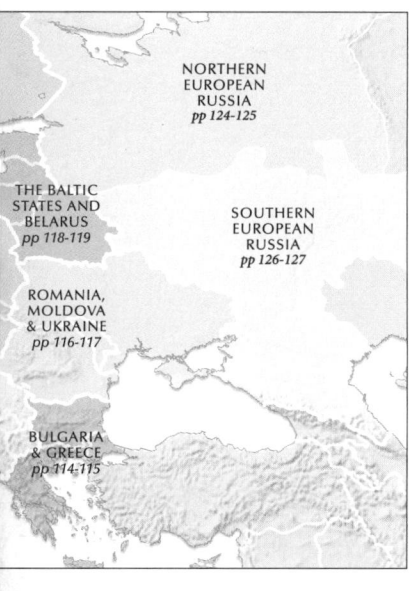

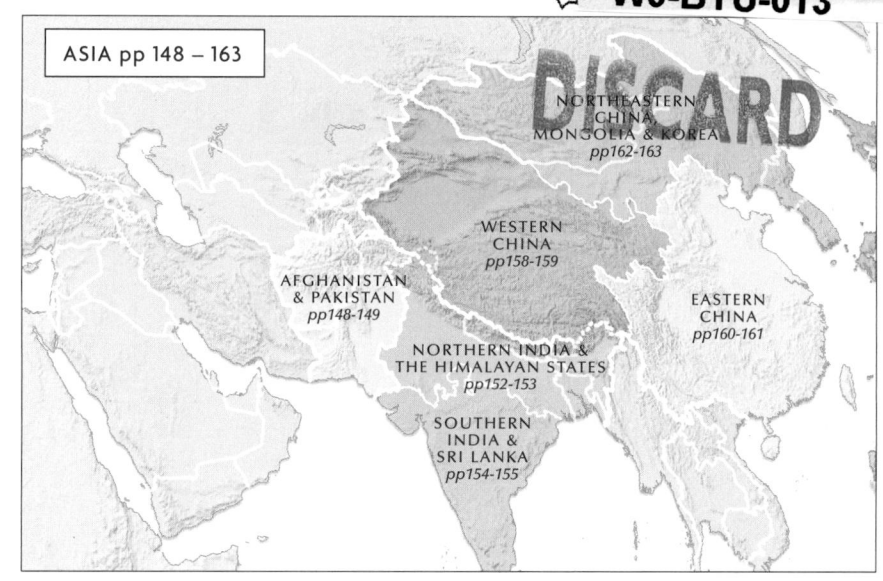

DISCARD

# CONCISE
# WORLD
# ATLAS

# CONCISE
# WORLD
# ATLAS

## EIGHTH EDITION

**Senior Cartographic Editor** Simon Mumford
**Cartographers** Suresh Kumar, Subhashree Bharati, Dheeraj Singh
**Index Editor** Simon Mumford **Index DTP** Rohan Sinha, Anita Kakar
**Production Editor** Kavita Varma **Senior Production Controller** Jude Crozier
**Jacket Design Development Manager** Sophia MTT
**Publishing Director** Jonathan Metcalf **Associate Publishing Director** Liz Wheeler **Art Director** Karen Self

## FIRST EDITION
### General Geographical Consultants
**Physical Geography** Denys Brunsden, Emeritus Professor, Department of Geography, King's College, London
**Human Geography** Professor J. Malcolm Wagstaff, Department of Geography, University of Southampton
**Place Names** Caroline Burgess, CartoConsulting Ltd., Reading
**Boundaries** International Boundaries Research Unit, Mountjoy Research Centre, University of Durham

### Digital Mapping Consultants
DK Cartopia developed by George Galfalvi and XMap Ltd., London
Professor Jan-Peter Muller, Department of Photogrammetry and Surveying, University College, London
Planets and information on the Solar System provided by Philip Eales and Kevin Tildsley, Planetary Visions Ltd., London

### Regional Consultants
**North America** Dr. David Green, Department of Geography, King's College, London • Jim Walsh, Head of Reference, Wessell Library, Tufts University, Medford, Massachusetts
**South America** Dr. David Preston, School of Geography, University of Leeds **Europe** Dr. Edward M. Yates, formerly of the Department of Geography, King's College, London
**Africa** Dr. Philip Amis, Development Administration Group, University of Birmingham • Dr. Ieuan Ll. Griffiths, Department of Geography, University of Sussex
Dr. Tony Binns, Department of Geography, University of Sussex
**Central Asia** Dr. David Turnock, Department of Geography, University of Leicester **South and East Asia** Dr. Jonathan Rigg, Department of Geography, University of Durham
**Australasia and Oceania** Dr. Robert Allison, Department of Geography, University of Durham

### Acknowledgments
**Digital terrain data** created by Eros Data Center, Sioux Falls, South Dakota, USA. Processed by GVS Images Ltd., California, USA and Planetary Visions Ltd., London, UK
Cambridge International Reference on Current Affairs (CIRCA), Cambridge, UK • Digitization by Robertson Research International, Swanley, UK • Peter Clark
British Isles maps generated from a dataset supplied by Map Marketing Ltd./European Map Graphics Ltd. in combination with DK Cartopia copyright data

## DORLING KINDERSLEY CARTOGRAPHY

**Editor-in-Chief** Andrew Heritage **Managing Cartographer** David Roberts **Senior Cartographic Editor** Roger Bullen
**Editorial Direction** Louise Cavanagh **Database Manager** Simon Lewis **Art Direction** Chez Picthall

### Cartographers
Pamela Alford • James Anderson • Caroline Bowie • Dale Buckton • Tony Chambers • Jan Clark • Bob Croser • Martin Darlison • Damien Demaj • Claire Ellam • Sally Gable
Jeremy Hepworth • Geraldine Horner • Chris Jackson • Christine Johnston • Julia Lunn • Michael Martin • Ed Merritt • James Mills-Hicks • Simon Mumford • John Plumer
John Scott • Ann Stephenson • Gail Townsley • Julie Turner • Sarah Vaughan • Jane Voss • Scott Wallace • Iorwerth Watkins • Bryony Webb • Alan Whitaker • Peter Winfield

**Digital Maps Created in DK Cartopia by**
Tom Coulson • Thomas Robertshaw
Philip Rowles • Rob Stokes
**Managing Editor**
Lisa Thomas
**Editors**
Thomas Heath • Wim Jenkins • Jane Oliver
Siobhan Ryan • Elizabeth Wyse
**Editorial Research**
Helen Dangerfield • Andrew Rebeiro-Hargrave
**Additional Editorial Assistance**
Debra Clapson • Robert Damon • Ailsa Heritage
Constance Novis • Jayne Parsons • Chris Whitwell

**Placenames Database Team**
Natalie Clarkson • Ruth Duxbury • Caroline Falce • John Featherstone • Dan Gardiner
Ciárán Hynes • Margaret Hynes • Helen Rudkin • Margaret Stevenson • Annie Wilson
**Senior Managing Art Editor**
Philip Lord
**Designers**
Scott David • Carol Ann Davis • David Douglas • Rhonda Fisher
Karen Gregory • Nicola Liddiard • Paul Williams
**Illustrations**
Ciárán Hughes • Advanced Illustration, Congleton, UK
**Picture Research**
Melissa Albany • James Clarke • Anna Lord
Christine Rista • Sarah Moule • Louise Thomas

This American Edition, 2020
First American Edition, 2001
Published in the United States by DK Publishing
1450 Broadway, Suite 801, New York, NY 10018

DK books are available at special discounts when purchased in bulk for
sales promotions, premiums, fund-raising, or educational use.
For details, contact: DK Publishing Special Markets,
1450 Broadway, Suite 801, New York, NY 10018
SpecialSales@dk.com

A catalog record for this book is available from the Library of Congress.

ISBN 978-1-4654-8054-5

Printed and bound in Latvia

A WORLD OF IDEAS:
**SEE ALL THERE IS TO KNOW**

**www.dk.com**

# Introduction

## EVERYTHING YOU NEED TO KNOW ABOUT OUR PLANET TODAY

For many, the outstanding legacy of the twentieth century was the way in which the Earth shrank. In the third millennium, it is increasingly important for us to have a clear vision of the world in which we live. The human population has increased fourfold since 1900. The last scraps of *terra incognita*— the polar regions and ocean depths—have been penetrated and mapped. New regions have been colonized and previously hostile realms claimed for habitation. The growth of air transportation and mass tourism allows many of us to travel farther, faster, and more frequently than ever before. In doing so we are given a bird's-eye view of the Earth's surface denied to our forebears.

At the same time, the amount of information about our world has grown enormously. Our multi-media environment hurls uninterrupted streams of data at us, on the printed page, through the airwaves, and across our television, computer, and phone screens; events from all corners of the globe reach us instantaneously and are witnessed as they unfold. Our sense of stability and certainty has been eroded; instead, we are aware that the world is in a constant state of flux and change. Natural disasters, man-made cataclysms, and conflicts between nations remind us daily of the enormity and fragility of our domain. The ongoing threat of international terrorism throws into very stark relief the difficulties that arise when trying to "know" or "understand" our planet and its many cultures.

The current crisis in our global culture has made the need greater than ever before for everyone to possess an atlas. DK's *Concise World Atlas* has been conceived to meet this need.
At its core, like all atlases, it seeks to define where places are located, to describe their main characteristics, and to map them in relation to other places. Every attempt has been made to produce information and maps that are as clear, accurate, and accessible as possible using the latest digital cartographic techniques. In addition, each page of the atlas provides a wealth of further information, bringing the maps to life. Using photographs, diagrams, at-a-glance maps, introductory text, and captions, the atlas builds up a detailed portrait of those features—cultural, political, economic, and geomorphological—that make each region unique, and which are also the main agents of change.

This eighth edition of the *Concise World Atlas* incorporates hundreds of revisions and updates affecting every map and every page, distilling the burgeoning mass of information available through modern technology into an extraordinarily detailed and reliable view of our world.

# CONTENTS

## THE WORLD

## ATLAS OF THE WORLD

### North America

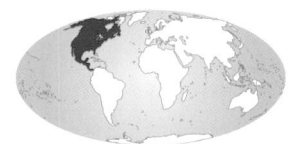

### South America

### Africa

# Europe

# Asia

# Australasia & Oceania

# INDEX–GAZETTEER

# Key to maps

## Regional

### Physical features

#### elevation

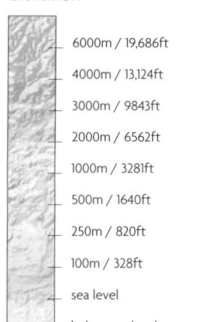

- 6000m / 19,686ft
- 4000m / 13,124ft
- 3000m / 9843ft
- 2000m / 6562ft
- 1000m / 3281ft
- 500m / 1640ft
- 250m / 820ft
- 100m / 328ft
- sea level
- below sea level

- ▲ elevation above sea level (mountain height)
- ▲ volcano
- ✕ pass
- ▼ elevation below sea level (depression depth)

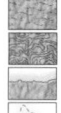

- sand desert
- lava flow
- coastline
- reef
- atoll

#### sea depth

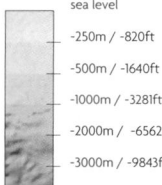

- sea level
- -250m / -820ft
- -500m / -1640ft
- -1000m / -3281ft
- -2000m / -6562ft
- -3000m / -9843ft

- ▲ seamount / guyot symbol
- ▼ undersea spot depth

### Drainage features

- main river
- secondary river
- tertiary river
- minor river
- main seasonal river
- secondary seasonal river
- canal
- waterfall
- rapids
- dam
- perennial lake
- seasonal lake
- perennial salt lake
- seasonal salt lake
- reservoir
- salt flat / salt pan
- marsh / salt marsh
- mangrove
- wadi
- ○ spring / well / waterhole / oasis

### Ice features

- ice cap / sheet
- ice shelf
- glacier / snowfield
- • • • summer pack ice limit
- ○ ○ ○ winter pack ice limit

### Communications

- ——— motorway / highway
- - - - - motorway / highway (under construction)
- ——— major road
- ——— minor road
- ⊣---← tunnel (road)
- ——— main railroad
- ——— minor railroad
- ⊣---← tunnel (railroad)
- ✈ international airport

### Borders

- ▬▬▬ full international border
- ▪ ▪ ▪ ▪ undefined international border
- ▬ ▪ ▬ ▪ disputed de facto border
- ▬ ▪ ▬ ▪ disputed territorial claim border
- ▬ ▪ ▬ ▪ indication of country extent (Pacific only)
- ▬ ▪ ▬ ▪ indication of dependent territory extent (Pacific only)
- •••••• demarcation/ cease fire line
- ▬▬▬ autonomous / federal region border
- ——— other 1st order internal administrative border
- ——— 2nd order internal administrative border

### Settlements

  built up area

#### settlement population symbols

- ▣ more than 5 million
- ◉ 1 million to 5 million
- ◉ 500,000 to 1 million
- ◎ 100,000 to 500,000
- ⊕ 50,000 to 100,000
- ○ 10,000 to 50,000
- ○ fewer than 10,000
- ▪ ◼ • country/dependent territory capital city
- ▪ ◉ • autonomous / federal region / other 1st order internal administrative center
- ▪ ◉ ⊕ 2nd order internal administrative center

### Miscellaneous features

- ∷∷∷∷ ancient wall
- ◇ site of interest
- • scientific station

### Graticule features

- ——— lines of latitude and longitude / Equator
- - - - - Tropics / Polar circles
- 45° degrees of longitude / latitude

### Typographic key

#### Physical features

landscape features ... *Namib Desert*
*Massif Central*
**ANDES**

headland ............. *Nordkapp*

elevation / volcano / pass ..... Mount Meru 4556 m

drainage features .... *Lake Geneva*

rivers / canals spring / well / waterhole / oasis / waterfall / rapids / dam ......... *Mekong*

ice features ........... *Vatnajökull*

sea features ........... Golfe de Lion
*Andaman Sea*
**INDIAN OCEAN**

undersea features ... *Barracuda Fracture Zone*

#### Regions

country ............... **ARMENIA**

dependent territory with parent state ..... NIUE (to NZ)

region outside feature area .......... ANGOLA

autonomous / federal region ........ MINAS GERAIS

other 1st order internal administrative region ................. **MINSKAYA VOBLASTS'**

2nd order internal administrative region ................ Vaucluse

cultural region ....... New England

#### Settlements

capital city ........... **BEIJING**

dependent territory capital city ........... FORT-DE-FRANCE

other settlements ... Chicago
Adana
**Tizi Ozou**
Yonezawa
Farnham

#### Miscellaneous

sites of interest / miscellaneous ........ Valley of the Kings

Tropics / Polar circles .......... *Antarctic Circle*

# How to use this Atlas

The atlas is organized by continent, moving eastward from the International Date Line. The opening section describes the world's structure, systems, and its main features. The Atlas of the World which follows, is a continent-by-continent guide to today's world, starting with a comprehensive insight into the physical, political, and economic structure of each continent, followed by integrated mapping and descriptions of each region or country.

## The world

The introductory section of the Atlas deals with every aspect of the planet, from physical structure to human geography, providing an overall picture of the world we live in. Complex topics such as the landscape of the Earth, climate, oceans, population, and economic patterns are clearly explained with the aid of maps and diagrams drawn from the latest information.

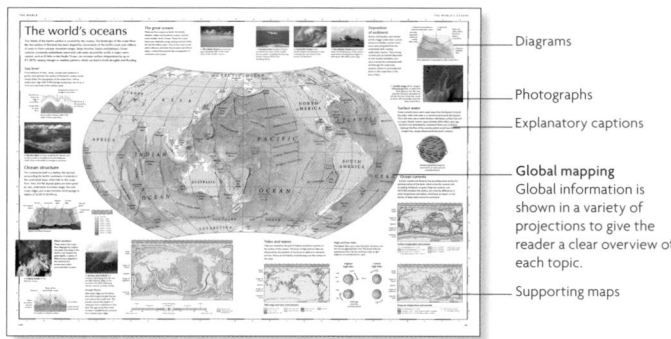

- Diagrams
- Photographs
- Explanatory captions
- **Global mapping** Global information is shown in a variety of projections to give the reader a clear overview of each topic.
- Supporting maps

## The political continent

The political portrait of the continent is a vital reference point for every continental section, showing the position of countries relative to one another, and the relationship between human settlement and geographic location. The complex mosaic of languages spoken in each continent is mapped, as is the effect of communications networks on the pattern of settlement.

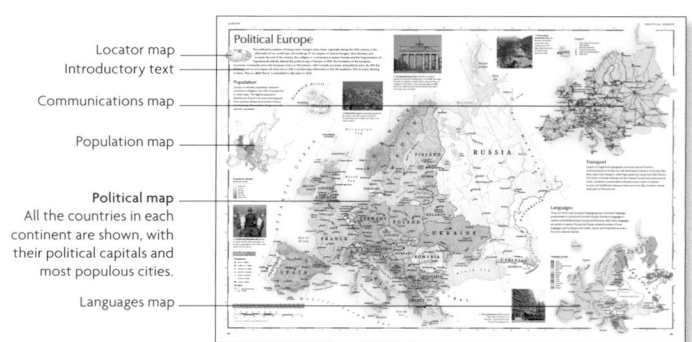

- Locator map
- Introductory text
- Communications map
- Population map
- **Political map** All the countries in each continent are shown, with their political capitals and most populous cities.
- Languages map

## Continental resources

The Earth's rich natural resources, including oil, gas, minerals, and fertile land, have played a key role in the development of society. These pages show the location of minerals and agricultural resources on each continent, and how they have been instrumental in dictating industrial growth and the varieties of economic activity across the continent.

- Mineral resources map
- Environmental issues map
- Land use map
- Industry map
- Comparative wealth map

# The physical continent

The astonishing variety of landforms, and the dramatic forces that created and continue to shape the landscape, are explained in the continental physical spread. Cross-sections, illustrations, and terrain maps highlight the different parts of the continent, showing how nature's forces have produced the landscapes we see today.

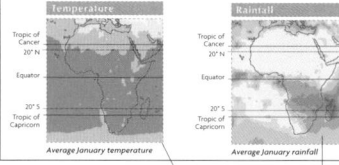

**Climate charts**
Rainfall and temperature charts clearly show the continental patterns of rainfall and temperature.

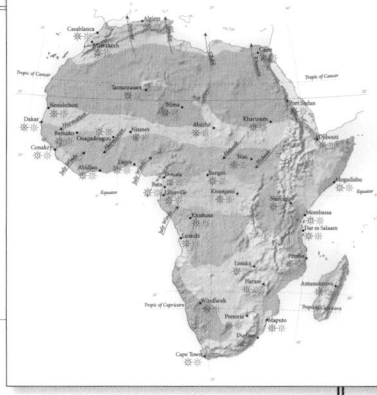

**Climate map**
Climatic regions vary across each continent. The map displays the differing climatic regions, as well as daily hours of sunshine at selected weather stations.

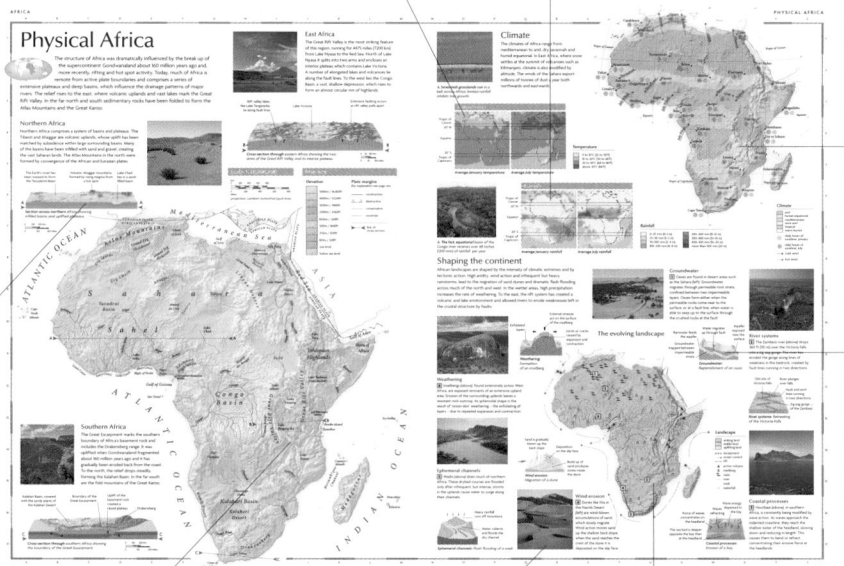

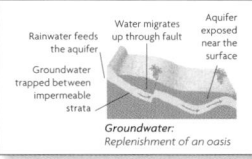

**Landform diagrams**
The complex formation of many typical landforms is summarized in these easy-to-understand illustrations.

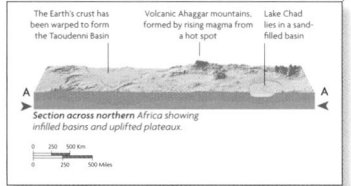

**Cross-sections**
Detailed cross-sections through selected parts of the continent show the underlying geomorphic structure.

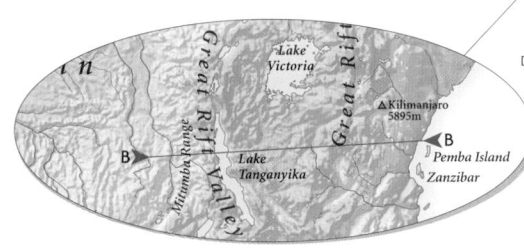

**Main physical map**
Detailed satellite data has been used to create an accurate and visually striking picture of the surface of the continent.

**Photographs**
A wide range of beautiful photographs bring the world's regions to life.

**Landscape evolution map**
The physical shape of each continent is affected by a variety of forces which continually sculpt and modify the landscape. This map shows the major processes which affect different parts of the continent.

**Key to transportation symbols**
❶ Extent of national paved road network.
❷ Extent of motorways, freeways, or major national highways.
❸ Extent of commercial railroad network.
❹ Extent of inland waterways navigable by commercial craft.

**The transport network**

| | | | |
|---|---|---|---|
| ❶ | 340,090 miles (544,144 km) | 4813 miles (7700 km) | ❷ |
| ❸ | 12,872 miles (20,592 km) | 2108 miles (3389 km) | ❹ |

New York's commercial success is tied historically to its transport connections. The Erie Canal, completed in 1825, opened up the Great Lakes and the interior to New York's markets and carried a stream of immigrants into the Midwest.

**Transportation network**
The differing extent of the transportation network for each region is shown here, along with key facts about the transportation system.

**Regional Locator**
This small map shows the location of each country in relation to its continent.

**Key to main map**
A key to the population symbols and land heights accompanies the main map.

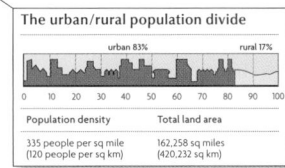

**World locator**
This locates the continent in which the region is found on a small world map.

**Land use map**
This shows the different types of land use which characterize the region, as well as indicating the principal agricultural activities.

**Map keys**
Each supporting map has its own key.

**Grid reference**
The framing grid provides a location reference for each place listed in the Index.

# Regional mapping

The main body of the Atlas is a unique regional map set, with detailed information on the terrain, the human geography of the region, and its infrastructure. Around the edge of the map, additional "at-a-glance" maps, give an instant picture of regional industry, land use, and agriculture. The detailed terrain map (shown in perspective), focuses on the main physical features of the region, and is enhanced by annotated illustrations, and photographs of the physical structure.

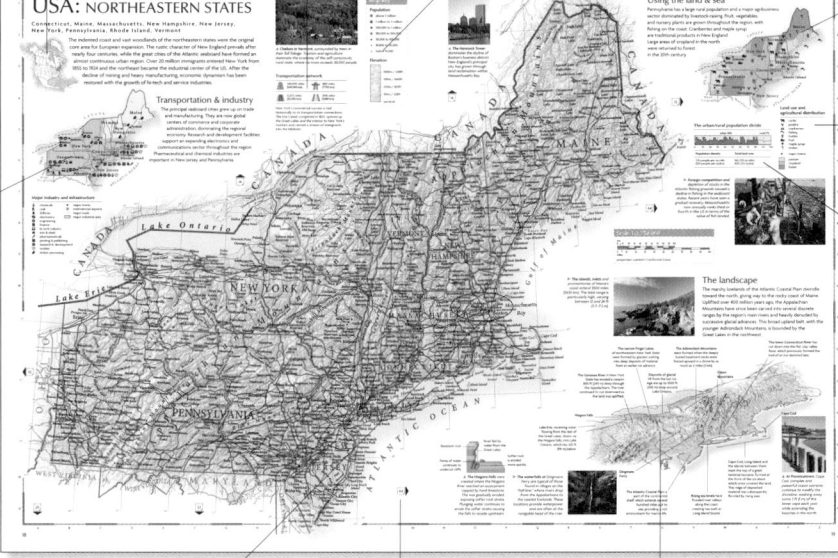

**The urban/rural population divide**

urban 83%    rural 17%

| Population density | Total land area |
|---|---|
| 335 people per sq mile (120 people per sq km) | 162,258 sq miles (420,232 sq km) |

**Urban/rural population divide**
The proportion of people in the region who live in urban and rural areas, as well as the overall population density and land area are clearly shown in these simple graphics.

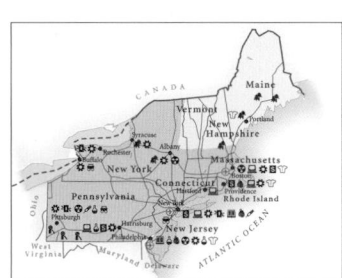

**Transportation and industry map**
The main industrial areas are mapped, and the most important industrial and economic activities of the region are shown.

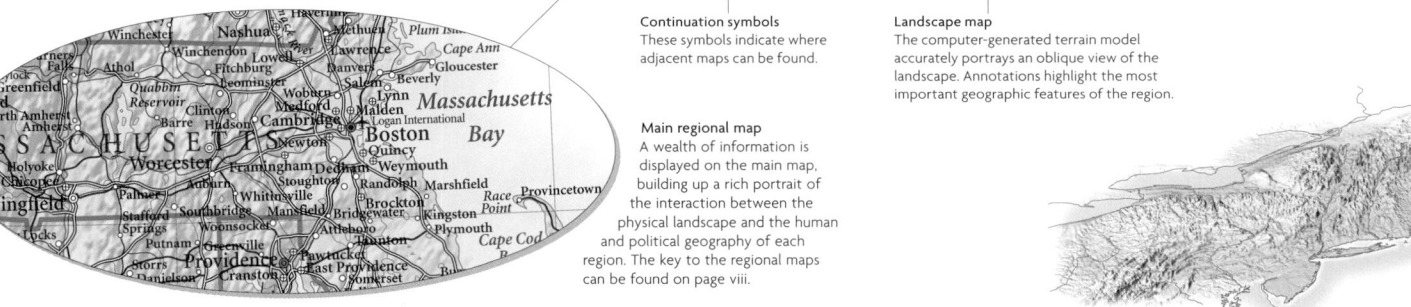

**Continuation symbols**
These symbols indicate where adjacent maps can be found.

**Main regional map**
A wealth of information is displayed on the main map, building up a rich portrait of the interaction between the physical landscape and the human and political geography of each region. The key to the regional maps can be found on page viii.

**Landscape map**
The computer-generated terrain model accurately portrays an oblique view of the landscape. Annotations highlight the most important geographic features of the region.

# The Solar System

Nine major planets, their satellites, and countless minor planets (asteroids) orbit the Sun to form the Solar System. The Sun, our nearest star, creates energy from nuclear reactions deep within its interior, providing all the light and heat which make life on Earth possible. The Earth is unique in the Solar System in that it supports life: its size, gravitational pull and distance from the Sun have all created the optimum conditions for the evolution of life. The planetary images seen here are composites derived from actual spacecraft images (not shown to scale).

## Orbits

All the Solar System's planets and dwarf planets orbit the Sun in the same direction and (apart from Pluto) roughly in the same plane. All the orbits have the shapes of ellipses (stretched circles). However, in most cases, these ellipses are close to being circular: only Pluto and Eris have very elliptical orbits. Orbital period (the time it takes an object to orbit the Sun) increases with distance from the Sun. The more remote objects not only have further to travel with each orbit, they also move more slowly.

Mercury

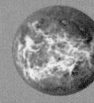
Venus

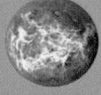
Earth

Mars

Ceres
*(dwarf planet)*
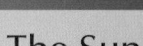

Jupiter

## The Sun

⊖ **Diameter:** *864,948 miles (1,392,000 km)*
● **Mass:** *1990 million million million million tons*

The Sun was formed when a swirling cloud of dust and gas contracted, pulling matter into its center. When the temperature at the center rose to 1,800,000°F (1,000,000°C), nuclear fusion – the fusing of hydrogen into helium, creating energy – occurred, releasing a constant stream of heat and light.

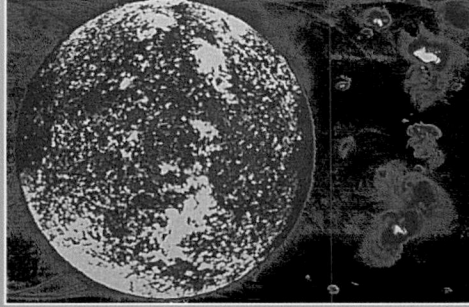

▲ *Solar flares are sudden bursts of energy from the Sun's surface. They can be 125,000 miles (200,000 km) long.*

## The formation of the Solar System

The cloud of dust and gas thrown out by the Sun during its formation cooled to form the Solar System. The smaller planets nearest the Sun are formed of minerals and metals. The outer planets were formed at lower temperatures, and consist of swirling clouds of gases.

## Solar eclipse

A solar eclipse occurs when the Moon passes between Earth and the Sun, casting its shadow on Earth's surface. During a total eclipse *(below)*, viewers along a strip of Earth's surface, called the area of totality, see the Sun totally blotted out for a short time, as the umbra (Moon's full shadow) sweeps over them. Outside this area is a larger one, where the Sun appears only partly obscured, as the penumbra (partial shadow) passes over.

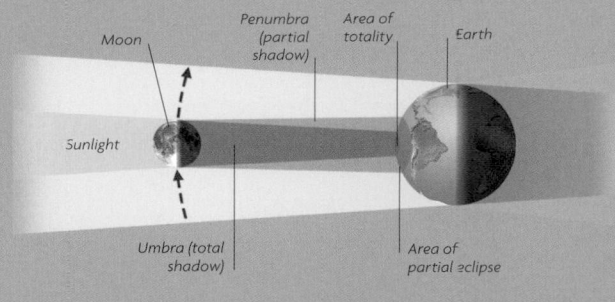

Moon

Penumbra *(partial shadow)*

Area of totality

Earth

Sunlight

Umbra *(total shadow)*

Area of partial eclipse

## PLANETS

|  | MERCURY | VENUS | EARTH | MARS | JUPITER | SATURN | URANUS | NEPTUNE |
|---|---|---|---|---|---|---|---|---|
| DIAMETER | 3029 miles (4875 km) | 7521 miles (12,104 km) | 7928 miles (12,756 km) | 4213 miles (6780 km) | 88,846 miles (142,984 km) | 74,898 miles (120,536 km) | 31,763 miles (51,118 km) | 30,775 miles (49,528 km) |
| AVERAGE DISTANCE FROM THE SUN | 36 mill. miles (57.9 mill. km) | 67.2 mill. miles (108.2 mill. km) | 93 mill. miles (149.6 mill. km) | 141.6 mill. miles (227.9 mill. km) | 483.6 mill. miles (778.3 mill. km) | 889.8 mill. miles (1431 mill. km) | 1788 mill. miles (2877 mill. km) | 2795 mill. miles (4498 mill. km) |
| ROTATION PERIOD | 58.6 days | 243 days | 23.93 hours | 24.62 hours | 9.93 hours | 10.65 hours | 17.24 hours | 16.11 hours |
| ORBITAL PERIOD | 88 days | 224.7 days | 365.26 days | 687 days | 11.86 years | 29.37 years | 84.1 years | 164.9 years |
| SURFACE TEMPERATURE | -292°F to 806°F (-180°C to 430°C) | 896°F (480°C) | -94°F to 131°F (-70°C to 55°C) | -184°F to 77 °F (-120°C to 25°C) | -160°F (-110°C) | -220°F (-140°C) | -320°F (-200°C) | -320°F (-200°C) |

## MAIN DWARF PLANETS

|  | CERES | PLUTO | ERIS |
|---|---|---|---|
| DIAMETER | 590 miles (950 km) | 1432 miles (2304 km) | 1429-1553 miles (2300-2500 km) |
| AVERAGE DISTANCE FROM THE SUN | 257 mill. miles (414 mill. km) | 3675 mill. miles (5915 mill. km) | 6344 mill. miles (10,210 mill. km) |
| ROTATION PERIOD | 9.1 hours | 6.38 days | not known |
| ORBITAL PERIOD | 4.6 years | 248.6 years | 557 years |
| SURFACE TEMPERATURE | -161°F (-107°C) | -380°F (-230°C) | -405°F (-243°C) |

## AVERAGE DISTANCE FROM THE SUN

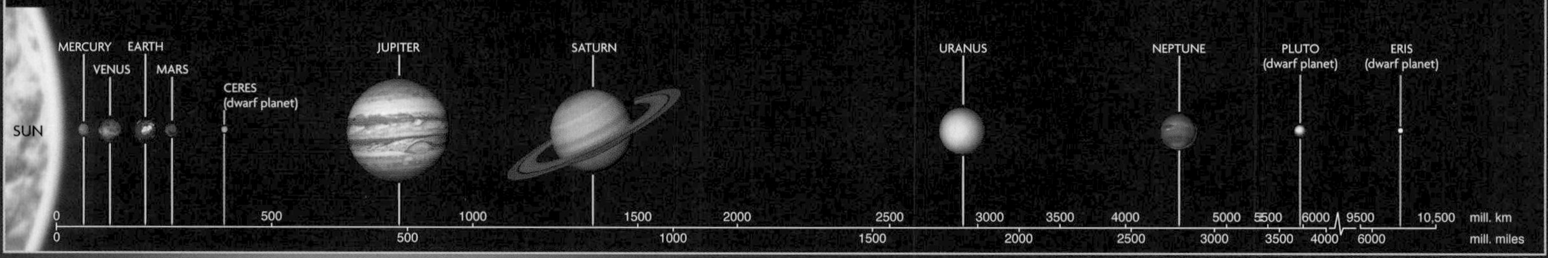

SUN · MERCURY · VENUS · EARTH · MARS · CERES (dwarf planet) · JUPITER · SATURN · URANUS · NEPTUNE · PLUTO (dwarf planet) · ERIS (dwarf planet)

0 · 500 · 1000 · 1500 · 2000 · 2500 · 3000 · 3500 · 4000 · 5000 · 5500 · 6000 · 9500 · 10,500 mill. km
0 · 500 · 1000 · 1500 · 2000 · 2500 · 3000 · 3500 · 4000 · 6000 mill. miles

Saturn

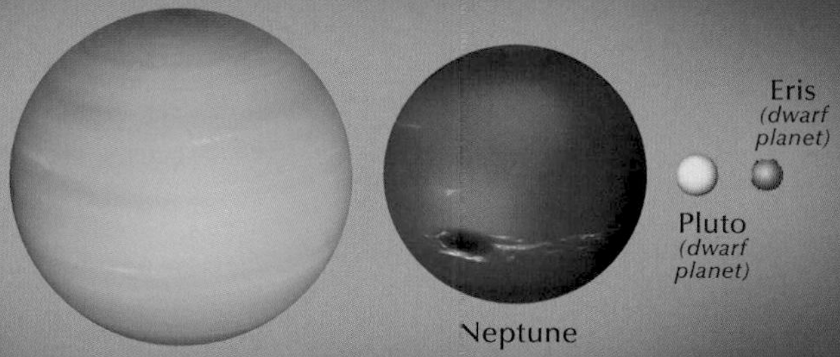

Uranus

Neptune

Pluto (dwarf planet)

Eris (dwarf planet)

## The Earth's Atmosphere

During the early stages of the Earth's formation, ash, lava, carbon dioxide, and water vapor were discharged onto the surface of the planet by constant volcanic eruptions. The water formed the oceans, while carbon dioxide entered the atmosphere or was dissolved in the oceans. Clouds, formed of water droplets, reflected some of the Sun's radiation back into space. The Earth's temperature stabilized and early life forms began to emerge, converting carbon dioxide into life-giving oxygen.

▲ *It is thought* that the gases that make up the Earth's atmosphere originated deep within the interior, and were released many millions of years ago during intense volcanic activity, similar to this eruption at Mount St. Helens.

## Space Debris

Millions of objects, remnants of planetary formation, circle the Sun in a zone lying between Mars and Jupiter: the asteroid belt. Fragments of asteroids break off to form meteoroids, which can reach the Earth's surface. Comets, composed of ice and dust, originated outside our Solar System. Their elliptical orbit brings them close to the Sun and into the inner Solar System.

▲ *Meteor Crater in* Arizona is 4200 ft (1300 m) wide and 660 ft (200 m) deep. It was formed over 10,000 years ago.

Possible and actual meteorite craters

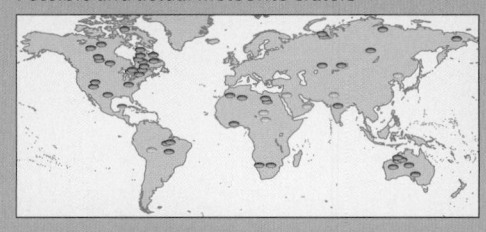

Map key
- Possible impact craters
- Meteorite impact craters

▲ *The orbit of* Halley's Comet brings it close to the Earth every 76 years. It last visited in 1986.

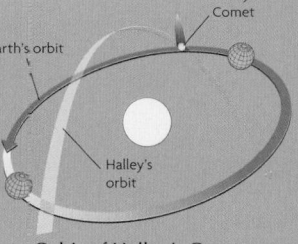

Halley's Comet · Earth's orbit · Halley's orbit

Orbit of Halley's Comet around the Sun

# The physical world

The Earth's surface is constantly being transformed: it is uplifted, folded, and faulted by tectonic forces; weathered and eroded by wind, water, and ice. Sometimes change is dramatic, the spectacular results of earthquakes or floods. More often it is a slow process lasting millions of years. A physical map of the world represents a snapshot of the ever-evolving architecture of the Earth. This terrain map shows the whole surface of the Earth, both above and below the sea.

## The world in section

These cross-sections around the Earth, one in the northern hemisphere; one straddling the Equator, reveal the limited areas of land above sea level in comparison with the extent of the sea floor. The greater erosive effects of weathering by wind and water limit the upward elevation of land above sea level, while the deep oceans retain their dramatic mountain and trench profiles.

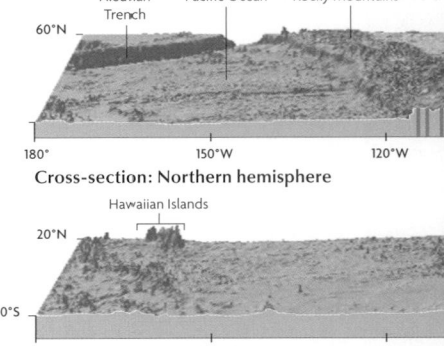

Cross-section: Northern hemisphere

Cross-section: Southern hemisphere

## Map key

**Elevation**

- 6000m / 19,686ft
- 4000m / 13,124ft
- 3000m / 9843ft
- 2000m / 6562ft
- 1000m / 3281ft
- 500m / 1640ft
- 250m / 820ft
- 100m / 328ft
- sea level
- below sea level

**Sea depth**

- sea level
- -250m / -820ft
- -2000m / -6562ft
- -4000m / -13,124ft

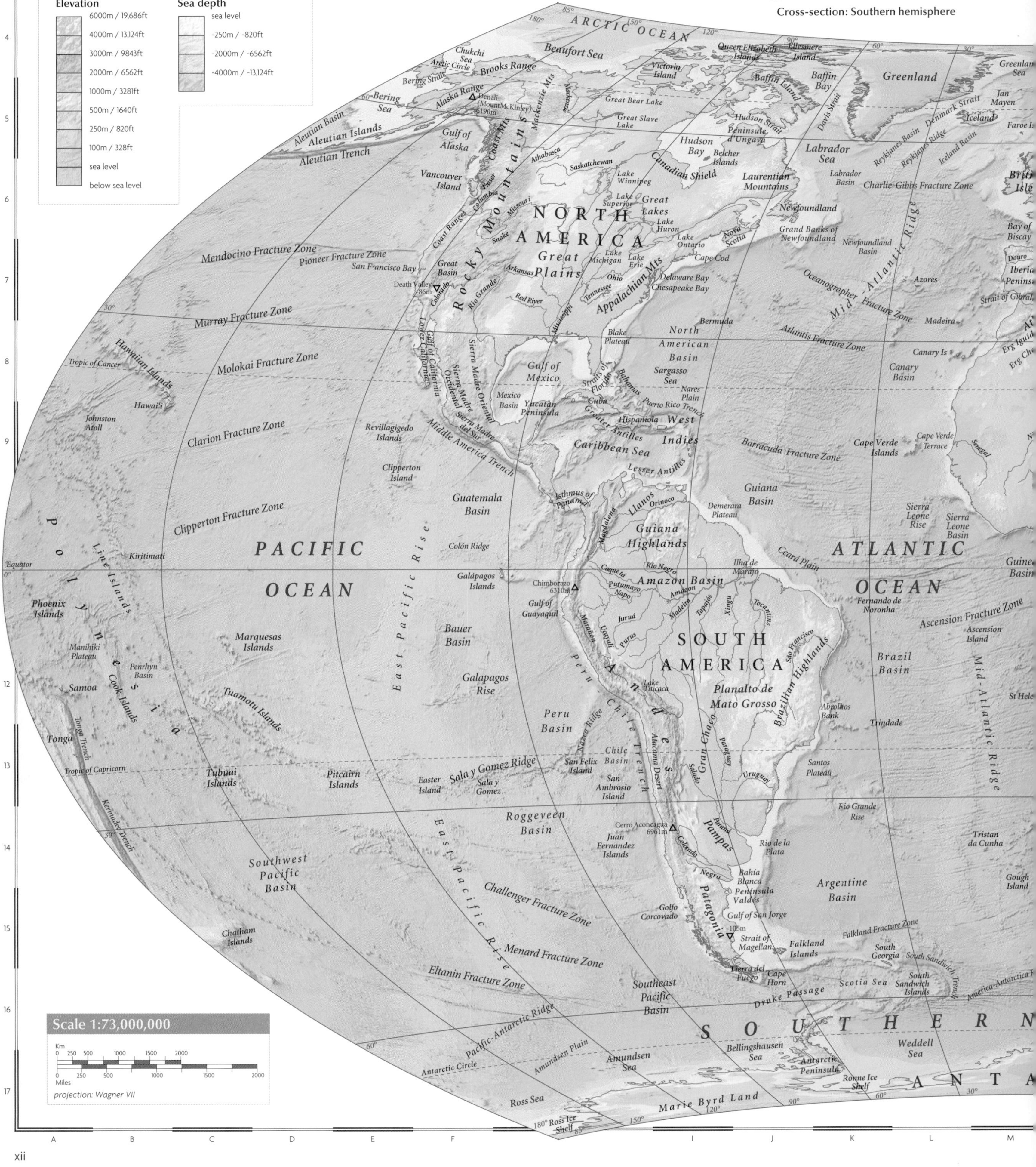

## Scale 1:73,000,000

Km 0 250 500 1000 1500 2000

Miles 0 250 500 1000 1500 2000

*projection: Wagner VII*

ARCTIC OCEAN

Chukchi Sea
Beaufort Sea
Arctic Circle
Brooks Range
Bering Strait
Bering Sea
Alaska Range
Denali (Mount McKinley) 6190m
Gulf of Alaska
Aleutian Basin
Aleutian Islands
Aleutian Trench
Vancouver Island
Coast Ranges
Rocky Mountains
Mendocino Fracture Zone
Pioneer Fracture Zone
San Francisco Bay
Great Basin
Death Valley -86m
Murray Fracture Zone
Molokai Fracture Zone
Tropic of Cancer
Hawaiian Islands
Hawai'i
Johnston Atoll
Clarion Fracture Zone
Revillagigedo Islands
Clipperton Island
Clipperton Fracture Zone
Sierra Madre Occidental
Sierra Madre Oriental
Sierra Madre del Sur
Mexico Basin
Gulf of California
Lower California
Colorado
Rio Grande
Red River
Great Plains
Snake
Missouri
Arkansas
Ohio
Tennessee
Mississippi
Yucatán Peninsula
Middle America Trench
Guatemala Basin
Colón Ridge
Galápagos Islands
Isthmus of Panamá

Mackenzie Mts
Great Bear Lake
Great Slave Lake
Athabasca
Saskatchewan
Lake Winnipeg
Canadian Shield
Hudson Bay
Belcher Islands
Lake Superior
Lake Michigan
Lake Huron
Lake Erie
Lake Ontario
Great Lakes
NORTH AMERICA
Appalachian Mts
Cape Cod
Delaware Bay
Chesapeake Bay
Blake Plateau
North American Basin
Sargasso Sea
Nares Plain
Bahamas
Cuba
Straits of Florida
Greater Antilles
Hispaniola
West Indies
Caribbean Sea
Lesser Antilles
Puerto Rico Trench

Victoria Island
Queen Elizabeth Islands
Ellesmere Island
Baffin Island
Baffin Bay
Hudson Strait
Peninsula d'Ungava
Laurentian Mountains
Newfoundland
Nova Scotia
Grand Banks of Newfoundland
Newfoundland Basin
Bermuda
Davis Strait
Labrador Sea
Labrador Basin
Greenland
Greenland Sea
Jan Mayen
Denmark Strait
Iceland
Faroe Is
Reykjanes Basin
Reykjanes Ridge
Iceland Basin
Charlie-Gibbs Fracture Zone
British Isles
Bay of Biscay
Douro
Iberian Peninsula
Strait of Gibraltar
Oceanographer Fracture Zone
Azores
Madeira
Atlantis Fracture Zone
Canary Is
Canary Basin
Cape Verde Islands
Cape Verde Terrace
Senegal
Barracuda Fracture Zone
Mid-Atlantic Ridge

PACIFIC OCEAN
East Pacific Rise
Polynesia
Line Islands
Kiritimati
Equator
Phoenix Islands
Manihiki Plateau
Penrhyn Basin
Cook Islands
Samoa
Tonga
Tonga Trench
Tropic of Capricorn
Kermadec Trench
Tubuai Islands
Marquesas Islands
Tuamotu Islands
Pitcairn Islands
Bauer Basin
Galápagos Rise
Peru Basin
Sala y Gomez Ridge
Easter Island
Sala y Gomez
San Felix Island
San Ambrosio Island
Roggeveen Basin
Southwest Pacific Basin
Chatham Islands
East Pacific Rise
Challenger Fracture Zone
Menard Fracture Zone
Eltanin Fracture Zone
Southeast Pacific Basin
Pacific-Antarctic Ridge
Antarctic Circle
Amundsen Plain
Amundsen Sea
Ross Sea
Ross Ice Shelf

Orinoco
Llanos
Guiana Highlands
Guiana Basin
Demerara Plateau
Ceará Plain
SOUTH AMERICA
Chimborazo 6310m
Gulf of Guayaquil
Amazon Basin
Caquetá
Putumayo
Napo
Amazon
Madeira
Tapajós
Xingu
Tocantins
São Francisco
Marañón
Ucayali
Juruá
Purus
Andes
Brazilian Highlands
Planalto de Mato Grosso
Brazil Basin
Abrolhos Bank
Trindade
Lake Titicaca
Peru-Chile Trench
Nazca Ridge
Atacama Desert
Chile Basin
Cerro Aconcagua 6961m
Juan Fernandez Islands
Gran Chaco
Paraná
Paraguay
Salado
Uruguay
Santos Plateau
Rio Grande Rise
Colorado
Pampas
Rio de la Plata
Argentine Basin
Bahía Blanca
Peninsula Valdés
Negra
Golfo Corcovado
Patagonia
Gulf of San Jorge
-105m
Strait of Magellan
Tierra del Fuego
Cape Horn
Falkland Islands
Falkland Fracture Zone
South Georgia
South Sandwich Islands
Scotia Sea
Drake Passage
Bellingshausen Sea
Antarctic Peninsula
Weddell Sea
Ronne Ice Shelf
Marie Byrd Land
SOUTHERN
ANTA

ATLANTIC OCEAN
Fernando de Noronha
Ascension Fracture Zone
Ascension Island
Guinea Basin
St Helena
Mid-Atlantic Ridge
Sierra Leone Rise
Sierra Leone Basin
Tristan da Cunha
Gough Island
South Sandwich Trench
American-Antarctic Ridge

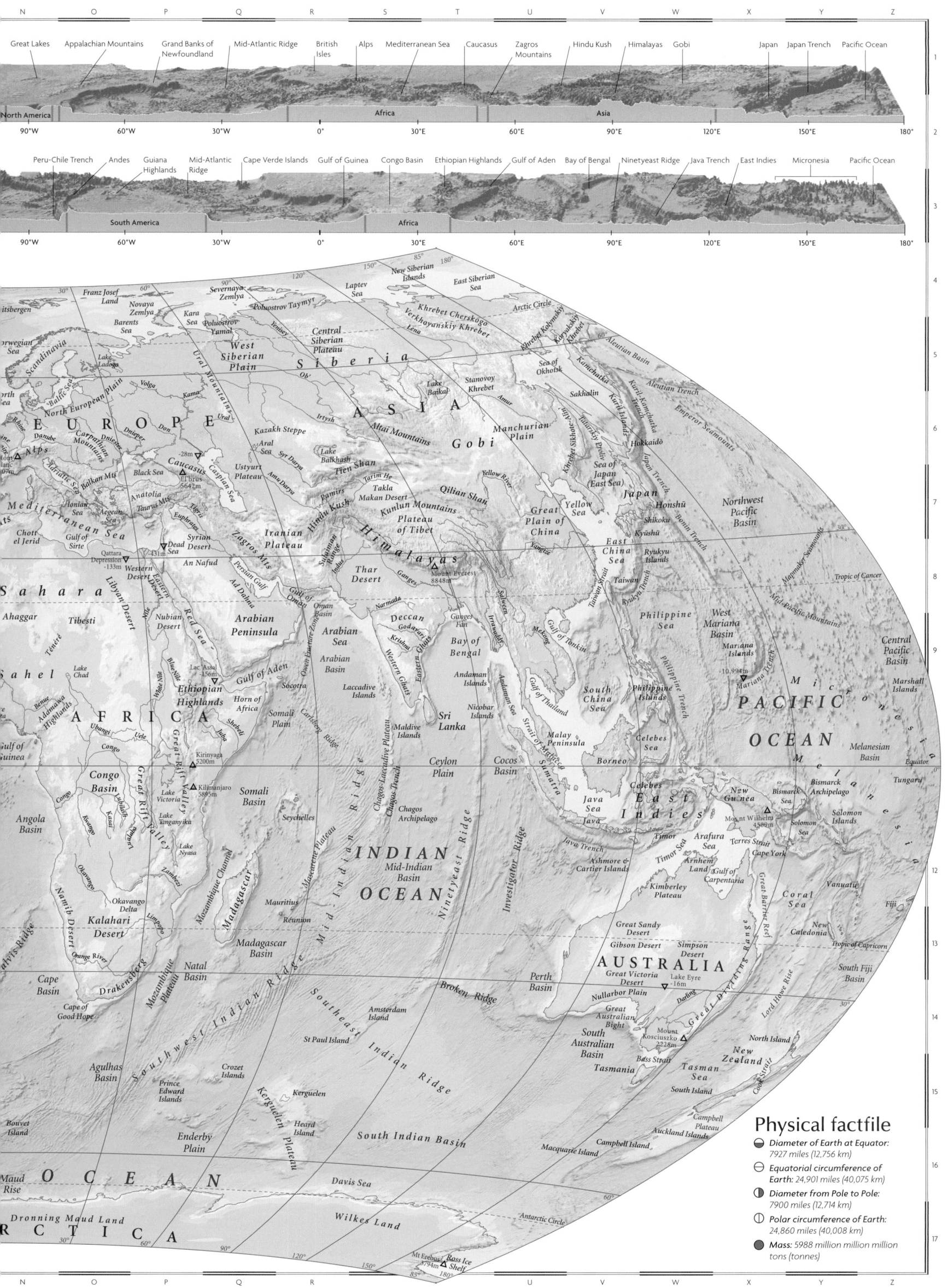

## Physical factfile

◗ *Diameter of Earth at Equator:*
7927 miles (12,756 km)

◖ *Equatorial circumference of Earth:* 24,901 miles (40,075 km)

◗ *Diameter from Pole to Pole:*
7900 miles (12,714 km)

◗ *Polar circumference of Earth:*
24,860 miles (40,008 km)

● *Mass:* 5988 million million million tons (tonnes)

# Structure of the Earth

The Earth as it is today is just the latest phase in a constant process of evolution which has occurred over the past 4.5 billion years. The Earth's continents are neither fixed nor stable; over the course of the Earth's history, propelled by currents rising from the intense heat at its center, the great plates on which they lie have moved, collided, joined together, and separated. These processes continue to mold and transform the surface of the Earth, causing earthquakes and volcanic eruptions and creating oceans, mountain ranges, deep ocean trenches, and island chains.

## Inside the Earth

The Earth's hot inner core is made up of solid iron, while the outer core is composed of liquid iron and nickel. The mantle nearest the core is viscous, whereas the rocky upper mantle is fairly rigid. The crust is the rocky outer shell of the Earth. Together, the upper mantle and the crust form the lithosphere.

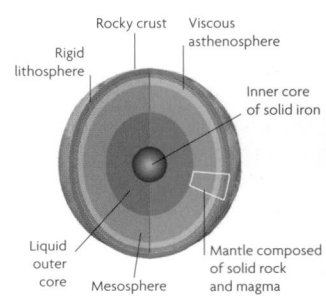

Rocky crust
Viscous asthenosphere
Rigid lithosphere
Inner core of solid iron
Liquid outer core
Mesosphere
Mantle composed of solid rock and magma

## The dynamic Earth

The Earth's crust is made up of eight major (and several minor) rigid continental and oceanic tectonic plates, which fit closely together. The positions of the plates are not static. They are constantly moving relative to one another. The type of movement between plates affects the way in which they alter the structure of the Earth. The oldest parts of the plates, known as shields, are the most stable parts of the Earth and little tectonic activity occurs here.

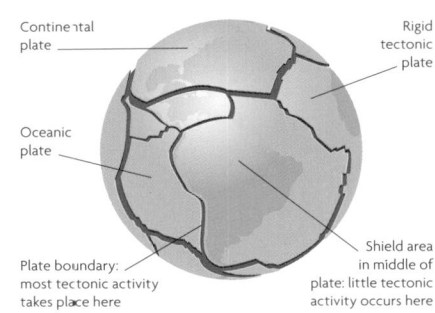

Continental plate
Rigid tectonic plate
Oceanic plate
Plate boundary: most tectonic activity takes place here
Shield area in middle of plate: little tectonic activity occurs here

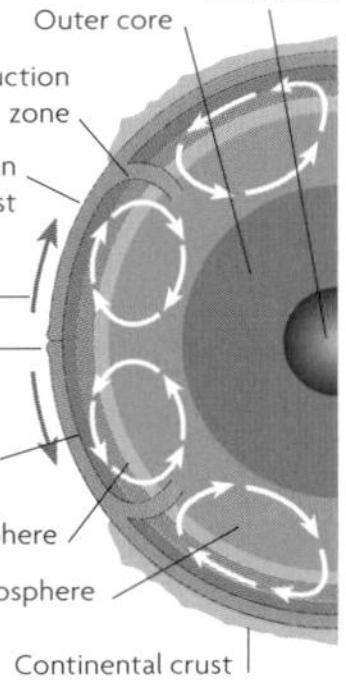

## Convection currents

Deep within the Earth, at its inner core, temperatures may exceed 8,100°F (4,500°C). This heat warms rocks in the mesosphere which rise through the partially molten mantle, displacing cooler rocks just below the solid crust, which sink, and are warmed again by the heat of the mantle. This process is continuous, creating convection currents which form the moving force beneath the Earth's crust.

Inner core
Outer core
Subduction zone
Ocean crust
Movement of plate
Mid-ocean ridge
Lithosphere
Asthenosphere
Mesosphere
Continental crust

## Plate boundaries

The boundaries between the plates are the areas where most tectonic activity takes place. Three types of movement occur at plate boundaries: the plates can either move toward each other, move apart, or slide past each other. The effect this has on the Earth's structure depends on whether the margin is between two continental plates, two oceanic plates, or an oceanic and continental plate.

## Mid-ocean ridges

Mid-ocean ridges are formed when two adjacent oceanic plates pull apart, allowing magma to force its way up to the surface, which then cools to form solid rock. Vast amounts of volcanic material are discharged at these mid-ocean ridges which can reach heights of 10,000 ft (3000 m).

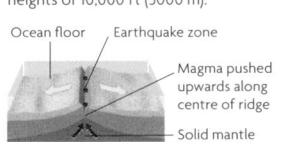

▲ *The Mid-Atlantic Ridge rises above sea level in Iceland, producing geysers and volcanoes.*

Ocean floor
Earthquake zone
Magma pushed upwards along centre of ridge
Solid mantle

*Formation of a mid-ocean ridge*

## Ocean plates meeting

△△ Oceanic crust is denser and thinner than continental crust; on average it is 3 miles (5 km) thick, while continental crust averages 18–24 miles (30–40 km). When oceanic plates of similar density meet, the crust is contorted as one plate overrides the other, forming deep sea trenches and volcanic island arcs above sea level.

▲ *Mount Pinatubo is an active volcano, lying on the Pacific "Ring of Fire."*

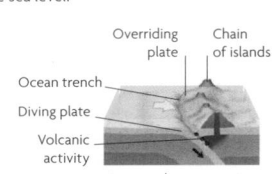

Overriding plate
Chain of islands
Ocean trench
Diving plate
Volcanic activity

*Ocean plates meeting to form an island arc*

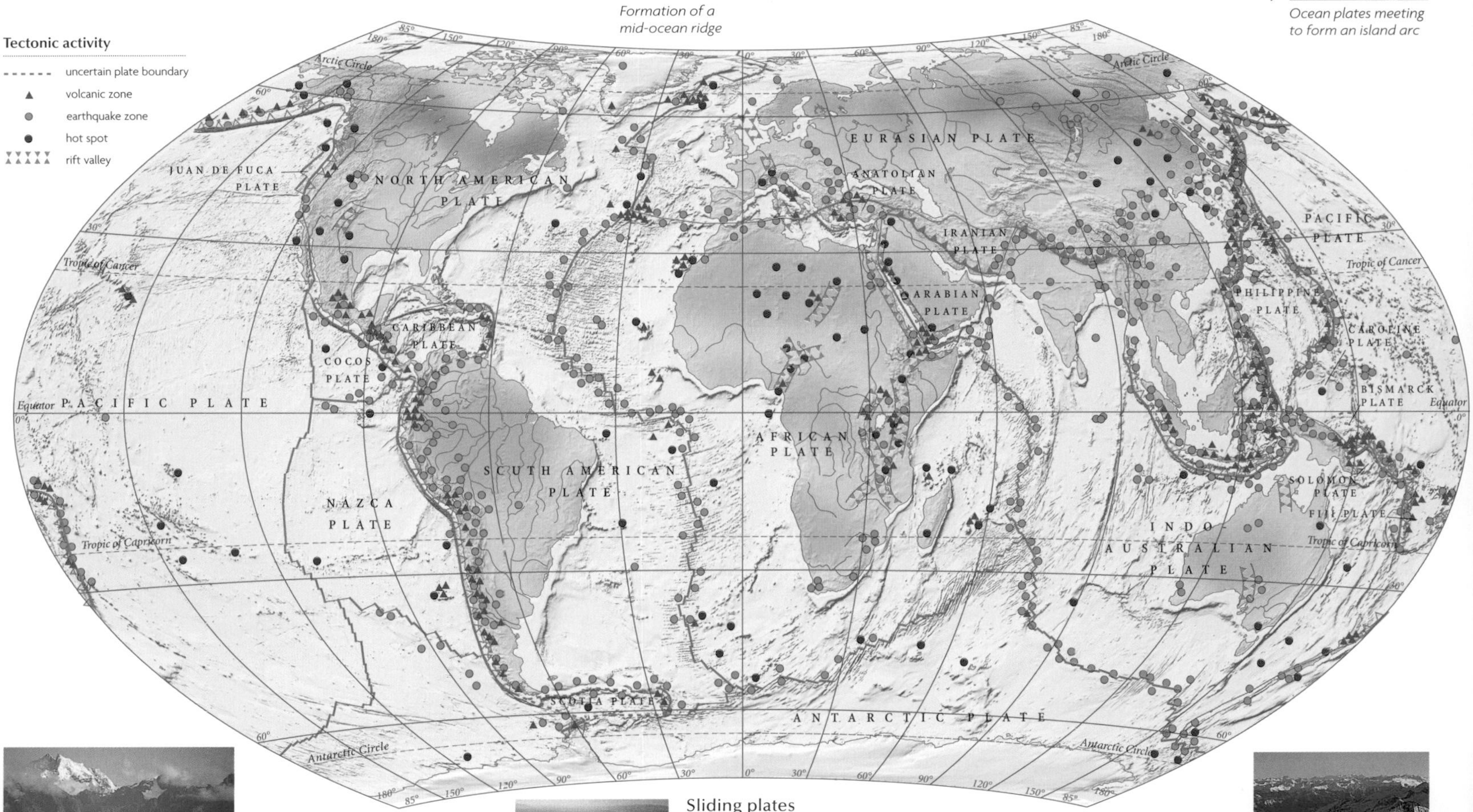

### Tectonic activity

- - - - - uncertain plate boundary
▲ volcanic zone
● earthquake zone
• hot spot
ᐱᐱᐱ rift valley

*Map labels:*
Arctic Circle
JUAN DE FUCA PLATE
NORTH AMERICAN PLATE
EURASIAN PLATE
ANATOLIAN PLATE
IRANIAN PLATE
PACIFIC PLATE
Tropic of Cancer
ARABIAN PLATE
PHILIPPINE PLATE
CARIBBEAN PLATE
CAROLINE PLATE
COCOS PLATE
BISMARCK PLATE
Equator PACIFIC PLATE
AFRICAN PLATE
INDO-AUSTRALIAN PLATE
SOLOMON PLATE
FIJI PLATE
SOUTH AMERICAN PLATE
NAZCA PLATE
Tropic of Capricorn
SCOTIA PLATE
ANTARCTIC PLATE
Antarctic Circle

## Diving plates

△△ When an oceanic and a continental plate meet, the denser oceanic plate is driven underneath the continental plate, which is crumpled by the collision to form mountain ranges. As the ocean plate plunges downward, it heats up, and molten rock (magma) is forced up to the surface.

◀ *The Andean mountain chain is the typical result of the impact of a diving plate.*

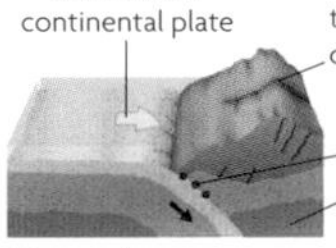

Oceanic plate dives under continental plate
Mountains thrust up by collision
Earthquake zone
Continental plate

*Diving plate*

## Sliding plates

When two plates slide past each other, friction is caused along the fault line which divides them. The plates do not move smoothly, and the uneven movement causes earthquakes.

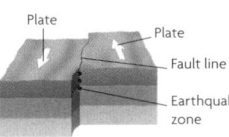

▲ *The deep fracture caused by the sliding plates of the San Andreas Fault can be clearly seen in parts of California.*

Plate
Plate
Fault line
Earthquake zone

*Sliding plates*

## Colliding plates

▲▲▲ When two continental plates collide, great mountain chains are thrust upward as the crust buckles and folds under the force of the impact.

▶ *The Alps were formed when the African Plate collided with the Eurasian Plate, about 65 million years ago.*

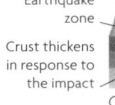

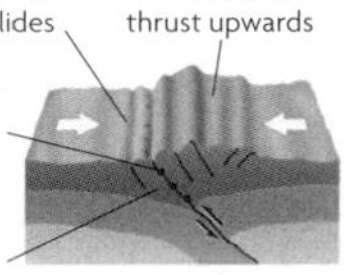

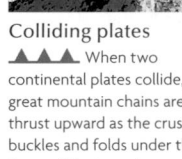

Plate buckles as it collides
Mountains thrust upwards
Earthquake zone
Crust thickens in response to the impact

*Continental plates colliding to form a mountain range*

# Continental drift

Although the plates which make up the Earth's crust move only a few inches in a year, over the millions of years of the Earth's history, its continents have moved many thousands of miles, to create new continents, oceans, and mountain chains

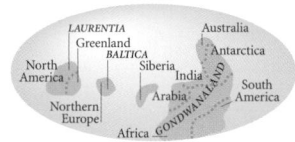

## 1: Cambrian period

570–510 million years ago. Most continents are in tropical latitudes. The supercontinent of Gondwanaland reaches the South Pole.

## 2: Devonian period

408–362 million years ago. The continents of Gondwanaland and Laurentia are drifting northward.

## 3: Carboniferous period

362–290 million years ago. The Earth is dominated by three continents; Laurentia, Angaraland, and Gondwanaland.

## 4: Triassic period

245–208 million years ago. All three major continents have joined to form the super-continent of Pangea.

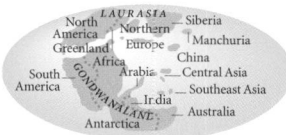

## 5: Jurassic period

208–145 million years ago. The super-continent of Pangea begins to break up, causing an overall rise in sea levels.

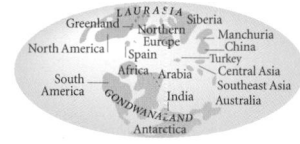

## 6: Cretaceous period

145–65 million years ago. Warm, shallow seas cover much of the land: sea levels are about 80 ft (25 m) above present levels.

## 7: Tertiary period

65–2 million years ago. Although the world's geography is becoming more recognizable, major events such as the creation of the Himalayan mountain chain, are still to occur during this period.

# Continental shields

The centers of the Earth's continents, known as shields, were established between 2500 and 500 million years ago; some contain rocks over three billion years old. They were formed by a series of turbulent events: plate movements, earthquakes, and volcanic eruptions. Since the Pre-Cambrian period, over 570 million years ago, they have experienced little tectonic activity, and today, these flat, low-lying slabs of solidified molten rock form the stable centers of the continents. They are bounded or covered by successive belts of younger sedimentary rock.

# The Hawaiian island chain

A hot spot lying deep beneath the Pacific Ocean pushes a plume of magma from the Earth's mantle up through the Pacific Plate to form volcanic islands. While the hot spot remains stationary, the plate on which the islands sit is moving slowly. A long chain of islands has been created as the plate passes over the hot spot.

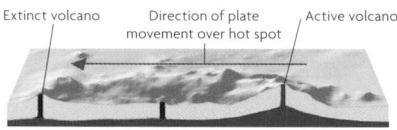

*Cross-section through the Hawaiian Islands*

## Evolution of the Hawaiian Islands

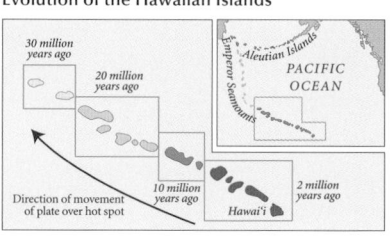

# Creation of the Himalayas

Between 10 and 20 million years ago, the Indian subcontinent, part of the ancient continent of Gondwanaland, collided with the continent of Asia. The Indo-Australian Plate continued to move northward, displacing continental crust and uplifting the Himalayas, the world's highest mountain chain.

### Movements of India

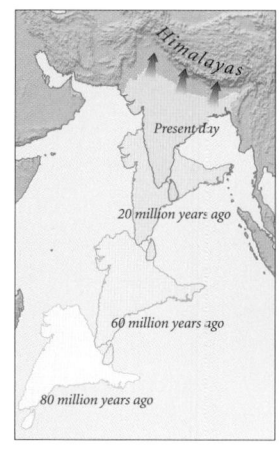

*Cross-section through the Himalayas*

▲ *The Himalayas were uplifted when the Indian subcontinent collided with Asia.*

# The Earth's geology

The Earth's rocks are created in a continual cycle. Exposed rocks are weathered and eroded by wind, water, and chemicals and deposited as sediments. If they pass into the Earth's crust they will be transformed by high temperatures and pressures into metamorphic rocks or they will melt and solidify as igneous rocks.

## Sandstone

[8] Sandstones are sedimentary rocks formed mainly in deserts, beaches, and deltas. Desert sandstones are formed of grains of quartz which have been well rounded by wind erosion.

▲ *Rock stacks of desert sandstone, at Bryce Canyon National Park, Utah, US.*

◀ *Extrusive igneous rocks are formed during volcanic eruptions, as here in Hawai'i.*

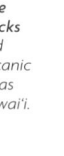

## Andesite

[7] Andesite is an extrusive igneous rock formed from magma which has solidified on the Earth's crust after a volcanic eruption.

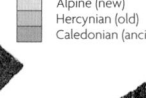

## Gneiss

[1] Gneiss is a metamorphic rock made at great depth during the formation of mountain chains, when intense heat and pressure transform sedimentary or igneous rocks.

▲ *Gneiss formations in Norway's Jotunheimen Mountains.*

◀ *Basalt columns at Giant's Causeway, Northern Ireland, UK.*

## Basalt

[2] Basalt is an igneous rock, formed when small quantities of magma lying close to the Earth's surface cool rapidly.

## Limestone

[3] Limestone is a sedimentary rock, which is formed mainly from the calcite skeletons of marine animals which have been compressed into rock.

▲ *Limestone hills, Guilin, China.*

## Coral

[4] Coral reefs are formed from the skeletons of millions of individual corals.

▲ *Great Barrier Reef, Australia.*

### Geological regions

- continental shield
- sedimentary cover
- coral formation
- igneous rock types

### Mountain ranges

- Alpine (new)
- Hercynian (old)
- Caledonian (ancient)

## Schist

[1] Schist is a metamorphic rock formed during mountain building, when temperature and pressure are comparatively high. Both mudstones and shales reform into schist under these conditions.

▶ *Schist formations in the Atlas Mountains, northwestern Africa.*

## Granite

[5] Granite is an intrusive igneous rock formed from magma which has solidified deep within the Earth's crust. The magma cools slowly, producing a coarse-grained rock.

▶ *Namibia's Namaqualand Plateau is formed of granite.*

# Shaping the landscape

The basic material of the Earth's surface is solid rock: valleys, deserts, soil, and sand are all evidence of the powerful agents of weathering, erosion, and deposit on which constantly shape and transform the Earth's landscapes. Water, either flowing continually in rivers or seas, or frozen and compacted into solid sheets of ice, has the most clearly visible impact on the Earth's surface. But wind can transport fragments of rock over huge distances and strip away protective layers of vegetation, exposing rock surfaces to the impact of extreme heat and cold.

## Coastal water

The world's coastlines are constantly changing; every day, tides deposit, sift and sort sand, and gravel on the shoreline. Over longer periods, powerful wave action erodes cliffs and headlands and carves out bays.

▶ *A low, wide* sandy beach on South Africa's Cape Peninsula is continually re-shaped by the action of the Atlantic waves.

▲ *The sheer chalk* cliffs at Seven Sisters in southern England are constantly under attack from waves.

## Water

Less than 2% of the world's water is on the land, but it is the most powerful agent of landscape change. Water, as rainfall, groundwater, and rivers, can transform landscapes through both erosion and deposition. Eroded material carried by rivers forms the world's most fertile soils.

▲ *Waterfalls such as* the Iguaçu Falls on the border between Argentina and southern Brazil, erode the underlying rock, causing the falls to retreat.

## Groundwater

In regions where there are porous rocks such as chalk, water is stored underground in large quantities; these reservoirs of water are known as aquifers. Rain percolates through topsoil into the underlying bedrock, creating an underground store of water. The limit of the saturated zone is called the water table.

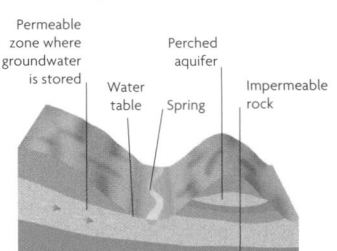

Permeable zone where groundwater is stored | Perched aquifer | Impermeable rock | Water table | Spring

*Storage of groundwater in an aquifer*

## World river systems

*drainage basin*

**World river systems:**
Sediment deposited annually per drainage basin

tons per sq mile per year — 9120 | 6080 | 1520 | 760 | 400 | 200 and less — 2400 | 1600 | tonnes per sq km per year

Rivers labeled on map: Yukon, Mackenzie, Nelson, Columbia, St. Lawrence, Colorado, Mississippi Missouri, Río Grande, Orinoco, Amazon, São Francisco, Paraná, Rhine, Danube, Volga, Ob', Yenisey, Lena, Amur, Niger, Nile, Tigris/Euphrates, Indus, Yellow River, Ganges Brahmaputra, Yangtze, Mekong, Congo, Zambezi, Orange, Murray Darling

ARCTIC OCEAN, ATLANTIC OCEAN, PACIFIC OCEAN, INDIAN OCEAN, Arctic Circle, Tropic of Cancer, Equator, Tropic of Capricorn, Antarctic Circle

## Rivers

Rivers erode the land by grinding and dissolving rocks and stones. Most erosion occurs in the river's upper course as it flows through highland areas. Rock fragments are moved along the river bed by fast-flowing water and deposited in areas where the river slows down, such as flat plains, or where the river enters seas or lakes.

### River valleys

Over long periods of time rivers erode uplands to form characteristic V-shaped valleys with smooth sides.

Resistant rock | River | Chemical erosion cuts valley in softer rock

*River valley erosion*

### Deltas

When a river deposits its load of silt and sediment (alluvium) on entering the sea, it may form a delta. As this material accumulates, it chokes the mouth of the river, forcing it to create new channels to reach the sea.

▶ *The Nile forms* a broad delta as it flows into the Mediterranean.

## Drainage basins

The drainage basin is the area of land drained by a major trunk river and its smaller branch rivers or tributaries. Drainage basins are separated from one another by natural boundaries known as watersheds.

Watershed | Major trunk river | Alps | Dolomites | Apennines | Tributary river | Delta | River mouth | Po Valley

*The drainage basin of the Po river, northern Italy.*

### Meanders

In their lower courses, rivers flow slowly. As they flow across the lowlands, they form looping bends called meanders.

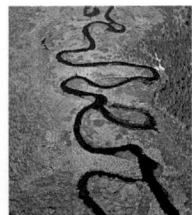

▲ *The Mississippi River* forms meanders as it flows across the southern US.

▲ *The meanders of* Utah's San Juan River have become deeply incised.

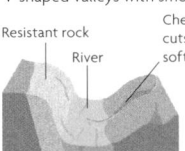

◀ *Mud is deposited* by China's Yellow River in its lower course.

### Deposition

When rivers have deposited large quantities of fertile alluvium, they are forced to find new channels through the alluvium deposits, creating braided river systems.

## Landslides

Heavy rain and associated flooding on slopes can loosen underlying rocks, which crumble, causing the top layers of rock and soil to slip.

▶ *A huge landslide* in the Swiss Alps has left massive piles of rocks and pebbles called scree.

## Gullies

In areas where soil is thin, rainwater is not effectively absorbed, and may flow overland. The water courses downhill in channels, or gullies, and may lead to rapid erosion of soil.

▲ *A deep gully* in the French Alps caused by the scouring of upper layers of turf.

# Ice

During its long history, the Earth has experienced a number of glacial episodes when temperatures were considerably lower than today. During the last Ice Age, 18,000 years ago, ice covered an area three times larger than it does today. Over these periods, the ice has left a remarkable legacy of transformed landscapes.

## Glaciers

Glaciers are formed by the compaction of snow into "rivers" of ice. As they move over the landscape, glaciers pick up and carry a load of rocks and boulders which erode the landscape they pass over, and are eventually deposited at the end of the glacier.

▲ *A massive glacier* advancing down a valley in southern Argentina.

## Post-glacial features

When a glacial episode ends, the retreating ice leaves many features. These include depositional ridges called moraines, which may be eroded into low hills known as drumlins; sinuous ridges called eskers; kames, which are rounded hummocks; depressions known as kettle holes; and windblown loess deposits.

## Glacial valleys

Glaciers can erode much more powerfully than rivers. They form steep-sided, flat-bottomed valleys with a typical U-shaped profile. Valleys created by tributary glaciers, whose floors have not been eroded to the same depth as the main glacial valley floor, are called hanging valleys

▲ *The U-shaped profile* and piles of morainic debris are characteristic of a valley once filled by a glacier.

▲ *A series of* hanging valleys high up in the Chilean Andes.

### Past and present world ice-cover and glacial features

*Post-glacial landscape features*

Kame terrace
Kettle hole
Esker
Braided river
Windblown loess
Retreating glacier
Drumlin
Terminal moraine
Glacial till
Bedrock

### Past and present world ice cover and glacial features

| | |
|---|---|
| extent of last Ice Age | present day ice cover |
| loess deposits | glacial field |
| post-glacial feature | |
| glacial feature | |

## Ice shattering

Water drips into fissures in rocks and freezes, expanding as it does so. The pressure weakens the rock, causing it to crack, and eventually to shatter into polygonal patterns.

▲ *Irregular polygons show* through the sedge-grass tundra in the Yukon, Canada.

▲ *The profile of* the Matterhorn has been formed by three cirques lying "back-to-back."

## Cirques

Cirques are basin-shaped hollows which mark the head of a glaciated valley. Where neighboring cirques meet, they are divided by sharp rock ridges called arêtes. It is these arêtes which give the Matterhorn its characteristic profile.

## Fjords

Fjords are ancient glacial valleys flooded by the sea following the end of a period of glaciation. Beneath the water, the valley floor can be 4000 ft (1300 m) deep.

▲ *A fjord fills* a former glacial valley in southern New Zealand.

## Periglaciation

Periglacial areas occur near to the edge of ice sheets. A layer of frozen ground lying just beneath the surface of the land is known as permafrost. When the surface melts in the summer, the water is unable to drain into the frozen ground, and so "creeps" downhill, a process known as solifluction.

# Wind

Strong winds can transport rock fragments great distances, especially where there is little vegetation to protect the rock. In desert areas, wind picks up loose, unprotected sand particles, carrying them over great distances. This powerfully abrasive debris is blasted at the surface by the wind, eroding the landscape into dramatic shapes.

### Prevailing winds and dust trajectories

**Prevailing winds**

| | |
|---|---|
| northeast trade | westerly |
| southeast trade | westerly |

| | |
|---|---|
| polar easterly | |
| polar easterly | |

**Dust trajectories**

→ trajectory of aeolian dust

### Hot and cold deserts

**Main desert types**

| | | |
|---|---|---|
| hot arid | semi-arid | cold polar |

# Temperature

Most of the world's deserts are in the tropics. The cold deserts which occur elsewhere are arid because they are a long way from the rain-giving sea. Rock in deserts is exposed because of lack of vegetation and is susceptible to changes in temperature; extremes of heat and cold can cause both cracks and fissures to appear in the rock.

## Deposition

The rocky, stony floors of the world's deserts are swept and scoured by strong winds. The smaller, finer particles of sand are shaped into surface ripples, dunes, or sand mountains, which rise to a height of 650 ft (200 m). Dunes usually form single lines, running perpendicular to the direction of the prevailing wind. These long, straight ridges can extend for over 100 miles (160 km).

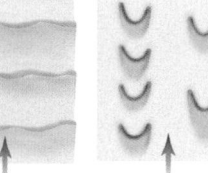

▲ *Barchan dunes in the* Arabian Desert.

▲ *Complex dune system in* the Sahara.

## Heat

Fierce sun can heat the surface of rock, causing it to expand more rapidly than the cooler, underlying layers. This creates tensions which force the rock to crack or break up. In arid regions, the evaporation of water from rock surfaces dissolves certain minerals within the water, causing salt crystals to form in small openings in the rock. The hard crystals force the openings to widen into cracks and fissures.

## Desert abrasion

Abrasion creates a wide range of desert landforms from faceted pebbles and wind ripples in the sand, to large-scale features such as yardangs (low, streamlined ridges), and scoured desert pavements.

Wind abrasion
Gravel
Faceted rock
Wind direction
Desert pavement
Sand desert
Wind rippling
Thermal fracturing

*Features of a desert surface*

## Dunes

Dunes are shaped by wind direction and sand supply. Where sand supply is limited, crescent-shaped barchan dunes are formed.

→ *Wind direction*

### Types of dune

*Transverse dune*

*Barchan dune*

*Linear dune*

*Star dune*

▲ *The cracked and* parched floor of Death Valley, California. This is one of the hottest deserts on Earth.

◄ *This dry valley* at Ellesmere Island in the Canadian Arctic is an example of a cold desert. The cracked floor and scoured slopes are features also found in hot deserts.

# The world's oceans

Two-thirds of the Earth's surface is covered by the oceans. The landscape of the ocean floor, like the surface of the land, has been shaped by movements of the Earth's crust over millions of years to form volcanic mountain ranges, deep trenches, basins, and plateaus. Ocean currents constantly redistribute warm and cold water around the world. A major warm current, such as El Niño in the Pacific Ocean, can increase surface temperature by up to 10°F (8°C), causing changes in weather patterns which can lead to both droughts and flooding.

## The great oceans

There are five oceans on Earth: the Pacific, Atlantic, Indian, and Southern oceans, and the much smaller Arctic Ocean. These five ocean basins are relatively young, having evolved within the last 80 million years. One of the most recent plate collisions, between the Eurasian and African plates, created the present-day arrangement of continents and oceans.

▲ *The Indian Ocean accounts for approximately 20% of the total area of the world's oceans.*

## Sea level

If the influence of tides, winds, currents, and variations in gravity were ignored, the surface of the Earth's oceans would closely follow the topography of the ocean floor, with an underwater ridge 3000 ft (915 m) high producing a rise of up to 3 ft (1 m) in the level of the surface water.

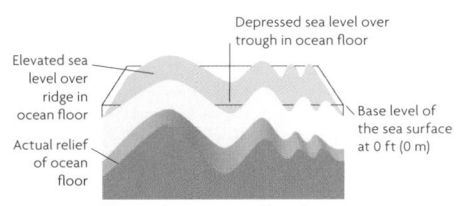

Elevated sea level over ridge in ocean floor
Depressed sea level over trough in ocean floor
Actual relief of ocean floor
Base level of the sea surface at 0 ft (0 m)

*How surface waters reflect the relief of the ocean floor*

▲ *The low relief of many small Pacific islands such as these atolls at Huahine in French Polynesia makes them vulnerable to changes in sea level.*

## Ocean structure

The continental shelf is a shallow, flat seabed surrounding the Earth's continents. It extends to the continental slope, which falls to the ocean floor. Here, the flat abyssal plains are interrupted by vast, underwater mountain ranges, the mid-ocean ridges, and ocean trenches which plunge to depths of 36,070 ft (10,994 m).

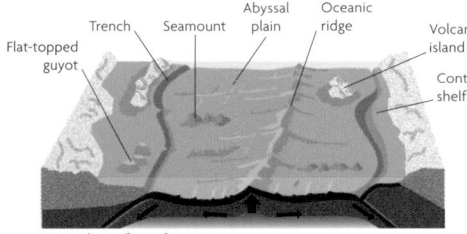

Flat-topped guyot
Trench
Seamount
Abyssal plain
Oceanic ridge
Volcanic island
Continental shelf

*Typical sea-floor features*

**Ocean depth**

| | |
|---|---|
| | Sea level |
| | 200m / 656ft |
| | 1000m / 3281ft |
| | 2000m / 6562ft |
| | 3000m / 9843ft |
| | 4000m / 13,124ft |
| | 5000m / 16,400ft |
| | 6000m / 19,686ft |

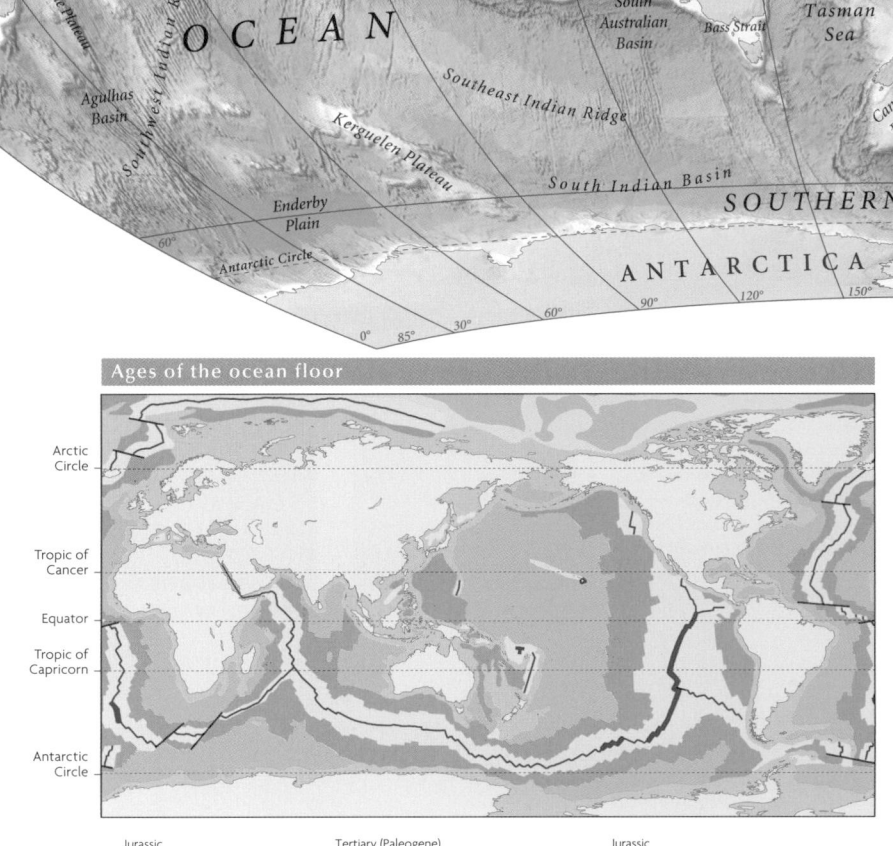

## Black smokers

These vents in the ocean floor disgorge hot, sulfur-rich water from deep in the Earth's crust. Despite the great depths, a variety of lifeforms have adapted to the chemical-rich environment which surrounds black smokers.

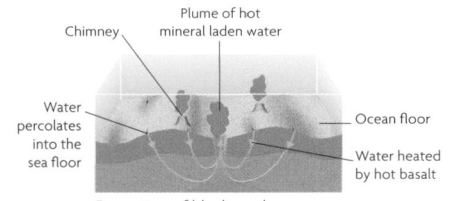

▲ *A black smoker in the Atlantic Ocean.*

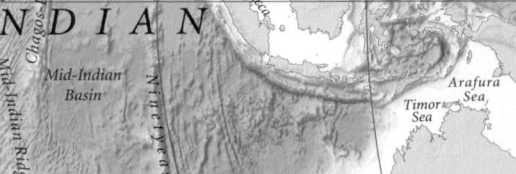

▲ *Surtsey, near Iceland, is a volcanic island lying directly over the Mid-Atlantic Ridge. It was formed in the 1960s following intense volcanic activity nearby.*

Chimney
Plume of hot mineral laden water
Water percolates into the sea floor
Ocean floor
Water heated by hot basalt

*Formation of black smokers*

## Ocean floors

Mid-ocean ridges are formed by lava which erupts beneath the sea and cools to form solid rock. This process mirrors the creation of volcanoes from cooled lava on the land. The ages of sea floor rocks increase in parallel bands outward from central ocean ridges.

**Ages of the ocean floor**

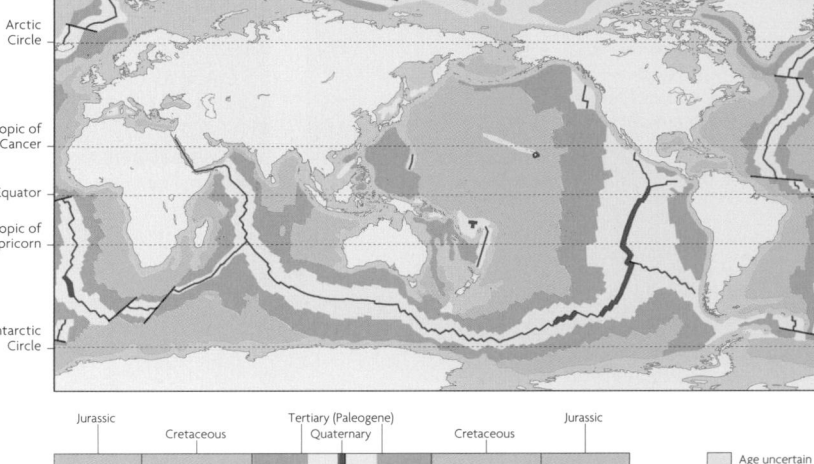

Arctic Circle
Tropic of Cancer
Equator
Tropic of Capricorn
Antarctic Circle

Jurassic
Cretaceous
Tertiary (Paleogene)
Quaternary
Cretaceous
Jurassic

| 208 | 145 | 65 | 23 | 0 | 23 | 65 | 145 | 208 |
|---|---|---|---|---|---|---|---|---|
| *million years old* | | | | Tertiary (Neogene) | | | | *million years old* |

Age uncertain
Continental shelf and island arcs

▲ *Currents in the* Southern Ocean *are driven by some of the world's fiercest winds, including the Roaring Forties, Furious Fifties, and Shrieking Sixties.*

▲ *The* Pacific Ocean *is the world's largest and deepest ocean, covering over one-third of the surface of the Earth.*

▲ *The* Atlantic Ocean *was formed when the landmasses of the eastern and western hemispheres began to drift apart 180 million years ago.*

## Deposition of sediment

Storms, earthquakes, and volcanic activity trigger underwater currents known as turbidity currents which scour sand and gravel from the continental shelf, creating underwater canyons. These strong currents pick up material deposited at river mouths and deltas, and carry it across the continental shelf and through the underwater canyons, where it is eventually laid down on the ocean floor in the form of fans.

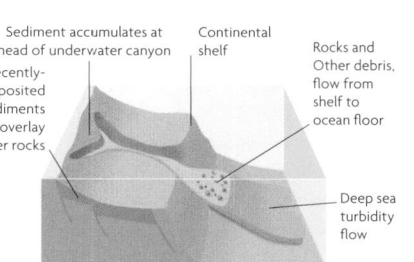

*How sediment is deposited on the ocean floor*

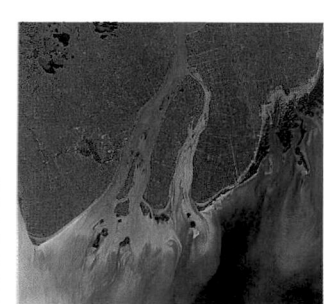

► *Satellite image of the Yangtze (Chang Jiang) Delta, in which the land appears red. The river deposits immense quantities of silt into the East China Sea, much of which will eventually reach the deep ocean floor.*

## Surface water

Ocean currents move warm water away from the Equator toward the poles, while cold water is, in turn, moved towards the Equator. This is the main way in wh ch the Earth distributes surface heat and is a major climatic control. Approximately 4000 million years ago, the Earth was dominated by oceans and there was no land to interrupt the flow of the currents, which would have flowed as straight lines, simply influenced by the Earth's rotation.

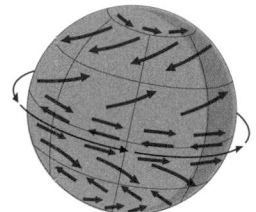

*Idealized globe showing the movement of water around a landless Earth.*

## Ocean currents

Surface currents are driven by the prevailing winds and by the spinning motion of the Earth, which drives the currents into circulating whirlpools, or gyres. Deep sea currents, over 330 ft (100 m) below the surface, are driven by differences in water temperature and salinity, which have an impact on the density of deep water and on its movement.

### Surface temperature and currents

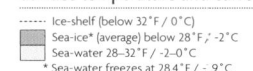

**Surface temperature and currents**

- - - - Ice-shelf (below 32°F / 0°C)
▨ Sea-ice* (average) below 28°F, -2°C
☐ Sea-water 28–32°F / -2–0°C
* Sea-water freezes at 28.4°F / -.9°C
☐ 32–50°F / 0–10°C
☐ 50–68°F / 10–20°C
☐ 68–86°F / 20–30°C
→ warm current
→ cold current

## Tides and waves

Tides are created by the pull of the Sun and Moon's gravity on the surface of the oceans. The levels of high and low tides are influenced by the position of the Moon in relation to the Earth and Sun. Waves are formed by wind blowing over the surface of the water.

### High and low tides

The highest tides occur when the Earth, the Moon and the Sun are aligned *(below left)*. The lowest tides are experienced when the Sun and Moon align at right angles to one another *(below right)*.

### Tidal range and wave environments

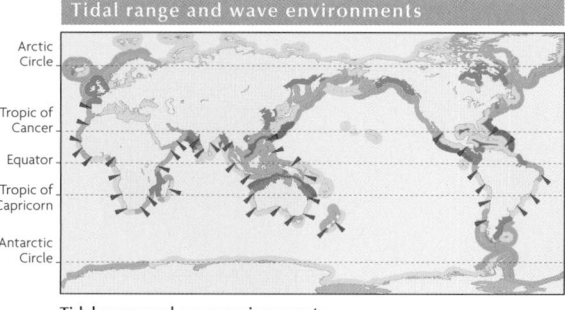

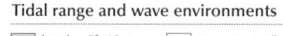

**Tidal range and wave environments**

☐ less than 7ft / 2m
☐ 7–13ft / 2–4m
☐ greater than 13ft / 4m
⇗ east coast swell
⇘ west coast swell
☐ tropical cyclone
☐ storm wave
☐ ice-shelf

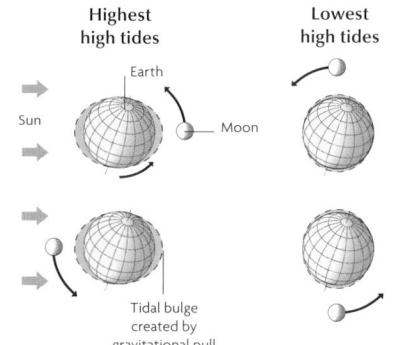

**Highest high tides**

Sun → → → Earth / Moon

Tidal bulge created by gravitational pull

**Lowest high tides**

### Deep sea temperature and currents

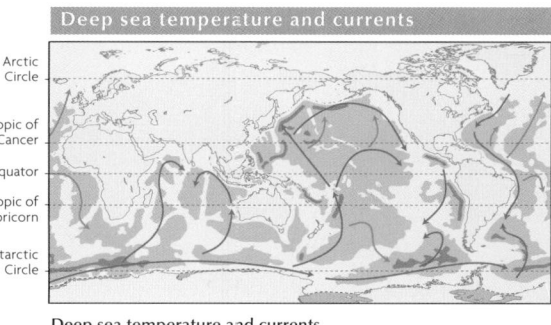

**Deep sea temperature and currents**

☐ Ice-shelf (below 32°F / 0°C)
☐ Sea-water 28–32°F / -2–0°C (below 16,400ft / 5000m)
☐ Sea-water 32–41°F /0–5°C (below 13,120ft / 4000m)
→ Primary currents
→ Secondary currents

# The global climate

The Earth's climatic types consist of stable patterns of weather conditions averaged out over a long period of time. Different climates are categorized according to particular combinations of temperature and humidity. By contrast, weather consists of short-term fluctuations in wind, temperature, and humidity conditions. Different climates are determined by latitude, altitude, the prevailing wind, and circulation of ocean currents. Longer-term changes in climate, such as global warming or the onset of ice ages, are punctuated by shorter-term events which comprise the day-to-day weather of a region, such as frontal depressions, hurricanes, and blizzards.

## The atmosphere, wind and weather

The Earth's atmosphere has been compared to a giant ocean of air which surrounds the planet. Its circulation patterns are similar to the currents in the oceans and are influenced by three factors; the Earth's orbit around the Sun and rotation about its axis, and variations in the amount of heat radiation received from the Sun. If both heat and moisture were not redistributed between the Equator and the poles, large areas of the Earth would be uninhabitable.

◀ Heavy fogs, as here in southern England, form as moisture-laden air passes over cold ground.

## Temperature

The world can be divided into three major climatic zones, stretching like large belts across the latitudes: the tropics which are warm; the cold polar regions and the temperate zones which lie between them. Temperatures across the Earth range from above 86°F (30°C) in the deserts to as low as -70°F (-55°C) at the poles. Temperature is also controlled by altitude; because air becomes cooler and less dense the higher it gets, mountainous regions are typically colder than those areas which are at, or close to, sea level.

## Global air circulation

Air does not simply flow from the Equator to the poles, it circulates in giant cells known as Hadley and Ferrel cells. As air warms it expands, becoming less dense and rising; this creates areas of low pressure. As the air rises it cools and condenses, causing heavy rainfall over the tropics and slight snowfall over the poles. This cool air then sinks, forming high pressure belts. At surface level in the tropics these sinking currents are deflected poleward as the westerlies and toward the equator as the trade winds. At the poles they become the polar easterlies.

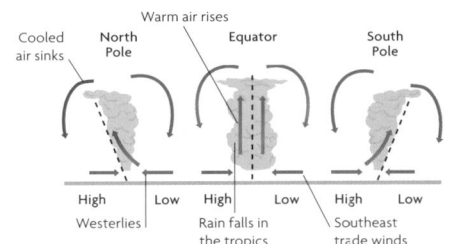

▲ The Antarctic pack ice expands its area by almost seven times during the winter as temperatures drop and surrounding seas freeze.

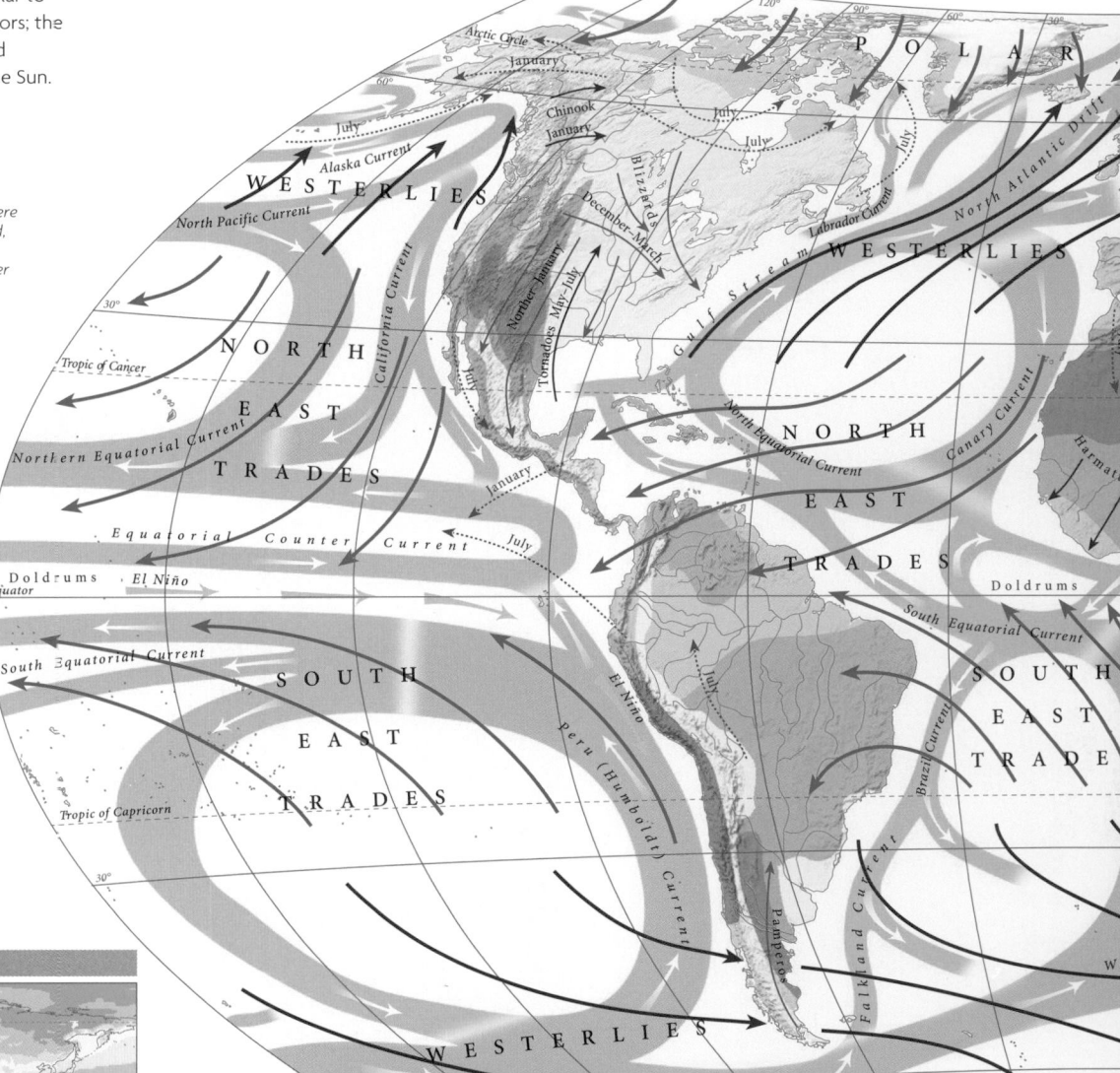

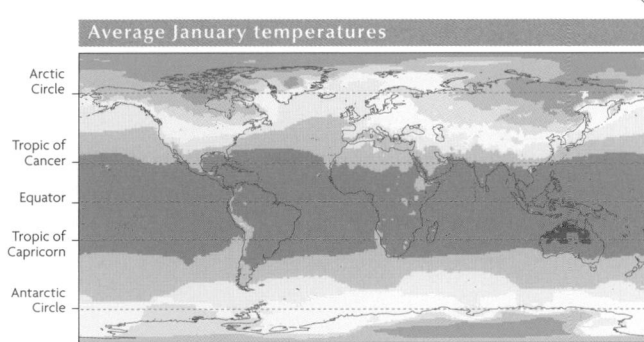

Average January temperatures

Arctic Circle
Tropic of Cancer
Equator
Tropic of Capricorn
Antarctic Circle

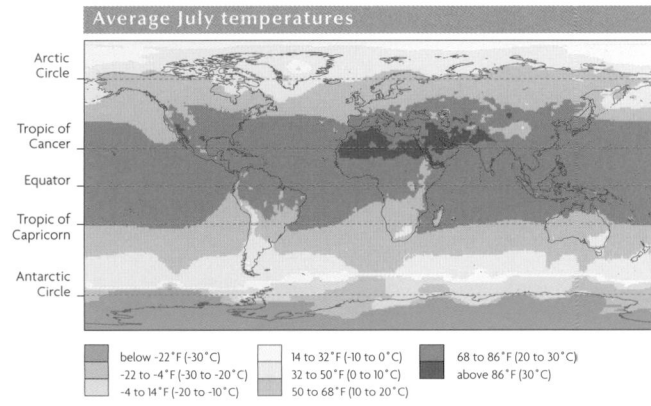

Average July temperatures

Arctic Circle
Tropic of Cancer
Equator
Tropic of Capricorn
Antarctic Circle

| | | |
|---|---|---|
| below -22°F (-30°C) | 14 to 32°F (-10 to 0°C) | 68 to 86°F (20 to 30°C) |
| -22 to -4°F (-30 to -20°C) | 32 to 50°F (0 to 10°C) | above 86°F (30°C) |
| -4 to 14°F (-20 to -10°C) | 50 to 68°F (10 to 20°C) | |

## Climatic change

The Earth is currently in a warm phase between ice ages. Warmer temperatures result in higher sea levels as more of the polar ice caps melt. Most of the world's population lives near coasts, so any changes which might cause sea levels to rise, could have a potentially disastrous impact.

▲ This ice fair, painted by Pieter Brueghel the Younger in the 17th century, shows the Little Ice Age which peaked around 300 years ago.

## The greenhouse effect

Gases such as carbon dioxide are known as "greenhouse gases" because they allow shortwave solar radiation to enter the Earth's atmosphere, but help to stop longwave radiation from escaping. This traps heat, raising the Earth's temperature. An excess of these gases, such as that which results from the burning of fossil fuels, helps trap more heat and can lead to global warming.

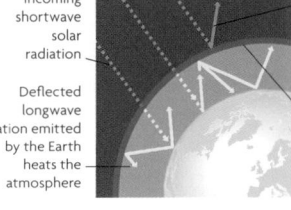

Incoming shortwave solar radiation

Deflected shortwave solar radiation

Deflected longwave radiation emitted by the Earth heats the atmosphere

Greenhouse gases prevent the escape of longwave radiation

◀ *The islands of the Caribbean, Mexico's Gulf coast and the southeastern US are often hit by hurricanes formed far out in the Atlantic.*

## Oceanic water circulation

In general, ocean currents parallel the movement of winds across the Earth's surface. Incoming solar energy is greatest at the Equator and least at the poles. So, water in the oceans heats up most at the Equator and flows poleward, cooling as it moves north or south toward the Arctic or Antarctic. The flow is eventually reversed and cold water currents move back toward the Equator. These ocean currents act as a vast system for moving heat from the Equator toward the poles and are a major influence on the distribution of the Earth's climates.

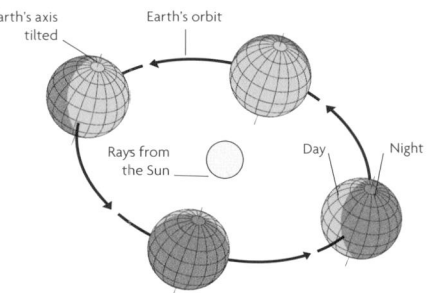

▲ *In marginal climatic zones years of drought can completely dry out the land and transform grassland to desert.*

### Map key

| Climate zones | | Ocean currents | Prevailing winds | Local winds |
|---|---|---|---|---|

- ice cap
- subarctic
- tundra
- continental
- temperate
- warm temperate
- mediterranean
- semi-arid
- arid
- hot humid
- humid equatorial
- tropical

Ocean currents: warm / cold

Prevailing winds: → warm / → cold

Local winds: → warm / → cold / → seasonal*

\* seasonal winds which can either be warm or cold

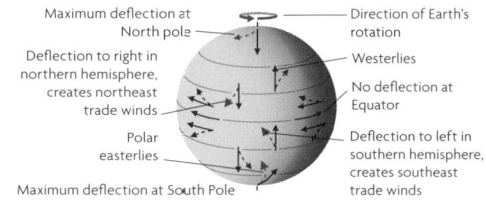

▲ *The wide range of environments found in the Andes is strongly related to their altitude, which modifies climatic influences. While the peaks are snow-capped, many protected interior valleys are semi-tropical.*

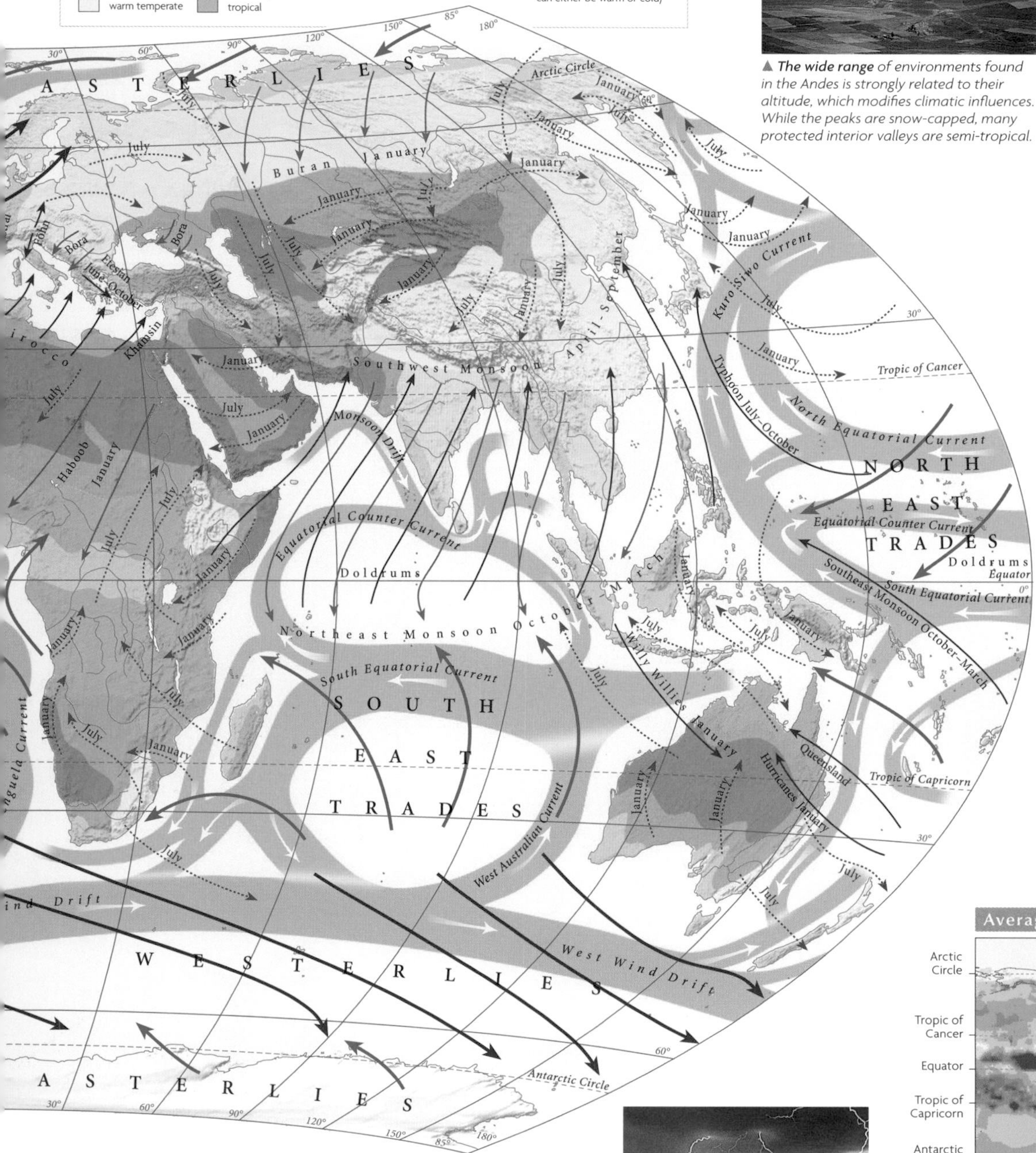

## Tilt and rotation

The tilt and rotation of the Earth during its annual orbit largely control the distribution of heat and moisture across its surface, which correspondingly controls its large-scale weather patterns. As the Earth annually rotates around the Sun, half its surface is receiving maximum radiation, creating summer and winter seasons. The angle of the Earth means that on average the tropics receive two and a half times as much heat from the Sun each day as the poles.

Earth's axis tilted — Earth's orbit

Rays from the Sun — Day — Night

## The Coriolis effect

The rotation of the Earth influences atmospheric circulation by deflecting winds and ocean currents. Winds blowing in the northern hemisphere are deflected to the right and those in the southern hemisphere are deflected to the left, creating large-scale patterns of wind circulation, such as the northeast and southeast trade winds and the westerlies. This effect is greatest at the poles and least at the Equator.

Maximum deflection at North pole — Direction of Earth's rotation

Deflection to right in northern hemisphere, creates northeast trade winds — Westerlies — No deflection at Equator

Polar easterlies — Deflection to left in southern hemisphere, creates southeast trade winds

Maximum deflection at South Pole

## Precipitation

When warm air expands, it rises and cools, and the water vapor it carries condenses to form clouds. Heavy, regular rainfall is characteristic of the equatorial region, while the poles are cold and receive only slight snowfall. Tropical regions have marked dry and rainy seasons, while in the temperate regions rainfall is relatively unpredictable.

▲ *Monsoon rains, which affect southern Asia from May to September, are caused by sea winds blowing across the warm land.*

▲ *Heavy tropical rainstorms occur frequently in Papua New Guinea, often causing soil erosion and landslides in cultivated areas.*

### Average January rainfall

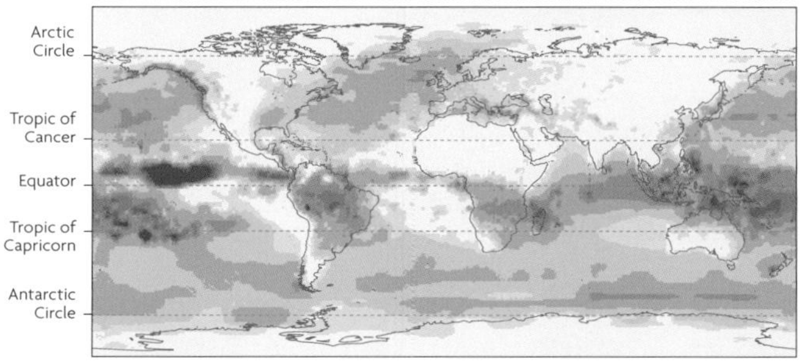

Arctic Circle
Tropic of Cancer
Equator
Tropic of Capricorn
Antarctic Circle

### Average July rainfall

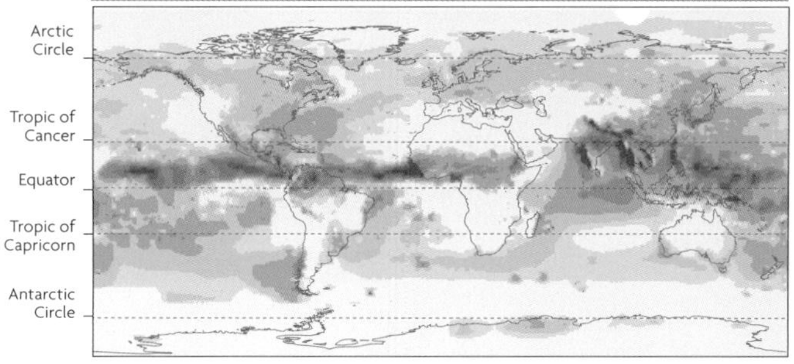

Arctic Circle
Tropic of Cancer
Equator
Tropic of Capricorn
Antarctic Circle

0–1 in (0–25 mm)
1–2 in (25–50 mm)
2–4 in (50–100 mm)
4–8 in (100–200 mm)
8–12 in (200–300 mm)
12–16 in (300–400 mm)
16–20 in (400–500 mm)
above 20 in (500 mm)

*(Map labels on main map:)*
EASTERLIES, Buran, Bora, Föhn, Bise, Sirocco, Khamsin, Haboob, Southwest Monsoon, April-September, Monsoon Drift, Kuro-Siwo Current, Typhoon July-October, Tropic of Cancer, NORTH EAST TRADES, North Equatorial Current, Equatorial Counter Current, Doldrums, Equator, South Equatorial Current, Southeast Monsoon October-March, SOUTH EAST TRADES, Northeast Monsoon October, Equatorial Counter Current, Doldrums, Willy Willies January, Queensland, Hurricanes January, Tropic of Capricorn, Benguela Current, West Australian Current, West Wind Drift, WESTERLIES, Antarctic Circle, EASTERLIES, Arctic Circle, January, July, March

▲ *The Atacama Desert in Chile is one of the driest places on Earth, with an average rainfall of less than 2 inches (50 mm) per year.*

▲ *The intensity of some blizzards in Canada and the northern US can give rise to snowdrifts as high as 10 ft (3 m).*

▲ *Violent thunderstorms occur along advancing cold fronts, when cold, dry air masses meet warm, moist air, which rises rapidly, its moisture condensing into thunderclouds. Rain and hail become electrically charged, causing lightning.*

## The rainshadow effect

When moist air is forced to rise by mountains, it cools and the water vapor falls as precipitation, either as rain or snow. Only the dry, cold air continues over the mountains, leaving inland areas with little or no rain. This is called the rainshadow effect and is one reason for the existence of the Mojave Desert in California, which lies east of the Coast Ranges.

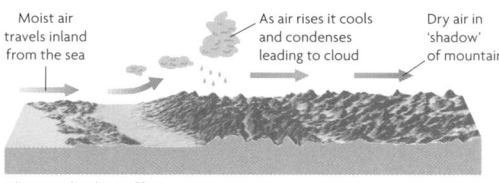

Moist air travels inland from the sea — As air rises it cools and condenses leading to cloud — Dry air in 'shadow' of mountain

*The rainshadow effect*

# Life on Earth

A unique combination of an oxygen-rich atmosphere and plentiful water is the key to life on Earth. Apart from the polar ice caps, there are few areas which have not been colonized by animals or plants over the course of the Earth's history. Plants process sunlight to provide them with their energy, and ultimately all the Earth's animals rely on plants for survival. Because of this reliance, plants are known as primary producers, and the availability of nutrients and temperature of an area is defined as its primary productivity, which affects the quantity and type of animals which are able to live there. This index is affected by climatic factors – cold and aridity restrict the quantity of life, whereas warmth and regular rainfall allow a greater diversity of species.

## Biogeographical regions

The Earth can be divided into a series of biogeographical regions, or biomes, ecological communities where certain species of plant and animal coexist within particular climatic conditions. Within these broad classifications, other factors including soil richness, altitude, and human activities such as urbanization, intensive agriculture, and deforestation, affect the local distribution of living species within each biome.

### Polar regions
A layer of permanent ice at the Earth's poles covers both seas and land. Very little plant and animal life can exist in these harsh regions.

### Tundra
A desolate region, with long, dark freezing winters and short, cold summers. With virtually no soil and large areas of permanently frozen ground known as permafrost, the tundra is largely treeless, though it is briefly clothed by small flowering plants in the summer months.

### Needleleaf forests
With milder summers than the tundra and less wind, these areas are able to support large forests of coniferous trees.

### Broadleaf forests
Much of the northern hemisphere was once covered by deciduous forests, which occurred in areas with marked seasonal variations. Most deciduous forests have been cleared for human settlement.

### Temperate rain forests
In warmer wetter areas, such as southern China, temperate deciduous forests are replaced by evergreen forest.

### Deserts
Deserts are areas with negligible rainfall. Most hot deserts lie within the tropics; cold deserts are dry because of their distance from the moisture-providing sea.

### Mediterranean
Hot, dry summers and short winters typify these areas, which were once covered by evergreen shrubs and woodland, but have now been cleared by humans for agriculture.

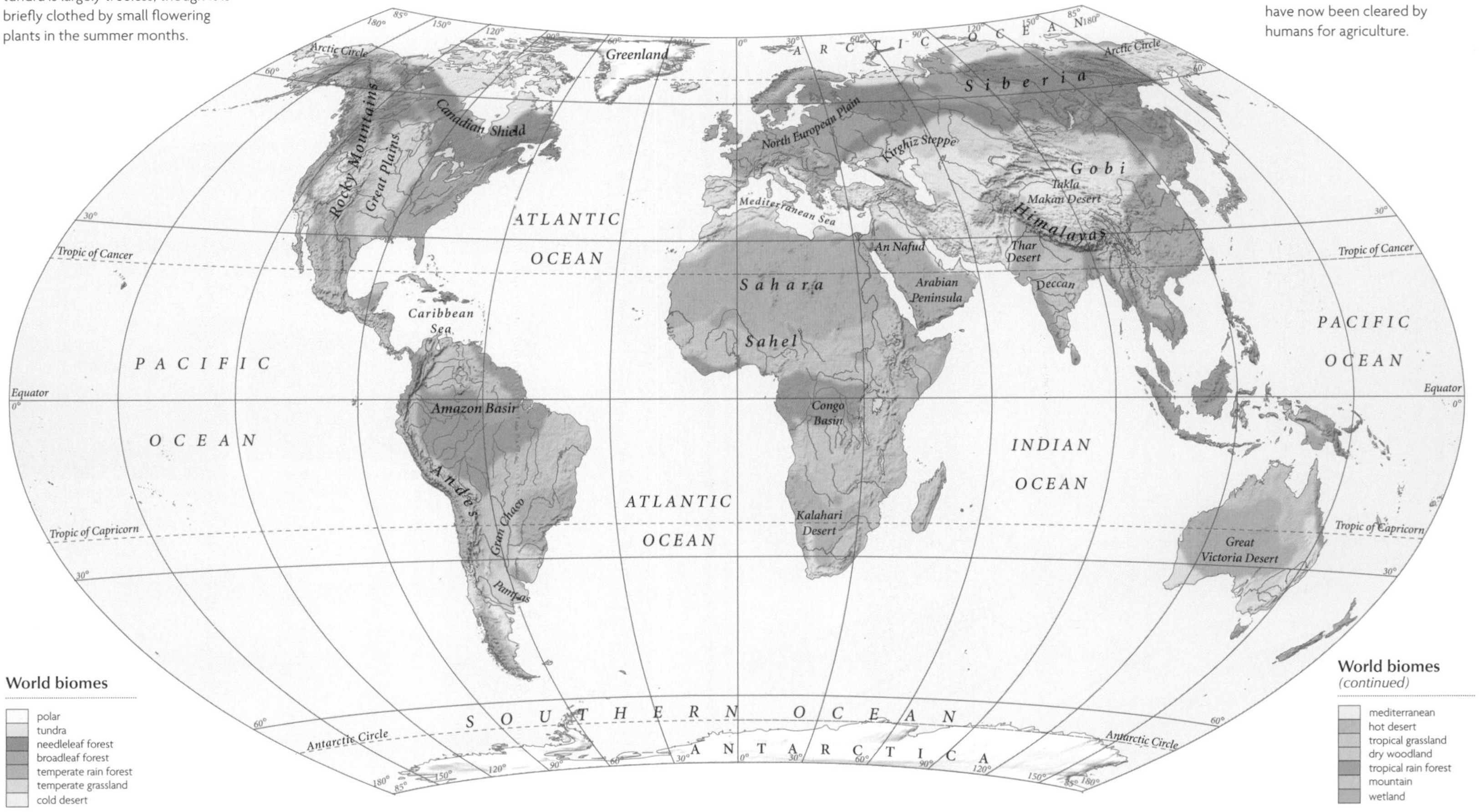

### World biomes
- polar
- tundra
- needleleaf forest
- broadleaf forest
- temperate rain forest
- temperate grassland
- cold desert

### World biomes
*(continued)*
- mediterranean
- hot desert
- tropical grassland
- dry woodland
- tropical rain forest
- mountain
- wetland

### Tropical and temperate grasslands
The major grassland areas are found in the centers of the larger continental landmasses. In Africa's tropical savannah regions, seasonal rainfall alternates with drought. Temperate grasslands, also known as steppes and prairies are found in the northern hemisphere, and in South America, where they are known as the pampas.

### Dry woodlands
Trees and shrubs, adapted to dry conditions, grow widely spaced from one another, interspersed by savannah grasslands.

### Tropical rain forests
Characterized by year-round warmth and high rainfall, tropical rain forests contain the highest diversity of plant and animal species on Earth.

### Mountains
Though the lower slopes of mountains may be thickly forested, only ground-hugging shrubs and other vegetation will grow above the tree line which varies according to both altitude and latitude.

### Wetlands
Rarely lying above sea level, wetlands are marshes, swamps, and tidal flats. Some, with their moist, fertile soils, are rich feeding grounds for fish and breeding grounds for birds. Others have little soil structure and are too acidic to support much plant and animal life.

# Biodiversity

The number of plant and animal species, and the range of genetic diversity within the populations of each species, make up the Earth's biodiversity. The plants and animals which are endemic to a region – that is, those which are found nowhere else in the world – are also important in determining levels of biodiversity. Human settlement and intervention have encroached on many areas of the world once rich in endemic plant and animal species. Increasing international efforts are being made to monitor and conserve the biodiversity of the Earth's remaining wild places.

## Animal adaptation

The degree of an animal's adaptability to different climates and conditions is extremely important in ensuring its success as a species. Many animals, particularly the largest mammals, are becoming restricted to ever-smaller regions as human development and modern agricultural practices reduce their natural habitats. In contrast, humans have been responsible – both deliberately and accidentally – for the spread of some of the world's most successful species. Many of these introduced species are now more numerous than the indigenous animal populations.

## Polar animals

The frozen wastes of the polar regions are able to support only a small range of species which derive their nutritional requirements from the sea. Animals such as the walrus *(left)* have developed insulating fat, stocky limbs, and double-layered coats to enable them to survive in the freezing conditions.

## Desert animals

Many animals which live in the extreme heat and aridity of the deserts are able to survive for days and even months with very little food or water. Their bodies are adapted to lose heat quickly and to store fat and water. The Gila monster *(above)* stores fat in its tail.

## Amazon rain forest

The vast Amazon Basin is home to the world's greatest variety of animal species. Animals are adapted to live at many different levels from the treetops to the tangled undergrowth which lies beneath the canopy. The sloth *(below)* hangs upside down in the branches. Its fur grows from its stomach to its back to enable water to run off quickly.

**Diversity of animal species**

**Number of animal species per country**

- more than 2000
- 1000–1999
- 700–999
- 400–699
- 200–399
- 100–199
- 0–99
- data not available

## Marine biodiversity

The oceans support a huge variety of different species, from the world's largest mammals like whales and dolphins down to the tiniest plankton. The greatest diversities occur in the warmer seas of continental shelves, where plants are easily able to photosynthesize, and around coral reefs, where complex ecosystems are found. On the ocean floor, nematodes can exist at a depth of more than 10,000 ft (3000 m) below sea level.

### High altitudes

Few animals exist in the rarefied atmosphere of the highest mountains. However, birds of prey such as eagles and vultures *(above)*, with their superb eyesight can soar as high as 23,000 ft (7000 m) to scan for prey below.

## Urban animals

The growth of cities has reduced the amount of habitat available to many species. A number of animals are now moving closer into urban areas to scavenge from the detritus of the modern city *(left)*. Rodents, particularly rats and mice, have existed in cities for thousands of years, and many insects, especially moths, quickly develop new coloring to provide them with camouflage.

## Endemic species

Isolated areas such as Australia and the island of Madagascar, have the greatest range of endemic species. In Australia, these include marsupials such as the kangaroo *(below)*, which carry their young in pouches on their bodies. Destruction of habitat, pollution, hunting, and predators introduced by humans, are threatening this unique biodiversity.

# Plant adaptation

Environmental conditions, particularly climate, soil type, and the extent of competition with other organisms, influence the development of plants into a number of distinctive forms. Similar conditions in quite different parts of the world create similar adaptations in the plants, which may then be modified by other, local, factors specific to the region.

### Cold conditions

In areas where temperatures rarely rise above freezing, plants such as lichens *(left)* and mosses grow densely, close to the ground.

## Rain forests

Most of the world's largest and oldest plants are found in rain forests; warmth and heavy rainfall provide ideal conditions for vast plants like the world's largest flower, the rafflesia *(left)*.

## Hot, dry conditions

Arid conditions lead to the development of plants whose surface area has been reduced to a minimum to reduce water loss. In cacti *(above)*, which can survive without water for months, leaves are minimal or not present at all.

## Ancient plants

Some of the world's most primitive plants still exist today, including algae, cycads, and many ferns *(above)*, reflecting the success with which they have adapted to changing conditions.

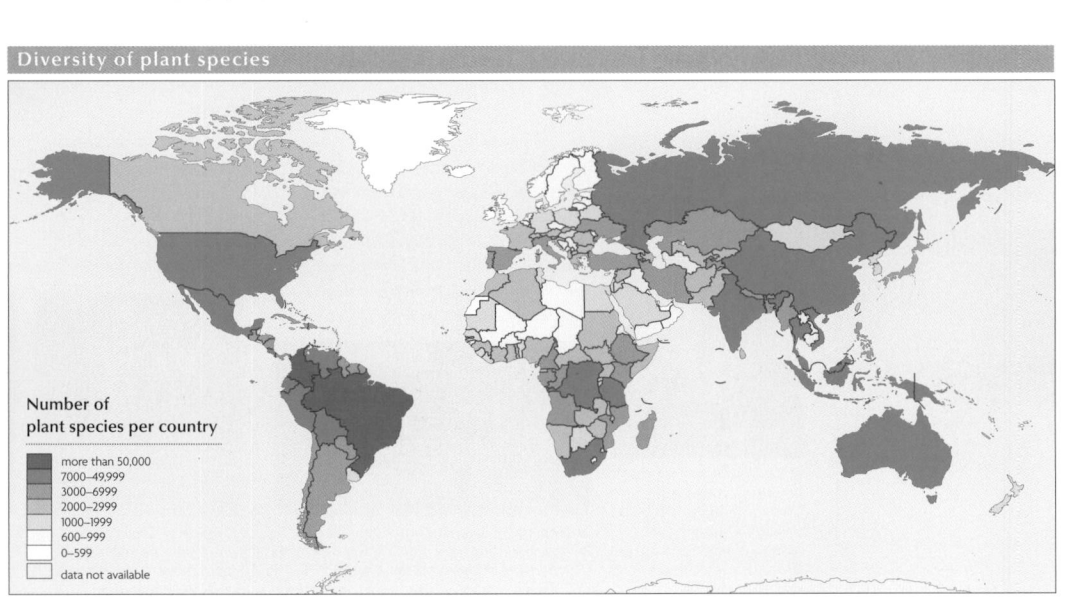

**Diversity of plant species**

**Number of plant species per country**

- more than 50,000
- 7000–49,999
- 3000–6999
- 2000–2999
- 1000–1999
- 600–999
- 0–599
- data not available

## Resisting predators

A great variety of plants have developed devices including spines *(above)*, poisons, stinging hairs, and an unpleasant taste or smell to deter animal predators.

## Weeds

Weeds such as bindweed *(above)* are fast-growing, easily dispersed, and tolerant of a number of different environments, enabling them to quickly colonize suitable habitats. They are among the most adaptable of all plants.

# Population and settlement

The Earth's population is projected to rise from its current level of about 7.7 billion to reach some 11 billion by 2050. The global distribution of this rapidly growing population is very uneven, and is dictated by climate, terrain, and natural and economic resources. The great majority of the Earth's people live in coastal zones, and along river valleys. Deserts cover over 20% of the Earth's surface, but support less than 5% of the world's population. It is estimated that over half of the world's population live in cities – most of them in Asia – as a result of mass migration from rural areas in search of jobs. Many of these people live in the so-called "megacities," some with populations as great as 40 million.

## Patterns of settlement

The past 200 years have seen the most radical shift in world population patterns in recorded history.

## Nomadic life

All the world's peoples were hunter-gatherers 10,000 years ago. Today nomads, who live by following available food resources, account for less than 0.0001% of the world's population. They are mainly pastoral herders, moving their livestock from place to place in search of grazing land.

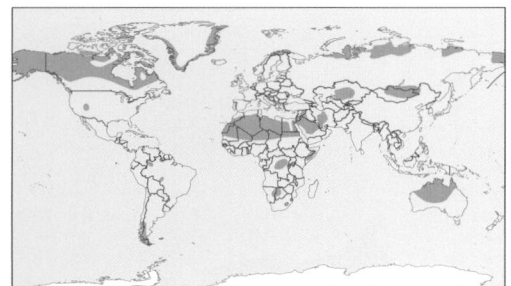

**Nomadic population**

◼ Nomadic population area

## The growth of cities

In 1900 there were only 14 cities in the world with populations of more than a million, mostly in the northern hemisphere. Today, as more and more people in the developing world migrate to towns and cities, there are over 70 cities whose population exceeds 5 million, and around 490 "million-cities."

**Million-cities in 1900**

**Million-cities in 1900**

• Cities over 1 million population

**Million-cities in 2005**

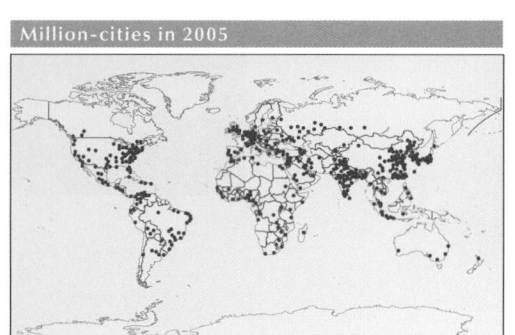

**Million-cities in 2005**

• Cities over 1 million population

## North America

The eastern and western seaboards of the US, with huge expanses of interconnected cities, towns, and suburbs, are vast, densely-populated megalopolises. Central America and the Caribbean also have high population densities. Yet, away from the coasts and in the wildernesses of northern Canada the land is very sparsely settled.

▲ *Vancouver on Canada's west coast, grew up as a port city. In recent years it has attracted many Asian immigrants, particularly from the Pacific Rim.*

▲ *North America's central plains, the continent's agricultural heartland, are thinly populated and highly productive.*

## Europe

With its temperate climate, and rich mineral and natural resources, Europe is generally very densely settled. The continent acts as a magnet for economic migrants from the developing world, and immigration is now widely restricted. Birthrates in Europe are generally low, and in some countries, such as Germany, the populations have stabilized at zero growth, with a fast-growing elderly population.

▲ *Many European cities, like Siena, once reflected the "ideal" size for human settlements. Modern technological advances have enabled them to grow far beyond the original walls.*

▲ *Within the densely-populated Netherlands the reclamation of coastal wetlands is vital to provide much-needed land for agriculture and settlement.*

**Population density**
**(inhabitants per sq mile)**

◼ 520–2600
◼ 260–520
◼ 130–260
◼ 52–130
◼ 26–52
◼ 13–26
◼ 3–13
◻ Fewer than 3

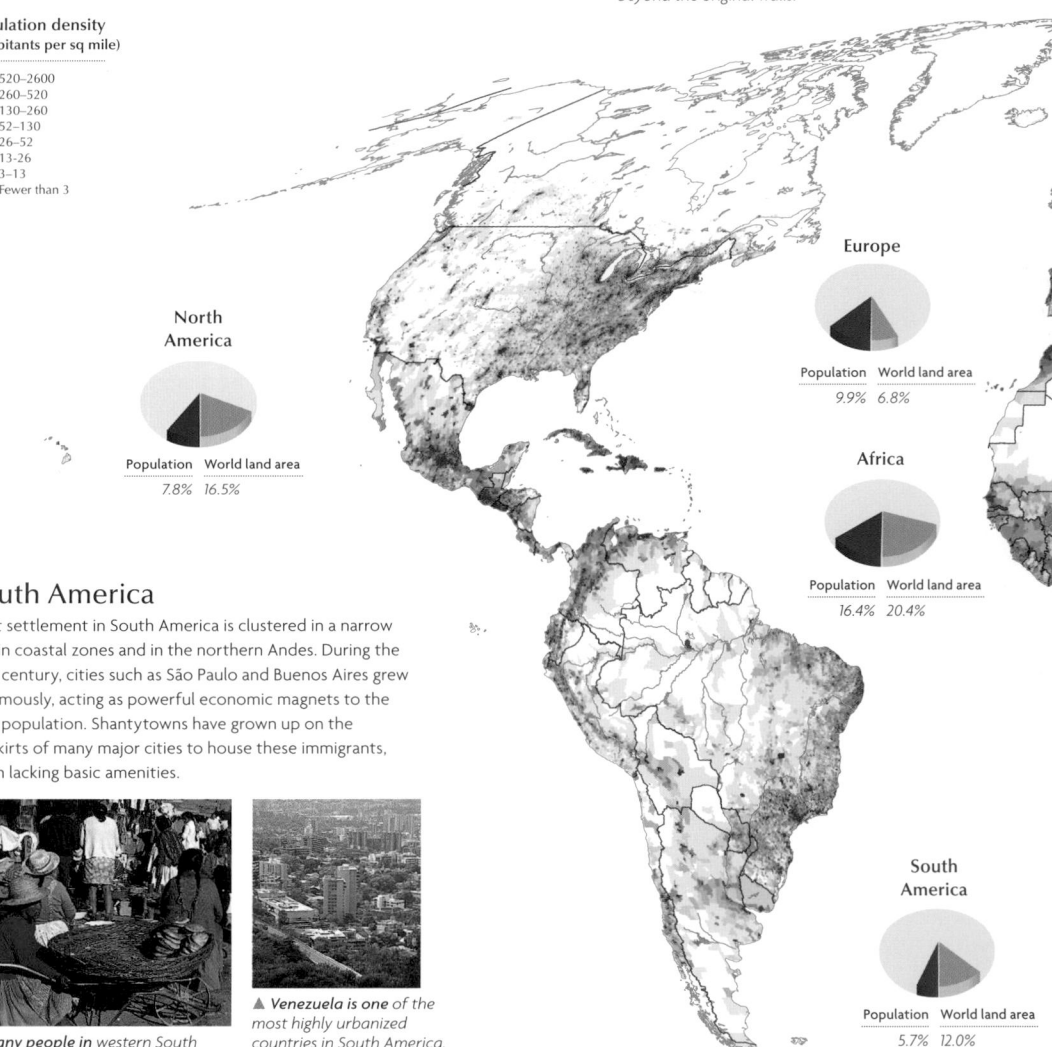

**North America**

Population 7.8%  World land area 16.5%

**Europe**

Population 9.9%  World land area 6.8%

**Africa**

Population 16.4%  World land area 20.4%

**South America**

Population 5.7%  World land area 12.0%

## South America

Most settlement in South America is clustered in a narrow belt in coastal zones and in the northern Andes. During the 20th century, cities such as São Paulo and Buenos Aires grew enormously, acting as powerful economic magnets to the rural population. Shantytowns have grown up on the outskirts of many major cities to house these immigrants, often lacking basic amenities.

▲ *Many people in western South America live at high altitudes in the Andes, both in cities and in villages such as this one in Bolivia.*

▲ *Venezuela is one of the most highly urbanized countries in South America, with nearly 90% of the population living in cities such as Caracas.*

## Africa

The arid climate of much of Africa means that settlement of the continent is sparse, focusing in coastal areas and fertile regions such as the Nile Valley. Africa still has a high proportion of nomadic agriculturalists, although many are now becoming settled, and the population is predominantly rural.

◀ *Cities such as Nairobi (above), Cairo, and Johannesburg have grown rapidly in recent years, although only Cairo has a significant population on a global scale.*

▲ *Traditional lifestyles and homes persist across much of Africa, which has a higher proportion of rural or village-based population than any other continent.*

## Asia

Most Asian settlement originally centered around the great river valleys such as the Indus, the Ganges, and the Yangtze. Today, almost 60% of the world's population lives in Asia, many in burgeoning cities – particularly in the economically-buoyant Pacific Rim countries. Even rural population densities are high in many countries; practices such as terracing in Southeast Asia making the most of the available land.

▲ *Many of China's cities are now vast urban areas with populations of more than 5 million people.*

▲ *This stilt village in Bangladesh is built to resist the regular flooding. Pressure on land, even in rural areas, forces many people to live in marginal areas.*

# Population structures

Population pyramids are an effective means of showing the age structures of different countries, and highlighting changing trends in population growth and decline. The typical pyramid for a country with a growing, youthful population, is broad-based *(left)*, reflecting a high birthrate and a far larger number of young rather than elderly people. In contrast, countries with populations whose numbers are stabilizing have a more balanced distribution of people in each age band, and may even have lower numbers of people in the youngest age ranges, indicating both a high life expectancy, and that the population is now barely replacing itself *(right)*. The Russian Federation *(center)* is suffering from a declining population, forcing the government to consider a number of measures, including tax incentives and immigration, in an effort to stabilize the population .

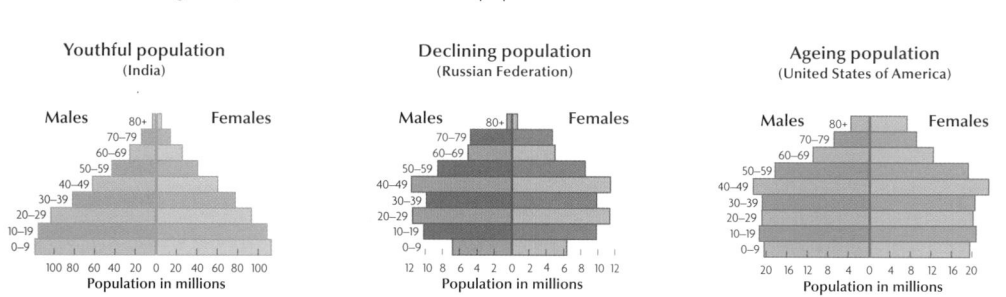

Youthful population (India) — Declining population (Russian Federation) — Ageing population (United States of America)

# Population growth

Improvements in food supply and advances in medicine have both played a major role in the remarkable growth in global population, which has increased five-fold over the last 150 years. Food supplies have risen with the mechanization of agriculture and improvements in crop yields. Better nutrition, together with higher standards of public health and sanitation, have led to increased longevity and higher birthrates.

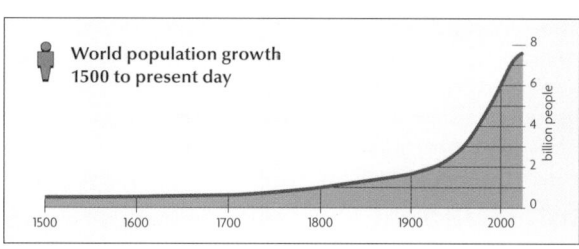
World population growth 1500 to present day

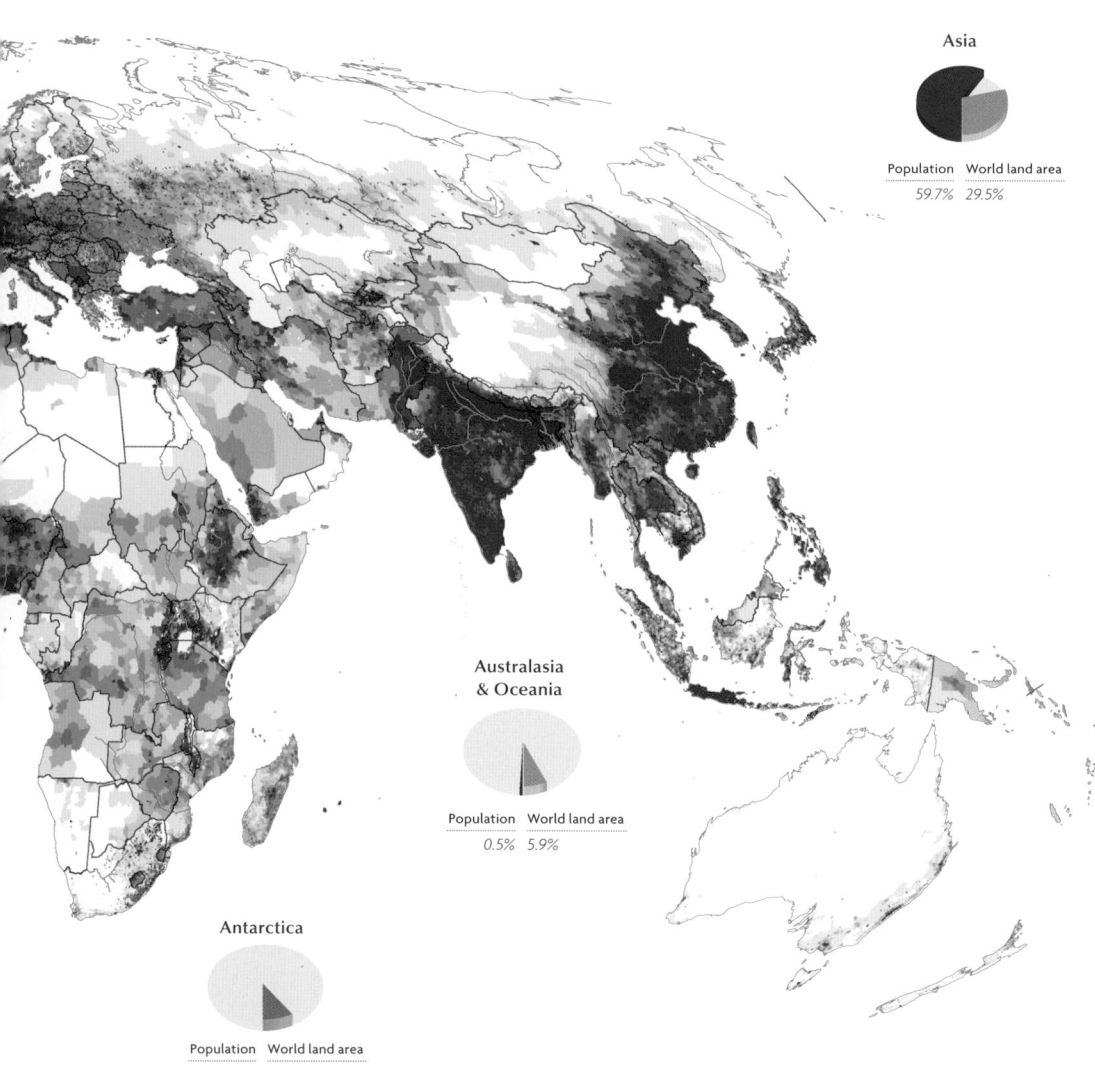

Asia — Population 59.7% World land area 29.5%

Australasia & Oceania — Population 0.5% World land area 5.9%

Antarctica — Population 0.0% World land area 9.2%

# World nutrition

Two-thirds of the world's food supply is consumed by the industrialized nations, many of which have a daily calorific intake far higher than is necessary for their populations to maintain a healthy body weight. In contrast, in the developing world, about 800 million people do not have enough food to meet their basic nutritional needs.

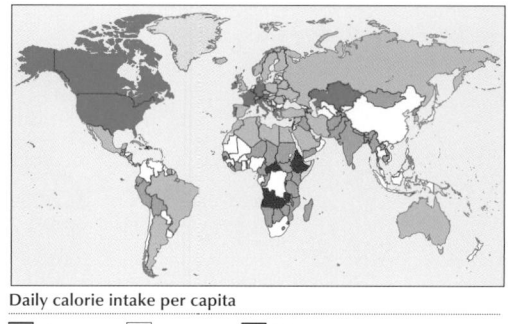

Daily calorie intake per capita — above 3500, 3000–3500, 2500–3000, 2000–2500, below 2000, data not available

# World life expectancy

Improved public health and living standards have greatly increased life expectancy in the developed world, where people can now expect to live twice as long as they did 100 years ago. In many of the world's poorest nations, inadequate nutrition and disease, means that the average life expectancy still does not exceed 45 years.

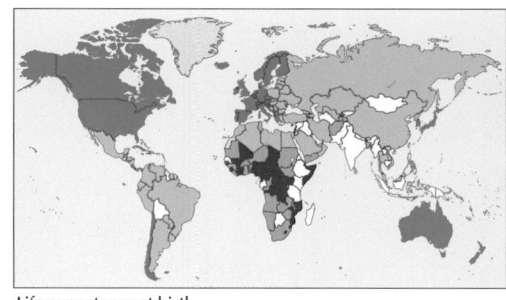

Life expectancy at birth — above 78 years, 71–78 years, 65–71 years, 60–65 years, below 60 years, data not available

# Australasia and Oceania

This is the world's most sparsely settled region. The peoples of Australia and New Zealand live mainly in the coastal cities, with only scattered settlements in the arid interior. The Pacific islands can only support limited populations because of their remoteness and lack of resources.

▶ *Brisbane, on Australia's Gold Coast is the most rapidly expanding city in the country. The great majority of Australia's population lives in cities near the coasts.*

◀ *The remote highlands of Papua New Guinea are home to a wide variety of peoples, many of whom still subsist by traditional hunting and gathering.*

# Average world birth rates

Birthrates are much higher in Africa, Asia, and South America than in Europe and North America. Increased affluence and easy access to contraception are both factors which can lead to a significant decline in a country's birthrate.

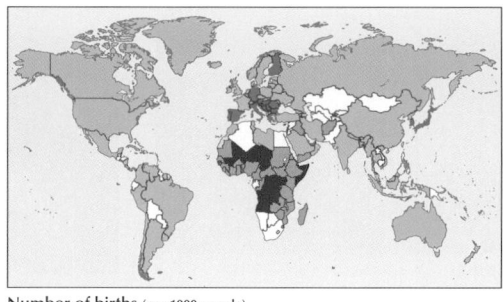

Number of births (per 1000 people) — above 40, 30–40, 20–30, 10–20, below 10, data not available

# World infant mortality

In parts of the developing world infant mortality rates are still high; access to medical services such as immunization, adequate nutrition, and the promotion of breast-feeding have been important in combating infant mortality.

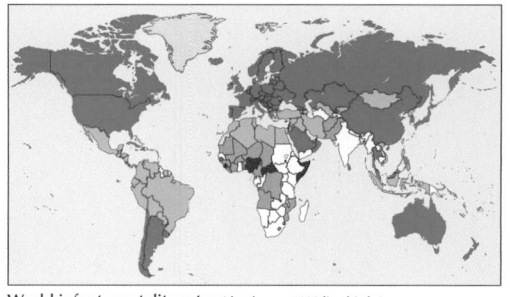
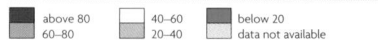

World infant mortality rates (deaths per 1000 live births) — above 80, 60–80, 40–60, 20–40, below 20, data not available

# The economic system

The wealthy countries of the developed world, with their aggressive, market-led economies and their access to productive new technologies and international markets, dominate the world economic system. At the other extreme, many of the countries of the developing world are locked in a cycle of national debt, rising populations, and unemployment. In 2008 a major financial crisis swept the world's banking sector leading to a huge downturn in the global economy. Despite this, China overtook Japan in 2010 to become the world's second largest economy.

## Trade blocs

International trade blocs are formed when groups of countries, often already enjoying close military and political ties, join together to offer mutually preferential terms of trade for both imports and exports. Increasingly, global trade is dominated by three main blocs: the EU, NAFTA, and ASEAN. They are supplanting older trade blocs such as the Commonwealth, a legacy of colonialism.

**Trade blocs**

EU / CACM / NAFTA / SADC / ASEAN / ECOWAS / LAIA / CEEAC

## International trade flows

World trade acts as a stimulus to national economies, encouraging growth. Over the last three decades, as heavy industries have declined, services – banking, insurance, tourism, airlines, and shipping – have taken an increasingly large share of world trade. Manufactured articles now account for nearly two-thirds of world trade; raw materials and food make up less than a quarter of the total.

**Shipping**
Ships carry 80% of international cargo, and extensive container ports, where cargo is stored, are vital links in the international transportation network.

**Multinationals**
Multinational companies are increasingly penetrating inaccessible markets. The reach of many American commodities is now global.

**Primary products**
Many countries, particularly in the Caribbean and Africa, are still reliant on primary products such as rubber and coffee, which makes them vulnerable to fluctuating prices.

**Service industries**
Service industries such as banking, tourism and insurance were the fastest-growing industrial sector in the last half of the 20th century. Lloyds of London is the center of the world insurance market.

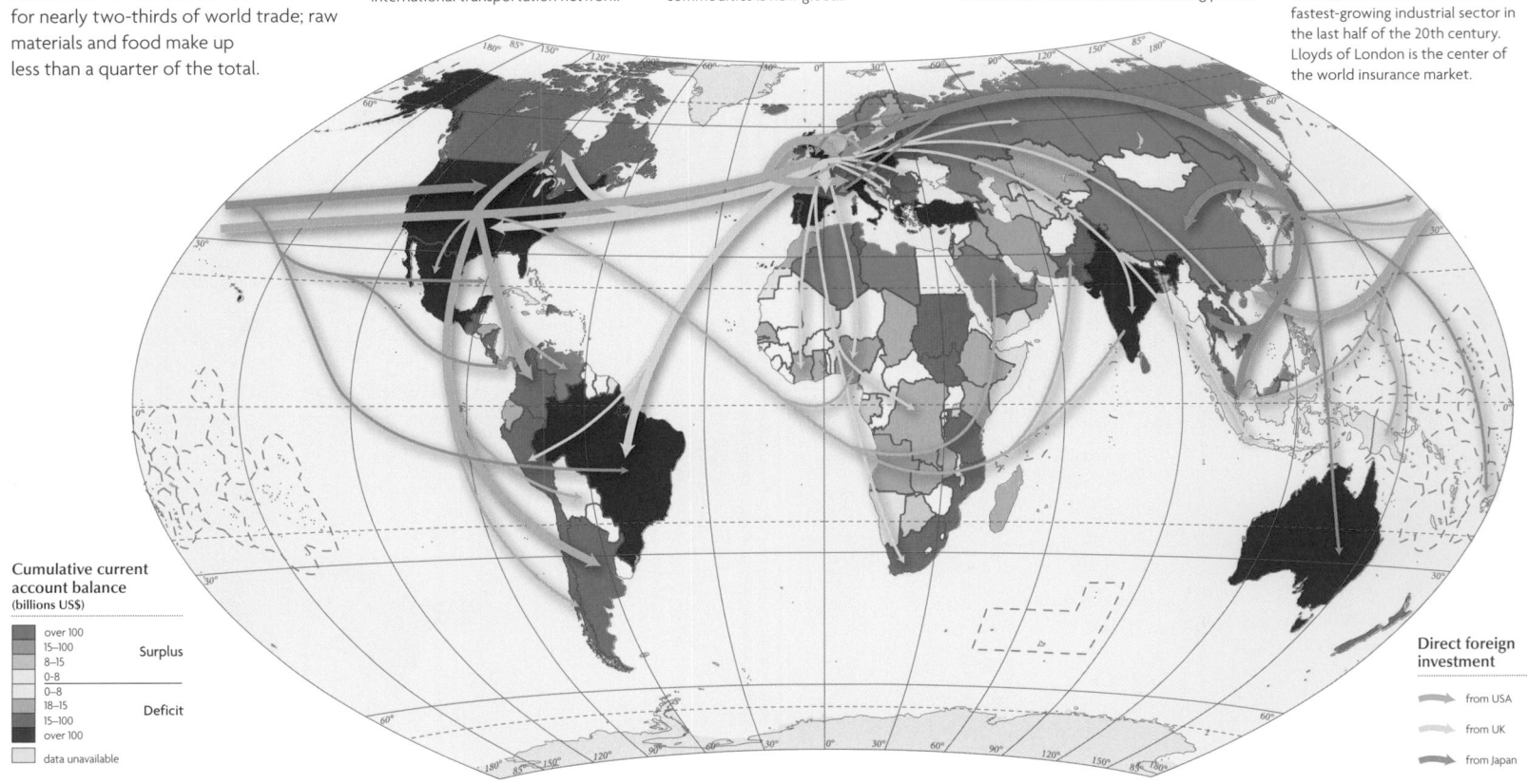

**Cumulative current account balance (billions US$)**

over 100 / 15–100 / 8–15 / 0–8 — Surplus
0–8 / 18–15 / 15–100 / over 100 — Deficit
data unavailable

**Direct foreign investment**
from USA
from UK
from Japan

## World money markets

The financial world has traditionally been dominated by three major centers – Tokyo, New York, and London, which house the headquarters of stock exchanges, multinational corporations and international banks. Their geographic location means that, at any one time in a 24-hour day, one major market is open for trading in shares, currencies, and commodities. Since the late 1980s, technological advances have enabled transactions between financial centers to occur at ever-greater speed, and new markets have sprung up throughout the world.

### New stock markets

New stock markets are now opening in many parts of the world, where economies have recently emerged from state controls. In Moscow and Beijing, and several countries in eastern Europe, newly-opened stock exchanges reflect the transition to market-driven economies.

### The developing world

International trade in capital and currency is dominated by the rich nations of the northern hemisphere. In parts of Africa and Asia, where exports of any sort are extremely limited, home-produced commodities are simply sold in local markets.

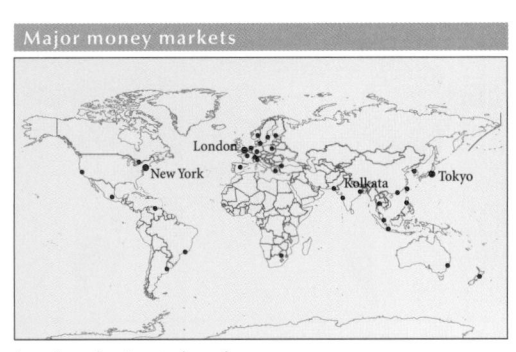

**Major money markets**

Location of major stock markets

● Major stock markets

▲ *The Tokyo Stock Market* crashed in 1990, leading to a slow-down in the growth of the world's most powerful economy, and a refocusing on economic policy away from export-led growth and toward the domestic market.

▲ *Dealers at the* Kolkata Stock Market. The Indian economy has been opened up to foreign investment and many multinationals now have bases there.

▲ *Markets have thrived* in communist Vietnam since the introduction of a liberal economic policy.

# World wealth disparity

A global assessment of Gross Domestic Product (GDP) by nation reveals great disparities. The developed world, with only a quarter of the world's population, has 80% of the world's manufacturing income. Civil war, conflict, and political instability further undermine the economic self-sufficiency of many of the world's poorest nations.

## Urban sprawl

Cities are expanding all over the developing world, attracting economic migrants in search of work and opportunities. In cities such as Rio de Janeiro, housing has not kept pace with the population explosion, and squalid shanty towns (favelas) rub shoulders with middle-class housing.

▲ **The favelas of** Rio de Janeiro sprawl over the hills surrounding the city.

## Agricultural economies

In parts of the developing world, people survive by subsistence farming – only growing enough food for themselves and their families. With no surplus product, they are unable to exchange goods for currency, the only means of escaping the poverty trap. In other countries, farmers have been encouraged to concentrate on growing a single crop for the export market. This reliance on cash crops leaves farmers vulnerable to crop failure and to changes in the market price of the crop.

## Urban decay

Although the US still dominates the global economy, it faces deficits in both the federal budget and the balance of trade. Vast discrepancies in personal wealth, high levels of unemployment, and the dismantling of welfare provisions throughout the 1980s have led to severe deprivation in several of the inner cities of North America's industrial heartland.

▲ **Cities such as** Detroit have been badly hit by the decline in heavy industry.

## Booming cities

Since the 1980s the Chinese government has set up special industrial zones, such as Shanghai, where foreign investment is encouraged through tax incentives. Migrants from rural China pour into these regions in search of work, creating "boomtown" economies.

◄ **Foreign investment has** encouraged new infrastructure development in cities like Shanghai.

## Economic "tigers"

The economic "tigers" of the Pacific Rim – China, Singapore, and South Korea – have grown faster than Europe and the US over the last decade. Their export- and service-led economies have benefited from stable government, low labor costs, and foreign investment.

▲ **Hong Kong, with** its fine natural harbor, is one of the most important ports in Asia.

### Comparative world wealth

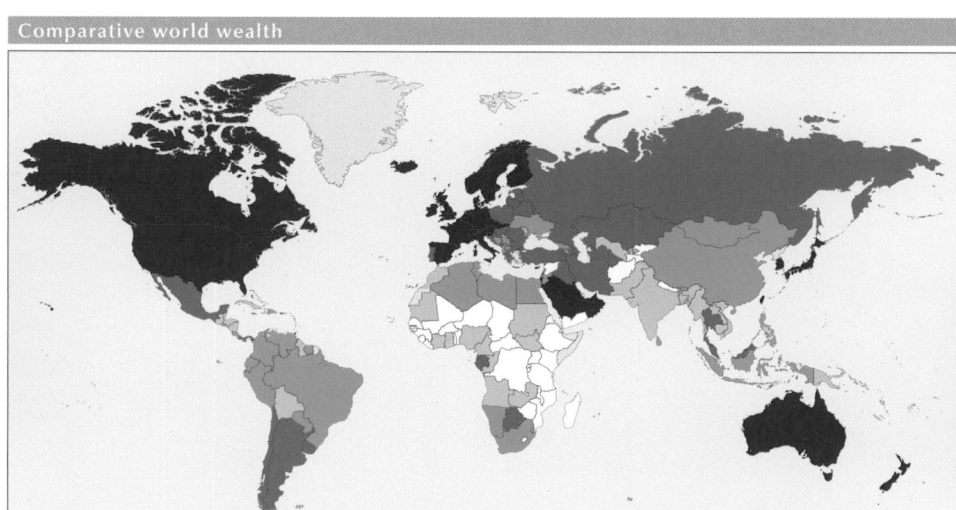

**World economies - average GNI per capita (US$)**

- above 30,000
- 16,000–30,000
- 8000–16,000
- 3500–8000
- below 3500
- data unavailable

▲ **The Ugandan uplands** are fertile, but poor infrastructure hampers the export of cash crops.

▲ **A shopping arcade** in Paris displays a great profusion of luxury goods.

## The affluent West

The capital cities of many countries in the developed world are showcases for consumer goods, reflecting the increasing importance of the service sector, and particularly the retail sector, in the world economy. The idea of shopping as a leisure activity is unique to the western world. Luxury goods and services attract visitors, who in turn generate tourist revenue.

# Tourism

In 2004, there were over 940 million tourists worldwide. Tourism is now the world's biggest single industry, employing over 130 million people, though frequently in low-paid unskilled jobs. While tourists are increasingly exploring inaccessible and less-developed regions of the world, the benefits of the industry are not always felt at a local level. There are also worries about the environmental impact of tourism, as the world's last wildernesses increasingly become tourist attractions.

▲ **Botswana's Okavango Delta** is an area rich in wildlife. Tourists go on safaris to the region, but the impact of tourism is controlled.

# Money flows

In 2008 a global financial crisis swept through the world's economic system. The crisis triggered the failure of several major financial institutions and lead to increased borrowing costs known as the "credit crunch". A consequent reduction in economic activity together with rising inflation forced many governments to introduce austerity measures to reduce borrowing and debt, particulary in Europe where massive "bailouts" were needed to keep some European single currency (Euro) countries solvent.

◄ **In rural Southeast Asia,** babies are given medical checks by UNICEF as part of a global aid program sponsored by the UN.

### Tourist arrivals

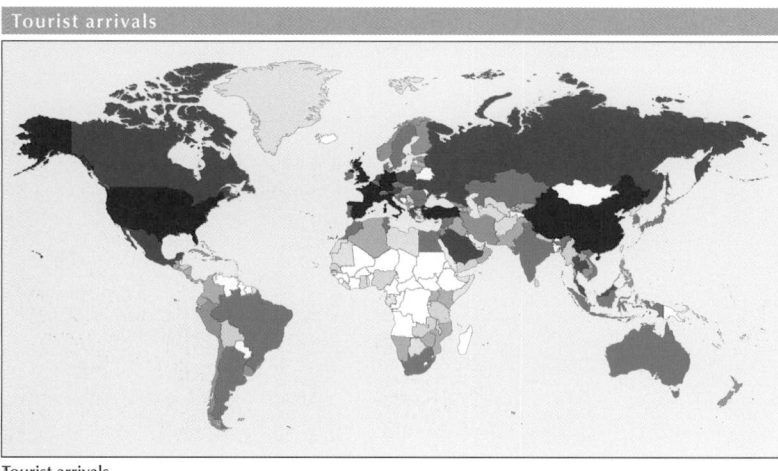

**Tourist arrivals**

- over 25 million
- 10–25 million
- 5–10 million
- 2.5–5 million
- 1–2.5 million
- 700,000–1 million
- under 700,000
- data unavailable

### External debt

**External debt** (as percentage of GNI)

- over 100%
- 70–100%
- 50–70%
- 30–50%
- 10–30%
- below 10%
- data unavailable

# The political world

There are 196 independent countries in the world today. With the exception of Antarctica, where territorial claims have been deferred by international treaty, every land area of the Earth's surface either belongs to, or is claimed by, one country or another. The largest country in the world is Russia, the smallest is Vatican City. Some 60 overseas dependent territories remain, administered variously by France, Australia, Denmark, New Zealand, Norway, Portugal, the UK, the US, and the Netherlands.

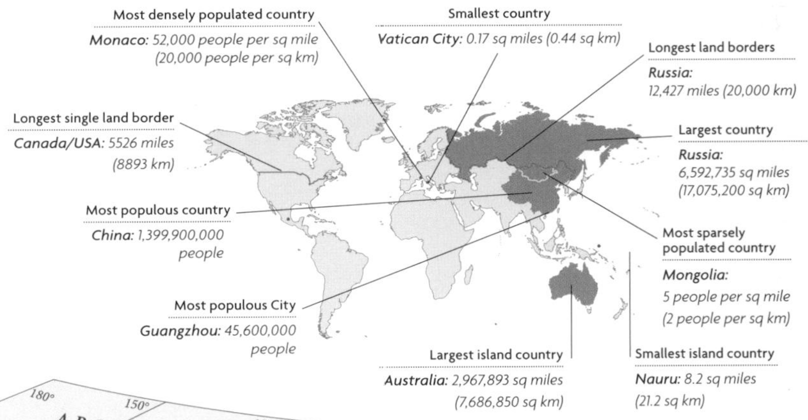

## International borders

The map shows three main types of boundary between states. Full borders represent internationally agreed and recognized territorial boundaries. Undefined borders exist where no fixed boundary between states has been demarcated; the boundaries indicated in this way show approximate areas of sovereignty. A disputed border is indicated where a *de facto* territorial boundary exists, which is not agreed or is subject to arbitration.

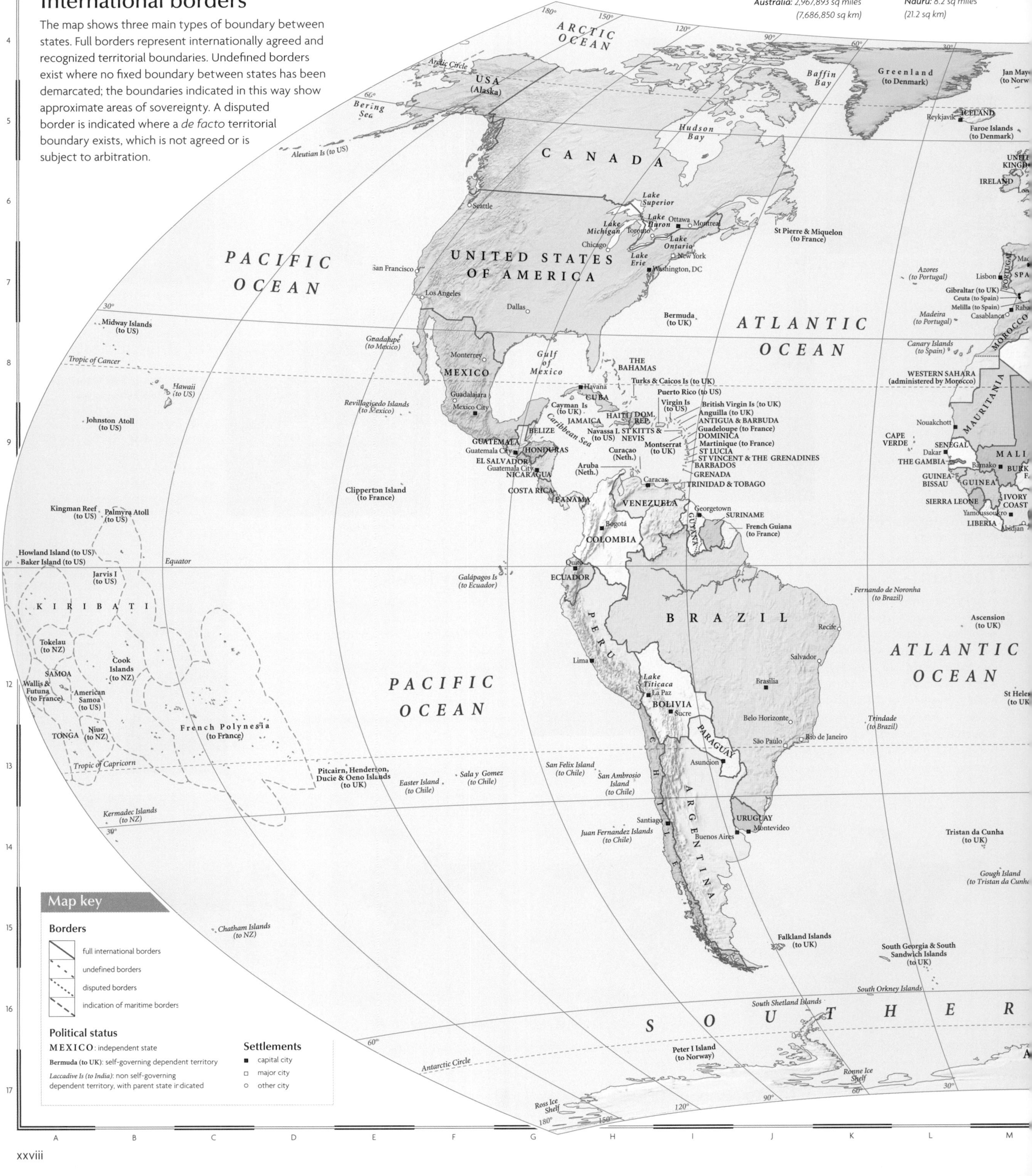

Most densely populated country
*Monaco:* 52,000 people per sq mile (20,000 people per sq km)

Smallest country
*Vatican City:* 0.17 sq miles (0.44 sq km)

Longest land borders
*Russia:* 12,427 miles (20,000 km)

Longest single land border
*Canada/USA:* 5526 miles (8893 km)

Largest country
*Russia:* 6,592,735 sq miles (17,075,200 sq km)

Most populous country
*China:* 1,399,900,000 people

Most sparsely populated country
*Mongolia:* 5 people per sq mile (2 people per sq km)

Most populous City
*Guangzhou:* 45,600,000 people

Largest island country
*Australia:* 2,967,893 sq miles (7,686,850 sq km)

Smallest island country
*Nauru:* 8.2 sq miles (21.2 sq km)

### Map key

#### Borders

- full international borders
- undefined borders
- disputed borders
- indication of maritime borders

#### Political status

MEXICO: independent state
**Bermuda (to UK):** self-governing dependent territory
*Laccadive Is (to India):* non self-governing dependent territory, with parent state indicated

#### Settlements

- ■ capital city
- □ major city
- ○ other city

### Map labels

ARCTIC OCEAN

Arctic Circle

Greenland (to Denmark)

Jan Mayen (to Norway)

Baffin Bay

ICELAND

Reykjavik

Faroe Islands (to Denmark)

USA (Alaska)

Bering Sea

Hudson Bay

CANADA

UNITED KINGDOM

IRELAND

Seattle

Lake Superior
Lake Huron
Lake Michigan
Lake Ontario
Lake Erie

Ottawa
Montreal
Toronto
New York

St Pierre & Miquelon (to France)

PACIFIC OCEAN

San Francisco

UNITED STATES OF AMERICA

Chicago
Washington, DC

Los Angeles

Dallas

Bermuda (to UK)

ATLANTIC OCEAN

Azores (to Portugal)

Lisbon

SPAIN

Gibraltar (to UK)
Ceuta (to Spain)
Melilla (to Spain)

Madeira (to Portugal)

Casablanca

MOROCCO

Midway Islands (to US)

Tropic of Cancer

Guadalupe (to Mexico)

Monterrey

Gulf of Mexico

MEXICO

Guadalajara

Mexico City

THE BAHAMAS

Turks & Caicos Is (to UK)

Canary Islands (to Spain)

WESTERN SAHARA (administered by Morocco)

Hawaii (to US)

Havana

CUBA

Puerto Rico (to US)

Virgin Is (to US)

British Virgin Is (to UK)
Anguilla (to UK)
ANTIGUA & BARBUDA

Nouakchott

MAURITANIA

Johnston Atoll (to US)

Revillagigedo Islands (to Mexico)

Cayman Is (to UK)

JAMAICA

HAITI DOM. REP.

Navassa I. (to US)

ST KITTS & NEVIS

BELIZE

Guadeloupe (to France)
DOMINICA
Martinique (to France)
ST LUCIA
ST VINCENT & THE GRENADINES
BARBADOS
GRENADA

CAPE VERDE

SENEGAL

Dakar

MALI

GUATEMALA

Guatemala City

HONDURAS

EL SALVADOR

Guatemala City

NICARAGUA

Curaçao (Neth.)

Aruba (Neth.)

Caracas

TRINIDAD & TOBAGO

THE GAMBIA

Bamako

BURKINA FASO

GUINEA-BISSAU

GUINEA

SIERRA LEONE

IVORY COAST

Yamoussoukro

LIBERIA

Abidjan

Clipperton Island (to France)

COSTA RICA

PANAMA

VENEZUELA

Georgetown

SURINAME

French Guiana (to France)

Kingman Reef (to US)

Palmyra Atoll (to US)

COLOMBIA

Bogotá

GUYANA

Howland Island (to US)

Baker Island (to US)

Equator

Galápagos Is (to Ecuador)

Quito

ECUADOR

Fernando de Noronha (to Brazil)

Jarvis I (to US)

KIRIBATI

PERU

BRAZIL

Recife

Ascension (to UK)

Tokelau (to NZ)

Lima

Lake Titicaca

La Paz

Brasília

ATLANTIC OCEAN

SAMOA

Cook Islands (to NZ)

Salvador

Wallis & Futuna (to France)

American Samoa (to US)

PACIFIC OCEAN

BOLIVIA

Sucre

Belo Horizonte

St Helena (to UK)

TONGA

Niue (to NZ)

French Polynesia (to France)

PARAGUAY

São Paulo

Rio de Janeiro

Trindade (to Brazil)

Tropic of Capricorn

Asunción

Pitcairn, Henderson, Ducie & Oeno Islands (to UK)

Easter Island (to Chile)

Sala y Gomez (to Chile)

San Felix Island (to Chile)

San Ambrosio Island (to Chile)

CHILE

ARGENTINA

URUGUAY

Tristan da Cunha (to UK)

Kermadec Islands (to NZ)

Santiago

Buenos Aires

Montevideo

Gough Island (to Tristan da Cunha)

Juan Fernandez Islands (to Chile)

Chatham Islands (to NZ)

Falkland Islands (to UK)

South Georgia & South Sandwich Islands (to UK)

South Orkney Islands

South Shetland Islands

SOUTHERN

Peter I Island (to Norway)

Antarctic Circle

Ross Ice Shelf

Ronne Ice Shelf

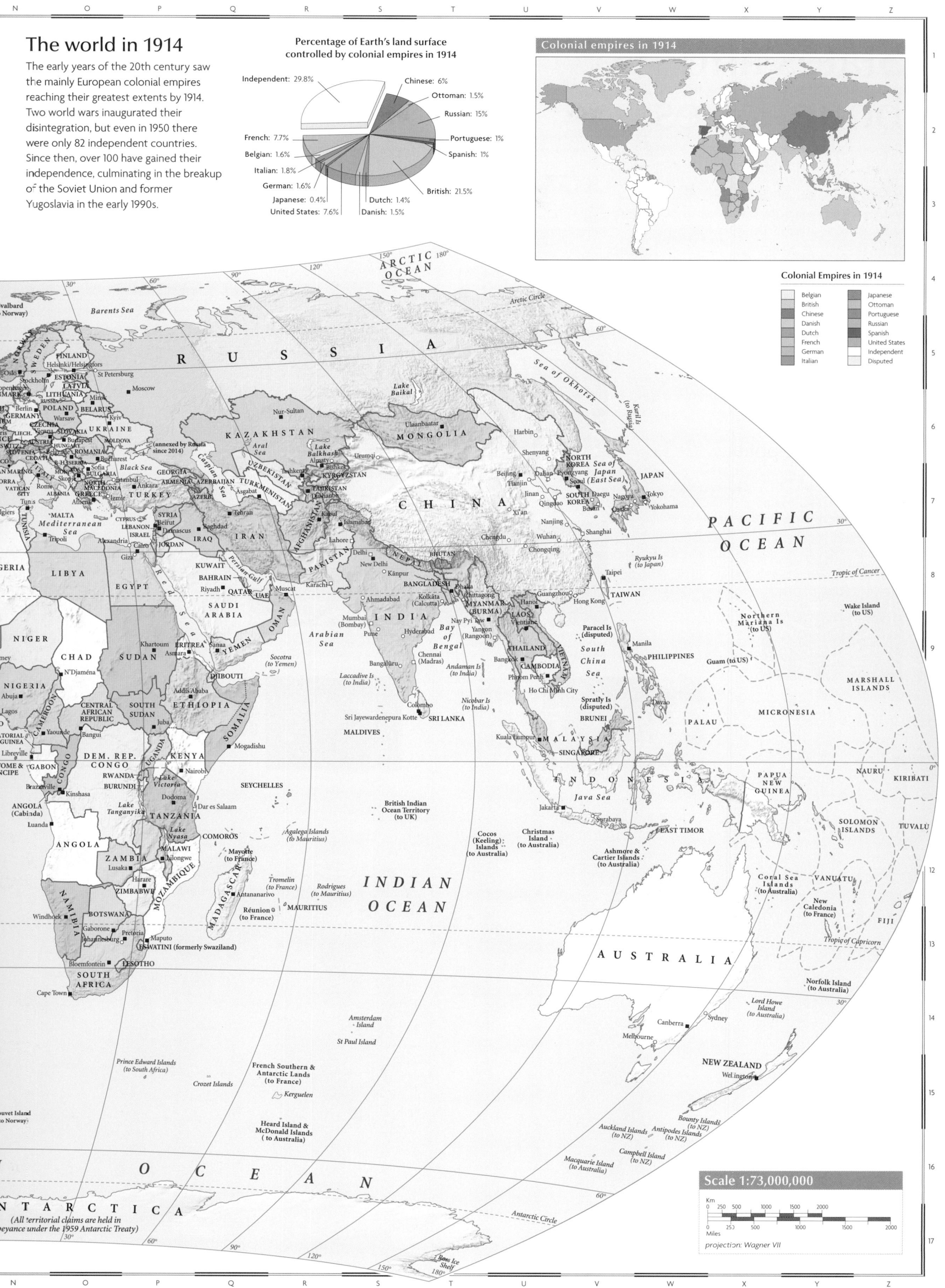

# The world in 1914

The early years of the 20th century saw the mainly European colonial empires reaching their greatest extents by 1914. Two world wars inaugurated their disintegration, but even in 1950 there were only 82 independent countries. Since then, over 100 have gained their independence, culminating in the breakup of the Soviet Union and former Yugoslavia in the early 1990s.

### Percentage of Earth's land surface controlled by colonial empires in 1914

- Independent: 29.8%
- Chinese: 6%
- Ottoman: 1.5%
- Russian: 15%
- Portuguese: 1%
- Spanish: 1%
- British: 21.5%
- Danish: 1.5%
- Dutch: 1.4%
- United States: 7.6%
- Japanese: 0.4%
- German: 1.6%
- Italian: 1.8%
- Belgian: 1.6%
- French: 7.7%

### Colonial empires in 1914

### Colonial Empires in 1914

- Belgian
- British
- Chinese
- Danish
- Dutch
- French
- German
- Italian
- Japanese
- Ottoman
- Portuguese
- Russian
- Spanish
- United States
- Independent
- Disputed

Scale 1:73,000,000

projection: Wagner VII

# States and boundaries

There are almost 200 sovereign states in the world today; in 1950 there were only 82. Over the last 65 years national self-determination has been a driving force for many states with a history of colonialism and oppression. As more borders have been added to the world map, the number of international border disputes has increased.

In many cases, where the impetus toward independence has been religious or ethnic, disputes with minority groups have also caused violent internal conflict. While many newly-formed states have moved peacefully toward independence, successfully establishing government by multiparty democracy, dictatorship by military regime or individual despot is often the result of the internal power-struggles which characterize the early stages in the lives of new nations.

## The nature of politics

Democracy is a broad term: it can range from the ideal of multiparty elections and fair representation to, in countries such as Singapore, a thin disguise for single-party rule. In despotic regimes, on the other hand, a single, often personal authority has total power; institutions such as parliament and the military are mere instruments of the dictator.

◀ The stars and stripes of the US flag are a potent symbol of the country's status as a federal democracy.

### Types of government
- Multiparty democracy for more than 10 yrs
- Multiparty democracy within last 10 yrs
- Single-party government
- Military regime
- Theocracy
- Monarchy
- Non-party system
- Transitional regime
- ⚔ Current civil unrest

## The changing world map
### Decolonization

In 1950, large areas of the world remained under the control of a handful of European countries *(page xxix)*. The process of decolonization had begun in Asia, where, following the Second World War, much of southern and southeastern Asia sought and achieved self-determination. In the 1960s, a host of African states achieved independence, so that by 1965, most of the larger tracts of the European overseas empires had been substantially eroded. The final major stage in decolonization came with the breakup of the Soviet Union and the Eastern bloc after 1990. The process continues today as the last toeholds of European colonialism, often tiny island nations, press increasingly for independence.

▲ Icons of communism, including statues of former leaders such as Lenin and Stalin, were destroyed when the Soviet bloc was dismantled in 1989, creating several new nations.

▲ Iran has been one of the modern world's few true theocracies; Islam has an impact on every aspect of political life.

▲ North Korea is an independent communist republic. Power was transferred directly to Kim Jong-un in 2012 following the death of his father Kim Jong-il.

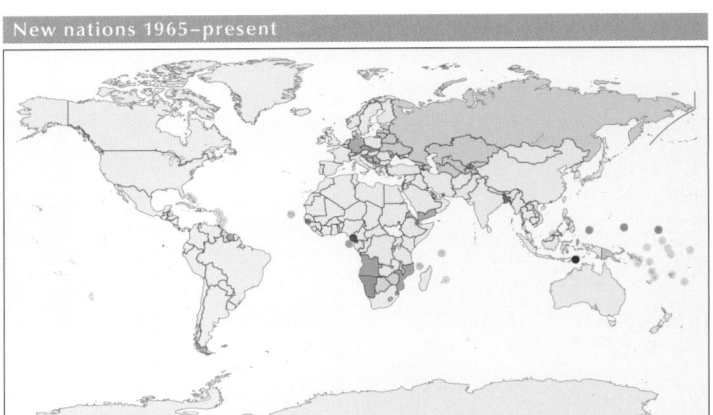
New nations 1945–1965

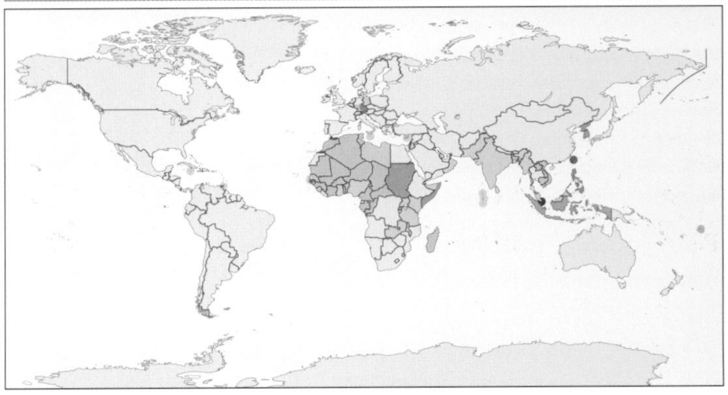

New nations 1965–present

### Administration at the time of independence
| | |
|---|---|
| Australia | Netherlands |
| Aust/NZ/UK | New Zealand |
| Belgium | Pakistan |
| China | Portugal |
| Czechoslovakia | South Africa |
| Egypt/UK | Spain |
| Ethiopia | Sudan |
| France | UK |
| France/UK | Unified country |
| Indonesia | USA |
| Italy | USSR |
| Japan | Yugoslavia |
| Malaysia | |

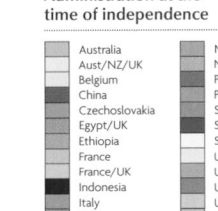
◀ Afghanistan has suffered decades of war and occupation resulting in widespread destruction. The hardline Taliban government were ousted by a US-led coalition in 2001 but efforts to stabilize the country are still continuing.

◀ In early 2011, Egypt underwent a revolution, part of the so called "Arab Spring," which resulted in the ousting of President Hosni Mubarak after nearly 30 years in power.

▲ In Brunei the Sultan has ruled by decree since 1962; power is closely tied to the royal family. The Sultan's brothers are responsible for finance and foreign affairs.

# Lines on the map

The determination of international boundaries can use a variety of criteria. Many of the borders between older states follow physical boundaries; some mirror religious and ethnic differences; others are the legacy of complex histories of conflict and colonialism, while others have been imposed by international agreements or arbitration.

## Post-colonial borders

When the European colonial empires in Africa were dismantled during the second half of the 20th century, the outlines of the new African states mirrored colonial boundaries. These boundaries had been drawn up by colonial administrators, often based on inadequate geographical knowledge. Such arbitrary boundaries were imposed on people of different languages, racial groups, religions, and customs. This confused legacy often led to civil and international war.

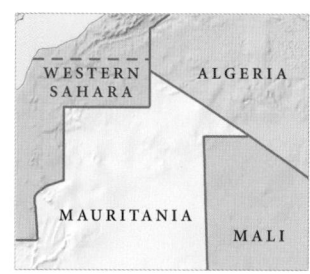

▲ *The conflict that* has plagued many African countries since independence has caused millions of people to become refugees.

## Physical borders

Many of the world's countries are divided by physical borders: lakes, rivers, mountains. The demarcation of such boundaries can, however, lead to disputes. Control of waterways, water supplies, and fisheries are frequent causes of international friction.

## Enclaves and exclaves

The shifting political map over the course of history has frequently led to anomalous situations. Parts of national territories may become isolated by territorial agreement, forming an enclave or exclave. For example, in Europe, Kaliningrad has been separated from the rest of Russia since the independence of the Baltic States, creating an exclave.

## Antarctica

When Antarctic exploration began a century ago, seven nations, Australia, Argentina, Britain, Chile, France, New Zealand, and Norway, laid claim to the new territory. In 1961 the Antarctic Treaty, now signed by 45 nations, agreed to hold all territorial claims in abeyance.

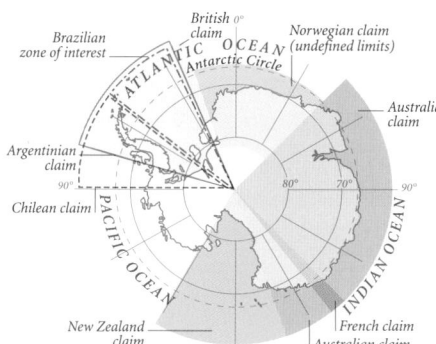

*Brazilian zone of interest*
*British claim*
*Norwegian claim (undefined limits)*
*Antarctic Circle*
*Australian claim*
*Argentinian claim*
*Chilean claim*
*New Zealand claim*
*French claim*
*Australian claim*
ATLANTIC OCEAN
PACIFIC OCEAN
INDIAN OCEAN

▲ *Since the independence* of Lithuania and Belarus, the peoples of the Russian exclave of Kaliningrad have become physically isolated.

## Geometric borders

Straight lines and lines of longitude and latitude have occasionally been used to determine international boundaries; and indeed the world's second longest continuous international boundary, between Canada and the USA follows the 49th Parallel for over one-third of its course. Many Canadian, American, and Australian internal administrative boundaries are similarly determined using a geometric solution.

CANADA
49th Parallel
UNITED STATES OF AMERICA

▲ *Different farming techniques* in Canada and the US clearly mark the course of the international boundary in this satellite map.

### World boundaries

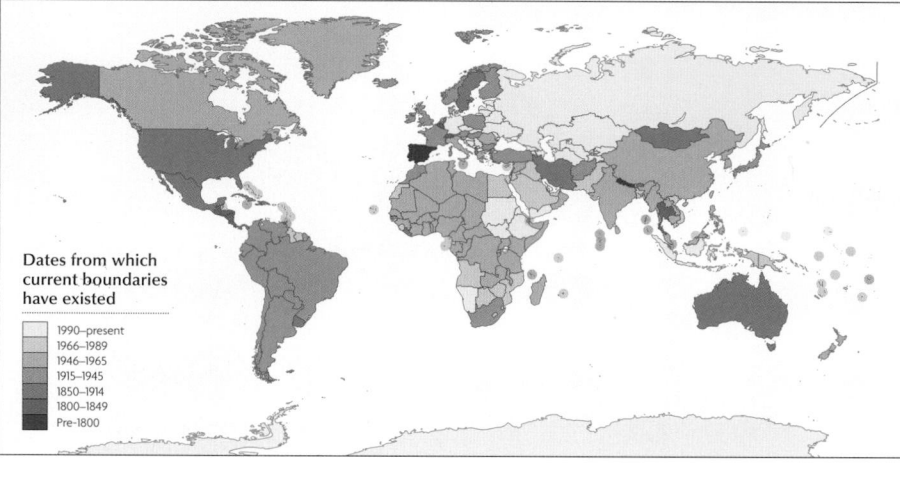

**Dates from which current boundaries have existed**
- 1990–present
- 1966–1989
- 1946–1965
- 1915–1945
- 1850–1914
- 1800–1849
- Pre-1800

## Lake borders

Countries which lie next to lakes usually fix their borders in the middle of the lake. Unusually the Lake Nyasa border between Malawi and Tanzania runs along Tanzania's shore.

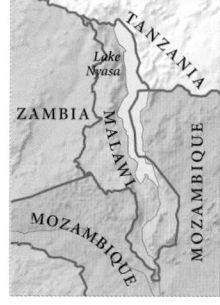

▲ *Complicated agreements* between colonial powers led to the awkward division of Lake Nyasa.

## River borders

Rivers alone account for one-sixth of the world's borders. Many great rivers form boundaries between a number of countries. Changes in a river's course and interruptions of its natural flow can lead to disputes, particularly in areas where water is scarce. The center of the river's course is the nominal boundary line.

▲ *The Danube forms* all or part of the border between nine European nations.

## Mountain borders

Mountain ranges form natural barriers and are the basis for many major borders, particularly in Europe and Asia. The watershed is the conventional boundary demarcation line, but its accurate determination is often problematic.

▲ *The Pyrenees form* a natural mountain border between France and Spain.

## Shifting boundaries – Poland

Borders between countries can change dramatically over time. The nations of eastern Europe have been particularly affected by changing boundaries. Poland is an example of a country whose boundaries have changed so significantly that it has literally moved around Europe. At the start of the 16th century, Poland was the largest nation in Europe. Between 1772 and 1795, it was absorbed into Prussia, Austria, and Russia, and it effectively ceased to exist. After the First World War, Poland became an independent country once more, but its borders changed again after the Second World War following invasions by both Soviet Russia and Nazi Germany.

▲ *In 1634, Poland* was the largest nation in Europe. Its eastern boundary reaching toward Moscow.

▲ *From 1772–1795, Poland* was gradually partitioned between Austria, Russia, and Prussia. Its eastern boundary receded by over 100 miles (160 km).

▲ *Following the First World War,* Poland was reinstated as an independent state, but it was less than half the size it had been in 1634.

▲ *After the Second World War,* the Baltic Sea border was extended westward, but much of the eastern territory was annexed by Russia.

# International disputes

There are more than 60 disputed borders or territories in the world today. Although many of these disputes can be settled by peaceful negotiation, some areas have become a focus for international conflict. Ethnic tensions have been a major source of territorial disagreement throughout history, as has the ownership of, and access to, valuable natural resources. The turmoil of the postcolonial era in many parts of Africa is partly a result of the 19th century "carve-up" of the continent, which created potential for conflict by drawing often arbitrary lines through linguistic and cultural areas.

## Jammu and Kashmir

Disputes over Jammu and Kashmir have caused three serious wars between India and Pakistan since 1947. Pakistan wishes to annex the largely Muslim territory, while India refuses to cede any territory or to hold a referendum, and also lays claim to the entire territory. Most international maps show the "line of control" agreed in 1972 as the *de facto* border. In addition, India has territorial disputes with neighboring China. The situation is further complicated by a Kashmiri independence movement, active since the late 1980s.

▲ *Indian army troops* maintain their positions in the mountainous terrain of northern Kashmir.

## North and South Korea

Since 1953, the *de facto* border between North and South Korea has been a cease-fire line which straddles the 38th Parallel and is designated as a demilitarized zone. Both countries have heavy fortifications and troop concentrations behind this zone.

▲ Heavy fortifications on the border between North and South Korea.

## Cyprus

Cyprus was partitioned in 1974, following an invasion by Turkish troops. The south is now the Greek Cypriot Republic of Cyprus, while the self-proclaimed Turkish Republic of Northern Cyprus is recognized only by Turkey.

▲ The so-called "green line" divides Cyprus into Greek and Turkish sectors.

### Conflicts and international disputes

- UN peacekeeping missions 2005–2015
- Major active land based territorial or border disputes
- Countries involved in internal conflict
- Active land based territorial or border disputes and internal conflict
- Disputed border

## The Falkland Islands

The British dependent territory of the Falkland Islands was invaded by Argentina in 1982, sparking a full-scale war with the UK. Tensions ran high during 2012 in the build up to the thirtieth anniversary of the conflict.

◄ British warships in Falkland Sound during the 1982 war with Argentina.

## Israel

Israel was created in 1948 following the 1947 UN Resolution (147) on Palestine. Until 1979 Israel had no borders, only cease-fire lines from a series of wars in 1948, 1967, and 1973. Treaties with Egypt in 1979 and Jordan in 1994 led to these borders being defined and agreed. Negotiations over Israeli settlements and Palestinian self-government have seen little effective progress since 2000.

- Palestinian control
- Mixed control
- Israeli settlement block
- Israeli settlement
- Palestinian settlement
- West Bank fence

## Former Yugoslavia

Following the disintegration in 1991 of the communist state of Yugoslavia, the breakaway states of Croatia and Bosnia and Herzegovina came into conflict with the "parent" state (consisting of Serbia and Montenegro). Warfare focused on ethnic and territorial ambitions in Bosnia. The tenuous Dayton Accord of 1995 sought to recognize the post-1990 borders, whilst providing for ethnic partition and required international peace-keeping troops to maintain the terms of the peace.

▲ Barbed-wire fences surround a settlement in the Golan Heights.

- Republika Srpska
- Federacija Bosne i Hercegovine
- Brčko Distrikt

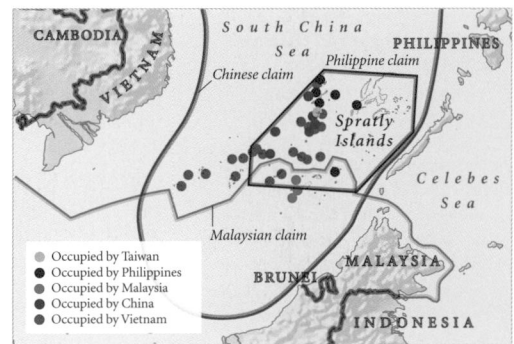
▲ Most claimant states have small military garrisons on the Spratly Islands.

## The Spratly Islands

The site of potential oil and natural gas reserves, the Spratly Islands in the South China Sea have been claimed by China, Vietnam, Taiwan, Malaysia, and the Philippines since the Japanese gave up a wartime claim in 1951.

- Occupied by Taiwan
- Occupied by Philippines
- Occupied by Malaysia
- Occupied by China
- Occupied by Vietnam

# ATLAS
## OF THE WORLD

THE MAPS IN THIS ATLAS ARE ARRANGED CONTINENT BY CONTINENT, STARTING

FROM THE INTERNATIONAL DATE LINE, AND MOVING EASTWARD. THE MAPS PROVIDE

A UNIQUE VIEW OF TODAY'S WORLD, COMBINING TRADITIONAL CARTOGRAPHIC

TECHNIQUES WITH THE LATEST REMOTE-SENSED AND DIGITAL TECHNOLOGY.

# North America

North America is the world's third largest continent with a total area of 9,358,340 sq miles

(24,238,000 sq km) including Greenland and the Caribbean islands.

It lies wholly within the Northern Hemisphere.

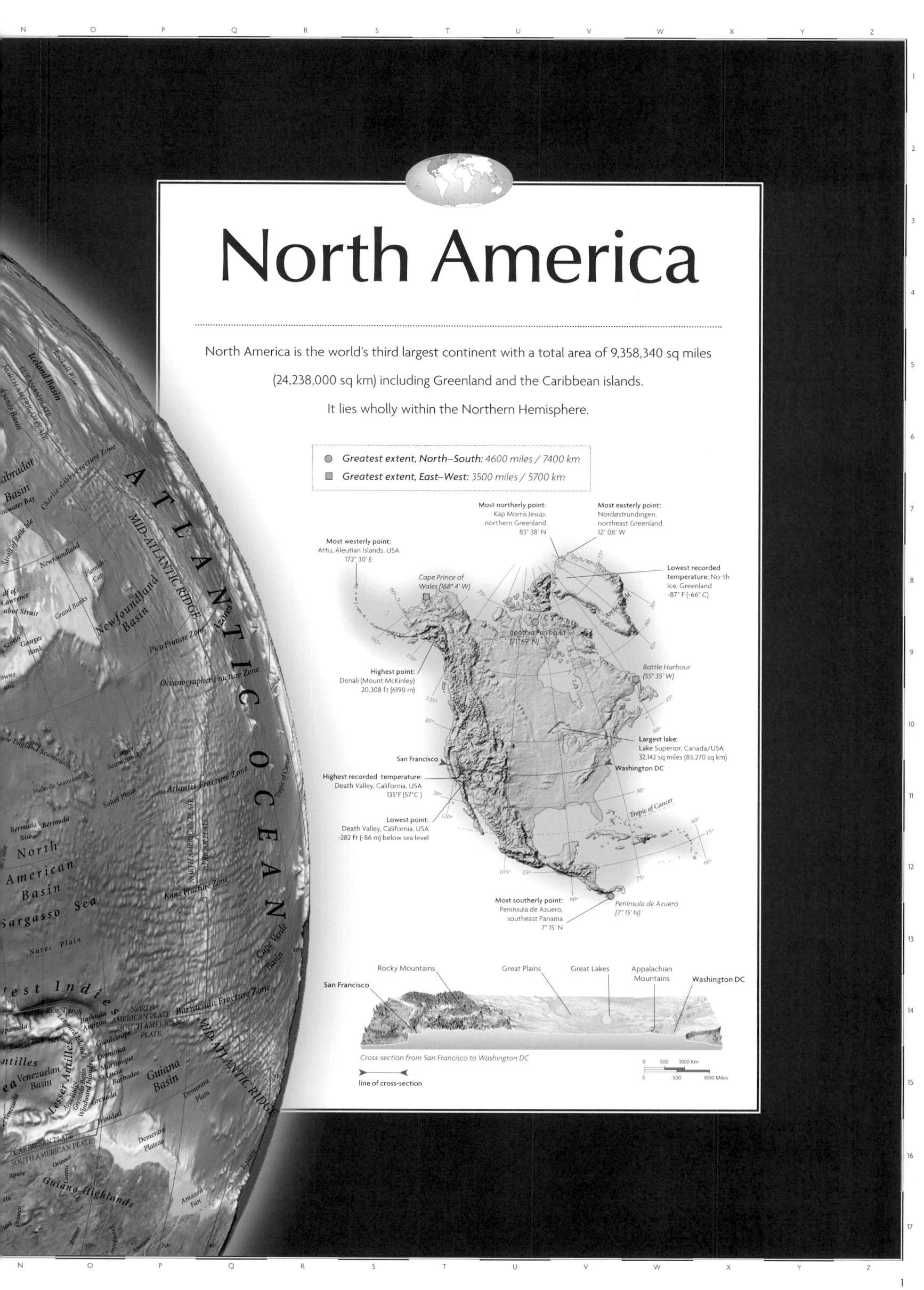

- **Greatest extent, North–South:** 4600 miles / 7400 km
- **Greatest extent, East–West:** 3500 miles / 5700 km

**Most northerly point:**
Kap Morris Jesup,
northern Greenland
83° 38' N

**Most easterly point:**
Nordøstrundingen,
northeast Greenland
12° 08' W

**Most westerly point:**
Attu, Aleutian Islands, USA
172° 30' E

**Lowest recorded
temperature:** North
Ice, Greenland
-87° F (-66° C)

Cape Prince of
Wales (168° 4' W)

Boothia Peninsula
(71° 59' N)

**Highest point:**
Denali (Mount McKinley)
20,308 ft (6190 m)

Battle Harbour
(55° 35' W)

San Francisco

**Largest lake:**
Lake Superior, Canada/USA
32,142 sq miles (83,270 sq km)

Washington DC

**Highest recorded temperature:**
Death Valley, California, USA
135°F (57°C )

Tropic of Cancer

**Lowest point:**
Death Valley, California, USA
-282 ft (-86 m) below sea level

**Most southerly point:**
Peninsula de Azuero,
southeast Panama
7° 15' N

Peninsula de Azuero
(7° 15' N)

Rocky Mountains   Great Plains   Great Lakes   Appalachian Mountains   Washington DC

San Francisco

*Cross-section from San Francisco to Washington DC*

line of cross-section

0   500   1000 Km
0   500   1000 Miles

*(globe relief map labels)*
Iceland Basin · Rockall Rise · EURASIAN PLATE · NORTH AMERICAN PLATE · Reykjanes Basin · Charlie-Gibbs Fracture Zone · Labrador · Basin · Roswater Bay · Strait of Belle Isle · Newfoundland · Flemish · Cap · Gulf of Lawrence · Cabot Strait · Grand Banks · Scotia · Georges · Bank · owns · ank · New England Seamounts · Corner · Seamounts · Nashville Seamount · Sohm Plain · Bermuda · Bermuda · Rise · North · American · Basin · Sargasso Sea · Nares Plain · West Indies · Puerto Rico Trench · spaniola · Puerto Rico · Nevis · Lesser Antilles · Venezuelan · Basin · Windward Islands · Grenada · Trinidad · Guiana · Basin · Demerara · Plain · Demerara · Plateau · CARIBBEAN PLATE · SOUTH AMERICAN PLATE · Guiana Highlands · Orinoco · Apure · Amazon · Amazon Fan · MID-ATLANTIC RIDGE · ATLANTIC OCEAN · Newfoundland · Basin · Pico Fracture Zone · Azores · Oceanographer Fracture Zone · Atlantis Fracture Zone · Tropic of Cancer · Kane Fracture Zone · NORTH AMERICAN PLATE · AFRICAN PLATE · Cape Verde · Basin · NORTH AMERICAN PLATE · SOUTH AMERICAN PLATE · Barracuda Fracture Zone · Guadeloupe · Barbuda · Antigua · Dominica · Martinique · St Lucia · Barbados · St Vincent

# Physical North America

The North American continent can be divided into a number of major structural areas: the Western Cordillera, the Canadian Shield, the Great Plains, and Central Lowlands, and the Appalachians. Other smaller regions include the Gulf Atlantic Coastal Plain which borders the southern coast of North America from the southern Appalachians to the Great Plains. This area includes the expanding Mississippi Delta. A chain of volcanic islands, running in an arc around the margin of the Caribbean Plate, lie to the east of the Gulf of Mexico.

## The Canadian Shield

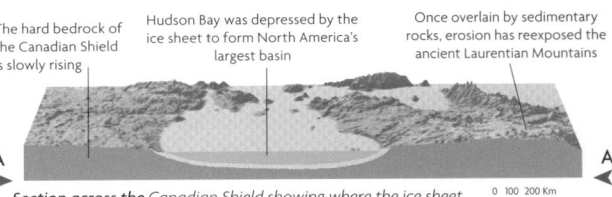

Spanning northern Canada and Greenland, this geologically stable plain forms the heart of the continent, containing rocks more than two billion years old. A long history of weathering and repeated glaciation has scoured the region, leaving flat plains, gentle hummocks, numerous small basins and lakes, and the bays and islands of the Arctic.

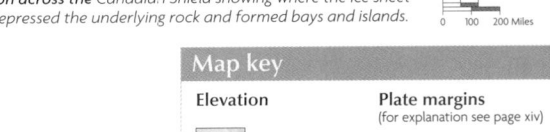

The hard bedrock of the Canadian Shield is slowly rising

Hudson Bay was depressed by the ice sheet to form North America's largest basin

Once overlain by sedimentary rocks, erosion has reexposed the ancient Laurentian Mountains

**Section across the** Canadian Shield showing where the ice sheet has depressed the underlying rock and formed bays and islands.

0  100  200 Km
0  100  200 Miles

## The Western Cordillera

About 80 million years ago the Pacific and North American plates collided, uplifting the Western Cordillera. This consists of the Aleutian, Coast, Cascade, and Sierra Nevada mountains, and the inland Rocky Mountains. These run parallel from the Arctic to Mexico.

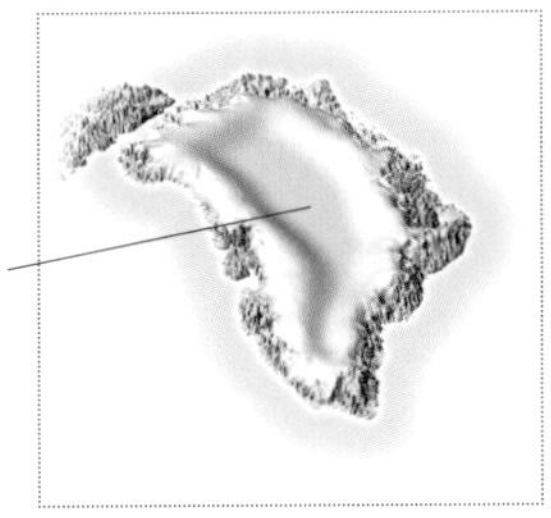

The weight of the ice sheet, 1.8 miles (3 km) thick, has depressed the land to 0.6 miles (1 km) below sea level

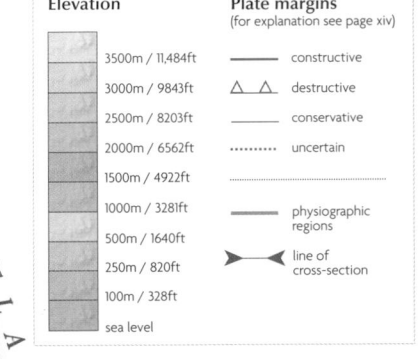

▲ **This computer-generated view** shows the ice-covered island of Greenland without its ice cap.

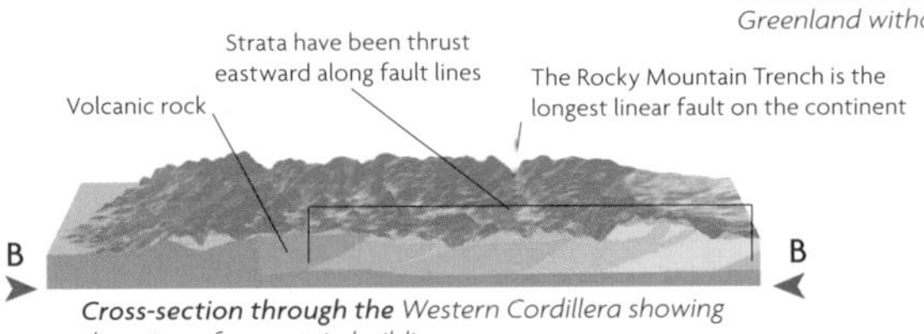

Strata have been thrust eastward along fault lines

Volcanic rock

The Rocky Mountain Trench is the longest linear fault on the continent

**Cross-section through the** Western Cordillera showing direction of mountain building.

0  50  100 Km
0  50  130 Miles

### Map key

**Elevation**

| | |
|---|---|
| | 3500m / 11,484ft |
| | 3000m / 9843ft |
| | 2500m / 8203ft |
| | 2000m / 6562ft |
| | 1500m / 4922ft |
| | 1000m / 3281ft |
| | 500m / 1640ft |
| | 250m / 820ft |
| | 100m / 328ft |
| | sea level |

**Plate margins**
(for explanation see page xiv)

constructive

△ △  destructive

conservative

.......... uncertain

............ physiographic regions

▶◀ line of cross-section

**Scale 1:42,000,000**

Km
0  200  400  600  800  1000
Miles
0  200  400  600  800  1000

projection: Lambert Azimuthal Equal Area

## The Great Plains & Central Lowlands

Deposits left by retreating glaciers and rivers have made this vast flat area very fertile. In the north this is the result of glaciation, with deposits up to one mile (1.7 km) thick, covering the basement rock. To the south and west, the massive Missouri/Mississippi river system has for centuries deposited silt across the plains, creating broad, flat floodplains and deltas.

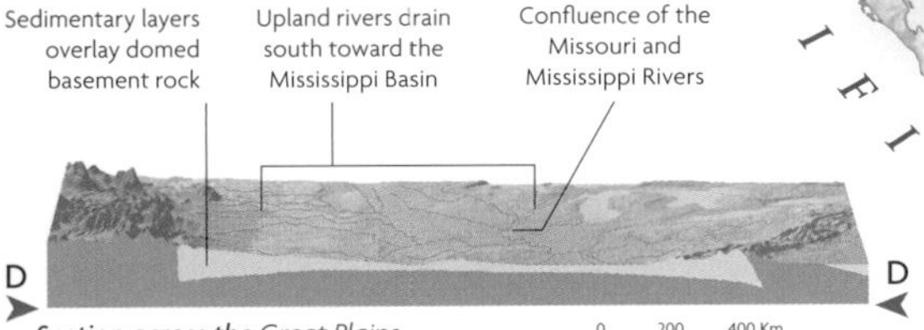

Sedimentary layers overlay domed basement rock

Upland rivers drain south toward the Mississippi Basin

Confluence of the Missouri and Mississippi Rivers

**Section across the** Great Plains and Central Lowlands showing river systems and structure.

0  200  400 Km
0  200  400 Miles

## The Appalachians

The Appalachian Mountains, uplifted about 400 million years ago, are some of the oldest in the world. They have been lowered and rounded by erosion and now slope gently toward the Atlantic across a broad coastal plain.

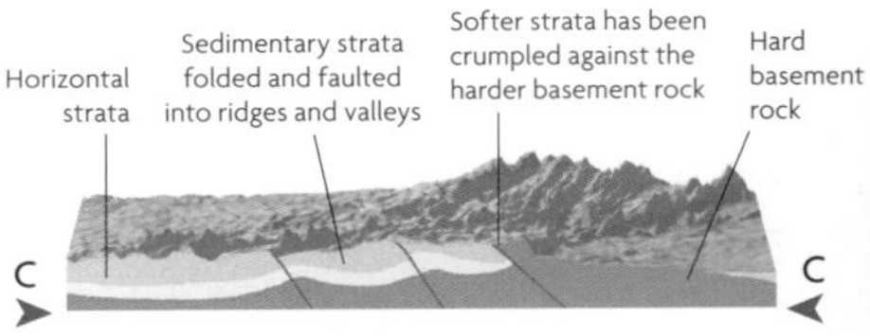

Horizontal strata

Sedimentary strata folded and faulted into ridges and valleys

Softer strata has been crumpled against the harder basement rock

Hard basement rock

**Cross-section through the** Appalachians showing the numerous folds, which have subsequently been weathered to create a rounded relief.

0  25  50 Km
0  25  50 Miles

### Map labels

ASIA

Bering Strait

Beaufort Sea

Bering Sea

Aleutian Islands

Gulf of Alaska

Brooks Range

Denali (Mt McKinley) 6190m

Mackenzie Delta

Aleutian Range   Alaska Range

Mackenzie Mountains

Mackenzie

Great Bear Lake

NORTH AMERICAN PLATE

PACIFIC PLATE

Coast Mountains

Great Slave Lake

Lake Athabasca

Reindeer Lake

WESTERN CORDILLERA

ROCKY MOUNTAINS

CANADIAN SHIELD

Greenland

ATLANTIC OCEAN

Baffin Bay

Baffin Island

Davis Strait

Foxe Basin

Hudson Strait

Labrador Sea

Labrador

Laurentian Mountains

Newfoundland

Hudson Bay

JUAN DE FUCA PLATE

Mount Rainier 4392m

Mount St Helens 2549m

Cascade Range

Sierra Nevada

San Joaquin Valley

San Andreas Fault

Great Basin

Great Salt Lake

Colorado

Colorado Plateau

Death Valley -86m

Grand Canyon

Mojave Desert

Sonoran Desert

Lower California

Gulf of California

Sierra Madre Occidental

Lake Winnipeg

Lake Manitoba

GREAT PLAINS

Missouri

Lake Superior

Lake Huron

Lake Michigan

Lake Erie

Lake Ontario

St Lawrence

GREAT LAKES

CENTRAL LOWLANDS

Arkansas

Ohio

Mississippi

Cape Cod

Nova Scotia

APPALACHIAN MOUNTAINS

APPALACHIANS

GULF ATLANTIC COASTAL PLAIN

Mississippi Delta

Rio Grande

Sierra Madre Oriental

Gulf of Mexico

Volcán Pico de Orizaba 5636m

Yucatan Peninsula

West Indies

Greater Antilles

Lesser Antilles

Caribbean Sea

Sierra Madre del Sur

NORTH AMERICAN PLATE

CARIBBEAN PLATE

Lake Nicaragua

Isthmus of Panama

CARIBBEAN PLATE

SOUTH AMERICAN PLATE

SOUTH AMERICA

PACIFIC OCEAN

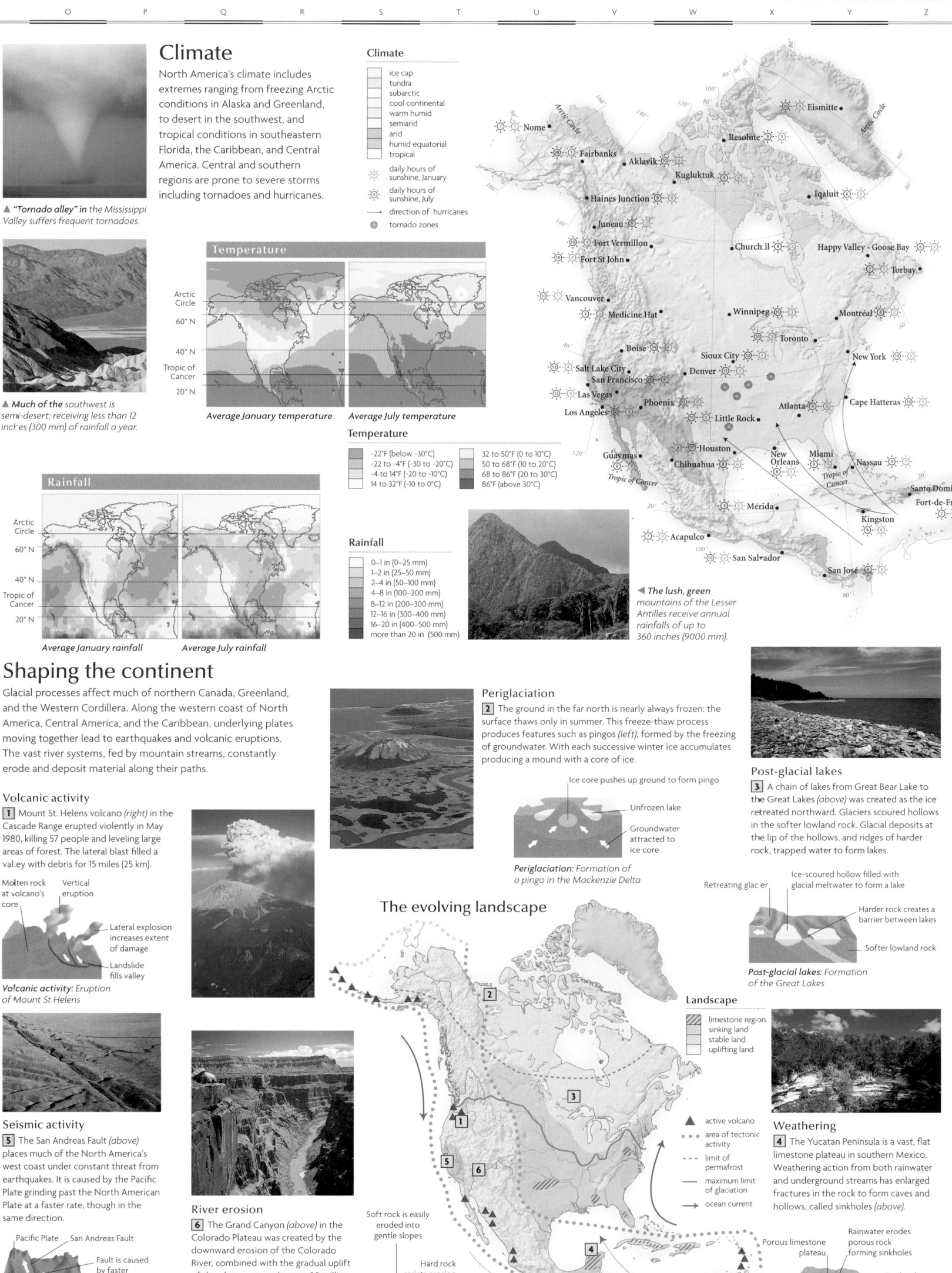

## Climate

North America's climate includes extremes ranging from freezing Arctic conditions in Alaska and Greenland, to desert in the southwest, and tropical conditions in southeastern Florida, the Caribbean, and Central America. Central and southern regions are prone to severe storms including tornadoes and hurricanes.

▲ *"Tornado alley" in the Mississippi Valley suffers frequent tornadoes.*

▲ *Much of the southwest is semi-desert; receiving less than 12 inches (300 mm) of rainfall a year.*

**Climate**
- ice cap
- tundra
- subarctic
- cool continental
- warm humid
- semiarid
- arid
- humid equatorial
- tropical

☼ daily hours of sunshine, January
☼ daily hours of sunshine, July
→ direction of hurricanes
⊙ tornado zones

### Temperature

*Average January temperature*

*Average July temperature*

**Temperature**
- -22°F (below -30°C)
- -22 to -4°F (-30 to -20°C)
- -4 to 14°F (-20 to -10°C)
- 14 to 32°F (-10 to 0°C)
- 32 to 50°F (0 to 10°C)
- 50 to 68°F (10 to 20°C)
- 68 to 86°F (20 to 30°C)
- 86°F (above 30°C)

Arctic Circle
60° N
40° N
Tropic of Cancer
20° N

### Rainfall

*Average January rainfall*

*Average July rainfall*

Arctic Circle
60° N
40° N
Tropic of Cancer
20° N

**Rainfall**
- 0–1 in (0–25 mm)
- 1–2 in (25–50 mm)
- 2–4 in (50–100 mm)
- 4–8 in (100–200 mm)
- 8–12 in (200–300 mm)
- 12–16 in (300–400 mm)
- 16–20 in (400–500 mm)
- more than 20 in (500 mm)

◄ *The lush, green mountains of the Lesser Antilles receive annual rainfalls of up to 360 inches (9000 mm).*

## Shaping the continent

Glacial processes affect much of northern Canada, Greenland, and the Western Cordillera. Along the western coast of North America, Central America, and the Caribbean, underlying plates moving together lead to earthquakes and volcanic eruptions. The vast river systems, fed by mountain streams, constantly erode and deposit material along their paths.

### Volcanic activity

**1** Mount St. Helens volcano *(right)* in the Cascade Range erupted violently in May 1980, killing 57 people and leveling large areas of forest. The lateral blast filled a valley with debris for 15 miles (25 km).

Molten rock at volcano's core
Vertical eruption
Lateral explosion increases extent of damage
Landslide fills valley

*Volcanic activity: Eruption of Mount St Helens*

### Seismic activity

**5** The San Andreas Fault *(above)* places much of the North America's west coast under constant threat from earthquakes. It is caused by the Pacific Plate grinding past the North American Plate at a faster rate, though in the same direction.

Pacific Plate
San Andreas Fault
Fault is caused by faster movement of Pacific Plate
North American Plate

*Seismic activity: Action of the San Andreas Fault*

### River erosion

**6** The Grand Canyon *(above)* in the Colorado Plateau was created by the downward erosion of the Colorado River, combined with the gradual uplift of the plateau, over the past 30 million years. The contours of the canyon formed as the softer rock layers eroded into gentle slopes, and the hard rock layers into cliffs. The depth varies from 3855–6560 ft (1175–2000 m).

Soft rock is easily eroded into gentle slopes
Hard rock resists erosion
Colorado River cuts down through rock

*River Erosion: Formation of the Grand Canyon*

### Periglaciation

**2** The ground in the far north is nearly always frozen: the surface thaws only in summer. This freeze-thaw process produces features such as pingos *(left)*; formed by the freezing of groundwater. With each successive winter ice accumulates producing a mound with a core of ice.

Ice core pushes up ground to form pingo
Unfrozen lake
Groundwater attracted to ice core

*Periglaciation: Formation of a pingo in the Mackenzie Delta*

### The evolving landscape

**Landscape**
- limestone region
- sinking land
- stable land
- uplifting land

▲ active volcano
⋯ area of tectonic activity
--- limit of permafrost
— maximum limit of glaciation
→ ocean current

### Post-glacial lakes

**3** A chain of lakes from Great Bear Lake to the Great Lakes *(above)* was created as the ice retreated northward. Glaciers scoured hollows in the softer lowland rock. Glacial deposits at the lip of the hollows, and ridges of harder rock, trapped water to form lakes.

Retreating glacier
Ice-scoured hollow filled with glacial meltwater to form a lake
Harder rock creates a barrier between lakes
Softer lowland rock

*Post-glacial lakes: Formation of the Great Lakes*

### Weathering

**4** The Yucatan Peninsula is a vast, flat limestone plateau in southern Mexico. Weathering action from both rainwater and underground streams has enlarged fractures in the rock to form caves and hollows, called sinkholes *(above)*.

Rainwater erodes porous rock forming sinkholes
Porous limestone plateau
Sea level
Underground stream further erodes rock

*Weathering: Water erosion on the Yucatan Peninsula*

# Political North America

Democracy is well established in some parts of the continent but is a recent phenomenon in others. The economically dominant nations of Canada and the US have a long democratic tradition but elsewhere, notably in the countries of Central America, political turmoil has been more common. In Nicaragua and Haiti, harsh dictatorships have only recently been superseded by democratically elected governments. North America's largest countries, Canada, Mexico, and the US have federal state systems, sharing political power between national and state governments. The US has intervened militarily on several occasions in Central America and the Caribbean to protect its strategic interests.

## Transportation

In the 19th century, railroads opened up the North American continent. Air transportation is now more common for long distance passenger travel, although railroads are still extensively used for bulk freight transportation. Waterways like the Mississippi River are important for the transportation of bulk materials, and the Panama Canal is a vital link between the Pacific and Atlantic Oceans. In the 20th century, road transportation increased massively, with the introduction of cheap, mass-produced motor cars and extensive highway construction.

◀ *This busy suburban interchange in Los Angeles is part of the US's Interstate freeway system. Construction of the 55,000 mile (88,500 km) freeway network began in the 1950s, and it now connects most major cities, and carries one-fifth of the US's road traffic.*

▲ *The 40 mile (65 km) long Panama Canal cuts through the Isthmus of Panama, a narrow strip of land connecting North and South America. Opened in 1914, the canal reduced the journey between the Atlantic and Pacific oceans by almost 8000 nautical miles (14,800 km).*

◀ *Low-density housing developments such as this one on the outskirts of Phoenix, Arizona, reflect the US's abundance of land and a dispersed population, dependent on the car for personal mobility.*

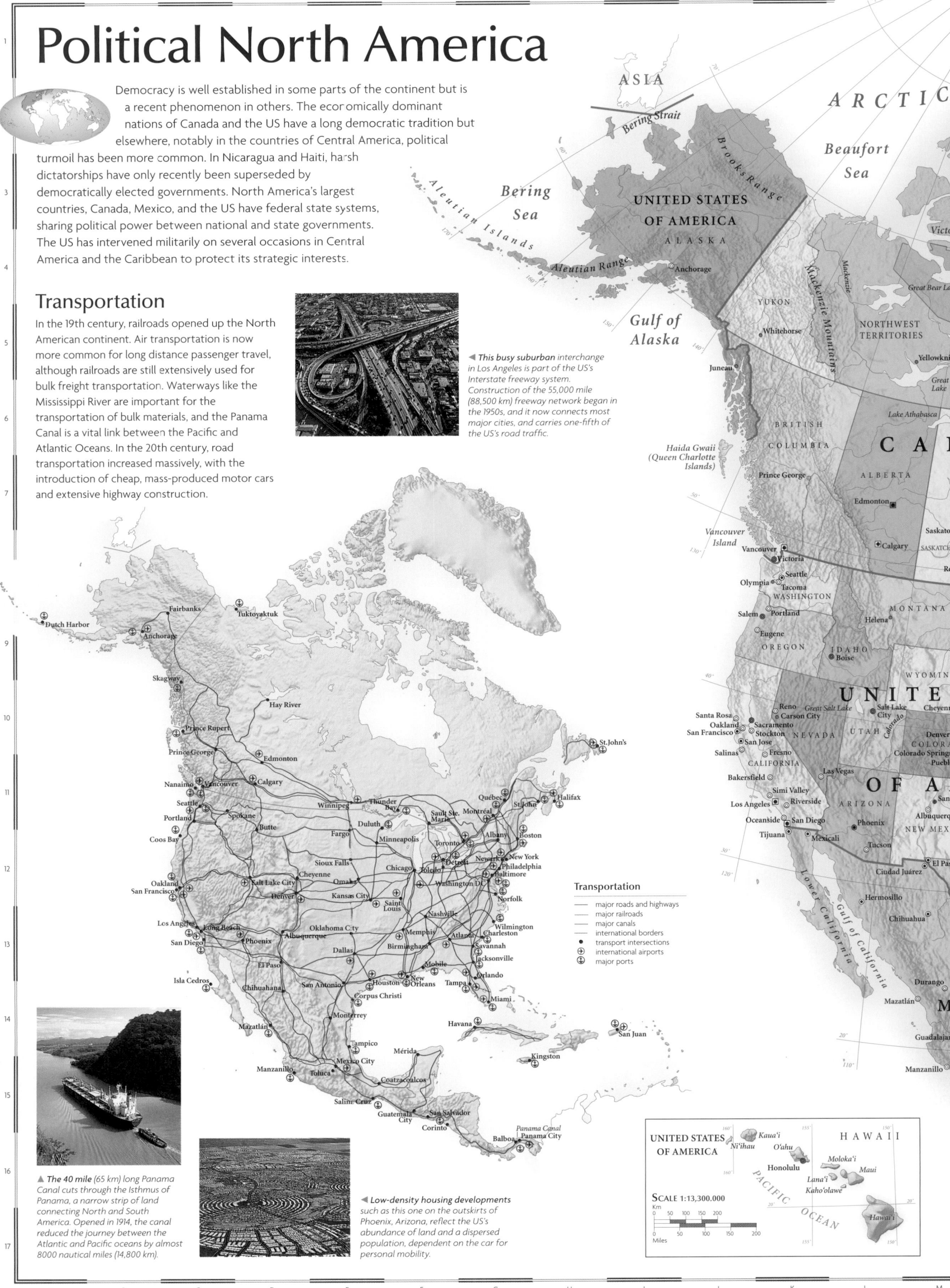

### Transportation

— major roads and highways
— major railroads
— major canals
— international borders
• transport intersections
⊕ international airports
⊕ major ports

UNITED STATES OF AMERICA

SCALE 1:13,300,000

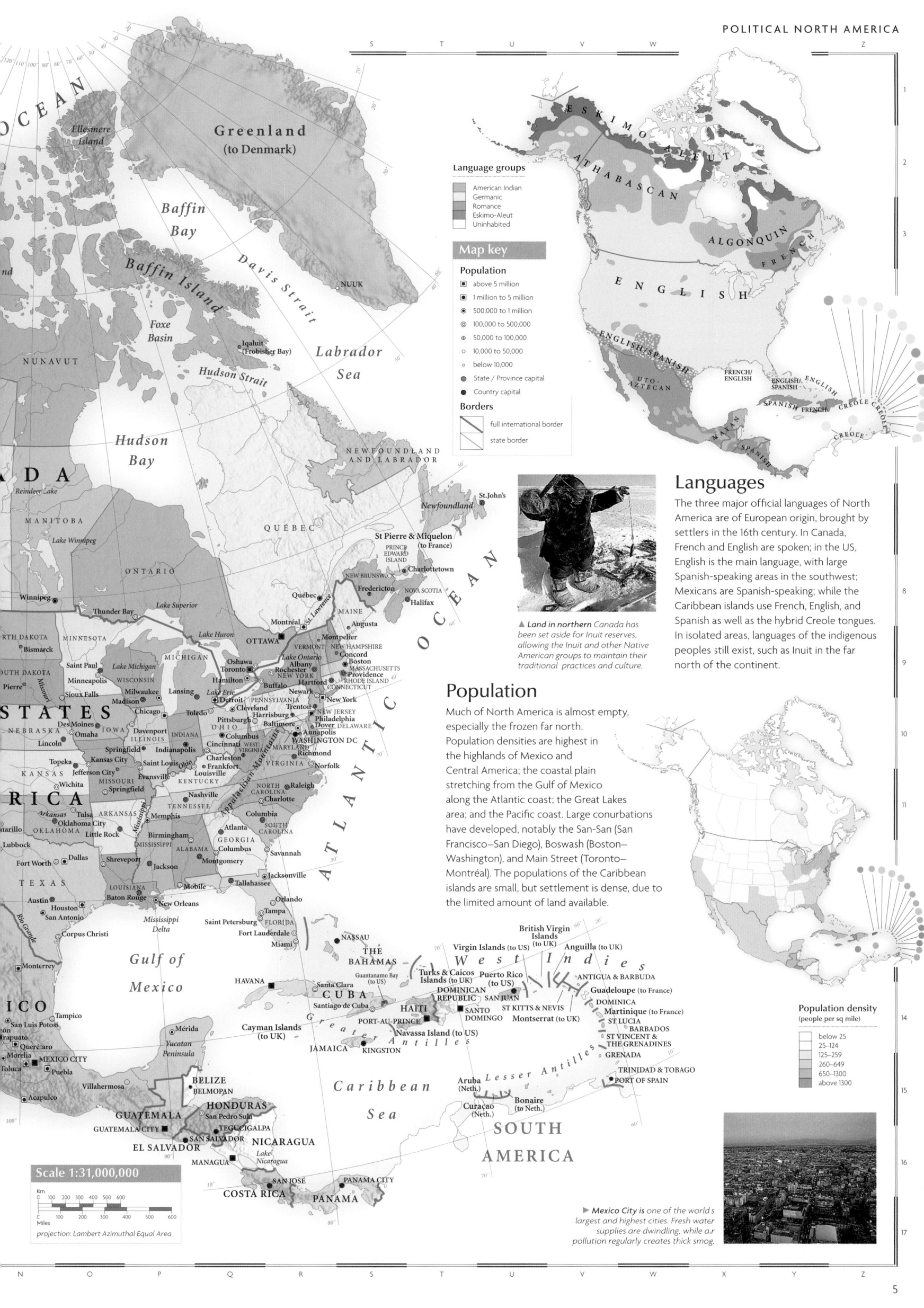

## Languages

The three major official languages of North America are of European origin, brought by settlers in the 16th century. In Canada, French and English are spoken; in the US, English is the main language, with large Spanish-speaking areas in the southwest; Mexicans are Spanish-speaking; while the Caribbean islands use French, English, and Spanish as well as the hybrid Creole tongues. In isolated areas, languages of the indigenous peoples still exist, such as Inuit in the far north of the continent.

▲ Land in northern Canada has been set aside for Inuit reserves, allowing the Inuit and other Native American groups to maintain their traditional practices and culture.

## Population

Much of North America is almost empty, especially the frozen far north. Population densities are highest in the highlands of Mexico and Central America; the coastal plain stretching from the Gulf of Mexico along the Atlantic coast; the Great Lakes area; and the Pacific coast. Large conurbations have developed, notably the San-San (San Francisco–San Diego), Boswash (Boston–Washington), and Main Street (Toronto–Montréal). The populations of the Caribbean islands are small, but settlement is dense, due to the limited amount of land available.

▶ Mexico City is one of the world's largest and highest cities. Fresh water supplies are dwindling, while air pollution regularly creates thick smog.

**Language groups**
- American Indian
- Germanic
- Romance
- Eskimo-Aleut
- Uninhabited

**Map key**

**Population**
- ▣ above 5 million
- ⊡ 1 million to 5 million
- ◉ 500,000 to 1 million
- ⊕ 100,000 to 500,000
- ⊕ 50,000 to 100,000
- ○ 10,000 to 50,000
- ∘ below 10,000
- ● State / Province capital
- ● Country capital

**Borders**
- full international border
- state border

**Population density**
(people per sq mile)
- below 25
- 25–124
- 125–259
- 260–649
- 650–1300
- above 1300

Scale 1:31,000,000

projection: Lambert Azimuthal Equal Area

# North American resources

The two northern countries of Canada and the US are richly endowed with natural resources that have helped to fuel economic development. The US is the world's largest economy, although today it is facing stiff competition from the Far East. Mexico has relied on oil revenues but there are hopes that the North American Free Trade Agreement (NAFTA), will encourage trade growth with Canada and the US. The poorer countries of Central America and the Caribbean depend largely on cash crops and tourism.

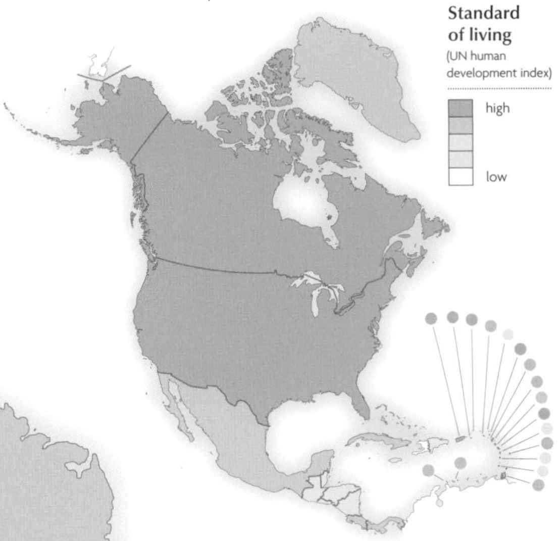

## Industry

The modern, industrialized economies of the US and Canada contrast sharply with those of Mexico, Central America, and the Caribbean. Manufacturing is especially important in the US; vehicle production is concentrated around the Great Lakes, while electronic and hi-tech industries are increasingly found in the western and southern states. Mexico depends on oil exports and assembly work, taking advantage of cheap labor. Many Central American and Caribbean countries rely heavily on agricultural exports.

◄ *After its purchase* from Russia in 1867, Alaska's frozen lands were largely ignored by the US. Oil reserves similar in magnitude to those in eastern Texas were discovered in Prudhoe Bay, Alaska in 1968. Freezing temperatures and a fragile environment hamper oil extraction.

## Standard of living

The US and Canada have one of the highest overall standards of living in the world. However, many people still live in poverty, especially in urban ghettos and some rural areas. Central America and the Caribbean are markedly poorer than their wealthier northern neighbors. Haiti is the poorest country in the western hemisphere.

**Standard of living**
(UN human development index)

high

low

▲ *South of San Francisco,* "Silicon Valley" is both a national and international center for hi-tech industries, electronic industries, and research institutions.

▲ *Multinational companies rely* on cheap labor and tax benefits to facilitate the assembly of vehicle parts in Mexican factories.

▲ *Fish such as* cod, flounder, and plaice are caught in the Grand Banks, off the Newfoundland coast, and processed in many North Atlantic coastal settlements.

▲ *The health of* the Wall Street stock market in New York is the standard measure of the state of the world's economy.

### Industry

| | |
|---|---|
| ✈ aerospace | ⚙ printing & publishing |
| ♠ brewing | ⚙ research & development |
| 🚗 car/vehicle manufacture | ⚓ shipbuilding |
| ♦ chemicals | ⚙ sugar processing |
| ☗ defense | ♠ textiles |
| ⚡ electronics | ⚒ timber processing |
| ⚙ engineering | ⚲ tobacco processing |
| 🎬 film industry | |
| S finance | ♠ coal |
| 🍴 food processing | ♦ oil |
| 💻 hi-tech industry | ♦ gas |
| ⚒ iron & steel | • industrial cities |
| 💊 pharmaceuticals | ⧄ major industrial areas |

**GNI per capita (US$)**

below 1999
2000–4999
5000–9999
10,000–19,999
20,000–24,999
above 25,000

### Map labels

ARCTIC OCEAN
Beaufort Sea
Bering Strait
RUSS. FED.
Bering Sea
Prudhoe Bay
Gulf of Alaska
USA
Baffin Bay
Greenland (to Denmark)
Labrador Sea
Hudson Strait
Hudson Bay
CANADA
Vancouver
Calgary
Seattle
Winnipeg
Portland
Montréal
Boston
Minneapolis
Toronto
Buffalo
Albany
Milwaukee
Detroit
New York
UNITED STATES OF AMERICA
Chicago
Cleveland
Pittsburgh
Philadelphia
Dayton
Baltimore
San Francisco
Denver
Kansas City
Saint Louis
Cincinnati
Wichita
Greensboro
Nashville
Charlotte
Tulsa
Los Angeles
Phoenix
Atlanta
San Diego
Dallas
Birmingham
Tijuana
Ciudad Juárez
El Paso
Houston
Jacksonville
New Orleans
Orlando
Tampa
Monterrey
Miami
Gulf of Mexico
PACIFIC OCEAN
ATLANTIC OCEAN
Guadalajara
Mexico City
MEXICO
West Indies
BAHAMAS
Havana
CUBA
Virgin Islands (to US)
British Virgin Islands (to UK)
Anguilla (to UK)
ST KITTS & NEVIS
ANTIGUA & BARBUDA
Turks & Caicos Islands (to UK)
Puerto Rico (to US)
San Juan
Guadeloupe (to France)
DOMINICA
Martinique (to France)
ST LUCIA
BARBADOS
ST VINCENT & THE GRENADINES
GRENADA
TRINIDAD & TOBAGO
Port of Spain
Cayman Islands (to UK)
JAMAICA
HAITI
DOMINICAN REPUBLIC
Port-au-Prince
Santo Domingo
Greater Antilles
Lesser Antilles
Navassa Island (to US)
Aruba (to Neth.)
Curaçao (to Neth.)
Bonaire (to Neth.)
Caribbean Sea
VENEZUELA
COLOMBIA
BELIZE
GUATEMALA
Guatemala City
HONDURAS
Tegucigalpa
EL SALVADOR
San Salvador
NICARAGUA
Managua
San José
COSTA RICA
Panama City
PANAMA

## Environmental issues

Many fragile environments are under threat throughout the region. In Haiti, all the primary rain forest has been destroyed, while air pollution from factories and cars in Mexico City is among the worst in the world. Elsewhere, industry and mining pose threats, particularly in the delicate arctic environment of Alaska where oil spills have polluted coastlines and decimated fish stocks.

## Mineral resources

Fossil fuels are exploited in considerable quantities throughout the continent. Coal mining in the Appalachians is declining but vast open pits exist further west in Wyoming. Oil and natural gas are found in Alaska, Texas, the Gulf of Mexico, and the Canadian West. Canada has large quantities of nickel, while Jamaica has considerable deposits of bauxite, and Mexico has large reserves of silver.

**Mineral resources**
- oil field
- gas field
- coal field
- bauxite
- copper
- gold
- iron
- lead
- nickel
- phosphates
- silver
- uranium

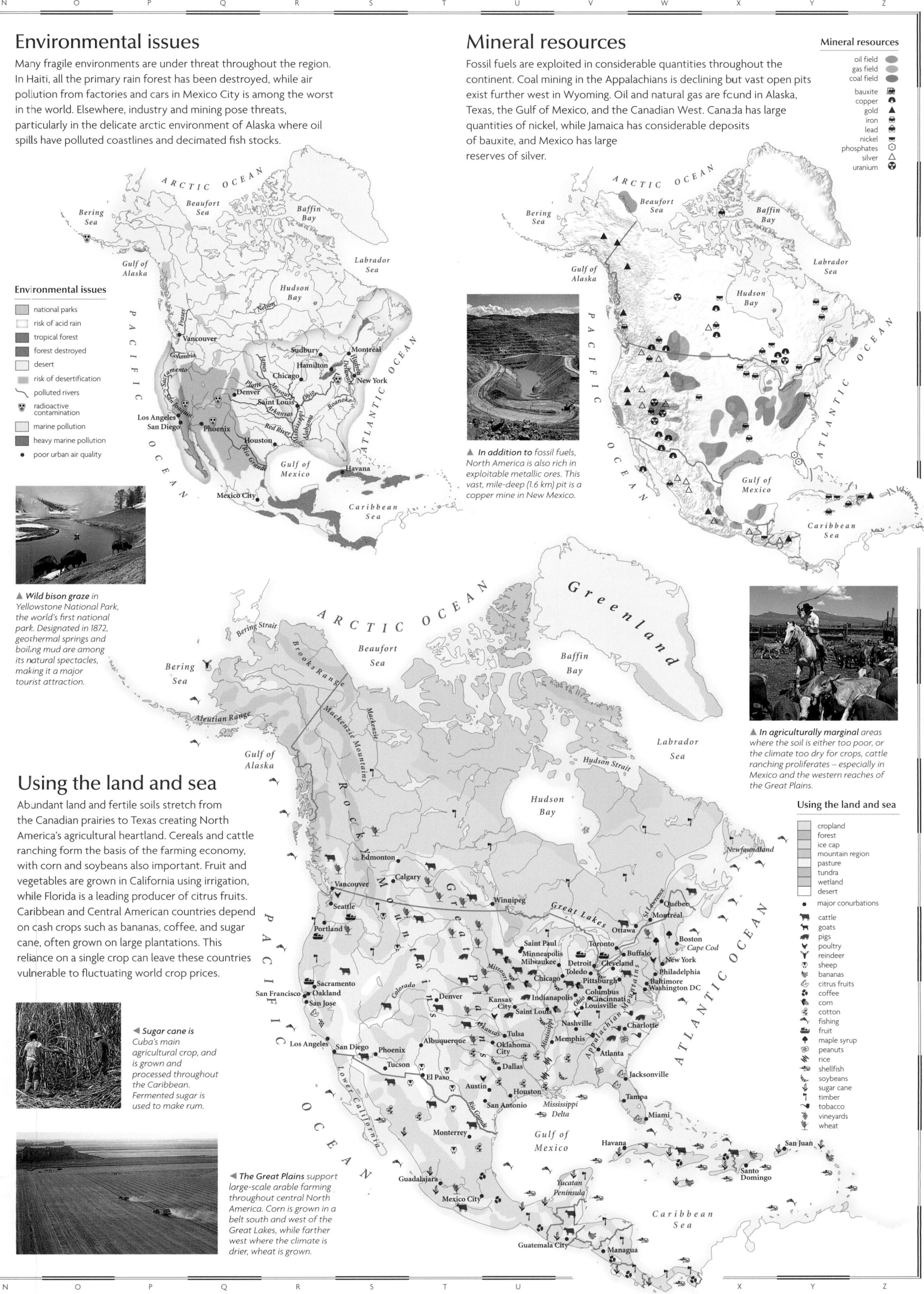

**Environmental issues**
- national parks
- risk of acid rain
- tropical forest
- forest destroyed
- desert
- risk of desertification
- polluted rivers
- radioactive contamination
- marine pollution
- heavy marine pollution
- poor urban air quality

▲ *Wild bison graze* in Yellowstone National Park, the world's first national park. Designated in 1872, geothermal springs and boiling mud are among its natural spectacles, making it a major tourist attraction.

▲ *In addition to* fossil fuels, North America is also rich in exploitable metallic ores. This vast, mile-deep (1.6 km) pit is a copper mine in New Mexico.

▲ *In agriculturally marginal* areas where the soil is either too poor, or the climate too dry for crops, cattle ranching proliferates – especially in Mexico and the western reaches of the Great Plains.

## Using the land and sea

Abundant land and fertile soils stretch from the Canadian prairies to Texas creating North America's agricultural heartland. Cereals and cattle ranching form the basis of the farming economy, with corn and soybeans also important. Fruit and vegetables are grown in California using irrigation, while Florida is a leading producer of citrus fruits. Caribbean and Central American countries depend on cash crops such as bananas, coffee, and sugar cane, often grown on large plantations. This reliance on a single crop can leave these countries vulnerable to fluctuating world crop prices.

**Using the land and sea**
- cropland
- forest
- ice cap
- mountain region
- pasture
- tundra
- wetland
- desert
- major conurbations
- cattle
- goats
- pigs
- poultry
- reindeer
- sheep
- bananas
- citrus fruits
- coffee
- corn
- cotton
- fishing
- fruit
- maple syrup
- peanuts
- rice
- shellfish
- soybeans
- sugar cane
- timber
- tobacco
- vineyards
- wheat

◀ *Sugar cane is* Cuba's main agricultural crop, and is grown and processed throughout the Caribbean. Fermented sugar is used to make rum.

◀ *The Great Plains* support large-scale arable farming throughout central North America. Corn is grown in a belt south and west of the Great Lakes, while farther west where the climate is drier, wheat is grown.

# Canada

Canada is the second largest country in the world, and with only about one-tenth of its land area inhabited, it is one of the most sparsely populated. Canada became a confederation in 1867, though Newfoundland did not join until 1949. As a founding member of the UN and of the Commonwealth, Canada has played an important role in international affairs. A constitutional crisis, focusing on the French-speaking Québécois, and Inuit, and Native American land rights, dominated politics in the 1990s. In 1999, part of the Northwest Territories, Nunavut, became a self-governing homeland for the Inuit.

◀ *The Selwyn Mountains* in northwestern Canada form part of the Rocky Mountains. The highest point, Keele Peak, rises to 9750 ft (2972 m).

## Transportation and industry

Abundant energy in the form of coal, oil, natural gas, and hydroelectric power underpins Canadian industry. Over 75% of manufacturing is concentrated in the Great Lakes–St. Lawrence region, including prospering aerospace, transportation, and hi-tech industries. Across Canada as a whole, manufacturing has developed around a diversified, high-quality resource base and a wide range of metallic and nonmetallic minerals.

◀ *Canada has one* of the world's highest rates of energy consumption per person. It is endowed with vast hydroelectric potential from which more than 60% of its electricity requirements are generated.

### Major industry and infrastructure

- ✈ aerospace
- 🚗 car manufacture
- ⚙ chemicals
- engineering
- 🍴 food processing
- 💻 hi-tech industry
- hydroelectric power
- 🛢 oil & gas
- ⛏ mining
- 🌲 timber processing
- ■ capital cities
- ● major towns
- ✈ international airports
- — major roads
- major industrial areas

### Transportation network

| | |
|---|---|
| 309,019 miles (497,375 km) | 10,500 miles (16,900 km) |
| 8049 miles (12,995 km) | 1864 miles (3000 km) |

*In recent years the road network has been expanded, especially links to remote areas. Meanwhile, for long-distance travel, air transportation now supersedes the declining rail network, which focuses mainly on east–west routes.*

## Using the land and sea

The majority of Canada's agricultural land is found in the prairies, which cover 140 million acres (57 million ha) and support wheat and grain-fed cattle. More specialized crops, such as fruit and vegetables, are grown in pockets of agricultural land in the east and west. Of Canada's many islands, only Prince Edward Island has notable farmland. Further north, boreal forests, exploited for timber, run in an almost unbroken arc, giving way to uncultivable tundra and ice sheets in the far north.

### The urban/rural population divide

urban 77%       rural 23%

0 10 20 30 40 50 60 70 80 90 100

| Population density | Total land area |
|---|---|
| 9 people per sq mile (3 people per sq km) | 3,559,294 sq miles (9,220,970 sq km) |

### Land use and agricultural distribution

- 🐄 cattle
- 🌾 cereals
- 🎣 fishing
- 🍎 fruit
- ⅃ timber
- ■ capital cities
- ● major towns

- pasture
- cropland
- forest
- wetland
- mountain region
- barren
- tundra

◀ *The climate and* topography of the prairies makes them ideally suited to farming. Long summer days, moderate temperatures, limited rainfall, and flat plains provide excellent conditions for wheat farming.

Scale 1:14,700,000

projection: Lambert Azimuthal Equal Area

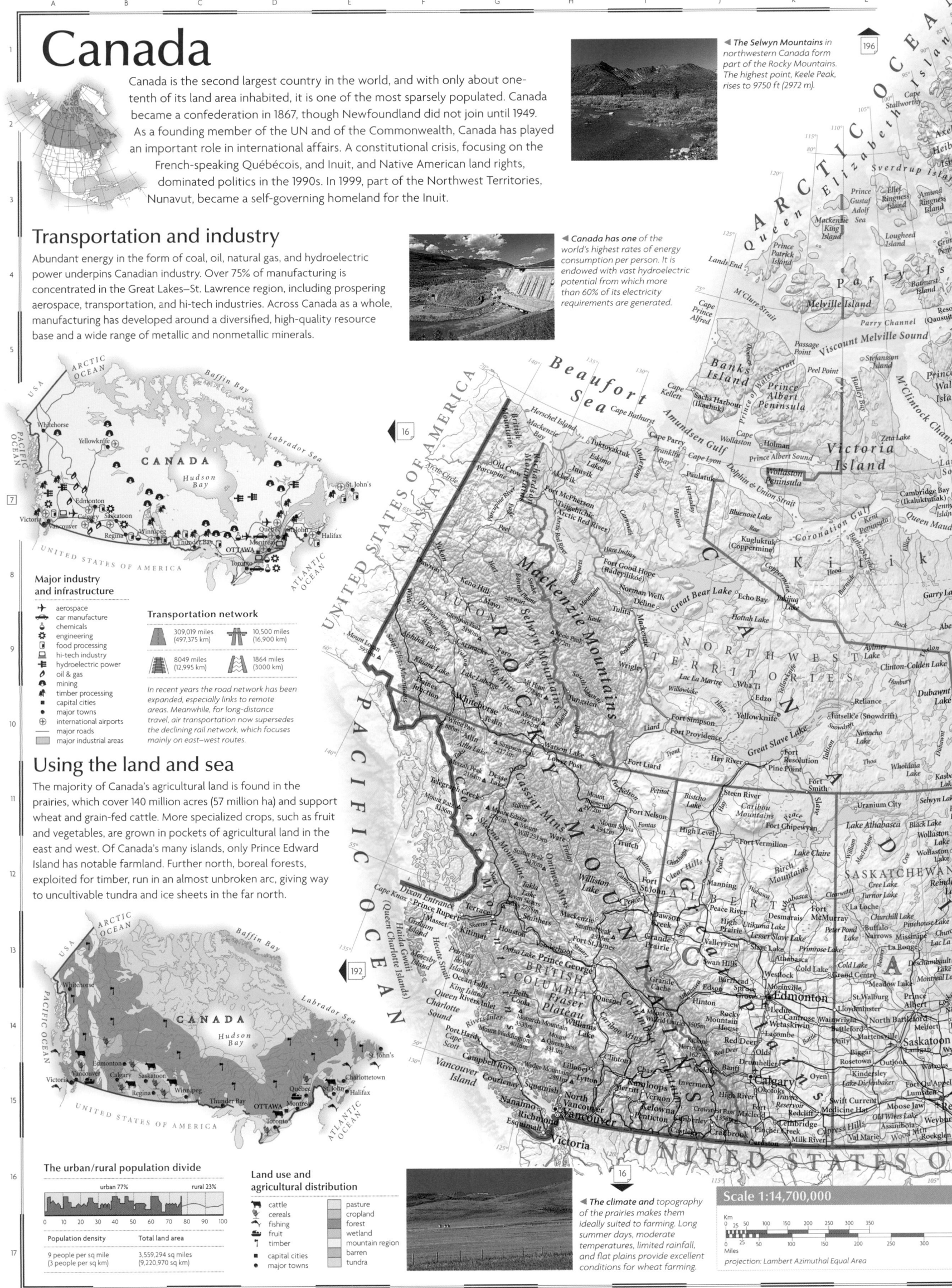

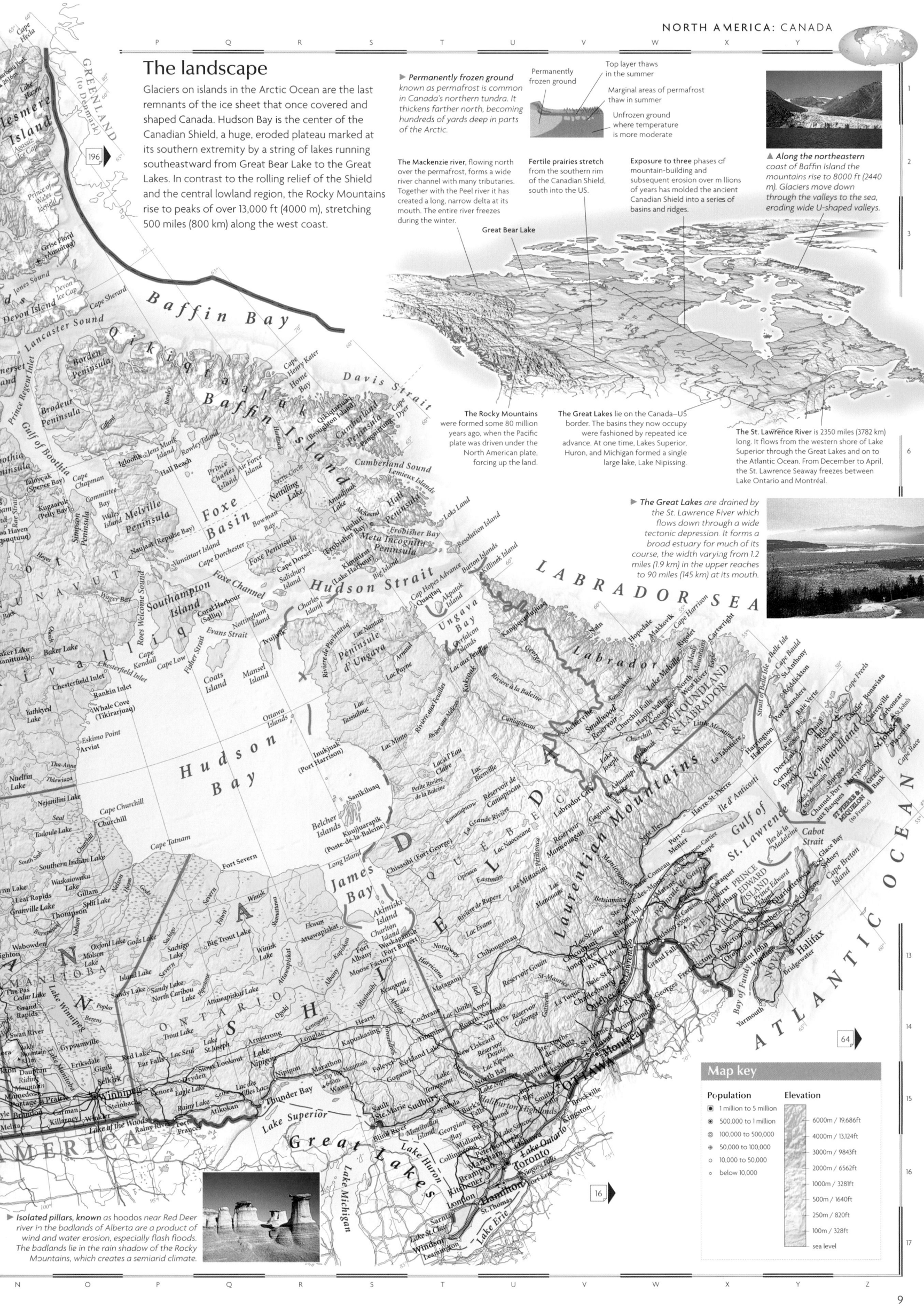

# The landscape

Glaciers on islands in the Arctic Ocean are the last remnants of the ice sheet that once covered and shaped Canada. Hudson Bay is the center of the Canadian Shield, a huge, eroded plateau marked at its southern extremity by a string of lakes running southeastward from Great Bear Lake to the Great Lakes. In contrast to the rolling relief of the Shield and the central lowland region, the Rocky Mountains rise to peaks of over 13,000 ft (4000 m), stretching 500 miles (800 km) along the west coast.

▶ **Permanently frozen ground** known as permafrost is common in Canada's northern tundra. It thickens farther north, becoming hundreds of yards deep in parts of the Arctic.

Permanently frozen ground

Top layer thaws in the summer

Marginal areas of permafrost thaw in summer

Unfrozen ground where temperature is more moderate

▲ **Along the northeastern** coast of Baffin Island the mountains rise to 8000 ft (2440 m). Glaciers move down through the valleys to the sea, eroding wide U-shaped valleys.

**The Mackenzie river,** flowing north over the permafrost, forms a wide river channel with many tributaries. Together with the Peel river it has created a long, narrow delta at its mouth. The entire river freezes during the winter.

**Fertile prairies stretch** from the southern rim of the Canadian Shield, south into the US.

**Exposure to three** phases of mountain-building and subsequent erosion over millions of years has molded the ancient Canadian Shield into a series of basins and ridges.

Great Bear Lake

**The Rocky Mountains** were formed some 80 million years ago, when the Pacific plate was driven under the North American plate, forcing up the land.

**The Great Lakes** lie on the Canada–US border. The basins they now occupy were fashioned by repeated ice advance. At one time, Lakes Superior, Huron, and Michigan formed a single large lake, Lake Nipissing.

**The St. Lawrence River** is 2350 miles (3782 km) long. It flows from the western shore of Lake Superior through the Great Lakes and on to the Atlantic Ocean. From December to April, the St. Lawrence Seaway freezes between Lake Ontario and Montréal.

▶ **The Great Lakes** are drained by the St. Lawrence River which flows down through a wide tectonic depression. It forms a broad estuary for much of its course, the width varying from 1.2 miles (1.9 km) in the upper reaches to 90 miles (145 km) at its mouth.

▶ **Isolated pillars, known** as hoodoos near Red Deer river in the badlands of Alberta are a product of wind and water erosion, especially flash floods. The badlands lie in the rain shadow of the Rocky Mountains, which creates a semiarid climate.

## Map key

**Population**
- ◉ 1 million to 5 million
- ◉ 500,000 to 1 million
- ⊙ 100,000 to 500,000
- ⊕ 50,000 to 100,000
- ○ 10,000 to 50,000
- ○ below 10,000

**Elevation**
- 6000m / 19,686ft
- 4000m / 13,124ft
- 3000m / 9843ft
- 2000m / 6562ft
- 1000m / 3281ft
- 500m / 1640ft
- 250m / 820ft
- 100m / 328ft
- sea level

# Canada:
## WESTERN PROVINCES

Alberta, British Columbia, Manitoba,
Saskatchewan, Yukon

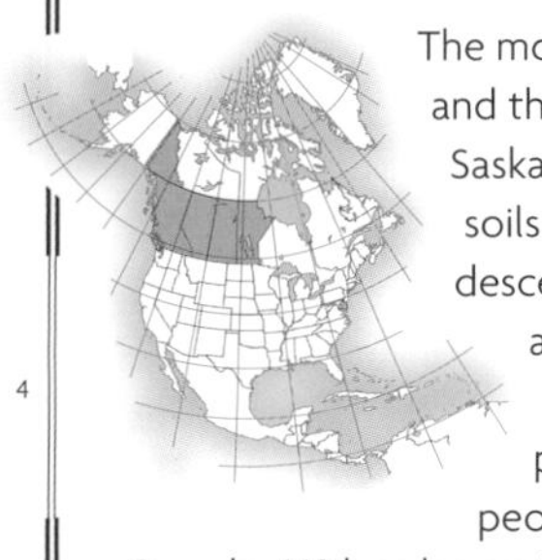

The mountains of the west coast, incorporating British Columbia
and the Yukon, descend into the vast, flat prairies of Alberta,
Saskatchewan, and Manitoba. The empty lands and fertile
soils of the prairie provinces attracted migrants, and the
descendants of early European immigrants still make up
a large proportion of the population. The mechanization
of agriculture has reduced the need for labor, and rural
population densities remain low. The majority of the
people live within 100 miles (160 km) of the southern
Canada–US border, and in British Columbia, one of the leading Canadian
provinces in terms of economic wealth. The Yukon, in the far
north, remains a relatively unspoiled wilderness, containing large,
untapped mineral reserves. This province has a significant population of
Native American people, many of whom maintain a traditional lifestyle.

## Using the land and sea

Wheat farming is the economic mainstay of Alberta, Manitoba, and
Saskatchewan, which contain 82% of farmland in Canada. Cattle
are also raised on the prairies. Forestry and fishing are the most
prominent resource-based industries in British Columbia. Despite
the mountainous terrain, fruit and specialized grains can be grown
in the Okanagan and Fraser valleys.

### Land use and agricultural distribution

- cattle
- cereals
- fishing
- fruit
- timber
- major towns
- pasture
- cropland
- forest
- wetland
- barren
- tundra

▲ Large, highly-mechanized and
often very specialized farms,
requiring huge investment but little
labor, characterize modern
farming in the prairies.

### The urban/rural population divide

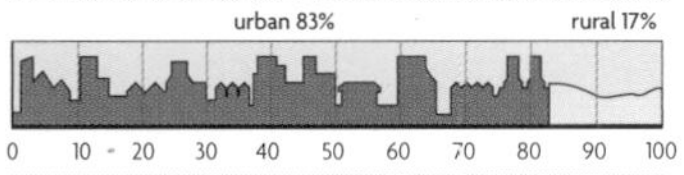

urban 83%     rural 17%

0  10  20  30  40  50  60  70  80  90  100

| Population density | Total land area |
|---|---|
| 8 people per sq mile (3 people per sq km) | 1,230,547 sq miles (3,187,120 sq km) |

## Transportation & industry

The western provinces contain a wealth of mineral resources.
Alberta holds the bulk of Canada's fossil fuels; the other
provinces contain reserves of metallic ores, such as zinc, lead,
and silver. Isolation from markets has slowed the development
of manufacturing, restricting it to the large cities like Vancouver,
Winnipeg, and Calgary. Hydroelectric power is widely exploited,
although there is increasing concern about potential
ecological damage.

### Major industry and infrastructure

- aerospace
- chemicals
- coal
- engineering
- food processing
- hydroelectric power
- mining
- oil & gas
- timber processing
- major towns
- international airports
- major roads
- major industrial areas

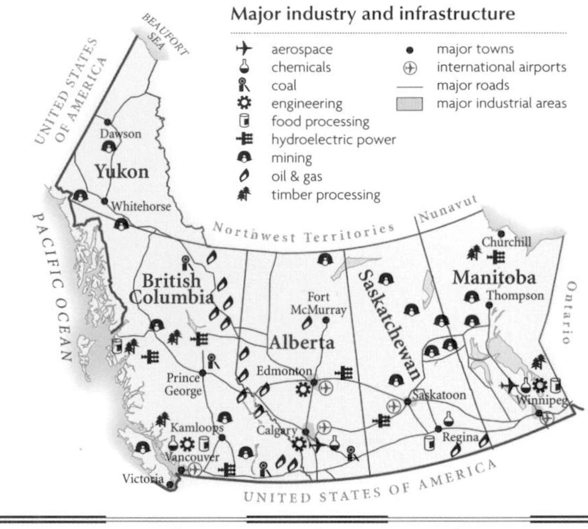

### Transportation network

- 82,438 miles (135,145 km)
- 6459 miles (10,401 km)
- 24,041 miles (38,694 km)
- None

The transportation network of
the western provinces is
dominated by east–west routes
that weave through mountain
passes and spread across the
plains. Access to some northern
areas is restricted to air travel.

▲ The Fraser River valley is a major
area of settlement in British
Columbia. Railroads cross the
Rocky Mountains via this valley.

▲ Established in 1907,
Jasper National Park lies
in the heart of the Rocky
Mountains. It is noted for
its spectacular alpine
scenery and contains
part of the large
Columbia Icefield.

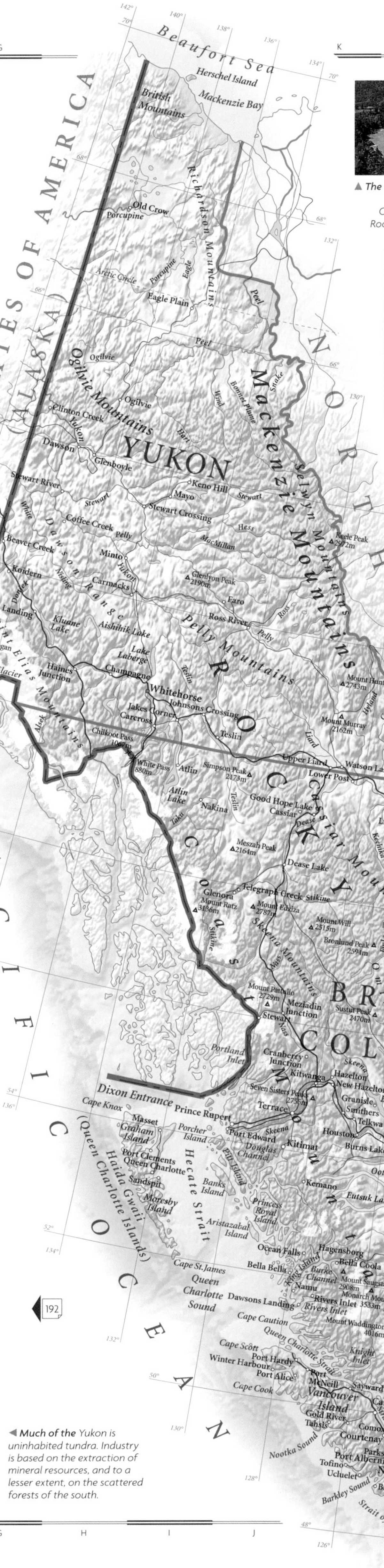

◄ Much of the Yukon is
uninhabited tundra. Industry
is based on the extraction of
mineral resources, and to a
lesser extent, on the scattered
forests of the south.

N O P Q R S T U V W X Y

# The landscape

The massive Rocky Mountains form a continental divide between rivers flowing eastward and westward. The interior plains lie east of the mountains, stretching from the Arctic Circle south into the US. Covered with glacial deposits from the last Ice Age, these are interspersed with hilly regions and long, steep escarpments.

## Map key

### Population
- ◉ 500,000 to 1 million
- ◎ 100,000 to 500,000
- ⊕ 50,000 to 100,000
- ○ 10,000 to 50,000
- ∘ below 10,000

### Elevation
- 6000m / 19,686ft
- 4000m / 13,124ft
- 3000m / 9843ft
- 2000m / 6562ft
- 1000m / 3281ft
- 500m / 1640ft
- 250m / 820ft
- 100m / 328ft
- sea level

## Scale 1:8,250,000

Km
0 25 50 100 150 200 250

Miles
0 25 50 100 150 200 250

*projection: Lambert Conformal Conic*

Mount Logan rises 19,551 ft (5959 m). It is the highest peak in Canada.

The Columbia Icefield in the Rocky Mountains is the source of two major rivers, the Athabasca and the North Saskatchewan.

The badlands of Alberta were created when east-flowing rivers, swollen by meltwater at the end of the last Ice Age, cut deep, wide canyons producing eroded, barren landscapes.

South Saskatchewan River

Vegetated island

River flow is diverted by deposited sediments

Bar

Sand flat

▲ *Braided rivers are* shallow and fast-flowing. The interlaced branches are formed when excess sediments, which can no longer be transported, are deposited. The sediments collect in the river channel forming bars and sand flats. Islands form when the bars are colonized by vegetation.

▲ *Across the tundra* of northern Manitoba, widespread permafrost inhibits water from permeating the soil. This causes rivers like the Churchill to flow in many channels, which can be frozen for up to six months during the winter.

The Nelson and Churchill rivers drain northward across the Canadian Shield to Hudson Bay. The shield covers three-fifths of Saskatchewan.

Setting Lake

The Rocky Mountain Trench is the longest linear fault in the world. It has formed a straight, flat-bottomed valley between 2–9 miles (4–15 km) wide, and up to 3280 ft (1000 m) deep.

Hundreds of islands dot the fjord-indented coast of British Columbia; the largest is Vancouver Island.

Three major passes cut through the Rocky Mountains: Yellowhead, Kicking Horse, and Crowsnest. They are all used as transportation routes through the mountains.

The Cypress Hills rise to 4806 ft (1465 m) above the surrounding plain. Having escaped the last glaciation they contain unique plant and animal life. The silvery lupine, bunchberry, and lodgepole pine all grow in the cool, moist climate of the hills.

The Alberta and Saskatchewan plains bear strong testament to past glaciations. The Assiniboine, Saskatchewan and Qu'Appelle rivers occupy flat-bottomed, steep-sided valleys eroded during the last Ice Age by glacial meltwater.

*Ancient granite outcrops,* part of the Canadian Shield, rise above the surface of Setting Lake, which was initially formed by meltwater from the last Ice Age.

The lowlands of Manitoba are a basin that once held the vast post-glacial Lake Agassiz, remnants of which include Lake Winnipeg, Lake Winnipegosis, and Lake Manitoba.

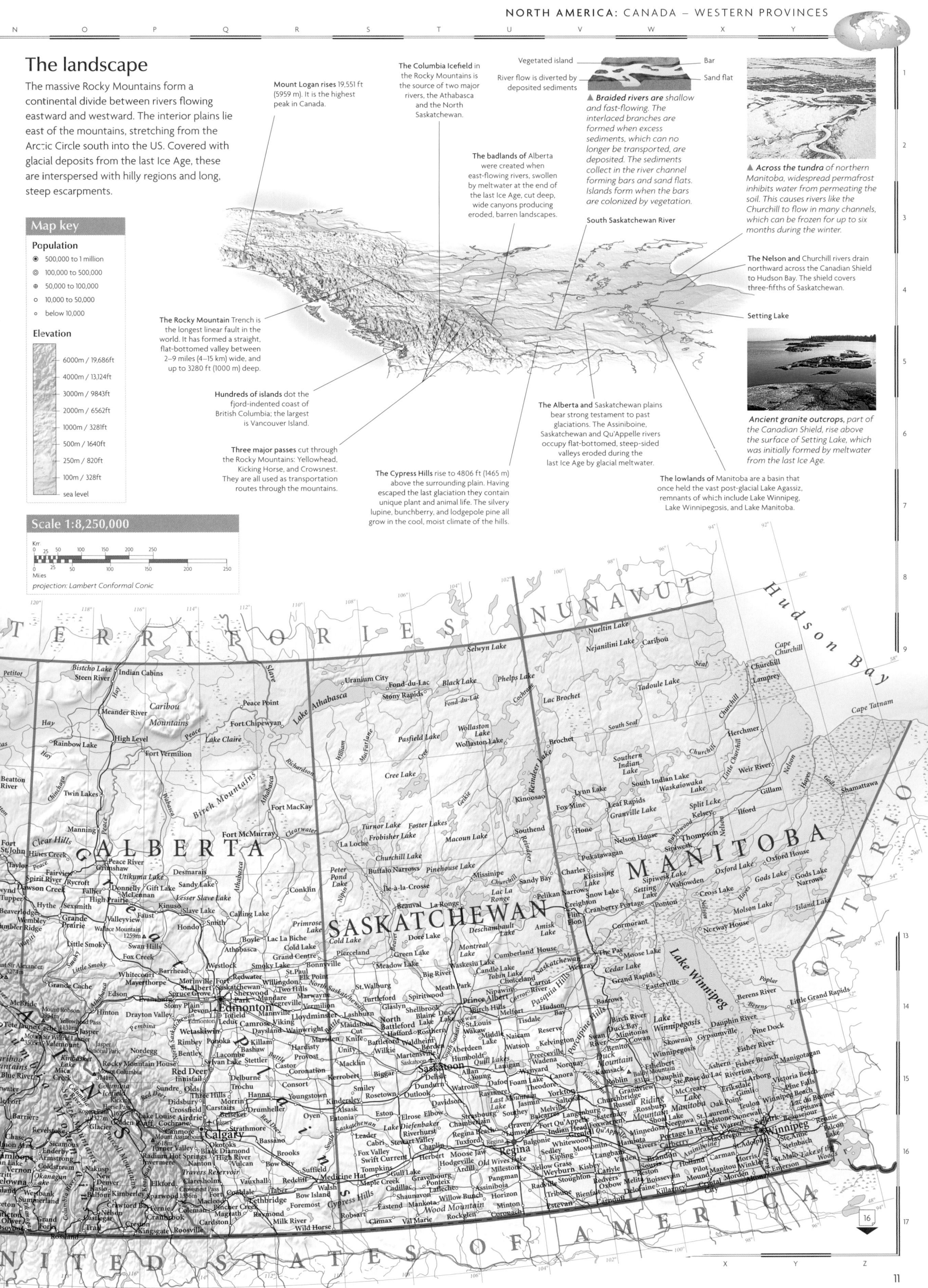

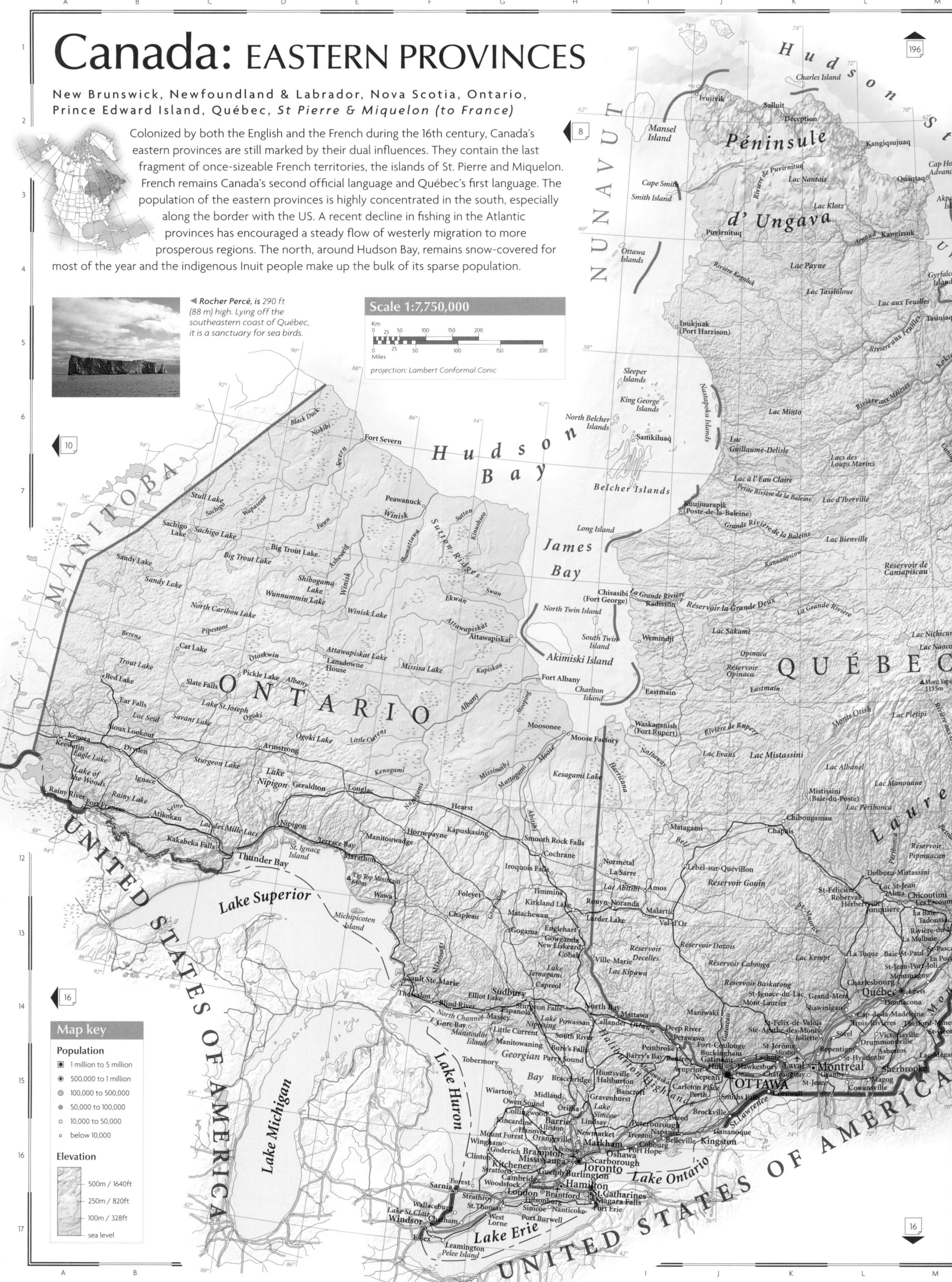

# Canada: EASTERN PROVINCES

New Brunswick, Newfoundland & Labrador, Nova Scotia, Ontario,
Prince Edward Island, Québec, *St Pierre & Miquelon (to France)*

Colonized by both the English and the French during the 16th century, Canada's eastern provinces are still marked by their dual influences. They contain the last fragment of once-sizeable French territories, the islands of St. Pierre and Miquelon. French remains Canada's second official language and Québec's first language. The population of the eastern provinces is highly concentrated in the south, especially along the border with the US. A recent decline in fishing in the Atlantic provinces has encouraged a steady flow of westerly migration to more prosperous regions. The north, around Hudson Bay, remains snow-covered for most of the year and the indigenous Inuit people make up the bulk of its sparse population.

◀ *Rocher Percé, is 290 ft (88 m) high. Lying off the southeastern coast of Québec, it is a sanctuary for sea birds.*

**Scale 1:7,750,000**

Km
0  25  50      100      150      200

Miles
0    25    50        100        150        200

projection: Lambert Conformal Conic

## Map key

**Population**
- 1 million to 5 million
- 500,000 to 1 million
- 100,000 to 500,000
- 50,000 to 100,000
- 10,000 to 50,000
- below 10,000

**Elevation**
- 500m / 1640ft
- 250m / 820ft
- 100m / 328ft
- sea level

# The landscape

Much of eastern Canada is part of the Canadian Shield. Glaciers have scoured the land leaving deposits that have dammed and diverted streams, to create a rocky landscape strewn with lakes and swamps. Much of the ground is subject to permafrost, which further impedes drainage. The uplands in the far east are the most northerly extension of the Appalachian mountain chain.

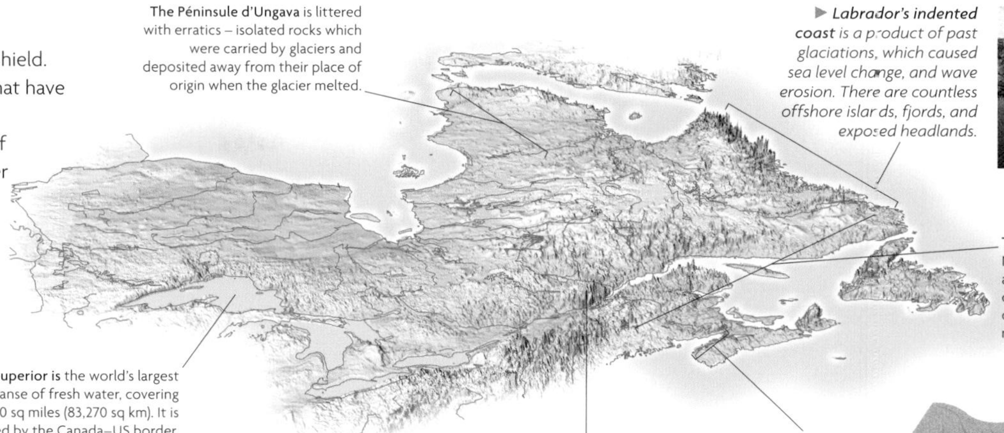

The Péninsule d'Ungava is littered with erratics – isolated rocks which were carried by glaciers and deposited away from their place of origin when the glacier melted.

▶ **Labrador's indented coast** is a product of past glaciations, which caused sea level change, and wave erosion. There are countless offshore islands, fjords, and exposed headlands.

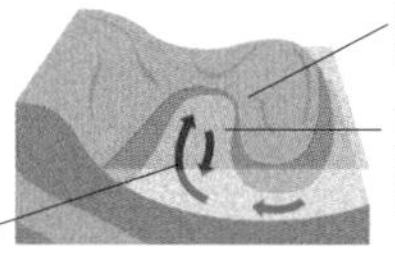

**The eroded highlands** of New Brunswick, Nova Scotia, and Newfoundland are part of the Appalachian mountain chain, formed over 400 million years ago.

**Lake Superior is** the world's largest expanse of fresh water, covering 32,150 sq miles (83,270 sq km). It is crossed by the Canada–US border.

**Bay of Fundy**
Tidal waters are channeled down the bay

Steep cliffs bound the bay

The bay is 94 miles (151 km) long

▲ **At the Bay** of Fundy, incoming waves are funneled down the long, narrow, steep-sided bay. These topographical features cause fast-flowing tides which can rise 70 ft (21 m).

▶ **The forested Laurentides Park** incorporates part of the Laurentian Mountains. Within its boundaries are over 1600 lakes.

Laurentides Park

▲ **The tides at** the Bay of Fundy are among the highest in the world. At low tide the tree-topped rocks have been likened to flowerpots.

# Transportation & industry

Both Québec and Ontario have a diversified manufacturing sector located in the south. Across the rest of the region, industry is largely based around local resources, which accounts for the large number of fish and timber processing plants and mines. Many of the fast-flowing rivers are also gradually being harnessed for hydroelectric power.

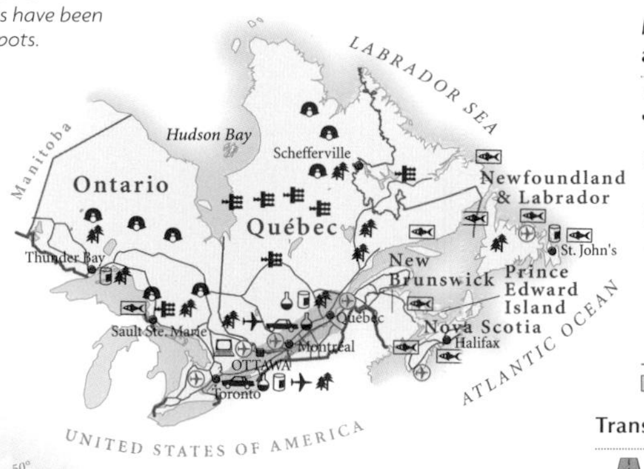

**Major industry and infrastructure**

- ✈ aerospace
- 🚗 vehicle manufacture
- 🧪 chemicals
- 🐟 fish processing
- 🍴 food processing
- 💻 hi-tech industry
- ⚡ hydroelectric power
- ⛏ mining
- 🌲 timber processing
- ● capital cities
- ● major towns
- ✈ international airports
- — major roads
- ▭ major industrial areas

**Transportation network**

- 84,522 miles (136,325 km)
- 1858 miles (2998 km)
- 20,602 miles (33,159 km)
- 376 miles (606 km)

The majority of Canada's large ports lie in the east. Since the 1960s the region's rail network has been steadily reduced; Newfoundland recently lost its last remaining line, the Long-Cross Island line.

▲ **Fish processing is** a major industry in the Atlantic provinces. Fogo Island, off Newfoundland, has barely a thousand inhabitants but it is able to sustain a number of cod canneries.

# Using the land & sea

With thin soils restricting farming to the south, the forests that grow in vast unbroken tracts across eastern Canada provide an important source of revenue. Coastal communities rely heavily on the rich fishing grounds of the Atlantic Ocean, although foreign competition and overfishing have resulted in strict policies to conserve stocks.

**The urban/rural population divide**

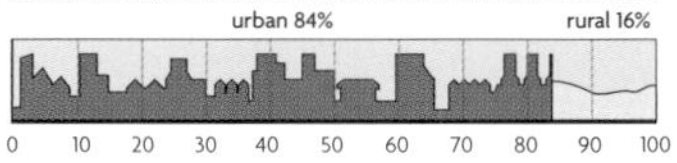

urban 84%          rural 16%

0  10  20  30  40  50  60  70  80  90  100

| Population density | Total land area |
|---|---|
| 21 people per sq mile (8 people per sq km) | 1,076,227 sq miles (2,787,431 sq km) |

**Land use and agricultural distribution**

- 🐄 cattle
- 🌾 cereals
- 🐟 fishing
- 🍎 fruit
- 🌲 timber
- ● capital cities
- ● major towns
- ▢ pasture
- ▢ cropland
- ▢ forest
- ▢ tundra

▶ **Prince Edward Island** is the only Atlantic province with notable agricultural land. The island is Canada's leading producer of potatoes.

# Southeastern Canada

## Southern Ontario, Southern Québec

The southern parts of Québec and Ontario form the economic heart of Canada. The two provinces are divided by their language and culture; in Québec, French is the main language, whereas English is spoken in Ontario. Separatist sentiment in Québec has led to a provincial referendum on the question of a sovereignty association with Canada. The region contains Canada's capital, Ottawa, and its two largest cities: Toronto, the center of commerce, and Montréal, the cultural and administrative heart of French Canada.

▲ *The port at* Montréal *is situated on the St. Lawrence Seaway. A network of 16 locks allows oceangoing vessels access to routes once plied by fur-trappers and early settlers.*

▶ *Niagara Falls lies on the border between Canada and the US. It comprises a system of two falls: American Falls, in New York, is separated from Horseshoe Falls, in Ontario, by Goat Island. Horseshoe Falls, seen here, plunges 184 ft (56 m) and is 2500 ft (762 m) wide.*

## Major industry and infrastructure

- car manufacture
- chemicals
- engineering
- finance
- food processing
- hi-tech industry
- mining
- iron & steel
- textiles
- paper industry
- timber processing
- capital cities
- major towns
- international airports
- major roads
- major industrial areas

## Transportation & industry

The cities of southern Québec and Ontario, and their hinterlands, form the heart of Canadian manufacturing industry. Toronto is Canada's leading financial center, and Ontario's motor and aerospace industries have developed around the city. A major center for nickel mining lies to the north of Toronto. Most of Québec's industry is located in Montréal, the oldest port in North America. Chemicals, paper manufacture, and the construction of transportation equipment are leading industrial activities.

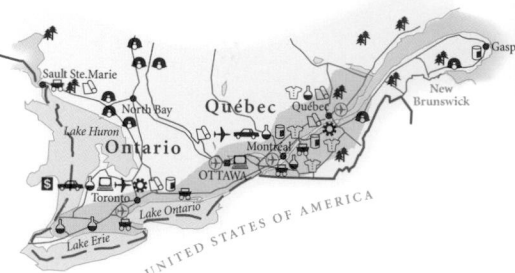

### Transportation network

*The opening of the St. Lawrence Seaway in 1959 finally allowed oceangoing ships (up to 24,000 tons (tonnes)) access to the interior of Canada, creating a vital trading route.*

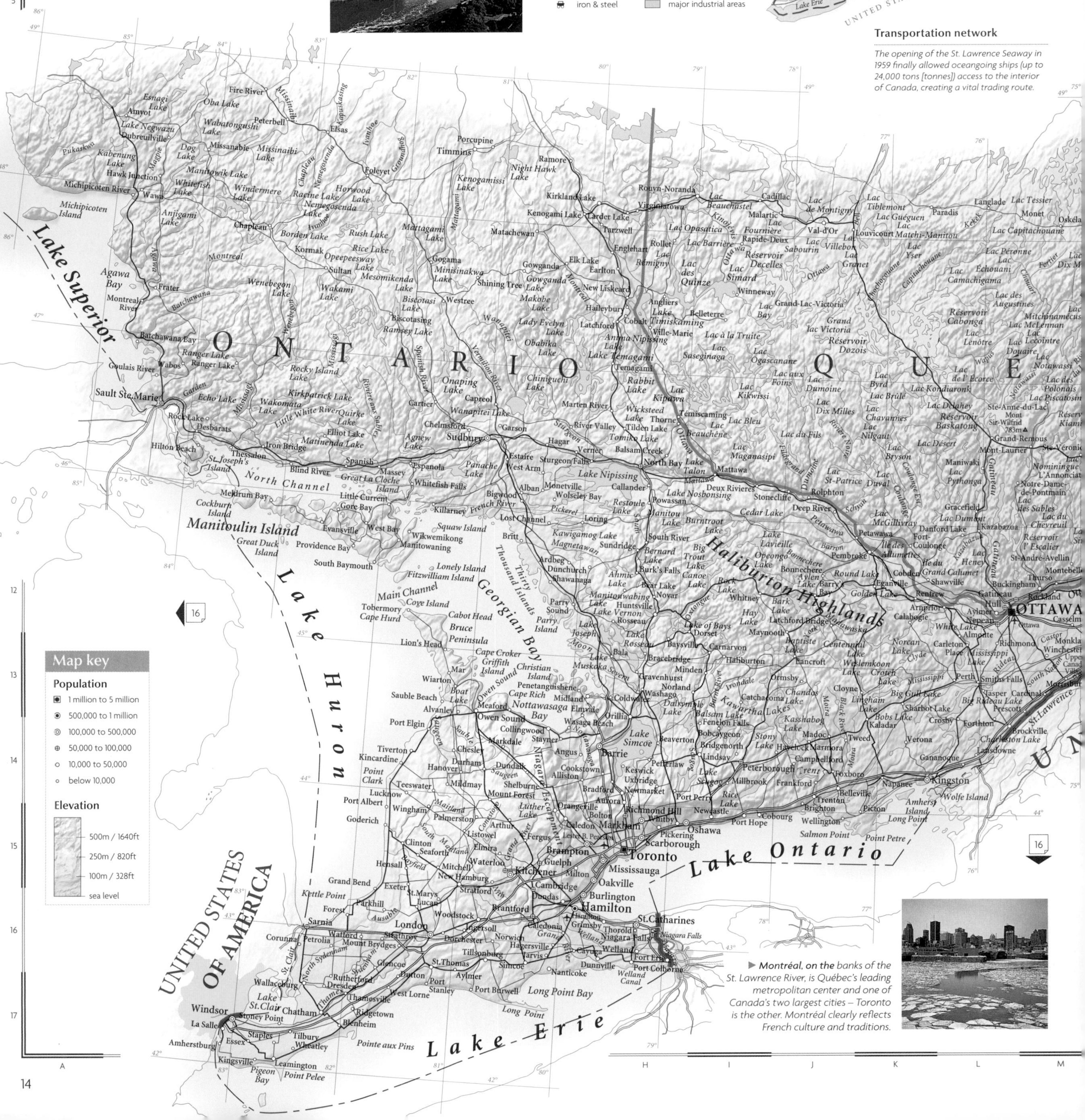

## Map key

### Population

- ⊞ 1 million to 5 million
- ◉ 500,000 to 1 million
- ◎ 100,000 to 500,000
- ⊕ 50,000 to 100,000
- ○ 10,000 to 50,000
- ○ below 10,000

### Elevation

- 500m / 1640ft
- 250m / 820ft
- 100m / 328ft
- sea level

▶ Montréal, *on the banks of the St. Lawrence River, is Québec's leading metropolitan center and one of Canada's two largest cities – Toronto is the other. Montréal clearly reflects French culture and traditions.*

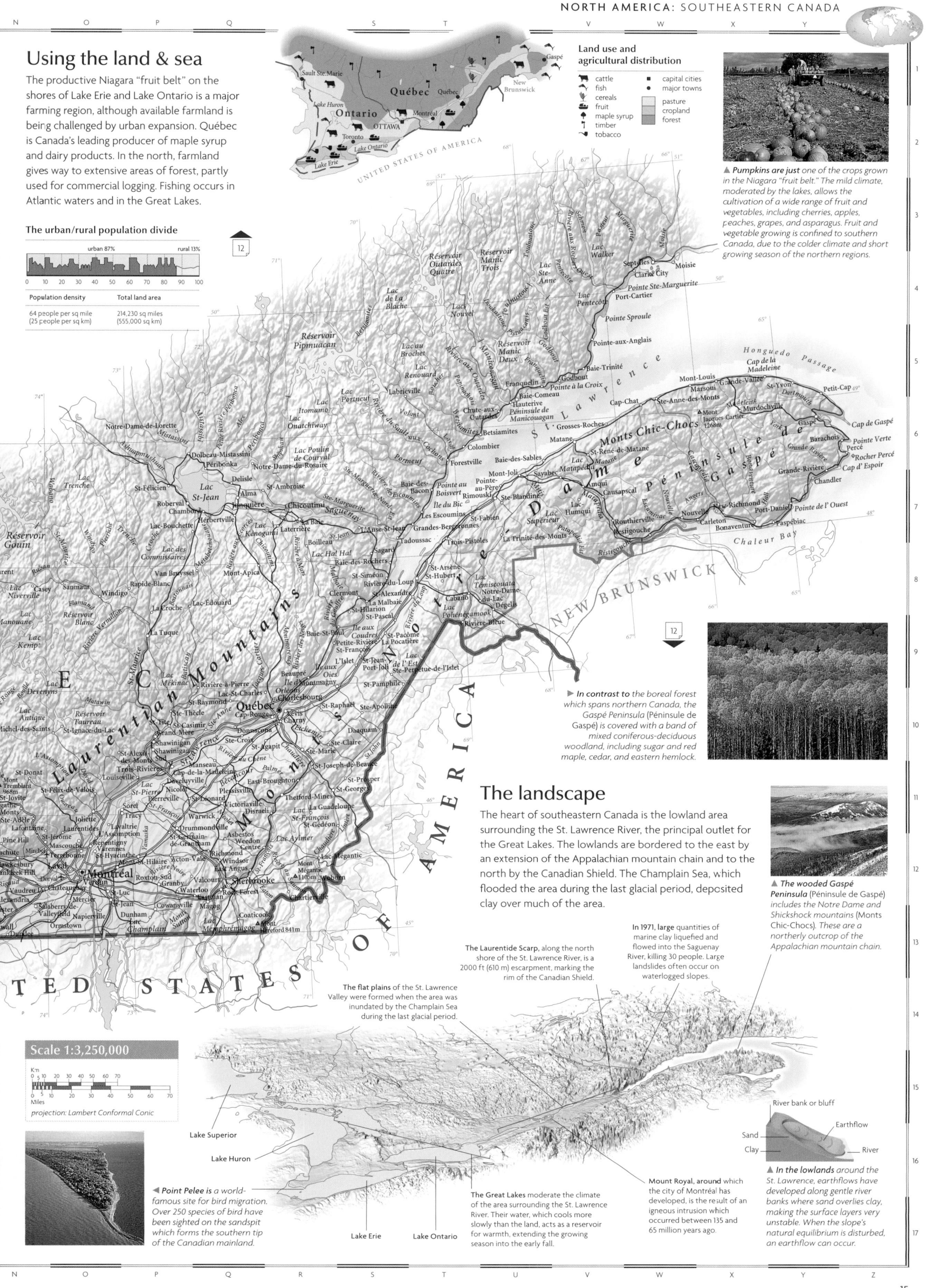

# Using the land & sea

The productive Niagara "fruit belt" on the shores of Lake Erie and Lake Ontario is a major farming region, although available farmland is being challenged by urban expansion. Québec is Canada's leading producer of maple syrup and dairy products. In the north, farmland gives way to extensive areas of forest, partly used for commercial logging. Fishing occurs in Atlantic waters and in the Great Lakes.

**The urban/rural population divide**

urban 87%    rural 13%

0  10  20  30  40  50  60  70  80  90  100

| Population density | Total land area |
|---|---|
| 64 people per sq mile (25 people per sq km) | 214,230 sq miles (555,000 sq km) |

**Land use and agricultural distribution**

- cattle
- fish
- cereals
- fruit
- maple syrup
- timber
- tobacco
- capital cities
- major towns
- pasture
- cropland
- forest

▲ *Pumpkins are just one of the crops grown in the Niagara "fruit belt." The mild climate, moderated by the lakes, allows the cultivation of a wide range of fruit and vegetables, including cherries, apples, peaches, grapes, and asparagus. Fruit and vegetable growing is confined to southern Canada, due to the colder climate and short growing season of the northern regions.*

▶ *In contrast to the boreal forest which spans northern Canada, the Gaspé Peninsula (Péninsule de Gaspé) is covered with a band of mixed coniferous-deciduous woodland, including sugar and red maple, cedar, and eastern hemlock.*

# The landscape

The heart of southeastern Canada is the lowland area surrounding the St. Lawrence River, the principal outlet for the Great Lakes. The lowlands are bordered to the east by an extension of the Appalachian mountain chain and to the north by the Canadian Shield. The Champlain Sea, which flooded the area during the last glacial period, deposited clay over much of the area.

▲ *The wooded Gaspé Peninsula (Péninsule de Gaspé) includes the Notre Dame and Shickshock mountains (Monts Chic-Chocs). These are a northerly outcrop of the Appalachian mountain chain.*

**In 1971, large** quantities of marine clay liquefied and flowed into the Saguenay River, killing 30 people. Large landslides often occur on waterlogged slopes.

**The Laurentide Scarp,** along the north shore of the St. Lawrence River, is a 2000 ft (610 m) escarpment, marking the rim of the Canadian Shield.

**The flat plains** of the St. Lawrence Valley were formed when the area was inundated by the Champlain Sea during the last glacial period.

Scale 1:3,250,000

projection: Lambert Conformal Conic

◀ *Point Pelee is a world-famous site for bird migration. Over 250 species of bird have been sighted on the sandspit which forms the southern tip of the Canadian mainland.*

**The Great Lakes** moderate the climate of the area surrounding the St. Lawrence River. Their water, which cools more slowly than the land, acts as a reservoir for warmth, extending the growing season into the early fall.

**Mount Royal, around** which the city of Montréal has developed, is the result of an igneous intrusion which occurred between 135 and 65 million years ago.

River bank or bluff / Earthflow / Sand / Clay / River

▲ *In the lowlands around the St. Lawrence, earthflows have developed along gentle river banks where sand overlies clay, making the surface layers very unstable. When the slope's natural equilibrium is disturbed, an earthflow can occur.*

15

# The United States of America

## COTERMINOUS US (FOR ALASKA AND HAWAII SEE PAGES 38–39)

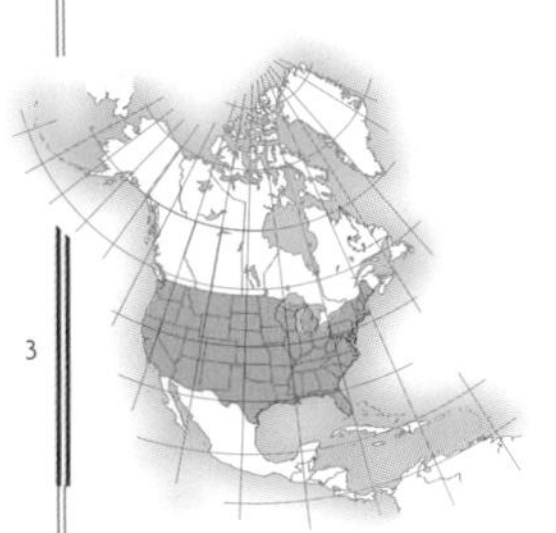

The US's progression from frontier territory to economic and political superpower has taken less than 200 years. The 48 coterminous states, along with the outlying states of Alaska and Hawaii, are part of a federal union, held together by the guiding principles of the US Constitution, which embodies the ideals of democracy and liberty for all. Abundant fertile land and a rich resource base fueled and sustained US economic development. With the spread of agriculture and the growth of trade and industry came the need for a larger workforce, which was supplied by millions of immigrants, many seeking an escape from poverty and political or religious persecution. Immigration continues today, particularly from Central America and Asia.

▲ *Washington DC was* established as the site for the nation's capital in 1790. It is home to the seat of national government, on Capitol Hill, as well as the President's official residence, the White House.

▶ *The clear waters* of Niagara Falls cascade 190 ft (58 m) into the gorge below. It is one of America's most famous spectacles and a leading tourist attraction. The falls are slowly receding and the gorge may one day stretch from Lake Ontario to Lake Erie.

▲ *Mount Rainier is a* dormant volcano in the Cascade Range, Washington. This 14,090 ft (4392 m) peak is flanked by the most extensive glacier outside Alaska.

Scale 1:12,700,000

projection: Lambert Azimuthal Equal Area

## Transportation & industry

The US has been the industrial powerhouse of the world since the Second World War, pioneering mass-production and the consumer lifestyle. Initially, heavy engineering and manufacturing in the northeast led the economy. Today, heavy industry has declined and the US economy is driven by service and financial industries, with the most important being defense, hi-tech, and electronics.

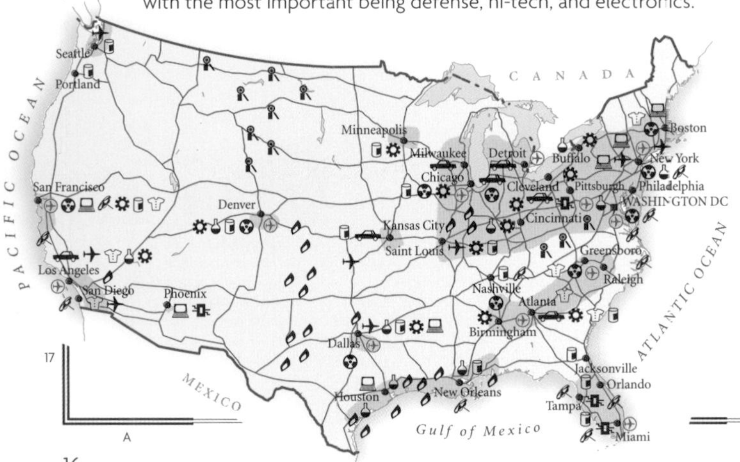

### Transportation network

| | |
|---|---|
| 3,875,040 miles (6,240,000 km) | 52,388 miles (84,361 km) |
| 148,308 miles (235,238 km) | 25,467 miles (41,009 km) |

*Transportation in the US is dominated by the car which, with the extensive Interstate Highway system, allows great personal mobility. Today, internal air flights between major cities provide the most rapid cross-country travel.*

### Major industry and infrastructure

- aerospace
- car manufacture
- chemicals
- coal
- electronics
- engineering
- food processing
- hi-tech industry
- oil & gas
- research & development
- textiles
- tourism
- capital cities
- major towns
- international airports
- major roads
- major industrial areas

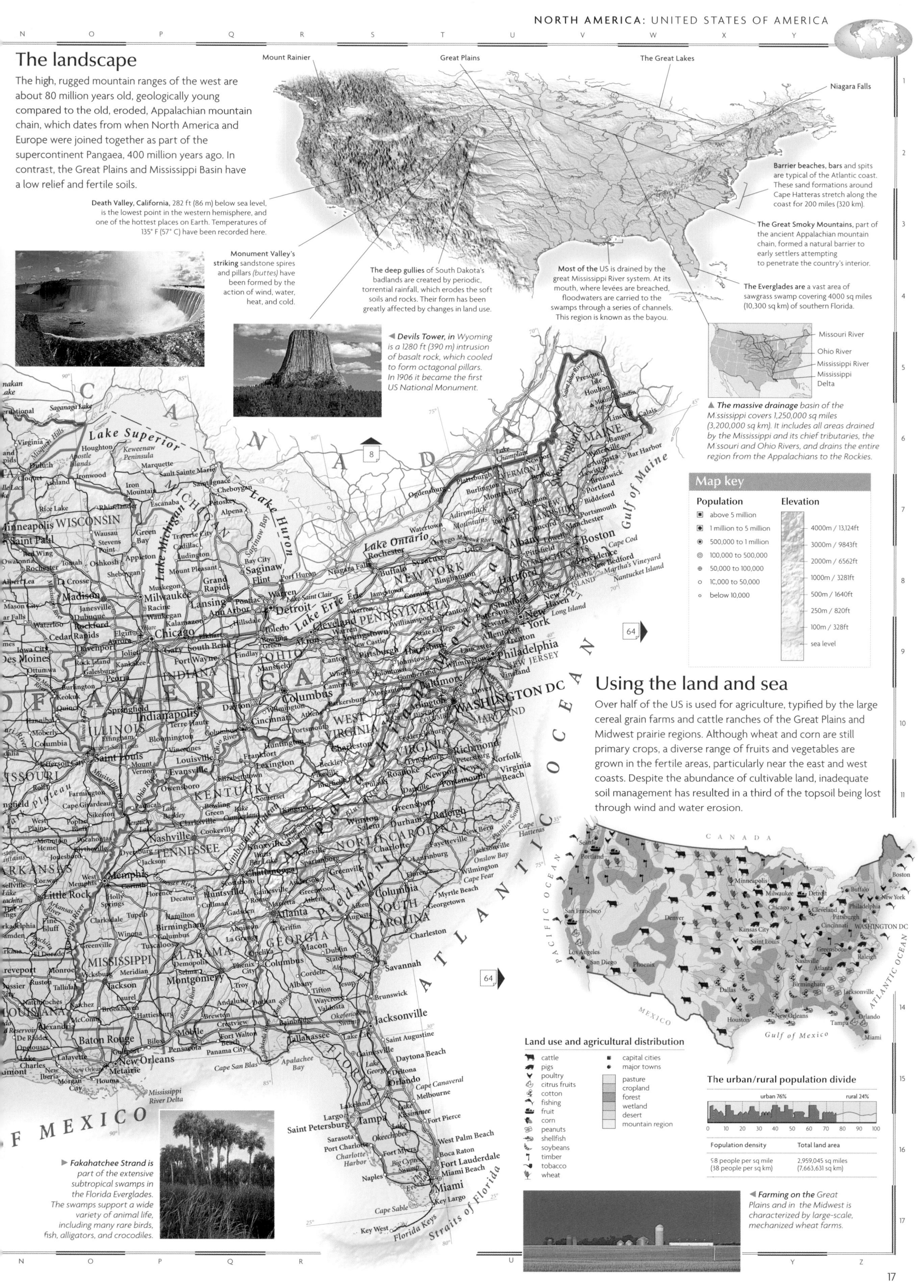

## The landscape

The high, rugged mountain ranges of the west are about 80 million years old, geologically young compared to the old, eroded, Appalachian mountain chain, which dates from when North America and Europe were joined together as part of the supercontinent Pangaea, 400 million years ago. In contrast, the Great Plains and Mississippi Basin have a low relief and fertile soils.

Mount Rainier

Great Plains

The Great Lakes

Niagara Falls

**Death Valley, California**, 282 ft (86 m) below sea level, is the lowest point in the western hemisphere, and one of the hottest places on Earth. Temperatures of 135° F (57° C) have been recorded here.

**Monument Valley's** striking sandstone spires and pillars *(buttes)* have been formed by the action of wind, water, heat, and cold.

**The deep gullies** of South Dakota's badlands are created by periodic, torrential rainfall, which erodes the soft soils and rocks. Their form has been greatly affected by changes in land use.

**Most of the US** is drained by the great Mississippi River system. At its mouth, where levées are breached, floodwaters are carried to the swamps through a series of channels. This region is known as the bayou.

**Barrier beaches,** bars and spits are typical of the Atlantic coast. These sand formations around Cape Hatteras stretch along the coast for 200 miles (320 km).

**The Great Smoky Mountains,** part of the ancient Appalachian mountain chain, formed a natural barrier to early settlers attempting to penetrate the country's interior.

**The Everglades are** a vast area of sawgrass swamp covering 4000 sq miles (10,300 sq km) of southern Florida.

◀ **Devils Tower, in** *Wyoming is a 1280 ft (390 m) intrusion of basalt rock, which cooled to form octagonal pillars. In 1906 it became the first US National Monument.*

Missouri River
Ohio River
Mississippi River
Mississippi Delta

▲ **The massive drainage** basin of the Mississippi covers 1,250,000 sq miles (3,200,000 sq km). It includes all areas drained by the Mississippi and its chief tributaries, the Missouri and Ohio Rivers, and drains the entire region from the Appalachians to the Rockies.

### Map key

**Population**
- ▣ above 5 million
- ▣ 1 million to 5 million
- ◉ 500,000 to 1 million
- ◎ 100,000 to 500,000
- ⊙ 50,000 to 100,000
- ⊙ 10,000 to 50,000
- ∘ below 10,000

**Elevation**
- 4000m / 13,124ft
- 3000m / 9843ft
- 2000m / 6562ft
- 1000m / 3281ft
- 500m / 1640ft
- 250m / 820ft
- 100m / 328ft
- sea level

## Using the land and sea

Over half of the US is used for agriculture, typified by the large cereal grain farms and cattle ranches of the Great Plains and Midwest prairie regions. Although wheat and corn are still primary crops, a diverse range of fruits and vegetables are grown in the fertile areas, particularly near the east and west coasts. Despite the abundance of cultivable land, inadequate soil management has resulted in a third of the topsoil being lost through wind and water erosion.

### Land use and agricultural distribution

- 🐄 cattle
- 🐖 pigs
- 🦃 poultry
- 🍊 citrus fruits
- cotton
- 🐟 fishing
- 🍎 fruit
- corn
- peanuts
- 🦐 shellfish
- soybeans
- 🌲 timber
- tobacco
- 🌾 wheat

- ■ capital cities
- ● major towns
- pasture
- cropland
- forest
- wetland
- desert
- mountain region

### The urban/rural population divide

urban 76%          rural 24%

0  10  20  30  40  50  60  70  80  90  100

| Population density | Total land area |
| --- | --- |
| 58 people per sq mile (38 people per sq km) | 2,959,045 sq miles (7,663,631 sq km) |

◀ *Farming on the Great Plains and in the Midwest is characterized by large-scale, mechanized wheat farms.*

▶ *Fakahatchee Strand is part of the extensive subtropical swamps in the Florida Everglades. The swamps support a wide variety of animal life, including many rare birds, fish, alligators, and crocodiles.*

# USA: NORTHEASTERN STATES

Connecticut, Maine, Massachusetts, New Hampshire, New Jersey, New York, Pennsylvania, Rhode Island, Vermont

The indented coast and vast woodlands of the northeastern states were the original core area for European expansion. The rustic character of New England prevails after nearly four centuries, while the great cities of the Atlantic seaboard have formed an almost continuous urban region. Over 20 million immigrants entered New York from 1855 to 1924 and the northeast became the industrial center of the US. After the decline of mining and heavy manufacturing, economic dynamism has been restored with the growth of hi-tech and service industries.

## Transportation & industry

The principal seaboard cities grew up on trade and manufacturing. They are now global centers of commerce and corporate administration, dominating the regional economy. Research and development facilities support an expanding electronics and communications sector throughout the region. Pharmaceutical and chemical industries are important in New Jersey and Pennsylvania.

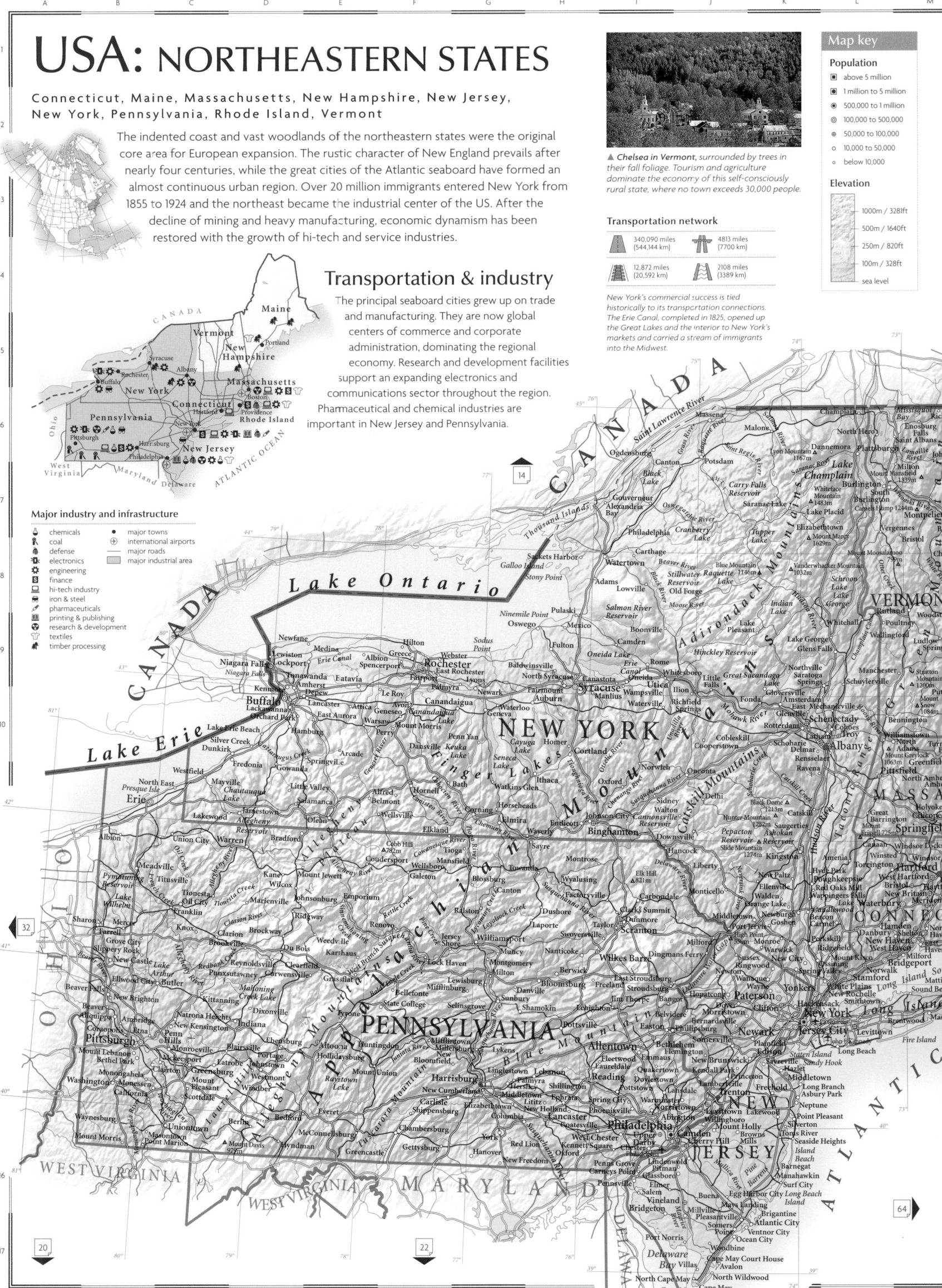

▲ *Chelsea in Vermont*, surrounded by trees in their fall foliage. Tourism and agriculture dominate the economy of this self-consciously rural state, where no town exceeds 30,000 people.

### Map key

**Population**

- ■ above 5 million
- ▣ 1 million to 5 million
- ◉ 500,000 to 1 million
- ⊚ 100,000 to 500,000
- ⊕ 50,000 to 100,000
- ○ 10,000 to 50,000
- ○ below 10,000

**Elevation**

- 1000m / 3281ft
- 500m / 1640ft
- 250m / 820ft
- 100m / 328ft
- sea level

### Transportation network

| | |
|---|---|
| 340,090 miles (544,144 km) | 4813 miles (7700 km) |
| 12,872 miles (20,592 km) | 2108 miles (3389 km) |

*New York's commercial success is tied historically to its transportation connections. The Erie Canal, completed in 1825, opened up the Great Lakes and the interior to New York's markets and carried a stream of immigrants into the Midwest.*

### Major industry and infrastructure

- chemicals
- coal
- defense
- electronics
- engineering
- finance
- hi-tech industry
- iron & steel
- pharmaceuticals
- printing & publishing
- research & development
- textiles
- timber processing
- major towns
- international airports
- major roads
- major industrial area

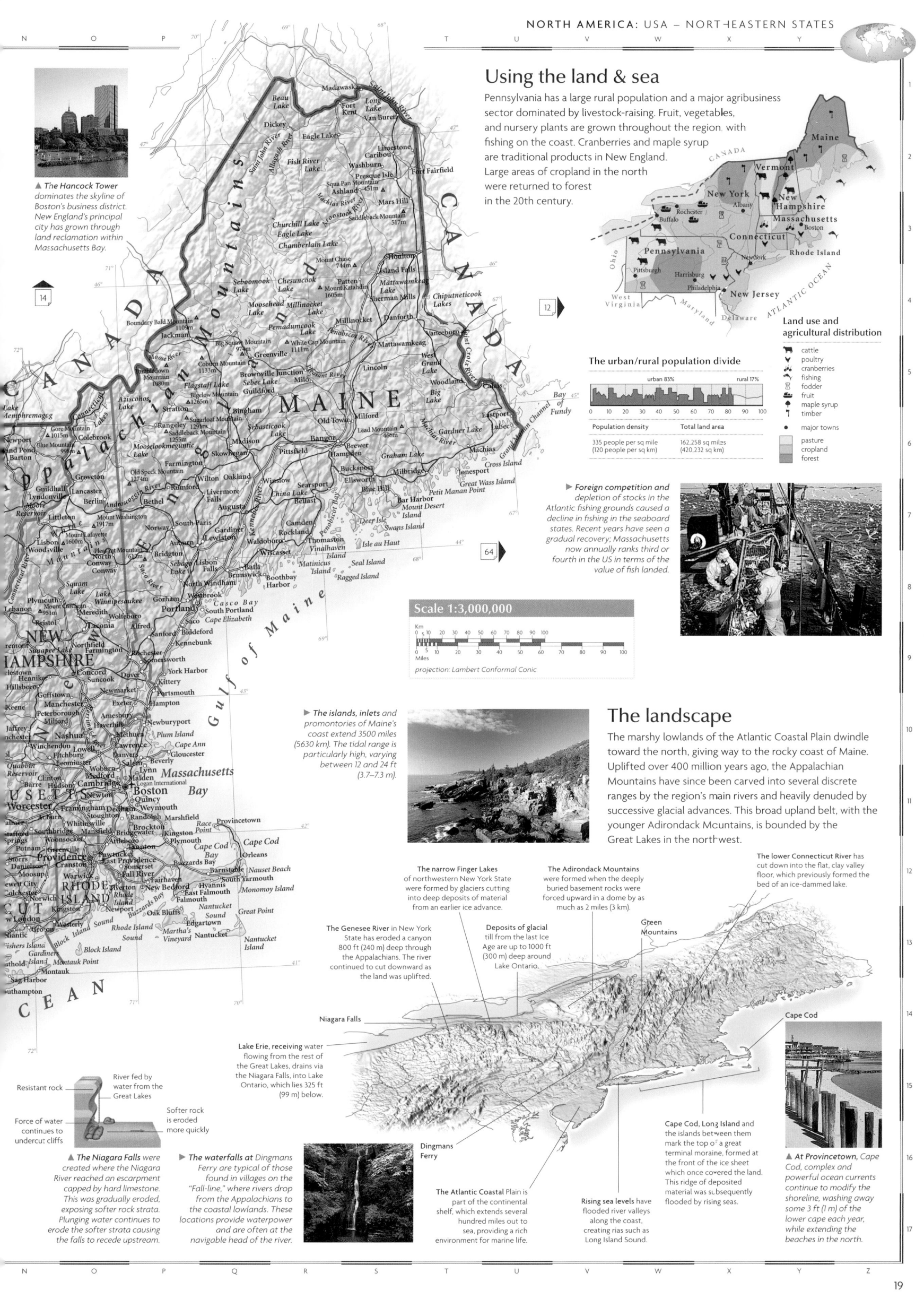

▲ *The Hancock Tower dominates the skyline of Boston's business district. New England's principal city has grown through land reclamation within Massachusetts Bay.*

## Using the land & sea

Pennsylvania has a large rural population and a major agribusiness sector dominated by livestock-raising. Fruit, vegetables, and nursery plants are grown throughout the region, with fishing on the coast. Cranberries and maple syrup are traditional products in New England. Large areas of cropland in the north were returned to forest in the 20th century.

### The urban/rural population divide

urban 83%    rural 17%

0  10  20  30  40  50  60  70  80  90  100

Population density
335 people per sq mile
(120 people per sq km)

Total land area
162,258 sq miles
(420,232 sq km)

### Land use and agricultural distribution

- cattle
- poultry
- cranberries
- fishing
- fodder
- fruit
- maple syrup
- timber
- major towns
- pasture
- cropland
- forest

▶ *Foreign competition and depletion of stocks in the Atlantic fishing grounds caused a decline in fishing in the seaboard states. Recent years have seen a gradual recovery; Massachusetts now annually ranks third or fourth in the US in terms of the value of fish landed.*

▶ *The islands, inlets and promontories of Maine's coast extend 3500 miles (5630 km). The tidal range is particularly high, varying between 12 and 24 ft (3.7–7.3 m).*

### Scale 1:3,000,000

Km
0  5 10  20  30  40  50  60  70  80  90  100

Miles
0  5  10  20  30  40  50  60  70  80  90  100

projection: Lambert Conformal Conic

## The landscape

The marshy lowlands of the Atlantic Coastal Plain dwindle toward the north, giving way to the rocky coast of Maine. Uplifted over 400 million years ago, the Appalachian Mountains have since been carved into several discrete ranges by the region's main rivers and heavily denuded by successive glacial advances. This broad upland belt, with the younger Adirondack Mountains, is bounded by the Great Lakes in the north-west.

The narrow Finger Lakes of northwestern New York State were formed by glaciers cutting into deep deposits of material from an earlier ice advance.

The Adirondack Mountains were formed when the deeply buried basement rocks were forced upward in a dome by as much as 2 miles (3 km).

The lower Connecticut River has cut down into the flat, clay valley floor, which previously formed the bed of an ice-dammed lake.

The Genesee River in New York State has eroded a canyon 800 ft (240 m) deep through the Appalachians. The river continued to cut downward as the land was uplifted.

Deposits of glacial till from the last Ice Age are up to 1000 ft (300 m) deep around Lake Ontario.

Green Mountains

Niagara Falls

Cape Cod

Lake Erie, receiving water flowing from the rest of the Great Lakes, drains via the Niagara Falls, into Lake Ontario, which lies 325 ft (99 m) below.

Cape Cod, Long Island and the islands between them mark the top of a great terminal moraine, formed at the front of the ice sheet which once covered the land. This ridge of deposited material was subsequently flooded by rising seas.

Resistant rock

River fed by water from the Great Lakes

Force of water continues to undercut cliffs

Softer rock is eroded more quickly

▲ *The Niagara Falls were created where the Niagara River reached an escarpment capped by hard limestone. This was gradually eroded, exposing softer rock strata. Plunging water continues to erode the softer strata causing the falls to recede upstream.*

▶ *The waterfalls at Dingmans Ferry are typical of those found in villages on the "Fall-line," where rivers drop from the Appalachians to the coastal lowlands. These locations provide waterpower and are often at the navigable head of the river.*

Dingmans Ferry

The Atlantic Coastal Plain is part of the continental shelf, which extends several hundred miles out to sea, providing a rich environment for marine life.

Rising sea levels have flooded river valleys along the coast, creating rias such as Long Island Sound.

▲ *At Provincetown, Cape Cod, complex and powerful ocean currents continue to modify the shoreline, washing away some 3 ft (1 m) of the lower cape each year, while extending the beaches in the north.*

# USA: MID-EASTERN STATES

Delaware, District of Columbia, Kentucky,
Maryland, North Carolina, South Carolina,
Tennessee, Virginia, West Virginia

Key events in American history took place n this diverse region, which became the front line between the North and the South during the Civil War of the 1860s. Strong regional contrasts exist between the fertile coastal plains, the isolated upcountry of the Appalachian Mountains, and the cotton-growing areas of the Mississippi lowlands to the west. While coal mining, a traditional industry in the Appalachians, has declined in recent years leaving much rural poverty, service industries elsewhere have increased, especially in Washington DC, the nation's capital.

## Transportation & industry

In the urbanized northeast, manufacturing remains important, alongside a burgeoning service sector. North Carolina is a major center for industrial research and development. Traditional industries include Tennessee whiskey and textiles in South Carolina. The decline of open-pit coal mining in the Appalachians has been hastened by environmental controls, although adventure-tourism is a flourishing new industry.

### Major industry and infrastructure

adventure-tourism, car manufacture, coal, electronics, engineering, finance, food processing, hi-tech industry, mining, research & development, textiles — capital cities, major towns, international airports, major roads, major industrial areas

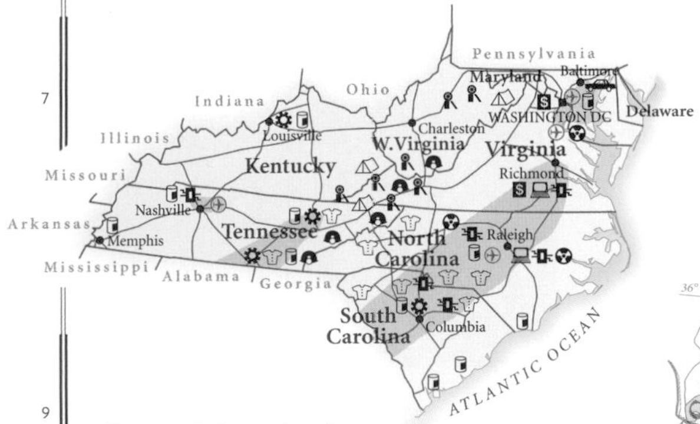

### Map key

**Population**
- 500,000 to 1 million
- 100,000 to 500,000
- 50,000 to 100,000
- 10,000 to 50,000
- below 10,000

**Elevation**
6000m / 19,686ft
4000m / 13,124ft
3000m / 9843ft
2000m / 6562ft
1000m / 3281ft
500m / 1640ft
250m / 820ft
100m / 328ft
sea level

**Scale 1:3,250,000**

projection: Lambert Conformal Conic

▲ *The Bluegrass region* of Kentucky centers on the town of Lexington. This exceptionally fertile rolling plain is well known for its thoroughbred horse-breeding ranches.

### Transportation network

452,218 miles (723,548 km)
5737 miles (8267 km)
18,336 miles (29,503 km)
4404 miles (7081 km)

Tennessee's rivers are part of an important inland bulk transportation network. Memphis connects with New Orleans in the south, and with cities as distant as Minneapolis, Sioux City, Chicago, and Pittsburgh, via the Mississippi and its tributaries.

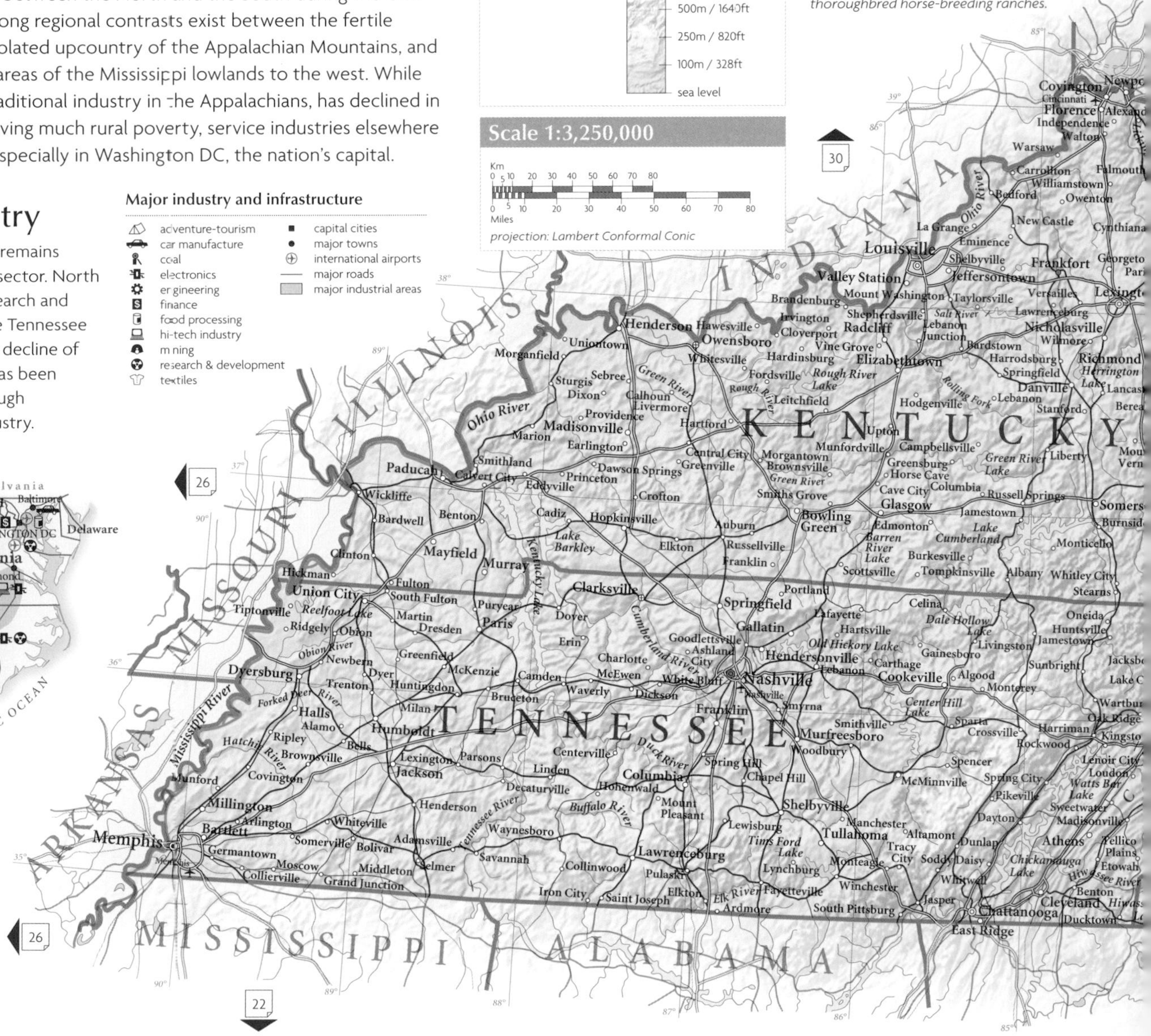

## The landscape

The eastern tributaries of the Mississippi drain the interior lowlands. The Cumberland Plateau and the parallel ranges of the Appalachians have been successively uplifted and eroded over time, with the eastern side reduced to a series of foothills known as the Piedmont. The broad coastal plain gradually falls away into salt marshes, lagoons, and offshore bars, broken by flooded estuaries along the shores of the Atlantic.

**Natural Bridge** in eastern Kentucky is an arch 78 ft (26 m) long and 65 ft (20 m) high. It has been shaped from resistant sandstone by gradual weathering processes, which removed the softer rock lying underneath.

**The Allegheny Mountains** form the northwestern edge of the Appalachian mountain chain. Continuous folding has formed rich seams of bituminous coal.

Appalachian Mountains

◄ *Farmland on the* eastern shores of Chesapeake Bay is sustained by artificial drainage. The area also provides refuge for a variety of waterfowl.

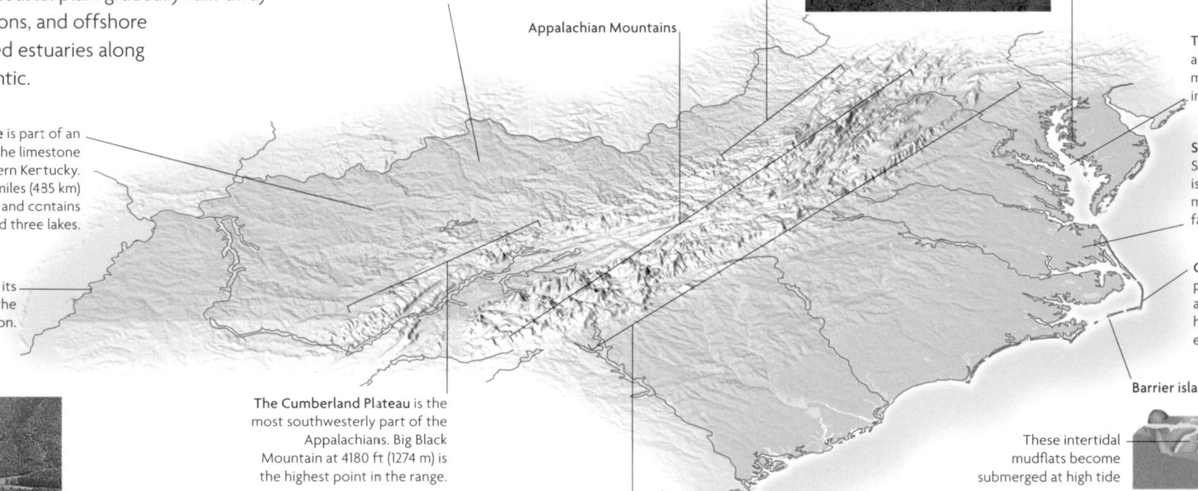

**The many inlets** of Chesapeake Bay are the flooded tributaries of the main river valley, which have been inundated by rising sea levels.

**The Mammoth Cave** is part of an extensive cave system in the limestone region of southwestern Kentucky. It stretches for over 300 miles (435 km) on five different levels and contains three rivers and three lakes.

**Salt marshes** such as Great Dismal Swamp, develop where the coast is sheltered. Vast areas of such marshland have been reclaimed for farmland and settlement.

**Cape Hatteras** is the easternmost point of an offshore barrier island, a wave-deposited sand-bar which has become permanent, establishing its own vegetation.

**The Mississippi River** and its tributary the Ohio River form the western border of the region.

Barrier islands

These intertidal mudflats become submerged at high tide

Tidal inlet
Barrier island

**The Cumberland Plateau** is the most southwesterly part of the Appalachians. Big Black Mountain at 4180 ft (1274 m) is the highest point in the range.

▲ *Barrier islands are* common along the coasts of North and South Carolina. As sea levels rise, wave action builds up ridges of sand and pebbles parallel to the coast, separated by lagoons or intertidal mud flats, which are flooded at high tide.

◄ *The Great Smoky Mountains* form the western escarpment of the Appalachians. The region is heavily forested, with over 130 species of tree.

**The Blue Ridge** mountains are a steep ridge, culminating in Mount Mitchell, the highest point in the Appalachians, at 6684 ft (2037 m).

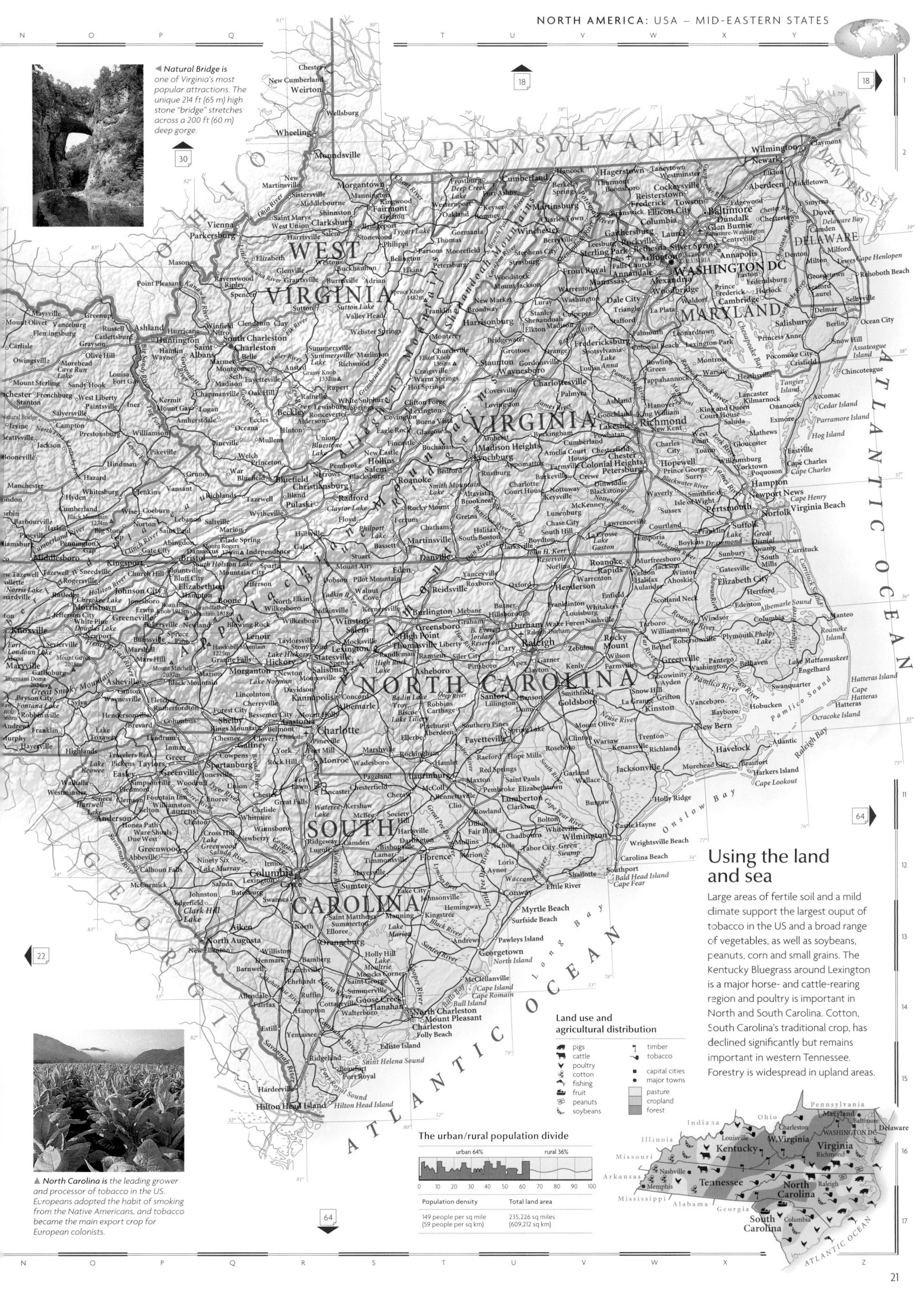

◀ *Natural Bridge is* one of Virginia's most popular attractions. The unique 214 ft (65 m) high stone "bridge" stretches across a 200 ft (60 m) deep gorge.

▲ *North Carolina is* the leading grower and processor of tobacco in the US. Europeans adopted the habit of smoking from the Native Americans, and tobacco became the main export crop for European colonists.

## Using the land and sea

Large areas of fertile soil and a mild climate support the largest ouput of tobacco in the US and a broad range of vegetables, as well as soybeans, peanuts, corn and small grains. The Kentucky Bluegrass around Lexington is a major horse- and cattle-rearing region and poultry is important in North and South Carolina. Cotton, South Carolina's traditional crop, has declined significantly but remains important in western Tennessee. Forestry is widespread in upland areas.

### Land use and agricultural distribution

- pigs
- cattle
- poultry
- cotton
- fishing
- fruit
- peanuts
- soybeans
- timber
- tobacco
- capital cities
- major towns
- pasture
- cropland
- forest

### The urban/rural population divide

urban 64%          rural 36%

Population density

149 people per sq mile
(59 people per sq km)

Total land area

235,226 sq miles
(609,212 sq km)

# USA: SOUTHERN STATES

### Alabama, Florida, Georgia, Louisiana, Mississippi

The South has maintained a separate identity and outlook throughout the history of the US. Defeat in the Civil War (1861–65) brought chronic poverty to the former confederate states, while the subsequent liberation of four million slaves began a struggle not resolved until the 1960s, when the Civil Rights movement achieved an end to legal racial segregation. Many parts of the South have experienced rapid change. Tourism and retirement communities, together with agriculture, have fueled growth in Florida, while defense-related industries have boosted the growth of cities such as Miami and Atlanta. Many people retain a strong attachment to their history and culture, evidenced by Creole-speaking Cajuns in Louisiania and Hispanic communities in South Florida.

## Transportation & industry

Florida's tourist trade is only part of a flourishing service sector, which has swelled the principal cities of the south. Petroleum and mineral extraction has made the Gulf Coast a major industrial region. Traditional textile production remains important in Georgia, while advanced new industries have grown from the NASA Space Program.

### Transportation network

| | |
|---|---|
| 🛣 | 441,625 miles (706,600 km) |
| 🛣 | 5116 miles (8186 km) |
| 🚉 | 16,597 miles (26,555 km) |
| ✈ | 6179 miles (9942 km) |

Atlanta's Hartsfield International airport is one of the busiest in the world. A dramatic rise in the use of regional air transportation has helped to integrate the major cities of the southern states.

◄ **The French Quarter** is the traditional cultural center of New Orleans. The city, extensively damaged by Hurricane Katrina in 2005, once thrived on the cotton trade but now relies mainly on tourism and on oil from the Gulf of Mexico.

### Major industry and infrastructure

- ✈ aerospace
- 🚗 car manufacture
- 🧪 chemicals
- coal
- defense
- electronics
- engineering
- food processing
- oil
- textiles
- tourism
- • major towns
- ⊕ international airports
- — major roads
- major industrial areas

## The landscape

The Blue Ridge mountains in the north are skirted by the gentle hills of the Piedmont, whose rivers drain south on to the great flat expanse of the coastal plain. Sandy barrier beaches and islands dominate the sea shore, tracing round the swampy limestone arm of Florida. In the west, the Mississippi meanders toward its delta, crossing the thickly mantled alluvial plain of the interior lowlands.

▲ **The cypress swamps** of the Mississippi Delta form in the backswamps behind the leveés of the river and in the multitude of subsiding delta basins.

**The Mississippi** is the world's third longest river and moves over 1000 million tons (tonnes) of sediment a year, creating deep alluvial plains. Flooding is a constant threat in lowland areas.

**The Yazoo River** flows parallel to the Mississippi through a common floodplain. The confluence of the rivers is deferred downstream because flood deposition has built the Mississippi channel up above the level of the Yazoo.

**Cathedral Caverns near** Huntsville in Alabama is a system of vast limestone caves, with a main opening 1000 ft (300 m) high and 150 ft (50 m) wide.

**At De Soto Falls**, Alabama, the Little River descends into the deepest canyon east of the Mississippi, with sheer cliff walls up to 700 ft (230 m) high.

**Brasstown Bald in** the Blue Ridge mountains of Georgia is the region's highest point, at 4784 ft (1458 m).

▲ **In Providence Canyon**, Georgia, the Chattahoochee River has cut straight down through the sandy bedrock, to leave sheer rock faces and pinnacles, which have been smoothed by subsequent weathering.

**Sandbars, deposited by** waves breaking offshore, form barrier beaches along much of the coastline, creating sheltered lagoons and salt marshes behind them.

**Across Florida the** coastal plain is mostly less than 75 ft (25 m) above sea level. The land is underlain by limestone, pitted with hollows which have been filled by over 10,000 lakes.

**The delta of the** Mississippi over 5000 years ago

**Delta lobe**

Present-day delta

**Lake Okeechobee is** actually a shallow, slow-moving river, 150 miles (240 km) long and 50 miles (80 km) wide.

▲ **Over the last** 5,000 years the lower course of the Mississippi has moved back and forth over great distances. These changes, caused by varying sediment loads and human modification, have resulted in a "bird's foot" delta with several lobes, each reflecting the river's different historic position

**The Everglades lie** in a limestone hollow formed over two million years ago, which has gradually become filled with swamp deposits.

**Florida Keys**

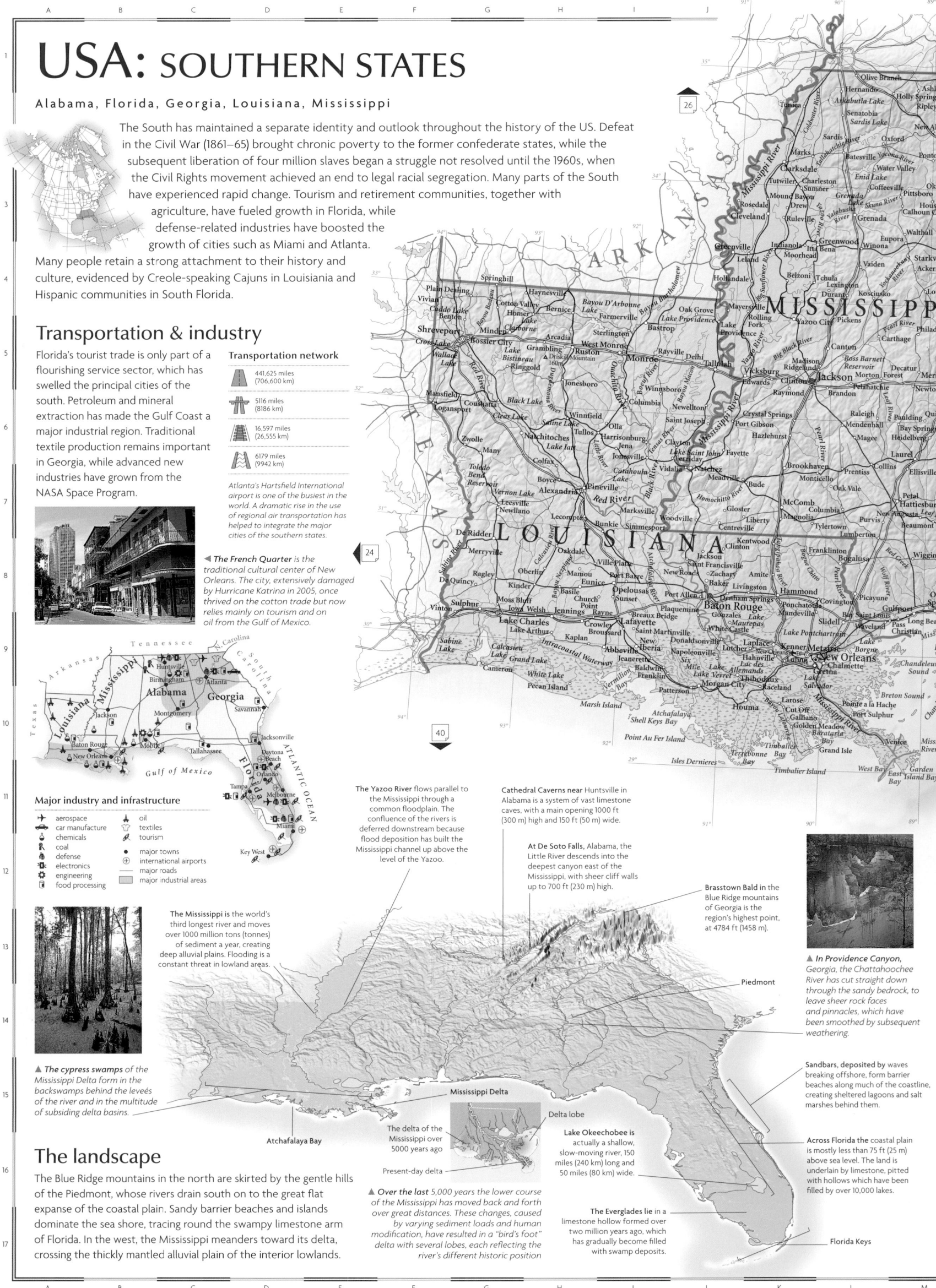

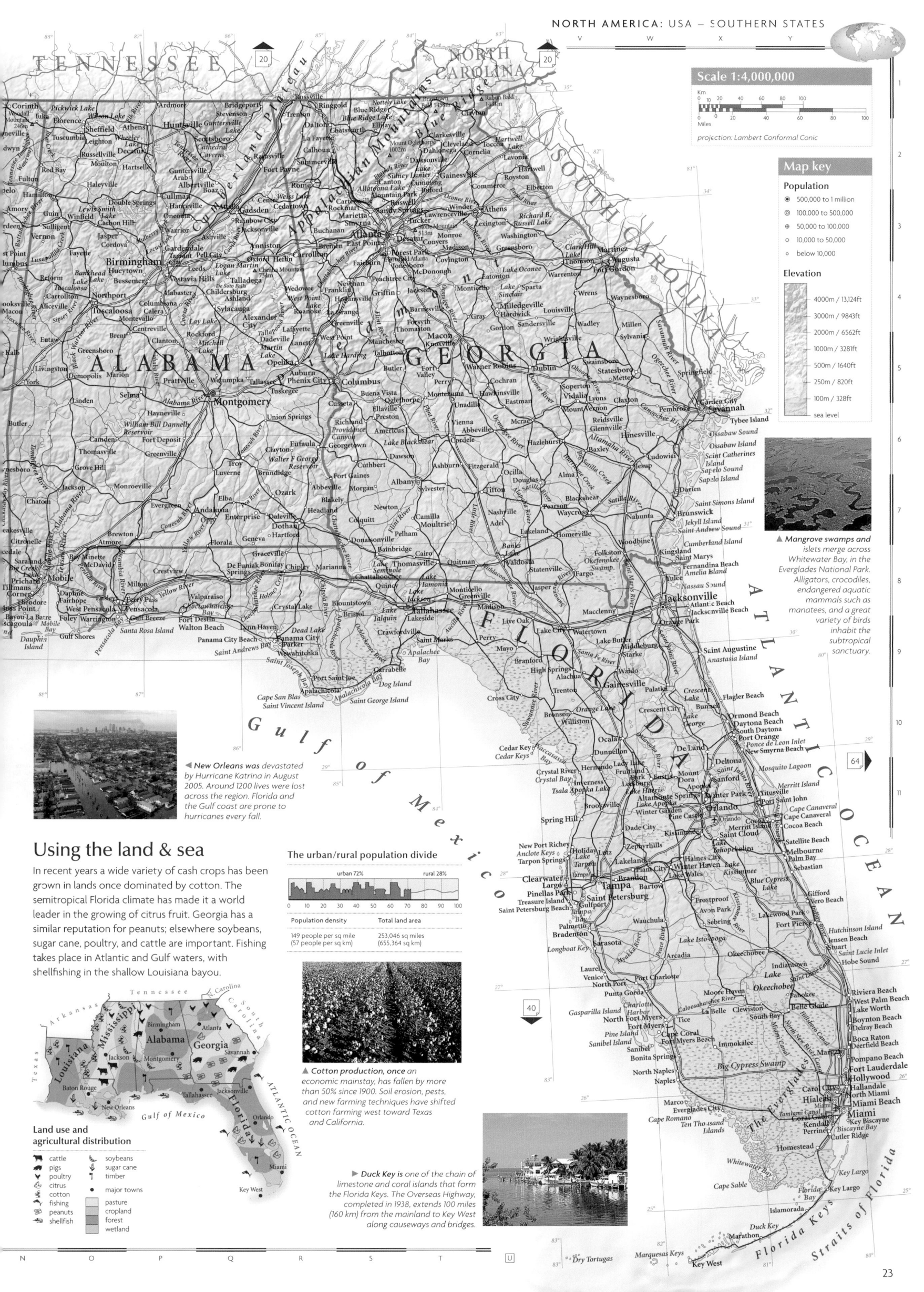

Scale 1:4,000,000

projection: Lambert Conformal Conic

**Map key**

Population
- 500,000 to 1 million
- 100,000 to 500,000
- 50,000 to 100,000
- 10,000 to 50,000
- below 10,000

Elevation
- 4000m / 13,124ft
- 3000m / 9843ft
- 2000m / 6562ft
- 1000m / 3281ft
- 500m / 1640ft
- 250m / 820ft
- 100m / 328ft
- sea level

▲ *Mangrove swamps and islets merge across Whitewater Bay, in the Everglades National Park. Alligators, crocodiles, endangered aquatic mammals such as manatees, and a great variety of birds inhabit the subtropical sanctuary.*

◄ *New Orleans was devastated by Hurricane Katrina in August 2005. Around 1200 lives were lost across the region. Florida and the Gulf coast are prone to hurricanes every fall.*

## Using the land & sea

In recent years a wide variety of cash crops has been grown in lands once dominated by cotton. The semitropical Florida climate has made it a world leader in the growing of citrus fruit. Georgia has a similar reputation for peanuts; elsewhere soybeans, sugar cane, poultry, and cattle are important. Fishing takes place in Atlantic and Gulf waters, with shellfishing in the shallow Louisiana bayou.

**The urban/rural population divide**

urban 72%    rural 28%

| Population density | Total land area |
|---|---|
| 149 people per sq mile (57 people per sq km) | 253,046 sq miles (655,364 sq km) |

▲ *Cotton production, once an economic mainstay, has fallen by more than 50% since 1900. Soil erosion, pests, and new farming techniques have shifted cotton farming west toward Texas and California.*

▶ *Duck Key is one of the chain of limestone and coral islands that form the Florida Keys. The Overseas Highway, completed in 1938, extends 100 miles (160 km) from the mainland to Key West along causeways and bridges.*

**Land use and agricultural distribution**
- cattle
- pigs
- poultry
- citrus
- cotton
- fishing
- peanuts
- shellfish
- soybeans
- sugar cane
- timber
- major towns
- pasture
- cropland
- forest
- wetland

# USA: Texas

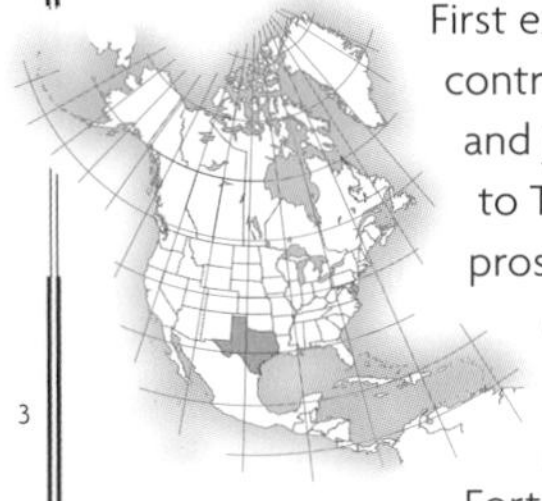

First explored by Spaniards moving north from Mexico in search of gold, Texas was controlled by Spain and then by Mexico, before becoming an independent republic in 1836, and joining the Union of States in 1845. During the 19th century, many migrants who came to Texas raised cattle on the abundant land; in the 20th century, they were joined by prospectors attracted by the promise of oil riches. Today, although natural resources, especially oil, still form the basis of its wealth, the diversified Texan economy includes thriving hi-tech and financial industries. The major urban centers, home to 80% of the population, lie in the south and east, and include Houston, the "oil-city," and Dallas–Fort Worth. Hispanic influences remain strong, especially in southern and western Texas.

▲ *Dallas was founded* in 1841 as a prairie trading post and its development was stimulated by the arrival of railroads. Cotton and then oil funded the town's early growth. Today, the modern, high rise skyline of Dallas reflects the city's position as a leading center of banking, insurance, and the petroleum industry in the southwest.

## Using the land

Cotton production and livestock-raising, particularly cattle, dominate farming, although crop failures and the demands of local markets have led to some diversification. Following the introduction of modern farming techniques, cotton production spread out from the east to the plains of western Texas. Cattle ranches are widespread, while sheep and goats are raised on the dry Edwards Plateau.

**Land use and agricultural distribution**

- cattle
- goats
- sheep
- cereals
- cotton
- major towns
  pasture
  cropland
  forest
  barren

**The urban/rural population divide**

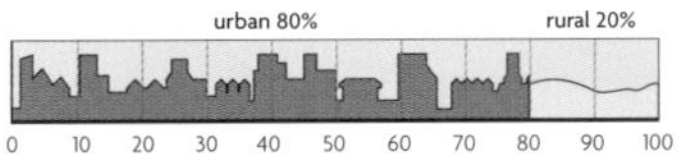

urban 80%    rural 20%

0 10 20 30 40 50 60 70 80 90 100

| Population density | Total land area |
|---|---|
| 84 people per sq mile (33 people per sq km) | 261,797 sq miles (678,028 sq km) |

▲ *The huge cattle* ranches of Texas developed during the 19th century when land was plentiful and could be acquired cheaply. Today, more cattle and sheep are raised in Texas than in any other state.

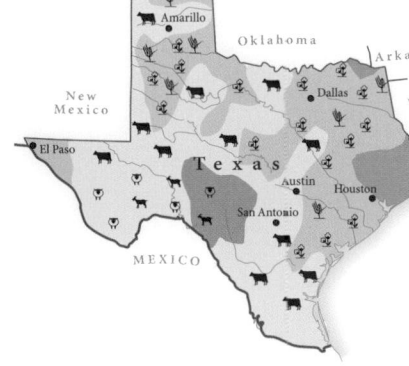

## The landscape

Texas is made up of a series of massive steps descending from the mountains and high plains of the west and northwest to the coastal lowlands in the southeast. Many of the state's borders are delineated by water. The Rio Grande flows from the Rocky Mountains to the Gulf of Mexico, marking the border with Mexico.

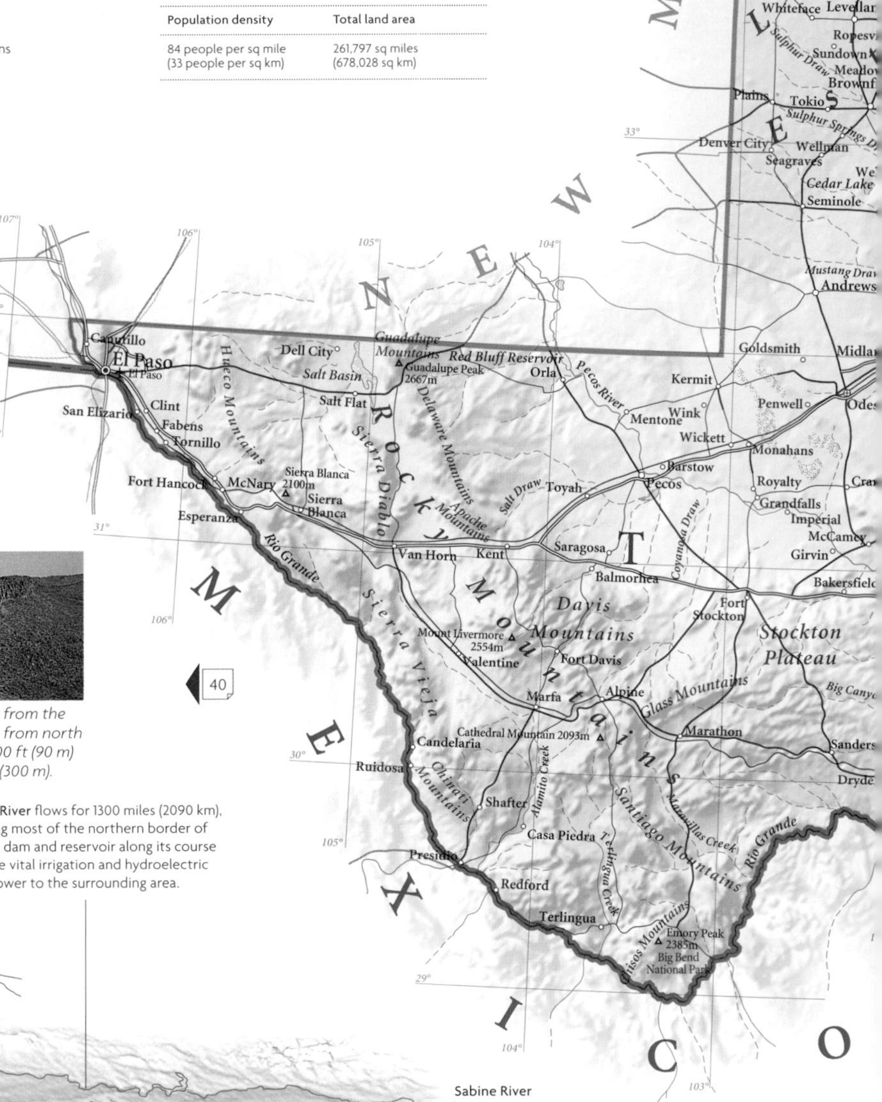

▲ *Cap Rock Escarpment* juts out from the plains, running 200 miles (320 km) from north to south. Its height varies from 300 ft (90 m) rising to sheer cliffs up to 1000 ft (300 m).

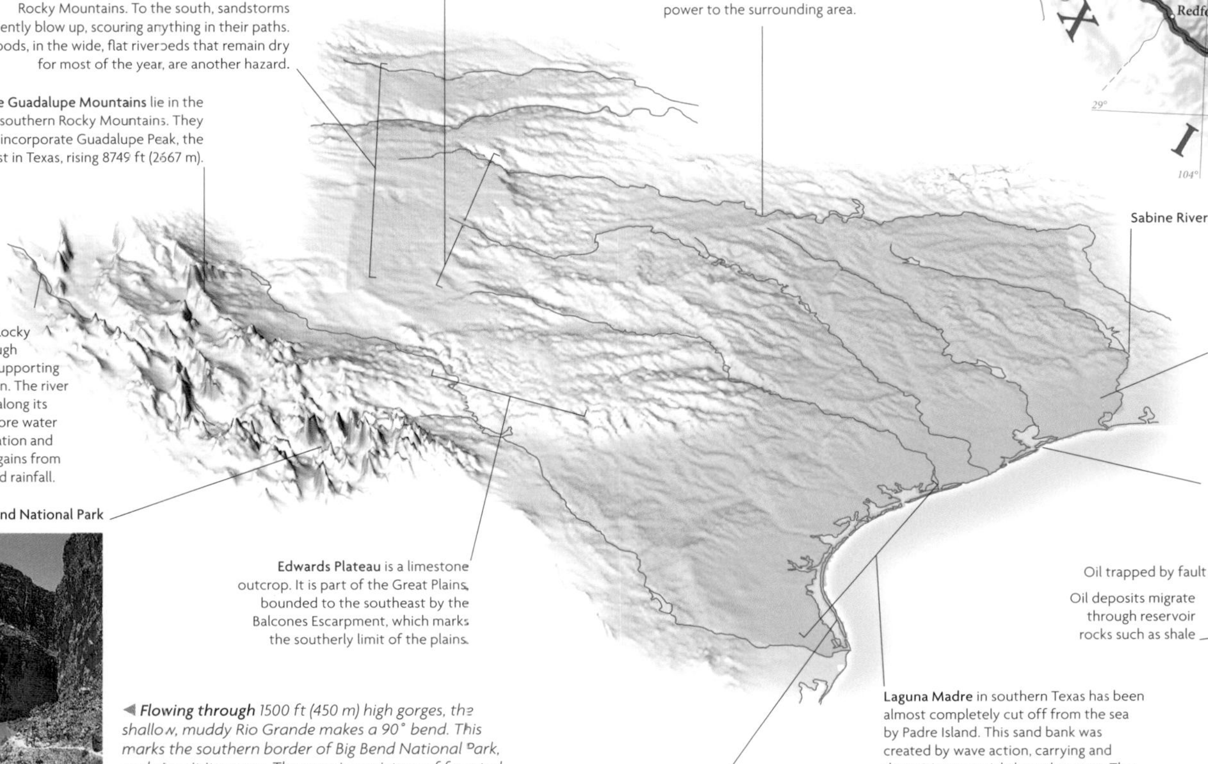

**The Llano Estacado** or Staked Plain in northern Texas is known for its harsh environment. In the north, freezing winds carrying ice and snow sweep down from the Rocky Mountains. To the south, sandstorms frequently blow up, scouring anything in their paths. Flash floods, in the wide, flat riverbeds that remain dry for most of the year, are another hazard.

**The Guadalupe Mountains** lie in the southern Rocky Mountains. They incorporate Guadalupe Peak, the highest in Texas, rising 8749 ft (2667 m).

**The Red River** flows for 1300 miles (2090 km), marking most of the northern border of Texas. A dam and reservoir along its course provide vital irrigation and hydroelectric power to the surrounding area.

**The Rio Grande** flows from the Rocky Mountains through semi-arid land, supporting sparse vegetation. The river actually shrinks along its course, losing more water through evaporation and seepage than it gains from its tributaries and rainfall.

**Big Bend National Park**

◄ *Flowing through* 1500 ft (450 m) high gorges, the shallow, muddy Rio Grande makes a 90° bend. This marks the southern border of Big Bend National Park, and gives it its name. The area is a mixture of forested mountains, deserts, and canyons.

**Edwards Plateau** is a limestone outcrop. It is part of the Great Plains, bounded to the southeast by the Balcones Escarpment, which marks the southerly limit of the plains.

**Laguna Madre** in southern Texas has been almost completely cut off from the sea by Padre Island. This sand bank was created by wave action, carrying and depositing material along the coast. The process is known as longshore drift.

**Padre Island**

**Sabine River**

**Extensive forests** of pine and cypress grow in the eastern corner of the coastal lowlands where the average rainfall is 45 inches (1145 mm) a year. This is higher than the rest of the state and over twice the average in the west.

**In the coastal** lowlands of southeastern Texas the Earth's crust is warping, causing the land to subside and allowing the sea to invade. Around Galveston, the rate of downward tilting is 6 inches (15 cm) per year. Erosion of the coast is also exacerbated by hurricanes.

**Oil deposits**

Oil accumulates beneath impermeable cap rock

Oil trapped by fault

Oil deposits migrate through reservoir rocks such as shale

Impermeable rock strata

Salt dome

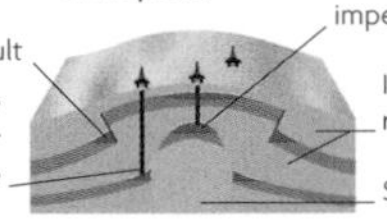

▲ *Oil deposits are* found beneath much of Texas. They collect as oil migrates upward through porous layers of rock until it is trapped, either by a cap of rock above a salt dome, or by a fault line which exposes impermeable rock through which the oil cannot rise.

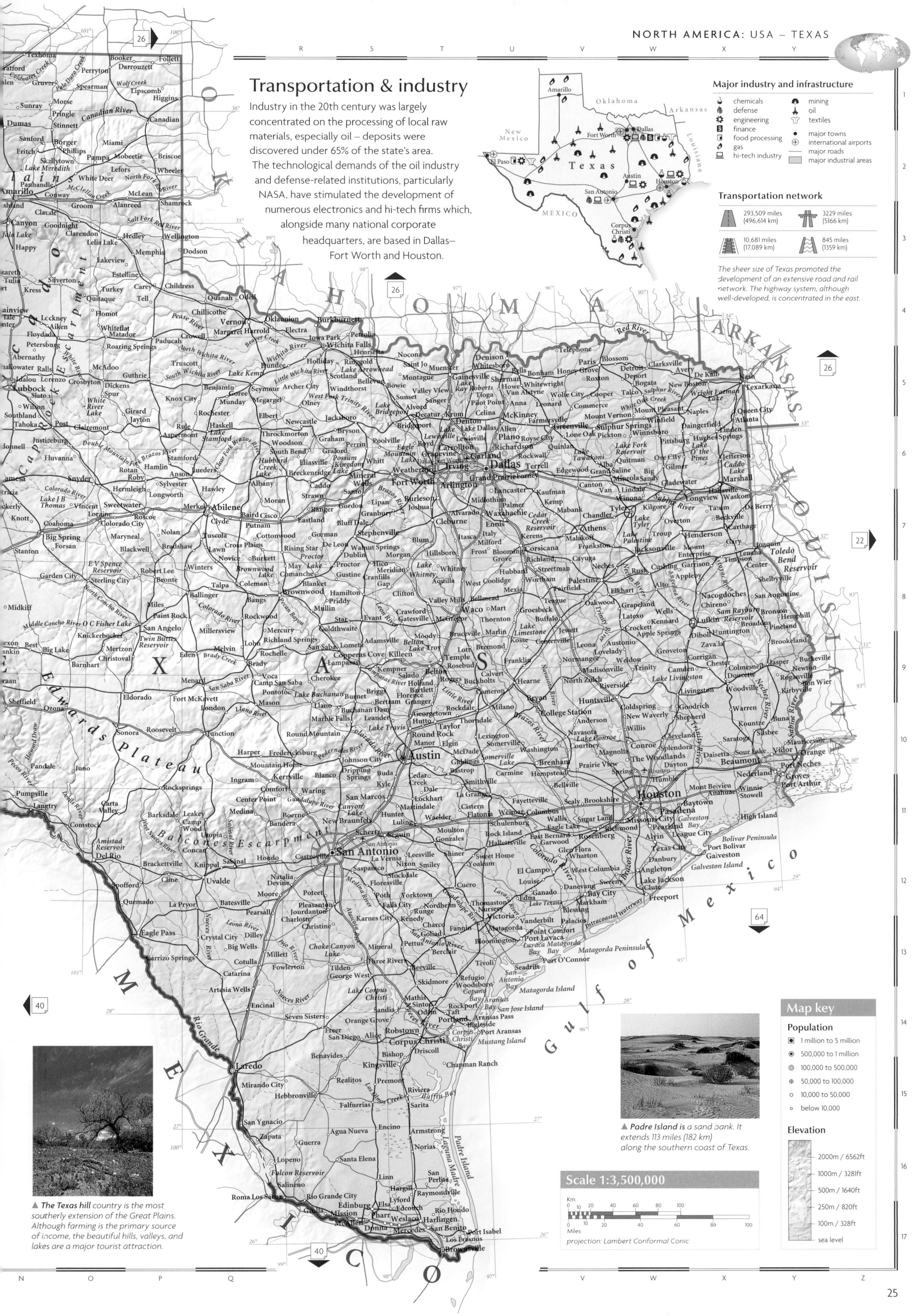

## Transportation & industry

Industry in the 20th century was largely concentrated on the processing of local raw materials, especially oil – deposits were discovered under 65% of the state's area. The technological demands of the oil industry and defense-related institutions, particularly NASA, have stimulated the development of numerous electronics and hi-tech firms which, alongside many national corporate headquarters, are based in Dallas–Fort Worth and Houston.

### Major industry and infrastructure

- chemicals
- defense
- engineering
- finance
- food processing
- gas
- hi-tech industry
- mining
- oil
- textiles
- major towns
- international airports
- major roads
- major industrial areas

### Transportation network

| | |
|---|---|
| 293,509 miles (496,614 km) | 3229 miles (5166 km) |
| 10,681 miles (17,089 km) | 845 miles (1359 km) |

The sheer size of Texas promoted the development of an extensive road and rail network. The highway system, although well-developed, is concentrated in the east.

▲ *The Texas hill* country is the most southerly extension of the Great Plains. Although farming is the primary source of income, the beautiful hills, valleys, and lakes are a major tourist attraction.

▲ *Padre Island is* a sand bank. It extends 113 miles (182 km) along the southern coast of Texas.

### Map key

#### Population
- 1 million to 5 million
- 500,000 to 1 million
- 100,000 to 500,000
- 50,000 to 100,000
- 10,000 to 50,000
- below 10,000

#### Elevation
- 2000m / 6562ft
- 1000m / 3281ft
- 500m / 1640ft
- 250m / 820ft
- 100m / 328ft
- sea level

Scale 1:3,500,000

projection: Lambert Conformal Conic

25

# USA: SOUTH MIDWESTERN STATES

### Arkansas, Kansas, Missouri, Oklahoma

The expansion of the US focused on this region in the mid-19th century. Settlers spread from the confluence of the Missouri and Mississippi rivers up onto the Great Plains. This treeless expanse, which early explorers had called the Great American Desert was turned into one of the world's richest agricultural regions. But periodic droughts, coupled with overintensive farming, led to the "dustbowl" soil erosion crisis of the 1930s, the abandonment of many farms, and a mass exodus to the west coast. The land has since recovered, although the mechanization of agriculture has led to a decline in the rural population. In recent years, suburban residential development has spread rapidly across the wooded Ozark Plateau in the east of the region.

## Transportation & industry

The processing of agricultural products, such as brewing and meatpacking, has been traditionally important in these states. In Kansas and Oklahoma, diversified manufacturing now supplements income from fossil fuels; Wichita has become a world center for aeronautical engineering, an industry which also employs many people in neighboring Missouri.

### Major industry and infrastructure

- ✈ aerospace
- ⚙ engineering
- S finance
- 🍴 food processing
- ◊ gas
- ⛏ mining
- ◓ oil
- 🚗 vehicle manufacture
- • major towns
- ⊕ international airports
- — major roads
- ▭ major industrial areas

▶ *Agricultural produce from the plains is moved by barges along the Mississippi. The river now carries a far greater tonnage of freight than any other waterway system in the US.*

### Transportation network

| | | | |
|---|---|---|---|
| 380,307 miles (608,491 km) | | 4068 miles (6508 km) | |
| 16,185 miles (25,896 km) | | 1994 miles (3208 km) | |

*The Arkansas River and its tributaries allow access to over half of the US's navigable inland waterways. A system of locks and dams along the river provides Tulsa, in Oklahoma, with a navigable water route to the Gulf of Mexico.*

### Map key

**Population**
- ◎ 100,000 to 500,000
- ⊕ 50,000 to 100,000
- ○ 10,000 to 50,000
- ○ below 10,000

**Elevation**
- 1000m / 3281ft
- 500m / 1640ft
- 250m / 820ft
- 100m / 328ft
- sea level

## The landscape

Most of the region consists of high, treeless plains, which gradually descend east from the Rocky Mountains. Drainage follows this slope, with rivers flowing toward the alluvial lowlands of the Mississippi in the southeast. Between the plains and the lowlands lie various ranges of wooded hills, including the deeply incised Ozark Plateau.

▲ *The Mississippi, North America's longest river, is joined by the Missouri, its main tributary, on a flood plain which spreads south to the Gulf of Mexico.*

**Collapsed limestone caverns** led to the formation of Big Basin in Kansas; a depression 100 ft (33 m) deep and 1 mile (1.6 km) wide.

**The Great Salt Plains** of northern Oklahoma cover 45 sq miles (116 sq km). The arid, white flats were left by the gradual evaporation of an ancient salt lake.

**Flint Hills is** the region's easternmost major escarpment. Steep, grassy uplands are interspersed with rocky, wooded ravines and outcrops of limestone and chert.

**Missouri River**

**The Ozark Plateau is** a wooded, hilly region of rivers and narrow, winding lakes. The Lake of the Ozarks was created by the damming of the Osage River in 1930.

**Crowleys Ridge is** a long, sandy ridge, rising from the Mississippi floodplain. It was formed over thousands of years by the deposition of sand blown eastward from the Great Plains.

### Scale 1:3,250,000

Km
0 5 10 20 30 40 50 60 70

Miles
0 5 10 20 30 40 50 60 70

*projection: Lambert Conformal Conic*

**Underground water reserves**

- WY
- NE
- CO
- KS / MO — Kansas
- NM
- OK / AR
- TX — Oklahoma
- Extent of the aquifer

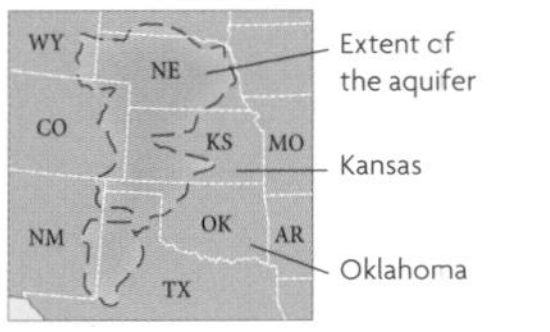

▲ *The Ogallala Aquifer, beneath the Great Plains, is the largest known source of underground water in the world. There is concern about the rapid depletion of this finite water supply by irrigation schemes.*

**Red River**

**Devil's Den is** a dry badland area. The rugged landscape, strewn with large boulders, is the eroded remnant of a spur extending from the Arbuckle Mountains to the west.

**Ouachita Mountains**

**Mississippi River**

▼ *Lake Ouachita, in Arkansas is one of a number of irregularly-shaped lakes found among the ridges of the Ouachita Mountains.*

▲ *The landscape of northeast Kansas is interlaced by rivers which have cut broad wooded valleys through the gentle hills. All the rivers in Kansas form part of the massive Missouri/Mississippi drainage basin.*

► *Gateway Arch*, in Saint Louis, Missouri, is 634 ft (192 m) high. The huge steel arch symbolizes the city's historic role as the "Gateway to the West".

## Using the land

The problems of a harsh continental climate, with severe winters and hot, dry summers, are partially offset by the rich soils of the plains. Kansas is a major cereal crop producer, ranking first in US production of wheat and sorghum. Rainfall increases toward the east, favoring the cultivation of soybeans, cotton, and rice, with corn concentrated in Missouri. Huge herds of cattle are raised in Oklahoma, Kansas, and Missouri.

▲ *A combine harvester* works the land on the great plains. A hundred years ago this region, also known as the prairies – the French word for pasture – was covered with tall, wild grasses.

**The urban/rural population divide**

urban 65%      rural 35%

0 10 20 30 40 50 60 70 80 90 100

| Population density | Total land area |
|---|---|
| 54 people per sq mile (21 people per sq km) | 271,436 sq miles (702,992 sq km) |

**Land use and agricultural distribution**

- 🐄 cattle
- 🦃 poultry
- 🌾 cereals
- 🌽 corn
- cotton
- fodder
- rice
- soybeans
- • major towns

pasture
cropland
forest

# USA: UPPER PLAINS STATES

## Iowa, Minnesota, Nebraska, North Dakota, South Dakota

Lying at the very heart of the North American continent, much of this region was acquired from France as part of the Louisiana Purchase in 1803. The area was largely bypassed by the early waves of westward migrants. When Europeans did settle, during the 19th century, they displaced the Native Americans who lived on the plains. The settlers planted arable crops and raised cattle on the immensely fertile prairie land, founding an agrarian tradition which flourishes today. Most of this region remains rural; of the five states, only in Minnesota has there been significant diversification away from agriculture and resource-based industries into the hi-tech and service sectors.

## Using the land

The popular image of these states as agricultural is entirely justified; prairies stretch uninterrupted across most of the area. Croplands fall into two regions: the wheat belt of the plains, and the corn belt of the central US. Cash crops, such as soybeans, are grown to supplement incomes. Livestock, particularly pigs and cattle, are raised throughout this region.

▶ *Dark, fertile prairie* soils in the southeast provide Minnesota's most productive farmland. Hot, humid summers create a long growing season for corn cultivation.

**The urban/rural population divide**

urban 64%  rural 36%

0  10  20  30  40  50  60  70  80  90  100

| Population density | Total land area |
|---|---|
| 31 people per sq mile (12 people per sq km) | 357,212 sq miles (925,143 sq km) |

**Land use and agricultural distribution**

- cattle
- pigs
- corn
- soybeans
- wheat
- major towns
- pasture
- cropland
- forest
- wetland

## Transportation & industry

Food processing and the production of farm machinery are supported by the large agricultural sector. Mineral exploitation is also an important activity: gold is mined in the ore-rich Black Hills of South Dakota, and both North Dakota and Nebraska are emerging as major petroleum producers.

▶ *Water erosion along* the Little Missouri River has carried away sedimentary deposits, creating rugged landscapes known as badlands.

**Transportation network**

| | |
|---|---|
| 504,522 miles (807,235 km) | 3422 miles (5475 km) |
| 16,940 miles (27,104 km) | 683 miles (1098 km) |

*Nebraska's central location has made it an important transportation artery for east–west traffic. Minnesota's road network radiates out from the hub of the twin cities, Minneapolis–Saint Paul.*

**Major industry and infrastructure**

- coal
- engineering
- electronics
- finance
- food processing
- oil & gas
- mining
- major towns
- international airports
- major roads
- major industrial areas

## The landscape

These states straddle the Great Plains and the lowlands of the central US, with Minnesota lying in a transition zone between the eastern forests and the prairies. The region was shaped by repeated ice advances and retreats, leaving a flat relief, broken only by the numerous lakes and broad river networks that drain the prairies.

Escarpment   Ridge
In permeable strata hollows are formed by small mudslides
Water flowing into gullies erodes back the escarpment

▲ *Badlands are formed* by stormwater run-off. This flows down the impermeable strata of the escarpment and saturates the permeable strata, leading to mudslides and the formation of gullies.

**The Minnesota landscape** contains many post-glacial features, including its numerous lakes, boulder-strewn hills, and mineral-rich deposits.

North Dakota Badlands

▲ *In the badlands* of North and South Dakota, horizontal layers of sandstone have been eroded by rivers, leaving a landscape of narrow gullies, sharp crests and pinnacles.

South Dakota Badlands

**Although it escaped** the last glaciation, the limestone bedrock of southeastern Minnesota has been eroded by surface and subterranean streams, leaving a network of underground caverns and steepsided valleys.

▲ *Chimney Rock is* a remnant of an ancient land surface, eroded by the North Platte River. The tip of its spire stands 500 ft (150 m) above the plain.

Missouri River

Mississippi River

◀ *In northeastern Iowa,* the Mississippi and its tributaries have deeply incised the underlying bedrock creating a hilly terrain, with bluffs standing 300 ft (90 m) above the valley.

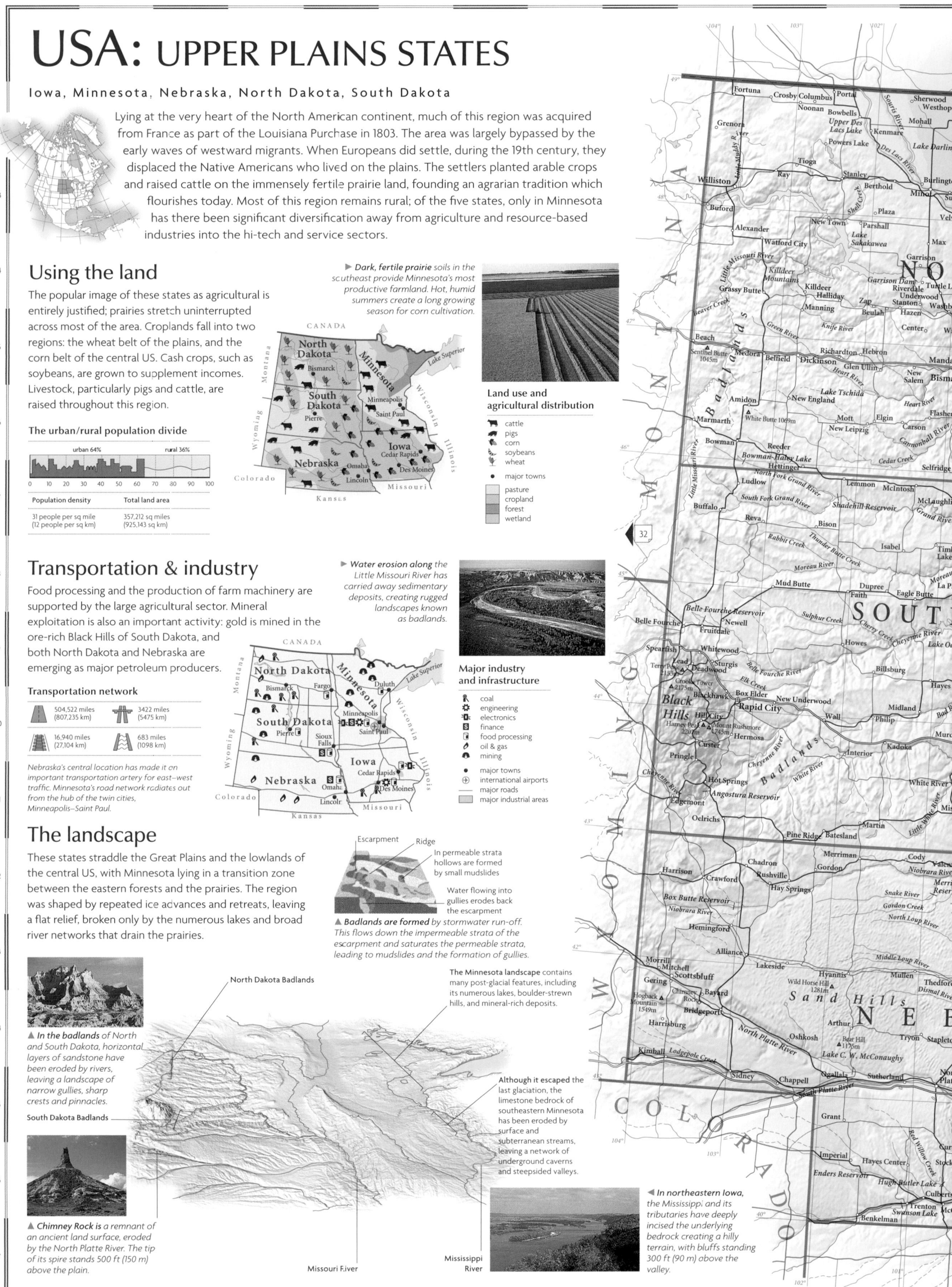

▶ **Along the shores** of Lake Superior in Minnesota, the average number of frostfree days can be as few as 90, and frosts may occur in any month of the year.

C A N A D A

**NORTH DAKOTA**

**SOUTH DAKOTA**

**MINNESOTA**

**IOWA**

**NEBRASKA**

**KANSAS**

**MISSOURI**

**WISCONSIN**

**ILLINOIS**

*Lake of the Woods*

*Lake Superior*

*Rainy Lake*

*Lake Winnibigoshish*

*Leech Lake*

*Mille Lacs Lake*

Minneapolis · Saint Paul

Duluth

Fargo · Moorhead

Sioux Falls

Sioux City

Des Moines

Omaha · Council Bluffs

Lincoln

Cedar Rapids

Davenport

Rochester

Waterloo

Dubuque

*Missouri River*

*Mississippi River*

*Red River*

*James River*

*Platte River*

*Des Moines River*

**Map key**

**Population**
- ◉ 100,000 to 500,000
- ⊕ 50,000 to 100,000
- ○ 10,000 to 50,000
- ○ below 10,000

**Elevation**

| | |
|---|---|
| | 2000m / 6562ft |
| | 1000m / 3281ft |
| | 500m / 1640ft |
| | 250m / 820ft |
| | 100m / 328ft |
| | sea level |

**Scale 1:3,500,000**

Km
0 20 40 60 80 100 120

Miles
0 20 40 60 80 100 120

projection: Lambert Conformal Conic

# USA: GREAT LAKES STATES

## Illinois, Indiana, Michigan, Ohio, Wisconsin

The states bordering the Great Lakes developed rapidly in the second half of the 19th century as a result of improvements in communications: railroads to the west and waterways to the south and east. Fertile land and good links with growing eastern seaboard cities encouraged the development of agriculture and food processing. Migrants from Europe and other parts of the US flooded into the region and for much of the 20th century the region's economy boomed. However, in recent years heavy industry has declined, earning the region the unwanted label the "Rustbelt."

## Transportation & industry

The Great Lakes region is the center of the US car industry. Since the early part of the 20th century, its prosperity has been closely linked to the fortunes of automobile manufacturing. Iron and steel production has expanded to meet demand from this industry. In the 1970s, nationwide recession, cheaper foreign competition in the automobile sector, pollution in and around the Great Lakes, and the collapse of the meatpacking industry, centered on Chicago, forced these states to diversify their industrial base. New industries have emerged, notably electronics, service, and finance industries.

### Transportation network

| | |
|---|---|
| 540,682 miles (865,091 km) | 6550 miles (10,480 km) |
| 24,928 miles (39,884 km) | 2330 miles (3748 km) |

Few areas of the US have a comparable system. Chicago is a principal transportation terminus with a dense network of roads, railroads, and Interstate freeways that radiates out from the city.

▶ *Ever since Ransom Olds* and Henry Ford started mass-producing automobiles in Detroit early in the 20th century, the city's name has become synonymous with the American automotive industry.

### Major industry and infrastructure

- car manufacture
- coal
- electronics
- engineering
- finance
- food processing
- iron & steel
- oil
- research & development
- textiles
- major towns
- international airports
- major roads
- major industrial areas

## The landscape

Much of this region shows the impact of glaciation which lasted until about 10,000 years ago, and extended as far south as Illinois and Ohio. Although the relief of the region slopes toward the Great Lakes, because the ice sheets blocked northerly drainage, most of the rivers today flow southward, forming part of the massive Mississippi/Missouri drainage basin.

◀ *The dunes near* Sleeping Bear Point rise 400 ft (120 m) from the banks of Lake Michigan. They are constantly being resculpted by wind action.

Lake Michigan

**The many lakes** and marshes of Wisconsin and Michigan are the result of glacial erosion and deposition which occurred during the last Ice Age.

**Southwestern Wisconsin** is known as a "driftless" area. Unlike most of the region, low hills protected it from erosion by the advancing ice sheet.

**Most of the** water used in northern Illinois is pumped from underground reservoirs. Due to increased demand, many areas now face a water shortage. Around Joliet, the water table was lowered by more than 700 ft (210 m) over the last century.

**Lake Erie is** the shallowest of the five Great Lakes. Its average depth is about 62 ft (19 m). Storms sweeping across from Canada erode its shores and cause the silting of its harbors.

**The Appalachian plateau** stretches eastward from Ohio. It is dissected by streams flowing west into the Mississippi and Ohio rivers.

Illinois plains

Mississippi River

Ohio River

**Relic landforms from** the last glaciation, such as shallow basins and ridges, cover all but the south of this region. Ridges, known as moraines, up to 300 ft (100 m) high, lie to the south of Lake Michigan.

**Unlike the level** prairie to the north, southern Indiana is relatively rugged. Limestone in the hills has been dissolved by water, producing features such as sinkholes and underground caves.

Glacial till

Present-day river or stream

Channels caused by outwash from melting glacier

Most recent till deposits

Older till sheet

Bedrock

▲ *The plains of* Illinois are characteristic of drift landscapes, scoured and flattened by glacial erosion and covered with fertile glacial deposits.

▲ *As a result* of successive glacial depositions, the total depth of till along the former southern margin of the Laurentide ice sheet can exceed 1300 ft (400 m).

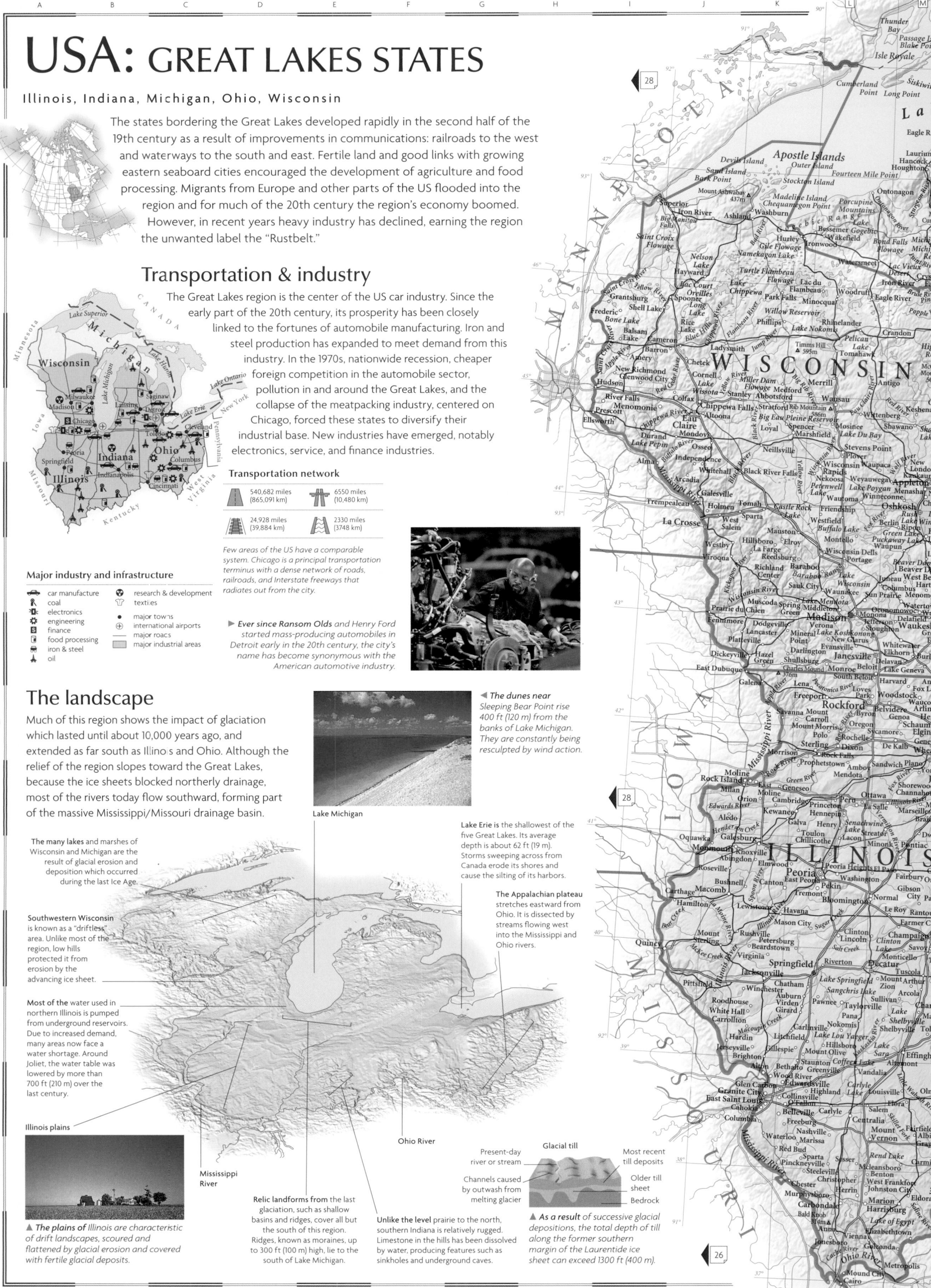

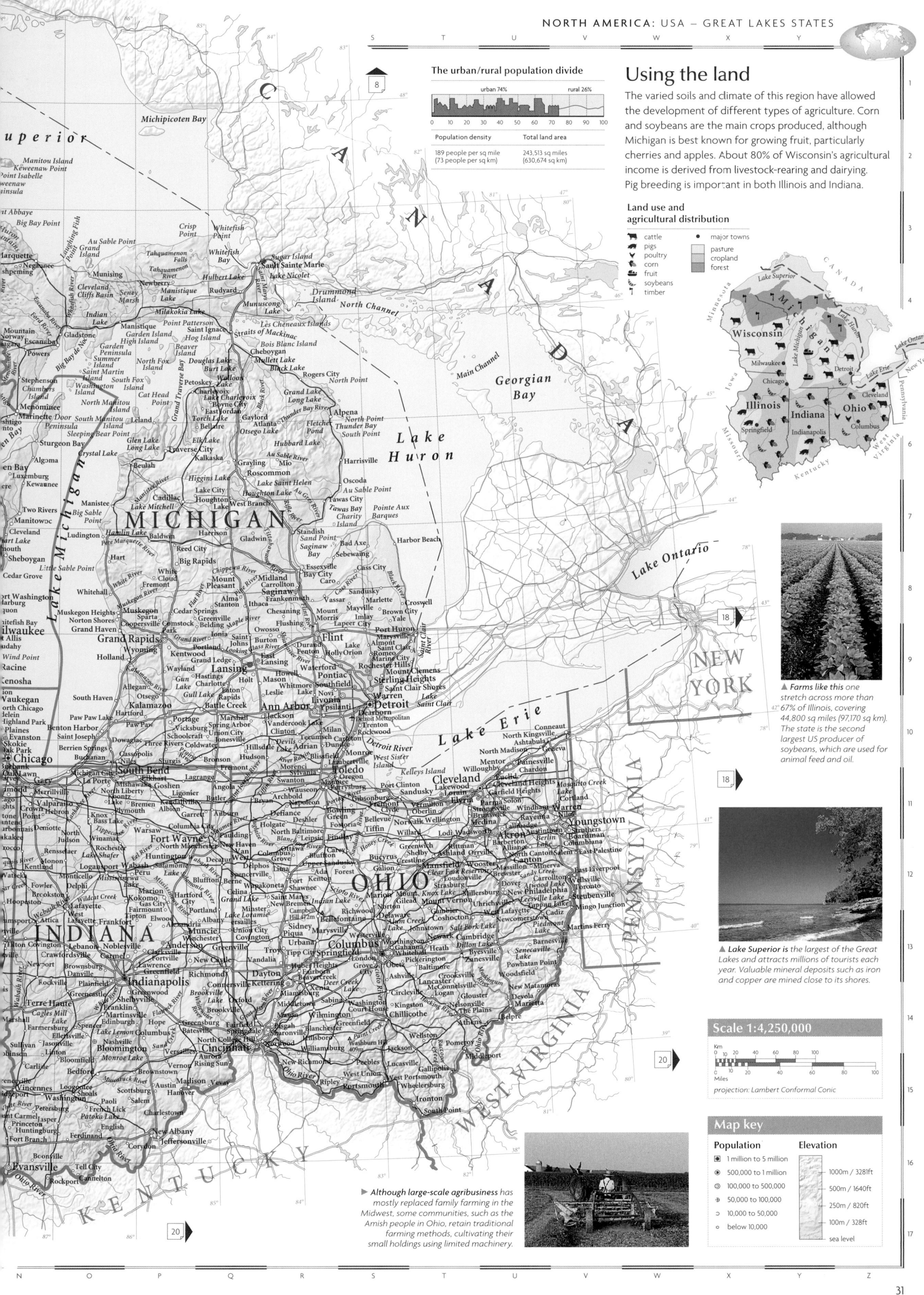

## The urban/rural population divide

urban 74%    rural 26%

0  10  20  30  40  50  60  70  80  90  100

| Population density | Total land area |
|---|---|
| 189 people per sq mile (73 people per sq km) | 243,513 sq miles (630,674 sq km) |

## Using the land

The varied soils and climate of this region have allowed the development of different types of agriculture. Corn and soybeans are the main crops produced, although Michigan is best known for growing fruit, particularly cherries and apples. About 80% of Wisconsin's agricultural income is derived from livestock-rearing and dairying. Pig breeding is important in both Illinois and Indiana.

### Land use and agricultural distribution

- cattle
- pigs
- poultry
- corn
- fruit
- soybeans
- timber
- major towns
- pasture
- cropland
- forest

▲ *Farms like this* one stretch across more than 67% of Illinois, covering 44,800 sq miles (97,170 sq km). The state is the second largest US producer of soybeans, which are used for animal feed and oil.

▲ *Lake Superior is* the largest of the Great Lakes and attracts millions of tourists each year. Valuable mineral deposits such as iron and copper are mined close to its shores.

## Scale 1:4,250,000

Km
0 10 20    40    60    80    100

Miles
0    20    40    60    80    100

projection: Lambert Conformal Conic

## Map key

### Population
- 1 million to 5 million
- 500,000 to 1 million
- 100,000 to 500,000
- 50,000 to 100,000
- 10,000 to 50,000
- below 10,000

### Elevation
- 1000m / 3281ft
- 500m / 1640ft
- 250m / 820ft
- 100m / 328ft
- sea level

▲ *Although large-scale agribusiness* has mostly replaced family farming in the Midwest, some communities, such as the Amish people in Ohio, retain traditional farming methods, cultivating their small holdings using limited machinery.

# USA: NORTH MOUNTAIN STATES

## Idaho, Montana, Oregon, Washington, Wyoming

The remoteness of the northwestern states, coupled with the rugged landscape, ensured that this was one of the last areas settled by Europeans in the 19th century. Fur-trappers and gold-prospectors followed the Snake River westward as it wound its way through the Rocky Mountains. The states of the northwest have pioneered many conservationist policies, with the first US National Park opened at Yellowstone in 1872. More recently, the Cascades and Rocky Mountains have become havens for adventure tourism. The mountains still serve to isolate the western seaboard from the rest of the continent. This isolation has encouraged West Coast cities to expand their trade links with countries of the Pacific Rim.

▲ The Snake River has cut down into the basalt of the Columbia Basin to form Hells Canyon, the deepest in the US, with cliffs up to 7900 ft (2408 m) high.

### Map key

**Population**
- ◉ 500,000 to 1 million
- ◉ 100,000 to 500,000
- ⊕ 50,000 to 100,000
- ○ 10,000 to 50,000
- ○ below 10,000

**Elevation**
- 4000m / 13,124ft
- 3000m / 9843ft
- 2000m / 6562ft
- 1000m / 3281ft
- 500m / 1640ft
- 250m / 820ft
- 100m / 328ft
- sea level

► Fine-textured, volcanic soils in the hilly Palouse region of eastern Washington are susceptible to erosion.

## Using the land

Wheat farming in the east gives way to cattle ranching as rainfall decreases. Irrigated farming in the Snake River valley produces large yields of potatoes and other vegetables. Dairying and fruit-growing take place in the wet western lowlands between the mountain ranges.

**The urban/rural population divide**

urban 74%    rural 26%

| Population density | Total land area |
|---|---|
| 26 people per sq mile (10 people per sq km) | 487,970 sq miles (1,263,716 sq km) |

**Scale 1:4,250,000**

Km
0 10 20 40 60 80 100

Miles
0 10 20 40 60 80 100

projection: Lambert Conformal Conic

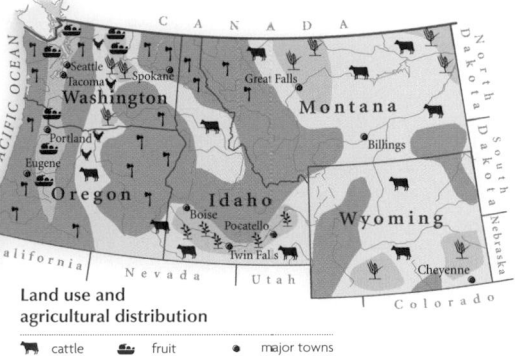

**Land use and agricultural distribution**

- 🐄 cattle
- 🦃 poultry
- 🌾 cereals
- 🍎 fruit
- 🥔 potatoes
- 🌲 timber
- • major towns
- pasture
- cropland
- forest

## Transportation & industry

Minerals and timber are extremely important in this region. Uranium, precious metals, copper, and coal are all mined, the latter in vast open-cast pits in Wyoming; oil and natural gas are extracted further north. Manufacturing, notably related to the aerospace and electronics industries, is important in western cities.

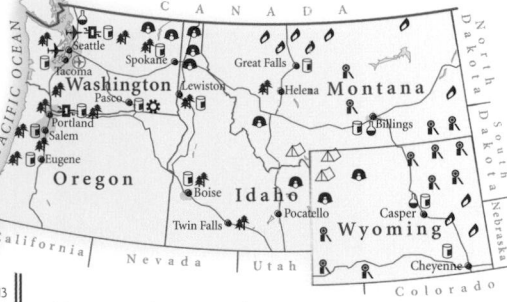

**Transportation network**

- 347,857 miles (556,571 km)
- 4200 miles (6720 km)
- 12,354 miles (19,766 km)
- 1108 miles (1782 km)

**Major industry and infrastructure**

- adventure tourism
- aerospace
- coal
- chemicals
- electronics
- food processing
- mining
- oil & gas
- timber processing
- • major towns
- ⊕ international airports
- major roads
- major industrial areas

The Union Pacific Railroad has been in service across Wyoming since 1867. The route through the Rocky Mountains is now shared with the Interstate 80, a major east–west highway.

◄ Seattle lies in one of Puget Sound's many inlets. The city receives oil and other resources from Alaska, and benefits from expanding trade across the Pacific.

◄ Crater Lake, Oregon, is 6 miles (10 km) wide and 1800 ft (600 m) deep. It marks the site of a volcanic cone, which collapsed after an eruption within the last 7000 years.

## The landscape

The Rocky Mountains are flanked by lower parallel ranges, which spread onto the Great Plains in the east and surmount the broad lava plateau which extends westward. The Cascade Range divides the Columbia Basin from the coastlands, where the low areas around Puget Sound are broken by the steep, volcanic Olympic Mountains and the wooded hills of the Coast Ranges.

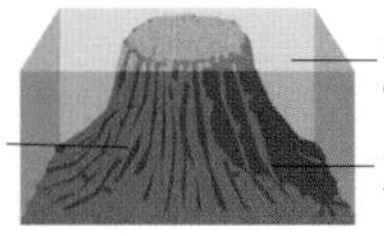

Molten rock cools, forming parallel columns
Surrounding strata eroded away
Molten rock wells up from the Earth's core

▲ **Devil's Tower in** *Wyoming is an igneous intrusion, formed below the Earth's surface. Molten rock intruded through cracks in the overlying strata and cooled. Over time, the softer rock layers have been eroded away, leaving only the tower standing.*

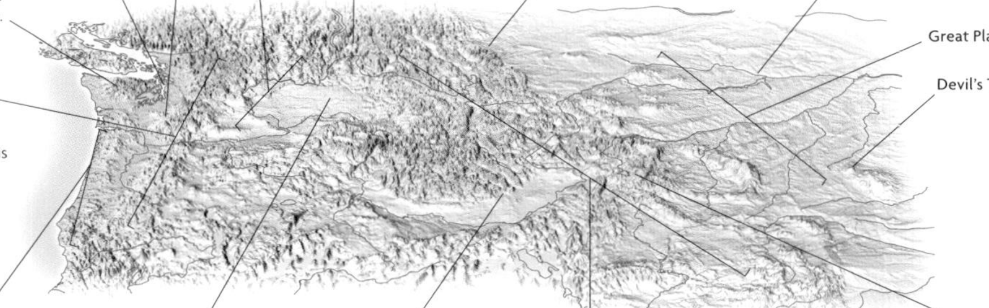

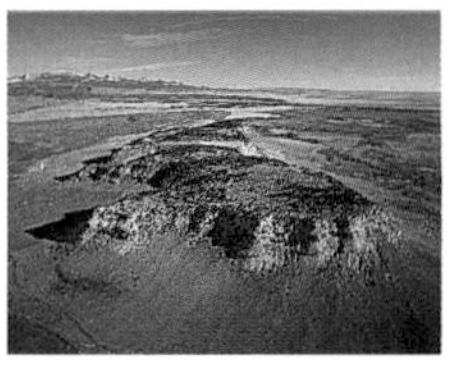

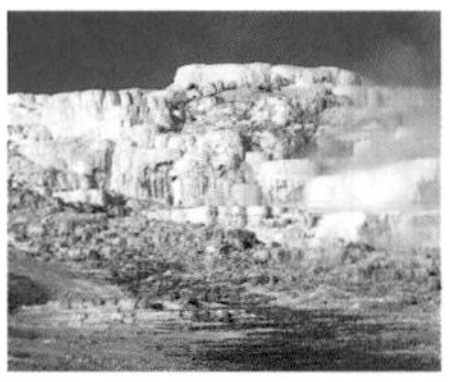

**Glacial valleys on** the seaward side of the Olympic Mountains receive about 142 inches (3600 mm) of rain per year, supporting the only true rain forest of the northern hemisphere.
Puget Sound
Mount St. Helens erupted in 1980, killing 57 people and devastating a huge area.
Columbia Basin
**Grand Coulee** and the lesser *coulées* (ravines) were cut by cataclysmic floods, from the release of an ice-dammed lake, at the end of the last Ice Age.
**The Continental Divide,** or watershed, crosses the Lewis Range. From here, rivers flow east to Hudson Bay, south to the Gulf of Mexico and west to the Pacific Ocean.
**The Cascades are** glacially scoured volcanic mountains, the highest of which is Mount Rainier, a dormant volcano at 14,409 ft (4392 m).
Coast Ranges
**The plateaus of** the Columbia and Snake rivers represent one of the world's largest accumulations of lava. Over 5 million years ago, successive flows of molten basalt buried the existing land surface by up to 450 ft (150 m).
**The contorted rock** shapes at "Craters of the Moon" National Monument in Idaho were left 2000 years ago by the sporadic upwelling of viscous lava from fissures in the basalt plateau.
Rocky Mountains
Great Plains
Devil's Tower

▶ ***Piney Buttes are** the remnants of an older, higher land surface gradually weathered and eroded into isolated outcrops with flat tops and steep sides.*

▲ ***Water from the** hot springs in Yellowstone National Park deposits minerals as it cools in rock pools. Long periods of deposition have created these rock terraces.*

CANADA
MONTANA
IDAHO
WYOMING
NORTH DAKOTA
SOUTH DAKOTA
NEBRASKA
UTAH
COLORADO
ROCKY MOUNTAINS
Great Plains
Helena
Great Falls
Billings
Missoula
Bozeman
Butte
Cheyenne
Casper
Laramie
Pocatello
Idaho Falls
Yellowstone Lake
Fort Peck Lake
Bighorn Basin
Great Divide Basin
Snake River Plain
Missouri River
Yellowstone River
Snake River
Bighorn Mountains
Laramie Mountains
Wind River Range
Absaroka Range
Salmon River Mountains
Bitterroot Range
Lewis Range
Big Belt Mountains
Piney Buttes

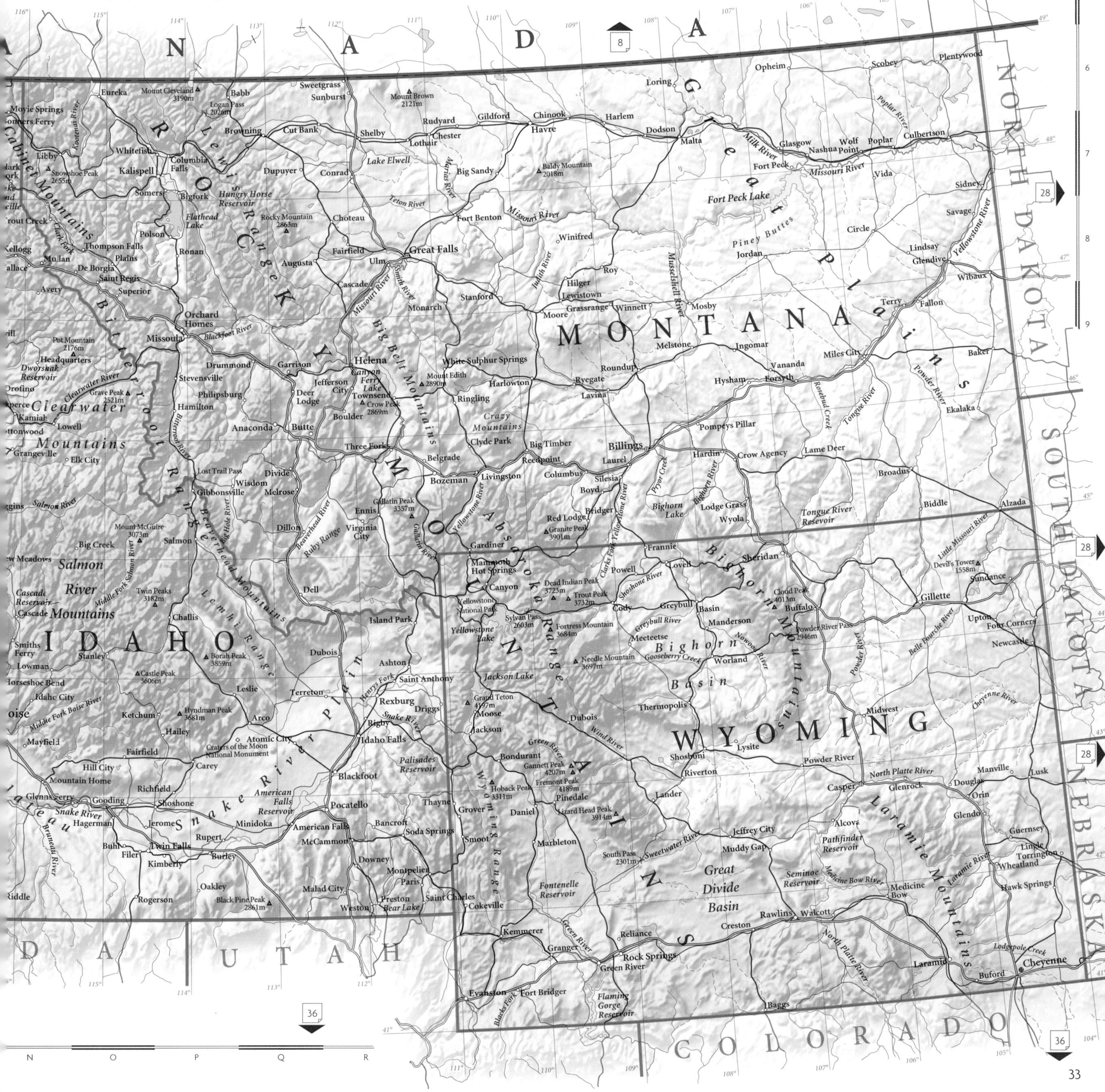

# USA: CALIFORNIA & NEVADA

The Gold Rush of 1849 attracted the first major wave of European settlers to the West Coast. The pleasant climate, beautiful scenery, and dynamic economy continue to attract immigrants – despite the ever-present danger of earthquakes – and California has become the US's most populous state. The overwhelmingly urban population is concentrated in the vast conurbations of Los Angeles, San Francisco, and San Diego; new immigrants include people from South Korea, the Philippines, Vietnam, and Mexico. Nevada's arid lands were initially exploited for minerals; in recent years, revenue from mining has been superseded by income from the tourist and gambling centers of Las Vegas and Reno.

## Map key

### Population
- ◼ 1 million to 5 million
- ◉ 500,000 to 1 million
- ◎ 100,000 to 500,000
- ⊕ 50,000 to 100,000
- ○ 10,000 to 50,000
- ∘ below 10,000

### Elevation
- 4000m / 13,124ft
- 3000m / 9843ft
- 2000m / 6562ft
- 1000m / 3281ft
- 500m / 1640ft
- 250m / 820ft
- 100m / 328ft
- sea level

### Scale 1:3,250,000

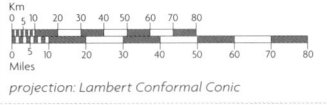

projection: Lambert Conformal Conic

## Transportation & industry

Nevada's rich mineral reserves ushered in a period of mining wealth which has now been replaced by revenue generated from gambling. California supports a broad set of activities including defense-related industries and research and development facilities. "Silicon Valley," near San Francisco, is a world leading center for micro-electronics, while tourism and the Los Angeles film industry also generate large incomes.

### Major industry and infrastructure
- ✈ aerospace
- 🚗 car manufacture
- defense
- 🎬 film industry
- S finance
- food processing
- gambling
- 🖳 hi-tech industry
- ⛏ mining
- pharmaceuticals
- research & development
- textiles
- tourism
- ● major towns
- ⊕ international airports
- — major roads
- ▨ major industrial areas

### Transportation network
- 211,459 miles (338,334 km)
- 2944 miles (4710 km)
- 7822 miles (12,595 km)
- 190 miles (360 km)

In California, the motor vehicle is a vital part of daily life, and an extensive freeway system runs throughout the state, cementing its position as the most important mode of transport.

◀ *Gambling was legalized in Nevada in 1931. Las Vegas has since become the center of this multimillion dollar industry.*

## The landscape

The broad Central Valley divides California's coastal mountains from the Sierra Nevada. The San Andreas Fault, running beneath much of the state, is the site of frequent earth tremors and sometimes more serious earthquakes. East of the Sierra Nevada, the landscape is characterized by the basin and range topography with stony deserts and many salt lakes.

Rising molten rock causes stretching of the Earth's crust

Extensive cracking (faulting) uplifted a series of ridges

As ridges are eroded they fill intervening valleys with sediments

▲ *Molten rock (magma) welling up to form a dome in the Earth's interior, causes the brittle surface rocks to stretch and crack. Some areas were uplifted to form mountains (ranges), while others sunk to form flat valleys (basins).*

◀ *The General Sherman sequoia tree in Sequoia National Park is around 2500 years old and at 275 ft (84 m) is one of the largest living things on earth.*

Most of California's agriculture is confined to the fertile and extensively irrigated Central Valley, running between the Coast Ranges and the Sierra Nevada. It incorporates the San Joaquin and Sacramento valleys.

The dramatic granitic rock formations of Half Dome and El Capitan, and the verdant coniferous forests, attract millions of visitors annually to Yosemite National Park in the Sierra Nevada.

Sierra Nevada

The Great Basin dominates most of Nevada's topography containing large open basins, punctuated by eroded features such as *buttes* and *mesas*. River flow tends to be seasonal, dependent upon spring showers and winter snow melt.

Wheeler Peak is home to some of the world's oldest trees, bristlecone pines, which live for up to 5000 years.

## Using the land

California is the leading agricultural producer in the US, although low rainfall makes irrigation essential. The long growing season and abundant sunshine allow many crops to be grown in the fertile Central Valley including grapes, citrus fruits, vegetables, and cotton. Almost 17 million acres (6.8 million hectares) of California's forests are used commercially. Nevada's arid climate and poor soil are largely unsuitable for agriculture; 85% of its land is state owned and large areas are used for underground testing of nuclear weapons.

### Land use and agricultural distribution
- 🐄 cattle
- citrus fruits
- fruit
- irrigation
- timber
- vineyards
- ● major towns
- pasture
- cropland
- forest
- desert

When the Hoover Dam across the Colorado River was completed in 1936, it created Lake Mead, one of the largest artificial lakes in the world, extending for 115 miles (285 km) upstream.

Amargosa Desert

The San Andreas Fault is a transverse fault which extends for 650 miles (1050 km) through California. Major earthquakes occur when the land either side of the fault moves at different rates. San Francisco was devastated by an earthquake in 1906.

Death Valley

▶ *Named by migrating settlers in 1849, Death Valley is the driest, hottest place in North America, as well as being the lowest point on land in the western hemisphere, at 282 ft (86 m) below sea level.*

The sparsely populated Mojave Desert receives less than 8 inches (200 mm) of rainfall a year. It is used extensively for weapons-testing and military purposes.

The Salton Sea was created accidentally between 1905 and 1907 when an irrigation channel from the Colorado River broke out of its banks and formed this salty 300 sq mile (777 sq km), landlocked lake.

▲ *The Sierra Nevada create a "rainshadow," preventing rain from reaching much of Nevada. Pacific air masses, passing over the mountains, are stripped of their moisture.*

▲ *Without considerable irrigation, this fertile valley at Palm Springs would still be part of the Sonoran Desert. California's farmers account for about 80% of the state's total water usage.*

### The urban/rural population divide

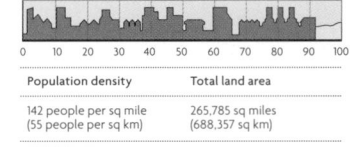

urban 92%          rural 8%

| Population density | Total land area |
|---|---|
| 142 people per sq mile (55 people per sq km) | 265,785 sq miles (688,357 sq km) |

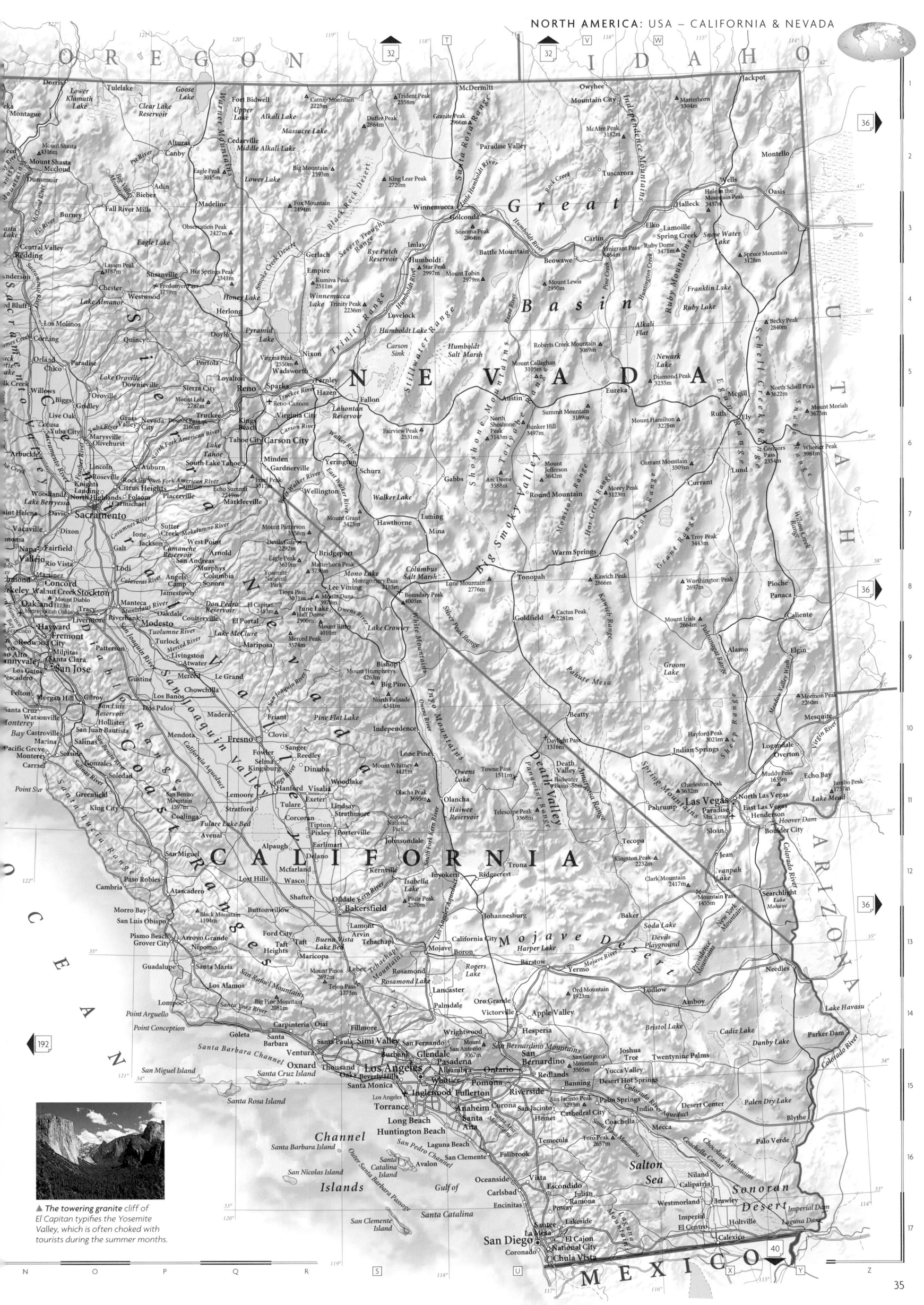

▲ The towering granite cliff of El Capitan typifies the Yosemite Valley, which is often choked with tourists during the summer months.

# USA: SOUTH MOUNTAIN STATES

## Arizona, Colorado, New Mexico, Utah

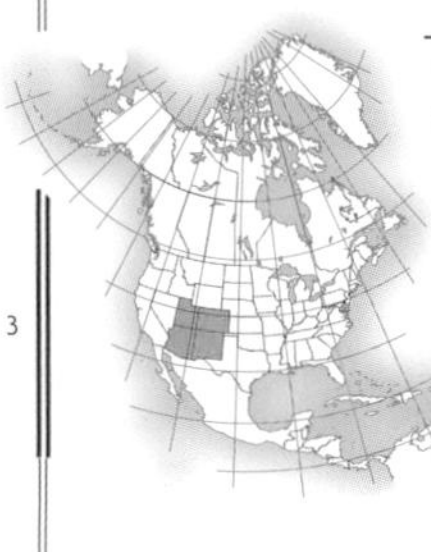

This arid region, characterized by expansive plateaus and spectacular canyons is home to several distinct peoples. The ruins of cliff dwellings built a thousand years ago by the Anasazi people still exist today, and native Americans own one-third of the land in Arizona. Spanish and Mexican conquest and settlement left a hispanic presence which is strongest in New Mexico. The Mormons, who came to the Great Salt Lake seeking religious freedom in 1847, were among the earliest Anglo-American settlers and now make up over 70% of Utah's population. The region's mineral wealth drove rapid development in the 20th century, yet the constraints of a fragile environment, including widespread water shortages, may limit prospects for growth.

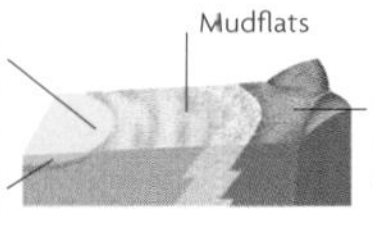

When water evaporates it leaves a salt pan

Mudflats

Lake is fed by seasonal snow melt

Water level of lake varies according to quantity of run-off received from snow melt

▲ *The Great Salt Lake is an ephemeral lake; it can remain dry for extended periods, leaving a pan of evaporated mineral salts in its center.*

## The landscape

The arid, rocky expanse of the Colorado Plateau is dissected by immense canyons of the Colorado River. Desert lies to the north and south and branches of the Rocky Mountains run east and west. The Great Salt Lake and Desert lie within the Great Basin, a barren region of parallel mountain ranges that extends into Arizona.

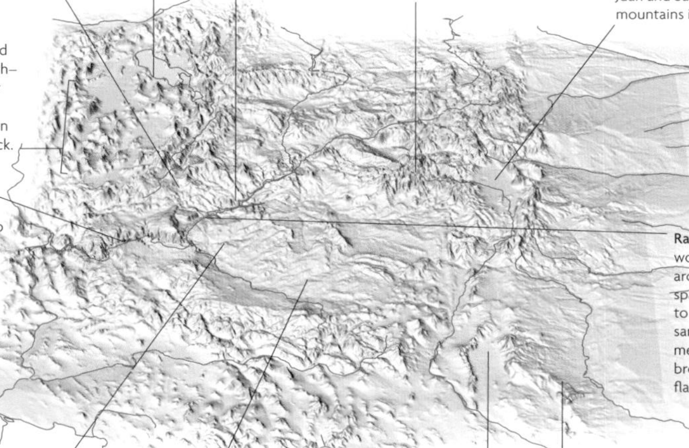

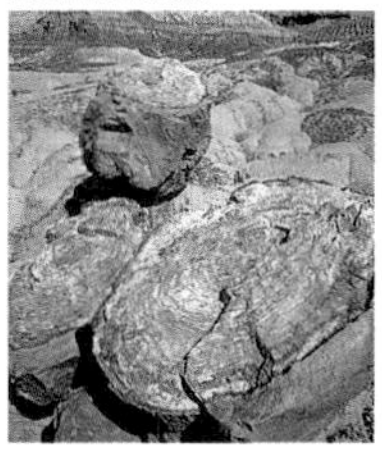

Over 13 million years of weathering has created thousands of spires and pinnacles from the alternating rock strata of Bryce Canyon.

Lake Powell

The Rio Grande has its source in several meltwater streams, which have cut deep valleys into the platform of the San Juan Mountains.

Sand dunes, 600 ft (180 m) high, have been deposited in San Luis Valley, by winds funnelled through the San Juan and Sangre de Cristo mountains in the Rockies.

The parallel basins and ridges, which run north–south along the Great Basin, reflect a major series of block-faults in the underlying bedrock.

Parts of the Grand Canyon, which cuts through the Colorado Plateau, are 16 miles (25 km) wide. The Colorado River has cut down 6262 ft (2000 m), exposing rock strata more than 2 billion years old.

Rainbow Bridge is the world's largest natural arch. The 309 ft (94 m) span probably began to grow when the sandstone spur of a meandering creek was breached during a flash flood.

The striking color effects seen in the Painted Desert come from minerals such as gypsum and haematite, combined with ambient heat and dust.

Petrified Forest

▶ *In the arid landscape of Petrified Forest National Park in Arizona, the grain of prehistoric trees has been preserved as a fossil imprint in the rocks. The bog-preserved trees were gradually turned to stone by seeping mineral-rich water.*

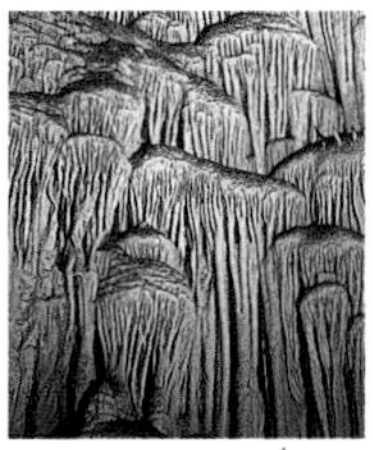

Shifting gypsum sands produce a constantly changing land surface, overwhelming plants and any other obstacles in Tularosa Valley.

▶ *The intricate stalactites of Carlsbad Caverns have grown with the seepage of calcium-rich water over the last 100,000 years. The huge caves are home to around 100,000 Mexican freetail bats..*

## Transportation & industry

New industries have helped reduce the region's dependence on the extraction of minerals and fossil fuels. Precision manufacture has grown rapidly, particularly in Arizona and Colorado. Salt Lake City and Denver are well-established financial centers and New Mexico, the main US producer of uranium, is a prominent region for nuclear research. Colorado is the most important US center for winter sports.

### Transportation network

| | | | |
|---|---|---|---|
| 232,434 miles (373,986 km) | | 4059 miles (6515 km) | |
| 8627 miles (13,881 km) | | none | |

The Colorado Rockies are crossed by 32 mountain passes, some as high as 12,183 ft (3713 m). The Eisenhower Tunnel west of Denver carries Interstate Highway 70 straight through the Continental Divide.

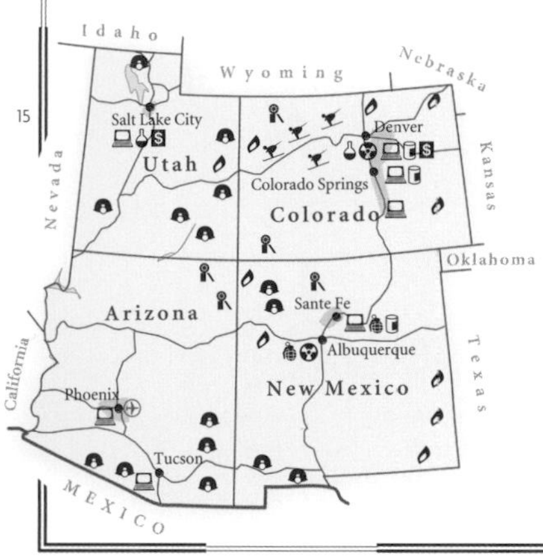

### Major industry and infrastructure

- chemicals
- coal
- defense
- finance
- food processing
- hi-tech industry
- oil & gas
- mining
- research & development
- winter sports
- • major towns
- ✈ international airports
- — major roads
- ▢ major industrial areas

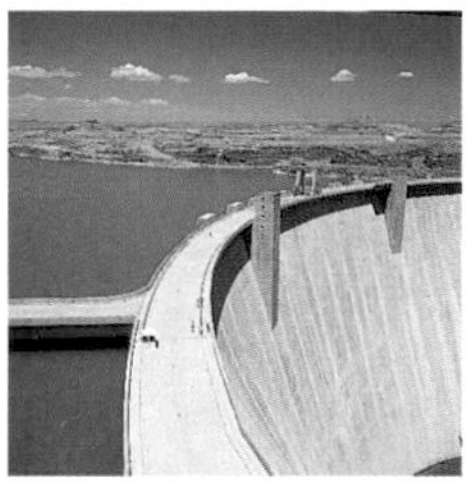

▲ *Glen Canyon Dam on the Colorado river was completed in 1964. it provides hydroelectric power and irrigation water as part of a long-term federal project to harness the river.*

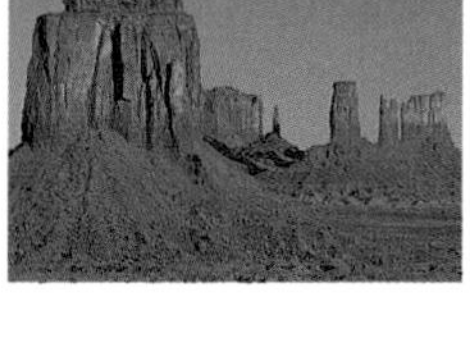

◀ *The flat tablelands (mesas), and the isolated pinnacles (buttes) which rise from the floor of Monument Valley are the resistant remnants of an earlier land surface, gradually cut back by erosion under arid conditions.*

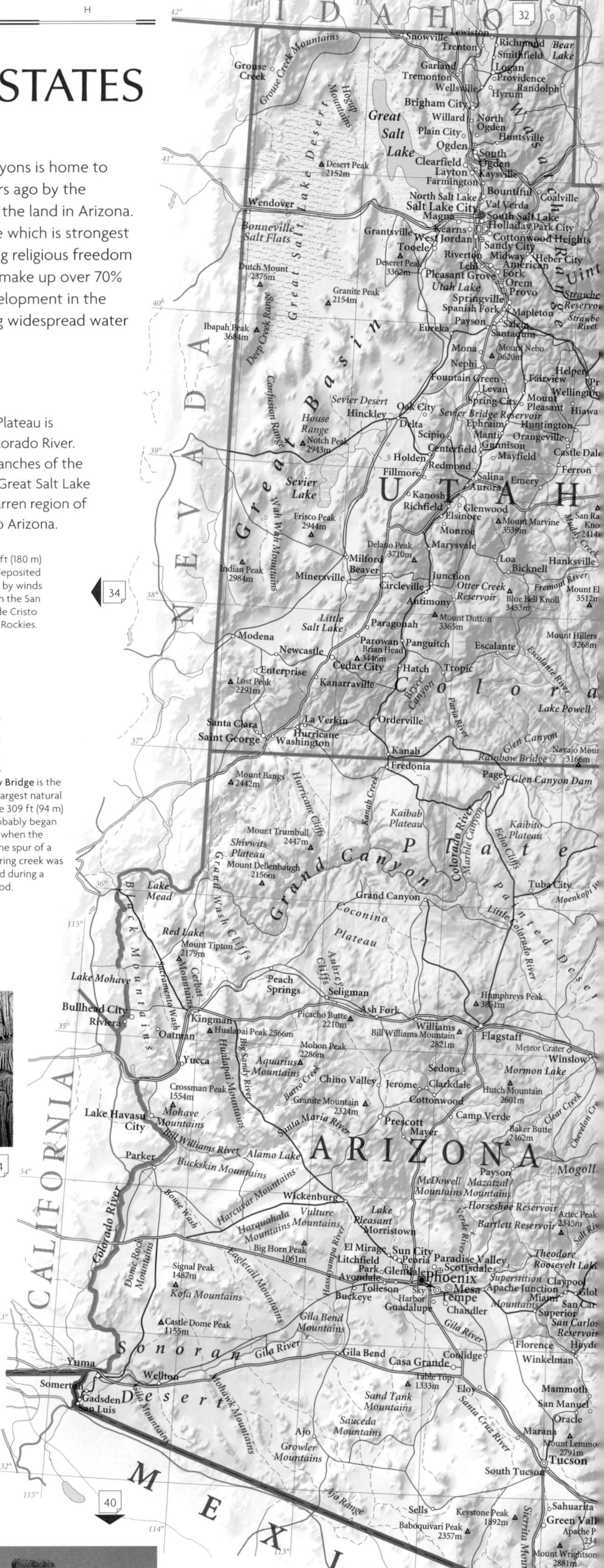

◀ *The Bonneville Salt Flats* are in the Great Salt Lake. Sodium chloride (salt), magnesium, and other minerals are commercially extracted from these flats.

### Scale 1:4,000,000

Km 0 10 20 40 60 80 100
Miles 0 10 20 40 60 80 100

*projection: Lambert Conformal Conic*

### Map key

**Population**
- ◉ 500,000 to 1 million
- ◎ 100,000 to 500,000
- ⊕ 50,000 to 100,000
- ○ 10,000 to 50,000
- ∘ below 10,000

**Elevation**
- 4000m / 13124ft
- 3000m / 9843ft
- 2000m / 6562ft
- 1000m / 3281ft
- 500m / 1640ft
- 250m / 820ft
- 100m / 328ft
- sea level

▲ *A glacially eroded* valley in Rocky Mountain National Park, Colorado. There are 1500 peaks exceeding 10,000 ft (3000 m) within the state, six times the number of major mountains found in the Swiss Alps.

## Using the land

Livestock, particularly cattle ranching, is the main source of agricultural income. The region has a long growing season and areas of rich soil, but depends heavily on water for irrigation. Crops include corn and wheat in eastern areas, and chili peppers, fruit, and cotton aided by additional irrigation.

### Land use and agricultural distribution

- 🐄 cattle
- 🌾 cereals
- cotton
- 🍎 fruit
- irrigation
- major towns
- pasture
- cropland
- forest
- desert

### The urban/rural population divide

urban 80%  rural 20%

| Population density | Total land area |
|---|---|
| 34 people per sq mile (13 people per sq km) | 424,852 sq miles (1,089,965 sq km) |

▶ *Cattle ranching was* introduced to New Mexico via Texas in the 19th century, and has become the principal agricultural land use across this region.

# USA: HAWAII

The 122 islands of the Hawaiian archipelago – which are part of Polynesia – are the peaks of the world's largest volcanoes. They rise approximately 6 miles (9.7 km) from the floor of the Pacific Ocean. The largest, the island of Hawai'i, remains highly active. Hawaii became the US's 50th state in 1959. A tradition of receiving immigrant workers is reflected in the islands' ethnic diversity, with peoples drawn from around the rim of the Pacific. Only 2% of the current population are native Polynesians.

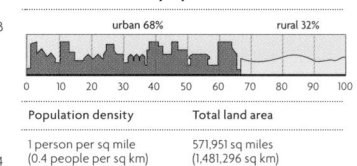

▲ The island of Moloka'i is formed from volcanic rock. Mature sand dunes cover the rocks in coastal areas.

## Transportation & industry

Tourism dominates the economy, with over 90% of the population employed in services. The naval base at Pearl Harbor is also a major source of employment. Industry is concentrated on the island of O'ahu and relies mostly on imported materials, while agricultural produce is processed locally.

### Transportation network

| | | | |
|---|---|---|---|
| 🛣 4102 miles (6600 km) | | 43 miles (69 km) | |
| none | | none | |

Hawaii relies on ocean-surface transportation. Honolulu is the main focus of this network, bringing foreign trade and the markets of mainland US to Hawaii's outer islands.

### Major industry and infrastructure

- 🏭 food processing
- ✠ military base
- textiles
- 🏄 tourism
- • major towns
- ⊕ international airports
- — major roads
- ▨ major industrial areas

◀ Haleakala's extinct volcanic crater is the world's largest. The giant caldera, containing many secondary cones, is 2000 ft (600 m) deep and 20 miles (32 km) in circumference.

## Using the land & sea

The volcanic soils are extremely fertile and the climate hot and humid on the lower slopes, supporting large commercial plantations growing sugar cane, bananas, pineapples, and other tropical fruit, as well as nursery plants and flowers. Some land is given to pasture, particularly for beef and dairy cattle.

### Land use and agricultural distribution

- 🐄 cattle
- 🐟 fishing
- 🍍 fruit
- sugar cane
- • major towns
- pasture
- cropland
- forest
- mountain region

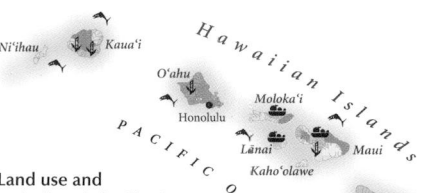

▶ The island of Kaua'i is one of the wettest places in the world, receiving some 450 inches (11,500 mm) of rain a year.

### Scale 1:4,000,000

Km 20 40 60 80 100
Miles 20 40 60 80 100

projection: Lambert Conformal Conic

### Map key

**Population**
- ◉ 100,000 to 500,000
- ⊕ 50,000 to 100,000
- ○ 10,000 to 50,000
- ○ below 10,000

**Elevation**
- 4000m / 13,124ft
- 3000m / 9843ft
- 2000m / 6562ft
- 1000m / 3281ft
- 500m / 1640ft
- 250m / 820ft
- 100m / 328ft
- sea level

## Using the land & sea

The ice-free coastline of Alaska provides access to salmon fisheries and more than 129 million acres (52.2 million ha) of forest. Most of Alaska is uncultivable, and around 90% of food is imported. Barley, hay, and hothouse products are grown around Anchorage, where dairy farming is also concentrated.

### The urban/rural population divide

| urban 68% | rural 32% |
|---|---|

0 10 20 30 40 50 60 70 80 90 100

| Population density | Total land area |
|---|---|
| 1 person per sq mile (0.4 people per sq km) | 571,951 sq miles (1,481,296 sq km) |

◀ A raft of timber from the Tongass forest is hauled by a tug, bound for the pulp mills of the Alaskan coast between Juneau and Ketchikan.

### The urban/rural population divide

| urban 89% | rural 11% |
|---|---|

0 10 20 30 40 50 60 70 80 90 100

| Population density | Total land area |
|---|---|
| 189 people per sq mile (73 people per sq km) | 6,423 sq miles (16,636 sq km) |

### Map key

**Population**
- ◉ 100,000 to 500,000
- ⊕ 50,000 to 100,000
- ○ 10,000 to 50,000
- ○ below 10,000

**Elevation**
- 4000m / 13,124ft
- 3000m / 9843ft
- 2000m / 6562ft
- 1000m / 3281ft
- 500m / 1640ft
- 250m / 820ft
- 100m / 328ft
- sea level

### Scale 1:9,000,000

Km 25 50 100 150 200 250
Miles 25 50 100 150 200 250

projection: Lambert Conformal Conic

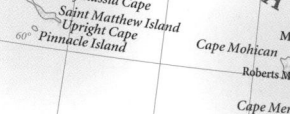

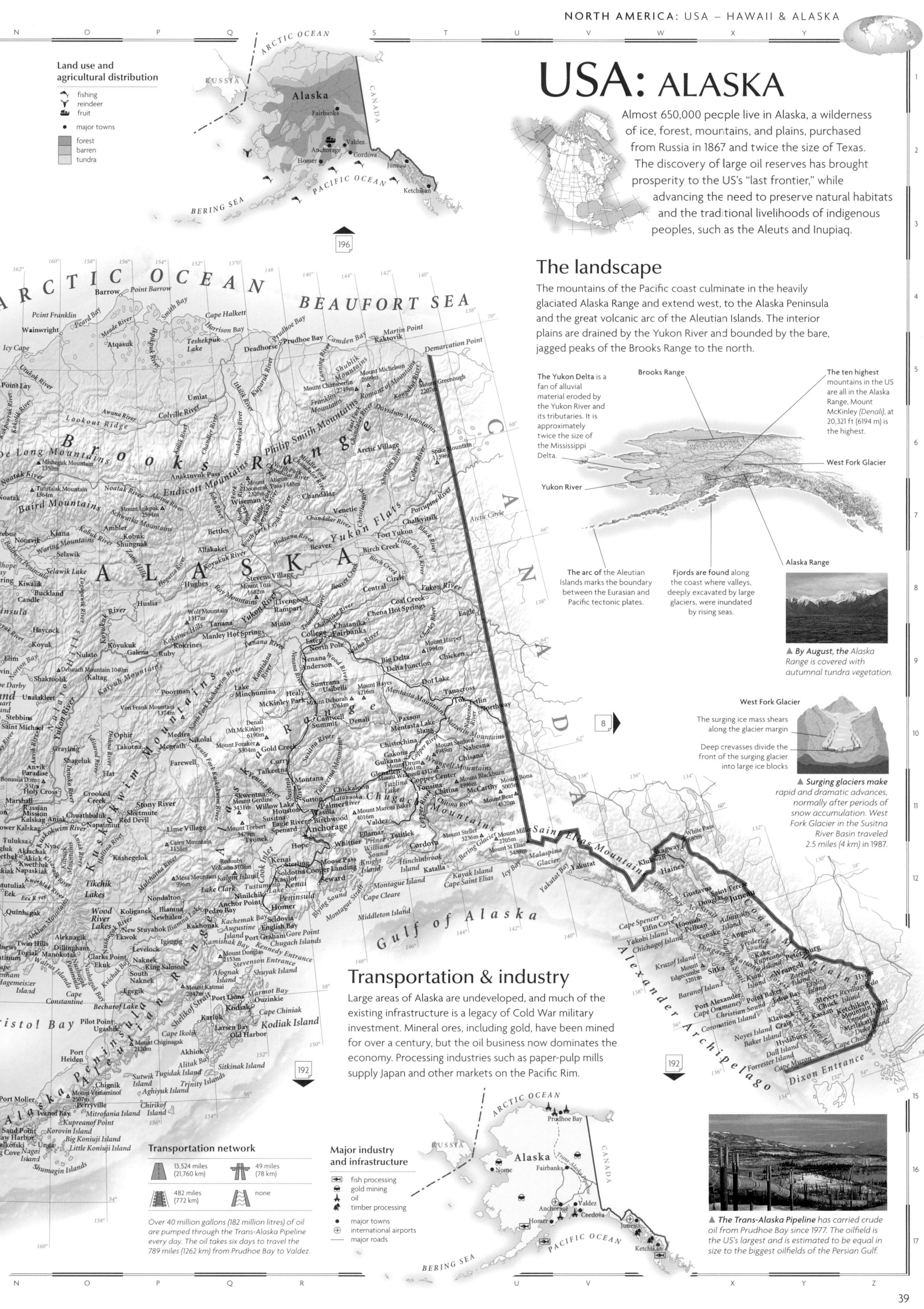

# USA: ALASKA

Almost 650,000 people live in Alaska, a wilderness of ice, forest, mountains, and plains, purchased from Russia in 1867 and twice the size of Texas. The discovery of large oil reserves has brought prosperity to the US's "last frontier," while advancing the need to preserve natural habitats and the traditional livelihoods of indigenous peoples, such as the Aleuts and Inupiaq.

## The landscape

The mountains of the Pacific coast culminate in the heavily glaciated Alaska Range and extend west, to the Alaska Peninsula and the great volcanic arc of the Aleutian Islands. The interior plains are drained by the Yukon River and bounded by the bare, jagged peaks of the Brooks Range to the north.

The Yukon Delta is a fan of alluvial material eroded by the Yukon River and its tributaries. It is approximately twice the size of the Mississippi Delta.

The ten highest mountains in the US are all in the Alaska Range, Mount McKinley *(Denali)*, at 20,321 ft (6194 m) is the highest.

Brooks Range

West Fork Glacier

Yukon River

Alaska Range

The arc of the Aleutian Islands marks the boundary between the Eurasian and Pacific tectonic plates.

Fjords are found along the coast where valleys, deeply excavated by large glaciers, were inundated by rising seas.

▲ **By August, the** *Alaska Range is covered with autumnal tundra vegetation.*

### West Fork Glacier

The surging ice mass shears along the glacier margin

Deep crevasses divide the front of the surging glacier into large ice blocks

▲ **Surging glaciers make** *rapid and dramatic advances, normally after periods of snow accumulation. West Fork Glacier in the Susitna River Basin traveled 2.5 miles (4 km) in 1987.*

## Transportation & industry

Large areas of Alaska are undeveloped, and much of the existing infrastructure is a legacy of Cold War military investment. Mineral ores, including gold, have been mined for over a century, but the oil business now dominates the economy. Processing industries such as paper-pulp mills supply Japan and other markets on the Pacific Rim.

### Land use and agricultural distribution

- fishing
- reindeer
- fruit
- major towns
- forest
- barren
- tundra

### Transportation network

| | |
|---|---|
| 13,524 miles (21,760 km) | 49 miles (78 km) |
| 482 miles (772 km) | none |

*Over 40 million gallons (182 million litres) of oil are pumped through the Trans-Alaska Pipeline every day. The oil takes six days to travel the 789 miles (1262 km) from Prudhoe Bay to Valdez.*

### Major industry and infrastructure

- fish processing
- gold mining
- oil
- timber processing
- major towns
- international airports
- major roads

▲ **The Trans-Alaska Pipeline** *has carried crude oil from Prudhoe Bay since 1977. The oilfield is the US's largest and is estimated to be equal in size to the biggest oilfields of the Persian Gulf.*

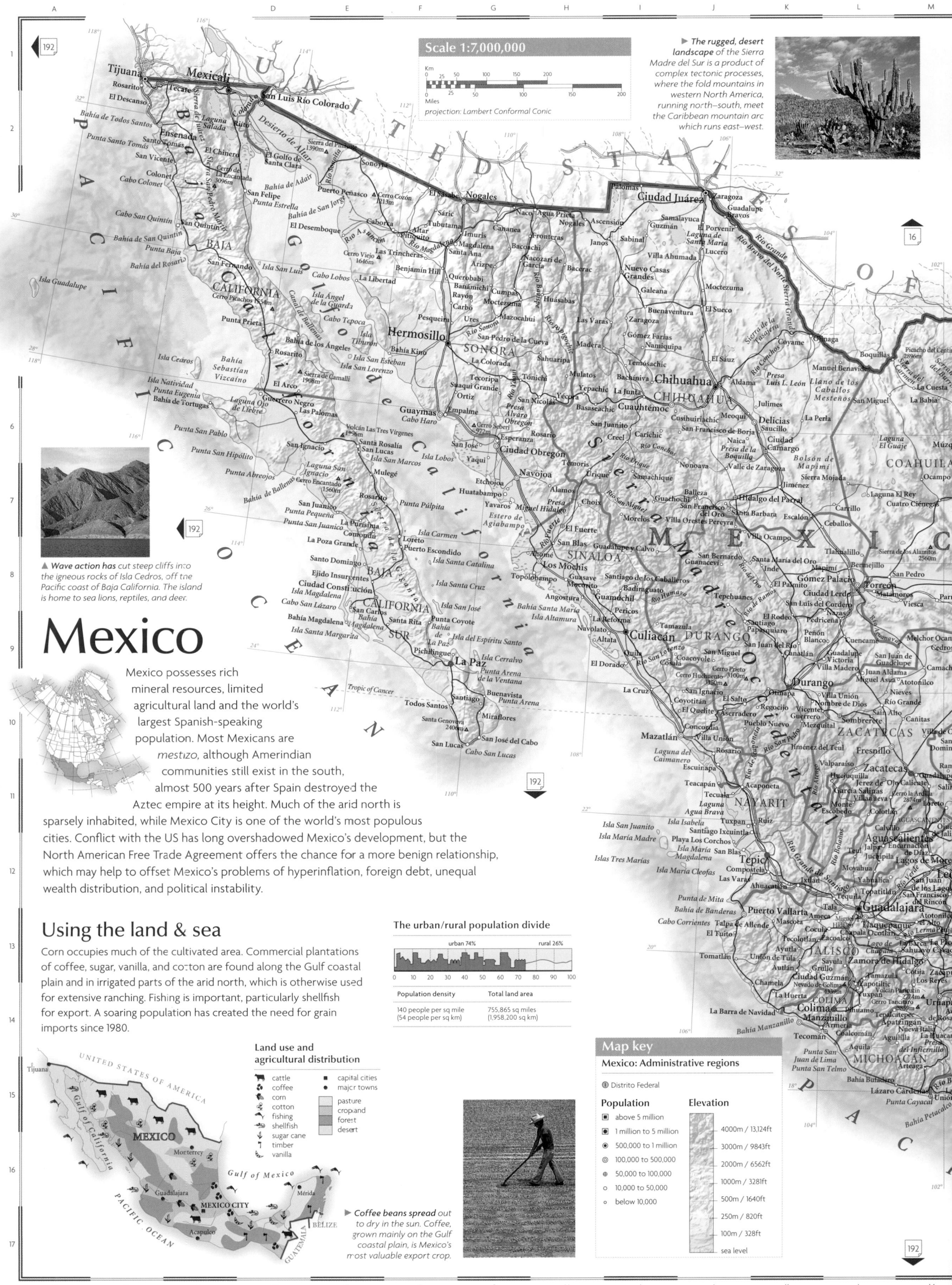

**Scale 1:7,000,000**

projection: Lambert Conformal Conic

▶ **The rugged, desert landscape** of the Sierra Madre del Sur is a product of complex tectonic processes, where the fold mountains in western North America, running north–south, meet the Caribbean mountain arc which runs east–west.

▲ **Wave action has** cut steep cliffs into the igneous rocks of Isla Cedros, off the Pacific coast of Baja California. The island is home to sea lions, reptiles, and deer.

# Mexico

Mexico possesses rich mineral resources, limited agricultural land and the world's largest Spanish-speaking population. Most Mexicans are *mestizo*, although Amerindian communities still exist in the south, almost 500 years after Spain destroyed the Aztec empire at its height. Much of the arid north is sparsely inhabited, while Mexico City is one of the world's most populous cities. Conflict with the US has long overshadowed Mexico's development, but the North American Free Trade Agreement offers the chance for a more benign relationship, which may help to offset Mexico's problems of hyperinflation, foreign debt, unequal wealth distribution, and political instability.

## Using the land & sea

Corn occupies much of the cultivated area. Commercial plantations of coffee, sugar, vanilla, and cotton are found along the Gulf coastal plain and in irrigated parts of the arid north, which is otherwise used for extensive ranching. Fishing is important, particularly shellfish for export. A soaring population has created the need for grain imports since 1980.

**The urban/rural population divide**

urban 74%    rural 26%

0  10  20  30  40  50  60  70  80  90  100

| Population density | Total land area |
| --- | --- |
| 140 people per sq mile (54 people per sq km) | 755,865 sq miles (1,958,200 sq km) |

### Land use and agricultural distribution

- cattle
- coffee
- corn
- cotton
- fishing
- shellfish
- sugar cane
- timber
- vanilla
- ■ capital cities
- • major towns
- pasture
- cropland
- forest
- desert

▶ **Coffee beans spread** out to dry in the sun. Coffee, grown mainly on the Gulf coastal plain, is Mexico's most valuable export crop.

## Map key

**Mexico: Administrative regions**

⊕ Distrito Federal

**Population**
- ▪ above 5 million
- ▪ 1 million to 5 million
- ◉ 500,000 to 1 million
- ◉ 100,000 to 500,000
- ◎ 50,000 to 100,000
- ○ 10,000 to 50,000
- ○ below 10,000

**Elevation**
- 4000m / 13,124ft
- 3000m / 9843ft
- 2000m / 6562ft
- 1000m / 3281ft
- 500m / 1640ft
- 250m / 820ft
- 100m / 328ft
- sea level

# The landscape

The great central plateau rises gently southward from the Rio Grande, isolated from the coastal plains by the Sierra Madre Oriental and Occidental. The two ranges converge from east and west respectively, culminating in high volcanic peaks around Mexico City. Further ranges of the Sierra Madre rise to the south of the Balsas basin, skirted by the low-lying Isthmus of Tehuantepec (*Istmo de Tehuantepec*) and Yucatan Peninsula.

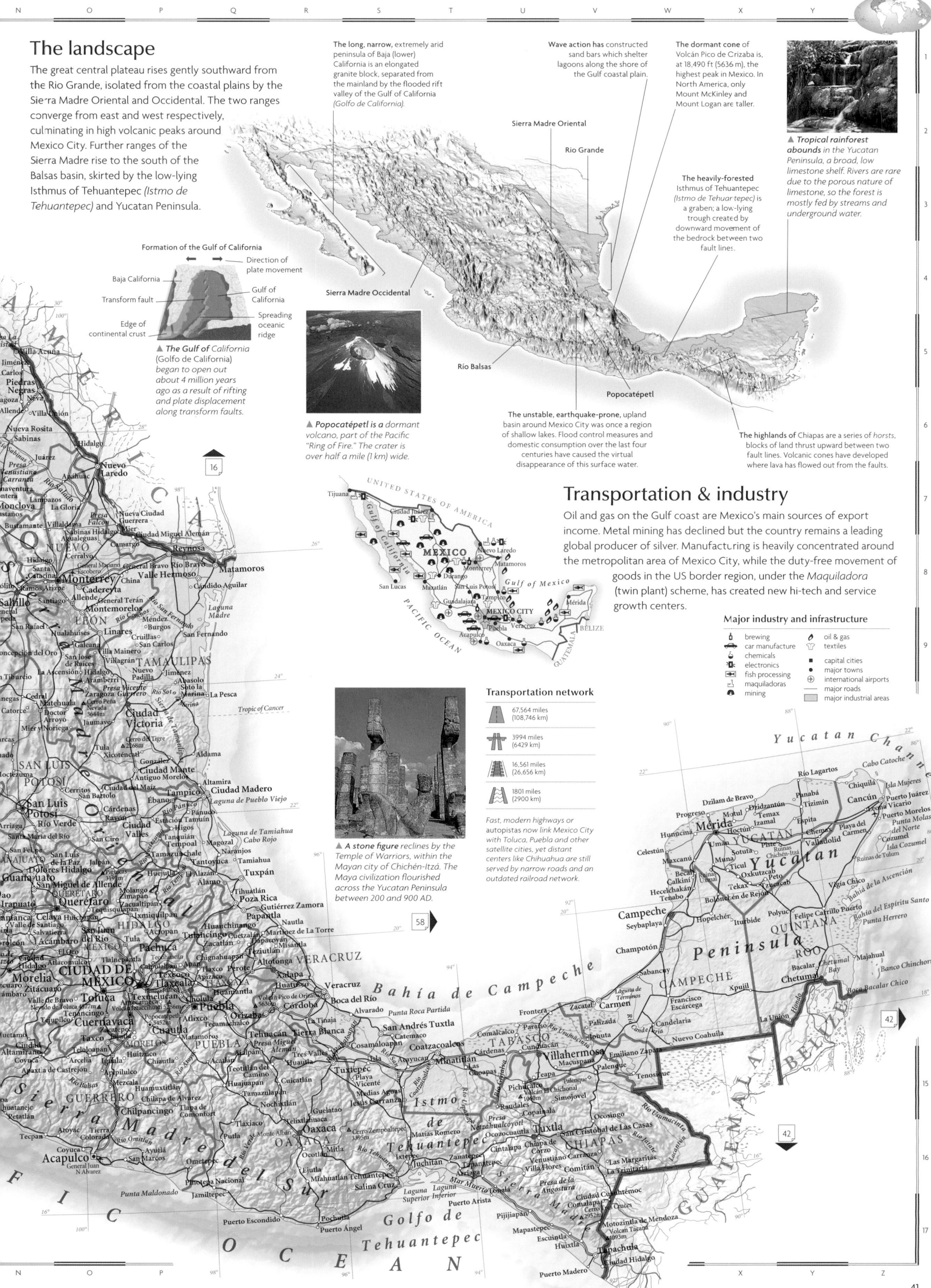

The long, narrow, extremely arid peninsula of Baja (lower) California is an elongated granite block, separated from the mainland by the flooded rift valley of the Gulf of California (*Golfo de California*).

Wave action has constructed sand bars which shelter lagoons along the shore of the Gulf coastal plain.

The dormant cone of Volcán Pico de Orizaba is, at 18,490 ft (5636 m), the highest peak in Mexico. In North America, only Mount McKinley and Mount Logan are taller.

▲ *Tropical rainforest abounds* in the Yucatan Peninsula, a broad, low limestone shelf. Rivers are rare due to the porous nature of limestone, so the forest is mostly fed by streams and underground water.

The heavily-forested Isthmus of Tehuantepec (*Istmo de Tehuar tepec*) is a graben; a low-lying trough created by downward movement of the bedrock between two fault lines.

Formation of the Gulf of California

Direction of plate movement
Baja California
Transform fault
Gulf of California
Edge of continental crust
Spreading oceanic ridge

▲ *The Gulf of California* (Golfo de California) began to open out about 4 million years ago as a result of rifting and plate displacement along transform faults.

▲ *Popocatépetl is a* dormant volcano, part of the Pacific "Ring of Fire." The crater is over half a mile (1 km) wide.

The unstable, earthquake-prone, upland basin around Mexico City was once a region of shallow lakes. Flood control measures and domestic consumption over the last four centuries have caused the virtual disappearance of this surface water.

The highlands of Chiapas are a series of *horsts*, blocks of land thrust upward between two fault lines. Volcanic cones have developed where lava has flowed out from the faults.

# Transportation & industry

Oil and gas on the Gulf coast are Mexico's main sources of export income. Metal mining has declined but the country remains a leading global producer of silver. Manufacturing is heavily concentrated around the metropolitan area of Mexico City, while the duty-free movement of goods in the US border region, under the *Maquiladora* (twin plant) scheme, has created new hi-tech and service growth centers.

## Major industry and infrastructure

- brewing
- car manufacture
- chemicals
- electronics
- fish processing
- maquiladoras
- mining
- oil & gas
- textiles
- capital cities
- major towns
- international airports
- major roads
- major industrial areas

## Transportation network

| | |
|---|---|
| 67,564 miles (108,746 km) | |
| 3994 miles (6429 km) | |
| 16,561 miles (26,656 km) | |
| 1801 miles (2900 km) | |

Fast, modern highways or autopistas now link Mexico City with Toluca, Puebla and other satellite cities, yet distant centers like Chihuahua are still served by narrow roads and an outdated railroad network.

▲ *A stone figure reclines by the Temple of Warriors, within the Mayan city of Chichén-Itzá. The Maya civilization flourished across the Yucatan Peninsula between 200 and 900 AD.*

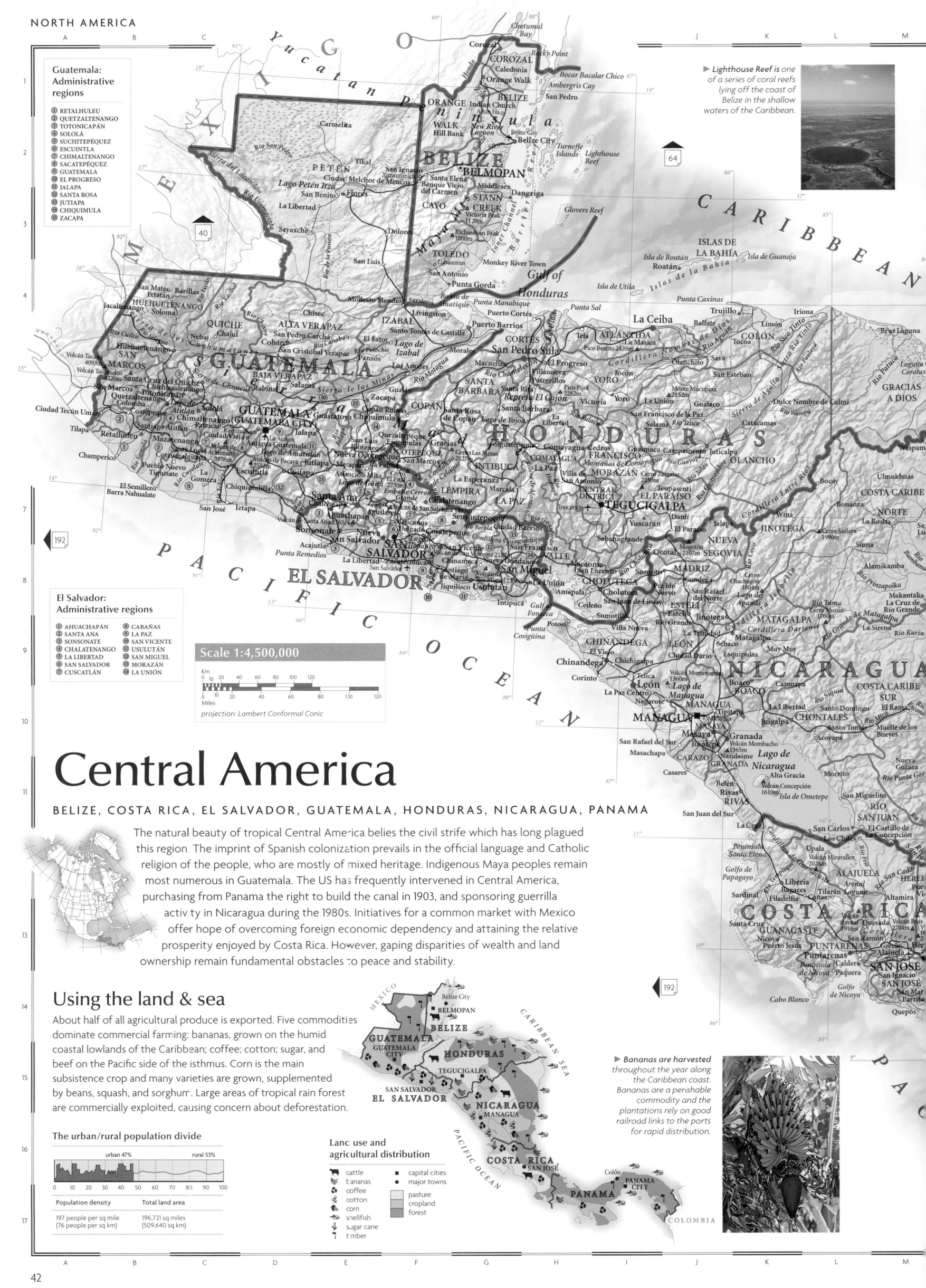

# Central America

**BELIZE, COSTA RICA, EL SALVADOR, GUATEMALA, HONDURAS, NICARAGUA, PANAMA**

The natural beauty of tropical Central America belies the civil strife which has long plagued this region. The imprint of Spanish colonization prevails in the official language and Catholic religion of the people, who are mostly of mixed heritage. Indigenous Maya peoples remain most numerous in Guatemala. The US has frequently intervened in Central America, purchasing from Panama the right to build the canal in 1903, and sponsoring guerrilla activity in Nicaragua during the 1980s. Initiatives for a common market with Mexico offer hope of overcoming foreign economic dependency and attaining the relative prosperity enjoyed by Costa Rica. However, gaping disparities of wealth and land ownership remain fundamental obstacles to peace and stability.

## Using the land & sea

About half of all agricultural produce is exported. Five commodities dominate commercial farming: bananas, grown on the humid coastal lowlands of the Caribbean; coffee; cotton; sugar, and beef on the Pacific side of the isthmus. Corn is the main subsistence crop and many varieties are grown, supplemented by beans, squash, and sorghum. Large areas of tropical rain forest are commercially exploited, causing concern about deforestation.

### The urban/rural population divide

urban 47%   rural 53%

| Population density | Total land area |
|---|---|
| 197 people per sq mile (76 people per sq km) | 196,721 sq miles (509,640 sq km) |

### Land use and agricultural distribution

- cattle
- bananas
- coffee
- cotton
- corn
- shellfish
- sugar cane
- timber
- ■ capital cities
- • major towns
- pasture
- cropland
- forest

**Guatemala: Administrative regions**
① RETALHULEU
② QUETZALTENANGO
③ TOTONICAPÁN
④ SOLOLÁ
⑤ SUCHITEPÉQUEZ
⑥ ESCUINTLA
⑦ CHIMALTENANGO
⑧ SACATEPÉQUEZ
⑨ GUATEMALA
⑩ EL PROGRESO
⑪ JALAPA
⑫ SANTA ROSA
⑬ JUTIAPA
⑭ CHIQUIMULA
⑮ ZACAPA

**El Salvador: Administrative regions**
① AHUACHAPÁN
② SANTA ANA
③ SONSONATE
④ CHALATENANGO
⑤ LA LIBERTAD
⑥ SAN SALVADOR
⑦ CUSCATLÁN
⑧ CABAÑAS
⑨ LA PAZ
⑩ SAN VICENTE
⑪ USULUTÁN
⑫ SAN MIGUEL
⑬ MORAZÁN
⑭ LA UNIÓN

Scale 1:4,500,000

projection: Lambert Conformal Conic

▶ *Lighthouse Reef is one of a series of coral reefs lying off the coast of Belize in the shallow waters of the Caribbean.*

▶ *Bananas are harvested throughout the year along the Caribbean coast. Bananas are a perishable commodity and the plantations rely on good railroad links to the ports for rapid distribution.*

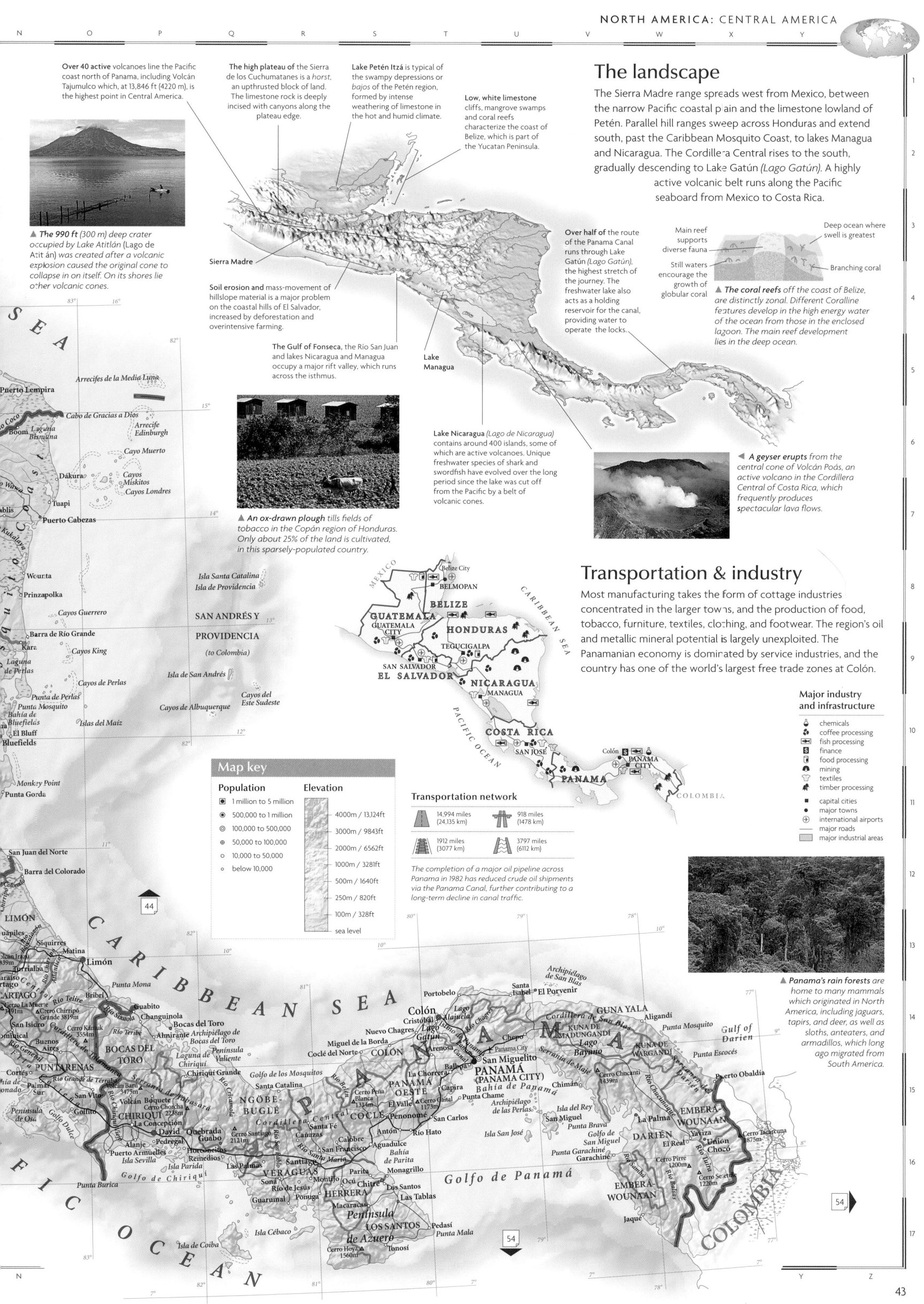

Over 40 active volcanoes line the Pacific coast north of Panama, including Volcán Tajumulco which, at 13,846 ft (4220 m), is the highest point in Central America.

▲ The 990 ft (300 m) deep crater occupied by Lake Atitlán (Lago de Atitlán) was created after a volcanic explosion caused the original cone to collapse in on itself. On its shores lie other volcanic cones.

Sierra Madre

The high plateau of the Sierra de los Cuchumatanes is a horst, an upthrusted block of land. The limestone rock is deeply incised with canyons along the plateau edge.

Lake Petén Itzá is typical of the swampy depressions or bajos of the Petén region, formed by intense weathering of limestone in the hot and humid climate.

Low, white limestone cliffs, mangrove swamps and coral reefs characterize the coast of Belize, which is part of the Yucatan Peninsula.

Soil erosion and mass-movement of hillslope material is a major problem on the coastal hills of El Salvador, increased by deforestation and overintensive farming.

The Gulf of Fonseca, the Río San Juan and lakes Nicaragua and Managua occupy a major rift valley, which runs across the isthmus.

Lake Managua

Lake Nicaragua (Lago de Nicaragua) contains around 400 islands, some of which are active volcanoes. Unique freshwater species of shark and swordfish have evolved over the long period since the lake was cut off from the Pacific by a belt of volcanic cones.

▲ An ox-drawn plough tills fields of tobacco in the Copán region of Honduras. Only about 25% of the land is cultivated, in this sparsely-populated country.

## The landscape

The Sierra Madre range spreads west from Mexico, between the narrow Pacific coastal plain and the limestone lowland of Petén. Parallel hill ranges sweep across Honduras and extend south, past the Caribbean Mosquito Coast, to lakes Managua and Nicaragua. The Cordillera Central rises to the south, gradually descending to Lake Gatún (Lago Gatún). A highly active volcanic belt runs along the Pacific seaboard from Mexico to Costa Rica.

Over half of the route of the Panama Canal runs through Lake Gatún (Lago Gatún), the highest stretch of the journey. The freshwater lake also acts as a holding reservoir for the canal, providing water to operate the locks.

Main reef supports diverse fauna

Still waters encourage the growth of globular coral

Deep ocean where swell is greatest

Branching coral

▲ The coral reefs off the coast of Belize, are distinctly zonal. Different Coralline features develop in the high energy water of the ocean from those in the enclosed lagoon. The main reef development lies in the deep ocean.

◀ A geyser erupts from the central cone of Volcán Poás, an active volcano in the Cordillera Central of Costa Rica, which frequently produces spectacular lava flows.

## Transportation & industry

Most manufacturing takes the form of cottage industries concentrated in the larger towns, and the production of food, tobacco, furniture, textiles, clothing, and footwear. The region's oil and metallic mineral potential is largely unexploited. The Panamanian economy is dominated by service industries, and the country has one of the world's largest free trade zones at Colón.

### Major industry and infrastructure
- chemicals
- coffee processing
- fish processing
- S finance
- food processing
- mining
- textiles
- timber processing

- capital cities
- major towns
- ⊕ international airports
- major roads
- major industrial areas

### Map key

**Population**
- ◉ 1 million to 5 million
- ◎ 500,000 to 1 million
- ◉ 100,000 to 500,000
- ⊕ 50,000 to 100,000
- ⊙ 10,000 to 50,000
- ○ below 10,000

**Elevation**
- 4000m / 13,124ft
- 3000m / 9843ft
- 2000m / 6562ft
- 1000m / 3281ft
- 500m / 1640ft
- 250m / 820ft
- 100m / 328ft
- sea level

### Transportation network

14,994 miles (24,135 km)

918 miles (1478 km)

1912 miles (3077 km)

3797 miles (6112 km)

The completion of a major oil pipeline across Panama in 1982 has reduced crude oil shipments via the Panama Canal, further contributing to a long-term decline in canal traffic.

▲ Panama's rain forests are home to many mammals which originated in North America, including jaguars, tapirs, and deer, as well as sloths, anteaters, and armadillos, which long ago migrated from South America.

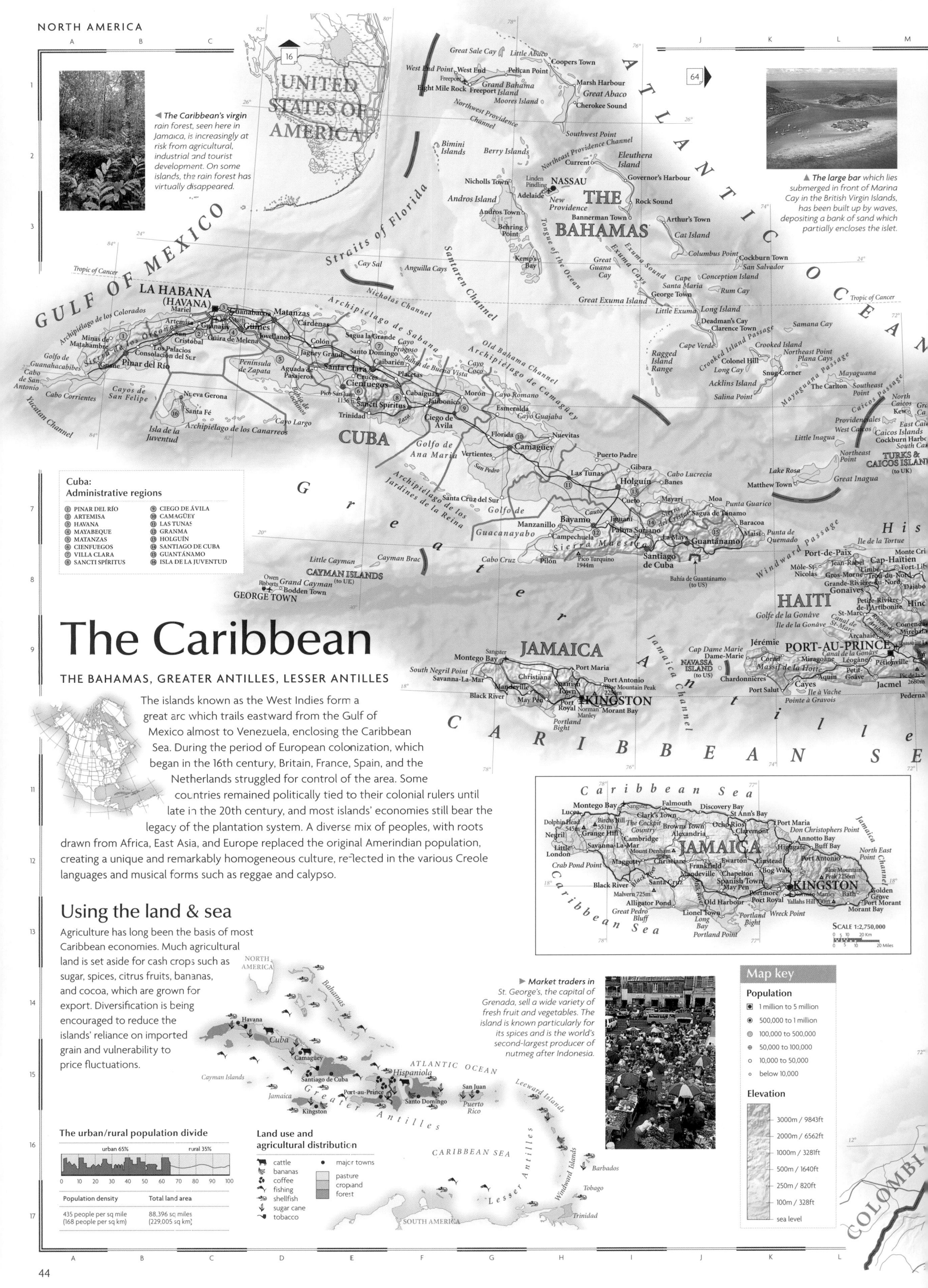

◄ **The Caribbean's virgin** rain forest, seen here in Jamaica, is increasingly at risk from agricultural, industrial and tourist development. On some islands, the rain forest has virtually disappeared.

▲ **The large bar** which lies submerged in front of Marina Cay in the British Virgin Islands, has been built up by waves, depositing a bank of sand which partially encloses the islet.

**Cuba:**
**Administrative regions**

① PINAR DEL RÍO
② ARTEMISA
③ HAVANA
④ MAYABEQUE
⑤ MATANZAS
⑥ CIENFUEGOS
⑦ VILLA CLARA
⑧ SANCTI SPÍRITUS
⑨ CIEGO DE ÁVILA
⑩ CAMAGÜEY
⑪ LAS TUNAS
⑫ GRANMA
⑬ HOLGUÍN
⑭ SANTIAGO DE CUBA
⑮ GUANTÁNAMO
⑯ ISLA DE LA JUVENTUD

# The Caribbean

## THE BAHAMAS, GREATER ANTILLES, LESSER ANTILLES

The islands known as the West Indies form a great arc which trails eastward from the Gulf of Mexico almost to Venezuela, enclosing the Caribbean Sea. During the period of European colonization, which began in the 16th century, Britain, France, Spain, and the Netherlands struggled for control of the area. Some countries remained politically tied to their colonial rulers until late in the 20th century, and most islands' economies still bear the legacy of the plantation system. A diverse mix of peoples, with roots drawn from Africa, East Asia, and Europe replaced the original Amerindian population, creating a unique and remarkably homogeneous culture, reflected in the various Creole languages and musical forms such as reggae and calypso.

## Using the land & sea

Agriculture has long been the basis of most Caribbean economies. Much agricultural land is set aside for cash crops such as sugar, spices, citrus fruits, bananas, and cocoa, which are grown for export. Diversification is being encouraged to reduce the islands' reliance on imported grain and vulnerability to price fluctuations.

▲ **Market traders in** St. George's, the capital of Grenada, sell a wide variety of fresh fruit and vegetables. The island is known particularly for its spices and is the world's second-largest producer of nutmeg after Indonesia.

**SCALE 1:2,750,000**

**The urban/rural population divide**

urban 65%   rural 35%

0  10  20  30  40  50  60  70  80  90  100

| Population density | Total land area |
| --- | --- |
| 435 people per sq mile (168 people per sq km) | 88,396 sq miles (229,005 sq km) |

**Land use and agricultural distribution**

- cattle
- bananas
- coffee
- fishing
- shellfish
- sugar cane
- tobacco
- major towns
- pasture
- cropland
- forest

### Map key

**Population**
- 1 million to 5 million
- 500,000 to 1 million
- 100,000 to 500,000
- 50,000 to 100,000
- 10,000 to 50,000
- below 10,000

**Elevation**
- 3000m / 9843ft
- 2000m / 6562ft
- 1000m / 3281ft
- 500m / 1640ft
- 250m / 820ft
- 100m / 328ft
- sea level

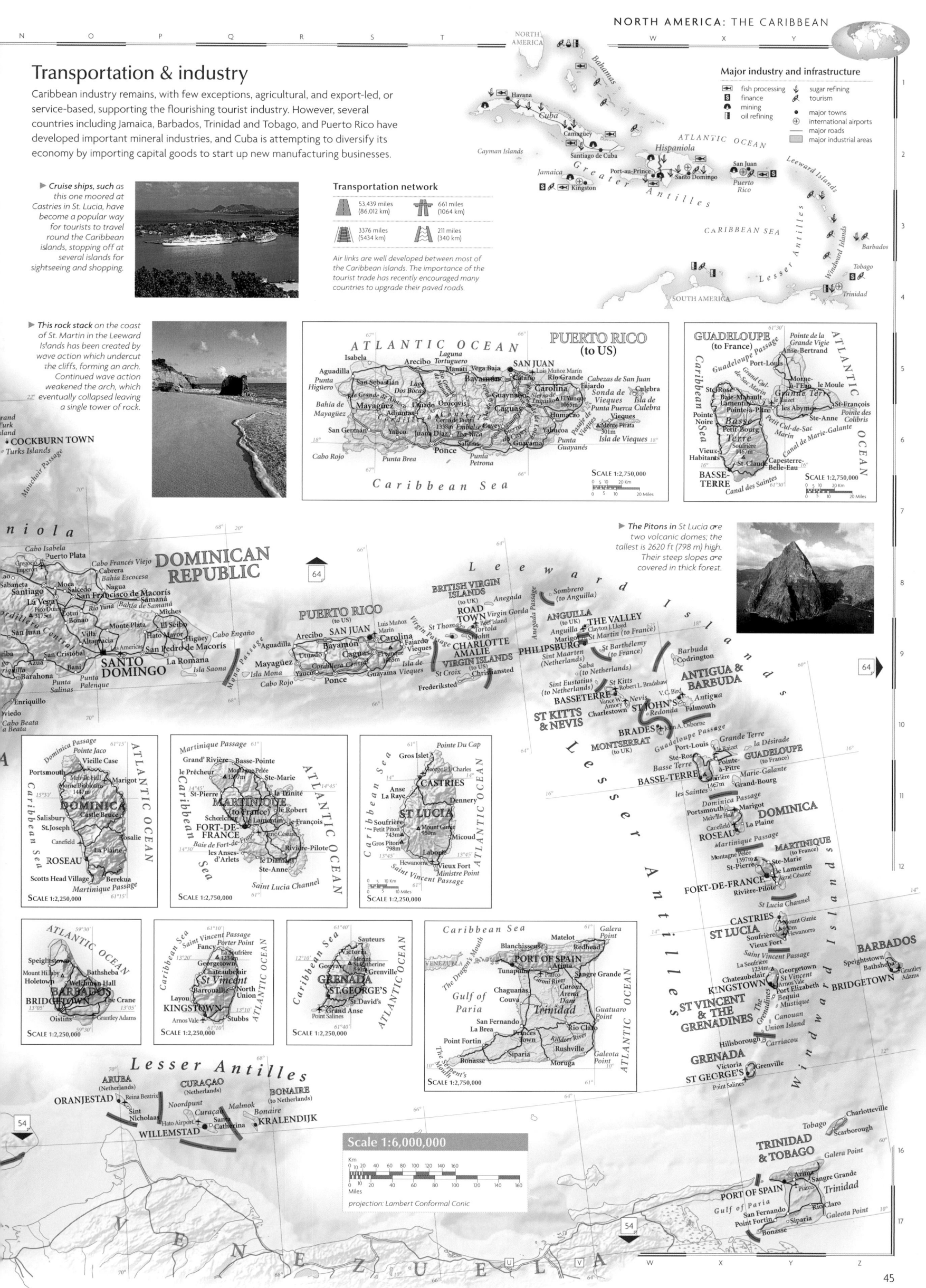

# Transportation & industry

Caribbean industry remains, with few exceptions, agricultural, and export-led, or service-based, supporting the flourishing tourist industry. However, several countries including Jamaica, Barbados, Trinidad and Tobago, and Puerto Rico have developed important mineral industries, and Cuba is attempting to diversify its economy by importing capital goods to start up new manufacturing businesses.

▶ **Cruise ships,** such as this one moored at Castries in St. Lucia, have become a popular way for tourists to travel round the Caribbean islands, stopping off at several islands for sightseeing and shopping.

## Major industry and infrastructure

- fish processing
- finance
- mining
- oil refining
- sugar refining
- tourism
- major towns
- international airports
- major roads
- major industrial areas

## Transportation network

| | |
|---|---|
| 53,439 miles (86,012 km) | 661 miles (1064 km) |
| 3376 miles (5434 km) | 211 miles (340 km) |

Air links are well developed between most of the Caribbean islands. The importance of the tourist trade has recently encouraged many countries to upgrade their paved roads.

▶ **This rock stack** on the coast of St. Martin in the Leeward Islands has been created by wave action which undercut the cliffs, forming an arch. Continued wave action weakened the arch, which eventually collapsed leaving a single tower of rock.

▶ **The Pitons** in St Lucia are two volcanic domes; the tallest is 2620 ft (798 m) high. Their steep slopes are covered in thick forest.

Scale 1:6,000,000

projection: Lambert Conformal Conic

# South America

Reaching from the humid tropics down into the cold south Atlantic, South America has an area of 6,886,000 sq miles (17,835,000 sq km). There are 12 separate countries, with the largest, Brazil, covering almost half the continent.

- **Greatest extent, North–South:** 4750 miles / 7640 km
- **Greatest extent, East–West:** 3100 miles / 4990 km

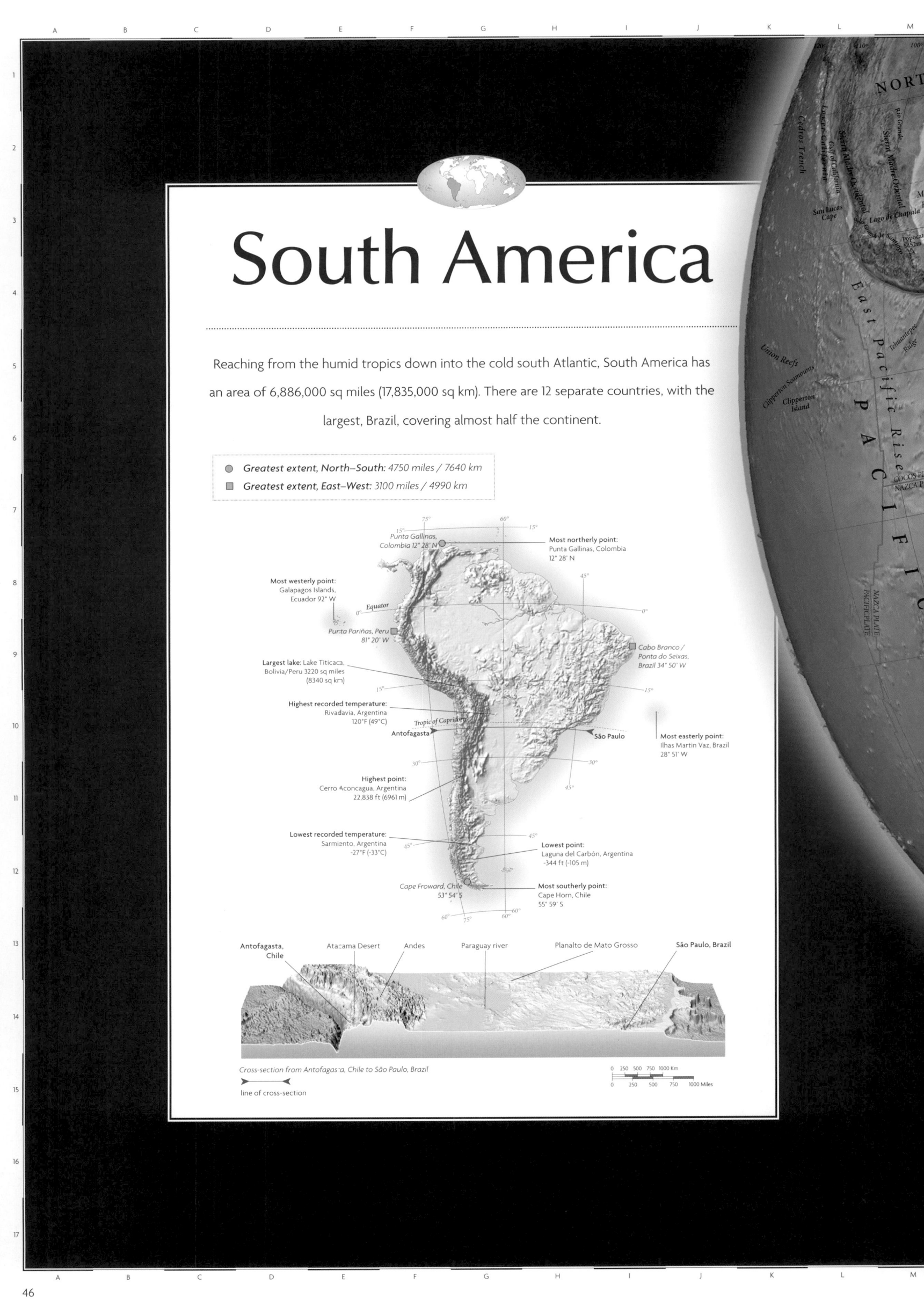

Punta Gallinas, Colombia 12° 28' N

**Most northerly point:**
Punta Gallinas, Colombia
12° 28' N

**Most westerly point:**
Galapagos Islands,
Ecuador 92° W

Equator

Punta Pariñas, Peru
81° 20' W

Cabo Branco /
Ponta do Seixas,
Brazil 34° 50' W

**Largest lake:** Lake Titicaca,
Bolivia/Peru 3220 sq miles
(8340 sq km)

**Highest recorded temperature:**
Rivadavia, Argentina
120°F (49°C)

**Antofagasta**

Tropic of Capricorn

São Paulo

**Most easterly point:**
Ilhas Martin Vaz, Brazil
28° 51' W

**Highest point:**
Cerro Aconcagua, Argentina
22,838 ft (6961 m)

**Lowest recorded temperature:**
Sarmiento, Argentina
-27°F (-33°C)

**Lowest point:**
Laguna del Carbón, Argentina
-344 ft (-105 m)

Cape Froward, Chile
53° 54' S

**Most southerly point:**
Cape Horn, Chile
55° 59' S

Antofagasta, Chile | Atacama Desert | Andes | Paraguay river | Planalto de Mato Grosso | São Paulo, Brazil

*Cross-section from Antofagasta, Chile to São Paulo, Brazil*

line of cross-section

0 250 500 750 1000 Km
0 250 500 750 1000 Miles

NORTH

East Pacific Rise

PACIFIC

Clipperton Seamounts

Clipperton Island

Union Reefs

Cedros Trench

COCOS PLATE
NAZCA PLATE

NAZCA PLATE
PACIFIC PLATE

Rio Grande

Sierra Madre Occidental

Sierra Madre Oriental

Gulf of California

Baja California

San Lucas Cape

Lago de Chapala

Popocatépetl 5452m

Mex
Bas

Tehuantepec
Ridge

AMERICA

Cape Canaveral

Apalachee Bay

Mississippi Fan
gbee Escarpment

Lake Okeechobee

**Gulf of Mexico**

Straits of Florida

Bahamas

Sargasso
Sea

*W e s t    I n d i e s*

Hatteras Plain

Nares Plain

Tropic of Cancer

Cape Verde
Basin

Cape Verde
Islands

Yucatan
Peninsula

Yucatan
Basin

Cayman Trench

Cuba

Great Bahama Bank

Puerto Rico Trench

Leeward Islands

NORTH AMERICAN PLATE
SOUTH AMERICAN PLATE

Gambia
Plain

*A T L A N T I C*

NORTH AMERICAN
PLATE
CARIBBEAN
PLATE

Gulf of
Honduras

Cayman Trough

Jamaica

Windward Passage

Hispaniola

*G r e a t e r    A n t i l l e s*

Puerto Rico

Nevis

Barbuda
Antigua
Guadeloupe

Dominica

AFRICAN PLATE

Doldrums Fracture Zone

Sierra
Andre del Sur

Middle America Trench

Nicaraguan Rise

**Caribbean Sea**

Punta
Gallinas

Cordillera de la Costa

Isla de
Margarita

*L e s s e r    A n t i l l e s*

Windward Islands

Grenada Basin

Saint Lucia
Barbados

Martinique

Grenada

Tobago

Trinidad

Demerara
Plain

*M I D - A T L A N T I C    R I D G E*

Guiana
Basin

Four North Fracture Zone

Saint Paul Fracture Zone

Equator

uatemala
Basin

Gulf of
Fonseca

Lake
Nicaragua

Mosquita
Gulf

Ismuth of Panama

Gulf of
Panama

Gulf of
Darien

Peninsula
de la Guajira

Gulf of Venezuela

Aruba
Curaçao

Bonaire

CARIBBEAN PLATE
SOUTH AMERICAN PLATE

Lake
Maracaibo

Apure

Arauca

Meta

Orinoco

Caroni

Orinoco

Caura

Esequibo

Ceará Plain

Colombian
Basin

*Cordillera Oriental*

*Cordillera Central*

*L l a n o s*

Ilha de
Maruajó

Amazon Fan

Peninsula
de Azuero

Colón Ridge

**Panama
Basin**

**Guiana Highlands**

Caricoeara

Tumuc-Humac Mountains

Araguari

Baía de
São Marcos

Atol
das Rocas

Fernando
de Noronha

Chimborazo
6268m

*Cordillera Occidental*

*Cordillera Real*

Serra
Parima

Vichada

Branco

Orinoco

Uaupés

Rio Negro

Japurá

Icá

Napo

Caquetá

Putumayo

Amazon

Marañón

Represa
Balbina

Amazon

Purus

Madeira

**Amazon Basin**

Juruá

Tapauá

Juruá

Juruá

Piauás

Amazon

Xingu

Tocantins

Xingu

Mexpana

Itapicuru

Serra Grande

Represa
de Tucuruí

Flanalto da
Borborema

Cabo Branco

Pernambuco
Plain

Represa de
Sobradinho

Represa de
Itaparica

alápagos
Islands

Gulf of
Guayaquil

Punta
Parinas

A
N
D
E
S

*S o u t h    A m e r i c a n    P l a t e*

*N A Z C A    P L A T E*

Lake
Titicaca

Lago Poopó

*Altiplano*

*Atacama Desert*

Ucayali

Purus

Madre de Dios

Beni

Guaporé

Mamoré

Jurua

**S O U T H**

**A M E R I C A**

*Chapada dos Parecis*

Pilcomayo

*Yungas*

Rio Grande

Rio Grande

Represa de
Itapú

Iguaçu

*Chapada das
Mangabeiras*

*Serra Geral
de Goiás*

Serra Formosa

Serra do Roncador

Araguaia

Aporé

Paranaíba

Rio Grande

*Serra do
Paranapiacaba*

São Francisco

Chapada Diamantina

*Serra do Espinhaço*

*B r a z i l i a n    H i g h l a n d s*

Jequitinhonha

Paracatu

Paraguaçu

Baía de
Todos os Santos

Abrolhos
Bank

Trindade Spur

*B r a z i l
B a s i n*

Peru
Basin

Mendaña Fracture Zone

Nazca Ridge

Chile
Basin

Islas de los
Desventurados

Planalto de
Mato Grosso

Pantanal

Taquari

Pilcomayo

Paraguay

Gran Chaco

Mesopotamia

Paraná

Rio Grande

Doce

*Serra do Mar*

Ilha de
São Sebastião

Ilha de
São Francisco

Tropic of Capricorn

Santos
Plateau

Easter
Island

Sala y Gomez Fracture Zone

Roggeveen
Basin

Juan Fernandez
Islands

Mar
Chiquita

Laguna

Nequén

Salado

Aconcagua
6959m

Chubut

Colorado

Río Negro

Chico

Desado

Lago
Buenos
Aires

*P a m p a s*

Embalse
de Río Negro

Río
Negro

Uruguay

Mirim
Lagoon

Lagoa
dos Patos

Cuchilla Grande

Río de la Plata

Bahía
Blanca

Golfo San Matías

Argentina
Plain

*A r g e n t i n e*

*B a s i n*

Falkland Escarpment

Maurice Ewing
Bank

South Georgia

South Sandwich Trench

EAST PACIFIC RISE

*E a s t    P a c i f i c    R i s e*

NAZCA PLATE
ANTARCTIC PLATE

Golfo Concepción

Archipiélago
de los Chonos

*P a t a g o n i a*

Chaco

Gulf of
San Jorge

Bahía
Grande

Strait of Magellan

Tierra
del Fuego

Cape Horn

Scotia Ridge

SOUTH AMERICAN PLATE
SCOTIA PLATE

*Scotia
Sea*

SCOTIA PLATE
ANTARCTIC PLATE

South Georgia Ridge

Sandwich
Islands

ANTARCTIC PLATE
PACIFIC PLATE

South Shetland Trench

South Shetland
Islands

South Orkney
Islands

South Sandwich Trench

Antarctic Circle

South Sandwich Trench

**Weddell
Sea**

*A N T A R C T I C A*

# Physical South America

Three major physiographic regions characterize South America. The oldest, the ancient Brazilian Shield and the smaller Guiana and Patagonian shields, form the stable core of the continent. Stretching along the entire west coast are the younger Andean fold mountains with many summits rising to 20,000 ft (6100 m). These two diverse regions are separated by a number of sedimentary basins carrying South America's large river systems to the sea. These include the massive Amazon Basin and the basin of the Gran Chaco.

## The Amazon Basin and Guiana Shield

The Amazon river occupies a large depression in the Earth's crust, formed by the uplift of the Andes. It is covered by thick volcanic deposits and layers of alluvium – these have been laid down by the Amazon's many tributaries. To the north is the smaller Guiana Shield.

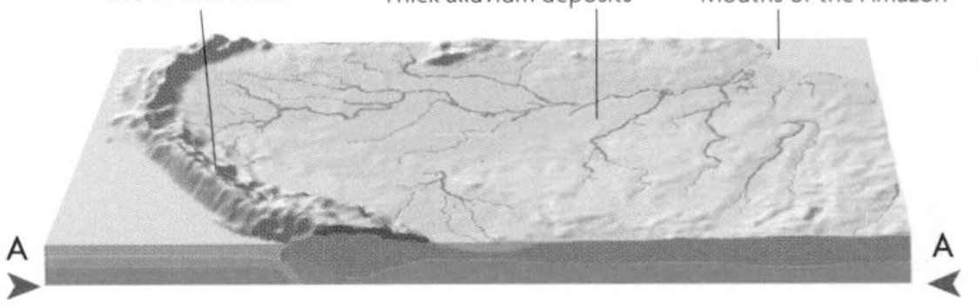

Headwaters of the Amazon rise in the Andes    Thick alluvium deposits    Mouths of the Amazon

**Section across northern** South America showing Amazon Basin and its drainage pattern.

0  500  1000 Km
0  500  1000 Miles

### Scale 1:30,500,000

Km
0   200   400   600   800
Miles
0   200   400   600   800

projection: Lambert Azimuthal Equal Area

## The Andean Uplands

The Andean Uplands run along the west coast of South America. They are being uplifted as the Nazca Plate is subducted beneath the South American Plate. They contain some of the world's largest volcanoes, such as Cotopaxi, and Lake Titicaca which occupies a dormant site. The far south has many large ice-sheets and a fragmented coastline.

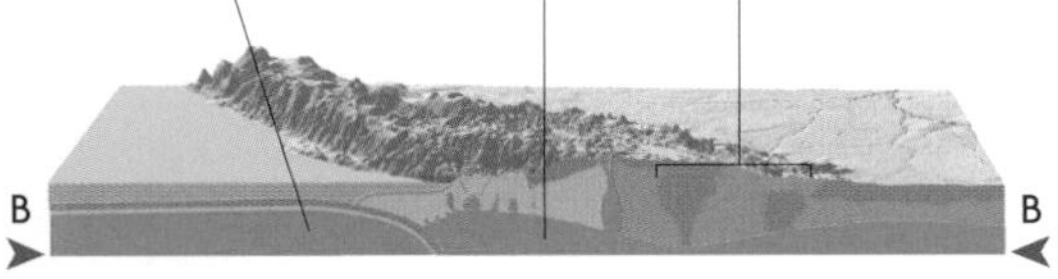

Nazca Plate    South American Plate    Volcanic intrusions

**Cross-section through the** Andes showing the subduction of the Nazca Plate beneath the South American Plate

0  200  400 Km
0  200  400 Miles

## The Brazilian Shield and Gran Chaco

The immense Brazilian Shield underlies more than one-third of South America. It is pitted with numerous volcanic intrusions, and a large basaltic plateau exists between the Paraná river and the Atlantic Ocean. The flat Gran Chaco lies to the west of the shield, covered by sedimentary deposits eroded from the Andes, and transported by South America's mighty rivers.

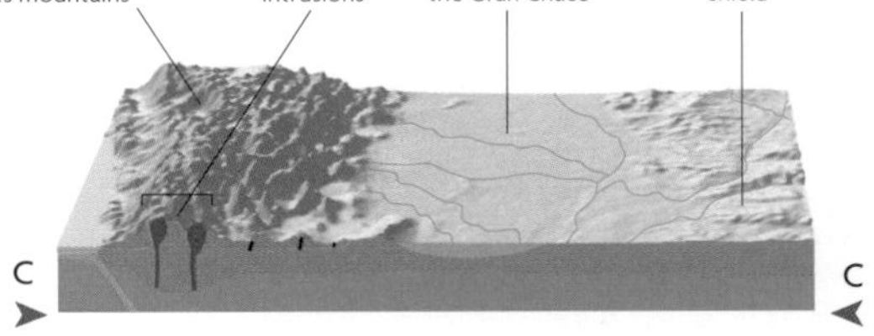

Young, folded Andes mountains    Volcanic intrusions    Major rivers drain to the south through the Gran Chaco    Ancient resistant shield

**Section across central** South America showing the flat basin of the Gran Chaco and the ancient Brazilian Shield.

0  200  400 Km
0  200  400 Miles

### Map key

**Elevation**

6000m / 19,686ft
4000m / 13,124ft
3000m / 9843ft
2000m / 6562ft
1000m / 3281ft
500m / 1640ft
250m / 820ft
100m / 328ft
sea level

**Plate margins**
(for explanation see page xiv)

———— constructive
△△ destructive
———— conservative
·········· uncertain
———— physiographic regions
◄► line of cross-section

### Map labels

Punta Gallinas
Gulf of Venezuela
Lake Maracaibo
Gulf of Darien
Gulf of Panama
Cauca
Magdalena
Cordillera Occidental
Cordillera Central
Cordillera Oriental
Llanos
Orinoco
Río Negro
Pakaraima Mountains
Macunimã
GUIANA SHIELD
Guiana Highlands
Tumuc-Humac Mountains
Japurá
Putumayo
Amazon
Amazon Basin
Represa Balbina
Amazon
Ilha de Marajó
Cotopaxi 5897m
Chimborazo 6268m
Gulf of Guayaquil
Marañón
Ucayali
Purus
Madeira
Tapajós
Xingu
Serra dos Carajás
Tocantins
Araguaia
Cabo de São Roque
Punta Negra
Nevado Huascarán 6768m
Madre de Dios
Serra do Cachimbo
Chapada dos Parecis
Guaporé
Serra Formosa
Planalto de Mato Grosso
Serra do Roncador
Serra Dourada
Tocantins
BRAZILIAN SHIELD
São Francisco
Represa de Sobradinho
Planalto da Borborema
ANDEAN SYSTEM
Lake Titicaca
Lago Poopó
Altiplano
Pantanal
Serra do Caiapó
Brazilian Highlands
Serra do Espinhaço
Atacama Desert
Pilcomayo
Gran Chaco
Paraguay
Paraná
Serra de Maracaju
Serra Geral
Serra do Mar
Serra da Mantiqueira
Cerro Ojos del Salado 6893m
Uruguay
Cerro Aconcagua 6961m
ANDES
Mesopotamia
Paraná
Lagoa dos Patos
Mirim Lagoon
PAMPAS
Salado
Río de la Plata
PATAGONIAN SHIELD
Colorado
Río Negro
Península Valdés
Isla de Chiloé
Lago Colhué Huapí
Chico
Gulf of San Jorge
Deseado
Golfo de Penas
Bahía Grande
Strait of Magellan
Tierra del Fuego
Falkland Islands
Cape Horn
Patagonia

PACIFIC OCEAN
ATLANTIC OCEAN
COCOS PLATE
NAZCA PLATE
SOUTH AMERICAN PLATE
ANTARCTIC PLATE
SCOTIA PLATE

# Climate

The climate of South America is influenced by three principal factors: the seasonal shift of high pressure air masses over the tropics, cold ocean currents along the western coast, affecting temperature and precipitation, and the mountain barrier produced by by the Andes, which creates a rain shadow over much of the south.

▲ *Mild winters and cool summers typify the extensive Pampas grasslands of Argentina.*

▲ *Chile's hyperarid Atacama Desert is renowned as one of the driest places on Earth.*

### Climate

- tundra
- cool continental
- warm humid
- semiarid
- arid
- humid equatorial
- tropical
- ☼ daily hours of sunshine, January
- ☼ daily hours of sunshine, July
- → cold wind

### Temperature

*Average January temperature*

*Average July temperature*

#### Temperature

- below -22°F (-30°C)
- -22 to -4°F (-30 to -20°C)
- -4 to 14°F (-20 to -10°C)
- 14 to 32°F (-10 to 0°C)
- 32 to 50°F (0 to 10°C)
- 50°F to 68°F (10 to 20°C)
- 68 to 86°F (20 to 30°C)
- above 86°F (30°C)

### Rainfall

*Average January rainfall*

*Average July rainfall*

#### Rainfall

- 0–1 in (0–25 mm)
- 1–2 in (25–50 mm)
- 2–4 in (50–100 mm)
- 4–8 in (100–200 mm)
- 8–12 in (200–300 mm)
- 12–16 in (300–400 mm)
- 16–20 in (400–500 mm)
- more than 20 in (500 mm)

▲ *Tropical conditions are found across over half of South America. When both rainfall and temperatures are high, hot humid rain forests prevail.*

# Shaping the continent

South America's active tectonic belt has been extensively folded over millions of years; landslides are still frequent in the mountains. The large river systems that erode the mountains flow across resistant shield areas, depositing sediment. Present-day glaciation affects the distinctive landscape of the far south.

## Mass movement

**6** Debris slides are common in the highlands of South America *(left)*. They occur where soil on a slope is saturated by rainwater and therefore less stable. The actual slides are often triggered by earthquakes.

- Scarp face left after soil has moved to the base of the slope
- Failure plane
- Toe of debris slide

*Mass movement: A section of a debris slide*

## Chemical weathering

**1** Table mountains *(left)* are the eroded remnants of an ancient upland. As water percolates along cracks in these high, flat-topped mountains it forms intricate cave systems. Chemical weathering also isolates large blocks which then collapse, accumulating as rockfalls at the foot of scarp slopes.

- Smooth summit dissected by deep gorges
- Rainfall
- Runoff surges down caverns as waterfalls

*Chemical weathering: Erosion of the Guyana Shield*

## The evolving landscape

## River systems

**2** Along the Amazon *(above)* there is a great variation in rates of erosion. As the headwaters of the Amazon flow down from the Andes, they erode and transport vast quantities of sediment, and are known as whitewaters. Across the shield areas erosion rates are very low. These rivers, carrying rotting vegetation, are called blackwaters.

- Whitewater river
- Blackwater river
- Little erosion in shield areas
- Confluence of whitewater with blackwater

*River systems: Suspended sediments in the Amazon*

## Folding

**5** Folding occurs beneath the surface under high temperatures and pressures. Rocks become sufficiently malleable to flow and not fracture as tectonic plates collide. In the Valley of the Moon in Chile *(above)*, anticlines (or upfolds) and synclines (or troughs) have been exploited by erosion.

- Fold axis
- Anticline
- Syncline
- Fold axis

*Folding: Synclines and anticlines*

## Deposition

**4** Large alluvial fans are found extensively across South America *(above)*. Confined mountain rivers, carrying large quantities of eroded material, emerge from a mountain gorge onto the plains, where they deposit their load in huge fans.

- Confined stream in the mountains
- Subsequent fan
- Mountain front
- Fan forms as stream emerges onto the plain

*Deposition: Formation of an alluvial fan*

### Landscape

- uplifting land
- stable land
- sinking land
- glacier
- → ocean current
- alluvial fan
- inselberg
- river

- Unstable front in deep water, where ice is fracturing
- Original extent of glacier
- Icebergs
- Stable front
- Glacier was grounded against a shoal

*Glaciation: Retreating glacier in Patagonia*

## Glaciation

**3** As fjord glaciers in Patagonia *(above)* retreat, they become grounded on shoals. In deeper water the base of the glacier becomes unstable, and icebergs break off (calve) until the glacier snout grounds once more.

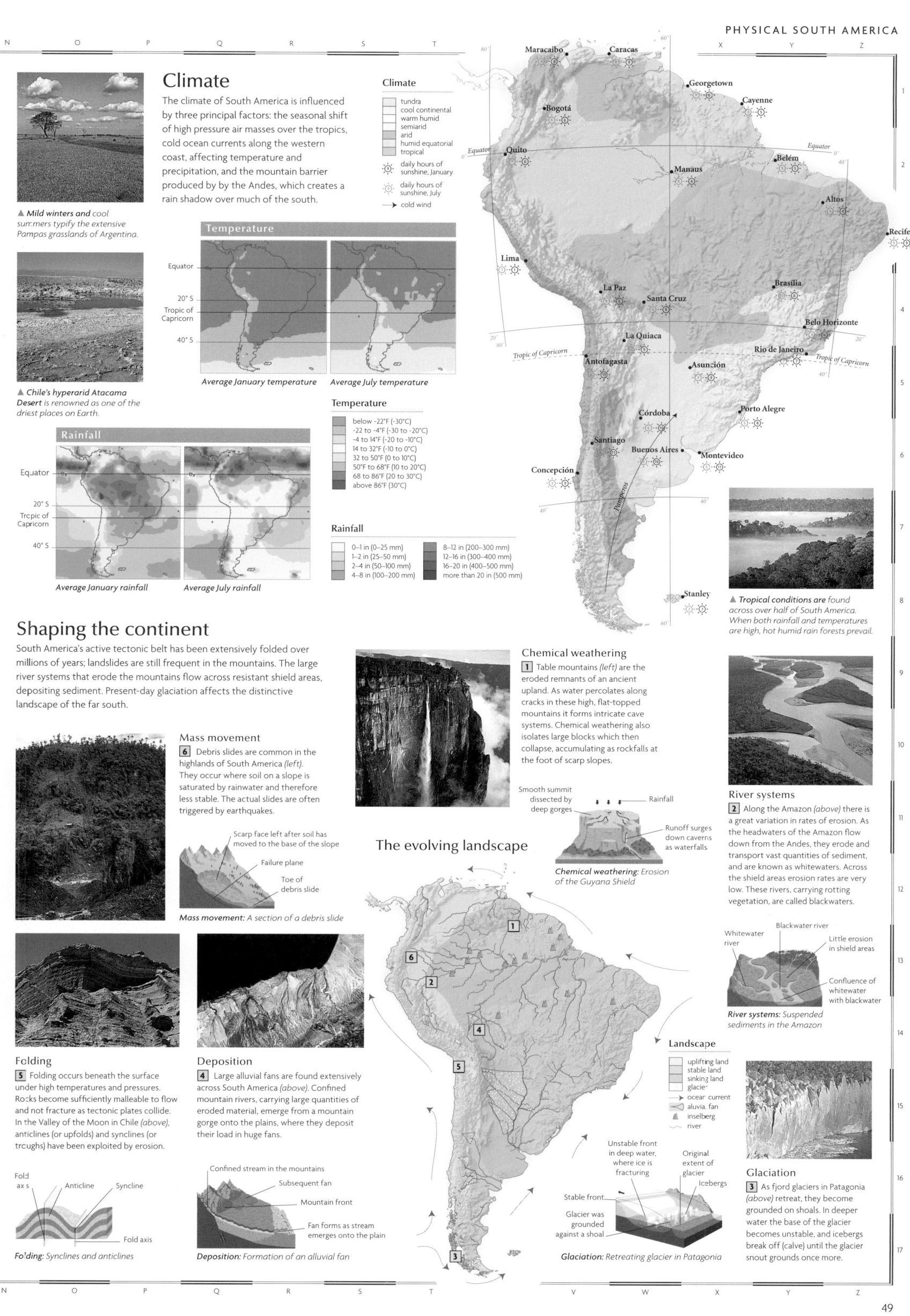

Maracaibo · Caracas · Georgetown · Cayenne · Bogotá · Quito · Manaus · Belém · Altos · Recife · Lima · La Paz · Santa Cruz · Brasília · Belo Horizonte · La Quiaca · Rio de Janeiro · Antofagasta · Asunción · Córdoba · Porto Alegre · Santiago · Buenos Aires · Montevideo · Concepción · Stanley

Equator · Tropic of Capricorn · Pampas

# Political South America

Modern South America's political boundaries have their origins in the territorial endeavors of explorers during the 16th century, who claimed almost the entire continent for Portugal and Spain. The Portuguese land in the east later evolved into the federal state of Brazil, while the Spanish vice-royalties eventually emerged as separate independent nation-states in the early 19th century. South America's growing population has become increasingly urbanized, with the growth of coastal cities into large conurbations like Rio de Janeiro and Buenos Aires. In Brazil, Argentina, Chile, and Uruguay, a succession of military dictatorships has given way to fragile, but strengthening, democracies.

◄ *Europe retains a* small foothold in South America. Kourou in French Guiana was the site chosen by the European Space Agency to launch the Ariane rocket. As a result of its status as a French overseas department, French Guiana is actually part of the European Union.

## Scale 1:24,000,000

Km
0  100  200  300  400  500  600  700  800

Miles
0  100  200  300  400  500  600  700  800

projection: Lambert Azimuthal Equal Area

## Transportation

Most major road and rail routes are confined to the coastal regions by the forbidding natural barriers of the Andes mountains and the Amazon Basin. Few major cross-continental routes exist, although Buenos Aires serves as a transportation center for the main rail links to La Paz and Valparaíso, while the construction of the Trans-Amazon and Pan-American Highways have made direct road travel possible from Recife to Lima and from Puerto Montt up the coast into central America. A new waterway project is proposed to transform the River Paraguay into a major shipping route, although it involves considerable wetland destruction.

► *South America's most* extensive rail network is centered on the Argentinian capital, Buenos Aires. The construction of new rail lines ouward from this important port, allowed the colonization of the Pampas lands for agriculture.

## Languages

Prior to European exploration in the 16th century, a diverse range of indigenous languages were spoken across the continent. With the arrival of Iberian settlers, Spanish became the dominant language, with Portuguese spoken in Brazil, and Native American languages such as Quechua and Guaraní, becoming concentrated in the continental interior. Today this pattern persists, although successive European colonization has led to Dutch being spoken in Suriname, English in Guyana, and French in French Guiana, while in large urban areas, Japanese and Chinese are increasingly common.

### Transportation

— major roads and highways
— major railroads
— international borders
• transport intersections
⊕ international airports
⊕ major ports

### Language groups

American Indian
Germanic
Romance

► *Chile's main port*, Valparaíso, is a vital national shipping center, in addition to playing a key role in the growing trade with Pacific nations. The country's awkward, elongated shape means that sea transportation is frequently used for internal travel and communications in Chile.

▲ *Indigenous South American* lifestyles have not been totally submerged by European cultures and languages. The continental interior, and particularly the Amazon Basin, is still home to many different ethnic peoples.

► *Lima's magnificent* cathedral reflects South America's colonial past with its unmistakably Spanish style. In July 1821, Peru became the last Spanish colony on the mainland to declare independence.

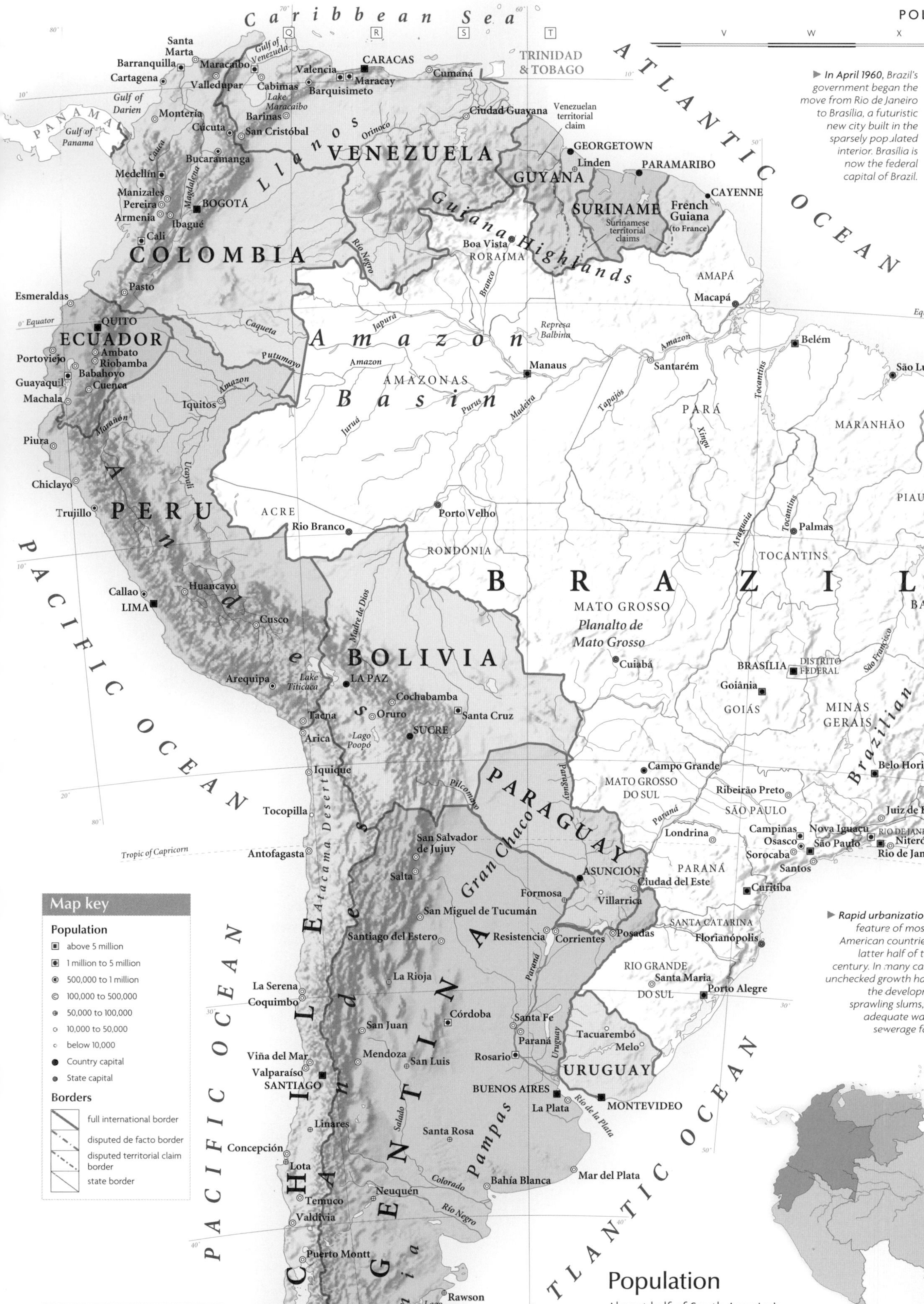

Caribbean Sea
ATLANTIC OCEAN
PACIFIC OCEAN
TRINIDAD & TOBAGO
Santa Marta
Barranquilla
Cartagena
Maracaibo
Gulf of Venezuela
Valencia
CARACAS
Maracay
Cumaná
Valledupar
Cabimas
Barquisimeto
Gulf of Darien
Montería
Lake Maracaibo
Barinas
PANAMA
Gulf of Panama
Cúcuta
San Cristóbal
Orinoco
Ciudad Guayana
Venezuelan territorial claim
Llanos
VENEZUELA
GEORGETOWN
Linden
GUYANA
PARAMARIBO
CAYENNE
SURINAME
Surinamese territorial claims
French Guiana (to France)
Bucaramanga
Medellín
Manizales
Pereira
Armenia
BOGOTÁ
Ibagué
Cali
Magdalena
Cauca
Guiana Highlands
Boa Vista
RORAIMA
Rio Negro
COLOMBIA
AMAPÁ
Macapá
Branco
Pasto
Esmeraldas
Equator
QUITO
ECUADOR
Ambato
Riobamba
Portoviejo
Babahoyo
Guayaquil
Cuenca
Machala
Caquetá
Japurá
Putumayo
Represa Balbina
Amazon Basin
Amazon
AMAZONAS
Manaus
Santarém
Belém
São Luís
Tocantins
Iquitos
Juruá
Purus
Madeira
Tapajós
PARÁ
Xingu
MARANHÃO
Fortaleza
Teresina
CEARÁ
RIO GRANDE DO NORTE
Natal
Marañón
Piura
Chiclayo
Trujillo
PERU
Ucayali
Andes
PARAÍBA
João Pessoa
PIAUÍ
PERNAMBUCO
Jaboatão
Recife
Araguaia
Palmas
ACRE
Rio Branco
Porto Velho
RONDÔNIA
TOCANTINS
Juazeiro
Represa de Sobradinho
ALAGOAS
Maceió
SERGIPE
Aracaju
BRAZIL
BAHIA
Callao
LIMA
Huancayo
Cusco
MATO GROSSO
Planalto de Mato Grosso
Madre de Dios
Salvador
BOLIVIA
Cuiabá
BRASÍLIA
DISTRITO FEDERAL
São Francisco
Goiânia
GOIÁS
Arequipa
Lake Titicaca
LA PAZ
Cochabamba
Santa Cruz
Tacna
Oruro
MINAS GERAIS
Brazilian Highlands
Arica
Lago Poopó
SUCRE
Iquique
Pilcomayo
PARAGUAY
Paraguay
Campo Grande
MATO GROSSO DO SUL
Belo Horizonte
Ribeirão Preto
Vitória
ESPÍRITO SANTO
Tocopilla
Atacama Desert
Gran Chaco
SÃO PAULO
Juiz de Fora
Paraná
Campinas
Nova Iguaçu
RIO DE JANEIRO
Niterói
Osasco
São Paulo
Rio de Janeiro
Sorocaba
Londrina
Tropic of Capricorn
Antofagasta
San Salvador de Jujuy
Salta
ASUNCIÓN
Santos
PARANÁ
Ciudad del Este
Curitiba
Formosa
Villarrica
San Miguel de Tucumán
SANTA CATARINA
Florianópolis
Santiago del Estero
Resistencia
Corrientes
Posadas
RIO GRANDE DO SUL
Santa Maria
Porto Alegre
La Rioja
La Serena
Coquimbo
Córdoba
Santa Fe
Paraná
Uruguay
Tacuarembó
Melo
San Juan
Viña del Mar
Valparaíso
SANTIAGO
Mendoza
San Luis
Rosario
URUGUAY
BUENOS AIRES
La Plata
MONTEVIDEO
Río de la Plata
CHILE
ARGENTINA
Linares
Salado
Santa Rosa
Pampas
Concepción
Lota
Colorado
Bahía Blanca
Mar del Plata
Neuquén
Temuco
Valdivia
Río Negro
Puerto Montt
Patagonia
Rawson
Lago Colhué Huapí
Chico
Gulf of San Jorge
Deseado
Golfo de Penas
Bahía Grande
Río Gallegos
Falkland Islands (to UK)
STANLEY
Punta Arenas
Strait of Magellan
Ushuaia
Beagle Channel
Cape Horn
Map key
Population
above 5 million
1 million to 5 million
500,000 to 1 million
100,000 to 500,000
50,000 to 100,000
10,000 to 50,000
below 10,000
Country capital
State capital
Borders
full international border
disputed de facto border
disputed territorial claim border
state border

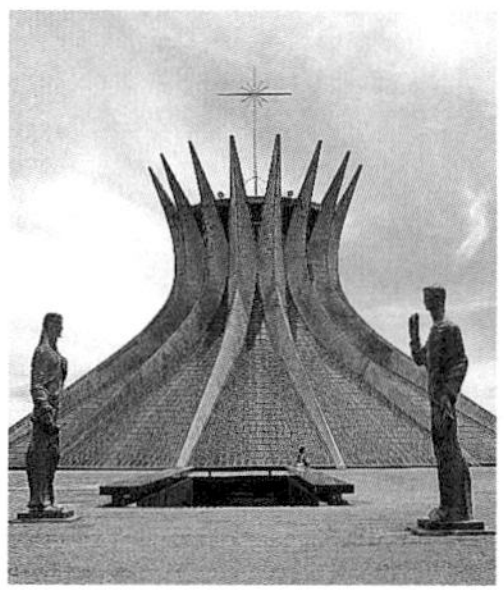

▶ **In April 1960,** Brazil's government began the move from Rio de Janeiro to Brasília, a futuristic new city built in the sparsely populated interior. Brasília is now the federal capital of Brazil.

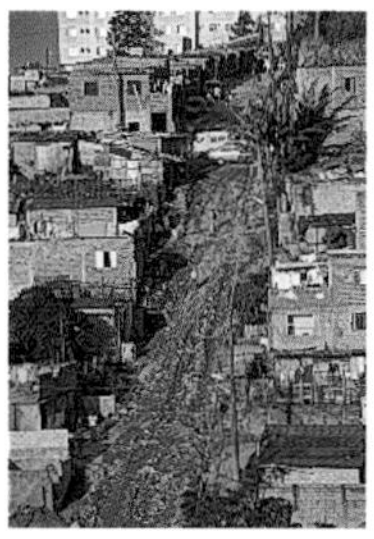

▶ **Rapid urbanization was** a feature of most South American countries in the latter half of the 20th century. In many cases, this unchecked growth has led to the development of sprawling slums, lacking adequate water and sewerage facilities.

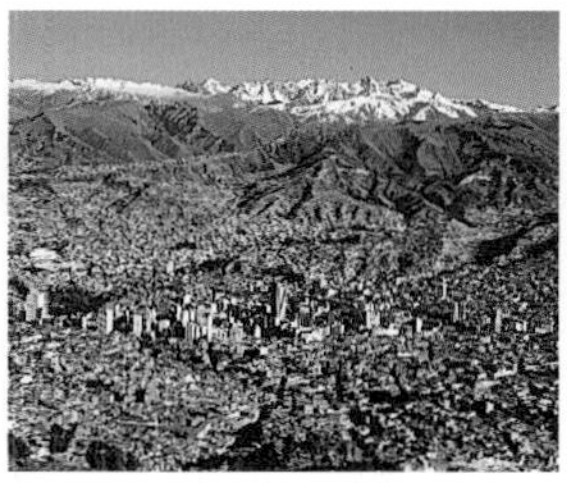

▲ **Perched high in** the Andes like many of the cities in western South America, La Paz, Bolivia is the world's highest capital city at over 11,500 ft (3500 m).

## Population

Almost half of South America's population lives in Brazil but, due to the large uninhabited expanses of the Amazon Basin, its overall population density is much lower than in other countries. During the 20th century the most important population trend was the movement from rural to urban areas, giving rise to great population concentrations in large cities like São Paulo, Rio de Janeiro, Caracas, Lima, Bogotá, and Buenos Aires.

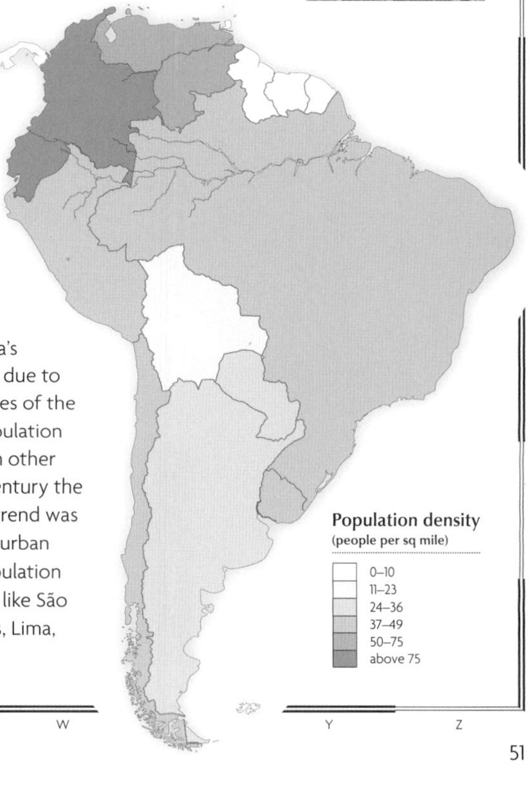

Population density
(people per sq mile)
0–10
11–23
24–36
37–49
50–75
above 75

# South American resources

Agriculture still provides the largest single form of employment in South America, although rural unemployment and poverty continue to drive people towards the huge coastal cities in search of jobs and opportunities. Mineral and fuel resources, although substantial, are distributed unevenly; few countries have both fossil fuels and minerals. To break industrial dependence on raw materials, boost manufacturing, and improve infrastructure, governments borrowed heavily from the World Bank in the 1960s and 1970s. This led to the accumulation of massive debts which are unlikely ever to be repaid. Today, Brazil dominates the continent's economic output, followed by Argentina. Recently, the less-developed western side of South America has benefited due to its geographical position; for example Chile is increasingly exporting raw materials to Japan.

◄ *Ciudad Guayana is a planned industrial complex in eastern Venezuela, built as an iron and steel center to exploit the nearby iron ore reserves.*

### Industry

| | | |
|---|---|---|
| ✈ | aerospace | ✎ pharmaceuticals |
| | brewing | 🖶 printing & publishing |
| | car/vehicle manufacture | ⚓ shipbuilding |
| | chemicals | ✿ sugar processing |
| | electronics | ▽ textiles |
| ✿ | engineering | ⚒ timber processing |
| S | finance | tobacco processing |
| | fish processing | wine |
| | food processing | ◊ oil |
| 💻 | hi-tech industry | ◊ gas |
| | iron & steel | |
| ▼ | meat processing | ● industrial cities |
| △ | metal refining | ▨ major industrial areas |
| | narcotics | |

▲ *The cold Peru Current flows north from the Antarctic along the Pacific coast of Peru, providing rich nutrients for one of the world's largest fishing grounds. However, over exploitation has severely reduced Peru's anchovy catch.*

## Standard of living

Wealth disparities throughout the continent create a wide gulf between affluent landowners and those afflicted by chronic poverty in inner city slums. The illicit production of cocaine, and the hugely influential drug barons who control its distribution, contribute to the violent disorder and corruption which affect northwestern South America, destabilizing local governments and economies.

**Standard of living**
(UN human development index)

low

high

▶ *Both Argentina and Chile are now exploring the southernmost tip of the continent in search of oil. Here in Punta Arenas, a drilling rig is being prepared for exploratory drilling in the Strait of Magellan.*

**GNI per capita (US$)**

below 999
1000–1999
2000–2999
3000–3999
4000–4999
above 5000

## Industry

Argentina and Brazil are South America's most industrialized countries and São Paulo is the continent's leading industrial center. Long-term government investment in Brazilian industry has encouraged a diverse industrial base; engineering, steel production, food processing, textile manufacture, and chemicals predominate. The illegal production of cocaine is economically significant in the Andean countries of Colombia and Bolivia. In Venezuela, the oil-dominated economy has left the country vulnerable to world oil price fluctuations. Food processing and mineral exploitation are common throughout the less industrially developed parts of the continent, including Bolivia, Chile, Ecuador, and Peru.

*Caribbean Sea*

PANAMA
*Gulf of Panama*

Barranquilla
Cartagena
Maracaibo
Barquisimeto
Caracas
Valencia
Ciudad Guayana

**VENEZUELA**

Georgetown
Paramaribo
**GUYANA**
**SURINAME**
French Guiana (to France)

Medellín
Bogotá
Cali
**COLOMBIA**

Quito
**ECUADOR**
Guayaquil
Iquitos

*A m a z o n*
Manaus

*B a s i n*

Belém

**B R A Z I L**

Fortaleza
Natal
Recife
Maceió
Salvador

Chiclayo
Chimbote
**PERU**
Lima
Cusco
Arequipa

**BOLIVIA**
La Paz
Sucre
Santa Cruz

Brasília

Belo Horizonte

Arica
Iquique
Chuquicamata

Antofagasta

**PARAGUAY**
Asunción
Ciudad del Este

São Paulo
Rio de Janeiro
Curitiba

San Miguel de Tucumán
Corrientes

Córdoba

Santa Fe
Rosario

Porto Alegre
Rio Grande

**URUGUAY**
Montevideo

Valparaíso
Mendoza
Santiago
Talca
Buenos Aires

Concepción

**ARGENTINA**

Bahía Blanca
Neuquén

Valdivia

Comodoro Rivadavia
*Gulf of San Jorge*

**Falkland Islands**
(to UK)

*Bahía Grande*

Punta Arenas
*Magellan*

Cape Horn

*PACIFIC OCEAN*

*ATLANTIC OCEAN*

# Environmental issues

The Amazon Basin is one of the last great wilderness areas left on Earth. The tropical rain forests which grow there are a valuable genetic resource, containing innumerable unique plants and animals. The forests are increasingly under threat from new and expanding settlements and "slash-and-burn" farming techniques, which clear land for the raising of beef cattle, causing land degradation and soil erosion.

▲ *Clouds of smoke* billow from the burning Amazon rainforest. Over 11,500 sq miles (30,000 sq km) of virgin rainforest are being cleared annually, destroying an ancient, irreplaceable, natural resource and biodiverse habitat.

### Environmental issues

- national parks
- tropical forest
- forest destroyed
- desert
- risk of desertification
- polluted rivers
- marine pollution
- heavy marine pollution
- poor urban air quality

# Using the land and sea

Many foods now common worldwide originated in South America. These include the potato, tomato, squash, and cassava. Today, large herds of beef cattle roam the temperate grasslands of the Pampas, supporting an extensive meatpacking trade in Argentina, Uruguay and Paraguay. Corn is grown as a staple crop across the continent and coffee is grown as a cash crop in Brazil and Colombia. Coca plants grown in Bolivia, Peru, and Colombia provide most of the world's cocaine. Fish and shellfish are caught off the western coast, especially anchovies off Peru, shrimps off Ecuador and pilchards off Chile.

◄ *South America, and* Brazil in particular, now leads the world in coffee production, mainly growing Coffea arabica in large plantations. Coffee beans are harvested, roasted and brewed to produce the world's second most popular drink, after tea.

◄ *The Pampas region* of southeast South America is characterized by extensive, flat plains, and populated by cattle and ranchers (gauchos). Argentina is a major world producer of beef, much of which is exported to the US for use in hamburgers.

◄ *High in the Andes,* hardy alpacas graze on the barren land. Alpacas are thought to have been domesticated by the Incas, whose nobility wore robes made from their wool. Today, they are still reared and prized for their soft, warm fleeces.

# Mineral resources

Over a quarter of the world's known copper reserves are found at the Chuquicamata mine in northern Chile, and other metallic minerals such as tin are found along the length of the Andes. The discovery of oil and gas at Venezuela's Lake Maracaibo in 1917 turned the country into one of the world's leading oil producers. In contrast, South America is virtually devoid of coal, the only significant deposit being on the peninsula of Guajira in Colombia.

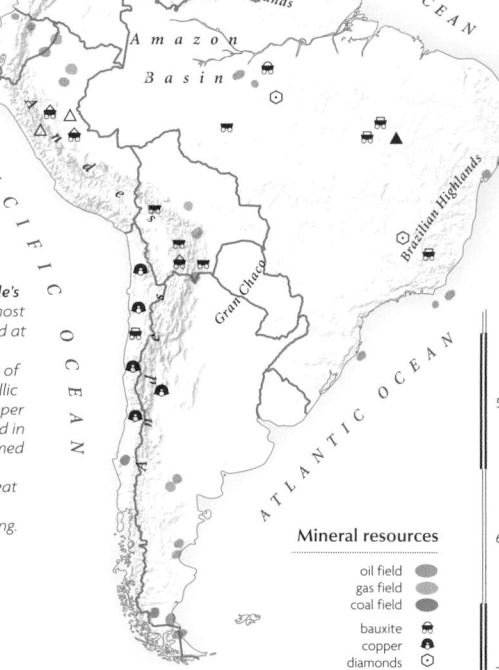

▲ *Copper is Chile's* largest export, most of which is mined at Chuquicamata. Along the length of the Andes, metallic minerals like copper and tin are found in abundance, formed by the excessive pressures and heat involved in mountain-building.

### Mineral resources

- oil field
- gas field
- coal field
- bauxite
- copper
- diamonds
- gold
- iron
- lead
- silver
- tin

### Using the land and sea

- barren land
- cropland
- desert
- forest
- mountain region
- pasture
- major conurbations
- cattle
- pigs
- sheep
- bananas
- corn
- citrus fruits
- cocoa
- cotton
- coffee
- fishing
- oil palms
- peanuts
- rubber
- shellfish
- soybeans
- sugar cane
- vineyards
- wheat

53

# Northern South America

COLOMBIA, GUYANA, SURINAME, VENEZUELA, French Guiana (to France)

Fringed by the Pacific and Atlantic oceans and the Caribbean Sea, South America's northern region has a rich range of natural resources, some exploited for centuries by colonial powers including the Spanish, French, Dutch, and British, others still to be fully explored. The prospects for further economic development in Colombia, Guyana, and Suriname are blighted by drug-related violence and political instability. Venezuela, despite huge incomes from its oil reserves, remains less developed in other industrial sectors. French Guiana is an overseas *département* of France, now seeking greater autonomy. Most of the major population centers, such as Bogotá, have grown up in the temperate conditions of the high Andes or, like Caracas, at strategic points along the Caribbean coast.

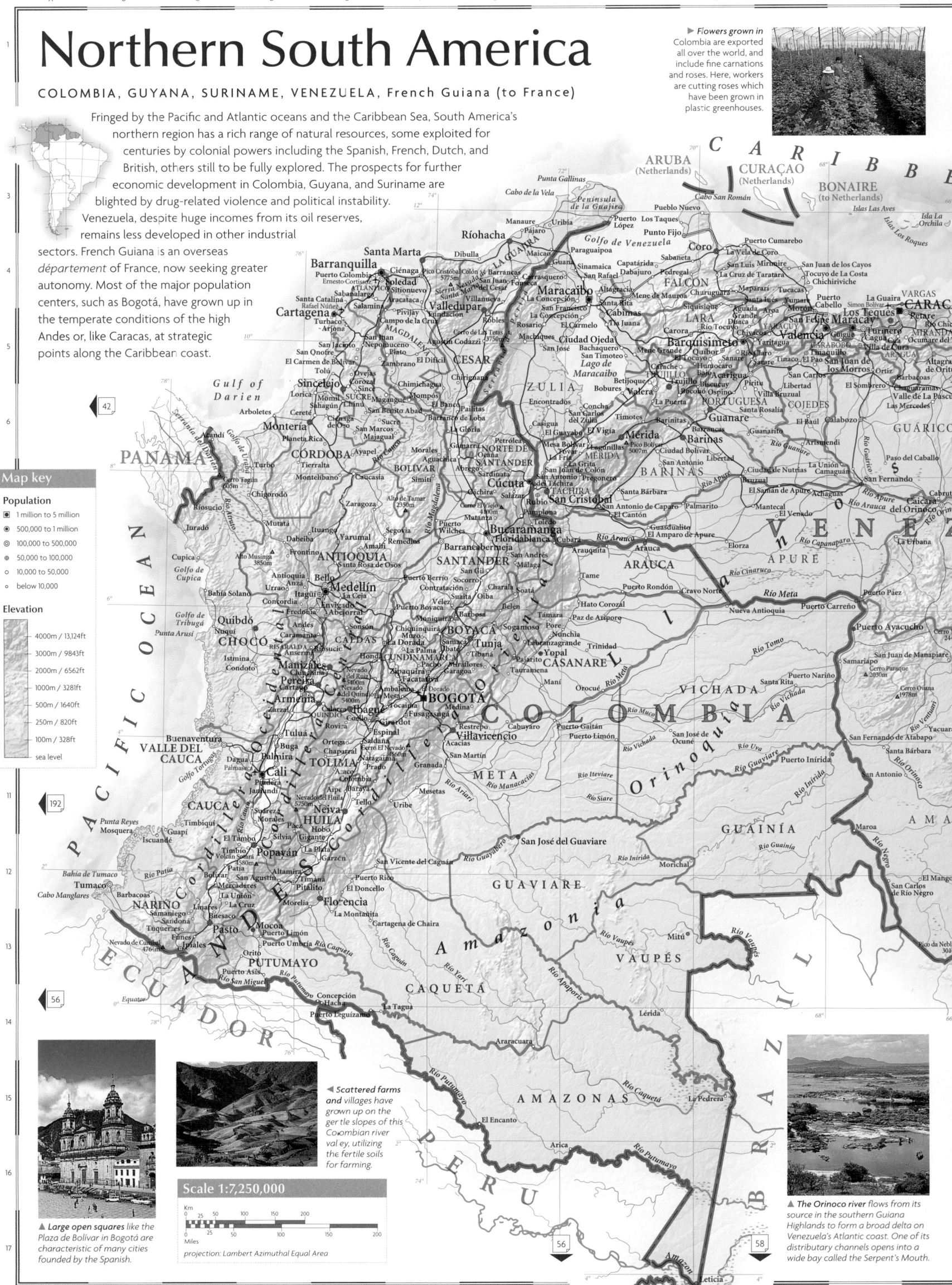

▶ *Flowers grown in* Colombia are exported all over the world, and include fine carnations and roses. Here, workers are cutting roses which have been grown in plastic greenhouses.

## Map key

**Population**
- ◉ 1 million to 5 million
- ◎ 500,000 to 1 million
- ◉ 100,000 to 500,000
- ⊕ 50,000 to 100,000
- ○ 10,000 to 50,000
- ∘ below 10,000

**Elevation**
- 4000m / 13,124ft
- 3000m / 9843ft
- 2000m / 6562ft
- 1000m / 3281ft
- 500m / 1640ft
- 250m / 820ft
- 100m / 328ft
- sea level

Scale 1:7,250,000

Km 0 25 50 100 150 200
Miles 0 25 50 100 150 200

projection: Lambert Azimuthal Equal Area

▲ *Large open squares* like the *Plaza de Bolívar* in Bogotá are characteristic of many cities founded by the Spanish.

◀ *Scattered farms and villages* have grown up on the gentle slopes of this Colombian river valley, utilizing the fertile soils for farming.

▲ *The Orinoco river* flows from its source in the southern Guiana Highlands to form a broad delta on Venezuela's Atlantic coast. One of its distributary channels opens into a wide bay called the Serpent's Mouth.

# Transportation & industry

Many mineral resources are mined in Colombia, including fuels, gold, and precious and semiprecious stones. Revenues from coffee and exports of illegal narcotics are crucial to the economy. Venezuela's major economic activity is the oil industry around Lake Maracaibo (Lago de Maracaibo). Sugar and bauxite are exported from Guyana and Suriname.

**Transportation network**

| | |
|---|---|
| 🛣 | 31,720 miles (51,054 km) |
| 🛤 | 3411 miles (5490 km) |
| 🚃 | 2448 miles (3940 km) |
| ⚓ | 22,429 miles (36,100 km) |

*Rivers are an important means of transportation in Colombia; many are extensively navigable. The Pan-American Highway runs through Colombia. In Venezuela, much infrastructure investment is linked to the oil industry.*

**Major industry and infrastructure**

- chemicals
- finance
- food processing
- iron & steel
- narcotics
- mining
- oil
- oil refining
- pharmaceuticals
- textiles
- timber processing
- ■ capital cities
- ● major towns
- ⊕ international airports
- major roads
- major industrial areas

▲ **Vast oil reserves** around Lake Maracaibo (Lago de Maracaibo) form the focus of Venezuelan industry. Incomes from oil are used to invest in other industries and in the development of infrastructure.

# Using the land

The Andean basins support cereals and potatoes. Livestock graze at higher altitudes and on the drier tropical grasslands known as the llanos; hardy goats are reared in scrubland areas. Grown at higher elevations, coffee is an important cash crop, as is cotton, sugar cane, bananas, citrus fruits, cocoa, and rice, farmed on the Caribbean lowlands. Coca is the most widely grown narcotic plant, with heroin poppies grown in Colombia and marijuana in lowland areas throughout the region.

**Land use and agricultural distribution**

- cattle
- goats
- bananas
- cereals
- coffee
- cotton
- sugar cane
- ■ capital cities
- ● major towns
- pasture
- cropland
- forest
- wetlands
- mountain region

**The urban/rural population divide**

urban 80%   rural 20%

| Population density | Total land area |
|---|---|
| 78 people per sq mile (30 people per sq km) | 1,111,317 sq miles (2,879,060 sq km) |

▲ **The Sierra Nevada** de Santa Marta is a granite massif which rises sharply from the Caribbean lowlands to snow-covered peaks, the tallest of which is 18,947 ft (5775 m) high.

# The landscape

At its northernmost reaches, in western Colombia and Venezuela, the great Andean mountain chain splits into three distinct ranges: the Cordillera Oriental, Cordillera Central, and Cordillera Occidental, intercut by a complex series of lesser ranges and basins. The relief becomes lower toward the coast and the interior plains of the northern Amazon Basin, rising again into the tropical hills of the Guiana Highlands.

**Lake Maracaibo** (Lago de Maracaibo) is not a true lake but a shallow inlet of the Caribbean Sea. It is the main source of Venezuela's oil.

**The drainage basin** of the Magdalena River and the Cauca, its main tributary, covers over 20% of Colombia's total surface area.

**In the Guiana Highlands,** Venezuela's most remote region, the ancient crystalline rocks contain deposits of iron ore, gold, and diamonds.

**Angel Falls** (Salto Ángel), at 3212 ft (979 m), is the world's highest waterfall.

**Igneous intrusions into** the crystalline plateau which forms most of central Guyana have led to the formation of the many rapids that characterize Guyana's rivers.

**Guiana Shield**
- Alluvial plains
- Inselbergs
- Table mountains

▲ **The Guiana Shield** is one of the oldest land surfaces in the world – probably formed more than 4 billion years ago. Chemical weathering over millions of years has created flat-topped table mountains and large numbers of inselbergs.

**Over 80% of** Suriname is covered by tropical rain forest.

Cordillera Occidental
Cordillera Central
Cordillera Oriental

**Colombia's eastern lowlands** are known locally as llanos, meaning grasslands.

▶ **The Potaru river** descends 741 ft (226 m) over a sandstone ledge at the Kaieteur Falls in Guyana.

Potaru river

**Most of the land** in French Guiana is low-lying; here, the rocks of the Guiana Highlands have been eroded by rivers flowing toward the sea.

# Western South America

## BOLIVIA, ECUADOR, PERU

The three states of Western South America share a similar geography and recent history. Dominated by the Inca empire until Spanish conquest in the 16th century, they achieved independence from Spain in the early 19th century. The precipitous terrain of the Andes presents severe difficulties for overland transportation and continues to be a barrier to national unity and stability. Although Ecuador is now a relatively stable democracy, the military is highly influential in Peru and Bolivia, while the drug trade and associated corruption discourages external aid and economic progress. Wealth and power are still largely concentrated in the hands of a small elite of families, who attained their position during the Spanish colonial period. Energy resources and political recognition for the indigenous peoples are becoming increasingly important issues, particularly in Bolivia.

## The landscape

Bolivia, Peru, and Ecuador each possess a high Andean mountain region and an eastern region consisting of tropical lowlands and the Andean slope leading down to them. Toward the south of the region, the mountains widen to form the high plateau of the Altiplano. Peru and Ecuador also have fertile, lowland coastal plains. A wide variety of environments include *selva* (tropical rain forest), *montaña* (mountain forest), and grassland.

*▲ There are many large and active volcanoes in the Andes. Magma generated in the heart of the volcano erupts in a huge cloud of ash. Ashfall deposits are common throughout the Andes and the rock produced is known as andesite. This is rapidly soaked by heavy rain, causing massive debris flows.*

Eruption column

Falling ash

Lava flows

Magma chamber

Subduction zone

Zone of magma generation

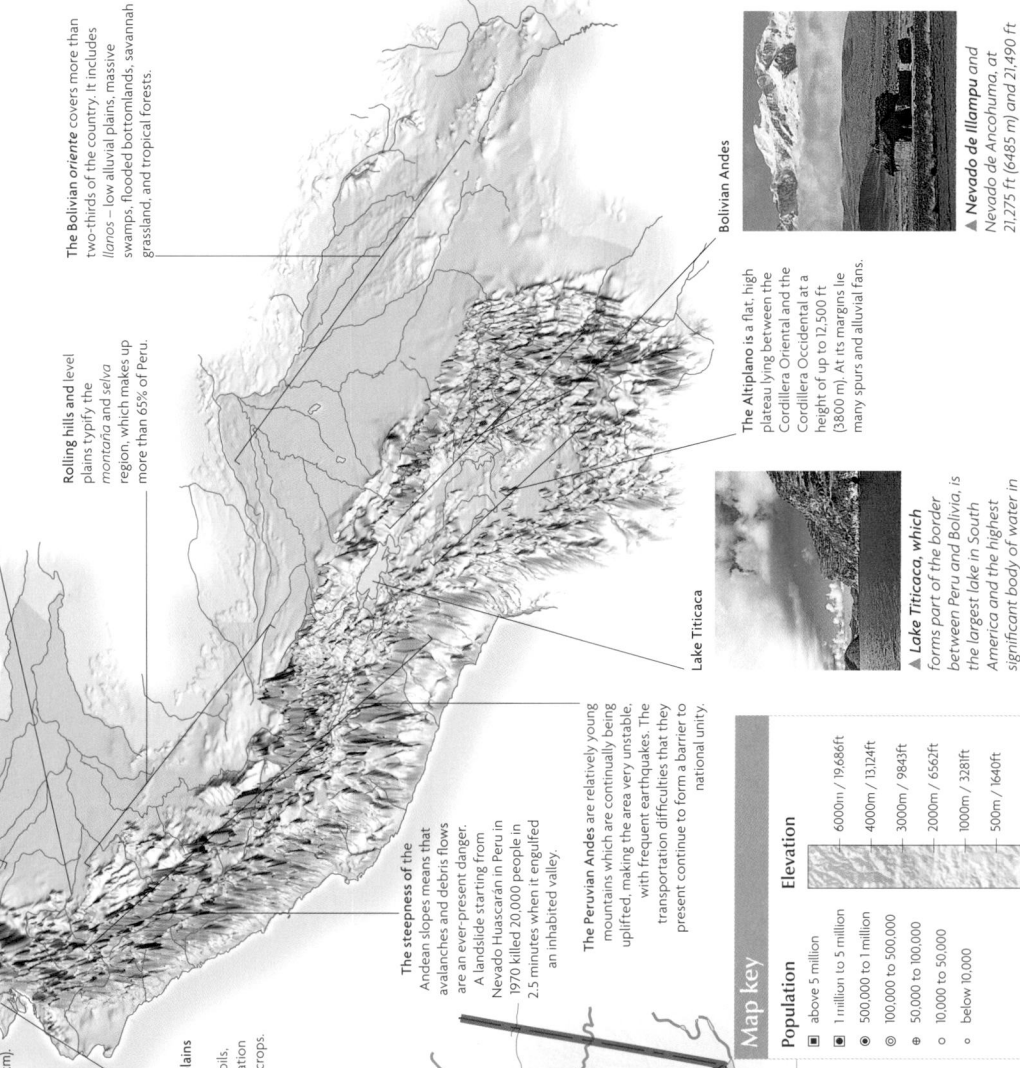

Bolivian Andes

*The Bolivian oriente covers more than two-thirds of the country. It includes llanos – low alluvial plains, massive swamps, flooded bottomlands, savannah grassland, and tropical forests.*

**Fast-flowing tributaries** of the Amazon, which rise in the Andes, run eastward through the front ranges to reach the tropical lowlands. They cut valleys so deep that tropical environments can be found extending well into mountainous areas.

**Rolling hills and level** plains typify the *montaña* and *selva* region, which makes up more than 65% of Peru.

**Much of eastern** Ecuador is covered by the tropical rain forest of the Amazon Basin.

**Cotopaxi is the world's** highest active volcano, with a peak 19,347 ft (5897 m) high. A massive eruption in 1877 caused a mudflow which destroyed everything in its path for 150 miles (240 km).

**The coastal floodplains** are the source of Ecuador's richest soils, enabling the cultivation of a wide range of crops.

**The steepness of the** Andean slopes means that avalanches and debris flows are an ever-present danger. A landslide starting from Nevado Huascarán in Peru in 1970 killed 20,000 people in 2.5 minutes when it engulfed an inhabited valley.

**The Peruvian Andes** are relatively young mountains which are continually being uplifted, making the area very unstable, with frequent earthquakes. The transportation difficulties that they present continue to form a barrier to national unity.

**The Altiplano** is a flat, high plateau lying between the Cordillera Oriental and the Cordillera Occidental at a height of up to 12,500 ft (3800 m). At its margins lie many spurs and alluvial fans.

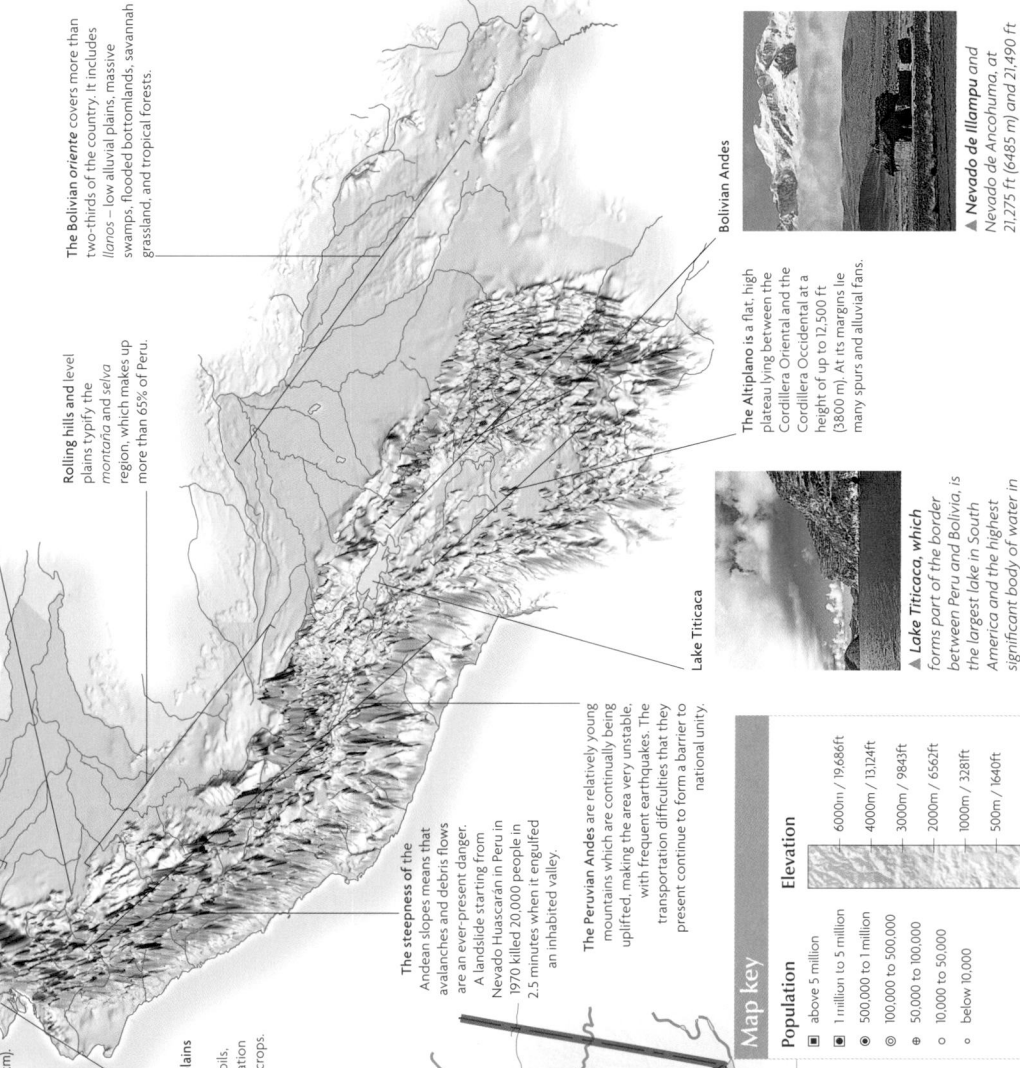

Lake Titicaca

*▲ Lake Titicaca, which forms part of the border between Peru and Bolivia, is the largest lake in South America and the highest significant body of water in the world at an altitude of 12,507 ft (3812 m).*

*▲ Nevado de Illampu and Nevado de Ancohuma, at 21,275 ft (6485 m) and 21,490 ft (6550 m) respectively, form Illampu, the highest mountain in the Bolivian Andes.*

Scale 1:8,500,000

projection: Lambert Azimuthal Equal Area

*▲ Ecuador's capital city, Quito, lies high in the Andes, nestling between snowcapped peaks. At 9350 ft (2850 m), Quito is the second highest capital in the world – La Paz in Bolivia is the highest.*

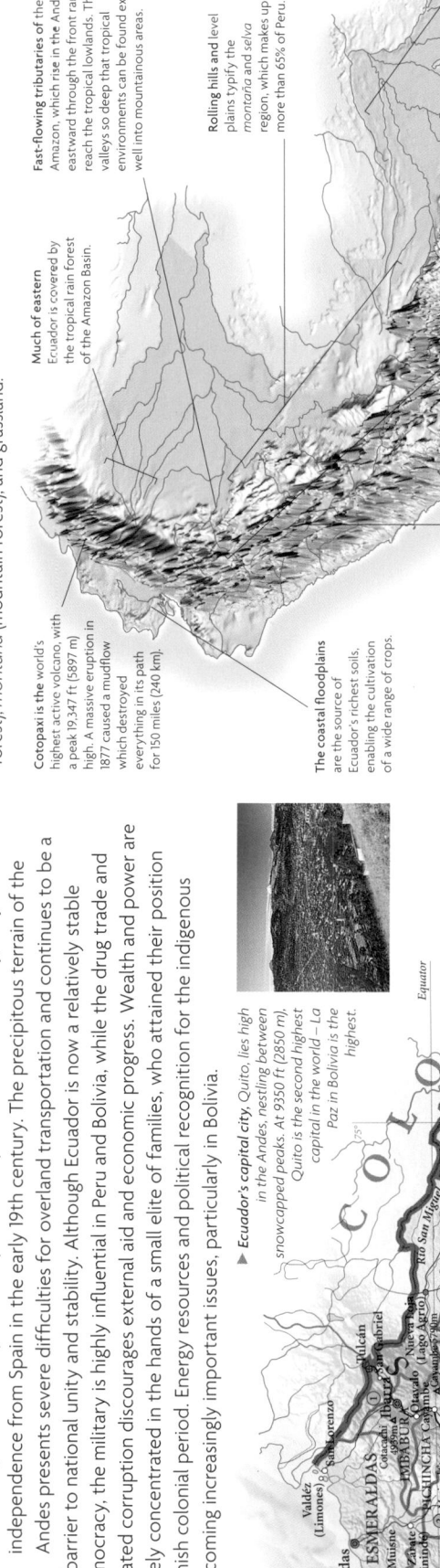

### Map key

**Population**

| | |
|---|---|
| ■ | above 5 million |
| ◉ | 1 million to 5 million |
| ◎ | 500,000 to 1 million |
| ⊙ | 100,000 to 500,000 |
| ⊕ | 50,000 to 100,000 |
| ○ | 10,000 to 50,000 |
| ○ | below 10,000 |

**Elevation**

| | |
|---|---|
| | 6000m / 19,686ft |
| | 4000m / 13,124ft |
| | 3000m / 9843ft |
| | 2000m / 6562ft |
| | 1000m / 3281ft |
| | 500m / 1640ft |
| | 250m / 820ft |
| | 100m / 328ft |
| | sea level |

Ecuador:
Administrative regions

① CARCHI
② SANTO DOMINGO DE LOS COLORADOS
③ TUNGURAHUA
④ BOLIVAR
⑤ SANTA ELENA
⑥ CHIMBORAZO

COLOMBIA

ECUADOR

PERU

BRAZIL

B O L I V I A

LORETO

SAN MARTIN

AMAZONAS

CAJAMARCA

LAMBAYEQUE

PIURA

TUMBES

Equator

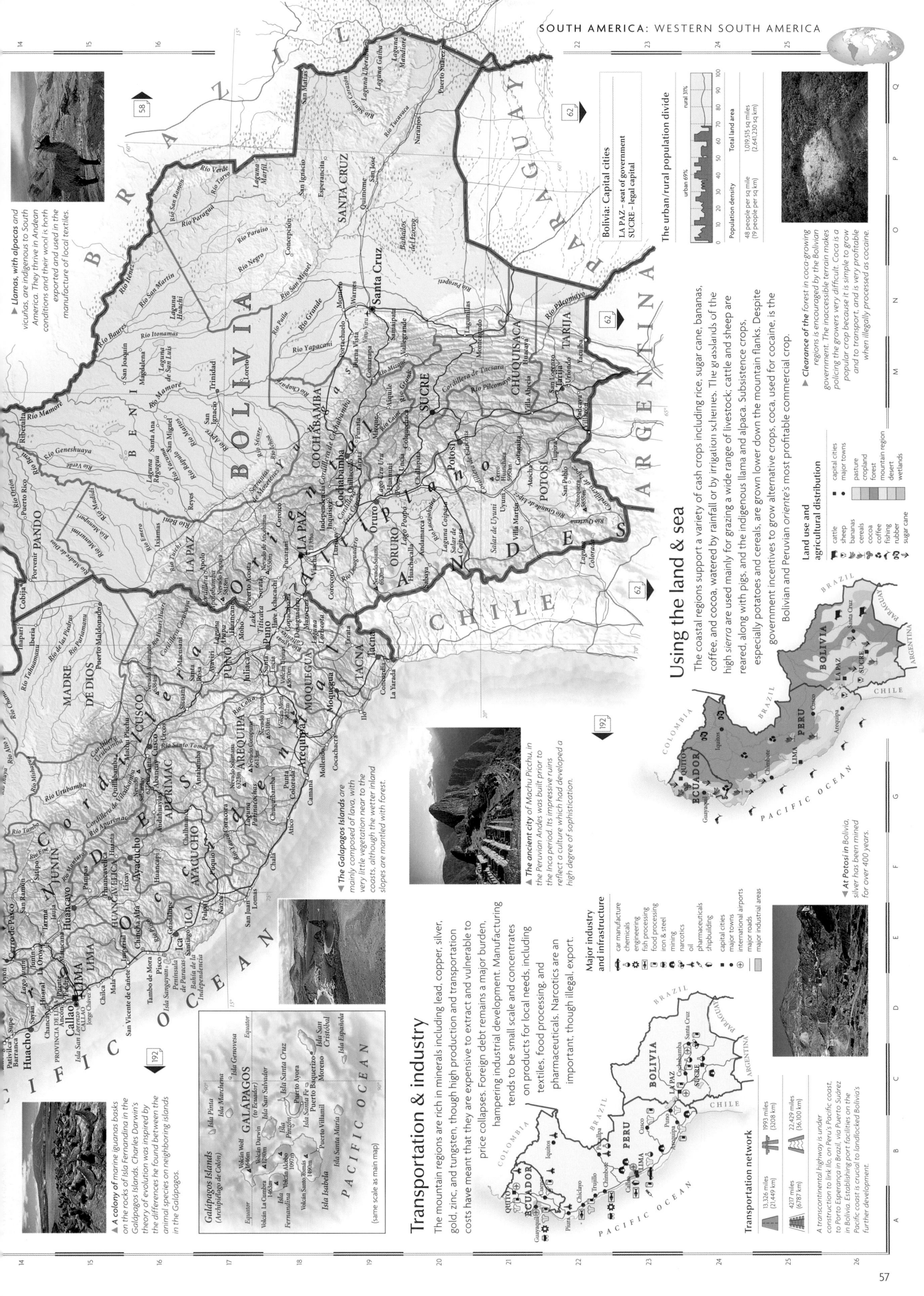

▲ **Llamas, with alpacas and vicuñas, are indigenous to South America. They thrive in Andean conditions and their wool is both exported and used in the manufacture of local textiles.**

▲ **A colony of marine iguanas basks on the rocks of Isla Fernandina in the Galápagos Islands. Charles Darwin's theory of evolution was inspired by the differences he found between the animal species on neighboring islands in the Galápagos.**

**Galápagos Islands**
(Archipiélago de Colón)

GALÁPAGOS
(to Ecuador)

(same scale as main map)

▼ **The Galápagos Islands are mainly composed of lava, with very little vegetation near to the coasts, although the wetter inland slopes are mantled with forest.**

▲ **The ancient city of Machu Picchu, in the Peruvian Andes was built prior to the Inca period. Its impressive ruins reflect a culture which had developed a high degree of sophistication.**

## Transportation & industry

The mountain regions are rich in minerals including lead, copper, silver, gold, zinc, and tungsten, though high production and transportation costs have meant that they are expensive to extract and vulnerable to price collapses. Foreign debt remains a major burden, hampering industrial development. Manufacturing tends to be small scale and concentrates on products for local needs, including textiles, food processing, and pharmaceuticals. Narcotics are an important, though illegal, export.

**Major industry and infrastructure**
- car manufacture
- chemicals
- engineering
- fish processing
- food processing
- iron & steel
- mining
- narcotics
- oil
- pharmaceuticals
- shipbuilding
- capital cities
- major towns
- international airports
- major roads
- major industrial areas

**Transportation network**
| | |
|---|---|
| 13,326 miles (21,449 km) | 1993 miles (3208 km) |
| 4217 miles (6787 km) | 22,429 miles (36,100 km) |

A transcontinental highway is under construction to link Ilo, on Peru's Pacific coast, to Porto Esperança in Brazil, via Puerto Suárez in Bolivia. Establishing port facilities on the Pacific coast is crucial to landlocked Bolivia's further development.

## Using the land & sea

The coastal regions support a variety of cash crops including rice, sugar cane, bananas, coffee, and cocoa, watered by rainfall or by irrigation schemes. The grasslands of the high sierra are used mainly for grazing a wide range of livestock; cattle and sheep are reared, along with pigs, and the indigenous llama and alpaca. Subsistence crops, especially potatoes and cereals, are grown lower down the mountain flanks. Despite government incentives to grow alternative crops, coca, used for cocaine, is the Bolivian and Peruvian oriente's most profitable commercial crop.

**Land use and agricultural distribution**
- cattle
- sheep
- bananas
- cereals
- cocoa
- coffee
- fishing
- rubber
- sugar cane
- capital cities
- major towns
- pasture
- cropland
- forest
- mountain region
- desert
- wetlands

▲ **Clearance of the forest in coca-growing regions is encouraged by the Bolivian government. The inaccessible terrain makes policing the growers very difficult. Coca is a popular crop because it is simple to grow and to transport, and is very profitable when illegally processed as cocaine.**

▲ **At Potosí in Bolivia, silver has been mined for over 400 years.**

**The urban/rural population divide**

urban 69%     rural 31%

| Population density | Total land area |
|---|---|
| 48 people per sq mile (19 people per sq km) | 1,019,515 sq miles (2,641,230 sq km) |

**Bolivia: Capital cities**
LA PAZ – seat of government
SUCRE – legal capital

# Brazil

Brazil is the largest country in South America, with a population of 191 million – almost half the combined total of the continent. The 26 states which make up the federal republic of Brazil are administered from the purpose-built capital, Brasília. Tropical rain forest, covering more than one-third of the country, contains rich natural resources, but great tracts are sacrificed to agriculture, industry and urban expansion on a daily basis. Most of Brazil's multiethnic population now live in cities, some of which are vast areas of urban sprawl; São Paulo is one of the world's biggest conurbations, with more than 20 million inhabitants. Although prosperity is a reality for some, many people still live in great poverty, and mounting foreign debts continue to damage Brazil's prospects of economic advancement.

## Using the land

Brazil has immense natural resources, including minerals and hardwoods, many of which are found in the fragile rain forest. Brazil is the world's leading coffee grower and a major producer of livestock, sugar, and orange juice concentrate. Soybeans for animal feed, particularly for poultry feed, have become the country's most significant crop.

**Land use and agricultural distribution**

- cattle
- pigs
- sheep
- citrus fruits
- coffee
- cotton
- soybeans
- sugar cane
- timber
- ● capital cities
- ● major towns

pasture
cropland
forest

## The landscape

The Amazon Basin, containing the largest area of tropical rain forest on Earth, covers nearly half of Brazil. It is bordered by two shield areas: in the south by the Brazilian Highlands, and in the north by the Guiana Highlands. The east coast is dominated by a great escarpment which runs for 1600 miles (2565 km).

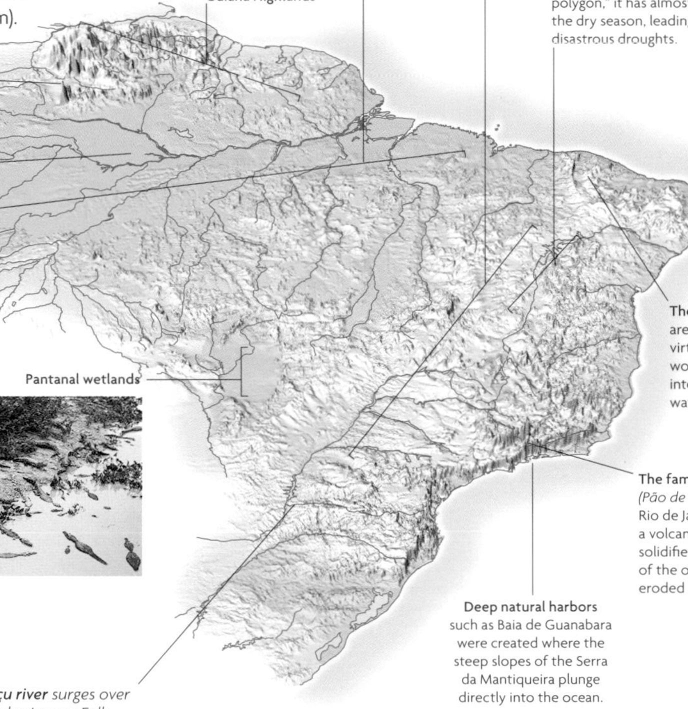

**The ancient Brazilian Highlands** have a varied topography. Their plateaus, hills, and deep valleys are bordered by highly-eroded mountains containing important mineral deposits. They are drained by three great river systems, the Amazon, the Paraguay–Paraná, and the São Francisco.

**The São Francisco Basin** has a climate unique in Brazil. Known as the "drought polygon," it has almost no rain during the dry season, leading to regular disastrous droughts.

**The Amazon Basin** is the largest river basin in the world. The Amazon river and over a thousand tributaries drain an area of 2,375,000 sq miles (6,150,000 sq km) and carry one-fifth of the world's fresh water out to sea.

**The northeastern scrublands** are known as the caatinga, a virtually impenetrable thorny woodland, sometimes intermixed with cacti where water is scarce.

**The famous Sugar** Loaf Mountain (Pão de Açúcar) which overlooks Rio de Janeiro is a fine example of a volcanic plug a domed core of solidified lava left after the slopes of the original volcano have eroded away.

**Deep natural harbors** such as Baía de Guanabara were created where the steep slopes of the Serra da Mantiqueira plunge directly into the ocean.

Brazil's highest mountain is the Pico da Neblina which was only discovered in 1962. It is 9888 ft (3014 m) high.

**The floodplains** which border the Amazon river are made up of a variety of different features including shallow lakes and swamps, mangrove forests in the tidal delta area, and fertile levees on river banks and point bars.

Guiana Highlands

Pantanal wetlands

▲ **The Pantanal region** in the south of Brazil is an extension of the Gran Chaco plain. The swamps and marshes of this area are renowned for their beauty, and abundant and unique wildlife, including wildfowl and these caimans, a type of crocodile.

▼ **The Iguaçu river** surges over the spectacular Iguaçu Falls (Saltos do Iguaçu) toward the Paraná river. Falls like these are increasingly under pressure from large-scale hydroelectric projects such as that at Itaipú.

▼ **The fecundity of** parts of Brazil's rain forest results from exceptionally high levels of rainfall and the quantities of silt deposited by the Amazon river system.

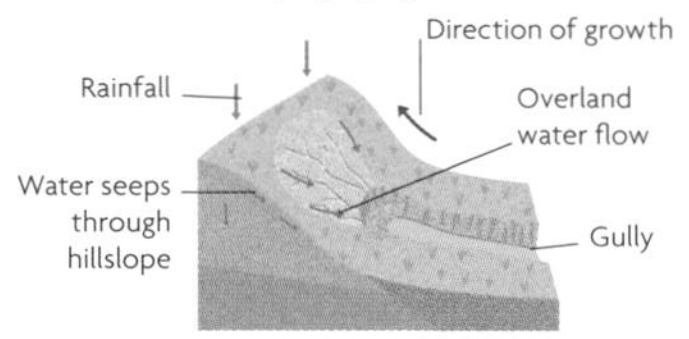

▼ **Large-scale gullies** are common in Brazil, particularly on hillslopes from which vegetation has been removed. Gullies grow headwards (up the slope), aided by a combination of erosion through water seepage and rainwater runoff.

Hillslope gullying

Direction of growth

Overland water flow

Gully

Rainfall

Water seeps through hillslope

### The urban/rural population divide

urban 78% — rural 22%

| Population density | Total land area |
|---|---|
| 55 people per sq mile (21 people per sq km) | 3,286,472 sq miles (8,511,970 sq km) |

### Map key

**Population**
- ■ above 5 million
- ◘ 1 million to 5 million
- ◙ 500,000 to 1 million
- ◉ 100,000 to 500,000
- ⊕ 50,000 to 100,000
- ○ 10,000 to 50,000
- ○ below 10,000

**Elevation**
- 3000m / 9843ft
- 2000m / 6562ft
- 1000m / 328ft
- 500m /1640ft
- 250m / 820ft
- 100m / 328ft
- sea level

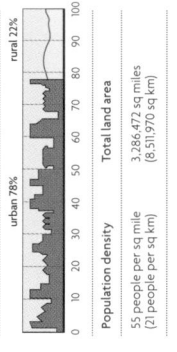

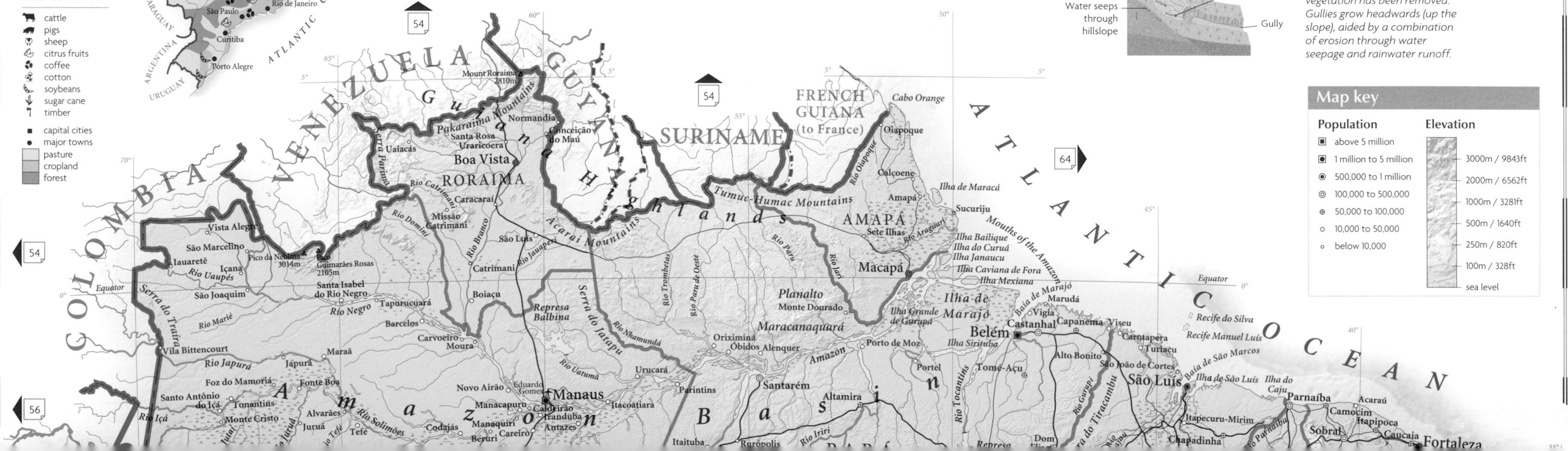

FRENCH GUIANA (to France)

SURINAME

VENEZUELA

COLOMBIA

PERU

BOLIVIA

PARAGUAY

ARGENTINA

URUGUAY

GUYANA

B r a z i l

A m a z o n

G u i a n a   H i g h l a n d s

B r a z i l i a n   H i g h l a n d s

ATLANTIC OCEAN

São Luís
Belém
Macapá
Manaus
Boa Vista
Fortaleza
Recife
Salvador
BRASÍLIA
Belo Horizonte
Rio de Janeiro
São Paulo
Curitiba
Porto Alegre

RORAIMA
AMAPÁ

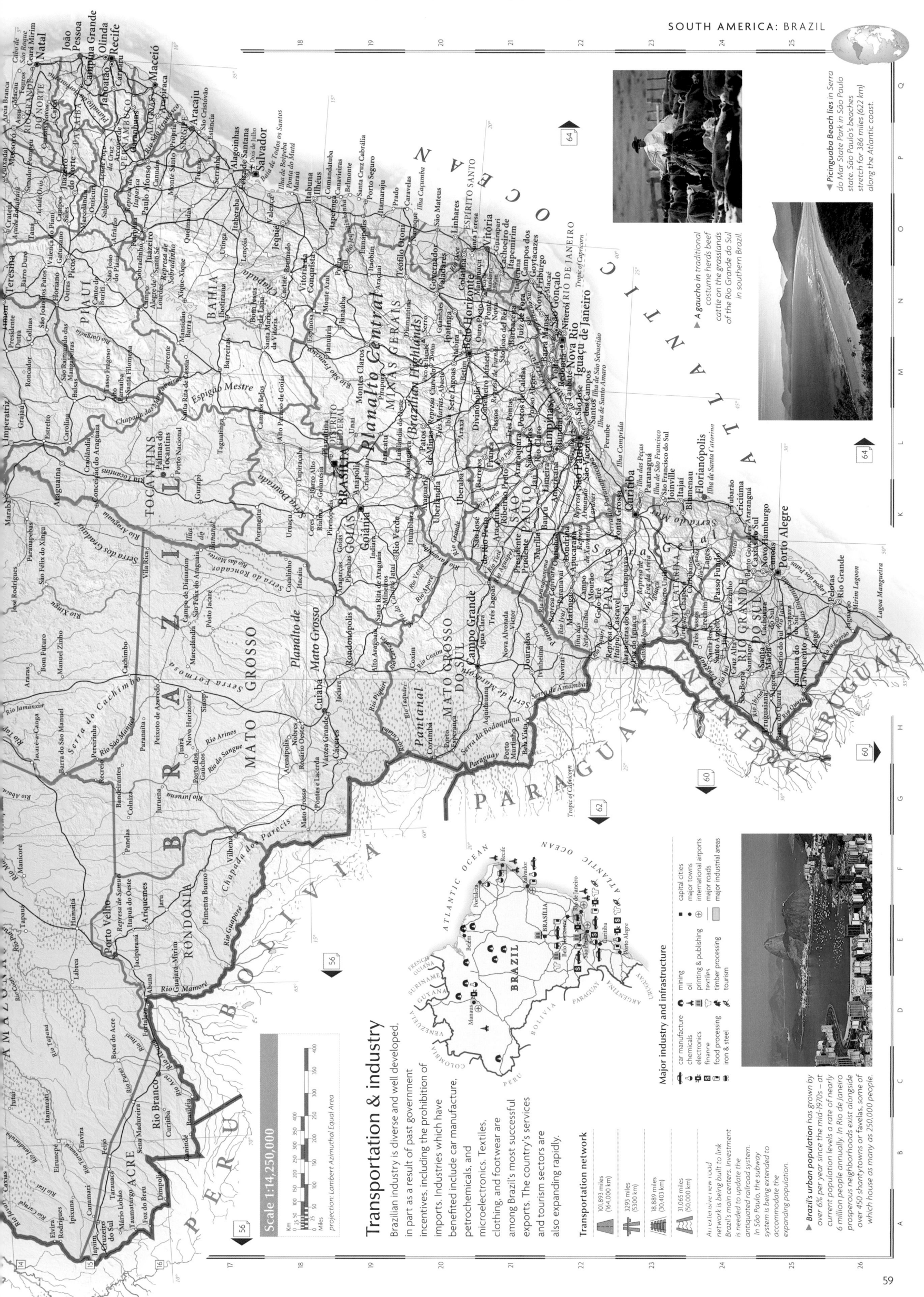

▲ *Picinguaba Beach lies in Serra do Mar State Park in São Paulo state. São Paulo's beaches stretch for 386 miles (622 km) along the Atlantic coast.*

▲ *A gaucho in traditional costume herds beef cattle on the grasslands of the Rio Grande do Sul in southern Brazil.*

# Transportation & industry

Brazilian industry is diverse and well developed, in part as a result of past government incentives, including the prohibition of imports. Industries which have benefited include car manufacture, petrochemicals, and microelectronics. Textiles, clothing, and footwear are among Brazil's most successful exports. The country's services and tourism sectors are also expanding rapidly.

## Transportation network

101,893 miles (164,000 km)

3293 miles (5300 km)

18,889 miles (30,403 km)

31,065 miles (50,000 km)

An extensive new road network is being built to link Brazil's main centers. Investment is needed to update the antiquated railroad system. In São Paulo, the subway system is being extended to accommodate the expanding population.

▶ Brazil's urban population has grown by over 6% per year since the mid-1970s – at current population levels a rate of nearly 6 million people annually. In Rio de Janeiro prosperous neighborhoods exist alongside over 450 shantytowns or favelas, some of which house as many as 250,000 people.

Scale 1:14,250,000

projection: Lambert Azimuthal Equal Area

## Major industry and infrastructure

car manufacture, chemicals, electronics, finance, food processing, iron & steel, mining, oil, printing & publishing, textiles, timber processing, tourism

capital cities, major towns, international airports, major roads, major industrial areas

59

# Eastern South America

## URUGUAY, NORTHEAST ARGENTINA, SOUTHEAST BRAZIL

The vast conurbations of Rio de Janeiro, São Paulo, and Buenos Aires form the core of South America's highly-urbanized eastern region. São Paulo state, with over 40 million inhabitants, is among the world's 20 most powerful economies, and São Paulo is the fastest growing city on the continent. Rio de Janeiro and Buenos Aires, transformed in the last hundred years from port cities to great metropolitan areas each with more than 10 million inhabitants, typify the unstructured growth and wealth disparities of South America's great cities. In Uruguay, over two fifths of the population lives in the capital, Montevideo, which faces Buenos Aires across the Plate River (*Rio de la Plata*). Immigration from the countryside has created severe pressure on the urban infrastructure, particularly on available housing, leading to a profusion of crowded shanty settlements (*favelas or barrios*).

## Using the land

Most of Uruguay and the Pampas of northern Argentina are devoted to the rearing of livestock, especially cattle and sheep, which are central to both countries' economies. Soybeans, first produced in Brazil's Rio Grande do Sul, are now more widely grown for large-scale export, as are cereals, sugar cane, and grapes. Subsistence crops, including potatoes, corn and sugar beets, are grown on the remaining arable land.

### Land use and agricultural distribution

- cattle
- sheep
- cereals
- coffee
- fruit
- soybeans
- sugar cane
- capital cities
- major towns
- pasture
- cropland
- forest
- wetlands
- barren land

▼ The rolling grasslands of Uruguay are ideally suited to the rearing of cattle. Beef is the country's main export commodity, valued at over one billion US dollars in 2006.

▲ Soybeans are harvested, pressed, and processed into soycake, which is used as animal feed. The cake is fed mainly to chickens on large-scale factory farms, and the growth in soy production has been an important factor in the expansion of the Brazilian poultry trade.

## Transportation & industry

Southeast Brazil is home to much of the important motor and capital goods industry, largely based around São Paulo; iron and steel production is also concentrated in this region. Uruguay's economy continues to be based mainly on the export of livestock products including meat and leather goods. Buenos Aires is Argentina's chief port, and the region has a varied and sophisticated economic base including service-based industries such as finance and publishing, as well as primary processing.

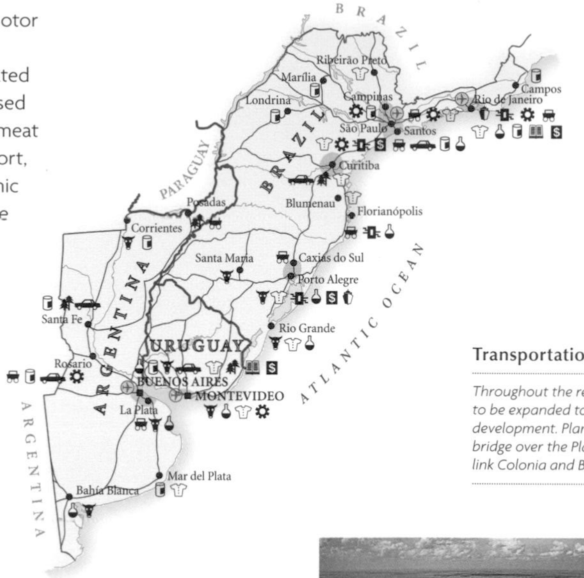

### Major industry and infrastructure

- car manufacture
- chemicals
- engineering
- finance
- food processing
- iron & steel
- meat processing
- printing & publishing
- shipbuilding
- textiles
- timber processing
- capital cities
- major towns
- international airports
- major roads
- major industrial areas

### Transportation network

*Throughout the region, road networks need to be expanded to cope with urban development. Plans are underway to build a bridge over the Plate River (Rio de la Plata) to link Colonia and Buenos Aires.*

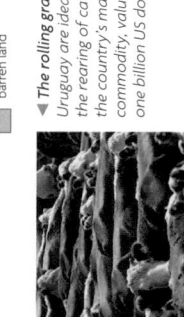

▲ The Itaipú dam on the Paraná river is one of the largest hydroelectric projects in the world, jointly financed by Brazil and Paraguay.

▶ Rio de Janeiro's annual carnival, Mardi Gras, which ushers in the start of Lent, is an extravagant five-day parade through the city, characterized by fantastically decorated floats, exuberant dancing, and samba music.

### Map key

**Population**
- ■ above 5 million
- ● 1 million to 5 million
- ◉ 500,000 to 1 million
- ◎ 100,000 to 500,000
- ○ 50,000 to 100,000
- ○ 10,000 to 50,000
- ○ below 10,000

**Elevation**
- 2000m / 6562ft
- 1000m / 3281ft
- 500m / 1640ft
- 250m / 820ft
- 100m / 328ft
- sea level

### Scale 1:7,000,000

projection: Lambert Azimuthal Equal Area

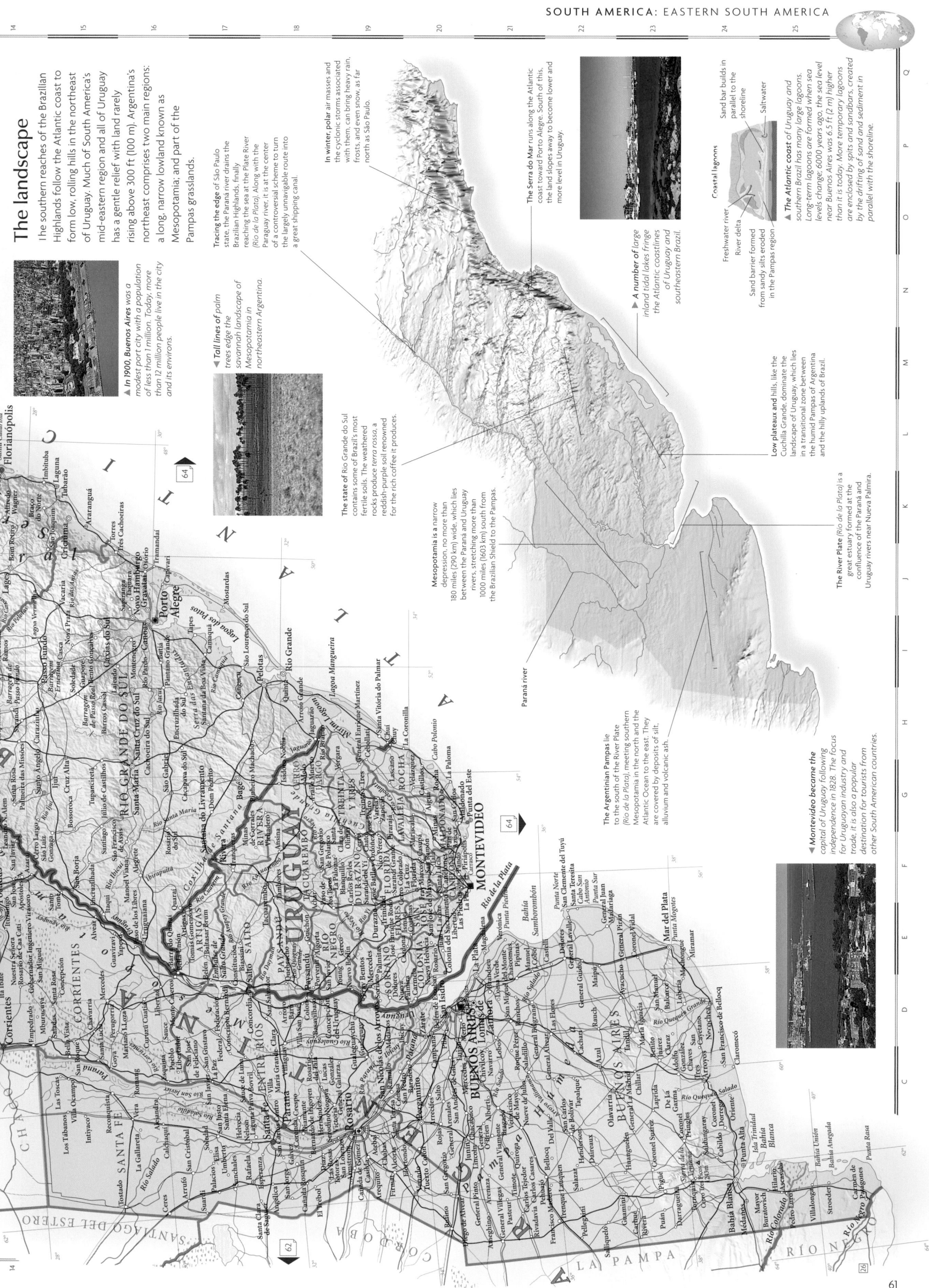

# The landscape

The southern reaches of the Brazilian Highlands follow the Atlantic coast to form low, rolling hills in the northeast of Uruguay. Much of South America's mid-eastern region and all of Uruguay has a gentle relief with land rarely rising above 300 ft (100 m). Argentina's northeast comprises two main regions: a long, narrow lowland known as Mesopotamia; and part of the Pampas grasslands.

▲ In 1900, Buenos Aires was a modest port city with a population of less than 1 million. Today, more than 12 million people live in the city and its environs.

Tracing the edge of São Paulo state, the Paraná river drains the Brazilian Highlands, finally reaching the sea at the Plate River (Río de la Plata). Along with the Paraguay river, it is at the center of a controversial scheme to turn the largely unnavigable route into a great shipping canal.

▼ Tall lines of palm trees edge the savannah landscape of Mesopotamia in northeastern Argentina.

In winter, polar air masses and the cyclonic storms associated with them, can bring heavy rain, frosts, and even snow, as far north as São Paulo.

The state of Rio Grande do Sul contains some of Brazil's most fertile soils. The weathered rocks produce terra rossa, a reddish-purple soil renowned for the rich coffee it produces.

The Serra do Mar runs along the Atlantic coast toward Porto Alegre. South of this, the land slopes away to become lower and more level in Uruguay.

▲ A number of large inland tidal lakes fringe the Atlantic coastlines of Uruguay and southeastern Brazil.

Coastal lagoons

Sand bars build in parallel to the shoreline
Saltwater
Freshwater river
River delta
Sand barrier formed from sandy silts eroded in the Pampas region

▲ The Atlantic coast of Uruguay and southern Brazil has many large lagoons. Long-term lagoons are formed when sea levels change; 6000 years ago, the sea level near Buenos Aires was 6.5 ft (2 m) higher than it is today. More temporary lagoons are enclosed by spits and sandbars, created by the drifting of sand and sediment in parallel with the shoreline.

Low plateaux and hills, like the Cuchilla Grande, dominate the landscape of Uruguay, which lies in a transitional zone between the humid Pampas of Argentina and the hilly uplands of Brazil.

Mesopotamia is a narrow depression, no more than 180 miles (290 km) wide, which lies between the Paraná and Uruguay rivers, stretching more than 1000 miles (1603 km) south from the Brazilian Shield to the Pampas.

The River Plate (Río de la Plata) is a great estuary formed at the confluence of the Paraná and Uruguay rivers near Nueva Palmira.

The Argentinian Pampas lie to the south of the River Plate (Río de la Plata), meeting southern Mesopotamia in the north and the Atlantic Ocean to the east. They are covered by deposits of silt, alluvium and volcanic ash.

▼ Montevideo became the capital of Uruguay following independence in 1828. The focus for Uruguayan industry and trade, it is also a popular destination for tourists from other South American countries.

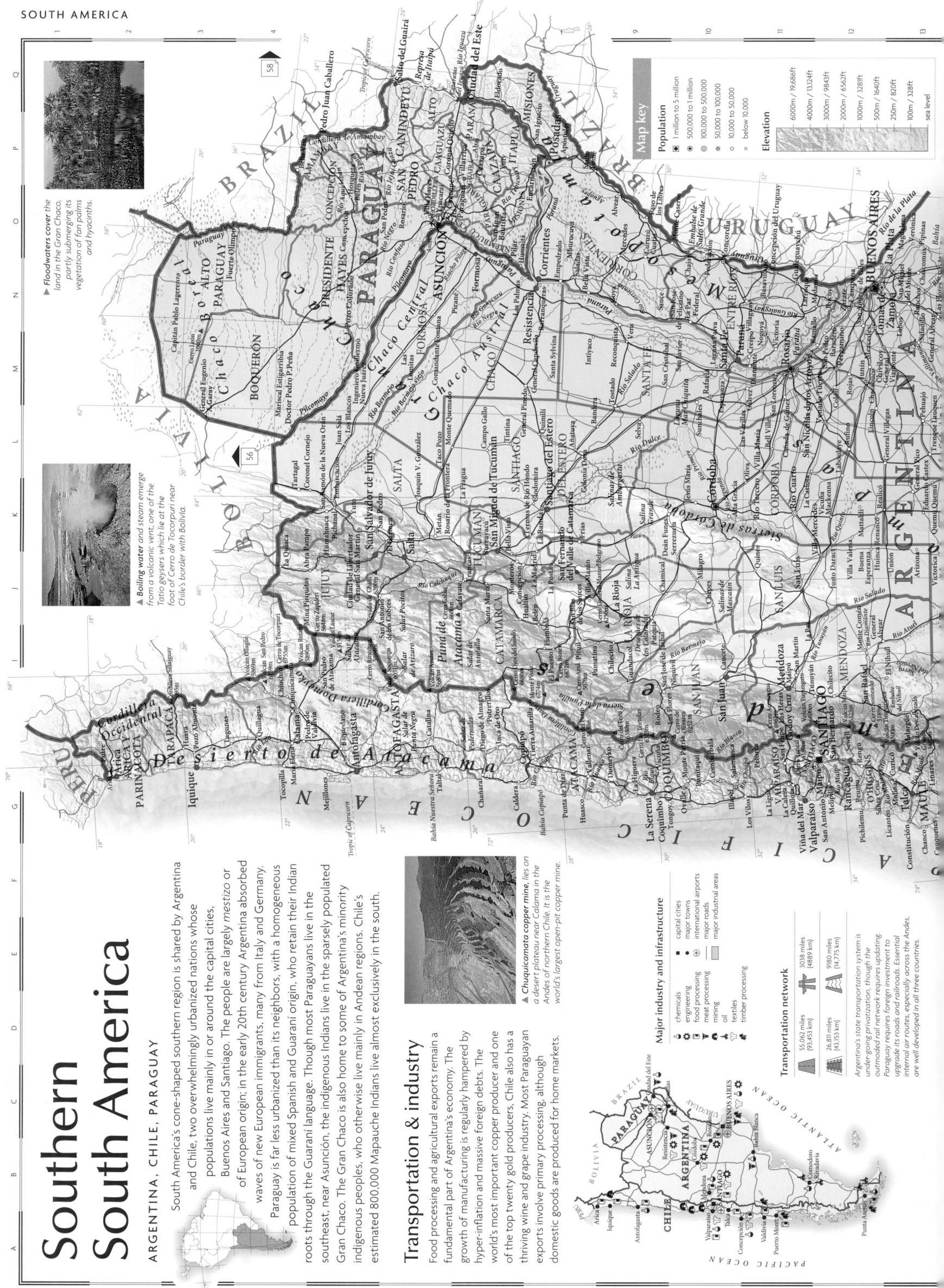

# Southern South America

## ARGENTINA, CHILE, PARAGUAY

South America's cone-shaped southern region is shared by Argentina and Chile, two overwhelmingly urbanized nations whose populations live mainly in or around the capital cities, Buenos Aires and Santiago. The people are largely *mestizo* or of European origin; in the early 20th century Argentina absorbed waves of new European immigrants, many from Italy and Germany. Paraguay is far less urbanized than its neighbors, with a homogeneous population of mixed Spanish and Guarani origin, who retain their Indian roots through the Guarani language. Though most Paraguayans live in the southeast, near Asunción, the indigenous Indians live in the sparsely populated Gran Chaco. The Gran Chaco is also home to some of Argentina's minority indigenous peoples, who otherwise live mainly in Andean regions. Chile's estimated 800,000 Mapuche Indians live almost exclusively in the south.

## Transportation & industry

Food processing and agricultural exports remain a fundamental part of Argentina's economy. The growth of manufacturing is regularly hampered by hyper-inflation and massive foreign debts. The world's most important copper producer and one of the top twenty gold producers, Chile also has a thriving wine and grape industry. Most Paraguayan exports involve domestic processing, although domestic goods are produced for home markets.

▶ *Floodwaters cover the land in the Gran Chaco, partly submerging its vegetation of fan palms and hyacinths.*

▲ *Boiling water and steam emerge from a volcanic vent, one of the Tatio geysers which lie at the foot of Cerro de Tocorpuri near Chile's border with Bolivia.*

▲ *Chuquicamata copper mine, lies on a desert plateau near Calama in the Andes of northern Chile. It is the world's largest open-pit copper mine.*

### Major industry and infrastructure

- chemicals
- engineering
- food processing
- meat processing
- mining
- oil
- textiles
- timber processing

⊙ capital cities
• major towns
⊕ international airports
— major roads
▨ major industrial areas

### Transportation network

| | | |
|---|---|---|
| 55,062 miles (93,453 km) | ✈ | 3038 miles (4889 km) |
| 26,811 miles (43,153 km) | ⊞ | 9180 miles (14,775 km) |

*Argentina's state transportation system is undergoing privatization, though the outmoded rail network requires updating. Paraguay requires foreign investment to upgrade its roads and railroads. Essential internal air routes, especially across the Andes, are well developed in all three countries.*

### Map key

**Population**
- ⊙ 1 million to 5 million
- ◉ 500,000 to 1 million
- ⊕ 100,000 to 500,000
- ⊙ 50,000 to 100,000
- ⊙ 10,000 to 50,000
- ∙ below 10,000

**Elevation**
- 6000m / 19,686ft
- 4000m / 13,124ft
- 3000m / 9843ft
- 2000m / 6562ft
- 1000m / 3281ft
- 500m / 1640ft
- 250m / 820ft
- 100m / 328ft
- sea level

## The landscape

The Andes run from north to south, forming a precipitous natural border between Chile and Argentina. East of the Andes are the scrublands of the Gran Chaco and the plains of the Pampas, which extend northward toward Paraguay. In the far southwest, Chile's indented Pacific coastline has many features typical of areas which have been affected by glaciation.

▲ Great blocks of ice break away from the jagged blue peaks of these ice mountains to form icebergs off the coast of Patagonia, Argentina's most southerly region.

▲ Charred tree stumps surround a cattle enclosure on the island of Tierra del Fuego in southern Argentina. Forest clearance to provide grazing land for cattle is of major environmental concern.

**The Atacama Desert** (Desierto de Atacama) in Chile is one of the driest places on Earth where some areas have never recorded any rain. It contains a number of salt lakes.

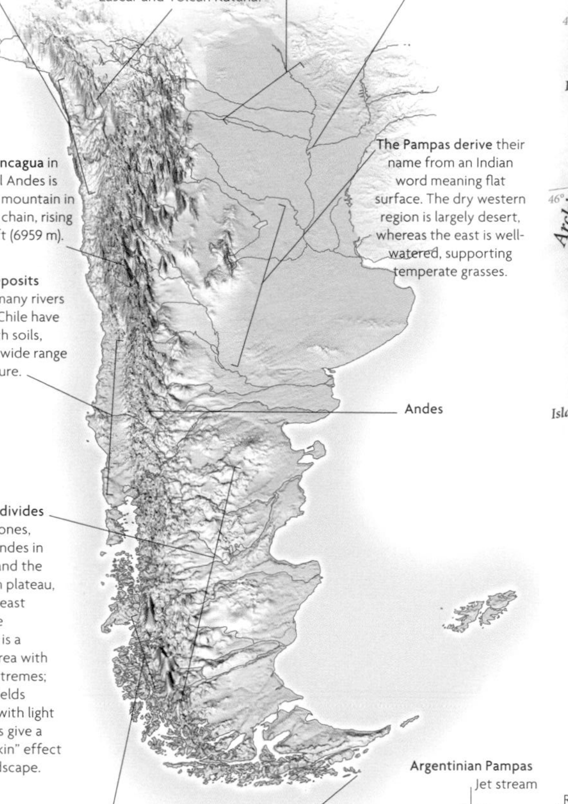

**The Gran Chaco** combines poor drainage, extremely hot temperatures and thorn-infested scrub to make it one of South America's most inhospitable regions.

**Landlocked Paraguay** relies on its river system for access to the sea and to produce hydroelectric power. The most important river system is the Paraguay–Paraná which provides links into neighboring countries including Brazil, Uruguay, and Argentina.

**Most of the highest** mountains in Chile's northern Andes are volcanoes like Volcán Lascar and Volcán Rutana.

**Alluvial deposits** from the many rivers in central Chile have created rich soils, ideal for a wide range of agriculture.

**Cerro Aconcagua** in the central Andes is the tallest mountain in the whole chain, rising to 22,834 ft (6959 m).

**Patagonia divides** into two zones, with the Andes in the west, and the lower main plateau, extending east toward the Atlantic. It is a desolate area with climatic extremes; dark lava fields scattered with light bunchgrass give a "leopard skin" effect to the landscape.

**The Patagonian ice sheet** is the world's third largest ice field, covering 6560 sq miles (17,000 sq km). Patagonia also contains many typical features from past glaciations. These include glacial lakes, U-shaped valleys, fjords, and deep-cut channels.

**Cape Horn** is the most southerly point of South America. The severity of the "Roaring Forties" winds makes the Horn one of the world's most treacherous shipping regions.

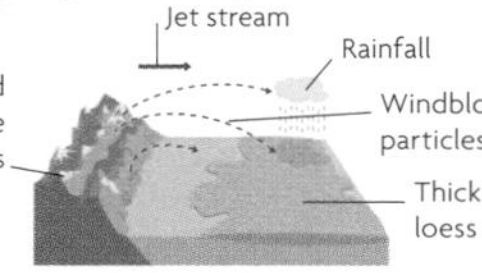

**The Pampas** derive their name from an Indian word meaning flat surface. The dry western region is largely desert, whereas the east is well-watered, supporting temperate grasses.

Andes

Ice-capped Andes are source of loess

Argentinian Pampas

Jet stream

Rainfall

Windblown particles

Thick layer of loess sediments

▲ A thick, fertile layer of loess lies in the basin underlying the Argentinian Pampas. It has been laid down following successive periods of glaciation. The minute loess particles are transported as dust and deposited by a downward air motion, or following rainfall.

## Using the land & sea

The rich plains of the Pampas support massive herds of cattle, producing meat, milk, and hides essential to the domestic and export markets of both Argentina and Paraguay. Wheat and fruit are Argentina's other major agricultural products. A wide range of soft fruits, citrus fruits, and more specialized crops such as walnuts, and grapes for wine and the table, are grown in Chile's fertile Central Valley, while the landscape to the south is dominated by forestry, mainly growing commercial radiata pine. Paraguay is self-sufficient in wheat and other staples. Cotton, coffee, tobacco, and oil sources such as soybeans, are the major export crops.

### The urban/rural population divide

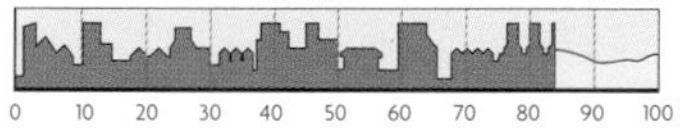

urban 84%        rural 16%

Population density

40 people per sq mile
(15 people per sq km)

Total land area

1,498,757 sq miles
(3,882,790 sq km)

### Land use and agricultural distribution

- capital cities
- major towns

- cattle
- sheep
- cereals
- fruit
- grapes
- timber
- fishing

- pasture
- cropland
- forest
- barren land
- mountain region
- desert

Scale 1:9,750,000

projection: Lambert Azimuthal Equal Area

# The Atlantic Ocean

The Atlantic is the youngest of the world's oceans, formed about 180 million years ago when the landmasses of the eastern and western hemispheres separated. Its underwater topography is dominated by the Mid-Atlantic Ridge, a huge mountain system running north to south along the center of the ocean. Although most of the ridge's peaks lie below the sea, some emerge as volcanic islands, like Iceland and the Azores. The Atlantic contains a wealth of resources, including substantial oil and gas reserves and rich fishing grounds. Until the 1950s, the north Atlantic was the world's busiest shipping route; cheaper air transportation and alternative routes have shifted patterns of world trade.

## Resources

Development of the oil and gas reserves in the Atlantic began in the 1940s around the Gulf of Mexico. Since then other areas have been exploited, including the North Sea, the west coast of Africa and the area east of Newfoundland and Nova Scotia. There is also extensive mining of sand, gravel, and shell deposits by the US and UK. For centuries, the north Atlantic's fishing grounds have been utilized more heavily than other oceans, leading to a serious decline in many fish stocks.

Resources (including wildlife)
- fish
- whales
- aggregates
- oil & gas
- major towns
- major ports

▲ Surtsey near Iceland, lies on the Mid-Atlantic Ridge. The island was formed in 1963 following a volcanic eruption caused by sea-floor spreading.

▲ On January 5 1993, the oil tanker Braer ran aground in the Shetland Islands, spilling 83,660 tons (85,000 tonnes) of light crude oil into the ocean, devastating the local marine ecosystem.

▲ Fishing in the seas around northwestern Europe dates back over 1500 years. The high nutrient content of the seas makes them ideal breeding grounds for many species of fish.

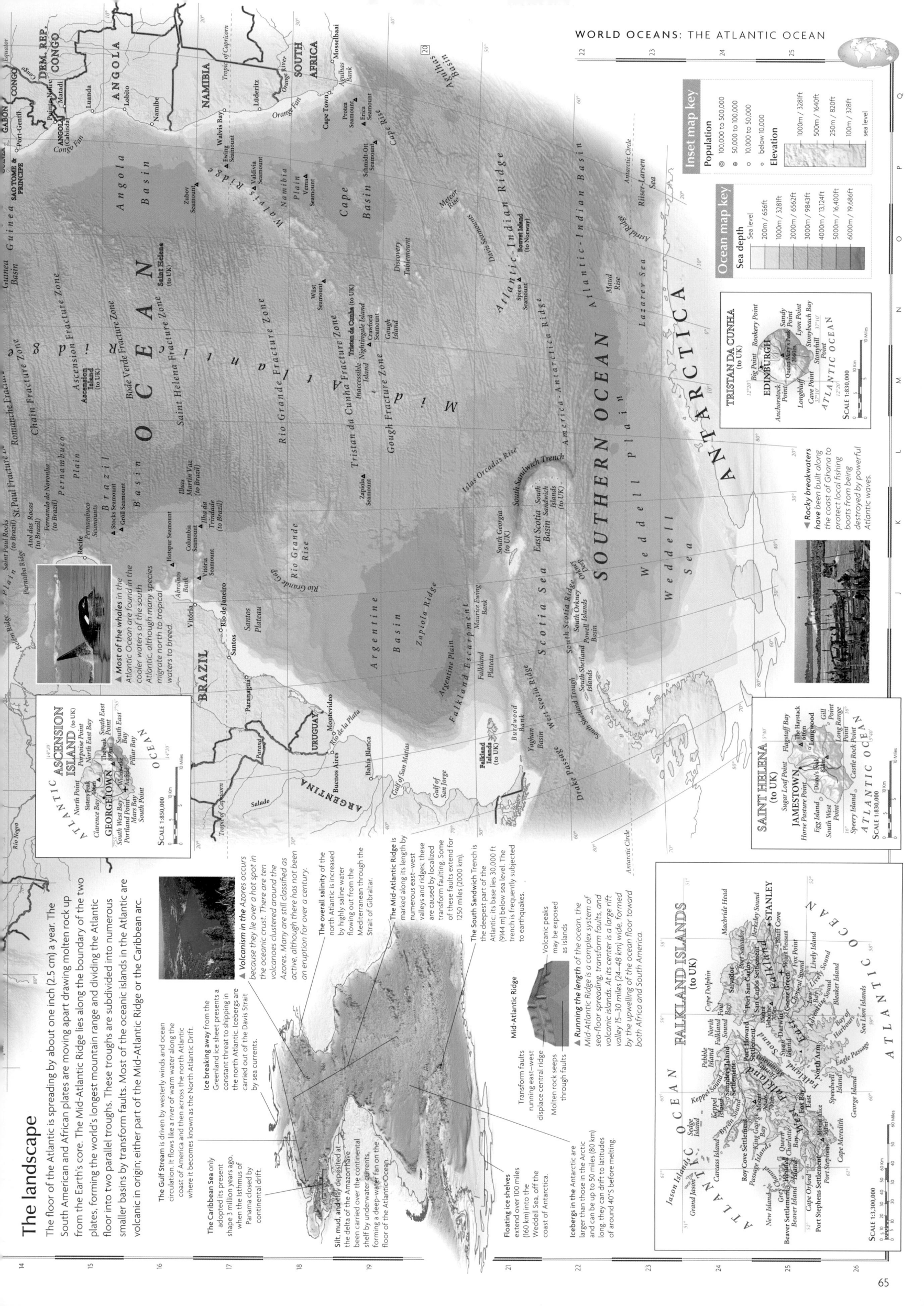

# The landscape

The floor of the Atlantic is spreading by about one inch (2.5 cm) a year. The South American and African plates are moving apart drawing molten rock up from the Earth's core. The Mid-Atlantic Ridge lies along the boundary of the two plates, forming the world's longest mountain range and dividing the Atlantic floor into two parallel troughs. These troughs are subdivided into numerous smaller basins by transform faults. Most of the oceanic islands in the Atlantic are volcanic in origin; either part of the Mid-Atlantic Ridge or the Caribbean arc.

**The Gulf Stream** is driven by westerly winds and ocean circulation. It flows like a river of warm water along the coast of America and then across the north Atlantic where it becomes known as the North Atlantic Drift.

**The Caribbean Sea** only adopted its present shape 3 million years ago, when the Isthmus of Panama closed by continental drift.

**Ice breaking away** from the Greenland ice sheet presents a constant threat to shipping in the north Atlantic. Icebergs are carried out of the Davis Strait by sea currents.

**Silt, mud, and clay** deposited at the delta of the Amazon have been carried over the continental shelf by underwater currents, forming a deep-water fan on the floor of the Atlantic Ocean.

**Floating ice shelves** extend over 100 miles (160 km) in the Weddell Sea, off the coast of Antarctica.

**Icebergs** in the Antarctic are larger than those in the Arctic and can be up to 50 miles (80 km) long, they can drift to latitudes of around 40°S before melting.

▲ *Volcanism in the Azores occurs because they lie over a hot spot in the oceanic crust. There are ten volcanoes clustered around the Azores. Many are still classified as active, although there has not been an eruption for over a century.*

**The overall salinity** of the north Atlantic is increased by highly saline water flowing out from the Mediterranean through the Strait of Gibraltar.

**The Mid-Atlantic Ridge** is marked along its length by numerous east–west valleys and ridges; these are caused by localized transform faulting. Some of these faults extend for 1250 miles (2000 km).

**The South Sandwich Trench** is the deepest part of the Atlantic; its base lies 30,000 ft (9144 m) below sea level. The trench is frequently subjected to earthquakes.

▲ *Running the length of the ocean, the Mid-Atlantic Ridge is a complex system of sea-floor spreading, transform faults, and volcanic islands. At its center is a large rift valley 15–30 miles (24–48 km) wide, formed by the upwelling of the ocean floor toward both Africa and South America.*

Volcanic peaks may be exposed as islands

**Mid-Atlantic Ridge**

Transform faults running east–west displace central ridge

Molten rock seeps through faults

▲ *Most of the whales in the Atlantic Ocean are found in the cooler waters of the south Atlantic, although many species migrate north to tropical waters to breed.*

▲ *Rocky breakwaters have been built along the coast of Ghana to protect local fishing boats from being destroyed by powerful Atlantic waves.*

## Inset map key

**Population**
- ◉ 100,000 to 500,000
- ⊕ 50,000 to 100,000
- ○ 10,000 to 50,000
- ○ below 10,000

**Elevation**
- 1000m / 3281ft
- 500m / 1640ft
- 250m / 820ft
- 100m / 328ft
- sea level

## Ocean map key

**Sea depth**
- 200m / 656ft
- 1000m / 3281ft
- 2000m / 6562ft
- 3000m / 9843ft
- 4000m / 13,124ft
- 5000m / 16,400ft
- 6000m / 19,686ft

### TRISTAN DA CUNHA (to UK)
Big Point, Rookery Point, Sandy Point, Lyon Point, Stonybeach Bay, The Peak, Queen Mary's Peak, Stonyhill, EDINBURGH, Anchorstock Point, Cave Point, Longbluff, South West Point
**ATLANTIC OCEAN**
SCALE 1:830,000

### SAINT HELENA (to UK)
Sugar Loaf Point, Flagstaff Bay, The Haystack, Horse Pasture Point, Diana's Peak, Longwood, Gill Point, Egg Island, Half Tree Hollow, JAMESTOWN, Long Range Point, South West Point, Castle Rock Point, Speery Island
**ATLANTIC OCEAN**
SCALE 1:830,000

### ASCENSION ISLAND (to UK)
North Point, Porpoise Point, South East Head, Sisters Peak, South East Bay, Clarence Bay, GEORGETOWN, Cat Hill, South West Bay, Portland Point, Pillar Bay, Mars Bay, South Point
**ATLANTIC OCEAN**
SCALE 1:850,000

### FALKLAND ISLANDS (to UK)
SCALE 1:3,300,000

*(Labels include: Jason Islands, Grand Jason, Steeple Jason, Carcass Island, Keppel Sound, Pebble Island, Saunders Island, Roy Cove Settlement, Passage Islands, New Island, Beaver Settlement, Weddell Island, Port Stephens Settlement, George Island, Cape Orford, Cape Meredith, Byron Sound, Port Howard, Falkland Sound, San Carlos Settlement, Goose Green, Darwin, Lafonia, Speedwell Island, Sea Lion Islands, Macbride Head, Berkeley Sound, STANLEY, Bluff Cove, Fitzroy, Port Salvador, Port San Carlos, Mount Usborne, Salvador, Lively Island, Bleaker Island, East Falkland, West Falkland, Bay of Harbours, Eagle Passage)*

ATLANTIC OCEAN

65

# Africa

The world's second largest continent, Africa covers an area of 11,712,434 sq miles (30,355,000 sq km). It has 54 separate countries, including Madagascar, Comoros, Mauritius, and the Seychelles in the Indian Ocean – the highest number of any continent.

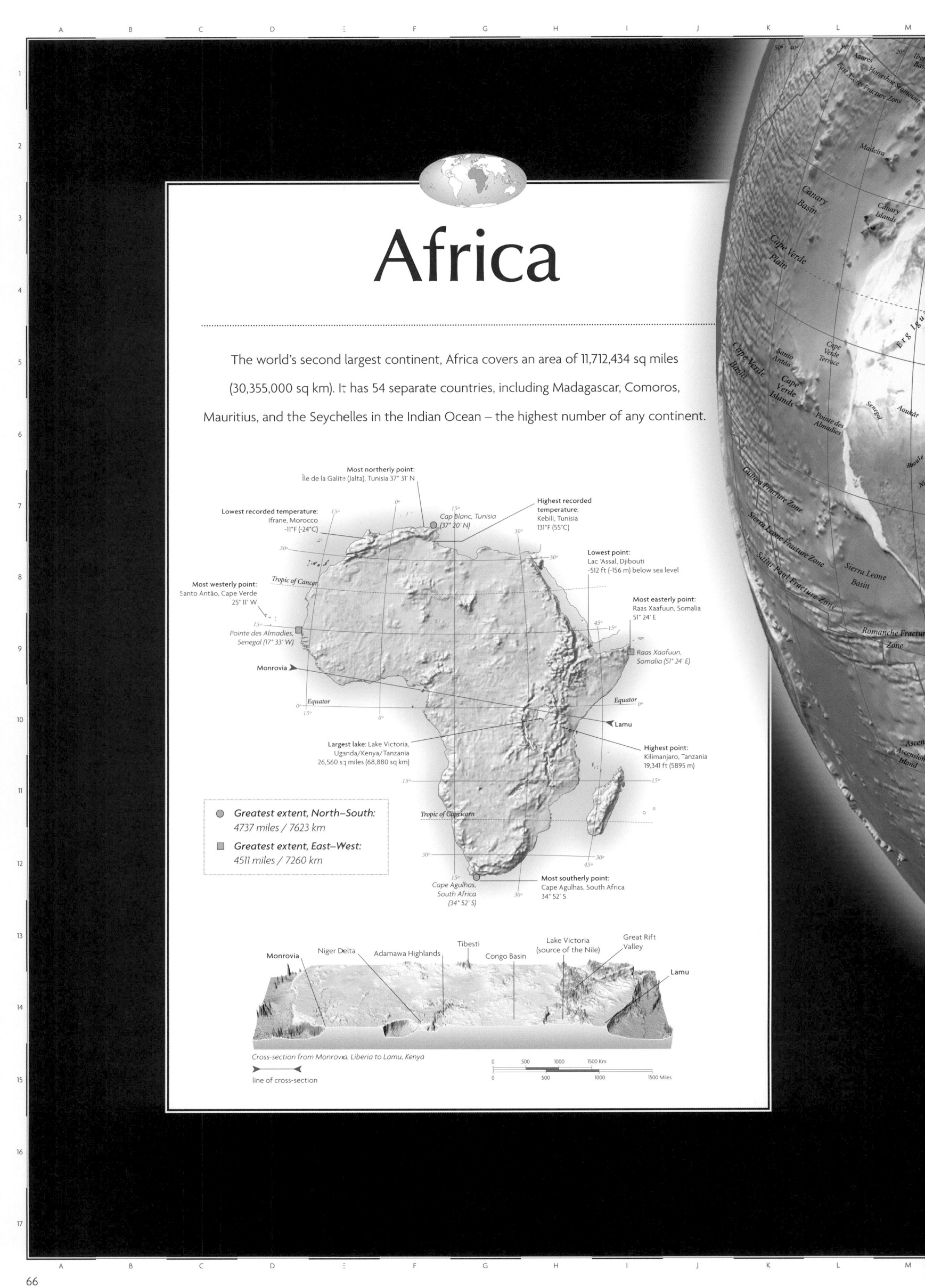

Most northerly point:
Île de la Galite (Jalta), Tunisia 37° 31' N

Lowest recorded temperature:
Ifrane, Morocco
-11°F (-24°C)

Highest recorded temperature:
Kebili, Tunisia
131°F (55°C)

Cap Blanc, Tunisia
(37° 20' N)

Lowest point:
Lac 'Assal, Djibouti
-512 ft (-156 m) below sea level

Most westerly point:
Santo Antão, Cape Verde
25° 11' W

Pointe des Almadies,
Senegal (17° 33' W)

Most easterly point:
Raas Xaafuun, Somalia
51° 24' E

Raas Xaafuun,
Somalia (51° 24' E)

Monrovia

Tropic of Cancer

Equator

Equator

Lamu

Largest lake: Lake Victoria,
Uganda/Kenya/Tanzania
26,560 sq miles (68,880 sq km)

Highest point:
Kilimanjaro, Tanzania
19,341 ft (5895 m)

Tropic of Capricorn

● **Greatest extent, North–South:**
4737 miles / 7623 km

■ **Greatest extent, East–West:**
4511 miles / 7260 km

Cape Agulhas,
South Africa
(34° 52' S)

Most southerly point:
Cape Agulhas, South Africa
34° 52' S

Cross-section from Monrovia, Liberia to Lamu, Kenya

Monrovia

Niger Delta

Adamawa Highlands

Tibesti

Congo Basin

Lake Victoria
(source of the Nile)

Great Rift
Valley

Lamu

line of cross-section

| 0 | 500 | 1000 | 1500 Km |
| 0 | 500 | 1000 | 1500 Miles |

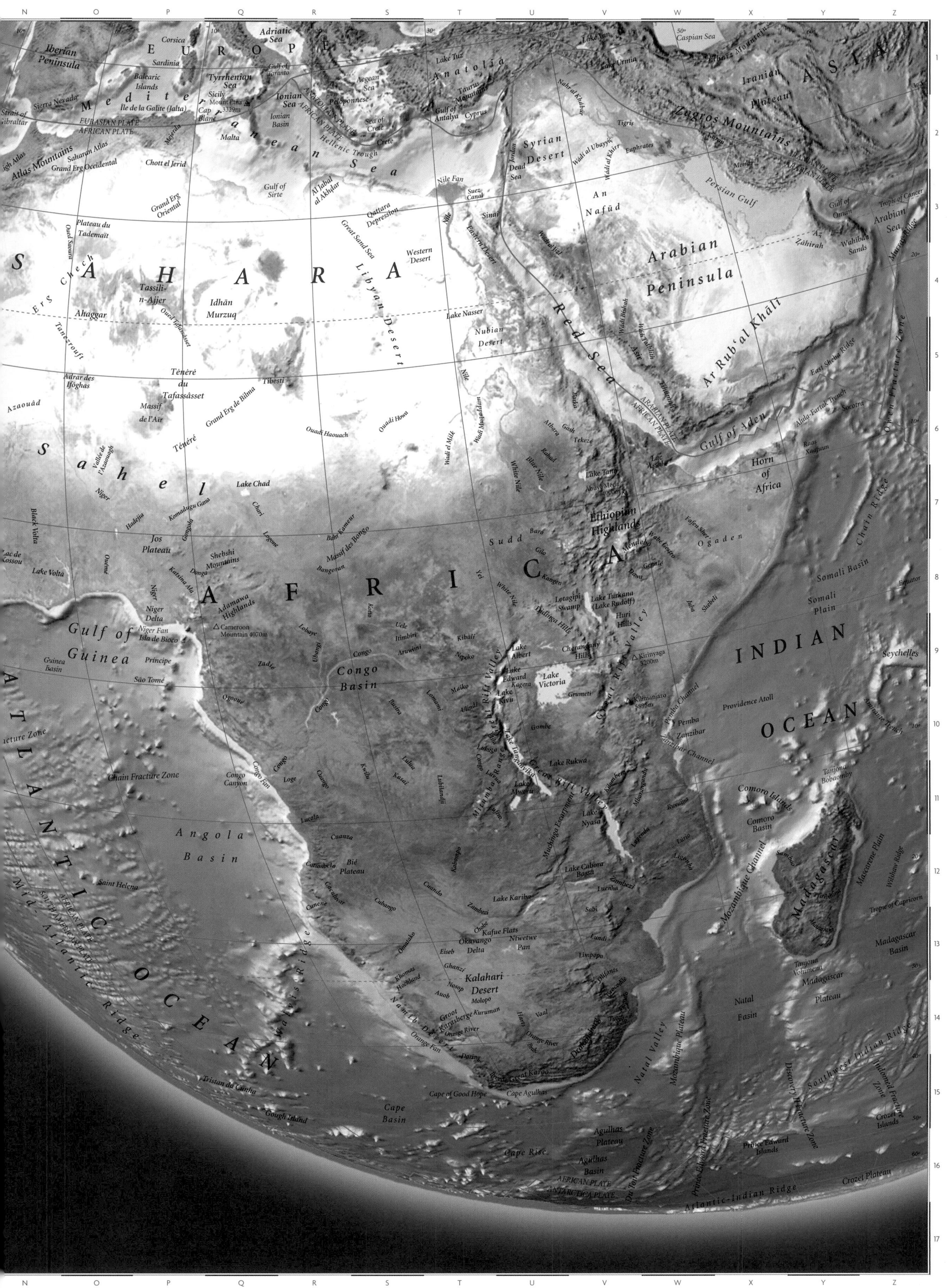

EUROPE

ASIA

**Iberian Peninsula**

Corsica
Sardinia
Balearic Islands

Adriatic Sea

Lake Van
Caspian Sea

Elburz Mountains

Sierra Nevada

Tyrrhenian Sea

Gulf of Taranto

Lake Tuz

Anatolia

Lake Urmia

Iranian Plateau

Mediterranean

Sicily
Mount Etna 3329m
Île de la Galite (Jalta)
Cap Blanc

Aegean Sea

Peloponnese

Taurus Mountains

Zagros Mountains

Strait of Gibraltar

EURASIAN PLATE
AFRICAN PLATE

Melilla

Ionian Sea

Ionian Basin

Sea of Crete

Gulf of Antalya

Cyprus

Nahr al Khābūr

Tigris

Mesopotamia

High Atlas
Atlas Mountains
Saharan Atlas
Grand Erg Occidental

Malta

Hellenic Trough

Syrian Desert

Wādī al Ubayyiḍ

Euphrates

Kārūn

Persian Gulf

Mendi

Chott el Jerid

Gulf of Sirte

Al Jabal al Akhḍar

Nile Fan

Dead Sea

Jordan

Wādī Khuḍr

Gulf of Oman

Plateau du Tademaït

Grand Erg Oriental

Qattara Depression

Suez Canal

Sinai

An Nafūd

Az Zāhirah

Arabian Sea

Oued Saoura

Western Desert

Eastern Desert

Wādī al Jiḍ

Wahībah Sands

Maxeira Ridge

**S A H A R A**

Chech

Tassili-n-Ajjer
Ahaggar

Idhān Murzuq

Libyan Desert

Lake Nasser

Nubian Desert

Red Sea

Arabian Peninsula

Ar Rub' al Khālī

Ers

Tanezrouft

Têněrě du Tafassâsset

Tibesti

Nile

ARABIAN PLATE
AFRICAN PLATE

East Sheba Ridge

Owen Fracture Zone

Azouâd

Adrar des Ifôghas

Massif de l'Air

Grand Erg de Bilma

Ouadi Haouach

Ouadi Howa

Tokar

Atbara

Gash

Socotra

Alula-Fartak Trench

Ras Xaafuun

**S a h e l**

Niger

Black Volta

Tanezrouft

Ténéré

Wadi el Milk

Lake Tana
Abay Wenz 6960m

Rahad

Tekezé

Gulf of Aden

Lac Assal

Horn of Africa

Lac de Kossou

Lake Volta

Jos Plateau

Komadugu Gana

Lake Chad

Chari

Bahr Keïta

White Nile

Blue Nile

Sudd

Bard

Gilo

Ethiopian Highlands

Gabal Elba

Mendebo

Gebele

Ogaden

Somali Basin

Oueme

Donga
Katsina Ala

Massif des Bongo

Bangoran

Yei

Kangen

Genale

Wabe Sheb

Shebeli

Somali Plain

Niger

Shebshi Mountains

**A F R I C A**

Komo

White Nile

Lotagipi Swamp

Gilo

Juba

Equator

Niger Delta
Gulf of Guinea

Adamawa Highlands

△ Cameroon Mountain 4070m

Lobaye

Ucle

Itimbiri

Aruwimi

Dadinga Hills

Lake Turkana (Lake Rudolf)

Huri Hills

Chain River

Isla de Bioco

Zadie

Uhangui

Kibali

Nzoko

Maiko

Charangani Hills

Kirinyaga 5200m

INDIAN

Seychelles

Guinea Basin

Príncipe

São Tomé

Ogooué

Congo

Congo Basin

Lomami

Ulindi

Lake Albert
Lake Edward
Lake Kivu

Lake Kagera

Lake Victoria

Grumeti

Kilimanjaro 5895m

OCEAN

Mascarene Plain

ATLANTIC

Fracture Zone

Congo

Congo

Congo Canyon

Loge

Kwilu

Kasai

Lukuga

Lake Tanganyika

Gombe

Pemba

Zanzibar

Pemba Channel

Zanzibar Channel

Providence Atoll

Comoro Basin

Mascarene Plateau

Chain Fracture Zone

Congo Fan

Lucala

Kwango

Lualaba

Luvua

Lake Mweru

Ruvuma

Tanjona Bobaomby

**Angola Basin**

Saint Helena

Cuanza

Bié Plateau

Kalahango

Kalungwishi

Lake Rukwa

Lake Nyasa

Lugenda

Usno

Lisangu

Comoro Islands

**Madagascar**

Cunene

Cubango

Zambezi

Chobe

Lake Cabora Bassa

Luenha

Sabi

Lundi

Zambezi

Lake Kariba

Tropic of Capricorn

Madagascar Basin

Okavango Delta

Kafue Flats

Ntwetwe Pan

Limpopo

Madagascar Plateau

Omambo

Eiseb

Ghanzi

**Kalahari Desert**

Molopo

Tsoilcho

Tanjona Vohimena

Madagascar Plateau

Khomas Hochland

Nosop

Auob

Groot

Kangsberge Kuruman

Vaal

Natal Basin

Namib Desert

Orange River

Haris

Orange River

Orange Fan

Darling

Great Karoo

Natal Valley

Mozambique Plateau

Drakensberg

Southwest Indian Ridge

**A T L A N T I C  O C E A N**

Walvis Ridge

Mid-Atlantic Ridge

AFRICAN PLATE

Tristan da Cunha

Gough Island

Cape of Good Hope

Cape Agulhas

Cape Basin

Cape Rise

Agulhas Plateau

Agulhas Basin

Prince Edward Islands

Del Cano Fracture Zone

Crozet Islands

AFRICAN PLATE
ANTARCTICA PLATE

Atlantic-Indian Ridge

Crozet Plateau

# Physical Africa

The structure of Africa was dramatically influenced by the break up of the supercontinent Gondwanaland about 160 million years ago and, more recently, rifting and hot spot activity. Today, much of Africa is remote from active plate boundaries and comprises a series of extensive plateaus and deep basins, which influence the drainage patterns of major rivers. The relief rises to the east, where volcanic uplands and vast lakes mark the Great Rift Valley. In the far north and south sedimentary rocks have been folded to form the Atlas Mountains and the Great Karoo.

## East Africa

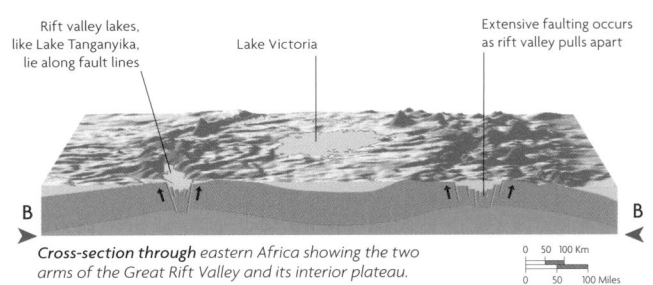

The Great Rift Valley is the most striking feature of this region, running for 4475 miles (7200 km) from Lake Nyasa to the Red Sea. North of Lake Nyasa it splits into two arms and encloses an interior plateau which contains Lake Victoria. A number of elongated lakes and volcanoes lie along the fault lines. To the west lies the Congo Basin, a vast, shallow depression, which rises to form an almost circular rim of highlands.

Rift valley lakes, like Lake Tanganyika, lie along fault lines

Lake Victoria

Extensive faulting occurs as rift valley pulls apart

B ◄                                                      B

*Cross-section through* eastern Africa showing the two arms of the Great Rift Valley and its interior plateau.

0    50    100 Km
0    50    100 Miles

## Northern Africa

Northern Africa comprises a system of basins and plateaus. The Tibesti and Ahaggar are volcanic uplands, whose uplift has been matched by subsidence within large surrounding basins. Many of the basins have been infilled with sand and gravel, creating the vast Saharan lands. The Atlas Mountains in the north were formed by convergence of the African and Eurasian plates.

The Earth's crust has been warped to form the Taoudenni Basin

Volcanic Ahaggar mountains, formed by rising magma from a hot spot

Lake Chad lies in a sand-filled basin

A ◄                                                      A ◄

*Section across northern* Africa showing infilled basins and uplifted plateaus.

0    250    500 Km
0    250    500 Miles

### Scale 1:40,000,000

Km
0    200    400    600    800
Miles
0    200    400    600    800

*projection: Lambert Azimuthal Equal Area*

### Map key

**Elevation**

5000m / 16,405ft
4000m / 13,124ft
3000m / 9843ft
2000m / 6562ft
1000m / 3281ft
500m / 1640ft
250m / 820ft
100m / 328ft
sea level
below sea level

**Plate margins**
(for explanation see page xiv)

constructive
destructive
conservative
uncertain
line of cross-section

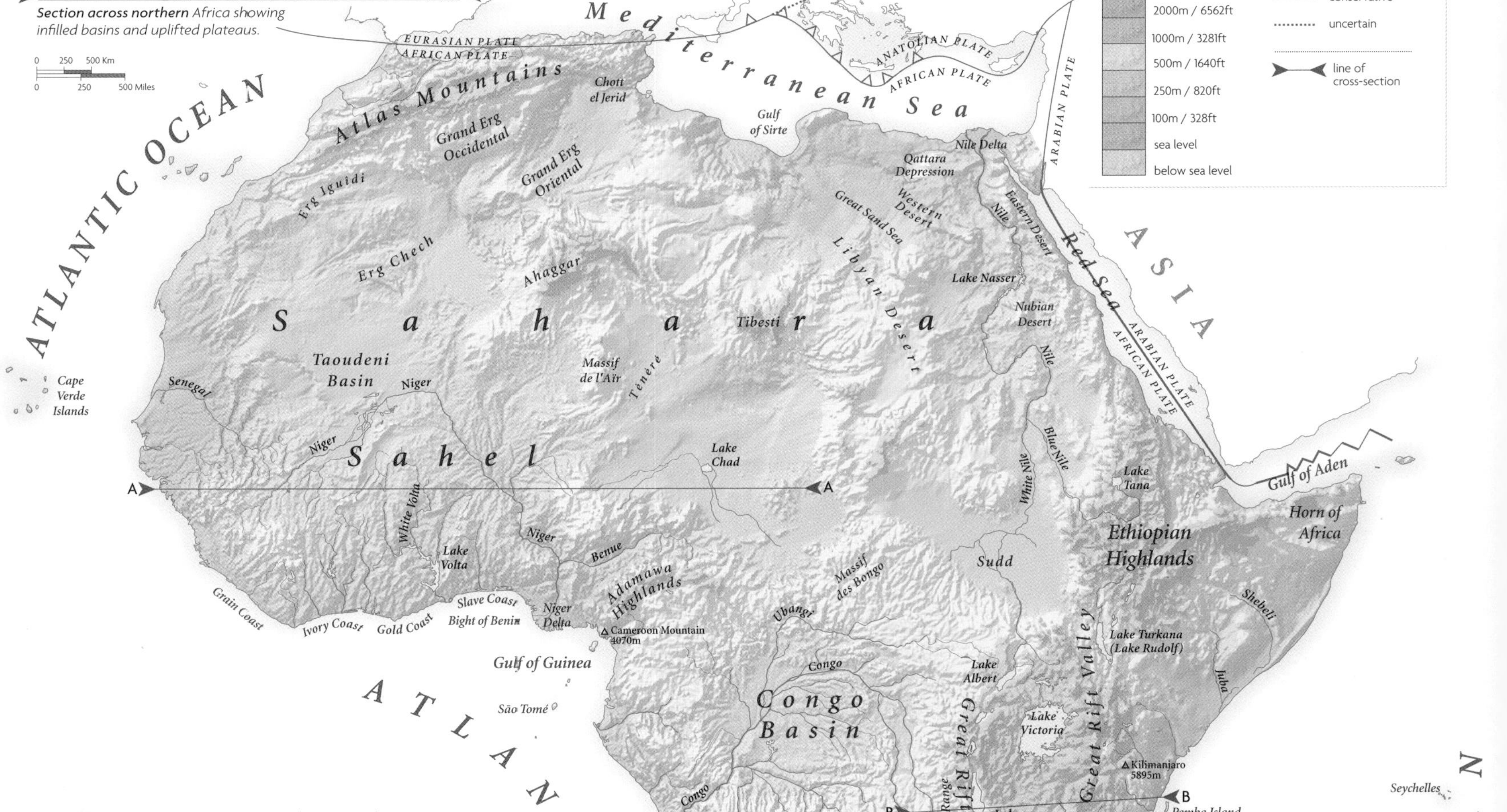

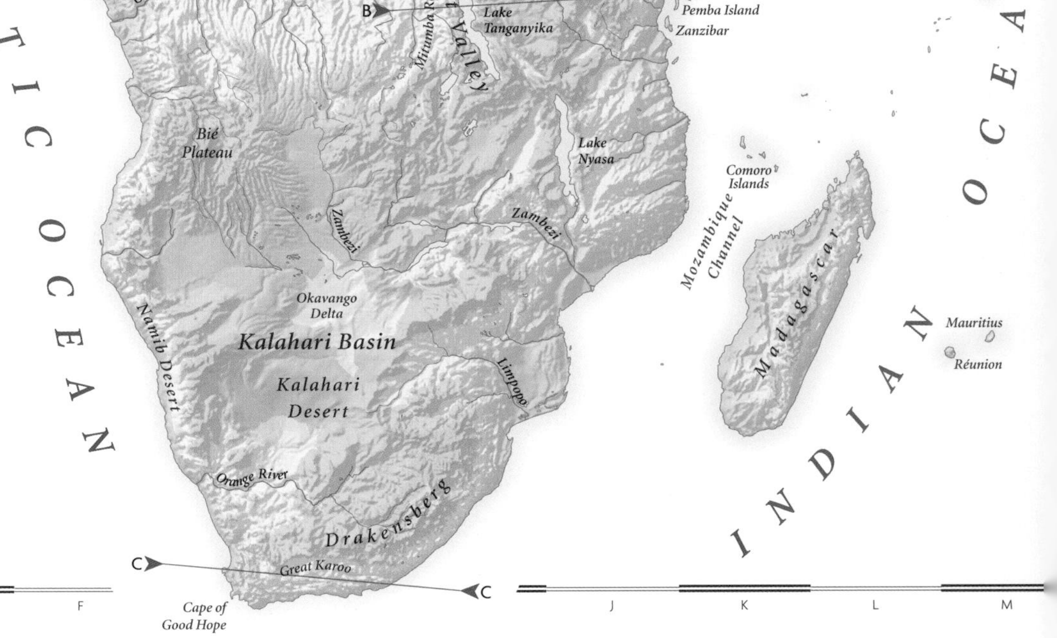

## Southern Africa

The Great Escarpment marks the southern boundary of Africa's basement rock and includes the Drakensberg range. It was uplifted when Gondwanaland fragmented about 160 million years ago and it has gradually been eroded back from the coast. To the north, the relief drops steadily, forming the Kalahari Basin. In the far south are the fold mountains of the Great Karoo.

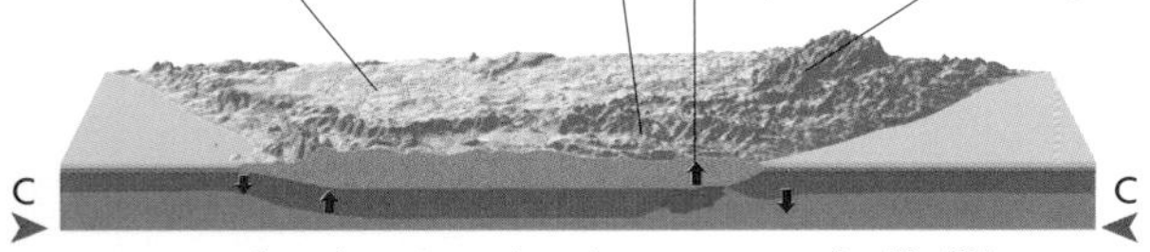

Kalahari Basin, covered with the sandy plains of the Kalahari Desert

Boundary of the Great Escarpment

Uplift of the basement rock created a raised plateau

Drakensberg

C ◄                                                      C ◄

*Cross-section through* southern Africa showing the boundary of the Great Escarpment.

0    100    200 Km
0    100    200 Miles

### Map labels

ATLANTIC OCEAN

Mediterranean Sea

EURASIAN PLATE
AFRICAN PLATE
ANATOLIAN PLATE
AFRICAN PLATE
ARABIAN PLATE

ASIA

Atlas Mountains

Grand Erg Occidental
Grand Erg Oriental
Chott el Jerid
Gulf of Sirte
Nile Delta
Qattara Depression
Western Desert
Great Sand Sea
Libyan Desert
Lake Nasser
Nubian Desert

Erg Iguidi
Erg Chech
Ahaggar
Tibesti

S  a  h  a  r  a

Taoudeni Basin
Niger
Massif de l'Air
Ténéré

Red Sea
ARABIAN PLATE
AFRICAN PLATE

Cape Verde Islands

Senegal
Niger
Sahel
Lake Chad

Lake Tana
Blue Nile
White Nile
Gulf of Aden

Horn of Africa

White Volta
Niger
Benue
Lake Volta

Ethiopian Highlands

Shebeli

A                                                        A

Grain Coast
Ivory Coast
Gold Coast
Slave Coast
Bight of Benin
Niger Delta
Adamawa Highlands
△ Cameroon Mountain 4070m

Massif des Bongo
Ubangi
Sudd

Lake Turkana (Lake Rudolf)
Juba

Gulf of Guinea

São Tomé

ATLANTIC OCEAN

Congo
Congo Basin
Congo

Lake Albert
Lake Victoria

Great Rift Valley

△ Kilimanjaro 5895m

Seychelles

B                                                        B
Mitumba Range
Lake Tanganyika

Pemba Island
Zanzibar

Bié Plateau

Lake Nyasa

Comoro Islands

Madagascar

Zambezi
Zambezi

Mozambique Channel

Namib Desert

Okavango Delta

Kalahari Basin
Kalahari Desert

Limpopo

Mauritius
Réunion

Orange River

Drakensberg

INDIAN OCEAN

C                                                        C
Great Karoo

Cape of Good Hope

# Climate

The climates of Africa range from mediterranean to arid, dry savannah, and humid equatorial. In East Africa, where snow settles at the summit of volcanoes such as Kilimanjaro, climate is also modified by altitude. The winds of the Sahara export millions of tonnes of dust a year both northward and eastward.

▲ *Savannah grasslands run in a belt across Africa; limited rainfall inhibits tree growth.*

## Temperature

**Temperature**
- 32 to 50°F (0 to 10°C)
- 50 to 68°F (10 to 20°C)
- 68 to 86°F (20 to 30°C)
- above 86°F (30°C)

*Average January temperature*   *Average July temperature*

▲ *The hot, equatorial basin of the Congo river receives over 48 inches (1200 mm) of rainfall per year.*

## Rainfall

**Rainfall**
- 0–1 in (0–25 mm)
- 1–2 in (25–50 mm)
- 2–4 in (50–100 mm)
- 4–8 in (100–200 mm)
- 8–12 in (200–300 mm)
- 12–16 in (300–400 mm)
- 16–20 in (400–500 mm)
- more than 20 in (500 mm)

*Average January rainfall*   *Average July rainfall*

**Climate**
- arid
- humid equatorial
- mediterranean
- semi-arid
- tropical
- warm humid
- daily hours of sunshine, January
- daily hours of sunshine, July
- cold wind
- hot wind

# Shaping the continent

African landscapes are shaped by the intensity of climatic extremes and by tectonic action. High aridity, wind action, and infrequent but heavy rainstorms, lead to the migration of sand dunes and dramatic flash flooding across much of the north and west. In the wetter areas, high precipitation increases the rate of weathering. To the east, the rift system has created a volcanic and lake environment and allowed rivers to erode weaknesses left in the crustal structure by faults.

## Weathering

**6** Inselbergs (above), found extensively across West Africa, are exposed remnants of an extensive upland area. Erosion of the surrounding uplands leaves a resistant rock outcrop. Its spheroidal shape is the result of "onion-skin" weathering – the exfoliating of layers – due to repeated expansion and contraction.

*Weathering: Formation of an inselberg*

External stresses act on the surface of the inselberg
Exfoliated layers
Joints or cracks caused by expansion and contraction

## Ephemeral channels

**5** Wadis (above) drain much of northern Africa. These drybed courses are flooded only after infrequent, but intense, storms in the uplands cause water to surge along their channels.

Heavy rainfall runs off mountains
Water collects and floods the dry channel

*Ephemeral channels: Flash flooding of a wadi*

## Wind erosion

**4** Dunes like this in the Namib Desert (left) are wind-blown accumulations of sand, which slowly migrate. Wind action moves sand up the shallow back slope; when the sand reaches the crest of the dune it is deposited on the slip face.

Sand is gradually blown up the back slope
Deposition on the slip face
Build up of sand produces strata inside the dune

*Wind erosion: Migration of a dune*

## Groundwater

**1** Oases are found in desert areas such as the Sahara (left). Groundwater migrates through permeable rock strata, confined between two impermeable layers. Oases form either when the permeable rocks come near to the surface, or at a fault line, when water is able to seep up to the surface through the crushed rocks at the fault.

## The evolving landscape

Rainwater feeds the aquifer
Water migrates up through fault
Aquifer exposed near the surface
Groundwater trapped between impermeable strata

*Groundwater: Replenishment of an oasis*

## River systems

**2** The Zambezi river (above) drops 360 ft (110 m) over the Victoria Falls into a zigzag gorge. The river has eroded the gorge along lines of weakness in the bedrock, created by fault lines running in two directions.

Old site of Victoria Falls
River plunges over falls
Fault and joint lines running in two directions
Zigzag gorge of the Zambezi

*River systems: Retreating of the Victoria Falls*

**Landscape**
- sinking land
- stable land
- uplifting land
- escarpment
- ocean current
- rift
- active volcano
- inselberg
- oasis
- river
- wadi
- waterfall

## Coastal processes

**3** Houtbaai (above), in southern Africa, is constantly being modified by wave action. As waves approach the indented coastline, they reach the shallow water of the headland, slowing down and reducing in length. This causes them to bend or refract, concentrating their erosive force at the headlands.

Wave energy dispersed in the bay
Waves refracting
Force of waves concentrates on the headland
The sea bed is deeper opposite the bay than at the headland

*Coastal processes: Erosion of a bay*

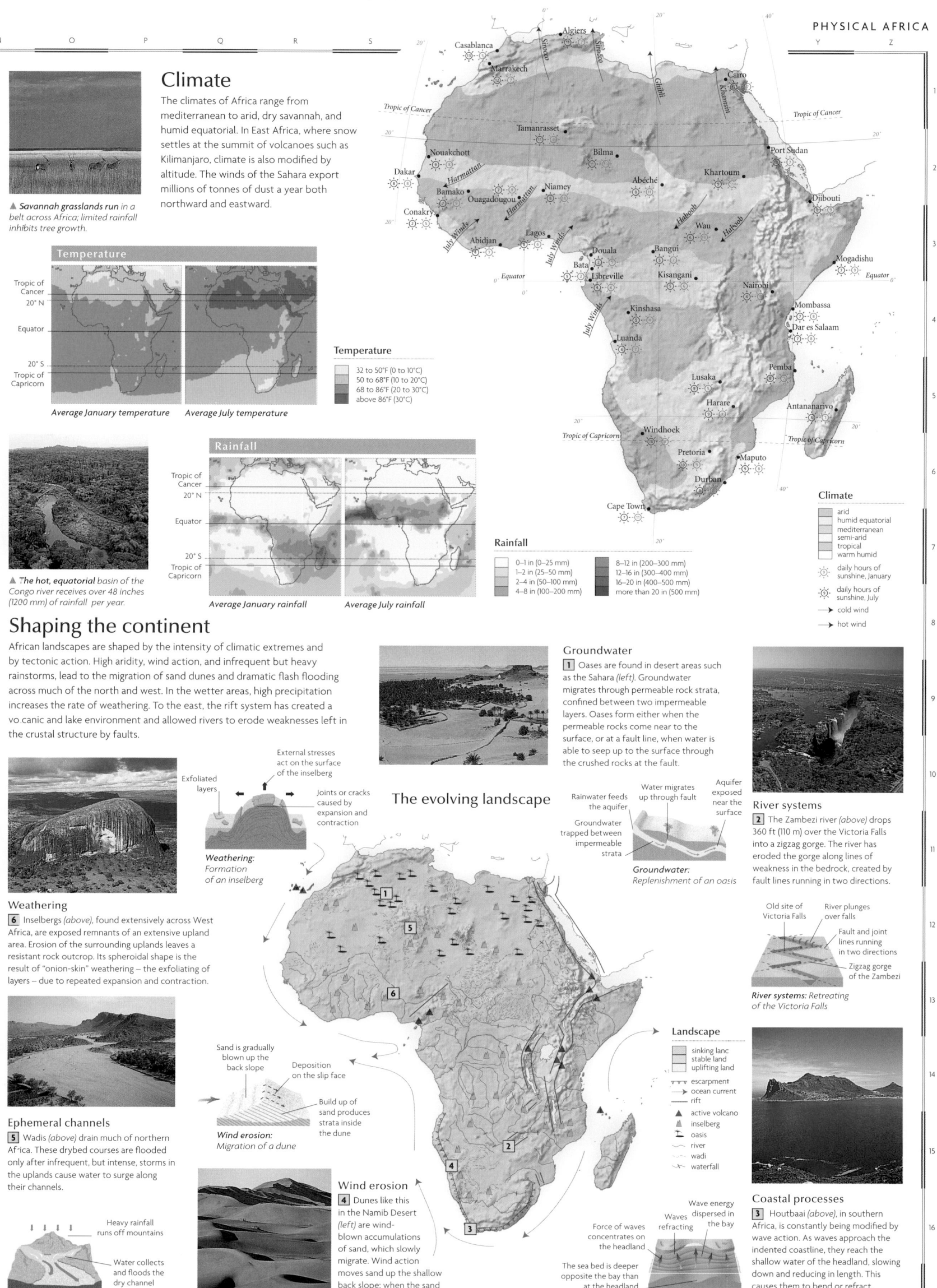

69

# Political Africa

The political map of modern Africa only emerged following the end of the Second World War. Over the next half-century, all of the countries formerly controlled by European powers gained independence from their colonial rulers – only Liberia and Ethiopia were never colonized. The postcolonial era has not been an easy period for many countries, but there have been moves toward multiparty democracy across much of the continent. In South Africa, democratic elections replaced the internationally-condemned apartheid system only in 1994. Other countries have still to find political stability; corruption in government, and ethnic tensions are serious problems. National infrastructures, based on the colonial transportation systems built to exploit Africa's resources, are often inappropriate for independent economic development.

## Languages

Three major world languages act as *lingua francas* across the African continent: Arabic in North Africa; English in southern and eastern Africa and Nigeria; and French in Central and West Africa, and in Madagascar. A huge number of African languages are spoken as well – over 2000 have been recorded, with more than 400 in Nigeria alone – reflecting the continuing importance of traditional cultures and values. In the north of the continent, the extensive use of Arabic reflects Middle Eastern influences while Bantu languages are widely-spoken across much of southern Africa.

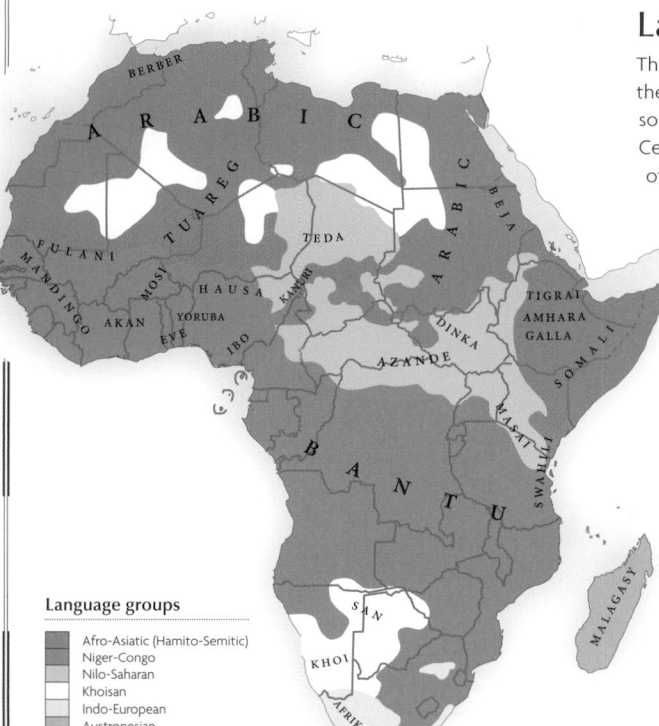

### Language groups
- Afro-Asiatic (Hamito-Semitic)
- Niger-Congo
- Nilo-Saharan
- Khoisan
- Indo-European
- Austronesian

### Official African languages

- French
- English
- Arabic
- Portuguese
- Swahili
- Amharic
- Spanish
- French/English
- French/Arabic
- French/Malagasy
- English/Swahili
- Arabic/Somali

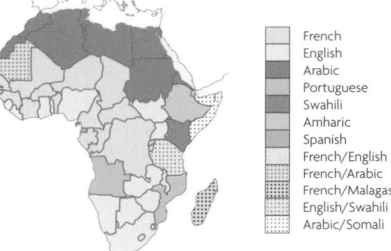

▲ *Islamic influences are evident throughout North Africa. The Great Mosque at Kairouan, Tunisia, is Africa's holiest Islamic place.*

▲ *In northeastern Nigeria, people speak Kanuri – a dialect of the Nilo-Saharan language group.*

## Transportation

African railroads were built to aid the exploitation of natural resources, and most offer passage only from the interior to the coastal cities, leaving large parts of the continent untouched – five landlocked countries have no railroads at all. The Congo, Nile, and Niger river networks offer limited access to land within the continental interior, but have a number of waterfalls and cataracts which prevent navigation from the sea. Many roads were developed in the 1960s and 1970s, but economic difficulties are making the maintenance and expansion of the networks difficult.

▶ *South Africa has the largest concentration of railroads in Africa. Over 20,000 miles (32,000 km) of routes have been built since 1870.*

▲ *Traditional means of transportation, such as the camel, are still widely used across the less accessible parts of Africa.*

◀ *The Congo river, though not suitable for river transportation along its entire length, forms a vital link for people and goods in its navigable inland reaches.*

### Transportation
- major roads and highways
- major railroads
- major canal
- international borders
- • transport intersections
- ⊕ international airports
- ⊕ major ports

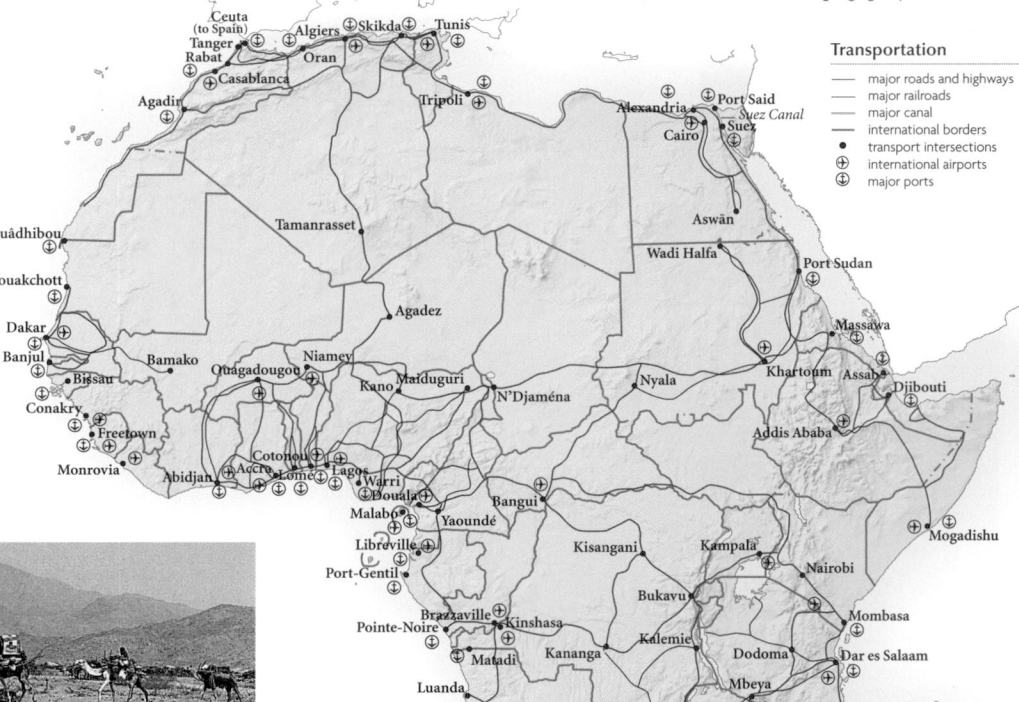

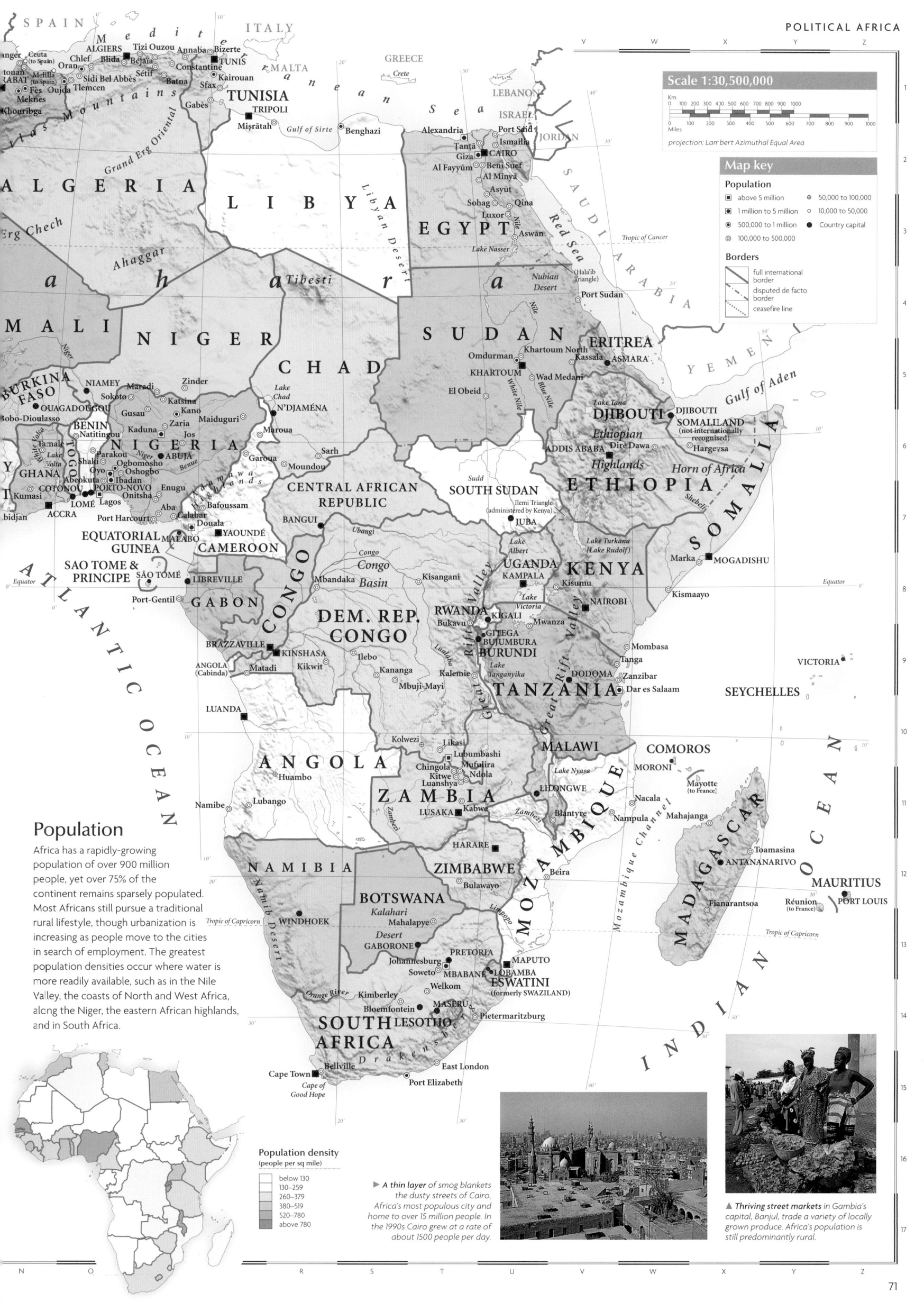

Map key

Population
- ■ above 5 million
- ▣ 1 million to 5 million
- ◉ 500,000 to 1 million
- ⊙ 100,000 to 500,000
- ⊕ 50,000 to 100,000
- ○ 10,000 to 50,000
- ● Country capital

Borders
- full international border
- disputed de facto border
- ceasefire line

## Population

Africa has a rapidly-growing population of over 900 million people, yet over 75% of the continent remains sparsely populated. Most Africans still pursue a traditional rural lifestyle, though urbanization is increasing as people move to the cities in search of employment. The greatest population densities occur where water is more readily available, such as in the Nile Valley, the coasts of North and West Africa, along the Niger, the eastern African highlands, and in South Africa.

Population density
(people per sq mile)
- below 130
- 130–259
- 260–379
- 380–519
- 520–780
- above 780

▶ A thin layer of smog blankets the dusty streets of Cairo, Africa's most populous city and home to over 15 million people. In the 1990s Cairo grew at a rate of about 1500 people per day.

▲ Thriving street markets in Gambia's capital, Banjul, trade a variety of locally grown produce. Africa's population is still predominantly rural.

# African resources

The economies of most African countries are dominated by subsistence and cash crop agriculture, with limited industrialization. Manufacturing is largely confined to South Africa. Many countries depend on a single resource, such as copper or gold, or a cash crop, such as coffee, for export income, which can leave them vulnerable to fluctuations in world commodity prices. In order to diversify their economies and develop a wider industrial base, investment from overseas is being actively sought by many African governments.

## Industry

Many African industries concentrate on the extraction and processing of raw materials. These include the oil industry, food processing, mining, and textile production. South Africa accounts for over half of the continent's industrial output with much of the remainder coming from the countries along the northern coast. Over 60% of Africa's workforce is employed in agriculture.

◀ The unspoiled natural splendor of wildlife reserves, like the Serengeti National Park in Tanzania, attract tourists to Africa from around the globe. The tourist industry in Kenya and Tanzania is particularly well developed, where it accounts for almost 10% of GNI.

## Standard of living

Since the 1960s most countries in Africa have seen significant improvements in life expectancy, healthcare, and education. However, 28 of the 30 most deprived countries in the world are African, and the continent as a whole lies well behind the rest of the world in terms of meeting many basic human needs.

**Standard of living**
(UN human development index)

- high
- low

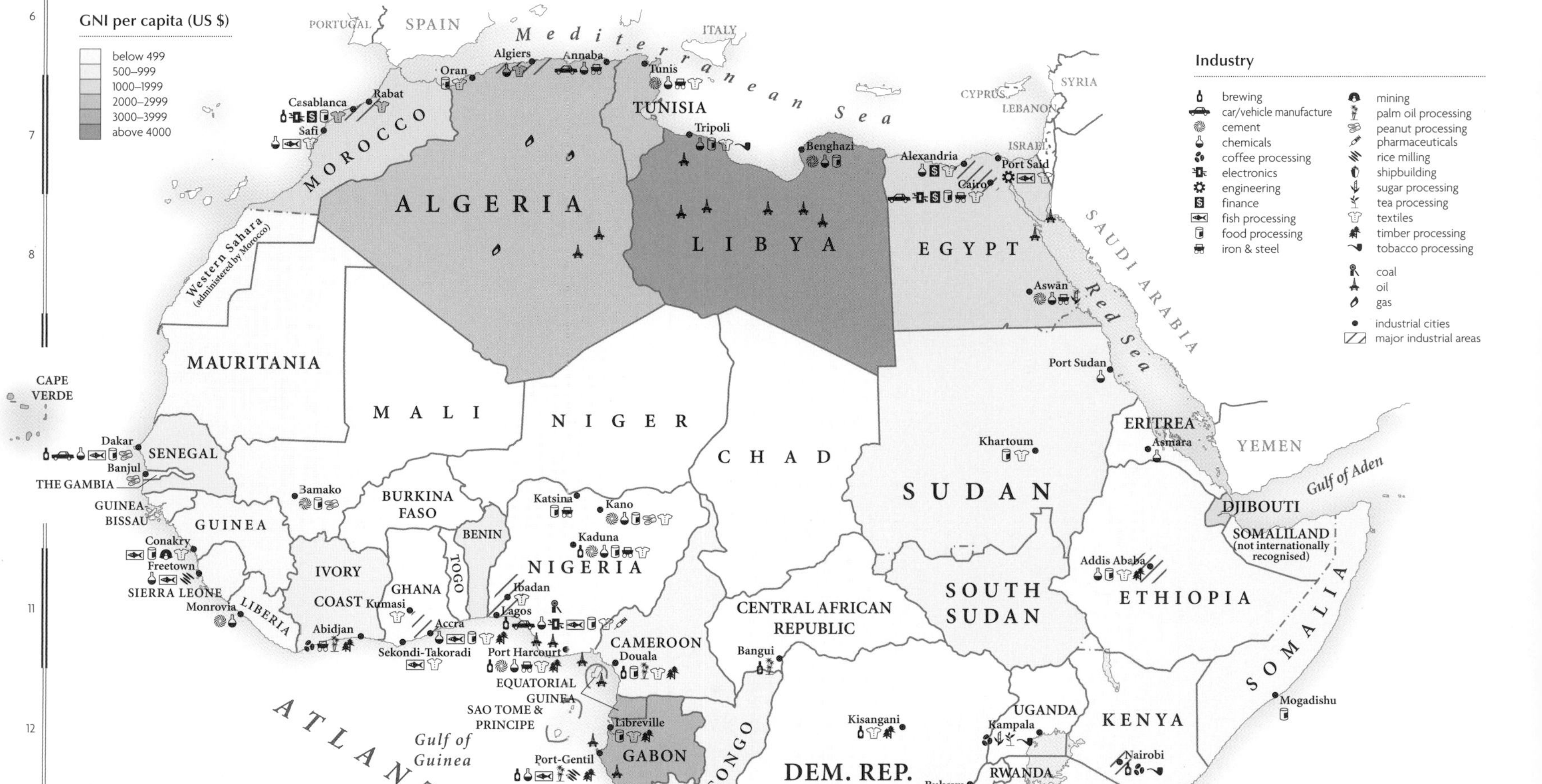

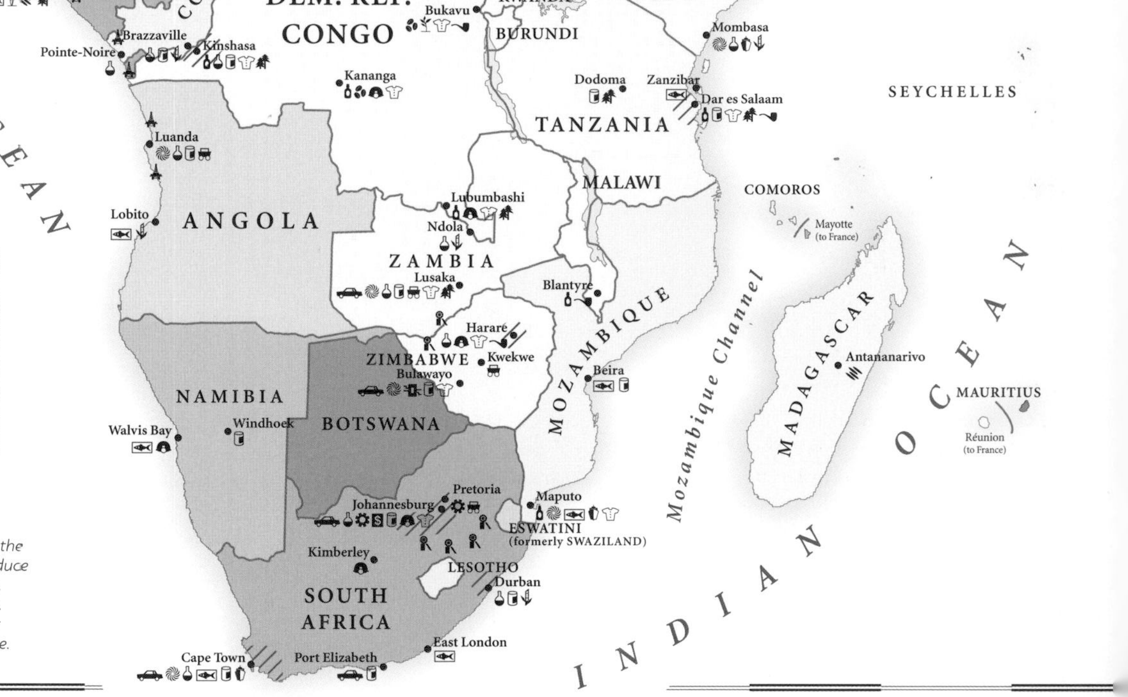

**GNI per capita (US $)**
- below 499
- 500–999
- 1000–1999
- 2000–2999
- 3000–3999
- above 4000

**Industry**

| | |
|---|---|
| brewing | mining |
| car/vehicle manufacture | palm oil processing |
| cement | peanut processing |
| chemicals | pharmaceuticals |
| coffee processing | rice milling |
| electronics | shipbuilding |
| engineering | sugar processing |
| finance | tea processing |
| fish processing | textiles |
| food processing | timber processing |
| iron & steel | tobacco processing |

- coal
- oil
- gas

- • industrial cities
- major industrial areas

◀ The discovery of oil in the swampy Niger Delta during the 1960s made Nigeria one of Africa's richer nations. As world oil prices fell in the 1980s, the Nigerian economy faltered.

▶ Exotic rugs and brightly colored textiles are sold in a street market along the banks of the river Nile in Luxor, Egypt.

◀ The Rössing uranium mines in Namibia are one of the largest in the world. Canada and Australia produce over half the world's uranium ore, used to fuel nuclear power plants. Elsewhere, South Africa and Niger also mine uranium on a large scale.

# Environmental issues

One of Africa's most serious environmental problems occurs in marginal areas such as the Sahel where scrub and forest clearance, often for cooking fuel, combined with overgrazing, are causing desertification. Game reserves in southern and eastern Africa have helped to preserve many endangered animals, although the needs of growing populations have led to conflict over land use, and poaching is a serious problem.

**Environmental issues**
- national parks
- tropical forest
- forest destroyed
- desert
- desertification
- polluted rivers
- radioactive contamination
- marine pollution
- heavy marine pollution
- • poor urban air quality

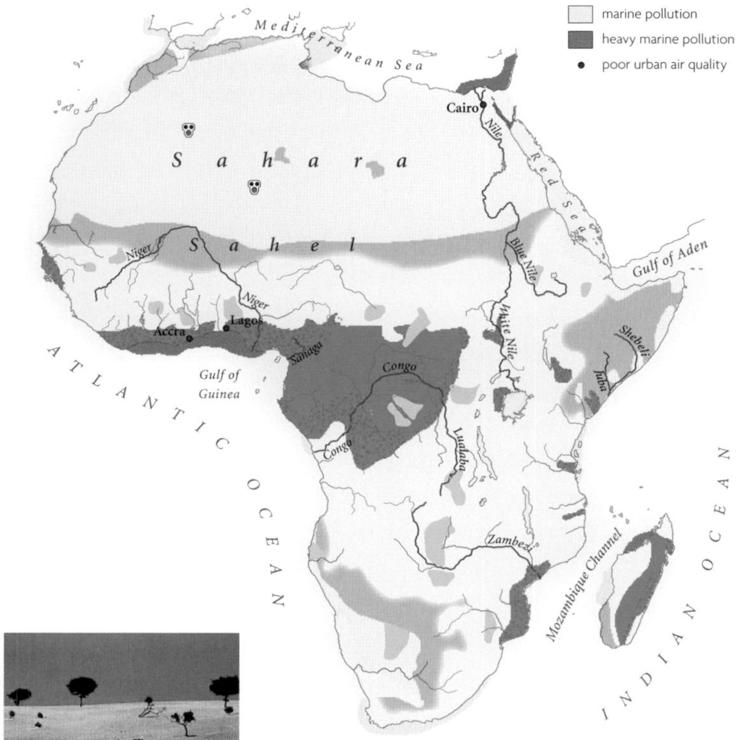

▲ *The Sahel's delicate* natural equilibrium is easily destroyed by the clearing of vegetation, drought, and overgrazing. This causes the Sahara to advance south, engulfing the savannah grasslands.

# Mineral resources

Africa's ancient plateaus contain some of the world's most substantial reserves of precious stones and metals. About 15% of the world's gold is mined in South Africa; Zambia has great copper deposits; and diamonds are mined in Botswana, Dem. Rep. Congo, and South Africa. Oil has brought great economic benefits to Algeria, Libya, and Nigeria.

**Mineral resources**
- oil field
- gas field
- coal field
- bauxite
- copper
- diamonds
- gold
- iron
- phosphates
- tin
- uranium

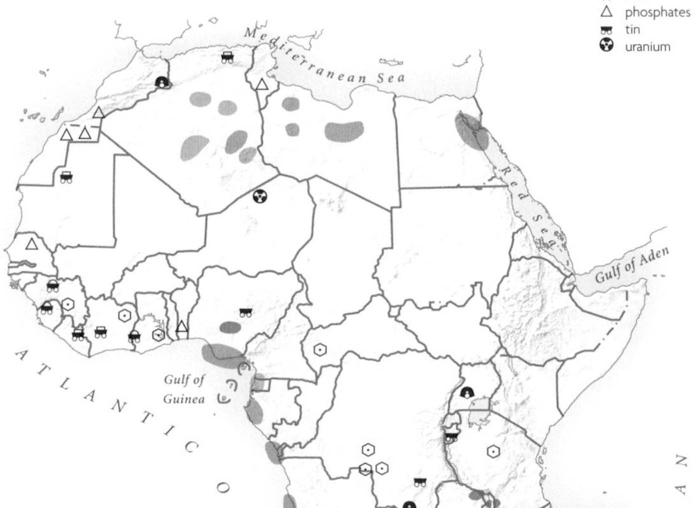

▲ *North and West* Africa have large deposits of white phosphate minerals, which are used in making fertilizers. Morocco, Senegal, and Tunisia are among the continent's leading producers.

▲ *Workers on a* tea plantation gather one of Africa's most important cash crops, providing a valuable source of income. Coffee, rubber, bananas, cotton, and cocoa are also widely grown as cash crops.

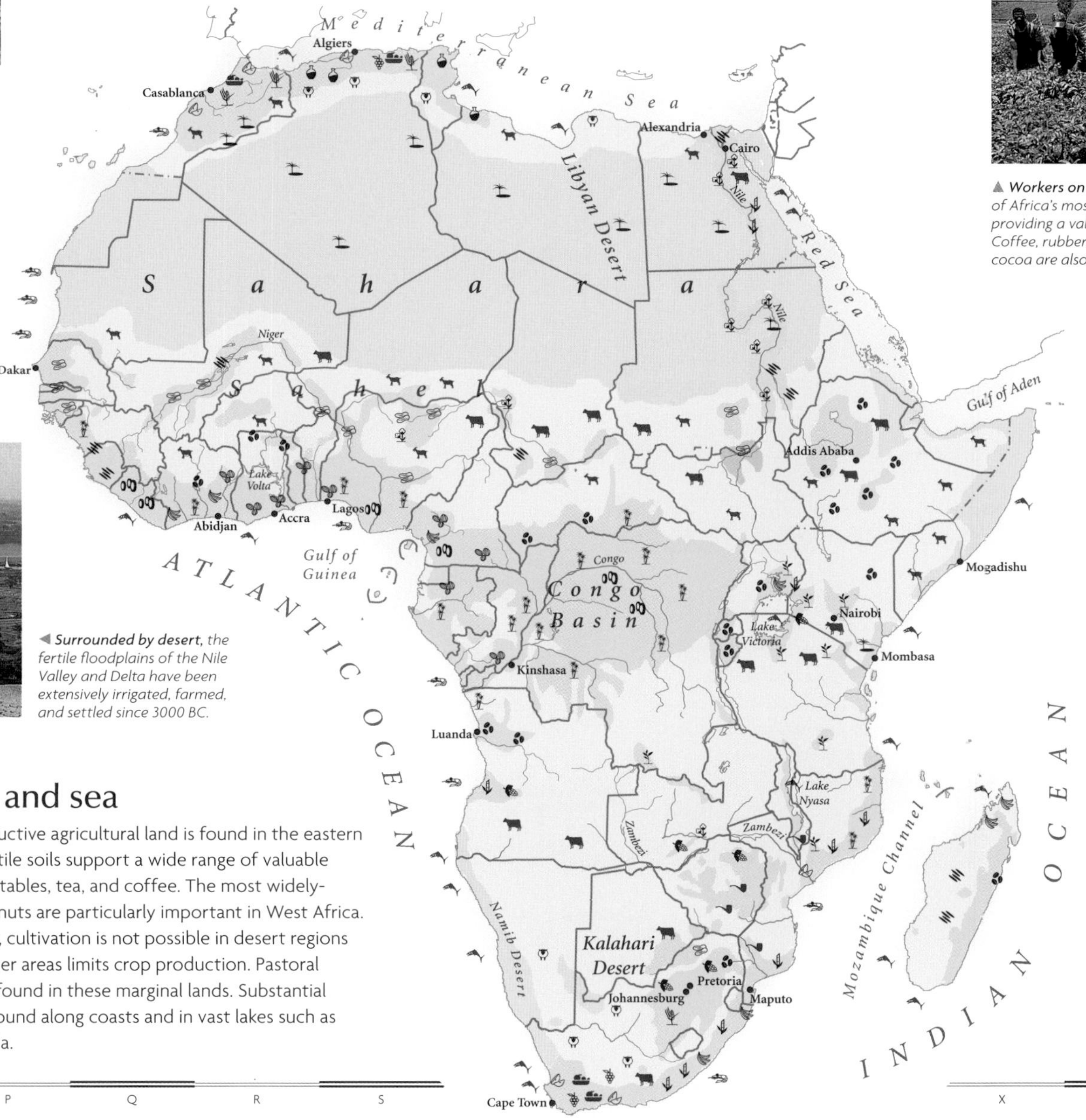

◄ *Surrounded by desert, the* fertile floodplains of the Nile Valley and Delta have been extensively irrigated, farmed, and settled since 3000 BC.

# Using the land and sea

Some of Africa's most productive agricultural land is found in the eastern volcanic uplands, where fertile soils support a wide range of valuable export crops including vegetables, tea, and coffee. The most widely-grown grain is corn and peanuts are particularly important in West Africa. Without intensive irrigation, cultivation is not possible in desert regions and unreliable rainfall in other areas limits crop production. Pastoral herding is most commonly found in these marginal lands. Substantial local fishing industries are found along coasts and in vast lakes such as Lake Nyasa and Lake Victoria.

**Using the land and sea**
- cropland
- desert
- forest
- pasture
- wetland
- • major conurbations
- cattle
- goats
- cereals
- sheep
- bananas
- corn
- citrus fruits
- cocoa
- cotton
- coffee
- dates
- fruit
- oil palms
- olives
- peanuts
- rice
- rubber
- shellfish
- sugar cane
- tea
- tobacco
- vineyards
- wheat

# North Africa

ALGERIA, EGYPT, LIBYA, MOROCCO, TUNISIA, Western Sahara

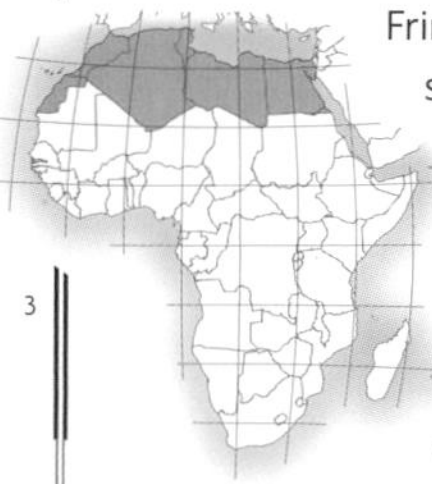

Fringed by the Mediterranean along the northern coast and by the arid Sahara in the south, North Africa reflects the influence of many invaders, both European and, most importantly, Arab, giving the region an almost universal Islamic flavor and a common Arabic language. The countries lying to the west of Egypt are often referred to as the Maghreb, an Arabic term for "west." Today, Morocco and Tunisia exploit their culture and landscape for tourism, while rich oil and gas deposits aid development in Libya and Algeria, despite political turmoil. Egypt, with its fertile, Nile-watered agricultural land and varied industrial base, is the most populous nation.

## The landscape

The Atlas Mountains, which extend across much of Morocco, northern Algeria, and Tunisia, are part of the fold mountain system which also runs through much of southern Europe. They recede to the south and east, becoming a steppe landscape before meeting the Sahara desert which covers more than 90% of the region. The sediments of the Sahara overlie an ancient plateau of crystalline rock, some of which is more than four billion years old.

▲ *These rock piles* in Algeria's Ahaggar mountains are the result of weathering caused by extremes of temperature. Great cracks or joints appear in the rocks, which are then worn and smoothed by the wind.

## Map key

### Population
- ■ above 5 million
- ■ 1 million to 5 million
- ◉ 500,000 to 1 million
- ◎ 100,000 to 500,000
- ◉ 50,000 to 100,000
- ○ 10,000 to 50,000
- ○ below 10,000

### Elevation
- 4000m / 13,124ft
- 3000m / 9843ft
- 2000m / 6562ft
- 1000m / 3281ft
- 500m / 1640ft
- 250m / 820ft
- 100m / 328ft
- sea level

### Scale 1:12,250,000

projection: Lambert Azimuthal Equal Area

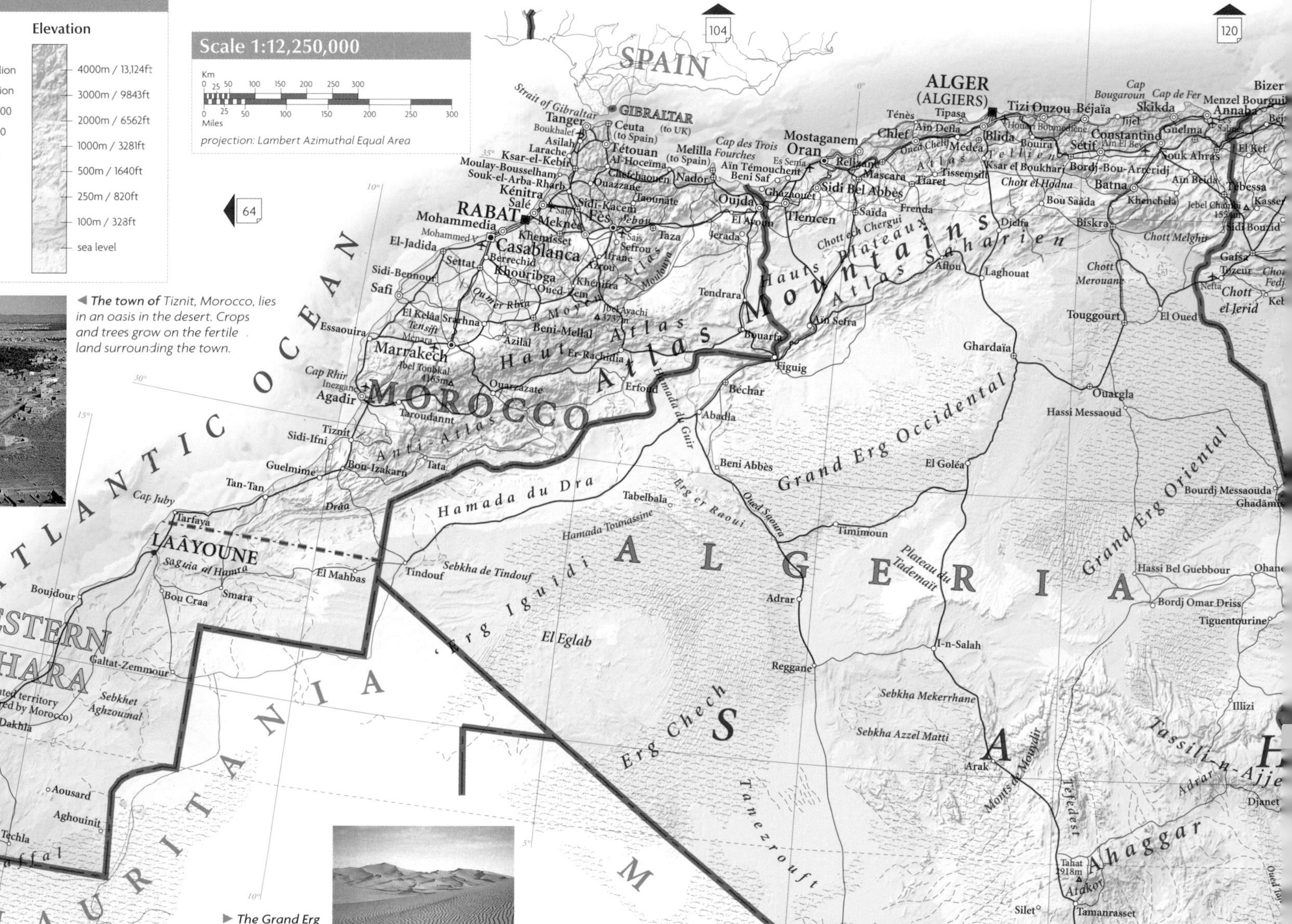

◀ *The town of* Tiznit, Morocco, lies in an oasis in the desert. Crops and trees grow on the fertile land surrounding the town.

▶ *The Grand Erg Occidental* is one of Algeria's great Saharan sand seas. Wind force and direction determines the nature of landforms such as the linear or seif dunes in the foreground.

## Using the land & sea

Sheltered valleys in the Atlas Mountains, the Nile Valley and Delta, and the Mediterranean coast are the main sources of good farming land. A wide variety of valuable crops including cereals, rice, and cotton, and woods such as cedar and cork, are grown. Typical Mediterranean crops such as olives, figs, dates, and citrus fruits also thrive in these areas. The Nile Valley is particularly fertile, and most of Egypt's population lives close to the river. Elsewhere, irrigation is essential to improve crop yields on the desert margins.

### Land use and agricultural distribution
- 🐐 goats
- 🐑 sheep
- 🌾 cereals
- 🍊 citrus fruits
- 🌳 cork
- 🌿 cotton
- 🌴 dates
- 🎣 fishing
- 🫒 olives
- 🍇 vineyards
- ■ capital cities
- ● major towns
- pasture
- cropland
- forest
- desert

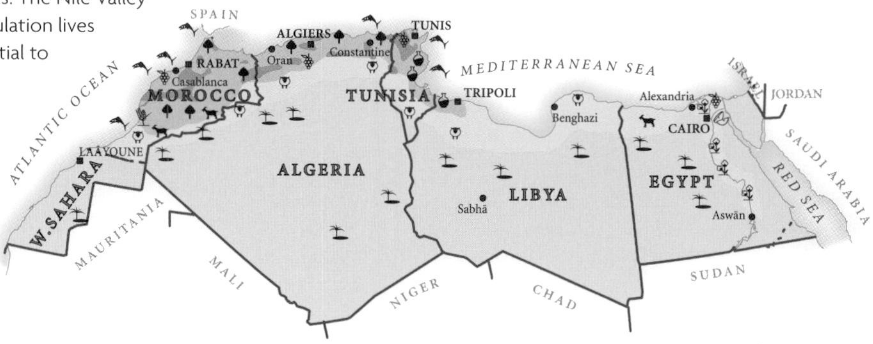

### The urban/rural population divide

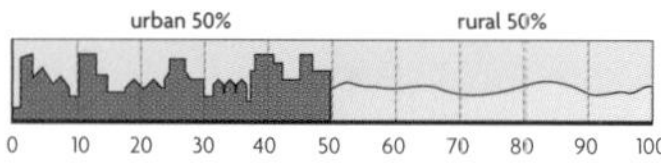

urban 50%     rural 50%

0  10  20  30  40  50  60  70  80  90  100

| Population density | Total land area |
|---|---|
| 65 people per sq mile (25 people per sq km) | 2,215,020 sq miles (5,738,394 sq km) |

▲ *Many North African* nomads, such as the Bedouin, maintain a traditional pastoral lifestyle on the desert fringes, moving their herds of sheep, goats, and camels from place to place – crossing country borders in order to find sufficient grazing land.

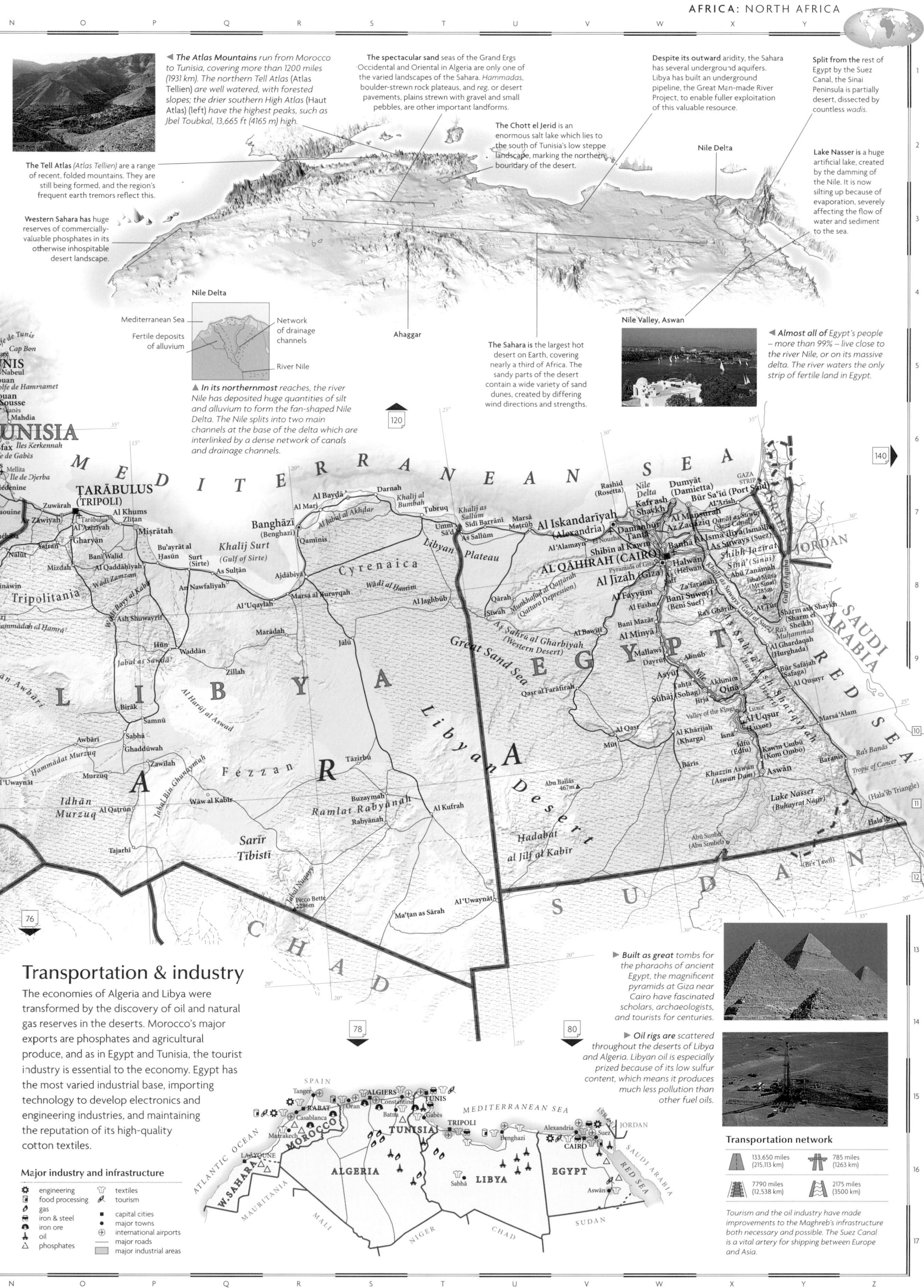

◄ *The Atlas Mountains* run from Morocco to Tunisia, covering more than 1200 miles (1931 km). The northern Tell Atlas (Atlas Tellien) are well watered, with forested slopes; the drier southern High Atlas (Haut Atlas) (left) have the highest peaks, such as Jbel Toubkal, 13,665 ft (4165 m) high.

*The Tell Atlas* (Atlas Tellien) are a range of recent, folded mountains. They are still being formed, and the region's frequent earth tremors reflect this.

*Western Sahara* has huge reserves of commercially-valuable phosphates in its otherwise inhospitable desert landscape.

The spectacular sand seas of the Grand Ergs Occidental and Oriental in Algeria are only one of the varied landscapes of the Sahara. *Hammadas*, boulder-strewn rock plateaus, and *reg*, or desert pavements, plains strewn with gravel and small pebbles, are other important landforms.

*The Chott el Jerid* is an enormous salt lake which lies to the south of Tunisia's low steppe landscape, marking the northern boundary of the desert.

Despite its outward aridity, the Sahara has several underground aquifers. Libya has built an underground pipeline, the Great Man-made River Project, to enable fuller exploitation of this valuable resource.

*Split from the rest* of Egypt by the Suez Canal, the Sinai Peninsula is partially desert, dissected by countless *wadis*.

*Lake Nasser* is a huge artificial lake, created by the damming of the Nile. It is now silting up because of evaporation, severely affecting the flow of water and sediment to the sea.

**Nile Delta**

Mediterranean Sea
Fertile deposits of alluvium
Network of drainage channels
River Nile

▲ *In its northernmost* reaches, the river Nile has deposited huge quantities of silt and alluvium to form the fan-shaped Nile Delta. The Nile splits into two main channels at the base of the delta which are interlinked by a dense network of canals and drainage channels.

*The Sahara* is the largest hot desert on Earth, covering nearly a third of Africa. The sandy parts of the desert contain a wide variety of sand dunes, created by differing wind directions and strengths.

Nile Valley, Aswan

◄ *Almost all of* Egypt's people – more than 99% – live close to the river Nile, or on its massive delta. The river waters the only strip of fertile land in Egypt.

# Transportation & industry

The economies of Algeria and Libya were transformed by the discovery of oil and natural gas reserves in the deserts. Morocco's major exports are phosphates and agricultural produce, and as in Egypt and Tunisia, the tourist industry is essential to the economy. Egypt has the most varied industrial base, importing technology to develop electronics and engineering industries, and maintaining the reputation of its high-quality cotton textiles.

## Major industry and infrastructure

- ⚙ engineering
- 🏭 food processing
- ⬡ gas
- iron & steel
- iron ore
- oil
- △ phosphates
- 🧵 textiles
- tourism
- ■ capital cities
- ● major towns
- ⊕ international airports
- major roads
- major industrial areas

▶ *Built as great* tombs for the pharaohs of ancient Egypt, the magnificent pyramids at Giza near Cairo have fascinated scholars, archaeologists, and tourists for centuries.

▶ *Oil rigs are* scattered throughout the deserts of Libya and Algeria. Libyan oil is especially prized because of its low sulfur content, which means it produces much less pollution than other fuel oils.

## Transportation network

| | | | |
|---|---|---|---|
| 🛣 133,650 miles (215,113 km) | 785 miles (1263 km) |
| 7790 miles (12,538 km) | 2175 miles (3500 km) |

*Tourism and the oil industry have made improvements to the Maghreb's infrastructure both necessary and possible. The Suez Canal is a vital artery for shipping between Europe and Asia.*

# West Africa

BENIN, BURKINA FASO, CAPE VERDE, THE GAMBIA, GHANA, GUINEA, GUINEA-BISSAU,
IVORY COAST, LIBERIA, MALI, MAURITANIA, NIGER, NIGERIA, SENEGAL, SIERRA LEONE, TOGO

West Africa is an immensely diverse region, encompassing the desert landscapes and mainly Muslim populations of the southern Saharan countries, and the tropical rain forests of the more humid south, with a great variety of local languages and cultures. The rich natural resources and accessibility of the area were quickly exploited by Europeans; most of the Africans taken by slave traders came from this region, causing serious depopulation. The very different influences of West Africa's leading colonial powers, Britain and France, remain today, reflected in the languages and institutions of the countries they once governed.

► The dry scrub of the Sahel is only suitable for grazing herd animals like these cattle in Mali.

## Transportation & industry

Abundant natural resources including oil and metallic minerals are found in much of West Africa, although investment is required for their further exploitation. Nigeria experienced an oil boom during the 1970s but subsequent growth has been sporadic. Most industry in other countries has a primary basis, including mining, logging, and food processing.

### Transportation network

| | |
|---|---|
| 62,154 miles (100,038 km) | 1037 miles (1669 km) |
| 6752 miles (10,867 km) | 10,192 miles (16,405 km) |

The road and rail systems are most developed near the coasts. Some of the landlocked countries remain disadvantaged by the difficulty of access to ports, and their poor road networks.

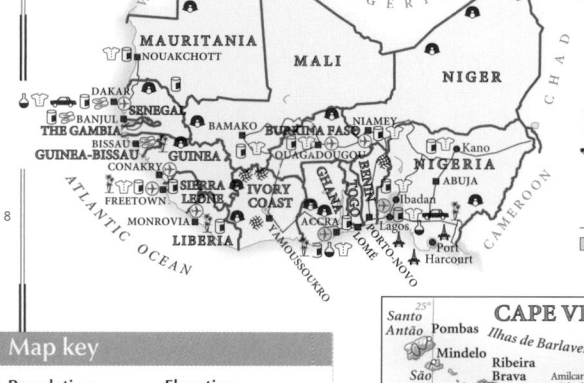

### Major industry and infrastructure

- chemicals
- cotton spinning
- food processing
- mining
- oil
- palm oil processing
- peanut processing
- textiles
- vehicle manufacture
- capital cities
- major towns
- ⊕ international airports
- major roads
- major industrial areas

### Map key

**Population**
- ■ Above 5 million
- ■ 1 million to 5 million
- ● 500,000 to 1 million
- ⊕ 100,000 to 500,000
- ⊕ 50,000 to 100,000
- ⊕ 10,000 to 50,000
- ○ below 10,000

**Elevation**
- 2000m / 6562ft
- 1000m / 3281ft
- 500m / 1640ft
- 250m / 820ft
- 100m / 328ft
- sea level

### CAPE VERDE

Santo Antão
Pombas
Mindelo
São Vicente
Ribeira Brava
São Nicolau
Ilhas de Barlavento
Pedra Lame
Amílcar Cabral
Sal
Boa Vista
João Barrosa

**ATLANTIC OCEAN**

Tarrafal
Fogo
São Filipe
Santiago
Maio
Maie
PRAIA
Ilhas de Sotavento

(same scale as main map)

◄ The southern regions of West Africa still contain great swathes of tropical rainforest, including some of the world's most prized hardwood trees, such as mahogany and iroko.

## Using the land & sea

The humid southern regions are most suitable for cultivation; in these areas, cash crops such as coffee, cotton, cocoa, and rubber are grown in large quantities. Peanuts are grown throughout West Africa. In the north, advancing desertification has made the Sahel increasingly uncultivable, and pastoral farming is more common. Great herds of sheep, cattle, and goats are grazed on the savannah grasses. Fishing is important in coastal and delta areas.

▲ The Gambia, mainland Africa's smallest country, produces great quantities of peanuts. Winnowing is used to separate the nuts from their stalks.

### Land use and agricultural distribution

- goats
- sheep
- cocoa
- coffee
- cotton
- oil palms
- peanuts
- rubber
- shellfish
- ■ capital cities
- ■ major towns
- pasture
- cropland
- forest
- desert

### The urban/rural population divide

urban 36%     rural 64%

0 10 20 30 40 50 60 70 80 90 100

| Population density | Total land area |
|---|---|
| 104 people per sq mile (40 people per sq km) | 2,337,137 sq miles (6,054,760 sq km) |

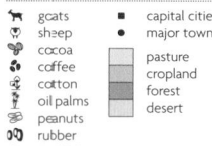

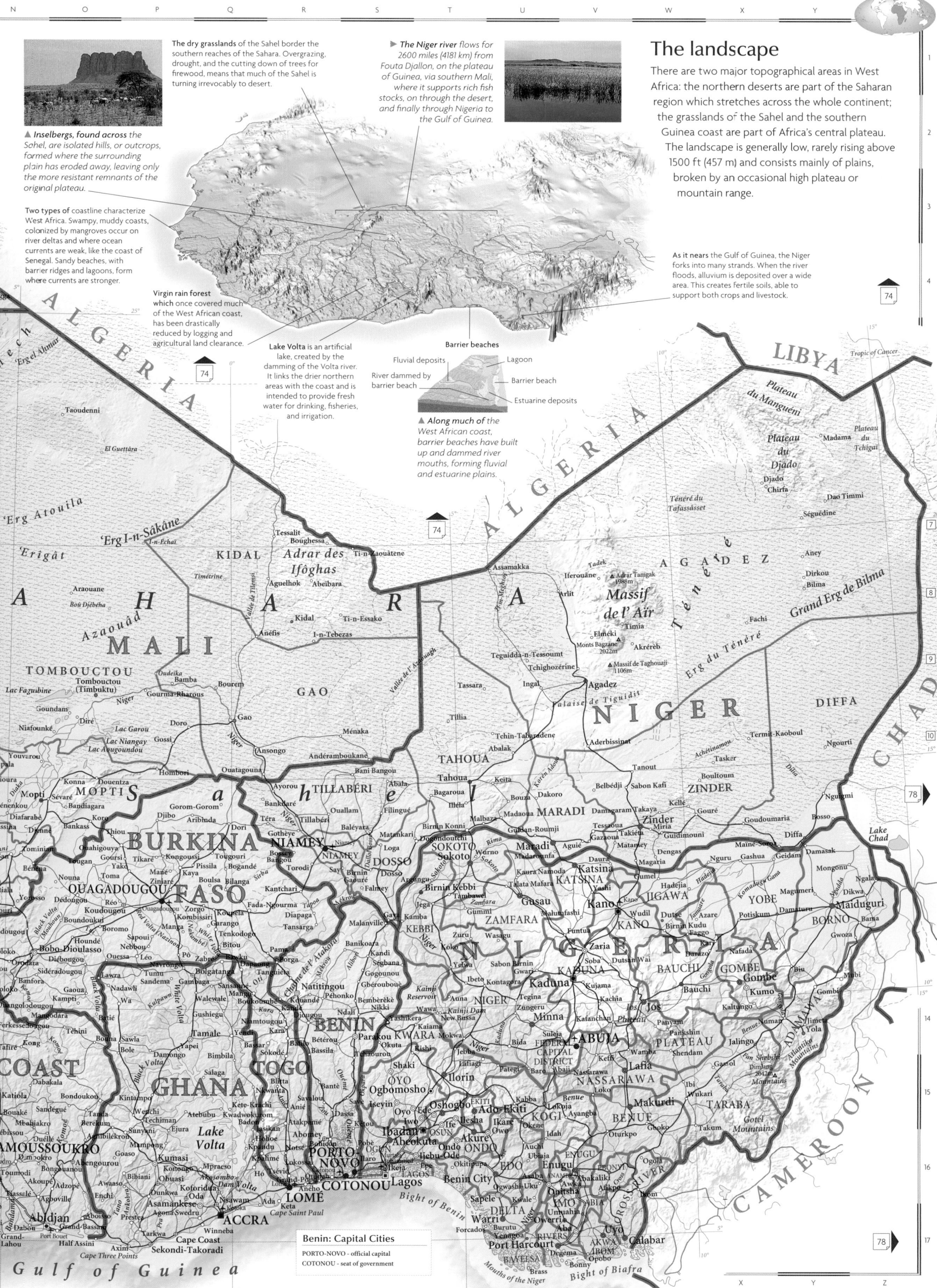

The dry grasslands of the Sahel border the southern reaches of the Sahara. Overgrazing, drought, and the cutting down of trees for firewood, means that much of the Sahel is turning irrevocably to desert.

► The Niger river flows for 2600 miles (4181 km) from Fouta Djallon, on the plateau of Guinea, via southern Mali, where it supports rich fish stocks, on through the desert, and finally through Nigeria to the Gulf of Guinea.

## The landscape

There are two major topographical areas in West Africa: the northern deserts are part of the Saharan region which stretches across the whole continent; the grasslands of the Sahel and the southern Guinea coast are part of Africa's central plateau. The landscape is generally low, rarely rising above 1500 ft (457 m) and consists mainly of plains, broken by an occasional high plateau or mountain range.

▲ Inselbergs, found across the Sahel, are isolated hills, or outcrops, formed where the surrounding plain has eroded away, leaving only the more resistant remnants of the original plateau.

Two types of coastline characterize West Africa. Swampy, muddy coasts, colonized by mangroves occur on river deltas and where ocean currents are weak, like the coast of Senegal. Sandy beaches, with barrier ridges and lagoons, form where currents are stronger.

Virgin rain forest which once covered much of the West African coast, has been drastically reduced by logging and agricultural land clearance.

Lake Volta is an artificial lake, created by the damming of the Volta river. It links the drier northern areas with the coast and is intended to provide fresh water for drinking, fisheries, and irrigation.

As it nears the Gulf of Guinea, the Niger forks into many strands. When the river floods, alluvium is deposited over a wide area. This creates fertile soils, able to support both crops and livestock.

Barrier beaches
Fluvial deposits — Lagoon
River dammed by barrier beach — Barrier beach
— Estuarine deposits

▲ Along much of the West African coast, barrier beaches have built up and dammed river mouths, forming fluvial and estuarine plains.

**Benin: Capital Cities**

PORTO-NOVO - official capital
COTONOU - seat of government

# Central Africa

CAMEROON, CENTRAL AFRICAN REPUBLIC, CHAD, CONGO, DEM. REP. CONGO, EQUATORIAL GUINEA, GABON, SAO TOME & PRINCIPE

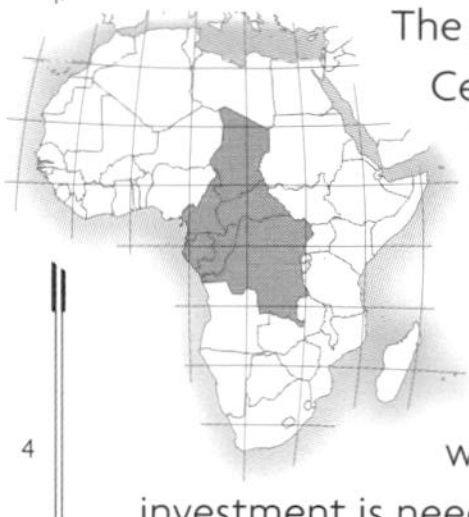

The great rain forest basin of the Congo river embraces most of remote Central Africa. The interior was largely unknown to Europeans until late in the 19th century, when its tribal kingdoms were split – principally between France and Belgium – with Sao Tome and Principe the lone Portuguese territory, and Equatorial Guinea controlled by Spain. Open democracy and regional economic integration are important goals for these nations – several of which have only recently emerged from restrictive regimes – and investment is needed to improve transportation infrastructures. Many of the small, but fast-growing and increasingly urban population, speak French, the regional *lingua franca*, along with several hundred Pygmy, Bantu, and Sudanic dialects.

## The landscape

Lake Chad lies in a desert basin bounded by the volcanic Tibesti mountains in the north, plateaus in the east and, in the south, the broad watershed of the Congo basin. The vast circular depression of the Congo is isolated from the coastal plain by the granite Massif du Chaillu. To the northwest, the volcanoes and fold mountains of the Cameroon Ridge *(Dorsale Camerounaise)* extend as islands into the Gulf of Guinea. The high fold mountains fringing the east of the Congo Basin fall steeply to the lakes of the Great Rift Valley.

◄ ***A plug of** resistant lava, at the southwestern end of the Cameroon Ridge (Dorsale Camerounaise), is all that remains of an eroded volcano.*

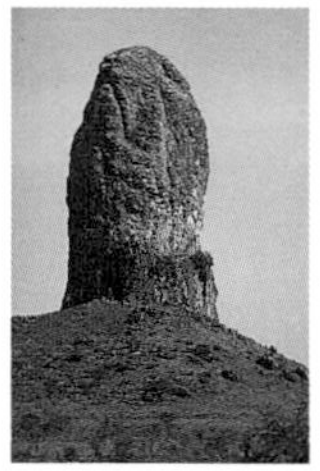

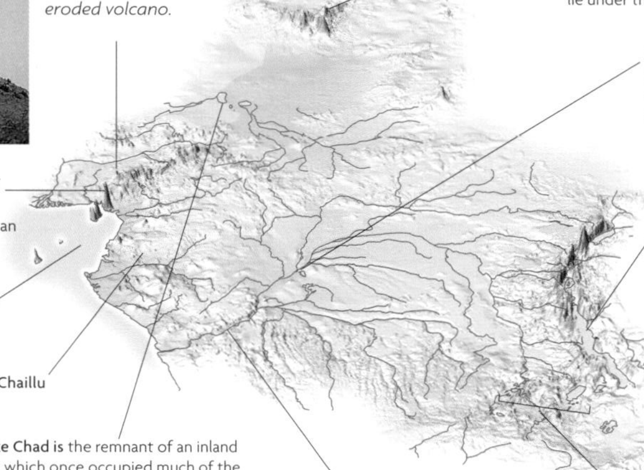

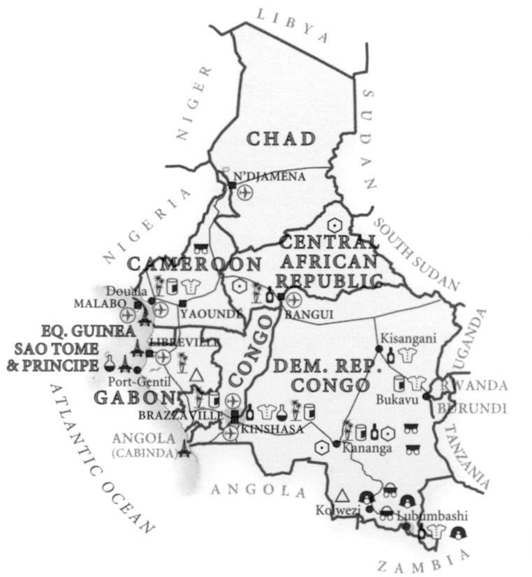

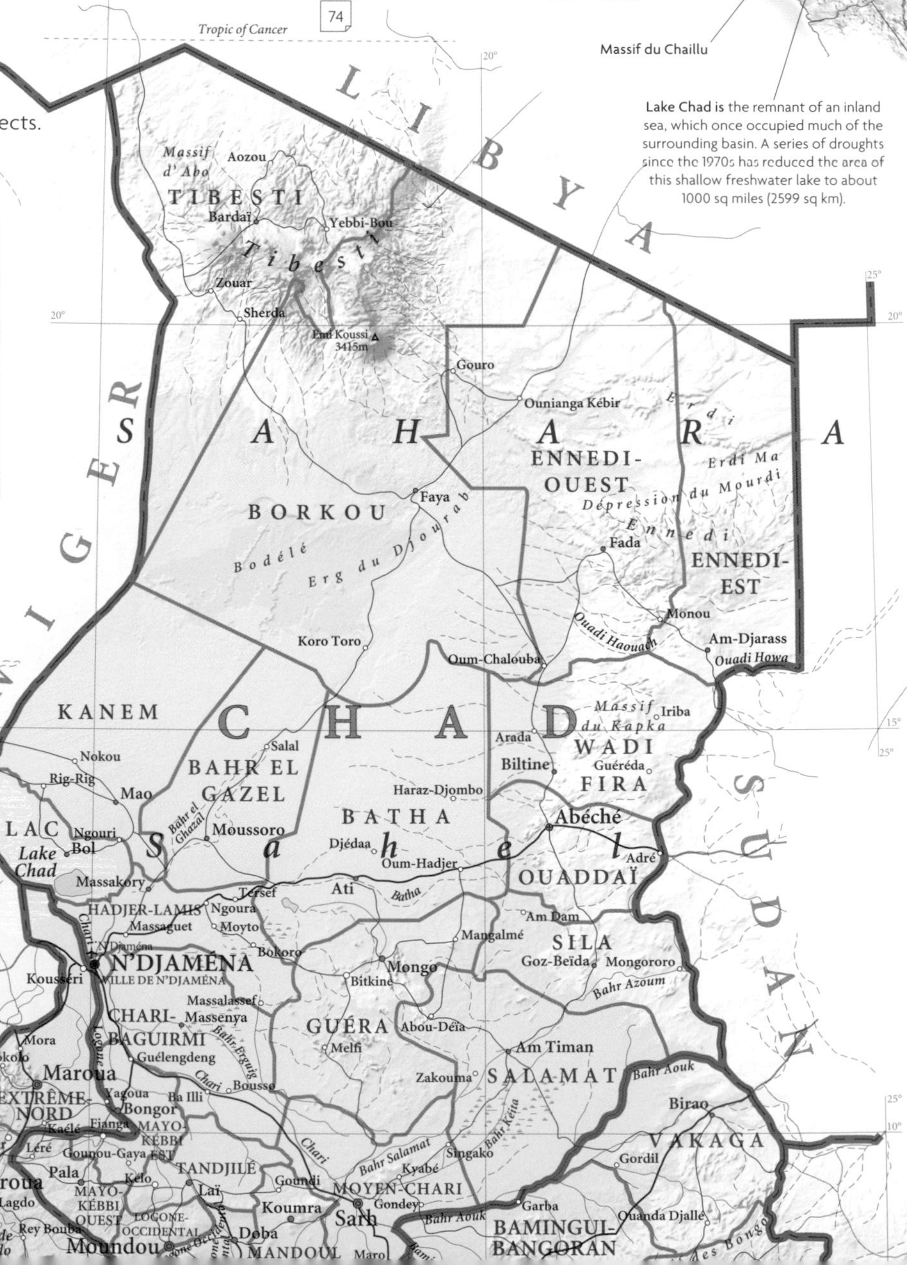

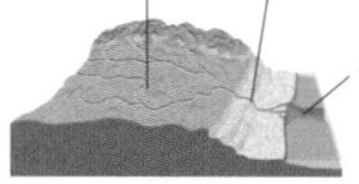

## Transportation & industry

Large reserves of valuable minerals are found in Central Africa: copper, cobalt, zinc, and diamonds are mined in Dem. Rep. Congo and manganese in Gabon. Congo, Cameroon, Gabon, and Equatorial Guinea have oil deposits and oil has also been recently discovered in Chad. Goods such as palm oil and rubber are processed for export.

▲ ***The ancient rocks** of Dem. Rep. Congo hold immense and varied mineral reserves. This open pit copper mine is at Kolwezi in the far south.*

Major industry and infrastructure

- brewing
- chemicals
- cobalt
- copper
- diamonds
- food processing
- manganese
- oil
- palm oil processing
- textiles
- tin

- capital cities
- major towns
- international airports
- major roads
- major industrial areas

Transportation network

| | |
|---|---|
| 102,747 miles (165,774 km) | 37 miles (60 km) |
| 3985 miles (6414 km) | 14,110 miles (22,710 km) |

*The Trans-Gabon railroad, which began operating in 1987, has opened up new sources of timber and manganese. Elsewhere, much investment is needed to update and improve road, rail, and water transportation.*

74

76

▲ ***The Congo river** flows sluggishly through the rain forest of the interior basin. Toward the coast, the river drops steeply in a series of waterfalls and cataracts. At this point, the erosional power of the river becomes so great that it has formed a deep submarine canyon offshore.*

▲ ***Virgin tropical rain** forest covers the Ruwenzori range on the borders of Dem. Rep. Congo and Uganda.*

▲ ***The vast sandflats** surrounding Lake Chad were once covered by water. Changing climatic patterns caused the lake to shrink, and desert now covers much of its previous area.*

### Scale 1:10,500,000

Km 0 25 50 100 150 200 250

Miles 0 25 50 100 150 200 250

projection: Lambert Azimuthal Equal Area

### Map key

Population

- 1 million to 5 million
- 500,000 to 1 million
- 100,000 to 500,000
- 50,000 to 100,000
- 10,000 to 50,000
- below 10,000

Elevation

- 4000m / 13,124ft
- 3000m / 9843ft
- 2000m / 6562ft
- 1000m / 3281ft
- 500m / 1640ft
- 250m / 820ft
- 100m / 328ft
- sea level

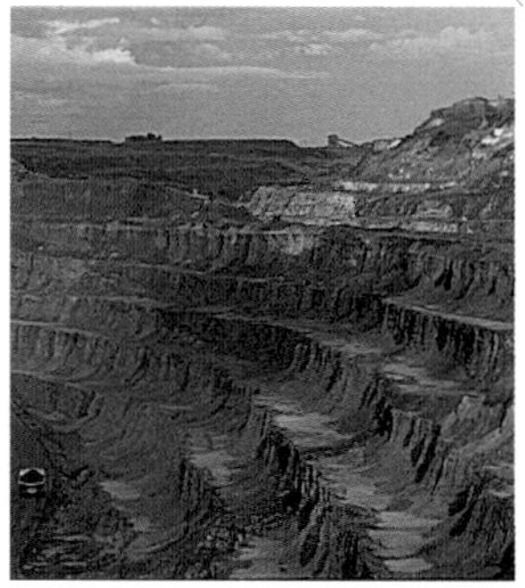

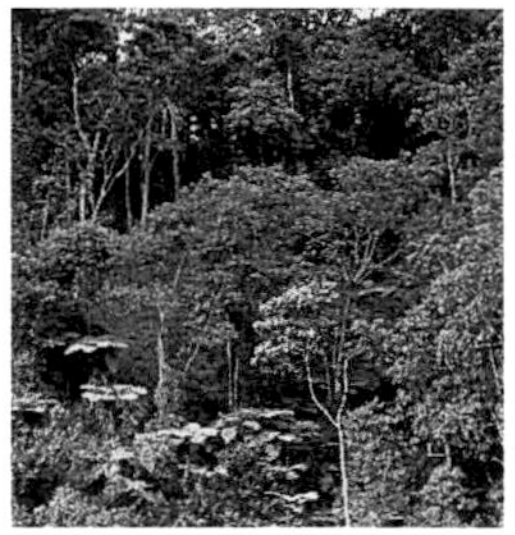

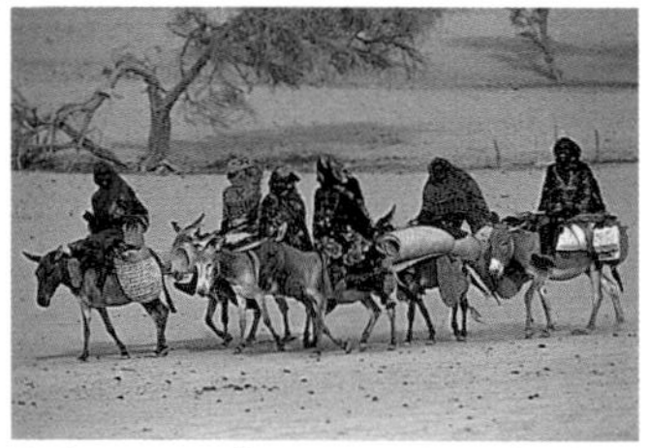

▲ *The great Congo river forms part of the border between Congo and Dem. Rep. Congo. The river is fast-flowing, and a series of falls and rapids means that it is only partly navigable.*

## Using the land

Cash crops for export include cocoa, coffee, and rubber. Shifting cultivation is widely practiced, and plantains are the staple food of the equatorial region, grown with yam and taro. Cassava, guinea corn (sorghum), and millet are the main subsistence crops in savannah areas. Cattle farming is limited to areas free of tsetse fly, and fish from the interior rivers are an important protein source.

### Land use and agricultural distribution

- cattle
- cocoa
- coffee
- cotton
- peanuts
- palms
- rubber
- timber
- capital cities
- major towns

- pasture
- cropland
- forest
- desert

▲ *High-quality timber is floated to Port-Gentil, Gabon, via the Ogooué river. Timber provides important export revenue for several countries, although there has been concern about the uncontrolled logging of rare tropical woods.*

### The urban/rural population divide

| urban 33% | rural 67% |
|---|---|

| Population density | Total land area |
|---|---|
| 43 people per sq mile (17 people per sq km) | 2,023,939 sq miles (5,243,364 sq km) |

# East Africa

BURUNDI, DJIBOUTI, ERITREA, ETHIOPIA, KENYA, RWANDA,
SOMALIA, SOUTH SUDAN, SUDAN, TANZANIA, UGANDA

The countries of East Africa divide into two distinct cultural regions. Sudan
and the "Horn" nations have been influenced by the Middle East; Ethiopia
was the home of one of the earliest Christian civilizations, and Sudan
reflects both Muslim and Christian influences. The southern countries
share a closer cultural affinity with other sub-Saharan nations. Some of
Africa's most densely populated countries lie in this region, and the
needs of a growing number of people have put pressure on marginal
lands and fragile environments. Although most East African economies
remain strongly agricultural, Kenya has developed a varied industrial base.

## The landscape

East Africa's most significant landscape
feature is the Great Rift Valley, which
formed during the most recent phase
of continental movement when the
rigid basement rocks cracked and
buckled. Great blocks of land were
raised and lowered, creating huge
flat-bottomed valleys and steep
escarpments, sometimes covered by
volcanic extrusions in highland areas.

▼ *This dome at* Gonder, in
Ethiopia, is a volcanic
intrusion, formed when
molten rock pushed up the
surface of the Earth and
then solidified, leaving an
outcrop of igneous rock.

▲ *The eastern arm of the Great Rift*
Valley is gradually being pulled apart;
however also because the forces on one side are
greater than the other causing the land
to slope. This affects regional drainage
which migrates down the slope.

Lava flows on uplifted areas either
side of the eastern branch of the
Great Rift Valley gave the Ethiopian
Highlands – a series of high, wide
plateaus – their distinctive rounded
appearance and fertile soils.

In contrast to the desert
conditions that prevail in
much of Sudan to the
north, annual rainfall in
the tropical wetlands of
the southern Sudd region
in South Sudan, can
sometimes exceed 40
inches (1000 mm).

The tiny countries of
Rwanda and Burundi are
mainly mountainous, with
large areas of inaccessible
tropical rain forest.

Lake Tanganyika lies 8202 ft
(2500 m) above sea level. It has a
depth of nearly 4700 ft (435 m).
The lake traces the valley floor for
some 400 miles (644 km) of the
western arm of the Great Rift Valley.

A vast plateau lies between the eastern and
western rift valleys in Kenya, Uganda, and
western Tanzania. It has been leveled by long
periods of erosion to form a peneplain, but is
dotted with inselbergs – outcrops of more
resistant rocks.

Lake Victoria occupies a vast basin between
the two arms of the Great Rift Valley. It is the
world's second largest lake in terms of
surface area, extending 26,560 sq miles
(68,880 sq km). The lake contains numerous
islands and coral reefs.

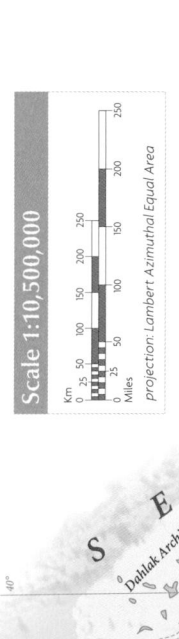

Kilimanjaro

▲ *An extinct volcano,*
Kilimanjaro is Africa's highest
mountain, rising 19,340 ft
(5895 m). Once famed for its
snow-capped peak, this has
almost competely melted due
to changing climatic conditions.

▲ *The Kassala region in*
eastern Sudan is watered
by the Atbara River, an
important tributary of the
Nile. Most of the population
is engaged in agriculture,
growing cotton and cereals.

Central block
slopes towards
main fault

Ephemeral lake forms
at far edge of slope

Boundary
fault

## Scale 1:10,500,000

km  0  25  50  100  150  200  250
Miles  0  25  50  100  150  200  250

projection: Lambert Azimuthal Equal Area

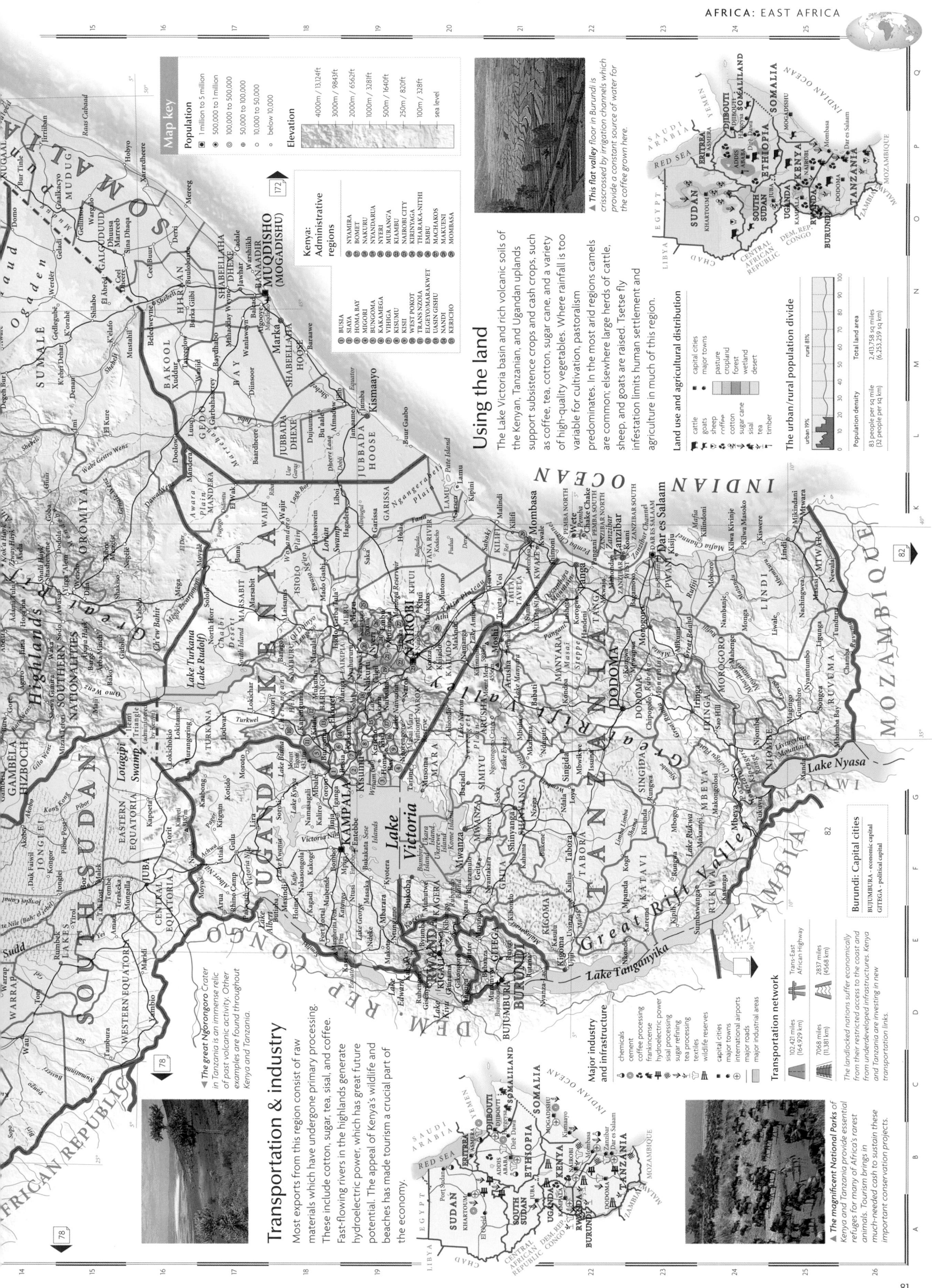

## Map key

**Population**
- ◉ 1 million to 5 million
- ⊙ 500,000 to 1 million
- ⊕ 100,000 to 500,000
- ⊕ 50,000 to 100,000
- ○ 10,000 to 50,000
- ∘ below 10,000

**Elevation**
- 4000m / 13,124ft
- 3000m / 9843ft
- 2000m / 6562ft
- 1000m / 328ft
- 500m / 1640ft
- 250m / 820ft
- 100m / 328ft
- sea level

**Kenya: Administrative regions**

1 NYAMIRA
2 BOMET
3 NAKURU
4 NYANDARUA
5 NYERI
6 MURANGA
7 KIAMBU
8 NAIROBI CITY
9 KIRINYAGA
10 THARAKA-NITHI
11 EMBU
12 MACHAKOS
13 MAKUENI
14 MOMBASA

1 BUSIA
2 SIAYA
3 HOMA BAY
4 MIGORI
5 BUNGOMA
6 KAKAMEGA
7 VIHIGA
8 KISUMU
9 KISII
10 WEST POKOT
11 TRANS NZOIA
12 ELGEYO/MARAKWET
13 UASIN GISHU
14 NANDI
15 KERICHO

▲ This flat valley floor in Burundi is crisscrossed by irrigation channels which provide a constant source of water for the coffee grown here.

## Using the land

The Lake Victoria basin and rich volcanic soils of the Kenyan, Tanzanian, and Ugandan uplands support subsistence crops and cash crops, such as coffee, tea, cotton, sugar cane, and a variety of high-quality vegetables. Where rainfall is too variable for cultivation, pastoralism predominates. In the most arid regions camels are common; elsewhere large herds of cattle, sheep, and goats are raised. Tsetse fly infestation limits human settlement and agriculture in much of this region.

**Land use and agricultural distribution**
- cattle
- goats
- sheep
- cotton
- sugar cane
- sisal
- tea
- timber
- capital cities
- major towns
- pasture
- cropland
- forest
- wetland
- desert

**The urban/rural population divide**
- urban 19%    rural 81%

**Population density**
83 people per sq mile
(32 people per sq km)

**Total land area**
2,413,758 sq miles
(6,253,259 sq km)

## Transportation & industry

Most exports from this region consist of raw materials which have undergone primary processing. These include cotton, sugar, tea, sisal, and coffee. Fast-flowing rivers in the highlands generate hydroelectric power, which has great future potential. The appeal of Kenya's wildlife and beaches has made tourism a crucial part of the economy.

▼ The great Ngorongoro Crater in Tanzania is an immense relic of past volcanic activity. Other examples are found throughout Kenya and Tanzania.

**Major industry and infrastructure**
- chemicals
- cement
- coffee processing
- frankincense
- hydroelectric power
- sisal processing
- sugar refining
- tea processing
- textiles
- wildlife reserves
- capital cities
- major towns
- international airports
- major roads
- major industrial areas

**Transportation network**
- Trans-East African Highway

| | |
|---|---|
| 102,421 miles (164,929 km) | |
| 7068 miles (11,381 km) | 2837 miles (4568 km) |

The landlocked nations suffer economically from their restricted access to the coast and from underdeveloped infrastructures. Kenya and Tanzania are investing in new transportation links.

▲ The magnificent National Parks of Kenya and Tanzania provide essential refuges for many of Africa's rarest animals. Tourism brings in much-needed cash to sustain these important conservation projects.

**Burundi: Capital cities**
BUJUMBURA – economic capital
GITEGA – political capital

# Southern Africa

ANGOLA, BOTSWANA, ESWATINI, LESOTHO, MALAWI, MOZAMBIQUE, NAMIBIA, SOUTH AFRICA, ZAMBIA, ZIMBABWE

Africa's vast southern plateau has been a contested homeland for disparate peoples for many centuries. The European incursion began with the slave trade and quickened in the 19th century, when the discovery of enormous mineral wealth secured South Africa's regional economic dominance. The struggle against white minority rule led to strife in Namibia, Zimbabwe, and the former Portuguese territories of Angola and Mozambique. South Africa's notorious apartheid laws, which denied basic human rights to more than 75% of the people, led to the state being internationally ostracized until 1994, when the first fully democratic elections inaugurated a new era of racial justice.

## Transportation & industry

South Africa, the world's largest exporter of gold, has a varied economy which generates about 75% of the region's income and draws migrant labor from neighboring states. Angola exports petroleum; Botswana and Namibia rely on diamond mining; and Zambia is seeking to diversify its economy to compensate for declining copper reserves.

▼ *Almost all new mining ventures in Zimbabwe are now subject to government control. This mine at Bindura in northeastern Zimbabwe produces nickel, one of the country's top three minerals in terms of economic value*

### Major industry and infrastructure

- car manufacture
- coal
- copper
- diamonds
- food processing
- gold
- oil
- textiles
- uranium
- wildlife reserves
- capital cities
- major towns
- international airports
- major roads
- major industrial areas

## The landscape

Most of southern Africa rests on a concave plateau comprising the Kalahari basin and a mountainous fringe, skirted by a coastal plain which widens out in Mozambique. The plateau extends north, toward the Planalto do Bié in Angola, the Congo Basin and the lake-filled troughs of the Great Rift Valley. The eastern region is drained by the Zambezi and Limpopo rivers, and the Orange is the major western river.

At Victoria Falls, the Zambezi river has cut a spectacular gorge taking advantage of large joints in the basalt, which were first formed as the lava cooled and contracted.

▶ *The fast-flowing Zambezi river cuts a deep, wide channel as it flows along the Zimbabwe/Zambia border.*

Lake Nyasa occupies one of the deep troughs of the Great Rift Valley, where the land has been displaced downward by as much as 3000 ft (920 m).

Great Rift Valley

Limpopo river

Bushveld intrusion

Volcanic lava, over 250 million years old, caps the peaks of the Drakensberg range, which lie on the mountainous rim of southern Africa's interior plateau.

The Okavango/Cubango River flows from the Planalto do bié to the swamplands of the Okavango Delta, one of the world's largest inland deltas, where it divides into countless distributary channels, feeding out into the desert.

Broad, flat-topped mountains characterize the Great Karoo, which have been cut from level rock strata under extremely arid conditions.

The mountains of the Little Karoo are composed of sedimentary rocks which have been substantially folded and faulted.

Thousands of years of evaporating water have produced the Etosha Pan, one of the largest salt flats in the world. Lake and river sediments in the area indicate that the region was once less arid.

Planalto do Bié

Khorixas, Namibia

Namib Desert

The Kalahari desert is the largest continuous sand surface in the world. Iron oxide gives a distinctive red color to the windblown sand, which, in eastern areas covers the bedrock by over 200 ft (60 m).

The Orange River, one of the longest in Africa, rises in Lesotho and is the only major river in the south which flows westward, rather than to the east coast.

▲ *Finger Rock, near Khorixas, Namibia is a remnant of a former land surface, which has been denuded by erosion over the last 5 million years. These occasional stacks of partially weathered rocks interrupt the plains of the dry southern interior.*

### Transportation network

| | |
|---|---|
| 84,213 miles (135,609 km) | 746 miles (1202 km) |
| 23,208 miles (37,372 km) | 3815 miles (6144 km) |

Southern Africa's Cape-gauge rail network is by far the largest in the continent. About two-thirds of the 20,000 mile (32,000 km) system lies within South Africa. Lines such as the Harare–Bulawayo route have become corridors for industrial growth.

▲ *Following a series of droughts, this baobab tree in Zimbabwe now stands alone in a field once filled by sugar cane. The thick trunk and small leaves of the baobab help it to conserve water, enabling it to survive even in drought conditions.*

## Map key

### Population
- 1 million to 5 million
- 500,000 to 1 million
- 100,000 to 500,000
- 50,000 to 100,000
- 10,000 to 50,000
- below 10,000

### Elevation
- 3000m / 9843ft
- 2000m / 6562ft
- 1000m / 3281ft
- 500m / 1640ft
- 250m / 820ft
- 100m / 328ft
- sea level

Granite
Chromite
Bushveld intrusion
Gabbro and peridotite
Magnetite
Platinum minerals

▲ *The Bushveld intrusion lies on South Africa's high "veld." Molten magma intruded into the Earth's crust creating a saucer-shaped feature, more than 180 miles (300 km) across, containing regular layers of precious minerals, overlain by a dome of granite.*

### South Africa: Capital cities
PRETORIA – administrative capital
CAPE TOWN – legislative capital
BLOEMFONTEIN – judicial capital

Scale 1:10,500,000

projection: Lambert Azimuthal Equal Area

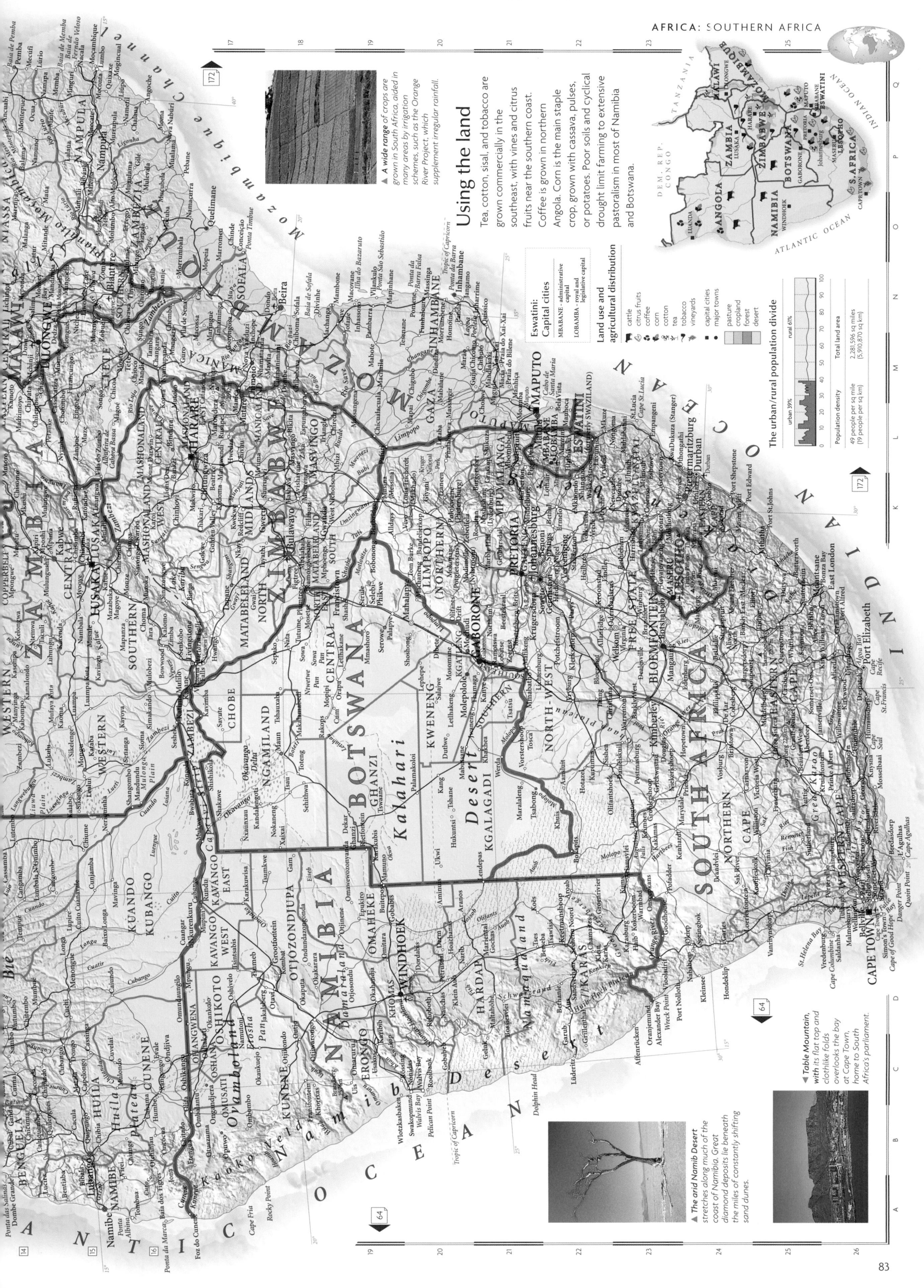

## Using the land

Tea, cotton, sisal, and tobacco are grown commercially in the southeast, with vines and citrus fruits near the southern coast. Coffee is grown in northern Angola. Corn is the main staple crop, grown with cassava, pulses, or potatoes. Poor soils and cyclical drought limit farming to extensive pastoralism in most of Namibia and Botswana.

▲ *A wide range of crops are grown in South Africa, aided in many areas by irrigation schemes, such as the Orange River Project, which supplement irregular rainfall.*

**Eswatini:**
Capital cities
MBABANE: administrative capital
LOBAMBA: royal and legislative capital

**Land use and agricultural distribution**

cattle
citrus fruits
coffee
corn
tea
tobacco
vineyards

capital cities
major towns

pasture
cropland
forest
desert

**The urban/rural population divide**

urban 39%   rural 61%

Population density
49 people per sq mile
(19 people per sq km)

Total land area
2,281,596 sq miles
(5,910,870 sq km)

▲ *The arid Namib Desert stretches along much of the coast of Namibia. Great diamond deposits lie beneath the miles of constantly shifting sand dunes.*

▲ *Table Mountain, with its flat top and clothlike folds overlooks the bay at Cape Town, home to South Africa's parliament.*

83

ARCTIC OCEAN

North Pole

Ellesmere Island

Greenland

King Frederik
VIII Land

Greenland
Sea

King Christian X Land

Laptev Sea

Ostrov
Rudolfa

Franz Josef Land

Severnaya
Zemlya

Poluostrov Taymyr

Kara Sea

Mys
Flissingsky

Novaya Zemlya

EURASIAN PLATE

NORTH AMERICAN PLATE

Spitsbergen

Bjørnøya

BARENTS
Sea

Poluostrov Yamal

Baydaratskaya Guba

Gulf of Ob

Yenisey

A S I

West Siberian
Plain

Ob'

Ob'

Jan Mayen Fracture Zone
Jan Mayen

Kolbeinsey Ridge

Arctic Circle

Denmark Strait

Iceland
Plateau

Bjargtangar

Reykjanes Ridge

Iceland

Vatnajökull

Iceland
Basin

Hatton Ridge

Rockall
Rise

Fení Ridge

Rockall Trough

Porcupine
Plain

ATLANTIC OCEAN

Azores-Biscay Rise

Charcot Seamounts

Thera Gap
Galicia
Bank

Iberian
Plain

Biscay
Plain

Bay of
Biscay

Iberian

Peninsula

Tagus Plain

Gorringe
Ridge

Horseshoe Seamounts

Cape
St Vincent

Cabo
da Roca

Guadiana

Douro

Duero

Sistema Central

Sierra Morena

Guadalquivir

Sistema Iberico

Ebro

Aragon

Cordillera Cantabrica

Miño

Júcar

Segura

Sistemas Béticos
Sierra Nevada

Punta de
Tarifa

Ampere Seamount

Seine Plain

Essine Seamount

Madeira

Dacia Seamount

Canary Islands

Agadir Canyon

Strait of
Gibraltar

Alboran Sea

Rif

Oued
Sebou

Oum er Rbia

Erg Iguidi

Middle Atlas

High Atlas

Atlas Mountains

Tell Atlas

Oued Chelif

Saharan Atlas

Chott el Jerid

Grand Erg Occidental

Grand Erg Oriental

Erg Chech

S A H A R A

A F R I C A

Norwegian Sea

Jan Mayen

Faroe-Iceland Ridge

Faroe Islands

Bill Baileys
Bank

Faroe-Shetland Trough

Shetland
Islands

Orkney Islands

Outer Hebrides

Ben Nevis
1343m

Grampian
Mountains

North Channel

British
Isles

Ireland

Shannon

Irish Sea

Snowdon
1085m

Celtic Sea

St George's
Channel

Celtic
Shelf

Bristol Channel

Land's End

Norwegian
Basin

Vøring Plateau

Tromsøflaket

North Cape

Nordkinn

Fugløya
Bank

Vesterålen

Lofoten

Traena
Bank

Kebnekaise
2117m

Torneträsk

Kjølen

Scandinavia

Gaustoppen
2469m

Ljungan

Ljusnan

Glåma

Viking Bank

North
Sea

Jutland
Bank

Great
Fisher
Bank

Dogger
Bank

Frisian Islands

Jutland

Skagerrak

Kattegat

Sjælland

Elbe

Odra

Warta

Vistula

Rhine

Meuse

Moselle

Seine

Loire

Vienne

Cher

Marne

Ardennes

Harz Forest

EUROPE

Dordogne

Lot

Garonne

Massif
Central

Cévennes

Loire

Saône

Mont Blanc
4807m

Lake Geneva

Lake Constance

Vosges

Rhine

Gulf of Lion

Ligurian
Sea

Corsica

Strait of Bonifacio

Sardinia

Algerian Basin

Balearic Islands

Gulf of
Valencia

M e d i t e r

Norwegian Trench

North European Plain

Pripet
Marshes

Neman

Bug

Dniester Podil's'ka Vysochina

Pivdennyy Buh

Dnieper Lowlands

Dniester

Prut

Tisza

Danube

Drava

Sava

Po

Moraya

Carpathian Mountains

Great
Hungarian
Plain

Lake Balaton

Bakony

Dinaric Alps

Apennines

Adriatic Sea

Corno Grande
2912m

Tiber

Adriatic
Basin

Tyrrhenian
Sea

Tyrrhenian
Basin

Gulf of
Taranto

Strait of Otranto

Lake
Scutari

Lake
Ohrid

Lake
Presba

Balkan Mountains

Maritsa

Rhodope Mountains

Gulf of
Thessaloniki

Mount Etna
3329m

Sicily

Malta

Strait of Sicily

Ionian Sea

Ionian Basin

Mediterranean Ridge

r a n e a n   S e a

Kola Peninsula

Ozero
Imandra

Murmansk Rise

Inarijärvi

Torniojoki

Kemijoki

White Sea

Timanskiy Kryazh

Mezen

Northern Dvina

Pechora

Ostrov
Kolguyev

Poluostrov
Kanin

Kolyma

Gulf of Bothnia

Oulujoki

Ozero
Vygozero

Onega Bay

Ozero
Vygozero

Vyg

Umeälven

Åland

Gulf of Finland

Gotland

Baltic Sea

Gulf of
Riga

Lake
Ladoga

Lake
Onega

Onega

Vaga

Lake
Peipus

Lake
Pskov

Msta

Lake Ilmen

Western Dvina

Dnieper

Desna

Seym

Dnieper

URAL

Mountains

Vychegda

Sukhona

Vyatka

Kama

Belaya

Ufa

Chusovaya

Kama

Tobol

Ozero
Chany

Ishim

Volga

Volga Upland

Central Russian Upland

Don

Khoper

Oka

Moskva

Moscow

Kiev
Reservoir

Kremenchuk
Reservoir

Black Sea Lowland

Sea of
Azov

Crimea

Kuban

Kerch Strait

Black Sea

EURASIAN PLATE
ANATOLIAN PLATE

Sea of
Marmara

Bosporus

Anatolia

Taurus Mountains

Gulf of
Antalya

Cyprus

Cyprus
Basin

Aegean Sea

Peloponnese

Myrtoan
Sea

Sea of Crete

Gávdos

Levantine Basin

Nile Fan

Gulf of
Sirte

Quattara Depression
-133m

Libyan Desert

Western Desert

Volga

Kuybyshev
Reservoir

Samara

Kirghiz Steppe

Caspian

Ural

Ural

Vergeni

Manych

Don

Sarpa

Yergeni

Gorky Reservoir

Rybinsk
Reservoir

Sheksna

Ozero
Beloye

Vologda

Sukhona

Bil'chug
Reservoir

Tsimlyansk
Reservoir

Denmark Strait

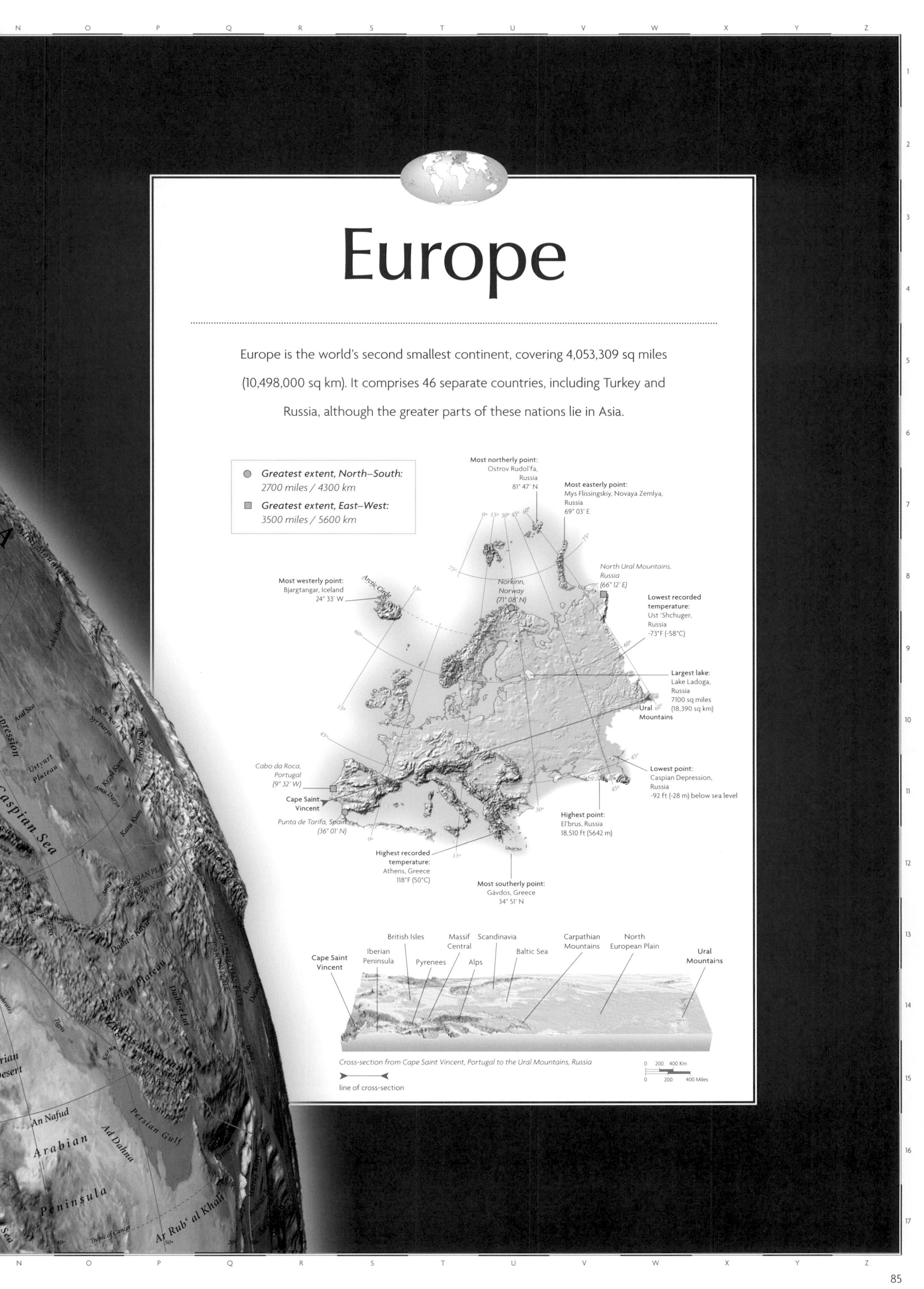

# Europe

Europe is the world's second smallest continent, covering 4,053,309 sq miles (10,498,000 sq km). It comprises 46 separate countries, including Turkey and Russia, although the greater parts of these nations lie in Asia.

● **Greatest extent, North–South:**
2700 miles / 4300 km

■ **Greatest extent, East–West:**
3500 miles / 5600 km

Most northerly point:
Ostrov Rudol'fa,
Russia
81° 47' N

Most easterly point:
Mys Flissingskiy, Novaya Zemlya,
Russia
69° 03' E

North Ural Mountains,
Russia
(66° 12' E)

Most westerly point:
Bjargtangar, Iceland
24° 33' W

Norkinn,
Norway
(71° 08' N)

Lowest recorded
temperature:
Ust 'Shchuger,
Russia
-73°F (-58°C)

Arctic Circle

Largest lake:
Lake Ladoga,
Russia
7100 sq miles
(18,390 sq km)

Ural
Mountains

Cabo da Roca,
Portugal
(9° 32' W)

Cape Saint
Vincent

Punta de Tarifa, Spain
(36° 01' N)

Lowest point:
Caspian Depression,
Russia
-92 ft (-28 m) below sea level

Highest point:
El'brus, Russia
18,510 ft (5642 m)

Highest recorded
temperature:
Athens, Greece
118°F (50°C)

Most southerly point:
Gávdos, Greece
34° 51' N

British Isles

Massif
Central

Scandinavia

Carpathian
Mountains

North
European Plain

Ural
Mountains

Iberian
Peninsula

Pyrenees

Alps

Baltic Sea

Cape Saint
Vincent

*Cross-section from Cape Saint Vincent, Portugal to the Ural Mountains, Russia*

line of cross-section

0   200   400 Km

0   200   400 Miles

# Physical Europe

The physical diversity of Europe belies its relatively small size. To the northwest and south it is enclosed by mountains. The older, rounded Atlantic Highlands of Scandinavia and the British Isles lie to the north and the younger, rugged peaks of the Alpine Uplands to the south. In between lies the North European Plain, stretching 2485 miles (4000 km) from The Fens in England to the Ural Mountains in Russia. South of the plain lies a series of gently folded sedimentary rocks separated by ancient plateaux, known as massifs.

## The North European Plain

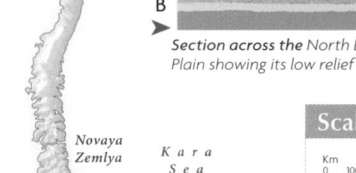

Rising less than 1000 ft (300 m) above sea level, the North European Plain strongly reflects past glaciation. Ridges of both coarse moraine and finer, windblown deposits have accumulated over much of the region. The ice sheet also diverted a number of river channels from their original courses.

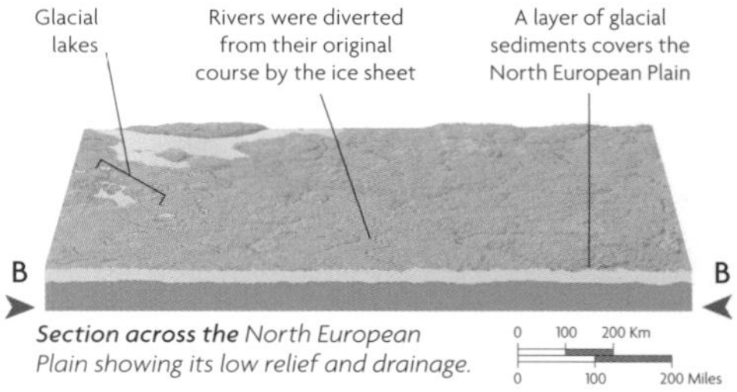

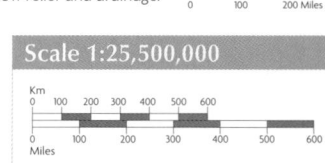

Glacial lakes

Rivers were diverted from their original course by the ice sheet

A layer of glacial sediments covers the North European Plain

**Section across the** North European Plain showing its low relief and drainage.

B — B

0   100   200 Km
0   100   200 Miles

## The Atlantic Highlands

The Atlantic Highlands were formed by compression against the Scandinavian Shield during the Caledonian mountain-building period over 500 million years ago. The highlands were once part of a continuous mountain chain, now divided by the North Sea and a submerged rift valley.

The Atlantic Highlands continue in the British Isles

Rift valley buried by sediments

North Sea

Atlantic Highlands in Norway

Rocks affected by ancient mountain-building

Scandinavian Shield

A — A

**Cross-section through** northeastern Europe showing the continuous mountain chain and rift valley system.

0   100   200 Km
0   100   200 Miles

### Scale 1:25,500,000

Km
0   100   200   300   400   500   600
0   100   200   300   400   500   600
Miles

projection: Lambert Azimuthal Equal Area

### Map key

**Elevation**

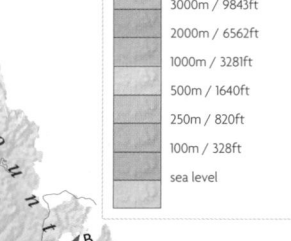

4000m / 13,124ft
3000m / 9843ft
2000m / 6562ft
1000m / 3281ft
500m / 1640ft
250m / 820ft
100m / 328ft
sea level

### Plate margins
(for explanation see page xiv)

—————— constructive
△    △ destructive
—————— conservative
.............. uncertain
—————— physiographic regions
▶— line of cross-section

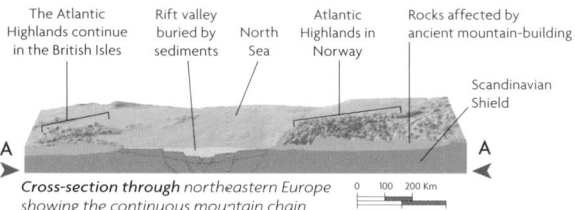

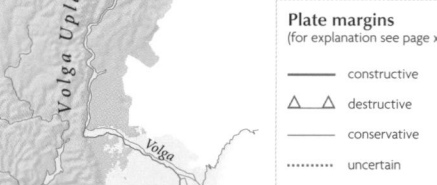

*Map labels:*

NORTH AMERICAN PLATE
EURASIAN PLATE
Iceland
Novaya Zemlya
Kara Sea
Barents Sea
Ostrov Kolguyev
Kola Peninsula
White Sea
Kölen
Norwegian Sea
Faroe Islands
Shetland Islands
Outer Hebrides
SCANDINAVIAN HIGHLANDS
SCANDINAVIAN SHIELD
Gulf of Bothnia
Northern Dvina
Lake Onega
Lake Ladoga
Ural Mountains
British Isles
ATLANTIC OCEAN
Ireland
Shannon
Vänern
Vättern
Gulf of Riga
Western Dvina
Britain
North Sea
Jutland
Baltic Sea
NORTH EUROPEAN PLAIN
Central Russian Upland
Volga Uplands
The Fens
Thames
English Channel
Rhine
Elbe
Oder
Vistula
Seine
Loire
Harz
Ardennes
PLATEAUX AND LOWLANDS
Danube
Carpathian Mountains
Dnieper
Dniester
Don
Volga
Caspian Sea
Bay of Biscay
Garonne
Massif Central
Rhône
Mt Blanc 4807 m
ALPINE UPLANDS
Po
Great Hungarian Plain
Danube
Sea of Azov
Crimea
Caucasus
El'brus 5642m
Douro
Pyrenees
Ebro
Corsica
Apennines
Adriatic Sea
Dinaric Alps
Balkan Mountains
Black Sea
ASIA
Iberian Peninsula
Guadalquivir
Balearic Islands
Sardinia
Tyrrhenian Sea
Vesuvius 1171m
EURASIAN PLATE
AFRICAN PLATE
Mediterranean Sea
Sicily
Etna 3329m
Ionian Sea
EURASIAN PLATE
ANATOLIAN PLATE
AFRICAN PLATE
Peloponnese
Aegean Sea
Crete

## The plateaus and lowlands

The uplifted plateaus or massifs of southern central Europe are the result of long-term erosion, later followed by uplift. They are the source areas of many of the rivers which drain Europe's lowlands. In some of the higher reaches, fractures have enabled igneous rocks from deep in the Earth to reach the surface.

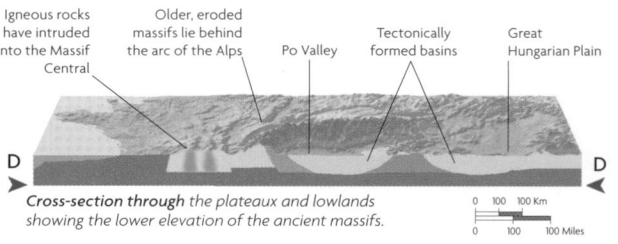

Igneous rocks have intruded into the Massif Central

Older, eroded massifs lie behind the arc of the Alps

Po Valley

Tectonically formed basins

Great Hungarian Plain

D — D

**Cross-section through** the plateaux and lowlands showing the lower elevation of the ancient massifs.

0   100   100 Km
0   100   100 Miles

## The Alpine Uplands

The collision of the African and European continents, which began about 65 million years ago, folded and then uplifted a series of mountain ranges running across southern Europe and into Asia. Two major lines of folding can be traced: one includes the Pyrenees, the Alps, and the Carpathian Mountains; the other incorporates the Apennines and the Dinaric Alps.

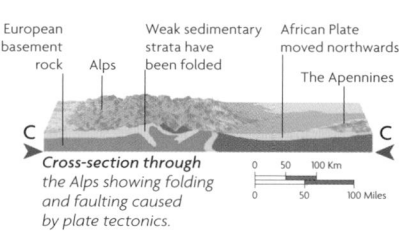

European basement rock

Alps

Weak sedimentary strata have been folded

African Plate moved northwards

The Apennines

C — C

**Cross-section through** the Alps showing folding and faulting caused by plate tectonics.

0   50   100 Km
0   50   100 Miles

# Climate

Europe experiences few extremes in either rainfall or temperature, with the exception of the far north and south. Along the west coast, the warm currents of the North Atlantic Drift moderate temperatures. Although east–west air movement is relatively unimpeded by relief, the Alpine Uplands halt the progress of north–south air masses, protecting most of the Mediterranean from cold, north winds.

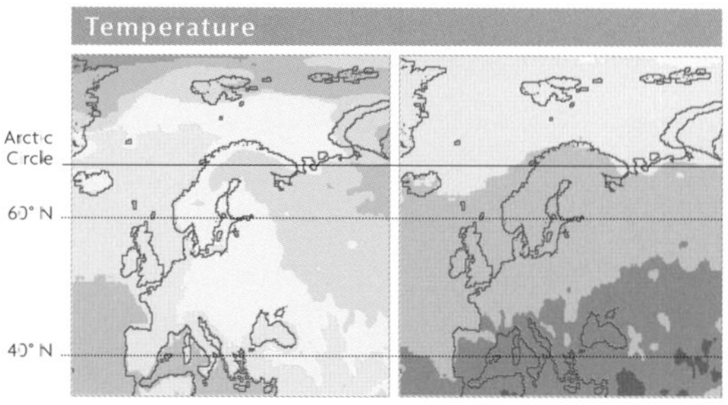

▲ *Frost grips northern* and eastern Europe during the long cold winters. Lakes and rivers frequently freeze.

## Temperature

*Average January temperature*

*Average July temperature*

### Temperature

| | |
|---|---|
| | below -22°F (-30°C) |
| | -22 to -4°F (-30 to -20°C) |
| | -4 to 14°F (-20 to -10°C) |
| | 14 to 32°F (-10 to 0°C) |
| | 32 to 50°F (0 to 10°C) |
| | 50 to 68°F (10 to 20°C) |
| | 68 to 86°F (20 to 30°C) |
| | above 86°F (30°C) |

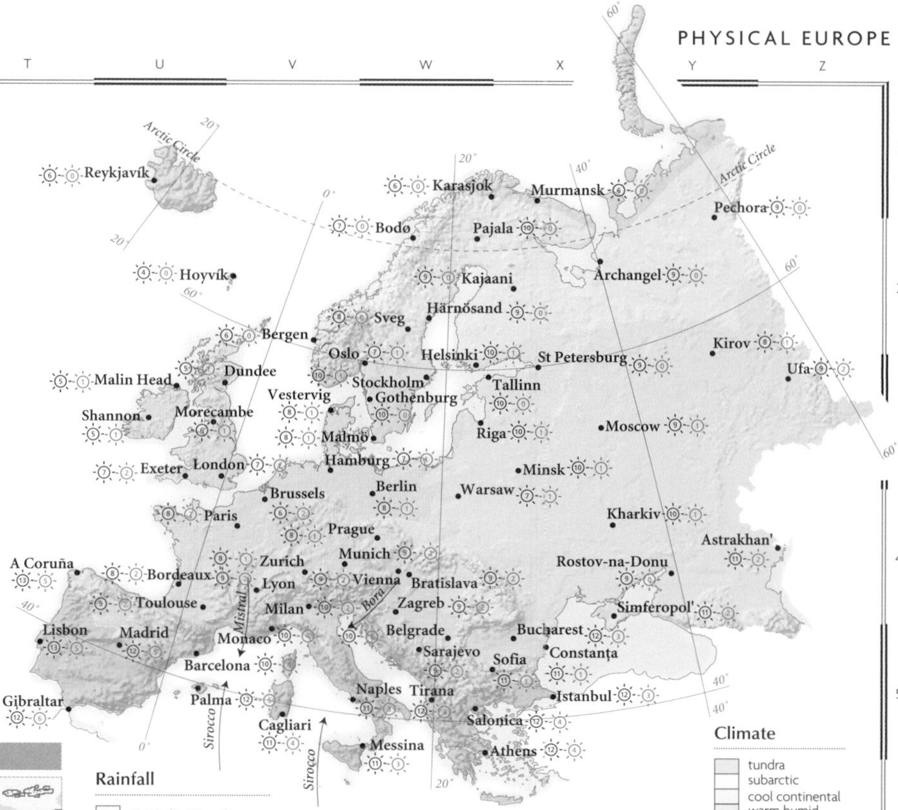

## Rainfall

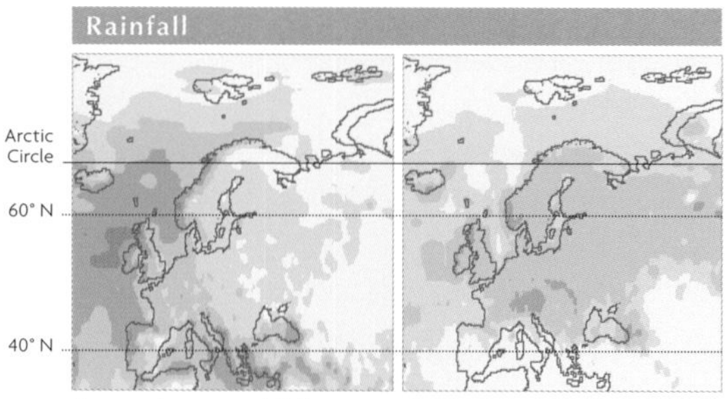

*Average January rainfall*

*Average July rainfall*

### Rainfall

| | |
|---|---|
| | 0–1 in (0–25 mm) |
| | 1–2 in (25–50 mm) |
| | 2–4 in (50–100 mm) |
| | 4–8 in (100–200 mm) |
| | 8–12 in (200–300 mm) |
| | 12–16 in (300–400 mm) |
| | 16–20 in (400–500 mm) |
| | more than 20 in (500 mm) |

▲ *Mild temperatures and frequent rainfall contribute to the fertile farming land found over much of northwestern Europe.*

### Climate

| | |
|---|---|
| | tundra |
| | subarctic |
| | cool continental |
| | warm humid |
| | mediterranean |
| | semi-arid |
| ☼ | daily hours of sunshine, January |
| ☼ | daily hours of sunshine, July |
| → | cold wind |
| → | hot wind |

▶ *Dusty Sirocco winds* from Africa help create the semiarid scrubland common across the Mediterranean coastlands of southern Europe.

# Shaping the continent

Successive Ice Ages have left many relict landforms across Europe. Present glaciers continue to carve peaks and valleys in the northern Atlantic Highlands and Alpine Uplands. Tectonic activity, both past and present, has shaped southern Europe and Iceland. Active volcanoes and earthquakes still occur in Italy and Greece. Europe's extensive coastline, particularly in the northwest, is constantly modified by wave action and fluvial deposits.

## Glaciation

1 Valley glaciers, such as this one *(left)* in Iceland, form in hollows at the top of valleys and flow downward, drawn by gravity. Their growth is dynamic; new snowfall constantly accumulates at the head of the glacier, while the snout melts, depositing material eroded and carried by the glacier.

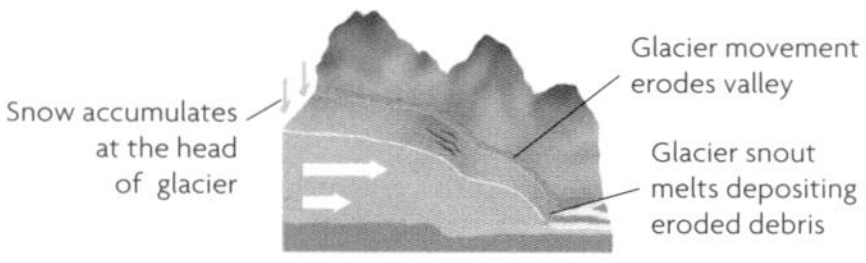

Snow accumulates at the head of glacier

Glacier movement erodes valley

Glacier snout melts depositing eroded debris

*Glaciation: Development of a glacier*

### Landscape

| | |
|---|---|
| | uplifting land |
| | stable land |
| | sinking land |
| | limestone region |
| | glacier |
| ▲ | active volcano |
| → | ocean current |
| • • • | area of tectonic activity |
| —— | maximum limit of glaciation |

## River systems

2 Rivers are continuously transporting eroded material toward the sea. Slow-moving, low-gradient rivers, like this one in western Russia *(above)*, deposit their alluvium load, infilling valleys creating a floodplain. Subsequent climatic and tectonic fluctuations may erode the floodplain to form terraces.

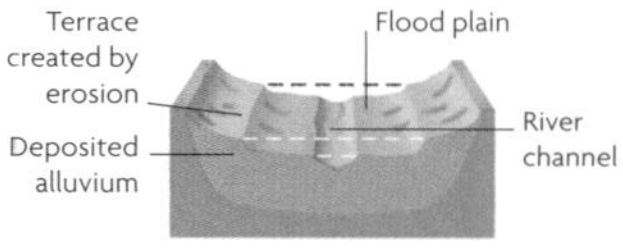

Terrace created by erosion

Flood plain

Deposited alluvium

River channel

*River systems: Formation of a flood plain and terraces*

## Coastal processes

5 Spits are narrow bands of sand or shingle, formed by longshore drift; a process whereby waves carry material along the beach. They usually form where the coastline changes direction, and their growth is then halted by an opposing river current, as at Spurn Head, in the British Isles *(left)*. Coastal features such as these are constantly being created and destroyed.

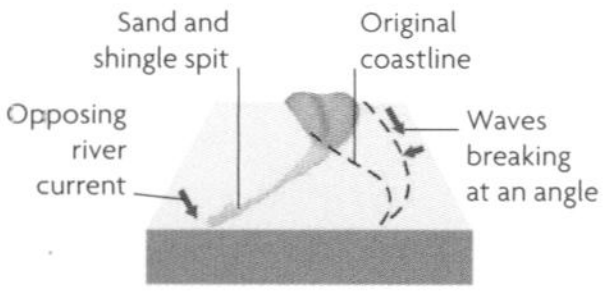

# The evolving landscape

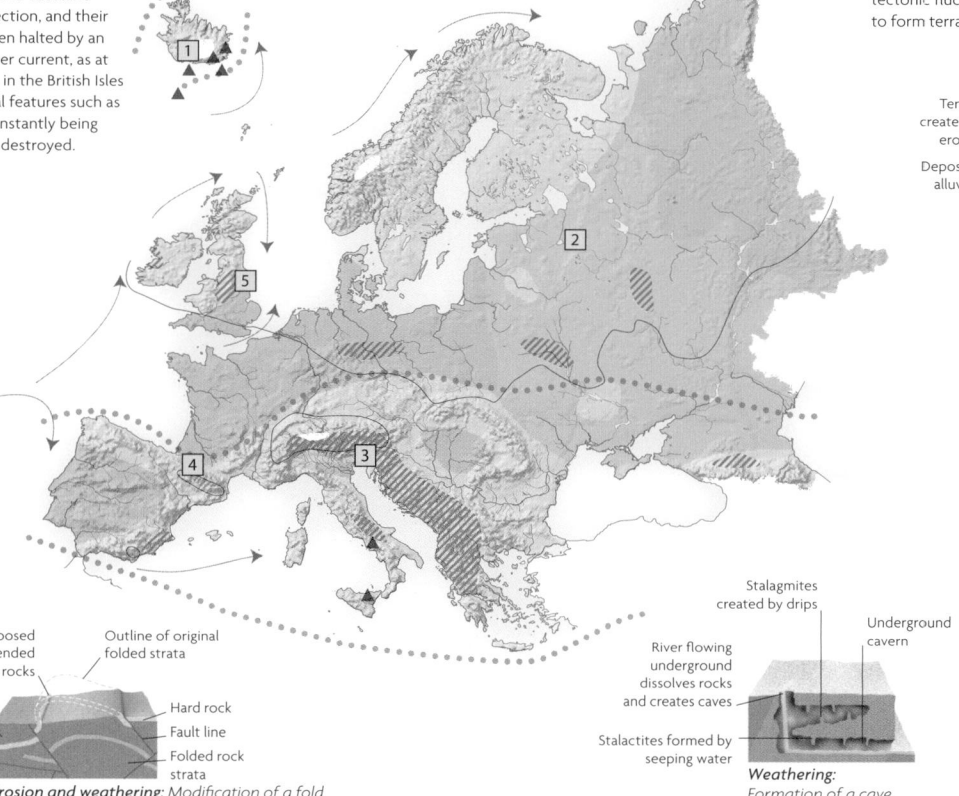

Sand and shingle spit

Original coastline

Opposing river current

Waves breaking at an angle

*Coastal processes: Formation of a spit*

## Erosion and weathering

4 Much of Europe was once subjected to folding and faulting, exposing hard and soft rock layers. Subsequent erosion and weathering has worn away the softer strata, leaving up-ended layers of hard rock as in the French Pyrenees *(above)*.

Exposed up-ended rocks

Outline of original folded strata

Soft rock

Hard rock

Fault line

Folded rock strata

*Erosion and weathering: Modification of a fold*

Stalagmites created by drips

Underground cavern

River flowing underground dissolves rocks and creates caves

Stalactites formed by seeping water

*Weathering: Formation of a cave*

## Weathering

3 As surface water filters through permeable limestone, the rock dissolves to form underground caves, like Postojna in the Karst region of Slovenia *(above)*. Stalactites grow downward as lime-enriched water seeps from roof fractures; stalagmites grow upward where drips splash down.

Map labels: Reykjavík, Hoyvík, Bergen, Malin Head, Shannon, Morecambe, Dundee, Vestervig, Oslo, Stockholm, Gothenburg, Sveg, Härnösand, Bodo, Karasjok, Pajala, Kajaani, Murmansk, Pechora, Archangel, Kirov, Ufa, Helsinki, St Petersburg, Tallinn, Riga, Moscow, Minsk, Kharkiv, Warsaw, Berlin, Hamburg, Brussels, London, Exeter, Paris, Prague, Munich, Vienna, Bratislava, Zagreb, Zurich, Lyon, Milan, Bordeaux, Toulouse, Madrid, Lisbon, A Coruña, Gibraltar, Palma, Barcelona, Monaco, Belgrade, Sarajevo, Sofia, Bucharest, Constanta, Simferopol', Rostov-na-Donu, Astrakhan', Kirov, Naples, Tirana, Salonica, Istanbul, Athens, Messina, Cagliari, Mistral, Bern, Sirocco, Arctic Circle

# Political Europe

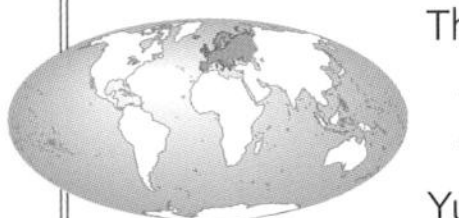

The political boundaries of Europe have changed many times, especially during the 20th century in the aftermath of two world wars, the break-up of the empires of Austria-Hungary, Nazi Germany and, towards the end of the century, the collapse of communism in eastern Europe and the fragmentation of Yugoslavia all radically altered the political map of Europe. In 1958, the formation of the European Economic Community (now the European Union or EU) started a shift towards economic and political union. By 2013 the EU had grown to encompass 28 states but in 2016 a membership referendum in the UK resulted in 52% of voters electing to leave. This so-called "Brexit" eventually took place on January 31st, 2020, when the UK officially left the EU.

▲ *The Brandenburg Gate* in Berlin is a potent symbol of German reunification. From 1961, the road beneath it ended in a wall, built to stop the flow of refugees to the West. It was opened again in 1989 when the wall was destroyed and East and West Germany were reunited.

## Population

Europe is a densely populated, urbanized continent; in Belgium over 90% of people live in urban areas. The highest population densities are found in an area stretching east from southern Britain and northern France, into Germany. The northern fringes are only sparsely populated.

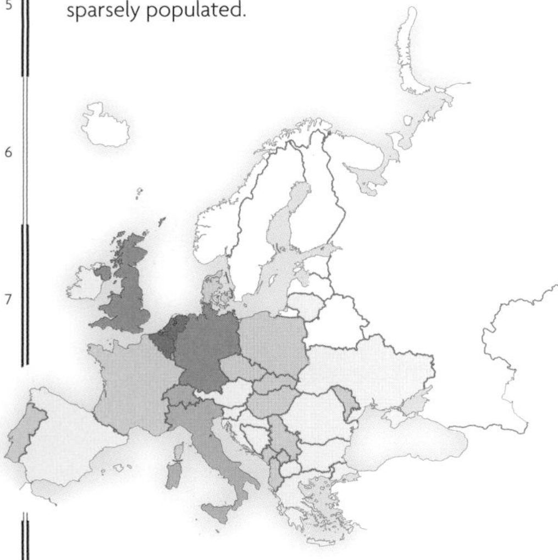

▲ *Demand for space* in densely populated European cities like London has led to the development of high-rise offices and urban sprawl.

### Population density
(people per sq mile)

- below 130
- 130–259
- 260–379
- 380–519
- 520–780
- above 780

▲ *Traditional lifestyles still* persist in many remote and rural parts of Europe, especially in the south, east, and in the far north.

### Map key

**Population**

- ▣ above 5 million
- ▪ 1 million to 5 million
- ◉ 500,000 to 1 million
- ◎ 100,000 to 500,000
- ⊕ 50,000 to 100,000
- ○ 10,000 to 50,000
- ● Country capital

**Borders**

full international border

### Scale 1:17,250,000

Km
0  100  200  300  400  500  600  700

Miles
0  100  200  300  400  500  600  700

projection: Lambert Azimuthal Equal Area

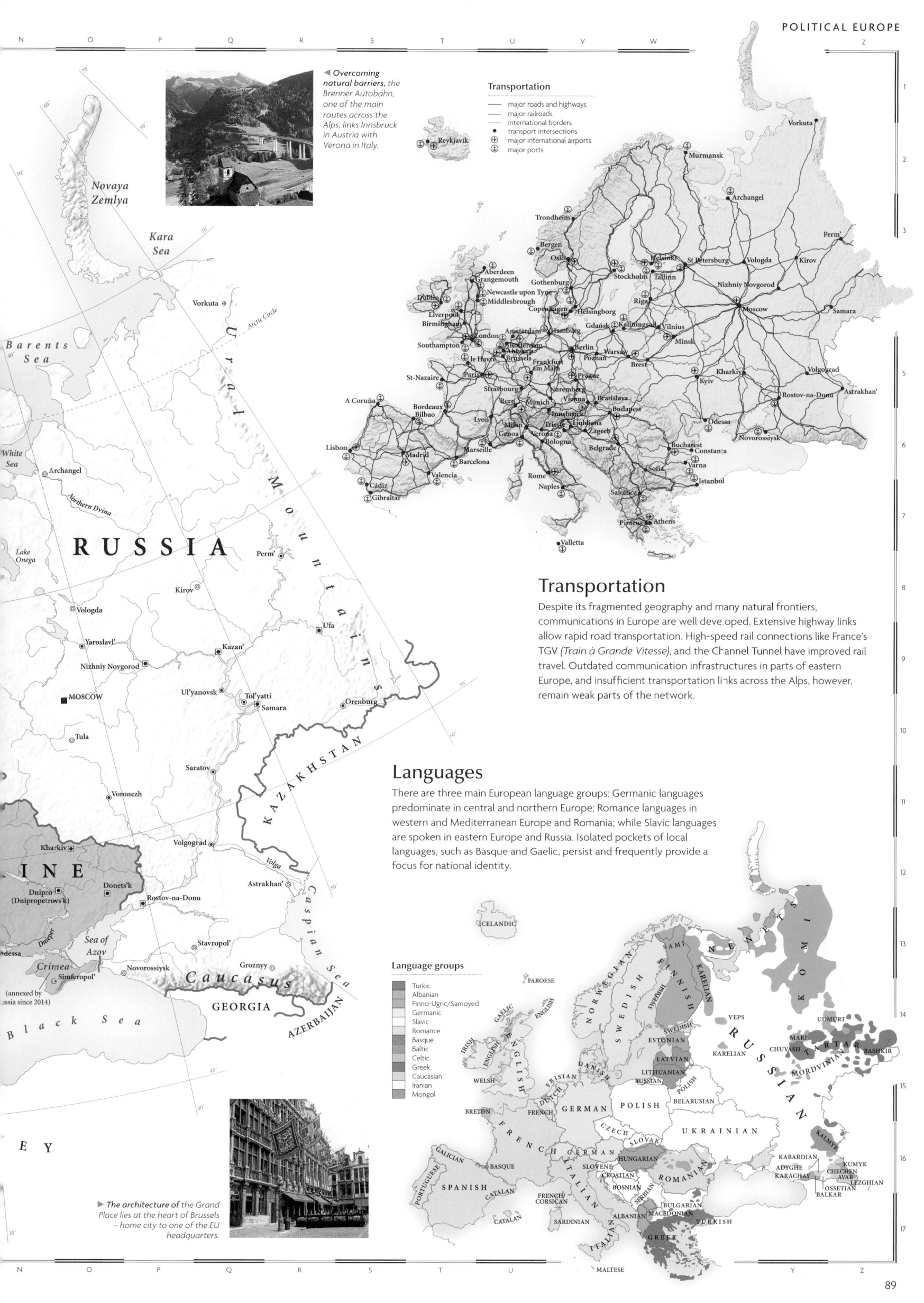

◀ *Overcoming natural barriers,* the Brenner Autobahn, one of the main routes across the Alps, links Innsbruck in Austria with Verona in Italy.

**Transportation**
- — major roads and highways
- — major railroads
- ······ international borders
- ● transport intersections
- ⊕ major international airports
- ⚓ major ports

## Transportation

Despite its fragmented geography and many natural frontiers, communications in Europe are well developed. Extensive highway links allow rapid road transportation. High-speed rail connections like France's TGV *(Train à Grande Vitesse),* and the Channel Tunnel have improved rail travel. Outdated communication infrastructures in parts of eastern Europe, and insufficient transportation links across the Alps, however, remain weak parts of the network.

## Languages

There are three main European language groups: Germanic languages predominate in central and northern Europe; Romance languages in western and Mediterranean Europe and Romania; while Slavic languages are spoken in eastern Europe and Russia. Isolated pockets of local languages, such as Basque and Gaelic, persist and frequently provide a focus for national identity.

**Language groups**
- Turkic
- Albanian
- Finno-Ugric/Samoyed
- Germanic
- Slavic
- Romance
- Basque
- Baltic
- Celtic
- Greek
- Caucasian
- Iranian
- Mongol

▶ *The architecture of* the Grand Place lies at the heart of Brussels – home city to one of the EU headquarters.

# European resources

Europe's large tracts of fertile, accessible land, combined with its generally temperate climate, have allowed a greater percentage of land to be used for agricultural purposes than in any other continent. Extensive coal and iron ore deposits were used to create steel and manufacturing industries during the 19th and 20th centuries. Today, although natural resources have been widely exploited, and heavy industry is of declining importance, the growth of hi-tech and service industries has enabled Europe to maintain its wealth.

## Industry

Europe's wealth was generated by the rise of industry and colonial exploitation during the 19th century. The mining of abundant natural resources made Europe the industrial center of the world. Adaptation has been essential in the changing world economy, and a move to service-based industries has been widespread except in eastern Europe, where heavy industry still dominates.

▲ *Other power sources* are becoming more attractive as fossil fuels run out; 16% of Europe's electricity is now provided by hydroelectric power.

▲ *Countries like Hungary* are still struggling to modernize inefficient factories left over from extensive, centrally-planned industrialization during the communist era.

◄ *Frankfurt am Main* is an example of a modern service-based city. The skyline is dominated by headquarters from the worlds of banking and commerce.

## Standard of living

Living standards in western Europe are among the highest in the world, although there is a growing sector of homeless, jobless people. Eastern Europeans have lower overall standards of living – a legacy of stagnated economies.

**Standard of living**
(UN human development index)

| | |
|---|---|
| | low |
| | |
| | high |
| | data not available |

▶ *Skiing brings millions* of tourists to the slopes each year, which means that even unproductive, marginal land is used to create wealth in the French, Swiss, Italian, and Austrian Alps.

**GNI per capita (US $)**

| | |
|---|---|
| | below 1999 |
| | 2000–4999 |
| | 5000–9999 |
| | 10,000–19,999 |
| | 20,000–24,999 |
| | above 25,000 |

**Industry**

| | | |
|---|---|---|
| → | aerospace | 🍴 food processing | 🍷 wine |
| 🍺 | brewing | 🖥 hi-tech industry | ⚒ coal |
| 🚗 | car/vehicle manufacture | ⚙ iron & steel | 🛢 oil |
| 🧪 | chemicals | 💊 pharmaceuticals | 🛢 gas |
| 🛡 | defense | ⑃ printing & publishing | |
| 🖥 | electronics | ⚓ shipbuilding | ● industrial cities |
| ⚙ | engineering | ✄ textiles | ▨ major industrial areas |
| $ | finance | 🌲 timber processing | |

*Map labels:*

ICELAND, Reykjavík, NORWAY, SWEDEN, FINLAND, RUSSIA, Murmansk, Archangel, Novaya Zemlya, Ostrov Kolguyev, Barents Sea, Norwegian Sea, Faroe Islands (to Denmark), Trondheim, Bergen, Oslo, Stockholm, Gothenburg, Gulf of Bothnia, Turku (Åbo), Helsinki (Helsingfors), Tallinn, St Petersburg, Cherepovets, Yaroslavl', Ivanovo, Nizhniy Novgorod, Kazan', Perm', Ufa, Moscow, Ryazan', Tula, Tol'yatti, Samara, Saratov, ESTONIA, Riga, LATVIA, LITHUANIA, Vilnius, RUSSIA (Kaliningrad), Minsk, BELARUS, Voronezh, Kursk, Volgograd, Rostov-na-Donu, KAZAKHSTAN, Caspian Sea, ATLANTIC OCEAN, IRELAND, Dublin, Belfast, Glasgow, UNITED KINGDOM, Newcastle upon Tyne, Liverpool, Manchester, Birmingham, Cardiff, London, North Sea, DENMARK, Copenhagen, Malmö, Hamburg, Gdańsk, POLAND, Poznań, Warsaw, Łódź, Amsterdam, NETH., Rotterdam, Berlin, Dresden, Leipzig, GERMANY, Cologne, Essen, Antwerp, BELG., Brussels, Liège, Lille, Rouen, Paris, Metz, Strasbourg, Frankfurt am Main, Stuttgart, Munich, LUX., Nantes, FRANCE, Zürich, SWITZ., Bordeaux, Lyon, Toulouse, Channel Islands, Bay of Biscay, A Coruña, Porto, PORTUGAL, Lisbon, Bilbao, SPAIN, Madrid, Seville, Barcelona, ANDORRA, Marseille, MONACO, Gibraltar (to UK), Ceuta (to Spain), Melilla (to Spain), MOROCCO, Balearic Islands, Corsica, Sardinia, ITALY, Turin, Genoa, Milan, Venice, Bologna, Rome, VATICAN CITY, SAN MARINO, Naples, Taranto, Palermo, Sicily, MALTA, Tyrrhenian Sea, Ionian Sea, Mediterranean Sea, Adriatic Sea, SLVN., Zagreb, CROATIA, BOSNIA & HERZ., SERBIA, MONT., KOSOVO, Belgrade, ALBANIA, NORTH MACEDONIA, GREECE, Salonica, Athens, Piraeus, Aegean Sea, Crete, Linz, Vienna, AUSTRIA, Bratislava, SLOVAKIA, Prague, CZECHIA, Katowice, Kraków, Budapest, HUNGARY, ROMANIA, Bucharest, Ploesti, Constanța, MOLDOVA, Odessa, UKRAINE, Kyiv, Dnipro, Kryvyy Rih, Kharkiv, Donets'k, BULGARIA, Sofia, Varna, Black Sea, TURKEY, Istanbul, GEORGIA, AZERBAIJAN, Baltic Sea

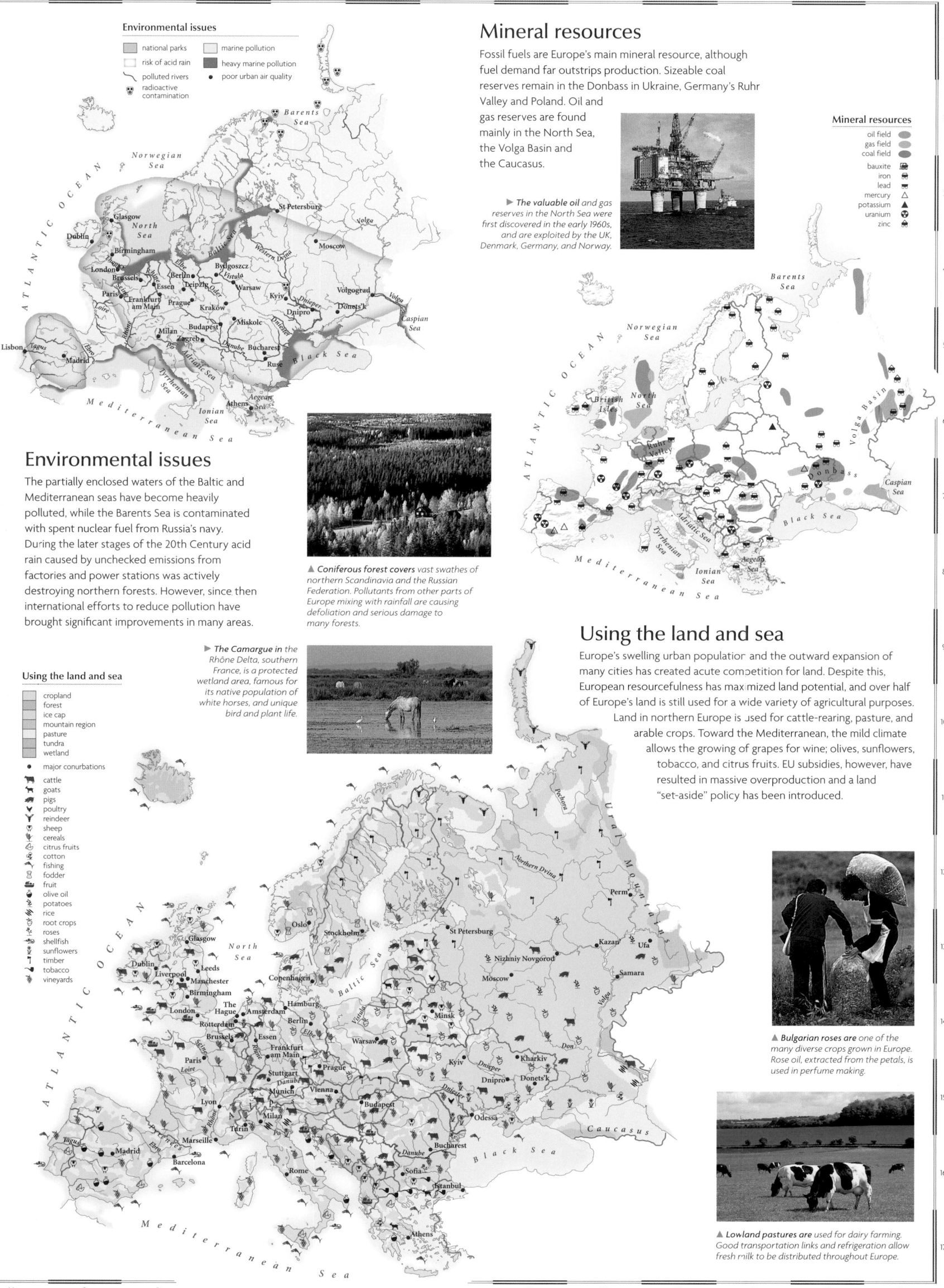

## Environmental issues

**Environmental issues**
- national parks
- risk of acid rain
- polluted rivers
- radioactive contamination
- marine pollution
- heavy marine pollution
- poor urban air quality

The partially enclosed waters of the Baltic and Mediterranean seas have become heavily polluted, while the Barents Sea is contaminated with spent nuclear fuel from Russia's navy. During the later stages of the 20th Century acid rain caused by unchecked emissions from factories and power stations was actively destroying northern forests. However, since then international efforts to reduce pollution have brought significant improvements in many areas.

▲ *Coniferous forest covers* vast swathes of northern Scandinavia and the Russian Federation. Pollutants from other parts of Europe mixing with rainfall are causing defoliation and serious damage to many forests.

▶ *The Camargue in the Rhône Delta, southern France, is a protected wetland area, famous for its native population of white horses, and unique bird and plant life.*

## Mineral resources

Fossil fuels are Europe's main mineral resource, although fuel demand far outstrips production. Sizeable coal reserves remain in the Donbass in Ukraine, Germany's Ruhr Valley and Poland. Oil and gas reserves are found mainly in the North Sea, the Volga Basin and the Caucasus.

▶ *The valuable oil and gas reserves in the North Sea were first discovered in the early 1960s, and are exploited by the UK, Denmark, Germany, and Norway.*

**Mineral resources**
- oil field
- gas field
- coal field
- bauxite
- iron
- lead
- mercury
- potassium
- uranium
- zinc

## Using the land and sea

Europe's swelling urban population and the outward expansion of many cities has created acute competition for land. Despite this, European resourcefulness has maximized land potential, and over half of Europe's land is still used for a wide variety of agricultural purposes. Land in northern Europe is used for cattle-rearing, pasture, and arable crops. Toward the Mediterranean, the mild climate allows the growing of grapes for wine; olives, sunflowers, tobacco, and citrus fruits. EU subsidies, however, have resulted in massive overproduction and a land "set-aside" policy has been introduced.

**Using the land and sea**
- cropland
- forest
- ice cap
- mountain region
- pasture
- tundra
- wetland
- major conurbations
- cattle
- goats
- pigs
- poultry
- reindeer
- sheep
- cereals
- citrus fruits
- cotton
- fishing
- fodder
- fruit
- olive oil
- potatoes
- rice
- root crops
- roses
- shellfish
- sunflowers
- timber
- tobacco
- vineyards

▲ *Bulgarian roses are* one of the many diverse crops grown in Europe. Rose oil, extracted from the petals, is used in perfume making.

▲ *Lowland pastures are* used for dairy farming. Good transportation links and refrigeration allow fresh milk to be distributed throughout Europe.

# Scandinavia, Finland & Iceland

## DENMARK, NORWAY, SWEDEN, FINLAND, ICELAND

Jutting into the Arctic Circle, this northern swath of Europe has some of the continent's harshest environments, but benefits from great reserves of oil, gas, and natural evergreen forests. While most early settlers came from the south, migrants to Finland came from the east, giving it a distinct language and culture. Since the late 19th century, the Scandinavian states have developed strong egalitarian traditions. Today, their welfare benefits systems are among the most extensive in the world, and standards of living are high. The Lapps, or Sami, maintain their traditional lifestyle in the northern regions of Norway, Sweden, and Finland.

## The landscape

Glaciers up to 10,000 ft (3000 m) deep covered most of Scandinavia and Finland during the last Ice Age. The effects of glaciation mark the entire landscape, from the mountains to the lowlands, across the tundra landscape of Lapland, and the lake districts of Sweden and Finland.

Geysers are a by-product of Iceland's volcanic activity. Geysir, Iceland's largest spring, gives them their name.

**Fjords**
▲ The fjords on the western coast of Norway were once gentle river valleys. Their deep floors and steep sides were carved out by glaciers during the last Ice Age, and they were later flooded by the sea.

The Lofoten Islands were one of the first areas exposed as the ice sheet melted.

Halti Mountain is Finland's highest point, at 4356 ft (1328 m).

Lapland, north of the Arctic Circle, is an area of undulating fells and plains known as tundra. The subsoil is permanently frozen and therefore impermeable. There are many peat bogs. Pools reappear in the summer when the surface thaws.

▲ Finland's landscape was fashioned by ice action. Glaciers gouged out its distinctive shallow lake basins, such as Oulujärvi, and left debris called moraines in their wake.

Oulujärvi

Area of maximum yearly uplift 0.3 in/yr (9 mm/yr)

▲ Scandinavia is still recovering from the last Ice Age, when ice depressed the land by 2000 ft (600 m). This gradual uplift is known as isostatic rebound.

Slower rates of uplift 0.1 in/yr (3 mm/yr)

Sjælland coast
▲ On the coast of Sjælland, these cliffs have been eroded by the sea, exposing layers of chalk and limestone.

## Using the land & sea

The cold climate, short growing season, poorly developed soil, steep slopes, and exposure to high winds across northern regions means that most agriculture is concentrated, with the population, in the south. Most of Finland and much of Norway and Sweden are covered by dense forests of pine, spruce, and birch, which supply the timber industries.

### Land use and agricultural distribution

- capital cities
- major towns
- pasture
- cropland
- forest
- mountain region
- tundra

- fishing
- pigs
- reindeer
- sheep
- cereals
- timber

### The urban/rural population divide

urban 77%   rural 23%

Population density
SI people per sq mile
(20 people per sq km)

Total land area
473,970 sq miles
(1,227,610 sq km)

**SCALE 1:9,000,000**

Projection: Lambert Conformal Conic

**Scale 1:5,500,000**

projection: Lambert Conformal Conic

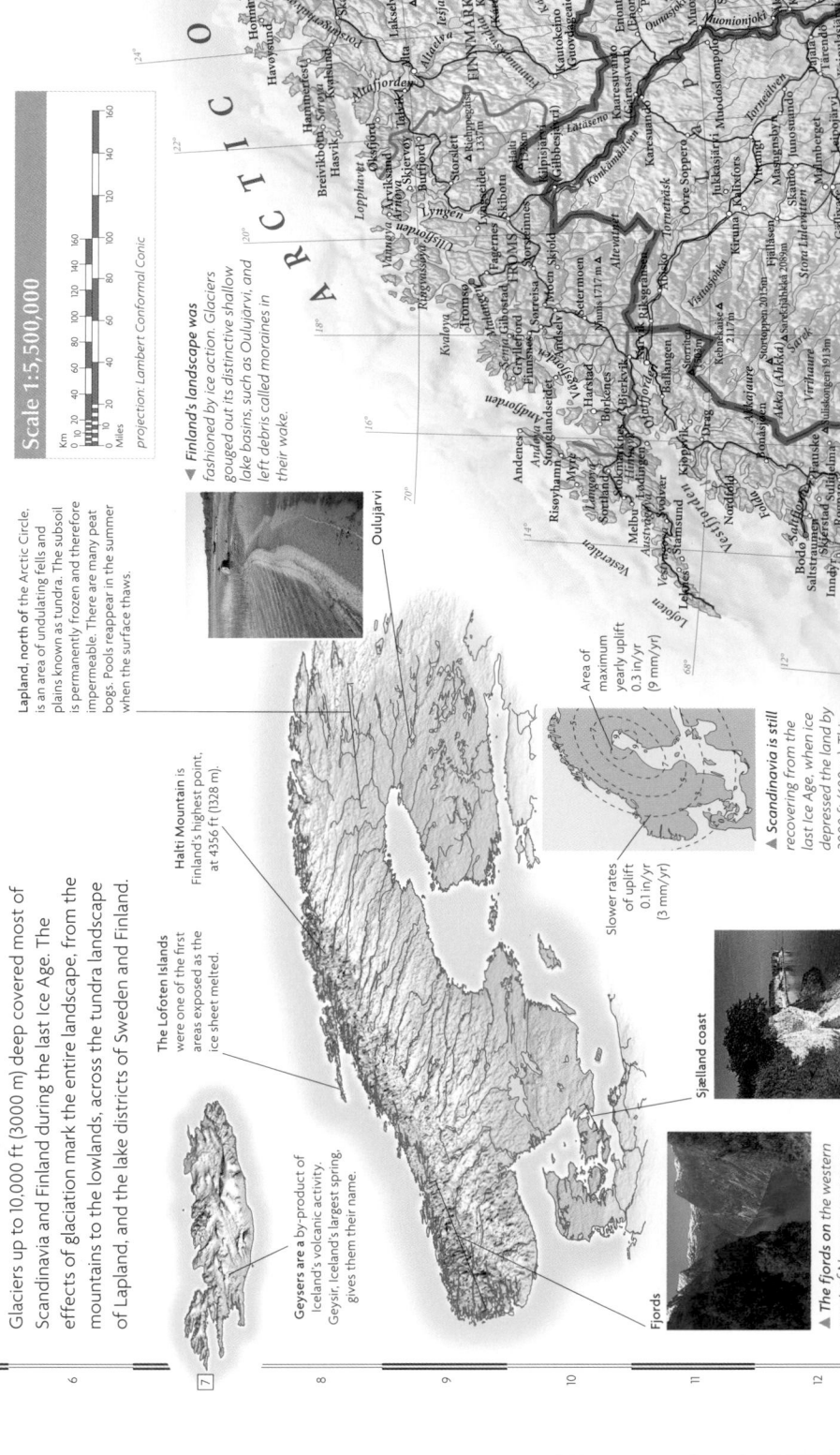

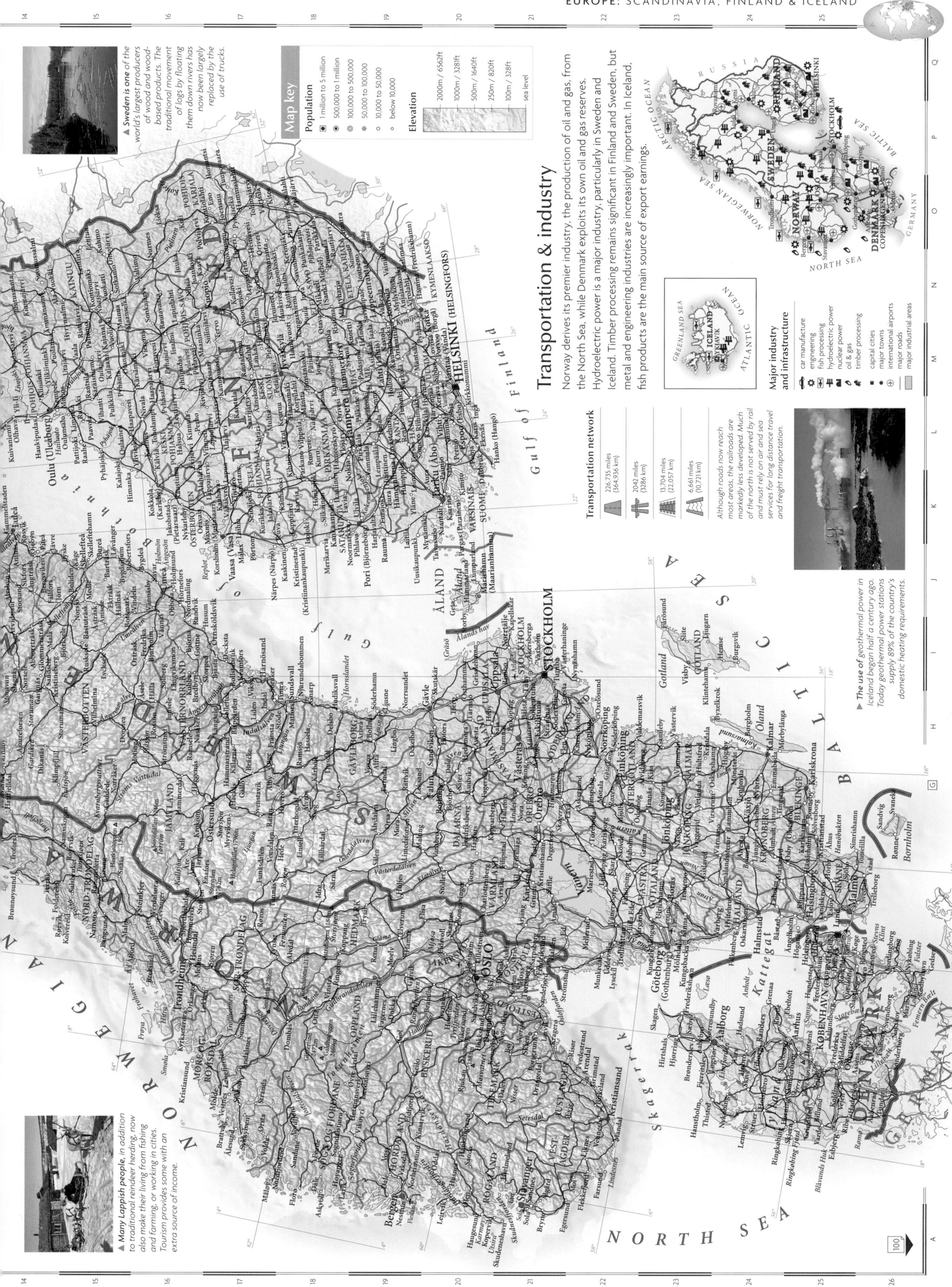

▲ *Sweden is one of the world's largest producers of wood and wood-based products. The traditional movement of logs by floating them down rivers has now been largely replaced by the use of trucks.*

## Map key

**Population**
- ● 1 million to 5 million
- ◉ 500,000 to 1 million
- ◎ 100,000 to 500,000
- ⊕ 50,000 to 100,000
- ○ 10,000 to 50,000
- ∘ below 10,000

**Elevation**
- 2000m / 6562ft
- 1000m / 3281ft
- 500m / 1640ft
- 250m / 820ft
- 100m / 328ft
- sea level

## Transportation & industry

Norway derives its premier industry, the production of oil and gas, from the North Sea, while Denmark exploits its own oil and gas reserves. Hydroelectric power is a major industry, particularly in Sweden and Iceland. Timber processing remains significant in Finland and Sweden, but metal and engineering industries are increasingly important. In Iceland, fish products are the main source of export earnings.

### Major industry and infrastructure
- car manufacture
- engineering
- fish processing
- hydroelectric power
- nuclear power
- oil & gas
- timber processing
- capital cities
- major towns
- international airports
- major roads
- major industrial areas

### Transportation network
- 226,735 miles (364,936 km)
- 2042 miles (3286 km)
- 13,704 miles (22,057 km)
- 6,661 miles (10,721 km)

Although roads now reach most areas, the railroads are markedly less developed. Much of the north is not served by rail and must rely on air and sea services for long distance travel and freight transportation.

▲ *The use of geothermal power in Iceland began half a century ago. Today geothermal power stations supply 89% of the country's domestic heating requirements.*

▲ *Many Lappish people, in addition to traditional reindeer herding, now also make their living from fishing and farming, or working in cities. Tourism provides some with an extra source of income.*

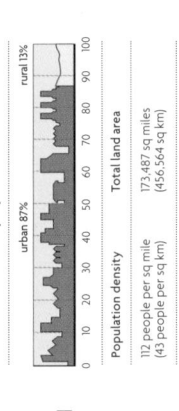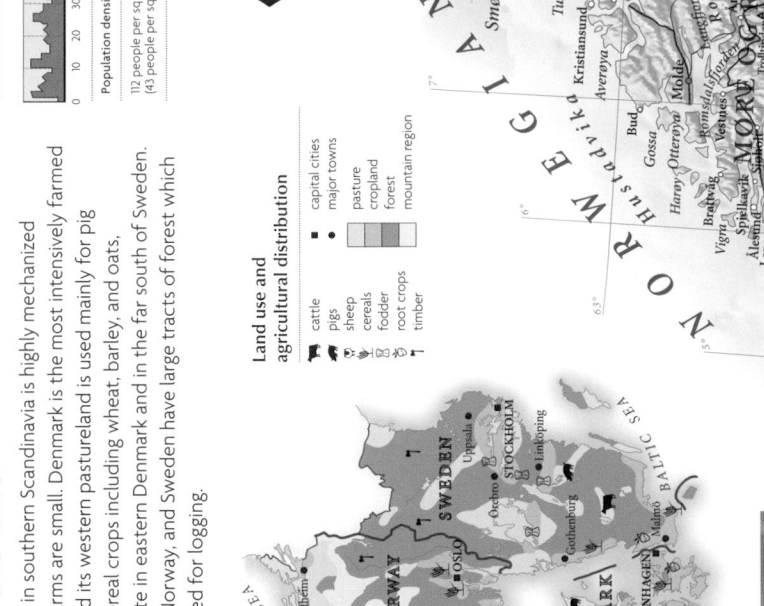

# Southern Scandinavia

## SOUTHERN NORWAY, SOUTHERN SWEDEN, DENMARK

Scandinavia's economic and political hub is the more habitable and accessible southern region. Many of the area's major cities are on the southern coasts, including Oslo and Stockholm, the capitals of Norway and Sweden. In Denmark, most of the population and the capital, Copenhagen, are located on its many islands. A cultural unity links the three Scandinavian countries. Their main languages, Danish, Swedish, and Norwegian, are mutually intelligible, and they all retain their monarchies, although the parliaments have legislative control.

## Using the land

Agriculture in southern Scandinavia is highly mechanized although farms are small. Denmark is the most intensively farmed country and its western pastureland is used mainly for pig farming. Cereal crops including wheat, barley, and oats, predominate in eastern Denmark and in the far south of Sweden. Southern Norway, and Sweden have large tracts of forest which are exploited for logging.

### The urban/rural population divide

urban 87%  rural 13%

Population density
112 people per sq mile
(43 people per sq km)

Total land area
173,487 sq miles
(456,564 sq km)

### Land use and agricultural distribution

- cattle
- pigs
- sheep
- cereals
- fodder
- root crops
- timber

capital cities
major towns
pasture
cropland
forest
mountain region

## The landscape

Southern Scandinavia, with the exception of Norway, has a flatter terrain than the rest of the region. Denmark and southern Sweden are both extensions of the North European Plain. In this area, because of glacial deposition rather than erosion, the soils are deeper and more fertile.

Acid rain, caused by industrial pollution carried north from elsewhere in Europe, harms plant and animal life in Scandinavian forests and lakes. The region's surface rocks lack lime to neutralize the acid, so making the problem more serious.

Denmark's flat and fertile soils are formed on glacial deposits between 100–160 ft (30–50 m) deep.

Vänern in Sweden is the largest lake in Scandinavia. It covers an area of 2080 sq miles (5390 sq km).

The lakes of southern Sweden remain from a period when the land was completely flooded. As the ice which covered the area melted, the land rose, leaving lakes in shallow, ice-scoured depressions. Sweden has over 90,000 lakes.

▲ Limestone pillars eroded by the sea dot the coast of Gotland and surrounding islands.

Distinctive low ridges, called eskers, are found across southern Sweden. They are formed from sand and gravel deposits left by retreating glaciers.

The peak of Glittertind in the Jotunheimen mountains is 8110 ft (2472 m) high.

▼ In the past, glaciers such as this one in Olden, Norway, were much larger. Today, many are retreating to yield the spectacular glacial scenery.

When the ice retreated the valley was flooded by the sea

Old valley floor

Erosion by glaciers deepened existing river valleys

Sea level

Sognefjorden

▲ Sognefjorden is the deepest of Norway's many fjords. It drops to 429 ft (1308 m) below sea level.

### Map key

Population
- 1 million to 5 million
- 500,000 to 1 million
- 100,000 to 500,000
- 50,000 to 100,000
- 10,000 to 50,000
- below 10,000

Elevation
2000m / 6562ft
1000m / 3281ft
500m / 1640ft
250m / 820ft
100m / 328ft

Scale 1:3,250,000
projection: Lambert Conformal Conic

▲ In Norway winters are longer and colder inland than in coastal areas, where the warm current of the North Atlantic Drift moderates the climate.

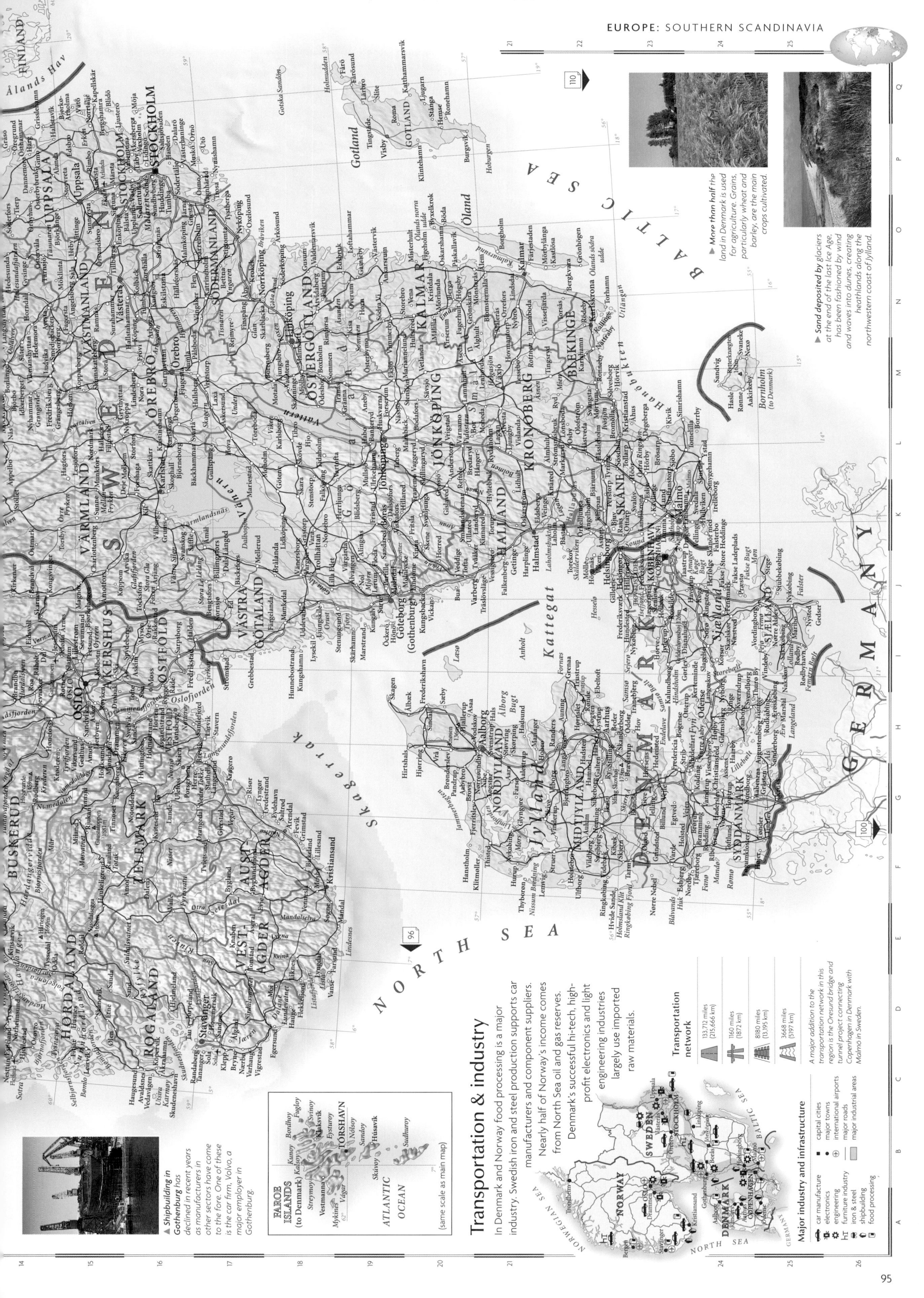

▲ *More than half the land in Denmark is used for agriculture. Grains, particularly wheat and barley, are the main crops cultivated.*

▲ *Sand deposited by glaciers at the end of the last Ice Age, has been fashioned by wind and waves into dunes, creating heathlands along the northwestern coast of Jylland.*

## Transportation & industry

In Denmark and Norway food processing is a major industry. Swedish iron and steel production supports car manufacturers and component suppliers. Nearly half of Norway's income comes from North Sea oil and gas reserves. Denmark's successful hi-tech, high-profit electronics and light engineering industries largely use imported raw materials.

### Transportation network

| | |
|---|---|
| 133,712 miles (215,666 km) | |
| 1160 miles (1872 km) | |
| 8180 miles (13,195 km) | |
| 3668 miles (5197 km) | |

*A major addition to the transportation network in this region is the Oresund bridge and tunnel project connecting Copenhagen in Denmark with Malmö in Sweden.*

### Major industry and infrastructure

- car manufacture
- electronics
- engineering
- furniture industry
- iron & steel
- shipbuilding
- food processing

- ● capital cities
- ■ major towns
- ⊕ international airports
- — major roads
- major industrial areas

▲ *Shipbuilding in Gothenburg has declined in recent years as manufacturers in other sectors have come to the fore. One of these is the car firm, Volvo, a major employer in Gothenburg.*

### FAROE ISLANDS
(to Denmark)

(same scale as main map)

# The British Isles

## UNITED KINGDOM, IRELAND

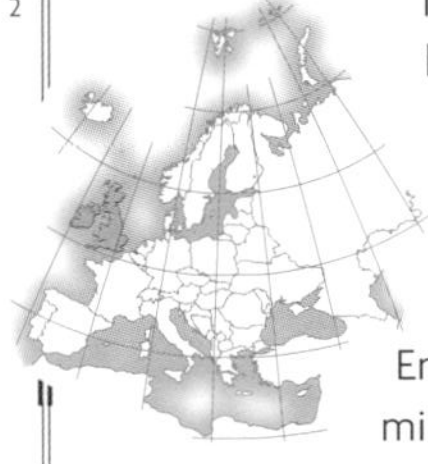

The British Isles have for centuries played a central role in European and world history. England, Wales, Scotland, and Northern Ireland together form the United Kingdom (UK), while the southern portion of Ireland is an independent country, self-governing since 1921. Although England has tended to be the politically and economically dominant partner in the UK, the Scots, Welsh, and Irish maintain independent cultures, distinct national identities and languages. Southeastern England is the most densely populated part of this crowded region, with over eight million people living in and around the London area.

## Transportation & industry

The British Isles' industrial base was founded primarily on coal, iron, and textiles, based largely in the north. Today, the most productive sectors include hi-tech industries clustered mainly in southeastern England, chemicals, finance, and the service sector, particularly tourism.

### Major industry and infrastructure

- car manufacture
- chemicals
- engineering
- hi-tech industry
- iron & steel
- tourism
- ◉ capital cities
- ● major towns
- ✈ international airports
- major roads
- major industrial areas

### Transportation network

| | |
|---|---|
| ▲ 285,947 miles (460,240 km) | 2033 miles (3578 km) |
| ▦ 11,825 miles (19,032km) | 3976 miles (6400 km) |

The UK's congested roads have become a major focus of environmental concern in recent years. No longer an island, the UK was finally linked to continental Europe by the Channel Tunnel in 1994.

## The landscape

Rugged uplands dominate the landscape of Scotland, Wales, and northern England. All the peaks in the British Isles over 4000 ft (1219 m) lie in highland Scotland. Lowland England rises into several ranges of rolling hills, including the older Mendips, and the Cotswolds and the Chilterns, which were formed at the same time as the Alps in southern Europe.

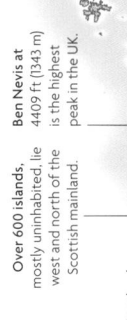
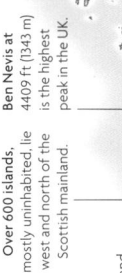

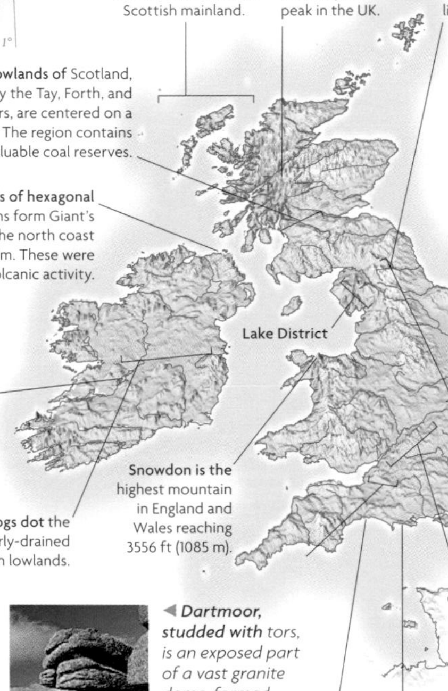

▲ *The valley of* Glen Coe *in the Scottish Highlands is a U-shaped valley, typical of the north and west of the British Isles, where glaciers shaped much of the landscape.*

Over 600 islands, mostly uninhabited, lie west and north of the Scottish mainland.

Ben Nevis at 4409 ft (1343 m) is the highest peak in the UK.

The Pennines, sometimes called "the backbone of England," are formed of limestones and grits.

▲ *Ullswater in the Lake District fills a deep valley formed by glacial erosion.*

The Fens are a low-lying area reclaimed from the sea.

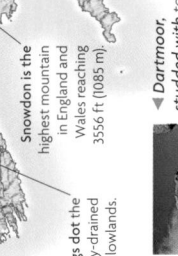

The Cotswold Hills are characterized by a series of limestone ridges overlooking clay vales.

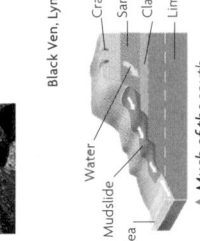
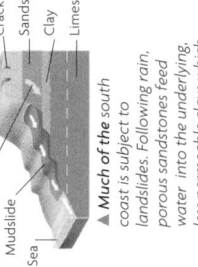
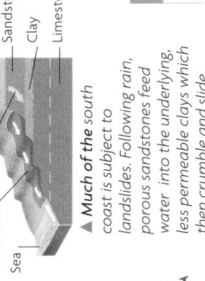
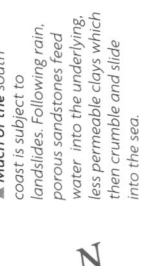

Durdle Door

▲ *Coastal erosion around the British Isles forms striking features such as this limestone arch, Durdle Door in Dorset.*

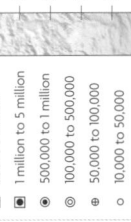

The lowlands of Scotland, drained by the Tay, Forth, and Clyde rivers, are centered on a rift valley. The region contains valuable coal reserves.

Thousands of hexagonal basalt columns form Giant's Causeway on the north coast of Antrim. These were created by volcanic activity.

Snowdon is the highest mountain in England and Wales reaching 3556 ft (1085 m).

Peat bogs dot the poorly-drained Irish lowlands.

The British Isles have no large-scale river systems. The Shannon is the longest at 230 miles (370 km).

▲ *Dartmoor, studded with* tors, *is an exposed part of a vast granite dome, formed when molten rock intruded into the Earth's crust.*

Black Ven, Lyme Regis

Cracks
Sandstone
Clay
Limestone
Water
Mudslide
Sea

▲ *Much of the south coast is subject to landslides. Following rain, porous sandstones feed water into the underlying, less permeable clays which then crumble and slide into the sea.*

### Map key

**Population**
- ■ above 5 million
- ◉ 1 million to 5 million
- ◎ 100,000 to 500,000
- ⊕ 50,000 to 100,000
- ● 10,000 to 50,000
- · below 10,000

**Elevation**
- 1000m / 3281ft
- 500m / 1640ft
- 250m / 820ft
- 100m / 328ft
- sea level

▼ *Clew Bay in western Ireland, is characteristic of the heavily indented west coast, where deep wide-mouthed bays separate the mountains of Mayo, Donegal, and Kerry as they thrust out into the Atlantic Ocean.*

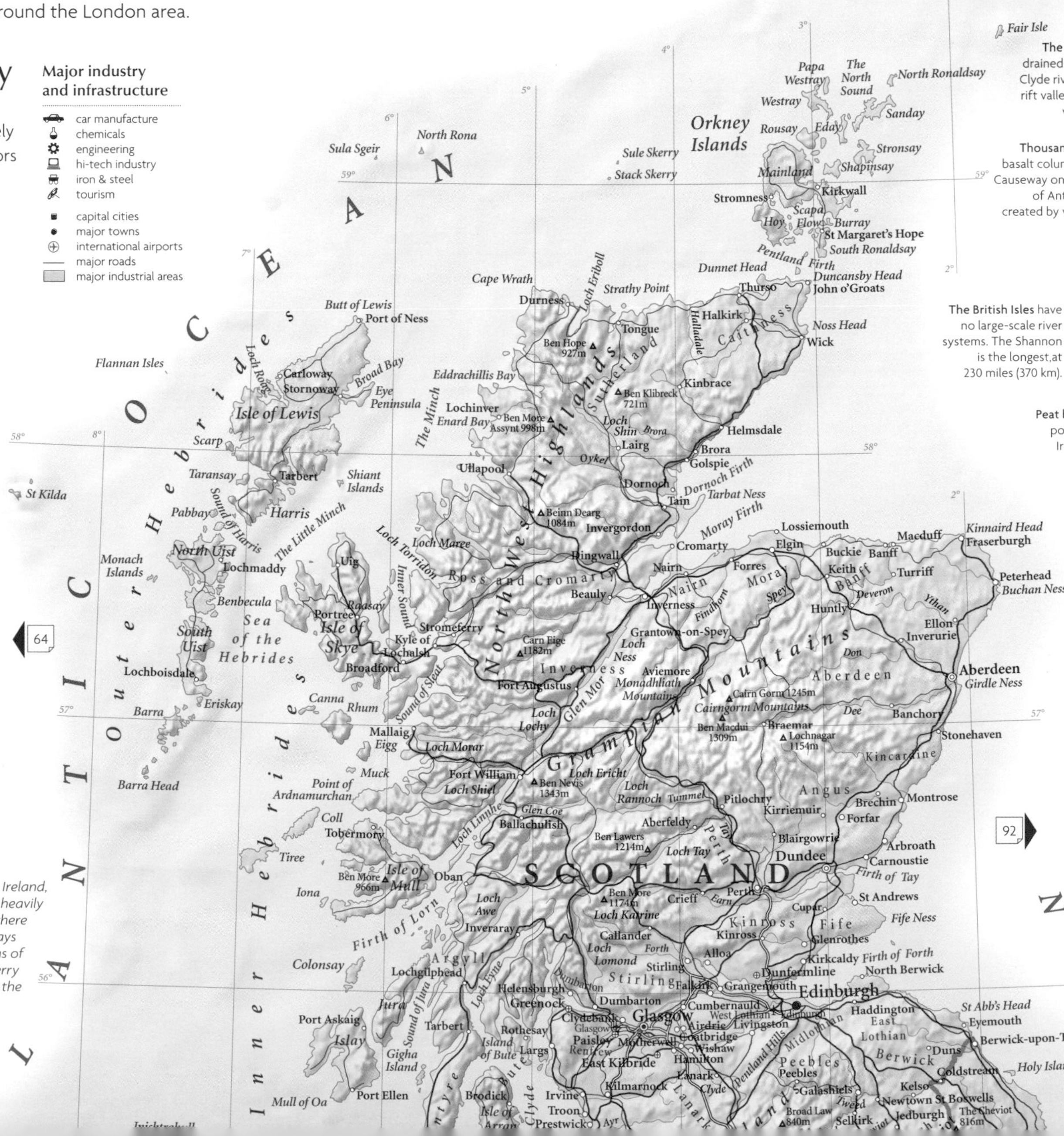

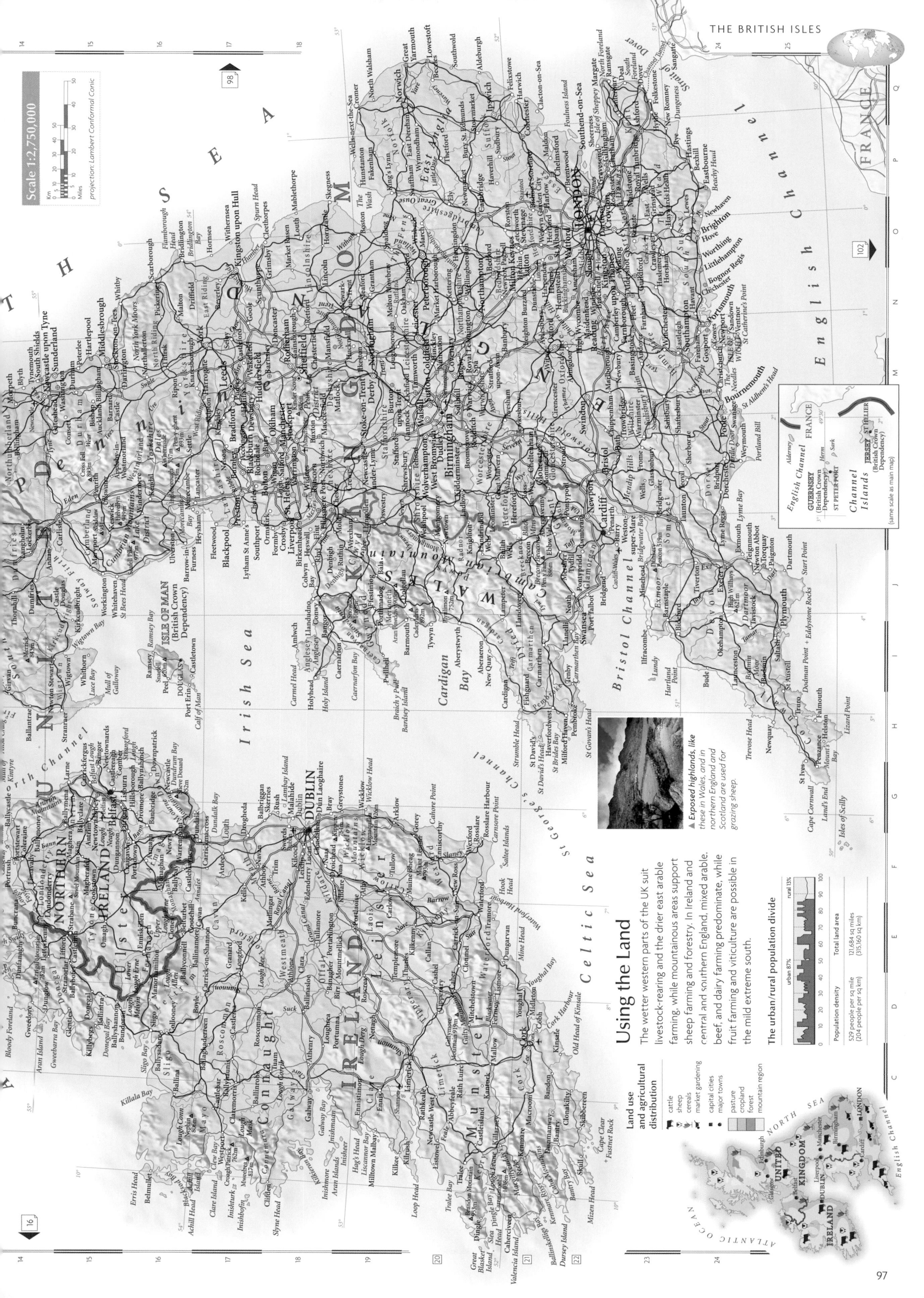

Scale 1:2,750,000

projection: Lambert Conformal Conic

## Using the Land

The wetter western parts of the UK suit livestock-rearing and the drier east arable farming, while mountainous areas support sheep farming and forestry. In Ireland and central and southern England, mixed arable, beef, and dairy farming predominate, while fruit farming and viticulture are possible in the mild extreme south.

▲ Exposed highlands, like these in Wales, and in northern England and Scotland are used for grazing sheep.

The urban/rural population divide

urban 87%     rural 13%

Population density     Total land area
529 people per sq mile     121,684 sq miles
(204 people per sq km)     (315,160 sq km)

Land use and agricultural distribution

cattle
sheep
cereals
market gardening
capital cities
major towns
pasture
cropland
forest
mountain region

# The Low Countries

## BELGIUM, LUXEMBOURG, NETHERLANDS

One of northwestern Europe's strategic crossroads, the Low Countries are united by a common history in which they have often been a battleground in European wars. For over a thousand years they were ruled by foreign powers. Even after they achieved independence, the three countries maintained close links, later forming the world's first totally free labor and goods market, the Benelux Economic Union, which became the core of the European Community (now the European Union or EU). These states have remained at the forefront of wider European cooperation; Brussels, The Hague, and Luxembourg are hosts to major institutions of the EU.

## The landscape

The main geographical regions of the Netherlands are the northern glacial heathlands, the low-lying lands of the Rhine and Maas/Meuse, the reclaimed polders, and the dune coast and islands. Belgium includes part of the Ardennes, together with the coalfields on its northern flanks, and the fertile Flanders plain.

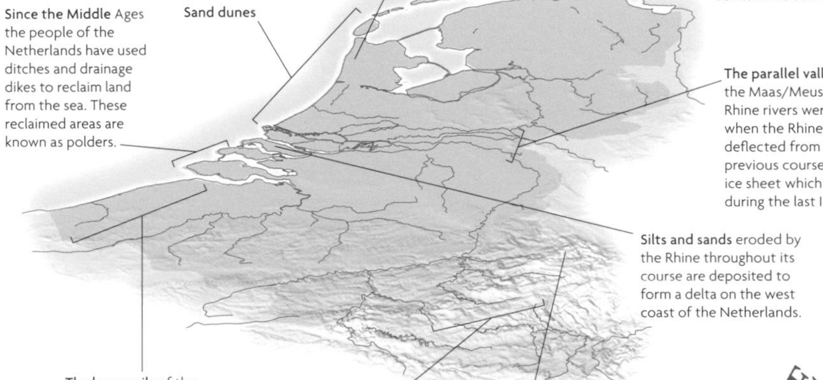

Since the Middle Ages the people of the Netherlands have used ditches and drainage dikes to reclaim land from the sea. These reclaimed areas are known as polders.

▲ **Extensive sand dune** systems along the coast have prevented flooding of the land. Behind the dunes, marshy land is drained to form polders, usable land suitable for agriculture.

Dune system

Sea | Polder | Drainage ditch

Sand dunes

The loess soils of the Flanders Plain in western Belgium provide excellent conditions for arable farming.

▼ **Uplifted and folded** 220 million years ago, the Ardennes have since been reduced to relatively level plateaus, then sharply incised by rivers such as the Maas/Meuse.

**Hautes Fagnes** is the highest part of Belgium. The bogs and streams in this upland region result from high rainfall and low temperatures.

Ardennes

**The parallel valleys** of the Maas/Meuse and Rhine rivers were created when the Rhine was deflected from its previous course by the ice sheet which formed during the last Ice Age.

Silts and sands eroded by the Rhine throughout its course are deposited to form a delta on the west coast of the Netherlands.

▲ **One-third of the** Netherlands lies below sea level and flooding is a constant threat. Much of the coast of the Netherlands was breached by the sea in the 15th century, creating its distinctive inlets and islands.

▼ **Heathlands, like these** at Schoorl, are found along the coast of the Netherlands. Much of the coast was breached by the sea in the 15th century, creating its distinctive inlets and islands.

Schoorl

## Transportation & industry

In the western Netherlands, a massive, sprawling industrialized zone encompasses many new hi-tech and service industries. Belgium's central region has emerged as the country's light manufacturing and services center. Luxembourg city is home to more than 160 banks and the European headquarters of many international companies.

### Major industry and infrastructure

- ✈ aerospace
- 🏦 finance
- ⚙ engineering
- 🖳 hi-tech industry
- ⚗ pharmaceuticals
- ✂ textiles
- ■ capital cities
- • major towns
- ⊕ international airports
- — major roads
- ▭ major industrial areas

*The Low Countries hold a key position on the North Sea, containing Europe's two largest ports, Rotterdam and Antwerp, which are connected to a comprehensive system of inland waterways.*

### Transportation network

| | | |
|---|---|---|
| ▲ 140,588 miles (226,281 km) | ✈ 2565 miles (4129 km) | 🚢 4134 miles (6653 km) |
| ▦ 4099 miles (6598 km) | | |

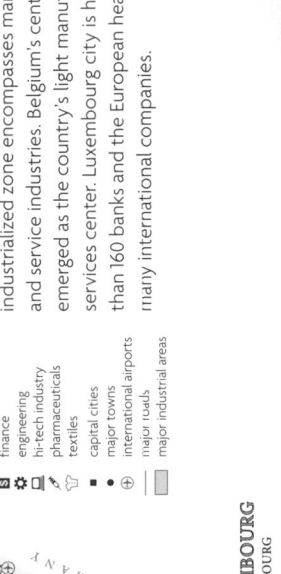

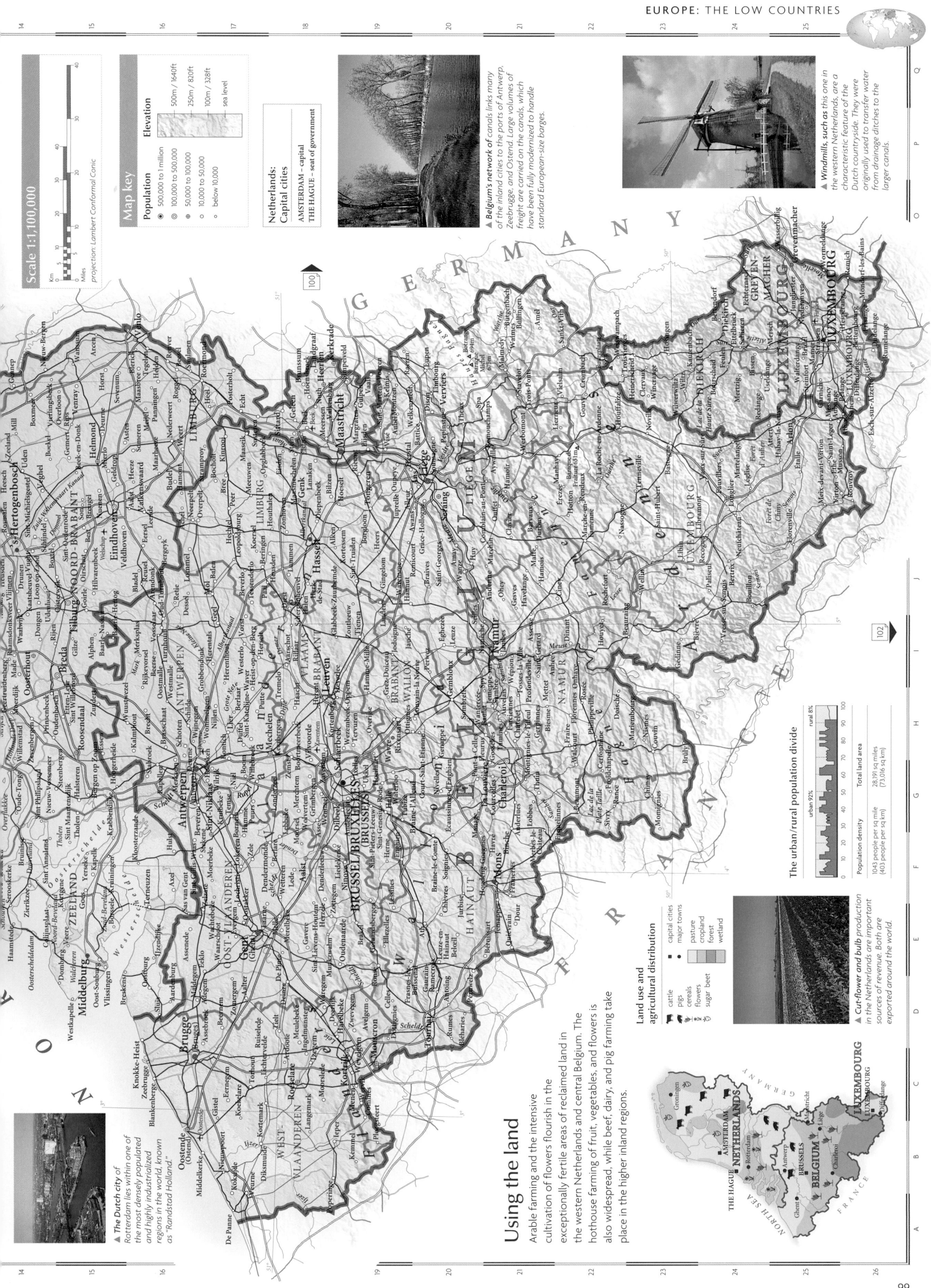

Scale 1:1,100,000

projection: Lambert Conformal Conic

## Map key

**Population**

- ⊙ 500,000 to 1 million
- ◎ 100,000 to 500,000
- ⊕ 50,000 to 100,000
- ○ 10,000 to 50,000
- ∘ below 10,000

**Elevation**

- 500m / 1640ft
- 250m / 820ft
- 100m / 328ft
- sea level

Netherlands:
Capital cities
AMSTERDAM – capital
THE HAGUE – seat of government

▲ Belgium's network of canals links many of the inland cities to the ports of Antwerp, Zeebrugge, and Ostend. Large volumes of freight are carried on the canals, which have been fully modernized to handle standard European-size barges.

▲ Windmills, such as this one in the western Netherlands, are a characteristic feature of the Dutch countryside. They were originally used to transfer water from drainage ditches to the larger canals.

# Using the land

Arable farming and the intensive cultivation of flowers flourish in the exceptionally fertile areas of reclaimed land in the western Netherlands and central Belgium. The hothouse farming of fruit, vegetables, and flowers is also widespread, while beef, dairy, and pig farming take place in the higher inland regions.

▲ The Dutch city of Rotterdam lies within one of the most densely populated and highly industrialized regions in the world, known as "Randstad Holland."

### The urban/rural population divide

rural 8%
urban 92%

Population density
1,043 people per sq mile
(403 people per sq km)

Total land area
28,191 sq miles
(73,016 sq km)

### Land use and agricultural distribution

- cattle
- pigs
- cereals
- flowers
- sugar beet
- capital cities
- major towns
- pasture
- cropland
- forest
- wetland

▲ Cut-flower and bulb production in the Netherlands are important sources of revenue. Both are exported around the world.

# Germany

Despite the devastation of its industry and infrastructure during the Second World War and its separation from eastern Germany during the Cold War, West Germany made a rapid recovery in the following generation to become Europe's most formidable economic power. When the Berlin Wall was dismantled in 1989, the two halves of Germany were politically united for the first time in 40 years. Complete social and economic unity remain a longer term goal, as East German industry and society adapt to a free market. Germany has been a key player in the creation of the European Union (EU) and in moves toward a single European currency.

## Using the land

Germany has a large, efficient agricultural sector, and produces more than three-quarters of its own food. The major crops grown are **cereals** and **sugar beet** on the more fertile soils, and root crops, rye, oats, and fodder on the poorer soils of the northern plains and central uplands. Southern Germany is also a principal producer of high quality wines. Vineyards cover the slopes surrounding the Rhine and its tributaries.

### Land use and agricultural distribution

- cattle
- pigs
- cereals
- sugar beet
- vineyards
- ● capital cities
- ● major towns

- pasture
- cropland
- forest

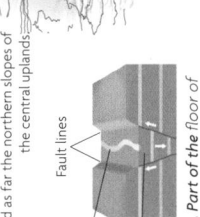

### The urban/rural population divide

urban 87%    rural 13%

| Population density | |
|---|---|
| 612 people per sq mile | (236 people per sq km) |

| Total land area | |
|---|---|
| 13,804 sq miles | (356,910 sq km) |

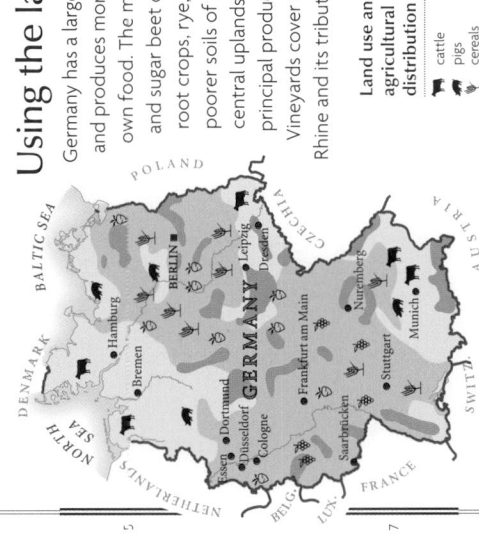

▲ *The Moselle river flows through the Rhine State Uplands (Rheinisches Schiefergebirge). During a period of uplift, preexisting river meanders were deeply incised, to form its present dramatic contours.*

## The landscape

The plains of northern Germany, the volcanic plateaus and mountains of the central uplands, and the Bavarian Alps are the three principal geographic regions in Germany. North to south the land rises steadily from barely 300 ft (90 m) in the plains to 6500 ft (2000 m) in the Bavarian Alps, which are a small but distinct region in the far south.

**The Harz Mountains** were formed 300 million years ago. They are block-faulted mountains, formed when a section of the Earth's crust was thrust up between two faults.

▲ *The Elbe flows in wide meanders across the north German plain to the North Sea. At its mouth it is 10 miles (16 km) wide.*

Elbe river

### Scale 1:2,500,000

Km 0 5 10 20 30 40 50 60 70
Miles 0 10 20 30 40 50 60 70

projection: Lambert Conformal Conic

**The Danube rises in the** Black Forest (Schwarzwald) and flows east, across a wide valley, on its course to the Black Sea.

**Zugspitze, the highest peak** in Germany at 9719 ft (2962 m), was formed during the Alpine mountain-building period, 30 million years ago.

Rhine Rift Valley

**The Rhine** is Germany's principal waterway and one of Europe's longest rivers, flowing 820 miles (1320 km).

▲ *Part of the floor of the Rhine Rift Valley was let down between two parallel faults in the Earth's crust.*

Fault lines

Rhine

Downfaulted block

▲ *Much of the landscape of northern Germany has been shaped by glaciation. During the last ice Age, the ice sheet advanced as far the northern slopes of the central uplands.*

Lüneburg Heath (Lüneburger Heide)

▲ *The heathlands of northern Germany are covered by glacial deposits of sandy outwash soil which makes them largely infertile. They support only sheep and solitary trees.*

**Müritz lake covers** 45 sq miles (117 sq km), but is only 108 ft (33 m) deep. It lies in a shallow valley formed by meltwater flowing out from a retreating ice sheet. These valleys are known as *Urstromtäler*.

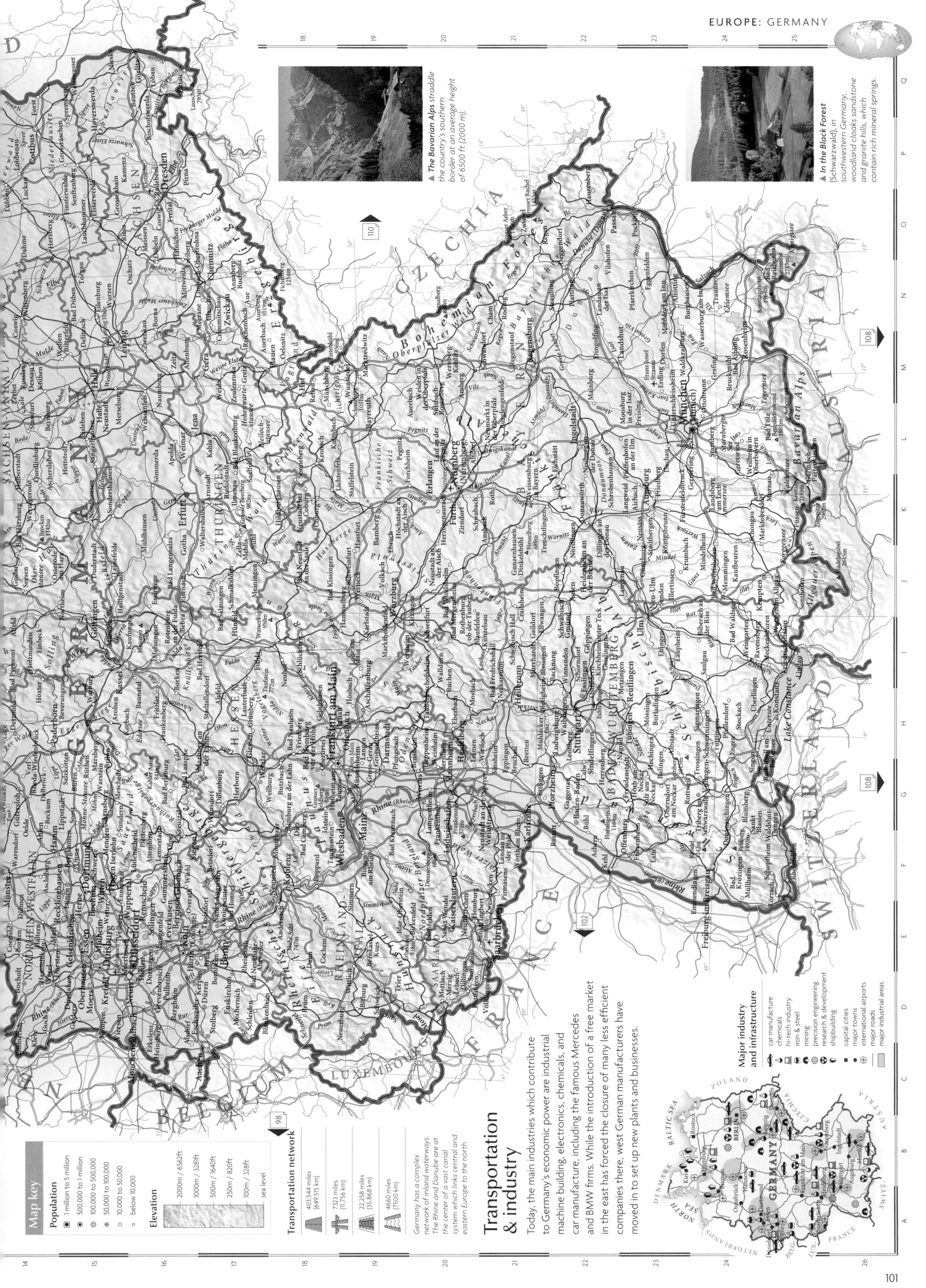

▲ *The Bavarian Alps* straddle the country's southern border at an average height of 6500 ft (2000 m).

▲ *In the Black Forest* (Schwarzwald), in southwestern Germany, woodland cloaks sandstone and granite hills, which contain rich mineral springs.

## Transportation & industry

Today, the main industries which contribute to Germany's economic power are industrial machine building, electronics, chemicals, and car manufacture, including the famous Mercedes and BMW firms. While the introduction of a free market in the east has forced the closure of many less efficient companies there, west German manufacturers have moved in to set up new plants and businesses.

*Germany has a complex network of inland waterways. The Rhine and Danube are at the center of a vast canal system which links central and eastern Europe to the north.*

### Transportation network

| | |
|---|---|
| 403,544 miles (649,515 km) | |
| 7323 miles (11,756 km) | |
| 22,258 miles (35,868 km) | |
| 4660 miles (7500 km) | |

### Major industry and infrastructure

- car manufacture
- chemicals
- hi-tech industry
- iron & steel
- mining
- precision engineering
- research & development
- shipbuilding
- capital cities
- major cities
- major towns
- international airports
- major roads
- major industrial areas

### Map key

**Population**

- 1 million to 5 million
- 500,000 to 1 million
- 100,000 to 500,000
- 50,000 to 100,000
- 10,000 to 50,000
- below 10,000

**Elevation**

- 2000m / 6562ft
- 1000m / 3281ft
- 500m / 1640ft
- 250m / 820ft
- 100m / 328ft
- sea level

# France

## FRANCE, MONACO

Europe's second largest nation and the founder of modern Republican government, France is a major center of culture and fashion, and a leading producer of both agricultural and industrial goods. It has played a leading role in European events for centuries, and remains a key player in the push toward European unity. The Paris Basin is the most highly populated area; Île de France is home to over 11 million people. Large parts of France remain thinly populated, particularly the mountainous Massif Central, Pyrenees, and southern Alps.

◀ The chalk cliffs of Normandy (Normandie) and southeastern England form part of a single geological region, now divided in two by the English Channel.

## The landscape

France's landscape was fashioned by two phases of mountain-building. The northwestern peninsula, the Massif Central, and the Vosges date from 220 million years ago. The complex folds of the Alps and Pyrenees, the gently-folded Jura, and the low-lying sedimentary areas of the Paris, Garonne, and Rhône basins started to form 65 million years ago.

The coast of Brittany (Bretagne) is highly indented where deep valleys in the northwestern peninsula were drowned by the sea.

The Normandy (Normandie) coastline is characterized by high chalk cliffs.

The coastline of France is 2141 miles (3427 km) long.

▲ The Paris Basin consists of a layered sequence of sedimentary rocks. Fertile soils over much of the area make good agricultural land.

The gently rounded summits of the Vosges are over 200 million years old.

The Biscay coast, like the Mediterranean, is characterized by flat sandy beaches, interspersed with lagoons.

Garonne Basin

The Dordogne region contains spectacular examples of limestone scenery including caves and gorges.

The Pyrenees form a natural border between France and Spain.

The ancient Massif Central, disturbed by the formation of the Alps, was subject to volcanism that only ceased during the last 10,000 years.

The folded Jura form low ridges and long narrow valleys.

The Alps were forced up during several phases of mountain-building beginning 65 million years ago.

Rhône Basin

Corsica's northeastern peninsula has dramatic cliffs of folded limestone.

Rhône Delta

Rhône

Delta plain

The marshes of the Camargue

◀ The volcanic landscape of the Auvergne where the cones of its extinct volcanoes have worn away to leave "plugs" of lava.

▲ Deposition in the Rhône Delta is wave-dominated. Sea currents carry river sediments extending the delta plain westwards.

## Transportation & industry

Today the main French growth industries are hi-tech, including micro-electronics, telecommunications and aerospace. Other important sectors are the nuclear industry, only rivalled in scale by that of the US, car manufacture, dominated by the giants Renault and Peugeot, and a highly diversified tourist industry.

### Major industry and infrastructure

✈ aerospace industry
🚗 car manufacture
⚗ chemicals
⚙ engineering
💻 hi-tech industry
⚛ nuclear power
🏖 tourism

■ capital cities
● major towns
⊕ international airports
— major roads
▢ major industrial areas

### Transportation network

| | | |
|---|---|---|
| 555,473 miles (894,050 km) | | 7305 miles (11,758 km) |
| 10,399 miles (16,737 km) | | 1159 miles (1863 km) |

The French TGV (Train à Grande Vitesse) leads the world in high-speed train technology, and provides a service which can be faster, door-to-door, than air travel.

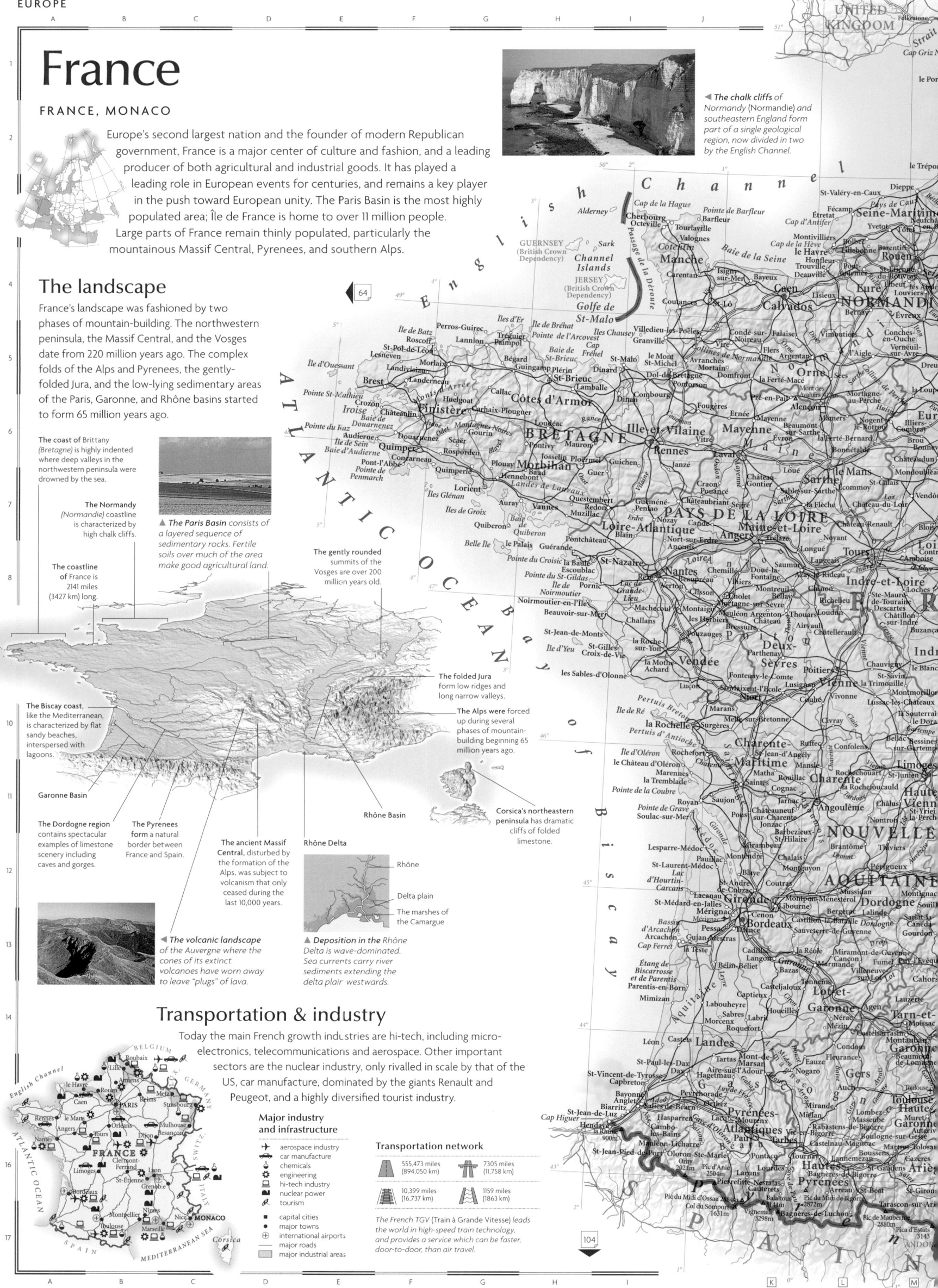

▶ *The climate in* northwestern Spain is milder in both summer and winter than in the rest of the country, creating a verdant environment, more commonly associated with northwestern Europe.

## Map key

### Population

- 1 million to 5 million
- 500,000 to 1 million
- 100,000 to 500,000
- 50,000 to 100,000
- 10,000 to 50,000
- below 10,000

### Elevation

| | |
|---|---|
| 3000m / 9843ft |
| 2000m / 6562ft |
| 1000m / 3281ft |
| 500m / 1640ft |
| 250m / 820ft |
| 100m / 328ft |
| sea level |

**Scale 1:3,000,000**

Km
0 5 10 20 30 40 50 60 70 80

Miles
0 5 10 20 30 40 50 60 70 80

*projection: Lambert Conformal Conic*

## The landscape

A vast plateau, the Meseta dominates the centre of the peninsula, enclosed by the Cordillera Cantábrica to the north and the Sierra Morena to the south. It is drained by three major rivers, the Douro/Duero, the Tagus, and the Guadalquivir. The peninsula experiences great variations in climate and rainfall, both regionally and locally.

▲ *The Pyrenees form* Iberia's northeastern boundary, running for 270 miles (440 km), dividing the peninsula from the rest of Europe.

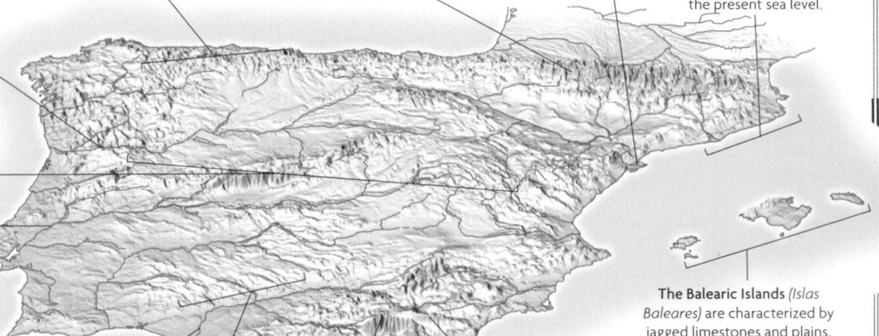

Cordillera Cantábrica

Douro/Duero river

The Meseta plateau averages 1970 ft (600 m) in height and is now largely dry and treeless.

Tagus River

**The Ebro river** has formed the peninsu a's largest delta. Recently, sediment flows have been seriously disturbed by nearby reservoirs.

**On the northeastern** coast sea level changes are evident from wave-cut beaches which rise up to 200 ft (60 m) above the present sea level.

The Balearic Islands *(Islas Baleares)* are characterized by jagged limestones and plains.

▶ *In the Sierra de los Filabres* deforestation and overgrazing, which cause soil erosion, have created semidesert badlands.

The Guadalquivir river brings vital irrigation water to the plains, and like many of Iberia's rivers, is prone to flooding.

Sierra Morena

The Sierra Nevada in southern Spain contain Iberia's highest peak, Mulhacén, which rises 11,418 ft (3481 m).

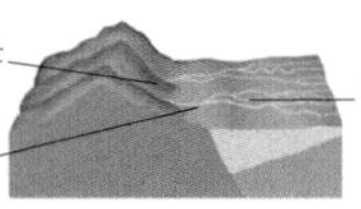

Mountain front

Weathered material

Pediment

▲ *Pediments are characteristic* of semiarid lands across Iberia. A pediment is a flat, low-lying, eroded platform, cut into the bedrock. Weathered material is transported by streams and deposited in broad fan shapes on the pediment.

Peñón de Alhucemas (to Spain)

Islas Chafarinas (to Spain)

Melilla (to Spain)

Isla de Alborán

Iboran Sea

# The Italian peninsula

## ITALY, SAN MARINO, VATICAN CITY

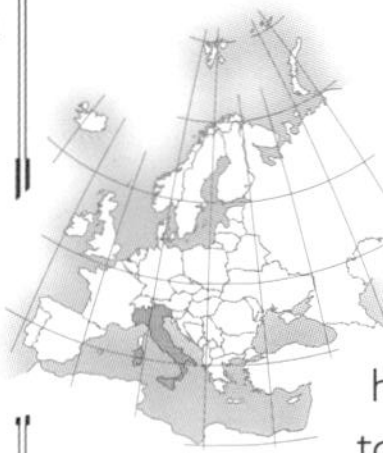

The Italian peninsula is a land of great contrasts. Until unification in 1861, Italy was a collection of independent states, whose competitiveness during the Renaissance resulted in the architectural and artistic magnificence of cities such as Rome, Florence, and Venice. The majority of Italy's population and economic activity is concentrated in the north, centered on the sophisticated industrial city of Milan. Southern Italy, the *Mezzogiorno*, has a harsh terrain, and remains far less developed than the north. Attempts to attract industry and investment in the south are frequently deterred by the entrenched network of organized crime and corruption.

## The landscape

The mainly mountainous and hilly Italian peninsula took its present form following a collision between the African and Eurasian tectonic plates. The Alps in the northwest rise to a high point of 15,772 ft (4807 m) at Mont Blanc (*Monte Bianco*) on the French border, while the Apennines (*Appennino*) form a rugged backbone, running along the entire length of the country.

▲ *The island of Sardinia* is an ancient land mass; an uplifted section of very old igneous rocks. Its rugged mountainous regions provide pasture for sheep and goats, while its valleys support some agriculture.

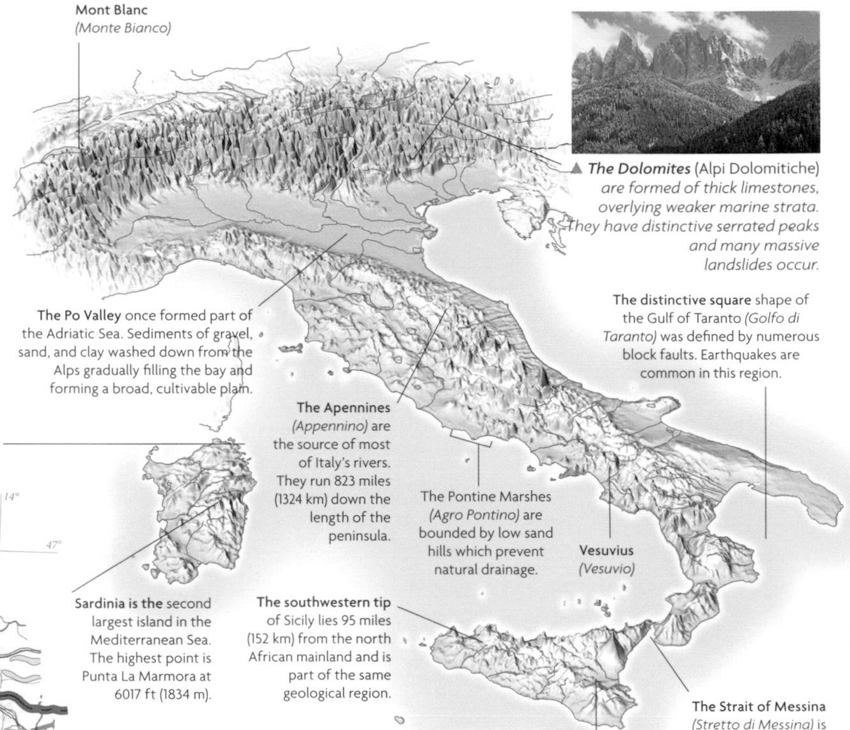

Mont Blanc (*Monte Bianco*)

Costa Smeralda

▲ *The Dolomites* (Alpi Dolomitiche) are formed of thick limestones, overlying weaker marine strata. They have distinctive serrated peaks and many massive landslides occur.

The *distinctive square* shape of the Gulf of Taranto (*Golfo di Taranto*) was defined by numerous block faults. Earthquakes are common in this region.

The **Apennines** (*Appennino*) are the source of most of Italy's rivers. They run 823 miles (1324 km) down the length of the peninsula.

The *Po Valley* once formed part of the Adriatic Sea. Sediments of gravel, sand, and clay washed down from the Alps gradually filling the bay and forming a broad, cultivable plain.

The **Pontine Marshes** (*Agro Pontino*) are bounded by low sand hills which prevent natural drainage.

**Sardinia is the second** largest island in the Mediterranean Sea. The highest point is Punta La Marmora at 6017 ft (1834 m).

The *Strait of Messina* (*Stretto di Messina*) is between 2 and 12 miles (3–19 km) wide, and is a rich fishing ground.

The *southwestern tip* of Sicily lies 95 miles (152 km) from the north African mainland and is part of the same geological region.

Vesuvius (*Vesuvio*)

**Sicily is the largest** island in the Mediterranean at 9926 sq miles (25,708 sq km).

Present-day crater has developed within the old crater of Monte Somma

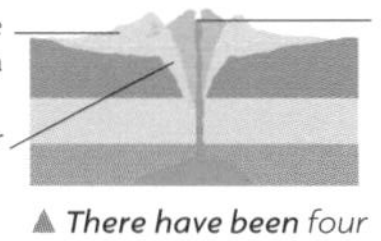

▲ *There have been* four volcanoes on the site of Vesuvius since volcanic activity began here more than 10,000 years ago.

Vesuvius (*Vesuvio*)
Monte Somma
Old crater

## Using the land

Italy produces 95% of its own food. The best farming land is in the Po Valley in northern Italy, where soft wheat and rice are grown. Irrigation is essential to agriculture in much of the south. Italy is a major producer and exporter of citrus fruits, olives, tomatoes, and wine.

### The urban/rural population divide

urban 67%
rural 33%

Population density
506 people per sq mile
(195 people per sq km)

Total land area
116,320 sq miles
(301,270 sq km)

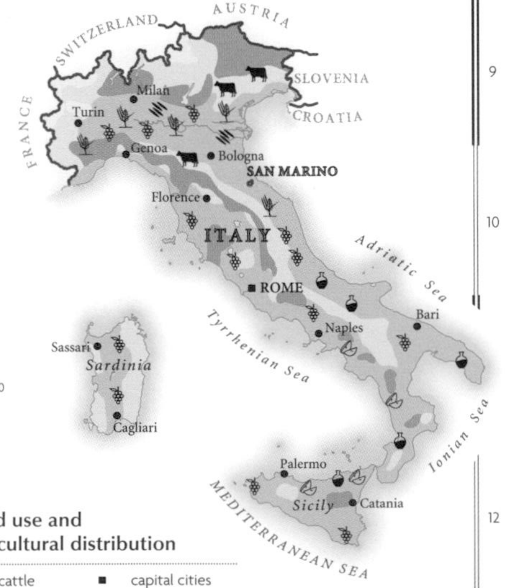

### Land use and agricultural distribution

- capital cities
- major towns
- cattle
- cereals
- citrus fruits
- olive oil
- rice
- vineyards
- pasture
- cropland
- forest
- mountain region

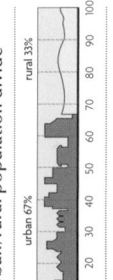
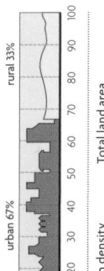
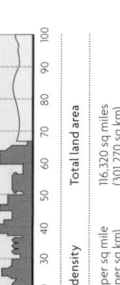

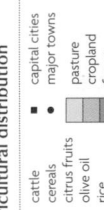
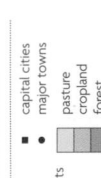

Scale 1:2,750,000

projection: Lambert Conformal Conic

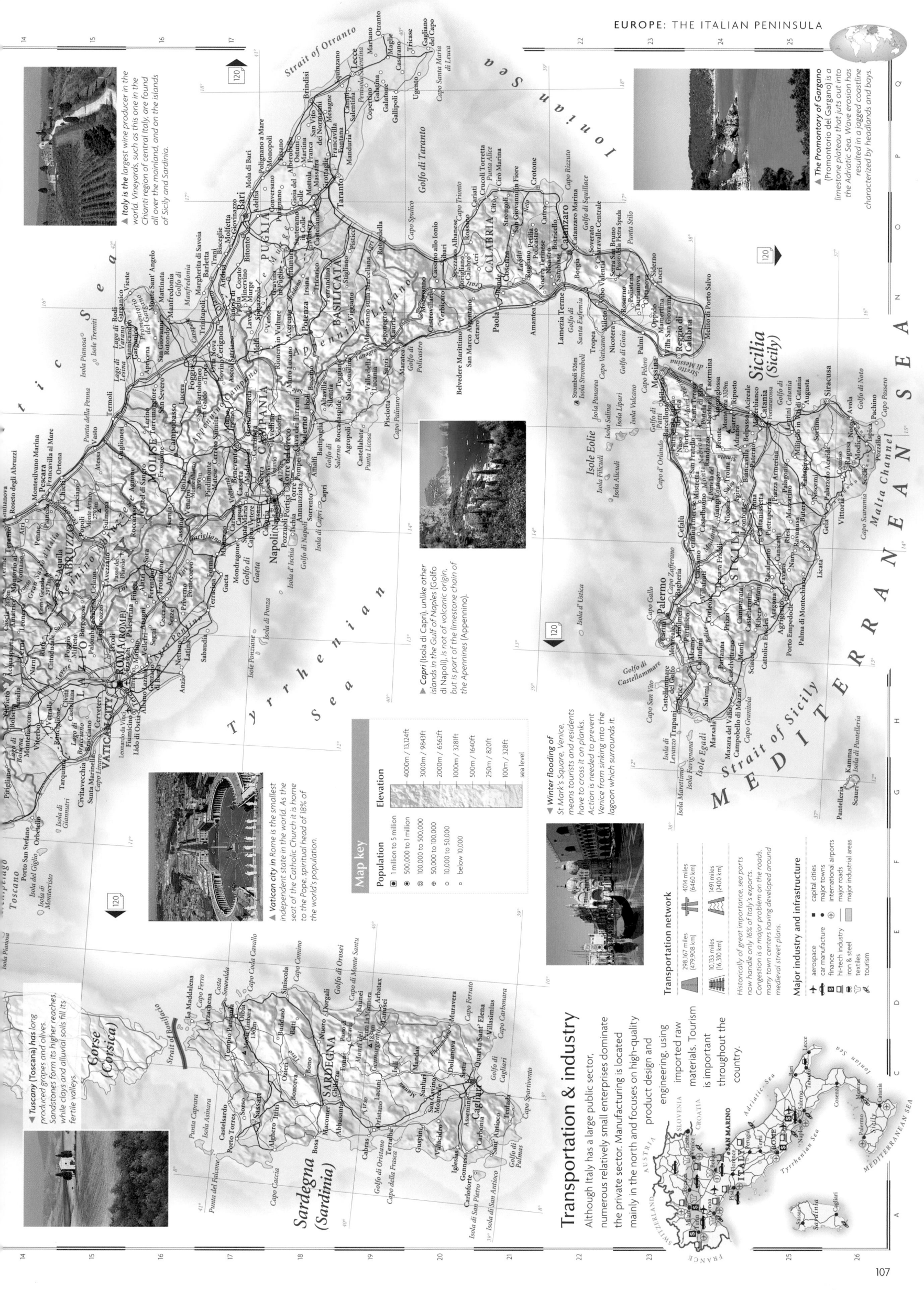

▲ **Italy is** the largest wine producer in the world. Vineyards, such as this one in the Chianti region of central Italy, are found all over the mainland, and on the islands of Sicily and Sardinia.

▲ **The Promontory of Gargano** (Promontorio del Gargano) is a limestone plateau that juts out into the Adriatic Sea. Wave erosion has resulted in a jagged coastline characterized by headlands and bays.

▲ **Capri** (Isola di Capri), unlike other islands in the Gulf of Naples (Golfo di Napoli), is not of volcanic origin, but is part of the limestone chain of the Apennines (Appennino).

▲ **Vatican city in** Rome is the smallest independent state in the world. As the seat of the Catholic Church it is home to the Pope, spiritual head of 18% of the world's population.

▼ **Winter flooding of** St Mark's Square, Venice, means tourists and residents have to cross it on planks. Action is needed to prevent Venice from sinking into the lagoon which surrounds it.

▲ **Tuscany (Toscana) has** long produced grapes and olives. Sandstones form its higher reaches, while clays and alluvial soils fill its fertile valleys.

## Map key

### Population

| | |
|---|---|
| ● | 1 million to 5 million |
| ◉ | 500,000 to 1 million |
| ◎ | 100,000 to 500,000 |
| ○ | 50,000 to 100,000 |
| ○ | 10,000 to 50,000 |
| ○ | below 10,000 |

### Elevation

| | |
|---|---|
| 4000m / 13,124ft | |
| 3000m / 9843ft | |
| 2000m / 6562ft | |
| 1000m / 3281ft | |
| 500m / 1640ft | |
| 250m / 820ft | |
| 100m / 328ft | |
| sea level | |

## Transportation & industry

Although Italy has a large public sector, numerous relatively small enterprises dominate the private sector. Manufacturing is located mainly in the north and focuses on high-quality product design and engineering, using imported raw materials. Tourism is important throughout the country.

### Transportation network

| | |
|---|---|
| 298,167 miles (479,908 km) | 4014 miles (6460 km) |
| 10,133 miles (16,310 km) | 1491 miles (2400 km) |

Historically of great importance, sea ports now handle only 16% of Italy's exports. Congestion is a major problem on the roads, many town centers having developed around medieval street plans.

### Major industry and infrastructure

| | |
|---|---|
| ✈ aerospace | ● capital cities |
| 🚗 car manufacture | ● major towns |
| finance | ✈ international airports |
| hi-tech industry | major roads |
| iron & steel | major industrial areas |
| textiles | |
| tourism | |

# The Alpine states

## AUSTRIA, LIECHTENSTEIN, SLOVENIA, SWITZERLAND

The Alpine countries of Austria, Switzerland, Liechtenstein, and Slovenia form a narrow strip across western Europe's geographical core, lying on the main north–south trading routes across the Alps. Switzerland, politically neutral since 1815, is an important international meeting place and houses one of the headquarters of the United Nations, it only became a member in 2002. Austria, once at the heart of the great Habsburg Empire has been a fully independent nation since 1955, and maintains a deserved reputation as an international center of culture. Slovenia declared independence from the former Yugoslavia in 1991 and despite initial economic hardship, is now starting to achieve the prosperity enjoyed by its Alpine neighbors.

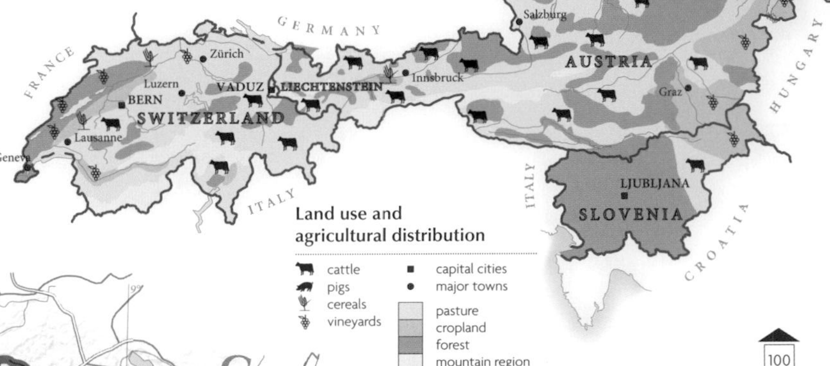

◀ *The Matterhorn, on the Swiss-Italian border, is one of the highest mountains in the Alps, at 14,692 ft (4478 m). The term "horn" refers to its distinctive peak, formed by three glaciers eroding hollows, known as cirques, in each of its sides.*

## Using the land

The Alpine region's mountainous terrain discourages cultivation over much of the land area. The primary agricultural activity is the raising of dairy and beef cattle on the pasture land of the lower mountain slopes. Austria is self-supporting in grains, and crops such as wheat, barley, and grapes are grown on the east Austrian lowlands. Woodlands are more prevalent in the eastern Alps; both Austria and Slovenia have large tracts of forest.

### Land use and agricultural distribution

- cattle
- pigs
- cereals
- vineyards
- ■ capital cities
- • major towns

pasture
cropland
forest
mountain region

## The landscape

The Alps occupy three-fifths of Switzerland, most of southern Austria and the northwest of Slovenia. They were formed by the collision of the African and Eurasian tectonic plates, which began 65 million years ago. Their complex geology is reflected in the differing heights and rock types of the various ranges. The Rhine flows along Liechtenstein's border with Switzerland, creating a broad floodplain in the north and west of Liechtenstein. In the far northeast and east are a number of lowland regions, including the Vienna Basin, Burgenland, and the plain of the Danube. Slovenia's major rivers largely flow across the lower eastern regions; in the west, the rivers flow underground through the limestone Karst region.

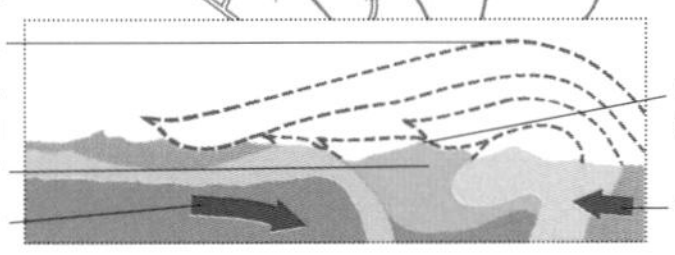

Original height after uplift and folding
Folded strata are overturned creating a *nappe*
Present-day height of Alps
Eurasian Plate
African Plate

▲ *The convergence of the African and Eurasian plates compressed and folded huge masses of rock strata. As the plates continued to move together, the folded strata were overturned, creating complex nappes. Much of the rock strata has since been eroded, resulting in the current topography of the Alps.*

▲ *Constricted as it cuts through ridges in the Alps, the Danube meanders across the lowlands, where uplift combined with river erosion has deepened meanders.*

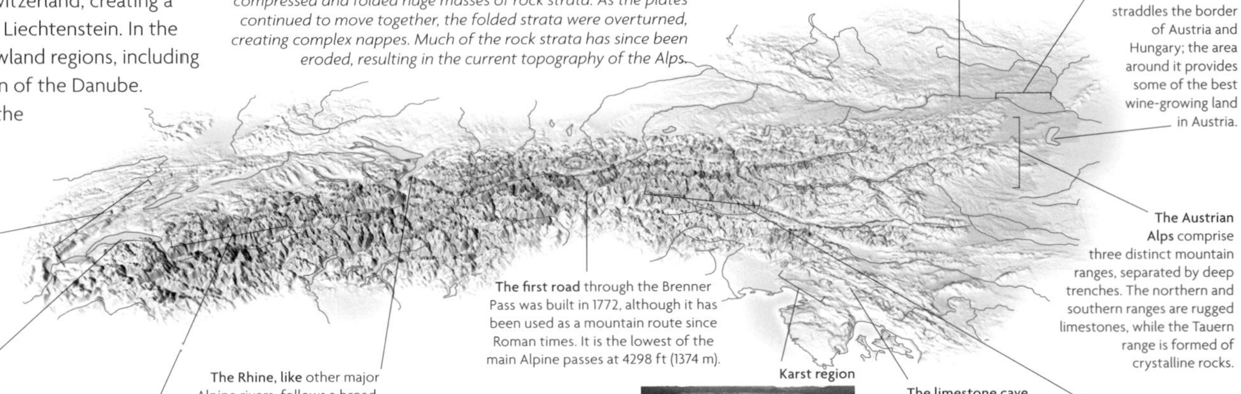

**The Vienna Basin** lies mainly below 390 ft (120 m). It gradually subsided and filled with sediment as the Alps were uplifted.

**Neusiedler See** straddles the border of Austria and Hungary; the area around it provides some of the best wine-growing land in Austria.

**The Austrian Alps** comprise three distinct mountain ranges, separated by deep trenches. The northern and southern ranges are rugged limestones, while the Tauern range is formed of crystalline rocks.

**The mountains of** the Jura form a natural border between Switzerland and France. Their marine limestones date from over 200 million years ago. When the Alps were formed the Jura were folded into a series of parallel ridges and troughs.

**Tectonic activity** has resulted in dramatic changes in land height over very short distances. Lake Geneva, lying at 1221 ft (372 m) is only 43 miles (70 km) away from the 15,772 ft (4807 m) peak of Mont Blanc, on the France–Italy border.

**The Bernese Alps** (*Berner Alpen*) contain the Aletsch, which at 15 miles (24 km) is the longest Alpine glacier.

**The Rhine, like** other major Alpine rivers, follows a broad, flat trough between the mountains. Along part of its course, the Rhine forms the boundary between Switzerland and Liechtenstein.

**The first road** through the Brenner Pass was built in 1772, although it has been used as a mountain route since Roman times. It is the lowest of the main Alpine passes at 4298 ft (1374 m).

Karst region

▶ *The deep, blue lakes of the Karst region are part of a drainage network which runs largely underground through this limestone area.*

**The limestone cave** system at Postojna extends for more than 10 miles (16 km) and includes caverns reaching 125 ft (40 m) in height and width.

**The Tauern range** in the central Austrian Alps contains the highest mountain in Austria, the towering Grossglockner, rising 12,461 ft (3798 m).

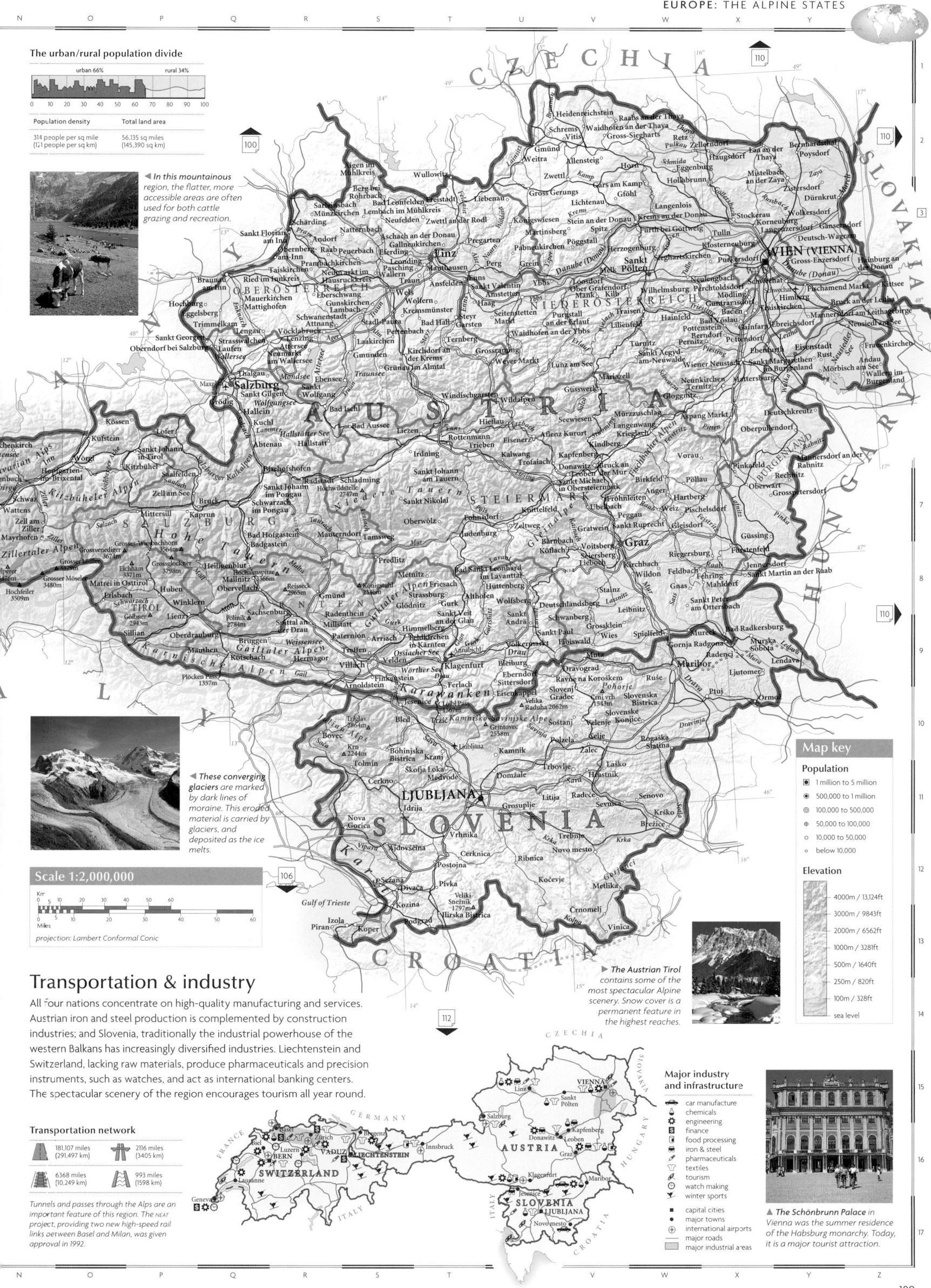

## The urban/rural population divide

urban 66%     rural 34%

0 10 20 30 40 50 60 70 80 90 100

| Population density | Total land area |
| --- | --- |
| 314 people per sq mile | 56,135 sq miles |
| (121 people per sq km) | (145,390 sq km) |

◀ *In this mountainous region, the flatter, more accessible areas are often used for both cattle grazing and recreation.*

◀ *These converging glaciers are marked by dark lines of moraine. This eroded material is carried by glaciers, and deposited as the ice melts.*

### Scale 1:2,000,000

Km
0 5 10 20 30 40 50 60

Miles
0 5 10 20 30 40 50 60

*projection: Lambert Conformal Conic*

## Transportation & industry

All four nations concentrate on high-quality manufacturing and services. Austrian iron and steel production is complemented by construction industries; and Slovenia, traditionally the industrial powerhouse of the western Balkans has increasingly diversified industries. Liechtenstein and Switzerland, lacking raw materials, produce pharmaceuticals and precision instruments, such as watches, and act as international banking centers. The spectacular scenery of the region encourages tourism all year round.

### Transportation network

| | | | |
| --- | --- | --- | --- |
| 181,107 miles (291,497 km) | | 2116 miles (3405 km) | |
| 6368 miles (10,249 km) | | 993 miles (1598 km) | |

*Tunnels and passes through the Alps are an important feature of this region. The NEAT project, providing two new high-speed rail links between Basel and Milan, was given approval in 1992.*

### Map key

**Population**
- 1 million to 5 million
- 500,000 to 1 million
- 100,000 to 500,000
- 50,000 to 100,000
- 10,000 to 50,000
- below 10,000

**Elevation**
- 4000m / 13,124ft
- 3000m / 9843ft
- 2000m / 6562ft
- 1000m / 3281ft
- 500m / 1640ft
- 250m / 820ft
- 100m / 328ft
- sea level

▶ *The Austrian Tirol contains some of the most spectacular Alpine scenery. Snow cover is a permanent feature in the highest reaches.*

### Major industry and infrastructure

- car manufacture
- chemicals
- engineering
- finance
- food processing
- iron & steel
- pharmaceuticals
- textiles
- tourism
- watch making
- winter sports

- ■ capital cities
- • major towns
- international airports
- major roads
- major industrial areas

▲ *The Schönbrunn Palace in Vienna was the summer residence of the Habsburg monarchy. Today, it is a major tourist attraction.*

# Central Europe

## CZECHIA (CZECH REPUBLIC), HUNGARY, POLAND, SLOVAKIA

When Slovakia and Czechia became separate countries in 1993, they joined Hungary and Poland in a new role as independent nation states, following centuries of shifting boundaries and imperial strife. This turbulent history bequeathed the region a rich cultural heritage, shared through the works of its many great writers and composers, and celebrated in the vibrant historic capitals of Prague, Budapest, and Warsaw. Having shaken off years of Soviet domination in 1989, these states are confronting the challenge of winning commercial investment to modernize outmoded industries as they integrate their economies with those of the European Union.

## The landscape

The forested Carpathian Mountains, uplifted with the Alps, lie southeast of the older Bohemian Massif, which contains the Sudeten and Krusné Hory (Erzgebirge) ranges. They divide the fertile plains of the Danube to the south and the Vistula (Wisła), which flows north across vast expanses of glacial deposits into the Baltic Sea.

## Transportation & industry

Heavy industry has dominated postwar life in Central Europe. Poland has large coal reserves, having inherited the Silesian coalfield from Germany after the Second World War, allowing the export of large quantities of coal, along with other minerals. Hungary specializes in consumer goods and services, while Slovakia's industrial base is still relatively small. Czechia's traditional glassworks and breweries bring some stability to its precarious Soviet-built manufacturing sector.

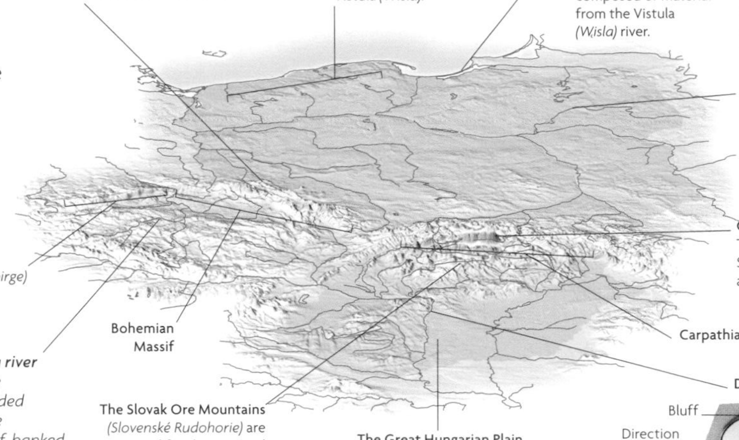

▲ The Biebrza river has left meanders and oxbow lakes as it flows across low-lying ground.

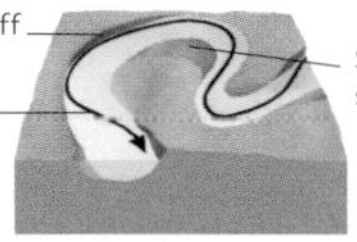

Longshore currents moving east along the Baltic coast have built a 40 mile (65 km) spit composed of material from the Vistula (Wisła) river.

Gerlachovský Štít, in the Tatra Mountains, is Slovakia's highest mountain, at 8711ft (2655 m).

Carpathian Mountains

Pomerania is a sandy coastal region of glacially-formed lakes stretching west from the Vistula (Wisła).

Hot mineral springs occur where geothermally heated water wells up through faults and fractures in the rocks of the Sudeten Mountains.

Danube river

The Great Hungarian Plain formed by the floodplain of the Danube is a mixture of steppe and cultivated land, covering nearly half of Hungary's total area.

The Slovak Ore Mountains (Slovenské Rudohorie) are noted for their mineral resources, including high-grade iron ore.

Bohemian Massif

Krušné Hory (Erzgebirge)

Slip-off slope

▲ Meanders form as rivers flow across plains at a low gradient. A steep cliff or bluff forms on the outside curve, and a gentler slip-off slope on the inside bend.

Bluff

Direction of flow

◀ The Berounka river cuts through the precipitous wooded landscape of the Bohemian Massif, banked by a broad floodplain.

### Major industry and infrastructure

car manufacture
chemicals
engineering
food processing
mining
shipbuilding
tourism

capital cities
major towns
international airports
major roads
major industrial areas

### Transportation network

| | |
|---|---|
| 213,997 miles (344,600 km) | 817 miles (1315 km) |
| 27,479 miles (44,249 km) | 3784 miles (6094 km) |

The huge growth of tourism and business has prompted major investment in the transportation infrastructure, with new roadbuilding schemes within and between the main cities of the region.

▲ Budapest, the capital of Hungary, straddles the Danube. It comprises the historic towns of Buda, on the west bank, and Pest, which contains the Parliament Building, seen here on the far bank.

## Map key

**Population**

- ◉ 1 million to 5 million
- ⊙ 500,000 to 1 million
- ◎ 100,000 to 500,000
- ⊕ 50,000 to 100,000
- ⊙ 10,000 to 50,000
- ○ below 10,000

**Elevation**

| | |
|---|---|
| | 2000m / 6562ft |
| | 1000m / 3281ft |
| | 500m / 1640ft |
| | 250m / 820ft |
| | 100m / 328ft |
| | sea level |

Scale 1:2,750,000

projection: Lambert Conformal Conic

▲ *The upper Dunajec river of Poland and eastern Slovakia forms a gorge through the Pieniny range of the Carpathian Mountains.*

## Using the land

Cereals, sugar beet, and potatoes are Central Europe's main crops, along with hops for the Czech breweries, sweet peppers for paprika, sunflowers and vines in milder areas. The plains of Poland and Hungary are wellsuited to livestock-rearing, while forestry is important in the mountains of Slovakia.

**Land use and agricultural distribution**

- ■ capital cities
- • major towns
- cattle
- pigs
- cereals
- root crops
- timber
- vineyards
- pasture
- cropland
- forest

▲ *Hay, used to feed livestock, is one of the major crops grown on the fertile foothills of Slovakia's Tatra Mountains.*

**The urban/rural population divide**

| | urban 65% | rural 35% |
|---|---|---|

| Population density | Total land area |
|---|---|
| 312 people per sq mile (120 people per sq km) | 201,561 sq miles (522,180 sq km) |

# Southeast Europe

ALBANIA, BOSNIA & HERZEGOVINA, CROATIA, KOSOVO, NORTH MACEDONIA, MONTENEGRO, SERBIA

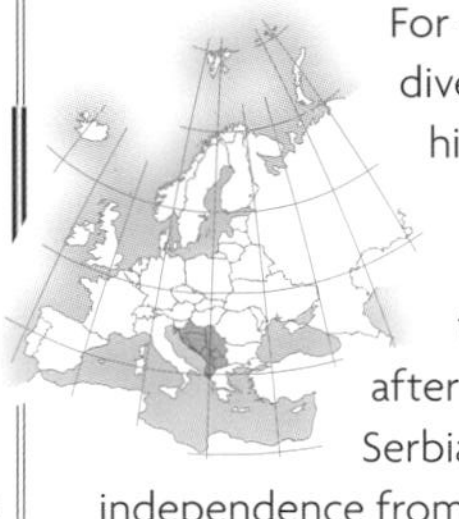

For 46 years the federation of Yugoslavia held together the most diverse ethnic region in Europe, along the picturesque mountain hinterland of the Dalmatian coast. Economic collapse resulted in internal tensions. In the early 1990s, civil war broke out in both Croatia and Bosnia as the ethnic populations struggled to establish their own exclusive territories. Peace was only restored by the UN after NATO launched air strikes in 1995. Montenegro voted to split from Serbia in 2006. More recently, Kosovo controversially declared independence from Serbia in 2008, although this may take some time to be fully recognized. Neighboring Albania is slowly improving its fragile economy but remains one of Europe's poorest nations.

## The landscape

The Tisza, Sava, and Drava Rivers drain the broad northern lowland, meeting the Danube after it crosses the Hungarian border. In the west, the Dinaric Alps divide the Adriatic Sea from the interior. Mainland valleys and elongated islands run parallel to the steep Dalmatian (Dalmacija) coastline, following alternating bands of resistant limestone.

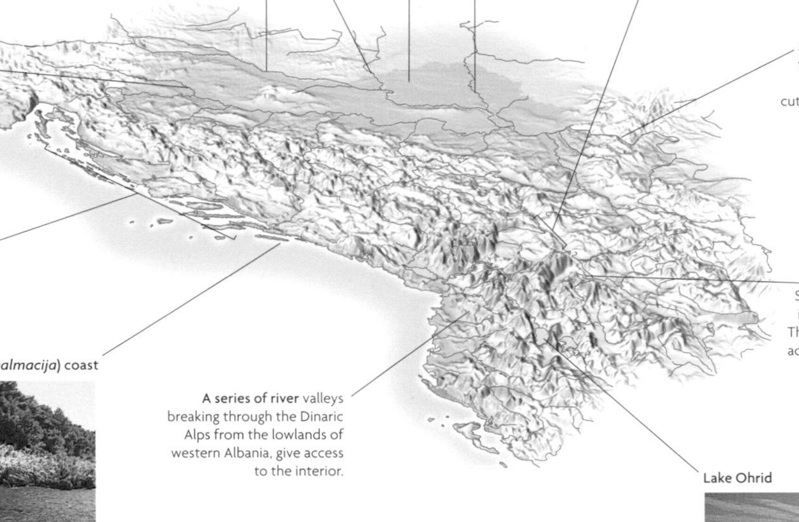

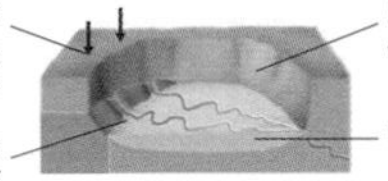

▲ Hot, dry summers and mild winters offer excellent conditions for viticulture in Montenegro. The precipitous Dinaric Alps have kept this region relatively isolated for centuries.

Scale 1:2,750,000

projection: Lambert Conformal Conic

Dalmatian (Dalmacija) coast

▲ Limestone cliffs along the Dalmatian (Dalmacija) shoreline are heavily eroded, as salt water dissolves the rock along existing horizontal cracks, or joints. This tends to form a platform of rock at the foot of the cliff.

The elongated islands, promontories and straits of the Dalmatian (Dalmacija) coast were formed as the Adriatic Sea rose to flood valleys running parallel to the shore.

Sava river

A series of river valleys breaking through the Dinaric Alps from the lowlands of western Albania, give access to the interior.

Drava river

At least 70% of the fresh water in the western Balkans drains eastward into the Black Sea, mostly via the Danube (Dunav).

The river floodplains of the Pannonian Basin are flanked by terraces of gravel and wind-blown glacial deposits known as loess.

Tisza river

Poljes in the Kosovo region

Sheer limestone walls enclose all sides
Flat polje floor
Underground drainage along joints in the rock
Spring at foot of cliff

▲ Rain and underground water dissolve limestone along massive vertical joints (cracks). This creates poljes: depressions several miles across with steep walls and broad, flat floors.

At Iron Gate (Derdap), on the border with Romania, the Danube narrows and cuts through foothills of the Balkan and Carpathian mountains, forming the deepest gorge in Europe.

A major earthquake at Skopje, North Macedonia, in 1963 killed 1000 people. The whole region lies on an active crustal plate margin.

Lake Ohrid

▲ Lake Ohrid borders Albania and North Macedonia. Ohrid is the deepest lake in the western Balkans, reaching depths of 938 ft (286 m).

## Map key

**Population**
- ● 1 million to 5 million
- ● 500,000 to 1 million
- ◉ 100,000 to 500,000
- ◎ 50,000 to 100,000
- ◌ 10,000 to 50,000
- ○ below 10,000

**Elevation**
- 2000m / 6562ft
- 1000m / 3281ft
- 500m / 1640ft
- 250m / 820ft
- 100m / 328ft
- sea level

▲ *The Tara river is one of Montenegro's major rivers. It flows into the Danube via the Drina and Sava rivers. Along its course the Tara has eroded spectacular gorges up to 3280 ft (1000 m) deep.*

## Transportation & industry

Processing industries based on the region's wealth of mineral reserves predominate in Albania and North Macedonia. In other regions, industrial plants have been commandeered, if not destroyed in the war and mineral extraction has severely declined. The fast-flowing rivers found throughout the Dinaric Alps are exploited to generate hydroelectric power.

▲ *The historic center of Mostar in southern Bosnia, with its famous 16th-century Turkish bridge, was destroyed by shelling during 1993. The bridge was rebuilt and opened again in 2004.*

In February 2008, Kosovo (a UN Protectorate within Serbia since 1999) declared independence. Although now recognized by numerous countries, this decision has proved controversial with other states wary of setting a precedent for separatist groups within their own borders. It is therefore likely to be some time before Kosovo becomes universally recognized.

**Transportation network**

| | |
|---|---|
| 🚗 46,996 miles (75,642 km) | ✈ 685 miles (1103 km) |
| 🚂 5413 miles (8713 km) | 🚢 879 miles (1415 km) |

The war has resulted in the destruction or disintegration of infrastructure for transportation, communications, and power supply, though this is now in the process of recovery.

**Major industry and infrastructure**
- ⚙ aluminum refining
- 🚗 car manufacture
- 🧪 chemicals
- ⚙ engineering
- 🍴 food processing
- ⛏ mining
- ⚡ hydroelectric power
- ⚓ shipbuilding
- 🧵 textiles
- 🪵 timber processing
- ● capital cities
- ■ major towns
- ✈ international airports
- — major roads

▲ *Industrial processing plants were established throughout Albania by the Hoxha regime, which collapsed in 1992. They remain incongruous among the villages of one of Europe's most conservative rural societies.*

▲ *The ancient Croatian port of Dubrovnik was one of the former Yugoslavia's most popular tourist resorts and an important point of access to the sea along the Dalmatian (Dalmacija) coast. Shelling of the old city by Serb forces in 1991 provoked international condemnation.*

## Land use and agricultural distribution

- 🐖 pigs
- 🐑 sheep
- 🌾 cereals
- 🍒 fruit
- 🫒 olives
- 🍬 sugar beet
- 🪵 timber
- 🍇 vineyards
- ■ capital cities
- • major towns
- pasture
- cropland
- forest
- mountain region

### The urban/rural population divide

urban 51%  rural 49%

| Population density | Total land area |
|---|---|
| 240 people per sq mile (93 people per sq km) | 95,038 sq miles (246,278 sq km) |

## Using the land

Crops of wheat, maize, sugar beet, vegetables, and fruit are widely grown. The hilly terrain is suited to forestry and livestock farming. The mild, Mediterranean climate of the coastal regions provides ideal conditions for growing vines and olives. Albania's largely agricultural economy has been adversely affected by the recent dismantling of state farms.

▼ *Sweet red peppers are dried in the sun, ready to make paprika. North Macedonia's economy is mainly agricultural and its fertile soils support a broad range of crops.*

113

# Bulgaria & Greece

Including EUROPEAN TURKEY

Greece is renowned as the original hearth of western civilization. The rugged terrain and numerous islands have profoundly affected its development, creating a strong agricultural and maritime tradition.

In the past 50 years, this formerly rural society has rapidly urbanized, with one third of the population now living in the capital, Athens, and in the northern city of Salonica. Bulgaria, dominated for centuries by the Ottoman Turks, became part of the eastern bloc after the Second World War, only slowly emerging from Soviet influence in 1989. Moves toward democracy led to some instability in Bulgaria and Greece, now outweighed by the challenge of integration with the European Union.

## Transportation & industry

Soviet investment introduced heavy industry into Bulgaria, and the processing of agricultural produce, such as tobacco, is important throughout the country. Both countries have substantial shipyards and Greece has one of the world's largest merchant fleets. Many small craft workshops, producing textiles and processed foods, are clustered around Greek cities. The service and construction sectors have profited from the successful tourist industry.

## The landscape

Bulgaria's Balkan mountains divide the Danubian Plain (Dunavska Ravnina) and Maritsa Basin, meeting the Black Sea in the east along sandy beaches. The steep Rhodope Mountains form a natural barrier with Greece, while the younger Pindus form a rugged central spine which descends into the Aegean Sea to give a vast archipelago of over 2000 islands, the largest of which is Crete.

Limestone rocks exposed by erosion of metamorphic rocks

Ancient metamorphic rock, formed miles below the surface

Younger limestones created in shallow seas

▲ *Mount Olympus is a composite of rocks formed by two major tectonic events. First the older metamorphic rocks were thrust over the limestones, then two million years ago regional warping and subsequent erosion, reexposed the limestone.*

*The Peloponnese consist of several mountainous peninsulas, linked to the mainland by the isthmus of Corinth. The Corinth Canal (Dióryga Korínthou), built in 1893, cuts through the isthmus, linking the Aegean and Ionian Seas.*

*Mount Olympus is the mythical home of the Greek Gods and, at 9570 ft (2917 m), is the highest mountain in Greece.*

The islands of Crete, Kythira, Kárpathos, and Rhodes are part of an arc which bends southeastward from the Peloponnese, forming the southern boundary of the Aegean.

▲ *Layers of black volcanic ash still cover the island of Santorini. This volcano last erupted 3500 years ago, but still shows signs of volcanic activity.*

▶ *The Arda river cuts through the Rhodope Mountains in rugged, rocky gorges.*

The Danube, Europe's second longest river, forms most of Bulgaria's northern border. The Danubian plain (Dunavska Ravnina), extending from the southern bank, is extremely fertile.

Balkan Mountains

Maritsa Basin

Pindus Mountains

Rhodes

Kárpathos

Crete

Kythira

Corinth Canal (Dióryga Korínthou)

Mount Olympus

Rhodope Mountains

Scale 1:2,750,000

projection: Lambert Conformal Conic

### Major industry and infrastructure

- chemicals
- engineering
- food processing
- shipbuilding
- textiles
- tourism
- capital cities
- major towns
- international airports
- major roads
- major industrial areas

### Transportation network

| | |
|---|---|
| 103,930 miles (167,630 km) | |
| 345 miles (557 km) | |
| 4346 miles (6995 km) | |
| 294 miles (474 km) | |

*Bulgaria's railroads require investment to revive an outdated infrastructure. In Greece, despite a developing road network, ferry-boats remain the most effective form of transportation in many areas.*

▲ *A towering pinnacle at Metéora in central Greece is home to the monastery of Roussánou. The 24 rock towers which dominate the plain of Thessaly (Thessalía) are remnants of an old plateau. Long-term weathering along fissures in the rock has worn away the rest of the plateau.*

BLACK SEA

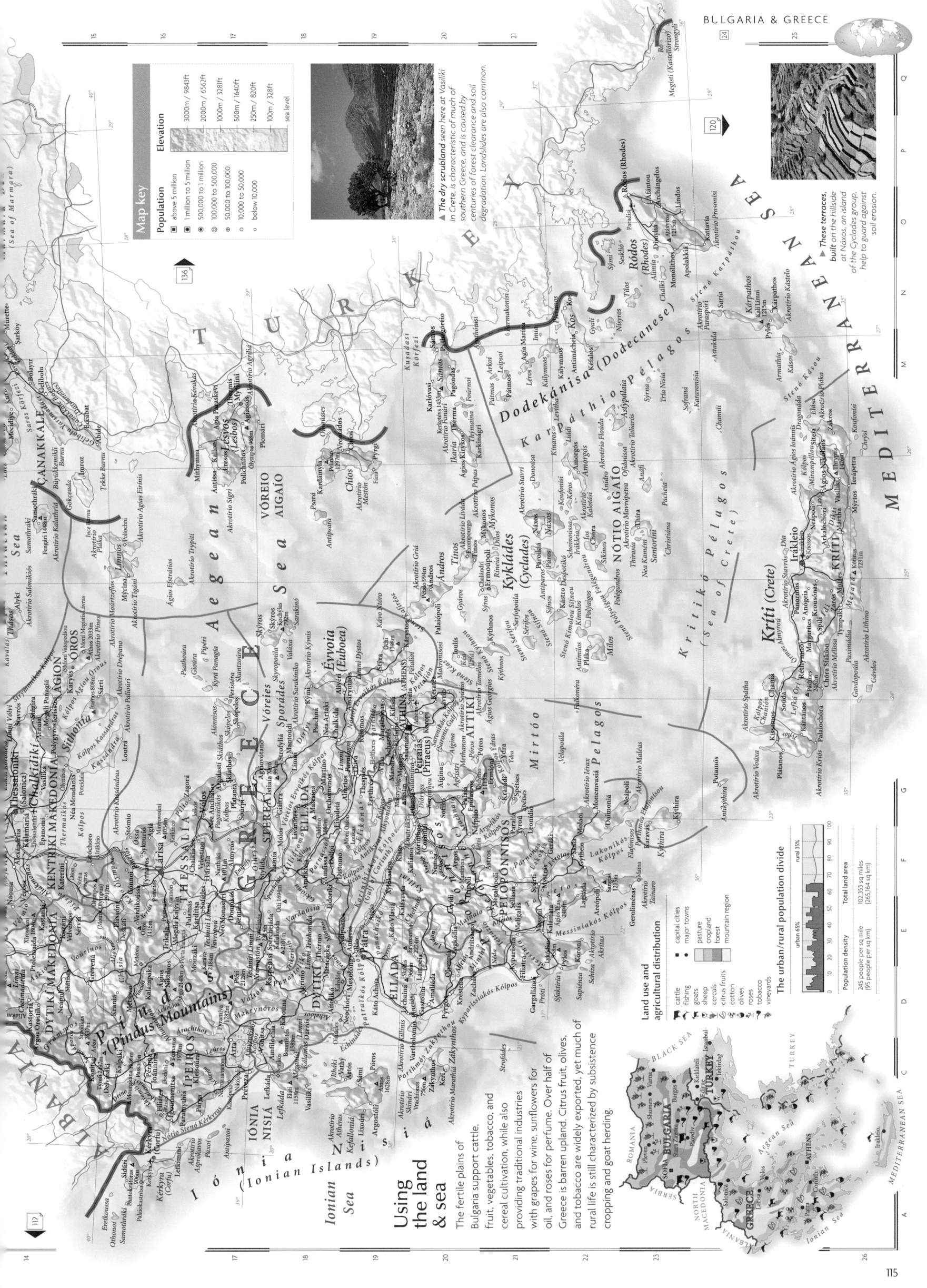

## Map key

**Elevation**

| 3000m / 9843ft |
| 2000m / 6562ft |
| 1000m / 3281ft |
| 500m / 1640ft |
| 250m / 820ft |
| 100m / 328ft |
| sea level |

**Population**

■ above 5 million
□ 1 million to 5 million
◉ 500,000 to 1 million
◎ 100,000 to 500,000
◉ 50,000 to 100,000
○ 10,000 to 50,000
○ below 10,000

▲ The dry scrubland seen here at Vasiliki in Crete, is characteristic of much of southern Greece, and is caused by centuries of forest clearance and soil degradation. Landslides are also common.

▲ These terraces, built on the hillside at Náxos, an island of the Cyclades group, help to guard against soil erosion.

## Using the land & sea

The fertile plains of Bulgaria support cattle, fruit, vegetables, tobacco, and cereal cultivation, while also providing traditional industries with grapes for wine, sunflowers for oil, and roses for perfume. Over half of Greece is barren upland. Citrus fruit, olives, and tobacco are widely exported, yet much of rural life is still characterized by subsistence cropping and goat herding.

### Land use and agricultural distribution

🐂 cattle
🐟 fishing
🐐 goats
🐑 sheep
🌾 cereals
🍊 citrus fruits
🌿 cotton
🫒 olives
🌹 roses
🍃 tobacco
🍇 vineyards

■ capital cities
• major towns

pasture
cropland
forest
mountain region

### The urban/rural population divide

urban 65%        rural 35%

| Population density | Total land area |
|---|---|
| 245 people per sq mile (95 people per sq km) | 102,353 sq miles (265,164 sq km) |

# Romania, Moldova & Ukraine

The industrial, social, and cultural make-up of Romania and the former Soviet states of Moldova and Ukraine still bear the imprint of their communist past. As part of the USSR, Ukraine was a leading agricultural, industrial, and energy producer. These industries, like those in Moldova and Romania, are now being reoriented more firmly toward western markets. As a result of shifting borders, and Soviet policy actively encouraging Russian immigration into other Soviet states like Ukraine and Moldova, all three countries now contain large numbers of foreign nationals. In 2014, Russia drew international condemnation by annexing the Ukrainian territory of Crimea.

## Using the land

The fertile black soils of Ukraine, often called "the breadbasket of Europe," have enabled the cultivation of a variety of cereals and vegetables, which are widely exported. Romania and Moldova also grow cereals, sunflowers, and vegetables, and are noted for the quality of their wines.

◄ *The fertile lands and tolerant climate of Moldova are ideally suited to growing grapes for wine.*

### The urban/rural population divide

| urban 65% | rural 35% |
| --- | --- |

| 0 | 10 | 20 | 30 | 40 | 50 | 60 | 70 | 80 | 90 | 100 |

| Population density | Total land area |
| --- | --- |
| 222 people per sq mile (86 people per sq km) | 334,947 sq miles (867,740 sq km) |

◄ *Glacial lakes are found throughout the Transylvanian Alps (Carpatii Meridionali), although the mountains no longer have any permanent snow cover.*

## Transportation & industry

Heavy industry using local raw materials characterizes much of this region. The industrial heartland of Ukraine, specializing in metal and machine-building industries, is based around its vast mineral reserves in the Donbass region. In Moldova, food processing draws on produce from its agricultural sector. Romanian industry relies both on local raw materials and imported iron, steel, and oil.

### Land use and agricultural distribution

- cattle
- pigs
- poultry
- sheep
- cereals
- cotton
- sugar beet
- sunflowers
- vineyards
- ■ capital cities
- ● major towns

- pasture
- cropland
- forest
- wetland

### Major industry and infrastructure

- car manufacture
- chemicals
- coal
- engineering
- food processing
- mining
- oil & gas
- textiles
- tourism

- ■ capital cities
- ● major towns
- ⊕ international airports
- — major roads
- major industrial areas

### Transportation network

| 170,707 miles (274,757 km) | 1170 miles (1883 km) |
| --- | --- |
| 21,474 miles (34,563 km) | 4130 miles (6647 km) |

*Increased industrialization has necessitated the upgrading of road and rail networks in all three countries. Modernization has tended to focus only on major cities and industrial areas.*

► *During the 1960s and 1970s, many industries, like this carbon factory, developed using the mineral resources on the flanks of the Transylvanian Alps (Carpatii Meridionali).*

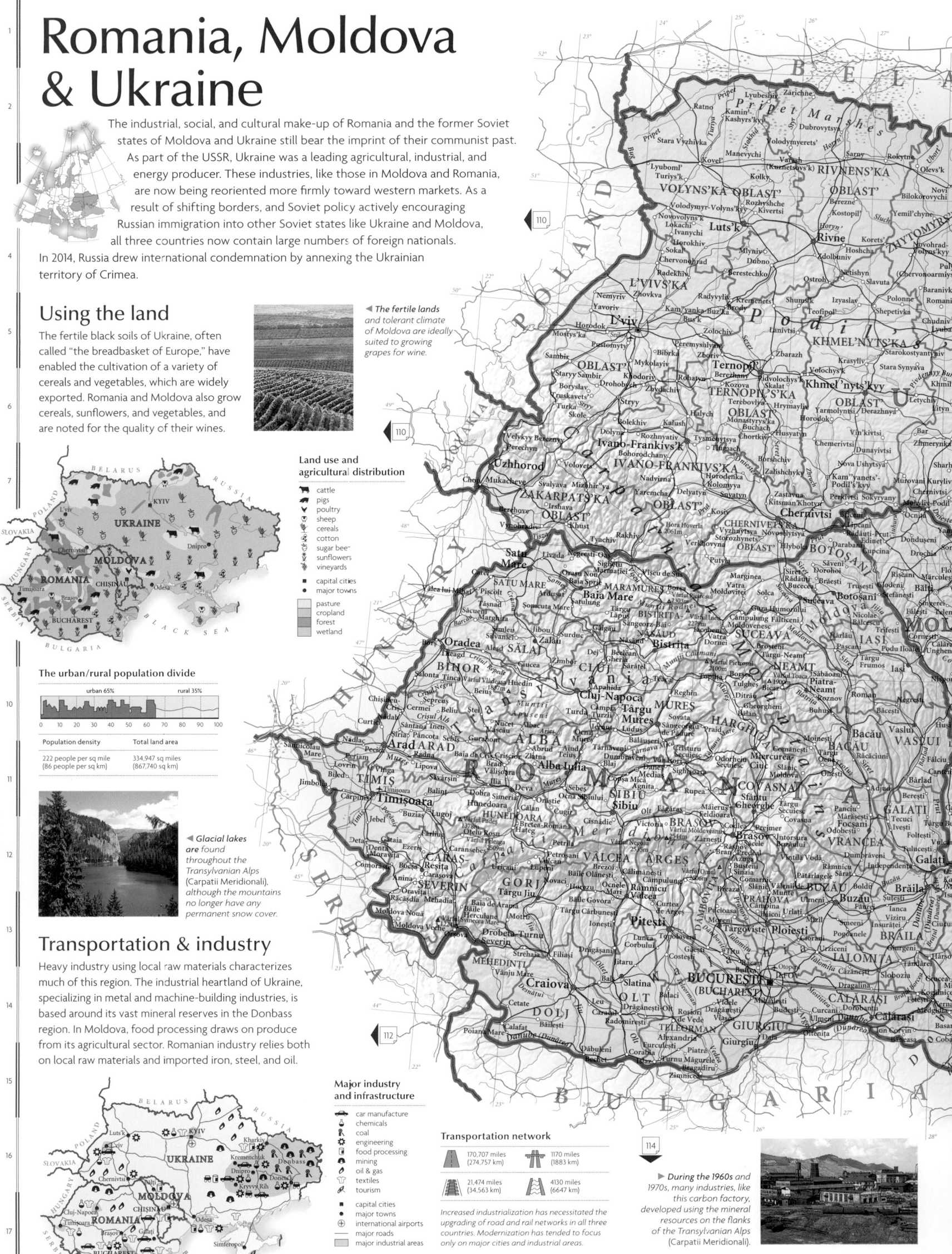

**Scale 1:3,500,000**

Km
0 5 10 20 30 40 50 60 70 80 90 100

Miles
0 5 10 20 30 40 50 60 70 80 90 100

*projection: Lambert Conformal Conic*

**Map key**

**Population**
- 1 million to 5 million
- 500,000 to 1 million
- 100,000 to 500,000
- 50,000 to 100,000
- 10,000 to 50,000
- below 10,000

**Elevation**
- 2000m / 6562ft
- 1000m / 3281ft
- 500m / 1640ft
- 250m / 820ft
- 100m / 328ft
- sea level

▲ *The Swallow's Nest castle at Yalta is one of many tourist resorts on the Crimean (Krym) coast, dubbed the "Russian Riviera."*

*(since 2014 the Ukrainian territory of Crimea has been annexed by Russia)*

**Old glaciated valley**

**Water has eroded a new post-glacial valley**

▲ *Balkas are common throughout Ukraine. They are large U-shaped valleys, formed during the last Ice Age, which contain narrower, deep valleys. These were incised by a sudden flow of water, following an icemelt.*

**Steppe landscape** covers two-thirds of Ukraine. These flat, treeless grasslands extend from central Europe to central Asia.

**Most of the** major rivers in southeastern Europe, like the Danube, the Dniester, and Dnieper flow south and east to the Black Sea.

**Counterclockwise currents** have created the sandspits which fringe the Sea of Azov.

**The Codrii Hills** dominate the landscape of central Moldova; they are intersected by deep, flat valleys and ravines.

**Uplifted and folded** at the same time as the Alps, some 250 miles (400 km) of the eastern Carpathian Mountains contain ancient volcanic cones and craters.

**The Apuseni Mountains** *(Muntii Apuseni)* are rich in mineral deposits, including gold and iron ore.

**Transylvanian Alps** *(Carpatii Meridionali)*

**The Danube forms** a natural border between Romania and Bulgaria.

**The three branches of the** Danube Delta *(Delta Dunării)* form a triangle of wetlands covering some 1950 sq miles (5050 sq km).

**At Kryms'ki Hory,** three flat-topped, parallel limestone ridges run 80 miles (128 km) along the southern coast of the Crimean (Krym) Peninsula.

## The landscape

Vast flat lowlands and gently rolling hills cover most of southeastern Europe. In the southwest, the Carpathian Mountains form a gentle arc. To the south of the Carpathian Mountains lies the Danube Plain, across which the Danube river flows to the Black Sea. To the north and east, the hills of Moldova level out into low plains, running east to the steppes of Ukraine.

▶ *Divided into crystalline massifs, the southern arm of the Carpathian Mountains, the Transylvanian Alps (Carpatii Meridionali), extend 170 miles (274 km) across southwestern Romania.*

# The Baltic states & Belarus

## BELARUS, ESTONIA, LATVIA, LITHUANIA, Kaliningrad

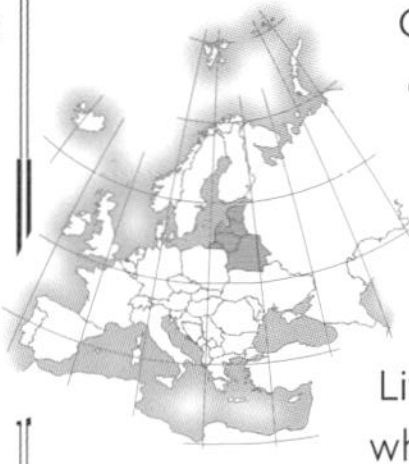

Occupying Europe's main corridor to Russia, the four distinct cultures of Estonia, Latvia, Lithuania, and Belarus share a history of struggle for nationhood against the interests of more powerful neighbors. As the first republics to declare their independence from the Soviet Union in 1990–91, the Baltic states of Estonia, Latvia, and Lithuania sought an economic role in the EU, while reaffirming their European cultural roots through the church and a strong musical tradition. Meanwhile, Belarus has shown economic and political allegiance to Russia by joining the Commonwealth of Independent States.

▲ *The seaport of Riga is Latvia's capital and the center of economic and cultural life. With a 32% Russian minority in Latvia, language and the right to national citizenship are key issues.*

## Using the land

Across the four nations cattle and pig farming are widespread, together with diverse arable crops, including flax for making linen, potatoes used to produce vodka, cereals, and other vegetables. Almost a third of the land is forested; demand for timber has increased the importance of forest management.

### Land use and agricultural distribution

- cattle
- pigs
- cereals
- flax
- potatoes
- timber
- capital cities
- major towns

- pasture
- cropland
- forest
- wetland

The urban/rural population divide

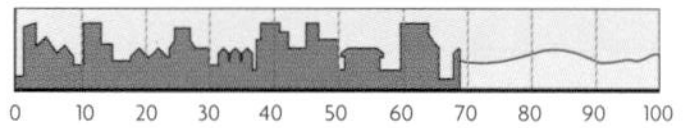

urban 69%
rural 31%

Population density
122 people per sq mile
(47 people per sq km)

Total land area
145,006 sq miles
(375,656 sq km)

▲ *A pine forest in northern Belarus. Conifers in the north give way to hardwood forest farther south. Timber mills are supplied with logs floated along the country's many navigable waterways.*

▲ *The Western Dvina river provides hydroelectric power and, during the summer months, access to the Baltic Sea. The lower course of the river freezes from December to April.*

### Map key

**Population**
- 1 million to 5 million
- 500,000 to 1 million
- 100,000 to 500,000
- 50,000 to 100,000
- 10,000 to 50,000
- below 10,000

**Elevation**
- 250m / 820ft
- 100m / 328ft
- sea level

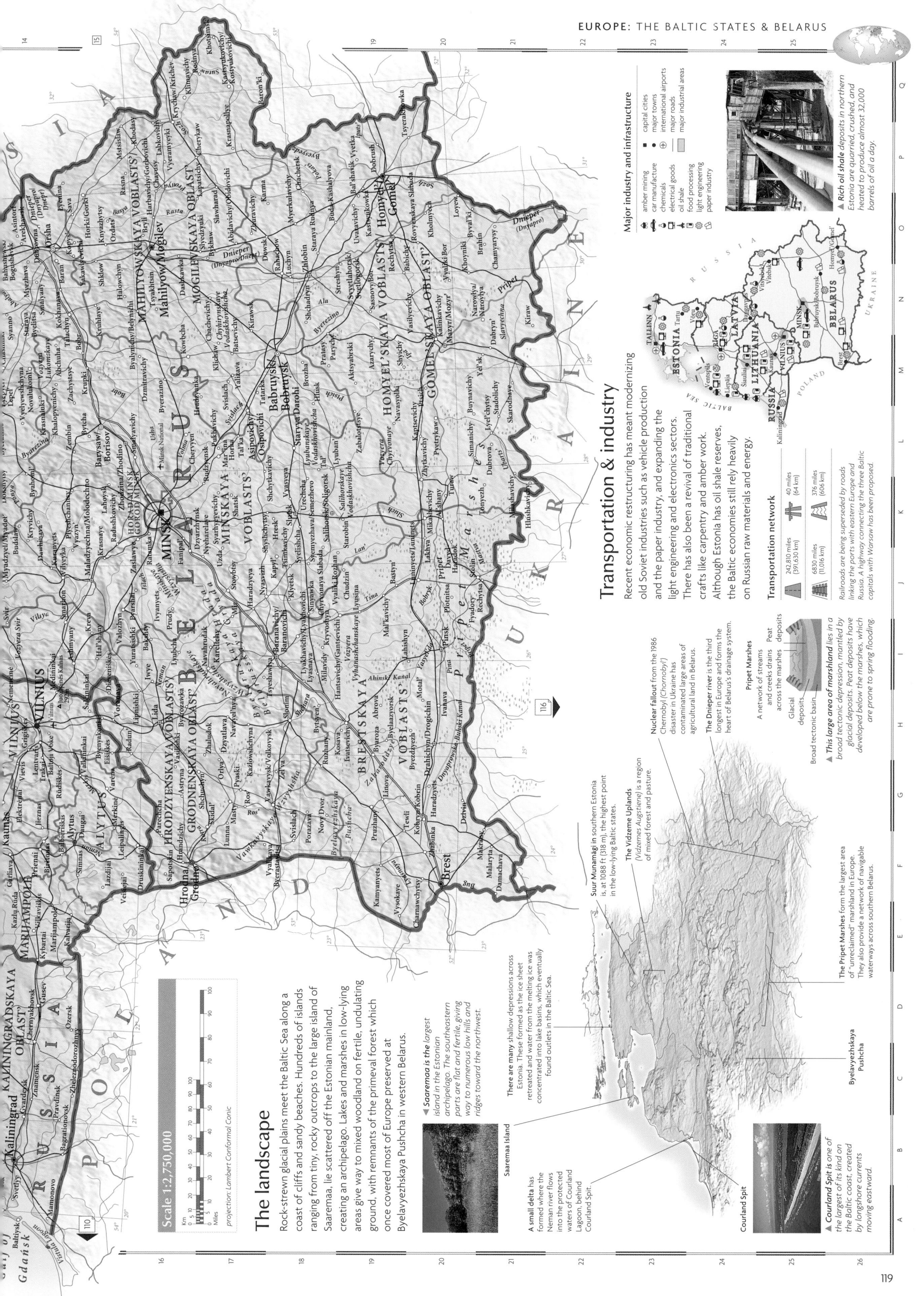

## The landscape

Rock-strewn glacial plains meet the Baltic Sea along a coast of cliffs and sandy beaches. Hundreds of islands ranging from tiny, rocky outcrops to the large island of Saaremaa, lie scattered off the Estonian mainland, creating an archipelago. Lakes and marshes in low-lying areas give way to mixed woodland on fertile, undulating ground, with remnants of the primeval forest which once covered most of Europe preserved at Byelavyezhskaya Pushcha in western Belarus.

**Scale 1:2,750,000**

projection: Lambert Conformal Conic

▼ *Saaremaa is the largest island in the Estonian archipelago. The southeastern parts are flat and fertile, giving way to numerous low hills and ridges toward the northwest.*

**There are many shallow depressions across Estonia. These formed as the ice sheet retreated and water from the melting ice was concentrated into lake basins, which eventually found outlets in the Baltic Sea.**

**Saaremaa Island**

**A small delta has formed where the Neman river flows into the protected waters of Courland Lagoon, behind Courland Spit.**

**Courland Spit**

▲ *Courland Spit is one of the largest of its kind on the Baltic coast, created by longshore currents moving eastward.*

**Byelavyezhskaya Pushcha**

The Pripet Marshes form the largest area of "unreclaimed" marshland in Europe. They also provide a network of navigable waterways across southern Belarus.

**Suur Munamägi** in southern Estonia is, at 1088 ft (318 m), the highest point in the low-lying Baltic states.

**The Vidzeme Uplands** (*Vidzemes Augstiene*) is a region of mixed forest and pasture.

**Nuclear fallout from** the 1986 Chernobyl (*Chornobyl*) disaster in Ukraine has contaminated large areas of agricultural land in Belarus.

**The Dnieper river** is the third longest in Europe and forms the heart of Belarus's drainage system.

**Pripet Marshes**
A network of streams and creeks drains across the marshes

Peat deposits

Glacial deposits.

Broad tectonic basin.

▲ *This large area of marshland lies in a broad tectonic depression, mantled by glacial deposits. Peat deposits have developed below the marshes, which are prone to spring flooding.*

## Transportation & industry

Recent economic restructuring has meant modernizing old Soviet industries such as vehicle production and the paper industry, and expanding the light engineering and electronics sectors. There has also been a revival of traditional crafts like carpentry and amber work. Although Estonia has oil shale reserves, the Baltic economies still rely heavily on Russian raw materials and energy.

**Transportation network**

| | |
|---|---|
| 243,810 miles (391,630 km) | 40 miles (64 km) |
| 6830 miles (11,016 km) | 376 miles (606 km) |

*Railroads are being superseded by roads linking the ports with eastern Europe and Russia. A highway connecting the three Baltic capitals with Warsaw has been proposed.*

**Major industry and infrastructure**

- amber mining
- car manufacture
- chemicals
- electrical goods
- oil shale
- food processing
- light engineering
- paper industry

- capital cities
- major towns
- ⊕ international airports
- major roads
- major industrial areas

▲ *Rich oil shale deposits in northern Estonia are quarried, crushed, and heated to produce almost 32,000 barrels of oil a day.*

# The Mediterranean

The Mediterranean Sea stretches over 2500 miles (4000 km) east to west, separating Europe from Africa. At its westernmost point it is connected to the Atlantic Ocean through the Strait of Gibraltar. In the east, the Suez canal, opened in 1869, gives passage to the Indian Ocean. In the northeast, linked by the Sea of Marmara, lies the Black Sea. The Mediterranean is bordered by almost 30 states and territories, and more than 100 million people live on its shores and islands. Throughout history, the Mediterranean has been a focal area for many great empires and civilizations, reflected in the variety of cultures found on its shores. Since the 1960s, development along the southern coast of Europe has expanded rapidly to accommodate increasing numbers of tourists and to enable the exploitation of oil and gas reserves. This has resulted in rising levels of pollution, threatening the future of the sea.

▲ *Monte Carlo is just one of the luxurious resorts scattered along the Riviera, which stretches along the coast from Cannes in France to La Spezia in Italy. The region's mild winters and hot summers have attracted wealthy tourists since the early 19th century.*

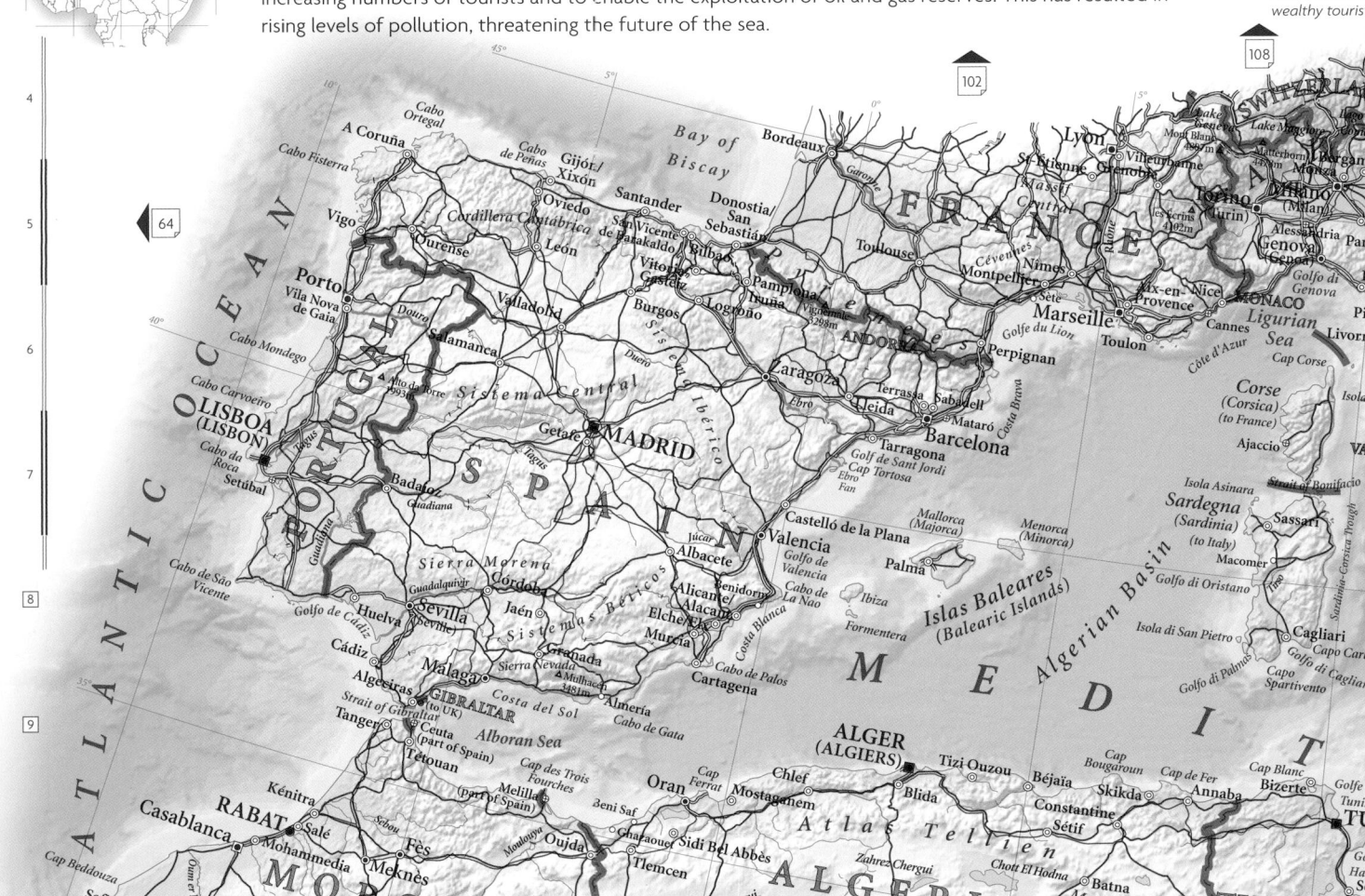

## The landscape

The Mediterranean Sea is almost totally landlocked, joined to the Atlantic Ocean through the Strait of Gibraltar, which is only 8 miles (13 km) wide. Lying on an active plate margin, sea floor movements have formed a variety of basins, troughs, and ridges. A submarine ridge running from Tunisia to the island of Sicily divides the Mediterranean into two distinct basins. The western basin is characterized by broad, smooth abyssal (or ocean) plains. In contrast, the eastern basin is dominated by a large ridge system, running east to west.

The narrow Strait of Gibraltar inhibits water exchange between the Mediterranean Sea and the Atlantic Ocean, producing a high degree of salinity and a low tidal range within the Mediterranean. The lack of tides has encouraged the build-up of pollutants in many semienclosed bays.

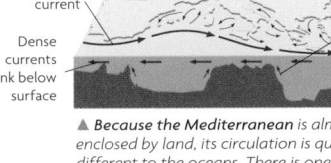

Main surface current

Denser, more saline currents flow back to Atlantic

Dense currents sink below surface

▲ *Because the Mediterranean is almost enclosed by land, its circulation is quite different to the oceans. There is one major current which flows in from the Atlantic and moves east. Currents flowing back to the Atlantic are denser and flow below the main current.*

Industrial pollution flowing from the Dnieper and Danube rivers has destroyed a large proportion of the fish population that used to inhabit the upper layers of the Black Sea.

The Ionian Basin is the deepest in the Mediterranean, reaching depths of 16,800 ft (5121 m).

The edge of the Eurasian Plate is edged by a continental shelf. In the Mediterranean Sea this is widest at the Ebro Fan where it extends 60 miles (96 km).

◀ *The Atlas Mountains are a range of fold mountains that lie in Morocco and Algeria. They run parallel to the Mediterranean, forming a topographical and climatic divide between the Mediterranean coast and the western Sahara.*

An arc of active submarine, island and mainland volcanoes, including Etna and Vesuvius, lie in and around southern Italy. The area is also susceptible to earthquakes and landslides.

Nutrient flows into the eastern Mediterranean, and sediment flows to the Nile Delta have been severely lowered by the building of the Aswan Dam across the Nile in Eygpt. This is causing the delta to shrink.

Oxygen in the Black Sea is dissolved only in its upper layers; at depths below 230–300 ft (70–100 m) the sea is "dead" and can support no lifeforms other than specially adapted bacteria.

The Suez Canal, opened in 1869, extends 100 miles (160 km) from Port Said to the Gulf of Suez.

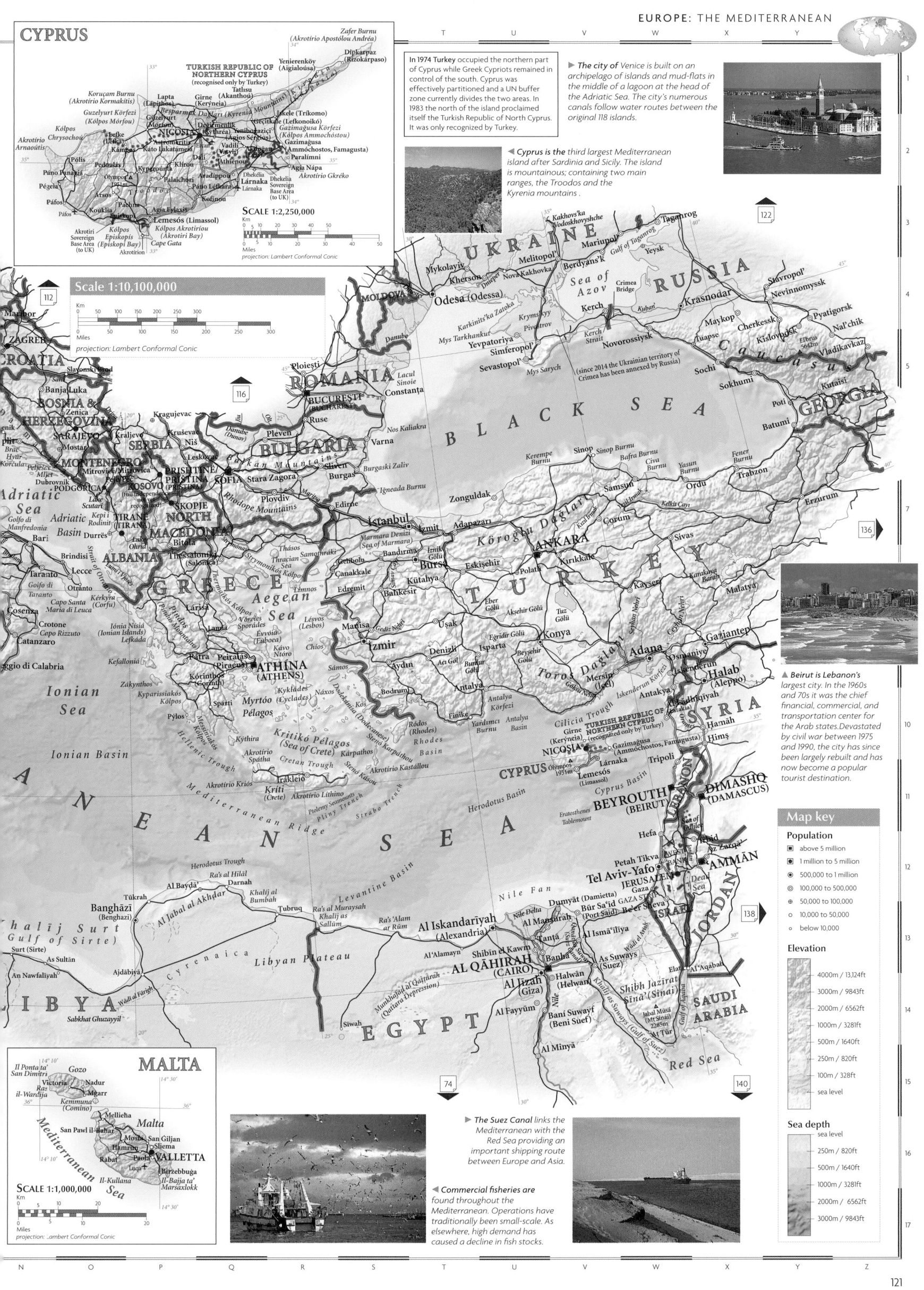

# CYPRUS

SCALE 1:2,250,000

projection: Lambert Conformal Conic

Scale 1:10,100,000

projection: Lambert Conformal Conic

In 1974 Turkey occupied the northern part of Cyprus while Greek Cypriots remained in control of the south. Cyprus was effectively partitioned and a UN buffer zone currently divides the two areas. In 1983 the north of the island proclaimed itself the Turkish Republic of North Cyprus. It was only recognized by Turkey.

► *The city of* Venice is built on an archipelago of islands and mud-flats in the middle of a lagoon at the head of the Adriatic Sea. The city's numerous canals follow water routes between the original 118 islands.

◄ *Cyprus is the* third largest Mediterranean island after Sardinia and Sicily. The island is mountainous; containing two main ranges, the Troodos and the Kyrenia mountains .

▲ *Beirut is Lebanon's* largest city. In the 1960s and 70s it was the chief financial, commercial, and transportation center for the Arab states.Devastated by civil war between 1975 and 1990, the city has since been largely rebuilt and has now become a popular tourist destination.

# MALTA

SCALE 1:1,000,000

projection: Lambert Conformal Conic

► *The Suez Canal* links the Mediterranean with the Red Sea providing an important shipping route between Europe and Asia.

◄ *Commercial fisheries are* found throughout the Mediterranean. Operations have traditionally been small-scale. As elsewhere, high demand has caused a decline in fish stocks.

## Map key

### Population

- ▪ above 5 million
- ◻ 1 million to 5 million
- ◉ 500,000 to 1 million
- ◎ 100,000 to 500,000
- ⊙ 50,000 to 100,000
- ○ 10,000 to 50,000
- ○ below 10,000

### Elevation

- 4000m / 13,124ft
- 3000m / 9843ft
- 2000m / 6562ft
- 1000m / 3281ft
- 500m / 1640ft
- 250m / 820ft
- 100m / 328ft
- sea level

### Sea depth

- sea level
- 250m / 820ft
- 500m / 1640ft
- 1000m / 3281ft
- 2000m / 6562ft
- 3000m / 9843ft

# Russia

The Cold War era of global relations was concluded in 1991 with the formal dissolution of the Soviet Union. Russia declared its separate sovereignty from the foundering communist empire following independence declarations from a number of former Soviet republics. As the leading member of the Commonwealth of Independent States, Russia has a central role in the development of post-Soviet Eurasia. Crossing 11 time zones, Russia is almost twice the size of the US, and with more than 150 ethnic minorities and 21 autonomous republics, regionalist dissent within its own territory remains a danger.

RUSSIA: ADMINISTRATIVE REGIONS

124–125
126–127

The administrative area names in European Russia have been omitted west of the Ural Mountains. Please refer to pages 124–125 and 126–127 where these areas are shown at a larger scale.

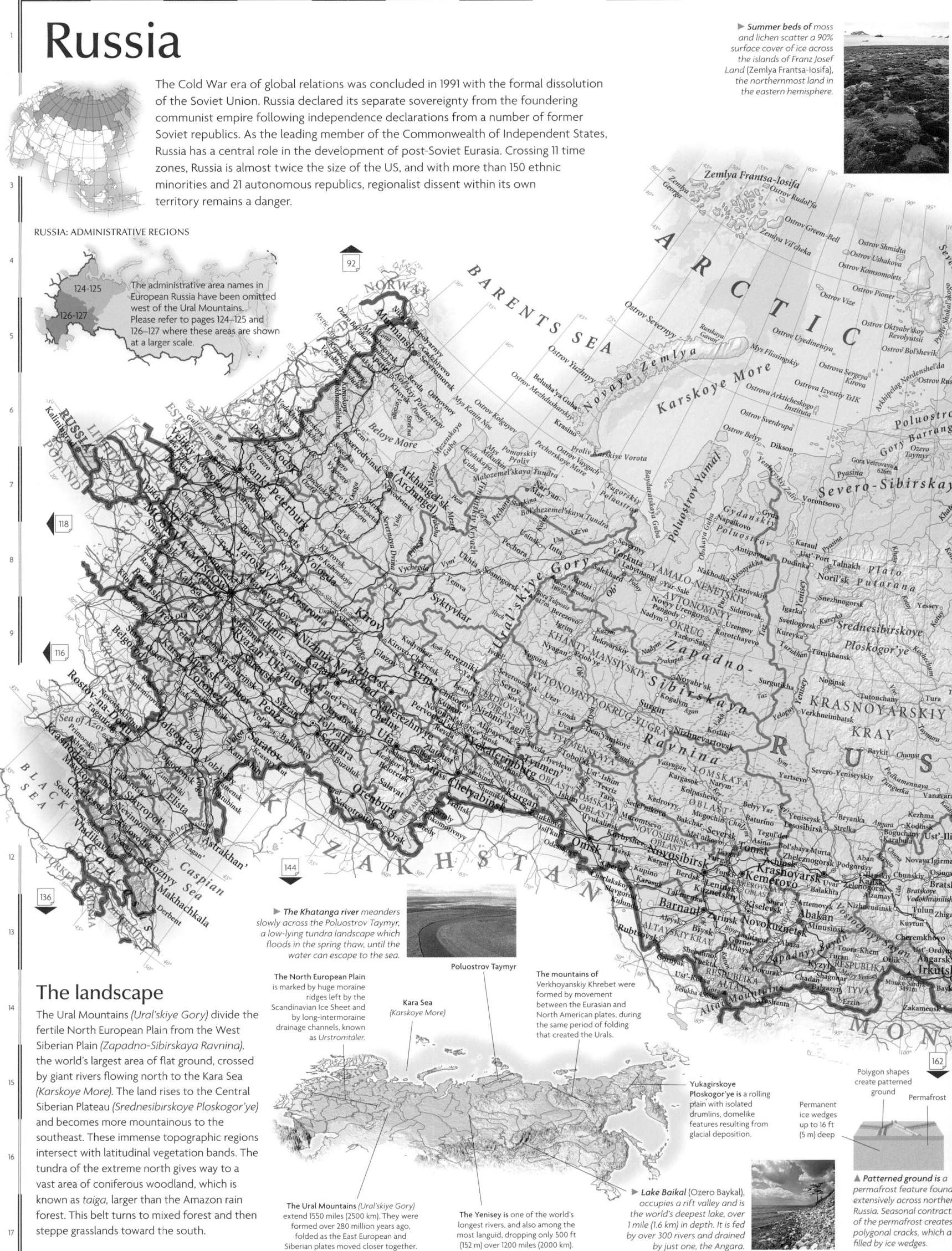

▶ *Summer beds of* moss and lichen scatter a 90% surface cover of ice across the islands of Franz Josef Land (Zemlya Frantsa-Iosifa), the northernmost land in the eastern hemisphere.

## The landscape

The Ural Mountains (*Ural'skiye Gory*) divide the fertile North European Plain from the West Siberian Plain (*Zapadno-Sibirskaya Ravnina*), the world's largest area of flat ground, crossed by giant rivers flowing north to the Kara Sea (*Karskoye More*). The land rises to the Central Siberian Plateau (*Srednesibirskoye Ploskogor'ye*) and becomes more mountainous to the southeast. These immense topographic regions intersect with latitudinal vegetation bands. The tundra of the extreme north gives way to a vast area of coniferous woodland, which is known as *taiga*, larger than the Amazon rain forest. This belt turns to mixed forest and then steppe grasslands toward the south.

▶ *The Khatanga river* meanders slowly across the Poluostrov Taymyr, a low-lying tundra landscape which floods in the spring thaw, until the water can escape to the sea.

Poluostrov Taymyr

The North European Plain is marked by huge moraine ridges left by the Scandinavian Ice Sheet and by long-intermoraine drainage channels, known as *Urstromtäler*.

Kara Sea
(*Karskoye More*)

The mountains of Verkhoyanskiy Khrebet were formed by movement between the Eurasian and North American plates, during the same period of folding that created the Urals.

The Ural Mountains (*Ural'skiye Gory*) extend 1550 miles (2500 km). They were formed over 280 million years ago, folded as the East European and Siberian plates moved closer together.

The Yenisey is one of the world's longest rivers, and also among the most languid, dropping only 500 ft (152 m) over 1200 miles (2000 km).

▶ *Lake Baikal* (Ozero Baykal), occupies a rift valley and is the world's deepest lake, over 1 mile (1.6 km) in depth. It is fed by over 300 rivers and drained by just one, the Angara.

Yukagirskoye Ploskogor'ye is a rolling plain with isolated drumlins, domelike features resulting from glacial deposition.

Permanent ice wedges up to 16 ft (5 m) deep

Polygon shapes create patterned ground

Permafrost

▲ *Patterned ground is* a permafrost feature found extensively across northern Russia. Seasonal contraction of the permafrost creates polygonal cracks, which are filled with ice wedges.

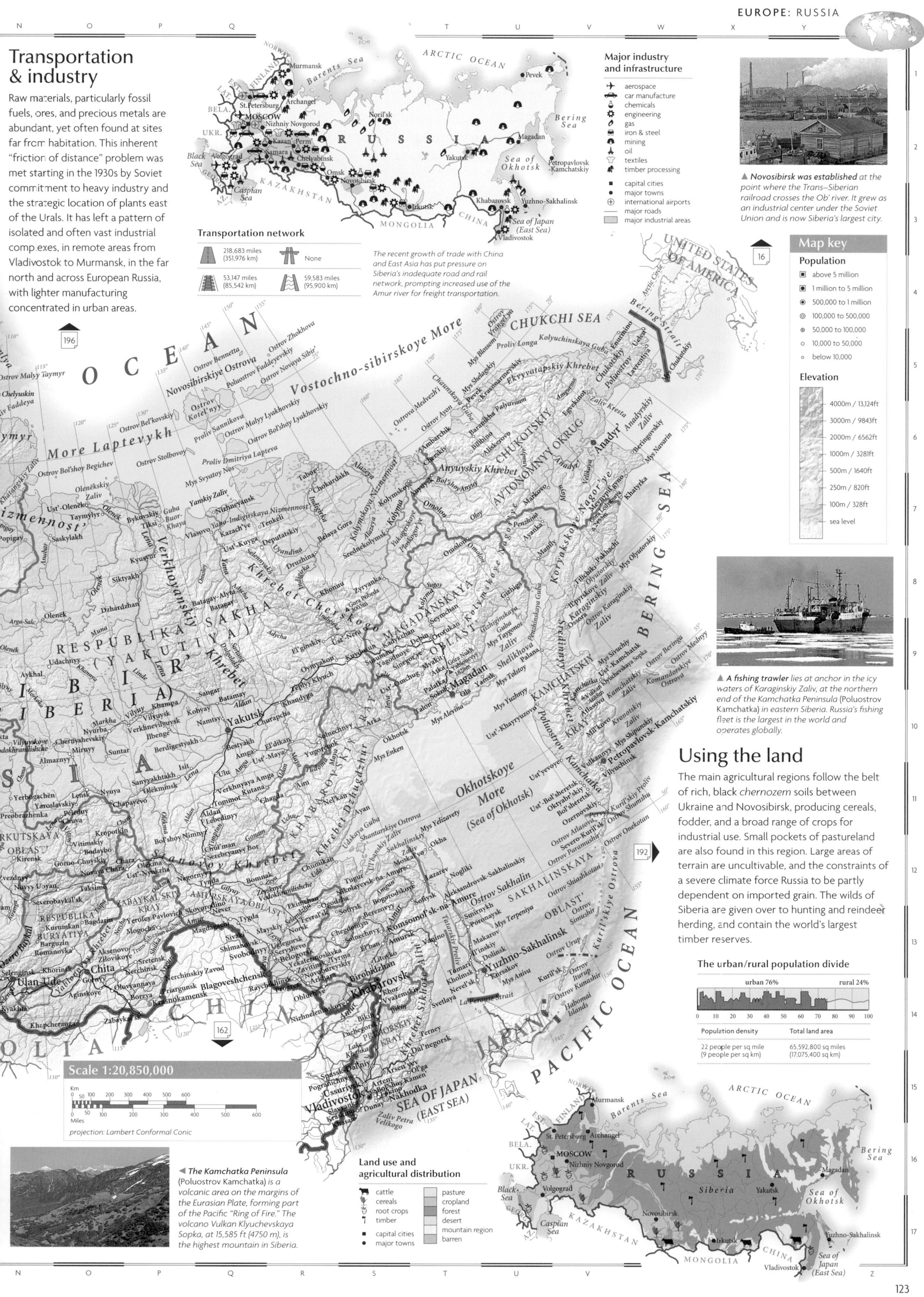

# Transportation & industry

Raw materials, particularly fossil fuels, ores, and precious metals are abundant, yet often found at sites far from habitation. This inherent "friction of distance" problem was met starting in the 1930s by Soviet commitment to heavy industry and the strategic location of plants east of the Urals. It has left a pattern of isolated and often vast industrial complexes, in remote areas from Vladivostok to Murmansk, in the far north and across European Russia, with lighter manufacturing concentrated in urban areas.

## Major industry and infrastructure

- aerospace
- car manufacture
- chemicals
- engineering
- gas
- iron & steel
- mining
- oil
- textiles
- timber processing
- capital cities
- major towns
- international airports
- major roads
- major industrial areas

## Transportation network

| | | | |
|---|---|---|---|
| 218,683 miles (351,976 km) | | None | |
| 53,147 miles (85,542 km) | | 59,583 miles (95,900 km) | |

The recent growth of trade with China and East Asia has put pressure on Siberia's inadequate road and rail network, prompting increased use of the Amur river for freight transportation.

▲ *Novosibirsk was established* at the point where the Trans–Siberian railroad crosses the Ob' river. It grew as an industrial center under the Soviet Union and is now Siberia's largest city.

## Map key

### Population

- ▣ above 5 million
- ◨ 1 million to 5 million
- ◉ 500,000 to 1 million
- ◎ 100,000 to 500,000
- ⊙ 50,000 to 100,000
- ⊙ 10,000 to 50,000
- ○ below 10,000

### Elevation

- 4000m / 13,124ft
- 3000m / 9843ft
- 2000m / 6562ft
- 1000m / 3281ft
- 500m / 1640ft
- 250m / 820ft
- 100m / 328ft
- sea level

▲ *A fishing trawler* lies at anchor in the icy waters of Karaginskiy Zaliv, at the northern end of the Kamchatka Peninsula (Poluostrov Kamchatka) in eastern Siberia. Russia's fishing fleet is the largest in the world and operates globally.

## Using the land

The main agricultural regions follow the belt of rich, black *chernozem* soils between Ukraine and Novosibirsk, producing cereals, fodder, and a broad range of crops for industrial use. Small pockets of pastureland are also found in this region. Large areas of terrain are uncultivable, and the constraints of a severe climate force Russia to be partly dependent on imported grain. The wilds of Siberia are given over to hunting and reindeer herding, and contain the world's largest timber reserves.

### The urban/rural population divide

| | |
|---|---|
| urban 76% | rural 24% |

0 10 20 30 40 50 60 70 80 90 100

| Population density | Total land area |
|---|---|
| 22 people per sq mile (9 people per sq km) | 65,592,800 sq miles (17,075,400 sq km) |

Scale 1:20,850,000

Km 0 50 100 200 300 400 500 600
Miles 0 50 100 200 300 400 500 600

projection: Lambert Conformal Conic

◀ *The Kamchatka Peninsula* (Poluostrov Kamchatka) is a volcanic area on the margins of the Eurasian Plate, forming part of the Pacific "Ring of Fire." The volcano Vulkan Klyuchevskaya Sopka, at 15,585 ft (4750 m), is the highest mountain in Siberia.

## Land use and agricultural distribution

- cattle
- cereals
- root crops
- timber
- capital cities
- major towns
- pasture
- cropland
- forest
- desert
- mountain region
- barren

# Northern European Russia

Reaching into the Arctic Circle, this region of lakeland, forest and tundra is historically bound to Europe by St Petersburg, the old imperial capital of Tsarist Russia and home to a third of the region's population. Communist rule from Moscow left the north politically marginalized, contributing to the present problems of outmoded industry, poor infrastructure and serious environmental neglect. However, with borders embracing Finland, Norway, the Baltic and the northern sea route to the Atlantic, the region's success in foreign trade is now of prime importance to the Russian economy.

## The landscape

The ancient bedrock of the Scandinavian Shield lies exposed across the glacially scoured Khibiny Mountains of the Kola Peninsula (Kol'skiy Poluostrov), becoming mantled with till toward the North European Plain. The Valdai Hills (Valdayskaya Vozvyshennost') form an important watershed for the plain's rivers, while thick forest veils a complicated topography of moraines, lakes, and ground disturbed by frost action. The Ural Mountains (Ural'skiye Gory) form a border with Asia in the east.

◄ *The Kola Peninsula* (Kol'skiy Poluostrov) is part of the Scandinavian Shield, an area of ancient bedrock underlying Scandinavia. Rocks in excess of 2500 million years old are exposed across the peninsula.

▲ *The Khibiny mountains* were formed by volcanic intrusions into the Scandinavian Shield, over 570 million years ago.

Kola Peninsula (Kol'skiy Poluostrov)

*Karst features*, including sinkholes, lakes, and caverns, are found in limestone outcrops across the plain of the Severnaya Dvina and Mezen' rivers.

*The low-lying plains* of the Pechora, Mezen', and Severnaya Dvina rivers were flooded by the sea while the land was still isostatically depressed following the last Ice Age, a process which has hidden the landforms created by glacial deposition.

Retreating glacier    Meltwater channels    Terminal moraine

▲ *Terminal moraines are* crescent-shaped ridges of glacial deposits, widely found in central Russia. Detritus is carried by the glacier and deposited at its terminus (snout) as it melts, marking the limit of the ice advance.

Ural Mountains (Ural'skiye Gory)

Two of Europe's biggest rivers, the Volga and Western Dvina, rise in the swampy uplands of the Valdai Hills (Valdayskaya Vozvyshennost'.)

◄ *Lake Onega* (Onezhskoye Ozero) is the remnant of a body of water which, 12,000 years ago, connected the White Sea (Beloye More) with the Gulf of Finland and the Baltic Sea.

## Using the land & sea

The cold climate confines agriculture mainly to southern and western provinces, where dairy farming predominates and arable land is given over to fodder crops as well as flax, potatoes, oats, and rye. Areas beyond the northern margins of cultivation are used for forestry, hunting, herding, and fishing, with some vegetables grown in hothouses around urban areas.

**Land use and agricultural distribution**

- cattle
- fishing
- reindeer
- timber
- fodder
- • major towns
- pasture
- cropland
- forest
- mountain region
- wetland
- tundra
- barren
- ice

**The urban/rural population divide**

urban 80%    rural 20%

0  10  20  30  40  50  60  70  80  90  100

Population density | Total land area

26 people per sq mile (10 people per sq km) | 829,398 sq miles (2,148,700 sq km)

◄ *Many rapids are* found along the 175 mile (280 km) course of the Sura river.

▶ *St. Peter and Paul* Fortress is the oldest building in St Petersburg, founded by Peter the Great in 1703 as a modern, European capital for Russia.

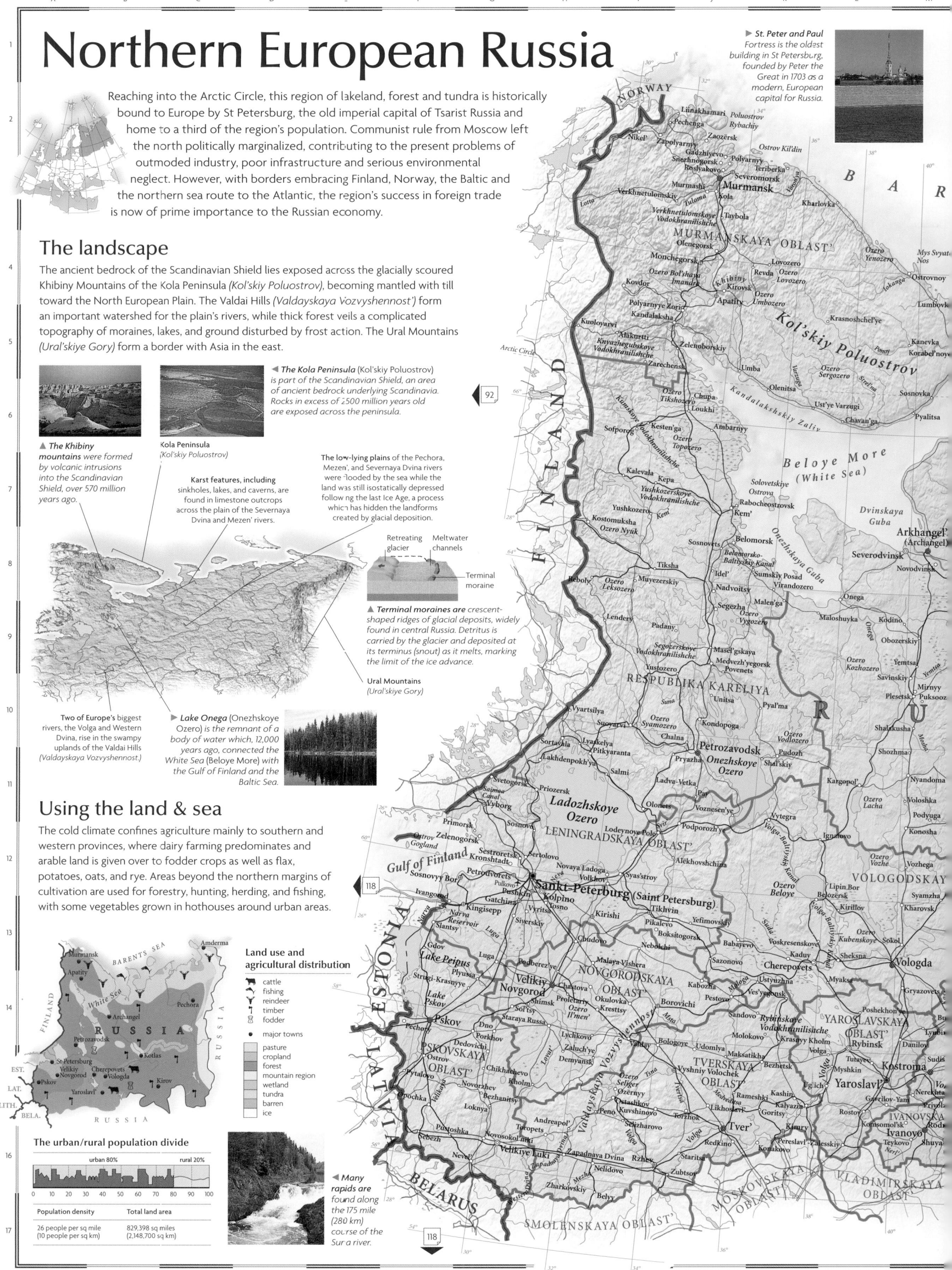

◄ *The Ural Mountains* (Ural'skiye Gory) form the traditional boundary between Europe and Asia. Elevations rarely exceed 6000 ft (1830 m). The region is extremely barren in the far northern latitudes.

**Scale 1:6,000,000**

Km 0 20 40 60 80 100 120 140
Miles 0 10 20 40 60 80 100 120 140

projection: Lambert Conformal Conic

## Map key

### Population
- ◉ 1 million to 5 million
- ◎ 500,000 to 1 million
- ⊙ 100,000 to 500,000
- ⊕ 50,000 to 100,000
- ○ 10,000 to 50,000
- ∘ below 10,000

### Elevation
- 1000m / 3281ft
- 500m / 1640ft
- 250m / 820ft
- 100m / 328ft
- sea level

## Transportation & industry

The ports of St. Petersburg, Murmansk, and Archangel serve a regional economy led by large-scale resource extraction. Nickel, iron ore, and apatite are mined in the Kola Peninsula (Kol'skiy Poluostrov), and fossil fuels in the Pechora Basin. Paper production is central to Archangel's vast timber industry, while St. Petersburg, drawing on ample labor, has become a major manufacturing center.

### Major industry and infrastructure
- chemicals
- coal
- defense
- engineering
- food processing
- hydroelectric power
- mining
- oil & gas
- textiles
- timber processing
- major towns
- international airports
- major roads
- major industrial areas

### Transportation network
- 53,700 miles (85,920 km)
- None
- 10,300 miles (16,572 km)
- 12,500 miles (20,000 km)

Railroads linking remote industrial centers with the region's ports are the principal means of supply, although the impressive system of canals, linking natural waterways, is used for freight haulage during the summer.

▶ *Ice forces the* port at St. Petersburg to close in winter, yet Murmansk, on the Barents Sea, remains open, its waters prevented from freezing by warmer ocean currents extending from the North Atlantic Drift.

► *Kaliningrad has been a Russian enclave since 1945. The port is an important center for Russia's Baltic fishing fleet.*

◄ *St Basil's Cathedral, completed in 1561, stands in Moscow's Red Square next to the Kremlin; the original fortified stronghold of the city.*

# Southern European Russia

This region, divided from Asia by desert, seas, and mountains, has exerted a powerful influence both east and west since the 13th century. Over 70 years of Communist rule produced a highly urbanized, industrial society dominated by Moscow, which was the capital of the Soviet Union until 1991. Almost two-thirds of Russia's population live in this core area, with a relatively high per capita share of its wealth. However, the rapid growth of a market economy has caused great social upheaval, with rising crime and political instability.

## The landscape

Ancient folds in the deep sedimentary strata of the North European Plain have created a sequence of high and low regions. The Central Russian Upland (*Srednerusskaya Vozvyshennost'*) in the west is deeply incised by rivers draining into the lowland of the Oka and Don rivers. In the east the Volga, Europe's longest river, flows south to the Caspian Sea, dividing the Volga Uplands (*Privolzhskaya Vozvyshennost'*) from the foothills of the Ural Mountains (*Ural'skiye Gory*). The Caucasus mountains and the Black Sea form a natural border to the southwest.

▲ *A plantation of Scots pine helps consolidate the loose sandy soils of the Meshchera Lowland (Meshcherskaya Nizmennost), which lies on the bed of an old glacial lake.*

The Smolensk-Moscow Upland (*Smolensko-Moskovskaya Vozvyshennost'*) is a series of terminal moraine ridges marking the southern extent of the last glaciation.

Glacial till covers the bedrock to the north of the North European Plain, giving a gentle surface relief.

The lowland of the Oka and Don rivers lies over a broad trough, between the upfolds of the Volga Uplands (*Privolzhskaya Vozvyshennost'*) to the east, and the Central Russian Upland (*Srednerusskaya Vozvyshennost'*) to the west.

The southern Ural mountains (*Ural'skiye Gory*) consist of several parallel ranges of ancient fold mountains running from north to south.

Central Russian Upland (*Srednerusskaya Vozvyshennost'*).

The floodplain of the Volga forms a long oasis of verdant vegetation, contrasting with the aridity of the surrounding Caspian hinterland.

The marshlands of the Volga Delta are visited by over 260 species of bird each year, migrating between South Africa and Arctic Siberia.

The Caspian Depression is a large downfold (or syncline) which became flooded, forming the Caspian Sea. The shoreline is 98 ft (30 m) below sea level.

**Salt dome**

Salt dome is forced up and through the rock strata

Sedimentary strata

Salts are forced upwards by denser overlying strata

▲ *Salt domes, rounded hills up to 500 ft (150 m) high, are produced as less dense rock salts are displaced under the extreme pressure of denser, overlying strata and forced up toward the surface creating domes. They are widespread in the Caspian Depression.*

◄ *The Caucasus mountains run from the Black Sea to the Caspian Sea. They include El'brus which, at 18,511 ft (5642 m), is the highest point in Europe. It is still uplifting at a rate of 0.4 inches (10 mm) per year.*

Drifting sand occupies large areas of the south, forming dunes up to 50 ft (15 m) high.

**Scale 1:6,000,000**

projection: Lambert Conformal Conic

**Map key**

**Population**
- ■ above 5 million
- ▣ 1 million to 5 million
- ◉ 500,000 to 1 million
- ◎ 100,000 to 500,000
- ⊕ 50,000 to 100,000
- ○ 10,000 to 50,000
- ○ below 10,000

**Elevation**
- 4000m / 13,124ft
- 3000m / 9843ft
- 2000m / 6562ft
- 1000m / 3281ft
- 500m / 1640ft
- 250m / 820ft
- 100m / 328ft
- sea level

## Using the land

In the cold, humid north and in the southern Urals (Ural'skiye Gory), small grains, potatoes, and flax are commonly rotated with legumes which support livestock farming. The rich chernozem (or black earth) areas support diverse crops such as sugar beet, hemp, sunflowers, millet, and vegetables. Further south, aridity restricts husbandry to extensive grazing, with intensive fruit and rice cultivation along the oasis of the Volga.

**The urban/rural population divide**

urban 71%     rural 29%

0  10  20  30  40  50  60  70  80  90  100

**Population density**
119 people per sq mile
(46 people per sq km)

**Total land area**
705,916 sq miles
(1,828,800 sq km)

**Land use and agricultural distribution**
- 🐑 sheep
- flax
- potatoes
- rice
- sunflowers
- sugar beet
- timber
- ● capital cities
- ● major towns
- pasture
- cropland
- forest
- wetland
- mountain region
- tundra

◀ Industrial plants are massed along the Volga. Environmental stress from decades of unbridled industrial development has prompted widespread concern about pollution levels.

## Transportation & industry

Manufacturing is largely based around Moscow and the Volga region, which became a major industrial area during the Second World War. Both Moscow and Nizhniy Novgorod are centers of skilled labor for light manufacturing and engineering. Most of Russia's main chemical plants are located along the Volga, and Tol'yatti is the site of one of the world's largest car factories. Processing and machine construction plants use oil, gas, and hydroelectric power from the Volga Basin and metallic minerals from the Urals (Ural'skiye Gory) and Kursk.

**Transportation network**

250,000 miles (402,000 km)     None

28,000 miles (44,800 km)     16,300 miles (26,080 km)

Seventy private and national flag airlines have been created from the reorganization of the state airline Aeroflot, which maintained the world's largest fleet of aircraft during the Soviet era.

**Major industry and infrastructure**
- aerospace
- car manufacture
- chemicals
- defense
- electronics
- engineering
- gas
- mining
- oil
- textiles
- ● capital cities
- ● major towns
- ⊕ international airports
- major roads
- major industrial areas

127

# Asia

Asia, the world's largest continent, covers 16,838,365 sq miles (43,608,000 sq km).
It comprises 49 separate countries, including 97% of Turkey and 72% of Russia.
Almost 60% of the world's population lives in Asia.

● *Greatest extent, North–South:*
4000 miles / 6440 km

■ *Greatest extent, East–West:*
6000 miles / 9650 km

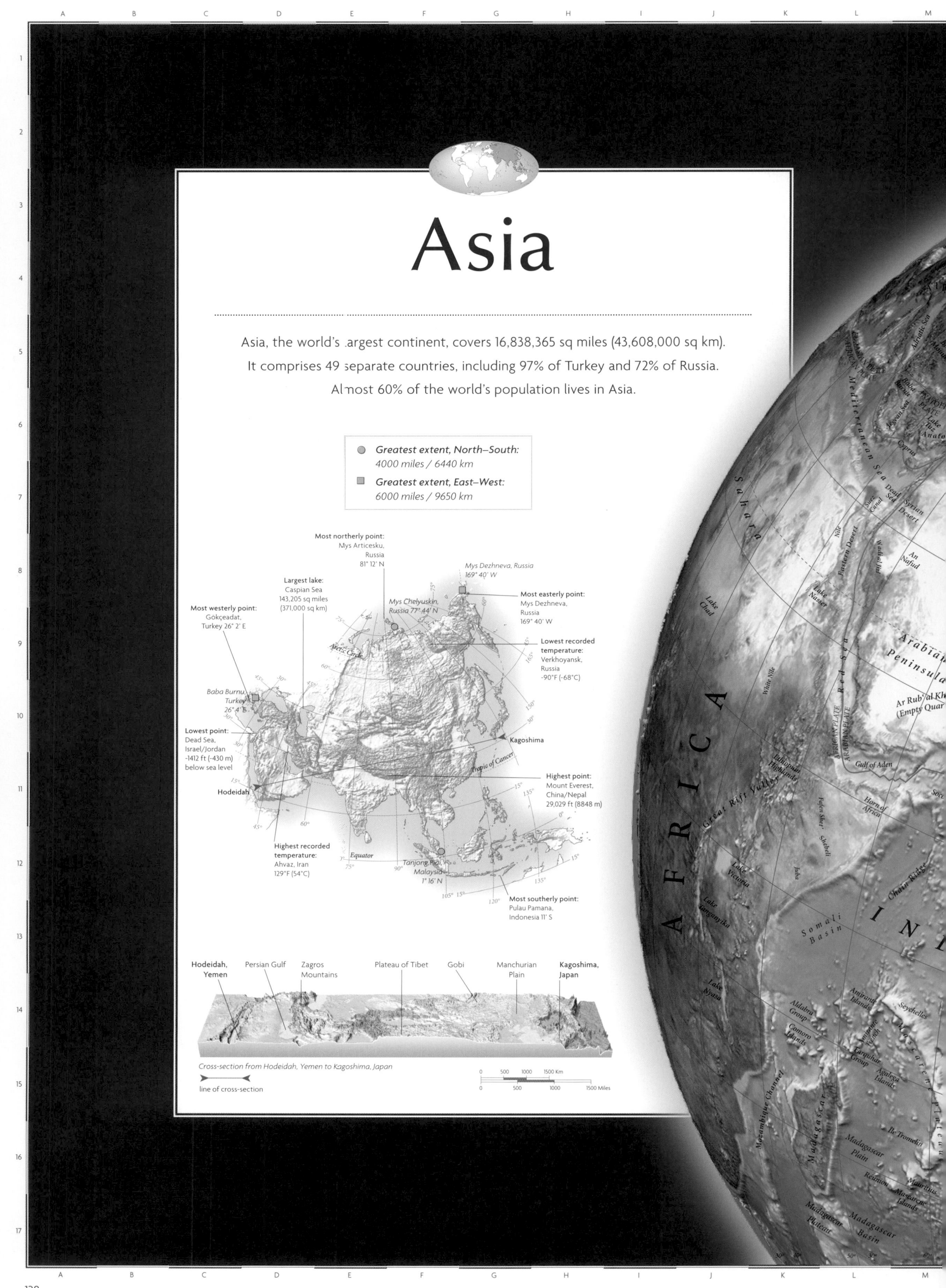

Most northerly point:
Mys Articesku,
Russia
81° 12′ N

Mys Dezhneva, Russia
169° 40′ W

Largest lake:
Caspian Sea
143,205 sq miles
(371,000 sq km)

Mys Chelyuskin,
Russia 77° 44′ N

Most easterly point:
Mys Dezhneva,
Russia
169° 40′ W

Most westerly point:
Gökçeadat,
Turkey 26° 2′ E

Lowest recorded
temperature:
Verkhoyansk,
Russia
-90°F (-68°C)

Baba Burnu,
Turkey
26° 4′ B

Lowest point:
Dead Sea,
Israel/Jordan
-1412 ft (-430 m)
below sea level

Kagoshima

**Hodeidah**

Highest point:
Mount Everest,
China/Nepal
29,029 ft (8848 m)

Highest recorded
temperature:
Ahvaz, Iran
129°F (54°C)

Equator

Tanjong Piai,
Malaysia
1° 16′ N

Most southerly point:
Pulau Pamana,
Indonesia 11° S

**Hodeidah,
Yemen** | Persian Gulf | Zagros
Mountains | Plateau of Tibet | Gobi | Manchurian
Plain | **Kagoshima,
Japan**

*Cross-section from Hodeidah, Yemen to Kagoshima, Japan*

line of cross-section

0 500 1000 1500 Km

0 500 1000 1500 Miles

ARCTIC OCEAN
North Pole
NORTH AMERICAN PLATE
EURASIAN PLATE

Norwegian Sea
Scandinavia
North Sea
Barents Sea
Gulf of Bothnia
North Cape
Kola Peninsula
Novaya Zemlya
Franz Josef Land
Severnaya Zemlya
Mys Chelyuskin
Laptev Sea
New Siberian Islands
East Siberian Sea
Long Strait
Bering Strait
Bering Sea
Chukot Range

EUROPE
Baltic Sea
Gulf of Finland
Lake Ladoga
Lake Onega
White Sea
Kara Sea
Poluostrov Yamal
Gydansky
North Siberian Lowland
Khrebet Cherskogo
Kotelny
Kolyma Range
Rhine

North European Plain
Central Russian Upland
Pechora
Poluostrov
Ob
Central Siberian Plateau
Lower Tunguska
Markha
Verkhoyanskiy Khrebet
Indigirka
Kolyma Range

Ural Mountains
West Siberian Plain
S i b e r i a
Stony Tunguska
Angara
Lena
Aldan
Sea of Okhotsk

Caspian Depression
Kazakh Steppe
Lake Zaysan
Altai Mountains
Lake Baikal
Stanovoy Khrebet
Zeya Reservoir
Amur

A S I A
Turan Lowland
Kara Kum
Lake Balkhash
Tien Shan
Dzungaria
Plateau of Mongolia
G o b i
Manchurian Plain
Lake Khanka

Caspian Sea
Great Salt Desert
EURASIAN PLATE
IRANIAN PLATE
Pamirs
Tarim Basin
Takla Makan Desert
Qaidam He
Lop Nur
Altun Shan
Nan Shan
Qilian Shan
Ordos Desert
Wutai Shan
Yellow River
Bo Hai
Korea Bay
Sea of Japan (East Sea)

Zagros Mountains
Iranian Plateau
Registán
Hindu Kush
Karakoram Range
Kunlun Mountains
Plateau of Tibet
Bayan Har Shan
Qinghai Hu
Han Shui
Yellow Sea
Jeju-do
Korea Strait

Strait of Hormuz
Gulf of Oman
Central Makran Range
IRANIAN PLATE
Thar Desert
Himalayas
Mount Everest 8848m
Siling Co
Nam Co
Brahmaputra
Hong Hu
Dongting Hu
Yangtze
Tai Hu
East China Sea

Arabian Sea
Gulf of Kachchh
Deccan
Vindhya Range
Satpura Range
Ganges
Damodar
Khasi Hills
Taiwan Strait
Taiwan

Arabian Basin
Western Ghats
Eastern Ghats
Bay of Bengal
Mouths of the Ganges
Arakan Yoma
Gulf of Tonkin
Hainan
Hainan Strait
Luzon Strait
Philippine Sea

Laccadive Islands
Malabar Coast
Coromandel Coast
Cape Comorin
Gulf of Mannar
Sri Lanka
Andaman Islands
Gulf of Martaban
Chao Phraya
Mekong
South China Sea
Luzon
Mindoro

I N D I A N   O C E A N
Maldives
Ceylon Plain
Andaman Sea
Nicobar Islands
Isthmus of Kra
Gulf of Thailand
Mouths of the Mekong
South China Basin
Palawan
Sulu Sea
Mindanao
Celebes Sea

PACIFIC OCEAN

Mid-Indian Basin
Ninetyeast Ridge
Cocos Basin
Sunda Trough
Malay Peninsula
Strait of Malacca
Anambas Islands
Natuna Islands
Sunda Shelf
G r e a t e r   S u n d a   I s l a n d s
Borneo
Gunung Kinabalu 4101m
Celebes
Molucca Sea
Halmahera
New Guinea Trench

Java Trench
Christmas Island
Java
Java Sea
Bali
Sunda Trough
Lesser Sunda
Flores Sea
Banda Sea
Arafura Sea
Torres Strait

AUSTRALIA

A B C D E F G H I J K

# Physical Asia

The structure of Asia can be divided into two distinct regions. The landscape of northern Asia consists of old mountain chains, shields, plateaus, and basins, like the Ural Mountains in the west and the Central Siberian Plateau to the east. To the south of this region, are a series of plateaus and basins, including the vast Plateau of Tibet and the Tarim Basin. In contrast, the landscapes of southern Asia are much younger, formed by tectonic activity beginning about 65 million years ago, leading to an almost continuous mountain chain running from Europe, across much of Asia, and culminating in the mighty Himalayan mountain belt, formed when the Indo-Australian Plate collided with the Eurasian Plate. They are still being uplifted today. North of the mountains lies a belt of deserts, including the Gobi and the Takla Makan. In the far south, tectonic activity has formed narrow island arcs, extending over 4000 miles (7000 km). To the west lies the Arabian Shield, once part of the African Plate. As it was rifted apart from Africa, the Arabian Plate collided with the Eurasian Plate, uplifting the Zagros Mountains.

## Coastal Lowlands and Island Arcs

The coastal plains that fringe Southeast Asia contain many large delta systems, caused by high levels of rainfall and erosion of the Himalayas, the Plateau of Tibet, and relict loess deposits. To the south is an extensive island archipelago, lying on the drowned Sunda Shelf. Most of these islands are volcanic in origin, caused by the subduction of the Indo-Australian Plate beneath the Eurasian Plate.

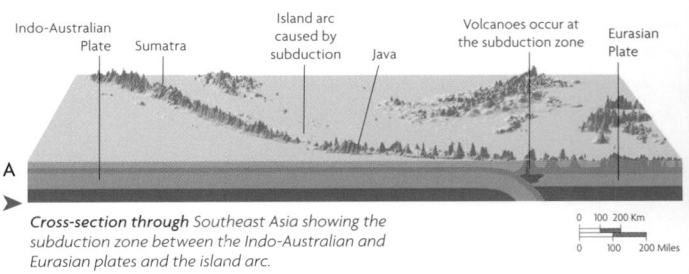

*Cross-section through Southeast Asia showing the subduction zone between the Indo-Australian and Eurasian plates and the island arc.*

0 100 200 Km
0 100 200 Miles

## The Indian Shield and Himalayan System

The large shield area beneath the Indian subcontinent is between 2.5 and 3.5 billion years old. As the floor of the southern Indian Ocean spread, it pushed the Indian Shield north. This was eventually driven beneath the Plateau of Tibet. This process closed up the ancient Tethys Sea and uplifted the world's highest mountain chain, the Himalayas. Much of the uplifted rock strata was from the seabed of the Tethys Sea, partly accounting for the weakness of the rocks and the high levels of erosion found in the Himalayas.

*Cross-section through the Himalayas showing thrust faulting of the rock strata.*

0 50 100 Km
0 50 100 Miles

## East Asian Plains and Uplands

Several, small, isolated shield areas, such as the Shandong Peninsula, are found in east Asia. Between these stable shield areas, large river systems like the Yangtze and the Yellow River have deposited thick layers of sediment, forming extensive alluvial plains. The largest of these is the Great Plain of China, the relief of which does not rise above 300 ft (100 m).

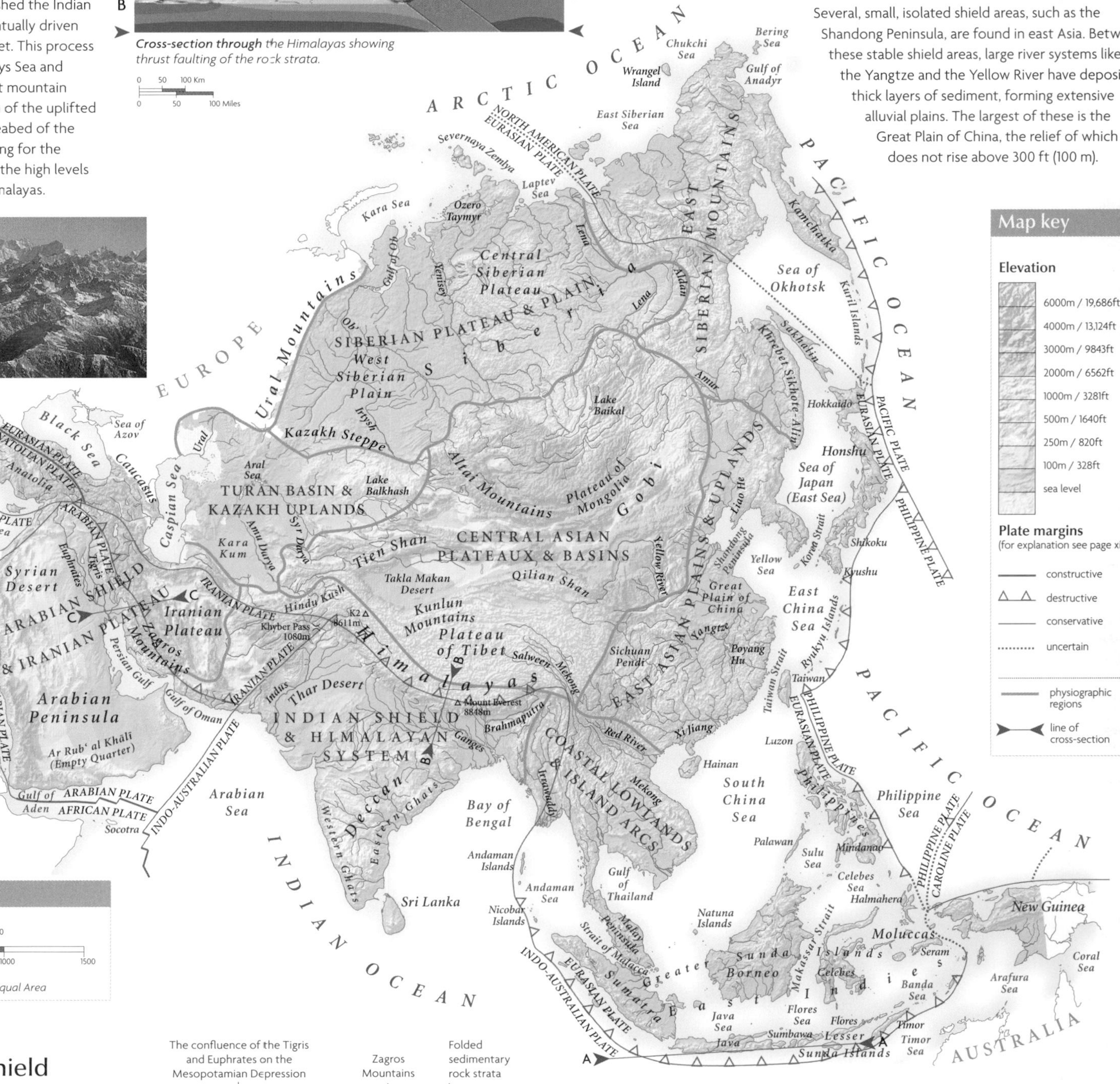

### Map key

**Elevation**

6000m / 19,686ft
4000m / 13,124ft
3000m / 9843ft
2000m / 6562ft
1000m / 3281ft
500m / 1640ft
250m / 820ft
100m / 328ft
sea level

**Plate margins**
(for explanation see page xiv)

━━━ constructive
△ △ destructive
━━━ conservative
········ uncertain
━━━ physiographic regions
▶◀ line of cross-section

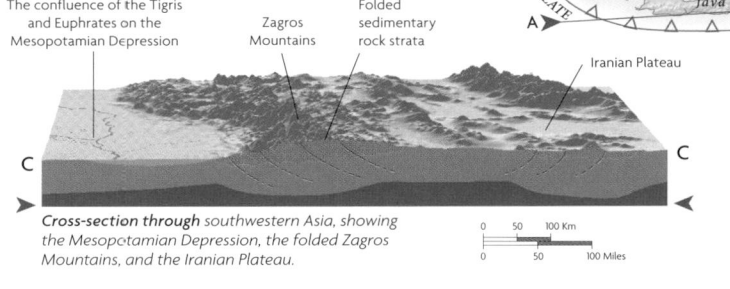

### Scale 1:63,000,000

Km
0 250 500 1000 1500
Miles
0 250 500 1000 1500

*projection: Lambert Azimuthal Equal Area*

## The Arabian Shield and Iranian Plateau

Approximately five million years ago, rifting of the continental crust split the Arabian Plate from the African Plate and flooded the Red Sea. As this rift spread, the Arabian Plate collided with the Eurasian Plate, transforming part of the Tethys seabed into the Zagros Mountains which run northwest-southeast across western Iran.

*Cross-section through southwestern Asia, showing the Mesopotamian Depression, the folded Zagros Mountains, and the Iranian Plateau.*

0 50 100 Km
0 50 100 Miles

# Climate

The climate of Asia exhibits marked differences from region to region, with freezing polar conditions in the north, hot and cold deserts in central regions and subtropical conditions throughout the south. Much of this variation can be attributed to enormous mountain barriers and internal depressions found across the continent. Monsoon winds, which reverse semiannually, cause alternate wet and dry seasons across southern Asia. These air masses moving north from the ocean are stripped of their moisture over the Himalayas causing arid conditions across the Plateau of Tibet. Both the south and east are susceptible to tropical cyclones or typhoons.

▲ *Tropical cyclones occur* principally during late summer and early fall. The intense winds and heavy rainfall can devastate entire villages.

### Temperature

*Average January temperature*

*Average July temperature*

### Temperature

| | |
|---|---|
| below -22°F (-30°C) | 32 to 50°F (0 to 10°C) |
| -22 to -4°F (-30 to -20°C) | 50 to 68°F (10 to 20°C) |
| -4 to 14°F (-20 to -10°C) | 68 to 86°F (20 to 30°C) |
| 14 to 32°F (-10 to 0°C) | above 86°F (30°C) |

### Climate

| Climate | Symbols |
|---|---|
| tundra | ☼ daily hours of sunshine, January |
| subarctic | ☀ daily hours of sunshine, July |
| cool continental | → cyclone |
| warm humid | → typhoon |
| mediterranean | → cold/dry monsoon |
| semi-arid | → warm/wet monsoon |
| arid | → cold wind |
| humid equatorial | |
| tropical | |

▶ *The Gobi Desert* experiences major extremes in climate, with winter temperatures sometimes falling below -40°C (-40°F) and summer temperatures exceeding 45°C (113°F).

### Rainfall

*Average January rainfall*

*Average July rainfall*

### Rainfall

| |
|---|
| 0–1 in (0 –25 mm) |
| 1–2 in (25–50 mm) |
| 2–4 in (50–100 mm) |
| 4–8 in (100–200 mm) |
| 8–12 in (200–300 mm) |
| 12–16 in (300–400 mm) |
| 16–20 in (400–500 mm) |
| more than 20 in (500 mm) |

◀ *Through India, the* southwest monsoon, which brings heavy rainfall from May to September, accounts for 80% of annual precipitation.

# Shaping the landscape

In the north, melting of extensive permafrost leads to typical periglacial features such as thermokarst. In the arid areas wind action transports sand creating extensive dune systems. An active tectonic margin in the south causes continued uplift, and volcanic and seismic activity, but also high rates of weathering and erosion. Across the continent, huge rivers erode and transport vast quantities of sediment depositing it on the plains or forming large deltas.

## River systems

**1** Vast river systems flow across Asia, many originating in the Himalayas and the Plateau of Tibet. Seasonal melting of snow and monsoon rains swell the river flow leading to flooding and erosion. The Yellow River *(right)* gets its color from the high level of eroded material from the loess plateau.

*River systems: erosion of the loess plateau by the yellow river*

## Chemical weathering

**2** Tower karsts are widespread across south China *(left)* and Vietnam. It is thought the karstic towers were formed under a soil cover, where small depressions in the limestone bedrock began to be weathered by soil water acids, eventually creating larger hollows. This process continued over millions of years, deepening the hollows and leaving steep-sided limestone hills.

*Chemical weathering: formation of tower karst*

## Sedimentation

**4** The Ganges/Brahmaputra is a tide-dominated delta *(below)*. The two rivers transport huge quantities of mountain sediment, which is deposited on the delta plain. This debris is then redistributed by tidal currents, to form extensions to the bars, beach ridges, and deltaic deposits.

*Sedimentation: the destruction of a delta*

## Volcanic activity

**3** Volcanic eruptions occur frequently across Southeast Asia's island arcs *(below)*. Low-level eruptions occur when groundwater, superheated by underlying magma, becomes pressurized, forcing hot fluid and rocks up through cracks in the volcanic cone. This is known as aphreatic eruption.

*Volcanic activity: a phreatic eruption*

### Landscape

| | |
|---|---|
| limestone region | ••• area of tectonic activity |
| sinking land | |
| stable land | --- limit of permafrost |
| uplifting land | |
| ▲ active volcano | → ocean current |

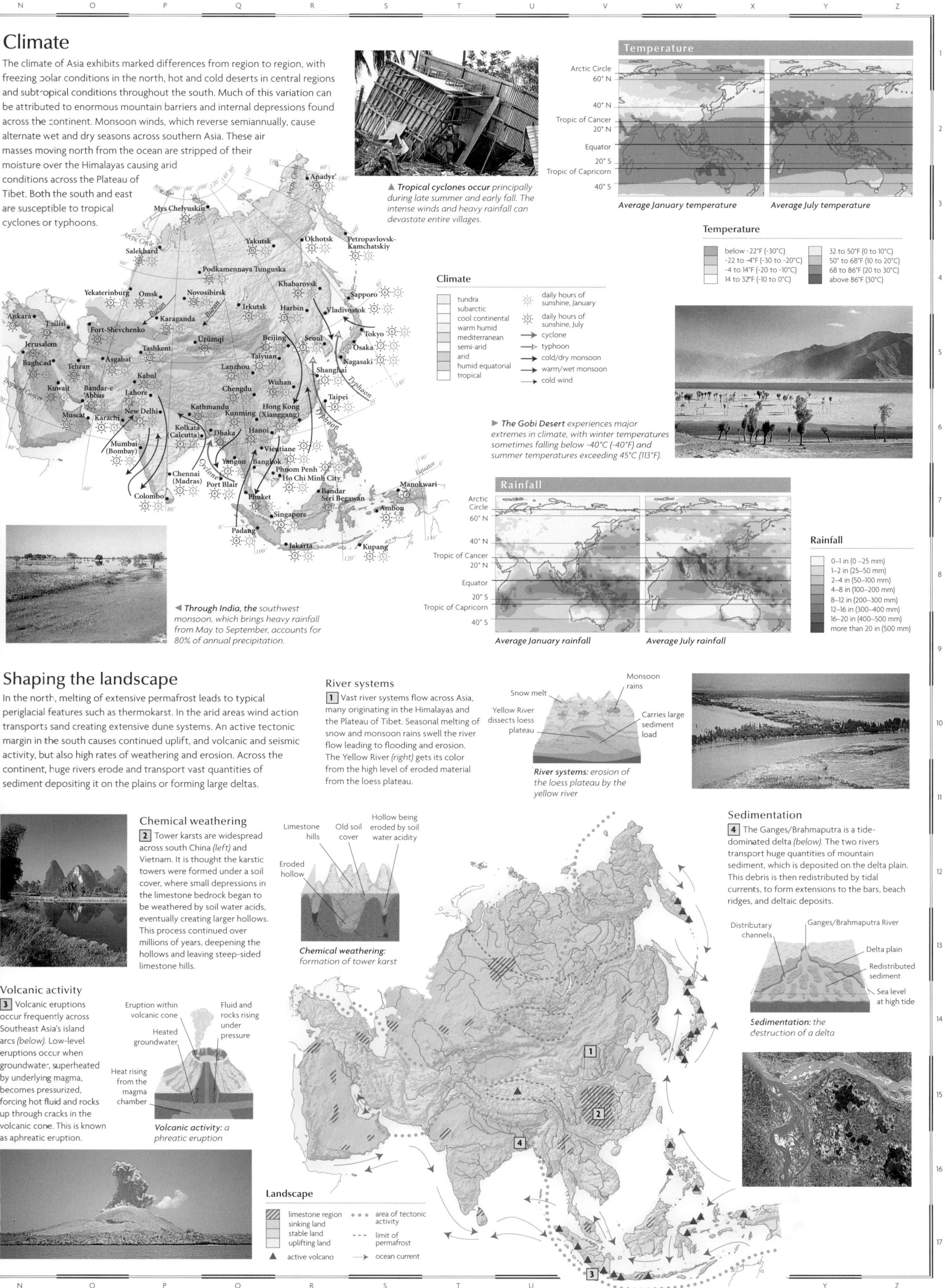

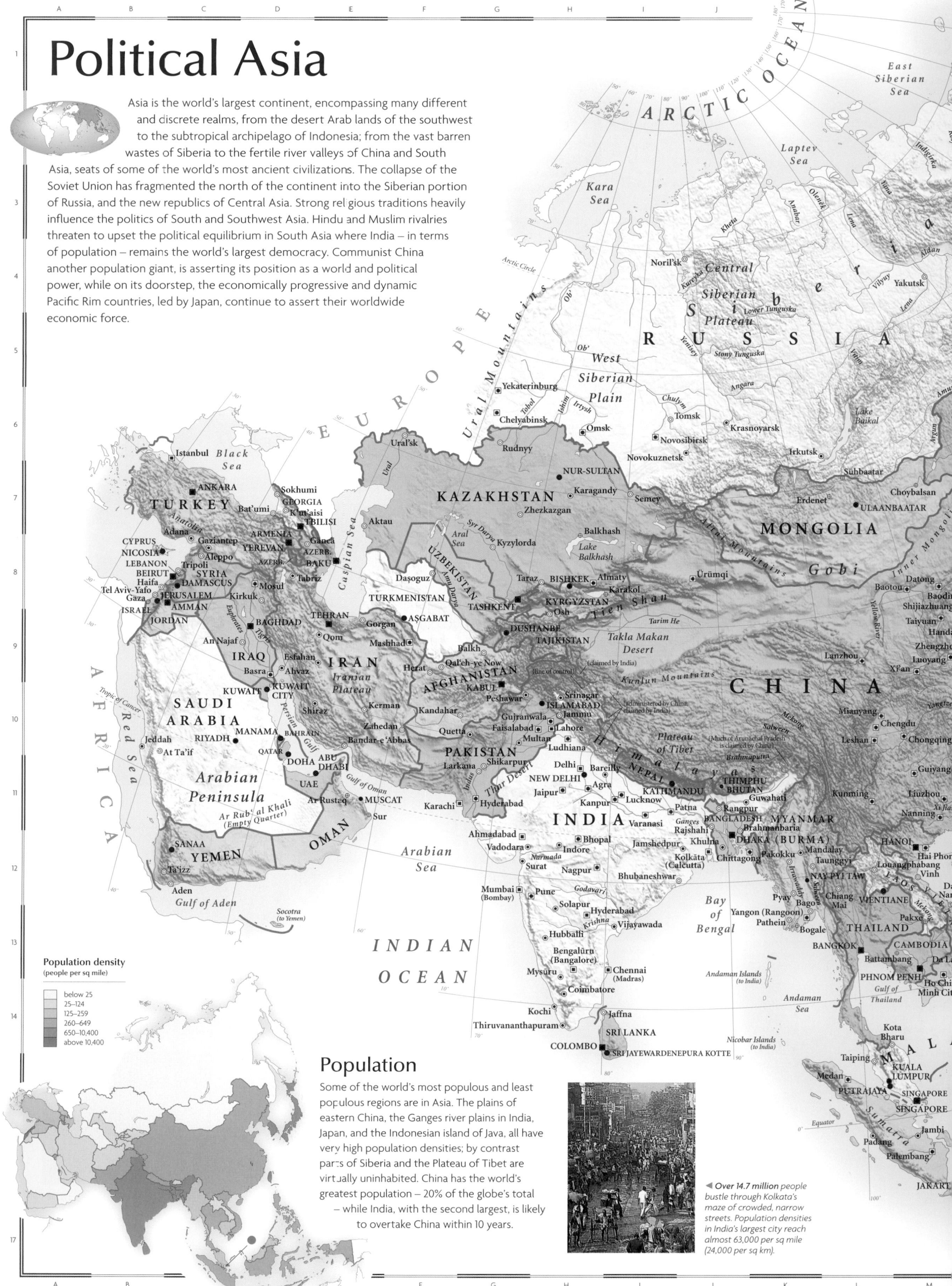

# Political Asia

Asia is the world's largest continent, encompassing many different and discrete realms, from the desert Arab lands of the southwest to the subtropical archipelago of Indonesia; from the vast barren wastes of Siberia to the fertile river valleys of China and South Asia, seats of some of the world's most ancient civilizations. The collapse of the Soviet Union has fragmented the north of the continent into the Siberian portion of Russia, and the new republics of Central Asia. Strong religious traditions heavily influence the politics of South and Southwest Asia. Hindu and Muslim rivalries threaten to upset the political equilibrium in South Asia where India – in terms of population – remains the world's largest democracy. Communist China another population giant, is asserting its position as a world and political power, while on its doorstep, the economically progressive and dynamic Pacific Rim countries, led by Japan, continue to assert their worldwide economic force.

## Population density
(people per sq mile)

- below 25
- 25–124
- 125–259
- 260–649
- 650–10,400
- above 10,400

## Population

Some of the world's most populous and least populous regions are in Asia. The plains of eastern China, the Ganges river plains in India, Japan, and the Indonesian island of Java, all have very high population densities; by contrast parts of Siberia and the Plateau of Tibet are virtually uninhabited. China has the world's greatest population – 20% of the globe's total – while India, with the second largest, is likely to overtake China within 10 years.

◄ Over 14.7 million people bustle through Kolkata's maze of crowded, narrow streets. Population densities in India's largest city reach almost 63,000 per sq mile (24,000 per sq km).

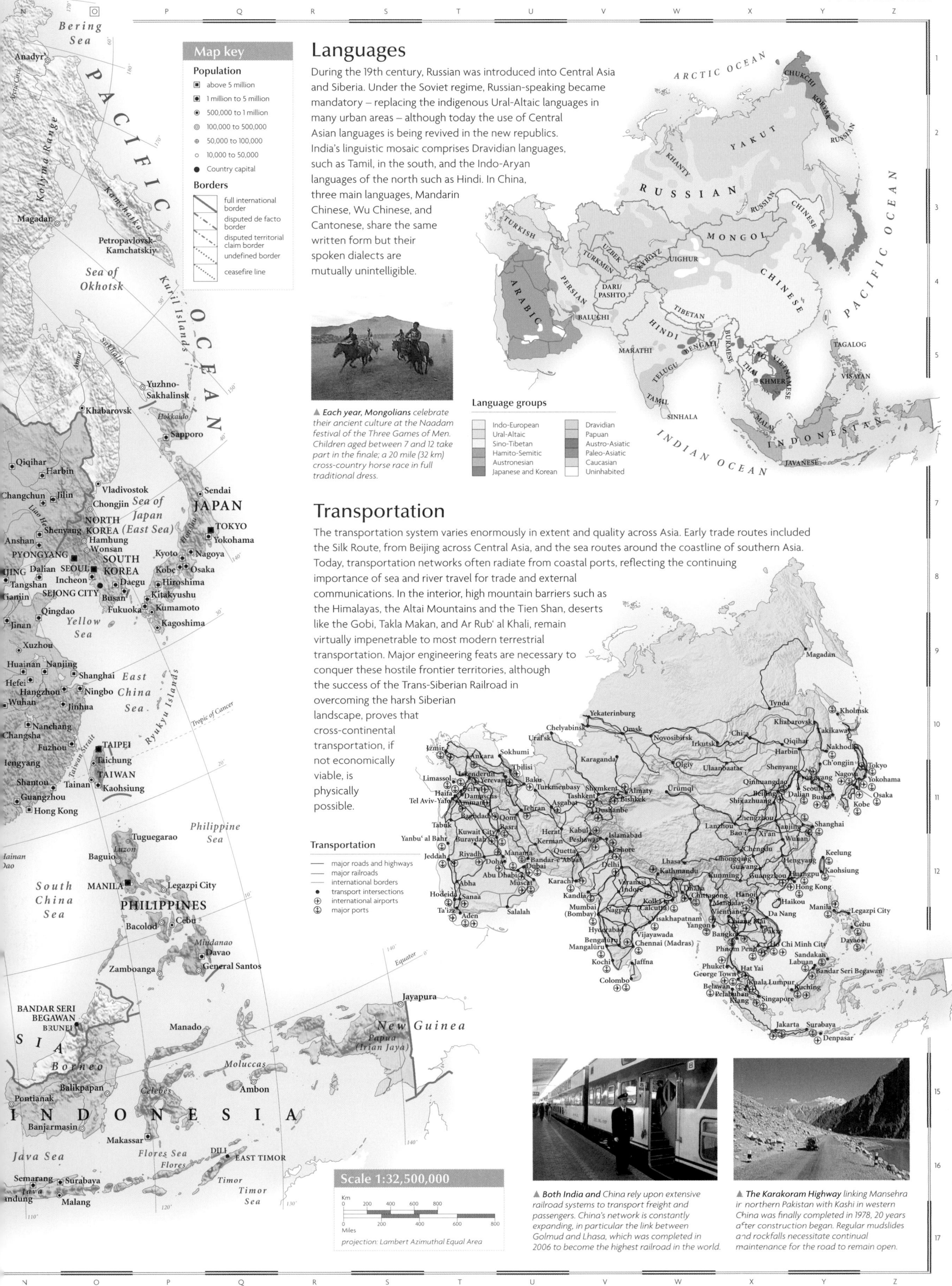

## Languages

During the 19th century, Russian was introduced into Central Asia and Siberia. Under the Soviet regime, Russian-speaking became mandatory – replacing the indigenous Ural-Altaic languages in many urban areas – although today the use of Central Asian languages is being revived in the new republics. India's linguistic mosaic comprises Dravidian languages, such as Tamil, in the south, and the Indo-Aryan languages of the north such as Hindi. In China, three main languages, Mandarin Chinese, Wu Chinese, and Cantonese, share the same written form but their spoken dialects are mutually unintelligible.

▲ *Each year, Mongolians* celebrate their ancient culture at the Naadam festival of the Three Games of Men. Children aged between 7 and 12 take part in the finale; a 20 mile (32 km) cross-country horse race in full traditional dress.

### Language groups

- Indo-European
- Ural-Altaic
- Sino-Tibetan
- Hamito-Semitic
- Austronesian
- Japanese and Korean
- Dravidian
- Papuan
- Austro-Asiatic
- Paleo-Asiatic
- Caucasian
- Uninhabited

## Transportation

The transportation system varies enormously in extent and quality across Asia. Early trade routes included the Silk Route, from Beijing across Central Asia, and the sea routes around the coastline of southern Asia. Today, transportation networks often radiate from coastal ports, reflecting the continuing importance of sea and river travel for trade and external communications. In the interior, high mountain barriers such as the Himalayas, the Altai Mountains and the Tien Shan, deserts like the Gobi, Takla Makan, and Ar Rub' al Khali, remain virtually impenetrable to most modern terrestrial transportation. Major engineering feats are necessary to conquer these hostile frontier territories, although the success of the Trans-Siberian Railroad in overcoming the harsh Siberian landscape, proves that cross-continental transportation, if not economically viable, is physically possible.

### Transportation

- —— major roads and highways
- —— major railroads
- —— international borders
- ● transport intersections
- ⊕ international airports
- ⊕ major ports

### Map key

**Population**
- ■ above 5 million
- ⊡ 1 million to 5 million
- ⊙ 500,000 to 1 million
- ⊚ 100,000 to 500,000
- ⊕ 50,000 to 100,000
- ○ 10,000 to 50,000
- ● Country capital

**Borders**
- full international border
- disputed de facto border
- disputed territorial claim border
- undefined border
- ceasefire line

Scale 1:32,500,000

projection: Lambert Azimuthal Equal Area

▲ *Both India and* China rely upon extensive railroad systems to transport freight and passengers. China's network is constantly expanding, in particular the link between Golmud and Lhasa, which was completed in 2006 to become the highest railroad in the world.

▲ *The Karakoram Highway* linking Mansehra in northern Pakistan with Kashi in western China was finally completed in 1978, 20 years after construction began. Regular mudslides and rockfalls necessitate continual maintenance for the road to remain open.

# Asian resources

Although agriculture remains the economic mainstay of most Asian countries, the number of people employed in agriculture has steadily declined, as new industries have been developed during the past 30 years. China, Indonesia, Malaysia, Thailand, and Turkey have all experienced far-reaching structural change in their economies, while the breakup of the Soviet Union has created a new economic challenge in the Central Asian republics. The countries of The Persian Gulf illustrate the rapid transformation from rural nomadism to modern, urban society which oil wealth has brought to parts of the continent. Asia's most economically dynamic countries, Japan, Singapore, South Korea, and Taiwan, fringe the Pacific Ocean and are known as the Pacific Rim. In contrast, other Southeast Asian countries like Laos and Cambodia remain both economically and industrially underdeveloped.

## Industry

East Asian industry leads the continent in both productivity and efficiency; electronics, hi-tech industries, car manufacture, and shipbuilding are important. The so-called economic "tigers" of the Pacific Rim are Japan, South Korea, and Taiwan and in recent years China has rediscovered its potential as an economic superpower. Heavy industries such as engineering, chemicals, and steel typify the industrial complexes along the corridor created by the Trans-Siberian Railroad, the Fergana Valley in Central Asia, and also much of the huge industrial plain of east China. The discovery of oil in the Persian Gulf has brought immense wealth to countries that previously relied on subsistence agriculture on marginal desert land.

### Industry

- ✈ aerospace
- 🍺 brewing
- 🚗 car/vehicle manufacture
- cement
- chemicals
- electronics
- engineering
- $ finance
- fish processing
- food processing
- hi-tech industry
- iron & steel
- pharmaceuticals
- printing & publishing
- shipbuilding
- sugar processing
- tea processing
- textiles
- timber processing
- tobacco processing
- coal
- oil
- gas
- ● industrial cities
- ▱ major industrial areas

## Standard of living

Despite Japan's high standards of living, and Southwest Asia's oil-derived wealth, immense disparities exist across the continent. Afghanistan remains one of the world's most underdeveloped nations, as do the mountain states of Nepal and Bhutan. Further rapid population growth is exacerbating poverty and overcrowding in many parts of India and Bangladesh.

### Standard of living
(UN human development index)

- low
- high

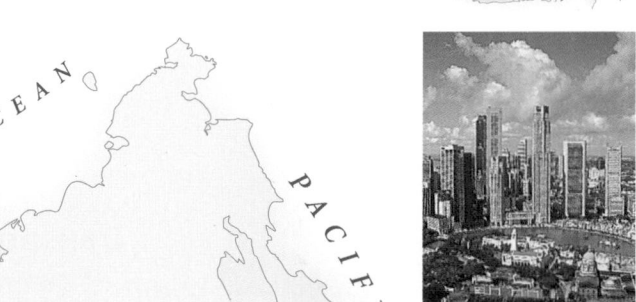

▲ On a small island at the southern tip of the Malay Peninsula lies Singapore, one of the Pacific Rim's most vibrant economic centers. Multinational banking and finance form the core of the city's wealth.

### GNI per capita (US$)

- below 1999
- 2000–4999
- 5000–9999
- 10,000–19,999
- 20,000–24,999
- above 25,000

▲ Iron and steel, engineering, and shipbuilding typify the heavy industry found in eastern China's industrial cities, especially the nation's leading manufacturing center, Shanghai.

◄ Traditional industries are still crucial to many rural economies across Asia. Here, on the Vietnamese coast, salt has been extracted from seawater by evaporation and is being loaded into a van to take to market.

ARCTIC OCEAN

PACIFIC OCEAN

RUSSIA

Yakutsk

Sea of Okhotsk

Trans-Siberian Railroad

Yekaterinburg
Chelyabinsk
Magnitogorsk
Omsk
Novosibirsk
Kemerovo
Krasnoyarsk
Novokuznetsk
Bratsk
Irkutsk
Khabarovsk
Vladivostok

KAZAKHSTAN
Karagandy

Ulaanbaatar
MONGOLIA

Harbin
Shenyang
NORTH KOREA
Pyongyang
JAPAN
Tokyo
Nagoya
Kobe

Istanbul
Izmir
Ankara
GEORGIA
Tbilisi
ARMENIA
Yerevan
AZERB.
Baku
TURKEY
CYPRUS
LEBANON
Beirut
SYRIA
Damascus
Tel Aviv-Yafo
ISRAEL
Amman
JORDAN
Baghdad
IRAQ
Kirkuk
Tehran
Isfahan
IRAN
Basra
Kuwait City
KUWAIT
SAUDI ARABIA
Ad Damman
BAHRAIN
QATAR
Abu Dhabi
UAE
Dubai
Jeddah
Riyadh
Persian Gulf
Gulf of Oman
OMAN
YEMEN
Gulf of Aden
Red Sea

Caspian Sea
Aral Sea
UZBEKISTAN
Tashkent
TURKMENISTAN
Asgabat
Dushanbe
TAJIKISTAN
KYRGYZSTAN
Fergana
Almaty
AFGHANISTAN
Rawalpindi
Lahore
PAKISTAN
Karachi
Ahmadabad
Indore
Mumbai (Bombay)
Nagpur
Delhi
Kanpur
Jamshedpur
INDIA
NEPAL
BHUTAN
BANGLADESH
Dhaka
Kolkata (Calcutta)
Chittagong
Bengaluru
Chennai (Madras)
SRI LANKA

Ürümqi
Beijing
Tianjin
Dalian
Seoul
SOUTH KOREA
Busan
Taiyuan
Jinan
Qingdao
Lanzhou
Zhengzhou
Nanjing
Shanghai
Xi'an
CHINA
Wuhan
Chengdu
Chongqing
Kunming
Guangzhou
Hong Kong
Taipei
TAIWAN

Mandalay
MYANMAR (BURMA)
Yangon (Rangoon)
Hanoi
LAOS
VIETNAM
THAILAND
Bangkok
CAMBODIA
Da Nang
South China Sea
Ho Chi Minh City
Manila
PHILIPPINES

Arabian Sea
INDIAN OCEAN

MALAYSIA
BRUNEI
Kuala Lumpur
Singapore
SINGAPORE
INDONESIA
Jakarta
Surabaya
EAST TIMOR

# Environmental issues

The transformation of Uzbekistan by the former Soviet Union into the world's fifth largest producer of cotton led to the diversion of several major rivers for irrigation. Starved of this water, the Aral Sea diminished in volume by over 90% since 1960, irreversibly altering the ecology of the area. Heavy industries in eastern China have polluted coastal waters, rivers, and urban air, while in Myanmar (Burma), Malaysia, and Indonesia, ancient hardwood rainforests are felled faster than they can regenerate.

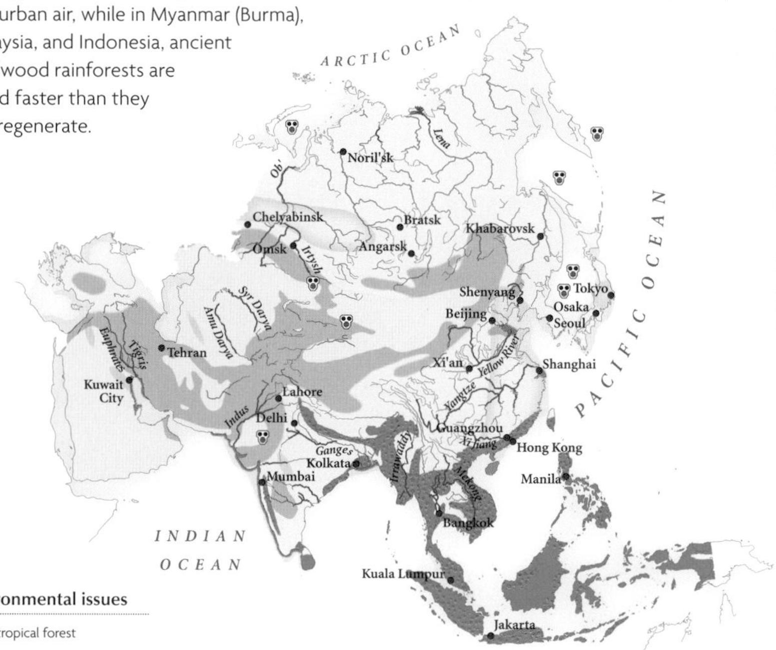

▲ *Although Siberia remains a quintessentially frozen, inhospitable wasteland, vast untapped mineral reserves – especially the oil and gas of the West Siberian Plain – have lured industrial development to the area since the 1950s and 1960s.*

**Environmental issues**
- tropical forest
- forest destroyed
- desert
- desertification
- acid rain
- polluted rivers
- marine pollution
- heavy marine pollution
- radioactive contamination
- poor urban air quality

◀ *Commercial logging activities in Borneo have placed great stress on the rainforest ecosystem. Government attempts to regulate the timber companies and control illegal logging have only been partially successful.*

# Mineral resources

At least 60% of the world's known oil and gas deposits are found in Asia; notably the vast oil fields of the Persian Gulf, and the less-exploited oil and gas fields of the Ob' basin in west Siberia. Immense coal reserves in Siberia and China have been utilized to support large steel industries. Southeast Asia has some of the world's largest deposits of tin, found in a belt running down the Malay Peninsula to Indonesia.

**Mineral resources**
- oil field
- gas field
- coal field
- chromite
- copper
- gold
- iron
- lead
- nickel
- platinum
- tin
- wolfram

# Using the land and sea

Vast areas of Asia remain uncultivated as a result of unsuitable climatic and soil conditions. In favourable areas such as river deltas, farming is intensive. Rice is the staple crop of most Asian countries, grown in paddy fields on waterlogged alluvial plains and terraced hillsides, and often irrigated for higher yields. Across the black earth region of the Eurasian steppe in southern Siberia and Kazakhstan, wheat farming is the dominant activity. Cash crops, like tea in Sri Lanka and dates in the Arabian Peninsula, are grown for export, and provide valuable income. The sovereignty of the rich fishing grounds in the South China Sea is disputed by China, Malaysia, Taiwan, the Philippines, and Vietnam, because of potential oil reserves.

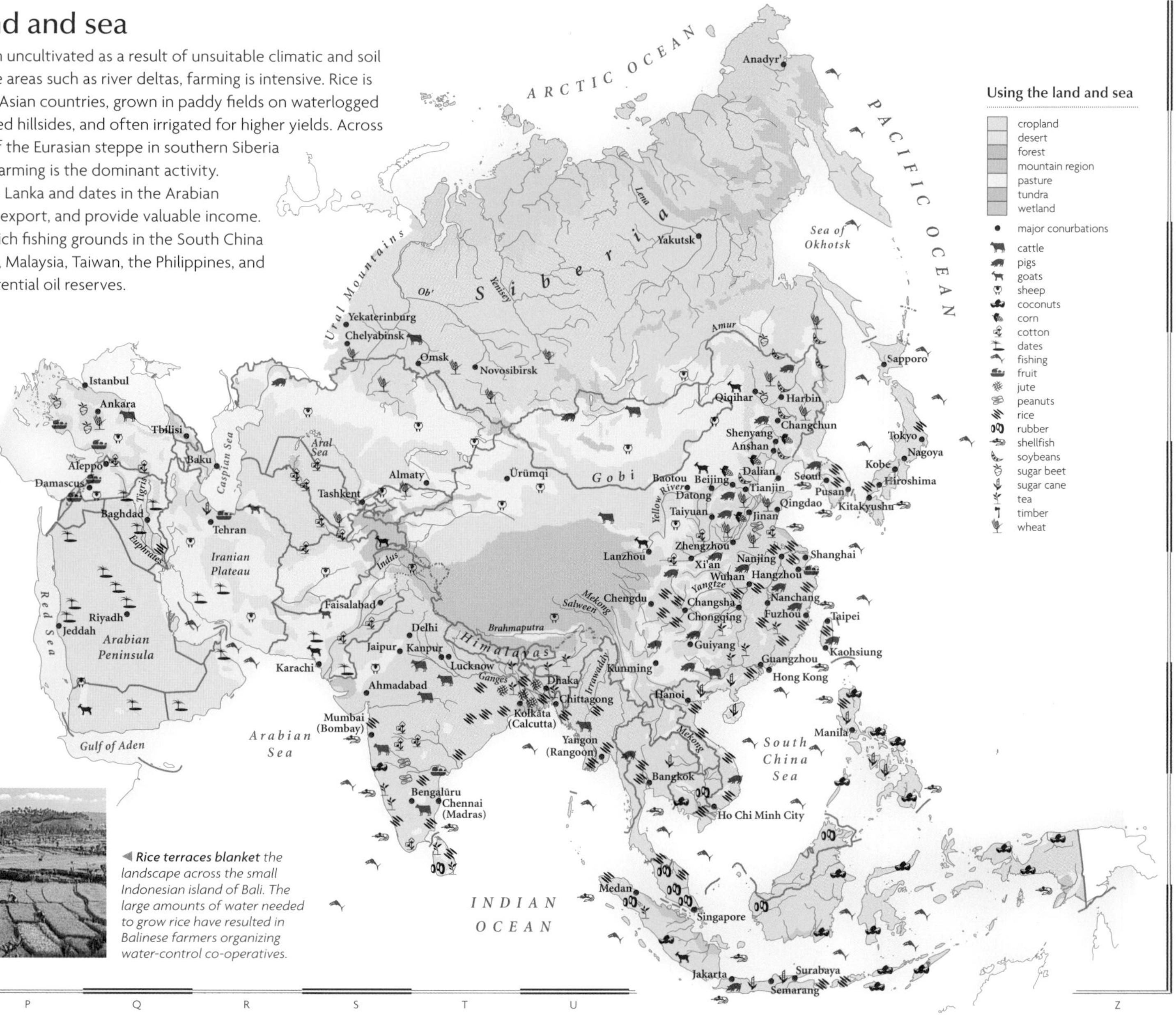

**Using the land and sea**
- cropland
- desert
- forest
- mountain region
- pasture
- tundra
- wetland
- major conurbations
- cattle
- pigs
- goats
- sheep
- coconuts
- corn
- cotton
- dates
- fishing
- fruit
- jute
- peanuts
- rice
- rubber
- shellfish
- soybeans
- sugar beet
- sugar cane
- tea
- timber
- wheat

▲ *Date palms have been cultivated in oases throughout the Arabian Peninsula since antiquity. In addition to the fruit, palms are used for timber, fuel, rope, and for making vinegar, syrup and a liquor known as arrack.*

◀ *Rice terraces blanket the landscape across the small Indonesian island of Bali. The large amounts of water needed to grow rice have resulted in Balinese farmers organizing water-control co-operatives.*

# Turkey & the Caucasus

ARMENIA, AZERBAIJAN, GEORGIA, TURKEY

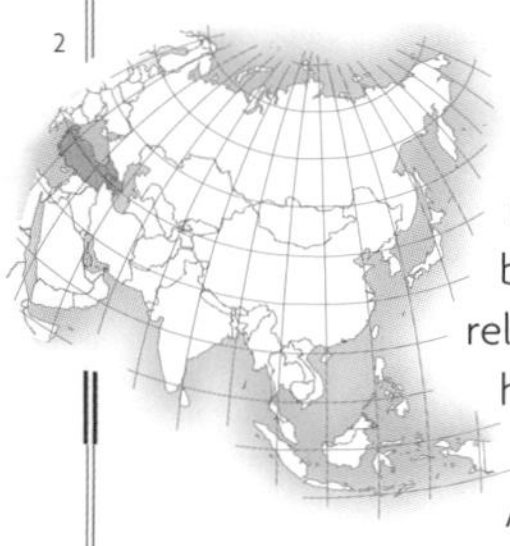

This region occupies the fragmented junction between Europe, Asia, and the Russian Federation. Sunni Islam provides a common identity for the secular state of Turkey, which the revered leader Kemal Atatürk established from the remnants of the Ottoman Empire after the First World War. Turkey has a broad resource base and expanding trade links with Europe, but the east is relatively undeveloped and strife between the state and a large Kurdish minority has yet to be resolved. Georgia is similarly challenged by ethnic separatism, while the Christian state of Armenia and the mainly Muslim and oil-rich Azerbaijan are locked in conflict over the territory of Nagornyy-Karabakh.

## Using the land & sea

Turkey is largely self-sufficient in food. The irrigated Black Sea coastlands have the world's highest yields of hazelnuts. Tobacco, cotton, sultanas, tea, and figs are the region's main cash crops and a great range of fruit and vegetables are grown. Wine grapes are among the labor-intensive crops which allow full use of limited agricultural land in the Caucasus. Sturgeon fishing is particularly important in Azerbaijan.

## Transportation & industry

Turkey leads the region's well diversified economy. Petrochemicals, textiles, engineering, and food processing are the main industries. Azerbaijan is able to export oil, while the other states rely heavily on hydroelectric power and imported fuel. Georgia produces precision machinery. War and earthquake damage have devastated Armenia's infrastructure.

▲ **Azerbaijan has substantial** oil reserves, located in and around the Caspian Sea. They were some of the earliest oilfields in the world to be exploited.

### Major industry and infrastructure

- ⚙ carpet weaving
- cement
- chemicals
- coal
- engineering
- food processing
- oil
- textiles
- tourism
- vehicle manufacture

- ■ capital cities
- ● major towns
- ⊕ international airports
- — major roads
- major industrial areas

### Land use and agricultural distribution

- cattle
- goats
- cotton
- fishing
- fruit
- hazelnuts
- olives
- sugar beet
- tobacco
- vineyards

- ■ capital cities
- ● major towns
- pasture
- cropland
- forest

### Transportation network

| | |
|---|---|
| 🛣 | 114,867 miles (184,882 km) |
| 🛣 | 5778 miles (9300 km) |
| 🚂 | 8120 miles (13,069 km) |
| ⛟ | 745 miles (1200 km) |

Physical and political barriers have severely limited communications between Armenia, Georgia and Azerbaijan. Turkey has a relatively well-developed transportation network.

### The urban/rural population divide

urban 72%   rural 28%

0 10 20 30 40 50 60 70 80 90 100

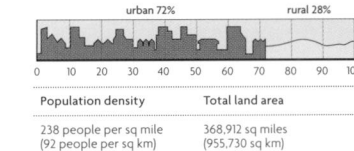

| Population density | Total land area |
|---|---|
| 238 people per sq mile (92 people per sq km) | 368,912 sq miles (955,730 sq km) |

▲ **For many centuries,** Istanbul has held tremendous strategic importance as a crucial gateway between Europe and Asia. Founded by the Greeks as Byzantium, the city became the center of the East Roman Empire and was known as Constantinople to the Romans. From the 15th century onward the city became the center of the great Ottoman Empire.

# The landscape

The deeply eroded hills and salty basins of the Anatolian Plateau are bordered by several mountain ranges along the Black Sea coast, and the limestone Taurus Mountains (*Toros Daglari*) in the south. A lowland trough divides the Caucasus and the Lesser Caucasus, which form a formidable barrier of peaks in the north.

Limestone weathering in the Anatolian Plateau

High plateau

Eroded gully

Layers of tephra

Remnant landforms

▲ **In central Turkey,** rainwater has chemically weathered away numerous layers of limestone, leaving isolated outcrops and pinnacles and deep eroded gullies.

▶ **The Caucasus are** fold mountains, which formed around the same time as the Taurus Mountains (Toros Daglari) around 65 million years ago and have since been modified by volcanic erruptions.

**Lava has flowed** over large areas of the Lesser Caucasus within the last five million years, producing extensive basalt plateaus.

**The earthquake that** struck Armenia in 1988 killed over 55,000 people and devastated the country's infrastructure.

**The volcanic cone** of Mount Ararat is the highest peak in Turkey, with an altitude of 16,853 ft (5137 m).

▶ **Since the 6th century** BC, the pinnacles and caves of east-central Anatolia have been utilized as dwellings. Many are still inhabited today.

▲ **The white rock terraces** at Pamukkale in western Turkey were formed when underground water, heated by volcanic activity, dissolved minerals in the rocks. When the water reached the surface and evaporated the minerals were left behind in these extraordinary formations.

**Long, parallel mountain** ranges run from east to west into the Aegean Sea, which has risen since the last Ice Age to form a drowned coastline of numerous islands and extended inlets.

**The straits of** the Bosporus and the Dardanelles, respectively linking the Black and Mediterranean seas with the Sea of Marmara, formed after the last Ice Age, when a rising sea level caused these former river valleys to be flooded.

**Many of the** rivers crossing the Anatolian Plateau never reach the sea, but drain into salt marshes and shallow salt lakes such as Lake Tuz (*Tuz Gölü*), where much of the water is lost to evaporation.

**The folded peaks of** the Taurus Mountains (*Toros Daglari*) were formed 60–65 million years ago, at the same time as the Alps. The rock is mainly limestone, with deep caves, gorges, and underground rivers.

**The Cilician Gates** (*Gülek Bogazi*), a major pass through the Taurus Mountains (*Toros Daglari*), is the point where streams flow from the interior plateau onto the lowland of Adana.

**Thick, temperate forest** veils the seaward slopes of the Kaçkar Daglari. The southern slopes, which lie in a rainshadow, are dry and barren.

**The granite massif** near Surami divides the lowlands of Georgia from the oil-rich basin of Azerbaijan's Kura river, which has built a large delta into the Caspian Sea.

**The shallow, saline** Lake Van (*Van Gölü*) is the largest lake in Turkey. Dry terraces mark a previous shoreline 181 ft (55 m) above the present water level.

## Map key

### Population
- above 5 million
- 1 million to 5 million
- 500,000 to 1 million
- 100,000 to 500,000
- 50,000 to 100,000
- 10,000 to 50,000
- below 10,000

### Elevation
- 4000m / 13,124ft
- 3000m / 9843ft
- 2000m / 6562ft
- 1000m / 3281ft
- 500m / 1640ft
- 250m / 820ft
- 100m / 328ft
- sea level

Scale 1:4,500,000

projection: Lambert Conformal Conic

▲ **The fisheries of** Azerbaijan are noted for their hauls of sturgeon, and the Caspian Sea accounts for 80% of the world's total catch. However, stocks are now under serious threat due to overfishing.

▲ **Traditional steam baths** are found throughout the region, and are used for socializing as well as for bathing.

# The Near East

**IRAQ, ISRAEL, JORDAN, LEBANON, SYRIA**

Some of the world's oldest civilizations developed in this region – the Fertile Crescent – which is venerated by Jews, Muslims, and Christians, but torn by competing religious, ethnic, and national claims to the land. Turkish Ottoman rule ended with the First World War and the region was divided into areas administered by Britain and France. The UN endorsed calls for a Jewish homeland in what was then Palestine and in 1948 the state of Israel was declared. Hostility towards the Jewish state led to a series of wars with its Arab neighbors. After 2000, attempts to broker peaceful resolutions with both the Palestinian population and with adjacent Arab states were hampered by a revival of Islamic militarism and conflicting international interests in the oil-rich region. This led to an Israeli retrenchment and culminated in a US-led invasion of Iraq in 2003, which toppled the Ba'athist regime of Saddam Hussein in the name of a "war on terror".

## Using the land & sea

Water scarcity limits cropland to the north and to areas watered principally by the Tigris, Euphrates, and Jordan rivers. In Israel, new irrigation techniques are allowing cultivation in the arid Negev. Wheat is the chief grain and large areas of scrub support livestock herding. Commercial produce includes dates, tobacco, citrus fruits, olives, grapes, and cotton, which is Syria's main export crop. Fishing is still important in the Mediterranean.

The urban/rural population divide

urban 70%     rural 30%

0 10 20 30 40 50 60 70 80 90 100

Population density: 217 people per sq mile (84 people per sq km)

Total land area: 325,460 sq miles (843,160 sq km)

Land use and agricultural distribution

- sheep
- cereals
- citrus fruits
- cotton
- dates
- fishing
- rice
- tobacco
- capital cities
- major towns
- pasture
- cropland
- wetland
- desert

## Transportation & industry

The petrochemical industry is well established, and central to the economies of Syria and Iraq, which was the world's second largest oil exporter before the war with Iran which began in 1980. Lebanon has traditionally been a center for commerce, while Israel has a well-diversified economy with an expanding tourist industry, despite few natural resources.

Transportation network

- 49,859 miles (80,249 km)
- 1365 miles (2197 km)
- 3826 miles (6158 km)
- 1171 miles (1885 km)

*Jordan's seaport of Al 'Aqabah is connected to Damascus in Syria by road and rail. This route to the Red Sea provides for large exports of phosphate and trade with states in the Persian Gulf.*

Major industry and infrastructure

- car manufacture
- cement
- chemicals
- electronics
- finance
- food processing
- iron & steel
- oil
- oil refining
- textiles
- capital cities
- major towns
- international airports
- major roads
- major industrial areas

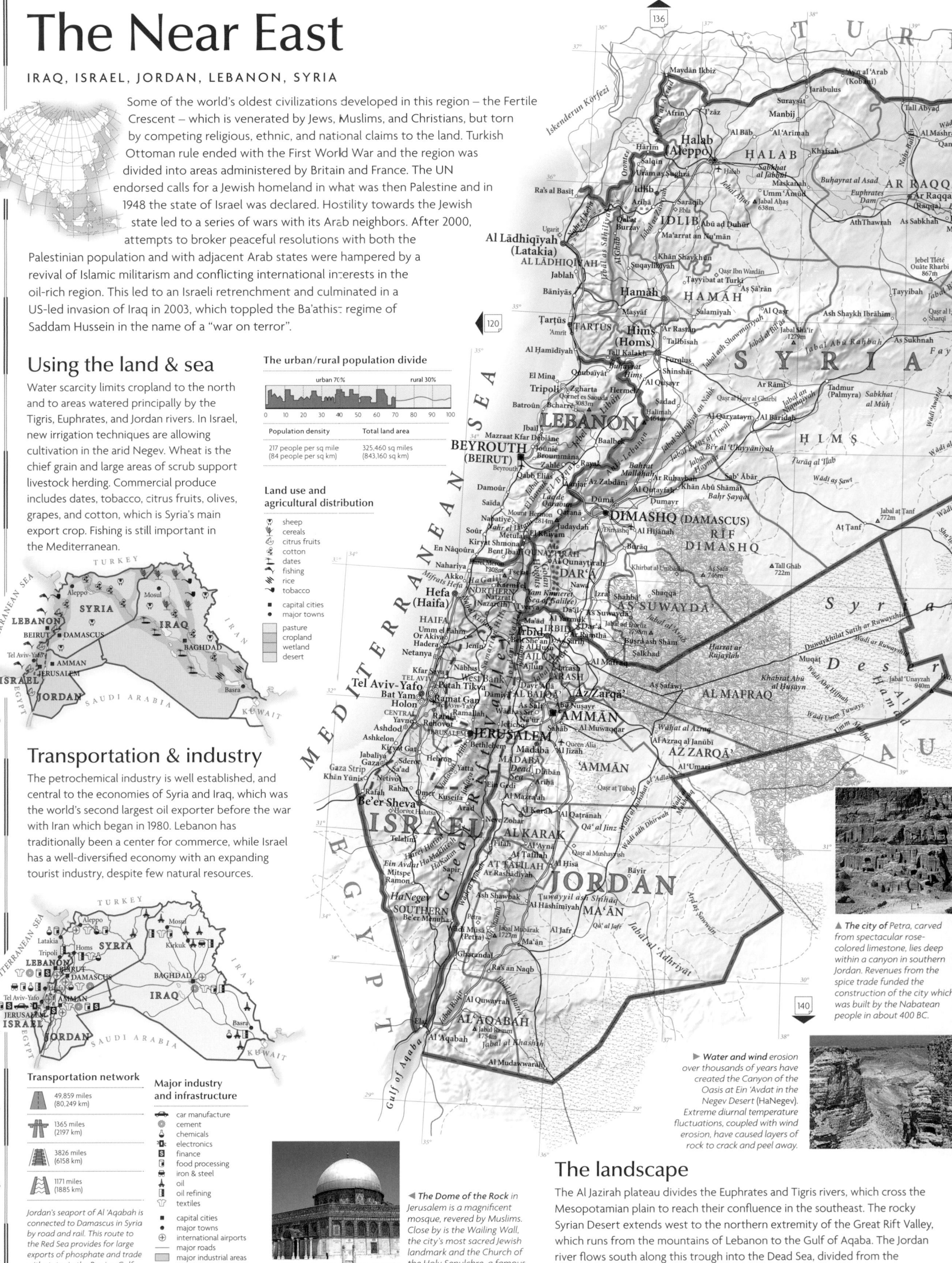

◀ *The Dome of the Rock in Jerusalem is a magnificent mosque, revered by Muslims. Close by is the Wailing Wall, the city's most sacred Jewish landmark and the Church of the Holy Sepulchre, a famous Christian place of worship.*

▲ *The city of Petra, carved from spectacular rose-colored limestone, lies deep within a canyon in southern Jordan. Revenues from the spice trade funded the construction of the city which was built by the Nabatean people in about 400 BC.*

▶ *Water and wind erosion over thousands of years have created the Canyon of the Oasis at Ein 'Avdat in the Negev Desert (HaNegev). Extreme diurnal temperature fluctuations, coupled with wind erosion, have caused layers of rock to crack and peel away.*

## The landscape

The Al Jazirah plateau divides the Euphrates and Tigris rivers, which cross the Mesopotamian plain to reach their confluence in the southeast. The rocky Syrian Desert extends west to the northern extremity of the Great Rift Valley, which runs from the mountains of Lebanon to the Gulf of Aqaba. The Jordan river flows south along this trough into the Dead Sea, divided from the Mediterranean coastal plain by a steep-sided plateau.

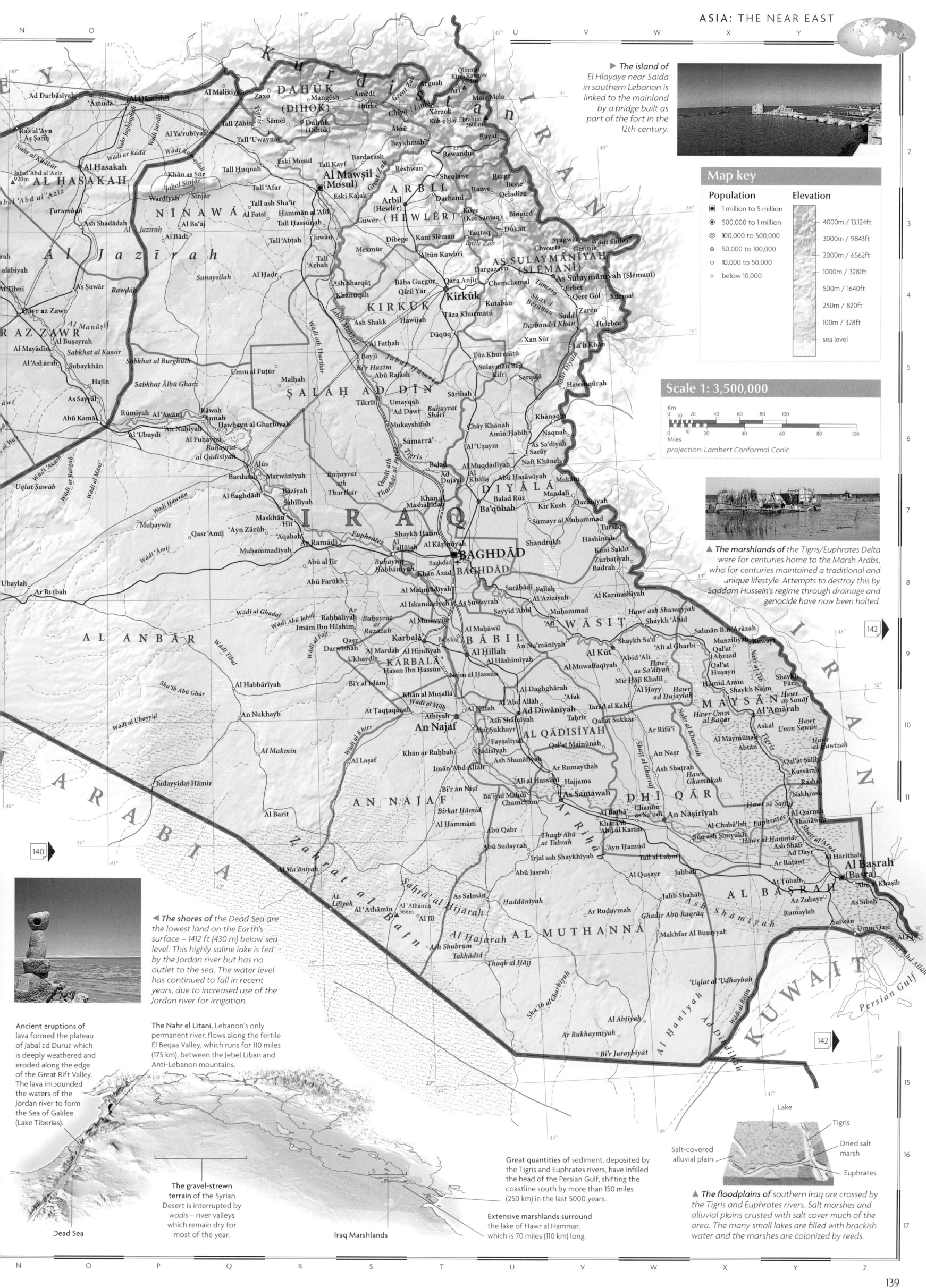

▶ The island of El Hlayaye near Saida in southern Lebanon is linked to the mainland by a bridge built as part of the fort in the 12th century.

## Map key

### Population
- ◼ 1 million to 5 million
- ◉ 500,000 to 1 million
- ◎ 100,000 to 500,000
- ⊕ 50,000 to 100,000
- ○ 10,000 to 50,000
- ∘ below 10,000

### Elevation
- 4000m / 13,124ft
- 3000m / 9843ft
- 2000m / 6562ft
- 1000m / 3281ft
- 500m / 1640ft
- 250m / 820ft
- 100m / 328ft
- sea level

### Scale 1: 3,500,000

Km  0  20  40  60  80  100
Miles  0  10  20  40  60  80  100

projection: Lambert Conformal Conic

▲ The marshlands of the Tigris/Euphrates Delta were for centuries home to the Marsh Arabs, who for centuries maintained a traditional and unique lifestyle. Attempts to destroy this by Saddam Hussein's regime through drainage and genocide have now been halted.

◀ The shores of the Dead Sea are the lowest land on the Earth's surface – 1412 ft (430 m) below sea level. This highly saline lake is fed by the Jordan river but has no outlet to the sea. The water level has continued to fall in recent years, due to increased use of the Jordan river for irrigation.

Ancient eruptions of lava formed the plateau of Jabal ad Duruz which is deeply weathered and eroded along the edge of the Great Rift Valley. The lava impounded the waters of the Jordan river to form the Sea of Galilee (Lake Tiberias).

Dead Sea

The Nahr el Litani, Lebanon's only permanent river, flows along the fertile El Beqaa Valley, which runs for 110 miles (175 km), between the Jebel Liban and Anti-Lebanon mountains.

The gravel-strewn terrain of the Syrian Desert is interrupted by wadis – river valleys which remain dry for most of the year.

Iraq Marshlands

Great quantities of sediment, deposited by the Tigris and Euphrates rivers, have infilled the head of the Persian Gulf, shifting the coastline south by more than 150 miles (250 km) in the last 5000 years.

Extensive marshlands surround the lake of Hawr al Hammar, which is 70 miles (110 km) long.

Lake
Tigris
Salt-covered alluvial plain
Dried salt marsh
Euphrates

▲ The floodplains of southern Iraq are crossed by the Tigris and Euphrates rivers. Salt marshes and alluvial plains crusted with salt cover much of the area. The many small lakes are filled with brackish water and the marshes are colonized by reeds.

# The Arabian Peninsula

BAHRAIN, KUWAIT, OMAN, QATAR, SAUDI ARABIA,
UNITED ARAB EMIRATES (UAE), YEMEN

Huge expanses of desert cover much of the Arabian Peninsula, limiting settlement to oases, the mountains along the Red Sea, and coastal belts. The most populous area is the fertile highlands of Yemen. The Islamic faith and Arabic language give the region a cultural and religious unity, and the Saudi city of Mecca (Makkah) is Islam's most holy place, visited by over two million pilgrims each year. More than half the world's oil reserves are contained in this region, and the exploitation of oil and gas has brought great wealth, particularly to Saudi Arabia. Yemen and Oman are the least developed of the Arabian states, with large rural populations. Within Saudi Arabia over 86% of the people live in urban areas.

## Using the land

Most of the Arabian Peninsula is unsuited to settled agriculture, making irrigation and land reclamation projects essential. The narrow coastal plain and isolated oases, commonly amounting to less than 1% of the land area, are used to cultivate grains, coffee, and exotic fruits. Goats, sheep, and camels are widespread throughout the region.

### The urban/rural population divide

urban 64%   rural 36%

| Population density | Total land area |
|---|---|
| 50 people per sq mile (19 people per sq km) | 1,147,856 sq miles (2,973,720 sq km) |

### Land use and agricultural distribution

- goats
- sheep
- cereals
- coffee
- dates
- fruit
- capital cities
- major towns
- pasture
- cropland
- desert

◀ The fertile soils of Yemen have encouraged settlement of almost all of the land from sea level up to the mountains at 10,000 ft (3050 m). In the higher reaches elaborate terraces have been constructed to facilitate crop cultivation.

## The landscape

A plateau more than 2500 ft (760 m) high extends across much of the Arabian Peninsula. The plateau slopes eastward from the massive, rifted escarpment along the coast of the Red Sea, to the shallow waters of the Persian Gulf. The interior is characterized by cuestas and valleys, drained by a system of wadis. A crescent of sand and gravel deserts lies to the east.

**The An Nafud Desert** is covered with barchan dunes varying between 30–100 ft (10–30 m) high. The "horns" of the crescent-shaped dunes reflect the direction in which they are being moved by the wind.

**Inselbergs are dotted** over a wide area of the Najd Plateau. These resistant remnants of the ancient basement rock are left standing when the softer weathered rock has been worn away.

▲ A sabkha is a flat, salt-encrusted plain which occurs near the coast just above the high water mark. Flooding by sea water leads to saturation of the land with saline-rich groundwater. As this evaporates, a cracked layer of sand, cemented together with salt, gypsum, and calcium carbonate is left behind.

Evaporation
Crusted layer left behind
Storm surge flooding
Normal level of tidal range
Salt wedge penetrates inland water

**Few areas in** the Arabian Peninsula have rivers flowing through them. Most are drained by ephemeral watercourses called wadis.

**The Hejaz** (Al Hijaz) and Asir mountains form part of the same geological region as the highlands of Sudan and Eritrea, to which they were once joined. They were separated when faulting opened the Red Sea, over 50 million years ago.

**Across the Najd Plateau** the flat relief is broken by mesas; steep-sided rock plateaus and cuestas; ridges with one steep and one gentle slope.

▲ Ar Rub' al Khali, also known as the Empty Quarter, is the most arid part of the Arabian Peninsula. It is the largest uninterrupted sand desert in the world. Ridges of sand up to 25 miles (40 km) long, run northeast–southwest, giving characteristic linear dunes.

**The Jabal an Nabi Shu'ayb** in Yemen is the highest point on the peninsula, rising to 12,336 ft (3760 m).

**The Arabian Shield** underpins the west of the peninsula. It is a fragment of the ancient continent, Gondwanaland, which was separated by rifting millions of years ago.

◀ Every Muslim must make at least one pilgrimage or hajj to Mecca (Makkah), in Saudi Arabia, during their lifetime. The cloth-covered shrine is called the Ka'bah, and is regarded by Muslims as the most sacred place on Earth.

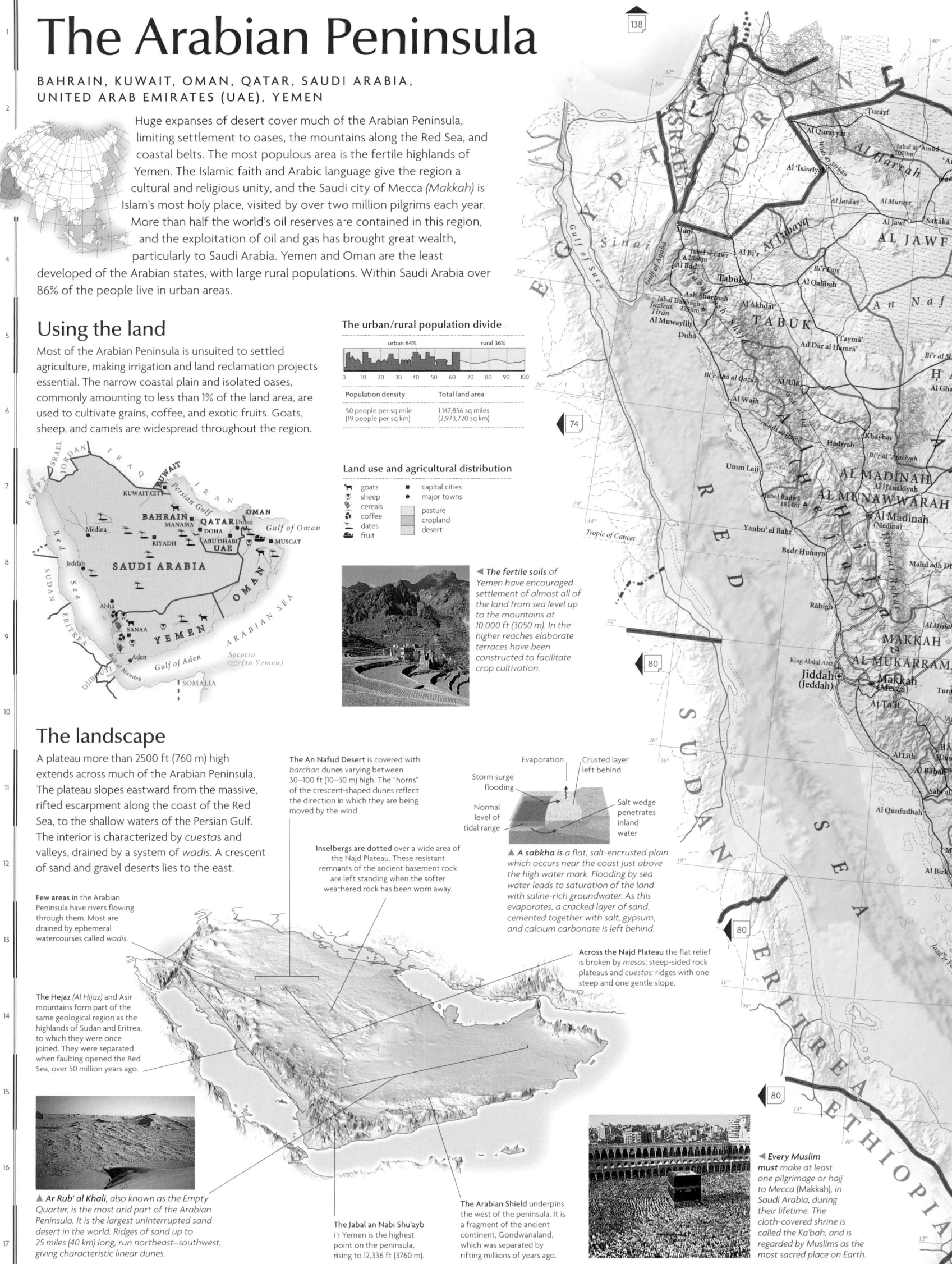

138

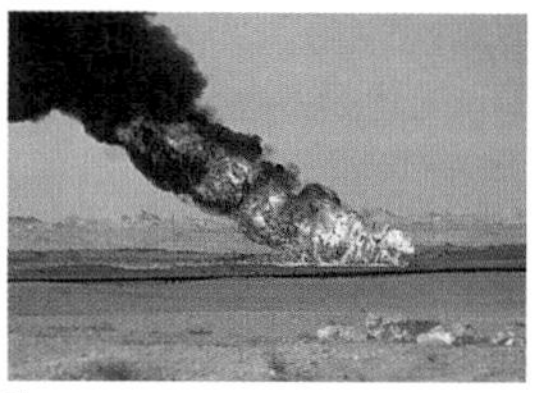

◀ Saudi Arabia contains the world's largest oil reserves, lying mainly along the Persian Gulf coast. Each day the region produces around 10 million barrels of oil. Here, in the desert, excess oil is being burnt off.

## Transportation & industry

The extraction and refining of oil and gas are the major industrial activities in the Arabian Peninsula. The region also has an active construction sector, with many Arab cities reflecting the wealth generated by the oil industry. The service sector is dominated by financial and technical institutions, which, like the construction sector, mainly serve the oil industry. Traditional handicrafts such as carpet-weaving are found in rural areas.

### Transportation network

| | |
|---|---|
| 44,832 miles (72,159 km) | 673 miles (1083 km) |
| 670 miles (1078 km) | none |

*Internal surface transportation is poorly developed across the peninsula. Along the coast, commercial routes have developed, but connections between bordering states rely on major airports.*

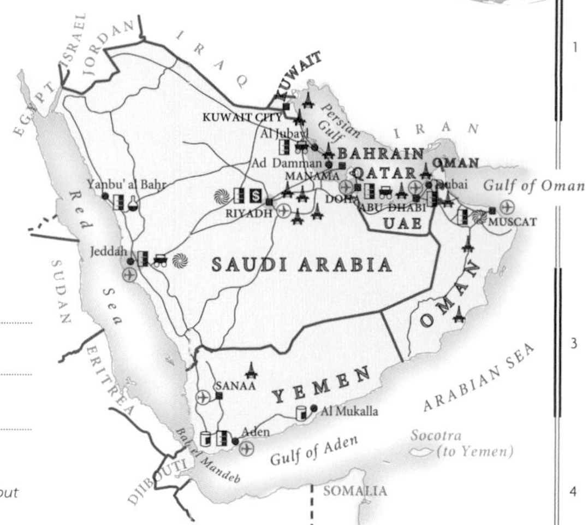

### Major industry and infrastructure

- cement
- chemicals
- iron & steel
- oil
- oil refining
- food processing
- capital cities
- major towns
- international airports
- major roads
- major industrial areas

142

80

## Map key

**Population**

- 1 million to 5 million
- 500,000 to 1 million
- 100,000 to 500,000
- 50,000 to 100,000
- 10,000 to 50,000
- below 10,000

**Elevation**

- 3000m / 9843ft
- 2000m / 6562ft
- 1000m / 3281ft
- 500m / 1640ft
- 250m / 820ft
- 100m / 328ft
- sea level

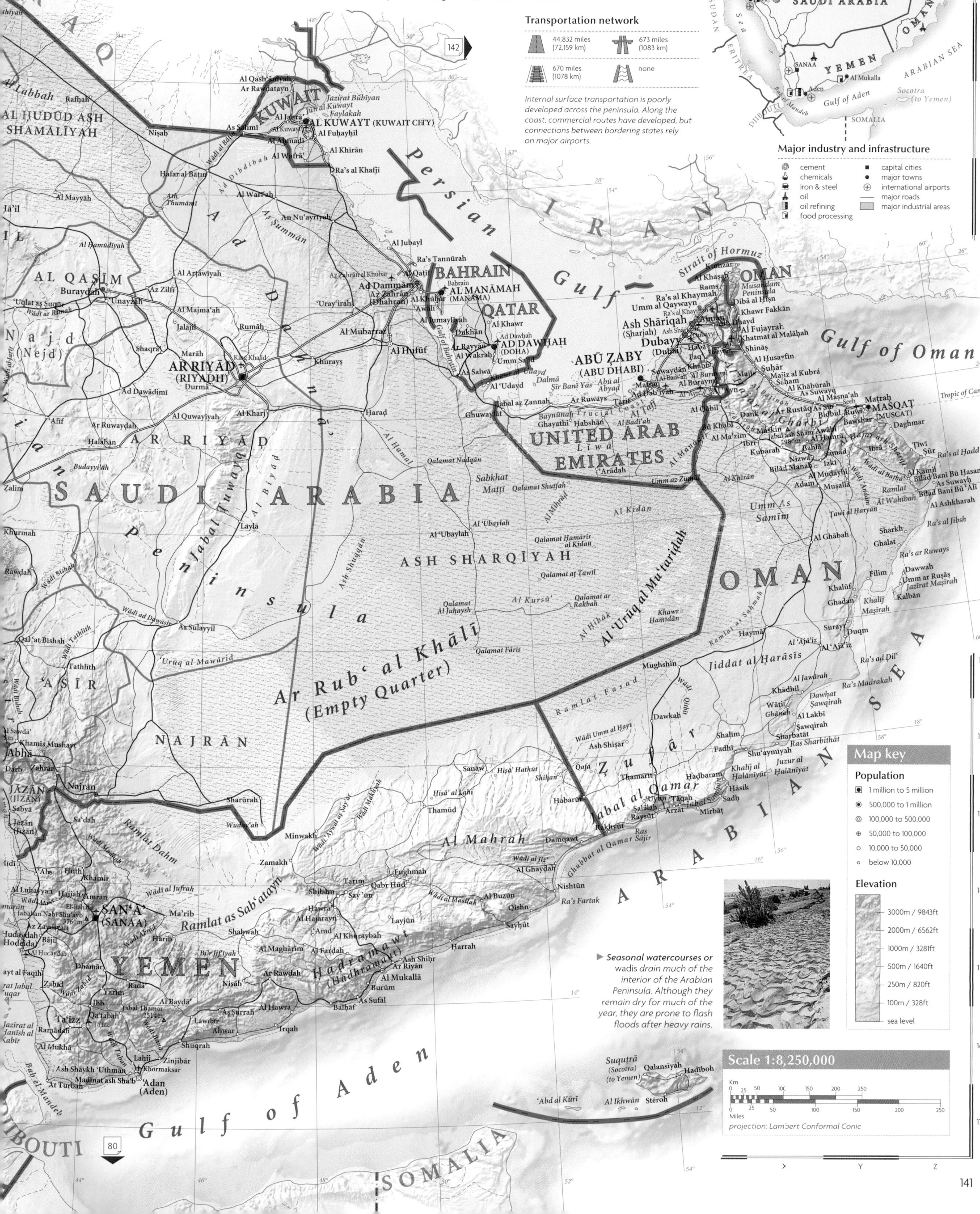

▶ Seasonal watercourses or wadis drain much of the interior of the Arabian Peninsula. Although they remain dry for much of the year, they are prone to flash floods after heavy rains.

**Scale 1:8,250,000**

Km 0 25 50 100 150 200 250
Miles 0 25 50 100 150 200 250

projection: Lambert Conformal Conic

# Iran & the Gulf states

## BAHRAIN, IRAN, KUWAIT, QATAR, UNITED ARAB EMIRATES (UAE)

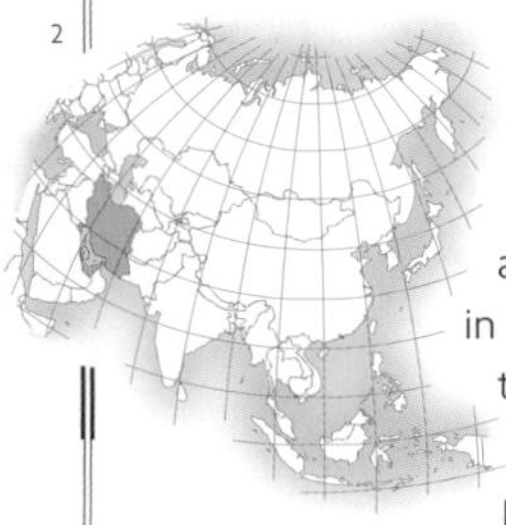

The discovery of oil in the Persian Gulf in the 1930s brought great wealth to the surrounding states. The revenue was largely used to modernize industry and infrastructure, initiating great social change in these formerly agrarian countries. Today, over 90% of the people in the Gulf states live in urban areas, and foreign nationals make up a sizeable proportion of the population in Kuwait, Qatar, and the United Arab Emirates. The importance of control of the oil reserves has led to a number of territorial disputes, including most recently the Iran–Iraq War (1980-88) and the First Gulf War (1991). Islam is practiced almost exclusively throughout the region and two distinct strands are found; Sunni Muslims in Qatar, Kuwait, and UAE, and Shi'a Muslims in Iran and Bahrain. In 1979 Iran became the world's largest theocracy.

## The landscape

The land rises steeply from the fragmented coastal lowlands bordering the Persian Gulf, to reach Iran's interior plateau, bounded by heavily eroded mountain chains. An unstable plate boundary runs northwest to southeast across Iran causing frequent earthquakes. On the sandy west coast of the Persian Gulf, the relief is generally flat, with patches of salt marsh. Bahrain consists of two groups of islands, which are mostly small and rocky.

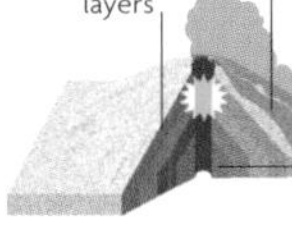

Pyroclastic layers    Lava flow

Lava flow layers

▲ *Qolleh-ye Damavand in the Elburz Mountains is a composite volcano. It comprises layers of lava and pyroclasts fragmentary rocks which accumulate on the slopes of the volcano after being ejected into the air.*

▲ *Marine sediments from deep beneath the ancient Tethys Sea have been uplifted to form the Elburz Mountains, which stretch along the shores of the Caspian Sea, northern Iran.*

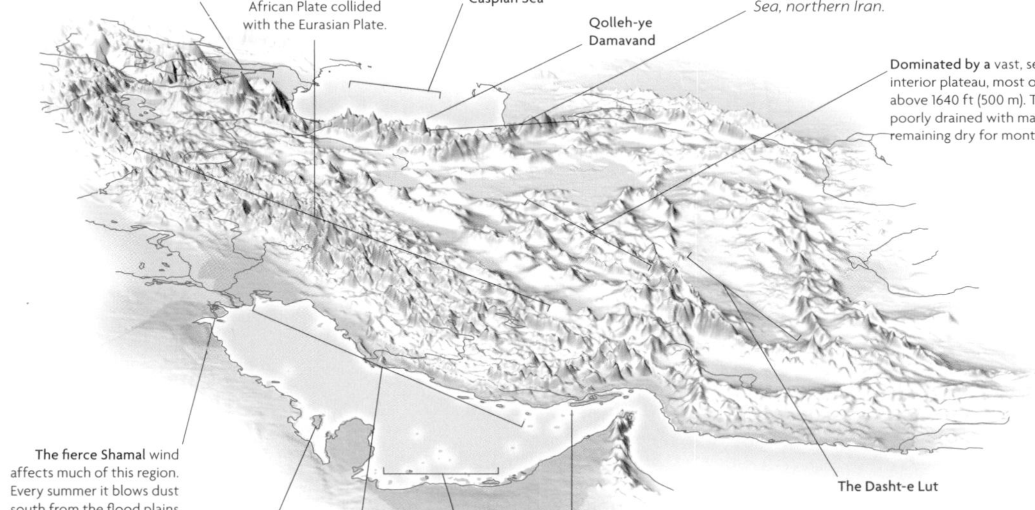

Lava and ash from previous volcanic activity covers a 200 mile (320 km) stretch from the border with Azerbaijan to the Caspian Sea.

Iran's two mountain chains, the Zagros and Elburz, were uplifted at the same time as the Alps in Europe, when the African Plate collided with the Eurasian Plate.

Caspian Sea

Qolleh-ye Damavand

Dominated by a vast, semi-arid interior plateau, most of Iran lies above 1640 ft (500 m). The region is poorly drained with many of its basins remaining dry for months at a time.

The fierce Shamal wind affects much of this region. Every summer it blows dust south from the flood plains of the Tigris and Euphrates, reducing visibility to such an extent that Kuwait International Airport is frequently forced to close.

The Dasht-e Lut

Autumn winds blowing across the Persian Gulf can reach speeds of up to 95 mph (150 kmph) causing severe storms, squalls, and waterspouts.

Prolific springs tapping artesian water make cultivation possible across the north of Bahrain's main island. This provides a sharp contrast to the sandy plains in the south and west.

The oilfields of the Persian Gulf are formed from marine shale deposits lying in sedimentary basins at the margins of the Zagros Mountains.

Numerous islands lie along the southern coast of the Persian Gulf. Some of these are salt domes, created when less dense salts were displaced and forced up to the surface by denser, overlying strata.

◀ *The Dasht-e Lut covers a large portion of eastern Iran with its dry, wind-eroded plain of scattered sandstone pillars and salty depressions. During the summer, temperatures soar, making it one of the world's hottest, driest places.*

## Using the land & sea

Along the coast of the Caspian Sea, desalinated water allows fruits and vegetables to be produced, although water shortages and desert soils still limit farming. Sheep are the most important livestock raised in Iran and commercial forests cover the northwest of the country. Shrimp stocks were decimated by pollution during the Gulf War, but fishing remains important for domestic and export markets.

◀ *All of the Gulf states have commercial fishing fleets. Before the discovery of oil, fishing was the region's leading industry.*

### Land use and agricultural distribution

- 🐐 goats
- 🐑 sheep
- 🌾 cereals
- 🍊 citrus fruits
- 🌱 cotton
- 🌴 dates
- 🐟 fishing
- 🌲 timber

- ■ capital cities
- ● major towns

pasture
cropland
forest
desert
wetland

### The urban/rural population divide

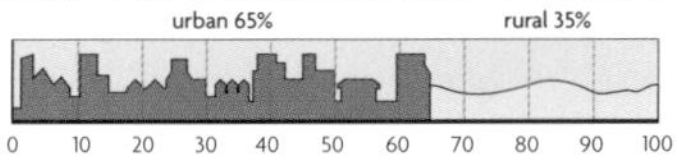

urban 65%    rural 35%

0  10  20  30  40  50  60  70  80  90  100

| Population density | Total land area |
|---|---|
| 112 people per sq mile (43 people per sq km) | 642,883 sq miles (1,665,500 sq km) |

◀ *The Kuwait Towers in the center of Kuwait are symbols of the vast wealth oil has brought to the country. Before 1960, the city had only one main street and was surrounded by a mud wall.*

◀ *Many volcanoes lie in Iran's 1200 mile (1930 km) volcanic belt, including the country's highest peak, the now-extinct Qolleh-ye Damavand at 18,600 ft (5671 m).*

146

▶ *Extensive oil and gas exploitation in the Gulf region has allowed the economic transformation of the Gulf states. Consequently, many of these states have a hugely improved per capita income compared to the 1960's.*

# Transportation & industry

Both onshore and offshore oil reserves are exploited throughout the region. Kuwait not only extracts but also refines 80% of its oil. Bahrain has diversified its economy to become the main commercial and financial center in the Persian Gulf. Iran produces a wide range of products: textile mills are widespread and carpet weaving is an important export industry.

## Major industry and infrastructure

- carpet manufacture
- chemicals
- S finance
- food processing
- oil
- oil refining
- textiles
- ■ capital city
- ● major towns
- ⊕ international airports
- — major roads
- major industrial areas

## Transportation network

| | |
|---|---|
| 63,543 miles (102,274 km) | 884 miles (1423 km) |
| 3822 miles (6151 km) | 562 miles (904 km) |

*Major towns and neighboring countries are linked by adequate road networks, although rural areas are less well served. Bahrain is linked to the mainland by a 15 mile (25 km) long causeway.*

## Map key

### Population

- ■ above 5 million
- ◉ 1 million to 5 million
- ◉ 500,000 to 1 million
- ⊕ 100,000 to 500,000
- ⊕ 50,000 to 100,000
- ○ 10,000 to 50,000
- ○ below 10,000

### Elevation

- 4000m / 13,124ft
- 3000m / 9843ft
- 2000m / 6562ft
- 1000m / 3281ft
- 500m / 1640ft
- 250m / 820ft
- 100m / 328ft
- sea level

### Scale 1:6,000,000

*projection: Lambert Conformal Conic*

148

TURKMENISTAN
AFGHANISTAN
PAKISTAN
I R A N
Caspian Sea
Gulf of Oman
Strait of Hormuz
Makran Coast
Tropic of Cancer

UNITED ARAB EMIRATES
OMAN
QATAR
BAHRAIN

143

# Kazakhstan

Abundant natural resources lie in the immense steppe grasslands, deserts, and central plateau of the former Soviet republic of Kazakhstan. An intensive program of industrial and agricultural development to exploit these resources during the Soviet era resulted in catastrophic industrial pollution, including fallout from nuclear testing and the shrinkage of the Aral Sea. Since independence, the government has encouraged foreign investment and liberalized the economy to promote growth. The adoption of Kazakh as the national language is intended to encourage a new sense of national identity in a state where living conditions for the majority remain harsh, both in cramped urban centers and impoverished rural areas.

## Transportation & industry

The single most important industry in Kazakhstan is mining, based around extensive oil deposits near the Caspian Sea, the world's largest chromium mine, and vast reserves of iron ore. Recent foreign investment has helped to develop industries including food processing and steel manufacture, and to expand the exploitation of mineral resources. The Russian space program is still based at Baykonyr, near Kyzylorda in central Kazakhstan.

**Major industry and infrastructure**

- ⚗ chemicals
- ⚙ engineering
- 🐟 fish processing
- 🍴 food processing
- 🏭 iron & steel
- △ metallurgy
- ⛏ mining
- ♠ oil
- ■ capital cities
- • major towns
- ✈ international airports
- — major roads
- major industrial areas

**Transportation network**

48,263 miles (77,680 km)

8483 miles (13,660 km)

3900 miles (2423 km)

*Industrial areas in the north and east are well-connected to Russia. Air and rail links with Germany and China have been established through foreign investment. Better access to Baltic ports is being sought.*

*◄ An open-pit coal mine in Kazakhstan. Foreign investment is being actively sought by the Kazakh government in order to fully exploit the potential of the country's rich mineral reserves.*

**Map key**

Population
- ◉ 1 million to 5 million
- ◉ 500,000 to 1 million
- ◎ 100,000 to 500,000
- ⊕ 50,000 to 100,000
- ◦ 10,000 to 50,000
- · below 10,000

Elevation
- 4000m / 13,124ft
- 3000m / 9843ft
- 2000m / 6562ft
- 1000m / 3281ft
- 500m / 1640ft
- 250m / 820ft
- 100m / 328ft
- sea level

## Using the land & sea

The rearing of large herds of sheep and goats on the steppe grasslands forms the core of Kazakh agriculture. Arable cultivation and cotton-growing in pasture and desert areas was encouraged during the Soviet era, but relative yields are low. The heavy use of fertilizers and the diversion of natural water sources for irrigation has degraded much of the land.

**The urban/rural population divide**

urban 56%   rural 44%

0 10 20 30 40 50 60 70 80 90 100

| Population density | Total land area |
| --- | --- |
| 16 people per sq mile (6 people per sq km) | 1,048,878 sq miles (2,717,300 sq km) |

**Land use and agricultural distribution**

- 🐄 cattle
- 🐐 goats
- 🐑 sheep
- 🌿 cotton
- 🐟 fishing
- 🌾 wheat
- ■ capital cities
- • major towns
- pasture
- cropland
- forest
- mountain region
- desert

*◄ The nomadic peoples who moved their herds around the steppe grasslands are now largely settled, although echoes of their traditional lifestyle, in particular their superb riding skills, remain.*

Scale 1:7,000,000

*projection: Lambert Conformal Conic*

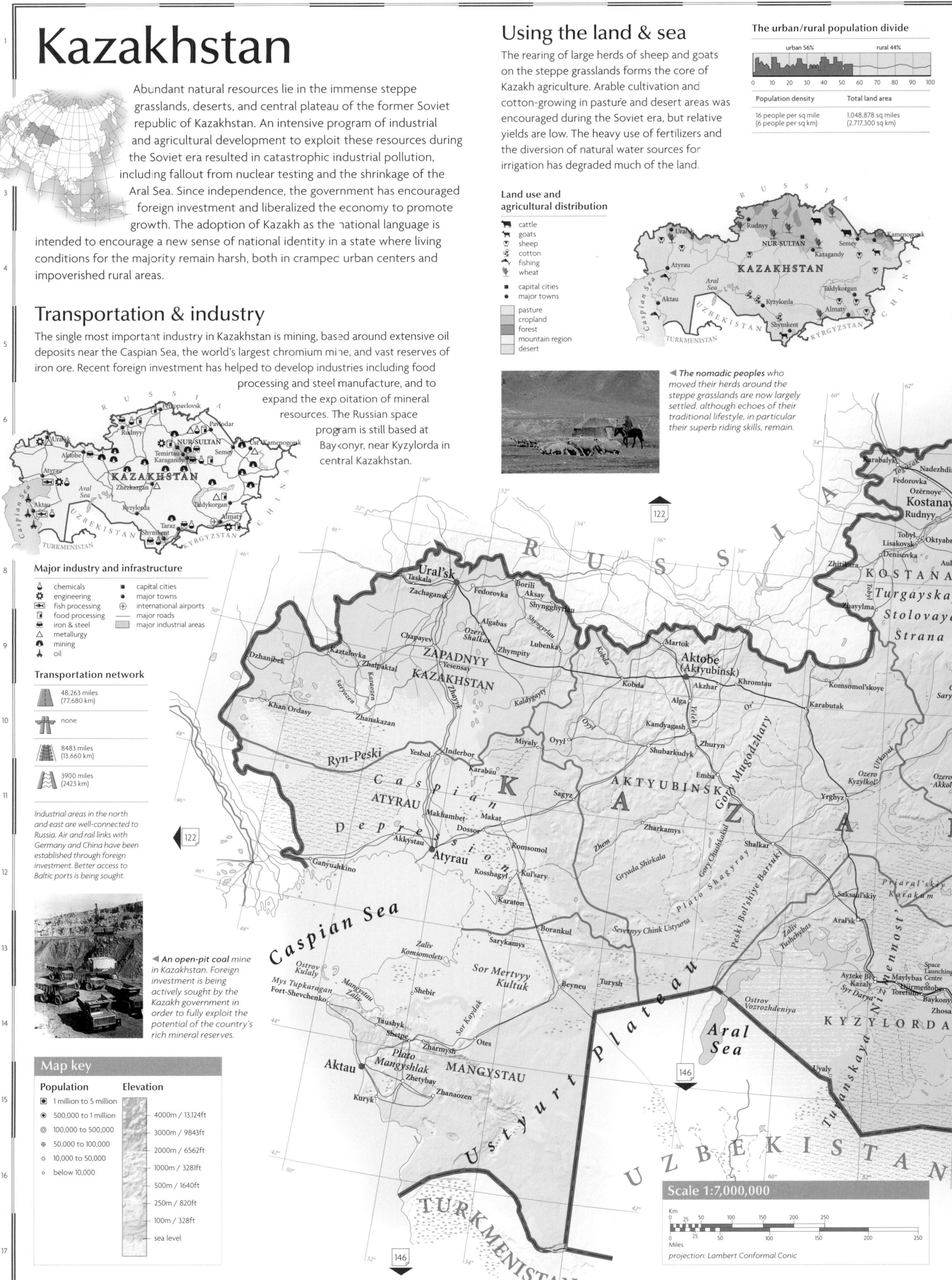

# The landscape

Stretching more than 1250 miles (2000 km) from the Caspian Sea in the west to China in the east, more than 40% of Kazakhstan is covered by steppe grasslands which give way to barren desert in the south. The land rises eastward towards the mineral-rich central plateau, to form the Altai Mountains.

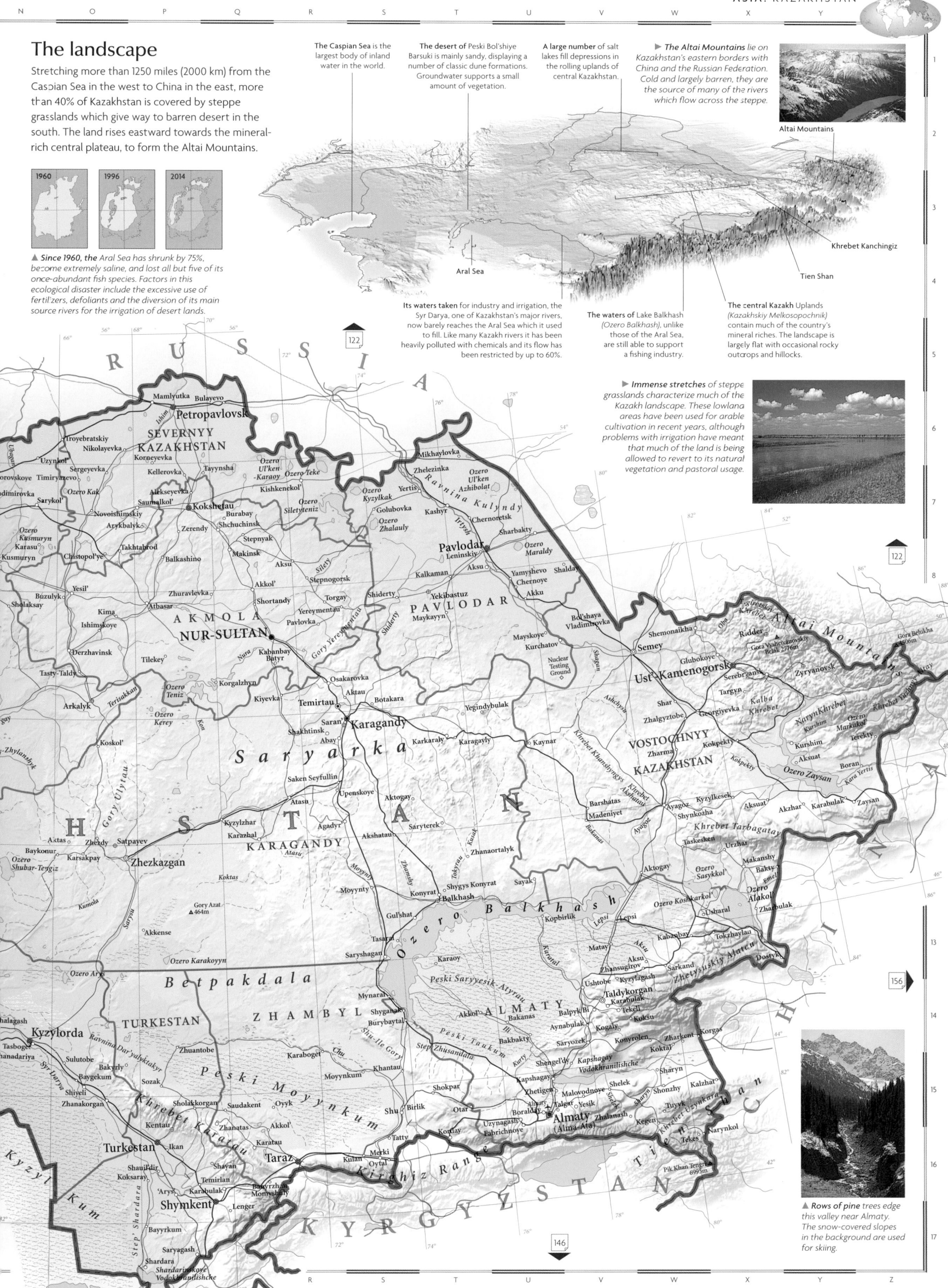

▲ **Since 1960, the** Aral Sea has shrunk by 75%, become extremely saline, and lost all but five of its once-abundant fish species. Factors in this ecological disaster include the excessive use of fertilizers, defoliants and the diversion of its main source rivers for the irrigation of desert lands.

**The Caspian Sea** is the largest body of inland water in the world.

**The desert of** Peski Bol'shiye Barsuki is mainly sandy, displaying a number of classic dune formations. Groundwater supports a small amount of vegetation.

**A large number** of salt lakes fill depressions in the rolling uplands of central Kazakhstan.

▶ **The Altai Mountains** lie on Kazakhstan's eastern borders with China and the Russian Federation. Cold and largely barren, they are the source of many of the rivers which flow across the steppe.

Altai Mountains

Khrebet Kanchingiz

Tien Shan

Aral Sea

**Its waters taken** for industry and irrigation, the Syr Darya, one of Kazakhstan's major rivers, now barely reaches the Aral Sea which it used to fill. Like many Kazakh rivers it has been heavily polluted with chemicals and its flow has been restricted by up to 60%.

**The waters of** Lake Balkhash (Ozero Balkhash), unlike those of the Aral Sea, are still able to support a fishing industry.

**The central Kazakh** Uplands (Kazakhskiy Melkosopochnik) contain much of the country's mineral riches. The landscape is largely flat with occasional rocky outcrops and hillocks.

▶ **Immense stretches** of steppe grasslands characterize much of the Kazakh landscape. These lowland areas have been used for arable cultivation in recent years, although problems with irrigation have meant that much of the land is being allowed to revert to its natural vegetation and pastoral usage.

▲ **Rows of pine** trees edge this valley near Almaty. The snow-covered slopes in the background are used for skiing.

145

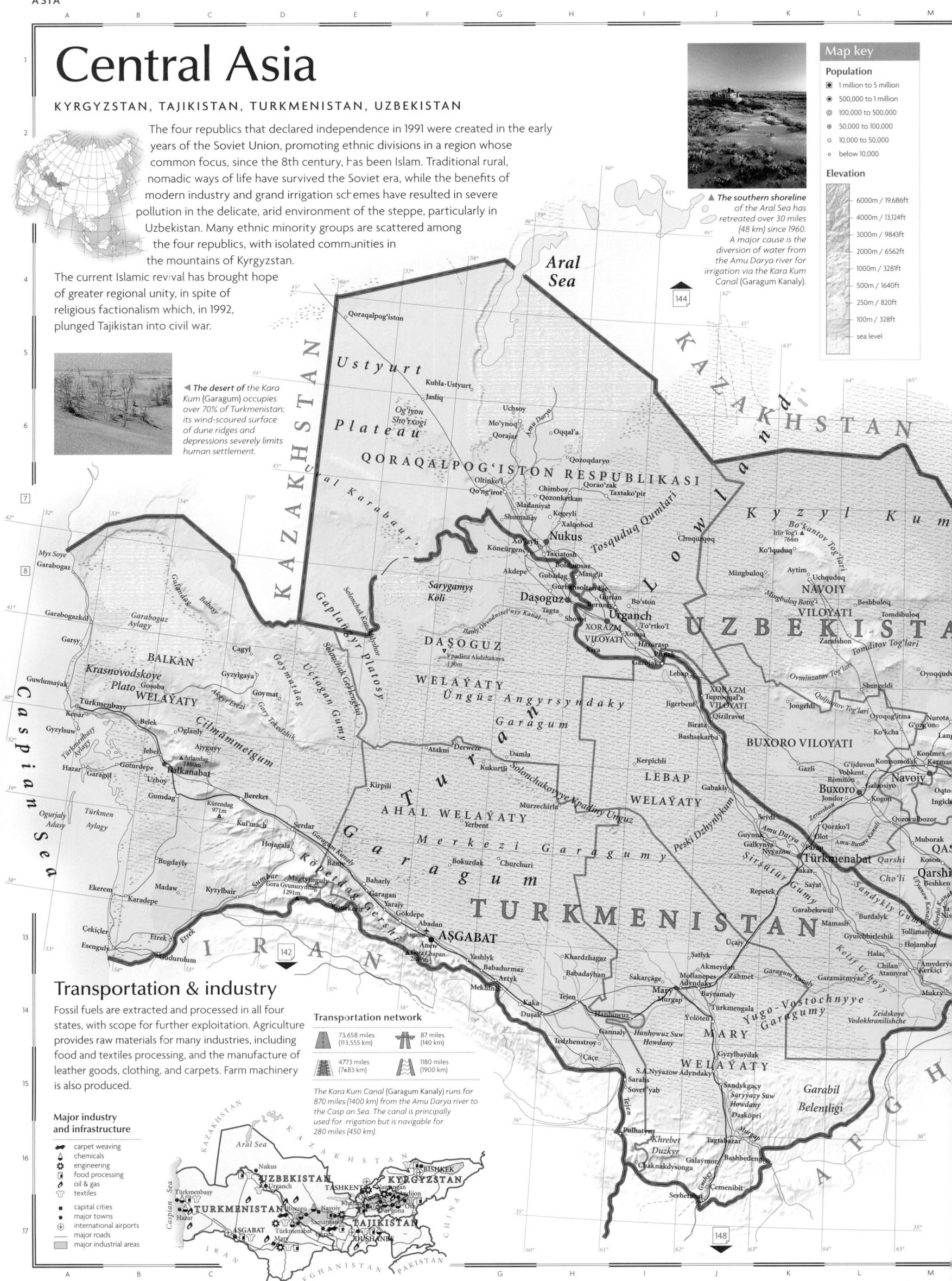

# Central Asia

## KYRGYZSTAN, TAJIKISTAN, TURKMENISTAN, UZBEKISTAN

The four republics that declared independence in 1991 were created in the early years of the Soviet Union, promoting ethnic divisions in a region whose common focus, since the 8th century, has been Islam. Traditional rural, nomadic ways of life have survived the Soviet era, while the benefits of modern industry and grand irrigation schemes have resulted in severe pollution in the delicate, arid environment of the steppe, particularly in Uzbekistan. Many ethnic minority groups are scattered among the four republics, with isolated communities in the mountains of Kyrgyzstan.

The current Islamic revival has brought hope of greater regional unity, in spite of religious factionalism which, in 1992, plunged Tajikistan into civil war.

◀ **The desert of** the Kara Kum (Garagum) occupies over 70% of Turkmenistan; its wind-scoured surface of dune ridges and depressions severely limits human settlement.

▲ **The southern shoreline** of the Aral Sea has retreated over 30 miles (48 km) since 1960. A major cause is the diversion of water from the Amu Darya river for irrigation via the Kara Kum Canal (Garagum Kanaly).

### Map key

**Population**
- ⊡ 1 million to 5 million
- ◉ 500,000 to 1 million
- ◎ 100,000 to 500,000
- ⊙ 50,000 to 100,000
- ○ 10,000 to 50,000
- ∘ below 10,000

**Elevation**
- 6000m / 19,686ft
- 4000m / 13,124ft
- 3000m / 9843ft
- 2000m / 6562ft
- 1000m / 3281ft
- 500m / 1640ft
- 250m / 820ft
- 100m / 328ft
- sea level

## Transportation & industry

Fossil fuels are extracted and processed in all four states, with scope for further exploitation. Agriculture provides raw materials for many industries, including food and textiles processing, and the manufacture of leather goods, clothing, and carpets. Farm machinery is also produced.

**Transportation network**

| | |
|---|---|
| 73,658 miles (113,555 km) | 87 miles (140 km) |
| 4773 miles (7683 km) | 1180 miles (1900 km) |

The Kara Kum Canal (Garagum Kanaly) runs for 870 miles (1400 km) from the Amu Darya river to the Caspian Sea. The canal is principally used for irrigation but is navigable for 280 miles (450 km).

### Major industry and infrastructure

- carpet weaving
- chemicals
- engineering
- food processing
- oil & gas
- textiles
- ● capital cities
- • major towns
- ⊕ international airports
- major roads
- major industrial areas

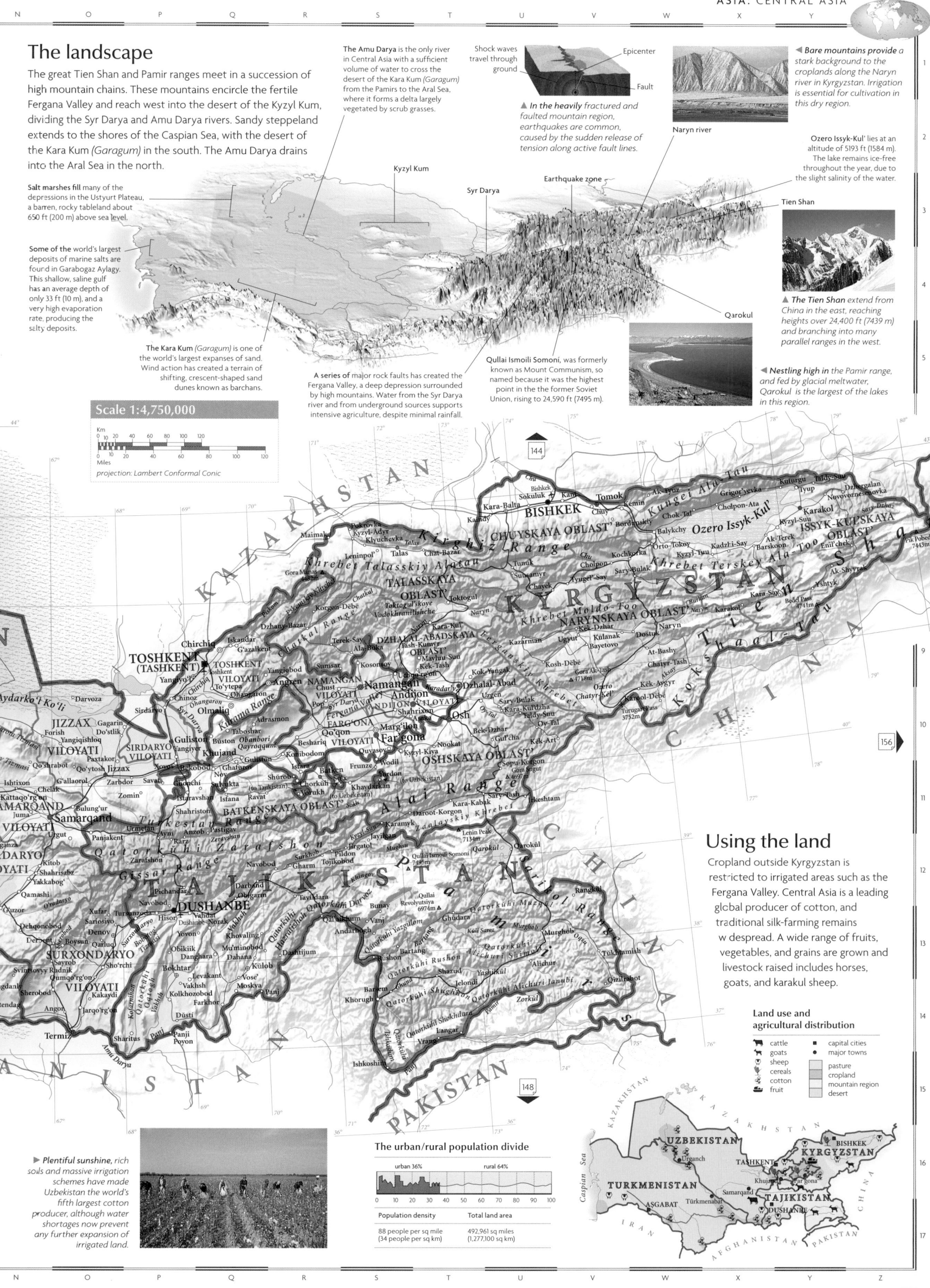

# The landscape

The great Tien Shan and Pamir ranges meet in a succession of high mountain chains. These mountains encircle the fertile Fergana Valley and reach west into the desert of the Kyzyl Kum, dividing the Syr Darya and Amu Darya rivers. Sandy steppeland extends to the shores of the Caspian Sea, with the desert of the Kara Kum (Garagum) in the south. The Amu Darya drains into the Aral Sea in the north.

Salt marshes fill many of the depressions in the Ustyurt Plateau, a barren, rocky tableland about 650 ft (200 m) above sea level.

Some of the world's largest deposits of marine salts are found in Garabogaz Aylagy. This shallow, saline gulf has an average depth of only 33 ft (10 m), and a very high evaporation rate, producing the salty deposits.

The Kara Kum (Garagum) is one of the world's largest expanses of sand. Wind action has created a terrain of shifting, crescent-shaped sand dunes known as barchans.

The Amu Darya is the only river in Central Asia with a sufficient volume of water to cross the desert of the Kara Kum (Garagum) from the Pamirs to the Aral Sea, where it forms a delta largely vegetated by scrub grasses.

▲ In the heavily fractured and faulted mountain region, earthquakes are common, caused by the sudden release of tension along active fault lines.

A series of major rock faults has created the Fergana Valley, a deep depression surrounded by high mountains. Water from the Syr Darya river and from underground sources supports intensive agriculture, despite minimal rainfall.

Qullai Ismoili Somoni, was formerly known as Mount Communism, so named because it was the highest point in the the former Soviet Union, rising to 24,590 ft (7495 m).

◀ Bare mountains provide a stark background to the croplands along the Naryn river in Kyrgyzstan. Irrigation is essential for cultivation in this dry region.

Ozero Issyk-Kul' lies at an altitude of 5193 ft (1584 m). The lake remains ice-free throughout the year, due to the slight salinity of the water.

▲ The Tien Shan extend from China in the east, reaching heights over 24,400 ft (7439 m) and branching into many parallel ranges in the west.

◀ Nestling high in the Pamir range, and fed by glacial meltwater, Qarokul is the largest of the lakes in this region.

Scale 1:4,750,000

projection: Lambert Conformal Conic

# Using the land

Cropland outside Kyrgyzstan is restricted to irrigated areas such as the Fergana Valley. Central Asia is a leading global producer of cotton, and traditional silk-farming remains widespread. A wide range of fruits, vegetables, and grains are grown and livestock raised includes horses, goats, and karakul sheep.

Land use and agricultural distribution

- cattle
- goats
- sheep
- cereals
- cotton
- fruit
- capital cities
- major towns
- pasture
- cropland
- mountain region
- desert

▶ Plentiful sunshine, rich soils and massive irrigation schemes have made Uzbekistan the world's fifth largest cotton producer, although water shortages now prevent any further expansion of irrigated land.

The urban/rural population divide

urban 36%    rural 64%

Population density
88 people per sq mile
(34 people per sq km)

Total land area
492,961 sq miles
(1,277,100 sq km)

A B C D E F G H I J K L M

# Afghanistan & Pakistan

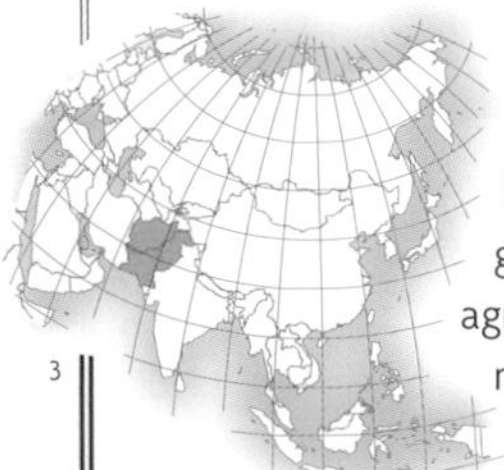

Pakistan was created by the partition of British India in 1947, becoming the western arm of a new Islamic state for Indian Muslims; the eastern sector, in Bengal, seceded to become the separate country of Bangladesh in 1971. Over half of Pakistan's 158 million people live in the Punjab, at the fertile head of the great Indus Basin. The river sustains a national economy based on irrigated agriculture, including cotton for the vital textiles industry. Afghanistan, a mountainous, landlocked country, with an ancient and independent culture, has been wracked by war since 1979. Factional strife escalated into an international conflict in late 2001, as US-led troops ousted the militant and fundamentally Islamist *taliban* regime as part of their "war on terror."

◀ *The town of* Bamyan lies high in the Hindu Kush west of Kabul. Between the 2nd and 5th centuries two huge statues of Buddha were carved into the nearby rock, the largest of which stood 125 ft (38 m) high. The statues were destroyed by the taliban regime in March 2001.

## Transportation & industry

Pakistan is highly dependent on the cotton textiles industry, although diversified manufacture is expanding around cities such as Karachi and Lahore. Afghanistan's limited industry is based mainly on the processing of agricultural raw materials and includes traditional crafts such as carpet weaving.

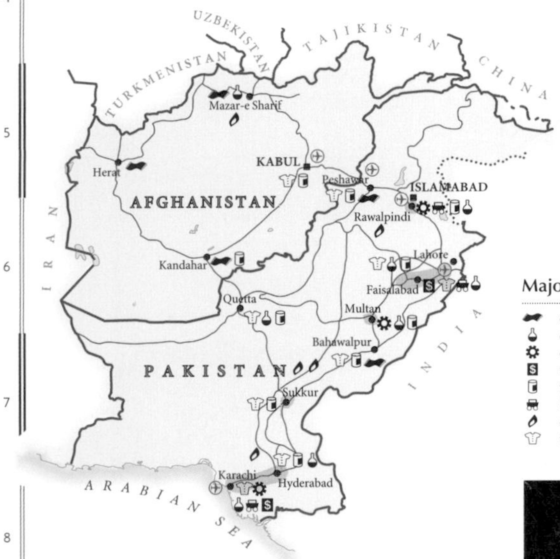

### Major industry and infrastructure

- carpet weaving
- chemicals
- engineering
- finance
- food processing
- iron & steel
- oil & gas
- textiles
- ■ capital cities
- ■ major towns
- ⊕ international airports
- — major roads
- major industrial areas

### Transportation network

| | |
|---|---|
| 96,154 miles (154,763 km) | |
| 211 miles (340 km) | |
| 4852 miles (7814 km) | |
| 745 miles (1200 km) | |

▶ *The Karakoram Highway* is one of the highest major roads in the world. It took over 24,000 workers almost 20 years to complete.

The Karakoram Highway was completed after 20 years of construction in 1978. It breaches the Himalayan mountain barrier providing a commercial motor route linking lowland Pakistan and China.

## The landscape

Afghanistan's topography is dominated by the mountains of the Hindu Kush, which spread south and west into numerous mountain spurs. The dry plateau of southwestern Afghanistan extends into Pakistan and the hills which overlook the great Indus Basin. In northern Pakistan the Hindu Kush, Himalayan, and Karakoram ranges meet to form one of the world's highest mountain regions.

◀ *The Hunza river* rises in the northern Karakoram Range, running for 120 miles (193 km) before joining the Gilgit river.

Hunza river

▶ *The arid Hindu Kush* makes much of Afghanistan uninhabitable, with over 50% of the land lying above 6500 ft (2000 m).

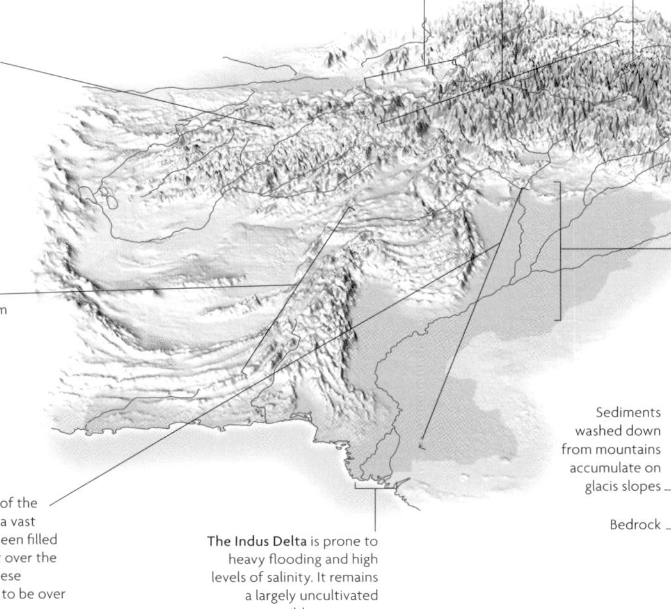

The plains and foothills which extend from the northern slopes of the Hindu Kush are part of the great grassy steppe lands of Central Asia.

Hindu Kush

K2 (Mount Godwin Austen), in the Karakoram Range, is the second highest mountain in the world, at an altitude of 28,251 ft (8611 m).

Some of the largest glaciers outside the polar regions are found in the Karakoram Range, including Siachen Glacier *(Siachen Muztagh),* which is 40 miles (72 km) long.

Himalayas

Frequent earthquakes mean that mountain-building processes are continuing in this region, as the Indo-Australian Plate drifts northward, colliding with the Eurasian Plate.

Mountain chains running southwest from the Hindu Kush into Pakistan form a barrier to the humid winds which blow from the Indian Ocean, creating arid conditions across southern Afghanistan.

The Indus Basin is part of the Indus-Ganges lowland, a vast depression which has been filled with layers of sediment over the last 50 million years. These deposits are estimated to be over 16,400 ft (5000 m) deep.

The Indus Delta is prone to heavy flooding and high levels of salinity. It remains a largely uncultivated wilderness area.

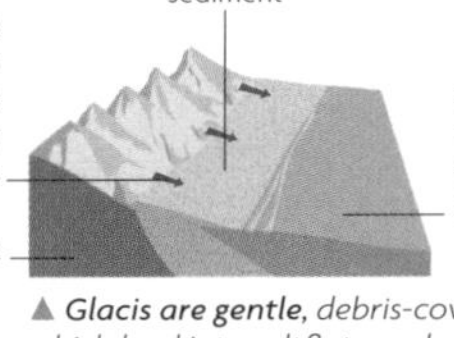

The soils of the Punjab plain are nourished by enormous quantities of sediment, carried from the Himalayas by the five tributaries of the Indus river.

Glacis covered by coarse-grained sediment

Sediments washed down from mountains accumulate on glacis slopes

Bedrock

Fine sediments deposited on salt flats are removed by wind erosion.

▲ *Glacis are gentle,* debris-covered slopes which lead into saltflats or deserts. They typically occur at the base of mountains in arid regions such as Afghanistan.

### Scale 1:5,000,000

Km
0 10 20 40 60 80 100 120 140 160

Miles
0 20 40 60 80 100 120 140 160

projection: Lambert Conformal Conic

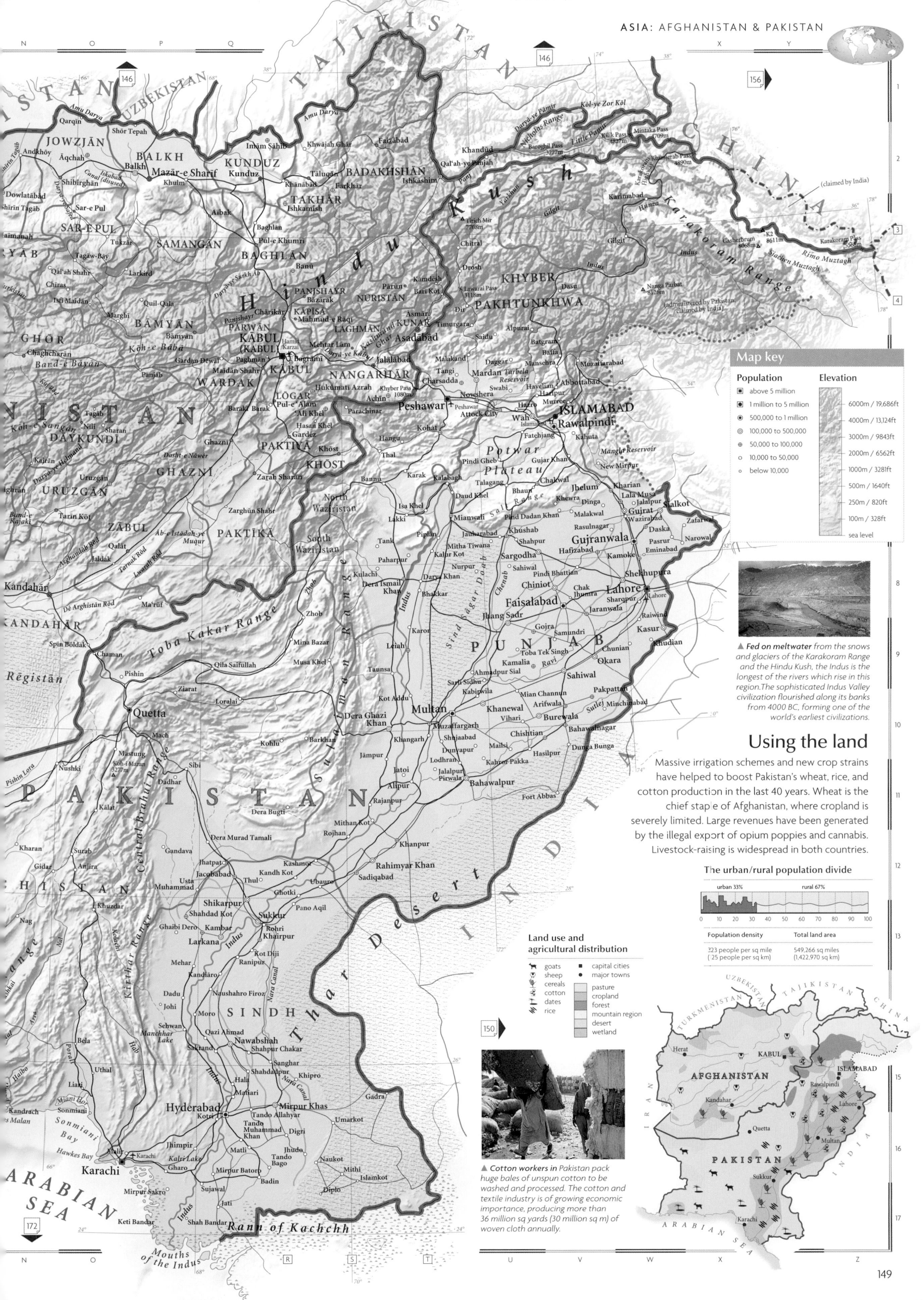

▲ Fed on meltwater from the snows and glaciers of the Karakoram Range and the Hindu Kush, the Indus is the longest of the rivers which rise in this region. The sophisticated Indus Valley civilization flourished along its banks from 4000 BC, forming one of the world's earliest civilizations.

## Using the land

Massive irrigation schemes and new crop strains have helped to boost Pakistan's wheat, rice, and cotton production in the last 40 years. Wheat is the chief staple of Afghanistan, where cropland is severely limited. Large revenues have been generated by the illegal export of opium poppies and cannabis. Livestock-raising is widespread in both countries.

### The urban/rural population divide

urban 33%    rural 67%

| Population density | Total land area |
|---|---|
| 323 people per sq mile (125 people per sq km) | 549,266 sq miles (1,422,970 sq km) |

### Land use and agricultural distribution

- goats
- sheep
- cereals
- cotton
- dates
- rice
- ■ capital cities
- • major towns
- pasture
- cropland
- forest
- mountain region
- desert
- wetland

▲ Cotton workers in Pakistan pack huge bales of unspun cotton to be washed and processed. The cotton and textile industry is of growing economic importance, producing more than 36 million sq yards (30 million sq m) of woven cloth annually.

### Map key

**Population**
- ▣ above 5 million
- ◉ 1 million to 5 million
- ◉ 500,000 to 1 million
- ⊕ 100,000 to 500,000
- ⊕ 50,000 to 100,000
- ○ 10,000 to 50,000
- ○ below 10,000

**Elevation**
- 6000m / 19,686ft
- 4000m / 13,124ft
- 3000m / 9843ft
- 2000m / 6562ft
- 1000m / 3281ft
- 500m / 1640ft
- 250m / 820ft
- 100m / 328ft
- sea level

# South Asia

**BANGLADESH, BHUTAN, INDIA, MALDIVES, NEPAL, PAKISTAN, SRI LANKA**

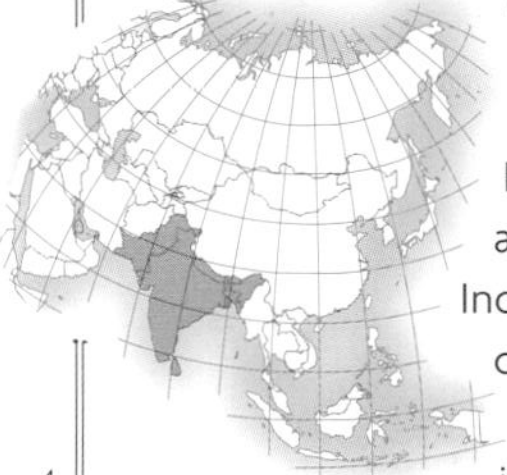

More than one-fifth of the world's population lives in the south Asian subcontinent. Great cultural diversity has come from a long succession of foreign invaders, including Hindu Aryans, Islamic Moguls, and the British, whose empire incorporated the princely states of the Maharajas and extended to the borders of Nepal and Bhutan in the Himalayas. Independent since 1947, India is the world's largest democracy, and at the current rate of growth, may overtake China as the world's most populous country during the 21st century. There are points of tension in the region over claims for independence by the Sikhs in the Indian Punjab and the long-standing dispute with Pakistan over Jammu and Kashmir in the north.

## The landscape

South Asia is effectively isolated from the rest of Asia by desert along the western flank of Pakistan, and a continuous wall of mountains, dominated by the Himalayas, to the north and east. The great basins of the Indus and Ganges separate this mountain fringe from the rolling plateau of the Indian peninsula, which is bordered by a line of coastal hills, the Eastern and Western Ghats.

**The Himalayas are** the highest and most extensive mountain system in the world. They were formed when the Indo-Australian Plate collided with the Eurasian Plate about 40 million years ago, thrusting up huge masses of land and creating a "ripple" effect, which formed lesser mountain ranges in Tibet and Southeast Asia. Mount Everest is the world's tallest mountain at 29,029 ft (8848 m).

**Almost all of Bangladesh** lies in the immense delta formed by the Ganges and the Brahmaputra which merge and flow out into the Bay of Bengal.

▼ *The Indus valley near Skardu in northern Pakistan has been partially infilled by great quantities of eroded sediment. Most of this is carried from the region's bare slopes by swollen rivers during the spring thaw and mass movement activity.*

*Ganges delta*

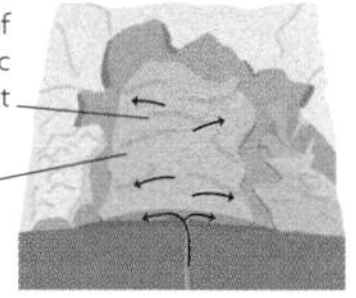

▲ *The Deccan plateau covers an area of more than 123,553 sq miles (320,000 sq km). It is formed of deep layers of volcanic basalt, reaching thicknesses of more than 9800 ft (3000 m) toward the coast. Distinctive stepped valleys cut in the basalt plateau by rivers are known as "traps."*

Deccan plateau

Layers of volcanic basalt

Stepped valleys or 'traps'

Eastern Ghats

**Coastal deposition has formed** many typical features along the western coast of Sri Lanka. These include spits and bars, sometimes enclosing lagoons.

**Trivandrum in southern India** normally receives the first of the monsoon rains, which are essential to south Asian agriculture and moderate the extreme summer heat. The monsoon then moves northward over a period of about two months.

**The Western Ghats are** formed by a fault scarp which runs unbroken for more than 930 miles (1500 km). They reach their highest point at the southern Cardamom Hills.

**The Indus river flows** more than 1970 miles (3180 km) from southwestern Tibet to its mouth on the Arabian Sea. It has an estimated catchment area of 450,000 sq miles (1,165,500 sq km).

**The coast of** western Pakistan is a staircase of folded rock strata caused by successive periods of rapid uplift.

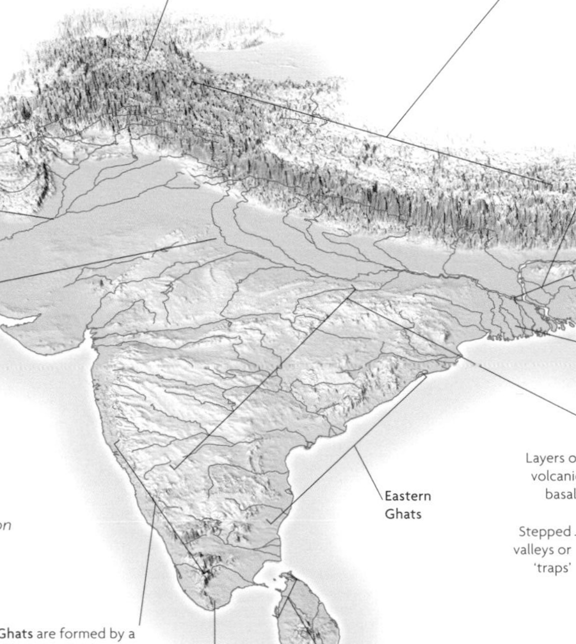

Bharatpur

▲ *Rivers flowing from the Himalayas into a broad depression in northern India have formed marshes around Bharatpur. They are now a sanctuary for numerous bird species.*

▼ *The towering Karakoram and Hindu Kush ranges, formed at the same time as the Himalayas, dominate Pakistan's northern borders. K2 on the border of northern Pakistan is the second highest mountain on Earth, at 28,251 ft (8611 m).*

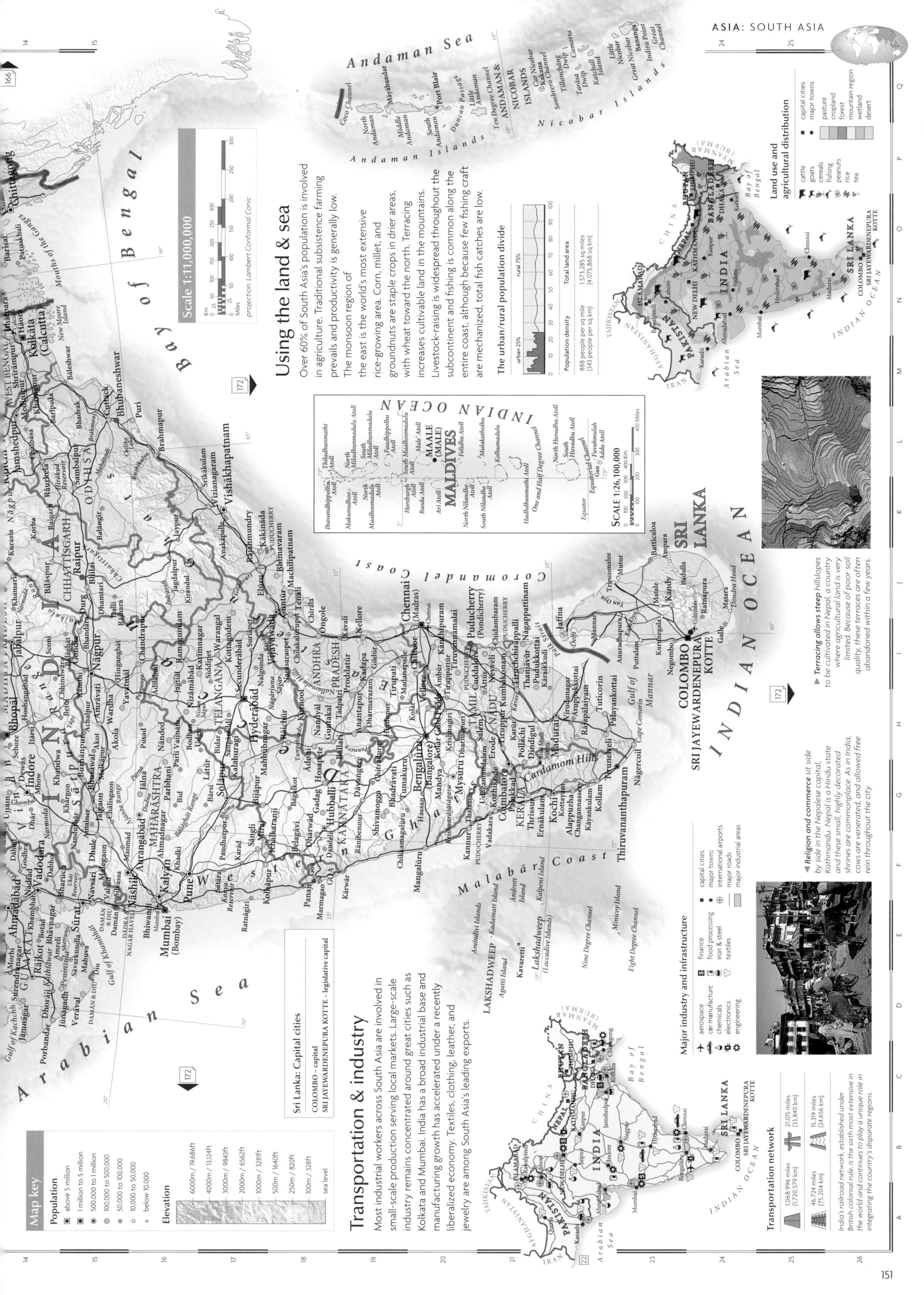

## Map Key

**Population**

- ■ above 5 million
- ■ 1 million to 5 million
- ◉ 500,000 to 1 million
- ◎ 100,000 to 500,000
- ⊙ 50,000 to 100,000
- ○ 10,000 to 50,000
- ○ below 10,000

**Elevation**

- 6000m / 19,686ft
- 4000m / 13,124ft
- 3000m / 9843ft
- 2000m / 6562ft
- 1000m / 328ft
- 500m / 1640ft
- 250m / 820ft
- 100m / 328ft
- sea level

**Scale 1:11,000,000**

projection: Lambert Conformal Conic

## Transportation & industry

Most industrial workers across South Asia are involved in small-scale production serving local markets. Large-scale industry remains concentrated around great cities such as Kolkata and Mumbai. India has a broad industrial base and manufacturing growth has accelerated under a recently liberalized economy. Textiles, clothing, leather, and jewelry are among South Asia's leading exports.

**Sri Lanka: Capital cities**

COLOMBO – capital
SRI JAYEWARDENEPURA KOTTE – legislative capital

## Major industry and infrastructure

- ✈ aerospace
- ⚙ car manufacture
- ⚗ chemicals
- ⌨ electronics
- ⚙ engineering
- $ finance
- 🍴 food processing
- ⚒ iron & steel
- ✂ textiles

- ● capital cities
- ■ major towns
- ✈ international airports
- major roads
- major industrial areas

## Transportation network

| | |
|---|---|
| 🚂 | 21,015 miles (33,840 km) |
| 🚂 | 15,339 miles (24,656 km) |
| 🚗 | 1,068,996 miles (1,720,579 km) |
| 🚗 | 46,724 miles (75,204 km) |

India's railroad network, established under British colonial rule is the sixth most extensive in the world and continues to play a unique role in integrating the country's disparate regions.

## Using the land & sea

Over 60% of South Asia's population is involved in agriculture. Traditional subsistence farming prevails and productivity is generally low. The monsoon region of the east is the world's most extensive rice-growing area. Corn, millet, and groundnuts are staple crops in drier areas, with wheat toward the north. Terracing increases cultivable land in the mountains. Livestock-raising is widespread throughout the subcontinent and fishing is common along the entire coast, although because few fishing craft are mechanized, total fish catches are low.

**The urban/rural population divide**

| Population density | Total land area |
|---|---|
| 888 people per sq mile (343 people per sq km) | 1,573,285 sq miles (4,075,868 sq km) |

rural 75%
urban 25%

## Land use and agricultural distribution

- capital cities
- major towns
- pasture
- cropland
- forest
- mountain region
- wetland
- desert

- cattle
- goats
- cereals
- peanuts
- rice
- tea
- fishing

▲ **Terracing allows steep hillslopes** to be cultivated in Nepal, a country where agricultural land is very limited. Because of poor soil quality, these terraces are often abandoned within a few years.

▼ **Religion and commerce** sit side by side in the Nepalese capital, Kathmandu. Nepal is a Hindu state and these small, highly decorated shrines are commonplace. As in India, cows are venerated, and allowed free rein throughout the city.

**MALDIVES**
MAALE (MALE)

SCALE 1:26,100,000

INDIAN OCEAN

Arabian Sea

Bay of Bengal

Andaman Sea

Andaman Islands

Nicobar Islands

ANDAMAN & NICOBAR ISLANDS

Laccadive Islands (Lakshadweep)

SRI LANKA

COLOMBO
SRI JAYEWARDENEPURA KOTTE

# Northern India & the Himalayan states

BANGLADESH, BHUTAN, NEPAL, Arunachal Pradesh, Assam, Bihar, Chandigarh, Delhi, Haryana, Himachal Pradesh, Jammu & Kashmir, Jharkhand, Manipur, Meghalaya, Mizoram, Nagaland, Punjab, Rajasthan, Sikkim, Tripura, Uttarakhand, Uttar Pradesh, West Bengal

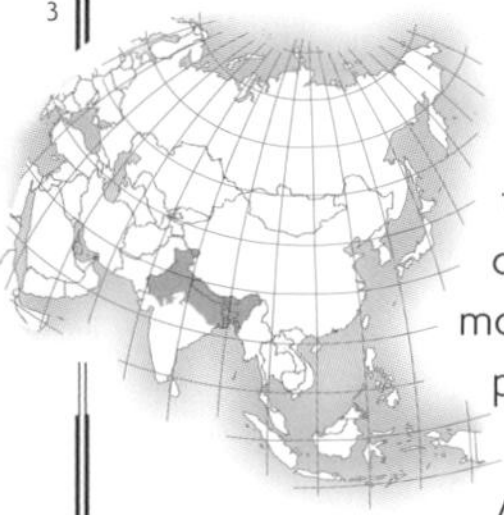

The Ganges and Brahmaputra river basins and the massive mountain barrier of the Himalayas define this region's landscape and have served to reinforce potent cultural and religious differences among its people. Hinduism pervades most aspects of national life and is a growing political force within India, a secular country which also encompasses the center of Sikhism at Amritsar and the world's largest Muslim minority. Nepal is a crowded mountain state, which faces severe ecological problems from deforestation, while the tiny Himalayan Buddhist kingdom of Bhutan is emerging from long-term isolation, to welcome selected visitors. The Muslim state of Bangladesh, formerly East Pakistan, is one of the world's most densely populated countries and one of the poorest, with more than 145 million people living largely on the massive Ganges/Brahmaputra delta. Many Bangladeshis live under threat of repeated, catastrophic floods.

◀ *The Golden Temple* in Amritsar, the most sacred shrine of the Sikh religion, was the scene of violent clashes between Sikh separatists and government forces in 1984.

## Scale 1:6,500,000

projection: Lambert Conformal Conic

## Map key

### Population
- ▣ 1 million to 5 million
- ◉ 500,000 to 1 million
- ◎ 100,000 to 500,000
- ◉ 50,000 to 100,000
- ◦ 10,000 to 50,000
- ∘ below 10,000

### Elevation
- 6000m / 19,686ft
- 4000m / 13,124ft
- 3000m / 9843ft
- 2000m / 6562ft
- 1000m / 3281ft
- 500m / 1640ft
- 250m / 820ft
- 100m / 328ft
- sea level

## Transportation & industry

Textiles, engineering, chemicals, and electronics are leading industries in north India. The plateau of Chota Nagpur provides ore for iron and steel production in the major industrial region northeast of Kolkata. Bangladesh processes jute and Nepal has a small manufacturing sector based on agricultural produce, while Bhutan's limited industry is concentrated in the southern lowland area.

### Major industry and infrastructure

- adventure tourism
- car manufacture
- chemicals
- coal
- electronics
- engineering
- finance
- food processing
- iron & steel
- jute processing
- oil
- tea processing
- textiles
- capital cities
- major towns
- international airports
- major roads
- major industrial areas

### Transportation network

*Over 60% of Bangladesh's internal trade is carried by boat. The country has a very disjointed land transportation network, with no bridges over the Brahmaputra and few road crossings on the Ganges river.*

N  O  P  Q  R  S  T  U  V  W  X  Y

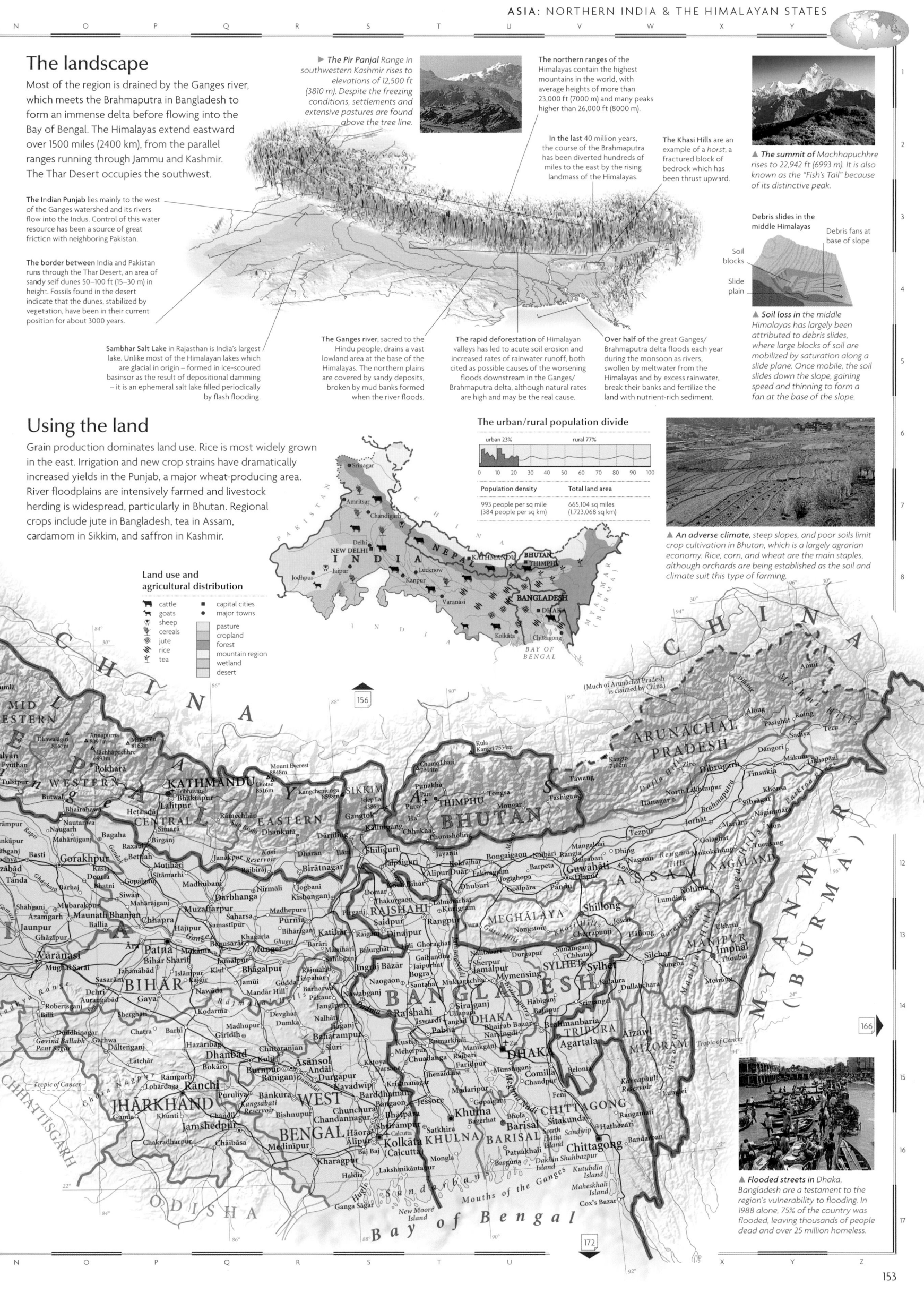

## The landscape

Most of the region is drained by the Ganges river, which meets the Brahmaputra in Bangladesh to form an immense delta before flowing into the Bay of Bengal. The Himalayas extend eastward over 1500 miles (2400 km), from the parallel ranges running through Jammu and Kashmir. The Thar Desert occupies the southwest.

**The Indian Punjab** lies mainly to the west of the Ganges watershed and its rivers flow into the Indus. Control of this water resource has been a source of great friction with neighboring Pakistan.

**The border between** India and Pakistan runs through the Thar Desert, an area of sandy seif dunes 50–100 ft (15–30 m) in height. Fossils found in the desert indicate that the dunes, stabilized by vegetation, have been in their current position for about 3000 years.

**Sambhar Salt Lake** in Rajasthan is India's largest lake. Unlike most of the Himalayan lakes which are glacial in origin – formed in ice-scoured basins or as the result of depositional damming – it is an ephemeral salt lake filled periodically by flash flooding.

▶ *The Pir Panjal* Range in southwestern Kashmir rises to elevations of 12,500 ft (3810 m). Despite the freezing conditions, settlements and extensive pastures are found above the tree line.

**The northern ranges** of the Himalayas contain the highest mountains in the world, with average heights of more than 23,000 ft (7000 m) and many peaks higher than 26,000 ft (8000 m).

**In the last** 40 million years, the course of the Brahmaputra has been diverted hundreds of miles to the east by the rising landmass of the Himalayas.

**The Khasi Hills** are an example of a *horst*, a fractured block of bedrock which has been thrust upward.

**The Ganges river**, sacred to the Hindu people, drains a vast lowland area at the base of the Himalayas. The northern plains are covered by sandy deposits, broken by mud banks formed when the river floods.

**The rapid deforestation** of Himalayan valleys has led to acute soil erosion and increased rates of rainwater runoff, both cited as possible causes of the worsening floods downstream in the Ganges/Brahmaputra delta, although natural rates are high and may be the real cause.

**Over half** of the great Ganges/Brahmaputra delta floods each year during the monsoon as rivers, swollen by meltwater from the Himalayas and by excess rainwater, break their banks and fertilize the land with nutrient-rich sediment.

▲ *The summit of* Machhapuchhre rises to 22,942 ft (6993 m). It is also known as the "Fish's Tail" because of its distinctive peak.

Debris slides in the middle Himalayas
Debris fans at base of slope
Soil blocks
Slide plain

▲ *Soil loss in* the middle Himalayas has largely been attributed to debris slides, where large blocks of soil are mobilized by saturation along a slide plane. Once mobile, the soil slides down the slope, gaining speed and thinning to form a fan at the base of the slope.

## Using the land

Grain production dominates land use. Rice is most widely grown in the east. Irrigation and new crop strains have dramatically increased yields in the Punjab, a major wheat-producing area. River floodplains are intensively farmed and livestock herding is widespread, particularly in Bhutan. Regional crops include jute in Bangladesh, tea in Assam, cardamom in Sikkim, and saffron in Kashmir.

### The urban/rural population divide

urban 23%          rural 77%

0  10  20  30  40  50  60  70  80  90  100

| Population density | Total land area |
|---|---|
| 993 people per sq mile (384 people per sq km) | 665,104 sq miles (1,723,068 sq km) |

▲ *An adverse climate*, steep slopes, and poor soils limit crop cultivation in Bhutan, which is a largely agrarian economy. Rice, corn, and wheat are the main staples, although orchards are being established as the soil and climate suit this type of farming.

### Land use and agricultural distribution

- cattle
- goats
- sheep
- cereals
- jute
- rice
- tea
- capital cities
- major towns
- pasture
- cropland
- forest
- mountain region
- wetland
- desert

▲ *Flooded streets in* Dhaka, Bangladesh are a testament to the region's vulnerability to flooding. In 1988 alone, 75% of the country was flooded, leaving thousands of people dead and over 25 million homeless.

# Southern India & Sri Lanka

SRI LANKA, Andhra Pradesh, Chhattisgarh, Dadra & Nagar Haveli, Daman & Diu, Goa, Gujarat, Karnataka, Kerala, Lakshadweep, Madhya Pradesh, Maharashtra, Odisha, Puducherry, Tamil Nadu, Telangana

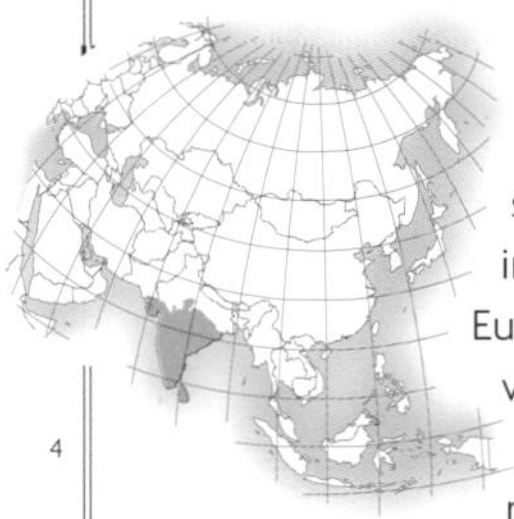

The unique and highly independent southern states reflect the diverse and decentralized nature of India, which has fourteen official languages. The southern half of the peninsula lay beyond the reach of early invaders from the north and retained the distinct and ancient culture of Dravidian peoples such as the Tamils, whose language is spoken in preference to Hindi throughout southern India. The interior plateau of southern India is less densely populated than the coastal lowlands, where the European colonial imprint is strongest. Urban and industrial growth is accelerating, but southern India's vast population remains predominantly rural. The island of Sri Lanka has two distinct cultural groups; the mainly Buddhist Sinhalese majority, and the Tamil minority whose struggle for a homeland in the northeast led to prolonged civil war.

## Using the land and sea

Rice is the main staple in the east, in Sri Lanka and along the humid Malabar Coast. Peanuts are grown on the Deccan plateau, with wheat, corn, and chickpeas, toward the north. Sri Lanka is a leading exporter of tea, coconuts and rubber. Cotton plantations supply local mills around Nagpur and Mumbai. Fishing supports many communities in Kerala and the Laccadive Islands.

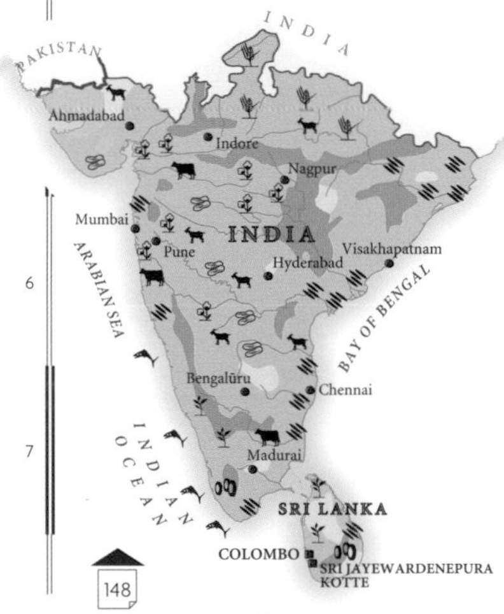

### Land use and agricultural distribution

cattle
goats
cotton
fishing
peanuts

rice
rubber
tea

capital cities
major towns

pasture
cropland
forest
wetland

## The landscape

The undulating Deccan plateau underlies most of southern India; it slopes gently down toward the east and is largely enclosed by the Ghats coastal hill ranges. The Western Ghats run continuously along the Arabian Sea coast, while the Eastern Ghats are interrupted by rivers which follow the slope of the plateau and flow across broad lowlands into the Bay of Bengal. The plateaus and basins of Sri Lanka's central highlands are surrounded by a broad plain.

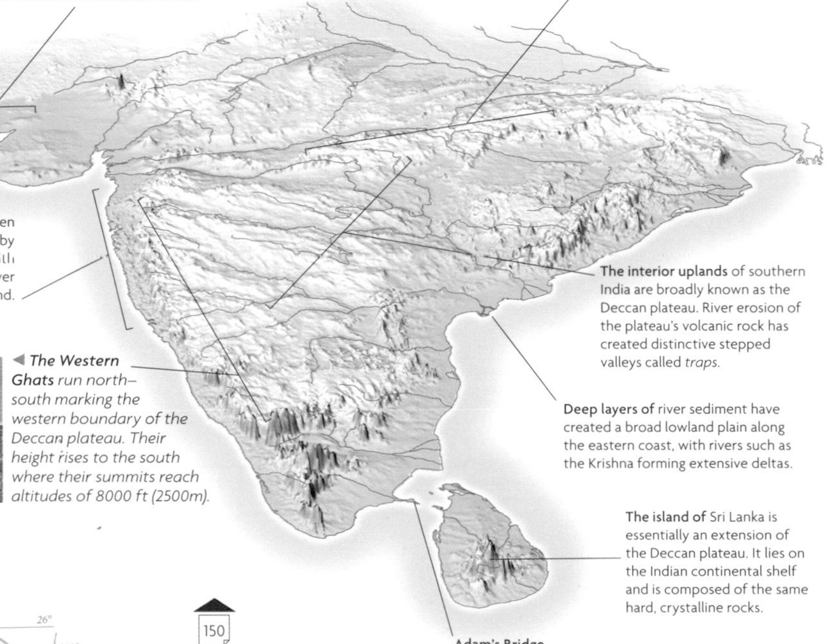

### The urban/rural population divide

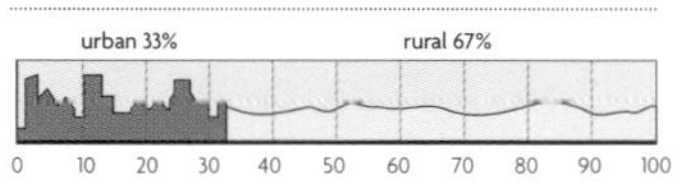

urban 33%    rural 67%

0  10  20  30  40  50  60  70  80  90  100

Population density       Total land area
730 people per sq mile   698,295 sq miles
(282 people per sq km)   (1,809,054 sq km)

**Along the northern** boundary of the Deccan plateau, old basement rocks are interspersed with younger sedimentary strata. This creates spectacular scarplands, cut by numerous waterfalls along the softer sedimentary strata.

**The interior uplands** of southern India are broadly known as the Deccan plateau. River erosion of the plateau's volcanic rock has created distinctive stepped valleys called traps.

**Deep layers** of river sediment have created a broad lowland plain along the eastern coast, with rivers such as the Krishna forming extensive deltas.

**The island of Sri Lanka** is essentially an extension of the Deccan plateau. It lies on the Indian continental shelf and is composed of the same hard, crystalline rocks.

**The Rann of Kachchh** tidal marshes encircle the low-lying Kachchh peninsula. For several months during the rainy season the water level of the marshes rises and Kachchh becomes an island.

**The Konkan coast**, which runs between Daman and Goa, is characterized by rocky lowlands, and bays with crescent-shaped beaches. Flooded river valleys known as *rias* extend inland.

▼ **The Western Ghats** run north–south marking the western boundary of the Deccan plateau. Their height rises to the south where their summits reach altitudes of 8000 ft (2500m).

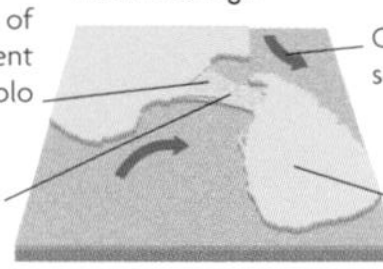

Ocean currents cause sediment build up

Sri Lanka

▲ **Adam's Bridge (Rama's Bridge)** is a chain of sandy shoals lying about 4 ft (1.2 m) under the sea between India and Sri Lanka. They once formed the world's longest tombolo, or land bridge, before the sea level began to rise several thousand years ago.

Adam's Bridge

Relict of ancient tombolo

Adam's Bridge

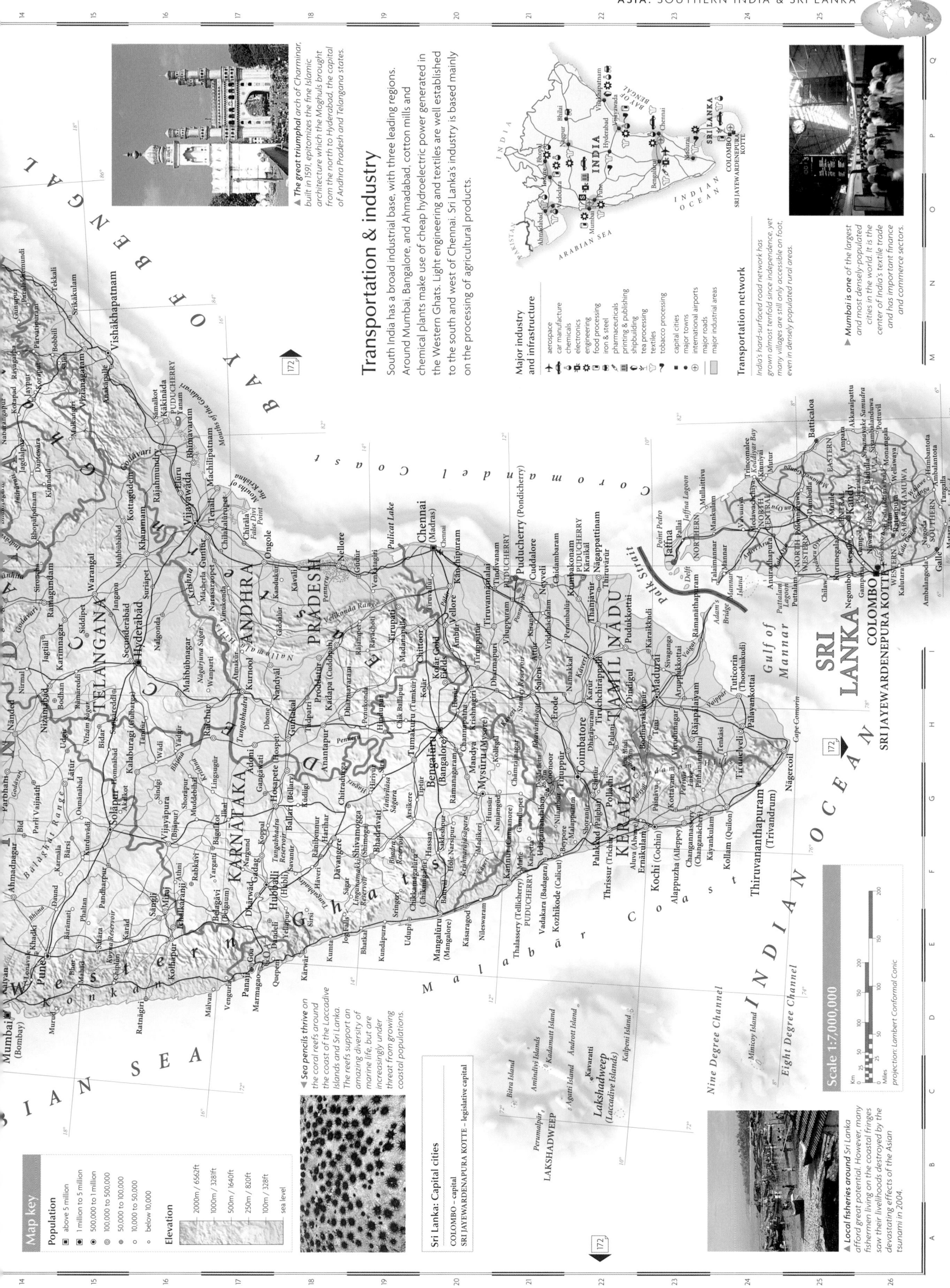

▲ The great triumphal arch of Charminar, built in 1591, epitomizes the fine Islamic architecture which the Moghuls brought from the north to Hyderabad, the capital of Andhra Pradesh and Telangana states.

## Transportation & industry

South India has a broad industrial base, with three leading regions. Around Mumbai, Bangalore, and Ahmadabad, cotton mills and chemical plants make use of cheap hydroelectric power generated in the Western Ghats. Light engineering and textiles are well established to the south and west of Chennai. Sri Lanka's industry is based mainly on the processing of agricultural products.

### Major industry and infrastructure

aerospace
car manufacture
chemicals
electronics
engineering
food processing
iron & steel
pharmaceuticals
printing & publishing
shipbuilding
tea processing
textiles
tobacco processing
capital cities
major towns
international airports
major roads
major industrial areas

### Transportation network

India's hard-surfaced road network has grown almost tenfold since independence, yet many villages are still only accessible on foot, even in densely populated rural areas.

▲ Mumbai is one of the largest and most densely-populated cities in the world. It is the center of India's textile trade and has important finance and commerce sectors.

▼ Sea pencils thrive on the coral reefs around the coast of the Laccadive Islands and Sri Lanka. The reefs support an amazing diversity of marine life, but are increasingly under threat from growing coastal populations.

### Sri Lanka: Capital cities

COLOMBO – capital
SRI JAYEWARDENAPURA KOTTE – legislative capital

▲ Local fisheries around Sri Lanka afford great potential. However, many fishermen living on the coastal fringes saw their livelihoods destroyed by the devastating effects of the Asian tsunami in 2004.

### Map key

**Population**
above 5 million
1 million to 5 million
500,000 to 1 million
100,000 to 500,000
50,000 to 100,000
10,000 to 50,000
below 10,000

**Elevation**
2000m / 6562ft
1000m / 3281ft
500m / 1640ft
250m / 820ft
100m / 328ft
sea level

Scale 1:7,000,000

Km
Miles
projection: Lambert Conformal Conic

# Mainland East Asia

## CHINA, MONGOLIA, NORTH KOREA, SOUTH KOREA, TAIWAN

China, the world's most populous nation, has an unbroken cultural history, longer than that of any other country, and is rapidly emerging as a leading world power. When Mao Zedong established Communist rule in 1949, China had become a backward feudal empire, stricken by civil war and over a century of European and Japanese incursions. The closed regime withstood the traumas of rapid industrialization, communal farming, and the brutal purges of the Cultural Revolution but, since the 1980s has introduced economic reforms, led by expanded foreign trade. China's population is heavily concentrated in the east and, despite accelerating urban growth, remains predominantly rural. One cultural group, the Han, make up over 90% of the people, while five "Autonomous Regions" have been established in the south and west for the main ethnic minorities.

## Transportation & industry

Large-scale industrial growth has always been a priority of the Communist government. Metals and machine production, chemicals, and engineering are among the leading industries, concentrated in the major cities of the east coast. Textiles and clothing manufacture, the main consumer goods sector, is relatively well dispersed, with a few significant centers such as Shanghai, Beijing, and Hong Kong.

### Major industry and infrastructure

- car manufacture
- chemicals
- electronics
- engineering
- finance
- food processing
- iron & steel
- shipbuilding
- textiles
- capital cities
- major towns
- international airports
- major roads
- major industrial areas

### Transportation network

| | |
|---|---|
| 829,790 miles (1,335,571 km) | 12,740 miles (20,506 km) |
| 43,976 miles (70,780 km) | 70,991 miles (114,262 km) |

Ever-increasing demand for rail transportation has led to major improvment and expansion of the network, notably the 690 mile ('100 km) link between Golmud and Lhasa opened in 2006.

◀ *Coal is China's* most abundant mineral resource. This mine at Fuxin in Liaoning province is used to provide coal for a nearby power station.

## The landscape

The East Asian landmass is arranged in three distinct levels, the highest of which is the Plateau of Tibet in the southwest. The arid uplands of northwestern China form a barren middle step. The main rivers flow eastward from these two platforms to the East China and South China sea coasts, across a broad region of alluvial lowlands and low hills.

◀ *Paektu-san, at 9023* ft (2750 m), is North Korea's highest peak; an extinct volcanic cone now filled by a crater lake.

**The loess plateau** of northern China is the world's greatest expanse of loess, a loose soil made up of wind-blown material. The plateau has been heavily eroded by tributaries of the Yellow River.

**The Gobi Desert** extends across the Nei Mongol Gaoyuan; a vast saucer-shaped upland surrounded by a rim of higher mountains.

**Shifting sand dunes** are found in the arid west of the northeast China Plain, while the eastern part of this great expanse is wet and swampy.

River-eroded fine soils
Thick blanket of loess

▲ *Because of its* very small grain-size, loess has been easily transported and deposited by winds which scour the plains, and in northern China, deposits of loess can be up to 3000 ft (1000 m) thick. Loess-based soils are very fertile, but clearing land for agriculture quickly destabilizes the soil and allows it to be eroded.

▲ *The Plateau of Tibet* occupies about a quarter of China's total area. The Yangtze, Mekong, Indus, and Brahmaputra rivers all originate in the south and east of the plateau.

Tarim Basin (*Tarim Pendi*)
Plateau of Tibet
Paektu-san
North China Plain
The Yangtze is China's longest river and the principal navigable waterway.
Sichuan Pendi

**The Himalayas extend** along the southwestern edge of the Plateau of Tibet, forming a continuous mountain barrier over 1500 miles (2500 km) long.

**Warm, humid conditions** have caused intensive erosion of south China's karst areas, producing spectacular jagged peaks and vast caves in the limestone.

◀ *Gansu province, through* which the ancient Silk Route passes on its way to the west, is characterized by extensive loess deposits which are terraced and used for crop cultivation.

◀ *Although it is* over 30 years since his death, the legacy of Chairman Mao Zedong, architect of the Great Proletariat Cultural Revolution, is still very much in evidence across China's landscape. In 1959 Mao launched a 20-year period of industrialization and socioeconomic realignment, rejecting western ideals and social codes.

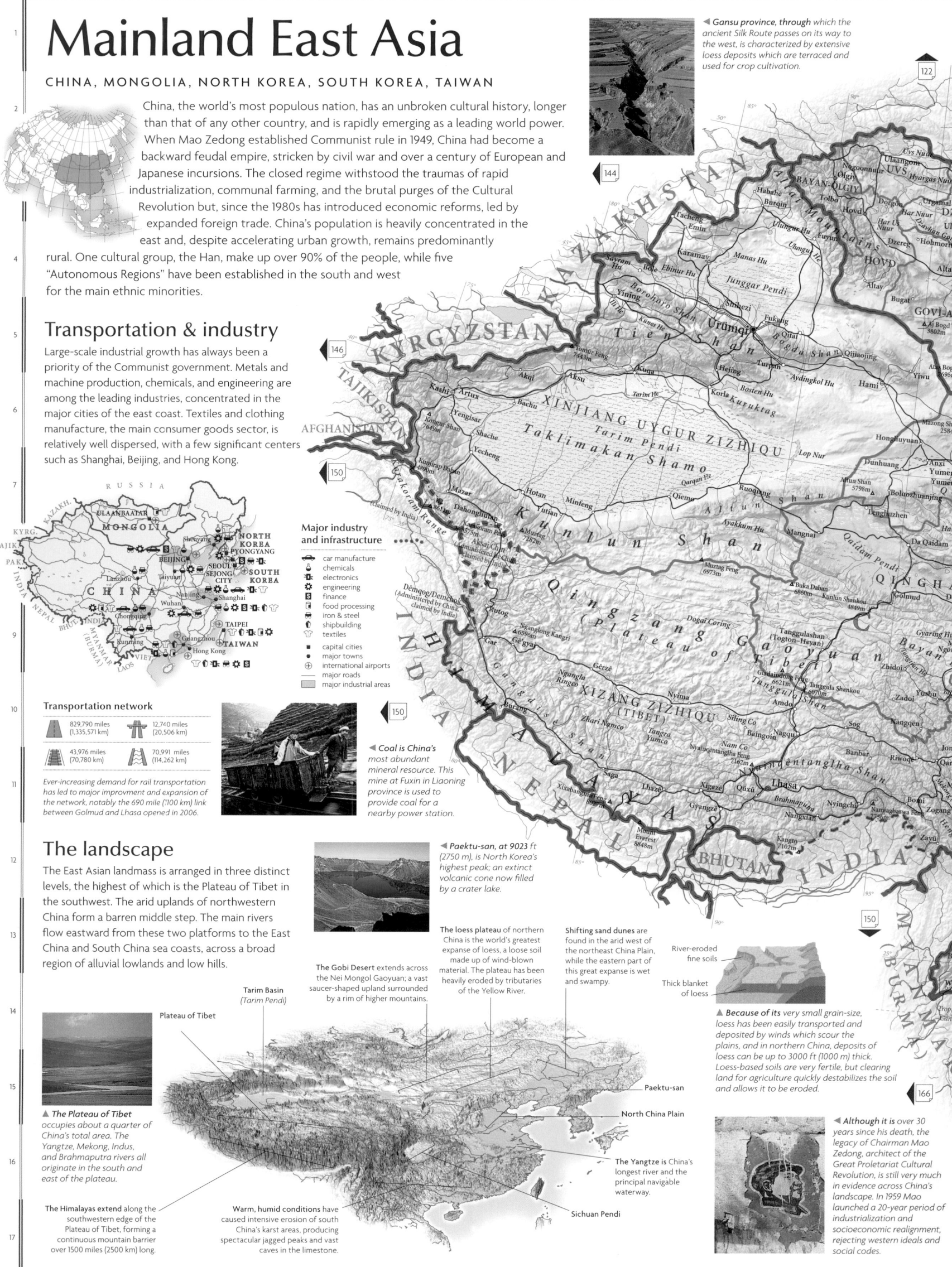

**Scale 1:14,000,000**

Km
0 25 50 100 150 200 250 300 350 400

Miles
0 25 50 100 150 200 250 300 350 400

projection: Lambert Conformal Conic

## Map key

### Population
- ▣ above 5 million
- ◉ 1 million to 5 million
- ◎ 500,000 to 1 million
- ⊕ 100,000 to 500,000
- ⊙ 50,000 to 100,000
- ○ 10,000 to 50,000
- ∘ below 10,000

### Elevation
- 6000m / 19,686ft
- 4000m / 13,124ft
- 3000m / 9843ft
- 2000m / 6562ft
- 1000m / 3281ft
- 500m / 1640ft
- 250m / 820ft
- 100m / 328ft
- sea level

## Using the land & sea

Around 90% of China is unsuitable for cultivation, being either climatically or topographically adverse, or lacking sufficiently fertile soils. Most of the west is used for nomadic herding, while farmland is concentrated in the eastern monsoon region, with rice grown in the tropical and subtropical south. Cereals and soybeans predominate as rainfall and temperatures decline further north.

### Land use and agricultural distribution
- pigs
- sheep
- corn
- cotton
- fishing
- fruit
- rice
- sugar cane
- soybeans
- ■ capital cities
- ● major towns
- pasture
- cropland
- forest
- mountain region

◀ **The Great Wall** of China remains one of the world's largest-ever construction projects, and is so vast that it is visible from space. Sections were added as late as 1640 and it runs for over 4000 miles (6400 km) from the Yellow Sea to Central Asia.

### The urban/rural population divide

urban 32%     rural 68%

0 10 20 30 40 50 60 70 80 90 100

| Population density | Total land area |
| --- | --- |
| 325 people per sq mile (125 people per sq km) | 4,288,672 sq miles (11,110,550 sq km) |

China and Taiwan claim all of each other's territory

# Western China

## Gansu, Ningxia, Qinghai, Tibet, Xinjiang

The plateaus and basins of China's dry, desolate western domain are sparsely populated and largely undeveloped, although they have rich mineral reserves; they also form a critical buffer zone for China, in a geographically important and culturally sensitive part of the Asian continent. Across most of the west, the Han Chinese are outnumbered by a range of cultural groups, including the Uygur, the largest group of the various seminomadic Muslim peoples from Central Asia. The remote, inhospitable Plateau of Tibet is the world's coldest and highest plateau. It has been occupied by the Chinese since 1950. Tibet is one of western China's five "Autonomous Regions," but its reclusive Buddhist culture has been systematically undermined by the Chinese government.

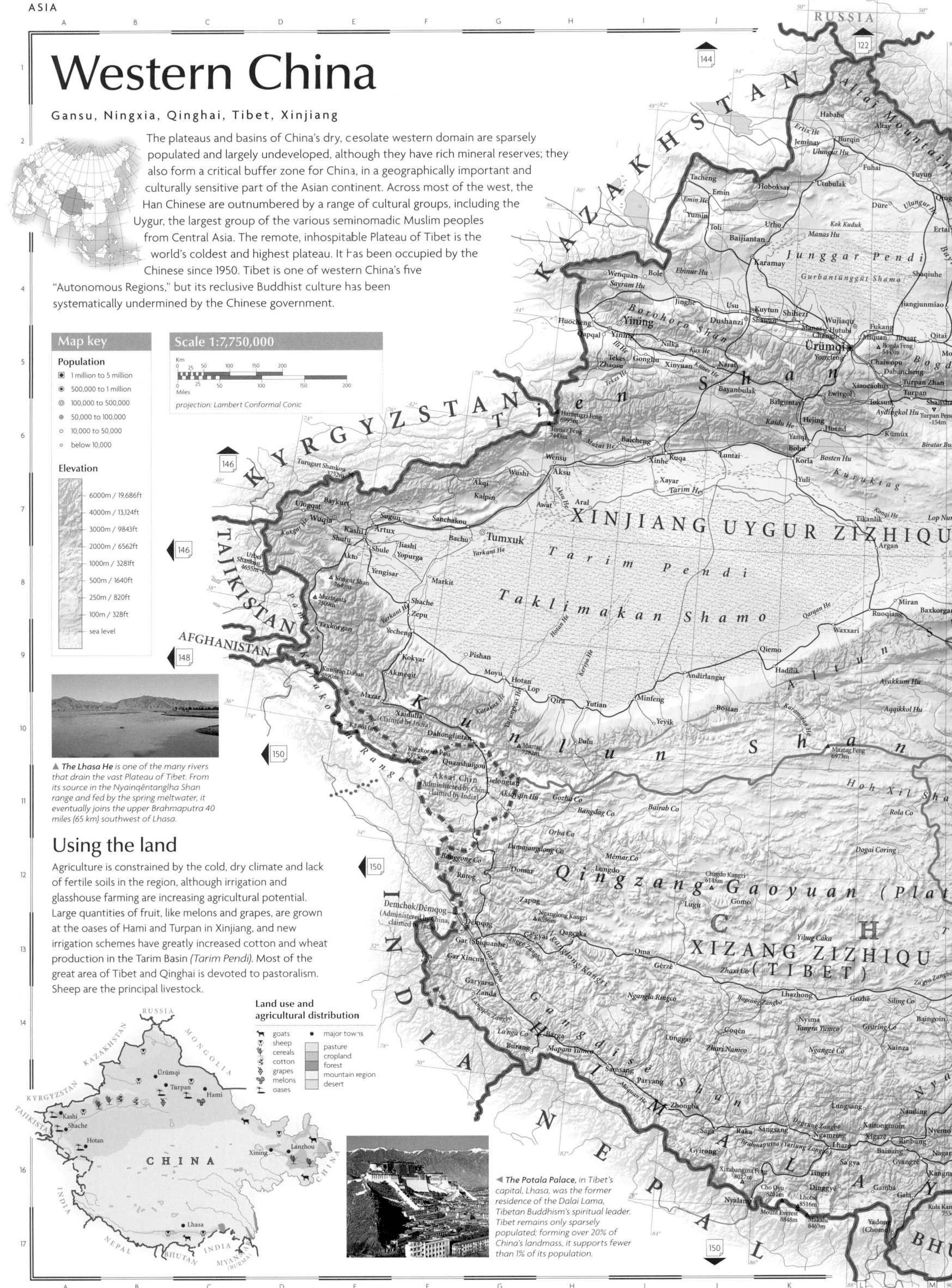

### Map key

**Population**
- ▣ 1 million to 5 million
- ◉ 500,000 to 1 million
- ◎ 100,000 to 500,000
- ⊕ 50,000 to 100,000
- ○ 10,000 to 50,000
- ∘ below 10,000

**Elevation**
- 6000m / 19,686ft
- 4000m / 13,124ft
- 3000m / 9843ft
- 2000m / 6562ft
- 1000m / 3281ft
- 500m / 1640ft
- 250m / 820ft
- 100m / 328ft
- sea level

Scale 1:7,750,000

projection: Lambert Conformal Conic

▲ **The Lhasa He** is one of the many rivers that drain the vast Plateau of Tibet. From its source in the Nyainqêntanglha Shan range and fed by the spring meltwater, it eventually joins the upper Brahmaputra 40 miles (65 km) southwest of Lhasa.

## Using the land

Agriculture is constrained by the cold, dry climate and lack of fertile soils in the region, although irrigation and glasshouse farming are increasing agricultural potential. Large quantities of fruit, like melons and grapes, are grown at the oases of Hami and Turpan in Xinjiang, and new irrigation schemes have greatly increased cotton and wheat production in the Tarim Basin (Tarim Pendi). Most of the great area of Tibet and Qinghai is devoted to pastoralism. Sheep are the principal livestock.

### Land use and agricultural distribution

- 🐐 goats
- 🐑 sheep
- 🌾 cereals
- ❀ cotton
- 🍇 grapes
- 🌿 melons
- ✿ oases
- ● major towns
- pasture
- cropland
- forest
- mountain region
- desert

◀ **The Potala Palace**, in Tibet's capital, Lhasa, was the former residence of the Dalai Lama, Tibetan Buddhism's spiritual leader. Tibet remains only sparsely populated; forming over 20% of China's landmass, it supports fewer than 1% of its population.

# The landscape

The Himalayas mark the southwestern edge of the Plateau of Tibet, an extreme mountain wilderness which occupies nearly a quarter of China's total area. A large structural depression, the Qaidam Pendi, lies at its northeastern edge. The Kunlun mountain chain isolates the plateau from the desert to the north, where the Tien Shan range forms a spur between the Tarim Basin (Tarim Pendi) and Dzungarian Basin (Junggar Pendi).

**Dzungarian Basin** (Junggar Pendi)

**The Tien Shan** reach elevations of over 24,419 ft (7435 m) and have permanent ice fields, from which large glaciers extend.

▶ **The Bogda Shan,** an eastward arm of the Tien Shan range, rise high above the Turpan Depression (Turpan Pendi).

**The Turpan Depression** (Turpan Pendi) is the lowest and hottest place in China. Temperatures can exceed 117°F (47°C) around the lake of Aydingkol Hu, which lies 505 ft (154 m) below sea level.

**Northwestern China is** largely a region of internal drainage. The Tarim He flows only as far as Lop Nur, where its water is lost by evapotranspiration from the lake and land surface.

**A vast glacial** lake filled much of the Tarim Basin (Tarim Pendi) during the last Ice Age. This area is now occupied by the Takla Makan Desert (Taklimakan Shamo). A remnant of the lake, Lop Nur, forms the eastern margin, where it is fed by the Tarim He.

◀ **The terrain of** the Plateau of Tibet consists of mountain peaks and open plateaus, dotted with brackish lakes. These are probably remnants of the Tethys Sea, which covered the area before it was uplifted following the collision of the Indo-Australian and Eurasian plates.

**Mount Everest is** the world's highest peak, at 29,029 ft (8848 m). The summit marks the border between China and Nepal.

**Sand dunes cover** western parts of the the basin of Qaidam Pendi. Strong winds frequently carry the sands east, threatening the agricultural areas around the lake of Qinghai Hu.

**Tarim Basin** (Tarim Pendi)

Barchan sand dunes in Takla Makan Desert (Taklimakan Shamo)

Oases at edge of basin

Lop Nur

▲ **The Tarim Basin** (Tarim Pendi) has no permanent rivers. Rainfall from the surrounding Plateau of Tibet and Tien Shan ranges drains into the basin's sand and gravel floor.

▲ **From its source,** high in eastern Qinghai, the Yellow River starts on a 3395 mile (5464 km) journey to the Yellow Sea.

# Transportation & industry

Oil extraction at Yumen and in the Dzungarian and Qaidam basins has led to the growth of the petrochemical industry and a range of heavy manufacturing plants in the cities of Lanzhou and Urumqi. Tibet, and most of Xinjiang, have little industry beyond traditional handicrafts, especially textiles at Hotan and Kashi, located along the ancient Silk Route. Nuclear and space-research testing are carried out at Lop Nur in Xinjiang.

## Transportation network

The construction of roads connecting Lhasa in Tibet with Sichuan, Qinghai, and Xinjiang was achieved in the 1950s, in spite of the extreme physical conditions of the Plateau of Tibet.

## Major industry and infrastructure

- agribusiness
- chemicals
- coal
- engineering
- food processing
- iron & steel
- nuclear testing
- oil
- textiles
- major towns
- major roads
- major industrial areas

# Eastern China

TAIWAN, Anhui, Beijing, Chongqing, Fujian, Guangdong, Guangxi, Guizhou, Hainan, Hebei, Henan, Hubei, Hunan, Jiangsu, Jiangxi, Shaanxi, Shandong, Shanghai, Shanxi, Sichuan, Tianjin, Yunnan, Zhejiang

The east is China's heartland. Massive industrial development since 1949 has transformed much of the densely populated rural landscape, in a region still prone to flooding and drought. Over 30 cities have populations of over a million, including the giant metropolis of Shanghai and the capital Beijing, which has been China's cultural and political center since the 13th century. The ethnically diverse southwest and the oil-rich interior provinces of Sichuan and Shaanxi have largely missed out on the remarkable economic growth occurring in designated free-trade areas along the coasts of the South and East China seas. The republic of Taiwan was established in 1949 by Chinese nationalists ousted from the mainland by the victorious Communist forces. Taiwan now has one of the strongest economies in the world but its sovereignty is not recognized by China. Hong Kong provides a major international trade link for China; a 99-year "lease" period of British control was concluded in 1997.

## Using the land & sea

This is a region of intensive cultivation. Wheat, millet, sorghum, and cotton are the main crops of the Yellow River basin. South from Sichuan, rice becomes the principal crop, grown with wheat, corn, and cotton along the Yangtze river. Tea is produced in the hills and sugar cane along the coast of the southeast, where flat land is limited. Pigs and poultry are raised in great numbers.

▲ North of the Qin Ling range in Shaanxi province, is an agriculturally fertile region covered with fine, wind-blown deposits and known as the loess plateau. The loose sediments are vulnerable to water erosion.

Land use and agricultural distribution

- cattle
- pigs
- cereals
- corn
- cotton
- fishing
- peanuts
- rice
- sugar cane
- tea
- capital cities
- major towns
- pasture
- cropland
- forest
- mountain region

▲ On the hills above the North China Plain, slopes are terraced to utilize the rich loess soils of the Taihang Shan range.

### Map key

**Population**
- above 5 million
- 1 million to 5 million
- 500,000 to 1 million
- 100,000 to 500,000
- 50,000 to 100,000
- 10,000 to 50,000
- below 10,000

**Elevation**
- 6000m / 19,686ft
- 4000m / 13,124ft
- 3000m / 9843ft
- 2000m / 6562ft
- 1000m / 3281ft
- 500m / 1640ft
- 250m / 820ft
- 100m / 328ft
- sea level

**Scale 1:8,500,000**

projection: Lambert Conformal Conic

◄ The former Portuguese territory of Macao, with its colonial architecture, bars and casinos, reverted to Chinese rule in 1999.

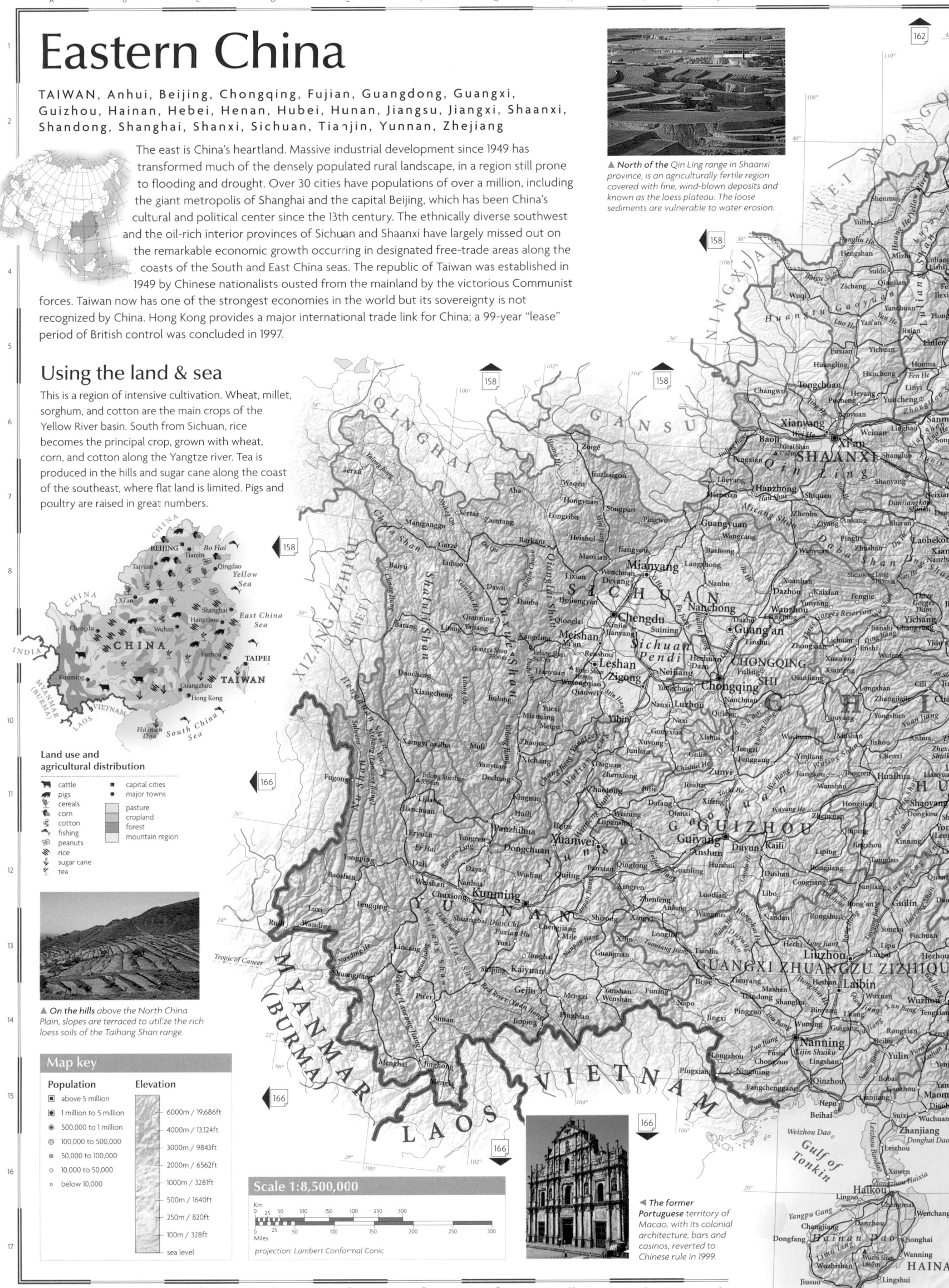

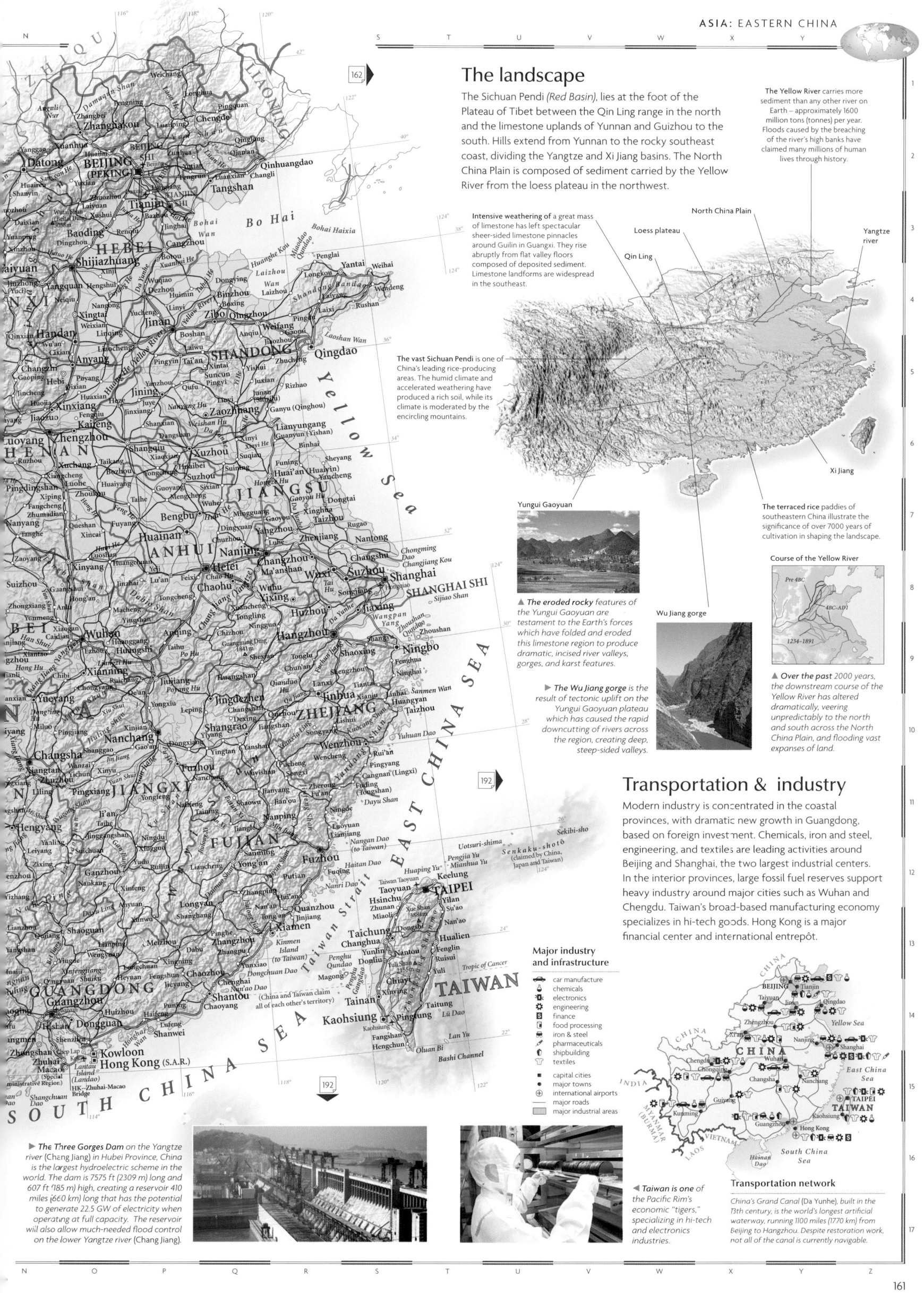

## The landscape

The Sichuan Pendi (*Red Basin*), lies at the foot of the Plateau of Tibet between the Qin Ling range in the north and the limestone uplands of Yunnan and Guizhou to the south. Hills extend from Yunnan to the rocky southeast coast, dividing the Yangtze and Xi Jiang basins. The North China Plain is composed of sediment carried by the Yellow River from the loess plateau in the northwest.

**The Yellow River** carries more sediment than any other river on Earth – approximately 1600 million tons (tonnes) per year. Floods caused by the breaching of the river's high banks have claimed many millions of human lives through history.

**Intensive weathering** of a great mass of limestone has left spectacular sheer-sided limestone pinnacles around Guilin in Guangxi. They rise abruptly from flat valley floors composed of deposited sediment. Limestone landforms are widespread in the southeast.

North China Plain

Loess plateau

Qin Ling

Yangtze river

**The vast Sichuan Pendi** is one of China's leading rice-producing areas. The humid climate and accelerated weathering have produced a rich soil, while its climate is moderated by the encircling mountains.

Xi Jiang

Yungui Gaoyuan

Wu Jiang gorge

**The terraced rice** paddies of southeastern China illustrate the significance of over 7000 years of cultivation in shaping the landscape.

▲ **The eroded rocky** features of the Yungui Gaoyuan are testament to the Earth's forces which have folded and eroded this limestone region to produce dramatic, incised river valleys, gorges, and karst features.

▶ **The Wu Jiang gorge** is the result of tectonic uplift on the Yungui Gaoyuan plateau which has caused the rapid downcutting of rivers across the region, creating deep, steep-sided valleys.

### Course of the Yellow River

Pre 4BC

4BC–AD1

1234–1891

▲ **Over the past** 2000 years, the downstream course of the Yellow River has altered dramatically, veering unpredictably to the north and south across the North China Plain, and flooding vast expanses of land.

## Transportation & industry

Modern industry is concentrated in the coastal provinces, with dramatic new growth in Guangdong, based on foreign investment. Chemicals, iron and steel, engineering, and textiles are leading activities around Beijing and Shanghai, the two largest industrial centers. In the interior provinces, large fossil fuel reserves support heavy industry around major cities such as Wuhan and Chengdu. Taiwan's broad-based manufacturing economy specializes in hi-tech goods. Hong Kong is a major financial center and international entrepôt.

**Major industry and infrastructure**

- car manufacture
- chemicals
- electronics
- engineering
- finance
- food processing
- iron & steel
- pharmaceuticals
- shipbuilding
- textiles

- ■ capital cities
- major towns
- ✈ international airports
- — major roads
- major industrial areas

▶ **The Three Gorges Dam** on the Yangtze river (Chang Jiang) in Hubei Province, China is the largest hydroelectric scheme in the world. The dam is 7575 ft (2309 m) long and 607 ft (185 m) high, creating a reservoir 410 miles (660 km) long that has the potential to generate 22.5 GW of electricity when operating at full capacity. The reservoir will also allow much-needed flood control on the lower Yangtze river (Chang Jiang).

◀ **Taiwan is one of** the Pacific Rim's economic "tigers," specializing in hi-tech and electronics industries.

### Transportation network

China's Grand Canal (Da Yunhe), built in the 13th century, is the world's longest artificial waterway, running 1100 miles (1770 km) from Beijing to Hangzhou. Despite restoration work, not all of the canal is currently navigable.

# Northeastern China, Mongolia & Korea

MONGOLIA, NORTH KOREA, SOUTH KOREA, Heilongjiang, Inner Mongolia, Jilin, Liaoning

This northerly region has been a domain of shifting borders and competing colonial powers for centuries. Mongolia was the heartland of Chinghiz Khan's vast Mongol empire in the 13th century, while northeastern China was home to the Manchus, China's last ruling dynasty (1644–1911). The mineral and forest wealth of the northeast helped make this China's principal region of heavy industry, although the outdated state factories now face decline. South Korea's state-led market economy has grown dramatically and Seoul is now one of the world's largest cities. The austere communist regime of North Korea has isolated itself from the expanding markets of the Pacific Rim and faces continuing economic stagnation.

▲ *The Eurasian steppe* stretches from the mouth of the Danube in Europe, to Mongolia. In Mongolia, nomadic people have lived in felt huts called yurts or gers, for thousands of years.

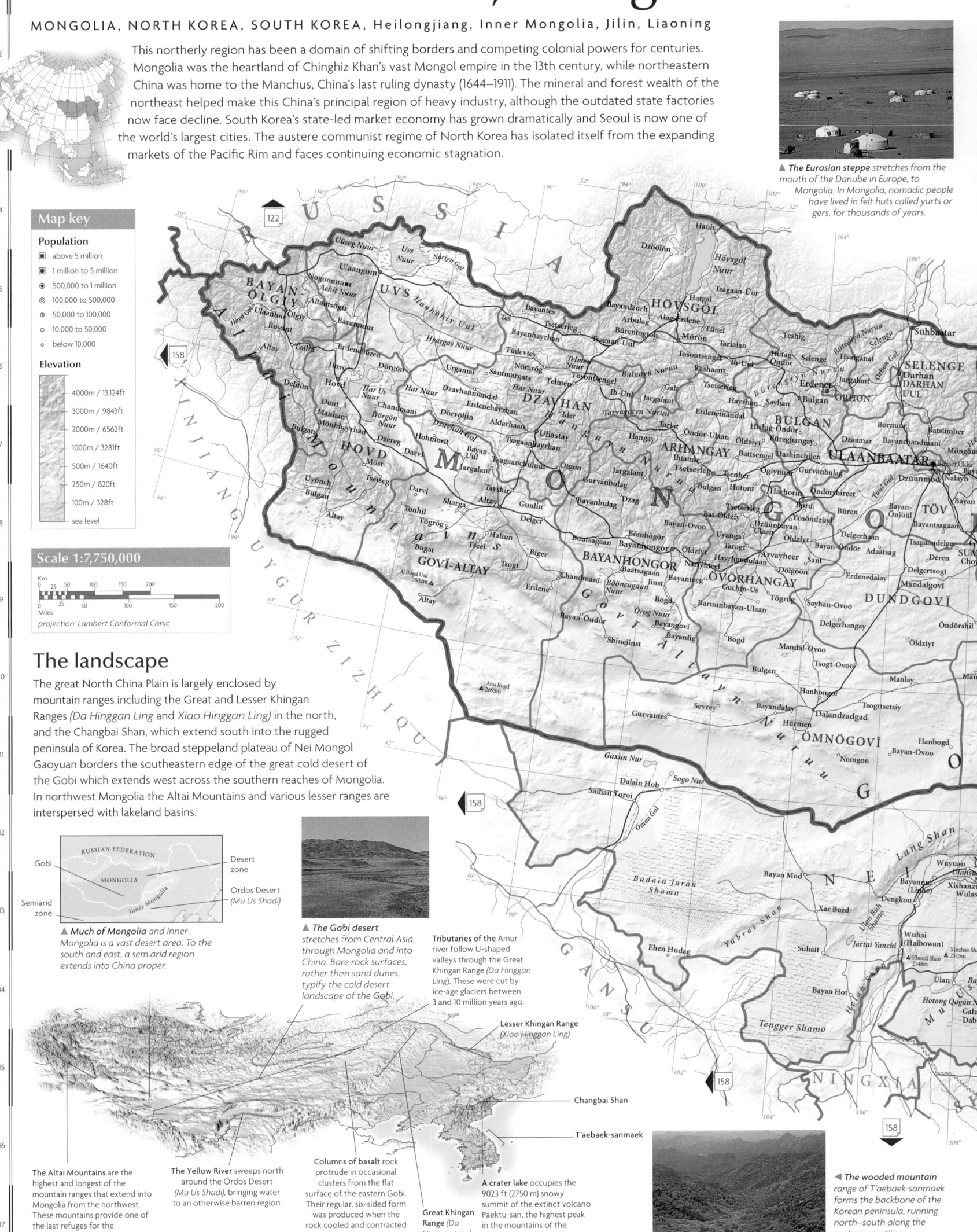

## Map key

### Population
■ above 5 million
◉ 1 million to 5 million
◎ 500,000 to 1 million
⊙ 100,000 to 500,000
⊕ 50,000 to 100,000
○ 10,000 to 50,000
○ below 10,000

### Elevation
4000m / 13,124ft
3000m / 9843ft
2000m / 6562ft
1000m / 3281ft
500m / 1640ft
250m / 820ft
100m / 328ft
sea level

## Scale 1:7,750,000

Km 0 25 50 100 150 200
Miles 0 50 100 150 200

projection: Lambert Conformal Conic

## The landscape

The great North China Plain is largely enclosed by mountain ranges including the Great and Lesser Khingan Ranges (*Da Hinggan Ling* and *Xiao Hinggan Ling*) in the north, and the Changbai Shan, which extend south into the rugged peninsula of Korea. The broad steppeland plateau of Nei Mongol Gaoyuan borders the southeastern edge of the great cold desert of the Gobi which extends west across the southern reaches of Mongolia. In northwest Mongolia the Altai Mountains and various lesser ranges are interspersed with lakeland basins.

▲ *Much of Mongolia* and Inner Mongolia is a vast desert area. To the south and east, a semiarid region extends into China proper.

▲ *The Gobi desert* stretches from Central Asia, through Mongolia and into China. Bare rock surfaces, rather than sand dunes, typify the cold desert landscape of the Gobi.

Tributaries of the Amur river follow U-shaped valleys through the Great Khingan Range (*Da Hinggan Ling*). These were cut by ice-age glaciers between 3 and 10 million years ago.

Lesser Khingan Range (*Xiao Hinggan Ling*)

Changbai Shan

T'aebaek-sanmaek

▲ *The wooded mountain* range of T'aebaek-sanmaek forms the backbone of the Korean peninsula, running north–south along the eastern coastline.

The Altai Mountains are the highest and longest of the mountain ranges that extend into Mongolia from the northwest. These mountains provide one of the last refuges for the endangered snow leopard.

The Yellow River sweeps north around the Ordos Desert (*Mu Us Shadi*), bringing water to an otherwise barren region.

Columns of basalt rock protrude in occasional clusters from the flat surface of the eastern Gobi. Their regular, six-sided form was produced when the rock cooled and contracted from its molten state.

Great Khingan Range (*Da Hinggan Ling*)

A crater lake occupies the 9023 ft (2750 m) snowy summit of the extinct volcano Paektu-san, the highest peak in the mountains of the Changbai Shan.

## Transportation & industry

North Korea's centrally-planned economy is strongly oriented toward heavy industry, while South Korea has a broad manufacturing base which includes textiles, steel, electronics, and one of the world's largest shipbuilding industries. Mongolia and Inner Mongolia's great mineral resource potential is largely undeveloped. The heavy industrial region around Shenyang produces iron, steel, chemicals, and cement on a massive scale.

**Major industry and infrastructure**
- car manufacture
- chemicals
- coal
- electronics
- engineering
- finance
- food processing
- iron & steel
- pharmaceuticals
- shipbuilding
- textiles
- ■ capital cities
- ● major towns
- ✈ international airports
- major roads
- major industrial areas

### Transportation network

*Liaoning has China's most comprehensive railroad network, the legacy of the Japanese occupation of Manchuria in the 20th century. The railroads are used primarily for freight transportation.*

▲ *Ulaanbaatar, the Mongolian capital bears many of the hallmarks of Soviet-style central planning, the result of economic and industrial assistance from the Soviet Union following Mongolian independence in 1921.*

▶ *While North Korea has remained politically and economically isolated from the rest of the world, South Korea has enjoyed immense economic growth. It has benefited considerably from US economic aid in the aftermath of the Korean war of 1950–1953.*

**South Korea: Capital cities**

SEOUL – capital
SEJONG CITY – administrative capital

## Using the land & sea

Mongolia and Inner Mongolia rely heavily on livestock farming, with only about 1% of the land area cultivated. Northeastern China produces wheat, corn, soybeans, and sugar beet. The cool climate limits the range of crops and large upland areas of the northeast remain forested. Rice is the staple food of North and South Korea. The latter has become a leading ocean-fishing nation.

**Land use and agricultural distribution**
- goats
- pigs
- sheep
- corn
- fishing
- rice
- soybeans
- sugar beet
- wheat
- ■ capital cities
- ● major towns
- pasture
- cropland
- forest
- mountain region
- desert

163

# Japan

In the years since the end of the Second World War, Japan has become the world's most dynamic industrial nation. The country comprises a string of over 4000 islands which lie in a great northeast to southwest arc in the northwest Pacific. Four major islands: Hokkaido, Honshu, Shikoku, and Kyushu are home to the great majority of Japan's population of 128 million people, although the mountainous terrain of the central region means that most cities are situated on the coast. A densely populated industrial belt stretches along much of Honshu's southern coast, including Japan's crowded capital, Tokyo. Alongside its spectacular economic growth and the increasing westernization of its cities, Japan still maintains a highly individual culture, reflected in its traditional food, formal behavioral codes, unique Shinto religion, and a deep reverence for the emperor.

## Using the land & sea

Although only about 11% of Japan is suitable for cultivation, substantial government support, a favorable climate and intensive farming methods enable the country to be virtually self-sufficient in rice production. Northern Hokkaido, the largest and most productive farming region, has an open terrain and climate similar to that of the American Midwest, and produces over half of Japan's cereal requirements. Farmers are being encouraged to diversify by growing fruit, vegetables, and wheat, as well as raising livestock.

### Land use and agricultural distribution

- cattle
- pigs
- fishing
- cereals
- citrus fruits
- fruit
- herbs
- rice
- root crops
- tobacco

- ■ capital cities
- • major towns

- pasture
- cropland
- forest

**The urban/rural population divide**

urban 78%      rural 22%

0  10  20  30  40  50  60  70  80  90  100

| Population density | Total land area |
|---|---|
| 885 people per sq mile (342 people per sq km) | 145,869 sq miles (377,800 sq km) |

► *Cutting terraces maximizes* the limited agricultural land, enabling Japan to produce large quantities of rice.

## The landscape

The islands of Japan lie on the Pacific "Ring of Fire," and form a series of clearly defined arcs. The largely mountainous landscape was formed very recently in geological terms. Volcanic eruptions and earthquakes continue to reshape the terrain and shake the country's complex infrastructure. There is no single continuous mountain range; the mountains divide into many small land blocks separated by lowlands and dissected by numerous river valleys.

Sea of Japan (East Sea)
Active volcanic island
Japan Trench (subduction zone)

▲ *Japan is part* of an arc of volcanic islands, formed by the Pacific Plate diving under the Eurasian Plate. This process generates intense stress which is periodically released as earthquakes.

◄ *Mount Fuji is* Japan's highest mountain, rising 12,388 ft (3776 m) above the Kanto Plain in the central region of Honshu. The flat land below is suitable for growing crops such as tea. Like many Japanese mountains, it is revered as a sacred site.

Mount Fuji

*A number of* rivers which emerge from the volcanic parts of northwestern Honshu are so highly acidic that their water is unsuitable for irrigation and consumption.

► *Trees cling to* the sheer slopes of the waterfalls on the northern island of Hokkaido. The island's climate is similar to that in northern Europe, with long, cold winters and short, warm summers.

In much of Kyushu the coast is subsiding, giving a highly indented coastline. In some places, former hilltops are barely visible above the current sea level.

*There are over* 60 active volcanoes – like Asahi-dake, Hokkaido's highest peak – throughout Japan. This accounts for more than 10% of the world's total.

The Inland Sea *(Seto-naikai)* has resulted from the depression of faulted blocks which has allowed sea water to invade the region between northern Shikoku and western Honshu.

Strong southeasterly winds blowing onshore during the winter create sand dunes which extend for miles along the eastern coasts.

Biwa-ko is the largest lake in Japan, covering 260 sq miles (673 sq km) in central Honshu. The depression in which it lies was created by recent faulting of the underlying rocks.

*Rising land on* the Pacific coast of Honshu leads to typical features such as raised beaches, some lying over 1000 ft (300 m) above sea level.

▼ *Autumnal trees near* Gifu, on central Honshu, create a spectacular display. Native trees on this island include camphor, pasania, Japanese evergreen oak, camellia, and holly.

► *The Kobe earthquake* in January 1995 highlighted Japan's vulnerability to earthquakes, despite technological advances. It shattered much of the infrastructure of this important port. More than 5000 people died as buildings and overhead highways collapsed and fires broke out.

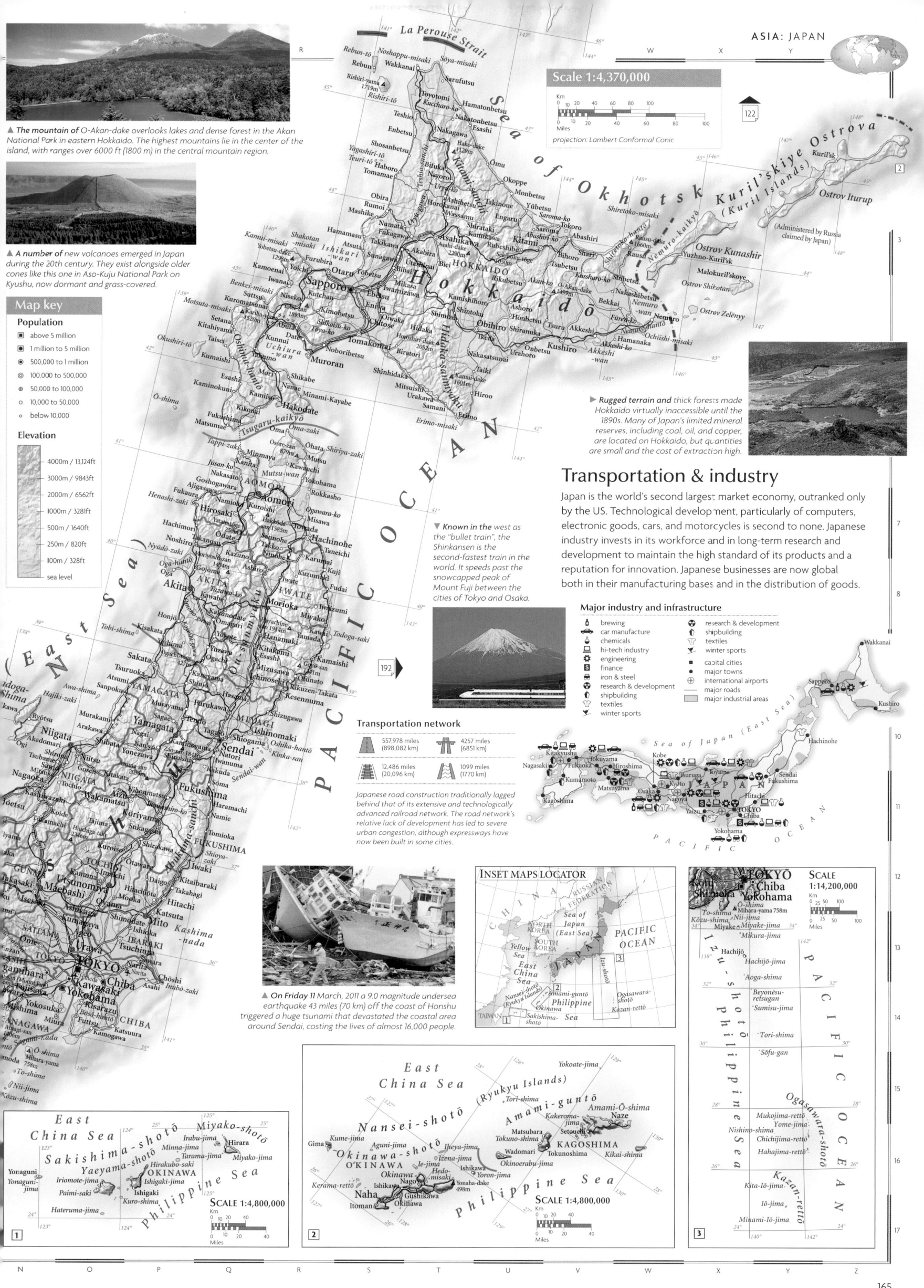

▲ The mountain of O-Akan-dake overlooks lakes and dense forest in the Akan National Park in eastern Hokkaido. The highest mountains lie in the center of the island, with ranges over 6000 ft (1800 m) in the central mountain region.

▲ A number of new volcanoes emerged in Japan during the 20th century. They exist alongside older cones like this one in Aso-Kuju National Park on Kyushu, now dormant and grass-covered.

**Map key**

**Population**
- above 5 million
- 1 million to 5 million
- 500,000 to 1 million
- 100,000 to 500,000
- 50,000 to 100,000
- 10,000 to 50,000
- below 10,000

**Elevation**
- 4000m / 13,124ft
- 3000m / 9843ft
- 2000m / 6562ft
- 1000m / 3281ft
- 500m / 1640ft
- 250m / 820ft
- 100m / 328ft
- sea level

Scale 1:4,370,000
projection: Lambert Conformal Conic

▶ Rugged terrain and thick forests made Hokkaido virtually inaccessible until the 1890s. Many of Japan's limited mineral reserves, including coal, oil, and copper, are located on Hokkaido, but quantities are small and the cost of extraction high.

## Transportation & industry

Japan is the world's second largest market economy, outranked only by the US. Technological development, particularly of computers, electronic goods, cars, and motorcycles is second to none. Japanese industry invests in its workforce and in long-term research and development to maintain the high standard of its products and a reputation for innovation. Japanese businesses are now global both in their manufacturing bases and in the distribution of goods.

**Major industry and infrastructure**
- brewing
- car manufacture
- chemicals
- hi-tech industry
- engineering
- finance
- iron & steel
- research & development
- shipbuilding
- textiles
- winter sports
- research & development
- shipbuilding
- textiles
- winter sports
- capital cities
- major towns
- international airports
- major roads
- major industrial areas

▼ Known in the west as the "bullet train", the Shinkansen is the second-fastest train in the world. It speeds past the snowcapped peak of Mount Fuji between the cities of Tokyo and Osaka.

**Transportation network**
557,978 miles (898,082 km)
4257 miles (6851 km)
12,486 miles (20,096 km)
1099 miles (1770 km)

Japanese road construction traditionally lagged behind that of its extensive and technologically advanced railroad network. The road network's relative lack of development has led to severe urban congestion, although expressways have now been built in some cities.

▲ On Friday 11 March, 2011 a 9.0 magnitude undersea earthquake 43 miles (70 km) off the coast of Honshu triggered a huge tsunami that devastated the coastal area around Sendai, costing the lives of almost 16,000 people.

INSET MAPS LOCATOR

SCALE 1:14,200,000

East China Sea — SCALE 1:4,800,000

Nansei-shotō (Ryukyu Islands) — SCALE 1:4,800,000

165

# Mainland Southeast Asia

CAMBODIA, LAOS, MYANMAR (BURMA), THAILAND, VIETNAM

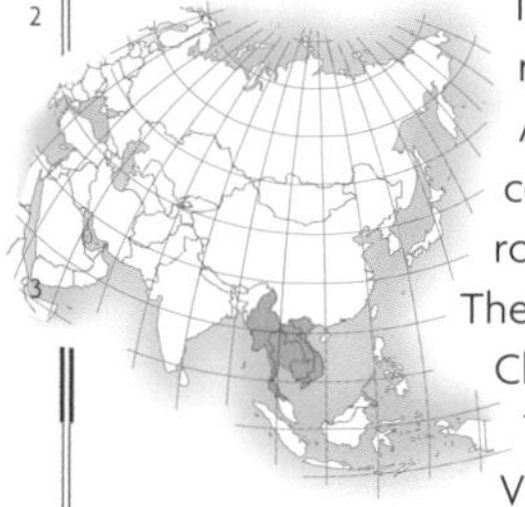

Thickly forested mountains, intercut by the broad valleys of five great rivers characterize the landscape of Southeast Asia's mainland countries. Agriculture remains the main activity for much of the population, which is concentrated in the river flood plains and deltas. Linked ethnic and cultural roots give the region a distinct identity. Most people on the mainland are Theravada Buddhists, and the Philippines is the only predominantly Christian country in Southeast Asia. Foreign intervention began in the 16th century with the opening of the spice trade; Cambodia, Laos and Vietnam were French colonies until the end of the Second World War, Myanmar (Burma) was under British control. Only Thailand was never colonized. Today, Thailand is poised to play a leading role in the economic development of the Pacific Rim, and Laos and Vietnam continues to mend the devastation of the Vietnam War, and to develop their economies. With ongoing political instability and a shattered infrastructure, Cambodia faces an uncertain future, while Myanmar (Burma) is seeking investment and the ending of its long isolation from the world community.

▲ *The Ayeyarwady (Irrawaddy) river is Myanmar's (Burma) vital central artery, watering the ricefields and providing a rich source of fish, as well as an important transport link, particularly for local traffic.*

## The landscape

A series of mountain ranges runs north–south through the mainland, formed as the result of the collision between the Eurasian Plate and the Indian subcontinent, which created the Himalayas. They are interspersed by the valleys of a number of great rivers. On their passage to the sea these rivers have deposited sediment, forming huge, fertile flood plains and deltas.

The coastline of the Isthmus of Kra

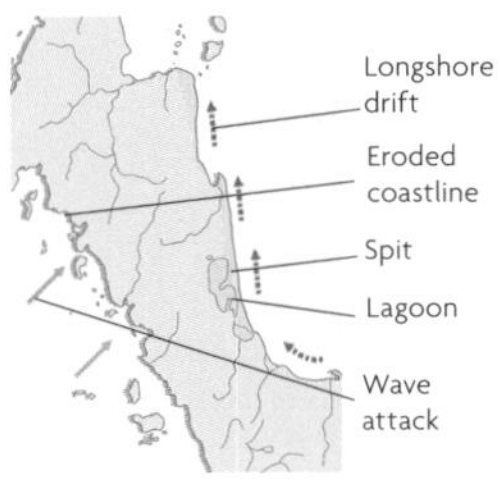

Longshore drift
Eroded coastline
Spit
Lagoon
Wave attack

◄ *The east and west coasts of the Isthmus of Kra differ greatly. The tectonically uplifting west coast is exposed to the harsh south-westerly monsoon and is heavily eroded. On the east coast, longshore currents produce depositional features such as spits and lagoons.*

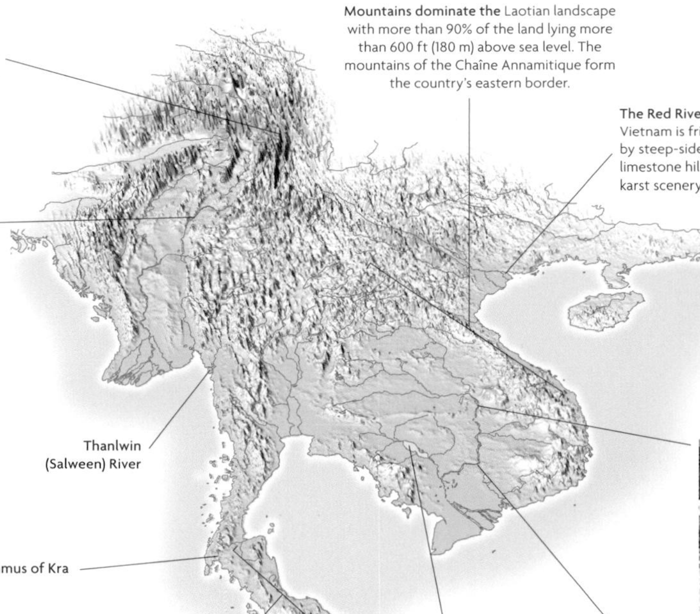

Hkakabo Razi is the highest point in mainland Southeast Asia. It rises 19,300 ft (5885 m) at the border between China and Myanmar (Burma).

Mountains dominate the Laotian landscape with more than 90% of the land lying more than 600 ft (180 m) above sea level. The mountains of the Chaîne Annamitique form the country's eastern border.

The Red River delta in northern Vietnam is fringed to the north by steep-sided, round-topped limestone hills, typical of karst scenery.

The Ayeyarwady (Irrawaddy) river runs virtually north–south, draining the plains of northern Myanmar (Burma). The Irrawaddy delta is the country's main rice-growing area.

Thanlwin (Salween) River

Isthmus of Kra

Malay Peninsula

Tonle Sap, a freshwater lake, drains into the Mekong delta via the Mekong river. It is the largest lake in Southeast Asia.

The Mekong river flows through southern China and Myanmar (Burma), then for much of its length forms the border between Laos and Thailand, flowing through Cambodia before terminating in a vast delta on the southern Vietnamese coast.

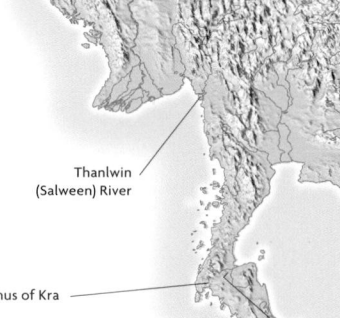

◄ *The fast-flowing waters of the Mekong river cascade over this waterfall in Champasak province in Laos. The force of the water erodes rocks at the base of the fall.*

▲ *The coast of the Isthmus of Kra, in southeast Thailand has many small, precipitous islands like these, formed by chemical erosion on limestone, which is weathered along vertical cracks. The humidity of the climate in Southeast Asia increases the rate of weathering.*

## Using the land and sea

The fertile flood plains of rivers such as the Mekong and Thanlwin (Salween), and the humid climate, enable the production of rice throughout the region. Cambodia, Laos, and Myanmar (Burma) still have substantial forests, producing hardwoods such as teak and rosewood. Cash crops include tropical fruits such as coconuts, bananas and pineapples, rubber, oil palm, sugar cane and the jute substitute, kenaf. Pigs and cattle are the main livestock raised. Large quantities of marine and freshwater fish are caught throughout the region.

▲ *Commercial logging – still widespread in Myanmar (Burma) – has now been stopped in Thailand because of over-exploitation of the tropical rainforest.*

### The urban/rural population divide

urban 30%    rural 70%

0  10  20  30  40  50  60  70  80  90  100

Population density
345 people per sq mile
(133 people per sq km)

Total land area
733,828 sq miles
(1,901,110 sq km)

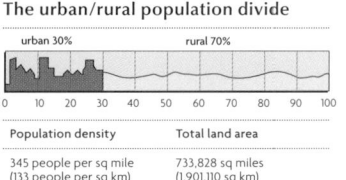

### Land use and agricultural distribution

- cattle
- pigs
- bananas
- coconuts
- fishing
- oil palms
- rice
- rubber
- sugar cane
- timber

- capital cities
- major towns

- pasture
- cropland
- forest
- wetland

# Transportation & industry

Industrial manufacturing has become increasingly important in Thailand and Vietnam in recent years. The assembling of component-based electrical and electronic goods is becoming more common throughout this region, with foreign companies benefiting from low labour costs and the upgrading of technology. The economies of Myanmar (Burma) and Cambodia are still based on agricultural produce and the processing of raw materials. Tin is the region's most important metal, and nickel, copper and chromite are also mined, although the quantities produced are not significant on a global scale. Thailand's successful tourist industry is the country's highest earner of foreign exchange.

## Transportation network

| | | | |
|---|---|---|---|
| 🛣 | 82,958 miles (133,524 km) | 🛤 | 267 miles (430 km) |
| 🚂 | 7500 miles (12,071 km) | ✈ | 28,585 miles (46,008 km) |

Transportation development has concentrated on the building of road networks. Water and sea transport remain important, although air links have improved, particularly in Thailand and the Philippines.

## Major industry and infrastructure

- ⚗ chemicals
- 💻 electronics
- ⚙ engineering
- 💲 finance
- 🍴 food processing
- ⛓ iron & steel
- 🛢 oil & gas
- ⛏ mining
- ⚓ shipbuilding
- 🧵 textiles
- 🌲 timber processing
- ■ capital cities
- • major towns
- ⊕ international airports
- — major roads
- major industrial areas

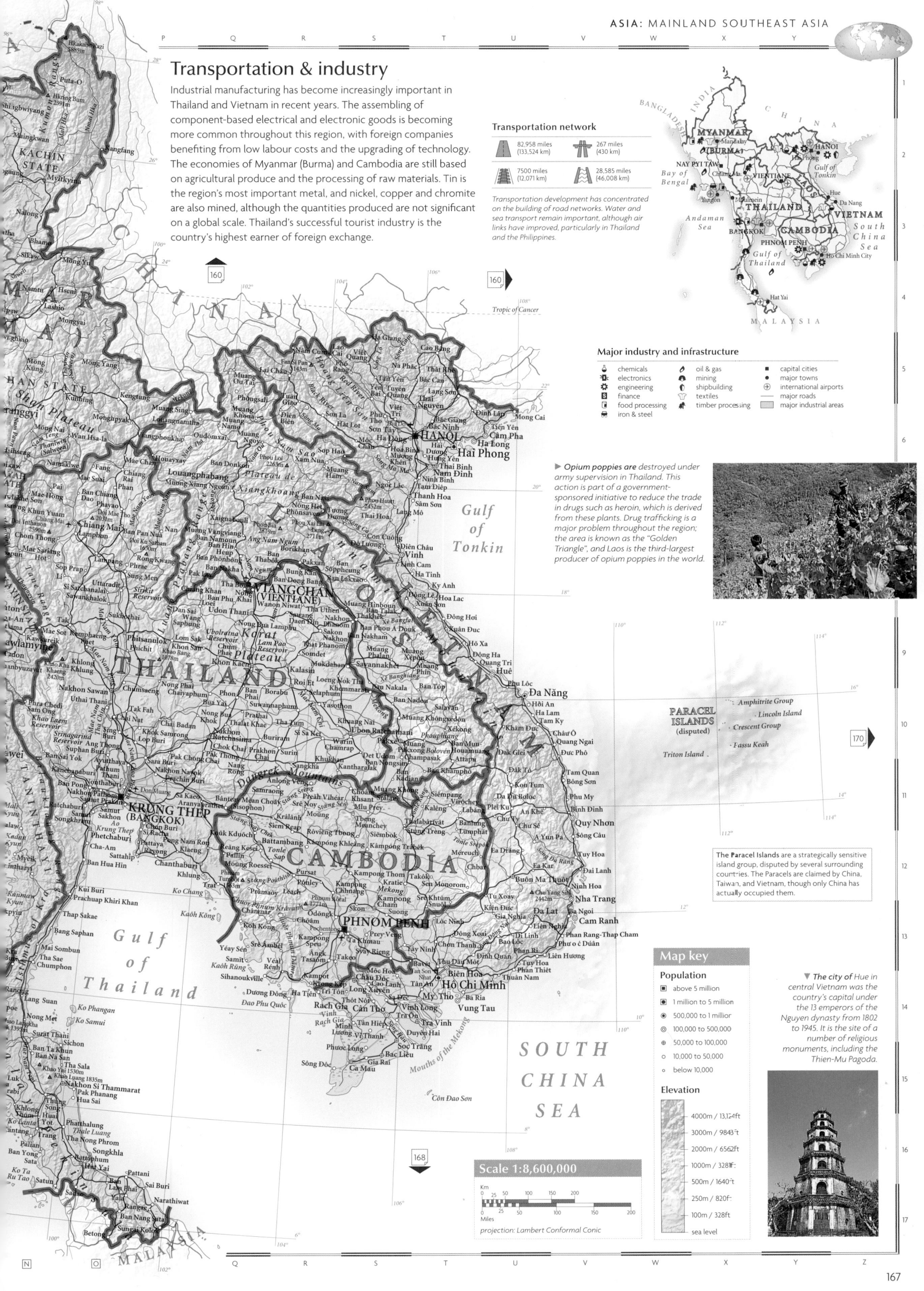

▶ Opium poppies are destroyed under army supervision in Thailand. This action is part of a government-sponsored initiative to reduce the trade in drugs such as heroin, which is derived from these plants. Drug trafficking is a major problem throughout the region; the area is known as the "Golden Triangle", and Laos is the third-largest producer of opium poppies in the world.

PARACEL ISLANDS (disputed)
- ∴ Amphitrite Group
- · Lincoln Island
- · Crescent Group
- · Passu Keah
- Triton Island ·

The Paracel Islands are a strategically sensitive island group, disputed by several surrounding countries. The Paracels are claimed by China, Taiwan, and Vietnam, though only China has actually occupied them.

## Map key

### Population
- ■ above 5 million
- ▣ 1 million to 5 million
- ◉ 500,000 to 1 million
- ◎ 100,000 to 500,000
- ⊙ 50,000 to 100,000
- ○ 10,000 to 50,000
- ∘ below 10,000

### Elevation
- 4000m / 13,124ft
- 3000m / 9843ft
- 2000m / 6562ft
- 1000m / 3281ft
- 500m / 1640ft
- 250m / 820ft
- 100m / 328ft
- sea level

▼ The city of Hue in central Vietnam was the country's capital under the 13 emperors of the Nguyen dynasty from 1802 to 1945. It is the site of a number of religious monuments, including the Thien-Mu Pagoda.

## Scale 1:8,600,000

projection: Lambert Conformal Conic

# Western Maritime Southeast Asia

## BRUNEI, INDONESIA, MALAYSIA, SINGAPORE

The world's largest archipelago, Indonesia's myriad islands stretch 3100 miles (5000 km) eastward across the Pacific, from the Malay Peninsula to western New Guinea. Only about 1500 of the 13,677 islands are inhabited and the huge, predominently Muslim population is unevenly distributed, with some two-thirds crowded onto the western islands of Java, Madura, and Bali. The national government is trying to resettle large numbers of people from these islands to other parts of the country to reduce population pressure there. Malaysia, split between the mainland and the east Malaysian states of Sabah and Sarawak on Borneo has a diverse population, as well as a fast-growing economy, although the pace of its development is still far outstripped by that of Singapore. This small island nation is the financial and commercial capital of Southeast Asia. The Sultanate of Brunei in northern Borneo, one of the world's last princely states, has an extremely high standard of living, based on its oil revenues.

## The landscape

Indonesia's western islands are characterized by rugged volcanic mountains cloaked with dense tropical forest, which slope down to coastal plains covered by thick alluvial swamps. The Sunda Shelf, an extension of the Eurasian Plate, lies between Java, Bali, Sumatra, and Borneo. These islands' mountains rise from a base below the sea, and they were once joined together by dry land, which has since been submerged by rising sea levels.

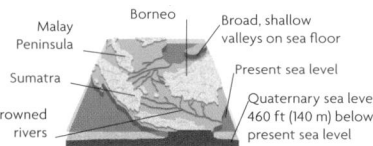

▲ *The Sunda Shelf* underlies this whole region. It is one of the largest submarine shelves in the world, covering an area of 714,285 sq miles (1,850,000 sq km). During the early Quaternary period, when sea levels were lower, the shelf was exposed.

◄ *On December 26*, 2004 a 9.2 magnitude earthquake off the coast of Sumatra triggered a devastating tsunami that was up to 90 ft (30 m) high in places. The death toll was estimated to be around 230,000 people from fourteen different countries around the Indian Ocean.

◄ *The river of* Sungai Mahakam cuts through the central highlands of Borneo, the third largest island in the world, with a total area of 290,000 sq miles (757,050 sq km). Although mountainous, Borneo is one of the most stable of the Indonesian islands, with little volcanic activity.

*Malay Peninsula has* a rugged east coast, but the west coast, fronting the Strait of Malacca, has many sheltered beaches and bays. The two coasts are divided by the Banjaran Titiwangsa, which run the length of the peninsula.

*The island of* Krakatau (Pulau Rakata), lying between Sumatra and Java, was all but destroyed in 1883, when the volcano erupted. The release of gas and dust into the atmosphere disrupted cloud cover and global weather patterns for several years.

Gunung Semeru

*Gunung Kinabalu is the* highest peak in Malaysia, rising 13,455 ft (4101 m).

*Indonesia has more* than 220 volcanoes, most of which are still active. They are strung out along the island arc from Sumatra through the Lesser Sunda Islands, into the Moluccas and Celebes.

## Transportation & industry

Singapore has a thriving economy based on international trade and finance. Annual trade through the port is among the highest of any in the world. Indonesia's western islands still depend on natural resources, particularly petroleum, gas, and wood, although the economy is rapidly diversifying with manufactured exports including garments, consumer electronics, and footwear. A high-profile aircraft industry has developed in Bandung on Java. Malaysia has a fast-growing and varied manufacturing sector, although oil, gas, and timber remain important resource-based industries.

► *Ranks of gleaming* skyscrapers, new motorways and infrastructure construction reflect the investment which is pouring into Southeast Asian cities like the Malaysian capital, Kuala Lumpur. Traditional housing and markets still exist amidst the new developments. Many of the city's inhabitants subsist at a level far removed from the prosperity implied by its outward modernity.

### Malaysia: Capital cities

KUALA LUMPUR – capital
PUTRAJAYA – administrative capital

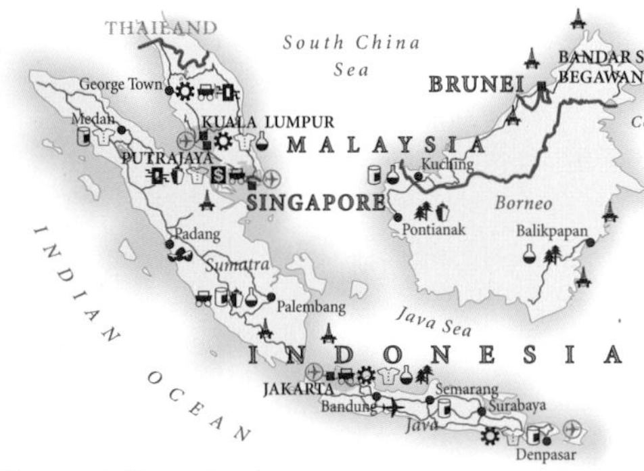

# Using the land and sea

Rice is the most important arable crop in Indonesia and Malaysia, and both countries manage to meet almost all of their domestic demand. Malaysian rubber accounts for 25% of world production and is the main cash crop, grown on plantations and small farms, along with oil palms and copra. Timber is exported from both Malaysia and Indonesia. Modern agricultural techniques enable Singapore to produce fruits and vegetables despite a shortage of suitable land.

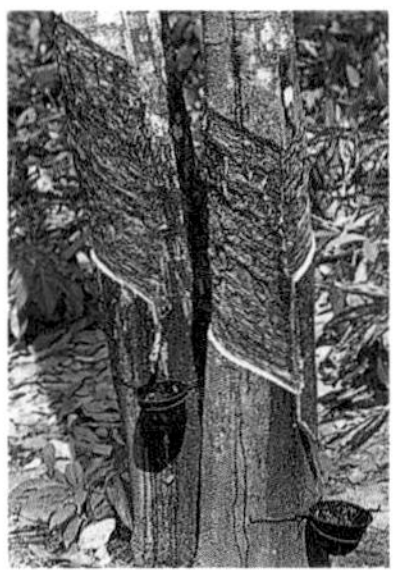

▶ Spiral cuts in the bark of this rubber palm show where it has been tapped. Sophisticated 'cloning' techniques mean that trees which produce consistently high quantities of rubber can be easily reproduced.

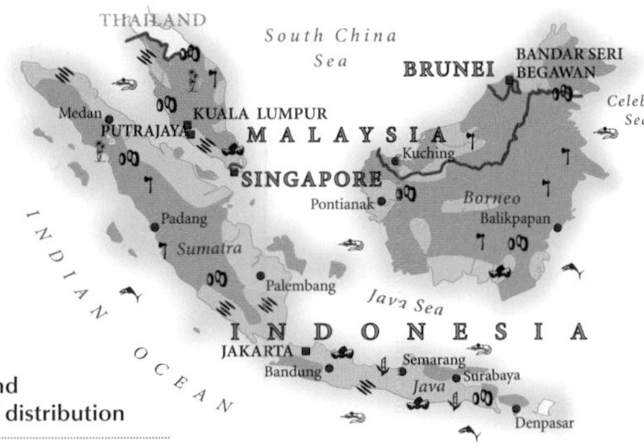

## Transportation network

165,272 miles (266,010 km)

958 miles (1,542 km)

5,061 miles (8,146 km)

18,070 miles (29,084 km)

Singapore's metro system, completed in 1991, is among the most efficient in the world. Malaysia has several fast, modern highways and most roads are paved. Indonesia's many islands make improvement of the shipping infrastructure a priority.

### Major industry and infrastructure

aerospace, copra processing, chemicals, electronics, engineering, finance, food processing, iron & steel, oil, ship building, timber processing, textiles

capital cities, major towns, international airports, major roads, major industrial areas

### Land use and agricultural distribution

coconuts, fishing, oil palms, rice, rubber, shellfish, sugar cane, timber, capital cities, major towns, pasture, cropland, forest, wetland

### The urban/rural population divide

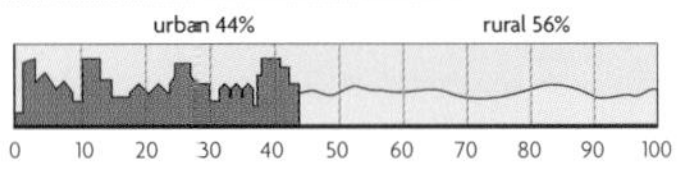

urban 44% · rural 56%

Population density
297 people per sq mile (115 people per sq km)

Total land area
828,356 sq miles (2,146,000 sq km)

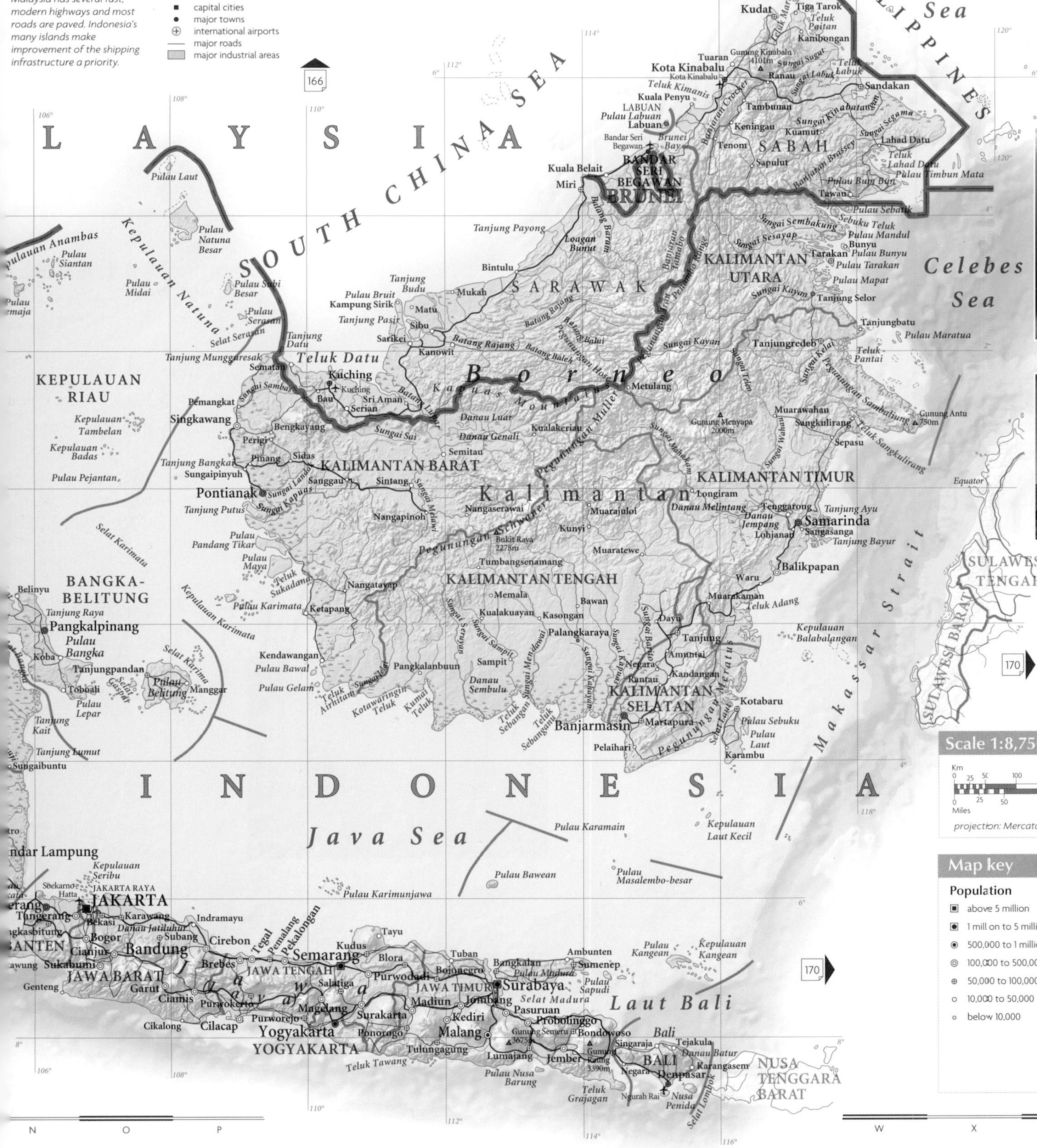

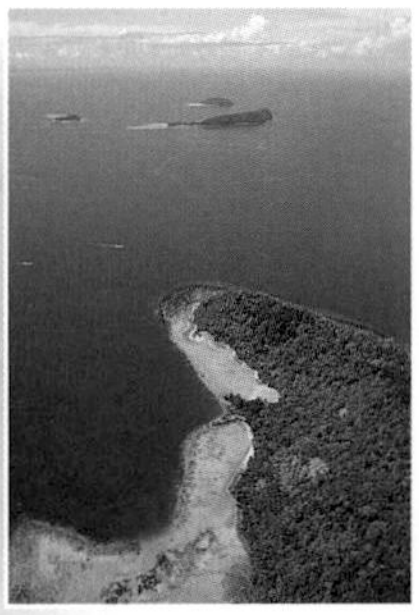

▼ This tiny island near Kota Kinabalu, in Sabah, eastern Malaysia, is a part of a designated national park. Thickly forested, it is surrounded by broad, sandy beaches and shallow inland seas.

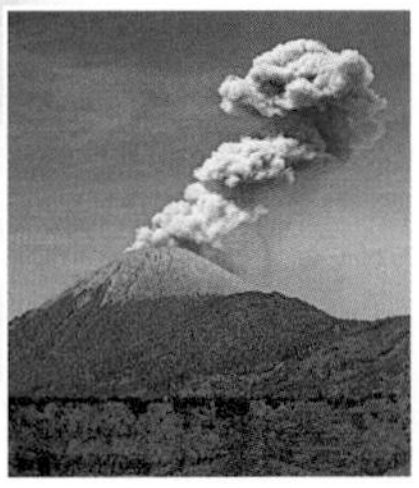

▲ The volcano of Gunung Semeru in eastern Java lies on the Pacific "Ring of Fire". It is part of the ancient Tennegger volcano and remains highly active.

## Scale 1:8,750,000

projection: Mercator

## Map key

### Population
above 5 million; 1 mill on to 5 million; 500,000 to 1 million; 100,000 to 500,000; 50,000 to 100,000; 10,000 to 50,000; below 10,000

### Elevation
4000m / 13,124ft; 3000m / 9843ft; 2000m / 6562ft; 1000m / 3281ft; 500m / 1640ft; 250m / 820ft; 100m / 328ft; sea level

# Eastern Maritime Southeast Asia

## EAST TIMOR, INDONESIA, PHILIPPINES

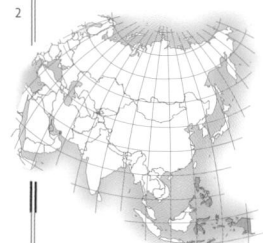

The Philippines takes its name from Philip II of Spain who was king when the islands were colonized during the 16th century. Almost 400 years of Spanish, and later US, rule have left their mark on the country's culture; English is widely spoken and over 90% of the population is Christian. The Philippines' economy is agriculturally based – inadequate infrastructure and electrical power shortages have so far hampered faster industrial growth. Indonesia's eastern islands are less economically developed than the rest of the country. Papua, which constitutes the western portion of New Guinea, is one of the world's last great wildernesses. After a long struggle, East Timor gained full autonomy from Indonesia in 2002.

▲ The traditional boat-shaped houses of the Toraja people in Sulawesi. Although now Christian, the Toraja still practice the animist traditions and rituals of their ancestors. They are famous for their elaborate funeral ceremonies and burial sites in cliffside caves.

## The landscape

Located on the Pacific "Ring of Fire" the Philippines' 7100 islands are subject to frequent earthquakes and volcanic activity. Their terrain is largely mountainous, with narrow coastal plains and interior valleys and plains. Luzon and Mindanao are by far the largest islands and comprise roughly 66% of the country's area. Indonesia's eastern islands are mountainous and dotted with volcanoes, both active and dormant.

▶ Lake Taal on the Philippines island of Luzon lies within the crater of an immense volcano that erupted twice in the 20th century, first in 1911 and again in 1965, causing the deaths of more than 3200 people.

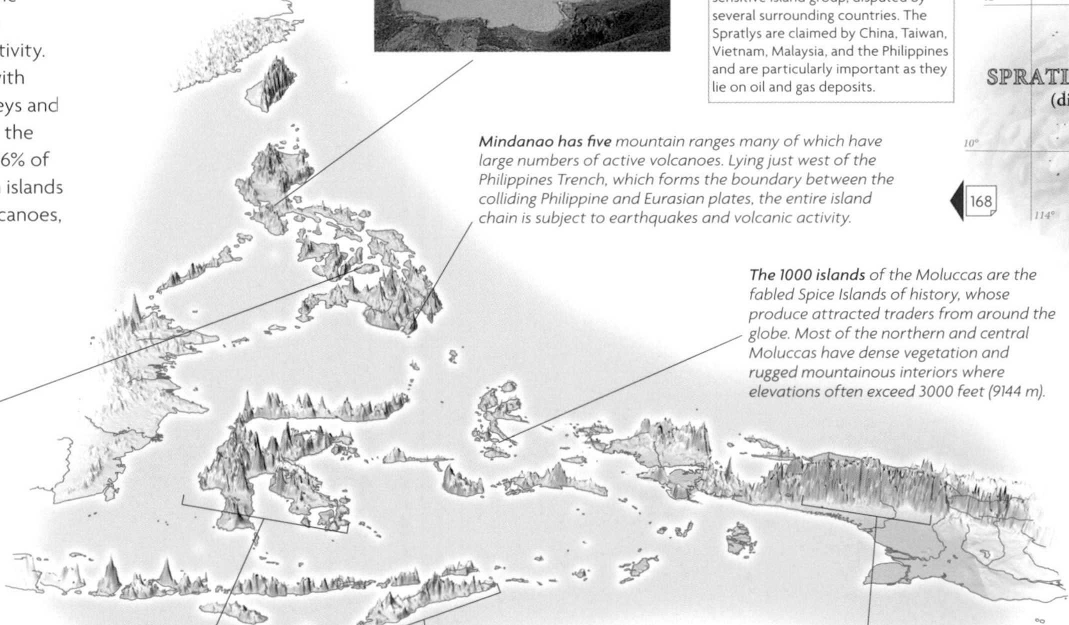

The Spratly Islands are a strategically sensitive island group, disputed by several surrounding countries. The Spratlys are claimed by China, Taiwan, Vietnam, Malaysia, and the Philippines and are particularly important as they lie on oil and gas deposits.

Mindanao has five mountain ranges many of which have large numbers of active volcanoes. Lying just west of the Philippines Trench, which forms the boundary between the colliding Philippine and Eurasian plates, the entire island chain is subject to earthquakes and volcanic activity.

The 1000 islands of the Moluccas are the fabled Spice Islands of history, whose produce attracted traders from around the globe. Most of the northern and central Moluccas have dense vegetation and rugged mountainous interiors where elevations often exceed 3000 feet (9144 m).

▲ Bohol in the southern Philippines is famous for its so-called "chocolate hills". There are more than 1000 of these regular mounds on the island. The hills are limestone in origin, the smoothed remains of an earlier cycle of erosion. Their brown appearance in the dry season gives them their name.

The four-pronged island of Celebes is the product of complex tectonic activity which ruptured and then reattached small fragments of the Earth's crust to form the island's many peninsulas.

Coral islands such as Timor in eastern Indonesia show evidence of very recent and dramatic movements of the Earth's plates. Reefs in Timor have risen by as much as 4000 ft (1300 m) in the last million years.

The Pegunungan Jayawijaya range in central Papua contains the world's highest range of limestone mountains, some with peaks more than 16,400 ft (5000 m) high. Heavy rainfall and high temperatures, which promote rapid weathering, have led to the creation of large underground caves and river systems such as the river of Sungai Baliem.

## Using the land and sea

Indonesia's eastern islands are less intensively cultivated than those in the west. Coconuts, coffee and spices such as cloves and nutmeg are the major commercial crops while rice, corn and soybeans are grown for local consumption. The Philippines' rich, fertile soils support year-round production of a wide range of crops. The country is one of the world's largest producers of coconuts and a major exporter of coconut products, including one-third of the world's copra. Although much of the arable land is given over to rice and corn, the main staple food crops, tropical fruits such as bananas, pineapples and mangos, and sugar cane are also grown for export.

◀ The terracing of land to restrict soil erosion and create flat surfaces for agriculture is a common practice throughout Southeast Asia, particularly where land is scarce. These terraces are on Luzon in the Philippines.

### Land use and agricultural distribution

- coconuts
- fishing
- rice
- rubber
- shellfish
- sugar cane
- ■ capital cities
- ● major towns

pasture
cropland
forest
wetland

### The urban/rural population divide

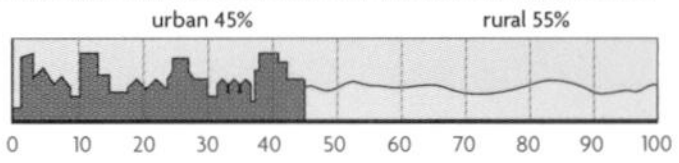

urban 45%   rural 55%

0  10  20  30  40  50  60  70  80  90  100

| Population density | Total land area |
| --- | --- |
| 258 people per sq mile (160 people per sq km) | 654,771 sq miles (1,053,755 sq km) |

▲ More than two-thirds of Papua's land area is heavily forested and the population of around 1.5 million live mainly in isolated tribal groups using more than 80 distinct languages.

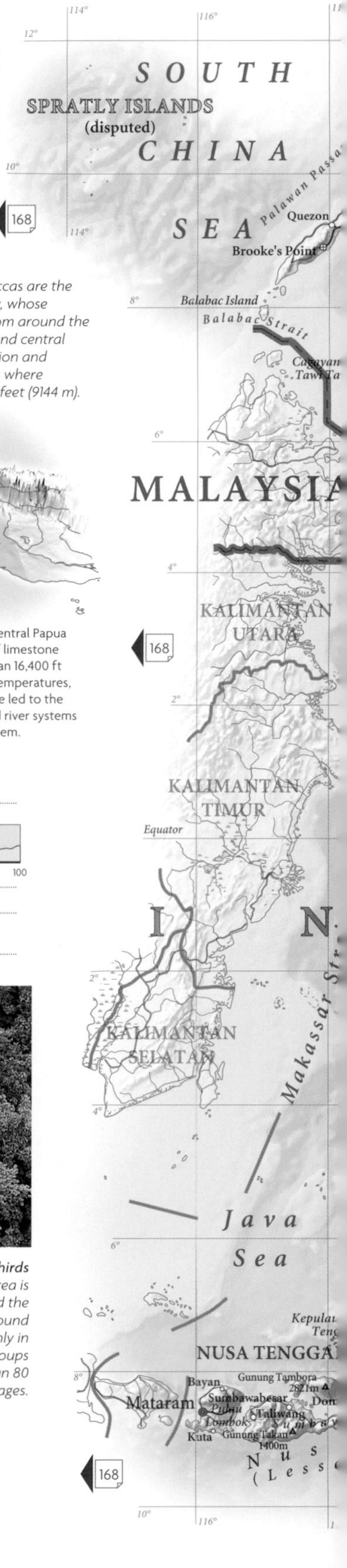

### Map labels

Luzon Strait
Luzon
Baguio
Philippine Sea
MANILA
South China Sea
PHILIPPINES
Cebu
Butuan
Sulu Sea
Mindanao
Zamboanga
Davao
MALAYSIA
Celebes Sea
Manado
PACIFIC OCEAN
Celebes
Halmahera
Maluku (Moluccas)
Ceram
Ambon
Makassar
Banda Sea
New Guinea
PAPUA NEW GUINEA
Jayapura
INDONESIA
Lombok
Sumbawa
Flores
Sumba
Timor
Kupang
DILI
EAST TIMOR
Arafura Sea
Timor Sea
INDIAN OCEAN

SOUTH CHINA SEA
SPRATLY ISLANDS (disputed)
Palawan Passage
Quezon
Brooke's Point
Balabac Island
Balabac Strait
Cagayan Tawi-Tawi
MALAYSIA
KALIMANTAN UTARA
KALIMANTAN TIMUR
Equator
KALIMANTAN SELATAN
Makassar Strait
Java Sea
Kepulauan
NUSA TENGGARA
Mataram
Bayan
Gunung Tambora
Sumbawabesar
Lombok
Kuta
Gunung
NUSA
168

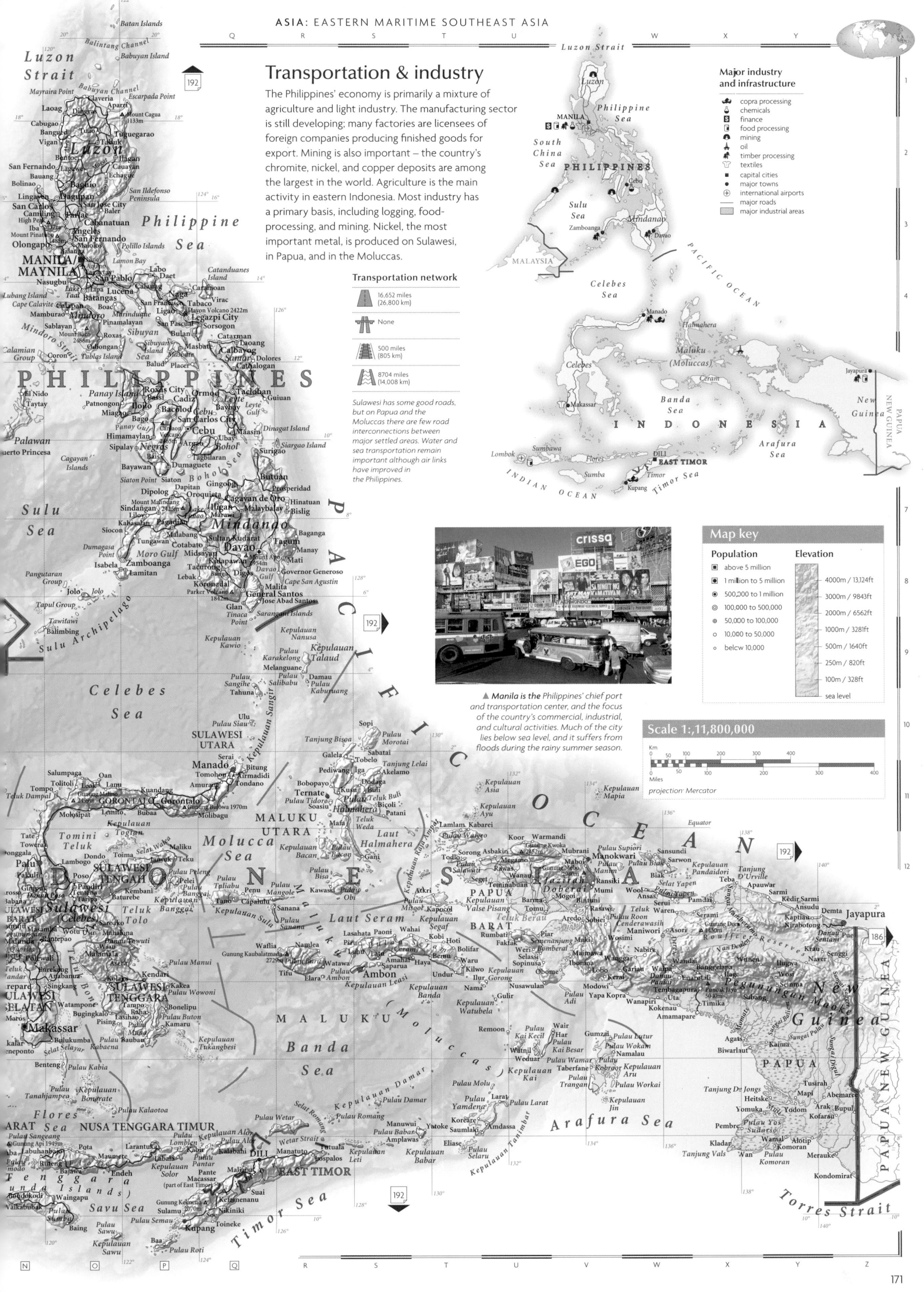

# Transportation & industry

The Philippines' economy is primarily a mixture of agriculture and light industry. The manufacturing sector is still developing; many factories are licensees of foreign companies producing finished goods for export. Mining is also important – the country's chromite, nickel, and copper deposits are among the largest in the world. Agriculture is the main activity in eastern Indonesia. Most industry has a primary basis, including logging, food-processing, and mining. Nickel, the most important metal, is produced on Sulawesi, in Papua, and in the Moluccas.

**Major industry and infrastructure**

- copra processing
- chemicals
- finance
- food processing
- mining
- oil
- timber processing
- textiles
- capital cities
- major towns
- international airports
- major roads
- major industrial areas

**Transportation network**

16,652 miles (26,800 km)

None

500 miles (805 km)

8704 miles (14,008 km)

Sulawesi has some good roads, but on Papua and the Moluccas there are few road interconnections between major settled areas. Water and sea transportation remain important although air links have improved in the Philippines.

▲ **Manila is the** Philippines' chief port and transportation center, and the focus of the country's commercial, industrial, and cultural activities. Much of the city lies below sea level, and it suffers from floods during the rainy summer season.

**Map key**

**Population**
- above 5 million
- 1 million to 5 million
- 500,200 to 1 million
- 100,000 to 500,000
- 50,000 to 100,000
- 10,000 to 50,000
- below 10,000

**Elevation**
- 4000m / 13,124ft
- 3000m / 9843ft
- 2000m / 6562ft
- 1000m / 3281ft
- 500m / 1640ft
- 250m / 820ft
- 100m / 328ft
- sea level

**Scale 1:,11,800,000**

Km
0  50  100  200  300  400

Miles
0  50  100  200  300  400

projection: Mercator

# The Indian Ocean

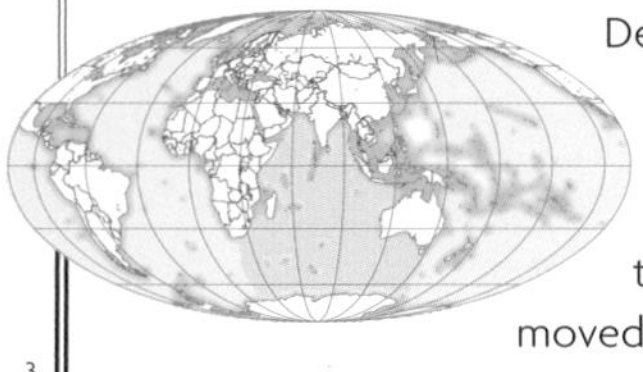

Despite being the smallest of the three major oceans, the evolution of the Indian Ocean was the most complex. The ocean basin was formed during the breakup of the supercontinent Gondwanaland, when the Indian subcontinent moved northeast, Africa moved west, and Australia separated from Antarctica. Like the Pacific Ocean, the warm waters of the Indian Ocean are punctuated by coral atolls and islands. About one-fifth of the world's population – over a billion people – live on its shores. In 2004, over 290,000 died and millions more were left homeless after a tsunami devastated large stretches of the ocean's coastline.

## The landscape

The Indian Ocean began forming about 150 million years ago, but in its present form it is relatively young, only about 36 million years old. Along the three subterranean mountain chains of its mid-ocean ridge the seafloor is still spreading. The Indian Ocean has fewer trenches than other oceans and only a narrow continental shelf around most of its surrounding land.

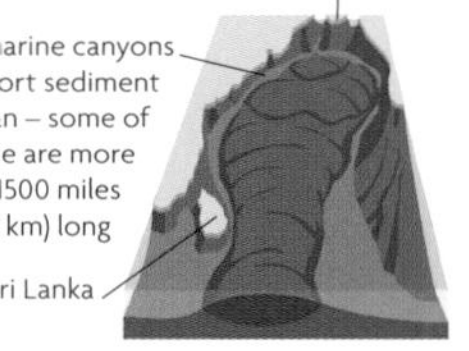

Sediments come from Ganges/ Brahmaputra river system

Submarine canyons transport sediment to fan – some of these are more than 1500 miles (2500 km) long

Sri Lanka

▲ **The Ganges Fan** is one of the world's largest submarine accumulations of sediment, extending far beyond Sri Lanka. It is fed by the Ganges/Brahmaputra river system, whose sediment is carried through a network of underwater canyons at the edge of the continental shelf.

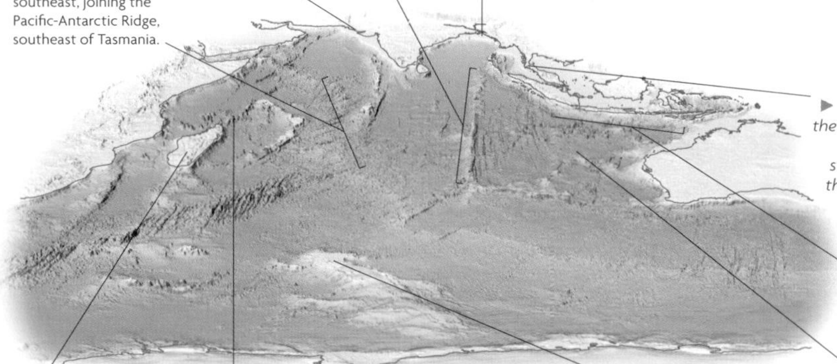

The mid-oceanic ridge runs from the Arabian Sea. It diverges east of Madagascar. One arm runs southwest to join the Mid-Atlantic Ridge, the other branches southeast, joining the Pacific-Antarctic Ridge, southeast of Tasmania.

The Ninetyeast Ridge takes its name from the line of longitude it follows. It is the world's longest and straightest under-sea ridge.

Two of the world's largest rivers flow into the Indian Ocean; the Indus and the Ganges/Brahmaputra. Both have deposited enormous fans of sediment.

Indus River

▶ A large proportion of the coast of Thailand, on the Isthmus of Kra, is stabilized by mangrove thickets. They act as an important breeding ground for wildlife.

The Java Trench is the world's longest, it runs 1600 miles (2570 km) from the southwest of Java, but is only 50 miles (80 km) wide.

The relief of Madagascar rises from a low-lying coastal strip in the east, to the central plateau. The plateau is also a major watershed separating Madagascar's three main river basins.

▶ The central group of the Seychelles are mountainous, granite islands. They have a narrow coastal belt and lush, tropical vegetation cloaks the highlands.

The Kerguelen Islands in the Southern Ocean were created by a hot spot in the Earth's crust. The islands were formed in succession as the Antarctic Plate moved slowly over the hot spot.

The circulation in the northern Indian Ocean is controlled by the monsoon winds. Biannually these winds reverse their pattern, causing a reversal in the surface currents and alternative high and low pressure conditions over Asia and Australia.

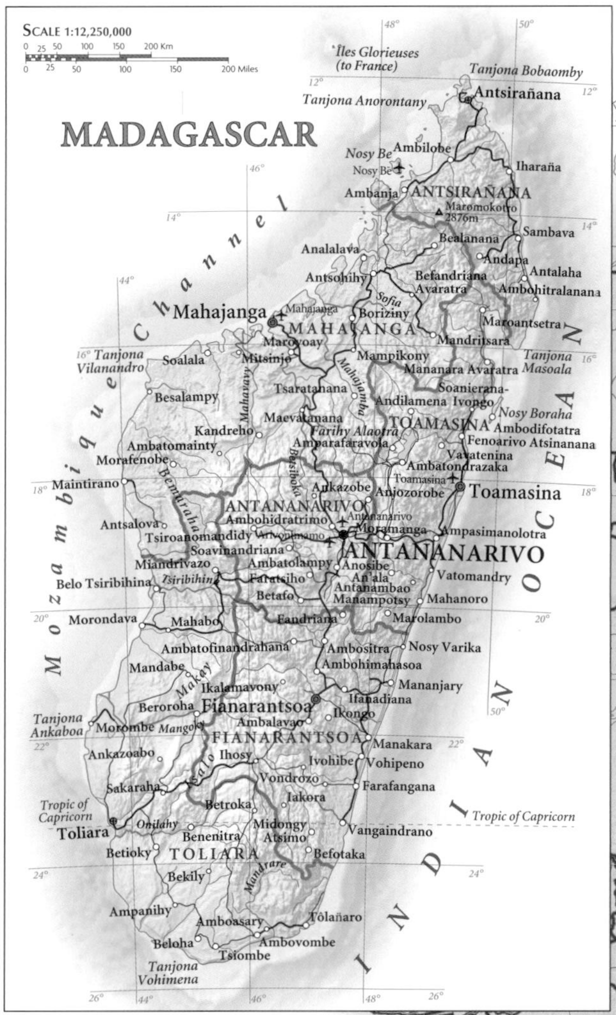

## Resources

Many of the small islands in the Indian Ocean rely exclusively on tuna-fishing and tourism to maintain their economies. Most fisheries are artisanal, although large-scale tuna-fishing does take place in the Seychelles, Mauritius and the western Indian Ocean. Other resources include oil in the Persian Gulf, pearls in the Red Sea, and tin from deposits off the shores of Myanmar, Thailand, and Indonesia.

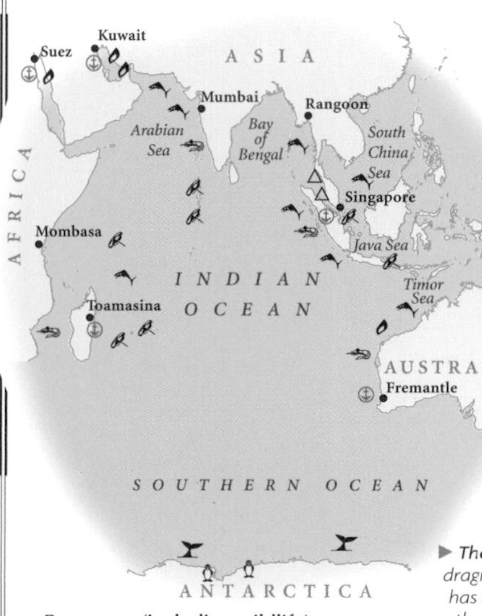

**Resources (including wildlife)**

| | | |
|---|---|---|
| fish | △ | tin deposits |
| penguins | | tourism |
| shellfish | ● | major towns |
| whales | ⊕ | major ports |
| oil & gas | | |

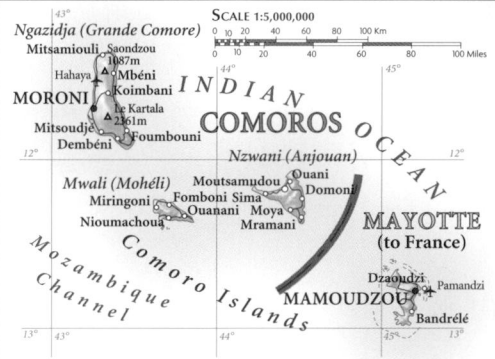

▶ The recent use of large dragnets for tuna-fishing has not only threatened the livelihoods of many small-scale fisheries, but also caused widespread environmental concern about the potential impact on other marine species.

SCALE 1:12,250,000

MADAGASCAR

SCALE 1:5,000,000

COMOROS
MORONI
MAYOTTE (to France)
MAMOUDZOU

SEYCHELLES
VICTORIA
SCALE 1:2,250,000

▲ Coral reefs support an enormous diversity of animal and plant life. Many species of tropical fish, like these squirrel fish, live and feed around the profusion of reefs and atolls in the Indian Ocean.

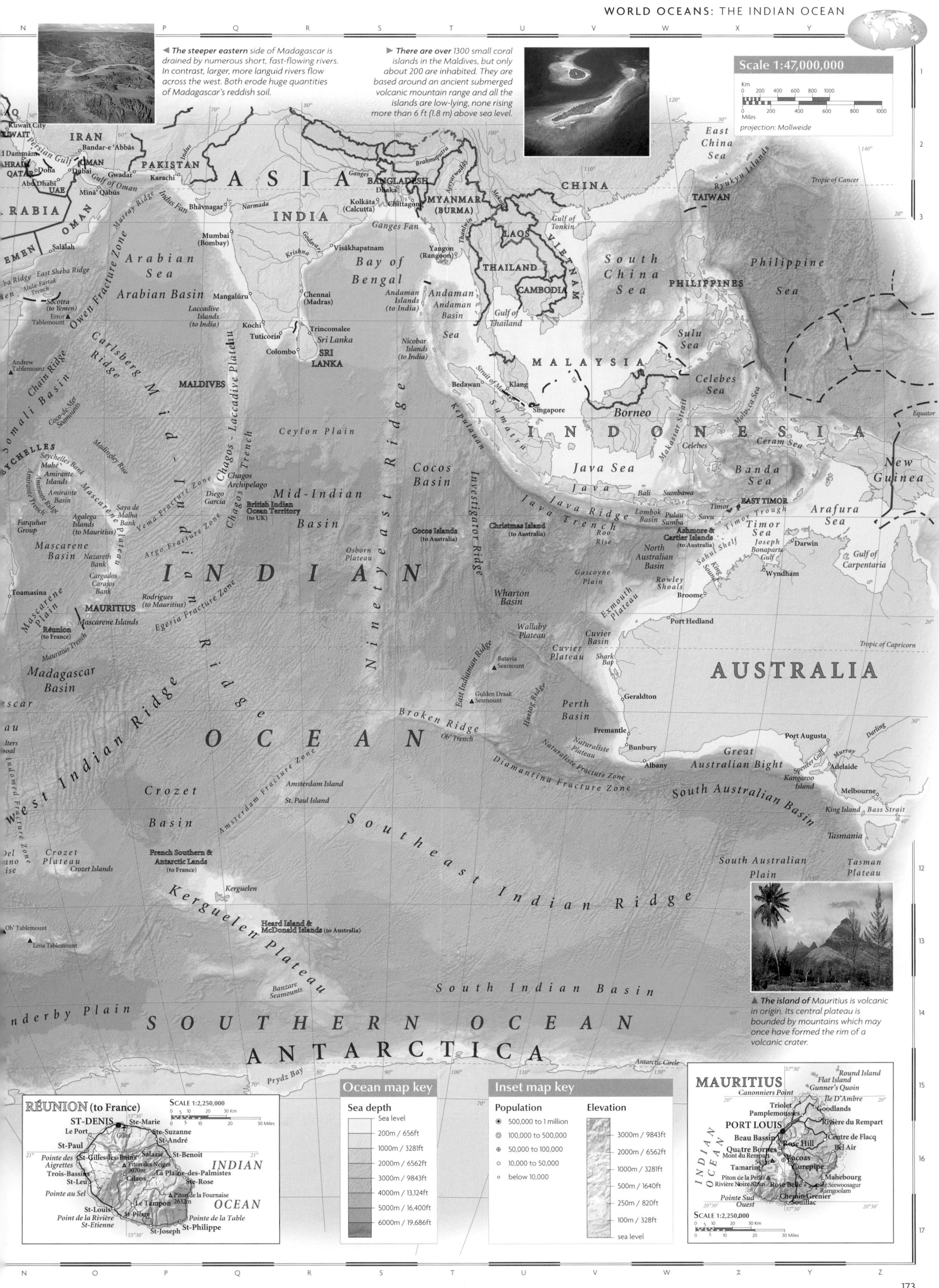

◀ *The steeper eastern* side of Madagascar is drained by numerous short, fast-flowing rivers. In contrast, larger, more languid rivers flow across the west. Both erode huge quantities of Madagascar's reddish soil.

▶ *There are over* 1300 small coral islands in the Maldives, but only about 200 are inhabited. They are based around an ancient submerged volcanic mountain range and all the islands are low-lying, none rising more than 6 ft (1.8 m) above sea level.

**Scale 1:47,000,000**

Km
0  200  400  600  800  1000

Miles
0  200  400  600  800  1000

*projection: Mollweide*

Kuwait City
KUWAIT
1 Dammām
BAHRAIN
QATAR Doha
Abu Dhabi UAE
ARABIA
YEMEN
Salālah

IRAN
OMAN Bandar-e 'Abbās
Gulf of Oman
Mina' Qābūs

PAKISTAN
Gwadar
Karachi

ASIA
Indus
INDIA
Narmada
Mumbai (Bombay)
Bhāvnagar
Gujarat
Krishna
Godavari

Ganges
BANGLADESH
Kolkāta (Calcutta)
Dhaka
Chittagong

MYANMAR (BURMA)
Brahmaputra
Irrawaddy
Yangon (Rangoon)

CHINA
LAOS
Mekong
THAILAND
VIETNAM
CAMBODIA
Gulf of Tonkin
Gulf of Thailand

TAIWAN
East China Sea
Ryukyu Islands
Tropic of Cancer

Murray Ridge
Indus Fan
Owen Fracture Zone

*Arabian Sea*
*Arabian Basin*
Mangalūru
Laccadive Islands (to India)
Kochi
Chennai (Madras)
Visākhapatnam

Bay of Bengal
Ganges Fan

Andaman Islands (to India)
Andaman Basin
Andaman Sea

South China Sea

Philippine Sea

PHILIPPINES

East Sheba Ridge
Socotra (to Yemen)
Error Tablemount
Alula-Fartak Trench

Andrew Tablemount

Carlsberg Ridge
Chain Ridge

Somali Basin

MALDIVES

Tuticorin
Trincomalee
Sri Lanka
SRI LANKA
Colombo

Nicobar Islands (to India)

Strait of Malacca
Bedawan
MALAYSIA
Klang
Singapore
Borneo

Sulu Sea
Celebes Sea

SEYCHELLES
Seychelles Bank
Mahé
Coco-de-Mer Seamounts
Amirante Islands
Amirante Basin
Amirante Trench

Madingley Rise
Mascarene Plateau

Chagos-Laccadive Plateau

Ceylon Plain

Vema Fracture Zone
Chagos Fracture Zone
Chagos Trench

Chagos Archipelago
Diego Garcia
British Indian Ocean Territory (to UK)

Mid-Indian Basin

Cocos Basin
Kepulauan
Sumatra

INDONESIA
Celebes
Java Sea
Java

Makassar Strait
Molucca Sea
Ceram Sea
Banda Sea

New Guinea

Equator

Farquhar Group
Agalega Islands (to Mauritius)
Saya de Malha Bank
Nazareth Bank
Cargados Carajos Bank

Argo Fracture Zone

INDIAN

Ninetyeast Ridge

Cocos Islands (to Australia)

Java Ridge
Java Trench

Christmas Island (to Australia)

Roo Rise
Lombok Basin
Bali
Sumbawa
Sumba
Savu
Timor
EAST TIMOR
Timor Sea
Timor Trough
Joseph Bonaparte Gulf
Darwin
Wyndham

Arafura Sea

Mascarene Basin

Mascarene Islands
MAURITIUS
Réunion (to France)

Osborn Plateau

Egeria Fracture Zone

Rodrigues (to Mauritius)

Wharton Basin

Gascoyne Plain
North Australian Basin

Ashmore & Cartier Islands (to Australia)
Sahul Shelf

Gulf of Carpentaria

Mauritius Trench

Madagascar Basin

Ninetyeast Ridge

Batavia Seamount
East Indiaman Ridge
Gulden Draak Seamount

Wallaby Plateau

Cuvier Plateau
Cuvier Basin

Shark Bay
Rowley Shoals
Esmouth Plateau
Broome
Port Hedland

AUSTRALIA

Tropic of Capricorn

OCEAN

Broken Ridge
Ob' Trench

Hantsu Ridge

Perth Basin
Geraldton

West Indian Ridge
Mid-Indian Ridge

Amsterdam Fracture Zone

Crozet Basin

Amsterdam Island
St. Paul Island

Naturaliste Plateau
Naturaliste Fracture Zone
Diamantina Fracture Zone

Fremantle
Bunbury

Great Australian Bight

Albany

South Australian Basin

Port Augusta
Spencer Gulf
Kangaroo Island
Adelaide
Melbourne

Darling
Murray

Crozet Plateau
Crozet Islands

French Southern & Antarctic Lands (to France)

Kerguelen

Southeast Indian Ridge

South Australian Plain

King Island
Tasmania
Bass Strait
Tasman Plateau

Ob' Tablemount
Lena Tablemount

Kerguelen Plateau

Heard Island & McDonald Islands (to Australia)

Banzare Seamounts

South Indian Basin

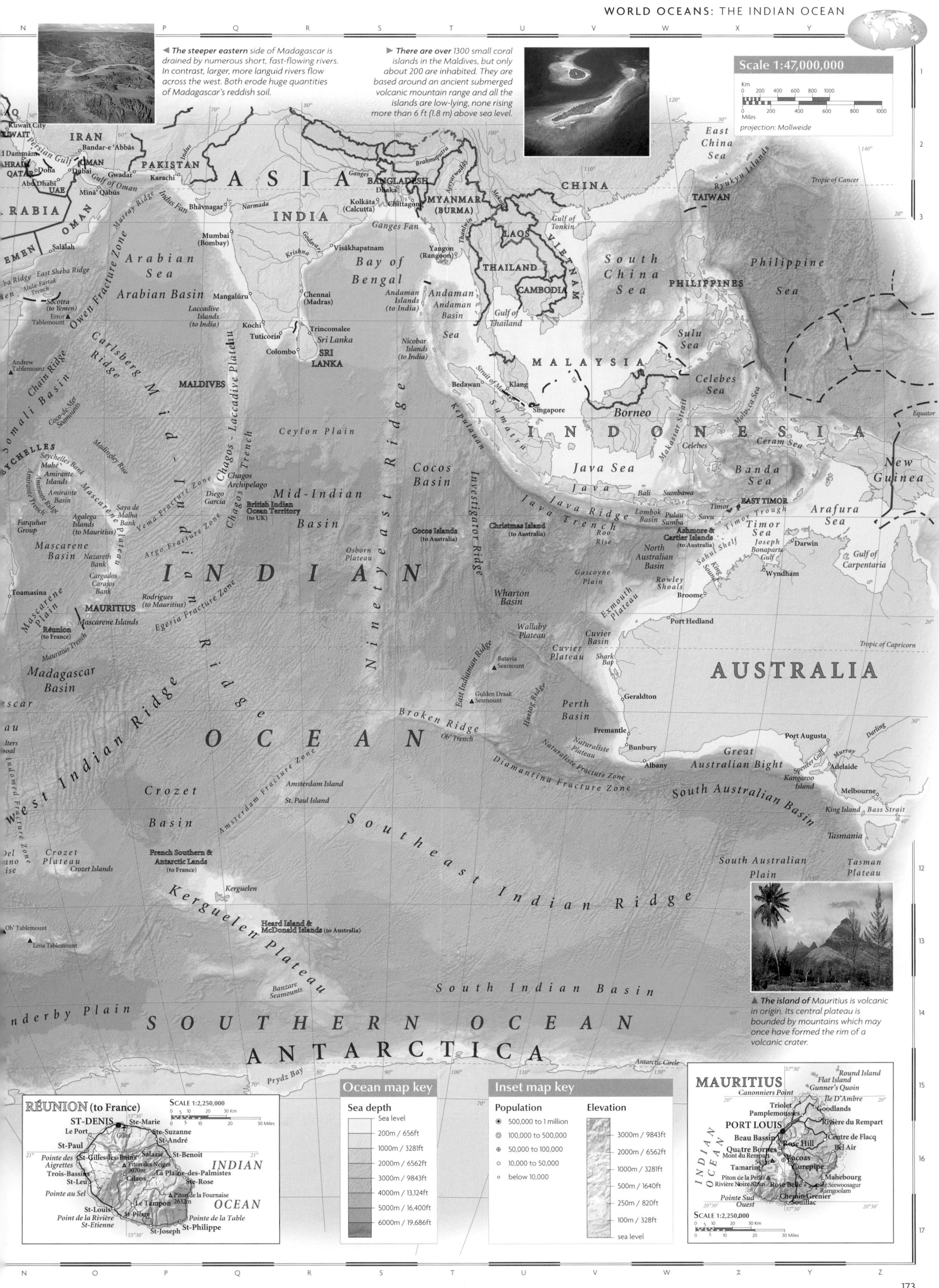

▲ *The island of* Mauritius is volcanic in origin. Its central plateau is bounded by mountains which may once have formed the rim of a volcanic crater.

Enderby Plain

SOUTHERN OCEAN

ANTARCTICA

Prydz Bay

Antarctic Circle

**Ocean map key**

**Sea depth**

Sea level
200m / 656ft
1000m / 3281ft
2000m / 6562ft
3000m / 9843ft
4000m / 13,124ft
5000m / 16,400ft
6000m / 19,686ft

**Inset map key**

**Population**
⦿ 500,000 to 1 million
◉ 100,000 to 500,000
⦾ 50,000 to 100,000
○ 10,000 to 50,000
○ below 10,000

**Elevation**
3000m / 9843ft
2000m / 6562ft
1000m / 3281ft
500m / 1640ft
250m / 820ft
100m / 328ft
sea level

**RÉUNION (to France)**
SCALE 1:2,250,000
0  5  10  20  30 Km
0  5  10  20  30 Miles

ST-DENIS
Le Port
St-Paul
Ste-Marie
Ste-Suzanne
St-André
Ste-Benoit
Salazie
St-Gilles-les-Bains
Piton des Neiges 3070m
Pointe des Aigrettes
Trois-Bassins
St-Leu
Cilaos
La Plaine-des-Palmistes
Ste-Rose
Pointe au Sel
INDIAN
Le Tampon 2632m
St-Louis
Piton de la Fournaise
OCEAN
St-Pierre
Pointe de la Table
Point de la Rivière St-Etienne
St-Joseph
St-Philippe

**MAURITIUS**
Round Island
Flat Island
Gunner's Quoin
Canonniers Point
Île D'Ambre
Triolet
Pamplemousses
Goodlands
Rivière du Rempart
PORT LOUIS
Beau Bassin
Centre de Flacq
Bel Air
Quatre Bornes
Mont du Rempart
Rose Hill
Tamarin
Vacoas
Curepipe
Piton de la Petite Rivière Noire 828m
INDIAN
OCEAN
Mahébourg
Rose Belle
Seewoosagur Ramgoolam
Souillac
Pointe Sud Ouest
Chemin Grenier

SCALE 1:2,250,000
0  5  10  20  30 Km
0  5  10  20  30 Miles

# Australasia & Oceania

Australasia and Oceania, covering a land area of

3,285,048 sq miles (8,508,238 sq km), takes in 14 countries

including the continent of Australia, New Zealand, Papua New Guinea,

and many island groups scattered across the Pacific Ocean.

**Greatest extent, North–South:**
2000 miles / 3200 km

**Greatest extent, East–West:**
2500 miles /4000 km

Most northerly point:
Eastern Island,
Midway Islands
28° 15′ N

Highest point:
Mount Wilhelm, Papua New Guinea
14,794 ft (4509 m)

Most easterly point:
Clipperton Island,
109° 12′ W

Highest recorded
temperature:
Oodnadatta, Australia
123°F (51°C)

Largest lake:
Lake Eyre, Australia
3430 sq miles (8884 sq km)

Lowest point:
Lake Eyre, Australia
-53 ft (-16 m) below sea level

Most westerly point:
Cape Inscription,
Australia 112° 57′ E

Cape York,
Australia
10° 41′ S

Ducie Island

Cape Byron,
Australia
153° 37′ E

*Tropic of Capricorn*

Lowest recorded
temperature:
Ranfurly, New Zealand
-14°F (-26°C)

Steep Point, Australia
113° 9′ E

Dirk Hartog
Island

South East Point,
Australia,
39° 10′ S

Most southerly point:
Macquarie Island,
Australia
54° 30′ S

Dirk Hartog
Island, Australia | Great Dividing
Range | New
Caledonia | New Zealand | Tonga | Tuamoto
Islands | Ducie Island,
Pitcairn Islands

*Cross-section from Dirk Hartog Island, Australia to Ducie Island, Pitcairn Islands*

line of cross-section

0  500  1000  1500 Km

0  500  1000  1500 Miles

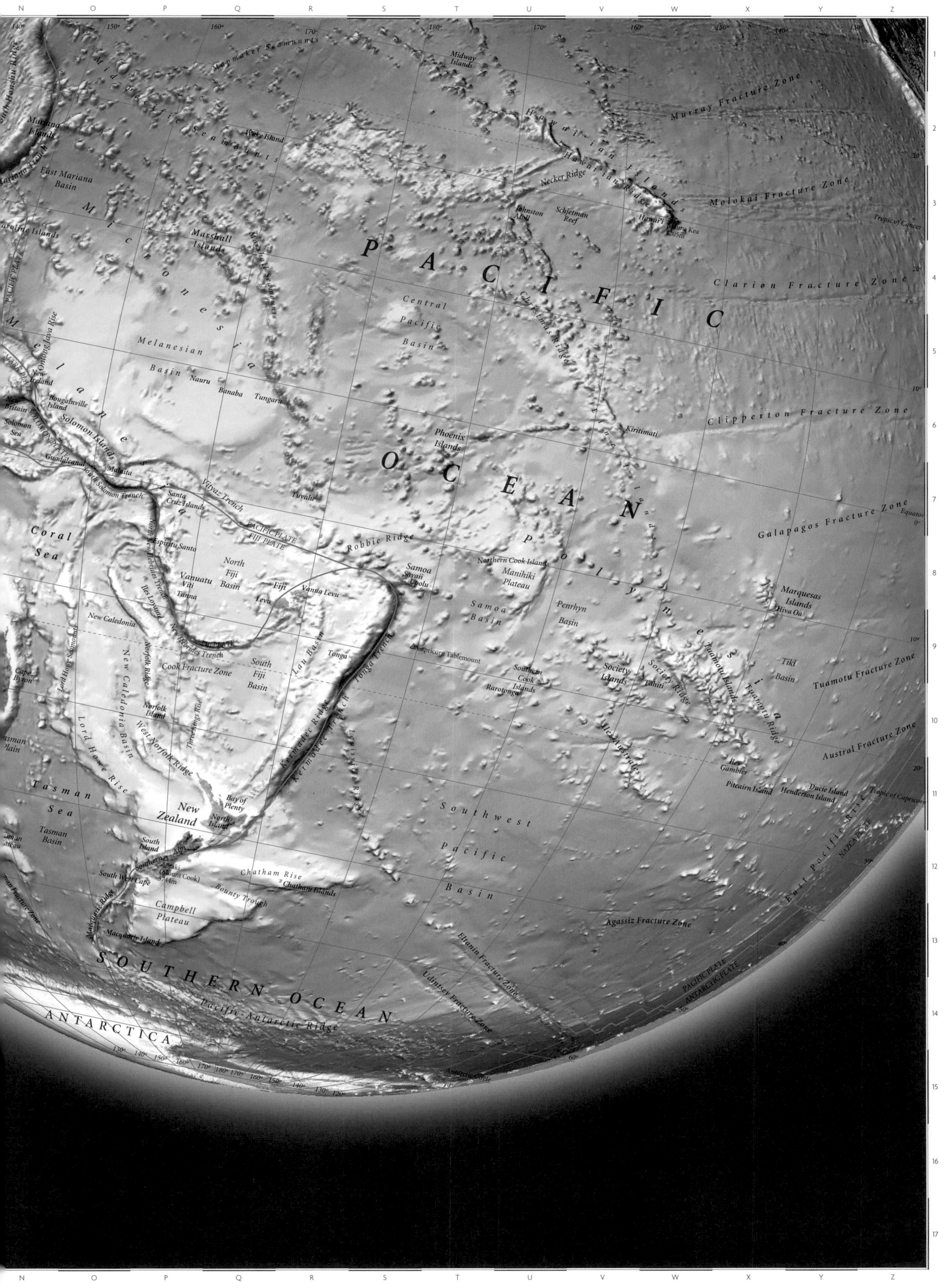

PACIFIC

OCEAN

SOUTHERN OCEAN

ANTARCTICA

Hawaiian Islands

Murray Fracture Zone

Molokai Fracture Zone

Tropic of Cancer

Clarion Fracture Zone

Clipperton Fracture Zone

Galapagos Fracture Zone

Equator

Tuamotu Fracture Zone

Austral Fracture Zone

Tropic of Capricorn

Mid-Pacific Seamounts

Musicians Seamounts

Midway Islands

Wake Island

Necker Ridge

Johnston Atoll

Schietman Reef

Hawaii Mauna Kea 4205m

Mariana Islands

East Mariana Basin

Caroline Islands

Marshall Islands

Micronesia

Melanesia

Melanesian Basin

Nauru

Banaba

Tungaru

Kiribati Seamounts

New Ireland

Bougainville Island

New Britain

Solomon Sea

Solomon Islands

Guadalcanal

Malaita

South Solomon Trench

North New Hebrides Trench

Santa Cruz Islands

Espiritu Santo

Vanuatu

Viti

Tanna

Iles Loyauté

New Caledonia

New Caledonia Basin

Norfolk Ridge

Norfolk Island

Three Kings Ridge

Cape Byron

Lord Howe Seamounts

Lord Howe Rise

Tasman Plain

Tasman Sea

Tasman Basin

New Zealand

South Island

North Island

Southern Alps

Aoraki (Mount Cook) 3724m

South West Cape

Campbell Plateau

Macquarie Ridge

Macquarie Island

Central Pacific Basin

Phoenix Islands

Tuvalu

Robbie Ridge

PACIFIC PLATE

FIJI PLATE

North Fiji Basin

Fiji

Levu

Vanua Levu

Samoa

Savaii

Upolu

Samoa Basin

Northern Cook Islands

Manihiki Plateau

Penrhyn Basin

Southern Cook Islands

Rarotonga

Society Islands

Society Ridge

Tahiti

Tuamotu Islands

Polynesia

Christmas Ridge

Line Islands

Kiritimati

Marquesas Islands

Hiva Oa

Tiki Basin

Rangiroa Ridge

Iles Australes

Iles Gambier

Pitcairn Island

Henderson Island

Ducie Island

New Hebrides Trench

Cook Fracture Zone

South Fiji Basin

Lau Basin

Tonga

Kermadec Ridge

Kermadec Trench

Tonga Trench

Louisville Ridge

Capricorn Tablemount

Bay of Plenty

Chatham Rise

Chatham Islands

Bounty Trough

Southwest Pacific Basin

Agassiz Fracture Zone

East Pacific Rise

NAZCA PLATE

Eltanin Fracture Zone

Udintsev Fracture Zone

Pacific-Antarctic Ridge

PACIFIC PLATE

ANTARCTIC PLATE

Antarctic Circle

# Political Australasia & Oceania

Vast expanses of ocean separate this geographically fragmented realm, characterized more by each country's isolation than by any political unity. Australia's and New Zealand's traditional ties with the United Kingdom, as members of the Commonwealth, are now being called into question as Australasian and Oceanian nations are increasingly looking to forge new relationships with neighboring Asian countries like Japan. External influences have featured strongly in the politics of the Pacific Islands; the various territories of Micronesia were largely under US control until the late 1980s, and France, New Zealand, the US, and the UK still have territories under colonial rule in Polynesia. Nuclear weapons-testing by Western superpowers was widespread during the Cold War period, but has now been discontinued.

◄ *Western Australia's mineral* wealth has transformed its state capital, Perth, into one of Australia's major cities. Perth is one of the world's most isolated cities – over 2500 miles (4000 km) from the population centers of the eastern seaboard.

Scale 1:35,500,000

*projection: Lambert Azimuthal Equal Area*

## Population

Density of settlement in the region is generally low. Australia is one of the least densely populated countries on Earth with over 80% of its population living within 25 miles (40 km) of the coast – mostly in the southeast of the country. New Zealand, and the island groups of Melanesia, Micronesia, and Polynesia, are much more densely populated, although many of the smaller islands remain uninhabited.

**Population density**
(people per sq mile)

| | |
|---|---|
| | below 10 |
| | 10–62 |
| | 63–130 |
| | 131–259 |
| | 260–519 |
| | 520–780 |
| | above 780 |

▲ *The myriad of* small coral islands that are scattered across the Pacific Ocean are often uninhabited, as they offer little shelter from the weather, often no fresh water, and only limited food supplies.

◄ *The planes of* the Australian Royal Flying Doctor Service are able to cover large expanses of barren land quickly, bringing medical treatment to the most inaccessible and far-flung places.

176

## Languages

English is spoken throughout Australia and New Zealand. In Australia, English has been superimposed on a mosaic of Aboriginal languages. In New Zealand, the indigenous language, Maori, is the official language besides English. In Papua New Guinea, Melanesian Pidgin has become a lingua franca alongside several hundred indigenous languages. Across the region, the indigenous languages can be grouped into (1) the Aboriginal languages of Australia, (2) the Papuan languages spoken mostly inland in Papua New Guinea, and (3) the widely dispersed Austronesian, which includes coastal languages of Papua New Guinea, New Zealand Maori, and languages of Oceania.

**Language groups**

- Australian
- Papuan
- Indo-European
- Austronesian

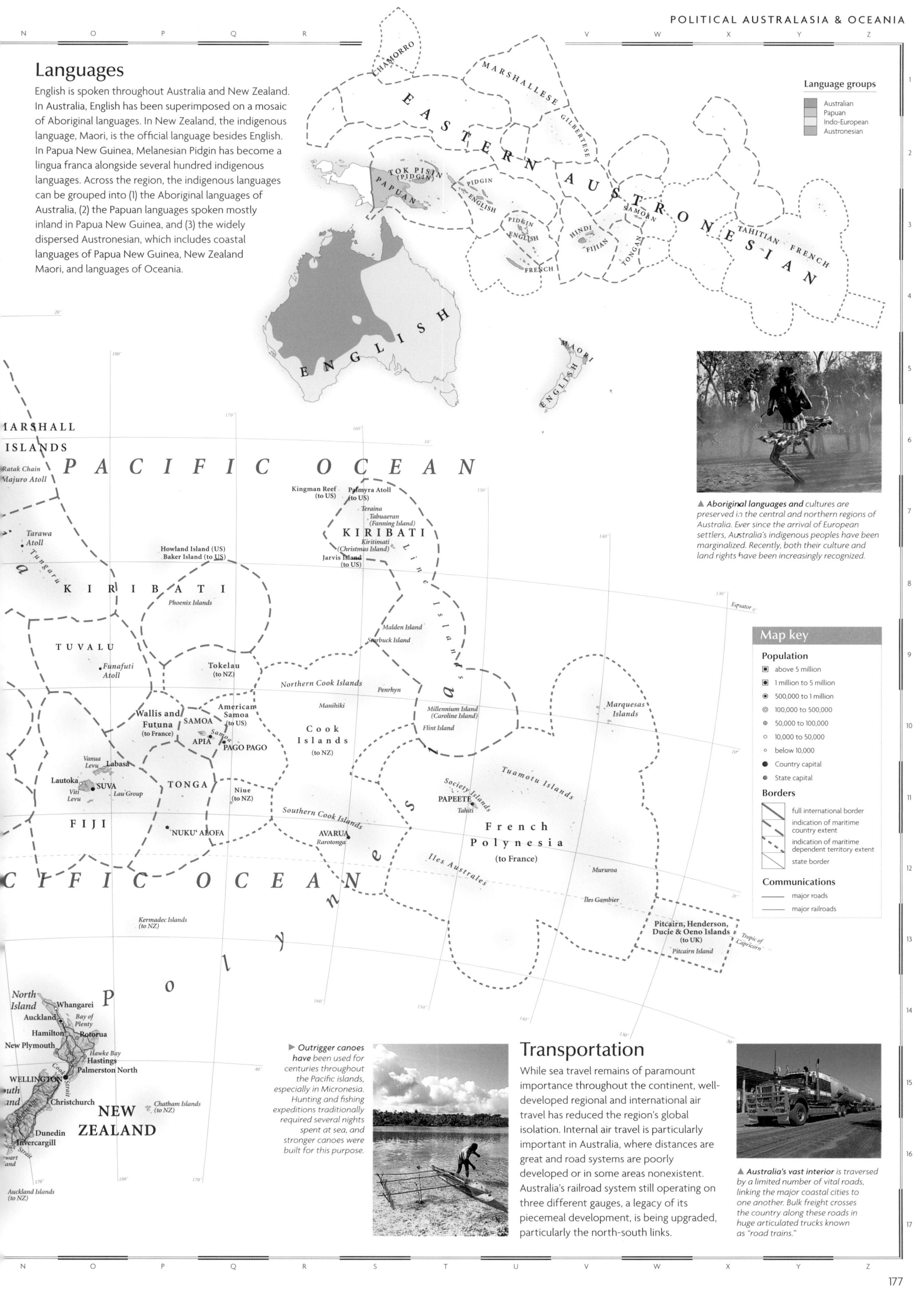

▲ *Aboriginal languages and* cultures are preserved in the central and northern regions of Australia. Ever since the arrival of European settlers, Australia's indigenous peoples have been marginalized. Recently, both their culture and land rights have been increasingly recognized.

**Map key**

**Population**

- ◼ above 5 million
- ◼ 1 million to 5 million
- ◉ 500,000 to 1 million
- ◎ 100,000 to 500,000
- ◍ 50,000 to 100,000
- ◦ 10,000 to 50,000
- ∘ below 10,000
- ● Country capital
- ● State capital

**Borders**

- full international border
- indication of maritime country extent
- indication of maritime dependent territory extent
- state border

**Communications**

- major roads
- major railroads

▶ *Outrigger canoes have* been used for centuries throughout the Pacific islands, especially in Micronesia. Hunting and fishing expeditions traditionally required several nights spent at sea, and stronger canoes were built for this purpose.

## Transportation

While sea travel remains of paramount importance throughout the continent, well-developed regional and international air travel has reduced the region's global isolation. Internal air travel is particularly important in Australia, where distances are great and road systems are poorly developed or in some areas nonexistent. Australia's railroad system still operating on three different gauges, a legacy of its piecemeal development, is being upgraded, particularly the north-south links.

▲ *Australia's vast interior is* traversed by a limited number of vital roads, linking the major coastal cities to one another. Bulk freight crosses the country along these roads in huge articulated trucks known as "road trains."

# Australasian & Oceanian resources

Natural resources are of major economic importance throughout Australasia and Oceania. Australia in particular is a major world exporter of raw materials such as coal, iron ore, and bauxite, while New Zealand's agricultural economy is dominated by sheep-raising. Trade with western Europe has declined significantly in the last 20 years, and the Pacific Rim countries of Southeast Asia are now the main trading partners, as well as a source of new settlers to the region. Australasia and Oceania's greatest resources are its climate and environment; tourism increasingly provides a vital source of income for the whole continent.

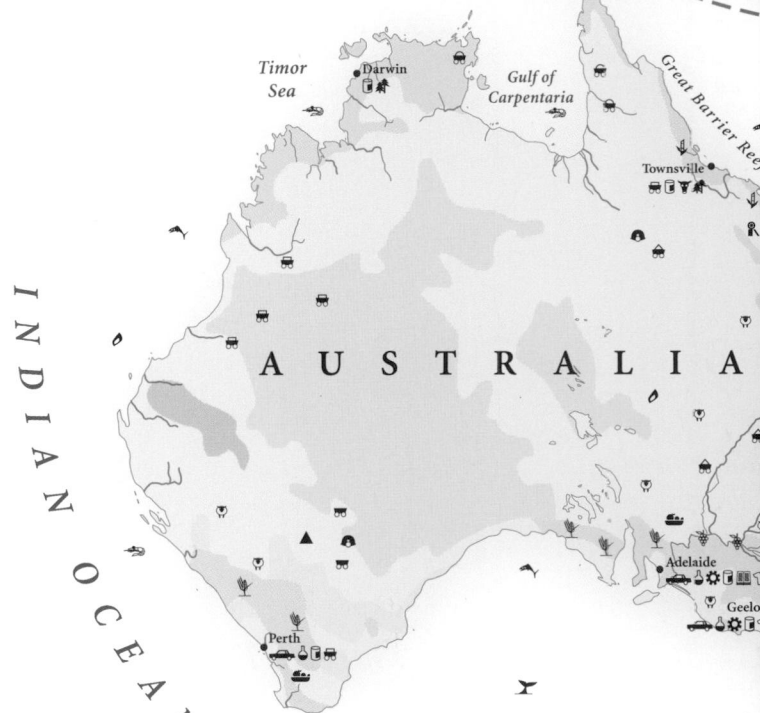

▲ **The largely unpolluted** waters of the Pacific Ocean support rich and varied marine life, much of which is farmed commercially. Here, oysters are gathered for market off the coast of New Zealand's South Island.

▶ **Huge flocks of** sheep are a common sight in New Zealand, where they outnumber people by 12 to 1. New Zealand is one of the world's largest exporters of wool and frozen lamb.

## Standard of living

In marked contrast to its neighbor, Australia, with one of the world's highest life expectancies and standards of living, Papua New Guinea is one of the world's least developed countries. In addition, high population growth and urbanization rates throughout the Pacific islands contribute to overcrowding. In Australia and New Zealand, the Aboriginal and Maori people have been isolated, although recently their traditional land ownership rights have begun to be legally recognized in an effort to ease their social and economic isolation, and to improve living standards.

### Standard of living
(UN human development index)

- low
- high
- figures unavailable

## Environmental issues

The prospect of rising sea levels poses a threat to many low-lying islands in the Pacific. The testing of nuclear weapons, once common throughout the region, was finally discontinued in 1996. Australia's ecological balance has been irreversibly altered by the introduction of alien species. Although it has the world's largest underground water reserve, the Great Artesian Basin, the availability of fresh water in Australia remains critical. Periodic droughts combined with overgrazing lead to desertification and increase the risk of devastating bush fires, and occasional flash floods.

### Environmental issues

- national parks
- tropical forest
- forest destroyed
- desert
- desertification
- polluted rivers
- radioactive contamination
- marine pollution
- heavy marine pollution
- poor urban air quality

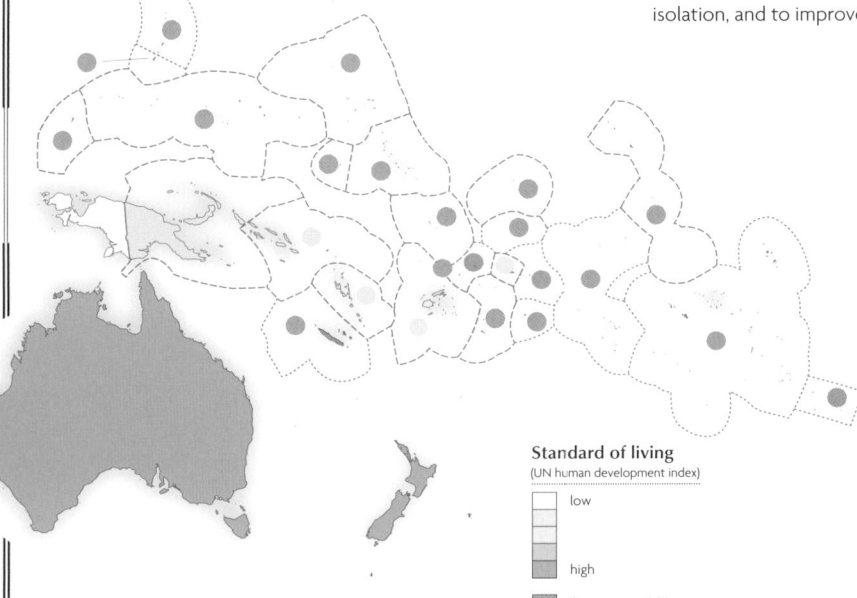

▲ **In 1946 Bikini Atoll,** in the Marshall Islands, was chosen as the site for Operation Crossroads – investigating the effects of atomic bombs upon naval vessels. Further nuclear tests continued until the early 1990s. The long-term environmental effects are unknown.

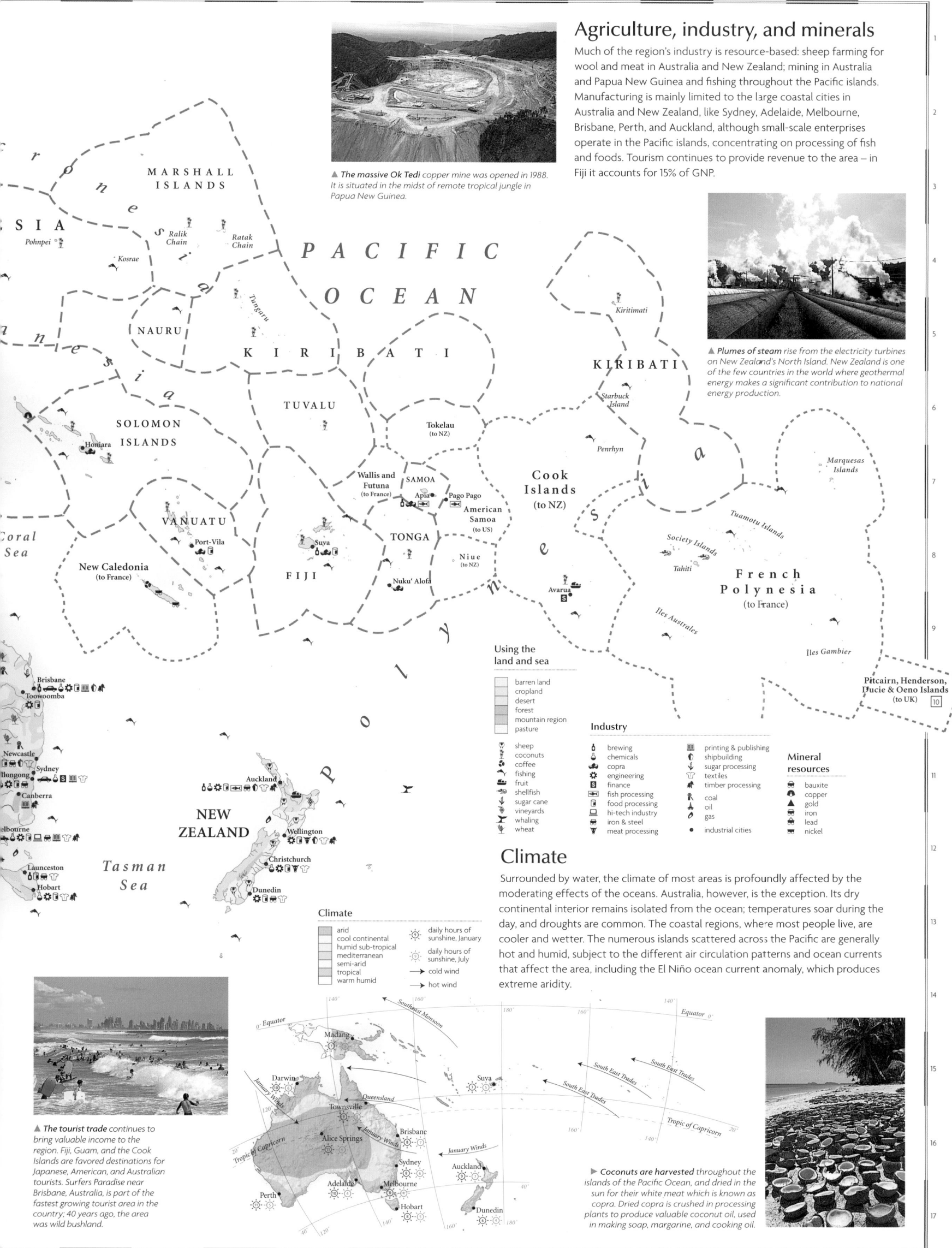

## Agriculture, industry, and minerals

Much of the region's industry is resource-based: sheep farming for wool and meat in Australia and New Zealand; mining in Australia and Papua New Guinea and fishing throughout the Pacific islands. Manufacturing is mainly limited to the large coastal cities in Australia and New Zealand, like Sydney, Adelaide, Melbourne, Brisbane, Perth, and Auckland, although small-scale enterprises operate in the Pacific islands, concentrating on processing of fish and foods. Tourism continues to provide revenue to the area – in Fiji it accounts for 15% of GNP.

▲ **The massive Ok Tedi** copper mine was opened in 1988. It is situated in the midst of remote tropical jungle in Papua New Guinea.

▲ **Plumes of steam** rise from the electricity turbines on New Zealand's North Island. New Zealand is one of the few countries in the world where geothermal energy makes a significant contribution to national energy production.

### Using the land and sea

- barren land
- cropland
- desert
- forest
- mountain region
- pasture

### Industry

- sheep
- coconuts
- coffee
- fishing
- fruit
- shellfish
- sugar cane
- vineyards
- whaling
- wheat

- brewing
- chemicals
- copra
- engineering
- finance
- fish processing
- food processing
- hi-tech industry
- iron & steel
- meat processing

- printing & publishing
- shipbuilding
- sugar processing
- textiles
- timber processing
- coal
- oil
- gas
- industrial cities

### Mineral resources

- bauxite
- copper
- gold
- iron
- lead
- nickel

## Climate

Surrounded by water, the climate of most areas is profoundly affected by the moderating effects of the oceans. Australia, however, is the exception. Its dry continental interior remains isolated from the ocean; temperatures soar during the day, and droughts are common. The coastal regions, where most people live, are cooler and wetter. The numerous islands scattered across the Pacific are generally hot and humid, subject to the different air circulation patterns and ocean currents that affect the area, including the El Niño ocean current anomaly, which produces extreme aridity.

### Climate

- arid
- cool continental
- humid sub-tropical
- mediterranean
- semi-arid
- tropical
- warm humid

- daily hours of sunshine, January
- daily hours of sunshine, July
- cold wind
- hot wind

▲ **The tourist trade** continues to bring valuable income to the region. Fiji, Guam, and the Cook Islands are favored destinations for Japanese, American, and Australian tourists. Surfers Paradise near Brisbane, Australia, is part of the fastest growing tourist area in the country; 40 years ago, the area was wild bushland.

▶ **Coconuts are harvested** throughout the islands of the Pacific Ocean, and dried in the sun for their white meat which is known as copra. Dried copra is crushed in processing plants to produce valuable coconut oil, used in making soap, margarine, and cooking oil.

# Australia

Australia is the world's smallest continent, a stable landmass lying between the Indian and Pacific oceans. Previously home to its aboriginal peoples only, since the end of the 18th century immigration has transformed the face of the country. Initially settlers came mainly from western Europe, particularly the UK, and for years Australia remained wedded to its British colonial past. More recent immigrants have come from eastern Europe, and from Asian countries such as Japan, South Korea, and Indonesia. Australia is now forging strong trading links with these "Pacific Rim" countries and its economic future seems to lie with Asia and the Americas, rather than Europe, its traditional partner.

◀ *Uluru (Ayers Rock)*, the world's largest free-standing rock, is a massive outcrop of red sandstone in Australia's desert center. Wind and sandstorms have ground the rock into the smooth curves seen here. Uluru is revered as a sacred site by many aboriginal peoples.

## Scale 1:11,500,000

projection: Lambert Conformal Conic

## Map key

**Population**

- ▣ 1 million to 5 million
- ◉ 500,000 to 1 million
- ◎ 100,000 to 500,000
- ⊕ 50,000 to 100,000
- ○ 10,000 to 50,000
- ∘ below 10,000

**Elevation**

- 2000m / 6562ft
- 1000m / 3281ft
- 500m / 1640ft
- 250m / 820ft
- 100m / 328ft
- sea level

## Using the land

Over 104 million sheep are dispersed in vast herds around the country, contributing to a major export industry. Cattle-ranching is important, particularly in the west. Wheat, and grapes for Australia's wine industry, are grown mainly in the south. Much of the country is desert, unsuitable for agriculture unless irrigation is used.

### The urban/rural population divide

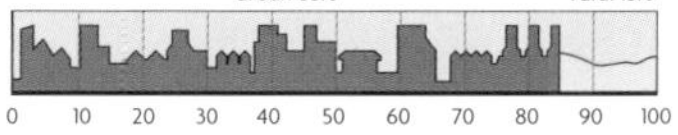

urban 85%                                    rural 15%

0  10  20  30  40  50  60  70  80  90  100

| Population density | Total land area |
|---|---|
| 6 people per sq mile (2 people per sq km) | 2,967,893 sq miles (7,686,850 sq km) |

### Land use and agricultural distribution

- 🐂 cattle
- 🐑 sheep
- 🌾 cereals
- sugar cane
- timber
- 🍇 vineyards
- ■ capital cities
- ■ major towns
- pasture
- cropland
- forest
- desert
- mountain region

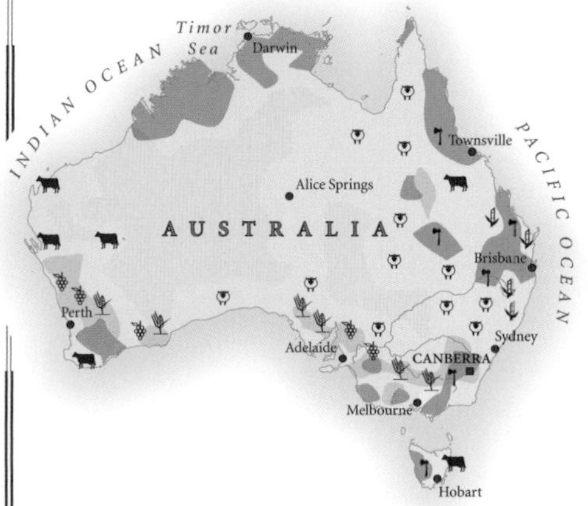

▲ *Lines of ripening* vines stretch for miles in Barossa Valley, a major wine-growing region near Adelaide.

## The landscape

Australia consists of many eroded plateaus, lying firmly in the middle of the Indo-Australian Plate. It is the world's flattest continent, and the driest, after Antarctica. The coasts tend to be more hilly and fertile, especially in the east. The mountains of the Great Dividing Range form a natural barrier between the eastern coastal areas and the flat, dry plains and desert regions of the Australian "outback."

▲ *The Great Barrier Reef* is the world's largest area of coral islands and reefs. It runs for about 1240 miles (2000 km) along the Queensland coast.

▲ *The Pinnacles are* a series of rugged sandstone pillars. Their strange shapes have been formed by water and wind erosion.

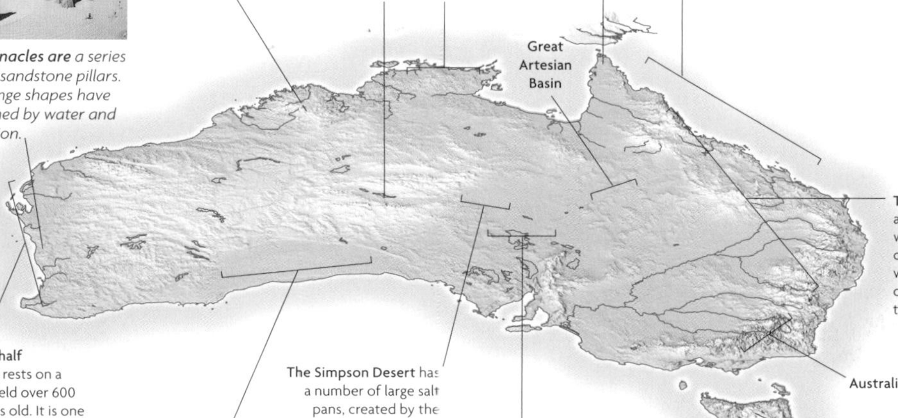

**The ancient Kimberley** Plateau is the source of some of Australia's richest mineral deposits, including diamonds.

**Uluru (Ayers Rock)**

**Arnhem Land**

**Great Artesian Basin**

**The tropical rain forest** of the Cape York Peninsula contains more than 600 different varieties of tree.

**More than half** of Australia rests on a uniform shield over 600 million years old. It is one of the Earth's original geological plates.

**The Simpson Desert** has a number of large salt pans, created by the evaporation of past rivers and now sourced by seasonal rains. Some are crusted with gypsum, but most are covered by common salt crystals.

**The Nullarbor Plain** is a low-lying limestone plateau which is so flat that the Trans-Australian Railway runs through it in a straight line for more than 300 miles (483 km).

**The Lake Eyre** basin, lying 51 ft (16 m) below sea level, is one of the largest inland drainage systems in the world, covering an area of more than 500,000 sq miles (1,300,000 sq km).

**The Great Dividing Range** forms a watershed between east- and west-flowing rivers. Erosion has created deep valleys, gorges, and waterfalls where rivers tumble over escarpments on their way to the sea.

**Australian Alps**

**Tasmania has the** same geological structure as the Australian Alps. During the last period of glaciation, 18,000 years ago, sea levels were some 300 ft (100 m) lower and it was joined to the mainland.

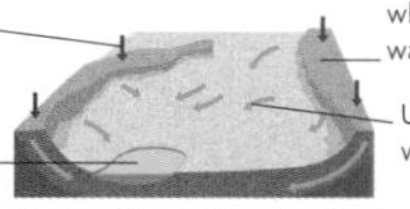

▲ *The Great Artesian Basin* underlies nearly 20% of the total area of Australia, providing a valuable store of underground water, essential to Australian agriculture. The ephemeral rivers which drain the northern part of the basin have highly braided courses and, in consequence, the area is known as "channel country."

▶ The Great Barrier Reef attracts thousands of tourists every year, drawn by the spectacular coral formations and exotic marine life.

▲ Lying on the border between New South Wales and Queensland, this summit is in the Great Dividing Range which splits the fertile eastern coast from the more arid interior.

## Transportation & industry

Extensive mineral reserves, including coal, iron ore, gold, bauxite, and copper, once formed the heart of Australian industry, along with agricultural products. In recent years, Australia has moved from being a primary producer to a largely service-based economy, particularly the rapidly developing tourist industry.

### Major industry and infrastructure

brewing
car manufacture
chemicals
coal
electronics
engineering
food processing
mining
oil & gas
tourism

■ capital cities
● major towns
✈ international airports
— major roads
major industrial areas

### The Transportation network

| | | | |
|---|---|---|---|
| 204,470 miles (329,100 km) | | 11,658 miles (18,619 km) | |
| 5911 miles (9514 km) | | 5197 miles (8366 km) | |

Well-developed air transportation links, including the Royal Flying Doctor Service, connect the sparsely populated center and west. Most freight travels in massive trucks known as "road trains."

▲ Sydney Harbour is one of the world's most spectacular natural harbors. Founded in 1788, Sydney was the first major settlement in Australia.

181

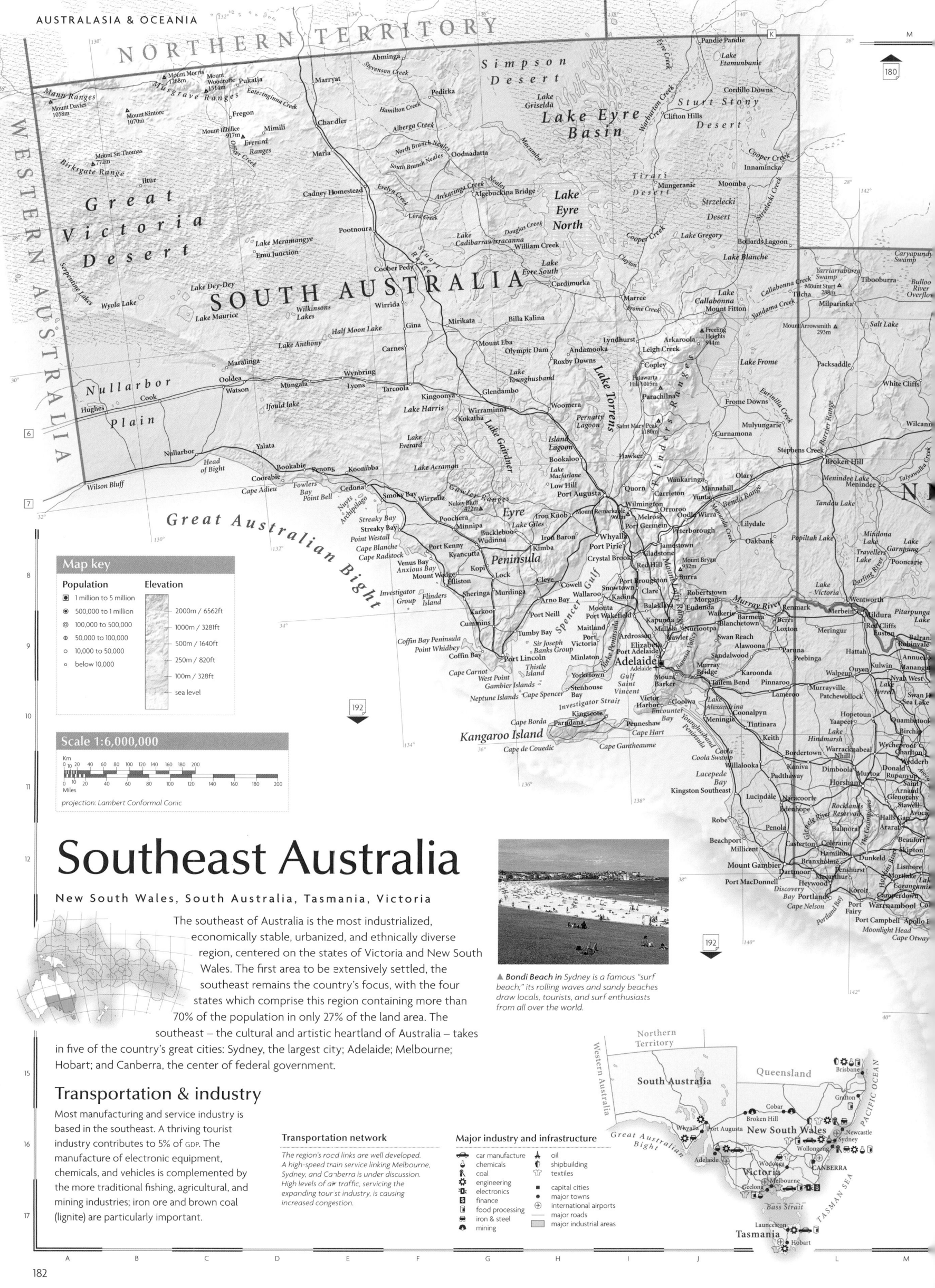

# Southeast Australia

## New South Wales, South Australia, Tasmania, Victoria

The southeast of Australia is the most industrialized, economically stable, urbanized, and ethnically diverse region, centered on the states of Victoria and New South Wales. The first area to be extensively settled, the southeast remains the country's focus, with the four states which comprise this region containing more than 70% of the population in only 27% of the land area. The southeast – the cultural and artistic heartland of Australia – takes in five of the country's great cities: Sydney, the largest city; Adelaide; Melbourne; Hobart; and Canberra, the center of federal government.

## Transportation & industry

Most manufacturing and service industry is based in the southeast. A thriving tourist industry contributes to 5% of GDP. The manufacture of electronic equipment, chemicals, and vehicles is complemented by the more traditional fishing, agricultural, and mining industries; iron ore and brown coal (lignite) are particularly important.

▲ **Bondi Beach in** Sydney is a famous "surf beach;" its rolling waves and sandy beaches draw locals, tourists, and surf enthusiasts from all over the world.

### Transportation network

*The region's road links are well developed. A high-speed train service linking Melbourne, Sydney, and Canberra is under discussion. High levels of air traffic, servicing the expanding tourist industry, is causing increased congestion.*

### Major industry and infrastructure

- car manufacture
- chemicals
- coal
- engineering
- electronics
- finance
- food processing
- iron & steel
- mining
- oil
- shipbuilding
- textiles
- capital cities
- major towns
- international airports
- major roads
- major industrial areas

### Map key

**Population**
- ▣ 1 million to 5 million
- ◉ 500,000 to 1 million
- ◎ 100,000 to 500,000
- ⊕ 50,000 to 100,000
- ○ 10,000 to 50,000
- ∘ below 10,000

**Elevation**
- 2000m / 6562ft
- 1000m / 3281ft
- 500m / 1640ft
- 250m / 820ft
- 100m / 328ft
- sea level

**Scale 1:6,000,000**

*projection: Lambert Conformal Conic*

## Using the land & sea

The western flanks of the Great Dividing Range and the northern deserts of South Australia support massive herds of sheep and cattle, while more intensive stockrearing occurs near the cities. Sugar cane is the most important industrial crop, and cereal grains including wheat, corn, barley, and sorghum are also grown. Grapes, citrus, and orchard fruits are among the wide range of fruit and vegetables cultivated in this region. Tasmania's forestry and fishing contributes to over one-third of the state's exports.

▲ The fertile Darling Downs, known as the "breadbasket of Australia," support a wide range of crops including cereals, sugar cane, and fruit.

▶ The Murray River has its source in the eastern uplands of the Great Dividing Range. Fed by melting snow, it runs for 1609 miles (2589 km), and has sufficient volume to reach the ocean southeast of Adelaide despite a minimal gradient for most of its lower reaches.

### The urban/rural population divide

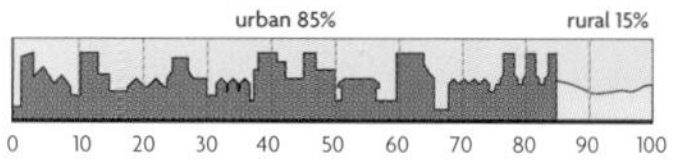

urban 85%    rural 15%

| Population density | Total land area |
|---|---|
| 18 people per sq mile (7 people per sq km) | 778,022 sq miles (2,015,600 sq km) |

### Land use and agricultural distribution

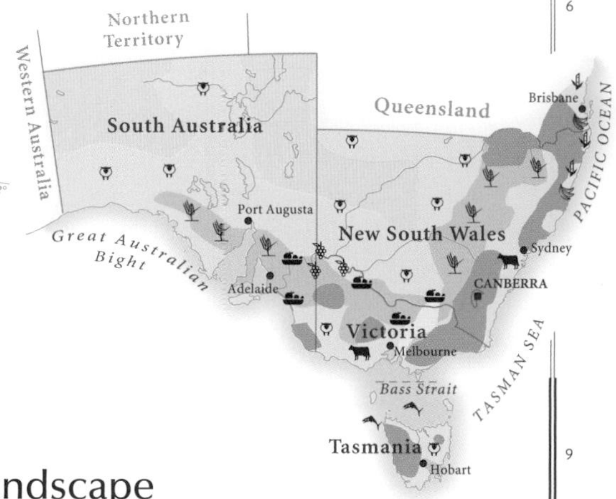

- cattle
- sheep
- bananas
- fishing
- fruit
- sugar cane
- vineyards
- wheat

- capital cities
- major towns

- pasture
- cropland
- forest
- desert
- mountain region

## The landscape

The southern half of the Great Dividing Range runs parallel to the eastern coast of Victoria and New South Wales as far as Tasmania, which, though divided from the mainland is part of the same mountain chain. South Australia comprises the Australian shield and half of the dry, flat Nullarbor Plain. The Murray/Darling river basin is the only major river system.

◀ The heavily folded Flinders Ranges is part of an arc of sedimentary rocks reaching northward from Kangaroo Island.

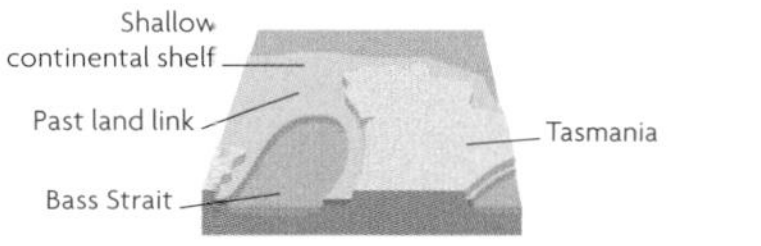

The Musgrave and Everard ranges form bare, rounded hills made up of ancient granite and gneiss.

Lake Eyre is the largest of southern Australia's dry lakes. Lying -51 ft (-16 m) below sea level, it has flooded only three times in the last century.

The Murray/Darling is Australia's longest river at 1703 miles (2739 km).

Shallow continental shelf
Past land link
Bass Strait
Tasmania

▲ Tasmania is part of Australia's eastern highlands, separated from the mainland by 155 miles (250 km) of the Bass Strait. In the recent geological past, dry land links between Tasmania and Victoria would have been possible during periods of world-wide glaciation, when the sea level was more than 180 ft (55 m) below that of present sea levels.

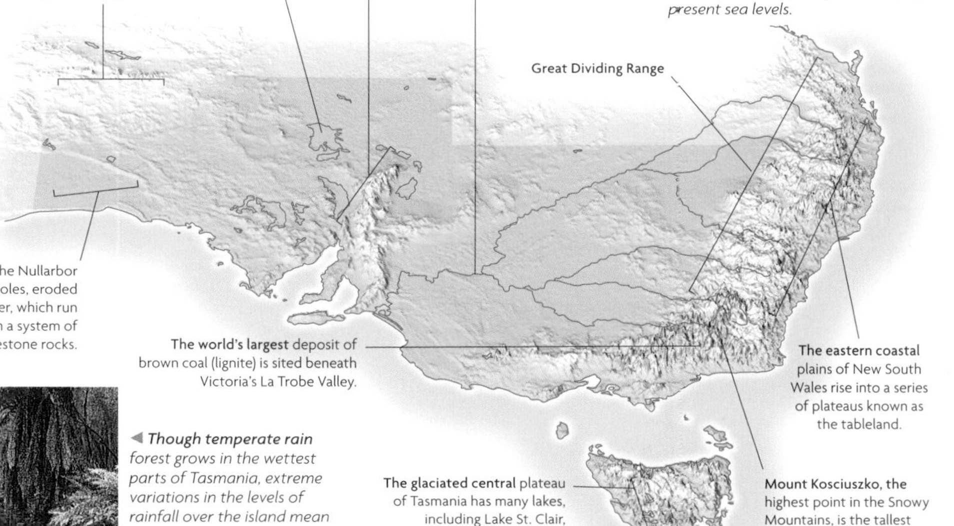

Great Dividing Range

The eastern part of the Nullarbor Plain has many sinkholes, eroded by rainwater, which run underground to form a system of long caves in the limestone rocks.

The world's largest deposit of brown coal (lignite) is sited beneath Victoria's La Trobe Valley.

◀ Though temperate rain forest grows in the wettest parts of Tasmania, extreme variations in the levels of rainfall over the island mean that some drier areas may experience forest fires.

The glaciated central plateau of Tasmania has many lakes, including Lake St. Clair, a piedmont lake more than 700 ft (200 m) deep.

The eastern coastal plains of New South Wales rise into a series of plateaus known as the tableland.

Mount Kosciuszko, the highest point in the Snowy Mountains, is the tallest mountain in Australia at 7316 ft (2228 m).

183

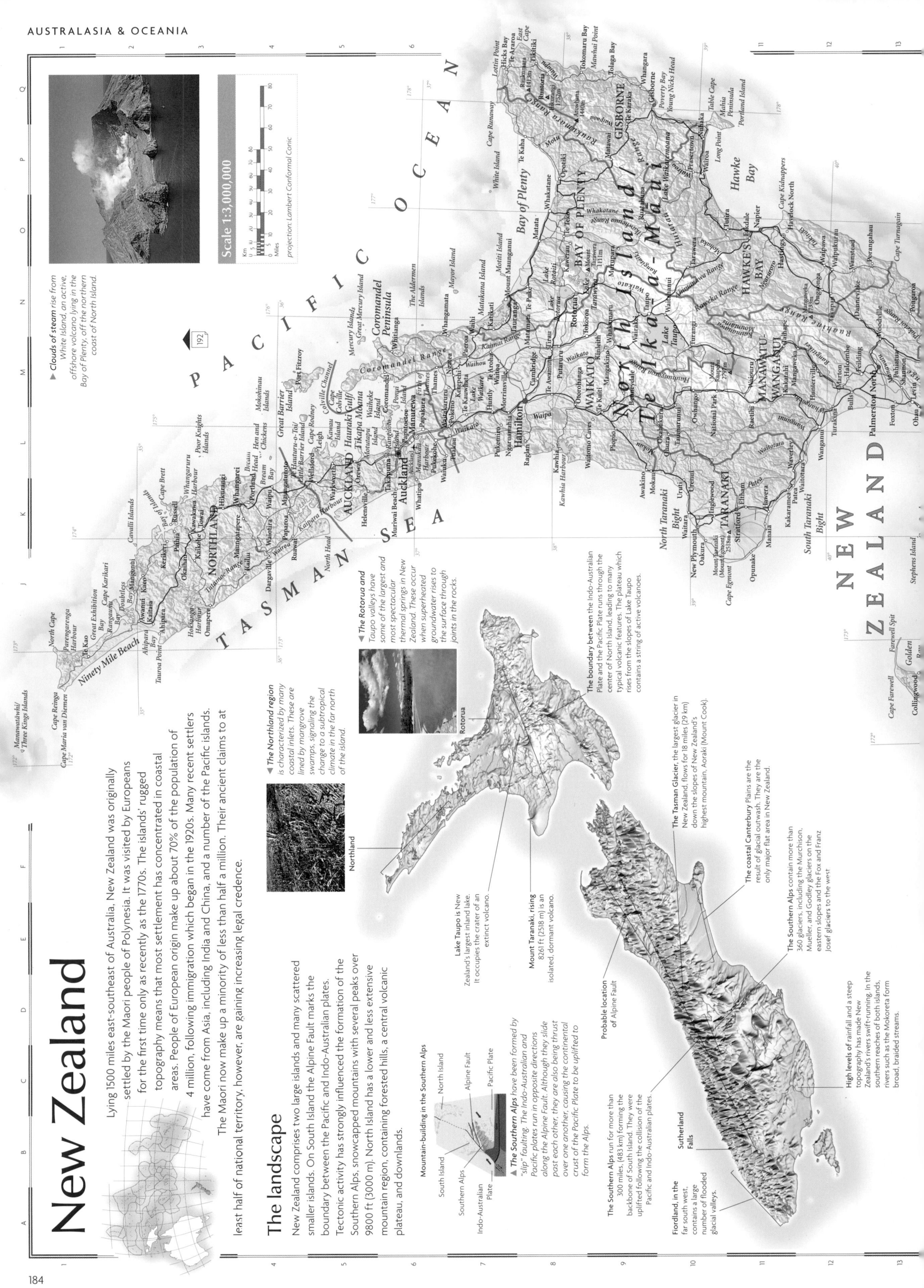

# New Zealand

Lying 1500 miles east-southeast of Australia, New Zealand was originally settled by the Maori people of Polynesia. It was visited by Europeans for the first time only as recently as the 1770s. The islands' rugged topography means that most settlement has concentrated in coastal areas. People of European origin make up about 70% of the population of 4 million, following immigration which began in the 1920s. Many recent settlers have come from Asia, including India and China, and a number of the Pacific islands. The Maori now make up a minority of less than half a million. Their ancient claims to at least half of national territory, however, are gaining increasing legal credence.

## The landscape

New Zealand comprises two large islands and many scattered smaller islands. On South Island the Alpine Fault marks the boundary between the Pacific and Indo-Australian plates. Tectonic activity has strongly influenced the formation of the Southern Alps, snowcapped mountains with several peaks over 9800 ft (3000 m). North Island has a lower and less extensive mountain region, containing forested hills, a central volcanic plateau, and downlands.

▲ Clouds of steam rise from White Island, an active, offshore volcano lying in the Bay of Plenty, off the northern coast of North Island.

Scale 1:3,000,000
projection: Lambert Conformal Conic

Mountain-building in the Southern Alps

North Island
Alpine Fault
Southern Alps
Pacific Plate
Indo-Australian Plate

▲ The Southern Alps have been formed by "slip" faulting. The Indo-Australian and Pacific plates run in opposite directions along the Alpine Fault. Although they slide past one another, they are also being thrust over one another, causing the continental crust of the Pacific Plate to be uplifted to form the Alps.

▼ The Rotorua and Taupo valleys have some of the largest and most spectacular thermal springs in New Zealand. These occur when superheated groundwater rises to the surface through joints in the rocks.

▲ The Northland region is characterized by many coastal inlets. These are lined by mangrove swamps, signaling the change to a subtropical climate in the far north of the island.

Northland

Rotorua

Lake Taupo is New Zealand's largest inland lake. It occupies the crater of an extinct volcano.

Mount Taranaki, rising 8261 ft (2518 m) is an isolated, dormant volcano.

The boundary between the Indo-Australian Plate and the Pacific Plate runs through the center of North Island, leading to many typical volcanic features. The plateau which rises from the slopes of Lake Taupo contains a string of active volcanoes.

Probable location of Alpine Fault

Fiordland, in the far south west, contains a large number of flooded glacial valleys.

Sutherland Falls

The Southern Alps run for more than 300 miles, (483 km) forming the backbone of South Island. They were uplifted following the collision of the Pacific and Indo-Australian plates.

High levels of rainfall and a steep topography has made New Zealand's rivers swift-running. In the southern reaches of both islands, rivers such as the Mokoreta form broad, braided streams.

The coastal Canterbury Plains are the result of glacial outwash. They are the only major flat area in New Zealand.

The Southern Alps contain more than 360 glaciers, including the Murchison, Mueller and Godley glaciers on the eastern slopes and the Fox and Franz Josef glaciers to the west.

The Tasman Glacier, the largest glacier in New Zealand, flows for 18 miles (29 km) down the slopes of New Zealand's highest mountain, Aoraki (Mount Cook).

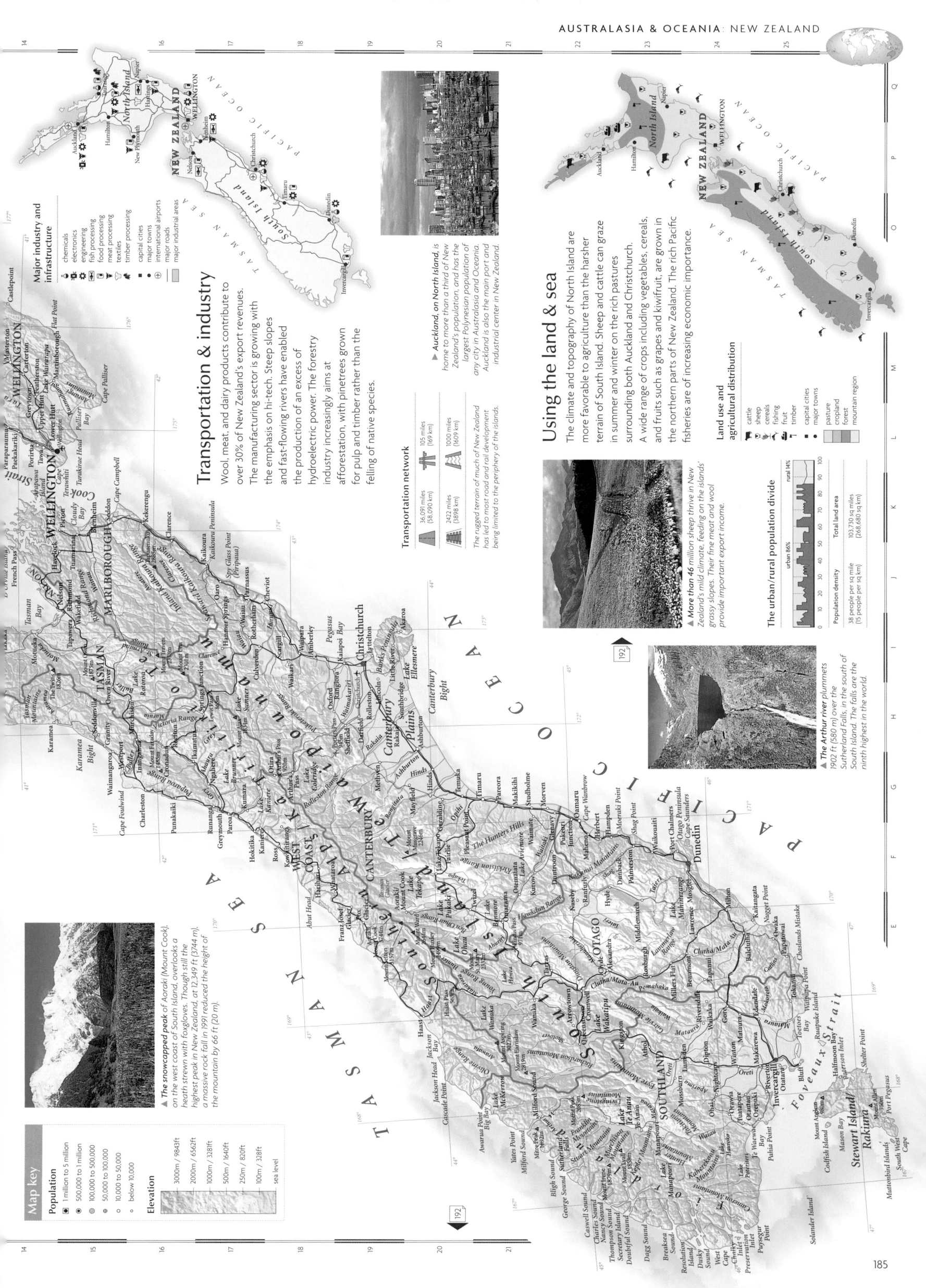

## Map key

**Population**
- 1 million to 5 million
- 500,000 to 1 million
- 100,000 to 500,000
- 50,000 to 100,000
- 10,000 to 50,000
- below 10,000

**Elevation**
- 3000m / 9843ft
- 2000m / 6562ft
- 1000m / 3281ft
- 500m / 1640ft
- 250m / 820ft
- 100m / 328ft
- sea level

▲ *The snowcapped peak* of Aoraki (Mount Cook), on the west coast of South Island, overlooks a heath strewn with foxgloves. Though still the highest peak in New Zealand, at 12,349 ft (3744 m), a massive rock fall in 1991 reduced the height of the mountain by 66 ft (20 m).

## Major industry and infrastructure

- chemicals
- electronics
- engineering
- fish processing
- food processing
- meat processing
- textiles
- timber processing
- capital cities
- major towns
- international airports
- major roads
- major industrial areas

## Transportation & industry

Wool, meat, and dairy products contribute to over 30% of New Zealand's export revenues. The manufacturing sector is growing with the emphasis on hi-tech. Steep slopes and fast-flowing rivers have enabled the production of an excess of hydroelectric power. The forestry industry increasingly aims at afforestation, with pinetrees grown for pulp and timber rather than the felling of native species.

▲ *Auckland, on North Island, is* home to more than a third of New Zealand's population, and has the largest Polynesian population of any city in Australasia and Oceania. Auckland is also the main port and industrial center in New Zealand.

### Transportation network

| | 105 miles (169 km) |
| --- | --- |
| 36,091 miles (58,090 km) | 1000 miles (1609 km) |
| 2422 miles (3898 km) | |

*The rugged terrain of much of New Zealand has led to most road and rail development being limited to the periphery of the islands.*

## Using the land & sea

The climate and topography of North Island are more favorable to agriculture than the harsher terrain of South Island. Sheep and cattle can graze in summer and winter on the rich pastures surrounding both Auckland and Christchurch. A wide range of crops including vegetables, cereals, and fruits such as grapes and kiwifruit, are grown in the northern parts of New Zealand. The rich Pacific fisheries are of increasing economic importance.

### Land use and agricultural distribution

- cattle
- sheep
- cereals
- fishing
- fruit
- timber
- capital cities
- major towns
- pasture
- cropland
- forest
- mountain region

▲ *More than 46 million sheep thrive in New* Zealand's mild climate, feeding on the islands' grassy slopes. Their fine meat and wool provide important export income.

▲ *The Arthur river plummets* 1902 ft (580 m) over the Sutherland Falls, in the south of South Island. The falls are the ninth highest in the world.

### The urban/rural population divide

urban 86% / rural 14%

| Population density | Total land area |
| --- | --- |
| 38 people per sq mile (15 people per sq km) | 103,730 sq miles (268,680 sq km) |

# Melanesia

FIJI, New Caledonia *(to France)*, PAPUA NEW GUINEA, SOLOMON ISLANDS, VANUATU

Lying in the southwest Pacific Ocean, northeast of Australia and south of the Equator, the islands of Melanesia form one of the three geographic divisions (along with Polynesia and Micronesia) of Oceania. Melanesia's name derives from the Greek melas, "black," and *nesoi,* "islands." Most of the larger islands are volcanic in origin. The smaller islands tend to be coral atolls and are mainly uninhabited. Rugged mountains, covered by dense rain forest, take up most of the land area. Melanesian's cultivate yams, taro, and sweet potatoes for local consumption and live in small, usually dispersed, homesteads.

▲ *Huli tribesmen from* Southern Highlands Province in Papua New Guinea parade in ceremonial dress, their powdered wigs decorated with exotic plumage and their faces and bodies painted with colored pigments.

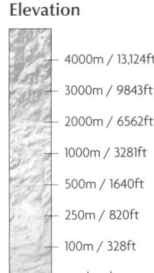

**Map key**

**Population**
- ⊚ 100,000 to 500,000
- ⊕ 50,000 to 100,000
- ⊙ 10,000 to 50,000
- ○ below 10,000

**Elevation**
- 4000m / 13,124ft
- 3000m / 9843ft
- 2000m / 6562ft
- 1000m / 3281ft
- 500m / 1640ft
- 250m / 820ft
- 100m / 328ft
- sea level

## Transportation & Industry

The processing of natural resources generates significant export revenue for the countries of Melanesia. The region relies mainly on copra, tuna, and timber exports, with some production of cocoa and palm oil. The islands have substantial mineral resources including the world's largest copper reserves on Bougainville Island; gold, and potential oil and natural gas. Tourism has become the fastest growing sector in most of the countries' economies.

◀ *On New Caledonia's* main island, relatively high interior plateaus descend to coastal plains. Nickel is the most important mineral resource, but the hills also harbor metallic deposits including chrome, cobalt, iron, gold, silver, and copper.

◀ *Lying close to* the banks of the Sepik river in northern Papua New Guinea, this building is known as the Spirit House. It is constructed from leaves and twigs, ornately woven and trimmed into geometric patterns. The house is decorated with a mask and topped by a carved statue.

▲ *On one of* Vanuatu's many islands, beach houses stand at the water's edge, surrounded by coconut palms and other tropical vegetation. The unspoilt beaches and tranquillity of its islands are drawing ever-larger numbers of tourists to Vanuatu.

**Transportation network**

| | | | |
|---|---|---|---|
| 🛣 | 1236 miles (1990 km) | 🛤 | None |
| 🚂 | 370 miles (595 km) | ✈ | 6924 miles (11,143 km) |

*As most of the islands of Melanesia lie off the major sea and air routes, services to and from the rest of the world are infrequent. Transportation by road on rugged terrain is difficult and expensive.*

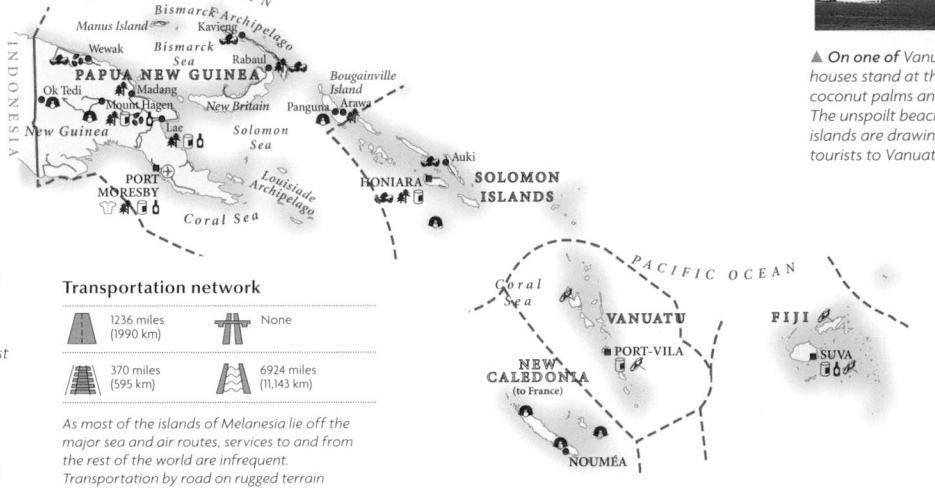

**Major industry and infrastructure**
- 🍶 beverages
- ☕ coffee processing
- copra processing
- 🍴 food processing
- ⛏ mining
- 👕 textiles
- 🌲 timber processing
- 🏖 tourism
- ■ capital cities
- ● major towns
- ✈ international airports
- — major roads

# The Landscape

Melanesia comprises high, volcanic islands, low coral islands and continental islands. New Guinea is part of the Australian continental platform, and is separated from it only by the shallow flooding of the Torres Strait. The plate margin of the Pacific and Indo-Australian plates cuts through mainland Papua New Guinea. Volcanic activity, resulting from the collision of these plates, has sculpted much of Melanesia's landscape.

**The Star Mountains** include some of the most remote terrain on Earth. The area is rich in gold and copper.

**The lowland plains** in the south and north of Papua New Guinea's main island are swampy, and contain some fertile alluvial soils. This contrasts with the mountainous islands in the rest of the country where soils are generally thin and nutrients are retained in the existing vegetation.

**Southern Papua New Guinea** is part of the Indo-Australian Plate. New Guinea only became separated physically from Australia about 8000 years ago following the flooding of the Torres Strait.

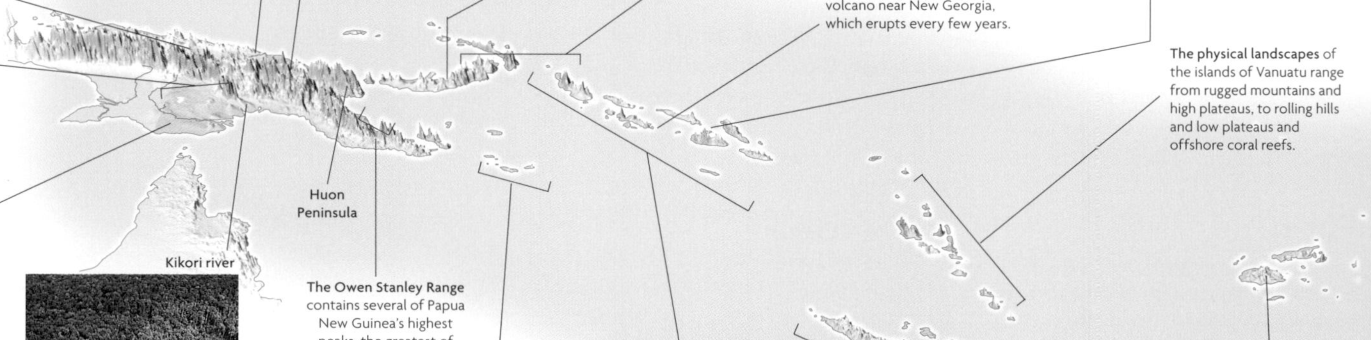

**The Sepik river** drains the lowlands north of the Central Range, flowing eastward into the Bismarck Sea.

**The Bismarck Range** is precipitous, rugged and covered in dense vegetation, rising to 14,793 ft (4509 m) at Mount Wilhelm in central Papua New Guinea.

**Huon Peninsula**

**Kikori river**

**The Owen Stanley Range** contains several of Papua New Guinea's highest peaks, the greatest of which is Mount Victoria at 13,200 ft (4035 m).

**The Louisiade Archipelago** contains 10 volcanic islands and numerous coral islets. Tagula Island is the largest of the islands, containing the archipelago's highest peak at 2645 ft (806 m).

**Most of Papua New Guinea's** outlying islands, including New Britain, Bougainville Island and New Ireland, are precipitous and of volcanic origin.

**Kavachi is an** active submarine volcano near New Georgia, which erupts every few years.

**The Solomon Islands** are mountainous continental-type islands with largely andesitic volcanoes.

**New Caledonia's main island** is surrounded by coral reef that extends from the Huon island group in the north, to Île des Pins in the south.

**The physical landscapes** of the islands of Vanuatu range from rugged mountains and high plateaus, to rolling hills and low plateaus and offshore coral reefs.

**Viti Levu, the** largest of Fiji's islands, contains the country's highest mountain, Mount Victoria at 4339 ft (1323 m).

◄ *The slopes of this extinct volcano near Talasea on the island of New Britain have been almost entirely colonized by rain forest vegetation.*

▲ *A series of coral reefs can be seen in the clear waters off Cape Esperance on the island of Guadalcanal in the Solomons.*

▶ *Papua New Guinea's rivers, though fairly short, carry extremely high sediment loads, largely due to soil erosion. This is caused by a combination of very steep slopes and heavy rainfall, and is made worse by forest clearance, particularly "slash and burn" techniques and road or mine operations.*

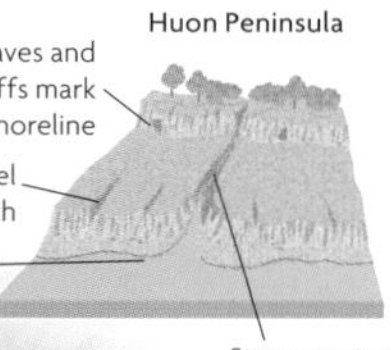

**Huon Peninsula**

Caves and undercut cliffs mark former shoreline

Former level of beach

Current beach

Stream cuts down through recently exposed land

**Uplift of the** land in tectonically active regions can lead to former coastlines being lifted beyond the reach of the sea. New cliffs and caves are formed at a lower level, and rivers cut down through the lower land to reach sea level once more.

# Using the land and sea

Almost 60% of the population of Melanesia is engaged in agriculture and animal husbandry at a subsistence level. Coconuts and cocoa are grown for export revenue. Over 80% of the land area is cloaked by tropical forest and woodlands, which have proved to be a rich timber source. In coastal areas, fishing, mainly for tuna, is a staple industry.

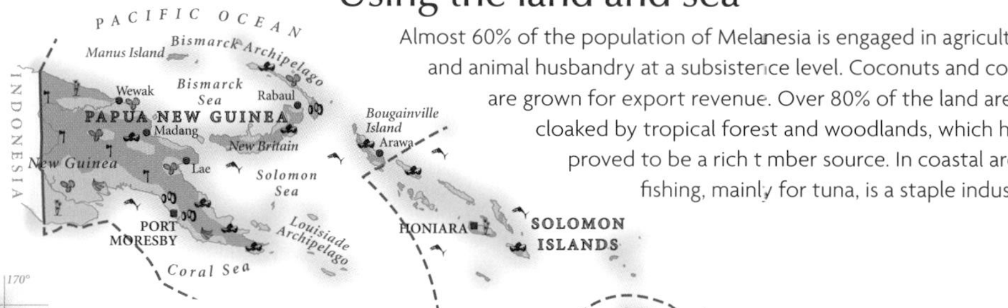

## The urban/rural population divide

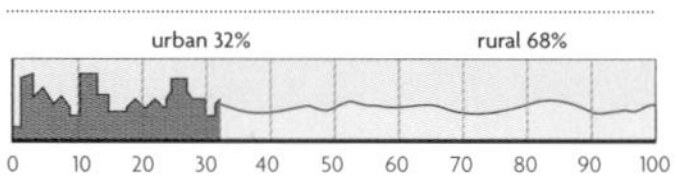

urban 32%     rural 68%

0  10  20  30  40  50  60  70  80  90  100

**Population density**

32 people per sq mile
(12 people per sq km)

**Total land area**

205,354 sq miles
(332,008 sq km)

◄ *Abaca Eco-tourist Park near Lautoka on the island of Viti Levu in western Fiji is one of a number of projects aimed at combining tourism with awareness about the environment. The government and people of Fiji are keen to protect the unique ecology of the islands and prevent further damage to the coral reefs. Until the recent ending of nuclear testing in the Pacific by Western nations, Fiji lay downwind of some of the main testing sites.*

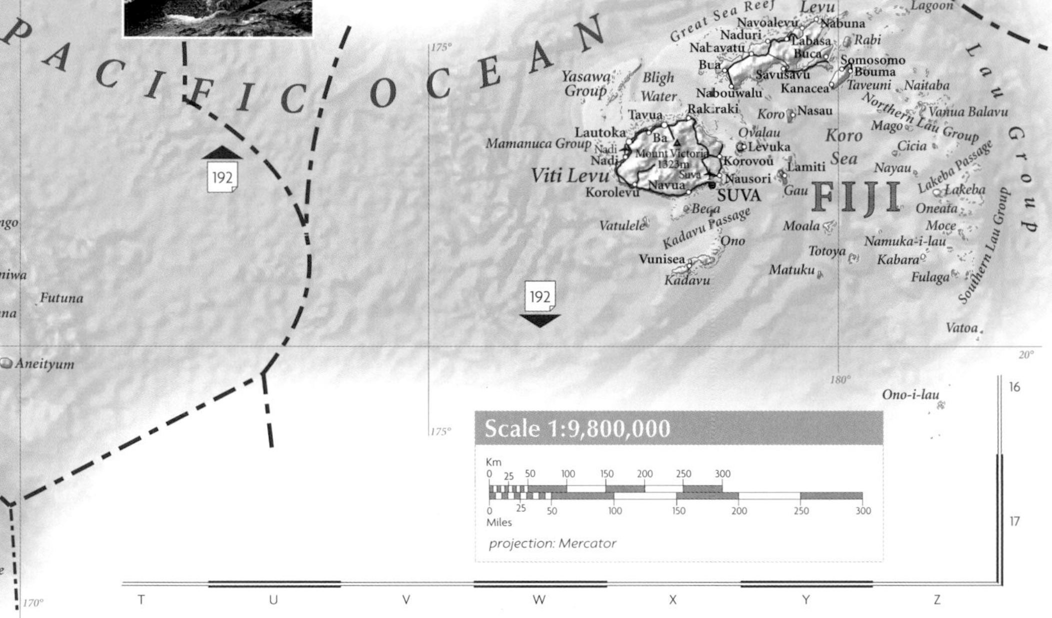

## Land use and agricultural distribution

- bananas
- cocoa
- coconuts
- fishing
- oil palms
- rubber
- timber
- ■ capital cities
- • major towns
- cropland
- forest
- wetland

**Scale 1:9,800,000**

Km
0  25  50  100  150  200  250  300

Miles
0  25  50  100  150  200  250  300

projection: Mercator

**PACIFIC OCEAN**

Manus Island
Bismarck Archipelago
Wewak
Bismarck Sea
Rabaul
**PAPUA NEW GUINEA**
Madang  New Britain
Bougainville Island
Arawa
New Guinea
Lae
Solomon Sea
**HONIARA**  **SOLOMON ISLANDS**
**PORT MORESBY**
Louisiade Archipelago
Coral Sea

Coral Sea
**VANUATU**
**PORT-VILA**
**FIJI**
**NEW CALEDONIA** (to France)
**SUVA**
**NOUMÉA**
PACIFIC OCEAN

**SOLOMON ISLANDS**
MALAITA
Sikaiana
Maramasike
Ulawa Island
Three Sisters Islands
Kirakira
San Cristobal
Star Harbour
**MAKIRA-ULAWA**
Tarapaina

Duff Islands
Reef Islands
Tinakula
**TEMOTU**
Nendö
Lata  Noka
Santa Cruz Islands
Utupua
Vanikolo
Anuta
Fatutaka
Tikopia

Torres Islands
Hiu
Toga
Ureparapara
Vanua Lava  Sola
**VANUATU**
Banks Islands
Gaua
Cape Cumberland
Nokuku  Naone
Port-Olry
**Espiritu Santo**  Navonda  Maéwo
Mount Tabwemasana 1879m  Ambae
Luganville
Malo  Pentecost
Bougainville Strait  Bwatnapne
Norsup
Unmet  Mount Marum 1270m  Ambrym
**Malekula**  Toak
Laman
Lamen Bay  Epi
Tongoa
Emae
Shepherd Islands
Nguna
Bauer Field  Paonangisu
**PORT-VILA**  Efate
Forari

*Coral Sea*

**NEW CALEDONIA** (to France)
*New Caledonia*
Huon
Récifs d'Entrecasteaux
Récif Petrie
Île Surprise
Grand Passage
Récif des Français
Île Art
Waala
Ile Balabio
Poum
Ouégoa
Koumac  Mont Panié 1628m
Kaala-Gomen  Hienghène
Voh  **PROVINCE NORD**
Koné  Ponérihouen
Poya  Houailou
Bourail  Canala
La Foa  Thio
**PROVINCE SUD**
La Tontouta  Yaté
Dumbéa  Mont-Dore
**NOUMÉA**
Vao  Île des Pins
Grand Récif Sud

Errromango
Unpongkor  Ipota
Aniwa
Isangel  Futuna
Tanna
Aneityum

Ouvéa
Fayaoué
Lifou
Wé
**PROVINCE DES ÎLES LOYAUTÉ**
Îles Loyauté
Ponérihouen
Tadine  Maré

Récifs de l'Astrolabe

**PACIFIC OCEAN**

**FIJI**
Cikobia
Vanua Levu
Qelelevu Lagoon
Nabuna
Great Sea Reef
Navoalevu
Naduri
Natavatu  Rabi
Labasa  Buca
Somosomo
Bligh Water  Savusavu  Taveuni  Naitaba
Yasawa Group  Nabouwalu  Kanacea
Tavua  Rakiraki  Koro  Nasau
Mamanuca Group  Ba  Koro  Northern Lau Group
Lautoka  Ovalau  Sea  Mago
Nadi  Levuka  Cicia
Viti Levu  Nausori  Lamiti
Koroleyu  **SUVA**  Gau  Nayau
Bega  Oneata
Vatulele  Moala  Moce
Kadavu Passage  Namuka-i-lau
Vunisea  Ono  Totoya  Kabara
**Kadavu**  Matuku  Fulaga
Vatoa
Ono-i-lau

Koro Sea
Lau Group
Lakeba Passage
Lakeba
Vanua Balavu
Southern Lau Group

# Micronesia

MARSHALL ISLANDS, MICRONESIA, NAJRU, PALAU,
Guam, Northern Mariana Islands, Wake Island

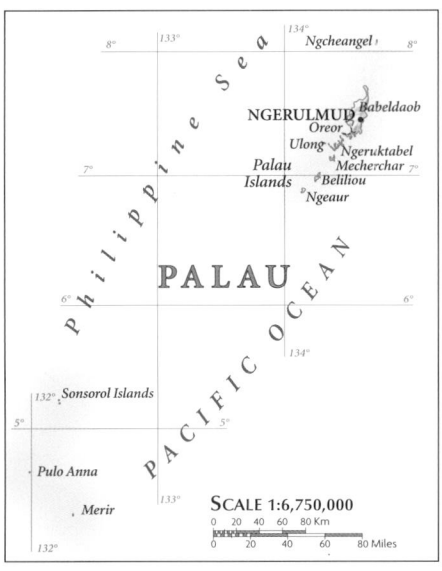

The Micronesian islands lie in the western reaches of the Pacific Ocean and are all part of the same volcanic zone. The Federated States of Micronesia is the largest group, with more than 600 atolls and forested volcanic islands in an area of more than 1120 sq miles (2900 sq km). Micronesia is a mixture of former colonies, overseas territories, and dependencies. Most of the region still relies on aid and subsidies to sustain economies limited by resources, isolation, and an emigrating population, drawn to New Zealand and Australia by the attractions of a western lifestyle.

## Palau

Palau is an archipelago of over 200 islands, only eight of which are inhabited. It was the last remaining UN trust territory in the Pacific, controlled by the US until 1994, when it became independent. The economy operates on a subsistence level, with coconuts and cassava the principal crops. Fishing licenses and tourism provide foreign currency.

SCALE 1:825,000

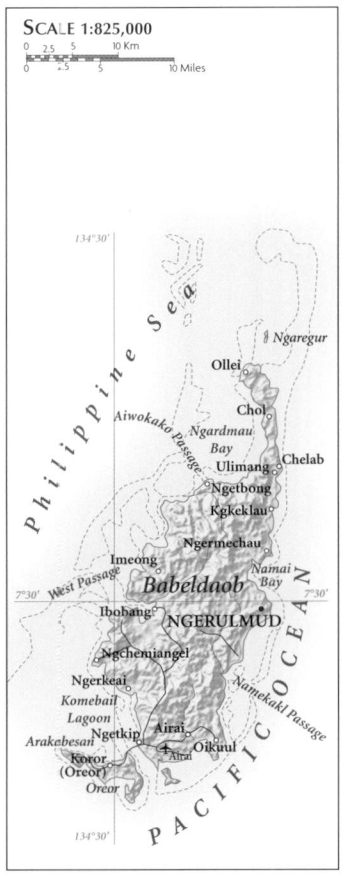

SCALE 1:6,750,000

◀ The tranquility of these coastal lagoons, at Inarajan in southern Guam, belies the fact that the island lies in a region where typhoons are common.

## Guam (to US)

Lying at the southern end of the Mariana Islands, Guam is an important US military base and tourist destination. Social and political life is dominated by the indigenous Chamorro, who make up just under half the population, although the increasing prevalence of western culture threatens Guam's traditional social stability.

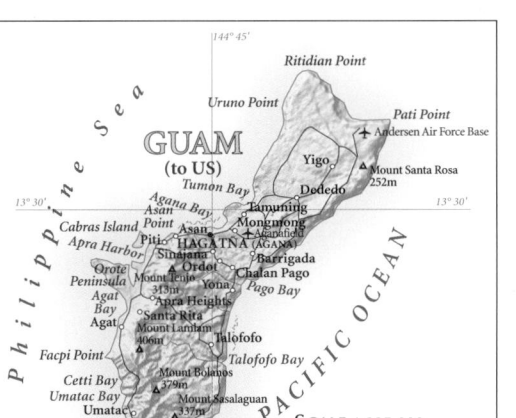

SCALE 1:925,000

## Northern Mariana Islands (to US)

A US Commonwealth territory, the Northern Marianas comprise the whole of the Mariana archipelago except for Guam. The islands retain their close links with the US and continue to receive American aid. Tourism, though bringing in much-needed revenue, has speeded the decline of the traditional subsistence economy. Most of the population lives on Saipan.

SCALE 1:550,000

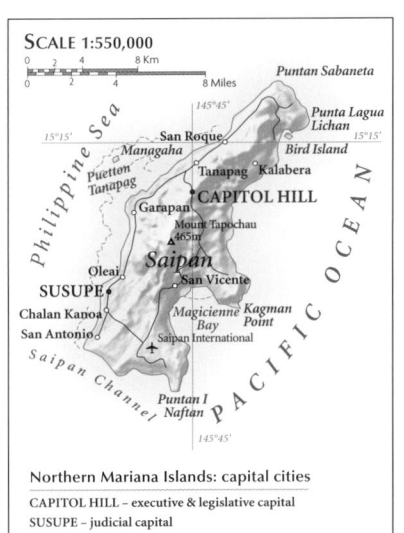

Northern Mariana Islands: capital cities
CAPITOL HILL – executive & legislative capital
SUSUPE – judicial capital

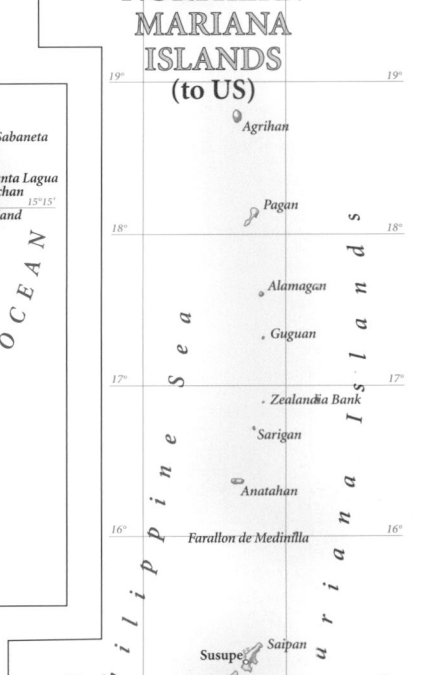

▲ The Palau Islands have numerous hidden lakes and lagoons. These sustain their own ecosystems which have developed in isolation. This has produced adaptations in the animals and plants that are often unique to each lake.

SCALE 1:5,500,000

## Micronesia

A mixture of high volcanic islands and low-lying coral atolls, the Federated States of Micronesia include all the Caroline Islands except Palau. Pohnpei, Kosrae, Chuuk, and Yap are the four main island cluster states, each of which has its own language, with English remaining the official language. Nearly half the population is concentrated on Pohnpei, the largest island. Independent since 1986, the islands continue to receive considerable aid from the US which supplements an economy based primarily on fishing and copra processing.

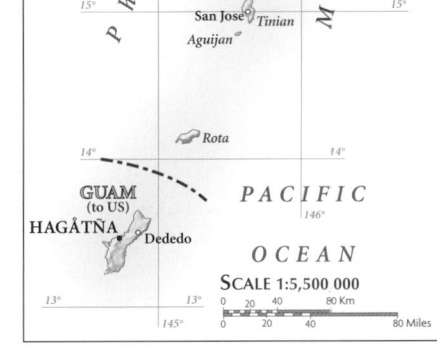

SCALE 1:925,000

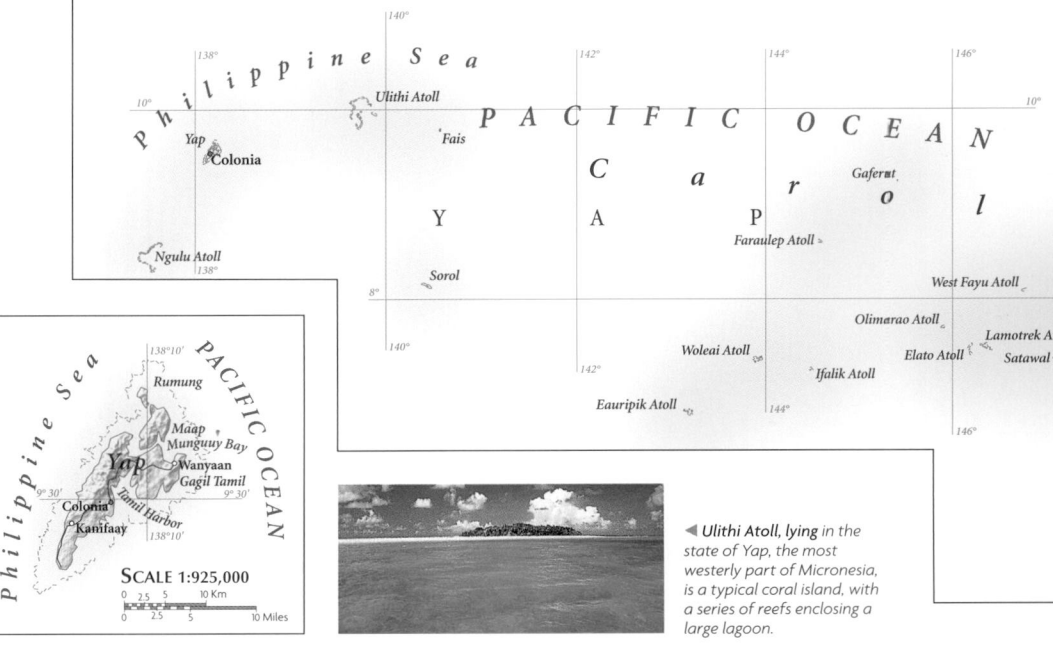

◀ Ulithi Atoll, lying in the state of Yap, the most westerly part of Micronesia, is a typical coral island, with a series of reefs enclosing a large lagoon.

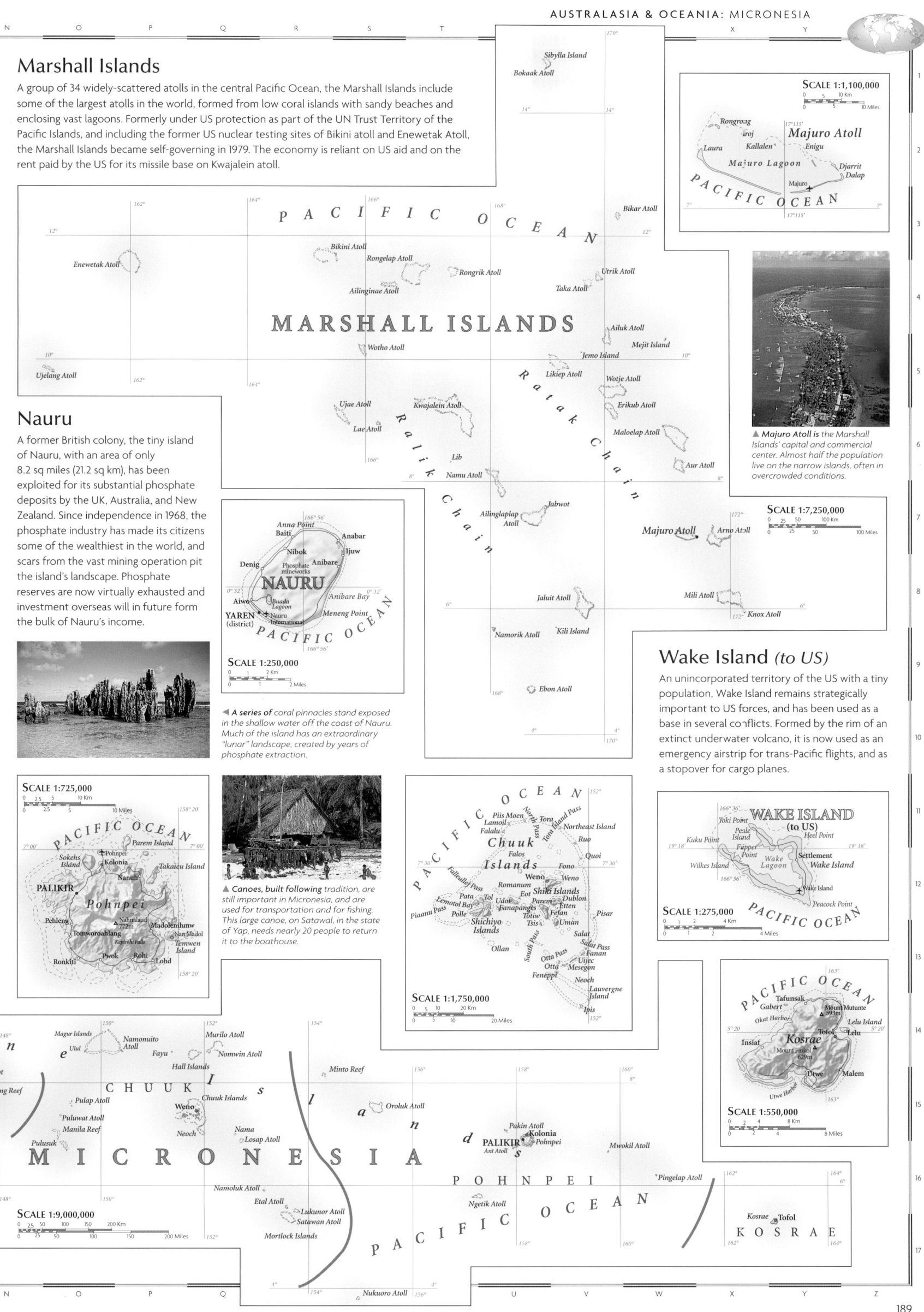

# Marshall Islands

A group of 34 widely-scattered atolls in the central Pacific Ocean, the Marshall Islands include some of the largest atolls in the world, formed from low coral islands with sandy beaches and enclosing vast lagoons. Formerly under US protection as part of the UN Trust Territory of the Pacific Islands, and including the former US nuclear testing sites of Bikini atoll and Enewetak Atoll, the Marshall Islands became self-governing in 1979. The economy is reliant on US aid and on the rent paid by the US for its missile base on Kwajalein atoll.

# Nauru

A former British colony, the tiny island of Nauru, with an area of only 8.2 sq miles (21.2 sq km), has been exploited for its substantial phosphate deposits by the UK, Australia, and New Zealand. Since independence in 1968, the phosphate industry has made its citizens some of the wealthiest in the world, and scars from the vast mining operation pit the island's landscape. Phosphate reserves are now virtually exhausted and investment overseas will in future form the bulk of Nauru's income.

▲ *Majuro Atoll is* the Marshall Islands' capital and commercial center. Almost half the population live on the narrow islands, often in overcrowded conditions.

◄ *A series of* coral pinnacles stand exposed in the shallow water off the coast of Nauru. Much of the island has an extraordinary "lunar" landscape, created by years of phosphate extraction.

▲ *Canoes, built following* tradition, are still important in Micronesia, and are used for transportation and for fishing. This large canoe, on Satawal, in the state of Yap, needs nearly 20 people to return it to the boathouse.

# Wake Island (to US)

An unincorporated territory of the US with a tiny population, Wake Island remains strategically important to US forces, and has been used as a base in several conflicts. Formed by the rim of an extinct underwater volcano, it is now used as an emergency airstrip for trans-Pacific flights, and as a stopover for cargo planes.

# Polynesia

KIRIBATI, TUVALU, Cook Islands, Easter Island, French Polynesia, Niue, Pitcairn Islands, Tokelau, Wallis & Futuna

The numerous island groups of Polynesia lie to the east of Australia, scattered over a vast area in the south Pacific. The islands are a mixture of low-lying coral atolls, some of which enclose lagoons, and the tips of great underwater volcanoes. The populations on the islands are small, and most people are of Polynesian origin, as are the Maori of New Zealand. Local economies remain simple, relying mainly on subsistence crops, mineral deposits, many now exhausted, fishing, and tourism.

SCALE 1:1,100,000

0      5      10 Km
0      5      10 Miles

## Kiribati

A former British colony, Kiribati became independent in 1979. Banaba's phosphate deposits ran out in 1980, following decades of exploitation by the British. Economic development remains slow and most agriculture is at a subsistence level, though coconuts provide export income, and underwater agriculture is being developed.

▶ With the exception of Banaba all the islands in Kiribati's three groups are low-lying, coral atolls. This aerial view shows the sparsely vegetated islands, intercut by many small lagoons.

## Tuvalu

A chain of nine coral atolls, 360 miles (579 km) long with a land area of just over 9 sq miles (23 sq km), Tuvalu is one of the world's smallest and most isolated states. As the Ellice Islands, Tuvalu was linked to the Gilbert Islands (now part of Kiribati) as a British colony until independence in 1978. Politically and socially conservative, Tuvaluans live by fishing and subsistence farming.

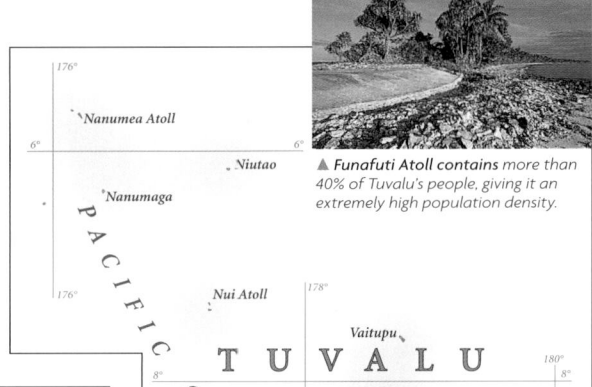

▲ Funafuti Atoll contains more than 40% of Tuvalu's people, giving it an extremely high population density.

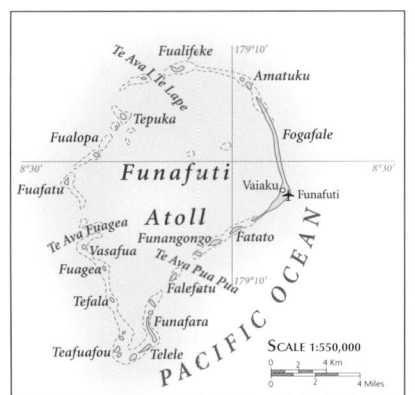

SCALE 1:550,000

0      2      4 Km
0      2      4 Miles

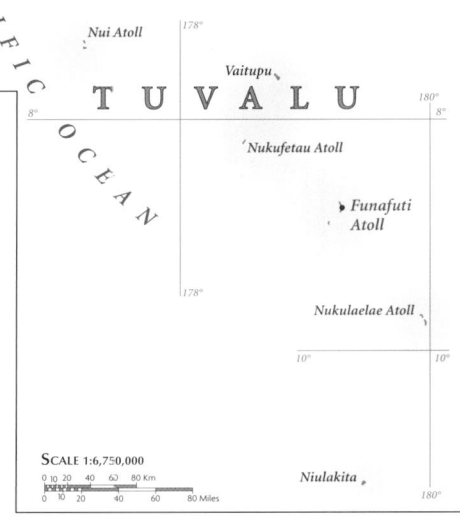

SCALE 1:6,750,000

0  10  20  40  60  80 Km
0  10  20  40  60  80 Miles

## Tokelau (to New Zealand)

A low-lying coral atoll, Tokelau is a dependent territory of New Zealand with few natural resources. Although a 1990 cyclone destroyed crops and infrastructure, a tuna cannery and the sale of fishing licenses have raised revenue and a catamaran link between the islands has increased their tourism potential. Tokelau's small size and economic weakness makes independence from New Zealand unlikely.

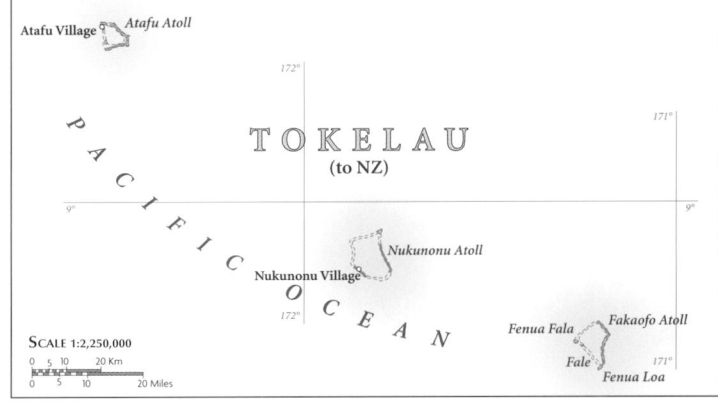

▲ Fishermen cast their nets to catch small fish in the shallow waters off Atafu Atoll, the most westerly island in Tokelau.

SCALE 1:2,250,000

0    5    10          20 Km
0    5    10          20 Miles

## Wallis & Futuna (to France)

In contrast to other French overseas territories in the south Pacific, the inhabitants of Wallis and Futuna have shown little desire for greater autonomy. A subsistence economy produces a variety of tropical crops, while foreign currency remittances come from expatriates and from the sale of licenses to Japanese and Korean fishing fleets.

SCALE 1:1,100,000

0      5      10 Km
0      5      10 Miles

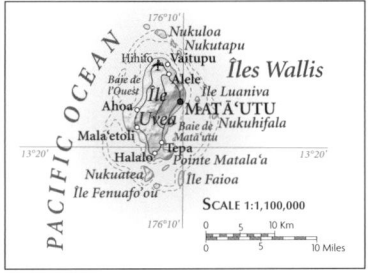

SCALE 1:1,100,000

0      5      10 Km
0      5      10 Miles

## Niue (to New Zealand)

Niue, the world's largest coral island, is self-governing but exists in free association with New Zealand. Tropical fruits are grown for local consumption; tourism and the sale of postage stamps provide foreign currency. The lack of local job prospects has led more than 10,000 Niueans to emigrate to New Zealand, which has now invested heavily in Niue's economy in the hope of reversing this trend.

▲ Palm trees fringe the white sands of a beach on Aitutaki in the Southern Cook Islands, where tourism is of increasing economic importance.

## Cook Islands (to New Zealand)

A mixture of coral atolls and volcanic peaks, the Cook Islands achieved self-government in 1965 but exist in free association with New Zealand. A diverse economy includes pearl and giant clam farming, and an ostrich farm, plus tourism and banking. A 1991 friendship treaty with France provides for French surveillance of territorial waters.

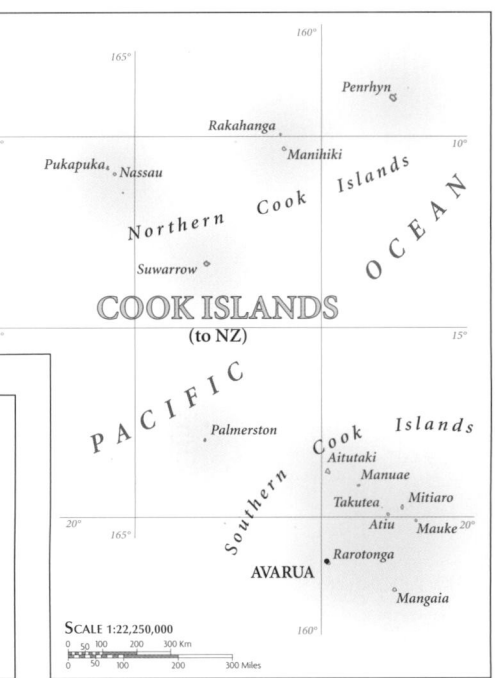

SCALE 1:22,250,000

0   50   100   200        300 Km
0   50   100   200        300 Miles

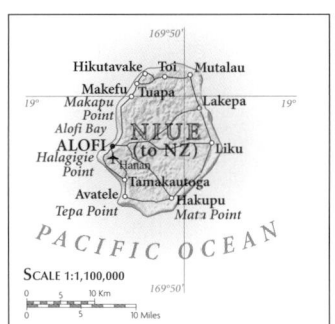

SCALE 1:1,100,000

0      5      10 Km
0      5      10 Miles

▲ Waves have cut back the original coastline, exposing a sandy beach, near Mutalau in the northeast corner of Niue.

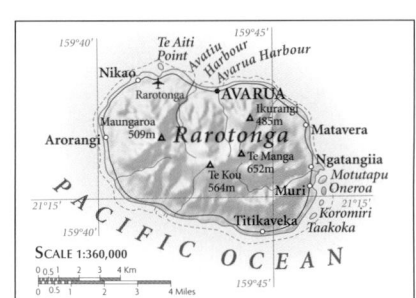

SCALE 1:360,000

0  0.5  1      2      3      4 Km
0  0.5  1      2      3      4 Miles

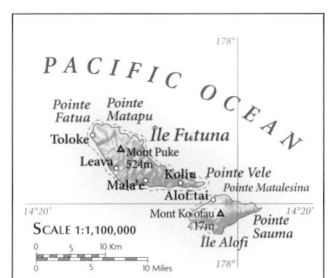

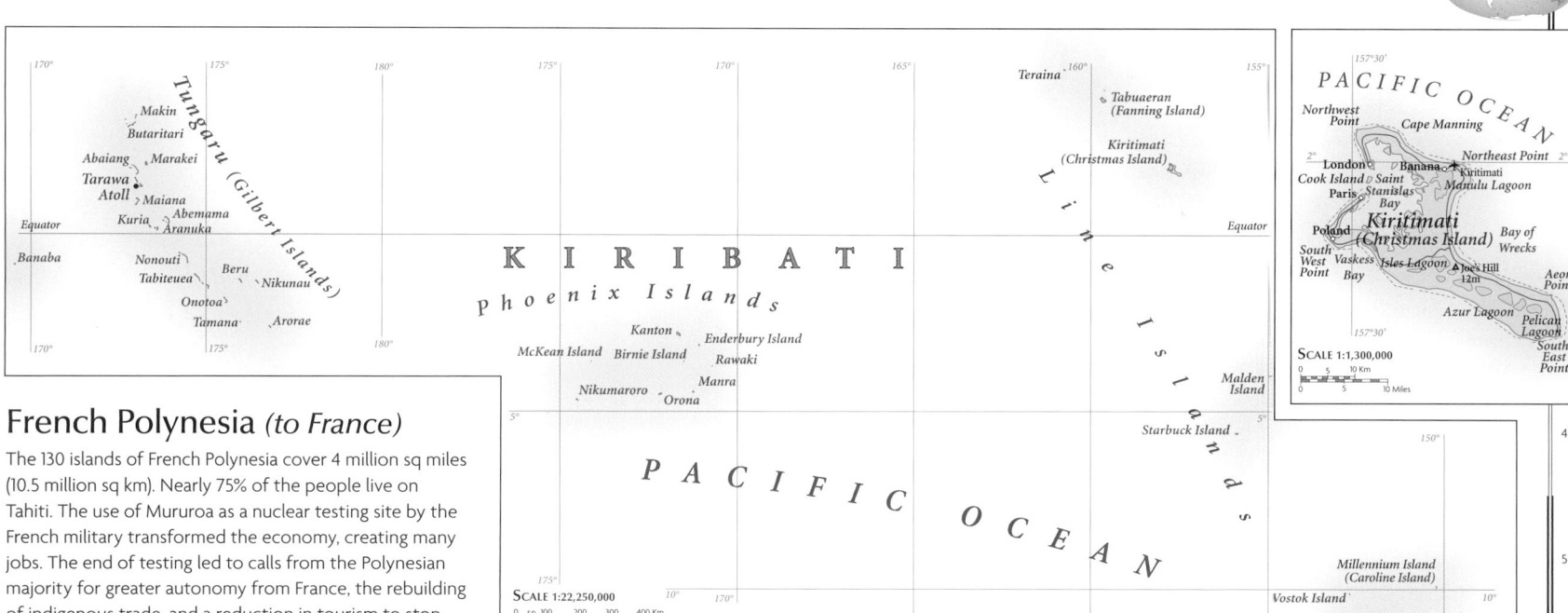

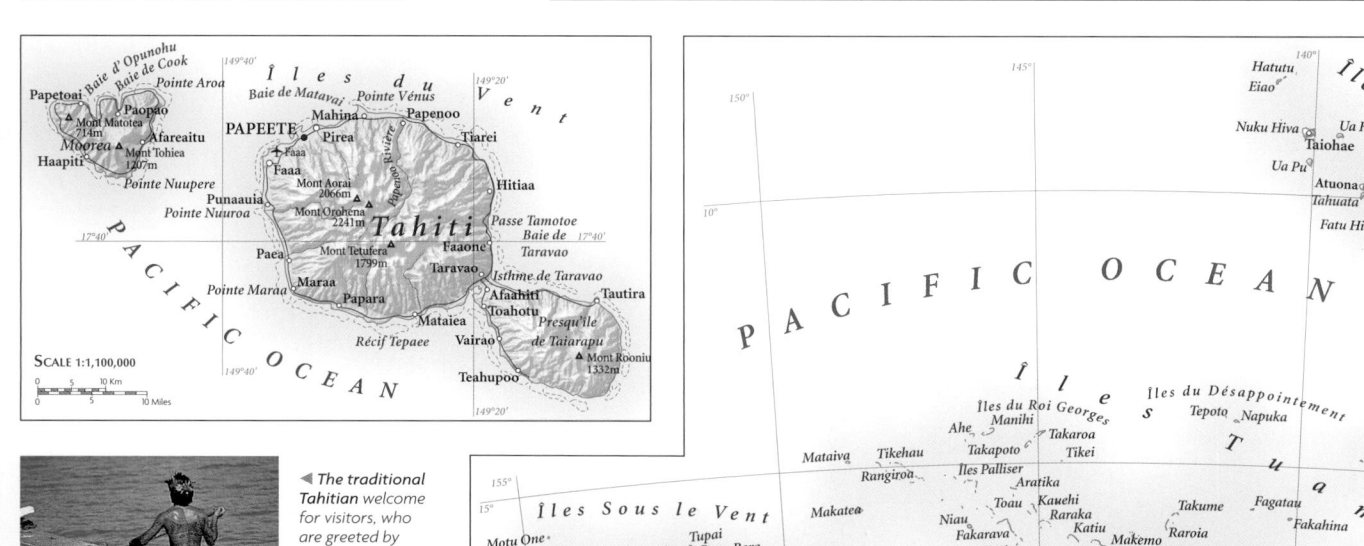

## French Polynesia (to France)

The 130 islands of French Polynesia cover 4 million sq miles (10.5 million sq km). Nearly 75% of the people live on Tahiti. The use of Mururoa as a nuclear testing site by the French military transformed the economy, creating many jobs. The end of testing led to calls from the Polynesian majority for greater autonomy from France, the rebuilding of indigenous trade, and a reduction in tourism to stop the erosion of the islands' traditional culture.

◀ The traditional Tahitian welcome for visitors, who are greeted by parties of canoes, has become a major tourist attraction.

## Pitcairn Group of Islands (to UK)

Britain's most isolated dependency, Pitcairn Island was first populated by mutineers from the HMS Bounty in 1790. Emigration is further depleting the already limited gene pool of the island's inhabitants, with associated social and health problems. Barter, fishing and subsistence farming form the basis of the economy whilst offshore mineral exploitation may boost the economy in future.

◀ The Pitcairn Islanders rely on regular airdrops from New Zealand and periodic visits by supply vessels to provide them with basic commodities.

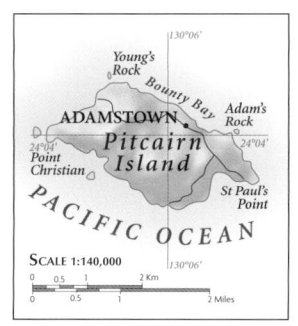

## Easter Island (to Chile)

One of the most easterly islands in Polynesia, Easter Island (Isla de Pascua) – also known as Rapa Nui, is part of Chile. The mainly Polynesian inhabitants support themselves by farming, which is mainly of a subsistence nature, and includes cattle rearing and crops such as sugar cane, bananas, corn, gourds, and potatoes. In recent years, tourism has become the most important source of income and the island sustains a small commercial airport.

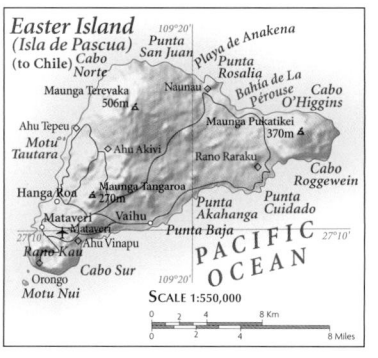

▲ The Naunau, a series of huge stone statues overlook Playa de Anakena, on Easter Island. Carved from a soft volcanic rock, they were erected between 400 and 900 years ago.

# The Pacific Ocean

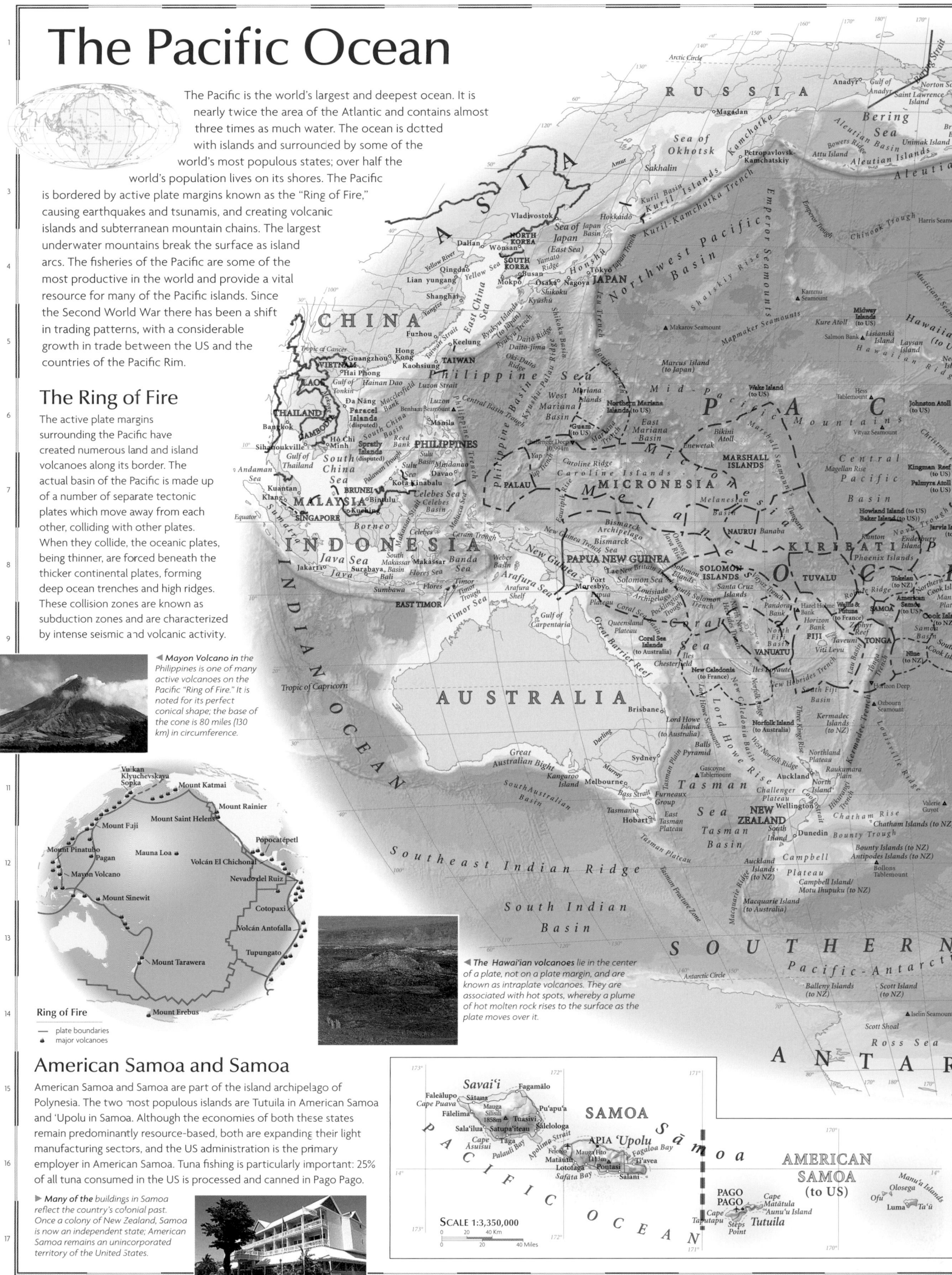

The Pacific is the world's largest and deepest ocean. It is nearly twice the area of the Atlantic and contains almost three times as much water. The ocean is dotted with islands and surrounded by some of the world's most populous states; over half the world's population lives on its shores. The Pacific is bordered by active plate margins known as the "Ring of Fire," causing earthquakes and tsunamis, and creating volcanic islands and subterranean mountain chains. The largest underwater mountains break the surface as island arcs. The fisheries of the Pacific are some of the most productive in the world and provide a vital resource for many of the Pacific islands. Since the Second World War there has been a shift in trading patterns, with a considerable growth in trade between the US and the countries of the Pacific Rim.

## The Ring of Fire

The active plate margins surrounding the Pacific have created numerous land and island volcanoes along its border. The actual basin of the Pacific is made up of a number of separate tectonic plates which move away from each other, colliding with other plates. When they collide, the oceanic plates, being thinner, are forced beneath the thicker continental plates, forming deep ocean trenches and high ridges. These collision zones are known as subduction zones and are characterized by intense seismic and volcanic activity.

◀ *Mayon Volcano in the Philippines is one of many active volcanoes on the Pacific "Ring of Fire." It is noted for its perfect conical shape; the base of the cone is 80 miles (130 km) in circumference.*

Ring of Fire

— plate boundaries
▲ major volcanoes

◀ *The Hawai'ian volcanoes lie in the center of a plate, not on a plate margin, and are known as intraplate volcanoes. They are associated with hot spots, whereby a plume of hot molten rock rises to the surface as the plate moves over it.*

## American Samoa and Samoa

American Samoa and Samoa are part of the island archipelago of Polynesia. The two most populous islands are Tutuila in American Samoa and 'Upolu in Samoa. Although the economies of both these states remain predominantly resource-based, both are expanding their light manufacturing sectors, and the US administration is the primary employer in American Samoa. Tuna fishing is particularly important: 25% of all tuna consumed in the US is processed and canned in Pago Pago.

▶ *Many of the buildings in Samoa reflect the country's colonial past. Once a colony of New Zealand, Samoa is now an independent state; American Samoa remains an unincorporated territory of the United States.*

SCALE 1:3,350,000

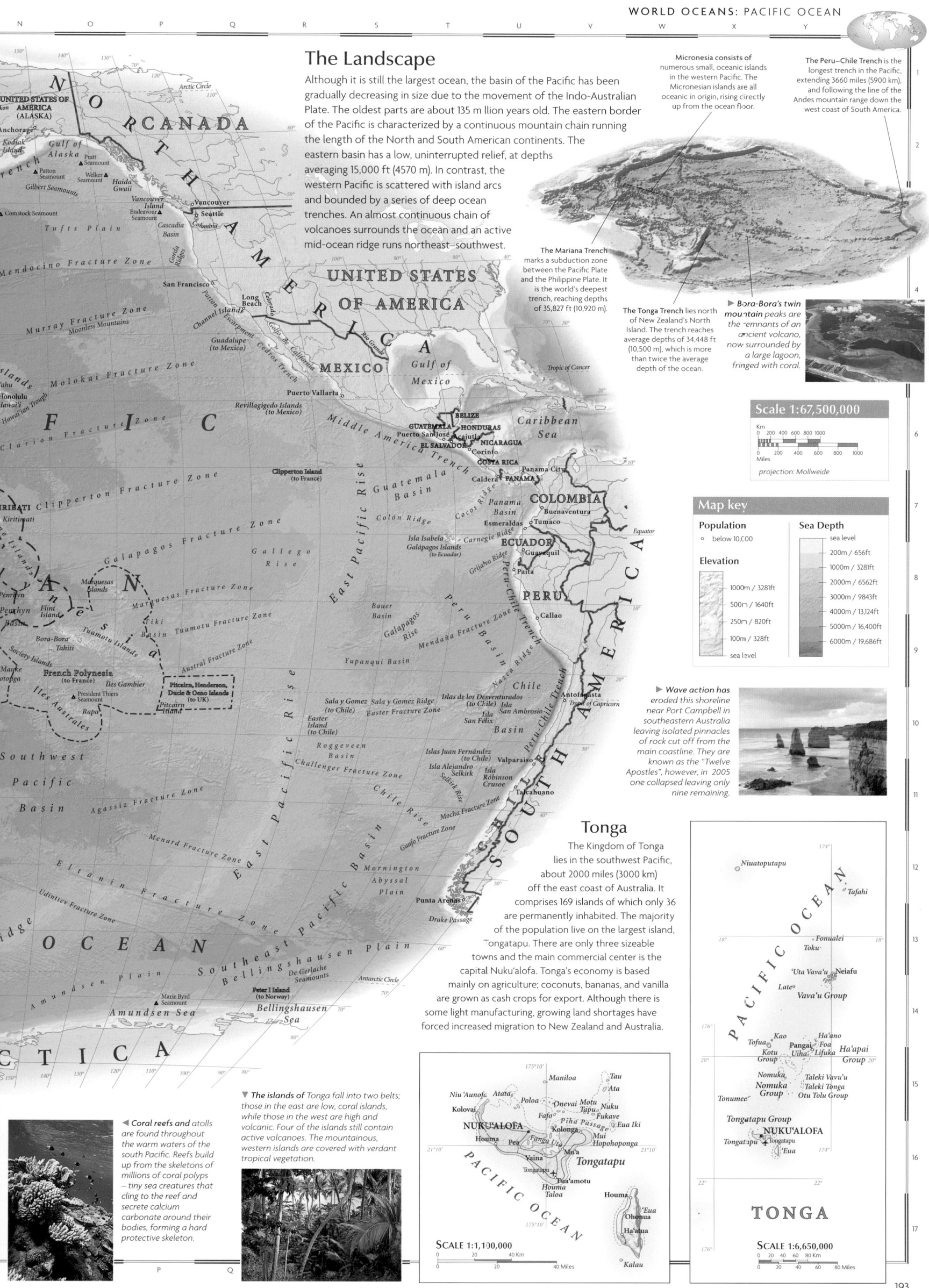

## The Landscape

Although it is still the largest ocean, the basin of the Pacific has been gradually decreasing in size due to the movement of the Indo-Australian Plate. The oldest parts are about 135 million years old. The eastern border of the Pacific is characterized by a continuous mountain chain running the length of the North and South American continents. The eastern basin has a low, uninterrupted relief, at depths averaging 15,000 ft (4570 m). In contrast, the western Pacific is scattered with island arcs and bounded by a series of deep ocean trenches. An almost continuous chain of volcanoes surrounds the ocean and an active mid-ocean ridge runs northeast–southwest.

Micronesia consists of numerous small, oceanic islands in the western Pacific. The Micronesian islands are all oceanic in origin, rising directly up from the ocean floor.

The Peru–Chile Trench is the longest trench in the Pacific, extending 3660 miles (5900 km), and following the line of the Andes mountain range down the west coast of South America.

The Mariana Trench marks a subduction zone between the Pacific Plate and the Philippine Plate. It is the world's deepest trench, reaching depths of 35,827 ft (10,920 m).

The Tonga Trench lies north of New Zealand's North Island. The trench reaches average depths of 34,448 ft (10,500 m), which is more than twice the average depth of the ocean.

▶ Bora-Bora's twin mountain peaks are the remnants of an ancient volcano, now surrounded by a large lagoon, fringed with coral.

Scale 1:67,500,000

Km
0 200 400 600 800 1000
Miles
0 200 400 600 800 1000

*projection: Mollweide*

### Map key

**Population**
○ below 10,000

**Elevation**
1000m / 3281ft
500m / 1640ft
250m / 820ft
100m / 328ft
sea level

**Sea Depth**
sea level
200m / 656ft
1000m / 3281ft
2000m / 6562ft
3000m / 9843ft
4000m / 13,124ft
5000m / 16,400ft
6000m / 19,686ft

▶ Wave action has eroded this shoreline near Port Campbell in southeastern Australia leaving isolated pinnacles of rock cut off from the main coastline. They are known as the "Twelve Apostles", however, in 2005 one collapsed leaving only nine remaining.

## Tonga

The Kingdom of Tonga lies in the southwest Pacific, about 2000 miles (3000 km) off the east coast of Australia. It comprises 169 islands of which only 36 are permanently inhabited. The majority of the population live on the largest island, Tongatapu. There are only three sizeable towns and the main commercial center is the capital Nuku'alofa. Tonga's economy is based mainly on agriculture; coconuts, bananas, and vanilla are grown as cash crops for export. Although there is some light manufacturing, growing land shortages have forced increased migration to New Zealand and Australia.

◀ Coral reefs and atolls are found throughout the warm waters of the south Pacific. Reefs build up from the skeletons of millions of coral polyps – tiny sea creatures that cling to the reef and secrete calcium carbonate around their bodies, forming a hard protective skeleton.

▼ The islands of Tonga fall into two belts; those in the east are low, coral islands, while those in the west are high and volcanic. Four of the islands still contain active volcanoes. The mountainous, western islands are covered with verdant tropical vegetation.

SCALE 1:1,100,000

SCALE 1:6,650,000

TONGA

# Antarctica

The ice-covered continent of Antarctica, which is the Earth's most southerly region, has drawn explorers and entrepreneurs seeking challenge and riches in its wintry lands for over 200 years. The extreme climate has deterred any large-scale settlement of the continent, and though commercial hunters built outposts in the past, habitation is now limited to scientific bases. The Antarctic Treaty, which came into force in 1961, provides for international governance and scientific cooperation in place of potential territorial conflict.

## Resources

Many ore minerals, including iron and gold, are found in the Antarctic, and there are also coal reserves in the Transantarctic Mountains. The severe conditions and environmental importance of the region mean that exploitation of potential mineral resources is both uneconomic and undesirable. The unique wildlife and landscape draw a small number of tourists annually.

### Resources (including wildlife)

- coal
- fish
- minerals
- oil & gas
- penguins
- seals
- whales
- polar research base

◀ **Most settlements in** Antarctica are research bases such as this one at Rothera on Adelaide Island, although there is a small Chilean settlement on King George Island.

## The landscape

There are two distinct parts to Antarctica: West Antarctica, a series of ice-covered, mountainous islands, joined together by the ice; and the high plateau of East Antarctica. The Ross Sea and the Weddell Sea are outliers of the Southern Ocean – deep bays partially covered by thick ice shelves.

◀ **On Elephant Island,** the coast is edged by glaciers, although the land is not permanently covered by ice.

▲ **Pack ice forms** out at sea in freezing temperatures. At the outer limits, grease ice congeals on the surface of the ocean. This is then spun around by wind and waves into irregular "pancakes," freezing and breaking up several times before bonding together again to form sea-ice sheets, which finally cement into enormous ice floes.

Grease ice  Pancake ice  Sea-ice sheet  Ice floe

**During the winter** the seas surrounding Antarctica freeze, increasing the size of the continent by 100%.

**Many volcanoes,** some of them still active, can be found in the mountains of the Antarctic Peninsula.

**The mountainous Antarctic Peninsula** is formed of rocks 65–225 million years old, overlain by more recent rocks and glacial deposits. It is connected to the Andes in South America by a submarine ridge.

**Nearly half – 44% – of the** Antarctic coastline is bounded by ice shelves, like the Ronne Ice Shelf, which float on the ocean. These are joined to the inland ice sheet by dome-shaped ice "rises."

**More than 30% of** Antarctic ice is contained in the Ross Ice Shelf.

◀ **The barren, flat-bottomed** Upper Wright Valley was once filled by a glacier, but is now dry, strewn with boulders and pebbles. In some dry valleys, there has been no rain for over 2 million years.

**High winds carrying** snow form huge snowdrifts. The erosive power of the wind-borne snow can also sculpt the ice sheet to produce landforms known as *sastrugi* which align with the direction of the wind.

**The Lambert Glacier** is the largest glacier system in the world, up to 50 miles (80 km) wide at its seaward limit, and reaching 180 miles (300 km) into the interior by way of the Prince Charles Mountains.

**Antarctica is the** highest continent on Earth, because of the great thickness of ice which overlays the land. In places the ice alone can each up to 15,700 ft (4800 m) thick. Much of the basement rock of west Antarctica lies below sea level, pushed down by the weight of the ice.

▲ **Large colonies of** seabirds live in the extremely harsh Antarctic climate. The Emperor penguins seen here, the smaller Adélie penguin, the Antarctic petrel, and the South Polar skua are the only birds that breed exclusively on the continent.

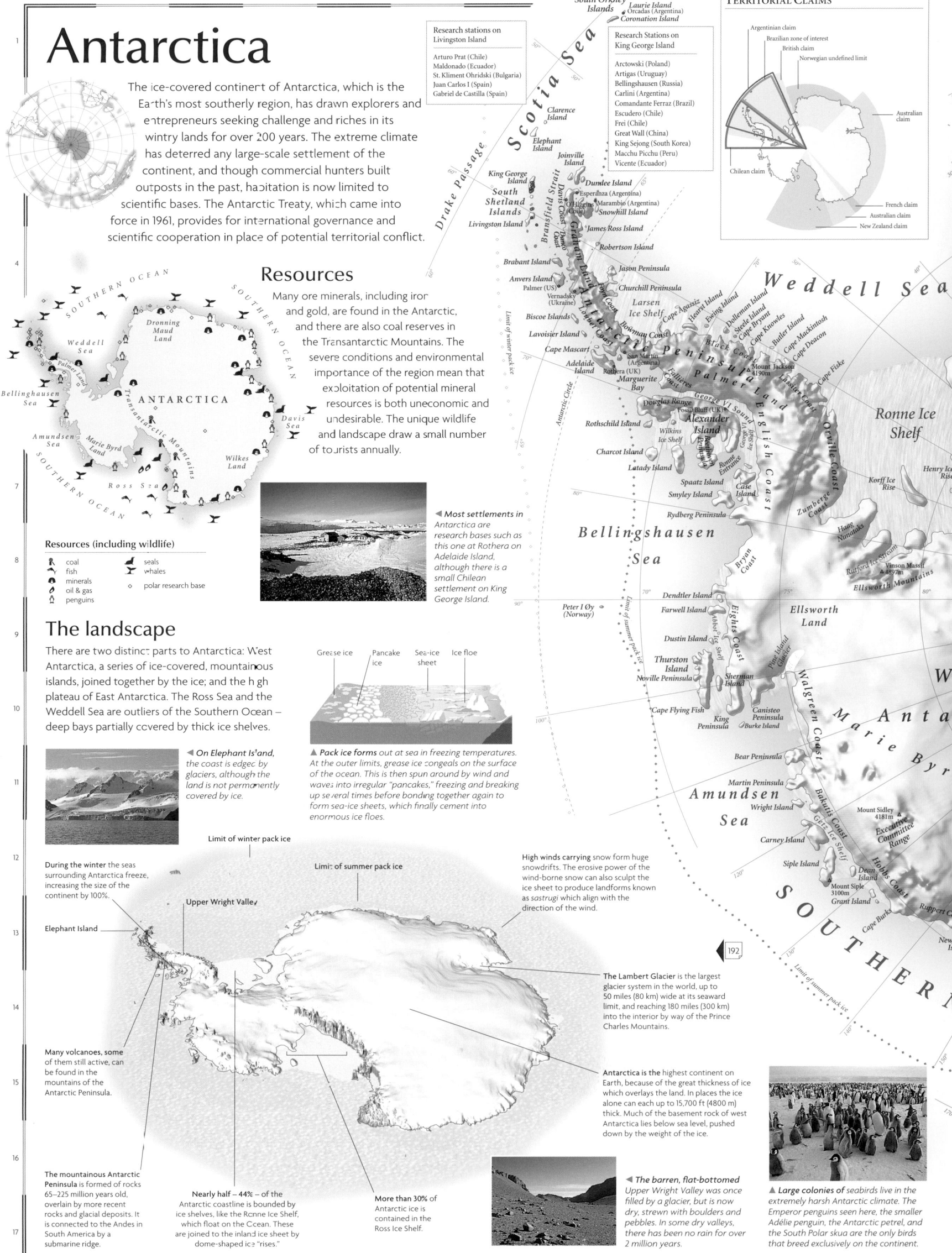

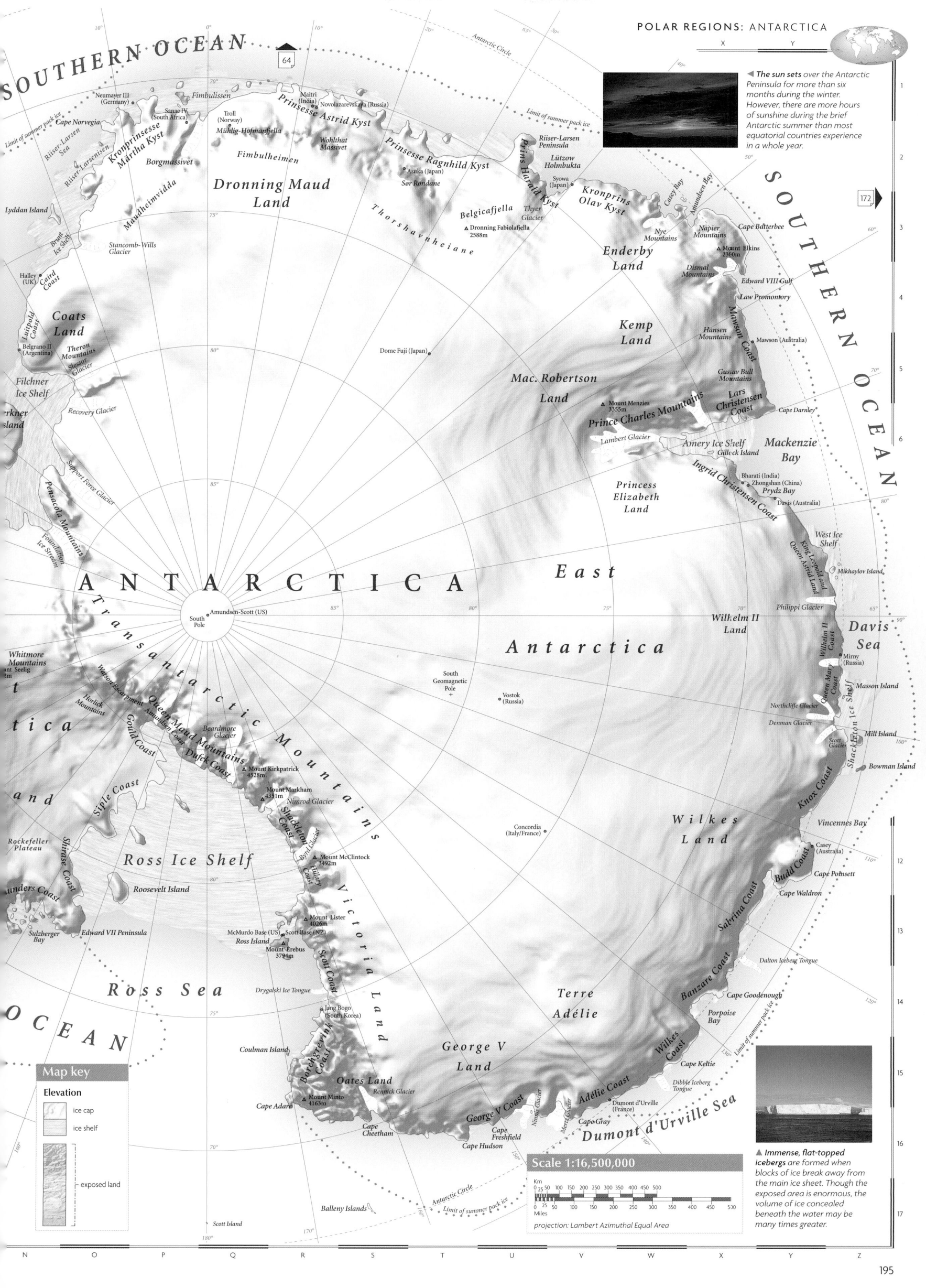

◀ **The sun sets** over the Antarctic Peninsula for more than six months during the winter. However, there are more hours of sunshine during the brief Antarctic summer than most equatorial countries experience in a whole year.

▲ **Immense, flat-topped icebergs** are formed when blocks of ice break away from the main ice sheet. Though the exposed area is enormous, the volume of ice concealed beneath the water may be many times greater.

Scale 1:16,500,000

projection: Lambert Azimuthal Equal Area

# The Arctic

Three continents, Asia, North America, and Europe, reach into the Arctic Circle at their northernmost limits, almost entirely encircling the Arctic Ocean. Despite the region's extraordinarily harsh climate, it has been inhabited for thousands of years by peoples such as the European Lapps, the Russian Nenet, and the North American Inuit, who draw a living from fishing, herding, and hunting. More recently, particularly in the Russian Arctic, opportunities to exploit oil and other mineral reserves have encouraged immigration. Pollution of the Arctic's unique ecology and damage to the traditional lifestyles of many native peoples have been the unfortunate results of this activity, and international cooperation is needed to safeguard the future of the region.

**Map key**

**Population**
- ▪ above 5 million
- ▪ 1 million to 5 million
- ⊙ 500,000 to 1 million
- ◎ 100,000 to 500,000
- ⊕ 50,000 to 100,000
- ○ 10,000 to 50,000
- ○ below 10,000

**Sea depth**
Sea level
- 200m / 656ft
- 1000m / 3281ft
- 2000m / 6562ft
- 3000m / 9843ft
- 4000m / 13,124ft
- 5000m / 16,400ft
- 6000m / 19,686ft

**Scale 1:23,500,000**

Km 0 100 200 300 400 500 600
Miles 0 100 200 300 400 500 600
*projection: Lambert Azimuthal Equal Area*

▲ *Windblown snow etches deep patterns in the ice sheet known as sastrugi. They align with the direction of the wind*

## Resources

Large quantities of coal, oil, and natural gas are to be found in the basins of the Arctic Ocean, and in northern Canada, Alaska, and Russia. The cost and difficulty of extraction and, more recently, awareness of damage to the environment, have limited exploitation to coastal regions. The unfrozen waters have stocks of fish including cod, flounder, and haddock. Quotas have now been put in place to restrict the number of fish caught annually. Reindeer are herded in large numbers by many of the native Arctic peoples. Most grain and vegetables are imported from elsewhere.

▲ *Icebreakers are ships with specially strengthened hulls, designed to break a path through the ice. They are used to keep important routes open during the winter, when falling temperatures cause much of the Arctic Ocean to freeze over.*

**Resources**
- 🗜 coal
- 🐟 fish
- ⛏ mining
- 🛢 oil & gas
- ☢ radioactive contamination
- ● major towns
- ⊕ major ports

## The landscape

The Arctic Ocean comprises two large ocean basins divided by three submarine ridges, the greatest of which, the Lomonosov Ridge, is a huge underwater mountain range which has an average height of more than 10,000 ft (3000 m). The lands which encircle the Arctic Ocean are underlain by great shield areas of ancient rocks, which were heavily glaciated during the last Ice Age.

◄ *Icebergs are constantly broken up and reshaped by wind and the oceans. This flat-topped iceberg has been undercut, leaving a craggy ice cliff.*

**The Canadian Shield** underlies almost all of the Canadian Arctic. It is a very stable plateau of ancient rock, now covered by glacial lakes and sediment, which supports tundra vegetation.

**The Arctic Ocean** is the world's smallest ocean with a total area of 5,440,000 sq miles (15,100,000 sq km).

**At a latitude** of more than 75° N, the Arctic Ocean is almost permanently covered by pack ice, though high winds and the movement of the seas may cause the ice to crack and break up.

**In the more** southerly reaches of the Arctic, like Siberia, much of the land is covered by permafrost. In the summer, higher temperatures warm the frozen ground, causing a number of typical phenomena. These include solifluction, the fast downhill movement of top soil layers; freeze/thaw activity, which patterns the ground into regular polygonal shapes, and the formation of large domes with a frozen ice core, known as pingos.

**A complex and** ancient mountain system, extending from the Queen Elizabeth Islands to eastern Greenland was formed more than 245 million years ago.

◄ *Much of Greenland is covered by a massive ice sheet more than 650,000 sq miles (1,683,400 sq km) in extent. The weight of the ice has depressed the central land area to form a basin lying more than 1000 ft (300 m) below sea level. Only at the edges of the island is bare rock visible.*

**Iceland has five** major glaciers, sustained by heavy snowfall. Parts of the ice cap cover active volcanoes, such as Bárdharbunga, which periodically erupt causing the melted ice to form a great lake at the glacier margins.

Lomonosov Ridge

Arctic ice shelf

Ice sheet · Iceberg
Crevasses occur at the edge of the ice sheet
Sea water melts the edge of the ice sheet

▲ *At the boundary of the Arctic ice shelves, sea water flows under the ice causing melting and forming crevasses on the surface. This eventually weakens blocks of ice which break away as icebergs. This process is known as calving.*

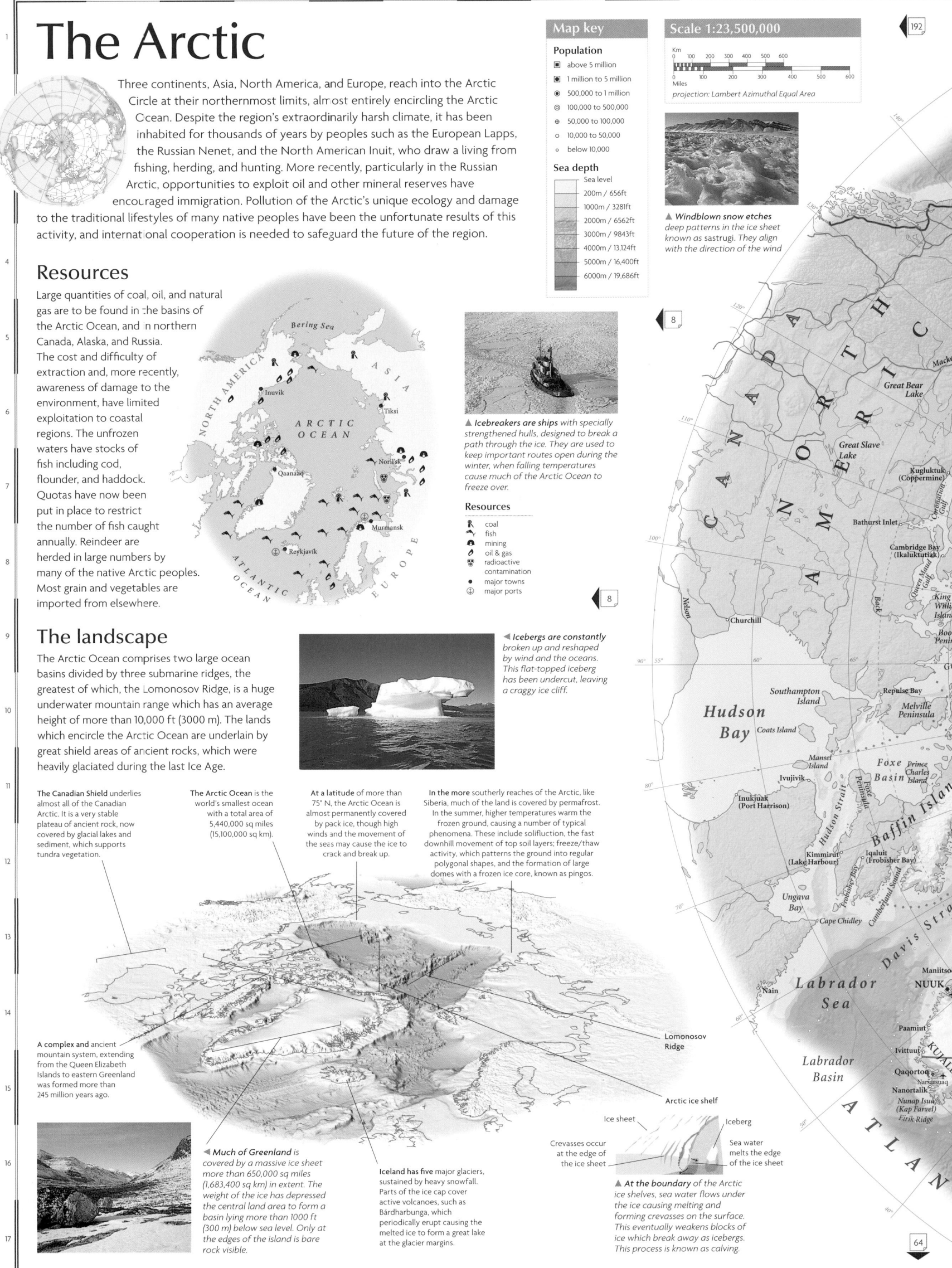

Bering Sea

NORTH AMERICA · ASIA

ARCTIC OCEAN

Inuvik · Tiksi · Noril'sk · Qaanaaq · Murmansk · Reykjavík

ATLANTIC OCEAN · EUROPE

NORTH AMERICA · CANADA

Mackenz... · Great Bear Lake · Great Slave Lake · Kugluktuk (Coppermine) · Coronation Gulf · Bathurst Inlet · Cambridge Bay (Ikaluktutiak) · Queen Maud Gulf · King William Island · Boothia Peninsu... · Back · Nelson

Churchill · Repulse Bay · Southampton Island · Melville Peninsula · Hudson Bay · Coats Island · Mansel Island · Foxe Basin · Prince Charles Island · Ivujivik · Inukjuak (Port Harrison) · Hudson Strait · Baffin Island · Kimmirut (Lake Harbour) · Iqaluit (Frobisher Bay) · Ungava Bay · Prince of Wales... · Cumberland Sound · Cape Chidley · Davis Strait

Nain · Labrador Sea · Maniitsoq · NUUK · Paamiut · Ivittuut · Qaqortoq · Narsarsuaq · Nanortalik · Nunap Isua (Kap Farvel) · Eirik Ridge · Labrador Basin · ATLANTIC

▲ **The aurora borealis** or Northern Lights are colored bands of light which appear in northern latitudes. Light is emitted when dust particles from the Sun react with gases in the Earth's atmosphere.

▲ **Polar bears range** for great distances over the Arctic pack ice in search of food. They are formidable hunters that live mainly on seals. In December and January, mother bears give birth to their cubs in dens dug deep beneath the snow.

# Geographical comparisons

## Largest countries

| | | |
|---|---|---|
| Russia | 6,592,735 sq miles | (17,075,200 sq km) |
| Canada | 3,855,171 sq miles | (9,984,670 sq km) |
| USA | 3,717,792 sq miles | (9,626,091 sq km) |
| China | 3,705,386 sq miles | (9,596,960 sq km) |
| Brazil | 3,286,470 sq miles | (8,511,965 sq km) |
| Australia | 2,967,893 sq miles | (7,686,850 sq km) |
| India | 1,269,339 sq miles | (3,287,590 sq km) |
| Argentina | 1,068,296 sq miles | (2,766,890 sq km) |
| Kazakhstan | 1,049,150 sq miles | (2,717,300 sq km) |
| Algeria | 919,590 sq miles | (2,381,740 sq km) |

## Smallest countries

| | | |
|---|---|---|
| Vatican City | 0.17 sq miles | (0.44 sq km) |
| Monaco | 0.75 sq miles | (1.95 sq km) |
| Nauru | 8 sq miles | (21 sq km) |
| Tuvalu | 10 sq miles | (26 sq km) |
| San Marino | 24 sq miles | (61 sq km) |
| Liechtenstein | 62 sq miles | (160 sq km) |
| Marshall Islands | 70 sq miles | (181 sq km) |
| St. Kitts & Nevis | 101 sq miles | (261 sq km) |
| Maldives | 116 sq miles | (300 sq km) |
| Malta | 122 sq miles | (316 sq km) |

## Largest islands

| | To the nearest 100 – or 10,000 for the largest | |
|---|---|---|
| Greenland | 840,000 sq miles | (2,170,000 sq km) |
| New Guinea | 312,000 sq miles | (808,000 sq km) |
| Borneo | 292,200 sq miles | (757,000 sq km) |
| Madagascar | 226,700 sq miles | (587,000 sq km) |
| Sumatra | 202,300 sq miles | (524,000 sq km) |
| Baffin Island | 183,800 sq miles | (476,000 sq km) |
| Honshu | 88,800 sq miles | (230,000 sq km) |
| Britain | 88,700 sq miles | (229,800 sq km) |
| Victoria Island | 81,900 sq miles | (212,000 sq km) |
| Ellesmere Island | 75,700 sq miles | (196,000 sq km) |

## Richest countries

| | GNI per capita, in US$ |
|---|---|
| Monaco | 168,004 |
| Liechtenstein | 134,660 |
| Switzerland | 81,130 |
| Norway | 76,160 |
| Luxembourg | 70,790 |
| Qatar | 60,510 |
| Iceland | 60,500 |
| USA | 59,160 |
| Denmark | 55,330 |
| Singapore | 54,530 |

## Poorest countries

| | GNI per capita, in US$ |
|---|---|
| Somalia | 88 |
| Burundi | 280 |
| Malawi | 320 |
| Niger | 360 |
| Central African Republic | 390 |
| Madagascar | 400 |
| Mozambique | 420 |
| Dem. Rep. Congo | 460 |
| Sierra Leone | 510 |
| Afghanistan | 560 |
| Burkina Faso | 590 |
| Uganda | 600 |

## Most populous countries

| | |
|---|---|
| China | 1,400,000,000 |
| India | 1,354,800,000 |
| USA | 330,200,000 |
| Indonesia | 266,900,000 |
| Brazil | 210,700,000 |
| Pakistan | 206,700,000 |
| Nigeria | 201,000,000 |
| Bangladesh | 167,600,000 |
| Russia | 146,800,000 |
| Mexico | 126,100,000 |

## Least populous countries

| | |
|---|---|
| Vatican City | 800 |
| Nauru | 11,000 |
| Tuvalu | 11,000 |
| Palau | 22,000 |
| San Marino | 34,000 |
| Liechtenstein | 38,000 |
| Monaco | 39,000 |
| Marshall Islands | 53,000 |
| St Kitts & Nevis | 56,000 |
| Dominica | 74,000 |
| Andorra | 77,000 |
| Seychelles | 95,000 |

## Most densely populated countries

| | | |
|---|---|---|
| Monaco | 52,000 people per sq mile | (20,000 per sq km) |
| Singapore | 24,576 people per sq mile | (9508 per sq km) |
| Bahrain | 5861 people per sq mile | (2266 per sq km) |
| Vatican City | 4706 people per sq mile | (1818 per sq km) |
| Maldives | 3828 people per sq mile | (1480 per sq km) |
| Malta | 3484 people per sq mile | (1350 per sq km) |
| Bangladesh | 3218 people per sq mile | (1243 per sq km) |
| Taiwan | 1895 people per sq mile | (732 per sq km) |
| Mauritius | 1811 people per sq mile | (699 per sq km) |
| Barbados | 1723 people per sq mile | (665 per sq km) |

## Most sparsely populated countries

| | | |
|---|---|---|
| Mongolia | 5 people per sq mile | (2 per sq km) |
| Namibia | 8 people per sq mile | (3 per sq km) |
| Australia | 8 people per sq mile | (3 per sq km) |
| Iceland | 9 people per sq mile | (3 per sq km) |
| Suriname | 9 people per sq mile | (4 per sq km) |
| Libya | 10 people per sq mile | (4 per sq km) |
| Guyana | 10 people per sq mile | (4 per sq km) |
| Canada | 10 people per sq mile | (4 per sq km) |
| Botswana | 11 people per sq mile | (4 per sq km) |
| Mauritania | 11 people per sq mile | (4 per sq km) |

## Most widely spoken languages

| | |
|---|---|
| 1. Chinese (Mandarin) | 6. Bengali |
| 2. Spanish | 7. Portuguese |
| 3. English | 8. Russian |
| 4. Arabic | 9. Japanese |
| 5. Hindi | 10. Lahnda/Punjabi |

## Largest conurbations

| | Urban area population |
|---|---|
| Guangzhou | 45,600,000 |
| Tokyo | 40,200,000 |
| Shanghai | 35,900,000 |
| Jakarta | 30,600,000 |
| Delhi | 29,400,000 |
| Manila | 25,200,000 |
| Mumbai | 24,700,000 |
| Seoul | 24,700,000 |
| Mexico City | 22,800,000 |
| New York | 22,400,000 |
| São Paulo | 22,200,000 |
| Cairo | 20,500,000 |
| Beijing | 20,400,000 |
| Dhaka | 19,500,000 |
| Lagos | 18,800,000 |
| Bangkok | 18,300,000 |
| Los Angeles | 17,800,000 |
| Osaka | 17,700,000 |
| Karachi | 17,300,000 |
| Moscow | 17,200,000 |
| Kolkatta | 16,600,000 |
| Buenos Aires | 16,300,000 |
| Istanbul | 15,800,000 |
| Tehran | 15,000,000 |
| London | 14,700,000 |

## Countries with the most land borders

| | |
|---|---|
| 14: China | (Afghanistan, Bhutan, India, Kazakhstan, Kyrgyzstan, Laos, Mongolia, Myanmar (Burma), Nepal, North Korea, Pakistan, Russia, Tajikistan, Vietnam) |
| 14: Russia | (Azerbaijan, Belarus, China, Estonia, Finland, Georgia, Kazakhstan, Latvia, Lithuania, Mongolia, North Korea, Norway, Poland, Ukraine) |
| 10: Brazil | (Argentina, Bolivia, Colombia, French Guiana, Guyana, Paraguay, Peru, Suriname, Uruguay, Venezuela) |
| 9: Congo, Dem. Rep. | (Angola, Burundi, Central African Republic, Congo, Rwanda, South Sudan, Tanzania, Uganda, Zambia) |
| 9: Germany | (Austria, Belgium, Czechia, Denmark, France, Luxembourg, Netherlands, Poland, Switzerland) |
| 8: Austria | (Czechia Germany, Hungary, Italy, Liechtenstein, Slovakia, Slovenia, Switzerland) |
| 8: France | (Andorra, Belgium, Germany, Italy, Luxembourg, Monaco, Spain, Switzerland) |
| 8: Tanzania | (Burundi, Dem. Rep. Congo, Kenya, Malawi, Mozambique, Rwanda, Uganda, Zambia) |
| 8: Turkey | (Armenia, Azerbaijan, Bulgaria, Georgia, Greece, Iran, Iraq, Syria) |
| 8: Zambia | (Angola, Botswana, Dem. Rep.Congo, Malawi, Mozambique, Namibia, Tanzania, Zimbabwe) |

## Longest rivers

| | | |
|---|---|---|
| Nile (NE Africa) | 4160 miles | (6695 km) |
| Amazon (South America) | 4049 miles | (6516 km) |
| Yangtze (China) | 3915 miles | (6299 km) |
| Mississippi/Missouri (USA) | 3710 miles | (5969 km) |
| Ob'-Irtysh (Russia) | 3461 miles | (5570 km) |
| Yellow River (China) | 3395 miles | (5464 km) |
| Congo (Central Africa) | 2900 miles | (4667 km) |
| Mekong (Southeast Asia) | 2749 miles | (4425 km) |
| Lena (Russia) | 2734 miles | (4400 km) |
| Mackenzie (Canada) | 2640 miles | (4250 km) |
| Yenisey (Russia) | 2541 miles | (4090km) |

## Highest mountains

| | Height above sea level | |
|---|---|---|
| Everest | 29,029 ft | (8848 m) |
| K2 | 28,253 ft | (8611 m) |
| Kangchenjunga I | 28,210 ft | (8598 m) |
| Makalu I | 27,767 ft | (8463 m) |
| Cho Oyu | 26,907 ft | (8201 m) |
| Dhaulagiri I | 26,796 ft | (8167 m) |
| Manaslu I | 26,783 ft | (8163 m) |
| Nanga Parbat I | 26,661 ft | (8126 m) |
| Annapurna I | 26,547 ft | (8091 m) |
| Gasherbrum I | 26,471 ft | (8068 m) |

## Largest bodies of inland water

| | With area and depth | |
|---|---|---|
| Caspian Sea | 143,243 sq miles (371,000 sq km) | 3215 ft (980 m) |
| Lake Superior | 31,151 sq miles (83,270 sq km) | 1289 ft (393 m) |
| Lake Victoria | 26,828 sq miles (69,484 sq km) | 328 ft (100 m) |
| Lake Huron | 23,436 sq miles (60,700 sq km) | 751 ft (229 m) |
| Lake Michigan | 22,402 sq miles (58,020 sq km) | 922 ft (281 m) |
| Lake Tanganyika | 12,703 sq miles (32,900 sq km) | 4700 ft (1435 m) |
| Great Bear Lake | 12,274 sq miles (31,790 sq km) | 1047 ft (319 m) |
| Lake Baikal | 11,776 sq miles (30,500 sq km) | 5712 ft (1741 m) |
| Great Slave Lake | 10,981 sq miles (28,440 sq km) | 459 ft (140 m) |
| Lake Erie | 9,915 sq miles (25,680 sq km) | 197 ft (60 m) |

## Deepest ocean features

| | | |
|---|---|---|
| Challenger Deep, Mariana Trench (Pacific) | 35,827 ft | (10,920 m) |
| Vityaz III Depth, Tonga Trench (Pacific) | 35,704 ft | (10,882 m) |
| Vityaz Depth, Kuril-Kamchatka Trench (Pacific) | 34,588 ft | (10,542 m) |
| Cape Johnson Deep, Philippine Trench (Pacific) | 34,441 ft | (10,497 m) |
| Kermadec Trench (Pacific) | 32,964 ft | (10,047 m) |
| Ramapo Deep, Japan Trench (Pacific) | 32,758 ft | (9984 m) |
| Milwaukee Deep, Puerto Rico Trench (Atlantic) | 30,185 ft | (9200 m) |
| Argo Deep, Torres Trench (Pacific) | 30,070 ft | (9165 m) |
| Meteor Depth, South Sandwich Trench (Atlantic) | 30,000 ft | (9144 m) |
| Planet Deep, New Britain Trench (Pacific) | 29,988 ft | (9140 m) |

## Greatest waterfalls

| | Mean flow of water | |
|---|---|---|
| Boyoma (Dem. Rep. Congo) | 600,400 cu. ft/sec | (17,000 cu.m/sec) |
| Khône (Laos/Cambodia) | 410,000 cu. ft/sec | (11,600 cu.m/sec) |
| Niagara (USA/Canada) | 195,000 cu. ft/sec | (5500 cu.m/sec) |
| Salto Grande (Uruguay) | 160,000 cu. ft/sec | (4500 cu.m/sec) |
| Paulo Afonso (Brazil) | 100,000 cu. ft/sec | (2800 cu.m/sec) |
| Salto do Urubupungá (Brazil) | 97,000 cu. ft/sec | (2750 cu.m/sec) |
| Iguaçu (Argentina/Brazil) | 62,000 cu. ft/sec | (1700 cu.m/sec) |
| Cachoeira do Maribondo (Brazil) | 53,000 cu. ft/sec | (1500 cu.m/sec) |
| Victoria (Zimbabwe) | 39,000 cu. ft/sec | (1100 cu.m/sec) |
| Murchison Falls (Uganda) | 42,000 cu. ft/sec | (1200 cu.m/sec) |
| Churchill (Canada) | 35,000 cu. ft/sec | (1000 cu.m/sec) |
| Kaveri Falls (India) | 33,000 cu. ft/sec | (900 cu.m/sec) |

## Highest waterfalls

| | * Indicates that the total height is a single leap | |
|---|---|---|
| Angel (Venezuela) | 3212 ft | (979 m) |
| Tugela (South Africa) | 3110 ft | (948 m) |
| Utigard (Norway) | 2625 ft | (800 m) |
| Mongefossen (Norway) | 2539 ft | (774 m) |
| Mtarazi (Zimbabwe) | 2500 ft | (762 m) |
| Yosemite (USA) | 2425 ft | (739 m) |
| Ostre Mardola Foss (Norway) | 2156 ft | (657 m) |
| Tyssestrengane (Norway) | 2119 ft | (646 m) |
| *Cuquenan (Venezuela) | 2001 ft | (610 m) |
| Sutherland (New Zealand) | 1903 ft | (580 m) |
| *Kjellfossen (Norway) | 1841 ft | (561 m) |

## Largest deserts

| NB – Most of Antarctica is a polar desert, with only 50mm of precipitation annually | | |
|---|---|---|
| Sahara | 3,450,000 sq miles | (9,065,000 sq km) |
| Gobi | 500,000 sq miles | (1,295,000 sq km) |
| Ar Rub al Khali | 289,600 sq miles | (750,000 sq km) |
| Great Victorian | 249,800 sq miles | (647,000 sq km) |
| Sonoran | 120,000 sq miles | (311,000 sq km) |
| Kalahari | 120,000 sq miles | (310,800 sq km) |
| Kara Kum | 115,800 sq miles | (300,000 sq km) |
| Takla Makan | 100,400 sq miles | (260,000 sq km) |
| Namib | 52,100 sq miles | (135,000 sq km) |
| Thar | 33,670 sq miles | (130,000 sq km) |

## Hottest inhabited places

| | | |
|---|---|---|
| Djibouti (Djibouti) | 86° F | (30 °C) |
| Tombouctou (Mali) | 84.7° F | (29.3 °C) |
| Tirunelveli (India) | | |
| Tuticorin (India) | | |
| Nellore (India) | 84.5° F | (29.2 °C) |
| Santa Marta (Colombia) | | |
| Aden (Yemen) | 84° F | (28.9 °C) |
| Madurai (India) | | |
| Niamey (Niger) | | |
| Hodeida (Yemen) | 83.8° F | (28.8 °C) |
| Ouagadougou (Burkina Faso) | | |
| Thanjavur (India) | | |
| Tiruchchirappalli (India) | | |

## Driest inhabited places

| | | |
|---|---|---|
| Aswân (Egypt) | 0.02 in | (0.5 mm) |
| Luxor (Egypt) | 0.03 in | (0.7 mm) |
| Arica (Chile) | 0.04 in | (1.1 mm) |
| Ica (Peru) | 0.1 in | (2.3 mm) |
| Antofagasta (Chile) | 0.2 in | (4.9 mm) |
| Al Minya (Egypt) | 0.2 in | (5.1 mm) |
| Asyut (Egypt) | 0.2 in | (5.2 mm) |
| Callao (Peru) | 0.5 in | (12.0 mm) |
| Trujillo (Peru) | 0.55 in | (14.0 mm) |
| Al Fayyum (Egypt) | 0.8 in | (19.0 mm) |

## Wettest inhabited places

| | | |
|---|---|---|
| Mawsynram (India) | 467 in | (11,862 mm) |
| Mount Waialeale (Hawaii, USA) | 460 in | (11,684 mm) |
| Cherrapunji (India) | 450 in | (11,430 mm) |
| Cape Debundsha (Cameroon) | 405 in | (10,290 mm) |
| Quibdo (Colombia) | 354 in | (8892 mm) |
| Buenaventura (Colombia) | 265 in | (6743 mm) |
| Monrovia (Liberia) | 202 in | (5131 mm) |
| Pago Pago (American Samoa) | 196 in | (4990 mm) |
| Mawlamyine (Myanmar [Burma]) | 191 in | (4852 mm) |
| Lae (Papua New Guinea) | 183 in | (4645 mm) |

# Standard time zones

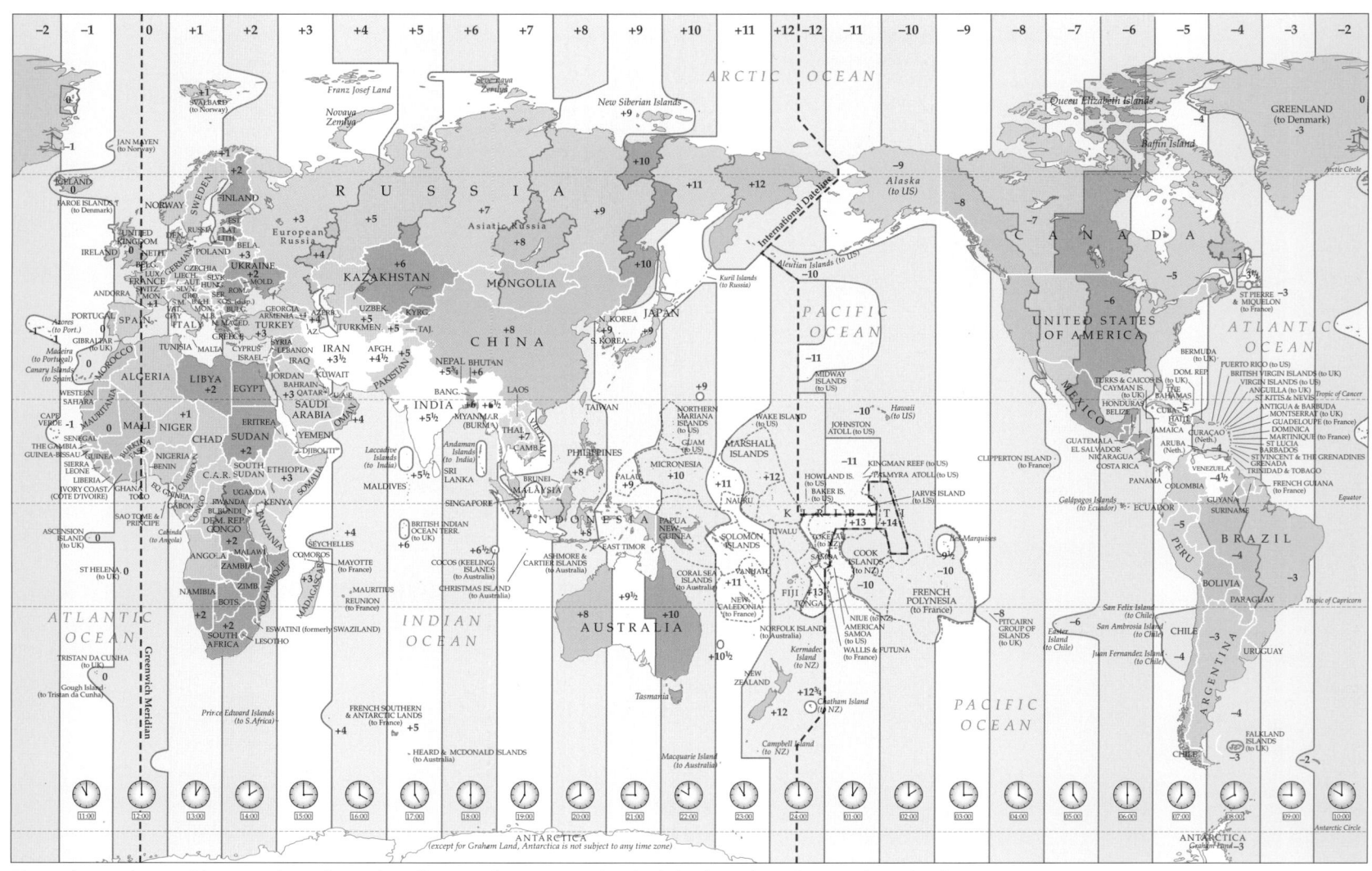

*The numbers at the top of the map indicate the number of hours each time zone is ahead or behind Coordinated Universal Time (UTC).*
*The clocks and 24-hour times given at the bottom of the map show the time in each time zone when it is 12:00 hours noon (UTC)*

## Time Zones

Because Earth is a rotating sphere, the Sun shines on only half of its surface at any one time. Thus, it is simultaneously morning, evening and night time in different parts of the world *(see diagram below)*. Because of these disparities, each country or part of a country adheres to a local time.

A region of Earth's surface within which a single local time is used is called a time zone. There are 24 one hour time zones around the world, arranged roughly in longitudinal bands.

## Standard Time

Standard time is the official local time in a particular country or part of a country. It is defined by the

**Day and night around the world**

time zone or zones associated with that country or region. Although time zones are arranged roughly in longitudinal bands, in many places the borders of a zone do not fall exactly on longitudinal meridians, as can be seen on the map *(above)*, but are determined by geographical factors or by borders between countries or parts of countries. Most countries have just one time zone and one standard time, but some large countries (such as the US, Canada, and Russia) are split between several time zones, so standard time varies across those countries. For example, the coterminous United States straddles four time zones and so has four standard times, called the Eastern, Central, Mountain, and Pacific standard times. China is unusual in that just one standard time is used for the whole country, even though it extends across 60° of longitude from west to east.

## Coordinated Universal Time (UTC)

Coordinated Universal Time (UTC) is a reference by which the local time in each time zone is set. For example, Australian Western Standard Time (the local time in Western Australia) is set 8 hours ahead of UTC (it is

UTC+8) whereas Eastern Standard Time in the United States is set 5 hours behind UTC (it is UTC-5). UTC is a successor to, and closely approximates, Greenwich Mean Time (GMT). However, UTC is based on an atomic clock, whereas GMT is determined by the Sun's position in the sky relative to the 0° longitudinal meridian, which runs through Greenwich, UK.

## The International Dateline

The International Dateline is an imaginary line from pole to pole that roughly corresponds to the 180° longitudinal meridian. It is an arbitrary marker between calendar days. The dateline is needed because of the use of local times around the world rather than a single universal time. When moving from west to east across the dateline, travelers have to set their watches back one day. Those traveling in the opposite direction, from east to west, must add a day.

## Daylight Saving Time

Daylight saving is a summertime adjustment to the local time in a country or region, designed to cause a higher proportion of its citizens' waking hours to pass during daylight. To follow the system, timepieces are advanced by an hour on a pre-decided date in spring and reverted back in the fall. About half of the world's nations use daylight saving.

# Countries of the World

There are currently 196 independent countries in the world and almost 60 dependencies. Antarctica is the only land area on Earth that is not officially part of, and does not belong to, any single country.

In 1950, the world comprised 82 countries. In the decades following, many more states came into being as they achieved independence from their former colonial rulers. Most recent additions were caused by the breakup of the former Soviet Union in 1991, and the former Yugoslavia in 1992, which swelled the ranks of independent states. In July 2011, South Sudan became the latest country to be formed after declaring independence from Sudan.

### Country factfile key

**Formation** Date of political origin or independence/ date current borders were established

**Population** Total population / population density – based on total *land* area

**Languages** An asterisk (*) denotes the official language(s)

**Calorie consumption** Average number of kilocalories consumed daily per person

## AFGHANISTAN
*Central Asia*

**Official name** Islamic Republic of Afghanistan
**Formation** 1919 / 1919
**Capital** Kabul
**Population** 36.4 million / 145 people per sq mile (56 people per sq km)
**Total area** 250,000 sq. miles (647,500 sq. km)
**Languages** Pashto*, Tajik, Dari*, Farsi, Uzbek, Turkmen
**Religions** Sunni Muslim 80%, Shi'a Muslim 19%, Other 1%
**Ethnic mix** Pashtun 38%, Tajik 25%, Hazara 19%, Uzbek and Turkmen 15%, Other 3%
**Government** Nonparty system
**Currency** Afghani = 100 puls
**Literacy rate** 32%
**Calorie consumption** 2090 kilocalories

## ALBANIA
*Southeast Europe*

**Official name** Republic of Albania
**Formation** 1912 / 1921
**Capital** Tirana
**Population** 2.9 million / 274 people per sq mile (106 people per sq km)
**Total area** 11,100 sq. miles (28,748 sq. km)
**Languages** Albanian*, Greek
**Religions** Muslim (mainly Sunni) 68%, Roman Catholic 12%, Albanian Orthodox 8%, Nonreligious 6%, Other 6%
**Ethnic mix** Albanian 98%, Greek 1%, Other 1%
**Government** Parliamentary system
**Currency** Lek = 100 qindarka (qintars)
**Literacy rate** 97%
**Calorie consumption** 3193 kilocalories

## ALGERIA
*North Africa*

**Official name** People's Democratic Republic of Algeria
**Formation** 1962 / 1962
**Capital** Algiers
**Population** 42 million / 46 people per sq mile (18 people per sq km)
**Total area** 919,590 sq. miles (2,381,740 sq. km)
**Languages** Arabic*, Tamazight* (Kabyle, Shawia, Tamashek), French
**Religions** Sunni Muslim 99%, Christian and Jewish 1%
**Ethnic mix** Arab 75%, Berber 24%, European and Jewish 1%
**Government** Transitional regime
**Currency** Algerian dinar = 100 centimes
**Literacy rate** 75%
**Calorie consumption** 3296 kilocalories

## ANDORRA
*Southwest Europe*

**Official name** Principality of Andorra
**Formation** 1278 / 1278
**Capital** Andorra la Vella
**Population** 77,000 / 428 people per sq mile (166 people per sq km)
**Total area** 181 sq. miles (468 sq. km)
**Languages** Spanish, Catalan*, French, Portuguese
**Religions** Roman Catholic 94%, Other 6%
**Ethnic mix** Spanish 46%, Andorran 28%, Other 18%, French 8%
**Government** Parliamentary system
**Currency** Euro = 100 cents
**Literacy rate** 99%
**Calorie consumption** Not available

## ANGOLA
*Southern Africa*

**Official name** Republic of Angola
**Formation** 1975 / 1975
**Capital** Luanda
**Population** 30.8 million / 64 people per sq mile (25 people per sq km)
**Total area** 481,351 sq. miles (1,246,700 sq. km)
**Languages** Portuguese*, Umbundu, Kimbundu, Kikongo
**Religions** Roman Catholic 40%, Protestant 38%, Nonreligious 12%, Other (including animist) 10%
**Ethnic mix** Ovimbundu 37%, Ambundu 25%, Other 25%, Bakongo 13%
**Government** Presidential system
**Currency** Readjusted kwanza = 100 lwei
**Literacy rate** 66%
**Calorie consumption** 2473 kilocalories

## ANTIGUA & BARBUDA
*West Indies*

**Official name** Antigua and Barbuda
**Formation** 1981 / 1981
**Capital** St. John's
**Population** 103,000 / 606 people per sq mile (234 people per sq km)
**Total area** 170 sq. miles (442 sq. km)
**Languages** English*, English patois
**Religions** Other Christian 49%, Other 19%, Anglican 19%, Seventh-day Adventist 13%
**Ethnic mix** Black African 87%, Mixed race 5%, Hispanic 3%, Other 3%, White 2%
**Government** Parliamentary system
**Currency** East Caribbean dollar = 100 cents
**Literacy rate** 99%
**Calorie consumption** 2417 kilocalories

## ARGENTINA
*South America*

**Official name** Republic of Argentina
**Formation** 1816 / 1816
**Capital** Buenos Aires
**Population** 44.7 million / 42 people per sq mile (16 people per sq km)
**Total area** 1,068,296 sq. miles (2,766,890 sq. km)
**Languages** Spanish*, Italian, Amerindian languages
**Religions** Roman Catholic 71%, Protestant 15%, Nonreligious 11%, Other 3%
**Ethnic mix** Indo-European 97%, Mestizo 2%, Amerindian 1%
**Government** Presidential system
**Currency** Argentine peso = 100 centavos
**Literacy rate** 99%
**Calorie consumption** 3229 kilocalories

## ARMENIA
*Southwest Asia*

**Official name** Republic of Armenia
**Formation** 1991 / 1991
**Capital** Yerevan
**Population** 2.9 million / 252 people per sq mile (97 people per sq km)
**Total area** 11,506 sq. miles (29,800 sq. km)
**Languages** Armenian*, Azeri, Russian
**Religions** Orthodox Christian 89%, Other 8%, Nonreligious 2%, Armenian Catholic Church 1%
**Ethnic mix** Armenian 98%, Other 1%, Yezidi 1%
**Government** Parliamentary system
**Currency** Dram = 100 luma
**Literacy rate** 99%
**Calorie consumption** 2928 kilocalories

## AUSTRALIA
*Australasia & Oceania*

**Official name** Commonwealth of Australia
**Formation** 1901 / 1901
**Capital** Canberra
**Population** 24.8 million / 8 people per sq mile (3 people per sq km)
**Total area** 2,967,893 sq. miles (7,686,850 sq. km)
**Languages** English*, Italian, Cantonese, Greek, Arabic, Vietnamese, Aboriginal languages
**Religions** Nonreligious 33%, Roman Catholic 26%, Other Christian 18%, Anglican 14%, Other 6%, Muslim 3%
**Ethnic mix** British 34%, Australian 27%, Other 21%, Irish 8%, Italian 4%, German 3%, Chinese 3%
**Government** Parliamentary system
**Currency** Australian dollar = 100 cents
**Literacy rate** 99%
**Calorie consumption** 3276 kilocalories

## AUSTRIA
*Central Europe*

**Official name** Republic of Austria
**Formation** 1918 / 1919
**Capital** Vienna
**Population** 8.8 million / 275 people per sq mile (106 people per sq km)
**Total area** 32,378 sq. miles (83,858 sq. km)
**Languages** German*, Croatian, Slovenian, Hungarian (Magyar)
**Religions** Roman Catholic 75%, Nonreligious 12%, Other Christian 8%, Muslim 4%, Other 1%
**Ethnic mix** Austrian 93%, Croat, Slovene, and Hungarian 6%, Other 1%
**Government** Parliamentary system
**Currency** Euro = 100 cents
**Literacy rate** 99%
**Calorie consumption** 3768 kilocalories

## AZERBAIJAN
*Southwest Asia*

**Official name** Republic of Azerbaijan
**Formation** 1991 / 1991
**Capital** Baku
**Population** 9.9 million / 296 people per sq mile (114 people per sq km)
**Total area** 33,436 sq. miles (86,600 sq. km)
**Languages** Azeri*, Russian
**Religions** Shi'a Muslim 68%, Sunni Muslim 26%, Russian Orthodox 3%, Armenian Apostolic Church (Orthodox) 2%, Other 1%
**Ethnic mix** Azeri 91%, Other 3%, Lazs 2%, Armenian 2%, Russian 2%
**Government** Presidential system
**Currency** New manat = 100 gopik
**Literacy rate** 99%
**Calorie consumption** 3118 kilocalories

## THE BAHAMAS
*West Indies*

**Official name** Commonwealth of The Bahamas
**Formation** 1973 / 1973
**Capital** Nassau
**Population** 399,000 / 103 people per sq mile (40 people per sq km)
**Total area** 5382 sq. miles (13,940 sq. km)
**Languages** English*, English Creole, French Creole
**Religions** Baptist 36%, Other 20%, Anglican 14%, Roman Catholic 12%, Pentecostal 9%, Seventh-day Adventist 5%, Methodist 4%
**Ethnic mix** Black African 85%, European 12%, Asian and Hispanic 3%
**Government** Parliamentary system
**Currency** Bahamian dollar = 100 cents
**Literacy rate** 96%
**Calorie consumption** 2670 kilocalories

## BAHRAIN
*Southwest Asia*

**Official name** Kingdom of Bahrain
**Formation** 1971 / 1971
**Capital** Manama
**Population** 1.6 million / 5861 people per sq mile (2266 people per sq km)
**Total area** 239 sq. miles (620 sq. km)
**Languages** Arabic*
**Religions** Muslim (mainly Shi'a) 70%, Other 30%
**Ethnic mix** Bahraini 46%, Asian 46%, Other Arab 5%, Other 3%
**Government** Mixed monarchical–parliamentary system
**Currency** Bahraini dinar = 1000 fils
**Literacy rate** 95%
**Calorie consumption** Not available

## BANGLADESH
*South Asia*

**Official name** People's Republic of Bangladesh
**Formation** 1971 / 1971
**Capital** Dhaka
**Population** 167 million / 3218 people per sq mile (1243 people per sq km)
**Total area** 55,598 sq. miles (144,000 sq. km)
**Languages** Bengali*, Urdu, Chakma, Marma (Magh), Garo, Khasi, Santhali, Tripuri, Mro
**Religions** Muslim (mainly Sunni) 90%, Hindu 9%, Other 1%
**Ethnic mix** Bengali 98%, Other 2%
**Government** Parliamentary system
**Currency** Taka = 100 poisha
**Literacy rate** 73%
**Calorie consumption** 2450 kilocalories

## BARBADOS
*West Indies*

**Official name** Barbados
**Formation** 1966 / 1966
**Capital** Bridgetown
**Population** 286,000 / 1723 people per sq mile (665 people per sq km)
**Total area** 166 sq. miles (430 sq. km)
**Languages** Bajan (Barbadian English), English*
**Religions** Anglican 24%, Nonreligious 21%, Other 21%, Pentecostal 20%, Seventh-day Adventist 6%, Methodist 4%, Roman Catholic 4%
**Ethnic mix** Black African 93%, Mixed race 3%, White 3%, Other 1%
**Government** Parliamentary system
**Currency** Barbados dollar = 100 cents
**Literacy rate** 99%
**Calorie consumption** 2937 kilocalories

## BELARUS
*Eastern Europe*

**Official name** Republic of Belarus
**Formation** 1991 / 1991
**Capital** Minsk
**Population** 9.5 million / 119 people per sq mile (46 people per sq km)
**Total area** 80,154 sq. miles (207,600 sq. km)
**Languages** Belarusian*, Russian*
**Religions** Orthodox Christian 73%, Roman Catholic 12%, Other 12%, Nonreligious 3%
**Ethnic mix** Belarussian 86%, Russian 8%, Polish 3%, Other 2%, Ukrainian 1%
**Government** Presidential system
**Currency** Belarussian rouble = 100 kopeks
**Literacy rate** 99%
**Calorie consumption** 3250 kilocalories

## BELGIUM
*Northwest Europe*

**Official name** Kingdom of Belgium
**Formation** 1830 / 1919
**Capital** Brussels
**Population** 11.5 million / 908 people per sq mile (350 people per sq km)
**Total area** 11,780 sq. miles (30,510 sq. km)
**Languages** Dutch*, French*, German*
**Religions** Roman Catholic 88%, Other 10%, Muslim 2%
**Ethnic mix** Fleming 58%, Walloon 33%, Other 6%, Italian 2%, Moroccan 1%
**Government** Parliamentary system
**Currency** Euro = 100 cents
**Literacy rate** 99%
**Calorie consumption** 3733 kilocalories

## BELIZE
*Central America*

**Official name** Belize
**Formation** 1981 / 1981
**Capital** Belmopan
**Population** 382,000 / 43 people per sq mile (17 people per sq km)
**Total area** 8867 sq. miles (22,966 sq. km)
**Languages** English Creole, Spanish, English*, Mayan, Garifuna (Carib)
**Religions** Roman Catholic 40%, Other Christian 34%, Nonreligious 16%, Other 10%
**Ethnic mix** Mestizo 49%, Creole 24%, Maya 10%, Other 7%, Garifuna 6%, Asian Indian 4%
**Government** Parliamentary system
**Currency** Belizean dollar = 100 cents
**Literacy rate** 75%
**Calorie consumption** 2751 kilocalories

## BENIN
*West Africa*

**Official name** Republic of Benin
**Formation** 1960 / 1960
**Capital** Porto-Novo (official), Cotonou (political)
**Population** 11.5 million / 269 people per sq mile (104 people per sq km)
**Total area** 43,483 sq. miles (112,620 sq. km)
**Languages** Fon, Bariba, Yoruba, Adja, Houeda, Somba, French*
**Religions** Indigenous beliefs and Voodoo 50%, Christian 30%, Muslim 20%
**Ethnic mix** Fon 41%, Other 21%, Adja 16%, Yoruba 12%, Bariba 10%
**Government** Presidential system
**Currency** CFA franc = 100 centimes
**Literacy rate** 33%
**Calorie consumption** 2619 kilocalories

## BHUTAN
*South Asia*

**Official name** Kingdom of Bhutan
**Formation** 1656 / 1865
**Capital** Thimphu
**Population** 817,000 / 45 people per sq mile (17 people per sq km)
**Total area** 18,147 sq. miles (47,000 sq. km)
**Languages** Dzongkha*, Nepali, Assamese
**Religions** Mahayana Buddhist 75%, Hindu 25%
**Ethnic mix** Drukpa 50%, Nepalese 35%, Other 15%
**Government** Mixed monarchical–parliamentary system
**Currency** Ngultrum = 100 chetrum
**Literacy rate** 57%
**Calorie consumption** Not available

## BOLIVIA
*South America*

**Official name** Plurinational State of Bolivia
**Formation** 1825 / 1938
**Capital** Sucre; La Paz (administrative)
**Population** 11.2 million / 27 people per sq mile (10 people per sq km)
**Total area** 424,162 sq. miles (1,098,580 sq. km)
**Languages** Aymara*, Quechua*, Spanish*
**Religions** Roman Catholic 77%, Protestant 16%, Nonreligious 4%, Other 3%
**Ethnic mix** Quechua 37%, Aymara 32%, Mixed race 13%, European 10%, Other 8%
**Government** Presidential system
**Currency** Boliviano = 100 centavos
**Literacy rate** 92%
**Calorie consumption** 2256 kilocalories

## BOSNIA & HERZEGOVINA
*Southeast Europe*

**Official name** Bosnia and Herzegovina
**Formation** 1992 / 1992
**Capital** Sarajevo
**Population** 3.5 million / 177 people per sq mile (68 people per sq km)
**Total area** 19,741 sq. miles (51,129 sq. km)
**Languages** Bosnian*, Serbian*, Croatian*
**Religions** Muslim (mainly Sunni) 53%, Orthodox Christian 35%, Roman Catholic 8%, Nonreligious 3%, Other 1%
**Ethnic mix** Bosniak 48%, Serb 34%, Croat 16%, Other 2%
**Government** Parliamentary system
**Currency** Marka = 100 pfeninga
**Literacy rate** 97%
**Calorie consumption** 3154 kilocalories

## BOTSWANA
*Southern Africa*

**Official name** Republic of Botswana
**Formation** 1966 / 1966
**Capital** Gaborone
**Population** 2.3 million / 11 people per sq mile (4 people per sq km)
**Total area** 231,803 sq. miles (600,370 sq. km)
**Languages** Setswana, English*, Shona, San, Khoikhoi, isiNdebele
**Religions** Christian (mainly Protestant) 80%, Nonreligious 15%, Traditional beliefs 4%, Other (including Muslim) 1%
**Ethnic mix** Tswana 79%, Kalanga 11%, Other 10%
**Government** Presidential system
**Currency** Pula = 100 thebe
**Literacy rate** 88%
**Calorie consumption** 2326 kilocalories

## BRAZIL
*South America*

**Official name** Federative Republic of Brazil
**Formation** 1822 / 1828
**Capital** Brasília
**Population** 211 million / 65 people per sq mile (25 people per sq km)
**Total area** 3,286,470 sq. miles (8,511,965 sq. km)
**Languages** Portuguese*, German, Italian, Spanish, Polish, Japanese, Amerindian languages
**Religions** Roman Catholic 61%, Protestant 26%, Nonreligious 8%, Other 5%
**Ethnic mix** White 48%, Mixed race 43%, Black 8%, Other 1%
**Government** Presidential system
**Currency** Real = 100 centavos
**Literacy rate** 92%
**Calorie consumption** 3263 kilocalories

## BRUNEI
*Southeast Asia*

**Official name** Brunei Darussalam
**Formation** 1984 / 1984
**Capital** Bandar Seri Begawan
**Population** 434,000 / 213 people per sq mile (32 people per sq km)
**Total area** 2228 sq. miles (5770 sq. km)
**Languages** Malay*, English, Chinese
**Religions** Muslim (mainly Sunni) 79%, Christian 9%, Buddhist 8%, Other 4%
**Ethnic mix** Malay 66%, Other 21%, Chinese 10%, Indigenous 3%
**Government** Monarchy
**Currency** Brunei dollar = 100 cents
**Literacy rate** 95%
**Calorie consumption** 2985 kilocalories

## BULGARIA
*Southeast Europe*

**Official name** Republic of Bulgaria
**Formation** 1908 / 1947
**Capital** Sofia
**Population** 7 million / 164 people per sq mile (63 people per sq km)
**Total area** 42,822 sq. miles (110,910 sq. km)
**Languages** Bulgarian*, Turkish, Roman
**Religions** Orthodox Christian 75%, Muslim 15%, Nonreligious 5%, Other 3%, Protestant 1%, Roman Catholic 1%
**Ethnic mix** Bulgarian 85%, Turkish 9%, Roma 5%, Other 1%
**Government** Parliamentary system
**Currency** Lev = 100 stotinki
**Literacy rate** 98%
**Calorie consumption** 2829 kilocalories

## BURKINA FASO
*West Africa*

**Official name** Burkina Faso
**Formation** 1960 / 1960
**Capital** Ouagadougou
**Population** 19.8 million / 187 people per sq mile (72 people per sq km)
**Total area** 105,869 sq. miles (274,200 sq. km)
**Languages** Mossi, Fulani, French*, Tuareg, Dyula, Songhai
**Religions** Muslim 61%, Roman Catholic 19%, Traditional beliefs 15%, Protestant 4%, Other and nonreligious 1%
**Ethnic mix** Mossi 48%, Other 21%, Peul 10%, Lobi 7%, Bobo 7%, Mandé 7%
**Government** Presidential system
**Currency** CFA franc = 100 centimes
**Literacy rate** 35%
**Calorie consumption** 2720 kilocalories

## BURUNDI
*Central Africa*

**Official name** Republic of Burundi
**Formation** 1962 / 1962
**Capital** Bujumbura (commercial); Gitega (political)
**Population** 11.2 million / 1131 people per sq mile (437 people per sq km)
**Total area** 10,745 sq. miles (27,830 sq. km)
**Languages** Kirundi*, French*, Kiswahili
**Religions** Roman Catholic 65%, Protestant 23%, Other 7%, Muslim 3%, Seventh-day Adventist 2%
**Ethnic mix** Hutu 85%, Tutsi 14%, Twa 1%
**Government** Presidential system
**Currency** Burundian franc = 100 centimes
**Literacy rate** 62%
**Calorie consumption** 1604 kilocalories

## CAMBODIA
*Southeast Asia*

**Official name** Kingdom of Cambodia
**Formation** 1953 / 1953
**Capital** Phnom Penh
**Population** 16.2 million / 238 people per sq mile (92 people per sq km)
**Total area** 69,900 sq. miles (181,040 sq. km)
**Languages** Khmer*, French, Chinese, Vietnamese, Cham
**Religions** Buddhist 97%, Muslim 2%, Other (mostly Christian) 1%
**Ethnic mix** Khmer 90%, Vietnamese 5%, Other 4%, Chinese 1%
**Government** Parliamentary system
**Currency** Riel = 100 sen
**Literacy rate** 81%
**Calorie consumption** 2477 kilocalories

## CAMEROON
*Central Africa*

**Official name** Republic of Cameroon
**Formation** 1960 / 1961
**Capital** Yaoundé
**Population** 24.7 million / 137 people per sq mile (53 people per sq km)
**Total area** 183,567 sq. miles (475,400 sq. km)
**Languages** Bamileke, Fang, Fulani, French*, English*
**Religions** Roman Catholic 35%, Traditional beliefs 25%, Muslim 22%, Protestant 18%
**Ethnic mix** Cameroon highlanders 31%, Other 21%, Equatorial Bantu 19%, Kirdi 11%, Fulani 10%, Northwestern Bantu 8%
**Government** Presidential system
**Currency** CFA franc = 100 centimes
**Literacy rate** 71%
**Calorie consumption** 2671 kilocalories

## CANADA
*North America*

**Official name** Canada
**Formation** 1867 / 1949
**Capital** Ottawa
**Population** 37 million / 10 people per sq mile (4 people per sq km)
**Total area** 3,855,171 sq. miles (9,984,670 sq. km)
**Languages** English*, French*, Chinese, Italian, German, Ukrainian, Portuguese, Inuktitut, Cree
**Religions** Roman Catholic 39%, Other Christian 28%, Nonreligious 24%, Other 6%, Muslim 3%
**Ethnic mix** European descent 80%, Asian 15%, First Nations and Métis 5%
**Government** Parliamentary system
**Currency** Canadian dollar = 100 cents
**Literacy rate** 99%
**Calorie consumption** 3494 kilocalories

## CAPE VERDE
*Atlantic Ocean*

**Official name** Republic of Cape Verde
**Formation** 1975 / 1975
**Capital** Praia
**Population** 553,000 / 355 people per sq mile (137 people per sq km)
**Total area** 1557 sq. miles (4033 sq. km)
**Languages** Portuguese Creole, Portuguese*
**Religions** Roman Catholic 97%, Other 2%, Protestant (Church of the Nazarene) 1%
**Ethnic mix** Mestiço 71%, African 28%, European 1%
**Government** Mixed presidential–parliamentary system
**Currency** Escudo = 100 centavos
**Literacy rate** 87%
**Calorie consumption** 2609 kilocalories

## CENTRAL AFRICAN REPUBLIC
*Central Africa*

**Official name** Central African Republic
**Formation** 1960 / 1960
**Capital** Bangui
**Population** 4.7 million / 20 people per sq mile (8 people per sq km)
**Total area** 240,534 sq. miles (622,984 sq. km)
**Languages** Sango*, Banda, Gbaya, French*
**Religions** Traditional beliefs 35%, Roman Catholic 25%, Protestant 25%, Muslim 15%
**Ethnic mix** Baya 33%, Banda 27%, Other 17%, Mandjia 13%, Sara 10%
**Government** Presidential system
**Currency** CFA franc = 100 centimes
**Literacy rate** 37%
**Calorie consumption** 1879 kilocalories

## CHAD
*Central Africa*

**Official name** Republic of Chad
**Formation** 1960 / 1960
**Capital** N'Djaména
**Population** 15.4 million / 32 people per sq mile (12 people per sq km)
**Total area** 495,752 sq. miles (1,284,000 sq. km)
**Languages** French*, Sara, Arabic*, Maba
**Religions** Muslim 51%, Christian 35%, Animist 7%, Traditional beliefs 7%
**Ethnic mix** Other 30%, Sara 28%, Mayo-Kebbi 12%, Arab 12%, Ouaddai 9%, Kanem-Bornou 9%
**Government** Presidential system
**Currency** CFA franc = 100 centimes
**Literacy rate** 22%
**Calorie consumption** 2110 kilocalories

## CHILE
*South America*

**Official name** Republic of Chile
**Formation** 1818 / 1883
**Capital** Santiago
**Population** 18.2 million / 63 people per sq mile (24 people per sq km)
**Total area** 292,258 sq. miles (756,950 sq. km)
**Languages** Spanish*, Amerindian languages
**Religions** Roman Catholic 64%, Protestant 17%, Nonreligious 16%, Other 3%
**Ethnic mix** Mestizo and European 95%, Mapuche 4%, Other Amerindian 1%
**Government** Presidential system
**Currency** Chilean peso = 100 centavos
**Literacy rate** 97%
**Calorie consumption** 2979 kilocalories

## CHINA
*East Asia*

**Official name** People's Republic of China
**Formation** 960 / 1999
**Capital** Beijing
**Population** 1.40 billion / 393 people per sq mile (152 people per sq km)
**Total area** 3,705,386 sq. miles (9,596,960 sq. km)
**Languages** Mandarin*, Wu, Cantonese, Hsiang, Min, Hakka, Kan
**Religions** Nonreligious or traditional beliefs 73%, Buddhist 16%, Other 7%, Christian 3%, Muslim 1%
**Ethnic mix** Han 92%, Other 4%, Zhuang 1%, Hui 1%, Manchu 1%, Uighur 1%
**Government** One-party state
**Currency** Renminbi (known as yuan) = 10 jiao = 100 fen
**Literacy rate** 95%
**Calorie consumption** 3108 kilocalories

## COLOMBIA
*South America*

**Official name** Republic of Colombia
**Formation** 1819 / 1903
**Capital** Bogotá
**Population** 49.5 million / 123 people per sq mile (48 people per sq km)
**Total area** 439,733 sq. miles (1,138,910 sq. km)
**Languages** Spanish*, Wayuu, Páez, and other Amerindian languages
**Religions** Roman Catholic 79%, Protestant 13%, Nonreligious 6%, Other 2%
**Ethnic mix** Mestizo 58%, White 20%, European–African 14%, African 4%, African–Amerindian 3%, Amerindian 1%
**Government** Presidential system
**Currency** Colombian peso = 100 centavos
**Literacy rate** 95%
**Calorie consumption** 2804 kilocalories

## COMOROS
*Indian Ocean*

**Official name** Union of the Comoros
**Formation** 1975 / 1975
**Capital** Moroni
**Population** 832,000 / 966 people per sq mile (373 people per sq km)
**Total area** 838 sq. miles (2170 sq. km)
**Languages** Arabic*, Comoran*, French*
**Religions** Muslim (mainly Sunni) 98%, Other 1%, Roman Catholic 1%
**Ethnic mix** Comoran 97%, Other 3%
**Government** Presidential system
**Currency** Comoros franc = 100 centimes
**Literacy rate** 49%
**Calorie consumption** 2139 kilocalories

## CONGO
*Central Africa*

**Official name** Republic of the Congo
**Formation** 1960 / 1960
**Capital** Brazzaville
**Population** 5.4 million / 41 people per sq mile (16 people per sq km)
**Total area** 132,046 sq. miles (342,000 sq. km)
**Languages** Kongo, Teke, Lingala, French*
**Religions** Traditional beliefs 50%, Roman Catholic 35%, Protestant 13%, Muslim 2%
**Ethnic mix** Bakongo 51%, Teke 17%, Other 16%, Mbochi 11%, Mbédé 5%
**Government** Presidential system
**Currency** CFA franc = 100 centimes
**Literacy rate** 79%
**Calorie consumption** 2208 kilocalories

## CONGO, DEM. REP.
*Central Africa*

**Official name** Democratic Republic of the Congo
**Formation** 1960 / 1960
**Capital** Kinshasa
**Population** 84 million / 96 people per sq mile (37 people per sq km)
**Total area** 905,563 sq. miles (2,345,410 sq. km)
**Languages** Kiswahili, Tshiluba, Kikongo, Lingala, French*
**Religions** Roman Catholic 50%, Protestant 20%, Traditional beliefs and other 10%, Muslim 10%, Kimbanguist 10%
**Ethnic mix** Other 55%, Mongo, Luba, Kongo, and Mangbetu-Azande 45%
**Government** Presidential system
**Currency** Congolese franc = 100 centimes
**Literacy rate** 77%
**Calorie consumption** 1585 kilocalories

## COSTA RICA
*Central America*

**Official name** Republic of Costa Rica
**Formation** 1838 / 1838
**Capital** San José
**Population** 5 million / 254 people per sq mile (98 people per sq km)
**Total area** 19,730 sq. miles (51,100 sq. km)
**Languages** Spanish*, English Creole, Bribri, Cabecar
**Religions** Roman Catholic 62%, Protestant 25%, Nonreligious 9%, Other 4%
**Ethnic mix** Mestizo and European 96%, Amerindian 3%, Black 1%
**Government** Presidential system
**Currency** Costa Rican colón = 100 céntimos
**Literacy rate** 97%
**Calorie consumption** 2848 kilocalories

## CROATIA
*Southeast Europe*

**Official name** Republic of Croatia
**Formation** 1991 / 1991
**Capital** Zagreb
**Population** 4.2 million / 192 people per sq mile (74 people per sq km)
**Total area** 21,831 sq. miles (56,542 sq. km)
**Languages** Croatian*
**Religions** Roman Catholic 84%, Nonreligious 7%, Orthodox Christian 4%, Other 3%, Muslim 2%
**Ethnic mix** Croat 92%, Serb 4%, Other 3%, Bosniak 1%
**Government** Parliamentary system
**Currency** Kuna = 100 lipa
**Literacy rate** 99%
**Calorie consumption** 3059 kilocalories

## CUBA
*West Indies*

**Official name** Republic of Cuba
**Formation** 1902 / 1902
**Capital** Havana
**Population** 11.5 million / 269 people per sq mile (104 people per sq km)
**Total area** 42,803 sq. miles (110,860 sq. km)
**Languages** Spanish*
**Religions** Nonreligious 49%, Roman Catholic 40%, Atheist 6%, Other 4%, Protestant 1%
**Ethnic mix** White 65%, Mixed race 25%, Black 10%
**Government** One-party state
**Currency** Cuban peso = 100 centavos
**Literacy rate** 99%
**Calorie consumption** 3409 kilocalories

## CYPRUS
*Southeast Europe*

**Official name** Republic of Cyprus
**Formation** 1960 / 1960
**Capital** Nicosia
**Population** 1.2 million / 336 people per sq mile (130 people per sq km)
**Total area** 3571 sq. miles (9250 sq. km)
**Languages** Greek*, Turkish*
**Religions** Orthodox Christian 78%, Muslim 18%, Other 4%
**Ethnic mix** Greek 81%, Turkish 11%, Other 8%
**Government** Presidential system
**Currency** Euro = 100 cents; (TRNC: Turkish lira = 100 kurus)
**Literacy rate** 99%
**Calorie consumption** 2649 kilocalories

## CZECHIA
*Central Europe*

**Official name** Czech Republic
**Formation** 1993 / 1993
**Capital** Prague
**Population** 10.6 million / 348 people per sq mile (134 people per sq km)
**Total area** 30,450 sq. miles (78,866 sq. km)
**Languages** Czech*, Slovak, Hungarian (Magyar)
**Religions** Nonreligious 72%, Roman Catholic 21%, Other 6%, Orthodox Christian 1%
**Ethnic mix** Czech 86%, Moravian 7%, Other 5%, Slovak 2%
**Government** Parliamentary system
**Currency** Czech koruna = 100 haleru
**Literacy rate** 99%
**Calorie consumption** 3256 kilocalories

## DENMARK
*Northern Europe*

**Official name** Kingdom of Denmark
**Formation** 950 / 1944
**Capital** Copenhagen
**Population** 5.8 million / 355 people per sq mile (137 people per sq km)
**Total area** 16,639 sq. miles (43,094 sq. km)
**Languages** Danish*
**Religions** Evangelical Lutheran 95%, Roman Catholic 3%, Muslim 2%
**Ethnic mix** Danish 96%, Other (including Scandinavian and Turkish) 3%, Faeroese and Inuit 1%
**Government** Parliamentary system
**Currency** Danish krone = 100 øre
**Literacy rate** 99%
**Calorie consumption** 3367 kilocalories

## DJIBOUTI
*East Africa*

**Official name** Republic of Djibouti
**Formation** 1977 / 1977
**Capital** Djibouti
**Population** 971,000 / 108 people per sq mile (42 people per sq km)
**Total area** 8494 sq. miles (22,000 sq. km)
**Languages** Somali, Afar, French*, Arabic*
**Religions** Muslim (mainly Sunni) 94%, Christian 6%
**Ethnic mix** Issa 60%, Afar 35%, Other 5%
**Government** Presidential system
**Currency** Djibouti franc = 100 centimes
**Literacy rate** 70%
**Calorie consumption** 2607 kilocalories

## DOMINICA
*West Indies*

**Official name** Commonwealth of Dominica
**Formation** 1978 / 1978
**Capital** Roseau
**Population** 74,000 / 255 people per sq mile (99 people per sq km)
**Total area** 291 sq. miles (754 sq. km)
**Languages** French Creole, English*
**Religions** Roman Catholic 62%, Protestant 30%, Nonreligious 6%, Other 2%
**Ethnic mix** Black 87%, Mixed race 9%, Carib 3%, Other 1%
**Government** Parliamentary system
**Currency** East Caribbean dollar = 100 cents
**Literacy rate** 88%
**Calorie consumption** 2931 kilocalories

## DOMINICAN REPUBLIC
*West Indies*

**Official name** Dominican Republic
**Formation** 1865 / 1865
**Capital** Santo Domingo
**Population** 10.9 million / 584 people per sq mile (225 people per sq km)
**Total area** 18,679 sq. miles (48,380 sq. km)
**Languages** Spanish*, French Creole
**Religions** Roman Catholic 57%, Protestant 23%, Nonreligious 18%, Other 2%
**Ethnic mix** Mixed race 73%, European 16%, Black African 11%
**Government** Presidential system
**Currency** Dominican Republic peso = 100 centavos
**Literacy rate** 94%
**Calorie consumption** 2614 kilocalories

## EAST TIMOR
*Southeast Asia*

**Official name** Democratic Republic of Timor-Leste
**Formation** 2002 / 2002
**Capital** Dili
**Population** 1.3 million / 230 people per sq mile (89 people per sq km)
**Total area** 5756 sq. miles (14,874 sq. km)
**Languages** Tetum (Portuguese/Austronesian)*, Bahasa Indonesia, Portuguese*
**Religions** Roman Catholic 96%, Protestant 2%, Other 2%
**Ethnic mix** Papuan groups approx 85%, Indonesian approx 13%, Chinese 2%
**Government** Parliamentary system
**Currency** US dollar = 100 cents
**Literacy rate** 58%
**Calorie consumption** 2131 kilocalories

## ECUADOR
*South America*

**Official name** Republic of Ecuador
**Formation** 1830 / 1942
**Capital** Quito
**Population** 16.9 million / 158 people per sq mile (61 people per sq km)
**Total area** 109,483 sq. miles (283,560 sq. km)
**Languages** Spanish*, Quechua, other Amerindian languages
**Religions** Roman Catholic 79%, Protestant 13%, Nonreligious 5%, Other 3%
**Ethnic mix** Mestizo 79%, Black African 7%, Amerindian 7%, White 6%, Other 1%
**Government** Presidential system
**Currency** US dollar = 100 cents
**Literacy rate** 94%
**Calorie consumption** 2344 kilocalories

## EGYPT
*North Africa*

**Official name** Arab Republic of Egypt
**Formation** 1936 / 1982
**Capital** Cairo
**Population** 99.4 million / 259 people per sq mile (100 people per sq km)
**Total area** 386,660 sq. miles (1,001,450 sq. km)
**Languages** Arabic*, French, English, Berber
**Religions** Muslim (mainly Sunni) 90%, Coptic Christian and other 10%
**Ethnic mix** Egyptian 99%, Other 1%
**Government** Presidential system
**Currency** Egyptian pound = 100 piastres
**Literacy rate** 71%
**Calorie consumption** 3522 kilocalories

## EL SALVADOR
*Central America*

**Official name** Republic of El Salvador
**Formation** 1841 / 1841
**Capital** San Salvador
**Population** 6.4 million / 800 people per sq mile (309 people per sq km)
**Total area** 8124 sq. miles (21,040 sq. km)
**Languages** Spanish*
**Religions** Roman Catholic 50%, Protestant 36%, Nonreligious 12%, Other 2%
**Ethnic mix** Mestizo 86%, White 13%, Other and Amerindian 1%
**Government** Presidential system
**Currency** Salvadorean colón = 100 centavos; and US dollar = 100 cents
**Literacy rate** 89%
**Calorie consumption** 2577 kilocalories

## EQUATORIAL GUINEA
*Central Africa*

**Official name** Republic of Equatorial Guinea
**Formation** 1968 / 1968
**Capital** Malabo
**Population** 1.3 million / 120 people per sq mile (46 people per sq km)
**Total area** 10,830 sq. miles (28,051 sq. km)
**Languages** Spanish*, Fang, Bubi, French*
**Religions** Roman Catholic 90%, Other 10%
**Ethnic mix** Fang 85%, Other 11%, Bubi 4%
**Government** Presidential system
**Currency** CFA franc = 100 centimes
**Literacy rate** 95%
**Calorie consumption** Not available

## ERITREA
*East Africa*

**Official name** State of Eritrea
**Formation** 1993 / 2018
**Capital** Asmara
**Population** 5.2 million / 115 people per sq mile (44 people per sq km)
**Total area** 46,842 sq. miles (121,320 sq. km)
**Languages** Tigrinya*, English*, Tigre, Afar, Arabic*, Saho, Bilen, Kunama, Nara, Hadareb
**Religions** Christian 50%, Muslim 48%, Other 2%
**Ethnic mix** Tigray 50%, Tigre 31%, Other 9%, Afar 5%, Saho 5%
**Government** Presidential system
**Currency** Nakfa = 100 cents
**Literacy rate** 70%
**Calorie consumption** 1640 kilocalories

## ESTONIA
*Northeast Europe*

**Official name** Republic of Estonia
**Formation** 1991 / 1991
**Capital** Tallinn
**Population** 1.3 million / 75 people per sq mile (29 people per sq km)
**Total area** 17,462 sq. miles (45,226 sq. km)
**Languages** Estonian*, Russian
**Religions** Nonreligious 45%, Orthodox Christian 25%, Lutheran 20%, Other 10%
**Ethnic mix** Estonian 70%, Russian 25%, Other 2%, Ukrainian 2%, Belarussian 1%
**Government** Parliamentary system
**Currency** Euro = 100 cents
**Literacy rate** 99%
**Calorie consumption** 3253 kilocalories

## ESWATINI (formerly Swaziland)
*Southern Africa*

**Official name** Kingdom of Eswatini
**Formation** 1968 / 1968
**Capital** Mbabane (administrative), Lobamba (royal and legislative)
**Population** 1.4 million / 211 people per sq mile (81 people per sq km)
**Total area** 6704 sq. miles (17,363 sq. km)
**Languages** English*, siSwati*, isiZulu, Xitsonga
**Religions** Traditional beliefs 40%, Other 30%, Roman Catholic 20%, Muslim 10%
**Ethnic mix** Swazi 97%, Other 3%
**Government** Monarchy
**Currency** Lilangeni = 100 cents
**Literacy rate** 83%
**Calorie consumption** 2329 kilocalories

## ETHIOPIA
*East Africa*

**Official name** Federal Democratic Republic of Ethiopia
**Formation** 1896 / 2018
**Capital** Addis Ababa
**Population** 108 million / 251 people per sq mile (97 people per sq km)
**Total area** 435,184 sq. miles (1,127,127 sq. km)
**Languages** Amharic*, Tigrinya, Galla, Sidamo, Somali, English, Arabic
**Religions** Orthodox Christian 44%, Muslim 34%, Protestant 18%, Traditional beliefs 3%, Other 1%
**Ethnic mix** Oromo 34%, Amhara 27%, Other 23%, Somali 6%, Tigray 6%, Sidama 4%
**Government** Parliamentary system
**Currency** Birr = 100 cents
**Literacy rate** 39%
**Calorie consumption** 2131 kilocalories

## FIJI
*Australasia & Oceania*

**Official name** Republic of Fiji
**Formation** 1970 / 1970
**Capital** Suva
**Population** 912,000 / 129 people per sq mile (50 people per sq km)
**Total area** 7054 sq. miles (18,270 sq. km)
**Languages** Fijian*, English*, Hindi*, Urdu, Tamil, Telugu
**Religions** Methodist 35%, Hindu 28%, Other Christian 21%, Roman Catholic 9%, Muslim 6%, Other and nonreligious 1%
**Ethnic mix** Melanesian 57%, Indian 38%, Other 5%
**Government** Parliamentary system
**Currency** Fiji dollar = 100 cents
**Literacy rate** 94%
**Calorie consumption** 2943 kilocalories

## FINLAND
*Northern Europe*

**Official name** Republic of Finland
**Formation** 1917 / 1947
**Capital** Helsinki
**Population** 5.5 million / 47 people per sq mile (18 people per sq km)
**Total area** 130,127 sq. miles (337,030 sq. km)
**Languages** Finnish*, Swedish*, Sámi
**Religions** Evangelical Lutheran 78%, Nonreligious 19%, Other 2%, Orthodox Christian 1%
**Ethnic mix** Finnish 93%, Other (including Sámi) 7%
**Government** Parliamentary system
**Currency** Euro = 100 cents
**Literacy rate** 99%
**Calorie consumption** 3368 kilocalories

## FRANCE
*Western Europe*

**Official name** French Republic
**Formation** 987 / 1919
**Capital** Paris
**Population** 65.2 million / 307 people per sq mile (119 people per sq km)
**Total area** 211,208 sq. miles (547,030 sq. km)
**Languages** French*, Provençal, German, Breton, Catalan, Basque
**Religions** Christian 51%, Nonreligious 40%, Muslim 6%, Other 2%, Jewish 1%
**Ethnic mix** French 86%, North African 5%, Black 5%, German (Alsace) 2%, Breton 1%, Other 1%
**Government** Mixed presidential–parliamentary system
**Currency** Euro = 100 cents
**Literacy rate** 99%
**Calorie consumption** 3482 kilocalories

## GABON
*Central Africa*

**Official name** Gabonese Republic
**Formation** 1960 / 1960
**Capital** Libreville
**Population** 2.1 million / 21 people per sq mile (8 people per sq km)
**Total area** 103,346 sq. miles (267,667 sq. km)
**Languages** Fang, French*, Punu, Sira, Nzebi, Mpongwe
**Religions** Christian (mainly Roman Catholic) 55%, Traditional beliefs 40%, Other 4%, Muslim 1%
**Ethnic mix** Fang 26%, Shira-punu 24%, Other 24%, Foreign residents 15%, Nzabi-duma 11%
**Government** Presidential system
**Currency** CFA franc = 100 centimes
**Literacy rate** 82%
**Calorie consumption** 2830 kilocalories

## GAMBIA
*West Africa*

**Official name** Republic of the Gambia
**Formation** 1965 / 1965
**Capital** Banjul
**Population** 2.2 million / 570 people per sq mile (220 people per sq km)
**Total area** 4363 sq. miles (11,300 sq. km)
**Languages** Mandinka, Fulani, Wolof, Jola, Soninke, English*
**Religions** Sunni Muslim 90%, Christian 8%, Traditional beliefs 2%
**Ethnic mix** Mandinka 42%, Fulani 18%, Wolof 16%, Jola 10%, Serahuli 9%, Other 5%
**Government** Presidential system
**Currency** Dalasi = 100 butut
**Literacy rate** 42%
**Calorie consumption** 2628 kilocalories

## GEORGIA
*Southwest Asia*

**Official name** Georgia
**Formation** 1991 / 1991
**Capital** Tbilisi
**Population** 3.9 million / 145 people per sq mile (56 people per sq km)
**Total area** 26,911 sq. miles (69,700 sq. km)
**Languages** Georgian*, Russian, Azeri, Armenian, Mingrelian, Ossetian, Abkhazian (* in Abkhazia)
**Religions** Orthodox Christian 89%, Muslim 9%, Roman Catholic 1%, Other 1%
**Ethnic mix** Georgian 87%, Azeri 6%, Armenian 4%, Other 2%, Russian 1%
**Government** Presidential system
**Currency** Lari = 100 tetri
**Literacy rate** 99%
**Calorie consumption** 2905 kilocalories

## GERMANY
*Northern Europe*

**Official name** Federal Republic of Germany
**Formation** 1871 / 1990
**Capital** Berlin
**Population** 82.3 million / 610 people per sq mile (235 people per sq km)
**Total area** 137,846 sq. miles (357,021 sq. km)
**Languages** German*, Turkish
**Religions** Nonreligious 36%, Roman Catholic 29%, Protestant 26%, Muslim 5%, Other 4%
**Ethnic mix** German 81%, Other European 10%, Other 4%, Turkish 3%, Polish 2%
**Government** Parliamentary system
**Currency** Euro = 100 cents
**Literacy rate** 99%
**Calorie consumption** 3499 kilocalories

## GHANA
*West Africa*

**Official name** Republic of Ghana
**Formation** 1957 / 1957
**Capital** Accra
**Population** 29.5 million / 332 people per sq mile (128 people per sq km)
**Total area** 92,100 sq. miles (238,540 sq. km)
**Languages** Twi, Fanti, Ewe, Ga, Adangbe, Gurma, Dagomba (Dagbani), English*
**Religions** Christian 71%, Muslim 18%, Nonreligious 5%, Traditional beliefs 5%, Other 1%
**Ethnic mix** Akan 47%, Gurma 17%, Ga-Dangme 14%, Other 9%, Ewe 7%, Guan 6%
**Government** Presidential system
**Currency** Cedi = 100 pesewas
**Literacy rate** 72%
**Calorie consumption** 3016 kilocalories

## GREECE
*Southeast Europe*

**Official name** Hellenic Republic
**Formation** 1829 / 1947
**Capital** Athens
**Population** 11.1 million / 220 people per sq mile (85 people per sq km)
**Total area** 50,942 sq. miles (131,940 sq. km)
**Languages** Greek*, Turkish, Macedonian, Albanian
**Religions** Orthodox Christian 90%, Nonreligious 4%, Other 4%, Muslim 2%
**Ethnic mix** Greek 98%, Other 2%
**Government** Parliamentary system
**Currency** Euro = 100 cents
**Literacy rate** 97%
**Calorie consumption** 3400 kilocalories

## GRENADA
*West Indies*

**Official name** Grenada
**Formation** 1974 / 1974
**Capital** St. George's
**Population** 108,000 / 824 people per sq mile (318 people per sq km)
**Total area** 131 sq. miles (340 sq. km)
**Languages** English*, English Creole
**Religions** Roman Catholic 68%, Anglican 17%, Other 15%
**Ethnic mix** Black African 82%, Mulatto (mixed race) 13%, East Indian 3%, Other 2%
**Government** Parliamentary system
**Currency** East Caribbean dollar = 100 cents
**Literacy rate** 99%
**Calorie consumption** 2447 kilocalories

## GUATEMALA
*Central America*

**Official name** Republic of Guatemala
**Formation** 1838 / 1838
**Capital** Guatemala City
**Population** 17.2 million / 411 people per sq mile (159 people per sq km)
**Total area** 42,042 sq. miles (108,890 sq. km)
**Languages** Quiché, Mam, Cakchiquel, Kekchi, Spanish*
**Religions** Roman Catholic 50%, Protestant 41%, Nonreligious 6%, Other 3%
**Ethnic mix** Amerindian 60%, Mestizo 30%, Other 10%
**Government** Presidential system
**Currency** Quetzal = 100 centavos
**Literacy rate** 81%
**Calorie consumption** 2419 kilocalories

## GUINEA
*West Africa*

**Official name** Republic of Guinea
**Formation** 1958 / 1958
**Capital** Conakry
**Population** 13.1 million / 138 people per sq mile (53 people per sq km)
**Total area** 94,925 sq. miles (245,857 sq. km)
**Languages** Pulaar, Malinké, Soussou, French*
**Religions** Muslim 89%, Christian 7%, Nonreligious 2%, Traditional beliefs and other 2%
**Ethnic mix** Peul 40%, Malinké 30%, Soussou 20%, Other 10%
**Government** Presidential system
**Currency** Guinea franc = 100 centimes
**Literacy rate** 32%
**Calorie consumption** 2566 kilocalories

## GUINEA-BISSAU
*West Africa*

**Official name** Republic of Guinea-Bissau
**Formation** 1974 / 1974
**Capital** Bissau
**Population** 1.9 million / 175 people per sq mile (68 people per sq km)
**Total area** 13,946 sq. miles (36,120 sq. km)
**Languages** Portuguese Creole, Balante, Fulani, Malinké, Portuguese*
**Religions** Muslim 54%, Christian 26%, Traditional beliefs 18%, Nonreligious 2%
**Ethnic mix** Balante 30%, Fulani 20%, Other 16%, Mandyako 14%, Mandinka 13%, Papel 7%
**Government** Presidential system
**Currency** CFA franc = 100 centimes
**Literacy rate** 46%
**Calorie consumption** 2292 kilocalories

## GUYANA
*South America*

**Official name** Cooperative Republic of Guyana
**Formation** 1966 / 1966
**Capital** Georgetown
**Population** 782,000 / 10 people per sq mile (4 people per sq km)
**Total area** 83,000 sq. miles (214,970 sq. km)
**Languages** English Creole, Hindi, Tamil, Amerindian languages, English*
**Religions** Christian 57%, Hindu 28%, Muslim 10%, Other 5%
**Ethnic mix** East Indian 43%, Black African 30%, Mixed race 17%, Amerindian 9%, Other 1%
**Government** Presidential system
**Currency** Guyanese dollar = 100 cents
**Literacy rate** 86%
**Calorie consumption** 2764 kilocalories

## HAITI
*West Indies*

**Official name** Republic of Haiti
**Formation** 1804 / 1844
**Capital** Port-au-Prince
**Population** 11.1 million / 1043 people per sq mile (403 people per sq km)
**Total area** 10,714 sq. miles (27,750 sq. km)
**Languages** French Creole*, French*
**Religions** Roman Catholic 55%, Protestant 28%, Other (including Voodoo) 16%, Nonreligious 1%
**Ethnic mix** Black African 95%, Mulatto (mixed race) and European 5%
**Government** Presidential system
**Currency** Gourde = 100 centimes
**Literacy rate** 49%
**Calorie consumption** 2091 kilocalories

## HONDURAS
*Central America*

**Official name** Republic of Honduras
**Formation** 1838 / 1838
**Capital** Tegucigalpa
**Population** 9.4 million / 218 people per sq mile (84 people per sq km)
**Total area** 43,278 sq. miles (112,090 sq. km)
**Languages** Spanish*, Garifuna (Carib), English Creole
**Religions** Roman Catholic 46%, Protestant 41%, Nonreligious 10%, Other 3%
**Ethnic mix** Mestizo 90%, Black African 5%, Amerindian 4%, White 1%
**Government** Presidential system
**Currency** Lempira = 100 centavos
**Literacy rate** 89%
**Calorie consumption** 2641 kilocalories

## HUNGARY
*Central Europe*

**Official name** Hungary
**Formation** 1918 / 1947
**Capital** Budapest
**Population** 9.7 million / 272 people per sq mile (105 people per sq km)
**Total area** 35,919 sq. miles (93,030 sq. km)
**Languages** Hungarian (Magyar)*
**Religions** Roman Catholic 56%, Nonreligious 21%, Presbyterian 13%, Other (mostly Protestant) 10%
**Ethnic mix** Magyar 92%, Roma 3%, Other 3%, German 2%
**Government** Parliamentary system
**Currency** Forint = 100 fillér
**Literacy rate** 99%
**Calorie consumption** 3037 kilocalories

## ICELAND
*Northwest Europe*

**Official name** Republic of Iceland
**Formation** 1944 / 1944
**Capital** Reykjavík
**Population** 338,000 / 9 people per sq mile (3 people per sq km)
**Total area** 39,768 sq. miles (103,000 sq. km)
**Languages** Icelandic*
**Religions** Evangelical Lutheran 70%, Other (mostly Christian) 10%, Nonreligious 6%, Roman Catholic 4%
**Ethnic mix** Icelandic 89%, Other 7%, Polish 3%, Danish 1%
**Government** Parliamentary system
**Currency** Icelandic króna = 100 aurar
**Literacy rate** 99%
**Calorie consumption** 3380 kilocalories

## INDIA
*South Asia*

**Official name** Republic of India
**Formation** 1947 / 1947
**Capital** New Delhi
**Population** 1.35 billion / 1180 people per sq mile (455 people per sq km)
**Total area** 1,269,338 sq. miles (3,287,590 sq. km)
**Languages** Hindi*, English*, Urdu, Bengali, Marathi, Telugu, Tamil, Bihari, Gujarati, Kanarese
**Religions** Hindu 81%, Muslim 13%, Christian 2%, Sikh 2%, Buddhist 1%, Other 1%
**Ethnic mix** Indo-Aryan 72%, Dravidian 25%, Mongoloid and other 3%
**Government** Parliamentary system
**Currency** Indian rupee = 100 paise
**Literacy rate** 69%
**Calorie consumption** 2459 kilocalories

## INDONESIA
*Southeast Asia*

**Official name** Republic of Indonesia
**Formation** 1949 / 1999
**Capital** Jakarta
**Population** 267 million / 385 people per sq mile (148 people per sq km)
**Total area** 741,096 sq. miles (1,919,440 sq. km)
**Languages** Javanese, Sundanese, Madurese, Bahasa Indonesia*, Dutch
**Religions** Sunni Muslim 87%, Protestant 7%, Roman Catholic 3%, Hindu 2%, Buddhist 1%
**Ethnic mix** Javanese 40%, Other 27%, Sundanese 16%, Coastal Malays 14%, Madurese 3%
**Government** Presidential system
**Currency** Rupiah = 100 sen
**Literacy rate** 95%
**Calorie consumption** 2777 kilocalories

## IRAN
*Southwest Asia*

**Official name** Islamic Republic of Iran
**Formation** 1502 / 1990
**Capital** Tehran
**Population** 82 million / 130 people per sq mile (50 people per sq km)
**Total area** 636,293 sq. miles (1,648,000 sq. km)
**Languages** Farsi*, Azeri, Luri, Gilaki, Mazanderani, Kurdish, Turkmen, Arabic, Baluchi
**Religions** Shi'a Muslim 90%, Sunni Muslim 9%, Other 1%
**Ethnic mix** Persian 51%, Azari 24%, Other 10%, Lur and Bakhtiari 8%, Kurdish 7%
**Government** Islamic theocracy
**Currency** Iranian rial = 100 dinars
**Literacy rate** 86%
**Calorie consumption** 3094 kilocalories

## IRAQ
*Southwest Asia*

**Official name** Republic of Iraq
**Formation** 1932 / 1990
**Capital** Baghdad
**Population** 39.3 million / 233 people per sq mile (90 people per sq km)
**Total area** 168,753 sq. miles (437,072 sq. km)
**Languages** Arabic*, Kurdish*, Turkic languages, Armenian, Assyrian
**Religions** Shi'a Muslim 60%, Sunni Muslim 35%, Other (including Christian) 5%
**Ethnic mix** Arab 80%, Kurdish 15%, Turkmen 3%, Other 2%
**Government** Parliamentary system
**Currency** New Iraqi dinar = 1000 fils
**Literacy rate** 44%
**Calorie consumption** 2545 kilocalories

## IRELAND
*Northwest Europe*

**Official name** Ireland
**Formation** 1922 / 1922
**Capital** Dublin
**Population** 4.8 million / 180 people per sq mile (70 people per sq km)
**Total area** 27,135 sq. miles (70,280 sq. km)
**Languages** English*, Irish*
**Religions** Roman Catholic 86%, Other Christian 6%, Nonreligious 6%, Muslim 1%, Other 1%
**Ethnic mix** Irish 86%, Other White 9%, Asian 2%, Other 2%, Black 1%
**Government** Parliamentary system
**Currency** Euro = 100 cents
**Literacy rate** 99%
**Calorie consumption** 3600 kilocalories

## ISRAEL
*Southwest Asia*

**Official name** State of Israel
**Formation** 1948 / 1994
**Capital** Jerusalem (not internationally recognized)
**Population** 8.5 million / 1083 people per sq mile (418 people per sq km)
**Total area** 8019 sq. miles (20,770 sq. km)
**Languages** Hebrew*, Arabic*, Yiddish, German, Russian, Polish, Romanian, Persian
**Religions** Jewish 81%, Muslim (mainly Sunni) 14%, Druze 2%, Christian 2%, Other and nonreligious 1%
**Ethnic mix** Jewish 81%, Arab 18%, Other 1%
**Government** Parliamentary system
**Currency** Shekel = 100 agorot
**Literacy rate** 98%
**Calorie consumption** 3610 kilocalories

## ITALY
*Southern Europe*

**Official name** Italian Republic
**Formation** 1861 / 1947
**Capital** Rome
**Population** 59.3 million / 522 people per sq mile (202 people per sq km)
**Total area** 116,305 sq. miles (301,230 sq. km)
**Languages** Italian*, German, French, Rhaeto-Romanic, Sardinian
**Religions** Roman Catholic 90%, Nonreligious 6%, Muslim 2%, Other Christian 2%
**Ethnic mix** Italian 92%, Other European 5%, Other 2%, North African (mainly Moroccan) 1%
**Government** Parliamentary system
**Currency** Euro = 100 cents
**Literacy rate** 99%
**Calorie consumption** 3579 kilocalories

## IVORY COAST
*West Africa*

**Official name** Republic of Côte d'Ivoire
**Formation** 1960 / 1960
**Capital** Yamoussoukro
**Population** 24.9 million / 203 people per sq mile (78 people per sq km)
**Total area** 124,502 sq. miles (322,460 sq. km)
**Languages** Akan, French*, Krou, Voltaique
**Religions** Muslim 43%, Nonreligious or traditional beliefs 23%, Roman Catholic 17%, Evangelical 12%, Other Christian 4%, Other 1%
**Ethnic mix** Akan 42%, Voltaique 18%, Mandé du Nord 17%, Krou 11%, Mandé du Sud 10%, Other 2%
**Government** Presidential system
**Currency** CFA franc = 100 centimes
**Literacy rate** 44%
**Calorie consumption** 2799 kilocalories

## JAMAICA
*West Indies*

**Official name** Jamaica
**Formation** 1962 / 1962
**Capital** Kingston
**Population** 2.9 million / 694 people per sq mile (268 people per sq km)
**Total area** 4243 sq. miles (10,990 sq. km)
**Languages** English Creole, English*
**Religions** Church of God 26%, Nonreligious 22%, Other Christian 21%, Seventh-day Adventist 12%, Pentecostal 11%, Other 8%
**Ethnic mix** Black African 92%, Mulatto (mixed race) 6%, East Indian 1%, Other 1%
**Government** Parliamentary system
**Currency** Jamaican dollar = 100 cents
**Literacy rate** 88%
**Calorie consumption** 2746 kilocalories

## JAPAN
*East Asia*

**Official name** Japan
**Formation** 1590 / 1972
**Capital** Tokyo
**Population** 127 million / 875 people per sq mile (338 people per sq km)
**Total area** 145,882 sq. miles (377,835 sq. km)
**Languages** Japanese*, Korean, Chinese
**Religions** Buddhist 50%, Nonreligious 23%, Shinto 16%, Christian 10%, Muslim 1%
**Ethnic mix** Japanese 99%, Other (mainly Korean) 1%
**Government** Parliamentary system
**Currency** Yen = 100 sen
**Literacy rate** 99%
**Calorie consumption** 2726 kilocalories

## JORDAN
*Southwest Asia*

**Official name** Hashemite Kingdom of Jordan
**Formation** 1946 / 1967
**Capital** Amman
**Population** 9.9 million / 288 people per sq mile (111 people per sq km)
**Total area** 35,637 sq. miles (92,300 sq. km)
**Languages** Arabic*
**Religions** Sunni Muslim 92%, Christian 6%, Other 2%
**Ethnic mix** Arab 98%, Circassian 1%, Armenian 1%
**Government** Monarchy
**Currency** Jordanian dinar = 1000 fils
**Literacy rate** 98%
**Calorie consumption** 3100 kilocalories

## KAZAKHSTAN
*Central Asia*

**Official name** Republic of Kazakhstan
**Formation** 1991 / 1991
**Capital** Nursultan
**Population** 18.4 million / 18 people per sq mile (7 people per sq km)
**Total area** 1,049,150 sq. miles (2,717,300 sq. km)
**Languages** Kazakh*, Russian, Ukrainian, German, Uzbek, Tatar, Uighur
**Religions** Muslim (mainly Sunni) 71%, Christian (mainly Orthodox) 26%, Nonreligious 3%
**Ethnic mix** Kazakh 63%, Russian 24%, Other 5%, Uzbek 3%, Ukrainian 2%, Uighur 1%, Tatar 1%, German 1%
**Government** Presidential system
**Currency** Tenge = 100 tiyn
**Literacy rate** 99%
**Calorie consumption** 3264 kilocalories

## KENYA
*East Africa*

**Official name** Republic of Kenya
**Formation** 1963 / 1963
**Capital** Nairobi
**Population** 51 million / 233 people per sq mile (90 people per sq km)
**Total area** 224,961 sq. miles (582,650 sq. km)
**Languages** Kiswahili*, English*, Kikuyu, Luo, Kalenjin, Kamba
**Religions** Other Christian 60%, Roman Catholic 23%, Muslim 11%, Other 4%, Nonreligious 2%
**Ethnic mix** Other 35%, Kikuyu 17%, Luhya 14%, Kalenjin 13%, Luo 11%, Kamba 10%
**Government** Presidential system
**Currency** Kenya shilling = 100 cents
**Literacy rate** 79%
**Calorie consumption** 2206 kilocalories

## KIRIBATI
*Australasia & Oceania*

**Official name** Republic of Kiribati
**Formation** 1979 / 1979
**Capital** Bairiki (Tarawa Atoll)
**Population** 118,000 / 431 people per sq mile (166 people per sq km)
**Total area** 277 sq. miles (717 sq. km)
**Languages** English*, Kiribati
**Religions** Roman Catholic 56%, Kiribati Protestant Church 34%, Mormon 5%, Baha'i 2%, Seventh-day Adventist 2%, Other 1%
**Ethnic mix** Micronesian 99%, Other 1%
**Government** Presidential system
**Currency** Australian dollar = 100 cents
**Literacy rate** 99%
**Calorie consumption** 3040 kilocalories

## KOSOVO (not yet recognised)
*Southeast Europe*

**Official name** Republic of Kosovo
**Formation** 2008 / 2008
**Capital** Prishtinë
**Population** 1.8 million / 427 people per sq mile (165 people per sq km)
**Total area** 4212 sq. miles (10,908 sq. km)
**Languages** Albanian*, Serbian*, Bosniak, Gorani, Roma, Turkish
**Religions** Muslim 92%, Roman Catholic 4%, Orthodox Christian 4%
**Ethnic mix** Albanian 92%, Serb 4%, Bosniak and Gorani 2%, Turkish 1%, Roma 1%
**Government** Parliamentary system
**Currency** Euro = 100 cents
**Literacy rate** 94%
**Calorie consumption** Not available

## KUWAIT
*Southwest Asia*

**Official name** State of Kuwait
**Formation** 1961 / 1961
**Capital** Kuwait City
**Population** 4.2 million / 610 people per sq mile (236 people per sq km)
**Total area** 6880 sq. miles (17,820 sq. km)
**Languages** Arabic*, English
**Religions** Sunni Muslim 45%, Shi'a Muslim 40%, Christian, Hindu, and other 15%
**Ethnic mix** Asian 39%, Kuwaiti 37%, Other Arab 21%, African 2%, Other 1%
**Government** Monarchy
**Currency** Kuwaiti dinar = 1000 fils
**Literacy rate** 96%
**Calorie consumption** 3501 kilocalories

## KYRGYZSTAN
*Central Asia*

**Official name** Kyrgyz Republic
**Formation** 1991 / 1991
**Capital** Bishkek
**Population** 6.1 million / 80 people per sq mile (31 people per sq km)
**Total area** 76,641 sq. miles (198,500 sq. km)
**Languages** Kyrgyz*, Russian*, Uzbek, Tatar, Ukrainian
**Religions** Muslim (mainly Sunni) 70%, Orthodox Christian 30%
**Ethnic mix** Kyrgyz 71%, Uzbek 14%, Russian 8%, Other 4%, Dungan 1%, Uighur 1%, Tajik 1%
**Government** Mixed presidential–parliamentary system
**Currency** Som = 100 tyiyn
**Literacy rate** 99%
**Calorie consumption** 2817 kilocalories

## LAOS
*Southeast Asia*

**Official name** Lao People's Democratic Republic
**Formation** 1953 / 1953
**Capital** Vientiane
**Population** 7 million / 79 people per sq mile (30 people per sq km)
**Total area** 91,429 sq. miles (236,800 sq. km)
**Languages** Lao*, Mon-Khmer, Yao, Vietnamese, Chinese, French
**Religions** Buddhist 67%, Other 31%, Christian 2%
**Ethnic mix** Lao Loum 66%, Lao Theung 30%, Lao Soung 2%, Other 2%
**Government** One-party state
**Currency** Kip = 100 at
**Literacy rate** 85%
**Calorie consumption** 2451 kilocalories

## LATVIA
*Northeast Europe*

**Official name** Republic of Latvia
**Formation** 1991 / 1991
**Capital** Riga
**Population** 1.9 million / 76 people per sq mile (29 people per sq km)
**Total area** 24,938 sq. miles (64,589 sq. km)
**Languages** Latvian*, Russian
**Religions** Orthodox Christian 31%, Roman Catholic 23%, Nonreligious 21%, Lutheran 19%, Other 6%
**Ethnic mix** Latvian 62%, Russian 27%, Belarussian 3%, Other 3%, Polish 2%, Ukrainian 2%, Lithuanian 1%
**Government** Parliamentary system
**Currency** Euro = 100 cents
**Literacy rate** 99%
**Calorie consumption** 3174 kilocalories

## LEBANON
*Southwest Asia*

**Official name** Republic of Lebanon
**Formation** 1941 / 1941
**Capital** Beirut
**Population** 6.1 million / 1544 people per sq mile (596 people per sq km)
**Total area** 4015 sq. miles (10,400 sq. km)
**Languages** Arabic*, French, Armenian, Assyrian
**Religions** Muslim 60%, Christian 39%, Other 1%
**Ethnic mix** Arab 95%, Armenian 4%, Other 1%
**Government** Parliamentary system
**Currency** Lebanese pound = 100 piastres
**Literacy rate** 91%
**Calorie consumption** 3066 kilocalories

## LESOTHO
*Southern Africa*

**Official name** Kingdom of Lesotho
**Formation** 1966 / 1966
**Capital** Maseru
**Population** 2.3 million / 196 people per sq mile (76 people per sq km)
**Total area** 11,720 sq. miles (30,355 sq. km)
**Languages** English*, Sesotho*, isiZulu
**Religions** Christian 90%, Traditional beliefs 10%
**Ethnic mix** Sotho 99%, European and Asian 1%
**Government** Parliamentary system
**Currency** Loti = 100 lisente; and South African rand = 100 cents
**Literacy rate** 77%
**Calorie consumption** 2529 kilocalories

## LIBERIA
*West Africa*

**Official name** Republic of Liberia
**Formation** 1847 / 1847
**Capital** Monrovia
**Population** 4.9 million / 132 people per sq mile (51 people per sq km)
**Total area** 43,000 sq. miles (111,370 sq. km)
**Languages** Kpelle, Vai, Bassa, Kru, Grebo, Kissi, Gola, Loma, English*
**Religions** Christian 86%, Muslim 12%, Nonreligious 1%, Traditional beliefs and other 1%
**Ethnic mix** Indigenous tribes (12 groups) 50%, Kpellé 20%, Bassa 14%, Gio 8%, Krou 6%, Other 2%
**Government** Presidential system
**Currency** Liberian dollar = 100 cents
**Literacy rate** 43%
**Calorie consumption** 2204 kilocalories

## LIBYA
*North Africa*

**Official name** State of Libya
**Formation** 1951 / 1951
**Capital** Tripoli
**Population** 6.5 million / 10 people per sq mile (4 people per sq km)
**Total area** 679,358 sq. miles (1,759,540 sq. km)
**Languages** Arabic*, Tuareg
**Religions** Muslim (mainly Sunni) 97%, Other 3%
**Ethnic mix** Arab and Berber 97%, Other 3%
**Government** Transitional regime
**Currency** Libyan dinar = 1000 dirhams
**Literacy rate** 90%
**Calorie consumption** 3211 kilocalories

## LIECHTENSTEIN
*Central Europe*

**Official name** Principality of Liechtenstein
**Formation** 1719 / 1719
**Capital** Vaduz
**Population** 38,000 / 613 people per sq mile (238 people per sq km)
**Total area** 62 sq. miles (160 sq. km)
**Languages** German*, Alemannish dialect, Italian
**Religions** Roman Catholic 78%, Protestant 9%, Muslim 6%, Nonreligious 5%, Orthodox Christian 1%, Other 1%
**Ethnic mix** Liechtensteiner 66%, Other 12%, Swiss 10%, Austrian 6%, German 3%, Italian 3%
**Government** Parliamentary system
**Currency** Swiss franc = 100 rappen/centimes
**Literacy rate** 99%
**Calorie consumption** Not available

## LITHUANIA
*Northeast Europe*

**Official name** Republic of Lithuania
**Formation** 1991 / 1991
**Capital** Vilnius
**Population** 2.9 million / 115 people per sq mile (44 people per sq km)
**Total area** 25,174 sq. miles (65,200 sq. km)
**Languages** Lithuanian*, Russian
**Religions** Roman Catholic 75%, Christian 14%, Nonreligious 6%, Orthodox Christian 3%, Other 2%
**Ethnic mix** Lithuanian 85%, Polish 7%, Russian 6%, Belarussian 1%, Other 1%
**Government** Parliamentary system
**Currency** Euro = 100 cents
**Literacy rate** 99%
**Calorie consumption** 3417 kilocalories

## LUXEMBOURG
*Northwest Europe*

**Official name** Grand Duchy of Luxembourg
**Formation** 1867 / 1867
**Capital** Luxembourg-Ville
**Population** 590,000 / 591 people per sq mile (228 people per sq km)
**Total area** 998 sq. miles (2586 sq. km)
**Languages** Luxembourgish*, German*, French*
**Religions** Roman Catholic 97%, Protestant, Orthodox Christian, and Jewish 3%
**Ethnic mix** Luxembourger 62%, Foreign residents 38%
**Government** Parliamentary system
**Currency** Euro = 100 cents
**Literacy rate** 99%
**Calorie consumption** 3539 kilocalories

## MADAGASCAR
*Indian Ocean*

**Official name** Republic of Madagascar
**Formation** 1960 / 1960
**Capital** Antananarivo
**Population** 26.3 million / 117 people per sq mile (45 people per sq km)
**Total area** 226,656 sq. miles (587,040 sq. km)
**Languages** Malagasy*, French*, English*
**Religions** Traditional beliefs 52%, Christian (mainly Roman Catholic) 41%, Muslim 7%
**Ethnic mix** Other Malay 46%, Merina 26%, Betsimisaraka 15%, Betsileo 12%, Other 1%
**Government** Mixed presidential–parliamentary system
**Currency** Ariary = 5 iraimbilanja
**Literacy rate** 72%
**Calorie consumption** 2052 kilocalories

## MALAWI
*Southern Africa*

**Official name** Republic of Malawi
**Formation** 1964 / 1964
**Capital** Lilongwe
**Population** 19.2 million / 529 people per sq mile (204 people per sq km)
**Total area** 45,745 sq. miles (118,480 sq. km)
**Languages** Chewa, Lomwe, Yao, Ngoni, English*
**Religions** Christian (mainly Protestant) 83%, Muslim 13%, Nonreligious 2%, Other 2%
**Ethnic mix** Bantu 99%, Other 1%
**Government** Presidential system
**Currency** Malawi kwacha = 100 tambala
**Literacy rate** 62%
**Calorie consumption** 2367 kilocalories

## MALAYSIA
*Southeast Asia*

**Official name** Malaysia
**Formation** 1963 / 1965
**Capital** Kuala Lumpur; Putrajaya (administrative)
**Population** 32 million / 252 people per sq mile (97 people per sq km)
**Total area** 127,316 sq. miles (329,750 sq. km)
**Languages** Bahasa Malaysia*, Malay, Chinese, Tamil, English
**Religions** Muslim (mainly Sunni) 62%, Buddhist 20%, Christian 9%, Hindu 6%, Other and nonreligious 3%
**Ethnic mix** Malay 50%, Chinese 22%, Indigenous tribes 12%, Other 9%, Indian 7%
**Government** Parliamentary system
**Currency** Ringgit = 100 sen
**Literacy rate** 94%
**Calorie consumption** 2916 kilocalories

## MALDIVES
*Indian Ocean*

**Official name** Republic of Maldives
**Formation** 1965 / 1965
**Capital** Male'
**Population** 444,000 / 3828 people per sq mile (1480 people per sq km)
**Total area** 116 sq. miles (300 sq. km)
**Languages** Dhivehi (Maldivian)*, Sinhala, Tamil, Arabic
**Religions** Sunni Muslim 94%, Hindu 3%, Christian 2%, Buddhist 1%
**Ethnic mix** Arab–Sinhalese–Malay 100%
**Government** Presidential system
**Currency** Rufiyaa = 100 laari
**Literacy rate** 99%
**Calorie consumption** 2732 kilocalories

## MALI
*West Africa*

**Official name** Republic of Mali
**Formation** 1960 / 1960
**Capital** Bamako
**Population** 19.1 million / 41 people per sq mile (16 people per sq km)
**Total area** 478,764 sq. miles (1,240,000 sq. km)
**Languages** Bambara, Fulani, Senufo, Soninke, French*
**Religions** Muslim (mainly Sunni) 90%, Traditional beliefs 6%, Christian 4%
**Ethnic mix** Bambara 52%, Other 14%, Fulani 11%, Saracolé 7%, Soninka 7%, Tuareg 5%, Mianka 4%
**Government** Presidential system
**Currency** CFA franc = 100 centimes
**Literacy rate** 33%
**Calorie consumption** 2890 kilocalories

## MALTA
*Southern Europe*

**Official name** Republic of Malta
**Formation** 1964 / 1964
**Capital** Valletta
**Population** 432,000 / 3484 people per sq mile (1350 people per sq km)
**Total area** 122 sq. miles (316 sq. km)
**Languages** Maltese*, English*
**Religions** Roman Catholic 98%, Other and nonreligious 2%
**Ethnic mix** Maltese 96%, Other 4%
**Government** Parliamentary system
**Currency** Euro = 100 cents
**Literacy rate** 93%
**Calorie consumption** 3378 kilocalories

## MARSHALL ISLANDS
*Australasia & Oceania*

**Official name** Republic of the Marshall Islands
**Formation** 1986 / 1986
**Capital** Majuro
**Population** 53,000 / 757 people per sq mile (293 people per sq km)
**Total area** 70 sq. miles (181 sq. km)
**Languages** Marshallese*, English*, Japanese, German
**Religions** Protestant 81%, Other 11%, Roman Catholic 8%
**Ethnic mix** Micronesian 90%, Other 10%
**Government** Presidential system
**Currency** US dollar = 100 cents
**Literacy rate** 98%
**Calorie consumption** Not available

## MAURITANIA
*West Africa*

**Official name** Islamic Republic of Mauritania
**Formation** 1960 / 1960
**Capital** Nouakchott
**Population** 4.5 million / 11 people per sq mile (4 people per sq km)
**Total area** 397,953 sq. miles (1,030,700 sq. km)
**Languages** Arabic*, Hassaniyah Arabic, Wolof, French
**Religions** Sunni Muslim 100%
**Ethnic mix** Maure 81%, Wolof 7%, Tukolor 5%, Other 4%, Soninka 3%
**Government** Presidential system
**Currency** Ouguiya = 5 khoums
**Literacy rate** 46%
**Calorie consumption** 2876 kilocalories

## MAURITIUS
*Indian Ocean*

**Official name** Republic of Mauritius
**Formation** 1968 / 1968
**Capital** Port Louis
**Population** 1.3 million / 1811 people per sq mile (699 people per sq km)
**Total area** 718 sq. miles (1860 sq. km)
**Languages** French Creole, Hindi, Urdu, Tamil, Chinese, English*, French
**Religions** Hindu 48%, Roman Catholic 26%, Muslim 17%, Other Christian 7%, Other 2%
**Ethnic mix** Indo-Mauritian 68%, Creole 27%, Sino-Mauritian 3%, Franco-Mauritian 2%
**Government** Parliamentary system
**Currency** Mauritian rupee = 100 cents
**Literacy rate** 93%
**Calorie consumption** 3065 kilocalories

## MEXICO
*North America*

**Official name** United Mexican States
**Formation** 1836 / 1848
**Capital** Mexico City
**Population** 127 million / 168 people per sq mile (64 people per sq km)
**Total area** 761,602 sq. miles (1,972,550 sq. km)
**Languages** Spanish*, Nahuatl, Mayan, Zapotec, Mixtec, Otomi, Totonac, Tzotzil, Tzeltal
**Religions** Roman Catholic 81%, Protestant 9%, Nonreligious 7%, Other 3%
**Ethnic mix** Mestizo 60%, Amerindian 30%, European 9%, Other 1%
**Government** Presidential system
**Currency** Mexican peso = 100 centavos
**Literacy rate** 95%
**Calorie consumption** 3072 kilocalories

## MICRONESIA
*Australasia & Oceania*

**Official name** Federated States of Micronesia
**Formation** 1986 / 1986
**Capital** Palikir (Pohnpei Island)
**Population** 106,000 / 391 people per sq mile (151 people per sq km)
**Total area** 271 sq. miles (702 sq. km)
**Languages** Trukese, Pohnpeian, Kosraean, Yapese, English*
**Religions** Roman Catholic 53%, Protestant 43%, Other 3%, Nonreligious 1%
**Ethnic mix** Chuukese 49%, Pohnpeian 24%, Other 14%, Kosraean 6%, Yapese 5%, Asian 2%
**Government** Nonparty system
**Currency** US dollar = 100 cents
**Literacy rate** 81%
**Calorie consumption** Not available

## MOLDOVA
*Southeast Europe*

**Official name** Republic of Moldova
**Formation** 1991 / 1991
**Capital** Chisinau
**Population** 4 million / 307 people per sq mile (119 people per sq km)
**Total area** 13,067 sq. miles (33,843 sq. km)
**Languages** Moldovan (Romanian)*, Ukrainian, Russian
**Religions** Orthodox Christian 92%, Other 6%, Nonreligious 2%
**Ethnic mix** Moldovan 76%, Ukrainian 9%, Russian 6%, Gagauz 4%, Romanian 2%, Bulgarian 2%, Other 1%
**Government** Parliamentary system
**Currency** Moldovan leu = 100 bani
**Literacy rate** 99%
**Calorie consumption** 2714 kilocalories

## MONACO
*Southern Europe*

**Official name** Principality of Monaco
**Formation** 1861 / 1861
**Capital** Monaco-Ville
**Population** 39,000 / 52,000 people per sq mile (20,000 people per sq km)
**Total area** 0.75 sq. miles (1.95 sq. km)
**Languages** French*, Italian, Monégasque, English
**Religions** Roman Catholic 89%, Protestant 6%, Other 5%
**Ethnic mix** French 47%, Other 21%, Italian 16%, Monégasque 16%
**Government** Mixed monarchical–parliamentary system
**Currency** Euro = 100 cents
**Literacy rate** 99%
**Calorie consumption** Not available

## MONGOLIA
*East Asia*

**Official name** Mongolia
**Formation** 1924 / 1924
**Capital** Ulan Bator
**Population** 3.1 million / 5 people per sq mile (2 people per sq km)
**Total area** 604,247 sq. miles (1,565,000 sq. km)
**Languages** Khalkha Mongolian*, Kazakh, Chinese
**Religions** Tibetan Buddhist 53%, Nonreligious 38%, Muslim 3%, Shamanist 3%, Christian 2%, Other 1%
**Ethnic mix** Khalkh 82%, Other 9%, Kazakh 4%, Dorvod 3%, Bayad 2%
**Government** Mixed presidential–parliamentary system
**Currency** Tugrik (tögrög) = 100 möngö
**Literacy rate** 98%
**Calorie consumption** 2510 kilocalories

## MONTENEGRO
*Southeast Europe*

**Official name** Montenegro
**Formation** 2006 / 2006
**Capital** Podgorica
**Population** 629,000 / 118 people per sq mile (46 people per sq km)
**Total area** 5332 sq. miles (13,812 sq. km)
**Languages** Montenegrin*, Serbian, Albanian, Bosniak, Croatian
**Religions** Orthodox Christian 74%, Muslim 20%, Roman Catholic 4%, Nonreligious 1%, Other 1%
**Ethnic mix** Montenegrin 43%, Serb 32%, Other 12%, Bosniak 8%, Albanian 5%
**Government** Parliamentary system
**Currency** Euro = 100 cents
**Literacy rate** 98%
**Calorie consumption** 3491 kilocalories

## MOROCCO
*North Africa*

**Official name** Kingdom of Morocco
**Formation** 1956 / 1969
**Capital** Rabat
**Population** 36.2 million / 210 people per sq mile (81 people per sq km)
**Total area** 172,316 sq. miles (446,300 sq. km)
**Languages** Arabic*, Tamazight (Berber)*, French, Spanish
**Religions** Muslim (mainly Sunni) 99%, Other (mostly Christian) 1%
**Ethnic mix** Arab 70%, Berber 29%, European 1%
**Government** Mixed monarchical–parliamentary system
**Currency** Moroccan dirham = 100 centimes
**Literacy rate** 69%
**Calorie consumption** 3403 kilocalories

## MOZAMBIQUE
*Southern Africa*

**Official name** Republic of Mozambique
**Formation** 1975 / 1975
**Capital** Maputo
**Population** 30.5 million / 101 people per sq mile (39 people per sq km)
**Total area** 309,494 sq. miles (801,590 sq. km)
**Languages** Makua, Xitsonga, Sena, Lomwe, Portuguese*
**Religions** Roman Catholic 28%, Nonreligious 19%, Muslim 18%, Traditional beliefs 16%, Pentecostal 11%, Other 8%
**Ethnic mix** Makua Lomwe 47%, Tsonga 23%, Malawi 12%, Shona 11%, Yao 4%, Other 3%
**Government** Presidential system
**Currency** New metical = 100 centavos
**Literacy rate** 56%
**Calorie consumption** 2283 kilocalories

## MYANMAR (BURMA)
*Southeast Asia*

**Official name** Republic of the Union of Myanmar
**Formation** 1948 / 1948
**Capital** Nay Pyi Taw
**Population** 53.9 million / 212 people per sq mile (82 people per sq km)
**Total area** 261,969 sq. miles (678,500 sq. km)
**Languages** Myanmar (Burmese)*, Shan, Karen, Rakhine, Chin, Yangbye, Kachin, Mon
**Religions** Buddhist 88%, Christian 6%, Muslim 4%, Animist 1%, Other 1%
**Ethnic mix** Burman (Bamah) 68%, Other 12%, Shan 9%, Karen 7%, Rakhine 4%
**Government** Presidential system
**Currency** Kyat = 100 pyas
**Literacy rate** 76%
**Calorie consumption** 2571 kilocalories

## NAMIBIA
*Southern Africa*

**Official name** Republic of Namibia
**Formation** 1990 / 1994
**Capital** Windhoek
**Population** 2.6 million / 8 people per sq mile (3 people per sq km)
**Total area** 318,694 sq. miles (825,418 sq. km)
**Languages** Ovambo, Kavango, English*, Bergdama, German, Afrikaans
**Religions** Christian 90%, Traditional beliefs 10%
**Ethnic mix** Ovambo 50%, Other tribes 22%, Kavango 9%, Damara 7%, Herero 7%, Other 5%
**Government** Presidential system
**Currency** Namibian dollar = 100 cents; and South African rand = 100 cents
**Literacy rate** 88%
**Calorie consumption** 2171 kilocalories

## NAURU
*Australasia & Oceania*

**Official name** Republic of Nauru
**Formation** 1968 / 1968
**Capital** None
**Population** 11,000 / 1358 people per sq mile (524 people per sq km)
**Total area** 8.1 sq. miles (21 sq. km)
**Languages** Nauruan*, Kiribati, Chinese, Tuvaluan, English*
**Religions** Nauruan Congregational Church 60%, Roman Catholic 35%, Other 5%
**Ethnic mix** Nauruan 93%, Chinese 5%, European 1%, Other Pacific islanders 1%
**Government** Nonparty system
**Currency** Australian dollar = 100 cents
**Literacy rate** 95%
**Calorie consumption** Not available

## NEPAL
*South Asia*

**Official name** Federal Democratic Republic of Nepal
**Formation** 1769 / 1769
**Capital** Kathmandu
**Population** 29.6 million / 560 people per sq mile (216 people per sq km)
**Total area** 54,363 sq. miles (140,800 sq. km)
**Languages** Nepali*, Maithili, Bhojpuri
**Religions** Hindu 82%, Buddhist 9%, Other (including Christian) 5%, Muslim 4%
**Ethnic mix** Other 52%, Chhetri 17%, Hill Brahman 12%, Magar 7%, Tharu 7%, Tamang 6%
**Government** Parliamentary system
**Currency** Nepalese rupee = 100 paisa
**Literacy rate** 60%
**Calorie consumption** 2673 kilocalories

## NETHERLANDS
*Northwest Europe*

**Official name** Kingdom of the Netherlands
**Formation** 1648 / 1839
**Capital** Amsterdam; The Hague (administrative)
**Population** 17.1 million / 1306 people per sq mile (504 people per sq km)
**Total area** 16,033 sq. miles (41,526 sq. km)
**Languages** Dutch*, Frisian
**Religions** Roman Catholic 36%, Other 34%, Protestant 27%, Muslim 3%
**Ethnic mix** Dutch 82%, Other 12%, Surinamese 2%, Turkish 2%, Moroccan 2%
**Government** Parliamentary system
**Currency** Euro = 100 cents
**Literacy rate** 99%
**Calorie consumption** 3228 kilocalories

## NEW ZEALAND
*Australasia & Oceania*

**Official name** New Zealand
**Formation** 1947 / 1947
**Capital** Wellington
**Population** 4.7 million / 45 people per sq mile (17 people per sq km)
**Total area** 103,737 sq. miles (268,680 sq. km)
**Languages** English*, Maori*
**Religions** Nonreligious 36%, Other Christian 16%, Anglican 15%, Roman Catholic 14%, Presbyterian 11%, Other 8%
**Ethnic mix** European 60%, Other 19%, Maori 14%, Chinese 4%, Samoan 3%
**Government** Parliamentary system
**Currency** New Zealand dollar = 100 cents
**Literacy rate** 99%
**Calorie consumption** 3137 kilocalories

## NICARAGUA
*Central America*

**Official name** Republic of Nicaragua
**Formation** 1838 / 1838
**Capital** Managua
**Population** 6.3 million / 137 people per sq mile (53 people per sq km)
**Total area** 49,998 sq. miles (129,494 sq. km)
**Languages** Spanish*, English Creole, Miskito
**Religions** Roman Catholic 50%, Protestant 40%, Nonreligious 7%, Other 3%
**Ethnic mix** Mestizo 69%, White 17%, Black 9%, Amerindian 5%
**Government** Presidential system
**Currency** Córdoba oro = 100 centavos
**Literacy rate** 78%
**Calorie consumption** 2638 kilocalories

## NIGER
*West Africa*

**Official name** Republic of Niger
**Formation** 1960 / 1960
**Capital** Niamey
**Population** 22.3 million / 46 people per sq mile (18 people per sq km)
**Total area** 489,188 sq. miles (1,267,000 sq. km)
**Languages** Hausa, Djerma, Fulani, Tuareg, Teda, French*
**Religions** Muslim 99%, Other (including Christian) 1%
**Ethnic mix** Hausa 55%, Djerma and Songhai 21%, Tuareg 9%, Peul 9%, Kanuri 5%, Other 1%
**Government** Presidential system
**Currency** CFA franc = 100 centimes
**Literacy rate** 31%
**Calorie consumption** 2547 kilocalories

## NIGERIA
*West Africa*

**Official name** Federal Republic of Nigeria
**Formation** 1960 / 1961
**Capital** Abuja
**Population** 201 million / 563 people per sq mile (217 people per sq km)
**Total area** 356,667 sq. miles (923,768 sq. km)
**Languages** Hausa, English*, Yoruba, Ibo
**Religions** Muslim 50%, Christian 40%, Traditional beliefs 10%
**Ethnic mix** Other 29%, Hausa 21%, Yoruba 21%, Ibo 18%, Fulani 11%
**Government** Presidential system
**Currency** Naira = 100 kobo
**Literacy rate** 51%
**Calorie consumption** 2700 kilocalories

## NORTH KOREA
*East Asia*

**Official name** Democratic People's Republic of Korea
**Formation** 1948 / 1953
**Capital** Pyongyang
**Population** 25.6 million / 551 people per sq mile (213 people per sq km)
**Total area** 46,540 sq. miles (120,540 sq. km)
**Languages** Korean*
**Religions** Atheist 100%
**Ethnic mix** Korean 100%
**Government** One-party state
**Currency** North Korean won = 100 chon
**Literacy rate** 99%
**Calorie consumption** 2094 kilocalories

## NORTH MACEDONIA
*Southeast Europe*

**Official name** Republic of North Macedonia
**Formation** 1991 / 1991
**Capital** Skopje
**Population** 2.1 million / 212 people per sq mile (82 people per sq km)
**Total area** 9781 sq. miles (25,333 sq. km)
**Languages** Macedonian*, Albanian*, Turkish, Romani, Serbian
**Religions** Orthodox Christian 65%, Muslim 33%, Other 2%
**Ethnic mix** Macedonian 64%, Albanian 25%, Turkish 4%, Roma 3%, Serb 2%, Other 2%
**Government** Mixed presidential–parliamentary system
**Currency** Macedonian denar = 100 deni
**Literacy rate** 98%
**Calorie consumption** 2949 kilocalories

## NORWAY
*Northern Europe*

**Official name** Kingdom of Norway
**Formation** 1905 / 1905
**Capital** Oslo
**Population** 5.4 million / 46 people per sq mile (18 people per sq km)
**Total area** 125,181 sq. miles (324,220 sq. km)
**Languages** Norwegian* (Bokmål "book language" and Nynorsk "new Norsk"), Sámi
**Religions** Evangelical Lutheran 88%, Other and nonreligious 8%, Muslim 2%, Pentecostal 1%, Roman Catholic 1%
**Ethnic mix** Norwegian 93%, Other 6%, Sámi 1%
**Government** Parliamentary system
**Currency** Norwegian krone = 100 øre
**Literacy rate** 99%
**Calorie consumption** 3485 kilocalories

## OMAN
*Southwest Asia*

**Official name** Sultanate of Oman
**Formation** 1951 / 1951
**Capital** Muscat
**Population** 4.8 million / 59 people per sq mile (23 people per sq km)
**Total area** 82,031 sq. miles (212,460 sq. km)
**Languages** Arabic*, Baluchi, Farsi, Hindi, Punjabi
**Religions** Other Muslim 50%, Ibadi Muslim 25%, Hindu 17%, other 8%
**Ethnic mix** Arab 54%, Bangladeshi 15%, Indian 15%, African and other 11%, Pakistani 5%
**Government** Monarchy
**Currency** Omani rial = 1000 baisa
**Literacy rate** 96%
**Calorie consumption** 3143 kilocalories

## PAKISTAN
*South Asia*

**Official name** Islamic Republic of Pakistan
**Formation** 1947 / 1971
**Capital** Islamabad
**Population** 207 million / 667 people per sq mile (257 people per sq km)
**Total area** 310,401 sq. miles (803,940 sq. km)
**Languages** Punjabi, Sindhi, Pashtu, Urdu*, Baluchi, Brahui
**Religions** Sunni Muslim 77%, Shi'a Muslim 20%, Hindu 2%, Christian 1%
**Ethnic mix** Punjabi 56%, Pathan (Pashtun) 15%, Sindhi 14%, Mohajir 7%, Baluchi 4%, Other 4%
**Government** Parliamentary system
**Currency** Pakistani rupee = 100 paisa
**Literacy rate** 57%
**Calorie consumption** 2440 kilocalories

## PALAU
*Australasia & Oceania*

**Official name** Republic of Palau
**Formation** 1994 / 1994
**Capital** Ngerulmud
**Population** 22,000 / 112 people per sq mile (43 people per sq km)
**Total area** 177 sq. miles (458 sq. km)
**Languages** Palauan*, English*, Japanese, Angaur, Tobi, Sonsorolese
**Religions** Roman Catholic 49%, Protestant 33%, Modekngei 9%, Other 8%, Nonreligious 1%
**Ethnic mix** Palauan 73%, Filipino 16%, Other Asian 7%, Other Micronesian 3%, Other 1%
**Government** Nonparty system
**Currency** US dollar = 100 cents
**Literacy rate** 97%
**Calorie consumption** Not available

## PANAMA
*Central America*

**Official name** Republic of Panama
**Formation** 1903 / 1903
**Capital** Panama City
**Population** 4.2 million / 143 people per sq mile (55 people per sq km)
**Total area** 30,193 sq. miles (78,200 sq. km)
**Languages** English Creole, Spanish*, Amerindian languages, Chibchan languages
**Religions** Roman Catholic 70%, Protestant 19%, Nonreligious 7%, Other 4%
**Ethnic mix** Mestizo 70%, Black 14%, White 10%, Amerindian 6%
**Government** Presidential system
**Currency** Balboa = 100 centésimos; and US dollar = 100 cents
**Literacy rate** 94%
**Calorie consumption** 2733 kilocalories

## PAPUA NEW GUINEA
*Australasia & Oceania*

**Official name** Independent State of Papua New Guinea
**Formation** 1975 / 1975
**Capital** Port Moresby
**Population** 8.4 million / 48 people per sq mile (19 people per sq km)
**Total area** 178,703 sq. miles (462,840 sq. km)
**Languages** Tok Pisin (Pidgin English)*, Papuan, English*, Hiri Motu*, 800 (est.) native languages
**Religions** Protestant 60%, Roman Catholic 37%, Other 3%
**Ethnic mix** Melanesian and mixed race 100%
**Government** Parliamentary system
**Currency** Kina = 100 toea
**Literacy rate** 63%
**Calorie consumption** 2193 kilocalories

## PARAGUAY
*South America*

**Official name** Republic of Paraguay
**Formation** 1811 / 1938
**Capital** Asunción
**Population** 6.9 million / 45 people per sq mile (17 people per sq km)
**Total area** 157,046 sq. miles (406,750 sq. km)
**Languages** Guaraní*, Spanish*, German
**Religions** Roman Catholic 89%, Protestant (including Mennonite) 7%, Other 3%, Nonreligious 1%
**Ethnic mix** Mestizo 91%, Other 7%, Amerindian 2%
**Government** Presidential system
**Currency** Guaraní = 100 céntimos
**Literacy rate** 95%
**Calorie consumption** 2589 kilocalories

## PERU
*South America*

**Official name** Republic of Peru
**Formation** 1824 / 1941
**Capital** Lima
**Population** 32.6 million / 66 people per sq mile (25 people per sq km)
**Total area** 496,223 sq. miles (1,285,200 sq. km)
**Languages** Spanish*, Quechua*, Aymara*
**Religions** Roman Catholic 76%, Protestant 17%, Nonreligious 4%, Other 3%
**Ethnic mix** Amerindian 45%, Mestizo 37%, White 15%, Other 3%
**Government** Presidential system
**Currency** New sol = 100 céntimos
**Literacy rate** 94%
**Calorie consumption** 2700 kilocalories

## PHILIPPINES
*Southeast Asia*

**Official name** Republic of the Philippines
**Formation** 1946 / 1946
**Capital** Manila
**Population** 106 million / 925 people per sq mile (357 people per sq km)
**Total area** 115,830 sq. miles (300,000 sq. km)
**Languages** Filipino*, English*, Tagalog, Cebuano, Ilocano, Hiligaynon, many other local languages
**Religions** Roman Catholic 81%, Other Christian 11%, Muslim 5%, Other 3%
**Ethnic mix** Other 34%, Tagalog 28%, Cebuano 13%, Ilocano 9%, Hiligaynon 8%, Bisaya 8%
**Government** Presidential system
**Currency** Philippine peso = 100 centavos
**Literacy rate** 96%
**Calorie consumption** 2570 kilocalories

## POLAND
*Northern Europe*

**Official name** Republic of Poland
**Formation** 1918 / 1945
**Capital** Warsaw
**Population** 38.1 million / 324 people per sq mile (125 people per sq km)
**Total area** 120,728 sq. miles (312,685 sq. km)
**Languages** Polish*
**Religions** Roman Catholic 87%, Nonreligious 7%, Other 5%, Orthodox Christian 1%
**Ethnic mix** Polish 97%, Silesian 2%, Other 1%
**Government** Parliamentary system
**Currency** Zloty = 100 groszy
**Literacy rate** 99%
**Calorie consumption** 3451 kilocalories

## PORTUGAL
*Southwest Europe*

**Official name** Portuguese Republic
**Formation** 1139 / 1640
**Capital** Lisbon
**Population** 10.3 million / 290 people per sq mile (112 people per sq km)
**Total area** 35,672 sq. miles (92,391 sq. km)
**Languages** Portuguese*
**Religions** Roman Catholic 88%, Nonreligious 7%, Other Christian 4%, Other 1%
**Ethnic mix** Portuguese 98%, African and other 2%
**Government** Parliamentary system
**Currency** Euro = 100 cents
**Literacy rate** 94%
**Calorie consumption** 3477 kilocalories

## QATAR
*Southwest Asia*

**Official name** State of Qatar
**Formation** 1971 / 1971
**Capital** Doha
**Population** 2.7 million / 636 people per sq mile (245 people per sq km)
**Total area** 4416 sq. miles (11,437 sq. km)
**Languages** Arabic*
**Religions** Muslim (mainly Sunni) 78%, Other 14%, Christian 8%
**Ethnic mix** Qatari 20%, Indian 20%, Other Arab 20%, Nepalese 13%, Filipino 10%, Other 10%, Pakistani 7%
**Government** Monarchy
**Currency** Qatar riyal = 100 dirhams
**Literacy rate** 93%
**Calorie consumption** Not available

## ROMANIA
*Southeast Europe*

**Official name** Romania
**Formation** 1878 / 1947
**Capital** Bucharest
**Population** 19.6 million / 220 people per sq mile (85 people per sq km)
**Total area** 91,699 sq. miles (237,500 sq. km)
**Languages** Romanian*, Hungarian (Magyar), Romani, German
**Religions** Orthodox Christian 86%, Other 8%, Roman Catholic 5%, Nonreligious 1%
**Ethnic mix** Romanian 89%, Magyar 7%, Roma 3%, Other 1%
**Government** Mixed presidential–parliamentary system
**Currency** New Romanian leu = 100 bani
**Literacy rate** 99%
**Calorie consumption** 3358 kilocalories

## RUSSIA
*Europe / Asia*

**Official name** Russian Federation / Russia
**Formation** 1480 / 1991
**Capital** Moscow
**Population** 147 million / 22 people per sq mile (8 people per sq km)
**Total area** 6,592,735 sq. miles (17,075,200 sq. km)
**Languages** Russian*, Tatar, Ukrainian, Chavash, various other national languages
**Religions** Orthodox Christian 71%, Nonreligious 15%, Muslim 11%, Other Christian 2%, Other 1%
**Ethnic mix** Russian 81%, Other 11%, Tatar 4%, Ukrainian 1%, Bashkir 1%, Chavash 1%, Chechen 1%
**Government** Mixed presidential–parliamentary system
**Currency** Russian rouble = 100 kopeks
**Literacy rate** 99%
**Calorie consumption** 3361 kilocalories

## RWANDA
*Central Africa*

**Official name** Republic of Rwanda
**Formation** 1962 / 1962
**Capital** Kigali
**Population** 12.5 million / 1298 people per sq mile (501 people per sq km)
**Total area** 10,169 sq. miles (26,338 sq. km)
**Languages** Kinyarwanda*, French*, Kiswahili, English*
**Religions** Roman Catholic 44%, Protestant 38%, Seventh-day Adventist 12%, Other and nonreligious 4%, Muslim 2%
**Ethnic mix** Hutu 85%, Tutsi 14%, Other (including Twa) 1%
**Government** Presidential system
**Currency** Rwanda franc = 100 centimes
**Literacy rate** 71%
**Calorie consumption** 2228 kilocalories

## ST KITTS & NEVIS
*West Indies*

**Official name** Federation of Saint Christopher and Nevis
**Formation** 1983 / 1983
**Capital** Basseterre
**Population** 56,000 / 403 people per sq mile (156 people per sq km)
**Total area** 101 sq. miles (261 sq. km)
**Languages** English*, English Creole
**Religions** Anglican 33%, Methodist 29%, Other 22%, Moravian 9%, Roman Catholic 7%
**Ethnic mix** Black 95%, Mixed race 3%, White 1%, Other and Amerindian 1%
**Government** Parliamentary system
**Currency** East Caribbean dollar = 100 cents
**Literacy rate** 98%
**Calorie consumption** 2492 kilocalories

## ST LUCIA
*West Indies*

**Official name** Saint Lucia
**Formation** 1979 / 1979
**Capital** Castries
**Population** 180,000 / 763 people per sq mile (295 people per sq km)
**Total area** 239 sq. miles (620 sq. km)
**Languages** English*, French Creole
**Religions** Roman Catholic 68%, Seventh-day Adventist 9%, Other Christian 9%, Pentecostal 6%, Nonreligious 5%, Rastafarian 2%, Other 1%
**Ethnic mix** Black 84%, Mulatto (mixed race) 12%, Asian 3%, Other 1%
**Government** Parliamentary system
**Currency** East Caribbean dollar = 100 cents
**Literacy rate** 95%
**Calorie consumption** 2595 kilocalories

## ST VINCENT & THE GRENADINES
*West Indies*

**Official name** Saint Vincent and the Grenadines
**Formation** 1979 / 1979
**Capital** Kingstown
**Population** 110,000 / 840 people per sq mile (324 people per sq km)
**Total area** 150 sq. miles (389 sq. km)
**Languages** English*, English Creole
**Religions** Other Christian 37%, Anglican 18%, Pentecostal 18%, Methodist 11%, Nonreligious 9%, Other 7%
**Ethnic mix** Black 73%, Mulatto (mixed race) 20%, Carib 4%, Asian 2%, Other 1%
**Government** Parliamentary system
**Currency** East Caribbean dollar = 100 cents
**Literacy rate** 88%
**Calorie consumption** 2968 kilocalories

## SAMOA
*Australasia & Oceania*

**Official name** Independent State of Samoa
**Formation** 1962 / 1962
**Capital** Apia
**Population** 198,000 / 181 people per sq mile (70 people per sq km)
**Total area** 1104 sq. miles (2860 sq. km)
**Languages** Samoan*, English*
**Religions** Other Christian 78%, Roman Catholic 20%, Other 2%
**Ethnic mix** Polynesian 91%, Euronesian 7%, Other 2%
**Government** Parliamentary system
**Currency** Tala = 100 sene
**Literacy rate** 99%
**Calorie consumption** 2960 kilocalories

## SAN MARINO
*Southern Europe*

**Official name** Republic of San Marino
**Formation** 1631 / 1631
**Capital** San Marino
**Population** 34,000 / 1417 people per sq mile (557 people per sq km)
**Total area** 23.6 sq. miles (61 sq. km)
**Languages** Italian*
**Religions** Roman Catholic 93%, Other and nonreligious 7%
**Ethnic mix** Sammarinese 88%, Italian 10%, Other 2%
**Government** Parliamentary system
**Currency** Euro = 100 cents
**Literacy rate** 99%
**Calorie consumption** Not available

## SAO TOME & PRINCIPE
*West Africa*

**Official name** Democratic Republic of Sao Tome and Principe
**Formation** 1975 / 1975
**Capital** São Tomé
**Population** 209,000 / 563 people per sq mile (218 people per sq km)
**Total area** 386 sq. miles (1001 sq. km)
**Languages** Portuguese Creole, Portuguese*
**Religions** Roman Catholic 56%, Nonreligious 21%, Other Christian 15%, Other 8%
**Ethnic mix** Black 90%, Portuguese and Creole 10%
**Government** Mixed presidential–parliamentary system
**Currency** Dobra = 100 céntimos
**Literacy rate** 90%
**Calorie consumption** 2400 kilocalories

## SAUDI ARABIA
*Southwest Asia*

**Official name** Kingdom of Saudi Arabia
**Formation** 1932 / 1932
**Capital** Riyadh
**Population** 33.6 million / 41 people per sq mile (16 people per sq km)
**Total area** 756,981 sq. miles (1,960,582 sq. km)
**Languages** Arabic*
**Religions** Sunni Muslim 85%, Shi'a Muslim 15%
**Ethnic mix** Arab 72%, Foreign residents (mostly south and southeast Asian) 20%, Afro-Asian 8%
**Government** Monarchy
**Currency** Saudi riyal = 100 halalat
**Literacy rate** 94%
**Calorie consumption** 3255 kilocalories

## SENEGAL
*West Africa*

**Official name** Republic of Senegal
**Formation** 1960 / 1960
**Capital** Dakar
**Population** 16.3 million / 219 people per sq mile (85 people per sq km)
**Total area** 75,749 sq. miles (196,190 sq. km)
**Languages** Wolof, Pulaar, Serer, Diola, Mandinka, Malinké, Soninké, French*
**Religions** Sunni Muslim 95%, Christian (mainly Roman Catholic) 4%, Traditional beliefs 1%
**Ethnic mix** Wolof 43%, Serer 15%, Peul 14%, Other 14%, Toucouleur 9%, Diola 5%
**Government** Presidential system
**Currency** CFA franc = 100 centimes
**Literacy rate** 52%
**Calorie consumption** 2456 kilocalories

## SERBIA
*Southeast Europe*

**Official name** Republic of Serbia
**Formation** 2006 / 2008
**Capital** Belgrade
**Population** 8.8 million / 294 people per sq mile (114 people per sq km)
**Total area** 29,905 sq. miles (77,453 sq. km)
**Languages** Serbian*, Hungarian (Magyar)
**Religions** Orthodox Christian 88%, Roman Catholic 4%, Nonreligious 4%, Muslim 2%, Other 2%
**Ethnic mix** Serb 87%, Magyar 4%, Other 3%, Roma 2%, Bosniak 2%, Croat 1%, Slovak 1%
**Government** Mixed presidential–parliamentary system
**Currency** Serbian dinar = 100 para
**Literacy rate** 99%
**Calorie consumption** 2728 kilocalories

## SEYCHELLES
*Indian Ocean*

**Official name** Republic of Seychelles
**Formation** 1976 / 1976
**Capital** Victoria
**Population** 95,000 / 913 people per sq mile (352 people per sq km)
**Total area** 176 sq. miles (455 sq. km)
**Languages** French Creole*, English*, French*
**Religions** Roman Catholic 84%, Anglican 6%, Other Christian 5%, Hindu 2%, Other and nonreligious 2%, Muslim 1%
**Ethnic mix** Creole 89%, Indian 5%, Other 4%, Chinese 2%
**Government** Presidential system
**Currency** Seychelles rupee = 100 cents
**Literacy rate** 92%
**Calorie consumption** 2426 kilocalories

## SIERRA LEONE
*West Africa*

**Official name** Republic of Sierra Leone
**Formation** 1961 / 1961
**Capital** Freetown
**Population** 7.7 million / 278 people per sq mile (108 people per sq km)
**Total area** 27,698 sq. miles (71,740 sq. km)
**Languages** Mende, Temne, Krio, English*
**Religions** Muslim 60%, Christian 30%, Traditional beliefs 10%
**Ethnic mix** Mende 35%, Temne 32%, Other 21%, Limba 8%, Kuranko 4%
**Government** Presidential system
**Currency** Leone = 100 cents
**Literacy rate** 32%
**Calorie consumption** 2404 kilocalories

## SINGAPORE
*Southeast Asia*

**Official name** Republic of Singapore
**Formation** 1965 / 1965
**Capital** Singapore
**Population** 5.8 million / 24,576 people per sq mile (9508 people per sq km)
**Total area** 250 sq. miles (648 sq. km)
**Languages** Mandarin*, Malay*, Tamil*, English*
**Religions** Christian 31%, Buddhist 28%, Nonreligious 14%, Muslim 13%, Taoist 9%, Hindu 4%, Other 1%
**Ethnic mix** Chinese 74%, Malay 14%, Indian 9%, Other 3%
**Government** Parliamentary system
**Currency** Singapore dollar = 100 cents
**Literacy rate** 97%
**Calorie consumption** Not available

## SLOVAKIA
*Central Europe*

**Official name** Slovak Republic
**Formation** 1993 / 1993
**Capital** Bratislava
**Population** 5.4 million / 285 people per sq mile (110 people per sq km)
**Total area** 18,859 sq. miles (48,845 sq. km)
**Languages** Slovak*, Hungarian (Magyar), Czech
**Religions** Roman Catholic 69%, Nonreligious 15%, Other Christian 11%, Greek Catholic (Uniate) 4%, Other 1%
**Ethnic mix** Slovak 87%, Magyar 9%, Roma 2%, Other 1%, Czech 1%
**Government** Parliamentary system
**Currency** Euro = 100 cents
**Literacy rate** 99%
**Calorie consumption** 2944 kilocalories

## SLOVENIA
*Central Europe*

**Official name** Republic of Slovenia
**Formation** 1991 / 1991
**Capital** Ljubljana
**Population** 2.1 million / 269 people per sq mile (104 people per sq km)
**Total area** 7820 sq. miles (20,253 sq. km)
**Languages** Slovenian*
**Religions** Roman Catholic 75%, Nonreligious 18%, Muslim 3%, Orthodox Christian 3%, Other (mostly Protestant) 1%
**Ethnic mix** Slovene 92%, Other 3%, Serb 2%, Croat 2%, Bosniak 1%
**Government** Parliamentary system
**Currency** Euro = 100 cents
**Literacy rate** 99%
**Calorie consumption** 3168 kilocalories

## SOLOMON ISLANDS
*Australasia & Oceania*

**Official name** Solomon Islands
**Formation** 1978 / 1978
**Capital** Honiara
**Population** 623,000 / 58 people per sq mile (22 people per sq km)
**Total area** 10,985 sq. miles (28,450 sq. km)
**Languages** English*, Pidgin English, Melanesian Pidgin, 120 (est.) native languages
**Religions** Church of Melanesia (Anglican) 34%, Roman Catholic 19%, South Seas Evangelical Church 17%, Methodist 11%, Other 19%
**Ethnic mix** Melanesian 93%, Polynesian 4%, Micronesian 2%, Other 1%
**Government** Parliamentary system
**Currency** Solomon Islands dollar = 100 cents
**Literacy rate** 77%
**Calorie consumption** 2391 kilocalories

## SOMALIA
*East Africa*

**Official name** Federal Republic of Somalia
**Formation** 1960 / 1960
**Capital** Mogadishu
**Population** 15.2 million / 63 people per sq mile (24 people per sq km)
**Total area** 246,199 sq. miles (637,657 sq. km)
**Languages** Somali*, Arabic*, English, Italian
**Religions** Sunni Muslim 99%, Christian 1%
**Ethnic mix** Somali 85%, Other 15%
**Government** Non-party system
**Currency** Somali shilin = 100 senti
**Literacy rate** 24%
**Calorie consumption** 1696 kilocalories

## SOUTH AFRICA
*Southern Africa*

**Official name** Republic of South Africa
**Formation** 1934 / 1994
**Capital** Pretoria (Tshwane); Cape Town; Bloemfontein
**Population** 57.4 million / 122 people per sq mile (47 people per sq km)
**Total area** 471,008 sq. miles (1,219,912 sq. km)
**Languages** English*, isiZulu*, isiXhosa*, Afrikaans*, Sepedi*, Setswana*, Sesotho*, Xitsonga*, siSwati*, Tshivenda*, isiNdebele*
**Religions** Christian 81%, Nonreligious 15%, Muslim 2%, Hindu 1%, Other 1%
**Ethnic mix** Black 80%, Colored 9%, White 9%, Asian 2%
**Government** Presidential system
**Currency** Rand = 100 cents
**Literacy rate** 94%
**Calorie consumption** 3022 kilocalories

## SOUTH KOREA
*East Asia*

**Official name** Republic of Korea
**Formation** 1948 / 1953
**Capital** Seoul; Sejong City (administrative)
**Population** 51.2 million / 1343 people per sq mile (519 people per sq km)
**Total area** 38,023 sq. miles (98,480 sq. km)
**Languages** Korean*
**Religions** Nonreligious 47%, Mahayana Buddhist 23%, Other Christian 18%, Roman Catholic 11%, Other 1%
**Ethnic mix** Korean 100%
**Government** Presidential system
**Currency** South Korean won = 100 chon
**Literacy rate** 99%
**Calorie consumption** 3334 kilocalories

## SOUTH SUDAN
*East Africa*

**Official name** Republic of South Sudan
**Formation** 2011 / 2011
**Capital** Juba
**Population** 12.9 million / 52 people per sq mile (20 people per sq km)
**Total area** 248,777 sq. miles (644,329 sq. km)
**Languages** Arabic, Dinka, Nuer, Zande, Bari, Shilluk, Lotuko, English*
**Religions** Over half of the population follow Christian or traditional beliefs.
**Ethnic mix** Dinka 40%, Nuer 15%, Bari 10%, Shilluk/Anwak 10%, Azande 10%, Arab 10%, Other 5%
**Government** Transitional regime
**Currency** South Sudan pound = 100 piastres
**Literacy rate** 37%
**Calorie consumption** Not available

## SPAIN
*Southwest Europe*

**Official name** Kingdom of Spain
**Formation** 1492 / 1713
**Capital** Madrid
**Population** 46.4 million / 241 people per sq mile (93 people per sq km)
**Total area** 194,896 sq. miles (504,782 sq. km)
**Languages** Spanish*, Catalan*, Galician*, Basque*
**Religions** Roman Catholic 71%, Nonreligious 26%, Other 3%
**Ethnic mix** Castilian Spanish 72%, Catalan 17%, Galician 6%, Basque 2%, Other 2%, Roma 1%
**Government** Parliamentary system
**Currency** Euro = 100 cents
**Literacy rate** 98%
**Calorie consumption** 3174 kilocalories

## SRI LANKA
*South Asia*

**Official name** Democratic Socialist Republic of Sri Lanka
**Formation** 1948 / 1948
**Capital** Colombo; Sri Jayewardenapura Kotte (adm.)
**Population** 21 million / 840 people per sq mile (324 people per sq km)
**Total area** 25,332 sq. miles (65,610 sq. km)
**Languages** Sinhala*, Tamil*, Sinhala-Tamil, English
**Religions** Buddhist 70%, Hindu 13%, Muslim 10%, Christian (mainly Roman Catholic) 7%
**Ethnic mix** Sinhalese 75%, Tamil 15%, Moor 9%, Other 1%
**Government** Mixed presidential–parliamentary system
**Currency** Sri Lanka rupee = 100 cents
**Literacy rate** 92%
**Calorie consumption** 2539 kilocalories

## SUDAN
*East Africa*

**Official name** Republic of the Sudan
**Formation** 1956 / 2011
**Capital** Khartoum
**Population** 41.5 million / 58 people per sq mile (22 people per sq km)
**Total area** 718,722 sq. miles (1,861,481 sq. km)
**Languages** Arabic*, Nubian, Beja, Fur, English*
**Religions** Nearly the whole population is Muslim (mainly Sunni)
**Ethnic mix** Arab 60%, Other 18%, Nubian 10%, Beja 8%, Fur 3%, Zaghawa 1%
**Government** Transitional regime
**Currency** New Sudanese pound = 100 piastres
**Literacy rate** 73%
**Calorie consumption** 2336 kilocalories

## SURINAME
*South America*

**Official name** Republic of Suriname
**Formation** 1975 / 1975
**Capital** Paramaribo
**Population** 568,000 / 9 people per sq mile (4 people per sq km)
**Total area** 63,039 sq. miles (163,270 sq. km)
**Languages** Sranan (creole), Dutch*, Javanese, Sarnami Hindi, Saramaccan, Chinese, Carib
**Religions** Christian 50%, Hindu 23%, Muslim 14%, Other 13%
**Ethnic mix** East Indian 27%, Creole 18%, Black 15%, Javanese 15%, Mixed race 13%, Other 12%
**Government** Mixed presidential–parliamentary system
**Currency** Surinamese dollar = 100 cents
**Literacy rate** 93%
**Calorie consumption** 2753 kilocalories

## SWEDEN
*Northern Europe*

**Official name** Kingdom of Sweden
**Formation** 1523 / 1921
**Capital** Stockholm
**Population** 10 million / 63 people per sq mile (24 people per sq km)
**Total area** 173,731 sq. miles (449,964 sq. km)
**Languages** Swedish*, Finnish, Sámi
**Religions** Evangelical Lutheran 75%, Other 13%, Muslim 5%, Other Protestant 5%, Roman Catholic 2%
**Ethnic mix** Swedish 86%, Foreign-born or first-generation immigrant 12%, Finnish and Sámi 2%
**Government** Parliamentary system
**Currency** Swedish krona = 100 ore
**Literacy rate** 99%
**Calorie consumption** 3179 kilocalories

## SWITZERLAND
*Central Europe*

**Official name** Swiss Confederation
**Formation** 1291 / 1857
**Capital** Bern
**Population** 8.5 million / 554 people per sq mile (214 people per sq km)
**Total area** 15,942 sq. miles (41,290 sq. km)
**Languages** German*, Swiss-German, French*, Italian*, Romansch*
**Religions** Roman Catholic 39%, Other Christian 34%, Nonreligious 21%, Muslim 5%, Other 1%
**Ethnic mix** German 64%, French 20%, Other 9.5%, Italian 6%, Romansch 0.5%
**Government** Parliamentary system
**Currency** Swiss franc = 100 rappen/centimes
**Literacy rate** 99%
**Calorie consumption** 3391 kilocalories

## SYRIA
*Southwest Asia*

**Official name** Syrian Arab Republic
**Formation** 1941 / 1967
**Capital** Damascus
**Population** 18.3 million / 258 people per sq mile (99 people per sq km)
**Total area** 71,498 sq. miles (184,180 sq. km)
**Languages** Arabic*, French, Kurdish, Armenian, Circassian, Turkic languages, Assyrian, Aramaic
**Religions** Sunni Muslim 74%, Alawi 12%, Christian 10%, Druze 3%, Other 1%
**Ethnic mix** Arab 90%, Kurdish 9%, Armenian, Turkmen, and Circassian 1%
**Government** Presidential system
**Currency** Syrian pound = 100 piastres
**Literacy rate** 85%
**Calorie consumption** 3106 kilocalories

## TAIWAN
*East Asia*

**Official name** Republic of China (ROC)
**Formation** 1949 / 1949
**Capital** Taibei (Taipei)
**Population** 23.6 million / 1895 people per sq mile (732 people per sq km)
**Total area** 13,892 sq. miles (35,980 sq. km)
**Languages** Amoy Chinese, Mandarin Chinese*, Hakka Chinese
**Religions** Buddhist, Confucianist, and Taoist 93%, Christian 5%, Other 2%
**Ethnic mix** Han Chinese (pre-20th-century migration) 84%, Han Chinese (20th-century migration) 14%, Aboriginal 2%
**Government** Presidential system
**Currency** Taiwan dollar = 100 cents
**Literacy rate** 99%
**Calorie consumption** 2997 kilocalories

## TAJIKISTAN
*Central Asia*

**Official name** Republic of Tajikistan
**Formation** 1991 / 1991
**Capital** Dushanbe
**Population** 9.1 million / 165 people per sq mile (64 people per sq km)
**Total area** 55,251 sq. miles (143,100 sq. km)
**Languages** Tajik*, Uzbek, Russian
**Religions** Sunni Muslim 95%, Shi'a Muslim 3%, Other 2%
**Ethnic mix** Tajik 84%, Uzbek 12%, Other 2%, Kyrgyz 1%, Russian 1%
**Government** Presidential system
**Currency** Somoni = 100 diram
**Literacy rate** 99%
**Calorie consumption** 2201 kilocalories

## TANZANIA
*East Africa*

**Official name** United Republic of Tanzania
**Formation** 1964 / 1964
**Capital** Dodoma
**Population** 59.1 million / 173 people per sq mile (67 people per sq km)
**Total area** 364,898 sq. miles (945,087 sq. km)
**Languages** Kiswahili*, Sukuma, Chagga, Nyamwezi, Hehe, Makonde, Yao, Sandawe, English*
**Religions** Christian 63%, Muslim 35%, Other 2%
**Ethnic mix** Native African (over 120 tribes) 99%, European, Asian, and Arab 1%
**Government** Presidential system
**Currency** Tanzanian shilling = 100 cents
**Literacy rate** 78%
**Calorie consumption** 2208 kilocalories

## THAILAND
*Southeast Asia*

**Official name** Kingdom of Thailand
**Formation** 1238 / 1907
**Capital** Bangkok
**Population** 69.2 million / 351 people per sq mile (135 people per sq km)
**Total area** 198,455 sq. miles (514,000 sq. km)
**Languages** Thai*, Chinese, Malay, Khmer, Mon, Karen, Miao
**Religions** Buddhist 94%, Muslim 5%, Other (including Christian) 1%
**Ethnic mix** Thai 83%, Chinese 12%, Malay 3%, Khmer and Other 2%
**Government** Parliamentary system
**Currency** Baht = 100 satang
**Literacy rate** 93%
**Calorie consumption** 2784 kilocalories

## TOGO
*West Africa*

**Official name** Togolese Republic
**Formation** 1960 / 1960
**Capital** Lomé
**Population** 8 million / 381 people per sq mile (147 people per sq km)
**Total area** 21,924 sq. miles (56,785 sq. km)
**Languages** Ewe, Kabye, Gurma, French*
**Religions** Christian 47%, Traditional beliefs 33%, Muslim 14%, Other 6%
**Ethnic mix** Ewe 46%, Other African 41%, Kabye 12%, European 1%
**Government** Presidential system
**Currency** CFA franc = 100 centimes
**Literacy rate** 64%
**Calorie consumption** 2454 kilocalories

## TONGA
*Australasia & Oceania*

**Official name** Kingdom of Tonga
**Formation** 1970 / 1970
**Capital** Nuku'alofa
**Population** 109,000 / 392 people per sq mile (151 people per sq km)
**Total area** 289 sq. miles (748 sq. km)
**Languages** English*, Tongan*
**Religions** Free Wesleyan 38%, Church of Jesus Christ of Latter-day Saints 17%, Roman Catholic 16%, Other Christian 16%, Free Church of Tonga 12%, Other 1%
**Ethnic mix** Tongan 98%, Other 2%
**Government** Mixed monarchical–parliamentary system
**Currency** Pa'anga (Tongan dollar) = 100 seniti
**Literacy rate** 99%
**Calorie consumption** Not available

## TRINIDAD & TOBAGO
*West Indies*

**Official name** Republic of Trinidad and Tobago
**Formation** 1962 / 1962
**Capital** Port-of-Spain
**Population** 1.4 million / 707 people per sq mile (273 people per sq km)
**Total area** 1980 sq. miles (5128 sq. km)
**Languages** English Creole, English*, Hindi, French, Spanish
**Religions** Protestant 38%, Roman Catholic 24%, Hindu 20%, Other 9%, Muslim 6%, Nonreligious 3%
**Ethnic mix** East Indian 38%, Black 36%, Mixed race 24%, White and Chinese 1%, Other 1%
**Government** Parliamentary system
**Currency** Trinidad and Tobago dollar = 100 cents
**Literacy rate** 99%
**Calorie consumption** 3052 kilocalories

## TUNISIA
*North Africa*

**Official name** Republic of Tunisia
**Formation** 1956 / 1956
**Capital** Tunis
**Population** 11.7 million / 195 people per sq mile (75 people per sq km)
**Total area** 63,169 sq. miles (163,610 sq. km)
**Languages** Arabic*, French
**Religions** Muslim (mainly Sunni) 98%, Christian 1%, Jewish 1%
**Ethnic mix** Arab and Berber 98%, Jewish 1%, European 1%
**Government** Mixed presidential–parliamentary system
**Currency** Tunisian dinar = 1000 millimes
**Literacy rate** 79%
**Calorie consumption** 3349 kilocalories

## TURKEY
*Asia / Europe*

**Official name** Republic of Turkey
**Formation** 1923 / 1939
**Capital** Ankara
**Population** 81.9 million / 276 people per sq mile (106 people per sq km)
**Total area** 301,382 sq. miles (780,580 sq. km)
**Languages** Turkish*, Kurdish, Arabic, Circassian, Armenian, Greek, Georgian, Ladino
**Religions** Muslim (mainly Sunni) 99%, Other 1%
**Ethnic mix** Turkish 70%, Kurdish 20%, Other 8%, Arab 2%
**Government** Presidential system
**Currency** Turkish lira = 100 kurus
**Literacy rate** 96%
**Calorie consumption** 3706 kilocalories

## TURKMENISTAN
*Central Asia*

**Official name** Turkmenistan
**Formation** 1991 / 1991
**Capital** Ashgabat
**Population** 5.9 million / 31 people per sq mile (12 people per sq km)
**Total area** 188,455 sq. miles (488,100 sq. km)
**Languages** Turkmen*, Uzbek, Russian, Kazakh, Tatar
**Religions** Sunni Muslim 89%, Orthodox Christian 9%, Other 2%
**Ethnic mix** Turkmen 85%, Other 6%, Uzbek 5%, Russian 4%
**Government** Presidential system
**Currency** New manat = 100 tenge
**Literacy rate** 99%
**Calorie consumption** 2840 kilocalories

## TUVALU
*Australasia & Oceania*

**Official name** Tuvalu
**Formation** 1978 / 1978
**Capital** Funafuti Atoll
**Population** 11,000 / 1100 people per sq mile (423 people per sq km)
**Total area** 10 sq. miles (26 sq. km)
**Languages** Tuvaluan*, Kiribati, English*
**Religions** Church of Tuvalu 91%, Other (mostly Protestant) 5%, Seventh-day Adventist 2%, Baha'i 2%
**Ethnic mix** Polynesian 96%, Micronesian 4%
**Government** Nonparty system
**Currency** Australian dollar = 100 cents; and Tuvaluan dollar = 100 cents
**Literacy rate** 95%
**Calorie consumption** Not available

## UGANDA
*East Africa*

**Official name** Republic of Uganda
**Formation** 1962 / 1962
**Capital** Kampala
**Population** 44.3 million / 575 people per sq mile (222 people per sq km)
**Total area** 91,135 sq. miles (236,040 sq. km)
**Languages** Luganda, Nkole, Chiga, Lango, Acholi, Teso, Lugbara, English*
**Religions** Roman Catholic 42%, Protestant 42%, Muslim (mainly Sunni) 12%, Other 3%, Nonreligious 1%
**Ethnic mix** Other 50%, Baganda 17%, Banyakole 10%, Basoga 9%, Iteso 7%, Bakiga 7%
**Government** Presidential system
**Currency** Uganda shilling = 100 cents
**Literacy rate** 70%
**Calorie consumption** 2130 kilocalories

## UKRAINE
*Eastern Europe*

**Official name** Ukraine
**Formation** 1991 / 1991
**Capital** Kiev
**Population** 44 million / 189 people per sq mile (73 people per sq km)
**Total area** 223,089 sq. miles (603,700 sq. km)
**Languages** Ukrainian*, Russian, Tatar
**Religions** Orthodox Christian 78%, Roman Catholic 10%, Nonreligious 7%, Other 5%
**Ethnic mix** Ukrainian 78%, Russian 17%, Other 4%, Belarussian 1%
**Government** Mixed presidential–parliamentary system
**Currency** Hryvna = 100 kopiykas
**Literacy rate** 99%
**Calorie consumption** 3138 kilocalories

## UNITED ARAB EMIRATES
*Southwest Asia*

**Official name** United Arab Emirates
**Formation** 1971 / 1972
**Capital** Abu Dhabi
**Population** 9.5 million / 294 people per sq mile (114 people per sq km)
**Total area** 32,000 sq. miles (82,880 sq. km)
**Languages** Arabic*, Farsi, Indian and Pakistani languages, English
**Religions** Muslim (mainly Sunni) 96%, Christian, Hindu, and other 4%
**Ethnic mix** Asian 60%, Emirian 25%, Other Arab 12%, European 3%
**Government** Monarchy
**Currency** UAE dirham = 100 fils
**Literacy rate** 90%
**Calorie consumption** 3280 kilocalories

## UNITED KINGDOM
*Northwest Europe*

**Official name** United Kingdom of Great Britain and Northern Ireland
**Formation** 1707 / 1922
**Capital** London
**Population** 66.6 million / 714 people per sq mile (276 people per sq km)
**Total area** 94,525 sq. miles (244,820 sq. km)
**Languages** English*, Welsh*, Scottish Gaelic, Irish
**Religions** Christian 64%, Nonreligious 28%, Muslim 5%, Other 2%, Hindu 1%
**Ethnic mix** White 87%, Indian and Pakistani 4%, Other 3%, Black 3%, Other Asian 2%, Bengali 1%
**Government** Parliamentary system
**Currency** Pound sterling = 100 pence
**Literacy rate** 99%
**Calorie consumption** 3424 kilocalories

## UNITED STATES
*North America*

**Official name** United States of America
**Formation** 1776 / 1959
**Capital** Washington D.C.
**Population** 330 million / 92 people per sq mile (36 people per sq km)
**Total area** 3,717,792 sq. miles (9,626,091 sq. km)
**Languages** English*, Spanish, Chinese, French, German, Tagalog, Vietnamese, Italian, Korean
**Religions** Protestant 47%, Nonreligious 23%, Roman Catholic 21%, Other 6%, Jewish 2%, Muslim 1%
**Ethnic mix** White 60%, Hispanic 17%, Black American/African 14%, Asian 6%, American Indians and Alaska Natives 2%, Pacific Islanders 1%
**Government** Presidential system
**Currency** US dollar = 100 cents
**Literacy rate** 99%
**Calorie consumption** 3682 kilocalories

## URUGUAY
*South America*

**Official name** Eastern Republic of Uruguay
**Formation** 1828 / 1828
**Capital** Montevideo
**Population** 3.5 million / 52 people per sq mile (20 people per sq km)
**Total area** 68,039 sq. miles (176,220 sq. km)
**Languages** Spanish*
**Religions** Roman Catholic 42%, Protestant 15%, Nonreligious 37%, Other 6%
**Ethnic mix** White 87%, Black 7%, Mestizo 5%, Other 1%
**Government** Presidential system
**Currency** Uruguayan peso = 100 centésimos
**Literacy rate** 99%
**Calorie consumption** 3050 kilocalories

## UZBEKISTAN
*Central Asia*

**Official name** Republic of Uzbekistan
**Formation** 1991 / 1991
**Capital** Tashkent
**Population** 32.4 million / 188 people per sq mile (72 people per sq km)
**Total area** 172,741 sq. miles (447,400 sq. km)
**Languages** Uzbek*, Russian, Tajik, Kazakh
**Religions** Sunni Muslim 88%, Orthodox Christian 9%, Other 3%
**Ethnic mix** Uzbek 80%, Russian 6%, Other 6%, Tajik 5%, Kazakh 3%
**Government** Presidential system
**Currency** Som = 100 tiyin
**Literacy rate** 99%
**Calorie consumption** 2760 kilocalories

## VANUATU
*Australasia & Oceania*

**Official name** Republic of Vanuatu
**Formation** 1980 / 1980
**Capital** Port Vila
**Population** 282,000 / 60 people per sq mile (23 people per sq km)
**Total area** 4710 sq. miles (12,200 sq. km)
**Languages** Bislama (Melanesian pidgin)*, English*, French*, other indigenous languages
**Religions** Other 33%, Presbyterian 28%, Anglican 15%, Seventh-day Adventist 12%, Roman Catholic 12%
**Ethnic mix** ni-Vanuatu 99%, Other 1%
**Government** Parliamentary system
**Currency** Vatu = 100 centimes
**Literacy rate** 85%
**Calorie consumption** 2836 kilocalories

## VATICAN CITY
*Southern Europe*

**Official name** State of the Vatican City
**Formation** 1929 / 1929
**Capital** Vatican City
**Population** 800 / 4706 people per sq mile (1818 people per sq km)
**Total area** 0.17 sq. miles (0.44 sq. km)
**Languages** Italian*, Latin*
**Religions** Roman Catholic 100%
**Ethnic mix** The current pope is Argentinian; most popes have been Italian. Cardinals are from many nationalities, but Italians form the largest group. Most resident lay persons are Italian.
**Government** Papal state
**Currency** Euro = 100 cents
**Literacy rate** 99%
**Calorie consumption** Not available

## VENEZUELA
*South America*

**Official name** Bolivarian Republic of Venezuela
**Formation** 1830 / 1830
**Capital** Caracas
**Population** 32.4 million / 95 people per sq mile (37 people per sq km)
**Total area** 352,143 sq. miles (912,050 sq. km)
**Languages** Spanish*, Amerindian languages
**Religions** Roman Catholic 73%, Protestant 17%, Nonreligious 7%, Other 3%
**Ethnic mix** Mestizo 69%, White 20%, Black 9%, Amerindian 2%
**Government** Presidential system
**Currency** Bolívar fuerte = 100 céntimos
**Literacy rate** 97%
**Calorie consumption** 2631 kilocalories

## VIETNAM
*Southeast Asia*

**Official name** Socialist Republic of Vietnam
**Formation** 1976 / 1976
**Capital** Hanoi
**Population** 96.5 million / 768 people per sq mile (297 people per sq km)
**Total area** 127,243 sq. miles (329,560 sq. km)
**Languages** Vietnamese*, Chinese, Thai, Khmer, Muong, Nung, Miao, Yao, Jarai
**Religions** Nonreligious 81%, Buddhist 9%, Roman Catholic 7%, Hoa Hao 1%, Cao Dai 1%, Other 1%
**Ethnic mix** Vietnamese 86%, Other 8%, Tay 2%, Thai 2%, Muong 1%, Khome 1%
**Government** One-party state
**Currency** Dông = 10 hao = 100 xu
**Literacy rate** 94%
**Calorie consumption** 2745 kilocalories

## YEMEN
*Southwest Asia*

**Official name** Republic of Yemen
**Formation** 1990 / 1990
**Capital** Sana
**Population** 28.9 million / 133 people per sq mile (51 people per sq km)
**Total area** 203,849 sq. miles (527,970 sq. km)
**Languages** Arabic*
**Religions** Sunni Muslim 55%, Shi'a Muslim 42%, Christian, Hindu, and Jewish 3%
**Ethnic mix** Arab 99%, Afro-Arab, Indian, Somali, and European 1%
**Government** Transitional regime
**Currency** Yemeni rial = 100 fils
**Literacy rate** 66%
**Calorie consumption** 2223 kilocalories

## ZAMBIA
*Southern Africa*

**Official name** Republic of Zambia
**Formation** 1964 / 1964
**Capital** Lusaka
**Population** 17.6 million / 62 people per sq mile (24 people per sq km)
**Total area** 290,584 sq. miles (752,614 sq. km)
**Languages** Bemba, Tonga, Nyanja, Lozi, Lala-Bisa, Nsenga, English*
**Religions** Protestant 75%, Roman Catholic 20%, Other (including Muslim) 3%, Nonreligious 2%
**Ethnic mix** Bemba 34%, Other African 26%, Tonga 16%, Nyanja 14%, Lozi 9%, European 1%
**Government** Presidential system
**Currency** New Zambian kwacha = 100 ngwee
**Literacy rate** 83%
**Calorie consumption** 1930 kilocalories

## ZIMBABWE
*Southern Africa*

**Official name** Republic of Zimbabwe
**Formation** 1980 / 1980
**Capital** Harare
**Population** 16.9 million / 113 people per sq mile (44 people per sq km)
**Total area** 150,803 sq. miles (390,580 sq. km)
**Languages** Shona, isiNdebele, English*
**Religions** Syncretic (Christian/traditional beliefs) 50%, Christian 25%, Traditional beliefs 24%, Other (including Muslim) 1%
**Ethnic mix** Shona 71%, Ndebele 16%, Other African 11%, White 1%, Asian 1%
**Government** Presidential system
**Currency** US $, South African rand, euro, UK £, Botswana pula, Australian $, Chinese yuan, Indian rupee, and Japanese yen are legal tender
**Literacy rate** 89%
**Calorie consumption** 2110 kilocalories

# GLOSSARY

This glossary lists all geographical, technical and foreign language terms which appear in the text, followed by a brief definition of the term. Any acronyms used in the text are also listed in full. Terms in italics are for cross-reference and indicate that the word is separately defined in the glossary.

## A

**Aboriginal** The original (indigenous) inhabitants of a country or continent. Especially used with reference to Australia.

**Abyssal plain** A broad plain found in the depths of the ocean, more than 10,000 ft (3000 m) below sea level.

**Acid rain** Rain, sleet, snow or mist which has absorbed waste gases from fossil-fuelled power stations and vehicle exhausts, becoming more acid. It causes severe environmental damage.

**Adaptation** The gradual evolution of plants and animals so that they become better suited to survive and reproduce in their *environment*.

**Afforestation** The planting of new forest in areas which were once forested but have been cleared.

**Agribusiness** A term applied to activities such as the growing of crops, rearing of animals or the manufacture of farm machinery, which eventually leads to the supply of agricultural produce at market.

**Air mass** A huge, homogeneous mass of air, within which horizontal patterns of temperature and *humidity* are consistent. Air masses are separated by *fronts*.

**Alliance** An agreement between two or more states, to work together to achieve common purposes.

**Alluvial fan** A large fan-shaped deposit of fine sediments deposited by a river as it emerges from a narrow, mountain valley onto a broad, open *plain*.

**Alluvium** Material deposited by rivers. Nowadays usually only applied to finer particles of silt and clay.

**Alpine** Mountain *environment*, between the *treeline* and the level of permanent snow cover.

**Alpine mountains** Ranges of mountains formed between 30 and 65 million years ago, by *folding*, in west and central Europe.

**Amerindian** A term applied to people *indigenous* to North, Central and South America.

**Animal husbandry** The business of rearing animals.

**Antarctic circle** The parallel which lies at *latitude* of 66° 32' S.

**Anticline** A geological *fold* that forms an arch shape, curving upwards in the rock *strata*.

**Anticyclone** An area of relatively high atmospheric pressure.

**Aquaculture** Collective term for the farming of produce derived from the sea, including fish-farming, the cultivation of shellfish, and plants such as seaweed.

**Aquifer** A body of rock which can absorb water. Also applied to any rock strata that have sufficient porosity to yield *groundwater* through wells or springs.

**Arable** Land which has been ploughed and is being used, or is suitable, for growing crops.

**Archipelago** A group or chain of islands.

**Arctic Circle** The parallel which lies at a *latitude* of 66° 32' N.

**Arête** A thin, jagged mountain ridge which divides two adjacent *cirques*, found in regions where *glaciation* has occurred.

**Arid** Dry. An area of low rainfall, where the rate of *evaporation* may be greater than that of *precipitation*. Often defined as those areas that receive less than one inch (25 mm) of rain a year. In these areas only drought-resistant plants can survive.

**Artesian well** A naturally occurring source of underground water, stored in an *aquifer*.

**Artisanal** Small-scale, manual operation, such as fishing, using little or no machinery.

**ASEAN** Association of Southeast Asian Nations. Established in 1967 to promote economic, social and cultural co-operation. Its members include Brunei, Indonesia, Malaysia, Philippines, Singapore and Thailand.

**Aseismic** A region where *earthquake* activity has ceased.

**Asteroid** A minor planet circling the Sun, mainly between the orbits of Mars and Jupiter.

**Asthenosphere** A zone of hot, partially melted rock, which underlies the *lithosphere*, within the Earth's *crust*.

**Atmosphere** The envelope of odourless, colourless and tasteless gases surrounding the Earth, consisting of *oxygen* (23%), *nitrogen* (75%), argon (1%), *carbon dioxide* (0.03%), as well as tiny proportions of other gases.

**Atmospheric pressure** The pressure created by the action of gravity on the gases surrounding the Earth.

**Atoll** A ring-shaped island or *coral reef* often enclosing a *lagoon* of sea water.

**Avalanche** The rapid movement of a mass of snow and ice down a steep slope. Similar movements of other materials are described as *rock avalanches* or *landslides* and *sand avalanches*.

## B

**Badlands** A landscape that has been heavily eroded and dissected by rainwater, and which has little or no vegetation.

**Back slope** The gentler windward slope of a sand *dune* or gentler slope of a *cuesta*.

**Bajos** An *alluvial fan* deposited by a river at the base of mountains and hills which encircle *desert* areas.

**Bar, coastal** An offshore strip of sand or shingle, either above or below the water. Usually parallel to the shore but sometimes crescent-shaped or at an oblique angle.

**Barchan** A crescent-shaped sand *dune*, formed where wind direction is very consistent. The horns of the crescent point downwind and where there is enough sand the barchan is mobile.

**Barrio** A Spanish term for the shanty towns – self-built settlements – which are clustered around many South and Central American cities (*see also Favela*).

**Basalt** Dark, fine-grained *igneous rock*. Formed near the Earth's surface from fast-cooling *lava*.

**Base level** The level below which flowing water cannot erode the land.

**Basement rock** A mass of ancient rock often of *Pre-Cambrian age*, covered by a layer of more recent *sedimentary rocks*. Commonly associated with *shield* areas.

**Beach** Lake or sea shore where waves break and there is an accumulation of loose material – mud, sand, shingle or pebbles.

**Bedrock** Solid, consolidated and relatively unweathered rock, found on the surface of the land or just below a layer of soil or *weathered* rock.

**Biodiversity** The quantity of animal or plant species in a given area.

**Biomass** The total mass of organic matter – plants and animals – in a given area. It is usually measured in kilogrammes per square metre. Plant biomass is proportionally greater than that of animals, except in cities.

**Biosphere** The zone just above and below the Earth's surface, where all plants and animals live.

**Blizzard** A severe windstorm with snow and sleet. Visibility is often severely restricted.

**Bluff** The steep bank of a *meander*, formed by the erosive action of a river.

**Boreal forest** Tracts of mainly coniferous forest found in northern *latitudes*.

**Breccia** A type of rock composed of sharp fragments, cemented by a fine-grained material such as clay.

**Butte** An isolated, flat-topped hill with steep or vertical sides, buttes are the eroded remnants of a former land surface.

## C

**Caatinga** Portuguese (Brazilian) term for thorny woodland growing in areas of pale granitic soils.

**CACM** Central American Common Market. Established in 1960 to further economic ties between its members, which are Costa Rica, El Salvador, Guatemala, Honduras and Nicaragua.

**Calcite** Hexagonal crystals of calcium carbonate.

**Caldera** A huge volcanic vent, often containing a number of smaller vents, and sometimes a crater lake.

**Carbon cycle** The transfer of carbon to and from the *atmosphere*. This occurs on land through *photosynthesis*. In the sea, *carbon dioxide* is absorbed, some returning to the air and some taken up into the bodies of sea creatures.

**Carbon dioxide** A colourless, odourless gas ($CO_2$) which makes up 0.03% of the *atmosphere*.

**Carbonation** The process whereby rocks are broken down by carbonic acid. Carbon dioxide in the air dissolves in rainwater, forming carbonic acid. *Limestone* terrain can be rapidly eaten away.

**Cash crop** A single crop grown specifically for export sale, rather than for local use. Typical examples include coffee, tea and citrus fruits.

**Cassava** A type of grain meal, used to produce tapioca. A staple crop in many parts of Africa.

**Castle kopje** Hill or rock outcrop, especially in southern Africa, where steep sides, and a summit composed of blocks, give a castle-like appearance.

**Cataracts** A series of stepped waterfalls created as a river flows over a band of hard, resistant rock.

**Causeway** A raised route through marshland or a body of water.

**CEEAC** Economic Community of Central African States. Established in 1983 to promote regional co-operation and if possible, establish a common market between 16 Central African nations.

**Chemical weathering** The chemical reactions leading to the decomposition of rocks. Types of chemical weathering include *carbonation*, *hydrolysis* and *oxidation*.

**Chernozem** A fertile soil, also known as 'black earth' consisting of a layer of dark topsoil, rich in decaying vegetation, overlying a lighter chalky layer.

**Cirque** Armchair-shaped basin, found in mountain regions, with a steep back, or rear, wall and a raised rock lip, often containing a lake (or *tarn*). The cirque floor has been eroded by a *glacier*, while the back wall is eroded both by the *glacier* and by *weathering*.

**Climate** The average weather conditions in a given area over a period of years, sometimes defined as 30 years or more.

**Cold War** A period of hostile relations between the USA and the Soviet Union and their allies after the Second World War.

**Composite volcano** Also known as a strato-volcano, the volcanic cone is composed of alternating deposits of *lava* and *pyroclastic* material.

**Compound** A substance made up of *elements* chemically combined in a consistent way.

**Condensation** The process whereby a gas changes into a liquid. For example, water vapour in the *atmosphere* condenses around tiny airborne particles to form droplets of water.

**Confluence** The point at which two rivers meet.

**Conglomerate** Rock composed of large, water-worn or rounded pebbles, held together by a natural cement.

**Coniferous forest** A forest type containing trees which are generally, but not necessarily, *evergreen* and have slender, needle-like leaves and which reproduce by means of seeds contained in a cone.

**Continental drift** The theory that the continents of today are fragments of one or more prehistoric *supercontinents* which have moved across the Earth's surface, creating ocean basins. The theory has been superseded by a more sophisticated one – *plate tectonics*.

**Continental shelf** An area of the continental crust, below sea level, which slopes gently. It is separated from the deep ocean by a much more steeply inclined *continental slope*.

**Continental slope** A steep slope running from the edge of the *continental shelf* to the ocean floor.

**Conurbation** A vast metropolitan area created by the expansion of towns and cities into a virtually continuous urban area.

**Cool continental** A rainy *climate* with warm summers [warmest month below 76°F (22°C)] and often severe winters [coldest month below 32°F (0°C)].

**Copra** The dried, white kernel of a coconut, from which coconut oil is extracted.

**Coral reef** An underwater barrier created by colonies of the coral polyp. Polyps secrete a protective skeleton of calcium carbonate, and reefs develop as live polyps build on the skeletons of dead generations.

**Core** The centre of the Earth, consisting of a dense mass of iron and nickel. It is thought that the outer core is molten or liquid, and that the hot inner core is solid due to extremely high pressures.

**Coriolis effect** A deflecting force caused by the rotation of the Earth. In the northern hemisphere a body, such as an *air mass* or ocean current, is deflected to the right, and in the southern hemisphere to the left. This prevents winds from blowing straight from areas of high to low pressure.

**Coulées** A US / Canadian term for a ravine formed by river *erosion*.

**Craton** A large block of the Earth's *crust* which has remained stable for a long period of *geological time*. It is made up of ancient *shield* rocks.

**Cretaceous** A period of *geological time* beginning about 145 million years ago and lasting until about 65 million years ago.

**Crevasse** A deep crack in a *glacier*.

**Crust** The hard, thin outer shell of the Earth. The crust floats on the *mantle*, which is softer and more dense. Under the oceans (oceanic crust) the crust is 3.7–6.8 miles (6–11 km) thick. Continental crust averages 18–24 miles (30–40 km).

**Crystalline rock** Rocks formed when molten *magma* crystallizes (*igneous rocks*) or when heat or pressure cause re-crystallization (*metamorphic rocks*). Crystalline rocks are distinct from *sedimentary rocks*.

**Cuesta** A hill which rises into a steep slope on one side but has a gentler gradient on its other slope.

**Cyclone** An area of low *atmospheric pressure*, occurring where the air is warm and relatively low in density, causing low level winds to spiral. *Hurricanes* and *typhoons* are tropical cyclones.

## D

**De facto**
1 Government or other activity that takes place, or exists in actuality if not by right.
2 A border, which exists in practice, but which is not officially recognized by all the countries it adjoins.

**Deciduous forest** A forest of trees which shed their leaves annually at a particular time or season. In *temperate* climates the fall of leaves occurs in the Autumn. Some *coniferous* trees, such as the larch, are deciduous. Deciduous vegetation contrasts with *evergreen*, which keeps its leaves for more than a year.

**Defoliant** Chemical spray used to remove foliage (leaves) from trees.

**Deforestation** The act of cutting down and clearing large areas of forest for human activities, such as agricultural land or urban development.

**Delta** Low-lying, fan-shaped area at a river mouth, formed by the *deposition* of successive layers of *sediment*. Slowing as it enters the sea, a river deposits sediment and may, as a result, split into numerous smaller channels, known as *distributaries*.

**Denudation** The combined effect of *weathering*, *erosion* and *mass movement*, which, over long periods, exposes underlying rocks.

**Deposition** The laying down of material that has accumulated:
(1) after being *eroded* and then transported by physical forces such as wind, ice or water;
(2) as organic remains, such as coal and coral;
(3) as the result of *evaporation* and chemical *precipitation*.

**Depression**
1 In climatic terms it is a large low pressure system.
2 A complex *fold*, producing a large valley, which incorporates both a *syncline* and an *anticline*.

**Desert** An *arid* region of low rainfall, with little vegetation or animal life, which is adapted to the dry conditions. The term is now applied not only to hot tropical and subtropical regions, but to arid areas of the continental interiors and to the ice deserts of the *Arctic* and *Antarctic*.

**Desertification** The gradual extension of *desert* conditions in *arid* or *semi-arid* regions, as a result of climatic change or human activity, such as over-grazing and *deforestation*.

**Despot** A ruler with absolute power. Despots are often associated with oppressive regimes.

**Detritus** Piles of rock deposited by an erosive agent such as a river or *glacier*.

**Distributary** A minor branch of a river, which does not rejoin the main stream, common at *deltas*.

**Diurnal** Daily, something that occurs each day. Diurnal temperature refers to the variation in temperature over the course of a full day and night.

**Divide** A US term describing the area of high ground separating two *drainage basins*.

**Donga** A steep-sided *gully*, resulting from *erosion* by a river or by floods.

**Dormant** A term used to describe a *volcano* which is not currently erupting. They differ from extinct volcanoes as dormant volcanoes are still considered likely to erupt in the future.

**Drainage basin** The area drained by a single river system, its boundary is marked by a *watershed* or *divide*.

**Drought** A long period of continuously low rainfall.

**Drumlin** A long, streamlined hillock composed of material deposited by a *glacier*. They often occur in groups known as swarms.

**Dune** A mound or ridge of sand, shaped, and often moved, by the wind. They are found in hot *deserts* and on low-lying coasts where onshore winds blow across sandy beaches.

**Dyke** A wall constructed in low-lying areas to contain floodwaters or protect from high tides.

## E

**Earthflow** The rapid movement of soil and other loose surface material down a slope, when saturated by water. Similar to a mudflow but not as fast-flowing, due to a lower percentage of water.

**Earthquake** Sudden movements of the Earth's *crust*, causing the ground to shake. Frequently occurring at *tectonic plate* margins. The shock, or series of shocks, spreads out from an *epicentre*.

**EC** The European Community (*see* EU).

**Ecosystem** A system of living organisms – plants and animals – interacting with their *environment*.

**ECOWAS** Economic Community of West African States. Established in 1975, it incorporates 16 West African states and aims to promote closer regional and economic co-operation.

**Element**
1 A constituent of the *climate* – *precipitation*, *humidity*, temperature, *atmospheric pressure* or wind.
2 A substance that cannot be separated into simpler substances by chemical means.

**El Niño** A climatic phenomenon, the El Niño effect occurs about 14 times each century and leads to major shifts in global air circulation. It is associated with unusually warm currents off the coasts of Peru, Ecuador and Chile. The anomaly can last for up to two years.

**Environment** The conditions created by the surroundings (both natural and artificial) within which an organism lives. In human geography the word includes the surrounding economic, cultural and social conditions.

**Eon (aeon)** Traditionally a long, but indefinite, period of *geological time*.

**Ephemeral** A non-permanent feature, often used in connection with seasonal rivers or lakes in dry areas.

**Epicentre** The point on the Earth's surface directly above the underground origin – or focus – of an *earthquake*.

**Equator** The line of *latitude* which lies equidistant between the North and South Poles.

**Erg** An extensive area of sand *dunes*, particularly in the Sahara Desert.

**Erosion** The processes which wear away the surface of the land. *Glaciers*, wind, rivers, waves and currents all carry debris which causes *erosion*. Some definitions also include *mass movement* due to gravity as an agent of erosion.

**Escarpment** A steep slope at the margin of a level, upland surface. In a landscape created by *folding*, escarpments (or scarps) frequently lie behind a more gentle backward slope.

**Esker** A narrow, winding ridge of sand and gravel deposited by streams of water flowing beneath or at the edge of a *glacier*.

**Erratic** A rock transported by a *glacier* and deposited some distance from its place of origin.

**Eustacy** A world-wide fall or rise in ocean levels.

**EU** The European Union. Established in 1965, it was formerly known as the EEC (European Economic Community) and then the EC (European Community). Its members are Austria, Belgium, Denmark, Finland, France, Germany, Greece, Ireland, Italy, Luxembourg, Netherlands, Portugal, Spain, Sweden and UK. It seeks to establish an integrated European common market and eventual federation.

**Evaporation** The process whereby a liquid or solid is turned into a gas or vapour. Also refers to the diffusion of water vapour into the *atmosphere* from exposed water surfaces such as lakes and seas.

**Evapotranspiration** The loss of moisture from the Earth's surface through a combination of *evaporation*, and *transpiration* from the leaves of plants.

**Evergreen** Plants with long-lasting leaves, which are not shed annually or seasonally.

**Exfoliation** A kind of *weathering* whereby scale-like flakes of rock are peeled or broken off by the development of salt crystals in water within the rocks. *Groundwater*, which contains dissolved salts, seeps to the surface and evaporates, precipitating a film of salt crystals, which expands causing fine cracks. As these grow, flakes of rock break off.

**Extrusive rock** *Igneous* rock formed when molten material (*magma*) pours forth at the Earth's surface and cools rapidly. It usually has a glassy texture.

## F

**Factionalism** The actions of one or more minority political group acting against the interests of the majority government.

**Fault** A fracture or crack in rock, where strains (*tectonic* movement) have caused blocks to move, vertically or laterally, relative to each other.

**Fauna** Collective name for the animals of a particular period of time, or region.

**Favela** Brazilian term for the shanty towns or self-built, temporary dwellings which have grown up around the edge of many South and Central American cities.

**Ferrel cell** A component in the global pattern of air circulation, which rises in the colder *latitudes* (60° N and S) and descends in warmer *latitudes* (30° N and S). The Ferrel cell forms part of the world's three-cell air circulation pattern, with the *Hadley* and Polar cells.

**Fissure** A deep crack in a rock or a *glacier*.

**Fjord** A deep, narrow inlet, created when the sea inundates the *U-shaped valley* created by a *glacier*.

**Flash flood** A sudden, short-lived rise in the water level of a river or stream, or surge of water down a dry river channel, or *wadi*, caused by heavy rainfall.

**Flax** A plant used to make linen.

**Flood plain** The broad, flat part of a river valley, adjacent to the river itself, formed by *sediment* deposited during flooding.

**Flora** The collective name for the plants of a particular period of time or region.

**Flow** The movement of a river within its banks, particularly in terms of the speed and volume of water.

**Fold** A bend in the rock *strata* of the Earth's *crust*, resulting from compression.

**Fossil** The remains, or traces, of a dead organism preserved in the Earth's *crust*.

**Fossil dune** A *dune* formed in a once-*arid* region which is now wetter. *Dunes* normally move with the wind, but in these cases vegetation makes them stable.

**Fossil fuel** Fuel – coal, natural gas or oil – composed of the fossilized remains of plants and animals.

**Front** The boundary between two *air masses*, which contrast sharply in temperature and *humidity*.

**Frontal depression** An area of low pressure caused by rising warm air. They are generally 600–1200 miles (1000–2000 km) in diameter. Within *depressions* there are both warm and cold fronts.

**Frost shattering** A form of *weathering* where water freezes in cracks, causing expansion. As temperatures fluctuate and the ice melts and refreezes, it eventually causes the rocks to shatter and fragments of rock to break off.

## G

**Gaucho** South American term for a stock herder or cowboy who works on the grassy *plains* of Paraguay, Uruguay and Argentina.

**Geological time-scale** The chronology of the Earth's history as revealed in its rocks. Geological time is divided into a number of periods: *eon*, era, period, epoch, age and chron (the shortest). These units are not of uniform length.

**Geosyncline** A concave fold (*syncline*) or large depression in the Earth's *crust*, extending hundreds of kilometres. This basin contains a deep layer of sediment, especially at its centre, from the land masses around it.

**Geothermal energy** Heat derived from hot rocks within the Earth's *crust* and resulting in hot springs, steam or hot rocks at the surface. The energy is generated by rock movements, and from the breakdown of radioactive elements occurring under intense pressure.

**GDP** Gross Domestic Product. The total value of goods and services produced by a country excluding income from foreign countries.

**Geyser** A jet of steam and hot water that intermittently erupts from vents in the ground in areas that are, or were, *volcanic*. Some geysers occasionally reach heights of 196 ft (60 m).

**Ghetto** An area of a city or region occupied by an overwhelming majority of people from one racial or religious group, who may be subject to persecution or containment.

**Glaciation** The growth of *glaciers* and *ice sheets*, and their impact on the landscape.

**Glacier** A body of ice moving downslope under the influence of gravity and consisting of compacted and frozen snow. A glacier is distinct from an *ice sheet*, which is wider and less confined by features of the landscape.

**Glacio-eustacy** A world-wide change in the level of the oceans, caused when the formation of *ice sheets* takes up water or when their melting returns water to the ocean. The formation of ice sheets in the *Pleistocene* epoch, for example, caused sea level to drop by about 320 ft (100 m).

**Glaciofluvial** To do with glacial *meltwater*, the landforms it creates and its processes; *erosion*, transportation and *deposition*. Glaciofluvial effects are more powerful and rapid where they occur within or beneath the *glacier*, rather than beyond its edge.

**Glacis** A gentle slope or *pediment*.

**Global warming** An increase in the average temperature of the Earth. At present the *greenhouse effect* is thought to contribute to this.

**GNP** Gross National Product. The total value of goods and services produced by a country.

**Gondwanaland** The *supercontinent* thought to have existed over 200 million years ago in the southern hemisphere. Gondwanaland is believed to have comprised today's Africa, Madagascar, Australia, parts of South America, *Antarctica* and the Indian subcontinent.

**Graben** A block of rock let down between two parallel *faults*. Where the graben occurs within a valley, the structure is known as a *rift valley*.

**Grease ice** Slicks of ice which form in *Antarctic* seas, when ice crystals are bonded together by wind and wave action.

**Greenhouse effect** A change in the temperature of the *atmosphere*. Short-wave solar radiation travels through the *atmosphere* unimpeded to the Earth's surface, whereas outgoing, long-wave terrestrial radiation is absorbed by materials that re-radiate it back to the Earth. Radiation trapped in this way, by water vapour, carbon dioxide and other 'greenhouse gases', keeps the Earth warm. As more *carbon dioxide* is released into the atmosphere by the burning of *fossil fuels*, the greenhouse effect may cause a global increase in temperature.

**Groundwater** Water that has seeped into the pores, cavities and cracks of rocks or into soil and water held in an *aquifer*.

**Gully** A deep, narrow channel eroded in the landscape by *ephemeral* streams.

**Guyot** A small, flat-topped submarine mountain, formed as a result of subsidence which occurs during *sea-floor spreading*.

**Gypsum** A soft mineral *compound* (hydrated calcium sulphate), used as the basis of many forms of plaster, including plaster of Paris.

## H

**Hadley cell** A large-scale component in the global pattern of air circulation. Warm air rises over the *Equator* and blows at high altitude towards the poles, sinking in subtropical regions (30° N and 30° S) and creating high pressure. The air then flows at the surface towards the *Equator* in the form of trade winds. There is one cell in each hemisphere. Named after G Hadley, who published his theory in 1735.

**Hamada** An Arabic word for a plateau of bare rock in a *desert*.

**Hanging valley** A tributary valley which ends suddenly, high above the bed of the main valley. The effect is found where the main valley has been more deeply eroded by a *glacier*, than has the tributary valley. A stream in a hanging valley will descend to the floor of the main valley as a waterfall or *cataract*.

**Headwards** The action of a river eroding back upstream, as opposed to the normal process of downstream *erosion*. Headwards erosion is often associated with *gullying*.

**Hoodos** Pinnacles of rock which have been worn away by *weathering* in *semi-arid* regions.

**Horst** A block of the Earth's *crust* which has been left upstanding by the sinking of adjoining blocks along fault lines.

**Hot spot** A region of the Earth's *crust* where high thermal activity occurs, often leading to volcanic eruptions. Hot spots often occur far from plate boundaries, but their movement is associated with *plate tectonics*.

**Humid equatorial** Rainy *climate* with no winter, where the coolest month is generally above 64°F (18°C).

**Humidity** The relative amount of moisture held in the Earth's *atmosphere*.

**Hurricane**
*1* A tropical *cyclone* occurring in the Caribbean and western North Atlantic.
*2* A wind of more than 65 knots (75 kmph).

**Hydro-electric power** Energy produced by harnessing the rapid movement of water down steep mountain slopes to drive turbines to generate electricity.

**Hydrolysis** The chemical breakdown of rocks in reaction with water, forming new compounds.

## I

**Ice Age** A period in the Earth's history when surface temperatures in the temperate *latitudes* were much lower and *ice sheets* expanded considerably. There have been *ice ages* from *Pre-Cambrian* times onwards. The most recent began two million years ago and ended 10,000 years ago.

**Ice cap** A permanent dome of ice in highland areas. The term ice cap is often seen as distinct from *ice sheet*, which denotes a much wider covering of ice; and is also used refer to the very extensive polar and Greenland ice caps.

**Ice floe** A large, flat mass of ice floating free on the ocean surface. It is usually formed after the break-up of winter ice by heavy storms.

**Ice sheet** A continuous, very thick layer of ice and snow. The term is usually used of ice masses which are continental in extent.

**Ice shelf** A floating mass of ice attached to the edge of a coast. The seaward edge is usually a sheer cliff up to 100 ft (30 m) high.

**Ice wedge** Massive blocks of ice up to 6.5 ft (2 m) wide at the top and extending 32 ft (10 m) deep. They are found in cracks in *polygonally-patterned* ground in *periglacial* regions.

**Iceberg** A large mass of ice in a lake or a sea, which has broken off from a floating *ice sheet* (an *ice shelf*) or from a *glacier*.

**Igneous rock** Rock formed when molten material, *magma*, from the hot, lower layers of the Earth's *crust*, cools, solidifies and crystallizes, either within the Earth's *crust* (*intrusive*) or on the surface (*extrusive*).

**IMF** International Monetary Fund. Established in 1944 as a UN agency, it contains 182 members around the world and is concerned with world monetary stability and economic development.

**Incised meander** A *meander* where the river, following its original course, cuts deeply into *bedrock*. This may occur when a mature, meandering river begins to erode its bed much more vigorously after the surrounding land has been uplifted.

**Indigenous** People, plants or animals native to a particular region.

**Infrastructure** The communications and services – roads, railways and telecommunications – necessary for the functioning of a country or region.

**Inselberg** An isolated, steep-sided hill, rising from a low *plain* in *semi-arid* and *savannah* landscapes. Inselbergs are usually composed of a rock, such as granite, which resists *erosion*.

**Interglacial** A period of global *climate*, between two *ice ages*, when temperatures rise and *ice sheets* and *glaciers* retreat.

**Intraplate volcano** A *volcano* which lies in the centre of one of the Earth's *tectonic plates*, rather than, as is more common, at its edge. They are thought to have been formed by a *hot spot*.

**Intrusion (intrusive igneous rock)** Rock formed when molten material, *magma*, penetrates existing rocks below the Earth's surface before cooling and solidifying. These rocks cool more slowly than extrusive rock and therefore tend to have coarser grains.

**Irrigation** The artificial supply of agricultural water to dry areas, often involving the creation of canals and the diversion of natural watercourses.

**Island arc** A curved chain of islands. Typically, such an arc fringes an ocean trench, formed at the margin between two *tectonic plates*. As one plate overrides another, *earthquakes* and volcanic activity are common and the islands themselves are often volcanic cones.

**Isostasy** The state of equilibrium which the Earth's *crust* maintains as its lighter and heavier parts float on the denser underlying mantle.

**Isthmus** A narrow strip of land connecting two larger landmasses or islands.

## J

**Jet stream** A narrow belt of westerly winds in the *troposphere*, at altitudes above 39,000 ft (12,000 m). Jet streams tend to blow more strongly in winter and include: the subtropical jet stream; the *polar* front jet stream in mid-*latitudes*; the *Arctic* jet stream; and the polar-night jet stream.

**Joint** A crack in a rock, formed where blocks of rock have not shifted relative to each other, as is the case with a *fault*. Joints are created by *folding*; by shrinkage in *igneous rock* as it cools or *sedimentary rock* as it dries out; and by the release of pressure in a rock mass when overlying materials are removed by *erosion*.

**Jute** A plant fibre used to make coarse ropes, sacks and matting.

## K

**Kame** A mound of stratified sand and gravel with steep sides, deposited in a *crevasse* by *meltwater* running over a *glacier*. When the ice retreats, this forms an undulating terrain of hummocks.

**Karst** A barren *limestone* landscape created by carbonic acid in streams and rainwater, in areas where *limestone* is close to the surface. Typical features include caverns, tower-like hills, *sinkholes* and flat limestone pavements.

**Kettle hole** A round hollow formed in a glacial deposit by a detached block of glacial ice, which later melted. They can fill with water to form kettle-lakes.

## L

**Lagoon** A shallow stretch of coastal salt-water behind a partial barrier such as a sandbank or *coral reef*. Lagoon is also used to describe the water encircled by an *atoll*.

**LAIA** Latin American Integration Association. Established in 1980, its members are Argentina, Bolivia, Brazil, Chile, Colombia, Ecuador, Mexico, Paraguay, Peru, Uruguay and Venezuela. It aims to promote economic co-operation between member states.

**Landslide** The sudden downslope movement of a mass of rock or earth on a slope, caused either by heavy rain; the impact of waves; an *earthquake* or human activity.

**Laterite** A hard red deposit left by *chemical weathering* in tropical conditions, and consisting mainly of oxides of iron and aluminium.

**Latitude** The angular distance from the *Equator*, to a given point on the Earth's surface. Imaginary lines of *latitude* running parallel to the Equator encircle the Earth, and are measured in degrees north or south of the Equator. The Equator is 0°, the poles 90° South and North respectively. Also called parallels.

**Laurasia** In the theory of *continental drift*, the northern part of the great *supercontinent* of *Pangaea*. Laurasia is said to consist of N America, Greenland and all of Eurasia north of the Indian subcontinent.

**Lava** The molten rock, *magma*, which erupts onto the Earth's surface through a *volcano*, or through a *fault* or crack in the Earth's *crust*. Lava refers to the rock both in its molten and in its later, solidified form.

**Leaching** The process whereby water dissolves minerals and moves them down through layers of soil or rock.

**Levée** A raised bank alongside the channel of a river. Levées are either human-made or formed in times of flood when the river overflows its channel, slows and deposits much of its *sediment* load.

**Lichen** An organism which is the symbiotic product of an algae and a fungus. Lichens form in tight crusts on stones and trees, and are resistant to extreme cold. They are often found in tundra regions.

**Lignite** Low-grade coal, also known as brown coal. Found in large deposits in eastern Europe.

**Limestone** A porous *sedimentary* rock formed from carbonate materials.

**Lingua franca** The language adopted as the common language between speakers whose native languages are different. This is common in former colonial states.

**Lithosphere** The rigid upper layer of the Earth, comprising the *crust* and the upper part of the *mantle*.

**Llanos** Vast grassland *plains* of northern South America.

**Loess** Fine-grained, yellow deposits of unstratified silts and sands. Loess is believed to be wind-carried *sediment* created in the last *Ice Age*. Some deposits may later have been redistributed by rivers. Loess-derived soils are of high quality, fertile and easy to work.

**Longitude** A division of the Earth which pinpoints how far east or west a given place is from the Prime Meridian (0°) which runs through the Royal Observatory at Greenwich, England (UK). Imaginary lines of longitude are drawn around the world from pole to pole. The world is divided into 360 degrees.

**Longshore drift** The transport of sand and silt along the coast, carried by waves hitting the beach at an angle.

## M

**Magma** Underground, molten rock, which is very hot and highly charged with gas. It is generated at great pressure, at depths 10 miles (16 km) or more below the Earth's surface. It can issue as *lava* at the Earth's surface or, more often, solidify below the surface as *intrusive igneous rock*.

**Mantle** The layer of the Earth between the *crust* and the *core*. It is about 1800 miles (2900 km) thick. The uppermost layer of the mantle is the soft, 125 mile (200 km) thick *asthenosphere* on which the more rigid *lithosphere* floats.

**Maquiladoras** Factories on the Mexico side of the Mexico/US border, which are allowed to import raw materials and components duty-free and use low-cost labour to assemble the goods, finally exporting them for sale in the US.

**Market gardening** The intensive growing of fruit and vegetables close to large local markets.

**Mass movement** Downslope movement of weathered materials such as rock, often helped by rainfall or glacial *meltwater*. Mass movement may be a gradual process or rapid, as in a *landslide* or rockfall.

**Massif** A single very large mountain or an area of mountains with uniform characteristics and clearly-defined boundaries.

**Meander** A loop-like bend in a river, which is found typically in the lower, mature reaches of a river but can form wherever the valley is wide and the slope gentle.

**Mediterranean climate** A temperate *climate* of hot, dry summers and warm, damp winters. This is typical of the western fringes of the world's continents in the warm temperate regions between *latitudes* of 30° and 40° (north and south).

**Meltwater** Water resulting from the melting of a *glacier* or *ice sheet*.

**Mesa** A broad, flat-topped hill, characteristic of *arid* regions.

**Mesosphere** A layer of the Earth's *atmosphere*, between the *stratosphere* and the *thermosphere*. Extending from about 25–50 miles (40–80 km) above the surface of the Earth.

**Mestizo** A person of mixed *Amerindian* and European origin.

**Metallurgy** The refining and working of metals.

**Metamorphic rocks** Rocks which have been altered from their original form, in terms of texture, composition and structure by intense heat, pressure, or by the introduction of new chemical substances – or a combination of more than one of these.

**Meteor** A body of rock, metal or other material, which travels through space at great speeds. Meteors are visible as they enter the Earth's *atmosphere* as shooting stars and fireballs.

**Meteorite** The remains of a *meteor* that has fallen to Earth.

**Meteoroid** A *meteor* which is still travelling in space, outside the Earth's *atmosphere*.

**Mezzogiorno** A term applied to the southern portion of Italy.

**Milankovitch hypothesis** A theory suggesting that there are a series of cycles which slightly alter the Earth's position when rotating about the Sun. The cycles identified all affect the amount of *radiation* the Earth receives at different *latitudes*. The theory is seen as a key factor in the cause of *ice ages*.

**Millet** A grain-crop, forming part of the staple diet in much of Africa.

**Mistral** A strong, dry, cold northerly or north-westerly wind, which blows from the Massif Central of France to the Mediterranean Sea. It is common in winter and its cold blasts can cause crop damage in the Rhône Delta, in France.

**Mohorovicic discontinuity (Moho)** The structural divide at the margin between the Earth's *crust* and the *mantle*. On average it is 20 miles (35 km) below the continents and 6 miles (10 km) below the oceans. The different densities of the *crust* and the mantle cause *earthquake* waves to accelerate at this point.

**Monarchy** A form of government in which the head of state is a single hereditary monarch. The monarch may be a mere figurehead, or may retain significant authority.

**Monsoon** A wind which changes direction bi-annually. The change is caused by the reversal of pressure over landmasses and the adjacent oceans. Because the inflowing moist winds bring rain, the term monsoon is also used to refer to the rains themselves. The term is derived from and most commonly refers to the seasonal winds of south and east Asia.

**Montaña** Mountain areas along the west coast of South America.

**Moraine** Debris, transported and deposited by a *glacier* or *ice sheet* in unstratified, mixed, piles of rock, boulders, pebbles and clay.

**Mountain-building** The formation of *fold* mountains by tectonic activity. Also known as orogeny, mountain-building often occurs on the margin where two *tectonic plates* collide. The periods when most mountain-building occurred are known as orogenic phases and lasted many millions of years.

**Mudflow** An *avalanche* of mud which occurs when a mass of soil is drenched by rain or melting snow. It is a type of *mass movement*, faster than an *earthflow* because it is lubricated by water.

## N

**Nappe** A mass of rocks which has been overfolded by repeated thrust *faulting*.

**NAFTA** The North American Free Trade Association. Established in 1994 between Canada, Mexico and the US to set up a free-trade zone.

**NASA** The National Aeronautics and Space Administration. It is a US government agency established in 1958 to develop manned and unmanned space programmes.

**NATO** The North Atlantic Treaty Organization. Established in 1949 to promote mutual defence and co-operation between its members, which are Belgium, Canada, Czech Republic, Denmark, France, Germany, Greece, Iceland, Italy, Luxembourg, the Netherlands, Norway, Portugal, Poland, Spain, Turkey, UK, and US.

**Nitrogen** The odourless, colourless gas which makes up 78% of the atmosphere. Within the soil, it is a vital nutrient for plants.

**Nomads (nomadic)** Wandering communities who move around in search of suitable pasture for their herds of animals.

**Nuclear fusion** A technique used to create a new nucleus by the merging of two lighter ones, resulting in the release of large quantities of energy.

## O

**Oasis** A fertile area in the midst of a *desert*, usually watered by an underground *aquifer*.

**Oceanic ridge** A mid-ocean ridge formed, according to the theory of *plate tectonics*, when plates drift apart and hot *magma* pours through to form new oceanic *crust*.

**Oligarchy** The government of a state by a small, exclusive group of people – such as an elite class or a family group.

**Onion-skin weathering** The *weathering* away or *exfoliation* of a rock or outcrop by the peeling off of surface layers.

**Oriente** A flatter region lying to the east of the Andes in South America.

**Outwash plain** *Glaciofluvial* material (typically clay, sand and gravel) carried beyond an ice sheet by *meltwater* streams, forming a broad, flat deposit.

**Oxbow lake** A crescent-shaped lake formed on a river *flood plain* when a river erodes the outside bend of a *meander*, making the neck of the *meander* narrower until the river cuts across the neck. The meander is cut off and is dammed off with sediment, creating an oxbow lake. Also known as a cut-off or mortlake.

**Oxidation** A form of *chemical weathering* where *oxygen* dissolved in water reacts with minerals in rocks – particularly iron – to form oxides. Oxidation causes brown or yellow staining on rocks, and eventually leads to the break down of the rock.

**Oxygen** A colourless, odourless gas which is one of the main constituents of the Earth's *atmosphere* and is essential to life on Earth.

**Ozone layer** A layer of enriched *oxygen* ($O_3$) within the stratosphere, mostly between 18–50 miles (30–80 km) above the Earth's surface. It is vital to the existence of life on Earth because it absorbs harmful shortwave ultraviolet radiation, while allowing beneficial longer wave ultraviolet radiation to penetrate to the Earth's surface.

## P

**Pacific Rim** The name given to the economically-dynamic countries bordering the Pacific Ocean.

**Pack ice** Ice masses more than 10 ft (3 m) thick which form on the sea surface and are not attached to a landmass.

**Pancake ice** Thin discs of ice, up to 8 ft (2.4 m) wide which form when slicks of *grease ice* are tossed together by winds and stormy seas.

**Pangaea** In the theory of continental drift, Pangaea is the original great land mass which, about 190 million years ago, began to split into Gondwanaland in the south and Laurasia in the north, separated by the Tethys Sea.

**Pastoralism** Grazing of livestock–usually sheep, goats or cattle. Pastoralists in many drier areas have traditionally been *nomadic*.

**Parallel** *see Latitude*.

**Peat** Ancient, partially-decomposed vegetation found in wet, boggy conditions where there is little *oxygen*. It is the first stage in the development of coal and is often dried for use as fuel. It is also used to improve soil quality.

**Pediment** A gently-sloping ramp of *bedrock* below a steeper slope, often found at mountain edges in *desert* areas, but also in other climatic zones. Pediments may include depositional elements such as *alluvial fans*.

**Peninsula** A thin strip of land surrounded on three of its sides by water. Large examples include Florida and Korea.

**Per capita** Latin term meaning 'for each person'.

**Periglacial** Regions on the edges of *ice sheets* or *glaciers* or, more commonly, cold regions experiencing intense frost action, *permafrost* or both. Periglacial climates bring long, freezing winters and short, mild summers.

**Permafrost** Permanently frozen ground, typical of *Arctic* regions. Although a layer of soil above the permafrost melts in summer, the melted water does not drain through the permafrost.

**Permeable rocks** Rocks through which water can seep, because they are either porous or cracked.

**Pharmaceuticals** The manufacture of medicinal drugs.

**Phreatic eruption** A volcanic eruption which occurs when *lava* combines with *groundwater*, superheating the water and causing a sudden emission of steam at the surface.

**Physical weathering (mechanical weathering)** The breakdown of rocks by physical, as opposed to chemical, processes. Examples include: changes in pressure or temperature; the effect of windblown sand; the pressure of growing salt crystals in cracks within rock; and the expansion and contraction of water within rock as it freezes and thaws.

**Pingo** A dome of earth with a core of ice, found in *tundra* regions. Pingos are formed either when *groundwater* freezes and expands, pushing up the land surface, or when trapped, freezing water in a lake expands and pushes up lake *sediments* to form the pingo dome.

**Placer** A belt of mineral-bearing rock *strata* lying at or close to the Earth's surface, from which minerals can be easily extracted.

**Plain** A flat, level region of land, often relatively low-lying.

**Plateau** A highland tract of flat land.

**Plate** *see Tectonic plates*.

**Plate tectonics** The study of *tectonic plates*, which helps to explain *continental drift*, mountain formation and volcanic activity. The movement of tectonic plates may be explained by the currents of rock rising and falling from within the Earth's *mantle*, as it heats up and then cools. The boundaries of the plates are known as plate margins and most mountains, *earthquakes* and *volcanoes* occur at these margins. Constructive margins are moving apart; destructive margins are crunching together and conservative margins are sliding past one another.

**Pleistocene** A period of *geological time* spanning from about 5.2 million years ago to 1.6 million years ago.

**Plutonic rock** *Igneous* rocks found deep below the surface. They are coarse-grained because they cooled and solidified slowly.

**Polar** The zones within the *Arctic* and *Antarctic* circles.

**Polje** A long, broad *depression* found in *karst* (*limestone*) regions

**Polygonal patterning** Typical ground patterning, found in areas where the soil is subject to severe frost action, often in *periglacial* regions.

**Porosity** A measure of how much water can be held within a rock or a soil. Porosity is measured as the percentage of holes or pores in a material, compared to its total volume. For example, the porosity of slate is less than 1%, whereas that of gravel is 25–35%.

**Prairies** Originally a French word for grassy *plains* with few or no trees.

**Pre-Cambrian** The earliest period of *geological time* dating from over 570 million years ago.

**Precipitation** The fall of moisture from the *atmosphere* onto the surface of the Earth, whether as dew, hail, rain, sleet or snow.

**Pyramidal peak** A steep, isolated mountain summit, formed when the back walls of three or more *cirques* are cut back and move towards each other. The cliffs around such a horned peak, or horn, are divided by sharp *arêtes*. The Matterhorn in the Swiss Alps is an example.

**Pyroclasts** Fragments of rock ejected during volcanic eruptions

## Q

**Quaternary** The current period of *geological time*, which started about 1.6 million years ago.

## R

**Radiation** The emission of energy in the form of particles or waves. Radiation from the sun includes heat, light, ultraviolet rays, gamma rays and X-rays. Only some of the solar energy radiated into space reaches the Earth.

**Rainforest** Dense forests in tropical zones with high rainfall, temperature and *humidity*. Strictly, the term applies to the equatorial rainforest in tropical lowlands with constant rainfall and no seasonal change. The Congo and Amazon basins are examples. The term is applied more loosely to lush forest in other climates. Within rainforests organic life is dense and varied: at least 40% of all plant and animal species are found here and there may be as many as 100 tree species per hectare.

**Rainshadow** An area which experiences low rainfall, because of its position on the leeward side of a mountain range.

**Reg** A large area of stony *desert*, where tightly-packed gravel lies on top of clayey sand. A reg is formed where the wind blows away the finer sand.

**Remote-sensing** Method of obtaining information about the *environment* using unmanned equipment, such as a satellite, which relays the information to a point where it is collected and used

**Resistance** The capacity of a rock to resist *denudation*, by processes such as *weathering* and *erosion*.

**Ria** A flooded *V-shaped river valley* or estuary, flooded by a rise in sea level (*eustacy*) or sinking land. It is shorter than a *fjord* and gets deeper as it meets the sea.

**Rift valley** A long, narrow depression in the Earth's *crust*, formed by the sinking of rocks between two *faults*.

**River channel** The trough which contains a river and is moulded by the flow of water within it

**Roche moutonée** A rock found in a glaciated valley. The side facing the flow of the *glacier* has been smoothed and rounded, while the other side has been left more rugged because the *glacier*, as it flows over it, has plucked out frozen fragments and carried them away.

**Runoff** Water draining from a land surface by flowing across it.

## S

**Sabkha** The floor of an isolated *depression* which occurs in an *arid environment* – usually covered by salt deposits and devoid of vegetation.

**SADC** Southern African Development Community. Established in 1992 to promote economic integration between its member states, which are Angola, Botswana, Lesotho, Malawi, Mauritius, Mozambique, Namibia, South Africa, Swaziland, Tanzania, Zambia and Zimbabwe.

**Salt plug** A rounded hill produced by the upward doming of rock *strata* caused by the movement of salt or other evaporite deposits under intense pressure.

**Sastrugi** Ice ridges formed by wind action. They lie parallel to the direction of the wind.

**Savannah** Open grassland found between the zone of *deserts*, and that of tropical *rainforests* in the tropics and subtropics. Scattered trees and shrubs are found in some kinds of savannah. A savannah *climate* usually has wet and dry seasons.

**Scarp** *see Escarpment*.

**Scree** Piles of rock fragments beneath a cliff or rock face, caused by mechanical *weathering*, especially *frost shattering*, where the expansion and contraction of freezing and thawing water within the rock, gradually breaks it up.

**Sea-floor spreading** The process whereby *tectonic plates* move apart, allowing hot *magma* to erupt and solidify. This forms a new sea floor and, ultimately, widens the ocean.

**Seamount** An isolated, submarine mountain or hill, probably of volcanic origin.

**Season** A period of time linked to regular changes in the weather, especially the intensity of solar *radiation*.

**Sediment** Grains of rock transported and deposited by rivers, sea, ice or wind.

**Sedimentary rocks** Rocks formed from the debris of pre-existing rocks or of organic material. They are found in many *environments* – on the ocean floor, on beaches, rivers and *deserts*. Organically-formed sedimentary rocks include coal and chalk. Other sedimentary rocks, such as flint, are formed by chemical processes. Most of these rocks contain *fossils*, which can be used to date them.

**Seif** A sand *dune* which lies parallel to the direction of the prevailing wind. Seifs form steep-sided ridges, sometimes extending for miles.

**Seismic activity** Movement within the Earth, such as an *earthquake* or *tremor*.

**Selva** A region of wet forest found in the Amazon Basin.

**Semi-arid, semi-desert** The *climate* and landscape which lies between *savannah* and *desert* or between savannah and a *mediterranean* climate. In semi-arid conditions there is a little more moisture than in a true *desert*; and more patches of drought-resistant vegetation can survive.

**Shale (marine shale)** A compacted *sedimentary rock*, with fine-grained particles. Marine shale is formed on the seabed. Fuel such as oil may be extracted from it.

**Sheetwash** Water which runs downhill in thin sheets without forming channels. It can cause *sheet erosion*.

**Sheet erosion** The washing away of soil by a thin film or sheet of water, known as *sheetwash*.

**Shield** A vast stable block of the Earth's *crust*, which has experienced little or no *mountain-building*.

**Sierra** The Spanish word for mountains.

**Sinkhole** A circular *depression* in a *limestone* region. They are formed by the collapse of an underground cave system or the *chemical weathering* of the *limestone*.

**Sisal** A plant-fibre used to make matting.

**Slash and burn** A farming technique involving the cutting down and burning of scrub forest, to create agricultural land. After a number of seasons this land is abandoned and the process is repeated. This practice is common in Africa and South America.

**Slip face** The steep leeward side of a sand *dune* or slope. Opposite side to a *back slope*.

**Soil** A thin layer of rock particles mixed with the remains of dead plants and animals. This occurs naturally on the surface of the Earth and provides a medium for plants to grow.

**Soil creep** The very gradual downslope movement of rock debris and soil, under the influence of gravity. This is a type of *mass movement*.

**Soil erosion** The wearing away of soil more quickly than it is replaced by natural processes. Soil can be carried away by wind as well as by water. Human activities, such as over-grazing and the clearing of land for farming, accelerate the process in many areas.

**Solar energy** Energy derived from the Sun. Solar energy is converted into other forms of energy. For example, the wind and waves, as well as the creation of plant material in photosynthesis, depend on solar energy.

**Solifluction** A kind of *soil creep*, where water in the surface layer has saturated the soil and rock debris which slips slowly downhill. It often happens where frozen top-layer deposits thaw, leaving frozen layers below them.

**Sorghum** A type of grass found in South America, similar to sugar cane. When refined it is used to make molasses.

**Spit** A thin linear deposit of sand or shingle extending from the sea shore. Spits are formed as angled waves shift sand along the beach, eventually extending a ridge of sand beyond a change in the angle of the coast. Spits are common where the coastline bends, especially at estuaries.

**Squash** A type of edible gourd.

**Stack** A tall, isolated pillar of rock near a coastline, created as wave action erodes away the adjacent rock.

**Stalactite** A tapering cylinder of mineral deposit, hanging from the roof of a cave in a *karst* area. It is formed by calcium carbonate, dissolved in water, which drips through the roof of a *limestone* cavern.

**Stalagmite** A cone of calcium carbonate, similar to a *stalactite*, rising from the floor of a *limestone* cavern and formed when drops of water fall from the roof of a *limestone* cave. If the water has dripped from a *stalactite* above the stalagmite, the two may join to form a continuous pillar.

**Staple crop** The main crop on which a country is economically and or physically reliant. For example, the major crop grown for large-scale local consumption in South Asia is rice.

**Steppe** Large areas of dry grassland in the northern hemisphere – particularly found in southeast Europe and central Asia.

**Strata** The plural of stratum, a distinct, virtually horizontal layer of deposited material, lying parallel to other layers.

**Stratosphere** A layer of the *atmosphere*, above the *troposphere*, extending from about 7–30 miles (11–50 km) above the Earth's surface. In the lower part of the stratosphere, the temperature is relatively stable and there is little moisture.

**Strike-slip fault** Occurs where plates move sideways past each other and blocks of rocks move horizontally in relation to each other, not up or down as in normal *faults*.

**Subduction zone** A region where two *tectonic plates* collide, forcing one beneath the other. Typically, a dense oceanic plate dips below a lighter continental plate, melting in the heat of the *asthenosphere*. This is why the zone is also called a destructive margins (*see Plate tectonics*). These zones are characterized by *earthquakes*, volcanoes, *mountain–building* and the development of oceanic trenches and *island arcs*.

**Submarine canyon** A steep-sided valley, which extends along the *continental shelf* to the ocean floor. Often formed by *turbidity currents*.

**Submarine fan** Deposits of silt and *alluvium*, carried by large rivers forming great fan-shaped deposits on the ocean floor.

**Subsistence agriculture** An agricultural practice, whereby enough food is produced to support the farmer and his dependents, but not providing any surplus to generate an income.

**Subtropical** A term applied loosely to *climates* which are nearly tropical or tropical for a part of the year – areas north or south of the *tropics* but outside the *temperate zone*.

**Supercontinent** A large continent that breaks up to form smaller continents or which forms when smaller continents merge. In the theory of *continental drift*, the supercontinents are *Pangaea*, *Gondwanaland* and *Laurasia*.

**Sustainable development** An approach to development, applied to economies across the world which exploit natural resources without destroying them or the *environment*.

**Syncline** A basin-shaped downfold in rock *strata*, created when the *strata* are compressed, for example where *tectonic plates* collide.

## T

**Tableland** A highland area with a flat or gently undulating surface.

**Taiga** The belt of *coniferous* forest found in the north of Asia and North America. The conifers are adapted to survive low temperatures and long periods of snowfall.

**Tarn** A Scottish term for a small mountain lake, usually found at the head of a *glacier*.

**Tectonic plates** Plates, or tectonic plates, are the rigid slabs which form the Earth's outer shell, the *lithosphere*. Eight big plates and several smaller ones have been identified.

**Temperate** A moderate *climate* without extremes of temperature, typical of the mid-*latitudes* between the *tropics* and the *polar* circles.

**Theocracy** A state governed by religious laws – today Iran is the world's largest theocracy.

**Thermokarst** Subsidence created by the thawing of ground ice in *periglacial* areas, creating depressions.

**Thermosphere** A layer of the Earth's *atmosphere* which lies above the *mesophere*, about 60–300 miles (100–500 km) above the Earth

**Terraces** Steps cut into steep slopes to create flat surfaces for cultivating crops. They also help reduce soil *erosion* on unconsolidated slopes. They are most common in heavily-populated parts of Southeast Asia.

**Till** Unstratified glacial deposits or drift left by a *glacier* or *ice sheet*. Till includes mixtures of clay, sand, gravel and boulders.

**Topography** The typical shape and features of a given area such as land height and terrain.

**Tombolo** A large sand *spit* which attaches part of the mainland to an island.

**Tornado** A violent, spiralling windstorm, with a centre of very low pressure. Wind speeds reach 200 mph (320 kmph) and there is often thunder and heavy rain.

**Transform fault** In *plate tectonics*, a *fault* of continental scale, occurring where two plates slide past each other, staying close together for example, the San Andreas Fault, USA. The jerky, uneven movement creates *earthquakes* but does not destroy or add to the Earth's *crust*

**Transpiration** The loss of water vapour through the pores (or stomata) of plants. The process helps to return moisture to the *atmosphere*.

**Trap** An area of fine-grained *igneous rock* which has been extruded and cooled on the Earth's surface in stages, forming a series of steps or terraces.

**Treeline** The line beyond which trees cannot grow, dependent on *latitude* and altitude, as well as local factors such as soil.

**Tremor** A slight *earthquake*.

**Trench (oceanic trench)** A long, deep trough in the ocean floor, formed, according to the theory of *plate tectonics*, when two plates collide and one dives under the other, creating a *subduction zone*.

**Tropics** The zone between the *Tropic of Cancer* and the *Tropic of Capricorn* where the *climate* is hot. Tropical climate is also applied to areas rather further north and south of the *Equator* where the climate is similar to that of the true tropics.

**Tropic of Cancer** A line of *latitude* or imaginary circle round the Earth, lying at 23° 28' N.

**Tropic of Capricorn** A line of *latitude* or imaginary circle round the Earth, lying at 23° 28' S.

**Troposphere** The lowest layer of the Earth's *atmosphere*. From the surface, it reaches a height of between 4–10 miles (7–16 km). It is the most turbulent zone of the atmosphere and accounts for the generation of most of the world's weather. The layer above it is called the *stratosphere*.

**Tsunami** A huge wave created by shock waves from an *earthquake* under the sea. Reaching speeds of up to 600 mph (960 kmph), the wave may increase to heights of 50 ft (15 m) on entering coastal waters; and it can cause great damage.

**Tundra** The treeless *plains* of the *Arctic Circle*, found south of the *polar* region of permanent ice and snow, and north of the belt of *coniferous* forests known as *taiga*. In this region of long, very cold winters, vegetation is usually limited to mosses, *lichens*, sedges and rushes, although flowers and dwarf shrubs blossom in the brief summer.

**Turbidity current** An oceanic feature. A turbidity current is a mass of *sediment*-laden water which has substantial erosive power. Turbidity currents are thought to contribute to the formation of *submarine canyons*.

**Typhoon** A kind of *hurricane* (or tropical cyclone) bringing violent winds and heavy rain, a typhoon can do great damage. They occur in the South China Sea, especially around the Philippines.

## U

**U-shaped valley** A river valley that has been deepened and widened by a *glacier*. They are characteristically flat-bottomed and steep-sided and generally much deeper than river valleys.

**UN** United Nations. Established in 1945, it contains 188 nations and aims to maintain international peace and security, and promote co-operation over economic, social, cultural and humanitarian problems.

**UNICEF** United Nations Children's Fund. A UN organization set up to promote family and child related programmes.

**Urstromtäler** A German word used to describe *meltwater* channels which flowed along the front edge of the advancing *ice sheet* during the last Ice Age, 18,000–20,000 years ago.

## V

**V-shaped valley** A typical valley eroded by a river in its upper course.

**Virgin rainforest** Tropical *rainforest* in its original state, untouched by human activity such as logging, clearance for agriculture, settlement or road building.

**Viticulture** The cultivation of grapes for wine.

**Volcano** An opening or vent in the Earth's *crust* where molten rock, *magma*, erupts. Volcanoes tend to be conical but may also be a crack in the Earth's surface or a hole blasted through a mountain. The magma is accompanied by other materials such as gas, steam and fragments of rock, or *pyroclasts*. They tend to occur on destructive or constructive *tectonic plate* margins.

## W-Z

**Wadi** The dry bed left by a torrent of water. Also classified as a *ephemeral* stream, found in *arid* and *semi-arid* regions, which are subject to sudden and often severe flash flooding.

**Warm humid climate** A rainy climate with warm summers and mild winters.

**Water cycle** The continuous circulation of water between the Earth's surface and the *atmosphere*. The processes include *evaporation* and *transpiration* of moisture into the atmosphere, and its return as *precipitation*, some of which flows into lakes and oceans.

**Water table** The upper level of *groundwater* saturation in permeable rock *strata*.

**Watershed** The dividing line between one *drainage basin* – an area where all streams flow into a single river system – and another. In the US, watershed also means the whole drainage basin of a single river system – its catchment area.

**Waterspout** A rotating column of water in the form of cloud, mist and spray which form on open water. Often has the appearance of a small *tornado*.

**Weathering** The decay and break-up of rocks at or near the Earth's surface, caused by water, wind, heat or ice, organic material or the *atmosphere*. *Physical weathering* includes the effects of frost and temperature changes. Biological weathering includes the effects of plant roots, burrowing animals and the acids produced by animals, especially as they decay after death. *Carbonation* and *hydrolysis* are among many kinds of *chemical weathering*.

# Geographical names

The following glossary lists all geographical terms occurring on the maps and in main-entry names in the Index-Gazetteer. These terms may precede, follow or be run together with the proper element of the name; where they precede it the term is reversed for indexing purposes - thus Poluostrov Yamal is indexed as Yamal, Poluostrov.

## Key

Geographical term
*Language*, Term

### A

Å *Danish, Norwegian*, River
Áb *Persian*, River
Adrar *Berber*, Mountains
Agía, Ágios *Greek*, Saint
Air *Indonesian*, River
Akrotírio *Greek*, Cape, point
Alpen *German*, Alps
Alt- *German*, Old
Altiplanicie *Spanish*, Plateau
Älv, -älven *Swedish*, River
-ån *Swedish*, River
Anse *French*, Bay
'Aqabat *Arabic*, Pass
Archipiélago *Spanish*, Archipelago
Arcipelago *Italian*, Archipelago
Arquipélago *Portuguese*, Archipelago
Arrecife(s) *Spanish*, Reef(s)
Aru *Tamil*, River
Augstiene *Latvian*, Upland
Auk#tuma *Lithuanian*, Upland
Aust- *Norwegian*, Eastern
Avtonomnyy Okrug *Russian*, Autonomous district
Áw *Kurdish*, River
'Ayn *Arabic*, Spring, well
'Ayoûn *Arabic*, Wells

### B

Baelt *Danish*, Strait
Bahía *Spanish*, Bay
Baír *Arabic*, River
Baía *Portuguese*, Bay
Baie *French*, Bay
Bañado *Spanish*, Marshy land
Bandao *Chinese*, Peninsula
Banjaran *Malay*, Mountain range
Barajı *Turkish*, Dam
Barragem *Portuguese*, Reservoir
Bassin *French*, Basin
Batang *Malay*, Stream
Beinn, Ben *Gaelic*, Mountain
-berg *Afrikaans, Norwegian*, Mountain
Besar *Indonesian, Malay*, Big
Birkat, Birket *Arabic*, Lake, well,
Boêazı *Turkish*, Strait, defile
Boka *Croatian, Serbian*, Bay
Bol'sh-aya, -iye, -oy, -oye *Russian*, Big
Botigh(i) *Uzbek*, Depression basin
-bre(en) *Norwegian*, Glacier
Bredning *Danish*, Bay
Bucht *German*, Bay
Bugt(en) *Danish*, Bay
Búiayrat *Arabic*, Lake, reservoir
Buieiret *Arabic*, Lake
Bukit *Malay*, Mountain
-bukta *Norwegian*, Bay
bukten *Swedish*, Bay
Bulag *Mongolian*, Spring
Bulak *Uighur*, Spring
Burnu *Turkish*, Cape, point
Buuraha *Somali*, Mountains

### C

Cabo *Portuguese*, Cape
Caka *Tibetan*, Salt lake
Canal *Spanish*, Channel
Cap *French*, Cape
Capo *Italian*, Cape, headland
Cascada *Portuguese*, Waterfall
Cayo(s) *Spanish*, Islet(s), rock(s)
Cerro *Spanish*, Hill
Chaîne *French*, Mountain range
Chapada *Portuguese*, Hills, upland
Chau *Cantonese*, Island
Cháy *Turkish*, River
Chhâk *Cambodian*, Bay
Chhu *Tibetan*, River
-chôsuji *Korean*, Reservoir
Chott *Arabic*, Depression, salt lake
Chûli *Uzbek*, Grassland, steppe
Ch'ün-tao *Chinese*, Island group
Chuôr Phnum *Cambodian*, Mountains
Ciudad *Spanish*, City, town

Co *Tibetan*, Lake
Colline(s) *French*, Hill(s)
Cordillera *Spanish*, Mountain range
Costa *Spanish*, Coast
Côte *French*, Coast
Coxilha *Portuguese*, Mountains
Cuchilla *Spanish*, Mountains

### D

Daban *Mongolian, Uighur*, Pass
Daêi *Azerbaijani, Turkish*, Mountain
Daêları *Azerbaijani, Turkish*, Mountains
-dake *Japanese*, Peak
-dal(en) *Norwegian*, Valley
Danau *Indonesian*, Lake
Dao *Chinese*, Island
Åao *Vietnamese*, Island
Daryá *Persian*, River
Daryácheh *Persian*, Lake
Dasht *Persian*, Desert, plain
Dawíat *Arabic*, Bay
Denizi *Turkish*, Sea
Dere *Turkish*, Stream
Desierto *Spanish*, Desert
Dili *Azerbaijani*, Spit
-do *Korean*, Island
Dooxo *Somali*, Valley
Düzü *Azerbaijani*, Steppe
-dwíp *Bengali*, Island

### E

-eilanden *Dutch*, Islands
Embalse *Spanish*, Reservoir
Ensenada *Spanish*, Bay
Erg *Arabic*, Dunes
Estany *Catalan*, Lake
Estero *Spanish*, Inlet
Estrecho *Spanish*, Strait
Étang *French*, Lagoon, lake
-ey *Icelandic*, Island
Ezero *Bulgarian, Macedonian*, Lake
Ezers *Latvian*, Lake

### F

Feng *Chinese*, Peak
-fjella *Norwegian*, Mountain
Fjord *Danish*, Fjord
-fjord(en) *Danish, Norwegian, Swedish*, fjord
-fjördhur *Icelandic*, Fjord
Fleuve *French*, River
Fliegu *Maltese*, Channel
-fljór *Icelandic*, River
-flói *Icelandic*, Bay
Forêt *French*, Forest

### G

-gan *Japanese*, Rock
-gang *Korean*, River
Ganga *Hindi, Nepali, Sinhala*, River
Gaoyuan *Chinese*, Plateau
Garagumy *Turkmen*, Sands
-gawa *Japanese*, River
-gebirge *German*, Mountain range
Ghadír *Arabic*, Well
Ghubbat *Arabic*, Bay
Gjiri *Albanian*, Bay
Gol *Mongolian*, River
Golfe *French*, Gulf
Golfo *Italian, Spanish*, Gulf
Göl(ü) *Turkish*, Lake
Golyam, -a *Bulgarian*, Big
Gora *Russian, Croatian, Serbian*, Mountain
Góra *Polish*, mountain
Gory *Russian*, Mountain
Gryada *Russian*, ridge
Guba *Russian*, Bay
-gundo *Korean*, island group
Gunung *Malay*, Mountain

### H

Íadd *Arabic*, Spit
-haehyôp *Korean*, Strait
Haff *German*, Lagoon
Hai *Chinese*, Bay, lake, sea
Haixia *Chinese*, Strait
Íammádah *Arabic*, Desert
Íammádat *Arabic*, Rocky plateau
Hámún *Persian*, Lake
-hantó *Japanese*, Peninsula
Hara *Belorusian*, Mountain
Har, Haré *Hebrew*, Mountain
Íarrat *Arabic*, Lava-field
Hav(et) *Danish, Swedish*, Sea
Hawr *Arabic*, Lake
Háyk' *Amharic*, Lake
He *Chinese*, River
-hegység *Hungarian*, Mountain range
Heide *German*, Heath, moorland
Helodrano *Malagasy*, Bay
Higashi- *Japanese*, East(ern)
Ií§á' *Arabic*, Well
Hka *Burmese*, River
-ho *Korean*, Lake
/olot *Hebrew*, Dunes
Hora *Bulgarian, Czech, Slovene, Ukrainian*, Mountain

Hory *Czech, Ukrainian* Mountain
Hrada *Belorusian*, Mountain, ridge
Hsi *Chinese*, River
Hu *Chinese*, Lake
Huk *Danish*, Point

### I

Île(s) *French*, Island(s)
Ilha(s) *Portuguese*, Island(s)
Ilhéu(s) *Portuguese*, Islet(s)
-isen *Norwegian*, Ice shelf
Imeni *Russian*, In the name of
Inish- *Gaelic*, Island
Insel(n) *German*, Island(s)
Irmaêi, Irmak *Turkish*, River
Isla(s) *Spanish*, Island(s)
Isola (Isole) *Italian*, Island(s)

### J

Jabal *Arabic*, Mountain
Jál *Arabic*, Ridge
-järv *Estonian*, Lake
-järvi *Finnish*, Lake
Jazá'ir *Arabic*, Islands
Jazírat *Arabic*, Island
Jazíreh *Persian*, Island
Jebel *Arabic*, Mountain
Jezero *Croatian, Serbian*, Lake
Jezioro *Polish*, Lake
Jiang *Chinese*, River
-jima *Japanese*, Island
Jiªní *Czech*, Southern
-jógi *Estonian*, River
-joki *Finnish*, River
-jökull *Icelandic*, Glacier
Jún *Arabic*, Bay
Juzur *Arabic*, Islands

### K

Kaikyó *Japanese*, Strait
-kaise *Lappish*, Mountain
Kali *Nepali*, River
Kalnas *Lithuanian*, Mountain
Kalns *Latvian*, Mountain
Kang *Chinese*, Harbour
Kangri *Tibetan*, Mountain(s)
Kaôh *Cambodian*, Island
Kapp *Norwegian*, Cape
Káto *Greek*, Lower
Kavír *Persian*, Desert
K'edi *Georgian*, Mountain range
Kediet *Arabic*, Mountain
Kepi *Albanian*, Cape, point
Kepulauan *Indonesian, Malay*, Island group
Khalíg, Khalíj *Arabic*, Gulf
Khawr *Arabic*, Inlet
Khola *Nepali*, River
Khrebet *Russian*, Mountain range
Ko *Thai*, Island
-ko *Japanese*, Inlet, lake
Kólpos *Greek*, Bay
-kopf *German*, Peak
Körfãzi *Azerbaijani*, Bay
Körfezi *Turkish*, Bay
Kõrgustik *Estonian*, Upland
Kosa *Russian, Ukrainian*, Spit
Koshi *Nepali*, River
Kou *Chinese*, River-mouth
Kowtal *Persian*, Pass
Kray *Russian*, Region, territory
Kryazh *Russian*, Ridge
Kuduk *Uighur*, Well
Kúh(há) *Persian*, Mountain(s)
-kul' *Russian*, Lake
Kûl(i) *Tajik, Uzbek*, Lake
-kundo *Korean*, Island group
-kysten *Norwegian*, Coast
Kyun *Burmese*, Island

### L

Laaq *Somali*, Watercourse
Lac *French*, Lake
Lacul *Romanian*, Lake
Lagh *Somali*, Stream
Lago *Italian, Portuguese, Spanish*, Lake
Lagoa *Portuguese*, Lagoon
Laguna *Italian, Spanish*, Lagoon, lake
Laht *Estonian*, Bay
Laut *Indonesian*, Sea
Lembalemba *Malagasy*, Plateau
Lerr *Armenian*, Mountain
Lerrnashght'a *Armenian*, Mountain range
Les *Czech*, Forest
Lich *Armenian*, Lake
Liehtao *Chinese*, Island group
Liqeni *Albanian*, Lake
Límni *Greek*, Lake
Ling *Chinese*, Mountain range
Llano *Spanish*, Plain, prairie
Lumi *Albanian*, River
Lyman *Ukrainian*, Estuary

### M

Madínat *Arabic*, City, town
Mae Nam *Thai*, River
-mägi *Estonian*, Hill
Maja *Albanian*, Mountain
Mal *Albanian*, Mountains

Mal-aya, -oye, -yy *Russian*, Small
-man *Korean*, Bay
Mar *Spanish*, Sea
Marios *Lithuanian*, Lake
Massif *French*, Mountains
Meer *German*, Lake
-meer *Dutch*, Lake
Melkosopochnik *Russian*, Plain
-meri *Estonian*, Sea
Mifra∞ *Hebrew*, Bay
Minami- *Japanese*, South(ern)
-misaki *Japanese*, Cape, point
Montagne(s) *French*, Mountain(s)
Montañas *Spanish*, Mountains
Mont(s) *French*, Mountain(s)
Monte *Italian, Portuguese*, Mountain
More *Russian*, Sea
Mörön *Mongolian*, River
Munkhafaç *Arabic*, Depression
Mys *Russian*, Cape, point

### N

-nada *Japanese*, Open stretch of water
Nadi *Bengali*, River
Nagor'ye *Russian*, Upland
Najal *Hebrew*, River
Nahr *Arabic*, River
Nam *Laotian*, River
Namakzár *Persian*, Salt desert
Né-a, -on, -os *Greek*, New
Nedre- *Norwegian*, Lower
-neem *Estonian*, Cape, point
Nehri *Turkish*, River
-nes *Norwegian*, Cape, point
Nevado *Spanish*, Mountain (snow-capped)
Nieder- *German*, Lower
Nishi- *Japanese*, West(ern)
-nísi *Greek*, Island
Nisoi *Greek*, Islands
Nizhn-eye, -iy, -iye, -yaya *Russian*, Lower
Nizmennost' *Russian*, Lowland, plain
Nord *Danish, French, German*, North
Norte *Portuguese, Spanish*, North
Nos *Bulgarian*, Point, spit
Nosy *Malagasy*, Island
Nov-a, -i, -o, *Russian, Croatian, Serbian*, New
Nov-aya, -o, -oye, -yy, -yye *Russian*, New
Now-a, -e, -y *Polish*, New
Nur *Mongolian*, Lake
Nuruu *Mongolian*, Mountains
Nuur *Mongolian*, Lake
Nyzovyna *Ukrainian*, Lowland, plain

### O

-ø *Danish*, Island
Ober- *German*, Upper
Oblast' *Russian*, Province
Órmos *Greek*, Bay
Orol(i) *Uzbek*, Island
Øster- *Norwegian*, Eastern
Ostrov(a) *Russian*, Island(s)
Otok *Croatian, Serbian*, Island
Oued *Arabic*, Watercourse
-oy *Faeroese*, Island
-øy(a) *Norwegian*, Island
Oya *Sinhala*, River
Ozero *Russian, Ukrainian*, Lake

### P

Passo *Italian*, Pass
Pegunungan *Indonesian, Malay*, Mountain range
Pélagos *Greek*, Sea
Pendi *Chinese*, Basin
Penisola *Italian*, Peninsula
Pertuis *French*, Strait
Peski *Russian*, Sands
Phanom *Thai*, Mountain
Phou *Laotian*, Mountain
Pi *Chinese*, Point
Pic *Catalan, French*, Peak
Pico *Portuguese, Spanish*, Peak
-piggen *Danish*, Peak
Pik *Russian*, Peak
Pivostriv *Ukrainian*, Peninsula
Planalto *Portuguese*, Plateau
Planina, Planini *Bulgarian, Macedonian, Croatian, Serbian*, Mountain range
Plato *Russian*, Plateau
Ploskogor'ye *Russian*, Upland
Poluostrov *Russian*, Peninsula
Ponta *Portuguese*, Point
Porthmós *Greek*, Strait
Pótamos *Greek*, River
Presa *Spanish*, Dam
Prokhod *Bulgarian*, Pass
Proliv *Russian*, Strait
Pulau *Indonesian Malay*, Island
Pulu *Malay*, Island
Punta *Spanish*, Point
Pushcha *Belorusian*, Forest
Puszcza *Polish*, Forest

### Q

Qá' *Arabic*, Depression
Qalamat *Arabic*, Well
Qatorkûh(i) *Tajik*, Mountain
Qiuling *Chinese*, Hills
Qolleh *Persian*, Mountain
Qu *Tibetan*, Stream
Quan *Chinese*, Well
Qulla(i) *Tajik*, Peak
Qundao *Chinese*, Island group

### R

Raas *Somali*, Cape
-rags *Latvian*, Cape
Ramlat *Arabic*, Sands
Ra's *Arabic*, Cape, headland, point
Ravnina *Bulgarian, Russian*, Plain
Récif *French*, Reef
Recife *Portuguese*, Reef
Reka *Bulgarian*, River
Represa (Rep.) *Portuguese, Spanish*, Reservoir
Reshteh *Persian*, Mountain range
Respublika *Russian*, Republic, first-order administrative division
Respublika(si) *Uzbek*, Republic, first-order administrative divis on
-retsugan *Japanese*, Chain of rocks
-rettó *Japanese*, Island chain
Riacho *Spanish*, Stream
Riban' *Malagasy*, Mountains
Rio *Portuguese*, River
Río *Spanish*, River
Riu *Catalan*, River
Rivier *Dutch*, River
Rivière *French*, River
Ród *Dari*, River
Rt *Croatian, Serbian*, Point
Rúd *Persian*, River
Rúdkháneh *Persian*, River
Rudohorie *Slovak*, Mountains
Ruisseau *French*, Stream

### S

-saar *Estonian*, Island
-saari *Finnish*, Island
Sabkhat *Arabic*, Salt marsh
Ságar(a) *Hindi*, Lake, reservoir
fiairá' *Arabic*, Desert
Saint, Sainte *French*, Saint
Salar *Spanish*, Salt-pan
Salto *Portuguese, Spanish*, Waterfall
Samudra *Sinhala*, Reservoir
-san *Japanese, Korean*, Mountain
-sanchi *Japanese*, Mountains
-sandur *Icelandic*, Beach
Sankt *German, Swedish*, Saint
-sanmaek *Korean*, Mountain range
-sanmyaku *Japanese*, Mountain range
San, Santa, Santo *Italian, Portuguese, Spanish*, Saint
São *Portuguese*, Saint
Sarír *Arabic*, Desert
Sebkha, Sebkhet *Arabic*, Depression, salt marsh
Sedlo *Czech*, Pass
See *German*, Lake
Selat *Indonesian*, Strait
Selatan *Indonesian*, Southern
-selkä *Finnish*, Lake, ridge
Selseleh *Persian*, Mountain range
Serra *Portuguese*, Mountain
Serranía *Spanish*, Mountain
-seto *Japanese*, Channel, strait
Sever-naya, -noye, -nyy, -o *Russian*, Northern
Sha'íb *Arabic*, Watercourse
Shákh *Kurdish*, Mountain
Shamo *Chinese*, Desert
Shan *Chinese*, Mountain(s)
Shankou *Chinese*, Pass
Shanmo *Chinese*, Mountain range
Sha√√ *Arabic*, Distributary
Shet' *Amharic*, River
Shi *Chinese*, Municipality
-shima *Japanese*, Island
Shiqqat *Arabic*, Depression
-shotó *Japanese*, Group of islands
Shuiku *Chinese*, Reservoir
Shûrkhog(i) *Uzbek*, Salt marsh
Sierra *Spanish*, Mountains
Sint *Dutch*, Saint
-sjø(en) *Norwegian*, Lake
-sjön *Swedish*, Lake
Solonchak *Russian*, Salt lake
Solonchakovyye Vpadiny *Russian*, Salt basin, wetlands
Sòn *Vietnamese*, Mountain
Sóng *Vietnamese*, River
Sør- *Norwegian*, Southern
-spitze *German*, Peak
Star-á, -é *Czech*, Old
Star-aya, -oye, -yy, -yye *Russian*, Old
Stenó *Greek*, Strait
Step' *Russian*, Steppe
‹tít *Slovak*, Peak
Stœng *Cambodian*, River
Stolovaya Strana *Russian*, Plateau
Stredné *Slovak*, Middle
Stüední *Czech*, Middle
Stretto *Italian*, Strait
Su Anbarı *Azerbaijani*, Reservoir
-suidó *Japanese*, Channel, strait
Sund *Swedish*, Sound, strait
Sungai *Indonesian, Malay*, River
Suu *Turkish*, River

### T

Tal *Mongolian*, Plain
Tandavan' *Malagasy*, Mountain range
Tangorombohitr' *Malagasy*, Mountain massif
Tanjung *Indonesian, Malay*, Cape, point
Tao *Chinese*, Island
Òaraq *Arabic*, Hills
Tassili *Berber*, Mountain, plateau
Tau *Russian*, Mountain(s)
Taungdan *Burmese*, Mountain range
Techniti Límni *Greek*, Reservoir
Tekojärvi *Finnish*, Reservoir
Teluk *Indonesian, Malay*, Bay
Tengah *Indonesian*, Middle
Terara *Amharic*, Mountain
Timur *Indonesian*, Eastern
-tind(an) *Norwegian*, Peak
Tizma(si) *Uzbek*, Mountain range, ridge
-tó *Japanese*, island
Tog *Somali*, Valley
-tóge *Japanese*, pass
Togh(i) *Uzbek*, mountain
Tônlé *Cambodian*, Lake
Top *Dutch*, Peak
-tunturi *Finnish*, Mountain
Òuráq *Arabic*, hills
Tur'at *Arabic*, Channel

### U

Udde(n) *Swedish*, Cape, point
'Uqlat *Arabic*, Well
Utara *Indonesian*, Northern
Uul *Mongolian*, Mountains

### V

Väin *Estonian*, Strait
Vallée *French*, Valley
Varful *Romanian*, Peak
-vatn *Icelandic*, Lake
-vatnet *Norwegian*, Lake
Velayat *Turkmen*, Province
-vesi *Finnish*, Lake
Vestre- *Norwegian*, Western
-vidda *Norwegian*, Plateau
-vík *Icelandic*, Bay
-viken *Swedish*, Bay, inlet
Vinh *Vietnamese*, Bay
Víztárloló *Hungarian*, Reservoir
Vodaskhovishcha *Belorusian*, Reservoir
Vodokhranilishche (Vdkhr.) *Russian*, Reservoir
Vodoskhovyshche (Vdskh.) *Ukrainian*, Reservoir
Volcán *Spanish*, Volcano
Vostochn-o, yy *Russian*, Eastern
Vozvyshennost' *Russian*, Upland, plateau
Vozyera *Belorusian*, Lake
Vpadina *Russian*, Depression
Vrchovina *Czech*, Mountains
Vrh *Croat, Slovene*, Peak
Vychodné *Slovak*, Eastern
Vysochyna *Ukrainian*, Upland
Vysoâina *Czech*, Upland

### W

Waadi *Somali*, Watercourse
Wâdí *Arabic* Watercourse
Wáiat, Wâhat *Arabic*, Oasis
Wald *German*, Forest
Wan *Chinese*, Bay
Way *Indonesian*, River
Webi *Somali*, River
Wenz *Amharic*, River
Wiloyat(i) *Uzbek*, Province
Wyæyna *Polish*, Upland
Wzgórza *Polish*, Upland
Wzvyshsha *Belorusian*, Upland

### X

Xé *Laotian*, River
Xi *Chinese*, Stream

### Y

-yama *Japanese*, Mountain
Yanchi *Chinese*, Salt lake
Yanhu *Chinese*, Salt lake
Yarımadası *Azerbaijani, Turkish*, Peninsula
Yaylası *Turkish*, Plateau
Yazovir *Bulgarian*, Reservoir
Yoma *Burmese*, Mountains
Ytre- *Norwegian*, Outer
Yu *Chinese*, Islet
Yunhe *Chinese*, Canal
Yuzhn-o, -yy *Russian*, Southern

### Z

-zaki *Japanese*, Cape, point
Zaliv *Bulgarian, Russian*, Bay
-zan *Japanese*, Mountain
Zangbo *Tibetan*, River
Zapadn-aya, -o, -yy *Russian*, Western
Západné *Slovak*, Western
Západní *Czech*, Western
Zatoka *Polish, Ukrainian*, Bay
-zee *Dutch*, Sea
Zemlya *Russian*, Earth, land
Zizhiqu *Chinese*, Autonomous region

100 MILE HOUSE – ABŪ SUDAYRAH

# INDEX

## GLOSSARY OF ABBREVIATIONS

This glossary provides a comprehensive guide to the abbreviations used in this Atlas, and in the Index.

### A
**abbrev.** abbreviated
**AD** Anno Domini
**Afg.** Afghanistan
**Afr.** Afrikaans
**Alb.** Albanian
**Amh.** Amharic
**anc.** ancient
**approx.** approximately
**Ar.** Arabic
**Arm.** Armenian
**ASEAN** Association of South East Asian Nations
**ASSR** Autonomous Soviet Socialist Republic
**Aust.** Australian
**Az.** Azerbaijani
**Azerb.** Azerbaijan

### B
**Basq.** Basque
**BC** before Christ
**Bel.** Belarusian
**Ben.** Bengali
**Ber.** Berber
**B-H** Bosnia-Herzegovina
**bn** billion (one thousand million)
**BP** British Petroleum
**Bret.** Breton
**Brit.** British
**Bul.** Bulgarian
**Bur.** Burmese

### C
**C** central
**C.** Cape
**°C** degrees Centigrade
**CACM** Central America Common Market
**Cam.** Cambodian
**Cant.** Cantonese
**CAR** Central African Republic
**Cast.** Castilian
**Cat.** Catalan
**CEEAC** Central America Common Market
**Chin.** Chinese
**CIS** Commonwealth of Independent States
**cm** centimetre(s)
**Com.** Comorian
**Cro.** Croatian
**Cz.** Czech
**Czech Rep.** Czech Republic

### D
**Dan.** Danish
**Dar.** Dari
**Div.** Divehi
**Dom. Rep.** Dominican Republic
**Dut.** Dutch

### E
**E** east
**EC** *see* EU
**EEC** *see* EU
**ECOWAS** Economic Community of West African States
**ECU** European Currency Unit
**EMS** European Monetary System
**Eng.** English
**est** estimated
**Est.** Estonian
**EU** European Union (previously European Community [EC], European Economic Community [EEC])

### F
**°F** degrees Fahrenheit
**Far.** Faroese
**Fij.** Fijian
**Fil.** Filipino
**Fin.** Finnish
**Fr.** French
**Fris.** Frisian
**ft** foot/feet

### G
**g** gram(s)
**Gael.** Gaelic
**Gal.** Galician
**GDP** Gross Domestic Product (the total value of goods and services produced by a country excluding income from foreign countries)
**Geor.** Georgian
**Ger.** German
**Gk** Greek
**GNP** Gross National Product (the total value of goods and services produced by a country)

### H
**Heb.** Hebrew
**HEP** hydro-electric power
**Hind.** Hindi
**hist.** historical
**Hung.** Hungarian

### I
**I.** Island
**Icel.** Icelandic
**in** inch(es)
**In.** Inuit (Eskimo)
**Ind.** Indonesian
**Intl** International
**Ir.** Irish
**Is** Islands
**It.** Italian

### J
**Jap.** Japanese

### K
**Kaz.** Kazakh
**kg** kilogram(s)
**Khm.** Khmer
**km** kilometre(s)
**km²** square kilometre (singular)
**Kor.** Korean
**Kurd.** Kurdish
**Kyr.** Kyrgyz

### L
**L.** Lake
**LAIA** Latin American Integration Association
**Lao.** Laotian
**Lapp.** Lappish
**Lat.** Latin
**Latv.** Latvian
**Liech.** Liechtenstein
**Lith.** Lithuanian
**Lus.** Lusatian
**Lux.** Luxembourg

### M
**m** million/metre(s)
**Mac.** Macedonian
**Mal.** Malay
**Malg.** Malagasy
**Malt.** Maltese
**Mar.** Marshallese
**mi.** mile(s)
**Mong.** Mongolian
**Mt.** Mountain
**Mts** Mountains

### N
**N** north
**NAFTA** North American Free Trade Agreement
**Nep.** Nepali
**Neth.** Netherlands
**Nic.** Nicaraguan
**Nor.** Norwegian
**N. Maced.** North Macedonia
**NZ** New Zealand

### P
**Pash.** Pashto
**Per.** Persian
**PNG** Papua New Guinea
**Pol.** Polish
**Poly.** Polynesian
**Port.** Portuguese
**prev.** previously

### R
**Rep.** Republic
**Res.** Reservoir
**Rmsch** Romansch
**Rom.** Romanian
**Rus.** Russian
**Russ. Fed.** Russian Federation

### S
**S** south
**SADC** Southern Africa Development Community
**Serb.** Serbian
**Sinh.** Sinhala
**Slvk** Slovak
**Slvn.** Slovene
**Som.** Somali
**Sp.** Spanish
**St., St** Saint
**Strs** Straits
**Swa.** Swahili
**Swe.** Swedish
**Switz.** Switzerland

### T
**Taj.** Tajik
**Tet.** Tetum
**Th.** Thai
**Thai.** Thailand
**Tib.** Tibetan
**Tig.** Tigrinyan
**Tong.** Tongan
**Turk.** Turkish
**Turkm.** Turkmenistan

### U
**UAE** United Arab Emirates
**Uigh.** Uighur
**UK** United Kingdom
**Ukr.** Ukrainian
**UN** United Nations
**Urd.** Urdu
**US/USA** United States of America
**USSR** Union of Soviet Socialist Republics
**Uzb.** Uzbek

### V
**var.** variant
**Vdkhr.** Vodokhranilishche (Russian for reservoir)
**Vdskh.** Vodoskhovyshche (Ukrainian for reservoir)
**Vtn.** Vietnamese

### W
**W** west
**Wel.** Welsh

THIS INDEX LISTS all the placenames and features shown on the regional and continental maps in this Atlas. Placenames are referenced to the largest scale map on which they appear. The policy followed throughout the Atlas is to use the local spelling or local name at regional level; commonly-used English language names may occasionally be added (in parentheses) where this is an aid to identification e.g. Firenze (Florence). English names, where they exist, have been used for all international features e.g. oceans and country names; they are also used on the continental maps and in the introductory World Today section; these are then fully cross-referenced to the local names found on the regional maps. The index also contains commonly-found alternative names and variant spellings, which are also fully cross-referenced.

All main entry names are those of settlements unless otherwise indicated by the use of italicized definitions or representative symbols, which are keyed at the foot of each page.

## 1


10 *M16* **100 Mile House** *var.* Hundred Mile House. British Columbia, SW Canada *51°39′N 121°19′W*
**25 de Mayo** *see* Veinticinco de Mayo
**26 Bakinskikh Komissarov** *see* Häsänabad
**26 Baku Komissarlary Adyndaky** *see* Uzboý


## A


**Aa** *see* Gauja
95 *G24* **Aabenraa** *var.* Åbenrå, *Ger.* Apenrade. Syddanmark, SW Denmark *55°03′N 09°26′E*
95 *G20* **Aabybro** *var.* Åbybro. Nordjylland, N Denmark *57°09′N 09°32′E*
101 *C16* **Aachen** *Dut.* Aken, *Fr.* Aix-la-Chapelle; *anc.* Aquae Grani, Aquisgranum. Nordrhein-Westfalen, W Germany *50°47′N 06°06′E*
**Aaiún** *see* Laâyoune
95 *M24* **Aakirkeby** *var.* Åkirkeby. Bornholm, E Denmark *55°04′N 14°56′E*
95 *G20* **Aalborg** *var.* Ålborg, Ålborg-Nørresundby; *anc.* Alburgum. Nordjylland, N Denmark *57°03′N 09°56′E*
**Aalborg Bugt** *see* Ålborg Bugt
101 *J21* **Aalen** Baden-Württemberg, S Germany *48°50′N 10°06′E*
95 *G21* **Aalestrup** *var.* Ålestrup. Midtjylland, NW Denmark *56°42′N 09°31′E*
98 *I11* **Aalsmeer** Noord-Holland, C Netherlands *52°17′N 04°43′E*
99 *F18* **Aalst** Oost-Vlaanderen, C Belgium *50°57′N 04°03′E*
99 *K18* **Aalst** *Fr.* Alost. Noord-Brabant, S Netherlands *51°23′N 05°29′E*
98 *O12* **Aalten** Gelderland, E Netherlands *51°56′N 06°35′E*
99 *D17* **Aalter** Oost-Vlaanderen, NW Belgium *51°05′N 03°28′E*
**Aanaar** *see* Inari
**Aanaarjävri** *see* Inarijärvi
93 *M17* **Äänekoski** Keski-Suomi, W Finland *62°34′N 25°45′E*
138 *H7* **Aanjar** *var.* ʻAnjar. C Lebanon *33°45′N 35°56′E*
83 *G21* **Aansluit** Northern Cape, N South Africa *26°41′S 22°24′E*
**Aar** *see* Aare
108 *F7* **Aarau** Aargau, N Switzerland *47°22′N 08°00′E*
108 *D8* **Aarberg** Bern, W Switzerland *47°19′N 07°54′E*
99 *D16* **Aardenburg** Zeeland, SW Netherlands *51°16′N 03°27′E*
108 *D8* **Aare** *var.* Aar. ≈ W Switzerland
108 *F7* **Aargau** *Fr.* Argovie. ◈ *canton* N Switzerland
95 *G22* **Aarhus** *var.* Århus. Midtjylland, C Denmark *56°09′N 10°11′E*
**Aarlen** *see* Arlon
95 *G21* **Aars** *var.* Års. Nordjylland, N Denmark *56°49′N 09°32′E*
99 *I17* **Aarschot** Vlaams Brabant, C Belgium *50°59′N 04°50′E*
197 *N13* **Aasiaat** *Dan.* Egedesminde. Qeqertalik, C Greenland *68°43′N 52°52′W*
**Aassi, Nahr el** *see* Orontes
**Aat** *see* Ath
150 *G7* **Aba** *prev.* Ngawa. Sichuan, C China *32°51′N 101°46′E*
79 *P16* **Aba** Orientale, NE Dem. Rep. Congo *03°52′N 30°14′E*
77 *V17* **Aba** Abia, S Nigeria *05°06′N 07°22′E*
140 *J6* **Abā al Qazāz, Bi'r** *well* NW Saudi Arabia
**Abā as Su'ūd** *see* Najrān
59 *G14* **Abacaxis, Rio** ≈ NW Brazil
**Abaco Island** *see* Great Abaco/Little Abaco
**Abaco Island** *see* Great Abaco, N Bahamas
142 *K10* **Ābādān** Khūzestān, SW Iran *30°24′N 48°18′E*
146 *F13* **Abadan** *prev.* Bezmein, Büzmeýin, *Rus.* Byuzmeyin. Ahal Welaýaty, C Turkmenistan *38°08′N 57°53′E*
143 *O10* **Ābādeh** Fārs, C Iran *31°06′N 52°40′E*
74 *H8* **Abadla** W Algeria *31°04′N 02°39′W*
59 *M20* **Abaeté** Minas Gerais, SE Brazil *19°10′S 45°24′W*
52 *P7* **Abaí** Caazapá, S Paraguay *25°58′S 55°54′W*
**Abai** *see* Blue Nile
191 *O2* **Abaiang** *var.* Apia; *prev.* Charlotte Island. *atoll* Tungaru, W Kiribati
**Abaj** *see* Abay
77 *U15* **Abaji** Federal Capital District, C Nigeria *08°35′N 06°54′E*
37 *O7* **Abajo Peak** ▲ Utah, W USA *37°51′N 109°28′W*
77 *V16* **Abakaliki** Ebonyi, SE Nigeria *06°18′N 08°07′E*
122 *K13* **Abakan** Respublika Khakasiya, S Russia *53°43′N 91°25′E*
77 *S11* **Abala** Tillabéri, SW Niger *14°55′N 03°27′E*
77 *U11* **Abalak** Tahoua, C Niger *15°28′N 06°18′E*
119 *N14* **Abalyanka** *Rus.* Obolyanka. ≈ N Belarus
122 *L12* **Aban** Krasnoyarskiy Kray, S Russia *56°41′N 96°04′E*
143 *P9* **Āb Anbār-e Kān Sorkh** Yazd, C Iran *31°22′N 53°38′E*
57 *G16* **Abancay** Apurímac, SE Peru *13°37′S 72°52′W*
190 *H2* **Abaokoro** *atoll* Tungaru, W Kiribati
**Abariringa** *see* Kanton
143 *P10* **Abarkūh** Yazd, C Iran *31°07′N 53°17′E*
165 *V3* **Abashiri** *var.* Abasiri. Hokkaidō, NE Japan *44°N 144°15′E*
165 *U3* **Abashiri-ko** ◎ Hokkaidō, NE Japan
**Abasiri** *see* Abashiri
41 *P10* **Abasolo** Tamaulipas, C Mexico *24°02′N 98°18′W*
186 *F9* **Abau** Central, S Papua New Guinea *10°04′S 148°34′E*
145 *R10* **Abay** *var.* Abaj. Karaganda, C Kazakhstan *49°38′N 72°50′E*
81 *I15* **Ābaya Hāyk'** *Eng.* Lake Margherita, *It.* Abbaia. ◎ SW Ethiopia
**Ābay Wenz** *see* Blue Nile
122 *K13* **Abaza** Respublika Khakasiya, S Russia *52°40′N 89°58′E*
**Abbaia** *see* Ābaya Hāyk'
143 *Q13* **Āb Bārīk** Fārs, S Iran
107 *C18* **Abbasanta** Sardegna, Italy, C Mediterranean Sea *40°08′N 08°49′E*
**Abbatis Villa** *see* Abbeville
30 *M3* **Abbaye, Point** *headland* Michigan, N USA *46°58′N 88°08′W*
**Abbazia** *see* Opatija
**Abbé, Lake** *see* Abhe, Lake
103 *N2* **Abbeville** *anc.* Abbatis Villa. Somme, N France *50°06′N 01°50′E*
23 *R7* **Abbeville** Alabama, S USA *31°35′N 85°16′W*
23 *U6* **Abbeville** Georgia, SE USA *31°58′N 83°18′W*
22 *I9* **Abbeville** Louisiana, S USA *29°58′N 92°08′W*
21 *P12* **Abbeville** South Carolina, SE USA *34°10′N 82°23′W*
97 *B20* **Abbeyfeale** *Ir.* Mainistir na Féile. SW Ireland *52°24′N 09°21′W*
106 *D8* **Abbiategrasso** Lombardia, NW Italy *45°24′N 08°55′E*
93 *I14* **Abborrträsk** Norrbotten, N Sweden *65°24′N 19°33′E*
194 *J9* **Abbot Ice Shelf** *ice shelf* Antarctica
10 *M17* **Abbotsford** British Columbia, SW Canada *49°02′N 122°18′W*
30 *K6* **Abbotsford** Wisconsin, N USA *44°57′N 90°19′W*
149 *U5* **Abbottabad** Khyber Pakhtunkhwa, NW Pakistan *34°12′N 73°15′E*
119 *M14* **Abchuha** *Rus.* Obchuga. Minskaya Voblasts', NW Belarus *54°30′N 29°22′E*
98 *I10* **Abcoude** Utrecht, C Netherlands *52°17′N 04°59′E*
139 *N2* **ʻAbd al ʻAzīz, Jabal** ▲▲ NE Syria
141 *U17* **ʻAbd al Kūrī** *island* SE Yemen
127 *U6* **Abdulino** Orenburgskaya Oblast', W Russia *53°37′N 53°39′E*
78 *J10* **Abéché** *var.* Abécher, Abeshr. Ouaddaï, SE Chad *13°49′N 20°49′E*
**Abécher** *see* Abéché
143 *S8* **Āb-e Garm va Sard** Khorāsān-e Janūbī, E Iran
77 *R8* **Abeïbara** Kidal, NE Mali *19°07′N 01°52′E*
105 *P5* **Abejar** Castilla y León, N Spain *41°48′N 02°47′W*
54 *E9* **Abejorral** Antioquia, W Colombia *05°48′N 75°28′W*
**Abela** *see* Ávila
**Abellinum** *see* Avellino
92 *Q2* **Abeløya** *island* Kong Karls Land, E Svalbard
80 *I13* **Ābeltī** Oromīya, C Ethiopia *08°09′N 37°31′E*
191 *O2* **Abemama** *var.* Apamama; *prev.* Roger Simpson Island. *atoll* Tungaru, W Kiribati
171 *Y15* **Abemaree** *var.* Abermarre. Papua, E Indonesia *07°03′S 140°10′E*
77 *O16* **Abengourou** E Ivory Coast *06°42′N 03°27′W*
**Åbenrå** *see* Aabenraa
101 *L22* **Abens** ≈ SE Germany
77 *S16* **Abeokuta** Ogun, SW Nigeria *07°07′N 03°21′E*
97 *I20* **Aberaeron** SW Wales, United Kingdom *52°15′N 04°15′W*
**Aberbrothock** *see* Arbroath
**Abercorn** *see* Mbala
29 *R6* **Abercrombie** North Dakota, N USA *46°25′N 96°42′W*
183 *T7* **Aberdeen** New South Wales, SE Australia *32°09′S 150°55′E*
11 *T15* **Aberdeen** Saskatchewan, S Canada *52°15′N 106°19′W*
83 *H25* **Aberdeen** Eastern Cape, S South Africa *32°30′S 24°00′E*
96 *L9* **Aberdeen** *anc.* Devana. NE Scotland, United Kingdom *57°10′N 02°04′W*
21 *X2* **Aberdeen** Maryland, NE USA *39°28′N 76°09′W*
23 *N3* **Aberdeen** Mississippi, S USA *33°49′N 88°32′W*
21 *T10* **Aberdeen** North Carolina, SE USA *35°07′N 79°25′W*
29 *P8* **Aberdeen** South Dakota, N USA *45°27′N 98°29′W*
32 *F8* **Aberdeen** Washington, NW USA *46°57′N 123°48′W*
96 *K9* **Aberdeen** *cultural region* NE Scotland, United Kingdom
8 *L8* **Aberdeen Lake** ◎ Nunavut, NE Canada
96 *J10* **Aberfeldy** C Scotland, United Kingdom *56°38′N 03°49′W*
97 *K21* **Abergavenny** *anc.* Gobannium. SE Wales, United Kingdom *51°50′N 03°W*
**Abergwaun** *see* Fishguard
**Abermarre** *see* Abemaree
25 *N5* **Abernathy** Texas, SW USA *33°49′N 101°50′W*
**Abersee** *see* Wolfgangsee
**Abertawe** *see* Swansea
**Aberteifi** *see* Cardigan
32 *I15* **Abert, Lake** ◎ Oregon, NW USA
97 *I20* **Aberystwyth** W Wales, United Kingdom *52°25′N 04°05′W*
**Abeshr** *see* Abéché
**Ábeskovvu** *see* Abisko
106 *F10* **Abetone** Toscana, C Italy *44°09′N 10°42′E*
125 *V5* **Abez'** Respublika Komi, NW Russia *66°32′N 61°41′E*
142 *M5* **Āb Garm** Qazvin, N Iran
141 *N12* **Abhā** ʻAsīr, SW Saudi Arabia *18°16′N 42°32′E*
142 *M5* **Abhar** Zanjān, NW Iran *36°05′N 49°18′E*
**Abhé Bad/Ābhē Bid Hāyk'** *see* Abhe, Lake
80 *K12* **Abhe, Lake** *var.* Lake Abbé, *Amh.* Ābhē Bid Hāyk', *Som.* Abhé Bad. ◎ Djibouti/Ethiopia
77 *V17* **Abia** ◈ *state* SE Nigeria
139 *V9* **ʻAbīd ʻAlī** Wāsiț, E Iraq *32°20′N 45°58′E*
119 *O17* **Abidavichy** *Rus.* Obidovichi. Mahilyowskaya Voblasts', E Belarus *53°20′N 30°25′E*
115 *L15* **Abide** Çanakkale, NW Turkey *40°04′N 26°13′E*
77 *N17* **Abidjan** S Ivory Coast *05°19′N 04°01′W*
27 *N4* **Abilene** Kansas, C USA *38°55′N 97°14′W*
25 *Q7* **Abilene** Texas, SW USA *32°27′N 99°44′W*
**Abindonia** *see* Abingdon
97 *M21* **Abingdon** *anc.* Abindonia. S England, United Kingdom *51°41′N 01°17′W*
30 *K12* **Abingdon** Illinois, N USA *40°48′N 90°24′W*
21 *P8* **Abingdon** Virginia, NE USA *36°42′N 81°59′W*
**Abingdon** *see* Pinta, Isla
18 *J15* **Abington** Pennsylvania, NE USA *40°06′N 75°05′W*
126 *K14* **Abinsk** Krasnodarskiy Kray, SW Russia *44°51′N 38°12′E*
37 *R9* **Abiquiu Reservoir** ▣ New Mexico, SW USA
**Āb-i-safed** *see* Safēd, Darya-ye
92 *I10* **Abisko** *Lapp.* Ábeskovvu. Norrbotten, N Sweden *68°21′N 18°50′E*
12 *G12* **Abitibi** ≈ Ontario, S Canada
12 *H12* **Abitibi, Lac** ◎ Ontario/Québec, S Canada
80 *J10* **Ābīy Ādī** Tigray, N Ethiopia *13°40′N 38°57′E*
118 *H6* **Abja-Paluoja** Viljandimaa, S Estonia *58°08′N 25°20′E*
137 *Q8* **Abkhazia** *Georg.* Apkhazeti. ◈ *autonomous republic* NW Georgia
182 *F1* **Abminga** South Australia *26°07′S 134°49′E*
75 *W9* **Abnūb** *var.* Abnûb. C Egypt *27°18′N 31°09′E*
**Abnûb** *see* Abnūb
**Åbo** *see* Turku
152 *G9* **Abohar** Punjab, N India *30°11′N 74°14′E*
77 *O17* **Aboisso** SE Ivory Coast *05°26′N 03°13′W*
78 *H5* **Abo, Massif d'** ▲▲ NW Chad
77 *R16* **Abomey** S Benin *07°14′N 02°00′E*
79 *F16* **Abong Mbang** Est, SE Cameroon *03°58′N 13°10′E*
111 *L23* **Abony** Pest, C Hungary *47°10′N 20°00′E*
78 *J11* **Abou-Déïa** Salamat, SE Chad *11°30′N 19°18′E*
**Aboudouhour** *see* Abū aḍ Ḍuhūr
**Abou Kémal** *see* Abū Kamāl
**Abou Simbel** *see* Abū Sunbul
137 *T12* **Abovyan** C Armenia *40°16′N 44°33′E*
141 *P15* **Abrād, Wādī** *seasonal river* W Yemen
**Abraham Bay** *see* The Carlton
104 *G10* **Abrantes** *var.* Abrántes. Santarém, C Portugal *39°28′N 08°12′W*
62 *J4* **Abra Pampa** Jujuy, N Argentina *22°47′S 65°41′W*
**Abrashlare** *see* Brezovo
54 *G7* **Abrego** Norte de Santander, N Colombia *08°08′N 73°14′W*
**Abrene** *see* Pytalovo
40 *C7* **Abreojos, Punta** *headland* NW Mexico *26°43′N 113°36′W*
65 *J16* **Abrolhos Bank** *undersea feature* W Atlantic Ocean *18°30′S 38°45′W*
119 *H19* **Abrova** *Rus.* Obrovo. Brestskaya Voblasts', SW Belarus *52°30′N 25°34′E*
116 *G11* **Abrud** *Ger.* Gross-Schlatten, *Hung.* Abrudbánya. Alba, SW Romania *46°16′N 23°05′E*
**Abrudbánya** *see* Abrud
118 *E6* **Abruka** *island* SW Estonia
107 *J15* **Abruzzese, Appennino** ▲▲ C Italy
107 *J14* **Abruzzo** ◈ *region* C Italy
141 *N14* **ʻAbs** *var.* Sūq ʻAbs. W Yemen *16°42′N 42°55′E*
33 *T12* **Absaroka Range** ▲▲ Montana/Wyoming, NW USA
137 *Z11* **Abşeron Yarımadası** *Rus.* Apsheronskiy Poluostrov. *peninsula* E Azerbaijan
143 *N6* **Āb Shīrīn** Eşfahān, C Iran *34°17′N 51°17′E*
139 *X10* **Abtān** Maysān, SE Iraq *31°37′N 47°06′E*
109 *R6* **Abtenau** Salzburg, NW Austria *47°33′N 13°21′E*
152 *E14* **Ābu** Rājasthān, N India *24°41′N 72°50′E*
164 *E12* **Abu** Yamaguchi, Honshū, SW Japan *34°30′N 131°26′E*
138 *I4* **Abū aḍ Ḍuhūr** *Fr.* Aboudouhour. Idlib, NW Syria *35°30′N 37°00′E*
143 *P17* **Abū al Abyaḍ** *island* C United Arab Emirates
138 *K10* **Abū al Ḩuşayn, Khabrat** ◎ N Jordan
139 *R8* **Abū al Jīr** Al Anbār, C Iraq *33°16′N 42°55′E*
139 *Y12* **Abū al Khaşīb** *var.* Abul Khasib. Al Başrah, SE Iraq *30°26′N 48°00′E*
139 *U12* **Abū at Tubrah, Thaqb** *well* S Iraq
**Abu Balâs** *see* Abu Ballās
75 *V11* **Abu Ballās** *var.* Abu Balâs. ▲ SW Egypt *24°28′N 27°36′E*
**Abu Dhabi** *see* Abū Ẓaby
139 *R8* **Abū Farūkh** Al Anbār, C Iraq *33°06′N 43°18′E*
80 *C12* **Abu Gabra** Eastern Darfur, W Sudan *11°02′N 26°50′E*
139 *P10* **Abū Ghār, Shaʻīb** *dry watercourse* S Iraq
80 *G7* **Abu Hamed** River Nile, N Sudan *19°32′N 33°20′E*
**Abū Ḩardān** *see* Hajīn
139 *T7* **Abū Ḩasāwīyah** Diyālá, E Iraq *33°52′N 44°47′E*
138 *K10* **Abū Ḩifnah, Wādī** *dry watercourse* N Jordan
77 *V15* **Abuja** ● (Nigeria) Federal Capital District, C Nigeria *09°04′N 07°28′E*
139 *R9* **Abū Jahaf, Wādī** *dry watercourse* C Iraq
56 *F12* **Abujao, Río** ≈ E Peru
139 *U12* **Abū Jasrah** Al Muthanná, S Iraq *30°43′N 44°50′E*
139 *O6* **Abū Kamāl** *Fr.* Abou Kémal. Dayr az Zawr, E Syria *34°29′N 40°56′E*
165 *P12* **Abukuma-sanchi** ▲▲ Honshū, C Japan
**Abula** *see* Ávila
**Abul Khasib** *see* Abū al Khaşīb
79 *K16* **Abumombazi** *var.* Abumonbazi. Equateur, N Dem. Rep. Congo *03°43′N 22°06′E*
**Abumonbazi** *see* Abumombazi
59 *D15* **Abunã** Rondônia, W Brazil *09°41′S 65°20′W*
56 *K13* **Abunã, Rio** *var.* Río Abuná. ≈ Bolivia/Brazil
138 *G10* **Abū Nuşayr** *var.* Abu Nuseir. ʻAmmān, W Jordan *32°03′N 35°58′E*
**Abu Nuseir** *see* Abū Nuşayr
139 *T12* **Abū Qabr** Al Muthanná, S Iraq *31°03′N 44°34′E*
138 *K5* **Abū Raḩbah, Jabal** ▲▲ C Syria
139 *S5* **Abū Rajāsh** Şalāḩ ad Dīn, N Iraq *34°47′N 43°36′E*
139 *W13* **Abū Raqrāq, Ghadīr** *well* S Iraq
152 *E14* **Ābu Road** Rājasthān, N India *24°29′N 72°47′E*
80 *I6* **Abu Shagara, Ras** *headland* NE Sudan *18°04′N 38°31′E*
**Abu Simbel** *see* Abū Sunbul
139 *U12* **Abū Sudayrah** Al Muthanná, S Iraq *30°55′N 44°58′E*




◆ Country
● Country Capital
◇ Dependent Territory
○ Dependent Territory Capital
◈ Administrative Regions
✈ International Airport
▲ Mountain
▲▲ Mountain Range
Volcano
≈ River
◎ Lake
▣ Reservoir

ABŪ ŞUKHAYR – AÍGIO


139 T10 **Abū Şukhayr** Al Qādisīyah, S Iraq 31°54′N 44°27′E
185 E18 **Abut Head** headland South Island, New Zealand 43°06′S 170°16′E
80 E9 **Abu 'Urug** Northern Kordofan, C Sudan 15°52′N 30°25′E
80 K12 **Ābuyē Mēda** ▲ C Ethiopia 10°28′N 39°44′E
80 D11 **Abu Zabad** Western Kordofan, C Sudan 12°21′N 29°16′E
143 P16 **Abū Z̧aby** , *Eng.* Abu Dhabi. ● (United Arab Emirates) Abū Z̧aby, C United Arab Emirates 24°30′N 54°20′E
75 X8 **Abū Zanīmah** E Egypt 29°01′N 33°08′E
95 N17 **Åby** Östergötland, S Sweden 58°40′N 16°10′E
**Abyaḑ, Al Baḩr al** *see* White Nile
**Åbybro** *see* Aabybro
80 D13 **Abyei** Southern Kordofan, S Sudan 09°35′N 28°28′E
**Abyla** *see* Ávila
**Abymes** *see* les Abymes
**Abyssinia** *see* Ethiopia
**Açâba** *see* Assaba
54 F11 **Acacias** Meta, C Colombia 03°59′N 73°46′W
58 L13 **Açailândia** Maranhão, E Brazil 04°51′S 47°26′W
**Acaill** *see* Achill Island
42 E8 **Acajutla** Sonsonate, W El Salvador 13°34′N 89°50′W
79 D17 **Acalayong** SW Equatorial Guinea 01°05′N 09°34′E
41 N13 **Acámbaro** Guanajuato, C Mexico 20°01′N 100°42′W
54 C6 **Acandí** Chocó, NW Colombia 08°32′N 77°20′W
104 H4 **A Cañiza** *var.* La Cañiza. Galicia, NW Spain 42°13′N 08°16′W
40 J11 **Acaponeta** Nayarit, C Mexico 22°30′N 105°21′W
40 J11 **Acaponeta, Río de** ∽ C Mexico
41 O16 **Acapulco** *var.* Acapulco de Juárez. Guerrero, S Mexico 16°51′N 99°53′W
**Acapulco de Juárez** *see* Acapulco
55 T13 **Acarai Mountains** *Sp.* Serra Acaraí. ⛰ Brazil/Guyana
**Acaraí, Serra** *see* Acarai Mountains
58 O13 **Acaraú** Ceará, NE Brazil 04°35′S 37°37′W
54 J6 **Acarigua** Portuguesa, N Venezuela 09°35′N 69°12′W
104 H2 **A Carreira** Galicia, NW Spain 43°21′N 08°12′W
42 C6 **Acatenango, Volcán de** 🌋 S Guatemala 14°30′N 90°52′W
41 Q15 **Acatlán** *var.* Acatlán de Osorio. Puebla, S Mexico 18°12′N 98°02′W
**Acatlán de Osorio** *see* Acatlán
41 S15 **Acayucan** *var.* Acayucán. Veracruz, E Mexico 17°59′N 94°58′W
**Accho** *see* Akko
21 Y5 **Accomac** Virginia, NE USA 37°43′N 75°41′N
77 Q17 **Accra** ● (Ghana)SE Ghana 05°33′N 00°15′W
97 L17 **Accrington** NW England, United Kingdom 53°46′N 02°21′W
61 B19 **Acebal** Santa Fe, C Argentina 33°14′S 60°50′W
168 H8 **Aceh** *off.* Daerah Istimewa Aceh, *var.* Acheen, Achin, Atchin, Atjeh. ◐ *autonomous district* NW Indonesia
107 M18 **Acerenza** Basilicata, S Italy 40°46′N 15°51′E
107 K17 **Acerra** *anc.* Acerrae. Campania, S Italy 40°56′N 14°22′E
**Acerrae** *see* Acerra
57 J17 **Achacachi** La Paz, W Bolivia 16°01′S 68°44′W
54 K7 **Achaguas** Apure, C Venezuela 07°46′N 68°14′W
154 H12 **Achalpur** *prev.* Elichpur, Ellichpur. Mahārāshtra, C India 21°19′N 77°30′E
61 F18 **Achar** Tacuarembó, C Uruguay 32°20′S 56°15′W
**Ach'ara** *see* Ajaria
115 H19 **Acharnés** *var.* Aharnes; *prev.* Akharnaí. Attikí, C Greece 38°09′N 23°58′E
**Ach'asar Lerr** *see* Achk'asari, Mta
**Acheen** *see* Aceh
99 K16 **Achel** Limburg, NE Belgium 51°15′N 05°31′E
115 D16 **Achelóos** *var.* Akhelóös, Aspropótamos; *anc.* Achelous. ∽ W Greece
**Achelous** *see* Achelóos
163 W8 **Acheng** Heilongjiang, NE China 45°32′N 126°56′E
109 N6 **Achenkirch** Tirol, W Austria 47°31′N 11°42′E
101 L24 **Achenpass** pass Austria/ Germany
109 N7 **Achensee** ◎ W Austria
101 F22 **Achern** Baden-Württemberg, SW Germany 48°37′N 08°04′E
115 C16 **Acherón** ∽ W Greece
77 W11 **Achétinamou** ∽ S Niger
152 J12 **Achhnera** Uttar Pradesh, N India 27°10′N 77°45′E
42 C7 **Achiguate, Río** ∽ S Guatemala
97 A16 **Achill Head** *Ir.* Ceann Acla. headland W Ireland 53°58′N 10°14′W
97 A16 **Achill Island** *Ir.* Acaill. island W Ireland
100 H11 **Achim** Niedersachsen, NW Germany 53°01′N 09°01′E
149 S5 **Achīn** Nangarhār, E Afghanistan 34°04′N 70°41′E
**Achin** *see* Aceh
122 K12 **Achinsk** Krasnoyarskiy Kray, S Russia 56°21′N 90°25′E
162 E5 **Achit Nuur** ◎ NW Mongolia
137 T11 **Achk'asari, Mta** *Arm.* Ach'asar Lerr. ▲ Armenia/ Georgia 41°09′N 43°55′E
126 K13 **Achuyevo** Krasnodarskiy Kray, SW Russia 46°00′N 38°01′E
81 F16 **Achwa** *var.* Aswa. ∽ N Uganda
136 E15 **Acıgöl** salt lake SW Turkey
107 L24 **Acireale** Sicilia, Italy, C Mediterranean Sea 37°36′N 15°10′E
**Aciris** *see* Agri
25 N7 **Ackerly** Texas, SW USA 32°31′N 101°43′W
22 M4 **Ackerman** Mississippi, S USA 33°18′N 89°10′W
29 W13 **Ackley** Iowa, C USA 42°33′N 93°03′W
44 J5 **Acklins Island** island SE The Bahamas
**Acla, Ceann** *see* Achill Head
62 H11 **Aconcagua, Cerro** ▲ W Argentina 32°36′S 69°53′W
**Açores/Açores, Arquipélago dos/Açores, Ilhas dos** *see* Azores
**Açores, Região Autónoma dos** *see* Azores
104 H2 **A Coruña** *Cast.* La Coruña, *Eng.* Corunna; *anc.* Caronium. Galicia, NW Spain 43°22′N 08°24′W
104 G2 **A Coruña** *Cast.* La Coruña. ◐ *province* Galicia, NW Spain
42 L10 **Acoyapa** Chontales, S Nicaragua 11°58′N 85°10′W
106 H13 **Acquapendente** Lazio, C Italy 42°44′N 11°52′E
106 J13 **Acquasanta Terme** Marche, C Italy 42°46′N 13°24′E
106 I13 **Acquasparta** Lazio, C Italy 42°41′N 12°31′E
106 C9 **Acqui Terme** Piemonte, NW Italy 44°41′N 08°28′E
**Acrae** *see* Palazzola Acreide
182 F7 **Acraman, Lake** salt lake South Australia
59 A15 **Acre** *off.* Estado do Acre. ◐ *state* W Brazil
**Acre** *see* Akko
59 C16 **Acre, Rio** ∽ W Brazil
107 N20 **Acri** Calabria, SW Italy 39°30′N 16°22′E
**Acte** *see* Ágion Óros
191 Y12 **Actéon, Groupe** island group Îles Tuamotu, SE French Polynesia
15 P12 **Acton-Vale** Québec, SE Canada 45°39′N 72°31′W
41 P13 **Actopan** *var.* Actopán. Hidalgo, C Mexico 20°19′N 98°59′W
**Açu** *see* Assu
**Acunum Acusio** *see* Montélimar
77 Q17 **Ada** SE Ghana 05°47′N 00°42′E
112 L8 **Ada** Vojvodina, N Serbia 45°48′N 20°08′E
29 R5 **Ada** Minnesota, N USA 47°18′N 96°31′W
31 R12 **Ada** Ohio, N USA 40°46′N 83°49′W
27 O12 **Ada** Oklahoma, C USA 34°47′N 96°41′W
162 L8 **Adaatsag** *var.* Tavin. Dundgovĭ, C Mongolia 46°27′N 105°43′E
**Ada Bazar** *see* Adapazarı
40 D3 **Adair, Bahía de** bay NW Mexico
104 M7 **Adaja** ∽ N Spain
38 H17 **Adak Island** island Aleutian Islands, Alaska, USA
**Adalia** *see* Antalya
**Adalia, Gulf of** *see* Antalya Körfezi
141 X9 **Adam** N Oman 22°22′N 57°30′E
**Adama** *see* Nazrēt
60 I8 **Adamantina** São Paulo, S Brazil 21°41′S 51°04′W
79 E14 **Adamaoua** *Eng.* Adamawa. ◐ *region* N Cameroon
68 F11 **Adamaoua, Massif d'** *Eng.* Adamawa Highlands. plateau NW Cameroon
77 Y14 **Adamawa** ◐ *state* E Nigeria
**Adamawa** *see* Adamaoua
**Adamawa Highlands** *see* Adamaoua, Massif d'
106 F6 **Adamello** ▲ N Italy 46°09′N 10°33′E
81 J14 **Ādamī Tulu** Oromīya, C Ethiopia 07°52′N 38°39′E
63 M23 **Adam, Mount** *var.* Monte Independencia. ▲ West Falkland, Falkland Islands 51°36′S 60°00′W
29 R16 **Adams** Nebraska, C USA 40°25′N 96°30′W
18 H8 **Adams** New York, NE USA 43°48′N 75°57′W
29 Q3 **Adams** North Dakota, N USA 48°23′N 98°01′W
155 I23 **Adam's Bridge** chain of shoals NW Sri Lanka
32 H10 **Adams, Mount** ▲ Washington, NW USA 46°12′N 121°29′W
**Adam's Peak** *see* Sri Pada
191 R16 **Adam's Rock** island Pitcairn Island, Pitcairn Islands
191 P16 **Adamstown** ○ (Pitcairn Islands)Pitcairn Island, Pitcairn Islands 25°04′S 130°05′W
20 G10 **Adamsville** Tennessee, S USA 35°14′N 88°23′W
25 S9 **Adamsville** Texas, SW USA 31°15′N 98°09′W
141 O17 **'Adan** *Eng.* Aden. SW Yemen 12°51′N 45°05′E
136 K16 **Adana** *var.* Seyhan. Adana, S Turkey 37°N 35°19′E
136 K16 **Adana** *var.* Seyhan. ◐ *province* S Turkey
**Adâncata** *see* Horlivka
169 V12 **Adang, Teluk** bay Borneo, C Indonesia
136 F11 **Adapazarı** *prev.* Ada Bazar. Sakarya, NW Turkey 40°49′N 30°24′E
80 H8 **Adarama** River Nile, NE Sudan 17°04′N 34°57′E
195 Q16 **Adare, Cape** cape Antarctica
**Ādavāni** *see* Ādoni
106 E6 **Adda** *anc.* Addua. ∽ N Italy
80 A13 **Adda** ∽ W South Sudan
143 Q17 **Aḑ Ḑab'īyah** Abū Z̧aby, C United Arab Emirates 24°17′N 54°08′E
143 O18 **Aḑ Ḑafrah** desert S United Arab Emirates
141 Q6 **Ad Dahnā'** desert E Saudi Arabia
74 A11 **Ad Dakhla** *var.* Dakhla. SW Western Sahara 23°46′N 15°56′W
**Ad Dalanj** *see* Dilling
**Ad Damar** *see* Ed Damer
**Ad Damazīn** *see* Ed Damazin
**Ad Dāmir** *see* Ed Damer
141 R6 **Ad Dammām** *var.* Dammām. Ash Sharqīyah, NE Saudi Arabia 26°23′N 50°05′E
173 N2 **Ad Dammām** desert NE Saudi Arabia
**Ad Dāmūr** *see* Damoûr
140 K5 **Ad Dār al Ḩamrā'** Tabūk, NW Saudi Arabia 27°22′N 37°46′E
140 M13 **Ad Darb** Jāzān, SW Saudi Arabia 17°45′N 42°15′E
139 N1 **Ad Darbāsīyah** *var.* Derbisīye. Al Ḩasakah, N Syria 37°06′N 40°42′E
141 O8 **Ad Dawādimī** Ar Riyāḑ, C Saudi Arabia 24°32′N 44°21′E
143 N16 **Ad Dawḩah** *Eng.* Doha. ● (Qatar) C Qatar 25°15′N 51°36′E
143 N16 **Ad Dawḩah** *Eng.* Doha. ✈ C Qatar 25°11′N 51°37′E
139 S6 **Ad Dawr** Şalāḩ ad Dīn, N Iraq 34°30′N 43°49′E
139 Y12 **Ad Dayr** *var.* Dayr, Shahbān. Al Başrah, E Iraq 30°45′N 47°36′E
**Addi Arkay** *see* Ādī Ārk'ay
**Ad Dībakah** *see* Dībege
139 X15 **Ad Dibdibah** physical region Iraq/Kuwait
**Aḑ Ḑiffah** *see* Libyan Plateau
**Addis Ababa** *see* Ādīs Ābeba
**Addison** *see* Webster Springs
139 U10 **Ad Dīwānīyah** *var.* Diwaniyah. C Iraq 32°00′N 44°57′E
**Ad Dīwānīyah** *see* Al Qādisīyah
**Addoo Atoll** *see* Addu Atoll
**Addua** *see* Adda
151 K22 **Addu Atoll** *var.* Addoo Atoll, Seenu Atoll. atoll S Maldives
**Ad Dujail** *see* Ad Dujayl
139 T7 **Ad Dujayl** *var.* Ad Dujail. Şalāḩ ad Dīn, N Iraq 33°49′N 44°16′E
**Ad Dulaym** *see* Al Anbār
**Ad Duwaym/Ad Duwēm** *see* Ed Dueim
99 D16 **Adegem** Oost-Vlaanderen, NW Belgium 51°12′N 03°31′E
23 U7 **Adel** Georgia, SE USA 31°08′N 83°25′W
29 U14 **Adel** Iowa, C USA 41°36′N 94°01′W
182 I9 **Adelaide** state capital South Australia 34°56′S 138°36′E
44 H2 **Adelaide** New Providence, N The Bahamas 24°59′N 77°30′W
182 I9 **Adelaide** ✈ South Australia 34°55′S 138°31′E
194 H6 **Adelaide Island** island Antarctica
181 P2 **Adelaide River** Northern Territory, N Australia 13°12′S 131°06′E
76 M10 **'Adel Bagrou** Hodh ech Chargui, SE Mauritania 15°33′N 07°04′W
186 D6 **Adelbert Range** ⛰ N Papua New Guinea
180 K3 **Adele Island** island Western Australia
107 O17 **Adelfia** Puglia, SE Italy 41°01′N 16°52′E
195 V16 **Adélie Coast** physical region Antarctica
195 V14 **Adélie, Terre** physical region Antarctica
**Adelnau** *see* Odolanów
**Adelsberg** *see* Postojna
**Aden** *see* Khormaksar
**Aden** *see* 'Adan
141 Q17 **Aden, Gulf of** gulf SW Arabian Sea
77 V10 **Aderbissinat** Agadez, C Niger 15°30′N 07°57′E
**Adhaim** *see* Al 'Uz̧aym
143 R16 **Adh Dhayd** *var.* Al Dhaid. Ash Shāriqah, NE United Arab Emirates 25°19′N 55°51′E
140 M4 **'Adhfā'** spring/well NW Saudi Arabia 29°15′N 41°24′E
138 I13 **'Ādhriyāt, Jabāl al** ⛰ S Jordan
80 I10 **Ādī Ārk'ay** *var.* Addi Arkay. Āmara, N Ethiopia 13°18′N 37°56′E
182 C7 **Adieu, Cape** headland South Australia 32°01′S 132°12′E
106 H8 **Adige** *Ger.* Etsch. ∽ N Italy
80 J10 **Ādīgrat** Tigray, N Ethiopia 14°17′N 39°27′E
154 I13 **Ādilabād** *var.* Ādilābād. Telangana, C India 19°40′N 78°31′E
35 P2 **Adin** California, W USA 41°10′N 120°57′W
171 V14 **Adi, Pulau** island E Indonesia
18 K8 **Adirondack Mountains** ⛰ New York, NE USA
80 J13 **Ādīs Ābeba** *Eng.* Addis Ababa. ● (Ethiopia) Ādīs Ābeba, C Ethiopia 8°59′N 38°43′E
80 J13 **Ādīs Ābeba** ✈ Ādīs Ābeba, C Ethiopia 08°58′N 38°53′E
80 I11 **Ādīs Zemen** Āmara, N Ethiopia 12°00′N 37°43′E
**Adi Ugri** *see* Mendefera
137 N15 **Adıyaman** Adıyaman, SE Turkey 37°46′N 38°15′E
137 N15 **Adıyaman** ◐ *province* S Turkey
116 L11 **Adjud** Vrancea, E Romania 46°07′N 27°10′E
45 T6 **Adjuntas** C Puerto Rico 18°10′N 66°42′W
**Adjuntas, Presa de las** *see* Vicente Guerrero, Presa
**Ādkup** *see* Erikub Atoll
126 L15 **Adler** Krasnodarskiy Kray, SW Russia 43°25′N 39°58′E
**Adler** *see* Orlice
108 G7 **Adliswil** Zürich, NW Switzerland 47°19′N 08°32′E
32 G7 **Admiralty Inlet** inlet Washington, NW USA
39 X13 **Admiralty Island** island Alexander Archipelago, Alaska, USA
186 E5 **Admiralty Islands** island group N Papua New Guinea
136 B14 **Adnan Menderes** ✈ (İzmir) İzmir, W Turkey 38°16′N 27°09′E
37 V6 **Adobe Creek Reservoir** ⊠ Colorado, C USA
77 T16 **Ado-Ekiti** Ekiti, SW Nigeria 07°42′N 05°13′E
**Adola** *see* Kibre Mengist
61 C23 **Adolfo González Chaues** Buenos Aires, E Argentina
155 H17 **Ādoni** *var.* Ādavāni. Andhra Pradesh, C India 15°38′N 77°16′E
102 K15 **Adour** *anc.* Aturus. ∽ SW France
**Adowa** *see* Ādwa
105 O15 **Adra** Andalucía, S Spain 36°45′N 03°01′W
107 L24 **Adrano** Sicilia, Italy, C Mediterranean Sea 37°39′N 14°49′E
74 I9 **Adrar** C Algeria 27°56′N 00°12′W
76 K7 **Adrar** ◐ *region* C Mauritania
74 L11 **Adrar** ⛰ SE Algeria
74 A12 **Adrar Souttouf** ⛰ SW Western Sahara
**Adrasman** *see* Adrasmon
147 Q10 **Adrasmon** *Rus.* Adrasman. NW Tajikistan 40°38′N 69°56′E
78 K10 **Adré** Ouaddaï, E Chad 13°26′N 22°14′E
106 H9 **Adria** *anc.* Atria, Hadria, Hatria. Veneto, NE Italy 45°03′N 12°04′E
31 R10 **Adrian** Michigan, N USA 41°54′N 84°02′W
29 S11 **Adrian** Minnesota, N USA 43°38′N 95°55′W
27 R5 **Adrian** Missouri, C USA 38°24′N 94°21′W
24 M2 **Adrian** Texas, SW USA 35°16′N 102°39′W
21 S4 **Adrian** West Virginia, NE USA 38°53′N 80°14′W
**Adrianople/Adrianopolis** *see* Edirne
121 P7 **Adriatic Basin** undersea feature Adriatic Sea, N Mediterranean Sea 42°00′N 17°30′E
**Adriatico, Mare** *see* Adriatic Sea
106 L13 **Adriatic Sea** *Alb.* Deti Adriatik, *It.* Mare Adriatico, *SCr.* Jadransko More, *Slvn.* Jadransko Morje. sea N Mediterranean Sea
**Adriatik, Deti** *see* Adriatic Sea
**Adua** *see* Ādwa
**Aduana del Sásabe** *see* El Sásabe
79 O17 **Adusa** Orientale, NE Dem. Rep. Congo 01°25′N 28°05′E
118 J13 **Adutiškis** Vilnius, E Lithuania 55°09′N 26°34′E
27 Y7 **Advance** Missouri, C USA 37°06′N 89°54′W
65 D25 **Adventure Sound** bay East Falkland, Falkland Islands
80 J10 **Ādwa** *var.* Adowa, *It.* Adua. Tigray, N Ethiopia 14°08′N 38°51′E
123 Q8 **Adycha** ∽ NE Russia
126 L14 **Adygeya, Respublika** ◐ *autonomous republic* SW Russia
**Adzhikui** *see* Ajyguýy
77 N17 **Adzopé** SE Ivory Coast 06°07′N 03°49′W
125 U4 **Adz'va** ∽ NW Russia
125 U5 **Adz'vavom** Respublika Komi, NW Russia 66°35′N 59°13′E
**Ædua** *see* Autun
115 K19 **Aegean Islands** island group Greece/Turkey
**Aegean North** *see* Vóreio Aigaío
115 I17 **Aegean Sea** *Gk.* Aigaíon Pelagos, Aigaío Pélagos, *Turk.* Ege Denizi. sea NE Mediterranean Sea
**Aegean South** *see* Nótio Aigaío
118 H3 **Aegviidu** *Ger.* Charlottenhof. Harjumaa, NW Estonia 59°17′N 25°37′E
**Aegyptus** *see* Egypt
**Aelana** *see* Al 'Aqabah
**Aelok** *see* Ailuk Atoll
**Aelōninae** *see* Ailinginae Atoll
**Aelōnlaplap** *see* Ailinglaplap Atoll
**Æmilia** *see* Emilia-Romagna
**Æmilianum** *see* Millau
**Aemona** *see* Ljubljana
**Aenaria** *see* Ischia
**Aeolian Islands** *see* Eolie, Isole
191 Z3 **Aeon Point** headland Kiritimati, NE Kiribati 01°46′N 157°11′W
**Æsernia** *see* Isernia
104 G3 **A Estrada** Galicia, NW Spain 42°41′N 08°29′W
115 C18 **Aetós** Itháki, Iónia Nísoi, Greece, C Mediterranean Sea 38°21′N 20°40′E
191 Q8 **Afaahiti** Tahiti, W French Polynesia 17°43′S 149°18′W
139 U10 **'Afak** Al Qādisīyah, C Iraq 32°04′N 45°17′E
**Afanasjevo** *see* Afanas'yevo
125 T14 **Afanas'yevo** *var.* Afanasjevo. Kirovskaya Oblast', NW Russia 58°55′N 53°13′E
**Afándou** *see* Afántou
115 O23 **Afántou** *var.* Afándou. Ródos, Dodekánisa, Greece, Aegean Sea 36°17′N 28°10′E
80 K11 **Āfar** ◐ *region* NE Ethiopia
**Afar Depression** *see* Danakil Desert
191 O7 **Afareaitu** Moorea, W French Polynesia 17°33′S 149°47′W
140 L7 **'Afarīyah, Bi'r al** well NW Saudi Arabia
**Afars et des Issas, Territoire Français des** *see* Djibouti
83 D22 **Affenrücken** //Karas, SW Namibia 28°05′S 15°49′E
148 M6 **Afghanistan** *off.* Islamic Republic of Afghanistan, *Dar.* Jamhūrī-ye Islāmī-ye Afghānistān, *Pash.* Dê Afghānistān Islāmī Jumhūriyat; *prev.* Republic of Afghanistan. ◆ *islamic state* C Asia
**Afghānistān, Jamhūrī-ye Islāmī-ye** *see* Afghanistan
**Afgoi** *see* Afgooye
81 N17 **Afgooye** *It.* Afgoi. Shabeellaha Hoose, S Somalia 02°09′N 45°07′E
141 N8 **'Afīf** Ar Riyāḑ, C Saudi Arabia 23°57′N 42°57′E
77 V17 **Afikpo** Ebonyi, S Nigeria 05°52′N 07°58′E
**Afiun Karahissar** *see* Afyon
109 V6 **Aflenz Kurort** Steiermark, E Austria 47°33′N 15°14′E
74 J6 **Aflou** N Algeria 34°09′N 02°06′E
81 L18 **Afmadow** Jubbada Hoose, S Somalia 0°24′N 42°04′E
39 Q14 **Afognak Island** island Alaska, USA
104 J2 **A Fonsagrada** Galicia, NW Spain 43°09′N 07°03′W
186 E9 **Afore** Northern, S Papua New Guinea 09°10′S 148°30′E
59 O15 **Afrânio** Pernambuco, E Brazil 08°32′S 40°54′W
66-67 **Africa** continent
68 L11 **Africa, Horn of** physical region Ethiopia/Somalia
172 K11 **Africana Seamount** undersea feature SW Indian Ocean 37°10′S 29°10′E
86 A14 **African Plate** tectonic plate
138 I2 **'Afrīn** Ḩalab, N Syria 36°31′N 36°51′E
136 M15 **Afşin** Kahramanmaraş, C Turkey 38°14′N 36°54′E
98 J7 **Afsluitdijk** dam N Netherlands
29 U15 **Afton** Iowa, C USA 41°01′N 94°12′W
29 W9 **Afton** Minnesota, N USA 44°54′N 92°46′W
27 R8 **Afton** Oklahoma, C USA 36°41′N 94°57′W
136 F14 **Afyon** *prev.* Afyonkarahisar. Afyon, W Turkey 38°46′N 30°32′E
136 F14 **Afyon** *var.* Afiun Karahissar, Afyonkarahisar. ◐ *province* W Turkey
**Afyonkarahisar** *see* Afyon
**Agadès** *see* Agadez
77 V10 **Agadez** *prev.* Agadès. Agadez, C Niger 16°57′N 07°56′E
77 W8 **Agadez** ◐ *region* N Niger
74 E8 **Agadir** SW Morocco 30°30′N 09°37′W
64 M9 **Agadir Canyon** undersea feature SE Atlantic Ocean 32°30′N 12°50′W
145 R12 **Agadyr'** Karaganda, C Kazakhstan 48°15′N 72°55′E
173 O7 **Agalega Islands** island group N Mauritius
42 K6 **Agalta, Sierra de** ⛰ E Honduras
122 I10 **Agan** ∽ C Russia
**Agana/Agaña** *see* Hagåtña
188 B15 **Agana Bay** bay NW Guam
171 Kk13 **Agano-gawa** ∽ Honshū, C Japan
188 B17 **Aga Point** headland S Guam
154 G9 **Agar** Madhya Pradesh, C India 23°44′N 76°01′E
81 I14 **Āgaro** Oromīya, C Ethiopia 07°52′N 36°36′E
153 V15 **Agartala** state capital Tripura, NE India 23°49′N 91°15′E
194 I5 **Agassiz, Cape** headland Antarctica 68°29′S 62°59′W
175 V13 **Agassiz Fracture Zone** tectonic feature S Pacific Ocean
9 N2 **Agassiz Ice Cap** Ice feature Nunavut, N Canada
188 B16 **Agat** W Guam 13°20′N 144°38′E
188 B16 **Agat Bay** bay W Guam
**Agatha** *see* Agde
115 M20 **Agathónisi** island Dodekánisa, Greece, Aegean Sea
171 X14 **Agats** Papua, E Indonesia 05°33′S 138°07′E
155 C21 **Agatti Island** island Lakshadweep, India, N Indian Ocean
38 D16 **Agattu Island** island Aleutian Islands, Alaska, USA
38 D16 **Agattu Strait** strait Aleutian Islands, Alaska, USA
14 B8 **Agawa** ∽ Ontario, S Canada
14 B8 **Agawa Bay** lake bay Ontario, S Canada
77 N17 **Agboville** SE Ivory Coast 05°55′N 04°15′W
**kelbadzhar** *see* Kälbäcär
103 P16 **Agde** *anc.* Agatha. Hérault, S France 43°19′N 03°29′E
103 P16 **Agde, Cap d'** headland S France 43°17′N 03°30′E
**Agedabia** *see* Ajdābiyā
102 L14 **Agen** *anc.* Aginnum. Lot-et-Garonne, SW France 44°12′N 00°37′E
**Agendicum** *see* Sens
165 O13 **Ageo** Saitama, Honshū, S Japan 35°58′N 139°36′E
109 R5 **Ager** ∽ N Austria
**Agere Hiywet** *see* Hägere Hiywet
108 G8 **Ägerisee** ◎ W Switzerland
142 M10 **Āghā Jārī** Khūzestān, SW Iran 30°48′N 49°45′E
39 P15 **Aghiyuk Island** island Alaska, USA
74 B12 **Aghouinit** SE Western Sahara 22°14′N 13°10′W
74 B10 **Aghzoumal, Sebkhet** *var.* Sebjet Agsumal. salt lake E Western Sahara
115 F15 **Agiá** *var.* Ayiá. Thessalía, C Greece 39°43′N 22°45′E
40 G7 **Agiabampo, Estero de** estuary NW Mexico
121 P3 **Agía Fýlaxis** *var.* Ayia Phyla. S Cyprus 34°43′N 33°02′E
115 M21 **Agía Marína** Léros, Dodekánisa, Greece, Aegean Sea 37°09′N 26°51′E
121 Q2 **Agía Nápa** *var.* Ayia Napa. E Cyprus 34°59′N 34°00′E
115 L16 **Agía Paraskeví** Lésvos, E Greece 39°13′N 26°19′E
115 J15 **Agías Eirínis, Akrotírio** headland Límnos, E Greece 39°47′N 25°21′E
**Agiasós** *see* Agiassós
115 L17 **Agiassós** *var.* Agiasós, Ayiásos, Ayiássos. Lésvos, E Greece 39°05′N 26°23′E
**Aginnum** *see* Agen
123 O14 **Aginskoye** Zabaykal'skiy Kray, S Russia 51°10′N 114°32′E
115 I14 **Ágion Óros** *Eng.* Mount Athos. ◐ *monastic republic* NE Greece
115 H14 **Ágion Óros** *var.* Akte, Aktí; *anc.* Acte. peninsula NE Greece
114 D13 **Ágios Achílleios** religious building Dytikí Makedonía, N Greece
115 J16 **Ágios Efstrátios** *var.* Áyios Evstrátios, Hagios Evstrátios. island E Greece 34°00′N 25°00′E
115 H20 **Ágios Geórgios** island Kykládes, Greece, Aegean Sea
**Ágios Geórgios** *see* Ro
115 E21 **Ágios Ilías** ▲ S Greece 36°57′N 22°19′E
115 K25 **Ágios Ioánnis, Akrotírio** headland Kríti, Greece, E Mediterranean Sea 35°19′N 25°46′E
115 L20 **Ágios Kírykos** *var.* Áyios Kírikos. Ikaría, Dodekánisa, Greece, Aegean Sea 37°34′N 26°15′E
115 K25 **Ágios Nikólaos** *var.* Áyios Nikólaos. Kríti, Greece, E Mediterranean Sea 35°12′N 25°43′E
115 D16 **Ágios Nikolaos** Thessalía, C Greece 39°33′N 21°21′E
115 H14 **Agíou Órous, Kólpos** gulf N Greece
107 K24 **Agira** *anc.* Agyrium. Sicilia, Italy, C Mediterranean Sea 37°39′N 14°32′E
115 G20 **Agkístri** island S Greece
114 G12 **Ágkistro** *var.* Angistro. ▲ NE Greece 41°21′N 23°29′E
103 O17 **Agly** ∽ S France
**Agnetheln** *see* Agnita
14 E10 **Agnew Lake** ◎ Ontario, S Canada
77 O16 **Agnibilékrou** E Ivory Coast 07°10′N 03°11′W
116 I11 **Agnita** *Ger.* Agnetheln, *Hung.* Szentágota. Sibiu, SW Romania 45°59′N 24°40′E
107 K15 **Agnone** Molise, C Italy 41°49′N 14°21′E
164 K14 **Ago** Mie, Honshū, SW Japan 34°18′N 136°50′E
106 C8 **Agogna** ∽ N Italy
**Agoitz** *see* Aoiz
**Agoiz** *see* Aoiz
77 P17 **Agona Swedru** *var.* Swedru. SE Ghana 05°31′N 00°42′W
**Agordat** *see* Ak'ordat
**Agosta** *see* Augusta
103 N15 **Agout** ∽ S France
152 J12 **Āgra** Uttar Pradesh, N India 27°09′N 78°E
**Agra and Oudh, United Provinces of** *see* Uttar Pradesh
**Agram** *see* Zagreb
105 U5 **Agramunt** Cataluña, NE Spain 41°48′N 01°07′E
105 Q5 **Agreda** Castilla y León, N Spain 41°51′N 01°55′W
137 S13 **Ağrı** *var.* Karaköse; *prev.* Karakılısse. Ağrı, NE Turkey 39°44′N 43°04′E
137 S13 **Ağrı** ◐ *province* NE Turkey
107 N19 **Agri** *anc.* Aciris. ∽ S Italy
107 J24 **Agrigento** *Gk.* Akragas; *prev.* Girgenti. Sicilia, Italy, C Mediterranean Sea 37°19′N 13°33′E
188 K4 **Agrihan** island N Northern Mariana Islands
115 L17 **Agriliá, Akrotírio** *prev.* Ákra Maléas. cape Lésvos, E Greece
115 D18 **Agrínio** *prev.* Agrinion. Dytikí Elláda, W Greece 38°38′N 21°25′E
**Agrinion** *see* Agrínio
115 G17 **Agriovótano** Évvoia, C Greece 39°00′N 23°18′E
107 L18 **Agropoli** Campania, S Italy 40°22′N 14°59′E
127 T3 **Agryz** Udmurtskaya Respublika, NW Russia 56°27′N 52°58′E
137 U11 **Ağstafa** *Rus.* Akstafa. NW Azerbaijan 41°06′N 45°28′E
137 X11 **Ağsu** *Rus.* Akhsu. C Azerbaijan
**Agsumal, Sebjet** *see* Aghzoumal, Sebkhet
40 J11 **Agua Brava, Laguna** lagoon W Mexico
54 F7 **Aguachica** Cesar, N Colombia 08°16′N 73°35′W
59 J20 **Água Clara** Mato Grosso do Sul, SW Brazil 20°21′S 52°58′W
44 D5 **Aguada de Pasajeros** Cienfuegos, C Cuba 22°23′N 80°51′W
54 J5 **Aguada Grande** Lara, N Venezuela 10°38′N 69°29′W
45 S5 **Aguadilla** W Puerto Rico 18°27′N 67°08′W
43 S16 **Aguadulce** Coclé, S Panama 08°16′N 80°31′W
104 L14 **Aguadulce** Andalucía, S Spain 37°15′N 04°59′W
41 O8 **Agualeguas** Nuevo León, NE Mexico 26°17′N 99°30′W
40 L9 **Aguanaval, Río** ∽ C Mexico
42 J5 **Aguán, Río** ∽ N Honduras
25 R16 **Agua Nueva** Texas, SW USA 26°57′N 98°34′W
60 J8 **Aguapeí, Rio** ∽ S Brazil
61 E14 **Aguapey, Río** ∽ NE Argentina
40 G3 **Agua Prieta** Sonora, NW Mexico 31°16′N 109°33′W
104 G5 **A Guarda** *var.* A Guardia, Laguardia, La Guardia. Galicia, NW Spain 41°54′N 08°53′W
**A Guardia** *see* A Guarda
56 E6 **Aguarico, Río** ∽ Ecuador/ Peru
55 O6 **Aguasay** Monagas, NE Venezuela 09°25′N 63°44′W
40 M12 **Aguascalientes** Aguascalientes, C Mexico 21°54′N 102°17′W
40 L12 **Aguascalientes** ◐ *state* C Mexico
57 I18 **Aguas Calientes, Río** ∽ S Peru
105 R7 **Aguasvivas** ∽ NE Spain
60 J7 **Água Vermelha, Represa de** ⊠ S Brazil
56 E12 **Aguaytía** Ucayali, C Peru 09°02′S 75°30′W
104 I5 **A Gudiña** *var.* La Gudiña. Galicia, NW Spain 42°04′N 07°08′W
104 G7 **Águeda** Aveiro, N Portugal 40°34′N 08°28′W
104 J8 **Águeda** ∽ Portugal/Spain
77 Q8 **Aguelhok** Kidal, NE Mali 19°18′N 00°50′E
77 V12 **Aguié** Maradi, S Niger 13°28′N 07°43′E
188 K8 **Aguijan** island S Northern Mariana Islands
104 M14 **Aguilar** *var.* Aguilar de la Frontera. Andalucía, S Spain 37°31′N 04°40′W
104 M3 **Aguilar de Campóo** Castilla y León, N Spain 42°47′N 04°15′W
**Aguilar de la Frontera** *see* Aguilar
42 F7 **Aguilares** San Salvador, C El Salvador 13°56′N 89°09′W
105 Q14 **Aguilas** Murcia, SE Spain 37°24′N 01°36′W
40 L15 **Aguililla** Michoacán, SW Mexico 18°43′N 102°45′W
**Agulhas** *see* L'Agulhas
172 J11 **Agulhas Bank** undersea feature SW Indian Ocean 35°30′S 21°00′E
172 K11 **Agulhas Basin** undersea feature SW Indian Ocean 47°00′S 27°00′E
83 F26 **Agulhas, Cape** *Afr.* Kaap Agulhas. headland SW South Africa 34°51′S 19°59′E
**Agulhas, Kaap** *see* Agulhas, Cape
60 O9 **Agulhas Negras, Pico das** ▲ SE Brazil 22°21′S 44°39′W
172 K11 **Agulhas Plateau** undersea feature SW Indian Ocean 40°00′S 26°00′E
165 S16 **Aguni-jima** island Nansei-shotō, SW Japan
**Agurain** *see* Salvatierra
54 G5 **Agustín Codazzi** *var.* Codazzi. Cesar, N Colombia 10°02′N 73°15′W
**Agyrium** *see* Agira
74 L12 **Ahaggar** *Eng.* Hoggar Mountains. high plateau region SE Algeria
74 L12 **Ahaggar** *Eng.* Hoggar Mountains. high plateau region SE Algeria
74 K14 **Ahaggar, Tassili oua-n-** *var.* Tassili du Hoggar, Tassili ta-n-Ahaggar. plateau S Algeria
**Ahaggar, Tassili ta-n-** *see* Ahaggar, Tassili oua-n-
146 E12 **Ahal Welaýaty** *Rus.* Akhalskiy Velayat. ◐ *province* C Turkmenistan
142 K2 **Ahar** Āz̄arbāyjān-e Sharqī, NW Iran 38°25′N 47°07′E
**Aharnes** *see* Acharnés
138 J3 **Aḩaş, Jabal** ▲ NW Syria
138 J3 **Aḩaş, Jebal** ⛰ W Syria
185 G16 **Ahaura** ∽ South Island, New Zealand
100 E13 **Ahaus** Nordrhein-Westfalen, NW Germany 52°04′N 07°01′E
191 U9 **Ahe** atoll Îles Tuamotu, C French Polynesia
184 N10 **Ahimanawa Range** ⛰ North Island, New Zealand
119 I19 **Ahinski Kanal** *Rus.* Oginskiy Kanal. canal SW Belarus
186 G10 **Ahioma** SE Papua New Guinea 10°20′S 150°35′E
184 I2 **Ahipara** Northland, North Island, New Zealand 35°11′S 173°07′E
184 I2 **Ahipara Bay** bay SE Tasman Sea
**Áhkájávrre** *see* Akkajaure
**Áhkká** *see* Akka
39 N13 **Ahklun Mountains** ⛰ Alaska, USA
137 R14 **Ahlat** Bitlis, E Turkey 38°45′N 42°28′E
101 F14 **Ahlen** Nordrhein-Westfalen, W Germany 51°46′N 07°53′E
154 D10 **Ahmadābād** *var.* Ahmedabad. Gujarāt, W India 23°03′N 72°40′E
143 R10 **Ahmadābād** Kermān, C Iran 35°51′N 59°36′E
**Ahmadi** *see* Al Aḩmadī
**Ahmad Khel** *see* Ḩasan Khēl
155 F14 **Ahmadnagar** *var.* Ahmednagar. Mahārāshtra, W India 19°08′N 74°48′E
149 T9 **Ahmadpur Sial** Punjab, E Pakistan 30°40′N 71°52′E
77 N5 **Aḩmar, 'Erg el** desert N Mali
80 K13 **Ahmar Mountains** ⛰ C Ethiopia
**Ahmedabad** *see* Ahmadābād
**Ahmednagar** *see* Ahmadnagar
114 N12 **Ahmetbey** Kırklareli, NW Turkey 41°26′N 27°35′E
14 H12 **Ahmic Lake** ◎ Ontario, S Canada
190 G12 **Ahoa** Île Uvea, E Wallis and Futuna 13°17′S 176°12′W
40 G8 **Ahomé** Sinaloa, C Mexico 25°55′N 109°10′W
21 X8 **Ahoskie** North Carolina, SE USA 36°17′N 76°59′W
101 D17 **Ahr** ∽ W Germany
143 N12 **Ahram** *var.* Ahrom. Būshehr, S Iran 28°52′N 51°18′E
100 J9 **Ahrensburg** Schleswig-Holstein, N Germany 53°41′N 10°14′E
**Ahrom** *see* Ahram
93 L17 **Ähtäri** Etelä-Pohjanmaa, W Finland 62°34′N 24°08′E
40 K12 **Ahuacatlán** Nayarit, C Mexico 21°02′N 104°30′W
42 E7 **Ahuachapán** Ahuachapán, W El Salvador 13°55′N 89°51′W
42 A9 **Ahuachapán** ◐ *department* W El Salvador
191 V16 **Ahu Akivi** *var.* Siete Moai. ancient monument Easter Island, Chile, E Pacific Ocean
191 W11 **Ahunui** atoll Îles Tuamotu, C French Polynesia
185 E20 **Ahuriri** ∽ South Island, New Zealand
95 L22 **Åhus** Skåne, S Sweden 55°55′N 14°18′E
**Ahu Tahira** *see* Ahu Vinapu
191 V16 **Ahu Tepeu** ancient monument Easter Island, Chile, E Pacific Ocean
191 V17 **Ahu Vinapu** *var.* Ahu Tahira. ancient monument Easter Island, Chile, E Pacific Ocean
142 L9 **Ahvāz** *var.* Ahwāz; *prev.* Nāsiri. Khūzestān, SW Iran 31°20′N 48°38′E
**Ahvenanmaa** *see* Åland
141 Q16 **Aḩwar** SW Yemen 13°34′N 46°41′E
**Ahwāz** *see* Ahvāz
94 H7 **Åi Åfjord** *var.* Årnes. Sør-Trøndelag, C Norway 63°57′N 10°12′E
149 P3 **Aībak** *var.* Haibak; *prev.* Āybak, Samangān. Samangān, NE Afghanistan 36°16′N 68°04′E
101 K22 **Aichach** Bayern, SE Germany 48°26′N 11°06′E
164 L14 **Aichi** *off.* Aichi-ken, *var.* Aiti. ◐ *prefecture* Honshū, SW Japan
**Aïdin** *see* Aydın
**Aidussina** *see* Ajdovščina
**Aifir, Clochán an** *see* Giant's Causeway
**Aigaíon Pelagos/Aigaío Pélagos** *see* Aegean Sea
109 S3 **Aigen im Mülkreis** Oberösterreich, N Austria 48°39′N 13°57′E
**Aigialoúsa** *see* Yenierenköy
115 G20 **Aígina** *var.* Aíyina, Egina. Aígina, C Greece 37°45′N 23°26′E
115 G20 **Aígina** island S Greece
115 E18 **Aígio** *var.* Egio; *prev.* Aíyion. Dytikí Elláda, S Greece 38°15′N 22°05′E


◆ Country
● Country Capital
◇ Dependent Territory
○ Dependent Territory Capital
◐ Administrative Regions
✈ International Airport
▲ Mountain
⛰ Mountain Range
🌋 Volcano
∽ River
◎ Lake
⊠ Reservoir

| | | |
|---|---|---|
| 108 | C10 | **Aigle** Vaud, SW Switzerland 46°20′N 06°58′E |
| 103 | P14 | **Aigoual, Mont** ▲ S France 44°09′N 03°34′E |
| 173 | O16 | **Aigrettes, Pointe des** *headland* W Réunion 21°02′S 55°14′E |
| 61 | G19 | **Aiguá** var. Aigua. Maldonado, S Uruguay 34°13′S 54°46′W |
| 103 | S13 | **Aigues** ✍ SE France |
| 103 | N10 | **Aigurande** Indre, C France 46°26′N 01°49′E |
| | | **Ai-hun** see Heihe |
| 163 | N10 | **Aikawa** Niigata, Sado, C Japan 38°04′N 138°15′E |
| 21 | Q13 | **Aiken** South Carolina, SE USA 33°34′N 81°44′W |
| 25 | N4 | **Aiken** Texas, SW USA 34°06′N 101°31′W |
| 160 | F13 | **Ailao Shan** ▲ SW China |
| 189 | R4 | **Ailinginae Atoll** var. Aelōninae. *atoll* Ralik Chain, SW Marshall Islands |
| 189 | T7 | **Ailinglaplap Atoll** var. Aelōnlaplap. *atoll* Ralik Chain, S Marshall Islands |
| | | **Aillionn, Loch** see Allen, Lough |
| 96 | H13 | **Ailsa Craig** *island* SW Scotland, United Kingdom |
| 189 | V5 | **Ailuk Atoll** var. Aelok. *atoll* Ratak Chain, NE Marshall Islands |
| 123 | R11 | **Aim** Khabarovskiy Kray, E Russia 58°45′N 134°08′E |
| 45 | Q12 | **Aimé Césaire** ✈ (Fort-de-France) C Martinique 14°34′N 61°00′W |
| 103 | R11 | **Ain** ◆ *department* E France |
| 103 | S10 | **Ain** ✍ E France |
| 118 | G7 | **Ainaži** Est. Heinaste, Ger. Hainasch. N Latvia |
| 74 | L6 | **Aïn Beïda** NE Algeria 35°50′N 07°25′E |
| 76 | K4 | **'Aïn Ben Tili** Tiris Zemmour, N Mauritania 25°58′N 09°30′W |
| 74 | J3 | **Aïn Defla** var. Aïn Eddefla. N Algeria 36°15′N 01°58′E |
| 74 | L5 | **Aïn Eddefla** see Aïn Defla |
| | | **Aïn El Bey** ✈ (Constantine) NE Algeria 36°15′N 06°36′E |
| 115 | C19 | **Aínos** ▲ Kefallonía, Iónia Nísoi, Greece, C Mediterranean Sea 38°08′N 20°39′E |
| 105 | T4 | **Ainsa** Aragón, NE Spain 42°25′N 00°08′E |
| 74 | I7 | **Aïn Sefra** NW Algeria 32°45′N 00°32′W |
| 29 | N13 | **Ainsworth** Nebraska, C USA 42°33′N 99°51′W |
| | | **Aintab** see Gaziantep |
| 74 | H5 | **Aïn Témouchent** N Algeria 35°18′N 01°09′W |
| 186 | C6 | **Aiome** Madang, N Papua New Guinea 05°08′S 144°45′E |
| | | **Aïoun el Atrous/Aïoun el Atroûss** see 'Ayoûn el 'Atroûs |
| 54 | E11 | **Aipe** Huila, C Colombia 03°15′N 75°17′W |
| 56 | D9 | **Aipena, Río** ✍ N Peru |
| 57 | L19 | **Aiquile** Cochabamba, C Bolivia 18°10′S 65°10′W |
| | | **Air** see Aïr, Massif de l' |
| 188 | E10 | **Airai** Babeldaob, C Palau |
| 188 | E10 | **Airai** ✈ (Oreor) Babeldaob, C Palau 07°22′N 134°34′E |
| 168 | I11 | **Airbangis** Sumatera, NW Indonesia 0°12′N 99°22′E |
| 11 | Q16 | **Airdrie** Alberta, SW Canada 51°20′N 114°00′W |
| 96 | I12 | **Airdrie** S Scotland, United Kingdom 55°52′N 03°59′W |
| | | **Air du Azbine** see Aïr, Massif de l' |
| 97 | M17 | **Aire** ✍ N England, United Kingdom |
| 102 | K15 | **Aire-sur-l'Adour** Landes, SW France 43°43′N 00°16′W |
| 103 | O1 | **Aire-sur-la-Lys** Pas-de-Calais, N France 50°39′N 02°24′E |
| 9 | Q6 | **Air Force Island** *island* Baffin Island, Nunavut, NE Canada |
| 169 | Q13 | **Airhitam, Teluk** *bay* Borneo, C Indonesia |
| 171 | Q11 | **Airmadidi** Sulawesi, C Indonesia 01°25′N 124°59′E |
| 77 | V8 | **Aïr, Massif de l'** ▲ Aïr, Aïr du Azbine, Asben. ▲ NC Niger |
| 108 | G10 | **Airolo** Ticino, S Switzerland 46°32′N 08°48′E |
| 102 | K9 | **Airvault** Deux-Sèvres, W France 46°51′N 00°07′W |
| 101 | K19 | **Aisch** ✍ S Germany |
| 10 | H7 | **Aishihik Lake** ✍ Yukon, W Canada |
| 103 | P3 | **Aisne** ◆ *department* N France |
| 103 | R4 | **Aisne** ✍ NE France |
| 109 | T4 | **Aist** ✍ N Austria |
| 114 | K13 | **Aisými** Anatolikí Makedonía kai Thráki, NE Greece 41°00′N 25°55′E |
| 105 | S11 | **Aitana** ▲ S Spain 38°39′N 00°15′W |
| 186 | B5 | **Aitape** var. Eitape. West Sepik, NW Papua New Guinea 03°10′S 142°17′E |
| | | **Aiti** see Aichi |
| 29 | V4 | **Aitkin** Minnesota, N USA 46°32′N 93°42′W |
| 115 | D18 | **Aitolikó** var. Etoliko; prev. Aitolikón. Dytikí Elláda, C Greece 38°26′N 21°21′E |
| | | **Aitolikón** see Aitolikó |
| 190 | L15 | **Aitutaki** *island* S Cook Islands |
| 116 | H11 | **Aiud** Ger. Strassburg, Hung. Nagyenyed; prev. Engeten. Alba, SW Romania 46°19′N 23°43′E |
| 118 | I9 | **Aiviekste** ✍ C Latvia |
| 189 | Q8 | **Aiwo** SW Nauru 0°32′S 166°54′E |
| 188 | E8 | **Aiwokako Passage** *passage* Babeldaob, N Palau |
| | | **Aix** see Aix-en-Provence |
| 103 | R13 | **Aix-en-Provence** var. Aix; anc. Aquae Sextiae. Bouches-du-Rhône, SE France 43°31′N 05°27′E |
| 103 | T11 | **Aix-les-Bains** Savoie, E France 45°40′N 05°55′E |
| | | **Aix-la-Chapelle** see Aachen |
| 186 | A6 | **Aiyang, Mount** ▲ NW Papua New Guinea 05°03′S 141°12′E |
| | | **Aíyina** see Aígina |
| | | **Aíyion** see Aígio |
| 153 | W15 | **Aizawl** *state capital* Mizoram, NE India 23°39′N 92°45′E |
| 118 | H9 | **Aizkraukle** S Latvia 56°39′N 25°07′E |
| 118 | C9 | **Aizpute** W Latvia 56°43′N 21°32′E |

| | | |
|---|---|---|
| 165 | O11 | **Aizuwakamatsu** Fukushima, Honshū, C Japan 37°30′N 139°58′E |
| 103 | X15 | **Ajaccio** Corse, France, C Mediterranean Sea 41°54′N 08°43′E |
| 133 | X15 | **Ajaccio, Golfe d'** *gulf* Corse, France, C Mediterranean Sea |
| 41 | Q13 | **Ajalpán** Puebla, S Mexico 18°26′N 97°20′W |
| 154 | F13 | **Ajanta Range** ▲ C India |
| 137 | R10 | **Ajaria** Georg. Ach'ara. ◆ *autonomous republic* SW Georgia |
| 93 | C14 | **Ajaureforsen** Västerbotten, N Sweden 65°31′N 15°44′E |
| 185 | H17 | **Ajax, Mount** ▲ South Island, New Zealand 43°13′S 172°06′E |
| 162 | F9 | **Aj Bogd Uul** ▲ SW Mongolia |
| 75 | R8 | **Ajdābiyā** var. Agedabia, Ajdabiyah. NE Libya 30°46′N 20°14′E |
| | | **Ajdābiyah** see Ajdābiyā |
| 109 | S12 | **Ajdovščina** Ger. Haidenschaft, It. Aidussina. W Slovenia 45°53′N 140°11′E |
| 165 | Q7 | **Ajigasawa** Aomori, Honshū, N Japan 40°46′N 140°12′E |
| | | **Ajijena** see El Geneina |
| 111 | H23 | **Ajka** Veszprém, W Hungary 47°18′N 17°32′E |
| | | **'Ajlūn** 'Ajlūn, N Jordan 32°20′N 35°45′E |
| 138 | G9 | **'Ajlūn, Jabal** ▲ W Jordan |
| | | **Ajluokta** see Drag |
| 143 | R15 | **'Ajmān** var. Ajman, 'Ujmān. 'Ajmān, NE United Arab Emirates 25°36′N 55°42′E |
| 152 | G12 | **Ajmer** var. Ajmere. Rājasthān, N India 26°29′N 74°40′E |
| | | **Ajmere** see Ajmer |
| | | **Akkerman** see Bilhorod-Dnistrovs'kyy |
| 127 | W8 | **Akkermanovka** Orenburgskaya Oblast', W Russia 51°11′N 58°03′E |
| 165 | V4 | **Akkeshi** Hokkaidō, NE Japan 43°03′N 144°49′E |
| 165 | V4 | **Akkeshi-ko** ☺ Hokkaidō, NE Japan |
| 165 | V5 | **Akkeshi-wan** *bay* NW Pacific Ocean |
| 138 | F8 | **Akko** Eng. Acre, Fr. Saint-Jean-d'Acre, Bibl. Accho, Ptolemaïs. N Israel 32°55′N 35°04′E |
| 98 | L6 | **Akkrum** Fryslân, N Netherlands 53°01′N 05°52′E |
| 145 | U8 | **Akku** Kaz. Aqqū; prev. Lebyazh'ye. Pavlodar, NE Kazakhstan 51°29′N 77°48′E |
| 144 | F12 | **Akkystau** Atyrau, W Kazakhstan 47°05′N 51°03′E |
| 8 | G6 | **Aklavik** Northwest Territories, NW Canada 68°15′N 135°00′W |
| 118 | B9 | **Akmenrags** prev. Akmeņrags. *headland* W Latvia 56°49′N 21°03′E |
| 158 | E9 | **Akmeqit** Xinjiang Uygur Zizhiqu, NW China 37°10′N 76°59′E |
| 144 | I10 | **Akmeydan** Mary Welayaty, C Turkmenistan 37°52′N 62°08′E |
| 145 | P9 | **Akmola** off. Akmolinskaya Oblast', Kaz. Aqmola Oblysy; prev. Tselinogradskaya Oblast. ◆ *province* C Kazakhstan |
| | | **Akmola** see Nur-Sultan |
| 127 | V8 | **Akmolinsk** see Nur-Sultan |
| | | **Akmolinskaya Oblast'** see Akmola |
| 118 | I11 | **Aknīste** S Latvia 56°09′N 25°43′E |
| | | **Aknavásár** see Târgu Ocna |
| 81 | G14 | **Akobo** Jonglei, E South Sudan 07°50′N 33°05′E |
| 81 | G14 | **Akobo** var. Akobowenz. ✍ Ethiopia/Sudan |
| | | **Akobowenz** see Akobo |
| 154 | H12 | **Akola** Mahārāshtra, C India 20°44′N 77°00′E |
| 81 | Q16 | **Akosombo Dam** *dam* SE Ghana |
| 164 | C15 | **Akune** Kagoshima, Kyūshū, SW Japan 32°00′N 130°13′E |
| | | **Akurdet** see Ak'ordat |
| 77 | Q16 | **Akure** SW Nigeria 07°18′N 05°13′E |
| 92 | I2 | **Akureyri** N Iceland 65°40′N 18°07′W |
| 38 | M17 | **Akutan Island** *island* Aleutian Islands, Alaska, USA |
| 77 | V17 | **Akwa Ibom** ◆ *state* SE Nigeria |
| | | **Akyab** see Sittwe |
| 127 | W7 | **Akzhar** Respublika Bashkortostan, W Russia 53°59′N 59°15′E |
| 144 | J10 | **Akzhar** prev. Novorossiyskiy, Novorossiyskoye. Aktyubinsk, NW Kazakhstan |
| 145 | S13 | **Akzhar** Kaz. Aqzhar. Vostochnyy Kazakhstan 47°36′N 83°38′E |
| 23 | P5 | **Alabama** off. State of Alabama, also known as Camellia State, Heart of Dixie, The Cotton State, Yellowhammer State. ◆ *state* S USA |
| 23 | P6 | **Alabama River** ✍ Alabama, S USA |
| 23 | P4 | **Alabaster** Alabama, S USA 33°14′N 86°49′W |
| 139 | U10 | **Al 'Abd Allāh** var. Al Abdullah. Al Qādisīyah, S Iraq 31°21′N 45°27′E |
| | | **Al Abdullah** see Al 'Abd Allāh |
| 139 | W14 | **Al Abţiyah** well S Iraq |
| 147 | S9 | **Ala-Buka** Dzhalal-Abadskaya Oblast', C Kyrgyzstan 41°23′N 71°32′E |
| 136 | J12 | **Alaca** Çorum, N Turkey 40°10′N 34°51′E |
| 136 | K10 | **Alaçam** Samsun, N Turkey 41°37′N 35°34′E |

| | | |
|---|---|---|
| 136 | I15 | **Aksaray** Aksaray, C Turkey 38°23′N 33°50′E |
| 136 | I15 | **Aksaray** ◆ *province* C Turkey |
| 144 | G8 | **Aksay** var. Aksaj, Kaz. Aqsay. Zapadnyy Kazakhstan, NW Kazakhstan 51°11′N 53°00′E |
| 127 | C11 | **Aksay** Volgogradskaya Oblast', SW Russia 47°59′N 43°54′E |
| 147 | W10 | **Ak-say** var. Toxkan He. ✍ China/Kyrgyzstan |
| | | **Aksay Kazakzu Zizhixian** see Aksay/Aksay |
| 158 | G11 | **Aksayqin Hu** ☺ NW China |
| 136 | G14 | **Akşehir** Konya, W Turkey 38°22′N 31°24′E |
| 136 | G14 | **Akşehir Gölü** ☺ C Turkey |
| 123 | F13 | **Aksenovo-Zilovskoye** Zabaykal'skiy Kray, S Russia 53°01′N 117°26′E |
| 145 | S12 | **Akshatau** Kaz. Akshataū; prev. Akchatau. Karaganda, C Kazakhstan 47°59′N 74°02′E |
| 145 | V11 | **Akshatau, Khrebet** ▲ SE Kazakhstan |
| 143 | Y8 | **Ak-Shyyrak** Issyk-Kul'skaya Oblast', E Kyrgyzstan 41°46′N 78°34′E |
| 158 | H7 | **Aksu** Xinjiang Uygur Zizhiqu, NW China 41°17′N 80°15′E |
| 145 | R8 | **Aksu** Kaz. Aqsū. Akmola, N Kazakhstan 52°31′N 72°00′E |
| 145 | W13 | **Aksu** Kaz. Aqsū. Almaty, SE Kazakhstan 45°31′N 79°28′E |
| 145 | T8 | **Aksu** var. Jermak, Kaz. Ermak; prev. Yermak. Pavlodar, NE Kazakhstan 52°03′N 76°55′E |
| 145 | V13 | **Aksu** Kaz. Aqsū. ✍ SE Kazakhstan |
| 158 | H7 | **Aksu** Xinjiang Uygur Zizhiqu, NW China 41°07′N 80°05′E |
| 80 | J10 | **Āksum** Tigray, N Ethiopia 14°06′N 38°42′E |
| 145 | O12 | **Aktas, Kaz.** Aqtas. Karaganda, C Kazakhstan 48°03′N 66°12′E |
| | | **Aktash** see Oqtosh |
| 147 | V9 | **Ak-Tash, Gora** ▲ C Kyrgyzstan |
| 145 | R10 | **Aktau** Kaz. Aqtaū. Karaganda, C Kazakhstan 50°13′N 73°06′E |
| 144 | E11 | **Aktau** Kaz. Aqtaū; prev. Shevchenko. Mangistau, W Kazakhstan 51°29′N 51°14′E |
| 144 | M11 | **Aktau, Khrebet** ▲ C Kazakhstan |
| 144 | F12 | **Aktau, Khrebet** ▲ C Kazakhstan |
| | | **Akte** see Ágion Óros |
| 145 | X7 | **Ak-Terek** Issyk-Kul'skaya Oblast', E Kyrgyzstan 42°14′N 77°46′E |
| | | **Akti** see Ágion Óros |
| | | **Aktjubinsk/Aktyubinsk** see Aktobe |
| 158 | E8 | **Aktobe** Xinjiang Uygur Zizhiqu, NW China 39°07′N 75°43′E |
| 144 | I10 | **Aktobe** var. Aktyubinsk. 37°52′N 62°08′E |
| 144 | G9 | **Aktyubinsk** see Aktyubinsk |
| | | **Aktyubinsk** off. Aktyubinskaya Oblast', Kaz. Aqtöbe Oblysy. ◆ *province* W Kazakhstan |
| | | **Aktyubinsk** see Aktobe |
| 119 | M18 | **Aktsyabrski** Rus. Oktyabr'skiy; prev. Karpilovka. Homyel'skaya Voblasts', SE Belarus 52°38′N 28°53′E |
| | | **Aktyubinsk off.** Aktyubinskaya Oblast', Kaz. Aqtöbe Oblysy. ◆ *province* W Kazakhstan |
| | | **Aktyubinsk** see Aktobe |
| 147 | W7 | **Ak-Tyuz** var. Aktyuz. Chuyskaya Oblast', N Kyrgyzstan 42°50′N 76°05′E |
| 79 | J17 | **Akula** Equateur, NW Dem. Rep. Congo 02°22′N 20°13′E |
| 38 | L16 | **Akun Island** *island* Aleutian Islands, Alaska, USA |
| 77 | T16 | **Akure** SW Nigeria 07°18′N 05°13′E |
| 12 | M3 | **Akpatok Island** *island* Nunavut, E Canada |
| 158 | G7 | **Akqi** Xinjiang Uygur Zizhiqu, NW China 40°51′N 78°20′E |
| 138 | I2 | **Akrād, Jabal al** ▲ N Syria |
| 74 | K8 | **Akragas** see Agrigento |
| 139 | S2 | **Akranes** Vesturland, W Iceland 64°19′N 22°01′W |
| 37 | V3 | **Akron** Colorado, C USA 40°09′N 103°12′W |
| 29 | R12 | **Akron** Iowa, C USA 42°50′N 96°33′W |
| 31 | U11 | **Akron** Ohio, N USA 41°05′N 81°31′W |
| 119 | N18 | **Aksa** Rus. Okta. 60°33′N 30°33′E |

| | | |
|---|---|---|
| 105 | S12 | **Alacant** var. Alicante. ◆ *province* Comunitat Valenciana, SE Spain |
| | | **Alacant** see Alicante |
| 23 | W9 | **Alachua** Florida, SE USA 29°48′N 82°29′W |
| 137 | S13 | **Aladağlar** ▲ W Turkey |
| 136 | K15 | **Ala Dağları** ▲ C Turkey |
| 162 | I5 | **Alag-Erdene** var. Manhan. Hövsgöl, N Mongolia 50°05′N 100°01′E |
| 127 | O16 | **Alagir** Respublika Severnaya Osetiya, SW Russia 43°04′N 44°07′E |
| 106 | B6 | **Alagna Valsesia** Valle d'Aosta, NW Italy 45°51′N 07°50′E |
| 103 | P12 | **Alagnon** ✍ C France |
| 59 | P16 | **Alagoas** off. Estado de Alagoas. ◆ *state* E Brazil |
| 59 | P17 | **Alagoinhas** Bahia, E Brazil 12°09′S 38°21′W |
| 105 | R8 | **Alagón** Aragón, NE Spain 41°46′N 01°07′W |
| 104 | J9 | **Alagón** ✍ W Spain |
| 93 | K16 | **Alahärmä** Etelä-Pohjanmaa, W Finland 63°15′N 22°50′E |
| 142 | K12 | **Al Ahmadi** var. Ahmadi, Al Aḩmadī. E Kuwait 29°02′N 48°04′E |
| | | **Al Ain** var. Alayor. see Al 'Ayn |
| 73 | Z8 | **Al 'Athāmīn** An Najaf, S Iraq 30°27′N 43°27′E |
| 139 | S13 | **Alatna River** ✍ Alaska, USA |
| 38 | P7 | **Alatna** ▲ Alaska, USA |
| 107 | J15 | **Alatri** Lazio, C Italy 41°43′N 13°21′E |
| 127 | P5 | **Alatyr'** Chuvashskaya Respublika, W Russia 54°50′N 46°28′E |
| 56 | C7 | **Alausí** Chimborazo, C Ecuador 02°11′S 78°52′W |
| | | **Álava** see Araba |
| 117 | T11 | **Alaverdi** N Armenia 41°06′N 44°37′E |
| | | **Alavo see Alavus** |
| 93 | N14 | **Ala-Vuoksi** Kainuu, E Finland 64°N 29°29′E |
| 93 | K17 | **Alavus** Swe. Alavo. Etelä-Pohjanmaa, W Finland 62°33′N 23°38′E |
| 182 | K9 | **Alawoona** South Australia 34°45′S 140°28′E |
| | | **Alaykel'/Alay-Kuu** see Kök-Art |
| 143 | R17 | **Al 'Ayn** var. Al Ain. Abū Ẓaby, E United Arab Emirates 24°13′N 55°44′E |
| 143 | R17 | **Al 'Ayn** var. Al Ain. Abū Ẓaby, E United Arab Emirates 24°16′N 55°31′E |
| 138 | G12 | **Al 'Aynā** Al Karak, W Jordan 30°59′N 35°43′E |
| | | **Alayor** see Alaior |
| 145 | X13 | **Al Awaynāt** SE Libya |
| 182 | K9 | **Al 'Uwaynāt** see Al 'Uwaynāt |
| 143 | R17 | **Al 'Ayn** see Al 'Ayn |
| 125 | S6 | **Alazeya** ✍ NE Russia |
| 139 | U8 | **Al 'Azīzīyah** var. Aziziya. Wāsiţ, E Iraq 32°54′N 45°05′E |
| 120 | M12 | **Al 'Azīzīyah** NW Libya 32°32′N 13°01′E |
| 138 | I10 | **Az Zarqā'** ✍ N Jordan 31°49′N 36°48′E |
| 99 | I16 | **Albertkanaal** *canal* N Belgium |
| 79 | P17 | **Albert, Lake** var. Albert Nyanza, Lac Mobutu Sese Seko. ☺ Uganda/Dem. Rep. Congo |
| 29 | V11 | **Albert Lea** Minnesota, N USA 43°39′N 93°22′W |
| 81 | F16 | **Albert Nile** ✍ NW Uganda |
| | | **Albert Nyanza** see Albert, Lake |
| 103 | T11 | **Albertville** Savoie, E France 45°40′N 06°24′W |
| | | **Albertville** see Kalemie |
| 23 | Q2 | **Albertville** Alabama, S USA 34°16′N 86°12′W |
| 102 | L13 | **Albi** anc. Albiga. Tarn, S France 43°56′N 02°09′E |
| 29 | W15 | **Albia** Iowa, C USA 41°01′N 92°48′W |
| 55 | X9 | **Albina** Marowijne, NE Suriname 05°29′N 54°08′W |
| 83 | A15 | **Albina, Ponta** *headland* SW Angola 15°53′S 11°45′E |
| 30 | M16 | **Albion** Illinois, N USA 38°22′N 88°03′W |
| 31 | P11 | **Albion** Indiana, N USA 41°24′N 85°25′W |
| 29 | P14 | **Albion** Nebraska, C USA 41°41′N 98°00′W |
| 18 | E9 | **Albion** New York, NE USA 43°13′N 78°09′W |
| 18 | B12 | **Albion** Pennsylvania, NE USA 41°53′N 80°18′W |
| 140 | J4 | **Al Bi'r** var. Bi'r Ibn Hirmās. Tabūk, NW Saudi Arabia 28°52′N 36°16′E |
| 140 | M12 | **Al Birk** Makkah al Mukarramah, SW Saudi Arabia 18°13′N 41°36′E |
| 141 | Q9 | **Al Biyāḍ** *desert* C Saudi Arabia |

| | | |
|---|---|---|
| 141 | P6 | **Al Arṭāwīyah** Ar Riyāḍ, N Saudi Arabia 26°34′N 45°20′E |
| 10 | D14 | **Alaska, Golfo de** *gulf* of Alaska, Gulf of |
| 137 | N5 | **Alaşehir** Manisa, W Turkey 38°19′N 28°30′E |
| 138 | G8 | **Al 'Ashārah** var. Ashara. Dayr az Zawr, E Syria 34°51′N 40°36′E |
| 141 | Z9 | **Al Ashkharah** var. Al Ashkhara. NE Oman 21°47′N 59°30′E |
| 39 | P8 | **Al 'Aẓimah** see 'Ammān |
| | | **Alaska** off. State of Alaska, also known as Land of the Midnight Sun, The Last Frontier, Seward's Folly; prev. Russian America. ◆ *state* NW USA |
| 10 | R8 | **Alaska, Gulf of** var. Golfo de Alasca. *gulf* Canada/USA |
| 39 | O15 | **Alaska Peninsula** *peninsula* Alaska, USA |
| 39 | Q11 | **Alaska Range** ▲ Alaska, USA |
| 106 | B10 | **Alassio** Liguria, NW Italy 44°01′N 08°12′E |
| 137 | Y12 | **Älät** Rus. Alyat; prev. Alyaty-Pristan'. SE Azerbaijan 39°57′N 49°24′E |
| | | **Alat** see Olot |
| 139 | S13 | **Al 'Athāmīn** An Najaf, S Iraq 30°27′N 43°27′E |
| 38 | P7 | **Alatna River** ✍ Alaska, USA |
| 75 | V9 | **Al Batrūn** see Batroûn |
| | | **Al Bawīţī** var. Bawiti. N Egypt 28°19′N 28°53′E |
| 121 | Q12 | **Al Baydā'** var. Beida. NE Libya 32°46′N 21°43′E |
| 141 | P16 | **Al Baydā'** var. Al Beida. SW Yemen 13°58′N 45°38′E |
| | | **Al Bedei'ah** see Al Badī'ah |
| 21 | S10 | **Al Beida** see Al Baydā' |
| | | **Albemarle** var. Albermarle. North Carolina, SE USA 35°21′N 80°12′W |
| | | **Albemarle Island** see Isabela, Isla |
| 21 | N8 | **Albemarle Sound** *inlet* W Atlantic Ocean |
| 106 | B10 | **Albenga** Liguria, NW Italy 44°04′N 08°13′E |
| 104 | L8 | **Alberche** ✍ C Spain |
| 103 | O17 | **Albères, Chaîne des** var. les Albères, Montes Albères. ▲ France/Spain |
| | | **Albères, Montes** see Albères, Chaîne des |
| 182 | F2 | **Alberga Creek** *seasonal river* South Australia |
| 104 | G7 | **Albergaria-a-Velha** Aveiro, N Portugal 40°42′N 08°28′W |
| 105 | S10 | **Alberic** Comunitat Valenciana, E Spain 39°07′N 00°31′W |
| 106 | E7 | **Alberobello** Puglia, SE Italy 40°47′N 17°14′E |
| 108 | J7 | **Alberschwende** Vorarlberg, W Austria 47°28′N 09°50′E |
| 103 | O3 | **Albert** Somme, N France 50°N 02°38′E |
| 11 | O12 | **Alberta** ◆ *province* SW Canada |
| | | **Albert Edward Nyanza** see Edward, Lake |
| 61 | C20 | **Alberti** Buenos Aires, E Argentina 35°03′S 60°15′W |
| 111 | K23 | **Albertirsa** Pest, C Hungary 47°15′N 19°36′E |

| | | |
|---|---|---|
| 20 | L8 | **Albany** Kentucky, S USA 36°42′N 85°08′W |
| 29 | U7 | **Albany** Minnesota, N USA 45°39′N 94°33′W |
| 27 | R2 | **Albany** Missouri, C USA 40°15′N 94°15′W |
| 18 | L10 | **Albany** *state capital* New York, NE USA 42°39′N 73°45′W |
| 32 | G12 | **Albany** Oregon, NW USA 44°38′N 123°06′W |
| 25 | Q6 | **Albany** Texas, SW USA 32°44′N 99°18′W |
| 12 | F10 | **Albany** ✍ Ontario, S Canada |
| | | **Alba Pompeia** see Alba |
| 133 | J6 | **Albă Bărídah** var. Barídah. Ḥimş, C Syria 34°55′N 37°39′E |
| 138 | Q11 | **Al Bardī** Al Anbār, S Iraq 31°16′N 42°28′E |
| 139 | V11 | **Al Batḥā** Dhī Qār, SE Iraq 31°06′N 45°54′E |
| 141 | X8 | **Al Bāţinah** var. Batinah. *coastal region* N Oman |
| 0 | H16 | **Albatross Plateau** *undersea feature* E Pacific Ocean 10°00′N 103°00′W |
| 75 | V9 | **Al Batrūn** see Batroûn |
| | | **Al Bawīţī** var. Bawiti. N Egypt 28°19′N 28°53′E |
| 121 | Q12 | **Al Baydā'** var. Beida. NE Libya 32°46′N 21°43′E |
| 141 | P16 | **Al Baydā'** var. Al Beida. SW Yemen 13°58′N 45°38′E |
| | | **Al Bedei'ah** see Al Badī'ah |
| 21 | S10 | **Al Beida** see Al Baydā' |
| | | **Albemarle** var. Albermarle. North Carolina, SE USA 35°21′N 80°12′W |
| | | **Albemarle Island** see Isabela, Isla |
| 21 | N8 | **Albemarle Sound** *inlet* W Atlantic Ocean |
| 106 | B10 | **Albenga** Liguria, NW Italy 44°04′N 08°13′E |

| | | |
|---|---|---|
| 105 | S11 | **Albacete** ◆ *province* Castilla-La Mancha, C Spain |
| 140 | I4 | **Al Bad'** Tabūk, NW Saudi Arabia 28°28′N 35°00′E |
| 104 | L7 | **Alba de Tormes** Castilla y León, N Spain 40°50′N 05°30′W |
| 139 | P3 | **Al Bādī** Nīnawá, N Iraq 35°57′N 41°37′E |
| 143 | V8 | **Al Badī'ah** ✈ (Abū Ẓaby) Abū Ẓaby, C United Arab Emirates 24°27′N 54°39′E |
| 143 | P17 | **Al Badī'ah** var. Al Bedei'ah; *spring/well* C United Arab Emirates 23°41′N 53°50′E |
| 139 | Q7 | **Al Baghdādī** var. Khān al Baghdādī. Al Anbār, SW Iraq 33°60′N 42°50′E |
| 139 | V14 | **Al Baḩah** Al Anbār, SW Iraq 30°00′N 44°20′E |
| 140 | M11 | **Al Bāḩah** var. Al Bāha. Al Bāḩah, SW Saudi Arabia 20°01′N 41°29′E |
| 140 | M11 | **Al Bāḩah** var. Minţaqat al Bāḩah. ◆ *province* W Saudi Arabia |
| | | **Al Baḩrayn** see Bahrain |
| 105 | S11 | **Albaida** Comunitat Valenciana, E Spain 38°51′N 00°31′W |
| 116 | H11 | **Alba Iulia** Ger. Weissenburg, Hung. Gyulafehérvár; prev. Bálgrad, Karlsburg, Károly-Fehérvár. Alba, W Romania 46°06′N 23°37′E |
| 105 | S11 | **Albaida** Comunitat Valenciana, E Spain 38°51′N 00°31′W |
| 122 | O10 | **Al Balqā'** ✍ Sverdlovskaya Oblast', C Russia 57°48′N 61°52′E |
| 5 | G23 | **Alappuzha** var. Alleppey. Kerala, SW India 09°30′N 76°22′E |
| 138 | F10 | **Alban** Tarn, S France |
| 105 | O15 | **Albán** Tarn, S France |
| 2 | K11 | **Alban, Lac** ☺ Québec, SE Canada |
| 113 | L20 | **Albania** off. Republic of Albania, Alb. Republika e Shqipërisë; prev. People's Socialist Republic of Albania. ◆ *republic* SE Europe |
| | | **Albania** see Vlorë |
| 180 | J14 | **Albany** Western Australia 35°03′S 117°54′E |
| 23 | S7 | **Albany** Georgia, SE USA 31°35′N 84°09′W |
| 31 | P13 | **Albany** Indiana, N USA 40°18′N 85°14′W |

105 O15 Albuñol Andalucía, S Spain 36°48′N 03°11′W
37 Q11 Albuquerque New Mexico, SW USA 35°05′N 106°38′W
141 W8 Al Buraymī var. Buraimi. N Oman 24°16′N 55°48′E
143 R17 Al Buraymī var. Buraimi. spring/well Oman/United Arab Emirates 24°27′N 55°33′E
  Al Burayqah see Marsá al Burayqah
  Alburgum see Aalborg
104 I10 Alburquerque Extremadura, W Spain 39°12′N 07°00′W
181 V14 Albury New South Wales, SE Australia 36°03′S 146°53′E
139 N5 Al Buşayrah Dayr az Zawr, E Syria 35°10′N 40°25′E
141 T14 Al Buzūn SE Yemen 15°40′N 50°53′E
93 G17 Alby Västernorrland, C Sweden 62°30′N 15°25′E
  Albyn, Glen see Mor, Glen
104 G12 Alcácer do Sal Setúbal, W Portugal 38°22′N 08°29′W
  Alcalá de Chisvert/Alcalá de Chivert see Alcalà de Xivert
104 K14 Alcalá de Guadaira Andalucía, S Spain 37°20′N 05°50′W
105 O8 Alcalá de Henares Ar. Alkal'a; anc. Complutum. Madrid, C Spain 40°28′N 03°22′W
104 K16 Alcalá de los Gazules Andalucía, S Spain 36°29′N 05°43′W
105 T8 Alcalà de Xivert var. Alcalá de Chisvert, Cast. Alcalá de Chivert. Comunitat Valenciana, E Spain 40°19′N 00°13′E
105 N14 Alcalá La Real Andalucía, S Spain 37°28′N 03°55′W
107 I23 Alcamo Sicilia, Italy, C Mediterranean Sea 37°58′N 12°58′E
105 T4 Alcanadre ☑ NE Spain
105 T8 Alcanar Cataluña, NE Spain 40°33′N 00°25′E
104 J5 Alcañices Castilla y León, N Spain 41°41′N 06°21′W
105 T7 Alcañiz Aragón, NE Spain 41°03′N 00°09′W
104 I9 Alcántara Extremadura, W Spain 39°42′N 06°54′W
104 J9 Alcántara, Embalse de ☑ W Spain
105 R13 Alcantarilla Murcia, SE Spain 37°59′N 01°12′W
105 P11 Alcaraz Castilla-La Mancha, C Spain 38°40′N 02°29′W
105 P12 Alcaraz, Sierra de ▲ C Spain
104 I12 Alcarrache ☑ SW Spain
105 T6 Alcarràs Cataluña, NE Spain 41°34′N 00°31′E
105 N14 Alcaudete Andalucía, S Spain 37°35′N 04°05′W
  Alcázar see Ksar-el-Kebir
105 O10 Alcázar de San Juan anc. Alce. Castilla-La Mancha, C Spain 39°24′N 03°12′W
  Alcazarquivir see Ksar-el-Kebir
  Alce see Alcázar de San Juan
57 B17 Alcedo, Volcán ⋒ Galapagos Islands, Ecuador, E Pacific Ocean 0°25′S 91°06′W
139 X12 Al Chabā'ish var. Al Kaba'ish. Dhī Qār, SE Iraq 30°58′N 47°02′E
117 Y7 Alchevs'k prev. Kommunarsk, Voroshilovsk. Luhans'ka Oblast', E Ukraine 48°29′N 38°52′E
  Alcira see Alzira
21 N9 Alcoa Tennessee, S USA 35°47′N 83°58′W
104 F9 Alcobaça Leiria, C Portugal 39°32′N 08°59′W
105 N8 Alcobendas Madrid, C Spain 40°32′N 03°38′W
105 P7 Alcolea del Pinar Castilla-La Mancha, C Spain 41°02′N 02°28′W
  Alcora see L'Alcora
104 H14 Alcoutim Faro, S Portugal 37°28′N 07°28′W
33 W15 Alcova Wyoming, C USA 42°33′N 106°40′W
105 S11 Alcoy var. Alcoi. Comunitat Valenciana, E Spain 38°42′N 00°29′W
105 Y9 Alcúdia Mallorca, Spain, W Mediterranean Sea 39°51′N 03°06′E
105 Y9 Alcúdia, Badia d' bay Mallorca, Spain, W Mediterranean Sea
172 M7 Aldabra Group island group SW Seychelles
139 U10 Al Daghghārah Bābil, C Iraq 32°10′N 44°57′E
40 J5 Aldama Chihuahua, N Mexico 28°50′N 105°52′W
41 P11 Aldama Tamaulipas, C Mexico 22°54′N 98°05′W
123 Q11 Aldan Respublika Sakha (Yakutiya), NE Russia 58°31′N 125°15′E
123 Q10 Aldan ☑ NE Russia
  Aldar see Aldarhaan
  al Dar al Baida see Rabat
162 G7 Aldarhaan var. Aldar. Dzavhan, W Mongolia 47°43′N 96°36′E
97 Q20 Aldeburgh E England, United Kingdom 52°12′N 01°35′E
  Aldeia Nova see Aldeia Nova de São Bento
104 H13 Aldeia Nova de São Bento var. Aldeia Nova. Beja, S Portugal 37°55′N 07°24′W
29 V11 Alden Minnesota, N USA 43°40′N 93°34′W
184 N6 Aldermen Islands, The island group NE New Zealand
97 L25 Alderney island Channel Islands
97 N22 Aldershot S England, United Kingdom 51°15′N 00°47′W
21 R6 Alderson West Virginia, NE USA 37°43′N 80°38′W
  Al Dhaid see Adh Dhayd


98 L5 Aldtsjerk Dutch. Oudkerk. Fryslân, N Netherlands 53°16′N 05°52′E
30 J11 Aledo Illinois, N USA 41°12′N 90°45′W
76 H9 Aleg Brakna, SW Mauritania 17°03′N 13°53′W
64 Q10 Alegranza island Islas Canarias, Spain, NE Atlantic Ocean
37 P12 Alegres Mountain ▲ New Mexico, SW USA 34°09′N 108°11′W
61 F15 Alegrete Rio Grande do Sul, S Brazil 29°46′S 55°46′W
61 C16 Alejandra Santa Fe, C Argentina 29°54′S 59°50′W
193 T11 Alejandro Selkirk, Isla island Islas Juan Fernández, Chile, E Pacific Ocean
124 I12 Alëkhovshchina Leningradskaya Oblast', NW Russia 60°22′N 33°57′E
39 O13 Aleknagik Alaska, USA 59°16′N 158°37′W
  Aleksandriya see Oleksandriya
126 L3 Aleksandrov Vladimirskaya Oblast', W Russia 56°24′N 38°42′E
113 N14 Aleksandrovac Serbia, C Serbia 43°28′N 21°05′E
127 R9 Aleksandrov Gay Saratovskaya Oblast', W Russia 50°08′N 48°34′E
127 U6 Aleksandrovka Orenburgskaya Oblast', W Russia 52°47′N 54°14′E
  Aleksandrovka see Oleksandrivka
125 V13 Aleksandrovsk Permskiy Kray, NW Russia 59°12′N 57°27′E
  Aleksandrovsk see Zaporizhzhya
127 N14 Aleksandrovskoye Stavropol'skiy Kray, SW Russia 44°43′N 42°56′E
123 T12 Aleksandrovsk-Sakhalinskiy Ostrov Sakhalin, Sakhalinskaya Oblast', SE Russia 50°55′N 142°12′E
110 J10 Aleksandrów Kujawski Kujawsko-pomorskie, C Poland 52°52′N 18°40′E
110 K12 Aleksandrów Łódzki Łódzkie, C Poland 51°49′N 19°19′E
114 J8 Aleksandŭr Stamboliyski, Yazovir ☑ N Bulgaria
  Alekseevka see Akkol', Akmola, Kazakhstan
  Alekseevka see Terekty
145 P7 Alekseyevka Kaz. Alekseevka. Akmola, N Kazakhstan 53°32′N 69°30′E
126 L9 Alekseyevka Belgorodskaya, W Russia 50°35′N 38°41′E
127 S7 Alekseyevka Samarskaya Oblast', W Russia 52°37′N 51°20′E
  Alekseyevka see Akkol', Akmola, Kazakhstan
  Alekseyevka see Terekty Vostochnyy Kazakhstan, Kazakhstan
127 R4 Alekseyevskoye Respublika Tatarstan, W Russia 55°18′N 50°11′E
126 K5 Aleksin Tul'skaya Oblast', W Russia 54°31′N 37°08′E
113 O14 Aleksinac Serbia, SE Serbia 43°33′N 21°43′E
190 G11 Alele Île Uvea, E Wallis and Futuna 13°14′S 176°09′W
95 N20 Älem Kalmar, S Sweden 56°57′N 16°25′E
102 L6 Alençon Orne, N France 48°26′N 00°04′E
58 I12 Alenquer Pará, NE Brazil 01°58′S 54°45′W
38 G10 'Alenuihaha Channel var. Alenuihaha Channel. channel Hawai'i, USA, C Pacific Ocean
95 C17 Ålgård Rogaland, S Norway 58°45′N 05°52′E
  Alep/Aleppo see Ḥalab
103 Y15 Aléria Corse, France, C Mediterranean Sea 42°06′N 09°29′E
197 Q11 Alert Ellesmere Island, Nunavut, N Canada 82°28′N 62°13′W
103 Q14 Alès prev. Alais. Gard, S France 44°08′N 04°05′E
116 G9 Aleşd Hung. Élesd. Bihor, W Romania 47°03′N 22°22′E
106 C9 Alessandria Fr. Alexandrie. Piemonte, N Italy 44°54′N 08°37′E
94 D9 Ålesund Møre og Romsdal, S Norway 62°28′N 06°11′E
108 E10 Aletschhorn ▲ SW Switzerland 46°33′N 08°01′E
197 S1 Aleutian Basin undersea feature Bering Sea 57°00′N 177°00′E
38 H17 Aleutian Islands island group Alaska, USA
39 P14 Aleutian Range ▲ Alaska, USA
0 B5 Aleutian Trench undersea feature S Bering Sea 51°00′N 177°00′W
123 T10 Alevina, Mys cape E Russia
15 Q6 Alex ☑ Québec, SE Canada
28 J3 Alexander North Dakota, N USA 47°48′N 103°38′W
39 W14 Alexander Archipelago island group Alaska, USA
  Alexanderbaai see Alexander Bay
83 D23 Alexander Bay Afr. Alexanderbaai. Northern Cape, W South Africa 28°40′S 16°30′E
23 Q5 Alexander City Alabama, S USA 32°56′N 85°57′W
194 J6 Alexander Island island Antarctica
  Alexander Range see Kirghiz Range
183 O12 Alexandra Victoria, SE Australia 37°12′S 145°43′E
185 D22 Alexandra Otago, South Island, New Zealand 45°15′S 169°25′E
115 F14 Alexándreia var. Alexándria. Kentrikí Makedonía, N Greece 40°38′N 22°27′E
  Alexandra Bay see Alexander Bay
95 M20 Älghult Kronoberg, S Sweden 56°59′N 15°34′E
105 S10 Alginet Comunitat Valenciana, E Spain 39°16′N 00°28′W
105 S12 Algodonales Andalucía, S Spain 36°54′N 05°24′W
83 I26 Algoa Bay bay S South Africa
105 N9 Algodor ☑ C Spain
31 N6 Algoma Wisconsin, N USA 44°36′N 87°24′W
29 Z14 Algona Iowa, C USA 43°04′N 94°13′W
21 O2 Algonac Michigan, N USA 42°36′N 82°32′W
20 L8 Algood Tennessee, S USA 36°12′N 85°27′W
105 O2 Algorta País Vasco, N Spain 43°21′N 03°01′W
61 E18 Algorta Río Negro, W Uruguay 32°26′S 57°18′W
15 N13 Alexandria Ontario, SE Canada 45°19′N 74°37′W
44 J12 Alexandria C Jamaica 18°18′N 77°21′W


116 J15 Alexandria Teleorman, S Romania 43°58′N 25°18′E
31 P13 Alexandria Indiana, N USA 40°15′N 85°40′W
20 M4 Alexandria Kentucky, C USA 38°59′N 84°22′W
22 H7 Alexandria Louisiana, S USA 31°19′N 92°27′W
29 T7 Alexandria Minnesota, N USA 45°54′N 95°22′W
29 Q11 Alexandria South Dakota, N USA 43°39′N 97°46′W
21 W4 Alexandria Virginia, NE USA 38°49′N 77°06′W
  Alexandria see Al Iskandarīyah
  Alexándria see Alexándreia
18 I7 Alexandria Bay New York, NE USA 44°20′N 75°54′W
182 J10 Alexandrina, Lake ☑ South Australia
114 K13 Alexandroúpoli var. Alexandroúpolis, Turk. Dedeağaç, Dedeagach. Anatolikí Makedonía kai Thráki, NE Greece 40°52′N 25°53′E
  Alexandroúpolis see Alexandroúpoli
10 L15 Alexis Creek British Columbia, SW Canada 52°06′N 123°25′W
122 I13 Aleysk Altayskiy Kray, S Russia 52°32′N 82°46′E
139 S8 Al Fallūjah var. Falluja. Al Anbār, C Iraq 33°21′N 43°46′E
105 R8 Alfambra ☑ E Spain
141 R15 Al Farḍah C Yemen
105 Q4 Alfaro La Rioja, N Spain 42°13′N 01°45′W
105 U5 Alfarràs Cataluña, NE Spain 41°50′N 00°34′E
  Al Fāshir see El Fasher
  Al Fashn see El Fashn
114 M7 Alfatar Silistra, NE Bulgaria 43°56′N 27°17′E
139 S5 Al Fatḥah Şalāḥ ad Dīn, C Iraq 35°06′N 43°34′E
139 Q3 Al Fatsī Nīnawá, N Iraq 36°04′N 42°39′E
139 Z13 Al Fāw var. Fao. Al Başrah, SE Iraq 29°55′N 48°26′E
75 W8 Al Fayyūm var. El Faiyûm. N Egypt 29°19′N 30°50′E
115 D20 Alfeiós prev. Alfiós; anc. Alpheius, Alpheus. ☑ S Greece
100 I13 Alfeld Niedersachsen, C Germany 51°58′N 09°49′E
  Alfiós see Alfeiós
  Alföld see Great Hungarian Plain
141 Q6 Al Furaywisah glacier S Norway
79 P9 Alfred Maine, NE USA 43°29′N 70°44′W
18 F11 Alfred New York, NE USA 42°15′N 77°46′W
61 K14 Alfredo Wagner Santa Catarina, S Brazil 27°40′S 49°22′W
94 M12 Alfta Gävleborg, C Sweden 61°20′N 16°05′E
140 K12 Al Fuḩayḩīl var. Fahaheel. SE Kuwait 29°01′N 48°05′E
139 Q6 Al Fuḩaymī Al Anbār, C Iraq 34°18′N 42°09′E
143 S16 Al Fujayrah var. Fujairah. Al Fujayrah, NE United Arab Emirates 25°09′N 56°18′E
143 S16 Al Fujayrah var. Fujairah. ✈ Al Fujayrah, NE United Arab Emirates 25°04′N 56°12′E
  Al-Furāt see Euphrates
144 I10 Alga Kaz. Algha. Aktyubinsk, NW Kazakhstan 49°54′N 57°19′E
144 Q9 Algabas Kaz. Alghabas. Zapadnyy Kazakhstan, NW Kazakhstan 50°47′N 52°23′E
  Algarve cultural region S Portugal
182 G3 Algebuckina Bridge South Australia 28°03′S 135°48′E
104 K16 Algeciras Andalucía, SW Spain 36°08′N 05°27′W
105 S10 Algemesí Comunitat Valenciana, E Spain 39°11′N 00°27′W
  Al-Genain see El Geneina
120 F9 Alger var. Algiers, El Djezair, Al Jazâ'ir. ● (Algeria) N Algeria 36°47′N 03°03′E
74 H9 Algeria off. Democratic and Popular Republic of Algeria, Ar. Al Jazâ'ir, El Djazaïr; prev. Algerian Republic. ◆ republic N Africa
120 J8 Algerian Basin var. Balearic Plain. undersea feature W Mediterranean Sea
  Algha see Alga
138 I4 Al Ghāb Valley NW Syria
141 X10 Al Ghābah var. Ghaba. C Oman 21°22′N 57°14′E
75 X9 Al Ghardaqah var. Ghurdaqah, Hurghada. E Egypt 27°17′N 33°47′E
141 U14 Al Ghaydah E Yemen 16°15′N 52°13′E
140 M6 Al Ghazālah Ḥā'il, NW Saudi Arabia 26°55′N 41°23′E
107 B17 Alghero Sardegna, Italy, C Mediterranean Sea 40°34′N 08°20′E
115 G18 Aliartos Stereá Elláda, C Greece 38°23′N 23°18′E
  Äli-Bayramli see Şirvan
114 F12 Alibey Barajı ☑ NW Turkey
77 S13 Alibori ☑ N Benin
112 M10 Alibunar Vojvodina, NE Serbia 45°06′N 20°59′E
105 S12 Alicante Cat. Alacant, Lat. Lucentum. Comunitat Valenciana, SE Spain 38°21′N 00°29′W
105 N9 Alicante ✈ Murcia, E Spain
  Alicante see Alacant
141 Z9 Al Kāmil NE Oman 22°14′N 58°15′E
83 I24 Alice Eastern Cape, S South Africa 32°47′S 26°50′E
25 S14 Alice Texas, SW USA 27°45′N 98°06′W
83 I25 Alicedale Eastern Cape, S South Africa 33°19′S 26°05′E
25 P5 Alice, Mount hill West Falkland, Falkland Islands
181 P20 Alice Springs Northern Territory, C Australia 23°42′S 133°52′E


139 Q4 Al Ḥaḍr var. Al Hadhar; anc. Hatra. Nīnawạ, NW Iraq 35°34′N 42°44′E
147 U13 Al Ḥajar al Gharbī ▲ N Oman
141 T13 Al Ḥajar ash Sharqī ▲ NE Oman
141 R15 Al Hajarayn C Yemen 15°29′N 48°24′E
138 L10 Al Ḥamād desert Jordan/Saudi Arabia
  Al Hamad see Syrian Desert
105 N15 Alhama de Granada Andalucía, S Spain 37°00′N 03°59′W
105 R13 Alhama de Murcia Murcia, SE Spain 37°51′N 01°25′W
35 T15 Alhambra California, W USA 34°08′N 118°06′W
138 H5 Al Ḥamīdīyah var. Hamidiyé. Ṭarṭūs, Syria 34°43′N 35°56′E
139 T12 Al Ḥammām var. An Najaf. S Iraq 31°09′N 44°04′E
141 X8 Al Ḥamrā' NE Oman 23°07′N 57°23′E
  Al Ḥamrā' see Al Ḥamādah al Ḥamrā'
141 O6 Al Ḥamūdīyah spring/well N Saudi Arabia 27°05′N 44°24′E
140 M7 Al Ḥanākīyah al Madīnah al Munawwarah, W Saudi Arabia 24°55′N 40°31′E
139 W14 Al Ḥanīyah escarpment Iraq/Saudi Arabia
139 T12 Al Ḥārithah var. Al Başrah, SE Iraq 30°43′N 47°44′E
140 L3 Al Ḥarrah desert NW Saudi Arabia
75 Q10 Al Ḥarūj al Aswad desert C Libya
  Al Hasaifin see Ḥ Ḥusayfin
139 N2 Al Ḥasakah var. Al Hasaka, Fr. Hassetché. Al Ḥasakah, NE Syria 36°22′N 40°44′E
139 O2 Al Ḥasakah off. Muḩāfaẕat al Ḥasakah, var. Al Hasakah, Āl Ḥasakah, Hasakah, Hassakeh. ◆ governorate NE Syria
  Al Hasakah see Al Ḥasakah
  Al Hasakah see 'Āmūda
68 G13 Al Hāshimīyah Ma'ān, S Jordan 30°30′N 35°46′E
141 R14 Al Ḥawrā' S Yemen 13°54′N 47°36′E
141 V10 Al Ḥayy var. Kut al Hai, Kūt al Ḥayy. Wāsiṭ, E Iraq 32°11′N 46°03′E
141 U11 Al Ḥibāk desert E Saudi Arabia
138 H8 Al Ḥijānah var. Hejjane, Hijanah. Rīf Dimashq, SW Syria 33°23′N 36°34′E
140 K7 Al Ḥijāz Eng. Hejaz. physical region NW Saudi Arabia
121 V13 al Ḥikmah, Ra's headland N Egypt 31°11′N 27°22′E
  Al Hilbeh see 'Ulayyāniyah, Bi'r al
139 T9 Al Ḥillah var. Hilla. Bābil, C Iraq 32°28′N 44°29′E
139 T9 Al Ḥindīyah var. Hindiya. Bābil, C Iraq 32°32′N 44°16′E
138 G12 Al Ḥisā Aṭ Ṭafīlah, W Jordan 30°49′N 35°58′E
74 G6 Al-Hoceïma var. al Hoceima, Al-Hoceima, Alhucemas; prev. Villa Sanjurjo. N Morocco 35°14′N 03°56′W
  Alhucemas, Peñon de see Al-Hoceïma
105 N17 Alhucemas, Peñon de island group S Spain
141 N15 Al Ḩudaydah Eng. Hodeida. W Yemen 15°N 42°50′E
138 H13 Al Ḩudaydah var. Hodeida. W Yemen 14°45′N 43°01′E
140 M4 Al Ḩudūd ash Shamālīyah var. Minṭaqat al Ḥudūd ash Shamālīyah, Eng. Northern Border Region. ◆ region N Saudi Arabia
141 S7 Al Ḩufūf var. Hofuf. Ash Sharqīyah, NE Saudi Arabia 25°21′N 49°34′E
  al-Hurma see Al Khurmah
141 X7 Al Ḩusayfin var. Al Hasaifin. N Oman 24°33′N 56°33′E
138 G9 Al Ḩuşn var. Husn. Irbid, N Jordan 32°29′N 35°53′E
138 L4 Al Jawārah oasis SE Oman
18 E12 Al Jawf Minṭaqat al Jawf. ◆ region N Saudi Arabia
18 D11 Al Jawf see Dawmat al Jandal
138 G9 Al Jawlān see Golan Heights
  Al Jazā'ir see Alger
104 L10 Al Jazīrah physical region Iraq/Syria
104 F14 Aljezur Faro, S Portugal 37°18′N 08°49′W
139 S13 Al Jīl S Iraq 30°28′N 43°57′E
75 W8 Al Jīzah Eng. Giza, var. El Gīza, Gizeh. N Egypt 30°01′N 31°13′E
138 G11 Al Jīzah var. Jiza. 'Ammān, N Jordan 31°42′N 35°57′E
115 F14 Aliákmon see Aliákmonas
  Aliákmonas prev. Aliákmon; anc. Haliacmon. ☑ N Greece
141 S6 Al Jubayl var. Al Jubail. Ash Sharqīyah, NE Saudi Arabia 27°N 49°36′E
139 W9 'Alī al Gharbī Maysān, E Iraq 32°28′N 46°42′E
139 U11 'Alī al Ḩassūnī Al Qādisīyah, S Iraq 32°N 44°50′E
141 N15 Al Jumaylīyah N Qatar 25°37′N 51°05′E
104 G3 Aljustrel Beja, S Portugal 37°52′N 08°10′W
138 I14 Al Kaba'ish see Al Chabā'ish
141 N5 Al Kāf see Al Kef
  Alkal'a see Alcalá de Henares
35 W4 Alkali Flat salt flat Nevada, W USA
35 Q1 Alkali Lake ☑ Nevada, W USA
28 J13 Al Kāmil NE Oman 22°14′N 58°15′E
28 J13 Al Karak var. El Karak, Kerak, Karak; anc. Kir Moab, Kir of Moab. Al Karak, W Jordan 31°11′N 35°42′E
138 G12 Al Karak off. Muḩāfaẕat al Karak. ◆ governorate W Jordan
44 J13 Alligator River ☑ North Carolina, USA
14 G14 Al-Kashaniya see Qash'aniyah


23 N4 Aliceville Alabama, S USA 33°07′N 88°09′W
147 U13 Alichur SE Tajikistan 37°49′N 73°45′E
147 U14 Alichuri Janubî, Qatorkŭhi Rus. Yuzhno-Alichurskiy Khrebet. ▲ SE Tajikistan
147 U13 Alichuri Shimolî, Qatorkŭhi Rus. Severo-Alichurskiy Khrebet. ▲ SE Tajikistan
107 K22 Alicudi, Isola island Isole Eolie, S Italy
43 W14 Aligandí Guna Yala, NE Panama 09°18′N 78°05′W
152 J11 Aligarh Uttar Pradesh, N India 27°54′N 78°04′E
142 M7 Alīgūdarz Lorestān, W Iran 33°24′N 49°19′E
163 U5 Alihe var. Oroqen Zizhiqi. Nei Mongol Zizhiqu, N China 50°34′N 123°42′E
0 F12 Alijos, Islas islets California, SW USA
149 R6 'Alī Kbel Pash. 'Alī Khēl. Paktīkā, E Afghanistan 33°55′N 69°49′E
149 R6 'Alī Khēl var. 'Alī Khel, Jaji; prev. 'Alī Kheyl. Paktiā, SE Afghanistan 33°55′N 69°46′E
  'Alī Khēl see 'Alī Kbel, Paktīkā, Afghanistan
120 M12 'Alī Khel see 'Alī Kheyl
  'Alī Kheyl see 'Alī Khēl
79 H19 Alima ☑ C Congo
  Al Imārāt al 'Arabīyahal Muttaḩidah see United Arab Emirates
115 N23 Alimía island Dodekánisa, Greece, Aegean Sea
55 V12 Alimimuni Piek ▲ S Suriname 02°26′N 55°46′W
79 K15 Alindao Basse-Kotto, S Central African Republic 04°58′N 21°16′E
95 J18 Alingsås Västra Götaland, S Sweden 57°55′N 12°30′E
81 K8 Alinjugul spring/well E Kenya 00°13′S 40°31′E
149 S11 Alipur Punjab, E Pakistan 29°22′N 70°59′E
153 T12 Alipur Duār West Bengal, NE India 26°29′N 89°44′E
18 B14 Aliquippa Pennsylvania, NE USA 40°36′N 80°15′W
80 L12 'Alī Sabieh var. 'Alī Sabīḩ. S Djibouti 11°07′N 42°44′E
  'Alī Sabīḩ see 'Alī Sabieh
140 K3 Al 'Īsāwīyah Al Jawf, NW Saudi Arabia 30°41′N 37°58′E
104 J10 Aliseda Extremadura, W Spain 39°25′N 06°42′W
121 U13 Al Iskandarīyah Eng. Alexandria. N Egypt 31°07′N 29°51′E
139 T8 Al Iskandarīyah Bābil, C Iraq 32°53′N 44°22′E
123 T6 Aliskerovo Chukotskiy Avtonomnyy Okrug, NE Russia 67°40′N 167°32′E
75 W7 Al Ismā'īlīya var. Ismailia, Ismâ'îlîya. N Egypt 30°32′N 32°13′E
114 H13 Alistráti Kentrikí Makedonía, NE Greece 41°03′N 23°58′E
39 P15 Alitak Bay bay Kodiak Island, Alaska, USA
  Al Ittiḩād see Madīnat ash Sha'b
115 H18 Alivéri var. Alivérion. Évvoia, C Greece 38°24′N 24°02′E
  Alivérion see Alivéri
11 T15 Allan Saskatchewan, S Canada 51°50′N 105°59′W
  Allanmyo see Aunglan
83 I22 Allanridge Free State, C South Africa 27°46′S 26°40′E
104 H4 Allariz Galicia, NW Spain 42°11′N 07°48′W
139 R11 Al Laṣaf var. Al Luşşuf. An Najaf, S Iraq 31°38′N 43°16′E
  Al Lathqiyah see Al Lādhiqiyah
23 S2 Allatoona Lake ☑ Georgia, SE USA
83 J19 Alldays Limpopo, NE South Africa 22°39′S 29°04′E
31 P10 Allegan Michigan, N USA 42°31′N 85°51′W
18 E14 Allegany Mountains ▲ New York/Pennsylvania, NE USA
18 E12 Allegheny Plateau ▲ New York/Pennsylvania, NE USA
18 D11 Allegheny Reservoir ☑ New York/Pennsylvania, NE USA
18 D12 Allegheny River ☑ New York/Pennsylvania, NE USA
22 K9 Allemands, Lac des ☑ Louisiana, S USA
25 U6 Allen Texas, SW USA 33°06′N 96°40′W
21 R14 Allendale South Carolina, SE USA 33°01′N 81°19′W
41 N6 Allende Coahuila, NE Mexico 28°22′N 100°50′W
41 O9 Allende Nuevo León, C Mexico 25°20′N 100°01′W
97 D16 Allen, Lough Ir. Loch Aillinn. ☑ NW Ireland
185 B26 Allen, Mount ▲ Stewart Island, Southland, SW New Zealand 47°05′S 167°49′E
139 N3 Allentsteig Niederösterreich, N Austria 48°40′N 15°24′E
18 I14 Allentown Pennsylvania, NE USA 40°37′N 75°30′W
141 N5 Alleppey see Alappuzha
105 P6 Alleppey see Alappuzha
99 K19 Alleur Liège, E Belgium 50°40′N 05°33′E
101 J25 Allgäuer Alpen ▲ Austria/Germany
28 J13 Alliance Nebraska, C USA 42°06′N 102°52′W
31 U12 Alliance Ohio, N USA 40°55′N 81°06′W
103 O10 Allier ◆ department C France
44 I14 Alligator Pond S Jamaica 17°52′N 77°34′W
181 Y9 Alligator River ☑ North Carolina, USA
14 G14 Alliston Ontario, S Canada 44°09′N 79°51′W


139 T8 Al Kāẕimīyah var. Al-Kadhimain, Kedhimain. Baghdād, C Iraq 33°22′N 44°20′E
99 I18 Alken Limburg, NE Belgium 50°52′N 05°19′E
141 X8 Al Khābūrah var. Khabura. N Oman 23°57′N 57°06′E
139 T7 Al Khālis Diyālá, C Iraq 33°51′N 44°33′E
  Al Khalīl see Hebron
75 Q8 Al Kharj Ar Riyāḍ, C Saudi Arabia 24°12′N 47°12′E
141 W6 Al Khaṣab var. Khasab. N Oman 26°11′N 56°18′E
  Al Khaur see Al Khawr
143 N15 Al Khawr var. Al Khaur, Al Khor. E Qatar 25°40′N 51°33′E
142 K12 Al Khirān var. Al Khiran. SE Kuwait 28°34′N 48°25′E
141 W9 Al Khirān spring/well NW Oman 22°3..′N 55°42′E
  Al-Khobar see Al Khubar
  Al Khor see Al Khawr
141 S6 Al Khubar var. Al-Khobar. Ash Sharqīyah, NE Saudi Arabia 26°00′N 50°00′E
120 M12 Al Khums var. Homs, Khoms, Khums. NW Libya 32°39′N 14°16′E
141 R15 Al Khuraybah C Yemen 15°05′N 48°17′E
140 M9 Al Khurmah var. al-Hurma. Makkah al Mukarramah, W Saudi Arabia 21°59′N 42°02′E
141 V9 Al Kidan desert NE Saudi Arabia
127 V4 Alkino-2 Respublika Bashkortostan, W Russia 54°30′N 55°40′E
98 H9 Alkmaar Noord-Holland, NW Netherlands 52°37′N 04°45′E
139 T10 Al Kūfah var. Kufa. An Najaf, S Iraq 32°02′N 44°25′E
75 T11 Al Kufrah SE Libya 24°11′N 23°19′E
141 T10 Al Kursū' desert E Saudi Arabia
139 V9 Al Kūt var. Kūt al 'Amārah, Kut al Imara. Wāsiṭ, E Iraq 32°30′N 45°51′E
  Al-Kuwait see Al Kuwayt
  Al Kuwayt see Kuwait
142 K11 Al Kuwayt Eng. Kuwait City, var. Kuwait, Al Kuwait; prev. Qurein. ● (Kuwait) E Kuwait 29°23′N 48°00′E
142 K11 Al Kuwayt ✈ C Kuwait 29°13′N 47°57′E
115 G19 Alkyonídon, Kólpos gulf C Greece
141 N4 Al Labbah physical region N Saudi Arabia
138 G4 Al Lādhiqīyah Eng. Latakia, Fr. Lattaquié; anc. Laodicea, Laodicea ad Mare. Al Lādhiqīyah, W Syria 35°31′N 35°47′E
138 H4 Al Lādhiqīyah off. Muḩāfaẕat al Lādhiqīyah, var. Al Lathqiyah, Latakia, Lattakia. ◆ governorate W Syria
19 R2 Allagash River ☑ Maine, NE USA
139 N2 Al Lajā physical region S Syria
143 S3 Allāh Dāgh, Reshteh-ye ▲ NE Iran
143 O18 Al Manādir var. Al Manādir. desert Oman/United Arab Emirates
141 X12 Al Lakbi S Oman 18°27′N 56°37′E
11 T15 Allan Saskatchewan, S Canada 51°50′N 105°59′W


140 L11 Al Līth Makkah al Mukarramah, SW Saudi Arabia 21°N 41°E
  Al Liwā' see Liwā
96 J12 Alloa C Scotland, United Kingdom 56°07′N 03°49′W
103 U14 Allos Alpes-de-Haute-Provence, SE France 44°16′N 06°37′E
108 D6 Allschwil Basel Landschaft, NW Switzerland 47°34′N 07°32′E
141 N14 Al Luḩayyah W Yemen 15°44′N 42°45′E
14 K12 Allumettes, Île des island Québec, SE Canada
  Al Lussuf see Al Laṣaf
109 S5 Alm ☑ N Austria
15 Q7 Alma Québec, SE Canada 48°32′N 71°41′W
27 S10 Alma Arkansas, C USA 35°28′N 94°13′W
23 V7 Alma Georgia, SE USA 31°32′N 82°27′W
27 P4 Alma Kansas, C USA 39°01′N 96°17′W
31 Q8 Alma Michigan, N USA 43°22′N 84°39′W
29 O17 Alma Nebraska, C USA 40°06′N 99°21′W
30 I7 Alma Wisconsin, N USA 44°21′N 91°55′W
139 R12 Alma well An Najaf, S Iraq
  Alma-Ata see Almaty
  Alma-Atinskaya Oblast' see Almaty
105 T5 Almacelles Cataluña, NE Spain 41°44′N 00°26′E
104 F11 Almada Setúbal, W Portugal 38°40′N 09°09′W
104 L11 Almadén Castilla-La Mancha, C Spain 38°47′N 04°50′W
66 L6 Almadies, Pointe des headland W Senegal 14°44′N 17°31′W
140 L7 Al Madīnah Eng. Medina. Al Madīnah al Munawwarah, W Saudi Arabia 24°25′N 39°29′E
140 L7 Al Madīnah al Munawwarah off. Minṭaqat al Madīnah. ◆ region W Saudi Arabia
138 H9 Al Mafraq var. Mafraq. Al Mafraq, N Jordan 32°20′N 36°12′E
138 J10 Al Mafraq off. Muḩāfaẕat al Mafraq. ◆ governorate NW Jordan
141 R15 Al Maghārim C Yemen 15°00′N 49°49′E
  Al Maghrib see Morocco
  al Maghribīyah, Al Mamlakah see Morocco
105 N11 Almagro Castilla-La Mancha, C Spain 38°54′N 03°43′W
139 T9 Al Maḩāwīl var. Khan al Maḩāwīl. Bābil, C Iraq 32°39′N 44°28′E
139 T8 Al Maḩmūdīyah var. Mahmudiya. Baghdād, C Iraq 33°04′N 44°22′E
141 P7 Al Majma'ah Ar Riyāḍ, C Saudi Arabia 25°55′N 45°20′E
139 Q11 Al Makmin well S Iraq
139 Q1 Al Mālikīyah var. Malkiye. Al Ḥasakah, N Syria 37°12′N 42°13′E
  Almalyk see Olmaliq
143 O18 Al Manādir var. Al Manādir. desert Oman/United Arab Emirates
142 L15 Al Manāmah Eng. Manama. ● (Bahrain) N Bahrain 26°13′N 50°33′E
  Al Manṣūr see Baghdād
35 O4 Almanor, Lake ☑ California, W USA
105 R11 Almansa Castilla-La Mancha, C Spain 38°52′N 01°06′W
75 W7 Al Manṣūrah var. Manṣûra, El Manṣûra. N Egypt 31°03′N 31°23′E
104 L8 Almanzor ▲ W Spain
105 P14 Almanzora ☑ SE Spain
139 S9 Al Mardah Karbalā', C Iraq 32°35′N 43°30′E
  Al-Marj see Al Marj
75 R7 Al Marj var. Barka, It. Barce. NE Libya 32°30′N 20°54′E
138 K9 Al Mashrafah Ar Raqqah, N Syria
141 X8 Al Maṣna'ah var. Al Muṣana'a. NE Oman 23°45′N 57°38′E
105 N12 Almassora var. Almazora. Comunitat Valenciana, E Spain 39°55′N 00°02′E
139 V13 Al Maṭanah S Iraq
44 F3 Al Mawṣil Eng. Mosul. Nīnawạ, N Iraq 36°20′N 43°08′E
139 N3 Al Mayādīn var. Mayadin, Fr. Meyadine. Dayr az Zawr, E Syria 35°00′N 40°31′E
139 X10 Al Maymūnah var. Maimuna. Maysān, SE Iraq 31°45′N 46°59′E
141 N5 Al Mayyah Ḥā'il, N Saudi Arabia
105 P6 Almazán Castilla y León, N Spain 41°29′N 02°31′W
141 W8 Al Ma'zim var. Al Ma'zam. NW Oman 23°38′N 56°16′E
123 N11 Almaznyy Respublika Sakha (Yakutiya), NE Russia 62°19′N 114°14′E
  Almazora see Almassora
105 T9 Almaty var. Alma-Ata. Almaty, SE Kazakhstan 43°19′N 76°55′E
145 U15 Almaty off. Almatinskaya Oblast', Kaz. Almaty Oblysy; prev. Alma-Ata, Alma-Atinskaya Oblast'. ◆ province SE Kazakhstan
145 S14 Almaty SE Kazakhstan
145 U15 Almaty ✈ Almaty, SE Kazakhstan 43°15′N 76°57′E
  Almaty Oblysy see Almaty
  al-Mawālīh see Al Muwayliḩ
185 B26 Al Mawṣil Eng. Mosul. Nīnawạ, N Iraq 36°20′N 43°08′E
139 T9 Al Mayādīn var. Mayadin, Fr. Meyadine. Dayr az Zawr, E Syria 35°00′N 40°31′E
139 X10 Al Maymūnah var. Maimuna. Maysān, SE Iraq 31°45′N 46°59′E
101 J25 Almeal E Germany
105 P6 Almazán Castilla y León, N Spain 41°29′N 02°31′W
141 W8 Al Ma'zim var. Al Ma'zam. NW Oman 23°38′N 56°16′E
123 N11 Almazora see Almassora
104 I7 Almazora see Almassora
98 O10 Almelo Overijssel, E Netherlands 52°22′N 06°42′E

ALMENARA – 'AMMAN


105 S9 **Almenara** Comunitat Valenciana, E Spain 39°46′N 00°14′W
105 P12 **Almenaras** ▲ S Spain 38°31′N 02°27′W
105 P5 **Almenar de Soria** Castilla y León, N Spain 41°41′N 02°12′W
104 J6 **Almendra, Embalse de** ⊠ Castilla y León, NW Spain
104 J11 **Almendralejo** Extremadura, W Spain 38°41′N 06°25′W
98 J10 **Almere** *var.* Almere-stad. Flevoland, C Netherlands 52°22′N 05°12′E
98 J10 **Almere-Buiten** Flevoland, C Netherlands 52°24′N 05°15′E
98 J10 **Almere-Haven** Flevoland, C Netherlands 52°20′N 05°13′E
**Almere-stad** *see* Almere
105 P15 **Almería** *Ar.* Al-Mariyya; *anc.* Unci, *Lat.* Portus Magnus. Andalucía, S Spain 36°50′N 02°26′W
105 P14 **Almería** ◈ *province* Andalucía, S Spain
105 P15 **Almería, Golfo de** *gulf* S Spain
127 S5 **Al'met'yevsk** Respublika Tatarstan, W Russia 54°53′N 52°20′E
95 L21 **Älmhult** Kronoberg, S Sweden 56°32′N 14°10′E
141 U9 **Al Miḩrāḑ** *desert* NE Saudi Arabia
**Al Mīnā'** *see* El Mina
104 L17 **Almina, Punta** *headland* Ceuta, Spain, N Africa 35°54′N 05°16′W
75 W9 **Al Minyā** *var.* El Minya, Minya. C Egypt 28°06′N 30°40′E
**Al Miqdādīyah** *see* Al Muqdādīyah
43 P14 **Almirante** Bocas del Toro, NW Panama 09°20′N 82°22′W
**Almirós** *see* Almyrós
140 M9 **Al Mislaḩ** *spring/well* W Saudi Arabia 22°46′N 40°47′E
**Almissa** *see* Omiš
104 G13 **Almodôvar** *var.* Almodóvar. Beja, S Portugal 37°31′N 08°03′W
104 M11 **Almodóvar del Campo** Castilla-La Mancha, C Spain 38°43′N 04°10′W
105 Q9 **Almodóvar del Pinar** Castilla-La Mancha, C Spain 39°44′N 01°55′W
31 S9 **Almont** Michigan, N USA 42°53′N 83°02′W
14 L13 **Almonte** Ontario, SE Canada 45°13′N 76°12′W
104 J14 **Almonte** Andalucía, S Spain 37°16′N 06°31′W
104 K9 **Almonte** ≈ W Spain
152 K9 **Almora** Uttarākhand, N India 29°36′N 79°40′E
104 M8 **Almorox** Castilla-La Mancha, C Spain 40°13′N 04°22′W
141 S7 **Al Mubarraz** Ash Sharqīyah, E Saudi Arabia 25°28′N 49°34′E
**Al Muḑaibī** *see* Al Muḑaybī
138 G15 **Al Mudawwarah** Ma'ān, SW Jordan 29°20′N 36°E
141 Y9 **Al Muḑaybī** *var.* Al Muḑaibī. NE Oman 22°35′N 58°08′E
**Almudébar** *see* Almudévar
105 S5 **Almudévar** *var.* Almudébar. Aragón, NE Spain 42°03′N 00°34′W
141 S15 **Al Mukallā** *var.* Mukalla. SE Yemen 14°36′N 49°07′E
141 N16 **Al Mukhā** *Eng.* Mocha. SW Yemen 13°18′N 43°17′E
105 N15 **Almuñécar** Andalucía, S Spain 36°44′N 03°41′W
139 U7 **Al Muqdādīyah** *var.* Al Miqdādīyah. Diyālá, C Iraq 33°58′N 44°58′E
140 L3 **Al Murayr** *spring/well* NW Saudi Arabia 30°06′N 39°54′E
136 M12 **Almus** Tokat, N Turkey 40°22′N 36°54′E
**Al Muşana'a** *see* Al Maşna'ah
139 T9 **Al Musayyib** *var.* Musaiyib. Bābil, C Iraq 32°47′N 44°20′E
139 V13 **Al Muthannā** *off.* Muḩāfaz at al Muthannā, *var.* As Samāwah. ◈ *governorate* S Iraq
139 V9 **Al Muwaffaqīyah** Wāsiţ, S Iraq 32°19′N 45°22′E
138 H10 **Al Muwaqqar** *var.* El Muwaqqar. 'Ammān, W Jordan 31°49′N 36°06′E
140 J5 **Al Muwayliḩ** *var.* al-Mawailih. Tabūk, NW Saudi Arabia 27°39′N 35°33′E
115 F17 **Almyrós** *var.* Almirós. Thessalía, C Greece 39°11′N 22°45′E
115 I24 **Almyroú, Órmos** *bay* Kríti, Greece, E Mediterranean Sea
**Al Nūwfalīyah** *see* An Nawfalīyah
96 L13 **Alnwick** N England, United Kingdom 55°27′N 01°44′W
**Al Obayyid** *see* El Obeid
**Al Odaid** *see* Al 'Udayd
190 B16 **Alofi** ○ (Niue) W Niue 19°01′S 169°55′E
190 A16 **Alofi Bay** *bay* W Niue, C Pacific Ocean
190 E13 **Alofi, Île** *island* S Wallis and Futuna
190 E13 **Alofitai** Île Alofi, W Wallis and Futuna 14°21′S 178°03′W
**Aloha State** *see* Hawaii
118 G7 **Aloja** N Latvia 57°47′N 24°53′E
153 X10 **Along** Arunāchal Pradesh, NE India 28°15′N 94°56′E
115 H16 **Alónnisos** *island* Vóreies Sporádes, Greece, Aegean Sea
104 M15 **Álora** Andalucía, S Spain 36°50′N 04°43′W
171 Q16 **Alor, Kepulauan** *island group* E Indonesia
171 Q16 **Alor, Pulau** *prev.* Ombai. *island* Kepulauan Alor, E Indonesia
171 O16 **Alor, Selat** *strait* Flores Sea/Savu Sea
168 J7 **Alor Setar** *var.* Alor Star, Alur Setar. Kedah, Peninsular Malaysia 06°06′N 100°23′E
**Alor Star** *see* Alor Setar
**Alost** *see* Aalst
154 F9 **Ālot** Madhya Pradesh, C India 23°56′N 75°40′E
186 G10 **Alotau** Milne Bay, SE Papua New Guinea 10°20′S 150°23′E
171 Y16 **Alotip** Papua, E Indonesia 08°07′S 140°06′E
**Al Oued** *see* El Oued
35 R12 **Alpaugh** California, W USA 35°52′N 119°29′W
**Alpen** *see* Alps
31 R6 **Alpena** Michigan, N USA 45°04′N 83°27′W
**Alpes** *see* Alps
103 S14 **Alpes-de-Haute-Provence** ◈ *department* SE France
103 U14 **Alpes-Maritimes** ◈ *department* SE France
181 W8 **Alpha** Queensland, E Australia 23°40′S 146°38′E
197 R9 **Alpha Cordillera** *var.* Alpha Ridge. *undersea feature* Arctic Ocean 85°30′N 125°00′W
**Alpha Ridge** *see* Alpha Cordillera
**Alpheius** *see* Alfeiós
99 I15 **Alphen** Noord-Brabant, S Netherlands 51°29′N 04°57′E
**Alphen** *see* Alphen aan den Rijn
98 H11 **Alphen aan den Rijn** *var.* Alphen. Zuid-Holland, C Netherlands 52°08′N 04°40′E
**Alpheus** *see* Alfeiós
**Alpi** *see* Alps
104 G10 **Alpiarça** Santarém, C Portugal 39°15′N 08°35′W
24 K10 **Alpine** Texas, SW USA 30°22′N 103°40′W
108 F8 **Alpnach** Unterwalden, W Switzerland 46°56′N 08°17′E
108 D11 **Alps** *Fr.* Alpes, *Ger.* Alpen, *It.* Alpi. ▲▲ C Europe
141 W8 **Al Qābil** *var.* Qabil. N Oman 23°55′N 55°50′E
**Al Qaḑārif** *see* Gedaref
75 P8 **Al Qaddāḩīyah** N Libya 31°21′N 15°16′E
139 V10 **Al Qādisīyah** *off.* Muḩāfaẓat al Qādisīyah, *var.* Ad Dīwānīyah. ◈ *governorate* S Iraq
121 V13 **Al Qāhirah** *Eng.* Cairo. ● (Egypt) N Egypt 30°01′N 31°18′E
140 K4 **Al Qalībah** Tabūk, NW Saudi Arabia 28°29′N 37°40′E
139 O1 **Al Qāmishlī** *var.* Kamishli, Qamishly. Al Ḩasakah, NE Syria 37°N 41°E
138 I6 **Al Qaryatayn** *var.* Qaryatayn, *Fr.* Qariateïne. Ḩimş, C Syria 34°13′N 37°13′E
142 K11 **Al Qash'ānīyah** *var.* Al-Kashaniya. NE Kuwait 29°59′N 47°42′E
141 N7 **Al Qaşīm** *var.* Minţaqat Qaşīm, Qassim. ◈ *region* C Saudi Arabia
75 V10 **Al Qaşr** *var.* Al Qaşr *var.* El Qasr. C Egypt 25°43′N 28°54′E
138 J5 **Al Qaşr** Ḩimş, C Syria 35°06′N 37°39′E
**Al Qaşr** *see* Al Qaşr
**Al Qaşrayn** *see* Kasserine
141 S6 **Al Qaţīf** Ash Sharqīyah, NE Saudi Arabia 26°27′N 50°01′E
138 G11 **Al Qaţrānah** *var.* El Qatrani, Qatrana. Al Karak, W Jordan 31°14′N 36°03′E
75 P11 **Al Qaţrūn** SW Libya 24°57′N 14°40′E
**Al Qayrawān** *see* Kairouan
**Al-Qsar al-Kbir** *see* Ksar-el-Kebir
**Al Qubayyāt** *see* Qoubaiyât
**Al Quds/Al Quds ash Sharīf** *see* Jerusalem
104 H12 **Alqueva, Barragem do** ⊠ Portugal/Spain
138 G8 **Al Qunayţirah** *var.* El Kuneitra, El Quneitra, Kuneitra, Qunaytra. Al Qunayţirah, SW Syria 33°08′N 35°49′E
138 G8 **Al Qunayţirah** *off.* Muḩāfaẓat al Qunayţirah, *var.* El Q'unaytirah, Qunaytirah, *Fr.* Kuneitra. ◈ *governorate* SW Syria
140 M11 **Al Qunfudhah** Makkah al Mukarramah, SW Saudi Arabia 19°19′N 41°03′E
140 K2 **Al Qurayyāt** Al Jawf, NW Saudi Arabia 31°25′N 37°26′E
139 Y11 **Al Qurnah** *var.* Kurna. Al Başrah, SE Iraq 31°01′N 47°27′E
75 Y10 **Al Quşayr** *var.* Al Quşair *var.* Qusair, Quseir. E Egypt 26°05′N 34°16′E
139 V12 **Al Quşayr** Al Muthannā, S Iraq 30°36′N 45°52′E
138 I6 **Al Quşayr** *var.* El Quseir, Quşayr, *Fr.* Kousseir. Ḩimş, W Syria 34°36′N 36°36′E
**Al Quşayr** *see* Al Quşayr
138 H7 **Al Quţayfah** *var.* Quţayfah, Qutayfe, Quteife, *Fr.* Koteifé. Rīf Dimashq, W Syria 33°44′N 36°33′E
141 P8 **Al Quwayīyah** Ar Riyāḑ, C Saudi Arabia 24°06′N 45°18′E
**Al Quwayr** *see* Guwêr
138 F14 **Al Quwayrah** *var.* El Quweira. Al 'Aqabah, SW Jordan 29°47′N 35°18′E
**Al Rayyan** *see* Ar Rayyān
**Al Ruweis** *see* Ar Ruways
95 G24 **Als** *Ger.* Alsen. *island* SW Denmark
103 U5 **Alsace** *cultural region* NE France
11 R16 **Alsask** Saskatchewan, S Canada 51°24′N 109°55′W
**Alsasua** *see* Altsasu
101 C16 **Alsdorf** Nordrhein-Westfalen, W Germany 50°52′N 06°09′E
10 G8 **Alsek** ≈ Canada/USA
**Alsen** *see* Als
101 F19 **Alsenz** ≈ W Germany
101 H17 **Alsfeld** Hessen, C Germany 50°45′N 09°14′E
119 K20 **Al'shany** *Rus.* Ol'shany. Brestskaya Voblasts', SW Belarus 52°05′N 27°21′E
**Alsókubin** *see* Dolný Kubín
118 C9 **Alsunga** W Latvia 56°59′N 21°31′E
**Alt** *see* Olt
92 K9 **Alta** *Fin.* Alattio. Finnmark, N Norway 69°58′N 23°17′E
29 T12 **Alta** Iowa, C USA 42°40′N 95°17′W
**Al Tabaqah** *see* Ath Thawrah
108 I7 **Altach** Vorarlberg, W Austria 47°22′N 09°39′E
92 K9 **Altaelva** *Lapp.* Álahea eatnu. ≈ N Norway
92 J8 **Altafjorden** *fjord* NE Norwegian Sea
62 K10 **Alta Gracia** Córdoba, C Argentina 31°42′S 64°25′W
42 K11 **Alta Gracia** Rivas, SW Nicaragua 11°35′N 85°38′W
54 H4 **Altagracia** Zulia, NW Venezuela 10°44′N 71°30′W
54 M5 **Altagracia de Orituco** Guárico, N Venezuela 09°54′N 66°24′W
**Altai** *see* Altai Mountains
129 T7 **Altai Mountains** *var.* Altai, *Chin.* Altay Shan, *Rus.* Altay. ▲▲ Asia/Europe
23 V6 **Altamaha River** ≈ Georgia, SE USA
58 J13 **Altamira** Pará, NE Brazil 03°13′S 52°15′W
54 D12 **Altamira** Huila, S Colombia 02°04′N 75°47′W
42 M13 **Altamira** Alajuela, N Costa Rica 10°25′N 84°21′W
41 Q11 **Altamira** Tamaulipas, C Mexico 22°25′N 97°55′W
30 L15 **Altamont** Illinois, N USA 39°03′N 88°45′W
27 Q7 **Altamont** Kansas, C USA 37°11′N 95°18′W
32 H16 **Altamont** Oregon, NW USA 42°12′N 121°44′W
20 K10 **Altamont** Tennessee, S USA 35°28′N 85°42′W
23 X11 **Altamonte Springs** Florida, SE USA 28°39′N 81°22′W
107 O17 **Altamura** *anc.* Lupatia. Puglia, SE Italy 40°50′N 16°33′E
40 H9 **Altamura, Isla** *island* C Mexico
**Altan** *see* Erdenehayrhan
**Altanbulag** *see* Bayanhayrhan
163 Q7 **Altan Emel** *var.* Xin Barag Youqi. Nei Mongol Zizhiqu, N China 48°37′N 116°40′E
**Altan-Ovoo** *see* Tsenher
163 N9 **Altanshiree** *var.* Chamdmani. Dornogovĭ, SE Mongolia 45°36′N 110°30′E
**Altanteel** *see* Dzereg
162 D5 **Altantsögts** *var.* Tsagaantüngi. Bayan-Ölgiy, NW Mongolia 49°06′N 90°26′E
40 F3 **Altar** Sonora, NW Mexico 30°41′N 111°53′W
**Altar, Desierto de** *see* Sonoran Desert
105 Q8 **Alta, Sierra** ▲ N Spain 40°29′N 01°36′W
40 H9 **Altata** Sinaloa, C Mexico 24°40′N 107°54′W
42 D4 **Alta Verapaz** *off.* Departamento de Alta Verapaz. ◈ *department* C Guatemala
**Alta Verapaz, Departamento de** *see* Alta Verapaz
107 L18 **Altavilla Silentia** Campania, S Italy 40°32′N 15°06′E
21 T7 **Altavista** Virginia, NE USA 37°06′N 79°17′W
158 L2 **Altay** Xinjiang Uygur Zizhiqu, NW China 47°51′N 88°06′E
162 D6 **Altay** *var.* Chihertey. Bayan-Ölgiy, W Mongolia 48°10′N 89°35′E
162 G8 **Altay** *prev.* Yösönbulag. Govĭ-Altay, W Mongolia 46°23′N 96°17′E
162 E8 **Altay** *var.* Bor-Üdzüür. Hovd, W Mongolia 45°46′N 92°13′E
**Altay** *see* Altai Mountains, Asia/Europe
**Altay** *see* Bayantes, Mongolia
122 J14 **Altay, Respublika** *var.* Gornyy Altay; *prev.* Gorno-Altayskaya Respublika. ◈ *autonomous republic* S Russia
**Altay Shan** *see* Altai Mountains
123 I13 **Altayskiy Kray** ◈ *territory* S Russia
**Altbetsche** *see* Bečej
101 L20 **Altdorf** Bayern, SE Germany 49°23′N 11°22′E
108 G8 **Altdorf** *var.* Altorf. Uri, C Switzerland 46°53′N 08°38′E
105 T11 **Altea** Comunitat Valenciana, E Spain 38°37′N 00°03′W
100 L10 **Alte Elde** ≈ N Germany
101 M16 **Altenburg** Thüringen, E Germany 50°59′N 12°27′E
**Altenburg** *see* Bucureşti, Romania
**Altenburg** *see* Baia de Criş, Romania
100 P12 **Alte Oder** ≈ NE Germany
104 H10 **Alter do Chão** Portalegre, C Portugal 39°12′N 07°40′W
92 I10 **Altevatnet** *Lapp.* Álttesjávri. ◎ N Norway
27 V12 **Altheimer** Arkansas, C USA 34°19′N 91°51′W
109 T9 **Althofen** Kärnten, S Austria 46°52′N 14°27′E
114 H7 **Altimir** Vratsa, NW Bulgaria 43°33′N 23°48′E
136 K11 **Altınkaya Barajı** ⊠ N Turkey
136 E13 **Altıntaş** Kütahya, W Turkey 39°05′N 30°07′E
57 K18 **Altiplano** *physical region* W South America
**Altkanischa** *see* Kanjiža
103 U7 **Altkirch** Haut-Rhin, NE France 47°37′N 07°14′E
**Altlublau** *see* Stará L'ubovňa
100 L12 **Altmark** *cultural region* N Germany
**Altmoldowa** *see* Moldova Veche
25 W8 **Alto** Texas, SW USA 31°39′N 95°04′W
104 H11 **Alto Alentejo** *physical region* S Portugal
59 I19 **Alto Araguaia** Mato Grosso, C Brazil 17°19′S 53°10′W
58 L12 **Alto Bonito** Pará, NE Brazil 01°48′S 46°18′W
83 O15 **Alto Molócuè** Zambézia, NE Mozambique 15°38′S 37°42′E
30 K15 **Alton** Illinois, N USA 38°55′N 90°10′W
27 W8 **Alton** Missouri, C USA 36°41′N 91°25′W
11 X17 **Altona** Manitoba, S Canada 49°06′N 97°35′W
18 E14 **Altoona** Pennsylvania, NE USA 40°32′N 78°23′W
30 J6 **Altoona** Wisconsin, N USA 44°48′N 91°22′W
62 N3 **Alto Paraguay** *off.* Departamento del Alto Paraguay. ◈ *department* N Paraguay
**Alto Paraguay, Departamento del** *see* Alto Paraguay
59 L17 **Alto Paraíso de Goiás** Goiás, S Brazil 14°04′S 47°15′W
62 P6 **Alto Paraná** *off.* Departamento del Alto Paraná. ◈ *department* E Paraguay
**Alto Paraná** *see* Paraná
**Alto Paraná, Departamento del** *see* Alto Paraná
59 L15 **Alto Parnaíba** Maranhão, E Brazil 09°08′S 45°56′W
56 H13 **Alto Purús, Río** ≈ E Peru
**Altorf** *see* Altdorf
63 H19 **Alto Río Senguer** *var.* Alto Río Senguerr. Chubut, S Argentina 45°01′S 70°55′W
**Alto Río Senguerr** *see* Alto Río Senguer
41 Q13 **Altotonga** Veracruz, E Mexico 19°46′N 97°14′W
101 N23 **Altötting** Bayern, SE Germany 48°12′N 12°37′E
**Altpasua** *see* Stara Pazova
**Altraga** *see* Bayandzürh
105 P3 **Altsasu** *Cast.* Alsasua. Navarra, N Spain 42°54′N 02°10′W
**Alt-Schwanenburg** *see* Gulbene
**Altsohl** *see* Zvolen
108 I7 **Altstätten** Sankt Gallen, NE Switzerland 47°22′N 09°33′E
**Álttesjávri** *see* Altevatnet
42 G1 **Altun Ha** *ruins* Belize, N Belize
139 S3 **Altūn Kawbrī** *var.* Āltūn Kūbrī. Kirkūk, N Iraq 35°50′N 44°10′E
**Āltūn Kūbrī** *see* Āltūn Kawbrī
158 D8 **Altun Shan** ▲ C China 39°19′N 93°37′E
158 L9 **Altun Shan** *var.* Altyn Tagh. ▲▲ NW China
35 P2 **Alturas** California, W USA 41°28′N 120°32′W
26 K12 **Altus** Oklahoma, C USA 34°39′N 99°21′W
26 K11 **Altus Lake** ⊠ Oklahoma, C USA
**Altvater** *see* Praděd
**Altyn Tagh** *see* Altun Shan
**Alu** *see* Shortland Island
**al-'Ubaila** *see* Al 'Ubaylah
139 O6 **Al 'Ubaydī** Al Anbār, W Iraq 34°22′N 41°15′E
141 T9 **Al 'Ubaylah** *var.* al-'Ubaila. Ash Sharqīyah, E Saudi Arabia 22°02′N 50°57′E
141 T9 **Al 'Ubaylah** *spring/well* E Saudi Arabia 22°02′N 50°56′E
**Al Ubayyiḑ** *see* El Obeid
141 T7 **Al 'Udayd** *var.* Al Odaid. Abū Z̧aby, W United Arab Emirates 24°34′N 51°27′E
118 J8 **Alūksne** *Ger.* Marienburg. NE Latvia 57°26′N 27°02′E
140 K6 **Al 'Ulā** Al Madīnah al Munawwarah, NW Saudi Arabia 26°39′N 37°55′E
173 N4 **Alula-Fartak Trench** *var.* Illaue Fartak Trench. *undersea feature* W Indian Ocean 14°04′N 51°47′E
138 I11 **Al 'Umarī** 'Ammān, E Jordan 37°30′N 31°30′E
31 S13 **Alum Creek Lake** ⊠ Ohio, N USA
63 H15 **Aluminé** Neuquén, C Argentina 39°15′S 71°00′W
95 O14 **Alunda** Uppsala, C Sweden 60°04′N 18°04′E
117 T14 **Alupka** Avtonomna Respublika Krym, S Ukraine 44°24′N 34°01′E
75 P8 **Al 'Uqaylah** N Libya 30°13′N 19°12′E
75 X10 **Al Uqşur** *Eng.* Luxor. E Egypt 25°39′N 32°39′E
**Al Urdunn** *see* Jordan
**Al Urdunn** *see* Jordan
**al Urdunīyah al Hāshimīyah, Al Mamlakah** *see* Jordan
168 J9 **Alur Panal** *bay* Sumatera, W Indonesia
**Alur Setar** *see* Alor Setar
141 V10 **Al 'Urūq al Mu'tariḑah** *salt lake* SE Saudi Arabia
139 Q7 **Ālūs** Al Anbār, C Iraq 34°05′N 42°27′E
117 T13 **Alushta** Avtonomna Respublika Krym, S Ukraine 44°41′N 34°24′E
**Aluva** *see* Alwaye
75 N11 **Al 'Uwaynāt** *var.* Al Awaynāt. SW Libya 25°47′N 10°34′E
139 T6 **Al 'Uẓaym** *var.* Adhaim. Diyālá, E Iraq 34°12′N 44°31′E
26 L8 **Alva** Oklahoma, C USA 36°48′N 98°40′W
104 H8 **Alva** ≈ N Portugal
95 J18 **Älvängen** Västra Götaland, S Sweden 57°56′N 12°09′E
14 F14 **Alvanley** Ontario, S Canada 44°33′N 81°05′W
41 S14 **Alvarado** Veracruz, E Mexico 18°47′N 95°45′W
25 T7 **Alvarado** Texas, SW USA 32°24′N 97°12′W
58 D13 **Alvarães** Amazonas, NW Brazil 03°13′S 64°53′W
40 G6 **Álvaro Obregón, Presa** ⊠ W Mexico
94 H10 **Alvdal** Hedmark, S Norway 62°07′N 10°39′E
94 K12 **Älvdalen** Dalarna, C Sweden 61°13′N 14°04′E
61 E15 **Alvear** Corrientes, NE Argentina 29°05′S 56°35′W
104 F10 **Alverca do Ribatejo** Lisboa, C Portugal 38°56′N 09°01′W
95 L20 **Alvesta** Kronoberg, S Sweden 56°52′N 14°34′E
25 W12 **Alvin** Texas, SW USA 29°25′N 95°14′W
94 O13 **Älvkarleby** Uppsala, C Sweden 60°34′N 17°30′E
25 S5 **Alvord** Texas, SW USA 33°22′N 97°39′W
93 G18 **Älvros** Jämtland, C Sweden 62°04′N 14°30′E
92 J13 **Älvsbyn** Norrbotten, N Sweden 65°41′N 21°00′E
142 K12 **Al Wafrā'** SE Kuwait 28°38′N 47°57′E
140 J6 **Al Wajh** Tabūk, NW Saudi Arabia 26°16′N 36°30′E
143 N16 **Al Wakrah** *var.* Wakra. C Qatar 25°09′N 51°36′E
138 M8 **al Walaj, Sha'īb** *dry watercourse* W Iraq
152 I11 **Alwar** Rājasthān, N India 27°32′N 76°35′E
141 Q5 **Al Wari'ah** Ash Sharqīyah, N Saudi Arabia 27°54′N 47°23′E
155 G22 **Alwaye** *var.* Aluva. Kerala, SW India 10°06′N 76°23′E
**Alxa Zuoqi** *see* Bayan Hot
**Alx Youqi** *see* Ehen Hudag
**Al Yaman** *see* Yemen
138 G9 **Al Yarmūk** Irbid, N Jordan 32°41′N 35°55′E
139 P2 **Al Ya'rubīyah** *var.* Tall Kūchak, Tall Kūshik. Al Ḩasakah, E Syria 36°48′N 42°01′E
**Alyat/Alyaty-Pristan'** *see* Ālāt
115 I14 **Alykí** *var.* Aliki. Thásos, N Greece 40°36′N 24°45′E
119 F14 **Alytus** *Pol.* Olita. Alytus, S Lithuania 54°24′N 24°02′E
119 F15 **Alytus** ◈ *province* S Lithuania
101 N23 **Alz** ≈ SE Germany
33 Y11 **Alzada** Montana, NW USA 45°00′N 104°24′W
122 L12 **Alzamay** Irkutskaya Oblast', S Russia 55°33′N 98°36′E
99 M25 **Alzette** ≈ S Luxembourg
105 S10 **Alzira** *var.* Alcira; *anc.* Saetabicula, Suero. Comunitat Valenciana, E Spain 39°10′N 00°27′W
**Al Zubair** *see* Az Zubayr
181 O8 **Amadeus, Lake** *seasonal lake* Northern Territory, C Australia
81 E15 **Amadi** Western Equatoria, SW South Sudan 05°32′N 30°20′E
9 R7 **Amadjuak Lake** ◎ Baffin Island, Nunavut, N Canada
95 J23 **Amager** *island* E Denmark
165 N14 **Amagi-san** ▲ Honshū, S Japan 34°51′N 138°57′E
171 S13 **Amahai** *var.* Masohi. Palau Seram, E Indonesia 03°19′S 128°56′E
38 M16 **Amak Island** *island* Alaska, USA
164 C15 **Amakusa** *prev.* Hondo. Kumamoto, Shimo-jima, SW Japan 32°28′N 130°12′E
164 B14 **Amakusa-nada** *gulf* SW Japan
95 J16 **Åmål** Västra Götaland, S Sweden 59°04′N 12°41′E
54 E8 **Amalfi** Antioquia, N Colombia 06°54′N 75°04′W
107 L18 **Amalfi** Campania, S Italy 40°37′N 14°35′E
115 D19 **Amaliáda** *var.* Amaliás. Dytikí Elláda, S Greece 37°48′N 21°21′E
**Amaliás** *see* Amaliáda
154 F12 **Amalner** Mahārāshtra, C India 21°03′N 75°04′E
171 W14 **Amamapare** Papua, E Indonesia 04°51′S 136°44′E
59 H21 **Amambaí, Serra de** *var.* Cordillera de Amambay, Serra de Amambay. ▲▲ Brazil/Paraguay
62 P4 **Amambay** *off.* Departamento del Amambay. ◈ *department* E Paraguay
**Amambay, Cordillera de** *see* Amambaí, Serra de
**Amambay, Departamento del** *see* Amambay
**Amambay, Serra de** *see* Amambaí, Serra de
165 U16 **Amami-guntō** *island group* SW Japan
165 V15 **Amami-Ō-shima** *island* S Japan
186 A5 **Amanab** West Sepik, NW Papua New Guinea 03°38′S 141°16′E
**Amānat al 'Āşimah** *see* Baghdād
106 J13 **Amandola** Marche, C Italy 42°58′N 13°22′E
107 N21 **Amantea** Calabria, SW Italy 39°06′N 16°05′E
191 W10 **Amanu** *island* Îles Tuamotu, C French Polynesia
58 J10 **Amapá** Amapá, NE Brazil 02°00′N 50°50′W
58 J11 **Amapá** *off.* Estado de Amapá; *prev.* Território de Amapá. ◈ *state* NE Brazil
**Amapá, Estado de** *see* Amapá
42 H8 **Amapala** Valle, S Honduras 13°16′N 87°39′W
**Amapá, Território de** *see* Amapá
80 J12 **Āmara** *var.* Amhara. ◈ N Ethiopia
**Amara** *see* Al 'Amārah
**'Amārah, Al** *see* Maysān
104 H6 **Amarante** Porto, N Portugal 41°16′N 08°05′W
166 M5 **Amarapura** Mandalay, C Myanmar (Burma) 21°54′N 96°01′E
**Amardalay** *see* Delgertsogt
104 I12 **Amareleja** Beja, S Portugal 38°12′N 07°13′W
35 V11 **Amargosa Range** ▲▲ California, W USA
25 N2 **Amarillo** Texas, SW USA 35°13′N 101°50′W
**Amarinthos** *see* Amárynthos
107 K15 **Amaro, Monte** ▲ C Italy 42°03′N 14°06′E
115 H18 **Amárynthos** *var.* Amarinthos. Évvoia, C Greece 38°24′N 23°53′E
**Amasia** *see* Amasya
136 K12 **Amasya** *anc.* Amasia. Amasya, N Turkey 40°37′N 35°50′E
136 K11 **Amasya** ◈ *province* N Turkey
42 F4 **Amatique, Bahía de** *bay* Gulf of Honduras, W Caribbean Sea
42 D6 **Amatitlán, Lago de** ◎ S Guatemala
107 J14 **Amatrice** Lazio, C Italy 42°38′N 13°19′E
190 C8 **Amatuku** *atoll* C Tuvalu
99 J20 **Amay** Liège, E Belgium 50°33′N 05°19′E
48 F7 **Amazon** *Sp.* Amazonas. ≈ Brazil/Peru
59 C14 **Amazonas** *off.* Estado do Amazonas. ◈ *state* N Brazil
54 G15 **Amazonas** *off.* Comisaria del Amazonas. ◈ *province* SE Colombia
56 C10 **Amazonas** *off.* Región de Amazonas. ◈ *region* N Peru
54 M12 **Amazonas** *off.* Territorio Amazonas. ◈ *federal territory* S Venezuela
**Amazonas** *see* Amazon
**Amazonas, Comisaria del** *see* Amazonas
**Amazonas, Estado do** *see* Amazonas
**Amazonas, Región de** *see* Amazonas
**Amazonas, Territorio** *see* Amazonas
48 F7 **Amazon Basin** *basin* N South America
47 V5 **Amazon Fan** *undersea feature* W Atlantic Ocean 05°00′N 47°30′W
54 H13 **Amazonía** *physical region* SW Colombia
58 K11 **Amazon, Mouths of the** *delta* NE Brazil
187 R13 **Ambae** *var.* Aoba, Omba. *island* C Vanuatu
152 I9 **Ambāla** Haryāna, NW India 30°19′N 76°49′E
155 J26 **Ambalangoda** Southern Province, SW Sri Lanka 06°14′N 80°03′E
155 K26 **Ambalantota** Southern Province, S Sri Lanka 06°07′N 81°01′E
172 I6 **Ambalavao** Fianarantsoa, C Madagascar 21°50′S 46°56′E
54 E10 **Ambalema** Tolima, C Colombia 04°49′N 74°48′W
79 E17 **Ambam** Sud, S Cameroon 02°23′N 11°17′E
172 J2 **Ambanja** Antsiranana, N Madagascar 13°40′S 48°27′E
123 T6 **Ambarchik** Respublika Sakha (Yakutiya), NE Russia 69°33′N 162°08′E
62 K9 **Ambargasta, Salinas de** *salt lake* C Argentina
124 J6 **Ambarnyy** Respublika Kareliya, NW Russia 65°53′N 33°44′E
56 C7 **Ambato** Tungurahua, C Ecuador 01°18′S 78°39′W
172 I6 **Ambato Finandrahana** Fianarantsoa, SE Madagascar
172 I5 **Ambatolampy** Antananarivo, C Madagascar 19°21′S 47°27′E
172 H4 **Ambatomainty** Mahajanga, W Madagascar 17°40′S 45°39′E
172 J4 **Ambatondrazaka** Toamasina, C Madagascar 17°49′S 48°28′E
101 L20 **Amberg** *var.* Amberg in der Oberpfalz. Bayern, SE Germany 49°26′N 11°52′E
**Amberg in der Oberpfalz** *see* Amberg
42 H1 **Ambergris Cay** *island* NE Belize
103 S11 **Ambérieu-en-Bugey** Ain, E France 45°57′N 05°21′E
185 I18 **Amberley** Canterbury, South Island, New Zealand 43°09′S 172°43′E
103 P11 **Ambert** Puy-de-Dôme, C France 45°33′N 03°45′E
**Ambianum** *see* Amiens
76 J11 **Ambidédi** Kayes, SW Mali 14°37′N 11°49′W
154 M10 **Ambikāpur** Chhattīsgarh, C India 23°09′N 83°12′E
172 J2 **Ambilobe** Antsiranana, N Madagascar 13°10′S 49°03′E
39 O7 **Ambler** Alaska, USA 67°05′N 157°51′W
**Amblève** *see* Amel
**Ambo** *see* Hägere Hiywet
172 I8 **Amboasary** Toliara, S Madagascar 25°01′S 46°23′E
172 J4 **Ambodifotatra** *var.* Ambodifototra. Toamasina, E Madagascar 16°59′S 49°51′E
**Amboenten** *see* Ambunten
172 I5 **Ambohidratrimo** Antananarivo, C Madagascar 18°48′S 47°26′E
172 I6 **Ambohimahasoa** Fianarantsoa, SE Madagascar 21°07′S 47°13′E
172 K3 **Ambohitralanana** Antsiranana, NE Madagascar 15°13′S 50°28′E
**Amboina** *see* Ambon
102 M8 **Amboise** Indre-et-Loire, C France 47°25′N 01°00′E
171 S13 **Ambon** *prev.* Amboina, Amboyna. Pulau Ambon, E Indonesia 03°41′S 128°10′E
171 S13 **Ambon, Pulau** *island* E Indonesia
81 I20 **Amboseli, Lake** ◎ Kenya/Tanzania
172 I6 **Ambositra** Fianarantsoa, SE Madagascar 20°31′S 47°15′E
172 I8 **Ambovombe** Toliara, S Madagascar 25°10′S 46°06′E
35 W14 **Amboy** California, W USA 34°33′N 115°44′W
30 L11 **Amboy** Illinois, N USA 41°42′N 89°19′W
**Amboyna** *see* Ambon
**Ambracia** *see* Árta
**Ambre, Cap d'** *see* Bobaomby, Tanjona
18 B14 **Ambridge** Pennsylvania, NE USA 40°33′N 80°11′W
**Ambrim** *see* Ambrym
82 A11 **Ambriz** Bengo, NW Angola 07°55′S 13°11′E
**Ambrizete** *see* N'Zeto
187 R13 **Ambrym** *var.* Ambrim. *island* C Vanuatu
169 T16 **Ambunten** *prev.* Amboenten. Pulau Madura, E Indonesia 06°55′S 113°45′E
186 B6 **Ambunti** East Sepik, NW Papua New Guinea 04°12′S 142°49′E
155 I20 **Āmbūr** Tamil Nādu, SE India 12°48′N 78°44′E
38 E17 **Amchitka Island** *island* Aleutian Islands, Alaska, USA
38 F17 **Amchitka Pass** *strait* Aleutian Islands, Alaska, USA
141 R15 **'Amd** C Yemen 15°10′N 47°58′E
78 J10 **Am Dam** Sila, E Chad 12°46′N 20°29′E
171 U16 **Amdassa** Pulau Yamdena, E Indonesia 07°40′S 131°24′E
125 U1 **Amderma** Nenetskiy Avtonomnyy Okrug, NW Russia 69°45′N 61°36′E
159 N14 **Amdo** Xizang Zizhiqu, W China 32°15′N 91°43′E
40 K13 **Ameca** Jalisco, SW Mexico 20°34′N 104°03′W
41 P14 **Amecameca** *var.* Amecameca de Juárez. México, C Mexico 19°08′N 98°48′W
**Amecameca de Juárez** *see* Amecameca
139 R1 **Amēdī** *Ar.* Al 'Amādiyah. Dahūk, N Iraq 37°09′N 43°27′E
61 A20 **Ameghino** Buenos Aires, E Argentina 34°51′S 62°28′W
99 M21 **Amel** *Fr.* Amblève. Liège, E Belgium 50°20′N 06°13′E
98 K4 **Ameland** *Fris.* It Amelân. *island* Waddeneilanden, N Netherlands
**Amelân, It** *see* Ameland
107 H14 **Amelia** Umbria, C Italy 42°33′N 12°26′E
21 V6 **Amelia Court House** Virginia, NE USA 37°20′N 77°59′W
23 W8 **Amelia Island** *island* Florida, SE USA
18 L12 **Amenia** New York, NE USA 41°51′N 73°31′W
**America** *see* United States of America
65 M21 **America-Antarctica Ridge** *undersea feature* S Atlantic Ocean
**America in Miniature** *see* Maryland
60 L9 **Americana** São Paulo, S Brazil 22°44′S 47°19′W
33 Q15 **American Falls** Idaho, NW USA 42°47′N 112°51′W
33 Q15 **American Falls Reservoir** ⊠ Idaho, NW USA
36 L3 **American Fork** Utah, W USA 40°24′N 111°47′W
192 K16 **American Samoa** ◇ US *unincorporated territory* W Polynesia
23 S6 **Americus** Georgia, SE USA 32°04′N 84°13′W
98 K12 **Amerongen** Utrecht, C Netherlands 52°00′N 05°30′E
98 K11 **Amersfoort** Utrecht, C Netherlands 52°09′N 05°23′E
97 N21 **Amersham** SE England, United Kingdom 51°40′N 00°37′W
30 I5 **Amery** Wisconsin, N USA 45°18′N 92°20′W
195 W6 **Amery Ice Shelf** *ice shelf* Antarctica
29 V13 **Ames** Iowa, C USA 42°01′N 93°37′W
19 P10 **Amesbury** Massachusetts, NE USA 42°51′N 70°55′W
**Amestratus** *see* Mistretta
115 F18 **Amfíkleia** *var.* Amfiklia. Stereá Elláda, C Greece 38°38′N 22°35′E
**Amfiklia** *see* Amfíkleia
115 D17 **Amfilochía** *var.* Amfilokhía. Dytikí Elláda, C Greece 38°52′N 21°09′E
**Amfilokhía** *see* Amfilochía
114 H13 **Amfípoli** *anc.* Amphipolis. *site of ancient city* Kentrikí Makedonía, NE Greece
115 F18 **Ámfissa** Stereá Elláda, C Greece 38°32′N 22°22′E
123 Q10 **Amga** Respublika Sakha (Yakutiya), NE Russia 60°55′N 131°45′E
123 Q11 **Amga** ≈ NE Russia
163 R7 **Amgalang** *var.* Xin Barag Zuoqi. Nei Mongol Zizhiqu, N China 48°12′N 118°15′E
123 V5 **Amguema** ≈ NE Russia
123 S12 **Amgun'** ≈ SE Russia
**Amhara** *see* Āmara
13 P15 **Amherst** Nova Scotia, SE Canada 45°50′N 64°14′W
18 M11 **Amherst** Massachusetts, NE USA 42°22′N 72°31′W
18 D10 **Amherst** New York, NE USA 42°57′N 78°47′W
24 M4 **Amherst** Texas, SW USA 33°59′N 102°24′W
21 U6 **Amherst** Virginia, NE USA 37°35′N 79°04′W
**Amherst** *see* Kyaikkami
14 C18 **Amherstburg** Ontario, S Canada 42°05′N 83°06′W
21 Q6 **Amherstdale** West Virginia, NE USA 37°46′N 81°46′W
14 K15 **Amherst Island** *island* Ontario, SE Canada
**Amida** *see* Diyarbakır
28 J6 **Amidon** North Dakota, N USA 46°29′N 103°19′W
103 O3 **Amiens** *anc.* Ambianum, Samarobriva. Somme, N France 49°54′N 02°18′E
139 P8 **'Āmij, Wādī** *var.* Wadi 'Amīq. *dry watercourse* W Iraq
136 L17 **Amik Ovası** ◎ S Turkey
76 E9 **Amilcar Cabral** ✈ Sal, NE Cape Verde
**Amilhayt, Wādī** *see* Umm al Ḩayt, Wādī
**Amíndaion/Amindeo** *see* Amýntaio
155 C21 **Amīndīvi Islands** *island group* Lakshadweep, India, N Indian Ocean
139 U6 **Āmin Ḩabīb** Diyālá, E Iraq 34°17′N 45°10′E
83 E20 **Aminuis** Omaheke, E Namibia 23°43′S 19°21′E
**'Amīq, Wadi** *see* 'Āmij, Wādī
142 J7 **Amīrābād** Īlām, NW Iran 33°20′N 46°16′E
**Amirante Bank** *see* Amirante Ridge
173 N6 **Amirante Basin** *undersea feature* W Indian Ocean 07°00′S 54°00′E
173 N6 **Amirante Islands** *var.* Amirantes Group. *island group* C Seychelles
173 N7 **Amirante Ridge** *var.* Amirante Bank. *undersea feature* W Indian Ocean 06°00′S 53°10′E
**Amirantes Group** *see* Amirante Islands
173 N7 **Amirante Trench** *undersea feature* W Indian Ocean 08°00′S 52°30′E
11 U13 **Amisk Lake** ◎ Saskatchewan, C Canada
**Amistad, Presa de la** *see* Amistad Reservoir
25 O12 **Amistad Reservoir** *var.* Presa de la Amistad. ⊠ Mexico/USA
**Amisus** *see* Samsun
22 K8 **Amite** *var.* Amite City. Louisiana, S USA 30°40′N 90°30′W
**Amite City** *see* Amite
27 T12 **Amity** Arkansas, C USA 34°15′N 93°27′W
154 H11 **Amla** *prev.* Amulla. Madhya Pradesh, C India 21°53′N 78°10′E
38 I17 **Amlia Island** *island* Aleutian Islands, Alaska, USA
97 I18 **Amlwch** NW Wales, United Kingdom 53°25′N 04°23′W
**Ammaia** *see* Portalegre
138 H10 **'Ammān** *var.* Amman; *anc.* Philadelphia, *Bibl.* Rabbah Ammon, Rabbath Ammon. ● (Jordan) 'Ammān, NW Jordan 31°57′N 35°56′E




◆ Country
● Country Capital
◇ Dependent Territory
○ Dependent Territory Capital
◈ Administrative Regions
✈ International Airport
▲ Mountain
▲▲ Mountain Range
Volcano
≈ River
◎ Lake
⊠ Reservoir

'Ammān – Antequera


138 H10 **'Ammān** *off.* Muḩāfaẓat 'Ammān; *prev.* Al 'Aşimah. ◆ *governorate* NW Jordan
**'Ammān, Muḩāfaẓat** *see* 'Ammān
93 N14 **Ämmänsaari** Kainuu, E Finland 64°51′N 28°58′E
92 H13 **Ammarnäs** Västerbotten, N Sweden 65°58′N 16°10′E
197 O15 **Ammassalik** *var.* Angmagssalik. Sermersooq, S Greenland 65°51′N 37°30′W
101 K24 **Ammer** ⚞ SE Germany
101 K24 **Ammersee** ◎ SE Germany
98 J13 **Ammerzoden** Gelderland, C Netherlands 51°46′N 05°07′E
**Ammóchostos** *see* Gazimağusa
**Ammóchostou, Kólpos** *see* Gazimağusa Körfezi
**Amnok-kang** *see* Yalu
**Amoea** *see* Portalegre
**Amoentai** *see* Amuntai
**Amoerang** *see* Amurang
143 O4 **Āmol** *var.* Amul. Māzandarān, N Iran 36°31′N 52°24′E
115 K21 **Amorgós** Amorgós, Kykládes, Greece, Aegean Sea 36°49′N 25°54′E
115 K22 **Amorgós** *island* Kykládes, Greece, Aegean Sea
23 N3 **Amory** Mississippi, S USA 33°58′N 88°29′W
12 I13 **Amos** Québec, SE Canada 48°34′N 78°08′W
95 G15 **Åmot** Buskerud, S Norway 59°52′N 09°55′E
95 E15 **Åmot** Telemark, S Norway 59°34′N 07°59′E
95 J15 **Åmotfors** Värmland, C Sweden 59°46′N 12°24′E
76 L10 **Amourj** Hodh ech Chargui, SE Mauritania 16°04′N 07°12′W
**Amoy** *see* Xiamen
172 H7 **Ampanihy** Toliara, SW Madagascar 24°40′S 44°45′E
155 L25 **Ampara** *var.* Amparai. Eastern Province, E Sri Lanka 07°17′N 81°41′E
172 J4 **Amparafaravola** Toamasina, E Madagascar 17°33′S 48°13′E
**Amparai** *see* Ampara
60 M9 **Amparo** São Paulo, S Brazil 22°40′S 46°49′W
172 J5 **Ampasimanolotra** Toamasina, E Madagascar 18°49′S 49°04′E
57 H17 **Ampato, Nevado** ▲ S Peru 15°52′S 71°51′W
101 L23 **Amper** ⚞ SE Germany
64 M9 **Ampère Seamount** *undersea feature* E Atlantic Ocean 35°05′N 13°00′W
**Amphipolis** *see* Amfípoli
167 X10 **Amphitrite Group** *Chin.* Xuande Qundao, *Viet.* Nhom An Vinh. *island group* N Paracel Islands
171 T16 **Amplawas** *var.* Emplawas. Pulau Babar, E Indonesia 08°01′S 129°42′E
105 U7 **Amposta** Cataluña, NE Spain 40°43′N 00°34′E
15 V7 **Amqui** Québec, SE Canada 48°28′N 67°27′W
141 O14 **'Amrān** W Yemen 15°39′N 43°59′E
**Amraoti** *see* Amrāvati
154 H12 **Amrāvati** *prev.* Amraoti. Mahārāshtra, C India 20°56′N 77°45′E
154 C11 **Amreli** Gujarāt, W India 21°36′N 71°20′E
108 H6 **Amriswil** Thurgau, NE Switzerland 47°33′N 09°18′E
138 H5 **'Amrīt** *ruins* Ţarţūs, W Syria
152 H7 **Amritsar** Punjab, N India 31°38′N 74°55′E
152 J10 **Amroha** Uttar Pradesh, N India 28°54′N 78°29′E
100 G7 **Amrum** *island* NW Germany
93 I15 **Åmsele** Västerbotten, N Sweden 64°31′N 19°24′E
98 I10 **Amstelveen** Noord-Holland, C Netherlands 52°18′N 04°50′E
98 I10 **Amsterdam** ● (Netherlands-official) Noord-Holland, C Netherlands 52°22′N 04°54′E
18 K10 **Amsterdam** New York, NE USA 42°56′N 74°11′W
173 Q11 **Amsterdam Fracture Zone** *tectonic feature* S Indian Ocean
173 R11 **Amsterdam Island** *island* NE French Southern and Antarctic Lands
109 U4 **Amstetten** Niederösterreich, N Austria 48°08′N 14°52′E
78 J11 **Am Timan** Salamat, SE Chad 11°02′N 20°17′E
146 L12 **Amu-Buxoro Kanali** *var.* Aral-Bukhorskiy Kanal. *canal* C Uzbekistan
139 O1 **'Āmūda** *var.* Amude, 'Āmūdah, Al Ḩasakah. Al Ḩasakah, N Syria 37°06′N 40°56′E
**'Āmūdah** *see* 'Āmūda
147 O15 **Amu Darya** *Rus.* Amudar'ya, *Taj.* Amu Daryo, *Turkm.* Amyderya, *Afg.* Āmū Daryā, *Uzb.* Amudaryo; *anc.* Oxus. ⚞ C Asia
**Amu-Dar'ya** *see* Amyderýa
**Amudar'ya/Amudaryo/Amu Daryo** *see* Amu Darya
**Amude** *see* 'Āmūda
140 L3 **'Amūd, Jabal al** ▲ NW Saudi Arabia 30°59′N 39°17′E
38 J17 **Amukta Island** *island* Aleutian Islands, Alaska, USA
38 I17 **Amukta Pass** *strait* Aleutian Islands, Alaska, USA
**Amul** *see* Āmol
**Amulla** *see* Amla
197 S10 **Amundsen Basin** *var.* Fram Basin. *undersea basin* Arctic Ocean
195 X3 **Amundsen Bay** *bay* Antarctica
195 P10 **Amundsen Coast** *physical region* Antarctica
193 O14 **Amundsen Plain** *undersea feature* S Pacific Ocean
195 Q9 **Amundsen-Scott** *research station* (US) Antarctica 89°59′S 10°00′E
194 J11 **Amundsen Sea** *sea* S Pacific Ocean
94 M12 **Amungen** ◎ C Sweden
169 U13 **Amuntai** *prev.* Amoentai. Borneo, C Indonesia 02°24′S 115°14′E
129 W6 **Amur** *Chin.* Heilong Jiang. ⚞ China/Russia
171 Q11 **Amurang** *prev.* Amoerang. Sulawesi, C Indonesia 01°12′N 124°37′E
105 O3 **Amurrio** País Vasco, N Spain 43°03′N 03°00′W
123 S13 **Amursk** Khabarovskiy Kray, SE Russia 50°13′N 136°34′E
123 Q12 **Amurskaya Oblast'** ◆ *province* SE Russia
80 G7 **'Amur, Wadi** ⚞ NE Sudan
115 C17 **Amvrakikós Kólpos** *gulf* W Greece
**Amvrosiyevka** *see* Amvrosiyivka
117 X8 **Amvrosiyivka** *Rus.* Amvrosiyevka. Donets'ka Oblast', SE Ukraine 47°46′N 38°30′E
146 M14 **Amyderýa** *Rus.* Amu-Dar'ya. Lebap Welaýaty, NE Turkmenistan 37°58′N 65°14′E
**Amyderya** *see* Amu Darya
114 E13 **Amýntaio** *var.* Amindeo; *prev.* Amíndaion. Dytikí Makedonía, N Greece 40°42′N 21°42′E
14 B6 **Amyot** Ontario, S Canada 48°28′N 84°58′W
191 U10 **Anaa** *atoll* Îles Tuamotu, C French Polynesia
**Anabanoea** *see* Anabanua
171 N14 **Anabanua** *prev.* Anabanoea. Sulawesi, C Indonesia 03°58′S 120°07′E
189 R8 **Anabar** NE Nauru 0°30′S 166°56′E
123 N8 **Anabar** ⚞ NE Russia
**An Abhainn Mhór** *see* Blackwater
55 O6 **Anaco** Anzoátegui, NE Venezuela 09°30′N 64°28′W
33 Q10 **Anaconda** Montana, NW USA 46°09′N 112°56′W
32 H7 **Anacortes** Washington, NW USA 48°30′N 122°36′W
26 M11 **Anadarko** Oklahoma, C USA 35°04′N 98°16′W
114 N12 **Ana Dere** ⚞ NW Turkey
104 G8 **Anadia** Aveiro, N Portugal 40°26′N 08°27′W
**Anadolu Dağları** *see* Doğu Karadeniz Dağları
123 V6 **Anadyr'** Chukotskiy Avtonomnyy Okrug, NE Russia 64°41′N 177°22′E
123 V6 **Anadyr'** ⚞ NE Russia
**Anadyr, Gulf of** *see* Anadyrskiy Zaliv
129 X4 **Anadyrskiy Khrebet** *var.* Chukot Range. ▲ NE Russia
123 W6 **Anadyrskiy Zaliv** *Eng.* Gulf of Anadyr. *gulf* NE Russia
115 K22 **Anáfi** *anc.* Anaphe. *island* Kykládes, Greece, Aegean Sea
107 J15 **Anagni** Lazio, C Italy 41°43′N 13°12′E
**'Ānah** *see* 'Annah
148 J7 **Anāh Darreh** *var.* Anar Dara. Farāh, W Afghanistan 32°45′N 61°38′E
35 T15 **Anaheim** California, W USA 33°50′N 117°54′W
10 L15 **Anahim Lake** British Columbia, SW Canada 52°26′N 125°13′W
38 B8 **Anahola** Kaua'i, Hawai'i, USA, C Pacific Ocean 22°09′N 159°19′W
41 O7 **Anáhuac** Nuevo León, NE Mexico 27°13′N 100°09′W
25 X11 **Anahuac** Texas, SW USA 29°44′N 94°41′W
155 G22 **Anai Mudi** ▲ S India 10°16′N 77°08′E
**Anaiza** *see* 'Unayzah
155 M15 **Anakāpalle** Andhra Pradesh, E India 17°42′N 83°06′E
191 W15 **Anakena, Playa de** *beach* Easter Island, Chile, E Pacific Ocean
39 Q7 **Anaktuvuk Pass** Alaska, USA 68°08′N 151°44′W
39 Q6 **Anaktuvuk River** ⚞ Alaska, USA
172 J3 **Analalava** Mahajanga, NW Madagascar 14°38′S 47°46′E
44 F6 **Ana María, Golfo de** *gulf* N Caribbean Sea
**Anambas Islands** *see* Anambas, Kepulauan
169 N8 **Anambas, Kepulauan** *var.* Anambas Islands. *island group* W Indonesia
77 U17 **Anambra** ◆ *state* SE Nigeria
29 N4 **Anamoose** North Dakota, N USA 47°50′N 100°14′W
29 Y13 **Anamosa** Iowa, C USA 42°06′N 91°17′W
136 H17 **Anamur** İçel, S Turkey 36°06′N 32°49′E
136 H17 **Anamur Burnu** *headland* S Turkey 36°03′N 32°49′E
154 O12 **Ānandapur** *var.* Anandpur. Odisha, E India 21°14′N 86°10′E
**Anandpur** *see* Ānandapur
155 H18 **Anantapur** Andhra Pradesh, S India 14°41′N 77°36′E
152 H5 **Anantnāg** *var.* Islamabad. Jammu and Kashmir, NW India 33°44′N 75°11′E
**Ananyev** *see* Anan'yiv
117 O9 **Anan'yiv** *Rus.* Ananyev. Odes'ka Oblast', SW Ukraine 47°43′N 29°51′E
126 J14 **Anapa** Krasnodarskiy Kray, SW Russia 44°55′N 37°20′E
**Anaphe** *see* Anáfi
59 K18 **Anápolis** Goiás, C Brazil 16°19′S 48°58′W
143 R10 **Anār** Kermān, C Iran 30°49′N 55°18′E
**Anár** *see* Inari
143 P7 **Anārak** Eşfahān, C Iran 33°21′N 53°43′E
**Anar Dara** *see* Anāh Darreh
**Anárjohka** *see* Inarijoki
23 X9 **Anastasia Island** *island* Florida, SE USA
188 K7 **Anatahan** *island* C Northern Mariana Islands
128 M6 **Anatolia** *plateau* C Turkey
86 F14 **Anatolian Plate** *tectonic feature* Asia/Europe
114 H13 **Anatolikí Makedonía kai Thráki** *Eng.* Macedonia East and Thrace. ◆ *region* NE Greece
**Anatom** *see* Aneityum
62 L8 **Añatuya** Santiago del Estero, N Argentina 28°28′S 62°52′W
**An Baile Meánach** *see* Ballymena
**Anbār, Muḩāfaẓat al** *see* Al Anbār
**An Bhearú** *see* Barrow
**An Bhóinn** *see* Boyne
**An Blascaod Mór** *see* Great Blasket Island
**An Cabhán** *see* Cavan
**An Caisleán Nua** *see* Newcastle
**An Caisleán Riabhach** *see* Castlerea, Ireland
**An Caisleán Riabhach** *see* Castlereagh
56 C13 **Ancash** *off.* Región de Ancash. ◆ *region* W Peru
**Ancash, Región de** *see* Ancash
**An Cathair** *see* Caher
102 J8 **Ancenis** Loire-Atlantique, NW France 47°23′N 01°10′W
**An Chanáil Ríoga** *see* Royal Canal
**An Cheacha** *see* Caha Mountains
39 R11 **Anchorage** Alaska, USA 61°13′N 149°52′W
39 R12 **Anchorage** ✕ Alaska, USA 61°08′N 150°00′W
39 Q13 **Anchor Point** Alaska, USA 59°46′N 151°49′W
**An Chorr Chríochach** *see* Cookstown
65 M24 **Anchorstock Point** *headland* W Tristan da Cunha 37°07′S 12°21′W
**An Clár** *see* Clare
**An Clochán** *see* Clifden
**An Clochán Liath** *see* Dunglow
23 U12 **Anclote Keys** *island group* Florida, SE USA
**An Cóbh** *see* Cobh
57 J17 **Ancohuma, Nevado de** ▲ W Bolivia 15°51′S 68°33′W
**An Comar** *see* Comber
57 D14 **Ancón** Provincia de Lima, W Peru 11°45′S 77°08′W
106 J12 **Ancona** Marche, C Italy 43°38′N 13°30′E
**Ancuabe** *see* Ancuabi
82 Q13 **Ancuabi** *var.* Ancuabe. Cabo Delgado, NE Mozambique 13°00′S 39°50′E
63 F17 **Ancud** *prev.* San Carlos de Ancud. Los Lagos, S Chile 41°53′S 73°50′W
63 G17 **Ancud, Golfo de** *gulf* S Chile
**Ancyra** *see* Ankara
163 V8 **Anda** Heilongjiang, NE China 46°25′N 125°20′E
57 G16 **Andahuaylas** Apurímac, S Peru 13°39′S 73°24′W
**An Daingean** *see* Dingle
153 R15 **Andāl** West Bengal, NE India 23°35′N 87°14′E
94 E9 **Åndalsnes** Møre og Romsdal, S Norway 62°33′N 07°42′E
104 K13 **Andalucía** *Eng.* Andalusia. ◆ *autonomous community* S Spain
23 P7 **Andalusia** Alabama, S USA 31°18′N 86°29′W
**Andalusia** *see* Andalucía
151 Q21 **Andaman and Nicobar Islands** *var.* Andamans and Nicobars. ◆ *union territory* India, NE Indian Ocean
173 T4 **Andaman Basin** *undersea feature* NE Indian Ocean 10°00′N 94°00′E
151 P19 **Andaman Islands** *island group* India, NE Indian Ocean
**Andamans and Nicobars** *see* Andaman and Nicobar Islands
173 T4 **Andaman Sea** *sea* NE Indian Ocean
57 K19 **Andamarca** Oruro, C Bolivia 18°46′S 67°31′W
182 H5 **Andamooka** South Australia 30°26′S 137°12′E
141 Y9 **'Andām, Wādī** *seasonal river* NE Oman
172 J3 **Andapa** Antsiranana, NE Madagascar 14°39′S 49°40′E
**Andarāb** *see* Banū
**Andarbag** *see* Andarbogh
147 S13 **Andarbogh** *Rus.* Andarbag, Anderbak. S Tajikistan 37°51′N 71°45′E
109 Z5 **Andau** Burgenland, E Austria 47°47′N 17°02′E
108 I10 **Andeer** Graubünden, S Switzerland 46°36′N 09°24′E
92 H9 **Andenes** Nordland, C Norway 69°18′N 16°10′E
99 J20 **Andenne** Namur, SE Belgium 50°29′N 05°06′E
77 S11 **Andéramboukane** Gao, E Mali 15°24′N 03°03′E
**Anderbak** *see* Andarbogh
99 G18 **Anderlecht** Brussels, C Belgium 50°50′N 04°18′E
99 G21 **Anderlues** Hainaut, S Belgium 50°24′N 04°16′E
108 G9 **Andermatt** Uri, C Switzerland 46°39′N 08°36′E
101 E17 **Andernach** *anc.* Antunnacum. Rheinland-Pfalz, SW Germany 50°26′N 07°24′E
188 D15 **Andersen Air Force Base** *air base* NE Guam 13°34′N 144°55′E
39 R9 **Anderson** Alaska, USA 64°20′N 149°11′W
35 N4 **Anderson** California, W USA 40°26′N 122°21′W
31 P13 **Anderson** Indiana, N USA 40°06′N 85°40′W
27 R8 **Anderson** Missouri, C USA 36°39′N 94°26′W
21 P11 **Anderson** South Carolina, SE USA 34°30′N 82°39′W
25 V10 **Anderson** Texas, SW USA 30°29′N 96°00′W
95 K20 **Anderstorp** Jönköping, S Sweden 57°17′N 13°38′E
54 D9 **Andes** Antioquia, W Colombia 05°40′N 75°56′W
47 P7 **Andes** ▲ W South America
29 P12 **Andes, Lake** ◎ South Dakota, N USA
92 H9 **Andfjorden** *fjord* E Norwegian Sea
155 H16 **Andhra Pradesh** ◆ *state* E India
98 J8 **Andijk** Noord-Holland, NW Netherlands 52°38′N 05°00′E
147 S10 **Andijon** *Rus.* Andizhan. Andijon Viloyati, E Uzbekistan 40°46′N 72°19′E
147 S10 **Andijon Viloyati** *Rus.* Andizhanskaya Oblast'. ◆ *province* E Uzbekistan
**Andikíthira** *see* Antikýthira
172 J4 **Andilamena** Toamasina, C Madagascar 17°00′S 48°35′E
142 L8 **Andīmeshk** *var.* Andimishk; *prev.* Salehābād. Khūzestān, SW Iran 32°30′N 48°26′E
**Andimishk** *see* Andīmeshk
**Andipáros** *see* Antíparos
**Andipaxi** *see* Antípaxoi
**Andípsara** *see* Antípsara
136 L16 **Andırın** Kahramanmaraş, S Turkey 37°33′N 36°18′E
158 J8 **Andirlangar** Xinjiang Uygur Zizhiqu, NW China 37°38′N 83°40′E
**Andírrion** *see* Antírrio
**Ándissa** *see* Ántissa
**Andizhan** *see* Andijon
**Andizhanskaya Oblast'** *see* Andijon Viloyati
149 N2 **Andkhvoy** *prev.* Andkhvoy. Fāryāb, N Afghanistan 36°56′N 65°08′E
105 Q2 **Andoain** País Vasco, N Spain 43°13′N 02°02′W
163 Y15 **Andong** *Jap.* Antō. E South Korea 36°34′N 128°44′E
109 R4 **Andorf** Oberösterreich, N Austria 48°22′N 13°33′E
105 S7 **Andorra** Aragón, NE Spain 40°59′N 00°27′W
105 V4 **Andorra** *off.* Principality of Andorra, *Cat.* Valls d'Andorra, *Fr.* Vallée d'Andorre. ◆ *monarchy* SW Europe
**Andorra** *see* Andorra la Vella
105 V4 **Andorra la Vella** *var.* Andorra, *Fr.* Andorre la Vielle, *Sp.* Andorra la Vieja. ● (Andorra) C Andorra 42°30′N 01°30′E
**Andorra la Vieja** *see* Andorra la Vella
**Andorra, Principality of** *see* Andorra
**Andorra, Valls d'/Andorra, Vallée d'** *see* Andorra
**Andorre la Vielle** *see* Andorra la Vella
97 M22 **Andover** S England, United Kingdom 51°13′N 01°28′W
27 N6 **Andover** Kansas, C USA 37°42′N 97°08′W
92 G10 **Andøya** *island* C Norway
60 I8 **Andradina** São Paulo, S Brazil 20°54′S 51°19′W
105 X9 **Andratx** Mallorca, Spain, W Mediterranean Sea 39°35′N 02°25′E
39 N10 **Andreafsky River** ⚞ Alaska, USA
38 H17 **Andreanof Islands** *island group* Aleutian Islands, Alaska, USA
124 H16 **Andreapol'** Tverskaya Oblast', W Russia 56°38′N 32°17′E
**Andreas, Cape** *see* Zafer Burnu
**Andreevka** *see* Kabanbay
21 N10 **Andrews** North Carolina, SE USA 35°19′N 83°49′W
21 T13 **Andrews** South Carolina, SE USA 33°27′N 79°33′W
24 M7 **Andrews** Texas, SW USA 32°19′N 102°34′W
173 N5 **Andrew Tablemount** *var.* Gora Andryu. *undersea feature* W Indian Ocean 06°45′N 50°30′E
**Andreyevka** *see* Kabanbay
107 N17 **Andria** Puglia, SE Italy 41°13′N 16°17′E
113 K16 **Andrijevica** E Montenegro 42°45′N 19°45′E
115 E20 **Andrítsaina** Pelopónnisos, S Greece 37°29′N 21°52′E
**An Droichead Nua** *see* Newbridge
**Andropov** *see* Rybinsk
115 J19 **Ándros** Ándros, Kykládes, Greece, Aegean Sea 37°49′N 24°54′E
115 J20 **Ándros** *island* Kykládes, Greece, Aegean Sea
19 O7 **Androscoggin River** ⚞ Maine/New Hampshire, NE USA
44 F3 **Andros Island** *island* NW The Bahamas
127 R7 **Androsovka** Samarskaya Oblast', W Russia 52°41′N 49°34′E
44 G3 **Andros Town** Andros Island, NW The Bahamas 24°40′N 77°47′W
155 D21 **Āndrott Island** *island* Lakshadweep, India, N Indian Ocean
117 N5 **Andrushivka** Zhytomyrs'ka Oblast', N Ukraine 50°01′N 29°02′E
111 K17 **Andrychów** Małopolskie, S Poland 49°51′N 19°18′E
**Andryu, Gora** *see* Andrew Tablemount
92 I10 **Andselv** Troms, N Norway 69°05′N 18°30′E
79 O17 **Andudu** Orientale, NE Dem. Rep. Congo 02°26′N 28°39′E
105 N13 **Andújar** *anc.* Illiturgis. Andalucía, SW Spain 38°02′N 04°03′W
82 C12 **Andulo** Bié, W Angola 11°29′S 16°43′E
103 Q14 **Anduze** Gard, S France 44°03′N 03°59′E
**An Earagail** *see* Errigal Mountain
95 L19 **Aneby** Jönköping, S Sweden 57°50′N 14°45′E
**Anécho** *see* Aného
77 Q9 **Anéfis** Kidal, NE Mali 18°05′N 00°38′E
45 U8 **Anegada** *island* NE British Virgin Islands
61 B25 **Anegada, Bahía** *bay* E Argentina
45 U9 **Anegada Passage** *passage* Anguilla/British Virgin Islands
77 R17 **Aného** *var.* Anécho; *prev.* Petit-Popo. S Togo 06°14′N 01°36′E
197 D17 **Aneityum** *var.* Anatom; *prev.* Kéamu. *island* S Vanuatu
117 N10 **Anenii Noi** *Rus.* Novyye Aneny. C Moldova 46°52′N 29°10′E
186 F7 **Anepmete** New Britain, E Papua New Guinea 05°47′S 148°37′E
105 U4 **Aneto** ▲ NE Spain 42°36′N 00°37′E
146 F13 **Änew** *Rus.* Annau. Ahal Welaýaty, C Turkmenistan 37°51′N 58°22′E
**Änewetak** *see* Enewetak Atoll
77 Y8 **Aney** Agadez, NE Niger 19°22′N 13°00′E
**An Fheoir** *see* Nore
122 L12 **Angara** ⚞ C Russia
122 M13 **Angarsk** Irkutskaya Oblast', S Russia 52°31′N 103°55′E
**Angaur** *see* Ngeaur
93 G17 **Ånge** Västernorrland, C Sweden 62°31′N 15°40′E
**Angel** *see* Úhlava
40 D4 **Ángel de la Guarda, Isla** *island* NW Mexico
171 O3 **Angeles** *off.* Angeles City. Luzon, N Philippines 15°16′N 120°37′E
**Angeles City** *see* Angeles
**Angel Falls** *see* Ángel, Salto
95 J22 **Ängelholm** Skåne, S Sweden 56°14′N 12°52′E
61 A17 **Angélica** Santa Fe, C Argentina 31°33′S 61°33′W
25 W8 **Angelina River** ⚞ Texas, SW USA
55 Q9 **Ángel, Salto** *Eng.* Angel Falls. *waterfall* E Venezuela
95 M15 **Ängelsberg** Västmanland, C Sweden 59°57′N 16°01′E
35 P8 **Angels Camp** California, W USA 38°03′N 120°31′W
109 W7 **Anger** Steiermark, SE Austria 47°16′N 15°41′E
**Angerapp** *see* Ozersk
**Angerburg** *see* Węgorzewo
93 H15 **Ångermanälven** ⚞ N Sweden
100 P11 **Angermünde** Brandenburg, NE Germany 53°02′N 13°59′E
102 K7 **Angers** *anc.* Juliomagus. Maine-et-Loire, NW France 47°30′N 00°33′W
15 W7 **Angers** ⚞ Québec, SE Canada
93 J16 **Ängesön** *island* N Sweden
**Angistro** *see* Ágkistro
114 H13 **Angítis** ⚞ NE Greece
167 R13 **Ângk Tasaôm** *prev.* Angtassom. Takeo, S Cambodia
185 C25 **Anglem, Mount** ▲ Stewart Island, Southland, SW New Zealand 46°44′S 167°56′E
97 I18 **Anglesey** *cultural region* NW Wales, United Kingdom
97 I18 **Anglesey** *island* NW Wales, United Kingdom
102 I15 **Anglet** Pyrénées-Atlantiques, SW France 43°29′N 01°30′W
25 W12 **Angleton** Texas, SW USA 29°10′N 95°27′W
**Anglia** *see* England
14 H9 **Angliers** Québec, SE Canada 47°33′N 79°17′W
**Anglo-Egyptian Sudan** *see* Sudan
**Angmagssalik** *see* Ammassalik
167 Q7 **Ang Nam Ngum** ◎ C Laos
79 N16 **Ango** Orientale, N Dem. Rep. Congo 04°01′N 25°52′E
83 Q15 **Angoche** Nampula, E Mozambique 16°10′S 39°58′E
63 G14 **Angol** Araucanía, C Chile 37°47′S 72°45′W
31 Q11 **Angola** Indiana, N USA 41°37′N 85°00′W
82 A9 **Angola** *off.* Republic of Angola; *prev.* People's Republic of Angola, Portuguese West Africa. ◆ *republic* SW Africa
65 P15 **Angola Basin** *undersea feature* E Atlantic Ocean 15°00′S 03°00′E
**Angola, People's Republic of** *see* Angola
**Angola, Republic of** *see* Angola
39 X13 **Angoon** Admiralty Island, Alaska, USA 57°33′N 134°30′W
147 O14 **Angor** Surkhondaryo Viloyati, S Uzbekistan 37°30′N 67°06′E
**Angora** *see* Ankara
186 C6 **Angoram** East Sepik, NW Papua New Guinea 04°04′S 144°04′E
40 H8 **Angostura** Sinaloa, C Mexico 25°18′N 108°10′W
**Angostura** *see* Ciudad Bolívar
41 U17 **Angostura, Presa de la** ⊠ SE Mexico
28 J11 **Angostura Reservoir** ⊠ South Dakota, N USA
102 L11 **Angoulême** *anc.* Iculisma. Charente, W France 45°39′N 00°10′E
102 K11 **Angoumois** *cultural region* W France
64 O2 **Angra do Heroísmo** Terceira, Azores, Portugal, NE Atlantic Ocean 38°40′N 27°14′W
60 O10 **Angra dos Reis** Rio de Janeiro, SE Brazil 22°59′S 44°17′W
**Angra Pequena** *see* Lüderitz
147 Q10 **Angren** Toshkent Viloyati, E Uzbekistan 41°05′N 70°18′E
**Angtassom** *see* Ângk Tasaôm
167 O10 **Ang Thong** *var.* Angthong. Ang Thong, C Thailand 14°35′N 100°25′E
**Angthong** *see* Ang Thong
79 M16 **Angu** Orientale, N Dem. Rep. Congo 03°38′N 24°14′E
105 S5 **Angüés** Aragón, NE Spain 42°07′N 00°10′W
45 V9 **Anguilla** ◇ *UK Overseas Territory* E West Indies
45 V9 **Anguilla** *island* E West Indies
44 F4 **Anguilla Cays** *islets* SW The Bahamas
**Angul** *see* Anugul
161 N1 **Anguli Nur** ◎ E China
79 O18 **Angumu** Orientale, E Dem. Rep. Congo 0°10′S 27°42′E
14 G14 **Angus** Ontario, S Canada 44°19′N 79°52′W
96 J10 **Angus** *cultural region* E Scotland, United Kingdom
59 K19 **Anhangüera** Goiás, S Brazil 18°12′S 48°19′W
99 I21 **Anhée** Namur, S Belgium 50°18′N 04°52′E
95 I21 **Anholt** *island* C Denmark
160 M11 **Anhua** *var.* Dongping. Hunan, S China 28°25′N 111°10′E
161 P8 **Anhui** *var.* Anhui Sheng, Anhwei, Wan. ◆ *province* E China
**AnhuiSheng/Anhwei Wan** *see* Anhui
39 O11 **Aniak** Alaska, USA 61°34′N 159°31′W
39 O12 **Aniak River** ⚞ Alaska, USA
**An Iarmhí** *see* Westmeath
189 R8 **Anibare** E Nauru 0°31′S 166°56′E
189 R8 **Anibare Bay** *bay* E Nauru, W Pacific Ocean
**Anicium** *see* le Puy
115 K22 **Ánidro** *island* Kykládes, Greece, Aegean Sea
77 R15 **Anié** C Togo 07°48′N 01°12′E
77 Q15 **Anié** ⚞ C Togo
102 J16 **Anie, Pic d'** ▲ SW France 42°56′N 00°44′W
127 Y7 **Anikhovka** Orenburgskaya Oblast', W Russia 51°27′N 60°17′E
14 G9 **Anima Nipissing Lake** ◎ Ontario, S Canada
37 O16 **Animas** New Mexico, SW USA 31°55′N 108°49′W
37 P16 **Animas Peak** ▲ New Mexico, SW USA 31°34′N 108°46′W
37 P16 **Animas Valley** *valley* New Mexico, SW USA
116 F13 **Anina** *Ger.* Steierdorf, *Hung.* Stájerlakanina; *prev.* Ştaierdorf-Anina, Steierdorf-Anina, Steyerlak-Anina. Caraş-Severin, SW Romania 45°05′N 21°51′E
29 U14 **Anita** Iowa, C USA 41°27′N 94°45′W
123 U14 **Aniva, Mys** *headland* Ostrov Sakhalin, SE Russia 46°02′N 143°25′E
187 S15 **Aniwa** *island* S Vanuatu
93 M19 **Anjalankoski** Kymenlaakso, S Finland 60°39′N 26°54′E
**'Anjar** *see* Aanjar
**Anjiangying** *see* Luanping
14 B8 **Anjigami Lake** ◎ Ontario, S Canada
149 N13 **Anjira** Baluchistan, SW Pakistan 28°19′N 66°19′E
164 K14 **Anjō** *var.* Anzyô. Aichi, Honshū, SW Japan 34°56′N 137°05′E
102 J8 **Anjou** *cultural region* NW France
**Anjouan** *see* Nzwani
172 J4 **Anjozorobe** Antananarivo, C Madagascar 18°22′S 47°52′E
163 W13 **Anju** W North Korea 39°36′N 125°44′E
98 M5 **Anjum** *Fris.* Eanjum. Fryslân, N Netherlands 53°22′N 06°09′E
172 G6 **Ankaboa, Tanjona** *prev./Fr.* Cap Saint-Vincent. *headland* W Madagascar 21°57′S 43°16′E
160 L7 **Ankang** *prev.* Xing'an. Shaanxi, C China 32°45′N 109°00′E
136 I12 **Ankara** *prev.* Angora; *anc.* Ancyra. ● (Turkey) Ankara, C Turkey 39°55′N 32°50′E
136 H12 **Ankara** ◆ *province* C Turkey
95 N19 **Ankarsrum** Kalmar, S Sweden 57°40′N 16°19′E
172 H6 **Ankazoabo** Toliara, SW Madagascar 22°18′S 44°30′E
172 I4 **Ankazobe** Antananarivo, C Madagascar 18°20′S 47°07′E
29 V14 **Ankeny** Iowa, C USA 41°43′N 93°37′W
167 V11 **An Khê** Gia Lai, C Vietnam 13°57′N 108°39′E
100 O9 **Anklam** Mecklenburg-Vorpommern, NE Germany 53°51′N 13°42′E
80 K13 **Änkober** Āmara, N Ethiopia 09°36′N 39°44′E
77 O17 **Ankobra** ⚞ S Ghana
79 N22 **Ankoro** Katanga, SE Dem. Rep. Congo 06°45′S 26°58′E
99 L24 **Anlier, Forêt d'** *forest* SE Belgium
160 I13 **Anlong** *var.* Xin'an. Guizhou, S China 25°05′N 105°29′E
**An Longfort** *see* Longford
167 R11 **Ânlong Vêng** Siem Reap, NW Cambodia 14°16′N 104°08′E
**An Lorgain** *see* Lurgan
161 N8 **Anlu** Hubei, C China 31°15′N 113°41′E
**An Mhí** *see* Meath
**An Mhuir Cheilteach** *see* Celtic Sea
**An Muileann gCearr** *see* Mullingar
93 F16 **Ånn** Jämtland, C Sweden 63°19′N 12°34′E
126 M8 **Anna** Voronezhskaya Oblast', W Russia 51°31′N 40°23′E
30 L17 **Anna** Illinois, N USA 37°27′N 89°15′W
25 U5 **Anna** Texas, SW USA 33°21′N 96°33′W
74 L5 **Annaba** *prev.* Bône. NE Algeria 36°55′N 07°47′E
**An Nabatīyah at Taḩtā** *see* Nabatîyé
101 N17 **Annaberg-Buchholz** Sachsen, E Germany 50°35′N 13°01′E
109 T9 **Annabichl** ✕ (Klagenfurt) Kärnten, S Austria 46°39′N 14°21′E
140 M5 **An Nafūd** *desert* NW Saudi Arabia
139 P6 **'Annah** *var.* 'Ānah. Al Anbār, NW Iraq 34°50′N 42°00′E
139 P6 **An Nāḩiyah** Al Anbār, W Iraq 34°24′N 41°33′E
139 T10 **An Najaf** *off.* Muḩāfa at an Najaf, *var.* Najaf. An Najaf, S Iraq 31°59′N 44°19′E
139 T10 **An Najaf** *off.* Muḩāfaẓ at an Najaf. ◆ *governorate* S Iraq
21 V5 **Anna, Lake** ◎ Virginia, NE USA
97 F16 **Annalee** ⚞ N Ireland
167 S9 **Annamite Mountains** *var.* annamses cordillera, *Fr.* Chaîne Annamitique, *Lao.* Phou Louang. ▲ C Laos
**Annamitique, Chaîne** *see* Annamite Mountains
**Annamses Cordillera** *see* Annamite Mountains
97 J14 **Annan** S Scotland, United Kingdom 55°N 03°20′W
29 U8 **Annandale** Minnesota, N USA 45°15′N 94°07′W
21 W4 **Annandale** Virginia, NE USA 38°48′N 77°10′W
189 Q7 **Anna Point** *headland* N Nauru 0°30′S 166°56′E
21 X3 **Annapolis** *state capital* Maryland, NE USA 38°59′N 76°30′W
188 A10 **Anna, Pulo** *island* S Palau
153 O10 **Annapurna** ▲ C Nepal 28°30′N 83°50′E
**An Nāqūrah** *see* En Nâqoûra
31 R10 **Ann Arbor** Michigan, N USA 42°17′N 83°45′W
**An Nás** *see* Naas
139 W12 **An Nāşirīyah** *var.* Nasiriya. Dhī Qār, SE Iraq 31°04′N 46°17′E
139 W11 **An Naşr** Dhī Qār, E Iraq 31°34′N 46°08′E
**Annau** *see* Änew
121 O13 **An Nawfalīyah** *var.* Al Nūwfalīyah. N Libya 30°46′N 17°48′E
19 P10 **Ann, Cape** *headland* Massachusetts, NE USA 42°39′N 70°35′W
180 I10 **Annean, Lake** ◎ Western Australia
**Anneciacum** *see* Annecy
103 T11 **Annecy** *anc.* Anneciacum. Haute-Savoie, E France 45°53′N 06°09′E
103 T11 **Annecy, Lac d'** ◎ E France
103 T10 **Annemasse** Haute-Savoie, E France 46°10′N 06°13′E
39 Z14 **Annette Island** *island* Alexander Archipelago, Alaska, USA
**An Nhon** *see* Binh Đinh
**An Nīl al Abyaḑ** *see* White Nile
**An Nīl al Azraq** *see* Blue Nile
23 Q3 **Anniston** Alabama, S USA 33°39′N 85°49′W
79 A19 **Annobón** *island* W Equatorial Guinea
103 R12 **Annonay** Ardèche, E France 45°15′N 04°40′E
44 K12 **Annotto Bay** C Jamaica 18°16′N 76°47′W
141 R5 **An Nu'ayrīyah** *var.* Nariya. Ash Sharqīyah, NE Saudi Arabia 27°30′N 48°30′E
182 M9 **Annuello** Victoria, SE Australia 34°54′S 142°50′E
139 Q10 **An Nukhayb** Al Anbār, S Iraq 32°02′N 42°15′E
139 U9 **An Nu'mānīyah** Wāsiţ, E Iraq 32°34′N 45°23′E
**Áno Arkhánai** *see* Archánes
115 J25 **Anógeia** *var.* Anogia, Anóyia. Kriti, Greece, E Mediterranean Sea 35°17′N 24°53′E
**Anogia** *see* Anógeia
29 V8 **Anoka** Minnesota, N USA 45°15′N 93°26′W
**An Ómaigh** *see* Omagh
172 I1 **Anorontany, Tanjona** *Fr.* Cap Saint-Sébastien. *headland* N Madagascar
172 J5 **Anosibe An'Ala** Toamasina, E Madagascar 19°24′S 48°11′E
**Anóyia** *see* Anógeia
**An Pointe** *see* Warrenpoint
161 P9 **Anqing** Anhui, E China 30°32′N 116°59′E
161 Q5 **Anqiu** Shandong, E China 36°25′N 119°10′E
**An Ráth** *see* Ráth Luirc
**An Ribhéar** *see* Kenmare River
**An Ros** *see* Rush
99 K19 **Ans** Liège, E Belgium 50°39′N 05°32′E
**Anşāb** *see* Nişāb
171 W12 **Ansas** Papua, E Indonesia 01°44′S 135°52′E
101 J20 **Ansbach** Bayern, SE Germany 49°18′N 10°36′E
**An Sciobairín** *see* Skibbereen
**An Scoil** *see* Skull
**An Seancheann** *see* Old Head of Kinsale
45 Y5 **Anse-Bertrand** Grande Terre, N Guadeloupe 16°28′N 61°31′W
172 H17 **Anse Boileau** Mahé, NE Seychelles 04°43′S 55°29′E
45 S11 **Anse La Raye** NW Saint Lucia 13°57′N 61°01′W
54 D9 **Anserma** Caldas, W Colombia 05°15′N 75°47′W
109 T4 **Ansfelden** Oberösterreich, N Austria 48°12′N 14°17′E
163 U12 **Anshan** Liaoning, NE China 41°06′N 122°55′E
160 J12 **Anshun** Guizhou, S China 26°15′N 105°58′E
61 F17 **Ansina** Tacuarembó, C Uruguay 31°58′S 55°28′W
29 O15 **Ansley** Nebraska, C USA 41°16′N 99°22′W
25 P6 **Anson** Texas, SW USA 32°45′N 99°55′W
77 Q10 **Ansongo** Gao, E Mali 15°39′N 00°33′E
**An Srath Bán** *see* Strabane
21 R5 **Ansted** West Virginia, NE USA 38°08′N 81°06′W
171 Y13 **Ansudu** Papua, E Indonesia 02°09′S 139°19′E
57 G15 **Anta** Cusco, S Peru 13°30′S 72°08′W
57 G16 **Antabamba** Apurímac, C Peru 14°23′S 72°54′W
**Antafalva** *see* Kovačica
136 L17 **Antakya** *anc.* Antioch, Antiochia. Hatay, S Turkey 36°12′N 36°10′E
172 K3 **Antalaha** Antsiranana, NE Madagascar 14°53′S 50°16′E
136 F17 **Antalya** *prev.* Adalia; *anc.* Attaleia, *Bibl.* Attalia. Antalya, SW Turkey 36°53′N 30°42′E
136 F17 **Antalya** ◆ *province* SW Turkey
136 F16 **Antalya** ✕ Antalya, SW Turkey 36°53′N 30°45′E
121 U10 **Antalya Basin** *undersea feature* E Mediterranean Sea
**Antalya, Gulf of** *see* Antalya Körfezi
136 F16 **Antalya Körfezi** *var.* Gulf of Adalia, *Eng.* Gulf of Antalya. *gulf* SW Turkey
172 J5 **Antanambao Manampotsy** Toamasina, E Madagascar 19°30′S 48°36′E
172 I5 **Antananarivo** *prev.* Tananarive. ● (Madagascar) Antananarivo, C Madagascar 18°52′S 47°30′E
172 I4 **Antananarivo** ◆ *province* C Madagascar
172 J5 **Antananarivo** ✕ Antananarivo, C Madagascar 18°52′S 47°30′E
**An tAonach** *see* Nenagh
194-195 **Antarctica** *continent*
194 I5 **Antarctic Peninsula** *peninsula* Antarctica
61 J15 **Antas, Rio das** ⚞ S Brazil
189 U16 **Ant Atoll** *atoll* Caroline Islands, E Micronesia
**An Teampall Mór** *see* Templemore
**Antep** *see* Gaziantep
104 M15 **Antequera** *anc.* Anticaria, Antiquaria. Andalucía, S Spain 37°01′N 04°34′W
**Antequera** *see* Oaxaca


◆ Country ● Country Capital ◇ Dependent Territory ○ Dependent Territory Capital ◆ Administrative Regions ✕ International Airport ▲ Mountain ▲ Mountain Range ⚠ Volcano ⚞ River ◎ Lake ⊠ Reservoir

ANTERO RESERVOIR – ARÉVALO


37 S5 **Antero Reservoir** ⊠ Colorado, C USA
26 M7 **Anthony** Kansas, C USA 37°10′N 98°02′W
37 R16 **Anthony** New Mexico, SW USA 32°00′N 106°36′W
182 D5 **Anthony, Lake** *salt lake* South Australia
74 E8 **Anti-Atlas** ▲▲ SW Morocco
103 U15 **Antibes** *anc.* Antipolis. Alpes-Maritimes, SE France 43°35′N 07°07′E
103 U15 **Antibes, Cap d'** *headland* SE France 43°33′N 07°08′E
**Anticaria** *see* Antequera
13 Q11 **Anticosti, Île d'** *Eng.* Anticosti Island. *island* Québec, E Canada
**Anticosti Island** *see* Anticosti, Île d'
102 K3 **Antifer, Cap d'** *headland* N France 49°43′N 00°10′E
30 L6 **Antigo** Wisconsin, N USA 45°10′N 89°10′W
13 Q15 **Antigonish** Nova Scotia, SE Canada 45°39′N 62°00′W
64 P11 **Antigua** Fuerteventura, Islas Canarias, NE Atlantic Ocean
45 X10 **Antigua** *island* S Antigua and Barbuda, Leeward Islands
**Antigua** *see* Antigua Guatemala
45 W9 **Antigua and Barbuda** ◆ *commonwealth republic* E West Indies
42 C6 **Antigua Guatemala** *var.* Antigua. Sacatepéquez, SW Guatemala 14°33′N 90°42′W
41 P11 **Antiguo Morelos** *var.* Antiguo-Morelos. Tamaulipas, C Mexico 22°35′N 99°08′W
115 F19 **Antíkyras, Kólpos** *gulf* C Greece
115 G24 **Antikýthira** *var.* Andikíthira. *island* S Greece
138 I7 **Anti-Lebanon** *var.* Jebel esh Sharqi, *Ar.* Al Jabal ash Sharqī, *Fr.* Anti-Liban. ▲▲ Lebanon/ Syria
**Anti-Liban** *see* Anti-Lebanon
115 M22 **Antimácheia** Kos, Dodekánisa, Greece 47°19′N 07°54′E
115 I22 **Antímilos** *island* Kykládes, Greece, Aegean Sea
36 L6 **Antimony** Utah, W USA 38°07′N 112°00′W
**An tInbhear Mór** *see* Arklow
30 M10 **Antioch** Illinois, N USA 42°28′N 88°06′W
**Antioch** *see* Antakya
102 I10 **Antioche, Pertuis d'** *inlet* W France
**Antiochia** *see* Antakya
54 D8 **Antioquia** Antioquia, C Colombia 06°36′N 75°53′W
54 E8 **Antioquia** *off.* Departamento de Antioquia. ◈ *province* C Colombia
**Antioquia, Departamento de** *see* Antioquia
115 J21 **Antíparos** *var.* Andipáros. *island* Kykládes, Greece, Aegean Sea
115 B17 **Antípaxoi** *var.* Andipaxi. *island* Iónia Nísiá, Greece, C Mediterranean Sea
122 J8 **Antipayuta** Yamalo-Nenetskiy Avtonomnyy Okrug, N Russia 69°08′N 76°43′E
192 L12 **Antipodes Islands** *island group* S New Zealand
**Antipolis** *see* Antibes
115 J18 **Antípsara** *var.* Andípsara. *island* E Greece
**Antiquaria** *see* Antequera
15 N10 **Antique, Lac** ◎ Québec, SE Canada
115 E18 **Antírrio** *var.* Andírrion. Dytikí Elláda, C Greece 38°20′N 21°46′E
115 K16 **Ántissa** *var.* Ándissa. Lésvos, E Greece 39°15′N 26°00′E
**An tIúr** *see* Newry
**Antivari** *see* Bar
56 C6 **Antizana** ▲ N Ecuador 0°29′S 78°08′W
27 Q13 **Antlers** Oklahoma, C USA 34°15′N 95°38′W
93 J14 **Antnäs** Norrbotten, N Sweden 65°32′N 21°53′E
**Antō** *see* Andong
62 G5 **Antofagasta** Antofagasta, N Chile 23°40′S 70°23′W
62 G6 **Antofagasta** *off.* Región de Antofagasta. ◈ *region* N Chile
**Antofagasta, Región de** *see* Antofagasta
62 I7 **Antofalla, Salar de** *salt lake* NW Argentina
99 D20 **Antoing** Hainaut, SW Belgium 50°34′N 03°26′E
43 S16 **Antón** Coclé, C Panama 08°23′N 80°15′W
24 M5 **Anton** Texas, SW USA 33°48′N 102°09′W
37 T11 **Anton Chico** New Mexico, SW USA 35°12′N 105°09′W
60 K12 **Antonina** Paraná, S Brazil 25°28′S 48°43′W
188 C16 **Antonio B. Won Pat International** ✈ (Agana) C Guam 13°28′N 144°48′E
103 O5 **Antony** Hauts-de-Seine, N France 48°45′N 02°17′E
**Antratsit** *see* Antratsyt
117 Y8 **Antratsyt** *Rus.* Antratsit. Luhans'ka Oblast', E Ukraine 48°07′N 39°05′E
97 G15 **Antrim** *Ir.* Aontroim. NE Northern Ireland, United Kingdom 54°43′N 06°13′W
97 G14 **Antrim** *Ir.* Aontroim. *cultural region* NE Northern Ireland, United Kingdom
97 G14 **Antrim Mountains** ▲▲ NE Northern Ireland, United Kingdom
172 H5 **Antsalova** Mahajanga, W Madagascar 18°40′S 44°37′E
**Antserana** *see* Antsirañana
**An tSionainn** *see* Shannon
172 J2 **Antsirañana** *var.* Antserana; *prev.* Antsirane, Diégo-Suarez. Antsirañana, N Madagascar 12°19′S 49°17′E
172 J2 **Antsirañana** ◈ *province* N Madagascar
**Antsirane** *see* Antsirañana
**An tSiúir** *see* Suir
118 I7 **Antsla** *Ger.* Anzen. Võrumaa, SE Estonia 57°52′N 26°33′E
**An tSláine** *see* Slaney
172 J3 **Antsohihy** Mahajanga, NW Madagascar 14°50′S 47°58′E
63 G14 **Antuco, Volcán** ⛰ C Chile 37°29′S 71°25′W
169 W10 **Antu, Gunung** ▲ Borneo, N Indonesia 0°57′N 118°51′E
**An Tullach** *see* Tullow
**An-tung** *see* Dandong
**Antunnacum** *see* Andernach
**Antwerp** *see* Antwerpen
99 G16 **Antwerpen** *Eng.* Antwerp, *Fr.* Anvers. Antwerpen, N Belgium 51°13′N 04°25′E
99 H16 **Antwerpen** *Eng.* Antwerp. ◈ *province* N Belgium
**An Uaimh** *see* Navan
154 N12 **Anugul** *var.* Angul. Odisha, E India 20°51′N 84°59′E
152 F9 **Anūpgarh** Rājasthān, NW India 29°10′N 73°14′E
154 K10 **Anūppur** Madhya Pradesh, C India 23°05′N 81°45′E
155 K24 **Anuradhapura** North Central Province, C Sri Lanka 08°20′N 80°25′E
**Anvers** *see* Antwerpen
194 G4 **Anvers Island** *island* Antarctica
39 N11 **Anvik** Alaska, USA 62°39′N 160°12′W
39 N10 **Anvik River** ≈ Alaska, USA
38 F17 **Anvil Peak** ▲ Semisopochnoi Island, Alaska, USA 51°59′N 179°36′E
**An Vinh, Nhom** *see* Amphitrite Group
159 P7 **Anxi** *var.* Yuanquan. Gansu, N China 40°32′N 95°50′E
182 F8 **Anxious Bay** *bay* South Australia
161 O5 **Anyang** Henan, C China 36°11′N 114°18′E
159 S11 **A'nyêmaqên Shan** ▲▲ C China
118 H12 **Anykščiai** Utena, E Lithuania 55°30′N 25°34′E
161 P13 **Anyuan** *var.* Xinshan. Jiangxi, S China 25°10′N 115°25′E
123 T7 **Anyuysk** Chukotskiy Avtonomnyy Okrug, NE Russia 68°22′N 161°33′E
123 T7 **Anyuyskiy Khrebet** ▲▲ NE Russia
54 D8 **Anzá** Antioquia, C Colombia 06°18′N 75°54′W
**Anzen** *see* Antsla
107 I16 **Anzio** Lazio, C Italy 41°28′N 12°38′E
55 O6 **Anzoátegui** *off.* Estado Anzoátegui. ◈ *state* NE Venezuela
**Anzoátegui, Estado** *see* Anzoátegui
147 P12 **Anzob** W Tajikistan 39°24′N 68°55′E
**Anzyō** *see* Anjō
**Aoba** *see* Ambae
165 X13 **Aoga-shima** *island* Izu-shotō, SE Japan
**Aohan Qi** *see* Xinhui
105 R3 **Aoiz** *Bas.* Agoitz, *var.* Agoiz. Navarra, N Spain 42°47′N 01°23′W
157 O11 **Ao Krung Thep** *var.* Krung Thep Mahanakhon, *Eng.* Bangkok. ● (Thailand) Bangkok, C Thailand 13°44′N 100°30′E
186 M9 **Aola** *var.* Tenaghau. Guadalcanal, C Solomon Islands 09°32′S 160°28′E
**Aolepān Aorōkin Maḷajel** *see* Marshall Islands
156 M15 **Ao Luk Nua** Krabi, SW Thailand 08°21′N 98°43′E
**Aomen Tebie Xingzhengqu** *see* Macao
172 N8 **Aomori** Aomori, Honshū, C Japan 40°50′N 140°43′E
172 N8 **Aomori** *off.* Aomori-ken. ◈ *prefecture* Honshū, C Japan
**Aomori-ken** *see* Aomori
**Aontroim** *see* Antrim
115 C15 **Aóos** *var.* Vijosa, Vijosë, *Alb.* Lumi i Vjosës. ≈ Albania/ Greece *see also* Vjosës, Lumi i
**Aóos** *see* Vjosës, Lumi i
191 Q7 **Aorai, Mont** ▲ Tahiti, W French Polynesia 17°36′S 149°29′W
135 E19 **Aoraki / Mount Cook** *var.* Mount Cook. Canterbury, South Island, New Zealand 43°47′S 170°06′E
135 E19 **Aoraki / Mount Cook** *prev.* Aorangi, *var.* Mount Cook. ▲ South Island, New Zealand 43°38′S 170°05′E
157 R13 **Aôral, Phnum** *prev.* Phnom Aural. ▲ W Cambodia 12°01′N 104°10′E
**Aorangi** *see* Aoraki / Mount Cook
185 L15 **Aorangi Mountains** ▲▲ North Island, New Zealand
134 H13 **Aorere** ≈ South Island, New Zealand
106 A7 **Aosta** *anc.* Augusta Praetoria. Valle d'Aosta, NW Italy 45°43′N 07°20′E
77 O11 **Aougoundou, Lac** ◎ S Mali
76 K9 **Aoukâr** *var.* Aouker. *plateau* C Mauritania
78 J13 **Aouk, Bahr** ≈ Central African Republic/Chad
**Aouker** *see* Aoukâr
74 B11 **Aousard** SE Western Sahara 22°42′N 14°22′W
164 H12 **Aoya** Tottori, Honshū, SW Japan 35°31′N 134°01′E
**Aoyang** *see* Shanggao
78 H5 **Aozou** Tibesti, N Chad 22°01′N 17°11′E
26 M11 **Apache** Oklahoma, C USA 34°57′N 98°21′W
36 L14 **Apache Junction** Arizona, SW USA 33°25′N 111°33′W
24 J9 **Apache Mountains** ▲▲ Texas, SW USA
36 M16 **Apache Peak** ▲ Arizona, SW USA 31°50′N 110°25′W
116 H10 **Apahida** Cluj, NW Romania 46°49′N 23°45′E
23 T9 **Apalachee Bay** *bay* Florida, SE USA
23 T3 **Apalachee River** ≈ Georgia, SE USA
23 S10 **Apalachicola** Florida, SE USA 29°43′N 84°58′W
23 S10 **Apalachicola Bay** *bay* Florida, SE USA
23 R9 **Apalachicola River** ≈ Florida, SE USA
**Apam** *see* Apan
**Apamama** *see* Abemama
41 P14 **Apan** *var.* Apam. Hidalgo, C Mexico 19°48′N 98°25′W
42 J8 **Apanás, Lago de** ◎ NW Nicaragua
54 H14 **Apaporis, Río** ≈ Brazil/ Colombia
185 C23 **Aparima** ≈ South Island, New Zealand
171 O1 **Aparri** Luzon, N Philippines 18°16′N 121°42′E
112 J9 **Apatin** Vojvodina, NW Serbia 45°40′N 19°01′E
124 J4 **Apatity** Murmanskaya Oblast', NW Russia 67°34′N 33°26′E
55 X9 **Apatou** NW French Guiana 05°10′N 54°22′W
40 M14 **Apatzingán** *var.* Apatzingán de la Constitución. Michoacán, SW Mexico 19°05′N 102°20′W
**Apatzingán de la Constitución** *see* Apatzingán
171 X12 **Apauwar** Papua, E Indonesia 01°36′S 138°10′E
**Apaxtla** *see* Apaxtla de Castrejón
41 O15 **Apaxtla de Castrejón** *var.* Apaxtla. Guerrero, S Mexico 18°06′N 99°55′W
118 J7 **Ape** NE Latvia 57°32′N 26°42′E
98 L11 **Apeldoorn** Gelderland, E Netherlands 52°13′N 05°57′E
**Apennines** *see* Appennino
**Apenrade** *see* Aabenraa
57 L17 **Apere, Río** ≈ C Bolivia
55 W11 **Apetina** Sipaliwini, SE Suriname 03°30′N 55°03′W
21 U9 **Apex** North Carolina, SE USA 35°43′N 78°51′W
79 M16 **Api** Orientale, N Dem. Rep. Congo 03°40′N 25°26′E
152 M9 **Api** ▲ NW Nepal 30°07′N 80°57′E
192 H16 **Apia** ● (Samoa) Upolu, SE Samoa 13°50′S 171°47′W
**Apia** *see* Abaiang
60 K11 **Apiaí** São Paulo, S Brazil 24°29′S 48°51′W
170 M16 **Api, Gunung** ▲ Pulau Sangeang, S Indonesia 08°09′S 119°03′E
187 N9 **Apio** Maramasike Island, N Solomon Islands 09°36′S 161°25′E
41 O15 **Apipilulco** Guerrero, S Mexico 18°11′N 99°40′W
41 P14 **Apizaco** Tlaxcala, S Mexico 19°26′N 98°09′W
**Ap'khazet'i** *see* Abkhazia
104 I4 **A Pobla de Trives** *Cast.* Puebla de Trives. Galicia, NW Spain 42°21′N 07°16′W
55 U9 **Apoera** Sipaliwini, NW Suriname 05°12′N 57°13′W
115 O23 **Apolakkiá** Ródos, Dodekánisa, Greece, Aegean Sea 36°02′N 27°48′E
101 L16 **Apolda** Thüringen, C Germany 51°02′N 11°31′E
192 H16 **Apolima Strait** *strait* C Pacific Ocean
182 M13 **Apollo Bay** Victoria, SE Australia 38°40′S 143°44′E
**Apollonia** *see* Sozopol
57 J16 **Apolo** La Paz, W Bolivia 14°48′S 68°31′W
57 J16 **Apolobamba, Cordillera** ▲▲ Bolivia/Peru
171 Q8 **Apo, Mount** ⛰ Mindanao, S Philippines 06°54′N 125°16′E
23 W11 **Apopka** Florida, SE USA 28°40′N 81°30′W
23 W11 **Apopka, Lake** ◎ Florida, SE USA
59 J19 **Aporé, Rio** ≈ SW Brazil
30 K2 **Apostle Islands** *island group* Wisconsin, N USA
61 F14 **Apóstoles** Misiones, NE Argentina 27°54′S 55°45′W
**Apostolos Andreas, Cape** *see* Zafer Burnu
**Apostólou Andréa, Akrotírio** *see* Zafer Burnu
117 S9 **Apostolove** *Rus.* Apostolovo. Dnipropetrovs'ka Oblast', E Ukraine 47°40′N 33°45′E
**Apostolovo** *see* Apostolove
17 S10 **Appalachian Mountains** ▲▲ E USA
95 K14 **Äppelbo** Dalarna, C Sweden 60°30′N 14°00′E
98 N7 **Appelscha** *Fris.* Appelskea. Fryslân, N Netherlands 52°57′N 06°19′E
**Appelskea** *see* Appelscha
106 G11 **Appennino** *Eng.* Apennines. ▲▲ Italy/San Marino
107 L17 **Appennino Campano** ▲▲ C Italy
108 I7 **Appenzell** Inner-Rhoden, NW Switzerland 47°20′N 09°25′E
55 V12 **Appikalo** Sipaliwini, S Suriname 02°07′N 56°16′W
98 O5 **Appingedam** Groningen, NE Netherlands 53°18′N 06°52′E
25 X8 **Appleby** Texas, SW USA 31°43′N 94°36′W
97 L15 **Appleby-in-Westmorland** Cumbria, NW England, United Kingdom 54°35′N 03°26′W
30 K10 **Apple River** ≈ Illinois, N USA
30 I5 **Apple River** ≈ Wisconsin, N USA
25 W9 **Apple Springs** Texas, SW USA 31°13′N 94°57′W
29 S8 **Appleton** Minnesota, N USA 45°12′N 96°01′W
30 M7 **Appleton** Wisconsin, N USA 44°17′N 88°24′W
27 S5 **Appleton City** Missouri, C USA 38°11′N 94°01′W
35 U14 **Apple Valley** California, W USA 34°30′N 117°11′W
29 V9 **Apple Valley** Minnesota, N USA 44°43′N 93°13′W
21 U6 **Appomattox** Virginia, NE USA 37°21′N 78°51′W
188 B16 **Apra Harbor** *harbor* W Guam
188 B16 **Apra Heights** W Guam
106 F6 **Aprica, Passo dell'** *pass* N Italy
107 M15 **Apricena** *anc.* Hadria Picena. Puglia, SE Italy 41°47′N 15°27′E
126 L14 **Apsheronsk** Krasnodarskiy Kray, SW Russia 44°27′N 39°45′E
**Apsheronskiy Poluostrov** *see* Abşeron Yarımadası
103 S15 **Apt** *anc.* Apta Julia. Vaucluse, SE France 43°54′N 05°24′E
**Apta Julia** *see* Apt
38 H12 **'Apua Point** *var.* Apua Point. *headland* Hawai'i, USA, C Pacific Ocean 19°15′N 155°13′W
60 I10 **Apucarana** Paraná, S Brazil 23°34′S 51°28′W
**Apulia** *see* Puglia
54 K8 **Apure** *off.* Estado Apure. ◈ *state* C Venezuela
**Apure, Estado** *see* Apure
54 J7 **Apure, Río** ≈ W Venezuela
57 F16 **Apurímac** *off.* Región de Apurímac. ◈ *region* C Peru
**Apurímac, Región de** *see* Apurímac
57 F15 **Apurímac, Río** ≈ S Peru
116 G10 **Apuseni, Munţii** ▲▲ W Romania
**Aqaba/'Aqaba** *see* Al 'Aqabah
138 F15 **Aqaba, Gulf of** *var.* Gulf of Elat, *Ar.* Khalīj al 'Aqabah; *anc.* Sinus Aelaniticus. *gulf* NE Red Sea
139 R7 **'Aqabah** Al Anbār, C Iraq 33°33′N 42°55′E
**'Aqabah, Khalīj al** *see* Aqaba, Gulf of
**'Aqabah, Muḩāfa at al** *see* Al 'Aqabah
149 O2 **Āqchah** *var.* Āqcheh. Jowzjān, N Afghanistan 37°N 66°07′E
**Āqcheh** *see* Āqchah
**Aqkengse** *see* Akkense
**Aqköl** *see* Akkol'
**Aqmola** *see* Nur-Sultan
**Aqmola Oblysy** *see* Akmola
158 L10 **Aqqikkol Hu** ◎ NW China
**Aqqū** *see* Akku
**Aqqystaū** *see* Akkystau
**'Aqrah** *see* Ākrē
**Aqsay** *see* Aksay
**Aqshataū** *see* Akshatau
**Aqsū** *see* Aksu
**Aqsūat** *see* Aksuat
**Aqtas** *see* Aktas
**Aqtaū** *see* Aktau
**Aqtöbe** *see* Aktobe
**Aqtöbe Oblysy** *see* Aktyubinsk
**Aqtoghay** *see* Aktogay
**Aquae Augustae** *see* Dax
**Aquae Calidae** *see* Bath
**Aquae Flaviae** *see* Chaves
**Aquae Grani** *see* Aachen
**Aquae Panoniae** *see* Baden
**Aquae Sextiae** *see* Aix-en-Provence
**Aquae Solis** *see* Bath
**Aquae Tarbelicae** *see* Dax
36 J11 **Aquarius Mountains** ▲▲ Arizona, SW USA
62 O5 **Aquidabán, Río** ≈ E Paraguay
59 H20 **Aquidauana** Mato Grosso do Sul, S Brazil 20°27′S 55°45′W
40 L15 **Aquila** Michoacán, S Mexico 18°36′N 103°32′W
**Aquila/Aquila degli Abruzzi** *see* L'Aquila
25 T8 **Aquilla** Texas, SW USA 31°51′N 97°13′W
44 L9 **Aquin** S Haiti 18°16′N 73°24′W
**Aquisgranum** *see* Aachen
102 J13 **Aquitaine** *cultural region* SW France
**Aqzhar** *see* Akzhar
153 F13 **Āra** *prev.* Arrah. Bihār, N India 25°34′N 84°40′E
105 S4 **Ara** ≈ NE Spain
23 P2 **Arab** Alabama, S USA 34°19′N 86°30′W
105 O3 **Araba** *var.* Álava. ◈ *province* País Vasco, N Spain
138 C12 **'Arabah, Wādī al** *Heb.* Ha'Arava. *dry watercourse* Israel/Jordan
117 U12 **Arabats'ka Strilka, Kosa** *spit* S Ukraine
117 U12 **Arabats'ka Zatoka** *gulf* S Ukraine
**'Arab, Baḩr** *see* Arab, Bahr el
80 C12 **Arab, Bahr el** *var.* Baḩr al 'Arab. ≈ S Sudan
56 E7 **Arabela, Río** ≈ N Peru
173 O4 **Arabian Basin** *undersea feature* N Arabian Sea 11°30′N 65°00′E
**Arabian Desert** *see* Aş Şaḩrā' ash Sharqīyah
141 N9 **Arabian Peninsula** *peninsula* SW Asia
85 P15 **Arabian Plate** *tectonic feature* Africa/Asia/Europe
141 W14 **Arabian Sea** *sea* NW Indian Ocean
**Arabicus, Sinus** *see* Red Sea
**'Arabī, Khalīj al** *see* Persian Gulf
**Arabistan** *see* Khūzestān
**'Arabīyah as Su'ūdīyah, Al Mamlakah al** *see* Saudi Arabia
138 I9 **'Arab, Jabal al** ▲ S Syria
**Arab Republic of Egypt** *see* Egypt
139 Y12 **Arab, Shatt al** *Ar.* Shaţţ al 'Arab, *Per.* Arvand Rūd. ≈ Iran/Iraq
136 I11 **Araç** Kastamonu, N Turkey 41°14′N 33°20′E
59 P16 **Aracaju** *state capital* Sergipe, E Brazil 10°45′S 37°07′W
54 F5 **Aracataca** Magdalena, N Colombia 10°38′N 74°09′W
58 P13 **Aracati** Ceará, E Brazil 04°32′S 37°45′W
60 J8 **Araçatuba** São Paulo, S Brazil 21°12′S 50°24′W
136 I11 **Araç Çayı** ≈ N Turkey
104 J13 **Aracena** Andalucía, S Spain 37°54′N 06°33′W
115 F20 **Árachnaío** ▲▲ S Greece
115 D16 **Árachthos** *var.* Arta, *prev.* Árakhthos; *anc.* Arachthus. ≈ W Greece
**Arachthus** *see* Árachthos
59 N19 **Araçuaí** Minas Gerais, SE Brazil 16°52′S 42°03′W
138 F11 **'Arad** Southern, S Israel 31°16′N 35°09′E
116 F11 **Arad** Arad, W Romania 46°12′N 21°20′E
116 F11 **Arad** ◈ *county* W Romania
78 J9 **Arada** Wadi Fira, NE Chad 15°00′N 20°38′E
143 P18 **'Arādah** Abū Z̧aby, S United Arab Emirates 22°57′N 53°24′E
**Aradhippou** *see* Aradíppou
121 Q3 **Aradíppou** *var.* Aradhippou. SE Cyprus 34°57′N 33°37′E
174 K5 **Arafura Sea** *Ind.* Laut Arafuru. *sea* W Pacific Ocean
174 L6 **Arafura Shelf** *undersea feature* C Arafura Sea
**Arafuru, Laut** *see* Arafura Sea
59 J18 **Aragarças** Goiás, C Brazil 15°55′S 52°12′W
**Aragats, Gora** *see* Aragats Lerr
137 T12 **Aragats Lerr** *Rus.* Gora Aragats. ▲ W Armenia 40°31′N 44°06′E
32 E14 **Arago, Cape** *headland* Oregon, NW USA 43°17′N 124°25′W
105 R6 **Aragón** *autonomous community* E Spain
105 Q4 **Aragón** ≈ NE Spain
107 I24 **Aragona** Sicilia, Italy, C Mediterranean Sea 37°25′N 13°37′E
105 Q7 **Aragoncillo** ▲ C Spain 40°59′N 02°01′W
54 L5 **Aragua** *off.* Estado Aragua. ◈ *state* N Venezuela
55 N6 **Aragua de Barcelona** Anzoátegui, NE Venezuela 09°30′N 64°51′W
55 O5 **Aragua de Maturín** Monagas, NE Venezuela 09°58′N 63°30′W
**Aragua, Estado** *see* Aragua
59 K15 **Araguaia, Río** *var.* Araguaya. ≈ C Brazil
59 K19 **Araguari** Minas Gerais, SE Brazil 18°38′S 48°13′W
58 J11 **Araguari, Rio** ≈ SW Brazil
**Araguaya** *see* Araguaia, Río
104 K14 **Arahal** Andalucía, S Spain 37°15′N 05°33′W
165 N11 **Arai** Niigata, Honshū, C Japan 37°02′N 138°17′E
**Árainn** *see* Inishmore
**Árainn Mhór** *see* Aran Island
**Ara Jovis** *see* Aranjuez
74 J11 **Arak** C Algeria 25°17′N 03°45′E
171 Y15 **Arak** Papua, E Indonesia 07°14′S 139°40′E
142 M7 **Arāk** *prev.* Sultānābād. Markazī, W Iran 34°07′N 49°39′E
188 D10 **Arakabesan** *island* Palau Islands, N Palau
55 S7 **Arakaka** NW Guyana 07°37′N 59°58′W
**Arakan State** *see* Rakhine State
**Arakan Yoma** *see* Rakhine Yoma
165 O10 **Arakawa** Niigata, Honshū, C Japan 38°06′N 139°25′E
**Árakhthos** *see* Árachthos
**Araks/Arak's** *see* Aras
158 H7 **Aral** Xinjiang Uygur Zizhiqu, NW China 40°40′N 81°19′E
**Aral** *see* Aralsk, Kazakhstan
**Aral** *see* Vose', Tajikistan
**Aral-Bukhorskiy Kanal** *see* Amu-Buxoro Kanali
137 T12 **Aralık** Iğdır, E Turkey 39°54′N 44°28′E
146 H5 **Aral Sea** *Kaz.* Aral Tengizi, *Rus.* Aral'skoye More, *Uzb.* Orol Dengizi. *inland sea* Kazakhstan/Uzbekistan
144 L13 **Aral'sk** *Kaz.* Aral. Kzylorda, SW Kazakhstan 46°48′N 61°40′E
**Aral'skoye More/Aral Tengizi** *see* Aral Sea
41 O10 **Aramberri** Nuevo León, NE Mexico 24°05′N 99°52′W
186 B8 **Aramia** ≈ SW Papua New Guinea
105 N5 **Aranda de Duero** Castilla y León, N Spain 41°40′N 03°41′W
112 M12 **Arandelovac** *prev.* Arandjelovac. Serbia, C Serbia 44°18′N 20°32′E
**Arandjelovac** *see* Arandelovac
97 J19 **Aran Fawddwy** ▲ NW Wales, United Kingdom 52°48′N 03°42′W
97 C14 **Aran Island** *Ir.* Árainn Mhór. *island* NW Ireland
97 A18 **Aran Islands** *island group* W Ireland
105 N9 **Aranjuez** *anc.* Ara Jovis. Madrid, C Spain 40°02′N 03°37′W
83 E20 **Aranos** Hardap, SE Namibia 24°10′S 19°08′E
25 U14 **Aransas Bay** *inlet* Texas, SW USA
25 T14 **Aransas Pass** Texas, SW USA 27°54′N 97°09′W
191 O3 **Aranuka** *prev.* Nanouki. *atoll* Tungaru, W Kiribati
143 N6 **Ārān-va-Bidgol** *var.* Golārā. Eşfahān, C Iran 34°03′N 51°30′E
167 Q11 **Aranyaprathet** Prachin Buri, S Thailand 13°42′N 102°32′E
**Aranyosasztal** *see* Zlatý Stôl
**Aranyosgyéres** *see* Câmpia Turzii
**Aranyosmarót** *see* Zlaté Moravce
164 C14 **Arao** Kumamoto, Kyūshū, SW Japan 32°58′N 130°26′E
77 O8 **Araouane** Tombouctou, N Mali 18°53′N 03°31′W
26 L10 **Arapaho** Oklahoma, C USA 35°34′N 98°57′W
29 N16 **Arapahoe** Nebraska, C USA 40°18′N 99°54′W
57 I16 **Arapa, Laguna** ◎ SE Peru
185 K14 **Arapawa Island** *island* C New Zealand
61 E17 **Arapey Grande, Río** ≈ N Uruguay
59 P16 **Arapiraca** Alagoas, E Brazil 09°45′S 36°40′W
140 M3 **'Ar'ar** Al Ḩudūd ash Shamālīyah, NW Saudi Arabia 31°N 41°E
54 G15 **Araracuara** Caquetá, S Colombia 0°36′S 72°24′W
61 K15 **Araranguá** Santa Catarina, S Brazil 28°56′S 49°30′W
60 L8 **Araraquara** São Paulo, S Brazil 21°46′S 48°08′W
59 O13 **Araras** Ceará, E Brazil 04°08′S 40°30′W
58 I14 **Araras** Pará, N Brazil 06°04′S 54°34′W
60 L9 **Araras** São Paulo, S Brazil 22°21′S 47°21′W
60 H11 **Araras, Serra das** ▲▲ S Brazil
137 U12 **Ararat** S Armenia 39°49′N 44°45′E
182 M12 **Ararat** Victoria, SE Australia 37°20′S 143°00′E
**Ārārat-e Bozorg, Kūh-e** *see* Büyük Ağrı Dağı
**Ararat, Mount** *see* Büyük Ağrı Dağı
140 M3 **'Ar'ar, Wādī** *dry watercourse* Iraq/Saudi Arabia
129 N7 **Aras** *Arm.* Arak's, *Az.* Araz Nehri, *Per.* Rūd-e Aras, *Rus.* Araks; *prev.* Araxes. ≈ SW Asia
**Aras de Alpuente** *see* Aras de los Olmos
105 R9 **Aras de los Olmos** *prev.* Aras de Alpuente. Comunitat Valenciana, E Spain 39°55′N 01°09′W
137 S13 **Aras Güneyi Dağları** ▲▲ NE Turkey
**Aras, Rūd-e** *see* Aras
191 U9 **Aratika** *atoll* Îles Tuamotu, C French Polynesia
**Aratürük** *see* Yiwu
54 I8 **Arauca** Arauca, NE Colombia 07°03′N 70°47′W
54 I8 **Arauca** *off.* Intendencia de Arauca. ◈ *province* NE Colombia
**Arauca, Intendencia de** *see* Arauca
63 G15 **Araucanía** *off.* Región de la Araucanía. ◈ *region* C Chile
**Araucanía, Región de la** *see* Araucanía
54 L7 **Arauca, Río** ≈ Colombia/ Venezuela
63 F14 **Arauco** Bío Bío, C Chile 37°15′S 73°22′W
63 F14 **Arauco, Golfo de** *gulf* S Chile
54 H8 **Arauquita** Arauca, C Colombia 06°57′N 71°19′W
**Arausio** *see* Orange
152 F13 **Arāvali Range** ▲▲ N India
185 C20 **Arawata** ≈ South Island, New Zealand
186 F7 **Arawe Islands** *island group* E Papua New Guinea
59 L20 **Araxá** Minas Gerais, SE Brazil 19°37′S 46°50′W
**Araxes** *see* Aras
55 O5 **Araya** Sucre, N Venezuela 10°34′N 64°15′W
**Araz Nehri** *see* Aras
105 R4 **Arba** ≈ N Spain
81 I15 **Ārba Minch'** Southern Nationalities, S Ethiopia 06°02′N 37°34′E
**'Arbat** *see* Erbet
**Arbat** *see* Erbet
107 D19 **Arbatax** Sardegna, Italy, C Mediterranean Sea 39°57′N 09°42′E
**Arbe** *see* Rab
**Arbela** *see* Arbīl
139 S3 **Arbīl** *Kurd.* Hewlêr, *var.* Erbil, Irbil, Hewlêr; *anc.* Arbela. Arbīl, N Iraq 36°12′N 44°01′E
139 S3 **Arbīl** *off.* Muḩāfaz at Arbīl, *var.* Irbil, *off. Kurd.* Parêzga-î Hewlêr, *Kurd.* Hewlêr. ◈ *governorate* N Iraq
**Arbīl, Muḩāfaz at** *see* Arbīl
95 M16 **Arboga** Västmanland, C Sweden 59°24′N 15°50′E
95 M16 **Arbogaån** ≈ C Sweden
103 S9 **Arbois** Jura, E France 46°54′N 05°45′E
54 D6 **Arboletes** Antioquia, NW Colombia 08°52′N 76°25′W
11 X15 **Arborg** Manitoba, S Canada 50°52′N 97°20′W
94 N12 **Arbrå** Gävleborg, C Sweden 61°27′N 16°21′E
96 K10 **Arbroath** *anc.* Aberbrothock. E Scotland, United Kingdom 56°34′N 02°35′W
35 N6 **Arbuckle** California, W USA 39°00′N 122°05′W
27 N12 **Arbuckle Mountains** ▲▲ Oklahoma, C USA
162 I5 **Arbulag** *var.* Mandal. Hövsgöl, N Mongolia 49°55′N 99°21′E
**Arbuzinka** *see* Arbuzynka
117 Q8 **Arbuzynka** *Rus.* Arbuzinka. Mykolayivs'ka Oblast', S Ukraine 47°54′N 31°19′E
103 U12 **Arc** ≈ E France
102 J13 **Arcachon** Gironde, SW France 44°40′N 01°11′W
102 J13 **Arcachon, Bassin d'** *inlet* SW France
18 E10 **Arcade** New York, NE USA 42°32′N 78°19′W
23 W14 **Arcadia** Florida, SE USA 27°13′N 81°51′W
22 H5 **Arcadia** Louisiana, S USA 32°33′N 92°55′W
30 J7 **Arcadia** Wisconsin, N USA 44°15′N 91°30′W
**Arcae Remorum** *see* Châlons-en-Champagne
44 L9 **Arcahaie** C Haiti 18°46′N 72°32′W
34 K3 **Arcata** California, W USA 40°51′N 124°06′W
35 U6 **Arc Dome** ▲ Nevada, W USA 38°52′N 117°20′W
107 J16 **Arce** Lazio, C Italy 41°35′N 13°34′E
41 O15 **Arcelia** Guerrero, S Mexico 18°20′N 100°16′W
99 M15 **Arcen** Limburg, SE Netherlands 51°28′N 06°10′E
115 J25 **Archánes** *var.* Áno Arkhánai, Epáno Archánes; *prev.* Epáno Arkhánai. Kríti, Greece, E Mediterranean Sea 35°12′N 25°10′E
**Archangel** *see* Arkhangel'sk
**Archangel Bay** *see* Chëshskaya Guba
115 O23 **Archángelos** *var.* Arhangelos, Arkhángelos. Ródos, Dodekánisa, Greece, Aegean Sea 36°13′N 28°07′E
114 F7 **Archar** ≈ NW Bulgaria
31 R11 **Archbold** Ohio, N USA 41°31′N 84°18′W
105 R12 **Archena** Murcia, SE Spain 38°07′N 01°17′W
25 R5 **Archer City** Texas, SW USA 33°36′N 98°37′W
104 M14 **Archidona** Andalucía, S Spain 37°06′N 04°23′W
65 B25 **Arch Islands** *island group* SW Falkland Islands
106 G13 **Arcidosso** Toscana, C Italy 42°52′N 11°30′E
103 Q5 **Arcis-sur-Aube** Aube, N France 48°32′N 04°09′E
182 F3 **Arckaringa Creek** *seasonal river* South Australia
106 G7 **Arco** Trentino-Alto Adige, N Italy 45°53′N 10°52′E
33 Q14 **Arco** Idaho, NW USA 43°38′N 113°18′W
30 M14 **Arcola** Illinois, N USA 39°39′N 88°19′W
105 P6 **Arcos de Jalón** Castilla y León, N Spain 41°12′N 02°13′W
104 K15 **Arcos de la Frontera** Andalucía, S Spain 36°45′N 05°49′W
104 G5 **Arcos de Valdevez** Viana do Castelo, N Portugal 41°51′N 08°25′W
59 P15 **Arcoverde** Pernambuco, E Brazil 08°23′S 37°W
102 H5 **Arcovest, Pointe de l'** *headland* NW France 48°49′N 02°58′W
**Arctic Mid Oceanic Ridge** *see* Gakkel Ridge
197 R8 **Arctic Ocean** *ocean*
8 G7 **Arctic Red River** ≈ Northwest Territories/ Yukon, NW Canada
**Arctic Red River** *see* Tsiigehtchic
39 S6 **Arctic Village** Alaska, USA 68°07′N 145°32′W
194 H1 **Arctowski** *research station (Poland)* South Shetland Islands, Antarctica 61°57′S 58°23′W
114 I12 **Arda** *var.* Ardhas, *Gk.* Ardas. ≈ Bulgaria/Greece *see also* Ardas
142 L2 **Ardabīl** *var.* Ardebil. Ardabīl, NW Iran 38°15′N 48°18′E
142 L2 **Ardabīl** *off.* Ostān-e Ardabīl. ◈ *province* NW Iran
**Ardabīl, Ostān-e** *see* Ardabīl
137 R11 **Ardahan** Ardahan, NE Turkey 41°08′N 42°41′E
137 S11 **Ardahan** ◈ *province* Ardahan, Turkey
143 P8 **Ardakān** Yazd, C Iran 32°20′N 53°59′E
94 E12 **Årdalstangen** Sogn Og Fjordane, S Norway 61°14′N 07°45′E
137 R11 **Ardanuç** Artvin, NE Turkey 41°07′N 42°04′E
114 L12 **Ardas** *var.* Ardhas, *Bul.* Arda. ≈ Bulgaria/Greece *see also* Arda
138 I13 **Arḑ aş Şawwān** *var.* Ardh es Suwwān. *plain* S Jordan
127 P5 **Ardatov** Respublika Mordoviya, W Russia 54°49′N 46°13′E
14 G12 **Ardbeg** Ontario, S Canada 45°38′N 80°05′W
**Ardeal** *see* Transylvania
**Ardebil** *see* Ardabīl
103 Q13 **Ardèche** ◈ *department* E France
103 Q13 **Ardèche** ≈ C France
97 F17 **Ardee** *Ir.* Baile Átha Fhirdhia. Louth, NE Ireland 53°52′N 06°33′W
103 Q3 **Ardennes** ◈ *department* NE France
99 J23 **Ardennes** *physical region* Belgium/France
137 Q11 **Ardeşen** Rize, NE Turkey 41°14′N 41°00′E
143 O7 **Ardestān** *var.* Ardistan. Eşfahān, C Iran 33°29′N 52°17′E
108 J9 **Ardez** Graubünden, SE Switzerland 46°47′N 10°09′E
**Ardhas** *see* Arda/Ardas
**Ardh es Suwwān** *see* Arḑ aş Şawwān
**Ardila** *see* Ardila, Ribeira de
104 I12 **Ardila, Ribeira de** *Sp.* Ardilla. ≈ Portugal/Spain *see also* Ardilla
**Ardila, Ribeira de** *see* Ardilla
11 T17 **Ardill** Saskatchewan, S Canada 49°56′N 105°49′W
104 I12 **Ardilla** *Port.* Ribeira de Ardila. ≈ Portugal/Spain *see also* Ardila, Ribeira de
40 M11 **Ardilla, Cerro la** ▲ C Mexico 22°15′N 102°33′W
114 J12 **Ardino** Kardzhali, S Bulgaria 41°38′N 25°22′E
**Ardistan** *see* Ardestān
183 P9 **Ardlethan** New South Wales, SE Australia 34°24′S 146°52′E
**Ard Mhacha** *see* Armagh
23 P1 **Ardmore** Alabama, S USA 34°59′N 86°51′W
27 N13 **Ardmore** Oklahoma, C USA 34°11′N 97°08′W
20 J10 **Ardmore** Tennessee, S USA 35°00′N 86°48′W
96 G10 **Ardnamurchan, Point of** *headland* N Scotland, United Kingdom 56°42′N 06°15′W
**Ardni** *see* Arnøya
99 C17 **Ardooie** West-Vlaanderen, W Belgium 50°59′N 03°10′E
182 I9 **Ardrossan** South Australia 34°27′S 137°54′E
116 H9 **Ardusat** *Hung.* Erdőszáda. Maramureş, N Romania 47°36′N 23°25′E
93 F16 **Åre** Jämtland, C Sweden 63°25′N 13°04′E
79 P16 **Arebi** Orientale, NE Dem. Rep. Congo 02°47′N 29°35′E
45 T5 **Arecibo** C Puerto Rico 18°29′N 66°44′W
171 V13 **Aredo** Papua Barat, E Indonesia 02°27′S 133°59′E
59 P14 **Areia Branca** Rio Grande do Norte, E Brazil 04°53′S 37°03′W
119 O14 **Arekhawsk** *Rus.* Orekhovsk. Vitsyebskaya Voblasts', N Belarus 54°42′N 30°30′E
**Arel** *see* Arlon
**Arelas/Arelate** *see* Arles
**Arenal, Embalse de** *see* Arenal Laguna
42 L12 **Arenal Laguna** *var.* Embalse de Arenal. ◎ NW Costa Rica
42 L13 **Arenal, Volcán** ⛰ NW Costa Rica 10°21′N 84°42′W
34 K6 **Arena, Point** *headland* California, W USA 38°57′N 123°44′W
59 H17 **Arenápolis** Mato Grosso, W Brazil 14°25′S 56°52′W
40 G10 **Arena, Punta** *headland* NW Mexico 23°28′N 109°24′W
104 L8 **Arenas de San Pedro** Castilla y León, N Spain 40°12′N 05°05′W
63 I24 **Arenas, Punta de** *headland* S Argentina 53°10′S 68°15′W
61 B20 **Arenaza** Buenos Aires, E Argentina 34°55′S 61°45′W
95 F17 **Arendal** Aust-Agder, S Norway 58°27′N 08°45′E
99 J16 **Arendonk** Antwerpen, N Belgium 51°18′N 05°06′E
43 T15 **Arenosa** West Panamá, C Panama 09°02′N 79°57′W
**Arensburg** *see* Kuressaare
105 W5 **Arenys de Mar** Cataluña, NE Spain 41°35′N 02°33′E
106 C9 **Arenzano** Liguria, NW Italy 44°25′N 08°43′E
115 F22 **Areópoli** *prev.* Areópolis. Pelopónnisos, S Greece 36°40′N 22°24′E
**Areópolis** *see* Areópoli
57 H18 **Arequipa** Arequipa, SE Peru 16°24′S 71°33′W
57 G17 **Arequipa** *off.* Región de Arequipa. ◈ *region* Arequipa SW Peru
**Arequipa, Región de** *see* Arequipa
61 B19 **Arequito** Santa Fe, C Argentina 33°09′S 61°28′W
104 M7 **Arévalo** Castilla y León, N Spain 41°04′N 04°44′W




◆ Country ● Country Capital ◇ Dependent Territory ○ Dependent Territory Capital ◈ Administrative Regions ✈ International Airport ▲ Mountain ▲▲ Mountain Range ⛰ Volcano ≈ River ◎ Lake ⊠ Reservoir

Arezzo – Asikaga


106 H12 **Arezzo** *anc.* Arretium. Toscana, C Italy *43°28′N 11°50′E*
105 Q4 **Arga** ≈ N Spain
**Argaeus** *see* Erciyes Dağı
115 G17 **Argalastí** Thessalía, C Greece *39°13′N 23°13′E*
105 O10 **Argamasilla de Alba** Castilla-La Mancha, C Spain *39°08′N 03°05′W*
158 L8 **Argan** Xinjiang Uygur Zizhiqu, NW China *40°09′N 88°16′E*
105 O8 **Arganda** Madrid, C Spain *40°19′N 03°26′W*
104 H8 **Arganil** Coimbra, N Portugal *40°13′N 08°03′W*
171 P6 **Argao** Cebu, C Philippines *09°52′N 123°33′E*
153 V15 **Argartala** Tripura, NE India
123 N9 **Arga-Sala** ≈ Respublika Sakha (Yakutiya), NE Russia
103 P17 **Argelès-sur-Mer** Pyrénées-Orientales, S France *42°33′N 03°01′E*
103 T15 **Argens** ≈ SE France
106 H9 **Argenta** Emilia-Romagna, N Italy *44°37′N 11°49′E*
102 K5 **Argentan** Orne, N France *48°45′N 00°01′W*
103 N12 **Argentat** Corrèze, C France *45°06′N 01°57′E*
106 A9 **Argentera** Piemonte, NE Italy *44°25′N 06°57′E*
103 N5 **Argenteuil** Val-d'Oise, N France *48°57′N 02°13′E*
62 K13 **Argentina** *off.* Argentine Republic. ◆ *republic* S South America
**Argentina Basin** *see* Argentine Basin
**Argentine Abyssal Plain** *see* Argentine Plain
65 I19 **Argentine Basin** *var.* Argentina Basin. *undersea feature* SW Atlantic Ocean *45°00′S 45°00′W*
65 I20 **Argentine Plain** *var.* Argentine Abyssal Plain. *undersea feature* SW Atlantic Ocean *47°31′S 50°00′W*
**Argentine Republic** *see* Argentina
**Argentine Rise** *see* Falkland Plateau
63 H22 **Argentino, Lago** ◎ S Argentina
102 K8 **Argenton-Château** Deux-Sèvres, W France *46°59′N 00°22′W*
102 M9 **Argenton-sur-Creuse** Indre, C France *46°34′N 01°32′E*
**Argentoratum** *see* Strasbourg
116 I12 **Argeș** ◈ *county* S Romania
116 K14 **Argeș** ≈ S Romania
**Arghandāb, Daryā-ye** *see* Arghandāb Rōd
149 O8 **Arghandāb Rōd** *prev.* Daryā-ye Arghandāb. ≈ SE Afghanistan
**Arghestān** *see* Dê Arghistān Rōd
**Arghistān** *see* Dê Arghistān Rōd
**Argirocastro** *see* Gjirokastër
80 E7 **Argo** Northern, N Sudan *19°31′N 30°25′E*
173 P7 **Argo Fracture Zone** *tectonic feature* C Indian Ocean
115 F20 **Argolikós Kólpos** *gulf* S Greece
103 R4 **Argonne** *physical region* NE France
115 F20 **Árgos** Pelopónnisos, S Greece *37°38′N 22°43′E*
**Argōsh** *see* Argush
115 D14 **Árgos Orestikó** Dytikí Makedonía, N Greece *40°27′N 21°15′E*
115 B19 **Argostóli** *var.* Argostólion. Kefallonía, Iónia Nísiá, Greece, C Mediterranean Sea *38°13′N 20°29′E*
**Argostólion** *see* Argostóli
**Argovie** *see* Aargau
35 O14 **Arguello, Point** *headland* California, W USA *34°34′N 120°39′W*
127 P16 **Argun** Chechenskaya Respublika, SW Russia *43°16′N 45°53′E*
157 T2 **Argun** *Chin.* Ergun He, *Rus.* Argun'. ≈ China/Russia
77 T12 **Argungu** Kebbi, NW Nigeria *12°45′N 04°24′E*
139 S1 **Argush** *Ar.* Argūsh, *var.* Argōsh. Dahūk, N Iraq *37°07′N 44°13′E*
**Argūsh** *see* Argush
**Arguut** *see* Guchin-Us
181 N3 **Argyle, Lake** *salt lake* Western Australia
96 G12 **Argyll** *cultural region* W Scotland, United Kingdom
**Argyrokastron** *see* Gjirokastër
162 I7 **Arhangay** ◈ *province* C Mongolia
**Arhangelos** *see* Archángelos
**Århus** *see* Aarhus
139 T1 **Arî** *Ar.* Ārī. Arbīl, E Iraq *37°07′N 44°34′E*
**Ārī** *see* Arî
**Aria** *see* Herāt
83 F22 **Ariamsvlei** //Karas, SE Namibia *28°08′S 19°50′E*
107 L17 **Ariano Irpino** Campania, S Italy *41°08′N 15°00′E*
54 F11 **Ariari, Río** ≈ C Colombia
151 K19 **Ari Atoll** *var.* Alifu Atoll. *atoll* C Maldives
77 P11 **Aribinda** N Burkina Faso *14°12′N 00°50′W*
62 G2 **Arica** *hist.* San Marcos de Arica. Arica y Parinacota, N Chile *18°31′S 70°18′W*
54 H16 **Arica** Amazonas, S Colombia *02°09′S 71°48′W*
62 G2 **Arica** ✈ Arica y Parinacota, N Chile *18°30′S 70°20′W*
62 H2 **Arica y Parinacota** ◈ *region* N Chile
114 E13 **Aridaía** *var.* Aridea, Aridhaía. Dytikí Makedonía, N Greece *40°59′N 22°04′E*
**Aridea** *see* Aridaía
172 I15 **Aride, Île** *island* Inner Islands, NE Seychelles
**Aridhaía** *see* Aridaía
103 N17 **Ariège** ◈ *department* S France
102 M16 **Ariège** *var.* la Riege. ≈ Andorra/France
116 H11 **Arieș** ≈ W Romania
149 U10 **Arifwala** Punjab, E Pakistan *30°15′N 73°08′E*
**Ariguaní** *see* El Difícil
138 G11 **Arīhā** Al Karak, W Jordan *31°25′N 35°47′E*
138 I3 **Arīḩā** *var.* Arīhā. Idlib, W Syria *35°50′N 36°36′E*
**Arīhā** *see* Arīḩā
**Arīḩā** *see* Jericho
37 W4 **Arikaree River** ≈ Colorado/Nebraska, C USA
112 L13 **Arilje** Serbia, W Serbia *43°45′N 20°06′E*
45 U14 **Arima** Trinidad, Trinidad and Tobago *10°38′N 61°17′W*
**Arime** *see* Al 'Arīmah
**Ariminum** *see* Rimini
59 H16 **Arinos, Rio** ≈ W Brazil
40 M14 **Ario de Rosales** *var.* Ario de Rosáles. Michoacán, SW Mexico *19°12′N 101°42′W*
**Ario de Rosáles** *see* Ario de Rosales
118 F12 **Ariogala** Kaunas, C Lithuania *55°16′N 23°30′E*
47 T7 **Aripuanã** ≈ W Brazil
59 E15 **Ariquemes** Rondônia, W Brazil *09°55′S 63°06′W*
121 W13 **'Arīsh, Wādī al** ≈ NE Egypt
54 K6 **Arismendi** Barinas, C Venezuela *08°29′N 68°22′W*
10 J14 **Aristazabal Island** *island* SW Canada
60 F13 **Aristóbulo del Valle** Misiones, NE Argentina *27°09′S 54°54′W*
172 I5 **Arivonimamo** ✈ (Antananarivo) Antananarivo, C Madagascar *19°00′S 47°11′E*
**Arixang** *see* Wenquan
105 Q6 **Ariza** Aragón, NE Spain *41°19′N 02°03′W*
62 I6 **Arizaro, Salar de** *salt lake* NW Argentina
105 O2 **Arizgoiti** *var.* Basauri. País Vasco, N Spain *43°13′N 02°54′W*
62 K13 **Arizona** San Luis, C Argentina *35°44′S 65°16′W*
36 J12 **Arizona** *off.* State of Arizona, *also known as* Copper State, Grand Canyon State. ◈ *state* SW USA
40 G4 **Arizpe** Sonora, NW Mexico *30°20′N 110°11′W*
95 J16 **Årjäng** Värmland, C Sweden *59°24′N 12°09′E*
143 P8 **Arjenān** Yazd, C Iran *32°19′N 53°48′E*
92 I13 **Arjeplog** *Lapp.* Árjepluovve. Norrbotten, N Sweden *66°04′N 18°E*
**Árjepluovve** *see* Arjeplog
54 E5 **Arjona** Bolívar, N Colombia *10°14′N 75°22′W*
105 N13 **Arjona** Andalucía, S Spain *37°56′N 04°04′W*
123 S10 **Arka** Khabarovskiy Kray, E Russia *60°04′N 142°17′E*
22 L2 **Arkabutla Lake** ⊠ Mississippi, S USA
127 O7 **Arkadak** Saratovskaya Oblast', W Russia *51°55′N 43°29′E*
27 T13 **Arkadelphia** Arkansas, C USA *34°07′N 93°06′W*
115 J25 **Arkalochóri** ; *prev.* Arkalokhórion. Kríti, Greece, E Mediterranean Sea *35°09′N 25°15′E*
**Arkalohori/Arkalokhórion** *see* Arkalochóri
145 O10 **Arkalyk** *Kaz.* Arqalyq. Kostanay, N Kazakhstan *50°17′N 66°51′E*
27 U10 **Arkansas** *off.* State of Arkansas, *also known as* The Land of Opportunity. ◈ *state* S USA
27 W14 **Arkansas City** Arkansas, C USA *33°36′N 91°12′W*
27 O7 **Arkansas City** Kansas, C USA *37°03′N 97°02′W*
16 K11 **Arkansas River** ≈ C USA
182 J5 **Arkaroola** South Australia *30°21′S 139°20′E*
**Arkhángelos** *see* Archángelos
124 L8 **Arkhangel'sk** *Eng.* Archangel. Arkhangel'skaya Oblast', NW Russia *64°32′N 40°40′E*
124 L9 **Arkhangel'skaya Oblast'** ◈ *province* NW Russia
127 O14 **Arkhangel'skoye** Stavropol'skiy Kray, SW Russia *44°37′N 44°03′E*
123 R14 **Arkhara** Amurskaya Oblast', S Russia *49°20′N 130°04′E*
97 G19 **Arklow** *Ir.* An tInbhear Mór. SE Ireland *52°48′N 06°09′W*
**Ark, Mountain of the** *see* Büyük Ağrı Dağı
115 M20 **Arkoí** *island* Dodekánisa, Greece, Aegean Sea
27 R11 **Arkoma** Oklahoma, C USA *35°19′N 94°27′W*
100 O7 **Arkona, Kap** *headland* NE Germany *54°40′N 13°24′E*
95 N17 **Arkösund** Östergötland, S Sweden *58°28′N 16°55′E*
122 J6 **Arkticheskogo Instituta, Ostrova** *island* N Russia
95 O15 **Arlanda** ✈ (Stockholm) Stockholm, C Sweden *59°40′N 17°58′E*
146 C11 **Arlandag** *Rus.* Gora Arlan. ▲ W Turkmenistan *39°39′N 54°28′E*
**Arlan, Gora** *see* Arlandag
105 O5 **Arlanza** ≈ N Spain
105 N5 **Arlanzón** ≈ N Spain
103 R15 **Arles** *var.* Arles-sur-Rhône; *anc.* Arelas, Arelate. Bouches-du-Rhône, SE France *43°41′N 04°38′E*
**Arles-sur-Rhône** *see* Arles
103 O17 **Arles-sur-Tech** Pyrénées-Orientales, S France *42°27′N 02°37′E*
29 U9 **Arlington** Minnesota, N USA *44°36′N 94°04′W*
29 R15 **Arlington** Nebraska, C USA *41°27′N 96°21′W*
32 J11 **Arlington** Oregon, NW USA *45°43′N 120°10′W*
29 R10 **Arlington** South Dakota, N USA *44°21′N 97°07′W*
20 E10 **Arlington** Tennessee, S USA *35°17′N 89°40′W*
25 T6 **Arlington** Texas, SW USA *32°44′N 97°05′W*
21 W4 **Arlington** Virginia, NE USA *38°54′N 77°09′W*
32 H7 **Arlington** Washington, NW USA *48°12′N 122°07′W*
30 M10 **Arlington Heights** Illinois, N USA *42°08′N 88°03′W*
77 U8 **Arlit** Agadez, C Niger *18°54′N 07°25′E*
99 L24 **Arlon** *Dut.* Aarlen, *Ger.* Arel, *Lat.* Orolaunum. Luxembourg, SE Belgium *49°41′N 05°49′E*
27 R7 **Arma** Kansas, C USA *37°32′N 94°42′W*
97 F16 **Armagh** *Ir.* Ard Mhacha. S Northern Ireland, United Kingdom *54°15′N 06°33′W*
97 F16 **Armagh** *cultural region* S Northern Ireland, United Kingdom
102 K15 **Armagnac** *cultural region* S France
103 Q7 **Armançon** ≈ C France
60 K10 **Armando Laydner, Represa** ⊠ S Brazil
115 M24 **Armathía** *island* SE Greece
137 T12 **Armavir** *prev.* Hoktemberyan, *Rus.* Oktemberyan. SW Armenia *40°09′N 43°58′E*
126 M14 **Armavir** Krasnodarskiy Kray, SW Russia *44°59′N 41°07′E*
54 E10 **Armenia** Quindío, W Colombia *04°32′N 75°40′W*
137 T12 **Armenia** *off.* Republic of Armenia, *Arm.* Hayastan, Hayastani Hanrapetut'yun, *prev.* Armenian Soviet Socialist Republic, *prev.* Armenian Soviet Socialist Republic. ◆ *republic* SW Asia
**Armenian Soviet Socialist Republic** *see* Armenia
**Armenian Soviet Socialist Republic** *see* Armenia
**Armenia, Republic of** *see* Armenia
**Armenierstadt** *see* Gherla
103 O1 **Armentières** Nord, N France *50°41′N 02°53′E*
40 K14 **Armería** Colima, SW Mexico *18°55′N 103°59′W*
183 T5 **Armidale** New South Wales, SE Australia *30°32′S 151°40′E*
29 P11 **Armour** South Dakota, N USA *43°19′N 98°21′W*
61 B18 **Armstrong** Santa Fe, C Argentina *32°46′S 61°39′W*
11 N16 **Armstrong** British Columbia, SW Canada *50°27′N 119°14′W*
12 D11 **Armstrong** Ontario, S Canada *50°20′N 89°02′W*
29 U11 **Armstrong** Iowa, C USA *43°24′N 94°28′W*
25 S16 **Armstrong** Texas, SW USA *26°55′N 97°47′W*
117 S11 **Armyans'k** *Rus.* Armyansk. Avtonomna Respublika Krym, S Ukraine *46°05′N 33°43′E*
115 H14 **Arnaía** *Cont.* Arnea. Kentrikí Makedonía, N Greece *40°30′N 23°36′E*
**Arnaouti, Cape/Arnaoútis** *see* Arnaoútis, Akrotírio
121 N2 **Arnaoútis, Akrotírio** *var.* Arnaoútis, Cape Arnaouti. *headland* W Cyprus *35°06′N 32°16′E*
12 L4 **Arnaud** ≈ Québec, E Canada
103 Q8 **Arnay-le-Duc** Côte d'Or, C France *47°08′N 04°27′E*
**Arnea** *see* Arnaía
105 Q4 **Arnedo** La Rioja, N Spain *42°14′N 02°05′W*
95 I14 **Årnes** Akershus, S Norway *60°07′N 11°28′E*
**Årnes** *see* Åi Åfjord
26 K9 **Arnett** Oklahoma, C USA *36°08′N 99°46′W*
98 L12 **Arnhem** Gelderland, SE Netherlands *51°59′N 05°54′E*
181 Q2 **Arnhem Land** *physical region* Northern Territory, N Australia
106 F11 **Arno** ≈ C Italy
**Arņo** *see* Arno Atoll
189 W7 **Arno Atoll** *var.* Arņo. *atoll* Ratak Chain, NE Marshall Islands
182 H8 **Arno Bay** South Australia *33°55′S 136°31′E*
35 Q8 **Arnold** California, W USA *38°15′N 120°19′W*
27 X5 **Arnold** Missouri, C USA *38°25′N 90°22′W*
29 N15 **Arnold** Nebraska, C USA *41°25′N 100°11′W*
109 R10 **Arnoldstein** *Slvn.* Pod Klošter. Kärnten, S Austria *46°34′N 13°43′E*
103 N9 **Arnon** ≈ C France
45 P14 **Arnos Vale** ✈ (Kingstown) Saint Vincent, SE Saint Vincent and the Grenadines *13°08′N 61°13′W*
92 I8 **Arnøya** *Lapp.* Árdni. *island* N Norway
14 L12 **Arnprior** Ontario, SE Canada *45°31′N 76°11′W*
101 G15 **Arnsberg** Nordrhein-Westfalen, W Germany *51°24′N 08°04′E*
101 K16 **Arnstadt** Thüringen, C Germany *50°50′N 10°57′E*
**Arnswalde** *see* Choszczno
54 K5 **Aroa** Yaracuy, N Venezuela *10°26′N 68°54′W*
83 E21 **Aroab** //Karas, SE Namibia *26°47′S 19°40′E*
**Ároania** *see* Chelmós
191 O6 **Aroa, Pointe** *headland* Moorea, W French Polynesia *17°27′S 149°45′W*
**Aroe Islands** *see* Aru, Kepulauan
101 H15 **Arolsen** Niedersachsen, C Germany *51°23′N 09°00′E*
106 C7 **Arona** Piemonte, NE Italy *45°45′N 08°33′E*
19 R3 **Aroostook River** ≈ Canada/USA
**Arop Island** *see* Long Island
38 M12 **Aropuk Lake** ◎ Alaska, USA
191 P4 **Arorae** *atoll* Tungaru, W Kiribati
190 G16 **Arorangi** Rarotonga, S Cook Islands *21°13′S 159°49′W*
108 I9 **Arosa** Graubünden, S Switzerland *46°48′N 09°42′E*
104 F4 **Arousa, Ría de** *estuary* E Atlantic Ocean
184 P8 **Arowhana** ▲ North Island, New Zealand *38°07′S 177°52′E*
137 V12 **Arp'a** *Az.* Arpaçay. ≈ Armenia/Azerbaijan
137 S11 **Arpaçay** Kars, NE Turkey *40°51′N 43°20′E*
**Arpaçay** *see* Arp'a
**Arqalyq** *see* Arkalyk
149 N14 **Arra** ≈ SW Pakistan
**Arrabona** *see* Győr
**Arrah** *see* Āra
**Ar Rahad** *see* Er Rahad
139 R9 **Ar Raḩḩālīyah** Al Anbār, C Iraq *32°53′N 43°21′E*
60 Q10 **Arraial do Cabo** Rio de Janeiro, SE Brazil *22°57′S 42°00′W*
104 H11 **Arraiolos** Évora, S Portugal *38°44′N 07°59′W*
139 R8 **Ar Ramādī** *var.* Ramadi, Rumadiya. Al Anbār, SW Iraq *33°27′N 43°19′E*
138 J6 **Ar Rāmī** Ḩimş, C Syria *34°32′N 37°54′E*
**Ar Rams** *see* Rams
138 H9 **Ar Ramthā** *var.* Ramtha. Irbid, N Jordan *32°34′N 36°00′E*
96 H13 **Arran, Isle of** *island* SW Scotland, United Kingdom
138 L3 **Ar Raqqah** *var.* Rakka, Raqqa; *anc.* Nicephorium. Ar Raqqah, N Syria *35°57′N 39°03′E*
138 L3 **Ar Raqqah** *off.* Muḩāfaẓat al Raqqah, *var.* Raqqah, *Fr.* Rakka. ◈ *governorate* N Syria
103 O2 **Arras** *anc.* Nemetocenna. Pas-de-Calais, N France *50°17′N 02°46′E*
105 P3 **Arrasate** *Cast.* Mondragón. País Vasco, N Spain *43°04′N 02°30′W*
138 G12 **Ar Rashādīyah** Aţ ţafīlah, W Jordan *30°42′N 35°38′E*
138 I5 **Ar Rastān** *var.* Rastâne. Ḩimş, W Syria *34°57′N 36°43′E*
139 X12 **Ar Raţāwī** Al Başrah, E Iraq *30°37′N 47°12′E*
102 L15 **Arrats** ≈ S France
141 N10 **Ar Rawḑah** Makkah al Mukarramah, S Saudi Arabia *21°19′N 42°48′E*
141 Q15 **Ar Rawḑah** S Yemen *14°26′N 47°14′E*
142 K11 **Ar Rawḑatayn** *var.* Raudhatain. N Kuwait *29°80′N 47°50′E*
143 N16 **Ar Rayyān** *var.* Al Rayyan. C Qatar *25°18′N 51°29′E*
102 L17 **Arreau** Hautes-Pyrénées, S France *42°55′N 00°21′E*
64 Q11 **Arrecife** *var.* Arrecife de Lanzarote, Puerto Arrecife. Lanzarote, Islas Canarias, NE Atlantic Ocean *28°57′N 13°33′W*
**Arrecife de Lanzarote** *see* Arrecife
43 P6 **Arrecife Edinburgh** *reef* NE Nicaragua
61 C19 **Arrecifes** Buenos Aires, E Argentina *34°06′S 60°09′W*
102 F6 **Arrée, Monts d'** ▲▲ NW France
**Ar Refā'ī** *see* Ar Rifā'ī
**Arretium** *see* Arezzo
**Arriaca** *see* Guadalajara
109 S9 **Arriach** Kärnten, S Austria *46°43′N 13°52′E*
41 T16 **Arriaga** Chiapas, SE Mexico *16°14′N 93°54′W*
41 N12 **Arriaga** San Luis Potosí, C Mexico *21°55′N 101°23′W*
139 W10 **Ar Rifā'ī** *var.* Ar Refā'ī. Dhī Qār, SE Iraq *31°47′N 46°07′E*
139 V12 **Ar Riḩāb** *salt flat* S Iraq
**Arriondas** *see* Les Arriondes
141 Q7 **Ar Riyāḑ** *Eng.* Riyadh. ● (Saudi Arabia) Ar Riyāḑ, C Saudi Arabia *24°50′N 46°50′E*
141 O8 **Ar Riyāḑ** *off.* Minţaqat ar Riyāḑ. ◈ *region* C Saudi Arabia
141 S15 **Ar Riyān** S Yemen *14°43′N 49°18′E*
**Arrö** *see* Ærø
61 H18 **Arroio Grande** Rio Grande do Sul, S Brazil *32°15′S 53°02′W*
102 K15 **Arros** ≈ S France
103 Q9 **Arroux** ≈ C France
25 R5 **Arrowhead, Lake** ⊠ Texas, SW USA
182 L5 **Arrowsmith, Mount** *hill* New South Wales, SE Australia
185 D21 **Arrowtown** Otago, South Island, New Zealand *44°57′S 168°51′E*
61 D17 **Arroyo Barú** Entre Ríos, E Argentina *31°52′S 58°26′W*
104 J10 **Arroyo de la Luz** Extremadura, W Spain *39°28′N 06°36′W*
63 J16 **Arroyo de la Ventana** Río Negro, SE Argentina *41°41′S 66°03′W*
35 P13 **Arroyo Grande** California, W USA *35°07′N 120°35′W*
**Ar Ru'ays** *see* Ar Ruways
141 R11 **Ar Rub' al Khālī** *Eng.* Empty Quarter, Great Sandy Desert. *desert* SW Asia
139 V13 **Ar Ruḑaymah** Al Muthanná, S Iraq *30°20′N 45°26′E*
61 A16 **Arrufó** Santa Fe, C Argentina *30°15′S 61°45′W*
138 I7 **Ar Ruḩaybah** *var.* Ruhaybeh, *Fr.* Rouhaïbé. Rīf Dimashq, W Syria *33°45′N 36°40′E*
139 V15 **Ar Rukhaymīyah** *well* S Iraq
139 U11 **Ar Rumaythah** *var.* Rumaitha. Al Muthanná, S Iraq *31°31′N 45°15′E*
141 X8 **Ar Rustāq** *var.* Rostak, Rustaq. N Oman *23°34′N 57°25′E*
139 N8 **Ar Ruţbah** *var.* Rutba. Al Anbār, SW Iraq *33°03′N 40°16′E*
140 M3 **Ar Rūthīyah** *spring/well* NW Saudi Arabia *31°18′N 41°23′E*
**ar-Ruwaida** *see* Ar Ruwayḑah
141 O8 **Ar Ruwayḑah** *var.* ar-Ruwaida. Jāzān, C Saudi Arabia *23°48′N 44°44′E*
143 N15 **Ar Ruways** *var.* Al Ruweis, Ar Ru'ays, Ruwais. N Qatar *26°08′N 51°13′E*
143 O17 **Ar Ruways** *var.* Ar Ru'ays. Abū Ẓaby, W United Arab Emirates *24°09′N 52°57′E*
**Års** *see* Aars
**Arsanias** *see* Murat Nehri
123 S15 **Arsen'yev** Primorskiy Kray, SE Russia *44°09′N 133°28′E*
155 G19 **Arsikere** Karnātaka, W India *13°20′N 76°13′E′N*
127 R3 **Arsk** Respublika Tatarstan, W Russia *56°07′N 49°54′E*
94 N10 **Årskogen** Gävleborg, C Sweden *62°07′N 17°19′E*
121 O3 **Ársos** C Cyprus *34°51′N 32°46′E*
94 N13 **Årsunda** Gävleborg, C Sweden *60°31′N 16°45′E*
115 C17 **Árta** *anc.* Ambracia. Ípeiros, W Greece *39°08′N 20°59′E*
105 Y9 **Artà** Mallorca, Spain, W Mediterranean Sea *39°42′N 03°20′E*
**Arta** *see* Árachthos
137 T12 **Artashat** S Armenia *39°57′N 44°34′E*
40 M15 **Arteaga** Michoacán, SW Mexico *18°22′N 102°18′W*
123 S15 **Artem** Primorskiy Kray, SE Russia *43°24′N 132°20′E*
44 C4 **Artemisa** Artemisa, W Cuba *22°49′N 82°47′W*
44 C4 **Artemisa** ◈ *province* W Cuba
**Artemivs'k** *see* Bakhmut
122 K13 **Artemovsk** Krasnoyarskiy Kray, S Russia *54°22′N 93°24′E*
105 U5 **Artesa de Segre** Cataluña, NE Spain *41°54′N 01°03′E*
37 U14 **Artesia** New Mexico, SW USA *32°50′N 104°24′W*
25 Q14 **Artesia Wells** Texas, SW USA *28°13′N 99°18′W*
108 G8 **Arth** Schwyz, C Switzerland *47°05′N 08°39′E*
14 F15 **Arthur** Ontario, S Canada *43°49′N 80°31′W*
30 M14 **Arthur** Illinois, N USA *39°42′N 88°28′W*
28 L14 **Arthur** Nebraska, C USA *41°35′N 101°42′W*
29 Q5 **Arthur** North Dakota, N USA *47°03′N 97°12′W*
185 B21 **Arthur** ≈ South Island, New Zealand
18 B13 **Arthur, Lake** ⊠ Pennsylvania, NE USA
183 N15 **Arthur River** ≈ Tasmania, SE Australia
185 G18 **Arthur's Pass** Canterbury, South Island, New Zealand *42°59′S 171°33′E*
185 G17 **Arthur's Pass** *pass* South Island, New Zealand
44 I3 **Arthur's Town** Cat Island, C The Bahamas *24°34′N 75°39′W*
44 M9 **Artibonite, Rivière de l'** ≈ C Haiti
61 E16 **Artigas** *prev.* San Eugenio, San Eugenio del Cuareim. Artigas, N Uruguay *30°25′S 56°28′W*
61 E16 **Artigas** ◈ *department* N Uruguay
194 H1 **Artigas** *research station (Uruguay)* Antarctica *61°57′S 58°23′W*
137 T11 **Art'ik** W Armenia *40°38′N 43°58′E*
187 O16 **Art, Île** *island* Îles Belep, W New Caledonia
103 O2 **Artois** *cultural region* N France
136 L12 **Artova** Tokat, N Turkey *40°04′N 36°17′E*
105 Y9 **Artrutx, Cap d'** *var.* Cabo Dartuch. *cape* Menorca, Spain, W Mediterranean Sea
**Artsiz** *see* Artsyz
117 N11 **Artsyz** *Rus.* Artsiz. Odes'ka Oblast', SW Ukraine *45°59′N 29°26′E*
158 E7 **Artux** Xinjiang Uygur Zizhiqu, NW China *39°40′N 76°10′E*
137 R11 **Artvin** Artvin, NE Turkey *41°12′N 41°48′E*
137 R11 **Artvın** ◈ *province* NE Turkey
146 G14 **Artyk** Ahal Welaýaty, C Turkmenistan *37°32′N 59°16′E*
79 Q16 **Aru** Orientale, NE Dem. Rep. Congo *02°53′N 30°50′E*
81 E17 **Arua** NW Uganda *03°02′N 30°56′E*
104 I4 **A Rúa de Valdeorras** *var.* La Rúa. Galicia, NW Spain *42°22′N 07°12′W*
**Aruângua** *see* Luangwa
45 O15 **Aruba** *var.* Oruba. ◇ *self-governing country of the Kingdom of the Netherlands* S West Indies
47 Q4 **Aruba** *island* Aruba, Lesser Antilles
**Aru Islands** *see* Aru, Kepulauan
171 W15 **Aru, Kepulauan** *Eng.* Aru Islands; *prev.* Aroe Islands. *island group* E Indonesia
153 W10 **Arunāchal Pradesh** *prev.* North East Frontier Agency, North East Frontier Agency of Assam. ◈ *state* NE India
**Arun Qi** *see* Naji
155 H23 **Aruppukkottai** Tamil Nādu, SE India *09°31′N 78°03′E*
81 I20 **Arusha** Arusha, N Tanzania *03°23′S 36°40′E*
81 I21 **Arusha** ◈ *region* E Tanzania
81 I20 **Arusha** ✈ Arusha, N Tanzania *03°26′S 37°07′E*
54 C9 **Arusí, Punta** *headland* NW Colombia *05°36′N 77°30′W*
155 J23 **Aruvi Aru** ≈ NW Sri Lanka
79 M17 **Aruwimi** *var.* Ituri (upper course). ≈ NE Dem. Rep. Congo
**Árva** *see* Orava
37 T4 **Arvada** Colorado, C USA *39°48′N 105°06′W*
**Arvand Rūd** *see* Arab, Shatt al
162 J8 **Arvayheer** Övörhangay, C Mongolia *46°13′N 102°47′E*
9 O10 **Arviat** *prev.* Eskimo Point. Nunavut, C Canada *61°10′N 94°15′W*
93 I14 **Arvidsjaur** Norrbotten, N Sweden *65°34′N 19°12′E*
95 J15 **Arvika** Värmland, C Sweden *59°41′N 12°38′E*
92 J8 **Årviksand** Troms, N Norway *70°10′N 20°30′E*
35 S13 **Arvin** California, W USA *35°12′N 118°52′W*
163 S8 **Arxan** Nei Mongol Zizhiqu, N China *47.11N 119.58′E*
145 P7 **Arykbalyk** *Kaz.* Aryqbalyq. Severnyy Kazakhstan, N Kazakhstan *53°00′N 68°11′E*
**Aryqbalyq** *see* Arykbalyk
145 P17 **'Arys'** *prev.* Arys'. Turkestan, S Kazakhstan *42°26′N 68°49′E*
**Arys'** *see* 'Arys'
**Arys** *see* Orzysz
**Arys Köli** *see* Arys, Ozero
145 O14 **Arys, Ozero** *Kaz.* Arys Köli. ◎ C Kazakhstan
107 D16 **Arzachena** Sardegna, Italy, C Mediterranean Sea *41°05′N 09°21′E*
127 O4 **Arzamas** Nizhegorodskaya Oblast', W Russia *55°25′N 43°51′E*
141 V13 **Arzāt** S Oman *17°00′N 54°18′E*
104 H3 **Arzúa** Galicia, NW Spain *42°55′N 08°10′W*
111 A16 **Aš** *Ger.* Asch. Karlovarský Kraj, W Czechia *50°18′N 12°12′E*
95 H15 **Ås** Akershus, S Norway *59°40′N 10°50′E*
**Åsa** *see* Asaa
95 H20 **Asaa** *var.* Åsa. Nordjylland, N Denmark *57°07′N 10°24′E*
83 E21 **Asab** //Karas, S Namibia *25°29′S 17°59′E*
77 U16 **Asaba** Delta, S Nigeria *06°10′N 06°44′E*
76 J10 **Assaba** *var.* Açâba. ◈ *region* S Mauritania
149 S4 **Asadābād** *var.* Asadābād; *prev.* Chaghasarāy. Kunar, E Afghanistan *34°52′N 71°09′E*
**Asadābād** *see* Asadābād
138 K3 **Asad, Buḩayrat al** *Eng.* Lake Assad. ◎ N Syria
63 H20 **Asador, Pampa del** *plain* S Argentina
165 P14 **Asahi** Chiba, Honshū, S Japan *35°43′N 140°38′E*
164 M11 **Asahi** Toyama, Honshū, SW Japan *36°56′N 137°34′E*
165 T13 **Asahi-dake** ▲ Hokkaidō, N Japan *43°42′N 142°50′E*
165 T3 **Asahikawa** Hokkaidō, N Japan *43°46′N 142°23′E*
147 S10 **Asaka** *Rus.* Assake; *prev.* Leninsk. Andijon Viloyati, E Uzbekistan *40°39′N 72°16′E*
77 P17 **Asamankese** SE Ghana *05°47′N 00°41′W*
188 B15 **Asan** W Guam *13°28′N 144°43′E*
188 B15 **Asan Point** *headland* W Guam
153 R15 **Āsānsol** West Bengal, NE India *23°40′N 86°59′E*
80 K12 **Āsayita** Āfar, NE Ethiopia *11°35′S 41°23′E*
171 T12 **Asbakin** Papua Barat, E Indonesia *0°45′S 131°40′E*
**Asben** *see* Aïr, Massif de l'
15 Q12 **Asbestos** Québec, SE Canada *45°46′N 71°56′W*
29 Y13 **Asbury** Iowa, C USA *42°30′N 90°45′W*
18 K15 **Asbury Park** New Jersey, NE USA *40°13′N 74°00′W*
41 Z12 **Ascención, Bahiá de la** *bay* NW Caribbean Sea
40 I3 **Ascensión** Chihuahua, N Mexico *31°07′N 107°59′W*
**Ascension** *see* Saint Helena, Ascension and Tristan da Cunha
65 M14 **Ascension Fracture Zone** *tectonic feature* C Atlantic Ocean
**Ascension Island** ◇ *dependency of St.Helena* C Atlantic Ocean
65 N16 **Ascension Island** *island* C Atlantic Ocean
**Asch** *see* Aš
109 S3 **Aschach an der Donau** Oberösterreich, N Austria *48°22′N 14°00′E*
101 H18 **Aschaffenburg** Bayern, SW Germany *49°58′N 09°10′E*
101 F14 **Ascheberg** Nordrhein-Westfalen, W Germany *51°46′N 07°36′E*
101 L14 **Aschersleben** Sachsen-Anhalt, C Germany *51°46′N 11°28′E*
106 G12 **Asciano** Toscana, C Italy *43°15′N 11°32′E*
106 J13 **Ascoli Piceno** *anc.* Asculum Picenum. Marche, C Italy *42°51′N 13°34′E*
107 M17 **Ascoli Satriano** *anc.* Asculub, Ausculum Apulum. Puglia, SE Italy *41°13′N 15°32′E*
108 G11 **Ascona** Ticino, S Switzerland *46°10′N 08°45′E*
**Asculub** *see* Ascoli Satriano
**Asculum Picenum** *see* Ascoli Piceno
80 L11 **'Aseb** *var.* Assab, *Amh.* Āseb. SE Eritrea *13°04′N 42°36′E*
95 M20 **Åseda** Kronoberg, S Sweden *57°10′N 15°20′E*
127 T6 **Asekeyevo** Orenburgskaya Oblast', W Russia *53°36′N 52°53′E*
81 J14 **Āsela** *var.* Asella, Aselle, Asselle. Oromīya, C Ethiopia *07°55′N 39°08′E*
93 H15 **Åsele** Västerbotten, N Sweden *64°10′N 17°20′E*
**Asella/Aselle** *see* Āsela
98 N7 **Assen** Drenthe, NE Netherlands *53°N 06°34′E*
94 K12 **Åsen** Dalarna, C Sweden *61°18′N 13°49′E*
114 J11 **Asenovgrad** *prev.* Stanimaka. Plovdiv, C Bulgaria *42°00′N 24°53′E*
171 O13 **Asera** Sulawesi, C Indonesia *03°24′S 121°42′E*
95 E17 **Åseral** Vest-Agder, S Norway *58°37′N 07°27′E*
118 J3 **Aseri** *var.* Asserien, *Ger.* Asserin. Ida-Virumaa, NE Estonia *59°29′N 26°51′E*
104 G3 **A Serra de Outes** Galicia, NW Spain *42°50′N 08°54′W*
40 J10 **Aserradero** Durango, W Mexico
146 F13 **Aşgabat** *Eng.* Ashgabat, *Rus.* Ashkhabad, Poltoratsk. ● (Turkmenistan) Ahal Welaýaty, C Turkmenistan *37°58′N 58°22′E*
146 F13 **Aşgabat** ✈ Ahal Welaýaty, C Turkmenistan *38°06′N 58°10′E*
95 H16 **Åsgårdstrand** Vestfold, S Norway *59°22′N 10°27′E*
**Ashara** *see* Al 'Ashārah
23 T6 **Ashburn** Georgia, SE USA *31°42′N 83°39′W*
185 G19 **Ashburton** Canterbury, South Island, New Zealand *43°55′S 171°47′E*
185 G19 **Ashburton** ≈ South Island, New Zealand
180 H8 **Ashburton River** ≈ Western Australia
145 V10 **Ashchysu** ≈ E Kazakhstan
10 M16 **Ashcroft** British Columbia, SW Canada *50°41′N 121°17′W*
138 E10 **Ashdod** *anc.* Azotos, *Lat.* Azotus. Central, W Israel *31°48′N 34°38′E*
27 S14 **Ashdown** Arkansas, C USA *33°40′N 94°09′W*
21 T9 **Asheboro** North Carolina, SE USA *35°42′N 79°50′W*
11 X15 **Ashern** Manitoba, S Canada *51°10′N 98°22′W*
21 P10 **Asheville** North Carolina, SE USA *35°36′N 82°33′W*
12 E8 **Asheweig** ≈ Ontario, C Canada
27 V9 **Ash Flat** Arkansas, C USA *36°13′N 91°36′W*
183 T4 **Ashford** New South Wales, SE Australia *29°18′S 151°09′E*
97 P22 **Ashford** SE England, United Kingdom *51°09′N 00°52′E*
36 K11 **Ash Fork** Arizona, SW USA *35°12′N 112°31′W*
**Ashgabat** *see* Aşgabat
27 T7 **Ash Grove** Missouri, C USA *37°19′N 93°35′W*
165 O12 **Ashikaga** *var.* Asikaga. Tochigi, Honshū, S Japan *36°21′N 139°26′E*
165 Q8 **Ashiro** Iwate, Honshū, C Japan *40°04′N 141°00′E*
164 F15 **Ashizuri-misaki** Shikoku, SW Japan
138 E10 **Ashkelon** *prev.* Ashqelon. Southern, C Israel *31°40′N 34°35′E*
**Ashkhabad** *see* Aşgabat
23 Q4 **Ashland** Alabama, S USA *33°16′N 85°50′W*
26 K7 **Ashland** Kansas, C USA *37°12′N 99°47′W*
21 P5 **Ashland** Kentucky, S USA *38°28′N 82°40′W*
19 S2 **Ashland** Maine, NE USA *46°36′N 68°24′W*
22 M1 **Ashland** Mississippi, S USA *34°51′N 89°10′W*
27 U4 **Ashland** Missouri, C USA *38°46′N 92°15′W*
29 S15 **Ashland** Nebraska, C USA *41°01′N 96°21′W*
31 T12 **Ashland** Ohio, N USA *40°52′N 82°19′W*
32 G15 **Ashland** Oregon, NW USA *42°11′N 122°42′W*
21 W6 **Ashland** Virginia, NE USA *37°45′N 77°28′W*
30 K3 **Ashland** Wisconsin, N USA *46°34′N 90°54′W*
20 I8 **Ashland City** Tennessee, S USA *36°16′N 87°05′W*
183 S4 **Ashley** New South Wales, SE Australia *29°21′S 149°49′E*
29 O7 **Ashley** North Dakota, N USA *46°00′N 99°22′W*
173 W7 **Ashmore and Cartier Islands** ◇ *Australian external territory* E Indian Ocean
119 I14 **Ashmyany** *Rus.* Oshmyany. Hrodzyenskaya Voblasts', W Belarus *54°24′N 25°57′E*
18 K12 **Ashokan Reservoir** ⊠ New York, NE USA
165 U4 **Ashoro** Hokkaidō, NE Japan *43°16′N 143°33′E*
**Ashqelon** *see* Ashkelon
**Ashraf** *see* Behshahr
139 O3 **Ash Shadādah** *var.* Ash Shaddādah, Jisr ash Shadadi, Shaddādī, Shedadi, Tell Shedadi. Al Ḩasakah, NE Syria *36°00′N 40°42′E*
**Ash Shaddādah** *see* Ash Shadādah
139 Y12 **Ash Shāfī** Al Başrah, E Iraq *30°49′N 47°30′E*
139 R4 **Ash Shakk** *var.* Shaykh. Şalāḩ ad Dīn, C Iraq *35°15′N 43°27′E*
**Ash Sham/Ash Shām** *see* Rīf Dimashq
139 T10 **Ash Shāmīyah** *var.* Shamiya. Al Qādisīyah, C Iraq *31°56′N 44°37′E*
139 Y13 **Ash Shāmīyah** *var.* Al Bādiyah al Janūbīyah. *desert* S Iraq
139 T11 **Ash Shanāfīyah** *var.* Ash Shināfīyah. Al Qādisīyah, S Iraq *31°35′N 44°38′E*
138 G13 **Ash Sharāh** *var.* Esh Sharā. ▲▲ W Jordan
143 R16 **Ash Shāriqah** *Eng.* Sharjah. Ash Shāriqah, NE United Arab Emirates *25°22′N 55°28′E*
143 R16 **Ash Shāriqah** *var.* Sharjah. ✈ Ash Shāriqah, NE United Arab Emirates *25°19′N 55°37′E*
140 I4 **Ash Sharmah** *var.* Šarma. Tabūk, NW Saudi Arabia *28°02′N 35°16′E*
139 R4 **Ash Sharqāţ** Nīnawýa, NW Iraq *35°31′N 43°15′E*
141 S10 **Ash Sharqīyah** *off.* Al Minţaqah ash Sharqīyah, *Eng.* Eastern Region. ◈ *region* E Saudi Arabia
**Ash Sharqīyah** *see* Al 'Ubaylah
139 W11 **Ash Shaţrah** *var.* Shatra. Dhī Qār, SE Iraq *31°26′N 46°10′E*
138 G13 **Ash Shawbak** Ma'ān, W Jordan *30°32′N 35°34′E*
138 L5 **Ash Shaykh Ibrāhīm** Ḩimş, C Syria *35°03′N 38°50′E*
141 O17 **Ash Shaykh 'Uthmān** SW Yemen *12°53′N 45°00′E*
141 S15 **Ash Shiḩr** SE Yemen *14°45′N 49°24′E*
**Ash Shināfīyah** *see* Ash Shanāfīyah
141 V12 **Ash Shişar** *var.* Shisur. SW Oman *18°13′N 53°35′E*
139 S13 **Ash Shubrūm** *well* S Iraq
141 R10 **Ash Shuqqān** *desert* E Saudi Arabia
75 O9 **Ash Shuwayrif** *var.* Ash Shwayrif. N Libya *29°54′N 14°16′E*
**Ash Shwayrif** *see* Ash Shuwayrif
31 U10 **Ashtabula** Ohio, N USA *41°54′N 80°46′W*
29 Q5 **Ashtabula, Lake** ⊠ North Dakota, N USA
137 T12 **Ashtarak** W Armenia *40°18′N 44°22′E*
142 M6 **Āshtīān** *var.* Āshtiyān. Markazī, W Iran *34°23′N 49°55′E*
**Āshtiyān** *see* Āshtīān
33 R13 **Ashton** Idaho, NW USA *44°04′N 111°27′W*
13 O10 **Ashuanipi Lake** ◎ Newfoundland and Labrador, E Canada
15 P6 **Ashuapmushuan** ≈ Québec, SE Canada
23 Q3 **Ashville** Alabama, S USA *33°50′N 86°15′W*
31 S14 **Ashville** Ohio, N USA *39°43′N 82°57′W*
30 K3 **Ashwabay, Mount** *hill* Wisconsin, N USA
128-129 **Asia** *continent*
171 T11 **Asia, Kepulauan** *island group* E Indonesia
154 N13 **Āsika** Odisha, E India *19°38′N 84°41′E*
**Asikaga** *see* Ashikaga


◆ Country
● Country Capital
◇ Dependent Territory
○ Dependent Territory Capital
◈ Administrative Regions
✈ International Airport
▲ Mountain
▲▲ Mountain Range
⩙ Volcano
≈ River
◎ Lake
⊠ Reservoir

ASIKKALA – ĀVAJ


93 M18 **Asikkala** *var.* Vääksy. Päijät-Häme, S Finland *61°09′N 25°36′E*
74 G5 **Asilah** N Morocco *35°32′N 06°04′W*
**'Aṣī, Nahr al** *see* Orontes
107 B16 **Asinara, Isola** *island* W Italy
122 J12 **Asino** Tomskaya Oblast', C Russia *56°56′N 86°02′E*
119 O14 **Asintorf** *Rus.* Osintorf. Vitsyebskaya Voblasts', N Belarus *54°43′N 30°35′E*
119 L17 **Asipovichy** *Rus.* Osipovichi. Mahilyowskaya Voblasts', C Belarus *53°18′N 28°40′E*
141 N12 **'Asīr** *off.* Minṭaqat 'Asīr. ◐ *region* SW Saudi Arabia
140 M11 **'Asīr** *Eng.* Asir. ▲▲ SW Saudi Arabia
**'Asīr, Minṭaqat** *see* 'Asīr
139 X10 **Askal** Maysān, E Iraq *31°45′N 47°07′E*
137 P13 **Aşkale** Erzurum, NE Turkey *39°56′N 40°39′E*
117 T11 **Askaniya-Nova** Khersons'ka Oblast', S Ukraine *46°27′N 33°54′E*
95 H15 **Asker** Akershus, S Norway *59°52′N 10°26′E*
95 L17 **Askersund** Örebro, C Sweden *58°55′N 14°55′E*
**Askī Kalak** *see* Eski Kaļak
95 I15 **Askim** Østfold, S Norway *59°15′N 11°10′E*
127 V3 **Askino** Respublika Bashkortostan, W Russia *56°07′N 56°39′E*
115 D14 **Áskio** ▲▲ N Greece
152 L9 **Askot** Uttarākhand, N India *29°44′N 80°20′E*
94 C12 **Askvoll** Sogn Og Fjordane, S Norway *61°21′N 05°04′E*
136 A13 **Aslan Burnu** *headland* W Turkey *38°44′N 26°43′E*
136 L16 **Aslantaş Barajı** ▣ S Turkey
149 S4 **Āsmār** Kunar, E Afghanistan *34°59′N 71°29′E*
**Asmara** *see* Asmera
80 I9 **Asmera** *Eng.* Asmara. ● (Eritrea) C Eritrea *15°15′N 38°58′E*
95 L21 **Åsnen** ◎ S Sweden
115 F19 **Asopós** ⁓ S Greece
171 W13 **Asori** Papua, E Indonesia *02°37′S 136°06′E*
80 G12 **Āsosa** Bīnishangul Gumuz, W Ethiopia *10°06′N 34°27′E*
32 M10 **Asotin** Washington, NW USA *46°18′N 117°03′W*
**Aspadana** *see* Eşfahān
**Aspang** *see* Aspang Markt
109 X6 **Aspang Markt** *var.* Aspang. Niederösterreich, E Austria *47°34′N 16°06′E*
105 S12 **Aspe** Comunitat Valenciana, E Spain *38°21′N 00°43′W*
37 R5 **Aspen** Colorado, C USA *39°12′N 106°49′W*
25 P6 **Aspermont** Texas, SW USA *33°08′N 100°14′W*
**Asphaltites, Lacus** *see* Dead Sea
**Aspinwall** *see* Colón
185 C20 **Aspiring, Mount** ▲ South Island, New Zealand *44°21′S 168°47′E*
115 B16 **Asprókavos, Akrotírio** *headland* Kérkyra, Iónia Nísiá, Greece, C Mediterranean Sea *39°22′N 20°07′E*
**Aspropótamos** *see* Achelóos
**Assab** *see* 'Aseb
138 L4 **As Sabkhah** *var.* Sabkha. Ar Raqqah, NE Syria *35°30′N 35°54′E*
139 U6 **As Sa'dīyah** Diyālá, E Iraq *34°11′N 45°09′E*
**Assad, Lake** *see* Asad, Buḩayrat al
138 I8 **Aş Şafā** ▲ S Syria *33°03′N 37°07′E*
138 I10 **Aş Şafāwī** Al Mafraq, N Jordan *37°12′N 32°30′E*
75 W8 **Aş Şaff** *var.* El Şaff. N Egypt *29°34′N 31°16′E*
139 N2 **Aş Şafīḩ** Al Ḩasakah, N Syria *36°42′N 40°12′E*
75 U9 **Aş Şaḩrā' al Gharbīyah** *var.* Sahara el Gharbîya, *Eng.* Western Desert. *desert* C Egypt
75 X9 **Aş Şaḩrā' ash Sharqīyah** *Eng.* Arabian Desert, Eastern Desert. *desert* E Egypt
**Assake** *see* Asaka
**As Salamīyah** *see* Salamīyah
141 Q4 **As Sālimī** *var.* Salemy. SW Kuwait *29°07′N 46°41′E*
67 W7 **'Assal, Lac** ◎ C Djibouti
75 T7 **As Sallūm** *var.* Salûm. NW Egypt *31°31′N 25°09′E*
139 T13 **As Salmān** Al Muthanná, S Iraq *30°29′N 44°34′E*
138 G10 **As Salţ** *var.* Salt. Al Balqā', NW Jordan *32°03′N 35°44′E*
142 M16 **As Salwā** *var.* Salwa, Salwah. S Qatar *24°44′N 50°52′E*
153 V12 **Assam** ◐ *state* NE India
**Assamaka** *see* Assamakka
77 T8 **Assamakka** *var.* Assamaka. Agadez, NW Niger *19°24′N 05°53′E*
139 U11 **As Samāwah** *var.* Samawa. Al Muthanná, S Iraq *31°17′N 45°06′E*
**As Samāwah** *see* Al Muthannā
**As Saqia al Hamra** *see* Saguia al Hamra
138 J4 **Aş Şā'rān** Ḩamāh, C Syria *35°15′N 37°28′E*
138 G9 **Aş Şarīḩ** Irbid, N Jordan *32°31′N 35°54′E*
21 Z5 **Assateague Island** *island* Maryland, NE USA
139 O6 **As Sayyāl** *var.* Sayyāl. Dayr az Zawr, E Syria *34°37′N 40°52′E*
99 G18 **Asse** Vlaams Brabant, C Belgium *50°55′N 04°12′E*
99 D16 **Assebroek** West-Vlaanderen, NW Belgium *51°12′N 03°16′E*
**Asselle** *see* Āsela
107 C20 **Assemini** Sardegna, Italy, C Mediterranean Sea *39°16′N 08°58′E*
99 E16 **Assenede** Oost-Vlaanderen, NW Belgium *51°15′N 03°43′E*
95 G24 **Assens** Syddtjylland, C Denmark *55°16′N 09°54′N*
**Asserien/Asserin** *see* Aseri
99 I21 **Assesse** Namur, SE Belgium *50°22′N 05°01′E*
141 Y8 **As Sīb** *var.* Seeb. NE Oman *23°40′N 58°03′E*
139 Z13 **As Sībah** *var.* Sibah. Al Başrah, SE Iraq *30°13′N 47°24′E*
11 T17 **Assiniboia** Saskatchewan, S Canada *49°39′N 105°59′W*
11 V15 **Assiniboine** ⁓ Manitoba, S Canada
11 P16 **Assiniboine, Mount** ▲ Alberta/British Columbia, SW Canada *50°54′N 115°43′W*
**Assiout** *see* Asyūţ
60 J9 **Assis** São Paulo, S Brazil *22°37′S 50°25′W*
106 I13 **Assisi** Umbria, C Italy *43°04′N 12°36′E*
**Assiut** *see* Asyūţ
**Assling** *see* Jesenice
**Assouan** *see* Aswān
59 P14 **Assu** *var.* Açu. Rio Grande do Norte, E Brazil *05°33′S 36°55′W*
**Assuan** *see* Aswān
142 K12 **Aş Şubayḩīyah** *var.* Subiyah. S Kuwait *28°55′N 47°57′E*
141 R16 **As Sufāl** S Yemen *14°06′N 48°42′E*
138 L5 **As Sukhnah** *var.* Sukhne, *Fr.* Soukhné. Ḩimş, C Syria *34°56′N 38°52′E*
139 U4 **As Sulaymānīyah** *var.* Sulaimaniya, *Kurd.* Slêmanî. As Sulaymānīyah, NE Iraq *35°32′N 45°27′E*
139 U4 **As Sulaymānīyah** *off.* Muḩāfaz at as Sulaymānīyah, *off. Kurd.* Parêzga-î Slêmanî, *Kurd.* Slêmanî. ◐ *governorate* N Iraq
**as Sulaymānīyah, Muḩāfaz at** *see* As Sulaymānīyah
141 P11 **As Sulayyil** Ar Riyāḑ, S Saudi Arabia *20°29′N 45°33′E*
121 O13 **As Sulţān** N Libya *31°01′N 17°21′E*
141 Q5 **Aş Şummān** *desert* N Saudi Arabia
141 Q16 **Aş Şurrah** SW Yemen *13°56′N 46°23′E*
139 N4 **Aş Şuwār** *var.* Şuwār. Dayr az Zawr, E Syria *35°31′N 40°37′E*
138 H9 **As Suwaydā'** *var.* El Suweida, Es Suweida, Suweida, *Fr.* Soueida. As Suwaydā', SW Syria *32°43′N 36°33′E*
138 H9 **As Suwaydā'** *off.* Muḩāfaẓat as Suwaydā', *var.* As Suwaydā, Suwaydá, Suweida. ◐ *governorate* S Syria
141 Z9 **As Suwayḩ** NE Oman *22°07′N 59°42′E*
141 X8 **As Suwayq** *var.* Suwaik. N Oman *23°49′N 57°30′E*
139 T8 **Aş Şuwayrah** *var.* Suwaira. Wāsiţ, E Iraq *32°57′N 44°47′E*
75 X8 **As Suways** *Eng.* Suez, *var.* El Suweis. NE Egypt *29°59′N 32°33′E*
**Asta Colonia** *see* Asti
**Astacus** *see* İzmit
115 M23 **Astakída** *island* SE Greece
**Astana** *see* Nur-Sultan
142 M3 **Āstāneh** *var.* Āstāneh-ye Ashrafīyeh. Gīlān, NW Iran *37°17′N 49°58′E*
**Āstāneh-ye Ashrafīyeh** *see* Āstāneh
**Asta Pompeia** *see* Asti
137 Y14 **Astara** S Azerbaijan *38°28′N 48°51′E*
**Astarabad** *see* Gorgān
99 L15 **Asten** Noord-Brabant, SE Netherlands *51°24′N 05°45′E*
**Asterābād** *see* Gorgān
106 C8 **Asti** *anc.* Asta Colonia, Asta Pompeia, Hasta Colonia, Hasta Pompeia. Piemonte, NW Italy *44°54′N 08°11′E*
**Astigi** *see* Écija
**Astipálaia** *see* Astypálaia
148 L16 **Astola Island** *island* SW Pakistan
152 H4 **Astor** Jammu and Kashmir, NW India *35°21′N 74°52′E*
104 K4 **Astorga** *anc.* Asturica Augusta. Castilla y León, N Spain *42°27′N 06°04′W*
32 F10 **Astoria** Oregon, NW USA *46°12′N 123°50′W*
0 F8 **Astoria Fan** *undersea feature* E Pacific Ocean *45°15′N 126°15′W*
95 J22 **Åstorp** Skåne, S Sweden *56°09′N 12°57′E*
**Astrabad** *see* Gorgān
127 Q13 **Astrakhan'** Astrakhanskaya Oblast', SW Russia *46°20′N 48°01′E*
**Astrakhan-Bazar** *see* Cälilabad
127 Q11 **Astrakhanskaya Oblast'** ◐ *province* SW Russia
93 J15 **Åsträsk** Västerbotten, N Sweden *64°38′N 20°00′E*
**Astrida** *see* Butare
65 O22 **Astrid Ridge** *undersea feature* S Atlantic Ocean
187 P15 **Astrolabe, Récifs de l'** *reef* C New Caledonia
121 P2 **Astromerítis** N Cyprus *35°09′N 33°02′E*
115 F20 **Ástros** Pelopónnisos, S Greece *37°24′N 22°43′E*
119 G16 **Astryna** *Rus.* Ostryna. Hrodzyenskaya Voblasts', W Belarus *53°44′N 24°33′E*
104 J2 **Asturías** *var.* Principado de Asturías. ◐ *autonomous community* NW Spain
**Asturias** *see* Oviedo
**Asturías, Principado de** *see* Asturías
**Asturica Augusta** *see* Astorga
115 L22 **Astypálaia** *var.* Astipálaia, *It.* Stampalia. *island* Kykládes, Greece, Aegean Sea
192 G16 **Āsuisui, Cape** *headland* Savai'i, W Samoa *13°44′S 172°29′W*
195 S2 **Asuka** *research station (Japan)* Antarctica *71°49′S 23°52′E*
62 O6 **Asunción** ● (Paraguay) Central, S Paraguay *25°17′S 57°36′W*
62 O6 **Asunción** ✈ Central, S Paraguay *25°15′S 57°40′W*
188 K3 **Asuncion Island** *island* N Northern Mariana Islands
42 E6 **Asunción Mita** Jutiapa, SE Guatemala *14°20′N 89°42′W*
**Asunción Nochixtlán** *see* Nochixtlán
40 E3 **Asunción, Río** ⁓ NW Mexico
95 M18 **Åsunden** ◎ S Sweden
118 K11 **Asvyeya** *Rus.* Osveya. Vitsyebskaya Voblasts', N Belarus *56°00′N 28°05′E*
**Aswa** *see* Achwa
75 X11 **Aswān** *var.* Assouan, Assuan, Aswān; *anc.* Syene. SE Egypt *24°03′N 32°59′E*
**Aswān** *see* Aswān
**Aswan Dam** *see* Khazzān Aswān
75 W9 **Asyūţ** *var.* Assiout, Assiut, Asyût, Siut; *anc.* Lycopolis. C Egypt *27°06′N 31°11′E*
**Asyût** *see* Asyūţ
193 W15 **Ata** *island* Tongatapu Group, SW Tonga
62 G8 **Atacama** *off.* Región de Atacama. ◐ *region* C Chile
**Atacama Desert** *see* Atacama, Desierto de
62 H4 **Atacama, Desierto de** *Eng.* Atacama Desert. *desert* N Chile
62 I6 **Atacama, Puna de** ▲▲ NW Argentina
**Atacama, Región de** *see* Atacama
62 I5 **Atacama, Salar de** *salt lake* N Chile
54 E11 **Ataco** Tolima, C Colombia *03°36′N 75°23′W*
190 H8 **Atafu Atoll** *island* NW Tokelau
190 H8 **Atafu Village** Atafu Atoll, NW Tokelau *08°40′S 172°40′W*
74 K12 **Atakor** ▲▲ SE Algeria
77 R14 **Atakora, Chaîne de l'** *var.* Atakora Mountains. ▲▲ N Benin
**Atakora Mountains** *see* Atakora, Chaîne de l'
77 R16 **Atakpamé** C Togo *07°32′N 01°08′E*
146 F11 **Atakui** Ahal Welaýaty, C Turkmenistan *40°04′N 58°03′E*
58 B13 **Atalaia do Norte** Amazonas, N Brazil *04°22′S 70°10′W*
146 M14 **Atamyrat** *prev.* Kerki. Lebap Welaýaty, E Turkmenistan *37°52′N 65°06′E*
76 I7 **Aţâr** Adrar, W Mauritania *20°30′N 13°03′W*
162 G10 **Atas Bogd** ▲ SW Mongolia *43°17′N 96°47′E*
35 P12 **Atascadero** California, W USA *35°28′N 120°40′W*
25 S13 **Atascosa River** ⁓ Texas, SW USA
145 R11 **Atasu** Karaganda, C Kazakhstan *48°42′N 71°38′E*
145 R12 **Atasu** ⁓ Karaganda, C Kazakhstan
193 V15 **Atata** *island* Tongatapu Group, S Tonga
136 H10 **Atatürk** ✈ (İstanbul) İstanbul, NW Turkey *40°58′N 28°50′E*
137 N16 **Atatürk Barajī** ▣ S Turkey
115 O23 **Atavýros** *prev.* Attavyros. Ródos, Dodekánisa, Aegean Sea *36°10′N 27°50′E*
115 O23 **Atávyros** *prev.* Attávyros. ▲ Ródos, Dodekánisa, Greece, Aegean Sea *36°10′N 27°50′E*
**Atax** *see* Aude
80 G8 **Atbara** *var.* 'Aţbārah. River Nile, NE Sudan *17°42′N 34°E*
80 H8 **Atbara** *var.* Nahr 'Aţbarah. ⁓ Eritrea/Sudan
**'Aţbārah/'Aţbarah, Nahr** *see* Atbara
145 P9 **Atbasar** Akmola, N Kazakhstan *51°49′N 68°18′E*
**At-Bashi** *see* At-Bashy
147 W9 **At-Bashy** *var.* At-Bashi. Narynskaya Oblast', C Kyrgyzstan *41°07′N 75°48′E*
22 I10 **Atchafalaya Bay** *bay* Louisiana, S USA
22 I8 **Atchafalaya River** ⁓ Louisiana, S USA
**Atchin** *see* Aceh
27 Q3 **Atchison** Kansas, C USA *39°31′N 95°07′W*
77 P16 **Atebubu** C Ghana *07°47′N 01°00′W*
105 Q6 **Ateca** Aragón, NE Spain *41°20′N 01°49′W*
40 K11 **Atengo, Río** ⁓ C Mexico
**Aternum** *see* Pescara
107 K15 **Atessa** Abruzzo, C Italy *42°03′N 14°25′E*
**Ateste** *see* Este
99 E19 **Ath** *var.* Aat. Hainaut, SW Belgium *50°38′N 03°47′E*
11 Q13 **Athabasca** Alberta, SW Canada *54°44′N 113°15′W*
11 Q12 **Athabasca** *var.* Athabaska. ⁓ Alberta, SW Canada
11 R10 **Athabasca, Lake** ◎ Alberta/Saskatchewan, SW Canada
**Athabaska** *see* Athabasca
115 C16 **Athamánon** ▲▲ C Greece
97 F17 **Athboy** *Ir.* Baile Átha Buí. E Ireland *53°38′N 06°55′W*
**Athenae** *see* Athína
97 C18 **Athenry** *Ir.* Baile Átha an Rí. W Ireland *53°19′N 08°49′W*
23 P2 **Athens** Alabama, S USA *34°48′N 86°58′W*
23 T3 **Athens** Georgia, SE USA *33°57′N 83°24′W*
31 T14 **Athens** Ohio, N USA *39°20′N 82°06′W*
20 M10 **Athens** Tennessee, S USA *35°27′N 84°38′W*
25 V7 **Athens** Texas, SW USA *32°12′N 95°51′W*
**Athens** *see* Athína
115 B18 **Athéras, Akrotírio** *headland* Kefallonía, Iónia Nísiá, Greece, C Mediterranean Sea *38°20′N 20°24′E*
181 W4 **Atherton** Queensland, NE Australia *17°18′S 145°29′E*
81 I19 **Athi** ⁓ S Kenya
121 Q2 **Athiénou** SE Cyprus *35°01′N 33°31′E*
115 H19 **Athína** *Eng.* Athens, *prev.* Athínai; *anc.* Athenae. ● (Greece) Attikí, C Greece *37°59′N 23°44′E*
**Athínai** *see* Athína
139 S10 **Athīyah** An Najaf, C Iraq *32°01′N 44°04′E*
97 D18 **Athlone** *Ir.* Baile Átha Luain. C Ireland *53°25′N 07°56′W*
155 F16 **Athni** Karnātaka, W India *16°43′N 75°04′E*
185 C23 **Athol** Southland, South Island, New Zealand *45°30′S 168°35′E*
19 N11 **Athol** Massachusetts, NE USA *42°35′N 72°11′W*
115 I15 **Áthos** ▲ NE Greece *40°10′N 24°21′E*
**Athos, Mount** *see* Ágion Óros
138 K3 **Ath Thawrah** *var.* Al Tabaqah. Ar Raqqah, N Syria *35°36′N 39°00′E*
141 P5 **Ath Thumāmī** *spring/well* N Saudi Arabia *27°56′N 45°06′E*
99 L25 **Athus** Luxembourg, SE Belgium *49°34′N 05°50′E*
97 E19 **Athy** *Ir.* Baile Átha Í. C Ireland *52°59′N 06°59′W*
78 I10 **Ati** Batha, C Chad *13°11′N 18°20′E*
81 F16 **Atiak** NW Uganda *03°14′N 32°05′E*
57 G17 **Atico** Arequipa, SW Peru *16°13′S 73°13′W*
105 O6 **Atienza** Castilla-La Mancha, C Spain *41°12′N 02°52′W*
39 Q6 **Atigun Pass** *pass* Alaska, USA
12 B12 **Atikokan** Ontario, S Canada *48°45′N 91°38′W*
13 O9 **Atikonak Lac** ◎ Newfoundland and Labrador, E Canada
42 C6 **Atitlán, Lago de** ◎ W Guatemala
190 L16 **Atiu** *island* S Cook Islands
**Atjeh** *see* Aceh
123 T9 **Atka** Magadanskaya Oblast', E Russia *60°45′N 151°35′E*
38 H17 **Atka** Atka Island, Alaska, USA *52°12′N 174°14′W*
38 H17 **Atka Island** *island* Aleutian Islands, Alaska, USA
127 O7 **Atkarsk** Saratovskaya Oblast', W Russia *52°15′N 43°48′E*
27 U11 **Atkins** Arkansas, C USA *35°15′N 92°56′W*
29 O13 **Atkinson** Nebraska, C USA *42°31′N 98°57′W*
171 T12 **Atkri** Papua Barat, E Indonesia *01°45′S 130°04′E*
41 O13 **Atlacomulco** *var.* Atlacomulco de Fabela. México, C Mexico *19°49′N 99°54′W*
**Atlacomulco de Fabela** *see* Atlacomulco
23 S3 **Atlanta** *state capital* Georgia, SE USA *33°45′N 84°23′W*
31 R6 **Atlanta** Michigan, N USA *45°01′N 84°07′W*
25 X6 **Atlanta** Texas, SW USA *33°06′N 94°09′W*
29 T15 **Atlantic** Iowa, C USA *41°24′N 95°00′W*
21 Y10 **Atlantic** North Carolina, SE USA *34°52′N 76°20′W*
23 W8 **Atlantic Beach** Florida, SE USA *30°19′N 81°24′W*
18 J17 **Atlantic City** New Jersey, NE USA *39°23′N 74°27′W*
172 L14 **Atlantic-Indian Basin** *undersea feature* SW Indian Ocean *60°00′S 15°00′E*
172 K13 **Atlantic-Indian Ridge** *undersea feature* SW Indian Ocean *53°00′S 15°00′E*
54 E4 **Atlántico** *off.* Departamento del Atlántico. ◐ *province* NW Colombia
64-55 **Atlantic Ocean** *ocean*
**Atlántico, Departamento del** *see* Atlántico
**Atlántico Norte, Región Autónoma** *see* Costa Caribe Norte
**Atlántico Sur, Región Autónoma** *see* Costa Caribe Sur
42 I5 **Atlántida** ◐ *department* N Honduras
77 Y15 **Atlantika Mountains** ▲▲ E Nigeria
64 J10 **Atlantis Fracture Zone** *tectonic feature* NW Atlantic Ocean
74 H7 **Atlas Mountains** ▲▲ NW Africa
123 V11 **Atlasova, Ostrov** *island* SE Russia
123 V10 **Atlasovo** Kamchatskiy Kray, E Russia *55°42′N 159°35′E*
120 G11 **Atlas Saharien** *var.* Saharan Atlas. ▲▲ Algeria/Morocco
**Atlas, Tell** *see* Atlas Tellien
120 H10 **Atlas Tellien** *Eng.* Tell Atlas. ▲▲ N Algeria
10 I9 **Atlin** British Columbia, W Canada *59°31′N 133°41′W*
10 I9 **Atlin Lake** ◎ British Columbia, W Canada
41 P14 **Atlixco** Puebla, S Mexico *18°55′N 98°26′W*
94 B11 **Atløyna** *island* S Norway
155 I17 **Ātmakūr** Andhra Pradesh, C India *15°52′N 78°42′E*
23 O8 **Atmore** Alabama, S USA *31°01′N 87°29′W*
101 J20 **Atmühl** ⁓ S Germany
94 H11 **Atna** ⁓ S Norway
164 E13 **Atō** Yamaguchi, Honshū, SW Japan *34°24′N 131°42′E*
57 L21 **Atocha** Potosí, S Bolivia *20°55′S 66°14′W*
27 P12 **Atoka** Oklahoma, C USA *34°22′N 96°08′W*
27 O12 **Atoka Lake** *var.* Atoka Reservoir. ▣ Oklahoma, C USA
**Atoka Reservoir** *see* Atoka Lake
33 Q14 **Atomic City** Idaho, NW USA *43°26′N 112°48′W*
40 L10 **Atotonilco** Zacatecas, C Mexico *24°12′N 102°46′W*
**Atotonilco** *see* Atotonilco el Alto
40 M13 **Atotonilco el Alto** *var.* Atotonilco. Jalisco, SW Mexico *20°35′N 102°30′W*
77 N7 **Atouila, 'Erg** *desert* N Mali
41 N16 **Atoyac** *var.* Atoyac de Alvarez. Guerrero, S Mexico *17°12′N 100°28′W*
**Atoyac de Alvarez** *see* Atoyac
41 P15 **Atoyac, Río** ⁓ S Mexico
39 O5 **Atqasuk** Alaska, USA *70°28′N 157°24′W*
**Atrak/Atrak, Rūd-e** *see* Etrek
95 J20 **Ätran** ⁓ S Sweden
54 C7 **Atrato, Río** ⁓ NW Colombia
**Atrek** *see* Etrek
107 K14 **Atri** Abruzzo, C Italy *42°35′N 13°59′E*
**Atria** *see* Adria
165 P9 **Atsumi** Yamagata, Honshū, C Japan *38°38′N 139°36′E*
165 S3 **Atsuta** Hokkaidō, NE Japan *43°28′N 141°24′E*
143 Q17 **Aţ Ţaff** *desert* C United Arab Emirates
138 G12 **Aţ Ţafīlah** *var.* Et Tafila, Tafila. Aţ Ţafīlah, W Jordan *30°52′N 35°36′E*
138 G12 **Aţ Ţafīlah** *off.* Muḩāfaẓat aţ Ţafīlah. ◐ *governorate* W Jordan
140 L10 **Aţ Ţā'if** Makkah al Mukarramah, W Saudi Arabia *21°50′N 40°50′E*
**Attaleia/Attalia** *see* Antalya
23 Q3 **Attalla** Alabama, S USA *34°01′N 86°05′W*
138 L2 **At Tall al Abyaḑ** *var.* Tall al Abyaḑ, Tell Abyad, *Fr.* Tell Abiad. Ar Raqqah, N Syria *36°36′N 34°00′E*
**At Ta'mīm** *see* Kirkūk
138 L7 **Aţ Ţanf** Ḩimş, S Syria *33°29′N 38°39′E*
163 N9 **Attanshiree** Dornogovĭ, SE Mongolia *45°36′N 110°30′E*
167 T10 **Attapu** *var.* Attopeu, Samakhixai. Attapu, S Laos *14°48′N 106°51′E*
139 S10 **At Ţaqţaqānah** An Najaf, C Iraq *32°03′N 43°54′E*
**Attávyros** *see* Atávyros
12 G9 **Attawapiskat** Ontario, C Canada *52°55′N 82°26′W*
12 F9 **Attawapiskat** ⁓ Ontario, S Canada
12 D9 **Attawapiskat Lake** ◎ Ontario, C Canada
**At Taybé** *see* Ţayyibah
101 F16 **Attendorn** Nordrhein-Westfalen, W Germany *51°07′N 07°54′E*
109 R5 **Attersee** Salzburg, NW Austria *47°55′N 13°31′E*
109 R5 **Attersee** ◎ N Austria
99 L24 **Attert** Luxembourg, SE Belgium *49°45′N 05°47′E*
138 M4 **At Tibnī** *var.* Tibnī. Dayr az Zawr, NE Syria *35°30′N 39°48′E*
31 N13 **Attica** Indiana, N USA *40°17′N 87°15′W*
18 E10 **Attica** New York, NE USA *42°51′N 78°13′W*
**Attica** *see* Attikí
13 N7 **Attikamagen Lake** ◎ Newfoundland and Labrador, E Canada
115 H20 **Attikí** *Eng.* Attica. ◐ *region* C Greece
19 O12 **Attleboro** Massachusetts, NE USA *41°55′N 71°15′W*
109 R5 **Attnang** Oberösterreich, N Austria *48°02′N 13°44′E*
149 U6 **Attock City** Punjab, E Pakistan *33°52′N 72°20′E*
**Attopeu** *see* Attapu
25 X8 **Attoyac River** ⁓ Texas, SW USA
38 D16 **Attu** Attu Island, Alaska, USA *52°53′N 173°18′E*
139 Y12 **Aţ Ţūbah** Al Başrah, E Iraq *30°29′N 47°28′E*
140 K4 **Aţ Ţubayq** *plain* Jordan/Saudi Arabia
38 C16 **Attu Island** *island* Aleutian Islands, Alaska, USA
75 X8 **Aţ Ţūr** *var.* El Ţûr. NE Egypt *28°14′N 33°36′E*
155 I21 **Āttūr** Tamil Nādu, SE India *11°34′N 78°39′E*
141 N17 **At Turbah** SW Yemen *12°42′N 43°31′E*
62 I12 **Atuel, Río** ⁓ C Argentina
191 X7 **Atuona** Hiva Oa, NE French Polynesia *09°47′S 139°03′W*
**Aturus** *see* Adour
95 M18 **Åtvidaberg** Östergötland, S Sweden *58°12′N 16°00′E*
35 P9 **Atwater** California, W USA *37°19′N 120°33′W*
29 T8 **Atwater** Minnesota, N USA *45°08′N 94°48′W*
26 I2 **Atwood** Kansas, C USA *39°48′N 101°03′W*
31 U12 **Atwood Lake** ▣ Ohio, N USA
127 P5 **Atyashevo** Respublika Mordoviya, W Russia *54°36′N 46°04′E*
144 F12 **Atyrau** *prev.* Gur'yev. Atyrau, W Kazakhstan *47°07′N 51°56′E*
144 E11 **Atyrau** *off.* Atyrauskaya Oblast', *var.Kaz.* Atyraū Oblysy; *prev.* Gur'yevskaya Oblast'. ◐ *province* W Kazakhstan
**Atyraū Oblysy/ Atyrauskaya Oblast'** *see* Atyrau
**Atyrauskaya Oblast'** *see* Atyrau
108 J7 **Au** Vorarlberg, NW Austria *47°19′N 10°01′E*
186 B4 **Aua Island** *island* NW Papua New Guinea
103 S16 **Aubagne** *anc.* Albania. Bouches-du-Rhône, SE France *43°17′N 05°35′E*
99 L25 **Aubange** Luxembourg, SE Belgium *49°35′N 05°49′E*
103 Q6 **Aube** ◐ *department* N France
103 R6 **Aube** ⁓ N France
99 L19 **Aubel** Liège, E Belgium *50°45′N 05°49′E*
103 Q13 **Aubenas** Ardèche, E France *44°37′N 04°24′E*
103 O8 **Aubigny-sur-Nère** Cher, C France *47°30′N 02°27′E*
103 O13 **Aubin** Aveyron, S France *44°30′N 02°18′E*
103 O13 **Aubrac, Monts d'** ▲▲ S France
36 J10 **Aubrey Cliffs** *cliff* Arizona, SW USA
23 R5 **Auburn** Alabama, S USA *32°37′N 85°30′W*
35 P6 **Auburn** California, W USA *38°53′N 121°03′W*
30 K14 **Auburn** Illinois, N USA *39°35′N 89°45′W*
31 Q11 **Auburn** Indiana, N USA *41°22′N 85°03′W*
20 J7 **Auburn** Kentucky, S USA *36°52′N 86°42′W*
19 P8 **Auburn** Maine, NE USA *44°05′N 70°15′W*
19 N11 **Auburn** Massachusetts, NE USA *42°11′N 71°47′W*
29 S16 **Auburn** Nebraska, C USA *40°23′N 95°50′W*
18 H10 **Auburn** New York, NE USA *42°55′N 76°31′W*
32 H8 **Auburn** Washington, NW USA *47°18′N 122°13′W*
103 N11 **Aubusson** Creuse, C France *45°58′N 02°10′E*
118 E10 **Auce** *Ger.* Autz. SW Latvia *56°28′N 22°54′E*
102 L15 **Auch** *Lat.* Augusta Auscorum, Elimberrum. Gers, S France *43°40′N 00°37′E*
77 U16 **Auchi** Edo, S Nigeria *07°01′N 06°17′E*
23 T9 **Aucilla River** ⁓ Florida/Georgia, SE USA
184 L6 **Auckland** Auckland, North Island, New Zealand *36°53′S 174°46′E*
184 K5 **Auckland** *off.* Auckland Region. ◐ *region* North Island, New Zealand
184 L6 **Auckland** ✈ Auckland, North Island, New Zealand *37°01′S 174°49′E*
192 J12 **Auckland Islands** *island group* S New Zealand
**Auckland Region** *see* Auckland
103 O16 **Aude** ◐ *department* S France
103 N16 **Aude** *anc.* Atax. ⁓ S France
**Audenarde** *see* Oudenaarde
**Audern** *see* Audru
102 E6 **Audierne** Finistère, NW France *48°01′N 04°30′W*
102 E6 **Audierne, Baie d'** *bay* NW France
103 U7 **Audincourt** Doubs, E France *47°29′N 06°50′E*
118 G5 **Audru** *Ger.* Audern. Pärnumaa, SW Estonia *58°24′N 24°22′E*
29 T14 **Audubon** Iowa, C USA *41°44′N 94°56′W*
101 N17 **Aue** Sachsen, E Germany *50°35′N 12°42′E*
100 H12 **Aue** ⁓ NW Germany
100 L9 **Auerbach** Bayern, SE Germany *49°41′N 11°41′E*
101 M17 **Auerbach** Sachsen, E Germany *50°30′N 12°24′E*
108 I10 **Auererrhein** ⁓ SW Switzerland
101 N17 **Auersberg** ▲ E Germany *50°30′N 12°42′E*
181 W9 **Augathella** Queensland, E Australia *25°54′S 146°38′E*
31 Q12 **Auglaize River** ⁓ Ohio, N USA
83 F22 **Augrabies Falls** *waterfall* W South Africa
31 R7 **Au Gres River** ⁓ Michigan, N USA
**Augsbourg** *see* Augsburg
101 K22 **Augsburg** *Fr.* Augsbourg; *anc.* Augusta Vindelicorum. Bayern, S Germany *48°22′N 10°54′E*
180 I14 **Augusta** Western Australia *34°18′S 115°10′E*
107 L25 **Augusta** *It.* Agosta. Sicilia, Italy, C Mediterranean Sea *37°14′N 15°14′E*
27 W11 **Augusta** Arkansas, C USA *35°16′N 91°21′W*
23 V3 **Augusta** Georgia, SE USA *33°29′N 81°58′W*
27 O6 **Augusta** Kansas, C USA *37°40′N 96°59′W*
19 Q7 **Augusta** *state capital* Maine, NE USA *44°20′N 69°44′W*
33 Q8 **Augusta** Montana, NW USA *47°28′N 112°23′W*
**Augusta** *see* London
**Augusta Auscorum** *see* Auch
**Augusta Emerita** *see* Mérida
**Augusta Praetoria** *see* Aosta
**Augusta Suessionum** *see* Soissons
**Augusta Trajana** *see* Stara Zagora
**Augusta Treverorum** *see* Trier
**Augusta Vangionum** *see* Worms
**Augusta Vindelicorum** *see* Augsburg
95 G24 **Augustenborg** *Ger.* Augustenburg. Syddanmark, SW Denmark *54°57′N 09°53′E*
**Augustenburg** *see* Augustenborg
39 Q13 **Augustine Island** *island* Alaska, USA
14 L9 **Augustines, Lac des** ◎ Québec, SE Canada
**Augustobona Tricassium** *see* Troyes
**Augustodunum** *see* Autun
**Augustodurum** *see* Bayeux
**Augustoritum Lemovicensium** *see* Limoges
110 O8 **Augustów** *Rus.* Avgustov. Podlaskie, NE Poland *53°52′N 22°58′E*
**Augustow Canal** *see* Augustowski, Kanał
110 O8 **Augustowski, Kanał** *Eng.* Augustow Canal, *Rus.* Avgustovskiy Kanal. *canal* NE Poland
180 I9 **Augustus, Mount** ▲ Western Australia *24°42′S 117°42′E*
**Aujuittuq** *see* Grise Fiord
186 M9 **Auki** Malaita, N Solomon Islands *08°48′S 160°45′E*
21 W8 **Aulander** North Carolina, SE USA *36°15′N 77°16′W*
180 L7 **Auld, Lake** *salt lake* C Western Australia
**Aulie Ata/Auliye-Ata** *see* Taraz
**Äūlīeköl** *see* Auliyekol'
144 M8 **Auliyekol'** *Kaz.* Äūlīeköl; *prev.* Semiozernoye. Kostanay, N Kazakhstan *52°22′N 64°06′E*
106 E10 **Aulla** Toscana, C Italy *44°15′N 10°00′E*
102 F6 **Aulne** ⁓ NW France
**Aulong** *see* Ulong
37 T3 **Ault** Colorado, C USA *40°34′N 104°43′W*
95 F22 **Aulum** *var.* avlum. Midtjylland, C Denmark *56°16′N 08°48′E*
103 N3 **Aumale** Seine-Maritime, N France *49°45′N 01°43′E*
**Auminzatau, Gory** *see* Ovminzatovo Tog'lari
77 T14 **Auna** Niger, W Nigeria *10°13′N 04°43′E*
166 L6 **Aunglan** *var.* Allanmyo, Myaydo. Magway, C Myanmar (Burma) *19°25′N 95°13′E*
95 H21 **Auning** Midtjylland, C Denmark *56°26′N 10°23′E*
192 K17 **'Aunu'u Island** *island* W American Samoa
83 E20 **Auob** *var.* Oup. ⁓ Namibia/South Africa
93 K19 **Aura** Varsinais-Suomi, SW Finland *60°37′N 22°35′E*
109 R5 **Aurach** ⁓ N Austria
**Aural, Phnom** *see* Aôral, Phnum
153 O14 **Aurangābād** Bihār, N India *24°46′N 84°23′E*
154 F13 **Aurangābād** Mahārāshtra, C India *19°52′N 75°22′E*
189 V7 **Aur Atoll** *atoll* E Marshall Islands
102 G7 **Auray** Morbihan, NW France *47°40′N 02°59′W*
94 G13 **Aurdal** Oppland, S Norway *60°51′N 09°25′E*
94 F8 **Aure** Møre og Romsdal, S Norway *63°16′N 08°31′E*
29 T12 **Aurelia** Iowa, C USA *42°42′N 95°26′W*
**Aurelia Aquensis** *see* Baden-Baden
**Aurelianum** *see* Orléans
120 J10 **Aurès, Massif de l'** ▲▲ NE Algeria
100 F10 **Aurich** Niedersachsen, NW Germany *53°28′N 07°28′E*
103 O13 **Aurillac** Cantal, C France *44°56′N 02°26′E*
**Aurine, Alpi** *see* Zillertaler Alpen
**Aurium** *see* Ourense
14 H15 **Aurora** Ontario, S Canada *44°00′N 79°26′W*
55 S8 **Aurora** NW Guyana *06°46′N 59°45′W*
37 T4 **Aurora** Colorado, C USA *39°42′N 104°51′W*
30 M11 **Aurora** Illinois, N USA *41°46′N 88°19′W*
31 Q15 **Aurora** Indiana, N USA *39°01′N 84°55′W*
29 W4 **Aurora** Minnesota, N USA *47°31′N 92°14′W*
27 S8 **Aurora** Missouri, C USA *36°58′N 93°43′W*
29 P16 **Aurora** Nebraska, C USA *40°52′N 98°00′W*
36 J5 **Aurora** Utah, W USA *38°55′N 111°55′W*
**Aurora** *see* San Francisco, Philippines
**Aurora** *see* Maéwo, Vanuatu
94 F10 **Aursjøen** ◎ S Norway
94 I9 **Aursunden** ◎ S Norway
83 D21 **Aus** //Karas, SW Namibia *26°38′S 16°19′E*
**Ausa** *see* Vic
14 E16 **Ausable** ⁓ Ontario, S Canada
31 O3 **Au Sable Point** *headland* Michigan, N USA *46°40′N 86°08′W*
31 S7 **Au Sable Point** *headland* Michigan, N USA *44°19′N 83°20′W*
31 R6 **Au Sable River** ⁓ Michigan, N USA
57 H16 **Ausangate, Nevado** ▲ C Peru *13°47′S 71°13′W*
**Auschwitz** *see* Oświęcim
**Ausculum Apulum** *see* Ascoli Satriano
105 Q4 **Ausejo** La Rioja, N Spain *42°21′N 02°10′W*
108 H7 **Ausser Rhoden** ◐ *canton* NE Switzerland
**Aussig** *see* Ústí nad Labem
95 F17 **Aust-Agder** ◐ *county* S Norway
92 P2 **Austfonna** *glacier* NE Svalbard
31 P15 **Austin** Indiana, N USA *38°45′N 85°48′W*
29 W11 **Austin** Minnesota, N USA *43°40′N 92°58′W*
35 U5 **Austin** Nevada, W USA *39°30′N 117°05′W*
25 S10 **Austin** *state capital* Texas, SW USA *30°16′N 97°45′W*
180 J10 **Austin, Lake** *salt lake* Western Australia
31 V11 **Austintown** Ohio, N USA *41°06′N 80°45′W*
25 V9 **Austonio** Texas, SW USA *31°09′N 95°39′W*
**Australes, Archipel des** *see* Australes, Îles
**Australes et Antarctiques Françaises, Terres** *see* French Southern and Antarctic Lands
191 T14 **Australes, Îles** *var.* Archipel des Australes, Îles Tubuai, Tubuai Islands, *Eng.* Austral Islands. *island group* SW French Polynesia
175 Y11 **Austral Fracture Zone** *tectonic feature* S Pacific Ocean
174 M8 **Australia** *continent*
181 O7 **Australia** *off.* Commonwealth of Australia. ◆ *commonwealth republic*
**Australia, Commonwealth of** *see* Australia
183 Q12 **Australian Alps** ▲▲ SE Australia
183 R11 **Australian Capital Territory** *prev.* Federal Capital Territory. ◐ *territory* SE Australia
**Australie, Bassin Nord de l'** *see* North Australian Basin
**Austral Islands** *see* Australes, Îles
**Austrava** *see* Ostrov
109 T6 **Austria** *off.* Republic of Austria, *Ger.* Österreich. ◆ *republic* C Europe
**Austria, Republic of** *see* Austria
92 K3 **Austurland** ◐ *region* SE Iceland
92 G10 **Austvågøya** *island* C Norway
**Ausuitoq** *see* Grise Fiord
58 G13 **Autazes** Amazonas, N Brazil *03°37′S 59°08′W*
102 M16 **Auterive** Haute-Garonne, S France *43°22′N 01°28′E*
**Autesiodorum** *see* Auxerre
103 N2 **Authie** ⁓ N France
**Autissiodorum** *see* Auxerre
40 K14 **Autlán** *var.* Autlán de Navarro. Jalisco, SW Mexico *19°48′N 104°20′W*
**Autlán de Navarro** *see* Autlán
**Autricum** *see* Chartres
103 Q9 **Autun** *anc.* Ædua, Augustodunum. Saône-et-Loire, C France *46°58′N 04°18′E*
**Autz** *see* Auce
99 H20 **Auvelais** Namur, S Belgium *50°27′N 04°38′E*
103 R12 **Auvergne-Rhône-Alpes** ◐ *region* E France
102 M12 **Auvézère** ⁓ W France
103 P7 **Auxerre** *anc.* Autesiodorum, Autissiodorum. Yonne, C France *47°48′N 03°35′E*
103 N2 **Auxi-le-Château** Pas-de-Calais, N France *50°14′N 02°06′E*
103 S8 **Auxonne** Côte d'Or, C France *47°12′N 05°22′E*
55 P9 **Auyan Tebuy** ▲ SE Venezuela *05°48′N 62°27′W*
103 O10 **Auzances** Creuse, C France *46°01′N 02°29′E*
27 U8 **Ava** Missouri, C USA *36°57′N 92°39′W*
142 M5 **Āvaj** Qazvin, N Iran


220

◆ Country
● Country Capital
◇ Dependent Territory
○ Dependent Territory Capital
◐ Administrative Regions
✈ International Airport
▲ Mountain
▲▲ Mountain Range
Volcano
⁓ River
◎ Lake
▣ Reservoir

Avaldsnes – Bagherhat


95 C15 **Avaldsnes** Rogaland, S Norway *59°21′N 05°16′E*
103 Q8 **Avallon** Yonne, C France *47°30′N 03°54′E*
102 K6 **Avaloirs, Mont des** ▲ NW France *48°27′N 00°11′W*
35 S16 **Avalon** Santa Catalina Island, California, W USA *33°20′N 118°19′W*
18 J17 **Avalon** New Jersey, NE USA *39°04′N 74°42′W*
13 V13 **Avalon Peninsula** *peninsula* Newfoundland and Labrador, E Canada
197 O12 **Avannaata** ◈ *municipality* NW Greenland
60 K10 **Avaré** São Paulo, S Brazil *23°06′S 48°57′W*
**Avaricum** *see* Bourges
190 H16 **Avarua** ○ (Cook Islands) Rarotonga, S Cook Islands *21°12′S 159°46′E*
190 H16 **Avarua Harbour** *harbor* Rarotonga, S Cook Islands
**Avasfelsőfalu** *see* Negreşti-Oaş
38 L17 **Avatanak Island** *island* Aleutian Islands, Alaska, USA
190 B16 **Avatele** S Niue *19°06′S 169°55′E*
190 H15 **Avatiu Harbour** *harbor* Rarotonga, S Cook Islands
**Avdeyevka** *see* Avdiyivka
114 J13 **Ávdira** Anatolikí Makedonía kai Thráki, NE Greece *40°58′N 24°58′E*
117 X8 **Avdiyivka** *Rus.* Avdeyevka. Donets'ka Oblast', SE Ukraine *48°06′N 37°46′E*
**Avdzaga** *see* Gurvanbulag
104 G6 **Ave** ≈ N Portugal
104 G7 **Aveiro** *anc.* Talabriga. Aveiro, W Portugal *40°38′N 08°40′W*
104 G7 **Aveiro** ◈ *district* N Portugal
**Avela** *see* Ávila
99 D18 **Avelgem** West-Vlaanderen, W Belgium *50°46′N 03°25′E*
61 D20 **Avellaneda** Buenos Aires, E Argentina *34°43′S 58°23′W*
107 L17 **Avellino** *anc.* Abellinum. Campania, S Italy *40°54′N 14°46′E*
35 Q12 **Avenal** California, W USA *36°00′N 120°07′W*
**Avenio** *see* Avignon
94 E8 **Averøya** *island* S Norway
107 K17 **Aversa** Campania, S Italy *40°58′N 14°13′E*
33 N9 **Avery** Idaho, NW USA *47°14′N 115°48′W*
25 W5 **Avery** Texas, SW USA *33°33′N 94°46′W*
**Aves, Islas de** *see* Las Aves, Islas
**Avesnes** *see* Avesnes-sur-Helpe
103 Q2 **Avesnes-sur-Helpe** *var.* Avesnes. Nord, N France *50°08′N 03°57′E*
64 G12 **Aves Ridge** *undersea feature* SE Caribbean Sea *14°00′N 63°30′W*
95 M14 **Avesta** Dalarna, C Sweden *60°09′N 16°10′E*
103 O14 **Aveyron** ◈ *department* S France
103 N14 **Aveyron** ≈ S France
107 J15 **Avezzano** Abruzzo, C Italy *42°02′N 13°26′E*
115 D16 **Avgó** ▲ C Greece *39°31′N 21°24′E*
**Avgustov** *see* Augustów
**Avgustovskiy Kanal** *see* Augustowski, Kanał
96 J9 **Aviemore** N Scotland, United Kingdom *57°06′N 04°01′W*
185 F21 **Aviemore, Lake** ◎ South Island, New Zealand
103 R15 **Avignon** *anc.* Avenio. Vaucluse, SE France *43°57′N 04°49′E*
104 M7 **Ávila** *var.* Avila; *anc.* Abela, Abula, Abyla, Avela. Castilla y León, C Spain *40°39′N 04°42′W*
104 L8 **Ávila** ◈ *province* Castilla y León, C Spain
104 K2 **Avilés** Asturias, NW Spain *43°33′N 05°55′W*
118 J4 **Avinurme** *Ger.* Awwinorm. Ida-Virumaa, NE Estonia *58°58′N 26°53′E*
104 H10 **Avis** Portalegre, C Portugal *39°03′N 07°53′W*
**Avlum** *see* Aulum
182 M11 **Avoca** Victoria, SE Australia *37°09′S 143°34′E*
29 T14 **Avoca** Iowa, C USA *41°27′N 95°20′W*
182 M11 **Avoca River** ≈ Victoria, SE Australia
107 L25 **Avola** Sicilia, Italy, C Mediterranean Sea *36°54′N 15°08′E*
18 F10 **Avon** New York, NE USA *42°53′N 77°41′W*
29 P12 **Avon** South Dakota, N USA *43°00′N 98°03′W*
97 M23 **Avon** ≈ S England, United Kingdom
97 L20 **Avon** ≈ C England, United Kingdom
36 K13 **Avondale** Arizona, SW USA *33°25′N 112°20′W*
23 X13 **Avon Park** Florida, SE USA *27°36′N 81°30′W*
102 J5 **Avranches** Manche, N France *48°42′N 01°21′W*
**Avveel** *see* Ivalojoki, Finland
186 M6 **Avuavu** *var.* Kolotambu. Guadalcanal, C Solomon Islands *09°52′S 160°25′E*
103 O3 **Avure** ≈ N France
**Avveel** *see* Ivalo, Finland
**Avvil** *see* Ivalo
77 O17 **Awaaso** *var.* Awaso. SW Ghana *06°10′N 02°18′W*
141 X8 **Awābī** *var.* Al 'Awābī. NE Oman *23°20′N 57°35′E*
184 L9 **Awakino** Waikato, North Island, New Zealand *38°40′S 174°37′E*
142 M15 **'Awālī** C Bahrain *26°07′N 50°33′E*
99 K19 **Awans** Liège, E Belgium *50°39′N 05°30′E*
184 I2 **Awanui** Northland, North Island, New Zealand *35°01′S 173°16′E*
148 M14 **Awaran** Baluchistan, SW Pakistan *26°31′N 65°10′E*
81 K16 **Awara Plain** *plain* NE Kenya
80 M13 **Āwarē** Sumalē, E Ethiopia *08°12′N 44°09′E*
138 M6 **'Awāriḍ, Wādī** *dry watercourse* E Syria
185 B20 **Awarua Point** *headland* South Island, New Zealand *44°15′S 168°03′E*
81 J14 **Āwasa** Southern Nationalities, S Ethiopia *06°54′N 38°26′E*
80 K13 **Āwash** Āfar, NE Ethiopia *08°59′N 40°16′E*
80 K12 **Āwash** *var.* Hawash. ≈ C Ethiopia
**Awaso** *see* Awaaso
158 H7 **Awat** Xinjiang Uygur Zizhiqu, NW China *40°36′N 80°22′E*
185 J15 **Awatere** ≈ South Island, New Zealand
75 O10 **Awbārī** SW Libya *26°35′N 12°46′E*
75 N9 **Awbārī, Idhān** *var.* Edeyen d'Oubari. *desert* Algeria/Libya
80 M12 **Awdal** *off.* Gobolka Awdal. ◈ N Somalia
80 C13 **Aweil** Northern Bahr el Ghazal, NW South Sudan *08°42′N 27°20′E*
96 H11 **Awe, Loch** ◎ W Scotland, United Kingdom
77 U16 **Awka** Anambra, SW Nigeria *06°12′N 07°04′E*
39 O6 **Awuna River** ≈ Alaska, USA
**Awwinorm** *see* Avinurme
**Ax** *see* Dax
**Axarfjördhur** *see* Öxarfjörður
103 N17 **Axat** Aude, S France *42°47′N 02°14′E*
99 F16 **Axel** Zeeland, SW Netherlands *51°16′N 03°55′E*
197 P9 **Axel Heiberg Island** *var.* Axel Heiburg. *island* Nunavut, N Canada
**Axel Heiburg** *see* Axel Heiberg Island
77 O17 **Axim** S Ghana *04°53′N 02°14′W*
114 F13 **Axiós** *var.* Vardar. ≈ Greece/North Macedonia *see also* Vardar
**Axiós** *see* Vardar
103 N17 **Ax-les-Thermes** Ariège, S France *42°43′N 01°49′E*
120 D11 **Ayachi, Jbel** ▲ C Morocco *32°30′N 05°00′W*
61 D22 **Ayacucho** Buenos Aires, E Argentina *37°09′S 58°30′W*
57 F15 **Ayacucho** Ayacucho, S Peru *13°10′S 74°15′W*
57 E16 **Ayacucho** *off.* Región de Ayacucho. ◈ *region* SW Peru
**Ayacucho, Región de** *see* Ayacucho
145 W11 **Ayagoz** *var.* Ayaguz, *Kaz.* Ayaköz; *prev.* Sergiopol. Vostochnyy Kazakhstan, E Kazakhstan *47°54′N 80°25′E*
145 V12 **Ayagoz** *var.* Ayaguz, *Kaz.* Ayaköz. ≈ E Kazakhstan
**Ayaguz** *see* Ayagoz
**Ayakagytma** *see* Oyoqog'itma
**Ayakkuduk** *see* Oyoqquduq
158 L10 **Ayakkum Hu** ◎ NW China
**Ayaköz** *see* Ayagoz
104 H14 **Ayamonte** Andalucía, S Spain *37°13′N 07°24′W*
123 S11 **Ayan** Khabarovskiy Kray, E Russia *56°27′N 138°09′E*
136 J10 **Ayancık** Sinop, N Turkey *41°56′N 34°35′E*
55 S9 **Ayanganna Mountain** ▲ C Guyana *05°21′N 59°54′W*
77 U16 **Ayangba** Kogi, C Nigeria *07°36′N 07°10′E*
123 U7 **Ayanka** Krasnoyarskiy Kray, E Russia *63°42′N 167°31′E*
54 E7 **Ayapel** Córdoba, NW Colombia *08°16′N 75°10′W*
136 H12 **Ayaş** Ankara, N Turkey *40°02′N 32°21′E*
57 I16 **Ayaviri** Puno, S Peru *14°53′S 70°35′W*
**Āybak** *see* Aībak
147 N10 **Aydarkoʻl Koʻli** *Rus.* Ozero Aydarkul'. ◎ C Uzbekistan
**Aydarkul', Ozero** *see* Aydarkoʻl Koʻli
21 W10 **Ayden** North Carolina, SE USA *35°28′N 77°25′W*
136 C15 **Aydın** *var.* Aïdin; *anc.* Tralles Aydin. Aydın, SW Turkey *37°51′N 27°51′E*
136 C15 **Aydın** *var.* Aïdin. ◈ *province* SW Turkey
136 I17 **Aydıncık** İçel, S Turkey *36°08′N 33°17′E*
136 C15 **Aydın Dağları** ▲▲ W Turkey
158 L6 **Aydingkol Hu** ◎ NW China
127 X7 **Aydyrlinskiy** Orenburgskaya Oblast', W Russia *52°03′N 59°54′E*
105 S4 **Ayerbe** Aragón, NE Spain *42°16′N 00°41′W*
**Ayers Rock** *see* Uluṟu
166 K8 **Ayeyarwady** *var.* Ayeyawady, Irrawaddy. ◈ *region* SW Myanmar (Burma)
166 L6 **Ayeyarwady** *var.* Irrawaddy. ≈ W Myanmar (Burma)
166 K8 **Ayeyarwady, Mouths of the** *var.* Mouths of the Irrawaddy. *delta* SW Myanmar (Burma)
**Ayeyawady** *see* Ayeyarwady
**Ayiá** *see* Agiá
**Ayia Napa** *see* Agía Nápa
**Ayia Phyla** *see* Agía Fýlaxis
**Ayiássos/Ayiásos** *see* Agiasos
**Áyios Evstrátios** *see* Ágios Efstrátios
**Áyios Kírikos** *see* Ágios Kírykos
**Áyios Nikólaos** *see* Ágios Nikólaos
80 I11 **Āykel** Āmara, N Ethiopia *12°33′N 37°01′E*
123 N9 **Aykhal** Respublika Sakha (Yakutiya), NE Russia *66°07′N 110°25′E*
14 J12 **Aylen Lake** ◎ Ontario, SE Canada
97 N21 **Aylesbury** SE England, United Kingdom *51°50′N 00°50′W*
105 O6 **Ayllón** Castilla y León, N Spain *41°25′N 03°23′W*
14 F17 **Aylmer** Ontario, S Canada *42°46′N 80°57′W*
15 L12 **Aylmer** Québec, SE Canada *45°23′N 75°51′W*
15 R12 **Aylmer, Lac** ◎ Québec, SE Canada
8 L9 **Aylmer Lake** ◎ Northwest Territories, NW Canada
145 V14 **Aynabulak** *Kaz.* Aynabulaq. Almaty, SE Kazakhstan *44°37′N 77°59′E*
**Aynabulaq** *see* Aynabulak
138 K2 **'Ayn al 'Arab** *Kurd.* Kobanî, Kobanê. Ḥalab, N Syria *36°55′N 38°21′E*
**Aynayn** *see* 'Aynīn
139 V12 **'Ayn Ḥamūd** Dhī Qār, S Iraq *30°51′N 45°37′E*
147 P12 **Ayní** *prev.* Varzimanor Ayni. W Tajikistan *39°24′N 68°30′E*
140 M10 **'Aynīn** *var.* Aynayn. *spring/well* SW Saudi Arabia *20°52′N 41°41′E*
21 U12 **Aynor** South Carolina, SE USA *33°59′N 79°11′W*
139 Q7 **'Ayn Zāzūh** Al Anbār, C Iraq *33°29′N 42°34′E*
153 N12 **Ayodhya** Uttar Pradesh, N India *26°47′N 82°12′E*
123 S6 **Ayon, Ostrov** *island* NE Russia
105 R11 **Ayora** Comunitat Valenciana, E Spain *39°04′N 01°04′W*
77 Q11 **Ayorou** Tillabéri, W Niger *14°45′N 00°54′E*
79 E16 **Ayos** Centre, S Cameroon *03°53′N 12°31′E*
76 L5 **'Ayoûn 'Abd el Mâlek** *well* N Mauritania
76 K10 **'Ayoûn el 'Atroûs** *var.* Aïoun el Atrous, Aïoun el Atroûss. Hodh el Gharbi, SE Mauritania *16°38′N 09°36′W*
96 I13 **Ayr** W Scotland, United Kingdom *55°28′N 04°38′W*
96 I13 **Ayr** ≈ W Scotland, United Kingdom
96 I13 **Ayrshire** *cultural region* SW Scotland, United Kingdom
63 G20 **Aysén** *off.* Región Aysén del General Carlos Ibañez del Campo. ◈ *region* S Chile
80 L12 **Āysha** Sumalē, E Ethiopia *10°36′N 42°31′E*
144 L14 **Ayteke Bi** *Kaz.* Zhangaqazaly; *prev.* Novokazalinsk. Kzylorda, SW Kazakhstan *45°53′N 62°10′E*
146 K8 **Aytim** Navoiy Viloyati, N Uzbekistan *42°15′N 63°25′E*
181 W4 **Ayton** Queensland, NE Australia *15°54′S 145°19′E*
114 M9 **Aytos** Burgas, E Bulgaria *42°43′N 27°14′E*
171 T11 **Ayu, Kepulauan** *island group* E Indonesia
167 U12 **A Yun Pa** *prev.* Cheo Reo. Gia Lai, S Vietnam *13°19′N 108°27′E*
169 V11 **Ayu, Tanjung** *headland* Borneo, N Indonesia *0°25′N 117°34′E*
41 P16 **Ayutlá** *var.* Ayutla de los Libres. Guerrero, S Mexico *16°51′N 99°16′W*
40 K13 **Ayutla** Jalisco, C Mexico *20°07′N 104°18′W*
**Ayutla de los Libres** *see* Ayutlá
167 O11 **Ayutthaya** *var.* Phra Nakhon Si Ayutthaya. Phra Nakhon Si Ayutthaya, C Thailand *14°20′N 100°35′E*
136 B13 **Ayvacık** Çanakkale, W Turkey *39°18′N 26°42′E*
99 L20 **Aywaille** Liège, E Belgium *50°28′N 05°40′E*
141 R13 **'Aywat aş Şay'ar, Wādī** *seasonal river* N Yemen
**Azaffal** *see* Azeffâl
105 T9 **Azahar, Costa del** *coastal region* E Spain
105 S6 **Azaila** Aragón, NE Spain *41°17′N 00°20′W*
104 F10 **Azambuja** Lisboa, C Portugal *39°04′N 08°52′W*
153 N13 **Āzamgarh** Uttar Pradesh, N India *26°03′N 83°10′E*
77 O9 **Azaouâd** *desert* C Mali
77 S10 **Azaouagh, Vallée de l'** *var.* Azaouak. ≈ W Niger
**Azaouak** *see* Azaouagh, Vallée de l'
61 F14 **Azara** Misiones, NE Argentina *28°03′S 55°42′W*
**Azaran** *see* Hashtrūd
**Azärbaycan/Azärbaycan Respublikasi** *see* Azerbaijan
**Āzarbāyjān-e Bākhtarī** *see* Āzarbāyjān-e Gharbī
142 I4 **Āzarbāyjān-e Gharbī** *off.* Ostān-e Āzarbāyjān-e Gharbī, *Eng.* West Azerbaijan; *prev.* Āzarbāyjān-e Bākhtarī. ◈ *province* NW Iran
**Āzarbāyjān-e Gharbī, Ostān-e** *see* Āzarbāyjān-e Gharbī
**Āzarbāyjān-e Khāvarī** *see* Āzarbāyjān-e Sharqī
142 J3 **Āzarbāyjān-e Sharqī** *off.* Ostān-e Āzarbāyjān-e Sharqī, *Eng.* East Azerbaijan; *prev.* Āzarbāyjān-e Khāvarī. ◈ *province* NW Iran
**Āzarbāyjān-e Sharqī, Ostān-e** *see* Āzarbāyjān-e Sharqī
77 W13 **Azare** Bauchi, N Nigeria *11°41′N 10°09′E*
119 M19 **Azarychy** *Rus.* Ozarichi. Homyel'skaya Voblasts', SE Belarus *52°31′N 29°19′E*
145 P13 **Azat, Gory** *hill* C Kazakhstan
102 L8 **Azay-le-Rideau** Indre-et-Loire, C France *47°16′N 00°25′E*
76 H7 **Azeffâl** *var.* Azaffal. *desert* Mauritania/Western Sahara
137 V12 **Azerbaijan** *off.* Republic of Azerbaijan, *Az.* Azärbaycan, Azärbaycan Respublikasi; *prev.* Azerbaijan SSR. ◆ *republic* SE Asia
**Azerbaijan, Republic of** *see* Azerbaijan
**Azerbaijan SSR** *see* Azerbaijan
74 F7 **Azilal** C Morocco *31°58′N 06°53′W*
**Azimabad** *see* Patna
19 O6 **Aziscohos Lake** ⊠ Maine, NE USA
**Azizbekov** *see* Vayk'
**Azizie** *see* Telish
**Aziziya** *see* Al 'Azīzīyah
127 T4 **Aznakayevo** Respublika Tatarstan, W Russia *54°55′N 53°15′E*
56 C8 **Azogues** Cañar, S Ecuador *02°44′S 78°48′W*
64 N2 **Azores** *Port.* Região Autónoma dos Açores. ◈ *autonomous region* Azores, W Portugal Europe
64 N2 **Azores** *var.* Açores, Ilhas dos Açores, *Port.* Arquipélago dos Açores. *island group* Portugal, NE Atlantic Ocean
64 L8 **Azores-Biscay Rise** *undersea feature* E Atlantic Ocean *19°00′W 42°40′N*
**Azotos/Azotus** *see* Ashdod
78 K11 **Azoum, Bahr** *seasonal river* SE Chad
126 L12 **Azov** Rostovskaya Oblast', SW Russia *47°07′N 39°26′E*
126 J13 **Azov, Sea of** *Rus.* Azovskoye More, *Ukr.* Azovs'ke More. *sea* NE Black Sea
**Azovs'ke More/Azovskoye More** *see* Azov, Sea of
138 I10 **Azraq, Wāḥat al** *oasis* N Jordan
**Āzro** *see* Ḥukūmatī Azrah
74 G6 **Azrou** C Morocco *33°30′N 05°12′W*
**Āzrow** *see* Ḥukūmatī Azrah
37 P8 **Aztec** New Mexico, SW USA *36°49′N 107°59′W*
36 M13 **Aztec Peak** ▲ Arizona, SW USA *33°48′N 110°54′W*
45 N9 **Azua** *var.* Azua de Compostela. S Dominican Republic *18°29′N 70°44′W*
**Azua de Compostela** *see* Azua
104 K12 **Azuaga** Extremadura, W Spain *38°16′N 05°40′W*
56 B8 **Azuay** ◈ *province* W Ecuador
164 C13 **Azuchi-Ō-shima** *island* SW Japan
105 O11 **Azuer** ≈ C Spain
43 S17 **Azuero, Península de** *peninsula* S Panama
62 I6 **Azufre, Volcán** *var.* Volcán Lastarria. ⛰ N Chile *25°16′S 68°35′W*
116 J12 **Azuga** Prahova, SE Romania *45°27′N 25°34′E*
61 C22 **Azul** Buenos Aires, E Argentina *36°46′S 59°50′W*
62 I8 **Azul, Cerro** ▲ NW Argentina *28°28′S 68°43′W*
56 E12 **Azul, Cordillera** ▲▲ C Peru
165 P11 **Azuma-san** ▲ Honshū, C Japan *37°44′N 140°05′E*
103 V15 **Azur, Côte d'** *coastal region* SE France
191 Z3 **Azur Lagoon** ◎ Kiritimati, E Kiribati
**'Azza** *see* Gaza
**Az Zāb al Kabīr** *see* Great Zab
138 H7 **Az Zabdānī** *var.* Zabadani. Rīf Dimashq, W Syria *33°45′N 36°07′E*
141 W8 **Aẓ Ẓāhirah** *desert* NW Oman
141 S6 **Aẓ Ẓahrān** *Eng.* Dhahran. Ash Sharqīyah, NE Saudi Arabia *26°18′N 50°02′E*
141 R6 **Aẓ Ẓahrān al Khubar** *var.* Dhahran Al Khobar. ✈ Ash Sharqīyah, NE Saudi Arabia *26°28′N 49°42′E*
75 W7 **Az Zaqāzīq** *var.* Zagazig. N Egypt *30°36′N 31°32′E*
138 H10 **Az Zarqā'** *var.* Zarqa. Az Zarqā', NW Jordan *32°04′N 36°06′E*
138 I11 **Az Zarqā'** *off.* Muḥāfaẓat az Zarqā', *var.* Zarqa. ◈ *governorate* N Jordan
75 O7 **Az Zāwiyah** *var.* Zawia. NW Libya *32°45′N 12°44′E*
141 N15 **Az Zaydīyah** W Yemen *15°20′N 43°03′E*
74 I11 **Azzel Matti, Sebkha** *var.* Sebkha Azz el Matti. *salt flat* C Algeria
141 P6 **Az Zilfī** Ar Riyāḍ, N Saudi Arabia *26°17′N 44°48′E*
139 Y13 **Az Zubayr** *var.* Al Zubair. Al Baṣrah, SE Iraq *30°24′N 47°45′E*
**Az Zuqur** *see* Jabal Zuqar, Jazirat


# B


187 X15 **Ba** *prev.* Mba. Viti Levu, W Fiji *17°35′S 177°40′E*
**Ba** *see* Da Răng, Sông
171 P17 **Baa** Pulau Rote, C Indonesia *10°44′S 123°06′E*
138 H7 **Baalbek** *var.* Ba'labakk; *anc.* Heliopolis. E Lebanon *34°00′N 36°15′E*
108 G8 **Baar** Zug, N Switzerland *47°12′N 08°32′E*
81 L17 **Baardheere** *var.* Bardere, *It.* Bardera. Gedo, SW Somalia *02°13′N 42°19′E*
**Baargaal** *see* Bargaal
99 I15 **Baarle-Hertog** Antwerpen, N Belgium *51°26′N 04°56′E*
99 I15 **Baarle-Nassau** Noord-Brabant, S Netherlands *51°27′N 04°56′E*
98 J11 **Baarn** Utrecht, C Netherlands *52°13′N 05°16′E*
162 H9 **Baatsagaan** *var.* Bayansayr. Bayanhongor, C Mongolia *45°36′N 99°27′E*
114 D13 **Baba** *var.* Buševa, *Gk.* Varnoús. ▲▲ North Macedonia/Greece
76 H10 **Bababé** Brakna, W Mauritania *16°22′N 13°57′W*
117 N13 **Babadag** Tulcea, SE Romania *44°53′N 28°47′E*
137 X10 **Babadağ** ▲ NE Azerbaijan *41°02′N 48°04′E*
146 H14 **Babadayhan** *Rus.* Babadaykhan; *prev.* Kirovsk. Ahal Welaýaty, C Turkmenistan *37°39′N 60°17′E*
**Babadaykhan** *see* Babadayhan
146 G14 **Babadurmaz** Ahal Welaýaty, C Turkmenistan *37°39′N 59°03′E*
114 M12 **Babaeski** Kırklareli, NW Turkey *41°26′N 27°06′E*
139 T4 **Bāba Gurgur** Kirkūk, N Iraq *35°34′N 44°18′E*
56 B7 **Babahoyo** *prev.* Bodegas. Los Ríos, C Ecuador *01°53′S 79°31′W*
149 P5 **Bābā, Kōh-e** ▲▲ C Afghanistan
171 N12 **Babana** Sulawesi, C Indonesia *02°03′S 119°13′E*
**Babao** *see* Qilian
171 Q12 **Babar, Kepulauan** *island group* E Indonesia
171 T12 **Babar, Pulau** *island* Kepulauan Babar, E Indonesia
**Bābāsar Pass** *see* Babusar Pass
**Babashy, Gory** *see* Babaşy
146 C9 **Babaşy** *Rus.* Gory Babashy. ▲ W Turkmenistan
168 M13 **Babat** Sumatera, W Indonesia *02°45′S 104°01′E*
**Babatag, Khrebet** *see* Bototog', Tizmasi
81 H21 **Babati** Manyara, NE Tanzania *04°12′S 35°45′E*
124 J13 **Babayevo** Vologodskaya Oblast', NW Russia *59°23′N 35°52′E*
127 Q15 **Babayurt** Respublika Dagestan, SW Russia *43°38′N 46°49′E*
33 P6 **Babb** Montana, NW USA *48°51′N 113°26′W*
29 X4 **Babbitt** Minnesota, N USA *47°42′N 91°56′W*
188 E9 **Babeldaob** *var.* Babeldaop, Babelthuap. *island* N Palau
**Babeldaop** *see* Babeldaob
141 N17 **Bab el Mandeb** *strait* Gulf of Aden/Red Sea
**Babelthuap** *see* Babeldaob
111 K17 **Babia Góra** *var.* Babia Hora. ▲ Poland/Slovakia *49°33′N 19°32′E*
**Babia Hora** *see* Babia Góra
**Babian Jiang** *see* Black River
**Babichi** *see* Babichy
119 N19 **Babichy** *Rus.* Babichi. Homyel'skaya Voblasts', SE Belarus *52°17′N 30°00′E*
139 U9 **Bābil** *off.* Muḥāfaẓat al Bābil, *var.* Babylon, Al Ḥillah. ◈ *governorate* S Iraq
**Bābil, Muḥāfaẓat at at** *see* Bābil
112 I10 **Babina Greda** Vukovar-Srijem, E Croatia *45°09′N 18°33′E*
10 K13 **Babine Lake** ◎ British Columbia, SW Canada
143 O4 **Bābol** *var.* Babul, Balfrush, Barfrush; *prev.* Barfurush. Māzandarān, N Iran *36°34′N 52°39′E*
143 O4 **Bābolsar** *var.* Babulsar; *prev.* Meshed-i-Sar. Māzandarān, N Iran *36°41′N 52°39′E*
36 L16 **Baboquivari Peak** ▲ Arizona, SW USA *31°46′N 111°36′W*
79 G15 **Baboua** Nana-Mambéré, W Central African Republic *05°46′N 14°47′E*
119 M17 **Babruysk** *Rus.* Bobruysk. Mahilyowskaya Voblasts', E Belarus *53°07′N 29°13′E*
**Babu** *see* Hezhou
**Babul** *see* Bābol
**Babulsar** *see* Bābolsar
113 O19 **Babuna** ▲▲ C North Macedonia
113 O19 **Babuna** ≈ C North Macedonia
152 G4 **Babusar Pass** *prev.* Bābāsar Pass. *pass* India/Pakistan
148 K7 **Bābūs, Dasht-e** *Pash.* Bebas, Dasht-i. ▲ W Afghanistan
171 O1 **Babuyan Channel** *channel* N Philippines
171 O1 **Babuyan Islands** *island* N Philippines
139 T9 **Babylon** *site of ancient city* C Iraq
**Babylon** *see* Bābil
112 J9 **Bač** *Ger.* Batsch. Vojvodina, NW Serbia *45°24′N 19°17′E*
58 M13 **Bacabal** Maranhão, E Brazil *04°15′S 44°45′W*
41 Y14 **Bacalar** Quintana Roo, SE Mexico *18°38′N 88°17′W*
41 Y14 **Bacalar Chico, Boca** *strait* SE Mexico
171 Q12 **Bacan, Kepulauan** *island group* E Indonesia
171 S12 **Bacan, Pulau** *prev.* Batjan. *island* Maluku, E Indonesia
116 L10 **Bacău** *Hung.* Bákó. Bacău, NE Romania *46°36′N 26°56′E*
116 K11 **Bacău** ◈ *county* E Romania
**Băc Bô, Vinh** *see* Tonkin, Gulf of
167 T5 **Băc Can** *var.* Bach Thong. Băc Thai, N Vietnam *22°07′N 105°50′E*
103 T5 **Baccarat** Meurthe-et-Moselle, NE France *48°27′N 06°46′E*
183 N12 **Bacchus Marsh** Victoria, SE Australia *37°41′S 144°30′E*
40 H4 **Bacerac** Sonora, NW Mexico *30°27′N 108°55′W*
116 L10 **Băceşti** Vaslui, E Romania *46°50′N 27°14′E*
167 T6 **Băc Giang** Ha Băc, N Vietnam *21°17′N 106°12′E*
54 I5 **Bachaquero** Zulia, NW Venezuela *09°57′N 71°09′W*
**Bacher** *see* Pohorje
118 M13 **Bacheykava** *Rus.* Bocheykovo. Vitsyebskaya Voblasts', N Belarus *55°01′N 29°09′E*
40 I5 **Bachíniva** Chihuahua, N Mexico *28°41′N 107°13′W*
**Bạch Quy, Đảo** *see* Passu Keah
**Bach Thong** *see* Băc Can
158 G8 **Bachu** Xinjiang Uygur Zizhiqu, NW China *39°46′N 78°30′E*
9 N8 **Back** ≈ Nunavut, N Canada
112 K10 **Bačka Palanka** *prev.* Palanka. Serbia, NW Serbia *44°22′N 20°57′E*
112 K8 **Bačka Topola** *Hung.* Topolya; *prev. Hung.* Bácstopolya. Vojvodina, N Serbia *45°48′N 19°39′E*
95 J17 **Bäckefors** Västra Götaland, S Sweden *58°49′N 12°07′E*
**Bäckermühle Schulzenmühle** *see* Żywiec
95 L16 **Bäckhammar** Värmland, C Sweden *59°09′N 14°13′E*
112 K9 **Bački Petrovac** *Hung.* Petrőcz; *prev.* Petrovac, Petrovácz. Vojvodina, NW Serbia *45°22′N 19°34′E*
101 I21 **Backnang** Baden-Württemberg, SW Germany *48°57′N 09°26′E*
167 S15 **Bac Liêu** *var.* Vinh Loi. Minh Hai, S Vietnam *09°17′N 105°44′E*
167 T6 **Băc Ninh** Ha Băc, N Vietnam *21°10′N 106°04′E*
40 G4 **Bacoachi** Sonora, NW Mexico *30°36′N 110°00′W*
171 P6 **Bacolod** *off.* Bacolod City. Negros, C Philippines *10°43′N 122°58′E*
**Bacolod City** *see* Bacolod
171 O4 **Baco, Mount** ▲ Mindoro, N Philippines *12°50′N 121°08′E*
111 K25 **Bácsalmás** Bács-Kiskun, S Hungary *46°07′N 19°20′E*
**Bácsjózseffalva** *see* Žednik
111 J24 **Bács-Kiskun** *off.* Bács-Kiskun Megye. ◈ *county* S Hungary
**Bács-Kiskun Megye** *see* Bács-Kiskun
**Bácsszenttamás** *see* Srbobran
**Bácstopolya** *see* Bačka Topola
**Bactra** *see* Balkh
**Bada** *see* Xilin
**Badagara** *see* Vadakara
101 M24 **Bad Aibling** Bayern, SE Germany *47°52′N 12°00′E*
162 I13 **Badain Jaran Shamo** *desert* N China
104 I11 **Badajoz** *anc.* Pax Augusta. Extremadura, W Spain *38°53′N 06°58′W*
104 J11 **Badajoz** ◈ *province* Extremadura, W Spain
149 S2 **Badakhshān** ◈ *province* NE Afghanistan
105 W6 **Badalona** *anc.* Baetulo. Cataluña, E Spain *41°27′N 02°15′E*
154 O11 **Bādāmpāhārh** *var.* Bādāmapāhārh. Odisha, E India *22°04′N 86°06′E*
169 O10 **Badas, Kepulauan** *island group* W Indonesia
109 S6 **Bad Aussee** Salzburg, E Austria *47°35′N 13°44′E*
31 S8 **Bad Axe** Michigan, N USA *43°48′N 83°00′W*
101 G16 **Bad Berleburg** Nordrhein-Westfalen, W Germany *51°03′N 08°24′E*
101 L17 **Bad Blankenburg** Thüringen, C Germany *50°43′N 11°19′E*
**Bad Borseck** *see* Borsec
101 G18 **Bad Camberg** Hessen, W Germany *50°18′N 08°15′E*
100 L8 **Bad Doberan** Mecklenburg-Vorpommern, N Germany *54°06′N 11°55′E*
101 N14 **Bad Düben** Sachsen, E Germany *51°35′N 12°34′E*
109 X4 **Baden** *var.* Baden bei Wien; *anc.* Aquae Panoniae, Thermae Pannonicae. Niederösterreich, NE Austria *48°01′N 16°14′E*
108 F9 **Baden** Aargau, N Switzerland *47°28′N 08°19′E*
101 G21 **Baden-Baden** *anc.* Aurelia Aquensis. Baden-Württemberg, SW Germany *48°46′N 08°14′E*
**Baden bei Wien** *see* Baden
101 G22 **Baden-Württemberg** *Fr.* Bade-Wurtemberg. ◈ *state* SW Germany
112 A10 **Baderna** Istra, NW Croatia *45°12′N 13°45′E*
**Bade-Wurtemberg** *see* Baden-Württemberg
101 H20 **Bad Fredrichshall** Baden-Württemberg, S Germany *49°13′N 09°15′E*
100 P11 **Bad Freienwalde** Brandenburg, NE Germany *52°47′N 14°04′E*
109 Q8 **Badgastein** *var.* Gastein. Salzburg, NW Austria *47°07′N 13°09′E*
**Badger State** *see* Wisconsin
148 L4 **Bādghīs** ◈ *province* NW Afghanistan
109 T5 **Bad Hall** Oberösterreich, N Austria *48°03′N 14°13′E*
101 J14 **Bad Harzburg** Niedersachsen, C Germany *51°52′N 10°34′E*
101 I16 **Bad Hersfeld** Hessen, C Germany *50°52′N 09°42′E*
98 I10 **Badhoevedorp** Noord-Holland, C Netherlands *52°21′N 04°46′E*
109 Q8 **Bad Hofgastein** Salzburg, NW Austria *47°11′N 13°07′E*
**Bad Homburg** *see* Bad Homburg vor der Höhe
101 G18 **Bad Homburg vor der Höhe** *var.* Bad Homburg. Hessen, W Germany *50°14′N 08°37′E*
101 E17 **Bad Honnef** Nordrhein-Westfalen, W Germany *50°39′N 07°13′E*
149 Q17 **Badin** Sindh, SE Pakistan *24°38′N 68°53′E*
21 S10 **Badin Lake** ⊠ North Carolina, SE USA
40 I8 **Badiraguato** Sinaloa, C Mexico *25°21′N 107°31′W*
109 R6 **Bad Ischl** Oberösterreich, N Austria *47°43′N 13°36′E*
**Badjawa** *see* Bajawa
**Badje-Sohppar** *see* Övre Soppero
101 J18 **Bad Kissingen** Bayern, SE Germany *50°12′N 10°04′E*
**Bad Königswart** *see* Lázně Kynžvart
101 F19 **Bad Kreuznach** Rheinland-Pfalz, SW Germany *49°51′N 07°52′E*
101 F24 **Bad Krozingen** Baden-Württemberg, SW Germany *47°55′N 07°43′E*
101 G16 **Bad Laasphe** Nordrhein-Westfalen, W Germany *50°57′N 08°24′E*
28 J6 **Badlands** *physical region* North Dakota/South Dakota, N USA
101 K16 **Bad Langensalza** Thüringen, C Germany *51°05′N 10°40′E*
109 T3 **Bad Leonfelden** Oberösterreich, N Austria *48°31′N 14°17′E*
101 I20 **Bad Mergentheim** Baden-Württemberg, SW Germany *49°30′N 09°46′E*
101 H17 **Bad Nauheim** Hessen, W Germany *50°22′N 08°45′E*
101 E17 **Bad Neuenahr-Ahrweiler** Rheinland-Pfalz, W Germany *50°33′N 07°07′E*
**Bad Neustadt** *see* Bad Neustadt an der Saale
101 J18 **Bad Neustadt an der Saale** *var.* Bad Neustadt. Bayern, C Germany *50°21′N 10°13′E*
**Badnur** *see* Betūl
100 H13 **Bad Oeynhausen** Nordrhein-Westfalen, NW Germany *52°12′N 08°48′E*
100 J9 **Bad Oldesloe** Schleswig-Holstein, N Germany *53°49′N 10°22′E*
77 Q16 **Badou** C Togo *07°37′N 00°37′E*
**Bad Polzin** *see* Połczyn-Zdrój
100 H13 **Bad Pyrmont** Niedersachsen, C Germany *51°58′N 09°16′E*
109 X9 **Bad Radkersburg** Steiermark, SE Austria *46°40′N 16°02′E*
139 V8 **Badrah** Wāsiţ, E Iraq *33°06′N 45°58′E*
**Badrah** *see* Tarialan
101 N24 **Bad Reichenhall** Bayern, SE Germany *47°43′N 12°52′E*
140 K8 **Badr Ḥunayn** Al Madīnah al Munawwarah, W Saudi Arabia *23°46′N 38°45′E*
152 K8 **Badrīnāth** ▲ N India *30°44′N 79°29′E*
28 M10 **Bad River** ≈ South Dakota, N USA
30 K4 **Bad River** ≈ Wisconsin, N USA
100 H13 **Bad Salzuflen** Nordrhein-Westfalen, NW Germany *52°06′N 08°45′E*
101 J16 **Bad Salzungen** Thüringen, C Germany *50°48′N 10°15′E*
109 V8 **Bad Sankt Leonhard im Lavanttal** Kärnten, S Austria *46°55′N 14°51′E*
100 K9 **Bad Schwartau** Schleswig-Holstein, N Germany *53°55′N 10°42′E*
101 L24 **Bad Tölz** Bayern, SE Germany *47°44′N 11°34′E*
181 U1 **Badu Island** *island* Queensland, NE Australia
155 K25 **Badulla** Uva Province, C Sri Lanka *06°59′N 81°03′E*
109 X5 **Bad Vöslau** Niederösterreich, NE Austria *47°58′N 16°13′E*
101 I24 **Bad Waldsee** Baden-Württemberg, S Germany *47°54′N 09°44′E*
35 U11 **Badwater Basin** *depression* California, W USA
101 J20 **Bad Windsheim** Bayern, C Germany *49°30′N 10°25′E*
101 J23 **Bad Wörishofen** Bayern, S Germany *48°00′N 10°36′E*
100 G10 **Bad Zwischenahn** Niedersachsen, NW Germany *53°10′N 08°01′E*
104 M13 **Baena** Andalucía, S Spain *36°37′N 04°20′W*
163 V15 **Baengnyong-do** *prev.* Paengnyŏng. *island* NW South Korea
**Baeterrae/Baeterrae Septimanorum** *see* Béziers
**Baetic Cordillera/Baetic Mountains** *see* Béticos, Sistemas
**Baetulo** *see* Badalona
57 K18 **Baeza** Napo, NE Ecuador *0°30′S 77°52′W*
105 N13 **Baeza** Andalucía, S Spain *38°00′N 03°28′W*
79 D15 **Bafang** Ouest, W Cameroon *05°10′N 10°11′E*
76 H12 **Bafatá** C Guinea-Bissau *12°09′N 14°38′W*
149 U5 **Baffa** Khyber Pakhtunkhwa, NW Pakistan *34°30′N 73°18′E*
197 O11 **Baffin Basin** *undersea feature* N Labrador Sea
197 N12 **Baffin Bay** *bay* Canada/Greenland
25 T15 **Baffin Bay** *inlet* Texas, SW USA
196 M12 **Baffin Island** *island* Nunavut, NE Canada
79 E15 **Bafia** Centre, C Cameroon *04°49′N 11°14′E*
77 R14 **Bafilo** NE Togo *09°23′N 01°20′E*
76 J12 **Bafing** ≈ W Africa
76 J12 **Bafoulabé** Kayes, W Mali *13°43′N 10°49′W*
79 D15 **Bafoussam** Ouest, W Cameroon *05°31′N 10°25′E*
143 R9 **Bāfq** Yazd, C Iran *31°35′N 55°21′E*
136 L10 **Bafra** Samsun, N Turkey *41°34′N 35°56′E*
136 L10 **Bafra Burnu** *headland* N Turkey *41°42′N 36°02′E*
143 S12 **Bāft** Kermān, S Iran *29°12′N 56°36′E*
79 N18 **Bafwabalinga** Orientale, NE Dem. Rep. Congo *0°52′N 26°55′E*
79 N18 **Bafwaboli** Orientale, NE Dem. Rep. Congo *0°36′N 26°08′E*
79 N17 **Bafwasende** Orientale, NE Dem. Rep. Congo *01°00′N 27°09′E*
42 K13 **Bagaces** Guanacaste, NW Costa Rica *10°31′N 85°18′W*
153 O12 **Bagaha** Bihār, N India *27°08′N 84°04′E*
155 F16 **Bāgalkot** Karnātaka, W India *16°11′N 75°42′E*
81 J22 **Bagamoyo** Pwani, E Tanzania *06°26′S 38°55′E*
**Bagan Datok** *see* Bagan Datuk
168 J8 **Bagan Datuk** *var.* Bagan Datok. Perak, Peninsular Malaysia *03°58′N 100°47′E*
171 R7 **Baganga** Mindanao, S Philippines *07°31′N 126°34′E*
168 J9 **Bagansiapiapi** *var.* Pasirpangarayan. Sumatera, W Indonesia *02°06′N 100°52′E*
162 M8 **Baganuur** *var.* Nüürst. Töv, C Mongolia *47°44′N 108°22′E*
**Bagaria** *see* Bagheria
77 T11 **Bagaroua** Tahoua, W Niger *14°34′N 04°24′E*
79 I20 **Bagata** Bandundu, W Dem. Rep. Congo *03°47′S 17°57′E*
**Bagdad** *see* Baghdad
123 O13 **Bagdarin** Respublika Buryatiya, S Russia *54°27′N 113°34′E*
61 G17 **Bagé** Rio Grande do Sul, S Brazil *31°22′S 54°06′W*
**Bagenalstown** *see* Muine Bheag
153 T16 **Bagerhat** *var.* Bagherhat. Khulna, S Bangladesh *22°40′N 89°48′E*
103 P16 **Bages et de Sigean, Étang de** ◎ S France
33 W17 **Baggs** Wyoming, C USA *41°02′N 107°39′W*
154 F11 **Bāgh** Madhya Pradesh, C India *22°22′N 74°49′E*
139 T8 **Baghdād** *var.* Bagdad, *Eng.* Baghdad. ● Baghdād, C Iraq *33°20′N 44°26′E*
139 T8 **Baghdād** *off.* Muḥāfaẓat Baghdād, *var.* Amānat al 'Āşimah. ◈ *governorate* C Iraq
139 T8 **Baghdād** ✈ (Baghdād) Baghdād, C Iraq *33°20′N 44°26′E*
**Baghdad** *see* Baghdād
**Baghdād, Muḥāfaẓat at** *see* Baghdād
**Bagherhat** *see* Bagerhat


◆ Country ● Country Capital ◇ Dependent Territory ○ Dependent Territory Capital ◈ Administrative Regions ✈ International Airport ▲ Mountain ▲▲ Mountain Range ⛰ Volcano ≈ River ◎ Lake ⊠ Reservoir

BAGHERIA – BANDA ATJEH


107 J23 **Bagheria** var. Bagaria. Sicilia, Italy, C Mediterranean Sea 38°05′N 13°31′E
143 S10 **Bāghīn** Kermān, C Iran 30°50′N 57°00′E
149 Q3 **Baghlān** Baghlān, NE Afghanistan 36°11′N 68°44′E
149 Q3 **Baghlān** var. Bāghlān. ◆ province NE Afghanistan
**Bāghlān** see Baghlān
148 M7 **Bāghrān** Helmand, S Afghanistan 32°55′N 64°57′E
29 T4 **Bagley** Minnesota, N USA 47°31′N 95°24′W
106 H10 **Bagnacavallo** Emilia-Romagna, C Italy 44°00′N 12°59′E
102 K16 **Bagnères-de-Bigorre** Hautes-Pyrénées, S France 43°04′N 00°09′E
102 L17 **Bagnères-de-Luchon** Hautes-Pyrénées, S France 42°46′N 00°34′E
106 F11 **Bagni di Lucca** Toscana, C Italy 44°01′N 10°38′E
106 H11 **Bagno di Romagna** Emilia-Romagna, C Italy 43°51′N 11°57′E
103 R14 **Bagnols-sur-Cèze** Gard, S France 44°10′N 04°37′E
162 M14 **Bag Nur** ◎ N China
166 L8 **Bago** var. Pegu. Bago, SW Myanmar (Burma) 17°18′N 96°31′E
171 P6 **Bago** off. Bago City. Negros, C Philippines 10°30′N 122°49′E
166 L7 **Bago** var. Pegu. ◆ region S Myanmar (Burma)
**Bago City** see Bago
76 M13 **Bagoé** ~ Ivory Coast/Mali
**Bagrāmē** see Bagrāmī
149 R5 **Bagrāmī** var. Bagrāmē. Kābōl, E Afghanistan 34°29′N 69°16′E
119 B14 **Bagrationovsk** Ger. Preussisch Eylau. Kaliningradskaya Oblast', W Russia 54°24′N 20°39′E
**Bagrax** see Bohu
**Bagrax Hu** see Bosten Hu
56 C10 **Bagua** Amazonas, NE Peru 05°37′S 78°36′W
171 O2 **Baguio** off. Baguio City. Luzon, N Philippines 16°25′N 120°36′E
**Baguio City** see Baguio
77 V9 **Bagzane, Monts** ▲ N Niger 17°48′N 08°43′E
**Bāḥah, Minṭaqat al** see Al Bāḥah
**Bahama Islands** see Bahamas, The
**Bahamas** see Bahamas, The
**Bahamas, Commonwealth of The** see Bahamas, The
0 L13 **Bahamas, The** var. Bahama Islands, Bahamas. ◆ island group N West Indies
44 H3 **Bahamas, The** off. Commonwealth of The Bahamas. ◆ commonwealth republic N West Indies
153 S15 **Baharampur** prev. Berhampore. West Bengal, NE India 24°06′N 88°19′E
146 E12 **Baharly** var. Bäherden, Rus. Bakharden; prev. Bakherden. Ahal Welaýaty, C Turkmenistan 38°30′N 57°18′E
149 U10 **Bahawalnagar** Punjab, E Pakistan 30°00′N 73°03′E
149 T11 **Bahawalpur** Punjab, E Pakistan 29°25′N 71°40′E
136 L16 **Bahçe** Osmaniye, S Turkey 37°14′N 36°34′E
160 J8 **Ba He** ~ C China
**Bäherden** see Baharly
59 N16 **Bahia** off. Estado da Bahia. ◆ state E Brazil
61 B24 **Bahía Blanca** Buenos Aires, E Argentina 38°43′S 62°19′W
40 L15 **Bahía Bufadero** Michoacán, SW Mexico
63 J19 **Bahía Bustamante** Chubut, SE Argentina 45°06′S 66°30′W
40 D5 **Bahía de los Ángeles** Baja California, NW Mexico
40 C6 **Bahía de Tortugas** Baja California Sur, NW Mexico 27°42′N 114°54′W
**Bahia, Estado da** see Bahia
42 J4 **Bahía, Islas de la** Eng. Bay Islands. island group N Honduras
40 E5 **Bahía Kino** Sonora, NW Mexico 28°48′N 111°55′W
40 E9 **Bahía Magdalena** var. Puerto Magdalena. Baja California Sur, NW Mexico 24°34′N 112°07′W
54 C8 **Bahía Solano** var. Ciudad Mutis, Solano. Chocó, W Colombia 06°13′N 77°27′W
80 I11 **Bahir Dar** var. Bahr Dar, Bahrdar Giyorgis. Āmara, N Ethiopia 11°34′N 37°23′E
141 X8 **Bahlā'** var. Bahlah, Bahlat. NW Oman 22°58′N 57°16′E
**Bāhla** see Bālān
**Bahlah/Bahlat** see Bahlā'
152 M11 **Bahraich** Uttar Pradesh, N India 27°35′N 81°36′E
143 M14 **Bahrain** off. Kingdom of Bahrain, Ar. Al Baḥrayn, Mamlakat al Baḥrayn, prev. Bahrein; anc. Tylos, Tyros. ◆ monarchy SW Asia
142 M14 **Bahrain** ✈ C Bahrain 26°15′N 50°39′E
142 M15 **Bahrain, Gulf of** gulf Persian Gulf, NW Arabian Sea
**Bahrain, Kingdom of** see Bahrain
138 I7 **Baḥrat Mallāḥah** ◎ W Syria
**Baḥrayn, Mamlakat al** see Bahrain
**Bahr Dar/Bahrdar Giyorgis** see Bahir Dar
**Bahrein** see Bahrain
**Bahr el, Azraq** see Blue Nile
**Bahr el Gebel** see Central Equatoria
**Bahr el Jebel** see Central Equatoria
80 E13 **Bahr ez Zaref** ~ Jonglei, E South Sudan
67 R8 **Bahr Kameur** ~ N Central African Republic
**Bahr Tabariya, Sea of** see Kinneret, Yam
143 W15 **Bāhū Kalāt** Sīstān va Balūchestān, SE Iran 25°42′N 61°28′E
118 N13 **Bahushewsk** Rus. Bogushëvsk. Vitsyebskaya Voblasts', NE Belarus 54°51′N 30°13′E
**Bai** see Tagāw-Bāy
116 G13 **Baia de Aramă** Mehedinți, SW Romania 45°00′N 22°43′E
116 G11 **Baia de Criș** Ger. Altenburg, Hung. Körösbánya. Hunedoara, SW Romania 46°10′N 22°41′E
83 A16 **Baia dos Tigres** Namibe, SW Angola 16°36′S 11°44′E
82 A13 **Baia Farta** Benguela, W Angola 12°38′S 13°12′E
116 H9 **Baia Mare** Ger. Frauenbach, Hung. Nagybánya; prev. Neustadt. Maramureș, NW Romania 47°40′N 23°35′E
116 H8 **Baia Sprie** Ger. Mittelstadt, Hung. Felsőbánya. Maramureș, NW Romania 47°40′N 23°42′E
78 G13 **Baïbokoum** Logone-Oriental, SW Chad 07°46′N 15°43′E
160 F12 **Baicao Ling** ▲ SW China
163 U9 **Baicheng** var. Pai-ch'eng; prev. T'aon-an. Jilin, NE China 45°32′N 122°51′E
158 I6 **Baicheng** var. Bay. Xinjiang Uygur Zizhiqu, NW China 41°49′N 81°45′E
116 J13 **Băicoi** Prahova, SE Romania 45°02′N 25°51′E
**Baidoa** see Baydhabo
15 U6 **Baie-Comeau** Québec, SE Canada 49°12′N 68°10′W
15 U6 **Baie-des-Sables** Québec, SE Canada 48°41′N 67°55′W
15 T7 **Baie-des-Bacon** Québec, SE Canada 48°31′N 69°17′W
15 S8 **Baie-des-Rochers** Québec, SE Canada 47°57′N 69°50′W
**Baie-du-Poste** see Mistissini
172 H17 **Baie Lazare** Mahé, NE Seychelles 04°45′S 55°29′E
45 Y5 **Baie-Mahault** Basse Terre, C Guadeloupe 16°16′N 61°35′W
15 R9 **Baie-St-Paul** Québec, SE Canada 47°27′N 70°30′W
15 V5 **Baie-Trinité** Québec, SE Canada 49°25′N 67°20′W
13 T11 **Baie Verte** Newfoundland and Labrador, SE Canada 49°55′N 56°12′W
**Baiguan** see Shangyu
**Baihe** see Erdaobaihe
139 U11 **Bā'ij al Mahdī** Al Muthannā, S Iraq 31°21′N 44°57′E
**Baiji** see Bayjī
**Baikal, Lake** see Baykal, Ozero
**Bailādila** see Kirandul
**Baile an Chaistil** see Ballycastle
**Baile an Róba** see Ballinrobe
**Baile an tSratha** see Ballintra
**Baile Átha an Rí** see Athenry
**Baile Átha Buí** see Athboy
**Baile Átha Cliath** see Dublin
**Baile Átha Fhirdhia** see Ardee
**Baile Átha Í** see Athy
**Baile Átha Luain** see Athlone
**Baile Átha Troim** see Trim
**Baile Brigín** see Balbriggan
**Baile Easa Dara** see Ballysadare
116 I13 **Băile Govora** Vâlcea, SW Romania 45°00′N 24°08′E
116 F13 **Băile Herculane** Ger. Herkulesbad, Hung. Herkulesfürdő. Caraș-Severin, SW Romania 44°51′N 22°24′E
**Baile Locha Riach** see Loughrea
**Baile Mhistéala** see Mitchelstown
**Baile Monaidh** see Ballymoney
105 N12 **Bailén** Andalucía, S Spain 38°06′N 03°46′W
**Baile na hInse** see Ballynahinch
**Baile na Lorgan** see Castleblayney
**Baile na Mainistreach** see Newtownabbey
**Baile Nua na hArda** see Newtownards
116 I12 **Băile Olănești** Vâlcea, SW Romania 45°14′N 24°18′E
116 H14 **Băilești** Dolj, SW Romania 44°01′N 23°20′E
163 N12 **Bailingmiao** var. Darhan Muminggan Lianheqi. Nei Mongol Zizhiqu, N China 41°41′N 110°25′E
58 K11 **Bailique, Ilha** island NE Brazil
103 O1 **Bailleul** Nord, N France 50°43′N 02°43′E
78 H12 **Ba Illi** Chari-Baguirmi, SW Chad 10°31′N 16°29′E
159 V12 **Bailong Jiang** ~ C China
82 C13 **Bailundo** Port. Vila Teixeira da Silva. Huambo, C Angola 12°12′S 15°52′E
159 T13 **Baima** var. Sêraitang. Qinghai, C China 32°55′N 100°44′E
**Baima** see Baxoi
186 C8 **Baimuru** Gulf, S Papua New Guinea 07°34′S 144°49′E
158 M16 **Bainang** Xizang Zizhiqu, W China 28°57′N 89°31′E
23 S8 **Bainbridge** Georgia, SE USA 30°54′N 84°33′W
171 O17 **Baing** Pulau Sumba, SE Indonesia 10°09′S 120°34′E
158 M14 **Baingoin** var. Pubao. Xizang Zizhiqu, W China 31°22′N 90°00′E
104 G2 **Baio** Galicia, NW Spain 43°08′N 08°58′W
104 G4 **Baiona** Galicia, NW Spain 42°06′N 08°49′W
163 V7 **Baiquan** Heilongjiang, NE China 47°37′N 126°04′E
**Bā'ir** see Bāyir
158 I11 **Bairab Co** ◎ W China
25 Q7 **Baird** Texas, SW USA 32°23′N 99°24′W
39 N7 **Baird Mountains** ▲ Alaska, USA
**Baireuth** see Bayreuth
190 H3 **Bairiki** Tarawa, NW Kiribati 01°20′N 173°01′E
**Bairin Youqi** see Daban
**Bairin Zuoqi** see Lindong
**Bairkum** see Bayyrkum
183 P12 **Bairnsdale** Victoria, SE Australia 37°51′S 147°38′E
171 P6 **Bais** Negros, S Philippines 09°36′N 123°07′E
102 L15 **Baïse** var. Baise. ~ S France
**Baise** see Baïse
163 W11 **Baishan** prev. Hunjiang. Jilin, NE China 41°57′N 126°31′E
**Baishan** see Mashan
118 F12 **Baisogala** Šiauliai, C Lithuania 55°38′N 23°44′E
189 Q7 **Baiti** N Nauru 0°30′S 166°55′E
**Baitou Shan** see Paektu-san
104 G13 **Baixo Alentejo** physical region S Portugal
64 P5 **Baixo, Ilhéu de** island Madeira, Portugal, NE Atlantic Ocean
83 E15 **Baixo Longa** Kuando Kubango, SE Angola 15°39′S 18°39′E
159 V10 **Baiyin** Gansu, C China 36°33′N 104°11′E
160 E8 **Baiyü** var. Jianshe. Sichuan, C China 30°37′N 97°15′E
161 N14 **Baiyun** ✈ (Guangzhou) Guangdong, S China 23°12′N 113°19′E
160 K4 **Baiyu Shan** ▲ C China
111 J25 **Baja** Bács-Kiskun, S Hungary 46°13′N 18°56′E
40 C4 **Baja California** ◆ state NW Mexico
40 C4 **Baja California** Eng. Lower California. peninsula NW Mexico
40 E9 **Baja California Sur** ◆ state NW Mexico
**Bājah** see Béja
**Bajan** see Bayan
191 V16 **Baja, Punta** headland Easter Island, Chile, E Pacific Ocean 27°10′S 109°21′W
40 B4 **Baja, Punta** headland NW Mexico 29°57′N 115°48′W
55 R5 **Baja, Punta** headland NE Venezuela
42 D5 **Baja Verapaz** off. Departamento de Baja Verapaz. ◆ department C Guatemala
**Baja Verapaz, Departamento de** see Baja Verapaz
171 N16 **Bajawa** prev. Badjawa. Flores, S Indonesia 08°46′S 120°59′E
153 S16 **Baj Baj** prev. Budge-Budge. West Bengal, E India 22°29′N 88°11′E
141 N15 **Bājil** W Yemen 15°05′N 43°16′E
183 U4 **Bajimba, Mount** ▲ New South Wales, SE Australia 29°19′S 152°04′E
112 K13 **Bajina Bašta** Serbia, W Serbia 43°58′N 19°33′E
153 U14 **Bajitpur** Dhaka, E Bangladesh 24°12′N 90°57′E
112 K8 **Bajmok** Vojvodina, NW Serbia 45°59′N 19°25′E
**Bajo Boquete** see Boquete
113 L17 **Bajram Curri** Kukës, N Albania 42°23′N 20°06′E
79 J14 **Bakala** Ouaka, C Central African Republic 06°03′N 20°31′E
127 T4 **Bakaly** Respublika Bashkortostan, W Russia 55°10′N 53°46′E
**Bakan** see Shimonoseki
145 U14 **Bakanas** Kaz. Baqanas. Almaty, SE Kazakhstan 44°50′N 76°13′E
145 V12 **Bakanas** Kaz. Baqanas. ~ E Kazakhstan
149 R4 **Bākārak** Panjshīr, NE Afghanistan 35°16′N 69°28′E
145 U14 **Bakbakty** Kaz. Baqbaqty. Almaty, SE Kazakhstan 44°36′N 76°41′E
122 J12 **Bakchar** Tomskaya Oblast', C Russia 56°58′N 81°59′E
76 I11 **Bakel** E Senegal 14°54′N 12°26′W
35 W13 **Baker** California, W USA 35°15′N 116°04′W
22 J8 **Baker** Louisiana, S USA 30°35′N 91°10′W
33 Y9 **Baker** Montana, NW USA 46°22′N 104°16′W
32 L12 **Baker** Oregon, NW USA 44°46′N 117°50′W
36 L12 **Baker Butte** ▲ Arizona, SW USA 34°24′N 111°22′W
192 L7 **Baker Island** US unincorporated territory Oceania, C Pacific Ocean
39 X15 **Baker Island** island Alexander Archipelago, Alaska, USA
9 N9 **Baker Lake** var. Qamanittuaq. Nunavut, N Canada 64°20′N 96°10′W
9 N9 **Baker Lake** ◎ Nunavut, N Canada
32 H6 **Baker, Mount** ▲ Washington, NW USA 48°46′N 121°48′W
35 R13 **Bakersfield** California, W USA 35°22′N 119°01′W
24 M9 **Bakersfield** Texas, SW USA 30°54′N 102°21′W
21 P9 **Bakersville** North Carolina, SE USA 36°01′N 82°09′W
**Bākhābī** see Bū Khābī
**Bakharden** see Baharly
**Bakhardok** see Bokurdak
143 U5 **Bākharz, Kūhhā-ye** ▲ NE Iran
152 D13 **Bākhāsar** Rājasthān, NW India 24°42′N 71°11′E
**Bakhchisaray** see Bakhchysaray
117 T13 **Bakhchysaray** Rus. Bakhchisaray. Avtonomna Respublika Krym, S Ukraine 44°44′N 33°53′E
**Bakherden** see Baharly
117 R3 **Bakhmach** Chernihivs'ka Oblast', N Ukraine 51°10′N 32°48′E
117 W7 **Bakhmut** prev. Artemivs'k. Donets'ka Oblast', E Ukraine 48°35′N 37°58′E
**Bākhtarān** see Kermānshāh
143 Q11 **Bakhtegān, Daryācheh-ye** ◎ C Iran
**Bakhty** see Bakty
137 Z11 **Bakı** Eng. Baku. ● (Azerbaijan) E Azerbaijan 40°24′N 49°51′E
80 M12 **Baki** Awdal, N Somalia 10°10′N 43°45′E
137 Z11 **Bakı** ✈ E Azerbaijan 40°26′N 49°55′E
136 C13 **Bakır Çayı** ~ W Turkey
92 L1 **Bakkafjörður** Austurland, NE Iceland 66°01′N 14°49′W
92 L1 **Bakkaflói** sea area W Norwegian Sea
92 L2 **Bakkagerði** Austurland, NE Iceland 65°32′N 13°46′W
81 I15 **Bako** Southern Nationalities, S Ethiopia 05°45′N 36°39′E
76 L15 **Bako** NW Ivory Coast 09°08′N 07°40′W
**Bákó** see Bacău
111 H23 **Bakony** Eng. Bakony Mountains, Ger. Bakonywald. ▲ W Hungary
**Bakony Mountains/Bakonywald** see Bakony
81 M16 **Bakool** off. Gobolka Bakool. ◆ region W Somalia
**Bakool, Gobolka** see Bakool
79 L15 **Bakouma** Mbomou, SE Central African Republic 05°42′N 22°43′E
127 N15 **Baksan** Kabardino-Balkarskaya Respublika, SW Russia 43°43′N 43°31′E
119 I16 **Bakshty** Hrodzyenskaya Voblasts', W Belarus 53°56′N 26°11′E
145 X12 **Bakty** prev. Bakhty. Vostochnyy Kazakhstan, E Kazakhstan 46°41′N 82°45′E
**Baku** see Bakı
194 K12 **Bakutis Coast** physical region Antarctica
**Bakwanga** see Mbuji-Mayi
145 O15 **Bakyrly** Turkestan, S Kazakhstan 44°30′N 67°41′E
14 H13 **Bala** Ontario, S Canada 45°01′N 79°37′W
136 I13 **Balâ** Ankara, C Turkey 39°34′N 33°07′E
97 J19 **Bala** NW Wales, United Kingdom 52°54′N 03°31′W
170 L7 **Balabac Island** island W Philippines
**Balabac, Selat** see Balabac Strait
169 V5 **Balabac Strait** var. Selat Balabac. strait Malaysia/Philippines
**Ba'labakk** see Baalbek
187 P16 **Balabio, Île** island Province Nord, W New Caledonia
116 I14 **Balaci** Teleorman, S Romania 44°21′N 24°55′E
139 S7 **Balad** Ṣalāḥ ad Dīn, N Iraq 34°00′N 44°07′E
139 U7 **Balad Rūz** Diyālā, E Iraq 33°42′N 45°04′E
154 J11 **Bālāghāt** Madhya Pradesh, C India 21°48′N 80°11′E
154 F13 **Bālāghāt Range** ▲ W India
103 X14 **Balagne** physical region Corse, France, C Mediterranean Sea
105 U5 **Balaguer** Cataluña, NE Spain 41°48′N 00°48′E
105 S3 **Balaïtous** var. Pic de Balaïtous. ▲ France/Spain 42°51′N 00°17′W
**Balaïtous, Pic de** see Balaïtous
**Bálák** see Ballangen
127 O3 **Balakhna** Nizhegorodskaya Oblast', W Russia 56°26′N 43°43′E
122 L12 **Balakhta** Krasnoyarskiy Kray, S Russia 55°22′N 91°24′E
182 I9 **Balaklava** South Australia 34°10′S 138°22′E
**Balakleya** see Balakliya
117 V6 **Balakliya** Rus. Balakleya. Kharkivs'ka Oblast', E Ukraine 49°27′N 36°53′E
127 Q7 **Balakovo** Saratovskaya Oblast', W Russia 52°03′N 47°47′E
83 P14 **Balama** Cabo Delgado, N Mozambique 13°18′S 38°39′E
169 U6 **Balambangan, Pulau** island East Malaysia
**Bālā Morghāb** see Bālā Murghāb
148 L3 **Bālā Murghāb** prev. Bālā Morghāb. Laghmān, NW Afghanistan 35°38′N 63°21′E
152 E11 **Bālān** prev. Bāhla. Rājasthān, NW India 27°45′N 71°32′E
116 J10 **Bălan** Hung. Balánbánya. Harghita, C Romania 46°39′N 25°47′E
**Balánbánya** see Bălan
171 O3 **Balanga** Luzon, N Philippines 14°40′N 120°32′E
154 M12 **Balāngīr** prev. Bolangir. Odisha, E India 20°41′N 83°30′E
127 N8 **Balashov** Saratovskaya Oblast', W Russia 51°32′N 43°14′E
**Balasore** see Bāleshwar
111 K21 **Balassagyarmat** Nógrád, N Hungary 48°06′N 19°17′E
29 S10 **Balaton** Minnesota, N USA 44°13′N 95°52′W
111 H24 **Balaton** var. Lake Balaton, Ger. Plattensee. ◎ W Hungary
111 I23 **Balatonfüred** var. Füred. Veszprém, W Hungary 46°59′N 17°53′E
**Balaton, Lake** see Balaton
116 I11 **Bălăușeri** Ger. Bladenmarkt, Hung. Balavásár. Mureș, C Romania 46°24′N 24°41′E
**Balavásár** see Bălăușeri
105 Q11 **Balazote** Castilla-La Mancha, C Spain 38°54′N 02°09′W
**Balázsfalva** see Blaj
119 F14 **Balbieriškis** Kaunas, S Lithuania 54°29′N 23°52′E
186 J7 **Balbi, Mount** ▲ Bougainville Island, NE Papua New Guinea 05°51′S 154°58′E
58 F11 **Balbina, Represa** ⊠ NW Brazil
43 T15 **Balboa** West Panamá, C Panama 08°55′N 79°36′W
97 G17 **Balbriggan** Ir. Baile Brigín. E Ireland 53°37′N 06°11′W
**Balbunar** see Kubrat
81 N17 **Balcad** Shabeellaha Dhexe, C Somalia 02°19′N 45°19′E
61 D23 **Balcarce** Buenos Aires, E Argentina 37°51′S 58°16′W
11 U16 **Balcarres** Saskatchewan, S Canada 50°49′N 103°31′W
114 O8 **Balchik** Dobrich, NE Bulgaria 43°25′N 28°11′E
185 E24 **Balclutha** Otago, South Island, New Zealand 46°15′S 169°45′E
25 Q12 **Balcones Escarpment** escarpment Texas, SW USA
18 F14 **Bald Eagle Creek** ~ Pennsylvania, NE USA
**Baldenburg** see Biały Bór
21 V12 **Bald Head Island** island North Carolina, SE USA
27 W10 **Bald Knob** Arkansas, C USA 35°18′N 91°34′W
30 K17 **Bald Knob** hill Illinois, N USA
**Baldohn** see Baldone
118 G9 **Baldone** Ger. Baldohn. W Latvia 56°46′N 24°18′E
22 I9 **Baldwin** Louisiana, S USA 29°50′N 91°32′W
31 P7 **Baldwin** Michigan, N USA 43°54′N 85°50′W
27 Q4 **Baldwin City** Kansas, C USA 38°43′N 95°12′W
39 N8 **Baldwin Peninsula** headland Alaska, USA 66°45′N 162°19′W
18 H9 **Baldwinsville** New York, NE USA 43°09′N 76°19′W
23 N2 **Baldwyn** Mississippi, S USA 34°30′N 88°38′W
11 W15 **Baldy Mountain** ▲ Manitoba, S Canada 51°29′N 100°46′W
33 T7 **Baldy Mountain** ▲ Montana, NW USA 48°09′N 109°39′W
37 O13 **Baldy Peak** ▲ Arizona, SW USA 33°56′N 109°37′W
**Bâle** see Basel
**Balearic Plain** see Algerian Basin
**Baleares** see Illes Baleares
105 X11 **Baleares, Islas** Eng. Balearic Islands. island group Spain, W Mediterranean Sea
**Baleares Major** see Mallorca
**Balearic Islands** see Baleares, Islas
**Balearis Minor** see Menorca
169 S9 **Baleh, Batang** ~ East Malaysia
12 J8 **Baleine, Grande Rivière de la** ~ Québec, E Canada
12 K7 **Baleine, Petite Rivière de la** ~ Québec, NE Canada
12 K7 **Baleine, Petite Rivière de la** ~ Québec, SE Canada
13 N6 **Baleine, Rivière à la** ~ Québec, E Canada
99 J16 **Balen** Antwerpen, N Belgium 51°12′N 05°12′E
171 O3 **Baler** Luzon, N Philippines 15°47′N 121°30′E
154 P11 **Bāleshwar** prev. Balasore. Odisha, E India 21°31′N 86°59′E
77 S12 **Baléyara** Tillabéri, W Niger 13°48′N 02°57′E
127 T1 **Balezino** Udmurtskaya Respublika, NW Russia 57°57′N 53°03′E
42 J4 **Balfate** Colón, N Honduras 15°47′N 86°24′W
11 O17 **Balfour** British Columbia, SW Canada 49°39′N 116°57′W
29 N3 **Balfour** North Dakota, N USA 47°55′N 100°34′W
**Balfrush** see Bābol
114 L9 **Balgarka** ▲ E Bulgaria 42°43′N 26°19′E
122 L14 **Balgazyn** Respublika Tyva, S Russia 50°53′N 95°12′E
11 U16 **Balgonie** Saskatchewan, S Canada 50°30′N 104°12′W
**Bălgrad** see Alba Iulia
81 J19 **Balguda** spring/well S Kenya 01°28′S 39°50′E
158 K6 **Balguntay** Xinjiang Uygur Zizhiqu, NW China 42°45′N 86°18′E
141 R16 **Balḥāf** S Yemen 14°02′N 48°16′E
152 F13 **Bāli** Rājasthān, N India 25°10′N 73°20′E
169 U17 **Bali** ◆ province S Indonesia
169 T17 **Bali** island C Indonesia
111 K16 **Balice** ✈ (Kraków) Małopolskie, S Poland 49°57′N 19°49′E
171 Y14 **Baliem, Sungai** ~ Papua, E Indonesia
136 C12 **Balıkesir** Balıkesir, W Turkey 39°38′N 27°52′E
136 C12 **Balıkesir** ◆ province NW Turkey
138 L3 **Balīkh, Nahr** ~ N Syria
169 V12 **Balikpapan** Borneo, C Indonesia 01°15′S 116°50′E
**Bali, Laut** see Bali Sea
171 N9 **Balimbing** Tawitawi, SW Philippines 05°10′N 120°00′E
186 B8 **Balimo** Western, SW Papua New Guinea 08°00′S 143°00′E
**Bálinc** see Balinț
101 H23 **Balingen** Baden-Württemberg, SW Germany 48°16′N 08°51′E
116 F11 **Balinț** Hung. Bálinc. Timiș, W Romania 45°48′N 21°54′E
171 O1 **Balintang Channel** channel N Philippines
**Bālis** see Maskanah
169 T16 **Bali Sea** Ind. Laut Bali. sea C Indonesia
98 K7 **Balk** Fryslân, N Netherlands 52°54′N 05°34′E
146 B11 **Balkanabat** Rus. Nebitdag. Balkan Welaýaty, W Turkmenistan 39°33′N 54°19′E
121 R6 **Balkan Mountains** Bul./SCr. Stara Planina. ▲ Bulgaria/Serbia
**Balkanskiy Welayat** see Balkan Welaýaty
146 B9 **Balkan Welaýaty** Rus. Balkanskiy Velayat. ◆ province W Turkmenistan
**Balkash** see Balkhash
145 P8 **Balkashino** Akmola, N Kazakhstan 52°36′N 68°46′E
**Balkash, Ozero** see Balkhash, Ozero
149 O2 **Balkh** anc. Bactra. Balkh, N Afghanistan 36°46′N 66°54′E
149 P2 **Balkh** ◆ province N Afghanistan
145 T13 **Balkhash** Kaz. Balqash, var. Balkash. Karaganda, SE Kazakhstan 46°52′N 74°55′E
**Balkhash, Lake** see Balkhash, Ozero
145 T13 **Balkhash, Ozero** var. Ozero Balkash, Eng. Lake Balkhash, Kaz. Balqash. ◎ SE Kazakhstan
**Balla Balla** see Mbalabala
96 H10 **Ballachulish** N Scotland, United Kingdom 56°40′N 05°10′W
180 M12 **Balladonia** Western Australia 32°21′S 123°32′E
97 C16 **Ballaghaderreen** Ir. Bealach an Doirín. C Ireland 53°51′N 08°29′W
92 H10 **Ballangen** Lapp. Bálák. Nordland, NW Norway 68°18′N 16°48′E
97 H14 **Ballantrae** W Scotland, United Kingdom 55°05′N 05°W
183 N12 **Ballarat** Victoria, SE Australia 37°36′S 143°51′E
180 K11 **Ballard, Lake** salt lake Western Australia
155 G17 **Ballari** var. Bellary. Karnātaka, S India 15°11′N 76°54′E
76 L11 **Ballé** Koulikoro, W Mali 15°18′N 08°31′W
40 D7 **Ballenas, Bahía de** bay NW Mexico
40 D5 **Ballenas, Canal de** channel NW Mexico
195 R17 **Balleny Islands** island group Antarctica
40 J7 **Balleza** var. San Pablo Balleza. Chihuahua, N Mexico 26°55′N 106°21′W
114 M13 **Ballı** Tekirdağ, NW Turkey 40°48′N 27°03′E
153 O13 **Ballia** Uttar Pradesh, N India 25°45′N 84°09′E
183 V4 **Ballina** New South Wales, SE Australia 28°50′S 153°37′E
97 C16 **Ballina** Ir. Béal an Átha. W Ireland 54°07′N 09°09′W
97 D16 **Ballinamore** Ir. Béal an Átha Móir. NW Ireland 54°03′N 07°47′W
97 D18 **Ballinasloe** Ir. Béal Átha na Sluaighe. W Ireland 53°20′N 08°13′W
25 P8 **Ballinger** Texas, SW USA 31°44′N 99°57′W
97 C17 **Ballinrobe** Ir. Baile an Róba. W Ireland 53°37′N 09°14′W
97 A21 **Ballinskelligs Bay** Ir. Bá na Scealg. inlet SW Ireland
97 D15 **Ballintra** Ir. Baile an tSratha. NW Ireland 54°35′N 08°07′W
103 T7 **Ballon d'Alsace** ▲ NE France 47°50′N 06°54′E
**Ballon de Guebwiller** see Grand Ballon
113 K21 **Ballsh** var. Ballshi. Fier, SW Albania 40°35′N 19°45′E
**Ballshi** see Ballsh
98 K4 **Ballum** Fryslân, N Netherlands 53°27′N 05°40′E
97 F16 **Ballybay** Ir. Béal Átha Beithe. N Ireland 54°08′N 06°54′W
97 E14 **Ballybofey** Ir. Bealach Féich. NW Ireland 54°49′N 07°47′W
97 G14 **Ballycastle** Ir. Baile an Chaistil. N Northern Ireland, United Kingdom 55°12′N 06°14′W
97 G15 **Ballyclare** Ir. Bealach Cláir. E Northern Ireland, United Kingdom 54°45′N 06°W
97 E16 **Ballyconnell** Ir. Béal Átha Conaill. N Ireland 54°07′N 07°35′W
97 C17 **Ballyhaunis** Ir. Beál Átha hAmhnais. W Ireland 53°45′N 08°45′W
97 G14 **Ballymena** Ir. An Baile Meánach. NE Northern Ireland, United Kingdom 54°52′N 06°17′W
97 F14 **Ballymoney** Ir. Baile Monaidh. NE Northern Ireland, United Kingdom 55°10′N 06°30′W
97 G15 **Ballynahinch** Ir. Baile na hInse. SE Northern Ireland, United Kingdom 54°24′N 05°54′W
97 D16 **Ballysadare** Ir. Baile Easa Dara. NW Ireland 54°13′N 08°30′W
97 D15 **Ballyshannon** Ir. Béal Átha Seanaidh. NW Ireland 54°30′N 08°11′W
63 H19 **Balmaceda** Aysén, S Chile 45°52′S 72°43′W
63 G23 **Balmaceda, Cerro** ▲ S Chile 51°27′S 73°26′W
111 N22 **Balmazújváros** Hajdú-Bihar, E Hungary 47°36′N 21°18′E
108 E10 **Balmhorn** ▲ SW Switzerland 46°27′N 07°41′E
182 L12 **Balmoral** Victoria, SE Australia 37°16′S 141°38′E
24 K9 **Balmorhea** Texas, SW USA 30°58′N 103°44′W
**Balneario Claromecó** see Claromecó
148 M12 **Balochistān** prev. Baluchestan, Beluchistan. ◆ province SW Pakistan
82 B13 **Balombo** Port. Norton de Matos, Vila Norton de Matos. Benguela, W Angola 12°21′S 14°46′E
82 B13 **Balombo** ~ W Angola
181 X10 **Balonne River** ~ Queensland, E Australia
152 E13 **Bālotra** Rājasthān, N India 25°50′N 72°21′E
145 V14 **Balpyk Bi** prev. Kirovskiy, Kaz. Kīrov. Almaty, SE Kazakhstan 44°54′N 78°13′E
**Balqā'/Balqā', Muḥāfaẓat al** see Al Balqā'
**Balqash** see Balkhash/Balkhash, Ozero
152 M12 **Balrāmpur** Uttar Pradesh, N India 27°25′N 82°10′E
182 M9 **Balranald** New South Wales, SE Australia 34°39′S 143°33′E
116 H14 **Balș** Olt, S Romania 44°20′N 24°06′E
14 H11 **Balsam Creek** Ontario, S Canada 46°26′N 79°10′W
30 I5 **Balsam Lake** Wisconsin, N USA 45°27′N 92°28′W
14 I14 **Balsam Lake** ◎ Ontario, SE Canada
59 M14 **Balsas** Maranhão, E Brazil 07°30′S 46°W
40 M15 **Balsas, Río** var. Río Mexcala. ~ S Mexico
43 W16 **Balsas, Río** ~ SE Panama
119 O18 **Bal'shavik** Rus. Bol'shevik. Homyel'skaya Voblasts', SE Belarus 52°34′N 30°53′E
95 O15 **Bålsta** Uppsala, C Sweden 59°31′N 17°32′E
108 E7 **Balsthal** Solothurn, NW Switzerland 47°18′N 07°42′E
117 O8 **Balta** Odes'ka Oblast', SW Ukraine 47°58′N 29°39′E
105 N5 **Baltanás** Castilla y León, N Spain 41°56′N 04°12′W
61 E16 **Baltasar Brum** Artigas, N Uruguay 30°44′S 57°19′W
116 M9 **Bălți** Rus. Bel'tsy. N Moldova 47°45′N 27°57′E
**Baltic Port** see Paldiski
118 B10 **Baltic Sea** Ger. Ostee, Rus. Baltiskoye More. sea N Europe
21 X3 **Baltimore** Maryland, NE USA 39°17′N 76°37′W
31 T13 **Baltimore** Ohio, N USA 39°48′N 82°33′W
21 X3 **Baltimore-Washington** ✈ Maryland, E USA 39°10′N 76°40′W
**Baltischport/Baltiski** see Paldiski
**Baltiskoye More** see Baltic Sea
119 A14 **Baltiysk** Ger. Pillau. Kaliningradskaya Oblast', W Russia 54°39′N 19°54′E
**Baltkrievija** see Belarus
119 H14 **Baltoji Voke** Vilnius, SE Lithuania 54°35′N 25°13′E
**Balūchestān va Sīstān** see Sīstān va Balūchestān
**Baluchistan** see Balochistan
171 P5 **Balud** Masbate, N Philippines 12°03′N 123°12′E
169 T9 **Balui, Batang** ~ East Malaysia
153 S13 **Bālurghat** West Bengal, NE India 25°12′N 88°50′E
118 J8 **Balvi** NE Latvia 57°07′N 27°14′E
147 W7 **Balykchy** Kyr. Ysyk-Köl; prev. Issyk-Kul', Rybach'ye. Issyk-Kul'skaya Oblast', NE Kyrgyzstan 42°29′N 76°08′E
56 B7 **Balzar** Guayas, W Ecuador 01°25′S 79°54′W
108 I8 **Balzers** S Liechtenstein 47°04′N 09°32′E
143 T12 **Bam** Kermān, SE Iran 29°08′N 58°27′E
77 Y13 **Bama** Borno, NE Nigeria 11°28′N 13°46′E
76 L12 **Bamako** ● (Mali) Capital District, SW Mali 12°39′N 08°02′W
77 P10 **Bamba** Gao, C Mali 17°03′N 01°19′W
42 M8 **Bambana, Río** ~ NE Nicaragua
79 J15 **Bambari** Ouaka, C Central African Republic 05°45′N 20°37′E
181 W5 **Bambaroo** Queensland, NE Australia 19°00′S 146°16′E
101 K19 **Bamberg** Bayern, SE Germany 49°54′N 10°53′E
21 R14 **Bamberg** South Carolina, SE USA 33°16′N 81°02′W
79 M16 **Bambesa** Orientale, N Dem. Rep. Congo 03°25′N 25°43′E
76 G11 **Bambey** W Senegal 14°43′N 16°26′W
79 H16 **Bambio** Sangha-Mbaéré, SW Central African Republic 03°57′N 16°54′E
83 I24 **Bamboesberge** ▲ S South Africa 31°24′S 26°10′E
79 D14 **Bamenda** Nord-Ouest, W Cameroon 05°55′N 10°09′E
10 K17 **Bamfield** Vancouver Island, British Columbia, SW Canada 48°48′N 125°05′W
**Bami** see Bamy
79 J14 **Bamingui** Bamingui-Bangoran, C Central African Republic 07°38′N 20°06′E
78 J13 **Bamingui** ~ N Central African Republic
78 J13 **Bamingui-Bangoran** ◆ prefecture N Central African Republic
143 V13 **Bampūr** Sīstān va Balūchestān, SE Iran 27°13′N 60°28′E
186 C8 **Bamu** ~ SW Papua New Guinea
146 E12 **Bamy** Rus. Bami. Ahal Welaýaty, C Turkmenistan 38°42′N 56°47′E
149 P4 **Bāmyān** prev. Bāmiān. Bāmyān, NE Afghanistan 34°50′N 67°50′E
149 O4 **Bāmyān** prev. Bāmiān. ◆ province C Afghanistan
**Bán** see Bánovce nad Bebravou
81 N17 **Banaadir** off. Gobolka Banaadir. ◆ region S Somalia
**Banaadir, Gobolka** see Banaadir
191 N3 **Banaba** var. Ocean Island. island Tungaru, W Kiribati
59 O14 **Banabuiú, Açude** ⊠ NE Brazil
57 O19 **Bañados del Izozog** salt lake SE Bolivia
97 D18 **Banagher** Ir. Beannchar. C Ireland 53°12′N 07°56′W
79 M17 **Banalia** Orientale, N Dem. Rep. Congo 01°33′N 25°23′E
76 L12 **Banamba** Koulikoro, W Mali 13°29′N 07°22′W
40 G4 **Banámichi** Sonora, NW Mexico 30°00′N 110°14′W
181 Y9 **Banana** Queensland, E Australia 24°33′S 150°07′E
191 Z2 **Banana** prev. Main Camp. Kiritimati, E Kiribati 02°00′N 157°25′W
59 K16 **Bananal, Ilha do** island C Brazil
23 Y12 **Banana River** lagoon Florida, SE USA
151 Q22 **Bananga** Andaman and Nicobar Islands, India, NE Indian Ocean 06°57′N 93°54′E
**Banaras** see Vārānasi
114 N13 **Banarlı** Tekirdağ, NW Turkey 41°04′N 27°21′E
152 H12 **Banās** ~ N India
75 Z11 **Banās, Rās** headland E Egypt 23°55′N 35°47′E
112 N10 **Banatski Karlovac** Vojvodina, NE Serbia 45°03′N 21°02′E
141 P16 **Banā, Wādī** dry watercourse SW Yemen
136 E14 **Banaz** Uşak, W Turkey 38°47′N 29°46′E
136 E14 **Banaz Çayı** ~ W Turkey
159 P14 **Banbar** var. Coka. Xizang Zizhiqu, W China 31°01′N 94°43′E
97 G15 **Banbridge** Ir. Droichead na Banna. SE Northern Ireland, United Kingdom 54°21′N 06°16′W
**Ban Bua Yai** see Bua Yai
97 M21 **Banbury** S England, United Kingdom 52°04′N 01°20′W
167 O7 **Ban Chiang Dao** Chiang Mai, NW Thailand 19°22′N 98°59′E
96 K9 **Banchory** NE Scotland, United Kingdom 58°05′N 00°35′W
14 J13 **Bancroft** Ontario, SE Canada 45°03′N 77°52′W
33 R15 **Bancroft** Idaho, NW USA 42°43′N 111°54′W
29 U11 **Bancroft** Iowa, C USA 43°17′N 94°13′W
154 I9 **Bānda** Madhya Pradesh, C India 24°01′N 78°59′E
152 L13 **Bānda** Uttar Pradesh, N India 25°28′N 80°20′E
168 F7 **Banda Aceh** var. Banda Atjeh; prev. Koetaradja, Kutaradja, Kutaraja. Sumatera, W Indonesia 05°30′N 95°20′E
**Banda Atjeh** see Banda Aceh




◆ Country ● Country Capital ◇ Dependent Territory ○ Dependent Territory Capital ◆ Administrative Regions ✈ International Airport ▲ Mountain ▲ Mountain Range ⌂ Volcano ~ River ◎ Lake ⊠ Reservoir

◆ Country    ● Country Capital    ◇ Dependent Territory    ○ Dependent Territory Capital    ♦ Administrative Regions    ✈ International Airport    ▲ Mountain    ▲ Mountain Range    ▲ Volcano    ≈ River    ☺ Lake    ⊞ Reservoir

BARROW-IN-FURNESS – BEAVER RIVER


97 J16 Barrow-in-Furness NW England, United Kingdom 54°07′N 03°14′W
180 G7 Barrow Island island Western Australia
39 O4 Barrow, Point headland Alaska, USA 71°23′N 156°28′W
11 V14 Barrows Manitoba, S Canada 52°49′N 101°36′W
97 J22 Barry S Wales, United Kingdom 51°24′N 03°18′W
14 J12 Barry's Bay Ontario, SE Canada 45°30′N 77°41′W
144 K14 Barsakel'mes, Ostrov island SW Kazakhstan
Baršć Łužyca see Forst
147 S14 Barsem S Tajikistan 37°36′N 71°43′E
145 V11 Barshatas Vostochnyy Kazakhstan, E Kazakhstan 48°13′N 78°33′E
155 F14 Bārsi Mahārāshtra, W India 18°14′N 75°42′E
100 I13 Barsinghausen Niedersachsen, C Germany 53°19′N 09°30′E
147 X8 Barskoon Issyk-Kul'skaya Oblast', E Kyrgyzstan 42°07′N 77°34′E
100 F10 Barssel Niedersachsen, NW Germany 53°10′N 07°46′E
35 U14 Barstow California, W USA 34°52′N 117°00′W
24 L8 Barstow Texas, SW USA 31°27′N 103°23′W
103 R6 Bar-sur-Aube Aube, NE France 48°13′N 04°43′E
Bar-sur-Ornain see Bar-le-Duc
103 Q6 Bar-sur-Seine Aube, N France 48°06′N 04°22′E
147 S13 Bartang S Tajikistan 38°06′N 71°48′E
147 T13 Bartang ≈ SE Tajikistan
Bartenstein see Bartoszyce
Bártfa/Bartfeld see Bardejov
100 N7 Barth Mecklenburg-Vorpommern, NE Germany 54°21′N 12°43′E
27 W13 Bartholomew, Bayou ≈ Arkansas/Louisiana, S USA
55 T8 Bartica N Guyana 06°24′N 58°36′W
136 H10 Bartın Bartın, NW Turkey 41°37′N 32°20′E
136 H10 Bartın ◈ province NW Turkey
181 W4 Bartle Frere ▲ Queensland, E Australia 17°15′S 145°43′E
27 P8 Bartlesville Oklahoma, C USA 36°44′N 95°59′W
29 P14 Bartlett Nebraska, C USA 41°51′N 98°32′W
20 E10 Bartlett Tennessee, S USA 35°12′N 89°52′W
25 T9 Bartlett Texas, SW USA 30°47′N 97°25′W
36 L13 Bartlett Reservoir ⊠ Arizona, SW USA
19 N6 Barton Vermont, NE USA 44°44′N 72°09′W
110 L7 Bartoszyce Ger. Bartenstein. Warmińsko-mazurskie, NE Poland 54°16′N 20°49′E
23 W12 Bartow Florida, SE USA 27°54′N 81°50′W
Bartschin see Barcin
168 J10 Barumun, Sungai ≈ Sumatera, W Indonesia
Barū, Nahr see Baro Wenz
169 S17 Barung, Nusa island S Indonesia
168 H9 Barus Sumatera, NW Indonesia 02°02′N 98°20′E
162 I9 Baruunbayan-Ulaan var. Höövör. Övörhangay, C Mongolia 45°10′N 101°19′E
Baruunsuu see Tsogttsetsiy
163 P8 Baruun-Urt Sühbaatar, E Mongolia 46°40′N 113°17′E
43 P15 Barú, Volcán var. Volcán de Chiriquí. 🌋 W Panama 08°49′N 82°32′W
99 K21 Barvaux Luxembourg, SE Belgium 50°21′N 05°30′E
42 M13 Barva, Volcán 🌋 NW Costa Rica 10°07′N 84°08′W
117 W6 Barvinkove Kharkivs'ka Oblast', E Ukraine 48°54′N 37°03′E
154 G11 Barwāh Madhya Pradesh, C India 22°17′N 76°01′E
Barwalde Neumark see Mieszkowice
154 F11 Barwāni Madhya Pradesh, C India 22°02′N 74°56′E
183 P5 Barwon River ≈ New South Wales, SE Australia
119 L15 Barysaw Rus. Borisov. Minskaya Voblasts', NE Belarus 54°14′N 28°30′E
127 Q6 Barysh Ul'yanovskaya Oblast', W Russia 53°32′N 47°06′E
117 Q4 Baryshivka Kyivs'ka Oblast', N Ukraine 50°21′N 31°21′E
114 G8 Barzia var. Bŭrziya. NW Bulgaria
79 J17 Basankusu Equateur, NW Dem. Rep. Congo 01°12′N 19°50′E
117 N11 Basarabeasca Rus. Bessarabka. SE Moldova 46°22′N 28°56′E
116 M14 Basarabi Constanţa, SW Romania 44°10′N 28°26′E
40 H6 Basaseachic Chihuahua, NW Mexico 28°18′N 108°13′W
Basauri see Arizgoiti
61 D18 Basavilbaso Entre Ríos, E Argentina 32°23′S 58°55′W
79 F21 Bas-Congo off. Région du Bas-Congo; prev. Bas-Zaïre. ◈ region SW Dem. Rep. Congo
108 E6 Basel Eng. Basle, Fr. Bâle. Basel Stadt, NW Switzerland 47°33′N 07°36′E
Baselland see Basel Landschaft
108 E7 Basel Landschaft prev. Baselland. ◈ canton NW Switzerland
108 E6 Basel Stadt ◈ canton NW Switzerland
143 T14 Bashākerd, Kūhhā-ye ▲▲ SE Iran
11 Q15 Bashaw Alberta, SW Canada 52°40′N 112°53′W
146 K16 Bashbedeng Mary Welaýaty, S Turkmenistan 35°44′N 63°07′E
161 T15 Bashi Channel Chin. Pa-shih Hai-hsia. channel Philippines/Taiwan
Bashkiria see Bashkortostan, Respublika
122 F11 Bashkortostan, Respublika prev. Bashkiria. ◈ autonomous republic W Russia
127 N6 Bashmakovo Penzenskaya Oblast', W Russia 53°13′N 43°00′E
146 J10 Bashsakarba Lebap Welaýaty, NE Turkmenistan 40°25′N 62°16′E
117 R9 Bashtanka Mykolayivs'ka Oblast', S Ukraine 47°24′N 32°27′E
22 H8 Basile Louisiana, S USA 30°29′N 92°36′W
107 M18 Basilicata ◈ region S Italy
33 V13 Basin Wyoming, C USA 44°22′N 108°02′W
97 N22 Basingstoke S England, United Kingdom 51°16′N 01°08′W
143 U8 Başīrān Khorāsān-e Janūbī, E Iran 31°57′N 59°07′E
112 B10 Baška It. Bescanuova. Primorje-Gorski Kotar, NW Croatia 44°58′N 14°46′E
137 T15 Başkale Van, SE Turkey 38°03′N 43°59′E
14 L10 Baskatong, Réservoir ⊠ Québec, SE Canada
137 O14 Baskil Elazığ, E Turkey 38°38′N 38°47′E
Basle see Basel
154 H9 Bāsoda Madhya Pradesh, C India 23°54′N 77°58′E
79 L17 Basoko Orientale, N Dem. Rep. Congo 01°14′N 23°26′E
Basque Country, The see País Vasco
Basra see Al Başrah
Basra see Al Başrah
Başrah, Muḩāfaẓat al see Al Başrah
103 U5 Bas-Rhin ◈ department NE France
Bassam see Grand-Bassam
11 Q16 Bassano Alberta, SW Canada 50°48′N 112°28′W
106 H7 Bassano del Grappa Veneto, NE Italy 45°45′N 11°45′E
77 Q15 Bassar var. Bassari. NW Togo 09°15′N 00°47′E
Bassari see Bassar
172 L9 Bassas da India island group W Madagascar
108 D7 Bassecourt Jura, W Switzerland 47°20′N 07°16′E
Bassein see Pathein
79 J15 Basse-Kotto ◈ prefecture S Central African Republic
45 Q11 Basse-Pointe N Martinique 14°52′N 61°07′W
76 H12 Basse Santa Su E The Gambia 13°18′N 14°10′W
Basse-Saxe see Niedersachsen
45 X6 Basse-Terre ○ (Guadeloupe) Basse Terre, SW Guadeloupe 16°08′N 61°40′W
45 V10 Basseterre ● (Saint Kitts and Nevis) Saint Kitts, Saint Kitts and Nevis 17°16′N 62°45′W
45 X6 Basse Terre island W Guadeloupe
29 O13 Bassett Nebraska, C USA 42°34′N 99°32′W
21 S7 Bassett Virginia, NE USA 36°45′N 79°59′W
37 N15 Bassett Peak ▲ Arizona, SW USA 32°30′N 110°16′W
76 M10 Bassikounou Hodh ech Chargui, SE Mauritania 15°55′N 05°59′W
77 R15 Bassila W Benin 08°25′N 01°58′E
Bass, Îlots de see Marotiri
31 O11 Bass Lake Indiana, N USA 41°12′N 86°35′W
183 O14 Bass Strait strait SE Australia
100 H11 Bassum Niedersachsen, NW Germany 52°52′N 08°44′E
29 X3 Basswood Lake ◎ Canada/USA
95 J21 Båstad Skåne, S Sweden 56°25′N 12°50′E
Baştah see Beste
153 N12 Basti Uttar Pradesh, N India 26°48′N 82°44′E
103 X14 Bastia Corse, France, C Mediterranean Sea 42°42′N 09°27′E
99 L23 Bastogne Luxembourg, SE Belgium 50°N 05°43′E
22 I5 Bastrop Louisiana, S USA 32°46′N 91°54′W
25 T11 Bastrop Texas, SW USA 30°07′N 97°21′W
93 J15 Bastuträsk Västerbotten, N Sweden 64°47′N 20°05′E
119 J19 Bastyn' Rus. Bostyn'. Brestskaya Voblasts', SW Belarus 52°23′N 26°45′E
Basuo see Dongfang
Basutoland see Lesotho
119 O15 Basya ≈ E Belarus
Bas-Zaïre see Bas-Congo
79 D17 Bata NW Equatorial Guinea 01°51′N 09°48′E
79 D17 Bata ✈ S Equatorial Guinea 01°55′N 09°48′E
Batae Coritanorum see Leicester
123 Q8 Batagay Respublika Sakha (Yakutiya), NE Russia 67°36′N 134°44′E
123 P8 Batagay-Alyta Respublika Sakha (Yakutiya), NE Russia 67°48′N 130°15′E
112 L10 Batajnica Vojvodina, N Serbia 44°55′N 20°17′E
136 H15 Bataklık Gölü ◎ S Turkey
114 H11 Batak, Yazovir ⊠ SW Bulgaria
152 H7 Batāla Punjab, N India 31°48′N 75°12′E
104 F9 Batalha Leiria, C Portugal 39°40′N 08°50′W
79 N17 Batama Orientale, NE Dem. Rep. Congo 0°54′N 26°25′E
123 Q10 Batamay Respublika Sakha (Yakutiya), NE Russia 63°28′N 129°33′E
160 F9 Batang var. Bazhong. Sichuan, C China 30°04′N 99°10′E
79 I14 Batangafo Ouham, NW Central African Republic 07°19′N 18°22′E
171 P8 Batangas off. Batangas City. Luzon, N Philippines 13°47′N 121°03′E
Batangas City see Batangas
Bătania see Battonya
171 Q10 Batan Islands island group N Philippines
60 L8 Batatais São Paulo, S Brazil 20°54′S 47°37′W
18 E10 Batavia New York, NE USA 43°00′N 78°11′W
Batavia see Jakarta
173 T9 Batavia Seamount undersea feature E Indian Ocean 27°42′S 100°36′E
126 L12 Bataysk Rostovskaya Oblast', SW Russia 47°10′N 39°46′E
14 B9 Batchawana ≈ Ontario, S Canada
14 B9 Batchawana Bay Ontario, S Canada 46°55′N 84°36′W
Bătdâmbâng see Battambang
79 G20 Batéké, Plateaux plateau S Congo
183 S11 Batemans Bay New South Wales, SE Australia 35°45′S 150°09′E
21 Q13 Batesburg South Carolina, SE USA 33°54′N 81°33′W
28 K12 Batesland South Dakota, N USA 43°05′N 102°07′W
27 V10 Batesville Arkansas, C USA 35°45′N 91°39′W
31 Q14 Batesville Indiana, N USA 39°18′N 85°13′W
22 L2 Batesville Mississippi, S USA 34°18′N 89°56′W
25 Q13 Batesville Texas, SW USA 28°56′N 99°38′W
44 L13 Bath E Jamaica 17°57′N 76°22′W
97 L22 Bath hist. Akermanceaster; anc. Aquae Calidae, Aquae Solis. SW England, United Kingdom 51°23′N 02°22′W
19 Q8 Bath Maine, NE USA 43°54′N 69°49′W
18 F11 Bath New York, NE USA 42°20′N 77°16′W
Bath see Berkeley Springs
78 I10 Batha off. Région du Batha. ◈ region C Chad
78 I10 Batha seasonal river C Chad
Batha, Région du see Batha
141 Y8 Baṭḥā', Wādī al dry watercourse NE Oman
152 H9 Bathinda Punjab, NW India 30°14′N 74°54′E
98 M11 Bathmen Overijssel, E Netherlands 52°15′N 06°16′E
45 Z14 Bathsheba E Barbados 13°13′N 59°31′W
183 R8 Bathurst New South Wales, SE Australia 33°32′S 149°35′E
13 O13 Bathurst New Brunswick, SE Canada 47°37′N 65°40′W
Bathurst see Banjul
8 H6 Bathurst, Cape headland Northwest Territories, NW Canada 70°33′N 128°00′W
196 L8 Bathurst Inlet Nunavut, N Canada 66°23′N 107°00′W
196 L8 Bathurst Inlet inlet Nunavut, N Canada
181 N1 Bathurst Island island Northern Territory, N Australia
197 O9 Bathurst Island island Parry Islands, Nunavut, N Canada
77 O14 Batié SW Burkina Faso 09°53′N 02°53′W
Batinah see Al Bāṭinah
141 Y9 Bāṭin, Wādī al dry watercourse SW Asia
15 P9 Batiscan ≈ Québec, SE Canada
136 F16 Batı Toroslar ▲▲ SW Turkey
Batjan see Bacan, Pulau
147 R11 Batken Batenskaya Oblast', SW Kyrgyzstan 40°03′N 70°50′E
Batken Oblasty see Batkenskaya Oblast'
147 Q11 Batkenskaya Oblast' Kyr. Batken Oblasty. ◈ province SW Kyrgyzstan
Batlle y Ordóñez see José Batlle y Ordóñez
183 Q10 Batlow New South Wales, SE Australia 35°32′S 148°09′E
137 Q15 Batman var. Iluh. Batman, SE Turkey 37°52′N 41°06′E
137 Q15 Batman ◈ province SE Turkey
74 L6 Batna NE Algeria 35°34′N 06°10′E
163 O7 Batnorov var. Dundbürd. Hentiy, E Mongolia 47°55′N 111°37′E
Batoe see Batu, Kepulauan
162 K7 Bat-Öldziy var. Övt. Övörhangay, C Mongolia 46°50′N 102°15′E
Bat-Öldziyt see Dzaamar
22 J8 Baton Rouge state capital Louisiana, S USA 30°28′N 91°09′W
79 G15 Batouri Est, E Cameroon 04°26′N 14°27′E
138 G14 Batra', Jibāl al ▲▲ S Jordan
138 G6 Batroûn var. Al Batrūn. N Lebanon 34°15′N 35°42′E
Batsch see Bač
Batsevichi see Batsevichy
119 M17 Batsevichy Rus. Batsevichi. Mahilyowskaya Voblasts', E Belarus 53°24′N 29°14′E
92 M7 Båtsfjord Finnmark, N Norway 70°37′N 29°42′E
Batshireet see Hentiy
162 L7 Batsümber var. Mandal. Töv, C Mongolia 48°24′N 106°47′E
167 Q12 Battambang var. Bătdâmbâng. Battambang, NW Cambodia 13°06′N 103°13′E
195 X3 Batterbee, Cape headland Antarctica
155 L24 Batticaloa Eastern Province, E Sri Lanka 07°44′N 81°43′E
99 L19 Battice Liège, E Belgium 50°39′N 05°50′E
107 L18 Battipaglia Campania, S Italy 40°36′N 14°59′E
11 R15 Battle ≈ Alberta/Saskatchewan, SW Canada
Battle Born State see Nevada
31 Q10 Battle Creek Michigan, N USA 42°20′N 85°10′W
27 T7 Battlefield Missouri, C USA 37°07′N 93°22′W
11 S15 Battleford Saskatchewan, S Canada 52°45′N 108°20′W
29 S6 Battle Lake Minnesota, N USA 46°16′N 95°42′W
35 U3 Battle Mountain Nevada, W USA 40°37′N 116°55′W
111 M25 Battonya Rom. Bătania. Békés, SE Hungary 46°16′N 21°00′E
162 J7 Battsengel var. Jargalant. Arhangay, C Mongolia 47°46′N 101°56′E
168 D11 Batu, Kepulauan prev. Batoe. island group W Indonesia
137 Q10 Bat'umi W Georgia 41°39′N 41°38′E
168 K10 Batu Pahat prev. Bandar Penggaram. Johor, Peninsular Malaysia 01°51′N 102°56′E
171 O12 Baturebe Sulawesi, N Indonesia 01°43′S 121°43′E
122 J12 Baturino Tomskaya Oblast', C Russia 57°46′N 85°08′E
117 R3 Baturyn Chernihivs'ka Oblast', N Ukraine 51°20′N 32°54′E
138 F10 Bat Yam Tel Aviv, C Israel 32°01′N 34°45′E
127 Q4 Batyrevo Chuvashskaya Respublika, W Russia 55°04′N 47°34′E
Batys Qazaqstan Oblysy see Zapadnyy Kazakhstan
102 F5 Batz, Île de island NW France
169 Q10 Bau Sarawak, East Malaysia 01°25′N 110°10′E
171 N2 Bauang Luzon, N Philippines 16°33′N 120°19′E
171 P14 Baubau var. Baoebaoe. Pulau Buton, C Indonesia 05°30′S 122°37′E
77 W14 Bauchi Bauchi, NE Nigeria 10°18′N 09°46′E
77 W14 Bauchi ◈ state C Nigeria
102 H7 Baud Morbihan, NW France 47°52′N 02°59′W
29 T2 Baudette Minnesota, N USA 48°42′N 94°36′W
193 S9 Bauer Basin undersea feature E Pacific Ocean 10°00′S 101°45′W
187 R14 Bauer Field var. Port Vila. ✈ (Port-Vila) Éfaté, C Vanuatu 17°42′S 168°21′E
13 T9 Bauld, Cape headland Newfoundland and Labrador, E Canada 51°35′N 55°22′W
103 T8 Baume-les-Dames Doubs, E France 47°22′N 06°20′E
101 I15 Baunatal Hessen, C Germany 51°15′N 09°25′E
107 D18 Baunei Sardegna, Italy, C Mediterranean Sea 40°04′N 09°36′E
57 M15 Baures, Río ≈ N Bolivia
60 K9 Bauru São Paulo, S Brazil 22°19′S 49°07′W
Baushar see Bawshar
118 G10 Bauska Ger. Bauske. S Latvia 56°25′N 24°11′E
Bauske see Bauska
101 Q15 Bautzen Lus. Budyšin. Sachsen, E Germany 51°11′N 14°29′E
145 Q16 Bauyrzhan Momyshuly Kaz. Baŭyrzhan Momyshuly; prev. Burnoye. Zhambyl, S Kazakhstan 42°36′N 70°46′E
Bauzanum see Bolzano
Bavaria see Bayern
109 N7 Bavarian Alps Ger. Bayrische Alpen. ▲▲ Austria/Germany
167 T13 Bavĕt Svay Rieng, S Cambodia 11°04′N 106°08′E
Bavière see Bayern
40 H4 Bavispe, Río ≈ NW Mexico
127 T5 Bavly Respublika Tatarstan, W Russia 54°20′N 53°21′E
169 P13 Bawal, Pulau island N Indonesia
169 T12 Bawan Borneo, C Indonesia 01°36′S 113°55′E
183 O12 Baw Baw, Mount ▲ Victoria, SE Australia 37°49′S 146°16′E
169 S15 Bawean, Pulau island S Indonesia
Bawīṭi see Al Bawīṭī
77 Q13 Bawku N Ghana 11°00′N 00°12′W
Bawlake see Bawlakhe
167 N7 Bawlakhe var. Bawlake. Kayah State, C Myanmar (Burma) 19°10′N 97°19′E
168 H11 Bawo Ofuloa Pulau Tanahmasa, W Indonesia 0°10′S 98°24′E
141 Y8 Bawshar var. Baushar. NE Oman 23°32′N 58°24′E
Baxian see Bazhou
Ba Xian see Bazhou
158 M8 Baxkorgan Xinjiang Uygur Zizhiqu, W China 39°05′N 90°00′E
23 V6 Baxley Georgia, SE USA 31°46′N 82°21′W
159 R15 Baxoi var. Baima. Xizang Zizhiqu, W China 30°01′N 96°53′E
29 W14 Baxter Iowa, C USA 41°49′N 93°09′W
29 U6 Baxter Minnesota, N USA 46°21′N 94°18′W
27 R8 Baxter Springs Kansas, C USA 37°01′N 94°45′W
81 M17 Bay off. Gobolka Bay. ◈ region SW Somalia
Bay see Baicheng
44 H7 Bayamo Granma, E Cuba 20°21′N 76°38′W
45 U5 Bayamón E Puerto Rico 18°24′N 66°09′W
163 W8 Bayan Heilongjiang, NE China 46°05′N 127°24′E
170 L16 Bayan prev. Bajan. Pulau Lombok, C Indonesia 08°16′S 116°28′E
162 M8 Bayan var. Maanĭt. Töv, C Mongolia 47°14′N 107°34′E
Bayan see Hölönbuyr, Dornod, Mongolia
Bayan see Ihhet, Dornogovĭ, Mongolia
Bayan see Bayan-Uul, Govĭ-Altay, Mongolia
Bayan see Bayanhutag, Hentiy, Mongolia
Bayan see Bürentogtoh, Hövsgol, Mongolia
152 I12 Bayāna Rājasthān, N India 26°55′N 77°18′E
149 N5 Bāyān, Band-e ▲▲ C Afghanistan
162 H8 Bayanbulag Bayanhongor, C Mongolia 46°46′N 98°07′E
Bayanbulag see Ömnödelger
158 J5 Bayanbulak Xinjiang Uygur Zizhiqu, W China 43°05′N 84°05′E
162 L7 Bayanchandmanĭ var. Ihsüüj. Töv, C Mongolia 48°12′N 106°23′E
162 J11 Bayandalay var. Dalay. Ömnögovĭ, S Mongolia 43°27′N 103°30′E
163 O9 Bayandelger var. Shireet. Sühbaatar, SE Mongolia 45°33′N 112°19′E
162 I5 Bayandzürh var. Altraga. Hövsgöl, N Mongolia 50°08′N 98°54′E
Bayan Gol see Dengkou, China
Bayangol see Bugat, Mongolia
162 I9 Bayangovĭ var. Örgön. Bayanhongor, C Mongolia 44°43′N 100°23′E
159 R12 Bayan Har Shan var. Bayan Khar. ▲▲ C China
162 G6 Bayanhayrhan var. Altanbulag. Dzavhan, N Mongolia 49°16′N 96°22′E
162 I8 Bayanhongor Bayanhongor, C Mongolia 46°08′N 100°42′E
162 H9 Bayanhongor ◈ province C Mongolia
162 K14 Bayan Hot var. Alxa Zuoqi. Nei Mongol Zizhiqu, N China 38°49′N 105°40′E
163 O8 Bayanhutag var. Bayan. Hentiy, C Mongolia 47°13′N 110°57′E
163 T9 Bayan Huxu var. Horqin Zuoyi Zhongqi. Nei Mongol Zizhiqu, N China 45°02′N 121°28′E
Bayan Khar see Bayan Har Shan
163 N12 Bayan Kuang prev. Bayan Obo. Nei Mongol Zizhiqu, N China 41°45′N 109°58′E
168 J7 Bayan Lepas ✈ (George Town) Pinang, Peninsular Malaysia 05°18′N 100°15′E
162 I10 Bayanlig var. Hatansuudal. Bayanhongor, C Mongolia 44°34′N 100°41′E
162 K13 Bayan Mod Nei Mongol Zizhiqu, N China 40°45′N 104°29′E
163 N8 Bayanmönh var. Ulaan-Ereg. Hentiy, E Mongolia 46°50′N 109°39′E
162 L12 Bayannur var. Linhe. Nei Mongol Zizhiqu, N China 40°46′N 107°27′E
Bayan Nuru see Xar Burd
162 E5 Bayannuur var. Tsul-Ulaan. Bayan-Ölgiy, W Mongolia 48°51′N 91°13′E
Bayan Obo see Bayan Kuang
43 V15 Bayano, Lago ◎ E Panama
162 C5 Bayan-Ölgiy ◈ province NW Mongolia
162 H9 Bayan-Öndör var. Bulgan. Bayanhongor, C Mongolia 44°48′N 98°39′E
162 K8 Bayan-Öndör var. Bumbat. Övörhangay, C Mongolia 46°30′N 104°08′E
162 L8 Bayan-Önjüül var. Ihhayrhan. Töv, C Mongolia 46°57′N 105°51′E
163 O7 Bayan-Ovoo var. Javhlant. Hentiy, E Mongolia 47°46′N 112°06′E
162 L11 Bayan-Ovoo var. Erdenetsogt. Ömnögovĭ, S Mongolia 42°54′N 106°16′E
Bayansayr see Baatsagaan
159 Q9 Bayan Shan ▲ C China 37°36′N 96°23′E
162 J9 Bayanteeg Övörhangay, C Mongolia 45°39′N 101°30′E
162 G5 Bayantes var. Altay. Dzavhan, N Mongolia 49°40′N 96°21′E
Bayantöhöm see Büren
162 M8 Bayantsagaan var. Dzogsool. Töv, C Mongolia 46°46′N 107°18′E
163 P7 Bayantümen var. Tsagaanders. Dornod, NE Mongolia 48°03′N 114°16′E
Bayan-Uhaa see Ih-Uul
163 R10 Bayan Ul var. Xi Ujimqin Qi. Nei Mongol Zizhiqu, N China 44°31′N 117°36′E
Bayan-Ulaan see Dzüünbayan-Ulaan
163 O7 Bayan-Uul var. Javarthushuu. Dornod, NE Mongolia 49°05′N 112°40′E
162 F7 Bayan-Uul var. Bayan. Govĭ-Altay, W Mongolia 47°05′N 95°13′E
162 M8 Bayanuur var. Tsul-Ulaan. Töv, C Mongolia 47°44′N 108°22′E
28 J14 Bayard Nebraska, C USA 41°45′N 103°19′W
37 P15 Bayard New Mexico, SW USA 32°45′N 108°07′W
103 T13 Bayard, Col pass SE France
Bayasgalant see Mönhhaan
136 J12 Bayat Çorum, N Turkey 40°34′N 34°07′E
171 P6 Bayawan Negros, C Philippines 09°22′N 122°50′E
143 R10 Bayāz Kermān, C Iran 30°41′N 55°29′E
171 Q6 Baybay Leyte, C Philippines 10°41′N 124°49′E
21 X10 Bayboro North Carolina, SE USA 35°08′N 76°49′W
137 P12 Bayburt Bayburt, NE Turkey 40°15′N 40°16′E
137 P12 Bayburt ◈ province NE Turkey
31 R8 Bay City Michigan, N USA 43°35′N 83°52′W
25 V12 Bay City Texas, SW USA 28°59′N 96°00′W
Baydarata Bay see Baydaratskaya Guba
122 J7 Baydaratskaya Guba var. Baydarata Bay. bay N Russia
81 M16 Baydhabo var. Baydhowa, Isha Baydhabo, It. Baidoa. Bay, SW Somalia 03°08′N 43°39′E
Baydhowa see Baydhabo
101 N21 Bayerischer Wald ▲▲ SE Germany
101 K21 Bayern Eng. Bavaria, Fr. Bavière. ◈ state SE Germany
147 V9 Bayetovo Narynskaya Oblast', C Kyrgyzstan 41°14′N 74°55′E
102 K4 Bayeux anc. Augustodurum. Calvados, N France 49°16′N 00°42′W
14 E15 Bayfield ≈ Ontario, S Canada
145 O15 Baygekum Kaz. Bäygequm. Kzylorda, S Kazakhstan 44°15′N 66°34′E
Bäygequm see Baygekum
136 C14 Bayındır İzmir, SW Turkey 38°12′N 27°40′E
138 H12 Bāyir var. Bā'ir. Ma'ān, S Jordan 30°46′N 36°40′E
Bay Islands see Bahía, Islas de la
139 R5 Bayjī var. Baiji. Şalāḩ ad Dīn, N Iraq 34°56′N 43°29′E
Baykadam see Saudakent
123 N13 Baykal, Ozero Eng. Lake Baikal. ◎ S Russia
123 M14 Baykal'sk Irkutskaya Oblast', S Russia 51°30′N 104°03′E
137 R15 Baykan Siirt, SE Turkey 38°08′N 41°43′E
139 S2 Baykhmah var. Bēkma. Arbīl, E Iraq 36°40′N 44°15′E
123 L11 Baykit Krasnoyarskiy Kray, C Russia 61°37′N 96°23′E
145 N12 Baykonur var. Baykonyr. Karaganda, C Kazakhstan 47°50′N 75°33′E
144 M14 Baykonyr var. Baykonur, Kaz. Bayqongyr; prev. Leninsk. Kyzylorda, S Kazakhstan 45°38′N 63°20′E
Baykonyr see Baykonur
158 E7 Baykurt Xinjiang Uygur Zizhiqu, W China 39°56′N 75°33′E
14 I9 Bay, Lac ◎ Québec, SE Canada
127 W6 Baymak Respublika Bashkortostan, W Russia 52°34′N 58°20′E
23 O8 Bay Minette Alabama, S USA 30°52′N 87°46′W
143 O17 Baynūnah desert W United Arab Emirates
184 O8 Bay of Plenty off. Bay of Plenty Region. ◈ region North Island, New Zealand
Bay of Plenty Region see Bay of Plenty
191 Z3 Bay of Wrecks bay Kiritimati, E Kiribati
Bayonnaise Rocks see Beyonēsu-retsugan
102 I15 Bayonne anc. Lapurdum. Pyrénées-Atlantiques, SW France 43°30′N 01°28′W
22 H4 Bayou D'Arbonne Lake ⊠ Louisiana, S USA
23 N9 Bayou La Batre Alabama, S USA 30°24′N 88°15′W
Bayou State see Mississippi
Bayqadam see Saudakent
Bayqongyr see Baykonyr
Bayram-Ali see Baýramaly
146 J14 Baýramaly var. Bayramaly; prev. Bayram-Ali. Mary Welaýaty, S Turkmenistan 37°33′N 62°08′E
101 L19 Bayreuth var. Baireuth. Bayern, SE Germany 49°57′N 11°34′E
Bayrische Alpen see Bavarian Alps
Bayrūt see Beyrouth
22 L9 Bay Saint Louis Mississippi, S USA 30°18′N 89°19′W
Baysān see Beit She'an
Bayshint see Öndörshireet
14 H13 Bays, Lake of ◎ Ontario, S Canada
22 M6 Bay Springs Mississippi, S USA 31°58′N 89°17′W
Bay State see Massachusetts
Baysun see Boysun
14 H13 Baysville Ontario, S Canada 45°10′N 79°03′W
141 N15 Bayt al Faqīh W Yemen 14°30′N 43°20′E
158 M4 Baytik Shan ▲▲ China/Mongolia
Bayt Laḩm see Bethlehem
25 W11 Baytown Texas, SW USA 29°43′N 94°59′W
169 V11 Bayur, Tanjung headland Borneo, N Indonesia 0°43′S 117°32′E
121 N14 Bayyal al Kabīr, Wādī dry watercourse NW Libya
145 P17 Bayyrkum Kaz. Bayyrqum; prev. Bairkum. Turkestan, S Kazakhstan 41°57′N 68°05′E
Bayyrqum see Bayyrkum
105 P14 Baza Andalucía, S Spain 37°30′N 02°45′W
137 X10 Bazardüzü Dağı Rus. Gora Bazardyuzyu. ▲ N Azerbaijan 41°13′N 47°50′E
Bazardyuzyu, Gora see Bazardüzü Dağı
Bazargic see Dobrich
83 N18 Bazaruto, Ilha do island SE Mozambique
102 K14 Bazas Gironde, SW France 44°27′N 00°11′W
105 O14 Baza, Sierra de ▲▲ S Spain
160 J8 Bazhong var. Bazhou. Sichuan, C China 31°55′N 106°44′E
Bazhong see Batang
161 P3 Bazhou prev. Baxian, Ba Xian. Hebei, E China 39°05′N 116°24′E
Bazhou see Bazhong
14 M9 Bazin ≈ Québec, SE Canada
Bazin see Pezinok
139 Q7 Bāzīyah Al Anbār, C Iraq 33°50′N 42°41′E
138 H6 Bcharré var. Bcharreh, Bsharrī, Bsherri. NE Lebanon 34°16′N 36°01′E
Bcharreh see Bcharré
28 J5 Beach North Dakota, N USA 46°55′N 104°00′W
182 K12 Beachport South Australia 37°29′S 140°03′E
97 O23 Beachy Head headland SE England, United Kingdom 50°44′N 00°16′E
18 K13 Beacon New York, NE USA 41°30′N 73°54′W
63 J25 Beagle Channel channel Argentina/Chile
181 O1 Beagle Gulf gulf Northern Territory, N Australia
Bealach an Doirín see Ballaghaderreen
Bealach Cláir see Ballyclare
Bealach Féich see Ballybofey
172 J3 Bealanana Mahajanga, NE Madagascar 14°33′S 48°44′E
Béal an Átha see Ballina
Béal an Átha Móir see Ballinamore
Béal an Mhuirhead see Belmullet
Béal Átha Beithe see Ballybay
Béal Átha Conaill see Ballyconnell
Béal Átha hAmhnais see Ballyhaunis
Béal Átha na Sluaighe see Ballinasloe
Béal Átha Seanaidh see Ballyshannon
Bealdovuopmi see Peltovuoma
Béal Feirste see Belfast
Béal Tairbirt see Belturbet
Beanna Boirche see Mourne Mountains
Beannchar see Banagher, Ireland
Beannchar see Bangor, Northern Ireland, UK
Beanntraí see Bantry
Bearalváhki see Berlevåg
23 N2 Bear Creek ≈ Alabama/Mississippi, S USA
30 J13 Bear Creek ≈ Illinois, N USA
27 U13 Bearden Arkansas, C USA 33°43′N 92°37′W
195 Q10 Beardmore Glacier glacier Antarctica
30 K13 Beardstown Illinois, N USA 40°01′N 90°25′W
28 L14 Bear Hill ▲ Nebraska, C USA 41°24′N 101°49′W
Bear Island see Bjørnøya
14 H12 Bear Lake Ontario, S Canada 45°28′N 79°31′W
36 M1 Bear Lake ◎ Idaho/Utah, NW USA
39 U11 Bear, Mount ▲ Alaska, USA 61°16′N 141°09′W
102 J16 Béarn cultural region SW France
194 J11 Bear Peninsula peninsula Antarctica
152 I7 Beas ≈ India/Pakistan
105 P3 Beasain País Vasco, N Spain 43°03′N 02°11′W
105 O12 Beas de Segura Andalucía, S Spain 38°16′N 02°54′W
45 N10 Beata, Cabo headland SW Dominican Republic 17°34′N 71°25′W
45 N10 Beata, Isla island SW Dominican Republic
64 F11 Beata Ridge undersea feature N Caribbean Sea 16°00′N 72°30′W
29 R17 Beatrice Nebraska, C USA 40°14′N 96°43′W
83 L16 Beatrice Mashonaland East, NE Zimbabwe 18°15′S 30°55′E
11 N11 Beatton ≈ British Columbia, W Canada
11 N11 Beatton River British Columbia, W Canada 57°35′N 121°45′W
35 V10 Beatty Nevada, W USA 36°53′N 116°44′W
21 N6 Beattyville Kentucky, S USA 37°33′N 83°44′W
173 X16 Beau Bassin W Mauritius 20°13′S 57°27′E
103 R15 Beaucaire Gard, S France 43°49′N 04°37′E
14 I8 Beauchastel, Lac ◎ Québec, SE Canada
14 I10 Beauchêne, Lac ◎ Québec, SE Canada
183 V3 Beaudesert Queensland, E Australia 28°00′S 152°27′E
182 M12 Beaufort Victoria, SE Australia 37°27′S 143°24′E
21 X11 Beaufort North Carolina, SE USA 34°44′N 76°41′W
21 R15 Beaufort South Carolina, SE USA 32°23′N 80°40′W
38 M11 Beaufort Sea sea Arctic Ocean
Beaufort-Wes see Beaufort West
83 G25 Beaufort West Afr. Beaufort-Wes. Western Cape, SW South Africa 32°21′S 22°35′E
103 N7 Beaugency Loiret, C France 47°46′N 01°38′E
19 R1 Beau Lake ◎ Maine, NE USA
96 I8 Beauly N Scotland, United Kingdom 57°29′N 04°29′W
99 G21 Beaumont Hainaut, S Belgium 50°12′N 04°13′E
185 E23 Beaumont Otago, South Island, New Zealand 45°48′S 169°32′E
22 M7 Beaumont Mississippi, S USA 31°10′N 88°55′W
25 X10 Beaumont Texas, SW USA 30°05′N 94°06′W
102 M15 Beaumont-de-Lomagne Tarn-et-Garonne, S France 43°54′N 01°00′E
102 L6 Beaumont-sur-Sarthe Sarthe, NW France 48°15′N 00°07′E
103 R8 Beaune Côte d'Or, C France 47°02′N 04°50′E
15 R9 Beaupré Québec, SE Canada 47°03′N 70°52′W
102 J8 Beaupréau Maine-et-Loire, NW France 47°13′N 00°57′W
99 I22 Beauraing Namur, SE Belgium 50°07′N 04°57′E
103 R12 Beaurepaire Isère, E France 45°20′N 05°03′E
11 Y16 Beausejour Manitoba, S Canada 50°04′N 96°30′W
103 N4 Beauvais anc. Bellovacum, Caesaromagus. Oise, N France 49°27′N 02°04′E
11 S13 Beauval Saskatchewan, C Canada 55°10′N 107°37′W
102 I9 Beauvoir-sur-Mer Vendée, NW France 46°54′N 02°03′W
39 R8 Beaver Alaska, USA 66°22′N 147°31′W
26 J8 Beaver Oklahoma, C USA 36°48′N 100°32′W
18 B14 Beaver Pennsylvania, NE USA 40°39′N 80°19′W
36 K6 Beaver Utah, W USA 38°16′N 112°38′W
10 L9 Beaver ≈ British Columbia/Yukon, W Canada
11 S13 Beaver ≈ Saskatchewan, C Canada
29 N17 Beaver City Nebraska, C USA 40°08′N 99°49′W
10 G6 Beaver Creek Yukon, W Canada 62°20′N 140°45′W
31 R14 Beavercreek Ohio, N USA 39°42′N 83°58′W
39 S8 Beaver Creek ≈ Alaska, USA
26 H3 Beaver Creek ≈ Kansas/Nebraska, C USA
28 J5 Beaver Creek ≈ Montana/North Dakota, N USA
29 Q14 Beaver Creek ≈ Nebraska, C USA
25 Q4 Beaver Creek ≈ Texas, SW USA
30 M8 Beaver Dam Wisconsin, N USA 43°28′N 88°49′W
30 M8 Beaver Dam Lake ◎ Wisconsin, N USA
18 B14 Beaver Falls Pennsylvania, NE USA 40°45′N 80°20′W
33 P12 Beaverhead Mountains ▲▲ Idaho/Montana, NW USA
33 Q12 Beaverhead River ≈ Montana, NW USA
65 A25 Beaver Island island W Falkland Islands
31 P5 Beaver Island island Michigan, N USA
27 S9 Beaver Lake ⊠ Arkansas, C USA
11 N13 Beaverlodge Alberta, W Canada 55°11′N 119°29′W
18 I8 Beaver River ≈ New York, NE USA




◆ Country ● Country Capital ◇ Dependent Territory ○ Dependent Territory Capital ◈ Administrative Regions ✈ International Airport ▲ Mountain ▲▲ Mountain Range 🌋 Volcano ≈ River ◎ Lake ⊠ Reservoir

BEAVER RIVER – BEOGRAD


26 J8 **Beaver River** ≈ Oklahoma, C USA
18 B13 **Beaver River** ≈ Pennsylvania, NE USA
65 A25 **Beaver Settlement** Beaver Island, W Falkland Islands 51°30′S 61°15′W
**Beaver State** *see* Oregon
14 H14 **Beaverton** Ontario, S Canada 44°24′N 79°07′W
32 G11 **Beaverton** Oregon, NW USA 45°29′N 122°49′W
152 G12 **Beāwar** Rājasthān, N India 26°08′N 74°22′E
**Bebas, Dasht-i** *see* Bābūs, Dasht-e
60 L8 **Bebedouro** São Paulo, S Brazil 20°58′S 48°28′W
101 I16 **Bebra** Hessen, C Germany 50°59′N 09°46′E
41 W12 **Becal** Campeche, SE Mexico 19°49′N 90°28′W
15 Q11 **Bécancour** ≈ Québec, SE Canada
97 Q19 **Beccles** E England, United Kingdom 52°27′N 01°32′E
112 L9 **Bečej** *Ger.* Altbetsche, *Hung.* Óbecse, Rácz-Becse; *prev.* Magyar-Becse, Stari Bečej. Vojvodina, N Serbia 45°36′N 20°02′E
104 I3 **Becerréa** Galicia, NW Spain 42°51′N 07°10′W
74 H7 **Béchar** *prev.* Colomb-Béchar. W Algeria 31°38′N 02°11′W
39 O14 **Becharof Lake** ◎ Alaska, USA
116 H15 **Bechet** *var.* Bechetu. Dolj, SW Romania 43°45′N 23°57′E
**Bechetu** *see* Bechet
21 R6 **Beckley** West Virginia, NE USA 37°46′N 81°12′W
101 G14 **Beckum** Nordrhein-Westfalen, W Germany 51°45′N 08°03′E
25 X7 **Beckville** Texas, SW USA 32°14′N 94°27′W
35 X4 **Becky Peak** ▲ Nevada, W USA 39°59′N 114°33′W
116 I9 **Beclean** *Hung.* Bethlen; *prev.* Betlen. Bistrița-Năsăud, N Romania 47°10′N 24°11′E
**Bécs** *see* Wien
111 H18 **Bečva** *Ger.* Betschau, *Pol.* Beczwa. ≈ E Czechia
**Beczwa** *see* Bečva
103 P15 **Bédarieux** Hérault, S France 43°37′N 03°10′E
120 B10 **Beddouza, Cap** *headland* W Morocco 32°35′N 09°16′W
80 I13 **Bedelē** Oromīya, C Ethiopia 08°25′N 36°21′E
147 Y8 **Bedel Pass** *Rus.* Pereval Bedel. *pass* China/Kyrgyzstan
**Bedel, Pereval** *see* Bedel Pass
95 H22 **Beder** Midtjylland, C Denmark 56°03′N 10°13′E
97 N20 **Bedford** E England, United Kingdom 52°08′N 00°29′W
31 O15 **Bedford** Indiana, N USA 38°51′N 86°29′W
29 U16 **Bedford** Iowa, C USA 40°40′N 94°43′W
20 L4 **Bedford** Kentucky, S USA 38°36′N 85°18′W
18 D15 **Bedford** Pennsylvania, NE USA 40°00′N 78°29′W
21 T6 **Bedford** Virginia, NE USA 37°20′N 79°31′W
97 N20 **Bedfordshire** *cultural region* E England, United Kingdom
127 N5 **Bednodem'yanovsk** Penzenskaya Oblast', W Russia 53°55′N 43°14′E
98 N5 **Bedum** Groningen, NE Netherlands 53°18′N 06°36′E
27 V11 **Beebe** Arkansas, C USA 35°04′N 91°52′W
**Beechy Group** *see* Chichijima-rettō
45 T9 **Beef Island** ✈ (Road Town) Tortola, E British Virgin Islands 18°25′N 64°31′W
**Beehive State** *see* Utah
99 L18 **Beek** Limburg, SE Netherlands 50°56′N 05°47′E
99 L18 **Beek** ✈ (Maastricht) Limburg, SE Netherlands 50°55′N 05°47′E
99 K14 **Beek-en-Donk** Noord-Brabant, S Netherlands 51°31′N 05°37′E
138 F13 **Be'er Menuha** *prev.* Be'ér Menuḥa. Southern, S Israel 30°22′N 35°09′E
**Be'ér Menuḥa** *see* Be'er Menuha
99 D16 **Beernem** West-Vlaanderen, NW Belgium 51°09′N 03°18′E
99 I16 **Beerse** Antwerpen, N Belgium 51°20′N 04°52′E
**Beersheba** *see* Be'er Sheva
138 E11 **Be'er Sheva** *var.* Beersheba, *Ar.* Bir es Saba; *prev.* Be'ér Sheva'. Southern, S Israel 31°15′N 34°47′E
**Be'ér Sheva'** *see* Be'er Sheva
98 J13 **Beesd** Gelderland, C Netherlands 51°52′N 05°12′E
99 M16 **Beesel** Limburg, SE Netherlands 51°16′N 06°02′E
83 J21 **Beestekraal** North-West, N South Africa 25°21′S 27°40′E
194 J7 **Beethoven Peninsula** *peninsula* Alexander Island, Antarctica
**Beetstersweach** *see* Beetsterzwaag
98 M6 **Beetsterzwaag** *Fris.* Beetstersweach. Fryslân, N Netherlands 53°03′N 06°04′E
25 S13 **Beeville** Texas, SW USA 28°25′N 97°47′W
79 J18 **Befale** Equateur, NW Dem. Rep. Congo 0°25′N 20°48′E
**Befandriana** *see* Befandriana Avaratra
172 J3 **Befandriana Avaratra** *var.* Befandriana, Befandriana Nord. Mahajanga, NW Madagascar 15°14′S 48°33′E
**Befandriana Nord** *see* Befandriana Avaratra
79 K18 **Befori** Equateur, N Dem. Rep. Congo 0°09′N 22°18′E
172 I7 **Befotaka** Fianarantsoa, S Madagascar 23°49′S 47°00′E
183 R11 **Bega** New South Wales, SE Australia 36°43′S 149°50′E
102 G5 **Bégard** Côtes d'Armor, NW France 48°37′N 03°18′W
112 M9 **Begejski Kanal** *canal* Vojvodina, NE Serbia
94 G13 **Begna** ≈ S Norway
**Begoml'** *see* Byahoml'
**Begovat** *see* Bekobod
153 Q13 **Begusarai** Bihār, NE India 25°25′N 86°08′E
143 R9 **Behābād** Yazd, C Iran 32°23′N 59°50′E
**Behagle** *see* Laï
55 Z10 **Béhague, Pointe** *headland* E French Guiana 04°38′N 51°52′W
**Behar** *see* Bihār
142 M10 **Behbahān** *var.* Behbehān. Khūzestān, SW Iran 30°38′N 50°07′E
**Behbehān** *see* Behbahān
44 G3 **Behring Point** Andros Island, W The Bahamas 24°28′N 77°44′W
143 P4 **Behshahr** *prev.* Ashraf. Māzandarān, N Iran 36°42′N 53°36′E
163 V6 **Bei'an** Heilongjiang, NE China 48°16′N 126°29′E
**Beibunar** *see* Sredishte
**Beibu Wan** *see* Tonkin, Gulf of
**Beida** *see* Al Bayḍā'
80 H13 **Beigi** Oromīya, C Ethiopia 09°13′N 34°48′E
160 L16 **Beihai** Guangxi Zhuangzu Zizhiqu, S China 21°29′N 109°10′E
159 Q10 **Bei Hulsan Hu** ◎ C China
161 N13 **Bei Jiang** ≈ S China
161 O2 **Beijing** *var.* Pei-ching, *prev. Eng.* Peking; *prev.* Pei-p'ing. ● (China) Beijing Shi, E China 39°58′N 116°23′E
161 P2 **Beijing** ✈ Beijing Shi, N China 39°54′N 116°22′E
**Beijing** *see* Beijing Shi, China
161 P3 **Beijing Daxing International Airport** ✈ Beijing Shi, N China 39°30′N 116°25′E
161 O2 **Beijing Shi** *var.* Beijing, Jing, Pei-ching, *Eng.* Peking; *prev.* Pei-p'ing. ⬖ *municipality* E China
76 G8 **Beïla** Trarza, W Mauritania 18°07′N 15°56′W
98 N7 **Beilen** Drenthe, NE Netherlands 52°52′N 06°27′E
160 L15 **Beiliu** *var.* Lingcheng. Guangxi Zhuangzu Zizhiqu, S China 22°50′N 110°22′E
159 O12 **Beilu He** ≈ W China
**Beilul** *see* Beylul
163 U12 **Beining** *prev.* Beizhen. Liaoning, NE China 41°34′N 121°51′E
96 H8 **Beinn Dearg** ▲ N Scotland, United Kingdom 57°47′N 04°52′W
**Beinn MacDuibh** *see* Ben Macdui
160 I12 **Beipan Jiang** ≈ S China
163 T12 **Beipiao** Liaoning, NE China 41°49′N 120°45′E
83 N17 **Beira** Sofala, C Mozambique 19°45′S 34°56′E
83 N17 **Beira** ✈ Sofala, C Mozambique 19°39′S 35°05′E
104 I7 **Beira Alta** *former province* N Portugal
104 H9 **Beira Baixa** *former province* C Portugal
104 G8 **Beira Litoral** *former province* N Portugal
**Beirut** *see* Beyrouth
**Beisān** *see* Beit She'an
11 Q16 **Beiseker** Alberta, SW Canada 51°20′N 113°34′W
**Beitai Ding** *see* Wutai Shan
83 K19 **Beitbridge** Matabeleland South, S Zimbabwe 22°10′S 30°02′E
**Beit Lekhem** *see* Bethlehem
138 G9 **Beit She'an** *Ar.* Baysān, Beisān; *anc.* Scythopolis, *prev.* Bet She'an. Northern, N Israel 32°30′N 35°30′E
116 G10 **Beiuș** *Hung.* Belényes. Bihor, NW Romania 46°40′N 22°21′E
**Beizhen** *see* Beining
104 H12 **Beja** *anc.* Pax Julia. Beja, SE Portugal 38°01′N 07°52′W
74 M5 **Béja** *var.* Bājah. N Tunisia 36°45′N 09°04′E
104 G13 **Beja** ⬖ *district* S Portugal
120 I9 **Béjaïa** *var.* Bejaïa, *Fr.* Bougie; *anc.* Saldae. NE Algeria 36°49′N 05°03′E
**Bejaïa** *see* Béjaïa
104 K8 **Béjar** Castilla y León, N Spain 40°24′N 05°45′W
**Bejraburi** *see* Phetchaburi
**Bekaa Valley** *see* El Beqaa
**Bekabad** *see* Bekobod
**Békás** *see* Bicaz
169 O15 **Bekasi** Jawa, C Indonesia 06°14′S 106°595′E
**Bek-Budi** *see* Qarshi
**Bekdaş/Bekdash** *see* Garabogaz
147 T10 **Bek-Dzhar** Oshskaya Oblast', SW Kyrgyzstan 40°22′N 73°08′E
111 N24 **Békés** *Rom.* Bichiș. Békés, SE Hungary 46°45′N 21°09′E
111 M24 **Békés** *off.* Békés Megye. ⬖ *county* SE Hungary
111 M24 **Békéscsaba** *Rom.* Bichiș-Ciaba. Békés, SE Hungary 46°40′N 21°05′E
**Békés Megye** *see* Békés
172 H7 **Bekily** Toliara, S Madagascar 24°12′S 45°20′E
165 W4 **Bekkai** *var.* Betsukai. Hokkaidō, NE Japan 43°23′N 145°07′E
**Bēkma** *see* Baykhmah
147 Q11 **Bekobod** *Rus.* Bekabad; *prev.* Begovat. Toshkent Viloyati, E Uzbekistan 40°17′N 69°11′E
127 O7 **Bekovo** Penzenskaya Oblast', W Russia 52°27′N 43°41′E
**Bel** *see* Beliu
152 M13 **Bela** Uttar Pradesh, N India 25°55′N 82°00′E
149 N15 **Bela** Baluchistan, SW Pakistan 26°12′N 66°20′E
79 F15 **Bélabo** Est, C Cameroon 04°54′N 13°10′E
112 N10 **Bela Crkva** *Ger.* Weisskirchen, *Hung.* Fehértemplom. Vojvodina, W Serbia 44°55′N 21°28′E
155 E17 **Belagāvi** *prev.* Belgaum. Karnātaka, W India 15°52′N 74°30′E
173 Y16 **Bel Air** *var.* Rivière Sèche. E Mauritius
104 L12 **Belalcázar** Andalucía, S Spain 38°33′N 05°07′W
113 P15 **Bela Palanka** Serbia, SE Serbia 43°13′N 22°19′E
119 H16 **Belarus** *off.* Republic of Belarus, *var.* Belorussia, *Bel.* Byelarus', *Latv.* Baltkrievija, Respublika Byelarus', *Rus.* Belorusskaya SSR, Belarus', Respublika Belarus'; *prev.* Belorussian SSR. ◆ *republic* E Europe
**Belarus'** *see* Belarus
**Belarus, Republic of** *see* Belarus
**Belarus', Respublika** *see* Belarus
**Belau** *see* Palau
59 H21 **Bela Vista** Mato Grosso do Sul, SW Brazil 22°04′S 56°25′W
83 L21 **Bela Vista** Maputo, S Mozambique 26°20′S 32°40′E
168 I8 **Belawan** Sumatera, W Indonesia 03°46′N 98°44′E
**Bĕla Woda** *see* Weisswasser
127 U4 **Belaya** ≈ W Russia
123 R7 **Belaya Gora** Respublika Sakha (Yakutiya), NE Russia 68°25′N 146°12′E
126 M11 **Belaya Kalitiva** Rostovskaya Oblast', SW Russia 48°09′N 40°43′E
125 R14 **Belaya Kholunitsa** Kirovskaya Oblast', NW Russia 58°54′N 50°52′E
**Belaya Tserkov'** *see* Bila Tserkva
77 V11 **Belbédji** Zinder, S Niger 14°35′N 08°00′E
111 K14 **Bełchatów** *var.* Belchatow. Łódzski, C Poland 51°23′N 19°20′E
**Belchatow** *see* Bełchatów
**Belcher, Îles** *see* Belcher Islands
12 H7 **Belcher Islands** *Fr.* Îles Belcher. *island group* Nunavut, SE Canada
105 S6 **Belchite** Aragón, NE Spain 41°18′N 00°45′W
29 O2 **Belcourt** North Dakota, N USA 48°50′N 99°44′W
31 P9 **Belding** Michigan, N USA 43°06′N 85°13′W
127 U5 **Belebey** Respublika Bashkortostan, W Russia 54°04′N 54°13′E
81 N16 **Beledweyne** *var.* Belet Huen, *It.* Belet Uen. Hiiraan, C Somalia 04°39′N 45°12′E
146 B10 **Belek** Balkan Welaýaty, W Turkmenistan 39°57′N 53°51′E
58 L12 **Belém** *var.* Pará. *state capital* Pará, N Brazil 01°27′S 48°29′W
65 I14 **Belém Ridge** *undersea feature* C Atlantic Ocean
62 I7 **Belén** Catamarca, NW Argentina 27°36′N 67°00′W
54 G9 **Belén** Boyacá, C Colombia 06°01′N 72°55′W
42 J11 **Belén** Rivas, SW Nicaragua 11°30′N 85°55′W
62 O5 **Belén** Concepción, C Paraguay 23°25′S 57°14′W
61 D16 **Belén** Salto, N Uruguay 30°47′S 57°47′W
37 R12 **Belen** New Mexico, SW USA 34°37′N 106°46′W
61 D20 **Belén de Escobar** Buenos Aires, E Argentina 34°21′S 58°47′W
114 J7 **Belene** Pleven, N Bulgaria 43°39′N 25°09′E
114 J7 **Belene, Ostrov** *island* N Bulgaria
43 R15 **Belén, Río** ≈ C Panama
**Belényes** *see* Beiuș
**Embalse de Belesar** *see* Belesar, Encoro de
104 H3 **Belesar, Encoro de** *Sp.* Embalse de Belesar. ⊠ NW Spain
**Belet Huen/Belet Uen** *see* Beledweyne
126 J5 **Belëv** Tul'skaya Oblast', W Russia 53°48′N 36°07′E
19 R7 **Belfast** Maine, NE USA 44°25′N 69°02′W
97 G15 **Belfast** *Ir.* Béal Feirste. ◐ E Northern Ireland, United Kingdom 54°35′N 05°55′W
97 G15 **Belfast Aldergrove** ✈ E Northern Ireland, United Kingdom 54°37′N 06°11′W
97 G15 **Belfast Lough** *Ir.* Loch Lao. *inlet* E Northern Ireland, United Kingdom
28 K5 **Belfield** North Dakota, N USA 46°53′N 103°12′W
103 U7 **Belfort** Territoire-de-Belfort, E France 47°38′N 06°52′E
**Belgard** *see* Białogard
**Belgaum** *see* Belagāvi
**Belgian Congo** *see* Congo (Democratic Republic of)
**België/Belgique** *see* Belgium
99 F20 **Belgium** *off.* Kingdom of Belgium, *Dut.* België, *Fr.* Belgique. ◆ *monarchy* NW Europe
**Belgium, Kingdom of** *see* Belgium
126 J8 **Belgorod** Belgorodskaya Oblast', W Russia 50°38′N 36°37′E
**Belgorod-Dnestrovskiy** *see* Bilhorod-Dnistrovs'kyy
126 J8 **Belgorodskaya Oblast'** ⬖ *province* W Russia
**Belgrad** *see* Beograd
29 T8 **Belgrade** Minnesota, N USA 45°27′N 94°59′W
33 S11 **Belgrade** Montana, NW USA 45°46′N 111°10′W
**Belgrade** *see* Beograd
**Belgrano, Cabo** *see* Meredith, Cape
195 N5 **Belgrano II** *research station (Argentina)* Antarctica 77°50′S 35°25′W
21 X9 **Belhaven** North Carolina, SE USA 35°36′N 76°50′W
107 I23 **Belice** *anc.* Hypsas. ≈ Sicilia, Italy, C Mediterranean Sea
**Belice** *see* Belize/Belize City
**Beli Drim** *see* Drini i Bardhë
**Beligrad** *see* Berat
188 C8 **Beliliou** *prev.* Peleliu. *island* S Palau
114 L8 **Beli Lom, Yazovir** ⊠ NE Bulgaria
112 I8 **Beli Manastir** *Hung.* Pélmonostor; *prev.* Monostor. Osijek-Baranja, NE Croatia 45°46′N 16°38′E
102 J13 **Bélin-Béliet** Gironde, SW France 44°30′N 00°48′W
79 F17 **Bélinga** Ogooué-Ivindo, NE Gabon 01°05′N 13°12′E
21 S4 **Belington** West Virginia, NE USA 39°01′N 79°57′W
127 O6 **Belinskiy** Penzenskaya Oblast', W Russia 52°58′N 43°25′E
169 N12 **Belinyu** Pulau Bangka, W Indonesia 01°37′S 105°45′E
169 O13 **Belitung, Pulau** *island* W Indonesia
116 F10 **Beliu** *Hung.* Bel. Arad, W Romania 46°31′N 21°57′E
114 I9 **Beli Vit** ≈ NW Bulgaria
42 G2 **Belize** *Sp.* Belice; *prev.* British Honduras, Colony of Belize. ◆ *commonwealth republic* Central America
42 F2 **Belize** *Sp.* Belice. ⬖ *district* NE Belize
42 G2 **Belize** ≈ Belize/Guatemala
**Belize** *see* Belize City
42 G2 **Belize City** *var.* Belize, *Sp.* Belice. Belize, NE Belize 17°29′N 88°10′W
42 G2 **Belize City** ✈ Belize, NE Belize 17°31′N 88°15′W
**Belize, Colony of** *see* Belize
**Beljak** *see* Villach
39 N16 **Belkofski** Alaska, USA 55°07′N 162°04′W
123 O6 **Bel'kovskiy, Ostrov** *island* Novosibirskiye Ostrova, NE Russia
14 J8 **Bell** ≈ Québec, SE Canada
10 J15 **Bella Bella** British Columbia, SW Canada 52°04′N 128°07′W
102 M10 **Bellac** Haute-Vienne, C France 46°07′N 01°04′E
10 K15 **Bella Coola** British Columbia, SW Canada 52°23′N 126°46′W
106 D6 **Bellagio** Lombardia, N Italy 45°58′N 09°15′E
31 P6 **Bellaire** Michigan, N USA 44°59′N 85°12′W
106 D6 **Bellano** Lombardia, N Italy 46°06′N 09°21′E
**Bellary** *see* Ballari
183 S5 **Bellata** New South Wales, SE Australia 29°58′S 149°49′E
61 D16 **Bella Unión** Artigas, N Uruguay 30°18′S 57°35′W
61 C14 **Bella Vista** Corrientes, NE Argentina 28°30′S 59°03′W
62 J7 **Bella Vista** Tucumán, N Argentina 27°05′S 65°19′W
62 P4 **Bella Vista** Amambay, C Paraguay 22°08′S 56°20′W
56 B10 **Bellavista** Cajamarca, N Peru 05°43′S 78°48′W
56 D11 **Bellavista** San Martín, N Peru 07°04′S 76°35′W
183 U6 **Bellbrook** New South Wales, SE Australia 30°48′S 152°32′E
27 V5 **Belle** Missouri, C USA 38°17′N 91°43′W
21 Q5 **Belle** West Virginia, NE USA 38°13′N 81°32′W
31 R13 **Bellefontaine** Ohio, N USA 40°22′N 83°45′W
18 F14 **Bellefonte** Pennsylvania, NE USA 40°54′N 77°43′W
28 J9 **Belle Fourche** South Dakota, N USA 44°40′N 103°50′W
28 J9 **Belle Fourche Reservoir** ⊠ South Dakota, N USA
28 K9 **Belle Fourche River** ≈ South Dakota/Wyoming, N USA
103 S10 **Bellegarde-sur-Valserine** Ain, E France 46°06′N 05°49′E
23 Y14 **Belle Glade** Florida, SE USA 26°40′N 80°40′W
102 G8 **Belle Île** *island* NW France
13 T9 **Belle Isle** *island* Belle Isle, Newfoundland and Labrador, E Canada
13 S10 **Belle Isle, Strait of** *strait* Newfoundland and Labrador, E Canada
**Bellenz** *see* Bellinzona
29 W14 **Belle Plaine** Iowa, C USA 41°54′N 92°16′W
29 V9 **Belle Plaine** Minnesota, N USA 44°39′N 93°47′W
14 I9 **Belleterre** Québec, SE Canada 47°24′N 78°40′W
14 J15 **Belleville** Ontario, SE Canada 44°10′N 77°22′W
103 R10 **Belleville** Rhône, E France 46°09′N 04°42′E
30 K15 **Belleville** Illinois, N USA 38°31′N 89°58′W
27 N3 **Belleville** Kansas, C USA 39°51′N 97°38′W
29 Z13 **Bellevue** Iowa, C USA 42°15′N 90°25′W
29 S15 **Bellevue** Nebraska, C USA 41°08′N 95°53′W
31 S11 **Bellevue** Ohio, N USA 41°16′N 82°50′W
25 S5 **Bellevue** Texas, SW USA 33°38′N 98°00′W
32 H8 **Bellevue** Washington, NW USA 47°36′N 122°12′W
55 Y11 **Bellevue de l'Inini, Montagnes** ▲▲ S French Guiana
103 S11 **Belley** Ain, E France 45°46′N 05°41′E
**Bellin** *see* Kangirsuk
183 V6 **Bellingen** New South Wales, SE Australia 30°27′S 152°53′E
97 L14 **Bellingham** N England, United Kingdom 55°09′N 02°16′W
32 H6 **Bellingham** Washington, NW USA 48°46′N 122°29′W
**Belling Hausen Mulde** *see* Southeast Pacific Basin
194 H2 **Bellingshausen** *research station (Russia)* South Shetland Islands, Antarctica 61°57′S 58°23′W
**Bellingshausen** *see* Motu One
**Bellingshausen Abyssal Plain** *see* Bellingshausen Plain
196 R14 **Bellingshausen Plain** *var.* Bellingshausen Abyssal Plain. *undersea feature* SE Pacific Ocean 64°00′S 90°00′W
194 I8 **Bellingshausen Sea** *sea* Antarctica
98 P6 **Bellingwolde** Groningen, NE Netherlands 53°07′N 07°10′E
108 H11 **Bellinzona** *Ger.* Bellenz. Ticino, S Switzerland 46°12′N 09°02′E
25 T8 **Bellmead** Texas, SW USA 31°36′N 97°02′W
54 E8 **Bello** Antioquia, W Colombia 06°19′N 75°34′W
61 B21 **Bellocq** Buenos Aires, E Argentina 35°55′S 61°32′W
**Bello Horizonte** *see* Belo Horizonte
186 L10 **Bellona** *var.* Mungiki. *island* S Solomon Islands
**Bellovacum** *see* Beauvais
182 D7 **Bell, Point** *headland* South Australia 32°13′S 133°08′E
20 F9 **Bells** Tennessee, S USA 35°42′N 89°05′W
25 U5 **Bells** Texas, SW USA 33°36′N 96°24′W
92 N3 **Bellsund** *inlet* SW Svalbard
106 H6 **Belluno** Veneto, NE Italy 46°08′N 12°13′E
62 L11 **Bell Ville** Córdoba, C Argentina 32°35′S 62°41′W
83 E26 **Bellville** Western Cape, SW South Africa 33°50′S 18°43′E
25 U11 **Bellville** Texas, SW USA 29°57′N 96°15′W
104 L12 **Belméz** Andalucía, S Spain 38°16′N 05°12′W
29 V12 **Belmond** Iowa, C USA 42°51′N 93°36′W
18 E11 **Belmont** New York, NE USA 42°14′N 78°02′W
21 R10 **Belmont** North Carolina, SE USA 35°13′N 81°01′W
59 O18 **Belmonte** Bahia, E Brazil 15°53′S 38°54′W
104 I8 **Belmonte** Castelo Branco, C Portugal 40°21′N 07°20′W
105 P10 **Belmonte** Castilla-La Mancha, C Spain 39°34′N 02°43′W
42 G2 **Belmopan** ● (Belize) Cayo, C Belize 17°13′N 88°48′W
97 B16 **Belmullet** *Ir.* Béal an Mhuirhead. Mayo, W Ireland 54°14′N 09°59′W
99 E20 **Belœil** Hainaut, SW Belgium 50°33′N 03°45′E
123 R13 **Belogorsk** Amurskaya Oblast', SE Russia 50°53′N 128°24′E
**Belogorsk** *see* Bilohirs'k
114 F7 **Belogradchik** Vidin, NW Bulgaria 43°37′N 22°42′E
172 H8 **Beloha** Toliara, S Madagascar 25°09′S 45°04′E
59 M20 **Belo Horizonte** *prev.* Bello Horizonte. *state capital* Minas Gerais, SE Brazil 19°54′S 43°54′W
26 M3 **Beloit** Kansas, C USA 39°27′N 98°06′W
30 L9 **Beloit** Wisconsin, N USA 42°31′N 89°01′W
**Belokorovichi** *see* Novi Bilokorovychi
124 J8 **Belomorsk** Respublika Kareliya, NW Russia 64°30′N 34°43′E
124 J8 **Belomorsko-Baltiyskiy Kanal** *Eng.* White Sea-Baltic Canal, White Sea Canal. *canal* NW Russia
153 V15 **Belonia** Tripura, NE India 23°15′N 91°25′E
**Beloozersk** *see* Byelaazyorsk
**Belopol'ye** *see* Bilopillya
105 O4 **Belorado** Castilla y León, N Spain 42°25′N 03°11′W
126 L14 **Belorechensk** Krasnodarskiy Kray, SW Russia 44°46′N 39°53′E
127 W5 **Beloretsk** Respublika Bashkortostan, W Russia 53°56′N 58°26′E
**Belorussia/Belorussian SSR** *see* Belarus
**Belorusskaya Gryada** *see* Byelaruskaya Hrada
**Belorusskaya SSR** *see* Belarus
**Beloshchel'ye** *see* Nar'yan-Mar
114 N8 **Beloslav** Varna, E Bulgaria 43°13′N 27°42′E
**Belostok** *see* Białystok
**Belo-sur-Tsiribihina** *see* Belo Tsiribihina
172 H5 **Belo Tsiribihina** *var.* Belo-sur-Tsiribihina. Toliara, W Madagascar 19°40′S 44°30′E
**Belovár** *see* Bjelovar
**Belovezhskaya, Pushcha** *see* Białowieska, Puszcza/Byelavyezhskaya, Pushcha
114 H10 **Belovo** Pazardzhik, C Bulgaria 42°10′N 24°01′E
**Belovodsk** *see* Bilovods'k
122 H9 **Beloyarskiy** Khanty-Mansiyskiy Avtonomnyy Okrug-Yugra, N Russia 63°40′N 66°31′E
124 K7 **Beloye More** *Eng.* White Sea. *sea* NW Russia
124 K13 **Beloye, Ozero** ◎ NW Russia
114 J10 **Belozem** Plovdiv, C Bulgaria 42°11′N 25°00′E
124 K13 **Belozërsk** Vologodskaya Oblast', NW Russia 59°59′N 37°49′E
108 D8 **Belp** Bern, W Switzerland 46°54′N 07°31′E
108 D8 **Belp** ✈ (Bern) Bern, C Switzerland 46°55′N 07°29′E
107 L24 **Belpasso** Sicilia, Italy, C Mediterranean Sea 37°35′N 14°59′E
31 U14 **Belpre** Ohio, N USA 39°14′N 81°34′W
98 M8 **Belterwijde** ◎ N Netherlands
27 R4 **Belton** Missouri, C USA 38°48′N 94°31′W
21 P11 **Belton** South Carolina, SE USA 34°31′N 82°29′W
25 T9 **Belton** Texas, SW USA 31°04′N 97°30′W
25 S9 **Belton Lake** ⊠ Texas, SW USA
**Bel'tsy** *see* Bălți
97 E16 **Belturbet** *Ir.* Béal Tairbirt. Cavan, N Ireland 54°06′N 07°26′W
**Beluchistan** *see* Balochistan
145 Z9 **Belukha, Gora** ▲ Kazakhstan/Russia 49°50′N 86°44′E
107 M20 **Belvedere Marittimo** Calabria, SW Italy 39°37′N 15°52′E
30 L10 **Belvidere** Illinois, N USA 42°15′N 88°50′W
18 J14 **Belvidere** New Jersey, NE USA 40°50′N 75°05′W
**Bely** *see* Belyy
127 V8 **Belyayevka** Orenburgskaya Oblast', W Russia 51°25′N 56°26′E
**Belynichi** *see* Byalynichy
124 H17 **Belyy** *var.* Bely, Beyj. Tverskaya Oblast', W Russia 55°51′N 32°57′E
126 I6 **Belyye Berega** Bryanskaya Oblast', W Russia 53°11′N 34°42′E
122 J6 **Belyy, Ostrov** *island* N Russia
122 J11 **Belyy Yar** Tomskaya Oblast', C Russia 58°26′N 84°57′E
100 N13 **Belzig** Brandenburg, NE Germany 52°09′N 12°37′E
22 K4 **Belzoni** Mississippi, S USA 33°10′N 90°29′W
172 H4 **Bemaraha** *var.* Plateau du Bemaraha. ▲▲ W Madagascar
**Bemaraha, Plateau du** *see* Bemaraha
82 B10 **Bembe** Uíge, NW Angola 07°03′S 14°25′E
77 S14 **Bembèrèkè** *var.* Bimbéréké. N Benin 10°10′N 02°41′E
104 K12 **Bembézar** ≈ SW Spain
104 J3 **Bembibre** Castilla y León, N Spain 42°37′N 06°25′W
29 T4 **Bemidji** Minnesota, N USA 47°27′N 94°53′W
98 L12 **Bemmel** Gelderland, SE Netherlands 51°53′N 05°54′E
171 T13 **Bemu** Pulau Seram, E Indonesia 03°21′S 129°58′E
**Benāb** *see* Bonāb
105 T5 **Benabarre** *var.* Benavarn. Aragón, NE Spain 42°06′N 00°28′E
**Benaco** *see* Garda, Lago di
79 L20 **Bena-Dibele** Kasai-Oriental, C Dem. Rep. Congo 04°01′S 22°50′E
105 R9 **Benagéber, Embalse de** E Spain
183 O11 **Benalla** Victoria, SE Australia 36°33′S 146°00′E
104 M14 **Benamejí** Andalucía, S Spain 37°16′N 04°33′W
**Benares** *see* Vārānasi
**Benavarn** *see* Benabarre
104 F10 **Benavente** Santarém, C Portugal 38°59′N 08°49′W
104 K5 **Benavente** Castilla y León, N Spain 42°N 05°40′W
25 S15 **Benavides** Texas, SW USA 27°36′N 98°24′W
96 F8 **Benbecula** *island* NW Scotland, United Kingdom
**Bencovazzo** *see* Benkovac
32 H13 **Bend** Oregon, NW USA 44°04′N 121°19′W
182 K7 **Benda Range** ▲▲ South Australia
183 T6 **Bendemeer** New South Wales, SE Australia 30°54′S 151°12′E
117 O10 **Bender** *var.* Tighina, *Rus.* Bendery. E Moldova 46°51′N 29°28′E
**Bender Beila/Bender Beyla** *see* Bandarbeyla
**Bender Cassim/Bender Qaasim** *see* Boosaaso
**Bendery** *see* Bender
183 N11 **Bendigo** Victoria, SE Australia 36°46′S 144°19′E
118 E10 **Bēne** SW Latvia 56°30′N 23°04′E
98 K13 **Beneden-Leeuwen** Gelderland, C Netherlands 51°52′N 05°32′E
101 L24 **Benediktenwand** ▲ S Germany 47°39′N 11°28′E
**Benemérita de San Cristóbal** *see* San Cristóbal
77 N12 **Bénéna** Ségou, S Mali 13°04′N 04°20′W
172 I7 **Benenitra** Toliara, S Madagascar 23°25′S 45°06′E
**Beneschau** *see* Benešov
**Beneški Zaliv** *see* Venice, Gulf of
111 D17 **Benešov** *Ger.* Beneschau. Středočeský Kraj, W Czechia 49°48′N 14°41′E
107 L17 **Benevento** *anc.* Beneventum, Malventum. Campania, S Italy 41°07′N 14°45′E
**Beneventum** *see* Benevento
173 S3 **Bengal, Bay of** *bay* N Indian Ocean
**Bengalooru** *see* Bengalūru
155 H19 **Bengalūru** *var.* Bengalooru; *prev.* Bangalore. *state capital* Karnātaka, S India 12°58′N 77°35′E
79 M17 **Bengamisa** Orientale, N Dem. Rep. Congo 0°58′N 25°11′E
**Bengasi** *see* Banghāzī
**Bengazi** *see* Banghāzī
161 P7 **Bengbu** *var.* Peng-pu. Anhui, E China 32°57′N 117°17′E
32 L9 **Benge** Washington, NW USA 46°55′N 118°01′W
**Benghazi** *see* Banghāzī
168 K10 **Bengkalis** Pulau Bengkalis, W Indonesia 01°27′N 102°10′E
168 K10 **Bengkalis, Pulau** *island* W Indonesia
169 Q10 **Bengkayang** Borneo, C Indonesia 0°45′N 109°28′E
168 K14 **Bengkulu** *prev.* Bengkoeloe, Benkoelen, Benkulen. Sumatera, W Indonesia 03°46′S 102°16′E
168 K13 **Bengkulu** *off.* Propinsi Bengkulu; *prev.* Bengkoeloe, Benkoelen, Benkulen. ⬖ *province* W Indonesia
**Bengkulu, Propinsi** *see* Bengkulu
82 A11 **Bengo** ⬖ *province* W Angola
95 J16 **Bengtsfors** Västra Götaland, S Sweden 59°03′N 12°14′E
82 B13 **Benguela** *var.* Benguella. Benguela, W Angola 12°35′S 13°30′E
83 A14 **Benguela** ⬖ *province* W Angola
**Benguella** *see* Benguela
138 F10 **Ben Gurion** ✈ Tel Aviv, C Israel 32°04′N 34°45′E
**Bengweulu, Lake** *see* Bangweulu, Lake
**Benha** *see* Banhā
192 F6 **Benham Seamount** *undersea feature* W Philippine Sea 15°48′N 124°15′E
96 H6 **Ben Hope** ▲ N Scotland, United Kingdom 58°25′N 04°36′W
79 P18 **Beni** Nord-Kivu, NE Dem. Rep. Congo 0°31′N 29°30′E
57 L15 **Beni** *var.* El Beni. ⬖ *department* N Bolivia
74 H8 **Beni Abbès** W Algeria 30°07′N 02°09′W
105 T8 **Benicarló** Comunitat Valenciana, E Spain 40°25′N 00°25′E
105 T9 **Benicasim** *var.* Benicàssim. Comunitat Valenciana, E Spain 40°03′N 00°03′E
**Benicàssim** *see* Benicasim
105 T12 **Benidorm** Comunitat Valenciana, SE Spain 38°33′N 00°09′W
**Beni Mazâr** *see* Banī Mazār
121 C11 **Beni-Mellal** C Morocco 32°20′N 06°21′W
77 R14 **Benin** *off.* Republic of Benin; *prev.* Dahomey. ◆ *republic* W Africa
77 S17 **Benin, Bight of** *gulf* W Africa
77 U16 **Benin City** Edo, SW Nigeria 06°23′N 05°40′E
**Benin, Republic of** *see* Benin
57 K16 **Beni, Río** ≈ N Bolivia
120 F10 **Beni Saf** *var.* Beni-Saf. NW Algeria 35°19′N 01°23′W
**Beni-Saf** *see* Beni Saf
**Benishangul** *see* Bīnshangul Gumuz
105 T11 **Benissa** Comunitat Valenciana, E Spain 38°43′N 00°03′E
**Beni Suef** *see* Banī Suwayf
11 V15 **Benito** Manitoba, S Canada 51°57′N 101°24′W
**Benito** *see* Uolo, Río
61 C23 **Benito Juárez** Buenos Aires, E Argentina 37°43′S 59°48′W
41 P14 **Benito Juárez Internacional** ✈ (México) México, S Mexico 19°24′N 99°02′W
25 P5 **Benjamin** Texas, SW USA 33°35′N 99°49′W
58 B13 **Benjamin Constant** Amazonas, N Brazil 04°22′S 70°02′W
40 F4 **Benjamín Hill** Sonora, NW Mexico 30°13′N 111°08′W
63 F19 **Benjamín, Isla** *island* Archipiélago de los Chonos, S Chile
164 Q4 **Benkei-misaki** *headland* Hokkaidō, NE Japan 42°49′N 140°10′E
28 L17 **Benkelman** Nebraska, C USA 40°04′N 101°30′W
96 I7 **Ben Klibreck** ▲ N Scotland, United Kingdom 58°15′N 04°23′W
**Benkoelen/Bengkoeloe** *see* Bengkulu
112 D13 **Benkovac** *It.* Bencovazzo. Zadar, SW Croatia 44°02′N 15°36′E
**Benkulen** *see* Bengkulu
96 I11 **Ben Lawers** ▲ C Scotland, United Kingdom 56°33′N 04°13′W
96 J9 **Ben Macdui** *var.* Beinn MacDuibh. ▲ C Scotland, United Kingdom 57°02′N 03°42′W
96 G11 **Ben More** ▲ W Scotland, United Kingdom 56°26′N 06°00′W
96 I11 **Ben More** ▲ C Scotland, United Kingdom 56°22′N 04°31′W
96 H7 **Ben More Assynt** ▲ N Scotland, United Kingdom 58°09′N 04°51′W
185 E20 **Benmore, Lake** ◎ South Island, New Zealand
98 L12 **Bennekom** Gelderland, SE Netherlands 52°00′N 05°40′E
123 Q5 **Bennetta, Ostrov** *island* Novosibirskiye Ostrova, NE Russia
21 T11 **Bennettsville** South Carolina, SE USA 34°36′N 79°40′W
96 H10 **Ben Nevis** ▲ N Scotland, United Kingdom 56°80′N 05°00′W
184 M9 **Benneydale** Waikato, North Island, New Zealand 38°31′S 175°22′E
**Bennichab** *see* Bennichchâb
76 H8 **Bennichchâb** *var.* Bennichab. Inchiri, W Mauritania 19°26′N 15°21′W
18 L10 **Bennington** Vermont, NE USA 42°51′N 73°09′W
185 E20 **Ben Ohau Range** ▲▲ South Island, New Zealand
83 J21 **Benoni** Gauteng, NE South Africa 26°04′S 28°18′E
172 J2 **Be, Nosy** *var.* Nossi-Bé. *island* NW Madagascar
**Bénoué** *see* Benue
42 F2 **Benque Viejo del Carmen** Cayo, W Belize 17°04′N 89°08′W
101 G19 **Bensheim** Hessen, W Germany 49°41′N 08°38′E
37 N16 **Benson** Arizona, SW USA 31°55′N 110°16′W
29 S8 **Benson** Minnesota, N USA 45°19′N 95°36′W
21 U10 **Benson** North Carolina, SE USA 35°22′N 78°33′W
171 N15 **Benteng** Pulau Selayar, C Indonesia 06°07′S 120°28′E
83 A14 **Bentiaba** Namibe, SW Angola 14°18′S 12°27′E
181 T4 **Bentinck Island** *island* Wellesley Islands, Queensland, N Australia
80 E13 **Bentiu** Unity, N South Sudan 09°14′N 29°49′E
138 G8 **Bent Jbaïl** *var.* Bint Jubayl. S Lebanon 33°07′N 35°26′E
11 Q15 **Bentley** Alberta, SW Canada 52°27′N 114°02′W
61 I15 **Bento Gonçalves** Rio Grande do Sul, S Brazil 29°12′S 51°34′W
27 U12 **Benton** Arkansas, C USA 34°34′N 92°35′W
30 L16 **Benton** Illinois, N USA 38°00′N 88°55′W
20 H7 **Benton** Kentucky, S USA 36°51′N 88°21′W
22 G5 **Benton** Louisiana, S USA 32°41′N 93°44′W
27 Y7 **Benton** Missouri, C USA 37°05′N 89°34′W
20 M10 **Benton** Tennessee, S USA 35°10′N 84°39′W
31 O10 **Benton Harbor** Michigan, N USA 42°07′N 86°27′W
27 S9 **Bentonville** Arkansas, C USA 36°23′N 94°13′W
77 V16 **Benue** ⬖ *state* SE Nigeria
78 F13 **Benue** *Fr.* Bénoué. ≈ Cameroon/Nigeria
163 V12 **Benxi** *prev.* Pen-ch'i, Penhsihu, Penki. Liaoning, NE China 41°20′N 123°45′E
**Benyakoni** *see* Byenyakoni
112 K10 **Beočin** Vojvodina, N Serbia 45°13′N 19°43′E
**Beodericsworth** *see* Bury St Edmunds
112 M11 **Beograd** *Eng.* Belgrade, *Ger.* Belgrad; *anc.* Singidunum. ● (Serbia) Serbia, N Serbia 44°48′N 20°27′E
112 L11 **Beograd** *Eng.* Belgrade. ✈ Serbia, N Serbia 44°45′N 20°21′E


◆ Country
● Country Capital
◇ Dependent Territory
○ Dependent Territory Capital
⬖ Administrative Regions
✈ International Airport
▲ Mountain
▲▲ Mountain Range
⛰ Volcano
≈ River
◎ Lake
⊠ Reservoir

BÉOUMI – BIG STONE GAP


76 M16 **Béoumi** C Ivory Coast 07°40′N 05°34′W
35 V3 **Beowawe** Nevada, W USA 40°33′N 116°31′W
164 E14 **Beppu** Ōita, Kyūshū, SW Japan 33°18′N 131°30′E
187 X15 **Beqa** *prev.* Mbengga. *island* W Fiji
45 Y14 **Bequia** *island* C Saint Vincent and the Grenadines
139 U4 **Beranan, Shax-î** *var.* Shākh-i Barānān. ⛰ E Iraq
113 L16 **Berane** *prev.* Ivangrad. E Montenegro 42°51′N 19°51′E
113 L21 **Berat** *var.* Berati, *SCr.* Beligrad. Berat, C Albania 40°43′N 19°58′E
113 L21 **Berat** ◈ *county* C Albania
**Berătău** *see* Berettyó
**Berati** *see* Berat
**Beraun** *see* Berounka, Czech Republic
**Beraun** *see* Beroun, Czech Republic
171 U13 **Berau, Teluk** *var.* MacCluer Gulf. *bay* Papua, E Indonesia
80 G8 **Berber** River Nile, NE Sudan 18°01′N 34°00′E
80 N12 **Berbera** Woqooyi Galbeed, NW Somalia 10°24′N 45°02′E
79 H16 **Berbérati** Mambéré-Kadéï, SW Central African Republic 04°14′N 15°50′E
**Berberia, Cabo de** *see* Barbaria, Cap de
55 T9 **Berbice River** ≈ NE Guyana
**Berchid** *see* Berrechid
103 N2 **Berck-Plage** Pas-de-Calais, N France 50°24′N 01°35′E
25 T13 **Berclair** Texas, SW USA 28°33′N 97°32′W
117 W10 **Berda** ≈ SE Ukraine
**Berdichev** *see* Berdychiv
123 P10 **Berdigestyakh** Respublika Sakha (Yakutiya), NE Russia 62°02′N 127°03′E
122 J12 **Berdsk** Novosibirskaya Oblast', C Russia 54°42′N 82°56′E
117 W10 **Berdyans'k** *Rus.* Berdyansk; *prev.* Osipenko. Zaporiz'ka Oblast', SE Ukraine 46°46′N 36°49′E
117 W10 **Berdyans'ka Kosa** *spit* SE Ukraine
117 V10 **Berdyans'ka Zatoka** *gulf* S Ukraine
117 N5 **Berdychiv** *Rus.* Berdichev. Zhytomyrs'ka Oblast', N Ukraine 49°54′N 28°39′E
20 M6 **Berea** Kentucky, S USA 37°34′N 84°18′W
**Beregovo/Beregszász** *see* Berehove
116 G8 **Berehove** *Cz.* Berehovo, *Hung.* Beregszász, *Rus.* Beregovo. Zakarpats'ka Oblast', W Ukraine 48°13′N 22°39′E
**Berehovo** *see* Berehove
186 D9 **Bereina** Central, S Papua New Guinea 08°29′S 146°30′E
146 C11 **Bereket** *prev. Rus.* Gazandzhyk, Kazandzhik, *Turkm.* Gazanjyk. Balkan Welaýaty, W Turkmenistan 39°17′N 55°27′E
45 O12 **Berekua** S Dominica 15°14′N 61°19′W
77 O16 **Berekum** W Ghana 07°27′N 02°35′W
**Berenice** *see* Baranīs
11 O14 **Berens** ≈ Manitoba/Ontario, C Canada
11 X14 **Berens River** Manitoba, C Canada 52°22′N 97°00′W
29 R12 **Beresford** South Dakota, N USA 43°02′N 96°45′W
116 J4 **Berestechko** Volyns'ka Oblast', NW Ukraine 50°21′N 25°06′E
116 M11 **Bereşti** Galaţi, E Romania 46°04′N 27°54′E
117 U6 **Berestova** ≈ E Ukraine
**Beretău** *see* Berettyó
111 N23 **Berettyó** *Rom.* Barcău; *prev.* Berătău, Beretău. ≈ Hungary/Romania
111 N23 **Berettyóújfalu** Hajdú-Bihar, E Hungary 47°15′N 21°33′E
**Berëza/Bereza Kartuska** *see* Byaroza
117 Q4 **Berezan'** Kyivs'ka Oblast', N Ukraine 50°18′N 31°30′E
117 Q10 **Berezanka** Mykolayivs'ka Oblast', S Ukraine 46°51′N 31°24′E
116 J6 **Berezhany** *Pol.* Brzeżany. Ternopil's'ka Oblast', W Ukraine 49°29′N 25°00′E
**Berezina** *see* Byarezina
**Berezino** *see* Byerazino
117 P10 **Berezivka** *Rus.* Berezovka. Odes'ka Oblast', SW Ukraine 47°12′N 30°56′E
117 Q2 **Berezna** Chernihivs'ka Oblast', NE Ukraine 51°35′N 31°50′E
116 L3 **Berezne** Rivnens'ka Oblast', NW Ukraine 51°00′N 26°46′E
117 R9 **Bereznehuvate** Mykolayivs'ka Oblast', S Ukraine 47°18′N 32°52′E
125 N10 **Bereznik** Arkhangel'skaya Oblast', NW Russia 62°50′N 42°40′E
125 U13 **Berezniki** Permskiy Kray, NW Russia 59°26′N 56°49′E
**Berëzovka** *see* Byarozawka, Belarus
**Berezovka** *see* Berezivka, Ukraine
122 H9 **Berezovo** Khanty-Mansiyskiy Avtonomnyy Okrug-Yugra, N Russia 63°48′N 64°38′E
127 O9 **Berezovskaya** Volgogradskaya Oblast', SW Russia 50°17′N 43°58′E
123 S13 **Berezovyy** Khabarovskiy Kray, E Russia 51°42′N 135°39′E
83 E25 **Berg** ≈ W South Africa
**Berg** *see* Berg bei Rohrbach
105 V4 **Berga** Cataluña, NE Spain 42°06′N 01°41′E
95 N20 **Berga** Kalmar, S Sweden 57°13′N 16°03′E
136 B13 **Bergama** İzmir, W Turkey 39°08′N 27°10′E
106 E7 **Bergamo** *anc.* Bergomum. Lombardia, N Italy 45°42′N 09°40′E
105 P3 **Bergara** País Vasco, N Spain 43°05′N 02°25′W
109 S3 **Berg bei Rohrbach** *var.* Berg. Oberösterreich, N Austria 48°34′N 14°02′E
100 O6 **Bergen** Mecklenburg-Vorpommern, NE Germany 54°25′N 13°25′E
101 I11 **Bergen** Niedersachsen, NW Germany 52°49′N 09°57′E
98 H8 **Bergen** Noord-Holland, NW Netherlands 52°40′N 04°42′E
94 C13 **Bergen** Hordaland, S Norway 60°24′N 05°19′E
**Bergen** *see* Mons
55 W9 **Berg en Dal** Brokopondo, C Suriname 05°15′N 55°20′W
99 G15 **Bergen op Zoom** Noord-Brabant, S Netherlands 51°30′N 04°17′E
102 L13 **Bergerac** Dordogne, SW France 44°51′N 00°30′E
99 J16 **Bergeyk** Noord-Brabant, S Netherlands 51°19′N 05°21′E
101 D16 **Bergheim** Nordrhein-Westfalen, W Germany 50°57′N 06°39′E
55 X10 **Bergi** Sipaliwini, E Suriname 04°36′N 54°24′W
101 E16 **Bergisch Gladbach** Nordrhein-Westfalen, W Germany 50°59′N 07°09′E
101 F14 **Bergkamen** Nordrhein-Westfalen, W Germany 51°32′N 07°41′E
95 N21 **Bergkvara** Kalmar, S Sweden 56°22′N 16°04′E
**Bergomum** *see* Bergamo
98 K13 **Bergse Maas** ≈ S Netherlands
95 P15 **Bergshamra** Stockholm, C Sweden 59°37′N 18°40′E
94 N10 **Bergsjö** Gävleborg, C Sweden 62°00′N 17°10′E
93 J14 **Bergsviken** Norrbotten, N Sweden 65°16′N 21°24′E
**Bergum** *see* Burgum
98 M6 **Bergumer Meer** ◎ N Netherlands
94 N12 **Bergviken** ◎ C Sweden
168 M11 **Berhala, Selat** *strait* Sumatera, W Indonesia
**Berhampore** *see* Baharampur
99 J17 **Beringen** Limburg, NE Belgium 51°04′N 05°14′E
39 T12 **Bering Glacier** *glacier* Alaska, USA
**Beringov Proliv** *see* Bering Strait
192 L2 **Bering Sea** *sea* N Pacific Ocean
38 L9 **Bering Strait** *Rus.* Beringov Proliv. *strait* Bering Sea/Chukchi Sea
**Berislav** *see* Beryslav
105 O15 **Berja** Andalucía, S Spain 36°51′N 02°56′W
94 H9 **Berkåk** Sør-Trøndelag, S Norway 62°50′N 10°01′E
98 N11 **Berkel** ≈ Germany/Netherlands
35 N8 **Berkeley** California, W USA 37°52′N 122°16′W
65 E24 **Berkeley Sound** *sound* NE Falkland Islands
21 V2 **Berkeley Springs** *var.* Bath. West Virginia, NE USA 39°38′N 78°14′W
195 N6 **Berkner Island** *island* Antarctica
114 G8 **Berkovitsa** Montana, NW Bulgaria 43°15′N 23°05′E
97 M22 **Berkshire** *former county* S England, United Kingdom
99 H17 **Berlaar** Antwerpen, N Belgium 51°08′N 04°39′E
**Berlanga** *see* Berlanga de Duero
105 P6 **Berlanga de Duero** *var.* Berlanga. Castilla y León, N Spain 41°28′N 02°51′W
0 I16 **Berlanga Rise** *undersea feature* E Pacific Ocean 08°30′N 93°30′W
99 F17 **Berlare** Oost-Vlaanderen, NW Belgium 51°02′N 04°01′E
104 E9 **Berlenga, Ilha da** *island* C Portugal
92 M7 **Berlevåg** *Lapp.* Bearalváhki. Finnmark, N Norway 70°51′N 29°04′E
100 O12 **Berlin** ● (Germany) Berlin, NE Germany 52°31′N 13°26′E
21 Z4 **Berlin** Maryland, NE USA 38°19′N 75°13′W
19 O7 **Berlin** New Hampshire, NE USA 44°27′N 71°13′W
18 D16 **Berlin** Pennsylvania, NE USA 39°54′N 78°57′W
30 L7 **Berlin** Wisconsin, N USA 43°57′N 88°59′W
100 O12 **Berlin** ◈ *state* NE Germany
**Berlinchen** *see* Barlinek
31 U12 **Berlin Lake** ⊠ Ohio, N USA
183 R11 **Bermagui** New South Wales, SE Australia 36°26′S 150°01′E
40 L8 **Bermejillo** Durango, C Mexico 25°55′N 103°39′W
62 L5 **Bermejo, Río** ≈ N Argentina
62 I10 **Bermejo, Río** ≈ W Argentina
62 M6 **Bermejo viejo, Río** ≈ N Argentina
105 P2 **Bermeo** País Vasco, N Spain 43°25′N 02°44′W
104 K6 **Bermillo de Sayago** Castilla y León, N Spain 41°22′N 06°08′W
106 E6 **Bermina, Pizzo** *Rmsch.* Piz Bernina. ▲ Italy/Switzerland 46°22′N 09°52′E *see also* Bermina, Piz
64 A12 **Bermuda** *var.* Bermuda Islands, Bermudas; *prev.* Somers Islands. ◇ *UK Overseas Territory* NW Atlantic Ocean
1 N11 **Bermuda** *var.* Great Bermuda, Long Island, Main Island. *island* Bermuda
**Bermuda Islands** *see* Bermuda
**Bermuda-New England Seamount Arc** *see* New England Seamounts
1 N11 **Bermuda Rise** *undersea feature* C Sargasso Sea 32°30′N 65°00′W
**Bermudas** *see* Bermuda
108 D8 **Bern** *Fr.* Berne. ● (Switzerland) Bern, W Switzerland 46°57′N 07°26′E
108 D9 **Bern** *Fr.* Berne. ◈ *canton* W Switzerland
37 R11 **Bernalillo** New Mexico, SW USA 35°18′N 106°33′W
14 H12 **Bernard Lake** ◎ Ontario, S Canada
61 B18 **Bernardo de Irigoyen** Santa Fe, NE Argentina 32°09′S 61°06′W
18 J14 **Bernardsville** New Jersey, NE USA 40°43′N 74°34′W
63 K14 **Bernasconi** La Pampa, C Argentina 37°55′S 63°44′W
100 O12 **Bernau** Brandenburg, NE Germany 52°41′N 13°36′E
102 L4 **Bernay** Eure, N France 49°05′N 00°36′E
101 L14 **Bernburg** Sachsen-Anhalt, C Germany 51°47′N 11°45′E
109 X5 **Berndorf** Niederösterreich, NE Austria 47°58′N 16°08′E
31 Q12 **Berne** Indiana, N USA 40°39′N 84°57′W
**Berne** *see* Bern
108 D10 **Berner Alpen** *var.* Berner Oberland, *Eng.* Bernese Oberland. ⛰ SW Switzerland
**Berner Oberland/Bernese Oberland** *see* Berner Alpen
109 Y2 **Bernhardsthal** Niederösterreich, N Austria 48°40′N 16°51′E
22 H4 **Bernice** Louisiana, S USA 32°49′N 92°39′W
27 Y8 **Bernie** Missouri, C USA 36°40′N 89°58′W
180 G9 **Bernier Island** *island* Western Australia
**Bernina Pass** *see* Bernina, Passo del
108 J10 **Bernina, Passo del** *Eng.* Bernina Pass. *pass* SE Switzerland
108 J10 **Bernina, Piz** *It.* Pizzo Bernina. ▲ Italy/Switzerland 46°22′N 09°55′E *see also* Bermina, Pizzo
**Bernina, Piz** *see* Bermina, Pizzo
99 E20 **Bernissart** Hainaut, SW Belgium 50°29′N 03°37′E
101 E18 **Bernkastel-Kues** Rheinland-Pfalz, W Germany 49°55′N 07°04′E
**Beroea** *see* Ḥalab
172 H6 **Beroroha** Toliara, SW Madagascar 21°40′S 45°10′E
**Béroubouay** *see* Gbéroubouè
111 C17 **Beroun** *Ger.* Beraun. Středočeský Kraj, W Czechia 49°58′N 14°05′E
111 C16 **Berounka** *Ger.* Beraun. ≈ W Czechia
113 Q18 **Berovo** E North Macedonia 41°45′N 22°50′E
74 F6 **Berrechid** *var.* Berchid. W Morocco 33°16′N 07°32′W
103 R15 **Berre, Étang de** ◎ SE France
103 S15 **Berre-l'Étang** Bouches-du-Rhône, SE France 43°28′N 05°10′E
182 K9 **Berri** South Australia 34°16′S 140°35′E
31 O10 **Berrien Springs** Michigan, N USA 41°57′N 86°20′W
183 O10 **Berrigan** New South Wales, SE Australia 35°41′S 145°50′E
103 N9 **Berry** *cultural region* C France
35 N7 **Berryessa, Lake** ◎ California, W USA
44 G2 **Berry Islands** *island group* N The Bahamas
27 T9 **Berryville** Arkansas, C USA 36°22′N 93°35′W
21 V3 **Berryville** Virginia, NE USA 39°08′N 77°59′W
83 D21 **Berseba** //Karas, S Namibia 26°00′S 17°46′E
117 O8 **Bershad'** Vinnyts'ka Oblast', C Ukraine 48°20′N 29°30′E
28 L3 **Berthold** North Dakota, N USA 48°16′N 101°48′W
37 T3 **Berthoud** Colorado, C USA 40°18′N 105°04′W
37 S4 **Berthoud Pass** *pass* Colorado, C USA
79 F15 **Bertoua** Est, E Cameroon 04°34′N 13°42′E
25 S10 **Bertram** Texas, SW USA 30°44′N 98°03′W
63 G22 **Bertrand, Cerro** ▲ S Argentina 50°00′S 73°27′W
99 J23 **Bertrix** Luxembourg, SE Belgium 49°52′N 05°15′E
191 P3 **Beru** *var.* Peru. *atoll* Tungaru, W Kiribati
**Beruni** *see* Beruniy
146 I9 **Beruniy** *var.* Biruni, *Rus.* Beruni. Qoraqalpog'iston Respublikasi, W Uzbekistan 41°48′N 60°39′E
58 F13 **Beruri** Amazonas, NW Brazil 03°44′S 61°13′W
18 H14 **Berwick** Pennsylvania, NE USA 41°03′N 76°13′W
96 K12 **Berwick** *cultural region* SE Scotland, United Kingdom
96 L12 **Berwick-upon-Tweed** N England, United Kingdom 55°46′N 02°W
117 S10 **Beryslav** *Rus.* Berislav. Khersons'ka Oblast', S Ukraine 46°51′N 33°26′E
**Berytus** *see* Beyrouth
172 H4 **Besalampy** Mahajanga, W Madagascar 16°43′S 44°29′E
103 T8 **Besançon** *anc.* Besontium, Vesontio. Doubs, E France 47°14′N 06°01′E
103 P10 **Besbre** ≈ C France
**Bescanuova** *see* Baška
**Besdan** *see* Bezdan
**Besed'** *see* Byesyedz'
147 R10 **Beshariq** *Rus.* Besharyk; *prev.* Kirovo. Far'gona Viloyati, E Uzbekistan 40°26′N 70°33′E
**Besharyk** *see* Beshariq
146 L9 **Beshbuloq** *Rus.* Beshulak. Navoiy Viloyati, N Uzbekistan 41°55′N 64°13′E
**Beshenkovichi** *see* Byeshankovichy
146 M13 **Beshkent** Qashqadaryo Viloyati, S Uzbekistan 38°47′N 65°42′E
**Beshulak** *see* Beshbuloq
112 L10 **Beška** Vojvodina, N Serbia 45°09′N 20°04′E
**Beskra** *see* Biskra
127 O16 **Beslan** Respublika Severnaya Osetiya, SW Russia 43°12′N 44°33′E
113 P16 **Besna Kobila** ▲ SE Serbia 42°30′N 22°16′E
137 N16 **Besni** Adıyaman, S Turkey 37°42′N 37°53′E
**Besontium** *see* Besançon
121 Q2 **Beşparmak Dağları** *Gk.* Pentadáktylos, *Eng.* Kyrenia Mountains. ⛰ N Cyprus
**Bessarabka** *see* Basarabeasca
92 O2 **Bessels, Kapp** *headland* C Svalbard 78°36′N 21°43′E
23 P4 **Bessemer** Alabama, S USA 33°24′N 86°57′W
30 K3 **Bessemer** Michigan, N USA 46°28′N 90°03′W
21 Q10 **Bessemer City** North Carolina, SE USA 35°16′N 81°16′W
102 M10 **Bessines-sur-Gartempe** Haute-Vienne, C France 46°06′N 01°22′E
99 K15 **Best** Noord-Brabant, S Netherlands 51°31′N 05°24′E
25 N9 **Best** Texas, SW USA 31°13′N 101°34′W
139 U2 **Beste** *Ar.* Basṭah. As Sulaymānīyah, E Iraq 36°20′N 45°14′E
125 O11 **Bestuzhevo** Arkhangel'skaya Oblast', NW Russia 61°36′N 43°54′E
123 M11 **Bestyakh** Respublika Sakha (Yakutiya), NE Russia 61°25′N 129°05′E
**Beszterce** *see* Bistriţa
**Besztercebánya** *see* Banská Bystrica
172 I5 **Betafo** Antananarivo, C Madagascar 19°50′S 46°50′E
104 H2 **Betanzos** Galicia, NW Spain 43°17′N 08°17′W
104 G2 **Betanzos, Ría de** *estuary* NW Spain
79 G15 **Bétaré Oya** Est, E Cameroon 05°34′N 14°09′E
105 S9 **Bétera** Comunitat Valenciana, E Spain 39°35′N 00°28′W
77 R15 **Bétérou** C Benin 09°13′N 02°18′E
83 K21 **Bethal** Mpumalanga, NE South Africa 26°27′S 29°28′E
30 K15 **Bethalto** Illinois, N USA 38°54′N 90°02′W
83 D21 **Bethanie** *var.* Bethanien, Bethany. //Karas, S Namibia 26°32′S 17°11′E
**Bethanien** *see* Bethanie
27 S2 **Bethany** Missouri, C USA 40°15′N 94°03′W
27 N10 **Bethany** Oklahoma, C USA 35°31′N 97°37′W
**Bethany** *see* Bethanie
39 N12 **Bethel** Alaska, USA 60°47′N 161°45′W
19 P7 **Bethel** Maine, NE USA 44°24′N 70°47′W
21 W9 **Bethel** North Carolina, SE USA 35°46′N 77°21′W
18 B15 **Bethel Park** Pennsylvania, NE USA 40°21′N 80°03′W
21 W3 **Bethesda** Maryland, NE USA 39°00′N 77°05′W
83 J22 **Bethlehem** Free State, C South Africa 28°12′S 28°16′E
18 I14 **Bethlehem** Pennsylvania, NE USA 40°36′N 75°22′W
138 F10 **Bethlehem** *var.* Beit Lekhem, *Ar.* Bayt Laḥm, *Heb.* Bet Leḥem. C West Bank 31°43′N 35°12′E
**Bethlen** *see* Beclean
83 I24 **Bethulie** Free State, C South Africa 30°30′S 25°59′E
103 O1 **Béthune** Pas-de-Calais, N France 50°32′N 02°38′E
102 M3 **Béthune** ≈ N France
104 M14 **Béticos, Sistemas** *var.* Sistema Penibético, *Eng.* Baetic Cordillera, Baetic Mountains. ⛰ S Spain
54 I6 **Betijoque** Trujillo, NW Venezuela 09°25′N 70°45′W
59 M20 **Betim** Minas Gerais, SE Brazil 19°56′S 44°10′W
190 H3 **Betio** Tarawa, W Kiribati 01°21′N 172°56′E
172 H7 **Betioky** Toliara, S Madagascar 23°42′S 44°22′E
**Bet Leḥem** *see* Bethlehem
**Betlen** *see* Beclean
167 O17 **Betong** Yala, SW Thailand 05°45′N 101°05′E
79 I16 **Bétou** Likouala, N Congo 03°08′N 18°31′E
145 P14 **Betpakdala** *Kaz.* Betpaqdala *prev.* Betpak-Dala. *plateau* S Kazakhstan
**Betpak-Dala** *see* Betpakdala
**Betpaqdala** *see* Betpakdala
172 H7 **Betroka** Toliara, S Madagascar 23°15′S 46°07′E
**Betschau** *see* Bečva
**Bet She'an** *see* Beit She'an
15 T6 **Betsiamites** Québec, SE Canada 48°56′N 68°40′W
15 T6 **Betsiamites** ≈ Québec, SE Canada
172 I4 **Betsiboka** ≈ N Madagascar
**Betsukai** *see* Bekkai
99 M25 **Bettembourg** Luxembourg, S Luxembourg 49°31′N 06°06′E
99 M23 **Bettendorf** Diekirch, NE Luxembourg 49°53′N 06°13′E
29 Z14 **Bettendorf** Iowa, C USA 41°31′N 90°31′W
**Bette, Pic** *see* Bette, Picco
75 R13 **Bette, Picco** *var.* Bikkū Bittī, Pic Bette. ▲ S Libya 22°02′N 19°07′E
153 P12 **Bettiah** Bihār, N India 26°49′N 84°30′E
39 Q7 **Bettles** Alaska, USA 66°54′N 151°40′W
95 N17 **Bettna** Södermanland, C Sweden 58°52′N 16°40′E
154 H11 **Betūl** *prev.* Badnur. Madhya Pradesh, C India 21°55′N 77°54′E
154 H9 **Betwa** ≈ C India
101 F16 **Betzdorf** Rheinland-Pfalz, W Germany 50°47′N 07°50′E
82 C9 **Béu** Uíge, NW Angola 06°15′S 15°32′E
31 P6 **Beulah** Michigan, N USA 43°35′N 83°52′W
28 L5 **Beulah** North Dakota, N USA 47°16′N 101°48′W
98 M8 **Beulakerwijde** ◎ N Netherlands
98 L13 **Beuningen** Gelderland, SE Netherlands 51°52′N 05°47′E
**Beuthen** *see* Bytom
103 N7 **Beuvron** ≈ C France
99 F16 **Beveren** Oost-Vlaanderen, N Belgium 51°13′N 04°15′E
21 T9 **B. Everett Jordan Reservoir** *var.* Jordan Lake. ⊠ North Carolina, SE USA
97 N17 **Beverley** E England, United Kingdom 53°51′N 00°26′W
**Beverley** *see* Beverly
99 J17 **Beverlo** Limburg, NE Belgium 51°06′N 05°14′E
19 P11 **Beverly** Massachusetts, NE USA 42°33′N 70°49′W
32 J9 **Beverly** *var.* Beverley. Washington, NW USA 46°50′N 119°57′W
35 S15 **Beverly Hills** California, W USA 34°02′N 118°25′W
101 I14 **Beverungen** Nordrhein-Westfalen, C Germany 51°39′N 09°22′E
98 H9 **Beverwijk** Noord-Holland, W Netherlands 52°29′N 04°40′E
108 C10 **Bex** Vaud, W Switzerland 46°15′N 07°00′E
97 P23 **Bexhill** *var.* Bexhill-on-Sea. SE England, United Kingdom 50°50′N 00°28′E
**Bexhill-on-Sea** *see* Bexhill
136 E17 **Bey Dağları** ⛰ SW Turkey
**Beyj** *see* Belyy
136 E10 **Beykoz** İstanbul, NW Turkey 41°09′N 29°06′E
76 K15 **Beyla** SE Guinea 08°43′N 08°41′W
137 X12 **Beyläqan** *prev.* Zhdanov. SW Azerbaijan 39°43′N 47°38′E
80 L10 **Beylul** *var.* Beilul. SE Eritrea 13°10′N 42°27′E
144 H14 **Beyneu** *Kaz.* Beyneū. Mangistau, SW Kazakhstan 45°20′N 55°11′E
**Beyneū** *see* Beyneu
165 X14 **Beyonēsu-retsugan** *Eng.* Bayonnaise Rocks. *island group* SE Japan
136 G12 **Beypazarı** Ankara, NW Turkey 40°10′N 31°56′E
155 F21 **Beypore** Kerala, SW India 11°10′N 75°49′E
138 G7 **Beyrouth** *var.* Bayrūt, *Eng.* Beirut; *anc.* Berytus. ● (Lebanon) W Lebanon 33°55′N 35°31′E
138 G7 **Beyrouth** ✈ W Lebanon 33°52′N 35°30′E
136 G15 **Beyşehir** Konya, SW Turkey 37°40′N 31°43′E
136 G15 **Beyşehir Gölü** ◎ C Turkey
108 J7 **Bezau** Vorarlberg, NW Austria 47°24′N 09°55′E
112 J8 **Bezdan** *Ger.* Besdan, *Hung.* Bezdán. Vojvodina, NW Serbia 45°51′N 19°00′E
**Bezdezh** *see* Byezdzyezh
124 G15 **Bezhanitsy** Pskovskaya Oblast', W Russia 56°57′N 29°53′E
124 K15 **Bezhetsk** Tverskaya Oblast', W Russia 57°47′N 36°42′E
103 P16 **Béziers** *anc.* Baeterrae, Baeterrae Septimanorum, Julia Beterrae. Hérault, S France 43°21′N 03°13′E
**Bezmein** *see* Abadan
**Bezwada** *see* Vijayawāda
154 P12 **Bhadrak** *var.* Bhadrakh. Odisha, E India 21°04′N 86°30′N
**Bhadrakh** *see* Bhadrak
155 F19 **Bhadra Reservoir** ⊠ SW India
155 F18 **Bhadrāvati** Karnātaka, SW India 13°52′N 75°43′E
153 R14 **Bhāgalpur** Bihār, NE India 25°14′N 86°59′E
**Bhairab** *see* Bhairab Bazar
153 U14 **Bhairab Bazar** *var.* Bhairab. Dhaka, C Bangladesh 24°04′N 91°00′E
153 O11 **Bhairahawā** Western, S Nepal 27°31′N 83°27′E
149 S8 **Bhakkar** Punjab, E Pakistan 31°40′N 71°08′E
153 P11 **Bhaktapur** Central, C Nepal 27°47′N 85°21′E
167 N3 **Bhamo** *var.* Banmo. Kachin State, N Myanmar (Burma) 24°15′N 97°15′E
**Bhāmragad** *see* Bhāmragarh
154 K13 **Bhāmragarh** *var.* Bhāmragad. Mahārāshtra, C India 19°28′N 80°39′E
154 J12 **Bhandāra** Mahārāshtra, C India 21°10′N 79°41′E
**Bhārat** *see* India
195 X7 **Bharati** *research station (India)* Antarctica 69°24′S 76°11′E
152 J12 **Bharatpur** *prev.* Bhurtpore. Rājasthān, N India 27°14′N 77°29′E
154 D11 **Bharūch** Gujarāt, W India 21°48′N 72°55′E
155 E18 **Bhatkal** Karnātaka, W India 13°59′N 74°34′E
153 O13 **Bhatni** *var.* Bhatni Junction. Uttar Pradesh, N India 26°23′N 83°56′E
**Bhatni Junction** *see* Bhatni
153 S16 **Bhātpāra** West Bengal, NE India 22°55′N 88°30′E
149 U7 **Bhaun** Punjab, E Pakistan 32°53′N 72°48′E
**Bhaunagar** *see* Bhāvnagar
**Bhavānīpātna** *see* Bhawānipatna
155 H21 **Bhavānīsāgar** ⊠ S India
154 D11 **Bhāvnagar** *prev.* Bhaunagar. Gujarāt, W India 21°46′N 72°14′E
154 M13 **Bhawānipatna** *var.* Bhavānīpātna. Odisha, E India 19°56′N 83°09′E
**Bheanntraí, Bá** *see* Bantry Bay
**Bheara, Béal an** *see* Gweebarra Bay
154 K12 **Bhilai** Chhattīsgarh, C India 21°12′N 81°26′E
152 G13 **Bhīlwāra** Rājasthān, N India 25°23′N 74°39′E
155 E14 **Bhīma** ≈ S India
155 K16 **Bhīmavaram** Andhra Pradesh, E India 16°34′N 81°35′E
154 I7 **Bhind** Madhya Pradesh, C India 26°33′N 78°47′E
152 E13 **Bhīnmāl** Rājasthān, N India 25°01′N 72°22′E
**Bhir** *see* Bīd
83 J25 **Bhisho** *prev.* Bisho. Eastern Cape, S South Africa 32°46′S 27°21′E *see also* Bhisho
154 D13 **Bhiwandi** Mahārāshtra, W India 19°21′N 73°08′E
152 H10 **Bhiwāni** Haryāna, N India 28°50′N 76°10′E
152 L13 **Bhognīpur** Uttar Pradesh, N India 26°12′N 79°48′E
153 U16 **Bhola** Barisal, S Bangladesh 22°40′N 91°36′E
154 H10 **Bhopāl** *state capital* Madhya Pradesh, C India 23°17′N 77°25′E
155 J14 **Bhopālpatnam** Chhattīsgarh, C India 18°51′N 80°22′E
155 E14 **Bhor** Mahārāshtra, W India 18°10′N 73°55′E
154 O12 **Bhubaneshwar** *prev.* Bhubaneswar, Bhuvaneshwar. *state capital* Odisha, E India 20°16′N 85°51′E
**Bhubaneswar** *see* Bhubaneshwar
154 B9 **Bhuj** Gujarāt, W India 23°16′N 69°40′E
**Bhuket** *see* Phuket
**Bhurtpore** *see* Bharatpur
**Bhusaval** *see* Bhusāwal
154 G12 **Bhusāwal** *prev.* Bhusaval. Mahārāshtra, C India 21°01′N 75°50′E
153 T12 **Bhutan** *off.* Kingdom of Bhutan, *var.* Druk-yul. ◆ *monarchy* S Asia
**Bhutan, Kingdom of** *see* Bhutan
**Bhuvaneshwar** *see* Bhubaneshwar
143 T15 **Bīābān, Kūh-e** ⛰ S Iran
77 V18 **Biafra, Bight of** *var.* Bight of Bonny. *bay* W Africa
171 W12 **Biak** Papua, E Indonesia 01°10′S 136°05′E
171 W12 **Biak, Pulau** *island* E Indonesia
110 P12 **Biała Podlaska** Lubelskie, E Poland 52°03′N 23°08′E
110 F7 **Białogard** *Ger.* Belgard. Zachodnio-pomorskie, NW Poland 54°01′N 15°59′E
110 P10 **Białowieska, Puszcza** *Bel.* Byelavyezhskaya Pushcha, *Rus.* Belovezhskaya Pushcha. *physical region* Belarus/Poland *see also* Byelavyezhskaya, Pushcha
**Białowieska, Puszcza** *see* Byelavyezhskaya Pushcha
110 G8 **Biały Bór** *Ger.* Baldenburg. Zachodnio-pomorskie, NW Poland 53°53′N 16°49′E
110 P9 **Białystok** *Rus.* Belostok, Bielostok. Podlaskie, NE Poland 53°08′N 23°09′E
107 L24 **Biancavilla** *prev.* Inessa. Sicilia, Italy, C Mediterranean Sea 37°38′N 14°52′E
**Bianco, Monte** *see* Blanc, Mont
**Bianjiang** *see* Xunke
76 L15 **Biankouma** W Ivory Coast 07°44′N 07°37′W
167 R7 **Bia, Phou** *var.* Pou Bia. ▲ C Laos 18°59′N 103°09′E
**Bia, Pou** *see* Bia, Phou
143 R5 **Biārjmand** Semnān, N Iran 36°05′N 55°50′E
105 P4 **Biarra** ≈ NE Spain
102 I15 **Biarritz** Pyrénées-Atlantiques, SW France 43°25′N 01°40′W
108 H10 **Biasca** Ticino, S Switzerland 46°22′N 08°59′E
61 E17 **Biassini** Salto, N Uruguay 31°18′S 57°05′W
**Biasteri** *see* Laguardia
165 S3 **Bibai** Hokkaidō, NE Japan 43°21′N 141°53′E
83 B15 **Bibala** *Port.* Vila Arriaga. Namibe, SW Angola 14°46′S 13°21′E
104 I4 **Bibéi** ≈ NW Spain
**Biberach** *see* Biberach an der Riss
101 I23 **Biberach an der Riss** *var.* Biberach, *Ger.* Biberach an der Riß. Baden-Württemberg, S Germany 48°06′N 09°48′E
108 E7 **Biberist** Solothurn, NW Switzerland 47°11′N 07°34′E
77 O16 **Bibiani** SW Ghana 06°28′N 02°20′W
112 C13 **Bibinje** Zadar, SW Croatia 44°04′N 15°17′E
**Biblical Gebal** *see* Jbaïl
116 I5 **Bibrka** *Pol.* Bóbrka, *Rus.* Bobrka. L'vivs'ka Oblast', NW Ukraine 49°39′N 24°16′E
117 N10 **Bîc** ≈ S Moldova
113 M18 **Bicaj** Kukës, NE Albania 42°00′N 20°24′E
116 K10 **Bicaz** *Hung.* Békás. Neamţ, NE Romania 46°53′N 26°05′E
183 Q16 **Bicheno** Tasmania, SE Australia 41°56′S 148°15′E
**Bichiş** *see* Békés
**Bichiş-Ciaba** *see* Békéscsaba
**Bichitra** *see* Phichit
137 P8 **Bich'vinta** *Prev.* Bichvint'a, *Rus.* Pitsunda. NW Georgia 43°12′N 40°21′E
**Bichvint'a** *see* Bich'vinta
15 T7 **Bic, Île du** *island* Québec, SE Canada
32 J10 **Bickleton** Washington, NW USA 46°00′N 120°16′W
36 L6 **Bicknell** Utah, W USA 38°20′N 111°32′W
171 S11 **Bicoli** Pulau Halmahera, E Indonesia 0°34′N 128°33′E
111 J22 **Bicske** Fejér, C Hungary 47°30′N 18°36′E
155 F14 **Bīd** *prev.* Bhir. Mahārāshtra, W India 19°17′N 75°22′E
77 U15 **Bida** Niger, C Nigeria 09°06′N 06°02′E
155 H15 **Bīdar** Karnātaka, C India 17°56′N 77°35′E
141 Y8 **Bidbid** NE Oman 23°25′N 58°08′E
19 P9 **Biddeford** Maine, NE USA 43°29′N 70°27′W
98 L9 **Biddinghuizen** Flevoland, C Netherlands 52°28′N 05°41′E
33 X11 **Biddle** Montana, NW USA 45°04′N 105°21′W
97 J23 **Bideford** SW England, United Kingdom 51°01′N 04°12′W
82 D13 **Bié** ◈ *province* C Angola
35 O2 **Bieber** California, W USA 41°07′N 121°09′W
110 O9 **Biebrza** ≈ NE Poland
165 T3 **Biei** Hokkaidō, NE Japan 43°33′N 142°28′E
108 D8 **Biel** *Fr.* Bienne. Bern, W Switzerland 47°09′N 07°16′E
100 G13 **Bielefeld** Nordrhein-Westfalen, NW Germany 52°01′N 08°32′E
108 D8 **Bieler See** *Fr.* Lac de Bienne. ◎ W Switzerland
**Bielitz/Bielitz-Biala** *see* Bielsko-Biała
106 C7 **Biella** Piemonte, N Italy 45°34′N 08°04′E
**Bielostok** *see* Białystok
111 J17 **Bielsko-Biała** *Ger.* Bielitz, Bielitz-Biala. Śląskie, S Poland 49°49′N 19°01′E
110 P10 **Bielsk Podlaski** Białystok, E Poland 52°45′N 23°11′E
**Bien Bien** *see* Điên Biên Phu
11 V17 **Bienfait** Saskatchewan, S Canada 49°06′N 102°47′W
167 T14 **Biên Hoa** Đông Nai, S Vietnam 10°58′N 106°50′E
**Bienne** *see* Biel
**Bienne, Lac de** *see* Bieler See
12 K8 **Bienville, Lac** ◎ Québec, C Canada
82 D13 **Bié, Planalto do** *var.* Bié Plateau. *plateau* C Angola
**Bié Plateau** *see* Bié, Planalto do
108 B9 **Bière** Vaud, W Switzerland 46°32′N 06°19′E
98 O4 **Bierum** Groningen, NE Netherlands 53°25′N 06°51′E
98 I13 **Biesbos** *var.* Biesbosch. *wetland* S Netherlands
**Biesbosch** *see* Biesbos
99 H21 **Biesme** Namur, S Belgium 50°19′N 04°43′E
101 H21 **Bietigheim-Bissingen** Baden-Württemberg, SW Germany 48°57′N 09°07′E
99 I23 **Bièvre** Namur, SE Belgium 49°56′N 05°01′E
79 D18 **Bifoun** Moyen-Ogooué, NW Gabon 0°15′S 10°24′E
165 T2 **Bifuka** Hokkaidō, NE Japan 44°28′N 142°20′E
136 C11 **Biga** Çanakkale, NW Turkey 40°13′N 27°14′E
136 C13 **Bigadiç** Balıkesir, W Turkey 39°24′N 28°08′E
26 J7 **Big Basin** *basin* Kansas, C USA
185 B20 **Big Bay** *bay* South Island, New Zealand
31 O5 **Big Bay de Noc** ◎ Michigan, N USA
31 N3 **Big Bay Point** *headland* Michigan, N USA 46°51′N 87°40′W
33 R10 **Big Belt Mountains** ⛰ Montana, NW USA
29 N10 **Big Bend Dam** *dam* South Dakota, N USA
24 K12 **Big Bend National Park** *national park* Texas, S USA
22 K5 **Big Black River** ≈ Mississippi, S USA
27 O3 **Big Blue River** ≈ Kansas/Nebraska, C USA
24 M10 **Big Canyon** ≈ Texas, SW USA
33 N12 **Big Creek** Idaho, NW USA 45°05′N 115°20′W
23 N8 **Big Creek Lake** ⊠ Alabama, S USA
23 X15 **Big Cypress Swamp** *wetland* Florida, SE USA
39 S9 **Big Delta** Alaska, USA 64°09′N 145°50′W
30 K6 **Big Eau Pleine Reservoir** ⊠ Wisconsin, N USA
19 P5 **Bigelow Mountain** ▲ Maine, NE USA 45°09′N 70°17′W
162 G9 **Biger** *var.* Jargalant. Govĭ-Altay, W Mongolia 45°39′N 97°10′E
29 U3 **Big Falls** Minnesota, N USA 48°13′N 93°48′W
33 P8 **Bigfork** Montana, NW USA 48°03′N 114°04′W
29 U3 **Big Fork River** ≈ Minnesota, N USA
11 S15 **Biggar** Saskatchewan, S Canada 52°03′N 107°59′W
180 L3 **Bigge Island** *island* Western Australia
35 O5 **Biggs** California, W USA 39°24′N 121°44′W
32 I11 **Biggs** Oregon, NW USA 45°39′N 120°49′W
14 K13 **Big Gull Lake** ◎ Ontario, SE Canada
37 P16 **Big Hachet Peak** ▲ New Mexico, SW USA 31°38′N 108°24′W
33 P11 **Big Hole River** ≈ Montana, NW USA
33 V13 **Bighorn Basin** *basin* Wyoming, C USA
33 U11 **Bighorn Lake** ◎ Montana/Wyoming, N USA
33 W13 **Bighorn Mountains** ⛰ Wyoming, C USA
36 J13 **Big Horn Peak** ▲ Arizona, SW USA 33°40′N 113°01′W
33 V11 **Bighorn River** ≈ Montana/Wyoming, NW USA
9 S7 **Big Island** *island* Nunavut, NE Canada
39 O16 **Big Koniuji Island** *island* Shumagin Islands, Alaska, USA
25 N9 **Big Lake** Texas, SW USA 31°12′N 101°29′W
19 T5 **Big Lake** ◎ Maine, NE USA
30 I3 **Big Manitou Falls** *waterfall* Wisconsin, N USA
35 R2 **Big Mountain** ▲ Nevada, W USA 41°18′N 119°03′W
108 G10 **Bignasco** Ticino, S Switzerland 46°21′N 08°37′E
29 R16 **Big Nemaha River** ≈ Nebraska, C USA
76 G12 **Bignona** SW Senegal 12°49′N 16°16′W
**Bigorra** *see* Tarbes
**Bigosovo** *see* Bihosava
35 S10 **Big Pine** California, W USA 37°09′N 118°18′W
35 Q14 **Big Pine Mountain** ▲ California, W USA 34°41′N 119°37′W
27 V6 **Big Piney Creek** ≈ Missouri, C USA
65 M24 **Big Point** *headland* N Tristan da Cunha 37°10′S 12°18′W
31 P8 **Big Rapids** Michigan, N USA 43°42′N 85°28′W
30 K6 **Big Rib River** ≈ Wisconsin, N USA
14 L14 **Big Rideau Lake** ◎ Ontario, SE Canada
11 T14 **Big River** Saskatchewan, C Canada 53°48′N 106°55′W
27 X5 **Big River** ≈ Missouri, C USA
31 N7 **Big Sable Point** *headland* Michigan, N USA 44°03′N 86°30′W
33 S7 **Big Sandy** Montana, NW USA 48°08′N 110°09′W
25 W6 **Big Sandy** Texas, SW USA 32°34′N 95°06′W
37 V5 **Big Sandy Creek** ≈ Colorado, C USA
29 Q16 **Big Sandy Creek** ≈ Nebraska, C USA
29 V5 **Big Sandy Lake** ◎ Minnesota, N USA
36 J11 **Big Sandy River** ≈ Arizona, SW USA
21 P5 **Big Sandy River** ≈ S USA
23 V6 **Big Satilla Creek** ≈ Georgia, SE USA
29 R12 **Big Sioux River** ≈ Iowa/South Dakota, N USA
35 U7 **Big Smoky Valley** *valley* Nevada, W USA
25 N7 **Big Spring** Texas, SW USA 32°15′N 101°30′W
19 Q5 **Big Squaw Mountain** ▲ Maine, NE USA 45°28′N 69°42′W
21 O7 **Big Stone Gap** Virginia, NE USA 36°52′N 82°45′W




◆ Country
● Country Capital
◇ Dependent Territory
○ Dependent Territory Capital
◈ Administrative Regions
✈ International Airport
▲ Mountain
⛰ Mountain Range
⊼ Volcano
≈ River
◎ Lake
⊠ Reservoir

Big Stone Lake – Blossom, Mys


29 Q8 **Big Stone Lake** ◎ Minnesota/South Dakota, N USA
22 K4 **Big Sunflower River** ≈ Mississippi, S USA
33 T11 **Big Timber** Montana, NW USA 45°50′N 109°57′W
12 D8 **Big Trout Lake** Ontario, C Canada 53°40′N 90°00′W
14 I12 **Big Trout Lake** ◎ Ontario, SE Canada
35 O2 **Big Valley Mountains** ▲▲ California, W USA
25 Q13 **Big Wells** Texas, SW USA 28°34′N 99°34′W
14 F11 **Bigwood** Ontario, S Canada 46°03′N 80°37′W
112 D11 **Bihać** ◈ Federacija Bosne I Hercegovine, NW Bosnia and Herzegovina
153 P14 **Bihār** *prev.* Behar. ◈ *state* N India
**Bihār** *see* Bihār Sharīf
81 F20 **Biharamulo** Kagera, NW Tanzania 02°37′S 31°20′E
153 R13 **Bihārīganj** Bihār, NE India 25°44′N 86°59′E
153 P14 **Bihār Sharīf** *var.* Bihār. Bihār, N India 25°13′N 85°31′E
116 F10 **Bihor** ◈ *county* NW Romania
165 V3 **Bihoro** Hokkaidō, NE Japan 43°50′N 144°05′E
118 K11 **Bihosava** *Rus.* Bigosovo. Vitsyebskaya Voblasts', NW Belarus 55°50′N 27°46′E
**Bijagos Archipelago** *see* Bijagós, Arquipélago dos
76 G13 **Bijagós, Arquipélago dos** *var.* Bijagos Archipelago. *island group* W Guinea-Bissau
**Bijāpur** *see* Vijayāpura
142 K5 **Bījār** Kordestān, W Iran 35°52′N 47°39′E
112 J11 **Bijeljina** Republika Srpska, NE Bosnia and Herzegovina 44°46′N 19°13′E
113 K15 **Bijelo Polje** E Montenegro 43°03′N 19°44′E
160 I11 **Bijie** Guizhou, S China 27°15′N 105°16′E
152 J10 **Bijnor** Uttar Pradesh, N India 29°22′N 78°09′E
152 F11 **Bīkāner** Rājasthān, NW India 28°01′N 73°22′E
189 V3 **Bikar Atoll** *var.* Pikaar. *atoll* Ratak Chain, N Marshall Islands
190 H3 **Bikeman** *atoll* Tungaru, W Kiribati
190 I3 **Bikenebu** Tarawa, W Kiribati
123 S14 **Bikin** Khabarovskiy Kray, SE Russia 46°45′N 134°06′E
123 S14 **Bikin** ≈ SE Russia
189 R3 **Bikini Atoll** *var.* Pikinni. *atoll* Ralik Chain, NW Marshall Islands
83 L17 **Bikita** Masvingo, E Zimbabwe 20°06′S 31°41′E
**Bikkū Bīttī** *see* Bette, Picco
79 I19 **Bikoro** Equateur, W Dem. Rep. Congo 0°45′S 18°09′E
141 Z9 **Bilād Banī Bū ʿAlī** NE Oman 22°02′N 59°18′E
141 Z9 **Bilād Banī Bū Ḩasan** NE Oman 22°09′N 59°14′E
141 X9 **Bilād Manaḩ** *var.* Manaḩ. NE Oman 22°44′N 57°36′E
77 Q12 **Bilanga** C Burkina Faso 12°35′N 00°08′W
152 F12 **Bilāra** Rājasthān, N India 26°10′N x73°48′E
152 K10 **Bilāri** Uttar Pradesh, N India 28°37′N 78°48′E
138 J5 **Bilʿās, Jabal al** ▲▲ C Syria
154 L11 **Bilāspur** Chhattīsgarh, C India 22°06′N 82°08′E
152 I8 **Bilāspur** Himāchal Pradesh, N India 31°18′N 76°48′E
168 J9 **Bila, Sungai** ≈ Sumatera, W Indonesia
137 Y13 **Biläsuvar** *Rus.* Bilyasuvar; *prev.* Pushkino. SE Azerbaijan 39°26′N 48°34′E
117 O5 **Bila Tserkva** *Rus.* Belaya Tserkov'. Kyivs'ka Oblast', N Ukraine 49°49′N 30°08′E
167 N11 **Bilauktaung Range** *var.* Thanintari Taungdan. ▲▲ Myanmar (Burma)/Thailand
105 O2 **Bilbao** *Basq.* Bilbo. País Vasco, N Spain 43°15′N 02°56′W
**Bilbo** *see* Bilbao
92 H2 **Bíldudalur** Vestfirðir, NW Iceland 65°40′N 23°35′W
113 I16 **Bileća** ◈ Republika Srpska, S Bosnia and Herzegovina
136 E12 **Bilecik** Bilecik, NW Turkey 39°59′N 29°54′E
136 F12 **Bilecik** ◈ *province* NW Turkey
116 E11 **Biled** *Ger.* Billed, *Hung.* Billéd. Timiş, W Romania 45°55′N 20°55′E
111 O15 **Biłgoraj** Lubelskie, E Poland 50°31′N 22°41′E
117 P11 **Bilhorod-Dnistrovs'kyy** *Rus.* Belgorod-Dnestrovskiy, *Rom.* Cetatea Albă, *prev.* Akkerman; *anc.* Tyras. Odes'ka Oblast', SW Ukraine 46°10′N 30°19′E
79 M16 **Bili** Orientale, N Dem. Rep. Congo 04°07′N 25°09′E
123 T6 **Bilibino** Chukotskiy Avtonomnyy Okrug, NE Russia 67°56′N 166°45′E
166 M8 **Bilin** Mon State, S Myanmar (Burma) 17°14′N 97°12′E
113 N21 **Bilisht** *var.* Bilishti. Korçë, SE Albania 40°36′N 21°00′E
**Bilishti** *see* Bilisht
183 N10 **Billabong Creek** *var.* Moulamein Creek. *seasonal river* New South Wales, SE Australia
182 G4 **Billa Kalina** South Australia 29°57′S 136°13′E
197 Q17 **Bill Baileys Bank** *undersea feature* N Atlantic Ocean 60°35′N 10°15′W
**Billed/Billéd** *see* Biled
153 N14 **Billi** Uttar Pradesh, N India 24°30′N 82°59′E
97 M15 **Billingham** N England, United Kingdom 54°36′N 01°17′W
33 U11 **Billings** Montana, NW USA 45°47′N 108°32′W
95 J16 **Billingsfors** Västra Götaland, S Sweden 58°57′N 12°14′E
**Bill of Cape Clear, The** *see* Clear, Cape
28 L9 **Billsburg** South Dakota, N USA 44°22′N 101°40′W
95 F23 **Billund** Syddtjylland, W Denmark 55°44′N 09°07′E
36 L11 **Bill Williams Mountain** ▲ Arizona, SW USA 35°12′N 112°12′W
36 I12 **Bill Williams River** ≈ Arizona, SW USA
77 Y8 **Bilma** Agadez, NE Niger 18°22′N 13°01′E
77 Y8 **Bilma, Grand Erg de** *desert* NE Niger
117 W9 **Bilmak** *prev.* Kuybysheve. Zaporiz'ka Oblast', SE Ukraine 47°20′N 36°41′E
181 Y9 **Biloela** Queensland, E Australia 24°27′S 150°31′E
112 G8 **Bilo Gora** ▲▲ N Croatia
117 U13 **Bilohirs'k** *Rus.* Belogorsk; *prev.* Karasubazar. Avtonomna Respublika Krym, S Ukraine 45°04′N 34°35′E
**Bilokorovychi** *see* Novi Bilokorovychi
**Bilokurakine** *see* Bilokurakyne
117 X5 **Bilokurakyne** *var.* Bilokurakine. Luhans'ka Oblast', E Ukraine 49°32′N 38°44′E
117 T3 **Bilopillya** *Rus.* Belopol'ye. Sums'ka Oblast', NE Ukraine 51°09′N 34°17′E
117 Y6 **Bilovods'k** *Rus.* Belovodsk. Luhans'ka Oblast', E Ukraine 49°11′N 39°34′E
22 M9 **Biloxi** Mississippi, S USA 30°24′N 88°53′W
117 R10 **Bilozerka** Khersons'ka Oblast', S Ukraine 46°36′N 32°23′E
117 W7 **Bilozers'ke** Donets'ka Oblast', E Ukraine 48°29′N 37°03′E
98 J11 **Bilthoven** Utrecht, C Netherlands 52°07′N 05°12′E
78 K9 **Biltine** Wadi Fira, E Chad 14°30′N 20°53′E
**Biltine, Préfecture de** *see* Wadi Fira
**Bilüü** *see* Ulaanhus
**Bilwi** *see* Puerto Cabezas
**Bilyasuvar** *see* Biläsuvar
117 O11 **Bilyayivka** Odes'ka Oblast', SW Ukraine 46°28′N 30°11′E
99 K18 **Bilzen** Limburg, NE Belgium 50°52′N 05°31′E
**Bimbéréké** *see* Bembèrèkè
183 R10 **Bimberi Peak** ▲ New South Wales, SE Australia 35°42′S 148°46′E
77 Q15 **Bimbila** E Ghana 08°54′N 00°05′E
79 I15 **Bimbo** Ombella-Mpoko, SW Central African Republic 04°19′N 18°27′E
44 F2 **Bimini Islands** *island group* W The Bahamas
154 I9 **Bīna** Madhya Pradesh, C India 24°09′N 78°10′E
143 T4 **Bīnālūd, Kūh-e** ▲▲ NE Iran
99 F20 **Binche** Hainaut, S Belgium 50°25′N 04°10′E
**Bindloe Island** *see* Marchena, Isla
83 L16 **Bindura** Mashonaland Central, NE Zimbabwe 17°20′S 31°21′E
105 T5 **Binefar** Aragón, NE Spain 41°51′N 00°17′E
83 J16 **Binga** Matabeleland North, W Zimbabwe 17°40′S 27°22′E
183 T5 **Bingara** New South Wales, SE Australia 29°54′S 150°36′E
101 F18 **Bingen am Rhein** Rheinland-Pfalz, SW Germany 49°58′N 07°54′E
26 M11 **Binger** Oklahoma, C USA 35°19′N 98°19′W
**Bingerau** *see* Węgrów
**Bin Ghalfān, Jazā'ir** *see* Ḩalāniyāt, Juzur al
19 Q6 **Bingham** Maine, NE USA 45°01′N 69°51′W
18 H11 **Binghamton** New York, NE USA 42°06′N 75°55′W
**Bin Ghanīmah, Jabal** *see* Bin Ghunaymah, Jabal
75 P11 **Bin Ghunaymah, Jabal** *var.* Jabal Bin Ghanīmah. ▲▲ C Libya
139 U3 **Bingird** As Sulaymānīyah, NE Iraq 36°03′N 45°03′E
**Bingmei** *see* Congjiang
137 P14 **Bingöl** Bingöl, E Turkey 38°54′N 40°29′E
137 P14 **Bingöl** ◈ *province* E Turkey
161 R6 **Binhai** *var.* Dongkan. Jiangsu, E China 34°00′N 119°51′E
167 V11 **Binh Định** *var.* An Nhon. Binh Định, C Vietnam 13°53′N 109°07′E
**Binh Sơn** *see* Châu Ô
**Binimani** *see* Bintimani
168 I8 **Binjai** Sumatera, W Indonesia 03°37′N 98°30′E
183 R6 **Binnaway** New South Wales, SE Australia 31°34′S 149°24′E
108 E6 **Binningen** Basel Landschaft, NW Switzerland 47°32′N 07°35′E
80 H12 **Bīnshangul Gumuz** *var.* Benishangul. ◈ W Ethiopia
168 J8 **Bintang, Banjaran** ▲▲ Peninsular Malaysia
168 M10 **Bintan, Pulau** *island* Kepulauan Riau, W Indonesia
76 J14 **Bintimani** *var.* Binimani. ▲ NE Sierra Leone 09°21′N 11°09′W
**Bint Jubayl** *see* Bent Jbaïl
169 S9 **Bintulu** Sarawak, East Malaysia 03°12′N 113°01′E
169 S9 **Bintuni** *prev.* Steenkool. Papua Barat, E Indonesia 02°03′S 133°45′E
163 W8 **Binxian** *prev.* Binzhou. Heilongjiang, NE China 45°44′N 127°27′E
160 K14 **Binyang** *var.* Binzhou. Guangxi Zhuangzu Zizhiqu, S China 23°15′N 108°40′E
161 Q4 **Binzhou** Shandong, E China 37°23′N 118°03′E
**Binzhou** *see* Binyang
**Binzhou** *see* Binxian
63 G14 **Bío Bío** *var.* Región del Bío Bío. ◈ *region* C Chile
**Bío Bío, Región del** *see* Bío Bío
63 G14 **Bío Bío, Río** ≈ C Chile
79 C16 **Bioco, Isla de** *var.* Bioko, *Eng.* Fernando Po, *Sp.* Fernando Póo; *prev.* Macías Nguema Biyogo. *island* NW Equatorial Guinea
112 D13 **Biograd na Moru** *It.* Zaravecchia. Zadar, SW Croatia 43°57′N 15°27′E
**Bioko** *see* Bioco, Isla de
113 F14 **Biokovo** ▲▲ S Croatia
**Biorra** *see* Birr
**Bipontium** *see* Zweibrücken
143 W13 **Bīrag, Kūh-e** ▲▲ SE Iran
75 O10 **Birāk** *var.* Brak. C Libya 27°32′N 14°17′E
139 S10 **Bi'r al Islām** Karbalā', C Iraq 32°15′N 43°40′E
154 N11 **Biramitrapur** *var.* Birmitrapur. Odisha, E India 22°24′N 84°42′E
139 T11 **Bi'r an Niṣf** An Najaf, S Iraq 31°22′N 44°07′E
78 L12 **Birao** Vakaga, NE Central African Republic 10°14′N 22°49′E
146 J10 **Birata** *Rus.* Darganata, Dargan-Ata. Lebap Welaýaty, NE Turkmenistan 40°30′N 62°09′E
158 M6 **Biratar Bulak** *well* NW China
153 R12 **Birātnagar** Eastern, SE Nepal 26°28′N 87°16′E
165 R5 **Biratori** Hokkaidō, NE Japan 42°35′N 142°07′E
39 S8 **Birch Creek** Alaska, USA 66°17′N 145°54′W
38 M11 **Birch Creek** ≈ Alaska, USA
11 T14 **Birch Hills** Saskatchewan, S Canada 52°58′N 105°22′W
182 M10 **Birchip** Victoria, SE Australia 36°01′S 142°55′E
29 X4 **Birch Lake** ◎ Minnesota, N USA
11 Q11 **Birch Mountains** ▲▲ Alberta, W Canada
11 V15 **Birch River** Manitoba, S Canada 52°22′N 101°03′W
44 H12 **Birchs Hill** *hill* W Jamaica
39 R11 **Birchwood** Alaska, USA 61°24′N 149°28′W
188 I5 **Bird Island** *island* S Northern Mariana Islands
137 N16 **Birecik** Şanlıurfa, S Turkey 37°03′N 37°59′E
152 M10 **Birendranagar** *var.* Surkhet. Mid Western, W Nepal 28°35′N 81°36′E
**Bir es Saba** *see* Be'er Sheva
74 A12 **Bir-Gandouz** SW Western Sahara 21°35′N 16°27′W
153 P12 **Birganj** Central, C Nepal 27°03′N 84°53′E
81 B14 **Biri** ≈ W South Sudan
**Bi'r Ibn Hirmās** *see* Al Bi'r
143 U8 **Bīrjand** Khorāsān-e Janūbī, E Iran 32°54′N 59°14′E
139 T11 **Birkat Ḩāmid** *well* S Iraq
95 F18 **Birkeland** Aust-Agder, S Norway 58°18′N 08°13′E
101 E19 **Birkenfeld** Rheinland-Pfalz, SW Germany 49°39′N 07°10′E
97 K18 **Birkenhead** NW England, United Kingdom 53°24′N 03°02′W
109 W7 **Birkfeld** Steiermark, SE Austria 47°21′N 15°40′E
182 A2 **Birksgate Range** ▲▲ South Australia
**Bîrlad** *see* Bârlad
145 S15 **Birlik** *var.* Novotroickoje, Novotroitskoye; *prev.* Brlik. Zhambyl, SE Kazakhstan 43°39′N 73°45′E
97 K20 **Birmingham** C England, United Kingdom 52°30′N 01°50′W
23 P4 **Birmingham** Alabama, S USA 33°30′N 86°47′W
97 M20 **Birmingham** ✕ C England, United Kingdom 52°27′N 01°46′W
**Birmitrapur** *see* Biramitrapur
**Bir Moghrein** *see* Bîr Mogreïn
76 J4 **Bîr Mogreïn** *var.* Bir Moghrein; *prev.* Fort-Trinquet. Tiris Zemmour, N Mauritania 25°10′N 11°35′W
191 S4 **Birnie Island** *atoll* Phoenix Islands, C Kiribati
77 S12 **Birnin Gaouré** *var.* Birni-Ngaouré. Dosso, SW Niger 12°59′N 03°02′E
**Birni-Ngaouré** *see* Birnin Gaouré
77 S12 **Birnin Kebbi** Kebbi, NW Nigeria 12°28′N 04°08′E
77 T12 **Birnin Konni** *var.* Birni-Nkonni. Tahoua, SW Niger 13°51′N 05°15′E
**Birni-Nkonni** *see* Birnin Konni
77 W13 **Birnin Kudu** Jigawa, N Nigeria 11°28′N 09°29′E
123 S16 **Birobidzhan** Yevreyskaya Avtonomnaya Oblast', SE Russia 48°42′N 132°55′E
97 D18 **Birr** *var.* Parsonstown, *Ir.* Biorra. C Ireland 53°06′N 07°55′W
183 P4 **Birrie River** ≈ New South Wales/Queensland, SE Australia
108 D7 **Birse** ≈ NW Switzerland
**Birsen** *see* Biržai
108 E6 **Birsfelden** Basel Landschaft, NW Switzerland 47°33′N 07°37′E
127 U4 **Birsk** Respublika Bashkortostan, W Russia 55°24′N 55°33′E
119 F14 **Birštonas** Kaunas, C Lithuania 54°37′N 24°00′E
75 X12 **Bi'r Ṭawīl** *disputed region* S Egypt / N Sudan
159 P14 **Biru** Xinjiang Uygur Zizhiqu, W China 31°30′N 93°56′E
**Biruni** *see* Beruniy
122 L12 **Biryusa** ≈ C Russia
122 L12 **Biryusinsk** Irkutskaya Oblast', C Russia 55°52′N 97°48′E
118 G10 **Biržai** *Ger.* Birsen. Panevėžys, NE Lithuania 56°12′N 24°47′E
121 P16 **Birżebbuġa** SE Malta 35°50′N 14°32′E
**Bisanthe** *see* Tekirdağ
171 R12 **Bisa, Pulau** *island* Maluku, E Indonesia
37 N17 **Bisbee** Arizona, SW USA 31°27′N 109°55′W
29 O2 **Bisbee** North Dakota, N USA 48°36′N 99°21′W
**Biscaia, Baía de** *see* Biscay, Bay of
102 I13 **Biscarrosse et de Parentis, Étang de** ◎ SW France
104 M1 **Biscay, Bay of** *Sp.* Golfo de Vizcaya, *Port.* Baía de Biscaia. *bay* France/Spain
23 Z16 **Biscayne Bay** *bay* Florida, SE USA
64 M7 **Biscay Plain** *undersea feature* SE Bay of Biscay 07°15′W 45°00′N
107 N17 **Bisceglie** Puglia, SE Italy 41°14′N 16°31′E
**Bischoflack** *see* Škofja Loka
**Bischofsburg** *see* Biskupiec
109 Q7 **Bischofshofen** Salzburg, NW Austria 47°25′N 13°13′E
101 P15 **Bischofswerda** Sachsen, E Germany 51°07′N 14°13′E
103 V5 **Bischwiller** Bas-Rhin, NE France 48°46′N 07°52′E
21 T10 **Biscoe** North Carolina, SE USA 35°20′N 79°46′W
194 G5 **Biscoe Islands** *island group* Antarctica
14 E9 **Biscotasi Lake** ◎ Ontario, S Canada
14 E9 **Biscotasing** Ontario, S Canada 47°16′N 82°04′W
54 J6 **Biscucuy** Portuguesa, NW Venezuela 09°22′N 69°59′W
99 M24 **Bissen** Luxembourg, C Luxembourg 49°47′N 06°04′E
114 K11 **Biser** Haskovo, S Bulgaria 41°52′N 25°59′E
113 D15 **Biševo** *It.* Busi. *island* SW Croatia
141 N12 **Bīshah, Wādī** *dry watercourse* C Saudi Arabia
147 U7 **Bishkek** *var.* Pishpek; *prev.* Frunze. ● (Kyrgyzstan) Chuyskaya Oblast', N Kyrgyzstan 42°54′N 74°27′E
147 U7 **Bishkek** ✕ Chuyskaya Oblast', N Kyrgyzstan 42°55′N 74°37′E
153 R16 **Bishnupur** West Bengal, NE India 23°05′N 87°20′E
**Bisho** *see* Bhisho
35 S9 **Bishop** California, W USA 37°22′N 118°24′W
25 S15 **Bishop** Texas, SW USA 27°36′N 97°49′W
97 L15 **Bishop Auckland** N England, United Kingdom 54°41′N 01°41′W
**Bishop's Lynn** *see* King's Lynn
97 O21 **Bishop's Stortford** E England, United Kingdom 51°45′N 00°11′E
21 S12 **Bishopville** South Carolina, SE USA 34°18′N 80°15′W
138 M5 **Bishrī, Jabal** ▲▲ E Syria
163 U4 **Bishui** Heilongjiang, NE China 52°06′N 123°42′E
81 G17 **Bisina, Lake** *prev.* Lake Salisbury. ◎ E Uganda
**Biskara** *see* Biskra
74 L6 **Biskra** *var.* Beskra, Biskara. NE Algeria 34°51′N 05°44′E
110 M8 **Biskupiec** *Ger.* Bischofsburg. Warmińsko-Mazurskie, NE Poland 53°52′N 20°57′E
171 R7 **Bislig** Mindanao, S Philippines 08°10′N 126°19′E
27 X6 **Bismarck** Missouri, C USA 37°46′N 90°37′W
28 M5 **Bismarck** *state capital* North Dakota, N USA 46°49′N 100°47′W
186 D5 **Bismarck Archipelago** *island group* NE Papua New Guinea
129 Z16 **Bismarck Plate** *tectonic feature* W Pacific Ocean
186 D7 **Bismarck Range** ▲▲ N Papua New Guinea
186 E6 **Bismarck Sea** *sea* W Pacific Ocean
137 P15 **Bismil** Dıyarbakır, SE Turkey 37°53′N 40°38′E
43 N6 **Bismuna, Laguna** *lagoon* NE Nicaragua
**Bisnulok** *see* Phitsanulok
171 R10 **Bisoa, Tanjung** *headland* Pulau Halmahera, N Indonesia 02°15′N 127°57′E
28 K7 **Bison** South Dakota, N USA 45°31′N 102°27′W
93 H17 **Bispgården** Jämtland, C Sweden 63°00′N 16°40′E
76 G13 **Bissau** ● (Guinea-Bissau) W Guinea-Bissau 11°52′N 15°39′W
76 G13 **Bissau** ✕ W Guinea-Bissau 11°53′N 15°41′W
**Bissojohka** *see* Børselv
76 G12 **Bissorã** W Guinea-Bissau 12°16′N 15°35′W
11 O10 **Bistcho Lake** ◎ Alberta, W Canada
22 G5 **Bistineau, Lake** ▣ Louisiana, S USA
**Bistrica** *see* Ilirska Bistrica
116 I9 **Bistriţa** *Ger.* Bistritz, *Hung.* Beszterce; *prev.* Nösen. Bistriţa-Năsăud, N Romania 47°10′N 24°31′E
116 K10 **Bistriţa** *Ger.* Bistritz. ≈ NE Romania
116 I9 **Bistriţa-Năsăud** ◈ *county* N Romania
**Bistritz** *see* Bistriţa
**Bistritz ober Pernstein** *see* Bystřice nad Pernštejnem
152 L11 **Biswān** Uttar Pradesh, N India 27°30′N 81°00′E
110 M7 **Bisztynek** Warmińsko-Mazurskie, NE Poland 54°05′N 20°53′E
79 E17 **Bitam** Woleu-Ntem, N Gabon 02°05′N 11°30′E
101 D18 **Bitburg** Rheinland-Pfalz, SW Germany 49°58′N 06°31′E
103 U4 **Bitche** Moselle, NE France 49°01′N 07°27′E
78 I11 **Bitkine** Guéra, C Chad 11°59′N 18°13′E
137 R15 **Bitlis** Bitlis, SE Turkey 38°23′N 42°04′E
137 R14 **Bitlis** ◈ *province* E Turkey
**Bitoeng** *see* Bitung
113 N20 **Bitola** *Turk.* Monastir; *prev.* Bitolj. S North Macedonia 41°01′N 21°22′E
**Bitolj** *see* Bitola
107 O17 **Bitonto** *anc.* Butuntum. Puglia, SE Italy 41°07′N 16°41′E
77 Q13 **Bitou** *var.* Bittou. SE Burkina Faso 11°19′N 00°17′W
155 C20 **Bitra Island** *island* Lakshadweep, India, N Indian Ocean
101 M14 **Bitterfeld** Sachsen-Anhalt, E Germany 51°37′N 12°18′E
32 O9 **Bitterroot Range** ▲▲ Idaho/Montana, NW USA
33 P10 **Bitterroot River** ≈ Montana, NW USA
107 D18 **Bitti** Sardegna, Italy, C Mediterranean Sea 40°30′N 09°31′E
**Bittou** *see* Bitou
171 Q11 **Bitung** *prev.* Bitoeng. Sulawesi, C Indonesia 01°28′N 125°13′E
60 I12 **Bituruna** Paraná, S Brazil 26°11′S 51°34′W
77 Y13 **Biu** Borno, E Nigeria 10°35′N 12°13′E
**Biumba** *see* Byumba
164 J13 **Biwa-ko** ◎ Honshū, SW Japan
171 X14 **Biwarlaut** Papua, E Indonesia 05°44′S 138°14′E
27 P10 **Bixby** Oklahoma, C USA 35°56′N 95°52′W
122 J13 **Biya** ≈ S Russia
122 J13 **Biysk** Altayskiy Kray, S Russia 52°34′N 85°09′E
164 H13 **Bizen** Okayama, Honshū, SW Japan 34°45′N 134°10′E
**Bizerta** *see* Bizerte
120 K10 **Bizerte** *Ar.* Banzart, *Eng.* Bizerta. N Tunisia 37°18′N 09°48′E
105 O2 **Bizkaia** *Cast.* Vizcaya. ◈ *province* País Vasco, N Spain
92 G2 **Bjargtangar** *headland* W Iceland 63°30′N 24°29′W
**Bjärnå** *see* Perniö
95 K22 **Bjärnum** Skåne, S Sweden 56°15′N 13°45′E
93 I16 **Bjästa** Västernorrland, C Sweden 63°12′N 18°30′E
113 I14 **Bjelašnica** ▲ SE Bosnia and Herzegovina 43°13′N 18°18′E
112 C10 **Bjelolasica** ▲ NW Croatia 45°13′N 14°56′E
112 F8 **Bjelovar** *Hung.* Belovár. Bjelovar-Bilogora, N Croatia 45°54′N 16°49′E
112 F8 **Bjelovar-Bilogora** *off.* Bjelovarsko-Bilogorska Županija. ◈ *province* NE Croatia
**Bjelovarsko-Bilogorska Županija** *see* Bjelovar-Bilogora
92 H10 **Bjerkvik** Nordland, C Norway 68°31′N 16°08′E
95 G21 **Bjerringbro** Midtjylland, NW Denmark 56°23′N 09°40′E
**Bjeshkët e Namuna** *see* North Albanian Alps
95 L14 **Björbo** Dalarna, C Sweden 60°28′N 14°44′E
95 I15 **Bjørkelangen** Akershus, S Norway 59°54′N 11°33′E
95 O14 **Björklinge** Uppsala, C Sweden 60°03′N 17°33′E
95 P14 **Bjørkø-Arholma** Stockholm, C Sweden 59°51′N 19°01′E
93 I14 **Björksele** Västerbotten, N Sweden 64°58′N 18°30′E
93 I16 **Björna** Västernorrland, C Sweden 63°34′N 18°38′E
95 C14 **Bjørnafjorden** *fjord* S Norway
95 L16 **Björneborg** Värmland, C Sweden 59°13′N 14°15′E
**Björneborg** *see* Pori
95 E14 **Bjornesfjorden** ◎ S Norway
92 M9 **Bjørnevatn** Finnmark, N Norway 69°40′N 29°57′E
197 T13 **Bjørnøya** *Eng.* Bear Island. *island* N Norway
93 I15 **Bjurholm** Västerbotten, N Sweden 63°57′N 19°16′E
95 J22 **Bjuv** Skåne, S Sweden 56°05′N 12°57′E
76 M12 **Bla** Ségou, W Mali 12°58′N 05°45′W
181 W8 **Blackall** Queensland, E Australia 24°26′S 145°32′E
29 V2 **Black Bay** *lake bay* Minnesota, N USA
27 N9 **Black Bear Creek** ≈ Oklahoma, C USA
97 K17 **Blackburn** NW England, United Kingdom 53°45′N 02°29′W
39 T11 **Blackburn, Mount** ▲ Alaska, USA 61°43′N 143°25′W
35 N5 **Black Butte Lake** ▣ California, W USA
194 J5 **Black Coast** *physical region* Antarctica
11 Q16 **Black Diamond** Alberta, SW Canada 50°42′N 114°09′W
18 K11 **Black Dome** ▲ New York, NE USA 42°16′N 74°07′W
113 L18 **Black Drin** *Alb.* Lumi i Drinit të Zi, *SCr.* Crni Drim. ≈ Albania/North Macedonia
29 U4 **Blackduck** Minnesota, N USA 47°45′N 94°33′W
12 D6 **Black Duck** ≈ Ontario, C Canada
33 R14 **Blackfoot** Idaho, NW USA 43°11′N 112°20′W
33 P9 **Blackfoot River** ≈ Montana, NW USA
**Black Forest** *see* Schwarzwald
28 J10 **Blackhawk** South Dakota, N USA 44°09′N 103°18′W
28 I10 **Black Hills** ▲▲ South Dakota/Wyoming, N USA
11 T10 **Black Lake** ◎ Saskatchewan, C Canada
22 G6 **Black Lake** ▣ Louisiana, S USA
31 Q5 **Black Lake** ◎ Michigan, N USA
18 I7 **Black Lake** ◎ New York, NE USA
26 F7 **Black Mesa** ▲ Oklahoma, C USA 37°00′N 103°07′W
21 P10 **Black Mountain** North Carolina, SE USA 35°37′N 82°19′W
35 P13 **Black Mountain** ▲ California, W USA 35°22′N 120°21′W
37 Q2 **Black Mountain** ▲ Colorado, C USA 40°47′N 107°23′W
96 K1 **Black Mountains** ▲▲ SE Wales, United Kingdom
36 H10 **Black Mountains** ▲▲ Arizona, SW USA
21 O7 **Black Mountains** ▲ Kentucky, E USA 36°54′N 82°53′W
33 Q16 **Black Pine Peak** ▲ Idaho, NW USA 42°07′N 113°07′W
97 K17 **Blackpool** NW England, United Kingdom 53°50′N 03°03′W
37 Q14 **Black Range** ▲▲ New Mexico, SW USA
44 I12 **Black River** W Jamaica 18°02′N 77°52′W
14 J14 **Black River** ≈ Ontario, SE Canada
129 U12 **Black River** *Chin.* Babian Jiang, Lixian Jiang, *Fr.* Rivière Noire, *Vtn.* Sông Đa. ≈ China/Vietnam
44 I12 **Black River** ≈ W Jamaica
39 T7 **Black River** ≈ Alaska, USA
37 N13 **Black River** ≈ Arizona, SW USA
27 X7 **Black River** ≈ Arkansas/Missouri, C USA
22 I7 **Black River** ≈ Louisiana, S USA
31 S8 **Black River** ≈ Michigan, N USA
31 Q5 **Black River** ≈ Michigan, N USA
18 I8 **Black River** ≈ New York, NE USA
21 T13 **Black River** ≈ South Carolina, SE USA
30 J7 **Black River** ≈ Wisconsin, N USA
30 J7 **Black River Falls** Wisconsin, N USA 44°18′N 90°51′W
35 R3 **Black Rock Desert** *desert* Nevada, W USA
**Black Sand Desert** *see* Garagum
21 S7 **Blacksburg** Virginia, NE USA 37°15′N 80°25′W
136 H10 **Black Sea** *var.* Euxine Sea, *Bul.* Cherno More, *Rom.* Marea Neagră, *Rus.* Chernoye More, *Turk.* Karadeniz, *Ukr.* Chorne More. *sea* Asia/Europe
117 Q10 **Black Sea Lowland** *Ukr.* Prychornomor'ska Nyzovyna. *depression* SE Europe
33 S17 **Blacks Fork** ≈ Wyoming, C USA
23 V7 **Blackshear** Georgia, SE USA 31°18′N 82°14′W
23 S6 **Blackshear, Lake** ▣ Georgia, SE USA
97 A16 **Blacksod Bay** *Ir.* Cuan an Fhóid Duibh. *inlet* W Ireland
21 V7 **Blackstone** Virginia, NE USA 37°04′N 78°00′W
77 O14 **Black Volta** *var.* Borongo, Mouhoun, Moun Hou, *Fr.* Volta Noire. ≈ W Africa
23 O5 **Black Warrior River** ≈ Alabama, S USA
181 X8 **Blackwater** Queensland, E Australia 23°34′S 148°51′E
97 D20 **Blackwater** *Ir.* An Abhainn Mhór. ≈ S Ireland
27 T4 **Blackwater River** ≈ Missouri, C USA
21 W7 **Blackwater River** ≈ Virginia, NE USA
**Blackwater State** *see* Nebraska
27 N8 **Blackwell** Oklahoma, C USA 36°48′N 97°16′W
25 P7 **Blackwell** Texas, SW USA 32°05′N 100°19′W
99 J15 **Bladel** Noord-Brabant, S Netherlands 51°22′N 05°13′E
**Bladenmarkt** *see* Bălăuşeri
114 G11 **Blagoevgrad** *prev.* Gorna Dzhumaya. Blagoevgrad, W Bulgaria 42°01′N 23°05′E
114 G11 **Blagoevgrad** ◈ *province* SW Bulgaria
123 Q14 **Blagoveshchensk** Amurskaya Oblast', SE Russia 50°19′N 127°30′E
127 V4 **Blagoveshchensk** Respublika Bashkortostan, W Russia 55°03′N 56°01′E
117 O8 **Blahovishchens'ke** *prev.* Ul'yanovka. Kirovohrads'ka Oblast', C Ukraine 48°18′N 30°15′E
102 I7 **Blain** Loire-Atlantique, NW France 47°26′N 01°47′W
29 V8 **Blaine** Minnesota, N USA 45°09′N 93°13′W
32 H6 **Blaine** Washington, NW USA 48°59′N 122°45′W
11 T15 **Blaine Lake** Saskatchewan, S Canada 52°49′N 106°48′W
29 S14 **Blair** Nebraska, C USA 41°32′N 96°07′W
96 J10 **Blairgowrie** C Scotland, United Kingdom 56°19′N 03°25′W
18 C15 **Blairsville** Pennsylvania, NE USA 40°25′N 79°12′W
116 H11 **Blaj** *Ger.* Blasendorf, *Hung.* Balázsfalva. Alba, SW Romania 46°10′N 23°57′E
64 F9 **Blake-Bahama Ridge** *undersea feature* W Atlantic Ocean 29°00′N 73°30′W
23 S7 **Blakely** Georgia, SE USA 31°22′N 84°55′W
64 E10 **Blake Plateau** *var.* Blake Terrace. *undersea feature* W Atlantic Ocean 31°00′N 79°00′W
30 M1 **Blake Point** *headland* Michigan, N USA 48°11′N 88°25′W
**Blake Terrace** *see* Blake Plateau
61 B24 **Blanca, Bahía** *bay* E Argentina
56 C12 **Blanca, Cordillera** ▲▲ W Peru
105 T12 **Blanca, Costa** *physical region* SE Spain
37 S7 **Blanca Peak** ▲ Colorado, C USA 37°34′N 105°29′W
24 I9 **Blanca, Sierra** ▲ Texas, SW USA 31°15′N 105°26′W
120 K9 **Blanc, Cap** *headland* N Tunisia 37°20′N 09°41′E
**Blanc, Cap** *see* Nouâdhibou, Râs
31 R12 **Blanchard River** ≈ Ohio, N USA
182 E8 **Blanche, Cape** *headland* South Australia 33°03′S 134°10′E
182 J4 **Blanche, Lake** ◎ South Australia
31 R14 **Blanchester** Ohio, N USA 39°17′N 83°59′W
182 J9 **Blanchetown** South Australia 34°21′S 139°36′E
45 U13 **Blanchisseuse** Trinidad, Trinidad and Tobago 10°47′N 61°18′W
103 T11 **Blanc, Mont** *It.* Monte Bianco. ▲ France/Italy 45°45′N 06°51′E
25 R11 **Blanco** Texas SW USA 30°06′N 98°25′W
42 K14 **Blanco, Cabo** *headland* NW Costa Rica 09°34′N 85°06′W
32 D14 **Blanco, Cape** *headland* Oregon, NW USA 42°49′N 124°33′W
62 H10 **Blanco, Río** ≈ W Argentina
56 F10 **Blanco, Río** ≈ NE Peru
15 O9 **Blanc, Réservoir** ▣ Québec, SE Canada
21 R7 **Bland** Virginia, NE USA 37°06′N 81°08′W
92 I2 **Blanda** ≈ N Iceland
37 O7 **Blanding** Utah, W USA 37°37′N 109°28′W
105 X5 **Blanes** Cataluña, NE Spain 41°41′N 02°48′E
103 N3 **Blangy-sur-Bresle** Seine-Maritime, N France 49°55′N 01°37′E
111 C18 **Blanice** *Ger.* Blanitz. ≈ SE Czechia
**Blanitz** *see* Blanice
99 C16 **Blankenberge** West-Vlaanderen, NW Belgium 51°19′N 03°08′E
101 D17 **Blankenheim** Nordrhein-Westfalen, W Germany 50°26′N 06°41′E
25 R8 **Blanket** Texas, SW USA 31°49′N 98°47′W
55 O3 **Blanquilla, Isla** *var.* La Blanquilla. *island* N Venezuela
**Blanquilla, La** *see* Blanquilla, Isla
61 F18 **Blanquillo** Durazno, C Uruguay 32°53′S 55°37′W
111 G18 **Blansko** *Ger.* Blanz. Jihomoravský Kraj, SE Czechia 49°22′N 16°39′E
83 N15 **Blantyre** *var.* Blantyre-Limbe. Southern, S Malawi 15°45′S 35°04′E
83 N15 **Blantyre** ✕ Southern, S Malawi 15°34′S 35°03′E
**Blantyre-Limbe** *see* Blantyre
**Blanz** *see* Blansko
98 J10 **Blaricum** Noord-Holland, C Netherlands 52°16′N 05°15′E
**Blasendorf** *see* Blaj
**Blatnitsa** *see* Durankulak
113 F15 **Blato** *It.* Blatta. Dubrovnik-Neretva, S Croatia 42°57′N 16°47′E
**Blatta** *see* Blato
108 E10 **Blatten** Valais, SW Switzerland 46°22′N 08°00′E
101 J20 **Blaufelden** Baden-Württemberg, SW Germany 49°21′N 10°01′E
95 E23 **Blåvands Huk** *headland* W Denmark 55°33′N 08°04′E
102 G6 **Blavet** ≈ NW France
102 J12 **Blaye** Gironde, SW France
183 R8 **Blayney** New South Wales, SE Australia 33°33′S 149°13′E
65 D25 **Bleaker Island** *island* SE Falkland Islands
109 T10 **Bled** *Ger.* Veldes. NW Slovenia 46°23′N 14°06′E
99 D20 **Bléharies** Hainaut, SW Belgium 50°31′N 03°25′E
109 U9 **Bleiburg** *Slvn.* Pliberk. Kärnten, S Austria 46°36′N 14°49′E
101 L17 **Bleiloch-stausee** ▣ C Germany
98 H12 **Bleiswijk** Zuid-Holland, W Netherlands 52°01′N 04°32′E
95 L22 **Blekinge** ◈ *county* S Sweden
14 D17 **Blenheim** Ontario, S Canada 42°20′N 81°59′W
185 K15 **Blenheim** Marlborough, South Island, New Zealand 41°32′S 174°E
99 M15 **Blerick** Limburg, SE Netherlands 51°22′N 06°10′E
**Blesae** *see* Blois
25 V13 **Blessing** Texas, SW USA 28°52′N 96°12′W
14 I10 **Bleu, Lac** ◎ Québec, SE Canada
**Blibba** *see* Blitta
120 H10 **Blida** *var.* El Boulaida, El Boulaïda. N Algeria 36°30′N 02°50′E
95 P15 **Blidö** Stockholm, C Sweden 59°37′N 18°55′E
95 K18 **Blidsberg** Västra Götaland, S Sweden 57°55′N 13°30′E
185 A21 **Bligh Sound** *sound* South Island, New Zealand
187 X14 **Bligh Water** *strait* NW Fiji
14 D11 **Blind River** Ontario, S Canada 46°12′N 82°59′W
31 R11 **Blissfield** Michigan, N USA 41°49′N 83°51′W
77 R15 **Blitta** *prev.* Blibba. C Togo 08°19′N 00°59′E
19 O13 **Block Island** *island* Rhode Island, NE USA
19 O13 **Block Island Sound** *sound* Rhode Island, NE USA
98 H10 **Bloemendaal** Noord-Holland, W Netherlands 52°23′N 04°39′E
83 H23 **Bloemfontein** *var.* Mangaung. ● (South Africa-judicial capital) Free State, C South Africa 29°07′S 26°14′E
83 I22 **Bloemhof** North-West, NW South Africa 27°39′S 25°37′E
102 M7 **Blois** *anc.* Blesae. Loir-et-Cher, C France 47°36′N 01°20′E
98 L8 **Blokzijl** Overijssel, N Netherlands 52°46′N 05°58′E
95 N20 **Blomstermåla** Kalmar, S Sweden 56°58′N 16°19′E
92 I2 **Blönduós** Norðurland Vestra, N Iceland 65°39′N 20°15′W
110 L11 **Błonie** Mazowieckie, C Poland 52°13′N 20°36′E
97 C14 **Bloody Foreland** *Ir.* Cnoc Fola. *headland* NW Ireland 55°09′N 08°18′W
31 N15 **Bloomfield** Indiana, N USA 39°01′N 86°58′W
29 X16 **Bloomfield** Iowa, C USA 40°45′N 92°24′W
27 Y8 **Bloomfield** Missouri, C USA 36°54′N 89°58′W
37 P9 **Bloomfield** New Mexico, SW USA 36°42′N 108°00′W
25 U7 **Blooming Grove** Texas, SW USA 32°05′N 96°43′W
29 W10 **Blooming Prairie** Minnesota, N USA 43°52′N 93°03′W
30 L13 **Bloomington** Illinois, N USA 40°28′N 88°59′W
31 O15 **Bloomington** Indiana, N USA 39°10′N 86°31′W
29 V9 **Bloomington** Minnesota, N USA 44°50′N 93°18′W
25 U13 **Bloomington** Texas, SW USA 28°39′N 96°53′W
18 H14 **Bloomsburg** Pennsylvania, NE USA 40°59′N 76°27′W
181 X7 **Bloomsbury** Queensland, NE Australia 20°47′S 148°35′E
169 R16 **Blora** Jawa, C Indonesia 06°55′S 111°29′E
18 G12 **Blossburg** Pennsylvania, NE USA 41°38′N 77°00′W
25 V5 **Blossom** Texas, SW USA 33°39′N 95°23′W
123 T5 **Blossom, Mys** *headland* Ostrov Vrangelya, NE Russia 70°49′N 178°49′E


◆ Country
● Country Capital
◇ Dependent Territory
○ Dependent Territory Capital
◈ Administrative Regions
✕ International Airport
▲ Mountain
▲▲ Mountain Range
Volcano
≈ River
◎ Lake
▣ Reservoir

# Blountstown – Boquillas del Carmen



23 R8 **Blountstown** Florida, SE USA 30°26′N 85°03′W
21 P8 **Blountville** Tennessee, S USA 36°31′N 82°19′W
21 Q9 **Blowing Rock** North Carolina, SE USA 36°15′N 81°53′W
108 J8 **Bludenz** Vorarlberg, W Austria 47°10′N 09°50′E
36 L6 **Blue Bell Knoll** ▲ Utah, W USA 38°11′N 111°31′W
23 Y12 **Blue Cypress Lake** ◎ Florida, SE USA
29 U11 **Blue Earth** Minnesota, N USA 43°38′N 94°06′W
21 Q7 **Bluefield** Virginia, NE USA 37°15′N 81°16′W
21 R7 **Bluefield** West Virginia, NE USA 37°16′N 81°13′W
43 N10 **Bluefields** Costa Caribe Sur, SE Nicaragua 12°01′N 83°47′W
43 N10 **Bluefields, Bahía de** *bay* W Caribbean Sea
29 Z14 **Blue Grass** Iowa, C USA 41°30′N 90°46′W
**Bluegrass State** *see* Kentucky
**Blue Hen State** *see* Delaware
19 S7 **Blue Hill** Maine, NE USA 44°25′N 68°36′W
29 P16 **Blue Hill** Nebraska, C USA 40°19′N 98°27′W
30 J5 **Blue Hills** *hill range* Wisconsin, N USA
34 L3 **Blue Lake** California, W USA 40°52′N 124°00′W
**Blue Law State** *see* Connecticut
37 Q6 **Blue Mesa Reservoir** ⊠ Colorado, C USA
27 S12 **Blue Mountain** ▲ Arkansas, C USA 34°42′N 94°04′W
19 O6 **Blue Mountain** ▲ New Hampshire, NE USA 44°48′N 71°26′W
18 K8 **Blue Mountain** ▲ New York, NE USA 43°52′N 74°24′W
18 H15 **Blue Mountain** *ridge* Pennsylvania, NE USA
44 H10 **Blue Mountain Peak** ▲ E Jamaica 18°02′N 76°34′W
183 S8 **Blue Mountains** ▲▲ New South Wales, SE Australia
32 L11 **Blue Mountains** ▲▲ Oregon/ Washington, NW USA
80 G12 **Blue Nile** ◈ *state* E Sudan
80 H12 **Blue Nile** *var.* Abai, Bahr el, Azraq, *Amh.* Ābay Wenz, *Ar.* An Nīl al Azraq. ≈ Ethiopia/ Sudan
8 J7 **Bluenose Lake** ◎ Nunavut, NW Canada
27 O3 **Blue Rapids** Kansas, C USA 39°39′N 96°38′W
23 S1 **Blue Ridge** Georgia, SE USA 34°51′N 84°19′W
17 S11 **Blue Ridge** *var.* Blue Ridge Mountains. ▲▲ North Carolina/Virginia, USA
23 S1 **Blue Ridge Lake** ⊠ Georgia, SE USA
**Blue Ridge Mountains** *see* Blue Ridge
11 N15 **Blue River** British Columbia, SW Canada 52°03′N 119°21′W
27 O12 **Blue River** ≈ Oklahoma, C USA
27 R4 **Blue Springs** Missouri, C USA 39°01′N 94°16′W
21 R6 **Bluestone Lake** ⊠ West Virginia, NE USA
185 C25 **Bluff** Southland, South Island, New Zealand 46°36′S 168°22′E
37 O8 **Bluff** Utah, W USA 37°15′N 109°36′W
21 P8 **Bluff City** Tennessee, S USA 36°28′N 82°15′W
65 E24 **Bluff Cove** East Falkland, Falkland Islands 51°45′S 58°11′W
25 S7 **Bluff Dale** Texas, SW USA 32°18′N 98°01′W
183 N15 **Bluff Hill Point** *headland* Tasmania, SE Australia 41°03′S 144°35′E
31 Q12 **Bluffton** Indiana, N USA 40°44′N 85°10′W
31 R12 **Bluffton** Ohio, N USA 40°54′N 83°53′W
25 T7 **Blum** Texas, SW USA 32°08′N 97°24′W
101 G24 **Blumberg** Baden-Württemberg, SW Germany 47°48′N 08°31′E
60 K13 **Blumenau** Santa Catarina, S Brazil 26°55′S 49°07′W
29 N9 **Blunt** South Dakota, N USA 44°30′N 99°58′E
32 H15 **Bly** Oregon, NW USA 42°22′N 121°04′W
39 R13 **Blying Sound** *sound* Alaska, USA
97 M14 **Blyth** N England, United Kingdom 55°07′N 01°30′W
35 Y16 **Blythe** California, W USA 33°35′N 114°36′W
27 Y9 **Blytheville** Arkansas, C USA 35°56′N 89°55′W
117 V7 **Blyznyuky** Kharkivs'ka Oblast', E Ukraine 48°51′N 36°32′E
95 G16 **Bø** Telemark, S Norway 59°24′N 09°04′E
76 I15 **Bo** S Sierra Leone 07°58′N 11°45′W
171 O4 **Boac** Marinduque, N Philippines 13°26′N 121°50′E
42 K10 **Boaco** Boaco, S Nicaragua 12°28′N 85°45′W
42 J10 **Boaco** ◈ *department* C Nicaragua
79 I15 **Boali** Ombella-Mpoko, SW Central African Republic 04°52′N 18°00′E
**Boalsert** *see* Bolsward
31 V12 **Boardman** Ohio, N USA 41°01′N 80°39′W
32 J11 **Boardman** Oregon, NW USA 45°50′N 119°42′W
14 F13 **Boat Lake** ◎ Ontario, S Canada
58 F10 **Boa Vista** *state capital* Roraima, NW Brazil 02°51′N 60°43′W
76 D9 **Boa Vista** *island* Ilhas de Barlavento, E Cape Verde
23 Q2 **Boaz** Alabama, S USA 34°12′N 86°10′W
160 L15 **Bobai** Guangxi Zhuangzu Zizhiqu, S China 22°09′N 109°57′E
172 J1 **Bobaomby, Tanjona** *Fr.* Cap d'Ambre. *headland* N Madagascar 11°58′S 49°13′E
155 M14 **Bobbili** Andhra Pradesh, E India 18°32′N 83°29′E
106 D9 **Bobbio** Emilia-Romagna, C Italy 44°48′N 09°27′E
14 I14 **Bobcaygeon** Ontario, SE Canada 44°32′N 78°33′W
**Bober** *see* Bóbr
103 O5 **Bobigny** Seine-St-Denis, N France 48°55′N 02°27′E
77 N13 **Bobo-Dioulasso** SW Burkina Faso 11°12′N 04°21′W
110 G8 **Bobolice** *Ger.* Bublitz. Zachodnio-pomorskie, NW Poland 53°56′N 16°37′E
83 J19 **Bobonong** Central, E Botswana 21°58′S 28°26′E
171 R11 **Bobopayo** Pulau Halmahera, E Indonesia 01°07′N 127°26′E
113 J15 **Bobotov Kuk** ▲ N Montenegro 43°06′N 19°00′E
114 G10 **Bobov Dol** *var.* Bobovdol. Kyustendil, W Bulgaria 42°21′N 22°59′E
**Bobovdol** *see* Bobov Dol
119 M15 **Bobr** Minskaya Voblasts', NW Belarus 54°20′N 29°16′E
119 M15 **Bobr** ≈ C Belarus
111 E14 **Bóbr** *Eng.* Bobrawa, *Ger.* Bober. ≈ SW Poland
**Bobrawa** *see* Bóbr
**Bobrik** *see* Bobryk
**Bobrinets** *see* Bobrynets'
**Bobrka/Bóbrka** *see* Bibrka
126 L8 **Bobrov** Voronezhskaya Oblast', W Russia 51°10′N 40°03′E
117 Q4 **Bobrovytsya** Chernihivs'ka Oblast', N Ukraine 50°43′N 31°24′E
**Bobruysk** *see* Babruysk
119 J19 **Bobryk** *Rus.* Bobrik. ≈ SW Belarus
117 Q8 **Bobrynets'** *Rus.* Bobrinets. Kirovohrads'ka Oblast', C Ukraine 48°02′N 32°10′E
14 K14 **Bobs Lake** ◎ Ontario, SE Canada
54 I6 **Bobures** Zulia, NW Venezuela 09°15′N 71°10′W
42 H1 **Boca Bacalar Chico** *headland* N Belize 15°05′N 82°12′W
112 G11 **Bočac** ◈ Republika Srpska, NW Bosnia and Herzegovina
41 R14 **Boca del Río** Veracruz, S Mexico 19°08′N 96°08′W
55 O4 **Boca de Pozo** Nueva Esparta, NE Venezuela 11°00′N 64°23′W
59 C15 **Boca do Acre** Amazonas, N Brazil 08°45′S 67°23′W
55 N12 **Boca Mavaca** Amazonas, S Venezuela 02°30′N 65°11′W
79 G14 **Bocaranga** Ouham-Pendé, W Central African Republic 07°07′N 15°40′E
23 Z15 **Boca Raton** Florida, SE USA 26°22′N 80°05′W
43 P14 **Bocas del Toro** Bocas del Toro, NW Panama 09°20′N 82°15′W
43 P15 **Bocas del Toro** *off.* Provincia de Bocas del Toro ◈ *province* NW Panama
43 P15 **Bocas del Toro, Archipiélago de** *island group* NW Panama
**Bocas del Toro, Provincia de** *see* Bocas del Toro
42 L7 **Bocay** Jinotega, N Nicaragua 14°19′N 85°08′W
105 N6 **Boceguillas** Castilla y León, N Spain 41°20′N 03°39′W
**Bocheykovo** *see* Bacheykava
111 L17 **Bochnia** Małopolskie, SE Poland 49°58′N 20°27′E
99 K16 **Bocholt** Limburg, NE Belgium 51°10′N 05°37′E
101 D14 **Bocholt** Nordrhein-Westfalen, W Germany 51°50′N 06°37′E
101 E15 **Bochum** Nordrhein-Westfalen, W Germany 51°29′N 07°13′E
103 Y15 **Bocognano** Corse, France, C Mediterranean Sea 42°04′N 09°03′E
54 I6 **Boconó** Trujillo, NW Venezuela 09°17′N 70°17′W
116 F12 **Bocşa** *Ger.* Bokschen, *Hung.* Boksánbánya. Caraş-Severin, SW Romania 45°23′N 21°47′E
79 H15 **Boda** Lobaye, SW Central African Republic 04°17′N 17°25′E
94 L12 **Boda** Dalarna, C Sweden 61°00′N 15°15′E
95 O20 **Böda** Kalmar, S Sweden 57°16′N 17°04′E
95 L19 **Bodafors** Jönköping, S Sweden 57°30′N 14°40′E
123 O12 **Bodaybo** Irkutskaya Oblast', E Russia 57°52′N 114°05′E
22 G5 **Bodcau, Bayou** *var.* Bodcau Creek. ≈ Louisiana, S USA
**Bodcau Creek** *see* Bodcau, Bayou
44 D8 **Bodden Town** *var.* Boddentown. Grand Cayman, SW Cayman Islands 19°20′N 81°14′W
**Boddentown** *see* Bodden Town
101 K14 **Bode** ≈ C Germany
34 L7 **Bodega Head** *headland* California, W USA 38°16′N 123°04′W
**Bodegas** *see* Babahoyo
98 H11 **Bodegraven** Zuid-Holland, C Netherlands 52°05′N 04°45′E
78 H8 **Bodélé** *depression* W Chad
92 J13 **Boden** Norrbotten, N Sweden 65°50′N 21°44′E
**Bodensee** *see* Constance, Lake, C Europe
65 M15 **Bode Verde Fracture Zone** *tectonic feature* E Atlantic Ocean
155 H14 **Bodhan** Telangana, C India 18°40′N 77°51′E
**Bodī** *see* Jinst
155 H22 **Bodināyakkanūr** Tamil Nādu, SE India 10°02′N 77°18′E
108 H10 **Bodio** Ticino, S Switzerland 46°23′N 08°55′E
**Bodjonegoro** *see* Bojonegoro
97 I24 **Bodmin** SW England, United Kingdom 50°29′N 04°43′W
97 I24 **Bodmin Moor** *moorland* SW England, United Kingdom
92 G12 **Bodø** Nordland, C Norway 67°17′N 14°22′E
59 H20 **Bodoquena, Serra da** ▲▲ SW Brazil
136 B16 **Bodrum** Muğla, SW Turkey 37°01′N 27°28′E
**Bodzafordulő** *see* Întorsura Buzăului
99 L14 **Boekel** Noord-Brabant, SE Netherlands 51°35′N 05°42′E
**Boeloekoemba** *see* Bulukumba
103 Q11 **Boën** Loire, E France 45°45′N 04°01′E
79 K18 **Boende** Equateur, C Dem. Rep. Congo 0°12′S 20°54′E
**Boeng Tônlé Sab** *see* Tonle Sap
25 R11 **Boerne** Texas, SW USA 29°47′N 98°44′W
**Boeroe** *see* Buru, Pulau
**Boetoeng** *see* Buton, Pulau
22 I5 **Boeuf River** ≈ Arkansas/ Louisiana, S USA
76 H14 **Boffa** W Guinea 10°12′N 14°02′W
**Bó Finne, Inis** *see* Inishbofin
**Boga** *see* Bogë
166 L9 **Bogale** Ayeyarwady, SW Myanmar (Burma) 16°16′N 95°21′E
22 L8 **Bogalusa** Louisiana, S USA 30°47′N 89°51′W
77 Q12 **Bogandé** C Burkina Faso 13°02′N 00°08′W
79 I15 **Bogangolo** Ombella-Mpoko, C Central African Republic 05°36′N 18°17′E
183 Q7 **Bogan River** ≈ New South Wales, SE Australia
25 W5 **Bogata** Texas, SW USA 33°28′N 95°12′W
111 D14 **Bogatynia** *Ger.* Reichenau. Dolnośląskie, SW Poland 50°53′N 14°55′E
136 K13 **Boğazlıyan** Yozgat, C Turkey 39°13′N 35°17′E
79 J17 **Bogbonga** Equateur, NW Dem. Rep. Congo 01°36′N 19°24′E
158 J14 **Bogcang Zangbo** ≈ W China
162 I9 **Bogd** *var.* Horiult. Bayanhongor, C Mongolia 45°09′N 100°50′E
162 J10 **Bogd** *var.* Hovd. Övörhangay, C Mongolia 44°43′N 102°08′E
158 L5 **Bogda Feng** ▲ NW China 43°51′N 88°14′E
114 I9 **Bogdan** ▲ C Bulgaria 42°37′N 24°28′E
113 Q20 **Bogdanci** SE North Macedonia 41°12′N 22°34′E
158 M5 **Bogda Shan** *var.* Po-ko-to Shan. ▲▲ NW China
113 K17 **Bogë** *var.* Boga. Shkodër, N Albania 42°25′N 19°38′E
**Bogeda'er** *see* Wenquan
**Bogendorf** *see* Łuków
95 G23 **Bogense** Syddtjylland, C Denmark 55°34′N 10°06′E
183 T3 **Boggabilla** New South Wales, SE Australia 28°37′S 150°21′E
183 S6 **Boggabri** New South Wales, SE Australia 30°44′S 150°00′E
186 D6 **Bogia** Madang, N Papua New Guinea 04°16′S 144°56′E
97 N23 **Bognor Regis** SE England, United Kingdom 50°47′N 00°41′W
**Bogodukhov** *see* Bohodukhiv
181 V15 **Bogong, Mount** ▲ Victoria, SE Australia 36°43′S 147°19′E
169 O16 **Bogor** *Dut.* Buitenzorg. Jawa, C Indonesia 06°34′S 106°45′E
126 L5 **Bogoroditsk** Tul'skaya Oblast', W Russia 53°46′N 38°09′E
127 O3 **Bogorodsk** Nizhegorodskaya Oblast', W Russia 56°06′N 43°29′E
**Bogorodskoje** *see* Bogorodskoye
123 S12 **Bogorodskoye** Khabarovskiy Kray, SE Russia 52°22′N 140°33′E
125 R15 **Bogorodskoye** *var.* Bogorodskoje. Kirovskaya Oblast', NW Russia 57°50′N 51°41′E
54 F10 **Bogotá** *prev.* Santa Fe, Santa Fe de Bogotá. ● (Colombia) Cundinamarca, C Colombia 04°38′N 74°05′W
153 T14 **Bogra** Rajshahi, N Bangladesh 24°52′N 89°28′E
**Bogschan** *see* Boldu
122 L12 **Boguchany** Krasnoyarskiy Kray, C Russia 58°20′N 97°20′E
126 M9 **Boguchar** Voronezhskaya Oblast', W Russia 49°57′N 40°34′E
76 H10 **Bogué** Brakna, SW Mauritania 16°36′N 14°15′W
22 K8 **Bogue Chitto** ≈ Louisiana/ Mississippi, S USA
**Bogushëvsk** *see* Bahushewsk
**Boguslav** *see* Bohuslav
44 K12 **Bog Walk** C Jamaica 18°06′N 77°01′W
161 Q3 **Bo Hai** *var.* Gulf of Chihli. *gulf* NE China
161 R3 **Bohai Haixia** *strait* NE China
161 Q3 **Bohai Wan** *bay* NE China
111 C17 **Bohemia** *Cz.* Čechy, *Ger.* Böhmen. W Czechia
111 B18 **Bohemian Forest** *Cz.* Ceský Les, Šumava, *Ger.* Böhmerwald. ▲▲ C Europe
**Bohemian-Moravian Highlands** *see* Českomoravská Vrchovina
77 R16 **Bohicon** S Benin 07°14′N 02°04′E
109 S11 **Bohinjska Bistrica** *Ger.* Wocheiner Feistritz. NW Slovenia 46°16′N 13°55′E
**Bohkká** *see* Pokka
**Böhmen** *see* Bohemia
**Böhmerwald** *see* Bohemian Forest
**Böhmisch-Krumau** *see* Český Krumlov
**Böhmisch-Leipa** *see* Česká Lípa
**Böhmisch-Mährische Höhe** *see* Českomoravská Vrchovina
**Böhmisch-Trübau** *see* Česká Třebová
117 U5 **Bohodukhiv** *Rus.* Bogodukhov. Kharkivs'ka Oblast', E Ukraine 50°10′N 35°32′E
171 Q6 **Bohol** *island* C Philippines
171 Q7 **Bohol Sea** *var.* Mindanao Sea. *sea* S Philippines
116 I7 **Bohorodchany** Ivano-Frankivs'ka Oblast', W Ukraine 48°46′N 24°31′E
**Böhöt** *see* Öndörshil
158 K6 **Bohu** *var.* Bagrax. Xinjiang Uygur Zizhiqu, NW China 42°00′N 86°28′E
111 I17 **Bohumín** *Ger.* Oderberg; *prev.* Neuoderberg, Nový Bohumín. Moravskoslezský Kraj, E Czechia 49°55′N 18°20′E
117 P6 **Bohuslav** *Rus.* Boguslav. Kyivs'ka Oblast', N Ukraine 49°33′N 30°53′E
58 F11 **Boiaçu** Roraima, N Brazil 0°27′S 61°46′W
107 K16 **Boiano** Molise, C Italy 41°28′N 14°28′E
15 R8 **Boilleau** Québec, SE Canada 48°06′N 70°49′W
59 O17 **Boipeba, Ilha de** *island* SE Brazil
104 G3 **Boiro** Galicia, NW Spain 42°39′N 08°53′W
31 Q5 **Bois Blanc Island** *island* Michigan, N USA
29 R7 **Bois de Sioux River** ≈ Minnesota, N USA
33 N14 **Boise** *var.* Boise City. *state capital* Idaho, NW USA 43°39′N 116°14′W
26 G8 **Boise City** Oklahoma, C USA 36°44′N 102°31′W
**Boise City** *see* Boise
33 N14 **Boise River, Middle Fork** ≈ Idaho, NW USA
**Bois, Lac des** *see* Woods, Lake of the
**Bois-le-Duc** *see* 's-Hertogenbosch
11 W17 **Boissevain** Manitoba, S Canada 49°14′N 100°02′W
15 T7 **Boisvert, Pointe au** *headland* Québec, SE Canada 48°34′N 69°07′W
100 K10 **Boizenburg** Mecklenburg-Vorpommern, N Germany 53°23′N 10°43′E
**Bojador** *see* Boujdour
113 K18 **Bojana** *Alb.* Bunë. ≈ Albania/Montenegro *see also* Bunë
**Bojana** *see* Bunë, Lumi i
143 S3 **Bojnūrd** *var.* Bujnurd. Khorāsān-e Shemālī, N Iran 37°31′N 57°24′E
169 R16 **Bojonegoro** *prev.* Bodjonegoro. Jawa, C Indonesia 07°06′S 111°50′E
189 T1 **Bokaak Atoll** *var.* Bokak, Taongi. *atoll* Ratak Chain, NE Marshall Islands
**Bokak** *see* Bokaak Atoll
146 K8 **Bo'kantov Tog'lari** *Rus.* Gory Bukantau. ▲▲ N Uzbekistan
153 Q15 **Bokāro** Jhārkhand, N India 23°46′N 85°55′E
79 I18 **Bokatola** Equateur, NW Dem. Rep. Congo 0°37′S 18°45′E
76 H13 **Boké** W Guinea 10°56′N 14°18′W
**Bokhara** *see* Buxoro
183 Q4 **Bokharra River** ≈ New South Wales/Queensland, SE Australia
147 P14 **Bokhtar** *prev.* Qŭrghonteppa, *Rus.* Kurgan-Tyube. SW Tajikistan 37°51′N 68°42′E
147 X8 **Bokonbayevo** *Kyr.* Kajisay; *prev.* Kadzhi-Say. Issyk-Kul'skaya Oblast', NE Kyrgyzstan 42°07′N 76°59′E
78 H11 **Bokoro** Hadjer-Lamis, W Chad 12°23′N 17°03′E
79 K19 **Bokota** Equateur, NW Dem. Rep. Congo 0°56′S 22°24′E
167 N13 **Bokpyin** Taninthayi, S Myanmar (Burma) 11°16′N 98°47′E
**Boksánbánya/Bokschen** *see* Bocşa
83 F21 **Bokspits** Kgalagadi, SW Botswana 26°50′S 20°41′E
79 K18 **Bokungu** Equateur, C Dem. Rep. Congo 0°41′S 22°19′E
146 F12 **Bokurdak** *Rus.* Bakhardok. Ahal Welaýaty, C Turkmenistan 38°51′N 58°34′E
78 G10 **Bol** Lac, W Chad 13°27′N 14°40′E
76 G13 **Bolama** SW Guinea-Bissau 11°35′N 15°30′W
**Bolangir** *see* Balāngīr
**Bolanos** *see* Bolanos, Mount, Guam
**Bolaños** *see* Bolaños de Calatrava, Spain
105 N11 **Bolaños de Calatrava** *var.* Bolaños. Castilla-La Mancha, C Spain 38°55′N 03°39′W
188 B17 **Bolanos, Mount** *var.* Bolanos. ▲ S Guam 13°18′N 144°41′E
40 L12 **Bolaños, Río** ≈ C Mexico
115 M14 **Bolayır** Çanakkale, NW Turkey 40°31′N 26°46′E
102 L3 **Bolbec** Seine-Maritime, N France 49°34′N 00°31′E
116 L13 **Boldu** *var.* Bogschan. Buzău, SE Romania 45°18′N 27°15′E
146 H8 **Boldumsaz** *prev.* Kalinin, Kalininsk, Porsy. Daşoguz Welaýaty, N Turkmenistan 42°12′N 59°33′E
158 I4 **Bole** *var.* Bortala. Xinjiang Uygur Zizhiqu, NW China 44°52′N 82°06′E
77 O15 **Bole** NW Ghana 09°02′N 02°29′W
79 J19 **Boleko** Equateur, W Dem. Rep. Congo 01°27′S 19°52′E
111 E14 **Bolesławiec** *Ger.* Bunzlau. Dolnośląskie, SW Poland 51°16′N 15°34′E
127 R4 **Bolgar** *prev.* Kuybyshev. Respublika Tatarstan, W Russia 54°58′N 49°03′E
77 P14 **Bolgatanga** N Ghana 10°45′N 00°52′W
**Bolgrad** *see* Bolhrad
117 N12 **Bolhrad** *Rus.* Bolgrad. Odes'ka Oblast', SW Ukraine 45°42′N 28°35′E
163 Y8 **Boli** Heilongjiang, NE China 45°45′N 130°32′E
79 I19 **Bolia** Bandundu, W Dem. Rep. Congo 01°34′S 18°24′E
93 J14 **Boliden** Västerbotten, N Sweden 64°52′N 20°20′E
171 T13 **Bolifar** Pulau Seram, E Indonesia 03°08′S 130°34′E
171 N2 **Bolinao** Luzon, N Philippines 16°22′N 119°52′E
54 C12 **Bolívar** Cauca, SW Colombia 01°52′N 76°56′W
27 T6 **Bolivar** Missouri, C USA 37°37′N 93°25′W
20 F10 **Bolivar** Tennessee, S USA 35°17′N 88°59′W
54 F7 **Bolívar** *off.* Departmento de Bolívar. ◈ *province* N Colombia
56 A13 **Bolívar** ◈ *province* C Ecuador
55 N9 **Bolívar** *off.* Estado Bolívar. ◈ *state* SE Venezuela
**Bolívar, Departmento de** *see* Bolívar
**Bolívar, Estado** *see* Bolívar
25 X12 **Bolivar Peninsula** *headland* Texas, SW USA 29°26′N 94°41′W
54 I6 **Bolívar, Pico** ▲ W Venezuela 08°33′N 71°05′W
57 K17 **Bolivia** *off.* Plurinational State of Bolivia; *prev.* Republic of Bolivia. ◆ *republic* W South America
**Bolivia, Plurinational State of** *see* Bolivia
**Bolivia, Republic of** *see* Bolivia
112 O13 **Boljevac** Serbia, E Serbia 43°50′N 21°57′E
**Bolkenhain** *see* Bolków
126 J5 **Bolkhov** Orlovskaya Oblast', W Russia 53°28′N 36°00′E
111 F14 **Bolków** *Ger.* Bolkenhain. Dolnośląskie, SW Poland 50°55′N 15°49′E
182 K3 **Bollards Lagoon** South Australia 28°58′S 140°52′E
103 R14 **Bollène** Vaucluse, SE France 44°16′N 04°45′E
94 N12 **Bollnäs** Gävleborg, C Sweden 61°18′N 16°27′E
181 W10 **Bollon** Queensland, C Australia 28°07′S 147°28′E
192 L12 **Bollons Tablemount** *undersea feature* S Pacific Ocean 49°40′S 176°10′W
93 H17 **Bollstabruk** Västernorrland, C Sweden 63°00′N 17°41′E
**Bolluilos de Par del Condado** *see* Bollulos Par del Condado
104 J14 **Bollulos Par del Condado** *var.* Bolluilos de Par del Condado. Andalucía, S Spain 37°20′N 06°32′W
95 K21 **Bolmen** ◎ S Sweden
137 T10 **Bolnisi** S Georgia 41°28′N 44°34′E
79 H19 **Bolobo** Bandundu, W Dem. Rep. Congo 02°10′S 16°17′E
106 G10 **Bologna** Emilia-Romagna, N Italy 44°30′N 11°20′E
124 I15 **Bologoye** Tverskaya Oblast', W Russia 57°54′N 34°04′E
79 J18 **Bolomba** Equateur, NW Dem. Rep. Congo 0°27′N 19°13′E
41 X13 **Bolónchén de Rejón** *var.* Bolonchén de Rejón. Campeche, SE Mexico 20°00′N 89°34′W
114 J13 **Boloústra, Akrotírio** *headland* NE Greece 40°56′N 24°58′E
167 L8 **Bolovén, Phouphiang** *Fr.* Plateau des Bolovens. *plateau* S Laos
**Bolovens, Plateau des** *see* Bolovén, Phouphiang
106 H13 **Bolsena** Lazio, C Italy 42°39′N 11°59′E
107 G14 **Bolsena, Lago di** ◎ C Italy
126 B3 **Bol'shakovo** *Ger.* Kreuzingen; *prev.* Gross-Skaisgirren. Kaliningradskaya Oblast', W Russia 54°53′N 21°38′E
**Bol'shaya Berëstovitsa** *see* Vyalikaya Byerastavitsa
127 S7 **Bol'shaya Chernigovka** Samarskaya Oblast', W Russia 52°07′N 50°49′E
127 S7 **Bol'shaya Glushitsa** Samarskaya Oblast', W Russia 52°22′N 50°29′E
124 J4 **Bol'shaya Imandra, Ozero** ◎ NW Russia
**Bol'shaya Khobda** *see* Kobda
126 M12 **Bol'shaya Martynovka** Rostovskaya Oblast', SW Russia 47°19′N 41°40′E
122 K12 **Bol'shaya Murta** Krasnoyarskiy Kray, C Russia 56°51′N 93°10′E
125 V4 **Bol'shaya Rogovaya** ≈ NW Russia
125 U7 **Bol'shaya Synya** ≈ NW Russia
145 V9 **Bol'shaya Vladimirovka** Vostochnyy Kazakhstan, E Kazakhstan 50°53′N 79°29′E
123 V11 **Bol'sheretsk** Kamchatskiy Kray, E Russia 52°20′N 156°24′E
127 W3 **Bol'sheust'ikinskoye** Respublika Bashkortostan, W Russia 56°00′N 58°13′E
**Bol'shevik** *see* Bal'shavik
122 L5 **Bol'shevik, Ostrov** *island* Severnaya Zemlya, N Russia
125 U4 **Bol'shezemel'skaya Tundra** *physical region* NW Russia
144 J13 **Bol'shiye Barsuki, Peski** *desert* SW Kazakhstan
123 T7 **Bol'shoy Anyuy** ≈ NE Russia
123 N7 **Bol'shoy Begichev, Ostrov** *island* NE Russia
123 S15 **Bol'shoye Kamen'** Primorskiy Kray, SE Russia 43°06′N 132°21′E
127 O4 **Bol'shoye Murashkino** Nizhegorodskaya Oblast', W Russia 55°46′N 44°48′E
127 W4 **Bol'shoy Iremel'** ▲ W Russia 54°31′N 58°47′E
127 R7 **Bol'shoy Irgiz** ≈ W Russia
123 Q6 **Bol'shoy Lyakhovskiy, Ostrov** *island* NE Russia
123 Q11 **Bol'shoy Nimnyr** Respublika Sakha (Yakutiya), NE Russia 57°55′N 125°34′E
**Bol'shoy Rozhan** *see* Vyaliki Rozhan
**Bol'shoy Uzen'** *see* Karaozen
40 K6 **Bolsón de Mapimí** ▲▲ NW Mexico
98 K6 **Bolsward** *Fris.* Boalsert. Fryslân, N Netherlands 53°04′N 05°31′E
105 T4 **Boltaña** Aragón, NE Spain 42°28′N 00°02′E
14 G15 **Bolton** Ontario, S Canada 43°52′N 79°45′W
97 K17 **Bolton** *prev.* Bolton-le-Moors. NW England, United Kingdom 53°35′N 02°26′W
21 V12 **Bolton** North Carolina, SE USA 34°22′N 78°26′W
**Bolton-le-Moors** *see* Bolton
136 G11 **Bolu** Bolu, NW Turkey 40°45′N 31°38′E
136 G11 **Bolu** ◈ *province* NW Turkey
186 G9 **Bolubolu** Goodenough Island, S Papua New Guinea 09°22′S 150°22′E
92 H1 **Bolungarvík** Vestfirðir, NW Iceland 66°09′N 23°17′W
159 O10 **Boluntay** Qinghai, W China 36°30′N 92°11′E
159 P8 **Boluozhuanjing**, Aksay Kazakzu Zizhixian. Gansu, N China 39°25′N 94°09′E
136 F14 **Bolvadin** Afyon, W Turkey 38°43′N 31°02′E
114 M10 **Bolyarovo** *prev.* Pashkeni. Yambol, E Bulgaria 42°09′N 26°49′E
106 G6 **Bolzano** *Ger.* Bozen; *anc.* Bauzanum. Trentino-Alto Adige, N Italy 46°30′N 11°22′E
79 F22 **Boma** Bas-Congo, W Dem. Rep. Congo 05°42′S 13°05′E
183 R12 **Bombala** New South Wales, SE Australia 36°54′S 149°15′E
104 F10 **Bombarral** Leiria, C Portugal 39°15′N 09°09′W
**Bombay** *see* Mumbai
171 U13 **Bomberai, Semenanjung** *cape* Papua Barat, E Indonesia
81 F18 **Bombo** S Uganda 0°36′N 32°33′E
162 I8 **Bömbögör** *var.* Dzadgay. Bayanhongor, C Mongolia 46°12′N 99°29′E
79 I17 **Bomboma** Equateur, NW Dem. Rep. Congo 02°23′N 19°03′E
59 I14 **Bom Futuro** Pará, N Brazil 06°27′S 54°44′W
159 Q15 **Bomi** *var.* Bowo, Zhamo. Xizang Zizhiqu, W China 29°43′N 96°12′E
79 N17 **Bomili** Orientale, NE Dem. Rep. Congo 01°45′N 27°01′E
59 N17 **Bom Jesus da Lapa** Bahia, E Brazil 13°16′S 43°23′W
60 Q8 **Bom Jesus do Itabapoana** Rio de Janeiro, SE Brazil 21°07′S 41°43′W
95 C15 **Bømlafjorden** *fjord* S Norway
95 B15 **Bømlo** *island* S Norway
12 Q12 **Bomnak** Amurskaya Oblast', SE Russia 54°43′N 128°50′E
79 I17 **Bomongo** Equateur, NW Dem. Rep. Congo 01°22′N 18°21′E
61 K14 **Bom Retiro** Santa Catarina, S Brazil 27°45′S 49°31′W
79 L15 **Bomu** *var.* Mbomou, Mbomu, M'Bomu. ≈ Central African Republic/ Dem. Rep. Congo
142 J3 **Bonāb** *var.* Benāb, Bunab. Āžarbāyjān-e Sharqī, N Iran 37°30′N 46°03′E
45 S9 **Bonaire** ◈ *special Municipality of the Netherlands* S Caribbean Sea
45 Q16 **Bonaire** *island* Lesser Antilles
39 U11 **Bona, Mount** ▲ Alaska, USA 61°22′N 141°45′W
183 Q12 **Bonang** Victoria, SE Australia 37°13′S 148°43′E
42 L7 **Bonanza** Costa Caribe Norte, NE Nicaragua 13°59′N 84°30′W
37 O4 **Bonanza** Utah, W USA 40°01′N 109°12′W
45 O9 **Bonao** C Dominican Republic 18°55′N 70°25′W
180 L3 **Bonaparte Archipelago** *island group* Western Australia
32 K6 **Bonaparte, Mount** ▲ Washington, NW USA 48°47′N 119°07′W
39 N11 **Bonasila Dome** ▲ Alaska, USA 62°24′N 160°28′W
45 T15 **Bonasse** Trinidad, Trinidad and Tobago 10°02′N 61°48′W
15 X7 **Bonaventure** Québec, SE Canada 48°03′N 65°30′W
15 X7 **Bonaventure** ≈ Québec, SE Canada
13 V11 **Bonavista** Newfoundland, Newfoundland and Labrador, SE Canada 48°38′N 53°08′W
13 U11 **Bonavista Bay** *inlet* NW Atlantic Ocean
79 E19 **Bonda** Ogooué-Lolo, C Gabon 0°50′S 12°28′E
127 N6 **Bondari** Tambovskaya Oblast', W Russia 52°58′N 42°02′E
106 G9 **Bondeno** Emilia-Romagna, C Italy 44°53′N 11°24′E
30 L4 **Bond Falls Flowage** ◎ Michigan, N USA
79 L16 **Bondo** Orientale, N Dem. Rep. Congo 03°52′N 23°41′E
171 N17 **Bondokodi** Pulau Sumba, S Indonesia 09°36′S 119°01′E
77 O15 **Bondoukou** E Ivory Coast 08°03′N 02°45′W
**Bondoukui/Bondoukuy** *see* Boundoukui
169 T17 **Bondowoso** Jawa, C Indonesia 07°54′S 113°50′E
33 S14 **Bondurant** Wyoming, C USA 43°14′N 110°26′W
**Bône** *see* Annaba, Algeria
**Bone** *see* Watampone, Indonesia
30 I5 **Bone Lake** ◎ Wisconsin, N USA
171 P14 **Bonelipu** Pulau Buton, C Indonesia 04°42′S 123°09′E
171 O15 **Bonerate, Kepulauan** *var.* Macan. *island group* C Indonesia
29 O12 **Bonesteel** South Dakota, N USA 43°01′N 98°55′W
62 I8 **Bonete, Cerro** ▲ N Argentina 27°58′S 68°22′W
171 O14 **Bone, Teluk** *bay* Sulawesi, C Indonesia
108 D6 **Bonfol** Jura, NW Switzerland 47°28′N 07°08′E
153 U12 **Bongaigaon** Assam, NE India 26°30′N 90°31′E
79 K17 **Bongandanga** Equateur, NW Dem. Rep. Congo 01°28′N 21°03′E
78 L13 **Bongo, Massif des** *var.* Chaîne des Mongos. ▲▲ NE Central African Republic
78 G12 **Bongor** Mayo-Kébbi Est, SW Chad 10°18′N 15°20′E
77 N16 **Bongouanou** E Ivory Coast 06°39′N 04°12′W
167 V11 **Bông Sơn** *var.* Hoai Nhơn. Bình Định, C Vietnam 14°28′N 109°00′E
25 U5 **Bonham** Texas, SW USA 33°36′N 96°12′W
**Bonhard** *see* Bonyhád
103 U6 **Bonhomme, Col du** *pass* NE France
103 Y16 **Bonifacio** Corse, France, C Mediterranean Sea 41°24′N 09°09′E
**Bonifacio, Bocche de/ Bonifacio, Bouches de** *see* Bonifacio, Strait of
103 Y16 **Bonifacio, Strait of** *Fr.* Bouches de Bonifacio, *It.* Bocche di Bonifacio. *strait* C Mediterranean Sea
23 Q8 **Bonifay** Florida, SE USA 30°49′N 85°42′W
**Bonin Islands** *see* Ogasawara-shotō
192 H5 **Bonin Trench** *undersea feature* NW Pacific Ocean
23 W15 **Bonita Springs** Florida, SE USA 26°19′N 81°48′W
42 I5 **Bonito, Pico** ▲ N Honduras 15°33′N 86°55′W
101 E17 **Bonn** Nordrhein-Westfalen, W Germany 50°44′N 07°06′E
92 H11 **Bonnåsjøen** Nordland, C Norway 67°35′N 15°39′E
14 J12 **Bonnechere** Ontario, SE Canada 45°39′N 77°36′W
14 J12 **Bonnechere** ≈ Ontario, SE Canada
33 N7 **Bonners Ferry** Idaho, NW USA 48°41′N 116°19′W
27 R4 **Bonner Springs** Kansas, C USA 39°03′N 94°52′W
102 L6 **Bonnétable** Sarthe, NW France 48°09′N 00°24′E
27 X6 **Bonne Terre** Missouri, C USA 37°55′N 90°33′W
10 J5 **Bonnet Plume** ≈ Yukon, NW Canada
102 M6 **Bonneval** Eure-et-Loir, C France 48°12′N 01°23′E
103 T10 **Bonneville** Haute-Savoie, E France 46°05′N 06°25′E
36 J3 **Bonneville Salt Flats** *salt flat* Utah, W USA
77 U18 **Bonny** Rivers, S Nigeria 04°25′N 07°13′E
**Bonny, Bight of** *see* Biafra, Bight of
37 W4 **Bonny Reservoir** ⊠ Colorado, C USA
11 R14 **Bonnyville** Alberta, SW Canada 54°16′N 110°46′W
107 C18 **Bono** Sardegna, Italy, C Mediterranean Sea 40°24′N 09°01′E
**Bononia** *see* Vidin, Bulgaria
**Bononia** *see* Boulogne-sur-Mer, France
107 B18 **Bonorva** Sardegna, Italy, C Mediterranean Sea 40°27′N 08°46′E
30 M15 **Bonpas Creek** ≈ Illinois, N USA
190 I3 **Bonriki** Tarawa, W Kiribati 01°23′N 173°09′E
183 T4 **Bonshaw** New South Wales, SE Australia 29°06′S 151°15′E
76 I16 **Bonthe** SW Sierra Leone 07°32′N 12°30′W
171 N2 **Bontoc** Luzon, N Philippines 17°04′N 120°58′E
25 Y9 **Bon Wier** Texas, SW USA 30°43′N 93°40′W
111 J25 **Bonyhád** *Ger.* Bonhard. Tolna, S Hungary 46°20′N 18°31′E
**Bonzabaai** *see* Bonza Bay
83 J25 **Bonza Bay** *Afr.* Bonzabaai. Eastern Cape, S South Africa 32°58′S 27°58′E
182 D7 **Bookabie** South Australia 31°49′S 132°41′E
182 H6 **Bookaloo** South Australia 31°56′S 137°21′E
37 P5 **Book Cliffs** *cliff* Colorado/ Utah, W USA
25 P1 **Booker** Texas, SW USA 36°27′N 100°32′W
76 K15 **Boola** SE Guinea 08°22′N 08°41′W
183 O8 **Booligal** New South Wales, SE Australia 33°56′S 144°54′E
99 G17 **Boom** Antwerpen, N Belgium 51°05′N 04°24′E
43 N6 **Boom** *var.* Boon. Costa Caribe Norte, NE Nicaragua 14°52′N 83°36′W
183 S3 **Boomi** New South Wales, SE Australia 28°43′S 149°35′E
**Boon** *see* Boom
162 H9 **Bööncagaan Nuur** ◎ S Mongolia
29 V13 **Boone** Iowa, C USA 42°04′N 93°52′W
21 Q8 **Boone** North Carolina, SE USA 36°13′N 81°41′W
27 S11 **Booneville** Arkansas, C USA 35°09′N 93°57′W
21 N6 **Booneville** Kentucky, S USA 37°26′N 83°45′W
23 N2 **Booneville** Mississippi, S USA 34°39′N 88°34′W
21 V3 **Boonsboro** Maryland, NE USA 39°30′N 77°39′W
34 L6 **Boonville** California, W USA 38°58′N 123°21′W
31 N16 **Boonville** Indiana, N USA 38°03′N 87°16′W
27 U4 **Boonville** Missouri, C USA 38°58′N 92°43′W
18 I9 **Boonville** New York, NE USA 43°28′N 75°17′W
80 M12 **Boorama** Awdal, NW Somalia 09°58′N 43°15′E
183 O6 **Booroondarra, Mount** *hill* New South Wales, SE Australia
183 N9 **Booroorban** New South Wales, SE Australia 34°55′S 144°45′E
183 R9 **Boorowa** New South Wales, SE Australia 34°26′S 148°42′E
99 H17 **Boortmeerbeek** Vlaams Brabant, C Belgium 50°58′N 04°27′E
80 P11 **Boosaaso** *var.* Bandar Kassim, Bender Qaasim, Bosaso, *It.* Bender Cassim. Bari, N Somalia 11°26′N 49°37′E
19 Q8 **Boothbay Harbor** Maine, NE USA 43°52′N 69°35′W
**Boothia Felix** *see* Boothia Peninsula
9 N6 **Boothia, Gulf of** *gulf* Nunavut, NE Canada
9 N6 **Boothia Peninsula** *prev.* Boothia Felix. *peninsula* Nunavut, NE Canada
79 E18 **Booué** Ogooué-Ivindo, NE Gabon 0°03′S 11°58′E
101 J21 **Bopfingen** Baden-Württemberg, S Germany 48°51′N 10°21′E
101 F18 **Boppard** Rheinland-Pfalz, W Germany 50°13′N 07°36′E
62 M4 **Boquerón** *off.* Departamento de Boquerón. ◈ *department* W Paraguay
**Boquerón, Departamento de** *see* Boquerón
43 P15 **Boquete** *var.* Bajo Boquete. Chiriquí, W Panama 08°45′N 82°26′W
40 J6 **Boquilla, Presa de la** ⊠ N Mexico
40 L5 **Boquillas** *var.* Boquillas del Carmen. Coahuila, NE Mexico 29°10′N 102°55′W
**Boquillas del Carmen** *see* Boquillas


◆ Country
● Country Capital
◇ Dependent Territory
○ Dependent Territory Capital
◈ Administrative Regions
✕ International Airport
▲ Mountain
▲▲ Mountain Range
⛰ Volcano
≈ River
◎ Lake
⊠ Reservoir

BOR – BRAZIL


112 P12 **Bor** Serbia, E Serbia 44°05′N 22°07′E
81 F15 **Bor** Jonglei, E South Sudan 06°12′N 31°33′E
95 L20 **Bor** Jönköping, S Sweden 57°04′N 14°10′E
136 J15 **Bor** Niğde, S Turkey 37°49′N 35°00′E
191 S10 **Bora-Bora** *island* Îles Sous le Vent, W French Polynesia
167 Q9 **Borabu** Maha Sarakham, E Thailand 16°01′N 103°06′E
172 K4 **Boraha, Nosy** *island* E Madagascar
33 P13 **Borah Peak** ▲ Idaho, NW USA 44°21′N 113°53′W
145 U16 **Boralday** *prev.* Burunday. Almaty, SE Kazakhstan 43°21′N 76°48′E
145 Y11 **Boran** *prev.* Buran. Vostochnyy Kazakhstan, E Kazakhstan 48°00′N 85°09′E
144 G13 **Borankul** *prev.* Opornyy. Mangistau, SW Kazakhstan 46°09′N 54°32′E
95 J19 **Borås** Västra Götaland, S Sweden 57°44′N 12°55′E
143 N11 **Borāzjān** *var.* Borazjān, Būshehr, S Iran 29°19′N 51°12′E
**Borazjan** *see* Borāzjān
58 G13 **Borba** Amazonas, N Brazil 04°39′S 59°35′W
104 H11 **Borba** Évora, S Portugal 38°48′N 07°28′W
**Borbetomagus** *see* Worms
55 O7 **Borbón** Bolívar, E Venezuela 07°55′N 64°03′W
59 Q15 **Borborema, Planalto da** *plateau* NE Brazil
116 M14 **Borcea, Braţul** ⚑ S Romania
**Borchalo** *see* Marneuli
195 R15 **Borchgrevink Coast** *physical region* Antarctica
137 Q11 **Borçka** Artvin, NE Turkey 41°24′N 41°38′E
98 N11 **Borculo** Gelderland, E Netherlands 52°07′N 06°31′E
182 G10 **Borda, Cape** *headland* South Australia 35°45′S 136°34′E
102 K13 **Bordeaux** *anc.* Burdigala. Gironde, SW France 44°49′N 00°33′W
11 T15 **Borden** Saskatchewan, S Canada 52°23′N 107°10′W
14 D8 **Borden Lake** ◎ Ontario, S Canada
9 N4 **Borden Peninsula** *peninsula* Baffin Island, Nunavut, NE Canada
182 K11 **Bordertown** South Australia 36°21′S 140°48′E
92 H2 **Borðeyri** Norðurland Vestra, NW Iceland 65°12′N 21°09′W
95 B18 **Bordhoy** *Dan.* Bordø. *island* NE Faroe Islands
106 B11 **Bordighera** Liguria, NW Italy 43°48′N 07°40′E
74 K5 **Bordj-Bou-Arreridj** *var.* Bordj Bou Arreridj, Bordj Bou Arréridj. N Algeria 36°02′N 04°49′E
74 L10 **Bordj Omar Driss** E Algeria 28°09′N 06°52′E
143 N13 **Bord Khūn** Hormozgān, S Iran
**Bordø** *see* Bordhoy
147 V7 **Bordunskiy** Chuyskaya Oblast', N Kyrgyzstan 42°37′N 75°31′E
95 M17 **Borensberg** Östergötland, S Sweden 58°33′N 15°15′E
**Borgå** *see* Porvoo
92 H3 **Borgarnes** Vesturland, W Iceland 64°33′N 21°55′W
93 G14 **Børgefjell** ▲▲ C Norway
98 O7 **Borger** Drenthe, NE Netherlands 52°54′N 06°48′E
25 N2 **Borger** Texas, SW USA 35°40′N 101°24′W
95 N20 **Borgholm** Kalmar, S Sweden 56°50′N 16°41′E
107 N22 **Borgia** Calabria, SW Italy 38°48′N 16°28′E
99 J18 **Borgloon** Limburg, NE Belgium 50°48′N 05°21′E
**Borg Massif** *see* Borgmassivet
195 P2 **Borgmassivet** *Eng.* Borg Massif. ▲▲ Antarctica
22 L9 **Borgne, Lake** ◎ Louisiana, S USA
106 C7 **Borgomanero** Piemonte, NE Italy 45°42′N 08°33′E
106 G10 **Borgo Panigale** ✈ (Bologna) Emilia-Romagna, N Italy 44°33′N 11°16′E
107 J15 **Borgorose** Lazio, C Italy 42°10′N 13°15′E
106 A9 **Borgo San Dalmazzo** Piemonte, N Italy 44°19′N 07°29′E
106 G11 **Borgo San Lorenzo** Toscana, C Italy 43°58′N 11°22′E
106 C7 **Borgosesia** Piemonte, NE Italy 45°41′N 08°21′E
106 E9 **Borgo Val di Taro** Emilia-Romagna, C Italy 44°29′N 09°48′E
106 G6 **Borgo Valsugana** Trentino-Alto Adige, N Italy 46°04′N 11°31′E
**Borhoyn Tal** *see* Dzamïn-Üüd
167 R8 **Borikhan** *var.* Borikhane. Bolikhamxai, C Laos 18°36′N 103°43′E
**Borikhane** *see* Borikhan
144 G8 **Borili** *prev.* Burlin. Zapadnyy Kazakhstan, NW Kazakhstan 51°25′N 52°42′E
**Borislav** *see* Boryslav
127 N8 **Borisoglebsk** Voronezhskaya Oblast', W Russia 51°23′N 42°00′E
**Borisov** *see* Barysaw
**Borisovgrad** *see* Parvomay
**Borispol'** *see* Boryspil'
172 I3 **Boriziny** *prev./Fr.* Port-Bergé. Mahajanga, NW Madagascar 15°31′S 47°40′E
105 Q5 **Borja** Aragón, NE Spain 41°50′N 01°32′W
**Borjas Blancas** *see* Les Borges Blanques
137 S10 **Borjomi** *Rus.* Borzhomi. C Georgia 41°50′N 43°24′E
118 L12 **Borkavichy** *Rus.* Borkovichi. Vitsyebskaya Voblasts', N Belarus 55°40′N 28°20′E
101 H16 **Borken** Hessen, C Germany 51°01′N 09°16′E
101 E14 **Borken** Nordrhein-Westfalen, W Germany 51°51′N 06°51′E
92 H10 **Borkenes** Troms, N Norway 68°46′N 16°10′E
78 H7 **Borkou** *off.* Région du Borkou. ◆ *region* N Chad
**Borkou, Région du** *see* Borkou
**Borkovichi** *see* Borkavichy
100 E9 **Borkum** *island* NW Germany
81 K17 **Bor, Lagh** *var.* Lak Bor. *dry watercourse* NE Kenya
**Bor, Lak** *see* Bor, Lagh
95 M14 **Borlänge** Dalarna, C Sweden 60°29′N 15°25′E
106 C9 **Bormida** ⚑ NW Italy
106 F6 **Bormio** Lombardia, N Italy 46°27′N 10°24′E
101 M16 **Borna** Sachsen, E Germany 51°07′N 12°30′E
98 O10 **Borne** Overijssel, E Netherlands 52°18′N 06°45′E
99 F17 **Bornem** Antwerpen, N Belgium 51°06′N 04°14′E
169 S10 **Borneo** *island* Brunei/Indonesia/Malaysia
101 E16 **Bornheim** Nordrhein-Westfalen, W Germany 50°46′N 06°58′E
95 L24 **Bornholm** *island* E Denmark
77 Y13 **Borno** ◆ *state* NE Nigeria
104 K15 **Bornos** Andalucía, S Spain 36°50′N 05°42′W
162 L7 **Bornuur** Töv, C Mongolia 48°28′N 106°15′E
117 O4 **Borodyanka** Kyivs'ka Oblast', N Ukraine 50°40′N 29°54′E
158 I5 **Borohoro Shan** ▲▲ NW China
77 O13 **Boromo** SW Burkina Faso 11°47′N 02°54′W
35 T13 **Boron** California, W USA 35°00′N 117°42′W
**Borongo** *see* Black Volta
**Boron'ki** *see* Baron'ki
**Borosjenő** *see* Ineu
**Borossebes** *see* Sebiş
76 L15 **Borotou** NW Ivory Coast 08°46′N 07°30′W
117 W6 **Borova** Kharkivs'ka Oblast', E Ukraine 49°22′N 37°39′E
114 H8 **Borovan** Vratsa, NW Bulgaria 43°25′N 23°45′E
124 I14 **Borovichi** Novgorodskaya Oblast', W Russia 58°24′N 33°56′E
**Borovlje** *see* Ferlach
112 J9 **Borovo** Vukovar-Srijem, NE Croatia 45°22′N 18°57′E
**Borovoye** *see* Burabay
126 K4 **Borovsk** Kaluzhskaya Oblast', W Russia 55°12′N 36°22′E
145 N7 **Borovskoy** Kostanay, N Kazakhstan 53°48′N 64°17′E
**Borovukha** *see* Baravukha
95 L23 **Borrby** Skåne, S Sweden 55°27′N 14°10′E
105 T9 **Borriana** *var.* Burriana. Comunitat Valenciana, E Spain 39°54′N 00°05′W
181 R3 **Borroloola** Northern Territory, N Australia 16°09′S 136°18′E
116 F9 **Borş** Bihor, NW Romania 47°07′N 21°49′E
116 I9 **Borşa** *Hung.* Borsa. Maramureş, N Romania 47°40′N 24°37′E
116 J10 **Borsec** *Ger.* Bad Borseck, *Hung.* Borszék. Harghita, C Romania 46°58′N 25°32′E
92 K8 **Børselv** *Lapp.* Bissojohka. Finnmark, N Norway 70°18′N 25°35′E
113 L23 **Borsh** *var.* Borshi. Vlorë, S Albania 40°04′N 19°51′E
**Borshchev** *see* Borshchiv
116 K7 **Borshchiv** *Pol.* Borszczów, *Rus.* Borshchev. Ternopil's'ka Oblast', W Ukraine 48°48′N 26°00′E
**Borshi** *see* Borsh
111 L20 **Borsod-Abaúj-Zemplén** *off.* Borsod-Abaúj-Zemplén Megye. ◆ *county* NE Hungary
**Borsod-Abaúj-Zemplén Megye** *see* Borsod-Abaúj-Zemplén
99 E15 **Borssele** Zeeland, SW Netherlands 51°26′N 03°45′E
**Borszczów** *see* Borshchiv
**Borszék** *see* Borsec
**Bortala** *see* Bole
103 O12 **Bort-les-Orgues** Corrèze, C France 45°28′N 02°31′E
**Bor u České Lípy** *see* Nový Bor
**Bor-Üdzüür** *see* Altay
143 N9 **Borūjen** Chahār Maḩall va Bakhtīārī, C Iran 32°N 51°09′E
142 L7 **Borūjerd** *var.* Burujird. Lorestān, W Iran 33°55′N 48°46′E
116 H6 **Boryslav** *Pol.* Borysław, *Rus.* Borislav. L'vivs'ka Oblast', NW Ukraine 49°18′N 23°28′E
**Borysław** *see* Boryslav
117 P4 **Boryspil'** *Rus.* Borispol'. Kyivs'ka Oblast', N Ukraine 50°21′N 30°59′E
117 P4 **Boryspil'** *Rus.* Borispol'. ✈ (Kyyiv) Kyivs'ka Oblast', N Ukraine 50°21′N 30°46′E
**Borzhomi** *see* Borjomi
117 R3 **Borzna** Chernihivs'ka Oblast', NE Ukraine 51°15′N 32°25′E
123 O14 **Borzya** Zabaykal'skiy Kray, S Russia 50°18′N 116°24′E
107 B18 **Bosa** Sardegna, Italy, C Mediterranean Sea 40°18′N 08°28′E
112 F10 **Bosanska Dubica** *var.* Kozarska Dubica. ◆ Republika Srpska, NW Bosnia and Herzegovina
112 G10 **Bosanska Gradiška** *var.* Gradiška. ◆ Republika Srpska, N Bosnia and Herzegovina
112 F10 **Bosanska Kostajnica** *var.* Srpska Kostajnica. ◆ Republika Srpska, NW Bosnia and Herzegovina
112 E11 **Bosanska Krupa** *var.* Krupa, Krupa na Uni. ◆ Federacija Bosne I Hercegovine, NW Bosnia and Herzegovina
112 H10 **Bosanski Brod** *var.* Srpski Brod. ◆ Republika Srpska, N Bosnia and Herzegovina
112 E10 **Bosanski Novi** *var.* Novi Grad. Republika Srpska, NW Bosnia and Herzegovina 45°03′N 16°23′E
112 E11 **Bosanski Petrovac** *var.* Petrovac. Federacija Bosne I Hercegovine, NW Bosnia and Herzegovina 44°34′N 16°21′E
112 I10 **Bosanski Šamac** *var.* Šamac. Republika Srpska, N Bosnia and Herzegovina 45°03′N 18°27′E
112 E12 **Bosansko Grahovo** *var.* Grahovo, Hrvatsko Grahovi. Federacija Bosne I Hercegovine, W Bosnia and Herzegovina 44°10′N 16°22′E
**Bosaso** *see* Boosaaso
186 B7 **Bosavi, Mount** ⚠ W Papua New Guinea 06°33′S 142°50′E
160 J14 **Bose** Guangxi Zhuangzu Zizhiqu, S China 23°55′N 106°32′E
161 Q5 **Boshan** Shandong, E China 36°32′N 117°47′E
113 P16 **Bosilegrad** *prev.* Bosiljgrad. Serbia, SE Serbia 42°30′N 22°30′E
**Bosiljgrad** *see* Bosilegrad
**Bösing** *see* Pezinok
98 H12 **Boskoop** Zuid-Holland, C Netherlands 52°04′N 04°40′E
111 G18 **Boskovice** *Ger.* Boskowitz. Jihomoravský Kraj, SE Czechia 49°30′N 16°39′E
**Boskowitz** *see* Boskovice
112 I10 **Bosna** ⚑ N Bosnia and Herzegovina
113 G14 **Bosne I Hercegovine, Federacija** ◆ *republic* Bosnia and Herzegovina
112 H12 **Bosnia and Herzegovina** *off.* Republic of Bosnia and Herzegovina. ◆ *republic* SE Europe
**Bosnia and Herzegovina, Republic of** *see* Bosnia and Herzegovina
79 J16 **Bosobolo** Equateur, NW Dem. Rep. Congo 04°11′N 19°55′E
165 O14 **Bōsō-hantō** *peninsula* Honshū, S Japan
**Bosora** *see* Buşrá ash Shām
**Bosphorus/Bosporus** *see* İstanbul Boğazı
**Bosporus Cimmerius** *see* Kerch Strait
**Bosporus Thracius** *see* İstanbul Boğazı
**Bosra** *see* Buşrá ash Shām
79 H14 **Bossangoa** Ouham, C Central African Republic 06°32′N 17°25′E
**Bossé Bangou** *see* Bossey Bangou
79 I15 **Bossembélé** Ombella-Mpoko, C Central African Republic 05°13′N 17°39′E
79 H15 **Bossentélé** Ouham-Pendé, W Central African Republic 05°36′N 16°37′E
77 R12 **Bossey Bangou** *var.* Bossé Bangou. Tillabéri, SW Niger 13°22′N 01°18′E
22 G5 **Bossier City** Louisiana, S USA 32°31′N 93°43′W
83 D20 **Bossiesvlei** Hardap, S Namibia 25°02′S 16°48′E
77 Y11 **Bosso** Diffa, SE Niger 13°42′N 13°18′E
61 F15 **Bossoroca** Rio Grande do Sul, S Brazil 28°45′S 54°54′W
158 J10 **Bostan** Xinjiang Uygur Zizhiqu, W China 41°20′N 83°15′E
142 K3 **Bostānābād** Āžarbāyjān-e Sharqī, N Iran 37°52′N 46°51′E
158 K6 **Bosten Hu** *var.* Bagrax Hu. ◎ NW China
97 O18 **Boston** *prev.* St.Botolph's Town. E England, United Kingdom 52°59′N 00°01′W
19 O11 **Boston** *state capital* Massachusetts, NE USA 42°22′N 71°04′W
146 I9 **Bo'ston** *Rus.* Bustan. Qoraqalpog'iston Respublikasi, W Uzbekistan 41°49′N 60°51′E
10 M17 **Boston Bar** British Columbia, SW Canada 49°54′N 121°22′W
27 T10 **Boston Mountains** ▲▲ Arkansas, C USA
15 P8 **Bostonnais** ⚑ Québec, SE Canada
**Bostyn'** *see* Bastyn'
112 J10 **Bosut** ⚑ E Croatia
154 C11 **Botād** Gujarāt, W India 22°12′N 71°44′E
145 S10 **Botakara** *Kas.* Botaqara; *prev.* Ul'yanovskiy. Karaganda, C Kazakhstan 50°05′N 73°45′E
183 T9 **Botany Bay** *inlet* New South Wales, SE Australia
**Botaqara** *see* Botakara
83 G18 **Boteti** *var.* Botletle. ⚑ N Botswana
114 J9 **Botev** ▲ C Bulgaria 42°45′N 24°57′E
114 H9 **Botevgrad** *prev.* Orkhaniye. Sofia, W Bulgaria 42°55′N 23°47′E
93 J16 **Bothnia, Gulf of** *Fin.* Pohjanlahti, *Swe.* Bottniska Viken. *gulf* N Baltic Sea
183 P17 **Bothwell** Tasmania, SE Australia 42°24′S 147°01′E
104 H5 **Boticas** Vila Real, N Portugal 41°41′N 07°40′W
55 W10 **Boti-Pasi** Sipaliwini, C Suriname 04°15′N 55°27′W
**Botletle** *see* Boteti
127 P16 **Botlikh** Chechenskaya Respublika, SW Russia 42°39′N 46°12′E
117 N10 **Botna** ⚑ E Moldova
116 I9 **Botoşani** *Hung.* Botosány. Botoşani, NE Romania 47°44′N 26°41′E
116 K8 **Botoşani** ◆ *county* NE Romania
**Botosány** *see* Botoşani
147 P12 **Bototog', Tizmasi** *Rus.* Khrebet Babatag. ▲▲ Tajikistan/Uzbekistan
161 P4 **Botou** *prev.* Bozhen. Hebei, E China 38°09′N 116°37′E
99 M20 **Botrange** ▲ E Belgium 50°30′N 06°03′E
107 O21 **Botricello** Calabria, SW Italy 38°56′N 16°51′E
83 I23 **Botshabelo** Free State, C South Africa 29°15′S 26°51′E
93 J15 **Botsmark** Västerbotten, N Sweden 64°15′N 20°15′E
83 G19 **Botswana** *off.* Republic of Botswana. ◆ *republic* S Africa
**Botswana, Republic of** *see* Botswana
29 N2 **Bottineau** North Dakota, N USA 48°50′N 100°28′W
**Bottniska Viken** *see* Bothnia, Gulf of
60 L9 **Botucatu** São Paulo, S Brazil 22°52′S 48°30′W
76 M16 **Bouaflé** C Ivory Coast 06°59′N 05°45′W
77 N16 **Bouaké** *var.* Bwake. C Ivory Coast 07°42′N 05°00′W
79 G14 **Bouar** Nana-Mambéré, W Central African Republic 05°58′N 15°38′E
74 H7 **Bouarfa** NE Morocco 32°33′N 01°54′W
111 B19 **Boubín** ▲ SW Czechia 49°00′N 13°51′E
79 I14 **Bouca** Ouham, W Central African Republic 06°57′N 18°18′E
15 T5 **Boucher** ⚑ Québec, SE Canada
103 R15 **Bouches-du-Rhône** ◆ *department* SE France
74 C9 **Bou Craa** *var.* Bu Craa. NW Western Sahara 26°32′N 12°52′W
77 O9 **Boû Djébéha** *oasis* C Mali
108 C8 **Boudry** Neuchâtel, W Switzerland 46°57′N 06°46′E
79 F21 **Bouenza** ◆ *department* S Congo
180 L2 **Bougainville, Cape** *cape* Western Australia
65 E24 **Bougainville, Cape** *headland* East Falkland, Falkland Islands 51°18′S 58°28′W
**Bougainville, Détroit de** *see* Bougainville Strait
186 J7 **Bougainville Island** *island* NE Papua New Guinea
186 I8 **Bougainville Strait** *strait* N Solomon Islands
187 Q13 **Bougainville Strait** *Fr.* Détroit de Bougainville. *strait* C Vanuatu
120 I9 **Bougaroun, Cap** *headland* NE Algeria 37°07′N 06°18′E
77 R8 **Boughessa** Kidal, NE Mali 20°05′N 02°13′E
**Bougie** *see* Béjaïa
76 L13 **Bougouni** Sikasso, SW Mali 11°25′N 07°28′W
99 J24 **Bouillon** Luxembourg, SE Belgium 49°47′N 05°04′E
74 K5 **Bouira** *var.* Bouïra. N Algeria 36°22′N 03°55′E
74 D8 **Bou-Izakarn** SW Morocco 29°12′N 09°43′W
74 B9 **Boujdour** *var.* Bojador. W Western Sahara 26°06′N 14°29′W
74 G5 **Boukhalef** ✈ (Tanger) N Morocco 35°45′N 05°53′W
**Boukombé** *see* Boukoumbé
77 R14 **Boukoumbé** *var.* Boukombé. C Benin 10°13′N 01°09′E
76 G6 **Boû Lanouâr** Dakhlet Nouâdhibou, W Mauritania 21°17′N 16°29′W
37 T4 **Boulder** Colorado, C USA 40°02′N 105°18′W
33 R10 **Boulder** Montana, NW USA 46°14′N 112°07′W
35 X12 **Boulder City** Nevada, W USA 35°58′N 114°49′W
181 T7 **Boulia** Queensland, C Australia 23°02′S 139°58′E
15 N10 **Boullé** ⚑ Québec, SE Canada
102 J9 **Boulogne** ⚑ NW France
**Boulogne** *see* Boulogne-sur-Mer
102 L16 **Boulogne-sur-Gesse** Haute-Garonne, S France 43°18′N 00°38′E
103 N1 **Boulogne-sur-Mer** *var.* Boulogne; *anc.* Bononia, Gesoriacum, Gessoriacum. Pas-de-Calais, N France 50°43′N 01°36′E
77 Q12 **Boulsa** C Burkina Faso 12°41′N 00°29′W
77 W11 **Boultoum** Zinder, C Niger 14°43′N 10°22′E
187 Y14 **Bouma** Taveuni, N Fiji 16°49′S 179°50′W
79 G16 **Boumba** ⚑ SE Cameroon
76 J9 **Boûmdeïd** *var.* Boumdeït. Assaba, S Mauritania 17°26′N 11°21′W
**Boumdeït** *see* Boûmdeïd
115 C17 **Boumistós** ▲ W Greece 38°48′N 20°59′E
77 O15 **Bouna** NE Ivory Coast 09°16′N 03°00′W
19 P4 **Boundary Bald Mountain** ▲ Maine, NE USA 45°45′N 70°10′W
35 S8 **Boundary Peak** ▲ Nevada, W USA 37°50′N 118°21′W
76 M14 **Boundiali** N Ivory Coast 09°30′N 06°31′W
79 G19 **Boundji** Cuvette, C Congo 01°05′S 15°18′E
77 O13 **Boundoukui** *var.* Bondoukui, Bondoukuy. W Burkina Faso 11°51′N 03°47′W
36 L2 **Bountiful** Utah, W USA 40°53′N 111°52′W
**Bounty Basin** *see* Bounty Trough
191 Q16 **Bounty Bay** *bay* Pitcairn Island, C Pacific Ocean
192 L12 **Bounty Islands** *island group* S New Zealand
175 Q13 **Bounty Trough** *var.* Bounty Basin. *undersea feature* S Pacific Ocean
187 P17 **Bourail** Province Sud, C New Caledonia 21°35′S 165°29′E
27 V5 **Bourbeuse River** ⚑ Missouri, C USA
103 Q9 **Bourbon-Lancy** Saône-et-Loire, C France 46°39′N 03°48′E
31 N11 **Bourbonnais** Illinois, N USA 41°08′N 87°52′W
103 O10 **Bourbonnais** *cultural region* C France
103 S7 **Bourbonne-les-Bains** Haute-Marne, N France 47°57′N 05°45′E
**Bourbon Vendée** *see* la Roche-sur-Yon
74 M8 **Bourdj Messaouda** E Algeria 30°18′N 09°19′E
77 Q10 **Bourem** Gao, C Mali 16°56′N 00°21′W
**Bourg** *see* Bourg-en-Bresse
103 N11 **Bourganeuf** Creuse, C France 45°57′N 01°47′E
**Bourgas** *see* Burgas
**Bourge-en-Bresse** *see* Bourg-en-Bresse
103 S10 **Bourg-en-Bresse** *var.* Bourg, Bourge-en-Bresse. Ain, E France 46°12′N 05°13′E
103 O8 **Bourges** *anc.* Avaricum. Cher, C France 47°06′N 02°24′E
103 T11 **Bourget, Lac du** ◎ E France
103 Q8 **Bourgogne** *cultural region* E France
103 R8 **Bourgogne-Franche-Comté** ◆ *region* E France
103 S11 **Bourgoin-Jallieu** Isère, E France 45°34′N 05°16′E
103 R14 **Bourg-St-Andéol** Ardèche, E France 44°24′N 04°36′E
103 U11 **Bourg-St-Maurice** Savoie, E France 45°37′N 06°49′E
108 C11 **Bourg St. Pierre** Valais, SW Switzerland 45°54′N 07°10′E
76 H8 **Boû Rjeïmât** *well* W Mauritania
183 P5 **Bourke** New South Wales, SE Australia 30°08′S 145°57′E
97 M24 **Bournemouth** S England, United Kingdom 50°43′N 01°54′W
99 M23 **Bourscheid** Diekirch, NE Luxembourg 49°55′N 06°04′E
74 K6 **Bou Saâda** *var.* Bou Saada. N Algeria 35°10′N 04°09′E
36 I13 **Bouse Wash** ⚑ Arizona, SW USA
103 N10 **Boussac** Creuse, C France 46°20′N 02°12′E
102 M16 **Boussens** Haute-Garonne, S France 43°11′N 00°58′E
78 H12 **Bousso** *prev.* Fort-Bretonnet. Chari-Baguirmi, S Chad 10°32′N 16°45′E
76 H9 **Boutilimit** Trarza, SW Mauritania 17°33′N 14°42′W
65 D21 **Bouvet Island** ◇ *Norwegian dependency* S Atlantic Ocean
77 U11 **Bouza** Tahoua, SW Niger 14°25′N 06°09′E
109 R10 **Bovec** *Ger.* Flitsch, *It.* Plezzo. NW Slovenia 46°21′N 13°33′E
98 J8 **Bovenkarspel** Noord-Holland, NW Netherlands 52°33′N 05°03′E
29 V5 **Bovey** Minnesota, N USA 47°18′N 93°25′W
32 M9 **Bovill** Idaho, NW USA 46°50′N 116°24′W
24 L4 **Bovina** Texas, SW USA 34°30′N 102°52′W
107 M17 **Bovino** Puglia, SE Italy 41°14′N 15°19′E
61 C17 **Bovril** Entre Ríos, E Argentina 31°24′S 59°25′W
28 L2 **Bowbells** North Dakota, N USA 48°48′N 102°15′W
11 Q16 **Bow City** Alberta, SW Canada 50°27′N 112°16′W
29 O8 **Bowdle** South Dakota, N USA 45°27′N 99°39′W
181 X6 **Bowen** Queensland, NE Australia 20°S 148°10′E
192 L2 **Bowers Ridge** *undersea feature* S Bering Sea 50°00′N 180°00′W
25 S5 **Bowie** Texas, SW USA 33°33′N 97°51′W
11 R17 **Bow Island** Alberta, SW Canada 49°53′N 111°24′W
**Bowkān** *see* Būkān
20 J7 **Bowling Green** Kentucky, S USA 37°00′N 86°29′W
27 V3 **Bowling Green** Missouri, C USA 39°21′N 91°11′W
31 R11 **Bowling Green** Ohio, N USA 41°22′N 83°40′W
21 W5 **Bowling Green** Virginia, NE USA 38°02′N 77°22′W
28 J6 **Bowman** North Dakota, N USA 46°11′N 103°26′W
9 Q7 **Bowman Bay** *bay* NW Atlantic Ocean
194 I5 **Bowman Coast** *physical region* Antarctica
28 J7 **Bowman-Haley Lake** ⊠ North Dakota, N USA
195 Z11 **Bowman Island** *island* Antarctica
**Bowo** *see* Bomi
183 S9 **Bowral** New South Wales, SE Australia 34°28′S 150°52′E
186 E8 **Bowutu Mountains** ▲▲ C Papua New Guinea
83 I16 **Bowwood** Southern, S Zambia 17°09′S 26°16′E
28 I12 **Box Butte Reservoir** ⊠ Nebraska, C USA
28 J10 **Box Elder** South Dakota, N USA 44°06′N 103°04′W
95 M18 **Boxholm** Östergötland, S Sweden 58°12′N 15°05′E
**Bo Xian/Boxian** *see* Bozhou
161 Q4 **Boxing** Shandong, E China 37°06′N 118°05′E
99 L14 **Boxmeer** Noord-Brabant, SE Netherlands 51°39′N 05°57′E
99 J14 **Boxtel** Noord-Brabant, S Netherlands 51°36′N 05°20′E
136 J10 **Boyabat** Sinop, N Turkey 41°27′N 34°45′E
54 F9 **Boyacá** *off.* Departamento de Boyacá. ◆ *province* C Colombia
**Boyacá, Departamento de** *see* Boyacá
117 O4 **Boyarka** Kyivs'ka Oblast', N Ukraine 50°19′N 30°20′E
22 H7 **Boyce** Louisiana, S USA 31°23′N 92°40′W
114 H8 **Boychinovtsi** Montana, NW Bulgaria 43°28′N 23°20′E
33 U11 **Boyd** Montana, NW USA 45°27′N 109°03′W
25 S6 **Boyd** Texas, SW USA 33°01′N 97°33′W
21 V8 **Boydton** Virginia, NE USA 36°40′N 78°26′W
**Boyer Ahmadī va Kohkīlūyeh** *see* Kohgīlūyeh va Bowyer Aḩmad
29 T13 **Boyer River** ⚑ Iowa, C USA
21 W8 **Boykins** Virginia, NE USA 36°35′N 77°11′W
117 X9 **Boykivs'ke** *prev.* Tel'manove. Donets'ka Oblast', E Ukraine 47°24′N 38°03′E
11 Q13 **Boyle** Alberta, SW Canada 54°38′N 112°45′W
97 D16 **Boyle** *Ir.* Mainistirna Búille. C Ireland 53°58′N 08°18′W
97 F17 **Boyne** *Ir.* An Bhóinn. ⚑ E Ireland
31 Q5 **Boyne City** Michigan, N USA 45°13′N 85°00′W
23 Z14 **Boynton Beach** Florida, SE USA 26°31′N 80°04′W
147 O13 **Boysun** *Rus.* Baysun. Surkhondaryo Viloyati, S Uzbekistan 38°14′N 67°08′E
**Bozau** *see* Întorsura Buzăului
136 B12 **Bozcaada** *Island* Çanakkale, NW Turkey
136 C14 **Boz Dağları** ▲▲ W Turkey
33 S11 **Bozeman** Montana, NW USA 45°40′N 111°02′W
**Bozen** *see* Bolzano
79 J16 **Bozene** Equateur, NW Dem. Rep. Congo 02°56′N 19°15′E
**Bozhen** *see* Botou
161 P7 **Bozhou** *var.* Boxian, Bo Xian. Anhui, E China 33°46′N 115°44′E
136 H16 **Bozkır** Konya, S Turkey 37°10′N 32°15′E
136 K13 **Bozok Yaylasī** *plateau* C Turkey
79 H14 **Bozoum** Ouham-Pendé, W Central African Republic 06°17′N 16°26′E
137 N16 **Bozova** Sanlıurfa, S Turkey 37°23′N 38°33′E
**Bozrah** *see* Buşrá ash Shām
136 E12 **Bozüyük** Bilecik, NW Turkey 39°55′N 30°02′E
106 B9 **Bra** Piemonte, NW Italy 44°42′N 07°51′E
194 G4 **Brabant Island** *island* Antarctica
99 I20 **Brabant Walloon** ◆ *province* C Belgium
113 F15 **Brač** *var.* Brach *It.* Brazza; *anc.* Brattia. *island* S Croatia
**Bracara Augusta** *see* Braga
107 H15 **Bracciano** Lazio, C Italy 42°04′N 12°12′E
107 H14 **Bracciano, Lago di** ◎ C Italy
14 H13 **Bracebridge** Ontario, S Canada 45°02′N 79°19′W
**Brach** *see* Brač
93 G17 **Bräcke** Jämtland, C Sweden 62°43′N 15°30′E
25 P12 **Brackettville** Texas, SW USA 29°19′N 100°27′W
97 N22 **Bracknell** S England, United Kingdom 51°26′N 00°46′W
61 K14 **Braço do Norte** Santa Catarina, S Brazil 28°16′S 49°11′W
116 G11 **Brad** *Hung.* Brád. Hunedoara, SW Romania 45°52′N 23°00′E
107 N18 **Bradano** ⚑ S Italy
23 V13 **Bradenton** Florida, SE USA 27°30′N 82°34′W
45 V10 **Brades** *de facto capital, de jure capital. Previous capital destroyed by volcano in 1995* Plymouth. ● (Montserrat) SW Montserrat 16°45′N 62°12′W
14 H14 **Bradford** Ontario, S Canada 44°09′N 79°34′W
97 L17 **Bradford** N England, United Kingdom 53°48′N 01°45′W
27 W10 **Bradford** Arkansas, C USA 35°25′N 91°27′W
18 D12 **Bradford** Pennsylvania, NE USA 41°57′N 78°38′W
27 T15 **Bradley** Arkansas, C USA 33°06′N 93°39′W
25 P7 **Bradshaw** Texas, SW USA 32°06′N 99°52′W
25 Q9 **Brady** Texas, SW USA 31°08′N 99°22′W
25 Q9 **Brady Creek** ⚑ Texas, SW USA
95 G22 **Brædstrup** Syddanmark, C Denmark 55°58′N 09°38′E
96 J10 **Braemar** NE Scotland, United Kingdom 57°12′N 02°52′W
116 K8 **Brăeşti** Botoşani, NW Romania 47°50′N 26°26′E
104 G5 **Braga** *anc.* Bracara Augusta. Braga, NW Portugal 41°32′N 08°26′W
104 G5 **Braga** ◆ *district* N Portugal
116 J15 **Bragadiru** Teleorman, S Romania 43°43′N 25°32′E
61 C20 **Bragado** Buenos Aires, E Argentina 35°10′S 60°29′W
104 J5 **Bragança** *Eng.* Braganza; *anc.* Julio Briga. Bragança, NE Portugal 41°47′N 06°46′W
104 I5 **Bragança** ◆ *district* N Portugal
60 N9 **Bragança Paulista** São Paulo, S Brazil 22°55′S 46°30′W
**Braganza** *see* Bragança
**Bragin** *see* Brahin
29 V7 **Braham** Minnesota, N USA 45°43′N 93°10′W
**Brahe** *see* Brda
**Brahestad** *see* Raahe
119 O20 **Brahin** *Rus.* Bragin. Homyel'skaya Voblasts', SE Belarus 51°47′N 30°16′E
153 U15 **Brahmanbaria** Chittagong, E Bangladesh 23°58′N 91°04′E
154 O12 **Brāhmani** ⚑ E India
154 N13 **Brahmapur** Odisha, E India 19°21′N 84°51′E
129 S10 **Brahmaputra** *var.* Padma, Tsangpo, *Ben.* Jamuna, *Chin.* Yarlung Zangbo Jiang, *Ind.* Bramaputra, Dihang, Siang. ⚑ S Asia
97 H19 **Braich y Pwll** *headland* NW Wales, United Kingdom 52°47′N 04°46′W
183 R10 **Braidwood** New South Wales, SE Australia 35°26′S 149°48′E
30 M11 **Braidwood** Illinois, N USA 41°16′N 88°12′W
116 M13 **Brăila** Brăila, E Romania 45°17′N 27°57′E
116 L13 **Brăila** ◆ *county* SE Romania
99 G19 **Braine-l'Alleud** Brabant Walloon, C Belgium 50°41′N 04°22′E
99 F19 **Braine-le-Comte** Hainaut, SW Belgium 50°37′N 04°08′E
29 U6 **Brainerd** Minnesota, N USA 46°22′N 94°10′W
99 J19 **Braives** Liège, E Belgium 50°37′N 05°09′E
83 H23 **Brak** ⚑ C South Africa
**Brak** *see* Birāk
99 E18 **Brakel** Oost-Vlaanderen, SW Belgium 50°50′N 03°48′E
98 J13 **Brakel** Gelderland, C Netherlands 51°49′N 05°05′E
76 H9 **Brakna** ◆ *region* S Mauritania
95 J17 **Brålanda** Västra Götaland, S Sweden 58°32′N 12°18′E
**Bramaputra** *see* Brahmaputra
95 F23 **Bramming** Syddtjylland, W Denmark 55°28′N 08°42′E
14 G15 **Brampton** Ontario, S Canada 43°42′N 79°46′W
100 F12 **Bramsche** Niedersachsen, NW Germany 52°25′N 07°58′E
116 J12 **Bran** *Ger.* Törzburg, *Hung.* Törcsvár. Braşov, S Romania 45°31′N 25°23′E
29 W8 **Branch** Minnesota, N USA 45°29′N 92°57′W
21 R14 **Branchville** South Carolina, SE USA 33°15′N 80°49′W
47 Y6 **Branco, Cabo** *headland* E Brazil 07°08′S 34°45′W
58 F11 **Branco, Rio** ⚑ N Brazil
108 J8 **Brand** Vorarlberg, W Austria 47°07′N 09°45′E
83 B18 **Brandberg** ▲ NW Namibia 21°20′S 14°22′E
95 H14 **Brandbu** Oppland, S Norway 60°24′N 10°30′E
95 F22 **Brande** Midtjylland, W Denmark 55°57′N 09°08′E
**Brandebourg** *see* Brandenburg
100 M12 **Brandenburg** *var.* Brandenburg an der Havel. Brandenburg, NE Germany 52°25′N 12°34′E
20 K5 **Brandenburg** Kentucky, S USA 38°00′N 86°11′W
100 N12 **Brandenburg** *off.* Freie und Hansestadt Hamburg, *Fr.* Brandebourg. ◆ *state* NE Germany
**Brandenburg an der Havel** *see* Brandenburg
83 I23 **Brandfort** Free State, C South Africa 28°42′S 26°28′E
11 W16 **Brandon** Manitoba, S Canada 49°50′N 99°57′W
23 V12 **Brandon** Florida, SE USA 27°56′N 82°17′W
22 L6 **Brandon** Mississippi, S USA 32°16′N 90°01′W
97 A20 **Brandon Mountain** *Ir.* Cnoc Bréanainn. ▲ SW Ireland 52°13′N 10°16′W
**Brandsen** *see* Coronel Brandsen
95 I14 **Brandval** Hedmark, S Norway 60°18′N 12°01′E
83 F24 **Brandvlei** Northern Cape, W South Africa 30°27′S 20°29′E
23 U9 **Branford** Florida, SE USA 29°57′N 82°54′W
110 K7 **Braniewo** *Ger.* Braunsberg. Warmińsko-mazurskie, N Poland 54°24′N 19°50′E
194 H3 **Bransfield Strait** *strait* Antarctica
37 U8 **Branson** Colorado, C USA 37°01′N 103°52′W
27 T8 **Branson** Missouri, C USA 36°38′N 93°13′W
14 G16 **Brantford** Ontario, S Canada 43°09′N 80°17′W
102 L12 **Brantôme** Dordogne, SW France 45°21′N 00°37′E
182 L12 **Branxholme** Victoria, SE Australia 37°51′S 141°48′E
**Brasil** *see* Brazil
59 C16 **Brasiléia** Acre, W Brazil 10°59′S 48°45′W
59 K18 **Brasília** ● (Brazil) Distrito Federal, C Brazil 15°45′S 47°57′W
**Brasil, República Federativa do** *see* Brazil
**Braslav** *see* Braslaw
118 J12 **Braslaw** *Pol.* Brasław, *Rus.* Braslav. Vitsyebskaya Voblasts', N Belarus 55°38′N 27°02′E
116 J12 **Braşov** *Ger.* Kronstadt, *Hung.* Brassó; *prev.* Oraşul Stalin. Braşov, C Romania 45°40′N 25°35′E
116 I12 **Braşov** ◆ *county* C Romania
77 U18 **Brass** Bayelsa, S Nigeria 04°19′N 06°21′E
99 H16 **Brasschaat** *var.* Brasschaet. Antwerpen, N Belgium 51°17′N 04°30′E
**Brasschaet** *see* Brasschaat
169 V8 **Brassey, Banjaran** *var.* Brassey Range. ▲▲ East Malaysia
**Brassey Range** *see* Brassey, Banjaran
**Brassó** *see* Braşov
23 T1 **Brasstown Bald** ▲ Georgia, SE USA 34°52′N 83°48′W
113 K22 **Brataj** Vlorë, SW Albania 40°18′N 19°37′E
114 J10 **Bratan** *var.* Morozov. ▲ C Bulgaria 42°31′N 25°08′E
114 H10 **Bratia** *var.* Bratiya. C Bulgaria 42°36′N 24°08′E
111 F21 **Bratislava** *Ger.* Pressburg, *Hung.* Pozsony. ● (Slovakia) Bratislavský Kraj, W Slovakia 48°10′N 17°10′E
111 H21 **Bratislavský Kraj** ◆ *region* W Slovakia
**Bratiya** *see* Bratia
122 M12 **Bratsk** Irkutskaya Oblast', C Russia 56°20′N 101°50′E
117 Q8 **Brats'ke** Mykolayivs'ka Oblast', S Ukraine 47°52′N 31°34′E
122 M13 **Bratskoye Vodokhranilishche** *Eng.* Bratsk Reservoir. ⊠ S Russia
**Bratsk Reservoir** *see* Bratskoye Vodokhranilishche
**Brattia** *see* Brač
94 D9 **Brattvåg** Møre og Romsdal, S Norway 62°36′N 06°21′E
112 K12 **Bratunac** ◆ Republika Srpska, E Bosnia and Herzegovina
114 J10 **Bratya Daskalovi** *prev.* Grozdovo. Stara Zagora, C Bulgaria 42°13′N 25°21′E
109 U2 **Braunau** ⚑ N Austria
**Braunau** *see* Braunau am Inn
109 Q4 **Braunau am Inn** *var.* Braunau. Oberösterreich, N Austria 48°16′N 13°03′E
**Braunsberg** *see* Braniewo
100 J13 **Braunschweig** *Eng./Fr.* Brunswick. Niedersachsen, N Germany 52°16′N 10°32′E
**Brava** *see* Baraawe
105 Y6 **Brava, Costa** *coastal region* NE Spain
43 V16 **Brava, Punta** *headland* E Panama 08°21′N 78°22′W
95 N17 **Bråviken** *inlet* S Sweden
56 B10 **Bravo, Cerro** ▲ N Peru 05°33′S 79°10′W
**Bravo del Norte, Río/ Bravo, Río** *see* Grande, Rio
35 X17 **Brawley** California, W USA 32°58′N 115°31′W
97 G18 **Bray** *Ir.* Bré. E Ireland 53°12′N 06°06′W
59 G16 **Brazil** *off.* Federative Republic of Brazil, *Port.* República Federativa do Brasil, *Sp.* Brasil; *prev.* United States of Brazil. ◆ *federal republic* South America


◆ Country
● Country Capital
◇ Dependent Territory
○ Dependent Territory Capital
◆ Administrative Regions
✈ International Airport
▲ Mountain
▲▲ Mountain Range
⚠ Volcano
⚑ River
◎ Lake
⊠ Reservoir

Brazil Basin – Buena Vista, Bahia de


65 K15 **Brazil Basin** *var.* Brazilian Basin, Brazil'skaya Kotlovina. *undersea feature* W Atlantic Ocean *15°00′S 25°00′W*
**Brazil, Federative Republic of** *see* Brazil
**Brazilian Basin** *see* Brazil Basin
**Brazilian Highlands** *see* Central, Planalto
**Brazil'skaya Kotlovina** *see* Brazil Basin
**Brazil, United States of** *see* Brazil
25 U10 **Brazos River** ≈ Texas, SW USA
**Brazza** *see* Brač
79 G21 **Brazzaville** ● (Congo) Capital District, S Congo *04°14′S 15°14′E*
79 G21 **Brazzaville** ✈ Pool, S Congo *04°15′S 15°15′E*
112 J11 **Brčko** Brčko Distrikt, NE Bosnia and Herzegovina *44°52′N 18°49′E*
110 H8 **Brda** *Ger.* Brahe. ≈ N Poland
**Bré** *see* Bray
185 A23 **Breaksea Sound** *sound* South Island, New Zealand
184 L4 **Bream Bay** *bay* North Island, New Zealand
184 L4 **Bream Head** *headland* North Island, New Zealand *35°51′S 174°35′E*
**Bréanainn, Cnoc** *see* Brandon Mountain
45 S6 **Brea, Punta** *headland* W Puerto Rico *17°56′N 66°55′W*
22 I9 **Breaux Bridge** Louisiana, S USA *30°16′N 91°54′W*
116 J13 **Breaza** Prahova, SE Romania *45°13′N 25°38′E*
169 P16 **Brebes** Jawa, C Indonesia *06°54′S 109°00′E*
96 K10 **Brechin** E Scotland, United Kingdom *56°45′N 02°38′W*
99 H15 **Brecht** Antwerpen, N Belgium *51°21′N 04°33′E*
37 S4 **Breckenridge** Colorado, C USA *39°28′N 106°02′W*
29 R6 **Breckenridge** Minnesota, N USA *46°15′N 96°35′W*
25 R6 **Breckenridge** Texas, SW USA *32°45′N 98°56′W*
97 J21 **Brecknock** *cultural region* SE Wales, United Kingdom
63 G25 **Brecknock, Península** *headland* S Chile *54°39′S 71°48′W*
111 G19 **Břeclav** *Ger.* Lundenburg. Jihomoravský Kraj, SE Czechiac *49°05′N 16°51′E*
97 J21 **Brecon** E Wales, United Kingdom *51°58′N 03°26′W*
97 J21 **Brecon Beacons** ▲▲ S Wales, United Kingdom
99 I14 **Breda** Noord-Brabant, S Netherlands *51°35′N 04°46′E*
95 K20 **Bredaryd** Jönköping, S Sweden *57°10′N 13°45′E*
83 F26 **Bredasdorp** Western Cape, SW South Africa *34°32′S 20°02′E*
93 H16 **Bredbyn** Västernorrland, N Sweden *63°28′N 18°04′E*
122 F11 **Bredy** Chelyabinskaya Oblast', C Russia *52°23′N 60°24′E*
99 K17 **Bree** Limburg, NE Belgium *51°08′N 05°36′E*
67 T15 **Breede** ≈ S South Africa
98 I7 **Breezand** Noord-Holland, NW Netherlands *52°52′N 04°47′E*
113 P18 **Bregalnica** ≈ E North Macedonia
108 I6 **Bregenz** *anc.* Brigantium. Vorarlberg, W Austria *47°31′N 09°46′E*
108 J7 **Bregenzer Wald** ▲▲ W Austria
114 F6 **Bregovo** Vidin, NW Bulgaria *44°07′N 22°40′E*
102 H5 **Bréhat, Île de** *island* NW France
92 H2 **Breiðafjörður** *bay* W Iceland
92 L3 **Breiðdalsvík** Austurland, E Iceland *64°48′N 14°02′W*
108 H9 **Breil** *Ger.* Brigels. Graubünden, S Switzerland *46°46′N 09°04′E*
92 J8 **Breivikbotn** Finnmark, N Norway *70°36′N 22°19′E*
94 I9 **Brekken** Sør-Trøndelag, S Norway *62°39′N 11°49′E*
94 G7 **Brekstad** Sør-Trøndelag, S Norway *63°42′N 09°40′E*
94 B10 **Bremangerlandet** *island* S Norway
**Brême** *see* Bremen
100 H11 **Bremen** *Fr.* Brême. Bremen, NW Germany *53°06′N 08°48′E*
23 R3 **Bremen** Georgia, SE USA *33°43′N 85°09′W*
31 O11 **Bremen** Indiana, N USA *41°24′N 86°07′W*
100 H10 **Bremen** *off.* Freie Hansestadt Bremen, *Fr.* Brême. ⬖ *state* N Germany
100 G9 **Bremerhaven** Bremen, NW Germany *53°33′N 08°35′E*
**Bremersdorp** *see* Manzini
32 G8 **Bremerton** Washington, NW USA *47°34′N 122°37′W*
100 H10 **Bremervörde** Niedersachsen, NW Germany *53°29′N 09°06′E*
25 U9 **Bremond** Texas, SW USA *31°10′N 96°40′W*
25 U10 **Brenham** Texas, SW USA *30°09′N 96°24′W*
108 M8 **Brenner** Tirol, W Austria *47°10′N 11°51′E*
**Brenner, Col du/Brennero, Passo del** *see* Brenner Pass
108 M8 **Brenner Pass** *var.* Brenner Sattel, *Fr.* Col du Brenner, *Ger.* Brennerpass, *It.* Passo del Brennero. *pass* Austria/Italy
**Brennerpass** *see* Brenner Pass
**Brenner Sattel** *see* Brenner Pass
108 G10 **Brenno** ≈ SW Switzerland
106 F7 **Breno** Lombardia, N Italy *45°58′N 10°18′E*
23 O5 **Brent** Alabama, S USA *32°54′N 87°10′W*
106 H7 **Brenta** ≈ NE Italy
97 P21 **Brentwood** E England, United Kingdom *51°38′N 00°21′E*
18 L14 **Brentwood** Long Island, New York, NE USA *40°46′N 73°12′W*
106 F7 **Brescia** *anc.* Brixia. Lombardia, N Italy *45°33′N 10°13′E*
99 D15 **Breskens** Zeeland, SW Netherlands *51°24′N 03°33′E*
**Breslau** *see* Wrocław
106 H5 **Bressanone** *Ger.* Brixen. Trentino-Alto Adige, N Italy *46°44′N 11°41′E*
96 M2 **Bressay** *island* NE Scotland, United Kingdom
102 K9 **Bressuire** Deux-Sèvres, W France *46°50′N 00°29′W*
119 F20 **Brest** *Pol.* Brześć nad Bugiem, *Rus.* Brest-Litovsk; *prev.* Brześć Litewski. Brestskaya Voblasts', SW Belarus *52°06′N 23°42′E*
102 F5 **Brest** Finistère, NW France *48°24′N 04°31′W*
**Brest-Litovsk** *see* Brest
112 A10 **Brestova** Istra, NW Croatia *45°09′N 14°13′E*
**Brestskaya Oblast'** *see* Brestskaya Voblasts'
119 G19 **Brestskaya Voblasts'** *prev. Rus.* Brestskaya Oblast'. ⬖ *province* SW Belarus
102 G6 **Bretagne** *Eng.* Brittany, *Lat.* Britannia Minor. ⬖ *region* NW France
116 G12 **Bretea-Română** *Hung.* Oláhbrettye; *prev.* Bretea-Romînă. Hunedoara, W Romania *45°39′N 23°00′E*
**Bretea-Romînă** *see* Bretea-Română
103 O3 **Breteuil** Oise, N France *49°37′N 02°18′E*
102 I10 **Breton, Pertuis** *inlet* W France
22 L10 **Breton Sound** *sound* Louisiana, S USA
184 K2 **Brett, Cape** *headland* North Island, New Zealand *35°11′S 174°21′E*
101 G21 **Bretten** Baden-Württemberg, SW Germany *49°01′N 08°42′E*
99 K15 **Breugel** Noord-Brabant, S Netherlands *51°30′N 05°30′E*
106 B6 **Breuil-Cervinia** *It.* Cervinia. Valle d'Aosta, NW Italy *45°57′N 07°37′E*
98 I11 **Breukelen** Utrecht, C Netherlands *52°11′N 05°01′E*
21 P10 **Brevard** North Carolina, SE USA *35°13′N 82°46′W*
38 L9 **Brevig Mission** Alaska, USA *65°19′N 166°29′W*
95 G16 **Brevik** Telemark, S Norway *59°05′N 09°42′E*
183 P5 **Brewarrina** New South Wales, SE Australia *30°01′S 146°50′E*
19 R6 **Brewer** Maine, NE USA *44°46′N 68°44′W*
29 T11 **Brewster** Minnesota, N USA *43°43′N 95°28′W*
29 N14 **Brewster** Nebraska, C USA *41°57′N 99°52′W*
31 U12 **Brewster** Ohio, N USA *40°42′N 81°36′W*
**Brewster, Kap** *see* Kangikajik
183 O8 **Brewster, Lake** ◎ New South Wales, SE Australia
23 P7 **Brewton** Alabama, S USA *31°06′N 87°04′W*
**Brezhnev** *see* Naberezhnyye Chelny
109 W12 **Brežice** *Ger.* Rann. E Slovenia *45°54′N 15°35′E*
114 G9 **Breznik** Pernik, W Bulgaria *42°45′N 22°54′E*
111 K19 **Brezno** *Ger.* Bries, Briesen, *Hung.* Breznóbánya; *prev.* Brezno nad Hronom. Banskobystrický Kraj, C Slovakia *48°49′N 19°40′E*
**Breznóbánya/Brezno nad Hronom** *see* Brezno
116 I12 **Brezoi** Vâlcea, SW Romania *45°18′N 24°15′E*
114 J10 **Brezovo** *prev.* Abrashlare. Plovdiv, C Bulgaria *42°19′N 25°05′E*
79 K14 **Bria** Haute-Kotto, C Central African Republic *06°30′N 22°00′E*
103 U13 **Briançon** *anc.* Brigantio. Hautes-Alpes, SE France *44°55′N 06°37′E*
36 K7 **Brian Head** ▲ Utah, W USA *37°40′N 112°49′W*
103 O7 **Briare** Loiret, C France *47°35′N 02°46′E*
183 V2 **Bribie Island** *island* Queensland, E Australia
43 O14 **Bribrí** Limón, E Costa Rica *09°37′N 82°51′W*
116 L8 **Briceni** *var.* Brinceni, *Rus.* Brichany. N Moldova *48°21′N 27°02′E*
**Bricgstow** *see* Bristol
**Brichany** *see* Briceni
99 M24 **Bridel** Luxembourg, C Luxembourg *49°40′N 06°03′E*
97 J22 **Bridgend** S Wales, United Kingdom *51°30′N 03°37′W*
14 I14 **Bridgenorth** Ontario, SE Canada *44°21′N 78°22′W*
23 Q1 **Bridgeport** Alabama, S USA *34°57′N 85°42′W*
35 R8 **Bridgeport** California, W USA *38°14′N 119°15′W*
18 L13 **Bridgeport** Connecticut, NE USA *41°10′N 73°12′W*
31 N15 **Bridgeport** Illinois, N USA *38°42′N 87°45′W*
28 J14 **Bridgeport** Nebraska, C USA *41°37′N 103°07′W*
25 S6 **Bridgeport** Texas, SW USA *33°12′N 97°45′W*
21 S3 **Bridgeport** West Virginia, NE USA *39°17′N 80°15′W*
25 S5 **Bridgeport, Lake** ▣ Texas, SW USA
33 U11 **Bridger** Montana, NW USA *45°16′N 108°55′W*
18 I17 **Bridgeton** New Jersey, NE USA *39°24′N 75°10′W*
180 J14 **Bridgetown** Western Australia *34°01′S 116°07′E*
45 Y14 **Bridgetown** ● (Barbados) SW Barbados *13°05′N 59°36′W*
183 P17 **Bridgewater** Tasmania, SE Australia *42°47′S 147°15′E*
13 P16 **Bridgewater** Nova Scotia, SE Canada *44°19′N 64°30′W*
19 P12 **Bridgewater** Massachusetts, NE USA *41°59′N 70°58′W*
29 Q11 **Bridgewater** South Dakota, N USA *43°33′N 97°30′W*
21 U5 **Bridgewater** Virginia, NE USA *38°22′N 78°58′W*
19 P8 **Bridgton** Maine, NE USA *44°04′N 70°43′W*
97 K23 **Bridgwater** SW England, United Kingdom *51°08′N 03°W*
97 K22 **Bridgwater Bay** *bay* SW England, United Kingdom
97 O16 **Bridlington** E England, United Kingdom *54°05′N 00°12′W*
97 O16 **Bridlington Bay** *bay* E England, United Kingdom
183 P15 **Bridport** Tasmania, SE Australia *41°03′S 147°26′E*
97 K24 **Bridport** S England, United Kingdom *50°44′N 02°43′W*
103 O5 **Brie** *cultural region* N France
**Brieg** *see* Brzeg
**Briel** *see* Brielle
98 G12 **Brielle** *var.* Briel, Bril, *Eng.* The Brill. Zuid-Holland, SW Netherlands *51°54′N 04°10′E*
108 E9 **Brienz** Bern, C Switzerland *46°45′N 08°00′E*
108 E9 **Brienzer See** ◎ SW Switzerland
**Bries/Briesen** *see* Brezno
**Brietzig** *see* Brzesko
103 S4 **Briey** Meurthe-et-Moselle, NE France *49°15′N 05°57′E*
108 E10 **Brig** *Fr.* Brigue, *It.* Briga. Valais, SW Switzerland *46°19′N 08°E*
**Briga** *see* Brig
101 G24 **Brigach** ≈ S Germany
18 K17 **Brigantine** New Jersey, NE USA *39°23′N 74°21′W*
**Brigantio** *see* Briançon
**Brigantium** *see* Bregenz
**Brigels** *see* Breil
25 S9 **Briggs** Texas, SW USA *30°52′N 97°55′W*
36 L1 **Brigham City** Utah, W USA *41°30′N 112°00′W*
14 J15 **Brighton** Ontario, SE Canada *44°01′N 77°44′W*
97 O23 **Brighton** SE England, United Kingdom *50°50′N 00°10′W*
37 T4 **Brighton** Colorado, C USA *39°58′N 104°46′W*
30 K15 **Brighton** Illinois, N USA *39°01′N 90°09′W*
103 T16 **Brignoles** Var, W France *43°25′N 06°03′E*
**Brigue** *see* Brig
105 O7 **Brihuega** Castilla-La Mancha, C Spain *40°45′N 02°52′W*
112 A10 **Brijuni** *It.* Brioni. *island group* NW Croatia
76 G12 **Brikama** W The Gambia *13°13′N 16°37′W*
**Bril** *see* Brielle
**Brill, The** *see* Brielle
101 G15 **Brilon** Nordrhein-Westfalen, W Germany *51°24′N 08°34′E*
**Brinceni** *see* Briceni
107 Q18 **Brindisi** *anc.* Brundisium, Brundusium. Puglia, SE Italy *40°39′N 17°55′E*
27 W11 **Brinkley** Arkansas, C USA *34°53′N 91°11′W*
**Brioni** *see* Brijuni
103 P12 **Brioude** *anc.* Brivas. Haute-Loire, C France *45°18′N 03°23′E*
**Briovera** *see* St-Lô
183 U2 **Brisbane** *state capital* Queensland, E Australia *27°30′S 153°E*
183 V2 **Brisbane** ✈ Queensland, E Australia *27°30′S 153°00′E*
25 P2 **Briscoe** Texas, SW USA *35°34′N 100°17′W*
106 H10 **Brisighella** Emilia-Romagna, C Italy *44°12′N 11°45′E*
108 G11 **Brissago** Ticino, S Switzerland *46°07′N 08°40′E*
97 K22 **Bristol** *anc.* Bricgstow. SW England, United Kingdom *51°27′N 02°35′W*
18 M12 **Bristol** Connecticut, NE USA *41°40′N 72°56′W*
23 R9 **Bristol** Florida, SE USA *30°25′N 84°58′W*
19 N9 **Bristol** New Hampshire, NE USA *43°34′N 71°42′W*
29 Q8 **Bristol** South Dakota, N USA *45°18′N 97°45′W*
21 P8 **Bristol** Tennessee, S USA *36°36′N 82°11′W*
18 M8 **Bristol** Vermont, NE USA *44°07′N 73°00′W*
39 N14 **Bristol Bay** *bay* Alaska, USA
97 I22 **Bristol Channel** *inlet* England/Wales, United Kingdom
35 W14 **Bristol Lake** ◎ California, W USA
27 P10 **Bristow** Oklahoma, C USA *35°49′N 96°23′W*
86 C10 **Britain** *var.* Great Britain. *island* United Kingdom
**Britannia Minor** *see* Bretagne
10 L12 **British Columbia** *Fr.* Colombie-Britannique. ⬖ *province* SW Canada
**British Guiana** *see* Guyana
**British Honduras** *see* Belize
173 Q7 **British Indian Ocean Territory** ◇ *UK Overseas Territory* C Indian Ocean
86 B9 **British Isles** *island group* NW Europe
10 I1 **British Mountains** ▲▲ Yukon, NW Canada
**British North Borneo** *see* Sabah
**British Solomon Islands Protectorate** *see* Solomon Islands
45 S8 **British Virgin Islands** *var* Virgin Islands. ◇ *UK Overseas Territory* E West Indies
83 J21 **Brits** North-West, N South Africa *25°39′S 27°47′E*
83 H24 **Britstown** Northern Cape, W South Africa *30°36′S 23°30′E*
14 F12 **Britt** Ontario, S Canada *45°46′N 80°34′W*
29 V12 **Britt** Iowa, C USA *43°06′N 93°48′W*
**Brittany** *see* Bretagne
29 Q7 **Britton** South Dakota, N USA *45°47′N 97°45′W*
**Briva Curretia** *see* Brive-la-Gaillarde
**Briva Isarae** *see* Pontoise
**Brivas** *see* Brioude
**Brive** *see* Brive-la-Gaillarde
102 M12 **Brive-la-Gaillarde** *prev.* Brive; *anc.* Briva Curretia. Corrèze, C France *45°09′N 01°31′E*
105 O4 **Briviesca** Castilla y León, N Spain *42°33′N 03°19′W*
**Brixen** *see* Bressanone
**Brixia** *see* Brescia
**Brlik** *see* Birlik
**Brněnský Kraj** *see* Jihomoravský Kraj
111 G18 **Brno** *Ger.* Brünn. Jihomoravský Kraj, SE Czechia *49°11′N 16°35′E*
96 G7 **Broad Bay** *bay* NW Scotland, United Kingdom
25 X8 **Broaddus** Texas, SW USA *31°18′N 94°16′W*
183 O12 **Broadford** Victoria, SE Australia *37°07′S 145°04′E*
96 G9 **Broadford** N Scotland, United Kingdom *57°14′N 05°54′W*
96 J13 **Broad Law** ▲ S Scotland, United Kingdom *55°30′N 03°22′W*
23 U3 **Broad River** ≈ Georgia, SE USA
21 N8 **Broad River** ≈ North Carolina/South Carolina, SE USA
181 Y8 **Broadsound Range** ▲▲ Queensland, E Australia
33 X11 **Broadus** Montana, NW USA *45°28′N 105°22′W*
21 U4 **Broadway** Virginia, NE USA *38°36′N 78°48′W*
118 E9 **Brocēni** SW Latvia *56°41′N 22°31′E*
11 U11 **Brochet** Manitoba, C Canada *57°55′N 101°40′W*
11 U10 **Brochet, Lac** ◎ Manitoba, C Canada
15 S5 **Brochet, Lac au** ◎ Québec, SE Canada
101 K14 **Brocken** ▲ C Germany *51°48′N 10°38′E*
19 O12 **Brockton** Massachusetts, NE USA *42°04′N 71°01′W*
14 L14 **Brockville** Ontario, SE Canada *44°35′N 75°44′W*
18 D13 **Brockway** Pennsylvania, NE USA *41°14′N 78°45′W*
**Brod/Bród** *see* Slavonski Brod
9 N5 **Brodeur Peninsula** *peninsula* Baffin Island, Nunavut, NE Canada
96 H13 **Brodick** W Scotland, United Kingdom *55°34′N 05°10′W*
**Brod na Savi** *see* Slavonski Brod
110 K9 **Brodnica** *Ger.* Buddenbrock. Kujawski-pomorskie, C Poland *53°15′N 19°23′E*
**Brod-Posavina** *see* Slavonski Brod-Posavina
**Brodsko-Posavska Županija** *see* Slavonski Brod-Posavina
116 J5 **Brody** L'vivs'ka Oblast', NW Ukraine *50°05′N 25°08′E*
98 I10 **Broek-in-Waterland** Noord-Holland, C Netherlands *52°27′N 04°59′E*
32 L13 **Brogan** Oregon, NW USA *44°15′N 117°34′W*
110 N10 **Brok** Mazowieckie, C Poland *52°42′N 21°53′E*
27 P9 **Broken Arrow** Oklahoma, C USA *36°03′N 95°47′W*
183 T9 **Broken Bay** *bay* New South Wales, SE Australia
29 N15 **Broken Bow** Nebraska, C USA *41°24′N 99°38′W*
27 R13 **Broken Bow** Oklahoma, C USA *34°01′N 94°44′W*
27 R12 **Broken Bow Lake** ▣ Oklahoma, C USA
182 L6 **Broken Hill** New South Wales, SE Australia *31°58′S 141°27′E*
173 S10 **Broken Ridge** *undersea feature* S Indian Ocean *31°30′S 95°00′E*
186 C6 **Broken Water Bay** *bay* W Bismarck Sea
55 W10 **Brokopondo** Brokopondo, NE Suriname *05°04′N 55°00′W*
55 W10 **Brokopondo** ⬖ *district* C Suriname
**Bromberg** *see* Bydgoszcz
95 L22 **Bromölla** Skåne, S Sweden *56°04′N 14°28′E*
97 L20 **Bromsgrove** W England, United Kingdom *52°20′N 02°03′W*
95 G20 **Brønderslev** Nordjylland, N Denmark *57°16′N 09°58′E*
106 D8 **Broni** Lombardia, N Italy *45°04′N 09°18′E*
10 K11 **Bronlund Peak** ▲ British Columbia, W Canada *57°27′N 126°43′W*
93 F14 **Brønnøysund** Nordland, C Norway *65°38′N 12°15′E*
23 V10 **Bronson** Florida, SE USA *29°25′N 82°38′W*
31 Q11 **Bronson** Michigan, N USA *41°52′N 85°11′W*
25 X8 **Bronson** Texas, SW USA *31°20′N 94°00′W*
107 L24 **Bronte** Sicilia, Italy, C Mediterranean Sea *37°47′N 14°50′E*
25 P8 **Bronte** Texas, SW USA *31°53′N 100°17′W*
25 Y9 **Brookeland** Texas, SW USA *31°05′N 93°57′W*
170 M7 **Brooke's Point** Palawan, W Philippines *08°54′N 117°54′E*
27 T3 **Brookfield** Missouri, C USA *39°46′N 93°04′W*
22 K7 **Brookhaven** Mississippi, S USA *31°34′N 90°26′W*
32 E16 **Brookings** Oregon, NW USA *42°03′N 124°16′W*
29 R10 **Brookings** South Dakota, N USA *44°15′N 96°46′W*
29 W14 **Brooklyn** Iowa, C USA *41°43′N 92°27′W*
29 U8 **Brooklyn Park** Minnesota, N USA *45°06′N 93°18′W*
21 U7 **Brookneal** Virginia, NE USA *37°03′N 78°56′W*
11 R16 **Brooks** Alberta, SW Canada *50°35′N 111°54′W*
25 V11 **Brookshire** Texas, SW USA *29°47′N 95°57′W*
38 L8 **Brooks Mountain** ▲ Alaska, USA *65°31′N 167°24′W*
38 M11 **Brooks Range** ▲▲ Alaska, USA
31 O12 **Brookston** Indiana, N USA *40°34′N 86°53′W*
23 V11 **Brooksville** Florida, SE USA *28°33′N 82°23′W*
23 N4 **Brooksville** Mississippi, S USA *33°13′N 88°34′W*
180 J13 **Brookton** Western Australia *32°24′S 117°04′E*
31 Q14 **Brookville** Indiana, N USA *39°25′N 85°00′W*
18 D13 **Brookville** Pennsylvania, NE USA *41°07′N 79°05′W*
31 Q14 **Brookville Lake** ▣ Indiana, N USA
180 K5 **Broome** Western Australia *17°58′S 122°15′E*
37 S4 **Broomfield** Colorado, C USA *39°55′N 105°05′W*
**Broos** *see* Orăştie
96 J7 **Brora** N Scotland, United Kingdom *57°59′N 04°00′W*
96 I7 **Brora** ≈ N Scotland, United Kingdom
95 F23 **Brørup** Syddtjylland, W Denmark *55°29′N 09°01′E*
95 L23 **Brösarp** Skåne, S Sweden *55°43′N 14°10′E*
116 J9 **Broşteni** Suceava, NE Romania *47°14′N 25°43′E*
102 M6 **Brou** Eure-et-Loir, C France *48°12′N 01°10′E*
**Broucsella** *see* Brussel/Bruxelles
**Broughton Bay** *see* Tongjosŏn-man
**Broughton Island** *see* Qikiqtarjuaq
138 G7 **Broummâna** C Lebanon *33°53′N 35°39′E*
22 I9 **Broussard** Louisiana, S USA *30°09′N 91°57′W*
98 E13 **Brouwersdam** *dam* SW Netherlands
98 E13 **Brouwershaven** Zeeland, SW Netherlands *51°44′N 03°50′E*
117 P4 **Brovary** Kyivs'ka Oblast', N Ukraine *50°30′N 30°45′E*
95 G20 **Brovst** Nordjylland, N Denmark *57°06′N 09°32′E*
31 S8 **Brown City** Michigan, N USA *43°12′N 82°50′W*
24 M6 **Brownfield** Texas, SW USA *33°11′N 102°16′W*
33 Q7 **Browning** Montana, NW USA *48°33′N 113°00′W*
33 R6 **Brown, Mount** ▲ Montana, NW USA *48°52′N 111°08′W*
0 M9 **Browns Bank** *undersea feature* NW Atlantic Ocean *42°40′N 66°05′W*
31 O14 **Brownsburg** Indiana, N USA *39°50′N 86°24′W*
18 J16 **Browns Mills** New Jersey, NE USA *39°58′N 74°33′W*
44 J12 **Browns Town** C Jamaica *18°28′N 77°22′W*
31 P15 **Brownstown** Indiana, N USA *38°52′N 86°02′W*
29 R8 **Browns Valley** Minnesota, N USA *45°36′N 96°49′W*
20 K7 **Brownsville** Kentucky, S USA *37°10′N 86°18′W*
20 F9 **Brownsville** Tennessee, S USA *35°35′N 89°15′W*
25 T17 **Brownsville** Texas, SW USA *25°56′N 97°28′W*
55 W10 **Brownsweg** Brokopondo, C Suriname
29 U9 **Brownton** Minnesota, N USA *44°43′N 94°21′W*
19 R5 **Brownville Junction** Maine, NE USA *45°20′N 69°04′W*
25 R8 **Brownwood** Texas, SW USA *31°42′N 98°59′W*
25 R8 **Brownwood Lake** ▣ Texas, SW USA
104 I9 **Brozas** Extremadura, W Spain *39°37′N 06°48′W*
119 M18 **Brozha** Mahilyowskaya Voblasts', E Belarus *52°57′N 29°07′E*
103 O2 **Bruay-en-Artois** Pas-de-Calais, N France *50°31′N 02°30′E*
103 P2 **Bruay-sur-l'Escaut** Nord, N France *50°24′N 03°33′E*
14 F13 **Bruce Peninsula** *peninsula* Ontario, S Canada
20 H9 **Bruceton** Tennessee, S USA *36°02′N 88°14′W*
25 T9 **Bruceville** Texas, SW USA *31°17′N 97°15′W*
101 G21 **Bruchsal** Baden-Württemberg, SW Germany *49°07′N 08°35′E*
109 Q7 **Bruck** Salzburg, NW Austria *47°18′N 12°51′E*
**Bruck** *see* Bruck an der Mur
109 Y4 **Bruck an der Leitha** Niederösterreich, NE Austria *48°02′N 16°47′E*
109 V7 **Bruck an der Mur** *var.* Bruck. Steiermark, C Austria *47°25′N 15°17′E*
101 M24 **Bruckmühl** Bayern, SE Germany *47°52′N 11°54′E*
168 E7 **Brueuh, Pulau** *island* NW Indonesia
**Bruges** *see* Brugge
108 F6 **Brugg** Aargau, NW Switzerland *47°29′N 08°13′E*
99 C16 **Brugge** *Fr.* Bruges. West-Vlaanderen, NW Belgium *51°13′N 03°14′E*
109 R9 **Bruggen** Kärnten, S Austria *46°46′N 13°13′E*
101 E16 **Brühl** Nordrhein-Westfalen, W Germany *50°50′N 06°55′E*
99 F14 **Bruinisse** Zeeland, SW Netherlands *51°40′N 04°04′E*
169 R9 **Bruit, Pulau** *island* East Malaysia
14 K10 **Brûlé, Lac** ◎ Québec, SE Canada
30 M4 **Brule River** ≈ Michigan/Wisconsin, N USA
99 H23 **Brûly** Namur, S Belgium *49°55′N 04°31′E*
59 N17 **Brumado** Bahia, E Brazil *14°14′S 41°38′W*
98 M11 **Brummen** Gelderland, E Netherlands *52°05′N 06°10′E*
94 H13 **Brumunddal** Hedmark, S Norway *60°54′N 11°00′E*
23 Q6 **Brundidge** Alabama, S USA *31°43′N 85°49′W*
**Brundisium/Brundusium** *see* Brindisi
33 N15 **Bruneau River** ≈ Idaho, NW USA
**Bruneck** *see* Brunico
169 T8 **Brunei** *off.* Brunei Darussalam, *Mal.* Negara Brunei Darussalam. ◆ *monarchy* SE Asia
169 T7 **Brunei Bay** *var.* Teluk Brunei. *bay* N Brunei
**Brunei Darussalam** *see* Brunei
**Brunei, Teluk** *see* Brunei Bay
**Brunei Town** *see* Bandar Seri Begawan
106 H5 **Brunico** *Ger.* Bruneck. Trentino-Alto Adige, N Italy *46°49′N 11°57′E*
**Brünn** *see* Brno
185 G17 **Brunner, Lake** ◎ South Island, New Zealand
99 M18 **Brunssum** Limburg, SE Netherlands *50°57′N 05°59′E*
23 W7 **Brunswick** Georgia, SE USA *31°09′N 81°30′W*
19 Q8 **Brunswick** Maine, NE USA *43°54′N 69°58′W*
21 V3 **Brunswick** Maryland, NE USA *39°18′N 77°37′W*
27 T3 **Brunswick** Missouri, C USA *39°25′N 93°07′W*
31 T11 **Brunswick** Ohio, N USA *41°14′N 81°50′W*
**Brunswick** *see* Braunschweig
63 H24 **Brunswick, Península** *headland* S Chile *53°30′S 71°27′W*
111 H17 **Bruntál** *Ger.* Freudenthal. Moravskoslezský Kraj, E Czechia *50°00′N 17°27′E*
195 N3 **Brunt Ice Shelf** *ice shelf* Antarctica
**Brusa** *see* Bursa
114 G7 **Brusartsi** Montana, NW Bulgaria *43°39′N 23°04′E*
37 U3 **Brush** Colorado, C USA *40°15′N 103°37′W*
42 M5 **Brus Laguna** Gracias a Dios, E Honduras *15°46′N 84°32′W*
60 K13 **Brusque** Santa Catarina, S Brazil *27°07′S 48°54′W*
**Brussa** *see* Bursa
99 E18 **Brussel** *var.* Brussels, *Fr.* Bruxelles, *Ger.* Brüssel; *anc.* Broucsella. ● (Belgium) Brussels, C Belgium *50°52′N 04°21′E* ***see also*** Bruxelles
**Brussel** *see* Bruxelles
**Brüssel/Brussels** *see* Brussel/Bruxelles
117 O5 **Brusyliv** Zhytomyrs'ka Oblast', N Ukraine *50°16′N 29°31′E*
183 Q12 **Bruthen** Victoria, SE Australia *37°43′S 147°49′E*
**Bruttium** *see* Calabria
**Brüx** *see* Most
99 E18 **Bruxelles** *var.* Brussels, *Dut.* Brussel, *Ger.* Brüssel; *anc.* Broucsella. ● Brussels, C Belgium *50°52′N 04°21′E* ***see also*** Brussel
**Bruxelles** *see* Brussel
54 J7 **Bruzual** Apure, W Venezuela *07°59′N 69°18′W*
31 Q11 **Bryan** Ohio, N USA *41°30′N 84°34′W*
25 U10 **Bryan** Texas, SW USA *30°40′N 96°23′W*
194 J4 **Bryan Coast** *physical region* Antarctica
122 L11 **Bryanka** Krasnoyarskiy Kray, C Russia *59°01′N 93°13′E*
117 Y7 **Bryanka** Luhans'ka Oblast', E Ukraine *48°30′N 38°45′E*
182 J8 **Bryan, Mount** ▲ South Australia *33°25′S 138°59′E*
126 I6 **Bryansk** Bryanskaya Oblast', W Russia *53°16′N 34°07′E*
126 H6 **Bryanskaya Oblast'** ⬖ *province* W Russia
194 J5 **Bryant, Cape** *headland* Antarctica
27 U8 **Bryant Creek** ≈ Missouri, C USA
36 K8 **Bryce Canyon** *canyon* Utah, W USA
119 O15 **Bryli** Mahilyowskaya Voblasts', E Belarus *53°54′N 30°33′E*
95 C17 **Bryne** Rogaland, S Norway *58°43′N 05°40′E*
25 R6 **Bryson** Texas, SW USA *33°09′N 98°23′W*
21 N10 **Bryson City** North Carolina, SE USA *35°26′N 83°27′W*
14 K11 **Bryson, Lac** ◎ Québec, SE Canada
126 K13 **Bryukhovetskaya** Krasnodarskiy Kray, SW Russia *45°49′N 38°01′E*
111 H15 **Brzeg** *Ger.* Brieg; *anc.* Civitas Altae Ripae. Opolskie, S Poland *50°52′N 17°27′E*
111 G14 **Brzeg Dolny** *Ger.* Dyhernfurth. Dolnośląskie, SW Poland *51°15′N 16°40′E*
**Brześć Litewski/Brześć nad Bugiem** *see* Brest
111 L17 **Brzesko** *Ger.* Brietzig. Małopolskie, SE Poland *49°59′N 20°34′E*
**Brzeżany** *see* Berezhany
110 K12 **Brzeziny** Łódzkie, C Poland *51°49′N 19°41′E*
**Brzostowica Wielka** *see* Vyalikaya Byerastavitsa
111 O17 **Brzozów** Podkarpackie, SE Poland *49°38′N 22°00′E*
**Bsharrī/Bsherri** *see* Bcharré
187 X14 **Bua** Vanua Levu, N Fiji *16°48′S 178°36′E*
95 J20 **Bua** Halland, S Sweden *57°14′N 12°07′E*
82 M13 **Bua** ≈ C Malawi
**Bua** *see* Čiovo
81 L18 **Bu'aale** *It.* Buale. Jubbada Dhexe, SW Somalia *0°52′N 42°37′E*
**Buache, Mount** *see* Mutunte, Mount
189 Q8 **Buada Lagoon** *lagoon* Nauru, C Pacific Ocean
186 M8 **Buala** Santa Isabel, E Solomon Islands *08°06′S 159°31′E*
**Buale** *see* Bu'aale
190 H1 **Buariki** *atoll* Tungaru, W Kiribati
167 Q10 **Bua Yai** *var.* Ban Bua Yai. Nakhon Ratchasima, E Thailand *15°35′N 102°25′E*
75 P8 **Bu'ayrāt al Ḩasūn** *var.* Buwayrāt al Hasūn. C Libya *31°22′N 15°41′E*
76 H13 **Buba** S Guinea-Bissau *11°36′N 14°55′W*
171 P11 **Bubaa** Sulawesi, N Indonesia *0°32′N 122°27′E*
81 D20 **Bubanza** NW Burundi *03°04′S 29°22′E*
83 K18 **Bubi** *prev.* Bubye. ≈ S Zimbabwe
142 L11 **Būbīyan, Jazīrat** *island* E Kuwait
**Bublitz** *see* Bobolice
**Bubye** *see* Bubi
187 Y13 **Buca** *prev.* Mbutha. Vanua Levu, N Fiji *16°39′S 179°51′E*
136 F16 **Bucak** Burdur, SW Turkey *37°28′N 30°37′E*
54 G8 **Bucaramanga** Santander, N Colombia *07°08′N 73°10′W*
107 M18 **Buccino** Campania, S Italy *40°37′N 15°25′E*
116 K9 **Bucecea** Botoşani, NE Romania *47°45′N 26°30′E*
116 J6 **Buchach** *Pol.* Buczacz. Ternopil's'ka Oblast', W Ukraine *49°04′N 25°23′E*
183 Q12 **Buchan** Victoria, SE Australia *37°26′S 148°11′E*
76 J17 **Buchanan** *prev.* Grand Bassa. SW Liberia *05°53′N 10°03′W*
23 R3 **Buchanan** Georgia, SE USA *33°48′N 85°11′W*
31 O11 **Buchanan** Michigan, N USA *41°49′N 86°21′W*
21 T6 **Buchanan** Virginia, NE USA *37°31′N 79°40′W*
25 R10 **Buchanan Dam** Texas, SW USA *30°42′N 98°24′W*
25 R10 **Buchanan, Lake** ▣ Texas, SW USA
96 L8 **Buchan Ness** *headland* NE Scotland, United Kingdom *57°28′N 01°46′W*
13 T12 **Buchans** Newfoundland and Labrador, SE Canada *48°49′N 56°53′W*
**Bucharest** *see* Bucureşti
101 H20 **Buchen** Baden-Württemberg, SW Germany *49°31′N 09°18′E*
100 I10 **Buchholz in der Nordheide** Niedersachsen, NW Germany *53°19′N 09°52′E*
108 F7 **Buchs** Aargau, N Switzerland *47°24′N 08°04′E*
108 I8 **Buchs** Sankt Gallen, NE Switzerland *47°10′N 09°28′E*
100 H13 **Bückeburg** Niedersachsen, NW Germany *52°16′N 09°03′E*
36 K14 **Buckeye** Arizona, SW USA *33°22′N 112°34′W*
**Buckeye State** *see* Ohio
21 S4 **Buckhannon** West Virginia, NE USA *38°59′N 80°14′W*
25 T9 **Buckholts** Texas, SW USA *30°52′N 97°07′W*
96 K8 **Buckie** NE Scotland, United Kingdom *57°39′N 02°56′W*
14 M12 **Buckingham** Québec, SE Canada *45°35′N 75°25′W*
21 U6 **Buckingham** Virginia, NE USA *37°33′N 78°34′W*
97 N21 **Buckinghamshire** *cultural region* SE England, United Kingdom
39 N8 **Buckland** Alaska, USA *65°58′N 161°07′W*
182 G7 **Buckleboo** South Australia *32°55′S 136°11′E*
26 K7 **Bucklin** Kansas, C USA *37°33′N 99°37′W*
27 T3 **Bucklin** Missouri, C USA *39°46′N 92°53′W*
36 I12 **Buckskin Mountains** ▲▲ Arizona, SW USA
19 R7 **Bucksport** Maine, NE USA *44°34′N 68°46′W*
82 A9 **Buco Zau** Cabinda, NW Angola *04°45′S 12°34′E*
**Bu Craa** *see* Bou Craa
116 K14 **Bucureşti** *Eng.* Bucharest, *Ger.* Bukarest, *prev.* Altenburg; *anc.* Cetatea Damboviţei. ● (Romania) Bucureşti, S Romania *44°27′N 26°06′E*
31 S12 **Bucyrus** Ohio, N USA *40°47′N 82°57′W*
**Buczacz** *see* Buchach
94 E9 **Bud** Møre og Romsdal, S Norway *62°55′N 06°55′E*
25 S11 **Buda** Texas, SW USA *30°05′N 97°50′W*
119 O18 **Buda-Kashalyova** *Rus.* Buda-Koshelëvo. Homyel'skaya Voblasts', SE Belarus *52°43′N 30°34′E*
**Buda-Koshelëvo** *see* Buda-Kashalyova
166 L4 **Budalin** Sagaing, C Myanmar (Burma) *22°24′N 95°08′E*
111 J22 **Budapest** *off.* Budapest Főváros, *SCr.* Budimpešta. ● (Hungary) Pest, N Hungary *47°30′N 19°03′E*
**Budapest Főváros** *see* Budapest
92 I2 **Búðardalur** Vesturland, W Iceland *65°07′N 21°45′W*
152 K11 **Budaun** Uttar Pradesh, N India *28°02′N 79°07′E*
141 O9 **Budayyi'ah** *oasis* C Saudi Arabia
195 Y12 **Budd Coast** *physical region* Antarctica
**Buddenbrock** *see* Brodnica
107 C17 **Budduso** Sardegna, Italy, C Mediterranean Sea *40°37′N 09°19′E*
97 I23 **Bude** SW England, United Kingdom *50°50′N 04°33′W*
22 J7 **Bude** Mississippi, S USA *31°27′N 90°51′W*
**Budějovický Kraj** *see* Jihočeský Kraj
99 K16 **Budel** Noord-Brabant, SE Netherlands *51°17′N 05°35′E*
100 I8 **Büdelsdorf** Schleswig-Holstein, N Germany *54°20′N 09°40′E*
127 O14 **Budënnovsk** Stavropol'skiy Kray, SW Russia *44°46′N 44°07′E*
116 K14 **Budeşti** Călăraşi, SE Romania *44°13′N 26°30′E*
**Budge-Budge** *see* Baj Baj
**Budgewoi** *see* Budgewoi Lake
183 T8 **Budgewoi Lake** *var.* Budgewoi. New South Wales, SE Australia *33°14′S 151°34′E*
**Budimpešta** *see* Budapest
79 J16 **Budjala** Equateur, NW Dem. Rep. Congo *02°39′N 19°42′E*
106 G10 **Budrio** Emilia-Romagna, C Italy *44°33′N 11°34′E*
**Budslav** *see* Budslaw
119 K14 **Budslaw** *Rus.* Budslav. Minskaya Voblasts', N Belarus *54°47′N 27°27′E*
**Budua** *see* Budva
169 R9 **Budu, Tanjung** *headland* East Malaysia *02°51′N 111°42′E*
113 J17 **Budva** *It.* Budua. W Montenegro *42°17′N 18°49′E*
**Budweis** *see* České Budějovice
**Budyšin** *see* Bautzen
79 D16 **Buea** Sud-Ouest, SW Cameroon *04°09′N 09°13′E*
103 S13 **Buëch** ≈ SE France
18 J17 **Buena** New Jersey, NE USA *39°30′N 74°55′W*
62 K12 **Buena Esperanza** San Luis, C Argentina *34°45′S 65°15′W*
54 C11 **Buenaventura** Valle del Cauca, W Colombia *03°54′N 77°02′W*
40 I4 **Buenaventura** Chihuahua, N Mexico *29°50′N 107°30′W*
57 M18 **Buena Vista** Santa Cruz, C Bolivia *17°28′S 63°37′W*
40 G10 **Buenavista** Baja California Sur, NW Mexico *23°39′N 109°41′W*
37 S5 **Buena Vista** Colorado, C USA *38°50′N 106°07′W*
23 S5 **Buena Vista** Georgia, SE USA *32°19′N 84°31′W*
21 T6 **Buena Vista** Virginia, NE USA *37°44′N 79°22′W*
44 F5 **Buena Vista, Bahia de** *bay* N Cuba




◆ Country
● Country Capital
◇ Dependent Territory
○ Dependent Territory Capital
⬖ Administrative Regions
✈ International Airport
▲ Mountain
▲▲ Mountain Range
Volcano
≈ River
◎ Lake
▣ Reservoir

◆ Country  ◇ Dependent Territory  ◈ Administrative Regions  ▲ Mountain  ◉ Volcano  ◎ Lake
● Country Capital  ○ Dependent Territory Capital  ★ International Airport  ▲ Mountain Range  ← River  ⊟ Reservoir

231

## Byron – Campos do Jordão


30 L10 **Byron** Illinois, N USA *42°06′N 89°15′W*
183 V4 **Byron Bay** New South Wales, SE Australia *28°39′S 153°34′E*
183 V4 **Byron, Cape** *headland* New South Wales, E Australia *28°37′S 153°40′E*
63 F21 **Byron, Isla** *island* S Chile
**Byron Island** *see* Nikunau
65 B24 **Byron Sound** *sound* NW Falkland Islands
**Byrranga, Gory** *see* Barranga, Gory
93 J14 **Byske** Västerbotten, N Sweden *64°58′N 21°10′E*
111 K18 **Bystrá** ▲ N Slovakia *49°10′N 19°49′E*
111 F18 **Bystřice nad Pernštejnem** *Ger.* Bistritz ober Pernstein. Vysočina, C Czechia *49°32′N 16°16′E*
**Bystrovka** *see* Kemin
111 G16 **Bystrzyca Kłodzka** *Ger.* Habelschwerdt. Wałbrzych, SW Poland *50°19′N 16°39′E*
111 I18 **Bytča** Žilinský Kraj, N Slovakia *49°15′N 18°32′E*
119 L15 **Bytcha** Minskaya Voblasts', NE Belarus *54°19′N 28°24′E*
**Byteń/Byten'** *see* Bytsyen'
111 J16 **Bytom** *Ger.* Beuthen. Śląskie, S Poland *50°21′N 18°51′E*
110 H7 **Bytów** *Ger.* Bütow. Pomorskie, N Poland *54°10′N 17°30′E*
119 H18 **Bytsyen'** *Pol.* Byteń, *Rus.* Byten'. Brestskaya Voblasts', SW Belarus *52°53′N 25°30′E*
81 E19 **Byumba** *var.* Biumba. N Rwanda *01°37′S 30°05′E*
**Byuzmeyin** *see* Abadan
119 O20 **Byval'ki** Homyel'skaya Voblasts', SE Belarus *51°51′N 30°38′E*
95 O20 **Byxelkrok** Kalmar, S Sweden *57°18′N 17°01′E*
**Byzantium** *see* İstanbul
**Bzīmah** *see* Buzaymah

# C

62 O6 **Caacupé** Cordillera, S Paraguay *25°23′S 57°05′W*
62 P6 **Caaguazú** *off.* Departamento de Caaguazú. ◈ *department* C Paraguay
**Caaguazú, Departamento de** *see* Caaguazú
82 C13 **Caála** *var.* Kaala, Robert Williams, *Port.* Vila Robert Williams. Huambo, C Angola *12°51′S 15°33′E*
62 P7 **Caazapá** Caazapá, S Paraguay *26°09′S 56°21′W*
62 P7 **Caazapá** *off.* Departamento de Caazapá. ◈ *department* SE Paraguay
**Caazapá, Departamento de** *see* Caazapá
81 P15 **Cabaad, Raas** *headland* C Somalia *06°13′N 49°01′E*
55 N10 **Cabadisocaña** Amazonas, S Venezuela *04°28′N 64°45′W*
44 F5 **Cabaiguán** Sancti Spíritus, C Cuba *22°04′N 79°32′W*
**Caballeria, Cabo** *see* Cavalleria, Cap de
37 Q14 **Caballo Reservoir** ⊠ New Mexico, SW USA
40 L6 **Caballos Mesteños, Llano de los** *plain* N Mexico
104 L2 **Cabanaquinta** Asturias, N Spain *43°10′N 05°37′W*
42 B9 **Cabañas** ◈ *department* E El Salvador
171 O3 **Cabanatuan** *off.* Cabanatuan City. Luzon, N Philippines *15°27′N 120°57′E*
**Cabanatuan City** *see* Cabanatuan
15 T8 **Cabano** Québec, SE Canada *47°40′N 68°56′W*
104 L11 **Cabeza del Buey** Extremadura, W Spain *38°44′N 05°13′W*
45 V5 **Cabezas de San Juan** *headland* E Puerto Rico *18°23′N 65°37′W*
105 N2 **Cabezón de la Sal** Cantabria, N Spain *43°19′N 04°14′W*
**Cabhán** *see* Cavan
61 B23 **Cabildo** Buenos Aires, E Argentina *38°28′S 61°50′W*
**Cabillonum** *see* Chalon-sur-Saône
54 H5 **Cabimas** Zulia, NW Venezuela *10°26′N 71°27′W*
82 A9 **Cabinda** *var.* Kabinda. Cabinda, NW Angola *05°34′S 12°12′E*
82 A9 **Cabinda** *var.* Kabinda. ◈ *province* NW Angola
33 N7 **Cabinet Mountains** ▲▲ Idaho/Montana, NW USA
82 B11 **Cabiri** Bengo, NW Angola *08°50′S 13°42′E*
63 J20 **Cabo Blanco** Santa Cruz, SE Argentina *47°13′S 65°43′W*
82 P13 **Cabo Delgado** *off.* Província de Capo Delgado. ◈ *province* NE Mozambique
14 L9 **Cabonga, Réservoir** ⊠ Québec, SE Canada
27 V7 **Cabool** Missouri, C USA *37°07′N 92°06′W*
183 V2 **Caboolture** Queensland, E Australia *27°05′S 152°50′E*
**Cabora Bassa, Lake** *see* Cahora Bassa, Albufeira de
40 F3 **Caborca** Sonora, NW Mexico *30°44′N 112°06′W*
**Cabo San Lucas** *see* San Lucas
27 V11 **Cabot** Arkansas, C USA *34°58′N 92°01′W*
14 F12 **Cabot Head** *headland* Ontario, S Canada *45°13′N 81°17′W*
13 R13 **Cabot Strait** *strait* E Canada
**Cabo Verde, Ilhas do** *see* Cape Verde
**Cabo Verde, Republic of** *see* Cape Verde
104 M14 **Cabra** Andalucía, S Spain *37°28′N 04°28′W*
107 B19 **Cabras** Sardegna, Italy, C Mediterranean Sea *39°55′N 08°30′E*
188 A15 **Cabras Island** *island* W Guam
45 O8 **Cabrera** N Dominican Republic *19°40′N 69°54′W*
104 J4 **Cabrera** 〰 NW Spain
105 X10 **Cabrera, Illa de** *anc.* Capraria. *island* Islas Baleares, Spain, W Mediterranean Sea
105 Q15 **Cabrera, Sierra** ▲▲ S Spain
11 S16 **Cabri** Saskatchewan, S Canada *50°38′N 108°28′W*
105 R10 **Cabriel** 〰 E Spain
54 M7 **Cabruta** Guárico, C Venezuela *07°39′N 66°19′W*
171 N2 **Cabugao** Luzon, N Philippines *17°55′N 120°29′E*
54 G10 **Cabuyaro** Meta, C Colombia *04°21′N 72°47′W*
60 I13 **Caçador** Santa Catarina, S Brazil *26°47′S 51°00′W*
42 G8 **Cacaguatique, Cordillera** *var.* Cordillera. ▲▲ NE El Salvador
112 L13 **Čačak** Serbia, C Serbia *43°52′N 20°23′E*
55 Y10 **Cacao** NE French Guiana *04°37′N 52°29′W*
61 H16 **Caçapava do Sul** Rio Grande do Sul, S Brazil *30°28′S 53°29′W*
21 U3 **Cacapon River** 〰 West Virginia, NE USA
107 J23 **Caccamo** Sicilia, Italy, C Mediterranean Sea *37°56′N 13°40′E*
107 A17 **Caccia, Capo** *headland* Sardegna, Italy, C Mediterranean Sea *40°34′N 08°09′E*
146 H15 **Çäçe** *var.* Chäche, *Rus.* Chaacha. Ahal Welaýaty, S Turkmenistan *36°49′N 60°33′E*
59 G18 **Cáceres** Mato Grosso, W Brazil *16°05′S 57°40′W*
104 J10 **Cáceres** *Ar.* Qazris. Extremadura, W Spain *39°29′N 06°23′W*
104 J9 **Cáceres** ◈ *province* Extremadura, W Spain
**Cachacrou** *see* Scotts Head Village
61 C21 **Cacharí** Buenos Aires, E Argentina *36°24′S 59°32′W*
26 L12 **Cache** Oklahoma, C USA *34°37′N 98°37′W*
10 M16 **Cache Creek** British Columbia, SW Canada *50°49′N 121°20′W*
35 N6 **Cache Creek** 〰 California, W USA
37 S3 **Cache La Poudre River** 〰 Colorado, C USA
**Cacheo** *see* Cacheu
27 W11 **Cache River** 〰 Arkansas, C USA
30 L17 **Cache River** 〰 Illinois, N USA
76 G12 **Cacheu** *var.* Cacheo. W Guinea-Bissau *12°12′N 16°10′W*
59 I15 **Cachimbo** Pará, NE Brazil *09°21′S 54°58′W*
59 H15 **Cachimbo, Serra do** ▲▲ C Brazil
82 D13 **Cachingues** Bié, C Angola *13°05′S 16°48′E*
54 G7 **Cáchira** Norte de Santander, N Colombia *07°44′N 73°07′W*
61 H16 **Cachoeira do Sul** Rio Grande do Sul, S Brazil *29°58′S 52°54′W*
59 O20 **Cachoeiro de Itapemirim** Espírito Santo, SE Brazil *20°51′S 41°07′W*
82 E12 **Cacolo** Lunda Sul, NE Angola *10°09′S 19°21′E*
83 C14 **Caconda** Huíla, C Angola *13°43′S 15°03′E*
82 A9 **Cacongo** Cabinda, NW Angola *05°13′S 12°08′E*
35 U9 **Cactus Peak** ▲ Nevada, W USA *37°42′N 116°51′W*
82 A11 **Cacuaco** Luanda, NW Angola *08°47′S 13°21′E*
83 B14 **Cacula** Huíla, SW Angola *14°33′S 14°04′E*
67 R12 **Caculuvar** 〰 SW Angola
59 O19 **Caçumba, Ilha** *island* SE Brazil
55 N10 **Cacuri** Amazonas, S Venezuela
81 N17 **Cadale** Shabeellaha Dhexe, E Somalia *02°48′N 46°19′E*
105 X4 **Cadaqués** Cataluña, NE Spain *42°17′N 03°16′E*
111 J18 **Čadca** *Hung.* Csaca. Žilinský Kraj, N Slovakia *49°27′N 18°46′E*
27 P13 **Caddo** Oklahoma, C USA *34°07′N 96°15′W*
25 R6 **Caddo** Texas, SW USA *32°42′N 98°40′W*
25 X6 **Caddo Lake** ⊠ Louisiana/Texas, SW USA
27 S12 **Caddo Mountains** ▲▲ Arkansas, C USA
41 O8 **Cadereyta** Nuevo León, NE Mexico *25°35′N 99°54′W*
97 J19 **Cader Idris** ▲ NW Wales, United Kingdom *52°43′N 03°57′W*
182 F3 **Cadibarrawirracanna, Lake** *salt lake* South Australia
14 I7 **Cadillac** Québec, SE Canada *48°12′N 78°23′W*
11 T17 **Cadillac** Saskatchewan, S Canada *49°43′N 107°41′W*
102 K13 **Cadillac** Gironde, SW France *44°37′N 00°16′W*
31 P7 **Cadillac** Michigan, N USA *44°15′N 85°23′W*
105 V4 **Cadí, Toretta de** *prev.* Torre de Cadí. ▲ NE Spain *42°16′N 01°38′E*
**Torre de Cadí** *see* Cadí, Toretta de
171 P5 **Cadiz** *off.* Cadiz City. Negros, C Philippines *10°58′N 123°18′E*
104 J15 **Cádiz** *anc.* Gades, Gadier, Gadir, Gadire. Andalucía, SW Spain *36°32′N 06°18′W*
20 H7 **Cadiz** Kentucky, S USA *36°52′N 87°50′W*
31 U13 **Cadiz** Ohio, N USA *40°16′N 81°00′W*
104 K15 **Cádiz** ◈ *province* Andalucía, SW Spain
104 I15 **Cadiz, Bahía de** *bay* SW Spain
**Cadiz City** *see* Cadiz
104 H15 **Cádiz, Golfo de** *Eng.* Gulf of Cadiz. *gulf* Portugal/Spain
**Cadiz, Gulf of** *see* Cádiz, Golfo de
35 X14 **Cadiz Lake** ◎ California, W USA
182 E2 **Cadney Homestead** South Australia *27°52′S 134°03′E*
**Cadurcum** *see* Cahors
83 F17 **Caecae** *var.* Xaixai. Ngamiland, NW Botswana *19°52′S 21°04′E*
102 K4 **Caen** Calvados, N France *49°10′N 00°20′W*
**Caene/Caenepolis** *see* Qīna
**Caerdydd** *see* Cardiff
**Caer Glou** *see* Gloucester
**Caer Gybi** *see* Holyhead
**Caerleon** *see* Chester
**Caer Luel** *see* Carlisle
97 I18 **Caernarfon** *var.* Caernarvon, Carnarvon. NW Wales, United Kingdom *53°08′N 04°16′W*
97 H18 **Caernarfon Bay** *bay* NW Wales, United Kingdom
97 I19 **Caernarvon** *cultural region* NW Wales, United Kingdom
**Caernarvon** *see* Caernarfon
**Caesaraugusta** *see* Zaragoza
**Caesarea Mazaca** *see* Kayseri
**Caesarobriga** *see* Talavera de la Reina
**Caesarodunum** *see* Tours
**Caesaromagus** *see* Beauvais
**Caesena** *see* Cesena
59 N17 **Caetité** Bahia, E Brazil *14°04′S 42°29′W*
62 J6 **Cafayate** Salta, N Argentina *26°02′S 66°00′W*
171 O2 **Cagayan** 〰 Luzon, N Philippines
171 Q7 **Cagayan de Oro** *off.* Cagayan de Oro City. Mindanao, S Philippines *08°29′N 124°38′E*
**Cagayan de Oro City** *see* Cagayan de Oro
170 M8 **Cagayan de Tawi Tawi** *island* S Philippines
171 N6 **Cagayan Islands** *island group* C Philippines
31 O14 **Cagles Mill Lake** ⊠ Indiana, N USA
106 I12 **Cagli** Marche, C Italy *43°33′N 12°39′E*
107 C20 **Cagliari** *anc.* Caralis. Sardegna, Italy, C Mediterranean Sea *39°15′N 09°06′E*
107 C20 **Cagliari, Golfo di** *gulf* Sardegna, Italy, C Mediterranean Sea
103 U15 **Cagnes-sur-Mer** Alpes-Maritimes, SE France *43°40′N 07°09′E*
54 L5 **Cagua** Aragua, N Venezuela *10°09′N 67°27′W*
171 O1 **Cagua, Mount** ▲ Luzon, N Philippines *18°10′N 122°03′E*
54 F13 **Caguán, Río** 〰 SW Colombia
45 U6 **Caguas** E Puerto Rico *18°14′N 66°02′W*
146 C9 **Çagyl** *Rus.* Chagyl. Balkan Welaýaty, NW Turkmenistan *40°48′N 55°21′E*
23 P5 **Cahaba River** 〰 Alabama, S USA
42 E5 **Cahabón, Río** 〰 C Guatemala
83 B15 **Cahama** Cunene, SW Angola *16°16′S 14°23′E*
97 B21 **Caha Mountains** *Ir.* An Cheacha. ▲▲ SW Ireland
97 D20 **Caher** *Ir.* An Cathair. S Ireland *52°21′N 07°58′W*
97 A21 **Caherciveen** *Ir.* Cathair Saidhbhín. SW Ireland *51°56′N 10°12′W*
30 K15 **Cahokia** Illinois, N USA *38°34′N 90°11′W*
83 L15 **Cahora Bassa, Albufeira de** *var.* Lake Cabora Bassa. ⊠ NW Mozambique
97 G20 **Cahore Point** *Ir.* Rinn Chathóir. *headland* SE Ireland *52°33′N 06°11′W*
102 M14 **Cahors** *anc.* Cadurcum. Lot, S France *44°26′N 01°27′E*
56 D9 **Cahuapanas, Río** 〰 N Peru
116 M12 **Cahul** *Rus.* Kagul. S Moldova *45°53′N 28°13′E*
**Cahul, Lacul** *see* Kahul, Ozero
83 N16 **Caia** Sofala, C Mozambique *17°50′S 35°21′E*
59 J19 **Caiapó, Serra do** ▲▲ C Brazil
44 F5 **Caibarién** Villa Clara, C Cuba *22°31′N 79°29′W*
55 O5 **Caicara** Monagas, NE Venezuela *09°52′N 63°38′W*
54 L5 **Caicara del Orinoco** Bolívar, C Venezuela *07°38′N 66°10′W*
59 P14 **Caicó** Rio Grande do Norte, E Brazil *06°25′S 37°04′W*
44 M6 **Caicos Islands** *island group* W Turks and Caicos Islands
44 L5 **Caicos Passage** *strait* The Bahamas/Turks and Caicos Islands
161 O9 **Caidian** *prev.* Hanyang. Hubei, C China *30°37′N 114°02′E*
**Caiffa** *see* Hefa
180 M12 **Caiguna** Western Australia *32°14′S 125°33′E*
**Caillí, Ceann** *see* Hag's Head
40 J11 **Caimanero, Laguna del** *var.* Laguna del Camaronero. *lagoon* E Pacific Ocean
117 N10 **Căinari** *Rus.* Kaynary. C Moldova *46°43′N 29°00′E*
57 L19 **Caine, Río** 〰 C Bolivia
**Caiphas** *see* Hefa
195 N4 **Caird Coast** *physical region* Antarctica
96 J9 **Cairn Gorm** ▲ C Scotland, United Kingdom *57°07′N 03°38′W*
96 J9 **Cairngorm Mountains** ▲▲ C Scotland, United Kingdom
39 P12 **Cairn Mountain** ▲ Alaska, USA *61°07′N 155°23′W*
181 W4 **Cairns** Queensland, NE Australia *16°51′S 145°43′E*
23 T8 **Cairo** Georgia, SE USA *30°52′N 84°12′W*
30 L17 **Cairo** Illinois, N USA *37°00′N 89°10′W*
75 V8 **Cairo** ✈ C Egypt *30°06′N 31°36′E*
**Cairo** *see* Al Qāhirah
**Caiseal** *see* Cashel
**Caisleán an Bharraigh** *see* Castlebar
**Caisleán na Finne** *see* Castlefinn
96 J6 **Caithness** *cultural region* N Scotland, United Kingdom
83 D15 **Caiundo** Kuando Kubango, S Angola *15°41′S 17°28′E*
56 C11 **Cajamarca** *prev.* Caxamarca. Cajamarca, NW Peru *07°09′S 78°32′W*
56 B11 **Cajamarca** *off.* Región de Cajamarca. ◈ *region* N Peru
**Cajamarca, Región de** *see* Cajamarca
103 N14 **Cajarc** Lot, S France *44°28′N 01°51′E*
42 G6 **Cajón, Represa El** ⊠ NW Honduras
58 N12 **Caju, Ilha do** *island* NE Brazil
159 R10 **Caka Yanhu** ◎ C China
112 E7 **Čakovec** *Ger.* Csakathurn, *Hung.* Csáktornya; *prev. Ger.* Tschakathurn. Medimurje, N Croatia *46°24′N 16°29′E*
77 V17 **Calabar** Cross River, S Nigeria *04°56′N 08°25′E*
14 K13 **Calabogie** Ontario, SE Canada *45°18′N 76°46′W*
54 L6 **Calabozo** Guárico, C Venezuela *08°58′N 67°28′W*
107 N20 **Calabria** *anc.* Bruttium. ◈ *region* SW Italy
104 M16 **Calaburra, Punta de** *headland* S Spain *36°30′N 04°38′W*
116 G14 **Calafat** Dolj, SW Romania *43°59′N 22°57′E*
**Calafate** *see* El Calafate
105 Q4 **Calahorra** La Rioja, N Spain *42°19′N 01°58′W*
103 N1 **Calais** Pas-de-Calais, N France *51°N 01°54′E*
19 T5 **Calais** Maine, NE USA *45°09′N 67°15′W*
**Calais, Pas de** *see* Dover, Strait of
**Calalen** *see* Kallalen
62 H4 **Calama** Antofagasta, N Chile *22°26′S 68°54′W*
**Calamianes** *see* Calamian Group
170 M5 **Calamian Group** *var.* Calamianes. *island group* W Philippines
105 R7 **Calamocha** Aragón, NE Spain *40°54′N 01°18′W*
29 N14 **Calamus River** 〰 Nebraska, C USA
116 G12 **Călan** *Ger.* Kalan, *Hung.* Pusztakalán. Hunedoara, SW Romania *45°45′N 22°59′E*
105 S7 **Calanda** Aragón, NE Spain *40°56′N 00°15′W*
168 F9 **Calang** Sumatera, W Indonesia *04°37′N 95°37′E*
171 N4 **Calapan** Mindoro, N Philippines *13°24′N 121°08′E*
**Călăras** *see* Călăraşi
116 M9 **Călăraşi** *var.* Călăras, *Rus.* Kalarash. C Moldova *47°19′N 28°13′E*
116 L14 **Călăraşi** Călăraşi, SE Romania *44°18′N 26°52′E*
116 K14 **Călăraşi** ◈ *county* SE Romania
54 E10 **Calarca** Quindío, W Colombia *04°31′N 75°38′W*
105 Q12 **Calasparra** Murcia, SE Spain *38°14′N 01°41′W*
107 I23 **Calatafimi** Sicilia, Italy, C Mediterranean Sea *37°54′N 12°52′E*
105 Q6 **Calatayud** Aragón, NE Spain *41°21′N 01°39′W*
171 O4 **Calauag** Luzon, N Philippines *13°57′N 122°18′E*
35 P8 **Calaveras River** 〰 California, W USA
171 N4 **Calavite, Cape** *headland* Mindoro, N Philippines *13°25′N 120°16′E*
171 Q8 **Calbayog** *off.* Calbayog City. Samar, C Philippines *12°08′N 124°36′E*
**Calbayog City** *see* Calbayog
22 G9 **Calcasieu Lake** ◎ Louisiana, S USA
22 H8 **Calcasieu River** 〰 Louisiana, S USA
56 B6 **Calceta** Manabí, W Ecuador *0°51′S 80°07′W*
61 B16 **Calchaquí** Santa Fe, C Argentina *29°56′S 60°14′W*
62 J6 **Calchaquí, Río** 〰 NW Argentina
58 J10 **Calçoene** Amapá, NE Brazil *02°29′N 51°01′W*
153 S16 **Calcutta** ✈ West Bengal, N India *22°30′N 88°20′E*
**Calcutta** *see* Kolkāta
54 E9 **Caldas** *off.* Departamento de Caldas. ◈ *province* W Colombia
104 F10 **Caldas da Rainha** Leiria, W Portugal *39°24′N 09°08′W*
**Caldas, Departamento de** *see* Caldas
104 G3 **Caldas de Reis** *var.* Caldas de Reyes. Galicia, NW Spain *42°36′N 08°39′W*
**Caldas de Reyes** *see* Caldas de Reis
58 F13 **Caldeirão** Amazonas, NW Brazil *03°18′S 60°22′W*
62 G7 **Caldera** Atacama, N Chile *27°05′S 70°48′W*
42 L14 **Caldera** Puntarenas, W Costa Rica *09°55′N 84°51′W*
105 N10 **Calderina** ▲ C Spain *39°18′N 03°49′W*
137 T13 **Çaldıran** Van, E Turkey *39°10′N 43°52′E*
32 M14 **Caldwell** Idaho, NW USA *43°39′N 116°41′W*
27 N8 **Caldwell** Kansas, C USA *37°01′N 97°36′W*
14 G15 **Caledon** Ontario, S Canada *43°51′N 79°58′W*
83 I23 **Caledon** *var.* Mohokare. 〰 Lesotho/South Africa
42 G1 **Caledonia** Corozal, N Belize *18°14′N 88°29′W*
14 G16 **Caledonia** Ontario, S Canada *43°04′N 79°57′W*
29 X11 **Caledonia** Minnesota, N USA *43°37′N 91°30′W*
105 X5 **Calella** *var.* Calella de la Costa. Cataluña, NE Spain *41°37′N 02°40′E*
**Calella de la Costa** *see* Calella
23 P4 **Calera** Alabama, S USA *33°06′N 86°45′W*
63 I19 **Caleta Olivia** Santa Cruz, SE Argentina *46°21′S 67°37′W*
35 X17 **Calexico** California, W USA *32°39′N 115°28′W*
97 H16 **Calf of Man** *island* SW Isle of Man
11 Q16 **Calgary** Alberta, SW Canada *51°05′N 114°05′W*
11 Q16 **Calgary** ✈ Alberta, SW Canada *51°15′N 114°03′W*
37 U5 **Calhan** Colorado, C USA *39°00′N 104°18′W*
64 O5 **Calheta** Madeira, Portugal, NE Atlantic Ocean *32°42′N 17°12′W*
23 R2 **Calhoun** Georgia, SE USA *34°30′N 84°57′W*
20 I6 **Calhoun** Kentucky, S USA *37°32′N 87°15′W*
22 M3 **Calhoun City** Mississippi, S USA *33°51′N 89°18′W*
21 P12 **Calhoun Falls** South Carolina, SE USA *34°05′N 82°36′W*
54 D11 **Cali** Valle del Cauca, W Colombia *03°24′N 76°30′W*
27 V9 **Calico Rock** Arkansas, C USA *36°07′N 92°08′W*
**calicut** *see* Kozhikode
35 Y9 **Caliente** Nevada, W USA *37°37′N 114°30′W*
27 U5 **California** Missouri, C USA *38°39′N 92°35′W*
18 B15 **California** Pennsylvania, NE USA *40°02′N 79°52′W*
35 Q12 **California** *off.* State of California, ***also known as*** El Dorado, The Golden State. ◈ *state* W USA
35 P11 **California Aqueduct** *aqueduct* California, W USA
35 T13 **California City** California, W USA *35°06′N 117°55′W*
40 F6 **California, Golfo de** *Eng.* Gulf of California; *prev.* Sea of Cortez. *gulf* W Mexico
**California, Gulf of** *see* California, Golfo de
137 Y13 **Cälilabad** *Rus.* Dzhalilabad; *prev.* Astrakhan-Bazar. S Azerbaijan *39°15′N 48°30′E*
116 I12 **Călimăneşti** Vâlcea, SW Romania *45°14′N 24°20′E*
116 J9 **Călimani, Munţii** ▲▲ N Romania
**Calinisc** *see* Cupcina
35 X17 **Calipatria** California, W USA *33°07′N 115°30′W*
**Calisia** *see* Kalisz
34 M7 **Calistoga** California, W USA *38°34′N 122°37′W*
83 G25 **Calitzdorp** Western Cape, SW South Africa *33°32′S 21°41′E*
41 W12 **Calkiní** Campeche, E Mexico *20°21′N 90°03′W*
182 K4 **Callabonna Creek** *var.* Tilcha Creek. *seasonal river* New South Wales/South Australia
182 J4 **Callabonna, Lake** ◎ South Australia
102 G5 **Callac** Côtes d'Armor, NW France *48°28′N 03°22′W*
35 U5 **Callaghan, Mount** ▲ Nevada, W USA *39°38′N 116°57′W*
**Callain** *see* Callan
97 E19 **Callan** *Ir.* Callain. S Ireland *52°33′N 07°23′W*
14 H11 **Callander** Ontario, S Canada *46°14′N 79°21′W*
96 I11 **Callander** C Scotland, United Kingdom *56°15′N 04°16′W*
98 H7 **Callantsoog** Noord-Holland, NW Netherlands *52°51′N 04°41′E*
57 D14 **Callao** Callao, W Peru *12°03′S 77°10′W*
57 D15 **Callao** *off.* Región del Callao. ◈ *region* W Peru
**Callao, Región del** *see* Callao
56 F11 **Callaria, Río** 〰 E Peru
**Callatis** *see* Mangalia
11 Q13 **Calling Lake** Alberta, W Canada *55°12′N 113°07′W*
**Callosa de Ensarriá** *see* Callosa d'En Sarrià
105 T11 **Callosa d'En Sarrià** *var.* Callosa de Ensarriá. Comunitat Valenciana, E Spain *38°40′N 00°08′W*
105 S12 **Callosa de Segura** Comunitat Valenciana, E Spain *38°07′N 00°53′W*
29 X11 **Calmar** Iowa, C USA *43°10′N 91°51′W*
**Calmar** *see* Kalmar
43 R16 **Calobre** Veraguas, C Panama *08°18′N 80°49′W*
23 X14 **Caloosahatchee River** 〰 Florida, SE USA
183 V2 **Caloundra** Queensland, E Australia *26°48′S 153°08′E*
**Calp** *see* Calpe
105 T11 **Calpe** *Cat.* Calp. Comunitat Valenciana, E Spain *38°39′N 00°03′E*
41 P14 **Calpulalpan** Tlaxcala, S Mexico *19°36′N 98°26′W*
107 K25 **Caltagirone** Sicilia, Italy, C Mediterranean Sea *37°14′N 14°31′E*
107 J24 **Caltanissetta** Sicilia, Italy, C Mediterranean Sea *37°30′N 14°01′E*
82 E11 **Caluango** Lunda Norte, NE Angola *08°16′S 19°36′E*
82 C12 **Calucinga** Bié, W Angola *11°18′S 16°12′E*
82 B12 **Calulo** Kwanza Sul, NW Angola *09°58′S 14°56′E*
83 B14 **Caluquembe** Huíla, W Angola *13°47′S 14°40′E*
80 Q11 **Caluula** Bari, NE Somalia *11°55′N 50°51′E*
102 K4 **Calvados** ◈ *department* N France
186 I10 **Calvados Chain, The** *island group* SE Papua New Guinea
25 U9 **Calvert** Texas, SW USA *30°58′N 96°40′W*
20 H7 **Calvert City** Kentucky, S USA *37°01′N 88°21′W*
103 X14 **Calvi** Corse, France, C Mediterranean Sea *42°34′N 08°44′E*
40 L12 **Calvillo** Aguascalientes, C Mexico *21°51′N 102°18′W*
83 F24 **Calvinia** Northern Cape, W South Africa *31°25′S 19°47′E*
104 K8 **Calvitero** ▲ W Spain *40°16′N 05°48′W*
101 G22 **Calw** Baden-Württemberg, SW Germany *48°43′N 08°43′E*
**Calydon** *see* Kalydón
105 N11 **Calzada de Calatrava** Castilla-La Mancha, C Spain *38°42′N 03°46′W*
**Cama** *see* Kama
82 C11 **Camabatela** Kwanza Norte, NW Angola *08°13′S 15°23′E*
64 Q5 **Camacha** Porto Santo, Madeira, Portugal, NE Atlantic Ocean *32°41′N 16°52′W*
14 L8 **Camachigama, Lac** ◎ Québec, SE Canada
40 M9 **Camacho** Zacatecas, C Mexico *24°23′N 102°20′W*
82 D13 **Camacupa** *var.* General Machado, *Port.* Vila General Machado. Bié, C Angola *12°S 17°31′E*
54 L7 **Camaguán** Guárico, C Venezuela *08°09′N 67°37′W*
44 G6 **Camagüey** *prev.* Puerto Príncipe. Camagüey, C Cuba *21°24′N 77°55′W*
44 G6 **Camagüey** ◈ *province* Cuba
44 G5 **Camagüey, Archipiélago de** *island group* C Cuba
40 D5 **Camalli, Sierra de** ▲ NW Mexico *28°21′N 113°26′W*
57 G18 **Camana** *var.* Camaná. Arequipa, SW Peru *16°37′S 72°42′W*
29 Z14 **Camanche** Iowa, C USA *41°47′N 90°15′W*
35 P8 **Camanche Reservoir** ⊠ California, W USA
61 I16 **Camaquã** Rio Grande do Sul, S Brazil *30°50′S 51°47′W*
61 H16 **Camaquã, Rio** 〰 S Brazil
64 P6 **Câmara de Lobos** Madeira, Portugal, NE Atlantic Ocean *32°38′N 16°59′W*
103 U16 **Camarat, Cap** *headland* SE France *43°12′N 06°42′E*
41 O8 **Camargo** Tamaulipas, C Mexico *26°16′N 98°49′W*
103 R15 **Camargue** *physical region* SE France
104 F2 **Camariñas** Galicia, NW Spain *43°07′N 09°10′W*
**Camaronero, Laguna del** *see* Caimanero, Laguna del
63 J18 **Camarones** Chubut, S Argentina *44°48′S 65°42′W*
63 J18 **Camarones, Bahía** *bay* S Argentina
104 J14 **Camas** Andalucía, S Spain *37°24′N 06°01′W*
167 S15 **Ca Mau** *var.* Quan Long. Minh Hai, S Vietnam *09°11′N 105°09′E*
82 E11 **Camaxilo** Lunda Norte, NE Angola *08°19′S 18°53′E*
104 G3 **Cambados** Galicia, NW Spain *42°31′N 08°49′W*
**Cambay, Gulf of** *see* Khambhāt, Gulf of
**Camberia** *see* Chambéry
97 N22 **Camberley** SE England, United Kingdom *51°21′N 00°45′W*
167 R12 **Cambodia** *off.* Kingdom of Cambodia, *var.* Democratic Kampuchea, Roat Kampuchea, *Cam.* Kampuchea, *Khm.* Kâmpŭchéa, Preăhréachéanachâkr Kâmpŭchéa; *prev.* People's Democratic Republic of Kampuchea. ◆ *republic* SE Asia
**Cambodia, Kingdom of** *see* Cambodia
102 I16 **Cambo-les-Bains** Pyrénées-Atlantiques, SW France *43°22′N 01°24′W*
103 P2 **Cambrai** *Flem.* Kambryk, *prev.* Cambray; *anc.* Cameracum. Nord, N France *50°10′N 03°14′E*
**Cambray** *see* Cambrai
104 H2 **Cambre** Galicia, NW Spain *43°18′N 08°21′W*
35 O12 **Cambria** California, W USA *35°33′N 121°04′W*
97 J20 **Cambrian Mountains** ▲▲ C Wales, United Kingdom
14 G16 **Cambridge** Ontario, S Canada *43°22′N 80°20′W*
44 I12 **Cambridge** W Jamaica *18°18′N 77°54′W*
184 M8 **Cambridge** Waikato, North Island, New Zealand *37°53′S 175°28′E*
97 O20 **Cambridge** *Lat.* Cantabrigia. E England, United Kingdom *52°12′N 00°07′E*
32 M12 **Cambridge** Idaho, NW USA *44°34′N 116°42′W*
30 K11 **Cambridge** Illinois, N USA *41°18′N 90°11′W*
21 Y4 **Cambridge** Maryland, NE USA *38°34′N 76°04′W*
19 O11 **Cambridge** Massachusetts, NE USA *42°21′N 71°05′W*
29 V7 **Cambridge** Minnesota, N USA *45°34′N 93°13′W*
29 N16 **Cambridge** Nebraska, C USA *40°18′N 100°10′W*
31 U13 **Cambridge** Ohio, NE USA *40°00′N 81°34′W*
8 L7 **Cambridge Bay** *var.* Ikaluktutiak. Victoria Island, Nunavut, NW Canada *68°56′N 105°09′W*
97 O20 **Cambridgeshire** *cultural region* E England, United Kingdom
105 U6 **Cambrils** *prev.* Cambrils de Mar. Cataluña, NE Spain *41°06′N 01°02′E*
**Cambrils de Mar** *see* Cambrils
**Cambundi-Catembo** *see* Nova Gaia
137 N11 **Çam Burnu** *headland* N Turkey *41°07′N 37°48′E*
183 S9 **Camden** New South Wales, SE Australia *34°04′S 150°40′E*
23 O6 **Camden** Alabama, S USA *31°59′N 87°17′W*
27 U14 **Camden** Arkansas, C USA *33°32′N 92°49′W*
21 Y3 **Camden** Delaware, NE USA *39°06′N 75°30′W*
19 R7 **Camden** Maine, NE USA *44°12′N 69°04′W*
18 I16 **Camden** New Jersey, NE USA *39°55′N 75°07′W*
18 I9 **Camden** New York, NE USA *43°21′N 75°45′W*
21 R12 **Camden** South Carolina, SE USA *34°16′N 80°36′W*
20 H8 **Camden** Tennessee, S USA *36°03′N 88°07′W*
25 X9 **Camden** Texas, SW USA *30°55′N 94°43′W*
39 S5 **Camden Bay** *bay* S Beaufort Sea
27 U6 **Camdenton** Missouri, C USA *38°01′N 92°44′W*
**Camellia State** *see* Alabama
18 M7 **Camels Hump** ▲ Vermont, NE USA *44°18′N 72°50′W*
117 N8 **Camenca** *Rus.* Kamenka. N Moldova *48°01′N 28°43′E*
**Cameracum** *see* Cambrai
22 G9 **Cameron** Louisiana, S USA *29°48′N 93°19′W*
25 T9 **Cameron** Texas, SW USA *30°51′N 96°58′W*
30 J5 **Cameron** Wisconsin, N USA *45°25′N 91°42′W*
10 M12 **Cameron** 〰 British Columbia, W Canada
185 A24 **Cameron Mountains** ▲▲ South Island, New Zealand
79 D15 **Cameroon** *off.* Republic of Cameroon, *Fr.* Cameroun, République du Cameroun. ◆ *republic* W Africa
79 D15 **Cameroon Mountain** ▲ SW Cameroon *04°12′N 09°00′E*
**Cameroon, Republic of** *see* Cameroon
**Cameroon Ridge** *see* Camerounaise, Dorsale
**Cameroun** *see* Cameroon
79 E14 **Camerounaise, Dorsale** *Eng.* Cameroon Ridge. *ridge* NW Cameroon
**Cameroun, République du** *see* Cameroon
136 B15 **Çamiçi Gölü** ◎ SW Turkey
171 N3 **Camiling** Luzon, N Philippines *15°41′N 120°22′E*
23 T7 **Camilla** Georgia, SE USA *31°13′N 84°12′W*
104 G5 **Caminha** Viana do Castelo, N Portugal *41°52′N 08°50′W*
35 P7 **Camino** California, W USA *38°43′N 120°39′W*
107 J24 **Cammarata** Sicilia, Italy, C Mediterranean Sea *37°36′N 13°39′E*
42 K10 **Camoapa** Boaco, S Nicaragua *12°25′N 85°30′W*
58 O13 **Camocim** Ceará, E Brazil *02°55′S 40°50′W*
106 D10 **Camogli** Liguria, NW Italy *44°21′N 09°10′E*
181 S5 **Camooweal** Queensland, C Australia *19°57′S 138°14′E*
55 Y11 **Camopi** E French Guiana *03°12′N 52°19′W*
151 Q22 **Camorta** *island* Nicobar Islands, India, NE Indian Ocean
42 I6 **Campamento** Olancho, C Honduras *14°36′N 86°38′W*
61 D19 **Campana** Buenos Aires, E Argentina *34°10′S 58°57′W*
63 F21 **Campana, Isla** *island* S Chile
104 K11 **Campanario** Extremadura, W Spain *38°52′N 05°36′W*
107 L17 **Campania** *Eng.* Champagne. ◈ *region* S Italy
27 Y8 **Campbell** Missouri, C USA *36°29′N 90°04′W*
185 K15 **Campbell, Cape** *headland* South Island, New Zealand *41°44′S 174°16′E*
14 J14 **Campbellford** Ontario, SE Canada *44°18′N 77°48′W*
31 R13 **Campbell Hill** *hill* Ohio, N USA
192 K13 **Campbell Island / Motu Ihupuku** *var.* Motu Ihupuku. *island* S New Zealand
175 P13 **Campbell Plateau** *undersea feature* SW Pacific Ocean *51°00′S 170°00′E*
10 K17 **Campbell River** Vancouver Island, British Columbia, SW Canada *49°59′N 125°18′W*
20 L6 **Campbellsville** Kentucky, S USA *37°20′N 85°21′W*
13 O13 **Campbellton** New Brunswick, SE Canada *48°00′N 66°41′W*
183 S9 **Campbelltown** New South Wales, SE Australia *34°04′S 150°46′E*
183 P16 **Campbell Town** Tasmania, SE Australia *41°57′S 147°30′E*
96 G13 **Campbeltown** W Scotland, United Kingdom *55°26′N 05°38′W*
41 W13 **Campeche** Campeche, SE Mexico *19°47′N 90°29′W*
41 W14 **Campeche** ◈ *state* SE Mexico
41 T14 **Campeche, Bahía de** *Eng.* Bay of Campeche. *bay* E Mexico
**Campeche, Banco de** *see* Campeche Bank
64 C11 **Campeche Bank** *Sp.* Banco de Campeche, Sonda de Campeche. *undersea feature* S Gulf of Mexico *22°00′N 90°00′W*
**Campeche, Bay of** *see* Campeche, Bahía de
**Campeche, Sonda de** *see* Campeche Bank
44 H7 **Campechuela** Granma, E Cuba *20°15′N 77°17′W*
182 M13 **Camperdown** Victoria, SE Australia *38°16′S 143°10′E*
167 U6 **Câm Pha** Quang Ninh, N Vietnam *21°04′N 107°20′E*
116 H10 **Câmpia Turzii** *Ger.* Jerischmarkt, *Hung.* Aranyosgyéres; *prev.* Cîmpia Turzii, Ghiriş, Gyéres. Cluj, NW Romania *46°33′N 23°53′E*
104 K12 **Campillo de Llerena** Extremadura, W Spain *38°30′N 05°48′W*
104 L15 **Campillos** Andalucía, S Spain *37°04′N 04°51′W*
116 J13 **Câmpina** *prev.* Cîmpina. Prahova, SE Romania *45°08′N 25°44′E*
59 Q15 **Campina Grande** Paraíba, E Brazil *07°15′S 35°50′W*
60 L9 **Campinas** São Paulo, S Brazil *22°54′S 47°06′W*
38 L10 **Camp Kulowiye** Saint Lawrence Island, Alaska, USA *63°15′N 168°45′W*
79 D17 **Campo** *var.* Kampo. Sud, SW Cameroon *02°22′N 09°50′E*
**Campo** *see* Ntem
59 N15 **Campo Alegre de Lourdes** Bahia, E Brazil *09°28′S 43°01′W*
107 L16 **Campobasso** Molise, C Italy *41°34′N 14°40′E*
107 H24 **Campobello di Mazara** Sicilia, Italy, C Mediterranean Sea *37°38′N 12°45′E*
**Campo Criptana** *see* Campo de Criptana
105 O10 **Campo de Criptana** *var.* Campo Criptana. Castilla-La Mancha, C Spain *39°25′N 03°07′W*
59 I16 **Campo de Diauarum** *var.* Pôsto Diuarum. Mato Grosso, W Brazil *11°08′S 53°16′W*
54 E5 **Campo de la Cruz** Atlántico, N Colombia *10°23′N 74°52′W*
105 P11 **Campo de Montiel** *physical region* C Spain
60 H12 **Campo Erê** Santa Catarina, S Brazil *26°24′S 53°04′W*
62 L7 **Campo Gallo** Santiago del Estero, N Argentina *26°32′S 62°51′W*
59 I20 **Campo Grande** *state capital* Mato Grosso do Sul, SW Brazil *20°24′S 54°35′W*
60 K12 **Campo Largo** Paraná, S Brazil *25°27′S 49°29′W*
58 N13 **Campo Maior** Piauí, E Brazil *04°50′S 42°12′W*
104 I10 **Campo Maior** Portalegre, C Portugal *39°01′N 07°04′W*
60 H10 **Campo Mourão** Paraná, S Brazil *24°01′S 52°24′W*
59 L17 **Campos Belos** Goiás, S Brazil *13°11′S 46°47′W*
60 N9 **Campos do Jordão** São Paulo, S Brazil *22°45′S 45°36′W*




◆ Country
● Country Capital
◇ Dependent Territory
○ Dependent Territory Capital
◈ Administrative Regions
✈ International Airport
▲ Mountain
▲▲ Mountain Range
⋀ Volcano
〰 River
◎ Lake
⊠ Reservoir

CAMPOS DOS GOYTACAZES – CARROLL


60 Q9 **Campos dos Goytacazes** Rio de Janeiro, SE Brazil 21°46′S 41°21′W
60 I13 **Campos Novos** Santa Catarina, S Brazil 27°22′S 51°11′W
59 O14 **Campos Sales** Ceará, E Brazil 07°01′S 40°21′W
25 Q9 **Camp San Saba** Texas, SW USA 30°57′N 99°16′W
21 N6 **Campton** Kentucky, S USA 37°44′N 83°35′W
116 I13 **Câmpulung** *prev.* Câmpulung-Muşcel, Cîmpulung. Argeş, S Romania 45°16′N 25°03′E
116 J9 **Câmpulung Moldovenesc** *var.* Cîmpulung Moldovenesc, *Ger.* Kimpolung, *Hung.* Hosszúmezjő. Suceava, NE Romania 47°32′N 25°34′E
**Câmpulung-Muşcel** *see* Câmpulung
**Campus Stellae** *see* Santiago de Compostela
36 L12 **Camp Verde** Arizona, SW USA 34°33′N 111°52′W
25 P11 **Camp Wood** Texas, SW USA 29°40′N 100°00′W
167 V13 **Cam Ranh** *prev.* Ba Ngoi. Khanh Hoa, S Vietnam 11°54′N 109°14′E
11 Q15 **Camrose** Alberta, SW Canada 53°01′N 112°48′W
**Camulodunum** *see* Colchester
136 B12 **Çan** Çanakkale, NW Turkey 40°03′N 27°03′E
18 L12 **Canaan** Connecticut, NE USA 42°00′N 73°17′W
11 O13 **Canada** ◆ *commonwealth republic* N North America
197 P6 **Canada Basin** *undersea feature* Arctic Ocean 80°00′N 145°00′W
61 B18 **Cañada de Gómez** Santa Fe, C Argentina 32°50′S 61°23′W
197 P6 **Canada Plain** *undersea feature* Arctic Ocean
61 A18 **Cañada Rosquín** Santa Fe, C Argentina 32°04′S 61°35′W
25 P1 **Canadian** Texas, SW USA 35°54′N 100°23′W
16 K12 **Canadian River** ≈ SW USA
8 L12 **Canadian Shield** *physical region* Canada
63 I18 **Cañadón Grande, Sierra** ▲▲ S Argentina
55 P9 **Canaima** Bolívar, SE Venezuela 09°41′N 72°33′W
136 B11 **Çanakkale** *var.* Dardanelli; *prev.* Chanak, Kale Sultanie. Çanakkale, W Turkey 40°09′N 26°25′E
136 B12 **Çanakkale** ◈ *province* NW Turkey
136 B11 **Çanakkale Boğazı** *Eng.* Dardanelles. *strait* NW Turkey
187 Q17 **Canala** Province Nord, C New Caledonia 21°31′S 165°57′E
59 A15 **Canamari** Amazonas, W Brazil 07°37′S 72°33′W
18 G10 **Canandaigua** New York, NE USA 42°52′N 77°14′W
18 F10 **Canandaigua Lake** ◎ New York, NE USA
40 G3 **Cananea** Sonora, NW Mexico 30°59′N 110°20′W
56 B8 **Cañar** ◈ *province* C Ecuador
64 N10 **Canarias, Islas** *Eng.* Canary Islands. ◈ *autonomous community* Spain, NE Atlantic Ocean
**Canaries Basin** *see* Canary Basin
44 C6 **Canarreos, Archipiélago de los** *island group* W Cuba
**Canary Islands** *see* Canarias, Islas
66 K3 **Canary Basin** *var.* Canaries Basin, Monaco Basin. *undersea feature* E Atlantic Ocean 30°00′N 25°00′W
42 L13 **Cañas** Guanacaste, NW Costa Rica 10°25′N 85°07′W
18 I10 **Canastota** New York, NE USA 43°04′N 75°45′W
40 K9 **Canatlán** Durango, C Mexico 24°33′N 104°45′W
104 J9 **Cañaveral** Extremadura, W Spain 39°47′N 06°24′W
23 Y11 **Canaveral, Cape** *headland* Florida, SE USA 28°27′N 80°31′W
59 O18 **Canavieiras** Bahia, E Brazil 15°44′S 38°58′W
43 R16 **Cañazas** Veraguas, W Panama 08°25′N 81°10′W
106 H6 **Canazei** Trentino-Alto Adige, N Italy 46°29′N 11°50′E
183 P6 **Canbelego** New South Wales, SE Australia 31°36′S 146°20′E
183 R10 **Canberra** ● (Australia) Australian Capital Territory, SE Australia 35°21′S 149°08′E
183 R10 **Canberra** ✈ Australian Capital Territory, SE Australia 35°19′S 149°12′E
35 P2 **Canby** California, W USA 41°27′N 120°51′W
29 S9 **Canby** Minnesota, N USA 44°42′N 96°17′W
103 N2 **Canche** ≈ N France
102 L13 **Cancon** Lot-et-Garonne, SW France 44°33′N 00°37′E
41 Z11 **Cancún** Quintana Roo, SE Mexico 21°05′N 86°48′W
104 K2 **Candás** Asturias, N Spain 43°35′N 05°45′W
102 J7 **Cande** Maine-et-Loire, NW France 47°33′N 01°03′W
41 W14 **Candelaria** Campeche, SE Mexico 18°10′N 91°00′W
24 J11 **Candelaria** Texas, SW USA 30°05′N 104°40′W
41 W15 **Candelaria, Río** ≈ Guatemala/Mexico
104 L8 **Candeleda** Castilla y León, N Spain 40°10′N 05°14′W
**Candia** *see* Irákleio
41 P8 **Cándido Aguilar** Tamaulipas, C Mexico 25°30′N 97°57′W
39 N8 **Candle** Alaska, USA 65°54′N 161°55′W
11 T14 **Candle Lake** Saskatchewan, C Canada 53°43′N 105°09′W
18 L13 **Candlewood, Lake** ⊠ Connecticut, NE USA
29 O3 **Cando** North Dakota, N USA 48°29′N 99°12′W
**Canea** *see* Chaniá
45 O12 **Canefield** ✈ (Roseau) SW Dominica 15°20′N 61°24′W
61 F20 **Canelones** *prev.* Guadalupe. Canelones, S Uruguay 34°32′S 56°17′W
61 E20 **Canelones** ◈ *department* S Uruguay
**Canendiyú** *see* Canindeyú
63 F14 **Cañete** Bío Bío, C Chile 37°48′S 73°25′W
105 Q9 **Cañete** Castilla-La Mancha, C Spain 40°03′N 01°39′W
**Cañete** *see* San Vicente de Cañete
27 P8 **Caney** Kansas, C USA 37°00′N 95°56′W
27 P8 **Caney River** ≈ Kansas/Oklahoma, C USA
105 S3 **Canfranc-Estación** Aragón, NE Spain 42°42′N 00°31′W
83 E14 **Cangamba** *Port.* Vila de Aljustrel. Moxico, E Angola 13°40′S 19°47′E
82 C12 **Cangandala** Malanje, NW Angola 09°47′S 16°27′E
104 G4 **Cangas** Galicia, NW Spain 42°16′N 08°46′W
104 J2 **Cangas del Narcea** Asturias, N Spain 43°10′N 06°32′W
**Cangas de Onís** *see* Cangues d'Onís
161 S11 **Cangnan** *var.* Lingxi. Zhejiang, SE China 27°29′N 120°23′E
82 C10 **Cangola** Uíge, NW Angola 07°54′S 15°57′E
83 E14 **Cangombe** Moxico, E Angola 14°27′S 20°05′E
63 H21 **Cangrejo, Cerro** ▲ S Argentina 49°19′S 72°18′W
61 H17 **Canguçu** Rio Grande do Sul, S Brazil 31°25′S 52°37′W
104 L2 **Cangues d'Onís** *var.* Cangas de Onís. Asturias, N Spain 43°21′N 05°08′W
161 P3 **Cangzhou** Hebei, E China 38°19′N 116°54′E
12 M7 **Caniapiscau** ≈ Québec, E Canada
12 M8 **Caniapiscau, Réservoir de** ⊠ Québec, C Canada
107 J24 **Canicattì** Sicilia, Italy, C Mediterranean Sea 37°22′N 13°51′E
136 L11 **Canik Dağları** ▲▲ N Turkey
105 P14 **Caniles** Andalucía, S Spain 37°24′N 02°41′W
59 B16 **Canindé** Acre, W Brazil 10°55′S 69°45′W
62 P6 **Canindeyú** *var.* Canendiyú, Canindiyú. ◈ *department* E Paraguay
**Canindiyú** *see* Canindeyú
194 J10 **Canisteo Peninsula** *peninsula* Antarctica
18 F11 **Canisteo River** ≈ New York, NE USA
40 M10 **Cañitas** *var.* Cañitas de Felipe Pescador. Zacatecas, C Mexico 23°35′N 102°39′W
**Cañitas de Felipe Pescador** *see* Cañitas
105 P15 **Canjáyar** Andalucía, S Spain 37°00′N 02°45′W
136 I12 **Çankırı** *var.* Chankiri; *anc.* Gangra, Germanicopolis. Çankın, N Turkey 40°36′N 33°35′E
136 I11 **Çankırı** *var.* Chankiri. ◈ *province* N Turkey
171 P6 **Canlaon Volcano** ⛰ Negros, C Philippines 10°24′N 123°05′E
11 P16 **Canmore** Alberta, SW Canada 51°07′N 115°18′W
96 F9 **Canna** *island* NW Scotland, United Kingdom
**Cannanore** *see* Kannur
31 O17 **Cannelton** Indiana, N USA 37°54′N 86°44′W
103 U15 **Cannes** Alpes-Maritimes, SE France 43°33′N 06°59′E
39 R5 **Canning River** ≈ Alaska, USA
106 C6 **Cannobio** Piemonte, NE Italy 46°04′N 08°39′E
97 L19 **Cannock** C England, United Kingdom 52°41′N 02°03′W
28 M6 **Cannonball River** ≈ North Dakota, N USA
29 W9 **Cannon Falls** Minnesota, N USA 44°30′N 92°54′W
18 I11 **Cannonsville Reservoir** ⊠ New York, NE USA
183 R12 **Cann River** Victoria, SE Australia 37°34′S 149°11′E
61 I16 **Canoas** Rio Grande do Sul, S Brazil 29°42′S 51°07′W
61 I14 **Canoas, Rio** ≈ S Brazil
14 I12 **Canoe Lake** ◎ Ontario, SE Canada
60 J12 **Canoinhas** Santa Catarina, S Brazil 26°12′S 50°24′W
37 T6 **Canon City** Colorado, C USA 38°25′N 105°14′W
55 P8 **Caño Negro** Bolívar, SE Venezuela
173 X15 **Canonniers Point** *headland* N Mauritius
23 W6 **Canoochee River** ≈ Georgia, SE USA
11 V15 **Canora** Saskatchewan, S Canada 51°38′N 102°28′W
45 Y14 **Canouan** *island* S Saint Vincent and the Grenadines
13 R15 **Canso** Nova Scotia, SE Canada 45°20′N 61°00′W
104 M3 **Cantabria** ◈ *autonomous community* N Spain
104 K3 **Cantábrica, Cordillera** ▲▲ N Spain
**Cantabrigia** *see* Cambridge
103 O12 **Cantal** ◈ *department* C France
105 N6 **Cantalejo** Castilla y León, N Spain 41°15′N 03°57′W
103 O12 **Cantal, Monts du** ▲▲ C France
104 G8 **Cantanhede** Coimbra, C Portugal 40°21′N 08°37′W
**Cantaño** *see* Cataño
55 O6 **Cantaura** Anzoátegui, NE Venezuela 09°22′N 64°24′W
116 M11 **Cantemir** *Rus.* Kantemir. S Moldova 46°17′N 28°12′E
97 Q22 **Canterbury** *hist.* Cantwaraburh; *anc.* Durovernum, *Lat.* Cantuaria. SE England, United Kingdom 51°17′N 01°05′E
185 F19 **Canterbury** *off.* Canterbury Region. ◈ *region* South Island, New Zealand
185 H20 **Canterbury Bight** *bight* South Island, New Zealand
185 H19 **Canterbury Plains** *plain* South Island, New Zealand
**Canterbury Region** *see* Canterbury
167 S14 **Cần Thơ** Cần Thơ, S Vietnam 10°03′N 105°46′E
104 K13 **Cantillana** Andalucía, S Spain 37°34′N 05°48′W
59 N15 **Canto do Buriti** Piauí, NE Brazil 08°07′S 43°00′W
23 S2 **Canton** Georgia, SE USA 34°14′N 84°29′W
30 K12 **Canton** Illinois, N USA 40°33′N 90°02′W
22 L5 **Canton** Mississippi, S USA 32°36′N 90°02′W
27 V2 **Canton** Missouri, C USA 40°07′N 91°31′W
18 J7 **Canton** New York, NE USA 44°36′N 75°10′W
21 O10 **Canton** North Carolina, SE USA 35°31′N 82°50′W
31 U12 **Canton** Ohio, N USA 40°48′N 81°23′W
26 L9 **Canton** Oklahoma, C USA 36°03′N 98°35′W
18 G12 **Canton** Pennsylvania, NE USA 41°38′N 76°49′W
29 R11 **Canton** South Dakota, N USA 43°19′N 96°33′W
25 V7 **Canton** Texas, SW USA 32°33′N 95°51′W
**Canton** *see* Guangzhou
**Canton Island** *see* Kanton
26 L9 **Canton Lake** ⊠ Oklahoma, C USA
106 D7 **Cantù** Lombardia, N Italy 45°44′N 09°98′E
**Cantuaria/Cantwaraburh** *see* Canterbury
39 R10 **Cantwell** Alaska, USA 63°23′N 148°57′W
59 O16 **Canudos** Bahia, E Brazil 09°51′S 39°08′W
47 T7 **Canumã, Rio** ≈ N Brazil
**Canusium** *see* Puglia, Canosa di
24 G7 **Canutillo** Texas, SW USA 31°53′N 106°34′W
25 N3 **Canyon** Texas, SW USA 34°58′N 101°56′W
33 S12 **Canyon** Wyoming, C USA 44°44′N 110°30′W
32 K13 **Canyon City** Oregon, NW USA 44°24′N 118°58′W
33 R10 **Canyon Ferry Lake** ◎ Montana, NW USA
25 S11 **Canyon Lake** ⊠ Texas, SW USA
167 T5 **Cao Băng** *var.* Caobang. Cao Băng, N Vietnam 22°40′N 106°16′E
**Caobang** *see* Cao Băng
160 J12 **Caodu He** ≈ S China
**Caohai** *see* Weining
167 S14 **Cao Lanh** Đông Thap, S Vietnam 10°35′N 105°25′E
82 C11 **Caombo** Malanje, NW Angola 08°42′S 16°33′E
**Caorach, Cuan na g** *see* Sheep Haven
**Caozhou** *see* Heze
171 Q12 **Capalulu** Pulau Mangole, E Indonesia 01°51′S 125°53′E
54 K8 **Capanaparo, Río** ≈ Colomiba/Venezuela
58 L12 **Capanema** Pará, NE Brazil 01°08′S 47°07′W
60 L10 **Capão Bonito do Sul** São Paulo, S Brazil 24°01′S 48°23′W
60 I13 **Capão Doce, Morro do** ▲ S Brazil 26°37′S 51°28′W
54 I4 **Capatárida** Falcón, N Venezuela 11°11′N 70°37′W
102 I15 **Capbreton** Landes, SW France 43°40′N 01°25′W
**Cap-Breton, Île du** *see* Cape Breton Island
15 W6 **Cap-Chat** Québec, SE Canada 49°04′N 66°43′W
15 P11 **Cap-de-la-Madeleine** Québec, SE Canada 46°22′N 72°31′W
103 N13 **Capdenac** Aveyron, S France 44°35′N 02°06′E
**Cap des Palmès** *see* Palmas, Cape
183 Q15 **Cape Barren Island** *island* Furneaux Group, Tasmania, SE Australia
65 O18 **Cape Basin** *undersea feature* S Atlantic Ocean 37°00′S 07°00′E
13 R14 **Cape Breton Island** *Fr.* Île du Cap-Breton. *island* Nova Scotia, SE Canada
23 Y11 **Cape Canaveral** Florida, SE USA 28°24′N 80°36′W
21 Y6 **Cape Charles** Virginia, NE USA 37°16′N 76°01′W
77 P17 **Cape Coast** *prev.* Cape Coast Castle, *var.* Oguaa. S Ghana 05°10′N 01°13′W
**Cape Coast Castle** *see* Cape Coast
19 Q12 **Cape Cod Bay** *bay* Massachusetts, NE USA
23 W15 **Cape Coral** Florida, SE USA 26°33′N 81°57′W
181 R4 **Cape Crawford Roadhouse** Northern Territory, N Australia 16°39′S 135°44′E
9 Q7 **Cape Dorset** *var.* Kingait. Baffin Island, Nunavut, NE Canada 76°14′N 76°32′W
21 N8 **Cape Fear River** ≈ North Carolina, SE USA
27 Y7 **Cape Girardeau** Missouri, C USA 37°19′N 89°31′W
21 T14 **Cape Island** *island* South Carolina, SE USA
186 A6 **Capella** ▲ NW Papua New Guinea 05°00′S 141°09′E
98 H12 **Capelle aan den IJssel** Zuid-Holland, SW Netherlands 51°56′N 04°36′E
83 C15 **Capelongo** Huíla, C Angola 14°45′S 15°02′E
18 J17 **Cape May** New Jersey, NE USA 38°54′N 74°54′W
18 J17 **Cape May Court House** New Jersey, NE USA 39°03′N 74°46′W
**Cape Palmas** *see* Harper
8 I16 **Cape Parry** Northwest Territories, N Canada 70°10′N 124°33′W
65 P19 **Cape Rise** *undersea feature* SW Indian Ocean 42°00′S 15°00′E
**Cape Saint Jacques** *see* Vung Tau
**Capesterre** *see* Capesterre-Belle-Eau
45 Y6 **Capesterre-Belle-Eau** *var.* Capesterre. Basse Terre, S Guadeloupe 16°03′N 61°34′W
83 D26 **Cape Town** *var.* Ekapa, *Afr.* Kaapstad, Kapstad. ● (South Africa-legislative capital) Western Cape, SW South Africa 33°56′S 18°28′E
83 E26 **Cape Town** ✈ Western Cape, SW South Africa 31°51′S 21°06′E
76 D9 **Cape Verde** *off.* Republic of Cabo Verde, *Port.* Cabo Verde, Ilhas do Cabo Verde. ◆ *republic* E Atlantic Ocean
64 L11 **Cape Verde Basin** *undersea feature* E Atlantic Ocean 15°00′N 30°00′W
66 K5 **Cape Verde Islands** *island group* E Atlantic Ocean
64 L10 **Cape Verde Plain** *undersea feature* E Atlantic Ocean 23°00′N 26°00′W
**Cape Verde Plateau/Cape Verde Rise** *see* Cape Verde Terrace
64 L11 **Cape Verde Terrace** *var.* Cape Verde Plateau, Cape Verde Rise. *undersea feature* E Atlantic Ocean 18°00′N 20°00′W
181 V2 **Cape York Peninsula** *peninsula* Queensland, N Australia
44 M8 **Cap-Haïtien** *var.* Le Cap. N Haiti 19°44′N 72°12′W
43 T15 **Capira** West Panamá, C Panama 08°48′N 79°51′W
14 K8 **Capitachouane** ≈ Québec, SE Canada
14 L8 **Capitachouane, Lac** ◎ Québec, SE Canada
37 T13 **Capitan** New Mexico, SW USA 33°33′N 105°34′W
194 G3 **Capitán Arturo Prat** *research station (Chile)* South Shetland Islands, Antarctica 62°24′S 59°42′W
37 S13 **Capitan Mountains** ▲▲ New Mexico, SW USA
62 M3 **Capitán Pablo Lagerenza** *var.* Mayor Pablo Lagerenza. Chaco, N Paraguay 19°55′S 60°46′W
37 T13 **Capitan Peak** ▲ New Mexico, SW USA 33°35′N 105°15′W
188 H5 **Capitol Hill** ● (Northern Mariana Islands-legislative capital) Saipan, S Northern Mariana Islands
60 I9 **Capivara, Represa** ⊠ S Brazil
61 J16 **Capivari** Rio Grande do Sul, S Brazil 30°08′S 50°32′W
113 H15 **Čapljina** Federicija Bosna I Hercegovina, S Bosnia and Herzegovina 43°07′N 17°42′E
83 M15 **Capoche** *var.* Kapoche. ≈ Mozambique/Zambia
**Capo Delgado, Província de** *see* Cabo Delgado
107 K17 **Capodichino** ✈ (Napoli) Campania, S Italy 40°53′N 14°15′E
**Capodistria** *see* Koper
106 E12 **Capraia, Isola di** *island* Arcipelago Toscano, C Italy
107 B16 **Caprara, Punta** *var.* Punta dello Scorno. *headland* Isola Asinara, W Italy 41°07′N 08°19′E
**Capraria** *see* Cabrera, Illa de
14 F10 **Capreol** Ontario, S Canada 46°43′N 80°56′W
107 K18 **Capri** Campania, S Italy 40°33′N 14°14′E
175 S9 **Capricorn Tablemount** *undersea feature* W Pacific Ocean 18°34′S 172°12′W
107 J18 **Capri, Isola di** *island* S Italy
**Caprivi Concession** *see* Caprivi Strip
83 F16 **Caprivi Strip** *Ger.* Caprivizipfel; *prev.* Caprivi Concession. *cultural region* NE Namibia
**Caprivizipfel** *see* Caprivi Strip
25 O5 **Cap Rock Escarpment** *cliffs* Texas, SW USA
15 R10 **Cap-Rouge** Québec, SE Canada 46°45′N 71°18′W
**Cap Saint-Jacques** *see* Vung Tau
38 F12 **Captain Cook** Hawaii, USA, C Pacific Ocean 19°30′N 155°55′W
183 R10 **Captains Flat** New South Wales, SE Australia 35°37′S 149°28′E
102 K14 **Captieux** Gironde, SW France 44°16′N 00°15′W
107 K17 **Capua** Campania, S Italy 41°06′N 14°13′E
54 F14 **Caquetá** *off.* Departamanto del Caquetá. ◈ *province* S Colombia
**Caquetá, Departamanto del** *see* Caquetá
54 E13 **Caquetá, Río** *var.* Rio Japurá, Yapurá. ≈ Brazil/Colombia *see also* Japurá, Rio
**Caquetá, Río** *see* Japurá, Rio
**CAR** *see* Central African Republic
**Cara** *see* Kara
57 I16 **Carabaya, Cordillera** ▲▲ E Peru
54 K5 **Carabobo** *off.* Estado Carabobo. ◈ *state* N Venezuela
**Carabobo, Estado** *see* Carabobo
116 I14 **Caracal** Olt, S Romania 44°07′N 24°18′E
58 F10 **Caracaraí** Rondônia, W Brazil 01°47′N 61°11′W
54 L5 **Caracas** ● (Venezuela) Distrito Federal, N Venezuela 10°29′N 66°54′W
54 I5 **Carache** Trujillo, N Venezuela 09°40′N 70°15′W
60 N10 **Caraguatatuba** São Paulo, S Brazil 23°37′S 45°24′W
48 I7 **Carajás, Serra dos** ▲▲ N Brazil
**Caralis** *see* Cagliari
54 E9 **Caramanta** Antioquia, W Colombia 05°36′N 75°38′W
171 P4 **Caramoan** Catanduanes Island, N Philippines 13°47′N 123°49′E
**Caramurat** *see* Mihail Kogălniceanu
116 F12 **Caransebeş** *Ger.* Karansebesch, *Hung.* Karánsebes. Caraş-Severin, SW Romania 45°23′N 22°13′E
**Carapella** *see* Carapelle
107 M16 **Carapelle** *var.* Carapella. ≈ SE Italy
55 O9 **Carapo** Bolívar, SE Venezuela
13 P13 **Caraquet** New Brunswick, SE Canada 47°48′N 64°59′W
**Caras** *see* Caraz
116 F12 **Caraşova** *Hung.* Krassóvár. Caraş-Severin, SW Romania 45°11′N 21°51′E
116 F12 **Caraş-Severin** ◈ *county* SW Romania
42 M5 **Caratasca, Laguna de** *lagoon* NE Honduras
58 C13 **Carauari** Amazonas, NW Brazil 04°55′S 66°57′W
**Caravaca** *see* Caravaca de la Cruz
105 Q12 **Caravaca de la Cruz** *var.* Caravaca. Murcia, SE Spain 38°06′N 01°51′W
106 E7 **Caravaggio** Lombardia, N Italy 45°31′N 09°39′E
107 C18 **Caravai, Passo di** *pass* Sardegna, Italy, C Mediterranean Sea
59 O19 **Caravelas** Bahia, E Brazil 17°45′S 39°15′W
56 C12 **Caraz** *var.* Caras. Ancash, W Peru 09°03′S 77°47′W
61 H14 **Carazinho** Rio Grande do Sul, S Brazil 28°16′S 52°46′W
42 J11 **Carazo** ◈ *department* SW Nicaragua
**Carballiño** *see* O Carballiño
104 G2 **Carballo** Galicia, NW Spain 43°13′N 08°41′W
11 W16 **Carberry** Manitoba, S Canada 49°52′N 99°20′W
40 F4 **Carbó** Sonora, NW Mexico 29°41′N 111°00′W
107 C20 **Carbonara, Capo** *headland* Sardegna, Italy, C Mediterranean Sea 39°06′N 09°31′E
37 Q5 **Carbondale** Colorado, C USA 39°24′N 107°12′W
30 L17 **Carbondale** Illinois, N USA 37°43′N 89°13′W
27 Q4 **Carbondale** Kansas, C USA 38°49′N 95°41′W
18 I13 **Carbondale** Pennsylvania, NE USA 41°34′N 75°30′W
13 V12 **Carbonear** Newfoundland, Newfoundland and Labrador, SE Canada 47°45′N 53°16′W
105 Q9 **Carboneras de Guadazaón** *var.* Carboneras de Guadazón. Castilla-La Mancha, C Spain 39°54′N 01°50′W
**Carboneras de Guadazón** *see* Carboneras de Guadazaón
23 O3 **Carbon Hill** Alabama, S USA 33°53′N 87°31′W
107 B20 **Carbonia** *var.* Carbonia Centro. Sardegna, Italy, C Mediterranean Sea 39°11′N 08°31′E
**Carbonia Centro** *see* Carbonia
63 I22 **Carbon, Laguna del** *depression* S Argentina
105 S10 **Carcaixent** Comunitat Valenciana, E Spain 39°08′N 00°28′W
**Carcaso** *see* Carcassonne
65 B24 **Carcass Island** *island* NW Falkland Islands
103 O16 **Carcassonne** *anc.* Carcaso. Aude, S France 43°13′N 02°21′E
105 R12 **Carche** ▲ S Spain 38°24′N 01°11′W
56 A13 **Carchi** ◈ *province* N Ecuador
10 I8 **Carcross** Yukon, W Canada 60°11′N 134°41′W
**Cardamomes, Chaîne des** *see* Krâvanh, Chuŏr Phnum
155 G22 **Cardamom Hills** ▲▲ SW India
**Cardamom Mountains** *see* Krâvanh, Chuŏr Phnum
104 M12 **Cardeña** Andalucía, S Spain 38°16′N 04°20′W
44 D4 **Cárdenas** Matanzas, W Cuba 23°02′N 81°12′W
41 O11 **Cárdenas** San Luis Potosí, C Mexico 22°03′N 99°30′W
41 U15 **Cárdenas** Tabasco, SE Mexico 18°00′N 93°21′W
63 H21 **Cardiel, Lago** ◎ S Argentina
97 K22 **Cardiff** *Wel.* Caerdydd. ◐ S Wales, United Kingdom 51°30′N 03°13′W
97 J22 **Cardiff-Wales** ✈ S Wales, United Kingdom 51°24′N 03°22′W
97 I21 **Cardigan** *Wel.* Aberteifi. SW Wales, United Kingdom 52°06′N 04°40′W
97 I20 **Cardigan** *cultural region* W Wales, United Kingdom
97 I20 **Cardigan Bay** *bay* W Wales, United Kingdom
19 N8 **Cardigan, Mount** ▲ New Hampshire, NE USA 43°39′N 71°52′W
14 M13 **Cardinal** Ontario, SE Canada 44°48′N 75°22′W
105 V5 **Cardona** Cataluña, NE Spain 41°55′N 01°41′E
61 E19 **Cardona** Soriano, SW Uruguay 33°53′S 57°18′W
105 V4 **Cardoner** ≈ NE Spain
11 Q17 **Cardston** Alberta, SW Canada 49°14′N 113°19′W
181 W5 **Cardwell** Queensland, NE Australia 18°24′S 146°06′E
116 G8 **Carei** *Ger.* Gross-Karol, Karol, *Hung.* Nagykároly; *prev.* Careii-Mari. Satu Mare, NW Romania 47°40′N 22°28′E
**Careii-Mari** *see* Carei
58 F13 **Careiro** Amazonas, NW Brazil 03°40′S 60°23′W
102 J4 **Carentan** Manche, N France 49°18′N 01°15′W
104 M2 **Cares** ≈ N Spain
33 P14 **Carey** Idaho, NW USA 43°17′N 113°58′W
31 S12 **Carey** Ohio, N USA 40°57′N 83°22′W
25 P4 **Carey** Texas, SW USA 34°28′N 100°18′W
180 L11 **Carey, Lake** ◎ Western Australia
173 O8 **Cargados Carajos Bank** *undersea feature* C Indian Ocean
102 G6 **Carhaix-Plouguer** Finistère, NW France 48°16′N 03°35′W
61 A22 **Carhué** Buenos Aires, E Argentina 37°10′S 62°45′W
55 O5 **Cariaco** Sucre, NE Venezuela 10°33′N 63°37′W
107 O20 **Cariati** Calabria, SW Italy 39°30′N 16°57′E
2 H17 **Caribbean Plate** *tectonic feature*
44 I11 **Caribbean Sea** *sea* W Atlantic Ocean
11 N15 **Cariboo Mountains** ▲▲ British Columbia, SW Canada
11 W9 **Caribou** Manitoba, C Canada 59°27′N 97°43′W
19 S2 **Caribou** Maine, NE USA 46°51′N 68°00′W
11 P10 **Caribou Mountains** ▲▲ Alberta, SW Canada
**Caribrod** *see* Dimitrovgrad
40 I6 **Carichic** Chihuahua, N Mexico 27°57′N 107°01′W
103 R3 **Carignan** Ardennes, N France 49°38′N 05°08′E
183 Q5 **Carinda** New South Wales, SE Australia 30°26′S 147°45′E
105 R6 **Cariñena** Aragón, NE Spain 41°20′N 01°13′W
107 I23 **Carini** Sicilia, Italy, C Mediterranean Sea 38°06′N 13°09′E
107 K17 **Carinola** Campania, S Italy 41°14′N 14°03′E
**Carinthi** *see* Kärnten
55 O5 **Caripe** Monagas, NE Venezuela 10°13′N 63°30′W
55 P5 **Caripito** Monagas, NE Venezuela 10°03′N 63°05′W
15 W7 **Carleton** Québec, SE Canada 48°07′N 66°07′W
31 S10 **Carleton** Michigan, N USA 42°03′N 83°23′W
13 O14 **Carleton, Mount** ▲ New Brunswick, SE Canada 47°10′N 66°54′W
14 L13 **Carleton Place** Ontario, SE Canada 45°08′N 76°09′W
35 V3 **Carlin** Nevada, W USA 40°40′N 116°09′W
194 H3 **Carlini** *research station (Argentina)* King George Island, Antarctica 62°14′S 58°40′W
30 K14 **Carlinville** Illinois, N USA 39°16′N 89°52′W
97 K14 **Carlisle** *anc.* Caer Luel, Luguvallium, Luguvallum. NW England, United Kingdom 54°54′N 02°55′W
27 V11 **Carlisle** Arkansas, C USA 34°46′N 91°45′W
31 N15 **Carlisle** Indiana, N USA 38°57′N 87°23′W
29 V14 **Carlisle** Iowa, C USA 41°30′N 93°29′W
21 N5 **Carlisle** Kentucky, S USA 38°19′N 84°02′W
18 F15 **Carlisle** Pennsylvania, NE USA 40°10′N 77°10′W
21 Q11 **Carlisle** South Carolina, SE USA 34°35′N 81°27′W
38 J17 **Carlisle Island** *island* Aleutian Islands, Alaska, USA
27 R7 **Carl Junction** Missouri, C USA 37°10′N 94°34′W
107 A20 **Carloforte** Sardegna, Italy, C Mediterranean Sea 39°10′N 08°17′E
**Carlopago** *see* Karlobag
61 B21 **Carlos Casares** Buenos Aires, E Argentina 35°39′S 61°28′W
61 E18 **Carlos Reyles** Durazno, C Uruguay 33°00′S 56°30′W
61 A21 **Carlos Tejedor** Buenos Aires, E Argentina 35°25′S 62°25′W
97 F19 **Carlow** *Ir.* Ceatharlach. SE Ireland 52°50′N 06°55′W
97 F19 **Carlow** *Ir.* Cheatharlach. *cultural region* SE Ireland
96 F7 **Carloway** NW Scotland, United Kingdom 58°17′N 06°48′W
35 U17 **Carlsbad** California, W USA 33°09′N 117°21′W
37 U15 **Carlsbad** New Mexico, SW USA 32°24′N 104°15′W
**Carlsbad** *see* Karlovy Vary
129 N13 **Carlsberg Ridge** *undersea feature* S Arabian Sea 06°00′N 61°00′E
**Carlsruhe** *see* Karlsruhe
29 W6 **Carlton** Minnesota, N USA 46°39′N 92°25′W
11 V17 **Carlyle** Saskatchewan, S Canada 49°39′N 102°18′W
30 L15 **Carlyle** Illinois, N USA 38°36′N 89°22′W
30 L15 **Carlyle Lake** ⊠ Illinois, N USA
10 H7 **Carmacks** Yukon, W Canada 62°04′N 136°21′W
106 B9 **Carmagnola** Piemonte, NW Italy 44°50′N 07°43′E
11 X16 **Carman** Manitoba, S Canada 49°32′N 97°59′W
**Carmana/Carmania** *see* Kermān
97 I21 **Carmarthen** SW Wales, United Kingdom 51°52′N 04°19′W
97 I21 **Carmarthen** *cultural region* SW Wales, United Kingdom
97 I22 **Carmarthen Bay** *inlet* SW Wales, United Kingdom
103 N14 **Carmaux** Tarn, S France 44°03′N 02°09′E
35 N11 **Carmel** California, W USA 36°32′N 121°54′W
31 O13 **Carmel** Indiana, N USA 39°58′N 86°07′W
18 L13 **Carmel** New York, NE USA 41°25′N 73°40′W
97 H18 **Carmel Head** *headland* NW Wales, United Kingdom 53°24′N 04°35′W
42 E2 **Carmelita** Petén, N Guatemala 17°33′N 90°11′W
61 D19 **Carmelo** Colonia, SW Uruguay 34°00′S 58°20′W
41 V14 **Carmen** *var.* Ciudad del Carmen. Campeche, SE Mexico 18°38′N 91°50′W
61 A25 **Carmen de Patagones** Buenos Aires, E Argentina 40°45′S 63°00′W
40 F8 **Carmen, Isla** *island* NW Mexico
40 M5 **Carmen, Sierra del** ▲▲ NW Mexico
30 M16 **Carmi** Illinois, N USA 38°05′N 88°09′W
35 O7 **Carmichael** California, W USA 38°36′N 121°21′W
**Carmiel** *see* Karmi'el
25 U11 **Carmine** Texas, SW USA 30°07′N 96°40′W
104 K14 **Carmona** Andalucía, S Spain 37°28′N 05°38′W
**Carmona** *see* Uíge
**Carnaro** *see* Kvarner
180 G9 **Carnarvon** Western Australia 24°57′S 113°38′E
14 I13 **Carnarvon** Ontario, SE Canada 45°03′N 78°41′W
83 G24 **Carnarvon** Northern Cape, W South Africa 30°59′S 22°08′E
**Carnarvon** *see* Caernarfon
180 K9 **Carnarvon Range** ▲▲ Western Australia
**Carn Domhnach** *see* Carndonagh
96 E13 **Carndonagh** *Ir.* Carn Domhnach. NW Ireland 55°15′N 07°15′W
11 V17 **Carnduff** Saskatchewan, S Canada 49°11′N 101°50′W
26 L11 **Carnegie** Oklahoma, C USA 35°06′N 98°36′W
180 L9 **Carnegie, Lake** *salt lake* Western Australia
193 U8 **Carnegie Ridge** *undersea feature* E Pacific Ocean 01°00′S 85°00′W
96 H9 **Carn Eige** ▲ N Scotland, United Kingdom 57°18′N 05°04′W
182 F5 **Carnes** South Australia 30°12′S 134°31′E
194 J12 **Carney Island** *island* Antarctica
18 H16 **Carneys Point** New Jersey, NE USA 39°38′N 75°29′W
**Carniche, Alpi** *see* Karnische Alpen
151 Q21 **Car Nicobar** *island* Nicobar Islands, India, NE Indian Ocean
79 H15 **Carnot** Mambéré-Kadéï, W Central African Republic 04°58′N 15°55′E
182 F10 **Carnot, Cape** *headland* South Australia 34°57′S 135°39′E
96 K11 **Carnoustie** E Scotland, United Kingdom 56°30′N 02°42′W
97 F20 **Carnsore Point** *Ir.* Ceann an Chairn. *headland* SE Ireland 52°10′N 06°22′W
8 H7 **Carnwath** ≈ Northwest Territories, NW Canada
31 R8 **Caro** Michigan, N USA 43°29′N 83°24′W
23 Z15 **Carol City** Florida, SE USA 25°56′N 80°15′W
59 L14 **Carolina** Maranhão, E Brazil 07°20′S 47°25′W
45 U5 **Carolina** E Puerto Rico 18°22′N 65°57′W
21 V12 **Carolina Beach** North Carolina, SE USA 34°02′N 77°53′W
**Caroline Island** *see* Millennium Island
189 N15 **Caroline Islands** *island group* C Micronesia
129 Z14 **Caroline Plate** *tectonic feature*
192 H7 **Caroline Ridge** *undersea feature* E Philippine Sea 08°00′N 150°00′E
**Carolopois** *see* Châlons-en-Champagne
45 V14 **Caroni Arena Dam** ⊠ Trinidad, Trinidad and Tobago
**Caronie, Monti** *see* Nebrodi, Monti
55 P7 **Caroní, Río** ≈ E Venezuela
45 U14 **Caroni River** ≈ Trinidad, Trinidad and Tobago
**Caronium** *see* A Coruña
54 J5 **Carora** Lara, N Venezuela 10°12′N 70°07′W
86 F12 **Carpathian Mountains** *var.* Carpathians, *Cz./Pol.* Karpaty, *Ger.* Karpaten. ▲▲ E Europe
**Carpathians** *see* Carpathian Mountains
**Carpathos/Carpathus** *see* Kárpathos
116 H12 **Carpaţii Meridionali** *var.* Alpi Transilvaniei, Carpaţii Sudici, *Eng.* South Carpathians, Transylvanian Alps, *Ger.* Südkarpaten, Transsylvanische Alpen, *Hung.* Déli-Kárpátok, Erdélyi-Havasok. ▲▲ C Romania
**Carpaţii Sudici** *see* Carpaţii Meridionali
174 L7 **Carpentaria, Gulf of** *gulf* N Australia
**Carpentoracte** *see* Carpentras
103 R14 **Carpentras** *anc.* Carpentoracte. Vaucluse, SE France 44°03′N 05°03′E
106 F9 **Carpi** Emilia-Romagna, N Italy 44°47′N 10°53′E
116 E11 **Cărpiniş** *Hung.* Gyertyámos. Timiş, W Romania 45°46′N 20°53′E
35 R14 **Carpinteria** California, W USA 34°24′N 119°30′W
23 S9 **Carrabelle** Florida, SE USA 29°51′N 84°39′W
**Carraig Aonair** *see* Fastnet Rock
**Carraig Fhearghais** *see* Carrickfergus
**Carraig Mhachaire Rois** *see* Carrickmacross
**Carraig na Siúire** *see* Carrick-on-Suir
**Carrantual** *see* Carrauntoohil
106 E10 **Carrara** Toscana, C Italy 44°05′N 10°07′E
61 F20 **Carrasco** ✈ (Montevideo) Canelones, S Uruguay 34°51′S 56°00′W
105 P9 **Carrascosa del Campo** Castilla-La Mancha, C Spain 40°02′N 02°35′W
54 H4 **Carrasquero** Zulia, NW Venezuela 11°00′N 72°01′W
183 O9 **Carrathool** New South Wales, SE Australia 34°25′S 145°30′E
**Carrauntohil** *see* Carrauntoohil
97 B21 **Carrauntoohil** *Ir.* Carrantual, Carrauntohil, Corrán Tuathail. ▲ SW Ireland 51°98′N 09°53′W
45 Y15 **Carriacou** *island* N Grenada
97 G15 **Carrickfergus** *Ir.* Carraig Fhearghais. NE Northern Ireland, United Kingdom 54°43′N 05°49′W
97 F16 **Carrickmacross** *Ir.* Carraig Mhachaire Rois. N Ireland 53°58′N 06°43′W
97 D16 **Carrick-on-Shannon** *Ir.* Cora Droma Rúisc. NW Ireland 53°37′N 08°05′W
97 E20 **Carrick-on-Suir** *Ir.* Carraig na Siúire. S Ireland 52°21′N 07°25′W
182 I7 **Carrieton** South Australia 32°27′S 138°33′E
40 L7 **Carrillo** Chihuahua, N Mexico 25°53′N 103°54′W
29 O4 **Carrington** North Dakota, N USA 47°27′N 99°07′W
104 M4 **Carrión** ≈ N Spain
104 M4 **Carrión de los Condes** Castilla y León, N Spain 42°20′N 04°37′W
25 P13 **Carrizo Springs** Texas, SW USA 28°33′N 99°54′W
37 S13 **Carrizozo** New Mexico, SW USA 33°38′N 105°52′W
29 T13 **Carroll** Iowa, C USA 42°04′N 94°52′W


◆ Country
● Country Capital
◇ Dependent Territory
○ Dependent Territory Capital
◈ Administrative Regions
✈ International Airport
▲ Mountain
▲▲ Mountain Range
⛰ Volcano
≈ River
◎ Lake
⊠ Reservoir

# Carrollton – Central Pacific Basin



23 N4 **Carrollton** Alabama, S USA 33°13′N 88°05′W
23 R3 **Carrollton** Georgia, SE USA 33°33′N 85°04′W
30 K14 **Carrollton** Illinois, N USA 39°18′N 90°24′W
20 L4 **Carrollton** Kentucky, S USA 38°41′N 85°09′W
31 R8 **Carrollton** Michigan, N USA 43°27′N 83°55′W
27 T3 **Carrollton** Missouri, C USA 39°20′N 93°30′W
31 U12 **Carrollton** Ohio, N USA 40°34′N 81°05′W
25 T6 **Carrollton** Texas, SW USA 32°57′N 96°53′W
11 U14 **Carrot** ≈ Saskatchewan, S Canada
11 U14 **Carrot River** Saskatchewan, C Canada 53°18′N 103°32′W
18 J7 **Carry Falls Reservoir** ▣ New York, NE USA
136 L11 **Çarşamba** Samsun, N Turkey 41°13′N 36°43′E
28 L6 **Carson** North Dakota, N USA 46°26′N 101°34′W
35 Q6 **Carson City** *state capital* Nevada, W USA 39°10′N 119°46′W
35 R6 **Carson River** ≈ Nevada, W USA
35 S5 **Carson Sink** *salt flat* Nevada, W USA
11 Q16 **Carstairs** Alberta, SW Canada 51°35′N 114°02′W
**Carstensz, Puntjak** *see* Jaya, Puncak
54 E5 **Cartagena** *var.* Cartagena de los Indes. Bolívar, NW Colombia 10°24′N 75°33′W
105 R13 **Cartagena** *anc.* Carthago Nova. Murcia, SE Spain 37°36′N 00°59′W
54 E13 **Cartagena de Chaira** Caquetá, S Colombia 01°19′N 74°52′W
**Cartagena de los Indes** *see* Cartagena
54 D10 **Cartago** Valle del Cauca, W Colombia 04°45′N 75°55′W
43 N14 **Cartago** Cartago, C Costa Rica 09°50′N 83°54′W
42 M14 **Cartago** *off.* Provincia de Cartago. ◈ *province* C Costa Rica
**Cartago, Provincia de** *see* Cartago
25 O11 **Carta Valley** Texas, SW USA 29°46′N 100°37′W
104 F10 **Cartaxo** Santarém, C Portugal 39°10′N 08°47′W
104 I14 **Cartaya** Andalucía, S Spain 37°16′N 07°09′W
**Carteret Islands** *see* Tulun Islands
29 S15 **Carter Lake** Iowa, C USA 41°17′N 95°55′W
23 S3 **Cartersville** Georgia, SE USA 34°10′N 84°48′W
185 M14 **Carterton** Wellington, North Island, New Zealand 41°01′S 175°30′E
30 J13 **Carthage** Illinois, N USA 40°25′N 91°09′W
22 L5 **Carthage** Mississippi, S USA 32°43′N 89°31′W
27 R7 **Carthage** Missouri, C USA 37°10′N 94°20′W
18 I8 **Carthage** New York, NE USA 43°58′N 75°36′W
21 T10 **Carthage** North Carolina, SE USA 35°21′N 79°27′W
20 K8 **Carthage** Tennessee, S USA 36°14′N 85°59′W
25 X7 **Carthage** Texas, SW USA 32°10′N 94°21′W
74 M5 **Carthage** ✈ (Tunis) N Tunisia 36°51′N 10°12′E
**Carthago Nova** *see* Cartagena
14 E10 **Cartier** Ontario, S Canada 46°40′N 81°31′W
13 S8 **Cartwright** Newfoundland and Labrador, E Canada 53°40′N 57°W
55 P9 **Caruana de Montaña** Bolívar, SE Venezuela 05°16′N 63°12′W
59 Q15 **Caruaru** Pernambuco, E Brazil 08°15′S 35°55′W
55 P5 **Carúpano** Sucre, NE Venezuela 10°39′N 63°14′W
**Carusbur** *see* Cherbourg
58 M12 **Carutapera** Maranhão, E Brazil 01°12′S 45°57′W
27 Y9 **Caruthersville** Missouri, C USA 36°11′N 89°40′W
103 O1 **Carvin** Pas-de-Calais, N France 50°31′N 03°00′E
58 E12 **Carvoeiro** Amazonas, NW Brazil 01°24′S 61°59′W
104 E10 **Carvoeiro, Cabo** *headland* C Portugal 39°19′N 09°27′W
21 U9 **Cary** North Carolina, SE USA 35°47′N 78°46′W
182 M3 **Caryapundy Swamp** *wetland* New South Wales/ Queensland, SE Australia
65 E24 **Carysfort, Cape** *headland* East Falkland, Falkland Islands 51°26′S 57°50′W
74 F6 **Casablanca** *Ar.* Dar-el-Beida. NW Morocco 33°39′N 07°31′W
60 M8 **Casa Branca** São Paulo, S Brazil 21°47′S 47°05′W
36 L14 **Casa Grande** Arizona, SW USA 32°52′N 111°45′W
106 C8 **Casale Monferrato** Piemonte, NW Italy 45°08′N 08°27′E
106 E8 **Casalpusterlengo** Lombardia, N Italy 45°10′N 09°37′E
54 H10 **Casanare** *off.* Intendencia de Casanare. ◈ *province* C Colombia
**Casanare, Intendencia de** *see* Casanare
55 P5 **Casanay** Sucre, NE Venezuela 10°30′N 63°25′W
24 K11 **Casa Piedra** Texas, SW USA 29°43′N 104°03′W
107 Q19 **Casarano** Puglia, SE Italy 40°01′N 18°10′E
42 J11 **Casares** Carazo, W Nicaragua 11°37′N 86°19′W
105 R10 **Casas Ibáñez** Castilla-La Mancha, C Spain 39°17′N 01°28′W
61 I14 **Casca** Rio Grande do Sul, S Brazil 28°39′S 51°55′W
172 I17 **Cascade** Mahé, NE Seychelles 04°39′S 55°29′E
33 N13 **Cascade** Idaho, NW USA 44°31′N 116°02′W
29 Y13 **Cascade** Iowa, C USA 42°18′N 91°00′W
33 R9 **Cascade** Montana, NW USA 47°15′N 111°46′W
185 B20 **Cascade Point** *headland* South Island, New Zealand 44°00′S 168°23′E
32 G13 **Cascade Range** ▲▲ Oregon/ Washington, NW USA
33 N12 **Cascade Reservoir** ▣ Idaho, NW USA
0 E8 **Cascadia Basin** *undersea feature* NE Pacific Ocean 47°00′N 127°30′W
104 E11 **Cascais** Lisboa, C Portugal 38°41′N 09°25′W
15 W7 **Cascapédia** ≈ Québec, SE Canada
59 I22 **Cascavel** Ceará, E Brazil 04°10′S 38°15′W
60 G11 **Cascavel** Paraná, S Brazil 24°56′S 53°28′W
106 I13 **Cascia** Umbria, C Italy 42°45′N 13°01′E
106 F11 **Cascina** Toscana, C Italy 43°40′N 10°33′E
19 Q8 **Casco Bay** *bay* Maine, NE USA
194 J7 **Case Island** *island* Antarctica
106 B8 **Caselle** ✈ (Torino) Piemonte, NW Italy 45°06′N 07°41′E
107 K17 **Caserta** Campania, S Italy 41°05′N 14°20′E
15 N8 **Casey** Québec, SE Canada 47°50′N 74°09′W
30 M14 **Casey** Illinois, N USA 39°18′N 87°59′W
195 Y12 **Casey** *research station (Australia)* Antarctica 65°58′S 111°04′E
195 W3 **Casey Bay** *bay* Antarctica
80 Q11 **Caseyr, Raas** *headland* NE Somalia 11°51′S 51°16′E
97 D20 **Cashel** *Ir.* Caiseal. S Ireland 52°31′N 07°53′W
54 G6 **Casigua** Zulia, W Venezuela 08°46′N 72°30′W
61 B19 **Casilda** Santa Fe, C Argentina 33°05′S 61°10′W
**Casim** *see* General Toshevo
183 V4 **Casino** New South Wales, SE Australia 28°50′S 153°02′E
107 J16 **Cassino** *prev.* San Germano; *anc.* Casinum. Lazio, C Italy 41°29′N 13°50′E
**Casinum** *see* Cassino
111 E17 **Čáslav** *Ger.* Tschaslau. Střední Čechy, C Czechia 49°54′N 15°23′E
56 C13 **Casma** Ancash, C Peru 09°30′S 78°18′W
167 S7 **Ca, Sông** ≈ N Vietnam
107 K17 **Casoria** Campania, S Italy 40°54′N 14°28′E
105 T6 **Caspe** Aragón, NE Spain 41°14′N 00°03′W
33 X15 **Casper** Wyoming, C USA 42°48′N 106°22′W
84 M10 **Caspian Depression** *Kaz.* Kaspīy Mangy Oypaty, *Rus.* Prikaspiyskaya Nizmennost'. *depression* Kazakhstan/Russia
130 D10 **Caspian Sea** *Az.* Xäzär Dänizi, *Kaz.* Kaspiy Tengizi, *Per.* Baḩr-e Khazar, Daryā-ye Khazar, Daryā-ye Māzandarān, *Rus.* Kaspiyskoye More. *inland sea* Asia/Europe
83 L14 **Cassacatiza** Tete, NW Mozambique 14°20′S 32°24′E
**Cassai** *see* Kasai
82 F13 **Cassamba** Moxico, E Angola 13°07′S 20°22′E
107 N20 **Cassano allo Ionio** Calabria, SE Italy 39°46′N 16°16′E
31 S8 **Cass City** Michigan, N USA 43°36′N 83°10′W
**Cassel** *see* Kassel
14 M13 **Casselman** Ontario, SE Canada 45°18′N 75°05′W
29 R5 **Casselton** North Dakota, N USA 46°53′N 97°10′W
**Cássia** *see* Santa Rita de Cassia
10 J9 **Cassiar** British Columbia, W Canada 59°16′N 129°40′W
10 K10 **Cassiar Mountains** ▲▲ British Columbia, W Canada
83 C15 **Cassinga** Huíla, SW Angola 15°08′S 16°05′E
29 T4 **Cass Lake** Minnesota, N USA 47°22′N 94°36′W
29 T4 **Cass Lake** ◎ Minnesota, N USA
31 P10 **Cassopolis** Michigan, N USA 41°56′N 86°00′W
31 S8 **Cass River** ≈ Michigan, N USA
27 S8 **Cassville** Missouri, C USA 36°42′N 93°52′W
**Castamoni** *see* Kastamonu
58 L12 **Castanhal** Pará, NE Brazil 01°16′S 47°55′W
104 G8 **Castanheira de Pêra** Leiria, C Portugal 40°01′N 08°12′W
41 N7 **Castaños** Coahuila, NE Mexico 26°48′N 101°26′W
108 I10 **Castasegna** Graubünden, SE Switzerland 46°21′N 09°30′E
106 D8 **Casteggio** Lombardia, N Italy 45°02′N 09°10′E
107 K23 **Castelbuono** Sicilia, Italy, C Mediterranean Sea 37°56′N 14°05′E
107 K15 **Castel di Sangro** Abruzzo, C Italy 41°46′N 14°03′E
106 H7 **Castelfranco Veneto** Veneto, NE Italy 45°40′N 11°55′E
102 K14 **Casteljaloux** Lot-et-Garonne, SW France 44°19′N 00°03′E
107 L18 **Castellabate** *var.* Santa Maria di Castellabate. Campania, S Italy 40°16′N 14°57′E
107 I23 **Castellammare del Golfo** Sicilia, Italy, C Mediterranean Sea 38°02′N 12°53′E
107 H22 **Castellammare, Golfo di** *gulf* Sicilia, Italy, C Mediterranean Sea
103 U15 **Castellane** Alpes-de-Haute-Provence, SE France 43°49′N 06°34′E
107 O18 **Castellaneta** Puglia, SE Italy 40°38′N 16°57′E
106 E9 **Castel l'Arquato** Emilia-Romagna, C Italy 44°52′N 09°51′E
61 E21 **Castelli** Buenos Aires, E Argentina 36°07′S 57°47′W
105 S8 **Castelló** *var.* Castellón. ◈ *province* Comunitat Valenciana, E Spain
105 T9 **Castelló de la Plana** *var.* Castellón, Castellón de la Plana. Comunitat Valenciana, E Spain 39°59′N 00°03′W
**Castellón** *see* Castelló
**Castellón** *see* Castelló de la Plana
**Castellón de la Plana** *see* Castelló de la Plana
105 S7 **Castellote** Aragón, NE Spain 40°46′N 00°18′W
103 N16 **Castelnaudary** Aude, S France 43°18′N 01°57′E
102 L16 **Castelnau-Magnoac** Hautes-Pyrénées, S France 43°18′N 00°30′E
106 F10 **Castelnovo ne' Monti** Emilia-Romagna, C Italy 44°26′N 10°24′E
**Castelnuovo** *see* Herceg-Novi
104 H9 **Castelo Branco** Castelo Branco, C Portugal 39°50′N 07°30′W
104 H8 **Castelo Branco** ◈ *district* C Portugal
104 I10 **Castelo de Vide** Portalegre, C Portugal 39°25′N 07°27′W
104 G9 **Castelo do Bode, Barragem do** ▣ C Portugal
106 G10 **Castel San Pietro Terme** Emilia-Romagna, C Italy 44°22′N 11°34′E
107 B17 **Castelsardo** Sardegna, Italy, C Mediterranean Sea 40°54′N 08°42′E
102 M14 **Castelsarrasin** Tarn-et-Garonne, S France 44°02′N 01°06′E
107 I24 **Casteltermini** Sicilia, Italy, C Mediterranean Sea 37°33′N 13°38′E
107 H24 **Castelvetrano** Sicilia, Italy, C Mediterranean Sea 37°40′N 12°46′E
182 L12 **Casterton** Victoria, SE Australia 37°37′S 141°22′E
102 J15 **Castets** Landes, SW France 43°55′N 01°08′W
106 H12 **Castiglione del Lago** Umbria, C Italy 43°07′N 12°02′E
106 F13 **Castiglione della Pescaia** Toscana, C Italy 42°46′N 10°53′E
106 F8 **Castiglione delle Stiviere** Lombardia, N Italy 45°24′N 10°31′E
104 M9 **Castilla-La Mancha** ◈ *autonomous community* NE Spain
105 N10 **Castilla Nueva** *cultural region* C Spain
105 N6 **Castilla Vieja** ◈ *cultural region* N Spain
104 L5 **Castilla y León** *var.* Castillia Leon. ◈ *autonomous community* NW Spain
**Castillia Leon** *see* Castilla y León
**Castillo de Locubim** *see* Castillo de Locubín
105 N14 **Castillo de Locubín** *var.* Castillo de Locubim. Andalucía, S Spain 37°32′N 03°56′W
102 K13 **Castillon-la-Bataille** Gironde, SW France 44°51′N 00°01′W
63 I19 **Castillo, Pampa del** *plain* S Argentina
61 G19 **Castillos** Rocha, SE Uruguay 34°12′S 53°52′W
97 B16 **Castlebar** *Ir.* Caisleán an Bharraigh. W Ireland 53°52′N 09°17′W
97 F16 **Castleblayney** *Ir.* Baile na Lorgan. N Ireland 54°07′N 06°44′W
45 O11 **Castle Bruce** E Dominica 15°24′N 61°26′W
36 M5 **Castle Dale** Utah, W USA 39°10′N 111°02′W
36 I14 **Castle Dome Peak** ▲ Arizona, SW USA 33°04′N 114°08′W
97 J14 **Castle Douglas** S Scotland, United Kingdom 54°56′N 03°56′W
97 E14 **Castlefinn** *Ir.* Caisleán na Finne. NW Ireland 54°47′N 07°35′W
97 M17 **Castleford** N England, United Kingdom 53°44′N 01°21′W
11 O17 **Castlegar** British Columbia, SW Canada 49°18′N 117°48′W
64 B12 **Castle Harbour** *inlet* Bermuda, NW Atlantic Ocean
21 V12 **Castle Hayne** North Carolina, SE USA 34°23′N 78°07′W
97 B20 **Castleisland** *Ir.* Oileán Ciarral. SW Ireland 52°12′N 09°30′W
183 N12 **Castlemaine** Victoria, SE Australia 37°06′S 144°13′E
37 R5 **Castle Peak** ▲ Colorado, C USA 39°00′N 106°51′W
33 O13 **Castle Peak** ▲ Idaho, NW USA 44°02′N 114°42′W
184 N13 **Castlepoint** Wellington, North Island, New Zealand 40°54′S 176°13′E
97 D17 **Castlerea** *Ir.* An Caisleán Riabhach. W Ireland 53°45′N 08°32′W
97 G15 **Castlereagh** *Ir.* An Caisleán Riabhach. N Northern Ireland, United Kingdom 54°33′N 05°53′W
183 R6 **Castlereagh River** ≈ New South Wales, SE Australia
37 T5 **Castle Rock** Colorado, C USA 39°22′N 104°51′W
30 K7 **Castle Rock Lake** ▣ Wisconsin, N USA
65 G25 **Castle Rock Point** *headland* S Saint Helena 16°02′S 05°45′W
97 I16 **Castletown** SE Isle of Man 54°05′N 04°39′W
29 R9 **Castlewood** South Dakota, N USA 44°43′N 97°01′W
11 R15 **Castor** Alberta, SW Canada 52°14′N 111°54′W
14 M13 **Castor** ≈ Ontario, SE Canada
27 X7 **Castor River** ≈ Missouri, C USA
**Castra Albiensium** *see* Castres
**Castra Regina** *see* Regensburg
103 N15 **Castres** *anc.* Castra Albiensium. Tarn, S France 43°36′N 02°15′E
98 H9 **Castricum** Noord-Holland, W Netherlands 52°33′N 04°40′E
45 S11 **Castries** ● (Saint Lucia) N Saint Lucia 14°01′N 60°59′W
60 J11 **Castro** Paraná, S Brazil 24°46′S 50°03′W
63 F17 **Castro** Los Lagos, W Chile 42°27′S 73°48′W
104 H7 **Castro Daire** Viseu, N Portugal 40°54′N 07°55′W
104 M13 **Castro del Río** Andalucía, S Spain 37°41′N 04°29′W
**Castrogiovanni** *see* Enna
104 H14 **Castro Marim** Faro, S Portugal 37°13′N 07°26′W
104 J2 **Castropol** Asturias, N Spain 43°30′N 07°01′W
105 O2 **Castro-Urdiales** *var.* Castro Urdiales. Cantabria, N Spain 43°23′N 03°11′W
104 G13 **Castro Verde** Beja, S Portugal 37°42′N 08°05′W
107 N19 **Castrovillari** Calabria, SW Italy 39°48′N 16°12′E
35 N10 **Castroville** California, W USA 36°46′N 121°46′W
25 R12 **Castroville** Texas, SW USA 29°21′N 98°52′W
104 K11 **Castuera** Extremadura, W Spain 38°44′N 05°33′W
61 F19 **Casupá** Florida, S Uruguay 34°09′S 55°38′W
185 A22 **Caswell Sound** *sound* South Island, New Zealand
137 Q13 **Çat** Erzurum, NE Turkey 39°40′N 41°03′E
42 K6 **Catacamas** Olancho, C Honduras 14°55′N 85°54′W
56 A10 **Catacaos** Piura, NW Peru 05°22′S 80°40′W
22 I7 **Catahoula Lake** ◎ Louisiana, S USA
137 S15 **Çatak** Van, SE Turkey 38°02′N 43°05′E
137 S15 **Çatak Çayi** ≈ SE Turkey
114 O12 **Çatalca** İstanbul, NW Turkey 41°09′N 28°28′E
114 O12 **Çatalca Yarimadasi** *physical region* NW Turkey
62 H6 **Catalina** Antofagasta, N Chile 25°19′S 69°37′W
**Catalonia** *see* Cataluña
105 U5 **Cataluña** *Cat.* Catalunya, *Eng.* Catalonia. ◈ *autonomous community* N Spain
**Catalunya** *see* Cataluña
62 I7 **Catamarca** *off.* Provincia de Catamarca. ◈ *province* NW Argentina
**Catamarca** *see* San Fernando del Valle de Catamarca
**Catamarca, Provincia de** *see* Catamarca
83 M16 **Catandica** Manica, C Mozambique 18°05′S 33°10′E
171 P4 **Catanduanes Island** *island* N Philippines
60 K8 **Catanduva** São Paulo, S Brazil 21°05′S 49°00′W
107 L24 **Catania** Sicilia, Italy, C Mediterranean Sea 37°31′N 15°04′E
107 M24 **Catania, Golfo di** *gulf* Sicilia, Italy, C Mediterranean Sea
45 U5 **Cataño** *var.* Cantaño. E Puerto Rico 18°26′N 66°06′W
107 O21 **Catanzaro** Calabria, SW Italy 38°53′N 16°36′E
107 O22 **Catanzaro Marina** *var.* Marina di Catanzaro. Calabria, S Italy 38°48′N 16°33′E
**Marina di Catanzaro** *see* Catanzaro Marina
25 Q14 **Catarina** Texas, SW USA 28°19′N 99°36′W
171 Q5 **Catarman** Samar, C Philippines 12°29′N 124°34′E
105 S10 **Catarroja** Comunitat Valenciana, E Spain 39°24′N 00°24′W
21 R11 **Catawba River** ≈ North Carolina/South Carolina, SE USA
171 Q5 **Catbalogan** Samar, C Philippines 11°49′N 124°55′E
14 I14 **Catchacoma** Ontario, SE Canada 44°43′N 78°19′W
41 S15 **Catemaco** Veracruz, SE Mexico 18°28′N 95°10′W
**Cathair na Mart** *see* Westport
**Cathair Saidhbhín** *see* Caherciveen
31 P5 **Cat Head Point** *headland* Michigan, N USA 45°11′N 85°37′W
23 Q2 **Cathedral Caverns** *cave* Alabama, S USA
35 V16 **Cathedral City** California, W USA 33°45′N 116°27′W
24 K10 **Cathedral Mountain** ▲ Texas, SW USA 30°10′N 103°39′W
32 G10 **Cathlamet** Washington, NW USA 46°12′N 123°24′W
76 G13 **Catió** S Guinea-Bissau 11°13′N 15°10′W
55 O10 **Catisimiña** Bolívar, SE Venezuela 04°07′N 63°40′W
44 J3 **Cat Island** *island* C The Bahamas
12 B9 **Cat Lake** Ontario, S Canada 51°47′N 91°52′W
21 P5 **Catlettsburg** Kentucky, S USA 38°24′N 82°37′W
185 D24 **Catlins** ≈ South Island, New Zealand
35 R1 **Catnip Mountain** ▲ Nevada, W USA 41°53′N 119°19′W
41 Z11 **Catoche, Cabo** *headland* SE Mexico 21°36′N 87°04′W
27 P9 **Catoosa** Oklahoma, C USA 36°11′N 95°45′W
41 N10 **Catorce** San Luis Potosí, C Mexico 23°42′N 100°49′W
63 I14 **Catriel** Río Negro, C Argentina 37°54′S 67°52′W
62 K13 **Catriló** La Pampa, C Argentina 36°28′S 63°20′W
58 F11 **Catrimani** Roraima, N Brazil 0°24′N 61°30′W
58 E10 **Catrimani, Rio** ≈ N Brazil
18 K11 **Catskill** New York, NE USA 42°13′N 73°52′W
18 K11 **Catskill Creek** ≈ New York, NE USA
18 J11 **Catskill Mountains** ▲▲ New York, NE USA
18 D11 **Cattaraugus Creek** ≈ New York, NE USA
**Cattaro** *see* Kotor
**Cattaro, Bocche di** *see* Kotorska, Boka
107 I24 **Cattolica Eraclea** Sicilia, Italy, C Mediterranean Sea 37°27′N 13°24′E
83 B14 **Catumbela** ≈ W Angola
83 N14 **Catur** Niassa, N Mozambique 13°50′S 35°43′E
82 C10 **Cauale** ≈ NE Angola
171 O2 **Cauayan** Luzon, N Philippines 16°55′N 121°46′E
54 C12 **Cauca** *off.* Departamento del Cauca. ◈ *province* SW Colombia
47 P5 **Cauca** ≈ SE Venezuela
**Cauca, Departamento del** *see* Cauca
58 P13 **Caucaia** Ceará, E Brazil 03°44′S 38°45′W
54 E7 **Cauca, Río** ≈ N Colombia
54 E7 **Caucasia** Antioquia, NW Colombia 07°59′N 75°13′W
137 Q8 **Caucasus** *Rus.* Kavkaz. ▲▲ Georgia/Russia
62 I10 **Caucete** San Juan, W Argentina 31°38′S 68°16′W
105 R11 **Caudete** Castilla-La Mancha, C Spain 38°42′N 01°00′W
103 P2 **Caudry** Nord, N France 50°07′N 03°24′E
82 D11 **Caungula** Lunda Norte, NE Angola 08°22′S 18°37′E
62 G13 **Cauquenes** Maule, C Chile 35°58′S 72°22′W
55 N8 **Caura, Río** ≈ C Venezuela
15 V7 **Causapscal** Québec, SE Canada 48°22′N 67°14′W
117 N10 **Căuşeni** *Rus.* Kaushany. E Moldova 46°37′N 29°21′E
102 M14 **Caussade** Tarn-et-Garonne, S France 44°10′N 01°31′E
102 K17 **Cauterets** Hautes-Pyrénées, S France 42°53′N 00°08′W
10 J15 **Caution, Cape** *headland* British Columbia, SW Canada 51°10′N 127°43′W
44 H7 **Cauto** ≈ E Cuba
**Cauvery** *see* Kāveri
102 L3 **Caux, Pays de** *physical region* N France
107 L18 **Cava de' Tirreni** Campania, S Italy 40°42′N 14°42′E
104 G6 **Cávado** ≈ N Portugal
**Cavaia** *see* Kavajë
103 R15 **Cavaillon** Vaucluse, SE France 43°51′N 05°01′E
103 U16 **Cavalaire-sur-Mer** Var, SE France 43°10′N 06°31′E
106 G6 **Cavalese** *Ger.* Gablös. Trentino-Alto Adige, N Italy 46°18′N 11°29′E
29 Q2 **Cavalier** North Dakota, N USA 48°47′N 97°37′W
76 L17 **Cavalla** *var.* Cavally, Cavally Fleuve. ≈ Ivory Coast/ Liberia
105 Y8 **Cavalleria, Cap de** *var.* Cabo Caballeria. *headland* Menorca, Spain, W Mediterranean Sea 40°04′N 04°06′E
184 K2 **Cavalli Islands** *island group* N New Zealand
**Cavally/Cavally Fleuve** *see* Cavalla
97 E16 **Cavan** *Ir.* Cabhán. N Ireland 54°N 07°21′W
97 E16 **Cavan** *Ir.* An Cabhán. *cultural region* N Ireland
106 H8 **Cavarzare** Veneto, NE Italy 45°08′N 12°05′E
27 W9 **Cave City** Arkansas, C USA 35°56′N 91°33′W
20 K7 **Cave City** Kentucky, S USA 37°08′N 85°57′W
65 M25 **Cave Point** *headland* S Tristan da Cunha
21 N5 **Cave Run Lake** ▣ Kentucky, S USA
58 K11 **Caviana de Fora, Ilha** *var.* Ilha Caviana. *island* N Brazil
**Caviana, Ilha** *see* Caviana de Fora, Ilha
113 I16 **Cavtat** *It.* Ragusavecchia. Dubrovnik-Neretva, SE Croatia 42°36′N 18°13′E
**Cawnpore** *see* Kānpur
**Caxamarca** *see* Cajamarca
58 A13 **Caxias** Amazonas, W Brazil 04°27′S 71°27′W
58 N13 **Caxias** Maranhão, E Brazil 04°53′S 43°20′W
61 I15 **Caxias do Sul** Rio Grande do Sul, S Brazil 29°14′S 51°10′W
42 J4 **Caxinas, Punta** *headland* N Honduras 16°01′N 86°02′W
82 B11 **Caxito** Bengo, NW Angola 08°34′S 13°38′E
136 F14 **Çay** Afyon, W Turkey 38°35′N 31°01′E
40 L15 **Cayacal, Punta** *var.* Punta Mongrove. *headland* S Mexico 17°55′N 102°09′W
56 C6 **Cayambe** Pichincha, N Ecuador 0°02′N 78°08′W
56 C6 **Cayambe** ▲ N Ecuador 0°00′S 77°58′W
21 R12 **Cayce** South Carolina, SE USA 33°58′N 81°04′W
55 Y10 **Cayenne** ○ (French Guiana) NE French Guiana 04°55′N 52°18′W
55 Y10 **Cayenne** ✈ NE French Guiana 04°55′N 52°18′W
44 K10 **Cayes** *var.* Les Cayes. SW Haiti 18°10′N 73°48′W
45 U6 **Cayey** C Puerto Rico 18°06′N 66°11′W
45 U6 **Cayey, Sierra de** ▲▲ E Puerto Rico
103 N14 **Caylus** Tarn-et-Garonne, S France 44°13′N 01°42′E
44 E8 **Cayman Brac** *island* E Cayman Islands
44 D8 **Cayman Islands** ◇ *UK Overseas Territory* W West Indies
64 D11 **Cayman Trench** *undersea feature* NW Caribbean Sea 19°00′N 80°00′W
47 O3 **Cayman Trough** *undersea feature* NW Caribbean Sea 18°00′N 81°00′W
80 O13 **Caynabo** Togdheer, N Somalia 08°55′N 46°28′E
42 F3 **Cayo** ◈ *district* SW Belize
**Cayo** *see* San Ignacio
43 N9 **Cayos Guerrero** *reef* E Nicaragua
43 O9 **Cayos King** *reef* E Nicaragua
44 E4 **Cay Sal** *islet* SW The Bahamas
14 G16 **Cayuga** Ontario, S Canada 42°57′N 79°49′W
25 V8 **Cayuga** Texas, SW USA 31°55′N 95°57′W
18 G10 **Cayuga Lake** ◎ New York, NE USA
104 K13 **Cazalla de la Sierra** Andalucía, S Spain 37°56′N 05°46′W
116 L14 **Căzăneşti** Ialomiţa, SE Romania 44°36′N 27°03′E
102 M16 **Cazères** Haute-Garonne, S France 43°15′N 01°11′E
112 E10 **Cazin** ◈ Federacija Bosne I Hercegovine, NW Bosnia and Herzegovina
82 G13 **Cazombo** Moxico, E Angola 11°54′S 22°56′E
105 O13 **Cazorla** Andalucía, S Spain 37°55′N 03°W
**Cazza** *see* Sušac
104 L4 **Cea** ≈ NW Spain
**Ceadâr-Lunga** *see* Ciadîr-Lunga
**Ceanannas** *see* Kells
**Ceann Toirc** *see* Kanturk
58 O13 **Ceará** *off.* Estado do Ceará. ◈ *state* C Brazil
**Ceará** *see* Fortaleza
**Ceara Abyssal Plain** *see* Ceará Plain
**Ceará, Estado do** *see* Ceará
59 Q14 **Ceará Mirim** Rio Grande do Norte, E Brazil 05°30′S 35°51′W
64 J13 **Ceará Plain** *var.* Ceara Abyssal Plain. *undersea feature* W Atlantic Ocean 0°00 36°30′W
64 I13 **Ceará Ridge** *undersea feature* C Atlantic Ocean
**Ceatharlach** *see* Carlow
43 Q17 **Cébaco, Isla** *island* SW Panama
40 K7 **Ceballos** Durango, C Mexico 26°33′N 104°07′W
61 G19 **Cebollatí** Rocha, E Uruguay 33°15′S 53°46′W
61 G19 **Cebollatí, Río** ≈ E Uruguay
105 P5 **Cebollera** ▲ N Spain 42°01′N 02°40′W
104 M8 **Cebreros** Castilla y León, N Spain 40°27′N 04°28′W
171 P6 **Cebu** *off.* Cebu City. Cebu, C Philippines 10°17′N 123°46′E
171 P6 **Cebu** *island* C Philippines
**Cebu City** *see* Cebu
107 J16 **Ceccano** Lazio, C Italy 41°34′N 13°20′E
**Čechy** *see* Bohemia
106 F12 **Cecina** Toscana, C Italy 43°19′N 10°31′E
26 K4 **Cedar Bluff Reservoir** ▣ Kansas, C USA
30 M8 **Cedarburg** Wisconsin, N USA 43°18′N 87°58′W
36 J7 **Cedar City** Utah, W USA 37°40′N 113°03′W
25 T11 **Cedar Creek** Texas, SW USA 30°04′N 97°30′W
28 L7 **Cedar Creek** ≈ North Dakota, N USA
25 U7 **Cedar Creek Reservoir** ▣ Texas, SW USA
29 W13 **Cedar Falls** Iowa, C USA 42°31′N 92°27′W
31 N8 **Cedar Grove** Wisconsin, N USA 43°31′N 87°48′W
21 Y6 **Cedar Island** *island* Virginia, NE USA
23 U11 **Cedar Key** Cedar Keys, Florida, SE USA 29°08′N 83°03′W
23 U11 **Cedar Keys** *island group* Florida, SE USA
11 V14 **Cedar Lake** ◎ Manitoba, C Canada
14 I11 **Cedar Lake** ◎ Ontario, SE Canada
24 M6 **Cedar Lake** ◎ Texas, SW USA
29 X13 **Cedar Rapids** Iowa, C USA 41°58′N 91°40′W
29 X14 **Cedar River** ≈ Iowa/ Minnesota, C USA
29 O14 **Cedar River** ≈ Nebraska, C USA
31 P8 **Cedar Springs** Michigan, N USA 43°13′N 85°33′W
23 R3 **Cedartown** Georgia, SE USA 34°00′N 85°16′W
27 O7 **Cedar Vale** Kansas, C USA 37°06′N 96°30′W
35 Q2 **Cedarville** California, W USA 41°30′N 120°10′W
104 H1 **Cedeira** Galicia, NW Spain 43°40′N 08°03′W
42 H8 **Cedeño** Choluteca, S Honduras 13°10′N 87°25′W
41 N10 **Cedral** San Luis Potosí, C Mexico 23°47′N 100°40′W
42 I6 **Cedros** Francisco Morazán, C Honduras 14°38′N 86°42′W
40 M9 **Cedros** Zacatecas, C Mexico 24°39′N 101°47′W
40 B5 **Cedros, Isla** *island* W Mexico
193 R5 **Cedros Trench** *undersea feature* E Pacific Ocean 27°45′N 115°45′W
182 E7 **Ceduna** South Australia 32°09′S 133°43′E
110 D10 **Cedynia** *Ger.* Zehden. Zachodnio-pomorskie, W Poland 52°54′N 14°15′E
80 P12 **Ceelaayo** Sanaag, N Somalia 11°18′N 49°20′E
81 O16 **Ceel Buur** *It.* El Bur. Galguduud, C Somalia 04°36′N 46°33′E
81 N15 **Ceel Dheere** *var.* Ceel Dher, *It.* El Dere. Galguduud, C Somalia 05°18′N 46°07′E
**Ceel Dher** *see* Ceel Dheere
80 O12 **Ceerigaabo** *var.* Erigabo, Erigavo. Sanaag, N Somalia 10°34′N 47°22′E
107 J23 **Cefalù** *anc.* Cephaloedium. Sicilia, Italy, C Mediterranean Sea 38°02′N 14°02′E
105 N6 **Cega** ≈ Castilla y León, N Spain
111 K23 **Cegléd** *prev.* Czegléd. Pest, C Hungary 47°10′N 19°47′E
113 N18 **Čegrane** W North Macedonia 41°50′N 20°59′E
105 Q13 **Cehegín** Murcia, SE Spain 38°04′N 01°48′W
136 K12 **Çekerek** Yozgat, N Turkey 40°04′N 35°30′E
146 B13 **Çekiçler** *Rus.* Chekishlyar, *Turkm.* Chekichler. Balkan Welaýaty, W Turkmenistan 37°35′N 53°52′E
107 J15 **Celano** Abruzzo, C Italy 42°06′N 13°33′E
104 H4 **Celanova** Galicia, NW Spain 42°09′N 07°58′W
42 F6 **Celaque, Cordillera de** ▲▲ W Honduras
41 N13 **Celaya** Guanajuato, C Mexico 20°32′N 100°48′W
**Celebes** *see* Sulawesi
192 F7 **Celebes Basin** *undersea feature* SE South China Sea 04°00′N 122°00′E
192 F7 **Celebes Sea** *Ind.* Laut Sulawesi. *sea* Indonesia/ Philippines
41 W12 **Celestún** Yucatán, E Mexico 20°50′N 90°22′W
31 Q12 **Celina** Ohio, N USA 40°34′N 84°35′W
20 L8 **Celina** Tennessee, S USA 36°32′N 85°30′W
25 U5 **Celina** Texas, SW USA 33°19′N 96°46′W
112 G11 **Čelinac Donji** Republika Srpska, N Bosnia and Herzegovina 44°43′N 17°19′E
109 V10 **Celje** *Ger.* Cilli. C Slovenia 46°16′N 15°14′E
111 G23 **Celldömölk** Vas, W Hungary 47°16′N 17°10′E
100 J12 **Celle** *var.* Zelle. Niedersachsen, N Germany 52°38′N 10°05′E
99 D19 **Celles** Hainaut, SW Belgium 50°42′N 03°25′E
104 I7 **Celorico da Beira** Guarda, N Portugal 40°38′N 07°24′W
**Celovec** *see* Klagenfurt
64 M7 **Celtic Sea** *Ir.* An Mhuir Cheilteach. *sea* SW British Isles
64 N7 **Celtic Shelf** *undersea feature* E Atlantic Ocean 07°00′W 49°15′N
114 L13 **Çeltik Gölu** ◎ NW Turkey
146 J17 **Çemenibit** *prev. Rus.* Chemenibit. Mary Welaýaty, S Turkmenistan 35°27′N 62°19′E
113 M14 **Čemerno** ▲▲ C Serbia
105 Q12 **Cenajo, Embalse del** ▣ S Spain
171 V13 **Cenderawasih, Teluk** *var.* Teluk Irian, Teluk Sarera. *bay* W Pacific Ocean
105 P4 **Cenicero** La Rioja, N Spain 42°29′N 02°38′W
106 E9 **Ceno** ≈ NW Italy
102 K13 **Cenon** Gironde, SW France 44°51′N 00°33′W
14 K13 **Centennial Lake** ◎ Ontario, SE Canada
**Centennial State** *see* Colorado
37 S7 **Center** Colorado, C USA 37°45′N 106°06′W
29 Q13 **Center** Nebraska, C USA 42°33′N 97°51′W
28 M5 **Center** North Dakota, N USA 47°07′N 101°18′W
25 X8 **Center** Texas, SW USA 31°49′N 94°10′W
29 W8 **Center City** Minnesota, N USA 45°25′N 92°48′W
36 L5 **Centerfield** Utah, W USA 39°07′N 111°49′W
20 K9 **Center Hill Lake** ▣ Tennessee, S USA
29 X13 **Center Point** Iowa, C USA 42°11′N 91°47′W
25 R11 **Center Point** Texas, SW USA 29°56′N 99°01′W
29 W16 **Centerville** Iowa, C USA 40°47′N 92°51′W
27 W7 **Centerville** Missouri, C USA 37°27′N 91°01′W
29 R12 **Centerville** South Dakota, N USA 43°07′N 96°57′W
20 I9 **Centerville** Tennessee, S USA 35°45′N 87°29′W
25 V9 **Centerville** Texas, SW USA 31°17′N 95°59′W
40 M5 **Centinela, Picacho del** ▲ NE Mexico 29°07′N 102°40′W
106 G9 **Cento** Emilia-Romagna, N Italy 44°43′N 11°16′E
**Centrafricaine, République** *see* Central African Republic
39 S8 **Central** Alaska, USA 65°34′N 144°48′W
37 P15 **Central** New Mexico, SW USA 32°46′N 108°09′W
83 H18 **Central** ◈ *district* E Botswana
138 E10 **Central** ◈ *district* C Israel
82 M13 **Central** ◈ *region* C Malawi
153 P12 **Central** ◈ *zone* C Nepal
186 E9 **Central** ◈ *province* S Papua New Guinea
63 I21 **Central** ◈ *department* C Paraguay
155 K25 **Central** ◈ *province* C Sri Lanka
83 J14 **Central** ◈ *province* C Zambia
117 P11 **Central** ✈ (Odesa) Odes'ka Oblast', SW Ukraine 46°26′N 30°41′E
**Central** *see* Centre
**Central** *see* Rennell and Bellona
79 H14 **Central African Republic** *var.* République Centrafricaine, *abbrev.* CAR; *prev.* Ubangi-Shari, Oubangui-Chari, Territoire de l'Oubangui-Chari. ◆ *republic* C Africa
192 C6 **Central Basin Trough** *undersea feature* W Pacific Ocean 16°45′N 130°00′E
**Central Borneo** *see* Kalimantan Tengah
149 P12 **Central Brahui Range** ▲▲ W Pakistan
**Central Celebes** *see* Sulawesi Tengah
29 Y13 **Central City** Iowa, C USA 42°12′N 91°31′W
20 I6 **Central City** Kentucky, S USA 37°17′N 87°07′W
29 P15 **Central City** Nebraska, C USA 41°04′N 97°59′W
48 D6 **Central, Cordillera** ▲▲ W Bolivia
54 D11 **Central, Cordillera** ▲▲ W Colombia
42 M13 **Central, Cordillera** ▲▲ C Costa Rica
45 N9 **Central, Cordillera** ▲▲ C Dominican Republic
43 R16 **Central, Cordillera** ▲▲ C Panama
45 S6 **Central, Cordillera** ▲▲ Puerto Rico
42 H7 **Central District** *var.* Tegucigalpa. ◈ *district* C Honduras
81 E16 **Central Equatoria** *var.* Bahr el Gebel, Bahr el Jebel. ◈ *state* S South Sudan
**Central Group** *see* Inner Islands
30 L15 **Centralia** Illinois, N USA 38°31′N 89°07′W
27 U4 **Centralia** Missouri, C USA 39°12′N 92°08′W
32 G9 **Centralia** Washington, NW USA 46°43′N 122°57′W
**Central Indian Ridge** *see* Mid-Indian Ridge
**Central Java** *see* Jawa Tengah
**Central Kalimantan** *see* Kalimantan Tengah
148 L14 **Central Makran Range** ▲▲ W Pakistan
192 K7 **Central Pacific Basin** *undersea feature* C Pacific Ocean 05°00′N 175°00′W




◆ Country
● Country Capital
◇ Dependent Territory
○ Dependent Territory Capital
◈ Administrative Regions
✈ International Airport
▲ Mountain
▲▲ Mountain Range
Volcano
≈ River
◎ Lake
▣ Reservoir

Central, Planalto – Chastova

59 M19 **Central, Planalto** *var.* Brazilian Highlands. ▲▲ E Brazil
32 F15 **Central Point** Oregon, NW USA 42°22′N 122°55′W
**Central Provinces and Berar** *see* Madhya Pradesh
186 B6 **Central Range** ▲▲ NW Papua New Guinea
**Central Russian Upland** *see* Srednerusskaya Vozvyshennost'
**Central Siberian Plateau/Central Siberian Uplands** *see* Srednesibirskoye Ploskogor'ye
104 K8 **Central, Sistema** ▲▲ C Spain
**Central Sulawesi** *see* Sulawesi Tengah
35 N3 **Central Valley** California, W USA 40°39′N 122°21′W
35 P8 **Central Valley** *valley* California, W USA
23 Q3 **Centre** Alabama, S USA 34°09′N 85°40′W
79 E15 **Centre** *Eng.* Central. ◈ *region* C Cameroon
173 Y16 **Centre de Flacq** E Mauritius 20°12′S 57°43′E
55 Y9 **Centre Spatial Guyanais** *space station* N French Guiana
102 M8 **Centre-Val de Loire** ◈ *region* N France
23 O5 **Centreville** Alabama, S USA 32°58′N 87°08′W
21 X3 **Centreville** Maryland, NE USA 39°03′N 76°04′W
22 J7 **Centreville** Mississippi, S USA 31°05′N 91°04′W
**Centum Cellae** *see* Civitavecchia
160 M14 **Cenxi** Guangxi Zhuangzu Zizhiqu, S China 22°58′N 111°00′E
**Ceos** *see* Kéa
**Cephaloedium** *see* Cefalù
**Cephalonia** *see* Kefalloniá
112 I9 **Čepin** *Hung.* Csepén. Osijek-Baranja, E Croatia 45°32′N 18°33′E
**Ceram** *see* Seram, Pulau
171 R13 **Ceram Sea** *Ind.* Laut Seram. *sea* E Indonesia
192 G8 **Ceram Trough** *undersea feature* W Pacific Ocean
**Cerasus** *see* Giresun
36 I10 **Cerbat Mountains** ▲▲ Arizona, SW USA
103 P17 **Cerbère, Cap** *headland* S France 42°28′N 03°15′E
104 F13 **Cercal do Alentejo** Setúbal, S Portugal 37°48′N 08°40′W
111 A18 **Čerchov** *Ger.* Czerkow. ▲ W Czechia 49°24′N 12°47′E
103 O13 **Cère** ~ C France
61 A16 **Ceres** Santa Fe, C Argentina 29°55′S 61°55′W
59 K18 **Ceres** Goiás, C Brazil 15°21′S 49°34′W
**Ceresio** *see* Lugano, Lago di
103 O17 **Céret** Pyrénées-Orientales, S France 42°30′N 02°44′E
54 E6 **Cereté** Córdoba, NW Colombia 08°54′N 75°51′W
172 I17 **Cerf, Île au** *island* Inner Islands, NE Seychelles
99 G22 **Cerfontaine** Namur, S Belgium 50°08′N 04°25′E
**Cergy-Pontoise** *see* Pontoise
107 N16 **Cerignola** Puglia, SE Italy 41°17′N 15°53′E
**Cerigo** *see* Kýthira
103 O9 **Cérilly** Allier, C France 46°38′N 02°51′E
136 I11 **Çerkeş** Çankin, N Turkey 40°51′N 32°52′E
136 D10 **Çerkezköy** Tekirdağ, NW Turkey 41°17′N 28°00′E
109 T12 **Cerknica** *Ger.* Zirknitz. SW Slovenia 45°48′N 14°21′E
109 S11 **Cerkno** W Slovenia 46°07′N 13°58′E
116 F10 **Cermei** *Hung.* Csermő. Arad, W Romania 46°33′N 21°51′E
137 O15 **Çermik** Dıyarbakır, SE Turkey 38°09′N 39°27′E
112 I10 **Cerna** Vukovar-Srijem, E Croatia 45°10′N 18°36′E
**Cernăuţi** *see* Chernivtsi
116 M14 **Cernavodă** Constanţa, SW Romania 44°20′N 28°03′E
103 U7 **Cernay** Haut-Rhin, NE France 47°49′N 07°11′E
**Černice** *see* Schwarzach
41 O8 **Cerralvo** Nuevo León, NE Mexico 26°10′N 99°40′W
40 G9 **Cerralvo, Isla** *island* NW Mexico
107 L16 **Cerreto Sannita** Campania, S Italy 41°17′N 14°39′E
113 L20 **Cërrik** *var.* Cerriku. Elbasan, C Albania 41°01′N 19°55′E
**Cerriku** *see* Cërrik
41 O11 **Cerritos** San Luis Potosí, C Mexico 22°25′N 100°16′W
60 K11 **Cerro Azul** Paraná, S Brazil 24°48′S 49°14′W
61 F18 **Cerro Chato** Treinta y Tres, E Uruguay 33°04′S 55°08′W
61 F19 **Cerro Colorado** Florida, S Uruguay 33°52′S 55°33′W
56 E13 **Cerro de Pasco** Pasco, C Peru 10°43′S 76°15′W
61 G14 **Cêrro Largo** Rio Grande do Sul, S Brazil 28°10′S 54°43′W
61 G18 **Cerro Largo** ◈ *department* NE Uruguay
42 E7 **Cerrón Grande, Embalse** ▣ N El Salvador
63 I14 **Cerros Colorados, Embalse** ◎ W Argentina
105 V5 **Cervera** Cataluña, NE Spain 41°40′N 01°16′E
104 M3 **Cervera del Pisuerga** Castilla y León, N Spain 42°51′N 04°30′W
105 Q5 **Cervera del Río Alhama** La Rioja, N Spain 42°01′N 01°58′W
107 H15 **Cerveteri** Lazio, C Italy 42°00′N 12°06′E
106 H10 **Cervia** Emilia-Romagna, N Italy 44°14′N 12°22′E
106 J7 **Cervignano del Friuli** Friuli-Venezia Giulia, NE Italy 45°49′N 13°18′E
107 L17 **Cervinara** Campania, S Italy 41°02′N 14°36′E
**Cervinia** *see* Breuil-Cervinia
82 L12 **Chambeshi** ~ NE Zambia
74 M6 **Chambi, Jebel** *var.* Jabal ash Sha'nabī. ▲ W Tunisia 35°16′N 08°39′E
15 Q7 **Chambord** Québec, SE Canada 48°25′N 72°02′W
139 U11 **Chamcham** Al Muthanná, S Iraq 31°17′N 45°05′E
**Chamchamāl** *see* Chemchemal
**Chamdmanī** *see* Altanshiree
40 J14 **Chamela** Jalisco, SW Mexico 19°31′N 105°02′W
42 G5 **Chamelecón, Río** ~ NW Honduras
62 J9 **Chamical** La Rioja, C Argentina 30°21′S 66°19′W
115 L23 **Chamili** *island* Kykládes, Greece, Aegean Sea
167 Q13 **Châmnar** Koh Kong, SW Cambodia 11°45′N 103°32′E
152 K9 **Chamoli** Uttarākhand, N India 30°22′N 79°19′E
103 U11 **Chamonix-Mont-Blanc** Haute-Savoie, E France 45°55′N 06°52′E
154 L11 **Chāmpa** Chhattisgarh, C India 22°02′N 82°42′E
10 H8 **Champagne** Yukon, W Canada 60°48′N 136°22′W
103 Q5 **Champagne** *cultural region* N France
**Champagne** *see* Campania
103 S9 **Champagnole** Jura, E France 46°44′N 05°55′E
30 M13 **Champaign** Illinois, N USA 40°07′N 88°15′W
167 S10 **Champasak** Champasak, S Laos 14°50′N 105°51′E
103 U6 **Champ de Feu** ▲ NE France 48°24′N 07°15′E
13 O7 **Champdoré, Lac** ◎ Québec, NE Canada
42 B6 **Champerico** Retalhuleu, SW Guatemala 14°18′N 91°54′W
108 C11 **Champéry** Valais, SW Switzerland 46°12′N 06°52′E
18 L6 **Champlain** New York, NE USA 44°58′N 73°25′W
18 L9 **Champlain Canal** *canal* New York, NE USA
15 P13 **Champlain, Lac** ◎ Québec, Canada/USA *see also* Champlain, Lake
18 L7 **Champlain, Lake** ◎ Canada/USA *see also* Champlain, Lac
103 S7 **Champlitte** Haute-Saône, E France 47°36′N 05°31′E
41 W13 **Champotón** Campeche, SE Mexico 19°18′N 90°43′W
104 G10 **Chamusca** Santarém, C Portugal 39°21′N 08°29′W
119 O20 **Chamyarysy** *Rus.* Chemerisy. Homyel'skaya Voblasts', SE Belarus 51°42′N 30°27′E
127 P5 **Chamzinka** Respublika Mordoviya, W Russia 54°22′N 45°22′E
**Chanáil Mhór, An** *see* Grand Canal
**Chanak** *see* Çanakkale
62 G7 **Chañaral** Atacama, N Chile 26°19′S 70°34′W
104 H13 **Chança, Rio** *var.* Chanza. ~ Portugal/Spain
57 D14 **Chancay** Lima, W Peru 11°36′S 77°14′W
**Chan-chiang/Chanchiang** *see* Zhanjiang
62 G13 **Chanco** Maule, C Chile 35°43′S 72°35′W
39 R7 **Chandalar** Alaska, USA 67°30′N 148°29′W
39 R6 **Chandalar River** ~ Alaska, USA
152 L10 **Chandan Chauki** Uttar Pradesh, N India 28°32′N 80°43′E
153 S16 **Chandannagar** *prev.* Chandernagore. West Bengal, E India 22°52′N 88°21′E
152 K10 **Chandausi** Uttar Pradesh, N India 28°27′N 78°43′E
22 M10 **Chandeleur Islands** *island group* Louisiana, S USA
22 M9 **Chandeleur Sound** *sound* N Gulf of Mexico
**Chandernagore** *see* Chandannagar
152 I8 **Chandīgarh** *state capital* Punjab, N India 30°41′N 76°51′E
153 Q16 **Chāndil** Jhārkhand, NE India 22°58′N 86°04′E
182 D2 **Chandler** South Australia 26°59′S 133°22′E
15 Y7 **Chandler** Québec, SE Canada 48°21′N 64°41′W
36 L14 **Chandler** Arizona, SW USA 33°18′N 111°50′W
27 O10 **Chandler** Oklahoma, C USA 35°43′N 96°54′W
25 V7 **Chandler** Texas, SW USA 32°18′N 95°28′W
39 Q6 **Chandler River** ~ Alaska, USA
56 H13 **Chandles, Río** ~ E Peru
162 H9 **Chandmanī** *var.* Talshand. Govĭ-Altayĭ, C Mongolia 45°21′N 98°00′E
162 F7 **Chandmanī** *var.* Urdgol. Hovd, W Mongolia 47°39′N 92°46′E
14 J13 **Chandos Lake** ◎ Ontario, SE Canada
153 U15 **Chandpur** Chittagong, C Bangladesh 23°13′N 90°43′E
154 I13 **Chandrapur** Mahārāshtra, C India 19°58′N 79°21′E
83 J15 **Changa** Southern, S Zambia 16°24′S 28°27′E
**Chang'an** *see* Rong'an, Guangxi Zhuangzu Zizhiqu, S China
**Changan** *see* Xi'an, Shaanxi, C China
**Changanācheri** *see* Changannassery
83 M19 **Changane** ~ S Mozambique
155 G23 **Changannassery** *var.* Changanācheri. Kerala, SW India 09°26′N 76°31′E
83 M16 **Changara** Tete, NW Mozambique 16°54′S 33°15′E
163 X11 **Changbai** *var.* Changbai Chaoxianzu Zizhixian. Jilin, NE China 41°25′N 128°08′E
**Changbai Chaoxianzu Zizhixian** *see* Changbai
163 X11 **Changbai Shan** ▲▲ NE China
163 V10 **Changchun** *var.* Ch'ang-ch'un; *prev.* Hsinking. *province capital* Jilin, NE China 43°53′N 125°18′E
**Ch'angch'un/Ch'ang-ch'un** *see* Changchun
160 M10 **Changde** Hunan, S China 29°04′N 111°42′E
161 S13 **Changhua** *var.* Zhanghua, *Jap.* Shōka. C Taiwan 24°06′N 120°31′E
168 L10 **Changi** ✈ (Singapore) E Singapore 01°22′N 103°58′E
158 L5 **Changji** Xinjiang Uygur Zizhiqu, NW China 44°02′N 87°12′E
160 L17 **Changjiang** *var.* Changjiang Lizu Zizhixian, Shiliu. Hainan, S China 19°16′N 109°09′E
157 R11 **Chang Jiang** *var.* Yangtze Kiang, *Eng.* Yangtze. ~ C China
157 N12 **Chang Jiang** *Eng.* Yangtze. ~ SW China
161 S8 **Changjiang Kou** *delta* E China
**Changjiang Lizu Zizhixian** *see* Changjiang
**Changkiakow** *see* Zhangjiakou
167 F12 **Chang, Ko** *island* S Thailand
161 Q2 **Changli** Hebei, E China 39°44′N 119°13′E
163 V10 **Changling** Jilin, NE China 44°15′N 124°03′E
**Changning** *see* Xunwu
161 N11 **Changsha** *var.* Ch'angsha, Ch'ang-sha. *province capital* Hunan, S China 28°10′N 113°E
**Ch'angsha/Ch'ang-sha** *see* Changsha
161 Q10 **Changshan** Zhejiang, SE China 28°54′N 118°30′E
163 V14 **Changshan Qundao** *island group* NE China
161 S8 **Changshu** *var.* Ch'ang-shu. Jiangsu, E China 31°39′N 120°45′E
**Ch'ang-shu** *see* Changshu
163 V11 **Changtu** Liaoning, NE China 42°50′N 123°59′E
43 P14 **Changuinola** Bocas del Toro, NW Panama 09°28′N 82°31′W
159 N9 **Changweiliang** Qinghai, W China 38°24′N 92°08′E
160 K6 **Changwu** *var.* Zhaoren. Shaanxi, C China 35°12′N 107°46′E
163 U13 **Changxing Dao** *island* N China
160 M9 **Changyang** *var.* Longzhouping. Hubei, C China 30°45′N 111°13′E
163 W14 **Changyŏn** SW North Korea 38°19′N 125°15′E
161 N5 **Changzhi** Shanxi, C China 36°10′N 113°02′E
161 R8 **Changzhou** Jiangsu, E China 31°45′N 119°58′E
115 H24 **Chaniá** *var.* Hania, Khaniá, *Eng.* Canea; *anc.* Cydonia. Kríti, Greece, E Mediterranean Sea 35°31′N 24°00′E
62 J5 **Chañi, Nevado de** ▲ NW Argentina 24°09′S 65°44′W
115 H24 **Chanión, Kólpos** *gulf* Kríti, Greece, E Mediterranean Sea
**Chankiri** *see* Çankırı
30 M11 **Channahon** Illinois, N USA 41°25′N 88°13′W
155 H20 **Channapatna** Karnātaka, E India 12°43′N 77°14′E
97 K26 **Channel Islands** *Fr.* Iles Normandes. *island group* S English Channel
35 R16 **Channel Islands** *island group* California, W USA
13 S13 **Channel-Port aux Basques** Newfoundland and Labrador, SE Canada 47°35′N 59°02′W
**Channel, The** *see* English Channel
97 Q23 **Channel Tunnel** *tunnel* France/United Kingdom
24 M2 **Channing** Texas, SW USA 35°41′N 102°21′W
**Chantabun/Chantaburi** *see* Chanthaburi
104 H3 **Chantada** Galicia, NW Spain 42°36′N 07°46′W
167 P12 **Chanthaburi** *var.* Chantabun, Chantaburi. Chantaburi, S Thailand 12°35′N 102°08′E
103 O4 **Chantilly** Oise, N France 49°12′N 02°28′E
139 V12 **Chanūn as Sa'ūdī** Dhī Qār, S Iraq 31°04′N 46°00′E
27 Q6 **Chanute** Kansas, C USA 37°40′N 95°27′W
**Chanza** *see* Chança, Rio
**Ch'ao-an/Chaochow** *see* Chaozhou
161 P8 **Chao Hu** ◎ E China
167 P11 **Chao Phraya, Mae Nam** ~ C Thailand
163 T8 **Chaor Hol** *prev.* Qulin Gol. ~ NE China
**Chaouèn** *see* Chefchaouen
161 P14 **Chaoyang** Guangdong, S China 23°17′N 116°33′E
163 T12 **Chaoyang** Liaoning, NE China 41°34′N 120°29′E
**Chaoyang** *see* Jiayin, Heilongjiang, China
**Chaoyang** *see* Huinan, Jilin China
161 Q14 **Chaozhou** *var.* Chaoan, Chao'an, Ch'ao-an; *prev.* Chaochow. Guangdong, SE China 23°42′N 116°36′E
58 N13 **Chapadinha** Maranhão, E Brazil 03°45′S 43°23′W
12 K12 **Chapais** Québec, SE Canada 49°47′N 74°54′W
40 L13 **Chapala** Jalisco, SW Mexico 20°20′N 103°10′W
40 L13 **Chapala, Lago de** ◎ C Mexico
146 F13 **Chapan, Gora** ▲ C Turkmenistan 37°48′N 58°03′E
57 M18 **Chapare, Río** ~ C Bolivia
54 E11 **Chaparral** Tolima, C Colombia 03°45′N 75°30′W
144 F9 **Chapayev** Zapadnyy Kazakhstan, NW Kazakhstan 50°12′N 51°09′E
123 O11 **Chapayevo** Respublika Sakha (Yakutiya), NE Russia 60°03′N 117°19′E
127 R6 **Chapayevsk** Samarskaya Oblast', W Russia 52°57′N 49°42′E
60 H13 **Chapecó** Santa Catarina, S Brazil 27°14′S 52°41′W
60 I13 **Chapecó, Rio** ~ S Brazil
20 J9 **Chapel Hill** Tennessee, S USA 35°38′N 86°40′W
44 J12 **Chapelton** C Jamaica 18°05′N 77°16′W
14 C8 **Chapleau** Ontario, SE Canada 47°50′N 83°24′W
14 D7 **Chapleau** ~ Ontario, S Canada
11 T16 **Chaplin** Saskatchewan, S Canada 50°27′N 106°37′W
126 M6 **Chaplygin** Lipetskaya Oblast', W Russia 53°13′N 39°58′E
117 S11 **Chaplynka** Khersons'ka Oblast', S Ukraine 46°20′N 33°34′E
9 O6 **Chapman, Cape** *headland* Nunavut, NE Canada 69°15′N 89°09′W
25 T15 **Chapman Ranch** Texas, SW USA 27°32′N 97°25′W
**Chapman's** *see* Okwa
21 P5 **Chapmanville** West Virginia, NE USA 37°58′N 82°01′W
28 K15 **Chappell** Nebraska, C USA 41°05′N 102°28′W
**Chapra** *see* Chhapra
56 D9 **Chapuli, Río** ~ N Peru
76 I6 **Châr** *well* N Mauritania
123 P12 **Chara** Zabaykal'skiy Kray, S Russia 56°57′N 118°05′E
123 O11 **Chara** ~ C Russia
54 G8 **Charala** Santander, C Colombia 06°17′N 73°09′W
41 N10 **Charcas** San Luis Potosí, C Mexico 23°09′N 101°10′W
25 T13 **Charco** Texas, SW USA 28°42′N 97°35′E
194 H7 **Charcot Island** *island* Antarctica
64 M8 **Charcot Seamounts** *undersea feature* E Atlantic Ocean 11°30′W 45°00′N
**Chardara** *see* Shardara
**Chardarinskoye Vodokhranilishche** *see* Shardarinskoye Vodokhranilishche
31 U11 **Chardon** Ohio, N USA 41°34′N 81°12′W
44 K9 **Chardonnières** SW Haiti 18°16′N 74°10′W
**Chardzhev** *see* Türkmenabat
**Chardzhevskaya Oblast** *see* Lebap Welaýaty
**Chardzhou/Chardzhui** *see* Türkmenabat
102 L11 **Charente** ◈ *department* W France
102 J11 **Charente** ~ W France
102 J10 **Charente-Maritime** ◈ *department* W France
137 U12 **Ch'arents'avan** C Armenia 40°23′N 44°41′E
106 B6 **Cervino, Monte** *var.* Matterhorn. ▲ Italy/Switzerland 46°00′N 07°39′E *see also* Matterhorn
**Cervino, Monte** *see* Matterhorn
103 Y14 **Cervione** Corse, France, C Mediterranean Sea 42°22′N 09°28′E
104 I1 **Cervo** Galicia, NW Spain 43°39′N 07°25′W
54 F5 **Cesar** *off.* Departamento del Cesar. ◈ *province* N Colombia
**Cesar, Departamento del** *see* Cesar
106 H10 **Cesena** *anc.* Caesena. Emilia-Romagna, N Italy 44°09′N 12°14′E
106 I10 **Cesenatico** Emilia-Romagna, N Italy 44°12′N 12°24′E
118 H8 **Cēsis** *Ger.* Wenden. C Latvia 57°19′N 25°17′E
111 D15 **Česká Lípa** *Ger.* Böhmisch-Leipa. Liberecký Kraj, N Czechia 50°43′N 14°35′E
111 F17 **Česká Třebová** *Ger.* Böhmisch-Trübau. Pardubický Kraj, C Czechia 49°54′N 16°27′E
111 D19 **České Budějovice** *Ger.* Budweis. Jihočeský Kraj, S Czechia 48°58′N 14°29′E
111 D19 **České Velenice** Jihočeský Kraj, S Czechia 48°49′N 14°57′E
**Česko** *see* Czechia
111 E18 **Českomoravská Vrchovina** *var.* Českomoravská Vysočina, *Eng.* Bohemian-Moravian Highlands, *Ger.* Böhmisch-Mährische Höhe. ▲▲ S Czechia
**Českomoravská Vysočina** *see* Českomoravská Vrchovina
**Česko Republika** *see* Czechia
111 C19 **Český Krumlov** *var.* Böhmisch-Krumau, *Ger.* Krummau. Jihočeský Kraj, S Czechia 48°48′N 14°18′E
**Český Les** *see* Bohemian Forest
112 F8 **Česma** ~ N Croatia
136 A14 **Çeşme** İzmir, W Turkey 38°19′N 26°20′E
**Cess** *see* Cestos
183 T8 **Cessnock** New South Wales, SE Australia 32°51′S 151°21′E
76 K17 **Cestos** *var.* Cess. ~ S Liberia
118 I9 **Cesvaine** E Latvia 56°58′N 26°15′E
116 G14 **Cetate** Dolj, SW Romania 44°06′N 23°01′E
**Cetatea Albă** *see* Bilhorod-Dnistrovs'kyy
**Cetatea Damboviţei** *see* Bucureşti
113 J17 **Cetinje** *It.* Cettigne. S Montenegro 42°23′N 18°55′E
107 N20 **Cetraro** Calabria, S Italy 39°30′N 15°59′E
**Cette** *see* Sète
188 A17 **Cetti Bay** *bay* SW Guam
**Cettigne** *see* Cetinje
104 L17 **Ceuta** *off.* Ciudad Autónoma de Ceuta, *var.* Sebta. Ceuta, N Africa 35°53′N 05°19′W
88 C16 **Ceuta** *autonomous city of Spain* Spain, N Africa
**Ceuta, Ciudad Autónoma de** *see* Ceuta
106 B9 **Ceva** Piemonte, NE Italy 44°24′N 08°01′E
103 P14 **Cévennes** ▲▲ S France
108 G10 **Cevio** Ticino, S Switzerland 46°18′N 08°36′E
136 K16 **Ceyhan** Adana, S Turkey 37°02′N 35°48′E
136 K17 **Ceyhan Nehri** ~ S Turkey
137 P17 **Ceylanpınar** Şanlıurfa, SE Turkey 36°53′N 40°02′E
**Ceylon** *see* Sri Lanka
173 R6 **Ceylon Plain** *undersea feature* N Indian Ocean 04°00′S 82°00′E
**Ceyre to the Caribs** *see* Marie-Galante
103 Q14 **Cèze** ~ S France
**Chaacha** *see* Çäçe
127 P6 **Chaadayevka** Penzenskaya Oblast', W Russia 53°07′N 45°55′E
167 O12 **Cha-Am** Phetchaburi, SW Thailand 12°48′N 99°58′E
143 W15 **Chābahār** *var.* Chāh Bahār, Chahbar. Sīstān va Balūchestān, SE Iran 25°21′N 60°38′E
**Chabaricha** *see* Khabarikha
61 B19 **Chabas** Santa Fe, C Argentina 33°16′S 61°23′W
103 T10 **Chablais** *physical region* E France
61 B20 **Chacabuco** Buenos Aires, E Argentina 34°40′S 60°27′W
42 K8 **Chachagón, Cerro** ▲ N Nicaragua 13°18′N 85°39′W
56 C10 **Chachapoyas** Amazonas, NW Peru 06°13′S 77°54′W
**Chäche** *see* Çäçe
119 O18 **Chachersk** *Rus.* Chechersk. Homyel'skaya Voblasts', SE Belarus 52°54′N 30°54′E
119 N16 **Chachevichy** *Rus.* Chechevichi. Mahilyowskaya Voblasts', E Belarus 53°31′N 29°51′E
61 B14 **Chaco** *off.* Provincia de Chaco. ◈ *province* NE Argentina
**Chaco** *see* Gran Chaco
62 M6 **Chaco Austral** *physical region* N Argentina
62 M3 **Chaco Boreal** *physical region* N Paraguay
62 M6 **Chaco Central** *physical region* N Argentina
39 Y15 **Chacon, Cape** *headland* Prince of Wales Island, Alaska, USA 54°41′N 132°00′W
**Chaco, Provincia de** *see* Chaco
78 H9 **Chad** *off.* Republic of Chad, *Fr.* Tchad. ◆ *republic* C Africa
122 K14 **Chadan** Respublika Tyva, S Russia 51°16′N 91°25′E
21 U12 **Chadbourn** North Carolina, SE USA 34°19′N 78°49′W
83 L14 **Chadiza** Eastern, E Zambia 14°04′S 32°27′E
67 Q7 **Chad, Lake** *Fr.* Lac Tchad. ◎ C Africa
**Chad, Republic of** *see* Chad
28 J12 **Chadron** Nebraska, C USA 42°48′N 102°57′W
**Chadyr-Lunga** *see* Ciadîr-Lunga
163 W14 **Chaeryŏng** SW North Korea 38°22′N 125°35′E
105 P17 **Chafarinas, Islas** *island group* S Spain
27 Y7 **Chaffee** Missouri, C USA 37°10′N 89°39′W
148 L12 **Chagai Hills** *var.* Chāh Gay. ▲▲ Afghanistan/Pakistan
123 Q11 **Chagda** Respublika Sakha (Yakutiya), NE Russia 58°43′N 130°38′E
**Chaghasarāy** *see* Asadābād
149 N5 **Chaghcharān** *var.* Chakhcharan, Cheghcheran, Qala Āhangarān. ◈ Ghōr, C Afghanistan
103 R9 **Chagny** Saône-et-Loire, C France 46°54′N 04°45′E
173 Q7 **Chagos Archipelago** *var.* Oil Islands. *island group* British Indian Ocean Territory
129 O15 **Chagos Bank** *undersea feature* C Indian Ocean 06°15′S 72°00′E
129 O14 **Chagos-Laccadive Plateau** *undersea feature* N Indian Ocean 03°00′S 73°00′E
173 Q7 **Chagos Trench** *undersea feature* N Indian Ocean 07°00′S 73°30′E
43 T14 **Chagres, Río** ~ C Panama
45 U14 **Chaguanas** Trinidad, Trinidad and Tobago 10°31′N 61°25′W
54 M6 **Chaguaramas** Guárico, N Venezuela 09°23′N 66°18′W
**Chagyl** *see* Çagyl
**Chahār Maḩāll and Bakhtiyārī** *see* Chahār Maḩāll va Bakhtīārī
142 M9 **Chahār Maḩāll va Bakhtīārī** *off.* Ostān-e Chahār Maḩāll va Bakhtīārī, *var.* Chahār Maḩāll and Bakhtiyārī. ◈ *province* SW Iran
**Chahār Maḩāll va Bakhtīārī, Ostān-e** *see* Chahār Maḩāll va Bakhtīārī
**Chāh Bahār/Chahbar** *see* Chābahār
143 V13 **Chāh Derāz** Sīstān va Balūchestān, SE Iran 27°07′N 60°01′E
**Chāh Gay** *see* Chagai Hills
167 P10 **Chai Badan** Lop Buri, C Thailand 15°08′N 101°03′E
153 Q16 **Chāībāsa** Jhārkhand, N India 22°31′N 85°50′E
79 E19 **Chaillu, Massif du** ▲ C Gabon
167 O10 **Chai Nat** *var.* Chainat, Jainat, Jayanath. Chai Nat, C Thailand 15°10′N 100°10′E
**Chainat** *see* Chai Nat
65 M14 **Chain Fracture Zone** *tectonic feature* E Atlantic Ocean
173 N5 **Chain Ridge** *undersea feature* W Indian Ocean 06°00′N 54°00′E
**Chairn, Ceann an** *see* Carnsore Point
158 L5 **Chaiwopu** Xinjiang Uygur Zizhiqu, W China 43°32′N 87°55′E
167 Q10 **Chaiyaphum** *var.* Jayabum. Chaiyaphum, C Thailand 15°46′N 101°55′E
62 N10 **Chajarí** Entre Ríos, E Argentina 30°45′S 57°57′W
42 C5 **Chajul** Quiché, W Guatemala 15°28′N 91°02′W
83 K16 **Chakari** Mashonaland West, N Zimbabwe 18°05′S 29°51′E
148 J9 **Chakhānsūr** Nīmrōz, SW Afghanistan 31°11′N 62°06′E
**Chakhānsūr** *see* Nīmrōz
**Chakhcharan** *see* Chaghcharān
149 V8 **Chak Jhumra** *var.* Jhumra. Punjab, E Pakistan 31°33′N 73°14′E
146 I16 **Chaknakdysonga** Ahal Welaýaty, S Turkmenistan 35°39′N 61°24′E
153 P16 **Chakradharpur** Jhārkhand, N India 22°42′N 85°38′E
152 J8 **Chakrāta** Uttarākhand, N India 30°42′N 77°52′E
149 U7 **Chakwal** Punjab, NE Pakistan 32°56′N 72°53′E
57 F17 **Chala** Arequipa, SW Peru 15°52′S 74°13′W
102 K12 **Chalais** Charente, W France 45°16′N 00°02′E
108 D10 **Chalais** Valais, SW Switzerland 46°18′N 07°37′E
115 J20 **Chalándri** *var.* Halandri; *prev.* Khalándrion. *prehistoric site* Sýros, Kykládes, Greece, Aegean Sea
188 H6 **Chalan Kanoa** Saipan, S Northern Mariana Islands 15°08′S 145°43′E
188 C16 **Chalan Pago** C Guam
**Chalap Dalam/Chalap Dalan** *see* Chehil Abdālān, Kōh-e
42 F7 **Chalatenango** Chalatenango, N El Salvador 14°04′N 88°53′W
42 A9 **Chalatenango** ◈ *department* NW El Salvador
83 P15 **Chalaua** Nampula, NE Mozambique 16°04′S 39°08′E
81 I16 **Chalbi Desert** *desert* N Kenya
42 D7 **Chalchuapa** Santa Ana, W El Salvador 13°59′N 89°41′W
**Chalcidice** *see* Chalkidikí
**Chalcis** *see* Chalkída
**Chälderän** *see* Siāh Chashmeh
103 N6 **Châlette-sur-Loing** Loiret, C France 48°01′N 02°45′E
15 X8 **Chaleur Bay** *Fr.* Baie des Chaleurs. *bay* New Brunswick/Québec, E Canada
**Chaleurs, Baie des** *see* Chaleur Bay
57 G16 **Chalhuanca** Apurímac, S Peru 14°17′S 73°15′W
154 F12 **Chālisgaon** Mahārāshtra, C India 20°29′N 75°10′E
115 N23 **Chálki** *island* Dodekánisa, Greece, Aegean Sea
115 F16 **Chalkiádes** Thessalía, C Greece 39°24′N 22°25′E
115 H18 **Chalkída** *var.* Halkida, *prev.* Khalkís; *anc.* Chalcis. Evvoia, E Greece 38°27′N 23°38′E
115 G14 **Chalkidikí** *var.* Khalkidhikí; *anc.* Chalcidice. *peninsula* NE Greece
185 A24 **Chalky Inlet** *inlet* South Island, New Zealand
39 S7 **Chalkyitsik** Alaska, USA 66°39′N 143°43′W
102 I9 **Challans** Vendée, NW France 46°51′N 01°52′W
57 K19 **Challapata** Oruro, SW Bolivia 18°50′S 66°45′W
192 H6 **Challenger Deep** *undersea feature* W Pacific Ocean 11°20′N 142°12′E
**Challenger Deep** *see* Mariana Trench
193 S11 **Challenger Fracture Zone** *tectonic feature* SE Pacific Ocean
192 K11 **Challenger Plateau** *undersea feature* E Tasman Sea
33 P13 **Challis** Idaho, NW USA 44°31′N 114°14′W
22 L9 **Chalmette** Louisiana, S USA 29°56′N 89°57′W
124 J11 **Chalna** Respublika Kareliya, NW Russia 61°53′N 33°59′E
103 Q5 **Châlons-en-Champagne** *prev.* Châlons-sur-Marne, *hist.* Arcae Remorum; *anc.* Carolopolis. Marne, NE France 48°58′N 04°22′E
**Châlons-sur-Marne** *see* Châlons-en-Champagne
103 R9 **Chalon-sur-Saône** *anc.* Cabillonum. Saône-et-Loire, C France 46°47′N 04°51′E
**Chaltel, Cerro** *see* Fitzroy, Monte
102 M11 **Châlus** Haute-Vienne, C France 45°38′N 01°00′E
143 N4 **Chālūs** Māzandarān, N Iran 36°40′N 51°25′E
101 N20 **Cham** Bayern, SE Germany 49°13′N 12°40′E
108 F7 **Cham** Zug, N Switzerland 47°11′N 08°28′E
37 R8 **Chama** New Mexico, SW USA 36°54′N 106°34′W
**Cha Mai** *see* Thung Song
83 E22 **Chamaites** //Karas, S Namibia 27°15′S 17°52′E
149 O9 **Chaman** Baluchistan, SW Pakistan 30°55′N 66°27′E
37 R9 **Chama, Rio** ~ New Mexico, SW USA
152 I6 **Chamba** Himāchal Pradesh, N India 32°33′N 76°10′E
81 I25 **Chamba** Ruvuma, S Tanzania 11°33′S 37°01′E
150 H12 **Chambal** ~ C India
11 U16 **Chamberlain** Saskatchewan, S Canada 50°49′N 105°29′W
29 O11 **Chamberlain** South Dakota, N USA 43°48′N 99°19′W
19 R3 **Chamberlain Lake** ◎ Maine, NE USA
39 S5 **Chamberlin, Mount** ▲ Alaska, USA 69°16′N 144°54′W
37 O11 **Chambers** Arizona, SW USA 35°11′N 109°25′W
18 F16 **Chambersburg** Pennsylvania, NE USA 39°54′N 77°39′W
31 N5 **Chambers Island** *island* Wisconsin, N USA
103 T11 **Chambéry** *anc.* Camberia. Savoie, E France 45°34′N 05°56′E
82 L12 **Chambeshi** Muchinga, NE Zambia 10°55′S 31°07′E
78 I12 **Chari** *var.* Shari. ~ Central African Republic/Chad
78 G11 **Chari-Baguirmi** *off.* Région du Chari-Baguirmi. ◈ *region* SW Chad
**Chari-Baguirmi, Région du** *see* Chari-Baguirmi
149 Q4 **Chārīkār** Parwān, NE Afghanistan 35°01′N 69°11′E
29 V15 **Chariton** Iowa, C USA 41°00′N 93°18′W
27 U3 **Chariton River** ~ Missouri, C USA
55 T7 **Charity** NW Guyana 07°22′N 58°34′W
31 R7 **Charity Island** *island* Michigan, N USA
**Chärjew** *see* Türkmenabat
**Chärjew Oblasty** *see* Lebap Welaýaty
**Charkhlik/Charkhliq** *see* Ruoqiang
99 G20 **Charleroi** Hainaut, S Belgium 50°25′N 04°27′E
11 V12 **Charles** Manitoba, C Canada 55°27′N 100°58′W
15 R10 **Charlesbourg** Québec, SE Canada 46°50′N 71°15′W
21 Y7 **Charles, Cape** *headland* Virginia, NE USA 37°09′N 75°57′W
29 W12 **Charles City** Iowa, C USA 43°04′N 92°40′W
21 W6 **Charles City** Virginia, NE USA 37°21′N 77°05′W
103 O5 **Charles de Gaulle** ✈ (Paris) Seine-et-Marne, N France 49°04′N 02°36′E
12 K1 **Charles Island** *island* Nunavut, NE Canada
**Charles Island** *see* Santa María, Isla
30 K9 **Charles Mound** *hill* Illinois, N USA
185 A22 **Charles Sound** *sound* South Island, New Zealand
185 G15 **Charleston** West Coast, South Island, New Zealand 41°54′S 171°25′E
27 S11 **Charleston** Arkansas, C USA 35°19′N 94°02′W
30 M14 **Charleston** Illinois, N USA 39°30′N 88°10′W
22 L3 **Charleston** Mississippi, S USA 34°00′N 90°03′W
27 Z7 **Charleston** Missouri, C USA 36°54′N 89°22′W
21 T15 **Charleston** South Carolina, SE USA 32°48′N 79°57′W
21 Q5 **Charleston** *state capital* West Virginia, NE USA 38°21′N 81°38′W
14 L14 **Charleston Lake** ◎ Ontario, SE Canada
35 W11 **Charleston Peak** ▲ Nevada, W USA 36°16′N 115°40′W
45 W10 **Charlestown** Nevis, Saint Kitts and Nevis 17°08′N 62°37′W
31 P16 **Charlestown** Indiana, N USA 38°27′N 85°40′W
18 M9 **Charlestown** New Hampshire, NE USA 43°14′N 72°23′W
21 V3 **Charles Town** West Virginia, NE USA 39°18′N 77°54′W
181 W9 **Charleville** Queensland, E Australia 26°25′S 146°18′E
103 R3 **Charleville-Mézières** Ardennes, N France 49°45′N 04°43′E
31 P5 **Charlevoix** Michigan, N USA 45°19′N 85°15′W
31 Q6 **Charlevoix, Lake** ◎ Michigan, N USA
39 T9 **Charley River** ~ Alaska, USA
64 J6 **Charlie-Gibbs Fracture Zone** *tectonic feature* N Atlantic Ocean
103 Q10 **Charlieu** Loire, E France 46°11′N 04°10′E
31 Q9 **Charlotte** Michigan, N USA 42°33′N 84°50′W
21 R10 **Charlotte** North Carolina, SE USA 35°14′N 80°51′W
20 I8 **Charlotte** Tennessee, S USA 36°11′N 87°18′W
25 R13 **Charlotte** Texas, SW USA 28°51′N 98°42′W
21 R10 **Charlotte** ✈ North Carolina, SE USA 35°12′N 80°54′W
45 T9 **Charlotte Amalie** *prev.* Saint Thomas. ○ (Virgin Islands (US)) Saint Thomas, N Virgin Islands (US) 18°22′N 64°56′W
21 U7 **Charlotte Court House** Virginia, NE USA 37°04′N 78°37′W
23 W14 **Charlotte Harbor** *inlet* Florida, SE USA
**Charlotte Island** *see* Abaiang
95 J15 **Charlottenberg** Värmland, C Sweden 59°53′N 12°17′E
**Charlottenhof** *see* Aegviidu
21 U5 **Charlottesville** Virginia, NE USA 38°02′N 78°29′W
13 Q14 **Charlottetown** *province capital* Prince Edward Island, Prince Edward Island, SE Canada 46°14′N 63°09′W
**Charlotte Town** *see* Roseau, Dominica
**Charlotte Town** *see* Gouyave, Grenada
45 Z16 **Charlotteville** Tobago, Trinidad and Tobago 11°16′N 60°33′W
182 M11 **Charlton** Victoria, SE Australia 36°18′S 143°19′E
12 H10 **Charlton Island** *island* Northwest Territories, C Canada
103 T6 **Charmes** Vosges, NE France 48°19′N 06°19′E
119 F19 **Charnawchytsy** *Rus.* Chernawchitsy. Brestskaya Voblasts', SW Belarus 52°13′N 23°44′E
15 R10 **Charny** Québec, SE Canada 46°43′N 71°15′W
149 T5 **Charsadda** Khyber Pakhtunkhwa, NW Pakistan 34°12′N 71°46′E
**Charshanga/Charshangngy/Charshangy** *see* Köýtendag
**Charsk** *see* Shar
181 W6 **Charters Towers** Queensland, NE Australia 20°02′S 146°20′E
15 R12 **Chartierville** Québec, SE Canada 45°19′N 71°13′W
102 M6 **Chartres** *anc.* Autricum, Civitas Carnutum. Eure-et-Loir, C France 48°27′N 01°27′E
**Charyn** *see* Sharyn
**Charyn** *see* Sharyn
61 D21 **Chascomús** Buenos Aires, E Argentina 35°34′S 58°01′W
11 N16 **Chase** British Columbia, SW Canada 50°49′N 119°41′W
21 U7 **Chase City** Virginia, NE USA 36°48′N 78°27′W
19 S4 **Chase, Mount** ▲ Maine, NE USA 46°06′N 68°30′W
118 M13 **Chashniki** Vitsyebskaya Voblasts', N Belarus 54°52′N 29°10′E
115 D15 **Chásia** ▲ C Greece
29 V9 **Chaska** Minnesota, N USA 44°47′N 93°36′W
185 D25 **Chaslands Mistake** *headland* South Island, New Zealand 46°37′S 169°21′E
125 R11 **Chasovo** Respublika Komi, NW Russia 61°58′N 50°34′E
**Chasovo** *see* Vazhgort
124 H14 **Chastova** Novgorodskaya Oblast', NW Russia 58°37′N 32°05′E

◆ Country
● Country Capital
◇ Dependent Territory
○ Dependent Territory Capital
◈ Administrative Regions
✈ International Airport
▲ Mountain
▲▲ Mountain Range
⊼ Volcano
~ River
◎ Lake
▣ Reservoir

Chāt – China Lake


143 R3 **Chāt** Golestān, N Iran 37°52′N 55°27′E
**Chatak** see Chhatak
**Chatang** see Zhanang
39 R9 **Chatanika** Alaska, USA 65°06′N 147°28′W
39 R9 **Chatanika River** ≈ Alaska, USA
147 T8 **Chat-Bazar** Talasskaya Oblast', NW Kyrgyzstan 42°29′N 72°37′E
45 Y14 **Châteaubelair** Saint Vincent, W Saint Vincent and the Grenadines 13°15′N 61°05′W
102 J7 **Châteaubriant** Loire-Atlantique, NW France 47°43′N 01°22′W
103 Q8 **Château-Chinon** Nièvre, C France 47°04′N 03°50′E
108 C10 **Château d'Oex** Vaud, W Switzerland 46°28′N 07°09′E
102 L7 **Château-du-Loir** Sarthe, NW France 47°40′N 00°25′E
102 M6 **Châteaudun** Eure-et-Loir, C France 48°04′N 01°20′E
102 K7 **Château-Gontier** Mayenne, NW France 47°49′N 00°42′W
15 O13 **Châteauguay** Québec, SE Canada 45°22′N 73°44′W
102 F6 **Châteaulin** Finistère, NW France 48°12′N 04°07′W
103 N9 **Châteaumeillant** Cher, C France 46°33′N 02°10′E
102 K11 **Châteauneuf-sur-Charente** Charente, W France 45°34′N 00°33′W
102 M7 **Château-Renault** Indre-et-Loire, C France 47°34′N 00°52′E
103 N9 **Châteauroux** prev. Indreville. Indre, C France 46°50′N 01°43′E
103 T5 **Château-Salins** Moselle, NE France 48°50′N 06°29′E
103 P4 **Château-Thierry** Aisne, N France 49°03′N 03°24′E
99 H21 **Châtelet** Hainaut, S Belgium 50°24′N 04°32′E
**Châtelherault** see Châtellerault
102 L9 **Châtellerault** var. Châtelherault. Vienne, W France 46°49′N 00°33′E
29 X10 **Chatfield** Minnesota, N USA 43°51′N 92°11′W
13 O14 **Chatham** New Brunswick, SE Canada 47°02′N 65°30′W
14 D17 **Chatham** Ontario, S Canada 42°24′N 82°11′W
97 P22 **Chatham** SE England, United Kingdom 51°23′N 00°31′E
30 K14 **Chatham** Illinois, N USA 39°40′N 89°42′W
21 T7 **Chatham** Virginia, NE USA 36°49′N 79°26′W
63 F22 **Chatham, Isla** island S Chile
175 R12 **Chatham Island** island Chatham Islands, New Zealand
**Chatham Island** see San Cristóbal, Isla
**Chatham Island Rise** see Chatham Rise
175 R12 **Chatham Islands** island group New Zealand, SW Pacific Ocean
175 Q12 **Chatham Rise** var. Chatham Island Rise. undersea feature S Pacific Ocean
39 X13 **Chatham Strait** strait Alaska, USA
**Chathóir, Rinn** see Cahore Point
102 M9 **Châtillon-sur-Indre** Indre, C France 46°58′N 01°10′E
103 Q7 **Châtillon-sur-Seine** Côte d'Or, C France 47°51′N 04°30′E
147 S8 **Chatkal** Uzb. Chotqol. ≈ Kyrgyzstan/Uzbekistan
147 R9 **Chatkal Range** Rus. Chatkal'skiy Khrebet. ▲▲ Kyrgyzstan/Uzbekistan
**Chatkal'skiy Khrebet** see Chatkal Range
23 N7 **Chatom** Alabama, S USA 31°28′N 88°15′W
**Chatrapur** see Chhatrapur
143 S10 **Chatrūd** Kermān, C Iran 30°39′N 56°57′E
23 S2 **Chatsworth** Georgia, SE USA 34°46′N 84°46′W
**Chāttagām** see Chittagong
23 S8 **Chattahoochee** Florida, SE USA 30°40′N 84°51′W
23 R8 **Chattahoochee River** ≈ SE USA
20 L10 **Chattanooga** Tennessee, S USA 35°05′N 85°16′W
147 V10 **Chatyr-Kël', Ozero** ◎ C Kyrgyzstan
147 W9 **Chatyr-Tash** Narynskaya Oblast', C Kyrgyzstan 40°54′N 76°22′E
15 R12 **Chaudière** ≈ Québec, SE Canada
167 S14 **Châu Đốc** var. Chauphu, Chau Phu. An Giang, S Vietnam 10°53′N 105°07′E
152 D13 **Chauhtan** prev. Chohtan. Rājasthān, NW India 25°27′N 71°08′E
166 L5 **Chauk** Magway, W Myanmar (Burma) 20°52′N 94°50′E
103 R6 **Chaumont** prev. Chaumont-en-Bassigny. Haute-Marne, N France 48°07′N 05°08′E
**Chaumont-en-Bassigny** see Chaumont
123 T5 **Chaunskaya Guba** bay NE Russia
103 P3 **Chauny** Aisne, N France 49°37′N 03°13′E
167 U10 **Châu Ô** var. Binh Son. Quang Ngai, C Vietnam 15°18′N 108°45′E
**Chau Phu** see Châu Đốc
102 I5 **Chausey, Îles** island group N France
**Chausy** see Chavusy
18 C11 **Chautauqua Lake** ◎ New York, NE USA
**ChâuThanh** see Ba Ria
102 L9 **Chauvigny** Vienne, W France 46°35′N 00°37′E
124 L6 **Chavan'ga** Murmanskaya Oblast', NW Russia 66°07′N 37°44′E
14 K10 **Chavannes, Lac** ◎ Québec, SE Canada
**Chavantes, Represa de** see Xavantes, Represa de
61 D15 **Chavarría** Corrientes, NE Argentina 28°57′S 58°35′W
**Chavash Respubliki** see Chuvashskaya Respublika
104 I5 **Chaves** anc. Aquae Flaviae. Vila Real, N Portugal 41°44′N 07°28′W
**Chávez, Isla** see Santa Cruz, Isla
82 G13 **Chavuma** North Western, NW Zambia 13°04′S 22°43′E
119 O16 **Chavusy** Rus. Chausy. Mahilyowskaya Voblasts', E Belarus 53°48′N 30°58′E
**Chayan** see Shayan
147 U8 **Chayek** Narynskaya Oblast', C Kyrgyzstan 41°54′N 74°28′E
139 T6 **Chāy Khānah** Diyālá, E Iraq 34°19′N 44°33′E
125 T16 **Chaykovskiy** Permskiy Kray, NW Russia 56°45′N 54°09′E
167 T12 **Chbar** Mondolkiri, E Cambodia 12°46′N 107°10′E
23 Q4 **Cheaha Mountain** ▲ Alabama, S USA 33°29′N 85°48′W
**Cheatharlach** see Carlow
21 S2 **Cheat River** ≈ NE USA
111 A16 **Cheb** Ger. Eger. Karlovarský Kraj, W Czechia 50°05′N 12°23′E
127 Q3 **Cheboksary** Chuvashskaya Respublika, W Russia 56°06′N 47°15′E
31 Q5 **Cheboygan** Michigan, N USA 45°40′N 84°28′W
**Chechaouèn** see Chefchaouen
**Chechenia** see Chechenskaya Respublika
127 O15 **Chechenskaya Respublika** Eng. Chechenia, Chechnia, Rus. Chechnya. ◈ autonomous republic SW Russia
67 N4 **Chech, Erg** desert Algeria/Mali
**Chechevichi** see Chachevichy
**Che-chiang** see Zhejiang
**Chechnia/Chechnya** see Chechenskaya Respublika
**Chech'ŏn** see Jecheon
111 L15 **Chęciny** Świętokrzyskie, S Poland 50°51′N 20°31′E
27 Q10 **Checotah** Oklahoma, C USA 35°28′N 95°31′W
13 R15 **Chedabucto Bay** inlet Nova Scotia, E Canada
**Cheduba Island** see Munaung Island
37 T5 **Cheesman Lake** ⊠ Colorado, C USA
195 S16 **Cheetham, Cape** headland Antarctica 70°26′S 162°40′E
74 G5 **Chefchaouen** var. Chaouèn, Chechaouèn, Sp. Xauen. N Morocco 35°10′N 05°16′W
**Chefoo** see Yantai
38 M12 **Chefornak** Alaska, USA 60°09′N 164°09′W
123 R13 **Chegdomyn** Khabarovskiy Kray, SE Russia 51°09′N 132°58′E
76 M4 **Chegga** Tiris Zemmour, NE Mauritania 25°27′N 05°49′W
**Cheghcheran** see Chaghcharān
32 G9 **Chehalis** Washington, NW USA 46°39′N 122°57′W
32 G9 **Chehalis River** ≈ Washington, NW USA
115 D14 **Cheimaditis, Límni** var. Límni Cheimaditis. ◎ N Greece
**Cheimadítis, Límni** see Cheimaditis, Límni
103 U15 **Cheiron, Mont** ▲ SE France 43°49′N 07°00′E
163 Y17 **Cheju** ✈ S South Korea 33°31′N 126°29′E
**Cheju** see Jeju
**Cheju-do** see Jeju-do
**Cheju-haehyeop** see Jeju-haehyeop
**Cheju Strait** see Jeju-haehyeop
**Chekiang** see Zhejiang
**Chekichler/Chekishlyar** see Çekiçler
188 F8 **Chelab** Babeldaob, N Palau
147 N11 **Chelak** Rus. Chelek. Samarqand Viloyati, C Uzbekistan 39°55′N 66°45′E
32 J7 **Chelan, Lake** ⊠ Washington, NW USA
**Chelek** see Chelak
**Cheleken** see Hazar
**Chélif/Chéliff** see Chelif, Oued
74 J5 **Chelif, Oued** var. Chélif, Chéliff, Chellif, Shellif. ≈ N Algeria
**Chelkar** see Shalkar
**Chelkar Ozero** see Shalkar, Ozero
**Chellif** see Chelif Oued
111 P14 **Chełm** Rus. Kholm. Lubelskie, SE Poland 51°08′N 23°29′E
110 I9 **Chełmno** Ger. Culm, Kulm. Kujawski-pomorskie, C Poland 53°21′N 18°27′E
115 E19 **Chelmós** var. Aroania. ▲ S Greece
14 F10 **Chelmsford** Ontario, S Canada 46°33′N 81°16′W
97 P21 **Chelmsford** E England, United Kingdom 51°44′N 00°28′E
110 J9 **Chełmża** Ger. Culmsee, Kulmsee. Kujawski-pomorskie, C Poland 53°11′N 18°34′E
27 Q8 **Chelsea** Oklahoma, C USA 36°32′N 95°25′W
18 M8 **Chelsea** Vermont, NE USA 43°58′N 72°29′W
97 L21 **Cheltenham** C England, United Kingdom 51°54′N 02°04′W
105 R9 **Chelva** Comunitat Valenciana, E Spain 39°45′N 01°00′W
122 G11 **Chelyabinsk** Chelyabinskaya Oblast', C Russia 55°12′N 61°25′E
122 F11 **Chelyabinskaya Oblast'** ◈ province C Russia
123 N5 **Chelyuskin, Mys** headland N Russia 77°42′N 104°13′E
41 Y12 **Chemax** Yucatán, SE Mexico 20°41′N 87°54′W
83 N16 **Chemba** Sofala, C Mozambique 17°11′S 34°53′E
82 J13 **Chembe** Luapula, NE Zambia 11°58′S 28°45′E
139 T4 **Chemchemal** Ar. Juwārtā, var. Chamchamāl. At Ta'mím, N Iraq 35°32′N 44°50′E
**Chemenibit** see Çemenibit
**Chemerisy** see Chamyarysy
116 K7 **Chemerivtsi** Khmel'nyts'ka Oblast', W Ukraine 49°00′N 26°21′E
102 J8 **Chemillé** Maine-et-Loire, NW France 47°15′N 00°42′W
173 X17 **Chemin Grenier** S Mauritius 20°29′S 57°28′E
101 N16 **Chemnitz** prev. Karl-Marx-Stadt. Sachsen, E Germany 50°50′N 12°55′E
**Chemulpo** see Incheon
32 H14 **Chemult** Oregon, NW USA 43°14′N 121°48′W
18 G12 **Chemung River** ≈ New York/Pennsylvania, NE USA
149 U8 **Chenāb** ≈ India/Pakistan
39 S9 **Chena Hot Springs** Alaska, USA 65°06′N 146°02′W
18 I11 **Chenango River** ≈ New York, NE USA
168 J7 **Chenderoh, Tasik** ◎ Peninsular Malaysia
15 Q11 **Chêne, Rivière du** ≈ Québec, SE Canada
32 L8 **Cheney** Washington, NW USA 47°29′N 117°34′W
26 M6 **Cheney Reservoir** ⊠ Kansas, C USA
**Chengchiatun** see Liaoyuan
**Ch'eng-chou/Chengchow** see Zhengzhou
161 P1 **Chengde** var. Jehol. Hebei, E China 41°N 117°57′E
160 I9 **Chengdu** var. Chengtu, Ch'eng-tu. province capital Sichuan, C China 30°41′N 104°03′E
161 Q14 **Chenghai** Guangdong, S China 23°30′N 116°42′E
**Chenghsien** see Zhengzhou
160 H13 **Chengjiang** Yunnan, SW China 24°40′N 102°55′E
**Chengjiang** see Taihe
160 L17 **Chengmai** var. Jinjiang. Hainan, S China 19°45′N 109°56′E
**Chengtu/Ch'eng-tu** see Chengdu
**Chengwen** see Chindu
159 W12 **Chengxian** var. Cheng Xiang. Gansu, C China 33°42′N 105°45′E
**Cheng Xiang** see Chengxian
**Chengyang** see Juxian
**Chengzhong** see Ningming
**Chenkiang** see Zhenjiang
155 J19 **Chennai** prev. Madras. state capital Tamil Nādu, S India 13°05′N 80°18′E
155 J19 **Chennai** ✈ Tamil Nādu, S India 13°07′N 80°13′E
103 R8 **Chenôve** Côte d'Or, C France 47°16′N 05°00′E
**Chenstokhov** see Częstochowa
160 L11 **Chenxi** var. Chenyang. Hunan, S China 28°02′N 110°15′E
**Chen Xian/Chenxian/Chen Xiang** see Chenzhou
**Chenyang** see Chenxi
161 N12 **Chenzhou** var. Chenxian, Chen Xian, Chen Xiang. Hunan, S China 25°51′N 113°01′E
163 X15 **Cheonan** Jap. Tenan; prev. Ch'ŏnan. W South Korea 36°51′N 127°11′E
163 W13 **Cheongju** prev. Chŏngju. W North Korea 37°44′N 125°13′E
**Cheo Reo** see A Yun Pa
114 I11 **Chepelare** Smolyan, S Bulgaria 41°44′N 24°41′E
114 I11 **Chepelarska Reka** ≈ S Bulgaria
56 B11 **Chepén** La Libertad, C Peru 07°15′S 79°23′W
62 J10 **Chepes** La Rioja, C Argentina 31°19′S 66°40′W
161 O15 **Chep Lap Kok** ✈ S China 22°23′N 114°11′E
43 U14 **Chepo** Panamá, C Panama 09°09′N 79°03′W
**Chepping Wycombe** see High Wycombe
125 R14 **Cheptsa** ≈ NW Russia
30 K3 **Chequamegon Point** headland Wisconsin, N USA 46°42′N 90°45′W
103 O8 **Cher** ◈ department C France
102 M8 **Cher** ≈ C France
**Cherangani Hills** see Cherangany Hills
81 H17 **Cherangany Hills** var. Cherangani Hills. ▲▲ W Kenya
21 S11 **Cheraw** South Carolina, SE USA 34°42′N 79°52′W
102 I3 **Cherbourg** anc. Carusbur. Manche, N France 49°40′N 01°36′W
127 R5 **Cherdakly** Ul'yanovskaya Oblast', W Russia 54°21′N 48°54′E
125 U12 **Cherdyn'** Permskiy Kray, NW Russia 60°21′N 56°39′E
124 J14 **Cherekha** ≈ W Russia
122 M13 **Cheremkhovo** Irkutskaya Oblast', S Russia 53°16′N 102°44′E
**Cheren** see Keren
124 K14 **Cherepovets** Vologodskaya Oblast', NW Russia 59°09′N 37°50′E
125 O11 **Cherevkovo** Arkhangel'skaya Oblast', NW Russia 61°45′N 45°16′E
74 I6 **Chergui, Chott ech** salt lake NW Algeria
**Cherikov** see Cherykaw
117 P6 **Cherkas'ka Oblast'** var. Cherkasy, Rus. Cherkasskaya Oblast'. ◈ province C Ukraine
**Cherkasskaya Oblast'** see Cherkas'ka Oblast'
**Cherkassy** see Cherkasy
117 Q6 **Cherkasy** Rus. Cherkassy. Cherkas'ka Oblast', C Ukraine 49°26′N 32°05′E
**Cherkasy** see Cherkas'ka Oblast'
126 M15 **Cherkessk** Karachayevo-Cherkesskaya Respublika, SW Russia 44°12′N 42°06′E
122 H12 **Cherlak** Omskaya Oblast', C Russia 54°06′N 74°59′E
122 H12 **Cherlakskoye** Omskaya Oblast', C Russia 53°42′N 74°23′E
125 U13 **Chermoz** Permskiy Kray, NW Russia 58°49′N 56°07′E
**Chernavchitsy** see Charnawchytsy
125 T3 **Chernaya** Nenetskiy Avtonomnyy Okrug, NW Russia 68°36′N 56°34′E
125 T4 **Chernaya** ≈ NW Russia
**Chernigov** see Chernihiv
**Chernigovskaya Oblast'** see Chernihivs'ka Oblast'
117 Q2 **Chernihiv** Rus. Chernigov. Chernihivs'ka Oblast', NE Ukraine 51°28′N 31°19′E
**Chernihiv** see Chernihivs'ka Oblast'
117 V9 **Chernihivka** Zaporiz'ka Oblast', SE Ukraine 47°11′N 36°10′E
117 P2 **Chernihivs'ka Oblast'** var. Chernihiv, Rus. Chernigovskaya Oblast'. ◈ province NE Ukraine
114 I9 **Cherni Osŭm** ≈ N Bulgaria
116 J8 **Chernivets'ka Oblast'** var. Chernivtsi, Rus. Chernovitskaya Oblast'. ◈ province W Ukraine
114 I9 **Cherni Vit** ≈ NW Bulgaria
114 G10 **Cherni Vrah**, Cherni Vrŭkh. ▲ W Bulgaria 42°33′N 23°18′E
**Cherni Vrŭkh** see Cherni Vrah
116 K8 **Chernivtsi** Ger. Czernowitz, Rom. Cernăuţi, Rus. Chernovtsy. Chernivets'ka Oblast', W Ukraine 48°18′N 25°55′E
115 M7 **Chernivtsi** Vinnyts'ka Oblast', C Ukraine 48°33′N 28°06′E
**Chernivtsi** see Chernivets'ka Oblast'
**Chernobyl'** see Chornobyl'
**Cherno More** see Black Sea
**Chernomorskoye** see Chornomors'ke
145 T7 **Chernoretsk** prev. Chernoretskoye. Pavlodar, NE Kazakhstan 52°51′N 76°37′E
**Chernoretskoye** see Chernoretsk
**Chernovitskaya Oblast'** see Chernivets'ka Oblast'
**Chernovtsy** see Chernivtsi
145 U8 **Chernoye** Pavlodar, NE Kazakhstan 51°40′N 77°33′E
**Chernoye More** see Black Sea
125 U16 **Chernushka** Permskiy Kray, NW Russia 56°30′N 56°07′E
117 N4 **Chernyakhiv** Rus. Chernyakhov. Zhytomyrs'ka Oblast', N Ukraine 50°30′N 28°38′E
**Chernyakhov** see Chernyakhiv
119 C14 **Chernyakhovsk** Ger. Insterburg. Kaliningradskaya Oblast', W Russia 54°36′N 21°49′E
126 K8 **Chernyanka** Belgorodskaya Oblast', W Russia 50°59′N 37°54′E
125 V5 **Chernyshëva, Gryada** ▲▲ NW Russia
144 J14 **Chernyshëva, Zaliv** gulf SW Kazakhstan
123 O10 **Chernyshevskiy** Respublika Sakha (Yakutiya), NE Russia 62°57′N 112°29′E
127 P13 **Chernyye Zemli** plain SW Russia
**Chërnyy Irtysh** see Ertix He, China/Kazakhstan
**Chërnyy Irtysh** see Kara Irtysh, Kazakhstan
127 V7 **Chernyy Otrog** Orenburgskaya Oblast', W Russia 52°03′N 56°09′E
29 T12 **Cherokee** Iowa, C USA 42°45′N 95°33′W
26 M8 **Cherokee** Oklahoma, C USA 36°45′N 98°22′W
25 R9 **Cherokee** Texas, SW USA 30°56′N 98°42′W
21 O8 **Cherokee Lake** ⊠ Tennessee, S USA
**Cherokees, Lake O' The** see Grand Lake O' The Cherokees
44 H1 **Cherokee Sound** Great Abaco, N The Bahamas 26°16′N 77°03′W
153 V13 **Cherrapunji** Meghālaya, NE India 25°16′N 91°42′E
28 L9 **Cherry Creek** ≈ South Dakota, N USA
18 J16 **Cherry Hill** New Jersey, NE USA 39°55′N 75°01′W
27 Q7 **Cherryvale** Kansas, C USA 37°16′N 95°33′W
21 Q10 **Cherryville** North Carolina, SE USA 35°22′N 81°22′W
**Cherski Range** see Cherskogo, Khrebet
123 T6 **Cherskiy** Respublika Sakha (Yakutiya), NE Russia 68°45′N 161°15′E
123 R8 **Cherskogo, Khrebet** var. Cherski Range. ▲▲ NE Russia
**Cherso** see Cres
126 L10 **Chertkovo** Rostovskaya Oblast', SW Russia 49°22′N 40°10′E
**Cherven'** see Chervyen'
114 H8 **Cherven Bryag** Pleven, N Bulgaria 43°16′N 24°06′E
**Chervonoarmiys'k** see Pulyny
**Chervonograd** see Chervonohrad
116 I4 **Chervonohrad** Rus. Chervonograd. L'vivs'ka Oblast', NW Ukraine 50°25′N 24°10′E
117 W6 **Chervonooskil's'ke Vodoskhovyshche** Rus. Krasnooskol'skoye Vodokhranilishche. ⊠ NE Ukraine
**Chervonoye, Ozero** see Chyrvonaye, Vozyera
**Chervonozavods'ke** see Zavods'ke
119 L16 **Chervyen'** Rus. Cherven'. Minskaya Voblasts', C Belarus 53°42′N 28°26′E
119 P16 **Cherykaw** Rus. Cherikov. Mahilyowskaya Voblasts', E Belarus 53°34′N 31°23′E
31 R9 **Chesaning** Michigan, N USA 43°10′N 84°07′W
21 X5 **Chesapeake Bay** inlet NE USA
**Chesha Bay** see Chëshskaya Guba
**Cheshevlya** see Tsyeshawlya
97 K18 **Cheshire** cultural region C England, United Kingdom
125 P5 **Chëshskaya Guba** var. Archangel Bay, Chesha Bay, Dvina Bay. bay NW Russia
14 F14 **Chesley** Ontario, S Canada 44°17′N 81°06′W
21 Q10 **Chesnee** South Carolina, SE USA 35°09′N 81°51′W
97 K18 **Chester** Wel. Caerleon, hist. Legaceaster, Lat. Deva, Devana Castra. C England, United Kingdom 53°12′N 02°54′W
35 O4 **Chester** California, W USA 40°18′N 121°14′W
30 K16 **Chester** Illinois, N USA 37°54′N 89°49′W
33 S7 **Chester** Montana, NW USA 48°30′N 110°59′W
18 I16 **Chester** Pennsylvania, NE USA 39°51′N 75°21′W
21 R11 **Chester** South Carolina, SE USA 34°43′N 81°14′W
25 X9 **Chester** Texas, SW USA 30°55′N 94°36′W
21 W6 **Chester** Virginia, NE USA 37°22′N 77°27′W
21 R11 **Chester** West Virginia, NE USA 40°34′N 80°33′W
97 M18 **Chesterfield** C England, United Kingdom 53°15′N 01°25′W
21 S11 **Chesterfield** South Carolina, SE USA 34°44′N 80°04′W
21 W6 **Chesterfield** Virginia, NE USA 37°22′N 77°31′W
192 J9 **Chesterfield, Îles** island group NW New Caledonia
9 O9 **Chesterfield Inlet** Nunavut, NW Canada 63°19′N 90°57′W
9 O9 **Chesterfield Inlet** inlet Nunavut, N Canada
21 Y3 **Chester River** ≈ Delaware/Maryland, NE USA
21 X3 **Chestertown** Maryland, NE USA 39°13′N 76°04′W
19 R4 **Chesuncook Lake** ◎ Maine, NE USA
30 J5 **Chetek** Wisconsin, N USA 45°19′N 91°37′W
13 R14 **Chéticamp** Nova Scotia, SE Canada 46°14′N 61°19′W
27 Q8 **Chetopa** Kansas, C USA 37°02′N 95°05′W
42 Y14 **Chetumal** var. Payo Obispo. Quintana Roo, SE Mexico 18°32′N 88°16′W
**Chetumal, Bahia/Chetumal, Bahía de** see Chetumal Bay
42 G1 **Chetumal Bay** var. Bahia Chetumal, Bahía de Chetumal. bay Belize/Mexico
10 M13 **Chetwynd** British Columbia, W Canada 55°42′N 121°36′W
38 M11 **Chevak** Alaska, USA 61°31′N 165°35′W
36 M12 **Chevelon Creek** ≈ Arizona, SW USA
185 J17 **Cheviot** Canterbury, South Island, New Zealand 42°48′S 173°17′E
96 L13 **Cheviot Hills** hill range England/Scotland, United Kingdom
96 L13 **Cheviot, The** ▲ NE England, United Kingdom 55°28′N 02°10′W
14 M11 **Chevreuil, Lac du** ◎ Québec, SE Canada
81 I16 **Ch'ew Bahir** var. Lake Stefanie. ◎ Ethiopia/Kenya
32 L7 **Chewelah** Washington, NW USA 48°16′N 117°42′W
26 K10 **Cheyenne** Oklahoma, C USA 35°37′N 99°43′W
33 Z17 **Cheyenne** state capital Wyoming, C USA 41°08′N 104°46′W
26 L5 **Cheyenne Bottoms** ◎ Kansas, C USA
16 J8 **Cheyenne River** ≈ South Dakota/Wyoming, N USA
37 W5 **Cheyenne Wells** Colorado, C USA 38°49′N 102°21′W
108 C9 **Cheyres** Vaud, W Switzerland 46°48′N 06°48′E
**Chezdi-Oşorheiu** see Târgu Secuiesc
153 P13 **Chhapra** prev. Chapra. Bihār, N India 25°50′N 84°42′E
153 V13 **Chhatak** var. Chatak. Sylhet, NE Bangladesh 25°02′N 91°33′E
154 J9 **Chhatarpur** Madhya Pradesh, C India 24°54′N 79°35′E
154 N13 **Chhatrapur** prev. Chatrapur. Odisha, E India 19°26′N 85°02′E
154 K2 **Chhattīsgarh** ◈ state E India
154 L12 **Chhattīsgarh** plain C India
154 I11 **Chhindwāra** Madhya Pradesh, C India 22°04′N 78°58′E
153 T12 **Chhukha** SW Bhutan 27°02′N 89°36′E
**Chia-i** see Chiayi
**Chiai** see Chiayi
**Chia-mu-ssu** see Jiamusi
83 B15 **Chiange** Port. Vila de Almoster. Huíla, SW Angola 15°44′S 13°54′E
**Chiang-hsi** see Jiangxi
**Chiang Kai-shek** see Taiwan Taoyuan
167 P8 **Chiang Khan** Loei, E Thailand 17°51′N 101°43′E
167 O7 **Chiang Mai** var. Chiangmai, Chiengmai, Kiangmai. Chiang Mai, NW Thailand 18°48′N 98°59′E
167 O7 **Chiang Mai** ✈ Chiang Mai, NW Thailand 18°44′N 98°53′E
**Chiangmai** see Chiang Mai
167 O6 **Chiang Rai** var. Chianpai, Chienrai, Muang Chiang Rai. Chiang Rai, NW Thailand 19°56′N 99°51′E
**Chiang-su** see Jiangsu
**Chianning/Chian-ning** see Nanjing
**Chianpai** see Chiang Rai
106 G12 **Chianti** cultural region C Italy
**Chiapa** see Chiapa de Corzo
41 U16 **Chiapa de Corzo** var. Chiapa. Chiapas, SE Mexico 16°42′N 92°59′W
41 V16 **Chiapas** ◈ state SE Mexico
106 J12 **Chiaravalle** Marche, C Italy 43°36′N 13°19′E
107 N22 **Chiaravalle Centrale** Calabria, SW Italy 38°40′N 16°25′E
106 E7 **Chiari** Lombardia, N Italy 45°33′N 10°00′E
108 H12 **Chiasso** Ticino, S Switzerland 45°51′N 09°02′E
137 S9 **Ch'iatura** C Georgia 42°13′N 43°11′E
41 P15 **Chiautla** var. Chiautla de Tapia. Puebla, S Mexico 18°16′N 98°31′W
**Chiautla de Tapia** see Chiautla
106 D10 **Chiavari** Liguria, NW Italy 44°19′N 09°19′E
106 E6 **Chiavenna** Lombardia, N Italy 46°19′N 09°22′E
161 S14 **Chiayi** var. Jiayi, Chia-i, Chiai, Kiayi, Jap. Kagi. C Taiwan 23°29′N 120°27′E
**Chiazza** see Piazza Armerina
165 O14 **Chiba** var. Tiba. Chiba, Honshū, S Japan 35°37′N 140°06′E
165 O13 **Chiba** off. Chiba-ken, var. Tiba. ◈ prefecture Honshū, S Japan
83 M18 **Chibabava** Sofala, C Mozambique 20°17′S 33°39′E
**Chiba-ken** see Chiba
161 O10 **Chibi** prev. Puqi. Hubei, C China 29°45′N 113°55′E
83 B15 **Chibia** Port. João de Almeida, Vila João de Almeida. Huíla, SW Angola 15°11′S 13°41′E
83 M18 **Chiboma** Sofala, C Mozambique 20°06′S 33°54′E
82 J12 **Chibondo** Luapula, N Zambia 10°42′S 28°42′E
82 K11 **Chibote** Luapula, NE Zambia 09°52′S 29°33′E
12 K12 **Chibougamau** Québec, SE Canada 49°56′N 74°24′W
164 H11 **Chiburi-jima** island Oki-shotō, SW Japan
83 M20 **Chibuto** Gaza, S Mozambique 24°40′S 33°33′E
31 N11 **Chicago** Illinois, N USA 41°51′N 87°39′W
31 N11 **Chicago Heights** Illinois, N USA 41°30′N 87°38′W
15 W6 **Chic-Chocs, Monts** Eng. Shickshock Mountains. ▲▲ Québec, SE Canada
39 W13 **Chichagof Island** island Alexander Archipelago, Alaska, USA
57 K20 **Chichas, Cordillera de** ▲▲ SW Bolivia
41 X12 **Chichén-Itzá, Ruinas** ruins Yucatán, SE Mexico
97 N23 **Chichester** SE England, United Kingdom 50°50′N 00°48′W
42 C5 **Chichicastenango** Quiché, W Guatemala 14°55′N 91°06′W
42 I9 **Chichigalpa** Chinandega, NW Nicaragua 12°35′N 87°04′W
**Ch'i-ch'i-ha-erh** see Qiqihar
165 X16 **Chichijima-rettō** Eng. Beechy Group. island group SE Japan
54 K4 **Chichiriviche** Falcón, N Venezuela 10°58′N 68°17′W
39 R11 **Chickaloon** Alaska, USA 61°48′N 148°27′W
20 L10 **Chickamauga Lake** ⊠ Tennessee, S USA
23 N7 **Chickasawhay River** ≈ Mississippi, S USA
26 M11 **Chickasha** Oklahoma, C USA 35°03′N 97°57′W
39 T9 **Chicken** Alaska, USA 64°04′N 141°56′W
104 J16 **Chiclana de la Frontera** Andalucía, S Spain 36°26′N 06°09′W
56 B11 **Chiclayo** Lambayeque, NW Peru 06°47′S 79°47′W
35 N5 **Chico** California, W USA 39°42′N 121°51′W
83 L15 **Chicoa** Tete, NW Mozambique 15°45′S 32°25′E
83 M20 **Chicomo** Gaza, S Mozambique 24°29′S 34°15′E
18 M11 **Chicopee** Massachusetts, NE USA 42°08′N 72°34′W
63 I19 **Chico, Río** ≈ SE Argentina
63 I21 **Chico, Río** ≈ S Argentina
27 W14 **Chicot, Lake** ◎ Arkansas, C USA
15 R7 **Chicoutimi** Québec, SE Canada 48°24′N 71°04′W
15 Q8 **Chicoutimi** ≈ Québec, SE Canada
83 L19 **Chicualacuala** Gaza, SW Mozambique 22°06′S 31°42′E
83 B14 **Chicuma** Benguela, C Angola 13°33′S 14°41′E
155 J21 **Chidambaram** Tamil Nādu, SE India 11°25′N 79°42′E
196 K13 **Chidley, Cape** headland Newfoundland and Labrador, E Canada 60°25′N 64°39′W
101 N24 **Chiemsee** ◎ SE Germany
**Chiengmai** see Chiang Mai
**Chienrai** see Chiang Rai
106 B8 **Chieri** Piemonte, NW Italy 45°01′N 07°49′E
106 F8 **Chiese** ≈ N Italy
107 K14 **Chieti** var. Teate. Abruzzo, C Italy 42°22′N 14°10′E
99 E19 **Chièvres** Hainaut, SW Belgium 50°34′N 03°49′E
163 S12 **Chifeng** var. Ulanhad. Nei Mongol Zizhiqu, N China 42°17′N 118°56′E
82 F13 **Chifumage** ≈ E Angola
82 M13 **Chifunda** Muchinga, NE Zambia 11°57′S 32°36′E
**Chiganak** see Shyganak
39 P15 **Chiginagak, Mount** ▲ Alaska, USA 57°10′N 157°00′W
**Chigirin** see Chyhyryn
**Chigirinskoye Vodokhranilishche** see Chyhyrynskaye Vodaskhovishcha
41 P13 **Chignahuapan** Puebla, S Mexico 19°52′N 98°03′W
39 O15 **Chignik** Alaska, USA 56°18′N 158°24′W
83 M19 **Chigombe** ≈ S Mozambique
54 D7 **Chigorodó** Antioquia, NW Colombia 07°42′N 76°45′W
83 M19 **Chigubo** Gaza, S Mozambique 22°50′S 33°30′E
**Chihertey** see Altay
**Chih-fu** see Yantai
148 M6 **Chihil Abdālān, Kōh-e** var. Chalap Dalam. ▲▲ C Afghanistan
**Chihli** see Hebei
**Chihli, Gulf of** see Bo Hai
40 J6 **Chihuahua** Chihuahua, NW Mexico 28°40′N 106°06′W
40 J6 **Chihuahua** ◈ state N Mexico
**Chiili** see Shiyeli
26 M7 **Chikaskia River** ≈ Kansas/Oklahoma, C USA
155 H19 **Chik Ballāpur** Karnātaka, W India 13°28′N 77°42′E
124 G15 **Chikhachevo** Pskovskaya Oblast', W Russia 57°17′N 29°51′E
155 F19 **Chikkamagalūru** prev. Chikmagalūr. Karnātaka, W India 13°20′N 75°46′E
**Chikmagalūr** see Chikkamagalūru
129 V7 **Chikoy** ≈ C Russia
83 J15 **Chikumbi** Lusaka, C Zambia 15°11′S 28°20′E
82 M13 **Chikwa** Muchinga, NE Zambia 11°39′S 32°45′E
**Chikwana** see Chikwawa
83 N15 **China Lake** var. Chikwana. Southern, S Malawi 16°03′S 34°48′E
155 J16 **Chilakalūrupet** Andhra Pradesh, E India 16°09′N 80°13′E
146 L14 **Chilan** Lebap Welaýaty, E Turkmenistan 37°57′N 64°58′E
**Chilapa** see Chilapa de Alvarez
41 P16 **Chilapa de Alvarez** var. Chilapa. Guerrero, S Mexico 17°38′N 99°11′W
155 J25 **Chilaw** North Western Province, W Sri Lanka 07°34′N 79°48′E
57 D15 **Chilca** Lima, W Peru 12°35′S 76°41′W
23 Q4 **Childersburg** Alabama, S USA 33°16′N 86°21′W
25 P4 **Childress** Texas, SW USA 34°25′N 100°14′W
63 G14 **Chile** off. Republic of Chile. ◆ republic SW South America
47 R10 **Chile Basin** undersea feature E Pacific Ocean 33°00′S 80°00′W
63 H20 **Chile Chico** Aysén, W Chile 46°34′S 71°44′W
62 I9 **Chilecito** La Rioja, NW Argentina 29°10′S 67°30′W
62 H12 **Chilecito** Mendoza, W Argentina 33°53′S 69°03′W
83 L14 **Chilembwe** Eastern, E Zambia 13°54′S 31°38′E
**Chile, Republic of** see Chile
193 S11 **Chile Rise** undersea feature SE Pacific Ocean 40°00′S 90°00′W
117 N13 **Chilia, Braţul** ≈ SE Romania
**Chilia-Nouă** see Kiliya
**Chilik** see Shelek
**Chilik** see Shelek
154 O13 **Chilika Lake** var. Chilka Lake. ◎ E India
82 J13 **Chililabombwe** Copperbelt, C Zambia 12°20′S 27°52′E
**Chi-lin** see Jilin
**Chilka Lake** see Chilika Lake
10 H9 **Chilkoot Pass** pass British Columbia, W Canada
**Chill Ala, Cuan** see Killala Bay
62 G13 **Chillán** Ñuble, C Chile 36°37′S 72°10′W
61 C22 **Chillar** Buenos Aires, E Argentina 37°16′S 59°58′W
**Chill Chiaráin, Cuan** see Kilkieran Bay
30 K12 **Chillicothe** Illinois, N USA 40°55′N 89°29′W
27 S3 **Chillicothe** Missouri, C USA 39°47′N 93°33′W
31 S14 **Chillicothe** Ohio, N USA 39°20′N 83°00′W
25 Q4 **Chillicothe** Texas, SW USA 34°15′N 99°31′W
10 M17 **Chilliwack** British Columbia, SW Canada 49°09′N 121°54′W
**Chill Mhantáin, Ceann** see Wicklow Head
**Chill Mhantáin, Sléibhte** see Wicklow Mountains
108 C10 **Chillon** Vaud, W Switzerland 46°24′N 06°56′E
**Chil'mamedkum, Peski/Chilmämetgum** see Çilmämmetgum
63 F17 **Chiloé, Isla de** var. Isla Grande de Chiloé. island W Chile
32 H15 **Chiloquin** Oregon, NW USA 42°33′N 121°33′W
41 O16 **Chilpancingo** var. Chilpancingo de los Bravos. Guerrero, S Mexico 17°33′N 99°30′W
**Chilpancingo de los Bravos** see Chilpancingo
97 N21 **Chiltern Hills** hill range S England, United Kingdom
30 M7 **Chilton** Wisconsin, N USA 44°04′N 88°10′W
82 F11 **Chiluage** Lunda Sul, NE Angola 09°32′S 21°48′E
82 N12 **Chilumba** prev. Deep Bay. Northern, N Malawi 10°27′S 34°12′E
**Chilung** see Keelung
83 N15 **Chilwa, Lake** var. Lago Chirua, Lake Shirwa. ◎ SE Malawi
167 R10 **Chi, Mae Nam** ≈ E Thailand
42 C6 **Chimaltenango** Chimaltenango, C Guatemala 14°40′N 90°48′W
42 A2 **Chimaltenango** off. Departamento de Chimaltenango. ◈ department S Guatemala
**Chimaltenango, Departamento de** see Chimaltenango
43 V15 **Chimán** Panamá, E Panama 08°42′N 78°35′W
83 M17 **Chimanimani** prev. Mandidzudzure, Melsetter. Manicaland, E Zimbabwe 19°48′S 32°52′E
99 G22 **Chimay** Hainaut, S Belgium 50°03′N 04°20′E
37 S10 **Chimayo** New Mexico, SW USA 36°00′N 105°55′W
**Chimbay** see Chimboy
56 A13 **Chimborazo** ◈ province C Ecuador
56 C7 **Chimborazo** ⛰ C Ecuador 01°29′S 78°50′W
56 C12 **Chimbote** Ancash, W Peru 09°04′S 78°34′W
146 H7 **Chimboy** Rus. Chimbay. Qoraqalpog'iston Respublikasi, NW Uzbekistan 43°03′N 59°52′E
186 D7 **Chimbu** var. Simbu. ◈ province C Papua New Guinea
54 F6 **Chimichagua** Cesar, N Colombia 09°19′N 73°51′W
**Chimishliya** see Cimişlia
**Chimkent** see Shymkent
28 I14 **Chimney Rock** rock Nebraska, C USA
83 M17 **Chimoio** Manica, C Mozambique 19°08′S 33°29′E
82 K11 **Chimpembe** Northern, NE Zambia 09°31′S 29°33′E
41 O8 **China** Nuevo León, NE Mexico 25°42′N 99°15′W
156 M9 **China** off. People's Republic of China, Chin. Zhonghua Renmin Gongheguo; prev. Chinese Empire. ◆ republic E Asia
19 Q7 **China Lake** ◎ Maine, NE USA




◆ Country
● Country Capital
◇ Dependent Territory
○ Dependent Territory Capital
◈ Administrative Regions
✈ International Airport
▲ Mountain
▲▲ Mountain Range
⛰ Volcano
≈ River
◎ Lake
⊠ Reservoir

CHINAMECA – CINEY


42 F8 **Chinameca** San Miguel, E El Salvador 13°30′N 88°20′W*
**Chi-nan/Chinan** *see* Jinan
42 H9 **Chinandega** Chinandega, NW Nicaragua 12°37′N 87°08′W
42 H9 **Chinandega** ⬖ *department* NW Nicaragua
**China, People's Republic of** *see* China
**China, Republic of** *see* Taiwan
24 J11 **Chinati Mountains** ⛰ Texas, SW USA
**Chinaz** *see* Chinoz
57 E15 **Chincha Alta** Ica, SW Peru 13°25′S 76°07′W
11 N11 **Chinchaga** 〰 Alberta, SW Canada
**Chin-chiang** *see* Quanzhou
**Chinchilla** *see* Chinchilla de Monte Aragón
105 Q11 **Chinchilla de Monte Aragón** *var.* Chinchilla. Castilla-La Mancha, C Spain 38°56′N 01°44′W
54 D10 **Chinchiná** Caldas, W Colombia 04°59′N 75°37′W
105 O8 **Chinchón** Madrid, C Spain 40°08′N 03°26′W
41 Z14 **Chinchorro, Banco** *island* SE Mexico
**Chin-chou/Chinchow** *see* Jinzhou
21 Z5 **Chincoteague** Assateague Island, Virginia, NE USA 37°55′N 75°22′W
83 O17 **Chinde** Zambézia, NE Mozambique 18°35′S 36°28′E
**Chin-do** *see* Jin-do
159 R13 **Chindu** *var.* Chengwen; *prev.* Chuqung. Qinghai, C China 33°19′N 97°08′E
**Chindwin** *see* Chindwinn
166 M2 **Chindwinn** *var.* Chindwin. 〰 N Myanmar (Burma)
**Chinese Empire** *see* China
**Chinghai** *see* Qinghai
**Ch'ing Hai** *see* Qinghai Hu, China
**Chingildi** *see* Shengeldi
**Chingirlau** *see* Shyngghyrlau
82 J13 **Chingola** Copperbelt, C Zambia 12°31′S 27°53′E
**Ching-Tao/Ch'ing-tao** *see* Qingdao
82 C13 **Chinguar** Huambo, C Angola 12°33′S 16°25′E
76 I7 **Chinguețți** *var.* Chinguetti. Adrar, C Mauritania 20°25′N 12°24′W
**Chinhae** *see* Jinhae
166 K4 **Chin Hills** ⛰ W Myanmar (Burma)
83 K16 **Chinhoyi** *prev.* Sinoia. Mashonaland West, N Zimbabwe 17°22′S 30°12′E
**Chinhsien** *see* Jinzhou
39 Q14 **Chiniak, Cape** *headland* Kodiak Island, Alaska, USA 57°37′N 152°10′W
14 G10 **Chiniguchi Lake** ◎ Ontario, S Canada
149 U8 **Chiniot** Punjab, NE Pakistan 31°40′N 73°00′E
**Chinju** *see* Jinju
**Chinkai** *see* Jinhae
78 M13 **Chinko** 〰 E Central African Republic
37 O9 **Chinle** Arizona, SW USA 36°09′N 109°33′W
**Chinmen Tao** *see* Kinmen Island
**Chinnchâr** *see* Shinshār
**Chinnereth** *see* Kinneret, Yam
164 C12 **Chino** *var.* Tino. Nagano, Honshū, S Japan 36°00′N 138°10′E
102 L8 **Chinon** Indre-et-Loire, C France 47°10′N 00°15′E
33 T7 **Chinook** Montana, NW USA 48°35′N 109°13′W
**Chinook State** *see* Washington
192 L4 **Chinook Trough** *undersea feature* N Pacific Ocean
36 K11 **Chino Valley** Arizona, SW USA 34°45′N 112°27′W
147 P10 **Chinoz** *Rus.* Chinaz. Toshkent Viloyati, E Uzbekistan 40°58′N 68°46′E
82 L12 **Chinsali** Muchinga, NE Zambia 10°33′S 32°05′E
166 K5 **Chin State** ⬖ *state* W Myanmar (Burma)
**Chinsura** *see* Chunchura
**Chin-tō** *see* Jin-do
54 E6 **Chinú** Córdoba, NW Colombia 09°07′N 75°25′W
99 K24 **Chiny, Forêt de** *forest* SE Belgium
83 M15 **Chioco** Tete, NW Mozambique 16°22′S 32°50′E
106 H8 **Chioggia** *anc.* Fossa Claudia. Veneto, NE Italy 45°14′N 12°17′E
114 H12 **Chionótrypa** ▲ NE Greece 41°16′N 24°06′E
115 L18 **Chíos** *var.* Hios, Khíos, *It.* Scio, *Turk.* Sakiz-Adasi. Chíos, E Greece 38°23′N 26°07′E
115 K18 **Chíos** *var.* Khíos. *island* E Greece
83 M14 **Chipata** *prev.* Fort Jameson. Eastern, E Zambia 13°40′S 32°42′E
83 C14 **Chipindo** Huíla, C Angola 13°53′S 15°47′E
23 R8 **Chipley** Florida, SE USA 30°46′N 85°32′W
155 D15 **Chiplūn** Mahārāshtra, W India 17°32′N 73°32′E
81 H22 **Chipogolo** Dodoma, C Tanzania 06°52′S 36°03′E
23 R8 **Chipola River** 〰 Florida, SE USA
97 L22 **Chippenham** S England, United Kingdom 51°28′N 02°07′W
30 J6 **Chippewa Falls** Wisconsin, N USA 44°56′N 91°25′W
30 J4 **Chippewa, Lake** ⊞ Wisconsin, N USA
31 Q8 **Chippewa River** 〰 Michigan, N USA
30 I6 **Chippewa River** 〰 Wisconsin, N USA
**Chipping Wycombe** *see* High Wycombe
114 G8 **Chiprovtsi** Montana, NW Bulgaria 43°23′N 22°53′E
19 T4 **Chiputneticook Lakes** *lakes* Canada/USA
56 D13 **Chiquián** Ancash, W Peru 10°09′S 78°08′W
41 Y11 **Chiquilá** Quintana Roo, SE Mexico 21°25′N 87°20′W
42 E6 **Chiquimula** Chiquimula, SE Guatemala 14°46′N 89°32′W
42 A3 **Chiquimula** *off.* Departamento de Chiquimula. ⬖ *department* SE Guatemala
**Chiquimula, Departamento de** *see* Chiquimula
42 D7 **Chiquimulilla** Santa Rosa, S Guatemala 14°06′N 90°23′W
54 F9 **Chiquinquirá** Boyacá, C Colombia 05°37′N 73°51′W
155 J17 **Chīrāla** Andhra Pradesh, E India 15°49′N 80°21′E
149 N4 **Chīras** Ghōr, N Afghanistan 35°15′N 65°39′E
152 H11 **Chirāwa** Rājasthān, N India 28°12′N 75°42′E
**Chirchik** *see* Chirchiq
147 Q9 **Chirchiq** *Rus.* Chirchik. Toshkent Viloyati, E Uzbekistan 41°30′N 69°32′E
147 P10 **Chirchiq** 〰 E Uzbekistan
**Chire** *see* Shire
83 L18 **Chiredzi** Masvingo, SE Zimbabwe 21°00′S 31°38′E
25 X8 **Chireno** Texas, SW USA 31°30′N 94°21′W
77 X7 **Chirfa** Agadez, NE Niger 21°01′N 12°41′E
37 O16 **Chiricahua Mountains** ⛰ Arizona, SW USA
37 O16 **Chiricahua Peak** ▲ Arizona, SW USA 31°51′N 109°17′W
54 F6 **Chiriguaná** Cesar, N Colombia 09°24′N 73°38′W
39 P15 **Chirikof Island** *island* Alaska, USA
43 P16 **Chiriquí** *off.* Provincia de Chiriquí. ⬖ *province* SW Panama
43 P17 **Chiriquí, Golfo de** *Eng.* Chiriqui Gulf. *gulf* SW Panama
43 P15 **Chiriquí Grande** Bocas del Toro, W Panama 08°58′N 82°08′W
**Chiriqui Gulf** *see* Chiriquí, Golfo de
43 P15 **Chiriquí, Laguna de** *lagoon* NW Panama
**Chiriquí, Provincia de** *see* Chiriquí
43 O16 **Chiriquí Viejo, Río** 〰 W Panama
**Chiriquí, Volcán de** *see* Barú, Volcán
83 N15 **Chiromo** Southern, S Malawi 16°32′S 35°07′E
114 J10 **Chirpan** Stara Zagora, C Bulgaria 42°12′N 25°20′E
43 N14 **Chirripó Atlántico, Río** 〰 E Costa Rica
**Chirripó, Cerro** *see* Chirripó Grande, Cerro
**Chirripó del Pacífico, Río** *see* Chirripó, Río
43 N14 **Chirripó Grande, Cerro** *var.* Cerro Chirripó. ▲ SE Costa Rica 09°31′N 83°28′W
43 N13 **Chirripó, Río** *var.* Río Chirripó del Pacífico. 〰 NE Costa Rica
**Chirua, Lago** *see* Chilwa, Lake
83 J15 **Chirundu** Southern, S Zambia 16°03′S 28°50′E
29 W8 **Chisago City** Minnesota, N USA 45°22′N 92°53′W
83 J14 **Chisamba** Central, C Zambia 15°00′S 28°22′E
39 T10 **Chisana** Alaska, USA 62°09′N 142°07′W
82 I13 **Chisasa** North Western, NW Zambia 12°09′S 25°30′E
12 I9 **Chisasibi** *prev.* Fort George. Québec, C Canada 53°50′N 79°01′W
42 D4 **Chisec** Alta Verapaz, C Guatemala 15°50′N 90°18′W
127 U5 **Chishmy** Respublika Bashkortostan, W Russia 54°33′N 55°21′E
29 V4 **Chisholm** Minnesota, N USA 47°29′N 92°52′W
149 U10 **Chishtian** *var.* Chishtian Mandi. Punjab, E Pakistan 29°44′N 72°54′E
**Chishtian Mandi** *see* Chishtian
160 I11 **Chishui He** 〰 C China
**Chisimaio/Chisimayu** *see* Kismaayo
117 N10 **Chişinău** *Rus.* Kishinev. ● (Moldova) C Moldova 47°N 28°51′E
117 N10 **Chişinău** ✈ S Moldova 46°54′N 28°56′E
**Chişinău-Criş** *see* Chişineu-Criş
116 F10 **Chişineu-Criş** *Hung.* Kisjenő; *prev.* Chişinău-Criş. Arad, W Romania 46°33′N 21°30′E
83 K14 **Chisomo** Central, C Zambia 13°30′S 30°37′E
106 A8 **Chisone** 〰 NW Italy
24 K12 **Chisos Mountains** ⛰ Texas, SW USA
39 T10 **Chistochina** Alaska, USA 62°34′N 144°39′W
127 R4 **Chistopol'** Respublika Tatarstan, W Russia 55°20′N 50°39′E
145 O8 **Chistopol'ye** Severnyy Kazakhstan, N Kazakhstan 52°37′N 67°14′E
123 O13 **Chita** Zabaykal'skiy Kray, S Russia 52°03′N 113°35′E
83 B16 **Chitado** Cunene, SW Angola 17°16′S 13°54′E
**Chitaldroog/Chitaldrug** *see* Chitradurga
83 C15 **Chitanda** 〰 S Angola
**Chitangwiza** *see* Chitungwiza
82 F10 **Chitato** Lunda Norte, NE Angola 07°23′S 20°46′E
83 C14 **Chitembo** Bié, C Angola 13°33′S 16°47′E
39 T11 **Chitina** Alaska, USA 61°31′N 144°26′W
39 T11 **Chitina River** 〰 Alaska, USA
82 M11 **Chitipa** Northern, NW Malawi 09°41′S 33°19′E
165 S4 **Chitose** *var.* Titose. Hokkaidō, NE Japan 42°51′N 141°40′E
155 G18 **Chitradurga** *prev.* Chitaldroog, Chitaldrug. Karnātaka, W India 14°16′N 76°23′E
149 T3 **Chitral** Khyber Pakhtunkhwa, NW Pakistan 35°51′N 71°47′E
43 S16 **Chitré** Herrera, S Panama 07°57′N 80°26′W
153 V16 **Chittagong** *Ben.* Chāttagām. Chittagong, SE Bangladesh 22°20′N 91°48′E
153 U16 **Chittagong** ⬖ *division* E Bangladesh
153 Q15 **Chittaranjan** West Bengal, NE India 23°52′N 86°40′E
152 G14 **Chittaurgarh** *var.* Chittorgarh. Rājasthān, N India 24°54′N 74°42′E
155 I19 **Chittoor** Andhra Pradesh, E India 13°13′N 79°06′E
**Chittorgarh** *see* Chittaurgarh
155 G21 **Chittūr** Kerala, SW India 10°42′N 76°46′E
83 K16 **Chitungwiza** *prev.* Chitangwiza. Mashonaland East, NE Zimbabwe 18°S 31°06′E
62 H4 **Chíuchíu** Antofagasta, N Chile 22°13′S 68°34′W
82 F12 **Chiumbe** *var.* Tshiumbe. 〰 Angola/Dem. Rep. Congo
83 F15 **Chiume** Moxico, E Angola 15°08′S 21°09′E
82 K13 **Chiundaponde** Muchinga, NE Zambia 12°14′S 30°40′E
106 H13 **Chiusi** Toscana, C Italy 43°00′N 11°56′E
54 J5 **Chivacoa** Yaracuy, N Venezuela 10°10′N 68°54′W
106 B8 **Chivasso** Piemonte, NW Italy 45°13′N 07°54′E
83 L17 **Chivhu** *prev.* Enkeldoorn. Midlands, C Zimbabwe 19°01′S 30°54′E
61 C20 **Chivilcoy** Buenos Aires, E Argentina 34°55′S 60°00′W
**Chiwei Yu** *see* Sekibi-sho
82 N12 **Chiweta** Northern, N Malawi 10°36′S 34°09′E
42 D4 **Chixoy, Río** *var.* Río Negro, Río Salinas. 〰 Guatemala/Mexico
82 H13 **Chizela** North Western, NW Zambia 13°11′S 24°59′E
125 O5 **Chizha** Nenetskiy Avtonomnyy Okrug, NW Russia 67°04′N 44°19′E
161 Q9 **Chizhou** *var.* Guichi. Anhui, E China 30°39′N 117°29′E
164 I12 **Chizu** Tottori, Honshū, SW Japan 35°15′N 134°14′E
**Chkalov** *see* Orenburg
74 J5 **Chlef** *var.* Ech Cheliff, Ech Chleff; *prev.* Al-Asnam, El Asnam, Orléansville. NW Algeria 36°11′N 01°21′E
115 G18 **Chlómo** ⛰ C Greece 38°36′N 22°57′E
111 M15 **Chmielnik** Świętokrzyskie, C Poland 50°37′N 20°43′E
167 S11 **Chŏâm Khsant** Preah Vihear, N Cambodia 14°13′N 104°56′E
62 G10 **Choapa, Río** *var.* Choapo. 〰 C Chile
**Choapas** *see* Las Choapas
**Choapo** *see* Choapa, Río
**Choarta** *see* Chwarta
83 H17 **Chobe** ⬖ *district* NE Botswana
67 T13 **Chobe** 〰 N Botswana
14 K8 **Chochocouane** 〰 Québec, SE Canada
110 E13 **Chocianów** *Ger.* Kotzenan. Dolnośląskie, SW Poland 51°23′N 15°55′E
54 C9 **Chocó** *off.* Departamento del Chocó. ⬖ *province* W Colombia
**Chocó, Departamento del** *see* Chocó
35 X16 **Chocolate Mountains** ⛰ California, W USA
21 W9 **Chocowinity** North Carolina, SE USA 35°33′N 77°03′W
27 N10 **Choctaw** Oklahoma, C USA 35°30′N 97°16′W
23 Q8 **Choctawhatchee Bay** *bay* Florida, SE USA
23 Q8 **Choctawhatchee River** 〰 Florida, SE USA
**Chodau** *see* Chodov
163 V14 **Ch'o-do** *island* SW North Korea
**Chodorów** *see* Khodoriv
111 A16 **Chodov** *Ger.* Chodau. Karlovarský Kraj, W Czechia 50°15′N 12°45′E
110 G10 **Chodzież** Wielkopolskie, C Poland 53°N 16°55′E
63 J15 **Choele Choel** Río Negro, C Argentina 39°19′S 65°42′W
83 L14 **Chofombo** Tete, NW Mozambique 14°43′S 31°48′E
**Chohtan** *see* Chauhtan
11 U14 **Choiceland** Saskatchewan, C Canada 53°28′N 104°26′W
186 K8 **Choiseul** ⬖ *province* NW Solomon Islands
186 K8 **Choiseul** *var.* Lauru. *island* NW Solomon Islands
63 M23 **Choiseul Sound** *sound* East Falkland, Falkland Islands
40 H7 **Choix** Sinaloa, C Mexico 26°43′N 108°20′W
110 D10 **Chojna** Zachodnio-pomorskie, W Poland 52°56′N 14°25′E
110 H8 **Chojnice** *Ger.* Konitz. Pomorskie, N Poland 53°41′N 17°34′E
111 F14 **Chojnów** *Ger.* Hainau, Haynau. Dolnośląskie, SW Poland 51°16′N 15°55′E
167 Q10 **Chok Chai** Nakhon Ratchasima, C Thailand 14°45′N 102°10′E
80 I12 **Ch'ok'ē** *var.* Choke Mountains. ⛰ NW Ethiopia
25 R13 **Choke Canyon Lake** ⊞ Texas, SW USA
**Choke Mountains** *see* Ch'ok'ē
**Chokpar** *see* Shokpar
147 W7 **Chok-Tal** *var.* Choktal. Issyk-Kul'skaya Oblast', E Kyrgyzstan 42°37′N 76°45′E
**Choktal** *see* Chok-Tal
**Chókué** *see* Chokwè
123 R7 **Chokurdakh** Respublika Sakha (Yakutiya), NE Russia 70°38′N 148°18′E
83 L20 **Chokwè** *var.* Chókué. Gaza, S Mozambique 24°27′S 32°55′E
188 F8 **Chol** Babeldaob, N Palau
160 E8 **Chola Shan** ⛰ C China
102 J8 **Cholet** Maine-et-Loire, NW France 47°03′N 00°52′W
63 H17 **Cholila** Chubut, W Argentina 42°33′S 71°28′W
**Cholo** *see* Thyolo
147 V8 **Cholpon** Narynskaya Oblast', C Kyrgyzstan 42°07′N 75°25′E
147 X7 **Cholpon-Ata** Issyk-Kul'skaya Oblast', E Kyrgyzstan 42°39′N 77°05′E
41 P14 **Cholula** Puebla, S Mexico 19°03′N 98°19′W
42 I8 **Choluteca** Choluteca, S Honduras 13°15′N 87°10′W
42 H8 **Choluteca** ⬖ *department* S Honduras
42 H8 **Choluteca, Río** 〰 SW Honduras
83 I15 **Choma** Southern, S Zambia 16°48′S 26°58′E
153 T11 **Chomo Lhari** ▲ NW Bhutan 27°59′N 89°24′E
167 N7 **Chom Thong** Chiang Mai, NW Thailand 18°25′N 98°44′E
111 B15 **Chomutov** *Ger.* Komotau. Ústecký Kraj, NW Czechia 50°28′N 13°24′E
123 N11 **Chona** 〰 C Russia
**Ch'ŏnan** *see* Cheonan
167 P11 **Chon Buri** *prev.* Bang Pla Soi. Chon Buri, S Thailand 13°24′N 100°59′E
56 B6 **Chone** Manabí, W Ecuador 0°44′S 80°04′W
**Chong'an** *see* Wuyishan
163 W13 **Ch'ŏngch'ŏn-gang** 〰 W North Korea
163 Y11 **Ch'ŏngjin** NE North Korea 41°48′N 129°44′E
**Chŏngju** *see* Cheongju
161 S8 **Chongming Dao** *island* E China
160 J10 **Chongqing** *var.* Ch'ung-ching, Ch'ung-ch'ing, Chungking, Pahsien, Tchongking, Yuzhou. Chongqing Shi, C China 29°34′N 106°27′E
**Chŏngup** *see* Chŏnju
161 O10 **Chongyang** *var.* Tiancheng. Hubei, C China 29°35′N 114°03′E
160 J15 **Chongzuo** *prev.* Taiping. Guangxi Zhuangzu Zizhiqu, S China 22°18′N 107°23′E
163 Y16 **Chŏnju** *prev.* Chŏnju, Chŏngup, *Jap.* Seiyu. SW South Korea 35°51′N 127°08′E
**Chŏnju** *see* Chŏnju
**Chŏnju** *see* Jeonju
**Chonnacht** *see* Connaught
**Chonogol** *see* Erdenetsagaan
63 F19 **Chonos, Archipiélago de los** *island group* S Chile
42 K10 **Chontales** ⬖ *department* S Nicaragua
167 T13 **Chơn Thanh** Sông Be, S Vietnam 11°25′N 106°38′E
158 K17 **Cho Oyu** *var.* Qowowuyag. ▲ China/Nepal 28°07′N 86°37′E
116 G7 **Chop** *Cz.* Čop, *Hung.* Csap. Zakarpats'ka Oblast', W Ukraine 48°26′N 22°13′E
21 Y3 **Choptank River** 〰 Maryland, NE USA
115 J22 **Chóra** *prev.* Íos. Íos, Kykládes, Greece, Aegean Sea 36°42′N 25°16′E
115 H25 **Chóra Sfakíon** *var.* Sfákia. Kríti, Greece, E Mediterranean Sea 35°12′N 24°05′E
**Chorcaí, Cuan** *see* Cork Harbour
43 P15 **Chorcha, Cerro** ▲ W Panama 08°39′N 82°07′W
**Chorku** *see* Chorkŭh
147 R11 **Chorkŭh** *Rus.* Chorku. N Tajikistan 40°04′N 70°30′E
97 K17 **Chorley** NW England, United Kingdom 53°40′N 02°38′W
**Chorne More** *see* Black Sea
117 R5 **Chornobay** Cherkas'ka Oblast', C Ukraine 49°40′N 32°20′E
117 O3 **Chornobyl'** *Rus.* Chernobyl'. Kyivs'ka Oblast', N Ukraine 51°17′N 30°15′E
117 P11 **Chornomors'k** *prev.* Illichivs'k. Odes'ka Oblast', SW Ukraine 46°18′N 30°36′E
117 R12 **Chornomors'ke** *Rus.* Chernomorskoye. Avtonomna Respublika Krym, S Ukraine 45°29′N 32°45′E
117 R4 **Chornukhy** Poltavs'ka Oblast', C Ukraine 50°15′N 32°57′E
**Chorokh/Chorokhi** *see* Çoruh Nehri
110 O9 **Choroszcz** Podlaskie, NE Poland 53°10′N 23°E
116 K6 **Chortkiv** *Rus.* Chortkov. Ternopil's'ka Oblast', W Ukraine 49°01′N 25°46′E
**Chortkov** *see* Chortkiv
**Chorum** *see* Çorum
110 M9 **Chorzele** Mazowieckie, C Poland 53°16′N 20°53′E
111 J16 **Chorzów** *Ger.* Königshütte; *prev.* Królewska Huta. Śląskie, S Poland 50°17′N 18°58′E
163 W12 **Ch'osan** N North Korea 40°45′N 125°52′E
**Chośebuz** *see* Cottbus
**Chōsen-kaikyō** *see* Korea Strait
164 P14 **Chōshi** *var.* Tyôsi. Chiba, Honshū, S Japan 35°44′N 140°48′E
63 H14 **Chos Malal** Neuquén, W Argentina 37°23′S 70°16′W
**Chosŏn-minjujuŭi-inmin-konghwaguk** *see* North Korea
110 E9 **Choszczno** *Ger.* Arnswalde. Zachodnio-pomorskie, NW Poland 53°10′N 15°24′E
153 O15 **Chota Nāgpur** *plateau* N India
33 R8 **Choteau** Montana, NW USA 47°48′N 112°40′W
**Chotqol** *see* Chatkal
14 M8 **Chouart** 〰 Québec, SE Canada
76 I7 **Choûm** Adrar, C Mauritania 21°19′N 12°59′W
27 Q9 **Chouteau** Oklahoma, C USA 36°11′N 95°20′W
21 X8 **Chowan River** 〰 North Carolina, SE USA
35 Q10 **Chowchilla** California, W USA 37°06′N 120°15′W
163 Q7 **Choybalsan** *var.* Hulstay. Dornod, NE Mongolia 48°25′N 114°56′E
163 P7 **Choybalsan** *prev.* Byan Tumen. Dornod, E Mongolia 48°03′N 114°32′E
162 M9 **Choyr** Govĭ Sumber, C Mongolia 46°20′N 108°21′E
185 I19 **Christchurch** Canterbury, South Island, New Zealand 43°31′S 172°39′E
97 M24 **Christchurch** S England, United Kingdom 50°44′N 01°45′W
185 I18 **Christchurch** ✈ Canterbury, South Island, New Zealand 43°28′S 172°33′E
44 J12 **Christiana** C Jamaica 18°13′N 77°29′W
83 H22 **Christiana** Free State, C South Africa 27°55′S 25°10′E
115 J23 **Christiána** *var.* Christiani. *island* Kykládes, Greece, Aegean Sea
**Christiani** *see* Christiána
**Christiania** *see* Oslo
14 G13 **Christian Island** *island* Ontario, S Canada
191 P16 **Christian, Point** *headland* Pitcairn Island, Pitcairn Islands 25°04′S 130°08′E
38 M11 **Christian River** 〰 Alaska, USA
**Christiansand** *see* Kristiansand
21 S7 **Christiansburg** Virginia, NE USA 37°07′N 80°26′W
95 G23 **Christiansfeld** Syddanmark, SW Denmark 55°21′N 09°30′E
**Christianshåb** *see* Qasigiannguit
39 X14 **Christian Sound** *inlet* Alaska, USA
45 T9 **Christiansted** Saint Croix, S Virgin Islands (US) 17°43′N 64°42′W
**Christiansund** *see* Kristiansund
25 R13 **Christine** Texas, SW USA 28°47′N 98°30′W
173 U7 **Christmas Island** ◇ *Australian external territory* E Indian Ocean
129 T17 **Christmas Island** *island* E Indian Ocean
**Christmas Island** *see* Kiritimati
192 M7 **Christmas Ridge** *undersea feature* C Pacific Ocean
30 L16 **Christopher** Illinois, N USA 37°58′N 89°03′W
25 P9 **Christoval** Texas, SW USA 31°09′N 100°30′W
111 F17 **Chrudim** Pardubický Kraj, C Czechia 49°58′N 15°49′E
115 K25 **Chrýsi** *island* SE Greece
121 N2 **Chrysochoús, Kólpos** *var.* Khrysokhou Bay. *bay* E Mediterranean Sea
121 N2 **Chrysochoús, Kólpos** *var.* Khrysokhou Bay. *bay* E Mediterranean Sea
114 I13 **Chrysoúpoli** *var.* Hrisoupoli; *prev.* Khrisoúpolis. Anatolikí Makedonía kai Thráki, NE Greece 40°59′N 24°42′E
111 K16 **Chrzanów** *var.* Chrzanow, *Ger.* Zaumgarten. Śląskie, S Poland 50°10′N 19°21′E
**Chu** *see* Shu
42 C5 **Chuacús, Sierra de** ⛰ W Guatemala
153 S15 **Chuadanga** Khulna, W Bangladesh 23°38′N 88°52′E
**Chuan** *see* Sichuan
**Ch'uan-chou** *see* Quanzhou
**Chuankou** *see* Minhe
39 O11 **Chuathbaluk** Alaska, USA 61°36′N 159°14′W
**Chubek** *see* Moskva
63 I17 **Chubut** *off.* Provincia de Chubut. ⬖ *province* S Argentina
**Chubut, Provincia de** *see* Chubut
63 I17 **Chubut, Río** 〰 SE Argentina
43 V15 **Chucanti, Cerro** ▲ E Panama 08°48′N 78°27′W
**Ch'u-chiang** *see* Shaoguan
43 W15 **Chucunaque, Río** 〰 E Panama
**Chudin** *see* Chudzin
116 M5 **Chudniv** Zhytomyrs'ka Oblast', N Ukraine 50°02′N 28°06′E
124 H13 **Chudovo** Novgorodskaya Oblast', W Russia 59°07′N 31°42′E
**Chudskoye Ozero** *see* Peipus, Lake
119 J18 **Chudzin** *Rus.* Chudin. Brestskaya Voblasts', SW Belarus 52°44′N 26°59′E
39 Q13 **Chugach Islands** *island group* Alaska, USA
39 S11 **Chugach Mountains** ⛰ Alaska, USA
164 G12 **Chūgoku-sanchi** ⛰ Honshū, SW Japan
**Chugqênsumdo** *see* Jigzhi
**Chuguyev** *see* Chuhuyiv
117 V5 **Chuhuyiv** *var.* Chuguyev. Kharkivs'ka Oblast', E Ukraine 49°51′N 36°44′E
61 H19 **Chuí** Rio Grande do Sul, S Brazil 33°45′S 53°23′W
**Chuí** *see* Chuy
**Chu-Iliyskiye Gory** *see* Gory Shu-Ile
**Chukai** *see* Cukai
**Chukchi Avtonomnyy Okrug** *see* Chukotskiy Avtonomnyy Okrug
**Chukchi Peninsula** *see* Chukotskiy Poluostrov
197 R6 **Chukchi Plain** *undersea feature* Arctic Ocean
197 R6 **Chukchi Plateau** *undersea feature* Arctic Ocean
197 R4 **Chukchi Sea** *Rus.* Chukotskoye More. *sea* Arctic Ocean
125 N14 **Chukhloma** Kostromskaya Oblast', NW Russia 58°42′N 42°39′E
**Chukotka** *see* Chukotskiy Avtonomnyy Okrug
**Chukot Range** *see* Anadyrskiy Khrebet
123 V6 **Chukotskiy Avtonomnyy Okrug** *var.* Chukchi Avtonomnyy Okrug, Chukotka. ⬖ *autonomous district* NE Russia
123 W5 **Chukotskiy, Mys** *headland* NE Russia 64°15′N 173°03′W
123 V5 **Chukotskiy Poluostrov** *Eng.* Chukchi Peninsula. *peninsula* NE Russia
**Chukotskoye More** *see* Chukchi Sea
**Chukurkak** *see* Chuqurqoq
**Chulakkurgan** *see* Sholakkorgan
35 U17 **Chula Vista** California, W USA 32°38′N 117°04′W
123 Q12 **Chul'man** Respublika Sakha (Yakutiya), NE Russia 56°50′N 124°47′E
56 B9 **Chulucanas** Piura, NW Peru 05°08′S 80°10′W
122 J12 **Chulym** 〰 C Russia
152 K6 **Chumar** Jammu and Kashmir, N India 32°38′N 78°36′E
114 K9 **Chumerna** ▲ C Bulgaria 42°45′N 25°58′E
123 R12 **Chumikan** Khabarovskiy Kray, E Russia 54°41′N 135°12′E
167 Q9 **Chum Phae** Khon Kaen, C Thailand 16°31′N 102°09′E
167 N13 **Chumphon** *var.* Jumporn. Chumphon, SW Thailand 10°30′N 99°11′E
167 O9 **Chumsaeng** *var.* Chum Saeng. Nakhon Sawan, C Thailand 15°52′N 100°18′E
**Chum Saeng** *see* Chumsaeng
122 L12 **Chuna** 〰 C Russia
161 R9 **Chun'an** *var.* Qiandaohu; *prev.* Pailing. Zhejiang, SE China 29°37′N 118°59′E
**Chunan** *see* Zhunan
**Chuncheng** *see* Yangchun
163 Y14 **Chuncheon** *Jap.* Shunsen; *prev.* Ch'unch'ŏn. N South Korea 37°52′N 127°48′E
**Ch'unch'ŏn** *see* Chuncheon
153 S16 **Chunchura** *prev.* Chinsura. West Bengal, NE India 22°54′N 88°20′E
**Chundzha** *see* Shonzhy
**Ch'ung-ch'ing/Ch'ung-ching** *see* Chongqing
163 Y15 **Chungju** *Jap.* Chūshū; *prev.* Ch'ungju. C South Korea 36°57′N 127°50′E
**Ch'ungju** *see* Chungju
**Chungking** *see* Chongqing
**Chungyang Shanmo** *see* Zhongyang Shanmo
149 V9 **Chunian** Punjab, E Pakistan 30°57′N 74°01′E
122 L12 **Chunskiy** Irkutskaya Oblast', S Russia 56°10′N 99°15′E
122 M11 **Chunya** 〰 C Russia
124 J6 **Chupa** Respublika Kareliya, NW Russia 66°15′N 33°02′E
125 P8 **Chuprovo** Respublika Komi, NW Russia 64°16′N 46°27′E
57 G17 **Chuquibamba** Arequipa, SW Peru 15°47′S 72°44′W
62 H4 **Chuquicamata** Antofagasta, N Chile 22°20′S 68°56′W
57 L21 **Chuquisaca** ⬖ *department* S Bolivia
**Chuquisaca** *see* Sucre
**Chuqung** *see* Chindu
146 I8 **Chuqurqoq** *Rus.* Chukurkak. Qoraqalpog'iston Respublikasi, NW Uzbekistan 42°44′N 61°33′E
127 T2 **Chur** Udmurtskaya Respublika, NW Russia 57°06′N 52°57′E
108 I9 **Chur** *Fr.* Coire, *It.* Coira, *Rmsch.* Cuera, Quera; *anc.* Curia Rhaetorum. Graubünden, E Switzerland 46°52′N 09°32′E
123 Q10 **Churapcha** Respublika Sakha (Yakutiya), NE Russia 61°59′N 132°06′E
11 V16 **Churchbridge** Saskatchewan, S Canada 50°55′N 101°53′W
21 O8 **Church Hill** Tennessee, S USA 36°31′N 82°42′W
11 X9 **Churchill** Manitoba, C Canada 58°46′N 94°10′W
11 X10 **Churchill** 〰 Manitoba/Saskatchewan, C Canada
13 P9 **Churchill** 〰 Newfoundland and Labrador, E Canada
11 Y9 **Churchill, Cape** *headland* Manitoba, C Canada 58°42′N 93°12′W
13 P9 **Churchill Falls** Newfoundland and Labrador, E Canada 53°38′N 54°00′W
11 S12 **Churchill Lake** ◎ Saskatchewan, C Canada
19 Q3 **Churchill Lake** ⊞ Maine, NE USA
194 I5 **Churchill Peninsula** *peninsula* Antarctica
22 H8 **Church Point** Louisiana, S USA 30°24′N 92°13′W
29 O3 **Churchs Ferry** North Dakota, N USA 48°15′N 99°12′W
146 G12 **Churchuri** Ahal Welaýaty, C Turkmenistan 38°55′N 59°13′E
21 T5 **Churchville** Virginia, NE USA 38°13′N 79°10′W
152 G10 **Chūru** Rājasthān, NW India 28°18′N 75°00′E
54 J4 **Churuguara** Falcón, N Venezuela 10°52′N 69°35′W
167 U11 **Chư Sê** Gia Lai, C Vietnam 13°38′N 108°06′E
144 J12 **Chushkakul, Gory** ⛰ SW Kazakhstan
**Chūshū** *see* Chungju
37 O9 **Chuska Mountains** ⛰ Arizona/New Mexico, SW USA
**Chu, Sông** *see* Sam, Nam
125 V14 **Chusovoy** Permskiy Kray, NW Russia 58°17′N 57°54′E
147 R10 **Chust** Namangan Viloyati, E Uzbekistan 40°58′N 71°12′E
**Chust** *see* Khust
15 U6 **Chute-aux-Outardes** Québec, SE Canada 49°07′N 68°25′W
117 U5 **Chutove** Poltavs'ka Oblast', C Ukraine 49°45′N 35°11′E
167 U11 **Chư Ty** *var.* Đưc Cơ. Gia Lai, C Vietnam 13°48′N 107°41′E
189 O15 **Chuuk** *var.* Truk. ⬖ *state* C Micronesia
189 P15 **Chuuk Islands** *var.* Hogoley Islands; *prev.* Truk Islands. *island group* Caroline Islands, C Micronesia
**Chuvashia** *see* Chuvashskaya Respublika
**Chuvashiya** *see* Chuvashskaya Respublika
127 P4 **Chuvashskaya Respublika** *var.* Chuvashiya, *Eng.* Chuvashia. ⬖ *autonomous republic* W Russia
**Chuwārtah** *see* Chwarta
**Chu Xian/Chuxian** *see* Chuzhou
160 G13 **Chuxiong** Yunnan, SW China 25°02′N 101°32′E
147 V7 **Chuy** Chuyskaya Oblast', N Kyrgyzstan 42°45′N 75°11′E
61 H19 **Chuy** *var.* Chuí. Rocha, E Uruguay 33°42′S 53°27′W
123 O11 **Chuya** Respublika Sakha (Yakutiya), NE Russia 59°30′N 112°26′E
**Chüy Oblasty** *see* Chuyskaya Oblast'
147 U8 **Chuyskaya Oblast'** *Kyr.* Chüy Oblasty. ⬖ *province* N Kyrgyzstan
161 Q7 **Chuzhou** *var.* Chuxian, Chu Xian. Anhui, E China 32°20′N 118°18′E
139 U3 **Chwarta** *Ar.* Juwārtā, *var.* Chwārtā, Choarta, Chuwārtah. As Sulaymānīyah, NE Iraq 35°11′N 45°59′E
**Chwārtā** *see* Chwarta
119 N16 **Chyhirynskaye Vodaskhovishcha** *Rus.* Chigirinskoye Vodokhranilishche. ⊞ E Belarus
117 R6 **Chyhyryn** *Rus.* Chigirin. Cherkas'ka Oblast', N Ukraine 49°03′N 32°40′E
119 J18 **Chyrvonaya Slabada** *Rus.* Krasnaya Slabada, Krasnaya Sloboda. Minskaya Voblasts', S Belarus 52°51′N 27°10′E
119 L19 **Chyrvonaye, Vozyera** *Rus.* Ozero Chervonoye. ◎ SE Belarus
117 Y8 **Chystyakove** *prev.* Torez. Donets'ka Oblast', SE Ukraine 48°00′N 38°38′E
117 N11 **Ciadîr-Lunga** *var.* Ceadâr-Lunga, *Rus.* Chadyr-Lunga. S Moldova 46°03′N 28°50′E
169 P16 **Ciamis** *prev.* Tjiamis. Jawa, C Indonesia 07°20′S 108°21′E
107 I16 **Ciampino** ✈ Lazio, C Italy 41°48′N 12°36′E
169 N16 **Cianjur** *prev.* Tjiandjoer. Jawa, C Indonesia 06°50′S 107°09′E
60 H10 **Cianorte** Paraná, S Brazil 23°42′S 52°31′W
**Ciarraí** *see* Kerry
112 N13 **Ćićevac** Serbia, E Serbia 43°44′N 21°25′E
187 Z14 **Cicia** *prev.* Thithia. *island* Lau Group, E Fiji
105 P4 **Cidacos** 〰 N Spain
136 I10 **Cide** Kastamonu, N Turkey 41°53′N 33°01′E
110 L10 **Ciechanów** *prev.* Zichenau. Mazowieckie, C Poland 52°53′N 20°37′E
110 O10 **Ciechanowiec** *Ger.* Rudelstadt. Podlaskie, E Poland 52°43′N 22°30′E
110 J10 **Ciechocinek** Kujawskio-pomorskie, C Poland 52°53′N 18°49′E
44 F6 **Ciego de Ávila** Ciego de Ávila, C Cuba 21°50′N 78°44′W
44 G6 **Ciego de Ávila** ⬖ *province* Cuba
54 F4 **Ciénaga** Magdalena, N Colombia 11°01′N 74°15′W
54 E6 **Ciénaga de Oro** Córdoba, NW Colombia 08°54′N 75°39′W
44 E5 **Cienfuegos** Cienfuegos, C Cuba 22°10′N 80°27′W
44 E5 **Cienfuegos** ⬖ *province* S Cuba
104 F4 **Cíes, Illas** *island group* NW Spain
111 P16 **Cieszanów** Podkarpackie, SE Poland 50°15′N 23°09′E
111 J17 **Cieszyn** *Cz.* Těšín, *Ger.* Teschen. Śląskie, S Poland 49°45′N 18°35′E
105 R12 **Cieza** Murcia, SE Spain 38°14′N 01°25′W
136 F13 **Çifteler** Eskişehir, W Turkey 39°25′N 31°00′E
105 P7 **Cifuentes** Castilla-La Mancha, C Spain 40°47′N 02°37′W
**Čiganak** *see* Shyganak
105 P9 **Cigüela** 〰 C Spain
136 H14 **Cihanbeyli** Konya, C Turkey 38°40′N 32°55′E
136 H14 **Cihanbeyli Yaylası** *plateau* C Turkey
104 L10 **Cíjara, Embalse de** ⊞ C Spain
169 P16 **Cikalong** Jawa, S Indonesia 07°46′S 108°13′E
169 N16 **Cikawung** Jawa, S Indonesia 06°49′S 105°29′E
187 Y13 **Cikobia** *prev.* Thikombia. *island* N Fiji
169 P17 **Cilacap** *prev.* Tjilatjap. Jawa, C Indonesia 07°44′S 109°E
173 O16 **Cilaos** C Réunion 21°08′S 55°28′E
137 S11 **Çıldır** Ardahan, NE Turkey 41°08′N 43°08′E
137 S11 **Çıldır Gölü** ◎ NE Turkey
160 M10 **Cili** Hunan, S China 29°24′N 110°59′E
**Cilician Gates** *see* Gülek Boğazı
121 V10 **Cilicia Trough** *undersea feature* E Mediterranean Sea
**Cill Airne** *see* Killarney
**Cill Chainnigh** *see* Kilkenny
**Cill Chaoi** *see* Kilkee
**Cill Choca** *see* Kilcock
**Cill Dara** *see* Kildare
105 N3 **Cilleruelo de Bezana** Castilla y León, N Spain 42°58′N 03°50′W
**Cilli** *see* Celje
**Cill Mhantáin** *see* Wicklow
**Cill Rois** *see* Kilrush
146 C11 **Çilmämmetgum** *Rus.* Peski Chil'mamedkum,, *Turkm.* Chilmämetgum. *desert* Balkan Welaýaty, W Turkmenistan
137 Z11 **Çilov Adası** *Rus.* Ostrov Zhiloy. *island* E Azerbaijan
26 J6 **Cimarron** Kansas, C USA 37°49′N 100°20′W
37 T9 **Cimarron** New Mexico, SW USA 36°30′N 104°55′W
26 M9 **Cimarron River** 〰 Kansas/Oklahoma, C USA
117 N11 **Cimişlia** *Rus.* Chimishliya. S Moldova 46°31′N 28°45′E
**Cîmpia Turzii** *see* Câmpia Turzii
**Cîmpina** *see* Câmpina
**Cîmpulung** *see* Câmpulung
**Cîmpulung Moldovenesc** *see* Câmpulung Moldovenesc
137 P15 **Çınar** Dıyarbakır, SE Turkey 37°45′N 40°22′E
54 J8 **Cinaruco, Río** 〰 Colombia/Venezuela
105 T5 **Cinca** 〰 NE Spain
112 G13 **Cincar** ▲ SW Bosnia and Herzegovina 43°55′N 17°05′E
31 Q15 **Cincinnati** Ohio, N USA 39°04′N 84°34′W
21 M4 **Cincinnati** ✈ Kentucky, S USA 39°03′N 84°39′W
**Cinco de Outubro** *see* Xá-Muteba
136 C15 **Çine** Aydın, SW Turkey 37°37′N 28°03′E
99 J21 **Ciney** Namur, SE Belgium 50°17′N 05°06′E


◆ Country
● Country Capital
◇ Dependent Territory
○ Dependent Territory Capital
⬖ Administrative Regions
✈ International Airport
▲ Mountain
⛰ Mountain Range
⩚ Volcano
〰 River
◎ Lake
⊞ Reservoir

CINFÃES – COLLEGE STATION


104 H6 **Cinfães** Viseu, N Portugal *41°04′N 08°06′W*

106 J12 **Cingoli** Marche, C Italy *43°25′N 13°09′E*

41 U16 **Cintalapa** *var.* Cintalapa de Figueroa. Chiapas, SE Mexico *16°42′N 93°40′W*

**Cintalapa de Figueroa** *see* Cintalapa

103 X14 **Cinto, Monte** ▲ Corse, France, C Mediterranean Sea *42°22′N 08°57′E*

**Cintra** *see* Sintra

105 Q5 **Cintruénigo** Navarra, N Spain *42°05′N 01°50′W*

**Cionn tSáile** *see* Kinsale

116 K13 **Ciorani** Prahova, SE Romania *44°49′N 26°25′E*

113 E14 **Čiovo** *It.* Bua. *island* S Croatia

**Cipiúr** *see* Kippure

63 I15 **Cipolletti** Río Negro, C Argentina *38°55′S 68°W*

120 L7 **Circeo, Capo** *headland* C Italy *41°15′N 13°03′E*

39 S8 **Circle** *var.* Circle City. Alaska, USA *65°51′N 144°04′W*

33 X8 **Circle** Montana, NW USA *47°25′N 105°32′W*

**Circle City** *see* Circle

31 S14 **Circleville** Ohio, N USA *39°36′N 82°57′W*

36 K6 **Circleville** Utah, W USA *38°10′N 112°16′W*

169 P16 **Cirebon** *prev.* Tjirebon. Jawa, S Indonesia *06°46′S 108°33′E*

97 L21 **Cirencester** *anc.* Corinium, Corinium Dobunorum. C England, United Kingdom *51°44′N 01°59′W*

**Cirkvenica** *see* Crikvenica

107 O20 **Cirò** Calabria, SW Italy *39°22′N 17°02′E*

107 O20 **Cirò Marina** Calabria, S Italy *39°21′N 17°07′E*

102 K14 **Ciron** 〰 SW France

**Cirquenizza** *see* Crikvenica

25 R7 **Cisco** Texas, SW USA *32°23′N 98°58′W*

116 I12 **Cisnădie** *Ger.* Heltau, *Hung.* Nagydisznód. Sibiu, SW Romania *45°42′N 24°09′E*

63 G18 **Cisnes, Río** 〰 S Chile

25 T11 **Cistern** Texas, SW USA *29°46′N 97°12′W*

104 L3 **Cistierna** Castilla y León, N Spain *42°47′N 05°08′W*

**Citharista** *see* la Ciotat

**Citlaltépetl** *see* Orizaba, Volcán Pico de

55 X10 **Citron** NW French Guiana *04°49′N 53°55′W*

23 N7 **Citronelle** Alabama, S USA *31°05′N 88°13′W*

35 O7 **Citrus Heights** California, W USA *38°42′N 121°18′W*

106 H7 **Cittadella** Veneto, NE Italy *45°37′N 11°46′E*

106 H13 **Città della Pieve** Umbria, C Italy *42°57′N 12°01′E*

106 H12 **Città di Castello** Umbria, C Italy *43°27′N 12°13′E*

107 I14 **Cittaducale** Lazio, C Italy *42°24′N 12°55′E*

107 N22 **Cittanova** Calabria, SW Italy *38°21′N 16°05′E*

**Cittavecchia** *see* Stari Grad

116 G10 **Ciucea** *Hung.* Csucsa. Cluj, NW Romania *46°58′N 22°50′E*

116 M13 **Ciucurova** Tulcea, SE Romania *44°57′N 28°24′E*

**Ciudad Acuña** *see* Villa Acuña

41 N15 **Ciudad Altamirano** Guerrero, S Mexico *18°20′N 100°40′W*

42 G7 **Ciudad Barrios** San Miguel, NE El Salvador *13°46′N 88°13′W*

54 I7 **Ciudad Bolívar** Barinas, NW Venezuela *08°22′N 70°37′W*

55 N7 **Ciudad Bolívar** *prev.* Angostura. Bolívar, E Venezuela *08°08′N 63°31′W*

40 K6 **Ciudad Camargo** Chihuahua, N Mexico *27°42′N 105°10′W*

40 E8 **Ciudad Constitución** Baja California Sur, NW Mexico *25°09′N 111°43′W*

**Ciudad Cortés** *see* Cortés

41 V17 **Ciudad Cuauhtémoc** Chiapas, SE Mexico *15°38′N 91°59′W*

42 J9 **Ciudad Darío** *var.* Dario. Matagalpa, W Nicaragua *12°42′N 86°10′W*

**Ciudad de Dolores Hidalgo** *see* Dolores Hidalgo

**Ciudad del Carmen** *see* Carmen

62 Q6 **Ciudad del Este** *prev.* Ciudad Presidente Stroessner, Presidente Stroessner, Puerto Presidente Stroessner. Alto Paraná, SE Paraguay *25°34′S 54°40′W*

62 K5 **Ciudad de Libertador General San Martín** *var.* Libertador General San Martín. Jujuy, C Argentina *23°50′S 64°45′W*

**Ciudad Delicias** *see* Delicias

41 O11 **Ciudad del Maíz** San Luis Potosí, C Mexico *22°26′N 99°36′W*

54 J7 **Ciudad de Nutrias** Barinas, NW Venezuela *08°03′N 69°17′W*

**Ciudad de Panama** *see* Panamá

55 P7 **Ciudad Guayana** *prev.* San Tomé de Guayana, Santo Tomé de Guayana. Bolívar, NE Venezuela *08°22′N 62°37′W*

40 K14 **Ciudad Guzmán** Jalisco, SW Mexico *19°40′N 103°30′W*

41 V17 **Ciudad Hidalgo** Chiapas, SE Mexico *14°40′N 92°11′W*

41 N14 **Ciudad Hidalgo** Michoacán, SW Mexico *19°40′N 100°34′W*

40 J3 **Ciudad Juárez** Chihuahua, N Mexico *31°39′N 106°26′W*

40 L8 **Ciudad Lerdo** Durango, C Mexico *25°34′N 103°30′W*

41 Q11 **Ciudad Madero** *var.* Villa Cecilia. Tamaulipas, C Mexico *22°18′N 97°56′W*

41 P11 **Ciudad Mante** Tamaulipas, C Mexico *22°43′N 99°02′W*

42 F2 **Ciudad Melchor de Mencos** *var.* Melchor de Mencos. Petén, NE Guatemala *17°03′N 89°12′W*

41 P8 **Ciudad Miguel Alemán** Tamaulipas, C Mexico *26°20′N 98°56′W*

**Ciudad Mutis** *see* Bahía Solano

40 G6 **Ciudad Obregón** Sonora, NW Mexico *27°32′N 109°53′W*

54 I5 **Ciudad Ojeda** Zulia, NW Venezuela *10°12′N 71°17′W*

55 P7 **Ciudad Piar** Bolívar, E Venezuela *07°25′N 63°19′W*

**Ciudad Porfirio Díaz** *see* Piedras Negras

**Ciudad Presidente Stroessner** *see* Ciudad del Este

**Ciudad Quesada** *see* Quesada

105 N11 **Ciudad Real** Castilla-La Mancha, C Spain *38°59′N 03°55′W*

105 N11 **Ciudad Real** ⬖ *province* Castilla-La Mancha, C Spain

104 J7 **Ciudad-Rodrigo** Castilla y León, N Spain *40°36′N 06°33′W*

42 A6 **Ciudad Tecún Umán** San Marcos, SW Guatemala *14°40′N 92°06′W*

**Ciudad Trujillo** *see* Santo Domingo

41 P12 **Ciudad Valles** San Luis Potosí, C Mexico *21°59′N 99°01′W*

41 O10 **Ciudad Victoria** Tamaulipas, C Mexico *23°44′N 99°07′W*

42 C6 **Ciudad Vieja** Suchitepéquez, S Guatemala *14°30′N 90°46′W*

116 L8 **Ciuhuru** *var.* Reuţel. 〰 N Moldova

105 Z8 **Ciutadella** *var.* Ciutadella de Menorca. Menorca, Spain, W Mediterranean Sea *40°N 03°50′E*

**Ciutadella Ciutadella de Menorca** *see* Ciutadella

136 L11 **Civa Burnu** *headland* N Turkey *41°22′N 36°39′E*

106 J7 **Cividale del Friuli** Friuli-Venezia Giulia, NE Italy *46°06′N 13°25′E*

107 H14 **Civita Castellana** Lazio, C Italy *42°16′N 12°24′E*

106 J12 **Civitanova Marche** Marche, C Italy *43°18′N 13°41′E*

**Civitas Altae Ripae** *see* Brzeg

**Civitas Carnutum** *see* Chartres

**Civitas Eburovicum** *see* Évreux

**Civitas Nemetum** *see* Speyer

107 G15 **Civitavecchia** *anc.* Centum Cellae, Trajani Portus. Lazio, C Italy *42°05′N 11°47′E*

102 L10 **Civray** Vienne, W France *46°10′N 00°18′E*

136 E14 **Çivril** Denizli, W Turkey *38°18′N 29°43′E*

161 O5 **Cixian** Hebei, E China *36°19′N 114°22′E*

137 R16 **Cizre** Şırnak, SE Turkey *37°21′N 42°11′E*

**Clacton** *see* Clacton-on-Sea

97 Q21 **Clacton-on-Sea** *var.* Clacton. E England, United Kingdom *51°48′N 01°09′E*

22 H5 **Claiborne, Lake** ⊠ Louisiana, S USA

102 L10 **Clain** 〰 W France

11 Q11 **Claire, Lake** ◎ Alberta, C Canada

25 O6 **Clairemont** Texas, SW USA *33°09′N 100°45′W*

34 M3 **Clair Engle Lake** ⊠ California, W USA

18 B15 **Clairton** Pennsylvania, NE USA *40°17′N 79°52′W*

32 F7 **Clallam Bay** Washington, NW USA *48°13′N 124°16′W*

103 P8 **Clamecy** Nièvre, C France *47°28′N 03°30′E*

23 P5 **Clanton** Alabama, S USA *32°50′N 86°37′W*

61 D17 **Clara** Entre Ríos, E Argentina *31°50′S 58°48′W*

97 E18 **Clara** *Ir.* Clóirtheach. C Ireland *53°20′N 07°36′W*

29 T9 **Clara City** Minnesota, N USA *44°57′N 95°22′W*

61 D23 **Claraz** Buenos Aires, E Argentina *37°56′S 59°18′W*

**Clár Chlainne Mhuiris** *see* Claremorris

182 I8 **Clare** South Australia *33°49′S 138°35′E*

97 C19 **Clare** *Ir.* An Clár. *cultural region* W Ireland

97 C18 **Clare** 〰 W Ireland

97 A16 **Clare Island** *Ir.* Cliara. *island* W Ireland

44 J12 **Claremont** C Jamaica *18°23′N 77°11′W*

29 W10 **Claremont** Minnesota, N USA *44°01′N 93°00′W*

19 N9 **Claremont** New Hampshire, NE USA *43°21′N 72°18′W*

27 Q9 **Claremore** Oklahoma, C USA *36°20′N 95°37′W*

97 C17 **Claremorris** *Ir.* Clár Chlainne Mhuiris. W Ireland *53°47′N 09°W*

185 J16 **Clarence** Canterbury, South Island, New Zealand *42°08′S 173°54′E*

185 J16 **Clarence** 〰 South Island, New Zealand

65 F15 **Clarence Bay** *bay* Ascension Island, C Atlantic Ocean

63 H25 **Clarence, Isla** *island* S Chile

194 H2 **Clarence Island** *island* South Shetland Islands, Antarctica

183 V5 **Clarence River** 〰 New South Wales, SE Australia

44 J5 **Clarence Town** Long Island, C The Bahamas *23°03′N 74°57′W*

27 W12 **Clarendon** Arkansas, C USA *34°41′N 91°19′W*

25 O3 **Clarendon** Texas, SW USA *34°57′N 100°54′W*

13 U12 **Clarenville** Newfoundland, Newfoundland and Labrador, SE Canada *48°10′N 54°00′W*

11 Q17 **Claresholm** Alberta, SW Canada *50°02′N 113°33′W*

29 T16 **Clarinda** Iowa, C USA *40°44′N 95°02′W*

55 N5 **Clarines** Anzoátegui, NE Venezuela *09°56′N 65°11′W*

29 V12 **Clarion** Iowa, C USA *42°43′N 93°43′W*

18 C13 **Clarion** Pennsylvania, NE USA *41°11′N 79°21′W*

193 O6 **Clarion Fracture Zone** *tectonic feature* NE Pacific Ocean

18 D13 **Clarion River** 〰 Pennsylvania, NE USA

29 Q9 **Clark** South Dakota, N USA *44°50′N 97°44′W*

36 K11 **Clarkdale** Arizona, SW USA *34°46′N 112°03′W*

15 W4 **Clarke City** Québec, SE Canada *50°09′N 66°36′W*

183 Q15 **Clarke Island** *island* Furneaux Group, Tasmania, SE Australia

181 X6 **Clarke Range** ▲▲ Queensland, E Australia

23 T2 **Clarkesville** Georgia, SE USA *34°36′N 83°31′W*

29 S9 **Clarkfield** Minnesota, N USA *44°48′N 95°49′W*

33 N7 **Clark Fork** Idaho, NW USA *48°06′N 116°10′W*

33 N8 **Clark Fork** 〰 Idaho/Montana, NW USA

21 P13 **Clark Hill Lake** *var.* J.Storm Thurmond Reservoir. ⊠ Georgia/South Carolina, SE USA

39 Q12 **Clark, Lake** ◎ Alaska, USA

35 W12 **Clark Mountain** ▲ California, W USA *35°30′N 115°34′W*

37 S3 **Clark Peak** ▲ Colorado, C USA *40°36′N 105°57′W*

14 D14 **Clark, Point** *headland* Ontario, S Canada *44°04′N 81°45′W*

21 S3 **Clarksburg** West Virginia, NE USA *39°16′N 80°22′W*

22 K2 **Clarksdale** Mississippi, S USA *34°12′N 90°34′W*

33 U12 **Clarks Fork Yellowstone River** 〰 Montana/Wyoming, NW USA

29 R14 **Clarkson** Nebraska, C USA *41°42′N 97°07′W*

39 O13 **Clarks Point** Alaska, USA *58°50′N 158°33′W*

18 I13 **Clarks Summit** Pennsylvania, NE USA *41°29′N 75°42′W*

32 M10 **Clarkston** Washington, NW USA *46°25′N 117°02′W*

44 J12 **Clark's Town** C Jamaica *18°25′N 77°32′W*

27 T10 **Clarksville** Arkansas, C USA *35°29′N 93°29′W*

31 P13 **Clarksville** Indiana, N USA *40°01′N 85°54′W*

20 I8 **Clarksville** Tennessee, S USA *36°32′N 87°22′W*

25 W5 **Clarksville** Texas, SW USA *33°37′N 95°04′W*

21 U8 **Clarksville** Virginia, NE USA *36°36′N 78°36′W*

21 U11 **Clarkton** North Carolina, SE USA *34°28′N 78°39′W*

61 C24 **Claromecó** *var.* Balneario Claromecó. Buenos Aires, E Argentina *38°51′S 60°01′W*

25 N3 **Claude** Texas, SW USA *35°06′N 101°22′W*

**Clausentum** *see* Southampton

171 O1 **Claveria** Luzon, N Philippines *18°36′N 121°04′E*

99 J20 **Clavier** Liège, E Belgium *50°27′N 05°21′E*

23 W6 **Claxton** Georgia, SE USA *32°09′N 81°54′W*

21 R4 **Clay** West Virginia, NE USA *38°28′N 81°17′W*

27 N3 **Clay Center** Kansas, C USA *39°22′N 97°08′W*

29 P16 **Clay Center** Nebraska, C USA *40°31′N 98°03′W*

21 Y2 **Claymont** Delaware, NE USA *39°48′N 75°27′W*

36 M14 **Claypool** Arizona, SW USA *33°24′N 110°50′W*

23 R6 **Clayton** Alabama, S USA *31°52′N 85°27′W*

23 T1 **Clayton** Georgia, SE USA *34°52′N 83°24′W*

22 J5 **Clayton** Louisiana, S USA *31°43′N 91°32′W*

27 X5 **Clayton** Missouri, C USA *38°39′N 90°21′W*

37 V9 **Clayton** New Mexico, SW USA *36°27′N 103°12′W*

21 V9 **Clayton** North Carolina, SE USA *35°39′N 78°27′W*

27 Q12 **Clayton** Oklahoma, C USA *34°35′N 95°21′W*

45 V9 **Clayton J. Lloyd** ✈ (The Valley) C Anguilla *18°12′N 63°02′W*

182 I4 **Clayton River** *seasonal river* South Australia

21 R7 **Claytor Lake** ⊠ Virginia, NE USA

27 P13 **Clear Boggy Creek** 〰 Oklahoma, C USA

97 B22 **Clear, Cape** *var.* The Bill of Cape Clear, *Ir.* Ceann Cléire. *headland* SW Ireland *51°25′N 09°31′W*

36 M12 **Clear Creek** 〰 Arizona, SW USA

39 S12 **Cleare, Cape** *headland* Montague Island, Alaska, USA *59°46′N 147°54′W*

18 E13 **Clearfield** Pennsylvania, NE USA *41°02′N 78°27′W*

36 L2 **Clearfield** Utah, W USA *41°06′N 112°03′W*

25 Q6 **Clear Fork Brazos River** 〰 Texas, SW USA

31 T12 **Clear Fork Reservoir** ⊠ Ohio, N USA

11 N12 **Clear Hills** ▲▲ Alberta, SW Canada

34 M6 **Clearlake** California, W USA *38°57′N 122°38′W*

29 V12 **Clear Lake** Iowa, C USA *43°07′N 93°27′W*

29 R9 **Clear Lake** South Dakota, N USA *44°45′N 96°40′W*

34 M6 **Clear Lake** ◎ California, W USA

22 G6 **Clear Lake** ⊠ Louisiana, S USA

35 P1 **Clear Lake Reservoir** ⊠ California, W USA

11 N16 **Clearwater** British Columbia, SW Canada *51°38′N 120°02′W*

23 U12 **Clearwater** Florida, SE USA *27°58′N 82°46′W*

11 R12 **Clearwater** 〰 Alberta/Saskatchewan, C Canada

27 W7 **Clearwater Lake** ⊠ Missouri, C USA

33 N10 **Clearwater Mountains** ▲▲ Idaho, NW USA

33 N10 **Clearwater River** 〰 Idaho, NW USA

29 S4 **Clearwater River** 〰 Minnesota, N USA

25 T7 **Cleburne** Texas, SW USA *32°21′N 97°24′W*

32 I9 **Cle Elum** Washington, NW USA *47°12′N 120°56′W*

97 O17 **Cleethorpes** E England, United Kingdom *53°34′N 00°02′W*

**Cléire, Ceann** *see* Clear, Cape

21 O11 **Clemson** South Carolina, SE USA *34°40′N 82°50′W*

21 Q4 **Clendenin** West Virginia, NE USA *38°29′N 81°21′W*

26 M9 **Cleo Springs** Oklahoma, C USA *36°25′N 98°25′W*

**Clerk Island** *see* Onotoa

181 X8 **Clermont** Queensland, E Australia *22°47′S 147°41′E*

15 S8 **Clermont** Québec, SE Canada *47°41′N 70°15′W*

103 O4 **Clermont** Oise, N France *49°23′N 02°26′E*

29 X12 **Clermont** Iowa, C USA *43°00′N 91°39′W*

103 P11 **Clermont-Ferrand** Puy-de-Dôme, C France *45°47′N 03°05′E*

103 Q15 **Clermont-l'Hérault** Hérault, S France *43°37′N 03°25′E*

99 M22 **Clervaux** Diekirch, N Luxembourg *50°03′N 06°02′E*

106 G6 **Cles** Trentino-Alto Adige, N Italy *46°22′N 11°04′E*

182 H8 **Cleve** South Australia *33°43′S 136°30′E*

**Cleve** *see* Kleve

23 T2 **Cleveland** Georgia, SE USA *34°36′N 83°45′W*

22 K3 **Cleveland** Mississippi, S USA *33°45′N 90°43′W*

31 T11 **Cleveland** Ohio, N USA *41°30′N 81°42′W*

27 O9 **Cleveland** Oklahoma, C USA *36°18′N 96°27′W*

20 L10 **Cleveland** Tennessee, S USA *35°10′N 84°51′W*

25 W10 **Cleveland** Texas, SW USA *30°19′N 95°06′W*

31 N7 **Cleveland** Wisconsin, N USA *43°58′N 87°45′W*

31 O4 **Cleveland Cliffs Basin** ◎ Michigan, N USA

31 U11 **Cleveland Heights** Ohio, N USA *41°30′N 81°34′W*

33 P6 **Cleveland, Mount** ▲ Montana, NW USA *48°55′N 113°51′W*

**Cleves** *see* Kleve

97 B16 **Clew Bay** *Ir.* Cuan Mó. *inlet* W Ireland

23 Y14 **Clewiston** Florida, SE USA *26°45′N 80°55′W*

**Cliara** *see* Clare Island

97 A17 **Clifden** *Ir.* An Clochán. Galway, W Ireland *53°29′N 10°14′W*

37 O14 **Clifton** Arizona, SW USA *33°03′N 109°18′W*

18 K14 **Clifton** New Jersey, NE USA *40°50′N 74°28′W*

25 S8 **Clifton** Texas, SW USA *31°43′N 97°36′W*

21 S6 **Clifton Forge** Virginia, NE USA *37°49′N 79°50′W*

182 I1 **Clifton Hills** South Australia *27°03′S 138°49′E*

11 S17 **Climax** Saskatchewan, S Canada *49°12′N 108°22′W*

21 O8 **Clinch River** 〰 Tennessee/Virginia, S USA

25 P12 **Cline** Texas, SW USA *29°14′N 100°07′W*

21 N10 **Clingmans Dome** ▲ North Carolina/Tennessee, SE USA *35°33′N 83°30′W*

24 H8 **Clint** Texas, SW USA *31°35′N 106°13′W*

10 M16 **Clinton** British Columbia, SW Canada *51°06′N 121°31′W*

14 E15 **Clinton** Ontario, S Canada *43°36′N 81°33′W*

27 U10 **Clinton** Arkansas, C USA *35°34′N 92°28′W*

30 L10 **Clinton** Illinois, N USA *40°09′N 88°57′W*

29 Z14 **Clinton** Iowa, C USA *41°50′N 90°11′W*

20 G7 **Clinton** Kentucky, S USA *36°39′N 89°00′W*

22 J8 **Clinton** Louisiana, S USA *30°52′N 91°01′W*

19 N11 **Clinton** Massachusetts, NE USA *42°25′N 71°40′W*

31 R10 **Clinton** Michigan, N USA *42°04′N 83°58′W*

22 K5 **Clinton** Mississippi, S USA *32°22′N 90°22′W*

27 S5 **Clinton** Missouri, C USA *38°22′N 93°51′W*

21 V10 **Clinton** North Carolina, SE USA *35°00′N 78°19′W*

26 L10 **Clinton** Oklahoma, C USA *35°31′N 98°58′W*

21 Q12 **Clinton** South Carolina, SE USA *34°28′N 81°52′W*

21 M9 **Clinton** Tennessee, S USA *36°07′N 84°08′W*

8 L9 **Clinton-Colden Lake** ◎ Northwest Territories, NW Canada

10 H5 **Clinton Creek** Yukon, NW Canada *64°24′N 140°35′W*

30 L13 **Clinton Lake** ⊠ Illinois, N USA

27 Q4 **Clinton Lake** ⊠ Kansas, N USA

21 T11 **Clio** South Carolina, SE USA *34°34′N 79°33′W*

193 O7 **Clipperton Fracture Zone** *tectonic feature* E Pacific Ocean

193 Q7 **Clipperton Island** *Fr.* Île Clipperton. ◇ *administered from France* E Pacific Ocean

46 K6 **Clipperton Island** *island* E Pacific Ocean

0 F16 **Clipperton Seamounts** *undersea feature* E Pacific Ocean *08°00′N 111°00′W*

102 J8 **Clisson** Loire-Atlantique, NW France *47°06′N 01°19′W*

62 K7 **Clodomira** Santiago del Estero, N Argentina *27°35′S 64°14′W*

**Cloich na Coillte** *see* Clonakilty

**Clóirtheach** *see* Clara

97 C21 **Clonakilty** *Ir.* Cloich na Coillte. SW Ireland *51°37′N 08°54′W*

181 T6 **Cloncurry** Queensland, C Australia *20°45′S 140°30′E*

97 F18 **Clondalkin** *Ir.* Cluain Dolcáin. E Ireland *53°19′N 06°24′W*

97 E16 **Clones** *Ir.* Cluain Eois. N Ireland *54°11′N 07°14′W*

97 D20 **Clonmel** *Ir.* Cluain Meala. S Ireland *52°21′N 07°42′W*

100 G11 **Cloppenburg** Niedersachsen, NW Germany *52°51′N 08°03′E*

29 W6 **Cloquet** Minnesota, N USA *46°43′N 92°27′W*

37 S14 **Cloudcroft** New Mexico, SW USA *32°57′N 105°44′W*

33 W12 **Cloud Peak** ▲ Wyoming, C USA *44°22′N 107°10′W*

185 K14 **Cloudy Bay** *inlet* South Island, New Zealand

21 R10 **Clover** South Carolina, SE USA *35°06′N 81°13′W*

34 M6 **Cloverdale** California, W USA *38°49′N 123°03′W*

20 J5 **Cloverport** Kentucky, S USA *37°50′N 86°37′W*

35 Q10 **Clovis** California, W USA *36°48′N 119°43′W*

37 W12 **Clovis** New Mexico, SW USA *34°22′N 103°12′W*

14 K13 **Cloyne** Ontario, SE Canada *44°48′N 77°09′W*

**Cluain Dolcáin** *see* Clondalkin

**Cluain Eois** *see* Clones

**Cluainín** *see* Manorhamilton

**Cluain Meala** *see* Clonmel

116 H10 **Cluj** ⬖ *county* NW Romania

**Cluj** *see* Cluj-Napoca

116 H10 **Cluj-Napoca** *Ger.* Klausenburg, *Hung.* Kolozsvár; *prev.* Cluj. Cluj, NW Romania *46°47′N 23°36′E*

**Clunia** *see* Feldkirch

103 R10 **Cluny** Saône-et-Loire, C France *46°25′N 04°38′E*

103 T10 **Cluses** Haute-Savoie, E France *46°04′N 06°34′E*

106 E7 **Clusone** Lombardia, N Italy *45°56′N 10°00′E*

25 W12 **Clute** Texas, SW USA *29°01′N 95°24′W*

185 D23 **Clutha River / Mata-Au** *var.* Mata-Au. 〰 South Island, New Zealand

97 J18 **Clwyd** *cultural region* NE Wales, United Kingdom

185 D22 **Clyde** Otago, South Island, New Zealand *45°12′S 169°21′E*

27 N3 **Clyde** Kansas, C USA *39°35′N 97°24′W*

29 P2 **Clyde** North Dakota, N USA *48°44′N 98°51′W*

31 S11 **Clyde** Ohio, N USA *41°18′N 82°58′W*

25 Q7 **Clyde** Texas, SW USA *32°24′N 99°29′W*

14 K13 **Clyde** 〰 Ontario, SE Canada

96 J13 **Clyde** 〰 W Scotland, United Kingdom

96 H12 **Clydebank** S Scotland, United Kingdom *55°54′N 04°24′W*

96 H13 **Clyde, Firth of** *inlet* S Scotland, United Kingdom

33 S11 **Clyde Park** Montana, NW USA *45°56′N 110°39′W*

35 W16 **Coachella** California, W USA *33°38′N 116°10′W*

35 W16 **Coachella Canal** *canal* California, W USA

40 I9 **Coacoyole** Durango, C Mexico *24°30′N 106°33′W*

25 N7 **Coahoma** Texas, SW USA *32°18′N 101°18′W*

10 K8 **Coal** 〰 Yukon, NW Canada

40 L14 **Coalcomán** *var.* Coalcomán de Matamoros. Michoacán, S Mexico *18°49′N 103°13′W*

**Coalcomán de Matamoros** *see* Coalcomán

39 T8 **Coal Creek** Alaska, USA *65°21′N 143°08′W*

11 Q17 **Coaldale** Alberta, SW Canada *49°42′N 112°36′W*

27 P12 **Coalgate** Oklahoma, C USA *34°33′N 96°15′W*

35 P11 **Coalinga** California, W USA *36°08′N 120°21′W*

10 L9 **Coal River** British Columbia, W Canada *59°38′N 126°45′W*

21 Q6 **Coal River** 〰 West Virginia, NE USA

36 M2 **Coalville** Utah, W USA *40°56′N 111°22′W*

58 E13 **Coari** Amazonas, N Brazil *04°08′S 63°07′W*

104 I7 **Côa, Rio** 〰 N Portugal

59 D14 **Coari, Rio** 〰 NW Brazil

**Coast** *see* Pwani

10 G12 **Coast Mountains** *Fr.* Chaîne Côtière. ▲▲ Canada/USA

16 C7 **Coast Ranges** ▲▲ W USA

96 I12 **Coatbridge** S Scotland, United Kingdom *55°52′N 04°01′W*

42 B6 **Coatepeque** Quetzaltenango, SW Guatemala *14°42′N 91°50′W*

18 H16 **Coatesville** Pennsylvania, NE USA *39°58′N 75°47′W*

15 Q13 **Coaticook** Québec, SE Canada *45°07′N 71°46′W*

9 P9 **Coats Island** *island* Nunavut, NE Canada

195 O4 **Coats Land** *physical region* Antarctica

41 T14 **Coatzacoalcos** *var.* Quetzalcoalco; *prev.* Puerto México. Veracruz, E Mexico *18°06′N 94°26′W*

41 S14 **Coatzacoalcos, Río** 〰 SE Mexico

116 M15 **Cobadin** Constanţa, SW Romania *44°05′N 28°13′E*

14 H9 **Cobalt** Ontario, S Canada *47°24′N 79°41′W*

42 D5 **Cobán** Alta Verapaz, C Guatemala *15°28′N 90°20′W*

183 O6 **Cobar** New South Wales, SE Australia *31°31′S 145°51′E*

18 F12 **Cobb Hill** ▲ Pennsylvania, NE USA *41°52′N 77°52′W*

0 D8 **Cobb Seamount** *undersea feature* E Pacific Ocean *47°00′N 131°00′W*

14 K12 **Cobden** Ontario, SE Canada *45°36′N 76°54′W*

97 D21 **Cobh** *Ir.* An Cóbh; *prev.* Cove of Cork, Queenstown. SW Ireland *51°51′N 08°17′W*

57 J14 **Cobija** Pando, NW Bolivia *11°04′S 68°49′W*

**Coblence/Coblenz** *see* Koblenz

18 J10 **Cobleskill** New York, NE USA *42°40′N 74°29′W*

14 I15 **Cobourg** Ontario, SE Canada *43°57′N 78°06′W*

181 P1 **Cobourg Peninsula** *headland* Northern Territory, N Australia *11°27′S 132°33′E*

183 O10 **Cobram** Victoria, SE Australia *35°56′S 145°36′E*

82 N13 **Cóbuè** Niassa, N Mozambique *12°08′S 34°46′E*

101 K18 **Coburg** Bayern, SE Germany *50°16′N 10°58′E*

19 Q5 **Coburn Mountain** ▲ Maine, NE USA *45°28′N 70°07′W*

57 H18 **Cocachacra** Arequipa, SW Peru *17°05′S 71°45′W*

59 J17 **Cocalinho** Mato Grosso, W Brazil *14°22′S 51°00′W*

**Cocanada** *see* Kākināda

105 S11 **Cocentaina** Comunitat Valenciana, E Spain *38°44′N 00°27′W*

57 L18 **Cochabamba** *hist.* Oropeza. Cochabamba, C Bolivia *17°23′S 66°10′W*

57 K18 **Cochabamba** ⬖ *department* C Bolivia

57 L18 **Cochabamba, Cordillera de** ▲▲ C Bolivia

101 E18 **Cochem** Rheinland-Pfalz, W Germany *50°09′N 07°09′E*

37 R6 **Cochetopa Hills** ▲▲ Colorado, C USA

**Cochin** *see* Kochi

44 D5 **Cochinos, Bahía de** *Eng.* Bay of Pigs. *bay* SE Cuba

37 O16 **Cochise Head** ▲ Arizona, SW USA *32°03′N 109°19′W*

23 U5 **Cochran** Georgia, SE USA *32°23′N 83°21′W*

11 P16 **Cochrane** Alberta, SW Canada *51°15′N 114°25′W*

12 G12 **Cochrane** Ontario, S Canada *49°04′N 81°02′W*

63 G20 **Cochrane** Aysén, S Chile *47°16′S 72°33′W*

11 U10 **Cochrane** 〰 Manitoba/Saskatchewan, C Canada

**Cochrane, Lago** *see* Pueyrredón, Lago

**Cocibolca** *see* Nicaragua, Lago de

**Cockade State** *see* Maryland

44 M6 **Cockburn Harbour** South Caicos, S Turks and Caicos Islands *21°28′N 71°30′W*

14 C11 **Cockburn Island** *island* Ontario, S Canada

44 J3 **Cockburn Town** San Salvador, E The Bahamas *24°01′N 74°31′W*

21 X2 **Cockeysville** Maryland, NE USA *39°29′N 76°34′W*

181 N12 **Cocklebiddy** Western Australia *32°02′S 125°54′E*

44 I12 **Cockpit Country, The** *physical region* W Jamaica

43 S16 **Coclé** *off.* Provincia de Coclé. ⬖ *province* C Panama

43 S15 **Coclé del Norte** Colón, C Panama *09°04′N 80°32′W*

**Coclé, Provincia de** *see* Coclé

23 Y12 **Cocoa** Florida, SE USA *28°23′N 80°44′W*

23 Y12 **Cocoa Beach** Florida, SE USA *28°19′N 80°36′W*

79 D17 **Cocobeach** Estuaire, NW Gabon *0°59′N 09°34′E*

44 G5 **Coco, Cayo** *island* C Cuba

151 Q19 **Coco Channel** *strait* Andaman Sea/Bay of Bengal

173 N6 **Coco-de-Mer Seamounts** *undersea feature* W Indian Ocean *0°30′N 56°00′E*

36 K10 **Coconino Plateau** *plain* Arizona, SW USA

43 N6 **Coco, Río** *var.* Río Wanki, Segoviao Wangkí. 〰 Honduras/Nicaragua

173 T7 **Cocos Basin** *undersea feature* E Indian Ocean *05°00′S 94°00′E*

188 B17 **Cocos Island** *island* S Guam

**Cocos Island Ridge** *see* Cocos Ridge

129 S17 **Cocos Islands** *island group* E Indian Ocean

173 T8 **Cocos (Keeling) Islands** ◇ *Australian external territory* E Indian Ocean

0 G15 **Cocos Plate** *tectonic feature*

193 T7 **Cocos Ridge** *var.* Cocos Island Ridge. *undersea feature* E Pacific Ocean *05°30′N 86°00′W*

40 K13 **Cocula** Jalisco, SW Mexico *20°22′N 103°50′W*

107 D17 **Coda Cavallo, Capo** *headland* Sardegna, Italy, C Mediterranean Sea *40°49′N 09°43′E*

58 E13 **Codajás** Amazonas, N Brazil *03°50′S 62°12′W*

**Codazzi** *see* Agustín Codazzi

19 Q12 **Cod, Cape** *headland* Massachusetts, NE USA *41°50′N 69°56′W*

185 B25 **Codfish Island** *island* SW New Zealand

106 H9 **Codigoro** Emilia-Romagna, N Italy *44°50′N 12°07′E*

13 P5 **Cod Island** *island* Newfoundland and Labrador, E Canada

116 J12 **Codlea** *Ger.* Zeiden, *Hung.* Feketehalom. Braşov, C Romania *45°43′N 25°27′E*

58 M13 **Codó** Maranhão, E Brazil *04°28′S 43°51′W*

106 E8 **Codogno** Lombardia, N Italy *45°10′N 09°42′E*

116 M10 **Codrii** *hill range* C Moldova

45 W9 **Codrington** Barbuda, Antigua and Barbuda *17°43′N 61°49′W*

106 J7 **Codroipo** Friuli-Venezia Giulia, NE Italy *45°58′N 13°00′E*

28 M12 **Cody** Nebraska, C USA *42°54′N 101°13′W*

33 U12 **Cody** Wyoming, C USA *43°31′N 109°04′W*

21 P7 **Coeburn** Virginia, NE USA *36°56′N 82°27′W*

54 E10 **Coello** Tolima, W Colombia *04°15′N 74°52′W*

**Coemba** *see* Cuemba

181 V2 **Coen** Queensland, NE Australia *14°03′S 143°16′E*

101 E14 **Coesfeld** Nordrhein-Westfalen, W Germany *51°55′N 07°10′E*

32 M8 **Coeur d'Alene** Idaho, NW USA *47°40′N 116°46′W*

32 M8 **Coeur d'Alene Lake** ⊠ Idaho, NW USA

98 O8 **Coevorden** Drenthe, NE Netherlands *52°39′N 06°45′E*

10 H6 **Coffee Creek** Yukon, W Canada *62°52′N 139°05′W*

30 L15 **Coffeen Lake** ⊠ Illinois, N USA

22 L3 **Coffeeville** Mississippi, S USA *33°58′N 89°40′W*

27 Q8 **Coffeyville** Kansas, C USA *37°02′N 95°37′W*

182 G9 **Coffin Bay** South Australia *34°39′S 135°30′E*

182 F9 **Coffin Bay Peninsula** *peninsula* South Australia

183 V5 **Coffs Harbour** New South Wales, SE Australia *30°18′S 153°08′E*

105 R10 **Cofrentes** Comunitat Valenciana, E Spain *39°14′N 01°04′W*

117 N10 **Cogîlnic** *Ukr.* Kohyl'nyk. 〰 Moldova/Ukraine

102 K11 **Cognac** *anc.* Compniacum. Charente, W France *45°42′N 00°19′W*

106 B7 **Cogne** Valle d'Aosta, NW Italy *45°37′N 07°27′E*

103 U16 **Cogolin** Var, SE France *43°15′N 06°30′E*

105 O7 **Cogolludo** Castilla-La Mancha, C Spain *40°58′N 03°05′W*

**Cohalm** *see* Rupea

92 K8 **Čohkarášša** *var.* Cuokkarašša. ▲ N Norway *69°57′N 24°38′E*

**Čohkkiras** *see* Jukkasjärvi

18 F11 **Cohocton River** 〰 New York, NE USA

18 L10 **Cohoes** New York, NE USA *42°46′N 73°42′W*

183 N10 **Cohuna** Victoria, SE Australia *35°51′S 144°15′E*

43 P17 **Coiba, Isla de** *island* SW Panama

63 H23 **Coig, Río** 〰 S Argentina

63 G19 **Coihaique** *var.* Coyhaique. Aysén, S Chile *45°32′S 72°00′W*

155 G21 **Coimbatore** Tamil Nādu, S India *11°N 76°57′E*

104 G8 **Coimbra** *anc.* Conimbria, Conimbriga. Coimbra, W Portugal *40°12′N 08°25′W*

104 G8 **Coimbra** ⬖ *district* N Portugal

104 L15 **Coín** Andalucía, S Spain *36°40′N 04°45′W*

**Coin de Mire** *see* Gunner's Quoin

57 J20 **Coipasa, Laguna** ◎ W Bolivia

57 J20 **Coipasa, Salar de** *salt lake* W Bolivia

**Coira/Coire** *see* Chur

**Coirib, Loch** *see* Corrib, Lough

54 K6 **Cojedes** *off.* Estado Cojedes. ⬖ *state* N Venezuela

**Cojedes, Estado** *see* Cojedes

42 F7 **Cojutepeque** Cuscatlán, C El Salvador *13°43′N 88°56′W*

**Coka** *see* Banbar

33 S16 **Cokeville** Wyoming, C USA *42°03′N 110°55′W*

182 M13 **Colac** Victoria, SE Australia *38°22′S 143°38′E*

59 O20 **Colatina** Espírito Santo, SE Brazil *19°35′S 40°37′W*

27 O13 **Colbert** Oklahoma, C USA *33°51′N 96°30′W*

100 L12 **Colbitz-Letzinger Heide** *heathland* N Germany

26 I3 **Colby** Kansas, C USA *39°24′N 101°04′W*

57 H17 **Colca, Río** 〰 SW Peru

97 P21 **Colchester** *hist.* Colneceaste; *anc.* Camulodunum. E England, United Kingdom *51°54′N 00°54′E*

19 N13 **Colchester** Connecticut, NE USA *41°34′N 72°17′W*

38 M16 **Cold Bay** Alaska, USA *55°11′N 162°43′W*

11 R14 **Cold Lake** Alberta, SW Canada *54°26′N 110°16′W*

11 R13 **Cold Lake** ◎ Alberta/Saskatchewan, S Canada

29 U8 **Cold Spring** Minnesota, N USA *45°27′N 94°25′W*

25 W10 **Coldspring** Texas, SW USA *30°34′N 95°10′W*

11 N17 **Coldstream** British Columbia, SW Canada *50°13′N 119°09′W*

96 L13 **Coldstream** SE Scotland, United Kingdom *55°39′N 02°19′W*

14 H13 **Coldwater** Ontario, S Canada *44°43′N 79°36′W*

26 K7 **Coldwater** Kansas, C USA *37°16′N 99°20′W*

31 Q10 **Coldwater** Michigan, N USA *41°56′N 85°00′W*

25 N1 **Coldwater Creek** 〰 Oklahoma/Texas, SW USA

22 K2 **Coldwater River** 〰 Mississippi, S USA

183 O9 **Coleambally** New South Wales, SE Australia *34°48′S 145°54′E*

19 O6 **Colebrook** New Hampshire, NE USA *44°52′N 71°27′W*

27 T5 **Cole Camp** Missouri, C USA *38°27′N 93°12′W*

39 T6 **Coleen River** 〰 Alaska, USA

11 P17 **Coleman** Alberta, SW Canada *49°36′N 114°26′W*

25 Q8 **Coleman** Texas, SW USA *31°50′N 99°27′W*

**Çölemerik** *see* Hakkâri

83 K22 **Colenso** KwaZulu/Natal, E South Africa *28°44′S 29°50′E*

182 L12 **Coleraine** Victoria, SE Australia *37°39′S 141°42′E*

97 F14 **Coleraine** *Ir.* Cúil Raithin. N Northern Ireland, United Kingdom *55°08′N 06°40′W*

185 G18 **Coleridge, Lake** ◎ South Island, New Zealand

83 H24 **Colesberg** Northern Cape, C South Africa *30°41′S 25°08′E*

22 H7 **Colfax** Louisiana, S USA *31°31′N 92°42′W*

32 L9 **Colfax** Washington, NW USA *46°52′N 117°21′W*

30 J6 **Colfax** Wisconsin, N USA *45°00′N 91°44′W*

63 I19 **Colhué Huapí, Lago** ◎ S Argentina

45 Z6 **Colibris, Pointe des** *headland* Grande Terre, E Guadeloupe *16°15′N 61°10′W*

106 D6 **Colico** Lombardia, N Italy *46°08′N 09°24′E*

99 E14 **Colijnsplaat** Zeeland, SW Netherlands *51°36′N 03°47′E*

40 L14 **Colima** Colima, S Mexico *19°13′N 103°46′W*

40 K14 **Colima** ⬖ *state* SW Mexico

40 L14 **Colima, Nevado de** ⩚ C Mexico *19°36′N 103°36′W*

59 M14 **Colinas** Maranhão, E Brazil *06°02′S 44°15′W*

96 F10 **Coll** *island* W Scotland, United Kingdom

105 N7 **Collado Villalba** *var.* Villalba. Madrid, C Spain *40°38′N 04°00′W*

183 R4 **Collarenebri** New South Wales, SE Australia *29°31′S 148°33′E*

37 P5 **Collbran** Colorado, C USA *39°14′N 107°57′W*

106 G12 **Colle di Val d'Elsa** Toscana, C Italy *43°26′N 11°06′E*

39 R9 **College** Alaska, USA *64°49′N 148°06′W*

32 K10 **College Place** Washington, NW USA *46°03′N 118°23′W*

25 U10 **College Station** Texas, SW USA *30°38′N 96°21′W*




◆ Country
● Country Capital
◇ Dependent Territory
○ Dependent Territory Capital
⬖ Administrative Regions
✈ International Airport
▲ Mountain
▲▲ Mountain Range
⩚ Volcano
〰 River
◎ Lake
⊠ Reservoir

Collerina – Corn Islands


183 P4 Collerina New South Wales, SE Australia 29°41′S 146°36′E
180 I13 Collie Western Australia 33°20′S 116°06′E
180 L4 Collier Bay bay Western Australia
21 F10 Collierville Tennessee, S USA 35°02′N 89°39′W
106 F11 Collina, Passo della pass C Italy
14 G14 Collingwood Ontario, S Canada 44°30′N 80°14′W
184 I13 Collingwood Tasman, South Island, New Zealand 40°40′S 172°40′E
22 L7 Collins Mississippi, S USA 31°39′N 89°33′W
30 K15 Collinsville Illinois, N USA 38°40′N 89°58′W
27 P9 Collinsville Oklahoma, C USA 36°21′N 95°50′W
20 H10 Collinwood Tennessee, S USA 35°10′N 87°44′W
Collipo see Leiria
63 G14 Collipulli Araucanía, C Chile 37°55′S 72°30′W
97 D16 Collooney Ir. Cúil Mhuine. NW Ireland 54°11′N 08°29′W
29 R10 Colman South Dakota, N USA 43°58′N 96°48′W
103 U6 Colmar Ger. Kolmar. Haut-Rhin, NE France 48°05′N 07°21′E
104 M15 Colmenar Andalucía, S Spain 36°54′N 04°20′W
Colmenar see Colmenar de Oreja
105 O9 Colmenar de Oreja var. Colmenar. Madrid, C Spain 40°06′N 03°25′W
105 N7 Colmenar Viejo Madrid, C Spain 40°39′N 03°46′W
25 X9 Colmesneil Texas, SW USA 30°54′N 94°25′W
Cöln see Köln
Colneceaste see Colchester
59 G15 Colniza Mato Grosso, W Brazil 09°16′S 59°25′W
Cologne see Köln
42 B6 Colomba Quetzaltenango, SW Guatemala 14°45′N 91°39′W
Colomb-Béchar see Béchar
54 E11 Colombia Huila, C Colombia 03°24′N 74°49′W
54 G10 Colombia off. Republic of Colombia. ◆ republic N South America
64 E12 Colombian Basin undersea feature SW Caribbean Sea 13°00′N 76°00′W
Colombia, Republic of see Colombia
Colombie-Britannique see British Columbia
15 T6 Colombier Québec, SE Canada 48°51′N 68°52′W
155 J25 Colombo ● (Sri Lanka - commercial capital) Western Province, W Sri Lanka 06°55′N 79°52′E
155 J25 Colombo ✈ Western Province, SW Sri Lanka 06°50′N 79°59′E
29 N11 Colome South Dakota, N USA 43°13′N 99°42′W
61 B19 Colón Buenos Aires, E Argentina 33°53′S 61°06′W
61 D18 Colon Entre Ríos, E Argentina 32°10′S 58°16′W
44 D5 Colón Matanzas, C Cuba 22°43′N 80°54′W
43 T14 Colón prev. Aspinwall. Colón, C Panama 09°04′N 80°33′W
42 K5 Colón ◈ department NE Honduras
43 S15 Colón off. Provincia de Colón. ◈ province N Panama
57 A16 Colón, Archipiélago de var. Islas de los Galápagos, Eng. Galapagos Islands, Tortoise Islands. island group Ecuador, E Pacific Ocean
44 K5 Colonel Hill Crooked Island, SE The Bahamas 22°43′N 74°12′W
40 C3 Colonet Baja California, NW Mexico 31°00′N 116°1′W
40 B3 Colonet, Cabo headland NW Mexico 30°57′N 116°19′W
188 G14 Colonia Yap, W Micronesia 09°29′N 138°06′E
61 D19 Colonia ◈ department SW Uruguay
Colonia see Kolonia, Micronesia
Colonia see Colonia del Sacramento, Uruguay
Colonia Agrippina see Köln
61 D20 Colonia del Sacramento var. Colonia. Colonia, SW Uruguay 34°29′S 57°48′W
62 L8 Colonia Dora Santiago del Estero, N Argentina 28°34′S 62°59′W
Colonia Julia Fanestris see Fano
21 W5 Colonial Beach Virginia, NE USA 38°15′N 76°57′W
21 V6 Colonial Heights Virginia, NE USA 37°15′N 77°24′W
Colón, Provincia de see Colón
193 S7 Colón Ridge undersea feature E Pacific Ocean 02°00′N 96°00′W
96 F12 Colonsay island W Scotland, United Kingdom
57 K22 Colorada, Laguna ⊚ SW Bolivia
37 R6 Colorado off. State of Colorado, also known as Centennial State, Silver State. ◈ state C USA
63 H22 Colorado, Cerro ▲ S Argentina 49°58′S 71°38′W
25 O7 Colorado City Texas, SW USA 32°24′N 100°51′W
36 M7 Colorado Plateau plateau W USA
61 A24 Colorado, Río ⪤ E Argentina
43 N12 Colorado, Río ⪤ NE Costa Rica
Colorado, Río see Colorado River
16 F12 Colorado River var. Río Colorado. ⪤ Mexico/USA
16 K14 Colorado River ⪤ Texas, SW USA
35 W15 Colorado River Aqueduct aqueduct California, W USA
44 A4 Colorados, Archipiélago de los island group NW Cuba
62 J9 Colorados, Desagües de los ⊚ W Argentina
37 T5 Colorado Springs Colorado, C USA 38°50′N 104°47′W
40 L11 Colotlán Jalisco, SW Mexico 22°08′N 103°15′W
57 L19 Colquechaca Potosí, C Bolivia 18°40′S 66°00′W
23 S7 Colquitt Georgia, SE USA 31°10′N 84°43′W
29 R11 Colton South Dakota, N USA 43°47′N 96°55′W
32 M10 Colton Washington, NW USA 46°34′N 117°10′W
35 P8 Columbia California, W USA 38°01′N 120°22′W
30 K16 Columbia Illinois, N USA 38°26′N 90°12′W
20 L7 Columbia Kentucky, S USA 37°05′N 85°19′W
22 I6 Columbia Louisiana, S USA 32°05′N 92°03′W
21 W3 Columbia Maryland, NE USA 39°13′N 76°51′W
22 L7 Columbia Mississippi, S USA 31°15′N 89°50′W
27 U4 Columbia Missouri, C USA 38°56′N 92°19′W
21 Y9 Columbia North Carolina, SE USA 35°55′N 76°15′W
18 G16 Columbia Pennsylvania, NE USA 40°01′N 76°30′W
21 Q12 Columbia state capital South Carolina, SE USA 34°00′N 81°02′W
20 I9 Columbia Tennessee, S USA 35°37′N 87°02′W
0 F9 Columbia ⪤ Canada/USA
32 K9 Columbia Basin basin Washington, NW USA
197 Q10 Columbia, Cape headland Ellesmere Island, Nunavut, NE Canada
31 Q12 Columbia City Indiana, N USA 41°09′N 85°29′W
21 W3 Columbia, District of ◈ federal district NE USA
33 P7 Columbia Falls Montana, NW USA 48°22′N 114°10′W
11 O15 Columbia Icefield ice field Alberta/British Columbia, S Canada
11 O15 Columbia, Mount ▲ Alberta/British Columbia, SW Canada 52°07′N 117°30′W
11 N15 Columbia Mountains ▲ British Columbia, SW Canada
23 P4 Columbiana Alabama, S USA 33°10′N 86°36′W
31 V12 Columbiana Ohio, N USA 40°53′N 80°41′W
32 M14 Columbia Plateau plateau Idaho/Oregon, NW USA
29 P7 Columbia Road Reservoir ⊠ South Dakota, N USA
65 K16 Columbia Seamount undersea feature C Atlantic Ocean 20°30′S 32°00′W
83 D25 Columbine, Cape headland SW South Africa 32°50′S 17°39′E
105 U9 Columbretes, Illes prev. Islas Columbretes. island group E Spain
Columbretes, Islas see Columbretes, Illes
23 R5 Columbus Georgia, SE USA 32°29′N 84°58′W
31 P14 Columbus Indiana, N USA 39°12′N 85°55′W
27 R7 Columbus Kansas, C USA 37°09′N 94°52′W
23 N4 Columbus Mississippi, S USA 33°30′N 88°25′W
33 U11 Columbus Montana, NW USA 45°38′N 109°15′W
29 Q15 Columbus Nebraska, C USA 41°25′N 97°22′W
37 Q16 Columbus New Mexico, SW USA 31°49′N 107°38′W
21 P10 Columbus North Carolina, SE USA 35°15′N 82°09′W
28 K2 Columbus North Dakota, N USA 48°52′N 102°47′W
31 S13 Columbus state capital Ohio, N USA 39°58′N 83°W
25 U11 Columbus Texas, SW USA 29°42′N 96°35′W
30 L8 Columbus Wisconsin, N USA 43°21′N 89°00′W
31 R12 Columbus Grove Ohio, N USA 40°55′N 84°03′W
29 Y15 Columbus Junction Iowa, C USA 41°16′N 91°21′W
44 J3 Columbus Point headland Cat Island, C The Bahamas 24°07′N 75°19′W
35 T8 Columbus Salt Marsh salt marsh Nevada, W USA
35 N6 Colusa California, W USA 39°10′N 122°03′W
32 L7 Colville Washington, NW USA 48°33′N 117°54′W
184 M5 Colville, Cape headland North Island, New Zealand 36°28′S 175°20′E
184 M5 Colville Channel channel North Island, New Zealand
39 P6 Colville River ⪤ Alaska, USA
97 J18 Colwyn Bay N Wales, United Kingdom 53°18′N 03°43′W
106 H9 Comacchio var. Commachio; anc. Comactium. Emilia-Romagna, N Italy 44°41′N 12°10′E
106 H9 Comacchio, Valli di lagoon Adriatic Sea, N Mediterranean Sea
Comactium see Comacchio
41 V17 Comalapa Chiapas, SE Mexico 15°42′N 92°06′W
41 U15 Comalcalco Tabasco, SE Mexico 18°16′N 93°05′W
63 H16 Comallo Río Negro, SW Argentina 40°58′S 70°13′W
26 M12 Comanche Oklahoma, C USA 34°22′N 97°57′W
25 R8 Comanche Texas, SW USA 31°55′N 98°36′W
194 H2 Comandante Ferraz research station (Brazil) King George Island, Antarctica61°57′S 58°23′W
62 N6 Comandante Fontana Formosa, N Argentina 25°19′S 59°42′W
63 I22 Comandante Luis Peidra Buena Santa Cruz, S Argentina 50°04′S 68°55′W
59 O18 Comandatuba Bahia, SE Brazil 15°13′S 39°00′W
116 K11 Comănești Hung. Kománfalva. Bacău, SW Romania 46°25′N 26°29′E
57 M19 Comarapa Santa Cruz, C Bolivia 17°53′S 64°30′W
116 J13 Comarnic Prahova, SE Romania 45°18′N 25°37′E
42 H6 Comayagua Comayagua, W Honduras 14°30′N 87°39′W
42 H6 Comayagua ◈ department W Honduras
42 I6 Comayagua, Montañas de ▲ C Honduras
21 R15 Combahee River ⪤ South Carolina, SE USA
62 G10 Combarbalá Coquimbo, C Chile 31°15′S 71°03′W
103 S7 Combeaufontaine Haute-Saône, E France 47°43′N 05°52′E
97 G15 Comber Ir. An Comar. E Northern Ireland, United Kingdom 54°33′N 05°45′W
99 K20 Comblain-au-Pont Liège, E Belgium 50°29′N 05°36′E
102 I6 Combourg Ille-et-Vilaine, NW France 48°21′N 01°44′W
44 M9 Comendador prev. Elías Piña. W Dominican Republic 18°53′N 71°42′W
Comer See see Como, Lago di
25 R11 Comfort Texas, SW USA 29°58′N 98°54′W
153 V15 Comilla Ben. Kumillā. Chittagong, E Bangladesh 23°28′N 91°10′E
99 B18 Comines Hainaut, W Belgium 50°46′N 02°58′E
Comino see Kemmuna
107 D18 Comino, Capo headland Sardegna, Italy, C Mediterranean Sea 40°32′N 09°49′E
107 K25 Comiso Sicilia, Italy, C Mediterranean Sea 36°57′N 14°37′E
41 V16 Comitán var. Comitán de Domínguez. Chiapas, SE Mexico 16°15′N 92°06′W
Comitán de Domínguez see Comitán
Commachio see Comacchio
Commander Islands see Komandorskiye Ostrova
103 O10 Commentry Allier, C France 46°18′N 02°46′E
23 T2 Commerce Georgia, SE USA 34°12′N 83°27′W
27 R8 Commerce Oklahoma, C USA 36°55′N 94°52′W
25 V5 Commerce Texas, SW USA 33°16′N 95°52′W
37 T4 Commerce City Colorado, C USA 39°45′N 104°54′W
103 S5 Commercy Meuse, NE France 48°46′N 05°36′E
55 W9 Commewijne var. Commewyne. ◈ district NE Suriname
Commewyne see Commewijne
15 P8 Commissaires, Lac des ⊚ Québec, SE Canada
64 A12 Commissioner's Point headland W Bermuda
9 O7 Committee Bay bay Nunavut, N Canada
106 D7 Como anc. Comum. Lombardia, N Italy 45°48′N 09°05′E
63 J19 Comodoro Rivadavia Chubut, SE Argentina 45°50′S 67°30′W
106 D6 Como, Lago di var. Lario, Eng. Lake Como, Ger. Comer See. ⊚ N Italy
Como, Lake see Como, Lago di
40 E7 Comondú Baja California Sur, NW Mexico 26°01′N 111°50′W
116 F12 Comorâște Hung. Komornok. Caraș-Severin, SW Romania 45°13′N 21°34′E
Comores, Union des see Comoros
155 G24 Comorin, Cape headland SE India 08°00′N 77°10′E
172 M8 Comoro Basin undersea feature SW Indian Ocean 14°00′S 44°00′E
172 K14 Comoro Islands island group W Indian Ocean
172 H13 Comoros off. Union of the Comoros, Fr. Union des Comores, Ar. Jumhūrīyat al Qamar al Muttaḥidah, Com. Udzima wa Komori; prev. Federal Islamic Republic of the Comoros. ◆ republic W Indian Ocean
Comoros, Federal Islamic Republic of the see Comoros
Comoros, Union of the see Comoros
10 L17 Comox Vancouver Island, British Columbia, SW Canada 49°40′N 124°55′W
103 O4 Compiègne Oise, N France 49°25′N 02°50′E
Complutum see Alcalá de Henares
Compniacum see Cognac
40 K12 Compostela Nayarit, C Mexico 21°12′N 104°52′W
Compostella see Santiago de Compostela
60 L11 Comprida, Ilha island S Brazil
117 N11 Comrat Rus. Komrat. S Moldova 46°18′N 28°40′E
25 O11 Comstock Texas, SW USA 29°39′N 101°10′W
31 P9 Comstock Park Michigan, N USA 43°00′N 85°40′W
193 N3 Comstock Seamount undersea feature N Pacific Ocean 48°15′N 156°55′W
Comum see Como
159 N17 Cona Xizang Zizhiqu, W China 27°59′N 91°54′E
76 H14 Conakry ● (Guinea) SW Guinea 09°31′N 13°43′W
76 H14 Conakry ✈ SW Guinea 09°37′N 13°32′W
Conamara see Connemara
Conca see Cuenca
25 Q12 Concan Texas, SW USA 29°27′N 99°43′W
102 F6 Concarneau Finistère, NW France 47°53′N 03°55′W
83 O17 Conceição Sofala, C Mozambique 18°47′S 36°18′E
59 K15 Conceição do Araguaia Pará, NE Brazil 08°15′S 49°15′W
58 F10 Conceição do Maú Roraima, W Brazil 03°35′N 59°52′W
61 D14 Concepción var. Concepcion. Corrientes, NE Argentina 28°25′S 57°54′W
62 J8 Concepción Tucumán, N Argentina 27°20′S 65°35′W
57 O17 Concepción Santa Cruz, E Bolivia 16°15′S 62°08′W
62 G13 Concepción Bío Bío, C Chile 36°47′S 73°01′W
54 E14 Concepción Putumayo, S Colombia 0°03′N 75°35′W
62 O5 Concepción var. Villa Concepción. Concepción, C Paraguay 23°26′S 57°24′W
62 O5 Concepción off. Departamento de Concepción. ◈ department E Paraguay
Concepción see La Concepción
Concepción de la Vega see La Vega
41 N9 Concepción del Oro Zacatecas, C Mexico 24°38′N 101°25′W
61 D18 Concepción del Uruguay Entre Ríos, E Argentina 32°30′S 58°15′W
Concepción, Departamento de see Concepción
42 K11 Concepción, Volcán ⩕ SW Nicaragua 11°31′N 85°37′W
44 J4 Conception Island island C The Bahamas
35 P14 Conception, Point headland California, W USA 34°27′N 120°28′W
54 H6 Concha Zulia, W Venezuela 09°02′N 71°45′W
60 L9 Conchas São Paulo, S Brazil 23°00′S 47°58′W
37 U11 Conchas Dam New Mexico, SW USA 35°21′N 104°11′W
37 U10 Conchas Lake ⊠ New Mexico, SW USA
102 M5 Conches-en-Ouche Eure, N France 49°00′N 01°00′E
37 N12 Concho Arizona, SW USA 34°28′N 109°33′W
40 J5 Conchos, Río ⪤ NW Mexico
41 O8 Conchos, Río ⪤ C Mexico
108 C8 Concise Vaud, W Switzerland 46°52′N 06°40′E
35 N8 Concord California, W USA 37°58′N 122°01′W
19 O9 Concord state capital New Hampshire, NE USA 43°10′N 71°32′W
21 R10 Concord North Carolina, SE USA 35°25′N 80°34′W
61 D17 Concordia Entre Ríos, E Argentina 31°25′S 58°W
60 I13 Concórdia Santa Catarina, S Brazil 27°14′S 52°01′W
54 D9 Concordia Antioquia, W Colombia 06°03′N 75°57′W
40 J10 Concordia Sinaloa, C Mexico 23°18′N 106°02′W
57 I19 Concordia Tacna, SW Peru 18°12′S 70°19′W
27 N3 Concordia Kansas, C USA 39°35′N 97°39′W
27 S4 Concordia Missouri, C USA 38°58′N 93°34′W
195 U12 Concordia research station (Italy/France) Antarctica 75°06′S 123°20′E
167 S7 Con Cuông Nghệ An, N Vietnam 19°02′N 104°54′E
167 T15 Côn Đao Sơn var. Con Son. island S Vietnam
Condate see Rennes, Ille-et-Vilaine, France
Condate see St-Claude, Jura, France
Condate see Montereau-Faut-Yonne, Seine-St-Denis, France
29 P8 Conde South Dakota, N USA 45°08′N 98°07′W
42 J8 Condega Estelí, NW Nicaragua 13°19′N 86°26′W
103 P2 Condé-sur-l'Escaut Nord, N France 50°27′N 03°36′E
102 K5 Condé-sur-Noireau Calvados, N France 48°52′N 00°31′W
Condivincum see Nantes
183 P8 Condobolin New South Wales, SE Australia 33°04′S 147°08′E
102 L15 Condom Gers, S France 43°56′N 00°23′E
32 J11 Condon Oregon, NW USA 45°15′N 120°10′W
54 D9 Condoto Chocó, W Colombia 05°06′N 76°37′W
23 P7 Conecuh River ⪤ Alabama/Florida, SE USA
106 H7 Conegliano Veneto, NE Italy 45°53′N 12°18′E
61 C19 Conesa Buenos Aires, E Argentina 33°36′S 60°21′W
14 F15 Conestogo ⪤ Ontario, S Canada
Confluentes see Koblenz
102 L10 Confolens Charente, W France 46°00′N 00°40′E
36 J4 Confusion Range ▲ Utah, W USA
62 N6 Confuso, Río ⪤ C Paraguay
21 R12 Congaree River ⪤ South Carolina, SE USA
160 K12 Congjiang var. Bingmei. Guizhou, S China 25°48′N 108°55′E
79 G18 Congo off. Republic of the Congo, Fr. République du Congo; prev. Middle Congo. ◆ republic C Africa
79 K19 Congo off. Democratic Republic of Congo, Fr. République Démocratique du Congo; prev. Zaire, Belgian Congo, Congo (Kinshasa). ◆ republic C Africa
67 T11 Congo var. Kongo, Fr. Zaire. ⪤ C Africa
Congo see Zaire (province) Angola
68 G12 Congo Basin drainage basin W Dem. Rep. Congo
67 Q11 Congo Canyon var. Congo Seavalley, Congo Submarine Canyon. undersea feature E Atlantic Ocean 06°00′S 11°50′E
Congo Cone see Congo Fan
Congo/Congo (Kinshasa) see Congo (Democratic Republic of)
65 P15 Congo Fan var. Congo Cone. undersea feature E Atlantic Ocean 06°00′S 09°00′E
Congo, Republic of the see Congo
Congo, République Démocratique du see Congo
Congo, République du see Congo (Republic of)
Congo Seavalley see Congo Canyon
Congo Submarine Canyon see Congo Canyon
Coni see Cuneo
63 H18 Cónico, Cerro ▲ SW Argentina 43°12′S 71°42′W
Conimbria/Conimbriga see Coimbra
Conjeeveram see Kānchīpuram
11 R13 Conklin Alberta, C Canada 55°36′N 111°06′W
24 M1 Conlen Texas, SW USA 36°16′N 102°10′W
Con, Loch see Conn, Lough
Connacht see Connaught
97 B17 Connaught var. Connacht, Ir. Chonnacht, Cúige. cultural region W Ireland
31 V10 Conneaut Ohio, N USA 41°56′N 80°32′W
18 L13 Connecticut off. State of Connecticut, also known as Blue Law State, Constitution State, Land of Steady Habits, Nutmeg State. ◈ state NE USA
19 N8 Connecticut ⪤ Canada/USA
19 O6 Connecticut Lakes lakes New Hampshire, NE USA
32 K9 Connell Washington, NW USA 46°39′N 118°51′W
97 B17 Connemara Ir. Conamara. physical region W Ireland
31 Q14 Connersville Indiana, N USA 39°38′N 85°15′W
97 B16 Conn, Lough Ir. Loch Con. ⊚ W Ireland
35 X6 Connors Pass pass Nevada, W USA
181 X7 Connors Range ▲ Queensland, E Australia
56 E7 Cononaco, Río ⪤ E Ecuador
29 W13 Conrad Iowa, C USA 42°13′N 92°52′W
33 R7 Conrad Montana, NW USA 48°10′N 111°58′W
25 W10 Conroe Texas, SW USA 30°19′N 95°28′W
25 V10 Conroe, Lake ⊠ Texas, SW USA
61 C17 Conscripto Bernardi Entre Ríos, E Argentina 31°03′S 59°05′W
59 M20 Conselheiro Lafaiete Minas Gerais, SE Brazil 20°40′S 43°48′W
Consentia see Cosenza
97 L14 Consett N England, United Kingdom 54°50′N 01°53′W
44 B5 Consolación del Sur Pinar del Río, W Cuba 22°32′N 83°32′W
Con Son see Côn Đao Sơn
11 R15 Consort Alberta, SW Canada 51°58′N 110°44′W
Constance see Konstanz
108 I6 Constance, Lake Ger. Bodensee. ⊚ C Europe
104 G9 Constância Santarém, C Portugal 39°29′N 08°22′W
117 N14 Constanța var. Küstendje, Eng. Constanza, Ger. Konstanza, Turk. Küstence. Constanța, SE Romania 44°09′N 28°37′E
116 L14 Constanța ◈ county SE Romania
Constantia see Coutances
Constantia see Konstanz
104 K13 Constantina Andalucía, S Spain 37°54′N 05°36′W
74 L5 Constantine var. Qacentina, Ar. Qoussantina. NE Algeria 36°23′N 06°44′E
39 O14 Constantine, Cape headland Alaska, USA 58°23′N 158°53′W
Constantinople see İstanbul
Constantiola see Oltenița
Constanz see Konstanz
Constanza see Constanța
62 G13 Constitución Maule, C Chile 35°20′S 72°28′W
61 D17 Constitución Salto, N Uruguay 31°05′S 57°51′W
Constitution State see Connecticut
105 N10 Consuegra Castilla-La Mancha, C Spain 39°28′N 03°36′W
181 X9 Consuelo Peak ▲ Queensland, E Australia 24°45′S 148°01′E
56 E11 Contamana Loreto, N Peru 07°19′S 75°04′W
Contrasto, Colle del see Contrasto, Portella del
107 K23 Contrasto, Portella del var. Colle del Contrasto. pass Sicilia, Italy, C Mediterranean Sea
54 G8 Contratación Santander, C Colombia 06°18′N 73°27′W
102 M8 Contres Loir-et-Cher, C France 47°24′N 01°30′E
107 O17 Conversano Puglia, SE Italy 40°58′N 17°07′E
27 U11 Conway Arkansas, C USA 35°05′N 92°27′W
19 O8 Conway New Hampshire, NE USA 43°58′N 71°05′W
21 U13 Conway South Carolina, SE USA 33°51′N 79°04′W
25 N2 Conway Texas, SW USA 35°10′N 101°23′W
27 U11 Conway, Lake ⊠ Arkansas, C USA
27 N7 Conway Springs Kansas, C USA 37°23′N 97°38′W
97 J18 Conwy N Wales, United Kingdom 53°17′N 03°51′W
23 T3 Conyers Georgia, SE USA 33°40′N 84°01′W
Coo see Kos
182 F4 Coober Pedy South Australia 29°01′S 134°47′E
181 P2 Cooinda Northern Territory, N Australia 12°54′S 132°31′E
182 B6 Cook South Australia 30°37′S 130°26′E
29 W4 Cook Minnesota, N USA 47°51′N 92°41′W
191 N6 Cook, Baie de bay Moorea, W French Polynesia
10 J16 Cook, Cape headland Vancouver Island, British Columbia, SW Canada 50°04′N 127°52′W
37 Q15 Cookes Peak ▲ New Mexico, SW USA 32°32′N 107°43′W
20 L8 Cookeville Tennessee, S USA 36°10′N 85°30′W
175 P9 Cook Fracture Zone tectonic feature S Pacific Ocean
Cook, Grand Récif de see Cook, Récif de
39 Q12 Cook Inlet inlet Alaska, USA
191 X2 Cook Island island Line Islands, E Kiribati
190 J14 Cook Islands ◇ self-governing entity in free association with New Zealand S Pacific Ocean
Cook, Mount see Aoraki / Mount Cook
Cook, Mount see Aoraki / Mount Cook
187 O15 Cook, Récif de var. Grand Récif de Cook. reef S New Caledonia
14 G14 Cookstown Ontario, S Canada 44°12′N 79°39′W
97 F15 Cookstown Ir. An Chorr Chríochach. C Northern Ireland, United Kingdom 54°39′N 06°45′W
185 K14 Cook Strait var. Raukawa. strait New Zealand
181 W3 Cooktown Queensland, NE Australia 15°28′S 145°15′E
183 P6 Coolabah New South Wales, SE Australia 31°03′S 146°42′E
182 J11 Coola Coola Swamp wetland South Australia
183 S7 Coolah New South Wales, SE Australia 31°49′S 149°43′E
183 P9 Coolamon New South Wales, SE Australia 34°49′S 147°13′E
183 T4 Coolatai New South Wales, SE Australia 29°16′S 150°45′E
180 K12 Coolgardie Western Australia 31°01′S 121°12′E
36 L14 Coolidge Arizona, SW USA 32°58′N 111°29′W
25 U8 Coolidge Texas, SW USA 31°45′N 96°39′W
183 Q11 Cooma New South Wales, SE Australia 36°16′S 149°09′E
Coomassie see Kumasi
183 R6 Coonabarabran New South Wales, SE Australia 31°19′S 149°18′E
182 J10 Coonalpyn South Australia 35°43′S 139°50′E
183 R6 Coonamble New South Wales, SE Australia 30°56′S 148°22′E
Coondapoor see Kundāpura
155 G21 Coonoor Tamil Nādu, SE India 11°21′N 76°46′E
29 U14 Coon Rapids Iowa, C USA 41°52′N 94°40′W
29 V8 Coon Rapids Minnesota, N USA 45°12′N 93°18′W
25 V5 Cooper Texas, SW USA 33°23′N 95°42′W
181 U9 Cooper Creek var. Barcoo, Cooper's Creek. seasonal river Queensland/South Australia
39 R12 Cooper Landing Alaska, USA 60°27′N 149°59′W
21 T14 Cooper River ⪤ South Carolina, SE USA
Cooper's Creek see Cooper Creek
44 H1 Coopers Town Great Abaco, N The Bahamas 26°46′N 77°27′W
18 J10 Cooperstown New York, NE USA 42°43′N 74°56′W
29 P4 Cooperstown North Dakota, N USA 47°26′N 98°07′W
31 P9 Coopersville Michigan, N USA 43°03′N 85°55′W
182 D7 Coorabie South Australia 31°57′S 132°18′E
23 Q3 Coosa River ⪤ Alabama/Georgia, S USA
32 E14 Coos Bay Oregon, NW USA 43°22′N 124°13′W
183 Q9 Cootamundra New South Wales, SE Australia 34°41′S 148°03′E
97 E16 Cootehill Ir. Muinchille. N Ireland 54°04′N 07°05′W
Čop see Chop
57 J17 Copacabana La Paz, W Bolivia 16°11′S 69°02′W
63 H14 Copahué, Volcán ⩕ C Chile 37°56′S 71°04′W
41 U16 Copainalá Chiapas, SE Mexico 17°04′N 93°13′W
32 F8 Copalis Beach Washington, NW USA 47°05′N 124°11′W
42 F6 Copán ◈ department W Honduras
Copán see Copán Ruinas
25 T14 Copano Bay bay NW Gulf of Mexico
42 F6 Copán Ruinas var. Copán. Copán, W Honduras 14°52′N 89°10′W
Copenhagen see København
107 Q19 Copertino Puglia, SE Italy 40°16′N 18°03′E
62 H7 Copiapó Atacama, N Chile 27°17′S 70°25′W
62 G8 Copiapó, Bahía bay N Chile
62 G7 Copiapó, Río ⪤ N Chile
114 M12 Çöpköy Edirne, NW Turkey 41°14′N 26°51′E
182 I5 Copley South Australia 30°36′S 138°26′E
106 H9 Copparo Emilia-Romagna, C Italy 44°53′N 11°53′E
55 V10 Coppename Rivier var. Koppename. ⪤ C Suriname
25 S9 Copperas Cove Texas, SW USA 31°07′N 97°54′W
82 J13 Copperbelt ◈ province C Zambia
39 S11 Copper Center Alaska, USA 61°57′N 145°21′W
8 K8 Coppermine ⪤ Northwest Territories/Nunavut, N Canada
Coppermine see Kugluktuk
39 T11 Copper River ⪤ Alaska, USA
Copper State see Arizona
116 I11 Copşa Mică Ger. Kleinkopisch, Hung. Kiskapus. Sibiu, C Romania 46°06′N 24°15′E
158 J14 Coqên Xizang Zizhiqu, W China 31°13′N 85°12′E
Coquilhatville see Mbandaka
32 E14 Coquille Oregon, NW USA 43°11′N 124°12′W
62 G9 Coquimbo Coquimbo, N Chile 30°57′S 71°18′W
62 G9 Coquimbo off. Región de Coquimbo. ◈ region C Chile
Coquimbo, Región de see Coquimbo
116 I15 Corabia Olt, S Romania 43°46′N 24°31′E
57 F17 Coracora Ayacucho, SW Peru 15°03′S 73°45′W
Cora Droma Rúisc see Carrick-on-Shannon
44 K9 Corail SW Haiti 18°34′N 73°53′W
183 V4 Coraki New South Wales, SE Australia 29°01′S 153°15′E
180 G8 Coral Bay Western Australia 23°02′S 113°51′E
23 Y16 Coral Gables Florida, SE USA 25°43′N 80°16′W
9 P8 Coral Harbour var. Salliq. Southampton Island, Nunavut, NE Canada 64°10′N 83°15′W
192 I9 Coral Sea sea SW Pacific Ocean
174 M7 Coral Sea Basin undersea feature N Coral Sea
192 H9 Coral Sea Islands ◇ Australian external territory SW Pacific Ocean
182 M12 Corangamite, Lake ⊚ Victoria, SE Australia
Corantijn Rivier see Courantyne River
18 B14 Coraopolis Pennsylvania, NE USA 40°28′N 80°08′W
107 N17 Corato Puglia, SE Italy 41°09′N 16°25′E
103 O17 Corbières ▲ S France
103 P8 Corbigny Nièvre, C France 47°15′N 03°42′E
21 N7 Corbin Kentucky, S USA 36°57′N 84°06′W
104 L14 Corbones ⪤ SW Spain
Corcaigh see Cork
35 R11 Corcoran California, W USA 36°06′N 119°33′W
47 T14 Corcovado, Golfo gulf S Chile
63 G18 Corcovado, Volcán ⩕ S Chile 43°13′S 72°45′W
104 F3 Corcubión Galicia, NW Spain 42°56′N 09°12′W
Corcyra Nigra see Korčula
60 Q9 Cordeiro Rio de Janeiro, SE Brazil 22°01′S 42°20′W
23 T6 Cordele Georgia, SE USA 31°59′N 83°49′W
26 L11 Cordell Oklahoma, C USA 35°17′N 98°59′W
103 N14 Cordes Tarn, S France 44°03′N 01°57′E
62 O6 Cordillera off. Departamento de la Cordillera. ◈ department C Paraguay
Cordillera see Cacaguatique, Cordillera
Cordillera, Departamento de la see Cordillera
182 K1 Cordillo Downs South Australia 26°44′S 140°37′E
62 K10 Córdoba Córdoba, C Argentina 31°25′S 64°11′W
41 R14 Córdoba Veracruz, E Mexico 18°55′N 96°55′W
104 M13 Córdoba var. Cordoba, Eng. Cordova; anc. Corduba. Andalucía, SW Spain 37°53′N 04°46′W
62 K11 Córdoba off. Provincia de Córdoba. ◈ province C Argentina
54 D7 Córdoba off. Departamento de Córdoba. ◈ province NW Colombia
104 L13 Córdoba ◈ province Andalucía, S Spain
Córdoba, Departamento de see Córdoba
Córdoba, Provincia de see Córdoba
62 K10 Córdoba, Sierras de ▲ C Argentina
23 O3 Cordova Alabama, S USA 33°45′N 87°10′W
39 S12 Cordova Alaska, USA 60°32′N 145°45′W
Cordova/Cordoba see Córdoba
Corduba see Córdoba
Corentyne River see Courantyne River
Corfu see Kérkyra
104 J9 Coria Extremadura, W Spain 39°59′N 06°32′W
104 J14 Coria del Río Andalucía, S Spain 37°18′N 06°04′W
183 S8 Coricudgy, Mount ▲ New South Wales, SE Australia 32°49′S 150°28′E
107 N20 Corigliano Calabro Calabria, SW Italy 39°36′N 16°32′E
Corinium/Corinium Dobunorum see Cirencester
23 N1 Corinth Mississippi, S USA 34°56′N 88°29′W
Corinth see Kórinthos
Corinth Canal see Korinthou, Dióryga
Corinth, Gulf of/Corinthiacus Sinus see Korinthiakós Kólpos
Corinthus see Kórinthos
42 I9 Corinto Chinandega, NW Nicaragua 12°29′N 87°14′W
97 C21 Cork Ir. Corcaigh. S Ireland 51°54′N 07°06′W
97 C21 Cork Ir. Corcaigh. cultural region SW Ireland
97 C21 Cork ✈ Cork, SW Ireland 51°52′N 08°25′W
97 D21 Cork Harbour Ir. Cuan Chorcaí. inlet SW Ireland
107 I23 Corleone Sicilia, Italy, C Mediterranean Sea 37°49′N 13°18′E
114 N13 Çorlu Tekirdağ, NW Turkey 41°11′N 27°48′E
114 N12 Çorlu Çayı ⪤ NW Turkey
Cormaiore see Courmayeur
11 V13 Cormorant Manitoba, C Canada 54°12′N 100°33′W
23 T2 Cornelia Georgia, SE USA 34°30′N 83°31′W
60 J10 Cornélio Procópio Paraná, S Brazil 23°07′S 50°40′W
55 V9 Corneliskondre Sipaliwini, N Suriname 05°21′N 56°10′W
30 J5 Cornell Wisconsin, N USA 45°09′N 91°10′W
13 S12 Corner Brook Newfoundland, Newfoundland and Labrador, E Canada 48°58′N 57°58′W
Corner Rise Seamounts see Corner Seamounts
64 I9 Corner Seamounts var. Corner Rise Seamounts. undersea feature NW Atlantic Ocean 35°30′N 51°30′W
116 M9 Cornești Rus. Korneshty. C Moldova 47°23′N 28°00′E
Corneto see Tarquinia
Cornhusker State see Nebraska
27 X8 Corning Arkansas, C USA 36°26′N 90°35′W
35 N5 Corning California, W USA 39°54′N 122°12′W
29 U15 Corning Iowa, C USA 40°58′N 94°46′W
18 G11 Corning New York, NE USA 42°08′N 77°03′W
Corn Islands see Maíz, Islas del


◆ Country
● Country Capital
◇ Dependent Territory
○ Dependent Territory Capital
◈ Administrative Regions
✈ International Airport
▲ Mountain
▲ Mountain Range
⩕ Volcano
⪤ River
⊚ Lake
⊠ Reservoir

CORNO GRANDE – CUETZALÁN DEL PROGRESO


107 J14 **Corno Grande** ▲ C Italy 42°26′N 13°29′E
15 N13 **Cornwall** Ontario, SE Canada 45°02′N 74°45′W
97 H25 **Cornwall** *cultural region* SW England, United Kingdom
97 G25 **Cornwall, Cape** *headland* SW England, United Kingdom 50°11′N 05°39′W
54 J4 **Coro** *prev.* Santa Ana de Coro. Falcón, NW Venezuela 11°27′N 69°41′W
57 J18 **Corocoro** La Paz, W Bolivia 17°10′S 68°28′W
57 K17 **Coroico** La Paz, W Bolivia 16°09′S 67°45′W
184 M5 **Coromandel** Waikato, North Island, New Zealand 36°47′S 175°30′E
155 K20 **Coromandel Coast** *coast* E India
184 M5 **Coromandel Peninsula** *peninsula* North Island, New Zealand
184 M6 **Coromandel Range** ▲▲ North Island, New Zealand
171 N5 **Coron** Busuanga Island, W Philippines 12°02′N 120°10′E
35 T15 **Corona** California, W USA 33°52′N 117°34′W
37 T12 **Corona** New Mexico, SW USA 34°15′N 105°36′W
11 U17 **Coronach** Saskatchewan, S Canada 49°07′N 105°33′W
35 U17 **Coronado** California, W USA 32°41′N 117°10′W
43 N15 **Coronado, Bahía de** *bay* S Costa Rica
11 R15 **Coronation** Alberta, SW Canada 52°06′N 111°25′W
8 K7 **Coronation Gulf** *gulf* Nunavut, N Canada
194 I1 **Coronation Island** *island* Antarctica
39 X14 **Coronation Island** *island* Alexander Archipelago, Alaska, USA
61 B18 **Coronda** Santa Fe, C Argentina 31°58′S 60°56′W
63 F14 **Coronel** Bío Bío, C Chile 37°01′S 73°08′W
61 D20 **Coronel Brandsen** *var.* Brandsen. Buenos Aires, E Argentina 35°08′S 58°15′W
62 K4 **Coronel Cornejo** Salta, N Argentina 22°46′S 63°49′W
61 B24 **Coronel Dorrego** Buenos Aires, E Argentina 38°38′S 61°15′W
62 P6 **Coronel Oviedo** Caaguazú, SE Paraguay 25°24′S 56°30′W
61 B23 **Coronel Pringles** Buenos Aires, E Argentina 37°56′S 61°25′W
61 B23 **Coronel Suárez** Buenos Aires, E Argentina 37°30′S 61°52′W
61 E22 **Coronel Vidal** Buenos Aires, E Argentina 37°28′S 57°45′W
55 V9 **Coronie** ◈ *district* NW Suriname
57 G17 **Coropuna, Nevado** ▲ S Peru 15°31′S 72°31′W
**Çorovoda** *see* Çorovodë
113 L22 **Çorovodë** *var.* Çorovoda. Berat, S Albania 40°29′N 20°15′E
183 P11 **Corowa** New South Wales, SE Australia 36°01′S 146°22′E
42 G1 **Corozal** Corozal, N Belize 18°23′N 88°23′W
54 E6 **Corozal** Sucre, NW Colombia 09°18′N 75°19′W
42 G1 **Corozal** ◈ *district* N Belize
25 T14 **Corpus Christi** Texas, SW USA 27°48′N 97°24′W
25 T14 **Corpus Christi Bay** *inlet* Texas, SW USA
25 R14 **Corpus Christi, Lake** ▣ Texas, SW USA
63 F16 **Corral** Los Ríos, C Chile 39°55′S 73°30′W
105 O9 **Corral de Almaguer** Castilla-La Mancha, C Spain 39°45′N 03°10′W
104 K6 **Corrales** Castilla y León, N Spain 41°22′N 05°44′W
37 R11 **Corrales** New Mexico, SW USA 35°11′N 106°37′W
**Corrán Tuathail** *see* Carrauntoohil
106 F9 **Correggio** Emilia-Romagna, C Italy 44°47′N 10°46′E
59 M16 **Corrente** Piauí, E Brazil 10°29′S 45°11′W
59 I19 **Correntes, Rio** ≈ SW Brazil
103 N12 **Corrèze** ◈ *department* C France
97 C17 **Corrib, Lough** *Ir.* Loch Coirib. ◎ W Ireland
61 C14 **Corrientes** Corrientes, NE Argentina 27°29′S 58°42′W
61 D15 **Corrientes** *off.* Provincia de Corrientes. ◈ *province* NE Argentina
44 A5 **Corrientes, Cabo** *headland* W Cuba 21°48′N 84°30′W
40 I13 **Corrientes, Cabo** *headland* SW Mexico 20°25′N 105°42′W
**Corrientes, Provincia de** *see* Corrientes
61 C16 **Corrientes, Río** ≈ NE Argentina
56 E8 **Corrientes, Río** ≈ Ecuador/Peru
25 W9 **Corrigan** Texas, SW USA 31°00′N 94°49′W
55 U9 **Corriverton** E Guyana 05°55′N 57°09′W
**Corriza** *see* Korçë
183 Q11 **Corryong** Victoria, SE Australia 36°14′S 147°54′E
103 F2 **Corse** *Eng.* Corsica. ◈ *region* France, C Mediterranean Sea
101 X13 **Corse** *Eng.* Corsica. *island* France, C Mediterranean Sea
103 Y12 **Corse, Cap** *headland* Corse, France, C Mediterranean Sea 43°01′N 09°25′E
103 X15 **Corse-du-Sud** ◈ *department* Corse, France, C Mediterranean Sea
29 P11 **Corsica** South Dakota, N USA 43°25′N 98°24′W
**Corsica** *see* Corse
25 U7 **Corsicana** Texas, SW USA 32°05′N 96°27′W
103 Y15 **Corte** Corse, France, C Mediterranean Sea 42°18′N 09°08′E
63 G16 **Corte Alto** Los Lagos, S Chile 40°58′S 73°04′W
104 I13 **Cortegana** Andalucía, S Spain 37°55′N 06°49′W
43 N15 **Cortés** *var.* Ciudad Cortés. Puntarenas, SE Costa Rica 08°59′N 83°32′W
42 G5 **Cortés** ◈ *department* NW Honduras
37 P8 **Cortez** Colorado, C USA 37°22′N 108°36′W
**Cortez, Sea of** *see* California, Golfo de
106 H6 **Cortina d'Ampezzo** Veneto, NE Italy 46°33′N 12°09′E
18 H11 **Cortland** New York, NE USA 42°34′N 76°09′W
31 V11 **Cortland** Ohio, N USA 41°19′N 80°43′W
106 H12 **Cortona** Toscana, C Italy 43°15′N 12°01′E
76 H13 **Corubal, Rio** ≈ E Guinea-Bissau
104 G10 **Coruche** Santarém, C Portugal 38°58′N 08°31′W
**Çoruh** *see* Rize
137 R11 **Çoruh Nehri** *Geor.* Chorokh, *Rus.* Chorokhi. ≈ Georgia/Turkey
136 K12 **Çorum** *var.* Chorum. Çorum, N Turkey 40°31′N 34°57′E
136 J12 **Çorum** *var.* Chorum. ◈ *province* N Turkey
59 H19 **Corumbá** Mato Grosso do Sul, S Brazil 19°S 57°35′W
14 D16 **Corunna** Ontario, S Canada 42°49′N 82°25′W
**Corunna** *see* A Coruña
32 F12 **Corvallis** Oregon, NW USA 44°35′N 122°36′W
64 M1 **Corvo** *var.* Ilha do Corvo. *island* Azores, Portugal, NE Atlantic Ocean
**Corvo, Ilha do** *see* Corvo
31 O16 **Corydon** Indiana, N USA 38°12′N 86°07′W
29 V16 **Corydon** Iowa, C USA 40°45′N 93°19′W
**Cos** *see* Kos
40 I9 **Cosalá** Sinaloa, C Mexico 24°25′N 106°39′W
41 R15 **Cosamaloapan** *var.* Cosamaloapan de Carpio. Veracruz, E Mexico 18°23′N 95°50′W
**Cosamaloapan de Carpio** *see* Cosamaloapan
107 N21 **Cosenza** *anc.* Consentia. Calabria, SW Italy 39°17′N 16°15′E
31 T13 **Coshocton** Ohio, N USA 40°16′N 81°53′W
42 H9 **Cosigüina, Punta** *headland* NW Nicaragua 12°53′N 87°42′W
29 T9 **Cosmos** Minnesota, N USA 44°56′N 94°42′W
103 O8 **Cosne-Cours-sur-Loire** Nièvre, C France 47°25′N 02°56′E
108 B9 **Cossonay** Vaud, W Switzerland 46°37′N 06°28′E
**Cossyra** *see* Pantelleria
42 K7 **Costa Caribe Norte** *prev.* Zelaya Norte, Región Autónoma Atlántico Norte. ◈ *autonomous region* NE Nicaragua
42 L10 **Costa Caribe Sur** *prev.* Zelaya Sur, Región Autónoma Atlántico Sur. ◈ *autonomous region* SE Nicaragua
47 R4 **Costa, Cordillera de la** *var.* Cordillera de Venezuela. ▲▲ N Venezuela
42 K13 **Costa Rica** *off.* Republic of Costa Rica. ◆ *republic* Central America
**Costa Rica, Republic of** *see* Costa Rica
43 N15 **Costeña, Fila** ▲▲ S Costa Rica
**Costermansville** *see* Bukavu
116 I14 **Costești** Argeș, SW Romania 44°40′N 24°53′E
37 S8 **Costilla** New Mexico, SW USA 36°58′N 105°31′W
35 O7 **Cosumnes River** ≈ California, W USA
101 O16 **Coswig** Sachsen, E Germany 51°07′N 13°36′E
101 M14 **Coswig** Sachsen-Anhalt, E Germany 51°53′N 12°26′E
**Cosyra** *see* Pantelleria
171 Q7 **Cotabato** Mindanao, S Philippines 07°13′N 124°12′E
56 C5 **Cotacachi** ▲ N Ecuador 0°29′N 78°17′W
57 L21 **Cotagaita** Potosí, S Bolivia 20°47′S 65°40′W
103 V15 **Côte d'Azur** *prev.* Nice. ✈ (Nice) Alpes-Maritimes, SE France 43°40′N 07°12′E
**Côte d'Ivoire** *see* Ivory Coast
**Côte d'Ivoire, Republic of the** *see* Ivory Coast
**Côte d'Ivoire, République de la** *see* Ivory Coast
103 R7 **Côte d'Or** ◈ *department* E France
103 R8 **Côte d'Or** *cultural region* C France
**Côte Française des Somalis** *see* Djibouti
102 J4 **Cotentin** *peninsula* N France
102 G6 **Côtes d'Armor** *prev.* Côtes-du-Nord. ◈ *department* NW France
**Côtes-du-Nord** *see* Côtes d'Armor
**Cöthen** *see* Köthen
**Côtière, Chaîne** *see* Coast Mountains
40 M13 **Cotija** *var.* Cotija de la Paz. Michoacán, SW Mexico 19°49′N 102°39′W
**Cotija de la Paz** *see* Cotija
77 R16 **Cotonou** *var.* Kotonu. ● (Benin-seat of government) S Benin 06°24′N 02°26′E
77 R16 **Cotonou** ✈ S Benin 06°31′N 02°18′E
56 B6 **Cotopaxi** *prev.* León. ◈ *province* C Ecuador
56 C6 **Cotopaxi** Ѧ N Ecuador 0°42′S 78°24′W
**Cotrone** *see* Crotone
97 L21 **Cotswold Hills** *var.* Cotswolds. *hill range* S England, United Kingdom
**Cotswolds** *see* Cotswold Hills
32 F13 **Cottage Grove** Oregon, NW USA 43°48′N 123°03′W
21 S14 **Cottageville** South Carolina, SE USA 32°55′N 80°28′W
101 P14 **Cottbus** *Lus.* Chośebuz; *prev.* Kottbus. Brandenburg, E Germany 51°42′N 14°22′E
27 U9 **Cotter** Arkansas, C USA 36°16′N 92°30′W
106 A9 **Cottian Alps** *Fr.* Alpes Cottiennes, *It.* Alpi Cozie. ▲▲ France/Italy
**Cottiennes, Alpes** *see* Cottian Alps
**Cotton State, The** *see* Alabama
22 G4 **Cotton Valley** Louisiana, S USA 32°49′N 93°25′W
36 L12 **Cottonwood** Arizona, SW USA 34°43′N 112°00′W
32 M10 **Cottonwood** Idaho, NW USA 46°01′N 116°20′W
29 S9 **Cottonwood** Minnesota, N USA 44°37′N 95°41′W
25 Q7 **Cottonwood** Texas, SW USA 32°12′N 99°14′W
27 O5 **Cottonwood Falls** Kansas, C USA 38°21′N 96°33′W
36 L3 **Cottonwood Heights** Utah, W USA 40°37′N 111°48′W
29 S10 **Cottonwood River** ≈ Minnesota, N USA
45 O9 **Cotuí** C Dominican Republic 19°04′N 70°10′W
25 Q13 **Cotulla** Texas, SW USA 28°27′N 99°15′W
**Cotyora** *see* Ordu
102 I11 **Coubre, Pointe de la** *headland* W France 45°39′N 01°23′W
18 E12 **Coudersport** Pennsylvania, NE USA 41°45′N 78°00′W
15 S9 **Coudres, Île aux** *island* Québec, SE Canada
182 G11 **Couedic, Cape de** *headland* South Australia 36°04′S 136°43′E
**Couentrey** *see* Coventry
102 I6 **Couesnon** ≈ NW France
32 H10 **Cougar** Washington, NW USA 46°03′N 122°18′W
102 L10 **Couhé** Vienne, W France 46°18′N 00°10′E
32 K8 **Coulee City** Washington, NW USA 47°36′N 119°18′W
195 Q15 **Coulman Island** *island* Antarctica
103 P5 **Coulommiers** Seine-et-Marne, N France 48°49′N 03°04′E
14 K11 **Coulonge** ≈ Québec, SE Canada
14 K11 **Coulonge Est** ≈ Québec, SE Canada
35 Q9 **Coulterville** California, W USA 37°41′N 120°10′W
38 M9 **Council** Alaska, USA 64°54′N 163°40′W
32 M12 **Council** Idaho, NW USA 44°45′N 116°26′W
29 S15 **Council Bluffs** Iowa, C USA 41°16′N 95°52′W
27 O5 **Council Grove** Kansas, C USA 38°41′N 96°29′W
27 O5 **Council Grove Lake** ▣ Kansas, C USA
32 G7 **Coupeville** Washington, NW USA 48°13′N 122°41′W
55 U12 **Courantyne River** *var.* Corantijn Rivier, Corentyne River. ≈ Guyana/Suriname
99 G21 **Courcelles** Hainaut, S Belgium 50°28′N 04°23′E
108 C7 **Courgenay** Jura, NW Switzerland 47°24′N 07°09′E
126 B2 **Courland Lagoon** *Ger.* Kurisches Haff, *Rus.* Kurskiy Zaliv. *lagoon* Lithuania/Russia
118 B12 **Courland Spit** *Lith.* Kuršių Nerija, *Rus.* Kurshskaya Kosa. *spit* Lithuania/Russia
106 A6 **Courmayeur** *prev.* Cormaiore. Valle d'Aosta, NW Italy 45°48′N 07°00′E
108 D7 **Courroux** Jura, NW Switzerland 47°22′N 07°23′E
10 K17 **Courtenay** Vancouver Island, British Columbia, SW Canada 49°40′N 124°58′W
21 W7 **Courtland** Virginia, NE USA 36°44′N 77°06′W
25 V10 **Courtney** Texas, SW USA 30°16′N 96°04′W
30 J4 **Court Oreilles, Lac** ◎ Wisconsin, N USA
**Courtrai** *see* Kortrijk
99 H19 **Court-Saint-Étienne** Walloon Brabant, C Belgium 50°38′N 04°34′E
22 G6 **Coushatta** Louisiana, S USA 32°00′N 93°20′W
172 I16 **Cousin** *island* Inner Islands, NE Seychelles
172 I16 **Cousine** *island* Inner Islands, NE Seychelles
102 J4 **Coutances** *anc.* Constantia. Manche, N France 49°04′N 01°27′W
102 K12 **Coutras** Gironde, SW France 45°01′N 00°07′W
45 U14 **Couva** Trinidad, Trinidad and Tobago 10°25′N 61°27′W
108 B8 **Couvet** Neuchâtel, W Switzerland 46°57′N 06°41′E
99 H22 **Couvin** Namur, S Belgium 50°03′N 04°30′E
116 K12 **Covasna** *Ger.* Kowasna, *Hung.* Kovászna. Covasna, E Romania 45°51′N 26°11′E
116 J11 **Covasna** ◈ *county* E Romania
14 E12 **Cove Island** *island* Ontario, S Canada
35 M5 **Covelo** California, W USA 39°46′N 123°16′W
97 M20 **Coventry** *anc.* Couentrey. C England, United Kingdom 52°25′N 01°30′W
**Cove of Cork** *see* Cobh
21 U5 **Covesville** Virginia, NE USA 37°52′N 78°41′W
104 I8 **Covilhã** Castelo Branco, E Portugal 40°17′N 07°30′W
23 T3 **Covington** Georgia, SE USA 33°34′N 83°52′W
31 N13 **Covington** Indiana, N USA 40°08′N 87°23′W
20 M3 **Covington** Kentucky, S USA 39°04′N 84°30′W
22 K8 **Covington** Louisiana, S USA 30°28′N 90°06′W
31 Q13 **Covington** Ohio, N USA 40°07′N 84°21′W
20 F9 **Covington** Tennessee, S USA 35°32′N 89°40′W
21 S6 **Covington** Virginia, NE USA 37°48′N 80°01′W
183 Q8 **Cowal, Lake** *seasonal lake* New South Wales, SE Australia
11 W15 **Cowan** Manitoba, S Canada 52°00′N 100°36′W
18 F12 **Cowanesque River** ≈ New York/Pennsylvania, NE USA
180 L12 **Cowan, Lake** ◎ Western Australia
15 P13 **Cowansville** Québec, SE Canada 45°13′N 72°44′W
182 H8 **Cowell** South Australia 33°43′S 136°53′E
97 M23 **Cowes** S England, United Kingdom 50°45′N 01°19′W
27 Q10 **Coweta** Oklahoma, C USA 35°57′N 95°39′W
0 D6 **Cowie Seamount** *undersea feature* NE Pacific Ocean 54°15′N 149°30′W
32 G10 **Cowlitz River** ≈ Washington, NW USA
21 Q11 **Cowpens** South Carolina, SE USA 35°01′N 81°48′W
183 R8 **Cowra** New South Wales, SE Australia 33°50′S 148°45′E
**Coxen Hole** *see* Roatán
59 I19 **Coxim** Mato Grosso do Sul, S Brazil 18°28′S 54°45′W
59 I19 **Coxim, Rio** ≈ SW Brazil
**Coxin Hole** *see* Roatán
153 V17 **Cox's Bazar** Chittagong, S Bangladesh 21°25′N 91°59′E
76 H14 **Coyah** Conakry, W Guinea 09°45′N 13°26′W
40 K5 **Coyame** Chihuahua, N Mexico 29°29′N 105°07′W
24 L9 **Coyanosa Draw** ≈ Texas, SW USA
**Coyhaique** *see* Coihaique
42 C7 **Coyolate, Río** ≈ S Guatemala
**Coyote State, The** *see* South Dakota
40 I10 **Coyotitán** Sinaloa, C Mexico 23°48′N 106°37′W
41 N15 **Coyuca** *var.* Coyuca de Catalán. Guerrero, S Mexico 18°21′N 100°39′W
41 O16 **Coyuca** *var.* Coyuca de Benítez. Guerrero, S Mexico 17°01′N 100°08′W
**Coyuca de Benítez/Coyuca de Catalán** *see* Coyuca
29 N15 **Cozad** Nebraska, C USA 40°52′N 99°58′W
158 L14 **Cozhê** Xizang Zizhiqu, W China 31°53′N 87°51′E
**Cozie, Alpi** *see* Cottian Alps
**Cozmeni** *see* Kitsman'
40 E3 **Cozón, Cerro** ▲ NW Mexico 31°16′N 112°29′W
41 Z12 **Cozumel** Quintana Roo, E Mexico 20°29′N 86°54′W
41 Z12 **Cozumel, Isla** *island* SE Mexico
32 K8 **Crab Creek** ≈ Washington, NW USA
44 H12 **Crab Pond Point** *headland* W Jamaica 18°07′N 78°01′W
**Cracovia/Cracow** *see* Kraków
83 I25 **Cradock** Eastern Cape, S South Africa 32°07′S 25°38′E
39 Y14 **Craig** Prince of Wales Island, Alaska, USA 55°29′N 133°04′W
37 Q3 **Craig** Colorado, C USA 40°31′N 107°33′W
97 F15 **Craigavon** C Northern Ireland, United Kingdom 54°28′N 06°25′W
21 T5 **Craigsville** Virginia, NE USA 38°07′N 79°21′W
101 J21 **Crailsheim** Baden-Württemberg, S Germany 49°07′N 10°04′E
116 H14 **Craiova** Dolj, SW Romania 44°19′N 23°49′E
10 K12 **Cranberry Junction** British Columbia, SW Canada 55°35′N 128°21′W
18 J8 **Cranberry Lake** ◎ New York, NE USA
11 V13 **Cranberry Portage** Manitoba, C Canada 54°34′N 101°22′W
11 P17 **Cranbrook** British Columbia, SW Canada 49°29′N 115°48′W
30 M5 **Crandon** Wisconsin, N USA 45°34′N 88°54′W
32 K14 **Crane** Oregon, NW USA 43°24′N 118°35′W
24 M9 **Crane** Texas, SW USA 31°23′N 102°22′W
**Crane** *see* The Crane
25 S8 **Cranfills Gap** Texas, SW USA 31°46′N 97°49′W
19 O12 **Cranston** Rhode Island, NE USA 41°46′N 71°26′W
**Cranz** *see* Zelenogradsk
59 L15 **Craolândia** Tocantins, E Brazil 07°17′S 47°23′W
102 J7 **Craon** Mayenne, NW France 47°52′N 00°57′W
195 V16 **Crary, Cape** *headland* Antarctica
**Crasna** *see* Kraszna
32 G14 **Crater Lake** ◎ Oregon, NW USA
33 P14 **Craters of the Moon National Monument** *national park* Idaho, NW USA
59 O14 **Crateús** Ceará, E Brazil 05°10′S 40°39′W
**Crathis** *see* Crati
107 N20 **Crati** *anc.* Crathis. ≈ S Italy
11 U16 **Craven** Saskatchewan, S Canada 50°44′N 104°50′W
54 I8 **Cravo Norte** Arauca, E Colombia 06°17′N 70°15′W
28 J12 **Crawford** Nebraska, C USA 42°40′N 103°24′W
25 T8 **Crawford** Texas, SW USA 31°31′N 97°26′W
11 O17 **Crawford Bay** British Columbia, SW Canada 49°39′N 116°44′W
65 M19 **Crawford Seamount** *undersea feature* S Atlantic Ocean 40°30′S 10°00′W
31 O13 **Crawfordsville** Indiana, N USA 40°02′N 86°52′W
23 S9 **Crawfordville** Florida, SE USA 30°10′N 84°22′W
97 O23 **Crawley** SE England, United Kingdom 51°07′N 00°12′W
33 S10 **Crazy Mountains** ▲▲ Montana, NW USA
11 T11 **Cree** ≈ Saskatchewan, C Canada
37 R7 **Creede** Colorado, C USA 37°51′N 106°55′W
40 I6 **Creel** Chihuahua, N Mexico 27°45′N 107°36′W
11 S11 **Cree Lake** ◎ Saskatchewan, C Canada
11 V13 **Creighton** Saskatchewan, C Canada 54°46′N 101°54′W
29 Q13 **Creighton** Nebraska, C USA 42°28′N 97°54′W
103 O4 **Creil** Oise, N France 49°16′N 02°29′E
106 E8 **Crema** Lombardia, N Italy 45°22′N 09°40′E
106 E8 **Cremona** Lombardia, N Italy 45°08′N 10°02′E
**Creole State** *see* Louisiana
112 M10 **Crepaja** *Hung.* Cserépalja. Vojvodina, N Serbia 45°02′N 20°36′E
103 O4 **Crépy-en-Valois** Oise, N France 49°13′N 02°54′E
112 B10 **Cres** *It.* Cherso. Primorje-Gorski Kotar, NW Croatia 44°57′N 14°24′E
112 A11 **Cres** *It.* Cherso; *anc.* Crexa. *island* W Croatia
32 H14 **Crescent** Oregon, NW USA 43°27′N 121°40′W
34 K1 **Crescent City** California, W USA 41°45′N 124°14′W
23 W10 **Crescent City** Florida, SE USA 29°25′N 81°30′W
167 X10 **Crescent Group** *Chin.* Yongle Qundao, *Viet.* Nhóm Lưỡi Liềm. *island group* C Paracel Islands
23 W10 **Crescent Lake** ◎ Florida, SE USA
29 X11 **Cresco** Iowa, C USA 43°22′N 92°06′W
61 B18 **Crespo** Entre Ríos, E Argentina 32°05′S 60°20′W
103 R13 **Crest** Drôme, E France 44°45′N 05°00′E
37 R5 **Crested Butte** Colorado, C USA 38°52′N 106°59′W
31 S12 **Crestline** Ohio, N USA 40°47′N 82°44′W
11 O17 **Creston** British Columbia, SW Canada 49°05′N 116°32′W
29 U15 **Creston** Iowa, C USA 41°03′N 94°21′W
33 V16 **Creston** Wyoming, C USA 41°40′N 107°43′W
37 S7 **Crestone Peak** ▲ Colorado, C USA 37°58′N 105°34′W
23 P8 **Crestview** Florida, SE USA 30°44′N 86°34′W
121 R10 **Cretan Trough** *undersea feature* Aegean Sea, C Mediterranean Sea
29 R16 **Crete** Nebraska, C USA 40°36′N 96°58′W
**Crete** *see* Kriti
103 O5 **Créteil** Val-de-Marne, N France 48°47′N 02°28′E
**Crete, Sea of/Creticum, Mare** *see* Kritikó Pélagos
105 X4 **Creus, Cap de** *headland* NE Spain 42°18′N 03°18′E
103 N10 **Creuse** ◈ *department* C France
102 L9 **Creuse** ≈ C France
103 T4 **Creutzwald** Moselle, NE France 49°13′N 06°41′E
105 S12 **Crevillent** *prev.* Crevillente. Comunitat Valenciana, E Spain 38°15′N 00°48′W
**Crevillente** *see* Crevillent
97 L18 **Crewe** C England, United Kingdom 53°05′N 02°27′W
21 V7 **Crewe** Virginia, NE USA 37°10′N 78°07′W
**Crexa** *see* Cres
43 Q15 **Cricamola, Río** ≈ NW Panama
61 K14 **Criciúma** Santa Catarina, S Brazil 28°39′S 49°23′W
96 J11 **Crieff** C Scotland, United Kingdom 56°22′N 03°49′W
112 B10 **Crikvenica** *It.* Cirquenizza; *prev.* Cirkvenica, Crjkvenica. Primorje-Gorski Kotar, NW Croatia 45°12′N 14°40′E
**Crimea/Crimean Oblast** *see* Krym, Avtonomna Respublika
101 M16 **Crimmitschau** *var.* Krimmitschau. Sachsen, E Germany 50°48′N 12°23′E
116 G11 **Crișcior** *Hung.* Kristyor. Hunedoara, W Romania 46°09′N 22°54′E
21 Y5 **Crisfield** Maryland, NE USA 37°58′N 75°51′W
31 P3 **Crisp Point** *headland* Michigan, N USA 46°45′N 85°15′W
59 L19 **Cristalina** Goiás, C Brazil 16°43′S 47°37′W
44 J7 **Cristal, Sierra del** ▲▲ E Cuba
43 T14 **Cristóbal** Colón, C Panama 09°18′N 79°52′W
54 F4 **Cristóbal Colón, Pico** ▲ N Colombia 10°52′N 73°46′W
**Cristur/Cristuru Săcuiesc** *see* Cristuru Secuiesc
116 I11 **Cristuru Secuiesc** *prev.* Cristur, Cristuru Săcuiesc, Sitaș Cristuru, *Ger.* Kreutz, *Hung.* Székelykeresztúr, Szitás-Keresztúr. Harghita, C Romania 46°17′N 25°02′E
116 F10 **Crișul Alb** *var.* Weisse Kreisch, *Ger.* Weisse Körös, *Hung.* Fehér-Körös. ≈ Hungary/Romania
116 F10 **Crișul Negru** *Ger.* Schwarze Körös, *Hung.* Fekete-Körös. ≈ Hungary/Romania
116 G10 **Crișul Repede** *var.* Schnelle Kreisch, *Ger.* Schnelle Körös, *Hung.* Sebes-Körös. ≈ Hungary/Romania
117 N10 **Criuleni** *Rus.* Kriulyany. C Moldova 47°12′N 29°09′E
**Crivadia Vulcanului** *see* Vulcan
**Crjkvenica** *see* Crikvenica
113 J17 **Crkvice** SW Montenegro 42°34′N 18°38′E
113 O17 **Crna Gora** *Alb.* Mali i Zi. ▲▲ North Macedonia/Serbia
**Crna Gora** *see* Montenegro
113 O20 **Crna Reka** ≈ S North Macedonia
**Crni Drim** *see* Black Drin
109 V10 **Črni vrh** ▲ NE Slovenia 46°28′N 15°14′E
109 V13 **Črnomelj** *Ger.* Tschernembl. SE Slovenia 45°32′N 15°12′E
97 A17 **Croagh Patrick** *Ir.* Cruach Phádraig. ▲ W Ireland 53°45′N 09°39′W
112 D9 **Croatia** *off.* Republic of Croatia, *Cro.* Hrvatska, Republika Hrvatska. ◆ *republic* SE Europe
**Croatia, Republic of** *see* Croatia
**Croce, Picco di** *see* Wilde Kreuzspitze
15 P8 **Croche** ≈ Québec, SE Canada
169 V7 **Crocker, Banjaran** *var.* Crocker Range. ▲▲ East Malaysia
**Crocker Range** *see* Crocker, Banjaran
25 V9 **Crockett** Texas, SW USA 31°21′N 95°30′W
67 V14 **Crocodile** *var.* Krokodil. ≈ N South Africa
**Crocodile** *see* Limpopo
20 I7 **Crofton** Kentucky, S USA 37°01′N 87°25′W
29 Q12 **Crofton** Nebraska, C USA 42°43′N 97°30′W
**Croia** *see* Krujë
103 R16 **Croisette, Cap** *headland* SE France 43°12′N 05°21′E
102 G8 **Croisic, Pointe du** *headland* NW France 47°16′N 02°42′W
103 S13 **Croix Haute, Col de la** *pass* E France
15 U5 **Croix, Pointe à la** *headland* Québec, SE Canada 49°16′N 67°46′W
14 F13 **Croker, Cape** *headland* Ontario, S Canada 44°56′N 80°57′W
181 P1 **Croker Island** *island* Northern Territory, N Australia
96 I8 **Cromarty** N Scotland, United Kingdom 57°40′N 04°02′W
99 M21 **Crombach** Liège, E Belgium 50°14′N 06°07′E
97 Q18 **Cromer** E England, United Kingdom 52°56′N 01°06′E
185 D22 **Cromwell** Otago, South Island, New Zealand 45°03′S 169°14′E
185 H16 **Cronadun** West Coast, South Island, New Zealand 42°03′S 171°52′E
39 O11 **Crooked Creek** Alaska, USA 61°52′N 158°06′W
44 K5 **Crooked Island** *island* SE The Bahamas
44 J5 **Crooked Island Passage** *channel* SE The Bahamas
32 I13 **Crooked River** ≈ Oregon, NW USA
29 R4 **Crookston** Minnesota, N USA 47°47′N 96°36′W
28 I10 **Crooks Tower** ▲ South Dakota, N USA 44°09′N 103°55′W
31 T14 **Crooksville** Ohio, N USA 39°46′N 82°05′W
183 R9 **Crookwell** New South Wales, SE Australia 34°28′S 149°27′E
14 L14 **Crosby** Ontario, SE Canada 44°39′N 76°13′W
97 K17 **Crosby** *var.* Great Crosby. NW England, United Kingdom 53°30′N 03°02′W
29 U6 **Crosby** Minnesota, N USA 46°30′N 93°58′W
28 K2 **Crosby** North Dakota, N USA 48°54′N 103°17′W
25 O5 **Crosbyton** Texas, SW USA 33°40′N 101°16′W
77 V16 **Cross** ≈ Cameroon/Nigeria
23 U10 **Cross City** Florida, SE USA 29°37′N 83°08′W
**Crossen** *see* Krosno Odrzańskie
27 V14 **Crossett** Arkansas, C USA 33°08′N 91°58′W
97 K15 **Cross Fell** ▲ N England, United Kingdom 54°42′N 02°30′W
11 P16 **Crossfield** Alberta, SW Canada 51°24′N 114°03′W
21 Q12 **Cross Hill** South Carolina, SE USA 34°18′N 81°58′W
19 U6 **Cross Island** *island* Maine, NE USA
11 X13 **Cross Lake** Manitoba, C Canada 54°38′N 97°35′W
22 F5 **Cross Lake** ▣ Louisiana, S USA
36 I12 **Crossman Peak** ▲ Arizona, SW USA 34°33′N 114°09′W
25 Q7 **Cross Plains** Texas, SW USA 32°07′N 99°10′W
77 V17 **Cross River** ◈ *state* SE Nigeria
20 L9 **Crossville** Tennessee, S USA 35°57′N 85°02′W
31 S8 **Croswell** Michigan, N USA 43°16′N 82°37′W
14 K13 **Crotch Lake** ◎ Ontario, SE Canada
**Croton/Crotona** *see* Crotone
107 O21 **Crotone** *var.* Cotrone; *anc.* Croton, Crotona. Calabria, SW Italy 39°05′N 17°07′E
33 V11 **Crow Agency** Montana, NW USA 45°35′N 107°28′W
183 U7 **Crowdy Head** *headland* New South Wales, SE Australia 31°52′S 152°45′E
25 Q4 **Crowell** Texas, SW USA 33°59′N 99°45′W
183 O6 **Crowl Creek** *seasonal river* New South Wales, SE Australia
22 H9 **Crowley** Louisiana, S USA 30°11′N 92°21′W
35 S9 **Crowley, Lake** ▣ California, W USA
27 X10 **Crowleys Ridge** *hill range* Arkansas, C USA
31 N11 **Crown Point** Indiana, N USA 41°25′N 87°22′W
37 P10 **Crownpoint** New Mexico, SW USA 35°40′N 108°09′W
33 R10 **Crow Peak** ▲ Montana, NW USA 46°17′N 111°54′W
11 P17 **Crowsnest Pass** *pass* Alberta/British Columbia, SW Canada
29 T6 **Crow Wing River** ≈ Minnesota, N USA
97 O22 **Croydon** SE England, United Kingdom 51°21′N 00°06′W
**Crozer, Mount** *see* Finkol, Mount
173 P11 **Crozet Basin** *undersea feature* S Indian Ocean 39°00′S 60°00′E
173 O12 **Crozet Islands** *island group* French Southern and Antarctic Lands
173 N12 **Crozet Plateau** *var.* Crozet Plateaus. *undersea feature* SW Indian Ocean 46°00′S 51°00′E
**Crozet Plateaus** *see* Crozet Plateau
102 E6 **Crozon** Finistère, NW France 48°14′N 04°31′W
**Cruacha Dubha, Na** *see* Macgillycuddy's Reeks
**Cruach Phádraig** *see* Croagh Patrick
116 M14 **Crucea** Constanța, SE Romania 44°30′N 28°18′E
44 E5 **Cruces** Cienfuegos, C Cuba 22°20′N 80°17′W
107 O20 **Crucoli Torretta** Calabria, SW Italy 39°26′N 17°03′E
41 P9 **Cruillas** Tamaulipas, C Mexico 24°43′N 98°26′W
64 K9 **Cruiser Tablemount** *undersea feature* E Atlantic Ocean 32°00′N 28°00′W
61 G14 **Cruz Alta** Rio Grande do Sul, S Brazil 28°38′S 53°38′W
44 G8 **Cruz, Cabo** *headland* S Cuba 19°50′N 77°43′W
60 N9 **Cruzeiro** São Paulo, S Brazil 22°33′S 44°59′W
60 H10 **Cruzeiro do Oeste** Paraná, S Brazil 23°45′S 53°03′W
59 A15 **Cruzeiro do Sul** Acre, W Brazil 07°40′S 72°39′W
23 U11 **Crystal Bay** *bay* Florida, SE USA NE Gulf of Mexico Atlantic Ocean
182 I8 **Crystal Brook** South Australia 33°24′S 138°10′E
11 X17 **Crystal City** Manitoba, S Canada 49°07′N 98°54′W
27 X5 **Crystal City** Missouri, C USA 38°13′N 90°22′W
25 P13 **Crystal City** Texas, SW USA 28°43′N 99°51′W
30 M4 **Crystal Falls** Michigan, N USA 46°06′N 88°20′W
23 Q8 **Crystal Lake** Florida, SE USA 30°26′N 85°41′W
31 O6 **Crystal Lake** ◎ Michigan, N USA
23 V11 **Crystal River** Florida, SE USA 28°54′N 82°35′W
37 Q5 **Crystal River** ≈ Colorado, C USA
22 K6 **Crystal Springs** Mississippi, S USA 31°59′N 90°21′W
**Csaca** *see* Čadca
**Csakathurn/Csáktornya** *see* Čakovec
**Csap** *see* Chop
**Csepén** *see* Čepin
**Cserépalja** *see* Crepaja
**Csermő** *see* Cermei
**Csíkszereda** *see* Miercurea-Ciuc
111 L24 **Csongrád** Csongrád, SE Hungary 46°42′N 20°09′E
111 L24 **Csongrád** *off.* Csongrád Megye. ◈ *county* SE Hungary
**Csongrád Megye** *see* Csongrád
111 H22 **Csorna** Győr-Moson-Sopron, NW Hungary 47°37′N 17°14′E
**Csucsa** *see* Ciucea
111 G25 **Csurgó** Somogy, SW Hungary 46°16′N 17°09′E
**Csurog** *see* Čurug
54 L5 **Cúa** Miranda, N Venezuela 10°14′N 66°58′W
82 C11 **Cuale** Malanje, NW Angola 08°22′S 16°10′E
67 T12 **Cuando** *var.* Kwando. ≈ S Africa
**Cuando Cubango** *see* Kuando Kubango
83 E16 **Cuangar** Kuando Kubango, S Angola 17°34′S 18°39′E
82 D11 **Cuango** Lunda Norte, NE Angola 09°10′S 17°59′E
82 C10 **Cuango** Uíge, NW Angola 06°20′S 16°42′E
82 C10 **Cuango** *var.* Kwango. ≈ Angola/Dem. Rep. Congo *see also* Kwango
**Cuango** *see* Kwango
**Cuan, Loch** *see* Strangford Lough
82 C12 **Cuanza** *var.* Kwanza. ≈ C Angola
**Cuanza Norte** *see* Kwanza Norte
**Cuanza Sul** *see* Kwanza Sul
61 E16 **Cuareim, Río** *var.* Rio Quaraí. ≈ Brazil/Uruguay *see also* Quaraí, Rio
**Cuareim, Río** *see* Quaraí, Rio
83 D15 **Cuatir** ≈ S Angola
40 M7 **Cuatro Ciénegas** *var.* Cuatro Ciénegas de Carranza. Coahuila, NE Mexico 27°00′N 102°03′W
**Cuatro Ciénegas de Carranza** *see* Cuatro Ciénegas
40 I6 **Cuauhtémoc** Chihuahua, N Mexico 28°22′N 106°52′W
41 P14 **Cuautla** Morelos, S Mexico 18°48′N 98°56′W
104 H12 **Cuba** Beja, S Portugal 38°10′N 07°54′W
27 W6 **Cuba** Missouri, C USA 38°03′N 91°24′W
37 R10 **Cuba** New Mexico, SW USA 36°01′N 106°57′W
44 E6 **Cuba** *off.* Republic of Cuba. ◆ *republic* W West Indies
47 O2 **Cuba** *island* W West Indies
82 B13 **Cubal** Benguela, W Angola 12°58′S 14°16′E
83 C15 **Cubango** *var.* Kuvango, *Port.* Vila Artur de Paiva, Vila da Ponte. Huíla, SW Angola 14°27′S 16°18′E
83 D16 **Cubango** *var.* Kavango, Kavengo, Kubango, Okavango, Okavanggo. ≈ S Africa *see also* Okavango
**Cubango** *see* Okavango
54 H8 **Cubará** Boyacá, N Colombia 07°01′N 72°07′W
**Cuba, Republic of** *see* Cuba
136 I12 **Çubuk** Ankara, N Turkey 40°13′N 33°02′E
83 D14 **Cuchi** Kuando Kubango, C Angola 14°40′S 16°58′E
42 C5 **Cuchumatanes, Sierra de los** ▲▲ W Guatemala
**Cuculaya, Rio** *see* Kukalaya, Rio
82 E12 **Cucumbi** *prev.* Trás-os-Montes. Lunda Sul, NE Angola 10°13′S 19°04′E
54 G7 **Cúcuta** *var.* San José de Cúcuta. Norte de Santander, N Colombia 07°55′N 72°31′W
31 N9 **Cudahy** Wisconsin, N USA 42°54′N 87°51′W
155 J21 **Cuddalore** Tamil Nādu, SE India 11°43′N 79°46′E
**Cuddapah** *see* Kadapa
104 M6 **Cuéllar** Castilla y León, N Spain 41°24′N 04°19′W
82 D13 **Cuemba** *var.* Coemba. Bié, C Angola 12°09′S 18°07′E
56 B8 **Cuenca** Azuay, S Ecuador 02°54′S 79°W
105 Q9 **Cuenca** *anc.* Conca. Castilla-La Mancha, C Spain 40°04′N 02°07′W
105 P9 **Cuenca** ◈ *province* Castilla-La Mancha, C Spain
40 L9 **Cuencamé** *var.* Cuencamé de Ceniceros. Durango, C Mexico 24°53′N 103°41′W
**Cuencamé de Ceniceros** *see* Cuencamé
105 Q8 **Cuenca, Serranía de** ▲▲ C Spain
**Cuera** *see* Chur
105 P5 **Cuerda del Pozo, Embalse de la** ▣ N Spain
41 O14 **Cuernavaca** Morelos, S Mexico 18°57′N 99°15′W
25 T12 **Cuero** Texas, SW USA 29°06′N 97°19′W
44 I7 **Cueto** Holguín, E Cuba 20°43′N 75°54′W
41 Q13 **Cuetzalán** *var.* Cuetzalán del Progreso. Puebla, S Mexico 20°00′N 97°27′W
**Cuetzalán del Progreso** *see* Cuetzalán




◆ Country
● Country Capital
◇ Dependent Territory
○ Dependent Territory Capital
◈ Administrative Regions
✈ International Airport
▲ Mountain
▲▲ Mountain Range
Ѧ Volcano
≈ River
◎ Lake
▣ Reservoir

Cuevas de Almanzora – Danxian/Dan Xian


105 Q14 **Cuevas de Almanzora** Andalucía, S Spain 37°19′N 01°52′W
**Cuevas de Vinromá** see Les Coves de Vinromá
116 H12 **Cugir** Hung. Kudzsir. Alba, SW Romania 45°48′N 23°25′E
59 H18 **Cuiabá** prev. Cuyabá. state capital Mato Grosso, SW Brazil 15°32′S 56°05′W
59 H19 **Cuiabá, Rio** ≈ SW Brazil
41 R15 **Cuicatlán** var. San Juan Bautista Cuicatlán. Oaxaca, SE Mexico 17°49′N 96°59′W
**Cuidad de Guatemala** see Guatemala
191 W16 **Cuidado, Punta** headland Easter Island, Chile, E Pacific Ocean 27°08′S 109°18′W
**Cúige** see Connaught
**Cúige Laighean** see Leinster
**Cúige Mumhan** see Munster
**Cuihua** see Daguan
98 L13 **Cuijck** Noord-Brabant, SE Netherlands 51°41′N 05°56′E
**Cúil an tSúdaire** see Portarlington
42 D7 **Cuilapa** Santa Rosa, S Guatemala 14°16′N 90°18′W
42 B5 **Cuilco, Río** ≈ W Guatemala
**Cúil Mhuine** see Collooney
**Cúil Raithin** see Coleraine
83 C14 **Cuima** Huambo, C Angola 13°16′S 15°39′E
83 E16 **Cuito** var. Kwito. ≈ SE Angola
**Cuito** see Kuito
83 E15 **Cuito Cuanavale** Kuando Kubango, E Angola 15°01′S 19°07′E
41 N14 **Cuitzeo, Lago de** ◎ C Mexico
27 W4 **Cuivre River** ≈ Missouri, C USA
**Çuka** see Çukë
168 L8 **Cukai** var. Chukai, Kemaman. Terengganu, Peninsular Malaysia 04°15′N 103°25′E
113 L23 **Çukë** var. Çuka. Vlorë, S Albania 39°50′N 20°01′E
**Cularo** see Grenoble
33 Y7 **Culbertson** Montana, NW USA 48°09′N 104°30′W
28 M16 **Culbertson** Nebraska, C USA 40°13′N 100°50′W
183 P10 **Culcairn** New South Wales, SE Australia 35°41′S 147°01′E
45 W5 **Culebra** var. Dewey. E Puerto Rico 18°19′N 65°17′W
45 W6 **Culebra, Isla de** island E Puerto Rico
37 T8 **Culebra Peak** ▲ Colorado, C USA 37°07′N 105°11′W
104 J5 **Culebra, Sierra de la** ▲ NW Spain
98 J12 **Culemborg** Gelderland, C Netherlands 51°57′N 05°17′E
137 V14 **Culfa** Rus. Dzhul'fa. SW Azerbaijan 38°58′N 45°37′E
183 P4 **Culgoa River** ≈ New South Wales/Queensland, SE Australia
40 I9 **Culiacán** var. Culiacán Rosales, Culiacán-Rosales. Sinaloa, C Mexico 24°48′N 107°25′W
**Culiacán-Rosales/Culiacán Rosales** see Culiacán
105 P14 **Cúllar-Baza** Andalucía, S Spain 37°35′N 02°34′W
105 S10 **Cullera** Comunitat Valenciana, E Spain 39°10′N 00°15′W
23 P3 **Cullman** Alabama, S USA 34°10′N 86°50′W
108 B10 **Cully** Vaud, W Switzerland 46°58′N 06°46′E
**Culm** see Chełmno
**Culmsee** see Chełmża
21 V4 **Culpeper** Virginia, NE USA 38°28′N 78°00′W
185 I17 **Culverden** Canterbury, South Island, New Zealand 42°46′S 172°51′E
83 H18 **Cum** var. Xhumo. Central, C Botswana 21°13′S 24°38′E
55 N5 **Cumaná** Sucre, NE Venezuela 10°29′N 64°12′W
55 O5 **Cumanacoa** Sucre, NE Venezuela 10°17′N 63°58′W
54 C13 **Cumbal, Nevado de** elevation S Colombia
21 O7 **Cumberland** Kentucky, S USA 36°55′N 83°00′W
21 U2 **Cumberland** Maryland, NE USA 39°40′N 78°47′W
21 V6 **Cumberland** Virginia, NE USA 37°31′N 78°16′W
187 P12 **Cumberland, Cape** var. Cape Nahoi. headland Espiritu Santo, N Vanuatu 14°39′S 166°35′E
11 V14 **Cumberland House** Saskatchewan, C Canada 53°57′N 102°21′W
23 W8 **Cumberland Island** island Georgia, SE USA
20 L7 **Cumberland, Lake** ⊠ Kentucky, S USA
9 R5 **Cumberland Peninsula** peninsula Baffin Island, Nunavut, NE Canada
2 N9 **Cumberland Plateau** plateau E USA
30 L1 **Cumberland Point** headland Michigan, N USA 47°51′N 89°14′W
21 O7 **Cumberland River** ≈ Kentucky/Tennessee, S USA
9 S6 **Cumberland Sound** inlet Baffin Island, Nunavut, NE Canada
96 I12 **Cumbernauld** S Scotland, United Kingdom 55°57′N 04°W
97 K15 **Cumbria** cultural region NW England, United Kingdom
97 K15 **Cumbrian Mountains** ▲▲ NW England, United Kingdom
23 S2 **Cumming** Georgia, SE USA 34°12′N 84°08′W
**Cummin in Pommern** see Kamień Pomorski
182 G9 **Cummins** South Australia 34°17′S 135°43′E
96 I13 **Cumnock** W Scotland, United Kingdom 55°32′N 04°28′W
40 G4 **Cumpas** Sonora, NW Mexico 30°N 109°48′W
136 H16 **Çumra** Konya, C Turkey 37°34′N 32°38′E
63 G15 **Cunco** Araucanía, C Chile 38°55′S 72°02′W
54 E9 **Cundinamarca** off. Departamento de Cundinamarca. ◈ province C Colombia
**Cundinamarca, Departamento de** see Cundinamarca
41 U15 **Cunduacán** Tabasco, SE Mexico 18°00′N 93°07′W
83 C16 **Cunene** ◈ province S Angola
83 A16 **Cunene** var. Kunene. ≈ Angola/Namibia see also Kunene
**Cunene** see Kunene
106 A9 **Cuneo** Fr. Coni. Piemonte, NW Italy 44°23′N 07°32′E
83 E15 **Cunjamba** Kuando Kubango, E Angola 15°22′S 20°07′E
181 V10 **Cunnamulla** Queensland, E Australia 28°09′S 145°44′E
**Čunusavvon** see Junosuando
**Cuokkarašša** see Čohkarášša
106 B7 **Cuorgne** Piemonte, NE Italy 45°23′N 07°34′E
96 K11 **Cupar** E Scotland, United Kingdom 56°19′N 03°01′W
116 L8 **Cupcina** Rus. Kupchino; prev. Calinisc, Kalinisk. N Moldova 48°07′N 27°22′E
54 C8 **Cupica** Chocó, W Colombia 06°43′N 77°31′W
54 C8 **Cupica, Golfo de** gulf W Colombia
112 N13 **Ćuprija** Serbia, E Serbia 43°57′N 21°21′E
**Cura** see Villa de Cura
45 P16 **Curaçao** island Lesser Antilles
56 H13 **Curanja, Río** ≈ E Peru
56 F7 **Curaray, Río** ≈ Ecuador/Peru
116 K14 **Curcani** Călărași, SE Romania 44°11′N 26°39′E
182 H4 **Curdimurka** South Australia 29°27′S 136°56′E
103 P7 **Cure** ≈ C France
173 Y16 **Curepipe** C Mauritius 20°19′S 57°31′E
55 R6 **Curiapo** Delta Amacuro, NE Venezuela 10°03′N 63°05′W
**Curia Rhaetorum** see Chur
62 G12 **Curicó** Maule, C Chile 35°00′S 71°15′W
**Curieta** see Krk
172 I15 **Curieuse** island Inner Islands, NE Seychelles
59 C16 **Curitiba** Acre, W Brazil 10°08′S 69°00′W
60 K12 **Curitiba** prev. Curytiba. state capital Paraná, S Brazil 25°25′S 49°25′W
60 J13 **Curitibanos** Santa Catarina, S Brazil 27°18′S 50°35′W
183 S6 **Curlewis** New South Wales, SE Australia 31°09′S 150°18′E
182 J6 **Curnamona** South Australia 31°39′S 139°35′E
83 A15 **Curoca** ≈ SW Angola
183 T6 **Currabubula** New South Wales, SE Australia 31°17′S 150°43′E
59 Q14 **Currais Novos** Rio Grande do Norte, E Brazil 06°12′S 36°30′W
35 W7 **Currant** Nevada, W USA 38°43′N 115°27′W
35 W6 **Currant Mountain** ▲ Nevada, W USA 38°56′N 115°19′W
44 H2 **Current** Eleuthera Island, C The Bahamas 25°24′N 76°44′W
27 W8 **Current River** ≈ Arkansas/Missouri, C USA
182 M14 **Currie** Tasmania, SE Australia 39°59′S 143°51′E
21 Y8 **Currituck** North Carolina, SE USA 36°29′N 76°02′W
21 Y8 **Currituck Sound** sound North Carolina, SE USA
39 R11 **Curry** Alaska, USA 62°36′N 150°00′W
**Curtbunar** see Tervel
116 I13 **Curtea de Argeș** var. Curtea-de-Arges. Argeș, S Romania 45°06′N 24°40′E
**Curtea-de-Arges** see Curtea de Argeș
116 E10 **Curtici** Ger. Kurtitsch, Hung. Kürtös. Arad, W Romania 46°21′N 21°17′E
104 H2 **Curtis** Galicia, NW Spain 43°09′N 08°10′W
28 M16 **Curtis** Nebraska, C USA 40°36′N 100°27′W
183 O14 **Curtis Group** island group Tasmania, SE Australia
181 Y8 **Curtis Island** island Queensland, SE Australia
58 K11 **Curuá, Ilha do** island NE Brazil
47 U7 **Curuá, Rio** ≈ N Brazil
59 A14 **Curuçá, Rio** ≈ NW Brazil
112 L9 **Čurug** Hung. Csurog. Vojvodina, N Serbia 45°30′N 20°02′E
61 D16 **Curuzú Cuatiá** Corrientes, NE Argentina 29°50′S 58°05′W
59 M19 **Curvelo** Minas Gerais, SE Brazil 18°45′S 44°27′W
18 E14 **Curwensville** Pennsylvania, NE USA 40°57′N 78°29′W
30 M3 **Curwood, Mount** ▲ Michigan, N USA 46°42′N 88°14′W
**Curytiba** see Curitiba
**Curzola** see Korčula
42 A10 **Cuscatlán** ◈ department C El Salvador
57 H15 **Cusco** var. Cuzco. Cusco, C Peru 13°35′S 72°02′W
57 H15 **Cusco** off. Región de Cusco, var. Cuzco. ◈ region C Peru
**Cusco, Región de** see Cusco
27 O9 **Cushing** Oklahoma, C USA 36°01′N 96°46′W
25 W8 **Cushing** Texas, SW USA 31°48′N 94°50′W
40 I6 **Cusihuiriachic** Chihuahua, N Mexico 28°16′N 106°46′W
103 P10 **Cusset** Allier, C France 46°08′N 03°27′E
23 S6 **Cusseta** Georgia, SE USA 32°18′N 84°46′W
28 J10 **Custer** South Dakota, N USA 43°46′N 103°36′W
**Cüstrin** see Kostrzyn
33 Q7 **Cut Bank** Montana, NW USA 48°38′N 112°20′W
**Cutch, Gulf of** see Kachchh, Gulf of
23 S6 **Cuthbert** Georgia, SE USA 31°46′N 84°47′W
11 S15 **Cut Knife** Saskatchewan, S Canada 52°40′N 108°54′W
23 Y16 **Cutler Ridge** Florida, SE USA 25°34′N 80°21′W
22 K10 **Cut Off** Louisiana, S USA 29°32′N 90°20′W
63 I15 **Cutral-Có** Neuquén, C Argentina 38°56′S 69°13′W
107 O21 **Cutro** Calabria, SW Italy 39°01′N 16°59′E
183 O4 **Cuttaburra Channels** seasonal river New South Wales, SE Australia
154 O12 **Cuttack** Odisha, E India 20°28′N 85°53′E
83 C15 **Cuvelai** Cunene, SW Angola 15°40′S 15°48′E
79 G18 **Cuvette** var. Région de la Cuvette. ◈ department C Congo
79 G18 **Cuvette-Ouest** ◈ department C Congo
**Cuvette, Région de la** see Cuvette
173 V9 **Cuvier Basin** undersea feature E Indian Ocean
173 U9 **Cuvier Plateau** undersea feature E Indian Ocean
82 B12 **Cuvo** ≈ W Angola
100 H9 **Cuxhaven** Niedersachsen, NW Germany 53°51′N 08°43′E
**Cuyabá** see Cuiabá
**Cuyuni, Río** see Cuyuni River
55 S8 **Cuyuni River** var. Río Cuyuni. ≈ Guyana/Venezuela
**Cuzco** see Cusco
97 K22 **Cwmbran** Wel. Cwmbrân. SW Wales, United Kingdom 51°39′N 03°W
**Cwmbrân** see Cwmbran
28 K15 **C. W. McConaughy, Lake** ⊠ Nebraska, C USA
81 D20 **Cyangugu** SW Rwanda 02°27′S 29°00′E
110 D11 **Cybinka** Ger. Ziebingen. Lubuskie, W Poland 52°11′N 14°46′E
**Cyclades** see Kykládes
**Cydonia** see Chaniá
**Cymru** see Wales
20 M5 **Cynthiana** Kentucky, S USA 38°22′N 84°18′W
11 S17 **Cypress Hills** ▲▲ Alberta/Saskatchewan, SW Canada
**Cypro-Syrian Basin** see Cyprus Basin
121 U11 **Cyprus** off. Republic of Cyprus, Gk. Kýpros, Kypriakí Dimokratía, Turk. Kıbrıs, Kıbrıs Cumhuriyeti. ◆ republic E Mediterranean Sea
84 L14 **Cyprus** Gk. Kypros, Turk. Kıbrıs. island E Mediterranean Sea
121 W11 **Cyprus Basin** var. Cypro-Syrian Basin. undersea feature E Mediterranean Sea 34°00′N 34°00′E
**Cyprus, Republic of** see Cyprus
75 S8 **Cyrenaica** ◈ cultural region NE Libya
**Cythera** see Kýthira
**Cythnos** see Kýthnos
110 F9 **Czaplinek** Ger. Tempelburg. Zachodnio-pomorskie, NW Poland 53°33′N 16°14′E
**Czarna Woda** see Wda
110 G8 **Czarne** Pomorskie, N Poland 53°40′N 17°00′E
110 G10 **Czarnków** Wielkopolskie, C Poland 52°55′N 16°32′E
111 E17 **Czechia** off. Czech Republic, Cz. Česko Republika, Česko. ◆ C Europe
**Czech Republic** see Czechia
**Czegléd** see Cegléd
110 G12 **Czempiń** Wielkopolskie, C Poland 52°10′N 16°46′E
**Czenstochau** see Częstochowa
**Czerkow** see Čerchov
**Czernowitz** see Chernivtsi
110 I8 **Czersk** Pomorskie, N Poland 53°48′N 17°58′E
111 J15 **Częstochowa** Ger. Czenstochau, Tschenstochau, Rus. Chenstokhov. Śląskie, S Poland 50°49′N 19°07′E
110 F10 **Człopa** Ger. Schloppe. Zachodnio-pomorskie, NW Poland 53°05′N 16°05′E
110 H8 **Człuchów** Ger. Schlochau. Pomorskie, NW Poland 53°41′N 17°20′E


# D


163 V9 **Da'an** var. Dalai. Jilin, NE China 45°28′N 124°18′E
15 S10 **Daaquam** Québec, SE Canada 46°36′N 70°03′W
**Daawo, Webi** see Dawa Wenz
54 I4 **Dabajuro** Falcón, NW Venezuela 11°00′N 70°41′W
77 N15 **Dabakala** NE Ivory Coast 08°19′N 04°24′W
163 S11 **Daban** var. Bairin Youqi. Nei Mongol Zizhiqu, N China 43°33′N 118°40′E
111 K23 **Dabas** Pest, C Hungary 47°36′N 19°22′E
160 L8 **Daba Shan** ▲▲ C China
**Dabba** see Daocheng
140 J5 **Dabbāgh, Jabal** ▲ NW Saudi Arabia 27°52′N 35°48′E
54 D8 **Dabeiba** Antioquia, NW Colombia 07°01′N 76°18′W
154 E11 **Dabhoi** Gujarāt, W India 22°08′N 73°28′E
161 P8 **Dabie Shan** ▲▲ C China
76 J13 **Dabola** C Guinea 10°48′N 11°02′W
77 N17 **Dabou** S Ivory Coast 05°20′N 04°23′W
162 M15 **Dabqig** prev. Uxin Qi. Nei Mongol Zizhiqu, N China 38°29′N 108°48′E
110 P8 **Dąbrowa Białostocka** Podlaskie, NE Poland 53°38′N 23°18′E
111 M16 **Dąbrowa Tarnowska** Małopolskie, S Poland 50°10′N 21°E
119 M20 **Dabryn'** Rus. Dobryn'. Homyel'skaya Voblasts', SE Belarus 51°46′N 29°12′E
159 P10 **Dabsan Hu** ◎ C China
161 Q13 **Dabu** var. Huliao. Guangdong, S China 24°19′N 116°07′E
116 H15 **Dăbuleni** Dolj, SW Romania 43°48′N 24°05′E
152 G9 **Dabwāli** Haryāna, NW India 29°56′N 74°40′E
**Dacca** see Dhaka
101 L23 **Dachau** Bayern, SE Germany 48°15′N 11°26′E
**Dachuan** see Dazhou
**Dacia Bank** see Dacia Seamount
64 M10 **Dacia Seamount** var. Dacia Bank. undersea feature E Atlantic Ocean 31°10′N 13°42′W
37 T3 **Dacono** Colorado, C USA 40°04′N 104°56′W
**Đắc Tô** see Đăk Tô
**Dacura** see Dákura
23 W12 **Dade City** Florida, SE USA 28°21′N 82°12′W
152 L10 **Dadeldhurā** var. Dandeldhura. Far Western, W Nepal 29°12′N 80°31′E
23 Q5 **Dadeville** Alabama, S USA 32°49′N 85°45′W
**Dadong** see Donggang
103 N15 **Dadou** ≈ S France
154 D12 **Dādra and Nagar Haveli** ◈ union territory W India
149 P14 **Dādu** Sindh, SE Pakistan 26°42′N 67°48′E
167 U11 **Da Du Boloc** Kon Tum, C Vietnam 14°06′N 107°40′E
160 G9 **Dadu He** ≈ C China
163 V15 **Daecheong-do** prev. Taechŏng-do. island NW South Korea
163 Y16 **Daegu** , Jap. Taikyū; prev. Taegu. SE South Korea 35°55′N 128°33′E
163 Y15 **Daejeon** , Jap. Taiden; prev. Taejŏn. C South Korea 36°20′N 127°28′E
**Daerah Istimewa Aceh** see Aceh
171 P4 **Daet** Luzon, N Philippines 14°06′N 122°57′E
160 I11 **Dafang** Guizhou, S China 27°07′N 105°40′E
**Dafeng** see Shanglin
153 W11 **Dafla Hills** ▲▲ NE India
11 U15 **Dafoe** Saskatchewan, S Canada 51°46′N 104°11′W
76 G10 **Dagana** N Senegal 16°28′N 15°35′W
**Dagana** see Massakory, Chad
**Dagana** see Dahana, Tajikistan
**Dagcagoin** see Zoigê
118 K11 **Dagda** SE Latvia 56°06′N 27°36′E
**Dagden** see Hiiumaa
**Dagden-Sund** see Soela Väin
127 P16 **Dagestan, Respublika** prev. Dagestanskaya ASSR, Eng. Daghestan. ◈ autonomous republic SW Russia
**Dagestanskaya ASSR** see Dagestan, Respublika
127 R17 **Dagestanskiye Ogni** Respublika Dagestan, SW Russia 42°09′N 48°08′E
**Dagezhen** see Fengning
185 A23 **Dagg Sound** sound South Island, New Zealand
**Daghestan** see Dagestan, Respublika
141 Y8 **Daghmar** NE Oman 23°09′N 59°01′E
**Dağliq Quarabağ** see Nagornyy Karabakh
**Dagö** see Hiiumaa
54 D11 **Dagua** Valle del Cauca, W Colombia 03°39′N 76°40′W
160 H11 **Daguan** var. Cuihua. Yunnan, SW China 27°42′N 103°51′E
171 N3 **Dagupan** off. Dagupan City. Luzon, N Philippines 16°05′N 120°21′E
**Dagupan City** see Dagupan
159 N16 **Dagzê** var. Dêqên. Xizang Zizhiqu, W China 29°38′N 91°15′E
147 Q13 **Dahana** Rus. Dagana, Dakhana. SW Tajikistan 38°03′N 69°51′E
163 V10 **Dahei Shan** ▲▲ N China
163 T7 **Da Hinggan Ling** Eng. Great Khingan Range. ▲▲ NE China
**Dahlac Archipelago** see Dahlak Archipelago
80 K9 **Dahlak Archipelago** var. Dahlac Archipelago. island group E Eritrea
23 T2 **Dahlonega** Georgia, SE USA 34°31′N 83°59′W
101 O14 **Dahme** Brandenburg, E Germany 52°10′N 13°47′E
100 O13 **Dahme** ≈ E Germany
141 O14 **Dahm, Ramlat** desert NW Yemen
154 E10 **Dāhod** prev. Dohad. Gujarāt, W India 22°48′N 74°18′E
**Dahomey** see Benin
158 G10 **Dahongliutan** Xinjiang Uygur Zizhiqu, NW China 35°59′N 79°12′E
**Dahra** see Dara
**Dahuaishu** see Hongtong
139 R2 **Dahūk** var. Dohuk, Kurd. Dihok, Dihŏk. Dahūk, N Iraq 36°52′N 43°01′E
139 R2 **Dahūk** off. Muḩāfaz at Dahūk, var. Dohuk, Kurd. Dihok, off. Kurd. Parêzga-î Dihok. ◈ governorate N Iraq
**Dahūk, Muḩāfaz at** see Dahūk
116 J15 **Daia** Giurgiu, S Romania 44°00′N 25°59′E
165 P12 **Daigo** Ibaraki, Honshū, S Japan 36°43′N 140°22′E
163 O13 **Dai Hai** ◎ N China
**Daihoku** see Taipei
186 M8 **Dai Island** island N Solomon Islands
166 M8 **Daik-U** Bago, SW Myanmar (Burma) 17°46′N 96°40′E
138 H9 **Dā'īl** Dar'ā, S Syria 32°45′N 36°08′E
167 U12 **Đại Lanh** Khanh Hoa, S Vietnam 12°49′N 109°20′E
161 Q13 **Daimao Shan** ▲▲ SE China
105 N11 **Daimiel** Castilla-La Mancha, C Spain 39°04′N 03°37′W
115 F22 **Daimoniá** Pelopónnisos, S Greece 36°38′N 22°54′E
**Dainan** see Tainan
25 W6 **Daingerfield** Texas, SW USA 33°03′N 94°42′W
**Daingin, Bá an** see Dingle Bay
159 R13 **Dainkognubma** Xizang Zizhiqu, W China 32°26′N 97°58′E
164 K14 **Daiō-zaki** headland Honshū, SW Japan 34°15′N 136°50′E
**Dairbhre** see Valencia Island
61 B22 **Daireaux** Buenos Aires, E Argentina 36°34′S 61°40′W
**Dairen** see Dalian
**Dairûţ** see Dayrūţ
25 X10 **Daisetta** Texas, SW USA 30°06′N 94°38′W
192 G5 **Daitō-jima** island group SW Japan
192 G5 **Daitō Ridge** undersea feature N Philippine Sea 25°30′N 133°00′E
161 N3 **Daixian** var. Dai Xian, Shangguan. Shanxi, C China 39°10′N 112°57′E
**Dai Xian** see Daixian
**Daiyue** see Shanyin
161 Q12 **Daiyun Shan** ▲▲ SE China
44 M8 **Dajabón** NW Dominican Republic 19°35′N 71°41′W
160 G8 **Dajin Chuan** ≈ C China
148 J6 **Dak** ◎ W Afghanistan
76 F11 **Dakar** ● (Senegal) W Senegal 14°44′N 17°27′W
76 F11 **Dakar** ✈ W Senegal 14°42′N 17°27′W
**Đak Glây** see Đak Glei
167 U10 **Đak Glei** prev. Đak Glây. Kon Tum, C Vietnam 15°05′N 107°42′E
**Dakhana** see Dahana
153 U16 **Dakhin Shahbazpur Island** island S Bangladesh
**Dakhla** see Ad Dakhla
76 F7 **Dakhlet Nouâdhibou** ◈ region NW Mauritania
**Đak Lap** see Kiên Đuc
**Đak Nông** see Gia Nghia
77 U11 **Dakoro** Maradi, S Niger 14°29′N 06°45′E
29 U12 **Dakota City** Iowa, C USA 42°42′N 94°13′W
29 R13 **Dakota City** Nebraska, C USA 42°25′N 96°25′W
**Đakovica** see Gjakovë
112 I10 **Đakovo** Ger. Djakovo, Hung. Diakovár. Osijek-Baranja, E Croatia 45°18′N 18°24′E
**Dakshin** see Deccan
167 U11 **Đăk Tô** var. Đăc Tô. Kon Tum, C Vietnam 14°35′N 107°55′E
43 N7 **Dákura** var. Dacura. Costa Caribe Norte, NE Nicaragua 14°22′N 83°13′W
95 I14 **Dal** Akershus, S Norway 60°19′N 11°16′E
82 E12 **Dala** Lunda Sul, E Angola 11°04′S 20°15′E
108 J8 **Dalaas** Vorarlberg, W Austria 47°08′N 10°03′E
76 I13 **Dalaba** W Guinea 10°47′N 12°12′W
**Dalai** see Da'an
162 I12 **Dalain Hob** var. Ejin Qi. Nei Mongol Zizhiqu, N China 41°59′N 101°04′E
**Dalai Nor** see Hulun Nur
163 Q11 **Dalai Nur** salt lake N China
**Dala-Jarna** see Järna
95 M14 **Dalälven** ≈ C Sweden
136 C16 **Dalaman** Muğla, SW Turkey 36°47′N 28°47′E
136 C16 **Dalaman** ✈ Muğla, SW Turkey 36°37′N 28°51′E
136 D16 **Dalaman Çayı** ≈ SW Turkey
162 K11 **Dalandzadgad** Ömnögovĭ, S Mongolia 43°35′N 104°23′E
95 D17 **Dalane** physical region S Norway
189 Z2 **Dalap-Uliga-Djarrit** var. Delap-Uliga-Darrit, D-U-D. island group Ratak Chain, SE Marshall Islands
94 J12 **Dalarna** prev. Kopparberg. ◈ county C Sweden
94 L13 **Dalarna** prev. Eng. Dalecarlia. cultural region C Sweden
95 P16 **Dalarö** Stockholm, C Sweden 59°07′N 18°25′E
167 U13 **Đa Lat** Lâm Đồng, S Vietnam 11°56′N 108°25′E
**Dalay** see Bayandalay
148 L12 **Dalbandin** var. Dal Bandin. Baluchistan, SW Pakistan 28°48′N 64°08′E
**Dal Bandin** see Dalbandin
95 J17 **Dalbosjön** lake bay S Sweden
181 Y10 **Dalby** Queensland, E Australia 27°11′S 151°12′E
94 D13 **Dale** Hordaland, S Norway 60°35′N 05°48′E
94 C12 **Dale** Sogn Og Fjordane, S Norway 61°22′N 05°24′E
32 K12 **Dale** Oregon, NW USA 44°58′N 118°56′W
25 T11 **Dale** Texas, SW USA 29°56′N 97°34′W
**Dalecarlia** see Dalarna
21 W4 **Dale City** Virginia, NE USA 38°38′N 77°18′W
20 L8 **Dale Hollow Lake** ⊠ Kentucky/Tennessee, S USA
98 O8 **Dalen** Drenthe, NE Netherlands 52°42′N 06°45′E
95 E15 **Dalen** Telemark, S Norway 59°25′N 07°58′E
166 K14 **Daletme** Chin State, W Myanmar (Burma) 21°44′N 92°48′E
23 Q7 **Daleville** Alabama, S USA 31°18′N 85°42′W
98 M9 **Dalfsen** Overijssel, E Netherlands 52°31′N 06°16′E
114 M8 **Dalgopol** var. Dŭlgopol. Varna, E Bulgaria 43°05′N 27°24′E
24 M1 **Dalhart** Texas, SW USA 36°05′N 102°31′W
13 O13 **Dalhousie** New Brunswick, SE Canada 48°03′N 66°22′W
152 I6 **Dalhousie** Himāchal Pradesh, N India 32°32′N 76°01′E
160 F12 **Dali** var. Xiaguan. Yunnan, SW China 25°34′N 100°11′E
121 P2 **Dáli** var. Dhali. C Cyprus 35°01′N 33°25′E
163 U14 **Dalian** var. Dairen, Dalien, Jay Dairen, Lüda, Ta-lien, Rus. Dalny. Liaoning, NE China 38°53′N 121°37′E
105 O15 **Dalías** Andalucía, S Spain 36°49′N 02°50′W
**Dalien** see Dalian
**Dalijan** see Delījān
112 J9 **Dalj** Hung. Dalja. Osijek-Baranja, E Croatia 45°29′N 19°00′E
**Dalja** see Dalj
32 F12 **Dallas** Oregon, NW USA 44°56′N 123°20′W
25 U6 **Dallas** Texas, SW USA 32°47′N 96°48′W
25 T7 **Dallas-Fort Worth** ✈ Texas, SW USA 32°37′N 97°16′W
154 K12 **Dalli Rājhara** var. Dhalli Rajhara. Chhattīsgarh, C India 20°32′N 81°10′E
39 X15 **Dall Island** island Alexander Archipelago, Alaska, USA
38 M12 **Dall Lake** ◎ Alaska, USA
**Dállogilli** see Korpilombolo
77 S12 **Dallol Bosso** seasonal river W Niger
141 U7 **Dalmā** island W United Arab Emirates
113 E14 **Dalmacija** Eng. Dalmatia, Ger. Dalmatien, It. Dalmazia. cultural region S Croatia
**Dalmatia/Dalmatien/Dalmazia** see Dalmacija
123 S15 **Dal'negorsk** Primorskiy Kray, SE Russia 44°27′N 135°30′E
**Dalny** see Dalian
76 M16 **Daloa** C Ivory Coast 06°56′N 06°28′W
160 J11 **Dalou Shan** ▲▲ S China
181 X7 **Dalrymple Lake** ◎ Queensland, E Australia
14 H14 **Dalrymple Lake** ◎ Ontario, S Canada
181 X7 **Dalrymple, Mount** ▲ Queensland, E Australia 21°01′S 148°34′E
93 K20 **Dalsbruk** Fin. Taalintehdas. Varsinais-Suomi, SW Finland 60°02′N 22°31′E
95 K19 **Dalsjöfors** Västra Götaland, S Sweden 57°43′N 13°05′E
95 J17 **Dals Långed** var. Långed. Västra Götaland, S Sweden 58°54′N 12°20′E
153 O15 **Dāltenganj** prev. Daltonganj. Jhārkhand, N India 24°02′N 84°07′E
23 R2 **Dalton** Georgia, SE USA 34°46′N 84°58′W
**Daltonganj** see Dāltenganj
195 X14 **Dalton Iceberg Tongue** ice feature Antarctica
92 J1 **Dalvík** Norðurland Eystra, N Iceland 65°58′N 18°31′W
**Dálvvadis** see Jokkmokk
35 N8 **Daly City** California, W USA 37°44′N 122°27′W
181 P2 **Daly River** ≈ Northern Territory, N Australia
181 Q3 **Daly Waters** Northern Territory, N Australia 16°21′S 133°22′E
119 F20 **Damachava** var. Damachova, Pol. Domaczewo, Rus. Domachëvo. Brestskaya Voblasts', SW Belarus 51°45′N 23°36′E
**Damachova** see Damachava
77 W11 **Damagaram Takaya** Zinder, S Niger 14°02′N 09°28′E
154 D12 **Damān** Damān and Diu, W India 20°25′N 72°58′E
154 B12 **Damān and Diu** ◈ union territory W India
75 V7 **Damanhûr** anc. Hermopolis Parva. N Egypt 31°03′N 30°28′E
161 O1 **Damaqun Shan** ▲▲ E China
79 I15 **Damara** Ombella-Mpoko, S Central African Republic 05°00′N 18°45′E
83 D18 **Damaraland** physical region C Namibia
171 S15 **Damar, Kepulauan** var. Baraf Daja Islands, Kepulauan Barat Daya. island group C Indonesia
168 J8 **Damar Laut** Perak, Peninsular Malaysia 04°13′N 100°36′E
171 S15 **Damar, Pulau** island Maluku, E Indonesia
**Damas** see Dimashq
77 Y12 **Damasak** Borno, NE Nigeria 13°10′N 12°40′E
**Damasco** see Dimashq
21 Q8 **Damascus** Virginia, NE USA 36°37′N 81°46′W
**Damascus** see Dimashq
77 X13 **Damaturu** Yobe, NE Nigeria 11°44′N 11°58′E
171 R9 **Damau** Pulau Kaburuang, N Indonesia 03°46′N 126°49′E
143 O5 **Damāvand, Kūh-e** ▲ N Iran 35°56′N 52°08′E
82 B10 **Damba** Uíge, NW Angola 06°44′S 15°20′E
114 M12 **Dambaslar** Tekirdağ, NW Turkey 41°13′N 27°13′E
116 J13 **Dâmbovița** prev. Dîmbovița. ◈ county SE Romania
116 J13 **Dâmbovița** prev. Dîmbovița. ≈ S Romania
173 Y15 **D'Ambre, Île** island NE Mauritius
155 K24 **Dambulla** Central Province, C Sri Lanka 07°51′N 80°40′E
44 K9 **Dame-Marie** SW Haiti 18°36′N 74°26′W
44 J9 **Dame Marie, Cap** headland SW Haiti 18°37′N 74°24′W
143 Q4 **Dāmghān** Semnān, N Iran 36°13′N 54°22′E
**Damietta** see Dumyāt
138 G10 **Dāmiyā** Al Balqā', NW Jordan 32°07′N 35°33′E
146 G11 **Damla** Daşoguz Welaýaty, N Turkmenistan 40°05′N 59°15′E
**Dammām** see Ad Dammām
100 G12 **Damme** Niedersachsen, NW Germany 52°31′N 08°12′E
153 R15 **Dāmodar** ≈ NE India
154 J9 **Damoh** Madhya Pradesh, C India 23°50′N 79°30′N
77 P15 **Damongo** NW Ghana 09°05′N 01°49′W
138 G7 **Damoûr** var. Ad Dāmūr. W Lebanon 33°36′N 35°30′E
171 N11 **Dampal, Teluk** bay Sulawesi, C Indonesia
180 H7 **Dampier** Western Australia 20°40′S 116°40′E
180 H6 **Dampier Archipelago** island group Western Australia
141 U14 **Damqawt** var. Damqut. E Yemen 16°35′N 52°39′E
159 O13 **Dam Qu** ≈ C China
**Damqut** see Damqawt
167 R13 **Dâmrei, Chuŏr Phnum** Fr. Chaîne de l'Éléphant. ▲▲ SW Cambodia
108 C7 **Damvant** Jura, NW Switzerland 47°22′N 06°55′E
**Damwâld** see Damwoude
98 L5 **Damwoude** Fris. Damwâld. Fryslân, N Netherlands 53°18′N 05°59′E
159 N15 **Damxung** var. Gongtang. Xizang Zizhiqu, W China 30°29′N 91°02′E
80 K11 **Danakil Desert** var. Afar Depression, Danakil Plain. desert E Africa
**Danakil Plain** see Danakil Desert
35 R8 **Dana, Mount** ▲ California, W USA 37°54′N 119°13′W
76 L16 **Danané** W Ivory Coast 07°16′N 08°09′W
167 U10 **Đa Nẵng** prev. Tourane. Quang Nam-Đa Nẵng, C Vietnam 16°04′N 108°14′E
160 G9 **Danba** var. Zhanggu, Tib. Rongzhag. Sichuan, C China 30°54′N 101°49′E
**Danborg** see Daneborg
18 L13 **Danbury** Connecticut, NE USA 41°21′N 73°27′W
25 W12 **Danbury** Texas, SW USA 29°13′N 95°20′W
35 X15 **Danby Lake** ◎ California, W USA
194 H4 **Danco Coast** physical region Antarctica
82 B11 **Dande** ≈ NW Angola
**Dandeldhura** see Dadeldhurā
155 E17 **Dandeli** Karnātaka, W India 15°18′N 74°42′E
183 O12 **Dandenong** Victoria, SE Australia 38°01′S 145°13′E
163 V13 **Dandong** var. Tan-tung; prev. An-tung. Liaoning, NE China 40°10′N 124°23′E
197 Q14 **Daneborg** var. Danborg. ◈ N Greenland
25 V12 **Danevang** Texas, SW USA 29°03′N 96°11′W
**Dänew** see Galkynyş
**Danfeng** see Shizong
14 L12 **Danford Lake** Québec, SE Canada 45°55′N 76°12′W
19 T4 **Danforth** Maine, NE USA 45°39′N 67°54′W
37 P3 **Danforth Hills** ▲▲ Colorado, C USA
**Dangara** see Danghara
159 V12 **Dangchang** Gansu, C China 34°01′N 104°19′E
159 P8 **Dangchengwan** var. Subei, Subei Mongolzu Zizhixian. Gansu, N China 39°33′N 94°50′E
82 B10 **Dange** Uíge, NW Angola 07°55′S 15°01′E
**Dangerous Archipelago** see Tuamotu, Îles
83 E26 **Danger Point** headland SW South Africa 34°37′S 19°20′E
147 Q13 **Danghara** Rus. Dangara. SW Tajikistan 38°05′N 69°14′E
159 P8 **Danghe Nanshan** ▲▲ W China
80 I12 **Dangila** var. Dänglā. Āmara, NW Ethiopia 11°08′N 36°51′E
159 P8 **Dangjin Shankou** pass N China
**Dangla** see Tanggula Shan, China
**Dang La** see Tanggula Shankou, China
**Dänglā** see Dangila, Ethiopia
**Dangme Chu** see Manās
153 Y11 **Dāngori** Assam, NE India 27°40′N 95°35′E
**Dangrek, Chaîne des** see Dangrek Mountains
**Dângrêk, Chuŏr Phnum** see Dangrek Mountains
167 S11 **Dangrek Mountains** Khm. Chuŏr Phnum Dângrêk, Thai. Thiu Khao Phanom Dong Rak, Fr. Chaîne des Dangrek. ▲▲ Cambodia/Thailand
42 G3 **Dangriga** prev. Stann Creek. Stann Creek, E Belize 16°59′N 88°13′W
161 P6 **Dangshan** Anhui, E China 34°22′N 116°21′E
33 T15 **Daniel** Wyoming, C USA 42°49′N 110°04′W
83 H22 **Daniëlskuil** Northern Cape, N South Africa 28°11′S 23°33′E
19 N12 **Danielson** Connecticut, NE USA 41°48′N 71°53′W
124 M15 **Danilov** Yaroslavskaya Oblast', W Russia 58°11′N 40°11′E
127 O9 **Danilovka** Volgogradskaya Oblast', SW Russia 50°21′N 44°03′E
**Danish West Indies** see Virgin Islands (US)
160 L7 **Dan Jiang** ≈ C China
160 M7 **Danjiangkou Shuiku** ⊠ C China
141 W8 **Dank** var. Dhank. NW Oman 23°34′N 56°16′E
152 J7 **Dankhar** Himāchal Pradesh, N India 32°08′N 78°12′E
126 L6 **Dankov** Lipetskaya Oblast', W Russia 53°17′N 39°07′E
42 J7 **Danlí** El Paraíso, S Honduras 14°02′N 86°34′W
**Danmark** see Denmark
**Danmark, Kongeriget** see Denmark
**Danmarksstraedet** see Denmark Strait
95 O14 **Dannemora** Uppsala, C Sweden 60°13′N 17°49′E
18 L6 **Dannemora** New York, NE USA 44°42′N 73°42′W
100 K11 **Dannenberg** Niedersachsen, N Germany 53°05′N 11°06′E
184 N12 **Dannevirke** Manawatu-Wanganui, North Island, New Zealand 40°14′S 176°05′E
21 U8 **Dan River** ≈ Virginia, NE USA
167 P8 **Dan Sai** Loei, C Thailand 17°15′N 101°04′E
18 F10 **Dansville** New York, NE USA 42°34′N 77°40′W
**Dantzig** see Gdańsk
86 E12 **Danube** Bul. Dunav, Cz. Dunaj, Ger. Donau, Hung. Duna, Rom. Dunărea, Ukr. Dunay. ≈ C Europe
**Danubian Plain** see Dunavska Ravnina
166 L8 **Danubyu** Ayeyarwady, SW Myanmar (Burma) 17°15′N 95°35′E
**Danum** see Doncaster
19 P11 **Danvers** Massachusetts, NE USA 42°34′N 70°54′W
27 T11 **Danville** Arkansas, C USA 35°03′N 93°22′W
31 N13 **Danville** Illinois, N USA 40°10′N 87°37′W
31 O14 **Danville** Indiana, N USA 39°45′N 86°31′W
29 Y15 **Danville** Iowa, C USA 40°52′N 91°18′W
20 M6 **Danville** Kentucky, S USA 37°40′N 84°49′W
18 G14 **Danville** Pennsylvania, NE USA 40°57′N 76°36′W
21 T6 **Danville** Virginia, NE USA 36°34′N 79°25′W
**Danxian/Dan Xian** see Danzhou


◆ Country ● Country Capital ◇ Dependent Territory ○ Dependent Territory Capital ◈ Administrative Regions ✈ International Airport ▲ Mountain ▲▲ Mountain Range Volcano ≈ River ◎ Lake ⊠ Reservoir

DANZHOU – DEMBĪ DOLO


160 L17 **Danzhou** *prev.* Danxian, Dan Xian, Nada. Hainan, S China 19°31′N 109°31′E
**Danzhou** *see* Yichuan
**Danzig** *see* Gdańsk
**Danziger Bucht** *see* Gdańsk, Gulf of
**Danzig, Gulf of** *see* Gdańsk, Gulf of
160 F10 **Daocheng** *var.* Jinzhu, *Tib.* Dabba. Sichuan, C China 29°05′N 100°14′E
**Daojiang** *see* Daoxian
**Daokou** *see* Huaxian
104 H7 **Dão, Rio** ↝ N Portugal
**Daosa** *see* Dausa
77 Y7 **Dao Timmi** Agadez, NE Niger 20°31′N 13°34′E
160 M13 **Daoxian** *var.* Daojiang. Hunan, S China 25°30′N 111°37′E
77 Q14 **Dapaong** N Togo 10°52′N 00°12′E
23 N8 **Daphne** Alabama, S USA 30°36′N 87°54′W
171 P7 **Dapitan** Mindanao, S Philippines 08°39′N 123°26′E
159 P9 **Da Qaidam** Qinghai, C China 37°50′N 95°18′E
163 V8 **Daqing** *var.* Sartu. Heilongjiang, NE China 46°35′N 125°00′E
163 O13 **Daqing Shan** ▲ N China
163 T11 **Daqin Tal** *var.* Naiman Qi. Nei Mongol Zizhiqu, N China 42°51′N 120°41′E
**Daqm** *see* Duqm
160 G8 **Da Qu** *var.* Do Qu. ↝ C China
139 T5 **Dāqūq** *var.* Tāwūq. Kirkūk, N Iraq 35°08′N 44°27′E
76 G10 **Dara** *var.* Dahra. NW Senegal 15°20′N 15°28′W
138 H9 **Dar'ā** *var.* Der'a, *Fr.* Déraa. Dar'ā, SW Syria 32°37′N 36°06′E
138 H8 **Dar'ā** *off.* Muḩāfaz̧at Dar'ā, *var.* Darā, Der'a, Derrá. ◆ *governorate* S Syria
143 Q12 **Dārāb** Fārs, S Iran 28°52′N 54°25′E
116 K8 **Darabani** Botoşani, NW Romania 48°10′N 26°39′E
**Daraj** *see* Dirj
**Dar'ā, Muḩāfaz̧at** *see* Dar'ā
142 M8 **Dārān** Eşfahān, W Iran 33°00′N 50°27′E
167 U12 **Da Răng, Sông** *var.* Ba. ↝ S Vietnam
**Daraut-Kurgan** *see* Daroot-Korgon
77 W13 **Darazo** Bauchi, E Nigeria 11°01′N 10°27′E
139 S3 **Darband** Arbīl, N Iraq 36°15′N 44°17′E
147 Q12 **Darband** *prev.* Komsomolobod, *Rus.* Komosolabad. C Tajikistan 38°51′N 69°54′E
139 V4 **Darband-i Khān, Sadd** *dam* NE Iraq
118 C11 **Darbėnai** Klaipėda, NW Lithuania 56°02′N 21°16′E
153 Q13 **Darbhanga** Bihār, N India 26°10′N 85°54′E
38 M9 **Darby, Cape** *headland* Alaska, USA 64°19′N 162°46′W
112 I9 **Darda** *Hung.* Dárda. Osijek-Baranja, E Croatia 45°37′N 18°41′E
**Dárda** *see* Darda
**Dardanë** *see* Kamenicë
27 T11 **Dardanelle** Arkansas, C USA 35°11′N 93°09′W
27 S11 **Dardanelle, Lake** ⊠ Arkansas, C USA
**Dardanelles** *see* Çanakkale Boğazı
**Dardanelli** *see* Çanakkale
**Dardo** *see* Kangding
**Dar-el-Beida** *see* Casablanca
136 M14 **Darende** Malatya, C Turkey 38°34′N 37°29′E
81 J22 **Dar es Salaam** Dar es Salaam, E Tanzania 06°51′S 39°18′E
81 J22 **Dar es Salaam** ✈ Dar es Salaam, E Tanzania 06°57′S 39°17′E
185 H18 **Darfield** Canterbury, South Island, New Zealand 43°29′S 172°07′E
106 F7 **Darfo** Lombardia, N Italy 45°54′N 10°12′E
80 B10 **Darfur** *var.* Darfur Massif. *cultural region* W Sudan
**Darfur Massif** *see* Darfur
**Darganata/Dargan-Ata** *see* Birata
143 T3 **Dargaz** *var.* Darreh Gaz; *prev.* Moḩammadābād. Khorāsān-e Raẕavī, NE Iran 37°28′N 59°08′E
139 U4 **Dargazayn** As Sulaymānīyah, NE Iraq 35°39′N 45°00′E
183 P12 **Dargo** Victoria, SE Australia 37°29′S 147°15′E
162 L6 **Darhan** Darhan Uul, N Mongolia 49°24′N 105°57′E
163 N8 **Darhan** Hentiy, C Mongolia 46°38′N 109°25′E
**Darhan** *see* Büreghangay
**Darhan Muminggan Lianheqi** *see* Bailingmiao
162 L6 **Darhan Uul** ◆ *province* N Mongolia
23 W7 **Darien** Georgia, SE USA 31°22′N 81°25′W
43 W16 **Darién** *off.* Provincia del Darién. ◆ *province* SE Panama
**Darién, Golfo del** *see* Darien, Gulf of
43 X14 **Darien, Gulf of** *Sp.* Golfo del Darién. *gulf* S Caribbean Sea
**Darien, Isthmus of** *see* Panama, Istmo de
**Darién, Provincia del** *see* Darién
42 K9 **Dariense, Cordillera** ▲ C Nicaragua
43 W15 **Darién, Serranía del** ▲ Colombia/Panama
163 P10 **Dariganga** *var.* Ovoot. Sühbaatar, SE Mongolia 45°08′N 113°51′E
**Dario** *see* Ciudad Darío
**Dariorigum** *see* Vannes
**Dariv** *see* Darvi
**Darj** *see* Dirj
**Darjeeling** *see* Dārjiling
153 S12 **Dārjiling** *prev.* Darjeeling. West Bengal, NE India 27°00′N 88°13′E
**Darkehnen** *see* Ozersk
159 S12 **Darlag** *var.* Gümai. Qinghai, C China 33°43′N 99°42′E
183 T3 **Darling Downs** *hill range* Queensland, E Australia
28 M2 **Darling, Lake** ⊠ North Dakota, N USA
180 I12 **Darling Range** ▲ Western Australia
182 L8 **Darling River** ↝ New South Wales, SE Australia
97 M15 **Darlington** N England, United Kingdom 54°31′N 01°34′W
21 T12 **Darlington** South Carolina, SE USA 34°19′N 79°53′W
30 K9 **Darlington** Wisconsin, N USA 42°41′N 90°08′W
110 G7 **Darłowo** Zachodnio-pomorskie, NW Poland 54°24′N 16°21′E
101 G19 **Darmstadt** Hessen, SW Germany 49°52′N 08°39′E
75 S7 **Darnah** *var.* Dérna. NE Libya 32°46′N 22°39′E
103 S6 **Darney** Vosges, NE France 48°06′N 05°58′E
182 M7 **Darnick** New South Wales SE Australia 32°52′S 143°38′E
195 Y6 **Darnley, Cape** *cape* Antarctica
105 R7 **Daroca** Aragón, NE Spain 41°07′N 01°25′W
147 S11 **Daroot-Korgon** *var.* Daraut-Kurgan. Oshskaya Oblast', SW Kyrgyzstan 39°35′N 72°13′E
61 A23 **Darregueira** *var.* Darregueira. Buenos Aires, E Argentina 37°40′S 63°12′W
**Darregueira** *see* Darregueira
**Darreh Gaz** *see* Dargaz
142 K7 **Darreh Shahr** *var.* Darreh-ye Shahr. Īlām, W Iran 33°10′N 47°18′E
**Darreh-ye Shahr** *see* Darreh Shahr
32 I7 **Darrington** Washington, NW USA 48°15′N 121°36′W
25 P1 **Darrouzett** Texas, SW USA 36°27′N 100°19′W
153 S15 **Darsana** *var.* Darshana. Khulna, N Bangladesh 23°32′N 88°49′E
**Darshana** *see* Darsana
100 M7 **Darss** *peninsula* NE Germany
100 M7 **Darsser Ort** *headland* NE Germany 54°28′N 12°31′E
97 J24 **Dart** ↝ SW England, United Kingdom
**Dartang** *see* Baqên
97 P22 **Dartford** SE England, United Kingdom 51°27′N 00°13′E
182 L12 **Dartmoor** Victoria, SE Australia 37°56′S 141°18′E
97 I24 **Dartmoor** *moorland* SW England, United Kingdom
13 Q15 **Dartmouth** Nova Scotia, SE Canada 44°40′N 63°35′W
97 J24 **Dartmouth** SW England, United Kingdom 50°21′N 03°34′W
15 Y6 **Dartmouth** ↝ Québec, SE Canada
183 Q11 **Dartmouth Reservoir** ◎ Victoria, SE Australia
**Dartuch, Cabo** *see* Artrutx, Cap d'
186 C9 **Daru** Western, SW Papua New Guinea 09°05′S 143°10′E
112 G9 **Daruvar** *Hung.* Daruvár. Bjelovar-Bilogora, NE Croatia 45°34′N 17°12′E
**Daruvár** *see* Daruvar
**Darvaza** *see* Derweze, Turkmenistan
**Darvaza** *see* Darvoza, Uzbekistan
**Darvazskiy Khrebet** *see* Darvoz, Qatorkŭhi
**Darvel Bay** *see* Lahad Datu, Teluk
**Darvel, Teluk** *see* Lahad Datu, Teluk
162 F8 **Darvi** *var.* Dariv. Govĭ-Altay, W Mongolia 46°20′N 94°11′E
162 F7 **Darvi** *var.* Bulgan. Hovd, W Mongolia 46°57′N 93°40′E
**Darvīshān** *see* Darwēshān
147 O10 **Darvoza** *Rus.* Darvaza. Jizzax Viloyati, C Uzbekistan 40°59′N 67°19′E
147 R13 **Darvoz, Qatorkŭhi** *Rus.* Darvazskiy Khrebet. ▲ C Tajikistan
148 L9 **Darwēshān** , *var.* Garmser; *prev.* Darvīshān. Helmand, S Afghanistan 31°02′N 64°12′E
63 J15 **Darwin** Río Negro, S Argentina 39°13′S 65°41′W
181 O1 **Darwin** *prev.* Palmerston, Port Darwin. *territory capital* Northern Territory, N Australia 12°28′S 130°52′E
65 D24 **Darwin** *var.* Darwin Settlement. East Falkland, Falkland Islands 51°51′S 58°55′W
62 H8 **Darwin, Cordillera** ▲ N Chile
**Darwin Settlement** *see* Darwin
57 B17 **Darwin, Volcán** ⛰ Galapagos Islands, Ecuador, E Pacific Ocean 0°12′S 91°17′W
149 S8 **Darya Khan** Punjab, E Pakistan 31°47′N 71°10′E
145 O15 **Dar'yalyktakyr, Ravnina** *plain* S Kazakhstan
143 T11 **Dārzīn** Kermān, S Iran 29°11′N 58°09′E
**Dashhowuz** *see* Daşoguz
**Dashhowuz Welayaty** *see* Daşoguz Welaýaty
162 K7 **Dashinchilen** *var.* Süüj. Bulgan, C Mongolia 47°49′N 104°06′E
119 O16 **Dashkawka** *Rus.* Dashkovka. Mahilyowskaya Voblasts', E Belarus 53°44′N 30°16′E
**Dashkhovuz** *see* Daşoguz Welaýaty
**Dashkhovuzskiy Velayat** *see* Daşoguz Welaýaty
**Dashköpri** *see* Daşköpri
**Dashkovka** *see* Dashkawka
148 J15 **Dasht** ↝ SW Pakistan
**Dasht-i** *see* Bābūs, Dasht-e
**Dashtidzhum** *see* Dashtijum
147 R13 **Dashtijum** *Rus.* Dashtidzhum. SW Tajikistan 38°06′N 70°11′E
149 W7 **Daska** Punjab, NE Pakistan 32°15′N 74°23′E
146 J16 **Daşköpri** *var.* Dashköpri, *Rus.* Tashkepri. Mary Welaýaty, S Turkmenistan 36°15′N 62°37′E
146 H8 **Daşoguz** *Rus.* Dashkhovuz, *Turkm.* Dashhowuz; *prev.* Tashauz. Daşoguz Welaýaty, N Turkmenistan 41°51′N 59°53′E
146 E9 **Daşoguz Welaýaty** *var.* Dashhowuz Welayaty, *Rus.* Dashkhovuz, Dashkhovuzskiy Velayat. ◆ *province* N Turkmenistan
**Đa, Sông** *see* Black River
77 R15 **Dassa** *var.* Dassa-Zoumé. S Benin 07°46′N 02°15′E
**Dassa-Zoumé** *see* Dassa
29 U8 **Dassel** Minnesota, N USA 45°06′N 94°18′W
152 H3 **Dastegil Sar** ▲ N India
136 C16 **Datça** Muğla, SW Turkey 36°46′N 27°40′E
165 R4 **Date** Hokkaidō, NE Japan 42°28′N 140°51′E
154 I8 **Datia** *prev.* Duttia. Madhya Pradesh, C India 25°41′N 78°28′E
**Dåtnejævrie** *see* Tunnsjøen
159 T10 **Datong** *var.* Datong Huizu Tuzu Zizhixian, Qiaotou Qinghai, C China 37°01′N 101°33′E
161 N2 **Datong** *var.* Tatung, Ta-t'ung. Shanxi, C China 40°09′N 113°17′E
**Datong** *see* Tong'an
159 S8 **Datong He** ↝ C China
**Datong Huizu Tuzu Zizhixian** *see* Datong
159 S9 **Datong Shan** ▲ C China
169 O10 **Datu, Tanjung** *headland* Indonesia/Malaysia 02°01′N 109°37′E
**Datu, Teluk** *see* Lahad Datu, Teluk
**Daua** *see* Dawa Wenz
172 H16 **Dauban, Mount** ▲ Silhouette, NE Seychelles
149 T7 **Daud Khel** Punjab, E Pakistan 32°52′N 71°35′E
119 G15 **Daugai** Alytus, S Lithuania 54°22′N 24°20′E
**Daugava** *see* Western Dvina
118 J11 **Daugavpils** *Ger.* Dünaburg; *prev. Rus.* Dvinsk. SE Latvia 55°53′N 26°34′E
**Dauka** *see* Dawkah
**Daulatabad** *see* Malāyer
101 D18 **Daun** Rheinland-Pfalz, W Germany 50°13′N 06°50′E
155 E14 **Daund** *prev.* Dhond. Mahārāshtra, W India 18°28′N 74°38′E
166 M12 **Daung Kyun** *island* S Myanmar (Burma)
11 W15 **Dauphin** Manitoba, S Canada 51°09′N 100°05′W
103 S13 **Dauphiné** *cultural region* E France
23 N9 **Dauphin Island** *island* Alabama, S USA
11 X15 **Dauphin River** Manitoba, S Canada 51°55′N 98°03′W
77 V12 **Daura** Katsina, N Nigeria 13°03′N 08°18′E
152 H12 **Dausa** *prev.* Daosa. Rājasthān, N India 26°51′N 76°21′E
**Dauwa** *see* Dawwah
**Dāvāçi** *see* Şabran
155 F18 **Dāvangere** Karnātaka, W India 14°30′N 75°52′E
171 Q8 **Davao** *off.* Davao City. Mindanao, S Philippines 07°06′N 125°36′E
**Davao City** *see* Davao
171 Q8 **Davao Gulf** *gulf* Mindanao, S Philippines
15 Q11 **Daveluyville** Québec, SE Canada 46°12′N 72°07′W
29 Z14 **Davenport** Iowa, C USA 41°31′N 90°35′W
32 L8 **Davenport** Washington, NW USA 47°39′N 118°09′W
43 P16 **David** Chiriquí, W Panama 08°26′N 82°26′W
15 O11 **David** ↝ Québec, SE Canada
29 R15 **David City** Nebraska, C USA 41°15′N 97°07′W
**David-Gorodok** *see* Davyd-Haradok
11 T16 **Davidson** Saskatchewan, S Canada 51°15′N 105°59′W
21 R10 **Davidson** North Carolina, SE USA 35°29′N 80°49′W
26 K12 **Davidson** Oklahoma, C USA 34°15′N 99°06′W
39 S6 **Davidson Mountains** ▲ Alaska, USA
172 M8 **Davie Ridge** *undersea feature* W Indian Ocean 17°10′S 41°45′E
182 A1 **Davies, Mount** ▲ South Australia 26°14′S 129°14′E
35 O7 **Davis** California, W USA 38°31′N 121°46′W
27 N12 **Davis** Oklahoma, C USA 34°30′N 97°07′W
195 Y7 **Davis** *research station* (Australia) Antarctica 68°30′S 78°15′E
194 H3 **Davis Coast** *physical region* Antarctica
18 C16 **Davis, Mount** ▲ Pennsylvania, NE USA 39°47′N 79°10′W
24 K9 **Davis Mountains** ▲ Texas, SW USA
195 Z9 **Davis Sea** *sea* Antarctica
65 O20 **Davis Seamounts** *undersea feature* S Atlantic Ocean
196 M13 **Davis Strait** *strait* Baffin Bay/Labrador Sea
127 U5 **Davlekanovo** Respublika Bashkortostan, W Russia 54°13′N 55°06′E
108 J9 **Davos** *Rmsch.* Tavau. Graubünden, E Switzerland 46°48′N 09°50′E
**Davvesiida** *see* Lebesby
119 J20 **Davyd-Haradok** *Pol.* Dawidgródek, *Rus.* David-Gorodok. Brestskaya Voblasts', SW Belarus 52°03′N 27°13′E
163 U12 **Dawa** Liaoning, NE China 40°55′N 122°02′E
141 O11 **Dawāsir, Wādī ad** *dry watercourse* S Saudi Arabia
81 K15 **Dawa Wenz** *var.* Daua, Webi Daawo. ↝ E Africa
**Dawaymah, Birkat ad** *see* Umm al Baqar, Hawr
167 N10 **Dawei** *var.* Tavoy, Htawei. Tanintharyi, S Myanmar (Burma) 14°02′N 98°12′E
119 K14 **Dawhinava** *Rus.* Dolginovo. Minskaya Voblasts', N Belarus 54°39′N 27°29′E
**Dawidgródek** *see* Davyd-Haradok
141 V12 **Dawkah** *var.* Dauka. SW Oman 18°32′N 54°03′E
**Dawlat Qaṭar** *see* Qatar
140 L3 **Dawmat al Jandal** *off.* Jawf, *var.* Al Jawf. Al Jawf, NW Saudi Arabia 29°51′N 39°49′E
24 M3 **Dawn** Texas, SW USA 34°54′N 102°10′W
**Dawo** *see* Maqên
140 M11 **Daws** Al Bāḩah, SW Saudi Arabia 20°19′N 41°12′E
10 H5 **Dawson** *var.* Dawson City. Yukon, NW Canada 64°04′N 139°24′W
23 S6 **Dawson** Georgia, SE USA 31°46′N 84°27′W
29 S9 **Dawson** Minnesota, N USA 44°55′N 96°03′W
**Dawson City** *see* Dawson
11 N13 **Dawson Creek** British Columbia, W Canada 55°45′N 120°07′W
10 H7 **Dawson Range** ▲ Yukon, W Canada
181 Y9 **Dawson River** ↝ Queensland, E Australia
10 J15 **Dawsons Landing** British Columbia, SW Canada 51°33′N 127°38′W
20 I7 **Dawson Springs** Kentucky, S USA 37°10′N 87°41′W
23 S2 **Dawsonville** Georgia, SE USA 34°28′N 84°07′W
160 G8 **Dawu** *var.* Xianshui. Sichuan, C China 30°55′N 101°08′E
**Dawu** *see* Maqên
**Dawukou** *see* Huinong
141 Y10 **Dawwah** *var.* Dauwa. W Oman 20°36′N 58°52′E
102 J15 **Dax** *var.* Ax; *anc.* Aquae Augustae, Aquae Tarbelicae. Landes, SW France 43°43′N 01°03′W
**Daxian** *see* Dazhou
**Daxiangshan** *see* Gangu
**Daxue** *see* Wencheng
160 G9 **Daxue Shan** ▲ C China
**Dayan** *see* Lijiang
160 G12 **Dayao** *var.* Jinbi. Yunnan, SW China 25°41′N 101°23′E
**Dayishan** *see* Gaoyou
**Dāykondī** *see* Dāykundī
149 O6 **Dāykundī** *prev.* Dāykondī. ◆ *province* C Afghanistan
183 N12 **Daylesford** Victoria, SE Australia 37°24′S 144°07′E
35 U10 **Daylight Pass** *pass* California, W USA
61 D17 **Daymán, Río** ↝ N Uruguay
**Dayong** *see* Zhangjiajie
**Dayr** *see* Ad Dayr
138 G10 **Dayr 'Allā** *var.* Deir 'Alla. Al Balqā', N Jordan 32°39′N 36°06′E
139 N4 **Dayr az Zawr** *var.* Deir ez Zor. Dayr az Zawr, E Syria 35°12′N 40°12′E
138 M5 **Dayr az Zawr** *off.* Muḩāfaz̧at Dayr az Zawr, *var.* Dayr Az-Zor. ◆ *governorate* E Syria
**Dayr az Zawr, Muḩāfaz̧at** *see* Dayr az Zawr
**Dayr Az-Zor** *see* Dayr az Zawr
75 W9 **Dayrūṭ** *var.* Dairût. C Egypt 27°34′N 30°48′E
11 Q15 **Daysland** Alberta, SW Canada 52°53′N 112°19′W
31 R14 **Dayton** Ohio, N USA 39°46′N 84°12′W
20 L10 **Dayton** Tennessee, S USA 35°30′N 85°01′W
25 W11 **Dayton** Texas, SW USA 30°03′N 94°53′W
32 L10 **Dayton** Washington, NW USA 46°19′N 117°58′W
23 X10 **Daytona Beach** Florida, SE USA 29°12′N 81°03′W
169 U12 **Dayu** Borneo, C Indonesia 01°59′S 115°04′E
161 O13 **Dayu Ling** ▲ S China
161 R7 **Da Yunhe** *Eng.* Grand Canal. *canal* E China
161 S11 **Dayu Shan** *island* SE China
160 K8 **Dazhou** *prev.* Dachuan, Daxian. Sichuan, C China 31°16′N 107°31′E
160 J9 **Dazhu** *var.* Zhuyang. Sichuan, C China 30°45′N 107°11′E
160 J9 **Dazu** *var.* Longgang. Chongqing Shi, C China 29°47′N 106°30′E
83 H24 **De Aar** Northern Cape, C South Africa 30°40′S 24°01′E
194 K5 **Deacon, Cape** *headland* Antarctica
39 R5 **Deadhorse** Alaska, USA 70°15′N 148°28′W
33 T12 **Dead Indian Peak** ▲ Wyoming, C USA 44°36′N 109°45′W
23 R9 **Dead Lake** ◎ Florida, SE USA
44 J4 **Deadman's Cay** Long Island, C The Bahamas 23°09′N 75°06′W
138 G11 **Dead Sea** *var.* Bahret Lut, Lacus Asphaltites, *Ar.* Al Baḩr al Mayyit, Baḩrat Lūt, *Heb.* Yam HaMelaḩ. *salt lake* Israel/Jordan
28 J9 **Deadwood** South Dakota, N USA 44°22′N 103°43′W
**Dē Afghānistān Islāmī Jumhūriyat** *see* Afghanistan
97 Q22 **Deal** SE England, United Kingdom 51°14′N 01°23′E
83 I22 **Dealesville** Free State, C South Africa 28°40′S 25°46′E
161 P10 **De'an** *var.* Puting. Jiangxi, S China 29°24′N 115°46′E
62 K9 **Deán Funes** Córdoba, C Argentina 30°25′S 64°22′W
194 L12 **Dean Island** *island* Antarctica
**Deanuvuotna** *see* Tanafjorden
31 S10 **Dearborn** Michigan, N USA 42°16′N 83°13′W
27 R3 **Dearborn** Missouri, C USA 39°31′N 94°46′W
**Deargget** *see* Tārendö
149 O8 **Dē Arghistān Rōd** *prev.* Arghestān, Arghistān. ↝ SE Afghanistan
32 K9 **Deary** Idaho, NW USA 46°46′N 118°33′W
32 M9 **Deary** Washington, NW USA 46°42′N 116°36′W
10 J10 **Dease** ↝ British Columbia, W Canada
10 J10 **Dease Lake** British Columbia, W Canada 58°28′N 130°04′W
35 U11 **Death Valley** California, W USA 36°25′N 116°50′W
35 U11 **Death Valley** *valley* California, W USA
92 M8 **Deatnu** *Fin.* Tenojoki, *Nor.* Tana. ↝ Finland/Norway *see also* Tana, Tenojoki
**Deatnu** *see* Tana
102 L4 **Deauville** Calvados, N France 49°21′N 00°06′E
117 X7 **Debal'tseve** *Rus.* Debal'tsevo. Donets'ka Oblast', SE Ukraine 48°21′N 38°26′E
**Debal'tsevo** *see* Debal'tseve
113 M19 **Debar** *Ger.* Dibra, *Turk.* Debre. W North Macedonia 41°32′N 20°33′E
39 O9 **Debauch Mountain** ▲ Alaska, USA 64°31′N 159°52′W
**De Behagle** *see* Laï
25 X7 **De Berry** Texas, SW USA 32°18′N 94°09′W
**Debessy** *see* Debesy
127 T2 **Debesy** *prev.* Debessy. Udmurtskaya Respublika, NW Russia 57°41′N 53°56′E
111 N16 **Dębica** Podkarpackie, SE Poland 50°04′N 21°24′E
**De Bildt** *see* De Bilt
98 J11 **De Bilt** *var.* De Bildt. Utrecht, C Netherlands 52°06′N 05°11′E
123 T9 **Debin** Magadanskaya Oblast', E Russia 62°18′N 150°42′E
110 N13 **Dęblin** *Rus.* Ivangorod. Lubelskie, E Poland 51°34′N 21°50′E
110 D10 **Dębno** Zachodnio-pomorskie, NW Poland 52°43′N 14°42′E
39 S10 **Deborah, Mount** ▲ Alaska, USA 63°38′N 147°13′W
33 N8 **De Borgia** Montana, NW USA 47°23′N 115°24′W
**Debra Birhan** *see* Debre Birhan
**Debra Marcos** *see* Debre Mark'os
**Debra Tabor** *see* Debre Tabor
**Debre** *see* Debar
80 J13 **Debre Birhan** *var.* Debra Birhan. Āmara, N Ethiopia 09°45′N 39°40′E
111 N22 **Debrecen** *Ger.* Debreczin, *Rom.* Debreţin; *prev.* Debreczen. Hajdú-Bihar, E Hungary 47°32′N 21°38′E
**Debreczen/Debreczin** *see* Debrecen
80 I12 **Debre Mark'os** *var.* Debra Marcos. Āmara, N Ethiopia 10°18′N 37°48′E
113 N19 **Debrešte** SW North Macedonia 41°29′N 21°20′E
80 J11 **Debre Tabor** *var.* Debra Tabor. Āmara, N Ethiopia 11°46′N 38°06′E
**Debreţin** *see* Debrecen
80 J13 **Debre Zeyt** Oromīya, C Ethiopia 08°41′N 39°00′E
113 L16 **Deçan** *Serb.* Dečane; *prev.* Dečani. W Kosovo 42°33′N 20°18′E
**Dečane** *see* Deçan
**Dečani** *see* Deçan
23 P2 **Decatur** Alabama, S USA 34°36′N 86°58′W
23 S3 **Decatur** Georgia, SE USA 33°46′N 84°18′W
30 L13 **Decatur** Illinois, N USA 39°50′N 88°57′W
31 Q12 **Decatur** Indiana, N USA 40°40′N 84°57′W
22 M5 **Decatur** Mississippi, S USA 32°26′N 89°06′W
29 S14 **Decatur** Nebraska, C USA 42°00′N 96°19′W
25 S6 **Decatur** Texas, SW USA 33°14′N 97°35′W
20 H9 **Decaturville** Tennessee, S USA 35°35′N 88°08′W
103 O13 **Decazeville** Aveyron, S France 44°34′N 02°18′E
155 H17 **Deccan** *Hind.* Dakshin. *plateau* C India
14 J8 **Decelles, Réservoir** ⊠ Québec, SE Canada
12 K2 **Déception** Québec, NE Canada 62°06′N 74°36′W
160 G11 **Dechang** *var.* Dezhou. Sichuan, C China 27°24′N 102°09′E
111 C15 **Děčín** *Ger.* Tetschen. Ústecký Kraj, NW Czechia 50°48′N 14°15′E
103 P9 **Decize** Nièvre, C France 46°51′N 03°25′E
98 I6 **De Cocksdorp** Noord-Holland, NW Netherlands 53°09′N 04°52′E
29 X11 **Decorah** Iowa, C USA 43°18′N 91°47′W
**Dedeagaç/Dedeagach** *see* Alexandroúpoli
188 C15 **Dededo** N Guam 13°30′N 144°51′E
98 N9 **Dedemsvaart** Overijssel, E Netherlands 52°36′N 06°28′E
19 O11 **Dedham** Massachusetts, NE USA 42°14′N 71°10′W
63 H19 **Dedo, Cerro** ▲ SW Argentina 44°46′S 71°48′W
77 O13 **Dédougou** W Burkina Faso 12°29′N 03°25′W
124 G15 **Dedovichi** Pskovskaya Oblast', W Russia 57°31′N 29°53′E
**Dedu** *see* Wudalianchi
155 J24 **Deduru Oya** ↝ W Sri Lanka
83 N14 **Dedza** Central, S Malawi 14°20′S 34°24′E
83 N14 **Dedza Mountain** ▲ C Malawi 14°22′S 34°16′E
96 K9 **Dee** ↝ NE Scotland, United Kingdom
97 J19 **Dee** *Wel.* Afon Dyfrdwy. ↝ England/Wales, United Kingdom
**Deep Bay** *see* Chilumba
21 T3 **Deep Creek Lake** ⊠ Maryland, NE USA
36 J4 **Deep Creek Range** ▲ Utah, W USA
27 P10 **Deep Fork River** ↝ Oklahoma, C USA
14 J11 **Deep River** Ontario, SE Canada 46°04′N 77°29′W
21 T10 **Deep River** ↝ North Carolina, SE USA
183 U4 **Deepwater** New South Wales, SE Australia 29°27′S 151°52′E
31 S14 **Deer Creek Lake** ◎ Ohio, N USA
23 Z15 **Deerfield Beach** Florida, SE USA 26°19′N 80°06′W
39 N8 **Deering** Alaska, USA 66°04′N 162°43′W
38 M16 **Deer Island** *island* Alaska, USA
19 S7 **Deer Isle** *island* Maine, NE USA
13 S11 **Deer Lake** Newfoundland and Labrador, SE Canada 49°11′N 57°27′N
99 D18 **Deerlijk** West-Vlaanderen, W Belgium 50°52′N 03°21′E
33 Q10 **Deer Lodge** Montana, NW USA 46°24′N 112°43′W
32 L8 **Deer Park** Washington, NW USA 47°55′N 117°28′W
29 U5 **Deer River** Minnesota, N USA 47°19′N 93°47′W
**Deés** *see* Dej
**Defeng** *see* Liping
31 R11 **Defiance** Ohio, N USA 41°17′N 84°21′W
23 Q8 **De Funiak Springs** Florida, SE USA 30°43′N 86°07′W
95 L23 **Degeberga** Skåne, S Sweden 55°48′N 14°06′E
104 H12 **Degebe, Ribeira** ↝ S Portugal
80 M13 **Degeh Bur** Sumalē, E Ethiopia 08°08′N 43°35′E
15 U9 **Dégelis** Québec, SE Canada 47°30′N 68°38′W
77 U17 **Degema** Rivers, S Nigeria 04°46′N 06°47′E
95 L16 **Degerfors** Örebro, C Sweden 59°14′N 14°26′E
193 R14 **De Gerlache Seamounts** *undersea feature* SE Pacific Ocean
101 N21 **Deggendorf** Bayern, SE Germany 48°50′N 12°58′E
80 I11 **Degoma** Āmara, N Ethiopia 12°22′N 37°36′E
**De Gordyk** *see* Gorredijk
27 T12 **De Gray Lake** ⊠ Arkansas, C USA
180 J6 **De Grey River** ↝ Western Australia
126 M10 **Degtevo** Rostovskaya Oblast', SW Russia 49°12′N 40°39′E
**Dehbārez** *see* Rūdān
**Deh Bid** *see* Şafāshahr
142 M10 **Deh Dasht** Kohkīlūyeh va Būyer AḨmad, SW Iran 30°49′N 50°36′E
148 K10 **Deh-e Shū** *var.* Deshu, Dīshū. Helmand, S Afghanistan 30°28′N 63°21′E
**Dehli** *see* Delhi
142 K8 **Dehlorān** Īlām, W Iran 32°41′N 47°18′E
147 N13 **Dehqonobod** *Rus.* Dekhkanabad. Qashqadaryo Viloyati, S Uzbekistan 38°24′N 66°31′E
152 J9 **Dehra Dūn** Uttaranchal, N India 30°19′N 78°04′E
153 O14 **Dehri** Bihār, N India 24°55′N 84°11′E
163 W9 **Dehui** Jilin, NE China 44°23′N 125°42′E
99 D17 **Deinze** Oost-Vlaanderen, NW Belgium 50°59′N 03°32′E
**Deir 'Alla** *see* Dayr 'Allā
**Deir ez Zor** *see* Dayr az Zawr
**Deirgeirt, Loch** *see* Derg, Lough
116 H9 **Dej** *Hung.* Dés; *prev.* Deés. Cluj, NW Romania 47°08′N 23°55′E
95 K15 **Deje** Värmland, C Sweden 59°35′N 13°29′E
171 Y15 **De Jongs, Tanjung** *headland* Papua, SE Indonesia 06°56′S 138°32′E
**De Jouwer** *see* Joure
30 M10 **De Kalb** Illinois, N USA 41°55′N 88°45′W
22 M5 **De Kalb** Mississippi, S USA 32°46′N 88°39′W
25 W5 **De Kalb** Texas, SW USA 33°30′N 94°34′W
83 G18 **Dekar** *var.* D'Kar. Ghanzi, NW Botswana 21°31′S 21°55′E
79 K20 **Dekese** Kasai-Occidental, C Dem. Rep. Congo 03°28′S 21°24′E
**Dekhkanabad** *see* Dehqonobod
79 I14 **Dékoa** Kémo, C Central African Republic 06°17′N 19°07′E
98 H6 **De Koog** Noord-Holland, NW Netherlands 53°06′N 04°43′E
30 M9 **Delafield** Wisconsin, N USA 43°03′N 88°22′W
61 C23 **De La Garma** Buenos Aires, E Argentina 37°58′S 60°25′W
14 K10 **Delahey, Lac** ◎ Québec, SE Canada
80 E11 **Delami** Southern Kordofan, C Sudan 11°51′N 30°30′E
23 X11 **De Land** Florida, SE USA 29°01′N 81°18′W
35 R12 **Delano** California, W USA 35°46′N 119°15′W
29 V8 **Delano** Minnesota, N USA 45°03′N 93°46′W
36 K6 **Delano Peak** ▲ Utah, W USA 38°22′N 112°21′W
**Delap-Uliga-Darrit** *see* Dalap-Uliga-Djarrit
**Delārām** *see* Dilārām
38 F17 **Delarof Islands** *island group* Aleutian Islands, Alaska, USA
30 M9 **Delavan** Wisconsin, N USA 42°37′N 88°37′W
31 S13 **Delaware** Ohio, N USA 40°18′N 83°06′W
18 I17 **Delaware** *off.* State of Delaware, *also known as* Blue Hen State, Diamond State, First State. ◆ *state* NE USA
18 I17 **Delaware Bay** *bay* NE USA
24 J8 **Delaware Mountains** ▲ Texas, SW USA
18 I12 **Delaware River** ↝ NE USA
27 Q3 **Delaware River** ↝ Kansas, C USA
18 J14 **Delaware Water Gap** *valley* New Jersey/Pennsylvania, NE USA
101 G14 **Delbrück** Nordrhein-Westfalen, W Germany 51°46′N 08°34′E
11 Q15 **Delburne** Alberta, SW Canada 52°09′N 113°11′W
172 M12 **Del Cano Rise** *undersea feature* SW Indian Ocean 45°15′S 44°15′E
113 Q18 **Delčevo** NE North Macedonia 41°57′N 22°45′E
**Delcommune, Lac** *see* Nzilo, Lac
98 O10 **Delden** Overijssel, E Netherlands 52°16′N 06°41′E
183 R12 **Delegate** New South Wales, SE Australia 37°04′S 148°57′E
**De Lemmer** *see* Lemmer
108 D7 **Delémont** *Ger.* Delsberg. Jura, NW Switzerland 47°22′N 07°21′E
25 R7 **De Leon** Texas, SW USA 32°06′N 98°33′W
115 F18 **Delfoí** Stereá Elláda, C Greece 38°28′N 22°31′E
98 G12 **Delft** Zuid-Holland, W Netherlands 52°01′N 04°22′E
155 J23 **Delft** *island* NW Sri Lanka
98 O5 **Delfzijl** Groningen, NE Netherlands 53°20′N 06°55′E
0 E9 **Delgada Fan** *undersea feature* NE Pacific Ocean 39°15′N 126°00′W
42 F7 **Delgado** San Salvador, SW El Salvador 13°44′N 89°07′W
82 Q12 **Delgado, Cabo** *headland* N Mozambique 10°41′S 40°40′E
162 G8 **Delger** *var.* Taygan. Govĭ-Altay, C Mongolia 46°20′N 97°22′E
163 O9 **Delgereh** *var.* Hongor. Dornogovĭ, SE Mongolia 45°49′N 111°20′E
162 J8 **Delgerhaan** *var.* Hujirt. Töv, C Mongolia 46°41′N 104°40′E
162 K9 **Delgerhangay** *var.* Hashaat. Dundgovĭ, C Mongolia 45°09′N 104°51′E
162 L9 **Delgertsogt** *var.* Amardalay. Dundgovĭ, C Mongolia 46°09′N 106°24′E
80 E6 **Delgo** Northern, N Sudan 20°08′N 30°35′E
159 R10 **Delhi** *var.* Delingha. Qinghai, C China 37°19′N 97°22′E
152 I10 **Delhi** *var.* Dehli, *Hind.* Dilli, *hist.* Shahjahanabad. *union territory capital* Delhi, N India 28°40′N 77°11′E
22 J5 **Delhi** Louisiana, S USA 32°28′N 91°29′W
18 J11 **Delhi** New York, NE USA 42°16′N 74°55′W
152 I10 **Delhi** ◆ *union territory* NW India
136 J17 **Deli Burnu** *headland* S Turkey 36°43′N 34°55′E
136 J12 **Delice Çayı** ↝ C Turkey
55 X10 **Délices** C French Guiana 04°45′N 53°45′W
40 J6 **Delicias** *var.* Ciudad Delicias. Chihuahua, N Mexico 28°09′N 105°22′W
143 N7 **Delījān** *var.* Dalijan, Diljan. Markazī, W Iran 34°02′N 50°39′E
112 P12 **Deli Jovan** ▲ E Serbia
**Déli-Kárpátok** *see* Carpaţii Meridionali
8 I8 **Délįne** *prev.* Fort Franklin. Northwest Territories, NW Canada 65°10′N 123°30′W
**Delingha** *see* Delhi
15 Q7 **Delisle** Québec, SE Canada 48°39′N 71°42′W
11 T15 **Delisle** Saskatchewan, S Canada 51°54′N 107°01′W
101 M15 **Delitzsch** Sachsen, E Germany 51°31′N 12°19′E
33 Q12 **Dell** Montana, NW USA 44°41′N 112°42′W
24 I7 **Dell City** Texas, SW USA 31°56′N 105°12′W
103 U7 **Delle** Territoire-de-Belfort, E France 47°30′N 07°00′E
36 J9 **Dellenbaugh, Mount** ▲ Arizona, SW USA 36°06′N 113°32′W
29 R11 **Dell Rapids** South Dakota, N USA 43°50′N 96°42′W
21 Y4 **Delmar** Maryland, NE USA 38°26′N 75°32′W
18 K11 **Delmar** New York, NE USA 42°37′N 73°49′W
100 G11 **Delmenhorst** Niedersachsen, NW Germany 53°03′N 08°38′E
112 C9 **Delnice** Primorje-Gorski Kotar, NW Croatia 45°24′N 14°49′E
37 R7 **Del Norte** Colorado, C USA 37°40′N 106°21′W
39 N6 **De Long Mountains** ▲ Alaska, USA
183 P16 **Deloraine** Tasmania, SE Australia 41°34′S 146°43′E
11 W17 **Deloraine** Manitoba, S Canada 49°12′N 100°28′W
31 O12 **Delphi** Indiana, N USA 40°35′N 86°40′W
31 Q12 **Delphos** Ohio, N USA 40°49′N 84°20′W
23 Z15 **Delray Beach** Florida, SE USA 26°27′N 80°04′W
25 O12 **Del Rio** Texas, SW USA 29°23′N 100°56′W
**Delsberg** *see* Delémont
94 N11 **Delsbo** Gävleborg, C Sweden 61°49′N 16°34′E
37 P6 **Delta** Colorado, C USA 38°44′N 108°04′W
36 K5 **Delta** Utah, W USA 39°21′N 112°34′W
77 T17 **Delta** ◆ *state* S Nigeria
55 Q6 **Delta Amacuro** *off.* Territorio Delta Amacuro. ◆ *federal district* NE Venezuela
**Delta Amacuro, Territorio** *see* Delta Amacuro
39 S9 **Delta Junction** Alaska, USA 64°02′N 145°43′W
23 X11 **Deltona** Florida, SE USA 28°54′N 81°15′W
183 T5 **Delungra** New South Wales, SE Australia 29°40′S 150°49′E
162 D6 **Delüün** *var.* Rashaant. Bayan-Ölgiy, W Mongolia 47°48′N 90°45′E
154 C12 **Delvāda** Gujarāt, W India 20°46′N 71°02′E
61 B21 **Del Valle** Buenos Aires, E Argentina 35°55′S 60°42′W
**Delvina** *see* Delvinë
115 C15 **Delvináki** *var.* Dhelvinákion; *prev.* Pogónion. Ípeiros, W Greece 39°57′N 20°28′E
113 L23 **Delvinë** *var.* Delvina, *It.* Delvino. Vlorë, S Albania 39°56′N 20°07′E
**Delvino** *see* Delvinë
116 I7 **Delyatyn** Ivano-Frankivs'ka Oblast', W Ukraine 48°32′N 24°38′E
127 U5 **Dëma** ↝ W Russia
105 O5 **Demanda, Sierra de la** ▲ W Spain
39 T5 **Demarcation Point** *headland* Alaska, USA 69°40′N 141°19′W
79 K21 **Demba** Kasai-Occidental, C Dem. Rep. Congo 05°24′S 22°16′E
172 H13 **Dembéni** Grande Comore, NW Comoros 11°50′S 43°25′E
79 M15 **Dembia** Mbomou, SE Central African Republic 05°08′N 24°25′E
**Dembidollo** *see* Dembī Dolo
80 H13 **Dembī Dolo** *var.* Dembidollo. Oromīya, C Ethiopia 08°33′N 34°49′E




◆ Country
● Country Capital
◇ Dependent Territory
○ Dependent Territory Capital
◆ Administrative Regions
✈ International Airport
▲ Mountain
▲ Mountain Range
⛰ Volcano
↝ River
◎ Lake
⊠ Reservoir

Demchok – Díon


152 K6 **Demchok** *var.* Dêmqog. China/India 32°30′N 79°42′E *see also* Dêmqog
152 L6 **Demchok** *var.* Dêmqog. *disputed region* China/India *see also* Dêmqog
98 I12 **De Meern** Utrecht, C Netherlands 52°06′N 05°00′E
99 I17 **Demer** ≈ C Belgium
64 H12 **Demerara Plain** *undersea feature* W Atlantic Ocean 10°00′N 48°00′W
64 H12 **Demerara Plateau** *undersea feature* W Atlantic Ocean
55 T9 **Demerara River** ≈ NE Guyana
126 H3 **Demidov** Smolenskaya Oblast', W Russia 55°15′N 31°30′E
37 Q15 **Deming** New Mexico, SW USA 32°17′N 107°46′W
32 H6 **Deming** Washington, NW USA 48°49′N 122°13′W
58 E10 **Demini, Rio** ≈ NW Brazil
136 D13 **Demirci** Manisa, W Turkey 39°03′N 28°40′E
113 P19 **Demir Kapija** *prev.* Železna Vrata. SE North Macedonia 41°25′N 22°15′E
114 N11 **Demirköy** Kırklareli, NW Turkey 41°48′N 27°49′E
100 N9 **Demmin** Mecklenburg-Vorpommern, NE Germany 53°53′N 13°03′E
23 O5 **Demopolis** Alabama, S USA 32°31′N 87°50′W
31 N11 **Demotte** Indiana, N USA 41°13′N 87°07′W
158 F13 **Dêmqog** *var.* Demchok. China/India 32°36′N 79°29′E *see also* Demchok
152 L6 **Dêmqog** *var.* Demchok. *disputed region* China/India *see also* Demchok
171 Y13 **Demta** Papua, E Indonesia 02°19′S 140°06′E
121 K11 **Dem'yanka** ≈ C Russia
124 H15 **Demyansk** Novgorodskaya Oblast', W Russia 57°39′N 32°31′E
122 H10 **Dem'yanskoye** Tyumenskaya Oblast', C Russia 59°39′N 69°15′E
103 P2 **Denain** Nord, N France 50°19′N 03°24′E
39 S10 **Denali** Alaska, USA 63°08′N 147°33′W
39 Q10 **Denali** *var.* Mount McKinley. ▲ Alaska, USA 63°04′N 151°00′W
81 M14 **Denan** Sumalē, E Ethiopia 06°40′N 43°31′E
**Denau** *see* Denov
97 J18 **Denbigh** *Wel.* Dinbych. NE Wales, United Kingdom 53°11′N 03°25′W
97 J18 **Denbigh** *cultural region* N Wales, United Kingdom
98 I6 **Den Burg** Noord-Holland, NW Netherlands 53°03′N 04°47′E
99 F18 **Dender** *Fr.* Dendre. ≈ W Belgium
99 F18 **Denderleeuw** Oost-Vlaanderen, NW Belgium 50°53′N 04°05′E
99 F17 **Dendermonde** *Fr.* Termonde. Oost-Vlaanderen, NW Belgium 51°02′N 04°08′E
**Dendre** *see* Dender
194 I9 **Dendtler Island** *island* Antarctica
98 P10 **Denekamp** Overijssel, E Netherlands 52°23′N 07°E
77 W12 **Dengas** Zinder, S Niger 13°15′N 09°43′E
**Dêngka** *see* Têwo
**Dêngkagoin** *see* Têwo
162 L13 **Dengkou** *var.* Bayan Gol. Nei Mongol Zizhiqu, N China 40°15′N 106°59′E
159 Q14 **Dêngqên** *var.* Gyamotang. Xizang Zizhiqu, W China 31°28′N 95°28′E
**Deng Xian** *see* Dengzhou
160 M7 **Dengzhou** *prev.* Deng Xian. Henan, C China 32°48′N 111°59′E
**Dengzhou** *see* Penglai
**Den Haag** *see* 's-Gravenhage
180 H10 **Denham** Western Australia 25°56′S 113°35′E
98 N9 **Den Ham** Overijssel, E Netherlands 52°30′N 06°31′E
44 J12 **Denham, Mount** ▲ C Jamaica 18°13′N 77°33′W
22 J8 **Denham Springs** Louisiana, S USA 30°29′N 90°57′W
98 I7 **Den Helder** Noord-Holland, NW Netherlands 52°54′N 04°45′E
105 T11 **Dénia** Comunitat Valenciana, E Spain 38°51′N 00°07′E
189 Q8 **Denig** W Nauru
183 N10 **Deniliquin** New South Wales, SE Australia 35°33′S 144°58′E
29 T14 **Denison** Iowa, C USA 42°00′N 95°22′W
25 U5 **Denison** Texas, SW USA 33°45′N 96°32′W
144 L8 **Denisovka** *prev.* Ordzhonikidze. Kostanay, N Kazakhstan 52°27′N 61°42′E
136 D15 **Denizli** Denizli, SW Turkey 37°46′N 29°05′E
136 D15 **Denizli** ◈ *province* SW Turkey
**Denjong** *see* Sikkim
183 S7 **Denman** New South Wales, SE Australia 32°24′S 150°43′E
195 Y10 **Denman Glacier** *glacier* Antarctica
21 R14 **Denmark** South Carolina, SE USA 33°19′N 81°08′W
95 G23 **Denmark** *off.* Kingdom of Denmark, *Dan.* Danmark, Kongeriget Danmark; *anc.* Hafnia. ◆ *monarchy* N Europe
**Denmark, Kingdom of** *see* Denmark
92 H1 **Denmark Strait** *var.* Danmarksstraedet. *strait* Greenland/Iceland
45 T11 **Dennery** E Saint Lucia 13°55′N 60°53′W
98 I7 **Den Oever** Noord-Holland, NW Netherlands 52°56′N 05°01′E
147 O13 **Denov** *Rus.* Denau. Surkhondaryo Viloyati, S Uzbekistan 38°20′N 67°48′E
169 U17 **Denpasar** *prev.* Paloe. Bali, C Indonesia 08°40′S 115°14′E
116 E12 **Denta** Timiş, W Romania 45°20′N 21°15′E
21 Y3 **Denton** Maryland, NE USA 38°53′N 75°50′W
25 T6 **Denton** Texas, SW USA 33°11′N 97°08′W
186 G9 **D'Entrecasteaux Islands** *island group* SE Papua New Guinea
37 T4 **Denver** *state capital* Colorado, C USA 39°45′N 105°W
37 T4 **Denver** ✕ Colorado, C USA 39°57′N 104°38′W
24 L6 **Denver City** Texas, SW USA 32°57′N 102°49′W
152 J9 **Deoband** Uttar Pradesh, N India 29°41′N 77°40′E
**Deoghar** *see* Devghar
163 X15 **Deokjeok-gundo** *prev.* Tŏkchŏk-kundo. *island group* NW South Korea
154 E13 **Deolāli** Mahārāshtra, W India 19°55′N 73°49′E
154 I10 **Deori** Madhya Pradesh, C India 23°09′N 78°39′E
153 O12 **Deoria** Uttar Pradesh, N India 26°31′N 83°48′E
99 A17 **De Panne** West-Vlaanderen, W Belgium 51°06′N 02°35′E
**Departamento del Quindío** *see* Quindío
**Departamento de Narino,** *see* Nariño
54 M5 **Dependencia Federal** *off.* Territorio Dependencia Federal. ◈ *federal dependency* N Venezuela
**Dependencia Federal, Territorio** *see* Dependencia Federal
30 M7 **De Pere** Wisconsin, N USA 44°26′N 88°03′W
18 D10 **Depew** New York, NE USA 42°54′N 78°41′W
99 E17 **De Pinte** Oost-Vlaanderen, NW Belgium 51°00′N 03°37′E
25 V5 **Deport** Texas, SW USA 33°31′N 95°19′W
123 Q8 **Deputatskiy** Respublika Sakha (Yakutiya), NE Russia 69°18′N 139°48′E
**Dêqên** *see* Dagzê
27 S13 **De Queen** Arkansas, C USA 34°02′N 94°20′W
22 G8 **De Quincy** Louisiana, S USA 30°27′N 93°25′W
81 J20 **Dera** *spring/well* S Kenya 02°39′S 39°52′E
**Der'a/Derá/Déraa** *see* Dar'ā
149 S10 **Dera Ghazi Khan** *var.* Dera Ghazikhan. Punjab, C Pakistan 30°01′N 70°37′E
**Dera Ghazikhan** *see* Dera Ghazi Khan
149 S8 **Dera Ismail Khan** Khyber Pakhtunkhwa, C Pakistan 31°51′N 70°56′E
**Ðeravica** *see* Gjeravicë
116 L6 **Derazhnya** Khmel'nyts'ka Oblast', W Ukraine 49°16′N 27°24′E
127 R17 **Derbent** Respublika Dagestan, SW Russia 42°01′N 48°16′E
147 N13 **Derbent** Surkhondaryo Viloyati, S Uzbekistan 38°15′N 66°59′E
**Derbisīye** *see* Ad Darbāsīyah
79 M15 **Derbissaka** Mbomou, SE Central African Republic 05°43′N 24°48′E
180 L4 **Derby** Western Australia 17°18′S 123°37′E
97 M19 **Derby** C England, United Kingdom 52°55′N 01°30′W
27 N7 **Derby** Kansas, C USA 37°33′N 97°16′W
97 L18 **Derbyshire** *cultural region* C England, United Kingdom
112 O11 **Derdap** *physical region* E Serbia
**Dereli** *see* Gönoi
162 L9 **Deren** *var.* Tsant. Dundgovĭ, C Mongolia 46°16′N 106°55′E
171 W13 **Derew** ≈ Papua, E Indonesia
127 R8 **Dergachi** Saratovskaya Oblast', W Russia 51°15′N 48°58′E
**Dergachi** *see* Derhachi
97 C19 **Derg, Lough** *Ir.* Loch Deirgeirt. ◎ W Ireland
117 V5 **Derhachi** *Rus.* Dergachi. Kharkivs'ka Oblast', E Ukraine 50°09′N 36°11′E
22 G8 **De Ridder** Louisiana, S USA 30°51′N 93°18′W
137 P16 **Derik** Mardin, SE Turkey 37°22′N 40°16′E
83 E20 **Derm** Hardap, C Namibia 23°38′S 18°12′E
**Dermentobe** *see* Diirmentobe
27 W14 **Dermott** Arkansas, C USA 33°31′N 91°26′W
**Dérna** *see* Darnah
**Dernberg, Cape** *see* Dolphin Head
22 J11 **Dernieres, Isles** *island group* Louisiana, S USA
102 I4 **Déroute, Passage de la** *strait* Channel Islands/France
**Derrá** *see* Dar'ā
81 O16 **Derri** *prev.* Dirri. Galguduud, C Somalia 04°15′N 46°31′E
**Derry** *see* Londonderry
**Dertona** *see* Tortona
**Dertosa** *see* Tortosa
80 H8 **Derudeb** Red Sea, NE Sudan 17°31′N 36°07′E
112 H10 **Derventa** Republika Srpska, N Bosnia and Herzegovina 44°57′N 17°55′E
183 O16 **Derwent Bridge** Tasmania, SE Australia 42°10′S 146°13′E
183 O17 **Derwent, River** ≈ Tasmania, SE Australia
146 F10 **Derweze** *Rus.* Darvaza. Ahal Welaýaty, C Turkmenistan 40°10′N 58°27′E
**Deržavinsk** *see* Derzhavinsk
145 O9 **Derzhavinsk** *var.* Deržavinsk. ◈ Akmola, C Kazakhstan
**Dés** *see* Dej
57 J18 **Desaguadero** Puno, S Peru 16°35′S 69°05′W
57 J18 **Desaguadero, Río** ≈ Bolivia/Peru
191 W9 **Désappointement, Îles du** *island group* Îles Tuamotu, C French Polynesia
27 W11 **Des Arc** Arkansas, C USA 34°58′N 91°30′W
14 C10 **Desbarats** Ontario, S Canada 46°20′N 83°52′W
62 H13 **Descabezado Grande, Volcán** ⚶ C Chile 35°34′S 70°40′W
102 L9 **Descartes** Indre-et-Loire, C France 46°58′N 00°40′E
11 T13 **Deschambault Lake** ◎ Saskatchewan, C Canada
**Deschnaer Koppe** *see* Velká Deštná
32 I11 **Deschutes River** ≈ Oregon, NW USA
80 J12 **Desē** *var.* Desse, *It.* Dessie. Āmara, N Ethiopia 11°02′N 39°39′E
63 I20 **Deseado, Río** ≈ S Argentina
106 F8 **Desenzano del Garda** Lombardia, N Italy 45°28′N 10°31′E
36 K3 **Deseret Peak** ▲ Utah, W USA 40°27′N 112°37′W
64 P6 **Deserta Grande** *island* Madeira, Portugal, NE Atlantic Ocean
64 P6 **Desertas, Ilhas** *island group* Madeira, Portugal, NE Atlantic Ocean
35 X16 **Desert Center** California, W USA 33°42′N 115°22′W
35 V15 **Desert Hot Springs** California, W USA 33°57′N 116°33′W
14 K10 **Désert, Lac** ◎ Québec, SE Canada
36 J2 **Desert Peak** ▲ Utah, W USA 41°03′N 113°22′W
31 R11 **Deshler** Ohio, N USA 41°12′N 83°55′W
**Deshu** *see* Deh-e Shū
**Desiderii Fanum** *see* St-Dizier
106 D7 **Desio** Lombardia, N Italy 45°37′N 09°12′E
115 E15 **Deskáti** *var.* Dheskáti. Dytikí Makedonía, N Greece 39°55′N 21°49′E
28 L2 **Des Lacs River** ≈ North Dakota, N USA
27 X6 **Desloge** Missouri, C USA 37°52′N 90°31′W
11 Q12 **Desmarais** Alberta, W Canada 55°58′N 113°56′W
29 Q10 **De Smet** South Dakota, N USA 44°23′N 97°33′W
29 V14 **Des Moines** *state capital* Iowa, C USA 41°36′N 93°37′W
17 N9 **Des Moines River** ≈ C USA
117 P4 **Desna** ≈ Russia/Ukraine
116 G14 **Desnățui** ≈ S Romania
63 F24 **Desolación, Isla** *island* S Chile
29 V14 **De Soto** Iowa, C USA 41°31′N 94°00′W
23 Q4 **De Soto Falls** *waterfall* Alabama, S USA
83 I25 **Despatch** Eastern Cape, S South Africa 33°48′S 25°28′E
105 N12 **Despeñaperros, Desfiladero de** *pass* S Spain
31 N10 **Des Plaines** Illinois, N USA 42°01′N 87°52′W
115 J21 **Despotikó** *island* Kykládes, Greece, Aegean Sea
112 N12 **Despotovac** Serbia, E Serbia 44°06′N 21°25′E
101 M14 **Dessau** Sachsen-Anhalt, E Germany 51°51′N 12°15′E
**Desse** *see* Desē
99 J16 **Dessel** Antwerpen, N Belgium 51°15′N 05°07′E
**Dessie** *see* Desē
**Destêrro** *see* Florianópolis
23 P9 **Destin** Florida, SE USA 30°23′N 86°30′W
**Deštná** *see* Velká Deštná
193 T10 **Desventurados, Islas de los** *island group* W Chile
103 N1 **Desvres** Pas-de-Calais, N France 50°41′N 01°48′E
116 E12 **Deta** *Ger.* Detta. Timiş, W Romania 45°24′N 21°14′E
101 H14 **Detmold** Nordrhein-Westfalen, W Germany 51°55′N 08°52′E
31 S10 **Detroit** Michigan, N USA 42°20′N 83°03′W
25 W5 **Detroit** Texas, SW USA 33°39′N 95°16′W
31 S10 **Detroit** ≈ Canada/USA
29 S6 **Detroit Lakes** Minnesota, N USA 46°49′N 95°49′W
31 S10 **Detroit Metropolitan** ✕ Michigan, N USA 42°12′N 83°16′W
**Detta** *see* Deta
167 S10 **Det Udom** Ubon Ratchathani, E Thailand 14°54′N 105°03′E
111 K20 **Detva** *Hung.* Gyeva. Bankobýstrický Kraj, C Slovakia 48°35′N 19°25′E
154 G13 **Deūlgaon Rāja** Mahārāshtra, C India 20°04′N 76°08′E
99 L15 **Deurne** Noord-Brabant, SE Netherlands 51°28′N 05°47′E
99 H16 **Deurne** ✕ (Antwerpen) Antwerpen, N Belgium 51°10′N 04°28′E
**Deutsch-Brod** *see* Havlíčkův Brod
**Deutschendorf** *see* Poprad
**Deutsch-Eylau** *see* Iława
109 Y6 **Deutschkreutz** Burgenland, E Austria 47°37′N 16°37′E
**Deutsch Krone** *see* Wałcz
**Deutschland/Deutschland, Bundesrepublik** *see* Germany
109 V9 **Deutschlandsberg** Steiermark, SE Austria 46°52′N 15°13′E
**Deutsch-Südwestafrika** *see* Namibia
109 Y3 **Deutsch-Wagram** Niederösterreich, E Austria 48°19′N 16°33′E
**Deux-Ponts** *see* Zweibrücken
14 I11 **Deux Rivieres** Ontario, SE Canada 46°13′N 78°16′W
102 K9 **Deux-Sèvres** ◈ *department* W France
116 G11 **Deva** *Ger.* Diemrich, *Hung.* Déva. Hunedoara, W Romania 45°55′N 22°55′E
**Déva** *see* Deva
**Deva** *see* Chester
**Devana** *see* Aberdeen
**Devana Castra** *see* Chester
**Đevđelija** *see* Gevgelija
136 L12 **Deveci Dağları** ▲▲ N Turkey
137 P15 **Devegeçidi Barajı** ⊠ SE Turkey
136 K15 **Develi** Kayseri, C Turkey 38°22′N 35°28′E
98 M11 **Deventer** Overijssel, E Netherlands 52°15′N 06°10′E
15 O10 **Devenyns, Lac** ◎ Québec, SE Canada
96 K8 **Deveron** ≈ NE Scotland, United Kingdom
153 R14 **Devghar** *prev.* Deoghar. Jhārkhand, NE India
27 R10 **Devil's Den** *plateau* Arkansas, C USA
35 R7 **Devils Gate** *pass* California, W USA
30 J2 **Devils Island** *island* Apostle Islands, Wisconsin, N USA
**Devil's Island** *see* Diable, Île du
29 P3 **Devils Lake** North Dakota, N USA 48°08′N 98°50′W
31 R10 **Devils Lake** ◎ Michigan, N USA
29 O3 **Devils Lake** ◎ North Dakota, N USA
35 W13 **Devils Playground** *desert* California, W USA
25 O11 **Devils River** ≈ Texas, SW USA
33 Y12 **Devils Tower** ▲ Wyoming, C USA 44°33′N 104°45′W
114 I11 **Devin** *prev.* Dovlen. Smolyan, S Bulgaria 41°45′N 24°24′E
25 R12 **Devine** Texas, SW USA 29°08′N 98°54′W
152 H13 **Devli** Rājasthān, N India 25°47′N 75°23′E
**Devne** *see* Devnya
114 N8 **Devnya** *prev.* Devne. Varna, E Bulgaria 43°15′N 27°35′E
31 U14 **Devola** Ohio, N USA 39°28′N 81°28′W
**Devoll** *see* Devollit, Lumi i
113 M21 **Devollit, Lumi i** *var.* Devoll. ≈ SE Albania
11 Q14 **Devon** Alberta, SW Canada 53°21′N 113°47′W
97 I23 **Devon** *cultural region* SW England, United Kingdom
197 N10 **Devon Island** *prev.* North Devon Island. *island* Parry Islands, Nunavut, NE Canada
183 O16 **Devonport** Tasmania, SE Australia 41°14′S 146°21′E
136 H11 **Devrek** Zonguldak, N Turkey 41°14′N 31°57′E
154 G10 **Dewās** Madhya Pradesh, C India 22°59′N 76°03′E
**De Westerein** *see* Zwaagwesteinde
27 P8 **Dewey** Oklahoma, C USA 36°48′N 95°56′W
**Dewey** *see* Culebra
98 M8 **De Wijk** Drenthe, NE Netherlands 52°41′N 06°13′E
27 W12 **De Witt** Arkansas, C USA 34°17′N 91°21′W
29 Z14 **De Witt** Iowa, C USA 41°49′N 90°32′W
29 R16 **De Witt** Nebraska, C USA 40°23′N 96°55′W
97 M17 **Dewsbury** N England, United Kingdom 53°42′N 01°37′W
161 Q10 **Dexing** Jiangxi, S China 28°51′N 117°36′E
27 Y8 **Dexter** Missouri, C USA 36°48′N 89°57′W
37 U14 **Dexter** New Mexico, SW USA 33°12′N 104°25′W
160 I8 **Deyang** Sichuan, C China 31°08′N 104°23′E
182 C4 **Dey-Dey, Lake** *salt lake* South Australia
143 S7 **Deyhūk** Khorāsān-e Janūbī, E Iran 33°18′N 57°30′E
**Deynau** *see* Galkynyş
**Deyyer** *see* Bandar-e Dayyer
142 L8 **Dezfūl** *var.* Dizful. Khūzestān, SW Iran 32°23′N 48°28′E
129 X4 **Dezhneva, Mys** *headland* NE Russia 66°08′N 169°40′W
161 P4 **Dezhou** Shandong, E China 37°28′N 116°18′E
**Dezhou** *see* Dechang
**Dezh Shāhpūr** *see* Marīvān
**Dhaalu Atoll** *see* South Nilandhe Atoll
**Dhahran** *see* Aẓ Ẓahrān
**Dhahran Al Khobar** *see* Aẓ Ẓahrān al Khubar
153 U14 **Dhaka** *prev.* Dacca. ● (Bangladesh) Dhaka, C Bangladesh 23°42′N 90°22′E
153 T15 **Dhaka** ◈ *division* C Bangladesh
**Dhali** *see* Dáli
**Dhalli Rajhara** *see* Dalli Rājhara
141 O15 **Dhamār** W Yemen 14°31′N 44°25′E
154 K12 **Dhamtari** Chhattīsgarh, C India 20°43′N 81°36′E
153 Q15 **Dhanbād** Jhārkhand, NE India 23°48′N 86°27′E
152 L10 **Dhangaḍhi** *var.* Dhangarhi. Far Western, W Nepal 28°45′N 80°38′E
**Dhangarhi** *see* Dhangaḍhi
**Dhank** *see* Ḍank
153 R12 **Dhankuṭā** Eastern, E Nepal 27°06′N 87°21′E
152 I6 **Dhaola Dhār** ▲▲ NE India
154 F10 **Dhār** Madhya Pradesh, C India 22°32′N 75°24′E
153 R12 **Dharān** *var.* Dharan Bazar. Eastern, E Nepal 26°51′N 87°18′E
**Dharan Bazar** *see* Dharān
155 H21 **Dhārāpuram** Tamil Nādu, SE India 10°45′N 77°33′E
155 H20 **Dharmapuri** Tamil Nādu, SE India 12°11′N 78°07′E
155 H18 **Dharmavaram** Andhra Pradesh, E India 14°27′N 77°44′E
154 M11 **Dharmjaygarh** Chhattīsgarh, C India 22°27′N 83°16′E
**Dharmsāla** *see* Dharmshāla
152 I7 **Dharmshāla** *prev.* Dharmsāla. Himāchal Pradesh, N India 32°14′N 76°24′E
155 F17 **Dhārwād** *prev.* Dharwar. Karnātaka, SW India 15°30′N 75°04′E
**Dharwar** *see* Dhārwād
**Dhaulagiri** *see* Dhawalāgiri
153 O10 **Dhawalāgiri** *var.* Dhaulagiri. ▲ C Nepal 28°45′N 83°27′E
81 L18 **Dheere Laaq** *var.* Lak Dera, *It.* Lach Dera. *seasonal river* Kenya/Somalia
75 N8 **Dhēhiba** *Lib.* Wāzin. SE Tunisia 31°58′N 10°43′E
**Dhekelia Sovereign Base Area** *see* Akrotiri and Dhekelia, Sovereign Base Areas of
**Dhelvinákion** *see* Delviňaki
113 M22 **Dhëmbelit, Maja e** ▲ S Albania 40°10′N 20°22′E
154 O12 **Dhenkānāl** Odisha, E India 20°40′N 85°36′E
**Dheskáti** *see* Deskáti
138 G11 **Dhībān** Mādabā, NW Jordan 31°30′N 35°47′E
**Dhidhimótikhon** *see* Didymóteicho
**Dhíkti Ori** *see* Díkti
139 W11 **Dhī Qār** *off.* Muḥāfaz at Dhī Qār, *var.* Al Muntafiq, An Nāṣiriyah. ◈ *governorate* SE Iraq
**Dhī Qār, Muḥāfaz at** *see* Dhī Qār
138 I12 **Dhirwah, Wādī adh** *dry watercourse* C Jordan
**Dhístomon** *see* Dístomo
**Dhivehi Raaje** *see* Maldives
**Dhivehi Raajjeyge Jumhooriyyaa** *see* Maldives
**Dhodhekánisos** *see* Dodekánisa
**Dhodhóni** *see* Dodóni
**Dhofar** *see* Ẓufār
**Dhomokós** *see* Domokós
**Dhond** *see* Daund
155 H17 **Dhone** Andhra Pradesh, C India 15°25′N 77°52′E
154 B11 **Dhorāji** Gujarāt, W India 21°44′N 70°27′E
**Dhráma** *see* Dráma
154 C10 **Dhrāngadhra** Gujarāt, W India 22°59′N 71°32′E
**Dhrepanon, Akrotírio** *see* Drépano, Akrotírio
153 T13 **Dhuburi** Assam, NE India 26°06′N 89°55′E
154 F12 **Dhule** *prev.* Dhulia. Mahārāshtra, C India 20°54′N 74°47′E
**Dhulia** *see* Dhule
**Dhún Dealgan, Cuan** *see* Dundalk Bay
**Dhún Droma, Cuan** *see* Dundrum Bay
**Dhún na nGall, Bá** *see* Donegal Bay
**Dhū Shaykh** *see* Qazānīyah
80 Q13 **Dhuudo** Bari, NE Somalia 09°21′N 50°19′E
81 N15 **Dhuusa Marreeb** *var.* Dusa Marreb, *It.* Dusa Mareb. Galguduud, C Somalia 05°33′N 46°24′E
115 J24 **Día** *island* SE Greece
55 Y9 **Diable, Île du** *var.* Devil's Island. *island* N French Guiana
15 N12 **Diable, Rivière du** ≈ Québec, SE Canada
35 N8 **Diablo, Mount** ▲ California, W USA 37°52′N 121°57′W
35 O9 **Diablo Range** ▲▲ California, W USA
24 I8 **Diablo, Sierra** ▲▲ Texas, SW USA
45 O11 **Diablotins, Morne** ▲ N Dominica 15°30′N 61°23′W
77 N11 **Diafarabé** Mopti, C Mali 14°09′N 05°01′W
77 N11 **Diaka** ≈ SW Mali
**Diakovár** *see* Đakovo
76 I12 **Dialakoto** S Senegal 13°21′N 13°19′W
61 B18 **Diamante** Entre Ríos, E Argentina 32°05′S 60°40′W
62 I12 **Diamante, Río** ≈ C Argentina
59 M19 **Diamantina** Minas Gerais, SE Brazil 18°17′S 43°37′W
59 N17 **Diamantina, Chapada** ▲ E Brazil
173 U11 **Diamantina Fracture Zone** *tectonic feature* E Indian Ocean
181 T8 **Diamantina River** ≈ Queensland/South Australia
38 D9 **Diamond Head** *headland* O'ahu, Hawai'i, USA 21°15′N 157°48′W
37 P2 **Diamond Peak** ▲ Colorado, C USA 40°56′N 108°56′W
35 W5 **Diamond Peak** ▲ Nevada, W USA 39°34′N 115°46′W
**Diamond State** *see* Delaware
76 J11 **Diamou** Kayes, SW Mali 14°04′N 11°16′W
95 I23 **Dianalund** Sjælland, C Denmark 55°32′N 11°30′E
65 G25 **Diana's Peak** ▲ C Saint Helena
160 M16 **Dianbai** *var.* Shuidong. Guangdong, S China 21°30′N 111°05′E
160 G13 **Dian Chi** ◎ SW China
106 B10 **Diano Marina** Liguria, NW Italy 43°55′N 08°06′E
163 V11 **Diaobingshan** *var.* Tiefa. Liaoning, NE China 42°25′N 123°39′E
**Diaoyu Dao** *see* Uotsuri-shima
**Diaoyutai** *see* Senkaku-shotō
77 R13 **Diapaga** E Burkina Faso 12°09′N 01°48′E
**Diarbekr** *see* Diyarbakır
107 J15 **Diavolo, Passo del** *pass* C Italy
61 B18 **Díaz** Santa Fe, C Argentina 32°22′S 61°05′W
141 W6 **Dibā al Ḥiṣn** *var.* Dibāh, Dibba. Ash Shāriqah, NE United Arab Emirates 25°35′N 56°16′E
**dibaga** *see* Dibege
**Dibāh** *see* Dibā al Ḥiṣn
79 L22 **Dibaya** Kasai-Occidental, S Dem. Rep. Congo 06°31′S 22°57′E
**Dibba** *see* Dibā al Ḥiṣn
195 W15 **Dibble Iceberg Tongue** *ice feature* Antarctica
139 S3 **Dibege** *Ar.* Ad Dibakah, *var.* Dibaga. Arbil, N Iraq 35°51′N 43°49′E
113 L19 **Dibër** ◈ *county* E Albania
83 I20 **Dibete** Central, SE Botswana 23°45′S 26°26′E
**Dibio** *see* Dijon
25 W9 **Diboll** Texas, SW USA 31°11′N 94°46′W
**Dibra** *see* Debar
153 X11 **Dibrugarh** Assam, NE India 27°29′N 94°49′E
54 G4 **Dibulla** La Guajira, N Colombia 11°14′N 73°22′W
25 O5 **Dickens** Texas, SW USA 33°38′N 100°51′W
19 R2 **Dickey** Maine, NE USA 47°04′N 69°05′W
30 K9 **Dickeyville** Wisconsin, N USA 42°37′N 90°36′W
28 K5 **Dickinson** North Dakota, N USA 46°54′N 102°48′W
0 E6 **Dickins Seamount** *undersea feature* NE Pacific Ocean 54°30′N 137°00′W
27 O13 **Dickson** Oklahoma, C USA 34°11′N 96°58′W
20 I9 **Dickson** Tennessee, S USA 36°04′N 87°23′W
**Dicle** *see* Tigris
**Dicsőszentmárton** *see* Târnăveni
98 M12 **Didam** Gelderland, E Netherlands 51°56′N 06°08′E
163 Y8 **Didao** Heilongjiang, NE China 45°22′N 130°48′E
76 L12 **Didiéni** Koulikoro, W Mali 13°48′N 08°01′W
**Didimo** *see* Dídymo
**Didimotiho** *see* Didymóteicho
81 K17 **Didimtu** *spring/well* NE Kenya 02°58′N 40°07′E
67 U9 **Didinga Hills** ▲▲ S Sudan
11 Q16 **Didsbury** Alberta, SW Canada 51°39′N 114°09′W
152 G11 **Dīdwāna** Rājasthān, N India 27°23′N 74°36′E
115 G20 **Dídymo** *var.* Didimo. ▲ S Greece 37°28′N 23°12′E
114 L12 **Didymóteicho** *var.* Dhidhimótikhon, Didimotiho. Anatolikí Makedonía kai Thráki, NE Greece 41°22′N 26°29′E
103 S13 **Die** Drôme, E France 44°46′N 05°21′E
77 O13 **Diébougou** SW Burkina Faso 11°00′N 03°12′W
**Diedenhofen** *see* Thionville
11 S16 **Diefenbaker, Lake** ⊠ Saskatchewan, S Canada
62 H7 **Diego de Almagro** Atacama, N Chile 26°24′S 70°10′W
63 F23 **Diego de Almagro, Isla** *island* S Chile
61 A20 **Diego de Alvear** Santa Fe, C Argentina 34°25′S 62°10′W
173 Q7 **Diego Garcia** *island* S British Indian Ocean Territory
**Diégo-Suarez** *see* Antsirañana
99 M23 **Diekirch** Diekirch, C Luxembourg 49°52′N 06°10′E
99 L23 **Diekirch** ◈ *district* N Luxembourg
76 K11 **Diéma** Kayes, W Mali 14°30′N 09°12′W
101 H15 **Diemel** ≈ W Germany
98 I10 **Diemen** Noord-Holland, C Netherlands 52°21′N 04°58′E
**Diemrich** *see* Deva
**Điện Biên** *see* Điện Biên Phu
167 R6 **Điện Biên Phu** *var.* Bien Bien, Điện Biên. Lai Châu, N Vietnam 21°23′N 103°02′E
167 S7 **Diễn Châu** Nghê An, N Vietnam 18°54′N 105°35′E
99 K18 **Diepenbeek** Limburg, NE Belgium 50°54′N 05°25′E
98 N11 **Diepenheim** Overijssel, E Netherlands 52°10′N 06°37′E
98 M10 **Diepenveen** Overijssel, E Netherlands 52°18′N 06°09′E
100 G12 **Diepholz** Niedersachsen, NW Germany 52°36′N 08°23′E
102 M3 **Dieppe** Seine-Maritime, N France 49°55′N 01°05′E
98 M12 **Dieren** Gelderland, E Netherlands 52°03′N 06°06′E
27 S13 **Dierks** Arkansas, C USA 34°07′N 94°01′W
99 J17 **Diest** Vlaams Brabant, C Belgium 50°58′N 05°03′E
108 F7 **Dietikon** Zürich, NW Switzerland 47°24′N 08°25′E
103 R13 **Dieulefit** Drôme, E France 44°30′N 05°01′E
103 T5 **Dieuze** Moselle, NE France 48°49′N 06°41′E
119 H15 **Dieveniškės** Vilnius, SE Lithuania 54°12′N 25°38′E
98 N7 **Diever** Drenthe, NE Netherlands 52°49′N 06°19′E
101 F17 **Diez** Rheinland-Pfalz, W Germany 50°22′N 08°01′E
77 Y12 **Diffa** Diffa, SE Niger 13°19′N 12°37′E
77 Y10 **Diffa** ◈ *region* SE Niger
99 L25 **Differdange** Luxembourg, SW Luxembourg 49°32′N 05°53′E
13 O16 **Digby** Nova Scotia, SE Canada 44°37′N 65°47′W
26 J5 **Dighton** Kansas, C USA 38°28′N 100°28′W
**Dignano d'Istria** *see* Vodnjan
103 T14 **Digne** *var.* Digne-les-Bains. Alpes-de-Haute-Provence, SE France 44°05′N 06°14′E
**Digne-les-Bains** *see* Digne
**Digoel** *see* Digul, Sungai
103 Q10 **Digoin** Saône-et-Loire, C France 46°30′N 04°E
171 Q8 **Digos** Mindanao, S Philippines 06°46′N 125°21′E
149 Q16 **Digri** Sindh, SE Pakistan 25°11′N 69°10′E
171 Y14 **Digul Barat, Sungai** ≈ Papua, E Indonesia
171 Y15 **Digul, Sungai** *prev.* Digoel. ≈ Papua, E Indonesia
171 Z14 **Digul Timur, Sungai** ≈ Papua, E Indonesia
153 X10 **Dihāng** ≈ NE India
**Dihang** *see* Brahmaputra
**Dihōk** *see* Dahūk
**Dihok** *see* Dahūk
**Dihok, Parēzga-i** *see* Dahūk
**Dishū** *see* Deh-e Shū
81 L17 **Diinsoor** Bay, S Somalia 02°28′N 43°00′E
144 M14 **Diirmentobe** *Kaz.* Diirmentōbe; *prev.* Dermentobe, Dyurment'yube. Kzyl-Orda, S Kazakhstan 45°46′N 63°42′E
**Diirmentōbe** *see* Diirmentobe
**Dijlah** *see* Tigris
99 H17 **Dijle** ≈ C Belgium
103 R8 **Dijon** *anc.* Dibio. Côte d'Or, C France 47°21′N 05°04′E
93 H14 **Dikanäs** Västerbotten, N Sweden 65°15′N 16°00′E
80 L12 **Dikhil** SW Djibouti 11°08′N 42°19′E
136 B13 **Dikili** İzmir, W Turkey 39°05′N 26°52′E
99 B17 **Diksmuide** *var.* Dixmuide, *Fr.* Dixmude. West-Vlaanderen, W Belgium 51°02′N 02°52′E
122 K7 **Dikson** Krasnoyarskiy Kray, N Russia 73°30′N 80°35′E
115 K25 **Díkti** *var.* Dhíkti Ori. ▲▲ Kríti, Greece, E Mediterranean Sea
77 Z13 **Dikwa** Borno, NE Nigeria 12°00′N 13°57′E
81 J15 **Dīla** Southern Nationalities, S Ethiopia 06°19′N 38°16′E
148 L7 **Dilārām** *prev.* Delārām. Nīmrōz, SW Afghanistan 32°11′N 63°27′E
99 G18 **Dilbeek** Vlaams Brabant, C Belgium 50°51′N 04°16′E
171 Q16 **Dili** *var.* Dilli, Dilly. ● (East Timor) N East Timor 08°33′S 125°34′E
77 Y11 **Dilia** *var.* Dillia. ≈ SE Niger
**Dilijan** *see* Delijan
167 U13 **Di Linh** Lâm Đông, S Vietnam 11°38′N 108°07′E
101 G16 **Dillenburg** Hessen, W Germany 50°45′N 08°16′E
25 Q13 **Dilley** Texas, SW USA 28°40′N 99°10′W
**Dilli** *see* Dili, East Timor
**Dilli** *see* Delhi, India
**Dillia** *see* Dilia
80 E11 **Dilling** *var.* Ad Dalanj. Southern Kordofan, C Sudan 12°02′N 29°41′E
101 D20 **Dillingen** Saarland, SW Germany 49°20′N 06°43′E
**Dillingen** *see* Dillingen an der Donau
101 J22 **Dillingen an der Donau** *var.* Dillingen. Bayern, S Germany 48°34′N 10°29′E
39 O13 **Dillingham** Alaska, USA 59°03′N 158°30′W
33 Q12 **Dillon** Montana, NW USA 45°14′N 112°38′W
21 T12 **Dillon** South Carolina, SE USA 34°25′N 79°22′W
31 T13 **Dillon Lake** ⊠ Ohio, N USA
**Dilly** *see* Dili
**Dilman** *see* Salmās
79 K24 **Dilolo** Katanga, S Dem. Rep. Congo 10°42′S 22°21′E
115 J20 **Dílos** *island* Kykládes, Greece, Aegean Sea
141 Y11 **Ḍil', Ra's aḍ** *headland* E Oman 19°12′N 57°53′E
29 R5 **Dilworth** Minnesota, N USA 46°53′N 96°38′W
138 H7 **Dimashq** *var.* Ash Shām, Esh Sham, *Eng.* Damascus, *Fr.* Damas, *It.* Damasco. ● (Syria) Rīf Dimashq, SW Syria 33°30′N 36°19′E
138 I7 **Dimashq** ✕ Rīf Dimashq, S Syria 33°30′N 36°19′E
**Dimashq, Muḥāfaẓat** *see* Rīf Dimashq
79 L21 **Dimbelenge** Kasai-Occidental, C Dem. Rep. Congo 05°36′S 23°04′E
77 N16 **Dimbokro** E Ivory Coast 06°43′N 04°46′W
182 L11 **Dimboola** Victoria, SE Australia 36°29′S 142°03′E
**Dîmbovița** *see* Dâmbovița
114 K11 **Dimitrovgrad** Haskovo, S Bulgaria 42°03′N 25°36′E
127 R5 **Dimitrovgrad** Ul'yanovskaya Oblast', W Russia 54°14′N 49°37′E
113 Q15 **Dimitrovgrad** *prev.* Caribrod. Serbia, SE Serbia 43°01′N 22°46′E
**Dimitrovo** *see* Pernik
**Dimlang** *see* Vogel Peak
24 M3 **Dimmitt** Texas, SW USA 34°32′N 102°20′W
114 F7 **Dimovo** Vidin, NW Bulgaria 43°46′N 22°47′E
59 A16 **Dimpolis** Acre, W Brazil 09°52′S 71°51′W
115 O23 **Dimyliá** Ródos, Dodekánisa, Greece, Aegean Sea 36°17′N 27°59′E
171 Q6 **Dinagat Island** *island* S Philippines
153 S13 **Dinajpur** Rajshahi, NW Bangladesh 25°38′N 88°40′E
102 I6 **Dinan** Côtes d'Armor, NW France 48°27′N 02°02′W
99 I21 **Dinant** Namur, S Belgium 50°16′N 04°55′E
136 E15 **Dinar** Afyon, SW Turkey 38°05′N 30°09′E
112 F13 **Dinara** ▲ W Croatia 43°49′N 16°42′E
**Dinara** *see* Dinaric Alps
102 I5 **Dinard** Ille-et-Vilaine, NW France 48°38′N 02°04′W
112 F13 **Dinaric Alps** *var.* Dinara. ▲▲ Bosnia and Herzegovina/Croatia
143 N10 **Dīnār, Kūh-e** ▲ C Iran 30°51′N 51°36′E
**Dinbych** *see* Denbigh
155 H22 **Dindigul** Tamil Nādu, SE India 10°23′N 78°E
83 M19 **Dindiza** Gaza, S Mozambique 23°22′S 33°28′E
79 H21 **Dinga** Bandundu, SW Dem. Rep. Congo 05°00′S 16°29′E
149 V7 **Dinga** Punjab, E Pakistan 32°38′N 73°45′E
**Dingchang** *see* Qinxian
158 L16 **Dinggyê** *var.* Gyangkar. Xizang Zizhiqu, W China 28°18′N 88°06′E
97 A20 **Dingle** *Ir.* An Daingean. SW Ireland 52°09′N 10°16′W
97 A20 **Dingle Bay** *Ir.* Bá an Daingin. *bay* SW Ireland
18 I13 **Dingmans Ferry** Pennsylvania, NE USA 41°12′N 74°51′W
101 N22 **Dingolfing** Bayern, SE Germany 48°37′N 12°28′E
171 O1 **Dingras** Luzon, N Philippines 18°06′N 120°43′E
76 J13 **Dinguiraye** N Guinea 11°19′N 10°49′W
96 I8 **Dingwall** N Scotland, United Kingdom 57°36′N 04°26′W
159 V10 **Dingxi** Gansu, C China 35°36′N 104°33′E
**Ding Xian** *see* Dingzhou
161 Q7 **Dingyuan** Anhui, E China 32°30′N 117°40′E
161 O3 **Dingzhou** *prev.* Ding Xian. Hebei, E China 38°31′N 114°52′E
167 U6 **Đinh Lập** Lang Sơn, N Vietnam 21°33′N 107°03′E
167 T13 **Đinh Quan** *var.* Tân Phu. Đông Nai, S Vietnam 11°11′N 107°20′E
100 E13 **Dinkel** ≈ Germany/Netherlands
101 J21 **Dinkelsbühl** Bayern, S Germany 49°06′N 10°18′E
101 D14 **Dinslaken** Nordrhein-Westfalen, W Germany 51°34′N 06°43′E
35 R11 **Dinuba** California, W USA 36°32′N 119°23′W
21 W7 **Dinwiddie** Virginia, NE USA 37°02′N 77°40′W
98 N13 **Dinxperlo** Gelderland, E Netherlands 51°51′N 06°30′E
**Dio** *see* Díon
**Diófás** *see* Nucet
76 M12 **Dioïla** Koulikoro, W Mali 12°28′N 06°43′W
115 F14 **Díon** *var.* Dio; *anc.* Dium. *site of ancient city* Kentrikí Makedonía, N Greece


◆ Country ◇ Dependent Territory ◈ Administrative Regions ▲ Mountain ⚶ Volcano ◎ Lake
● Country Capital ○ Dependent Territory Capital ✕ International Airport ▲▲ Mountain Range ≈ River ⊠ Reservoir

DIOULOULOU – DOUGLAS


76 G12 **Dioulouloù** SW Senegal 13°00′N 16°34′W
77 N11 **Dioura** Mopti, W Mali 14°48′N 05°20′W
76 G11 **Diourbel** W Senegal 14°39′N 16°12′W
152 L10 **Dipāyal** Far Western, W Nepal 29°09′N 80°46′E
121 R1 **Dipkarpaz** *Gk.* Rizokárpaso. NE Cyprus 35°36′N 34°23′E
149 R17 **Diplo** Sindh, SE Pakistan 24°29′N 69°36′E
171 P7 **Dipolog** *var.* Dipolog City. Mindanao, S Philippines 08°31′N 123°20′E
**Dipolog City** *see* Dipolog
185 C23 **Dipton** Southland, South Island, New Zealand 45°55′S 168°21′E
77 O10 **Diré** Tombouctou, C Mali 16°12′N 03°31′W
80 L13 **Dīrē Dawa** Dirē Dawa, E Ethiopia 09°35′N 41°53′E
**Dirfis** *see* Dírfys
115 H18 **Dírfys** *var.* Dirfis. ▲ Évvoia, C Greece
75 N9 **Dirj** *var.* Daraj, Darj. W Libya 30°09′N 10°26′E
180 G10 **Dirk Hartog Island** *island* Western Australia
77 Y8 **Dirkou** Agadez, NE Niger 18°45′N 13°00′E
181 X11 **Dirranbandi** Queensland, E Australia 28°37′S 148°13′E
**Dirri** *see* Derri
**Dirschau** *see* Tczew
37 N6 **Dirty Devil River** ≈ Utah, W USA
32 E10 **Disappointment, Cape** *headland* Washington, NW USA 46°16′N 124°06′W
180 L8 **Disappointment, Lake** *salt lake* Western Australia
183 R12 **Disaster Bay** *bay* New South Wales, SE Australia
44 J11 **Discovery Bay** C Jamaica 18°27′N 77°24′W
182 K13 **Discovery Bay** *inlet* SE Australia
67 Y15 **Discovery II Fracture Zone** *tectonic feature* SW Indian Ocean
**Discovery Seamount/ Discovery Seamounts** *see* Discovery Tablemounts
65 O19 **Discovery Tablemounts** *var.* Discovery Seamount, Discovery Seamounts. *undersea feature* SW Atlantic Ocean 42°00′S 00°10′E
108 G9 **Disentis** *Rmsch.* Mustér. Graubünden, S Switzerland 46°43′N 08°52′E
39 O10 **Dishna River** ≈ Alaska, USA
**Disko Bugt** *see* Qeqertarsuup Tunua
195 X4 **Dismal Mountains** ▲ Antarctica
28 M14 **Dismal River** ≈ Nebraska, C USA
**Disna** *see* Dzisna
99 L19 **Dison** Liège, E Belgium 50°37′N 05°52′E
153 V12 **Dispur** *state capital* Assam, NE India 26°03′N 91°52′E
15 R11 **Disraeli** Québec, SE Canada 45°58′N 71°21′W
115 F18 **Dístomo** *prev.* Dhístomon. Stereá Elláda, C Greece 38°25′N 22°40′E
**Dístos, Límni** *see* Dýstos, Límni
59 L18 **Distrito Federal** *Eng.* Federal District. ◈ *federal district* C Brazil
41 P14 **Distrito Federal** ◈ *federal district* S Mexico
54 L4 **Distrito Federal** *off.* Territorio Distrito Federal. ◈ *federal district* N Venezuela
**Distrito Federal, Territorio** *see* Distrito Federal
116 J10 **Ditrău** *Hung.* Ditró. Harghita, C Romania 46°49′N 25°31′E
**Ditró** *see* Ditrău
154 B12 **Diu** Damān and Diu, W India 20°42′N 70°59′E
**Dium** *see* Díon
109 S13 **Divača** SW Slovenia 45°40′N 13°58′E
102 K5 **Dives** ≈ N France
33 Q11 **Divide** Montana, NW USA 45°44′N 112°47′W
**Divin** *see* Dzivin
83 N18 **Divinhe** Sofala, E Mozambique 20°41′S 34°46′E
59 L20 **Divinópolis** Minas Gerais, SE Brazil 20°08′S 44°55′W
127 N13 **Divnoye** Stavropol'skiy Kray, SW Russia 45°54′N 43°18′E
76 M17 **Divo** S Ivory Coast 05°50′N 05°22′W
**Divodurum Mediomatricum** *see* Metz
137 N13 **Divriği** Sivas, C Turkey 39°23′N 38°06′E
**Diwaniyah** *see* Ad Dīwānīyah
14 J10 **Dix Milles, Lac** ◎ Québec, SE Canada
14 M8 **Dix Milles, Lac des** ◎ Québec, SE Canada
**Dixmude/Dixmuide** *see* Diksmuide
35 N7 **Dixon** California, W USA 38°19′N 121°49′W
30 L10 **Dixon** Illinois, N USA 41°51′N 89°26′W
20 I6 **Dixon** Kentucky, S USA 37°30′N 87°39′W
27 V6 **Dixon** Missouri, C USA 37°59′N 92°05′W
37 S9 **Dixon** New Mexico, SW USA 36°10′N 105°49′W
39 Y15 **Dixon Entrance** *strait* Canada/USA
18 D14 **Dixonville** Pennsylvania, NE USA 40°43′N 79°01′W
137 T13 **Diyadin** Ağrı, E Turkey 39°33′N 43°41′E
139 V7 **Diyālá** *off.* Muḩāfaz at Diyālá, *var.* Ba'qūbah. ◈ *governorate* E Iraq
**Diyālá, Muḩāfaz at** *see* Diyālá
**Diyālá, Nahr** *see* Sīrvān, Rūdkhāneh-ye
139 V5 **Diyālá, Sirwan Nahr** *var.* Rudkhaneh-ye Sīrvān, Sīrwān. ≈ Iran/Iraq *see also* Sīrvān, Rūdkhaneh-ye
137 P15 **Diyarbakır** *var.* Diarbekr; *anc.* Amida. Diyarbakır, SE Turkey 37°55′N 40°14′E
137 P15 **Diyarbakır** *var.* Diarbekr. ◈ *province* SE Turkey
**Dizful** *see* Dezfūl
79 F16 **Dja** ≈ SE Cameroon
**Djadié** *see* Zadié
77 X7 **Djado** Agadez, NE Niger 21°00′N 12°11′E
77 X6 **Djado, Plateau du** ▲ NE Niger
**Djailolo** *see* Halmahera, Pulau
**Djajapura** *see* Jayapura
**Djakarta** *see* Jakarta
**Djakovo** *see* Đakovo
79 G20 **Djambala** Plateaux, C Congo 02°32′S 14°43′E
**Djambi** *see* Jambi
**Djambi** *see* Hari, Batang
74 M9 **Djanet** E Algeria 28°43′N 08°57′E
**Djanet** *see* Ohanet
**Djaul** *see* Dyaul Island
**Djawa** *see* Jawa
**Djéblé** *see* Jablah
78 I10 **Djédaa** Batha, C Chad 13°31′N 18°34′E
74 J6 **Djelfa** *var.* El Djelfa. N Algeria 34°43′N 03°14′E
79 M14 **Djéma** Haut-Mbomou, E Central African Republic 06°04′N 25°20′E
**Djember** *see* Jember
**Djeneponto** *see* Jeneponto
77 N12 **Djenné** *var.* Jenné. Mopti, C Mali 13°55′N 04°31′W
**Djérablous** *see* Jarābulus
**Djerba** *see* Djerba, Île de
75 N7 **Djerba, Île de** *var.* Djerba, Jazīrat Jarbah. *island* E Tunisia
79 F15 **Djérem** ≈ C Cameroon
**Djevdjelija** *see* Gevgelija
77 P11 **Djibo** N Burkina Faso 14°09′N 01°38′W
80 L12 **Djibouti** *Fr.* République de Djibouti, *var.* Jibuti. ● (Djibouti) E Djibouti 11°33′N 42°55′E
80 L12 **Djibouti** *off.* Republic of Djibouti, *var.* Jibuti; *prev.* French Somaliland, French Territory of the Afars and Issas, *Fr.* Côte Française des Somalis, Territoire Français des Afars et des Issas. ◆ *republic* E Africa
80 L12 **Djibouti** ✈ C Djibouti 11°29′N 42°54′E
**Djibouti, Republic of** *see* Djibouti
**Djibouti, République de** *see* Djibouti
**Djidjel/Djidjelli** *see* Jijel
**Djidji** *see* Ivando
55 W10 **Djoemoe** Sipaliwini, C Suriname 04°00′N 55°27′W
**Djokjakarta** *see* Yogyakarta
79 K21 **Djoku-Punda** Kasai-Occidental, S Dem. Rep. Congo 05°27′S 20°58′E
79 K18 **Djolu** Equateur, N Dem. Rep. Congo 0°35′N 22°30′E
**Djombang** *see* Jombang
**Djorče Petrov** *see* Đorče Petrov
79 F17 **Djoua** ≈ Congo/Gabon
77 R14 **Djougou** W Benin 09°42′N 01°38′E
79 F16 **Djoum** Sud, S Cameroon 02°38′N 12°51′E
78 I8 **Djourab, Erg du** *desert* N Chad
79 P17 **Djugu** Orientale, NE Dem. Rep. Congo 01°55′N 30°31′E
**Djumbir** *see* Ďumbier
92 L3 **Djúpivogur** Austurland, SE Iceland 64°40′N 14°18′W
94 L13 **Djura** Dalarna, C Sweden 60°37′N 15°00′E
**Djurdjevac** *see* Đurđevac
**D'Kar** *see* Dekar
197 U6 **Dmitriya Lapteva, Proliv** *strait* N Russia
126 J7 **Dmitriyev-L'govskiy** Kurskaya Oblast', W Russia 52°08′N 35°09′E
**Dmitriyevsk** *see* Makiyivka
126 K3 **Dmitrov** Moskovskaya Oblast', W Russia 56°23′N 37°30′E
**Dmitrovichi** *see* Dzmitravichy
126 J6 **Dmitrovsk-Orlovskiy** Orlovskaya Oblast', W Russia 52°28′N 35°01′E
117 R3 **Dmytrivka** Chernihivs'ka Oblast', N Ukraine 50°56′N 32°57′E
**Dnepr** *see* Dnieper
**Dneprodzerzhinskoye Vodokhranilishche** *see* Dniprodzerzhyns'ke Vodoskhovyshche
**Dnepropetrovskaya Oblast'** *see* Dnipropetrovs'ka Oblast'
**Dneprorudnoye** *see* Dniprorudne
**Dneprovskiy Liman** *see* Dniprovs'kyy Lyman
**Dneprovsko-Bugskiy Kanal** *see* Dnyaprowska-Buhski Kanal
**Dnestr** *see* Dniester
**Dnestrovskiy Liman** *see* Dnistrovs'kyy Lyman
86 H11 **Dnieper** *Bel.* Dnyapro, *Rus.* Dnepr, *Ukr.* Dnipro. ≈ E Europe
117 P3 **Dnieper Lowland** *Bel.* Prydnyaprowskaya Nizina, *Ukr.* Prydniprovs'ka Nyzovyna. *lowlands* Belarus/Ukraine
116 M8 **Dniester** *Rom.* Nistru, *Rus.* Dnestr, *Ukr.* Dnister; *anc.* Tyras. ≈ Moldova/Ukraine
117 U7 **Dnipro** *prev.* Dnipropetrovs'k, Yekaterinoslav. Dnipropetrovs'ka Oblast', E Ukraine 48°28′N 35°E
**Dnipro** *see* Dnieper
**Dniprodzerzhyns'k** *see* Kam"yans'ke
117 T7 **Dniprodzerzhyns'ke Vodoskhovyshche** *Rus.* Dneprodzerzhinskoye Vodokhranilishche. ▣ C Ukraine
117 U8 **Dnipropetrovs'k** ✈ Dnipropetrovs'ka Oblast', S Ukraine 48°20′N 35°04′E
**Dnipropetrovs'k** *see* Dnipro
117 T7 **Dnipropetrovs'ka Oblast'** *var.* Dnipropetrovs'k, *Rus.* Dnepropetrovskaya Oblast'. ◈ *province* E Ukraine
117 U9 **Dniprorudne** *Rus.* Dneprorudnoye. Zaporiz'ka Oblast', SE Ukraine 47°21′N 35°00′E
117 Q11 **Dniprovs'kyy Lyman** *Rus.* Dneprovskiy Liman. *bay* S Ukraine
**Dnister** *see* Dniester
117 O11 **Dnistrovs'kyy Lyman** *Rus.* Dnestrovskiy Liman. *inlet* S Ukraine
124 G14 **Dno** Pskovskaya Oblast', W Russia 57°48′N 29°58′E
**Dnyapro** *see* Dnieper
119 H20 **Dnyaprowska-Buhski Kanal** *Rus.* Dneprovsko-Bugskiy Kanal. *canal* SW Belarus
13 O14 **Doaktown** New Brunswick, SE Canada 46°34′N 66°06′W
78 H13 **Doba** Logone-Oriental, S Chad 08°40′N 16°50′E
118 E9 **Dobele** *Ger.* Doblen. W Latvia 56°36′N 23°14′E
101 N16 **Döbeln** Sachsen, E Germany 51°07′N 13°07′E
171 U12 **Doberai, Jazirah** *Dut.* Vogelkop. *peninsula* Papua Barat, E Indonesia
110 F10 **Dobiegniew** *Ger.* Lubuskie, Woldenberg Neumark. Lubuskie, W Poland 52°58′N 15°43′E
**Doblen** *see* Dobele
81 K18 **Dobli** *spring/well* SW Somalia 0°24′N 41°18′E
112 H11 **Doboj** Republika Srpska, N Bosnia and Herzegovina 44°45′N 18°03′E
143 R12 **Doborjī** *var.* Fürg. Fārs, S Iran 28°16′N 55°13′E
110 L8 **Dobre Miasto** *Ger.* Guttstadt. Warmińsko-mazurskie, NE Poland 53°59′N 20°25′E
114 N7 **Dobrich** *Rom.* Bazargic; *prev.* Tolbukhin. Dobrich, NE Bulgaria 43°35′N 27°49′E
114 N7 **Dobrich** ◈ *province* NE Bulgaria
126 M8 **Dobrinka** Lipetskaya Oblast', W Russia 52°10′N 40°30′E
126 M7 **Dobrinka** Volgogradskaya Oblast', SW Russia 50°52′N 41°48′E
**Dobrla Vas** *see* Eberndorf
111 I15 **Dobrodzień** *Ger.* Guttentag. Opolskie, S Poland 50°43′N 18°24′E
**Dobrogea** *see* Dobruja
117 W7 **Dobropillya** *Rus.* Dobropol'ye. Donets'ka Oblast', SE Ukraine 48°25′N 37°02′E
**Dobropol'ye** *see* Dobropillya
117 P8 **Dobrovelychkivka** Kirovohrads'ka Oblast', C Ukraine 48°22′N 31°12′E
**Dobrudja/Dobrudzha** *see* Dobruja
114 O7 **Dobruja** *var.* Dobrudja, *Bul.* Dobrudzha, *Rom.* Dobrogea. *physical region* Bulgaria/Romania
119 P19 **Dobrush** Homyel'skaya Voblasts', SE Belarus 52°25′N 31°19′E
125 U14 **Dobryanka** Permskiy Kray, NW Russia 58°28′N 56°27′E
117 P2 **Dobryanka** Chernihivs'ka Oblast', N Ukraine 52°03′N 31°09′E
**Dobryn'** *see* Dabryn'
21 R8 **Dobson** North Carolina, SE USA 36°25′N 80°45′W
59 N20 **Doce, Rio** ≈ SE Brazil
93 I16 **Docksta** Västernorrland, C Sweden 63°06′N 18°22′E
41 N10 **Doctor Arroyo** Nuevo León, NE Mexico 23°40′N 100°09′W
62 L4 **Doctor Pedro P. Peña** Boquerón W Paraguay 22°22′S 62°23′W
171 S11 **Dodaga** Pulau Halmahera, E Indonesia 01°06′N 128°10′E
155 G21 **Dodda Betta** ▲ S India 11°28′N 76°44′E
**Dodecanese** *see* Dodekánisa
115 M22 **Dodekánisa** *var.* Nóties Sporádes, *Eng.* Dodecanese; *prev.* Dhodhekánisos, Dodekanisos. *island group* SE Greece
**Dodekanisos** *see* Dodekánisa
26 J6 **Dodge City** Kansas, C USA 37°45′N 100°01′W
30 K9 **Dodgeville** Wisconsin, N USA 42°57′N 90°08′W
97 H25 **Dodman Point** *headland* SW England, United Kingdom 50°13′N 04°47′W
81 J14 **Dodola** Oromīya, C Ethiopia 07°00′N 39°15′E
81 H22 **Dodoma** ● (Tanzania) Dodoma, C Tanzania 06°11′S 35°45′E
81 H22 **Dodoma** ◈ *region* C Tanzania
115 C16 **Dodóni** *var.* Dhodhóni. *site of ancient city* Ípeiros, W Greece
33 U7 **Dodson** Montana, NW USA 48°25′N 108°18′W
25 P3 **Dodson** Texas, SW USA 34°46′N 100°01′W
98 M12 **Doesburg** Gelderland, E Netherlands 52°01′N 06°08′E
98 N12 **Doetinchem** Gelderland, E Netherlands 51°58′N 06°17′E
158 L12 **Dogai Coring** *var.* Lake Montcalm. ◎ W China
137 N15 **Doğanşehir** Malatya, C Turkey 38°07′N 37°54′E
84 E9 **Dogger Bank** *undersea feature* C North Sea 55°00′N 03°00′E
23 S10 **Dog Island** *island* Florida, SE USA
14 C7 **Dog Lake** ◎ Ontario, S Canada
106 B9 **Dogliani** Piemonte, NE Italy 44°33′N 07°55′E
164 H11 **Dōgo** *island* Oki-shotō, SW Japan
143 N10 **Do Gonbadān** *var.* Dow Gonbadān, Gonbadān. Kohkīlūyeh va Būyer AHmad, SW Iran 30°12′N 50°48′E
77 S12 **Dogondoutchi** Dosso, SW Niger 13°36′N 04°03′E
137 T13 **Doğubayazıt** Ağrı, E Turkey 39°33′N 44°07′E
137 P12 **Doğu Karadeniz Dağları** *var.* Anadolu Dağları. ▲ NE Turkey
158 K16 **Dogxung Zangbo** ≈ W China
**Doha** *see* Ad Dawḩah
**Doha** *see* Ad Dawḩah
**Dohad** *see* Dāhod
**Dohuk** *see* Dahūk
**Dohuk** *see* Dahūk
159 N16 **Doilungdêqên** *var.* Namka. Xizang Zizhiqu, W China 29°41′N 90°58′E
114 F12 **Doïráni, Límni** *var.* Limni Doïranis, *Bul.* Ezero Doyransko. ◎ N Greece
**Doire** *see* Londonderry
99 H22 **Doische** Namur, S Belgium 50°09′N 04°43′E
59 P17 **Dois de Julho** ✈ (Salvador) Bahia, NE Brazil 12°04′S 38°58′W
60 H12 **Dois Vizinhos** Paraná, S Brazil 25°47′S 53°03′W
80 H10 **Doka** Gedaref, E Sudan 13°30′N 35°47′E
**Doka** *see* Kéita, Bahr
**Dokan** *see* Dūkān
94 H13 **Dokka** Oppland, S Norway 60°49′N 10°04′E
98 L5 **Dokkum** Fryslân, N Netherlands 53°20′N 06°E
98 L5 **Dokkumer Ee** ≈ N Netherlands
76 K13 **Doko** NE Guinea 11°46′N 08°58′W
**Dokshitsy** *see* Dokshytsy
118 K13 **Dokshytsy** *Rus.* Dokshitsy. Vitsyebskaya Voblasts', N Belarus 54°54′N 27°46′E
117 X8 **Dokuchaievs'k** *var.* Dokuchayevsk. Donets'ka Oblast', SE Ukraine 47°43′N 37°41′E
**Dokuchayevsk** *see* Dokuchaievs'k
**Dolak, Pulau** *see* Yos Sudarso, Pulau
29 P9 **Doland** South Dakota, N USA 44°51′N 98°06′W
63 J18 **Dolavón** Chaco, S Argentina 43°16′S 65°44′W
15 P5 **Dolbeau** Québec, SE Canada 48°52′N 72°15′W
15 P5 **Dolbeau-Mistassini** Québec, SE Canada 48°54′N 72°13′W
102 I5 **Dol-de-Bretagne** Ille-et-Vilaine, NW France 48°33′N 01°45′W
64 J13 **Doldrums Fracture Zone** *tectonic feature* W Atlantic Ocean
103 S8 **Dôle** Jura, E France 47°05′N 05°30′E
97 J19 **Dolgellau** NW Wales, United Kingdom 52°45′N 03°54′W
**Dolginovo** *see* Dawhinava
**Dolgi, Ostrov** *see* Dolgiy, Ostrov
125 U2 **Dolgiy, Ostrov** *var.* Ostrov Dolgi. *island* NW Russia
162 J9 **Dolgöön** Övörhangay, C Mongolia 45°57′N 103°14′E
107 C20 **Dolianova** Sardegna, Italy, C Mediterranean Sea 39°23′N 09°08′E
**Dolina** *see* Dolyna
123 T13 **Dolinsk** Ostrov Sakhalin, Sakhalinskaya Oblast', SE Russia 47°20′N 142°52′E
**Dolinskaya** *see* Dolyns'ka
79 F21 **Dolisie** *prev.* Loubomo. Niari, S Congo 04°12′S 12°41′E
116 G14 **Dolj** ◈ *county* SW Romania
98 P5 **Dollard** *bay* NW Germany
194 J5 **Dolleman Island** *island* Antarctica
114 K8 **Dolna Oryahovitsa** *var.* Dolna Oryakhovitsa. Veliko Tarnovo, N Bulgaria 43°09′N 25°44′E
**Dolna Oryakhovitsa** *see* Dolna Oryahovitsa
114 N9 **Dolni Chiflik** Varna, E Bulgaria 42°59′N 27°43′E
114 I8 **Dolni Dabnik** *var.* Dolni Dŭbnik. Pleven, N Bulgaria 43°24′N 24°25′E
**Dolni Dŭbnik** *see* Dolni Dabnik
114 F8 **Dolni Lom** Vidin, NW Bulgaria 43°31′N 22°46′E
**Dolnja Lendava** *see* Lendava
129 F14 **Dolnośląskie** ◈ *province* SW Poland
111 K18 **Dolný Kubín** *Hung.* Alsókubin. Žilinský Kraj, N Slovakia 49°12′N 19°17′E
106 H8 **Dolo** Veneto, NE Italy 45°25′N 12°06′E
**Dolomites/Dolomiti** *see* Dolomitiche, Alpi
106 H6 **Dolomitiche, Alpi** *var.* Dolomiti, *Eng.* Dolomites. ▲ NE Italy
**Dolonnur** *see* Duolun
**Doloon** *see* Tsogt-Ovoo
61 E21 **Dolores** Buenos Aires, E Argentina 36°21′S 57°39′W
42 E3 **Dolores** Petén, N Guatemala 16°33′N 89°26′W
171 Q5 **Dolores** Samar, C Philippines 12°01′N 125°27′E
105 S12 **Dolores** Comunitat Valenciana, E Spain 38°09′N 00°45′W
61 D19 **Dolores** Soriano, SW Uruguay 33°34′S 58°15′W
41 N12 **Dolores Hidalgo** *var.* Ciudad de Dolores Hidalgo. Guanajuato, C Mexico 21°10′N 100°55′W
8 J7 **Dolphin and Union Strait** *strait* Northwest Territories/ Nunavut, N Canada
65 D23 **Dolphin, Cape** *headland* East Falkland, Falkland Islands 51°15′S 58°57′W
44 H12 **Dolphin Head** *hill* W Jamaica
83 B21 **Dolphin Head** *var.* Cape Dernberg. *headland* SW Namibia 25°33′S 14°36′E
110 G12 **Dolsk** *Ger.* Dolzig. Weilkopolskie, C Poland 51°59′N 17°03′E
167 S8 **Đô Lương** Nghê An, N Vietnam 18°51′N 105°19′E
116 I6 **Dolyna** *Rus.* Dolina. Ivano-Frankivs'ka Oblast', W Ukraine 48°58′N 24°01′E
117 R8 **Dolyns'ka** *Rus.* Dolinskaya. Kirovohrads'ka Oblast', S Ukraine 48°06′N 32°46′E
**Dolzig** *see* Dolsk
**Domachëvo/Domaczewo** *see* Damachava
117 P9 **Domanivka** Mykolayivs'ka Oblast', S Ukraine 47°40′N 30°56′E
153 S13 **Domar** Rajshahi, N Bangladesh 26°08′N 88°57′E
108 I9 **Domat/Ems** Graubünden, S Switzerland 46°50′N 09°28′E
111 A18 **Domažlice** *Ger.* Taus. Plzeňský Kraj, W Czechia 49°26′N 12°54′E
127 X8 **Dombarovskiy** Orenburgskaya Oblast', W Russia 50°53′N 59°18′E
94 G10 **Dombås** Oppland, S Norway 62°04′N 09°07′E
83 M17 **Dombe** Manica, C Mozambique 19°59′S 33°24′E
82 A13 **Dombe Grande** Benguela, C Angola 12°57′S 13°07′E
103 R10 **Dombes** *physical region* E France
111 I25 **Dombóvár** Tolna, S Hungary 46°24′N 18°09′E
99 D14 **Domburg** Zeeland, SW Netherlands 51°34′N 03°30′E
58 L13 **Dom Eliseu** Pará, NE Brazil 04°02′S 47°31′W
**Domel Island** *see* Letsôk-aw Kyun
103 O11 **Dôme, Puy de** ▲ C France 45°46′N 03°00′E
36 H13 **Dome Rock Mountains** ▲ Arizona, SW USA
**Domesnes, Cape** *see* Kolkasrags
62 G8 **Domeyko** Atacama, N Chile 28°58′S 70°54′W
62 H5 **Domeyko, Cordillera** ▲ N Chile
102 K5 **Domfront** Orne, N France 48°35′N 00°39′W
171 X13 **Dom, Gunung** ▲ Papua, E Indonesia 02°41′S 137°00′E
45 X11 **Dominica** *off.* Commonwealth of Dominica. ◆ *republic* E West Indies
47 S3 **Dominica** *island* Dominica
**Dominica Channel** *see* Martinique Passage
**Dominica, Commonwealth of** *see* Dominica
43 N15 **Dominical** Puntarenas, SE Costa Rica 09°16′N 83°52′W
**Dominicana, República** *see* Dominican Republic
45 Q8 **Dominican Republic** *Sp.* República Dominicana. ◆ *republic* C West Indies
45 X11 **Dominica Passage** *passage* E Caribbean Sea
99 K14 **Dommel** ≈ S Netherlands
81 O14 **Domo** Sumalē, E Ethiopia 07°53′N 46°55′E
126 L4 **Domodedovo** ✈ (Moskva) Moskovskaya Oblast', W Russia 55°19′N 37°55′E
106 C6 **Domodossola** Piemonte, NE Italy 46°07′N 08°20′E
115 F17 **Domokós** *var.* Dhomokós. Stereá Elláda, C Greece 39°07′N 22°18′E
172 I14 **Domoni** Anjouan, SE Comoros 12°15′S 44°39′E
61 G16 **Dom Pedrito** Rio Grande do Sul, S Brazil 31°00′S 54°40′W
**Dompoe** *see* Dompu
170 M16 **Dompu** *prev.* Dompoe. Sumbawa, C Indonesia 08°30′S 118°28′E
**Domschale** *see* Domžale
62 H13 **Domuyo, Volcán** ▲ W Argentina 36°36′S 70°22′W
109 U11 **Domžale** *Ger.* Domschale. C Slovenia 46°09′N 14°33′E
127 O10 **Don** *var.* Duna, Tanais. ≈ SW Russia
96 K9 **Don** ≈ NE Scotland, United Kingdom
182 M11 **Donald** Victoria, SE Australia 36°27′S 143°03′E
22 J9 **Donaldsonville** Louisiana, S USA 30°06′N 90°59′W
23 S8 **Donalsonville** Georgia, SE USA 31°02′N 84°52′W
**Donau** *see* Danube
101 G23 **Donaueschingen** Baden-Württemberg, SW Germany 47°57′N 08°30′E
101 K22 **Donaumoos** *wetland* S Germany
101 K22 **Donauwörth** Bayern, S Germany 48°43′N 10°46′E
109 U7 **Donawitz** Steiermark, SE Austria 47°23′N 15°00′E
117 X7 **Donbass** *industrial region* Russia/Ukraine
104 K11 **Don Benito** Extremadura, W Spain 38°57′N 05°52′W
97 M17 **Doncaster** *anc.* Danum. N England, United Kingdom 53°32′N 01°07′W
44 K12 **Don Christophers Point** *headland* C Jamaica 18°19′N 76°48′W
55 V9 **Donderkamp** Sipaliwini, NW Suriname 05°18′N 56°22′W
82 B12 **Dondo** Kwanza Norte, NW Angola 09°40′S 14°24′E
171 O12 **Dondo** Sulawesi, N Indonesia 0°54′S 121°33′E
83 N17 **Dondo** Sofala, C Mozambique 19°41′S 34°45′E
155 K26 **Dondra Head** *headland* S Sri Lanka 05°57′N 80°33′E
**Donduşani** *see* Donduşeni
116 M8 **Donduşeni** *var.* Donduşani, *Rus.* Dondyushany. N Moldova 48°13′N 27°38′E
**Dondyushany** *see* Donduşeni
97 D15 **Donegal** *Ir.* Dún na nGall. Donegal, NW Ireland 54°39′N 08°06′W
97 D14 **Donegal** *Ir.* Dún na nGall. *cultural region* NW Ireland
97 C15 **Donegal Bay** *Ir.* Bá Dhún na nGall. *bay* NW Ireland
84 K10 **Donets** ≈ Russia/Ukraine
117 X8 **Donets'k** *Rus.* Donetsk; *prev.* Stalino. Donets'ka Oblast', E Ukraine 47°58′N 37°50′E
117 W8 **Donets'k** ✈ Donets'ka Oblast', E Ukraine 48°03′N 37°44′E
**Donets'k** *see* Donets'ka Oblast'
117 W8 **Donets'ka Oblast'** *var.* Donets'k, *Rus.* Donetskaya Oblast'; *prev. Rus.* Stalins'kaya Oblast'. ◈ *province* SE Ukraine
**Donetskaya Oblast'** *see* Donets'ka Oblast'
67 P8 **Donga** ≈ Cameroon/ Nigeria
157 O13 **Dongchuan** Yunnan, SW China 26°09′N 103°10′E
161 Q14 **Dongchuan Dao** *prev.* Dongshan Dao. *island* SE China
**Dong Dao** *see* Lincoln Island
99 I14 **Dongen** Noord-Brabant, S Netherlands 51°38′N 04°56′E
160 K17 **Dongfang** *var.* Basuo. Hainan, S China 19°05′N 108°40′E
163 Z7 **Dongfanghong** Heilongjiang, NE China 46°13′N 133°13′E
163 W11 **Dongfeng** Jilin, NE China 42°39′N 125°33′E
171 N12 **Donggala** Sulawesi, C Indonesia 0°40′S 119°44′E
163 V13 **Donggang** *var.* Dadong; *prev.* Donggou. Liaoning, NE China 39°52′N 124°08′E
**Donggou** *see* Donggang
161 O14 **Dongguan** Guangdong, S China 23°03′N 113°43′E
167 T9 **Đông Hà** Quang Tri, C Vietnam 16°45′N 107°10′E
163 Y14 **Donghae** *prev.* Tonghae. NE South Korea 37°26′N 129°09′E
**Dong Hai** *see* East China Sea
160 M16 **Donghai Dao** *island* S China
**Dong He** *see* Omon Gol
**Donghe** *see* Wangcang
167 T9 **Đông Hơi** Quang Binh, C Vietnam 17°32′N 106°35′E
**Donghua** *see* Huating
**Donghuang** *see* Xishui
108 H10 **Dongio** Ticino, S Switzerland 46°27′N 08°58′E
**Dongkan** *see* Binhai
160 L11 **Dongkou** Hunan, S China 27°06′N 110°35′E
167 S8 **Đông Lê** Quang Binh, C Vietnam 17°52′N 105°49′E
**Dongliao** *see* Liaoyuan
**Dong-nai** *see* Đông Nai, Sông
167 U13 **Đông Nai, Sông** *var.* Dong-nai, Dong Noi, Donnai. ≈ S Vietnam
161 N14 **Dongnan Qiuling** *plateau* SE China
163 Y9 **Dongning** Heilongjiang, NE China 44°01′N 131°03′E
**Dong Noi** *see* Đông Nai, Sông
83 C14 **Dongo** Huíla, C Angola 14°35′S 15°51′E
80 E7 **Dongola** *var.* Donqola, Dunqulah. Northern, N Sudan 19°10′N 30°27′E
79 I17 **Dongou** Likouala, NE Congo 02°05′N 18°E
**Đông Phu** *see* Đông Xoai
**Dongping** *see* Anhua
**Dong Rak, Thiu Khao Phanom** *see* Dangrek Mountains
**Dongshan Dao** *see* Dongchuan Dao
**Dongsheng** *see* Ordos
161 S13 **Dongshi** *Jap.* Tōsei; *prev.* Tungshih. N Taiwan 24°13′N 120°54′E
161 R7 **Dongtai** Jiangsu, E China 32°50′N 120°22′E
161 N10 **Dongting Hu** *var.* Tung-t'ing Hu. ◎ S China
161 P10 **Dongxiang** *var.* Xiaogang. Jiangxi, S China 28°16′N 116°32′E
167 T13 **Đông Xoai** *var.* Đông Phu. Sông Be, S Vietnam 11°31′N 106°55′E
161 Q4 **Dongying** Shandong, E China 37°27′N 118°01′E
27 X8 **Doniphan** Missouri, C USA 36°39′N 90°51′W
**Donja Lužica** *see* Niederlausitz
10 G7 **Donjek** ≈ Yukon, W Canada
112 E11 **Donji Lapac** Lika-Senj, W Croatia 44°33′N 15°58′E
112 H8 **Donji Miholjac** Osijek-Baranja, NE Croatia 45°45′N 18°10′E
112 P12 **Donji Milanovac** Serbia, E Serbia 44°27′N 22°06′E
112 G12 **Donji Vakuf** *var.* Srbobran. ◈ Federacija Bosne I Hercegovine, C Bosnia and Herzegovina
98 M6 **Donkerbroek** Fryslân, N Netherlands 52°58′N 05°15′E
167 P11 **Don Muang** ✈ (Krung Thep) Nonthaburi, C Thailand 13°51′N 100°40′E
25 S17 **Donna** Texas, SW USA 26°10′N 98°03′W
15 Q10 **Donnacona** Québec, SE Canada 46°41′N 71°46′W
**Donnai** *see* Đông Nai, Sông
29 Y16 **Donnellson** Iowa, C USA 40°38′N 91°33′W
11 O13 **Donnelly** Alberta, W Canada 55°42′N 117°06′W
35 P6 **Donner Pass** *Pass* California, W USA
101 F19 **Donnersberg** ▲ W Germany 49°37′N 07°54′E
**Donoso** *see* Miguel de la Borda
105 P2 **Donostia** País Vasco, N Spain 43°19′N 01°59′W
115 K21 **Donoúsa** *var.* Donoússa. *island* Kykládes, Greece, Aegean Sea
**Donoússa** *see* Donoúsa
35 P8 **Don Pedro Reservoir** ▣ California, W USA
**Donqola** *see* Dongola
126 L5 **Donskoy** Tul'skaya Oblast', W Russia 54°02′N 38°27′E
81 L16 **Doolow** Sumalē, E Ethiopia 04°10′N 42°05′E
39 Q7 **Doonerak, Mount** ▲ Alaska, USA 67°54′N 150°33′W
98 J12 **Doorn** Utrecht, C Netherlands 52°02′N 05°21′E
**Doornik** *see* Tournai
31 N6 **Door Peninsula** *peninsula* Wisconsin, N USA
80 P13 **Dooxo Nugaaleed** *var.* Nogal Valley. *valley* E Somalia
**Do Qu** *see* Da Qu
106 B7 **Dora Baltea** *anc.* Duria Major. ≈ NW Italy
180 K7 **Dora, Lake** *salt lake* Western Australia
106 A8 **Dora Riparia** *anc.* Duria Minor. ≈ NW Italy
**Dorbiljin** *see* Emin
**Dorbod/Dorbod Mongolzu Zizhixian** *see* Taikang
**Dorbod Mongolzu Zizhixian** *see* Taikang
113 N18 **Đorče Petrov** *var.* Djorče Petrov, Gorče Petrov. N Macedonia 42°01′N 21°21′E
14 F16 **Dorchester** Ontario, S Canada 43°00′N 81°04′W
97 L24 **Dorchester** *anc.* Durnovaria. S England, United Kingdom 50°43′N 02°26′W
9 P7 **Dorchester, Cape** *headland* Baffin Island, Nunavut, NE Canada 65°25′N 77°25′W
83 D19 **Dordabis** Khomas, C Namibia 22°57′S 17°39′E
102 L12 **Dordogne** ◈ *department* SW France
103 N12 **Dordogne** ≈ W France
98 H13 **Dordrecht** *var.* Dordt, Dort. Zuid-Holland, SW Netherlands 51°48′N 04°40′E
**Dordt** *see* Dordrecht
103 P11 **Dore** ≈ C France
11 S13 **Doré Lake** Saskatchewan, C Canada 54°37′N 107°36′W
103 O12 **Dore, Monts** ▲ C France
101 M23 **Dorfen** Bayern, SE Germany 48°16′N 12°06′E
107 D18 **Dorgali** Sardegna, Italy, C Mediterranean Sea 40°18′N 09°34′E
159 N11 **Dorgê Co** *var.* Elsen Nur. ◎ C China
162 E6 **Dörgön** *var.* Seer. Hovd, W Mongolia 48°18′N 92°37′E
162 F7 **Dörgön Nuur** ◎ NW Mongolia
77 Q12 **Dori** N Burkina Faso 14°03′N 00°02′W
83 E24 **Doring** ≈ S South Africa
101 E16 **Dormagen** Nordrhein-Westfalen, W Germany 51°06′N 06°49′E
103 P4 **Dormans** Marne, N France 49°03′N 03°44′E
108 E6 **Dornach** Solothurn, NW Switzerland 47°29′N 07°37′E
**Dorna Watra** *see* Vatra Dornei
108 J7 **Dornbirn** Vorarlberg, W Austria 47°25′N 09°46′E
96 I7 **Dornoch** N Scotland, United Kingdom 57°52′N 04°01′W
96 J7 **Dornoch Firth** *inlet* N Scotland, United Kingdom
163 P7 **Dornod** ◈ *province* E Mongolia
163 N10 **Dornogovĭ** ◈ *province* SE Mongolia
77 P10 **Doro** Tombouctou, S Mali 16°07′N 00°57′W
116 L14 **Dorobanţu** Călăraşi, S Romania 44°15′N 26°55′E
111 J22 **Dorog** Komárom-Esztergom, N Hungary 47°43′N 18°42′E
126 I4 **Dorogobuzh** Smolenskaya Oblast', W Russia 54°56′N 33°16′E
116 K8 **Dorohoi** Botoşani, NE Romania 47°57′N 26°24′E
93 H15 **Dorotea** Västerbotten, N Sweden 64°17′N 16°30′E
**Dorpat** *see* Tartu
180 G10 **Dorre Island** *island* Western Australia
183 U5 **Dorrigo** New South Wales, SE Australia 30°22′S 152°43′E
35 N1 **Dorris** California, W USA 41°58′N 121°54′W
14 H13 **Dorset** Ontario, SE Canada 45°12′N 78°52′W
97 K23 **Dorset** *cultural region* S England, United Kingdom
101 E14 **Dorsten** Nordrhein-Westfalen, W Germany 51°38′N 06°58′E
**Dort** *see* Dordrecht
101 F15 **Dortmund** Nordrhein-Westfalen, W Germany 51°31′N 07°28′E
100 F12 **Dortmund-Ems-Kanal** *canal* W Germany
136 L17 **Dörtyol** Hatay, S Turkey 36°51′N 36°11′E
**Do Rūd** *see* Dow Rūd
79 O15 **Doruma** Orientale, N Dem. Rep. Congo 04°35′N 27°43′E
15 O12 **Dorval** ✈ (Montréal) Québec, SE Canada 45°27′N 73°46′W
162 F7 **Dörvöljin** *var.* Buga. Dzavhan, W Mongolia 47°42′N 94°53′E
45 T5 **Dos Bocas, Lago** ▣ C Puerto Rico
104 K14 **Dos Hermanas** Andalucía, S Spain 37°16′N 05°55′W
**Dospad Dagh** *see* Rhodope Mountains
35 P10 **Dos Palos** California, W USA 37°00′N 120°39′W
114 I11 **Dospat** Smolyan, S Bulgaria 41°39′N 24°10′E
114 H11 **Dospat, Yazovir** ▣ SW Bulgaria
100 M11 **Dosse** ≈ NE Germany
77 S12 **Dosso** Dosso, SW Niger 13°03′N 03°10′E
77 S12 **Dosso** ◈ *region* SW Niger
144 G12 **Dossor** Atyrau, SW Kazakhstan 47°31′N 53°01′E
147 O10 **Do'stlik** Jizzax Viloyati, C Uzbekistan 40°37′N 67°59′E
147 V9 **Dostuk** Narynskaya Oblast', C Kyrgyzstan 41°19′N 75°40′E
145 X13 **Dostyk** *prev.* Druzhba. Almaty, SE Kazakhstan 45°15′N 82°29′E
23 R7 **Dothan** Alabama, S USA 31°13′N 85°23′W
39 T9 **Dot Lake** Alaska, USA 63°39′N 144°10′W
118 F12 **Dotnuva** Kaunas, C Lithuania 55°23′N 23°53′E
99 D19 **Dottignies** Hainaut, W Belgium 50°43′N 03°16′E
103 P2 **Douai** *prev.* Douay; *anc.* Duacum. Nord, N France 50°22′N 03°04′E
14 L9 **Douaire, Lac** ◎ Québec, SE Canada
79 D16 **Douala** *var.* Duala. Littoral, W Cameroon 04°04′N 09°43′E
79 D16 **Douala** ✈ Littoral, W Cameroon 03°57′N 09°48′E
102 F6 **Douarnenez** Finistère, NW France 48°05′N 04°20′W
102 E6 **Douarnenez, Baie de** *bay* NW France
**Douay** *see* Douai
25 O6 **Double Mountain Fork Brazos River** ≈ Texas, SW USA
23 O3 **Double Springs** Alabama, S USA 34°09′N 87°24′W
103 T8 **Doubs** ◈ *department* E France
108 C8 **Doubs** ≈ France/ Switzerland
185 A22 **Doubtful Sound** *sound* South Island, New Zealand
184 J2 **Doubtless Bay** *bay* North Island, New Zealand
25 X9 **Doucette** Texas, SW USA 30°48′N 94°25′W
102 K8 **Doué-la-Fontaine** Maine-et-Loire, NW France 47°12′N 00°16′W
77 O11 **Douentza** Mopti, S Mali 14°59′N 02°57′W
65 E24 **Douglas** East Falkland, Falkland Islands
97 I16 **Douglas** ○ (Isle of Man) E Isle of Man 54°09′N 04°28′W




◆ Country ● Country Capital ◇ Dependent Territory ○ Dependent Territory Capital ◈ Administrative Regions ✈ International Airport ▲ Mountain ▲ Mountain Range ▲ Volcano ≈ River ◎ Lake ▣ Reservoir

Douglas – D'Urville, Tanjung


83 H23 **Douglas** Northern Cape, C South Africa 29°04′S 23°47′E
39 X13 **Douglas** Alexander Archipelago, Alaska, USA 58°12′N 134°18′W
37 O17 **Douglas** Arizona, SW USA 31°20′N 109°32′W
23 U7 **Douglas** Georgia, SE USA 31°30′N 82°51′W
33 Y15 **Douglas** Wyoming, C USA 42°48′N 105°23′W
21 O7 **Douglas Cape** *headland* Alaska, N USA 64°59′N 166°41′W
10 J14 **Douglas Channel** *channel* British Columbia, W Canada
182 G3 **Douglas Creek** *seasonal river* South Australia
31 P5 **Douglas Lake** ◎ Michigan, N USA
21 O9 **Douglas Lake** ⊠ Tennessee, S USA
39 Q13 **Douglas, Mount** ▲ Alaska, USA 58°51′N 153°31′W
194 I6 **Douglas Range** ▲ Alexander Island, Antarctica
161 S14 **Douliu** *prev.* Touliu. C Taiwan 23°44′N 120°27′E
103 O2 **Doullens** Somme, N France 50°09′N 02°21′E
**Douma** *see* Dūmā
79 F15 **Doumé** Est, E Cameroon 04°14′N 13°27′E
99 E21 **Dour** Hainaut, S Belgium 50°24′N 03°47′E
59 K18 **Dourada, Serra** ▲ S Brazil
59 I21 **Dourados** Mato Grosso do Sul, S Brazil 22°09′S 54°52′W
103 N5 **Dourdan** Essonne, N France 48°33′N 01°58′E
104 I6 **Douro** *Sp.* Duero. ⇝ Portugal/Spain *see also* Duero
**Douro** *see* Duero
104 G6 **Douro Litoral** *former province* N Portugal
**Douvres** *see* Dover
102 K15 **Douze** ⇝ SW France
183 P17 **Dover** Tasmania, SE Australia 43°19′S 147°01′E
97 Q22 **Dover** *Fr.* Douvres, *Lat.* Dubris Portus. SE England, United Kingdom 51°08′N 01°E
21 Y3 **Dover** *state capital* Delaware, NE USA 39°09′N 75°31′W
19 P9 **Dover** New Hampshire, NE USA 43°10′N 70°50′W
18 J14 **Dover** New Jersey, NE USA 40°51′N 74°33′W
31 U12 **Dover** Ohio, N USA 40°31′N 81°28′W
20 H8 **Dover** Tennessee, S USA 36°30′N 87°50′W
97 Q23 **Dover, Strait of** *var.* Straits of Dover, *Fr.* Pas de Calais. *strait* England, United Kingdom/France
**Dover, Straits of** *see* Dover, Strait of
**Dovlen** *see* Devin
94 G11 **Dovre** Oppland, S Norway 61°59′N 09°16′E
94 G10 **Dovrefjell** *plateau* S Norway
**Dovsk** *see* Dowsk
117 Z8 **Dovzhans'k** *prev.* Sverdlovs'k, Imeni Sverdlova Rudnik. Luhans'ka Oblast', E Ukraine 48°05′N 39°37′E
83 M14 **Dowa** Central, C Malawi 13°40′S 33°55′E
31 O10 **Dowagiac** Michigan, N USA 41°58′N 86°06′W
**Dow Gonbadān** *see* Do Gonbadān
148 M2 **Dowlatābād** Fāryāb, N Afghanistan 36°30′N 64°51′E
97 G16 **Down** *cultural region* SE Northern Ireland, United Kingdom
33 R16 **Downey** Idaho, NW USA 42°25′N 112°06′W
35 P5 **Downieville** California, W USA 39°34′N 120°49′W
97 G16 **Downpatrick** *Ir.* Dún Pádraig. SE Northern Ireland, United Kingdom 54°20′N 05°43′W
26 M3 **Downs** Kansas, C USA 39°30′N 98°33′W
18 J12 **Downsville** New York, NE USA 42°03′N 74°59′W
142 L7 **Dow Rūd** *var.* Do Rūd, Durud. Lorestān, W Iran 33°28′N 49°04′E
29 V12 **Dows** Iowa, C USA 42°39′N 93°30′W
119 O17 **Dowsk** *Rus.* Dovsk. Homyel'skaya Voblasts', SE Belarus 53°09′N 30°28′E
35 Q4 **Doyle** California, W USA 40°00′N 120°06′W
18 I15 **Doylestown** Pennsylvania, NE USA 40°18′N 75°08′W
**Doyransko, Ezero** *see* Dojran, Lake
114 I8 **Doyrentsi** Lovech, N Bulgaria 43°13′N 24°46′E
164 G11 **Dōzen** *island* Oki-shotō, SW Japan
14 K9 **Dozois, Réservoir** ⊠ Québec, SE Canada
74 D9 **Drâa** *seasonal river* S Morocco
**Drâa, Hammada du** *see* Dra, Hamada du
**Drabble** *see* José Enrique Rodó
117 Q5 **Drabiv** Cherkas'ka Oblast', C Ukraine 49°57′N 32°10′E
**Drable** *see* José Enrique Rodó
103 S13 **Drac** ⇝ E France
**Drač/Draç** *see* Durrës
60 I8 **Dracena** São Paulo, S Brazil 21°27′S 51°30′W
98 M6 **Drachten** Fryslân, N Netherlands 53°07′N 06°06′E
92 H11 **Drag** *Lapp.* Ájluokta. Nordland, C Norway 68°02′N 16°E
116 L14 **Dragalina** Călăraşi, SE Romania 44°26′N 27°19′E
116 I14 **Draganesti-Olt** Olt, S Romania 44°06′N 25°00′E
116 J14 **Drăgăneşti-Vlaşca** Teleorman, S Romania 44°05′N 25°39′E
116 I13 **Drăgăşani** Vâlcea, SW Romania 44°40′N 24°16′E
114 G9 **Dragoman** Sofia, W Bulgaria 42°32′N 22°56′E
115 L25 **Dragonáda** *island* SE Greece
**Dragonera, Isla** *see* Sa Dragonera
45 T14 **Dragon's Mouths, The** *strait* Trinidad and Tobago/Venezuela
95 J23 **Dragør** Sjælland, E Denmark 55°36′N 12°42′E
114 F10 **Dragovishtitsa** Kyustendil, W Bulgaria 42°22′N 22°39′E
103 U15 **Draguignan** Var, SE France 43°31′N 06°31′E
74 E9 **Dra, Hamada du** *var.* Hammada du Drâa, Haut Plateau du Dra. *plateau* W Algeria
**Dra, Haut Plateau du** *see* Dra, Hamada du
119 H19 **Drahichyn** *Pol.* Drohiczyn Poleski, *Rus.* Drogichin. Brestskaya Voblasts', SW Belarus 52°11′N 25°10′E
29 N4 **Drake** North Dakota, N USA 47°54′N 100°23′W
83 K23 **Drakensberg** ▲▲ Lesotho/South Africa
194 F3 **Drake Passage** *passage* Atlantic Ocean/Pacific Ocean
114 L8 **Dralfa** Tŭrgovishte, N Bulgaria 43°17′N 26°25′E
114 I12 **Dráma** *var.* Dhráma. Anatolikí Makedonía kai Thráki, NE Greece 41°09′N 24°10′E
**Dramburg** *see* Drawsko Pomorskie
95 H15 **Drammen** Buskerud, S Norway 59°44′N 10°12′E
95 H15 **Drammensfjorden** *fjord* S Norway
92 H1 **Drangajökull** ▲ NW Iceland 66°13′N 22°18′W
95 F16 **Drangedal** Telemark, S Norway 59°05′N 09°05′E
92 I2 **Drangsnes** Vestfirðir, NW Iceland 65°42′N 21°27′W
**Drann** *see* Dravinja
109 T10 **Drau** *var.* Drava, *Eng.* Drave, *Hung.* Dráva. ⇝ C Europe *see also* Drava
**Drau** *see* Drava
84 I11 **Drava** *var.* Drau, *Eng.* Drave, *Hung.* Dráva. ⇝ C Europe *see also* Drau
**Drava** *see* Drau
**Dráva/Drave** *see* Drau/Drava
109 W10 **Dravinja** *Ger.* Drann. ⇝ NE Slovenia
109 V9 **Dravograd** *Ger.* Unterdrauburg; *prev.* Spodnji Dravograd. N Slovenia 46°36′N 15°00′E
110 F10 **Drawa** ⇝ NW Poland
110 F9 **Drawno** Zachodnio-pomorskie, NW Poland 53°12′N 15°44′E
110 F9 **Drawsko Pomorskie** *Ger.* Dramburg. Zachodnio-pomorskie, NW Poland 53°32′N 15°48′E
29 R3 **Drayton** North Dakota, N USA 48°34′N 97°10′W
11 P14 **Drayton Valley** Alberta, SW Canada 53°13′N 115°00′W
186 B6 **Dreikikir** East Sepik, NW Papua New Guinea 03°42′S 142°46′E
**Dreikirchen** *see* Teiuş
98 N7 **Drenthe** ◆ *province* NE Netherlands
115 H15 **Drépano, Akrotírio** *var.* Akrotírio Dhrepanon. *headland* N Greece 39°56′N 23°57′E
**Drepanum** *see* Trapani
14 D17 **Dresden** Ontario, S Canada 42°34′N 82°09′W
101 O16 **Dresden** Sachsen, E Germany 51°03′N 13°43′E
20 G8 **Dresden** Tennessee, S USA 36°17′N 88°42′W
118 M11 **Dretun'** Vitsyebskaya Voblasts', N Belarus 55°41′N 29°13′E
102 M5 **Dreux** *anc.* Drocae, Durocasses. Eure-et-Loir, C France 48°44′N 01°23′E
94 I11 **Drevsjø** Hedmark, S Norway 61°52′N 12°01′E
22 K3 **Drew** Mississippi, S USA 33°48′N 90°31′W
110 F10 **Drezdenko** *Ger.* Driesen. Lubuskie, W Poland 52°51′N 15°50′E
98 J12 **Driebergen** *var.* Driebergen-Rijsenburg. Utrecht, C Netherlands 52°03′N 05°17′E
**Driebergen-Rijsenburg** *see* Driebergen
**Driesen** *see* Drezdenko
97 N16 **Driffield** E England, United Kingdom 54°00′N 00°28′W
65 D25 **Driftwood Point** *headland* East Falkland, Falkland Islands 52°15′S 59°00′W
33 S14 **Driggs** Idaho, NW USA 43°44′N 111°06′W
**Drin** *see* Drinit, Lumi i
112 K12 **Drina** ⇝ Bosnia and Herzegovina/Serbia
**Drin, Gulf of** *see* Drinit, Gjiri i
113 M16 **Drini i Bardhë** *Serb.* Beli Drim. ⇝ Albania/Serbia
113 K18 **Drinit, Gjiri i** *var.* Pellg i Drinit, *Eng.* Gulf of Drin. *gulf* NW Albania
113 L17 **Drinit, Lumi i** *var.* Drin. ⇝ NW Albania
**Drinit, Pellg i** *see* Drinit, Gjiri i
**Drinit të Zi, Lumi i** *see* Black Drin
113 L22 **Drino** *var.* Drino, Drínos Pótamos, *Alb.* Lumi i Drinos. ⇝ Albania/Greece
**Drinos, Lumi i/Drínos Pótamos** *see* Drino
25 S11 **Dripping Springs** Texas, SW USA 30°11′N 98°04′W
25 S15 **Driscoll** Texas, SW USA 27°40′N 97°45′W
22 H5 **Driskill Mountain** ▲ Louisiana, S USA 32°25′N 92°54′W
**Drissa** *see* Drysa
94 G10 **Driva** ⇝ S Norway
112 E13 **Drniš** *It.* Šibenik-Knin. Šibenik-Knin, S Croatia 43°51′N 16°10′E
95 H15 **Drøbak** Akershus, S Norway 59°40′N 10°40′E
116 G13 **Drobeta-Turnu Severin** *prev.* Turnu Severin. Mehedinţi, SW Romania 44°39′N 22°40′E
**Drocae** *see* Dreux
116 M8 **Drochia** *Rus.* Drokiya. N Moldova 48°02′N 27°46′E
97 F17 **Drogheda** *Ir.* Droichead Átha. NE Ireland 53°43′N 06°21′W
**Drogichin** *see* Drahichyn
**Drogobych** *see* Drohobych
**Drohiczyn Poleski** *see* Drahichyn
116 H6 **Drohobych** *Pol.* Drohobycz, *Rus.* Drogobych. L'vivs'ka Oblast', NW Ukraine 49°22′N 23°33′E
**Drohobycz** *see* Drohobych
**Droichead Átha** *see* Drogheda
**Droicheadna Bandan** *see* Bandon
**Droichead na Banna** *see* Banbridge
**Droim Mór** *see* Dromore
**Drokiya** *see* Drochia
103 R13 **Drôme** ◆ *department* E France
103 S13 **Drôme** ⇝ E France
97 G15 **Dromore** *Ir.* Droim Mór. SE Northern Ireland, United Kingdom 54°25′N 06°09′W
106 A9 **Dronero** Piemonte, NE Italy 44°28′N 07°25′E
102 L12 **Dronne** ⇝ SW France
195 T3 **Dronning Fabiolafjella** *var.* Mount Victor. ▲ Antarctica 72°49′S 33°01′E
195 Q3 **Dronning Maud Land** *physical region* Antarctica
98 K6 **Dronrijp** *Fris.* Dronryp. Fryslân, N Netherlands 53°12′N 05°37′E
**Dronryp** *see* Dronrijp
98 L9 **Dronten** Flevoland, C Netherlands 52°31′N 05°41′E
**Drontheim** *see* Trondheim
102 L13 **Dropt** ⇝ SW France
149 T4 **Drosh** Khyber Pakhtunkhwa, NW Pakistan 35°33′N 71°48′E
**Drossen** *see* Ośno Lubuskie
**Drug** *see* Durg
**Drujba** *see* Pitnak
118 I12 **Drūkšiai** ◎ NE Lithuania
**Druk-yul** *see* Bhutan
11 Q16 **Drumheller** Alberta, SW Canada 51°28′N 112°42′W
33 Q10 **Drummond** Montana, NW USA 46°39′N 113°12′W
31 R4 **Drummond Island** *island* Michigan, N USA
**Drummond Island** *see* Tabiteuea
21 X7 **Drummond, Lake** ◎ Virginia, NE USA
15 P12 **Drummondville** Québec, SE Canada 45°52′N 72°28′W
39 T11 **Drum, Mount** ▲ Alaska, USA 62°11′N 144°37′W
27 O9 **Drumright** Oklahoma, C USA 35°59′N 96°36′W
99 J14 **Drunen** Noord-Brabant, S Netherlands 51°41′N 05°08′E
**Druskienniki** *see* Druskininkai
119 F15 **Druskininkai** *Pol.* Druskienniki. Alytus, S Lithuania 54°00′N 24°00′E
98 K13 **Druten** Gelderland, SE Netherlands 51°53′N 05°37′E
118 K11 **Druya** Vitsyebskaya Voblasts', NW Belarus 55°47′N 27°27′E
117 S2 **Druzhba** Sums'ka Oblast', NE Ukraine 52°01′N 33°56′E
**Druzhba** *see* Dostyk, Kazakhstan
**Druzhba** *see* Pitnak, Uzbekistan
123 R7 **Druzhina** Respublika Sakha (Yakutiya), NE Russia 68°01′N 144°58′E
117 X7 **Druzhkivka** Donets'ka Oblast', E Ukraine 48°38′N 37°31′E
112 E12 **Drvar** Federacija Bosne I Hercegovine, W Bosnia and Herzegovina 44°21′N 16°24′E
113 G15 **Drvenik** Split-Dalmacija, SE Croatia 43°10′N 17°13′E
114 K9 **Dryanovo** Gabrovo, N Bulgaria 42°58′N 25°28′E
26 G7 **Dry Cimarron River** ⇝ Kansas/Oklahoma, C USA
12 B11 **Dryden** Ontario, C Canada 49°48′N 92°48′W
24 M11 **Dryden** Texas, SW USA 30°01′N 102°06′W
195 Q14 **Drygalski Ice Tongue** *ice feature* Antarctica
118 L11 **Drysa** *Rus.* Drissa. ⇝ N Belarus
23 V17 **Dry Tortugas** *island* Florida, SE USA
79 D15 **Dschang** Ouest, W Cameroon 05°28′N 10°02′E
54 J5 **Duaca** Lara, N Venezuela 10°22′N 69°08′W
**Duacum** *see* Douai
**Duala** *see* Douala
45 N9 **Duarte, Pico** ▲ C Dominican Republic 19°02′N 70°57′W
140 J5 **Dubā** Tabūk, NW Saudi Arabia 27°26′N 35°42′E
**Dubai** *see* Dubayy
117 N9 **Dubăsari** *Rus.* Dubossary. NE Moldova 47°16′N 29°07′E
117 N9 **Dubăsari Reservoir** ⊠ NE Moldova
8 M10 **Dubawnt** ⇝ Nunavut, NW Canada
8 L9 **Dubawnt Lake** ◎ Northwest Territories/Nunavut, N Canada
30 L6 **Du Bay, Lake** ⊠ Wisconsin, N USA
141 U7 **Dubayy** *Eng.* Dubai. Dubayy, NE United Arab Emirates 25°11′N 55°18′E
141 W7 **Dubayy** *Eng.* Dubai. ✈ Dubayy, NE United Arab Emirates 25°15′N 55°22′E
183 R7 **Dubbo** New South Wales, SE Australia 32°16′S 148°41′E
108 G7 **Dübendorf** Zürich, NW Switzerland 47°23′N 08°37′E
97 F18 **Dublin** *Ir.* Baile Átha Cliath; *anc.* Eblana. ● (Ireland) Dublin, E Ireland 53°20′N 06°15′W
23 U5 **Dublin** Georgia, SE USA 32°32′N 82°54′W
25 R7 **Dublin** Texas, SW USA 32°05′N 98°20′W
97 G18 **Dublin** *Ir.* Baile Átha Cliath; *anc.* Eblana. *cultural region* E Ireland
97 G18 **Dublin Airport** ✈ Dublin, E Ireland 53°25′N 06°18′W
189 V12 **Dublon** *var.* Tonoas. *island* Chuuk Islands, C Micronesia
126 K2 **Dubna** Moskovskaya Oblast', W Russia 56°45′N 37°09′E
111 G19 **Dubňany** *Ger.* Dubnian. Jihomoravský Kraj, SE Czechia 48°54′N 17°00′E
**Dubnian** *see* Dubňany
111 I19 **Dubnica nad Váhom** *Hung.* Máriatölgyes; *prev.* Dubnicz. Trenčiansky Kraj, W Slovakia 48°58′N 18°10′E
**Dubnicz** *see* Dubnica nad Váhom
116 K4 **Dubno** Rivnens'ka Oblast', NW Ukraine 50°28′N 25°40′E
33 R13 **Dubois** Idaho, NW USA 44°10′N 112°13′W
18 D13 **Du Bois** Pennsylvania, NE USA 41°07′N 78°45′W
33 T14 **Dubois** Wyoming, C USA 43°31′N 109°37′W
**Dubossary** *see* Dubăsari
127 O10 **Dubovka** Volgogradskaya Oblast', SW Russia 49°10′N 44°49′E
76 H14 **Dubréka** SW Guinea 09°48′N 13°31′W
14 B7 **Dubreuilville** Ontario, S Canada 48°21′N 84°31′W
**Dubris Portus** *see* Dover
119 L20 **Dubrova** Homyel'skaya Voblasts', SE Belarus 51°47′N 28°13′E
**Dubrovačko-Neretvanska Županija** *see* Dubrovnik-Neretva
126 I5 **Dubrovka** Bryanskaya Oblast', W Russia 53°44′N 33°27′E
113 H16 **Dubrovnik** *It.* Ragusa. Dubrovnik-Neretva, SE Croatia 42°40′N 18°06′E
113 I16 **Dubrovnik** ✈ Dubrovnik-Neretva, SE Croatia 42°34′N 18°17′E
113 F16 **Dubrovnik-Neretva** *off.* Dubrovačko-Neretvanska Županija. ◆ *province* SE Croatia
**Dubrovno** *see* Dubrowna
116 L2 **Dubrovytsya** Rivnens'ka Oblast', NW Ukraine 51°34′N 26°37′E
119 O14 **Dubrowna** *Rus.* Dubrovno. Vitsyebskaya Voblasts', N Belarus 54°35′N 30°41′E
29 Z13 **Dubuque** Iowa, C USA 42°30′N 90°40′W
118 E12 **Dubysa** ⇝ C Lithuania
**Đưc Co** *see* Chu Ty
191 V12 **Duc de Gloucester, Îles du** *Eng.* Duke of Gloucester Islands. *island group* C French Polynesia
111 C15 **Duchcov** *Ger.* Dux. Ústecký Kraj, NW Czechia 50°37′N 13°45′E
37 N3 **Duchesne** Utah, W USA 40°09′N 110°24′W
191 P17 **Ducie Island** *atoll* E Pitcairn Group of Islands
11 W15 **Duck Bay** Manitoba, S Canada 52°11′N 100°08′W
23 X17 **Duck Key** *island* Florida Keys, Florida, SE USA
11 T14 **Duck Lake** Saskatchewan, S Canada 52°52′N 106°12′W
11 V15 **Duck Mountain** ▲▲ Manitoba, S Canada
20 I9 **Duck River** ⇝ Tennessee, S USA
20 M10 **Ducktown** Tennessee, S USA 35°01′N 84°24′W
167 U10 **Đưc Phô** Quang Ngai, C Vietnam 14°56′N 108°55′E
**Đưc Tho** *see* Lin Camh
**Đưc Trong** *see* Liên Nghia
**D-U-D** *see* Dalap-Uliga-Djarrit
153 N15 **Dūddhinagar** *var.* Dūdhi. Uttar Pradesh, N India 24°09′N 83°15′E
99 M25 **Dudelange** *var.* Forge du Sud, *Ger.* Dudelingen. Luxembourg, S Luxembourg 49°28′N 06°05′E
**Dudelingen** *see* Dudelange
101 J15 **Duderstadt** Niedersachsen, C Germany 51°31′N 10°16′E
**Dūdhi** *see* Dūddhinagar
122 K8 **Dudinka** Krasnoyarskiy Kray, N Russia 69°27′N 86°13′E
97 L20 **Dudley** C England, United Kingdom 52°30′N 02°05′W
154 G13 **Dudna** ⇝ C India
76 L16 **Duékoué** W Ivory Coast 06°50′N 05°22′W
104 M5 **Dueñas** Castilla y León, N Spain 41°52′N 04°33′W
104 K4 **Duerna** ⇝ NW Spain
105 O6 **Duero** *Port.* Douro. ⇝ Portugal/Spain *see also* Douro
**Duero** *see* Douro
**Duesseldorf** *see* Düsseldorf
21 P12 **Due West** South Carolina, SE USA 34°19′N 82°23′W
195 P11 **Dufek Coast** *physical region* Antarctica
99 H17 **Duffel** Antwerpen, C Belgium 51°06′N 04°30′E
35 S2 **Duffer Peak** ▲ Nevada, W USA 41°40′N 118°45′W
187 Q9 **Duff Islands** *island group* E Solomon Islands
**Dufour, Pizzo/Dufour, Punta** *see* Dufour Spitze
108 E12 **Dufour Spitze** *It.* Pizzo Dufour, Punta Dufour. ▲ Italy/Switzerland 45°54′N 07°50′E
112 D9 **Duga Resa** Karlovac, C Croatia 45°25′N 15°30′E
22 H5 **Dugdemona River** ⇝ Louisiana, S USA
154 J12 **Duggīpar** Mahārāshtra, C India 21°06′N 80°10′E
112 B13 **Dugi Otok** *var.* Isola Grossa, *It.* Isola Lunga. *island* W Croatia
113 F14 **Dugopolje** Split-Dalmacija, S Croatia 43°35′N 16°35′E
160 L8 **Du He** ⇝ C China
54 M11 **Duida, Cerro** ▲ S Venezuela 03°21′N 65°45′W
**Duinekerke** *see* Dunkerque
101 E15 **Duisburg** *prev.* Duisburg-Hamborn. Nordrhein-Westfalen, W Germany 51°25′N 06°47′E
**Duisburg-Hamborn** *see* Duisburg
99 F14 **Duiveland** *island* SW Netherlands
98 M12 **Duiven** Gelderland, E Netherlands 51°57′N 06°02′E
139 W10 **Dujaylah, Hawr ad** ◎ S Iraq
160 H9 **Dujiangyan** *var.* Guanxian, Guan Xian. Sichuan, C China 31°01′N 103°40′E
81 L18 **Dujuuma** Shabeellaha Hoose, S Somalia 01°04′N 42°37′E
139 T3 **Dūkān** *Ar.* Dokan, *var.* Dokan. As Sulaymānīyah, E Iraq 35°55′N 44°58′E
**Dūkān** *see* Dūkan
39 Z14 **Duke Island** *island* Alexander Archipelago, Alaska, USA
**Dukelský Priesmy/ Dukelský Průsmyk** *see* Dukla Pass
**Duke of Gloucester Islands** *see* Duc de Gloucester, Îles du
81 F14 **Duk Faiwil** Jonglei, E South Sudan 07°30′N 31°27′E
141 T7 **Dukhān** C Qatar 25°29′N 50°48′E
**Dukhan Heights** *see* Dukhān, Jabal
143 N16 **Dukhān, Jabal** *var.* Dukhan Heights. *hill range* S Qatar
127 Q7 **Dukhovnitskoye** Saratovskaya Oblast', W Russia 52°31′N 48°32′E
126 H4 **Dukhovshchina** Smolenskaya Oblast', W Russia 55°15′N 32°22′E
**Dukielska, Przełęcz** *see* Dukla Pass
111 N17 **Dukla** Podkarpackie, SE Poland 49°33′N 21°40′E
**Duklai Hág** *see* Dukla Pass
111 N18 **Dukla Pass** *Cz.* Dukelský Průsmyk, *Ger.* Dukla-Pass, *Hung.* Duklai Hág, *Pol.* Przełęcz Dukielska, *Slvk.* Dukelský Priesmy. *pass* Poland/Slovakia
**Dukla-Pass** *see* Dukla Pass
**Dukou** *see* Panzhihua
118 I12 **Dūkštas** Utena, E Lithuania 55°32′N 26°21′E
**Dulaan** *see* Herlenbayan-Ulaan
159 R10 **Dulan** *var.* Qagan Us. Qinghai, C China 36°11′N 97°51′E
37 R8 **Dulce** New Mexico, SW USA 36°55′N 107°00′W
43 N16 **Dulce, Golfo** *gulf* S Costa Rica
**Dulce, Golfo** *see* Izabal, Lago de
42 K6 **Dulce Nombre de Culmí** Olancho, C Honduras 15°09′N 85°37′W
62 L9 **Dulce, Río** ⇝ C Argentina
123 Q9 **Dulgalakh** ⇝ NE Russia
**Dŭlgopol** *see* Dalgopol
153 V14 **Dullabchara** Assam, NE India 24°25′N 92°22′E
20 D3 **Dulles** ✈ (Washington DC)Virginia, NE USA 39°00′N 77°27′W
101 E14 **Dülmen** Nordrhein-Westfalen, W Germany 51°51′N 07°17′E
114 M7 **Dulovo** Silistra, NE Bulgaria 43°51′N 27°10′E
29 W5 **Duluth** Minnesota, N USA 46°47′N 92°06′W
138 H7 **Dūmā** *Fr.* Douma. Rīf Dimashq, SW Syria 33°33′N 36°24′E
171 O8 **Dumagasa Point** *headland* Mindanao, S Philippines 07°01′N 121°54′E
171 P6 **Dumaguete** *var.* Dumaguete City. Negros, C Philippines 09°16′N 123°17′E
**Dumaguete City** *see* Dumaguete
168 J10 **Dumai** Sumatera, W Indonesia 01°39′N 101°28′E
183 T4 **Dumaresq River** ⇝ New South Wales/Queensland, SE Australia
27 W13 **Dumas** Arkansas, C USA 33°53′N 91°29′W
25 N1 **Dumas** Texas, SW USA 35°51′N 101°57′W
138 I7 **Dumayr** Rīf Dimashq, W Syria 33°36′N 36°28′E
96 I12 **Dumbarton** W Scotland, United Kingdom 55°57′N 04°35′W
96 I12 **Dumbarton** *cultural region* C Scotland, United Kingdom
187 Q17 **Dumbéa** Province Sud, S New Caledonia 22°11′S 166°27′E
111 K19 **Ďumbier** *Ger.* Djumbir, *Hung.* Gyömbér. ▲ C Slovakia 48°54′N 19°36′E
116 I11 **Dumbrăveni** *Ger.* Elisabethstedt, *Hung.* Erzsébetváros; *prev.* Ebesfalva, Eppeschdorf, Ibaşfalău. Sibiu, C Romania 46°14′N 24°34′E
116 L12 **Dumbrăveni** Vrancea, E Romania 45°31′N 27°09′E
97 J14 **Dumfries** S Scotland, United Kingdom 55°04′N 03°37′W
97 J14 **Dumfries** *cultural region* SW Scotland, United Kingdom
153 R15 **Dumka** Jhārkhand, NE India 24°17′N 87°15′E
**Dümmer** *see* Dümmersee
100 G12 **Dümmersee** *var.* Dümmer. ◎ NW Germany
14 J11 **Dumoine** ⇝ Québec, SE Canada
14 J10 **Dumoine, Lac** ◎ Québec, SE Canada
195 V16 **Dumont d'Urville** *research station (France)* Antarctica 66°24′S 139°38′E
195 W15 **Dumont d'Urville Sea** *sea* S Pacific Ocean
14 K11 **Dumont, Lac** ◎ Québec, SE Canada
75 W7 **Dumyāt** *var.* Dumyât, *Eng.* Damietta. N Egypt 31°26′N 31°48′E
**Duna** *see* Danube, C Europe
**Düna** *see* Western Dvina
**Duna** *see* Don, Russian Federation
**Dünaburg** *see* Daugavpils
111 J24 **Dunaföldvár** Tolna, C Hungary 46°48′N 18°55′E
**Dunaj** *see* Wien, Austria
**Dunaj** *see* Danube, C Europe
111 L18 **Dunajec** ⇝ S Poland
111 H21 **Dunajská Streda** *Hung.* Dunaszerdahely. Trnavský Kraj, W Slovakia 48°N 17°28′E
**Dunapentele** *see* Dunaújváros
**Dunărea** *see* Danube
116 M13 **Dunărea Veche, Braţul** ⇝ SE Romania
117 N13 **Dunării, Delta** *delta* SE Romania
**Dunaszerdahely** *see* Dunajská Streda
111 J23 **Dunaújváros** *prev.* Dunapentele, Sztálinváros. Fejér, C Hungary 47°N 18°55′E
**Dunav** *see* Danube
114 J8 **Dunavska Ravnina** *Eng.* Danubian Plain. *lowlands* N Bulgaria
114 G7 **Dunavtsi** Vidin, NW Bulgaria 43°54′N 22°49′E
123 S15 **Dunay** Primorskiy Kray, SE Russia 42°53′N 132°20′E
**Dunay** *see* Danube
**Dunayevtsy** *see* Dunayivtsi
116 L7 **Dunayivtsi** *Rus.* Dunayevtsy. Khmel'nyts'ka Oblast', NW Ukraine 48°56′N 26°50′E
185 F22 **Dunback** Otago, South Island, New Zealand 45°22′S 170°37′E
10 L17 **Duncan** Vancouver Island, British Columbia, SW Canada 48°46′N 123°10′W
37 O15 **Duncan** Arizona, SW USA 32°43′N 109°06′W
26 M12 **Duncan** Oklahoma, C USA 34°30′N 97°57′W
**Duncan Island** *see* Pinzón, Isla
151 Q20 **Duncan Passage** *strait* Andaman Sea/Bay of Bengal
96 K6 **Duncansby Head** *headland* N Scotland, United Kingdom 58°37′N 03°01′W
14 G12 **Dunchurch** Ontario, S Canada 45°36′N 79°54′W
118 D7 **Dundaga** NW Latvia 57°29′N 22°19′E
14 G14 **Dundalk** Ontario, S Canada 44°11′N 80°22′W
97 F16 **Dundalk** *Ir.* Dún Dealgan. Louth, NE Ireland 54°01′N 06°25′W
21 X3 **Dundalk** Maryland, NE USA 39°15′N 76°31′W
97 F16 **Dundalk Bay** *Ir.* Cuan Dhún Dealgan. *bay* NE Ireland
14 G16 **Dundas** Ontario, S Canada 43°16′N 79°55′W
180 L12 **Dundas, Lake** *salt lake* Western Australia
**Dundbürd** *see* Batnorov
**Dún Dealgan** *see* Dundalk
15 N13 **Dundee** Québec, SE Canada 45°01′N 74°27′W
83 K22 **Dundee** KwaZulu/Natal, E South Africa 28°09′S 30°12′E
96 K11 **Dundee** E Scotland, United Kingdom 56°28′N 03°W
31 R10 **Dundee** Michigan, N USA 41°57′N 83°39′W
25 R5 **Dundee** Texas, SW USA 33°43′N 98°52′W
194 H3 **Dundee Island** *island* Antarctica
162 L9 **Dundgovi** ◆ *province* C Mongolia
97 G16 **Dundrum Bay** *Ir.* Cuan Dhún Droma. *inlet* NW Irish Sea
11 T15 **Dundurn** Saskatchewan, S Canada 51°43′N 106°27′W
**Dund-Us** *see* Hovd
**Dund-Us** *see* Hovd
185 F23 **Dunedin** Otago, South Island, New Zealand 45°52′S 170°31′E
183 R7 **Dunedoo** New South Wales, SE Australia 32°04′S 149°23′E
97 D14 **Dunfanaghy** *Ir.* Dún Fionnachaidh. NW Ireland 55°11′N 07°59′W
96 J12 **Dunfermline** C Scotland, United Kingdom 56°04′N 03°29′W
**Dún Fionnachaidh** *see* Dunfanaghy
149 V10 **Dunga Bunga** Punjab, E Pakistan 29°51′N 73°19′E
97 F15 **Dungannon** *Ir.* Dún Geanainn. C Northern Ireland, United Kingdom 54°31′N 06°46′W
**Dun Garbháin** *see* Dungarvan
152 F15 **Dūngarpur** Rājasthān, N India 23°50′N 73°43′E
97 E21 **Dungarvan** *Ir.* Dun Garbháin. Waterford, S Ireland 52°05′N 07°37′W
101 N21 **Dungau** *cultural region* SE Germany
**Dún Geanainn** *see* Dungannon
97 P23 **Dungeness** *headland* SE England, United Kingdom 50°55′N 00°58′E
63 I23 **Dungeness, Punta** *headland* S Argentina 52°25′S 68°25′W
**Dunglow** *see* Dunglow
97 D14 **Dunglow** *var.* Dungloe, *Ir.* An Clochán Liath. Donegal, NW Ireland 54°57′N 08°22′W
183 T7 **Dungog** New South Wales, SE Australia 32°24′S 151°45′E
79 O16 **Dungu** Orientale, NE Dem. Rep. Congo 03°40′N 28°32′E
168 L8 **Dungun** *var.* Kuala Dungun. Terengganu, Peninsular Malaysia 04°47′N 103°26′E
80 I6 **Dungunab** Red Sea, NE Sudan 21°10′N 37°09′E
15 P13 **Dunham** Québec, SE Canada 45°08′N 72°48′W
**Dunheved** *see* Launceston
**Dunholme** *see* Durham
163 X10 **Dunhua** Jilin, NE China 43°22′N 128°12′E
159 P8 **Dunhuang** Gansu, N China 40°10′N 94°40′E
182 L12 **Dunkeld** Victoria, SE Australia 37°41′S 142°19′E
103 O1 **Dunkerque** *Eng.* Dunkirk, *Flem.* Duinekerke; *prev.* Dunquerque. Nord, N France 51°06′N 02°34′E
97 K23 **Dunkery Beacon** ▲ SW England, United Kingdom 51°10′N 03°36′W
18 C11 **Dunkirk** New York, NE USA 42°28′N 79°19′W
**Dunkirk** *see* Dunkerque
77 P17 **Dunkwa** SW Ghana 05°59′N 01°45′W
97 G18 **Dún Laoghaire** *Eng.* Dunleary; *prev.* Kingstown. E Ireland 53°17′N 06°08′W
29 S14 **Dunlap** Iowa, C USA 41°51′N 95°36′W
20 L10 **Dunlap** Tennessee, S USA 35°22′N 85°23′W
**Dunleary** *see* Dún Laoghaire
**Dún Mánmhaí** *see* Dunmanway
97 B21 **Dunmanway** *Ir.* Dún Mánmhaí. Cork, SW Ireland 51°43′N 09°07′W
18 I13 **Dunmore** Pennsylvania, NE USA 41°25′N 75°37′W
21 U10 **Dunn** North Carolina, SE USA 35°18′N 78°36′W
**Dún na nGall** *see* Donegal
23 V11 **Dunnellon** Florida, SE USA 29°03′N 82°27′W
96 J6 **Dunnet Head** *headland* N Scotland, United Kingdom 58°40′N 03°27′W
29 N14 **Dunning** Nebraska, C USA 41°49′N 100°04′W
65 B24 **Dunnose Head Settlement** West Falkland, Falkland Islands 51°24′S 60°29′W
14 G17 **Dunnville** Ontario, S Canada 42°54′N 79°36′W
**Dún Pádraig** *see* Downpatrick
**Dunquerque** *see* Dunkerque
**Dunqulah** *see* Dongola
96 L12 **Duns** SE Scotland, United Kingdom 55°46′N 02°13′W
29 N2 **Dunseith** North Dakota, N USA 48°48′N 100°03′W
35 N2 **Dunsmuir** California, W USA 41°12′N 122°19′W
97 N21 **Dunstable** *Lat.* Durocobrivae. E England, United Kingdom 51°53′N 00°32′W
185 D21 **Dunstan Mountains** ▲▲ South Island, New Zealand
103 O9 **Dun-sur-Auron** Cher, C France 46°52′N 02°40′E
185 F21 **Duntroon** Canterbury, South Island, New Zealand 44°52′S 170°40′E
149 T10 **Dunyāpur** Punjab, E Pakistan 29°48′N 71°48′E
163 U5 **Duobukur He** ⇝ NE China
163 R12 **Duolun** *var.* Dolonnur. Nei Mongol Zizhiqu, N China 42°11′N 116°30′E
114 G10 **Dupnitsa** *prev.* Marek, Stanke Dimitrov. Kyustendil, W Bulgaria 42°16′N 23°07′E
28 L8 **Dupree** South Dakota, N USA 45°03′N 101°36′W
33 Q7 **Dupuyer** Montana, NW USA 48°13′N 112°34′W
141 Y11 **Duqm** *var.* Daqm. E Oman 19°42′N 57°40′E
63 F23 **Duque de York, Isla** *island* S Chile
181 N4 **Durack Range** ▲▲ Western Australia
136 K10 **Durağan** Sinop, N Turkey 41°26′N 35°03′E
103 S15 **Durance** ⇝ SE France
31 R9 **Durand** Michigan, N USA 42°54′N 83°58′W
30 I6 **Durand** Wisconsin, N USA 44°37′N 91°56′W
40 K10 **Durango** *var.* Victoria de Durango. Durango, W Mexico 24°03′N 104°38′W
105 P3 **Durango** País Vasco, N Spain 43°10′N 02°38′W
37 Q8 **Durango** Colorado, C USA 37°13′N 107°51′W
40 J9 **Durango** ◆ *state* C Mexico
114 O7 **Durankulak** *Rom.* Răcari; *prev.* Blatnitsa, Duranulac. Dobrich, NE Bulgaria 43°41′N 28°31′E
22 L4 **Durant** Mississippi, S USA 33°04′N 89°51′W
27 P13 **Durant** Oklahoma, C USA 33°59′N 96°24′W
**Duranulac** *see* Durankulak
105 N6 **Duratón** ⇝ N Spain
61 E19 **Durazno** *var.* San Pedro de Durazno. Durazno, C Uruguay 33°22′S 56°31′W
61 E19 **Durazno** ◆ *department* C Uruguay
**Durazzo** *see* Durrës
83 K23 **Durban** *var.* Port Natal. KwaZulu/Natal, E South Africa 29°51′S 31°E
83 K23 **Durban** ✈ KwaZulu/Natal, E South Africa 29°55′S 31°01′E
118 C9 **Durbe** *Ger.* Durben. W Latvia 56°34′N 21°22′E
**Durben** *see* Durbe
99 K21 **Durbuy** Luxembourg, SE Belgium 50°21′N 05°27′E
105 N15 **Dúrcal** Andalucía, S Spain 37°00′N 03°24′W
112 F8 **Đurđevac** *Ger.* Sankt Georgen, *Hung.* Szentgyörgy; *prev.* Djurdjevac, Gjurgjevac. Koprivnica-Križevci, N Croatia 46°02′N 17°03′E
113 K15 **Đurđevica Tara** N Montenegro 43°09′N 19°18′E
97 L24 **Durdle Door** *natural arch* S England, United Kingdom
158 L3 **Düre** Xinjiang Uygur Zizhiqu, W China 46°30′N 88°26′E
101 D16 **Düren** *anc.* Marcodurum. Nordrhein-Westfalen, W Germany 50°48′N 06°30′E
154 K12 **Durg** *prev.* Drug. Chhattisgarh, C India 21°12′N 81°20′E
153 U13 **Durgapur** Dhaka, N Bangladesh 25°10′N 90°41′E
153 R15 **Durgāpur** West Bengal, NE India 23°30′N 87°20′E
14 F14 **Durham** Ontario, S Canada 44°10′N 80°48′W
97 M14 **Durham** *hist.* Dunholme. N England, United Kingdom 54°47′N 01°34′W
21 U9 **Durham** North Carolina, SE USA 36°N 78°54′W
97 L15 **Durham** *cultural region* N England, United Kingdom
168 J10 **Duri** Sumatera, W Indonesia 01°13′N 101°13′E
**Duria Major** *see* Dora Baltea
**Duria Minor** *see* Dora Riparia
**Durlas** *see* Thurles
141 P8 **Durmā** Ar Riyāḑ, C Saudi Arabia 24°37′N 46°06′E
96 H6 **Durness** N Scotland, United Kingdom 58°34′N 04°46′W
109 Y3 **Dürnkrut** Niederösterreich, E Austria 48°28′N 16°50′E
**Durnovaria** *see* Dorchester
**Durobrivae** *see* Rochester
**Durocasses** *see* Dreux
**Durocobrivae** *see* Dunstable
**Durocortorum** *see* Reims
**Durostorum** *see* Silistra
**Durovernum** *see* Canterbury
113 K20 **Durrës** *var.* Durrësi, Dursi, *It.* Durazzo, *SCr.* Drač, *Turk.* Draç. Durrës, W Albania 41°20′N 19°26′E
113 K19 **Durrës** ◆ *county* W Albania
**Durrësi** *see* Durrës
97 A21 **Dursey Island** *Ir.* Oileán Baoi. *island* SW Ireland
**Dursi** *see* Durrës
**Duru** *see* Wuchuan
**Durud** *see* Dow Rūd
114 P12 **Durusu** İstanbul, NW Turkey 41°18′N 28°41′E
114 O12 **Durusu Gölü** ◎ NW Turkey
138 I9 **Durūz, Jabal ad** ▲ SW Syria 37°00′N 32°30′E
**D'Urville Island** *see* Rangitoto ki te Tonga / D'Urville Island
171 X12 **D'Urville, Tanjung** *headland* Papua, E Indonesia 01°26′S 137°52′E


◆ Country
● Country Capital
◇ Dependent Territory
○ Dependent Territory Capital
◆ Administrative Regions
✈ International Airport
▲ Mountain
▲▲ Mountain Range
Volcano
⇝ River
◎ Lake
⊠ Reservoir

DUŞAK – EGYPT


146 H14 **Duşak** *Rus.* Dushak. Ahal Welaýaty, S Turkmenistan 37°15′N 59°57′E
**Dusa Mareb/Dusa Marreb** *see* Dhuusa Marreeb
118 I11 **Dusetos** Utena, NE Lithuania 55°44′N 25°49′E
**Dushak** *see* Duşak
160 K12 **Dushan** Guizhou, S China 25°50′N 107°36′E
147 P13 **Dushanbe** *var.* Dyushambe; *prev.* Stalinabad, *Taj.* Stalinobod. ● (Tajikistan) W Tajikistan 38°35′N 68°44′E
147 P13 **Dushanbe** ✈ W Tajikistan 38°31′N 68°49′E
137 T9 **Dusheti** *prev.* Dushet'i. E Georgia 42°07′N 44°44′E
**Dushet'i** *see* Dusheti
18 H13 **Dushore** Pennsylvania, NE USA 41°30′N 76°23′W
185 A23 **Dusky Sound** *sound* South Island, New Zealand
101 E15 **Düsseldorf** *var.* Duesseldorf. Nordrhein-Westfalen, W Germany 51°14′N 06°49′E
147 P14 **Dūstí** *Rus.* Dusti. SW Tajikistan 37°22′N 68°41′E
194 I9 **Dustin Island** *island* Antarctica
**Dutch East Indies** *see* Indonesia
**Dutch Guiana** *see* Suriname
38 L17 **Dutch Harbor** Unalaska Island, Alaska, USA 53°51′N 166°33′W
36 J3 **Dutch Mount** ▲ Utah, W USA 40°16′N 113°56′W
**Dutch New Guinea** *see* Papua
83 H20 **Dutlwe** Kweneng, S Botswana 23°58′S 23°56′E
67 V16 **Du Toit Fracture Zone** *tectonic feature* SW Indian Ocean
125 U8 **Dutovo** Respublika Komi, NW Russia 63°45′N 56°38′E
77 V13 **Dutsan Wai** *var.* Dutsen Wai. Kaduna, C Nigeria 10°49′N 08°15′E
77 W13 **Dutse** Jigawa, N Nigeria 11°43′N 09°25′E
**Dutsen Wai** *see* Dutsan Wai
**Duttia** *see* Datia
14 E17 **Dutton** Ontario, S Canada 42°40′N 81°28′W
36 L7 **Dutton, Mount** ▲ Utah, W USA 38°00′N 112°10′W
83 J25 **Dutywa** *prev.* Idutywa. Eastern Cape, SE South Africa 32°06′S 28°20′E *see also* Dutywa
162 E7 **Duut** Hovd, W Mongolia 47°28′N 91°52′E
14 K11 **Duval, Lac** ◎ Québec, SE Canada
127 W3 **Duvan** Respublika Bashkortostan, W Russia 55°42′N 57°56′E
138 L9 **Duwaykhilat Satīḩ ar Ruwayshid** *seasonal river* SE Jordan
**Dux** *see* Duchcov
160 J13 **Duyang Shan** ▲▲ S China
167 T14 **Duyên Hai** Tra Vinh, S Vietnam 09°39′N 106°28′E
160 K12 **Duyun** Guizhou, S China 26°16′N 107°29′E
136 G11 **Düzce** Düzce, NW Turkey 40°51′N 31°09′E
136 K14 **Düzce** ◈ *province* NW Turkey
**Duzdab** *see* Zāhedān
**Duzenkyr, Khrebet** *see* Duzkyr, Khrebet
146 I16 **Duzkyr, Khrebet** *prev.* Khrebet Duzenkyr. ▲▲ S Turkmenistan
**Dvina Bay** *see* Chëshskaya Guba
**Dvinsk** *see* Daugavpils
124 L7 **Dvinskaya Guba** *bay* NW Russia
112 E10 **Dvor** Sisak-Moslavina, C Croatia 45°05′N 16°22′E
117 W5 **Dvorichna** Kharkivs'ka Oblast', E Ukraine 49°52′N 37°43′E
111 F16 **Dvůr Králové nad Labem** *Ger.* Königinhof an der Elbe. Královéhradecký Kraj, N Czechia 50°27′N 15°50′E
154 A10 **Dwārka** Gujarāt, W India 22°14′N 68°58′E
30 M12 **Dwight** Illinois, N USA 41°05′N 88°25′W
98 N8 **Dwingeloo** Drenthe, NE Netherlands 52°49′N 06°20′E
33 N10 **Dworshak Reservoir** ⊠ Idaho, NW USA
**Dyal** *see* Dyaul Island
**Dyanev** *see* Galkynyş
**Dyatlovo** *see* Dzyatlava
186 G5 **Dyaul Island** *var.* Djaul, Dyal. *island* NE Papua New Guinea
20 G8 **Dyer** Tennessee, S USA 36°04′N 88°59′W
9 S5 **Dyer, Cape** *headland* Baffin Island, Nunavut, NE Canada 66°37′N 61°13′W
20 F8 **Dyersburg** Tennessee, S USA 36°02′N 89°21′W
29 Y13 **Dyersville** Iowa, C USA 42°29′N 91°07′W
97 I21 **Dyfed** *cultural region* SW Wales, United Kingdom
**Dyfrdwy, Afon** *see* Dee
**Dyhernfurth** *see* Brzeg Dolny
111 E19 **Dyje** *var.* Thaya. ⤳ Austria/Czechia *see also* Thaya
**Dyje** *see* Thaya
117 T5 **Dykan'ka** Poltavs'ka Oblast', C Ukraine 49°48′N 34°33′E
127 N16 **Dykhtau** ▲ SW Russia 43°01′N 42°56′E
111 A16 **Dyleń** *Ger.* Tillenberg. ▲ NW Czechia 49°58′N 12°31′E
110 K9 **Dylewska Góra** ▲ N Poland 53°33′N 19°57′E
117 O4 **Dymer** Kyivs'ka Oblast', N Ukraine 50°50′N 30°20′E
**Dymytrov** *see* Myrnohrad
111 O17 **Dynów** Podkarpackie, SE Poland 49°49′N 22°14′E
29 X13 **Dysart** Iowa, C USA 42°10′N 92°18′W
**Dysna** *see* Dzisna
115 H18 **Dýstos, Límni** *var.* Límni Dístos. ◎ Évvoia, C Greece
115 D18 **Dytikí Elláda** *Eng.* Greece West, *var.* Dytikí Ellás. ◈ *region* C Greece
**Dytikí Ellás** *see* Dytikí Elláda
115 C14 **Dytikí Makedonía** *Eng.* Macedonia West. ◈ *region* N Greece
**Dyurment'yube** *see* Diirmentobe
127 U4 **Dyurtyuli** Respublika Bashkortostan, W Russia 55°31′N 54°49′E
**Dyushambe** *see* Dushanbe
162 K7 **Dzaamar** *var.* Bat-Öldziyt. Töv, C Mongolia 48°10′N 104°49′E
**Dzaanhushuu** *see* Ihtamir
**Dza Chu** *see* Mekong
**Dzadgay** *see* Bömbögör
162 H8 **Dzag** Bayanhongor, C Mongolia 46°54′N 99°11′E
**Dzalaa** *see* Shinejinst
163 O11 **Dzamïn-Üüd** *var.* Borhoyn Tal. Dornogovĭ, SE Mongolia 43°43′N 111°53′E
172 J14 **Dzaoudzi** E Mayotte 12°48′S 45°18′E
**Dzaudzhikau** *see* Vladikavkaz
162 G7 **Dzavhan** ◈ *province* NW Mongolia
162 G7 **Dzavhan Gol** ⤳ NW Mongolia
162 G6 **Dzavhanmandal** *var.* Nuga. Dzavhan, W Mongolia 48°17′N 95°07′E
**Dzegstey** *see* Ögiynuur
162 E7 **Dzereg** *var.* Altanteel. Hovd, W Mongolia 47°05′N 92°57′E
127 O3 **Dzerzhinsk** Nizhegorodskaya Oblast', W Russia 56°20′N 43°22′E
**Dzerzhinsk** *see* Dzyarzhynsk
**Dzerzhinskiy** *see* Nar'yan-Mar
**Dzerzhinskoye** *see* Tokzhaylau
**Dzerzhinskoye** *see* Tokzhaylau
**Dzerzhyns'k** *see* Torets'k
**Dzerzhyns'k** *see* Romaniv
**Džetygara** *see* Zhitikara
**Dzhailgan** *see* Jayilgan
**Dzhalagash** *see* Zhalagash
147 T10 **Dzhalal-Abad** *Kyr.* Jalal-Abad. Dzhalal-Abadskaya Oblast', W Kyrgyzstan 40°56′N 73°00′E
147 S9 **Dzhalal-Abadskaya Oblast'** *Kyr.* Jalal-Abad Oblasty. ◈ *province* W Kyrgyzstan
**Dzhalilabad** *see* Cälilabad
**Dzhambeyty** *see* Zhympity
**Dzhambul** *see* Taraz
**Dzhambulskaya Oblast'** *see* Zhambyl
144 D9 **Dzhanibek** *prev.* Dzhanybek, *Kaz.* Zhänibek. Zapadnyy Kazakhstan, W Kazakhstan 49°27′N 46°51′E
**Dzhankel'dy** *see* Jongeldi
117 T12 **Dzhankoy** Avtonomna Respublika Krym, S Ukraine 45°40′N 34°20′E
**Dzhansugurov** *see* Zhansugirov
147 R9 **Dzhany-Bazar** *var.* Yangibazar. Dzhalal-Abadskaya Oblast', W Kyrgyzstan 41°40′N 70°49′E
**Dzhanybek** *see* Dzhanibek
123 P8 **Dzhardzhan** Respublika Sakha (Yakutiya), NE Russia 68°47′N 123°51′E
**Dzharkurgan** *see* Jarqo'rg'on
117 S11 **Dzharylhats'ka Zatoka** *gulf* S Ukraine
**Dzhayilgan** *see* Jayilgan
**Dzhebel** *see* Jebel
**Dzhelandy** *see* Jelondi
147 Y7 **Dzhergalan** *Kyr.* Jyrgalan. Issyk-Kul'skaya Oblast', NE Kyrgyzstan 42°37′N 78°56′E
**Dzhetysay** *see* Zhetysay
**Dzhezkazgan** *see* Zhezkazgan
**Dzhigirbent** *see* Jigerbent
**Dzhirgatal'** *see* Jirgatol
**Dzhizak** *see* Jizzax
**Dzhizakskaya Oblast'** *see* Jizzax Viloyati
123 P8 **Dzhugdzhur, Khrebet** ▲▲ E Russia
**Dzhul'fa** *see* Culfa
**Dzhuma** *see* Juma
**Dzhungarskiy Alatau** *see* Zhetysuskiy Alatau
**Dzhusaly** *see* Zhosaly
146 J12 **Dzhynlykum, Peski** *desert* E Turkmenistan
110 L9 **Działdowo** Warmińsko-Mazurskie, C Poland 53°13′N 20°12′E
111 L16 **Działoszyce** Świętokrzyskie, C Poland 50°21′N 20°19′E
41 X11 **Dzidzantún** Yucatán, E Mexico
111 G15 **Dzierżoniów** *Ger.* Reichenbach. Dolnośląskie, SW Poland 50°43′N 16°40′E
41 X11 **Dzilam de Bravo** Yucatán, E Mexico 21°24′N 88°52′W
118 L12 **Dzisna** *Rus.* Disna. Vitsyebskaya Voblasts', N Belarus 55°33′N 28°13′E
118 K12 **Dzisna** *Lith.* Dysna, *Rus.* Disna. ⤳ Belarus/Lithuania
119 G20 **Dzivin** *Rus.* Divin. Brestskaya Voblasts', SW Belarus 51°58′N 24°33′E
119 M15 **Dzmitravichy** *Rus.* Dmitrovichi. Minskaya Voblasts', C Belarus 53°58′N 29°14′E
**Dzogsool** *see* Bayantsagaan
162 I5 **Dzöölön** *var.* Rinchinlhumbe. Hövsgöl, N Mongolia 51°06′N 99°40′E
129 S8 **Dzungaria** *var.* Sungaria, Zungaria. *physical region* W China
**Dzungarian Basin** *see* Junggar Pendi
**Dzür** *see* Tes
162 J8 **Dzüünbayan-Ulaan** *var.* Bayan-Ulaan. Övörhangay, C Mongolia 46°38′N 102°30′E
**Dzüünbulag** *see* Matad, Dornod, Mongolia
**Dzüünbulag** *see* Uulbayan, Sühbaatar, Mongolia
162 L8 **Dzuunmod** Töv, C Mongolia 47°45′N 107°00′E
**Dzuunmod** *see* Ider
**Dzüün Soyonĭ Nuruu** *see* Vostochnyy Sayan
**Dzüyl** *see* Tonhil
**Dzvina** *see* Western Dvina
119 I16 **Dzyarzhynsk** *Rus.* Dzerzhinsk; *prev.* Kaydanovo. Minskaya Voblasts', C Belarus 53°41′N 27°09′E
119 H17 **Dzyatlava** *Pol.* Zdzięcioł, *Rus.* Dyatlovo. Hrodzyenskaya Voblasts', W Belarus 53°27′N 25°23′E


# E


**E** *see* Hubei
**Éadan Doire** *see* Edenderry
167 U12 **Ea Drăng** *var.* Ea H'leo. Đăc Lăc, S Vietnam 13°09′N 108°14′E
37 W6 **Eads** Colorado, C USA 38°28′N 102°46′W
37 O13 **Eagar** Arizona, SW USA 34°05′N 109°17′W
39 T8 **Eagle** Alaska, USA 64°47′N 141°12′W
13 S8 **Eagle** ⤳ Newfoundland and Labrador, E Canada
10 I3 **Eagle** ⤳ Yukon, NW Canada
29 T7 **Eagle Bend** Minnesota, N USA 46°10′N 95°02′W
28 M8 **Eagle Butte** South Dakota, N USA 44°58′N 101°13′W
29 V12 **Eagle Grove** Iowa, C USA 42°39′N 93°54′W
19 R2 **Eagle Lake** Maine, NE USA 47°01′N 68°35′W
25 U11 **Eagle Lake** Texas, SW USA 29°35′N 96°19′W
12 A11 **Eagle Lake** ◎ Ontario, S Canada
35 P3 **Eagle Lake** ◎ California, W USA
19 R3 **Eagle Lake** ◎ Maine, NE USA
29 Y3 **Eagle Mountain** ▲ Minnesota, N USA 47°54′N 90°33′W
25 T6 **Eagle Mountain Lake** ⊠ Texas, SW USA
37 S9 **Eagle Nest Lake** ⊠ New Mexico, SW USA
25 P13 **Eagle Pass** Texas, SW USA 28°44′N 100°31′W
65 C25 **Eagle Passage** *passage* SW Atlantic Ocean
35 Q2 **Eagle Peak** ▲ California, W USA 41°16′N 120°12′W
35 R8 **Eagle Peak** ▲ California, W USA 38°11′N 119°22′W
37 P13 **Eagle Peak** ▲ New Mexico, SW USA 33°39′N 109°36′W
10 I4 **Eagle Plain** Yukon, NW Canada 66°23′N 136°42′W
32 G15 **Eagle Point** Oregon, NW USA 42°28′N 122°48′W
186 P10 **Eagle Point** *headland* SE Papua New Guinea 10°31′S 149°53′E
39 R11 **Eagle River** Alaska, USA 61°18′N 149°38′W
30 M2 **Eagle River** Michigan, N USA 47°24′N 88°18′W
30 L4 **Eagle River** Wisconsin, N USA 45°56′N 89°15′W
21 S6 **Eagle Rock** Virginia, NE USA 37°40′N 79°46′W
36 J13 **Eagletail Mountains** ▲▲ Arizona, SW USA
**Ea H'leo** *see* Ea Drăng
167 U12 **Ea Kar** Đăc Lăc, S Vietnam 12°47′N 108°26′E
**Eanjum** *see* Anjum
**Eanodat** *see* Enontekiö
12 B10 **Ear Falls** Ontario, C Canada 50°38′N 93°13′W
27 X10 **Earle** Arkansas, C USA 35°16′N 90°28′W
35 R12 **Earlimart** California, W USA 35°52′N 119°17′W
20 I6 **Earlington** Kentucky, S USA 37°16′N 87°30′W
14 H8 **Earlton** Ontario, S Canada 47°41′N 79°46′W
29 T13 **Early** Iowa, C USA 42°27′N 95°09′W
96 J11 **Earn** ⤳ N Scotland, United Kingdom
185 C21 **Earnslaw, Mount** ▲ South Island, New Zealand 44°34′S 168°26′E
24 M4 **Earth** Texas, SW USA 34°13′N 102°24′W
21 P11 **Easley** South Carolina, SE USA 34°49′N 82°36′W
**East** *see* Est
**East Açores Fracture Zone** *see* East Azores Fracture Zone
97 P19 **East Anglia** *physical region* E England, United Kingdom
15 Q12 **East Angus** Québec, SE Canada 45°29′N 71°39′W
195 V8 **East Antarctica** *prev.* Greater Antarctica. *physical region* Antarctica
18 E10 **East Aurora** New York, NE USA 42°44′N 78°36′W
**East Australian Basin** *see* Tasman Basin
**East Azerbaijan** *see* Āzarbāyjān-e Sharqī
64 L9 **East Azores Fracture Zone** *var.* East Açores Fracture Zone. *tectonic feature* E Atlantic Ocean
22 M11 **East Bay** *bay* Louisiana, S USA
25 V11 **East Bernard** Texas, SW USA 29°32′N 96°04′W
29 V8 **East Bethel** Minnesota, N USA 45°24′N 93°14′W
**East Borneo** *see* Kalimantan Timur
97 P23 **Eastbourne** SE England, United Kingdom 50°46′N 00°16′E
15 R11 **East-Broughton** Québec, SE Canada 46°14′N 71°05′W
44 M6 **East Caicos** *island* E Turks and Caicos Islands
184 R7 **East Cape** *headland* North Island, New Zealand 37°40′S 178°31′E
174 M4 **East Caroline Basin** *undersea feature* SW Pacific Ocean 04°00′N 146°45′E
192 P4 **East China Sea** *Chin.* Dong Hai. *sea* W Pacific Ocean
97 P19 **East Dereham** E England, United Kingdom 52°41′N 00°57′E
30 J9 **East Dubuque** Illinois, N USA 42°29′N 90°38′W
11 S17 **Eastend** Saskatchewan, S Canada 49°29′N 108°48′W
193 S10 **Easter Fracture Zone** *tectonic feature* E Pacific Ocean
**Easter Island** *see* Pascua, Isla de
153 Q12 **Eastern** ◈ *zone* E Nepal
155 K25 **Eastern** ◈ *province* E Sri Lanka
83 L13 **Eastern** ◈ *province* E Zambia
83 H24 **Eastern Cape** *off.* Eastern Cape Province, *Afr.* Oos-Kaap. ◈ *province* SE South Africa
**Eastern Cape Province** *see* Eastern Cape
**Eastern Desert** *see* Aş Şaḩrā' ash Sharqīyah
81 F15 **Eastern Equatoria** ◈ *state* SE South Sudan
**Eastern Euphrates** *see* Murat Nehri
155 J17 **Eastern Ghats** ▲▲ SE India
186 E7 **Eastern Highlands** ◈ *province* C Papua New Guinea
**Eastern Region** *see* Ash Sharqīyah
**Eastern Sayans** *see* Vostochnyy Sayan
**Eastern Scheldt** *see* Oosterschelde
**Eastern Sierra Madre** *see* Madre Oriental, Sierra
**Eastern Transvaal** *see* Mpumalanga
11 W14 **Easterville** Manitoba, C Canada 53°06′N 99°53′W
**Easterwâlde** *see* Oosterwolde
63 M23 **East Falkland** *var.* Isla Soledad. *island* E Falkland Islands
19 P12 **East Falmouth** Massachusetts, NE USA 41°34′N 70°31′W
**East Fayu** *see* Fayu
**East Flanders** *see* Oost-Vlaanderen
39 S6 **East Fork Chandalar River** ⤳ Alaska, USA
29 U12 **East Fork Des Moines River** ⤳ Iowa/Minnesota, C USA
**East Frisian Islands** *see* Ostfriesische Inseln
18 K10 **East Glenville** New York, NE USA 42°53′N 73°55′W
29 R4 **East Grand Forks** Minnesota, N USA 47°54′N 97°59′W
97 O23 **East Grinstead** SE England, United Kingdom 51°08′N 00°00′W
18 M12 **East Hartford** Connecticut, NE USA 41°45′N 72°36′W
18 M13 **East Haven** Connecticut, NE USA 41°16′N 72°52′W
173 T9 **East Indiaman Ridge** *undersea feature* E Indian Ocean
129 V16 **East Indies** *island group* SE Asia
**East Java** *see* Jawa Timur
31 Q6 **East Jordan** Michigan, N USA 45°09′N 85°07′W
**East Kalimantan** *see* Kalimantan Timur
**East Kazakhstan** *see* Vostochnyy Kazakhstan
96 I12 **East Kilbride** S Scotland, United Kingdom 55°46′N 04°10′W
25 R7 **Eastland** Texas, SW USA 32°23′N 98°50′W
31 Q9 **East Lansing** Michigan, N USA 42°44′N 84°28′W
35 X11 **East Las Vegas** Nevada, W USA 36°05′N 115°02′W
97 M23 **Eastleigh** S England, United Kingdom 50°58′N 01°22′W
31 V12 **East Liverpool** Ohio, N USA 40°37′N 80°34′W
83 J25 **East London** *Afr.* Oos-Londen; *prev.* Emonti, Port Rex. Eastern Cape, S South Africa 33°S 27°54′E
96 K12 **East Lothian** *cultural region* SE Scotland, United Kingdom
12 I10 **Eastmain** Québec, E Canada 52°11′N 78°27′W
12 J10 **Eastmain** ⤳ Québec, C Canada
15 P13 **Eastman** Québec, SE Canada 45°19′N 72°18′W
23 U6 **Eastman** Georgia, SE USA 32°12′N 83°10′W
175 O3 **East Mariana Basin** *undersea feature* W Pacific Ocean
30 K11 **East Moline** Illinois, N USA 41°30′N 90°26′W
186 H7 **East New Britain** ◈ *province* E Papua New Guinea
29 T15 **East Nishnabotna River** ⤳ Iowa, C USA
197 V12 **East Novaya Zemlya Trough** *var.* Novaya Zemlya Trough. *undersea feature* W Kara Sea
**East Nusa Tenggara** *see* Nusa Tenggara Timur
21 X4 **Easton** Maryland, NE USA 38°46′N 76°04′W
18 I14 **Easton** Pennsylvania, NE USA 40°41′N 75°13′W
193 R16 **East Pacific Rise** *undersea feature* E Pacific Ocean 20°00′S 115°00′W
**East Pakistan** *see* Bangladesh
31 V12 **East Palestine** Ohio, N USA 40°49′N 80°32′W
30 L12 **East Peoria** Illinois, N USA 40°40′N 89°34′W
23 S3 **East Point** Georgia, SE USA 33°40′N 84°26′W
19 U6 **Eastport** Maine, NE USA 44°54′N 66°59′W
27 Z8 **East Prairie** Missouri, C USA 36°46′N 89°23′W
19 O12 **East Providence** Rhode Island, NE USA 41°48′N 71°20′W
20 L11 **East Ridge** Tennessee, S USA 35°00′N 85°15′W
97 N16 **East Riding** *cultural region* N England, United Kingdom
18 F9 **East Rochester** New York, NE USA 43°06′N 77°29′W
30 K15 **East Saint Louis** Illinois, N USA 38°35′N 90°07′W
65 K21 **East Scotia Basin** *undersea feature* SE Scotia Sea
129 Y8 **East Sea** *var.* Sea of Japan, *Rus.* Yapanskoye More. *Sea* NW Pacific Ocean *see also* Japan, Sea of
186 B6 **East Sepik** ◈ *province* NW Papua New Guinea
173 N4 **East Sheba Ridge** *undersea feature* W Arabian Sea 14°30′N 56°15′E
**East Siberian Sea** *see* Vostochno-Sibirskoye More
18 I14 **East Stroudsburg** Pennsylvania, NE USA 41°00′N 75°10′W
**East Tasmanian Rise/East Tasmania Plateau/East Tasmania Rise** *see* East Tasman Plateau
192 I12 **East Tasman Plateau** *var.* East Tasmanian Rise, East Tasmania Plateau, East Tasmania Rise. *undersea feature* SW Tasman Sea
64 L7 **East Thulean Rise** *undersea feature* N Atlantic Ocean
171 R16 **East Timor** ◆ *country* S Indonesia
21 Y6 **Eastville** Virginia, NE USA 37°22′N 75°58′W
35 R7 **East Walker River** ⤳ California/Nevada, W USA
182 D1 **Eateringinna Creek** ⤳ South Australia
37 T3 **Eaton** Colorado, C USA 40°31′N 104°42′W
15 Q12 **Eaton** ⤳ Québec, SE Canada
11 S16 **Eatonia** Saskatchewan, S Canada 51°13′N 109°22′W
31 Q10 **Eaton Rapids** Michigan, N USA 42°30′N 84°39′W
23 U4 **Eatonton** Georgia, SE USA 33°19′N 83°23′W
32 H9 **Eatonville** Washington, NW USA 46°51′N 122°19′W
30 J6 **Eau Claire** Wisconsin, N USA 44°50′N 91°30′W
12 J7 **Eau Claire, Lac à l'** ◎ Québec, SE Canada
**Eau Claire, Lac à L'** *see* St. Clair, Lake
30 L6 **Eau Claire River** ⤳ Wisconsin, N USA
188 J16 **Eauripik Atoll** *atoll* Caroline Islands, C Micronesia
192 H7 **Eauripik Rise** *undersea feature* W Pacific Ocean 03°00′N 142°00′E
102 K15 **Eauze** Gers, S France 43°52′N 00°06′E
41 P11 **Ébano** San Luis Potosí, C Mexico 22°16′N 98°26′W
97 K21 **Ebbw Vale** SE Wales, United Kingdom 51°48′N 03°13′W
79 E17 **Ebebiyin** NE Equatorial Guinea 02°08′N 11°15′E
95 H22 **Ebeltoft** Midtjylland, C Denmark 56°11′N 10°42′E
109 X5 **Ebenfurth** Niederösterreich, E Austria 47°53′N 16°22′E
18 D14 **Ebensburg** Pennsylvania, NE USA 40°28′N 78°44′W
109 S5 **Ebensee** Oberösterreich, N Austria 47°48′N 13°46′E
101 H20 **Eberbach** Baden-Württemberg, SW Germany 49°28′N 08°58′E
121 U8 **Eber Gölü** *salt lake* C Turkey
109 U9 **Eberndorf** *Slvn.* Dobrla Vas. Kärnten, S Austria 46°33′N 14°35′E
109 R4 **Eberschwang** Oberösterreich, N Austria 48°09′N 13°37′E
100 O11 **Eberswalde-Finow** Brandenburg, E Germany 52°50′N 13°48′E
**Ebesfalva** *see* Dumbrăveni
165 T4 **Ebetsu** *var.* Ebetu. Hokkaidō, NE Japan 43°08′N 141°37′E
**Ebetu** *see* Ebetsu
**Ebinayon** *see* Evinayong
158 I4 **Ebinur Hu** ◎ NW China
138 I3 **Ebla** *Ar.* Tell Mardīkh. *site of ancient city* Idlib, NW Syria
**Eblana** *see* Dublin
108 H7 **Ebnat** Sankt Gallen, NE Switzerland 47°16′N 09°07′E
107 L18 **Eboli** Campania, S Italy 40°37′N 15°03′E
79 E16 **Ebolowa** Sud, S Cameroon 02°56′N 11°11′E
79 N21 **Ebombo** Kasai-Oriental, C Dem. Rep. Congo 05°42′S 26°07′E
189 T9 **Ebon Atoll** *var.* Epoon. *atoll* Ralik Chain, S Marshall Islands
**Ebora** *see* Évora
**Eboracum** *see* York
**Eborodunum** *see* Yverdon
101 J19 **Ebrach** Bayern, C Germany 49°49′N 10°30′E
109 X5 **Ebreichsdorf** Niederösterreich, E Austria 47°58′N 16°24′E
105 S6 **Ebro** ⤳ NE Spain
105 N3 **Ebro, Embalse del** ⊠ N Spain
120 G7 **Ebro Fan** *undersea feature* W Mediterranean Sea
**Eburacum** *see* York
**Ebusus** *see* Ibiza
**Ebusus** *see* Eivissa
99 F20 **Écaussinnes-d'Enghien** Hainaut, SW Belgium 50°34′N 04°10′E
**Ecbatana** *see* Hamadān
21 Q6 **Eccles** West Virginia, NE USA 37°46′N 81°16′W
115 L14 **Eceabat** Çanakkale, NW Turkey 40°12′N 26°22′E
171 O2 **Echague** Luzon, N Philippines 16°42′N 121°37′E
**Ech Cheliff/Ech Chleff** *see* Chlef
**Echeng** *see* Ezhou
115 C18 **Echinádes** *island group* W Greece
114 J12 **Echínos** *var.* Ehinos, Ekhínos. Anatolikí Makedonía kai Thráki, NE Greece 41°16′N 25°00′E
**Echizen** *see* Takefu
164 J12 **Echizen-misaki** *headland* Honshū, SW Japan 35°59′N 135°57′E
**Echmiadzin** *see* Vagharshapat
8 J8 **Echo Bay** Northwest Territories, NW Canada 66°04′N 118°W
35 Y11 **Echo Bay** Nevada, W USA 36°19′N 114°27′W
36 L9 **Echo Cliffs** *cliff* Arizona, SW USA
14 C10 **Echo Lake** ◎ Ontario, S Canada
35 Q7 **Echo Summit** ▲ California, W USA 38°47′N 120°06′W
14 L8 **Échouani, Lac** ◎ Québec, SE Canada
99 L17 **Echt** Limburg, SE Netherlands 51°07′N 05°52′E
101 H22 **Echterdingen** ✈ (Stuttgart) Baden-Württemberg, SW Germany 48°40′N 09°13′E
99 N24 **Echternach** Grevenmacher, E Luxembourg 49°49′N 06°25′E
183 N11 **Echuca** Victoria, SE Australia 36°10′S 144°20′E
104 L14 **Écija** *anc.* Astigi. Andalucía, SW Spain 37°33′N 05°04′W
**Eckengraf** *see* Viesīte
100 I7 **Eckernförde** Schleswig-Holstein, N Germany 54°28′N 09°49′E
100 J7 **Eckernförder Bucht** *inlet* N Germany
102 L7 **Écommoy** Sarthe, NW France 47°51′N 00°15′E
14 L10 **Écorce, Lac de l'** ◎ Québec, SE Canada
15 Q8 **Écorces, Rivière aux** ⤳ Québec, SE Canada
56 C7 **Ecuador** *off.* Republic of Ecuador. ◆ *republic* NW South America
**Ecuador, Republic of** *see* Ecuador
95 I17 **Ed** Västra Götaland, S Sweden 58°55′N 11°55′E
**Ed** *see* 'Īdī
98 I9 **Edam** Noord-Holland, C Netherlands 52°30′N 05°02′E
96 K4 **Eday** *island* NE Scotland, United Kingdom
25 S17 **Edcouch** Texas, SW USA 26°17′N 97°57′W
80 C11 **Ed Da'ein** Eastern Darfur, W Sudan 11°25′N 26°08′E
80 G11 **Ed Damazin** *var.* Ad Damazīn. Blue Nile, E Sudan 11°45′N 34°20′E
80 G8 **Ed Damer** *var.* Ad Dāmir, Ad Damar. River Nile, NE Sudan 17°37′N 33°59′E
80 E8 **Ed Debba** Northern, N Sudan 18°02′N 30°56′E
80 F10 **Ed Dueim** *var.* Ad Duwaym, Ad Duwēm. White Nile, C Sudan 13°38′N 32°36′E
183 Q16 **Eddystone Point** *headland* Tasmania, SE Australia 41°01′S 148°18′E
97 I25 **Eddystone Rocks** *rocks* SW England, United Kingdom
29 W15 **Eddyville** Iowa, C USA 41°09′N 92°37′W
20 H7 **Eddyville** Kentucky, S USA 37°03′N 88°02′W
98 L12 **Ede** Gelderland, C Netherlands 52°03′N 05°40′E
77 T16 **Ede** Osun, SW Nigeria 07°40′N 04°21′E
79 D16 **Edéa** Littoral, SW Cameroon 03°47′N 10°08′E
111 M20 **Edelény** Borsod-Abaúj-Zemplén, NE Hungary 48°18′N 20°40′E
183 R12 **Eden** New South Wales, SE Australia 37°04′S 149°51′E
21 T8 **Eden** North Carolina, SE USA 36°29′N 79°46′W
25 P9 **Eden** Texas, SW USA 31°13′N 99°51′W
97 K14 **Eden** ⤳ NW England, United Kingdom
83 I23 **Edenburg** Free State, C South Africa 29°45′S 25°57′E
185 D24 **Edendale** Southland, South Island, New Zealand 46°18′S 168°48′E
97 E18 **Edenderry** *Ir.* Éadan Doire. Offaly, C Ireland 53°21′N 07°03′W
182 L11 **Edenhope** Victoria, SE Australia 37°04′S 141°15′E
21 X8 **Edenton** North Carolina, SE USA 36°04′N 76°39′W
101 G16 **Eder** ⤳ NW Germany
101 H15 **Edersee** ◎ W Germany
114 E13 **Édessa** *var.* Édhessa. Kentrikí Makedonía, N Greece 40°48′N 22°03′E
**Edessa** *see* Şanlıurfa
**Edfu** *see* Idfu
29 P16 **Edgar** Nebraska, C USA 40°22′N 97°58′W
19 P13 **Edgartown** Martha's Vineyard, Massachusetts, NE USA 41°23′N 70°30′W
39 X13 **Edgecumbe, Mount** ▲ Baranof Island, Alaska, USA 57°03′N 135°45′W
21 Q13 **Edgefield** South Carolina, SE USA 33°50′N 81°57′W
29 P6 **Edgeley** North Dakota, N USA 46°19′N 98°42′W
28 I11 **Edgemont** South Dakota, N USA 43°18′N 103°49′W
92 O3 **Edgeøya** *island* S Svalbard
27 Q4 **Edgerton** Kansas, C USA 38°45′N 95°00′W
29 S10 **Edgerton** Minnesota, N USA 43°52′N 96°07′W
21 X3 **Edgewood** Maryland, NE USA 39°20′N 76°21′W
25 V6 **Edgewood** Texas, SW USA 32°42′N 95°53′W
**Édhessa** *see* Édessa
29 V9 **Edina** Minnesota, N USA 44°53′N 93°21′W
27 U2 **Edina** Missouri, C USA 40°10′N 92°10′W
25 S17 **Edinburg** Texas, SW USA 26°18′N 98°10′W
65 M24 **Edinburgh** *var.* Settlement of Edinburgh. ○ (Tristan da Cunha) NW Tristan da Cunha 37°03′S 12°18′W
96 J12 **Edinburgh** ◐ S Scotland, United Kingdom 55°57′N 03°13′W
31 P14 **Edinburgh** Indiana, N USA 39°19′N 86°00′W
96 J12 **Edinburgh** ✈ S Scotland, United Kingdom 55°57′N 03°22′W
116 L8 **Edineţ** *var.* Edineţi, *Rus.* Yedintsy. NW Moldova 48°10′N 27°18′E
**Edineţi** *see* Edineţ
**Edingen** *see* Enghien
136 B9 **Edirne** *Eng.* Adrianople; *anc.* Adrianopolis, Hadrianopolis. Edirne, NW Turkey 41°40′N 26°34′E
136 B11 **Edirne** ◈ *province* NW Turkey
18 K15 **Edison** New Jersey, NE USA 40°31′N 74°24′W
21 S15 **Edisto Island** South Carolina, SE USA 32°34′N 80°17′W
21 R14 **Edisto River** ⤳ South Carolina, SE USA
33 S10 **Edith, Mount** ▲ Montana, NW USA 46°25′N 111°10′W
27 N10 **Edmond** Oklahoma, C USA 35°40′N 97°30′W
32 H8 **Edmonds** Washington, NW USA 47°48′N 122°22′W
11 Q14 **Edmonton** *province capital* Alberta, SW Canada 53°34′N 113°25′W
20 K7 **Edmonton** Kentucky, S USA 36°59′N 85°39′W
11 Q14 **Edmonton** ✈ Alberta, SW Canada 53°22′N 113°43′W
29 P3 **Edmore** North Dakota, N USA 48°22′N 98°26′W
13 N13 **Edmundston** New Brunswick, SE Canada 47°22′N 68°20′W
25 U12 **Edna** Texas, SW USA 29°00′N 96°41′W
39 X14 **Edna Bay** Kosciusko Island, Alaska, USA 55°54′N 133°40′W
77 U16 **Edo** ◈ *state* S Nigeria
106 F6 **Edolo** Lombardia, N Italy 46°13′N 10°20′E
64 L6 **Edoras Bank** *undersea feature* C Atlantic Ocean
96 G7 **Edrachillis Bay** *bay* NW Scotland, United Kingdom
136 B12 **Edremit** Balıkesir, NW Turkey 39°34′N 27°01′E
136 B12 **Edremit Körfezi** *gulf* NW Turkey
95 P14 **Edsbro** Stockholm, C Sweden 59°54′N 18°30′E
95 N18 **Edsbruk** Kalmar, S Sweden 58°01′N 16°30′E
94 M12 **Edsbyn** Gävleborg, C Sweden 61°22′N 15°45′E
11 O14 **Edson** Alberta, SW Canada 53°36′N 116°28′W
62 K13 **Eduardo Castex** La Pampa, C Argentina 35°55′S 64°18′W
58 F12 **Eduardo Gomes** ✈ (Manaus) Amazonas, NW Brazil 03°55′S 35°15′W
**Edwardesabad** *see* Bannu
67 U9 **Edward, Lake** *var.* Albert Edward Nyanza, Edward Nyanza, Lac Idi Amin, Lake Rutanzige. ◎ Uganda/Dem. Rep. Congo
**Edward Nyanza** *see* Edward, Lake
22 K5 **Edwards** Mississippi, S USA 32°19′N 90°36′W
25 O10 **Edwards Plateau** *plain* Texas, SW USA
30 J11 **Edwards River** ⤳ Illinois, N USA
30 K15 **Edwardsville** Illinois, N USA 38°48′N 89°57′W
195 X4 **Edward VIII Gulf** *bay* Antarctica
195 O13 **Edward VII Peninsula** *peninsula* Antarctica
10 J11 **Edziza, Mount** ▲ British Columbia, W Canada 57°43′N 130°39′W
23 H16 **Edzo** *prev.* Rae-Edzo. Northwest Territories, NW Canada 62°44′N 115°55′W
39 N12 **Eek** Alaska, USA 60°13′N 162°01′W
99 D16 **Eeklo** *var.* Eekloo. Oost-Vlaanderen, NW Belgium 51°11′N 03°34′E
**Eekloo** *see* Eeklo
39 N12 **Eek River** ⤳ Alaska, USA
98 N6 **Eelde** Drenthe, NE Netherlands 53°07′N 06°30′E
34 L5 **Eel River** ⤳ California, W USA
31 P12 **Eel River** ⤳ Indiana, N USA
**Eems** *see* Ems
98 O4 **Eemshaven** Groningen, NE Netherlands 53°28′N 06°50′E
98 O5 **Eems Kanaal** *canal* NE Netherlands
98 M11 **Eerbeek** Gelderland, E Netherlands 52°07′N 06°04′E
99 C17 **Eernegem** West-Vlaanderen, W Belgium 51°08′N 03°03′E
99 J15 **Eersel** Noord-Brabant, S Netherlands 51°22′N 05°19′E
**Eesti** *see* Estonia
**Eesti Vabariik** *see* Estonia
187 R14 **Efate** *var.* Éfaté, *Fr.* Vaté; *prev.* Sandwich Island. *island* C Vanuatu
**Efate** *see* Efate
109 S4 **Eferding** Oberösterreich, N Austria 48°18′N 14°00′E
30 M15 **Effingham** Illinois, N USA 39°07′N 88°32′W
117 N15 **Eforie-Nord** Constanța, SE Romania 44°04′N 28°37′E
117 N15 **Eforie-Sud** Constanța, E Romania 44°00′N 28°38′E
**Efyrnwy, Afon** *see* Vyrnwy
**Eg** *see* Hentiy
107 G23 **Egadi, Isole** *island group* S Italy
35 X6 **Egan Range** ▲▲ Nevada, W USA
14 K12 **Eganville** Ontario, SE Canada 45°33′N 77°03′W
**Ege Denizi** *see* Aegean Sea
**Egedesminde** *see* Aasiaat
39 O14 **Egegik** Alaska, USA 58°13′N 157°22′W
111 L21 **Eger** *Ger.* Erlau. Heves, NE Hungary 47°54′N 20°22′E
**Eger** *see* Cheb, Czech Republic
**Eger** *see* Ohre, Czech Republic/Germany
173 P8 **Egeria Fracture Zone** *tectonic feature* W Indian Ocean
95 C17 **Egersund** Rogaland, S Norway 58°27′N 06°01′E
108 J7 **Egg** Vorarlberg, NW Austria 47°27′N 09°55′E
101 H14 **Egge-gebirge** ▲▲ C Germany
109 Q4 **Eggelsberg** Oberösterreich, N Austria 48°04′N 13°00′E
109 W2 **Eggenburg** Niederösterreich, NE Austria 48°29′N 15°49′E
101 N22 **Eggenfelden** Bayern, SE Germany 48°24′N 12°45′E
18 J17 **Egg Harbor City** New Jersey, NE USA 39°31′N 74°39′W
65 G25 **Egg Island** *island* W Saint Helena
183 N14 **Egg Lagoon** Tasmania, SE Australia 39°42′S 143°57′E
99 I20 **Éghezée** Namur, C Belgium 50°36′N 04°55′E
92 L2 **Egilsstaðir** Austurland, E Iceland 65°14′N 14°21′W
**Egina** *see* Aígina
**Egindibulaq** *see* Yegindybulak
**Egio** *see* Aígio
103 N12 **Égletons** Corrèze, C France 45°24′N 02°01′E
98 H9 **Egmond aan Zee** Noord-Holland, NW Netherlands 52°37′N 04°37′E
**Egmont** *see* Taranaki, Mount
184 J10 **Egmont, Cape** *headland* North Island, New Zealand 39°18′S 173°44′E
**Egoli** *see* Johannesburg
136 I15 **Eğridir Gölü** ◎ W Turkey
**Eğri Palanka** *see* Kriva Palanka
95 G23 **Egtved** Syddanmark, C Denmark 55°34′N 09°18′E
123 U5 **Egvekinot** Chukotskiy Avtonomnyy Okrug, NE Russia 66°13′N 178°55′W
75 V9 **Egypt** *off.* Arab Republic of Egypt, *Ar.* Mişr, Jumhūrīyat Mişr al 'Arabīyah; *prev.* United Arab Republic; *anc.* Aegyptus. ◆ *republic* NE Africa




◆ Country ● Country Capital ◇ Dependent Territory ○ Dependent Territory Capital ◈ Administrative Regions ✈ International Airport ▲ Mountain ▲▲ Mountain Range Volcano ⤳ River ◎ Lake ⊠ Reservoir

Egypt, Lake Of – Emerson


30 L17 **Egypt, Lake Of** ⊠ Illinois, N USA
162 I14 **Ehen Hudag** *var.* Alx Youqi. Nei Mongol Zizhiqu, N China 39°12′N 101°40′E
164 F14 **Ehime** *off.* Ehime-ken. ◈ *prefecture* Shikoku, SW Japan
**Ehime-ken** *see* Ehime
101 I23 **Ehingen** Baden-Württemberg, S Germany 48°16′N 09°43′E
**Ehinos** *see* Echínos
21 R14 **Ehrhardt** South Carolina, SE USA 33°06′N 81°00′W
108 L7 **Ehrwald** Tirol, W Austria 47°24′N 10°52′E
191 W6 **Eiao** *island* Îles Marquises, NE French Polynesia
105 P2 **Eibar** País Vasco, N Spain 43°11′N 02°28′W
98 O11 **Eibergen** Gelderland, E Netherlands 52°06′N 06°39′E
109 V9 **Eibiswald** Steiermark, SE Austria 46°40′N 15°15′E
109 P8 **Eichham** ▲ SW Austria 47°04′N 12°24′E
101 J15 **Eichsfeld** *hill range* C Germany
101 K21 **Eichstätt** Bayern, SE Germany 48°53′N 11°11′E
100 H8 **Eider** ≈ N Germany
94 E13 **Eidfjord** Hordaland, S Norway 60°26′N 07°05′E
94 D13 **Eidfjorden** *fjord* S Norway
94 F9 **Eidsvåg** Møre og Romsdal, S Norway 62°46′N 08°00′E
95 I14 **Eidsvoll** Akershus, S Norway 60°19′N 11°14′E
92 N2 **Eidsvollfjellet** ▲ NW Svalbard 79°13′N 13°23′E
**Eier-Berg** *see* Suur Munamägi
101 D18 **Eifel** *plateau* W Germany
108 E9 **Eiger** ▲ C Switzerland 46°33′N 08°02′E
96 G10 **Eigg** *island* W Scotland, United Kingdom
155 D24 **Eight Degree Channel** *channel* India/Maldives
44 G1 **Eight Mile Rock** Grand Bahama Island, N The Bahamas 26°28′N 78°43′W
194 J9 **Eights Coast** *physical region* Antarctica
180 K6 **Eighty Mile Beach** *beach* Western Australia
99 L18 **Eijsden** Limburg, SE Netherlands 50°47′N 05°41′E
95 G15 **Eikeren** ◎ S Norway
**Eil** *see* Eyl
**Eilat** *see* Elat
183 O12 **Eildon** Victoria, SE Australia 37°17′S 145°57′E
183 O12 **Eildon, Lake** ◎ Victoria, SE Australia
80 E8 **Eilei** Northern Kordofan, C Sudan 16°33′N 30°54′E
101 N15 **Eilenburg** Sachsen, E Germany 51°28′N 12°37′E
**Eil Malk** *see* Mecherchar
94 H13 **Eina** Oppland, S Norway 60°37′N 10°37′E
138 E12 **Ein Avdat** *prev.* En 'Avedat. *well* S Israel
101 I14 **Einbeck** Niedersachsen, C Germany 51°49′N 09°52′E
99 K15 **Eindhoven** Noord-Brabant, S Netherlands 51°26′N 05°30′E
108 G8 **Einsiedeln** Schwyz, NE Switzerland 47°07′N 08°45′E
**Eipel** *see* Ipel'
**Éire** *see* Ireland
**Éireann, Muir** *see* Irish Sea
**Eirik Outer Ridge** *see* Eirik Ridge
64 I6 **Eirik Ridge** *var.* Eirik Outer Ridge. *undersea feature* E Labrador Sea
92 I3 **Eiríksjökull** ▲ C Iceland 64°47′N 20°23′W
59 B14 **Eirunepé** Amazonas, N Brazil 06°38′S 69°53′W
99 L17 **Eisden** Limburg, NE Belgium 51°05′N 05°42′E
83 F18 **Eiseb** ≈ Botswana/Namibia
**Eisen** *see* Yeongcheon
101 J16 **Eisenach** Thüringen, C Germany 50°59′N 10°19′E
**Eisenburg** *see* Vasvár
109 U6 **Eisenerz** Steiermark, SE Austria 47°33′N 14°53′E
100 Q13 **Eisenhüttenstadt** Brandenburg, E Germany 52°09′N 14°36′E
109 U10 **Eisenkappel** *Slvn.* Železna Kapela. Kärnten, S Austria 46°27′N 14°33′E
**Eisenmarkt** *see* Hunedoara
109 Y5 **Eisenstadt** Burgenland, E Austria 47°50′N 16°32′E
**Eishū** *see* Yeongju
119 H15 **Eišiškes** Vilnius, SE Lithuania 54°10′N 24°59′E
101 L15 **Eisleben** Sachsen-Anhalt, C Germany 51°32′N 11°33′E
190 I3 **Eita** Tarawa, W Kiribati 01°21′N 173°05′E
**Eitape** *see* Aitape
105 V11 **Eivissa** *var.* Iviza, *Cast.* Ibiza; *anc.* Ebusus. Ibiza, Spain, W Mediterranean Sea 38°54′N 01°26′E
**Eivissa** *see* Ibiza
105 R4 **Ejea de los Caballeros** Aragón, NE Spain 42°07′N 01°09′W
40 E8 **Ejido Insurgentes** Baja California Sur, NW Mexico 25°18′N 111°51′W
**Ejin Qi** *see* Dalain Hob
**Ejmiadzin/Ejmiatsin** *see* Vagharshapat
77 P16 **Ejura** C Ghana 07°23′N 01°22′W
41 R16 **Ejutla** *var.* Ejutla de Crespo. Oaxaca, SE Mexico 16°33′N 96°40′W
**Ejutla de Crespo** *see* Ejutla
33 Y10 **Ekalaka** Montana, NW USA 45°52′N 104°32′W
**Ekapa** *see* Cape Town
**Ekaterinodar** *see* Krasnodar
93 L20 **Ekenäs** *Fin.* Tammisaari. Uusimaa, SW Finland 60°00′N 23°30′E
146 B13 **Ekerem** *Rus.* Okarem. Balkan Welaýaty, W Turkmenistan 38°06′N 53°52′E
184 M13 **Eketahuna** Manawatu-Wanganui, North Island, New Zealand 40°41′S 175°40′E
**Ekhínos** *see* Echínos
**Ekiatapskiy Khrebet** *see* Ekvyvatapskiy Khrebet
**Ekibastuz** *see* Yekibastuz
123 R13 **Ekimchan** Amurskaya Oblast', SE Russia 53°04′N 132°56′E
95 O15 **Ekoln** ◎ C Sweden
80 I7 **Ekowit** Red Sea, NE Sudan 18°46′N 37°07′E
95 L19 **Eksjö** Jönköping, S Sweden 57°40′N 15°00′E
93 I15 **Ekträsk** Västerbotten, N Sweden 64°28′N 19°49′E
39 O13 **Ekuk** Alaska, USA 58°48′N 158°25′W
123 U5 **Ekvyvatapskiy Khrebet** *prev.* Ekiatapskiy Khrebet. ▲▲ NE Russia
12 F9 **Ekwan** ≈ Ontario, C Canada
39 O13 **Ekwok** Alaska, USA 59°21′N 157°28′W
166 M6 **Ela** Mandalay, C Myanmar (Burma) 19°37′N 96°15′E
**El Aaiun** *see* El Ayoun
81 N15 **Ēl Ābrēd** Sumalē, E Ethiopia 05°33′N 45°12′E
115 F22 **Elafónisos** *island* S Greece
115 F22 **Elafonísou, Porthmós** *strait* S Greece
**El-Aïoun** *see* El Ayoun
**El 'Alamein** *see* Al 'Alamayn
41 Q12 **El Alazán** Veracruz, C Mexico 21°06′N 97°43′W
57 J18 **El Alto** *var.* La Paz. ✈ (La Paz) La Paz, W Bolivia 16°31′S 68°07′W
**Elam** *see* Īlām
**El Amparo** *see* El Amparo de Apure
54 I8 **El Amparo de Apure** *var.* El Amparo. Apure, C Venezuela 07°07′N 70°47′W
171 R13 **Elara** Pulau Ambelau, E Indonesia 03°49′S 127°10′E
**El Araïch/El Araïche** *see* Larache
40 D6 **El Arco** Baja California, NW Mexico 28°03′N 113°25′W
**El 'Arîsh** *see* Al 'Arīsh
115 L25 **Elása** *island* SE Greece
**El Asnam** *see* Chlef
**Elassón** *see* Elassóna
115 E15 **Elassóna** *prev.* Elassón. Thessalía, C Greece 39°53′N 22°10′E
105 N2 **El Astillero** Cantabria, N Spain 43°23′N 03°45′W
138 F14 **Elat** *var.* Eilat, Elath. Southern, S Israel 29°33′N 34°57′E
**Elat, Gulf of** *see* Aqaba, Gulf of
**Elath** *see* Elat, Israel
**Elath** *see* Al 'Aqabah, Jordan
115 C17 **Eláti** ▲ Lefkáda, Iónia Nisiá, Greece, C Mediterranean Sea 38°43′N 20°38′E
188 L16 **Elato Atoll** *atoll* Caroline Islands, C Micronesia
80 C7 **El'Atrun** Northern Darfur, NW Sudan 18°11′N 26°40′E
74 H6 **El Ayoun** *var.* El Aaiun, El-Aïoun, La Youne. NE Morocco 34°39′N 02°29′W
137 N14 **Elâzığ** *var.* Elâzig, Elâziz. Elâzığ, E Turkey 38°41′N 39°14′E
137 O14 **Elâzığ** *var.* Elâzig, Elâziz. ◈ *province* C Turkey
**Elâzig/Elâziz** *see* Elâzığ
23 Q7 **Elba** Alabama, S USA 31°24′N 86°04′W
106 E13 **Elba, Isola d'** *island* Archipelago Toscano, C Italy
123 S13 **El'ban** Khabarovskiy Kray, E Russia 50°03′N 136°34′E
54 F6 **El Banco** Magdalena, N Colombia 09°00′N 74°01′W
**El Barco** *see* O Barco
104 L8 **El Barco de Ávila** Castilla y León, N Spain 40°21′N 05°31′W
**El Barco de Valdeorras** *see* O Barco
138 H7 **El Barouk, Jabal** ▲▲ C Lebanon
113 L20 **Elbasan** *var.* Elbasani. Elbasan, C Albania 41°07′N 20°04′E
113 L20 **Elbasan** ◈ *county* C Albania
**Elbasani** *see* Elbasan
54 K6 **El Baúl** Cojedes, C Venezuela 08°59′N 68°16′W
86 D11 **Elbe** *Cz.* Labe. ≈ Czechia/Germany
100 L13 **Elbe-Havel-Kanal** *canal* E Germany
100 K9 **Elbe-Lübeck-Kanal** *canal* N Germany
**El Beni** *see* Beni
138 H7 **El Beqaa** *var.* Al Biqā', Bekaa Valley. *valley* E Lebanon
25 R6 **Elbert** Texas, SW USA 33°15′N 98°58′W
37 R5 **Elbert, Mount** ▲ Colorado, C USA 39°07′N 106°26′W
23 U3 **Elberton** Georgia, SE USA 34°06′N 82°52′W
100 K11 **Elbe-Seiten-Kanal** *canal* N Germany
102 M4 **Elbeuf** Seine-Maritime, N France 49°16′N 01°01′E
**Elbing** *see* Elbląg
136 M15 **Elbistan** Kahramanmaraş, S Turkey 38°14′N 37°11′E
110 K7 **Elbląg** *var.* Elblag, *Ger.* Elbing. Warmińsko-Mazurskie, NE Poland 54°10′N 19°25′E
43 N10 **El Bluff** Costa Caribe Sur, SE Nicaragua 12°00′N 83°40′W
63 H17 **El Bolsón** Río Negro, W Argentina 41°59′S 71°35′W
105 P11 **El Bonillo** Castilla-La Mancha, C Spain 38°57′N 02°32′W
**El Bordo** *see* Patía
**El Boulaida/El Boulaïda** *see* Blida
11 T16 **Elbow** Saskatchewan, S Canada 51°07′N 106°30′W
29 S7 **Elbow Lake** Minnesota, N USA 45°59′N 95°58′W
127 N16 **El'brus** *var.* Gora El'brus. ▲ SW Russia 42°29′E 43°21′N
**El'brus, Gora** *see* El'brus
126 M15 **El'brusskiy** Karachayevo-Cherkesskaya Respublika, SW Russia 43°36′N 42°06′E
**El Buhayrat** *see* Lakes
**El Bur** *see* Ceel Buur
98 L10 **Elburg** Gelderland, E Netherlands 52°27′N 05°46′E
105 O6 **El Burgo de Osma** Castilla y León, C Spain 41°36′N 03°04′W
**Elburz Mountains** *see* Alborz, Reshteh-ye Kūhhā-ye
35 V17 **El Cajon** California, W USA 32°46′N 116°52′W
63 H22 **El Calafate** *var.* Calafate. Santa Cruz, S Argentina 50°20′S 72°13′W
55 Q8 **El Callao** Bolívar, E Venezuela 07°18′N 61°48′W
25 U12 **El Campo** Texas, SW USA 29°12′N 96°16′W
54 I7 **El Cantón** Barinas, W Venezuela 07°23′N 71°10′W
35 Q8 **El Capitan** ▲ California, W USA 37°46′N 119°39′W
54 H5 **El Carmelo** Zulia, NW Venezuela 10°20′N 71°48′W
62 J5 **El Carmen** Jujuy, NW Argentina 24°24′S 65°16′W
54 E5 **El Carmen de Bolívar** Bolívar, NW Colombia 09°43′N 75°07′W
55 O8 **El Casabe** Bolívar, SE Venezuela 06°26′N 63°35′W
42 M12 **El Castillo de La Concepción** Río San Juan, SE Nicaragua 11°01′N 84°24′W
**El Cayo** *see* San Ignacio
35 X17 **El Centro** California, W USA 32°47′N 115°33′W
55 N6 **El Chaparro** Anzoátegui, NE Venezuela 09°12′N 65°03′W
105 S12 **Elche** *var.* Elx; *anc.* Ilici, *Lat.* Illicis. Comunitat Valenciana, E Spain 38°16′N 00°41′W
105 Q12 **Elche de la Sierra** Castilla-La Mancha, C Spain 38°27′N 02°03′W
41 U15 **El Chichónal, Volcán** ☒ SE Mexico 17°20′N 93°12′W
40 C2 **El Chinero** Baja California, NW Mexico
181 R1 **Elcho Island** *island* Wessel Islands, Northern Territory, N Australia
63 H18 **El Corcovado** Chubut, SW Argentina 43°31′S 71°30′W
105 R12 **Elda** Comunitat Valenciana, E Spain 38°29′N 00°47′W
100 M10 **Elde** ≈ NE Germany
98 L12 **Elden** Gelderland, E Netherlands 51°57′N 05°53′E
81 J16 **El Der** *spring/well* S Ethiopia 03°55′N 39°48′E
**El Dere** *see* Ceel Dheere
40 B2 **El Descanso** Baja California, NW Mexico 32°08′N 116°51′W
40 E3 **El Desemboque** Sonora, NW Mexico 30°33′N 112°59′W
54 F5 **El Difícil** *var.* Ariguaní. Magdalena, N Colombia 09°55′N 74°12′W
123 R10 **El'dikan** Respublika Sakha (Yakutiya), NE Russia 60°46′N 135°04′E
**El Djelfa** *see* Djelfa
**El Djezair** *see* Alger
29 X15 **Eldon** Iowa, C USA 40°55′N 92°13′W
27 U5 **Eldon** Missouri, C USA 38°21′N 92°34′W
54 E13 **El Doncello** Caquetá, S Colombia 01°43′N 75°17′W
29 W13 **Eldora** Iowa, C USA 42°21′N 93°06′W
60 G12 **Eldorado** Misiones, NE Argentina 26°24′S 54°38′W
40 I9 **El Dorado** Sinaloa, C Mexico 24°19′N 107°23′W
27 U14 **El Dorado** Arkansas, C USA 33°12′N 92°40′W
30 M17 **Eldorado** Illinois, N USA 37°48′N 88°26′W
27 O6 **El Dorado** Kansas, C USA 37°51′N 96°52′W
26 K12 **Eldorado** Oklahoma, C USA 34°28′N 99°39′W
25 O9 **Eldorado** Texas, SW USA 30°53′N 100°37′W
55 Q8 **El Dorado** Bolívar, E Venezuela 06°45′N 61°37′W
54 F10 **El Dorado** ✈ (Bogotá) Cundinamarca, C Colombia 01°15′N 71°52′W
**El Dorado** *see* California
27 O6 **El Dorado Lake** ⊠ Kansas, C USA
27 S6 **El Dorado Springs** Missouri, C USA 37°53′N 94°01′W
81 H18 **Eldoret** Uasin Gishu, W Kenya 0°31′N 35°17′E
29 Z14 **Eldridge** Iowa, C USA 41°39′N 90°34′W
95 J21 **Eldsberga** Halland, S Sweden 56°36′N 13°00′E
25 R4 **Electra** Texas, SW USA 34°01′N 98°55′W
37 Q7 **Electra Lake** ⊠ Colorado, C USA
38 B8 **'Ele'ele** *var.* Eleele. Kaua'i, Hawaii, USA, C Pacific Ocean 21°54′N 159°35′W
**Eleele** *see* 'Ele'ele
**Elefantes** *see* Lepelle
115 H19 **Elefsína** *prev.* Elevsís. Attikí, C Greece 38°02′N 23°33′E
115 G19 **Eléftheres** *anc.* Eleutherae. *site of ancient city* Attikí/Stereá Elláda, C Greece
114 I13 **Eleftheroúpoli** *prev.* Elevtheroúpolis. Anatolikí Makedonía kai Thráki, NE Greece 40°55′N 24°15′E
74 F10 **El Eglab** ▲▲ SW Algeria
118 F10 **Eleja** C Latvia 56°24′N 23°41′E
**Elek** *see* Yelek
119 G14 **Elektrėnai** Vilnius, SE Lithuania 54°47′N 24°35′E
126 L3 **Elektrostal'** Moskovskaya Oblast', W Russia 55°47′N 38°24′E
**Elemi Triangle** *see* Ilemi Triangle
54 G16 **El Encanto** Amazonas, S Colombia 01°45′S 73°12′W
37 R14 **Elephant Butte Reservoir** ⊠ New Mexico, SW USA
**Éléphant, Chaîne de l'** *see* Dâmrei, Chuŏr Phmun
194 G2 **Elephant Island** *island* South Shetland Islands, Antarctica
**Elephant River** *see* Olifants
**El Escorial** *see* San Lorenzo de El Escorial
**Élesd** *see* Aleşd
114 F11 **Eleshnitsa** ≈ W Bulgaria
137 S13 **Eleşkirt** Ağrı, E Turkey 39°22′N 42°48′E
42 F5 **El Estor** Izabal, E Guatemala 15°37′N 89°22′W
**Eleutherae** *see* Eléftheres
44 I2 **Eleuthera Island** *island* N The Bahamas
37 S5 **Elevenmile Canyon Reservoir** ⊠ Colorado, C USA
27 W8 **Eleven Point River** ≈ Arkansas/Missouri, C USA
**Elevsís** *see* Elefsína
**Elevtheroúpolis** *see* Eleftheroúpoli
**El Faiyûm** *see* Al Fayyūm
80 B10 **El Fasher** *var.* Al Fāshir. Northern Darfur, W Sudan 13°37′N 25°22′E
**El Fashn** *see* Al Fashn
**El Ferrol/El Ferrol del Caudillo** *see* Ferrol
39 W13 **Elfin Cove** Chichagof Island, Alaska, USA 58°09′N 136°16′W
105 W4 **El Fluvià** ≈ NE Spain
40 H7 **El Fuerte** Sinaloa, W Mexico 26°28′N 108°35′W
80 D11 **El Fula** Western Kordofan, C Sudan 11°44′N 28°20′E
**El Gedaref** *see* Gedaref
80 A10 **El Geneina** *var.* Ajjinena, Al-Genain, Al Junaynah. Western Darfur, W Sudan 13°27′N 22°30′E
96 J8 **Elgin** NE Scotland, United Kingdom 57°39′N 03°20′W
30 M10 **Elgin** Illinois, N USA 42°02′N 88°16′W
29 P14 **Elgin** Nebraska, C USA 41°58′N 98°04′W
35 Y9 **Elgin** Nevada, W USA 37°19′N 114°30′W
28 L6 **Elgin** North Dakota, N USA 46°24′N 101°51′W
26 M12 **Elgin** Oklahoma, C USA 34°46′N 98°17′W
25 T10 **Elgin** Texas, SW USA 30°21′N 97°22′W
123 R9 **El'ginskiy** Respublika Sakha (Yakutiya), NE Russia 64°27′N 141°57′E
**El Gîza** *see* Al Jīzah
74 J8 **El Goléa** *var.* Al Golea. C Algeria 30°35′N 02°59′E
40 D2 **El Golfo de Santa Clara** Sonora, NW Mexico 31°48′N 114°40′W
81 G18 **Elgon, Mount** ▲ E Uganda 01°07′N 34°29′E
94 I10 **Elgpiggen** ▲ S Norway 62°13′N 11°18′E
105 T4 **El Grado** Aragón, NE Spain 42°09′N 00°13′E
40 L6 **El Guaje, Laguna** ⊠ NE Mexico
54 H6 **El Guayabo** Zulia, W Venezuela 08°37′N 72°20′W
77 O6 **El Gueṭṭâra** *oasis* N Mali
76 J6 **El Ḥammâmi** *desert* N Mauritania
76 M5 **El Ḥank** *cliff* N Mauritania
**El Haseke** *see* Al Ḥasakah
80 H10 **El Hawata** Gedaref, E Sudan 13°25′N 34°42′E
**El Higo** *see* Higos
114 L10 **Elhovo** *var.* Elkhovo; *prev.* Kizilagach. Yambol, E Bulgaria 42°10′N 26°34′E
171 T16 **Eliase** Pulau Selaru, E Indonesia 08°16′S 130°49′E
**Elías Piña** *see* Comendador
25 R6 **Eliasville** Texas, SW USA 32°55′N 98°46′W
**Elichpur** *see* Achalpur
37 V13 **Elida** New Mexico, SW USA 33°57′N 103°39′W
115 F18 **Elikónas** ▲▲ C Greece
67 T10 **Elila** ≈ W Dem. Rep. Congo
39 N9 **Elim** Alaska, USA 64°37′N 162°15′W
**Elimberrum** *see* Auch
**Eliocroca** *see* Lorca
61 B16 **Elisa** Santa Fe, C Argentina 30°42′S 61°04′W
**Elisabethstedt** *see* Dumbrăveni
**Élisabethville** *see* Lubumbashi
127 O13 **Elista** Respublika Kalmykiya, SW Russia 46°18′N 44°09′E
182 I9 **Elizabeth** South Australia 34°44′S 138°39′E
21 Q3 **Elizabeth** West Virginia, NE USA 39°04′N 81°24′W
19 Q9 **Elizabeth, Cape** *headland* Maine, NE USA 43°34′N 70°12′W
21 Y8 **Elizabeth City** North Carolina, SE USA 36°18′N 76°16′W
21 P8 **Elizabethton** Tennessee, S USA 36°22′N 82°15′W
30 M17 **Elizabethtown** Illinois, N USA 37°24′N 88°21′W
20 K6 **Elizabethtown** Kentucky, S USA 37°41′N 85°51′W
18 L7 **Elizabethtown** New York, NE USA 44°13′N 73°38′W
21 U11 **Elizabethtown** North Carolina, SE USA 34°36′N 78°36′W
18 G15 **Elizabethtown** Pennsylvania, NE USA 40°08′N 76°36′W
74 E6 **El-Jadida** *prev.* Mazagan. W Morocco 33°15′N 08°27′W
**El Jafr** *see* Jafr, Qā' al
80 F11 **El Jebelein** White Nile, E Sudan 12°38′N 32°51′E
110 N8 **Ełk** *Ger.* Lyck. Warmińsko-mazurskie, NE Poland 53°51′N 22°20′E
110 O8 **Ełk** ≈ NE Poland
29 Y12 **Elkader** Iowa, C USA 42°51′N 91°24′W
80 G9 **El Kamlin** Gezira, C Sudan 15°03′N 33°11′E
33 N11 **Elk City** Idaho, NW USA 45°50′N 115°28′W
26 K10 **Elk City** Oklahoma, C USA 35°24′N 99°24′W
27 P7 **Elk City Lake** ⊠ Kansas, C USA
34 M5 **Elk Creek** California, W USA 39°34′N 122°34′W
28 J10 **Elk Creek** ≈ South Dakota, N USA
74 M5 **El Kef** *var.* Al Kāf, Le Kef. NW Tunisia 36°13′N 08°44′E
74 F7 **El Kelâa Srarhna** *var.* Kal al Sraghna. C Morocco 32°05′N 07°20′W
**El Kerak** *see* Al Karak
11 P17 **Elkford** British Columbia, SW Canada 49°58′N 114°57′W
**El Khalil** *see* Hebron
80 E7 **El Khandaq** Northern, N Sudan 18°34′N 30°34′E
**El Khârga** *see* Al Khārijah
31 P11 **Elkhart** Indiana, N USA 41°40′N 85°58′W
26 H7 **Elkhart** Kansas, C USA 37°00′N 101°51′W
25 V8 **Elkhart** Texas, SW USA 31°37′N 95°34′W
30 M7 **Elkhart Lake** ◎ Wisconsin, N USA
**El Khartûm** *see* Khartoum
37 Q3 **Elkhead Mountains** ▲▲ Colorado, C USA
18 I12 **Elk Hill** ▲ Pennsylvania, NE USA 41°42′N 75°33′W
138 G8 **El Khiyam** *var.* Al Khiyām, Khiam. S Lebanon 33°12′N 35°42′E
29 S15 **Elkhorn** Nebraska, C USA 41°17′N 96°13′W
30 M9 **Elkhorn** Wisconsin, N USA 42°40′N 88°34′W
29 R14 **Elkhorn River** ≈ Nebraska, C USA
127 O16 **El'khotovo** Respublika Severnaya Osetiya, SW Russia 43°18′N 44°17′E
**Elkhovo** *see* Elhovo
21 R8 **Elkin** North Carolina, SE USA 36°14′N 80°51′W
21 S4 **Elkins** West Virginia, NE USA 38°56′N 79°53′W
195 X3 **Elkins, Mount** ▲ Antarctica 66°25′S 53°54′E
14 G8 **Elk Lake** Ontario, S Canada 47°44′N 80°19′W
31 P6 **Elk Lake** ◎ Michigan, N USA
18 F12 **Elkland** Pennsylvania, NE USA 41°59′N 77°16′W
35 W3 **Elko** Nevada, W USA 40°48′N 115°46′W
11 R14 **Elk Point** Alberta, SW Canada 53°52′N 110°49′W
29 R12 **Elk Point** South Dakota, N USA 42°42′N 96°37′W
29 V8 **Elk River** Minnesota, N USA 45°18′N 93°34′W
20 J10 **Elk River** ≈ Alabama/Tennessee, S USA
21 R4 **Elk River** ≈ West Virginia, NE USA
20 I7 **Elkton** Kentucky, S USA 36°49′N 87°11′W
21 Y2 **Elkton** Maryland, NE USA 39°37′N 75°50′W
29 R10 **Elkton** South Dakota, N USA 44°14′N 96°28′W
20 I10 **Elkton** Tennessee, S USA 35°01′N 86°51′W
21 U5 **Elkton** Virginia, NE USA 38°22′N 78°35′W
**El Kuneitra** *see* Al Qunayṭirah
81 L15 **El Kure** Somali, E Ethiopia 05°37′N 42°05′E
**Elláda** *see* Greece
80 D12 **El Lagowa** Western Kordofan, C Sudan 11°23′N 29°10′E
39 S12 **Ellamar** Alaska, USA 60°54′N 146°37′W
**Ellás** *see* Greece
23 S6 **Ellaville** Georgia, SE USA 32°14′N 84°18′W
197 P9 **Ellef Ringnes Island** *island* Nunavut, N Canada
29 V10 **Ellendale** Minnesota, N USA 43°53′N 93°19′W
29 P7 **Ellendale** North Dakota, N USA 45°57′N 98°33′W
36 M6 **Ellen, Mount** ▲ Utah, W USA 38°06′N 110°48′W
32 I9 **Ellensburg** Washington, NW USA 47°00′N 124°34′W
18 K12 **Ellenville** New York, NE USA 41°43′N 74°24′W
**Ellep** *see* Lib
21 T10 **Ellerbe** North Carolina, SE USA 35°04′N 79°45′W
197 P10 **Ellesmere Island** *island* Queen Elizabeth Islands, Nunavut, N Canada
185 H19 **Ellesmere, Lake** ◎ South Island, New Zealand
97 K18 **Ellesmere Port** C England, United Kingdom 53°17′N 02°54′W
31 O14 **Ellettsville** Indiana, N USA 39°13′N 86°37′W
99 E19 **Ellezelles** Hainaut, SW Belgium 50°44′N 03°40′E
8 L7 **Ellice** ≈ Nunavut, NE Canada
**Ellice Islands** *see* Tuvalu
**Ellichpur** *see* Achalpur
21 W3 **Ellicott City** Maryland, NE USA 39°16′N 76°48′W
23 S2 **Ellijay** Georgia, SE USA 34°42′N 84°28′W
27 W7 **Ellington** Missouri, C USA 37°14′N 90°58′W
**Ellinikí Dimokratía** *see* Greece
26 L5 **Ellinwood** Kansas, C USA 38°21′N 98°34′W
83 J24 **Elliot** Eastern Cape, SE South Africa 31°20′S 27°51′E
14 D10 **Elliot Lake** Ontario, S Canada 46°24′N 82°38′W
181 X6 **Elliot, Mount** ▲ Queensland, E Australia 19°36′S 147°02′E
21 T5 **Elliott Knob** ▲ Virginia, NE USA 38°10′N 79°18′W
26 K4 **Ellis** Kansas, C USA 38°56′N 99°33′W
182 F8 **Elliston** South Australia 33°40′S 134°56′E
22 M7 **Ellisville** Mississippi, S USA 31°36′N 89°12′W
105 V5 **El Llobregat** ≈ NE Spain
96 L9 **Ellon** NE Scotland, United Kingdom 57°22′N 02°06′W
**Ellore** *see* Elūru
21 S13 **Elloree** South Carolina, SE USA 33°34′N 80°37′W
26 M4 **Ellsworth** Kansas, C USA 38°45′N 98°15′W
19 S7 **Ellsworth** Maine, NE USA 44°32′N 68°25′W
30 I6 **Ellsworth** Wisconsin, N USA 44°44′N 92°29′W
26 M11 **Ellsworth, Lake** ⊠ Oklahoma, C USA
194 K9 **Ellsworth Land** *physical region* Antarctica
194 L9 **Ellsworth Mountains** ▲▲ Antarctica
101 J21 **Ellwangen** Baden-Württemberg, S Germany 48°58′N 10°07′E
18 B14 **Ellwood City** Pennsylvania, NE USA 40°49′N 80°15′W
108 H8 **Elm** Glarus, NE Switzerland 46°55′N 09°09′E
32 G9 **Elma** Washington, NW USA 47°00′N 123°24′W
121 V13 **El Maḥalla el Kubra** *var.* Al Maḥallah al Kubrá, Mahalla el Kubra. N Egypt 30°59′N 31°10′E
74 E9 **El Mahbas** *var.* Mahbés. SW Western Sahara 27°26′N 09°09′W
63 H17 **El Maitén** Chubut, W Argentina 42°03′S 71°10′W
136 E16 **Elmalı** Antalya, SW Turkey 36°43′N 29°19′E
80 G10 **El Manaqil** Gezira, C Sudan 14°12′N 33°01′E
54 M12 **El Mango** Amazonas, S Venezuela 01°55′N 66°35′W
**El Manṣûra** *see* Al Manṣūrah
55 P8 **El Manteco** Bolívar, E Venezuela 07°27′N 62°32′W
29 O16 **Elm Creek** Nebraska, C USA 40°43′N 99°22′W
**El Mediyya** *see* Médéa
77 V9 **Elméki** Agadez, C Niger 17°52′N 08°07′E
108 K7 **Elmen** Tirol, W Austria 47°22′N 10°34′E
18 I16 **Elmer** New Jersey, NE USA 39°34′N 75°09′W
138 G6 **El Mina** *var.* Al Mīnā'. N Lebanon 34°28′N 35°49′E
**El Minya** *see* Al Minyā
14 F15 **Elmira** Ontario, S Canada 43°35′N 80°34′W
18 G11 **Elmira** New York, NE USA 42°06′N 76°50′W
36 K13 **El Mirage** Arizona, SW USA 33°36′N 112°19′W
29 O7 **Elm Lake** ⊠ South Dakota, N USA
**El Moján** *see* San Rafael
105 N7 **El Molar** Madrid, C Spain 40°43′N 03°35′W
76 L7 **El Mrâyer** *well* C Mauritania
76 L5 **El Mreiti** *well* N Mauritania
76 L8 **El Mreyyé** *desert* E Mauritania
29 P8 **Elm River** ≈ North Dakota/South Dakota, N USA
100 I9 **Elmshorn** Schleswig-Holstein, N Germany 53°45′N 09°39′E
80 D12 **El Muglad** Western Kordofan, C Sudan 11°02′N 27°44′E
**El Muwaqqar** *see* Al Muwaqqar
14 G14 **Elmvale** Ontario, S Canada 44°34′N 79°53′W
30 K12 **Elmwood** Illinois, N USA 40°46′N 89°58′W
26 J8 **Elmwood** Oklahoma, C USA 36°37′N 100°31′W
103 P17 **Elne** *anc.* Illiberis. Pyrénées-Orientales, S France 42°36′N 02°58′E
54 F11 **El Nevado, Cerro** *elevation* C Colombia
171 N5 **El Nido** Palawan, W Philippines 11°10′N 119°25′E
62 I12 **El Nihuil** Mendoza, W Argentina 34°58′S 68°40′W
75 W7 **El Nouzha** ✈ (Alexandria) N Egypt 31°06′N 29°58′E
80 E10 **El Obeid** *var.* Al Obayyid, Al Ubayyiḍ. Northern Kordofan, C Sudan 13°11′N 30°10′E
41 O13 **El Oro** México, S Mexico 19°51′N 100°07′W
56 B8 **El Oro** ◈ *province* SW Ecuador
61 B19 **Elortondo** Santa Fe, C Argentina 33°42′S 61°37′W
54 J8 **Elorza** Apure, C Venezuela 07°02′N 69°30′W
**El Ouâdi** *see* El Oued
74 L7 **El Oued** *var.* Al Oued, El Ouâdi, El Wad. NE Algeria 33°20′N 06°53′E
36 L15 **Eloy** Arizona, SW USA 32°47′N 111°33′W
55 Q7 **El Palmar** Bolívar, E Venezuela 08°01′N 61°53′W
40 K8 **El Palmito** Durango, W Mexico 25°40′N 104°59′W
55 P7 **El Pao** Bolívar, E Venezuela 08°03′N 62°40′W
54 K5 **El Pao** Cojedes, N Venezuela 09°40′N 68°08′W
42 J7 **El Paraíso** El Paraíso, S Honduras 13°51′N 86°31′W
42 I7 **El Paraíso** ◈ *department* SE Honduras
30 L12 **El Paso** Illinois, N USA 40°44′N 89°01′W
24 G8 **El Paso** Texas, SW USA 31°45′N 106°30′W
24 G8 **El Paso** ✈ Texas, SW USA 31°48′N 106°24′W
105 U7 **El Perelló** Cataluña, NE Spain 40°53′N 00°43′E
55 P5 **El Pilar** Sucre, NE Venezuela 10°31′N 63°12′W
42 F7 **El Pital, Cerro** ▲ El Salvador/Honduras 14°19′N 89°06′W
35 Q9 **El Portal** California, W USA 37°40′N 119°46′W
40 J3 **El Porvenir** Chihuahua, N Mexico 31°15′N 105°48′W
43 U14 **El Porvenir** Guna Yala, N Panama 09°33′N 78°56′W
105 W6 **El Prat de Llobregat** Cataluña, NE Spain 41°20′N 02°05′E
42 H5 **El Progreso** Yoro, NW Honduras 15°25′N 87°49′W
42 A2 **El Progreso** *off.* Departamento de El Progreso. ◈ *department* C Guatemala
**El Progreso** *see* Guastatoya
**El Progreso, Departamento de** *see* El Progreso
104 L9 **El Puente del Arzobispo** Castilla-La Mancha, C Spain 39°48′N 05°10′W
104 J15 **El Puerto de Santa María** Andalucía, S Spain 36°36′N 06°13′W
62 I8 **El Puesto** Catamarca, NW Argentina 27°57′S 67°37′W
**El Qaṣr** *see* Al Qaṣr
**El Qatrani** *see* Al Qaṭrānah
40 I10 **El Quelite** Sinaloa, C Mexico 23°37′N 106°26′W
62 G9 **Elqui, Río** ≈ N Chile
**El Q'unayṭirah** *see* Al Qunayṭirah
**El Quneitra** *see* Al Qunayṭirah
**El Quseir** *see* Al Quṣayr
**El Quweira** *see* Al Quwayrah
141 O15 **El-Rahaba** ✈ (Ṣan'ā') W Yemen 15°28′N 44°12′E
42 M10 **El Rama** Costa Caribe Sur, SE Nicaragua 12°09′N 84°15′W
43 W16 **El Real** *var.* El Real de Santa María. Darién, SE Panama 08°06′N 77°42′W
**El Real de Santa María** *see* El Real
26 M10 **El Reno** Oklahoma, C USA 35°32′N 95°57′W
40 K9 **El Rodeo** Durango, C Mexico 25°12′N 104°35′W
104 J13 **El Ronquillo** Andalucía, S Spain 37°43′N 06°09′W
11 S16 **Elrose** Saskatchewan, S Canada 51°07′N 107°59′W
30 K8 **Elroy** Wisconsin, N USA 43°43′N 90°16′W
25 S17 **Elsa** Texas, SW USA 26°17′N 97°59′W
**El Şaff** *see* Aş Şaff
40 J10 **El Salto** Durango, C Mexico 23°47′N 105°22′W
42 D8 **El Salvador** *off.* Republic of El Salvador, *Sp.* República de El Salvador. ◆ *republic* Central America
**El Salvador, República de** *see* El Salvador
**El Salvador, Republic of** *see* El Salvador
54 K7 **El Samán de Apure** Apure, C Venezuela 07°54′N 68°44′W
14 D7 **Elsas** Ontario, S Canada 48°31′N 82°53′W
40 F3 **El Sásabe** *var.* Aduana del Sásabe. Sonora, NW Mexico 31°27′N 111°31′W
40 J5 **El Sáuz** Chihuahua, N Mexico 29°03′N 106°15′W
27 W4 **Elsberry** Missouri, C USA 39°10′N 90°46′W
45 P9 **El Seibo** *var.* Santa Cruz de El Seibo, Santa Cruz del Seibo. E Dominican Republic 18°45′N 69°04′W
42 B7 **El Semillero Barra Nahualate** Escuintla, SW Guatemala 14°01′N 91°28′W
**Elsene** *see* Ixelles
**Elsen Nur** *see* Dorgê Co
36 L6 **Elsinore** Utah, W USA 38°40′N 112°09′W
**Elsinore** *see* Helsingør
99 L18 **Elsloo** Limburg, SE Netherlands 50°57′N 05°46′E
60 G13 **El Soberbio** Misiones, NE Argentina 27°15′S 54°05′W
55 N6 **El Socorro** Guárico, C Venezuela 09°00′N 65°42′W
54 L6 **El Sombrero** Guárico, N Venezuela 09°25′N 67°06′W
98 L10 **Elspeet** Gelderland, E Netherlands 52°19′N 05°47′E
98 L12 **Elst** Gelderland, E Netherlands 51°55′N 05°51′E
101 O15 **Elsterwerda** Brandenburg, E Germany 51°27′N 13°32′E
40 J4 **El Sueco** Chihuahua, N Mexico 29°53′N 106°24′W
**El Suweida** *see* As Suwaydā'
**El Suweis** *see* As Suways
54 D12 **El Tambo** Cauca, SW Colombia 02°25′N 76°50′W
175 T13 **Eltanin Fracture Zone** *tectonic feature* SE Pacific Ocean
105 X5 **El Ter** ≈ NE Spain
184 K11 **Eltham** Taranaki, North Island, New Zealand 39°26′S 174°25′E
55 O6 **El Tigre** Anzoátegui, NE Venezuela 08°55′N 64°15′W
**El Tigrito** *see* San José de Guanipa
54 J5 **El Tocuyo** Lara, N Venezuela 09°48′N 69°51′W
127 Q10 **El'ton** Volgogradskaya Oblast', SW Russia 49°07′N 46°50′E
32 K10 **Eltopia** Washington, NW USA 46°33′N 118°59′W
**El Toro** *see* Mare de Déu del Toro
61 A18 **El Trébol** Santa Fe, C Argentina 32°12′S 61°40′W
40 J13 **El Tuito** Jalisco, SW Mexico 20°19′N 105°22′W
**El Ṭûr** *see* Aṭ Ṭūr
**Eluan Pi** *see* Oluan Bi
155 K16 **Elūru** *prev.* Ellore. Andhra Pradesh, E India 16°45′N 81°10′E
118 H13 **Elva** *Ger.* Elwa. Tartumaa, SE Estonia 58°13′N 26°25′E
37 R9 **El Vado Reservoir** ⊠ New Mexico, SW USA
43 S15 **El Valle** Coclé, C Panama 08°39′N 80°08′W
104 I11 **Elvas** Portalegre, C Portugal 38°53′N 07°10′W
54 K7 **El Venado** Apure, C Venezuela 07°25′N 68°46′W
105 V6 **El Vendrell** Cataluña, NE Spain 41°13′N 01°32′E
94 I13 **Elverum** Hedmark, S Norway 60°54′N 11°33′E
42 I9 **El Viejo** Chinandega, NW Nicaragua 12°39′N 87°11′W
54 G7 **El Viejo, Cerro** ▲ C Colombia 07°31′N 72°56′W
54 H6 **El Vigía** Mérida, NW Venezuela 08°38′N 71°39′W
105 Q4 **El Villar de Arnedo** La Rioja, N Spain 42°19′N 02°05′W
59 A14 **Elvira** Amazonas, W Brazil 07°12′S 69°56′W
**Elwa** *see* Elva
**El Wad** *see* El Oued
81 K17 **El Wak** Mandera, NE Kenya 02°46′N 40°57′E
33 R7 **Elwell, Lake** ⊠ Montana, NW USA
31 P13 **Elwood** Indiana, N USA 40°16′N 85°50′W
27 R3 **Elwood** Kansas, C USA 39°43′N 94°52′W
29 N16 **Elwood** Nebraska, C USA 40°35′N 99°51′W
**Elx** *see* Elche
97 O20 **Ely** E England, United Kingdom 52°24′N 00°15′E
29 X4 **Ely** Minnesota, N USA 47°54′N 91°52′W
35 X6 **Ely** Nevada, W USA 39°15′N 114°53′W
**El Yopal** *see* Yopal
31 T11 **Elyria** Ohio, N USA 41°22′N 82°06′W
45 S9 **El Yunque** ▲ E Puerto Rico 18°15′N 65°46′W
101 F23 **Elz** ≈ SW Germany
187 R14 **Emae** *island* Shepherd Islands, C Vanuatu
118 I5 **Emajõgi** *Ger.* Embach. ≈ SE Estonia
**Emāmrūd** *see* Shāhrūd
**Emām Şāḩeb** *see* Imām Şāḩib
**Emam Saheb** *see* Imām Şāḩib
**Emāmshahr** *see* Shāhrūd
95 M20 **Emån** ≈ S Sweden
144 J11 **Emba** *Kaz.* Embi. Aktyubinsk, W Kazakhstan 48°50′N 58°10′E
**Emba** *see* Zhem
**Embach** *see* Emajõgi
62 K5 **Embarcación** Salta, N Argentina 23°15′S 64°05′W
30 M15 **Embarras River** ≈ Illinois, N USA
**Embi** *see* Emba
81 I19 **Embu** Embu, C Kenya 0°32′N 37°28′E
100 E10 **Emden** Niedersachsen, NW Germany 53°22′N 07°12′E
160 H9 **Emei Shan** ▲ Sichuan, C China 29°32′N 103°21′E
29 Q4 **Emerado** North Dakota, N USA 47°55′N 97°21′W
181 X8 **Emerald** Queensland, E Australia 23°33′S 148°11′E
**Emerald Isle** *see* Montserrat
57 J15 **Emero, Río** ≈ W Bolivia
11 Y17 **Emerson** Manitoba, S Canada 49°01′N 97°07′W


◆ Country
● Country Capital
◇ Dependent Territory
○ Dependent Territory Capital
◈ Administrative Regions
✈ International Airport
▲ Mountain
▲▲ Mountain Range
☒ Volcano
≈ River
◎ Lake
⊠ Reservoir

EMERSON – ESTATS, PICO D'

29 T15 Emerson Iowa, C USA 41°00′N 95°22′W
29 R13 Emerson Nebraska, C USA 42°16′N 96°43′W
36 M5 Emery Utah, W USA 38°54′N 111°16′W
Emesa see Ḥimṣ
136 E13 Emet Kütahya, W Turkey 39°22′N 29°15′E
186 B8 Emeti Western, SW Papua New Guinea 07°54′S 143°18′E
35 V3 Emigrant Pass pass Nevada, W USA
78 I6 Emi Koussi ▲ N Chad 19°52′N 18°34′E
Emilia see Emilia-Romagna
41 V15 Emiliano Zapata Chiapas, SE Mexico 17°42′N 91°46′W
106 E9 Emilia-Romagna prev. Emilia; anc. Æmilia. ◆ region N Italy
158 J3 Emin var. Dorbiljin. Xinjiang Uygur Zizhiqu, NW China 46°30′N 83°42′E
149 W8 Eminabad Punjab, E Pakistan 32°02′N 73°51′E
21 L5 Eminence Kentucky, S USA 38°22′N 85°10′W
27 W7 Eminence Missouri, C USA 37°09′N 91°22′W
114 N9 Emine, Nos headland E Bulgaria 42°43′N 27°53′E
158 I3 Emin He ≈ NW China
186 G4 Emirau Island island N Papua New Guinea
136 F13 Emirdağ Afyon, W Turkey 39°01′N 31°09′E
83 K22 eMkhondo prev. Piet Retief. Mpumalanga, E South Africa 27°00′S 30°49′E see also Piet Retief
95 M21 Emmaboda Kalmar, S Sweden 56°36′N 15°30′E
118 E5 Emmaste Hiiumaa, W Estonia 58°43′N 22°36′E
18 I15 Emmaus Pennsylvania, NE USA 40°32′N 75°28′W
183 U4 Emmaville New South Wales, SE Australia 29°26′S 151°38′E
108 E9 Emme ≈ W Switzerland
98 L8 Emmeloord Flevoland, N Netherlands 52°43′N 05°46′E
98 O8 Emmen Drenthe, NE Netherlands 52°48′N 06°57′E
108 F8 Emmen Luzern, C Switzerland 47°03′N 08°14′E
101 F23 Emmendingen Baden-Württemberg, SW Germany 48°07′N 07°51′E
98 P8 Emmer-Compascuum Drenthe, NE Netherlands 52°47′N 07°03′E
101 D14 Emmerich Nordrhein-Westfalen, W Germany 51°49′N 06°16′E
29 U12 Emmetsburg Iowa, C USA 43°06′N 94°40′W
32 M14 Emmett Idaho, NW USA 43°52′N 116°30′W
38 M10 Emmonak Alaska, USA 62°46′N 164°31′W
Emona see Ljubljana
Emonti see East London
24 L12 Emory Peak ▲ Texas, SW USA 29°15′N 103°18′W
40 F6 Empalme Sonora, NW Mexico 27°57′N 110°49′W
83 L23 Empangeni KwaZulu/Natal, E South Africa 28°45′S 31°54′E
61 C14 Empedrado Corrientes, NE Argentina 27°59′S 58°47′W
192 K3 Emperor Seamounts undersea feature NW Pacific Ocean 42°00′N 170°00′E
192 L3 Emperor Trough undersea feature N Pacific Ocean
35 R4 Empire Nevada, W USA 40°26′N 119°21′W
Empire State of the South see Georgia
Emplawas see Amplawas
106 F11 Empoli Toscana, C Italy 43°43′N 10°57′E
27 P5 Emporia Kansas, C USA 38°24′N 96°10′W
21 W7 Emporia Virginia, NE USA 36°42′N 77°33′W
18 E13 Emporium Pennsylvania, NE USA 41°31′N 78°14′W
Empty Quarter see Ar Rub' al Khālī
100 E10 Ems Dut. Eems. ≈ NW Germany
100 F13 Emsdetten Nordrhein-Westfalen, NW Germany 52°11′N 07°32′E
Ems-Hunte Canal see Küstenkanal
100 F10 Ems-Jade-Kanal canal NW Germany
100 F11 Emsland cultural region NW Germany
182 D3 Emu Junction South Australia 28°39′S 132°13′E
163 T3 Emur He ≈ NE China
55 R8 Enachu Landing NW Guyana 06°09′N 60°02′W
93 F16 Enafors Jämtland, C Sweden 63°17′N 12°24′E
94 N11 Enånger Gävleborg, C Sweden 61°30′N 17°10′E
96 G7 Enard Bay bay NW Scotland, United Kingdom
Enareträsk see Inarijärvi
171 X14 Enarotali Papua, E Indonesia 03°55′S 136°21′E
En 'Avedat see Ein Avdat
165 T2 Enbetsu Hokkaidō, NE Japan 44°44′N 141°47′E
61 H16 Encantadas, Serra das ▲ S Brazil
40 E7 Encantado, Cerro ▲ NW Mexico 26°46′N 112°33′W
62 P7 Encarnación Itapúa, S Paraguay 27°20′S 55°50′W
40 M12 Encarnación de Díaz Jalisco, SW Mexico 21°33′N 102°13′W
77 O17 Enchi SW Ghana 05°53′N 02°48′W
25 Q14 Encinal Texas, SW USA 28°02′N 99°21′W
35 U17 Encinitas California, W USA 33°02′N 117°17′W
25 S16 Encino Texas, SW USA 26°58′N 98°06′W
54 H6 Encontrados Zulia, NW Venezuela 09°04′N 72°16′W
182 I10 Encounter Bay inlet South Australia
61 F15 Encruzilhada Rio Grande do Sul, S Brazil 28°58′S 55°31′W
61 H16 Encruzilhada do Sul Rio Grande do Sul, S Brazil 30°30′S 52°32′W
111 M20 Encs Borsod-Abaúj-Zemplén, NE Hungary 48°21′N 21°09′E
193 P3 Endeavour Seamount undersea feature N Pacific Ocean 48°15′N 129°04′W
181 V1 Endeavour Strait strait Queensland, NE Australia
171 O16 Endeh Flores, S Indonesia 08°48′S 121°37′E
95 G23 Endelave island C Denmark
191 T4 Enderbury Island atoll Phoenix Islands, C Kiribati
11 N16 Enderby British Columbia, SW Canada 50°34′N 119°09′W
195 W4 Enderby Land physical region Antarctica
173 N14 Enderby Plain undersea feature S Indian Ocean
29 Q6 Enderlin North Dakota, N USA 46°37′N 97°36′W
Endersdorf see Jędrzejów
28 K16 Enders Reservoir ⊠ Nebraska, C USA
18 H11 Endicott New York, NE USA 42°06′N 76°03′W
39 P7 Endicott Mountains ▲ Alaska, USA
118 I5 Endla Raba wetland C Estonia
117 T9 Enerhodar Zaporiz'ka Oblast', SE Ukraine 47°30′N 34°40′E
57 F14 Ene, Río ≈ C Peru
189 N4 Enewetak Atoll var. Ānewetak, Eniwetok. atoll Ralik Chain, W Marshall Islands
114 L13 Enez Edirne, NW Turkey 40°44′N 26°05′E
21 W8 Enfield North Carolina, SE USA 36°10′N 77°40′W
186 B7 Enga ◆ province W Papua New Guinea
45 Q9 Engaño, Cabo headland E Dominican Republic 18°36′N 68°19′W
164 U3 Engaru Hokkaidō, NE Japan 44°06′N 143°30′E
108 F9 Engelberg Unterwalden, C Switzerland 46°51′N 08°25′E
21 Y9 Engelhard North Carolina, SE USA 35°30′N 76°00′W
127 P8 Engel's Saratovskaya Oblast', W Russia 51°27′N 46°09′E
101 G24 Engen Baden-Württemberg, SW Germany 47°52′N 08°46′E
Engeten see Aiud
168 K15 Enggano, Pulau island W Indonesia
80 J8 Enghershatu ▲ N Eritrea 16°41′N 38°21′E
99 F19 Enghien Dut. Edingen. Hainaut, SW Belgium 50°42′N 04°03′E
27 V12 England Arkansas, C USA 34°32′N 91°58′W
97 M20 England Lat. Anglia. ◆ national region England, United Kingdom
14 H8 Englehart Ontario, S Canada 47°50′N 79°52′W
37 T4 Englewood Colorado, C USA 39°39′N 104°59′W
31 O16 English Indiana, N USA 38°20′N 86°28′W
39 Q13 English Bay Alaska, USA 59°21′N 151°55′W
English Bazar see Ingrāj Bāzār
97 N25 English Channel var. The Channel, Fr. la Manche. channel NW Europe
194 J7 English Coast physical region Antarctica
105 S11 Enguera Comunitat Valenciana, E Spain 38°58′N 00°42′W
118 E8 Engure W Latvia 57°09′N 23°13′E
118 E8 Engures Ezers ⊚ NW Latvia
137 R9 Enguri Rus. Inguri. ≈ NW Georgia
Engyum see Gangi
26 M9 Enid Oklahoma, C USA 36°25′N 97°53′W
22 L3 Enid Lake ⊠ Mississippi, S USA
189 Y2 Enigu island Ratak Chain, SE Marshall Islands
Enikale Strait see Kerch Strait
147 Z8 Enil'chek Issyk-Kul'skaya Oblast', E Kyrgyzstan 42°04′N 79°01′E
115 F17 Enipéfs ≈ C Greece
165 S4 Eniwa Hokkaidō, NE Japan 42°53′N 141°14′E
Eniwetok see Enewetak Atoll
Enjiang see Yongfeng
Enkeldoorn see Chivhu
123 S11 Enken, Mys prev. Mys Enkan. headland NE Russia 58°29′N 141°27′E
Enkan, Mys see Enken, Mys
98 J8 Enkhuizen Noord-Holland, NW Netherlands 52°34′N 05°03′E
109 Q4 Enknach ≈ N Austria
95 N15 Enköping Uppsala, C Sweden 59°38′N 17°05′E
107 K24 Enna var. Castrogiovanni, Henna. Sicilia, Italy, C Mediterranean Sea 37°34′N 14°16′E
80 D11 En Nahud Western Kordofan, C Sudan 12°41′N 28°28′E
138 F8 En Nâqoûra var. An Nāqūrah. SW Lebanon 33°06′N 33°30′E
En Nazira see Natzrat
73 K8 Ennedi plateau NE Chad
101 E15 Ennepetal Nordrhein-Westfalen, W Germany 51°18′N 07°23′E
183 P4 Enngonia New South Wales, SE Australia 29°19′S 145°52′E
97 C19 Ennis Ir. Inis. Clare, W Ireland 52°50′N 08°59′W
33 R11 Ennis Montana, NW USA 45°21′N 111°45′W
25 U7 Ennis Texas, SW USA 32°19′N 96°37′W
97 F20 Enniscorthy Ir. Inis Córthaidh. SE Ireland 52°30′N 06°34′W
97 E15 Enniskillen var. Inniskilling, Ir. Inis Ceithleann. SW Northern Ireland, United Kingdom 54°21′N 07°38′W
97 B19 Ennistimon Ir. Inis Díomáin. Clare, W Ireland 52°57′N 09°17′W
109 T4 Enns Oberösterreich, N Austria 48°13′N 14°28′E
109 T4 Enns ≈ C Austria
93 O16 Eno Pohjois-Karjala, SE Finland 62°45′N 30°15′E
24 M5 Enochs Texas, SW USA 33°51′N 102°46′W
93 N17 Enonkoski Etelä-Savo, E Finland 62°04′N 28°53′E
92 K10 Enontekiö N. Sami Eanodat, Swe. Enontekis. Lappi, N Finland 68°25′N 23°40′E
Enontekis see Enontekiö
21 Q11 Enoree South Carolina, SE USA 34°39′N 81°58′W
21 P11 Enoree River ≈ South Carolina, SE USA
18 M6 Enosburg Falls Vermont, NE USA 44°54′N 72°50′W
171 N13 Enrekang Sulawesi, C Indonesia 03°33′S 119°46′E
45 N10 Enriquillo SW Dominican Republic 17°57′N 71°13′W
45 N9 Enriquillo, Lago ⊚ SW Dominican Republic
98 L9 Ens Flevoland, N Netherlands 52°39′N 05°49′E
98 P11 Enschede Overijssel, E Netherlands 52°13′N 06°55′E
40 B2 Ensenada Baja California, NW Mexico 31°52′N 116°32′W
101 E20 Ensheim ✈ (Saarbrücken) Saarland, W Germany 49°13′N 07°09′E
160 L9 Enshi Hubei, C China 30°16′N 109°26′E
164 L14 Enshū-nada gulf SW Japan
23 O8 Ensley Florida, SE USA 30°31′N 87°16′W
Enso see Svetogorsk
81 F18 Entebbe S Uganda 0°07′N 32°30′E
81 F18 Entebbe ✈ C Uganda 0°04′N 32°29′E
101 M18 Entenbühl ▲ Czechia/Germany 50°09′N 12°10′E
98 N10 Enter Overijssel, E Netherlands 52°19′N 06°34′E
23 Q7 Enterprise Alabama, S USA 31°19′N 85°50′W
32 L11 Enterprise Oregon, NW USA 45°25′N 117°18′W
36 J7 Enterprise Utah, W USA 37°33′N 113°42′W
32 J8 Entiat Washington, NW USA 47°39′N 120°15′W
105 P15 Entinas, Punta de las headland S Spain 36°40′N 02°44′W
108 F8 Entlebuch Luzern, W Switzerland 47°02′N 08°04′E
108 F8 Entlebuch valley C Switzerland
63 I22 Entrada, Punta headland S Argentina
103 O13 Entraygues-sur-Truyère Aveyron, S France 44°39′N 02°36′E
187 O14 Entrecasteaux, Récifs d' reef N New Caledonia
61 C17 Entre Ríos off. Provincia de Entre Ríos. ◆ province NE Argentina
42 K7 Entre Ríos, Cordillera ▲ Honduras/Nicaragua
Entre Ríos, Provincia de see Entre Ríos
104 G9 Entroncamento Santarém, C Portugal 39°28′N 08°28′W
77 V16 Enugu Enugu, S Nigeria 06°24′N 07°24′E
77 U16 Enugu ◆ state SE Nigeria
123 V5 Enurmino Chukotskiy Avtonomnyy Okrug, NE Russia 66°46′N 171°40′W
54 E9 Envigado Antioquia, W Colombia 06°09′N 75°38′W
59 B15 Envira Amazonas, W Brazil 07°12′S 69°59′W
Enyélé see Enyellé
79 I16 Enyellé var. Enyélé. Likouala, NE Congo 02°49′N 18°02′E
101 H21 Enz ≈ SW Germany
165 N13 Enzan var. Kōshū. Yamanashi, Honshū, S Japan 35°44′N 138°43′E
104 I2 Eo ≈ NW Spain
Eochaill see Youghal
Eochaille, Cuan see Youghal Bay
107 K22 Eolie, Isole var. Isole Lipari, Eng. Aeolian Islands, Lipari Islands. island group S Italy
189 U12 Eot island Chuuk, C Micronesia
Epáno Archánes/Epáno Arkhánai see Archánes
115 G14 Epanomí Kentrikí Makedonía, N Greece 40°25′N 22°57′E
98 M10 Epe Gelderland, E Netherlands 52°21′N 05°59′E
77 S16 Epe Lagos, S Nigeria 06°37′N 04°01′E
79 I17 Epéna Likouala, NE Congo 01°28′N 17°29′E
Eperies/Eperjes see Prešov
103 Q4 Épernay anc. Sparnacum. Marne, N France 49°02′N 03°58′E
36 L5 Ephraim Utah, W USA 39°21′N 111°35′W
18 H15 Ephrata Pennsylvania, NE USA 40°09′N 76°08′W
32 J8 Ephrata Washington, NW USA 47°19′N 119°33′W
187 R14 Epi var. Épi. island C Vanuatu
Épi see Epi
105 R6 Épila Aragón, NE Spain 41°34′N 01°19′W
103 T6 Épinal Vosges, NE France 48°10′N 06°28′E
Epiphania see Ḥamāh
Epirus see Ípeiros
121 P3 Episkopí SW Cyprus 34°37′N 32°53′E
Episkopi Bay see Episkopís, Kólpos
121 P3 Episkopís, Kólpos var. Episkopi Bay. bay SE Cyprus
121 P3 Episkopís, Kólpos var. Episkopi Bay. bay SE Cyprus
Epoon see Ebon Atoll
Eporedia see Ivrea
Eppeschdorf see Dumbrăveni
101 H21 Eppingen Baden-Württemberg, SW Germany 49°09′N 08°54′E
83 E18 Epukiro Omaheke, E Namibia 21°40′S 19°09′E
29 Y13 Epworth Iowa, C USA 42°27′N 90°55′W
143 O10 Eqlīd var. Iqlid. Fārs, C Iran 30°54′N 52°40′E
Equality State see Wyoming
79 J18 Equateur off. Région de l' Equateur. ◆ region N Dem. Rep. Congo
Equateur, Région de l' see Equateur
151 K22 Equatorial Channel channel S Maldives
79 B17 Equatorial Guinea off. Equatorial Guinea, Republic of, Sp. República de Guinea Ecuatoria, Guinea Ecuatorial. ◆ republic C Africa
Equatorial Guinea, Republic of see Equatorial Guinea
121 V11 Eratosthenes Tablemount undersea feature E Mediterranean Sea 33°48′N 32°53′E
Erautini see Johannesburg
136 L12 Erbaa Tokat, N Turkey 40°42′N 36°37′E
101 E19 Erbeskopf ▲ W Germany 49°43′N 07°04′E
139 U4 Erbet Ar. 'Arbat, var. Arbat. As Sulaymānīyah, NE Iraq 35°26′N 45°34′E
Erbil see Arbil
121 P2 Ercan ✈ (Nicosia) N Cyprus 35°07′N 33°30′E
Ercegnovi see Herceg-Novi
137 T14 Erçek Gölü ⊚ E Turkey
137 S14 Erciş Van, E Turkey 39°02′N 43°21′E
136 K14 Erciyes Dağı anc. Argaeus. ▲ C Turkey 38°32′N 35°28′E
111 J22 Érd Ger. Hanselbeck. Pest, C Hungary 47°22′N 18°56′E
163 X11 Erdaobaihe prev. Baihe. Jilin, NE China 42°24′N 128°09′E
159 O12 Erdaogou Qinghai, W China 34°30′N 92°50′E
163 X11 Erdao Jiang ≈ NE China
Erdăt-Sângeorz see Sângeorgiu de Pădure
136 C11 Erdek Balıkesir, NW Turkey 40°24′N 27°47′E
Erdély see Transylvania
Erdélyi-Havasok see Carpații Meridionali
136 J17 Erdemli İçel, S Turkey 36°35′N 34°19′E
163 O10 Erdene var. Ulaan-Uul. Dornogovĭ, SE Mongolia 44°21′N 111°06′E
162 H9 Erdene var. Sangiyn Dalay. Govĭ-Altay, C Mongolia 45°12′N 97°51′E
162 E6 Erdenebüren var. Har-Us. Hovd, W Mongolia 48°30′N 91°25′E
162 K9 Erdenedalay var. Sangiyn Dalay. Dundgovĭ, C Mongolia 45°59′N 104°58′E
162 G7 Erdenehayrhan var. Altan. Dzavhan, W Mongolia 48°05′N 95°48′E
162 J7 Erdenemandal var. Öldziyt. Arhangay, C Mongolia 48°30′N 101°25′E
162 K6 Erdenet Orhon, N Mongolia 49°01′N 104°07′E
163 Q9 Erdenetsagaan var. Chonogol. Sühbaatar, E Mongolia 45°55′N 115°19′E
162 I8 Erdenetsogt Bayanhongor, C Mongolia 46°27′N 100°53′E
Erdenetsogt see Bayan-Ovoo
78 K7 Erdi plateau NE Chad
78 L7 Erdi Ma desert NE Chad
101 M23 Erding Bayern, SE Germany 48°18′N 11°54′E
Erdőszáda see Ardusat
Erdőszentgyörgy see Sângeorgiu de Pădure
102 I7 Erdre ≈ NW France
195 R13 Erebus, Mount ⚠ Ross Island, Antarctica 78°11′S 165°09′E
61 H14 Erechim Rio Grande do Sul, S Brazil 27°35′S 52°15′W
163 O7 Ereen Davaanĭ Nuruu ▲ NE Mongolia
163 Q6 Ereentsav Dornod, NE Mongolia 49°51′N 115°41′E
136 I16 Ereğli Konya, S Turkey 37°30′N 34°02′E
115 A15 Ereíkoussa island Iónia Nisiá, Greece, C Mediterranean Sea
163 O11 Erenhot var. Erlian. Nei Mongol Zizhiqu, NE China 43°35′N 112°E
104 M6 Eresma ≈ N Spain
115 K17 Eresós var. Eressós. Lésvos, E Greece 39°11′N 25°57′E
Eressós see Eresós
Ereymentaū see Yereymentau
99 K21 Érezée Luxembourg, SE Belgium 50°16′N 05°34′E
74 G7 Erfoud SE Morocco 31°29′N 04°18′W
101 D16 Erft ≈ W Germany
101 K16 Erfurt Thüringen, C Germany 50°59′N 11°02′E
137 P15 Ergani Diyarbakır, SE Turkey 38°17′N 39°44′E
Ergel see Hatanbulag
Ergene Çayı see Ergene Irmağı
136 C10 Ergene Irmağı var. Ergene Çayı. ≈ NW Turkey
118 J9 Ērgļi C Latvia 56°55′N 25°38′E
78 H11 Erguig, Bahr ≈ SW Chad
163 S5 Ergun var. Labudalin; prev. Ergun Youqi. Nei Mongol Zizhiqu, N China 50°13′N 120°09′E
Ergun see Gegan Gol
Ergun He see Argun
Ergun Youqi see Ergun
Ergun Zuoqi see Gegan Gol
160 F12 Er Hai ⊚ SW China
104 K4 Ería ≈ NW Spain
80 H8 Eriba Kassala, NE Sudan 16°37′N 36°04′E
96 I6 Eriboll, Loch inlet NW Scotland, United Kingdom
65 Q18 Erica Seamount undersea feature SW Indian Ocean 38°15′S 14°30′E
107 H23 Erice Sicilia, Italy, C Mediterranean Sea 38°02′N 12°35′E
104 E10 Ericeira Lisboa, C Portugal 38°58′N 09°25′W
96 H10 Ericht, Loch ⊚ C Scotland, United Kingdom
26 J11 Erick Oklahoma, C USA 35°13′N 99°52′W
18 B11 Erie Pennsylvania, NE USA 42°07′N 80°04′W
18 E9 Erie Canal canal New York, NE USA
Érié, Lac see Erie, Lake
31 T10 Erie, Lake Fr. Lac Érié. ⊚ Canada/USA
Erigabo see Ceerigaabo
77 N8 'Erîgât desert N Mali
Erigavo see Ceerigaabo
92 P2 Erik Eriksenstretet strait E Svalbard
11 X15 Eriksdale Manitoba, S Canada 50°52′N 98°07′W
189 V6 Erikub Atoll var. Ādkup. atoll Ratak Chain, C Marshall Islands
102 G4 Er, Îles d' island group NW France
Erimanthos see Erýmanthos
165 T6 Erimo Hokkaidō, NE Japan 42°01′N 143°07′E
165 T6 Erimo-misaki headland Hokkaidō, NE Japan 41°57′N 143°12′E
20 H8 Erin Tennessee, S USA 36°19′N 87°42′W
96 E9 Eriskay island NW Scotland, United Kingdom
Erithraí see Erythrés
80 I9 Eritrea off. State of Eritrea, Tig. Iertra, Hagera Iertra. ◆ transitional government E Africa
Eritrea, State of see Eritrea
Erivan see Yerevan
101 D16 Erkelenz Nordrhein-Westfalen, W Germany 51°04′N 06°19′E
95 P15 Erken ⊚ C Sweden
101 K19 Erlangen Bayern, S Germany 49°36′N 11°E
160 G9 Erlang Shan ▲ C China 29°56′N 102°24′E
Erlau see Eger
109 V5 Erlauf ≈ NE Austria
181 Q8 Erldunda Roadhouse Northern Territory, N Australia 25°13′S 133°13′E
Erlian see Erenhot
27 T15 Erling, Lake ⊠ Arkansas, USA
109 O8 Erlsbach Tirol, W Austria 46°54′N 12°15′E
Ermak see Aksu
98 K10 Ermelo Gelderland, C Netherlands 52°18′N 05°38′E
83 K21 Ermelo Mpumalanga, NE South Africa 26°32′S 29°59′E
136 H17 Ermenek Karaman, S Turkey 36°38′N 32°55′E
Érmihályfalva see Valea lui Mihai
115 G20 Ermióni Pelopónnisos, S Greece 37°24′N 23°15′E
115 J20 Ermoúpoli var. Hermoupolis; prev. Ermoúpolis. Sýyros, Kykládes, Greece, Aegean Sea 37°26′N 24°55′E
Ermoúpolis see Ermoúpoli
Ernabella see Pukatja
155 G22 Ernākulam Kerala, SW India 10°04′N 76°18′E
102 J6 Ernée Mayenne, NW France 48°18′N 00°54′W
61 H14 Ernestina, Barragem ⊠ S Brazil
54 E4 Ernesto Cortissoz ✈ (Barranquilla) Atlántico, N Colombia
155 H21 Erode Tamil Nādu, SE India 11°21′N 77°43′E
Eroj see Iroj
83 C19 Erongo ◆ region W Namibia
99 F21 Erquelinnes Hainaut, S Belgium 50°18′N 04°08′E
74 G7 Er-Rachidia var. Ksar al Soule. E Morocco 31°58′N 04°22′W
80 E11 Er Rahad var. Ar Rahad. Northern Kordofan, C Sudan 12°43′N 30°39′E
Er Ramle see Ramla
83 O15 Errego Zambézia, NE Mozambique 16°02′S 37°11′E
105 Q2 Errenteria Cast. Rentería. País Vasco, N Spain 43°17′N 01°54′W
Er Rif/Er Riff see Rif
97 D14 Errigal Mountain Ir. An Earagail. ▲ N Ireland 55°03′N 08°09′W
97 A15 Erris Head Ir. Ceann Iorrais. headland W Ireland 54°18′N 10°01′W
187 S15 Erromango island S Vanuatu
Error Guyot see Error Tablemount
173 O4 Error Tablemount var. Error Guyot. undersea feature W Indian Ocean 10°20′N 56°05′E
80 G11 Er Roseires Blue Nile, E Sudan 11°52′N 34°23′E
Erseka see Ersekë
113 M22 Ersekë var. Erseka, Kolonjë. Korçë, SE Albania 40°19′N 20°39′E
Érsekújvár see Nové Zámky
29 S4 Erskine Minnesota, N USA 47°42′N 96°00′W
103 V6 Erstein Bas-Rhin, NE France 48°24′N 07°39′E
108 G9 Erstfeld Uri, C Switzerland 46°49′N 08°41′E
158 M3 Ertai Xinjiang Uygur Zizhiqu, NW China 46°04′N 90°06′E
126 M7 Ertil' Voronezhskaya Oblast', W Russia 51°51′N 40°46′E
Ertis see Irtysh, C Asia
Ertis see Irtyshsk, Kazakhstan
158 K2 Ertix He Rus. Chërnyy Irtysh. ≈ China/Kazakhstan
21 P9 Erwin North Carolina, SE USA 35°19′N 78°40′W
Erydropótamos see Erythropótamos
115 E19 Erýmanthos var. Erimanthos. ▲ S Greece 37°57′N 21°51′E
115 G19 Erythrés prev. Erithraí. Stereá Elláda, C Greece 38°18′N 23°20′E
114 L12 Erythropótamos Bul. Byala Reka, var. Erydropótamos. ≈ Bulgaria/Greece
160 F12 Eryuan var. Yuhu. Yunnan, SW China 26°09′N 100°01′E
109 U6 Erzbach ≈ W Austria
Erzerum see Erzurum
101 N17 Erzgebirge Cz. Krušné Hory, Eng. Ore Mountains. ▲ Czechia/Germany see also Krušné Hory
Erzgebirge see Krušné Hory
122 L14 Erzin Respublika Tyva, S Russia 50°17′N 95°03′E
137 O13 Erzincan var. Erzinjan. Erzincan, E Turkey 39°44′N 39°30′E
137 N13 Erzincan var. Erzinjan. ◆ province NE Turkey
Erzinjan see Erzincan
Erzsébetváros see Dumbrăveni
137 Q13 Erzurum prev. Erzerum. Erzurum, NE Turkey 39°57′N 41°17′E
137 Q12 Erzurum prev. Erzerum. ◆ province NE Turkey
186 G9 Esa'ala Normanby Island, SE Papua New Guinea 09°45′S 150°47′E
165 T2 Esashi Hokkaidō, NE Japan 44°57′N 142°32′E
165 Q9 Esashi var. Esasi. Iwate, Honshū, C Japan 39°13′N 141°11′E
165 Q5 Esasho Hokkaidō, N Japan 41°52′N 140°07′E
Esasi see Esashi
95 F23 Esbjerg Syddtjylland, W Denmark 55°28′N 08°28′E
Esbo see Espoo
36 L7 Escalante Utah, W USA 37°46′N 111°36′W
36 M7 Escalante River ≈ Utah, W USA
14 L12 Escalier, Réservoir l' ⊠ Québec, SE Canada
40 K7 Escalón Chihuahua, N Mexico 26°43′N 104°20′W
104 M8 Escalona Castilla-La Mancha, C Spain 40°10′N 04°24′W
23 O8 Escambia River ≈ Florida, SE USA
31 N5 Escanaba Michigan, N USA 45°45′N 87°03′W
31 N4 Escanaba River ≈ Michigan, N USA
105 R8 Escandón, Puerto de pass E Spain
41 W14 Escárcega Campeche, SE Mexico 18°33′N 90°41′W
171 O1 Escarpada Point headland Luzon, N Philippines 18°28′N 122°10′E
23 N8 Escatawpa River ≈ Alabama/Mississippi, S USA
103 P2 Escaut ≈ N France
Escaut see Scheldt
99 M25 Esch-sur-Alzette Luxembourg, S Luxembourg 49°30′N 05°59′E
101 J15 Eschwege Hessen, C Germany 51°10′N 10°03′E
101 D16 Eschweiler Nordrhein-Westfalen, W Germany 50°49′N 06°16′E
Esclaves, Grand Lac des see Great Slave Lake
45 O8 Escocesa, Bahía bay N Dominican Republic
43 W15 Escocés, Punta headland NE Panama 08°50′N 77°37′W
35 U17 Escondido California, W USA 33°07′N 117°05′W
42 M10 Escondido, Río ≈ SE Nicaragua
15 S7 Escoumins, Rivière des ≈ Québec, SE Canada
194 G3 Escudero research station (Chile) King George Island, Antarctica 62°12′S 58°57′W
37 O13 Escudilla Mountain ▲ Arizona, SW USA 33°57′N 109°07′W
40 J11 Escuinapa var. Escuinapa de Hidalgo. Sinaloa, C Mexico 22°50′N 105°46′W
Escuinapa de Hidalgo see Escuinapa
42 C6 Escuintla Escuintla, S Guatemala 14°17′N 90°46′W
41 V17 Escuintla Chiapas, SE Mexico 15°20′N 92°40′W
42 A2 Escuintla off. Departamento de Escuintla. ◆ department S Guatemala
Escuintla, Departamento de see Escuintla
15 W7 Escuminac ≈ Québec, SE Canada
79 D16 Eséka Centre, SW Cameroon 03°40′N 10°48′E
136 I12 Esenboğa ✈ (Ankara) Ankara, C Turkey 40°05′N 33°01′E
136 D17 Eşen Çayı ≈ SW Turkey
146 B13 Esenguly Rus. Gasan-Kuli. Balkan Welaýaty, W Turkmenistan 37°29′N 53°57′E
105 T4 Ésera ≈ NE Spain
143 N8 Eşfahān Eng. Isfahan; anc. Aspadana. Eşfahān, C Iran 32°41′N 51°41′E
143 O7 Eşfahān off. Ostān-e Eşfahān. ◆ province C Iran
Eşfahān, Ostān-e see Eşfahān
105 N5 Esgueva ≈ N Spain
Eshkamesh see Ishkamish
Eshkāshem see Ishkāshim
83 L23 Eshowe KwaZulu/Natal, E South Africa 28°53′S 31°28′E
143 T5 'Eshqābād Khorāsān-e Razavī, NE Iran 36°00′N 59°01′E
Esh Sham see Rif Dimashq
Esh Sharā see Ash Sharāh
Esik see Yesik
Esil see Yesil'
Esil see Ishim, Kazakhstan/Russian Federation
183 V2 Esk Queensland, E Australia 27°15′S 152°23′E
184 O11 Eskdale Hawke's Bay, North Island, New Zealand 39°24′S 176°51′E
Eski Dzhumaya see Targovishte
92 L2 Eskifjörður Austurland, E Iceland 65°04′N 14°01′W
139 S3 Eski Kalak var. Askī Kalak, Kalak. Arbīl, N Iraq 36°16′N 43°40′E
95 N16 Eskilstuna Södermanland, C Sweden 59°22′N 16°31′E
8 H6 Eskimo Lakes ⊚ Northwest Territories, NW Canada
9 O10 Eskimo Point headland Nunavut, E Canada 61°19′N 93°49′W
Eskimo Point see Arviat
139 Q2 Eski Mosul Nīnawá, N Iraq 36°31′N 42°45′E
Eski-Nookat see Nookat
136 F12 Eskişehir var. Eskishehr. Eskişehir, W Turkey 39°46′N 30°30′E
136 F13 Eskişehir var. Eski shehr. ◆ province NW Turkey
Eskishehr see Eskişehir
104 K5 Esla ≈ NW Spain
Eslāmābād see Eslāmābād-e Gharb
142 J6 Eslāmābād-e Gharb var. Eslāmābād; prev. Harunabad, Shāhābād. Kermānshāhān, W Iran 34°08′N 46°35′E
Eslām Qal'eh see Islām Qal'ah
95 K23 Eslöv Skåne, S Sweden 55°50′N 13°20′E
143 S12 Esmā'īlābād Kermān, S Iran 28°48′N 56°39′E
143 U8 Esmā'īlābād Khorāsān-e Jonūbī, E Iran 35°20′N 60°30′E
136 D14 Eşme Uşak, W Turkey 38°26′N 28°59′E
44 G6 Esmeralda Camagüey, E Cuba 21°51′N 78°10′W
63 F21 Esmeralda, Isla island S Chile
56 B5 Esmeraldas Esmeraldas, N Ecuador 0°55′N 79°40′W
56 B5 Esmeraldas ◆ province NW Ecuador
Esna see Isnā
14 B6 Esnagi Lake ⊚ Ontario, S Canada
143 V14 Espakeh Sīstān va Balūchestān, SE Iran 26°54′N 60°09′E
103 O13 Espalion Aveyron, S France 44°31′N 02°45′E
España see Spain
España, Reino de see Spain
14 E11 Espanola Ontario, S Canada 46°15′N 81°46′W
37 S10 Espanola New Mexico, SW USA 35°59′N 106°04′W
57 C18 Española, Isla var. Hood Island. island Galapagos Islands, Ecuador, E Pacific Ocean
104 M13 Espejo Andalucía, S Spain 37°40′N 04°34′W
94 C13 Espeland Hordaland, S Norway 60°22′N 05°27′E
100 G12 Espelkamp Nordrhein-Westfalen, NW Germany 52°22′N 08°37′E
38 M8 Espenberg, Cape headland Alaska, USA 66°33′N 163°36′W
180 L13 Esperance Western Australia 33°49′S 121°52′E
186 L9 Esperance, Cape headland Guadacanal, C Solomon Islands 09°09′S 159°38′E
57 P18 Esperancita Santa Cruz, E Bolivia
61 B17 Esperanza Santa Fe, C Argentina 31°29′S 61°00′W
40 G6 Esperanza Sonora, NW Mexico 27°37′N 109°51′W
24 H9 Esperanza Texas, SW USA 31°09′N 105°40′W
194 H3 Esperanza research station (Argentina) Antarctica 63°29′S 56°53′W
104 E12 Espichel, Cabo headland S Portugal 38°25′N 09°15′W
54 E10 Espinal Tolima, C Colombia 04°08′N 74°53′W
48 K10 Espinhaço, Serra do ▲ SE Brazil
104 G6 Espinho Aveiro, N Portugal 41°01′N 08°38′W
59 N18 Espinosa Minas Gerais, SE Brazil 14°58′S 42°49′W
103 O15 Espinouse ▲ S France
60 Q8 Espírito Santo off. Estado do Espírito Santo. ◆ state E Brazil
Espírito Santo, Estado do see Espírito Santo
187 P13 Espiritu Santo var. Santo. island W Vanuatu
41 Z13 Espíritu Santo, Bahía del bay SE Mexico
40 F9 Espíritu Santo, Isla del island NW Mexico
41 Y12 Espita Yucatán, SE Mexico 21°00′N 88°17′W
15 Y7 Espoir, Cap d' headland Québec, SE Canada 48°24′N 64°21′W
Esponsede/Esponsende see Esposende
93 L20 Espoo Swe. Esbo. Uusimaa, S Finland 60°10′N 24°42′E
104 G5 Esposende var. Esponsede, Esponsende. Braga, N Portugal 41°32′N 08°47′W
83 M18 Espungabera Manica, SW Mozambique 20°29′S 32°48′E
63 H17 Esquel Chubut, SW Argentina 42°55′S 71°20′W
10 L17 Esquimalt Vancouver Island, British Columbia, SW Canada 48°26′N 123°27′W
61 C16 Esquina Corrientes, NE Argentina 30°00′S 59°30′W
42 E6 Esquipulas Chiquimula, SE Guatemala 14°36′N 89°22′W
42 K9 Esquipulas Matagalpa, C Nicaragua 12°30′N 85°55′W
94 I8 Essandsjøen ⊚ S Norway
74 E7 Essaouira prev. Mogador. W Morocco 31°33′N 09°40′W
Esseg see Osijek
Es Semara see Smara
99 G15 Essen Antwerpen, N Belgium 51°28′N 04°28′E
101 E15 Essen var. Essen an der Ruhr. Nordrhein-Westfalen, W Germany 51°28′N 07°01′E
Essen an der Ruhr see Essen
74 I5 Es Senia ✈ (Oran) NW Algeria 35°34′N 00°42′W
55 T8 Essequibo Islands island group N Guyana
55 T11 Essequibo River ≈ C Guyana
14 C18 Essex Ontario, S Canada 42°10′N 82°50′W
29 T16 Essex Iowa, C USA 40°49′N 95°18′W
97 P21 Essex cultural region E England, United Kingdom
31 R8 Essexville Michigan, N USA 43°37′N 83°50′W
101 H22 Esslingen var. Esslingen am Neckar. Baden-Württemberg, SW Germany 48°45′N 09°19′E
Esslingen am Neckar see Esslingen
103 N6 Essonne ◆ department N France
Es Suweida see As Suwaydā'
79 F16 Est Eng. East. ◆ region SE Cameroon
104 I11 Estaca de Bares, Punta de point NW Spain
24 M5 Estacado, Llano plain New Mexico/Texas, SW USA
41 P12 Estación Tamuín San Luis Potosí, C Mexico 22°00′N 98°44′W
63 K25 Estados, Isla de los prev. Eng. Staten Island. island S Argentina
Estado Vargas see Vargas
143 P12 Eşţahbān Fārs, S Iran
14 F11 Estaire Ontario, S Canada 46°19′N 80°47′W
59 P16 Estância Sergipe, E Brazil 11°15′S 37°28′W
37 S12 Estancia New Mexico, SW USA 34°45′N 106°03′W
104 G7 Estarreja Aveiro, N Portugal 40°45′N 08°35′W
102 M17 Estats, Pica d' Sp. Pico d'Estats. ▲ France/Spain 42°39′N 01°24′E
Estats, Pico d' see Estats, Pica d'



◆ Country
● Country Capital
◇ Dependent Territory
○ Dependent Territory Capital
◆ Administrative Regions
✈ International Airport
▲ Mountain
▲ Mountain Range
⚠ Volcano
≈ River
⊚ Lake
⊠ Reservoir

Estcourt – Faroe Islands


83 K23 **Estcourt** KwaZulu/Natal, E South Africa *29°00′S 29°53′E*
106 H8 **Este** *anc.* Ateste. Veneto, NE Italy *45°14′N 11°40′E*
42 J9 **Estelí** Estelí, NW Nicaragua *13°05′N 86°21′W*
42 J9 **Estelí** ⬖ *department* NW Nicaragua
105 Q4 **Estella** *Bas.* Lizarra. Navarra, N Spain *42°41′N 02°02′W*
29 R9 **Estelline** South Dakota, N USA *44°34′N 96°54′W*
25 P4 **Estelline** Texas, SW USA *34°33′N 100°26′W*
104 L14 **Estepa** Andalucía, S Spain *37°17′N 04°52′W*
104 L16 **Estepona** Andalucía, S Spain *36°26′N 05°09′W*
39 R9 **Ester** Alaska, USA *64°49′N 148°03′W*
11 V16 **Esterhazy** Saskatchewan, S Canada *50°40′N 102°02′W*
37 S3 **Estes Park** Colorado, C USA *40°22′N 105°31′W*
11 V17 **Estevan** Saskatchewan, S Canada *49°07′N 103°05′W*
29 T11 **Estherville** Iowa, C USA *43°24′N 94°49′W*
21 R15 **Estill** South Carolina, SE USA *32°45′N 81°14′W*
103 Q6 **Estissac** Aube, N France *48°17′N 03°51′E*
15 T9 **Est, Lac de l'** ◎ Québec, SE Canada
**Estland** *see* Estonia
11 S16 **Eston** Saskatchewan, S Canada *51°09′N 198°42′W*
118 G5 **Estonia** *off.* Republic of Estonia, *Est.* Eesti Vabariik, Eesti, *Ger.* Estland, *Latv.* Igaunija; *prev.* Estonian SSR, *Rus.* Estonskaya SSR. ◆ *republic* NE Europe
**Estonian SSR** *see* Estonia
**Estonia, Republic of** *see* Estonia
**Estonskaya SSR** *see* Estonia
104 E11 **Estoril** Lisboa, W Portugal *38°42′N 09°23′W*
59 L14 **Estreito** Maranhão, E Brazil *06°34′S 47°22′W*
104 I8 **Estrela, Serra da** ▲▲ C Portugal
40 D3 **Estrella, Punta** *headland* NW Mexico *30°53′N 114°45′W*
104 F10 **Estremadura** *cultural and historical region* W Portugal
**Estremadura** *see* Extremadura
104 H11 **Estremoz** Évora, S Portugal *38°50′N 07°35′W*
79 D18 **Estuaire** *off.* Province de l'Estuaire, *var.* L'Estuaire. ⬖ *province* NW Gabon
**Estuaire, Province de l'** *see* Estuaire
83 L22 **Eswatini** *off.* Kingdom of Eswatini; *prev.* Swaziland. ◆ *monarchy* S Africa
**Eswatini, Kingdom of** *see* Eswatini
**Eszék** *see* Osijek
111 I22 **Esztergom** *Ger.* Gran; *anc.* Strigonium. Komárom-Esztergom, N Hungary *47°47′N 18°44′E*
152 K11 **Etah** Uttar Pradesh, N India *27°33′N 78°39′E*
189 R17 **Etal Atoll** *atoll* Mortlock Islands, C Micronesia
99 K24 **Étalle** Luxembourg, SE Belgium *49°41′N 05°36′E*
103 N6 **Étampes** Essonne, N France *48°26′N 02°10′E*
182 J1 **Etamunbanie, Lake** *salt lake* South Australia
103 N1 **Étaples** Pas-de-Calais, N France *50°31′N 01°39′E*
152 K12 **Etāwah** Uttar Pradesh, N India *26°46′N 79°01′E*
15 R10 **Etchemin** ≈ Québec, SE Canada
**Etchmiadzin** *see* Vagharshapat
40 G7 **Etchojoa** Sonora, NW Mexico *26°54′N 109°37′W*
93 L19 **Etelä-Karjala** *Swe.* Södra Karelen, *Eng.* South Karelia. ⬖ *region* S Finland
83 B16 **Etengua** Kunene, NW Namibia *17°24′S 13°05′E*
99 K25 **Éthe** Luxembourg, SE Belgium *49°34′N 05°32′E*
11 W15 **Ethelbert** Manitoba, S Canada *51°30′N 100°22′W*
80 H12 **Ethiopia** *off.* Federal Democratic Republic of Ethiopia, *Amh.* Ītyop'iya, Yeĭtyop'iya Fēdēralawī Dēmokrasīyawī Rīpeblīk; *prev.* Abyssinia, People's Democratic Republic of Ethiopia. ◆ *republic* E Africa
**Ethiopia, Federal Democratic Republic of** *see* Ethiopia
80 I13 **Ethiopian Highlands** *var.* Ethiopian Plateau. *plateau* N Ethiopia
**Ethiopian Plateau** *see* Ethiopian Highlands
**Ethiopia, People's Democratic Republic of** *see* Ethiopia
34 M2 **Etna** California, W USA *41°25′N 122°53′W*
18 B14 **Etna** Pennsylvania, NE USA *40°29′N 79°55′W*
94 G12 **Etna** ≈ S Norway
107 L24 **Etna, Monte** *Eng.* Mount Etna. ▲ Sicilia, Italy, C Mediterranean Sea *37°46′N 15°00′E*
**Etna, Mount** *see* Etna, Monte
95 C15 **Etne** Hordaland, S Norway *59°40′N 05°55′E*
**Etoliko** *see* Aitolikó
39 Y14 **Etolin Island** *island* Alexander Archipelago, Alaska, USA
38 L12 **Etolin Strait** *strait* Alaska, USA
83 C17 **Etosha Pan** *salt lake* N Namibia
79 G18 **Etoumbi** Cuvette-Ouest, NW Congo *0°01′N 14°57′E*
20 M10 **Etowah** Tennessee, S USA *35°19′N 84°31′W*
23 S2 **Etowah River** ≈ Georgia, SE USA
146 B13 **Etrek** *var.* Gyzyletrek, *Rus.* Kizyl-Atrek. Balkan Welaýaty, W Turkmenistan *37°40′N 54°44′E*
146 C13 **Etrek** *Per.* Rūd-e Atrak, *Rus.* Atrak, Atrek. ≈ Iran/Turkmenistan
102 L3 **Étretat** Seine-Maritime, N France *49°46′N 00°23′E*
114 H9 **Etropole** Sofia, W Bulgaria *42°50′N 24°00′E*
**Etsch** *see* Adige
**Et Tafila** *see* Aţ Ţafīlah
99 M23 **Ettelbrück** Diekirch, C Luxembourg *49°51′N 06°06′E*
189 V12 **Etten** *atoll* Chuuk Islands, C Micronesia
99 H14 **Etten-Leur** Noord-Brabant, S Netherlands *51°34′N 04°37′E*
76 G7 **Et Tîdra** *var.* Ile Tîdra. *island* Dakhlet Nouâdhibou, NW Mauritania
101 G21 **Ettlingen** Baden-Württemberg, SW Germany *48°57′N 08°25′E*
102 M2 **Eu** Seine-Maritime, N France *50°01′N 01°24′E*
193 W16 **'Eua** *prev.* Middleburg Island. *island* Tongatapu Group, SE Tonga
193 W15 **Eua Iki** *island* Tongatapu Group, S Tonga
**Euboea** *see* Évvoia
181 O12 **Eucla** Western Australia *31°41′S 128°51′E*
31 U11 **Euclid** Ohio, N USA *41°34′N 81°33′W*
27 W14 **Eudora** Arkansas, C USA *33°06′N 91°15′W*
27 Q4 **Eudora** Kansas, C USA *38°56′N 95°06′W*
182 J9 **Eudunda** South Australia *34°11′S 139°03′E*
23 R6 **Eufaula** Alabama, S USA *31°53′N 85°09′W*
27 Q11 **Eufaula** Oklahoma, C USA *35°16′N 95°36′W*
27 Q11 **Eufaula Lake** *var.* Eufaula Reservoir. ⊠ Oklahoma, C USA
**Eufaula Reservoir** *see* Eufaula Lake
32 F13 **Eugene** Oregon, NW USA *44°03′N 123°05′W*
40 B6 **Eugenia, Punta** *headland* NW Mexico *27°48′N 115°03′W*
183 Q8 **Eugowra** New South Wales, SE Australia *33°28′S 148°21′E*
104 I2 **Eume** ≈ NW Spain
104 H2 **Eume, Encoro do** ⊠ NW Spain
**Eumolpias** *see* Plovdiv
59 O18 **Eunápolis** Bahia, SE Brazil *16°20′S 39°36′W*
22 H8 **Eunice** Louisiana, S USA *30°29′N 92°25′W*
37 W15 **Eunice** New Mexico, SW USA *32°26′N 103°09′W*
99 M19 **Eupen** Liège, E Belgium *50°38′N 06°02′E*
130 B10 **Euphrates** *Ar.* Al-Furāt, *Turk.* Firat Nehri. ≈ SW Asia
138 L3 **Euphrates Dam** *dam* N Syria
22 M4 **Eupora** Mississippi, S USA *33°32′N 89°16′W*
93 K19 **Eura** Satakunta, SW Finland *61°07′N 22°12′E*
93 K19 **Eurajoki** Satakunta, SW Finland *61°13′N 21°45′E*
0-1 **Eurasian Plate** *tectonic feature*
102 L4 **Eure** ⬖ *department* N France
102 M4 **Eure** ≈ N France
102 M6 **Eure-et-Loir** ⬖ *department* C France
34 K3 **Eureka** California, W USA *40°47′N 124°12′W*
27 P6 **Eureka** Kansas, C USA *37°51′N 96°17′W*
33 O6 **Eureka** Montana, NW USA *48°52′N 115°03′W*
35 V5 **Eureka** Nevada, W USA *39°31′N 115°58′W*
29 O7 **Eureka** South Dakota, N USA *45°46′N 99°37′W*
36 L4 **Eureka** Utah, W USA *39°57′N 112°07′W*
32 K10 **Eureka** Washington, NW USA *46°21′N 118°41′W*
27 S9 **Eureka Springs** Arkansas, C USA *36°25′N 93°45′W*
182 K6 **Eurinilla Creek** *seasonal river* South Australia
183 O11 **Euroa** Victoria, SE Australia *36°46′S 145°35′E*
172 M9 **Europa, Île** *island* W Madagascar
104 L3 **Europa, Picos de** ▲▲ N Spain
104 L16 **Europa Point** *headland* S Gibraltar *36°07′N 05°20′W*
84-85 **Europe** *continent*
98 F12 **Europoort** Zuid-Holland, W Netherlands *51°59′N 04°08′E*
**Euskadi** *see* País Vasco
101 D17 **Euskirchen** Nordrhein-Westfalen, W Germany *50°40′N 06°47′E*
23 W11 **Eustis** Florida, SE USA *28°51′N 81°41′W*
182 M9 **Euston** New South Wales, SE Australia *34°34′S 142°45′E*
23 N5 **Eutaw** Alabama, S USA *32°50′N 87°53′W*
100 K8 **Eutin** Schleswig-Holstein, N Germany *54°08′N 10°38′E*
10 K14 **Eutsuk Lake** ⊠ British Columbia, SW Canada
**Euxine Sea** *see* Black Sea
83 C16 **Evale** Cunene, SW Angola *16°36′S 15°46′E*
37 T3 **Evans** Colorado, C USA *40°22′N 104°41′W*
11 P14 **Evansburg** Alberta, SW Canada *53°34′N 114°57′W*
29 X13 **Evansdale** Iowa, C USA *42°28′N 92°16′W*
183 V4 **Evans Head** New South Wales, SE Australia *29°07′S 153°27′E*
12 J11 **Evans, Lac** ◎ Québec, SE Canada
37 S5 **Evans, Mount** ▲ Colorado, C USA *39°15′N 106°10′W*
9 Q6 **Evans Strait** *strait* Nunavut, N Canada
31 N10 **Evanston** Illinois, N USA *42°02′N 87°41′W*
33 S17 **Evanston** Wyoming, C USA *41°16′N 110°57′W*
14 D11 **Evansville** Manitoulin Island, Ontario, S Canada *45°48′N 82°34′W*
31 N16 **Evansville** Indiana, N USA *37°58′N 87°33′W*
30 L9 **Evansville** Wisconsin, N USA *42°46′N 89°16′W*
25 S8 **Evant** Texas, SW USA *31°28′N 98°09′W*
143 P13 **Evaz** Fārs, S Iran *27°48′N 53°58′E*
29 W4 **Eveleth** Minnesota, N USA *47°27′N 92°32′W*
182 E3 **Evelyn Creek** *seasonal river* South Australia
181 Q2 **Evelyn, Mount** ▲ Northern Territory, N Australia *13°28′S 132°50′E*
122 K10 **Evenkiyskiy Avtonomnyy Okrug** ⬖ *autonomous district* Krasnoyarskiy Kray, N Russia
183 R13 **Everard, Cape** *headland* Victoria, SE Australia *37°48′S 149°21′E*
182 F6 **Everard, Lake** *salt lake* South Australia
182 C2 **Everard Ranges** ▲▲ South Australia
153 R11 **Everest, Mount** *Chin.* Qomolangma Feng, *Nep.* Sagarmāthā. ▲ China/Nepal *27°59′N 86°57′E*
18 E15 **Everett** Pennsylvania, NE USA *40°00′N 78°22′W*
32 H7 **Everett** Washington, NW USA *47°59′N 122°12′W*
99 E17 **Evergem** Oost-Vlaanderen, NW Belgium *51°07′N 03°43′E*
23 X16 **Everglades City** Florida, SE USA *25°51′N 81°22′W*
23 Y16 **Everglades, The** *wetland* Florida, SE USA
23 P7 **Evergreen** Alabama, S USA *31°25′N 86°55′W*
37 T4 **Evergreen** Colorado, C USA *39°37′N 105°19′W*
**Evergreen State** *see* Washington
97 L21 **Evesham** C England, United Kingdom *52°06′N 01°57′W*
103 T10 **Évian-les-Bains** Haute-Savoie, E France *46°22′N 06°34′E*
93 K16 **Evijärvi** Etelä-Pohjanmaa, W Finland *63°22′N 23°30′E*
79 D17 **Evinayong** *var.* Ebinayon, Evinayoung. C Equatorial Guinea *01°28′N 10°17′E*
**Evinayoung** *see* Evinayong
115 E18 **Évinos** ≈ C Greece
95 E17 **Evje** Aust-Agder, S Norway *58°35′N 07°49′E*
**Evmolpia** *see* Plovdiv
104 H11 **Évora** *anc.* Ebora, *Lat.* Liberalitas Julia. Évora, C Portugal *38°34′N 07°54′W*
104 G11 **Évora** ⬖ *district* S Portugal
102 M4 **Évreux** *anc.* Civitas Eburovicum. Eure, N France *49°02′N 01°10′E*
102 K6 **Évron** Mayenne, NW France *48°10′N 00°24′W*
114 L13 **Évros** *Bul.* Maritsa, *Turk.* Meriç; *anc.* Hebrus. ≈ SE Europe *see also* Maritsa/Meriç
**Évros** *see* Meriç
**Évros** *see* Maritsa
115 F21 **Evrótas** ≈ S Greece
103 O5 **Évry** Essonne, N France *48°38′N 02°34′E*
25 O8 **E. V. Spence Reservoir** ⊠ Texas, SW USA
115 I18 **Évvoia** *Lat.* Euboea. *island* C Greece
38 D9 **'Ewa Beach** *var.* Ewa Beach. O'ahu, Hawaii, USA, C Pacific Ocean *21°19′N 158°00′W*
**Ewa Beach** *see* 'Ewa Beach
32 L9 **Ewan** Washington, NW USA *47°06′N 117°46′W*
44 K12 **Ewarton** C Jamaica *18°11′N 77°06′W*
81 J18 **Ewaso Ng'iro** *var.* Nyiro. ≈ C Kenya
29 P13 **Ewing** Nebraska, C USA *42°13′N 98°20′W*
194 J5 **Ewing Island** *island* Antarctica
65 P17 **Ewing Seamount** *undersea feature* E Atlantic Ocean *23°20′S 08°45′E*
158 L6 **Ewirgol** Xinjiang Uygur Zizhiqu, W China *42°56′N 87°39′E*
79 G19 **Ewo** Cuvette-Ouest, W Congo *0°55′S 14°49′E*
27 S3 **Excelsior Springs** Missouri, C USA *39°20′N 94°13′W*
97 J23 **Exe** ≈ SW England, United Kingdom
194 L12 **Executive Committee Range** ▲▲ Antarctica
14 E16 **Exeter** Ontario, S Canada *43°19′N 81°26′W*
97 J24 **Exeter** *anc.* Isca Damnoniorum. SW England, United Kingdom *50°43′N 03°31′W*
35 R11 **Exeter** California, W USA *36°17′N 119°08′W*
19 P10 **Exeter** New Hampshire, NE USA *42°57′N 70°55′W*
**Exin** *see* Kcynia
29 T14 **Exira** Iowa, C USA *41°36′N 94°55′W*
97 J23 **Exmoor** *moorland* SW England, United Kingdom
21 Y6 **Exmore** Virginia, NE USA *37°31′N 75°48′W*
180 G8 **Exmouth** Western Australia *22°01′S 114°06′E*
97 J24 **Exmouth** SW England, United Kingdom *50°36′N 03°25′W*
180 G8 **Exmouth Gulf** *gulf* Western Australia
173 V8 **Exmouth Plateau** *undersea feature* E Indian Ocean
83 K23 **eXobho** *prev.* Ixopo. KwaZulu/Natal, E South Africa *30°10′S 30°05′E*
115 J20 **Exompourgo** *ancient monument* Tínos, Kykládes, Greece, Aegean Sea
104 I10 **Extremadura** *var.* Estremadura. ⬖ *autonomous community* W Spain
78 F12 **Extrême-Nord** *Eng.* Extreme North. ⬖ *region* N Cameroon
**Extreme North** *see* Extrême-Nord
44 I3 **Exuma Cays** *islets* C The Bahamas
44 I3 **Exuma Sound** *sound* C The Bahamas
81 H20 **Eyasi, Lake** ◎ N Tanzania
95 F17 **Eydehavn** Aust-Agder, S Norway *58°31′N 08°53′E*
96 L12 **Eyemouth** SE Scotland, United Kingdom *55°52′N 02°07′W*
96 G7 **Eye Peninsula** *peninsula* NW Scotland, United Kingdom
80 Q13 **Eyl** *It.* Eil. Nugaal, E Somalia *08°03′N 49°49′E*
103 N11 **Eymoutiers** Haute-Vienne, C France *45°45′N 01°43′E*
**Eyo (lower course)** *see* Uolo, Río
29 X10 **Eyota** Minnesota, N USA *44°00′N 92°13′W*
182 H2 **Eyre Basin, Lake** *salt lake* South Australia
182 I1 **Eyre Creek** *seasonal river* Northern Territory/South Australia
174 L9 **Eyre, Lake** *salt lake* South Australia
185 C22 **Eyre Mountains** ▲▲ South Island, New Zealand
182 H3 **Eyre North, Lake** *salt lake* South Australia
182 G7 **Eyre Peninsula** *peninsula* South Australia
182 H4 **Eyre South, Lake** *salt lake* South Australia
95 B18 **Eysturoy** *Dan.* Østerø. *island* N Faroe Islands
61 D20 **Ezeiza** ✈ (Buenos Aires) Buenos Aires, E Argentina *34°49′S 58°30′W*
**Ezeres** *see* Ezeriş
116 F12 **Ezeriş** *Hung.* Ezeres. Caraş-Severin, W Romania *45°21′N 21°55′E*
161 O9 **Ezhou** *prev.* Echeng. Hubei, C China *30°23′N 114°52′E*
125 R11 **Ezhva** Respublika Komi, NW Russia *61°45′N 50°43′E*
136 B12 **Ezine** Çanakkale, NW Turkey *39°46′N 26°20′E*
**Ezo** *see* Hokkaidō
**Ezra/Ezraa** *see* Izra'


# F


191 P7 **Faaa** Tahiti, W French Polynesia *17°32′S 149°36′W*
191 P7 **Faaa** ✈ (Papeete) Tahiti, W French Polynesia *17°31′S 149°36′W*
95 H24 **Faaborg** *var.* Fåborg. Syddtjylland, C Denmark *55°06′N 10°10′E*
151 K19 **Faadhippolhu Atoll** *var.* Fadiffolu, Lhaviyani Atoll. *atoll* N Maldives
191 U10 **Faaite** *atoll* Îles Tuamotu, C French Polynesia
191 Q8 **Faaone** Tahiti, W French Polynesia *17°39′S 149°18′W*
24 H8 **Fabens** Texas, SW USA *31°30′N 106°09′W*
94 H12 **Fåberg** Oppland, S Norway *61°15′N 10°21′E*
**Fåborg** *see* Faaborg
106 I12 **Fabriano** Marche, C Italy *43°20′N 12°54′E*
145 U16 **Fabrichnoye** *prev.* Fabrichnyy. Almaty, SE Kazakhstan *43°12′N 76°19′E*
**Fabrichnyy** *see* Fabrichnoye
54 F10 **Facatativá** Cundinamarca, C Colombia *04°49′N 74°22′W*
77 X9 **Fachi** Agadez, C Niger *18°01′N 11°36′E*
188 B16 **Facpi Point** *headland* W Guam
18 I13 **Factoryville** Pennsylvania, NE USA *41°34′N 75°45′W*
78 K8 **Fada** Ennedi-Ouest, E Chad *17°14′N 21°32′E*
77 Q13 **Fada-Ngourma** E Burkina Faso *12°05′N 00°26′E*
123 N6 **Faddeya, Zaliv** *bay* N Russia
123 Q5 **Faddeyevskiy, Poluostrov** *island* Novosibirskiye Ostrova, NE Russia
141 W12 **Fadhī** S Oman *17°54′N 55°30′E*
**Fadiffolu** *see* Faadhippolhu Atoll
106 H10 **Faenza** *anc.* Faventia. Emilia-Romagna, N Italy *44°17′N 11°53′E*
**Faeroe-Iceland Ridge** *see* Faroe-Iceland Ridge
**Faeroe Islands** *see* Faroe Islands
**Færøerne** *see* Faroe Islands
**Faeroe-Shetland Trough** *see* Faroe-Shetland Trough
104 H6 **Fafe** Braga, N Portugal *41°27′N 08°11′W*
80 K13 **Fafen Shet'** ≈ E Ethiopia
193 V15 **Fafo** *island* Tongatapu Group, S Tonga
192 I16 **Fagaloa Bay** *bay* Upolu, E Samoa
192 H15 **Fagamālo** Savai'i, N Samoa *13°27′S 172°22′W*
116 I12 **Făgăraş** *Ger.* Fogarasch, *Hung.* Fogaras. Braşov, C Romania *45°50′N 24°59′E*
191 W10 **Fagatau** *prev.* Fangatau. *atoll* Îles Tuamotu, C French Polynesia
191 X12 **Fagataufa** *prev.* Fangataufa. *island* Îles Tuamotu, SE French Polynesia
95 M20 **Fagerhult** Kalmar, S Sweden *57°07′N 15°40′E*
94 G13 **Fagernes** Oppland, S Norway *60°59′N 09°14′E*
92 I9 **Fagernes** Troms, N Norway *69°31′N 19°16′E*
95 M14 **Fagersta** Västmanland, C Sweden *59°59′N 15°49′E*
77 W13 **Faggo** *var.* Foggo. Bauchi, N Nigeria *11°22′N 09°55′E*
**Faghman** *see* Fughmah
**Fagibina, Lake** *see* Faguibine, Lac
63 J25 **Fagnano, Lago** ◎ S Argentina
99 G22 **Fagne** *hill range* S Belgium
77 N10 **Faguibine, Lac** *var.* Lake Fagibina. ◎ NW Mali
**Fahaheel** *see* Al Fuḩayḩīl
**Fahlun** *see* Falun
143 U12 **Fahraj** Kermān, SE Iran *29°00′N 59°00′E*
64 P5 **Faial** Madeira, Portugal, NE Atlantic Ocean *32°47′N 16°53′W*
64 N2 **Faial** *var.* Ilha do Faial. *island* Azores, Portugal, NE Atlantic Ocean
**Faial, Ilha do** *see* Faial
108 G10 **Faido** Ticino, S Switzerland *46°30′N 08°48′E*
**Faifo** *see* Hôi An
**Failaka Island** *see* Faylakah
190 G12 **Faioa, Île** *island* N Wallis and Futuna
181 W8 **Fairbairn Reservoir** ⊠ Queensland, E Australia
39 R9 **Fairbanks** Alaska, USA *64°48′N 147°47′W*
21 U12 **Fair Bluff** North Carolina, SE USA *34°18′N 79°02′W*
31 R14 **Fairborn** Ohio, N USA *39°48′N 84°03′W*
23 S3 **Fairburn** Georgia, SE USA *33°34′N 84°34′W*
30 M12 **Fairbury** Illinois, N USA *40°45′N 88°30′W*
29 Q17 **Fairbury** Nebraska, C USA *40°08′N 97°10′W*
29 T9 **Fairfax** Minnesota, N USA *44°31′N 94°43′W*
27 O8 **Fairfax** Oklahoma, C USA *36°34′N 96°42′W*
21 R14 **Fairfax** South Carolina, SE USA *32°57′N 81°14′W*
35 N8 **Fairfield** California, W USA *38°14′N 122°03′W*
33 O14 **Fairfield** Idaho, NW USA *43°20′N 114°45′W*
30 M16 **Fairfield** Illinois, N USA *38°22′N 88°23′W*
29 X15 **Fairfield** Iowa, C USA *41°00′N 91°57′W*
33 R8 **Fairfield** Montana, NW USA *47°36′N 111°59′W*
31 Q14 **Fairfield** Ohio, N USA *39°21′N 84°34′W*
25 U8 **Fairfield** Texas, SW USA *31°43′N 96°10′W*
27 T7 **Fair Grove** Missouri, C USA *37°22′N 93°09′W*
19 P12 **Fairhaven** Massachusetts, NE USA *41°38′N 70°51′W*
23 N8 **Fairhope** Alabama, S USA *30°31′N 87°54′W*
96 L4 **Fair Isle** *island* NE Scotland, United Kingdom
185 F20 **Fairlie** Canterbury, South Island, New Zealand *44°06′S 170°50′E*
29 U11 **Fairmont** Minnesota, N USA *43°40′N 94°27′W*
29 Q16 **Fairmont** Nebraska, C USA *40°37′N 97°36′W*
21 S3 **Fairmont** West Virginia, NE USA *39°28′N 80°08′W*
31 P13 **Fairmount** Indiana, N USA *40°25′N 85°39′W*
18 H10 **Fairmount** New York, NE USA *43°03′N 76°14′W*
29 R7 **Fairmount** North Dakota, N USA *46°02′N 96°36′W*
37 S5 **Fairplay** Colorado, C USA *39°13′N 106°00′W*
18 F9 **Fairport** New York, NE USA *43°06′N 77°26′W*
11 O12 **Fairview** Alberta, W Canada *56°03′N 118°28′W*
26 L9 **Fairview** Oklahoma, C USA *36°16′N 98°29′W*
36 L4 **Fairview** Utah, W USA *39°37′N 111°26′W*
35 T6 **Fairview Peak** ▲ Nevada, W USA *39°13′N 118°09′W*
188 H14 **Fais** *atoll* Caroline Islands, W Micronesia
149 U8 **Faisalabad** *prev.* Lyallpur. Punjab, NE Pakistan *31°26′N 73°06′E*
**Faisaliya** *see* Fayşalīyah
28 L8 **Faith** South Dakota, N USA *45°01′N 102°02′W*
149 S2 **Faīẕābād** *var.* Feiẕābād, Faizābād, Feyzābād, Fyzabad; *prev.* Feyẕābād. Badakhshān, NE Afghanistan *37°06′N 70°34′E*
153 N12 **Faizābād** Uttar Pradesh, N India *26°46′N 82°08′E*
45 S9 **Fajardo** E Puerto Rico *18°20′N 65°39′W*
139 R9 **Fajj, Wādī al** *dry watercourse* S Iraq
140 K4 **Fajr, Bi'r** *well* NW Saudi Arabia
191 W10 **Fakahina** *atoll* Îles Tuamotu, C French Polynesia
190 L10 **Fakaofo Atoll** *island* SE Tokelau
191 U10 **Fakarava** *atoll* Îles Tuamotu, C French Polynesia
127 T2 **Fakel** Udmurtskaya Respublika, NW Russia *57°35′N 53°00′E*
97 P19 **Fakenham** E England, United Kingdom *52°50′N 00°51′E*
171 U13 **Fakfak** Papua Barat, E Indonesia *02°55′S 132°17′E*
153 T12 **Fakīragrām** Assam, NE India *26°22′N 90°15′E*
114 M10 **Fakiyska Reka** ≈ SE Bulgaria
95 J24 **Fakse** Sjælland, SE Denmark *55°16′N 12°08′E*
95 J24 **Fakse Bugt** *bay* SE Denmark
95 J24 **Fakse Ladeplads** Sjælland, SE Denmark *55°14′N 12°11′E*
163 V11 **Faku** Liaoning, NE China *42°30′N 123°27′E*
76 J14 **Falaba** N Sierra Leone *09°54′N 11°22′W*
102 K5 **Falaise** Calvados, N France *48°52′N 00°12′W*
114 H12 **Falakró** ▲ NE Greece
189 T12 **Falalu** *island* Chuuk, C Micronesia
166 L4 **Falam** Chin State, W Myanmar (Burma) *22°58′N 93°45′E*
143 N8 **Falāvarjān** Eşfahān, C Iran *32°33′N 51°28′E*
116 M11 **Fălciu** Vaslui, E Romania *46°19′N 28°10′E*
54 I4 **Falcón** *off.* Estado Falcón. ⬖ *state* NW Venezuela
106 J12 **Falconara Marittima** Marche, C Italy *43°37′N 13°23′E*
**Falcone, Capo del** *see* Falcone, Punta del
107 A16 **Falcone, Punta del** *var.* Capo del Falcone. *headland* Sardegna, Italy, C Mediterranean Sea *40°57′N 8°12′E*
**Falcón, Estado** *see* Falcón
11 Y16 **Falcon Lake** Manitoba, S Canada *49°44′N 95°18′W*
**Falcon Lake** *see* Falcón, Presa/Falcon Reservoir
41 O7 **Falcón, Presa** *var.* Falcon Lake, Falcon Reservoir. ⊠ Mexico/USA *see also* Falcon Reservoir
**Falcón, Presa** *see* Falcon Reservoir
25 Q16 **Falcon Reservoir** *var.* Falcon Lake, Presa Falcón. ⊠ Mexico/USA *see also* Falcón, Presa
**Falcon Reservoir** *see* Falcón, Presa
190 L10 **Fale** *island* Fakaofo Atoll, SE Tokelau
192 F15 **Faleālupo** Savai'i, NW Samoa *13°30′S 172°46′W*
190 B10 **Falefatu** *island* Funafuti Atoll, C Tuvalu
192 G15 **Fālelima** Savai'i, NW Samoa *13°30′S 172°41′W*
95 N18 **Falerum** Östergötland, S Sweden *58°07′N 16°15′E*
**Faleshty** *see* Făleşti
116 M9 **Făleşti** *Rus.* Faleshty. NW Moldova *47°33′N 27°43′E*
25 S15 **Falfurrias** Texas, SW USA *27°17′N 98°10′W*
11 O13 **Falher** Alberta, W Canada *55°45′N 117°18′W*
**Falkenau an der Eger** *see* Sokolov
95 J21 **Falkenberg** Halland, S Sweden *56°55′N 12°30′E*
**Falkenberg** *see* Niemodlin
**Falkenburg in Pommern** *see* Złocieniec
100 N12 **Falkensee** Brandenburg, NE Germany *52°34′N 13°04′E*
96 J12 **Falkirk** C Scotland, United Kingdom *56°N 03°48′W*
65 I20 **Falkland Escarpment** *undersea feature* SW Atlantic Ocean *50°00′S 45°00′W*
63 K24 **Falkland Islands** *var.* Falklands, Islas Malvinas. ◇ *UK Overseas Territory* SW Atlantic Ocean
47 W14 **Falkland Islands** *island group* SW Atlantic Ocean
65 I20 **Falkland Plateau** *var.* Argentine Rise. *undersea feature* SW Atlantic Ocean *51°00′S 50°00′W*
**Falklands** *see* Falkland Islands
63 M23 **Falkland Sound** *var.* Estrecho de San Carlos. *strait* C Falkland Islands
**Falknov nad Ohří** *see* Sokolov
115 H21 **Falkonéra** *island* S Greece
95 K18 **Falköping** Västra Götaland, S Sweden *58°10′N 13°31′E*
139 U8 **Fallāḩ** Wāsiţ, E Iraq *32°58′N 45°09′E*
35 U16 **Fallbrook** California, W USA *33°22′N 117°15′W*
189 U12 **Falleallej Pass** *passage* Chuuk Islands, C Micronesia
93 J14 **Fällfors** Västerbotten, N Sweden *65°07′N 20°46′E*
194 I6 **Fallières Coast** *physical region* Antarctica
100 I11 **Fallingbostel** Niedersachsen, NW Germany *52°52′N 09°42′E*
33 X9 **Fallon** Montana, NW USA *46°49′N 105°07′W*
35 S5 **Fallon** Nevada, W USA *39°29′N 118°47′W*
19 O12 **Fall River** Massachusetts, NE USA *41°42′N 71°09′W*
27 P6 **Fall River Lake** ⊠ Kansas, C USA
35 O3 **Fall River Mills** California, W USA *41°00′N 121°28′W*
21 W4 **Falls Church** Virginia, NE USA *38°53′N 77°11′W*
29 S17 **Falls City** Nebraska, C USA *40°03′N 95°36′W*
25 S12 **Falls City** Texas, SW USA *28°58′N 98°01′W*
**Falluja** *see* Al Fallūjah
77 S12 **Falmey** Dosso, SW Niger *12°29′N 02°58′E*
45 W10 **Falmouth** Antigua, Antigua and Barbuda *17°02′N 61°47′W*
44 J11 **Falmouth** W Jamaica *18°28′N 77°39′W*
97 H25 **Falmouth** SW England, United Kingdom *50°08′N 05°04′W*
20 M4 **Falmouth** Kentucky, S USA *38°40′N 84°20′W*
19 P13 **Falmouth** Massachusetts, NE USA *41°31′N 70°36′W*
21 W5 **Falmouth** Virginia, NE USA *38°19′N 77°28′W*
189 U12 **Falos** *island* Chuuk, C Micronesia
83 E26 **False Bay** *Afr.* Valsbaai. *bay* SW South Africa
155 K17 **False Divi Point** *headland* E India *15°46′N 80°43′E*
38 M16 **False Pass** Unimak Island, Alaska, USA *54°52′N 163°15′W*
154 P12 **False Point** *headland* E India *20°23′N 86°52′E*
105 U6 **Falset** Cataluña, NE Spain *41°08′N 00°49′E*
95 I25 **Falster** *island* SE Denmark
116 K9 **Fălticeni** *Hung.* Falticsén. Suceava, NE Romania *47°27′N 26°20′E*
**Falticsén** *see* Fălticeni
94 M13 **Falun** *var.* Fahlun. Kopparberg, C Sweden *60°36′N 15°36′E*
**Famagusta** *see* Gazimağusa
**Famagusta Bay** *see* Gazimağusa Körfezi
62 I8 **Famatina** La Rioja, NW Argentina *28°58′S 67°46′W*
99 J21 **Famenne** *physical region* SE Belgium
77 X15 **Fan** ≈ E Nigeria
76 M12 **Fana** Koulikoro, SW Mali *12°45′N 06°55′W*
115 K19 **Fána** *ancient harbor* Chíos, SE Greece
189 V13 **Fanan** *island* Chuuk, C Micronesia
189 U12 **Fanapanges** *island* Chuuk, C Micronesia
115 L20 **Fanári, Akrotírio** *headland* Ikaría, Dodekánisa, Greece, Aegean Sea *37°40′N 26°21′E*
45 Q13 **Fancy** Saint Vincent, Saint Vincent and the Grenadines *13°22′N 61°10′W*
172 I5 **Fandriana** Fianarantsoa, SE Madagascar *20°14′S 47°21′E*
167 O6 **Fang** Chiang Mai, NW Thailand *19°56′N 99°14′E*
80 E13 **Fangak** Jonglei, E South Sudan *09°05′N 30°52′E*
**Fangatau** *see* Fagatau
**Fangataufa** *see* Fagataufa
193 V15 **Fanga Uta** *bay* S Tonga
161 N7 **Fangcheng** Henan, C China *33°18′N 113°03′E*
**Fangcheng** *see* Fangchenggang
160 K15 **Fangchenggang** *var.* Fangcheng Gezu Zizhixian; *prev.* Fangcheng. Guangxi Zhuangzu Zizhiqu, S China *21°49′N 108°21′E*
**Fangcheng Gezu Zizhixian** *see* Fangchenggang
161 S15 **Fangshan** S Taiwan *22°19′N 120°41′E*
163 X8 **Fangzheng** Heilongjiang, NE China *45°50′N 128°50′E*
**Fani** *see* Fanit, Lumi i
119 K16 **Fanipal'** *Rus.* Fanipol'. Minskaya Voblasts', C Belarus *53°45′N 27°20′E*
**Fanipol'** *see* Fanipal'
113 D22 **Fanit, Lumi i** *var.* Fani. ≈ N Albania
25 T13 **Fannin** Texas, SW USA *28°41′N 97°13′W*
**Fanning Island** *see* Tabuaeran
94 G8 **Fannrem** Sør-Trøndelag, S Norway *63°16′N 09°48′E*
106 I11 **Fano** *anc.* Colonia Julia Fanestris, Fanum Fortunae. Marche, C Italy *43°50′N 13°E*
95 E23 **Fanø** *island* W Denmark
167 R5 **Fan Si Pan** ▲ N Vietnam *22°18′N 103°36′E*
**Fanum Fortunae** *see* Fano
**Fao** *see* Al Fāw
141 W7 **Faq'** *var.* Al Faqa. Dubayy, E United Arab Emirates *24°42′N 55°37′E*
**Farab** *see* Farap
185 G16 **Faraday, Mount** ▲ South Island, New Zealand *42°01′S 171°37′E*
79 P16 **Faradje** Orientale, NE Dem. Rep. Congo *03°45′N 29°43′E*
**Faradofay** *see* Tôlañaro
172 I7 **Farafangana** Fianarantsoa, SE Madagascar *22°50′S 47°50′E*
148 J7 **Farāh** *var.* Farah, Fararud. Farāh, W Afghanistan *32°22′N 62°07′E*
148 K7 **Farāh** ⬖ *province* W Afghanistan
148 J7 **Farāh Rōd** ≈ W Afghanistan
188 K7 **Farallon de Medinilla** *island* C Northern Mariana Islands
188 J2 **Farallon de Pajaros** *var.* Uracas. *island* N Northern Mariana Islands
76 J14 **Faranah** Haute-Guinée, S Guinea *10°02′N 10°44′W*
146 K12 **Farap** *Rus.* Farab. Lebap Welaýaty, NE Turkmenistan *39°15′N 63°32′E*
**Fararud** *see* Farāh
**Farasan Islands** *see* Farasān, Jazā'ir
140 M13 **Farasān, Jazā'ir** *Eng.* Farasan Islands. *island group* SW Saudi Arabia
172 I5 **Faratsiho** Antananarivo, C Madagascar *19°24′S 46°57′E*
188 K15 **Faraulep Atoll** *atoll* Caroline Islands, C Micronesia
99 H20 **Farciennes** Hainaut, S Belgium *50°26′N 04°33′E*
105 O14 **Fardes** ≈ S Spain
191 S10 **Fare** Huahine, W French Polynesia *16°42′S 151°01′W*
97 M23 **Fareham** S England, United Kingdom *50°51′N 01°10′W*
39 P11 **Farewell** Alaska, USA *62°35′N 153°59′W*
184 H13 **Farewell, Cape** *headland* South Island, New Zealand *40°30′S 172°39′E*
**Farewell, Cape** *see* Nunap Isua
184 I13 **Farewell Spit** *spit* South Island, New Zealand
95 I17 **Färgelanda** Västra Götaland, S Sweden *58°34′N 11°59′E*
**Farghona, Wodii/Farghona Valley** *see* Fergana Valley
**Farghona Wodiysi** *see* Fergana Valley
23 V8 **Fargo** Georgia, SE USA *30°42′N 82°33′W*
29 R5 **Fargo** North Dakota, N USA *46°53′N 96°47′W*
147 S10 **Far'gona** *Rus.* Fergana; *prev.* Novyy Margilan. Far'gona Viloyati, E Uzbekistan *40°28′N 71°44′E*
147 R10 **Farg'ona Viloyati** *Rus.* Ferganskaya Oblast'. ⬖ *province* E Uzbekistan
29 V10 **Faribault** Minnesota, N USA *44°18′N 93°16′W*
152 J11 **Farīdābād** Haryāna, N India *28°26′N 77°190′E*
152 H8 **Farīdkot** Punjab, NW India *30°42′N 74°47′E*
153 T15 **Faridpur** Dhaka, C Bangladesh *23°29′N 89°50′E*
121 P14 **Fārigh, Wādī al** ≈ N Libya
172 I4 **Farihy Alaotra** ◎ C Madagascar
94 M11 **Färila** Gävleborg, C Sweden *61°48′N 15°55′E*
104 E9 **Farilhões** *island* C Portugal
76 G12 **Farim** NW Guinea-Bissau *12°30′N 15°09′W*
**Farish** *see* Forish
141 T11 **Fāris, Qalamat** *well* SE Saudi Arabia
95 N21 **Färjestaden** Kalmar, S Sweden *56°38′N 16°30′E*
149 R2 **Farkhār** Takhār, NE Afghanistan *36°39′N 69°43′E*
147 Q14 **Farkhor** *Rus.* Parkhar. SW Tajikistan *37°32′N 69°22′E*
116 F12 **Fârliug** *prev.* Fîrliug, *Hung.* Furluk. Caraş-Severin, SW Romania *45°21′N 21°55′E*
115 M21 **Farmakonísi** *island* Dodekánisa, Greece, Aegean Sea
30 M13 **Farmer City** Illinois, N USA *40°14′N 88°38′W*
31 N14 **Farmersburg** Indiana, N USA *39°14′N 87°21′W*
25 U6 **Farmersville** Texas, SW USA *33°09′N 96°21′W*
22 H5 **Farmerville** Louisiana, S USA *32°46′N 92°24′W*
29 X16 **Farmington** Iowa, C USA *40°37′N 91°43′W*
19 Q6 **Farmington** Maine, NE USA *44°40′N 70°09′W*
29 V9 **Farmington** Minnesota, N USA *44°39′N 93°09′W*
27 X6 **Farmington** Missouri, C USA *37°46′N 90°26′W*
19 O9 **Farmington** New Hampshire, NE USA *43°23′N 71°04′W*
37 P9 **Farmington** New Mexico, SW USA *36°44′N 108°13′W*
36 L2 **Farmington** Utah, W USA *40°58′N 111°53′W*
21 W9 **Farmville** North Carolina, SE USA *35°37′N 77°36′W*
21 U6 **Farmville** Virginia, NE USA *37°17′N 78°25′W*
97 N22 **Farnborough** S England, United Kingdom *51°17′N 00°46′W*
97 N22 **Farnham** S England, United Kingdom *51°13′N 00°49′W*
10 J7 **Faro** Yukon, W Canada *62°15′N 133°30′W*
104 G14 **Faro** Faro, S Portugal *37°01′N 07°56′W*
95 Q18 **Fårö** Gotland, SE Sweden *57°55′N 19°10′E*
104 G14 **Faro** ⬖ *district* S Portugal
78 F13 **Faro** ≈ Cameroon/Nigeria
104 G14 **Faro** ✈ Faro, S Portugal *37°02′N 08°01′W*
64 M5 **Faroe-Iceland Ridge** *var.* Faeroe-Iceland Ridge. *undersea ridge* NW Norwegian Sea
86 C8 **Faroe Islands** *var.* Faeroe Islands. *island group* N Atlantic Ocean


◆ Country
● Country Capital
◇ Dependent Territory
○ Dependent Territory Capital
⬖ Administrative Regions
✈ International Airport
▲ Mountain
▲▲ Mountain Range
Volcano
≈ River
◎ Lake
⊠ Reservoir

# Faroe Islands – Foam Lake



64 M5 **Faroe Islands** var. Faeroe Islands, Dan. Færøerne, Faer. Føroyar. Self-governing territory of Denmark N Atlantic Ocean
64 N6 **Faroe-Shetland Trough** var. Faeroe-Shetland Trough. trough NE Atlantic Ocean
**Faro, Punta del** see Peloro, Capo
95 Q18 **Fårösund** Gotland, SE Sweden 57°51′N 19°02′E
173 N7 **Farquhar Group** island group S Seychelles
18 B13 **Farrell** Pennsylvania, NE USA 41°12′N 80°28′W
152 K11 **Farrukhābād** Uttar Pradesh, N India 27°24′N 79°34′E
143 P11 **Fārs** off. Ostān-e Fārs; anc. Persis. ◈ province S Iran
115 F16 **Fársala** Thessalía, C Greece 39°17′N 22°23′E
143 R4 **Farsīān** Golestán, N Iran
**Fars, Khalīj-e** see Persian Gulf
95 G21 **Farsø** Nordjylland, N Denmark 56°47′N 09°21′E
**Fārs, Ostān-e** see Fārs
95 D18 **Farsund** Vest-Agder, S Norway 58°05′N 06°49′E
141 U14 **Fartak, Ra's** headland E Yemen 15°34′N 52°19′E
60 H13 **Fartura, Serra da** ▲ S Brazil
**Farvel, Kap** see Nunap Isua
24 L4 **Farwell** Texas, SW USA 34°23′N 103°03′W
194 I9 **Farwell Island** island Antarctica
152 L9 **Far Western** ◈ zone W Nepal
148 M3 **Fāryāb** ◈ province N Afghanistan
143 P12 **Fasā** Fārs, S Iran 28°55′N 53°39′E
141 U12 **Fasad, Ramlat** desert SW Oman
107 P17 **Fasano** Puglia, SE Italy 40°50′N 17°21′E
92 L3 **Fáskrúðsfjörður** Austurland, E Iceland 64°55′N 14°01′W
117 O5 **Fastiv** Rus. Fastov. Kyivs'ka Oblast', NW Ukraine 50°08′N 29°59′E
97 B22 **Fastnet Rock** Ir. Carraig Aonair. island SW Ireland
**Fastov** see Fastiv
190 C9 **Fatato** island Funafuti Atoll, C Tuvalu
152 K12 **Fatehgarh** Uttar Pradesh, N India 27°22′N 79°38′E
149 U6 **Fatehjang** Punjab, E Pakistan 33°33′N 72°43′E
152 G11 **Fatehpur** Rājasthān, N India 27°59′N 74°58′E
152 L13 **Fatehpur** Uttar Pradesh, N India 25°56′N 80°55′E
126 J7 **Fatezh** Kurskaya Oblast', W Russia 52°01′N 35°51′E
76 G11 **Fatick** W Senegal 14°19′N 16°27′W
104 G9 **Fátima** Santarém, W Portugal 39°37′N 08°39′W
136 M11 **Fatsa** Ordu, N Turkey 41°02′N 37°31′E
**Fatshan** see Foshan
190 D12 **Fatua, Pointe** var. Pointe Nord. headland Île Futuna, S Wallis and Futuna
191 X7 **Fatu Hiva** island Îles Marquises, NE French Polynesia
**Fatunda** see Fatundu
79 H21 **Fatundu** var. Fatunda. Bandundu, W Dem. Rep. Congo 04°08′S 17°13′E
29 O8 **Faulkton** South Dakota, N USA 45°02′N 99°07′W
116 L13 **Făurei** prev. Filimon Sîrbu. Brăila, SE Romania 45°05′N 27°15′E
92 G12 **Fauske** Nordland, C Norway 67°15′N 15°27′E
11 P13 **Faust** Alberta, W Canada 55°19′N 115°33′W
99 L23 **Fauvillers** Luxembourg, SE Belgium 49°52′N 05°40′E
107 J24 **Favara** Sicilia, Italy, C Mediterranean Sea 37°19′N 13°40′E
**Faventia** see Faenza
107 G23 **Favignana, Isola** island Isole Egadi, S Italy
12 D8 **Fawn** ~ Ontario, SE Canada
92 H3 **Faxaflói** Eng. Faxa Bay. bay W Iceland
**Faxa Bay** see Faxaflói
78 I7 **Faya** prev. Faya-Largeau, Largeau. Borkou, N Chad 17°58′N 19°06′E
**Faya-Largeau** see Faya
187 Q16 **Fayaoué** Province des Îles Loyauté, C New Caledonia 20°41′S 166°31′E
138 M5 **Fayḍāt** hill range E Syria
23 O3 **Fayette** Alabama, S USA 33°40′N 87°49′W
29 X12 **Fayette** Iowa, C USA 42°50′N 91°48′W
22 J6 **Fayette** Mississippi, S USA 31°42′N 91°03′W
27 U4 **Fayette** Missouri, C USA 39°09′N 92°40′W
27 S9 **Fayetteville** Arkansas, C USA 36°04′N 94°10′W
21 U10 **Fayetteville** North Carolina, SE USA 35°03′N 78°53′W
20 J10 **Fayetteville** Tennessee, S USA 35°08′N 86°33′W
25 U11 **Fayetteville** Texas, SW USA 29°52′N 96°40′W
21 R5 **Fayetteville** West Virginia, NE USA 38°03′N 81°09′W
141 R4 **Faylakah** var. Failaka Island. island E Kuwait
139 T10 **Fayṣalīyah** var. Faisaliya. Al Qādisīyah, S Iraq 31°48′N 44°36′E
189 P15 **Fayu** var. East Fayu. island Hall Islands, C Micronesia
152 G8 **Fāzilka** Punjab, NW India 30°26′N 74°04′E
**Fdérick** see Fdérik
76 I6 **Fdérik** var. Fdérick, Fr. Fort Gouraud. Tiris Zemmour, NW Mauritania 22°40′N 12°41′W
**Feabhail, Loch** see Foyle, Lough
97 B20 **Feale** ~ SW Ireland
21 V12 **Fear, Cape** headland Bald Head Island, North Carolina, SE USA 33°50′N 77°57′W
35 O6 **Feather River** ~ California, W USA
185 M14 **Featherston** Wellington, North Island, New Zealand 41°07′S 175°28′E
102 L3 **Fécamp** Seine-Maritime, N France 49°45′N 00°22′E
**Fédala** see Mohammedia
61 D17 **Federación** Entre Ríos, E Argentina 31°00′S 57°55′W
61 D17 **Federal** Entre Ríos, E Argentina 30°55′S 58°45′W
77 T15 **Federal Capital District** ◆ capital territory C Nigeria
**Federal Capital Territory** see Australian Capital Territory
**Federal District** see Distrito Federal
21 Y4 **Federalsburg** Maryland, NE USA 38°41′N 75°46′W
74 M6 **Fedjaj, Chott el** var. Chott el Fejaj, Shaṭṭ al Fijāj. salt lake C Tunisia
94 B13 **Fedje** island S Norway
144 M7 **Fedorovka** Kostanay, N Kazakhstan 51°12′N 52°00′E
127 U6 **Fedorovka** Respublika Bashkortostan, W Russia 53°09′N 55°07′E
**Fëdory** see Fyadory
117 U11 **Fedotova Kosa** spit SE Ukraine
189 V13 **Fefan** atoll Chuuk Islands, C Micronesia
111 O21 **Fehérgyarmat** Szabolcs-Szatmár-Bereg, E Hungary 47°59′N 22°29′E
**Fehér-Körös** see Crişul Alb
**Fehértemplom** see Bela Crkva
**Fehérvölgy** see Albac
100 L7 **Fehmarn** island N Germany
95 H25 **Fehmarn Belt** Dan. Femern Bælt, Ger. Fehmarnbelt. strait Denmark/Germany see also Femern Bælt
**Fehmarnbelt** see Fehmarn Belt/Femer Bælt
109 X8 **Fehring** Steiermark, SE Austria 46°56′N 16°00′E
59 B15 **Feijó** Acre, W Brazil 08°07′S 70°27′W
184 M12 **Feilding** Manawatu-Wanganui, North Island, New Zealand 40°15′S 175°34′E
**Feira** see Feira de Santana
59 O17 **Feira de Santana** var. Feira. Bahia, E Brazil 12°17′S 38°53′W
109 X7 **Feistritz** ~ SE Austria
**Feistritz** see Ilirska Bistrica
161 P8 **Feixi** var. Shangpai; prev. Shangpaihe. Anhui, E China 31°40′N 117°08′E
**Feizābād** see Faizābād
**Fejaj, Chott el** see Fedjaj, Chott el
111 I23 **Fejér** off. Fejér Megye. ◈ county W Hungary
**Fejér Megye** see Fejér
95 I24 **Fejø** island SE Denmark
136 K15 **Feke** Adana, S Turkey 37°49′N 35°55′E
**Feketehalom** see Codlea
**Fekete-Körös** see Crişul Negru
105 Y9 **Felanitx** Mallorca, Spain, W Mediterranean Sea 39°28′N 03°08′E
109 T3 **Feldaist** ~ N Austria
109 W8 **Feldbach** Steiermark, SE Austria 46°58′N 15°53′E
101 F24 **Feldberg** ▲ SW Germany 47°52′N 08°01′E
116 J12 **Feldioara** Ger. Marienburg, Hung. Földvár. Braşov, C Romania 45°49′N 25°36′E
108 I7 **Feldkirch** anc. Clunia. Vorarlberg, W Austria 47°15′N 09°38′E
109 S9 **Feldkirchen in Kärnten** Slvn. Trg. Kärnten, S Austria 46°42′N 14°01′E
**Félegyháza** see Kiskunfélegyháza
192 H16 **Feleolo** ✈ (Āpia) Upolu, C Samoa 13°49′S 171°59′W
104 H6 **Felgueiras** Porto, N Portugal 41°22′N 08°12′W
**Felicitas Julia** see Lisboa
172 J16 **Félicité** island Inner Islands, NE Seychelles
151 K20 **Felidhu Atoll** atoll C Maldives
41 Y13 **Felipe Carrillo Puerto** Quintana Roo, SE Mexico 19°34′N 88°02′W
97 Q21 **Felixstowe** E England, United Kingdom 51°58′N 01°20′E
103 N11 **Felletin** Creuse, C France 45°53′N 02°12′E
**Fellin** see Viljandi
**Felsőbánya** see Baia Sprie
**Felsőmuzslya** see Mužlja
**Felsővisó** see Vişeu de Sus
35 N10 **Felton** California, W USA 37°03′N 122°04′W
106 H7 **Feltre** Veneto, NE Italy 46°01′N 11°55′E
95 H25 **Femer Bælt** Dan. Fehmarn Belt, Ger. Fehmarnbelt. strait Denmark/Germany see also Fehmarn Belt
95 I24 **Femø** island SE Denmark
94 I10 **Femunden** ◎ S Norway
104 H2 **Fene** Galicia, NW Spain 43°28′N 08°10′W
14 I14 **Fenelon Falls** Ontario, SE Canada 44°34′N 78°43′W
189 U13 **Feneppi** atoll Chuuk Islands, C Micronesia
137 O11 **Fener Burnu** headland N Turkey 41°07′N 39°26′E
**Fénérive** see Fenoarivo Atsinanana
115 J14 **Fengári** ▲ Samothráki, E Greece 40°27′N 25°37′E
163 V13 **Fengcheng** var. Feng-cheng, Fenghwangcheng. Liaoning, NE China 40°28′N 124°01′E
**Fengcheng** see Lianjiang
**Feng-cheng** see Fengcheng
160 K11 **Fenggang** var. Longquan. Guizhou, S China 27°57′N 107°42′E
161 S9 **Fenghua** Zhejiang, SE China 29°40′N 121°25′E
**Fenghwangcheng** see Fengcheng
**Fengjiaba** see Wangcang
160 L9 **Fengjie** var. Yong'an. Sichuan, C China 31°03′N 109°31′E
160 M14 **Fengkai** var. Jiangkou. Guangdong, S China 23°26′N 111°28′E
161 T13 **Fenglin** Jap. Hōrin. C Taiwan 23°52′N 121°30′E
161 P1 **Fengning** prev. Dagezhen. Hebei, E China 41°12′N 116°37′E
160 E13 **Fengqing** var. Fengshan. Yunnan, SW China 24°38′N 99°54′E
161 O6 **Fengqiu** Henan, C China 35°02′N 114°24′E
161 Q2 **Fengrun** Hebei, E China 39°50′N 118°10′E
**Fengshan** see Luoyuan, Fujian, China
**Fengshan** see Fengqing, Yunnan, China
163 T4 **Fengshui Shan** ▲ NE China 52°20′N 123°22′E
161 P14 **Fengshun** Guangdong, S China 23°51′N 116°11′E
**Fengtien** see Liaoning, China
**Fengtien** see Shenyang, China
160 J7 **Fengxian** var. Feng Xian; prev. Shuangshipu. Shaanxi, C China 33°50′N 106°33′E
**Feng Xian** see Fengxian
**Fengxiang** see Luobei
**Fengyizhen** see Maoxian
163 P13 **Fengzhen** Nei Mongol Zizhiqu, N China 40°25′N 113°09′E
160 M6 **Fen He** ~ C China
153 V15 **Feni** Chittagong, E Bangladesh 23°00′N 91°24′E
186 I6 **Feni Islands** island group NE Papua New Guinea
38 H17 **Fenimore Pass** strait Aleutian Islands, Alaska, USA
84 B9 **Feni Ridge** undersea feature N Atlantic Ocean 53°45′N 18°00′W
**Fennern** see Vändra
30 J9 **Fennimore** Wisconsin, N USA 42°58′N 90°39′W
172 J4 **Fenoarivo Atsinanana** prev./Fr. Fénérive. Toamasina, E Madagascar 20°52′S 46°52′E
95 I24 **Fensmark** Sjælland, SE Denmark 55°17′N 11°48′E
97 O19 **Fens, The** wetland E England, United Kingdom
31 R9 **Fenton** Michigan, N USA 42°48′N 83°42′W
190 K10 **Fenua Fala** island SE Tokelau
190 F12 **Fenuafo'ou, Île** island E Wallis and Futuna
190 L10 **Fenua Loa** island Fakaofo Atoll, E Tokelau
160 M4 **Fenyang** Shanxi, C China 37°14′N 111°40′E
117 U13 **Feodosiya** var. Kefe, It. Kaffa; anc. Theodosia. Avtonomna Respublika Krym, S Ukraine 45°03′N 35°24′E
94 I10 **Feragen** ◎ S Norway
74 L5 **Fer, Cap de** headland NE Algeria 37°05′N 07°10′E
31 O16 **Ferdinand** Indiana, N USA 38°13′N 86°51′W
**Ferdinand** see Montana, Bulgaria
**Ferdinand** see Mihail Kogălniceanu, Romania
**Ferdinandsberg** see Oţelu Roşu
143 T7 **Ferdows** var. Firdaus; prev. Tūn. Khorāsān-e Jonūbī, E Iran 34°00′N 58°09′E
103 Q5 **Fère-Champenoise** Marne, N France 48°45′N 03°59′E
**Ferencz-József Csúcs** see Gerlachovský štít
107 J16 **Ferentino** Lazio, C Italy 41°40′N 13°16′E
114 L13 **Féres** Anatolikí Makedonía kai Thráki, NE Greece 40°54′N 26°12′E
**Fergana** see Farg'ona
147 S10 **Fergana Valley** var. Farghona Valley, Rus. Ferganskaya Dolina, Taj. Wodii Farghona, Uzb. Farghona Wodiysi. basin Tajikistan/Uzbekistan
**Ferganskaya Dolina** see Fergana Valley
**Ferganskaya Oblast'** see Farg'ona Viloyati
147 U9 **Ferganskiy Khrebet** ▲▲ C Kyrgyzstan
14 F15 **Fergus** Ontario, S Canada 43°42′N 80°22′W
29 S6 **Fergus Falls** Minnesota, N USA 46°15′N 96°02′W
186 G9 **Fergusson Island** var. Kaluwawa. island SE Papua New Guinea
111 K22 **Ferihegy** ✈ (Budapest) Budapest, C Hungary 47°25′N 19°13′E
113 N17 **Ferizaj** Serb. Uroševac. C Kosovo 42°23′N 21°09′E
77 N14 **Ferkessédougou** N Ivory Coast 09°36′N 05°12′W
109 T10 **Ferlach** Slvn. Borovlje. Kärnten, S Austria 46°31′N 14°18′E
97 E16 **Fermanagh** cultural region SW Northern Ireland, United Kingdom
106 J13 **Fermo** anc. Firmum Picenum. Marche, C Italy 43°09′N 13°44′E
104 J6 **Fermoselle** Castilla y León, N Spain 41°19′N 06°24′W
97 D20 **Fermoy** Ir. Mainistir Fhear Maí. SW Ireland 52°08′N 08°16′W
23 W8 **Fernandina Beach** Amelia Island, Florida, SE USA 30°40′N 81°27′W
57 A17 **Fernandina, Isla** var. Narborough Island. island Galapagos Islands, Ecuador, E Pacific Ocean
47 Y5 **Fernando de Noronha** island E Brazil
**Fernando Po/Fernando Póo** see Bioco, Isla de
60 J7 **Fernandópolis** São Paulo, S Brazil 20°18′S 50°13′W
104 M13 **Fernán Núñez** Andalucía, S Spain 37°40′N 04°44′W
83 Q14 **Fernão Veloso, Baia de** bay NE Mozambique
34 K3 **Ferndale** California, W USA 40°34′N 124°16′W
32 H6 **Ferndale** Washington, NW USA 48°51′N 122°35′W
11 P17 **Fernie** British Columbia, SW Canada 49°30′N 115°00′W
35 R5 **Fernley** Nevada, W USA 39°35′N 119°15′W
**Ferozepore** see Firozpur
107 N18 **Ferrandina** Basilicata, S Italy 40°30′N 16°25′E
106 G9 **Ferrara** anc. Forum Alieni. Emilia-Romagna, N Italy 44°50′N 11°36′E
120 F9 **Ferrat, Cap** headland NW Algeria 35°52′N 00°24′W
107 D20 **Ferrato, Capo** headland Sardegna, Italy, C Mediterranean Sea 39°18′N 09°37′E
104 G12 **Ferreira do Alentejo** Beja, S Portugal 38°04′N 08°06′W
56 B11 **Ferreñafe** Lambayeque, W Peru 06°42′S 79°45′W
108 C12 **Ferret** Valais, SW Switzerland 45°57′N 07°04′E
102 I13 **Ferret, Cap** headland W France 44°37′N 01°15′W
22 I6 **Ferriday** Louisiana, S USA 31°37′N 91°33′W
**Ferro** see Hierro
107 D16 **Ferro, Capo** headland Sardegna, Italy, C Mediterranean Sea 41°09′N 09°31′E
104 H2 **Ferrol** var. El Ferrol; prev. El Ferrol del Caudillo. Galicia, NW Spain 43°29′N 08°14′W
56 B12 **Ferrol, Península de** peninsula W Peru
36 M5 **Ferron** Utah, W USA 39°05′N 111°07′W
21 S7 **Ferrum** Virginia, NE USA 36°54′N 80°01′W
23 O8 **Ferry Pass** Florida, SE USA 30°30′N 87°12′W
**Ferryville** see Menzel Bourguiba
29 S4 **Fertile** Minnesota, N USA 47°32′N 96°16′W
**Fertő** see Neusiedler See
**Ferwerd** see Ferwert
98 L5 **Ferwert** Dutch. Ferwerd. Fryslân, N Netherlands 53°21′N 05°47′E
74 G6 **Fès** Eng. Fez. N Morocco 34°06′N 04°57′W
79 I22 **Feshi** Bandundu, SW Dem. Rep. Congo 06°08′S 18°12′E
29 O4 **Fessenden** North Dakota, N USA 47°36′N 99°37′W
**Festenberg** see Twardogóra
27 X5 **Festus** Missouri, C USA 38°13′N 90°24′W
116 M14 **Feteşti** Ialomiţa, SE Romania 44°22′N 27°51′E
136 D17 **Fethiye** Muğla, SW Turkey 36°37′N 29°08′E
96 M1 **Fetlar** island NE Scotland, United Kingdom
95 I15 **Fetsund** Akershus, S Norway 59°55′N 11°03′E
15 I5 **Feuilles, Lac aux** ◎ Québec, E Canada
12 L5 **Feuilles, Rivière aux** ~ Québec, E Canada
99 M23 **Feulen** Diekirch, C Luxembourg 49°52′N 06°03′E
103 Q11 **Feurs** Loire, E France 45°44′N 04°14′E
95 F18 **Fevik** Aust-Agder, S Norway 58°22′N 08°40′E
123 R13 **Fevral'sk** Amurskaya Oblast', SE Russia 52°25′N 131°06′E
**Feyzābād** see Faizābād
**Feyẓābād** see Fayẓābād
**Fez** see Fès
75 Q11 **Fezzan** ◈ cultural region C Libya
97 J19 **Ffestiniog** NW Wales, United Kingdom 52°55′N 03°54′W
**Fhóid Duibh, Cuan an** see Blacksod Bay
62 I8 **Fiambalá** Catamarca, NW Argentina 27°45′S 67°37′W
172 I6 **Fianarantsoa** Fianarantsoa, C Madagascar 21°27′S 47°05′E
172 H6 **Fianarantsoa** ◈ province SE Madagascar
78 G12 **Fianga** Mayo-Kébbi Est, SW Chad 09°57′N 15°09′E
**Ficce** see Fichē
80 J12 **Fichē** It. Ficce. Oromīya, C Ethiopia 09°48′N 38°43′E
101 N17 **Fichtelberg** ▲ Czechia/Germany 50°26′N 12°57′E
101 M18 **Fichtelgebirge** ▲▲ SE Germany
101 M19 **Fichtelnaab** ~ SE Germany
106 E9 **Fidenza** Emilia-Romagna, N Italy 44°52′N 10°04′E
113 K21 **Fier** var. Fieri. Fier, SW Albania 40°44′N 19°34′E
113 K21 **Fier** ◈ county W Albania
**Fieri** see Fier
**Fierza** see Fierzë
113 L17 **Fierzë** var. Fierza. Shkodër, N Albania 42°15′N 20°02′E
113 L17 **Fierzës, Liqeni i** ◎ N Albania
108 F10 **Fiesch** Valais, SW Switzerland 46°25′N 08°09′E
106 G11 **Fiesole** Toscana, C Italy 43°50′N 11°18′E
138 G12 **Fīfah** Aṭ Ṭafīlah, W Jordan 30°55′N 35°25′E
96 K11 **Fife** var. Kingdom of Fife. cultural region E Scotland, United Kingdom
**Fife, Kingdom of** see Fife
96 K11 **Fife Ness** headland E Scotland, United Kingdom 56°16′N 02°35′W
**Fifteen Twenty Fracture Zone** see Barracuda Fracture Zone
103 N13 **Figeac** Lot, S France 44°37′N 02°01′E
95 N19 **Figeholm** Kalmar, SE Sweden 57°12′N 16°34′E
**Figig** see Figuig
83 J18 **Figtree** Matabeleland South, SW Zimbabwe 20°24′S 28°21′E
104 F8 **Figueira da Foz** Coimbra, W Portugal 40°09′N 08°51′W
105 X4 **Figueres** Cataluña, E Spain 42°16′N 02°57′E
74 H7 **Figuig** var. Figig. E Morocco 32°09′N 01°13′W
**Fijājj, Shaṭṭ al** see Fedjaj, Chott el
187 Y15 **Fiji** off. Republic of Fiji, prev. Sovereign Democratic Republic of Fiji, prev. Republic of the Fiji Islands, Fij. Viti. ◆ republic SW Pacific Ocean
192 K9 **Fiji** island group SW Pacific Ocean
**Fiji Islands, Republic of the** see Fiji
175 Q8 **Fiji Plate** tectonic feature
**Fiji, Republic of** see Fiji
**Fiji, Sovereign Democratic Republic of** see Fiji
105 P14 **Filabres, Sierra de los** ▲▲ SE Spain
83 K18 **Filabusi** Matabeleland South, S Zimbabwe 20°34′S 29°20′E
42 K13 **Filadelfia** Guanacaste, W Costa Rica 10°28′N 85°33′W
111 K20 **Fil'akovo** Hung. Fülek. Banskobystrický Kraj, C Slovakia 48°15′N 19°53′E
195 N5 **Filchner Ice Shelf** ice shelf Antarctica
14 J11 **Fildegrand** ~ Québec, SE Canada
33 O15 **Filer** Idaho, NW USA 42°34′N 114°36′W
**Filevo** see Varbitsa
116 H14 **Filiaşi** Dolj, SW Romania 44°32′N 23°31′E
115 B16 **Filiátes** Ípeiros, W Greece 39°38′N 20°16′E
115 D21 **Filiatrá** Pelopónnisos, S Greece 37°09′N 21°35′E
107 K22 **Filicudi, Isola** island Isole Eolie, S Italy
141 Y10 **Filim** E Oman 20°37′N 58°11′E
**Filimon Sîrbu** see Făurei
77 S11 **Filingué** Tillabéri, W Niger 14°21′N 03°22′E
**Filiouri** see Líssos
114 I13 **Filippoi** anc. Philippi. site of ancient city Anatolikí Makedonía kai Thráki, NE Greece
95 L15 **Filipstad** Värmland, C Sweden 59°44′N 14°10′E
108 I9 **Filisur** Graubünden, S Switzerland 46°40′N 09°43′E
94 E12 **Fillefjell** ▲ S Norway
35 R14 **Fillmore** California, W USA 34°23′N 118°56′W
36 K5 **Fillmore** Utah, W USA 38°57′N 112°19′W
14 J10 **Fils, Lac du** ◎ Québec, SE Canada
**Filyos Çayı** see Yenice Çayı
**Fimbul Ice Shelf** see Fimbulisen
195 Q2 **Fimbutheimen** physical region Antarctica
106 G9 **Finale Emilia** Emilia-Romagna, C Italy 44°50′N 11°17′E
106 C10 **Finale Ligure** Liguria, NW Italy 44°11′N 08°22′E
105 P14 **Fiñana** Andalucía, S Spain 37°09′N 02°47′W
21 S6 **Fincastle** Virginia, NE USA 37°30′N 79°54′W
99 M25 **Findel** ✈ (Luxembourg) Luxembourg, C Luxembourg 49°39′N 06°16′E
96 J9 **Findhorn** ~ N Scotland, United Kingdom
31 R12 **Findlay** Ohio, N USA 41°02′N 83°40′W
18 G11 **Finger Lakes** ◎ New York, NE USA
83 L14 **Fingoè** Tete, NW Mozambique 15°10′S 31°51′E
136 E17 **Finike** Antalya, SW Turkey 36°18′N 30°08′E
102 F6 **Finistère** ◈ department NW France
186 D7 **Finisterre Range** ▲▲ N Papua New Guinea
181 Q8 **Finke** Northern Territory, N Australia 25°37′S 134°35′E
109 S10 **Finkenstein** Kärnten, S Austria 46°34′N 13°53′E
189 Y15 **Finkol, Mount** var. Mount Crozer. ▲ Kosrae, E Micronesia 05°18′N 163°00′E
93 L17 **Finland** off. Republic of Finland, Fin. Suomen Tasavalta, Suomi, Swe. Finland, Republiken Finland. ◆ republic N Europe
124 F12 **Finland, Gulf of** Est. Soome Laht, Fin. Suomenlahti, Ger. Finnischer Meerbusen, Rus. Finskiy Zaliv, Swe. Finska Viken. gulf E Baltic Sea
**Finland, Republic of** see Finland
10 L11 **Finlay** ~ British Columbia, W Canada
183 O10 **Finley** New South Wales, SE Australia 35°41′S 145°33′E
29 Q4 **Finley** North Dakota, N USA 47°30′N 97°50′W
**Finnischer Meerbusen** see Finland, Gulf of
92 K9 **Finnmark** ◈ county N Norway
92 K9 **Finnmarksvidda** physical region N Norway
92 I9 **Finnsnes** Troms, N Norway 69°16′N 18°00′E
186 E7 **Finschhafen** Morobe, C Papua New Guinea 06°35′S 147°51′E
94 E13 **Finse** Hordaland, S Norway 60°35′N 07°33′E
**Finska Viken/Finskiy Zaliv** see Finland, Gulf of
95 M17 **Finspång** Östergötland, S Sweden 58°42′N 15°45′E
108 F10 **Finsteraarhorn** ▲ Switzerland 46°33′N 08°07′E
101 O14 **Finsterwalde** Brandenburg, E Germany 51°38′N 13°43′E
185 A23 **Fiordland** physical region South Island, New Zealand
106 E9 **Fiorenzuola d'Arda** Emilia-Romagna, C Italy 44°57′N 09°53′E
**Firat Nehri** see Euphrates
**Firdaus** see Ferdows
18 M14 **Fire Island** island New York, NE USA
106 G11 **Firenze** Eng. Florence; anc. Florentia. Toscana, C Italy 43°47′N 11°15′E
106 G10 **Firenzuola** Toscana, C Italy 44°07′N 11°22′E
14 C6 **Fire River** Ontario, S Canada 48°46′N 83°34′W
**Firliug** see Fărliug
61 B19 **Firmat** Santa Fe, C Argentina 33°29′S 61°29′W
103 Q12 **Firminy** Loire, E France 45°22′N 04°18′E
**Firmum Picenum** see Fermo
152 J12 **Fīrozābād** Uttar Pradesh, N India 27°09′N 78°24′E
152 G8 **Fīrozpur** var. Ferozepore. Punjab, NW India 30°55′N 74°38′E
**First State** see Delaware
143 O12 **Fīrūzābād** Fārs, S Iran 28°51′N 52°35′E
**Fischamend** see Fischamend Markt
109 Y4 **Fischamend Markt** var. Fischamend. Niederösterreich, NE Austria 48°08′N 16°37′E
109 W6 **Fischbacher Alpen** ▲▲ E Austria
**Fischhausen** see Primorsk
83 D21 **Fish** var. Vis. ~ S Namibia
83 F24 **Fish** Afr. Vis. ~ SW South Africa
11 X15 **Fisher Branch** Manitoba, S Canada 51°09′N 97°34′W
11 X15 **Fisher River** Manitoba, S Canada 51°25′N 97°23′W
19 N13 **Fishers Island** island New York, NE USA
37 U8 **Fishers Peak** ▲ Colorado, C USA 37°06′N 104°27′W
9 P9 **Fisher Strait** strait Nunavut, N Canada
97 H21 **Fishguard** Wel. Abergwaun. SW Wales, United Kingdom 51°59′N 04°49′W
19 R2 **Fish River Lake** ◎ Maine, NE USA
194 K6 **Fiske, Cape** headland Antarctica 74°27′S 60°28′W
103 P4 **Fismes** Marne, N France 49°19′N 03°41′E
104 F3 **Fisterra, Cabo** headland NW Spain 42°53′N 09°16′W
19 N11 **Fitchburg** Massachusetts, NE USA 42°34′N 71°48′W
96 L3 **Fitful Head** headland NE Scotland, United Kingdom 59°57′N 01°24′W
95 C14 **Fitjar** Hordaland, S Norway 59°55′N 05°19′E
192 H16 **Fito, Mauga** ▲ Upolu, C Samoa 13°57′S 171°42′W
23 U6 **Fitzgerald** Georgia, SE USA 31°42′N 83°15′W
180 M5 **Fitzroy Crossing** Western Australia 18°10′S 125°40′E
63 G21 **Fitzroy, Monte** var. Cerro Chaltel. ▲ S Argentina 49°18′S 73°06′W
181 Y8 **Fitzroy River** ~ Queensland, E Australia
180 L5 **Fitzroy River** ~ Western Australia
14 E12 **Fitzwilliam Island** island Ontario, S Canada
107 J15 **Fiuggi** Lazio, C Italy 41°47′N 13°16′E
**Fiume** see Rijeka
107 H15 **Fiumicino** Lazio, C Italy 41°46′N 12°13′E
**Fiumicino** see Leonardo da Vinci
106 E10 **Fivizzano** Toscana, C Italy 44°13′N 10°06′E
79 O21 **Fizi** Sud-Kivu, E Dem. Rep. Congo 04°15′S 28°57′E
**Fizuli** see Füzuli
92 I11 **Fjällåsen** Norrbotten, N Sweden 67°31′N 20°08′E
95 G20 **Fjerritslev** Nordjylland, N Denmark 57°06′N 09°17′E
**F.J.S.** see Franz Josef Strauss
95 L16 **Fjugesta** Örebro, C Sweden 59°10′N 14°50′E
**Fladstrand** see Frederikshavn
37 V5 **Flagler** Colorado, C USA 39°17′N 103°04′W
23 X10 **Flagler Beach** Florida, SE USA 29°28′N 81°07′W
36 L11 **Flagstaff** Arizona, SW USA 35°12′N 111°39′W
65 H24 **Flagstaff Bay** bay N Saint Helena, C Atlantic Ocean
19 P5 **Flagstaff Lake** ◎ Maine, NE USA
94 E13 **Flåm** Sogn Og Fjordane, S Norway 60°51′N 07°06′E
15 O8 **Flamand** ~ Québec, SE Canada
30 J5 **Flambeau River** ~ Wisconsin, N USA
97 O16 **Flamborough Head** headland E England, United Kingdom 54°06′N 00°03′W
100 N13 **Fläming** hill range NE Germany
16 H8 **Flaming Gorge Reservoir** ⊠ Utah/Wyoming, NW USA
**Flanders** see Vlaanderen
**Flandre** see Vlaanderen
29 R10 **Flandreau** South Dakota, N USA 44°03′N 96°36′W
96 D6 **Flannan Isles** island group NW Scotland, United Kingdom
28 M6 **Flasher** North Dakota, N USA 46°25′N 101°12′W
93 G15 **Flåsjön** ◎ N Sweden
39 O11 **Flat** Alaska, USA 62°27′N 158°00′W
92 H1 **Flateyri** Vestfirðir, NW Iceland 66°03′N 23°28′W
33 P8 **Flathead Lake** ◎ Montana, NW USA
173 Y15 **Flat Island** Fr. Île Plate. island N Mauritius
25 T11 **Flatonia** Texas, SW USA 29°41′N 97°06′W
185 M14 **Flat Point** headland North Island, New Zealand 41°12′S 176°03′E
27 X6 **Flat River** Missouri, C USA 37°51′N 90°31′W
31 P8 **Flat River** ~ Michigan, N USA
31 P14 **Flatrock River** ~ Indiana, N USA
32 E6 **Flattery, Cape** headland Washington, NW USA 48°22′N 124°43′W
64 B12 **Flatts Village** var. The Flatts Village. C Bermuda 32°19′N 64°44′W
108 H7 **Flawil** Sankt Gallen, NE Switzerland 47°25′N 09°12′E
97 N22 **Fleet** S England, United Kingdom 51°16′N 00°50′W
97 K16 **Fleetwood** NW England, United Kingdom 53°55′N 03°02′W
18 H15 **Fleetwood** Pennsylvania, NE USA 40°27′N 75°49′W
95 D18 **Flekkefjord** Vest-Agder, S Norway 58°17′N 06°40′E
21 N5 **Flemingsburg** Kentucky, S USA 38°26′N 83°43′W
18 J15 **Flemington** New Jersey, NE USA 40°30′N 74°51′W
64 I7 **Flemish Cap** undersea feature NW Atlantic Ocean 47°00′N 45°00′W
95 N16 **Flen** Södermanland, C Sweden 59°04′N 16°39′E
100 I6 **Flensburg** Schleswig-Holstein, N Germany 54°47′N 09°26′E
100 J6 **Flensburger Förde** inlet Denmark/Germany
102 K5 **Flers** Orne, N France 48°45′N 00°34′W
95 C14 **Flesland** ✈ (Bergen) Hordaland, S Norway 60°18′N 05°15′E
**Flessingue** see Vlissingen
21 P10 **Fletcher** North Carolina, SE USA 35°24′N 82°29′W
31 R6 **Fletcher Pond** ◎ Michigan, N USA
102 L15 **Fleurance** Gers, S France 43°50′N 00°39′E
108 B8 **Fleurier** Neuchâtel, W Switzerland 46°55′N 06°37′E
99 H20 **Fleurus** Hainaut, S Belgium 50°28′N 04°33′E
103 N7 **Fleury-les-Aubrais** Loiret, C France 47°55′N 01°55′E
98 K10 **Flevoland** ◈ province C Netherlands
**Flickertail State** see North Dakota
108 H9 **Flims** Glarus, NE Switzerland 46°50′N 09°16′E
182 F8 **Flinders Island** island Investigator Group, South Australia
183 P14 **Flinders Island** island Furneaux Group, Tasmania, SE Australia
182 I6 **Flinders Ranges** ▲▲ South Australia
181 U5 **Flinders River** ~ Queensland, NE Australia
11 V13 **Flin Flon** Manitoba, C Canada 54°47′N 101°51′W
97 K18 **Flint** NE Wales, United Kingdom 53°15′N 03°10′W
31 R9 **Flint** Michigan, N USA 43°01′N 83°41′W
97 J18 **Flint** cultural region NE Wales, United Kingdom
27 O7 **Flint Hills** hill range Kansas, C USA
191 Y6 **Flint Island** island Line Islands, E Kiribati
23 S4 **Flint River** ~ Georgia, SE USA
31 R9 **Flint River** ~ Michigan, N USA
189 X12 **Flipper Point** headland C Wake Island 19°18′N 166°37′E
94 I13 **Flisa** Hedmark, S Norway 60°36′N 12°02′E
94 J13 **Flisa** ~ S Norway
122 J5 **Flissingskiy, Mys** headland Novaya Zemlya, NW Russia 76°43′N 69°01′E
**Flitsch** see Bovec
105 U6 **Flix** Cataluña, NE Spain 41°13′N 00°32′E
95 J19 **Floda** Västra Götaland, S Sweden 57°47′N 12°20′E
101 O16 **Flöha** ~ E Germany
25 O4 **Flomot** Texas, SW USA 34°13′N 100°58′W
29 V5 **Floodwood** Minnesota, N USA 46°55′N 92°55′W
30 M15 **Flora** Illinois, N USA 38°40′N 88°29′W
103 P14 **Florac** Lozère, S France 44°18′N 03°35′E
23 Q8 **Florala** Alabama, S USA 31°00′N 86°19′W
103 S4 **Florange** Moselle, NE France 49°21′N 06°06′E
**Floreana, Isla** see Santa María, Isla
23 O2 **Florence** Alabama, S USA 34°48′N 87°40′W
36 L14 **Florence** Arizona, SW USA 33°01′N 111°23′W
37 T6 **Florence** Colorado, C USA 38°20′N 105°06′W
27 O5 **Florence** Kansas, C USA 38°13′N 96°56′W
20 M4 **Florence** Kentucky, S USA 39°00′N 84°37′W
32 E13 **Florence** Oregon, NW USA 43°58′N 124°06′W
21 T12 **Florence** South Carolina, SE USA 34°12′N 79°44′W
25 S9 **Florence** Texas, SW USA 30°50′N 97°47′W
**Florence** see Firenze
54 E13 **Florencia** Caquetá, S Colombia 01°37′N 75°37′W
99 H21 **Florennes** Namur, S Belgium 50°15′N 04°36′E
**Florentia** see Firenze
63 J18 **Florentino Ameghino, Embalse** ◎ S Argentina
99 J24 **Florenville** Luxembourg, SE Belgium 49°42′N 05°19′E
42 E3 **Flores** Petén, N Guatemala 16°55′N 89°56′W
61 E19 **Flores** ◈ department S Uruguay
171 O16 **Flores** island Nusa Tenggara, C Indonesia
64 M1 **Flores** island Azores, Portugal, NE Atlantic Ocean
**Floreshty** see Floreşti
**Flores, Lago de** see Petén Itzá, Lago
**Flores, Laut** see Flores Sea
171 N15 **Flores Sea** Ind. Laut Flores. sea C Indonesia
116 M8 **Floreşti** Rus. Floreshty. N Moldova 47°52′N 28°19′E
25 S12 **Floresville** Texas, SW USA 29°09′N 98°10′W
59 N14 **Floriano** Piauí, E Brazil 06°45′S 43°00′W
61 K14 **Florianópolis** prev. Desterro. state capital Santa Catarina, S Brazil 27°35′S 48°32′W
44 G6 **Florida** Camagüey, C Cuba 21°32′N 78°14′W
61 F19 **Florida** Florida, S Uruguay 34°04′S 56°14′W
61 F19 **Florida** ◈ department S Uruguay
23 U9 **Florida** off. State of Florida, also known as Peninsular State, Sunshine State. ◈ state SE USA
23 Y17 **Florida Bay** bay Florida, SE USA
54 G8 **Floridablanca** Santander, N Colombia 07°04′N 73°06′W
23 Y17 **Florida Keys** island group Florida, SE USA
37 Q16 **Florida Mountains** ▲▲ New Mexico, SW USA
64 D10 **Florida, Straits of** strait Atlantic Ocean/Gulf of Mexico
114 D13 **Flórina** var. Phlórina. Dytikí Makedonía, N Greece 40°48′N 21°26′E
27 X4 **Florissant** Missouri, C USA 38°48′N 90°20′W
94 C11 **Florø** Sogn Og Fjordane, S Norway 61°36′N 05°04′E
115 L22 **Floúda, Akrotírio** headland Astypálaia, Kykládes, Greece, Aegean Sea 36°38′N 26°23′E
21 S7 **Floyd** Virginia, NE USA 36°55′N 80°22′W
25 N4 **Floydada** Texas, SW USA 33°58′N 101°20′W
**Flüela Wisshorn** see Weisshorn
98 K7 **Fluessen** ◎ N Netherlands
105 S5 **Flúmen** ~ NE Spain
107 C20 **Flumendosa** ~ Sardegna, Italy, C Mediterranean Sea
31 R9 **Flushing** Michigan, N USA 43°03′N 83°51′W
**Flushing** see Vlissingen
25 O6 **Fluvanna** Texas, SW USA 32°54′N 101°06′W
186 B8 **Fly** ~ Indonesia/Papua New Guinea
194 I10 **Flying Fish, Cape** headland Thurston Island, Antarctica 72°00′S 102°25′W
**Flylân** see Vlieland
**Fly River** see Fly
193 Y15 **Foa** island Ha'apai Group, C Tonga
11 U15 **Foam Lake** Saskatchewan, S Canada 51°38′N 103°31′W




◆ Country
● Country Capital
◇ Dependent Territory
○ Dependent Territory Capital
◈ Administrative Regions
✈ International Airport
▲ Mountain
▲▲ Mountain Range
Volcano
~ River
◎ Lake
⊠ Reservoir

FOČA – FRENCH SOMALILAND


113 J14 **Foča** *var.* Srbinje. SE Bosnia and Herzegovina 43°32′N 18°46′E
116 L12 **Focşani** Vrancea, E Romania 45°45′N 27°13′E
190 G8 **Fogafale** *island* C Tuvalu
**Fogaras/Fogarasch** *see* Făgăraş
107 M16 **Foggia** Puglia, SE Italy 41°28′N 15°31′E
**Foggo** *see* Faggo
76 D10 **Fogo** *island* Ilhas de Sotavento, SW Cape Verde
13 U11 **Fogo Island** *island* Newfoundland and Labrador, E Canada
109 U7 **Fohnsdorf** Steiermark, SE Austria 47°13′N 14°40′E
100 G7 **Föhr** *island* NW Germany
104 F14 **Fóia** ▲ S Portugal 37°19′N 08°39′W
14 I10 **Foins, Lac aux** ⊛ Québec, SE Canada
103 N17 **Foix** Ariège, S France 42°58′N 01°39′E
126 I5 **Fokino** Bryanskaya Oblast', W Russia 53°22′N 34°22′E
123 S15 **Fokino** Primorskiy Kray, W Russia 42°58′N 132°25′E
**Fola, Cnoc** *see* Bloody Foreland
129 P8 **Fōlādī, Kōh-e** ▲ E Afghanistan 34°38′N 67°32′E
94 E13 **Folarskardnuten** ▲ S Norway 60°34′N 07°18′E
92 G11 **Folda** *prev.* Foldafjorden. *fjord* C Norway
**Foldafjorden** *see* Folda
93 F14 **Foldereid** Nord-Trøndelag, C Norway 64°58′N 12°09′E
**Földvár** *see* Feldioara
115 J22 **Folégandros** *island* Kykládes, Greece, Aegean Sea
23 O9 **Foley** Alabama, S USA 30°24′N 87°40′W
29 U7 **Foley** Minnesota, N USA 45°39′N 93°54′W
14 E7 **Foleyet** Ontario, S Canada 48°15′N 82°26′W
95 D14 **Folgefonna** *glacier* S Norway
106 I13 **Foligno** Umbria, C Italy 42°58′N 12°40′E
97 Q23 **Folkestone** SE England, United Kingdom 51°05′N 01°11′E
23 W8 **Folkston** Georgia, SE USA 30°49′N 82°00′W
94 H10 **Folldal** Hedmark, S Norway 62°08′N 10°00′E
25 P1 **Follett** Texas, SW USA 36°25′N 100°08′W
106 F13 **Follonica** Toscana, C Italy 42°55′N 10°45′E
21 T15 **Folly Beach** South Carolina, SE USA 32°39′N 79°56′W
35 O7 **Folsom** California, W USA 38°40′N 121°11′W
116 M12 **Folteşti** Galaţi, E Romania 45°45′N 28°00′E
172 H14 **Fomboni** Mohéli, S Comoros 12°18′S 43°46′E
18 K10 **Fonda** New York, NE USA 42°57′N 74°24′W
11 S10 **Fond-du-Lac** Saskatchewan, C Canada 59°20′N 107°09′W
30 M8 **Fond du Lac** Wisconsin, N USA 43°48′N 88°27′W
11 T10 **Fond-du-Lac** ≈ Saskatchewan, C Canada
107 C18 **Fonni** Sardegna, Italy, C Mediterranean Sea 40°07′N 09°17′E
189 V12 **Fono** *island* Chuuk, C Micronesia
54 G4 **Fonseca** La Guajira, N Colombia 10°53′N 72°51′W
**Fonseca, Golfo de** *see* Fonseca, Gulf of
42 H8 **Fonseca, Gulf of** *Sp.* Golfo de Fonseca. *gulf* C Central America
103 O6 **Fontainebleau** Seine-et-Marne, N France 48°24′N 02°42′E
63 G19 **Fontana, Lago** ⊛ W Argentina
21 N10 **Fontana Lake** ⊠ North Carolina, SE USA
107 L24 **Fontanarossa** ✈ (Catania) Sicilia, Italy, C Mediterranean Sea 37°28′N 15°04′E
11 N11 **Fontas** ≈ British Columbia, W Canada
58 D12 **Fonte Boa** Amazonas, N Brazil 02°32′S 66°01′W
102 J10 **Fontenay-le-Comte** Vendée, NW France 46°28′N 00°48′W
33 T16 **Fontenelle Reservoir** ⊠ Wyoming, C USA
193 Y14 **Fonualei** *island* Vava'u Group, N Tonga
111 H24 **Fonyód** Somogy, W Hungary 46°43′N 17°32′E
**Foochow** *see* Fuzhou
39 Q10 **Foraker, Mount** ▲ Alaska, USA 62°57′N 151°24′W
187 R14 **Forari** Éfaté, C Vanuatu 17°42′S 168°33′E
103 U4 **Forbach** Moselle, NE France 49°11′N 06°54′E
183 Q8 **Forbes** New South Wales, SE Australia 33°24′S 148°00′E
77 T17 **Forcados** Delta, S Nigeria 05°16′N 05°25′E
103 S14 **Forcalquier** Alpes-de-Haute-Provence, SE France 43°57′N 05°46′E
101 K19 **Forchheim** Bayern, SE Germany 49°43′N 11°07′E
35 R13 **Ford City** California, W USA 35°09′N 119°27′W
94 D11 **Førde** Sogn Og Fjordane, S Norway 61°27′N 05°51′E
31 N4 **Ford River** ≈ Michigan, N USA
183 O4 **Fords Bridge** New South Wales, SE Australia 29°44′S 145°25′E
20 J6 **Fordsville** Kentucky, S USA 37°36′N 86°39′W
27 U13 **Fordyce** Arkansas, C USA 33°49′N 92°23′W
76 I14 **Forécariah** SW Guinea 09°28′N 13°06′W
197 O14 **Forel, Mont** ▲ SE Greenland 66°55′N 36°45′W
11 R17 **Foremost** Alberta, SW Canada 49°30′N 111°34′W
14 D16 **Forest** Ontario, S Canada 43°05′N 82°00′W
22 L5 **Forest** Mississippi, S USA 32°22′N 89°30′W
31 S12 **Forest** Ohio, N USA 40°47′N 83°26′W
29 V11 **Forest City** Iowa, C USA 43°15′N 93°38′W
21 Q10 **Forest City** North Carolina, SE USA 35°19′N 81°52′W
32 G11 **Forest Grove** Oregon, NW USA 45°31′N 123°06′W
183 P17 **Forestier Peninsula** *peninsula* Tasmania, SE Australia
29 V8 **Forest Lake** Minnesota, N USA 45°16′N 92°59′W
23 S3 **Forest Park** Georgia, SE USA 33°37′N 84°22′W
29 Q3 **Forest River** ≈ North Dakota, N USA
15 T6 **Forestville** Québec, SE Canada 48°45′N 69°04′W
103 Q11 **Forez, Monts du** ▲▲ C France
96 K10 **Forfar** E Scotland, United Kingdom 56°38′N 02°54′W
26 J8 **Forgan** Oklahoma, C USA 36°54′N 100°32′W
**Forge du Sud** *see* Dudelange
101 J24 **Forggensee** ⊛ S Germany
147 N10 **Forish** *Rus.* Farish. Jizzax Viloyati, C Uzbekistan 40°33′N 66°52′E
20 F9 **Forked Deer River** ≈ Tennessee, S USA
32 F7 **Forks** Washington, NW USA 47°57′N 124°22′W
92 N2 **Forlandsundet** *sound* W Svalbard
106 H10 **Forlì** *anc.* Forum Livii. Emilia-Romagna, N Italy 44°14′N 12°02′E
29 Q7 **Forman** North Dakota, N USA 46°07′N 97°39′W
97 K17 **Formby** NW England, United Kingdom 53°34′N 03°05′W
105 V11 **Formentera** *anc.* Ophiusa, *Lat.* Frumentum. *island* Islas Baleares, Spain, W Mediterranean Sea
**Formentor, Cabo de** *see* Formentor, Cap de
105 Y9 **Formentor, Cap de** *var.* Cabo de Formentor, Cape Formentor. *headland* Mallorca, Spain, W Mediterranean Sea 39°57′N 03°12′E
**Formentor, Cape** *see* Formentor, Cap de
107 J16 **Formia** Lazio, C Italy 41°16′N 13°37′E
62 O7 **Formosa** Formosa, NE Argentina 26°07′S 58°14′W
62 M6 **Formosa** *off.* Provincia de Formosa. ◈ *province* NE Argentina
**Formosa/Formo'sa** *see* Taiwan
**Formosa, Provincia de** *see* Formosa
59 I17 **Formosa, Serra** ▲▲ C Brazil
**Formosa Strait** *see* Taiwan Strait
95 H21 **Fornæs** *headland* C Denmark 56°26′N 10°57′E
25 U6 **Forney** Texas, SW USA 32°45′N 96°28′W
106 E9 **Fornovo di Taro** Emilia-Romagna, C Italy 44°42′N 10°07′E
117 T14 **Foros** Avtonomna Respublika Krym, S Ukraine 44°24′N 33°47′E
**Føroyar** *see* Faroe Islands
96 J8 **Forres** NE Scotland, United Kingdom 57°32′N 03°38′W
27 X11 **Forrest City** Arkansas, C USA 35°01′N 90°48′W
39 Y15 **Forrester Island** *island* Alexander Archipelago, Alaska, USA
25 N7 **Forsan** Texas, SW USA 32°06′N 101°22′W
181 V5 **Forsayth** Queensland, NE Australia 18°31′S 143°37′E
95 L19 **Forserum** Jönköping, S Sweden 57°42′N 14°28′E
95 K15 **Forshaga** Värmland, C Sweden 59°33′N 13°29′E
93 L19 **Forssa** Kanta-Häme, S Finland 60°49′N 23°40′E
101 Q14 **Forst** *Lus.* Baršć Łužyca. Brandenburg, E Germany 51°43′N 14°38′E
183 U7 **Forster-Tuncurry** New South Wales, SE Australia 32°11′S 152°30′E
23 T4 **Forsyth** Georgia, SE USA 33°00′N 83°57′W
27 T8 **Forsyth** Missouri, C USA 36°41′N 93°07′W
33 W10 **Forsyth** Montana, NW USA 46°16′N 106°40′W
149 U11 **Fort Abbas** Punjab, E Pakistan 29°12′N 73°00′E
12 G10 **Fort Albany** Ontario, C Canada 52°15′N 81°35′W
56 L13 **Fortaleza** Pando, N Bolivia 09°48′S 65°29′W
58 P13 **Fortaleza** *prev.* Ceará. *state capital* Ceará, NE Brazil 03°45′S 38°35′W
59 D16 **Fortaleza** Rondônia, W Brazil 08°45′S 64°06′W
56 C13 **Fortaleza, Río** ≈ W Peru
**Fort-Archambault** *see* Sarh
21 U3 **Fort Ashby** West Virginia, NE USA 39°30′N 78°46′W
96 I9 **Fort Augustus** N Scotland, United Kingdom 57°14′N 04°38′W
**Fort-Bayard** *see* Zhanjiang
33 S8 **Fort Benton** Montana, NW USA 47°49′N 110°40′W
35 Q1 **Fort Bidwell** California, W USA 41°50′N 120°07′W
34 L5 **Fort Bragg** California, W USA 39°25′N 123°48′W
31 N16 **Fort Branch** Indiana, N USA 38°15′N 87°34′W
**Fort-Bretonnet** *see* Bousso
33 T17 **Fort Bridger** Wyoming, C USA 41°18′N 110°19′W
**Fort-Cappolani** *see* Tidjikja
**Fort-Carnot** *see* Ikongo
**Fort Charlet** *see* Ohanet
**Fort-Chimo** *see* Kuujjuaq
11 R10 **Fort Chipewyan** Alberta, C Canada 58°42′N 111°08′W
**Fort Cobb Lake** *see* Fort Cobb Reservoir
26 L11 **Fort Cobb Reservoir** *var.* Fort Cobb Lake. ⊠ Oklahoma, C USA
37 T3 **Fort Collins** Colorado, C USA 40°35′N 105°05′W
14 K12 **Fort-Coulonge** Québec, SE Canada 45°50′N 76°45′W
**Fort-Crampel** *see* Kaga Bandoro
**Fort-Dauphin** *see* Tôlañaro
24 K10 **Fort Davis** Texas, SW USA 30°35′N 103°54′W
37 O10 **Fort Defiance** Arizona, SW USA 35°44′N 109°04′W
45 Q12 **Fort-de-France** *prev.* Fort-Royal. ○ (Martinique) W Martinique 14°36′N 61°05′W
45 P12 **Fort-de-France, Baie de** *bay* W Martinique
**Fort de Kock** *see* Bukittinggi
23 P6 **Fort Deposit** Alabama, S USA 31°58′N 86°34′W
29 U13 **Fort Dodge** Iowa, C USA 42°30′N 94°10′W
13 S10 **Forteau** Québec, E Canada 51°30′N 56°55′W
106 E11 **Forte dei Marmi** Toscana, C Italy 43°59′N 10°10′E
14 H17 **Fort Erie** Ontario, S Canada 42°55′N 78°56′W
180 H7 **Fortescue River** ≈ Western Australia
19 S2 **Fort Fairfield** Maine, NE USA 46°45′N 67°51′W
**Fort-Foureau** *see* Kousséri
12 A11 **Fort Frances** Ontario, S Canada 48°37′N 93°23′W
**Fort Franklin** *see* Déljne
23 R7 **Fort Gaines** Georgia, SE USA 31°36′N 85°03′W
37 T8 **Fort Garland** Colorado, C USA 37°22′N 105°24′W
21 P5 **Fort Gay** West Virginia, NE USA 38°06′N 82°35′W
**Fort George** *see* Chisasibi
**Fort George** *see* La Grande Rivière
27 Q10 **Fort Gibson** Oklahoma, C USA 35°48′N 95°15′W
27 Q9 **Fort Gibson Lake** ⊠ Oklahoma, C USA
8 H7 **Fort Good Hope** *var.* Rádeyilikóé. Northwest Territories, NW Canada 66°16′N 128°37′W
23 V4 **Fort Gordon** Georgia, SE USA 33°25′N 82°09′W
**Fort Gouraud** *see* Fdérik
96 I11 **Forth** ≈ C Scotland, United Kingdom
**Fort Hall** *see* Murang'a
24 H8 **Fort Hancock** Texas, SW USA 31°18′N 105°49′W
**Fort Hertz** *see* Puta-O
96 K12 **Forth, Firth of** *estuary* E Scotland, United Kingdom
14 L14 **Forthton** Ontario, SE Canada 44°43′N 75°31′W
14 M8 **Fortier** ≈ Québec, SE Canada
**Fortín General Eugenio Garay** *see* General Eugenio A. Garay
**Fort Jameson** *see* Chipata
**Fort Johnston** *see* Mangochi
19 R1 **Fort Kent** Maine, NE USA 47°15′N 68°33′W
**Fort-Lamy** *see* N'Djaména
23 Z15 **Fort Lauderdale** Florida, SE USA 26°07′N 80°09′W
21 R11 **Fort Lawn** South Carolina, SE USA 34°43′N 80°46′W
8 H10 **Fort Liard** *var.* Liard. Northwest Territories, W Canada 60°14′N 123°28′W
44 M8 **Fort-Liberté** NE Haiti 19°42′N 71°51′W
21 N9 **Fort Loudoun Lake** ⊠ Tennessee, S USA
37 T3 **Fort Lupton** Colorado, C USA 40°04′N 104°48′W
11 R12 **Fort MacKay** Alberta, C Canada 57°12′N 111°41′W
11 Q17 **Fort Macleod** *var.* MacLeod. Alberta, SW Canada 49°44′N 113°24′W
29 Y16 **Fort Madison** Iowa, C USA 40°37′N 91°15′W
**Fort Manning** *see* Mchinji
25 P9 **Fort McKavett** Texas, SW USA 30°50′N 100°07′W
11 R12 **Fort McMurray** Alberta, C Canada 56°44′N 111°23′W
8 G7 **Fort McPherson** *var.* McPherson. Northwest Territories, NW Canada 67°29′N 134°50′W
21 R11 **Fort Mill** South Carolina, SE USA 35°00′N 80°57′W
**Fort-Millot** *see* Ngouri
37 U3 **Fort Morgan** Colorado, C USA 40°14′N 103°48′W
23 W14 **Fort Myers** Florida, SE USA 26°39′N 81°52′W
23 W15 **Fort Myers Beach** Florida, SE USA 26°27′N 81°57′W
10 M10 **Fort Nelson** British Columbia, W Canada 58°48′N 122°44′W
10 M10 **Fort Nelson** ≈ British Columbia, W Canada
**Fort Norman** *see* Tulita
23 Q2 **Fort Payne** Alabama, S USA 34°23′N 85°43′W
33 W7 **Fort Peck** Montana, NW USA 48°00′N 106°28′W
33 V8 **Fort Peck Lake** ⊠ Montana, NW USA
23 Y13 **Fort Pierce** Florida, SE USA 27°28′N 80°20′W
29 N10 **Fort Pierre** South Dakota, N USA 44°21′N 100°22′W
81 E18 **Fort Portal** SW Uganda 0°39′N 30°17′E
8 J10 **Fort Providence** *var.* Providence. Northwest Territories, W Canada 61°21′N 117°39′W
11 U16 **Fort Qu'Appelle** Saskatchewan, S Canada 50°50′N 103°52′W
**Fort-Repoux** *see* Akjoujt
8 K10 **Fort Resolution** *var.* Resolution. Northwest Territories, W Canada 61°10′N 113°39′W
33 T13 **Fortress Mountain** ▲ Wyoming, C USA 44°20′N 109°51′W
**Fort Rosebery** *see* Mansa
**Fort Rousset** *see* Owando
**Fort-Royal** *see* Fort-de-France
**Fort Rupert** *see* Waskaganish
8 H13 **Fort St. James** British Columbia, SW Canada 54°26′N 124°15′W
11 N12 **Fort St. John** British Columbia, W Canada 56°16′N 120°52′W
**Fort Sandeman** *see* Zhob
11 Q14 **Fort Saskatchewan** Alberta, SW Canada 53°42′N 113°12′W
27 R6 **Fort Scott** Kansas, C USA 37°52′N 94°43′W
12 E6 **Fort Severn** Ontario, C Canada 56°N 87°40′W
31 R12 **Fort Shawnee** Ohio, N USA 40°41′N 84°08′W
144 E14 **Fort-Shevchenko** Mangistau, W Kazakhstan 44°29′N 50°16′E
**Fort-Sibut** *see* Sibut
8 I10 **Fort Simpson** *var.* Simpson. Northwest Territories, W Canada 61°52′N 121°23′W
8 I10 **Fort Smith** Northwest Territories, W Canada 60°01′N 111°55′W
27 R10 **Fort Smith** Arkansas, C USA 35°23′N 94°24′W
37 T13 **Fort Stanton** New Mexico, SW USA 33°28′N 105°31′W
24 L9 **Fort Stockton** Texas, SW USA 30°54′N 102°54′W
37 U12 **Fort Sumner** New Mexico, SW USA 34°28′N 104°15′W
26 K8 **Fort Supply** Oklahoma, C USA 36°34′N 99°34′W
26 K8 **Fort Supply Lake** ⊠ Oklahoma, C USA
29 O10 **Fort Thompson** South Dakota, N USA 44°01′N 99°22′W
**Fort-Trinquet** *see* Bîr Mogreïn
105 R12 **Fortuna** Murcia, SE Spain 38°11′N 01°07′W
34 K3 **Fortuna** California, W USA 40°35′N 124°07′W
28 J2 **Fortuna** North Dakota, N USA 48°53′N 103°46′W
23 T5 **Fort Valley** Georgia, SE USA 32°33′N 83°53′W
11 P11 **Fort Vermilion** Alberta, W Canada 58°22′N 115°59′W
**Fort Victoria** *see* Masvingo
31 P13 **Fortville** Indiana, N USA 39°55′N 85°51′W
23 P9 **Fort Walton Beach** Florida, SE USA 30°24′N 86°37′W
31 P12 **Fort Wayne** Indiana, N USA 41°08′N 85°08′W
96 H10 **Fort William** N Scotland, United Kingdom 56°49′N 05°07′W
25 T6 **Fort Worth** Texas, SW USA 32°44′N 97°19′W
28 M7 **Fort Yates** North Dakota, N USA 46°05′N 100°37′W
39 S7 **Fort Yukon** Alaska, USA 66°35′N 145°05′W
**Forum Alieni** *see* Ferrara
**Forum Julii** *see* Fréjus
**Forum Livii** *see* Forlì
143 Q15 **Forūr-e Bozorg, Jazīreh-ye** *island* S Iran
94 H7 **Fosen** *physical region* S Norway
161 N14 **Foshan** *var.* Fatshan, Fo-shan, Namhoi. Guangdong, S China 23°03′N 113°08′E
**Fo-shan** *see* Foshan
**Fossa Claudia** *see* Chioggia
106 B9 **Fossano** Piemonte, NW Italy 44°33′N 07°43′E
99 H21 **Fosses-la-Ville** Namur, S Belgium 50°24′N 04°42′E
32 J12 **Fossil** Oregon, NW USA 45°01′N 120°14′W
**Foss Lake** *see* Foss Reservoir
106 I11 **Fossombrone** Marche, C Italy 43°42′N 12°48′E
26 K10 **Foss Reservoir** *var.* Foss Lake. ⊠ Oklahoma, C USA
29 S4 **Fosston** Minnesota, N USA 47°34′N 95°45′W
183 O13 **Foster** Victoria, SE Australia 38°40′S 146°15′E
11 T12 **Foster Lakes** ⊛ Saskatchewan, C Canada
31 S12 **Fostoria** Ohio, N USA 41°09′N 83°25′W
79 D19 **Fougamou** Ngounié, C Gabon 01°16′S 10°30′E
102 J6 **Fougères** Ille-et-Vilaine, NW France 48°21′N 01°12′W
**Fou-hsin** *see* Fuxin
27 S14 **Fouke** Arkansas, C USA 33°15′N 93°53′W
96 K2 **Foula** *island* NE Scotland, United Kingdom
65 D24 **Foul Bay** *bay* East Falkland, Falkland Islands
97 P21 **Foulness Island** *island* SE England, United Kingdom
185 F15 **Foulwind, Cape** *headland* South Island, New Zealand 41°45′S 171°28′E
79 E15 **Foumban** Ouest, NW Cameroon 05°43′N 10°50′E
172 H13 **Foumbouni** Grande Comore, NW Comoros 11°49′S 43°30′E
195 N8 **Foundation Ice Stream** *glacier* Antarctica
37 T6 **Fountain** Colorado, C USA 38°40′N 104°42′W
36 L4 **Fountain Green** Utah, W USA 39°37′N 111°37′W
21 P11 **Fountain Inn** South Carolina, SE USA 34°41′N 82°12′W
27 S11 **Fourche LaFave River** ≈ Arkansas, C USA
33 Z13 **Four Corners** Wyoming, C USA 44°04′N 104°08′W
103 Q2 **Fourmies** Nord, N France 50°01′N 04°03′E
38 J17 **Four Mountains, Islands of** *island group* Aleutian Islands, Alaska, USA
173 P17 **Fournaise, Piton de la** ⛰ SE Réunion 21°14′S 55°43′E
14 J8 **Fournière, Lac** ⊛ Québec, SE Canada
115 L20 **Foúrnoi** *island* Dodekánisa, Greece, Aegean Sea
64 K13 **Four North Fracture Zone** *tectonic feature* W Atlantic Ocean
**Fouron-Saint-Martin** *see* Sint-Martens-Voeren
30 L3 **Fourteen Mile Point** *headland* Michigan, N USA 46°59′N 89°07′W
**Fou-shan** *see* Fushun
76 I13 **Fouta Djallon** *var.* Futa Jallon. ▲▲ W Guinea
185 C25 **Foveaux Strait** *strait* S New Zealand
35 Q11 **Fowler** California, W USA 36°35′N 119°40′W
37 U6 **Fowler** Colorado, C USA 38°07′N 104°01′W
31 N12 **Fowler** Indiana, N USA 40°36′N 87°20′W
182 D7 **Fowlers Bay** *bay* South Australia
25 R13 **Fowlerton** Texas, SW USA 28°27′N 98°48′W
142 M3 **Fowman** *var.* Fuman, Fumen. Gīlān, NW Iran 37°15′N 49°19′E
65 C25 **Fox Bay East** West Falkland, Falkland Islands
65 C25 **Fox Bay West** West Falkland, Falkland Islands
14 J14 **Foxboro** Ontario, SE Canada 44°16′N 77°23′W
11 O14 **Fox Creek** Alberta, W Canada 54°25′N 116°57′W
64 G5 **Foxe Basin** *sea* Nunavut, N Canada
64 G5 **Foxe Channel** *channel* Nunavut, N Canada
95 I16 **Foxen** ⊛ C Sweden
9 Q7 **Foxe Peninsula** *peninsula* Baffin Island, Nunavut, NE Canada
185 E19 **Fox Glacier** West Coast, South Island, New Zealand 43°28′S 170°00′E
38 L17 **Fox Islands** *island* Aleutian Islands, Alaska, USA
30 M10 **Fox Lake** Illinois, N USA 42°24′N 88°10′W
35 R3 **Fox Mountain** ▲ Nevada, W USA 41°01′N 119°30′W
65 E25 **Fox Point** *headland* East Falkland, Falkland Islands 51°55′S 58°24′W
30 M11 **Fox River** ≈ Illinois/Wisconsin, N USA
30 L7 **Fox River** ≈ Wisconsin, N USA
184 L13 **Foxton** Manawatu-Wanganui, North Island, New Zealand 40°27′S 175°18′E
11 S16 **Fox Valley** Saskatchewan, S Canada 50°29′N 109°29′W
11 W16 **Foxwarren** Manitoba, S Canada 50°30′N 101°09′W
97 E14 **Foyle, Lough** *Ir.* Loch Feabhail. *inlet* N Ireland
194 H5 **Foyn Coast** *physical region* Antarctica
104 I2 **Foz** Galicia, NW Spain 43°33′N 07°16′W
60 I12 **Foz do Areia, Represa de** ⊠ S Brazil
59 A16 **Foz do Breu** Acre, W Brazil 09°21′S 72°41′W
83 A16 **Foz do Cunene** Namibe, SW Angola 17°11′S 11°52′E
60 G12 **Foz do Iguaçu** Paraná, S Brazil 25°33′S 54°31′W
58 C12 **Foz do Mamoriá** Amazonas, NW Brazil 02°28′S 66°06′W
105 T6 **Fraga** Aragón, NE Spain 41°32′N 00°21′E
44 F5 **Fragoso, Cayo** *island* C Cuba
61 G18 **Fraile Muerto** Cerro Largo, NE Uruguay 32°30′S 54°30′W
99 H21 **Fraire** Namur, S Belgium 50°16′N 04°30′E
99 L21 **Fraiture, Baraque de** *hill* SE Belgium
**Frakštát** *see* Hlohovec
**Fram Basin** *see* Amundsen Basin
99 F20 **Frameries** Hainaut, S Belgium 50°25′N 03°41′E
19 O11 **Framingham** Massachusetts, NE USA 42°15′N 71°24′W
60 L7 **Franca** São Paulo, S Brazil 20°33′S 47°27′W
**Française, République** *see* France
187 O15 **Français, Récif des** *reef* W New Caledonia
107 K14 **Francavilla al Mare** Abruzzo, C Italy 42°25′N 14°16′E
107 P18 **Francavilla Fontana** Puglia, SE Italy 40°32′N 17°35′E
102 M8 **France** *off.* French Republic, *Fr.* République Française, *It./Sp.* Francia; *prev.* Gaul, Gaule, *Lat.* Gallia. ◆ *republic* W Europe
45 O8 **Francés Viejo, Cabo** *headland* NE Dominican Republic 19°39′N 69°57′W
79 F19 **Franceville** *var.* Massoukou, Masuku. Haut-Ogooué, E Gabon 01°40′S 13°31′E
79 F19 **Franceville** ✈ Haut-Ogooué, E Gabon 01°38′S 13°24′E
**Francfort** *see* Frankfurt am Main
**Francia** *see* France
29 O11 **Francis Case, Lake** ⊠ South Dakota, N USA
60 H12 **Francisco Beltrão** Paraná, S Brazil 26°05′S 53°04′W
**Francisco l. Madero** *see* Villa Madero
61 A21 **Francisco Madero** Buenos Aires, E Argentina 35°52′S 62°03′W
42 H6 **Francisco Morazán** *prev.* Tegucigalpa. ◈ *department* C Honduras
83 J18 **Francistown** North East, NE Botswana 21°08′S 27°31′E
**Franconian Forest** *see* Frankenwald
**Franconian Jura** *see* Fränkische Alb
98 K6 **Franeker** *Fris.* Frentsjer. Fryslân, N Netherlands 53°11′N 05°33′E
**Frankenalb** *see* Fränkische Alb
101 H16 **Frankenberg** Hessen, C Germany 51°04′N 08°49′E
101 J20 **Frankenhöhe** *hill range* C Germany
31 R8 **Frankenmuth** Michigan, N USA 43°19′N 83°44′W
101 F20 **Frankenstein** *hill* W Germany
**Frankenstein/Frankenstein in Schlesien** *see* Ząbkowice Śląskie
101 G20 **Frankenthal** Rheinland-Pfalz, W Germany 49°32′N 08°22′E
101 L18 **Frankenwald** *Eng.* Franconian Forest. ▲▲ C Germany
44 J12 **Frankfield** C Jamaica 18°08′N 77°22′W
14 J14 **Frankford** Ontario, SE Canada 44°12′N 77°36′W
31 O13 **Frankfort** Indiana, N USA 40°16′N 86°30′W
27 O3 **Frankfort** Kansas, C USA 39°42′N 96°25′W
20 L5 **Frankfort** *state capital* Kentucky, S USA 38°12′N 84°52′W
**Frankfort on the Main** *see* Frankfurt am Main
**Frankfurt** *see* Frankfurt am Main, Germany
**Frankfurt** *see* Słubice, Poland
101 G18 **Frankfurt am Main** *var.* Frankfurt, *Fr.* Francfort; *prev. Eng.* Frankfort on the Main. Hessen, SW Germany 50°07′N 08°41′E
100 Q12 **Frankfurt an der Oder** Brandenburg, E Germany 52°20′N 14°32′E
101 L21 **Fränkische Alb** *var.* Frankenalb, *Eng.* Franconian Jura. ▲▲ S Germany
101 I18 **Fränkische Saale** ≈ C Germany
101 L19 **Fränkische Schweiz** *hill range* C Germany
23 R4 **Franklin** Georgia, SE USA 33°15′N 85°06′W
31 P14 **Franklin** Indiana, N USA 39°29′N 86°02′W
20 J7 **Franklin** Kentucky, S USA 36°42′N 86°35′W
22 I9 **Franklin** Louisiana, S USA 29°48′N 91°30′W
29 O17 **Franklin** Nebraska, C USA 40°06′N 98°57′W
21 N10 **Franklin** North Carolina, SE USA 35°12′N 83°23′W
18 C13 **Franklin** Pennsylvania, NE USA 41°24′N 79°49′W
20 J9 **Franklin** Tennessee, S USA 35°55′N 86°52′W
25 U9 **Franklin** Texas, SW USA 31°02′N 96°30′W
21 X7 **Franklin** Virginia, NE USA 36°41′N 76°58′W
21 T4 **Franklin** West Virginia, NE USA 38°39′N 79°21′W
30 M9 **Franklin** Wisconsin, N USA 42°53′N 88°00′W
8 I6 **Franklin Bay** *inlet* Northwest Territories, N Canada
32 K7 **Franklin D. Roosevelt Lake** ⊠ Washington, NW USA
35 W4 **Franklin Lake** ⊛ Nevada, W USA
185 B22 **Franklin Mountains** ▲▲ South Island, New Zealand
39 R5 **Franklin Mountains** ▲▲ Alaska, USA
39 N4 **Franklin, Point** *headland* Alaska, USA 70°54′N 158°48′W
183 O17 **Franklin River** ≈ Tasmania, SE Australia
22 K8 **Franklinton** Louisiana, S USA 30°51′N 90°09′W
21 U9 **Franklinton** North Carolina, SE USA 36°06′N 78°27′W
**Frankstadt** *see* Frenštát pod Radhoštěm
25 V7 **Frankston** Texas, SW USA 32°03′N 95°30′W
33 U12 **Frannie** Wyoming, C USA 44°57′N 108°37′W
15 U5 **Franquelin** Québec, SE Canada 49°17′N 67°52′W
15 U5 **Franquelin** ≈ Québec, SE Canada
83 C18 **Fransfontein** Kunene, NW Namibia 20°12′S 15°01′E
93 H17 **Fränsta** Västernorrland, C Sweden 62°30′N 16°06′E
122 J3 **Frantsa-Iosifa, Zemlya** *Eng.* Franz Josef Land. *island group* N Russia
185 E18 **Franz Josef Glacier** West Coast, South Island, New Zealand 43°22′S 170°11′E
**Franz Josef Land** *see* Frantsa-Iosifa, Zemlya
**Franz-Josef Spitze** *see* Gerlachovský štít
101 L23 **Franz Josef Strauss** *abbrev.* F.J.S.. ✈ (München) Bayern, SE Germany 48°07′N 11°43′E
107 A19 **Frasca, Capo della** *headland* Sardegna, Italy, C Mediterranean Sea 39°46′N 08°27′E
107 I15 **Frascati** Lazio, C Italy 41°48′N 12°41′E
11 N14 **Fraser** ≈ British Columbia, SW Canada
83 G24 **Fraserburg** Western Cape, SW South Africa 31°55′S 21°31′E
96 L8 **Fraserburgh** NE Scotland, United Kingdom 57°42′N 02°20′W
181 Z9 **Fraser Island** *var.* Great Sandy Island. *island* Queensland, E Australia
10 L14 **Fraser Lake** British Columbia, SW Canada 54°00′N 124°45′W
10 L15 **Fraser Plateau** *plateau* British Columbia, SW Canada
184 P10 **Frasertown** Hawke's Bay, North Island, New Zealand 38°58′S 177°25′E
99 E19 **Frasnes-lez-Buissenal** Hainaut, SW Belgium 50°40′N 03°37′E
108 I7 **Frastanz** Vorarlberg, NW Austria 47°13′N 09°38′E
14 B8 **Frater** Ontario, S Canada 47°19′N 84°28′W
**Frauenbach** *see* Baia Mare
**Frauenburg** *see* Saldus, Latvia
**Frauenburg** *see* Frombork, Poland
108 H6 **Frauenfeld** Thurgau, NE Switzerland 47°34′N 08°54′E
109 Z5 **Frauenkirchen** Burgenland, E Austria 47°50′N 15°57′E
61 D19 **Fray Bentos** Río Negro, W Uruguay 33°09′S 58°14′W
61 F19 **Fray Marcos** Florida, S Uruguay 34°13′S 55°43′W
29 S6 **Frazee** Minnesota, N USA 46°42′N 95°40′W
104 M5 **Frechilla** Castilla y León, N Spain 42°08′N 04°50′W
30 I4 **Frederic** Wisconsin, N USA 45°42′N 92°30′W
95 G23 **Fredericia** Syddanmark, C Denmark 55°34′N 09°47′E
21 W3 **Frederick** Maryland, NE USA 39°25′N 77°25′W
26 L12 **Frederick** Oklahoma, C USA 34°24′N 99°03′W
29 P7 **Frederick** South Dakota, N USA 45°49′N 98°31′W
29 X12 **Fredericksburg** Iowa, C USA 42°58′N 92°12′W
25 R10 **Fredericksburg** Texas, SW USA 30°17′N 98°52′W
21 W5 **Fredericksburg** Virginia, NE USA 38°16′N 77°27′W
39 X13 **Frederick Sound** *sound* Alaska, USA
27 X6 **Fredericktown** Missouri, C USA 37°33′N 90°19′W
60 H13 **Frederico Westphalen** Rio Grande do Sul, S Brazil 27°22′S 53°20′W
13 O15 **Fredericton** *province capital* New Brunswick, SE Canada 45°57′N 66°40′W
**Frederiksborgs Amt** *see* Hovedstaden
**Frederikshåb** *see* Paamiut
95 H19 **Frederikshavn** *prev.* Fladstrand. Nordjylland, N Denmark 57°28′N 10°33′E
95 J22 **Frederikssund** Hovedstaden, E Denmark 55°51′N 12°05′E
45 T9 **Frederiksted** Saint Croix, S Virgin Islands (US) 17°41′N 64°51′W
95 I22 **Frederiksværk** *var.* Frederiksværk og Hanehoved. Hovedstaden, E Denmark 55°58′N 12°02′E
**Frederiksværk og Hanehoved** *see* Frederiksværk
54 E9 **Fredonia** Antioquia, W Colombia 05°57′N 75°42′W
36 K8 **Fredonia** Arizona, SW USA 36°57′N 112°31′W
27 P7 **Fredonia** Kansas, C USA 37°32′N 95°50′W
18 C11 **Fredonia** New York, NE USA 42°26′N 79°19′W
35 P4 **Fredonyer Pass** *pass* California, W USA
93 I15 **Fredrika** Västerbotten, N Sweden 64°03′N 18°25′E
95 L14 **Fredriksberg** Dalarna, C Sweden 60°07′N 14°23′E
**Fredrikshald** *see* Halden
**Fredrikshamn** *see* Hamina
95 H16 **Fredrikstad** Østfold, S Norway 59°12′N 10°57′E
30 K16 **Freeburg** Illinois, N USA 38°25′N 89°54′W
18 K15 **Freehold** New Jersey, NE USA 40°14′N 74°14′W
18 H14 **Freeland** Pennsylvania, NE USA 41°01′N 75°54′W
182 J5 **Freeling Heights** ▲ South Australia 30°09′S 139°24′E
35 Q7 **Freel Peak** ▲ California, W USA 38°52′N 119°52′W
11 Z9 **Freels, Cape** *headland* Newfoundland and Labrador, E Canada 49°16′N 53°30′W
29 Q11 **Freeman** South Dakota, N USA 43°21′N 97°26′W
44 G1 **Freeport** Grand Bahama Island, N The Bahamas 26°28′N 78°43′W
30 L10 **Freeport** Illinois, N USA 42°18′N 89°37′W
25 W12 **Freeport** Texas, SW USA 28°57′N 95°21′W
44 G1 **Freeport** ✈ Grand Bahama Island, N The Bahamas 26°31′N 78°48′W
25 R14 **Freer** Texas, SW USA 27°52′N 98°37′W
83 I22 **Free State** *off.* Free State Province; *prev.* Orange Free State, *Afr.* Oranje Vrystaat. ◈ *province* C South Africa
**Free State** *see* Maryland
**Free State Province** *see* Free State
76 G15 **Freetown** ● (Sierra Leone) W Sierra Leone 08°27′N 13°16′W
172 J16 **Frégate** *island* Inner Islands, NE Seychelles
104 J12 **Fregenal de la Sierra** Extremadura, W Spain 38°10′N 06°39′W
182 C2 **Fregon** South Australia 26°44′S 132°03′E
102 H5 **Fréhel, Cap** *headland* NW France 48°41′N 02°21′W
94 F8 **Frei** Møre og Romsdal, S Norway 63°02′N 07°47′E
194 H2 **Frei** *research station (Chile)* King George Island, Antarctica
194 H2 **Frei** *research station (Chile)* King George Island, Antarctica 61°12′S 58°57′W
101 O16 **Freiberg** Sachsen, E Germany 50°55′N 13°21′E
101 O16 **Freiberger Mulde** ≈ E Germany
**Freiburg** *see* Freiburg im Breisgau, Germany
**Freiburg** *see* Fribourg, Switzerland
101 F23 **Freiburg im Breisgau** *var.* Freiburg, *Fr.* Fribourg-en-Brisgau. Baden-Württemberg, SW Germany 48°N 07°52′E
**Freiburg in Schlesien** *see* Świebodzice
**Freie Hansestadt Bremen** *see* Bremen
**Freie und Hansestadt Hamburg** *see* Brandenburg
101 L22 **Freising** Bayern, SE Germany 48°24′N 11°45′E
109 T3 **Freistadt** Oberösterreich, N Austria 48°31′N 14°31′E
**Freistadtl** *see* Hlohovec
101 O16 **Freital** Sachsen, E Germany 51°00′N 13°40′E
**Freiwaldau** *see* Jeseník
104 J6 **Freixo de Espada à Cinta** Bragança, N Portugal 41°05′N 06°49′W
103 U15 **Fréjus** *anc.* Forum Julii. Var, SE France 43°26′N 06°44′E
180 I13 **Fremantle** Western Australia 32°07′S 115°44′E
35 N9 **Fremont** California, W USA 37°34′N 122°01′W
31 Q11 **Fremont** Indiana, N USA 41°43′N 84°54′W
29 W15 **Fremont** Iowa, C USA 41°12′N 92°26′W
31 P8 **Fremont** Michigan, N USA 43°28′N 85°56′W
29 R15 **Fremont** Nebraska, C USA 41°25′N 96°30′W
31 S11 **Fremont** Ohio, N USA 41°21′N 83°08′W
33 T14 **Fremont Peak** ▲ Wyoming, C USA 43°07′N 109°37′W
36 M6 **Fremont River** ≈ Utah, W USA
21 O9 **French Broad River** ≈ Tennessee, S USA
21 N5 **Frenchburg** Kentucky, S USA 37°58′N 83°37′W
18 C12 **French Creek** ≈ Pennsylvania, NE USA
32 K15 **Frenchglen** Oregon, NW USA 42°49′N 118°55′W
55 Y10 **French Guiana** *var.* Guiana, Guyane. ◇ *French overseas department* N South America
**French Guinea** *see* Guinea
31 O15 **French Lick** Indiana, N USA 38°33′N 86°37′W
185 J14 **French Pass** Marlborough, South Island, New Zealand 40°57′S 173°49′E
191 T11 **French Polynesia** *Fr.* Polynésie Française. ◇ *overseas country of France* S Pacific Ocean
**French Republic** *see* France
14 F11 **French River** ≈ Ontario, S Canada
**French Somaliland** *see* Djibouti


◆ Country
● Country Capital
◇ Dependent Territory
○ Dependent Territory Capital
◈ Administrative Regions
✈ International Airport
▲ Mountain
▲▲ Mountain Range
⛰ Volcano
≈ River
⊛ Lake
⊠ Reservoir

FRENCH SOUTHERN AND ANTARCTIC LANDS – GANI


173 P12 French Southern and Antarctic Lands prev. French Southern and Antarctic Territories, Fr. Terres Australes et Antarctiques Françaises. ◆ French overseas territory S Indian Ocean
French Southern and Antarctic Territories see French Southern and Antarctic Lands
French Sudan see Mali
French Territory of the Afars and Issas see Djibouti
French Togoland see Togo
74 J6 Frenda NW Algeria 35°04′N 01°03′E
111 I18 Frenštát pod Radhoštěm Ger. Frankstadt. Moravskoslezský Kraj, E Czechia 49°33′N 18°10′E
Frentsjer see Franeker
76 M17 Fresco S Ivory Coast 05°03′N 05°31′W
195 U16 Freshfield, Cape headland Antarctica
40 L10 Fresnillo var. Fresnillo de González Echeverría. Zacatecas, C Mexico 23°11′N 102°53′W
Fresnillo de González Echeverría see Fresnillo
35 Q10 Fresno California, W USA 36°45′N 119°48′W
Freu, Cabo del see Freu, Cap des
105 Y9 Freu, Cap des var. Cabo del Freu. cape Mallorca, Spain, W Mediterranean Sea
101 G22 Freudenstadt Baden-Württemberg, SW Germany 48°28′N 08°25′E
Freudenthal see Bruntál
183 Q17 Freycinet Peninsula peninsula Tasmania, SE Australia
76 H14 Fria W Guinea 10°27′N 13°38′W
83 A17 Fria, Cape headland NW Namibia 18°32′S 12°00′E
35 Q10 Friant California, W USA 36°56′N 119°44′W
62 K8 Frías Catamarca, N Argentina 28°41′S 65°00′W
108 D9 Fribourg Ger. Freiburg. Fribourg, W Switzerland 46°50′N 07°10′E
108 C9 Fribourg Ger. Freiburg. ◆ canton W Switzerland
Fribourg-en-Brisgau see Freiburg im Breisgau
32 G7 Friday Harbor San Juan Islands, Washington, NW USA 48°31′N 123°01′W
Friedau see Ormož
101 K23 Friedberg Bayern, S Germany 48°21′N 10°58′E
101 H18 Friedberg Hessen, W Germany 50°19′N 08°46′E
Friedeberg Neumark see Strzelce Krajeńskie
Friedek-Mistek see Frýdek-Místek
Friedland see Pravdinsk
101 I24 Friedrichshafen Baden-Württemberg, S Germany 47°39′N 09°29′E
Friedrichstadt see Jaunjelgava
29 Q16 Friend Nebraska, C USA 40°37′N 97°16′W
Friendly Islands see Tonga
55 V9 Friendship Coronie, N Suriname 05°50′N 56°16′W
30 L7 Friendship Wisconsin, N USA 43°58′N 89°48′W
109 T8 Friesach Kärnten, S Austria 46°58′N 14°24′E
Friesche Eilanden see Frisian Islands
101 F22 Friesenheim Baden-Württemberg, SW Germany 48°27′N 07°56′E
Friesische Inseln see Frisian Islands
Friesland see Fryslân
60 Q10 Frio, Cabo headland SE Brazil 23°01′S 41°59′W
24 M3 Friona Texas, SW USA 34°38′N 102°43′W
42 L12 Frío, Río ∽ N Costa Rica
25 R13 Frio River ∽ Texas, SW USA
99 M25 Frisange Luxembourg, S Luxembourg 49°31′N 06°12′E
Frisches Haff see Vistula Lagoon
36 J6 Frisco Peak ▲ Utah, W USA 38°31′N 113°17′W
84 F9 Frisian Islands Dut. Friesche Eilanden, Ger. Friesische Inseln. island group N Europe
18 L12 Frissell, Mount ▲ Connecticut, NE USA 42°01′N 73°25′W
95 J19 Fristad Västra Götaland, S Sweden 57°50′N 13°01′E
25 N2 Fritch Texas, SW USA 35°38′N 101°36′W
95 J19 Fritsla Västra Götaland, S Sweden 57°33′N 12°47′E
101 H16 Fritzlar Hessen, C Germany 51°09′N 09°16′E
106 H6 Friuli-Venezia Giulia ◆ region NE Italy
196 L13 Frobisher Bay inlet Baffin Island, Nunavut, NE Canada
Frobisher Bay see Iqaluit
11 S12 Frobisher Lake ◎ Saskatchewan, C Canada
94 G7 Frohavet sound C Norway
Frohenbruck see Veselí nad Lužnicí
109 V7 Frohnleiten Steiermark, SE Austria 47°17′N 15°20′E
99 G22 Froidchapelle Hainaut, S Belgium 50°10′N 04°18′E
127 O9 Frolovo Volgogradskaya Oblast', SW Russia 49°46′N 43°38′E
110 K7 Frombork Ger. Frauenburg. Warmińsko-Mazurskie, NE Poland 54°21′N 19°40′E
97 L22 Frome SW England, United Kingdom 51°15′N 02°22′W
182 I4 Frome Creek seasonal river South Australia
182 J6 Frome Downs South Australia 31°17′S 139°48′E
182 J5 Frome, Lake salt lake South Australia
Fronicken see Wronki
104 H10 Fronteira Portalegre, C Portugal 39°03′N 07°39′W
40 M7 Frontera Coahuila, NE Mexico 26°55′N 101°27′W
41 U14 Frontera Tabasco, SE Mexico 18°32′N 92°39′W
40 G3 Fronteras Sonora, NW Mexico 30°51′N 109°35′W
103 Q16 Frontignan Hérault, S France 43°27′N 03°45′E
54 D8 Frontino Antioquia, NW Colombia 06°46′N 76°10′W
21 V4 Front Royal Virginia, NE USA 38°56′N 78°13′W
107 J16 Frosinone anc. Frusino. Lazio, C Italy 41°38′N 13°22′E
107 K16 Frosolone Molise, C Italy 41°34′N 14°25′E
25 U7 Frost Texas, SW USA 32°04′N 96°48′W
21 U2 Frostburg Maryland, NE USA 39°39′N 78°55′W
23 X13 Frostproof Florida, SE USA 27°45′N 81°31′W
Frostviken see Kvarnbergsvattnet
95 M15 Frövi Örebro, C Sweden 59°28′N 15°24′E
94 F7 Frøya island W Norway
37 P5 Fruita Colorado, C USA 39°10′N 108°42′W
28 J9 Fruitdale South Dakota, N USA 44°39′N 103°38′W
23 W11 Fruitland Park Florida, SE USA 28°51′N 81°54′W
Frumentum see Formentera
147 S11 Frunze Batkenskaya Oblast', SW Kyrgyzstan 40°07′N 71°40′E
Frunze see Bishkek
Frunzivka see Zakharivka
Frusino see Frosinone
108 E9 Frutigen Bern, W Switzerland 46°35′N 07°38′E
111 I17 Frýdek-Místek Ger. Friedek-Mistek. Moravskoslezský Kraj, E Czechia 49°40′N 18°22′E
Fryslân see Friesland
98 K6 Fryslân prev. Friesland. ◆ province N Netherlands
193 V16 Fua'amotu Tongatapu, S Tonga 21°15′S 175°08′W
190 A9 Fuafatu island Funafuti Atoll, C Tuvalu
190 A9 Fuagea island Funafuti Atoll, C Tuvalu
190 B8 Fualifeke atoll C Tuvalu
190 A8 Fualopa island Funafuti Atoll, C Tuvalu
151 K22 Fuammulah var. Fuammulah, Gnaviyani. atoll S Maldives
Fuammulah see Fuammulah
161 R11 Fu'an Fujian, SE China 27°11′N 119°42′E
Fu-chien see Fujian
Fu-chou see Fuzhou
164 G13 Fuchū var. Hutyû. Hiroshima, Honshū, SW Japan 34°35′N 133°12′E
160 M13 Fuchuan var. Fuyang. Guangxi Zhuangzu Zizhiqu, S China 24°56′N 111°15′E
161 R9 Fuchun Jiang ∽ SE China
165 R8 Fudai Iwate, Honshū, C Japan 39°59′N 141°50′E
161 S11 Fuding var. Tongshan. Fujian, SE China 27°21′N 120°10′E
81 J20 Fudua spring/well S Kenya 02°13′S 39°43′E
104 M16 Fuengirola Andalucía, S Spain 36°32′N 04°38′W
104 J12 Fuente de Cantos Extremadura, W Spain 38°15′N 06°18′W
104 J11 Fuente del Maestre Extremadura, W Spain 38°31′N 06°26′W
104 L12 Fuente Obejuna Andalucía, S Spain 38°15′N 05°25′W
104 L6 Fuentesaúco Castilla y León, N Spain 41°14′N 05°30′W
62 O3 Fuerte Olimpo var. Olimpo. Alto Paraguay, NE Paraguay 21°02′S 57°51′W
40 H8 Fuerte, Río ∽ C Mexico
64 Q11 Fuerteventura island Islas Canarias, Spain, NE Atlantic Ocean
141 S14 Fughmah var. Faghman, Fugma. C Yemen 16°08′N 49°23′E
92 M2 Fuglehuken headland W Svalbard 78°54′N 10°30′E
Fuglø see Fugloy
95 B18 Fugloy Dan. Fuglø. island NE Faroe Islands
197 T15 Fugløya Bank undersea feature E Norwegian Sea 71°00′N 19°20′E
Fugma see Fughmah
160 E11 Fugong Yunnan, SW China 27°00′N 98°48′E
81 K16 Fugugo spring/well NE Kenya 03°19′N 39°39′E
158 L2 Fuhai var. Burultokay. Xinjiang Uygur Zizhiqu, NW China 47°15′N 87°39′E
161 P10 Fu He ∽ S China
Fuhkien see Fujian
100 J9 Fuhlsbüttel ✈ (Hamburg) Hamburg, N Germany 53°37′N 09°57′E
101 L14 Fuhne ∽ C Germany
Fu-hsin see Fuxin
Fujairah see Al Fujayrah
164 M14 Fuji var. Huzi. Shizuoka, Honshū, S Japan 35°08′N 138°39′E
161 Q12 Fujian var. Fu-chien, Fuhkien, Fukien, Min, Fujian Sheng. ◆ province SE China
160 I9 Fu Jiang ∽ C China
Fujian Sheng see Fujian
164 M14 Fujieda var. Huzieda. Shizuoka, Honshū, S Japan 34°54′N 138°15′E
Fuji, Mount/Fujiyama see Fuji-san
163 Y7 Fujin Heilongjiang, NE China 47°12′N 132°01′E
164 M13 Fujinomiya var. Huzinomiya. Shizuoka, Honshū, S Japan 35°16′N 138°33′E
164 N13 Fuji-san var. Fujiyama, Eng. Mount Fuji. ▲ Honshū, SE Japan 35°23′N 138°44′E
165 N14 Fujisawa var. Huzisawa. Kanagawa, Honshū, S Japan 35°22′N 139°29′E
165 T3 Fukagawa var. Hukagawa. Hokkaidō, NE Japan 43°44′N 142°03′E
158 L5 Fukang Xinjiang Uygur Zizhiqu, W China 44°07′N 87°55′E
165 P7 Fukaura Aomori, Honshū, C Japan 40°38′N 139°55′E
193 W15 Fukave island Tongatapu Group, S Tonga
Fukien see Fujian
164 J13 Fukuchiyama var. Hukutiyama. Kyōto, Honshū, SW Japan 35°19′N 135°08′E
Fukue see Gotō
164 A13 Fukue-jima island Gotō-rettō, SW Japan
164 K12 Fukui var. Hukui. Fukui, Honshū, SW Japan 36°03′N 136°12′E
164 K12 Fukui off. Fukui-ken, var. Hukui. ◆ prefecture Honshū, SW Japan
Fukui-ken see Fukui
164 D13 Fukuoka var. Hukuoka, hist. Najima. Fukuoka, Kyūshū, SW Japan 33°36′N 130°24′E
164 D13 Fukuoka off. Fukuoka-ken, var. Hukuoka. ◆ prefecture Kyūshū, SW Japan
Fukuoka-ken see Fukuoka
165 Q6 Fukushima Hokkaidō, NE Japan 41°27′N 140°14′E
165 Q12 Fukushima off. Fukushima-ken, var. Hukusima. ◆ prefecture Honshū, C Japan
Fukushima-ken see Fukushima
164 G13 Fukuyama var. Hukuyama. Hiroshima, Honshū, SW Japan 34°29′N 133°21′E
76 G13 Fulacunda C Guinea-Bissau 11°44′N 15°03′W
187 Z15 Fulaga island Lau Group, E Fiji
101 I17 Fulda Hessen, C Germany 50°33′N 09°41′E
29 S10 Fulda Minnesota, N USA 43°52′N 95°36′W
101 I16 Fulda ∽ C Germany
Fülek see Fil'akovo
Fuli see Jixian
Fulin see Hanyuan
160 K10 Fuling Chongqing Shi, C China 29°45′N 107°23′E
35 T15 Fullerton California, SE USA 33°53′N 117°55′W
29 P15 Fullerton Nebraska, C USA 41°21′N 97°58′W
108 M8 Fulpmes Tirol, W Austria 47°11′N 11°22′E
20 G8 Fulton Kentucky, S USA 36°31′N 88°52′W
23 N2 Fulton Mississippi, S USA 34°16′N 88°24′W
27 V4 Fulton Missouri, C USA 38°50′N 91°57′W
18 H9 Fulton New York, NE USA 43°18′N 76°22′W
Fuman/Fumen see Fowman
103 R3 Fumay Ardennes, N France 49°58′N 04°42′E
102 M13 Fumel Lot-et-Garonne, SW France 44°31′N 00°58′E
190 B10 Funafara atoll C Tuvalu
190 C9 Funafuti ✈ Funafuti Atoll, C Tuvalu 08°30′S 179°12′E
190 C9 Funafuti Atoll ● (Tuvalu) atoll C Tuvalu
Funan see Fusui
190 B9 Funangongo atoll C Tuvalu
93 F17 Funäsdalen Jämtland, C Sweden 62°33′N 12°33′E
64 O6 Funchal Madeira, Portugal, NE Atlantic Ocean 32°40′N 16°55′W
64 P5 Funchal ✈ Madeira, Portugal, NE Atlantic Ocean 32°38′N 16°53′W
54 F5 Fundación Magdalena, N Colombia 10°31′N 74°09′W
104 I8 Fundão var. Fundão. Castelo Branco, C Portugal 40°08′N 07°30′W
Fundão see Fundão
13 O16 Fundy, Bay of bay Canada/USA
Fünen see Fyn
54 C13 Fúnes Nariño, SW Colombia 0°59′N 77°27′W
Fünfkirchen see Pécs
83 M19 Funhalouro Inhambane, S Mozambique 23°04′S 34°24′E
161 R6 Funing Jiangsu, E China 33°43′N 119°47′E
160 I14 Funing var. Xinhua. Yunnan, SW China 23°35′N 105°41′E
160 M7 Funiu Shan ▲▲ C China
77 U13 Funtua Katsina, N Nigeria 11°31′N 07°19′E
161 R12 Fuqing Fujian, SE China 25°40′N 119°23′E
83 M14 Furancungo Tete, NW Mozambique 14°51′S 33°39′E
116 I15 Furculeşti Teleorman, S Romania 43°51′N 25°07′E
Füred see Balatonfüred
165 W4 Füren-ko ◎ Hokkaidō, NE Japan
Fürg see Doborjī
Furluk see Fârliug
Fürmanov/Furmanovka see Moyynkum
Furmanovo see Zhalpaktal
59 L20 Furnas, Represa de ⊞ SE Brazil
183 Q14 Furneaux Group island group Tasmania, SE Australia
Furnes see Veurne
160 J10 Furong Jiang ∽ S China
138 I5 Furqlus Ḩimş, W Syria 34°40′N 37°02′E
100 F12 Fürstenau Niedersachsen, NW Germany 52°30′N 07°40′E
109 X8 Fürstenfeld Steiermark, SE Austria 47°03′N 16°05′E
101 L23 Fürstenfeldbruck Bayern, S Germany 48°10′N 11°16′E
100 P12 Fürstenwalde Brandenburg, NE Germany 52°22′N 14°04′E
101 K20 Fürth Bayern, S Germany 49°29′N 10°59′E
109 W3 Furth bei Göttweig Niederösterreich, NW Austria 48°22′N 15°33′E
165 R3 Furubira Hokkaidō, NE Japan 43°14′N 140°38′E
94 L12 Furudal Dalarna, C Sweden 61°10′N 15°07′E
164 L12 Furukawa var. Hida. Gifu, Honshū, SW Japan 36°13′N 137°11′E
165 Q10 Furukawa var. Hurukawa, Ōsaki. Miyagi, Honshū, C Japan 38°36′N 140°57′E
54 F10 Fusagasugá Cundinamarca, C Colombia 04°22′N 74°21′W
Fusan see Busan
Fushë-Arëzi/Fushë-Arrësi see Fushë-Arrëz
113 L18 Fushë-Arrëz var. Fushë-Arëzi, Fushë-Arrësi. Shkodër, N Albania 42°05′N 20°01′E
113 N16 Fushë Kosovë Serb. Kosovo Polje. C Kosovo 42°40′N 21°07′E
Fushë-Kruja see Fushë-Krujë
113 K19 Fushë-Krujë var. Fushë-Kruja. Durrës, C Albania 41°30′N 19°43′E
163 V12 Fushun var. Fou-shan, Fu-shun. Liaoning, NE China 41°50′N 123°54′E
Fu-shun see Fushun
Fusin see Fuxin
108 G10 Fusio Ticino, S Switzerland 46°27′N 08°39′E
163 X11 Fusong Jilin, NE China 42°20′N 127°17′E
101 K24 Füssen Bayern, S Germany 47°34′N 10°43′E
160 K15 Fusui var. Xinning; prev. Funan. Guangxi Zhuangzu Zizhiqu, S China 22°39′N 107°49′E
Futa Jallon see Fouta Djallon
63 G18 Futaleufú Los Lagos, S Chile 43°14′S 71°50′W
112 K10 Futog Vojvodina, NW Serbia 45°15′N 19°43′E
165 O14 Futtsu var. Huttu. Chiba, Honshū, S Japan 35°11′N 139°52′E
187 S15 Futuna island S Vanuatu
190 D12 Futuna, Île island S Wallis and Futuna
161 Q11 Futun Xi ∽ SE China
160 L5 Fuxian var. Fu Xian. Shaanxi, C China 36°03′N 109°19′E
Fuxian see Wafangdian
Fu Xian see Fuxian
160 G13 Fuxian Hu ◎ SW China
163 U12 Fuxin var. Fou-hsin, Fu-hsin, Fusin. Liaoning, NE China 41°59′N 121°40′E
Fuxing see Wangmo
161 P7 Fuyang Anhui, E China 32°52′N 115°51′E
Fuyang see Fuchuan
161 O4 Fuyang He ∽ E China
163 U7 Fuyu Heilongjiang, NE China 47°48′N 124°26′E
163 Z6 Fuyuan Heilongjiang, NE China 48°20′N 134°22′E
Fuyu/Fu-yü see Songyuan
158 M3 Fuyun var. Koktokay. Xinjiang Uygur Zizhiqu, NW China 46°58′N 89°30′E
111 L22 Füzesabony Heves, E Hungary 47°46′N 20°25′E
161 R12 Fuzhou var. Foochow, Fu-chou. province capital Fujian, SE China 26°09′N 119°17′E
161 P11 Fuzhou prev. Linchuan. Jiangxi, S China 27°58′N 116°20′E
137 W13 Füzuli Rus. Fizuli. SW Azerbaijan 39°33′N 47°09′E
119 I20 Fyadory Rus. Fëdory. Brestskaya Voblasts', SW Belarus 51°57′N 26°24′E
95 G23 Fyn Ger. Fünen. island C Denmark
96 H12 Fyne, Loch inlet W Scotland, United Kingdom
95 E16 Fyresvatnet ◎ S Norway
Fyzabad see Faizābād


# G


Gaafu Alifu Atoll see North Huvadhu Atoll
81 O14 Gaalkacyo var. Galka'yo, It. Galcaio. Mudug, C Somalia 06°42′N 47°24′E
145 J11 Gabakly Rus. Kabakly. Lebap Welaýaty, NE Turkmenistan 39°45′N 62°30′E
114 H8 Gabare Vratsa, NW Bulgaria 43°20′N 23°57′E
102 K15 Gabas ∽ SW France
Gabasumdo see Tongde
35 T7 Gabbs Nevada, W USA 38°51′N 117°55′W
82 B12 Gabela Kwanza Sul, W Angola 10°50′S 14°21′E
Gaberones see Gaborone
189 X14 Gabert island Caroline Islands, E Micronesia
74 M7 Gabès var. Qābis. E Tunisia 33°53′N 10°03′E
74 M6 Gabès, Golfe de Ar. Khalīj Qābis. gulf E Tunisia
Gablonz an der Neisse see Jablonec nad Nisou
Gablös see Cavalese
79 E18 Gabon off. Gabonese Republic, Fr. République Gabonaise. ◆ republic C Africa
Gabonaise, République see Gabon
Gabonese Republic see Gabon
83 I20 Gaborone prev. Gaberones. ● (Botswana) South East, SE Botswana 24°42′S 25°50′E
83 I20 Gaborone ✈ South East, SE Botswana 24°45′S 25°49′E
104 K8 Gabriel y Galán, Embalse de ⊞ W Spain
143 U15 Gābrik, Rūd-e ∽ SE Iran
114 J9 Gabrovo Gabrovo, N Bulgaria 42°54′N 25°19′E
114 J9 Gabrovo ◆ province N Bulgaria
76 H12 Gabú prev. Nova Lamego. E Guinea-Bissau 12°16′N 14°09′W
29 O6 Gackle North Dakota, N USA 46°34′N 99°07′W
113 I15 Gacko Republika Srpska, S Bosnia and Herzegovina 43°08′N 18°29′E
155 F17 Gadag Karnātaka, W India 15°25′N 75°37′E
93 G15 Gäddede Jämtland, C Sweden 64°30′N 14°15′E
159 S12 Gadê var. Kequ; prev. Pagqên. Qinghai, C China 33°56′N 99°49′E
Gades/Gadier/Gadir/Gadire see Cádiz
105 P15 Gádor, Sierra de ▲▲ S Spain
149 S15 Gadra Sindh, SE Pakistan 25°39′N 70°28′E
23 Q3 Gadsden Alabama, S USA 34°00′N 86°00′W
36 H15 Gadsden Arizona, SW USA 32°33′N 114°45′W
Gadyach see Hadyach
124 J3 Gadzhiyevo Murmanskaya Oblast', NW Russia 69°16′N 33°20′E
79 H15 Gadzi Mambéré-Kadéï, SW Central African Republic 04°46′N 16°42′E
116 J13 Găeşti Dâmboviţa, S Romania 44°42′N 25°19′E
107 J17 Gaeta Lazio, C Italy 41°12′N 13°35′E
107 J17 Gaeta, Golfo di var. Gulf of Gaeta. gulf C Italy
Gaeta, Gulf of see Gaeta, Golfo di
188 L14 Gaferut atoll Caroline Islands, W Micronesia
21 Q10 Gaffney South Carolina, SE USA 35°03′N 81°40′W
Gäfle see Gävle
Gäfleborg see Gävleborg
74 M6 Gafsa var. Qafşah. W Tunisia 34°25′N 08°52′E
Gafurov see Ghafurov
126 J3 Gagarin prev. Gzhatsk. Smolenskaya Oblast', W Russia 55°33′N 35°00′E
147 O10 Gagarin Jizzax Viloyati, C Uzbekistan 40°40′N 68°04′E
116 M12 Găgăuzia ◆ cultural region S Moldova
101 G21 Gaggenau Baden-Württemberg, SW Germany 48°48′N 08°19′E
188 F16 Gagil Tamil var. Gagil-Tomil. island Caroline Islands, W Micronesia
Gagil-Tomil see Gagil Tamil
127 O4 Gagino Nizhegorodskaya Oblast', W Russia 55°18′N 45°01′E
107 Q19 Gagliano del Capo Puglia, SE Italy 39°49′N 18°22′E
94 L13 Gagnef Dalarna, C Sweden 60°34′N 15°04′E
76 M17 Gagnoa C Ivory Coast 06°11′N 05°56′W
13 N10 Gagnon Québec, E Canada 51°56′N 68°16′W
Gago Coutinho see Lumbala N'Guimbo
137 P8 Gagra NW Georgia 43°17′N 40°18′E
31 S13 Gahanna Ohio, N USA 40°01′N 82°52′W
143 R13 Gahkom Hormozgān, S Iran 28°14′N 55°48′E
Gahnpa see Ganta
57 Q19 Gaíba, Laguna ◎ E Bolivia
153 T13 Gaibandha var. Gaibanda. Rajshahi, NW Bangladesh 25°21′N 89°36′E
Gaibhlte, Cnoc Mór na n see Galtymore Mountain
109 R9 Gail ∽ S Austria
101 I21 Gaildorf Baden-Württemberg, S Germany 48°41′N 10°08′E
103 N15 Gaillac var. Gaillac-sur-Tarn. Tarn, S France 43°54′N 01°54′E
Gaillac-sur-Tarn see Gaillac
Gaillimh see Galway
Gaillimhe, Cuan na see Galway Bay
109 Q9 Gailtaler Alpen ▲▲ S Austria
63 J17 Gaimán Chaco, S Argentina 43°15′S 65°30′W
20 K8 Gainesboro Tennessee, S USA 36°20′N 85°41′W
23 V10 Gainesville Florida, SE USA 29°39′N 82°19′W
23 T2 Gainesville Georgia, SE USA 34°18′N 83°49′W
27 U8 Gainesville Missouri, C USA 36°37′N 92°28′W
25 T5 Gainesville Texas, SW USA 33°39′N 97°08′W
109 X5 Gainfarn Niederösterreich, NE Austria 47°59′N 16°11′E
97 N18 Gainsborough E England, United Kingdom 53°24′N 00°48′W
182 G6 Gairdner, Lake salt lake South Australia
Gaissane see Gáissát
92 L8 Gáissát var. Gaissane. ▲▲ N Norway
43 T15 Gaital, Cerro ▲ C Panama 08°37′N 80°04′W
21 W3 Gaithersburg Maryland, NE USA 39°08′N 77°13′W
163 U13 Gaizhou Liaoning, NE China 40°24′N 122°17′E
Gaizina Kalns see Gaiziņkalns
118 H7 Gaiziņkalns var. Gaizina Kalns. ▲ E Latvia 56°51′N 25°58′E
Gajac see Villeneuve-sur-Lot
197 T10 Gakkel Ridge var. Arctic Mid Oceanic Ridge; prev. Nansen Cordillera. seamount range Arctic Ocean
39 S10 Gakona Alaska, USA 62°21′N 145°16′W
Galaassiya see Galaosiyo
114 K10 Galabovo Gŭlŭbovo. Stara Zagora, C Bulgaria 42°08′N 25°51′E
Ğalāğil see Jalājil
Galam, Pulau see Gelam, Pulau
62 J6 Galán, Cerro ▲ NW Argentina 25°54′S 66°45′W
111 H21 Galanta Hung. Galánta. Trnavský Kraj, W Slovakia 48°12′N 17°45′E
146 L11 Galaosiyo Rus. Galaassiya. Buxoro Viloyati, C Uzbekistan 39°53′N 64°25′E
57 B17 Galápagos off. Provincia de Galápagos. ◆ province W Ecuador, E Pacific Ocean
193 P8 Galapagos Fracture Zone tectonic feature E Pacific Ocean
Galapagos Islands see Colón, Archipiélago de
Galápagos, Islas de los see Colón, Archipiélago de
Galápagos, Provincia de see Galápagos
193 S9 Galapagos Rise undersea feature E Pacific Ocean 15°00′S 97°00′W
96 K13 Galashiels SE Scotland, United Kingdom 55°37′N 02°49′W
116 M12 Galaţi Ger. Galatz. Galaţi, E Romania 45°27′N 28°00′E
116 L12 Galaţi ◆ county E Romania
107 Q19 Galatina Puglia, SE Italy 40°10′N 18°10′E
107 Q19 Galatone Puglia, SE Italy 40°09′N 18°05′E
Galatz see Galaţi
21 R8 Galax Virginia, NE USA 36°40′N 80°56′W
146 J16 Galaýmor Rus. Kala-i-Mor. Mary Welaýaty, S Turkmenistan 35°40′N 62°28′E
Galcaio see Gaalkacyo
64 P11 Gáldar Gran Canaria, Islas Canarias, NE Atlantic Ocean 28°09′N 15°40′W
94 F11 Galdhøpiggen ▲ S Norway 61°30′N 08°08′E
40 I4 Galeana Chihuahua, N Mexico 30°08′N 107°38′W
41 O9 Galeana Nuevo León, NE Mexico 24°45′N 99°59′W
60 P9 Galeão ✈ (Rio de Janeiro) Rio de Janeiro, SE Brazil 22°48′S 43°16′W
171 R10 Galela Pulau Halmahera, E Indonesia 01°52′N 127°48′E
39 O9 Galena Alaska, USA 64°43′N 156°55′W
30 K10 Galena Illinois, N USA 42°25′N 90°25′W
27 R7 Galena Kansas, C USA 37°04′N 94°38′W
27 T8 Galena Missouri, C USA 36°45′N 93°30′W
45 V15 Galeota Point headland Trinidad, Trinidad and Tobago 10°07′N 60°59′W
105 P13 Galera Andalucía, S Spain 37°45′N 02°33′W
45 Y16 Galera Point headland Trinidad, Trinidad and Tobago 10°49′N 60°54′W
56 A5 Galera, Punta headland NW Ecuador 0°49′N 80°03′W
30 K12 Galesburg Illinois, N USA 40°57′N 90°22′W
30 J7 Galesville Wisconsin, N USA 44°04′N 91°21′W
18 F12 Galeton Pennsylvania, NE USA 41°43′N 77°38′W
116 H9 Gâlgău Hung. Galgó; prev. Gîlgău. Sălaj, NW Romania 47°17′N 23°43′E
Galgó see Gâlgău
Galgóc see Hlohovec
81 N15 Galguduud off. Gobolka Galguduud. ◆ region E Somalia
Galguduud, Gobolka see Galguduud
137 Q9 Gali W Georgia 42°40′N 41°39′E
125 N14 Galich Kostromskaya Oblast', NW Russia 58°21′N 42°21′E
114 H7 Galiche Vratsa, NW Bulgaria 43°36′N 23°53′E
104 H3 Galicia anc. Gallaecia. ◆ autonomous community NW Spain
64 M8 Galicia Bank undersea feature E Atlantic Ocean 11°45′W 42°40′N
Galilee see HaGalil
181 W7 Galilee, Lake ◎ Queensland, NE Australia
Galilee, Sea of see Kinneret, Yam
106 E11 Galileo Galilei ✈ (Pisa) Toscana, C Italy 43°40′N 10°22′E
31 S12 Galion Ohio, N USA 40°43′N 82°47′W
67 P2 Galite, Île de la var. Jalta. island N Tunisia
Galka'yo see Gaalkacyo
146 K12 Galkynyş prev. Rus. Deynau, Dyanev, Turkm. Dänew. Lebap Welaýaty, NE Turkmenistan 39°16′N 63°10′E
80 H11 Gallabat Gedaref, E Sudan 12°57′N 36°10′E
Gallaecia see Galicia
147 O11 G'allaorol Jizzax Viloyati, C Uzbekistan 40°01′N 67°30′E
106 C7 Gallarate Lombardia, NW Italy 45°39′N 08°47′E
27 S2 Gallatin Missouri, C USA 39°54′N 93°57′W
20 J8 Gallatin Tennessee, S USA 36°22′N 86°28′W
33 R11 Gallatin Peak ▲ Montana, NW USA 45°22′N 111°21′W
33 R12 Gallatin River ∽ Montana/Wyoming, NW USA
155 J26 Galle prev. Point de Galle. Southern Province, SW Sri Lanka 06°04′N 80°12′E
105 S5 Gállego ∽ NE Spain
193 Q8 Gallego Rise undersea feature E Pacific Ocean 02°00′S 115°00′W
Gallegos see Río Gallegos
63 H23 Gallegos, Río ∽ Argentina/Chile
Gallia see France
22 K10 Galliano Louisiana, S USA 29°26′N 90°18′W
114 G13 Gallikós ∽ N Greece
37 S12 Gallinas Peak ▲ New Mexico, SW USA 34°14′N 105°47′W
54 H3 Gallinas, Punta headland NE Colombia 12°27′N 71°44′W
37 T11 Gallinas River ∽ New Mexico, SW USA
107 Q19 Gallipoli Puglia, SE Italy 40°08′N 18°E
Gallipoli see Gelibolu
Gallipoli Peninsula see Gelibolu Yarımadası
31 T15 Gallipolis Ohio, N USA 38°49′N 82°14′W
92 J12 Gällivare Lapp. Váhtjer. Norrbotten, N Sweden 67°08′N 20°39′E
109 T4 Gallneukirchen Oberösterreich, N Austria 48°22′N 14°25′E
93 G17 Gällö Jämtland, C Sweden 62°57′N 15°15′E
105 Q7 Gallo ∽ C Spain
107 I23 Gallo, Capo headland Sicilia, Italy, C Mediterranean Sea 38°13′N 13°18′E
37 P13 Gallo Mountains ▲▲ New Mexico, SW USA
18 G8 Galloo Island island New York, NE USA
97 H15 Galloway, Mull of headland S Scotland, United Kingdom 54°37′N 04°54′W
37 P10 Gallup New Mexico, SW USA 35°32′N 108°45′W
105 R5 Gallur Aragón, NE Spain 41°51′N 01°21′W
Galma see Guelma
163 N9 Galshar var. Buyant. Hentiy, C Mongolia 46°15′N 110°50′E
162 I6 Galt var. Ider. Hövsgöl, C Mongolia 48°45′N 99°52′E
35 O8 Galt California, W USA 38°13′N 121°19′W
74 C10 Galtat-Zemmour C Western Sahara 25°07′N 12°21′W
95 G22 Galten Midtjylland, C Denmark 56°09′N 09°54′E
Galtern see Kultsjön
97 D20 Galtymore Mountain Ir. Cnoc Mór na nGaibhlte. ▲ S Ireland 52°21′N 08°09′W
97 D20 Galty Mountains Ir. Na Gaibhlte. ▲▲ S Ireland
30 K11 Galva Illinois, N USA 41°10′N 90°02′W
25 X12 Galveston Texas, SW USA 29°17′N 94°48′W
25 W11 Galveston Bay inlet Texas, SW USA
25 W12 Galveston Island island Texas, SW USA
61 B18 Gálvez Santa Fe, C Argentina 32°03′S 61°14′W
97 C18 Galway Ir. Gaillimh. W Ireland 53°16′N 09°03′W
97 B18 Galway Ir. Gaillimh. cultural region W Ireland
97 B18 Galway Bay Ir. Cuan na Gaillimhe. bay W Ireland
83 F18 Gam Otjozondjupa, NE Namibia 20°10′S 20°51′E
164 L14 Gamagōri Aichi, Honshū, SW Japan 34°49′N 137°15′E
54 F7 Gamarra Cesar, N Colombia 08°21′N 73°46′W
Gámas see Kaamanen
158 L17 Gamba Xizang Zizhiqu, W China 28°13′N 88°32′E
Gamba see Zamtang
77 P14 Gambaga NE Ghana 10°32′N 00°28′W
80 G13 Gambēla Gambēla Hizboch, W Ethiopia 08°09′N 34°15′E
81 H14 Gambēla Hizboch ◆ federal region W Ethiopia
38 K10 Gambell Saint Lawrence Island, Alaska, USA 63°44′N 171°41′W
76 I12 Gambia Fr. Gambie. ∽ W Africa
64 K12 Gambia Plain undersea feature E Atlantic Ocean
Gambia, Republic of The see Gambia, The
76 E12 Gambia, The off. Republic of The Gambia. ◆ republic W Africa
Gambie see Gambia
31 T13 Gambier Ohio, N USA 40°22′N 82°24′W
191 Y13 Gambier, Îles island group E French Polynesia
182 G10 Gambier Islands island group South Australia
79 H19 Gamboma Plateaux, E Congo 01°53′S 15°51′E
79 G16 Gamboula Mambéré-Kadéï, SW Central African Republic 04°09′N 15°12′E
37 P10 Gamerco New Mexico, SW USA 35°34′N 108°45′W
137 V12 Gamış Dağı ▲ W Azerbaijan 40°18′N 46°15′E
Gamlakarleby see Kokkola
95 N18 Gamleby Kalmar, S Sweden 57°54′N 16°25′E
Gammelstad see Gammelstaden
93 J14 Gammelstaden var. Gammelstad. Norrbotten, N Sweden 65°38′N 22°05′E
Gammouda see Sidi Bouzid
155 J25 Gampaha Western Province, W Sri Lanka 07°05′N 80°00′E
155 K25 Gampola Central Province, C Sri Lanka 07°10′N 80°34′E
167 S5 Gâm, Sông ∽ N Vietnam
92 L7 Gamvik Finnmark, N Norway 71°04′N 28°08′E
150 H13 Gan Addu Atoll, C Maldives
Gan see Gansu, China
Gan see Jiangxi, China
Ganaane see Juba
37 O10 Ganado Arizona, SW USA 35°42′N 109°31′W
25 U12 Ganado Texas, SW USA 29°02′N 96°30′W
14 L14 Gananoque Ontario, SE Canada 44°21′N 76°11′W
Ganāveh see Bandar-e Gonāveh
137 V11 Gäncä Rus. Gyandzha; prev. Kirovabad, Yelisavetpol. W Azerbaijan 40°42′N 46°23′E
Ganchi see Ghonchí
Gand see Gent
82 B13 Ganda var. Mariano Machado, Port. Vila Mariano Machado. Benguela, W Angola 13°02′S 14°40′E
79 L22 Gandajika Kasai-Oriental, S Dem. Rep. Congo 06°42′S 24°01′E
153 O12 Gandak Nep. Nārāyāni. ∽ India/Nepal
13 U11 Gander Newfoundland and Labrador, SE Canada 48°56′N 54°33′W
13 U11 Gander ✈ Newfoundland and Labrador, E Canada 49°03′N 54°49′W
100 G11 Ganderkesee Niedersachsen, NW Germany 53°01′N 08°33′E
105 T7 Gandesa Cataluña, NE Spain 41°03′N 00°26′E
154 B10 Gāndhīdhām Gujarāt, W India 23°08′N 70°05′E
154 D10 Gāndhīnagar state capital Gujarāt, W India 23°12′N 72°37′E
154 F9 Gāndhi Sāgar ◎ C India
105 T11 Gandia prev. Gandía. Comunitat Valenciana, E Spain 38°59′N 00°11′W
Gandía see Gandia
159 O10 Gang Qinghai, W China
152 G9 Gangānagar Rājasthān, NW India 29°54′N 73°56′E
152 I12 Gangāpur Rājasthān, N India 26°30′N 76°49′E
153 S17 Ganga Sāgar West Bengal, NE India 21°39′N 88°05′E
Gangavathi see Gangāwati
155 G17 Gangāwati var. Gangavathi. Karnātaka, C India 15°26′N 76°35′E
159 S9 Gangca var. Shaliuhe. Qinghai, C China 37°21′N 100°09′E
158 H14 Gangdisê Shan Eng. Kailas Range. ▲▲ W China
103 Q15 Ganges Hérault, S France 43°57′N 03°42′E
153 P13 Ganges Ben. Padma. ∽ Bangladesh/India see also Padma
Ganges see Padma
Ganges Cone see Ganges Fan
173 S3 Ganges Fan var. Ganges Cone. undersea feature N Bay of Bengal 12°00′N 87°00′E
153 U17 Ganges, Mouths of the delta Bangladesh/India
107 K23 Gangi anc. Engyum. Sicilia, Italy, C Mediterranean Sea 37°48′N 14°13′E
163 Y14 Gangneung Jap. Kōryō; prev. Kangnŭng. NE South Korea 37°47′N 128°51′E
152 K8 Gangotri Uttarākhand, N India 30°56′N 79°02′E
Gangra see Çankırı
153 S11 Gangtok state capital Sikkim, N India 27°20′N 88°39′E
159 W11 Gangu var. Daxiangshan. Gansu, C China 34°38′N 105°18′E
163 U5 Gan He ∽ NE China
171 S12 Gani Pulau Halmahera, E Indonesia 0°45′S 128°13′E




◆ Country ● Country Capital ◇ Dependent Territory ○ Dependent Territory Capital ◆ Administrative Regions ✈ International Airport ▲ Mountain ▲▲ Mountain Range Ж Volcano ∽ River ◎ Lake ⊞ Reservoir

GAN JIANG – GERMAN SOUTHWEST AFRICA


161 O12 **Gan Jiang** ≈ S China
163 U11 **Ganjig** var. Horqin Zuoyi Houqi. Nei Mongol Zizhiqu, N China 42°53′N 122°22′E
146 H15 **Gannaly** Ahal Welaýaty, S Turkmenistan 37°02′N 60°43′E
163 U7 **Gannan** Heilongjiang, NE China 47°58′N 123°36′E
103 P10 **Gannat** Allier, C France 46°06′N 03°12′E
33 T14 **Gannett Peak** ▲ Wyoming, C USA 43°10′N 109°39′W
29 O10 **Gannvalley** South Dakota, N USA 44°01′N 98°59′W
**Ganqu** see Lhünzhub
109 Y3 **Gänserndorf** Niederösterreich, NE Austria 48°21′N 16°43′E
**Gansos, Lago dos** see Goose Lake
159 T9 **Gansu** var. Gan, Gansu Sheng, Kansu. ◈ province N China
**Gansu Sheng** see Gansu
76 K16 **Ganta** var. Gahnpa. NE Liberia 07°15′N 08°59′W
182 H11 **Gantheaume, Cape** headland South Australia 36°04′S 137°28′E
**Gantsevichi** see Hantsavichy
161 Q6 **Ganyu** var. Qingkou. Jiangsu, E China 34°52′N 119°11′E
144 D12 **Ganyushkino** Atyrau, SW Kazakhstan 46°38′N 49°12′E
161 O12 **Ganzhou** Jiangxi, S China 25°51′N 114°59′E
**Ganzhou** see Zhangye
77 Q10 **Gao** Gao, E Mali 16°16′N 00°03′E
77 R10 **Gao** ◈ region SE Mali
161 O10 **Gao'an** Jiangxi, S China 28°24′N 115°27′E
**Gaocheng** see Litang
**Gaoleshan** see Xianfeng
161 N5 **Gaoping** Shanxi, C China 35°51′N 112°55′E
159 S8 **Gaotai** Gansu, N China 39°22′N 99°44′E
**Gaoth Dobhair** see Gweedore
77 O14 **Gaoua** SW Burkina Faso 10°18′N 03°12′W
76 I13 **Gaoual** N Guinea 11°44′N 13°14′W
**Gaoxiong** see Kaohsiung
161 R7 **Gaoyou** var. Dayishan. Jiangsu, E China 32°48′N 119°26′E
161 R7 **Gaoyou Hu** ◎ E China
160 M15 **Gaozhou** Guangdong, S China 21°56′N 110°49′E
103 T13 **Gap** anc. Vapincum. Hautes-Alpes, SE France 44°33′N 06°05′E
146 E9 **Gaplaňgyr Platosy** Rus. Plato Kaplangky. ridge Turkmenistan/Uzbekistan
156 G13 **Gar** var. Shiquanhe. Xizang Zizhiqu, W China 32°31′N 80°04′E
**Gar** see Gar Xincun
**Garabekevyul** see Garabekewül
146 L13 **Garabekewül** Rus. Garabekevyul, Karabekaul. Lebap Welaýaty, E Turkmenistan 38°31′N 64°04′E
146 K15 **Garabil Belentligi** Rus. Vozvyshennost' Karabil'. ▲▲ S Turkmenistan
146 A8 **Garabogaz** Rus. Bekdash. Balkan Welaýaty, NW Turkmenistan 41°33′N 52°33′E
146 B9 **Garabogaz Aylagy** Rus. Zaliv Kara-Bogaz-Gol. bay NW Turkmenistan
146 A9 **Garabogazköl** Rus. Kara-Bogaz-Gol. Balkan Welaýaty, NW Turkmenistan 41°03′N 52°52′E
43 V16 **Garachiné** Darién, SE Panama 08°03′N 78°22′W
43 V16 **Garachiné, Punta** headland SE Panama 08°05′N 78°23′W
146 K12 **Garagan** Rus. Karagan. Ahal Welaýaty, C Turkmenistan 38°16′N 57°34′E
54 G10 **Garagoa** Boyacá, C Colombia 05°05′N 73°20′W
146 A11 **Garagöl'** Rus. Karagel'. Balkan Welaýaty, W Turkmenistan 39°24′N 53°13′E
146 F12 **Garagum** var. Garagumy, Qara Qum, Eng. Black Sand Desert, Kara Kum; prev. Peski Karakumy. desert C Turkmenistan
146 E12 **Garagum Kanaly** var. Kara Kum Canal, Rus. Karagumskiy Kanal, Karakumskiy Kanal. canal C Turkmenistan
**Garagumy** see Garagum
183 S4 **Garah** New South Wales, SE Australia 29°07′S 149°37′E
64 O11 **Garajonay** ▲ Gomera, Islas Canarias, NE Atlantic Ocean 28°07′N 17°14′W
76 L13 **Garalo** Sikasso, SW Mali 10°58′N 07°26′W
**Garam** see Hron, Slovakia
146 L14 **Garamätnyýaz** Rus. Karamet-Niyaz. Lebap Welaýaty, E Turkmenistan 37°45′N 64°28′E
**Garamszentkereszt** see Žiar nad Hronom
77 Q13 **Garango** S Burkina Faso 11°45′N 00°30′W
59 Q15 **Garanhuns** Pernambuco, E Brazil 08°53′S 36°28′W
188 H5 **Garapan** Saipan, S Northern Mariana Islands 15°12′S 145°43′E
**Gárassavvon** see Karesuando
**Gárassavon** see Kaaresuvanto
78 J13 **Garba** Bamingui-Bangoran, N Central African Republic 09°09′N 20°24′E
**Garba** see Jiulong
81 L16 **Garbahaarrey** It. Garba Harre. Gedo, SW Somalia 03°14′N 42°18′E
**Garba Harre** see Garbahaarrey
81 J18 **Garba Tula** Isiolo, C Kenya 0°31′N 38°35′E
27 N9 **Garber** Oklahoma, C USA 36°26′N 97°35′W
34 L4 **Garberville** California, W USA 40°07′N 123°48′W
**Garbo** see Lhozhag
100 I12 **Garbsen** Niedersachsen, N Germany 52°25′N 09°36′E
60 K9 **Garça** São Paulo, S Brazil 22°14′S 49°36′W
104 L10 **García de Solá, Embalse de** ⊠ C Spain
103 Q14 **Gard** ◈ department S France
103 Q14 **Gard** ≈ S France
106 F7 **Garda, Lago di** var. Benaco, Eng. Lake Garda, Ger. Gardasee. ◎ NE Italy
**Garda, Lake** see Garda, Lago di
149 Q5 **Gardan Dēwāl** var. Gardan Divāl, Gardan Diwal. Wardak, C Afghanistan 34°30′N 68°15′E
**Gardan Divāl** see Gardan Dēwāl
**Gardan Diwal** see Gardan Dēwāl
103 S15 **Gardanne** Bouches-du-Rhône, SE France 43°27′N 05°28′E
**Gardasee** see Garda, Lago di
100 L12 **Gardelegen** Sachsen-Anhalt, C Germany 52°31′N 11°25′E
14 B10 **Garden** ≈ Ontario, S Canada
23 X6 **Garden City** Georgia, SE USA 32°06′N 81°09′W
26 I6 **Garden City** Kansas, C USA 37°57′N 100°54′W
27 S5 **Garden City** Missouri, C USA 38°34′N 94°12′W
25 N8 **Garden City** Texas, SW USA 31°51′N 101°30′W
23 P3 **Gardendale** Alabama, S USA 33°39′N 86°48′W
31 P5 **Garden Island** island Michigan, N USA
22 M11 **Garden Island Bay** bay Louisiana, S USA
31 O5 **Garden Peninsula** peninsula Michigan, N USA
**Garden State, The** see New Jersey
95 I14 **Gardermoen** Akershus, S Norway 60°10′N 11°04′E
**Gardeyz/Gardez** see Gardēz
149 Q6 **Gardēz** var. Gardeyz, Gordiaz; prev. Gardīz. Paktīyā, E Afghanistan 33°35′N 69°14′E
93 G14 **Gardiken** ◎ N Sweden
19 Q7 **Gardiner** Maine, NE USA 44°13′N 69°46′W
33 S12 **Gardiner** Montana, NW USA 45°02′N 110°42′W
19 N13 **Gardiners Island** island New York, NE USA
**Gardner Island** see Nikumaroro
19 T6 **Gardner Lake** ◎ Maine, NE USA
35 Q6 **Gardnerville** Nevada, W USA 38°55′N 119°44′W
**Gardo** see Qardho
106 F7 **Gardone Val Trompia** Lombardia, N Italy 45°40′N 10°11′E
**Garegasnjárga** see Karigasniemi
38 F17 **Gareloi Island** island Aleutian Islands, Alaska, USA
**Gares** see Puente la Reina
106 B10 **Garessio** Piemonte, NE Italy 44°14′N 08°01′E
32 M9 **Garfield** Washington, NW USA 47°00′N 117°07′W
31 U11 **Garfield Heights** Ohio, N USA 41°25′N 81°36′W
**Gargaliani** see Gargaliánoi
115 D21 **Gargaliánoi** var. Gargaliani. Pelopónnisos, S Greece 37°04′N 21°38′E
107 N15 **Gargàno, Promontorio del** headland SE Italy 41°51′N 16°11′E
108 J8 **Gargellen** Graubünden, W Switzerland 46°57′N 09°55′E
93 I14 **Gargnäs** Västerbotten, N Sweden 65°19′N 18°00′E
118 C11 **Gargždai** Klaipėda, W Lithuania 55°42′N 21°24′E
154 J13 **Garhchiroli** Mahārāshtra, C India 20°14′N 79°58′E
153 O15 **Garhwa** Jhārkhand, N India 24°07′N 83°52′E
171 V13 **Gariau** Papua Barat, E Indonesia 03°43′S 134°54′E
83 E24 **Garies** Northern Cape, W South Africa 30°30′S 18°00′E
107 K17 **Garigliano** ≈ C Italy
81 K19 **Garissa** Garissa, E Kenya 0°27′S 39°39′E
21 V11 **Garland** North Carolina, SE USA 34°45′N 78°25′W
25 T6 **Garland** Texas, SW USA 32°50′N 96°37′W
36 L1 **Garland** Utah, W USA 41°43′N 112°07′W
106 D8 **Garlasco** Lombardia, N Italy 45°12′N 08°59′E
119 F14 **Garliava** Kaunas, S Lithuania 54°49′N 23°52′E
**Garm** see Gharm
142 M9 **Garm, Āb-e** var. Rūd-e Khersān. ≈ SW Iran
**Garmik** see Germik
101 K25 **Garmisch-Partenkirchen** Bayern, S Germany 47°30′N 11°05′E
143 O5 **Garmsār** prev. Qishlaq. Semnān, N Iran 35°18′N 52°22′E
**Garmser** see Darwēshān
29 V12 **Garner** Iowa, C USA 43°06′N 93°36′W
21 U9 **Garner** North Carolina, SE USA 35°42′N 78°36′W
27 Q5 **Garnett** Kansas, C USA 38°16′N 95°15′W
99 M25 **Garnich** Luxembourg, SW Luxembourg 49°37′N 05°57′E
182 M8 **Garnpung, Lake** salt lake New South Wales, SE Australia
**Garoe** see Garoowe
**Garoet** see Garut
153 U13 **Gāro Hills** hill range NE India
102 K13 **Garonne** anc. Garumna. ≈ S France
80 P13 **Garoowe** var. Garoe. Nugaal, N Somalia 08°24′N 48°29′E
78 F12 **Garoua** var. Garua. Nord, N Cameroon 09°17′N 13°22′E
79 G14 **Garoua Boulaï** Est, E Cameroon 05°54′N 14°33′E
77 O10 **Garou, Lac** ◎ C Mali
95 L16 **Garphyttan** Örebro, C Sweden 59°18′N 14°54′E
29 R11 **Garretson** South Dakota, N USA 43°43′N 96°30′W
31 Q11 **Garrett** Indiana, N USA 41°21′N 85°08′W
33 Q10 **Garrison** Montana, NW USA 46°32′N 112°46′W
28 M4 **Garrison** North Dakota, N USA 47°36′N 101°25′W
25 X8 **Garrison** Texas, SW USA 31°49′N 94°29′W
28 L4 **Garrison Dam** dam North Dakota, N USA
104 J9 **Garrovillas** Extremadura, W Spain 39°43′N 06°33′W
**Garrygala** see Magtymguly
8 L8 **Garry Lake** ◎ Nunavut, N Canada
**Gars** see Gars am Kamp
109 W3 **Gars am Kamp** var. Gars. Niederösterreich, NE Austria 48°35′N 15°40′E
81 K20 **Garsen** Tana River, S Kenya 02°16′S 40°07′E
**Garshy** see Garşy
14 F10 **Garson** Ontario, S Canada 46°33′N 80°51′W
109 T5 **Garsten** Oberösterreich, N Austria 48°00′N 14°24′E
146 A9 **Garşy** var. Garshy, Rus. Karshi. Balkan Welaýaty, NW Turkmenistan 40°45′N 52°50′E
**Gartar** see Qianning
102 M10 **Gartempe** ≈ C France
**Gartog** see Markam
**Garua** see Garoua
83 D21 **Garub** //Karas, SW Namibia 26°33′S 16°00′E
**Garumna** see Garonne
169 P16 **Garut** prev. Garoet. Jawa, C Indonesia 07°15′S 107°55′E
185 C20 **Garvie Mountains** ▲▲ South Island, New Zealand
110 N12 **Garwolin** Mazowieckie, E Poland 51°54′N 21°36′E
25 U12 **Garwood** Texas, SW USA 29°25′N 96°24′W
158 G13 **Gar Xincun** prev. Gar. Xizang Zizhiqu, W China 32°04′N 80°01′E
31 N11 **Gary** Indiana, N USA 41°36′N 87°21′W
25 X7 **Gary** Texas, SW USA 32°00′N 94°21′W
158 G13 **Gar Zangbo** ≈ W China
160 F8 **Garzê** Sichuan, C China 31°40′N 99°58′E
54 E12 **Garzón** Huila, S Colombia 02°14′N 75°37′W
**Gasan-Kuli** see Esenguly
31 P13 **Gas City** Indiana, N USA 40°29′N 85°36′W
102 K15 **Gascogne** Eng. Gascony. cultural region S France
26 V5 **Gasconade River** ≈ Missouri, C USA
**Gascony** see Gascogne
180 H9 **Gascoyne Junction** Western Australia 25°06′S 115°10′E
173 V8 **Gascoyne Plain** undersea feature E Indian Ocean
180 H9 **Gascoyne River** ≈ Western Australia
192 J11 **Gascoyne Tablemount** undersea feature N Tasman Sea 36°30′S 156°30′E
67 U6 **Gash** var. Nahr al Qāsh. ≈ W Sudan
149 X3 **Gasherbrum** ▲ NE Pakistan 35°39′N 76°34′E
**Gas Hu** see Gas Hure Hu
77 X12 **Gashua** Yobe, NE Nigeria 12°55′N 11°10′E
159 N9 **Gas Hure Hu** var. Gas Hu. ◎ C China
**Gásluokta** see Kjøpsvik
186 G7 **Gasmata** New Britain, E Papua New Guinea 06°12′S 150°25′E
23 V14 **Gasparilla Island** island Florida, SE USA
169 O13 **Gaspar, Selat** strait W Indonesia
15 Y6 **Gaspé** Québec, SE Canada 48°50′N 64°33′W
15 Z6 **Gaspé, Cap de** headland Québec, SE Canada 48°45′N 64°10′W
15 X6 **Gaspé, Péninsule de** var. Péninsule de la Gaspésie. peninsula Québec, SE Canada
**Gaspésie, Péninsule de la** see Gaspé, Péninsule de
77 W15 **Gassol** Taraba, E Nigeria 08°28′N 10°24′E
**Gastein** see Badgastein
21 R10 **Gastonia** North Carolina, SE USA 35°14′N 81°12′W
21 V8 **Gaston, Lake** ⊠ North Carolina/Virginia, SE USA
115 D19 **Gastoúni** Dytikí Elláda, S Greece 37°51′N 21°15′E
63 I17 **Gastre** Chubut, S Argentina 42°20′S 69°10′W
**Gat** see Ghāt
105 P15 **Gata, Cabo de** cape S Spain
121 P3 **Gata, Cape** Gk. Akrotírio Gátas. headland S Cyprus 34°34′N 33°03′E
105 T11 **Gata de Gorgos** Comunitat Valenciana, E Spain 38°45′N 00°06′E
116 E12 **Gătaia** Ger. Gataja, Hung. Gátalja; prev. Gáttája. Timiș, W Romania 45°24′N 21°26′E
**Gataja/Gátalja** see Gătaia
**Gátas, Akrotírio** see Gata, Cape
104 J8 **Gata, Sierra de** ▲▲ W Spain
124 G13 **Gatchina** Leningradskaya Oblast', NW Russia 59°34′N 30°06′E
21 P8 **Gate City** Virginia, NE USA 36°38′N 82°37′W
97 M14 **Gateshead** NE England, United Kingdom 54°57′N 01°37′W
21 X8 **Gatesville** North Carolina, SE USA 36°24′N 76°46′W
25 S8 **Gatesville** Texas, SW USA 31°26′N 97°46′W
14 L12 **Gatineau** Québec, SE Canada 45°29′N 75°40′W
14 L11 **Gatineau** ≈ Ontario/Québec, SE Canada
21 N9 **Gatlinburg** Tennessee, S USA 35°42′N 83°30′W
**Gatooma** see Kadoma
**Gättája** see Gătaia
43 T14 **Gatún, Lago** ⊠ C Panama
59 N14 **Gaturiano** Piauí, NE Brazil 06°53′S 41°45′W
97 O22 **Gatwick** ✈ (London) SE England, United Kingdom 51°10′N 00°12′W
187 Y14 **Gau** prev. Ngau. island C Fiji
187 R12 **Gaua** var. Santa Maria. Island Banks Island, N Vanuatu
104 L16 **Gaucín** Andalucía, S Spain 36°31′N 05°19′W
118 J8 **Gauja** Ger. Aa. ≈ Estonia/Latvia
118 I7 **Gaujiena** NE Latvia 57°31′N 26°24′E
94 H9 **Gauldalen** valley S Norway
21 R5 **Gauley River** ≈ West Virginia, NE USA
**Gaul/Gaule** see France
99 D19 **Gaurain-Ramecroix** Hainaut, SW Belgium 50°35′N 03°31′E
95 F15 **Gaustatoppen** ▲ S Norway 59°50′N 08°39′E
83 J21 **Gauteng** off. Gauteng Province; prev. Pretoria-Witwatersrand-Vereeniging. ◈ province NE South Africa
**Gauteng** see Johannesburg, South Africa
**Gauteng** see Germiston, South Africa
**Gauteng Province** see Gauteng
137 U11 **Gavarr** prev. Kamo. C Armenia 40°21′N 45°07′E
143 P14 **Gāvbandī** Hormozgān, S Iran 27°07′N 53°21′E
115 H25 **Gavdopoúla** island SE Greece
115 H26 **Gávdos** island SE Greece
102 K16 **Gave de Pau** var. Gave-de-Pay. ≈ SW France
**Gave-de-Pay** see Gave de Pau
102 J16 **Gave d'Oloron** ≈ SW France
99 E18 **Gavere** Oost-Vlaanderen, NW Belgium 50°56′N 03°41′E
94 N13 **Gävle** var. Gäfle; prev. Gefle. Gävleborg, C Sweden 60°41′N 17°09′E
94 M11 **Gävleborg** var. Gäfleborg, Gefleborg. ◈ county C Sweden
94 O13 **Gävlebukten** bay C Sweden
124 L16 **Gavrilov-Yam** Yaroslavskaya Oblast', W Russia 57°19′N 39°52′E
182 I9 **Gawler** South Australia 34°38′S 138°44′E
182 G7 **Gawler Ranges** hill range South Australia
**Gawso** see Goaso
162 H11 **Gaxun Nur** ◎ N China
153 P14 **Gaya** Bihār, N India 24°48′N 85°E
77 S13 **Gaya** Dosso, SW Niger 11°52′N 03°28′E
**Gaya** see Kyjov
31 Q6 **Gaylord** Michigan, N USA 45°01′N 84°40′W
29 U9 **Gaylord** Minnesota, N USA 44°33′N 94°13′W
181 Y9 **Gayndah** Queensland, E Australia 25°37′S 151°31′E
125 T12 **Gayny** Komi-Permyatskiy Okrug, NW Russia 60°19′N 54°15′E
**Gaysin** see Haysyn
**Gayvorno** see Hayvoron
138 E11 **Gaza** Ar. Ghazzah, Heb. 'Azza. NE Gaza Strip 31°30′N 34°E
83 L20 **Gaza** off. Província de Gaza. ◈ province SW Mozambique
**Gaz-Achak** see Gazojak
147 Q9 **G'azalkent** Rus. Gazalkent. Toshkent Viloyati, E Uzbekistan 41°30′N 69°46′E
**Gazalkent** see G'azalkent
**Gazandzhyk/Gazanjyk** see Bereket
77 V12 **Gazaoua** Maradi, S Niger 13°28′N 07°54′E
**Gaza, Província de** see Gaza
138 E11 **Gaza Strip** Ar. Qiţā' Ghazzah. disputed region SW Asia
136 M16 **Gaziantep** var. Gazi Antep; prev. Aintab, Antep. Gaziantep, S Turkey 37°04′N 37°21′E
136 M17 **Gaziantep** var. Gazi Antep. ◈ province S Turkey
**Gazi Antep** see Gaziantep
114 M13 **Gaziköy** Tekirdağ, NW Turkey 40°45′N 27°18′E
121 Q2 **Gazimağusa** var. Famagusta, Gk. Ammóchostos. E Cyprus 35°07′N 33°57′E
121 Q2 **Gazimağusa Körfezi** var. Famagusta Bay, Gk. Kólpos Ammóchostou. bay E Cyprus
146 K11 **Gazli** Buxoro Viloyati, C Uzbekistan 40°09′N 63°28′E
146 I9 **Gazojak** Rus. Gaz-Achak. Lebap Welaýaty, NE Turkmenistan 41°12′N 61°24′E
79 K15 **Gbadolite** Equateur, NW Dem. Rep. Congo 04°14′N 20°59′E
76 K16 **Gbanga** var. Gbarnga. N Liberia 07°02′N 09°30′W
**Gbarnga** see Gbanga
77 S14 **Gbéroubouè** var. Béroubouay. N Benin 10°35′N 02°47′E
77 W16 **Gboko** Benue, S Nigeria 07°21′N 08°57′E
**Gcuwa** see Butterworth
110 J7 **Gdańsk** Fr. Dantzig, Ger. Danzig. Pomorskie, N Poland 54°22′N 18°35′E
**Gdan'skaya Bukhta/Gdańsk, Gulf of** see Gdańsk, Gulf of
**Gdańska, Zakota** see Gdańsk, Gulf of
110 J6 **Gdańsk, Gulf of** var. Gulf of Danzig, Ger. Danziger Bucht, Pol. Zakota Gdańska, Rus. Gdan'skaya Bukhta. gulf N Poland
**Gdingen** see Gdynia
124 F13 **Gdov** Pskovskaya Oblast', W Russia 58°43′N 27°51′E
110 I6 **Gdynia** Ger. Gdingen. Pomorskie, N Poland 54°31′N 18°30′E
26 M10 **Geary** Oklahoma, C USA 35°37′N 98°19′W
**Geavvú** see Kevo
76 H12 **Gêba, Rio** ≈ C Guinea-Bissau
136 E11 **Gebze** Kocaeli, NW Turkey 40°48′N 29°26′E
121 R2 **Geçitkale** var. Lefkonico, Gk. Lefkoniko. NE Cyprus 35°16′N 33°44′E
80 H10 **Gedaref** var. Al Qaḍārif, El Gedaref. Gedaref, E Sudan 14°03′N 35°24′E
80 H10 **Gedaref** ◈ state E Sudan
80 B11 **Gedid Ras el Fil** Southern Darfur, W Sudan 12°45′N 25°45′E
99 I23 **Gedinne** Namur, SE Belgium 49°57′N 04°55′E
136 E13 **Gediz** Kütahya, W Turkey 39°04′N 29°25′E
136 C14 **Gediz Nehri** ≈ W Turkey
81 N14 **Gedlegubē** Sumalē, E Ethiopia 06°53′N 45°08′E
81 L17 **Gedo** off. Gobolka Gedo. ◈ region SW Somalia
**Gedo, Gobolka** see Gedo
95 I25 **Gedser** Sjælland, SE Denmark 54°34′N 11°57′E
99 I16 **Geel** var. Gheel. Antwerpen, N Belgium 51°10′N 04°59′E
183 N13 **Geelong** Victoria, SE Australia 38°10′S 144°21′E
**Ge'e'mu** see Golmud
99 I14 **Geertruidenberg** Noord-Brabant, S Netherlands 51°43′N 04°52′E
100 H10 **Geeste** ≈ NW Germany
100 J10 **Geesthacht** Schleswig-Holstein, N Germany 53°25′N 10°22′E
183 P17 **Geeveston** Tasmania, SE Australia 43°12′S 146°54′E
**Gefle** see Gävle
**Gefleborg** see Gävleborg
163 S5 **Gegan Gol** prev. Ergun, Gen He, Zuoqi. NE China
163 T5 **Gegen Gol** prev. Ergun Zuoqi, Genhe. Nei Mongol Zizhiqu, N China 50°48′N 121°30′E
163 S6 **Gegen He** ≈ NE China
158 G13 **Gê'gyai** Xizang Zizhiqu, W China 32°29′N 81°04′E
77 X12 **Geidam** Yobe, NE Nigeria 12°52′N 11°55′E
11 T11 **Geikie** ≈ Saskatchewan, C Canada
94 F13 **Geilo** Buskerud, S Norway 60°32′N 08°13′E
94 E10 **Geiranger** Møre og Romsdal, S Norway 62°07′N 07°12′E
101 I22 **Geislingen** var. Geislingen an der Steige. Baden-Württemberg, SW Germany 48°37′N 09°50′E
**Geislingen an der Steige** see Geislingen
81 F20 **Geita** Geita, NW Tanzania 02°52′S 32°12′E
95 G15 **Geithus** Buskerud, S Norway 59°56′N 09°58′E
160 H14 **Gejiu** var. Kochiu. Yunnan, S China 23°22′N 103°07′E
**Gëkdepe** see Gökdepe
146 E9 **Gekleňgkui, Solonchak** var. Solonchak Goklenkuy. salt marsh NW Turkmenistan
81 D14 **Gel** ≈ C South Sudan
107 K25 **Gela** prev. Terranova di Sicilia. Sicilia, Italy, C Mediterranean Sea 37°05′N 14°15′E
81 N14 **Geladī** SE Ethiopia 06°58′N 46°24′E
169 P13 **Gelam, Pulau** var. Pulau Galam. island N Indonesia
**Gelaozu Miaozu Zhizhixian** see Wuchuan
98 L11 **Gelderland** prev. Eng. Guelders. ◈ province E Netherlands
98 J13 **Geldermalsen** Gelderland, C Netherlands 51°53′N 05°17′E
101 D14 **Geldern** Nordrhein-Westfalen, W Germany 51°31′N 06°19′E
99 K15 **Geldrop** Noord-Brabant, SE Netherlands 51°25′N 05°34′E
99 L17 **Geleen** Limburg, SE Netherlands 50°57′N 05°49′E
126 K14 **Gelendzhik** Krasnodarskiy Kray, SW Russia 44°34′N 38°06′E
**Gelib** see Jilib
136 B11 **Gelibolu** Eng. Gallipoli. Çanakkale, NW Turkey 40°25′N 26°41′E
115 L14 **Gelibolu Yarımadası** Eng. Gallipoli Peninsula. peninsula NW Turkey
81 O14 **Gellinsor** Galguduud, C Somalia 06°25′N 46°44′E
101 H18 **Gelnhausen** Hessen, C Germany 50°12′N 09°12′E
101 E14 **Gelsenkirchen** Nordrhein-Westfalen, W Germany 51°30′N 07°05′E
83 C20 **Geluk** Hardap, SW Namibia 24°35′S 15°48′E
99 H20 **Gembloux** Namur, Belgium 50°34′N 04°42′E
79 J16 **Gemena** Equateur, NW Dem. Rep. Congo 03°13′N 19°49′E
99 L14 **Gemert** Noord-Brabant, SE Netherlands 51°33′N 05°41′E
136 E11 **Gemlik** Bursa, NW Turkey 40°26′N 29°10′E
**Gem of the Mountains** see Idaho
106 J6 **Gemona del Friuli** Friuli-Venezia Giulia, NE Italy 46°18′N 13°12′E
**Gem State** see Idaho
**Genalē Wenz** see Juba
169 R11 **Genali, Danau** ◎ Borneo, N Indonesia
99 G19 **Genappe** Walloon Brabant, C Belgium 50°39′N 04°27′E
137 P14 **Genç** Bingöl, E Turkey 38°44′N 40°35′E
**Genck** see Genk
98 M9 **Genemuiden** Overijssel, E Netherlands 52°38′N 06°03′E
63 K14 **General Acha** La Pampa, C Argentina 37°25′S 64°38′W
61 C21 **General Alvear** Buenos Aires, E Argentina 36°03′S 60°01′W
62 I12 **General Alvear** Mendoza, W Argentina 34°59′S 67°40′W
61 B20 **General Arenales** Buenos Aires, E Argentina 34°21′S 61°20′W
61 D21 **General Belgrano** Buenos Aires, E Argentina 35°47′S 58°30′W
41 O8 **General Bravo** Nuevo León, NE Mexico 25°47′N 99°04′W
62 M7 **General Capdevila** Chaco, N Argentina 27°25′S 61°30′W
**General Carrera, Lago** see Buenos Aires, Lago
41 N9 **General Cepeda** Coahuila, NE Mexico 25°18′N 101°24′W
63 K15 **General Conesa** Río Negro, E Argentina 40°06′S 64°26′W
61 G18 **General Enrique Martínez** Treinta y Tres, E Uruguay 33°13′S 53°47′W
62 L3 **General Eugenio A. Garay** var. Fortín General Eugenio Garay; prev. Yrendagüé. Nueva Asunción, NW Paraguay 20°30′S 61°56′W
61 C18 **General Galarza** Entre Ríos, E Argentina 32°43′S 59°24′W
61 E22 **General Guido** Buenos Aires, E Argentina 36°36′S 57°45′W
**General José F.Uriburu** see Zárate
61 E22 **General Juan Madariaga** Buenos Aires, E Argentina 37°00′S 57°09′W
41 O16 **General Juan N Alvarez** ✈ (Acapulco) Guerrero, S Mexico 16°47′N 99°47′W
61 B22 **General La Madrid** Buenos Aires, E Argentina 37°17′S 61°20′W
61 E21 **General Lavalle** Buenos Aires, E Argentina 36°25′S 56°56′W
**General Machado** see Camacupa
62 I8 **General Manuel Belgrano, Cerro** ▲ W Argentina 29°05′S 67°05′W
41 O8 **General Mariano Escobero** ✈ (Monterrey) Nuevo León, NE Mexico 25°47′N 100°00′W
61 B20 **General O'Brien** Buenos Aires, E Argentina 34°54′S 60°45′W
62 K13 **General Pico** La Pampa, C Argentina 35°43′S 63°45′W
62 M7 **General Pinedo** Chaco, N Argentina 27°17′S 61°20′W
61 B20 **General Pinto** Buenos Aires, E Argentina 34°45′S 61°50′W
61 E22 **General Pirán** Buenos Aires, E Argentina 37°16′S 57°46′W
43 N15 **General, Río** ≈ S Costa Rica
63 I15 **General Roca** Río Negro, C Argentina 39°00′S 67°35′W
171 Q8 **General Santos** off. General Santos City. Mindanao, S Philippines 06°10′N 125°10′E
**General Santos City** see General Santos
41 O9 **General Terán** Nuevo León, NE Mexico 25°18′N 99°40′W
114 N7 **General Toshevo** Rom. I.G.Duca; prev. Casim, Kasimköj. Dobrich, NE Bulgaria 43°43′N 28°04′E
61 B20 **General Viamonte** Buenos Aires, E Argentina 35°01′S 61°00′W
61 A20 **General Villegas** Buenos Aires, E Argentina 35°02′S 63°01′W
**Gênes** see Genova
18 E11 **Genesee River** ≈ New York/Pennsylvania, NE USA
30 K11 **Geneseo** Illinois, N USA 41°27′N 90°08′W
18 F10 **Geneseo** New York, NE USA 42°48′N 77°46′W
57 L14 **Geneshuaya, Río** ≈ N Bolivia
23 Q8 **Geneva** Alabama, S USA 31°01′N 85°51′W
30 M10 **Geneva** Illinois, N USA 41°53′N 88°18′W
29 Q16 **Geneva** Nebraska, C USA 40°31′N 97°36′W
18 G10 **Geneva** New York, NE USA 42°52′N 76°58′W
31 U10 **Geneva** Ohio, NE USA 41°48′N 80°53′W
**Geneva** see Genève
108 B10 **Geneva, Lake** Fr. Lac de Genève, Lac Léman, le Léman, Ger. Genfer See. ◎ France/Switzerland
108 A10 **Genève** Eng. Geneva, Ger. Genf, It. Ginevra. Genève, SW Switzerland 46°13′N 06°09′E
108 A11 **Genève** Eng. Geneva, Ger. Genf, It. Ginevra. ◈ canton SW Switzerland
108 A10 **Genève** ✈ Vaud, SW Switzerland 46°13′N 06°06′E
**Genève, Lac de** see Geneva, Lake
**Genf** see Genève
**Genfer See** see Geneva, Lake
**Genhe** see Gegen Gol
**Gen He** see Gegan Gol
**Genichesk** see Heniches'k
104 L14 **Genil** ≈ S Spain
99 K18 **Genk** var. Genck. Limburg, NE Belgium 50°58′N 05°30′E
164 C13 **Genkai-nada** gulf Kyūshū, SW Japan
107 C19 **Gennargentu, Monti del** ▲▲ Sardegna, Italy, C Mediterranean Sea
99 M14 **Gennep** Limburg, SE Netherlands 51°43′N 05°58′E
30 M10 **Genoa** Illinois, N USA 42°06′N 88°41′W
29 Q15 **Genoa** Nebraska, C USA 41°27′N 97°43′W
**Genoa** see Genova
**Genoa, Gulf of** see Genova, Golfo di
106 D10 **Genova** Eng. Genoa, Fr. Gênes; anc. Genua. Liguria, NW Italy 44°28′N 09°E
106 D10 **Genova, Golfo di** Eng. Gulf of Genoa. gulf NW Italy
57 C17 **Genovesa, Isla** var. Tower Island. island Galapagos Islands, Ecuador, E Pacific Ocean
**Genshū** see Wonju
99 E17 **Gent** Eng. Ghent, Fr. Gand. Oost-Vlaanderen, NW Belgium 51°02′N 03°42′E
169 N16 **Genteng** Jawa, C Indonesia 07°21′S 106°20′E
100 M12 **Genthin** Sachsen-Anhalt, E Germany 52°24′N 12°10′E
27 R9 **Gentry** Arkansas, C USA 36°16′N 94°28′W
**Genua** see Genova
107 I15 **Genzano di Roma** Lazio, C Italy 41°42′N 12°42′E
163 Y17 **Geogeum-do** prev. Kōgūm-do. island S South Korea
163 Z16 **Geogeum-do** Jap. Kyōsai-tō; prev. Kŏje-do. island S South Korea
**Geokchay** see Göyçay
**Geok-Tepe** see Gökdepe
122 I3 **Georga, Zemlya** Eng. George Land. island Zemlya Frantsa-Iosifa, N Russia
83 G26 **George** Western Cape, S South Africa 33°57′S 22°28′E
29 S11 **George** Iowa, C USA 43°20′N 96°00′W
13 O5 **George** ≈ Newfoundland and Labrador/Québec, E Canada
**George F L Charles** see Vigie
65 C25 **George Island** island S Falkland Islands
183 R10 **George, Lake** ◎ New South Wales, SE Australia
81 E18 **George, Lake** ◎ SW Uganda
23 W10 **George, Lake** ◎ Florida, SE USA
18 L8 **George, Lake** ⊠ New York, NE USA
**George Land** see Georga, Zemlya
**Georgenburg** see Jurbarkas
**George River** see Kangiqsualujjuaq
64 G8 **Georges Bank** undersea feature W Atlantic Ocean 41°15′N 67°30′W
185 A21 **George Sound** sound South Island, New Zealand
65 F15 **Georgetown** ○ (Ascension Island) NW Ascension Island 17°56′S 14°25′W
181 V5 **Georgetown** Queensland, NE Australia 18°17′S 143°37′E
183 P15 **George Town** Tasmania, SE Australia 41°04′S 146°48′E
44 D8 **George Town** var. Georgetown. ○ (Cayman Islands) Grand Cayman, SW Cayman Islands 19°16′N 81°23′W
55 T8 **Georgetown** ● (Guyana) N Guyana 06°46′N 58°10′W
168 I7 **George Town** var. Penang, Pinang. Pinang, Peninsular Malaysia 05°28′N 100°20′E
45 Y14 **Georgetown** Saint Vincent, Saint Vincent and the Grenadines 13°19′N 61°09′W
44 I4 **George Town** Great Exuma Island, C The Bahamas 23°28′N 75°47′W
21 Y4 **Georgetown** Delaware, NE USA 38°39′N 75°22′W
23 R6 **Georgetown** Georgia, SE USA 31°52′N 85°04′W
20 M5 **Georgetown** Kentucky, S USA 38°13′N 84°30′W
21 T13 **Georgetown** South Carolina, SE USA 33°23′N 79°18′W
25 S10 **Georgetown** Texas, SW USA 30°39′N 97°42′W
55 T8 **Georgetown** ✈ N Guyana 06°46′N 58°10′W
**Georgetown** see George Town
**Georgetown** see Janjanbureh
195 U16 **George V Coast** physical region Antarctica
194 J7 **George VI Ice Shelf** ice shelf Antarctica
194 J6 **George VI Sound** sound Antarctica
195 T15 **George V Land** physical region Antarctica
25 S14 **George West** Texas, SW USA 28°21′N 98°08′W
137 R9 **Georgia** off. Georgia, Geor. Sakartvelo, Rus. Gruzinskaya SSR, Gruziya; prev. Georgian SSR, Republic of Georgia. ◆ republic SW Asia
23 S5 **Georgia** off. State of Georgia, also known as Empire State of the South, Peach State. ◈ state SE USA
14 F12 **Georgian Bay** lake bay Ontario, S Canada
**Georgian SSR** see Georgia
**Georgia, Republic of** see Georgia
10 L17 **Georgia, Strait of** strait British Columbia, W Canada
**Georgi Dimitrov** see Kostenets
**Georgi Dimitrov, Yazovir** see Koprinka, Yazovir
**Georgiu-Dezh** see Liski
145 W10 **Georgiyevka** Vostochnyy Kazakhstan, E Kazakhstan 49°19′N 81°35′E
**Georgiyevka** see Korday
127 N15 **Georgiyevsk** Stavropol'skiy Kray, SW Russia 44°07′N 43°22′E
100 G13 **Georgsmarienhütte** Niedersachsen, NW Germany 52°13′N 08°02′E
101 M16 **Gera** Thüringen, E Germany 50°51′N 12°13′E
101 K16 **Gera** ≈ C Germany
99 E19 **Geraardsbergen** Oost-Vlaanderen, SW Belgium 50°47′N 03°53′E
115 F21 **Geráki** Pelopónnisos, S Greece 36°56′N 22°46′E
27 W5 **Gerald** Missouri, C USA 38°24′N 91°20′W
47 V8 **Geral de Goiás, Serra** ▲ E Brazil
185 G20 **Geraldine** Canterbury, South Island, New Zealand 44°06′S 171°14′E
180 H11 **Geraldton** Western Australia 28°48′S 114°40′E
12 E11 **Geraldton** Ontario, S Canada 49°44′N 86°59′W
60 J12 **Geral, Serra** ▲ S Brazil
103 U6 **Gérardmer** Vosges, NE France 48°05′N 06°54′E
**Gerasa** see Jarash
**Gerdauen** see Zheleznodorozhnyy
39 Q11 **Gerdine, Mount** ▲ Alaska, USA 61°40′N 152°21′W
136 H11 **Gerede** Bolu, N Turkey 40°48′N 32°13′E
136 H11 **Gerede Çayı** ≈ N Turkey
**Gereshk** see Girishk
101 L24 **Geretsried** Bayern, S Germany 47°51′N 11°28′E
105 P14 **Gérgal** Andalucía, S Spain 37°07′N 02°34′W
28 I14 **Gering** Nebraska, C USA 41°49′N 103°39′W
35 R3 **Gerlach** Nevada, W USA 40°38′N 119°21′W
**Gerlachfalvi Csúcs/Gerlachovka** see Gerlachovský štít
111 L18 **Gerlachovský štít** var. Gerlachovka, Ger. Gerlsdorfer Spitze, Hung. Gerlachfalvi Csúcs; prev. Stalinov Štít, Ger. Franz-Josef Spitze, Hung. Ferencz-Jósef Csúcs. ▲ N Slovakia 49°12′N 20°09′E
108 E8 **Gerlafingen** Solothurn, NW Switzerland 47°10′N 07°35′E
**Gerlsdorfer Spitze** see Gerlachovský štít
**Germak** see Germik
**German East Africa** see Tanzania
**Germanicopolis** see Çankırı
**Germanicum, Mare/German Ocean** see North Sea
**Germanovichi** see Hyermanavichy
**German Southwest Africa** see Namibia


◆ Country ● Country Capital ◇ Dependent Territory ○ Dependent Territory Capital ◈ Administrative Regions ✈ International Airport ▲ Mountain ▲▲ Mountain Range Volcano ≈ River ◎ Lake ⊠ Reservoir
253

GERMANTOWN – GOLDENER TISCH


20 E10 **Germantown** Tennessee, S USA 35°06′N 89°51′W
101 I15 **Germany** off. Federal Republic of Germany, Bundesrepublik Deutschland, Ger. Deutschland. ◆ federal republic N Europe
**Germany, Federal Republic of** see Germany
101 L23 **Germering** Bayern, SE Germany 48°07′N 11°22′E
139 V3 **Germik** Ar. Garmik, var. Germak. As Sulaymānīyah, E Iraq 35°49′N 46°09′E
83 J21 **Germiston** var. Gauteng. Gauteng, NE South Africa 26°15′S 28°10′E
**Gernika** see Gernika-Lumo
105 P2 **Gernika-Lumo** var. Gernika, Guernica, Guernica y Lumo. País Vasco, N Spain 43°19′N 02°40′W
164 L12 **Gero** Gifu, Honshū, SW Japan 35°48′N 137°15′E
115 F22 **Geroliménas** Pelopónnisos, S Greece 36°28′N 22°25′E
**Gerona** see Girona
99 H21 **Gerpinnes** Hainaut, S Belgium 50°20′N 04°38′E
102 L15 **Gers** ◈ department S France
102 L14 **Gers** ≈ S France
**Gerunda** see Girona
158 I13 **Gêrzê** var. Luring. Xizang Zizhiqu, W China 32°19′N 84°05′E
136 K10 **Gerze** Sinop, N Turkey 41°48′N 35°13′E
**Gesoriacum** see Boulogne-sur-Mer
**Gessoriacum** see Boulogne-sur-Mer
99 J21 **Gesves** Namur, SE Belgium 50°24′N 05°04′E
93 J20 **Geta** Åland, SW Finland 60°22′N 19°49′E
105 N8 **Getafe** Madrid, C Spain 40°18′N 03°44′W
95 J21 **Getinge** Halland, S Sweden 56°46′N 12°42′E
18 F16 **Gettysburg** Pennsylvania, NE USA 39°49′N 77°13′W
29 N8 **Gettysburg** South Dakota, N USA 45°00′N 99°57′W
194 K12 **Getz Ice Shelf** ice shelf Antarctica
137 S15 **Gevaş** Van, SE Turkey 38°16′N 43°05′E
**Gevgeli** see Gevgelija
113 Q20 **Gevgelija** var. Đevđelija, Djevdjelija, Turk. Gevgeli. SE Macedonia 41°09′N 22°30′E
103 T10 **Gex** Ain, E France 46°21′N 06°02′E
92 I3 **Geysir** physical region SW Iceland
136 F11 **Geyve** Sakarya, NW Turkey 40°32′N 30°18′E
80 G10 **Gezira** ◈ state E Sudan
109 V3 **Gföhl** Niederösterreich, N Austria 48°30′N 15°27′E
83 H22 **Ghaap Plateau** Afr. Ghaapplato. plateau C South Africa
**Ghaapplato** see Ghaap Plateau
**Ghaba** see Al Ghābah
138 J8 **Ghāb, Tall** ▲ SE Syria 33°09′N 37°48′E
139 Q9 **Ghadaf, Wādī al** dry watercourse C Iraq
**Ghadamès** see Ghadāmis
74 M9 **Ghadāmis** var. Ghadamès, Rhadames. W Libya 30°08′N 09°30′E
141 Y10 **Ghadan** E Oman 20°20′N 57°58′E
75 O10 **Ghaddūwah** C Libya 26°36′N 14°26′E
147 Q11 **Ghafurov** Rus. Gafurov; prev. Sovetabad. NW Tajikistan 40°13′N 69°42′E
153 N12 **Ghāghara** ≈ S Asia
149 P13 **Ghaibi Dero** Sindh, SE Pakistan 27°35′N 67°42′E
141 Y10 **Ghalat** E Oman 21°06′N 58°51′E
139 W11 **Ghamūkah, Hawr** ◎ S Iraq
77 P15 **Ghana** off. Republic of Ghana. ◆ republic W Africa
141 X12 **Ghānah** spring/well S Oman 18°35′N 56°34′E
**Ghanongga** see Ranongga
**Ghansi/Ghansiland** see Ghanzi
83 F18 **Ghanzi** var. Khanzi. Ghanzi, W Botswana 21°39′S 21°38′E
83 G19 **Ghanzi** var. Ghansi, Ghansiland, Khanzi. ◈ district C Botswana
67 T14 **Ghanzi** var. Knanzi. ≈ Botswana/South Africa
**Ghap'an** see Kapan
138 F13 **Gharandal** Al'Aqabah, SW Jordan 30°12′N 35°18′E
139 U14 **Gharbīyah, Sha'īb al** ≈ S Iraq
**Gharbt, Jabal al** see Liban, Jebel
74 K7 **Ghardaïa** N Algeria 32°30′N 03°44′E
147 R12 **Gharm** Rus. Garm. C Tajikistan 39°03′N 70°25′E
149 P17 **Gharo** Sindh, SE Pakistan 24°44′N 67°35′E
139 W10 **Gharrāf, Shaṭṭ al** ≈ S Iraq
**Gharvān** see Gharyān
75 O7 **Gharyān** var. Gharvān. NW Libya 32°10′N 13°01′E
74 M11 **Ghāt** var. Gat. SW Libya 24°58′N 10°11′E
**Ghawdex** see Gozo
141 U8 **Ghayathi** Abū Ẓaby, W United Arab Emirates 23°51′N 53°01′E
**Ghazāl, Baḥr al** see Ghazal, Bahr el
78 H9 **Ghazal, Bahr el** var. Soro. seasonal river C Chad
80 E13 **Ghazal, Bahr el** var. Baḥr al Ghazāl. ≈ N South Sudan
74 H6 **Ghazaouet** NW Algeria 35°08′N 01°50′W
152 J10 **Ghāziābād** Uttar Pradesh, N India 28°42′N 77°28′E
153 O13 **Ghāzīpur** Uttar Pradesh, N India 25°36′N 83°36′E
149 Q6 **Ghaznī** var. Ghazni. Ghaznī, E Afghanistan 33°31′N 68°24′E
149 P7 **Ghaznī** ◈ province SE Afghanistan
**Ghazzah** see Gaza
**Gheel** see Geel
**Ghelîzâne** see Relizane
**Ghent** see Gent
**Gheorghe Brațul** see Sfântu Gheorghe, Brațul
**Gheorghe Gheorghiu-Dej** see Onești
116 J10 **Gheorgheni** prev. Gheorghieni, Sîn-Miclăuș, Ger. Niklasmarkt, Hung. Gyergyószentmiklós. Harghita, C Romania 46°43′N 25°36′E
**Gheorghieni** see Gheorgheni
116 H10 **Gherla** Ger. Neuschliss, Hung. Szamosújvár; prev. Armenierstadt. Cluj, NW Romania 47°02′N 23°55′E
**Gheweifat** see Ghuwayfāt
**Ghilan** see Gīlān
107 C18 **Ghilarza** Sardegna, Italy, C Mediterranean Sea 40°09′N 08°50′E
**Ghilizane** see Relizane
**Ghimbi** see Gīmbī
**Ghiriș** see Câmpia Turzii
103 Y15 **Ghisonaccia** Corse, France, C Mediterranean Sea 42°00′N 09°25′E
147 Q11 **Ghonchí** Rus. Ganchi. NW Tajikistan 39°57′N 69°10′E
148 M5 **Ghōr** var. Ghowr, Gōwr. ◈ province C Afghanistan
153 T13 **Ghoraghat** Rajshahi, NW Bangladesh 25°18′N 89°20′E
**Ghōrīān** see Ghōriyān
148 J5 **Ghōriyān** var. Ghūrīān, Ghōrīān. Herāt, W Afghanistan 34°20′N 61°25′E
149 R13 **Ghotki** Sindh, SE Pakistan 28°00′N 69°21′E
**Ghowr** see Ghōr
147 T13 **Ghŭdara** var. Gudara, Rus. Kudara. SE Tajikistan 38°28′N 72°39′E
153 R13 **Ghugri** ≈ N India
147 S14 **Ghund** Rus. Gunt. ≈ SE Tajikistan
**Ghurābīyah, Sha'īb al** see Gharbīyah, Sha'īb al
**Ghurdaqah** see Al Ghardaqah
**Ghūrīān** see Ghōriyān
141 T8 **Ghuwayfāt** var. Gheweifat. Abū Ẓaby, W United Arab Emirates 24°06′N 51°40′E
121 O14 **Ghuzayyil, Sabkhat** salt lake N Libya
126 J3 **Ghzatsk** Smolenskaya Oblast', W Russia 55°33′N 35°00′E
115 G17 **Giáltra** Évvoia, C Greece 38°21′N 22°58′E
**Giamame** see Jamaame
167 U13 **Gia Nghia** var. Đak Nông. Đăc Lăc, S Vietnam 11°58′N 107°42′E
114 F13 **Giannitsá** var. Yiannitsá. Kentrikí Makedonía, N Greece 40°49′N 22°24′E
107 F14 **Giannutri, Isola di** island Archipelago Toscano, C Italy
96 F13 **Giant's Causeway** Ir. Clochán an Aifir. lava flow N Northern Ireland, United Kingdom
167 S15 **Gia Rai** Minh Hai, S Vietnam 09°14′N 105°28′E
107 L24 **Giarre** Sicilia, Italy, C Mediterranean Sea 37°44′N 15°12′E
44 I7 **Gibara** Holguín, E Cuba 21°09′N 76°11′W
29 O16 **Gibbon** Nebraska, C USA 40°45′N 98°50′W
32 K11 **Gibbon** Oregon, NW USA 45°40′N 118°22′W
33 P11 **Gibbonsville** Idaho, NW USA 45°33′N 113°55′W
64 A13 **Gibbs Hill** hill S Bermuda
92 I9 **Gibostad** Troms, N Norway 69°21′N 18°01′E
104 I14 **Gibraleón** Andalucía, S Spain 37°23′N 06°58′W
104 L16 **Gibraltar** ○ (Gibraltar) S Gibraltar 36°08′N 05°21′W
104 L16 **Gibraltar** ◇ UK Overseas Territory SW Europe
**Gibraltar, Détroit de/Gibraltar, Estrecho de** see Gibraltar, Strait of
104 J17 **Gibraltar, Strait of** Fr. Détroit de Gibraltar, Sp. Estrecho de Gibraltar. strait Atlantic Ocean/Mediterranean Sea
31 S11 **Gibsonburg** Ohio, N USA 41°22′N 83°19′W
30 M13 **Gibson City** Illinois, N USA 40°27′N 88°24′W
180 L8 **Gibson Desert** desert Western Australia
10 L17 **Gibsons** British Columbia SW Canada 49°24′N 123°32′W
149 N12 **Gidar** Baluchistan, SW Pakistan 28°16′N 66°00′E
155 I17 **Giddalūr** Andhra Pradesh, E India 15°24′N 78°54′E
25 U10 **Giddings** Texas, SW USA 30°12′N 96°59′W
27 Y8 **Gideon** Missouri, C USA 36°27′N 89°55′W
81 I15 **Gīdolē** Southern Nationalities, S Ethiopia 05°31′N 37°26′E
**Giebnegáisi** see Kebnekaise
118 H13 **Giedraičiai** Utena, E Lithuania 55°05′N 25°16′E
103 O7 **Gien** Loiret, C France 47°40′N 02°37′E
101 G17 **Giessen** Hessen, W Germany 50°35′N 08°41′E
98 O6 **Gieten** Drenthe, NE Netherlands 53°00′N 06°43′E
23 Y13 **Gifford** Florida, SE USA 27°40′N 80°24′W
9 O5 **Gifford** ≈ Baffin Island, Nunavut, NE Canada
100 J12 **Gifhorn** Niedersachsen, N Germany 52°28′N 10°33′E
11 P13 **Gift Lake** Alberta, W Canada 55°49′N 115°57′W
**Giftokastro** see Tsiganskо Gradishte
164 L13 **Gifu** var. Gihu. Gifu, Honshū, SW Japan 35°24′N 136°46′E
164 K13 **Gifu** off. Gifu-ken, var. Gihu. ◈ prefecture Honshū, SW Japan
**Gifu-ken** see Gifu
126 M13 **Gigant** Rostovskaya Oblast', SW Russia 46°29′N 41°18′E
40 E8 **Giganta, Sierra de la** ▲▲ NW Mexico
54 E12 **Gigante** Huila, S Colombia 02°24′N 75°34′W
114 I7 **Gigen** Pleven, N Bulgaria 43°40′N 24°31′E
**Giggiga** see Jijiga
96 G12 **Gigha Island** island SW Scotland, United Kingdom
107 E14 **Giglio, Isola del** island Archipelago Toscano, C Italy
**Gihu** see Gifu
146 L11 **G'ijduvon** Rus. Gizhduvon. Buxoro Viloyati, C Uzbekistan 40°06′N 64°38′E
104 L2 **Gijón** var. Xixón. Asturias, NW Spain 43°32′N 05°40′W
81 D20 **Gikongoro** SW Rwanda 02°30′S 29°32′E
36 K14 **Gila Bend** Arizona, SW USA 32°57′N 112°43′W
36 J14 **Gila Bend Mountains** ▲▲ Arizona, SW USA
36 I15 **Gila Mountains** ▲▲ Arizona, SW USA
37 N14 **Gila Mountains** ▲▲ Arizona, SW USA
142 M4 **Gīlān** off. Ostān-e Gīlān, var. Ghilan, Guilan. ◈ province NW Iran
**Gīlān, Ostān-e** see Gīlān
36 L14 **Gila River** ≈ Arizona, SW USA
**gilbbesjavri** see Kilpisjärvi
29 W4 **Gilbert** Minnesota, N USA 47°29′N 92°27′W
**Gilbert Islands** see Tungaru
10 L16 **Gilbert, Mount** ▲ British Columbia, SW Canada 50°49′N 124°03′W
181 U4 **Gilbert River** ≈ Queensland, NE Australia
0 C6 **Gilbert Seamounts** undersea feature NE Pacific Ocean 52°50′N 150°10′W
33 S7 **Gildford** Montana, NW USA 48°34′N 110°21′W
83 P15 **Gilé** Zambézia, NE Mozambique 16°10′S 38°17′E
30 K4 **Gile Flowage** ◎ Wisconsin, N USA
182 G7 **Giles, Lake** salt lake South Australia
**Gilf Kebir Plateau** see Haḍabat al Jilf al Kabīr
183 R6 **Gilgandra** New South Wales, SE Australia 31°43′S 148°39′E
**Gilgău** see Gâlgău
81 I19 **Gilgil** Nakuru, SW Kenya 0°29′S 36°19′E
183 S4 **Gil Gil Creek** ≈ New South Wales, SE Australia
149 V3 **Gilgit** Jammu and Kashmir, NE Pakistan 35°54′N 74°20′E
149 V3 **Gilgit** ≈ N Pakistan
11 X11 **Gillam** Manitoba, C Canada 56°25′N 94°45′W
95 J22 **Gilleleje** Hovedstaden, E Denmark 56°05′N 12°17′E
30 K14 **Gillespie** Illinois, N USA 39°07′N 89°49′W
27 W13 **Gillett** Arkansas, C USA 34°07′N 91°22′W
33 X12 **Gillette** Wyoming, C USA 44°17′N 105°30′W
97 P22 **Gillingham** SE England, United Kingdom 51°24′N 00°33′E
195 X6 **Gillock Island** island Antarctica
173 O16 **Gillot** ✈ (St-Denis) N Réunion 20°53′S 55°31′E
65 H25 **Gill Point** headland E Saint Helena 15°59′S 05°38′W
30 M12 **Gilman** Illinois, N USA 40°44′N 87°58′W
25 W6 **Gilmer** Texas, SW USA 32°44′N 94°58′W
**Gilolo** see Halmahera, Pulau
81 G14 **Gīlo Wenz** ≈ SW Ethiopia
35 O10 **Gilroy** California, W USA 37°00′N 121°34′W
123 Q12 **Gilyuy** ≈ SE Russia
99 I14 **Gilze** Noord-Brabant, S Netherlands 51°33′N 04°56′E
165 R16 **Gima** Okinawa, Kume-jima, SW Japan
80 H13 **Gīmbī** It. Ghimbi. Oromīya, C Ethiopia 09°13′N 35°39′E
163 Y15 **Gimcheon** prev. Kimch'ŏn. C South Korea 36°08′N 128°06′E
163 Z16 **Gimhae** prev. Kim Hae. ✈ (Busan) SE South Korea 35°10′N 128°57′E
45 T12 **Gimie, Mount** ▲ C Saint Lucia 13°51′N 61°00′W
11 X16 **Gimli** Manitoba, S Canada 50°39′N 97°00′W
**Gimma** see Jīma
95 O14 **Gimo** Uppsala, C Sweden 60°11′N 18°12′E
102 L15 **Gimone** ≈ S France
**Gimpoe** see Gimpu
171 N12 **Gimpu** prev. Gimpoe. Sulawesi, C Indonesia 01°38′S 120°00′E
182 F5 **Gina** South Australia 29°56′S 134°33′E
**Ginevra** see Genève
99 J19 **Gingelom** Limburg, NE Belgium 50°46′N 05°09′E
180 I12 **Gingin** Western Australia 31°22′S 115°51′E
171 Q7 **Gingoog** Mindanao, S Philippines 08°47′N 125°05′E
81 K14 **Gīnīr** Oromīya, C Ethiopia 07°12′N 40°43′E
**Giohar** see Jawhar
107 O17 **Gióia del Colle** Puglia, SE Italy 40°47′N 16°56′E
107 M22 **Gioia, Golfo di** gulf S Italy
**Giona** see Gkióna
115 I16 **Gioúra** island Vóreies Sporádes, Greece, Aegean Sea
107 O17 **Giovinazzo** Puglia, SE Italy 41°11′N 16°40′E
**Gipeswic** see Ipswich
105 P3 **Gipuzkoa** Cast. Guipúzcoa. ◈ province País Vasco, N Spain
**Giran** see Ilan
30 K14 **Girard** Illinois, N USA 39°27′N 89°46′W
27 R7 **Girard** Kansas, C USA 37°30′N 94°50′W
25 O6 **Girard** Texas, SW USA 33°18′N 100°38′W
54 E10 **Girardot** Cundinamarca, C Colombia 04°19′N 74°47′W
172 M7 **Giraud Seamount** undersea feature SW Indian Ocean 09°57′S 46°55′E
83 A15 **Giraul** ≈ SW Angola
96 L9 **Girdle Ness** headland NE Scotland, United Kingdom 57°09′N 02°04′W
137 N11 **Giresun** var. Kerasunt; anc. Cerasus, Pharnacia. Giresun, NE Turkey 40°55′N 38°35′E
137 N12 **Giresun** var. Kerasunt. ◈ province NE Turkey
137 N12 **Giresun Dağları** ▲▲ N Turkey
**Girga** see Jirjā
**Girgeh** see Jirjā
**Girgenti** see Agrigento
153 Q15 **Girīdīh** Jhārkhand, NE India 24°10′N 86°20′E
183 P6 **Girilambone** New South Wales, SE Australia 31°19′S 146°57′E
**Girin** see Jilin
148 M8 **Girishk** var. Gereshk. Helmand, SW Afghanistan 31°50′N 64°32′E
121 W10 **Girne** Gk. Kerýneia, Kyrenia. N Cyprus 35°20′N 33°20′E
**Giron** see Kiruna
105 X5 **Girona** var. Gerona; anc. Gerunda. Cataluña, NE Spain 41°59′N 02°49′E
105 W5 **Girona** var. Gerona. ◈ province Cataluña, NE Spain
102 J12 **Gironde** ◈ department SW France
102 J11 **Gironde** estuary SW France
105 V5 **Gironella** Cataluña, NE Spain 42°02′N 01°53′E
103 N15 **Girou** ≈ S France
97 H14 **Girvan** W Scotland, United Kingdom 55°14′N 04°53′W
24 M9 **Girvin** Texas, SW USA 31°05′N 102°24′W
184 Q9 **Gisborne** Gisborne, North Island, New Zealand 38°41′S 178°01′E
184 P9 **Gisborne** off. Gisborne District. ◈ unitary authority North Island, New Zealand
**Gisborne District** see Gisborne
**Giseifu** see Uijeongbu
**Gisenye** see Gisenyi
81 D19 **Gisenyi** var. Gisenye. NW Rwanda 01°42′S 29°18′E
95 K20 **Gislaved** Jönköping, S Sweden 57°19′N 13°30′E
103 N4 **Gisors** Eure, N France 49°18′N 01°46′E
**Gissar** see Hisor
147 P12 **Gissar Range** Rus. Gissarskiy Khrebet. ▲▲ Tajikistan/Uzbekistan
**Gissarskiy Khrebet** see Gissar Range
99 B16 **Gistel** West-Vlaanderen, W Belgium 51°09′N 02°58′E
108 F9 **Giswil** Obwalden, C Switzerland 46°49′N 08°11′E
115 B16 **Gitánes** ancient monument Ípeiros, W Greece
81 E20 **Gitarama** C Rwanda 02°05′S 29°45′E
81 E20 **Gitega** ● (Burundi-political capital) Gitega, C Burundi 03°20′S 29°56′E
**Githio** see Gýtheio
108 H11 **Giubiasco** Ticino, S Switzerland 46°11′N 09°01′E
106 K13 **Giulianova** Abruzzi, C Italy 42°45′N 13°58′E
**Giulie, Alpi** see Julian Alps
**Giumri** see Gyumri
116 M13 **Giurgeni** Ialomița, SE Romania 44°45′N 27°48′E
116 J15 **Giurgiu** Giurgiu, S Romania 43°54′N 25°58′E
116 J14 **Giurgiu** ◈ county SE Romania
95 F22 **Give** Syddanmark, C Denmark 55°51′N 09°15′E
103 R2 **Givet** Ardennes, N France 50°08′N 04°50′E
103 R11 **Givors** Rhône, E France 45°35′N 04°47′E
83 K19 **Giyani** Limpopo, NE South Africa 23°20′S 30°37′E
80 I13 **Giyon** Oromīya, C Ethiopia 08°31′N 37°56′E
**Giza** see Al Jīzah
75 V8 **Giza, Pyramids of** ancient monument N Egypt
**Gizhduvon** see G'ijduvon
123 U8 **Gizhiga** Magadanskaya Oblast', E Russia 61°58′N 160°16′E
123 T9 **Gizhiginskaya Guba** bay E Russia
186 K8 **Gizo** Gizo, NW Solomon Islands 08°03′S 156°49′E
110 N7 **Giżycko** Ger. Lötzen. Warmińsko-Mazurskie, NE Poland 54°03′N 21°48′E
**Gízymałów** see Hrymayliv
113 M17 **Gjakovë** Serb. Đakovica. W Kosovo 42°22′N 20°30′E
94 F12 **Gjende** ◎ S Norway
113 L16 **Gjeravicë** Serb. Đeravica. ▲ S Serbia 42°33′N 20°08′E
95 F17 **Gjerstad** Aust-Agder, S Norway 58°54′N 09°03′E
113 O17 **Gjilan** Serb. Gnjilane. E Kosovo 42°27′N 21°28′E
**Gjinokastër** see Gjirokastër
113 L23 **Gjirokastër** var. Gjirokastra; prev. Gjinokastër, Gk. Argyrokastron, It. Argirocastro. Gjirokastër, S Albania 40°04′N 20°09′E
113 L22 **Gjirokastër** ◈ county S Albania
**Gjirokastra** see Gjirokastër
9 N7 **Gjoa Haven** var. Uqsuqtuuq. King William Island, Nunavut, NW Canada 68°38′N 95°57′W
94 H13 **Gjøvik** Oppland, S Norway 60°47′N 10°40′E
113 J22 **Gjuhëzës, Kepi i** headland SW Albania 40°25′N 19°19′E
**Gjurgjevac** see Đurđevac
115 E18 **Gkióna** var. Giona. ▲▲ C Greece
121 R3 **Gkréko, Akrotírio** var. Cape Greco, Pidálion. cape E Cyprus
99 I18 **Glabbeek-Zuurbemde** Vlaams Brabant, C Belgium 50°54′N 04°58′E
13 R14 **Glace Bay** Cape Breton Island, Nova Scotia, SE Canada 46°12′N 59°57′W
11 O16 **Glacier** British Columbia, SW Canada 51°12′N 117°33′W
39 W12 **Glacier Bay** inlet Alaska, USA
32 I7 **Glacier Peak** ▲ Washington, NW USA 48°06′N 121°06′W
159 N13 **Gladaindong Feng** ▲ C China 33°24′N 91°00′E
21 Q7 **Glade Spring** Virginia, NE USA 36°47′N 81°46′W
43 W7 **Gladewater** Texas, SW USA 32°32′N 94°57′W
181 Y8 **Gladstone** Queensland, E Australia 23°52′S 151°16′E
182 I8 **Gladstone** South Australia 33°16′S 138°21′E
11 X16 **Gladstone** Manitoba, S Canada 50°12′N 98°56′W
31 O5 **Gladstone** Michigan, N USA 45°51′N 87°01′W
27 R4 **Gladstone** Missouri, C USA 39°12′N 94°33′W
31 Q7 **Gladwin** Michigan, N USA 43°58′N 84°29′W
95 J15 **Glafsfjorden** ◎ C Sweden
92 H2 **Gláma** physical region NW Iceland
94 I12 **Gláma** var. Glommen. ≈ S Norway
112 F13 **Glamoč** Federacija Bosne I Hercegovine, NE Boznia and Herzegovina 44°01′N 16°51′E
97 J22 **Glamorgan** cultural region S Wales, United Kingdom
95 G24 **Glamsbjerg** Syddtjylland, C Denmark 55°17′N 10°07′E
171 Q8 **Glan** Mindanao, S Philippines 05°49′N 125°11′E
109 T9 **Glan** ≈ SE Austria
101 F19 **Glan** ≈ W Germany
95 M17 **Glan** ◎ S Sweden
**Glaris** see Glarus
108 H9 **Glarner Alpen** Eng. Glarus Alps. ▲▲ E Switzerland
108 H8 **Glarus** Glarus, E Switzerland 47°03′N 09°04′E
108 H9 **Glarus** Fr. Glaris. ◈ canton C Switzerland
**Glarus Alps** see Glarner Alpen
27 N3 **Glasco** Kansas, C USA 39°21′N 97°50′W
96 I12 **Glasgow** S Scotland, United Kingdom 55°53′N 04°15′W
20 K7 **Glasgow** Kentucky, S USA 37°00′N 85°54′W
27 T4 **Glasgow** Missouri, C USA 39°13′N 92°51′W
33 W7 **Glasgow** Montana, NW USA 48°12′N 106°37′W
21 T6 **Glasgow** Virginia, NE USA 37°37′N 79°27′W
96 I12 **Glasgow** ✈ W Scotland, United Kingdom 55°52′N 04°27′W
11 S14 **Glaslyn** Saskatchewan, S Canada 53°20′N 108°18′W
18 I16 **Glassboro** New Jersey, NE USA 39°40′N 75°05′W
24 L10 **Glass Mountains** ▲▲ Texas, SW USA
97 K23 **Glastonbury** SW England, United Kingdom 51°09′N 02°43′W
**Glatz** see Kłodzko
101 N16 **Glauchau** Sachsen, E Germany 50°48′N 12°32′E
**Glavn'a Morava** see Velika Morava
**Glavnik** see Gllamnik
127 T1 **Glazov** Udmurtskaya Respublika, NW Russia 58°06′N 52°38′E
**Głda** see Gwda
109 U8 **Gleinalpe** ▲▲ SE Austria
109 W8 **Gleisdorf** Steiermark, SE Austria 47°07′N 15°43′E
**Gleiwitz** see Gliwice
39 S11 **Glenallen** Alaska, USA 62°06′N 145°33′W
102 F7 **Glénan, Îles** island group NW France
185 G21 **Glenavy** Canterbury, South Island, New Zealand 44°53′S 171°04′E
10 H5 **Glenboyle** Yukon, NW Canada 63°55′N 138°43′W
21 X3 **Glen Burnie** Maryland, NE USA 39°09′N 76°37′W
36 L8 **Glen Canyon** canyon Utah, W USA
36 L8 **Glen Canyon Dam** dam Arizona, SW USA
30 K15 **Glen Carbon** Illinois, N USA 38°45′N 89°58′W
14 E17 **Glencoe** Ontario, S Canada 42°44′N 81°42′W
83 K22 **Glencoe** KwaZulu/Natal, E South Africa 28°10′S 30°15′E
29 U9 **Glencoe** Minnesota, N USA 44°46′N 94°09′W
96 H10 **Glen Coe** valley N Scotland, United Kingdom
36 K13 **Glendale** Arizona, SW USA 33°32′N 112°11′W
35 S15 **Glendale** California, W USA 34°09′N 118°20′W
182 G5 **Glendambo** South Australia 30°59′S 135°45′E
33 Y8 **Glendive** Montana, NW USA 47°08′N 104°42′W
33 Y15 **Glendo** Wyoming, C USA 42°27′N 105°01′W
55 S10 **Glendor Mountains** C Guyana
182 K12 **Glenelg River** ≈ South Australia/Victoria, SE Australia
29 P4 **Glenfield** North Dakota, N USA 47°25′N 98°33′W
25 V12 **Glen Flora** Texas, SW USA 29°22′N 96°12′W
181 P7 **Glen Helen** Northern Territory, N Australia 23°45′S 132°46′E
183 U5 **Glen Innes** New South Wales, SE Australia 29°42′S 151°45′E
31 P6 **Glen Lake** ◎ Michigan, N USA
10 I7 **Glenlyon Peak** ▲ Yukon, W Canada 62°32′N 134°51′W
37 N16 **Glenn, Mount** ▲ Arizona, SW USA 31°55′N 110°00′W
33 N15 **Glenns Ferry** Idaho, NW USA 42°57′N 115°18′W
23 W6 **Glennville** Georgia, SE USA 31°56′N 81°55′W
10 J10 **Glenora** British Columbia, W Canada 57°52′N 131°16′W
182 M11 **Glenorchy** Victoria, SE Australia 36°56′S 142°39′E
183 V5 **Glenreagh** New South Wales, SE Australia 30°04′S 153°00′E
33 X15 **Glenrock** Wyoming, C USA 42°51′N 105°52′W
96 K11 **Glenrothes** E Scotland, United Kingdom 56°11′N 03°09′W
18 L9 **Glens Falls** New York, NE USA 43°18′N 73°38′W
97 D14 **Glenties** Ir. Na Gleannta. Donegal, NW Ireland 54°47′N 08°17′W
28 L5 **Glen Ullin** North Dakota, N USA 46°49′N 101°49′W
21 R4 **Glenville** West Virginia, NE USA 38°57′N 80°51′W
27 T12 **Glenwood** Arkansas, C USA 34°19′N 93°33′W
29 S15 **Glenwood** Iowa, C USA 41°03′N 95°44′W
29 T7 **Glenwood** Minnesota, N USA 45°39′N 95°23′W
36 L5 **Glenwood** Utah, W USA 38°45′N 111°59′W
30 I5 **Glenwood City** Wisconsin, N USA 45°04′N 92°11′W
37 Q4 **Glenwood Springs** Colorado, C USA 39°33′N 107°21′W
108 F10 **Gletsch** Valais, S Switzerland 46°34′N 08°21′E
**Glevum** see Gloucester
29 U14 **Glidden** Iowa, C USA 42°03′N 94°43′W
112 E9 **Glina** var. Banijska Palanka. Sisak-Moslavina, NE Croatia 45°19′N 16°07′E
94 F11 **Glittertind** ▲ S Norway 61°24′N 08°19′E
111 J16 **Gliwice** Ger. Gleiwitz. Śląskie, S Poland 50°19′N 18°49′E
113 N16 **Gllamnik** Serb. Glavnik. N Kosovo 42°53′N 21°10′E
36 M14 **Globe** Arizona, SW USA 33°24′N 110°47′W
**Globino** see Hlobyne
108 L9 **Glockturm** ▲ SW Austria 46°54′N 10°42′E
116 L9 **Glodeni** Rus. Glodyany. N Moldova 47°47′N 27°33′E
109 S9 **Glödnitz** Kärnten, S Austria 46°57′N 14°03′E
**Glodyany** see Glodeni
**Glogau** see Głogów
109 W6 **Gloggnitz** Niederösterreich, E Austria 47°41′N 15°57′E
110 F13 **Głogów** Ger. Glogau, Glogow. Dolnośląskie, SW Poland 51°40′N 16°04′E
**Glogow** see Głogów
111 I16 **Głogówek** Ger. Oberglogau. Opolskie, S Poland 50°21′N 17°51′E
92 G12 **Glomfjord** Nordland, C Norway 66°49′N 14°00′E
**Glomma** see Gláma
**Glommen** see Gláma
93 I14 **Glommersträsk** Norrbotten, N Sweden 65°17′N 19°40′E
172 I1 **Glorieuses, Îles** Eng. Glorioso Islands. island group (to France) N Madagascar
**Glorioso Islands** see Glorieuses, Îles
65 C25 **Glorious Hill** hill East Falkland, Falkland Islands
38 J12 **Glory of Russia Cape** headland Saint Matthew Island, Alaska, USA 60°36′N 172°57′W
22 J7 **Gloster** Mississippi, S USA 31°12′N 91°01′W
183 U7 **Gloucester** New South Wales, SE Australia 32°01′S 152°00′E
186 F7 **Gloucester** New Britain, E Papua New Guinea 05°30′S 148°30′E
97 L21 **Gloucester** hist. Caer Glou, Lat. Glevum. C England, United Kingdom 51°53′N 02°14′W
19 P10 **Gloucester** Massachusetts, NE USA 42°36′N 70°36′W
21 X6 **Gloucester** Virginia, NE USA 37°26′N 76°33′W
97 K21 **Gloucestershire** cultural region C England, United Kingdom
31 T14 **Glouster** Ohio, N USA 39°30′N 82°04′W
42 H3 **Glovers Reef** reef E Belize
18 K10 **Gloversville** New York, NE USA 43°03′N 74°20′W
110 K12 **Głowno** Łódź, C Poland 51°58′N 19°43′E
111 H16 **Głubczyce** Ger. Leobschütz. Opolskie, S Poland 50°13′N 17°50′E
126 L11 **Glubokiy** Rostovskaya Oblast', SW Russia 48°34′N 40°16′E
145 W9 **Glubokoye** Vostochnyy Kazakhstan, E Kazakhstan 50°08′N 82°16′E
**Glubokoye** see Hlybokaye
111 H16 **Głuchołazy** Ger. Ziegenhais. Opolskie, S Poland 50°20′N 17°23′E
100 I9 **Glückstadt** Schleswig-Holstein, N Germany 53°47′N 09°26′E
**Glukhov** see Hlukhiv
**Glushkevichi** see Hlushkavichy
**Glusk/Glussk** see Hlusk
**Glybokaya** see Hlyboka
95 F21 **Glyngøre** Midtjylland, NW Denmark 56°45′N 08°55′E
127 Q9 **Gmelinka** Volgogradskaya Oblast', SW Russia 50°50′N 46°51′E
109 R8 **Gmünd** Kärnten, S Austria 46°56′N 13°32′E
109 U2 **Gmünd** Niederösterreich, N Austria 48°47′N 14°59′E
**Gmünd** see Schwäbisch Gmünd
109 S5 **Gmunden** Oberösterreich, N Austria 47°56′N 13°48′E
**Gmundner See** see Traunsee
94 N10 **Gnarp** Gävleborg, C Sweden 62°03′N 17°19′E
109 W8 **Gnas** Steiermark, SE Austria 46°53′N 15°48′E
**Gnaviyani** see Fuammulah
**Gnesen** see Gniezno
95 O16 **Gnesta** Södermanland, C Sweden 59°05′N 17°20′E
110 H11 **Gniezno** Ger. Gnesen. Weilkopolskie, C Poland 52°33′N 17°35′E
**Gnjilane** see Gjilan
95 K20 **Gnosjö** Jönköping, S Sweden 57°22′N 13°44′E
155 E17 **Goa** prev. Old Goa, Vela Goa, Velha Goa. Goa, W India 15°31′N 73°56′E
155 E17 **Goa** var. Old Goa. ◈ state W India
**Goabddális** see Kåbdalis
42 H7 **Goascorán, Río** ≈ El Salvador/Honduras
77 O16 **Goaso** var. Gawso. W Ghana 06°49′N 02°27′W
81 K14 **Goba** Oromīya, C Ethiopia 07°02′N 39°58′E
83 C20 **Gobabeb** Erongo, W Namibia 23°36′S 15°03′E
83 E19 **Gobabis** Omaheke, E Namibia 22°25′S 18°58′E
**Gobannium** see Abergavenny
64 M7 **Goban Spur** undersea feature NW Atlantic Ocean
63 H21 **Gobernador Gregores** Santa Cruz, S Argentina 48°43′S 70°21′W
61 F14 **Gobernador Ingeniero Virasoro** Corrientes, NE Argentina 28°06′S 56°00′W
162 L12 **Gobi** desert China/Mongolia
164 I14 **Gobō** Wakayama, Honshū, SW Japan 33°52′N 135°09′E
**Gobolka Awdal** see Awdal
**Gobolka Sool** see Sool
101 D14 **Goch** Nordrhein-Westfalen, W Germany 51°41′N 06°10′E
83 E20 **Gochas** Hardap, S Namibia 24°54′S 18°43′E
155 I14 **Godāvari** var. Godavari. ≈ C India
**Godavari** see Godāvari
155 L16 **Godāvari, Mouths of the** delta E India
15 V5 **Godbout** Québec, SE Canada 49°19′N 67°37′W
15 U5 **Godbout** ≈ Québec, SE Canada
15 U5 **Godbout Est** ≈ Québec, SE Canada
27 N6 **Goddard** Kansas, C USA 37°39′N 97°34′W
14 E15 **Goderich** Ontario, S Canada 43°43′N 81°43′W
**Godhavn** see Qeqertarsuaq
154 E10 **Godhra** Gujarāt, W India 22°49′N 73°40′E
**Göding** see Hodonín
111 K22 **Gödöllő** Pest, N Hungary 47°36′N 19°20′E
62 H11 **Godoy Cruz** Mendoza, W Argentina 32°59′S 68°49′W
11 Y11 **Gods** ≈ Manitoba, C Canada
11 X13 **Gods Lake** ◎ Manitoba, C Canada
11 Y13 **Gods Lake Narrows** Manitoba, C Canada 54°29′N 94°21′W
**Godthaab/Godthåb** see Nuuk
**Godwin Austen, Mount** see K2
**Goede Hoop, Kaap de** see Good Hope, Cape of
**Goedgegun** see Nhlangano
**Goeie Hoop, Kaap die** see Good Hope, Cape of
13 O7 **Goélands, Lac aux** ◎ Québec, SE Canada
98 E13 **Goeree** island SW Netherlands
99 F15 **Goes** Zeeland, SW Netherlands 51°30′N 03°55′E
**Goettingen** see Göttingen
19 O10 **Goffstown** New Hampshire, NE USA 43°01′N 71°34′W
14 E8 **Gogama** Ontario, S Canada 47°42′N 81°44′W
30 L3 **Gogebic, Lake** ◎ Michigan, N USA
30 K3 **Gogebic Range** hill range Michigan/Wisconsin, N USA
**Gogi Lerr** see Gogi, Mount
137 V13 **Gogi, Mount** Arm. Gogi Lerr, Az. Küküdağ. ▲ Armenia/Azerbaijan 39°33′N 45°35′E
124 F12 **Gogland, Ostrov** island NW Russia
111 I15 **Gogolin** Opolskie, S Poland 50°28′N 18°04′E
**Gogonou** see Gogounou
77 S14 **Gogounou** var. Gogonou. N Benin 10°50′N 02°50′E
152 I10 **Gohāna** Haryāna, N India 29°06′N 76°43′E
59 K18 **Goianésia** Goiás, C Brazil 15°21′S 49°02′W
59 K18 **Goiânia** prev. Goyania. state capital Goiás, C Brazil 16°43′S 49°18′W
59 K18 **Goiás** Goiás, C Brazil 15°57′S 50°07′W
59 J18 **Goiás** off. Estado de Goiás; prev. Goiaz, Goyaz. ◈ state C Brazil
**Goiás, Estado de** see Goiás
**Goiaz** see Goiás
**Goidhoo Atoll** see Horsburgh Atoll
159 R14 **Goinsargoin** Xizang Zizhiqu, W China 31°56′N 98°04′E
60 H10 **Goio-Erê** Paraná, SW Brazil 24°08′S 53°07′W
99 I15 **Goirle** Noord-Brabant, S Netherlands 51°31′N 05°04′E
104 H8 **Góis** Coimbra, N Portugal 40°10′N 08°06′W
165 Q8 **Gojōme** Akita, Honshū, NW Japan 39°55′N 140°07′E
149 U9 **Gojra** Punjab, E Pakistan 31°10′N 72°43′E
136 A11 **Gökçeada** var. Imroz Adasī, Gk. Imbros. island NW Turkey
**Gökçeada** see İmroz
146 F13 **Gökdepe** Rus. Gëkdepe, Geok-Tepe. Ahal Welaýaty, C Turkmenistan 38°05′N 58°08′E
136 I10 **Gökırmak** ≈ N Turkey
**Goklenkuy, Solonchak** see Geklengkui, Solonchak
136 C16 **Gökova Körfezi** gulf SW Turkey
136 K15 **Göksu** ≈ S Turkey
136 L15 **Göksun** Kahramanmaraş, C Turkey 38°03′N 36°30′E
136 I17 **Göksu Nehri** ≈ S Turkey
83 J16 **Gokwe** Midlands, NW Zimbabwe 18°13′S 28°55′E
94 F13 **Gol** Buskerud, S Norway 60°42′N 08°57′E
153 X12 **Golāghāt** Assam, NE India 26°31′N 93°54′E
110 H10 **Gołańcz** Wielkopolskie, C Poland 52°57′N 17°17′E
138 G8 **Golan Heights** Ar. Al Jawlān, Heb. HaGolan. ▲▲ SW Syria
**Golārā** see Ārān-va-Bidgol
**Golaya Pristan** see Hola Prystan'
143 T11 **Golbāf** Kermān, C Iran 29°51′N 57°44′E
136 M15 **Gölbaşı** Adıyaman, S Turkey 37°46′N 37°40′E
109 P9 **Gölbner** ▲ SW Austria 46°51′N 12°31′E
30 M17 **Golconda** Illinois, N USA 37°20′N 88°29′W
35 T3 **Golconda** Nevada, W USA 40°56′N 117°29′W
136 E11 **Gölcük** Kocaeli, NW Turkey 40°44′N 29°50′E
108 I7 **Goldach** Sankt Gallen, NE Switzerland 47°28′N 09°28′E
110 N7 **Gołdap** Ger. Goldap. Warmińsko-Mazurskie, NE Poland 54°19′N 22°23′E
32 E15 **Gold Beach** Oregon, NW USA 42°25′N 124°27′W
**Goldberg** see Złotoryja
183 V3 **Gold Coast** cultural region Queensland, E Australia
68 D12 **Gold Coast** coastal region S Ghana
39 R10 **Gold Creek** Alaska, USA 62°48′N 149°40′W
11 O16 **Golden** British Columbia, SW Canada 51°19′N 116°58′W
37 T4 **Golden** Colorado, C USA 39°40′N 105°12′W
184 I13 **Golden Bay** bay South Island, New Zealand
27 R7 **Golden City** Missouri, C USA 37°23′N 94°05′W
32 I11 **Goldendale** Washington, NW USA 45°49′N 120°49′W
**Goldener Tisch** see Zlatý Stôl




◆ Country
● Country Capital
◇ Dependent Territory
○ Dependent Territory Capital
◈ Administrative Regions
✈ International Airport
▲ Mountain
▲▲ Mountain Range
⛰ Volcano
≈ River
◎ Lake
⊠ Reservoir

Golden Grove – Grand Rapids


44 L13 **Golden Grove** E Jamaica 17°56′N 76°17′W
14 J12 **Golden Lake** ◎ Ontario, SE Canada
22 K10 **Golden Meadow** Louisiana, S USA 29°22′N 90°15′W
**Golden Sands** see Zlatni Pyasatsi
**Golden State, The** see California
83 K16 **Golden Valley** Mashonaland West, N Zimbabwe 18°11′S 29°50′E
35 U9 **Goldfield** Nevada, W USA 37°42′N 117°15′W
**Goldingen** see Kuldīga
**Goldmarkt** see Zlatna
10 K17 **Gold River** Vancouver Island, British Columbia, SW Canada 49°41′N 126°05′W
21 V10 **Goldsboro** North Carolina, SE USA 35°23′N 78°00′W
24 M8 **Goldsmith** Texas, SW USA 31°58′N 102°36′W
25 R8 **Goldthwaite** Texas, SW USA 31°28′N 98°35′W
137 R11 **Göle** Ardahan, NE Turkey 40°47′N 42°36′E
**Golema Ada** see Ostrovo
114 H9 **Golema Planina** ▲▲ W Bulgaria
114 F9 **Golemi Vrah** var. Golemi Vrŭkh. ▲ W Bulgaria 42°41′N 22°38′E
**Golemi Vrŭkh** see Golemi Vrah
110 D8 **Goleniów** Ger. Gollnow. Zachodnio-pomorskie, NW Poland 53°34′N 14°48′E
143 R3 **Golestān** off. Ostān-e Golestān. ◈ province N Iran
**Golestān, Ostān-e** see Golestān
35 Q14 **Goleta** California, W USA 34°26′N 119°50′W
43 O16 **Golfito** Puntarenas, SE Costa Rica 08°42′N 83°10′W
25 T13 **Goliad** Texas, SW USA 28°40′N 97°26′W
113 L14 **Golija** ▲▲ SW Serbia
**Golinka** see Gongbo'gyamda
113 O16 **Goljak** ▲▲ SE Serbia
136 M12 **Gölköy** Ordu, N Turkey 40°42′N 37°37′E
**Gollel** see Lavumisa
109 X3 **Göllersbach** ∿ NE Austria
**Gollnow** see Goleniów
**Golmo** see Golmud
159 P10 **Golmud** var. Ge'e'mu, Golmo, Chin. Ko-erh-mu. Qinghai, C China 36°23′N 94°56′E
103 Y14 **Golo** ∿ Corse, France, C Mediterranean Sea
**Golovanevsk** see Holovanivs'k
**Golovchin** see Halowchyn
39 N9 **Golovin** Alaska, USA 64°33′N 162°54′W
142 M7 **Golpāyegān** var. Gulpaigan. Eşfahān, W Iran 33°23′N 50°18′E
**Golshan** see Ţabas
**Gol'shany** see Hal'shany
96 J7 **Golspie** N Scotland, United Kingdom 57°59′N 03°56′W
112 O11 **Golubac** Serbia, NE Serbia 44°38′N 21°36′E
110 J9 **Golub-Dobrzyń** Kujawski-pomorskie, C Poland 53°07′N 19°03′E
145 S7 **Golubovka** Pavlodar, N Kazakhstan 53°07′N 74°11′E
82 B11 **Golungo Alto** Kwanza Norte, NW Angola 09°10′S 14°45′E
114 M8 **Golyama Kamchia** var. Golyama Kamchiya. ∿ E Bulgaria
**Golyama Kamchiya** see Golyama Kamchia
114 L8 **Golyama Reka** ∿ N Bulgaria
**Golyama Syutka** see Golyama Syutkya
114 H11 **Golyama Syutkya** var. Golyama Syutka. ▲ SW Bulgaria 41°55′N 24°03′E
114 I12 **Golyam Perelik** ▲ S Bulgaria 41°37′N 24°34′E
114 I11 **Golyam Persenk** ▲ S Bulgaria 41°50′N 24°33′E
79 P19 **Goma** Nord-Kivu, NE Dem. Rep. Congo 01°36′S 29°08′E
153 N13 **Gomati** var. Gumti. ∿ N India
77 X14 **Gombe** Gombe, E Nigeria 10°19′N 11°02′E
67 U10 **Gombe** var. Igombe. ∿ E Tanzania
77 Y14 **Gombi** Adamawa, E Nigeria 10°07′N 12°45′E
**Gombroon** see Bandar-e 'Abbās
**Gomel'** see Homyel'
**Gomel'skaya Oblast'** see Homyel'skaya Voblasts'
64 N11 **Gomera** island Islas Canarias, Spain, NE Atlantic Ocean
40 I5 **Gómez Farías** Chihuahua, N Mexico 29°25′N 107°46′W
40 L8 **Gómez Palacio** Durango, C Mexico 25°39′N 103°30′W
158 J13 **Gomo** Xizang Zizhiqu, W China 33°37′N 86°40′E
143 T6 **Gonābād** var. Gunabad. Khorāsān-e Razavī, NE Iran 36°30′N 59°18′E
44 L8 **Gonaïves** var. Les Gonaïves. N Haiti 19°26′N 72°41′W
123 Q12 **Gonam** ∿ NE Russia
44 L9 **Gonâve, Canal de la** var. Canal de Sud. channel N Caribbean Sea
44 K9 **Gonâve, Golfe de la** gulf N Caribbean Sea
**Gonāveh** see Bandar-e Gonāveh
44 K9 **Gonâve, Île de la** island C Haiti
**Gonbadān** see Do Gonbadān
143 Q3 **Gonbad-e Kāvūs** var. Gunbad-i-Qawus. Golestān, N Iran 37°15′N 55°11′E
152 M12 **Gonda** Uttar Pradesh, N India 27°08′N 81°58′E
**Gondar** see Gonder
80 I11 **Gonder** var. Gondar. Āmara, NW Ethiopia 12°36′N 37°27′E
78 J13 **Gondey** Moyen-Chari, S Chad 09°07′N 19°10′E
154 J12 **Gondia** Mahārāshtra, C India 21°27′N 80°12′E
104 G6 **Gondomar** Porto, NW Portugal 41°10′N 08°35′W
136 C12 **Gönen** Balıkesir, W Turkey 40°06′N 27°39′E
136 C12 **Gönen Çayı** ∿ NW Turkey
159 O15 **Gongbo'gyamda** var. Golinka. Xizang Zizhiqu, W China 30°03′N 93°10′E
**Gongchang** see Longxi
159 N16 **Gonggar** var. Gyixong. Xizang Zizhiqu, W China 29°18′N 90°56′E
160 G9 **Gongga Shan** ▲ C China 29°50′N 101°55′E
159 T10 **Gonghe** var. Qabqa. Qinghai, C China 36°20′N 100°46′E
**Gongjiang** see Yudu
158 I5 **Gongliu** var. Tokkuztara. Xinjiang Uygur Zizhiqu, NW China 43°29′N 82°16′E
77 W14 **Gongola** ∿ E Nigeria
**Gongoleh State** see Jonglei
183 P5 **Gongolgon** New South Wales, SE Australia 30°19′S 146°57′E
159 Q6 **Gongpoquan** Gansu, N China 41°45′N 100°27′E
**Gongquan** see Gongxian
**Gongtang** see Damxung
160 I10 **Gongxian** var. Gongquan, Gong Xian. Sichuan, C China 28°25′N 104°51′E
**Gong Xian** see Gongxian
157 V10 **Gongzhuling** prev. Huaide. Jilin, NE China 43°30′N 124°48′E
159 S14 **Gonjo** Xizang Zizhiqu, W China 30°51′N 98°16′E
107 B20 **Gonnesa** Sardegna, Italy, C Mediterranean Sea 39°15′N 08°27′E
**Gonni/Gónnos** see Gónnoi
115 F15 **Gónnoi** var. Gonni, Gónnos; prev. Derelí. Thessalía, C Greece 39°52′N 22°27′E
**Gōnoura** see Iki
35 O11 **Gonzales** California, W USA 36°30′N 121°26′W
22 J9 **Gonzales** Louisiana, S USA 30°14′N 90°55′W
25 T12 **Gonzales** Texas, SW USA 29°31′N 97°29′W
41 P11 **González** Tamaulipas, C Mexico 22°50′N 98°25′W
21 V6 **Goochland** Virginia, NE USA 37°42′N 77°54′W
195 X14 **Goodenough, Cape** headland Antarctica 66°15′S 126°35′E
186 F9 **Goodenough Island** var. Morata. island SE Papua New Guinea
39 N8 **Goodhope Bay** bay Alaska, USA
83 D26 **Good Hope, Cape of** Afr. Kaap de Goede Hoop, Kaap die Goeie Hoop. headland SW South Africa 34°19′S 18°25′E
10 K10 **Good Hope Lake** British Columbia, W Canada 59°15′N 129°18′W
83 E23 **Goodhouse** Northern Cape, W South Africa 28°54′S 18°13′E
33 O15 **Gooding** Idaho, NW USA 42°56′N 114°42′W
26 H3 **Goodland** Kansas, C USA 39°20′N 101°43′W
173 Y15 **Goodlands** NW Mauritius 20°02′S 57°39′E
20 J8 **Goodlettsville** Tennessee, S USA 36°19′N 86°42′W
39 N13 **Goodnews** Alaska, USA 59°07′N 161°35′W
25 O3 **Goodnight** Texas, SW USA 35°00′N 101°07′W
183 Q4 **Goodooga** New South Wales, SE Australia 29°09′S 147°30′E
29 N4 **Goodrich** North Dakota, N USA 47°24′N 100°07′W
25 W10 **Goodrich** Texas, SW USA 30°36′N 94°57′W
29 X10 **Goodview** Minnesota, N USA 44°04′N 91°42′W
26 H8 **Goodwell** Oklahoma, C USA 36°36′N 101°38′W
97 N17 **Goole** E England, United Kingdom 53°43′N 00°46′W
183 O8 **Goolgowi** New South Wales, SE Australia 34°00′S 145°43′E
182 I10 **Goolwa** South Australia 35°31′S 138°43′E
181 Y11 **Goondiwindi** Queensland, E Australia 28°33′S 150°22′E
98 O11 **Goor** Overijssel, E Netherlands 52°13′N 06°33′E
**Goose Bay** see Happy Valley-Goose Bay
33 V13 **Gooseberry Creek** ∿ Wyoming, C USA
21 S14 **Goose Creek** South Carolina, SE USA 32°58′N 80°01′W
63 M23 **Goose Green** var. Prado del Ganso. East Falkland, Falkland Islands 51°52′S 59°W
16 D8 **Goose Lake** var. Lago dos Gansos. ◎ California/Oregon, W USA
29 Q4 **Goose River** ∿ North Dakota, N USA
153 T16 **Gopalganj** Dhaka, S Bangladesh 23°00′N 89°48′E
153 O12 **Gopālganj** Bihār, N India 26°28′N 84°26′E
**Gopher State** see Minnesota
101 I22 **Göppingen** Baden-Württemberg, SW Germany 48°42′N 09°39′E
110 G13 **Góra** Ger. Guhrau. Dolnośląskie, SW Poland 51°40′N 16°03′E
110 M12 **Góra Kalwaria** Mazowieckie, C Poland 52°00′N 21°14′E
153 O12 **Gorakhpur** Uttar Pradesh, N India 26°45′N 83°23′E
**Gora Kyuren** see Kürendag
113 J14 **Goražde** Federacija Bosne I Hercegovine, SE Bosnia and Herzegovina 43°39′N 18°58′E
**Gorbovichi** see Harbavichy
**Gorče Petrov** see Đorče Petrov
0 E9 **Gorda Ridges** undersea feature NE Pacific Ocean 41°30′N 128°00′W
**Gordiaz** see Gardēz
78 K12 **Gordil** Vakaga, N Central African Republic 09°37′N 21°42′E
23 U5 **Gordon** Georgia, SE USA 32°52′N 83°19′W
28 K12 **Gordon** Nebraska, C USA 42°48′N 102°12′W
25 R7 **Gordon** Texas, SW USA 32°32′N 98°21′W
28 L13 **Gordon Creek** ∿ Nebraska, C USA
63 I25 **Gordon, Isla** island S Chile
183 O17 **Gordon, Lake** ◎ Tasmania, SE Australia
183 O17 **Gordon River** ∿ Tasmania, SE Australia
21 V5 **Gordonsville** Virginia, NE USA 38°08′N 78°11′W
78 H13 **Goré** Logone-Oriental, S Chad 07°55′N 16°38′E
80 H13 **Gorē** Oromīya, C Ethiopia 08°08′N 35°33′E
185 D24 **Gore** Southland, South Island, New Zealand 46°06′S 168°58′E
14 D11 **Gore Bay** Manitoulin Island, Ontario, S Canada 45°54′N 82°28′W
25 Q5 **Goree** Texas, SW USA 33°28′N 99°31′W
137 O11 **Görele** Giresun, NE Turkey 41°00′N 39°00′E
19 N6 **Gore Mountain** ▲ Vermont, NE USA 44°55′N 71°47′W
39 R13 **Gore Point** headland Alaska, USA 59°12′N 150°57′W
37 R4 **Gore Range** ▲▲ Colorado, C USA
97 F19 **Gorey** Ir. Guaire. Wexford, SE Ireland 52°40′N 06°18′W
143 R12 **Gorgāb** Kermān, S Iran
143 Q4 **Gorgān** var. Astarabad, Astrabad, Gurgan, prev. Asterābād; anc. Hyrcania. Golestān, N Iran 36°53′N 54°28′E
143 Q4 **Gorgān, Rūd-e** ∿ N Iran
76 I10 **Gorgol** ◈ region S Mauritania
106 D12 **Gorgona, Isola di** island Archipelago Toscano, C Italy
19 P8 **Gorham** Maine, NE USA 43°41′N 70°27′W
137 T10 **Gori** C Georgia 42°00′N 44°07′E
98 I13 **Gorinchem** var. Gorkum. Zuid-Holland, C Netherlands 51°50′N 04°59′E
137 V13 **Goris** SE Armenia 39°31′N 46°20′E
124 K16 **Goritsy** Tverskaya Oblast', W Russia 57°09′N 36°44′E
106 J7 **Gorizia** Ger. Görz. Friuli-Venezia Giulia, NE Italy 45°57′N 13°37′E
116 G13 **Gorj** ◈ county SW Romania
109 W12 **Gorjanci** var. Uskočke Planine, Žumberak, Žumberačko Gorje, Ger. Uskokengebirge; prev. Sichelburger Gerbirge. ▲ Croatia/Slovenia Europe see also Žumberačko Gorje
**Görkau** see Jirkov
**Gorki** see Horki
**Gor'kiy** see Nizhniy Novgorod
**Gorkum** see Gorinchem
95 I23 **Gørlev** Sjælland, E Denmark 55°33′N 11°14′E
111 M17 **Gorlice** Małopolskie, S Poland 49°40′N 21°09′E
101 Q15 **Görlitz** Sachsen, E Germany 51°09′N 14°58′E
**Görlitz** see Zgorzelec
**Gorlovka** see Horlivka
25 R7 **Gorman** Texas, SW USA 32°12′N 98°40′W
21 T3 **Gormania** West Virginia, NE USA 39°16′N 79°18′W
**Gorna Dzhumaya** see Blagoevgrad
114 K8 **Gorna Oryahovitsa** , Gorna Oryahovitsa. Veliko Tŭrnovo, N Bulgaria 43°07′N 25°40′E
**Gorna Oryakhovitsa** see Gorna Oryahovitsa
114 J8 **Gorna Studena** Veliko Tŭrnovo, N Bulgaria 43°26′N 25°21′E
**Gornja Mužlja** see Mužlja
109 X9 **Gornja Radgona** Ger. Oberradkersburg. NE Slovenia 46°39′N 16°00′E
112 M13 **Gornji Milanovac** Serbia, C Serbia 44°01′N 20°26′E
112 G13 **Gornji Vakuf** var. Uskoplje. Federacija Bosne I Hercegovine, SW Bosnia and Herzegovina 43°55′N 17°34′E
122 J13 **Gorno-Altaysk** Respublika Altay, S Russia 51°59′N 85°56′E
**Gorno-Altayskaya Respublika** see Altay, Respublika
123 N12 **Gorno-Chuyskiy** Irkutskaya Oblast', C Russia 57°33′N 111°38′E
125 V14 **Gornozavodsk** Permskiy Kray, NW Russia 58°21′N 58°24′E
125 V14 **Gornozavodsk** Ostrov Sakhalin, Sakhalinskaya Oblast', SE Russia 46°34′N 141°52′E
122 I13 **Gornyak** Altayskiy Kray, S Russia 50°58′N 81°24′E
127 R8 **Gornyy** Saratovskaya Oblast', W Russia 51°42′N 48°26′E
**Gornyy Altay** see Altay, Respublika
127 O10 **Gornyy Balykley** Volgogradskaya Oblast', SW Russia 49°37′N 45°03′E
80 I13 **Gorozh'an** ▲ W Ethiopia 09°09′N 37°16′E
116 J7 **Gorodenka** var. Horodenka. Ivano-Frankivs'ka Oblast', W Ukraine 48°41′N 25°28′E
127 O3 **Gorodets** Nizhegorodskaya Oblast', W Russia 56°36′N 43°27′E
**Gorodets** see Haradzyets
**Gorodeya** see Haradzyeya
127 P6 **Gorodishche** Penzenskaya Oblast', W Russia 53°17′N 45°39′E
**Gorodishche** see Horodyshche
**Gorodnya** see Horodnya
**Gorodok** see Haradok
**Gorodok/Gorodok Yagellonski** see Horodok
126 M13 **Gorodovikovsk** Respublika Kalmykiya, SW Russia 46°07′N 41°56′E
186 D7 **Goroka** Eastern Highlands, C Papua New Guinea 06°02′S 145°22′E
**Gorokhov** see Horokhiv
127 N3 **Gorokhovets** Vladimirskaya Oblast', W Russia 56°12′N 42°40′E
77 Q11 **Gorom-Gorom** NE Burkina Faso 14°27′N 00°14′W
171 U13 **Gorong, Kepulauan** island group E Indonesia
83 M17 **Gorongosa** Sofala, C Mozambique 18°40′S 34°03′E
171 P11 **Gorontalo** Sulawesi, C Indonesia 0°33′N 123°05′E
**Gorontalo, Teluk** see Tomini, Teluk
110 L7 **Górowo Iławeckie** Ger. Landsberg. Warmińsko-Mazurskie, NE Poland 54°18′N 20°30′E
98 M7 **Gorredijk** Fris. De Gordyk. Fryslân, N Netherlands 53°00′N 06°04′E
84 C14 **Gorringe Ridge** undersea feature E Atlantic Ocean 36°40′N 11°35′W
98 M11 **Gorssel** Gelderland, E Netherlands 52°12′N 06°13′E
109 T8 **Görtschitz** ∿ S Austria
**Goryany** see Harany
**Goryn** see Horyn'
145 S15 **Gory Shu-Ile** Kaz. Shū-Ile Taūlary; prev. Chu-Iliyskiye Gory. ▲▲ S Kazakhstan
**Görz** see Gorizia
110 E10 **Gorzów Wielkopolski** Ger. Landsberg, Landsberg an der Warthe. Lubuskie, W Poland 52°44′N 15°12′E
146 B10 **Goşabo** var. Goshoba, Rus. Koshoba. Balkan Welaýaty, NW Turkmenistan 40°28′N 54°11′E
108 G9 **Göschenen** Uri, C Switzerland 46°40′N 08°36′E
165 O11 **Gosen** Niigata, Honshū, C Japan 37°45′N 139°11′E
163 Y13 **Goseong** prev. Kosŏng. SE North Korea 38°41′N 128°14′E
183 T8 **Gosford** New South Wales, SE Australia 33°25′S 151°18′E
31 P11 **Goshen** Indiana, N USA 41°34′N 85°49′W
18 K13 **Goshen** New York, NE USA 41°24′N 74°17′W
**Goshoba** see Goşabo
**Goshoba** see Goşoba
165 Q7 **Goshogawara** var. Gosyogawara. Aomori, Honshū, C Japan 40°47′N 140°24′E
**Goshquduq Qum** see Tosquduq Qumlari
101 J14 **Goslar** Niedersachsen, C Germany 51°55′N 10°25′E
27 Y9 **Gosnell** Arkansas, C USA 35°57′N 89°58′W
146 B10 **Goşoba** var. Goshoba, Rus. Koshoba. Balkanskiy Velayat, NW Turkmenistan 40°28′N 54°11′E
112 C11 **Gospić** Lika-Senj, C Croatia 44°32′N 15°21′E
97 N23 **Gosport** S England, United Kingdom 50°48′N 01°08′W
94 D9 **Gossa** island S Norway
108 H7 **Gossau** Sankt Gallen, NE Switzerland 47°25′N 09°16′E
99 G20 **Gosselies** var. Goss'lies. Hainaut, S Belgium 50°28′N 04°26′E
77 P10 **Gossi** Tombouctou, C Mali 15°44′N 01°19′W
**Goss'lies** see Gosselies
113 N18 **Gostivar** W North Macedonia 41°48′N 20°55′E
**Gostomel'** see Hostomel'
110 G12 **Gostyń** var. Gostyn. Wielkopolskie, C Poland 51°52′N 17°00′E
**Gostyn** see Gostyń
110 K11 **Gostynin** Mazowieckie, C Poland 52°25′N 19°27′E
**Gosyogawara** see Goshogawara
95 J18 **Göta Älv** ∿ S Sweden
95 N17 **Göta kanal** canal S Sweden
95 K18 **Götaland** cultural region S Sweden
95 H17 **Göteborg** Eng. Gothenburg. Västra Götaland, S Sweden 57°43′N 11°58′E
77 X16 **Gotel Mountains** ▲▲ E Nigeria
95 K17 **Götene** Västra Götaland, S Sweden 58°32′N 13°29′E
**Gotera** see San Francisco
101 K16 **Gotha** Thüringen, C Germany 50°57′N 10°43′E
29 N15 **Gothenburg** Nebraska, C USA 40°57′N 100°09′W
**Gothenburg** see Göteborg
77 R12 **Gothèye** Tillabéri, SW Niger 13°52′N 01°27′E
**Gothland** see Gotland
95 P19 **Gotland** var. Gothland, Gottland. ◈ county SE Sweden
95 O18 **Gotland** island SE Sweden
164 A14 **Gotō** var. Hukue; prev. Fukue. Nagasaki, Fukue-jima, SW Japan 32°41′N 128°52′E
164 B13 **Gotō-rettō** island group SW Japan
114 H12 **Gotse Delchev** prev. Nevrokop. Blagoevgrad, SW Bulgaria 41°33′N 23°42′E
95 P17 **Gotska Sandön** island SE Sweden
108 G9 **Gotthard Base Tunnel** tunnel Switzerland
101 I15 **Göttingen** var. Goettingen. Niedersachsen, C Germany 51°33′N 09°55′E
**Gottland** see Gotland
93 I16 **Gottne** Västernorrland, C Sweden 63°27′N 18°25′E
**Gottschee** see Kočevje
**Gottwaldov** see Zlín
146 B11 **Goturdepe** Rus. Koturdepe. Balkan Welaýaty, W Turkmenistan 39°32′N 53°39′E
108 I7 **Götzis** Vorarlberg, NW Austria 47°21′N 09°40′E
98 H12 **Gouda** Zuid-Holland, C Netherlands 52°01′N 04°42′E
76 I11 **Goudiri** var. Goudiry. E Senegal 14°12′N 12°41′W
**Goudiry** see Goudiri
77 X12 **Goudoumaria** Diffa, S Niger 13°28′N 11°15′E
15 R9 **Gouffre, Rivière du** ∿ Québec, SE Canada
65 M19 **Gough Fracture Zone** tectonic feature S Atlantic Ocean
65 M19 **Gough Island** island Tristan da Cunha, S Atlantic Ocean
15 N8 **Gouin, Réservoir** ⊠ Québec, SE Canada
14 B10 **Goulais River** Ontario, S Canada 46°41′N 84°22′W
183 R9 **Goulburn** New South Wales, SE Australia 34°45′S 149°44′E
183 O11 **Goulburn River** ∿ Victoria, SE Australia
195 O10 **Gould Coast** physical region Antarctica
**Goulimine** see Guelmime
114 F13 **Gouménissa** Kentrikí Makedonía, N Greece 40°56′N 22°27′E
77 O10 **Goundam** Tombouctou, NW Mali 16°27′N 03°39′W
78 H12 **Goundi** Mandoul, S Chad 09°22′N 17°21′E
78 G12 **Gounou-Gaya** Mayo-Kébbi Est, SW Chad 09°37′N 15°30′E
**Gourci** see Goursi
**Gourcy** see Goursi
102 M13 **Gourdon** Lot, S France 44°45′N 01°22′E
77 W11 **Gouré** Zinder, SE Niger 13°59′N 10°16′E
102 G6 **Gourin** Morbihan, NW France 48°07′N 03°37′W
77 P10 **Gourma-Rharous** Tombouctou, C Mali 16°54′N 01°55′W
103 N4 **Gournay-en-Bray** Seine-Maritime, N France 49°29′N 01°42′E
78 J6 **Gouro** Ennedi-Ouest, N Chad 19°26′N 19°36′E
77 O12 **Goursi** var. Gourci, Gourcy. NW Burkina Faso 13°13′N 02°20′W
104 H8 **Gouveia** Guarda, N Portugal 40°29′N 07°35′W
18 I7 **Gouverneur** New York, NE USA 44°20′N 75°27′W
99 L21 **Gouvy** Luxembourg, E Belgium 50°10′N 05°55′E
45 R14 **Gouyave** var. Charlotte Town. NW Grenada 12°10′N 61°44′W
**Goverla, Gora** see Hoverla, Hora
59 N20 **Governador Valadares** Minas Gerais, SE Brazil 18°51′S 41°57′W
171 R8 **Governor Generoso** Mindanao, S Philippines 06°36′N 126°06′E
44 I2 **Governor's Harbour** Eleuthera Island, C The Bahamas 25°11′N 76°15′W
162 F9 **Govĭ-Altay** ◈ province SW Mongolia
162 I10 **Govĭ Altayn Nuruu** ▲▲ S Mongolia
154 L9 **Govind Ballabh Pant Sāgar** ⊠ C India
152 I7 **Govind Sāgar** ⊠ NE India
162 M8 **Govĭ-Sumber** ◈ province C Mongolia
**Govurdak** see Magdanly
18 D11 **Gowanda** New York, NE USA 42°25′N 78°55′W
148 J10 **Gowd-e Zerah, Dasht-e** marsh SW Afghanistan
14 F8 **Gowganda** Ontario, S Canada 47°41′N 80°46′W
14 G8 **Gowganda Lake** ◎ Ontario, S Canada
**Gōwr** see Ghōr
29 U13 **Gowrie** Iowa, C USA 42°16′N 94°17′W
**Gowurdak** see Magdanly
61 C15 **Goya** Corrientes, NE Argentina 29°10′S 59°15′W
**Goyania** see Goiânia
**Goyaz** see Goiás
137 X11 **Göyçay** Rus. Geokchay. C Azerbaijan 40°38′N 47°44′E
137 V11 **Göygöl**; prev. Xanlar. NW Azerbaijan 40°37′N 46°18′E
146 D10 **Goymat** Rus. Koymat. Balkan Welaýaty, NW Turkmenistan 40°23′N 55°45′E
146 D10 **Goymatdag, Gory** Rus. Gory Koymatdag. hill range Balkan Welaýaty, NW Turkmenistan
136 F12 **Göynük** Bolu, NW Turkey 40°24′N 30°45′E
165 R9 **Goyō-san** ▲ Honshū, C Japan 39°12′N 141°40′E
78 K11 **Goz Beïda** Sila, SE Chad 12°06′N 21°22′E
146 M10 **G'ozg'on** Rus. Gazgan. Navoiy Viloyati, C Uzbekistan 40°36′N 65°29′E
158 H11 **Gozha Co** ◎ W China
121 O15 **Gozo** var. Ghawdex. island N Malta
80 H9 **Gōz Regeb** Kassala, NE Sudan 16°03′N 35°33′E
83 H25 **Graaff-Reinet** Eastern Cape, S South Africa 32°15′S 24°32′E
**Graasten** see Gråsten
76 L17 **Grabo** SW Ivory Coast 04°57′N 07°30′W
112 P11 **Grabovica** Serbia, E Serbia 44°30′N 22°29′E
110 I13 **Grabów nad Prosną** Wielkopolskie, C Poland 51°30′N 18°06′E
108 I8 **Grabs** Sankt Gallen, NE Switzerland 47°10′N 09°27′E
112 D12 **Gračac** Zadar, SW Croatia 44°18′N 15°52′E
112 I11 **Gračanica** Federacija Bosne I Hercegovine, NE Bosnia and Herzegovina 44°41′N 18°20′E
14 L11 **Gracefield** Québec, SE Canada 46°06′N 76°03′W
99 K19 **Grâce-Hollogne** Liège, E Belgium 50°38′N 05°30′E
23 R8 **Graceville** Florida, SE USA 30°57′N 85°31′W
29 R8 **Graceville** Minnesota, N USA 45°34′N 96°25′W
42 G6 **Gracias** Lempira, W Honduras 14°35′N 88°35′W
**Gracias** see Lempira
42 L5 **Gracias a Dios** ◈ department E Honduras
43 O6 **Gracias a Dios, Cabo de** headland Honduras/Nicaragua 15°00′N 83°10′W
64 O2 **Graciosa** var. Ilha Graciosa. island Azores, Portugal, NE Atlantic Ocean
64 Q11 **Graciosa** island Islas Canarias, Spain, NE Atlantic Ocean
**Graciosa, Ilha** see Graciosa
112 I11 **Gradačac** Federacija Bosne I Hercegovine, N Bosnia and Herzegovina 44°51′N 18°24′E
59 J15 **Gradaús, Serra dos** ▲▲ C Brazil
104 L3 **Gradefes** Castilla y León, N Spain 42°37′N 05°14′W
**Gradiška** see Bosanska Gradiška
**Gradizhsk** see Hradyz'k
106 J7 **Grado** Friuli-Venezia Giulia, NE Italy 45°41′N 13°24′E
**Grado** see Grau
113 P19 **Gradsko** C North Macedonia 41°34′N 21°56′E
37 V11 **Grady** New Mexico, SW USA 34°49′N 103°19′W
**Grad Zagreb** see Zagreb
29 T12 **Graettinger** Iowa, C USA 43°14′N 94°45′W
101 M23 **Grafing** Bayern, SE Germany 48°01′N 11°57′E
25 S6 **Graford** Texas, SW USA 32°56′N 98°15′W
183 V5 **Grafton** New South Wales, SE Australia 29°41′S 152°55′E
29 Q3 **Grafton** North Dakota, N USA 48°24′N 97°24′W
21 S3 **Grafton** West Virginia, NE USA 39°21′N 80°03′W
21 T9 **Graham** North Carolina, SE USA 36°05′N 79°25′W
25 R6 **Graham** Texas, SW USA 33°07′N 98°36′W
**Graham Bell Island** see Greem-Bell, Ostrov
10 I13 **Graham Island** island Queen Charlotte Islands, British Columbia, SW Canada
19 S6 **Graham Lake** ◎ Maine, NE USA
194 H4 **Graham Land** physical region Antarctica
37 N15 **Graham, Mount** ▲ Arizona, SW USA 32°42′N 109°52′W
**Grahamstad** see Grahamstown
83 I25 **Grahamstown** Afr. Grahamstad. Eastern Cape, S South Africa 33°18′S 26°32′E
**Grahovo** see Bosansko Grahovo
68 C12 **Grain Coast** coastal region S Liberia
169 S17 **Grajagan, Teluk** bay Jawa, S Indonesia
59 L14 **Grajaú** Maranhão, E Brazil 05°50′S 45°12′W
58 M13 **Grajaú, Rio** ∿ NE Brazil
110 O8 **Grajewo** Podlaskie, NE Poland 53°38′N 22°26′E
95 F24 **Gram** Syddanmark, SW Denmark 55°18′N 09°03′E
103 N13 **Gramat** Lot, S France 44°45′N 01°45′E
22 H5 **Grambling** Louisiana, S USA 32°31′N 92°43′W
115 C14 **Grámmos** ▲ Albania/Greece
96 I9 **Grampian Mountains** ▲▲ C Scotland, United Kingdom
182 L12 **Grampians, The** ▲▲ Victoria, SE Australia
98 O9 **Gramsbergen** Overijssel, E Netherlands 52°37′N 06°39′E
113 L21 **Gramsh** var. Gramshi. Elbasan, C Albania 40°52′N 20°12′E
**Gramshi** see Gramsh
**Gran** see Esztergom, Hungary
**Gran** see Hron
54 F11 **Granada** Meta, C Colombia 03°33′N 73°44′W
42 J10 **Granada** Granada, SW Nicaragua 11°55′N 85°58′W
105 N14 **Granada** Andalucía, S Spain 37°13′N 03°41′W
37 W6 **Granada** Colorado, C USA 38°00′N 102°18′W
42 J11 **Granada** ◈ department SW Nicaragua
105 N14 **Granada** ◈ province Andalucía, S Spain
63 I21 **Gran Antiplanicie Central** plain S Argentina
97 E17 **Granard** Ir. Gránard. C Ireland 53°47′N 07°30′W
**Gránard** see Granard
63 J20 **Gran Bajo** basin S Argentina
63 J15 **Gran Bajo del Gualicho** basin E Argentina
63 I21 **Gran Bajo de San Julián** basin SE Argentina
25 S7 **Granbury** Texas, SW USA 32°27′N 97°47′W
15 P12 **Granby** Québec, SE Canada 45°23′N 72°44′W
27 S8 **Granby** Missouri, C USA 36°55′N 94°14′W
37 S3 **Granby, Lake** ⊠ Colorado, C USA
64 O12 **Gran Canaria** var. Grand Canary. island Islas Canarias, Spain, NE Atlantic Ocean
47 T11 **Gran Chaco** var. Chaco. lowland plain South America
45 R14 **Grand Anse** SW Grenada 12°01′N 61°45′W
**Grand-Anse** see Portsmouth
44 G1 **Grand Bahama Island** island N The Bahamas
**Grand Balé** see Tui
103 U7 **Grand Ballon** Ger. Ballon de Guebwiller. ▲ NE France 47°53′N 07°06′E
13 T13 **Grand Bank** Newfoundland, Newfoundland and Labrador, SE Canada 47°06′N 55°48′W
64 I7 **Grand Banks of Newfoundland** undersea feature NW Atlantic Ocean 45°00′N 40°00′W
**Grand Bassa** see Buchanan
77 N17 **Grand-Bassam** var. Bassam. SE Ivory Coast 05°14′N 03°45′W
14 E16 **Grand Bend** Ontario, S Canada 43°17′N 81°46′W
76 L17 **Grand-Bérébi** var. Grand-Béréby. SW Ivory Coast 04°38′N 06°55′W
**Grand-Béréby** see Grand-Bérébi
45 X11 **Grand-Bourg** Marie-Galante, SE Guadeloupe 15°53′N 61°19′W
44 M6 **Grand Caicos** var. Middle Caicos. island C Turks and Caicos Islands
14 K12 **Grand Calumet, Île du** island Québec, SE Canada
97 E18 **Grand Canal** Ir. An Chanáil Mhór. canal C Ireland
**Grand Canal** see Da Yunhe
**Grand Canary** see Gran Canaria
36 K10 **Grand Canyon** Arizona, SW USA 36°01′N 112°10′W
36 J9 **Grand Canyon** canyon Arizona, SW USA
**Grand Canyon State** see Arizona
44 D8 **Grand Cayman** island SW Cayman Islands
11 R14 **Grand Centre** Alberta, SW Canada 54°25′N 110°13′W
76 L17 **Grand Cess** SE Liberia 04°36′N 08°12′W
108 D12 **Grand Combin** ▲ S Switzerland 45°58′N 07°27′E
32 K8 **Grand Coulee** Washington, NW USA 47°56′N 119°00′W
32 J8 **Grand Coulee** valley Washington, NW USA
45 X5 **Grand Cul-de-Sac Marin** bay N Guadeloupe
**Grand Duchy of Luxembourg** see Luxembourg
63 I22 **Grande, Bahía** bay S Argentina
11 N14 **Grande Cache** Alberta, W Canada 53°53′N 119°07′W
103 U12 **Grande Casse** ▲ E France 45°22′N 06°50′E
**Grande Comore** see Ngazidja
61 G18 **Grande, Cuchilla** hill range E Uruguay
45 S5 **Grande de Añasco, Río** ∿ W Puerto Rico
**Grande de Chiloé, Isla** see Chiloé, Isla de
58 J12 **Grande de Gurupá, Ilha** river island NE Brazil
57 K21 **Grande de Lipez, Río** ∿ SW Bolivia
45 U6 **Grande de Loíza, Río** ∿ E Puerto Rico
45 T5 **Grande de Manatí, Río** ∿ C Puerto Rico
42 L9 **Grande de Matagalpa, Río** ∿ C Nicaragua
40 K12 **Grande de Santiago, Río** var. Santiago. ∿ C Mexico
43 O15 **Grande de Térraba, Río** var. Río Térraba. ∿ SE Costa Rica
12 J9 **Grande Deux, Réservoir la** ⊠ Québec, E Canada
61 O10 **Grande, Ilha** island SE Brazil
11 O13 **Grande Prairie** Alberta, W Canada 55°10′N 118°52′W
74 I8 **Grand Erg Occidental** desert W Algeria
74 L9 **Grand Erg Oriental** desert Algeria/Tunisia
57 M18 **Grande, Río** ∿ C Bolivia
59 J20 **Grande, Río** ∿ S Brazil
2 F15 **Grande, Río** var. Río Bravo, Sp. Río Bravo del Norte, Bravo del Norte. ∿ Mexico/USA
15 Y7 **Grande-Rivière** Québec, SE Canada 48°27′N 64°37′W
15 Y6 **Grande Rivière** ∿ Québec, SE Canada
44 M8 **Grande-Rivière-du-Nord** N Haiti 19°36′N 72°10′W
62 K9 **Grande, Salina** var. Gran Salitral. salt lake C Argentina
15 S7 **Grandes-Bergeronnes** Québec, SE Canada 48°16′N 69°32′W
47 W6 **Grande, Serra** ▲ W Brazil
40 K4 **Grande, Sierra** ▲▲ N Mexico
103 S12 **Grandes Rousses** ▲▲ E France
63 K17 **Grandes, Salinas** salt lake E Argentina
103 T5 **Grand Est** ◈ region NE France
45 Y5 **Grande Terre** island E West Indies
15 X5 **Grande-Vallée** Québec, SE Canada 49°14′N 65°08′W
45 Y5 **Grande Vigie, Pointe de la** headland Grande Terre, N Guadeloupe 16°31′N 61°27′W
13 N14 **Grand Falls** New Brunswick, SE Canada 47°02′N 67°46′W
13 T11 **Grand Falls** Newfoundland, Newfoundland and Labrador, SE Canada 48°57′N 55°48′W
24 L9 **Grandfalls** Texas, SW USA 31°20′N 102°51′W
21 P9 **Grandfather Mountain** ▲ North Carolina, SE USA 36°06′N 81°48′W
26 L13 **Grandfield** Oklahoma, C USA 34°15′N 98°40′W
11 N17 **Grand Forks** British Columbia, SW Canada 49°02′N 118°30′W
29 R4 **Grand Forks** North Dakota, N USA 47°54′N 97°03′W
31 O9 **Grand Haven** Michigan, N USA 43°03′N 86°13′W
**Grandichi** see Hrandzichy
29 P15 **Grand Island** Nebraska, C USA 40°55′N 98°20′W
31 O3 **Grand Island** island Michigan, N USA
22 K10 **Grand Isle** Louisiana, S USA 29°12′N 90°00′W
65 A23 **Grand Jason** island Jason Islands, NW Falkland Islands
37 P5 **Grand Junction** Colorado, C USA 39°03′N 108°33′W
20 F10 **Grand Junction** Tennessee, S USA 35°03′N 89°11′W
14 J9 **Grand-Lac-Victoria** Québec, SE Canada 47°33′N 77°28′W
14 J9 **Grand lac Victoria** ◎ Québec, SE Canada
77 N17 **Grand-Lahou** var. Grand Lahu. S Ivory Coast 05°09′N 05°01′W
**Grand Lahu** see Grand-Lahou
37 S3 **Grand Lake** Colorado, C USA 40°15′N 105°49′W
13 S11 **Grand Lake** ◎ Newfoundland and Labrador, E Canada
22 G9 **Grand Lake** ◎ Louisiana, S USA
31 R5 **Grand Lake** ◎ Michigan, N USA
31 Q13 **Grand Lake** ⊠ Ohio, N USA
27 R9 **Grand Lake O' The Cherokees** var. Lake O' The Cherokees. ⊠ Oklahoma, C USA
31 Q9 **Grand Ledge** Michigan, N USA 42°45′N 84°45′W
102 I8 **Grand-Lieu, Lac de** ◎ NW France
19 U6 **Grand Manan Channel** channel Canada/USA
13 O15 **Grand Manan Island** island New Brunswick, SE Canada
29 Y4 **Grand Marais** Minnesota, N USA 47°45′N 90°19′W
15 P10 **Grand-Mère** Québec, SE Canada 46°36′N 72°41′W
37 P5 **Grand Mesa** ▲ Colorado, C USA
108 C10 **Grand Muveran** ▲ W Switzerland 46°16′N 07°12′E
104 G12 **Grândola** Setúbal, S Portugal 38°10′N 08°34′W
**Grand Paradis** see Gran Paradiso
187 O15 **Grand Passage** passage N New Caledonia
77 R16 **Grand-Popo** S Benin 06°19′N 01°50′E
29 Z3 **Grand Portage** Minnesota, N USA 48°00′N 89°36′W
25 T6 **Grand Prairie** Texas, SW USA 32°45′N 97°00′W
11 W14 **Grand Rapids** Manitoba, C Canada 53°12′N 99°19′W
31 P9 **Grand Rapids** Michigan, N USA 42°57′N 86°40′W
29 V5 **Grand Rapids** Minnesota, N USA 47°14′N 93°31′W



◆ Country ● Country Capital ◇ Dependent Territory ○ Dependent Territory Capital ◈ Administrative Regions ✈ International Airport ▲ Mountain ▲▲ Mountain Range Volcano River ◎ Lake ⊠ Reservoir
255

Grand-Remous – Grundy

14 L10 **Grand-Remous** Québec, SE Canada 46°36′N 75°53′W
14 F15 **Grand River** ≈ Ontario, S Canada
31 P9 **Grand River** ≈ Michigan, N USA
27 T3 **Grand River** ≈ Missouri, C USA
28 M7 **Grand River** ≈ South Dakota, N USA
45 Q11 **Grand' Rivière** N Martinique 14°52′N 61°11′W
32 F11 **Grand Ronde** Oregon, NW USA 45°03′N 123°43′W
32 L11 **Grand Ronde River** ≈ Oregon/Washington, NW USA
**Grand-Saint-Bernard, Col du** *see* Great Saint Bernard Pass
25 V6 **Grand Saline** Texas, SW USA 32°40′N 95°42′W
55 X10 **Grand-Santi** W French Guiana 04°19′N 54°24′W
**Grandsee** *see* Grandson
172 J16 **Grand Sœur** *island* Les Sœurs, NE Seychelles
108 B9 **Grandson** *prev.* Grandsee. Vaud, W Switzerland 46°49′N 06°39′E
33 S14 **Grand Teton** ▲ Wyoming, C USA 43°44′N 110°48′W
31 P5 **Grand Traverse Bay** *lake bay* Michigan, N USA
45 N6 **Grand Turk** ○ (Turks and Caicos Islands) Grand Turk Island, S Turks and Caicos Islands 21°24′N 71°08′W
45 N6 **Grand Turk Island** *island* SE Turks and Caicos Islands
103 S13 **Grand Veymont** ▲ E France 44°51′N 05°32′E
11 W15 **Grandview** Manitoba, S Canada 51°11′N 100°41′W
27 R4 **Grandview** Missouri, C USA 38°53′N 94°31′W
36 I10 **Grand Wash Cliffs** *cliff* Arizona, SW USA
14 J8 **Granet, Lac** ◎ Québec, SE Canada
95 L14 **Grangärde** Dalarna, C Sweden 60°15′N 15°00′E
44 H12 **Grange Hill** W Jamaica 18°19′N 78°11′W
96 J12 **Grangemouth** C Scotland, United Kingdom 56°01′N 03°44′W
25 T10 **Granger** Texas, SW USA 30°43′N 97°26′W
32 J10 **Granger** Washington, NW USA 46°20′N 120°11′W
33 T17 **Granger** Wyoming, C USA 41°37′N 109°58′W
**Granges** *see* Grenchen
95 L14 **Grängesberg** Dalarna, C Sweden 60°06′N 15°00′E
33 N11 **Grangeville** Idaho, NW USA 45°55′N 116°07′W
10 K13 **Granisle** British Columbia, SW Canada 54°55′N 126°14′W
30 K15 **Granite City** Illinois, N USA 38°42′N 90°09′W
29 S9 **Granite Falls** Minnesota, N USA 44°48′N 95°33′W
21 Q9 **Granite Falls** North Carolina, SE USA 35°48′N 81°25′W
36 K12 **Granite Mountain** ▲ Arizona, SW USA 34°38′N 112°34′W
33 T12 **Granite Peak** ▲ Montana, NW USA 45°09′N 109°48′W
35 T2 **Granite Peak** ▲ Nevada, W USA 41°40′N 117°35′W
36 J3 **Granite Peak** ▲ Utah, W USA 40°09′N 113°18′W
**Granite State** *see* New Hampshire
107 H24 **Granitola, Capo** *headland* Sicilia, Italy, C Mediterranean Sea 37°33′N 12°39′E
185 H15 **Granity** West Coast, South Island, New Zealand 41°37′S 171°53′E
**Gran Lago** *see* Nicaragua, Lago de
63 J18 **Gran Laguna Salada** ◎ S Argentina
44 H7 **Granma** ◈ *province* SE Cuba
**Gran Malvina** *see* West Falkland
95 L18 **Gränna** Jönköping, S Sweden 58°02′N 14°30′E
105 W5 **Granollers** *var.* Granollérs. Cataluña, NE Spain 41°37′N 02°18′E
**Granollérs** *see* Granollers
106 A7 **Gran Paradiso** *Fr.* Grand Paradis. ▲ NW Italy 45°31′N 07°13′E
**Gran Pilastro** *see* Hochfeiler
**Gran Salitral** *see* Grande, Salina
**Gran San Bernardo, Passo di** *see* Great Saint Bernard Pass
**Gran Santiago** *see* Santiago
107 J14 **Gran Sasso d'Italia** ▲▲ C Italy
100 N11 **Gransee** Brandenburg, NE Germany 53°00′N 13°10′E
28 L15 **Grant** Nebraska, C USA 40°50′N 101°43′W
27 R1 **Grant City** Missouri, C USA 40°29′N 94°25′W
97 N19 **Grantham** E England, United Kingdom 52°55′N 00°39′W
65 D24 **Grantham Sound** *sound* East Falkland, Falkland Islands
194 K13 **Grant Island** *island* Antarctica
45 Z14 **Grantley Adams** ✈ (Bridgetown) SE Barbados 13°04′N 59°29′W
35 S7 **Grant, Mount** ▲ Nevada, W USA 38°34′N 118°47′W
96 J9 **Grantown-on-Spey** N Scotland, United Kingdom 57°11′N 03°53′W
35 W8 **Grant Range** ▲▲ Nevada, W USA
37 Q11 **Grants** New Mexico, SW USA 35°09′N 107°50′W
30 I4 **Grantsburg** Wisconsin, N USA 45°47′N 92°40′W
32 F15 **Grants Pass** Oregon, NW USA 42°26′N 123°20′W
36 K3 **Grantsville** Utah, W USA 40°36′N 112°27′W
21 R4 **Grantsville** West Virginia, NE USA 38°55′N 81°07′W
102 I5 **Granville** Manche, N France 48°50′N 01°35′W
11 V12 **Granville Lake** ◎ Manitoba, C Canada
25 V8 **Grapeland** Texas, SW USA 31°29′N 95°28′W
25 T6 **Grapevine** Texas, SW USA 32°55′N 97°04′W
83 K20 **Graskop** Mpumalanga, NE South Africa 24°58′S 30°49′E
95 P14 **Gräsö** Uppsala, C Sweden 60°22′N 18°30′E
93 I19 **Gräsö** *island* C Sweden
103 U15 **Grasse** Alpes-Maritimes, SE France 43°42′N 06°52′E
18 E14 **Grassflat** Pennsylvania, NE USA 41°00′N 78°04′W
33 U9 **Grassrange** Montana, NW USA 47°02′N 108°48′W
18 J6 **Grass River** ≈ New York, NE USA
35 P6 **Grass Valley** California, W USA 39°12′N 121°04′W
183 N14 **Grassy** Tasmania, SE Australia 40°03′S 144°04′E
28 K4 **Grassy Butte** North Dakota, N USA 47°20′N 103°13′W
21 R5 **Grassy Knob** ▲ West Virginia, NE USA 38°04′N 80°31′W
95 G24 **Gråsten** *var.* Graasten. Syddanmark, SW Denmark 54°55′N 09°37′E
95 J18 **Grästorp** Västra Götaland, S Sweden 58°20′N 12°40′E
**Gratianopolis** *see* Grenoble
109 V8 **Gratwein** Steiermark, SE Austria 47°08′N 15°20′E
**Gratz** *see* Graz
104 K2 **Grau** *var.* Grado. Asturias, N Spain 43°23′N 06°04′W
108 I9 **Graubünden** *Fr.* Grisons, *It.* Grigioni. ◈ *canton* SE Switzerland
**Graudenz** *see* Grudziądz
103 N15 **Graulhet** Tarn, S France 43°45′N 01°58′E
105 T4 **Graus** Aragón, NE Spain 42°11′N 00°21′E
61 I16 **Gravataí** Rio Grande do Sul, S Brazil 29°55′S 51°00′W
98 L13 **Grave** Noord-Brabant, SE Netherlands 51°45′N 05°45′E
11 T17 **Gravelbourg** Saskatchewan, S Canada 49°53′N 106°33′W
103 N1 **Gravelines** Nord, N France 51°00′N 02°07′E
**Graven** *see* Grez-Doiceau
14 H13 **Gravenhurst** Ontario, S Canada 44°55′N 79°22′W
33 O10 **Grave Peak** ▲ Idaho, NW USA 46°24′N 114°43′W
102 I11 **Grave, Pointe de** *headland* W France 45°33′N 01°04′W
183 S4 **Gravesend** New South Wales, SE Australia 29°37′S 150°15′E
97 P22 **Gravesend** SE England, United Kingdom 51°27′N 00°24′E
107 N17 **Gravina in Puglia** Puglia, SE Italy 40°48′N 16°25′E
103 S8 **Gray** Haute-Saône, E France 47°28′N 05°34′E
23 T4 **Gray** Georgia, SE USA 33°00′N 83°31′W
195 V16 **Gray, Cape** *headland* Antarctica 67°30′N 143°30′E
32 F9 **Grayland** Washington, NW USA 46°46′N 124°07′W
39 N10 **Grayling** Alaska, USA 62°55′N 160°07′W
31 Q6 **Grayling** Michigan, N USA 44°40′N 84°43′W
32 F9 **Grays Harbor** *inlet* Washington, NW USA
21 O5 **Grayson** Kentucky, S USA 38°21′N 82°59′W
37 S4 **Grays Peak** ▲ Colorado, C USA 39°37′N 105°49′W
30 M16 **Grayville** Illinois, N USA 38°15′N 87°59′W
109 V8 **Graz** *prev.* Gratz. Steiermark, SE Austria 47°05′N 15°23′E
104 L15 **Grazalema** Andalucía, S Spain 36°46′N 05°23′W
113 P15 **Grdelica** Serbia, SE Serbia 42°54′N 22°05′E
44 H1 **Great Abaco** *var.* Abaco Island. *island* N The Bahamas
**Great Admiralty Island** *see* Manus Island
**Great Alfold** *see* Great Hungarian Plain
**Great Ararat** *see* Büyük Ağrı Dağı
181 U8 **Great Artesian Basin** *lowlands* Queensland, C Australia
181 O12 **Great Australian Bight** *bight* S Australia
64 E11 **Great Bahama Bank** *undersea feature* E Gulf of Mexico 23°15′N 78°00′W
184 M4 **Great Barrier Island** *island* N New Zealand
181 X4 **Great Barrier Reef** *reef* Queensland, NE Australia
18 L11 **Great Barrington** Massachusetts, NE USA 42°11′N 73°20′W
0 F10 **Great Basin** *basin* W USA
8 I8 **Great Bear Lake** *Fr.* Grand Lac de l'Ours. ◎ Northwest Territories, NW Canada
**Great Belt** *see* Storebælt
26 L5 **Great Bend** Kansas, C USA 38°22′N 98°47′W
**Great Bermuda** *see* Bermuda
97 A20 **Great Blasket Island** *Ir.* An Blascaod Mór. *island* SW Ireland
**Great Britain** *see* Britain
151 Q23 **Great Channel** *channel* Andaman Sea/Indian Ocean
166 J10 **Great Coco Island** *island* SW Myanmar (Burma)
**Great Crosby** *see* Crosby
21 X7 **Great Dismal Swamp** *wetland* North Carolina/Virginia, SE USA
33 V16 **Great Divide Basin** *basin* Wyoming, C USA
181 W7 **Great Dividing Range** ▲▲ NE Australia
14 D12 **Great Duck Island** *island* Ontario, S Canada
**Great Elder Reservoir** *see* Waconda Lake
44 G8 **Greater Antilles** *island group* West Indies
129 V16 **Greater Sunda Islands** *var.* Sunda Islands. *island group* Indonesia
184 I1 **Great Exhibition Bay** *inlet* North Island, New Zealand
44 H4 **Great Exuma Island** *island* C The Bahamas
33 R8 **Great Falls** Montana, NW USA 47°30′N 111°18′W
21 R11 **Great Falls** South Carolina, SE USA 34°34′N 80°54′W
84 F9 **Great Fisher Bank** *undersea feature* C North Sea 57°00′N 04°00′E
**Great Glen** *see* Mor, Glen
**Great Grimsby** *see* Grimsby
44 I4 **Great Guana Cay** *island* C The Bahamas
64 I5 **Great Hellefiske Bank** *undersea feature* N Atlantic Ocean
111 L24 **Great Hungarian Plain** *var.* Great Alfold, Plain of Hungary, *Hung.* Alföld. *plain* SE Europe
44 L7 **Great Inagua** *var.* Inagua Islands. *island* S The Bahamas
**Great Indian Desert** *see* Thar Desert
83 G25 **Great Karoo** *var.* Great Karoo High Veld, *Afr.* Groot Karoo, Hoë Karoo. *plateau region* S South Africa
**Great Karroo** *see* Great Karoo
**Great Kei** *see* Nciba
**Great Khingan Range** *see* Da Hinggan Ling
14 E11 **Great La Cloche Island** *island* Ontario, S Canada
183 P16 **Great Lake** ◎ Tasmania, SE Australia
**Great Lake** *see* Tonle Sap
11 R15 **Great Lakes** *lakes* Ontario, Canada/USA
**Great Lakes State** *see* Michigan
97 L20 **Great Malvern** W England, United Kingdom 52°07′N 02°19′W
184 M5 **Great Mercury Island** *island* N New Zealand
**Great Meteor Seamount** *see* Great Meteor Tablemount
64 K10 **Great Meteor Tablemount** *var.* Great Meteor Seamount. *undersea feature* E Atlantic Ocean 30°00′N 28°30′W
31 Q14 **Great Miami River** ≈ Ohio, N USA
151 Q24 **Great Nicobar** *island* Nicobar Islands, India, NE Indian Ocean
97 O19 **Great Ouse** *var.* Ouse. ≈ E England, United Kingdom
183 Q17 **Great Oyster Bay** *bay* Tasmania, SE Australia
44 I13 **Great Pedro Bluff** *headland* W Jamaica 17°51′N 77°44′W
21 T12 **Great Pee Dee River** ≈ North Carolina/South Carolina, SE USA
129 W9 **Great Plain of China** *plain* E China
0 F12 **Great Plains** *var.* High Plains. *plains* Canada/USA
37 W6 **Great Plains Reservoirs** ⊠ Colorado, C USA
19 Q13 **Great Point** *headland* Nantucket Island, Massachusetts, NE USA 41°23′N 70°03′W
68 I13 **Great Rift Valley** *var.* Rift Valley. *depression* Asia/Africa
81 I23 **Great Ruaha** ≈ S Tanzania
18 K10 **Great Sacandaga Lake** ⊠ New York, NE USA
108 C12 **Great Saint Bernard Pass** *Fr.* Col du Grand-Saint-Bernard, *It.* Passo del Gran San Bernardo. *pass* Italy/Switzerland
44 F1 **Great Sale Cay** *island* N The Bahamas
**Great Salt Desert** *see* Kavīr, Dasht-e
36 K1 **Great Salt Lake** *salt lake* Utah, W USA
36 J3 **Great Salt Lake Desert** *plain* Utah, W USA
26 M8 **Great Salt Plains Lake** ⊠ Oklahoma, C USA
75 T9 **Great Sand Sea** *desert* Egypt/Libya
180 L6 **Great Sandy Desert** *desert* Western Australia
**Great Sandy Desert** *see* Ar Rub' al Khālī
**Great Sandy Island** *see* Fraser Island
187 Y13 **Great Sea Reef** *reef* Vanua Levu, N Fiji
38 H17 **Great Sitkin Island** *island* Aleutian Islands, Alaska, USA
8 J10 **Great Slave Lake** *Fr.* Grand Lac des Esclaves. ◎ Northwest Territories, NW Canada
21 O10 **Great Smoky Mountains** ▲▲ North Carolina/Tennessee, SE USA
10 L11 **Great Snow Mountain** ▲ British Columbia, W Canada 57°22′N 124°08′W
**Great Socialist People's Libyan Arab Jamahiriya** *see* Libya
64 A12 **Great Sound** *sound* Bermuda, NW Atlantic Ocean
180 M10 **Great Victoria Desert** *desert* South Australia/Western Australia
194 H2 **Great Wall** *research station (China)* South Shetland Islands, Antarctica 61°57′S 58°23′W
19 T7 **Great Wass Island** *island* Maine, NE USA
97 Q19 **Great Yarmouth** *var.* Yarmouth. E England, United Kingdom 52°37′N 01°44′E
139 S1 **Great Zab** *Ar.* Az Zāb al Kabīr, *Kurd.* Zē-i Bādīnān, *Turk.* Büyükzap Suyu. ≈ Iraq/Turkey
95 I17 **Grebbestad** Västra Götaland, S Sweden 58°42′N 11°15′E
**Grebenka** *see* Hrebinka
42 M13 **Grecia** Alajuela, C Costa Rica 10°04′N 84°19′W
61 E18 **Greco** Río Negro, W Uruguay 32°49′S 57°03′W
**Greco, Cape** *see* Gkréko, Akrotíri
104 L8 **Gredos, Sierra de** ▲▲ W Spain
18 F9 **Greece** New York, NE USA 43°12′N 77°41′W
115 E17 **Greece** *off.* Hellenic Republic, *Gk.* Ellás, Ellás, Ellinikí Dimokratía; *anc.* Hellas. ◆ *republic* SE Europe
**Greece Central** *see* Stereá Elláda
**Greece West** *see* Dytikí Elláda
37 T3 **Greeley** Colorado, C USA 40°21′N 104°41′W
29 P14 **Greeley** Nebraska, C USA 41°33′N 98°31′W
122 K3 **Greem-Bell, Ostrov** *Eng.* Graham Bell Island. *island* Zemlya Frantsa-Iosifa, N Russia
30 M6 **Green Bay** Wisconsin, N USA 44°32′N 88°W
31 N6 **Green Bay** *lake bay* Michigan/Wisconsin, N USA
21 S5 **Greenbrier River** ≈ West Virginia, NE USA
29 S2 **Greenbush** Minnesota, N USA 48°42′N 96°10′W
183 R12 **Green Cape** *headland* New South Wales, SE Australia 37°15′S 150°03′E
31 O14 **Greencastle** Indiana, N USA 39°38′N 86°51′W
18 F16 **Greencastle** Pennsylvania, NE USA 39°47′N 77°43′W
27 T2 **Green City** Missouri, C USA 40°16′N 92°57′W
21 O9 **Greeneville** Tennessee, S USA 36°10′N 82°50′W
35 O11 **Greenfield** California, W USA 36°19′N 121°15′W
31 P14 **Greenfield** Indiana, N USA 39°47′N 85°46′W
29 U15 **Greenfield** Iowa, C USA 41°18′N 94°27′W
18 M11 **Greenfield** Massachusetts, NE USA 42°33′N 72°34′W
27 S7 **Greenfield** Missouri, C USA 37°25′N 93°50′W
31 S14 **Greenfield** Ohio, N USA 39°21′N 83°22′W
20 G8 **Greenfield** Tennessee, S USA 36°09′N 88°48′W
30 M9 **Greenfield** Wisconsin, N USA 42°55′N 87°59′W
27 T9 **Green Forest** Arkansas, C USA 36°19′N 93°24′W
37 T7 **Greenhorn Mountain** ▲ Colorado, C USA 37°50′N 104°59′W
**Green Island** *see* Lü Dao
186 I6 **Green Islands** *var.* Nissan Islands. *island group* NE Papua New Guinea
11 S14 **Green Lake** Saskatchewan, C Canada 54°15′N 107°51′W
30 L8 **Green Lake** ◎ Wisconsin, N USA
197 O14 **Greenland** *Dan.* Grønland, *Inuit* Kalaallit Nunaat. ◇ *Danish self-governing territory* NE North America
84 D4 **Greenland** *island* NE North America
197 R13 **Greenland Plain** *undersea feature* N Greenland Sea
197 R14 **Greenland Sea** *sea* Arctic Ocean
37 R4 **Green Mountain Reservoir** ⊠ Colorado, C USA
18 M8 **Green Mountains** ▲▲ Vermont, NE USA
**Green Mountain State** *see* Vermont
96 H12 **Greenock** W Scotland, United Kingdom 55°57′N 04°45′W
39 T5 **Greenough, Mount** ▲ Alaska, USA 69°15′N 141°37′W
186 A6 **Green River** West Sepik, NW Papua New Guinea 03°54′S 141°08′E
37 N5 **Green River** Utah, W USA 39°00′N 110°07′W
33 U17 **Green River** Wyoming, C USA 41°33′N 109°27′W
16 H9 **Green River** ≈ W USA
30 K11 **Green River** ≈ Illinois, N USA
20 J7 **Green River** ≈ Kentucky, C USA
28 K5 **Green River** ≈ North Dakota, N USA
37 N6 **Green River** ≈ Utah, W USA
33 T16 **Green River** ≈ Wyoming, C USA
20 L7 **Green River Lake** ⊠ Kentucky, S USA
23 O5 **Greensboro** Alabama, S USA 32°42′N 87°36′W
23 U3 **Greensboro** Georgia, SE USA 33°34′N 83°10′W
21 T9 **Greensboro** North Carolina, SE USA 36°04′N 79°48′W
31 P14 **Greensburg** Indiana, N USA 39°20′N 85°28′W
26 K6 **Greensburg** Kansas, C USA 37°36′N 99°17′W
20 L7 **Greensburg** Kentucky, S USA 37°14′N 85°30′W
18 C15 **Greensburg** Pennsylvania, NE USA 40°18′N 79°32′W
36 O13 **Greens Peak** ▲ Arizona, SW USA 34°06′N 109°34′W
21 V12 **Green Swamp** *wetland* North Carolina, SE USA
21 O4 **Greenup** Kentucky, S USA 38°34′N 82°49′W
36 M16 **Green Valley** Arizona, SW USA 31°49′N 111°00′W
76 K17 **Greenville** *var.* Sino, Sinoe. SE Liberia 05°01′N 09°03′W
23 P6 **Greenville** Alabama, S USA 31°49′N 86°37′W
23 T8 **Greenville** Florida, SE USA 30°28′N 83°37′W
23 S4 **Greenville** Georgia, SE USA 33°03′N 84°42′W
30 L15 **Greenville** Illinois, N USA 38°53′N 89°24′W
20 I7 **Greenville** Kentucky, S USA 37°11′N 87°11′W
19 Q5 **Greenville** Maine, NE USA 45°26′N 69°36′W
31 P9 **Greenville** Michigan, N USA 43°10′N 85°15′W
22 J4 **Greenville** Mississippi, S USA 33°24′N 91°03′W
21 W9 **Greenville** North Carolina, SE USA 35°36′N 77°23′W
31 Q13 **Greenville** Ohio, N USA 40°06′N 84°37′W
19 O12 **Greenville** Rhode Island, NE USA 41°52′N 71°33′W
21 P11 **Greenville** South Carolina, SE USA 34°51′N 82°24′W
25 U6 **Greenville** Texas, SW USA 33°09′N 96°07′W
31 T12 **Greenwich** Ohio, N USA 41°01′N 82°31′W
27 S11 **Greenwood** Arkansas, C USA 35°13′N 94°15′W
31 O14 **Greenwood** Indiana, N USA 39°38′N 86°06′W
22 K4 **Greenwood** Mississippi, S USA 33°30′N 90°11′W
21 P12 **Greenwood** South Carolina, SE USA 34°11′N 82°10′W
21 Q12 **Greenwood, Lake** ⊠ South Carolina, SE USA
21 P11 **Greer** South Carolina, SE USA 34°56′N 82°13′W
27 V10 **Greers Ferry Lake** ⊠ Arkansas, C USA
27 S13 **Greeson, Lake** ⊠ Arkansas, C USA
45 N8 **Gregorio Luperón** ✈ N Dominican Republic 19°43′N 70°43′W
29 O12 **Gregory** South Dakota, N USA 43°11′N 99°26′W
182 J3 **Gregory, Lake** *salt lake* South Australia
180 J9 **Gregory Lake** ◎ Western Australia
181 V5 **Gregory Range** ▲▲ Queensland, E Australia
**Greifenberg/Greifenberg in Pommern** *see* Gryfice
**Greifenhagen** *see* Gryfino
100 O8 **Greifswald** Mecklenburg-Vorpommern, NE Germany 54°04′N 13°24′E
100 O8 **Greifswalder Bodden** *bay* NE Germany
109 U4 **Grein** Oberösterreich, N Austria 48°14′N 14°50′E
101 M17 **Greiz** Thüringen, C Germany 50°40′N 12°11′E
125 V14 **Gremyachinsk** Permskiy Kray, NW Russia 58°33′N 57°52′E
**Grenå** *see* Grenaa
95 H21 **Grenaa** *var.* Grenå. Midtjylland, C Denmark 56°25′N 10°53′E
22 L3 **Grenada** Mississippi, S USA 33°46′N 89°48′W
45 W15 **Grenada** ◆ *commonwealth republic* SE West Indies
47 S4 **Grenada** *island* Grenada
47 R4 **Grenada Basin** *undersea feature* W Atlantic Ocean 13°30′N 62°00′W
22 L3 **Grenada Lake** ⊠ Mississippi, S USA
45 Y14 **Grenadines, The** *island group* Grenada/St Vincent and the Grenadines
108 D7 **Grenchen** *Fr.* Granges. Solothurn, NW Switzerland 47°13′N 07°24′E
183 Q9 **Grenfell** New South Wales, SE Australia 33°54′S 148°09′E
11 V16 **Grenfell** Saskatchewan, S Canada 50°24′N 102°56′W
92 J1 **Grenivík** Norðurland Eystra, N Iceland 65°57′N 18°10′W
103 S12 **Grenoble** *anc.* Cularo, Gratianopolis. Isère, E France 45°11′N 05°42′E
28 J2 **Grenora** North Dakota, N USA 48°36′N 103°57′W
92 N8 **Grense-Jakobselv** Finnmark, N Norway 69°46′N 30°39′E
45 S14 **Grenville** E Grenada 12°07′N 61°37′W
32 G11 **Gresham** Oregon, NW USA 45°30′N 122°25′W
**Gresk** *see* Hresk
106 B7 **Gressoney-St-Jean** Valle d'Aosta, NW Italy 45°48′N 07°49′E
22 K9 **Gretna** Louisiana, S USA 29°54′N 90°03′W
21 T7 **Gretna** Virginia, NE USA 36°57′N 79°21′W
98 F13 **Grevelingen** *inlet* S North Sea
100 F13 **Greven** Nordrhein-Westfalen, NW Germany 52°07′N 07°38′E
115 D15 **Grevená** Dytikí Makedonía, N Greece 40°05′N 21°26′E
101 D16 **Grevenbroich** Nordrhein-Westfalen, W Germany 51°06′N 06°34′E
99 N24 **Grevenmacher** Grevenmacher, E Luxembourg 49°41′N 06°27′E
99 M24 **Grevenmacher** ◈ *district* E Luxembourg
100 K9 **Grevesmühlen** Mecklenburg-Vorpommern, N Germany 53°52′N 11°12′E
185 H16 **Grey** ≈ South Island, New Zealand
33 V12 **Greybull** Wyoming, C USA 44°29′N 108°03′W
33 U13 **Greybull River** ≈ Wyoming, C USA
65 A24 **Grey Channel** *sound* Falkland Islands
**Greyerzer See** *see* Gruyère, Lac de la
13 T10 **Grey Islands** *island group* Newfoundland and Labrador, E Canada
18 L10 **Greylock, Mount** ▲ Massachusetts, NE USA 42°38′N 73°09′W
185 G17 **Greymouth** West Coast, South Island, New Zealand 42°29′S 171°14′E
181 U10 **Grey Range** ▲▲ New South Wales/Queensland, E Australia
97 G18 **Greystones** *Ir.* Na Clocha Liatha. E Ireland 53°08′N 06°05′W
185 M14 **Greytown** Wellington, North Island, New Zealand 41°04′S 175°29′E
83 K23 **Greytown** KwaZulu/Natal, E South Africa 29°04′S 30°35′E
**Greytown** *see* San Juan del Norte
99 H19 **Grez-Doiceau** *Dut.* Graven. Walloon Brabant, C Belgium 50°43′N 04°41′E
115 J19 **Griá, Akrotírio** *headland* Ándros, Kykládes, Greece, Aegean Sea 37°54′N 24°57′E
127 N8 **Gribanovskiy** Voronezhskaya Oblast', W Russia 51°27′N 41°53′E
78 I13 **Gribingui** ≈ N Central African Republic
35 O6 **Gridley** California, W USA 39°21′N 121°41′W
83 G23 **Griekwastad** *var.* Griquatown. Northern Cape, C South Africa 28°50′S 23°16′E
23 S4 **Griffin** Georgia, SE USA 33°15′N 84°17′W
183 O9 **Griffith** New South Wales, SE Australia 34°18′S 146°04′E
14 F13 **Griffith Island** *island* Ontario, S Canada
21 W10 **Grifton** North Carolina, SE USA 35°22′N 77°26′W
**Grigioni** *see* Graubünden
119 H14 **Grigiškės** Vilnius, SE Lithuania 54°42′N 25°00′E
117 N10 **Grigoriopol** C Moldova 47°09′N 29°18′E
147 X7 **Grigor'yevka** Issyk-Kul'skaya Oblast', E Kyrgyzstan 42°43′N 77°27′E
193 U8 **Grijalva Ridge** *undersea feature* E Pacific Ocean
41 U15 **Grijalva, Río** *var.* Tabasco. ≈ Guatemala/Mexico
98 N5 **Grijpskerk** Groningen, NE Netherlands 53°15′N 06°18′E
83 C22 **Grillenthal** //Karas, SW Namibia 26°55′S 15°24′E
79 J15 **Grimari** Ouaka, C Central African Republic 05°44′N 20°02′E
**Grimaylov** *see* Hrymayliv
99 G18 **Grimbergen** Vlaams Brabant, C Belgium 50°56′N 04°22′E
183 N15 **Grim, Cape** *headland* Tasmania, SE Australia 40°42′S 144°42′E
100 N8 **Grimmen** Mecklenburg-Vorpommern, NE Germany 54°06′N 13°03′E
14 G16 **Grimsby** Ontario, S Canada 43°12′N 79°35′W
97 O17 **Grimsby** *prev.* Great Grimsby. E England, United Kingdom 53°35′N 00°05′W
92 J1 **Grímsey** *var.* Grimsey. *island* N Iceland
**Grimsey** *see* Grímsey
11 O12 **Grimshaw** Alberta, W Canada 56°11′N 117°37′W
95 F18 **Grimstad** Aust-Agder, S Norway 58°20′N 08°35′E
92 H4 **Grindavík** Suðurnes, W Iceland 65°57′N 18°10′W
108 F9 **Grindelwald** Bern, S Switzerland 46°37′N 08°04′E
95 F23 **Grindsted** Syddtjylland, W Denmark 55°46′N 08°56′E
29 W14 **Grinnell** Iowa, C USA 41°44′N 92°43′W
109 U10 **Grintovec** ▲ N Slovenia 46°21′N 14°31′E
**Griquatown** *see* Griekwastad
9 N4 **Grise Fiord** *var* Aujuittuq. Northwest Territories, Ellesmere Island, N Canada 76°10′N 83°15′W
182 H1 **Griselda, Lake** *salt lake* South Australia
**Grisons** *see* Graubünden
95 P14 **Grisslehamn** Stockholm, C Sweden 60°04′N 18°50′E
29 T15 **Griswold** Iowa, C USA 41°14′N 95°08′W
102 M1 **Griz Nez, Cap** *headland* N France 50°51′N 01°34′E
112 P13 **Grljan** Serbia, E Serbia 43°52′N 22°18′E
112 E11 **Grmeč** ▲ NW Bosnia and Herzegovina
99 H16 **Grobbendonk** Antwerpen, N Belgium 51°12′N 04°41′E
**Grobin** *see* Grobiņa
118 C10 **Grobiņa** *Ger.* Grobin. W Latvia 56°32′N 21°12′E
83 K20 **Groblersdal** Mpumalanga, NE South Africa 25°15′S 29°25′E
83 G23 **Groblershoop** Northern Cape, W South Africa 28°51′S 22°01′E
**Gródek Jagielloński** *see* Horodok
109 Q6 **Grödig** Salzburg, W Austria 47°42′N 13°06′E
111 H15 **Grodków** Opolskie, S Poland 50°42′N 17°23′E
**Grodnenskaya Oblast'** *see* Hrodzyenskaya Voblasts'
**Grodno** *see* Hrodna
110 L12 **Grodzisk Mazowiecki** Mazowieckie, C Poland 52°09′N 20°38′E
110 F12 **Grodzisk Wielkopolski** Wielkopolskie, C Poland 52°13′N 16°21′E
**Grodzyanka** *see* Hradzyanka
98 O12 **Groenlo** Gelderland, E Netherlands 52°02′N 06°36′E
83 E22 **Groenrivier** //Karas, SE Namibia 27°27′S 18°52′E
25 U8 **Groesbeck** Texas, SW USA 31°31′N 96°35′W
98 L13 **Groesbeek** Gelderland, SE Netherlands 51°47′N 05°56′E
102 G7 **Groix, Îles de** *island group* NW France
110 M12 **Grójec** Mazowieckie, C Poland 51°51′N 20°52′E
65 K15 **Gröll Seamount** *undersea feature* C Atlantic Ocean 12°54′S 33°24′W
100 E13 **Gronau** *var.* Gronau in Westfalen. Nordrhein-Westfalen, NW Germany 52°13′N 07°02′E
**Gronau in Westfalen** *see* Gronau
93 F15 **Grong** Nord-Trøndelag, C Norway 64°29′N 12°19′E
95 N22 **Grönhögen** Kalmar, S Sweden 56°16′N 16°09′E
98 N5 **Groningen** Groningen, NE Netherlands 53°13′N 06°35′E
55 W9 **Groningen** Saramacca, N Suriname 05°45′N 55°31′W
98 N5 **Groningen** ◈ *province* NE Netherlands
**Grønland** *see* Greenland
108 H11 **Grono** Graubünden, S Switzerland 46°15′N 09°07′E
95 M20 **Grönskåra** Kalmar, S Sweden 57°04′N 15°45′E
25 O2 **Groom** Texas, SW USA 35°12′N 101°06′W
35 W9 **Groom Lake** ◎ Nevada, W USA
83 H25 **Groot** ≈ S South Africa
181 S2 **Groote Eylandt** *island* Northern Territory, N Australia
98 M6 **Grootegast** Groningen, NE Netherlands 53°11′N 06°12′E
83 D17 **Grootfontein** Otjozondjupa, N Namibia 19°32′S 18°05′E
83 E22 **Groot Karasberge** ▲▲ S Namibia
**Groot Karoo** *see* Great Karoo
**Groot-Kei** *see* Nciba
15 V6 **Grosses-Roches** Québec, SE Canada 48°55′N 67°06′W
109 V2 **Gross-Siegharts** Niederösterreich, N Austria 48°48′N 15°25′E
45 T10 **Gros Islet** N Saint Lucia 14°04′N 60°57′W
44 L8 **Gros-Morne** NW Haiti 19°45′N 72°46′W
13 S11 **Gros Morne** ▲ Newfoundland, Newfoundland and Labrador, E Canada 49°38′N 57°45′W
103 R9 **Grosne** ≈ C France
45 S12 **Gros Piton** ▲ SW Saint Lucia 13°48′N 61°04′W
**Grossa, Isola** *see* Dugi Otok
**Grossbetschkerek** *see* Zrenjanin
**Grosse Isper** *see* Grosse Ysper
**Grosse Kokel** *see* Târnava Mare
101 M21 **Grosse Laaber** *var.* Grosse Laber. ≈ SE Germany
**Grosse Laber** *see* Grosse Laaber
**Grosse Morava** *see* Velika Morava
101 O15 **Grossenhain** Sachsen, E Germany 51°18′N 13°31′E
109 Y4 **Grossenzersdorf** Niederösterreich, NE Austria 48°12′N 16°33′E
101 O21 **Grosser Arber** ▲ SE Germany 49°07′N 13°10′E
101 K17 **Grosser Beerberg** ▲ C Germany 50°39′N 10°45′E
101 G18 **Grosser Feldberg** ▲ W Germany 50°13′N 08°28′E
109 O8 **Grosser Löffler** *It.* Monte Lovello. ▲ Austria/Italy 47°02′N 11°56′E
109 N8 **Grosser Möseler** *var.* Mesule. ▲ Austria/Italy 47°01′N 11°52′E
100 J8 **Grosser Plöner See** ◎ N Germany
101 O21 **Grosser Rachel** ▲ SE Germany 48°59′N 13°23′E
**Grosser Sund** *see* Suur Väin
109 P8 **Grosses Wiesbachhorn** *var.* Wiesbachhorn. ▲ W Austria 47°09′N 12°44′E
106 F13 **Grosseto** Toscana, C Italy 42°45′N 11°07′E
101 M22 **Grosse Vils** ≈ SE Germany
109 U4 **Grosse Ysper** *var.* Grosse Isper. ≈ N Austria
101 G19 **Gross-Gerau** Hessen, W Germany 49°55′N 08°28′E
109 U3 **Gross Gerungs** Niederösterreich, N Austria 48°33′N 14°58′E
109 P8 **Grossglockner** ▲ W Austria 47°05′N 12°39′E
**Grosskanizsa** *see* Nagykanizsa
**Gross-Karol** *see* Carei
**Grosskikinda** *see* Kikinda
109 W9 **Grossklein** Steiermark, SE Austria 46°43′N 15°24′E
**Grosskoppe** *see* Velká Deštná
**Grossmeseritsch** *see* Velké Meziříčí
**Grossmichel** *see* Michalovce
101 H19 **Grossostheim** Bayern, C Germany 49°54′N 09°03′E
109 X7 **Grosspetersdorf** Burgenland, SE Austria 47°15′N 16°19′E
109 T5 **Grossraming** Oberösterreich, C Austria 47°54′N 14°34′E
101 P14 **Grossräschen** Brandenburg, E Germany 51°34′N 14°00′E
**Grossrauschenbach** *see* Revúca
**Gross-Sankt-Johannis** *see* Suure-Jaani
**Gross-Schlatten** *see* Abrud
**Gross-Skaisgirren** *see* Bol'shakovo
**Gross-Steffelsdorf** *see* Rimavská Sobota
**Gross Strehlitz** *see* Strzelce Opolskie
109 O8 **Grossvenediger** ▲ W Austria 47°07′N 12°19′E
**Grosswardein** *see* Oradea
**Gross Wartenberg** *see* Syców
109 U11 **Grosuplje** C Slovenia 46°00′N 14°36′E
99 H17 **Grote Nete** ≈ N Belgium
94 E10 **Grotli** Oppland, S Norway 62°02′N 07°36′E
19 N13 **Groton** Connecticut, NE USA 41°20′N 72°03′W
29 P8 **Groton** South Dakota, N USA 45°27′N 98°06′W
107 P18 **Grottaglie** Puglia, SE Italy 40°32′N 17°26′E
107 L17 **Grottaminarda** Campania, S Italy 41°04′N 15°02′E
106 K13 **Grottammare** Marche, C Italy 43°00′N 13°52′E
21 U5 **Grottoes** Virginia, NE USA 38°16′N 78°49′W
98 L6 **Grou** *Dutch.* Grouw. Fryslân, N Netherlands 53°07′N 05°51′E
13 N10 **Groulx, Monts** ▲▲ Québec, E Canada
14 E7 **Groundhog** ≈ Ontario, S Canada
36 J1 **Grouse Creek** Utah, W USA 41°41′N 113°52′W
36 J1 **Grouse Creek Mountains** ▲▲ Utah, W USA
**Grouw** *see* Grou
27 R8 **Grove** Oklahoma, C USA 36°35′N 94°46′W
31 S13 **Grove City** Ohio, N USA 39°52′N 83°05′W
18 B13 **Grove City** Pennsylvania, NE USA 41°09′N 80°02′W
23 O6 **Grove Hill** Alabama, S USA 31°42′N 87°46′W
33 S15 **Grover** Wyoming, C USA 42°48′N 110°57′W
35 P13 **Grover City** California, W USA 35°08′N 120°37′W
25 Y11 **Groves** Texas, SW USA 29°57′N 93°55′W
19 O7 **Groveton** New Hampshire, NE USA 44°35′N 71°28′W
25 W9 **Groveton** Texas, SW USA 31°04′N 95°08′W
36 J15 **Growler Mountains** ▲▲ Arizona, SW USA
**Grozdovo** *see* Bratya Daskalovi
127 P16 **Groznyy** Chechenskaya Respublika, SW Russia 43°20′N 45°43′E
**Grubeshov** *see* Hrubieszów
112 G9 **Grubišno Polje** Bjelovar-Bilogora, NE Croatia 45°42′N 17°09′E
**Grudovo** *see* Sredets
110 J9 **Grudziądz** *Ger.* Graudenz. Kujawsko-pomorskie, C Poland 53°29′N 18°45′E
25 R17 **Grulla** *var.* La Grulla. Texas, SW USA 26°15′N 98°37′W
40 K14 **Grullo** Jalisco, SW Mexico 19°45′N 104°15′W
67 V10 **Grumeti** ≈ N Tanzania
95 K16 **Grums** Värmland, C Sweden 59°22′N 13°11′E
109 S5 **Grünau im Almtal** Oberösterreich, N Austria 47°51′N 13°56′E
101 H17 **Grünberg** Hessen, W Germany 50°36′N 08°57′E
**Grünberg/Grünberg in Schlesien** *see* Zielona Góra
92 H3 **Grundarfjördur** Vestfirdir, W Iceland 64°55′N 23°15′W
21 P7 **Grundy** Virginia, NE USA 37°17′N 82°06′W



◆ Country
● Country Capital
◇ Dependent Territory
○ Dependent Territory Capital
◈ Administrative Regions
✈ International Airport
▲ Mountain
▲▲ Mountain Range
Volcano
≈ River
◎ Lake
⊠ Reservoir

◆ Country    ◊ Dependent Territory    ♦ Administrative Regions    ▲ Mountain    ⊠ Volcano    ◊ Lake
● Country Capital    ○ Dependent Territory Capital    ✈ International Airport    ▲ Mountain Range    ♦ River    ⊡ Reservoir

GYDANSKIY POLUOSTROV – HANNA


122 J7 **Gydanskiy Poluostrov** *Eng.* Gyda Peninsula. *peninsula* N Russia
**Gyda Peninsula** *see* Gydanskiy Poluostrov
**Gyêgu** *see* Yushu
163 W15 **Gyeonggi-man** *prev.* Kyŏnggi-man. *bay* NW South Korea
163 Z16 **Gyeongju** *Jap.* Keishū; *prev.* Kyŏngju. SE South Korea 35°49′N 129°09′E
**Gyéres** *see* Câmpia Turzii
**Gyergyószentmiklós** *see* Gheorgheni
**Gyergyótölgyes** *see* Tulgheş
**Gyertyámos** *see* Cărpiniş
**Gyeva** *see* Detva
**Gyigang** *see* Zayü
**Gyixong** *see* Gonggar
95 I23 **Gyldenløveshøy** *hill range* C Denmark
181 Z10 **Gympie** Queensland, E Australia 26°05′S 152°40′E
166 L7 **Gyobingauk** Bago, SW Myanmar (Burma) 18°14′N 95°39′E
111 M23 **Gyomaendrőd** Békés, SE Hungary 46°56′N 20°50′E
**Gyömbér** *see* Ďumbier
111 L22 **Gyöngyös** Heves, NE Hungary 47°44′N 19°49′E
111 H22 **Győr** *Ger.* Raab, *Lat.* Arrabona. Győr-Moson-Sopron, NW Hungary 47°41′N 17°40′E
111 G22 **Győr-Moson-Sopron** *off.* Győr-Moson-Sopron Megye. ◈ *county* NW Hungary
**Győr-Moson-Sopron Megye** *see* Győr-Moson-Sopron
11 X15 **Gypsumville** Manitoba, S Canada 51°47′N 98°38′W
12 M4 **Gyrfalcon Islands** *island group* Northwest Territories, NE Canada
95 N14 **Gysinge** Gävleborg, C Sweden 60°16′N 16°55′E
115 F22 **Gýtheio** *var.* Githio; *prev.* Yíthion. Pelopónnisos, S Greece 36°46′N 22°34′E
146 L13 **Gyuichbirleshik** Lebap Welaýaty, E Turkmenistan 38°10′N 64°33′E
111 N24 **Gyula** *Rom.* Jula. Békés, SE Hungary 46°39′N 21°17′E
**Gyulafehérvár** *see* Alba Iulia
**Gyulovo** *see* Roza
137 T11 **Gyumri** *var.* Giumri, *Rus.* Kumayri; *prev.* Aleksandropol', Leninakan. W Armenia 40°48′N 43°51′E
146 D13 **Gyunuzyndag, Gora** ▲ Balkan Welaýaty, W Turkmenistan 38°15′N 56°25′E
146 J15 **Gyzylbaydak** *Rus.* Krasnoye Znamya. Mary Welaýaty, S Turkmenistan 36°51′N 62°24′E
**Gyzyletrek** *see* Etrek
146 D10 **Gyzylgaýa** *Rus.* Kizyl-Kaya. Balkan Welaýaty, NW Turkmenistan 40°37′N 55°15′E
146 A10 **Gyzylsuw** *Rus.* Kizyl-Su. Balkan Welaýaty, W Turkmenistan 39°49′N 53°00′E
**Gyzyrlabat** *see* Serdar
**Gzhatsk** *see* Gagarin

# H

153 T12 **Ha** W Bhutan 27°17′N 89°22′E
**Haabai** *see* Ha'apai Group
99 H17 **Haacht** Vlaams Brabant, C Belgium 50°58′N 04°38′E
109 T4 **Haag** Niederösterreich, NE Austria 48°07′N 14°32′E
194 L8 **Haag Nunataks** ▲▲ Antarctica
92 N2 **Haakon VII Land** *physical region* NW Svalbard
98 O11 **Haaksbergen** Overijssel, E Netherlands 52°09′N 06°45′E
99 E14 **Haamstede** Zeeland, SW Netherlands 51°43′N 03°45′E
193 Y15 **Ha'ano** *island* Ha'apai Group, C Tonga
193 Y15 **Ha'apai Group** *var.* Haabai. *island group* C Tonga
93 L15 **Haapajärvi** Pohjois-Pohjanmaa, C Finland 63°45′N 25°20′E
93 L17 **Haapamäki** Pirkanmaa, C Finland 62°11′N 24°32′E
93 L15 **Haapavesi** Pohjois-Pohjanmaa, C Finland 64°09′N 25°25′E
191 N7 **Haapiti** Moorea, W French Polynesia 17°33′S 149°52′W
118 F4 **Haapsalu** *Ger.* Hapsal. Läänemaa, W Estonia 58°58′N 23°32′E
**Ha'Arava** *see* 'Arabah, Wādī al
95 G24 **Haarby** *var.* Hårby. Syddtjylland, C Denmark 55°13′N 10°07′E
98 H10 **Haarlem** *prev.* Harlem. Noord-Holland, W Netherlands 52°23′N 04°39′E
185 D19 **Haast** West Coast, South Island, New Zealand 43°53′S 169°02′E
185 C20 **Haast** 〰 South Island, New Zealand
185 D20 **Haast Pass** *pass* South Island, New Zealand
193 W16 **Ha'atua** 'Eau, E Tonga 21°23′S 174°57′W
149 P15 **Hab** 〰 SW Pakistan
141 W7 **Haba** *var.* Al Haba. Dubayy, NE United Arab Emirates 25°01′N 55°37′E
158 K2 **Habahe** *var.* Kaba. Xinjiang Uygur Zizhiqu, NW China 48°04′N 86°20′E
141 U13 **Ḩabarūt** *var.* Habrut. SW Oman 17°19′N 52°45′E
81 J18 **Habaswein** Isiolo, NE Kenya 01°01′N 39°27′E
99 L24 **Habay-la-Neuve** Luxembourg, SE Belgium 49°43′N 05°38′E
139 S8 **Ḩabbānīyah, Buḩayrat** ◎ C Iraq
**Habelschwerdt** *see* Bystrzyca Kłodzka
153 V14 **Habiganj** Sylhet, NE Bangladesh 24°23′N 91°25′E
163 Q12 **Habirag** Nei Mongol Zizhiqu, N China 42°18′N 115°40′E
95 L19 **Habo** Västra Götaland, S Sweden 57°55′N 14°05′E
123 V14 **Habomai Islands** *island group* Kuril'skiye Ostrova, SE Russia
165 S2 **Haboro** Hokkaidō, NE Japan 44°19′N 141°42′E
153 S16 **Habra** West Bengal, NE India 22°39′N 88°17′E
**Habrut** *see* Ḩabarūt
143 P17 **Ḩabshān** Abū Ẓaby, C United Arab Emirates 23°51′N 53°34′E
54 E14 **Hacha** Putumayo, S Colombia 0°02′S 75°30′W
165 X13 **Hachijō-jima** *island* Izu-shotō, SE Japan
164 L12 **Hachiman** Gifu, Honshū, SW Japan 35°46′N 136°57′E
165 P7 **Hachimori** Akita, Honshū, C Japan 40°22′N 139°59′E
165 R7 **Hachinohe** Aomori, Honshū, C Japan 40°30′N 141°29′E
165 X13 **Hachiōji** Tōkyō, Hachijō-jima, SE Japan 35°40′N 139°20′E
137 Y12 **Hacıqabul** *prev.* Qazimämmäd. SE Azerbaijan 40°03′N 48°56′E
93 G17 **Hackås** Jämtland, C Sweden 62°55′N 14°31′E
18 K14 **Hackensack** New Jersey, NE USA 40°51′N 73°57′W
75 U12 **Ḩaḑabat al Jilf al Kabīr** *var.* Gilf Kebir Plateau. *plateau* SW Egypt
**Hadama** *see* Nazrēt
141 W13 **Ḩadbaram** S Oman 17°27′N 55°13′E
139 U13 **Ḩaddānīyah** *well* S Iraq
96 K12 **Haddington** SE Scotland, United Kingdom 55°59′N 02°46′W
141 Z8 **Ḩadd, Ra's al** *headland* NE Oman 22°28′N 59°58′E
**Haded** *see* Xadeed
77 W12 **Hadejia** Jigawa, N Nigeria 12°22′N 10°02′E
77 W12 **Hadejia** 〰 N Nigeria
138 F9 **Hadera** *var.* Khadera; *prev.* Ḩadera. Haifa, N Israel 32°26′N 34°55′E
**Ḩadera** *see* Hadera
**Hadersleben** *see* Haderslev
95 G24 **Haderslev** *Ger.* Hadersleben. Syddanmark, SW Denmark 55°15′N 09°30′E
151 J21 **Hadhdhunmathi Atoll** *atoll* S Maldives
**Hadhramaut** *see* Ḩaḑramawt
141 W17 **Hadīboh** Suquṭrā, SE Yemen 12°38′N 54°05′E
158 K9 **Hadilik** Xinjiang Uygur Zizhiqu, W China 37°51′N 86°10′E
136 H16 **Hadım** Konya, S Turkey 36°58′N 32°27′E
140 K7 **Hadīyah** Al Madīnah al Munawwarah, W Saudi Arabia 25°36′N 38°31′E
8 L5 **Hadley Bay** *bay* Victoria Island, Nunavut, N Canada
167 S6 **Ha Đông** *var.* Hadong. Ha Tây, N Vietnam 20°58′N 105°46′E
**Hadong** *see* Ha Đông
141 R15 **Ḩaḑramawt** *Eng.* Hadhramaut. ▲▲ S Yemen
**Hadria** *see* Adria
**Hadrianopolis** *see* Edirne
**Hadria Picena** *see* Apricena
95 G22 **Hadsten** Midtjylland, C Denmark 56°19′N 10°03′E
95 G21 **Hadsund** Nordjylland, N Denmark 56°43′N 10°08′E
117 S4 **Hadyach** *Rus.* Gadyach. Poltavs'ka Oblast', NE Ukraine 50°21′N 34°00′E
114 N9 **Hadzhiyska Reka** *var.* Khadzhiyska Reka. 〰 E Bulgaria
112 I13 **Hadžići** Federacija Bosne I Hercegovine, SE Bosnia and Herzegovina 43°49′N 18°12′E
163 W14 **Haeju** S North Korea 38°04′N 125°40′E
**Haerbin/Haerhpin/Ha-erh-pin** *see* Harbin
141 P5 **Ḩafar al Bāţın** Ash Sharqīyah, N Saudi Arabia 28°25′N 45°59′E
11 T15 **Hafford** Saskatchewan, S Canada 52°43′N 107°19′W
136 M13 **Hafik** Sivas, N Turkey 39°53′N 37°24′E
149 V8 **Hafizabad** Punjab, E Pakistan 32°03′N 73°42′E
92 H4 **Hafnarfjörður** Höfuðborgarsvæðið, W Iceland 64°03′N 21°57′W
**Hafnia** *see* Denmark
**Hafnia** *see* København
**Hafren** *see* Severn
**Hafun** *see* Xaafuun
**Hafun, Ras** *see* Xaafuun, Raas
80 G10 **Hag 'Abdullah** Sinnar, E Sudan 13°59′N 33°35′E
81 K18 **Hagadera** Garissa, E Kenya 0°06′N 40°23′E
138 G8 **HaGalil** *Eng.* Galilee. ▲▲ N Israel
14 G10 **Hagar** Ontario, S Canada 46°27′N 80°22′W
155 G18 **Hagari** *var.* Vedāvati. 〰 W India
188 B16 **Hagåtña** , *var.* Agaña. ○ (Guam) NW Guam 13°27′N 144°45′E
100 M13 **Hagelberg** *hill* NE Germany
39 N14 **Hagemeister Island** *island* Alaska, USA
101 F15 **Hagen** Nordrhein-Westfalen, W Germany 51°22′N 07°27′E
100 K10 **Hagenow** Mecklenburg-Vorpommern, N Germany 53°27′N 11°10′E
10 K15 **Hagensborg** British Columbia, SW Canada 52°24′N 126°24′W
**Hagera Iertra** *see* Eritrea
80 I13 **Hāgere Hiywet** *var.* Agere Hiywet, Ambo. Oromīya, C Ethiopia 09°00′N 37°55′E
33 O15 **Hagerman** Idaho, NW USA 42°48′N 114°53′W
37 U14 **Hagerman** New Mexico, SW USA 33°07′N 104°19′W
21 V2 **Hagerstown** Maryland, NE USA 39°39′N 77°44′W
14 G16 **Hagersville** Ontario, S Canada 42°58′N 80°03′W
102 J15 **Hagetmau** Landes, SW France 43°40′N 00°36′W
95 K14 **Hagfors** Värmland, C Sweden 60°03′N 13°45′E
93 G16 **Häggenås** Jämtland, C Sweden 63°24′N 14°53′E
164 E12 **Hagi** Yamaguchi, Honshū, SW Japan 34°25′N 131°22′E
167 S5 **Ha Giang** Ha Giang, N Vietnam 22°50′N 104°58′E
**Hagios Evstrátios** *see* Ágios Efstrátios
**HaGolan** *see* Golan Heights
103 T4 **Hagondange** Moselle, NE France 49°16′N 06°06′E
97 B18 **Hag's Head** *Ir.* Ceann Caillí. *headland* W Ireland 52°56′N 09°29′W
102 I3 **Hague, Cap de la** *headland* N France 49°43′N 01°56′W
103 V5 **Haguenau** Bas-Rhin, NE France 48°49′N 07°47′E
165 X16 **Hahajima-rettō** *island group* SE Japan
15 R8 **Há Há ! Lac** ◎ Québec, SE Canada
172 H13 **Hahaya** ✈ (Moroni) Grande Comore, NW Comoros
22 K9 **Hahnville** Louisiana, S USA 29°58′N 90°24′W
83 E22 **Haib** //Karas, S Namibia 28°12′S 18°19′E
**Haibak** *see* Aībak
149 N15 **Haibo** 〰 SW Pakistan
**Haibowan** *see* Wuhai
163 U12 **Haicheng** Liaoning, NE China 40°53′N 122°45′E
**Haicheng** *see* Haifeng
**Haicheng** *see* Haiyuan
**Haida** *see* Nový Bor
10 H14 **Haida Gwaii** *prev.* Queen Charlotte Islands, *Fr.* Îles de la Reine-Charlotte. *island group* British Columbia, SW Canada
**Haidarabad** *see* Hyderābād
**Haidenschaft** *see* Ajdovščina
167 T6 **Hai Dương** Hai Hưng, N Vietnam 20°56′N 106°21′E
138 F9 **Haifa** ◈ *district* NW Israel
**Haifa** *see* Hefa
**Haifa, Bay of** *see* Mifrats Hefa
161 P14 **Haifeng** *var.* Haicheng. Guangdong, S China 22°56′N 115°19′E
**Haifong** *see* Hai Phong
161 P3 **Hai He** 〰 E China
**Haikang** *see* Leizhou
160 L17 **Haikou** *var.* Hai-k'ou, Hoihow, *Fr.* Hoï-Hao. *province capital* Hainan, S China 20°N 110°17′E
**Hai-k'ou** *see* Haikou
140 M6 **Ḩā'il** Ḩā'il, NW Saudi Arabia 27°N 42°50′E
141 N5 **Ḩā'il** *off.* Minṭaqah Ḩā'il. ◈ *region* N Saudi Arabia
163 S6 **Hailar He** 〰 NE China
33 P14 **Hailey** Idaho, NW USA 43°31′N 114°18′W
14 H9 **Haileybury** Ontario, S Canada 47°27′N 79°39′W
163 X9 **Hailin** Heilongjiang, NE China 44°37′N 129°24′E
**Ḩā'il, Minṭaqah** *see* Ḩā'il
**Hailong** *see* Meihekou
93 K14 **Hailuoto** *Swe.* Karlö. *island* W Finland
**Haima** *see* Haymā'
**Haimen** *see* Taizhou
160 M17 **Hainan** *var.* Hainan Sheng, Qiong. ◈ *province* S China
160 K17 **Hainan Dao** *island* S China
**Hainan Sheng** *see* Hainan
**Hainan Strait** *see* Qiongzhou Haixia
**Hainasch** *see* Ainaži
**Hainau** *see* Chojnów
99 E20 **Hainaut** ◈ *province* SW Belgium
**Hainburg** *see* Hainburg an der Donau
109 Z4 **Hainburg an der Donau** *var.* Hainburg. Niederösterreich, NE Austria 48°09′N 16°57′E
39 W12 **Haines** Alaska, USA 59°13′N 135°27′W
32 L12 **Haines** Oregon, NW USA 44°53′N 117°56′W
23 W12 **Haines City** Florida, SE USA 28°06′N 81°37′W
10 H8 **Haines Junction** Yukon, W Canada 60°45′N 137°30′W
109 W4 **Hainfeld** Niederösterreich, NE Austria 48°03′N 15°47′E
101 N16 **Hainichen** Sachsen, E Germany 50°58′N 13°08′E
**Hai Ninh** *see* Mong Cai
167 T6 **Hai Phong** *var.* Haifong, Haiphong. N Vietnam 20°50′N 106°41′E
**Haiphong** *see* Hai Phong
161 S12 **Haitan Dao** *island* SE China
44 K8 **Haiti** *off.* Republic of Haiti, *Fr.* Haïti, République d' Haïti. ◆ *republic* C West Indies
**Haïti** *see* Haiti
**Haiti, Republic of** *see* Haiti
35 T11 **Haiwee Reservoir** ⊞ California, W USA
80 I7 **Haiya** Red Sea, NE Sudan 18°17′N 36°21′E
159 T10 **Haiyan** *var.* Sanjiaocheng. Qinghai, W China 36°55′N 100°54′E
160 M13 **Haiyang Shan** ▲▲ S China
159 V10 **Haiyuan** Ningxia, N China 36°32′N 105°31′E
**Hajda** *see* Nový Bor
111 M22 **Hajdú-Bihar** *off.* Hajdú-Bihar Megye. ◈ *county* E Hungary
**Hajdú-Bihar Megye** *see* Hajdú-Bihar
111 N22 **Hajdúböszörmény** Hajdú-Bihar, E Hungary 47°39′N 21°32′E
111 N22 **Hajdúhadház** Hajdú-Bihar, E Hungary 47°40′N 21°40′E
111 N21 **Hajdúnánás** Hajdú-Bihar, E Hungary 47°50′N 21°26′E
111 N22 **Hajdúszoboszló** Hajdú-Bihar, E Hungary 47°27′N 21°24′E
142 I3 **Ḩājī Ebrāhīm, Kūh-e** ▲ Iran/Iraq 36°53′N 44°56′E
165 O9 **Hajiki-zaki** *headland* Sado, C Japan 38°19′N 138°28′E
139 O5 **Hajīn** *var.* Hajîne, Abū Ḩardān. Dayr az Zawr, E Syria 34°45′N 40°49′E
**Hajîne** *see* Hajīn
153 P13 **Hājīpur** Bihār, N India 25°41′N 85°13′E
141 N14 **Ḩajjah** W Yemen 15°43′N 43°33′E
139 U11 **Ḩajjama** Al Muthanná, S Iraq 31°24′N 45°20′E
143 R12 **Ḩājjīābād** Hormozgān, C Iran
139 U14 **Ḩājj, Thaqb al** *well* S Iraq
113 L16 **Hajla** ▲ E Montenegro
110 P10 **Hajnówka** *Ger.* Hermhausen. Podlaskie, NE Poland 52°45′N 23°32′E
**Haka** *see* Hakha
**Hakapehi** *see* Punaauia
**Hakâri** *see* Hakkâri
138 F12 **HaKatan, HaMakhtesh** *prev.* HaMakhtesh HaQatan. ▲▲ S Israel
166 K4 **Hakha** *var.* Haka. Chin State, W Myanmar (Burma) 22°42′N 93°41′E
137 T16 **Hakkâri** *var.* Çölemerik, Hakâri. Hakkâri, SE Turkey 37°36′N 43°45′E
137 T16 **Hakkâri** *var.* Hakkari. ◈ *province* SE Turkey
**Hakkari** *see* Hakkâri
92 J12 **Hakkas** Norrbotten, N Sweden 66°53′N 21°36′E
164 J14 **Hakken-zan** ▲ Honshū, SW Japan 34°11′N 135°57′E
165 R7 **Hakkōda-san** ▲ Honshū, C Japan 40°40′N 140°49′E
165 T2 **Hako-dake** ▲ Hokkaidō, NE Japan 44°40′N 142°22′E
165 R5 **Hakodate** Hokkaidō, NE Japan 41°46′N 140°43′E
164 L11 **Hakui** Ishikawa, Honshū, SW Japan 36°55′N 136°46′E
190 B16 **Hakupu** SE Niue 19°06′S 169°50′E
164 L12 **Haku-san** ▲ Honshū, SW Japan 36°07′N 136°45′E
**Hakusan** *see* Mattō
**Hal** *see* Halle
149 Q15 **Hala** Sindh, SE Pakistan 25°47′N 68°28′E
138 J3 **Ḩalab** *Eng.* Aleppo, *Fr.* Alep; *anc.* Beroea. Ḩalab, NW Syria 36°14′N 37°10′E
138 J3 **Ḩalab** *off.* Muḩāfaẓat Ḩalab, *var.* Aleppo, Halab. ◈ *governorate* NW Syria
138 J3 **Ḩalab** ✈ Ḩalab, NW Syria 36°12′N 37°10′E
**Halab** *see* Ḩalab
141 O8 **Ḩalabān** *var.* Halibān. Ar Riyāḑ, C Saudi Arabia 23°29′N 44°20′E
**Ḩalabja** *see* Hełebce
**Ḩalabjah** *see* Hełebce
**Ḩalab, Muḩāfaẓat** *see* Ḩalab
146 L13 **Halaç** *Rus.* Khalach. Lebap Welaýaty, E Turkmenistan 38°05′N 64°46′E
190 A16 **Halagigie Point** *headland* W Niue
75 Z11 **Halaib** SE Egypt 22°10′N 36°33′E
76 Z11 **Hala'ib Triangle** ◈ *disputed region* S Egypt / N Sudan
190 G12 **Halalo** Île Uvea, N Wallis and Futuna 13°21′S 176°11′W
167 U10 **Ha Lam** Quang Nam-Đa Năng, C Vietnam 15°42′N 108°24′E
**Halandri** *see* Chalándri
141 X13 **Ḩalāniyāt, Juzur al** *var.* Jazā'ir Bin Ghalfān, *Eng.* Kuria Muria Islands. *island group* S Oman
141 W13 **Ḩalānīyāt, Khalīj al** *Eng.* Kuria Muria Bay. *bay* S Oman
**Halas** *see* Kiskunhalas
38 G11 **Hālawa** *var.* Halawa. Hawaii, USA, C Pacific Ocean 20°13′N 155°46′W
**Halawa** *see* Hālawa
38 F9 **Hālawa, Cape** *var.* Cape Halawa. *headland* Moloka'i, Hawai'i, USA 21°09′N 156°43′W
**Cape Halawa** *see* Hālawa, Cape
**Halban** *see* Tsetserleg
101 K14 **Halberstadt** Sachsen-Anhalt, C Germany 51°54′N 11°04′E
184 M12 **Halcombe** Manawatu-Wanganui, North Island, New Zealand 40°09′S 175°30′E
95 I16 **Halden** *prev.* Fredrikshald. Østfold, S Norway 59°08′N 11°20′E
100 L13 **Haldensleben** Sachsen-Anhalt, C Germany 52°18′N 11°25′E
**Háldi** *see* Halti
153 S17 **Haldia** West Bengal, NE India 22°04′N 88°02′E
152 K10 **Haldwāni** Uttarākhand, N India 29°13′N 79°31′E
163 P9 **Haldzan** Sühbaatar, E Mongolia 46°10′N 112°57′E
163 P9 **Haldzan** *var.* Hatavch. Sühbaatar, E Mongolia 46°10′N 112°57′E
38 F10 **Haleakalā** *var.* Haleakala. *crater* Maui, Hawai'i, USA
**Haleakala** *see* Haleakalā
25 N4 **Hale Center** Texas, SW USA 34°03′N 101°50′W
99 J18 **Halen** Limburg, NE Belgium 50°35′N 05°08′E
23 O2 **Haleyville** Alabama, S USA 34°13′N 87°37′W
77 O17 **Half Assini** SW Ghana 05°03′N 02°57′W
35 R8 **Half Dome** ▲ California, W USA 37°46′N 119°27′W
185 C25 **Halfmoon Bay** *var.* Oban. Stewart Island, Southland, New Zealand 46°53′S 168°08′E
182 E5 **Half Moon Lake** *salt lake* South Australia
163 S8 **Halhgol** *var.* Tsagaannuur. Dornod, E Mongolia 47°30′N 118°45′E
163 R7 **Halhgol** Dornod, E Mongolia 47°57′N 118°07′E
**Haliacmon** *see* Aliákmonas
**Halibān** *see* Ḩalabān
14 I13 **Haliburton** Ontario, SE Canada 45°03′N 78°20′W
14 I12 **Haliburton Highlands** *var.* Madawaska Highlands. *hill range* Ontario, SE Canada
13 Q15 **Halifax** *province capital* Nova Scotia, SE Canada 44°38′N 63°35′W
97 L17 **Halifax** N England, United Kingdom 53°44′N 01°52′W
21 W8 **Halifax** North Carolina, SE USA 36°19′N 77°37′W
21 U7 **Halifax** Virginia, NE USA 36°46′N 78°55′W
13 Q15 **Halifax** ✈ Nova Scotia, SE Canada 44°33′N 63°48′W
143 T13 **Halīl Rūd** *seasonal river* SE Iran
138 I6 **Ḩalīmah** ▲ Lebanon/Syria 34°12′N 36°37′E
162 G8 **Haliun** Govĭ-Altay, W Mongolia 45°55′N 96°06′E
118 I3 **Haljala** *Ger.* Halljal. Lääne-Virumaa, N Estonia 59°25′N 26°18′E
39 Q4 **Halkett, Cape** *headland* Alaska, USA 70°48′N 152°11′W
**Halkida** *see* Chalkída
96 J6 **Halkirk** N Scotland, United Kingdom 58°30′N 03°29′W
15 X7 **Hall** 〰 Québec, SE Canada
**Hall** *see* Schwäbisch Hall
93 H15 **Hälla** Västerbotten, N Sweden 63°56′N 17°20′E
96 J6 **Halladale** 〰 N Scotland, United Kingdom
95 J21 **Halland** ◈ *county* S Sweden
23 Z15 **Hallandale** Florida, SE USA 25°58′N 80°09′W
95 K22 **Hallandsås** *physical region* S Sweden
9 P6 **Hall Beach** *var* Sanirajak. Nunavut, N Canada 68°10′N 81°56′W
99 G19 **Halle** *Fr.* Hal. Vlaams Brabant, C Belgium 50°44′N 04°14′E
101 M15 **Halle** *var.* Halle an der Saale. Sachsen-Anhalt, C Germany 51°28′N 11°58′E
**Halle an der Saale** *see* Halle
35 W3 **Halleck** Nevada, W USA 40°57′N 115°27′W
95 L15 **Hällefors** Örebro, C Sweden 59°46′N 14°30′E
95 N16 **Hälleforsnäs** Södermanland, C Sweden 59°10′N 16°30′E
109 Q6 **Hallein** Salzburg, N Austria 47°41′N 13°06′E
101 L15 **Halle-Neustadt** Sachsen-Anhalt, C Germany 51°29′N 11°54′E
25 U12 **Hallettsville** Texas, SW USA 29°27′N 96°57′W
195 N4 **Halley** *research station (UK)* Antarctica 75°42′S 26°30′W
28 L4 **Halliday** North Dakota, N USA 47°19′N 102°19′W
37 S2 **Halligan Reservoir** ⊞ Colorado, C USA
100 G7 **Halligen** *island group* N Germany
94 G13 **Hallingdal** *valley* S Norway
38 J12 **Hall Island** *island* Alaska, USA
**Hall Island** *see* Maiana
189 P15 **Hall Islands** *island group* C Micronesia
118 H6 **Halliste** 〰 S Estonia
**Halljal** *see* Haljala
93 I15 **Hällnäs** Västerbotten, N Sweden 64°20′N 19°41′E
29 R2 **Hallock** Minnesota, N USA 48°47′N 96°56′W
9 S6 **Hall Peninsula** *peninsula* Baffin Island, Nunavut, NE Canada
20 F9 **Halls** Tennessee, S USA 35°52′N 89°24′W
95 M16 **Hallsberg** Örebro, C Sweden 59°05′N 15°07′E
181 N5 **Halls Creek** Western Australia 18°17′S 127°39′E
182 L12 **Halls Gap** Victoria, SE Australia 37°09′S 142°30′E
95 N15 **Hallstahammar** Västmanland, C Sweden 59°37′N 16°13′E
109 R6 **Hallstatt** Salzburg, W Austria 47°32′N 13°39′E
109 R6 **Hallstätter See** ◎ C Austria
95 P14 **Hallstavik** Stockholm, C Sweden 60°12′N 18°45′E
25 X7 **Hallsville** Texas, SW USA 32°31′N 94°30′W
103 P1 **Halluin** Nord, N France 50°46′N 03°07′E
171 S12 **Halmahera, Laut** *Eng.* Halmahera Sea. *sea* E Indonesia
171 R11 **Halmahera, Pulau** *prev.* Djailolo, Gilolo, Jailolo. *island* E Indonesia
**Halmahera Sea** *see* Halmahera, Laut
95 J21 **Halmstad** Halland, S Sweden 56°41′N 12°49′E
167 T6 **Ha Long** *prev.* Hông Gai, *var.* Hon Gai, Hongay. Quang Ninh, N Vietnam 20°57′N 107°06′E
119 N15 **Halowchyn** *Rus.* Golovchin. Mahilyowskaya Voblasts', E Belarus 54°04′N 29°55′E
95 H20 **Hals** Nordjylland, N Denmark 57°00′N 10°19′E
94 F8 **Halsa** Møre og Romsdal, S Norway 63°04′N 08°13′E
119 I15 **Hal'shany** *Rus.* Gol'shany. Hrodzyenskaya Voblasts', W Belarus 54°15′N 26°01′E
**Hälsingborg** *see* Helsingborg
29 R5 **Halstad** Minnesota, N USA 47°21′N 96°49′W
27 N6 **Halstead** Kansas, C USA 38°00′N 97°30′W
99 G15 **Halsteren** Noord-Brabant, S Netherlands 51°32′N 04°16′E
93 L16 **Halsua** Keski-Pohjanmaa, W Finland 63°28′N 24°10′E
101 E14 **Haltern** Nordrhein-Westfalen, W Germany 51°45′N 07°10′E
92 J9 **Halti** *var.* Haltiatunturi, *Lapp.* Háldi. ▲ Finland/Norway 69°18′N 21°19′E
**Haltiatunturi** *see* Halti
75 W8 **Ḩalwān** *var.* Helwan. N Egypt 29°51′N 31°20′E
116 J6 **Halych** Ivano-Frankivs'ka Oblast', W Ukraine 49°08′N 24°44′E
**Halycus** *see* Platani
103 P3 **Ham** Somme, N France 49°46′N 03°03′E
**Hama** *see* Ḩamāh
164 F12 **Hamada** Shimane, Honshū, SW Japan 34°54′N 132°07′E
142 L6 **Hamadān** *anc.* Ecbatana. Hamadān, W Iran 34°51′N 48°31′E
142 L6 **Hamadān** *off.* Ostān-e Hamadān. ◈ *province* W Iran
**Hamadān, Ostān-e** *see* Hamadān
138 I5 **Ḩamāh** *var.* Hama; *anc.* Epiphania, *Bibl.* Hamath. Ḩamāh, W Syria 35°09′N 36°44′E
138 I5 **Ḩamāh** *off.* Muḩāfaẓat Ḩamāh, *var.* Hama. ◈ *governorate* C Syria
**Ḩamāh, Muḩāfaẓat** *see* Ḩamāh
1665 S3 **Hamamasu** Hokkaidō, NE Japan 43°37′N 141°24′E
164 L14 **Hamamatsu** *var.* Hamamatu. Shizuoka, Honshū, S Japan 34°43′N 137°46′E
**Hamamatu** *see* Hamamatsu
165 W14 **Hamanaka** Hokkaidō, NE Japan 43°05′N 145°05′E
164 L14 **Hamana-ko** ◎ Honshū, S Japan
94 I13 **Hamar** *prev.* Storhammer. Hedmark, S Norway 60°57′N 10°55′E
141 U10 **Ḩamārīr al Kidan, Qalamat** *well* E Saudi Arabia
164 I12 **Hamasaka** Hyōgo, Honshū, SW Japan 35°37′N 134°27′E
**Hamath** *see* Ḩamāh
165 T1 **Hamatonbetsu** Hokkaidō, NE Japan 45°07′N 142°21′E
155 K26 **Hambantota** Southern Province, SE Sri Lanka 06°07′N 81°07′E
**Hambourg** *see* Hamburg
100 J9 **Hamburg** Hamburg, N Germany 53°33′N 10°03′E
27 V14 **Hamburg** Arkansas, C USA 33°13′N 91°50′W
29 S16 **Hamburg** Iowa, C USA 40°36′N 95°39′W
18 D10 **Hamburg** New York, NE USA 42°40′N 78°49′W
100 I10 **Hamburg** *Fr.* Hambourg. ◈ *state* N Germany
148 K5 **Hamdam Āb, Dasht-e** *Pash.* Dasht-i Hamdamab. ▲▲ W Afghanistan
**Hamdamab, Dasht-i** *see* Hamdam Āb, Dasht-e
18 M13 **Hamden** Connecticut, NE USA 41°23′N 72°55′W
140 K6 **Ḩamḑ, Wādī al** *dry watercourse* W Saudi Arabia
93 K18 **Hämeenkyrö** Pirkanmaa, W Finland 61°39′N 23°10′E
93 L19 **Hämeenlinna** *Swe.* Tavastehus. Kanta-Häme, S Finland 61°N 24°25′E
**HaMela h, Yam** *see* Dead Sea
**Hamelin** *see* Hameln
100 I13 **Hameln** *Eng.* Hamelin. Niedersachsen, N Germany 52°07′N 09°22′E
180 I8 **Hamersley Range** ▲▲ Western Australia
163 Y12 **Hamgyŏng-sanmaek** ▲▲ N North Korea
163 X13 **Hamhŭng** C North Korea 39°53′N 127°31′E
159 O6 **Hami** *var.* Ha-mi, *Uigh.* Kumul, Qomul. Xinjiang Uygur Zizhiqu, NW China 42°48′N 93°27′E
**Ha-mi** *see* Hami
139 X10 **Ḩāmid Amīn** Maysān, E Iraq 32°06′N 46°53′E
141 W11 **Hamīdān, Khawr** *oasis* SE Saudi Arabia
114 L12 **Hamidiye** Edirne, NW Turkey 41°09′N 26°40′E
**Hamîdîyé** *see* Al Ḩamīdīyah
149 Q5 **Hamid Karzai** ✈ Kābul, E Afghanistan 34°31′N 69°11′E
182 L12 **Hamilton** Victoria, SE Australia 37°45′S 142°04′E
64 B12 **Hamilton** ○ (Bermuda) C Bermuda 32°18′N 64°48′W
14 G16 **Hamilton** Ontario, S Canada 43°15′N 79°50′W
184 M7 **Hamilton** Waikato, North Island, New Zealand 37°49′S 175°16′E
96 I12 **Hamilton** S Scotland, United Kingdom 55°47′N 04°03′W
23 N3 **Hamilton** Alabama, S USA 34°08′N 87°59′W
38 M10 **Hamilton** Alaska, USA 62°54′N 163°53′W
30 J13 **Hamilton** Illinois, N USA 40°24′N 91°20′W
27 S3 **Hamilton** Missouri, C USA 39°44′N 94°00′W
33 P10 **Hamilton** Montana, NW USA 46°15′N 114°09′W
25 S8 **Hamilton** Texas, SW USA 31°42′N 98°08′W
14 G16 **Hamilton** ✈ Ontario, SE Canada 43°12′N 79°54′W
64 I6 **Hamilton Bank** *undersea feature* SE Labrador Sea
182 E1 **Hamilton Creek** *seasonal river* South Australia
13 R8 **Hamilton Inlet** *inlet* Newfoundland and Labrador, E Canada
27 T12 **Hamilton, Lake** ⊞ Arkansas, C USA
35 W6 **Hamilton, Mount** ▲ Nevada, W USA 39°15′N 115°30′W
75 S8 **Ḩamīm, Wādī al** 〰 NE Libya
93 N19 **Hamina** *Swe.* Fredrikshamn. Kymenlaakso, S Finland 60°33′N 27°15′E
11 W16 **Hamiota** Manitoba, S Canada 50°13′N 100°37′W
152 L13 **Hamīrpur** Uttar Pradesh, N India 25°57′N 80°08′E
**Hamïs Musait** *see* Khamīs Mushayṭ
21 T11 **Hamlet** North Carolina, SE USA 34°52′N 79°41′W
25 P6 **Hamlin** Texas, SW USA 32°52′N 100°07′W
21 P5 **Hamlin** West Virginia, NE USA 38°16′N 82°07′W
31 O7 **Hamlin Lake** ◎ Michigan, N USA
101 F14 **Hamm** *var.* Hamm in Westfalen. Nordrhein-Westfalen, W Germany 51°39′N 07°49′E
**Ḩammāmāt, Khalīj al** *see* Hammamet, Golfe de
75 N5 **Hammamet, Golfe de** *Ar.* Khalīj al Ḩammāmāt. *gulf* NE Tunisia
139 R3 **Ḩammān al 'Alīl** Nīnawé, N Iraq 36°07′N 43°15′E
139 X12 **Ḩammār, Hawr al** ◎ SE Iraq
93 J20 **Hammarland** Åland, SW Finland 60°13′N 19°45′E
93 H16 **Hammarstrand** Jämtland, C Sweden 63°07′N 16°27′E
93 O17 **Hammaslahti** Pohjois-Karjala, SE Finland 62°26′N 29°58′E
99 F17 **Hamme** Oost-Vlaanderen, NW Belgium 51°06′N 04°08′E
100 H10 **Hamme** 〰 NW Germany
95 G22 **Hammel** Midtjylland, C Denmark 56°15′N 09°53′E
101 I18 **Hammelburg** Bayern, C Germany 50°06′N 09°50′E
99 H18 **Hamme-Mille** Walloon Brabant, C Belgium 50°48′N 04°42′E
100 H10 **Hamme-Oste-Kanal** *canal* NW Germany
93 G16 **Hammerdal** Jämtland, C Sweden 63°34′N 15°19′E
92 K8 **Hammerfest** Finnmark, N Norway 70°40′N 23°44′E
101 D14 **Hamminkeln** Nordrhein-Westfalen, W Germany 51°43′N 06°36′E
**Hamm in Westfalen** *see* Hamm
26 K10 **Hammon** Oklahoma, C USA 35°37′N 99°22′W
31 N11 **Hammond** Indiana, N USA 41°35′N 87°30′W
22 K8 **Hammond** Louisiana, S USA 30°30′N 90°27′W
99 K20 **Hamoir** Liège, E Belgium 50°28′N 05°35′E
99 J21 **Hamois** Namur, SE Belgium 50°21′N 05°09′E
99 K16 **Hamont** Limburg, NE Belgium 51°15′N 05°33′E
185 F22 **Hampden** Otago, South Island, New Zealand 45°18′S 170°49′E
19 R6 **Hampden** Maine, NE USA 44°44′N 68°51′W
97 M23 **Hampshire** *cultural region* S England, United Kingdom
13 O15 **Hampton** New Brunswick, SE Canada 45°30′N 65°50′W
27 U14 **Hampton** Arkansas, C USA 33°33′N 92°28′W
29 V12 **Hampton** Iowa, C USA 42°44′N 93°12′W
19 P10 **Hampton** New Hampshire, NE USA 42°55′N 70°48′W
21 R14 **Hampton** South Carolina, SE USA 32°52′N 81°06′W
21 P8 **Hampton** Tennessee, S USA 36°16′N 82°10′W
21 X7 **Hampton** Virginia, NE USA 37°02′N 76°23′W
94 L11 **Hamra** Gävleborg, C Sweden 61°40′N 15°00′E
80 D10 **Hamrat esh Sheikh** Northern Kordofan, C Sudan 14°38′N 27°56′E
139 S5 **Ḩamrīn, Jabal** ▲▲ N Iraq
121 P16 **Ħamrun** C Malta 35°53′N 14°28′E
**Ham Thuân Nam** *see* Thuân Nam
**Hāmūn, Daryācheh-ye** *see* Şābirī, Hāmūn-e
**Hāmūn, Daryācheh-ye** *see* Şāberī, Hāmūn-e/Sīstān, Daryācheh-ye
**Hamwih** *see* Southampton
38 G10 **Hāna** *var.* Hana. Maui, Hawaii, USA, C Pacific Ocean 20°45′N 155°59′W
**Hana** *see* Hāna
21 S14 **Hanahan** South Carolina, SE USA 32°55′N 80°01′W
38 B8 **Hanalei** Kaua'i, Hawaii, USA, C Pacific Ocean 22°12′N 159°30′W
165 Q9 **Hanamaki** Iwate, Honshū, C Japan 39°25′N 141°04′E
38 F10 **Hanamanioa, Cape** *headland* Maui, Hawai'i, USA 20°34′N 156°22′W
190 B16 **Hanan** ✈ (Alofi) SW Niue
101 H18 **Hanau** Hessen, W Germany 50°06′N 08°56′E
162 M11 **Hanbogd** *var.* Ih Bulag. Ömnögovĭ, S Mongolia 43°04′N 107°43′E
8 L9 **Hanbury** 〰 Northwest Territories, NW Canada
**Hânceşti** *see* Hînceşti
10 M15 **Hanceville** British Columbia, SW Canada 51°54′N 122°56′W
23 P3 **Hanceville** Alabama, S USA 34°03′N 86°46′W
**Hancewicze** *see* Hantsavichy
160 L6 **Hancheng** Shaanxi, C China 35°22′N 110°27′E
21 V2 **Hancock** Maryland, NE USA 39°42′N 78°10′W
30 M3 **Hancock** Michigan, N USA 47°07′N 88°34′W
29 S8 **Hancock** Minnesota, N USA 45°30′N 95°47′W
18 I12 **Hancock** New York, NE USA 41°57′N 75°15′W
80 Q12 **Handa** Bari, NE Somalia 10°35′N 51°09′E
161 O5 **Handan** *var.* Han-tan. Hebei, E China 36°35′N 114°28′E
95 P16 **Handen** Stockholm, C Sweden 59°12′N 18°09′E
81 J22 **Handeni** Tanga, E Tanzania 05°25′S 38°04′E
37 Q7 **Handies Peak** ▲ Colorado, C USA 37°54′N 107°30′W
111 J19 **Handlová** *Ger.* Krickerhäu, *Hung.* Nyitrabánya; *prev.* Kriegerhaj. Trenčiansky Kraj, C Slovakia 48°45′N 18°45′E
165 O13 **Haneda** ✈ (Tōkyō) Tōkyō, Honshū, S Japan 35°33′N 139°45′E
138 F13 **HaNegev** *Eng.* Negev. *desert* S Israel
**Hanfeng** *see* Kaixian
35 Q11 **Hanford** California, W USA 36°19′N 119°39′W
191 V16 **Hanga Roa** Easter Island, Chile, E Pacific Ocean 27°09′S 109°26′W
162 I7 **Hangay** *var.* Hunt. Arhangay, C Mongolia 47°49′N 99°24′E
162 H7 **Hangayn Nuruu** ▲▲ C Mongolia
**Hang-chou/Hangchow** *see* Hangzhou
95 K20 **Hånger** Jönköping, S Sweden 57°06′N 13°58′E
**Hangö** *see* Hanko
161 R9 **Hangzhou** *var.* Hang-chou, Hangchow. *province capital* Zhejiang, SE China 30°18′N 120°07′E
162 J4 **Hanh** *var.* Turt. Hövsgöl, N Mongolia 51°30′N 100°40′E
162 F5 **Hanhöhiy Uul** ▲▲ NW Mongolia
162 K10 **Hanhongor** *var.* Ögöömör. Ömnögovĭ, S Mongolia 43°47′N 104°31′E
146 I14 **Hanhowuz** *Rus.* Khauz-Khan. Ahal Welaýaty, S Turkmenistan 37°15′N 61°12′E
146 I14 **Hanhowuz Suw Howdany** *Rus.* Khauzkhanskoye Vodoranilishche. ⊞ S Turkmenistan
137 P15 **Hani** Dıyarbakır, SE Turkey 38°26′N 40°23′E
**Hania** *see* Chaniá
141 R11 **Ḩanīsh al Kabīr, Jazīrat al** *island* SW Yemen
**Hanka, Lake** *see* Khanka, Lake
93 M17 **Hankasalmi** Keski-Suomi, C Finland 62°25′N 26°27′E
29 R7 **Hankinson** North Dakota, N USA 46°04′N 96°54′W
93 K20 **Hanko** *Swe.* Hangö. Uusimaa, SW Finland 59°50′N 23°E
**Han-kou/Han-k'ou/Hankow** *see* Wuhan
36 M6 **Hanksville** Utah, W USA 38°21′N 110°43′W
152 K6 **Hanle** Jammu and Kashmir, NW India 32°46′N 79°01′E
185 I17 **Hanmer Springs** Canterbury, South Island, New Zealand 42°31′S 172°49′E
11 R16 **Hanna** Alberta, SW Canada 51°38′N 111°56′W




◆ Country
● Country Capital
◇ Dependent Territory
○ Dependent Territory Capital
◈ Administrative Regions
✈ International Airport
▲ Mountain
▲▲ Mountain Range
Volcano
〰 River
◎ Lake
⊞ Reservoir

◆ Country  ● Country Capital  ◇ Dependent Territory  ○ Dependent Territory Capital  ◇ Administrative Regions  ✈ International Airport  ▲ Mountain  ▲ Mountain Range  ☆ Volcano  ಌ River  ⊗ Lake  ⊠ Reservoir

# Hebrides, Sea of the – Hinis



96 *F9* **Hebrides, Sea of the** *sea* NW Scotland, United Kingdom
13 *P5* **Hebron** Newfoundland and Labrador, E Canada *58°15′N 62°45′W*
31 *N11* **Hebron** Indiana, N USA *41°19′N 87°12′W*
29 *Q17* **Hebron** Nebraska, C USA *40°10′N 97°35′W*
28 *L5* **Hebron** North Dakota, N USA *46°54′N 102°03′W*
138 *F11* **Hebron** *var.* Al Khalīl, El Khalil, *Heb.* Hevron; *anc.* Kiriath-Arba. S West Bank *31°30′N 35°E*
**Hebrus** *see* Évros/Maritsa/Meriç
95 *N14* **Heby** Västmanland, C Sweden *59°56′N 16°53′E*
10 *I14* **Hecate Strait** *strait* British Columbia, W Canada
41 *W12* **Hecelchakán** Campeche, SE Mexico *20°09′N 90°04′W*
160 *K13* **Hechi** *var.* Jinchengjiang. Guangxi Zhuangzu Zizhiqu, S China *24°39′N 108°02′E*
101 *H23* **Hechingen** Baden-Württemberg, S Germany *48°20′N 08°58′E*
99 *K17* **Hechtel** Limburg, NE Belgium *51°07′N 05°24′E*
160 *J9* **Hechuan** *var.* Heyang. Chongqing Shi, C China *30°02′N 106°15′E*
29 *P7* **Hecla** South Dakota, N USA *45°52′N 98°09′W*
9 *N1* **Hecla, Cape** *headland* Nunavut, N Canada *82°00′N 64°00′W*
29 *T9* **Hector** Minnesota, N USA *44°44′N 94°43′W*
93 *F17* **Hede** Jämtland, C Sweden *62°25′N 13°33′E*
**Hede** *see* Sheyang
95 *M14* **Hedemora** Dalarna, C Sweden *60°18′N 15°58′E*
92 *K13* **Hedenäset** *Finn.* Hietaniemi. Norrbotten, N Sweden *66°12′N 23°40′E*
95 *G23* **Hedensted** Syddanmark, C Denmark *55°47′N 09°43′E*
95 *N14* **Hedesunda** Gävleborg, C Sweden *60°25′N 17°00′E*
95 *N14* **Hedesundafjärden** ◎ C Sweden
25 *O3* **Hedley** Texas, SW USA *34°52′N 100°39′W*
94 *I12* **Hedmark** ◈ *county* S Norway
165 *T16* **Hedo-misaki** *headland* Okinawa, SW Japan *26°55′N 128°15′E*
29 *X15* **Hedrick** Iowa, C USA *41°10′N 92°18′W*
99 *L16* **Heel** Limburg, SE Netherlands *51°12′N 06°01′E*
189 *Y12* **Heel Point** *point* Wake Island
98 *H9* **Heemskerk** Noord-Holland, W Netherlands *52°31′N 04°40′E*
98 *M10* **Heerde** Gelderland, E Netherlands *52°24′N 06°02′E*
98 *L7* **Heerenveen** *Fris.* It Hearrenfean. Fryslân, N Netherlands *52°57′N 05°55′E*
98 *I8* **Heerhugowaard** Noord-Holland, NW Netherlands *52°40′N 04°50′E*
92 *O3* **Heer Land** *physical region* C Svalbard
99 *M18* **Heerlen** Limburg, SE Netherlands *50°55′N 06°E*
99 *J19* **Heers** Limburg, NE Belgium *50°46′N 05°17′E*
**Heerwegen** *see* Polkowice
98 *K13* **Heesch** Noord-Brabant, S Netherlands *51°44′N 05°32′E*
99 *K15* **Heeze** Noord-Brabant, SE Netherlands *51°23′N 05°35′E*
138 *F8* **Hefa** *var.* Haifa, *hist.* Caiffa, Caiphas; *anc.* Sycaminum. Haifa, N Israel *32°49′N 34°59′E*
**Hefa, Mifraz** *see* Mifrats Hefa
161 *Q8* **Hefei** *var.* Hofei, *hist.* Luchow. *province capital* Anhui, E China *31°51′N 117°20′E*
23 *R3* **Heflin** Alabama, S USA *33°39′N 85°35′W*
163 *X7* **Hegang** Heilongjiang, NE China *47°18′N 130°16′E*
164 *L10* **Hegura-jima** *island* SW Japan
**Heguri-jima** *see* Heigun-tō
**Hei** *see* Heilongjiang
100 *H8* **Heide** Schleswig-Holstein, N Germany *54°12′N 09°06′E*
101 *G20* **Heidelberg** Baden-Württemberg, SW Germany *49°24′N 08°41′E*
83 *J21* **Heidelberg** Gauteng, NE South Africa *26°31′S 28°21′E*
22 *M6* **Heidelberg** Mississippi, S USA *31°53′N 88°58′W*
**Heidenheim** *see* Heidenheim an der Brenz
101 *J22* **Heidenheim an der Brenz** *var.* Heidenheim. Baden-Württemberg, S Germany *48°41′N 10°09′E*
109 *U2* **Heidenreichstein** Niederösterreich, N Austria *48°53′N 15°07′E*
164 *F14* **Heigun-tō** *var.* Heguri-jima. *island* SW Japan
163 *W5* **Heihe** *prev.* Ai-hun. Heilongjiang, NE China *50°13′N 127°29′E*
162 *S8* **Hei He** ≈ C China
**Hei-ho** *see* Nagqu
83 *J22* **Heilbron** Free State, N South Africa *27°17′S 27°58′E*
101 *H21* **Heilbronn** Baden-Württemberg, SW Germany *49°09′N 09°13′E*
**Heiligenbeil** *see* Mamonovo
109 *Q8* **Heiligenblut** Tirol, W Austria *47°04′N 12°50′E*
100 *K7* **Heiligenhafen** Schleswig-Holstein, N Germany *54°22′N 10°57′E*
**Heiligenkreuz** *see* Žiar nad Hronom
101 *J15* **Heiligenstadt** Thüringen, C Germany *51°22′N 10°09′E*
163 *W8* **Heilongjiang** *var.* Hei, Heilongjiang Sheng, Hei-lung-chiang, Heilungkiang. ◈ *province* NE China
**Heilong Jiang** *see* Amur
**Heilongjiang Sheng** *see* Heilongjiang
98 *H9* **Heiloo** Noord-Holland, NW Netherlands *52°36′N 04°43′E*
**Heilsberg** *see* Lidzbark Warmiński
**Hei-lung-chiang/Heilungkiang** *see* Heilongjiang
**Heimaæy** *see* Heimaey
92 *I4* **Heimaey** *var.* Heimaæy. *island* S Iceland
94 *H8* **Heimdal** Sør-Trøndelag, S Norway *63°21′N 10°23′E*
**Heinaste** *see* Ainaži
93 *N17* **Heinävesi** Etelä-Savo, E Finland *62°22′N 28°42′E*
99 *M22* **Heinerscheid** Diekirch, N Luxembourg *50°06′N 06°05′E*
98 *M10* **Heino** Overijssel, E Netherlands *52°26′N 06°13′E*
93 *M18* **Heinola** Päijät-Häme, S Finland *61°13′N 26°05′E*
101 *C16* **Heinsberg** Nordrhein-Westfalen, W Germany *51°02′N 06°01′E*
163 *U12* **Heishan** Liaoning, NE China *41°43′N 122°12′E*
160 *H8* **Heishui** *var.* Luhua. Sichuan, C China *32°08′N 102°54′E*
99 *H17* **Heist-op-den-Berg** Antwerpen, C Belgium *51°04′N 04°43′E*
**Heitō** *see* Pingtung
171 *X15* **Heitske** Papua, E Indonesia *07°02′S 138°45′E*
**Hejanah** *see* Al Hījānah
**Hejaz** *see* Al Ḩijāz
160 *M14* **He Jiang** ≈ S China
**Hejiayan** *see* Lüeyang
158 *K6* **Hejing** Xinjiang Uygur Zizhiqu, NW China *42°21′N 86°19′E*
**Héjjasfalva** *see* Vânători
**Heka** *see* Hoika
137 *N14* **Hekimhan** Malatya, C Turkey *38°50′N 37°56′E*
92 *J4* **Hekla** ▲ S Iceland *63°56′N 19°42′W*
**Hekou** *see* Yanshan, Jiangxi, China
**Hekou** *see* Yajiang, Sichuan, China
110 *J6* **Hel** *Ger.* Hela. Pomorskie, N Poland *54°35′N 18°48′E*
**Hela** *see* Hel
93 *F17* **Helagsfjället** ▲ C Sweden *62°57′N 12°31′E*
159 *W8* **Helan** *var.* Xigang. Ningxia, N China *38°33′N 106°21′E*
162 *K14* **Helan Shan** ▲▲ N China
99 *M16* **Helden** Limburg, SE Netherlands *51°20′N 06°00′E*
139 *V4* **Hełebce** *Ar.* Ḩalabjah, *var* Haļabja. As Sulaymānīyah, NE Iraq *35°11′N 45°59′E*
27 *X12* **Helena** Arkansas, C USA *34°32′N 90°34′W*
33 *R10* **Helena** *state capital* Montana, NW USA *46°36′N 112°02′W*
96 *H12* **Helensburgh** W Scotland, United Kingdom *56°00′N 04°45′W*
184 *K5* **Helensville** Auckland, North Island, New Zealand *36°42′S 174°26′E*
95 *L20* **Helgasjön** ◎ S Sweden
100 *G8* **Helgoland** *Eng.* Heligoland. *island* NW Germany
**Helgoland Bay** *see* Helgoländer Bucht
100 *G8* **Helgoländer Bucht** *var.* Helgoland Bay, Heligoland Bight. *bay* NW Germany
**Heligoland** *see* Helgoland
**Heligoland Bight** *see* Helgoländer Bucht
**Heliopolis** *see* Baalbek
92 *I4* **Hella** Suðurland, SW Iceland *63°51′N 20°24′W*
**Hellas** *see* Greece
143 *N11* **Ḩelleh, Rūd-e** ≈ S Iran
98 *N10* **Hellendoorn** Overijssel, E Netherlands *52°22′N 06°27′E*
**Hellenic Republic** *see* Greece
121 *Q10* **Hellenic Trough** *undersea feature* Aegean Sea, C Mediterranean Sea *22°00′E 35°30′N*
94 *E10* **Hellesylt** Møre og Romsdal, S Norway *62°06′N 06°51′E*
98 *F13* **Hellevoetsluis** Zuid-Holland, SW Netherlands *51°49′N 04°08′E*
105 *Q12* **Hellín** Castilla-La Mancha, C Spain *38°31′N 01°43′W*
115 *H19* **Hellinikon** ✈ (Athína) Attikí, C Greece *37°53′N 23°43′E*
32 *M12* **Hells Canyon** *valley* Idaho/Oregon, NW USA
148 *L9* **Helmand** ◈ *province* S Afghanistan
**Helmand, Daryā-ye** *see* Hīrmand, Rūd-e
**Helmand, Daryā-ye** *see* Helmand Rōd
148 *K10* **Helmand Rōd** *prev.* Daryā-ye Helmand, *var.* Helmand Rūd. ≈ Afghanistan/Iran *see also* Hīrmand, Rūd-e
**Helmand Rūd** *see* Helmand Rōd
**Helmantica** *see* Salamanca
101 *K15* **Helme** ≈ C Germany
99 *L15* **Helmond** Noord-Brabant, S Netherlands *51°29′N 05°41′E*
96 *J7* **Helmsdale** N Scotland, United Kingdom *58°06′N 03°36′W*
100 *K13* **Helmstedt** Niedersachsen, N Germany *52°14′N 11°01′E*
163 *Y10* **Helong** Jilin, NE China *42°38′N 129°01′E*
36 *M4* **Helper** Utah, W USA *39°40′N 110°52′W*
100 *O10* **Helpter Berge** *hill* NE Germany
95 *J22* **Helsingborg** *prev.* Hälsingborg. Skåne, S Sweden *56°N 12°48′E*
**Helsingfors** *see* Helsinki
95 *J22* **Helsingør** *Eng.* Elsinore. Hovedstaden, E Denmark *56°03′N 12°38′E*
93 *M20* **Helsinki** *Swe.* Helsingfors ● (Finland) Uusimaa, S Finland *60°18′N 24°58′E*
97 *H25* **Helston** SW England, United Kingdom *50°04′N 05°17′W*
**Heltau** *see* Cisnădie
61 *C17* **Helvecia** Santa Fe, C Argentina *31°09′S 60°09′W*
97 *K15* **Helvellyn** ▲ NW England United Kingdom *54°31′N 03°00′W*
**Helvetia** *see* Switzerland
**Helwân** *see* Ḩalwān
97 *N21* **Hemel Hempstead** E England, United Kingdom *51°46′N 00°28′W*
35 *U16* **Hemet** California, W USA *33°45′N 116°58′W*
28 *J13* **Hemingford** Nebraska, C USA *42°18′N 103°02′W*
21 *T13* **Hemingway** South Carolina, SE USA *33°45′N 79°25′W*
92 *G13* **Hemnesberget** Nordland, C Norway *66°14′N 13°40′E*
25 *Y8* **Hemphill** Texas, SW USA *31°21′N 93°50′W*
25 *V11* **Hempstead** Texas, SW USA *30°06′N 96°06′W*
95 *P20* **Hemse** Gotland, SE Sweden *57°12′N 18°22′E*
94 *F13* **Hemsedal** *valley* S Norway
161 *N6* **Henan** *var.* Henan Sheng, Honan, Yu. ◈ *province* C China
184 *L4* **Hen and Chickens** *island group* N New Zealand
**Henan Mongolzu Zizhixian/Henan Sheng** *see* Yêgainnyin
105 *O7* **Henares** ≈ C Spain
165 *P7* **Henashi-zaki** *headland* Honshū, C Japan *40°37′N 139°51′E*
102 *I16* **Hendaye** Pyrénées-Atlantiques, SW France *43°22′N 01°46′W*
136 *F11* **Hendek** Sakarya, NW Turkey *40°47′N 30°45′E*
61 *B21* **Henderson** Buenos Aires, E Argentina *36°18′S 61°43′W*
20 *I5* **Henderson** Kentucky, S USA *37°50′N 87°35′W*
35 *X11* **Henderson** Nevada, W USA *36°02′N 114°58′W*
21 *V8* **Henderson** North Carolina, SE USA *36°20′N 78°26′W*
20 *G10* **Henderson** Tennessee, S USA *35°27′N 88°40′W*
25 *W7* **Henderson** Texas, SW USA *32°11′N 94°48′W*
30 *J12* **Henderson Creek** ≈ Illinois, N USA
186 *M9* **Henderson Field** ✈ (Honiara) Guadalcanal, C Solomon Islands *09°28′S 160°02′E*
191 *O17* **Henderson Island** *atoll* N Pitcairn Group of Islands
21 *O10* **Hendersonville** North Carolina, SE USA *35°19′N 82°28′W*
20 *J8* **Hendersonville** Tennessee, S USA *36°18′N 86°37′W*
143 *O14* **Hendorābī, Jazīreh-ye** *island* S Iran
55 *V10* **Hendrik Top** *var.* Hendriktop. *elevation* C Suriname
**Hendriktop** *see* Hendrik Top
**Hendū Kosh** *see* Hindu Kush
14 *L12* **Heney, Lac** ◎ Québec, SE Canada
**Hengchow** *see* Hengyang
161 *S15* **Hengch'un** S Taiwan *22°09′N 120°43′E*
159 *R16* **Hengduan Shan** ▲▲ SW China
98 *N12* **Hengelo** Gelderland, E Netherlands *52°03′N 06°19′E*
98 *O10* **Hengelo** Overijssel, E Netherlands *52°16′N 06°46′E*
**Hengnan** *see* Hengyang
161 *N11* **Hengshan** Hunan, S China *27°17′N 112°51′E*
160 *L4* **Hengshan** Shaanxi, C China *37°57′N 109°17′E*
161 *O4* **Hengshui** Hebei, E China *37°42′N 115°39′E*
161 *N12* **Hengyang** *var.* Hengnan, Heng-yang; *prev.* Hengchow. Hunan, S China *26°55′N 112°34′E*
**Heng-yang** *see* Hengyang
117 *U11* **Heniches'k** *Rus.* Genichesk. Khersons'ka Oblast', S Ukraine *46°10′N 34°49′E*
21 *Z4* **Henlopen, Cape** *headland* Delaware, NE USA *38°48′N 75°06′W*
**Henna** *see* Enna
94 *M10* **Hennan** Gävleborg, C Sweden *62°01′N 15°55′E*
102 *G7* **Hennebont** Morbihan, NW France *47°48′N 03°17′W*
30 *L11* **Hennepin** Illinois, N USA *41°14′N 89°21′W*
26 *M9* **Hennessey** Oklahoma, C USA *36°06′N 97°54′W*
100 *N12* **Hennigsdorf** *var.* Hennigsdorf bei Berlin. Brandenburg, NE Germany *52°37′N 13°13′E*
**Hennigsdorf bei Berlin** *see* Hennigsdorf
19 *N9* **Henniker** New Hampshire, NE USA *43°10′N 71°47′W*
25 *S5* **Henrietta** Texas, SW USA *33°49′N 98°13′W*
**Henrique de Carvalho** *see* Saurimo
30 *L12* **Henry** Illinois, N USA *41°06′N 89°21′W*
21 *Y7* **Henry, Cape** *headland* Virginia, NE USA *36°55′N 76°01′W*
27 *P10* **Henryetta** Oklahoma, C USA *35°26′N 95°58′W*
194 *M7* **Henry Ice Rise** *ice cap* Antarctica
9 *R5* **Henry Kater, Cape** *headland* Baffin Island, Nunavut, NE Canada *69°09′N 66°45′W*
33 *R13* **Henrys Fork** ≈ Idaho, NW USA
14 *E15* **Hensall** Ontario, S Canada *43°25′N 81°28′W*
100 *J9* **Henstedt-Ulzburg** Schleswig-Holstein, N Germany *53°45′N 09°59′E*
163 *N7* **Hentiy** *var.* Batshireet, Eg. ◈ *province* N Mongolia
162 *M7* **Hentiyn Nuruu** ▲▲ N Mongolia
183 *P10* **Henty** New South Wales, SE Australia *35°33′S 147°03′E*
**Henzada** *see* Hinthada
**Heping** *see* Huishui
101 *G19* **Heppenheim** Hessen, W Germany *49°39′N 08°38′E*
32 *J11* **Heppner** Oregon, NW USA *45°21′N 119°32′W*
160 *L15* **Hepu** *var.* Lianzhou. Guangxi Zhuangzu Zizhiqu, S China *21°40′N 109°12′E*
**Heracleum** *see* Irákleio
92 *J2* **Heraðsvötn** C Iceland
**Herakleion** *see* Irákleio
148 *K5* **Herāt** *var.* Herat; *anc.* Aria. Herāt, W Afghanistan *34°23′N 62°11′E*
148 *J5* **Herāt** ◈ *province* W Afghanistan
103 *P14* **Hérault** ◈ *department* S France
103 *P15* **Hérault** ≈ S France
11 *T16* **Herbert** Saskatchewan, S Canada *50°27′N 107°09′W*
185 *F22* **Herbert** Otago, South Island, New Zealand *45°14′S 170°48′E*
38 *J17* **Herbert Island** *island* Aleutian Islands, Alaska, USA
**Herbertshöhe** *see* Kokopo
15 *Q7* **Hérbertville** Québec, SE Canada *48°23′N 71°42′W*
101 *G17* **Herborn** Hessen, W Germany *50°40′N 08°18′E*
113 *I17* **Herceg-Novi** *It.* Castelnuovo; *prev.* Ercegnovi. SW Montenegro *42°28′N 18°35′E*
11 *X10* **Herchmer** Manitoba, C Canada *57°25′N 94°12′W*
186 *E8* **Hercules Bay** *bay* E Papua New Guinea
92 *K2* **Herðubreið** C Iceland *65°12′N 16°26′W*
42 *M13* **Heredia** Heredia, C Costa Rica *10°N 84°06′W*
42 *M12* **Heredia** *off.* Provincia de Heredia. ◈ *province* N Costa Rica
**Heredia, Provincia de** *see* Heredia
97 *K21* **Hereford** W England, United Kingdom *52°04′N 02°43′W*
24 *M3* **Hereford** Texas, SW USA *34°49′N 102°25′W*
15 *Q13* **Hereford, Mont** ▲ Québec, SE Canada *45°04′N 71°38′W*
97 *K21* **Herefordshire** *cultural region* W England, United Kingdom
191 *U11* **Hereheretue** *atoll* Îles Tuamotu, C French Polynesia
105 *N10* **Herencia** Castilla-La Mancha, C Spain *39°22′N 03°12′W*
99 *H18* **Herent** Vlaams Brabant, C Belgium *50°54′N 04°40′E*
99 *I16* **Herentals** *var.* Herenthals. Antwerpen, N Belgium *51°11′N 04°50′E*
**Herenthals** *see* Herentals
99 *H17* **Herenthout** Antwerpen, N Belgium *51°09′N 04°45′E*
95 *J23* **Herfølge** Sjælland, E Denmark *55°25′N 12°09′E*
100 *G13* **Herford** Nordrhein-Westfalen, NW Germany *52°07′N 08°41′E*
27 *O5* **Herington** Kansas, C USA *38°37′N 96°55′W*
108 *H7* **Herisau** *Fr.* Hérisau. Ausser Rhoden, NE Switzerland *47°23′N 09°17′E*
**Hérisau** *see* Herisau
**Héristal** *see* Herstal
99 *J18* **Herk-de-Stad** Limburg, NE Belgium *50°57′N 05°12′E*
**Herkulesbad/Herkulesfürdő** *see* Băile Herculane
162 *M8* **Herlenbayan-Ulaan** *var.* Dulaan. Hentiy, C Mongolia *47°09′N 108°48′E*
**Herlen Gol/Herlen He** *see* Kerulen
35 *Q4* **Herlong** California, W USA *40°07′N 120°06′W*
97 *L26* **Herm** *island* Channel Islands
109 *R9* **Hermagor** *Slvn.* Šmohor. Kärnten, S Austria *46°37′N 13°24′E*
29 *S7* **Herman** Minnesota, N USA *45°49′N 96°08′W*
96 *L1* **Herma Ness** *headland* NE Scotland, United Kingdom *60°51′N 00°55′W*
27 *V4* **Hermann** Missouri, C USA *38°43′N 91°26′W*
181 *Q8* **Hermannsburg** Northern Territory, N Australia *23°59′S 132°55′E*
**Hermannstadt** *see* Sibiu
94 *E12* **Hermansverk** Sogn Og Fjordane, S Norway *61°11′N 06°52′E*
138 *H6* **Hermel** *var.* Hirmil. NE Lebanon *34°23′N 36°19′E*
**Hermhausen** *see* Hajnówka
183 *P6* **Hermidale** New South Wales, SE Australia *31°36′S 146°42′E*
55 *X9* **Herminadorp** Sipaliwini, NE Suriname *05°05′N 54°22′W*
32 *K11* **Hermiston** Oregon, NW USA *45°50′N 119°17′W*
27 *T6* **Hermitage** Missouri, C USA *37°57′N 93°21′W*
186 *D4* **Hermit Islands** *island group* N Papua New Guinea
25 *O7* **Hermleigh** Texas, SW USA *32°37′N 100°44′W*
138 *G7* **Hermon, Mount** *Ar.* Jabal ash Shaykh. ▲ S Syria *35°30′N 33°30′E*
**Hermopolis Parva** *see* Damanhūr
28 *J10* **Hermosa** South Dakota, N USA *43°49′N 103°12′W*
40 *F5* **Hermosillo** Sonora, NW Mexico *28°59′N 110°53′W*
**Hermoupolis** *see* Ermoúpoli
111 *N20* **Hernád** *var.* Hornád, *Ger.* Kundert. ≈ Hungary/Slovakia
61 *C18* **Hernández** Entre Ríos, E Argentina *32°21′S 60°02′W*
23 *V11* **Hernando** Florida, SE USA *28°54′N 82°22′W*
22 *L1* **Hernando** Mississippi, S USA *34°49′N 89°59′W*
105 *Q2* **Hernani** País Vasco, N Spain *43°16′N 01°59′W*
99 *F19* **Herne** Vlaams Brabant, C Belgium *50°45′N 04°03′E*
101 *E14* **Herne** Nordrhein-Westfalen, W Germany *51°32′N 07°12′E*
95 *F22* **Herning** Midtjylland, W Denmark *56°08′N 08°59′E*
**Hernösand** *see* Härnösand
121 *U11* **Herodotus Basin** *undersea feature* E Mediterranean Sea
121 *Q12* **Herodotus Trough** *undersea feature* C Mediterranean Sea
29 *T11* **Heron Lake** Minnesota, N USA *43°48′N 95°18′W*
**Herowābād** *see* Khalkhāl
95 *G16* **Herre** Telemark, S Norway *59°06′N 09°34′E*
29 *N7* **Herreid** South Dakota, N USA *45°49′N 100°04′W*
101 *H22* **Herrenberg** Baden-Württemberg, S Germany *48°36′N 08°52′E*
104 *L14* **Herrera** Andalucía, S Spain *37°22′N 04°50′W*
43 *R17* **Herrera** *off.* Provincia de Herrera. ◈ *province* S Panama
104 *L10* **Herrera del Duque** Extremadura, W Spain *39°10′N 05°03′W*
104 *M4* **Herrera de Pisuerga** Castilla y León, N Spain *42°35′N 04°20′W*
**Herrera, Provincia de** *see* Herrera
41 *Z13* **Herrero, Punta** *headland* SE Mexico *19°15′N 87°28′W*
183 *P16* **Herrick** Tasmania, SE Australia *41°07′S 147°53′E*
30 *L17* **Herrin** Illinois, N USA *37°48′N 89°01′W*
20 *M6* **Herrington Lake** ⊠ Kentucky, S USA
95 *K18* **Herrljunga** Västra Götaland, S Sweden *58°05′N 13°02′E*
103 *N16* **Hers** ≈ S France
10 *I1* **Herschel Island** *island* Yukon, NW Canada
99 *I17* **Herselt** Antwerpen, C Belgium *51°04′N 04°53′E*
18 *G15* **Hershey** Pennsylvania, NE USA *40°17′N 76°39′W*
99 *K19* **Herstal** *Fr.* Héristal. Liège, E Belgium *50°40′N 05°38′E*
97 *O21* **Hertford** E England, United Kingdom *51°48′N 00°05′W*
21 *X8* **Hertford** North Carolina, SE USA *36°11′N 76°30′W*
97 *O21* **Hertfordshire** *cultural region* E England, United Kingdom
181 *Z9* **Hervey Bay** Queensland, E Australia *25°17′S 152°48′E*
101 *O14* **Herzberg** Brandenburg, E Germany *51°42′N 13°15′E*
99 *E18* **Herzele** Oost-Vlaanderen, NW Belgium *50°52′N 03°52′E*
101 *K20* **Herzogenaurach** Bayern, SE Germany *49°34′N 10°52′E*
109 *W4* **Herzogenburg** Niederösterreich, NE Austria *48°18′N 15°43′E*
**Herzogenbusch** *see* 's-Hertogenbosch
103 *N2* **Hesdin** Pas-de-Calais, N France *50°21′N 02°00′E*
160 *K14* **Heshan** Guangxi Zhuangzu Zizhiqu, S China *23°45′N 108°58′E*
159 *X10* **Heshui** *var.* Xihuachi. Gansu, C China *35°42′N 108°06′E*
99 *M25* **Hespérange** Luxembourg, SE Luxembourg *49°34′N 06°10′E*
35 *U14* **Hesperia** California, W USA *34°25′N 117°17′W*
37 *P7* **Hesperus Mountain** ▲ Colorado, C USA *37°27′N 108°05′W*
10 *J6* **Hess** ≈ Yukon, NW Canada
**Hesse** *see* Hessen
101 *J21* **Hesselberg** ▲ S Germany *49°04′N 10°32′E*
95 *I22* **Hesselo** *island* E Denmark
101 *H17* **Hessen** *Eng./Fr.* Hesse. ◈ *state* C Germany
192 *L6* **Hess Tablemount** *undersea feature* C Pacific Ocean *17°49′N 174°15′W*
27 *N6* **Hesston** Kansas, C USA *38°08′N 97°25′W*
93 *G15* **Hestkjøltoppen** ▲ C Norway *64°21′N 13°57′E*
97 *K18* **Heswall** NW England, United Kingdom *53°20′N 03°06′W*
153 *P12* **Hetaudā** Central, C Nepal
**Hétfalu** *see* Săcele
28 *K7* **Hettinger** North Dakota, N USA *46°00′N 102°38′W*
101 *L14* **Hettstedt** Sachsen-Anhalt, C Germany *51°39′N 11°31′E*
92 *P3* **Heuglin, Kapp** *headland* SE Svalbard *78°15′N 22°49′E*
163 *W17* **Heuksan-jedo** *var.* Hŭksan-gundo. *island group* SW South Korea
187 *N10* **Heuru** Makira-Ulawa, SE Solomon Islands *10°13′S 161°25′E*
99 *J17* **Heusden** Limburg, NE Belgium *51°02′N 05°17′E*
98 *J13* **Heusden** Noord-Brabant, S Netherlands *51°43′N 05°05′E*
102 *K3* **Hève, Cap de la** *headland* N France *49°28′N 00°13′W*
99 *H18* **Heverlee** Vlaams Brabant, C Belgium *50°52′N 04°41′E*
111 *L22* **Heves** Heves, NE Hungary *47°36′N 20°17′E*
111 *L22* **Heves** *off.* Heves Megye. ◈ *county* NE Hungary
**Heves Megye** *see* Heves
**Hevron** *see* Hebron
45 *Y13* **Hewanorra** ✈ (Saint Lucia) S Saint Lucia *13°44′N 60°57′W*
**Hewlêr** *see* Arbīl
**Hewlêr** *see* Arbīl
**Hewlêr, Parêzga-î** *see* Arbīl
**Hexian** *see* Hezhou
160 *L6* **Heyang** Shaanxi, C China *35°14′N 110°02′E*
**Heyang** *see* Hechuan
**Heydebrech** *see* Kędzierzyn-Kozle
**Heydekrug** *see* Šilutė
**Heyin** *see* Guide
97 *K16* **Heysham** NW England, United Kingdom *54°02′N 02°54′W*
161 *O14* **Heyuan** *var.* Yuancheng. Guangdong, S China *23°41′N 114°45′E*
182 *L12* **Heywood** Victoria, SE Australia *38°09′S 141°38′E*
180 *K3* **Heywood Islands** *island group* Western Australia
161 *O6* **Heze** *var.* Caozhou. Shandong, E China *35°16′N 115°27′E*
159 *U11* **Hezheng** Gansu, C China *35°29′N 103°36′E*
160 *M13* **Hezhou** *var.* Babu; *prev.* Hexian. Guangxi Zhuangzu Zizhiqu, S China *24°33′N 11°30′E*
159 *U11* **Hezuo** Gansu, C China *34°55′N 102°49′E*
23 *Z16* **Hialeah** Florida, SE USA *25°51′N 80°16′W*
27 *Q3* **Hiawatha** Kansas, C USA *39°51′N 95°34′W*
36 *M4* **Hiawatha** Utah, W USA *39°28′N 111°00′W*
29 *V4* **Hibbing** Minnesota, N USA *47°24′N 92°55′W*
183 *N17* **Hibbs, Point** *headland* Tasmania, SE Australia *42°37′S 145°15′E*
**Hibernia** *see* Ireland
20 *F8* **Hickman** Kentucky, S USA *36°33′N 89°11′W*
21 *Q9* **Hickory** North Carolina, SE USA *35°44′N 81°20′W*
21 *Q9* **Hickory, Lake** ◎ North Carolina, SE USA
184 *Q7* **Hicks Bay** Gisborne, North Island, New Zealand *37°36′S 178°18′E*
25 *S8* **Hico** Texas, SW USA *31°58′N 98°01′W*
**Hida** *see* Furukawa
165 *T4* **Hidaka** Hokkaidō, NE Japan *42°53′N 142°24′E*
164 *I12* **Hidaka** Hyōgo, Honshū, SW Japan *35°27′N 134°43′E*
165 *T5* **Hidaka-sanmyaku** ▲▲ Hokkaidō, NE Japan
41 *O6* **Hidalgo** *var.* Villa Hidalgo. Coahuila, NE Mexico *27°46′N 99°54′W*
41 *N8* **Hidalgo** Nuevo León, NE Mexico *29°59′N 100°27′W*
41 *O10* **Hidalgo** Tamaulipas, C Mexico *24°16′N 99°28′W*
41 *O13* **Hidalgo** ◈ *state* C Mexico
40 *J7* **Hidalgo del Parral** *var.* Parral. Chihuahua, N Mexico *26°58′N 105°40′W*
100 *N7* **Hiddensee** *island* NE Germany
80 *G6* **Hidiglib, Wadi** ≈ NE Sudan
109 *U6* **Hieflau** Salzburg, E Austria *47°36′N 14°34′E*
187 *P16* **Hienghène** Province Nord, C New Caledonia *20°43′S 164°54′E*
**Hierosolyma** *see* Jerusalem
64 *N12* **Hierro** *var.* Ferro. *island* Islas Canarias, Spain, NE Atlantic Ocean
**Hietaniemi** *see* Hedenäset
164 *G13* **Higashi-Hiroshima** *var.* Higasihirosima. Hiroshima, Honshū, SW Japan *34°27′N 132°43′E*
164 *C12* **Higashi-suidō** *strait* SW Japan
**Higasihirosima** *see* Higashi-Hiroshima
25 *P1* **Higgins** Texas, SW USA *36°06′N 100°01′W*
31 *P7* **Higgins Lake** ◎ Michigan, N USA
27 *S4* **Higginsville** Missouri, C USA *39°04′N 93°43′W*
**High Atlas** *see* Haut Atlas
30 *M5* **High Falls Reservoir** ⊠ Wisconsin, N USA
44 *K12* **Highgate** C Jamaica *18°16′N 76°53′W*
25 *X11* **High Island** Texas, SW USA *29°35′N 94°24′W*
31 *O5* **High Island** *island* Michigan, N USA
30 *K15* **Highland** Illinois, N USA *38°44′N 89°40′W*
31 *N10* **Highland Park** Illinois, N USA *42°10′N 87°48′W*
21 *O10* **Highlands** North Carolina, SE USA *35°04′N 83°10′W*
11 *O11* **High Level** Alberta, W Canada *58°31′N 117°08′W*
29 *O9* **Highmore** South Dakota, N USA *44°29′N 99°26′W*
171 *N3* **High Peak** ▲ Luzon, N Philippines *15°28′N 120°07′E*
**High Plains** *see* Great Plains
21 *S9* **High Point** North Carolina, SE USA *35°58′N 80°00′W*
18 *J13* **High Point** *hill* New Jersey, NE USA
11 *P13* **High Prairie** Alberta, W Canada *55°27′N 116°28′W*
11 *Q16* **High River** Alberta, SW Canada *50°35′N 113°50′W*
21 *S9* **High Rock Lake** ⊠ North Carolina, SE USA
23 *V9* **High Springs** Florida, SE USA *29°49′N 82°36′W*
**High Veld** *see* Great Karoo
97 *J24* **High Willhays** ▲ SW England, United Kingdom *50°39′N 03°58′W*
97 *N22* **High Wycombe** *prev.* Chepping Wycombe, Chipping Wycombe. SE England, United Kingdom *51°38′N 00°46′W*
41 *P12* **Higos** *var.* El Higo. Veracruz, E Mexico *21°48′N 98°25′W*
102 *I16* **Higuer, Cap** *headland* NE Spain *43°23′N 01°46′W*
45 *R5* **Higüero, Punta** *headland* W Puerto Rico *18°21′N 67°15′W*
45 *P9* **Higüey** *var.* Salvaleón de Higüey. E Dominican Republic *18°40′N 68°43′W*
190 *G11* **Hihifo** ✈ (Matā'utu) Île Uvea, N Wallis and Futuna
81 *N16* **Hiiraan** *off.* Gobolka Hiiraan. ◈ *region* C Somalia
**Hiiraan, Gobolka** *see* Hiiraan
118 *E4* **Hiiumaa** *var.* Hiiumaa Maakond. ◈ *province* W Estonia
118 *D4* **Hiiumaa** *Ger.* Dagden, *Swe.* Dagö. *island* W Estonia
**Hiiumaa Maakond** *see* Hiiumaa
**Hijanah** *see* Al Hījānah
105 *S6* **Híjar** Aragón, NE Spain *41°10′N 00°27′W*
191 *V10* **Hikueru** *atoll* Îles Tuamotu, C French Polynesia
184 *K3* **Hikurangi** Northland, North Island, New Zealand *35°37′S 174°16′E*
184 *Q8* **Hikurangi** ▲ North Island, New Zealand *37°55′S 177°59′E*
192 *L11* **Hikurangi Trench** *var.* Hikurangi Trough. *undersea feature* SW Pacific Ocean
**Hikurangi Trough** *see* Hikurangi Trench
190 *B15* **Hikutavake** NW Niue
121 *Q12* **Hilāl, Ra's al** *headland* N Libya *32°55′N 22°09′E*
61 *A24* **Hilario Ascasubi** Buenos Aires, E Argentina *39°22′S 62°39′W*
101 *K17* **Hildburghausen** Thüringen, C Germany *50°26′N 10°44′E*
101 *E15* **Hilden** Nordrhein-Westfalen, W Germany *51°12′N 06°56′E*
100 *I13* **Hildesheim** Niedersachsen, N Germany *52°09′N 09°57′E*
33 *T9* **Hilger** Montana, NW USA *47°15′N 109°18′W*
153 *S13* **Hili** *var.* Hilli. Rajshahi, NW Bangladesh *25°16′N 89°04′E*
**Hilla** *see* Al Ḩillah
45 *O14* **Hillaby, Mount** ▲ N Barbados *13°12′N 59°34′W*
**Ḩillah, Al** *see* Bābil
95 *K19* **Hillared** Västra Götaland, S Sweden *57°37′N 13°10′E*
195 *R12* **Hillary Coast** *physical region* Antarctica
42 *G2* **Hill Bank** Orange Walk, N Belize *17°36′N 88°43′W*
33 *O14* **Hill City** Idaho, NW USA *43°18′N 115°03′W*
26 *K3* **Hill City** Kansas, C USA *39°23′N 99°51′W*
29 *V5* **Hill City** Minnesota, N USA *46°59′N 93°36′W*
28 *J10* **Hill City** South Dakota, N USA *43°54′N 103°33′W*
65 *C24* **Hill Cove Settlement** West Falkland, Falkland Islands
98 *H10* **Hillegom** Zuid-Holland, W Netherlands *52°18′N 04°35′E*
95 *J22* **Hillerød** Hovedstaden, E Denmark *55°56′N 12°19′E*
36 *M7* **Hillers, Mount** ▲ Utah, W USA *37°53′N 110°42′W*
**Hilli** *see* Hili
29 *R11* **Hills** Minnesota, N USA *43°31′N 96°21′W*
30 *L14* **Hillsboro** Illinois, N USA *39°09′N 89°29′W*
27 *N5* **Hillsboro** Kansas, C USA *38°21′N 97°12′W*
27 *X5* **Hillsboro** Missouri, C USA *38°13′N 90°33′W*
19 *N10* **Hillsboro** New Hampshire, NE USA *43°06′N 71°52′W*
37 *Q14* **Hillsboro** New Mexico, SW USA *32°55′N 107°33′W*
29 *R4* **Hillsboro** North Dakota, N USA *47°25′N 97°03′W*
31 *R14* **Hillsboro** Ohio, N USA *39°12′N 83°36′W*
32 *G11* **Hillsboro** Oregon, NW USA *45°32′N 122°59′W*
25 *T8* **Hillsboro** Texas, SW USA *32°01′N 97°08′W*
30 *K8* **Hillsboro** Wisconsin, N USA *43°40′N 90°21′W*
23 *Y14* **Hillsboro Canal** *canal* Florida, SE USA
45 *Y15* **Hillsborough** Carriacou, N Grenada *12°28′N 61°28′W*
97 *G15* **Hillsborough** E Northern Ireland, United Kingdom *54°27′N 06°06′W*
21 *U9* **Hillsborough** North Carolina, SE USA *36°04′N 79°06′W*
31 *Q10* **Hillsdale** Michigan, N USA *41°55′N 84°37′W*
183 *O8* **Hillston** New South Wales, SE Australia *33°30′S 145°33′E*
21 *R7* **Hillsville** Virginia, NE USA *36°46′N 80°44′W*
96 *L2* **Hillswick** NE Scotland, United Kingdom *60°28′N 01°37′W*
**Hill Tippera** *see* Tripura
38 *H11* **Hilo** Hawaii, USA, C Pacific Ocean *19°42′N 155°04′W*
18 *F9* **Hilton** New York, NE USA *43°17′N 77°47′W*
14 *C10* **Hilton Beach** Ontario, S Canada *46°14′N 83°51′W*
21 *R16* **Hilton Head Island** South Carolina, SE USA *32°13′N 80°45′W*
21 *R16* **Hilton Head Island** *island* South Carolina, SE USA
99 *J15* **Hilvarenbeek** Noord-Brabant, S Netherlands *51°29′N 05°08′E*
98 *J11* **Hilversum** Noord-Holland, C Netherlands *52°14′N 05°10′E*
152 *J7* **Himāchal Pradesh** ◈ *state* NW India
**Himalaya/Himalaya Shan** *see* Himalayas
152 *M9* **Himalayas** *var.* Himalaya, *Chin.* Himalaya Shan. ▲▲ S Asia
171 *P6* **Himamaylan** Negros, C Philippines *10°04′N 122°52′E*
93 *K15* **Himanka** Pohjois-Pohjanmaa, W Finland *64°04′N 23°40′E*
**Himara** *see* Himarë
113 *L23* **Himarë** *var.* Himara. Vlorë, S Albania *40°06′N 19°45′E*
138 *M2* **Ḩimār, Wādī al** *dry watercourse* N Syria
154 *D9* **Himatnagar** Gujarāt, W India *23°38′N 73°02′E*
109 *Y4* **Himberg** Niederösterreich, E Austria *48°05′N 16°27′E*
164 *I13* **Himeji** *var.* Himezi. Hyōgo, Honshū, SW Japan *34°47′N 134°32′E*
164 *E14* **Hime-jima** *island* SW Japan
**Himezi** *see* Himeji
164 *L13* **Himi** Toyama, Honshū, SW Japan *36°54′N 136°59′E*
109 *S9* **Himmelberg** Kärnten, S Austria *46°45′N 14°01′E*
138 *I5* **Ḩimş** *var.* Homs; *anc.* Emesa. Ḩimş, C Syria *34°44′N 36°43′E*
138 *K6* **Ḩimş** *off.* Muḩāfaẓat Hims, *var.* Homs. ◈ *governorate* C Syria
138 *I5* **Ḩimş, Buḩayrat** *var.* Buhayrat Qattinah. ◎ W Syria
171 *R7* **Hinatuan** Mindanao, S Philippines *08°21′N 126°19′E*
117 *N10* **Hînceşti** *var.* Hânceşti; *prev.* Kotovsk. C Moldova *46°48′N 28°33′E*
44 *M9* **Hinche** C Haiti *19°07′N 72°00′W*
181 *X5* **Hinchinbrook Island** *island* Queensland, NE Australia
39 *S12* **Hinchinbrook Island** *island* Alaska, USA
97 *M19* **Hinckley** C England, United Kingdom *52°33′N 01°21′W*
29 *V7* **Hinckley** Minnesota, N USA *46°01′N 92°57′W*
36 *K5* **Hinckley** Utah, W USA *39°21′N 112°39′W*
18 *J9* **Hinckley Reservoir** ⊠ New York, NE USA
79 *E21* **Hinda** Kouilou, S Congo *04°37′S 12°02′E*
152 *I12* **Hindaun** Rājasthān, N India *26°44′N 77°02′E*
**Hindenburg/Hindenburg in Oberschlesien** *see* Zabrze
**Hindiya** *see* Al Hindīyah
21 *O6* **Hindman** Kentucky, S USA *37°20′N 82°58′W*
182 *L10* **Hindmarsh, Lake** ◎ Victoria, SE Australia
185 *G19* **Hinds** Canterbury, South Island, New Zealand *44°01′S 171°33′E*
185 *G19* **Hinds** ≈ South Island, New Zealand
95 *H23* **Hindsholm** *island* C Denmark
149 *S4* **Hindu Kush** *Per.* Hendū Kosh. ▲▲ Afghanistan/Pakistan
155 *H19* **Hindupur** Andhra Pradesh, E India *13°46′N 77°33′E*
11 *O12* **Hines Creek** Alberta, W Canada *56°14′N 118°36′W*
23 *W6* **Hinesville** Georgia, SE USA *31°51′N 81°36′W*
154 *I12* **Hinganghāt** Mahārāshtra, C India *20°32′N 78°52′E*
149 *N15* **Hingol** ≈ SW Pakistan
154 *H13* **Hingoli** Mahārāshtra, C India *19°45′N 77°08′E*
137 *R13* **Hınıs** Erzurum, E Turkey *39°22′N 41°44′E*


◆ Country
● Country Capital
◇ Dependent Territory
○ Dependent Territory Capital
◈ Administrative Regions
✈ International Airport
▲ Mountain
▲▲ Mountain Range
Volcano
≈ River
◎ Lake
⊠ Reservoir

92 O2 **Hinlopenstretet** *strait* N Svalbard

92 G10 **Hinnøya** *Lapp.* Iinnasuolu. *island* C Norway

108 H10 **Hinterrhein** ♒ SW Switzerland

166 L8 **Hinthada** *var.* Henzada. Ayeyarwady, SW Myanmar (Burma) 17°36′N 95°26′E

11 O14 **Hinton** Alberta, SW Canada 53°24′N 117°35′W

26 M10 **Hinton** Oklahoma, C USA 35°28′N 98°21′W

21 R6 **Hinton** West Virginia, NE USA 37°42′N 80°54′W

**Hios** *see* Chíos

41 N8 **Hipólito** Coahuila, NE Mexico 25°42′N 101°22′W

**Hipponium** *see* Vibo Valentia

164 B13 **Hirado** Nagasaki, Hirado-shima, SW Japan 33°22′N 129°31′E

164 B13 **Hirado-shima** *island* SW Japan

165 P16 **Hirakubo-saki** *headland* Ishigaki-jima, SW Japan 24°36′N 124°19′E

154 M11 **Hirākud Reservoir** ☒ E India

**Hir al Gharbi, Qasr al** *see* Ḥayr al Gharbī, Qaṣr al

165 Q16 **Hirara** Okinawa, Miyako-jima, SW Japan 24°48′N 125°17′E

**Hir Ash Sharqī, Qasr al** *see* Ḥayr ash Sharqī, Qaṣr al

164 G12 **Hirata** Shimane, Honshū, SW Japan 35°25′N 132°45′E

136 I13 **Hirfanlı Barajı** ☒ C Turkey

155 G18 **Hiriyūr** Karnātaka, W India 13°58′N 76°33′E

**Hīrlau** *see* Hârlău

148 K10 **Hirmand, Rūd-e** *var.* Daryā-ye Helmand. Helmand, Daryā-ye Afghanistan/Iran *see also* ♒ Helmand, Daryā-ye

**Hirmil** *see* Hermel

165 T5 **Hiroo** Hokkaidō, NE Japan 42°16′N 143°16′E

165 Q7 **Hirosaki** Aomori, Honshū, C Japan 40°34′N 140°28′E

164 G13 **Hiroshima** *var.* Hirosima. Hiroshima, Honshū, SW Japan 34°23′N 132°26′E

164 F13 **Hiroshima** *off.* Hiroshima-ken, *var.* Hirosima-ken. ♦ *prefecture* Honshū, SW Japan

**Hiroshima-ken** *see* Hiroshima

**Hirosima** *see* Hiroshima

**Hirschberg/Hirschberg im Riesengebirge/Hirschberg in Schlesien** *see* Jelenia Góra

103 Q3 **Hirson** Aisne, N France 49°56′N 04°05′E

**Hirşova** *see* Hârșova

95 G19 **Hirtshals** Nordjylland, N Denmark 57°35′N 09°58′E

152 H10 **Hisār** Haryāna, NW India 29°10′N 75°45′E

114 I10 **Hisarya** *var.* Khisarya. Plovdiv, C Bulgaria 42°33′N 24°43′E

162 K7 **Hishig Öndör** *var.* Maanit. Bulgan, C Mongolia 48°17′N 103°32′E

186 E9 **Hisiu** Central, SW Papua New Guinea 09°20′S 146°48′E

147 P13 **Hisor** *Rus.* Gissar. W Tajikistan 38°34′N 68°29′E

**Hispalis** *see* Sevilla

**Hispana/Hispania** *see* Spain

44 M7 **Hispaniola** *island* Dominican Republic/Haiti

64 F11 **Hispaniola Basin** *var.* Hispaniola Trough. *undersea feature* NW Atlantic Ocean

**Hispaniola Trough** *see* Hispaniola Basin

**Histonium** *see* Vasto

139 R7 **Ḥīt** Al Anbār, SW Iraq 33°38′N 42°50′E

165 P14 **Hita** Ōita, Kyūshū, SW Japan 33°19′N 130°55′E

165 P12 **Hitachi** *var.* Hitati. Ibaraki, Honshū, S Japan 36°40′N 140°42′E

165 P12 **Hitachiōta** Ibaraki, Honshū, S Japan 36°32′N 140°31′E

97 O21 **Hitchin** E England, United Kingdom 51°57′N 00°17′W

191 Q7 **Hitiaa** Tahiti, W French Polynesia 17°35′S 149°17′W

164 D15 **Hitoyoshi** *var.* Hitoyosi. Kumamoto, Kyūshū, SW Japan 32°12′N 130°48′E

**Hitoyosi** *see* Hitoyoshi

94 F7 **Hitra** *prev.* Hitteren. *island* S Norway

**Hitteren** *see* Hitra

187 Q11 **Hiu** Torres Islands, N Vanuatu

165 O11 **Hiuchiga-take** ▲ Honshū, S Japan 36°57′N 139°18′E

191 X7 **Hiva Oa** *island* Îles Marquises, N French Polynesia

20 M10 **Hiwassee Lake** ☒ North Carolina, SE USA

20 M10 **Hiwassee River** ♒ SE USA

95 H20 **Hjallerup** Nordjylland, N Denmark

95 M16 **Hjälmaren** *Eng.* Lake Hjalmar. ⊚ C Sweden

**Hjalmar, Lake** *see* Hjälmaren

95 C14 **Hjellestad** Hordaland, S Norway 60°15′N 05°13′E

95 D16 **Hjelmeland** Rogaland, S Norway 59°12′N 06°07′E

94 G10 **Hjerkinn** Oppland, S Norway 62°13′N 09°37′E

95 L18 **Hjo** Västra Götaland, S Sweden 58°18′N 14°17′E

95 G19 **Hjørring** Nordjylland, N Denmark 57°28′N 09°59′E

167 O1 **Hkakabo Razi** ▲ Myanmar (Burma)/China 28°17′N 97°47′E

166 M2 **Hkamti** *var.* Singkaling Hkamti. Sagaing, N Myanmar (Burma) 26°00′N 95°43′E

167 N1 **Hkring Bum** ▲ N Myanmar (Burma) 26°51′N 97°16′E

83 L21 **Hlathikulu** *var.* Hlatikulu. S Eswatini 26°58′S 31°19′E

**Hlatikulu** *see* Hlathikulu

**Hliboka** *see* Hlyboka

111 F17 **Hlinsko** *var.* Hlinsko v Čechách. Pardubický Kraj, C Czechia 49°46′N 15°54′E

**Hlinsko v Čechách** *see* Hlinsko

117 S6 **Hlobyne** *Rus.* Globino. Poltavs'ka Oblast', NE Ukraine 49°24′N 33°16′E


111 H20 **Hlohovec** *Ger.* Freistadtl, *Hung.* Galgóc; *prev.* Frakštát. Trnavský Kraj, W Slovakia 48°26′N 17°48′E

83 J23 **Hlotse** *var.* Leribe. NW Lesotho 28°55′S 28°01′E

111 I17 **Hlučín** *Ger.* Hultschin, *Pol.* Hulczyn. Moravskoslezský Kraj, E Czechia 49°54′N 18°11′E

117 S2 **Hlukhiv** *Rus.* Glukhov. Sums'ka Oblast', NE Ukraine 51°40′N 33°53′E

119 K21 **Hlushkevichy** *Rus.* Glushkevichi. Homyel'skaya Voblasts', SE Belarus 51°34′N 27°47′E

119 L18 **Hlusk** *Rus.* Glusk, Glussk. Mahilyowskaya Voblasts', E Belarus 52°54′N 28°41′E

116 K8 **Hlyboka** *Ger.* Hliboka, *Rus.* Glybokaya. Chernivets'ka Oblast', W Ukraine 48°05′N 25°55′E

118 K13 **Hlybokaye** *Rus.* Glubokoye. Vitsyebskaya Voblasts', N Belarus 55°08′N 27°41′E

77 Q16 **Ho** SE Ghana 06°36′N 00°28′E

167 S6 **Hoa Binh** Hoa Binh, N Vietnam 20°49′N 105°20′E

83 E20 **Hoachanas** Hardap, C Namibia 23°55′S 18°04′E

167 T8 **Hoa Lac** Quang Binh, C Vietnam 17°14′N 106°24′E

167 S5 **Hoàng Liên Son** ▲ N Vietnam

**Hoàng Sa, Qu n Ɖ o** *see* Paracel Islands

83 B17 **Hoanib** ♒ NW Namibia

33 S15 **Hoback Peak** ▲ Wyoming, C USA 43°04′N 110°34′W

183 P17 **Hobart** *prev.* Hobarton, Hobart Town. *state capital* Tasmania, SE Australia 42°54′S 147°18′E

26 L11 **Hobart** Oklahoma, C USA 35°03′N 99°04′W

183 P17 **Hobart** ✈ Tasmania, SE Australia 42°52′S 147°28′E

**Hobart/Hobart Town** *see* Hobart

37 W14 **Hobbs** New Mexico, SW USA 32°42′N 103°08′W

194 L12 **Hobbs Coast** *physical region* Antarctica

23 Z14 **Hobe Sound** Florida, SE USA 27°03′N 80°08′W

**Hobicauriكány** *see* Uricani

54 G8 **Hobo** Huila, S Colombia 02°34′N 75°28′W

99 G16 **Hoboken** Antwerpen, N Belgium 51°11′N 04°22′E

158 K3 **Hoboksar** *var.* Hoboksar Mongol Zizhixian. Xinjiang Uygur Zizhiqu, W China 46°48′N 85°42′E

**Hoboksar Mongol Zizhixian** *see* Hoboksar

95 G21 **Hobro** Nordjylland, N Denmark 56°39′N 09°48′E

21 X10 **Hobucken** North Carolina, SE USA 35°15′N 76°31′W

95 G20 **Hoburgen** *headland* SE Sweden 56°54′N 18°07′E

81 P15 **Hobyo** *It.* Obbia. Mudug, E Somalia 05°16′N 48°24′E

109 R8 **Hochalmspitze** ▲ SW Austria 47°00′N 13°19′E

109 S7 **Hochburg** Oberösterreich, N Austria 48°10′N 12°57′E

108 F8 **Hochdorf** Luzern, W Switzerland 47°10′N 08°16′E

109 N8 **Hochfeiler** *It.* Gran Pilastro. ▲ Austria/Italy 46°59′N 11°42′E

167 T14 **Hồ Chí Minh** *var.* Ho Chi Minh City; *prev.* Saigon. S Vietnam 10°46′N 106°43′E

167 T14 **Hồ Chí Minh City** *see* Hồ Chí Minh

109 O7 **Höchst** Vorarlberg, NW Austria 47°28′N 09°40′E

**Höchstadt** *see* Höchstadt an der Aisch

101 K19 **Höchstadt an der Aisch** *var.* Höchstadt. Bayern, C Germany 49°43′N 10°48′E

109 L9 **Hochwilde** *It.* L'Altissima. ▲ Austria/Italy 46°45′N 11°00′E

109 S7 **Hochwildstelle** ▲ C Austria 47°21′N 13°53′E

31 T14 **Hocking River** ♒ Ohio, N USA

**Hoctún** *see* Hoctún

41 X12 **Hoctún** *var.* Hoctún. Yucatán, E Mexico 20°48′N 89°14′W

82 K6 **Hodgenville** Kentucky, S USA 37°34′N 85°45′W

11 T17 **Hodgeville** Saskatchewan, S Canada 50°06′N 106°55′W

76 J7 **Hodh ech Chargui** ♦ *region* E Mauritania

76 J10 **Hodh el Gharbi** *var.* Hodh el Garbi. ♦ *region* S Mauritania

111 L25 **Hódmezővásárhely** Csongrád, SE Hungary 46°27′N 20°18′E

74 J6 **Hodna, Chott El** *var.* Chott el-Hodna, *Ar.* Shatt al-Hodna. *salt lake* N Algeria

**Hodna, Chott el-/Hodna, Shatt al-** *see* Hodna, Chott El

111 G19 **Hodonín** *Ger.* Göding. Jihomoravský Kraj, SE Czechia 48°52′N 17°07′E

99 D16 **Hoegaarden** Vlaams Brabant, C Belgium 50°46′N 04°28′E

**Hoë Karoo** *see* Great Karoo

98 I9 **Hoek van Holland** *Eng.* Hook of Holland. Zuid-Holland, W Netherlands 52°00′N 04°07′E

98 L13 **Hoenderloo** Gelderland, E Netherlands 52°03′N 05°46′E

99 L18 **Hoensbroek** Limburg, SE Netherlands 50°55′N 05°55′E

163 Y11 **Hoeryŏng** NE North Korea 42°23′N 129°46′E

98 M11 **Hoeselt** Limburg, NE Belgium 50°50′N 05°30′E

98 L11 **Hoevelaken** Gelderland, C Netherlands 52°10′N 05°27′E

**Hoey** *see* Huy

101 M18 **Hof** Bayern, SE Germany 50°19′N 11°55′E

**Höfdhakaupstadhur** *see* Skagaströnd

**Hofei** *see* Hefei


101 G18 **Hofheim am Taunus** Hessen, W Germany 50°04′N 08°27′E

**Hofmark** *see* Odorheiu Secuiesc

31 L3 **Höfn** Austurland, SE Iceland 64°14′N 15°17′W

94 N13 **Hofors** Gävleborg, C Sweden 60°31′N 16°21′E

92 J1 **Hofsjökull** *glacier* C Iceland

92 J6 **Hofsós** Norðurland Vestra, N Iceland 65°54′N 19°24′W

164 E13 **Hōfu** Yamaguchi, Honshū, SW Japan 34°01′N 131°34′E

92 I4 **Höfuðborgarsvæðið** ♦ *region* SW Iceland

95 J22 **Höganäs** Skåne, S Sweden 56°12′N 12°39′E

183 P14 **Hogan Group** *island group* Tasmania, SE Australia

23 R4 **Hogansville** Georgia, SE USA 33°10′N 84°55′W

39 P8 **Hogatza River** ♒ Alaska, USA

28 I14 **Hogback Mountain** ▲ Nebraska, C USA 41°40′N 103°44′W

95 G14 **Hegevarde** ▲ S Norway 60°19′N 09°27′E

**Høgfors** *see* Karkkila

**Hoggar** *see* Ahaggar

**Hoggar Mountains** *see* Ahaggar

**Hoggar, Tassili du** *see* Ahaggar, Tassili oua-n-Ahaggar

31 P5 **Hog Island** *island* Michigan, N USA

21 Y6 **Hog Island** *island* Virginia, NE USA

**Hogoley Islands** *see* Chuuk Islands

95 N20 **Högsby** Kalmar, S Sweden 57°10′N 16°03′E

36 K1 **Hogup Mountains** ▲ Utah, W USA

101 E17 **Hohe Acht** ▲ W Germany 50°23′N 07°00′E

**Hohenelbe** *see* Vrchlabí

108 I7 **Hohenems** Vorarlberg, W Austria 47°23′N 09°43′E

**Hohenmauth** *see* Vysoké Mýto

**Hohensalza** *see* Inowrocław

**Hohenstadt** *see* Zábřeh

**Hohenstein in Ostpreussen** *see* Olsztynek

20 I9 **Hohenwald** Tennessee, S USA 35°33′N 87°31′W

101 L17 **Hohenwarte-Stausee** ☒ C Germany

**Hohes Venn** *see* Hautes Fagnes

109 Q8 **Hohe Tauern** ▲ W Austria

163 O13 **Hohhot** *var.* Huhehot, Huhohaote, *Mong.* Kukukhoto; *prev.* Kweisui, Kwesui. Nei Mongol Zizhiqu, N China 40°49′N 111°37′E

162 F7 **Hohó** *var.* Sayn-Ust. Govĭ-Altay, W Mongolia 47°23′N 94°19′E

103 U6 **Hohneck** ▲ NE France 48°04′N 07°01′E

77 Q16 **Hohoe** E Ghana 07°08′N 00°32′E

164 E12 **Hōhoku** Yamaguchi, Honshū, SW Japan 34°15′N 130°56′E

159 O11 **Hoh Sai Hu** ⊚ C China

159 N11 **Hoh Xil Hu** ⊚ C China

158 L11 **Hoh Xil Shan** ▲ W China

167 U10 **Hội An** *prev.* Faifo. Quang Nam-Đa Nẵng, C Vietnam 15°54′N 108°19′E

**Hoï-Hao/Hoihow** *see* Haikou

159 S11 **Hoika** *prev.* Heka. Qinghai, W China 35°49′N 99°50′E

81 F17 **Hoima** W Uganda 01°25′N 31°22′E

146 H14 **Hojagala** Balkan Welaýaty, W Turkmenistan 38°46′N 56°14′E

146 M13 **Hojambaz** *Rus.* Khodzhambas, Lebap Welaýaty, E Turkmenistan 38°11′N 64°33′E

95 H23 **Højby** Syddjylland, C Denmark 55°20′N 10°27′E

95 F24 **Højer** Syddjylland, SW Denmark 54°57′N 08°43′E

164 E14 **Hōjō** *var.* Hôzyô. Ehime, Shikoku, SW Japan 33°58′N 132°47′E

184 J3 **Hokianga Harbour** *inlet* SE Tasman Sea

185 F17 **Hokitika** West Coast, South Island, New Zealand 42°44′S 170°58′E

165 T3 **Hokkaidō** *prev.* Ezo, Yeso, Yezo. *island* NE Japan

111 H18 **Hokksund** Buskerud, S Norway 59°45′N 09°55′E

143 S4 **Hokmābād** Khorāsān-e Razavī, N Iran 36°37′N 57°34′E

**Hokō** *see* Pohang

**Hoko-guntō/Hoko-shotō** *see* Penghu Qundao

94 F13 **Hol** Buskerud, S Norway 60°36′N 08°18′E

81 K19 **Hola** Tana River, SE Kenya 01°06′S 40°01′E

117 R11 **Hola Prystan'** *Rus.* Golaya Pristan. Khersons'ka Oblast', S Ukraine 46°31′N 32°31′E

95 I23 **Holbæk** Sjælland, E Denmark 55°42′N 11°42′E

183 P10 **Holbrook** New South Wales, SE Australia 35°45′S 147°18′E

37 N11 **Holbrook** Arizona, SW USA 34°54′N 110°09′W

27 S5 **Holden** Missouri, C USA 38°42′N 93°59′W

36 K5 **Holden** Utah, W USA 39°06′N 112°16′W

26 O11 **Holdenville** Oklahoma, C USA 35°05′N 96°25′W

29 O16 **Holdrege** Nebraska, C USA 40°26′N 99°22′W

155 K18 **Hole in the Mountain Peak** ▲ Nevada, W USA

9 R5 **Hone Bay** *bay* Baffin Bay, Nunavut, NE Canada

38 D9 **Honolulu** *state capital* O'ahu, Hawaii, USA, C Pacific Ocean 21°18′N 157°51′W

20 Y16 **Homestead** Florida, SE USA 25°28′N 80°28′W


44 I7 **Holguín** ♦ *province* SE Cuba

23 V12 **Holiday** Florida, SE USA 28°11′N 82°44′W

39 N7 **Holitna River** ♒ Alaska, USA

94 J13 **Höljes** Värmland, C Sweden 60°53′N 12°34′E

109 X3 **Hollabrunn** Niederösterreich, NE Austria 48°33′N 16°06′E

36 L3 **Holladay** Utah, W USA 40°39′N 111°49′W

11 X16 **Holland** Manitoba, S Canada 49°36′N 98°49′W

31 O9 **Holland** Michigan, N USA 42°47′N 86°06′W

25 T9 **Holland** Texas, SW USA 30°52′N 97°24′W

**Holland** *see* Netherlands

22 K4 **Hollandale** Mississippi, S USA 33°10′N 90°51′W

**Hollandia** *see* Jayapura

**Hollands Diep** *see* Hollands Diep

99 H14 **Hollands Diep** *var.* Hollandsch Diep. *channel* SW Netherlands

**Holleschau** *see* Holešov

25 R5 **Holliday** Texas, SW USA 33°49′N 98°41′W

18 E15 **Hollidaysburg** Pennsylvania, NE USA 40°24′N 78°22′W

21 S6 **Hollins** Virginia, NE USA 37°20′N 79°56′W

26 J12 **Hollis** Oklahoma, C USA 34°43′N 99°54′W

35 O10 **Hollister** California, W USA 36°51′N 121°25′W

27 T8 **Hollister** Missouri, C USA 36°37′N 93°13′W

93 M19 **Hollola** Päijät-Häme, S Finland 61°N 25°32′E

98 K4 **Hollum** Fryslân, N Netherlands 53°27′N 05°38′E

95 I23 **Hollviken** *prev.* Höllviksnäs. Skåne, S Sweden 55°25′N 12°57′E

**Höllviksnäs** *see* Höllviken

36 W6 **Holly** Colorado, C USA 38°03′N 102°07′W

31 R9 **Holly** Michigan, N USA 42°47′N 83°37′W

21 S14 **Holly Hill** South Carolina, SE USA 33°19′N 80°24′W

21 W11 **Holly Ridge** North Carolina, SE USA 34°31′N 77°31′W

22 L1 **Holly Springs** Mississippi, S USA 34°46′N 89°27′W

23 Z15 **Hollywood** Florida, SE USA 26°00′N 80°09′W

6 J6 **Holman** Victoria Island, Northwest Territories, N Canada 70°42′N 117°45′W

92 I2 **Hólmavík** Vestfirðir, NW Iceland 65°42′N 21°43′W

30 J7 **Holmen** Wisconsin, N USA 43°57′N 91°14′W

23 R8 **Holmes Creek** ♒ Alabama/Florida, SE USA

95 H16 **Holmestrand** Vestfold, S Norway 59°29′N 10°20′E

93 J16 **Holmön** *island* N Sweden

95 E22 **Holmsland Klit** *beach* W Denmark

93 J16 **Holmsund** Västerbotten, N Sweden 63°42′N 20°26′E

95 Q18 **Holmudden** *headland* SE Sweden 57°59′N 19°14′E

138 F10 **Holon** *var.* Kholon; *prev.* Holon. Tel Aviv, C Israel 32°01′N 34°46′E

161 O7 **Hong He** ♒ C China

161 N9 **Hong He** ♒ C China

160 L11 **Hongjiang** Hunan, S China 27°09′N 109°58′E

**Hongjiang** *see* Wangcang

160 I15 **Hong Kong** *off.* Hong Kong Special Administrative Region, *var.* Xianggang, Tebie Xingzhengqu. S China 22°17′N 114°09′E

160 M15 **Hong Kong** ☒ S China 22°17′N 114°09′E

**Hong Kong S.A.R.** *see* Hong Kong

**Hong Kong Special Administrative Region** *see* Hong Kong

160 L9 **Hongliu He** ♒ C China

160 L8 **Hongliu He** ♒ C China

159 P8 **Hongliuwan** *var.* Aksay, Aksay Kazakzu Zizhixian. Gansu, N China 39°25′N 94°09′E

159 S7 **Hongliuyuan** Gansu, N China 41°02′N 95°24′E

161 S8 **Hongqiao** ✈ (Shanghai) Shanghai Shi, E China 31°28′N 121°08′E

160 K14 **Hongshui He** ♒ S China

160 M5 **Hongtong** *var.* Dahuaishu. Shanxi, C China 36°30′N 111°42′E

93 J15 **Hongü** Wakayama, Honshū, SW Japan 33°50′N 135°42′E

163 X13 **Hongwŏn** E North Korea 40°03′N 127°58′E

160 H7 **Hongyuan** *var.* Qiongxi; *prev.* Hurama. Sichuan, C China 32°48′N 102°40′E

161 Q12 **Hongze Hu** *var.* Hung-tse Hu. ⊚ E China

186 L9 **Honiara** ● (Solomon Islands) Guadalcanal, C Solomon Islands 09°27′S 159°56′E

165 N13 **Honjō** *var.* Honzyô. Akita, Honshū, C Japan 39°23′N 140°03′E

81 K18 **Honkajoki** Satakunta, SW Finland 62°00′N 22°15′E

95 F19 **Hönö** Västra Götaland, S Sweden 57°42′N 11°37′E

**Honshū** *var.* Hondo, Honsyū. *island* SW Japan

**Honsyū** *see* Honshū

**Honte** *see* Westerschelde

**Honzyô** *see* Honjō

8 K8 **Hood** ♒ Nur avut, NW Canada

32 H11 **Hood, Mount** ▲ Oregon, NW USA 45°22′N 121°41′W

32 H11 **Hood River** Oregon, NW USA 45°43′N 121°31′W

98 H10 **Hoofddorp** Noord-Holland, W Netherlands 52°18′N 04°41′E

99 G15 **Hoogerheide** Noord-Brabant, S Netherlands 51°25′N 04°19′E

98 N8 **Hoogezand-Sappemeer** Groningen, NE Netherlands 53°10′N 06°47′E

98 J8 **Hoogkarspel** Noord-Holland, W Netherlands 52°42′N 04°59′E

98 N5 **Hoogkerk** Groningen, NE Netherlands 53°13′N 06°30′E

98 L13 **Hoog-Keppel Zuid-Holland, SW Netherlands 51°51′N 04°23′E

98 N8 **Hoogeveen** D enthe, NE Netherlands 52°43′N 06°28′E

98 O12 **Hoogeveensche Vaart** *canal* NE Netherlands

164 U4 **Honbetsu** Hokkaidō, NE Japan 43°09′N 143°46′E

54 E9 **Honda** Tolima, C Colombia 05°12′N 74°45′W

42 G1 **Hondo** *see* Honshū

**Hondo** *see* Amakusa

42 G6 **Honduras** *off.* Republic of Honduras. ♦ *republic* Central America

42 H4 **Honduras, Golfo de** *see* Honduras, Gulf of

42 H4 **Honduras, Gulf of** *Sp.* Golfo de Honduras. *gulf* W Caribbean Sea

**Honduras, Republic of** *see* Honduras

11 V12 **Hone** Manitoba, C Canada 56°13′N 101°12′W

21 P12 **Honea Path** South Carolina, SE USA 34°27′N 82°23′W

95 H14 **Honefoss** Buskerud, S Norway 60°10′N 10°15′E

31 S12 **Honey Creek** ♒ Ohio, N USA

25 V5 **Honey Grove** Texas, SW USA 33°34′N 95°54′W

34 Q5 **Honey Lake** ⊚ California, W USA

10 M7 **Honfleur** Calvados, N France 49°25′N 00°14′E

**Hong'an** *prev.* Huang'an. Hubei, C China 31°20′N 114°43′E

**Hongay** *see* Ha Long

**Hông Gai** *see* Ha Long

**Hong Hai** *var.* bay N South China Sea

**Hông Hà, Sông** *see* Red River


195 O10 **Horlick Mountains** ▲ Antarctica

117 X7 **Horlivka** *Rom.* Adâncata, *Rus.* Gorlovka. Donets'ka Oblast', E Ukraine 48°19′N 38°04′E

143 V11 **Hormak** Sīstān va Balūchestān, SE Iran 30°00′N 60°50′E

143 R13 **Hormozgân** *off.* Ostān-e Hormozgân. ♦ *province* S Iran

**Hormozgân, Ostān-e** *see* Hormozgân

141 W6 **Hormoz, Tangeh-ye** *see* Hormuz, Strait of

143 P16 **Hormoz, Tangeh-ye** *var.* Strait of Ormuz, *Per.* Tangeh-ye Hormoz. *strait* Iran/Oman

109 W2 **Horn** Niederösterreich, NE Austria 48°40′N 15°40′E

95 M18 **Horn** Östergötland, S Sweden

8 J9 **Horn** ♒ Northwest Territories, NW Canada

92 J6 **Hornafjörður** *fjord* S Iceland

**Horn, Cape** *see* Hornos, Cabo de

97 O18 **Horncastle** E England, United Kingdom 53°12′N 00°07′W

95 N14 **Horndal** Dalarna, C Sweden N Sweden 63°13′N 19°03′E

93 I16 **Hörnefors** Västerbotten, N Sweden 63°37′N 19°54′W

18 F11 **Hornell** New York, NE USA 42°19′N 77°38′W

12 F12 **Hornepayne** Ontario, S Canada 49°14′N 84°48′W

94 D10 **Horníndalsvatnet** ⊚ S Norway

101 G22 **Hornisgrinde** ▲ SW Germany 48°37′N 08°13′E

22 M9 **Horn Island** *island* Mississippi, S USA

**Hornja Łužica** *see* Oberlausitz

63 J26 **Hornos, Cabo de** *Eng.* Cape Horn. *headland* S Chile 55°52′S 67°00′W

117 S10 **Hornostayivka** Khersons'ka Oblast', S Ukraine 46°59′N 33°42′E

183 T9 **Hornsby** New South Wales, SE Australia 33°44′S 151°08′E

97 O16 **Hornsea** E England, United Kingdom 53°54′N 00°10′W

94 O11 **Hornslandet** *peninsula* C Sweden

95 H22 **Hornslet** Midtjylland, C Denmark 56°19′N 10°20′E

92 O4 **Hornsundtind** ▲ S Svalbard 76°54′N 16°07′E

**Horochów** *see* Horokhiv

**Horodenka** *see* Gorodenka

137 Q2 **Horodnya** *Rus.* Chernihivs'ka Oblast', NE Ukraine 51°54′N 31°30′E

116 K6 **Horodok** Khmel'nyts'ka Oblast', W Ukraine 49°10′N 26°34′E

116 H5 **Horodok** *Pol.* Gródek Jagielloński, *Rus.* Gorodok Yagellonskiy. L'vivs'ka Oblast', NW Ukraine 49°48′N 23°39′E

117 Q6 **Horodyshche** *Rus.* Gorodishche. Cherkas'ka Oblast', C Ukraine 49°19′N 31°27′E

165 T3 **Horokanai** Hokkaidō, NE Japan 44°02′N 142°08′E

116 J4 **Horokhiv** *Pol.* Horochów, *Rus.* Gorokhov. Volyns'ka Oblast', NW Ukraine 50°31′N 24°50′E

165 T4 **Horoshiri-dake** *var.* Horosiri Dake. ▲ Hokkaidō, N Japan 42°43′N 142°41′E

**Horosiri Dake** *see* Horoshiri-dake

111 C17 **Hořovice** *Ger.* Horowitz. Středni Čechy, W Czechia 49°49′N 13°53′E

**Horowitz** *see* Hořovice

**Horqin Zuoyi Houqi** *see* Ganjig

**Horqin Zuoyi Zhongqi** *see* Bayan Huxu

62 O5 **Horqueta** Concepción, C Paraguay 23°24′S 56°53′W

55 O12 **Horqueta Minas** Amazonas, S Venezuela 02°23′N 67°01′W

95 J20 **Horred** Västra Götaland, S Sweden 57°22′N 12°25′E

151 J22 **Horsburgh Atoll** *var.* Goidhoo Atoll. *atoll* N Maldives

20 K7 **Horse Cave** Kentucky, S USA 37°10′N 85°54′W

37 V6 **Horse Creek** ♒ Colorado, C USA

27 S6 **Horse Creek** ♒ Missouri, C USA

18 G11 **Horseheads** New York, NE USA 42°10′N 76°49′W

37 P13 **Horse Mount** ▲ New Mexico, SW USA 33°58′N 108°10′W

95 G22 **Horsens** Syddanmark, C Denmark 55°53′N 09°53′E

33 N13 **Horseshoe Bend** Idaho, NW USA 43°55′N 116°11′W

33 L13 **Horseshoe Reservoir** ☒ Arizona, SW USA

64 M9 **Horseshoe Seamounts** *undersea feature* E Atlantic Ocean

182 L11 **Horsham** Victoria, SE Australia 36°44′S 142°13′E

97 O23 **Horsham** SE England, United Kingdom 51°04′N 00°21′W

99 M15 **Horst** Limburg, SE Netherlands 51°30′N 06°01′E

64 N2 **Horta** Faial, Azores, Portugal, NE Atlantic Ocean 38°31′N 28°37′W

105 S12 **Hortas, Cap de l'** *Cast.* Cabo Huertas. *headland* SE Spain 15°57′S 05°46′W

65 F25 **Horse Pasture Point** ▲ W Saint Helena 15°57′S 05°46′W

116 H13 **Horezu** Vâlcea, SW Romania 45°06′N 24°00′E

108 G7 **Horgen** Zürich, N Switzerland 47°16′N 08°36′E

**Horgo** *see* Tariat

137 S6 **Hörin** *see* Fenglin

165 P16 **Honjō** *var.* Honzyô. (see above)

**Horishni Plavni** *prev.* Komsomol'sk Poltavs'ka Oblast', C Ukraine (see above)

11 U17 **Horizon** Saskatchewan, S Canada 49°33′N 105°05′W

192 K9 **Horizon Bank** *undersea feature* W Pacific Ocean

192 L10 **Horizon Deep** *undersea feature* W Pacific Ocean

95 L14 **Hörken** Örebro, C Sweden 60°03′N 14°15′E

95 H16 **Horten** Vestfold, S Norway 59°25′N 10°30′E

111 M23 **Hortobágy-Berettyó** ♒ E Hungary

27 Q3 **Horton** Kansas, C USA 39°39′N 95°31′W

◆ Country
● Country Capital
◇ Dependent Territory
○ Dependent Territory Capital
◆ Administrative Regions
✈ International Airport
▲ Mountain
▲▲ Mountain Range
🌋 Volcano
♒ River
⊚ Lake
☒ Reservoir

261

**8 I7 Horton** ✕ Northwest Territories, NW Canada
**95 I23 Hørve** Sjælland, E Denmark 55°46′N 11°28′E
**95 L22 Hörvik** Blekinge, S Sweden 56°01′N 14°45′E
**Horvot Haluza** *see* Horvot Halutsa
**14 E7 Horwood Lake** ◎ Ontario, S Canada
**116 K4 Horyn′** *Rus.* Goryn.
**81 I14 Hosa′ina** *var.* Hosseina, *It.* Hosanna. Southern Nationalities, S Ethiopia 07°38′N 37°58′E
**Hosanna** *see* Hosa′ina
**155 G17 Hosapete** *prev.* Hospet. Karnātaka, C India 15°16′N 76°20′E
**101 H18 Hösbach** Bayern, C Germany 50°00′N 09°12′E
**Hose Mountains** *see* Hose, Pegunungan
**169 T9 Hose, Pegunungan** *var.* Hose Mountains. ▲ East Malaysia
**148 L15 Hoshab** Baluchistan, SW Pakistan 26°01′N 63°51′E
**154 H10 Hoshangābād** Madhya Pradesh, C India 22°44′N 77°45′E
**116 L4 Hoshcha** Rivnens′ka Oblast′, NW Ukraine 50°37′N 26°38′E
**152 H7 Hoshiārpur** Punjab, NW India 31°30′N 75°59′E
**Höshööt** *see* Öldziyt
**99 M23 Hosingen** Diekirch, NE Luxembourg 50°01′N 06°05′E
**186 G4 Hoskins** New Britain, E Papua New Guinea 05°28′S 150°25′E
**Hospet** *see* Hosapete
**104 K4 Hospital de Órbigo** Castilla y León, N Spain 42°27′N 05°53′W
**Hospitalet** *see* L′Hospitalet de Llobregat
**92 N13 Hossa** Kainuu, E Finland 65°28′N 29°36′E
**Hosseina** *see* Hosa′ina
**Hosszúmezjő** *see* Câmpulung Moldovenesc
**63 I25 Hoste, Isla** island S Chile
**117 O4 Hostomel′** *Rus.* Gostomel′. Kyivs′ka Oblast′, N Ukraine 50°41′N 30°15′E
**155 H20 Hosūr** Tamil Nādu, SE India 12°45′N 77°51′E
**167 N8 Hot** Chiang Mai, NW Thailand 18°07′N 98°34′E
**158 G10 Hotan** *var.* Khotan, *Chin.* Ho-t′ien. Xinjiang Uygur Zizhiqu, NW China 37°10′N 79°51′E
**158 H9 Hotan He** ❧ NW China
**83 G22 Hotazel** Northern Cape, North Africa 27°12′S 22°58′E
**37 Q5 Hotchkiss** Colorado, C USA 38°47′N 107°43′W
**35 V7 Hot Creek Range** ▲ Nevada, W USA
**Hote** *see* Hoti
**171 T13 Hoti** *var.* Hote. Pulau Seram, E Indonesia 02°58′S 130°19′E
**Ho-t′ien** *see* Hotan
**Hotin** *see* Khotyn
**93 H15 Hoting** Jämtland, C Sweden 64°07′N 16°14′E
**162 L14 Hotong Qagan Nur** ◎ N China
**162 J8 Hotont** Arhangay, C Mongolia 47°21′N 102°27′E
**27 T12 Hot Springs** Arkansas, C USA 34°31′N 93°03′W
**28 J11 Hot Springs** South Dakota, N USA 43°26′N 103°29′W
**21 S5 Hot Springs** Virginia, NE USA 38°00′N 79°50′W
**35 Q4 Hot Springs Peak** ▲ California, W USA 40°23′N 120°06′W
**27 T12 Hot Springs Village** Arkansas, C USA 34°39′N 93°03′W
**Hotspur Bank** *see* Hotspur Seamount
**65 J16 Hotspur Seamount** *var.* Hotspur Bank. undersea feature C Atlantic Ocean 18°00′S 35°00′W
**8 I8 Hottah Lake** ◎ Northwest Territories, NW Canada
**44 K9 Hotte, Massif de la** ▲ SW Haiti
**99 K21 Hotton** Luxembourg, SE Belgium 50°16′N 05°25′E
**Hötzing** *see* Hateg
**187 P17 Houaïlou** Province Nord, C New Caledonia 21°17′S 165°37′E
**74 K7 Houari Boumédiène** ✕ (Alger) N Algeria 36°38′N 03°15′E
**167 P6 Houay Xai** *var.* Ban Houayxay. Bokèo, N Laos 20°17′N 100°27′E
**103 N5 Houdan** Yvelines, N France 48°48′N 01°36′E
**99 F20 Houdeng-Goegnies** *var.* Houdeng-Gœgnies. Hainaut, S Belgium 50°29′N 04°10′E
**102 K14 Houeillès** Lot-et-Garonne, SW France 44°15′N 00°02′E
**99 L22 Houffalize** Luxembourg, SE Belgium 50°08′N 05°47′E
**30 M3 Houghton** Michigan, N USA 47°07′N 88°34′W
**31 Q7 Houghton Lake** Michigan, N USA 44°18′N 84°45′W
**31 Q7 Houghton Lake** ◎ Michigan, N USA
**19 T3 Houlton** Maine, NE USA 46°09′N 67°50′W
**160 M5 Houma** Shanxi, C China 35°36′N 111°23′E
**193 U16 Houma** Tongatapu, S Tonga 21°18′S 174°54′W
**22 J10 Houma** Louisiana, S USA 29°35′N 90°44′W
**196 V16 Houma Taloa** headland Tongatapu, S Tonga
**77 O13 Houndé** SW Burkina Faso 11°34′N 03°31′W
**102 J12 Hourtin-Carcans, Lac d′** ◎ SW France
**36 I5 House Range** ▲ Utah, W USA
**10 K13 Houston** British Columbia, SW Canada 54°24′N 126°39′W
**22 I7 Houston** Alaska, USA 61°37′N 149°50′W
**29 U10 Houston** Minnesota, N USA 43°45′N 91°34′W
**22 M3 Houston** Mississippi, S USA 33°54′N 89°00′W
**27 V7 Houston** Missouri, C USA 37°19′N 91°59′W

**25 W11 Houston** Texas, SW USA 29°46′N 95°22′W
**25 W11 Houston** ✕ Texas, SW USA 30°03′N 95°18′W
**98 J12 Houten** Utrecht, C Netherlands 52°02′N 05°11′E
**99 K17 Houthalen** Limburg, NE Belgium 51°02′N 05°22′E
**99 I22 Houyet** Namur, SE Belgium 50°10′N 05°00′E
**95 H22 Hov** Midtjylland, C Denmark 55°54′N 10°13′E
**95 L17 Hov** Västra Götaland, S Sweden 58°12′N 14°13′E
**.162 E6 Hovd** *var.* Khovd, Kobdo *prev.* Jirgalanta. Hovd, W Mongolia 47°59′N 91°41′E
**.162 I10 Hovd** *var.* Dund-Us. Hovd, W Mongolia 48°06′N 91°22′E
**.162 E6 Hovd** *var.* Khovd, Kobdo *var.* Dund-Us. Hovd, W Mongolia 48°06′N 91°22′E
**.162 E7 Hovd** ◆ province W Mongolia
**Hovd** *see* Bogd
**.162 C5 Hovd Gol** ❧ NW Mongolia
**97 O23 Hove** SE England, United Kingdom 50°49′N 00°11′W
**95 I22 Hovedstaden** *off.* Frederiksborgs Amt. ◆ county E Denmark
**29 N6 Hoven** South Dakota, N USA 45°12′N 99°47′W
**.116 I8 Hoverla, Hora** *Rus.* Gora Goverla. ▲ W Ukraine 48°09′N 24°30′E
**95 M21 Hovmantorp** Kronoberg, S Sweden 56°47′N 15°08′E
**.163 N11 Hövsgöl** Dornogovi, SE Mongolia 43°35′N 109°40′E
**.162 I5 Hövsgöl** ◆ province N Mongolia
**Hovsgol, Lake** *see* Hövsgöl Nuur
**.162 J5 Hövsgöl Nuur** *var.* Lake Hovsgol. ◎ N Mongolia
**78 L9 Howa, Ouadi** *var.* Wādi Howar. ❧ Chad/Sudan *see also* Howar, Wādi
**Howa, Ouadi** *see* Howar, Wādi
**114 P7 Howard** Kansas, C USA 37°27′N 96°16′W
**29 Q10 Howard** South Dakota, N USA 43°58′N 97°31′W
**25 N10 Howard Draw** valley Texas, SW USA
**80 M8 Howard Lake** Minnesota, N USA 45°03′N 94°03′W
**78 J8 Howar, Wādi** *var.* Ouadi Howa. ❧ Chad/Sudan *see also* Howa, Ouadi
**Howar, Wādi** *see* Howa, Ouadi
**25 U5 Howe** Texas, SW USA 33°29′N 96°38′W
**183 R12 Howe, Cape** headland New South Wales/Victoria, SE Australia 37°30′S 149°58′E
**31 R9 Howell** Michigan, N USA 42°36′N 83°55′W
**28 L9 Howes** South Dakota, N USA 44°34′N 102°03′W
**83 K23 Howick** KwaZulu/Natal, E South Africa 29°29′S 30°13′E
**167 T9 Hồ Xá** *prev.* Vinh Linh. Quang Tri, C Vietnam 17°02′N 107°03′E
**27 W9 Hoxie** Arkansas, C USA 36°03′N 90°58′W
**26 J3 Hoxie** Kansas, C USA 39°21′N 100°27′W
**101 I14 Höxter** Nordrhein-Westfalen, W Germany 51°46′N 09°22′E
**158 K6 Hoxud** *var.* Tewulike. Xinjiang Uygur Zizhiqu, NW China 42°18′N 86°51′E
**96 J3 Hoy** island N Scotland, United Kingdom
**43 S17 Hoya, Cerro** ▲ S Panama 07°22′N 80°38′W
**94 D12 Høyanger** Sogn Og Fjordane, S Norway 61°13′N 06°05′E
**101 P15 Hoyerswerda** *Lus.* Wojerecy. Sachsen, E Germany 51°27′N 14°18′E
**164 R14 Hōyo-kaikyō** *var.* Hayasui-seto. strait SW Japan
**104 J8 Hoyos** Extremadura, W Spain 40°10′N 06°43′W
**29 W4 Hoyt Lakes** Minnesota, N USA 47°31′N 92°08′W
**95 V2 Hoyvík** Streymoy, N Faroe Islands
**137 O14 Hozat** Tunceli, E Turkey 39°09′N 39°13′E
**Hözyö** *see* Hōjō
**167 N8 Hpa-An** *var.* Pa-an. Kayin State, S Myanmar (Burma) 16°51′N 97°37′E
**167 N8 Hpapun** *var.* Papun. Kayin State, S Myanmar (Burma) 18°05′N 97°26′E
**167 N8 Hpasawng** *var.* Pasawng. Kayah State, C Myanmar (Burma) 18°50′N 97°16′E
**Hpyu** *see* Phyu
**111 F16 Hradec Králové** *Ger.* Königgrätz. Královéhradecký Kraj, N Czechia 50°13′N 15°50′E
**Hradecký Kraj** *see* Královéhradecký Kraj
**111 B16 Hradiště** *Ger.* Burgstadlberg. ▲ NW Czechia 50°12′N 13°04′E
**117 R6 Hradyz′k** *Rus.* Gradizhsk. Poltavs′ka Oblast′, NE Ukraine 49°14′N 33°05′E
**119 M16 Hradzyanka** *Rus.* Grodzyanka. Mahilyowskaya Voblasts′, E Belarus 53°33′N 28°41′E
**119 F16 Hrandzichy** *Rus.* Grandichi. Hrodzyenskaya Voblasts′, W Belarus 53°43′N 23°49′E
**111 H18 Hranice** *Ger.* Mährisch-Weisskirchen. Olomoucký Kraj, E Czechia 49°34′N 17°44′E
**112 I13 Hrasnica** Federacija Bosna I Hercegovina, SE Bosnia and Herzegovina 43°48′N 18°19′E
**111 V11 Hrastnik** C Slovenia 46°09′N 15°08′E
**137 U12 Hrazdan** *Rus.* Razdan. C Armenia 40°30′N 44°50′E
**137 T12 Hrazdan** *var.* Zanga, *Rus.* Razdan. ❧ C Armenia
**117 R5 Hrebinka** *Rus.* Grebenka. Poltavs′ka Oblast′, NE Ukraine 50°08′N 32°27′E
**119 K17 Hresk** *Rus.* Gresk. Minskaya Voblasts′, C Belarus 53°10′N 27°23′E
**119 F16 Hrodna** *Rus., Pol.* Grodno Hrodzyenskaya Voblasts′, W Belarus 53°40′N 23°50′E
**Hrisoupoli** *see* Chrysoúpoli

**119 F16 Hrodzyenskaya Voblasts′** *Rus.* Grodnenskaya Oblast′. ◆ province W Belarus
**111 J21 Hron** *Ger.* Gran, *Hung.* Garam. ❧ C Slovakia
**111 Q14 Hrubieszów** *Rus.* Grubeshov. Lubelskie, E Poland 50°49′N 23°53′E
**112 F13 Hrvace** Split-Dalmacija, SE Croatia 43°46′N 16°35′E
**112 F10 Hrvatska Kostajnica** *var.* Kostajnica. Sisak-Moslavina, C Croatia 45°14′N 16°35′E
**Hrvatska, Republika** *see* Croatia
**116 K6 Hrymayliv** *Pol.* Gzymałów, *Rus.* Grimaylov. Ternopil′s′ka Oblast′, W Ukraine 49°18′N 26°02′E
**167 N4 Hseni** *var.* Hsenwi. Shan State, E Myanmar (Burma) 23°20′N 97°59′E
**Hsenwi** *see* Hseni
**167 N6 Hsihseng** Shan State, C Myanmar (Burma) 20°07′N 97°17′E
**161 S13 Hsincha** *var.* Xinzhu. N Taiwan 24°48′N 120°59′E
**Hsing-K′ai Hu** *see* Khanka, Lake
**Hsi-nirg/Hsining** *see* Xining
**Hsinking** *see* Changchun
**Hsin-yang** *see* Xinyang
**Hsinying** *see* Xinying
**167 N4 Hsipaw** Shan State, C Myanmar (Burma) 22°32′N 97°12′E
**Hsu-chou** *see* Xuzhou
**Hsüeh Shan** *see* Xue Shan
**Htawei** *see* Dawei
**83 B18 Huab** ❧ W Namibia
**57 M21 Huacaya** Chuquisaca, S Bolivia 20°45′S 63°42′W
**57 J19 Huachacalla** Oruro, S Bolivia 18°47′S 68°23′W
**159 X9 Huachi** *var.* Rouyuan, Rouyuanchengzi. Gansu, C China 36°24′N 107°58′E
**57 N16 Huachi, Laguna** ◎ N Bolivia
**57 D14 Huacho** Lima, W Peru 11°05′S 77°36′W
**163 Y7 Huachuan** Heilongjiang, NE China 47°00′S 130°21′E
**163 P12 Huade** Nei Mongol Zizhiqu, N China 41°52′N 113°58′E
**163 W10 Huadian** Jilin, NE China 42°59′N .26°38′E
**56 I11 Huagaruncho, Cordillera** ▲ C Peru
**Hua Hin** *see* Ban Hua Hin
**191 S10 Huahine** island Îles Sous le Vent, W French Polynesia
**Huahua, Rio** *see* Wawa, Río
**167 R8 Huai** ❧ E Thailand
**161 Q7 Huai′an** *var.* Qingjiang. Jiangsu, E China 33°33′N 119°03′E
**161 P6 Huaibei** Anhui, E China 34°00′N 116°48′E
**Huaide** *see* Gongzhuling
**157 T10 Huaihua** Hunan, S China 27°36′N .09°57′E
**161 N14 Huaiji** Guangdong, S China 23°54′N 112°12′E
**111 O2 Huailai** *var.* Shacheng. Hebei, E China 40°22′N 115°34′E
**161 P7 Huainan** *var.* Huai-nan, Hwainan. Anhui, E China 32°37′N 116°57′E
**Huai-nan** *see* Huainan
**161 O5 Huairen** *var.* Yunzhong. Shanxi, C China 35°28′N 109°29′E
**161 O7 Huaiyang** Henan, C China 33°44′N 114°53′E
**161 Q7 Huaiyin** Jiangsu, E China 33°31′N 119°03′E
**157 N16 Huai Yot** Trang, SW Thailand 07°45′N 99°36′E
**41 Q15 Huajuapan** *var.* Huajuapan de León. Oaxaca, SE Mexico 17°50′N 97°48′W
**Huajuapan de León** *see* Huajuapan
**41 O9 Hualahuises** Nuevo León, NE Mexico 24°56′N 99°42′W
**36 I11 Hualapai Mountains** ▲ Arizona, SW USA
**36 I11 Hualapai Peak** ▲ Arizona, SW USA 35°04′N 113°54′W
**62 J7 Hualfín** Catamarca, N Argentina 27°15′S 66°53′W
**161 T13 Hualien** *var.* Hualian, Hwalien. *Jap.* Karen. C Taiwan 23°11′N 121°35′E
**56 C11 Huallaga, Río** ❧ N Peru
**41 Q14 Huamantla** Tlaxcala, S Mexico 19°18′N 97°57′W
**82 C13 Huambo** *Port.* Nova Lisboa. Huambo, C Angola 12°48′S 15°45′E
**82 B13 Huambo** ◆ province C Angola
**41 P15 Huamuxtitlán** Guerrero, S Mexico 17°49′N 98°34′W
**163 Y8 Huanan** Heilongjiang, NE China 46°11′N 130°43′E
**63 H17 Huancache, Sierra** ▲ W Argentina
**57 I17 Huancané** Puno, SE Peru 15°10′S 69°44′W
**57 F15 Huancapi** Ayacucho, C Peru 13°40′S 74°05′S
**56 E15 Huancavelica** Huancavelica, SW Peru 12°45′S 75°03′W
**56 E15 Huancavelica** *off.* Región de Huancavelica. ◆ region W Peru
**Huancavelica, Región de** *see* Huancavelica
**57 E14 Huancayo** Junín, C Peru 12°03′S 75°14′W
**57 K20 Huanchaca, Cerro** ▲ S Bolivia 20°12′S 66°35′W
**Huancheng** *see* Huanxian
**56 C12 Huandoy, Nevado** ▲ W Peru 08°58′S 77°33′W
**Huang′an** *see* Hong′an
**161 O8 Huangchuan** Henan, C China 32°07′N 115°02′E
**161 O9 Huanggang** Hubei, C China 30°27′N 114°53′E
**Huang Hai** *see* Yellow Sea
**157 Q8 Huang He** *var.* Yellow River. ❧ C China
**161 Q4 Huanghe Kou** delta E China

**160 L5 Huangheyan** *see* Madoi
**160 L5 Huangling** Shaanxi, C China 35°30′N 109°14′E
**161 O9 Huangpi** Hubei, C China 30°53′N 114°24′E
**161 Q9 Huangshan** *var.* Tunxi. Anhui, E China 30°14′N 115°E
**161 O9 Huangshi** *var.* Huang-shih, Hwangshih. Hubei, C China 30°14′N 115°E
**160 L5 Huangtu Gaoyuan** plateau C China
**61 B22 Huanguelén** Buenos Aires, E Argentina 37°02′S 61°57′W
**161 S10 Huangyan** Zhejiang, SE China 28°38′N 121°15′E
**159 T10 Huangyuan** Qinghai, C China 36°40′N 101°12′E
**159 T10 Huangzhong** *var.* Lushar. Qinghai, C China 36°30′N 101°32′E
**163 W12 Huanren** *var.* Huanren Manzu Zizhixian. Liaoning, NE China 41°16′N 125°25′E
**Huanren Manzu Zizhixian** *see* Huanren
**57 F15 Huanta** Ayacucho, C Peru 12°54′S 74°13′W
**56 E13 Huánuco** Huánuco, C Peru 09°58′S 76°16′W
**56 D13 Huánuco** *off.* Región de Huánuco. ◆ region C Peru
**Huánuco, Región de** *see* Huánuco
**57 K19 Huanuni** Oruro, W Bolivia 18°15′S 66°48′W
**159 X9 Huanxian** *var.* Huancheng. Gansu, C China 36°30′N 107°20′E
**161 S12 Huaping Yu** *prev.* Huap′ing Yu. island N Taiwan
**62 H3 Huara** Tarapacá, N Chile 19°59′S 69°42′W
**57 D14 Huaral** Lima, W Peru 11°31′S 77°10′W
**Huarás** *see* Huaraz
**56 D13 Huaraz** *var.* Huarás. Ancash, W Peru 09°31′S 77°32′W
**57 I16 Huari Huari, Río** ❧ S Peru
**56 C13 Huarmey** Ancash, W Peru 10°03′S 78°08′W
**56 D8 Huasaga, Río** ❧ Ecuador/Peru
**167 O15 Hua Sai** Nakhon Si Thammarat, SW Thailand 08°02′N 100°18′E
**56 D12 Huascarán, Nevado** ▲ W Peru 09°01′S 77°27′W
**62 G8 Huasco** Atacama, N Chile 28°30′S 71°15′W
**62 G8 Huasco, Río** ❧ C Chile
**159 S11 Huashixia** Qinghai, W China
**57 G8 Huatabampo** Sonora, NW Mexico 26°49′N 109°40′W
**159 W10 Huating** *var.* Donghua. Gansu, C China 35°13′N 106°39′E
**167 S7 Huatt, Phou** ▲ N Vietnam 19°45′N 104°41′E
**41 Q14 Huatusco** *var.* Huatusco de Chicuellar. Veracruz, C Mexico 19°13′N 96°57′W
**Huatusco de Chicuellar** *see* Huatusco
**41 P13 Huauchinango** Puebla, S Mexico 20°11′N 98°04′W
**41 R15 Huautla** *var.* Huautla de Jiménez. Oaxaca, SE Mexico 18°10′N 96°51′W
**Huautla de Jiménez** *see* Huautla
**161 O5 Huaxian** *var.* Daokou, Hua Xian. Henan, C China 35°33′N 114°30′E
**Hua Xian** *see* Huaxian
**Huazanga** *see* Shexian
**41 O13 Huichapán** Hidalgo, C Mexico 20°24′N 99°40′W
**Huicheng** *see* Shexian
**163 W13 Huich′ŏn** C North Korea 40°09′N 126°17′E
**82 A10 Huíla** ◆ province SW Angola
**54 E12 Huila** *off.* Departamento del Huila. ◆ province S Colombia
**Huila, Departamento del** *see* Huila
**54 D11 Huila, Nevado del** elevation C Colombia
**83 B15 Huíla Plateau** plateau S Angola
**160 G12 Huili** Sichuan, C China 26°39′N 102°13′E
**161 P4 Huimin** Shandong, E China 37°29′N 117°30′E
**163 W11 Huinan** *var.* Chaoyang. Jilin, NE China 42°40′N 126°03′E
**62 K12 Huinca Renancó** Córdoba, C Argentina 34°51′S 64°22′W
**159 V10 Huining** *var.* Huishi. Gansu, C China 35°42′N 105°01′E
**159 W8 Huinong** *var.* Dawukou. Ningxia, N China 39°04′N 106°22′E
**Huishi** *see* Huining
**160 I11 Huishui** *var.* Heping. Guizhou, S China 26°07′N 106°39′E
**95 N15 Huittinen** *Swed.* Vittis. SW Finland 61°11′N 22°40′E
**41 O15 Huitzuco** *var.* Huitzuco de los Figueroa. Guerrero, S Mexico 18°18′N 99°20′W
**Huitzuco de los Figueroa** *see* Huitzuco
**159 W11 Huixian** Hui Xian. Gansu, C China 33°48′N 106°02′E
**41 V17 Huixtla** Chiapas, SE Mexico 15°09′N 92°30′W
**160 I10 Huize** *var.* Zhongping. Yunnan, SW China 26°28′N 103°18′E
**98 J9 Huizen** Noord-Holland, C Netherlands 52°17′N 05°15′E
**161 O14 Huizhou** Guangdong, S China 23°02′N 114°28′E
**162 J6 Hujirt** Arhangay, C Mongolia 48°49′N 101°20′E
**162 J6 Hujirt** Tsetserleg, Övörhangay, Mongolia
**Hujirt** *see* Delgerhaan, Töv, Mongolia

**104 J7 Huebra** ❧ W Spain
**24 H8 Hueco Mountains** ▲ Texas, SW USA
**116 G10 Huedin** *Hung.* Bánffyhunyad. Cluj, NW Romania 46°52′N 23°02′E
**40 L9 Huehuento, Cerro** ▲ C Mexico 23°46′N 105°42′W
**42 B5 Huehuetenango** Huehuetenango, W Guatemala 15°19′N 91°26′W
**42 B4 Huehuetenango** *off.* Departamento de Huehuetenango. ◆ department W Guatemala
**Huehuetenango, Departamento de** *see* Huehuetenango
**41 L12 Huejotzingo**
**41 L11 Huejuquilla** Jalisco, SW Mexico 22°40′N 103°52′W
**41 P12 Huejutla** *var.* Huejutla de Reyes. Hidalgo, C Mexico 21°10′N 98°25′N
**Huejutla de Reyes** *see* Huejutla
**Huejutla var.**
**102 G6 Huelgoat** Finistère, NW France 48°23′N 03°45′W
**105 O13 Huelma** Andalucía, S Spain 37°39′N 03°28′W
**104 I14 Huelva** *anc.* Onuba. Andalucía, SW Spain 37°15′N 06°56′W
**104 I13 Huelva** ◆ province Andalucía, SW Spain
**104 J13 Huelva** ❧ SW Spain
**105 Q14 Huércal-Overa** Andalucía, S Spain 37°23′N 01°56′W
**37 Q9 Huerfano Mountain** ▲ New Mexico, SW USA 36°25′N 107°50′W
**37 T7 Huerfano River** ❧ Colorado, C USA
**105 R6 Huerva** ❧ N Spain
**105 S4 Huesca** *anc.* Osca. Aragón, NE Spain 42°08′N 00°25′W
**105 T4 Huesca** ◆ province Aragón, NE Spain
**105 P13 Huéscar** Andalucía, S Spain 37°39′N 02°32′W
**41 N15 Huetamo** *var.* Huetamo de Núñez. Michoacán, SW Mexico 18°36′N 100°54′W
**Huetamo de Núñez** *see* Huetamo
**105 P8 Huete** Castilla-La Mancha, C Spain 40°09′N 02°42′W
**23 P4 Hueytown** Alabama, S USA 33°27′N 87°00′W
**28 L16 Hugh Butler Lake** ◎ Nebraska, C USA
**181 V6 Hughenden** Queensland, NE Australia 20°57′S 144°16′E
**182 A6 Hughes** South Australia 30°41′S 129°31′E
**39 P8 Hughes** Alaska, USA 66°03′N 154°15′W
**26 K12 Hughes** Arkansas, C USA 34°57′N 90°28′W
**21 U15 Hughesville** Maryland, NE USA
**27 U12 Hugo** Colorado, C USA 39°08′N 103°28′W
**27 Q13 Hugo** Oklahoma, C USA 34°01′N 95°31′W
**29 S8 Hugo Lake** ◎ Oklahoma, C USA
**26 H7 Hugoton** Kansas, C USA 37°11′N 101°22′W
**161 R13 Hui′an** *var.* Luocheng. Fujian, SE China 25°06′N 118°45′E
**184 O13 Huiarau Range** ▲ North Island, New Zealand
**83 E20 Huib-Hoch Plateau** plateau S Namibia
**41 O13 Huichapán** Hidalgo, C Mexico 20°24′N 99°40′W
**Huicheng** *see* Shexian
**163 W13 Huich′ŏn** C North Korea 40°09′N 126°17′E
**82 A10 Huíla** ◆ province SW Angola
**54 E12 Huila** *off.* Departamento del Huila. ◆ province S Colombia
**Huila, Departamento del** *see* Huila
**54 D11 Huila, Nevado del** elevation C Colombia
**83 B15 Huíla Plateau** plateau S Angola
**160 G12 Huili** Sichuan, C China 26°39′N 102°13′E
**161 P4 Huimin** Shandong, E China 37°29′N 117°30′E
**163 W11 Huinan** *var.* Chaoyang. Jilin, NE China 42°40′N 126°03′E
**62 K12 Huinca Renancó** Córdoba, C Argentina 34°51′S 64°22′W
**159 V10 Huining** *var.* Huishi. Gansu, C China 35°42′N 105°01′E
**159 W8 Huinong** *var.* Dawukou. Ningxia, N China 39°04′N 106°22′E
**Huishi** *see* Huining

**83 G20 Hukuntsi** Kgalagadi, SW Botswana 23°59′S 21°44′E
**Hukuoka** *see* Fukuoka
**Hukusima** *see* Fukushima
**Hukutiyama** *see* Fukuchiyama
**Hukuyama** *see* Fukuyama
**163 W8 Hulan** Heilongjiang, NE China 45°59′N 126°37′E
**31 Q4 Hulan He** ❧ NE China
**6 L12 Hulbert Lake** ◎ Michigan, N USA
**183 N15 Hulin** Heilongjiang, NE China 45°48′N 133°06′E
**Hulian** *see* Dabu
**Hulingol** *see* Huolin Gol
**99 F16 Hulst** Zeeland, SW Netherlands 51°17′N 04°03′E
**Hulstay** *see* Choybalsan
**Hultschin** *see* Hlučín
**163 M19 Hultsfred** Kalmar, S Sweden 57°30′N 15°50′E
**163 T13 Huludao** *prev.* Jinxi, Lianshan. Liaoning, NE China 40°46′N 120°47′E
**Hulun** *see* Hulun Buir
**163 S6 Hulun Buir** *var.* Hailar; *prev.* Hulun. Nei Mongol Zizhiqu, N China 49°15′N 119°41′E
**Hu-lun Ch′ih** *see* Hulun Nur
**163 Q9 Hulun Nur** *var.* Hu-lun Ch′ih; *prev.* Dalai Nor. ◎ NE China
**117 V8 Hulyaypole** *Rus.* Gulyaypole. Zaporiz′ka Oblast′, SE Ukraine 47°41′N 36°01′E
**163 V4 Huma** Heilongjiang, NE China 51°40′N 126°38′E
**45 V6 Humacao** E Puerto Rico 18°09′N 65°50′W
**163 U4 Huma He** ❧ NE China
**62 J5 Humahuaca** Jujuy, N Argentina 23°13′S 65°20′W
**59 N2 Humaitá** Amazonas, N Brazil 07°33′S 63°01′W
**62 N7 Humaitá** Ñeembucú, S Paraguay 27°02′S 58°31′W
**83 H26 Humansdorp** Eastern Cape, S South Africa 34°01′S 24°45′E
**27 S6 Humansville** Missouri, C USA 37°47′N 93°34′W
**23 C16 Humbe** Cunene, SW Angola 16°37′S 14°52′E
**97 N17 Humber** estuary E England, United Kingdom
**97 M17 Humberside** cultural region E England, United Kingdom
**Humberto** *see* Umberto
**181 Z8 Humbert River** Northern Territory, N Australia 29°58′S 130°15′E
**25 W11 Humble** Texas, SW USA
**11 U15 Humboldt** Saskatchewan, S Canada 52°13′N 105°09′W
**29 U12 Humboldt** Iowa, C USA 42°42′N 94°13′W
**26 L7 Humboldt** Kansas, C USA 37°48′N 95°26′W
**29 S17 Humboldt** Nebraska, C USA 40°09′N 95°56′W
**20 I9 Humboldt** Tennessee, S USA 35°49′N 88°55′W
**34 K3 Humboldt Bay** bay California, W USA
**35 S4 Humboldt Lake** ◎ Nevada, W USA
**35 S4 Humboldt River** ❧ Nevada, W USA
**35 T5 Humboldt Salt Marsh** wetland Nevada, W USA
**183 P11 Hume, Lake** ◎ New South Wales/Victoria, SE Australia
**41 Q13 Humenné** *Ger.* Homenau, *Hung.* Homonna. Prešovský Kraj, E Slovakia 48°57′N 21°54′E
**29 V15 Humeston** Iowa, C USA 40°51′N 93°30′W
**54 J5 Humocaro Bajo** Lara, N Venezuela 09°41′N 70°00′W
**29 Q14 Humphrey** Nebraska, C USA 41°38′N 97°29′W
**35 S9 Humphreys, Mount** ▲ California, W USA
**36 L11 Humphreys Peak** ▲ Arizona, SW USA 35°18′N 111°40′W
**111 E17 Humpolec** *Ger.* Gumpolds, Humpoletz. Vysočina, C Czechia 49°33′N 15°22′E
**Humpoletz** *see* Humpolec
**K19 Humppila** Kanta-Häme, S Finland 60°54′N 23°21′E
**158 K2 Humptulips** Washington, NW USA 47°13′N 123°57′W
**A7 Humuya, Río** ❧ W Honduras
**Hūn** N Libya 29°06′N 15°56′E
**91 I1 Húnaflói** bay NW Iceland
**160 M11 Hunan** *var.* Hunan Sheng, Xiang. ◆ province S China
**163 Y10 Hunchun** Jilin, NE China 42°51′N 130°21′E
**95 I22 Hundested** *var.* Hund ested. E Denmark 55°58′N 11°53′E
**Hundred Mile House** *see* 100 Mile House
**116 G12 Hunedoara** *Ger.* Eisenmarkt, *Hung.* Vajdahunyad. Hunedoara, SW Romania 45°45′N 22°54′E
**116 G12 Hunedoara** ◆ county W Romania
**116 H11 Hünfeld** Hessen, C Germany 50°40′N 09°46′E
**Hungarian People′s Republic** *see* Hungary
**111 H23 Hungary** *off.* Hungarian Rep., *Ger.* Ungarn, *Hung.* Magyarország, *Rom.* Ungaria, *SCr.* Mađarska, *Ukr.* Uhorshchyna; *prev.* Hungarian People′s Republic. ◆ republic C Europe
**Hungary, Plain of** *see* Great Hungarian Plain
**Hungiy** *see* Urgamal
**159 X13 Hüngnam** E North Korea 39°50′N 127°38′E
**33 P8 Hungry Horse Reservoir** ◎ Montana, NW USA
**Hungt′ou** *see* Lan Yu
**Hung-tse Hu** *see* Hongze Hu

**101 E19 Hunsrück** ▲ W Germany
**97 P18 Hunstanton** E England, United Kingdom 52°57′N 00°27′E
**155 G20 Hunsür** Karnātaka, E India 12°18′N 76°15′E
**Hunt** *see* Hangay
**100 G13 Hunte** ❧ NW Germany
**29 Q5 Hunter** North Dakota, N USA 47°10′N 97°11′W
**25 S11 Hunter** Texas, SW USA 29°47′N 98°01′W
**185 D20 Hunter** ❧ South Island, New Zealand
**183 N15 Hunter Island** island Tasmania, SE Australia
**18 K11 Hunter Mountain** ▲ New York, NE USA 42°10′N 74°13′W
**185 B23 Hunter Mountains** ▲ South Island, New Zealand
**183 S7 Hunter River** ❧ New South Wales, SE Australia
**32 L7 Hunters** Washington, NW USA 48°07′N 118°13′W
**185 F20 Hunters Hills, The** ▲ hill range South Island, New Zealand
**184 M12 Hunterville** Manawatu-Wanganui, North Island, New Zealand
**31 N16 Huntingburg** Indiana, N USA 38°18′N 86°57′W
**97 O20 Huntingdon** E England, United Kingdom 52°20′N 00°12′W
**18 E15 Huntingdon** Pennsylvania, NE USA 40°28′N 78°00′W
**20 G9 Huntingdon** Tennessee, S USA 36°00′N 88°25′W
**97 O20 Huntingdonshire** cultural region C England, United Kingdom
**31 P12 Huntington** Indiana, N USA 40°52′N 85°30′W
**32 L13 Huntington** Oregon, NW USA 44°22′N 117°18′W
**25 X9 Huntington** Texas, SW USA 31°16′N 94°34′W
**36 M5 Huntington** Utah, W USA 39°19′N 110°57′W
**21 P5 Huntington** West Virginia, NE USA 38°25′N 82°27′W
**35 T16 Huntington Beach** California, W USA 33°39′N 118°00′W
**35 W4 Huntington Creek** ❧ Nevada, W USA
**184 L7 Huntly** Waikato, North Island, New Zealand 37°34′S 175°09′E
**96 K8 Huntly** NE Scotland, United Kingdom 57°25′N 02°48′W
**10 K8 Hunt, Mount** ▲ Yukon, NW Canada 61°29′N 130°10′W
**14 H12 Huntsville** Ontario, S Canada 45°20′N 79°14′W
**23 P2 Huntsville** Alabama, S USA 34°44′N 86°35′W
**27 S9 Huntsville** Arkansas, C USA 36°04′N 93°46′W
**27 U3 Huntsville** Missouri, C USA 39°27′N 92°31′W
**20 M8 Huntsville** Tennessee, S USA 36°25′N 84°30′W
**25 V10 Huntsville** Texas, SW USA 30°43′N 95°34′W
**36 L2 Huntsville** Utah, W USA 41°15′N 111°45′W
**41 W12 Hunucmá** Yucatán, SE Mexico 21°01′N 89°53′W
**149 W3 Hunza** ❧ NE Pakistan
**Hunza** *see* Karimabad
**158 H4 Hunze** *var.* Oostermoers Vaart ❧ NE Netherlands
**Huocheng** *var.* Shuiding. Xinjiang Uygur Zizhiqu, NW China 44°03′N 80°49′E
**161 N6 Huojia** Henan, C China 35°14′N 113°38′E
**163 S9 Huolin Gol** *prev.* Hulingol. Nei Mongol Zizhiqu, N China 45°32′N 119°38′E
**186 N14 Huon** reef N New Caledonia
**186 E7 Huon Peninsula** headland C Papua New Guinea 06°24′S 147°50′E
**Huoshao Dao** *see* Lü Dao
**Huoshao Tao** *see* Lan Yu
**Hupeh/Hupei** *see* Hubei
**Hurama** *see* Hongua
**95 H14 Hurdalsjøen** *prev.* Hurdalssjøen. ◎ S Norway
**Hurdalssjøen** *see* Hurdalsjøen
**14 E13 Hurd, Cape** headland Ontario, S Canada 45°12′N 81°43′W
**98 L5 Hurdegaryp** *Dutch.* Hardegarijp. Fryslân, N Netherlands 53°13′N 05°57′E
**29 N4 Hurdsfield** North Dakota, N USA 47°26′N 99°55′W
**Hüremt** *see* Sayhan, Bulgan, Mongolia
**Hüremt** *see* Taragt, Övörhangay, Mongolia
**Hurghada** *see* El Ghardaqah
**81 H17 Huri Hills** ▲ NW Kenya
**67 V9 Hürká** *see* Harka
**92 I1 Húrká** *var.* Hürkay, *var.*
**93 R1 Hurke** *Ar.* Hürkay, *var.* Hărka, N Iraq 37°03′N 43°39′E
**33 P15 Hurley** New Mexico, SW USA 32°42′N 108°07′W
**30 K4 Hurley** Wisconsin, N USA 46°25′N 90°11′W
**21 Y4 Hurlock** Maryland, NE USA 38°37′N 75°51′W
**162 K11 Hürmen** *Ar.* Tsoohor. Ömnögovi, S Mongolia 43°13′N 104°04′E
**29 P10 Huron** South Dakota, N USA 44°22′N 98°13′W
**31 S6 Huron, Lake** ◎ Canada/USA
**31 N3 Huron Mountains** hill range Michigan, N USA
**20 J8 Hurricane** West Virginia, NE USA 38°25′N 82°10′W
**36 J8 Hurricane** Utah, W USA 37°10′N 113°18′W
**23 V6 Hurricane Cliffs** cliff Arizona, SW USA
**23 V6 Hurricane Creek** ❧ Georgia, SE USA
**94 E12 Hurrungane** ▲ S Norway
**101 E16 Hürth** Nordrhein-Westfalen, W Germany 50°52′N 06°49′E
**95 F21 Hurup** Midtjylland, NW Denmark 56°46′N 08°26′E
**117 T14 Hurzuf** Avtonomna Respublika Krym, S Ukraine 44°33′N 34°18′E
**Hus** *see* Huşi
**95 B19 Húsavík** *Dan.* Husevig. Sandoy, C Faroe Islands 65°24′N 06°38′W

◆ Country
● Country Capital
◇ Dependent Territory
◑ Dependent Territory Capital
◆ Administrative Regions
✕ International Airport
▲ Mountain
▲ Mountain Range
▨ Volcano
❧ River
◎ Lake
▨ Reservoir

HÚSAVÍK – INDIANAPOLIS


92 K1 **Húsavík** Norðurland Eystra, NE Iceland 66°03′N 17°20′W
**Husevig** see Húsavík
116 M10 **Huşi** var. Huş. Vaslui, E Romania 46°40′N 28°05′E
95 L19 **Huskvarna** Jönköping, S Sweden 57°47′N 14°15′E
39 P8 **Huslia** Alaska, USA 65°42′N 156°24′W
**Husn** see Al Ḥuṣn
95 C15 **Husnes** Hordaland, S Norway 59°52′N 05°46′E
94 D8 **Hustadvika** sea area S Norway
**Husté** see Khust
100 H7 **Husum** Schleswig-Holstein, N Germany 54°29′N 09°04′E
93 I16 **Husum** Västernorrland, C Sweden 63°21′N 19°12′E
116 K6 **Husyatyn** Ternopil's'ka Oblast', W Ukraine 49°04′N 26°10′E
**Huszt** see Khust
**Hutag** see Hutag-Öndör
162 K6 **Hutag-Öndör** var. Hutag. Bulgan, N Mongolia 49°22′N 102°50′E
26 M6 **Hutchinson** Kansas, C USA 38°03′N 97°56′W
29 U9 **Hutchinson** Minnesota, N USA 44°53′N 94°22′W
23 Y13 **Hutchinson Island** island Florida, SE USA
36 L11 **Hutch Mountain** ▲ Arizona, SW USA 34°49′N 111°22′W
141 O14 **Ḥūth** NW Yemen 16°14′N 44°E
186 I7 **Hutjena** Buka Island, NE Papua New Guinea 05°19′S 154°40′E
109 T8 **Hüttenberg** Kärnten, S Austria 46°58′N 14°33′E
25 T10 **Hutto** Texas, SW USA 30°32′N 97°33′W
**Huttu** see Futtsu
108 E8 **Huttwil** Bern, W Switzerland 47°06′N 07°48′E
158 K5 **Hutubi** Xinjiang Uygur Zizhiqu, NW China 44°10′N 86°51′E
161 N4 **Hutuo He** 🌊 C China
**Hutyû** see Fuchū
185 E20 **Huxley, Mount** ▲ South Island, New Zealand 44°02′S 169°42′E
99 J20 **Huy** Dut. Hoei, Hoey. Liège, E Belgium 50°32′N 05°14′E
161 R8 **Huzhou** var. Wuxing. Zhejiang, SE China 30°52′N 120°06′E
**Huzi** see Fuji
**Huzieda** see Fujieda
**Huzinomiya** see Fujinomiya
**Huzisawa** see Fujisawa
92 I2 **Hvammstangi** Norðurland Vestra, N Iceland 65°22′N 20°54′W
92 K4 **Hvannadalshnúkur** var. Hvannadalshnúkur. ⛰ S Iceland 64°01′N 16°39′W
**Hvannadalshnúkur** see Hvannadalshnúkur
113 E15 **Hvar** It. Lesina. Split-Dalmacija, S Croatia 43°10′N 16°27′E
113 F15 **Hvar** It. Lesina; anc. Pharus. island S Croatia
117 T13 **Hvardiys'ke** Rus. Gvardeyskoye. Avtonomna Respublika Krym, S Ukraine 45°08′N 34°01′E
92 I4 **Hveragerði** Suðurland, SW Iceland 64°00′N 21°13′W
95 E22 **Hvide Sande** Midtjylland, W Denmark 56°00′N 08°08′E
92 I3 **Hvítá** 🌊 C Iceland
95 G15 **Hvittingfoss** Buskerud, S Norway 59°28′N 10°00′E
92 I4 **Hvolsvöllur** Suðurland, SW Iceland 63°44′N 20°12′W
**Hwach'ŏn-chŏsuji** see Paro-ho
**Hwainan** see Huainan
**Hwalien** see Hualien
83 I16 **Hwange** prev. Wankie. Matabeleland North, W Zimbabwe 18°18′S 26°31′E
**Hwang-Hae** see Yellow Sea
**Hwangshih** see Huangshi
83 L17 **Hwedza** Mashonaland East, E Zimbabwe 18°35′S 31°35′E
63 G20 **Hyades, Cerro** ▲ S Chile 46°57′S 73°09′W
162 K6 **Hyalganat** var. Selenge. Bulgan, N Mongolia 49°34′N 104°18′E
19 Q12 **Hyannis** Massachusetts, NE USA 41°38′N 70°15′W
28 L13 **Hyannis** Nebraska, C USA 42°00′N 101°45′W
162 F6 **Hyargas Nuur** ◎ NW Mongolia
**Hybla/Hybla Major** see Paternò
39 Y14 **Hydaburg** Prince of Wales Island, Alaska, USA 55°10′N 132°44′W
185 F22 **Hyde** Otago, South Island, New Zealand 45°17′S 170°17′E
21 O7 **Hyden** Kentucky, S USA 37°08′N 83°23′W
18 K12 **Hyde Park** New York, NE USA 41°46′N 73°52′W
39 Z14 **Hyder** Alaska, USA 55°55′N 130°01′W
155 I15 **Hyderābād** var. Haidarabad. state capital Telangana/Andhra Pradesh, C India 17°22′N 78°26′E
149 Q16 **Hyderabad** var. Haidarabad. Sindh, SE Pakistan 25°26′N 68°22′E
103 T16 **Hyères** Var, SE France 43°07′N 06°08′E
103 T16 **Hyères, Îles d'** island group S France
118 K12 **Hyermanavichy** Rus. Germanovichi. Vitsyebskaya Voblasts', N Belarus 55°24′N 27°48′E
163 X12 **Hyesan** NE North Korea 41°18′N 128°13′E
10 K8 **Hyland** 🌊 Yukon, NW Canada
95 K20 **Hyltebruk** Halland, S Sweden 57°N 13°14′E
18 D16 **Hyndman** Pennsylvania, NE USA 39°49′N 78°42′W
33 P14 **Hyndman Peak** ▲ Idaho, NW USA 43°45′N 114°07′W
164 I13 **Hyōgo** off. Hyōgo-ken. ◆ prefecture Honshū, SW Japan
**Hyōgo-ken** see Hyōgo
**Hypsas** see Belice
**Hyrcania** see Gorgān
36 L1 **Hyrum** Utah, W USA 41°37′N 111°51′W
93 N14 **Hyrynsalmi** Kainuu, C Finland 64°41′N 28°30′E
33 V10 **Hysham** Montana, NW USA 46°16′N 107°14′W
11 N13 **Hythe** Alberta, W Canada 55°18′N 119°44′W
97 Q23 **Hythe** SE England, United Kingdom 51°05′N 01°04′E
**Hyvinge** see Hyvinkää
93 L19 **Hyvinkää** Swe. Hyvinge. Uusimaa, S Finland 60°37′N 24°50′E

# I

116 J9 **Iacobeni** Ger. Jakobeny. Suceava, NE Romania 47°24′N 25°20′E
**Iader** see Zadar
172 I7 **Iakora** Fianarantsoa, SE Madagascar 23°04′S 46°40′E
116 K14 **Ialomiţa** var. Jalomitsa. ◆ county SE Romania
116 K14 **Ialomiţa** 🌊 SE Romania
117 N10 **Ialoveni** Rus. Yaloveny. C Moldova 46°57′N 28°47′E
117 N11 **Ialpug** var. Ialpugul Mare, Rus. Yalpug. 🌊 Moldova/ Ukraine
**Ialpugul Mare** see Ialpug
23 T8 **Iamonia, Lake** ◎ Florida, SE USA
116 L13 **Ianca** Brăila, SE Romania 45°06′N 27°29′E
116 M10 **Iaşi** Ger. Jassy. Iaşi, NE Romania 47°08′N 27°38′E
116 L9 **Iaşi** Ger. Jassy, Yassy. ◆ county NE Romania
114 J13 **Íasmos** Anatolikí Makedonía kai Thráki, NE Greece 41°07′N 25°12′E
22 H6 **Iatt, Lake** ⊠ Louisiana, S USA
58 B11 **Iauretê** Amazonas, NW Brazil 0°37′N 69°10′W
171 N3 **Iba** Luzon, N Philippines 15°25′N 119°55′E
77 S16 **Ibadan** Oyo, SW Nigeria 07°22′N 04°01′E
54 E10 **Ibagué** Tolima, C Colombia 04°27′N 75°14′W
60 J10 **Ibaiti** Paraná, S Brazil 23°49′S 50°15′W
36 J4 **Ibapah Peak** ▲ Utah, W USA 39°51′N 113°55′W
**Ibar** see Ibër
165 P13 **Ibaraki** off. Ibaraki-ken. ◆ prefecture Honshū, S Japan
**Ibaraki-ken** see Ibaraki
56 C5 **Ibarra** var. San Miguel de Ibarra. Imbabura, N Ecuador 0°23′S 78°08′W
**Ibaşfalău** see Dumbrăveni
141 O16 **Ibb** W Yemen 13°55′N 44°10′E
100 F13 **Ibbenbüren** Nordrhein-Westfalen, NW Germany 52°17′N 07°43′E
79 H16 **Ibenga** 🌊 N Congo
113 M15 **Ibër** Serb. Ibar. 🌊 C Serbia
57 I14 **Iberia** Madre de Dios, E Peru 11°21′S 69°36′W
**Iberia** see Spain
66 M1 **Iberian Basin** undersea feature E Atlantic Ocean 39°00′N 16°00′W
**Iberian Mountains** see Ibérico, Sistema
84 D12 **Iberian Peninsula** physical region Portugal/Spain
64 M8 **Iberian Plain** undersea feature E Atlantic Ocean 13°30′W 43°45′N
**Ibérica, Cordillera** see Ibérico, Sistema
105 P6 **Ibérico, Sistema** var. Cordillera Ibérica, Eng. Iberian Mountains. ▲ NE Spain
12 K7 **Iberville Lac d'** ◎ Québec, NE Canada
77 T14 **Ibeto** Niger, W Nigeria 10°30′N 05°07′E
77 W15 **Ibi** Taraba, C Nigeria 08°13′N 09°46′E
105 S11 **Ibi** Comunitat Valenciana, E Spain 38°38′N 00°35′W
59 L20 **Ibiá** Minas Gerais, SE Brazil 19°30′S 46°31′W
61 F15 **Ibicuí, Rio** 🌊 S Brazil
61 C19 **Ibicuy** Entre Ríos, E Argentina 33°44′S 59°10′W
61 F16 **Ibirapuitã** 🌊 S Brazil
105 V10 **Ibiza** var. Iviza, Cast. Eivissa; anc. Ebusus. island Islas Baleares, Spain, W Mediterranean Sea
**Ibiza** see Eivissa
138 J4 **Ibn Wardān, Qaşr** ruins Ḥamāh, C Syria
**Ibo** see Sassandra
188 E9 **Ibobang** Babeldaob, N Palau
171 V13 **Ibonma** Papua Barat, E Indonesia 03°27′S 133°30′E
59 N17 **Ibotirama** Bahia, E Brazil 12°13′S 43°12′W
141 Y8 **Ibrā** NE Oman 22°45′N 58°30′E
127 Q4 **Ibresi** Chuvashskaya Respublika, W Russia 55°22′N 47°04′E
141 X8 **'Ibrī** NW Oman 23°12′N 56°28′E
164 C16 **Ibusuki** Kagoshima, Kyūshū, SW Japan 31°15′N 130°40′E
57 E16 **Ica** Ica, SW Peru 14°02′S 75°48′W
57 E16 **Ica** off. Región de Ica. ◆ region SW Peru
58 C11 **Içana** Amazonas, NW Brazil 0°22′N 67°25′W
**Ica, Región de** see Ica
**Icaria** see Ikaría
58 B13 **Içá, Rio** var. Río Putumayo. 🌊 NW South America see also Putumayo, Río
**Içá, Rio** see Putumayo, Río
136 I17 **İçel** prev. İchili; prev. Mersin. ◆ province S Turkey
**İçel** see Mersin
92 I3 **Iceland** off. Republic of Iceland, Dan. Island, Icel. Ísland, Lýðveldið Ísland. ◆ republic N Atlantic Ocean
86 B6 **Iceland** island N Atlantic Ocean
64 L5 **Iceland Basin** undersea feature N Atlantic Ocean 61°00′N 19°00′W
**Icelandic Plateau** see Iceland Plateau
197 Q15 **Iceland Plateau** var. Icelandic Plateau. undersea feature S Greenland Sea 12°00′W 69°30′N
**Iceland, Republic of** see Iceland
155 E16 **Ichalkaranji** Mahārāshtra, W India 16°42′N 74°28′E
164 D15 **Ichifusa-yama** ▲ Kyūshū, SW Japan 32°18′N 131°05′E
**Ichili** see İçel
164 K13 **Ichinomiya** var. Itinomiya. Aichi, Honshū, SW Japan 35°18′N 136°48′E
165 Q9 **Ichinoseki** var. Itinoseki. Iwate, Honshū, C Japan 38°56′N 141°08′E
117 U12 **Ichki** prev. Sovyets'kyy. Avtonomna Respublika Krym, S Ukraine 45°20′N 34°54′E
117 R3 **Ichnya** Chernihivs'ka Oblast', NE Ukraine 50°52′N 32°24′E
57 L17 **Ichoa, Río** 🌊 C Bolivia
**Iconium** see Konya
**Iculisma** see Angoulême
39 U12 **Icy Bay** inlet Alaska, USA
39 N5 **Icy Cape** headland Alaska, USA 70°19′N 161°52′W
39 W13 **Icy Strait** strait Alaska, USA
27 R13 **Idabel** Oklahoma, C USA 33°54′N 94°50′W
29 T13 **Ida Grove** Iowa, C USA 42°21′N 95°28′W
77 U16 **Idah** Kogi, S Nigeria 07°06′N 06°45′E
33 N13 **Idaho** off. State of Idaho, also known as Gem of the Mountains, Gem State. ◆ state NW USA
33 N14 **Idaho City** Idaho, NW USA 43°48′N 115°51′W
33 R14 **Idaho Falls** Idaho, NW USA 43°28′N 112°01′W
25 N5 **Idalou** Texas, SW USA 33°40′N 101°40′W
104 I9 **Idanha-a-Nova** Castelo Branco, C Portugal 39°55′N 07°15′W
101 E19 **Idar-Oberstein** Rheinland-Pfalz, SW Germany 49°43′N 07°19′E
118 J3 **Ida-Virumaa** var. Ida-Viru Maakond. ◆ province NE Estonia
**Ida-Viru Maakond** see Ida-Virumaa
124 J8 **Idel'** Respublika Kareliya, NW Russia 64°08′N 34°12′E
79 C15 **Idenao** Sud-Ouest, SW Cameroon 04°04′N 09°01′E
**Idensalmi** see Iisalmi
162 I6 **Ider** var. Dzuunmod. Hövsgöl, C Mongolia 48°09′N 97°22′E
**Ider** see Galt
75 X10 **Idfū** var. Edfu. SE Egypt 24°55′N 32°52′E
**Ídhi Óros** see Ídi
**Ídhra** see Ýdra
80 L10 **'Īdī** var. Ed. SE Eritrea 13°54′N 41°39′E
168 H7 **Idi** Sumatera, W Indonesia 05°00′N 98°00′E
115 I25 **Ídi** var. Ídhi Óros. ▲ Kríti, Greece, E Mediterranean Sea
**Idi Amin, Lac** see Edward, Lake
106 G10 **Idice** 🌊 N Italy
76 G9 **Idini** Trarza, W Mauritania 17°58′N 15°40′W
79 J21 **Idiofa** Bandundu, SW Dem. Rep. Congo 05°00′S 19°38′E
39 O10 **Iditarod River** 🌊 Alaska, USA
**Idjavuotna** see Ifjord
95 M14 **Idkerberget** Dalarna, C Sweden 60°22′N 15°15′E
138 I3 **Idlib** Idlib, NW Syria 35°57′N 36°38′E
138 I4 **Idlib** off. Muḥāfaẓat Idlib. ◆ governorate NW Syria
**Idlib, Muḥāfaẓat** see Idlib
**Idra** see Ýdra
94 J11 **Idre** Dalarna, C Sweden 61°52′N 12°45′E
**Idria** see Idrija
109 S11 **Idrija** It. Idria. W Slovenia 46°00′N 14°59′E
101 G18 **Idstein** Hessen, W Germany 50°10′N 08°16′E
**Idutywa** see Dutywa
**Idzhevan** see Ijevan
118 G9 **Iecava** S Latvia 56°36′N 24°10′E
165 T16 **Ie-jima** var. Ii-shima. island Nansei-shotō, SW Japan
99 B18 **Ieper** Fr. Ypres. West-Vlaanderen, W Belgium 50°51′N 02°53′E
115 K25 **Ierápetra** Kríti, Greece, E Mediterranean Sea 35°00′N 25°45′E
115 G22 **Iérax, Akrotírio** headland S Greece 36°45′N 23°06′E
**Ierisós** see Ierissós
115 H14 **Ierissós** var. Ierisós. Kentrikí Makedonía, N Greece 40°24′N 23°53′E
116 I11 **Iernut** Hung. Radnót. Mureş, C Romania 46°27′N 24°15′E
**Iertra** see Eritrea
106 J12 **Iesi** var. Jesi. Marche, C Italy 43°33′N 13°16′E
92 K9 **Iešjavri** ◎ N Norway
**Iesolo** see Jesolo
188 K16 **Ifalik Atoll** atoll Caroline Islands, C Micronesia
172 I6 **Ifanadiana** Fianarantsoa, SE Madagascar 21°19′S 47°39′E
77 T16 **Ife** Osun, SW Nigeria 07°25′N 04°31′E
77 V8 **Iferouâne** Agadez, N Niger 19°05′N 08°24′E
**Iferten** see Yverdon
92 L8 **Ifjord** Lapp. Idjavuotna. Finnmark, N Norway 70°27′N 27°06′E
77 R8 **Ifôghas, Adrar des** var. Adrar des Iforas. ▲ NE Mali
**Iforas, Adrar des** see Ifôghas, Adrar des
182 D6 **Ifould lake** salt lake South Australia
74 G6 **Ifrane** C Morocco 33°31′N 05°09′W
171 S11 **Iga** Pulau Halmahera, E Indonesia 01°23′N 128°17′E
81 G18 **Iganga** SE Uganda 0°34′N 33°27′E
60 L7 **Igarapava** São Paulo, S Brazil 20°01′S 47°46′W
122 K9 **Igarka** Krasnoyarskiy Kray, N Russia 67°31′N 86°33′E
**Igaunija** see Estonia
137 T12 **Iğdır** ◆ province NE Turkey
**I.G.Duca** see General Toshevo
**Igel** see Jihlava
94 N11 **Iggesund** Gävleborg, C Sweden 61°38′N 17°04′E
39 P7 **Igikpak, Mount** ▲ Alaska, USA 67°28′N 154°55′W
39 P13 **Igiugig** Alaska, USA 59°19′N 155°53′W
**Iglau/Iglawa/Igława** see Jihlava
107 B20 **Iglesias** Sardegna, Italy, C Mediterranean Sea 39°20′N 08°34′E
127 V4 **Iglino** Respublika Bashkortostan, W Russia 54°51′N 56°29′E
**Igló** see Spišská Nová Ves
9 O6 **Igloolik** Nunavut, N Canada 69°24′N 81°55′W
12 B11 **Ignace** Ontario, S Canada 49°26′N 91°40′W
118 I12 **Ignalina** Utena, E Lithuania 55°20′N 26°10′E
127 Q5 **Ignatovka** Ul'yanovskaya Oblast', W Russia 53°56′N 47°40′E
124 K12 **Ignatovo** Vologodskaya Oblast', NW Russia 60°47′N 37°51′E
114 N11 **İğneada** Kırklareli, NW Turkey 41°54′N 27°58′E
121 S7 **İğneada Burnu** headland NW Turkey 41°54′N 28°03′E
**Igombe** see Gombe
115 B16 **Igoumenítsa** Ípeiros, W Greece 39°30′N 20°16′E
127 T2 **Igra** Udmurtskaya Respublika, NW Russia 57°30′N 53°01′E
122 H9 **Igrim** Khanty-Mansiyskiy Avtonomnyy Okrug-Yugra, N Russia 63°09′N 64°33′E
60 G12 **Iguaçu, Rio** Sp. Río Iguazú. 🌊 Argentina/Brazil see also Iguazú, Río
**Iguaçu, Rio** see Iguazú, Río
59 I22 **Iguaçu, Salto do** Sp. Cataratas del Iguazú; prev. Victoria Falls. waterfall Argentina/Brazil see also Iguazú, Cataratas del
**Iguaçu, Salto do** see Iguazú, Cataratas del
41 O15 **Iguala** var. Iguala de la Independencia. Guerrero, S Mexico 18°21′N 99°31′W
105 V5 **Igualada** Cataluña, NE Spain 41°35′N 01°37′E
**Iguala de la Independencia** see Iguala
60 G12 **Iguazú, Cataratas del** Port. Salto do Iguaçu; prev. Victoria Falls. waterfall Argentina/ Brazil see also Iguaçu, Salto do
**Iguazú, Cataratas del** see Iguaçu, Salto do
62 Q6 **Iguazú, Río** var. Río Iguaçu. 🌊 Argentina/Brazil see also Iguaçu, Rio
**Iguazú, Río** see Iguaçu, Rio
79 D19 **Iguéla** prev. Iguéla. Ogooué-Maritime, SW Gabon 02°00′S 09°23′E
**Iguéla** see Iguéla
**Iguid, Erg** see Iguîdi, 'Erg
67 M5 **Iguîdi, 'Erg** var. Erg Iguid. desert Algeria/Mauritania
172 K2 **Iharaña** prev. Vohémar. Antsiranana, NE Madagascar 13°22′S 50°00′E
151 K18 **Ihavandhippolhu Atoll** var. Ihavandiffulu Atoll. atoll N Maldives
**Ihavandiffulu Atoll** see Ihavandhippolhu Atoll
**Ih Bulag** see Hanbogd
165 T16 **Iheya-jima** island Nansei-shotō, SW Japan
**Ihhayrhan** see Bayan-Önjüül
163 N9 **Ihhet** var. Bayan. Dornogovĭ, SE Mongolia 46°15′N 110°16′E
172 I6 **Ihosy** Fianarantsoa, S Madagascar 22°23′S 46°09′E
**Ihsüüj** see Bayanchandmanĭ
162 I7 **Ihtamir** var. Dzaanhushuu. Arhangay, C Mongolia 47°36′N 101°06′E
114 H10 **Ihtiman** Sofia, W Bulgaria 42°26′N 23°49′E
**Ihupuku, Motu** see Campbell Island / Motu Ihupuku
162 H6 **Ih-Uul** var. Bayan-Uhaa. Dzavhan, C Mongolia 48°41′N 98°46′E
162 J6 **Ih-Uul** var. Selenge. Hövsgöl, N Mongolia 49°25′N 101°30′E
93 L14 **Ii** Pohjois-Pohjanmaa, C Finland 65°18′N 25°23′E
164 M13 **Iida** Nagano, Honshū, S Japan 35°32′N 137°48′E
93 M14 **Iijoki** 🌊 C Finland
**Iinnasuolu** see Hinnøya
118 J4 **Iisaku** Ger. Isaak. Ida-Virumaa, NE Estonia 59°06′N 27°19′E
93 M16 **Iisalmi** var. Idensalmi. Pohjois-Savo, C Finland 63°32′N 27°10′E
**Ii-shima** see Ie-jima
165 N11 **Iiyama** Nagano, Honshū, S Japan 36°52′N 138°22′E
77 S16 **Ijebu-Ode** Ogun, SW Nigeria 06°46′N 03°57′E
137 U11 **Ijevan** Rus. Idzhevan. N Armenia 40°53′N 45°07′E
98 H9 **IJmuiden** Noord-Holland, W Netherlands 52°28′N 04°38′E
98 M12 **IJssel** var. Yssel. 🌊 Netherlands
98 J8 **IJsselmeer** prev. Zuider Zee. ◎ N Netherlands
98 L9 **IJsselmuiden** Overijssel, E Netherlands 52°34′N 05°55′E
98 I12 **IJsselstein** Utrecht, C Netherlands 52°01′N 05°02′E
61 G14 **Ijuí** Rio Grande do Sul, S Brazil 28°23′S 53°55′W
61 G14 **Ijuí, Rio** 🌊 S Brazil
189 R8 **Ijuw** NE Nauru 0°30′S 166°57′E
99 E16 **IJzendijke** Zeeland, SW Netherlands 51°20′N 03°36′E
99 A18 **Ijzer** 🌊 W Belgium
**Ikaahuk** see Sachs Harbour
93 K18 **Ikaalinen** Pirkanmaa, W Finland 61°46′N 23°05′E
172 I6 **Ikalamavony** Fianarantsoa, SE Madagascar 21°10′S 46°35′E
**Ikaluktutiak** see Cambridge Bay
185 G16 **Ikamatua** West Coast, South Island, New Zealand 42°16′S 171°42′E
145 P16 **Ikan** prev. Staroikan. Turkestan, S Kazakhstan 43°09′N 68°34′E
77 U16 **Ikare** Ondo, SW Nigeria 07°36′N 05°52′E
115 L20 **Ikaría** var. Kariot, Nicaria, Nikaria; anc. Icaria. island Dodekánisa, Greece, Aegean Sea
95 F22 **Ikast** Midtjylland, W Denmark 56°09′N 09°10′E
184 O9 **Ikawhenua Range** ▲ North Island, New Zealand
165 U4 **Ikeda** Hokkaidō, NE Japan 42°54′N 143°25′E
164 H14 **Ikeda** Tokushima, Shikoku, SW Japan 34°00′N 133°47′E
77 S16 **Ikeja** Lagos, SW Nigeria 06°36′N 03°16′E
79 L19 **Ikela** Equateur, C Dem. Rep. Congo 01°11′S 23°16′E
164 C13 **Iki** prev. Gōnoura. Nagasaki, Iki, SW Japan 33°44′N 129°41′E
164 C13 **Iki** island SW Japan
127 O13 **Iki Burul** Respublika Kalmykiya, SW Russia 45°48′N 44°44′E
137 P11 **İkizdere** Rize, NE Turkey 40°47′N 40°34′E
39 P14 **Ikolik, Cape** headland Kodiak Island, Alaska, USA 57°12′N 154°46′W
77 V17 **Ikom** Cross River, SE Nigeria 05°57′N 08°43′E
172 I6 **Ikongo** prev. Fort-Carnot. Fianarantsoa, SE Madagascar 21°52′S 47°27′E
39 P5 **Ikpikpuk River** 🌊 Alaska, USA
190 H1 **Iku** prev. Lone Tree Islet. atoll Tungaru, W Kiribati
164 I12 **Ikuno** Hyōgo, Honshū, SW Japan 35°13′N 134°48′E
190 H16 **Ikurangi** ▲ Rarotonga, S Cook Islands 21°12′S 159°45′W
171 X14 **Ilaga** Papua, E Indonesia 03°54′S 137°30′E
171 O2 **Ilagan** Luzon, N Philippines 17°08′N 121°54′E
142 J7 **Īlām** var. Elam. Īlām, W Iran 33°37′N 46°27′E
153 R12 **Ilām** Eastern, E Nepal 26°52′N 87°58′E
142 J8 **Īlām** off. Ostān-e Īlām. ◆ province W Iran
**Īlām, Ostān-e** see Īlām
161 T13 **Ilan** Jap. Giran. N Taiwan 24°45′N 121°44′E
146 G9 **Ilanly Obvodnitel'nyy Kanal** canal N Turkmenistan
122 L12 **Ilanskiy** Krasnoyarskiy Kray, S Russia 56°16′N 95°59′E
108 H9 **Ilanz** Graubünden, S Switzerland 46°46′N 09°10′E
77 S16 **Ilaro** Ogun, SW Nigeria 06°52′N 03°01′E
57 I17 **Ilave** Puno, S Peru 16°07′S 69°40′W
110 K8 **Iława** Ger. Deutsch-Eylau. Warmińsko-Mazurskie, NE Poland 53°36′N 19°35′E
121 P16 **Il-Bajja ta' Marsaxlokk** var. Marsaxlokk Bay. bay SE Malta
123 P10 **Ilbenge** Respublika Sakha (Yakutiya), NE Russia 62°52′N 124°13′E
**Ile** see Ile/Ili He
**Ile** see Ili He
11 S13 **Île-à-la-Crosse** Saskatchewan, C Canada 55°29′N 108°00′W
79 J21 **Ilebo** prev. Port-Francqui. Kasai-Occidental, W Dem. Rep. Congo 04°19′S 20°32′E
103 N5 **Île-de-France** ◆ region N France
**Ilek** see Yelek
81 H15 **Ilemi Triangle** prev. Elemi Triangle. disputed region Kenya/South Sudan
**Ilerda** see Lleida
77 T16 **Ilesha** Osun, SW Nigeria 07°35′N 04°49′E
187 Q16 **Îles Loyauté, Province des** ◆ province E New Caledonia
11 X12 **Ilford** Manitoba, C Canada 56°02′N 95°48′W
116 K14 **Ilfov** ◆ county S Romania
97 I23 **Ilfracombe** SW England, United Kingdom 51°12′N 04°10′W
136 I11 **Ilgaz Dağları** ▲ N Turkey
136 G15 **Ilgın** Konya, W Turkey 38°16′N 31°57′E
60 I7 **Ilha Solteira** São Paulo, S Brazil 20°28′S 51°19′W
104 G7 **Ílhavo** Aveiro, N Portugal 40°36′N 08°40′W
59 O18 **Ilhéus** Bahia, E Brazil 14°50′S 39°06′W
129 R7 **Ili** var. Ile, Chin. Ili He, Rus. Reka Ili. 🌊 China/ Kazakhstan see also Ili He
116 G11 **Ilia** Hung. Marosillye. Hunedoara, SW Romania 45°57′N 22°40′E
39 P13 **Iliamna** Alaska, USA 59°42′N 154°49′W
39 P13 **Iliamna Lake** ◎ Alaska, USA
137 N13 **Iliç** Erzincan, C Turkey 39°27′N 38°34′E
**Il'ichevsk** see Şärur, Azerbaijan
**Ilici** see Elche
37 V2 **Iliff** Colorado, C USA 40°46′N 103°04′W
171 Q7 **Iligan** off. Iligan City. Mindanao, S Philippines 08°12′N 124°16′E
171 Q7 **Iligan Bay** bay S Philippines
**Iligan City** see Iligan
158 I5 **Ili He** var. Ili, Kaz. Ile, Rus. Reka Ili. 🌊 China/ Kazakhstan see also Ile
**Ili He** see Ili
56 C6 **Iliniza** ▲ N Ecuador 0°37′S 78°41′W
**Ilinski** see Il'inskiy
125 U14 **Il'inskiy** var. Ilinski. Permskiy Kray, NW Russia 58°33′N 55°31′E
125 U14 **Il'inskiy** Ostrov Sakhalin, Sakhalinskaya Oblast', SE Russia 47°59′N 142°14′E
18 I10 **Ilion** New York, NE USA 43°01′N 75°02′W
38 E9 **'Ilio Point** var. Ilio Point. headland Moloka'i, Hawai'i, USA 21°13′N 157°15′W
**Ilio Point** see 'Ilio Point
109 T13 **Ilirska Bistrica** prev. Bistrica, Ger. Feistritz, Illyrisch-Feistritz, It. Villa del Nevoso. SW Slovenia 45°34′N 14°12′E
137 Q16 **Ilisu Barajı** ⊠ SE Turkey
155 G17 **Ilkal** Karnātaka, C India 15°59′N 76°08′E
97 M19 **Ilkeston** C England, United Kingdom 52°59′N 01°18′W
121 O16 **Il-Kullana** headland SW Malta 35°49′N 14°26′E
108 J8 **Ill** 🌊 W Austria
103 U6 **Ill** 🌊 NE France
62 G10 **Illapel** Coquimbo, C Chile 31°40′S 71°13′W
**Illaue Fartak Trench** see Alula-Fartak Trench
182 C2 **Illbillee, Mount** ▲ South Australia 27°01′S 132°13′E
102 I6 **Ille-et-Vilaine** ◆ department NW France
77 T11 **Illéla** Tahoua, SW Niger 14°25′N 05°10′E
101 J24 **Iller** 🌊 S Germany
101 J23 **Illertissen** Bayern, S Germany 48°13′N 10°08′E
105 X9 **Illes Balears** ◇ autonomous community E Spain
105 N8 **Illescas** Castilla-La Mancha, C Spain 40°08′N 03°51′W
**Ille-sur-la-Têt** see Ille-sur-Têt
103 O17 **Ille-sur-Têt** var. Ille-sur-la-Têt. Pyrénées-Orientales, S France 42°40′N 02°37′E
**Illiberis** see Elne
**Illichivs'k** see Illichivs'k, Ukraine
**Illicis** see Elche
102 M6 **Illiers-Combray** Eure-et-Loir, C France 43°18′N 01°15′E
30 K12 **Illinois** off. State of Illinois, also known as Prairie State, Sucker State. ◆ state C USA
30 J13 **Illinois River** 🌊 Illinois, N USA
117 N6 **Illintsi** Vinnyts'ka Oblast', C Ukraine 49°07′N 29°13′E
**Illiturgis** see Andújar
74 M10 **Illizi** SE Algeria 26°30′N 08°28′E
27 Y7 **Illmo** Missouri, C USA 37°13′N 89°30′W
**Illuro** see Lorca
**Illuro** see Mataró
**Illyrisch-Feistritz** see Ilirska Bistrica
101 K16 **Ilm** 🌊 C Germany
101 K17 **Ilmenau** Thüringen, C Germany 50°40′N 10°55′E
124 H14 **Il'men', Ozero** ◎ NW Russia
57 H18 **Ilo** Moquegua, SW Peru 17°42′S 71°20′W
171 O6 **Iloilo** off. Iloilo City. Panay Island, C Philippines 10°42′N 122°34′E
**Iloilo City** see Iloilo
112 K10 **Ilok** Hung. Újlak. Vojvodina, NW Serbia 45°12′N 19°22′E
93 O16 **Ilomantsi** Pohjois-Karjala, SE Finland 62°40′N 30°55′E
42 F8 **Ilopango, Lago de** volcanic lake C El Salvador
77 T15 **Ilorin** Kwara, W Nigeria 08°32′N 04°35′E
117 X8 **Ilovays'k** Rus. Ilovaysk. Donets'ka Oblast', SE Ukraine 47°55′N 38°14′E
**Ilovaysk** see Ilovays'k
127 O10 **Ilovlya** Volgogradskaya Oblast', SW Russia 49°45′N 44°19′E
127 O10 **Ilovlya** 🌊 SW Russia
121 N15 **Il-Ponta ta' San Dimitri** var. Ras San Dimitri, San Dimitri Point. headland Gozo, NW Malta 36°04′N 14°12′E
126 K14 **Il'skiy** Krasnodarskiy Kray, SW Russia 44°52′N 38°26′E
182 B2 **Iltur** South Australia 27°33′S 130°31′E
171 Y13 **Ilugwa** Papua, E Indonesia 03°42′S 139°09′E
**Iluh** see Batman
118 I11 **Ilūkste** SE Latvia 55°58′N 26°21′E
196 N13 **Ilulissat** Dan. Jakobshavn. Avannaata, C Greenland 68°13′N 51°06′W
171 Y13 **Ilur** Pulau Gorong, E Indonesia 04°00′S 131°25′E
32 F10 **Ilwaco** Washington, NW USA 46°19′N 124°03′W
**Il'yaly** see Gurbansoltan Eje
**Ilyasbaba Burnu** see Tekke Burnu
125 U9 **Ilych** 🌊 NW Russia
101 O21 **Ilz** 🌊 SE Germany
111 M14 **Iłża** Radom, SE Poland 51°09′N 21°15′E
164 G13 **Imabari** var. Imaharu. Ehime, Shikoku, SW Japan 34°04′N 132°59′E
**Imaharu** see Imabari
165 O12 **Imaichi** var. Imaiti. Tochigi, Honshū, S Japan 36°43′N 139°41′E
**Imaiti** see Imaichi
164 K12 **Imajō** Fukui, Honshū, SW Japan 35°45′N 136°10′E
139 R9 **Imām Ibn Hāshim** Karbalā', C Iraq 32°46′N 43°21′E
149 Q2 **Imām Ṣāḥib** var. Emam Saheb, Hazarat Imam; prev. Emām Ṣāḥeb. Kunduz, NE Afghanistan 37°11′N 68°55′E
139 T11 **Imān 'Abd Allāh** Al Qādisīyah, S Iraq 31°36′N 44°34′E
164 F15 **Imano-yama** ▲ Shikoku, SW Japan 32°51′N 132°48′E
164 C13 **Imari** Saga, Kyūshū, SW Japan 33°18′N 129°51′E
**Imarssuak Mid-Ocean Seachannel** see Imarssuak Seachannel
64 J6 **Imarssuak Seachannel** var. Imarssuak Mid-Ocean Seachannel. channel N Atlantic Ocean
93 N18 **Imatra** Etelä-Karjala, SE Finland 61°14′N 28°50′E
164 K13 **Imazu** Shiga, Honshū, SW Japan 35°25′N 136°00′E
56 C6 **Imbabura** ◆ province N Ecuador
55 R9 **Imbaimadai** W Guyana 05°44′N 60°23′W
61 K14 **Imbituba** Santa Catarina, S Brazil 28°15′S 48°44′W
27 W9 **Imboden** Arkansas, C USA 36°12′N 91°10′W
**Imbros** see Gökçeada
**Imeni 26 Bakinskikh Komissarov** see Uzboý
125 N13 **Imeni Babushkina** Vologodskaya Oblast', NW Russia 59°40′N 43°04′E
126 J7 **Imeni Karla Libknekhta** Kurskaya Oblast', W Russia 51°36′N 35°28′E
**Imeni Mollanepesa** see Mollanepes Adyndaky
**Imeni S. A. Niyazova** see S. A.Nyýazow Adyndaky
**Imeni Sverdlova Rudnik** see Dovzhans'k
188 E9 **Imeong** Babeldaob, N Palau
81 L14 **Īmī** Sumalē, E Ethiopia 06°27′N 42°10′E
115 M21 **Imia** Turk. Kardak. island Dodekánisa, Greece, Aegean Sea
**Imishli** see İmişli
137 X12 **İmişli** Rus. Imishli. C Azerbaijan 39°54′N 48°04′E
163 X14 **Imjin-gang** 🌊 North Korea/South Korea
35 S3 **Imlay** Nevada, W USA 40°39′N 118°10′W
31 S9 **Imlay City** Michigan, N USA 43°01′N 83°04′W
23 X15 **Immokalee** Florida, SE USA 26°24′N 81°25′W
77 U17 **Imo** ◆ state SE Nigeria
106 G10 **Imola** Emilia-Romagna, N Italy 44°22′N 11°43′E
186 A5 **Imonda** West Sepik, NW Papua New Guinea 03°21′S 141°10′E
**Imoschi** see Imotski
113 G14 **Imotski** It. Imoschi. Split-Dalmacija, SE Croatia 43°28′N 17°13′E
59 L14 **Imperatriz** Maranhão, NE Brazil 05°32′S 47°28′W
106 B10 **Imperia** Liguria, NW Italy 43°53′N 08°03′E
57 E15 **Imperial** Lima, W Peru 13°04′S 76°21′W
35 X17 **Imperial** California, W USA 32°51′N 115°34′W
28 L16 **Imperial** Nebraska, C USA 40°30′N 101°37′W
24 M9 **Imperial** Texas, SW USA 31°15′N 102°40′W
35 Y17 **Imperial Dam** dam California, W USA
79 I17 **Impfondo** Likouala, NE Congo 01°37′N 18°04′E
153 X14 **Imphāl** state capital Manipur, NE India 24°47′N 93°55′E
103 P9 **Imphy** Nièvre, C France 46°55′N 03°16′E
106 G11 **Impruneta** Toscana, C Italy 43°42′N 11°16′E
115 K15 **İmroz** var. Gökçeada. Çanakkale, NW Turkey 40°06′N 25°50′E
**Imroz Adası** see Gökçeada
108 L7 **Imst** Tirol, W Austria 47°14′N 10°45′E
40 F3 **Imuris** Sonora, NW Mexico 30°48′N 110°52′W
164 M13 **Ina** Nagano, Honshū, S Japan 35°52′N 137°58′E
65 M18 **Inaccessible Island** island W Tristan da Cunha
115 F20 **Ínachos** 🌊 S Greece
188 H6 **I Naftan, Puntan** headland Saipan, S Northern Mariana Islands
**Inagua Islands** see Great Inagua
**Inagua Islands** see Little Inagua
185 H15 **Inangahua** West Coast, South Island, New Zealand 41°51′S 171°58′E
57 I14 **Iñapari** Madre de Dios, E Peru 11°00′S 69°34′W
188 B17 **Inarajan** SE Guam 13°16′N 144°45′E
92 L10 **Inari** N. Sami. Anár, Inari Sami Aanaar. Lappi, N Finland 68°54′N 27°06′E
92 L10 **Inarijärvi** Lapp. Aanaarjävri, Swe. Enareträsk. ◎ N Finland
92 L9 **Inarijoki** Lapp. Anárjohka. 🌊 Finland/Norway
**Ināu** see Ineu
165 P11 **Inawashiro-ko** var. Inawasiro Ko. ◎ Honshū, C Japan
**Inawasiro Ko** see Inawashiro-ko
105 X9 **Inca** Mallorca, Spain, W Mediterranean Sea 39°43′N 02°54′E
62 H7 **Inca de Oro** Atacama, N Chile 26°45′S 69°54′W
115 J15 **İnce Burnu** cape NW Turkey
136 K9 **İnce Burnu** headland N Turkey 42°06′N 34°57′E
136 I17 **İncekum Burnu** headland S Turkey 36°13′N 33°57′E
163 X15 **Incheon** , Jap. Jinsen; prev. Chemulpo, Inch'ŏn. NW South Korea 37°27′N 126°41′E
161 X15 **Incheon** ✈ (Seoul) NW South Korea 37°37′N 126°42′E
76 G7 **Inchiri** ◆ region NW Mauritania
**Inch'ŏn** see Incheon
83 M17 **Inchope** Manica, C Mozambique 19°09′S 33°54′E
**Incoronata** see Kornat
103 Y15 **Incudine, Monte** ▲ Corse, France, C Mediterranean Sea 41°52′N 09°13′E
60 M10 **Indaiatuba** São Paulo, S Brazil 23°03′S 47°14′W
93 H17 **Indal** Västernorrland, C Sweden 62°36′N 17°06′E
93 H17 **Indalsälven** 🌊 C Sweden
40 K8 **Inde** Durango, C Mexico 25°55′N 105°10′W
**Indefatigable Island** see Santa Cruz, Isla
35 S10 **Independence** California, W USA 36°48′N 118°14′W
29 X13 **Independence** Iowa, C USA 42°28′N 91°42′W
27 P7 **Independence** Kansas, C USA 37°13′N 95°43′W
20 M4 **Independence** Kentucky, S USA 38°56′N 84°32′W
27 R4 **Independence** Missouri, C USA 39°04′N 94°27′W
21 R8 **Independence** Virginia, NE USA 36°38′N 81°11′W
30 J7 **Independence** Wisconsin, N USA 44°21′N 91°25′W
197 R12 **Independence Fjord** fjord N Greenland
**Independence Island** see Malden Island
35 W2 **Independence Mountains** ▲ Nevada, W USA
57 K18 **Independencia** Cochabamba, C Bolivia 17°08′S 66°52′W
57 E16 **Independencia, Bahía de la** bay W Peru
**Independencia, Monte** see Adam, Mount
116 M12 **Independenţa** Galaţi, SE Romania 45°29′N 27°45′E
**Inderagiri** see Indragiri, Sungai
144 F11 **Inderbor** prev. Inderborskiy. Atyrau, W Kazakhstan 48°35′N 51°45′E
**Inderborskiy** see Inderbor
151 I14 **India** off. Republic of India, var. Indian Union, Union of India, Hind. Bhārat. ◆ republic S Asia
**India** see Indija
18 D14 **Indiana** Pennsylvania, NE USA 40°37′N 79°09′W
31 N13 **Indiana** off. State of Indiana, also known as Hoosier State. ◆ state N USA
31 O14 **Indianapolis** state capital Indiana, N USA 39°46′N 86°09′W


◆ Country
● Country Capital
◇ Dependent Territory
○ Dependent Territory Capital
◈ Administrative Regions
✈ International Airport
▲ Mountain
▲ Mountain Range
⛰ Volcano
🌊 River
◎ Lake
⊠ Reservoir

INDIAN CABINS – ITAITUBA


11 O10 **Indian Cabins** Alberta, W Canada 59°51´N 117°06´W
42 G1 **Indian Church** Orange Walk, N Belize 17°47´N 88°39´W
**Indian Desert** *see* Thar Desert
11 U16 **Indian Head** Saskatchewan, S Canada 50°32´N 103°41´W
31 O4 **Indian Lake** ⊛ Michigan, N USA
18 K9 **Indian Lake** ⊛ New York, NE USA
31 R13 **Indian Lake** ⊠ Ohio, N USA
172-173 **Indian Ocean** *ocean*
29 V15 **Indianola** Iowa, C USA 41°21´N 93°33´W
22 K4 **Indianola** Mississippi, S USA 33°27´N 90°39´W
36 J6 **Indian Peak** ▲ Utah, W USA 38°18´N 113°52´W
23 Y13 **Indian River** *lagoon* Florida, SE USA
35 W10 **Indian Springs** Nevada, W USA 36°33´N 115°40´W
23 Y14 **Indiantown** Florida, SE USA 27°01´N 80°29´W
**Indian Union** *see* India
59 K19 **Indiara** Goiás, S Brazil 17°12´S 50°09´W
**India, Republic of** *see* India
**India, Union of** *see* India
125 Q4 **Indiga** Nenetskiy Avtonomnyy Okrug, NW Russia 67°40´N 49°01´E
123 R9 **Indigirka** ≋ NE Russia
112 L10 **Inđija** *Hung.* India; *prev.* Indjija. Vojvodina, N Serbia 45°03´N 20°04´E
35 V16 **Indio** California, W USA 33°42´N 116°13´W
42 M12 **Indio, Río** ≋ SE Nicaragua
152 I10 **Indira Gandhi** ✈ (Delhi) Delhi, N India
151 Q23 **Indira Point** *headland* Andaman and Nicobar Island, India, NE Indian Ocean 6°54´N 93°54´E
**Indjija** *see* Inđija
129 Q13 **Indo-Australian Plate** *tectonic feature*
173 N11 **Indomed Fracture Zone** *tectonic feature* SW Indian Ocean
170 L12 **Indonesia** *off.* Republic of Indonesia, *Ind.* Republik Indonesia; *prev.* Dutch East Indies, Netherlands East Indies, United States of Indonesia. ◆ *republic* SE Asia
**Indonesian Borneo** *see* Kalimantan
**Indonesia, Republic of** *see* Indonesia
**Indonesia, Republik** *see* Indonesia
**Indonesia, United States of** *see* Indonesia
154 G10 **Indore** Madhya Pradesh, C India 22°42´N 75°51´E
168 L11 **Indragiri, Sungai** *var.* Batang Kuantan, Inderagiri. ≋ Sumatera, W Indonesia
**Indramajoe/Indramaju** *see* Indramayu
169 P15 **Indramayu** *prev.* Indramajoe, Indramaju. Jawa, C Indonesia 06°22´S 108°20´E
155 K14 **Indrāvati** ≋ S India
103 N9 **Indre** ◐ *department* C France
102 M8 **Indre** ≋ C France
94 D13 **Indre Ålvik** Hordaland, S Norway 60°26´N 06°27´E
102 L8 **Indre-et-Loire** ◐ *department* C France
**Indreville** *see* Châteauroux
152 G3 **Indus** *Chin.* Yindu He; *prev.* Yin-tu Ho. ≋ S Asia
**Indus Cone** *see* Indus Fan
173 P3 **Indus Fan** *var.* Indus Cone. *undersea feature* N Arabian Sea 16°00´N 66°30´E
149 P17 **Indus, Mouths of the** *delta* S Pakistan
83 I24 **Indwe** Eastern Cape, SE South Africa 31°28´S 27°20´E
136 I10 **İnebolu** Kastamonu, N Turkey 41°57´N 33°45´E
77 P8 **I-n-Échaï** *oasis* C Mali
114 M13 **İnecik** Tekirdağ, NW Turkey 40°55´N 27°16´E
136 E12 **İnegöl** Bursa, NW Turkey 40°06´N 29°31´E
**Inessa** *see* Biancavilla
116 F10 **Ineu** *Hung.* Borosjenő; *prev.* Inău. Arad, W Romania 46°26´N 21°51´E
**Ineul/Ineu, Vîrful** *see* Ineu, Vârful
116 J9 **Ineu, Vârful** *var.* Ineul; *prev.* Vîrful Ineu. ▲ N Romania 47°31´N 24°52´E
21 P6 **Inez** Kentucky, S USA 37°53´N 82°33´W
74 E8 **Inezgane** ✈ (Agadir) W Morocco 30°35´N 09°27´W
41 T17 **Inferior, Laguna** *lagoon* S Mexico
40 M15 **Infiernillo, Presa del** ⊠ S Mexico
**Infiesto** *see* L'Infiestu
93 L20 **Ingå** *Fin.* Inkoo. Uusimaa, S Finland 60°01´N 24°05´E
77 U10 **Ingal** *var.* I-n-Gall. Agadez, C Niger 16°52´N 06°57´E
**I-n-Gall** *see* Ingal
99 C18 **Ingelmunster** West-Vlaanderen, W Belgium 50°12´N 03°15´E
79 I18 **Ingende** Equateur, W Dem. Rep. Congo 0°15´S 18°58´E
62 L5 **Ingeniero Guillermo Nueva Juárez** Formosa, N Argentina 23°55´S 61°50´W
63 H16 **Ingeniero Jacobacci** Río Negro, C Argentina 41°18´S 69°35´W
14 F16 **Ingersoll** Ontario, S Canada 43°03´N 80°53´W
**Ingettolgoy** *see* Selenge
181 W5 **Ingham** Queensland, NE Australia 18°35´S 146°12´E
146 M11 **Ingichka** Samarqand Viloyati, C Uzbekistan 39°46´N 65°56´E
97 L16 **Ingleborough** ▲ N England, United Kingdom 54°07´N 02°22´W
25 T14 **Ingleside** Texas, SW USA 27°52´N 97°12´W
184 K10 **Inglewood** Taranaki, North Island, New Zealand 39°07´S 174°13´E
35 S15 **Inglewood** California, W USA 33°57´N 118°21´W
101 L21 **Ingolstadt** Bayern, S Germany 48°46´N 11°26´E
33 V9 **Ingomar** Montana, NW USA 46°34´N 107°21´W
13 R14 **Ingonish Beach** Cape Breton Island, Nova Scotia, SE Canada 46°42´N 60°22´W
153 S14 **Ingrāj Bāzār** *prev.* English Bazar. West Bengal, NE India 25°00´N 88°10´E
25 Q11 **Ingram** Texas, SW USA 30°04´N 99°14´W
195 X7 **Ingrid Christensen Coast** *physical region* Antarctica
74 K14 **I-n-Guezzam** S Algeria 19°35´N 05°49´E
**Ingulets** *see* Inhulets'
**Inguri** *see* Enguri
**Ingushetia/Ingushetiya Respublika** *see* Ingushetiya, Respublika
127 O15 **Ingushetiya, Respublika** *var.* Respublika Ingushetiya, *Eng.* Ingushetia. ◐ *autonomous republic* SW Russia
83 N20 **Inhambane** Inhambane, SE Mozambique 23°52´S 35°31´E
83 M20 **Inhambane** *off.* Província de Inhambane. ◐ *province* S Mozambique
**Inhambane, Província de** *see* Inhambane
83 N17 **Inhaminga** Sofala, C Mozambique 18°24´S 35°00´E
83 N20 **Inharrime** Inhambane, SE Mozambique 24°29´S 35°01´E
83 M18 **Inhassoro** Inhambane, E Mozambique 21°32´S 35°13´E
117 S9 **Inhulets'** *Rus.* Ingulets. Dnipropetrovs'ka Oblast', E Ukraine 47°43´N 33°16´E
117 R10 **Inhulets'** *Rus.* Ingulets. ≋ S Ukraine
105 Q10 **Iniesta** Castilla-La Mancha, C Spain 39°27´N 01°45´W
**I-ning** *see* Yining
54 K11 **Inírida, Río** ≋ E Colombia
**Inis** *see* Ennis
**Inis Ceithleann** *see* Enniskillen
**Inis Córthaidh** *see* Enniscorthy
**Inis Díomáin** *see* Ennistimon
97 A17 **Inishbofin** *Ir.* Inis Bó Finne. *island* W Ireland
97 B18 **Inisheer** *var.* Inishere, *Ir.* Inis Oírr. *island* W Ireland
**Inishere** *see* Inisheer
97 B18 **Inishmaan** *Ir.* Inis Meáin. *island* W Ireland
97 A18 **Inishmore** *Ir.* Árainn. *island* W Ireland
96 E13 **Inishtrahull** *Ir.* Inis Trá Tholl. *island* NW Ireland
97 A17 **Inishturk** *Ir.* Inis Toirc. *island* W Ireland
**Inkoo** *see* Ingå
185 J16 **Inland Kaikoura Range** ▲▲ South Island, New Zealand
**Inland Sea** *see* Seto-naikai
21 P11 **Inman** South Carolina, SE USA 35°03´N 82°05´W
108 L7 **Inn** ≋ C Europe
197 O11 **Innaanganeq** *var.* Kap York. *headland* NW Greenland 75°54´N 66°27´W
182 K2 **Innamincka** South Australia 27°47´S 140°45´E
92 G12 **Inndyr** Nordland, C Norway 67°01´N 14°00´E
42 G3 **Inner Channel** *inlet* SE Belize
96 F11 **Inner Hebrides** *island group* W Scotland, United Kingdom
172 H15 **Inner Islands** *var.* Central Group. *island group* NE Seychelles
**Inner Mongolia/Inner Mongolian Autonomous Region** *see* Nei Mongol Zizhiqu
109 I7 **Inner Rhoden** *former canton* Appenzell. ◐ NW Switzerland
96 G8 **Inner Sound** *strait* NW Scotland, United Kingdom
100 J13 **Innerste** ≋ C Germany
181 W5 **Innisfail** Queensland, NE Australia 17°29´S 146°03´E
11 Q15 **Innisfail** Alberta, SW Canada 52°01´N 113°59´W
**Inniskilling** *see* Enniskillen
39 O11 **Innoko River** ≋ Alaska, USA
**Innsbruch** *see* Innsbruck
108 M7 **Innsbruck** *var.* Innsbruch. Tirol, W Austria 47°17´N 11°25´E
79 I19 **Inongo** Bandundu, W Dem. Rep. Congo 01°55´S 18°20´E
**Inoucdjouac** *see* Inukjuak
**Inowrazlaw** *see* Inowrocław
110 I10 **Inowrocław** *Ger.* Hohensalza; *prev.* Inowrazlaw. Kujawski-pomorskie, C Poland 52°47´N 18°15´E
57 K18 **Inquisivi** La Paz, W Bolivia 16°55´S 67°10´W
**Inrin** *see* Yunlin
77 O8 **I-n-Sâkâne, 'Erg** *desert* N Mali
74 J10 **I-n-Salah** *var.* In Salah. C Algeria 27°11´N 02°31´E
127 O5 **Insar** Respublika Mordoviya, W Russia 53°52´N 44°26´E
189 X15 **Insiaf** Kosrae, E Micronesia
94 L13 **Insjön** Dalarna, C Sweden 60°40´N 15°05´E
**Insterburg** *see* Chernyakhovsk
**Insula** *see* Lille
116 L13 **Însurăţei** Brăila, SE Romania 44°55´N 27°40´E
125 V6 **Inta** Respublika Komi, NW Russia 66°00´N 60°10´E
77 R9 **I-n-Tebezas** Kidal, E Mali 17°58´N 01°51´E
**Interamna** *see* Teramo
**Interamna Nahars** *see* Terni
28 L11 **Interior** South Dakota, N USA 43°42´N 101°57´W
108 E9 **Interlaken** Bern, SW Switzerland 46°41´N 07°51´E
29 V2 **International Falls** Minnesota, N USA 48°38´N 93°26´W
167 O7 **Inthanon, Doi** ▲ NW Thailand 18°33´N 98°29´E
42 G7 **Intibucá** ◐ *department* SW Honduras
42 G8 **Intipucá** La Unión, SE El Salvador 13°10´N 88°03´W
61 B15 **Intiyaco** Santa Fe, C Argentina 28°43´S 60°04´W
116 K12 **Întorsura Buzăului** *Ger.* Bozau, *Hung.* Bodzafordulő. Covasna, E Romania 45°40´N 26°02´E
22 H9 **Intracoastal Waterway** *inland waterway system* Louisiana, S USA
25 V13 **Intracoastal Waterway** *inland waterway system* Texas, SW USA
108 G11 **Intragna** Ticino, S Switzerland 46°12´N 08°42´E
165 P14 **Inubō-zaki** *headland* Honshū, S Japan 35°42´N 140°51´E
164 E14 **Inukai** Ōita, Kyūshū, SW Japan 33°05´N 131°37´E
12 I5 **Inukjuak** *var.* Inoucdjouac; *prev.* Port Harrison. Québec, NE Canada 58°28´N 77°58´W
63 I24 **Inútil, Bahía** *bay* S Chile
**Inuuvik** *see* Inuvik
11 R8 **Inuvik** *var.* Inuuvik. Northwest Territories, NW Canada 68°25´N 133°35´W
164 L13 **Inuyama** Aichi, Honshū, SW Japan 35°23´N 136°56´E
56 G13 **Inuya, Río** ≋ E Peru
125 U13 **In'va** ≋ NW Russia
96 H11 **Inveraray** W Scotland, United Kingdom 56°13´N 05°05´W
185 C24 **Invercargill** Southland, South Island, New Zealand 46°25´S 168°22´E
183 T5 **Inverell** New South Wales, SE Australia 29°46´S 151°10´E
96 I8 **Invergordon** N Scotland, United Kingdom 57°42´N 04°02´W
11 P16 **Invermere** British Columbia, SW Canada 50°30´N 116°00´W
13 R14 **Inverness** Cape Breton Island, Nova Scotia, SE Canada 46°14´N 61°19´W
96 I8 **Inverness** N Scotland, United Kingdom 57°27´N 04°15´W
23 V11 **Inverness** Florida, SE USA 28°50´N 82°19´W
96 I9 **Inverness** *cultural region* NW Scotland, United Kingdom
96 K9 **Inverurie** NE Scotland, United Kingdom 57°14´N 02°14´W
182 F8 **Investigator Group** *island group* South Australia
173 T7 **Investigator Ridge** *undersea feature* E Indian Ocean 11°30´S 98°10´E
182 H10 **Investigator Strait** *strait* South Australia
29 R11 **Inwood** Iowa, C USA 43°16´N 96°25´W
123 S10 **Inya** ≋ E Russia
**Inyanga** *see* Nyanga
83 J17 **Inyathi** Matabeleland North, SW Zimbabwe 19°39´S 28°54´E
35 T12 **Inyokern** California, W USA 35°37´N 117°48´W
35 T10 **Inyo Mountains** ▲▲ California, W USA
127 P6 **Inza** Ul'yanovskaya Oblast', W Russia 53°51´N 46°21´E
127 W5 **Inzer** Respublika Bashkortostan, W Russia 54°11´N 57°37´E
127 N7 **Inzhavino** Tambovskaya Oblast', W Russia 52°18´N 42°28´E
115 C16 **Ioánnina** *var.* Janina, Yannina. Ípeiros, W Greece 39°39´N 20°52´E
164 B17 **Iō-jima** *var.* Iwojima. *island* Nansei-shotō, SW Japan
124 L4 **Iokan'ga** ≋ NW Russia
27 Q6 **Iola** Kansas, C USA 37°55´N 95°24´W
**Iolcus** *see* Iolkós
115 G16 **Iolkós** *anc.* Iolcus. *site of ancient city* Thessalía, C Greece
**Iolotan'** *see* Ýolöten
83 A16 **Iona** Namibe, SW Angola 16°54´S 12°39´E
96 F11 **Iona** *island* W Scotland, United Kingdom
116 M15 **Ion Corvin** Constanţa, SE Romania 44°07´N 27°50´E
35 P7 **Ione** California, W USA 38°21´N 120°55´W
116 I13 **Ioneşti** Vâlcea, SW Romania 44°52´N 24°12´E
31 Q9 **Ionia** Michigan, N USA 42°59´N 85°04´W
**Ionia Basin** *see* Ionian Basin
121 O10 **Ionian Basin** *var.* Ionia Basin. *undersea feature* Ionian Sea, C Mediterranean Sea 36°00´N 20°00´E
115 B17 **Iónia Nisiá** *Eng.* Ionian Islands. ◐ *region* W Greece
115 B17 **Iónia Nisiá** *var.* Iónioi Nísoi, *Eng.* Ionian Islands. *island group* W Greece
**Ionian Islands** *see* Iónia Nisiá/Iónioi Nísoi
121 O10 **Ionian Sea** *Gk.* Iónio Pélagos, *It.* Mar Ionio. *sea* C Mediterranean Sea
**Iónioi Nísoi** *see* Iónia Nisiá
**Ionio, Mar/Iónio Pélagos** *see* Ionian Sea
**Iordan** *see* Yordon
137 U10 **Iori** *var.* Qabırrı. ≋ Azerbaijan/Georgia
**Iorrais, Ceann** *see* Erris Head
115 J22 **Íos** *var.* Nio. *island* Kykládes, Greece, Aegean Sea
**Íos** *see* Chóra
165 U15 **Io-Tori-shima** *prev.* Tori-shima. *island* Izu-shotō, SE Japan
22 G9 **Iowa** Louisiana, S USA 30°12´N 93°00´W
29 V13 **Iowa** *off.* State of Iowa, *also known as* Hawkeye State. ◐ *state* C USA
29 Y14 **Iowa City** Iowa, C USA 41°40´N 91°32´W
29 V13 **Iowa Falls** Iowa, C USA 42°31´N 93°15´W
25 R4 **Iowa Park** Texas, SW USA 33°57´N 98°40´W
29 Y14 **Iowa River** ≋ Iowa, C USA
119 M19 **Ipa** ≋ SE Belarus
59 N20 **Ipatinga** Minas Gerais, SE Brazil 19°32´S 42°30´W
127 N13 **Ipatovo** Stavropol'skiy Kray, SW Russia 45°40´N 42°51´E
115 C16 **Ípeiros** *Eng.* Epirus. ◐ *region* W Greece
111 J21 **Ipel'** *var.* Ipoly, *Ger.* Eipel. ≋ Hungary/Slovakia
54 C13 **Ipiales** Nariño, SW Colombia 0°52´N 77°38´W
189 V14 **Ipis** *atoll* Chuuk Islands, C Micronesia
59 A14 **Ipixuna** Amazonas, W Brazil 06°57´S 71°42´W
168 J8 **Ipoh** Perak, Peninsular Malaysia 04°36´N 101°02´E
**Ipoly** *see* Ipel'
187 S15 **Ipota** Erromango, S Vanuatu 18°54´S 169°19´E
79 K14 **Ippy** Ouaka, C Central African Republic 06°17´N 21°13´E
114 L13 **İpsala** Edirne, NW Turkey 40°56´N 26°23´E
**Ipsario** *see* Ypsário
183 V3 **Ipswich** Queensland, E Australia 27°28´S 152°40´E
97 Q20 **Ipswich** *hist.* Gipeswic. E England, United Kingdom 52°05´N 01°08´E
29 O8 **Ipswich** South Dakota, N USA 45°24´N 99°00´W
**Iput'** *see* Iputs'
119 P18 **Iputs'** *Rus.* Iput'. ≋ Belarus/Russia
9 R7 **Iqaluit** *prev.* Frobisher Bay. *province capital* Baffin Island, Nunavut, NE Canada 63°44´N 68°28´W
**Iqlid** *see* Eqlīd
62 G3 **Iquique** Tarapacá, N Chile 20°15´S 70°08´W
56 G8 **Iquitos** Loreto, N Peru 03°51´S 73°13´W
25 N9 **Iraan** Texas, SW USA 30°52´N 101°52´W
79 K14 **Ira Banda** Haute-Kotto, E Central African Republic 05°57´N 22°05´E
165 P16 **Irabu-jima** *island* Miyako-shotō, SW Japan
55 Y9 **Iracoubo** N French Guiana 05°28´N 53°15´W
60 H13 **Iraí** Rio Grande do Sul, S Brazil 27°15´S 53°17´W
114 G12 **Irákleia** Kentrikí Makedonía, N Greece 41°09´N 23°16´E
115 J21 **Irákleia** *island* Kykládes, Greece, Aegean Sea
115 J25 **Irákleio** *var.* Herakleion, *Eng.* Candia; *prev.* Iráklion. Kríti, Greece, E Mediterranean Sea 35°20´N 25°08´E
115 F15 **Irákleio** *anc.* Heracleum. *castle* Kentrikí Makedonía, N Greece
115 J25 **Irákleio** ✈ Kríti, Greece, E Mediterranean Sea 35°20´N 25°10´E
**Iráklion** *see* Irákleio
143 O7 **Iran** *off.* Islamic Republic of Iran, *Per.* Jomhūrī-ye Eslāmī-ye Īrān; *prev.* Persia. ◆ *republic* SW Asia
58 F13 **Iranduba** Amazonas, NW Brazil 03°19´S 60°09´W
85 P13 **Iranian Plate** *tectonic feature*
143 Q9 **Iranian Plateau** *var.* Plateau of Iran. *plateau* N Iran
**Iran, Islamic Republic of** *see* Iran
**Īrān, Jomhūrī-ye Eslāmī-ye,** *see* Iran
**Iran Mountains** *see* Iran, Pegunungan
169 U9 **Iran, Pegunungan** *var.* Iran Mountains. ▲▲ Indonesia/Malaysia
**Iran, Plateau of** *see* Iranian Plateau
143 W13 **Īrānshahr** Sīstān va Balūchestān, SE Iran 27°14´N 60°40´E
55 P5 **Irapa** Sucre, NE Venezuela 10°37´N 62°35´W
41 N13 **Irapuato** Guanajuato, C Mexico 20°40´N 101°23´W
139 R7 **Iraq** *off.* Republic of Iraq, *Ar.* 'Irāq, Jumhūrīyat al 'Irāq. ◆ *republic* SW Asia
**'Irāq** *see* Iraq
**'Irāq, Jumhūrīyat al** *see* Iraq
**Iraq, Republic of** *see* Iraq
60 J12 **Irati** Paraná, S Brazil 25°25´S 50°38´W
105 R3 **Irati** ≋ N Spain
125 T8 **Irayël'** Respublika Komi, NW Russia 64°28´N 55°20´E
43 N13 **Irazú, Volcán** ⛰ C Costa Rica 09°57´N 83°52´W
**Irbenskiy Zaliv/Irbes Šaurums** *see* Irbe Strait
118 D7 **Irbe Strait** *Est.* Kura Kurk, *Latv.* Irbes Šaurums, Irbenskiy Zaliv; *prev. Est.* Irbe Väin. *strait* Estonia/Latvia
**Irbe Väin** *see* Irbe Strait
138 G9 **Irbid** Irbid, N Jordan 32°33´N 35°51´E
138 G9 **Irbid** *off.* Muḩāfaẓat Irbid. ◐ *governorate* N Jordan
**Irbid, Muḩāfaẓat** *see* Irbid
**Irbil** *see* Arbīl
**Irbīl** *see* Arbīl
109 S6 **Irdning** Steiermark, SE Austria 47°29´N 14°04´E
79 I18 **Irebu** Equateur, W Dem. Rep. Congo 0°32´S 17°44´E
97 D17 **Ireland** *Ir.* Éire. ◆ *republic* NW Europe
84 C9 **Ireland** *Lat.* Hibernia. *island* Ireland/United Kingdom
64 A12 **Ireland Island North** *island* W Bermuda
64 A12 **Ireland Island South** *island* W Bermuda
125 V15 **Iren'** ≋ NW Russia
185 A22 **Irene, Mount** ▲ South Island, New Zealand 45°04´S 167°24´E
**Irgalem** *see* Yirga 'Alem
**Irgiz** *see* Yrghyz
**Irian** *see* New Guinea
**Irian Barat** *see* Papua
**Irian Jaya** *see* Papua
**Irian Jaya Barat** *see* Papua Barat
**Irian, Teluk** *see* Cenderawasih, Teluk
78 K9 **Iriba** Wadi Fira, NE Chad 15°10´N 22°11´E
127 X7 **Iriklinskoye Vodokhranilishche** ⊠ W Russia
81 H23 **Iringa** Iringa, C Tanzania 07°49´S 35°39´E
81 H23 **Iringa** ◐ *region* S Tanzania
165 O16 **Iriomote-jima** *island* Sakishima-shotō, SW Japan
42 L4 **Iriona** Colón, NE Honduras 15°55´N 85°10´W
47 U7 **Iriri** ≋ N Brazil
58 I13 **Iriri, Rio** ≋ C Brazil
**Iris** *see* Yeşilırmak
35 W9 **Irish, Mount** ▲ Nevada, W USA 37°39´N 115°22´W
97 H17 **Irish Sea** *Ir.* Muir Éireann. *sea* C British Isles
139 U12 **Irjal ash Shaykhīyah** Al Muthanná, S Iraq 30°49´N 44°58´E
147 U11 **Irkeshtam** Oshskaya Oblast', SW Kyrgyzstan 39°39´N 73°49´E
122 M13 **Irkutsk** Irkutskaya Oblast', S Russia 52°18´N 104°15´E
122 M12 **Irkutskaya Oblast'** ◐ *province* S Russia
**Irlir, Gora** *see* Irlir Tog'i
146 K8 **Irlir Tog'i** *var.* Gora Irlir. ▲ N Uzbekistan 42°43´N 63°24´E
**Irminger Basin** *see* Reykjanes Basin
21 R12 **Irmo** South Carolina, SE USA 34°05´N 81°10´W
102 E6 **Iroise** *sea* NW France
189 X2 **Iroj** *var.* Eroj. *island* Ratak Chain, SE Marshall Islands
182 H7 **Iron Baron** South Australia 33°01´S 137°13´E
14 C10 **Iron Bridge** Ontario, S Canada 46°16´N 83°12´W
20 H10 **Iron City** Tennessee, S USA 35°01´N 87°34´W
14 I13 **Irondale** ≋ Ontario, SE Canada
182 H7 **Iron Knob** South Australia 32°46´S 137°08´E
30 M5 **Iron Mountain** Michigan, N USA 45°51´N 88°03´W
30 M4 **Iron River** Michigan, N USA 46°05´N 88°38´W
30 J3 **Iron River** Wisconsin, N USA 46°34´N 91°22´W
27 X6 **Ironton** Missouri, C USA 37°37´N 90°40´W
31 S15 **Ironton** Ohio, N USA 38°32´N 82°40´W
30 K4 **Ironwood** Michigan, N USA 46°27´N 90°10´W
12 H12 **Iroquois Falls** Ontario, S Canada 48°47´N 80°41´W
31 N12 **Iroquois River** ≋ Illinois/Indiana, N USA
164 M15 **Irō-zaki** *headland* Honshū, S Japan 34°36´N 138°49´E
**Irpen'** *see* Irpin'
117 O4 **Irpin'** *Rus.* Irpen'. Kyivs'ka Oblast', N Ukraine 50°31´N 30°16´E
117 O4 **Irpin'** *Rus.* Irpen'. ≋ N Ukraine
141 Q16 **'Irqah** SW Yemen 13°42´N 47°21´E
**Irrawaddy** *see* Ayeyarwady
**Irrawaddy** *see* Ayeyarwady
**Irrawaddy, Mouths of the** *see* Ayeyarwady, Mouths of the
117 N4 **Irsha** ≋ N Ukraine
116 H7 **Irshava** Zakarpats'ka Oblast', W Ukraine 48°19´N 23°03´E
107 N18 **Irsina** Basilicata, S Italy 40°42´N 16°18´E
**Irtish** *see* Yertis
**Irtysh** *see* Yertis
**Irtyshsk** *see* Yertis
79 P17 **Irumu** Orientale, E Dem. Rep. Congo 01°27´N 29°52´E
105 Q2 **Irun** *Cast.* Irún. País Vasco, N Spain 43°20´N 01°48´W
**Irún** *see* Irun
**Iruña** *see* Pamplona
105 Q3 **Irurtzun** Navarra, N Spain 42°55´N 01°50´W
96 I13 **Irvine** W Scotland, United Kingdom 55°37´N 04°40´W
21 N6 **Irvine** Kentucky, S USA 37°42´N 83°59´W
25 T6 **Irving** Texas, SW USA 32°47´N 96°57´W
20 K5 **Irvington** Kentucky, S USA 37°52´N 86°16´W
164 C15 **Isa** *prev.* Ōkuchi, Ôkuti. Kagoshima, Kyūshū, SW Japan 32°04´N 130°36´E
**Isaak** *see* Iisaku
28 L8 **Isabel** South Dakota, N USA 45°21´N 101°25´W
186 L8 **Isabel** *off.* Isabel Province. ◐ *province* N Solomon Islands
171 O8 **Isabela** Basilan Island, SW Philippines 06°41´N 122°00´E
45 S5 **Isabela** W Puerto Rico 18°30´N 67°02´W
45 N8 **Isabela, Cabo** *headland* NW Dominican Republic 19°54´N 71°03´W
57 A18 **Isabela, Isla** *var.* Albemarle Island. *island* Galapagos Islands, Ecuador, E Pacific Ocean
40 I12 **Isabela, Isla** *island* C Mexico
42 K9 **Isabella, Cordillera** ▲▲ NW Nicaragua
35 S12 **Isabella Lake** ⊠ California, W USA
31 N2 **Isabelle, Point** *headland* Michigan, N USA 47°20´N 87°56´W
**Isabel Province** *see* Isabel
**Isabel Segunda** *see* Vieques
116 M13 **Isaccea** Tulcea, E Romania 45°16´N 28°28´E
92 H1 **Ísafjarðardjúp** *inlet* NW Iceland
92 H1 **Ísafjarðardjúp** *inlet* NW Iceland
92 H1 **Ísafjörður** Vestfirðir, NW Iceland 66°04´N 23°09´W
164 C14 **Isahaya** Nagasaki, Kyūshū, SW Japan 32°51´N 130°02´E
149 S7 **Isa Khel** Punjab, E Pakistan 32°39´N 71°20´E
172 H7 **Isalo** *var.* Massif de L'Isalo. ▲▲ SW Madagascar
79 K20 **Isandja** Kasai-Occidental, C Dem. Rep. Congo 03°03´S 21°57´E
187 R15 **Isangel** Tanna, S Vanuatu 19°34´S 169°17´E
79 M18 **Isangi** Orientale, C Dem. Rep. Congo 0°46´N 24°15´E
101 L24 **Isar** ≋ Austria/Germany
101 M23 **Isar-Kanal** *canal* SE Germany
**Isbarta** *see* İsparta
**Isca Damnoniorum** *see* Exeter
107 K18 **Ischia** *var.* Isola d'Ischia; *anc.* Aenaria. Campania, S Italy 40°44´N 13°57´E
107 J18 **Ischia, Isola d'** *island* S Italy
54 B12 **Iscuandé** *var.* Santa Bárbara. Nariño, SW Colombia 02°32´N 78°00´W
164 K14 **Ise** Mie, Honshū, SW Japan 34°29´N 136°43´E
100 J12 **Ise** ≋ N Germany
95 I23 **Isefjord** *fjord* E Denmark
**Iseghem** *see* Izegem
192 M14 **Iselin Seamount** *undersea feature* S Pacific Ocean 72°30´S 179°00´W
**Isenhof** *see* Püssi
106 E7 **Iseo** Lombardia, N Italy 45°40´N 10°03´E
103 U12 **Iseran, Col de l'** *pass* E France
103 S11 **Isère** ◐ *department* E France
103 S12 **Isère** ≋ E France
101 F15 **Iserlohn** Nordrhein-Westfalen, W Germany 51°23´N 07°42´E
107 K16 **Isernia** *var.* Æsernia. Molise, C Italy 41°35´N 14°14´E
165 N12 **Isesaki** Gunma, Honshū, S Japan 36°19´N 139°11´E
129 Q5 **Iset'** ≋ C Russia
77 S15 **Iseyin** Oyo, W Nigeria 07°56´N 03°33´E
**Isfahan** *see* Eşfahān
147 Q11 **Isfana** Batkenskaya Oblast', SW Kyrgyzstan 39°51´N 69°31´E
147 R11 **Isfara** N Tajikistan 40°06´N 70°34´E
149 O4 **Isfi Maidān** Ghōr, N Afghanistan 35°09´N 66°16´E
92 O3 **Isfjorden** *fjord* W Svalbard
**Isgender** *see* Kul'mach
**Isha Baydhabo** *see* Baydhabo
125 V11 **Isherim, Gora** ▲ NW Russia 61°06´N 59°09´E
127 Q5 **Isheyevka** Ul'yanovskaya Oblast', W Russia 54°27´N 48°18´E
165 P16 **Ishigaki** Okinawa, Ishigaki-jima, SW Japan 24°20´N 124°09´E
165 P16 **Ishigaki-jima** *island* Sakishima-shotō, SW Japan
165 R3 **Ishikari-wan** *bay* Hokkaidō, NE Japan
165 S16 **Ishikawa** *var.* Isikawa. Okinawa, Okinawa, SW Japan 26°25´N 127°47´E
164 K11 **Ishikawa** *off.* Ishikawa-ken, *var.* Isikawa. ◐ *prefecture* Honshū, SW Japan
**Ishikawa-ken** *see* Ishikawa
122 H11 **Ishim** Tyumenskaya Oblast', C Russia 56°13´N 69°25´E
127 V6 **Ishimbay** Respublika Bashkortostan, W Russia 53°21´N 56°03´E
145 O9 **Ishimskoye** Akmola, C Kazakhstan 51°23´N 67°07´E
165 Q10 **Ishinomaki** *var.* Isinomaki. Miyagi, Honshū, C Japan 38°26´N 141°17´E
165 P13 **Ishioka** *var.* Isioka. Ibaraki, Honshū, S Japan 36°11´N 140°16´E
149 Q3 **Ishkamish** *prev.* Eshkamesh. Takhār, NE Afghanistan 36°25´N 69°11´E
149 T2 **Ishkāshim** *prev.* Eshkāshem. Badakhshān, NE Afghanistan 36°43´N 71°34´E
**Ishkashim** *see* Ishkoshim
**Ishkashimskiy Khrebet** *see* Ishkoshim, Qatorkŭhi
147 S15 **Ishkoshim** *Rus.* Ishkashim. S Tajikistan 36°46´N 71°35´E
147 S15 **Ishkoshim, Qatorkŭhi** *Rus.* Ishkashimskiy Khrebet. ▲▲ SE Tajikistan
31 N4 **Ishpeming** Michigan, N USA 46°29´N 87°40´W
147 N11 **Ishtixon** *Rus.* Ishtykhan. Samarqand Viloyati, C Uzbekistan 39°59´N 66°28´E
**Ishtykhan** *see* Ishtixon
**Ishurdi** *see* Iswardi
61 G17 **Isidoro Noblia** Cerro Largo, NE Uruguay 31°58´S 54°09´W
102 J4 **Isigny-sur-Mer** Calvados, N France 49°20´N 01°06´W
**Isikawa** *see* Ishikawa
136 C11 **Işıklar Dağı** ▲▲ NW Turkey
107 C19 **Isili** Sardegna, Italy, C Mediterranean Sea 39°46´N 09°06´E
122 H12 **Isil'kul'** Omskaya Oblast', C Russia 54°52´N 71°07´E
**Isinomaki** *see* Ishinomaki
**Isioka** *see* Ishioka
81 I18 **Isiolo** Isiolo, C Kenya 0°20´N 37°36´E
79 O16 **Isiro** Orientale, NE Dem. Rep. Congo 02°51´N 27°47´E
92 P2 **Isispynten** *headland* NE Svalbard 79°51´N 26°44´E
123 P11 **Isit** Respublika Sakha (Yakutiya), NE Russia 60°53´N 125°32´E
149 O2 **Iskabad Canal** *canal* N Afghanistan
147 Q9 **Iskandar** *Rus.* Iskander. Toshkent Viloyati, E Uzbekistan 41°32´N 69°46´E
**Iskander** *see* Iskandar
114 G10 **Iskar** *var.* Iskăr, Iskŭr. ≋ NW Bulgaria
**Iskăr** *see* Iskar
114 H10 **Iskar, Yazovir** *var.* Yazovir Iskŭr; *prev.* Yazovir Stalin. ⊠ W Bulgaria
121 Q2 **İskele** *Gk.* Tríkomo. E Cyprus 35°16´N 33°54´E
136 K17 **İskenderun** *Eng.* Alexandretta. Hatay, S Turkey 36°34´N 36°10´E
138 H2 **İskenderun Körfezi** *Eng.* Gulf of Alexandretta. *gulf* S Turkey
136 J11 **İskilip** Çorum, N Turkey 40°45´N 34°28´E
**Iski-Nauket** *see* Nookat
114 J11 **Iskra** *prev.* Popovo. Haskovo, S Bulgaria 41°55´N 25°12´E
**Iskŭr** *see* Iskar
**Iskŭr, Yazovir** *see* Iskar, Yazovir
41 S15 **Isla** Veracruz, SE Mexico 18°01´N 95°30´W
119 J15 **Islach** *Rus.* Isloch'. ≋ C Belarus
104 H14 **Isla Cristina** Andalucía, S Spain 37°12´N 07°20´W
**Isla de León** *see* San Fernando
149 U6 **Islamabad** ● (Pakistan) Federal Capital Territory Islamabad, NE Pakistan 33°40´N 73°08´E
149 V6 **Islamabad** ✈ Federal Capital Territory Islamabad, NE Pakistan 33°40´N 73°08´E
**Islamabad** *see* Anantnāg
149 R17 **Islamkot** Sindh, SE Pakistan 24°37´N 70°04´E
23 Y17 **Islamorada** Florida Keys, Florida, SE USA 24°55´N 80°37´W
153 P14 **Islāmpur** Bihār, N India 25°09´N 85°13´E
148 J4 **Islām Qal'ah** *var.* Eslām Qal'eh. Herāt, W Afghanistan 34°41´N 61°03´E
18 K16 **Island Beach** *spit* New Jersey, NE USA
19 S4 **Island Falls** Maine, NE USA 45°59´N 68°16´W
**Island/Ísland** *see* Iceland
182 H6 **Island Lagoon** ⊛ South Australia
11 Y13 **Island Lake** ⊛ Manitoba, C Canada
29 W5 **Island Lake Reservoir** ⊠ Minnesota, N USA
33 R13 **Island Park** Idaho, NW USA 44°27´N 111°21´W
19 N6 **Island Pond** Vermont, NE USA 44°48´N 71°51´W
184 K2 **Islands, Bay of** *inlet* North Island, New Zealand
103 R7 **Is-sur-Tille** Côte d'Or, C France 47°34´N 05°03´E
42 J3 **Islas de la Bahía** ◐ *department* N Honduras
65 L20 **Islas Orcadas Rise** *undersea feature* S Atlantic Ocean
96 F12 **Islay** *island* SW Scotland, United Kingdom
116 I15 **Islaz** Teleorman, S Romania 43°44´N 24°45´E
29 V7 **Isle** Minnesota, N USA 46°08´N 93°28´W
102 M12 **Isle** ≋ W France
97 I16 **Isle of Man** ◇ *British Crown Dependency* NW Europe
97 I16 **Isle of Man** *island* NW Europe
21 X7 **Isle of Wight** Virginia, NE USA 36°54´N 76°41´W
97 M24 **Isle of Wight** *cultural region* S England, United Kingdom
191 Y3 **Isles Lagoon** ⊛ Kiritimati, E Kiribati
37 R11 **Isleta Pueblo** New Mexico, SW USA 34°54´N 106°40´W
**Isloch'** *see* Islach
117 U13 **Islyam-Terek** *prev.* Kirovs'ke. Avtonomna Respublika Krym, S Ukraine 45°13´N 35°12´E
61 E19 **Ismael Cortinas** Flores, S Uruguay 33°57´S 57°05´W
**Ismailia** *see* Al Ismā'īlīya
**Ismâ'ilîya** *see* Al Ismā'īlīya
**Ismailly** *see* İsmayıllı
137 X11 **İsmayıllı** *Rus.* Ismailly. N Azerbaijan 40°47´N 48°09´E
**Ismid** *see* İzmit
147 S12 **Ismoili Somoní, Qullai** *prev.* Qullai Kommunizm. ▲ E Tajikistan
75 X10 **Isnā** *var.* Esna. SE Egypt 25°16´N 32°30´E
93 K18 **Isojoki** Etelä-Pohjanmaa, W Finland 62°07´N 22°00´E
82 M12 **Isoka** Muchinga, NE Zambia 10°08´S 32°43´E
**Isola d'Ischia** *see* Ischia
**Isola d'Istria** *see* Izola
**Isonzo** *see* Soča
15 U4 **Isoukustouc** ≋ Québec, SE Canada
136 F15 **İsparta** *var.* Isbarta. Isparta, SW Turkey 37°46´N 30°32´E
136 F15 **Isparta** *var.* Isbarta. ◐ *province* SW Turkey
114 M7 **Isperih** *var.* Isperikh; *prev.* Kemanlar. Razgrad, N Bulgaria 43°43´N 26°49´E
**Isperikh** *see* Isperih
107 L26 **Ispica** Sicilia, Italy, C Mediterranean Sea 36°47´N 14°55´E
148 J14 **Ispikan** Baluchistan, SW Pakistan 26°21´N 62°15´E
137 Q12 **İspir** Erzurum, NE Turkey 40°29´N 41°02´E
138 E12 **Israel** *off.* State of Israel, *var.* Medinat Israel, *Heb.* Yisra'el, Medinat Yisra'el. ◆ *republic* SW Asia
**Israel, State of** *see* Israel
**Issa** *see* Vis
55 S9 **Issano** C Guyana 05°49´N 59°28´W
76 M16 **Issia** SW Ivory Coast 06°33´N 06°33´W
**Issiq Köl** *see* Issyk-Kul', Ozero
103 P11 **Issoire** Puy-de-Dôme, C France 45°33´N 03°15´E
103 N9 **Issoudun** *anc.* Uxellodunum. Indre, C France 46°57´N 01°59´E
81 H22 **Issuna** Singida, C Tanzania 05°24´S 34°48´E
**Issyk** *see* Yesik
**Issyk-Kul'** *see* Balykchy
147 X7 **Issyk-Kul', Ozero** *var.* Issiq Köl, *Kyr.* Ysyk-Köl. ⊛ E Kyrgyzstan
147 X7 **Issyk-Kul'skaya Oblast'** *Kyr.* Ysyk-Köl Oblasty. ◐ *province* E Kyrgyzstan
149 Q7 **Īstādah-ye Muqur, Āb-e-** ⊛ SE Afghanistan
136 D11 **İstanbul** *Bul.* Tsarigrad, *Eng.* Istanbul, *prev.* Constantinople; *anc.* Byzantium. Istanbul, NW Turkey 41°02´N 28°57´E
114 P12 **İstanbul** ◐ *province* NW Turkey
114 P12 **İstanbul Boğazı** *var.* Bosporus Thracius, *Eng.* Bosphorus, Bosporus, *Turk.* Karadeniz Boğazi. *strait* NW Turkey
147 P11 **Istaravshan** *prev.* Ŭroteppa, *Rus.* Ura-Tyube. NW Tajikistan 39°55´N 68°57´E
**Istarska Županija** *see* Istra
115 G19 **Isthmía** Pelopónnisos, S Greece 37°55´N 23°02´E
115 G17 **Istiaía** Évvoia, C Greece 38°57´N 23°09´E
54 D9 **Istmina** Chocó, W Colombia 05°09´N 76°42´W
23 W13 **Istokpoga, Lake** ⊛ Florida, SE USA
112 A9 **Istra** *off.* Istarska Županija. ◐ *province* NW Croatia
112 I10 **Istra** *Eng.* Istria, *Ger.* Istrien. *cultural region* NW Croatia
103 R15 **Istres** Bouches-du-Rhône, SE France 43°30´N 04°59´E
**Istria/Istrien** *see* Istra
153 T15 **Iswardi** *var.* Ishurdi. Rajshahi, W Bangladesh 24°10´N 89°04´E
127 V7 **Isyangulovo** Respublika Bashkortostan, W Russia 52°10´N 56°38´E
62 O6 **Itá** Central, S Paraguay 25°29´S 57°21´W
59 O17 **Itaberaba** Bahia, E Brazil 12°34´S 40°21´W
59 M20 **Itabira** *prev.* Presidente Vargas. Minas Gerais, SE Brazil 19°39´S 43°14´W
59 O18 **Itabuna** Bahia, E Brazil 14°48´S 39°18´W
59 J18 **Itacaiu** Mato Grosso, S Brazil 14°49´S 51°21´W
58 G12 **Itacoatiara** Amazonas, N Brazil 03°06´S 58°22´W
54 D9 **Itagüí** Antioquia, W Colombia 06°12´N 75°40´W
60 D13 **Itá Ibaté** Corrientes, NE Argentina 27°27´S 57°24´W
60 G11 **Itaipú, Represa de** ⊠ Brazil/Paraguay
58 H13 **Itaituba** Pará, NE Brazil 04°15´S 55°56´W




◆ Country
● Country Capital
◇ Dependent Territory
○ Dependent Territory Capital
◐ Administrative Regions
✈ International Airport
▲ Mountain
▲▲ Mountain Range
⛰ Volcano
≋ River
⊛ Lake
⊠ Reservoir

ITAJAÍ – JÁSZBERÉNY


60 K13 **Itajaí** Santa Catarina, S Brazil 26°50′S 48°39′W
**Italia/Italiana, Republica/Italian Republic, The** *see* Italy
**Italian Somaliland** *see* Somalia
25 T7 **Italy** Texas, SW USA 32°10′N 96°52′W
106 G12 **Italy** *off.* The Italian Republic, *It.* Italia, Repubblica Italiana. ◆ *republic* S Europe
59 O19 **Itamaraju** Bahia, E Brazil 16°58′S 39°32′W
59 C14 **Itamarati** Amazonas, W Brazil 06°13′S 68°17′W
59 M19 **Itambé, Pico de** ▲ SE Brazil 18°23′S 43°21′W
164 J13 **Itami** ✈ (Ōsaka) Ōsaka, Honshū, SW Japan 34°47′N 135°24′E
115 H15 **Ítamos** ▲ N Greece 40°06′N 23°51′E
153 W11 **Itānagar** *state capital* Arunāchal Pradesh, NE India 27°02′N 93°38′E
**Itany** *see* Litani
59 N19 **Itaobim** Minas Gerais, SE Brazil 16°34′S 41°27′W
59 P15 **Itaparica, Represa de** ⊠ E Brazil
58 M13 **Itapecuru-Mirim** Maranhão, E Brazil 03°24′S 44°20′W
60 Q8 **Itaperuna** Rio de Janeiro, SE Brazil 21°14′S 41°51′W
59 O18 **Itapetinga** Bahia, E Brazil 15°17′S 40°16′W
60 L10 **Itapetininga** São Paulo, S Brazil 23°36′S 48°07′W
60 K10 **Itapeva** São Paulo, S Brazil 23°58′S 48°54′W
47 W6 **Itapicuru, Rio** ≈ NE Brazil
58 O13 **Itapipoca** Ceará, E Brazil 03°29′S 39°35′W
60 M9 **Itapira** São Paulo, S Brazil 22°25′S 46°46′W
60 K8 **Itápolis** São Paulo, S Brazil 21°36′S 48°43′W
60 K10 **Itaporanga** São Paulo, S Brazil 23°43′S 49°28′W
62 P7 **Itapúa** *off.* Departamento de Itapúa. ⬖ *department* SE Paraguay
**Itapúa, Departamento de** *see* Itapúa
59 E15 **Itapuã do Oeste** Rondônia, W Brazil 09°21′S 63°07′W
61 E15 **Itaqui** Rio Grande do Sul, S Brazil 29°10′S 56°28′W
60 K10 **Itararé** São Paulo, S Brazil 24°07′S 49°16′W
60 K10 **Itararé, Rio** ≈ S Brazil
154 H11 **Itārsi** Madhya Pradesh, C India 22°39′N 77°48′E
25 T7 **Itasca** Texas, SW USA 32°09′N 97°09′W
**Itassi** *see* Vieille Case
60 D13 **Itatí** Corrientes, NE Argentina 27°16′S 58°15′W
60 K10 **Itatinga** São Paulo, S Brazil 23°08′S 48°36′W
115 F18 **Itéas, Kólpos** *gulf* C Greece
57 N15 **Iténez, Río** *var.* Río Guaporé. ≈ Bolivia/Brazil *see also* Río Guaporé
**Iténez, Río** *see* Guaporé, Rio
54 H11 **Iteviate, Río** ≈ C Colombia
100 I13 **Ith** *hill range* C Germany
31 Q8 **Ithaca** Michigan, N USA 43°17′N 84°36′W
18 H11 **Ithaca** New York, NE USA 42°26′N 76°30′W
115 C18 **Itháki** *island* Iónia Nísiá, Greece, C Mediterranean Sea
**Itháki** *see* Vathy
**It Hearrenfean** *see* Heerenveen
79 L17 **Itimbiri** ≈ N Dem. Rep. Congo
**Itinomiya** *see* Ichinomiya
**Itinoseki** *see* Ichinoseki
39 Q5 **Itkilik River** ≈ Alaska, USA
164 M11 **Itoigawa** Niigata, Honshū, C Japan 37°02′N 137°53′E
15 R6 **Itomamo, Lac** ◎ Québec, SE Canada
165 S17 **Itoman** Okinawa, SW Japan 26°05′N 127°40′E
102 M5 **Iton** ≈ N France
57 M16 **Itonamas Río** ≈ NE Bolivia
**Itoupé, Mont** *see* Sommet Tabulaire
**Itseqqortoormiit** *see* Ittoqqortoormiit
22 K4 **Itta Bena** Mississippi, S USA 33°30′N 90°19′W
107 B17 **Ittiri** Sardegna, Italy, C Mediterranean Sea 40°36′N 08°34′E
197 Q14 **Ittoqqortoormiit** *var.* Itseqqortoormiit, *Dan.* Scoresbysund, *Eng.* Scoresby Sound. Sermersooq, C Greenland 70°33′N 21°52′W
60 M10 **Itu** São Paulo, S Brazil 23°17′S 47°16′W
54 D8 **Ituango** Antioquia, NW Colombia 07°07′N 75°46′W
59 A14 **Ituí, Rio** ≈ NW Brazil
79 O20 **Itula** Sud-Kivu, E Dem. Rep. Congo 03°30′S 27°50′E
59 K19 **Itumbiara** Goiás, C Brazil 18°25′S 49°15′W
55 T9 **Ituni** E Guyana 05°24′N 58°18′W
41 X13 **Iturbide** Campeche, SE Mexico 19°41′N 89°29′W
**Ituri** *see* Aruwimi
123 V13 **Iturup, Ostrov** *island* Kuril'skiye Ostrova, SE Russia
60 L7 **Ituverava** São Paulo, S Brazil 20°22′S 47°48′W
59 C15 **Ituxi, Rio** ≈ W Brazil
61 E14 **Ituzaingó** Corrientes, NE Argentina 27°34′S 56°44′W
**Ītyop'iya** *see* Ethiopia
101 K18 **Itz** ≈ C Germany
100 I9 **Itzehoe** Schleswig-Holstein, N Germany 53°56′N 09°31′E
23 N2 **Iuka** Mississippi, S USA 34°48′N 88°11′W
60 I11 **Ivaiporã** Paraná, S Brazil 24°16′S 51°46′W
60 I11 **Ivaí, Rio** ≈ S Brazil
92 L10 **Ivalo** *Lapp.* Avveel, Avvil. Lappi, N Finland 68°34′N 27°29′E
92 L10 **Ivalojoki** *Lapp.* Avveel. ≈ N Finland
119 H20 **Ivanava** *Pol.* Janów, Janów Poleski, *Rus.* Ivanovo. Brestskaya Voblasts', SW Belarus 52°09′N 25°32′E
79 F18 **Ivando** *var.* Djidji. ≈ Congo/Gabon
**Ivangorod** *see* Dęblin
**Ivangrad** *see* Berane
183 N7 **Ivanhoe** New South Wales, SE Australia 32°55′S 144°21′E
29 S9 **Ivanhoe** Minnesota, N USA 44°27′N 96°15′W
14 D8 **Ivanhoe** ≈ Ontario, S Canada
112 E8 **Ivanić-Grad** Sisak-Moslavina, N Croatia 45°43′N 16°23′E
117 T10 **Ivanivka** Khersons'ka Oblast', S Ukraine 46°43′N 34°28′E
117 P10 **Ivanivka** Odes'ka Oblast', SW Ukraine 46°57′N 30°26′E
113 L14 **Ivanjica** Serbia, C Serbia 43°36′N 20°14′E
112 G11 **Ivanjska** *var.* Potkozarje. Republika Srpska, NW Bosnia and Herzegovina 44°54′N 17°04′E
111 H21 **Ivanka** ✈ (Bratislava) Bratislavský Kraj, W Slovakia 48°10′N 17°13′E
117 O3 **Ivankiv** *Rus.* Ivankov. Kyivs'ka Oblast', N Ukraine 50°55′N 29°53′E
**Ivankov** *see* Ivankiv
39 O15 **Ivanof Bay** Alaska, USA 55°55′N 159°28′W
116 J7 **Ivano-Frankivs'k** *Ger.* Stanislau, *Pol.* Stanisławów, *Rus.* Ivano-Frankovsk; *prev.* Stanislav. Ivano-Frankivs'ka Oblast', W Ukraine 48°55′N 24°45′E
**Ivano-Frankivs'k** *see* Ivano-Frankivs'ka Oblast'
116 I7 **Ivano-Frankivs'ka Oblast'** *var.* Ivano-Frankivs'k, *Rus.* Ivano-Frankovskaya Oblast'; *prev.* Stanislavskaya Oblast'. ⬖ *province* W Ukraine
**Ivano-Frankovsk** *see* Ivano-Frankivs'k
**Ivano-Frankovskaya Oblast'** *see* Ivano-Frankivs'ka Oblast'
124 M16 **Ivanovo** Ivanovskaya Oblast', W Russia 57°02′N 40°58′E
**Ivanovo** *see* Ivanava
124 M16 **Ivanovskaya Oblast'** ⬖ *province* W Russia
35 X12 **Ivanpah Lake** ◎ California, W USA
112 E7 **Ivanšćica** ▲▲ NE Croatia
127 R7 **Ivanteyevka** Saratovskaya Oblast', W Russia 52°13′N 49°06′E
**Ivantsevichi/Ivatsevichi** *see* Ivatsevichy
116 I4 **Ivanychi** Volyns'ka Oblast', NW Ukraine 50°37′N 24°22′E
119 H18 **Ivatsevichy** *Pol.* Iwacewicze, *Rus.* Ivantsevichi, Ivatsevichi. Brestskaya Voblasts', SW Belarus 52°43′N 25°21′E
114 L12 **Ivaylovgrad** Haskovo, S Bulgaria 41°32′N 26°06′E
114 K11 **Ivaylovgrad, Yazovir** ⊠ S Bulgaria
122 G9 **Ivdel'** Sverdlovskaya Oblast', C Russia 60°42′N 60°07′E
**Ivenets** *see* Ivyanyets
116 L12 **Ivești** Galați, E Romania 45°27′N 28°00′E
**Ivgovuotna** *see* Lyngen
**Ivigtut** *see* Ivittuut
79 F18 **Ivindo** ≈ Gabon
59 I21 **Ivinheima** Mato Grosso do Sul, SW Brazil 22°16′S 53°52′W
196 M15 **Ivittuut** *var.* Ivigtut. Sermersooq, S Greenland 61°12′N 48°10′W
**Iviza** *see* Eivissa/Ibiza
172 I6 **Ivohibe** Fianarantsoa, SE Madagascar 22°28′S 46°53′E
**Ivoire, Côte d'** *see* Ivory Coast
76 L15 **Ivory Coast** *off.* Republic of Côte d'Ivoire, *Fr.* Côte d'Ivoire, République de la Côte d'Ivoire. ◆ *republic* W Africa
68 C12 **Ivory Coast** *Fr.* Côte d'Ivoire. *coastal region* S Ivory Coast
95 L22 **Ivösjön** ◎ S Sweden
106 B7 **Ivrea** *anc.* Eporedia. Piemonte, NW Italy 45°28′N 07°52′E
12 J2 **Ivujivik** Québec, NE Canada 62°26′N 77°49′W
119 J16 **Ivyanyets** *Rus.* Ivenets. Minskaya Voblasts', C Belarus 53°53′N 26°45′E
**Iv'ye** *see* Iwye
**Iwacewicze** *see* Ivatsevichy
165 R8 **Iwaizumi** Iwate, Honshū, NE Japan 39°48′N 141°46′E
165 P12 **Iwaki** Fukushima, Honshū, N Japan 37°01′N 140°52′E
164 F13 **Iwakuni** Yamaguchi, Honshū, SW Japan 34°08′N 132°06′E
165 S4 **Iwamizawa** Hokkaidō, NE Japan 43°12′N 141°47′E
165 R4 **Iwanai** Hokkaidō, NE Japan 42°51′N 140°21′E
165 Q10 **Iwanuma** Miyagi, Honshū, C Japan 38°06′N 140°51′E
164 L14 **Iwata** Shizuoka, Honshū, S Japan 34°42′N 137°51′E
165 R8 **Iwate** Iwate, Honshū, N Japan 40°03′N 141°12′E
165 R8 **Iwate** *off.* Iwate-ken. ⬖ *prefecture* Honshū, C Japan
**Iwate-ken** *see* Iwate
77 S16 **Iwo** Oyo, SW Nigeria 07°21′N 03°58′E
**Iwojima** *see* Iō-jima
119 I16 **Iwye** *Pol.* Iwje, *Rus.* Iv'ye. Hrodzyenskaya Voblasts', W Belarus 53°56′N 25°46′E
42 C4 **Ixcán, Río** ≈ Guatemala/Mexico
99 G18 **Ixelles** *Dut.* Elsene. Brussels, C Belgium 50°49′N 04°21′E
57 J16 **Ixiamas** La Paz, NW Bolivia 13°45′S 68°10′W
41 O13 **Ixmiquilpan** *var.* Ixmiquilpán. Hidalgo, C Mexico 20°30′N 99°15′W
**Ixmiquilpán** *see* Ixmiquilpan
**Ixopo** *see* eXobho
**Ixtaccíhuatal, Volcán** *see* Iztaccíhuatl, Volcán
40 M16 **Ixtapa** Guerrero, S Mexico 17°38′N 101°29′W
41 S16 **Ixtepec** Oaxaca, SE Mexico 16°32′N 95°03′W
40 K12 **Ixtlán** *var.* Ixtlán del Río. Nayarit, C Mexico 21°02′N 104°21′W
**Ixtlán del Río** *see* Ixtlán
122 H11 **Iyevlevo** Tyumenskaya Oblast', C Russia 57°36′N 67°20′E
164 F14 **Iyo** Ehime, Shikoku, SW Japan 33°43′N 132°42′E
164 E14 **Iyo-nada** *sea* S Japan
42 E4 **Izabal** *off.* Departamento de Izabal. ⬖ *department* E Guatemala
**Izabal, Departamento de** *see* Izabal
42 F5 **Izabal, Lago de** *prev.* Golfo Dulce. ◎ E Guatemala
143 O9 **Īzad Khvāst** Fārs, C Iran 31°31′N 52°09′E
41 X12 **Izamal** Yucatán, SE Mexico 20°58′N 89°00′W
138 I2 **I'zāz** Ḥalab, NW Syria 36°35′N 37°03′E
127 Q16 **Izberbash** Respublika Dagestan, SW Russia 42°32′N 47°51′E
99 C18 **Izegem** *prev.* Iseghem. West-Vlaanderen, W Belgium 50°55′N 03°13′E
142 M9 **Īzeh** Khūzestān, SW Iran 31°48′N 49°49′E
165 T16 **Izena-jima** *island* Nansei-shotō, SW Japan
114 N10 **Izgrev** Burgas, E Bulgaria 42°09′N 27°49′E
127 T2 **Izhevsk** *prev.* Ustinov. Udmurtskaya Respublika, NW Russia 56°48′N 53°12′E
125 S7 **Izhma** Respublika Komi, NW Russia 64°56′N 53°52′E
125 S7 **Izhma** ≈ NW Russia
141 X8 **Izkī** NE Oman 22°45′N 57°36′E
**Izmail** *see* Izmayil
117 N13 **Izmayil** *Rus.* Izmail. Odes'ka Oblast', SW Ukraine 45°19′N 28°49′E
136 B14 **İzmir** *prev.* Smyrna. İzmir, W Turkey 38°25′N 27°10′E
136 C14 **İzmir** *prev.* Smyrna. ⬖ *province* W Turkey
136 E11 **İzmit** *var.* Ismid; *anc.* Astacus. Kocaeli, NW Turkey 40°47′N 29°55′E
104 M14 **Iznájar** Andalucía, S Spain 37°17′N 04°16′W
104 M14 **Iznajar, Embalse de** ⊠ S Spain
105 N14 **Iznalloz** Andalucía, S Spain 37°23′N 03°31′W
136 E11 **İznik** Bursa, NW Turkey 40°27′N 29°43′E
136 E12 **İznik Gölü** ◎ NW Turkey
126 M14 **Izobil'nyy** Stavropol'skiy Kray, SW Russia 45°22′N 41°40′E
109 S13 **Izola** *It.* Isola d'Istria. SW Slovenia 45°31′N 13°40′E
138 H9 **Izra'** *var.* Ezra, Ezraa. Dar'ā, S Syria 32°52′N 36°15′E
41 P14 **Iztaccíhuatl, Volcán** *var.* Volcán Ixtaccíhuatal. ⛰ S Mexico 19°07′N 98°37′W
42 C7 **Iztapa** Escuintla, SE Guatemala 13°58′N 90°42′W
**Izúcar de Matamoros** *see* Matamoros
165 N14 **Izu-hantō** *peninsula* Honshū, S Japan
**Izuhara** *see* Tsushima
164 J14 **Izumiōtsu** Ōsaka, Honshū, SW Japan 34°29′N 135°25′E
164 I14 **Izumisano** Ōsaka, Honshū, SW Japan 34°23′N 135°18′E
164 G12 **Izumo** Shimane, Honshū, SW Japan 35°22′N 132°46′E
192 H5 **Izu Trench** *undersea feature* NW Pacific Ocean
122 K6 **Izvestiy TsIK, Ostrova** *island* N Russia
114 G10 **Izvor** Pernik, W Bulgaria 42°27′N 22°53′E
116 L5 **Izyaslav** Khmel'nyts'ka Oblast', W Ukraine 50°08′N 26°53′E
117 W6 **Izyum** Kharkivs'ka Oblast', E Ukraine 49°12′N 37°19′E


# J


93 M18 **Jaala** Kymenlaakso, S Finland 61°04′N 26°30′E
140 J5 **Jabal ash Shifā** *desert* NW Saudi Arabia
141 U8 **Jabal az̧ Z̧annah** *var.* Jebel Dhanna. Abū Z̧aby, W United Arab Emirates 24°10′N 52°36′E
138 E11 **Jabalīya** *var.* Jabāliyah. NE Gaza Strip 31°32′N 34°29′E
**Jabāliyah** *see* Jabalīya
105 N11 **Jabalón** ≈ C Spain
154 J10 **Jabalpur** *prev.* Jubbulpore. Madhya Pradesh, C India 23°10′N 79°59′E
141 N15 **Jabal Zuqar, Jazīrat** *var.* Az Zuqur. *island* SW Yemen
**Jabar** *see* Jawa Barat
**Jabat** *see* Jabwot
138 J3 **Jabbūl, Sabkhat al** *sabkha* NW Syria
181 P1 **Jabiru** Northern Territory, N Australia 12°44′S 132°48′E
138 H4 **Jablah** *var.* Jeble, *Fr.* Djéblé. Al Lādhiqīyah, W Syria 35°00′N 36°00′E
112 C11 **Jablanac** Lika-Senj, W Croatia 44°43′N 14°54′E
113 H14 **Jablanica** Federacija Bosne I Hercegovine, SW Bosnia and Herzegovina 43°39′N 17°43′E
113 M20 **Jablanica** *Alb.* Mali i Jablanicës. *var.* Malet e Jablanicës. ▲ Albania/North Macedonia *see also* Jabllanicës, Mali i
**Jablanicës, Malet e** *see* Jablanica/Jabllanicës, Mali i
113 M20 **Jabllanicës, Mali i**, *Mac.* Jablanica. ▲ Albania/North Macedonia *see also* Jablanica
111 E15 **Jablonec nad Nisou** *Ger.* Gablonz an der Neisse. Liberecký Kraj, N Czechia 50°44′N 15°10′E
**Jabłonków/Jablunkau** *see* Jablunkov
110 J9 **Jabłonowo Pomorskie** Kujawski-pomorskie, C Poland 53°24′N 19°08′E
111 J17 **Jablunkov** *Ger.* Jablunkau, *Pol.* Jabłonków. Moravskoslezský Kraj, E Czechia 49°35′N 18°46′E
59 Q15 **Jaboatão** Pernambuco, E Brazil 08°05′S 35°W
60 L8 **Jaboticabal** São Paulo, S Brazil 21°15′S 48°17′W
189 U7 **Jabwot** *var.* Jabat, Jebat, Jōwat. *island* Ralik Chain, S Marshall Islands
105 S4 **Jaca** Aragón, NE Spain 42°34′N 00°33′W
42 B4 **Jacaltenango** Huehuetenango, W Guatemala 15°39′N 91°46′W
59 G14 **Jacaré-a-Canga** Pará, NE Brazil 05°59′S 57°32′W
60 N10 **Jacareí** São Paulo, S Brazil 23°18′S 45°55′W
59 I18 **Jaciara** Mato Grosso, W Brazil 15°59′S 54°57′W
59 E15 **Jaciparaná** Rondônia, W Brazil 09°20′S 64°28′W
19 P5 **Jackman** Maine, NE USA 45°35′N 70°14′W
35 X1 **Jackpot** Nevada, W USA 41°57′N 114°41′W
20 M8 **Jacksboro** Tennessee, S USA 36°19′N 84°11′W
25 S6 **Jacksboro** Texas, SW USA 33°13′N 98°11′W
23 N7 **Jackson** Alabama, S USA 31°30′N 87°53′W
35 P7 **Jackson** California, W USA 38°19′N 120°46′W
23 T4 **Jackson** Georgia, SE USA 33°17′N 83°58′W
21 O6 **Jackson** Kentucky, S USA 37°32′N 83°24′W
22 J8 **Jackson** Louisiana, S USA 30°50′N 91°13′W
31 Q10 **Jackson** Michigan, N USA 42°15′N 84°24′W
29 T11 **Jackson** Minnesota, N USA 43°38′N 95°00′W
22 K5 **Jackson** *state capital* Mississippi, S USA 32°19′N 90°12′W
27 Y7 **Jackson** Missouri, C USA 37°23′N 89°40′W
21 W8 **Jackson** North Carolina, SE USA 36°24′N 77°25′W
31 T15 **Jackson** Ohio, NE USA 39°03′N 82°40′W
20 G9 **Jackson** Tennessee, S USA 35°37′N 88°50′W
33 S14 **Jackson** Wyoming, C USA 43°28′N 110°45′W
185 C19 **Jackson Bay** *bay* South Island, New Zealand
186 E9 **Jackson Field** ✈ (Port Moresby) Central/National Capital District, S Papua New Guinea 09°28′S 147°12′E
185 C20 **Jackson Head** *headland* South Island, New Zealand 43°57′S 168°38′E
23 S8 **Jackson, Lake** ◎ Florida, SE USA
33 S13 **Jackson Lake** ◎ Wyoming, C USA
194 J6 **Jackson, Mount** ▲ Antarctica 71°43′S 63°45′W
37 U3 **Jackson Reservoir** ◎ Colorado, C USA
23 Q3 **Jacksonville** Alabama, S USA 33°48′N 85°45′W
27 V11 **Jacksonville** Arkansas, C USA 34°52′N 92°08′W
23 W8 **Jacksonville** Florida, SE USA 30°20′N 81°39′W
30 K14 **Jacksonville** Illinois, N USA 39°43′N 90°13′W
21 W11 **Jacksonville** North Carolina, SE USA 34°45′N 77°26′W
25 W7 **Jacksonville** Texas, SW USA 31°57′N 95°16′W
23 X9 **Jacksonville Beach** Florida, SE USA 30°17′N 81°23′W
44 L9 **Jacmel** *var.* Jaquemel. S Haiti 18°13′N 72°33′W
**Jacob** *see* Nkayi
149 Q12 **Jacobabad** Sindh, SE Pakistan 28°16′N 68°30′E
55 T11 **Jacobs Ladder Falls** *waterfall* S Guyana
45 O11 **Jaco, Pointe** *headland* N Dominica 15°38′N 61°25′W
15 Q9 **Jacques-Cartier** ≈ Québec, SE Canada
13 P11 **Jacques-Cartier, Détroit de** *var.* Jacques-Cartier Passage. *strait* Gulf of St. Lawrence/St. Lawrence River, Canada
15 W6 **Jacques-Cartier, Mont** ▲ Québec, SE Canada 48°58′N 66°00′W
**Jacques-Cartier Passage** *see* Jacques-Cartier, Détroit de
61 H16 **Jacuí, Rio** ≈ S Brazil
60 L11 **Jacupiranga** São Paulo, S Brazil 24°42′S 48°00′W
100 G10 **Jade** ≈ NW Germany
100 G10 **Jadebusen** *bay* NW Germany
**Jadotville** *see* Likasi
**Jadransko More/Jadransko Morje** *see* Adriatic Sea
105 O7 **Jadraque** Castilla-La Mancha, C Spain 40°55′N 02°55′W
95 I22 **Jægerspris** Hovedstaden, E Denmark 55°52′N 11°59′E
56 C10 **Jaén** Cajamarca, N Peru 05°45′S 78°51′W
105 N13 **Jaén** Andalucía, SW Spain 37°46′N 03°48′W
105 N13 **Jaén** ⬖ *province* Andalucía, S Spain
95 C17 **Jæren** *physical region* S Norway
155 J23 **Jaffna** Northern Province, N Sri Lanka 09°42′N 80°03′E
155 K23 **Jaffna Lagoon** *lagoon* N Sri Lanka
19 N10 **Jaffrey** New Hampshire, NE USA 42°46′N 72°00′W
138 H13 **Jafr, Qā' al** *var.* El Jafr. *salt pan* S Jordan
152 J9 **Jagādhri** Haryāna, N India 30°11′N 77°18′E
118 H4 **Jägala** *var.* Jägala Jõgi, *Ger.* Jaggowal. ≈ NW Estonia
**Jägala Jõgi** *see* Jägala
**Jagannath** *see* Puri
**Jagatsinghapur** *see* Kannur
155 L14 **Jagdalpur** Chhattīsgarh, C India 19°07′N 82°04′E
163 U5 **Jagdaqi** Nei Mongol Zizhiqu, N China 50°26′N 124°03′E
**Jägerndorf** *see* Krnov
**Jaggowal** *see* Jägala
139 O2 **Jaghjaghah, Nahr** ≈ N Syria
112 N13 **Jagodina** *prev.* Svetozarevo. Serbia, C Serbia 43°59′N 21°15′E
112 K12 **Jagodnja** ▲▲ W Serbia
101 I20 **Jagst** ≈ SW Germany
155 I14 **Jagtiāl** Telangana, C India 18°49′N 78°53′E
61 H18 **Jaguarão** Rio Grande do Sul, S Brazil 32°30′S 53°25′W
61 H18 **Jaguarão, Rio** *var.* Río Yaguarón. ≈ Brazil/Uruguay
60 K11 **Jaguariaíva** Paraná, S Brazil 24°15′S 49°44′W
44 D5 **Jagüey Grande** Matanzas, W Cuba 22°31′N 81°07′W
153 P14 **Jahānābād** Bihār, N India 25°13′N 84°59′E
**Jahra** *see* Al Jahrā'
143 P12 **Jahrom** *var.* Jahrum. Fārs, S Iran 28°35′N 53°32′E
**Jahrum** *see* Jahrom
**Jailolo** *see* Halmahera, Pulau
**Jainat** *see* Chai Nat
**Jainti** *see* Jayanti
152 H12 **Jaipur** *prev.* Jeypore. *state capital* Rājasthān, N India 26°54′N 75°47′E
153 T14 **Jaipurhat** *var.* Joypurhat. Rajshahi, NW Bangladesh 25°04′N 89°06′E
152 D11 **Jaisalmer** Rājasthān, NW India 26°55′N 70°56′E
154 O12 **Jājapur** *var.* Jajpur, Panikoilli. Odisha, E India 18°54′N 82°36′E
143 R4 **Jājarm** Khorāsān-e Shemālī, NE Iran 36°58′N 56°26′E
112 G12 **Jajce** Federacija Bosne I Hercegovine, W Bosnia and Herzegovina 44°20′N 17°16′E
**Jaji** *see* 'Alī Khēl
**Jajpur** *see* Jājapur
83 D17 **Jakalsberg** Otjozondjupa, N Namibia 19°23′S 17°28′E
169 O15 **Jakarta** *prev.* Djakarta, *Dut.* Batavia. ● (Indonesia) Jawa, C Indonesia 06°08′S 106°45′E
10 I8 **Jakes Corner** Yukon, W Canada 60°18′N 134°00′W
152 H9 **Jākhal** Haryāna, NW India 29°46′N 75°51′E
**Jakobeny** *see* Iacobeni
**Jakobshavn** *see* Ilulissat
93 K16 **Jakobstad** *Fin.* Pietarsaari. Österbotten, W Finland 63°41′N 22°40′E
**Jakobstadt** *see* Jēkabpils
113 O18 **Jakupica** ▲▲ C North Macedonia
37 W15 **Jal** New Mexico, SW USA 32°07′N 103°10′W
141 P7 **Jalājil** *var.* Ğalāğil. Ar Riyāḑ, C Saudi Arabia 25°43′N 45°22′E
149 S5 **Jalālābād** *var.* Jalalabad, Jelalabad. Nangarhār, E Afghanistan 34°26′N 70°28′E
**Jalal-Abad** *see* Dzhalal-Abad, Dzhalal-Abadskaya Oblast'
**Jalal-Abad Oblasty** *see* Dzhalal-Abadskaya Oblast'
149 V7 **Jalalpur** Punjab, E Pakistan 32°39′N 74°11′E
149 T11 **Jalalpur Pirwala** Punjab, E Pakistan 29°30′N 71°20′E
152 H8 **Jalandhar** *prev.* Jullundur. Punjab, N India 31°20′N 75°37′E
42 J7 **Jalán, Río** ≈ S Honduras
42 E6 **Jalapa** Jalapa, C Guatemala 14°39′N 89°59′W
42 J7 **Jalapa** Nueva Segovia, NW Nicaragua 13°56′N 86°11′W
42 A3 **Jalapa** *off.* Departamento de Jalapa. ⬖ *department* SE Guatemala
**Jalapa, Departamento de** *see* Jalapa
42 E6 **Jalapa, Río** ≈ SE Guatemala
143 X13 **Jālaq** Sīstān va Balūchestān, SE Iran
93 K17 **Jalasjärvi** Etelä-Pohjanmaa, W Finland 62°30′N 22°50′E
149 O8 **Jaldak** Zābul, SE Afghanistan 32°00′N 66°45′E
60 J7 **Jales** São Paulo, S Brazil 20°15′S 50°34′W
154 P11 **Jaleshwar** *var.* Jaleswar. Odisha, NE India 21°51′N 87°15′E
**Jaleswar** *see* Jaleshwar
154 F12 **Jalgaon** Mahārāshtra, C India 21°01′N 75°34′E
139 W12 **Jalībah** Dhī Qār, S Iraq 30°37′N 46°31′E
139 W13 **Jalīb Shahāb** Al Muthannā, S Iraq 30°26′N 46°09′E
77 X15 **Jalingo** Taraba, E Nigeria 08°54′N 11°22′E
40 K13 **Jalisco** ⬖ *state* SW Mexico
154 G13 **Jālna** Mahārāshtra, W India 19°50′N 75°53′E
**Jalomitsa** *see* Ialomița
105 R5 **Jalón** ≈ N Spain
152 E13 **Jālor** Rājasthān, N India 25°21′N 72°43′E
112 K11 **Jalovik** Serbia, W Serbia 44°37′N 19°48′E
40 L12 **Jalpa** Zacatecas, C Mexico 21°40′N 103°W
153 S12 **Jalpāiguri** West Bengal, NE India 26°43′N 88°24′E
41 O12 **Jalpán** *var.* Jalpan. Querétaro de Arteaga, C Mexico 21°13′N 99°28′W
**Jalpan** *see* Jalpán
**Jalta** *see* Galite, Île de la
75 S9 **Jālū** *var.* Jūlā. NE Libya 29°02′N 21°33′E
189 U8 **Jaluit Atoll** *var.* Jālwōj. *atoll* Ralik Chain, S Marshall Islands
**Jālwōj** *see* Jaluit Atoll
81 L18 **Jamaame** *It.* Giamame; *prev.* Margherita. Jubbada Hoose, S Somalia 0°00′N 42°43′E
77 W13 **Jamaare** ≈ NE Nigeria
44 G9 **Jamaica** ◆ *commonwealth republic* W West Indies
47 P3 **Jamaica** *island* W West Indies
44 I9 **Jamaica Channel** *channel* Haiti/Jamaica
153 T14 **Jamalpur** Dhaka, N Bangladesh 24°54′N 89°57′E
153 Q14 **Jamālpur** Bihār, NE India 25°19′N 86°30′E
168 L9 **Jamaluang** *var.* Jemaluang. Johor, Peninsular Malaysia 02°15′N 103°50′E
59 I14 **Jamanxim, Rio** ≈ C Brazil
56 B8 **Jambeli, Canal de** *channel* S Ecuador
99 I20 **Jambes** Namur, SE Belgium 50°26′N 04°51′E
168 L12 **Jambi** *var.* Telanaipura; *prev.* Djambi. Sumatera, W Indonesia 01°34′S 103°37′E
168 K12 **Jambi** *off.* Propinsi Jambi, *var.* Djambi. ⬖ *province* W Indonesia
**Jambi, Propinsi** *see* Jambi
**Jamdena** *see* Yamdena, Pulau
12 H8 **James Bay** *bay* Ontario/Québec, E Canada
63 F19 **James, Isla** *island* Archipiélago de los Chonos, S Chile
181 Q8 **James Ranges** ▲▲ Northern Territory, C Australia
29 P8 **James River** ≈ North Dakota/South Dakota, N USA
21 X7 **James River** ≈ Virginia, NE USA
194 H4 **James Ross Island** *island* Antarctica
182 I8 **Jamestown** South Australia 33°13′S 138°36′E
65 G25 **Jamestown** ○ (Saint Helena) NW Saint Helena 15°56′S 05°44′W
35 P8 **Jamestown** California, W USA 37°57′N 120°25′W
20 L7 **Jamestown** Kentucky, S USA 36°58′N 85°03′W
18 D11 **Jamestown** New York, NE USA 42°05′N 79°15′W
29 P5 **Jamestown** North Dakota, N USA 46°54′N 98°42′W
20 L8 **Jamestown** Tennessee, S USA 36°24′N 84°58′W
**Jamestown** *see* Holetown
15 N10 **Jamet** ≈ Québec, SE Canada
41 Q17 **Jamiltepec** *var.* Santiago Jamiltepec. Oaxaca, SE Mexico 16°18′N 97°51′W
95 F20 **Jammerbugten** *bay* Skagerrak, E North Sea
152 H6 **Jammu** *prev.* Jummoo. *state capital* Jammu and Kashmir, NW India 32°43′N 74°54′E
152 I5 **Jammu and Kashmir** *var.* Jammu-Kashmir, Kashmir. ⬖ *state* NW India
149 V4 **Jammu and Kashmir** ⬖ *disputed region* India/Pakistan
**Jammu-Kashmir** *see* Jammu and Kashmir
154 B10 **Jāmnagar** *prev.* Navanagar. Gujarāt, W India 22°28′N 70°06′E
149 S11 **Jampur** Punjab, E Pakistan 29°38′N 70°40′E
93 L18 **Jämsä** Keski-Suomi, C Finland 61°51′N 25°10′E
93 L18 **Jämsänkoski** Keski-Suomi, C Finland 61°54′N 25°10′E
153 Q16 **Jamshedpur** Jhārkhand, NE India 22°47′N 86°12′E
94 K9 **Jämtland** ⬖ *county* C Sweden
153 Q14 **Jamūi** Bihār, NE India 24°57′N 86°14′E
**Jamuna** *see* Brahmaputra
153 T14 **Jamuna Nadi** ≈ N Bangladesh
**Jamundá** *see* Nhamundá, Rio
54 D11 **Jamundí** Valle del Cauca, SW Colombia 03°16′N 76°31′W
153 Q12 **Janakpur** Central, C Nepal 26°45′N 85°55′E
59 N18 **Janaúba** Minas Gerais, SE Brazil 15°47′S 43°16′W
58 K11 **Janaucu, Ilha** *island* NE Brazil
143 Q7 **Jandaq** Eşfahān, C Iran 34°04′N 54°26′E
64 Q11 **Jandia, Punta de** *headland* Fuerteventura, Islas Canarias, Spain, NE Atlantic Ocean 28°03′N 14°32′W
59 B14 **Jandiatuba, Rio** ≈ NW Brazil
105 N12 **Jándula** ≈ S Spain
29 V10 **Janesville** Minnesota, N USA 44°07′N 93°43′W
30 L9 **Janesville** Wisconsin, N USA 42°42′N 89°02′W
83 N20 **Jangamo** Inhambane, SE Mozambique 24°04′S 35°25′E
155 J14 **Jangaon** Telangana, C India 17°43′N 79°11′E
195 R14 **Jang Bogo** *research station* (*South Korea*) Antarctica 74°37′S 164°13′E
153 S14 **Jangīpur** West Bengal, NE India 24°31′N 88°03′E
**Janina** *see* Ioánnina
**Janischken** *see* Joniškis
112 J11 **Janja** NE Bosnia and Herzegovina 44°40′N 19°15′E
76 H12 **Janjanbureh** *prev.* Georgetown. E The Gambia 13°33′N 14°49′W
**Jankovac** *see* Jánoshalma
197 Q15 **Jan Mayen** ◇ *constituent part of Norway* N Atlantic Ocean
84 D5 **Jan Mayen** *island* N Atlantic Ocean
197 R15 **Jan Mayen Fracture Zone** *tectonic feature* Greenland Sea/Norwegian Sea
197 R15 **Jan Mayen Ridge** *undersea feature* Greenland Sea/Norwegian Sea 69°00′N 08°00′W
40 H3 **Janos** Chihuahua, N Mexico 30°50′N 108°10′W
111 K25 **Jánoshalma** *SCr.* Jankovac. Bács-Kiskun, S Hungary 46°19′N 19°16′E
**Janów** *see* Ivanava, Belarus
110 H10 **Janowiec Wielkopolski** *Ger.* Janowitz. Kujawski-pomorskie, C Poland 52°47′N 17°30′E
**Janowitz** *see* Janowiec Wielkopolski
**Janow/Janów** *see* Jonava, Lithuania
111 O15 **Janów Lubelski** Lubelski, E Poland 50°42′N 22°24′E
**Janów Poleski** *see* Ivanava
83 H25 **Jansenville** Eastern Cape, S South Africa 32°56′S 24°40′E
59 M18 **Januária** Minas Gerais, SE Brazil 15°28′S 44°23′W
**Janūbīyah, Al Bādiyah al** *see* Ash Shāmīyah
102 I7 **Janzé** Ille-et-Vilaine, NW France 47°55′N 01°28′W
154 F10 **Jaora** Madhya Pradesh, C India 23°40′N 75°10′E
131 Y9 **Japan** *var.* Nippon, *Jap.* Nihon. ◆ *monarchy* E Asia
129 Y9 **Japan** *island group* E Asia
192 H4 **Japan Basin** *undersea feature* N Sea of Japan 40°00′N 135°00′E
129 Y8 **Japan, Sea of** *var.* East Sea, *Rus.* Yapanskoye More. *sea* NW Pacific Ocean *see also* East Sea
192 H4 **Japan Trench** *undersea feature* NW Pacific Ocean 37°00′N 143°00′E
**Japen** *see* Yapen, Pulau
59 A15 **Japiim** *var.* Máncio Lima. Acre, W Brazil 08°00′S 73°39′W
58 D12 **Japurá** Amazonas, N Brazil 01°43′S 66°14′W
58 C12 **Japurá, Rio** *var.* Río Caquetá, Yapurá. ≈ Brazil/Colombia *see also* Caquetá, Río
**Japurá, Rio** *see* Caquetá, Río
43 W17 **Jaqué** Darién, SE Panama 07°31′N 78°09′W
**Jaquemel** *see* Jacmel
**Jarablos** *see* Jarābulus
138 K2 **Jarābulus** *var.* Jarablos, Jerablus, *Fr.* Djérablous. Ḥalab, N Syria 36°51′N 38°02′E
60 K13 **Jaraguá do Sul** Santa Catarina, S Brazil 26°29′S 49°07′W
104 K9 **Jaraicejo** Extremadura, W Spain 39°40′N 05°49′W
104 K9 **Jaráiz de la Vera** Extremadura, W Spain 40°04′N 05°45′W
105 O7 **Jarama** ≈ C Spain
63 J20 **Jaramillo** Santa Cruz, SE Argentina 47°10′S 67°07′W
**Jarandilla de la Vega** *see* Jarandilla de la Vera
104 K8 **Jarandilla de la Vera** *var.* Jarandilla de la Vega. Extremadura, W Spain 40°08′N 05°39′W
149 V9 **Jaranwala** Punjab, E Pakistan 31°20′N 73°26′E
138 G9 **Jarash** *var.* Jerash; *anc.* Gerasa. Jarash, NW Jordan 32°17′N 35°54′E
**Jarbah, Jazīrat** *see* Djerba, Île de
94 N13 **Järbo** Gävleborg, C Sweden 60°43′N 16°40′E
**Jardan** *see* Yordon
44 F7 **Jardines de la Reina, Archipiélago de los** *island group* C Cuba
162 I8 **Jargalant** Bayanhongor, C Mongolia 47°14′N 99°43′E
162 K6 **Jargalant** Bulgan, N Mongolia 49°09′N 104°19′E
162 G7 **Jargalant** *var.* Buyanbat. Govĭ-Altay, W Mongolia 47°00′N 95°57′E
162 I6 **Jargalant** *var.* Orgil. Hövsgöl, C Mongolia 48°31′N 99°19′E
**Jargalant** *see* Battsengel
**Jargalant** *see* Bulgan, Bayan-Ölgiy, Mongolia
**Jargalant** *see* Biger, Govĭ-Altay, Mongolia
**Jarīd, Shaṭṭ al** *see* Jerid, Chott el
58 I11 **Jari, Rio** *var.* Jary. ≈ N Brazil
141 N7 **Jarīr, Wādī al** *dry watercourse* C Saudi Arabia
**Jarja** *see* Yur'ya
94 L13 **Järna** *var.* Dala-Jarna. Dalarna, C Sweden 60°31′N 14°22′E
95 O16 **Järna** Stockholm, C Sweden 59°05′N 17°35′E
102 K11 **Jarnac** Charente, W France 45°41′N 00°10′W
110 H12 **Jarocin** Wielkopolskie, C Poland 51°59′N 17°30′E
111 F16 **Jaroměř** *Ger.* Jermer. Královéhradecký Kraj, N Czechia 50°22′N 15°55′E
**Jaroslau** *see* Jarosław
111 O16 **Jarosław** *Ger.* Jaroslau, *Rus.* Yaroslav. Podkarpackie, SE Poland 50°01′N 22°41′E
93 F16 **Järpen** Jämtland, C Sweden 63°21′N 13°30′E
147 O14 **Jarqo'rg'on** *Rus.* Dzharkurgan. Surkhondaryo Viloyati, S Uzbekistan 37°31′N 67°20′E
139 P2 **Jarrāh, Wadi** *dry watercourse* NE Syria
**Jars, Plain of** *see* Xiangkhoang, Plateau de
162 K14 **Jartai Yanchi** ◎ N China
59 E16 **Jaru** Rondônia, W Brazil 10°24′S 62°45′W
**Jarud Qi** *see* Lubei
118 I4 **Järva-Jaani** *Ger.* Sankt-Johannis. Järvamaa, N Estonia 59°03′N 25°54′E
118 G5 **Järvakandi** *Ger.* Jerwakant. Raplamaa, NW Estonia 58°45′N 24°49′E
118 H4 **Järvamaa** *var.* Järva Maakond. ⬖ *province* N Estonia
**Järva Maakond** *see* Järvamaa
93 L19 **Järvenpää** Uusimaa, S Finland 60°29′N 25°06′E
14 G17 **Jarvis** Ontario, S Canada 42°53′N 80°06′W
177 R8 **Jarvis Island** ◇ *US unincorporated territory* C Pacific Ocean
94 M11 **Järvsö** Gävleborg, C Sweden 61°43′N 16°25′E
**Jary** *see* Jari, Rio
112 M9 **Jaša Tomić** Vojvodina, NE Serbia 45°27′N 20°51′E
112 D12 **Jasenice** Zadar, SW Croatia 44°15′N 15°33′E
138 I11 **Jashshat al 'Adlah, Wādī al** *dry watercourse* C Jordan
77 Q16 **Jasikan** E Ghana 07°24′N 00°28′E
**Jāsk** *see* Bandar-e Jāsk
146 F6 **Jasliq** *Rus.* Zhaslyk. Qoraqalpog'iston Respublikasi, NW Uzbekistan 43°57′N 57°30′E
111 N17 **Jasło** Podkarpackie, SE Poland 49°45′N 21°28′E
11 U16 **Jasmin** Saskatchewan, S Canada 51°11′N 103°34′W
65 A23 **Jason Islands** *island group* NW Falkland Islands
194 I4 **Jason Peninsula** *peninsula* Antarctica
31 N15 **Jasonville** Indiana, N USA 39°09′N 87°12′W
11 O15 **Jasper** Alberta, SW Canada 52°55′N 118°05′W
14 L13 **Jasper** Ontario, SE Canada 44°50′N 75°57′W
23 O3 **Jasper** Alabama, S USA 33°49′N 87°16′W
27 T9 **Jasper** Arkansas, C USA 36°00′N 93°11′W
23 U8 **Jasper** Florida, SE USA 30°31′N 82°57′W
31 N16 **Jasper** Indiana, N USA 38°22′N 86°57′W
29 R11 **Jasper** Minnesota, N USA 43°51′N 96°24′W
27 S7 **Jasper** Missouri, C USA 37°20′N 94°18′W
20 K10 **Jasper** Tennessee, S USA 35°04′N 85°36′W
25 Y9 **Jasper** Texas, SW USA 30°55′N 94°00′W
11 O15 **Jasper National Park** *national park* Alberta/British Columbia, SW Canada
**Jassy** *see* Iaşi
113 N14 **Jastrebac** ▲▲ SE Serbia
112 D9 **Jastrebarsko** Zagreb, N Croatia 45°40′N 15°40′E
**Jastrow** *see* Jastrowie
110 G9 **Jastrowie** *Ger.* Jastrow. Wielkopolskie, C Poland 53°25′N 16°48′E
111 J17 **Jastrzębie-Zdrój** Śląskie, S Poland 49°58′N 18°34′E
111 L22 **Jászapáti** Jász-Nagykun-Szolnok, E Hungary 47°30′N 20°10′E
111 L22 **Jászberény** Jász-Nagykun-Szolnok, E Hungary 47°30′N 19°56′E


◆ Country
● Country Capital
◇ Dependent Territory
○ Dependent Territory Capital
⬖ Administrative Regions
✈ International Airport
▲ Mountain
▲▲ Mountain Range
⛰ Volcano
≈ River
◎ Lake
⊠ Reservoir

Jász-Nagykun-Szolnok – José Pedro Varela


111 L23 **Jász-Nagykun-Szolnok** off. Jász-Nagykun-Szolnok Megye. ◈ county E Hungary
**Jász-Nagykun-Szolnok Megye** see Jász-Nagykun-Szolnok
59 J19 **Jataí** Goiás, C Brazil 17°58′S 51°45′W
58 G12 **Jatapu, Serra do** ▲▲ N Brazil
41 W16 **Jatate, Río** ≈ SE Mexico
**Jateng** see Jawa Tengah
149 P17 **Jati** Sindh, SE Pakistan 24°20′N 68°18′E
44 F6 **Jatibonico** Sancti Spíritus, C Cuba 21°56′N 79°11′W
169 O16 **Jatiluhur, Danau** ⊛ Jawa, S Indonesia
**Jatim** see Jawa Timur
**Jativa** see Xàtiva
149 S11 **Jatoi** prev. Jattoi. Punjab, E Pakistan 29°29′N 70°58′E
**Jattoi** see Jatoi
60 L9 **Jaú** São Paulo, S Brazil 22°11′S 48°35′W
58 F11 **Jauaperi, Rio** ≈ N Brazil
99 I19 **Jauche** Walloon Brabant, C Belgium 50°42′N 04°55′E
**Jauer** see Jawor
**Jauf** see Dawmat al Jandal
149 U7 **Jauharabad** Punjab, E Pakistan 32°16′N 72°17′E
57 E14 **Jauja** Junín, C Peru 11°48′S 75°30′W
41 O10 **Jaumave** Tamaulipas, C Mexico 23°28′N 99°22′W
118 H10 **Jaunjelgava** Ger. Friedrichstadt. S Latvia 56°38′N 25°03′E
**Jaunlatgale** see Pytalovo
118 I8 **Jaunpiebalga** NE Latvia 57°10′N 26°02′E
118 E9 **Jaunpils** C Latvia 56°45′N 23°03′E
153 N13 **Jaunpur** Uttar Pradesh, N India 25°44′N 82°41′E
29 N8 **Java** South Dakota, N USA 45°29′N 99°54′W
**Java** see Jawa
105 R9 **Javalambre** ▲ E Spain 40°02′N 01°06′W
173 V7 **Java Ridge** undersea feature E Indian Ocean
59 A14 **Javari, Rio** var. Yavarí. ≈ Brazil/Peru
**Javarthushuu** see Bayan-Uul
169 Q15 **Java Sea** Ind. Laut Jawa. sea W Indonesia
173 U7 **Java Trench** var. Sunda Trench. undersea feature E Indian Ocean
143 Q10 **Javazm** var. Jowzam. Kermān, C Iran 30°31′N 55°01′E
105 T11 **Jávea** var. Xàbia. Comunitat Valenciana, E Spain 38°48′N 00°10′E
**Javhlant** see Bayan-Ovoo
63 G20 **Javier, Isla** island S Chile
113 L14 **Javor** ▲▲ Bosnia and Herzegovina/Serbia
111 K20 **Javorie** Hung. Jávoros. ▲ S Slovakia 48°26′N 19°16′E
**Jávoros** see Javorie
93 J14 **Jävre** Norrbotten, N Sweden 65°07′N 21°31′E
192 E8 **Jawa** Eng. Java; prev. Djawa. island C Indonesia
169 O16 **Jawa Barat** off. Propinsi Jawa Barat, var. Jabar, Eng. West Java. ◈ province S Indonesia
**Jawa Barat, Propinsi** see Jawa Barat
**Jawa, Laut** see Java Sea
139 R3 **Jawān** Nīnawýa, NW Iraq 35°57′N 43°03′E
169 P16 **Jawa Tengah** off. Propinsi Jawa Tengah, var. Jateng, Eng. Central Java. ◈ province S Indonesia
**Jawa Tengah, Propinsi** see Jawa Tengah
169 R16 **Jawa Timur** off. Propinsi Jawa Timur, var. Jatim, Eng. East Java. ◈ province S Indonesia
**Jawa Timur, Propinsi** see Jawa Timur
81 N17 **Jawhar** var. Jowhar, It. Giohar. Shabeellaha Dhexe, S Somalia 02°37′N 45°30′E
111 F14 **Jawor** Ger. Jauer. Dolnośląskie, SW Poland 51°01′N 16°11′E
**Jaworów** see Yavoriv
111 J16 **Jaworzno** Śląskie, S Poland 50°13′N 19°11′E
**Jaxartes** see Syr Darya
27 R9 **Jay** Oklahoma, C USA 36°25′N 94°49′W
**Jayabum** see Chaiyaphum
**Jayanath** see Chai Nat
153 T12 **Jayanti** prev. Jainti. West Bengal, NE India 26°45′N 89°40′E
171 X14 **Jaya, Puncak** prev. Puntjak Carstensz, Puntjak Sukarno. ▲ Papua, E Indonesia 04°00′S 137°10′E
171 Z13 **Jayapura** var. Djajapura, Dut. Hollandia; prev. Kotabaru, Sukarnapura. Papua, E Indonesia 02°37′S 140°39′E
**Jay Dairen** see Dalian
**Jayhawker State** see Kansas
147 S12 **Jayilgan** Rus. Dzhailgan, Dzhayilgan. C Tajikistan 39°17′N 71°32′E
155 L14 **Jaypur** var. Jeypore, Jeypur. Odisha, E India 18°54′N 82°36′E
25 O6 **Jayton** Texas, SW USA 33°16′N 100°35′W
**Jazā'ir, Al** see Algeria
141 N13 **Jāzān** var. Jīzān, Qīzān. Jāzān, SW Saudi Arabia 17°50′N 42°50′E
141 N13 **Jāzān** var. Minṭaqat Jīzān. ◈ region SW Saudi Arabia
143 U13 **Jaz Mūrīān, Hāmūn-e** ⊛ SE Iran
138 M4 **Jazrah** Ar Raqqah, C Syria 35°56′N 39°02′E
138 G6 **Jbaïl** var. Jebeil, Jubayl, Jubeil; anc. Biblical Gebal, Bybles. W Lebanon 34°00′N 35°45′E
25 O7 **J. B. Thomas, Lake** ⊠ Texas, SW USA
**Jdaïdé** see Judaydah
35 X12 **Jean** Nevada, W USA 35°45′N 115°20′W
22 I9 **Jeanerette** Louisiana, S USA 29°54′N 91°39′W
44 L8 **Jean-Rabel** NW Haiti 19°48′N 73°05′W
143 T12 **Jebāl Bārez, Kūh-e** ▲▲ SE Iran
**Jebat** see Jabwot
77 T15 **Jebba** Kwara, W Nigeria 09°04′N 04°50′E
**Jebeil** see Jbaïl
116 E12 **Jebel** Hung. Széphely; prev. Hung. Zsebely. Timiș, W Romania 45°33′N 21°14′E
146 B11 **Jebel** Rus. Dzhebel. Balkan Welaýaty, W Turkmenistan 39°42′N 54°10′E
**Jebel, Bahr el** see White Nile
**Jebel Dhanna** see Jabal az Ẓannah
**Jeble** see Jablah
163 Y15 **Jecheon** Jap. Teisen; prev. Chech'ŏn. N South Korea 37°06′N 128°15′E
96 K13 **Jedburgh** SE Scotland, United Kingdom 55°29′N 02°34′W
**Jeddah** see Jiddah
111 L15 **Jędrzejów** Ger. Endersdorf. Świętokrzyskie, C Poland 50°39′N 20°18′E
100 K12 **Jeetze** var. Jeetzel. ≈ C Germany
**Jeetzel** see Jeetze
29 U14 **Jefferson** Iowa, C USA 42°01′N 94°22′W
21 Q8 **Jefferson** North Carolina, SE USA 36°24′N 81°33′W
25 X6 **Jefferson** Texas, SW USA 32°45′N 94°21′W
30 M9 **Jefferson** Wisconsin, N USA 43°01′N 88°48′W
27 U5 **Jefferson City** state capital Missouri, C USA 38°33′N 92°13′W
33 R10 **Jefferson City** Montana, NW USA 46°24′N 112°01′W
21 N9 **Jefferson City** Tennessee, S USA 36°07′N 83°29′W
35 U7 **Jefferson, Mount** ▲ Nevada, W USA 38°49′N 116°54′W
32 H12 **Jefferson, Mount** ▲ Oregon, NW USA 44°40′N 121°48′W
20 L5 **Jeffersontown** Kentucky, S USA 38°11′N 85°33′W
31 P16 **Jeffersonville** Indiana, N USA 38°16′N 85°45′W
33 V15 **Jeffrey City** Wyoming, C USA 42°29′N 107°49′W
77 T13 **Jega** Kebbi, NW Nigeria 12°15′N 04°21′E
**Jehol** see Chengde
163 X17 **Jeju** Jap. Saishū; prev. Cheju. S South Korea 33°31′N 126°34′E
163 Y17 **Jeju-do** Jap. Saishū; prev. Cheju-do, Quelpart. island S South Korea
163 Y17 **Jeju-haehyeop** Eng. Cheju Strait; prev. Cheju-haehyeop. strait S South Korea
62 P5 **Jejuí-Guazú, Río** ≈ E Paraguay
118 I10 **Jēkabpils** Ger. Jakobstadt. S Latvia 56°30′N 25°56′E
23 W7 **Jekyll Island** island Georgia, SE USA
169 R13 **Jelai, Sungai** ≈ Borneo, N Indonesia
**Jelalabad** see Jalālābād
111 H14 **Jelcz-Laskowice** Dolnośląskie, SW Poland 51°01′N 17°24′E
111 E14 **Jelenia Góra** Ger. Hirschberg, Hirschberg im Riesengebirge, Hirschberg in Riesengebirge, Hirschberg in Schlesien. Dolnośląskie SW Poland 50°54′N 15°48′E
153 S11 **Jelep La** pass N India
118 F9 **Jelgava** Ger. Mitau. C Latvia 56°38′N 23°47′E
112 L13 **Jelica** ▲▲ C Serbia
20 M8 **Jellico** Tennessee, S USA 36°33′N 84°06′W
95 G23 **Jelling** Syddanmark, C Denmark 55°45′N 09°24′E
147 T14 **Jelondi** prev. Dzhelandy. SE Tajikistan 37°34′N 72°35′E
169 N9 **Jemaja, Pulau** island W Indonesia
**Jemaluang** see Jamaluang
99 E20 **Jemappes** Hainaut, S Belgium 50°27′N 03°53′E
169 S17 **Jember** prev. Djember. Jawa, C Indonesia 08°07′S 113°45′E
99 I20 **Jemeppe-sur-Sambre** Namur, S Belgium 50°27′N 04°41′E
37 R10 **Jemez Pueblo** New Mexico, SW USA 35°36′N 106°43′W
158 K2 **Jeminay** var. Tuotiereke. Xinjiang Uygur Zizhiqu, NW China 47°28′N 85°49′E
189 U5 **Jemo Island** atoll Ratak Chain, C Marshall Islands
169 U11 **Jempang, Danau** ⊛ Borneo, N Indonesia
101 L16 **Jena** Thüringen, C Germany 50°56′N 11°35′E
22 I6 **Jena** Louisiana, S USA 31°40′N 92°07′W
108 I8 **Jenaz** Graubünden, SE Switzerland 46°56′N 09°43′E
109 N7 **Jenbach** Tirol, W Austria 47°24′N 11°47′E
171 N15 **Jeneponto** prev. Djeneponto. Sulawesi, C Indonesia 05°41′S 119°42′E
138 F9 **Jenin** N West Bank 32°28′N 35°17′E
21 P7 **Jenkins** Kentucky, S USA 37°10′N 82°37′W
27 P9 **Jenks** Oklahoma, C USA 36°01′N 95°58′W
**Jenné** see Djenné
109 X8 **Jennersdorf** Burgenland, SE Austria 46°57′N 16°08′E
22 H9 **Jennings** Louisiana, S USA 30°13′N 92°39′W
11 N7 **Jenny Lind Island** island Nunavut, N Canada
23 Y13 **Jensen Beach** Florida, SE USA 27°15′N 80°13′W
9 P6 **Jens Munk Island** island Nunavut, NE Canada
163 Y15 **Jeonju** Jap. Zenshū; prev. Chŏnju. SW South Korea 35°51′N 127°08′E
59 O17 **Jequié** Bahia, E Brazil 13°52′S 40°06′W
59 O18 **Jequitinhonha, Rio** ≈ E Brazil
**Jerablus** see Jarābulus
74 H6 **Jerada** NE Morocco 34°16′N 02°07′W
**Jerash** see Jarash
44 K9 **Jérémie** SW Haiti 18°39′N 74°11′W
**Jeréz** see Jerez de García Salinas, Mexico
**Jerez** see Jeréz de la Frontera, Spain
40 L11 **Jerez de García Salinas** var. Jeréz. Zacatecas, C Mexico 22°40′N 103°00′W
104 J15 **Jerez de la Frontera** var. Jerez; prev. Xeres. Andalucía, SW Spain 36°41′N 06°08′W
104 I12 **Jerez de los Caballeros** Extremadura, W Spain 38°20′N 06°45′W
**Jergucati** see Jorgucat
138 G10 **Jericho** Ar. Arīḥā, Heb. Yeriḥo. E West Bank 31°51′N 35°27′E
74 M7 **Jerid, Chott el** var. Shaṭṭ al Jarīd. salt lake SW Tunisia
183 O10 **Jerilderie** New South Wales, SE Australia 35°24′S 145°43′E
**Jerischmarkt** see Câmpia Turzii
92 K11 **Jerisjärvi** ⊛ NW Finland
**Jermak** see Aksu
**Jermentau** see Yereymentau
**Jermer** see Jaroměř
36 K11 **Jerome** Arizona, SW USA 34°45′N 112°06′W
33 O15 **Jerome** Idaho, NW USA 42°43′N 114°31′W
97 L26 **Jersey** island Channel Islands, NW Europe
18 K14 **Jersey City** New Jersey, NE USA 40°42′N 74°01′W
18 F13 **Jersey Shore** Pennsylvania, NE USA 41°12′N 77°13′W
30 K14 **Jerseyville** Illinois, N USA 39°07′N 90°19′W
104 K8 **Jerte** ≈ W Spain
138 F10 **Jerusalem** Ar. Al Quds, Al Quds ash Sharīf, Heb. Yerushalayim; anc. Hierosolyma. ● (Israel-not internationally recognised) Jerusalem, NE Israel 31°47′N 35°13′E
138 G10 **Jerusalem** ◈ district E Israel
183 S10 **Jervis Bay** New South Wales, SE Australia 35°09′S 150°42′E
183 S10 **Jervis Bay Territory** ◈ territory SE Australia
**Jerwakant** see Järvakandi
109 S10 **Jesenice** Ger. Assling. NW Slovenia 46°26′N 14°01′E
111 H16 **Jeseník** Ger. Freiwaldau. Olomoucký Kraj, E Czechia 50°14′N 17°12′E
**Jesi** see Iesi
106 I8 **Jesolo** var. Iesolo. Veneto, NE Italy 45°32′N 12°37′E
**Jesselton** see Kota Kinabalu
95 I14 **Jessheim** Akershus, S Norway 60°07′N 11°10′E
153 T15 **Jessore** Khulna, W Bangladesh 23°10′N 89°12′E
23 W6 **Jesup** Georgia, SE USA 31°36′N 81°54′W
41 S15 **Jesús Carranza** Veracruz, SE Mexico 17°30′N 95°01′W
62 K10 **Jesús María** Córdoba, C Argentina 30°59′S 64°05′W
26 K6 **Jetmore** Kansas, C USA 38°05′N 99°55′W
103 Q2 **Jeumont** Nord, N France 50°18′N 04°06′E
95 H14 **Jevnaker** Oppland, S Norway 60°15′N 10°25′E
**Jewe** see Jõhvi
25 V9 **Jewett** Texas, SW USA 31°21′N 96°08′W
19 N12 **Jewett City** Connecticut, NE USA 41°36′N 71°58′W
**Jeypore** see Jaipur, Rājasthān, India
**Jeypore/Jeypur** see Jaypur, Orissa, India
113 L17 **Jezercës, Maja e** ▲ N Albania 42°27′N 19°49′E
111 B18 **Jezerní Hora** ▲ SW Czechia 49°10′N 13°11′E
154 F10 **Jhābua** Madhya Pradesh, C India 22°44′N 74°37′E
152 H14 **Jhālāwār** Rājasthān, N India 24°37′N 76°12′E
**Jhang/Jhang Sadar** see Jhang Sadr
149 U9 **Jhang Sadr** var. Jhang, Jhang Sadar. Punjab, NE Pakistan 31°16′N 72°19′E
152 J13 **Jhānsi** Uttar Pradesh, N India 25°27′N 78°34′E
153 O16 **Jhārkhand** ◈ state NE India
154 M11 **Jhārsuguda** Odisha, E India 21°56′N 84°04′E
149 V7 **Jhelum** Punjab, NE Pakistan 32°55′N 73°42′E
129 P9 **Jhelum** ≈ E Pakistan
**Jhenaidaha** see Jhenida
153 T15 **Jhenida** var. Jhenaidaha. Dhaka, W Bangladesh 23°34′N 89°39′E
149 P16 **Jhimpir** Sindh, SE Pakistan 25°00′N 68°01′E
**Jhind** see Jīnd
149 R16 **Jhudo** Sindh, SE Pakistan 24°58′N 69°18′E
**Jhumra** see Chak Jhumra
152 H11 **Jhunjhunūn** Rājasthān, N India 28°05′N 75°30′E
**Ji** see Hebei, China
**Ji** see Jilin, China
**Jiading** see Xinfeng
153 S14 **Jiāganj** West Bengal, NE India 24°18′N 88°07′E
**Jiaji** see Qionghai
160 J7 **Jialing Jiang** ≈ C China
163 Y7 **Jiamusi** var. Chia-mu-ssu, Kiamusze. Heilongjiang, NE China 46°46′N 130°19′E
161 O11 **Ji'an** Jiangxi, S China 27°08′N 115°00′E
163 W12 **Ji'an** Jilin, NE China 41°04′N 126°07′E
163 T13 **Jianchang** Liaoning, NE China 40°48′N 119°51′E
**Jianchang** see Nancheng
**Jiancheng** see Jianyang
160 F11 **Jianchuan** var. Jinhuan. Yunnan, SW China 26°28′N 99°49′E
158 M4 **Jiangjunmiao** Xinjiang Uygur Zizhiqu, W China 44°42′N 90°06′E
160 K11 **Jiangkou** var. Shuangjiang. Guizhou, S China 27°46′N 108°53′E
**Jiangkou** see Fengkai
161 Q12 **Jiangle** var. Guyong. Fujian, SE China 26°44′N 117°26′E
161 N15 **Jiangmen** Guangdong, S China 22°35′N 113°02′E
**Jiangna** see Yanshan
161 Q10 **Jiangshan** Zhejiang, SE China 28°41′N 118°33′E
161 Q7 **Jiangsu** var. Chiang-su, Jiangsu Sheng, Kiangsu, Su. ◈ province E China
**Jiangsu** see Nanjing
**Jiangsu Sheng** see Jiangsu
161 O11 **Jiangxi** var. Chiang-hsi, Gan, Jiangxi Sheng, Kiangsi. ◈ province S China
**Jiangxi Sheng** see Jiangxi
160 I8 **Jiangyou** prev. Zhongba. Sichuan, C China 31°52′N 104°52′E
161 N9 **Jianli** var. Rongcheng. Hubei, C China 29°51′N 112°50′E
161 Q11 **Jian'ou** Fujian, SE China 27°04′N 118°20′E
163 S12 **Jianping** var. Yebaishou. Liaoning, NE China 41°13′N 119°37′E
**Jianshe** see Baiyü
160 L9 **Jianshi** var. Yezhou. Hubei, C China 30°37′N 109°42′E
**Jiantang** see Xamgyi'nyilha
129 V11 **Jian Xi** ≈ SE China
161 Q11 **Jianyang** Fujian, SE China 27°20′N 118°01′E
160 I9 **Jianyang** var. Jiancheng. Sichuan, C China 30°22′N 104°31′E
163 X10 **Jiaohe** Jilin, NE China 43°41′N 127°20′E
**Jiaojiang** see Taizhou
**Jiaoxian** see Jiaozhou
161 R5 **Jiaozhou** prev. Jiaoxian. Shandong, E China 36°17′N 120°00′E
161 N6 **Jiaozuo** Henan, C China 35°14′N 113°13′E
**Jiashan** see Mingguang
158 F8 **Jiashi** var. Baren, Payzawat. Xinjiang Uygur Zizhiqu, NW China 39°27′N 76°45′E
154 L9 **Jiāwān** Madhya Pradesh, C India 24°20′N 82°17′E
161 S9 **Jiaxing** Zhejiang, SE China 30°44′N 120°46′E
**Jiayi** see Chiayi
163 X6 **Jiayin** var. Chaoyang. Heilongjiang, NE China 48°51′N 130°24′E
159 R8 **Jiayuguan** Gansu, N China 39°47′N 98°14′E
**Jibhalanta** see Uliastay
138 M4 **Jibli** Ar Raqqah, C Syria 35°49′N 39°23′E
116 H9 **Jibou** Hung. Zsibó. Sălaj, NW Romania 47°15′N 23°17′E
141 Z9 **Jibsh, Ra's al** headland E Oman 21°20′N 59°23′E
**Jibuti** see Djibouti
**Jibuti** see Djibouti
111 E15 **Jičín** Ger. Jitschin. Královéhradecký Kraj, N Czechia 50°27′N 15°20′E
140 K10 **Jiddah** Eng. Jeddah. (Saudi Arabia) Makkah al Mukarramah, W Saudi Arabia 21°34′N 39°13′E
141 W11 **Jiddat al Ḥarāsīs** desert C Oman
**Jiesjavrre** see Iešjavri
160 M4 **Jiexiu** Shanxi, C China 37°00′N 111°50′E
161 P14 **Jieyang** Guangdong, S China 23°32′N 116°20′E
119 F14 **Jieznas** Kaunas, S Lithuania 54°37′N 24°10′E
**Jifa', Bi'r** see Jif'īyah, Bi'r
141 P15 **Jif'īyah, Bi'r** var. Bi'r Jifa'. well C Yemen
77 W13 **Jigawa** ◈ state N Nigeria
146 J10 **Jigerbent** Rus. Dzhigirbent. Lebap Welaýaty, NE Turkmenistan 40°44′N 61°56′E
44 I7 **Jiguaní** Granma, E Cuba 20°24′N 76°26′W
159 T12 **Jigzhi** var. Chugqênsumdo. Qinghai, C China 33°23′N 101°25′E
**Jih-k'a-tse** see Xigazê
111 E18 **Jihlava** Ger. Iglau, Pol. Igława. Vysočina, S Czechia 49°22′N 15°36′E
111 E18 **Jihlava** var. Igel, Ger. Iglawa. ≈ Vysočina, C Czechia
**Jihlavský Kraj** see Vysočina
111 C18 **Jihočeský Kraj** prev. Budějovický Kraj. ◈ region Czechia
111 G19 **Jihomoravský Kraj** prev. Brněnský Kraj. ◈ region SE Czechia
74 L5 **Jijel** var. Djidjel; prev. Djidjelli. NE Algeria 36°50′N 05°43′E
116 L9 **Jijia** ≈ N Romania
80 L13 **Jijiga** It. Giggiga. Sumalē, E Ethiopia 09°21′N 42°53′E
105 S12 **Jijona** var. Xixona. Comunitat Valenciana, E Spain 38°34′N 00°29′W
81 L18 **Jilib** It. Gelib. Jubbada Dhexe, S Somalia 0°18′N 42°48′E
163 W10 **Jilin** var. Chi-lin, Girin, Kirin; prev. Yungki, Yunki. Jilin, NE China 43°46′N 126°32′E
163 W10 **Jilin** var. Chi-lin, Girin, Ji, Jilin Sheng, Kirin. ◈ province NE China
163 W11 **Jilin Hada Ling** ▲▲ NE China
**Jilin Sheng** see Jilin
163 S4 **Jiliu He** ≈ NE China
105 Q6 **Jiloca** ≈ N Spain
**Jilong** see Keelung
81 I14 **Jīma** var. Jimma, It. Gimma. Oromīya, C Ethiopia 07°42′N 36°51′E
44 M9 **Jimaní** W Dominican Republic 18°29′N 71°49′W
116 E11 **Jimbolia** Ger. Hatzfeld, Hung. Zsombolya. Timiș, W Romania 45°47′N 20°43′E
104 K16 **Jimena de la Frontera** Andalucía, S Spain 36°27′N 05°28′W
40 K7 **Jiménez** Chihuahua, N Mexico 27°09′N 104°54′W
41 N5 **Jiménez** Coahuila, NE Mexico 29°05′N 100°40′W
41 P9 **Jiménez** var. Santander Jiménez. Tamaulipas, C Mexico 24°11′N 98°29′W
40 L10 **Jiménez del Teul** Zacatecas, C Mexico 23°13′N 103°46′W
77 Y14 **Jimeta** Adamawa, E Nigeria 09°16′N 12°25′E
**Jimma** see Jīma
158 M5 **Jimsar** Xinjiang Uygur Zizhiqu, NW China 44°05′N 88°48′E
18 I14 **Jim Thorpe** Pennsylvania, NE USA 40°51′N 75°43′W
**Jin** see Shanxi
**Jin** see Tianjin Shi
161 P5 **Jinan** var. Chinan, Chi-nan, Tsinan. province capital Shandong, E China 36°43′N 116°58′E
**Jin'an** see Songpan
**Jinbi** see Dayao
159 T8 **Jinchang** Gansu, N China 38°31′N 102°07′E
161 N5 **Jincheng** Shanxi, C China 35°30′N 112°52′E
**Jincheng** see Wuding
**Jinchengjiang** see Hechi
152 I9 **Jīnd** prev. Jhind. Haryāna, NW India 29°29′N 76°22′E
183 Q11 **Jindabyne** New South Wales, SE Australia 36°28′S 148°36′E
163 X17 **Jin-do** Jap. Chin-tō; prev. Chin-do. island SW South Korea
111 O18 **Jindřichův Hradec** Ger. Neuhaus. Jihočeský Kraj, S Czechia 49°09′N 15°01′E
**Jing** see Beijing Shi
**Jing** see Jinghe, China
159 X10 **Jingchuan** Gansu, C China 35°20′N 107°45′E
161 Q10 **Jingdezhen** Jiangxi, S China 29°18′N 117°18′E
161 O12 **Jinggangshan** Jiangxi, S China 26°36′N 114°11′E
161 P3 **Jinghai** Tianjin Shi, E China 38°53′N 116°45′E
158 I4 **Jinghe** var. Jing. Xinjiang Uygur Zizhiqu, NW China 44°35′N 82°55′E
160 K6 **Jing He** ≈ C China
160 F15 **Jinghong** var. Yunjinghong. Yunnan, SW China 22°03′N 100°56′E
160 M9 **Jingmen** Hubei, C China 30°58′N 112°09′E
163 X10 **Jingpo Hu** ⊛ NE China
160 M8 **Jing Shan** ▲▲ C China
159 V9 **Jingtai** var. Yitiaoshan. Gansu, C China 37°12′N 104°06′E
160 J14 **Jingxi** var. Xinjing. Guangxi Zhuangzu Zizhiqu, S China 23°10′N 106°22′E
**Jing Xian** see Jingzhou, Hunan, China
163 W11 **Jingyu** Jilin, NE China 42°23′N 126°48′E
159 V10 **Jingyuan** var. Wulan. Gansu, C China 36°35′N 104°40′E
160 M9 **Jingzhou** prev. Shashi, Sha-shih, Shasi. Hubei, C China 30°21′N 112°09′E
160 L12 **Jingzhou** var. Jing Xian, Jingzhou Miaouzu Dongzu Zizhixian, Quyang. Hunan, S China 26°35′N 109°40′E
**Jingzhou Miaouzu Dongzu Zizhixian** see Jingzhou
163 Z16 **Jinhae** Jap. Chinkai; prev. Chinhae. S South Korea 35°06′N 128°48′E
**Jinhe** see Jinping
161 R10 **Jinhua** Zhejiang, SE China 29°15′N 119°36′E
**Jinhuan** see Jianchuan
161 P5 **Jining** Shandong, E China 35°25′N 116°35′E
**Jining** see Ulan Qab
81 G18 **Jinja** S Uganda 0°27′N 33°14′E
161 R13 **Jinjiang** var. Qingyang. Fujian, SE China 24°53′N 118°36′E
161 O11 **Jin Jiang** ≈ S China
**Jinjiang** see Chengmai
163 Y16 **Jinju** prev. Chinju, Jap. Shinshū. S South Korea 35°12′N 128°06′E
171 V15 **Jin, Kepulauan** island group E Indonesia
**Jinmen Dao** see Kinmen Island
42 J9 **Jinotega** Jinotega, NW Nicaragua 13°03′N 85°59′W
42 K7 **Jinotega** ◈ department N Nicaragua
42 J11 **Jinotepe** Carazo, SW Nicaragua 11°50′N 86°10′W
160 L13 **Jinping** var. Sanjiang. Guizhou, S China 26°42′N 109°13′E
160 H14 **Jinping** var. Jinhe. Yunnan, SW China 22°47′N 103°12′E
**Jinsen** see Incheon
160 J11 **Jinsha** Guizhou, S China 27°24′N 106°16′E
160 M10 **Jinshi** Hunan, S China 29°42′N 111°46′E
**Jinshi** see Xinning
162 I9 **Jinst** var. Bodī. Bayanhongor, C Mongolia 45°25′N 100°33′E
159 R7 **Jinta** Gansu, N China 40°01′N 98°57′E
161 Q12 **Jin Xi** ≈ SE China
**Jinxi** see Huludao
**Jinxian** see Jinzhou
161 P6 **Jinxiang** Shandong, E China 35°08′N 116°19′E
161 P8 **Jinzhai** var. Meishan. Anhui, E China 31°42′N 115°47′E
161 N4 **Jinzhong** var. Yuci. Shanxi, C China 37°34′N 112°45′E
163 T12 **Jinzhou** var. Chin-chou, Chinchow; prev. Chinhsien. Liaoning, NE China 41°07′N 121°06′E
163 U14 **Jinzhou** prev. Jinxian. Liaoning, NE China 39°04′N 121°45′E
**Jinzhu** see Daocheng
138 H12 **Jinz, Qā' al** ⊛ C Jordan
47 S8 **Jiparaná, Rio** ≈ W Brazil
56 A7 **Jipijapa** Manabí, W Ecuador 01°23′S 80°35′W
42 F8 **Jiquilisco** Usulután, S El Salvador 13°19′N 88°35′W
**Jirgalanta** see Hovd
147 S12 **Jirgatol** Rus. Dzhirgatal'. C Tajikistan 39°13′N 71°09′E
75 X10 **Jirjā** var. Girga, Girgeh, Jirjā. C Egypt 26°17′N 31°58′E
**Jirjā** see Jirjā
111 B15 **Jirkov** Ger. Görkau. Ústecký Kraj, NW Czechia 50°30′N 13°27′E
143 T12 **Jīroft** var. Sabzawaran, Sabzvārān. Kermān, SE Iran 28°40′N 57°40′E
81 P14 **Jirriiban** Mudug, E Somalia 07°15′N 48°55′E
160 L11 **Jishou** Hunan, S China 28°20′N 109°43′E
**Jisr ash Shadadi** see Ash Shadādah
116 I14 **Jitaru** Olt, S Romania 44°27′N 24°32′E
**Jitschin** see Jičín
116 H14 **Jiu** Ger. Schil, Schyl, Hung. Zsil, Zsily. ≈ S Romania
161 R11 **Jiufeng Shan** ▲▲ SE China
161 P9 **Jiujiang** Jiangxi, S China 29°45′N 115°59′E
161 O10 **Jiuling Shan** ▲▲ S China
160 G10 **Jiulong** var. Garba, Tib. Gyaisi. Sichuan, C China 29°00′N 101°30′E
161 Q13 **Jiulong Jiang** ≈ SE China
161 Q12 **Jiulong Xi** ≈ SE China
159 R8 **Jiuquan** var. Suzhou. Gansu, N China 39°47′N 98°30′E
160 K17 **Jiusuo** Hainan, S China 18°25′N 109°55′E
163 W10 **Jiutai** Jilin, NE China 44°01′N 125°51′E
160 K13 **Jiuwan Dashan** ▲▲ S China
160 I7 **Jiuzhaigou** var. Nongle; prev. Nanping. Sichuan, C China 33°25′N 104°05′E
148 I16 **Jiwani** Baluchistan, SW Pakistan 25°05′N 61°46′E
163 Y8 **Jixi** Heilongjiang, NE China 45°17′N 131°01′E
163 Y7 **Jixian** var. Fuli. Heilongjiang, NE China 46°38′N 131°04′E
160 M5 **Jixian** var. Ji Xian. Shanxi, C China 36°15′N 110°41′E
**Ji Xian** see Jixian
**Jiza** see Al Jīzah
**Jīzān** see Jāzān
**Jīzān, Minṭaqat** see Jāzān
140 K6 **Jizl, Wādī al** dry watercourse W Saudi Arabia
164 H12 **Jizō-zaki** headland Honshū, SW Japan 35°34′N 133°16′E
141 U14 **Jiz', Wādī al** dry watercourse E Yemen
147 O11 **Jizzax** Rus. Dzhizak. Jizzax Viloyati, C Uzbekistan 40°08′N 67°47′E
147 N10 **Jizzax Viloyati** Rus. Dzhizakskaya Oblast'. ◈ province C Uzbekistan
60 I13 **Joaçaba** Santa Catarina, S Brazil 27°08′S 51°30′W
**Joal** see Joal-Fadiout
76 F11 **Joal-Fadiout** prev. Joal. W Senegal 14°09′N 16°50′W
76 E10 **João Barrosa** Boa Vista, E Cape Verde 16°01′N 22°44′W
**João Belo** see Xai-Xai
**João de Almeida** see Chibia
59 Q15 **João Pessoa** prev. Paraíba. state capital Paraíba, E Brazil 07°06′S 34°53′W
25 X7 **Joaquin** Texas, SW USA 31°58′N 94°03′W
62 K6 **Joaquín V. González** Salta, N Argentina 25°06′S 64°07′W
**Joazeiro** see Juazeiro
**Job'urg** see Johannesburg
109 O7 **Jochberger Ache** ≈ W Austria
**Jo-ch'iang** see Ruoqiang
92 K12 **Jock** Norrbotten, N Sweden 66°40′N 22°45′E
42 I5 **Jocón** Yoro, N Honduras 15°17′N 86°55′W
105 O13 **Jódar** Andalucía, S Spain 37°51′N 03°18′W
152 F12 **Jodhpur** Rājasthān, NW India 26°17′N 73°02′E
99 I19 **Jodoigne** Walloon Brabant, C Belgium 50°43′N 04°52′E
93 O16 **Joensuu** Pohjois-Karjala, SE Finland 62°36′N 29°45′E
37 W4 **Joes** Colorado, C USA 39°36′N 102°40′W
191 Z3 **Joe's Hill** hill Kiritimati, NE Kiribati
165 N11 **Jōetsu** var. Zyôetu. Niigata, Honshū, C Japan 37°09′N 138°13′E
83 M18 **Jofane** Inhambane, S Mozambique 21°16′S 34°21′E
153 R12 **Jogbani** Bihār, NE India 26°23′N 87°16′E
118 I5 **Jõgeva** Ger. Laisholm. Jõgevamaa, E Estonia 58°48′N 26°28′E
118 I4 **Jõgevamaa** off. Jõgeva Maakond. ◈ province E Estonia
**Jõgeva Maakond** see Jõgevamaa
155 E18 **Jog Falls** Waterfall Karnātaka, W India
143 S4 **Joghatāy** Khorāsān-e Razavī, NE Iran 36°34′N 57°00′E
153 U12 **Jogīghopa** Assam, NE India 26°14′N 90°35′E
152 I7 **Jogindarnagar** Himāchal Pradesh, N India 31°51′N 76°47′E
**Jogjakarta** see Yogyakarta
164 L11 **Jōhana** Toyama, Honshū, SW Japan 36°30′N 136°53′E
83 J21 **Johannesburg** var. Egoli, Erautini, Gauteng, abbrev. Job'urg. Gauteng, NE South Africa 26°10′S 28°02′E
35 T13 **Johannesburg** California, W USA 35°20′N 117°37′W
**Johannisburg** see Pisz
149 P14 **Johi** Sindh, SE Pakistan 26°46′N 67°28′E
55 T13 **Johi Village** S Guyana 01°48′N 58°33′W
45 W10 **John A. Osborne** ✈ (Plymouth) E Montserrat 16°45′N 62°09′W
32 K13 **John Day** Oregon, NW USA 44°25′N 118°57′W
32 I11 **John Day River** ≈ Oregon, NW USA
18 L14 **John F Kennedy** ✈ (New York) Long Island, New York, NE USA 40°39′N 73°45′W
21 V8 **John H. Kerr Reservoir** var. Buggs Island Lake, Kerr Lake. ⊠ North Carolina/Virginia, SE USA
37 V6 **John Martin Reservoir** ⊠ Colorado, C USA
96 K6 **John o'Groats** N Scotland, United Kingdom 58°38′N 03°03′W
27 P5 **John Redmond Reservoir** ⊠ Kansas, C USA
39 Q7 **John River** ≈ Alaska, USA
26 H6 **Johnson** Kansas, C USA 37°33′N 101°46′W
18 M7 **Johnson** Vermont, NE USA 44°39′N 72°40′W
18 D13 **Johnsonburg** Pennsylvania, NE USA 41°28′N 78°37′W
18 H11 **Johnson City** New York, NE USA 42°06′N 75°54′W
21 P8 **Johnson City** Tennessee, S USA 36°18′N 82°21′W
25 R10 **Johnson City** Texas, SW USA 30°17′N 98°27′W
35 S12 **Johnsondale** California, W USA 35°58′N 118°32′W
10 I8 **Johnsons Crossing** Yukon, W Canada 60°30′N 133°15′W
21 T13 **Johnsonville** South Carolina, SE USA 33°50′N 79°26′W
21 Q13 **Johnston** South Carolina, SE USA 33°49′N 81°48′W
192 M6 **Johnston Atoll** ◇ US unincorporated territory C Pacific Ocean
175 Q3 **Johnston Atoll** atoll C Pacific Ocean
30 L17 **Johnston City** Illinois, N USA 37°49′N 88°55′W
180 K12 **Johnston, Lake** salt lake Western Australia
31 S13 **Johnstown** Ohio, N USA 40°08′N 82°39′W
18 D15 **Johnstown** Pennsylvania, NE USA 40°20′N 78°56′W
168 L10 **Johor** var. Johore. ◈ state Peninsular Malaysia
**Johor Baharu** see Johor Bahru
168 K10 **Johor Bahru** var. Johor Baharu, Johore Bahru. Johor, Peninsular Malaysia 01°29′N 103°44′E
**Johore** see Johor
**Johore Bahru** see Johor Bahru
118 K3 **Jõhvi** Ger. Jewe. Ida-Virumaa, NE Estonia 59°21′N 27°25′E
103 P7 **Joigny** Yonne, C France 47°58′N 03°24′E
**Joinvile** see Joinville
60 K12 **Joinville** var. Joinvile. Santa Catarina, S Brazil 26°20′S 48°55′W
103 R6 **Joinville** Haute-Marne, N France 48°26′N 05°07′E
194 H3 **Joinville Island** island Antarctica
41 O15 **Jojutla** var. Jojutla de Juárez. Morelos, S Mexico 18°38′N 99°10′W
**Jojutla de Juárez** see Jojutla
92 I12 **Jokkmokk** Lapp. Dálvvadis. Norrbotten, N Sweden 66°35′N 19°57′E
92 L2 **Jökuldalur** ≈ E Iceland
92 K2 **Jökulsá á Fjöllum** ≈ NE Iceland
**Jokyakarta** see Yogyakarta
30 M11 **Joliet** Illinois, N USA 41°33′N 88°05′W
15 O11 **Joliette** Québec, SE Canada 46°02′N 73°27′W
171 O8 **Jolo** Jolo Island, SW Philippines 06°02′N 121°00′E
94 D11 **Jølstervatnet** ⊛ S Norway
169 S16 **Jombang** prev. Djombang. Jawa, S Indonesia 07°33′S 112°14′E
159 R14 **Jomda** Xizang Zizhiqu, W China 31°26′N 98°09′E
118 G13 **Jonava** Ger. Janow, Pol. Janów. Kaunas, C Lithuania 55°05′N 24°19′E
146 L11 **Jondor** Rus. Zhondor. Buxoro Viloyati, C Uzbekistan 39°46′N 64°11′E
159 V11 **Jonê** var. Liulin. Gansu, C China 34°36′N 103°39′E
27 X9 **Jonesboro** Arkansas, C USA 35°50′N 90°42′W
23 S4 **Jonesboro** Georgia, SE USA 33°31′N 84°21′W
30 L17 **Jonesboro** Illinois, N USA 37°25′N 89°19′W
22 H5 **Jonesboro** Louisiana, S USA 32°14′N 92°43′W
21 P8 **Jonesboro** Tennessee, S USA 36°17′N 82°28′W
19 T6 **Jonesport** Maine, NE USA 44°33′N 67°35′W
0 J4 **Jones Sound** channel Nunavut, N Canada
22 I6 **Jonesville** Louisiana, S USA 31°37′N 91°49′W
31 Q10 **Jonesville** Michigan, N USA 41°58′N 84°39′W
21 Q11 **Jonesville** South Carolina, SE USA 34°49′N 81°38′W
146 K10 **Jongeldi** Rus. Dzhankel'dy. Buxoro Viloyati, C Uzbekistan 40°50′N 63°16′E
81 F14 **Jonglei** Jonglei, E South Sudan 06°54′N 31°19′E
81 F14 **Jonglei** var. Gongoleh State. ◈ state E South Sudan
81 F14 **Jonglei Canal** canal E South Sudan
118 F11 **Joniškėlis** Panevėžys, N Lithuania 56°02′N 24°10′E
118 F10 **Joniškis** Ger. Janischken. Šiaulai, N Lithuania 56°15′N 23°36′E
95 L19 **Jönköping** Jönköping, S Sweden 57°45′N 14°10′E
95 K20 **Jönköping** ◈ county S Sweden
15 Q7 **Jonquière** Québec, SE Canada 48°25′N 71°16′W
41 V15 **Jonuta** Tabasco, SE Mexico 18°04′N 92°03′W
102 K12 **Jonzac** Charente-Maritime, W France 45°26′N 00°25′W
27 R7 **Joplin** Missouri, C USA 37°04′N 94°31′W
33 W8 **Jordan** Montana, NW USA 47°18′N 106°54′W
138 H12 **Jordan** off. Hashemite Kingdom of Jordan, Ar. Al Mamlakah al Urdunīyah al Hāshimīyah, Al Urdun; prev. Transjordan. ◆ monarchy SW Asia
138 G9 **Jordan** Ar. Al Urdun, Heb. HaYarden. ≈ SW Asia
**Jordan Lake** see B. Everett Jordan Reservoir
111 K17 **Jordanów** Małopolskie, S Poland 49°39′N 19°51′E
32 M15 **Jordan Valley** Oregon, NW USA 42°59′N 117°03′W
138 G9 **Jordan Valley** valley N Israel
57 D15 **Jorge Chávez Internacional** var. Lima. ✈ (Lima) Provincia de Lima, W Peru 12°07′S 77°01′W
113 L23 **Jorgucat** var. Jergucati, Jorgucati. Gjirokastër, S Albania 39°57′N 20°14′E
**Jorgucati** see Jorgucat
153 X12 **Jorhāt** Assam, NE India 26°45′N 94°09′E
93 J14 **Jörn** Västerbotten, N Sweden 65°03′N 20°04′E
37 R14 **Jornada Del Muerto** valley New Mexico, SW USA
93 N17 **Joroinen** Etelä-Savo, E Finland 62°11′N 27°50′E
95 C16 **Jørpeland** Rogaland, S Norway 59°01′N 06°04′E
77 W14 **Jos** Plateau, C Nigeria 09°59′N 08°57′E
171 Q8 **Jose Abad Santos** var. Trinidad. Mindanao, S Philippines 05°51′N 125°35′E
61 F19 **José Batlle y Ordóñez** var. Batlle y Ordóñez. Florida, C Uruguay 33°28′S 55°08′W
63 H18 **José de San Martín** Chubut, S Argentina 44°04′S 70°29′W
61 E19 **José Enrique Rodó** var. Rodó, José E.Rodo; prev. Drabble, Drable. Soriano, SW Uruguay 33°43′S 57°33′W
**José E.Rodo** see José Enrique Rodó
**Josefsdorf** see Žabalj
44 C4 **José Martí** ✈ (La Habana) Cuidad de La Habana, N Cuba 23°03′N 82°22′W
61 F19 **José Pedro Varela** var. José P.Varela. Lavalleja, S Uruguay 33°30′S 54°28′W




◆ Country
● Country Capital
◇ Dependent Territory
○ Dependent Territory Capital
◈ Administrative Regions
✈ International Airport
▲ Mountain
▲▲ Mountain Range
Volcano
≈ River
⊛ Lake
⊠ Reservoir

JOSEPH BONAPARTE GULF – KALE SULTANIE


181 N2 **Joseph Bonaparte Gulf** *gulf* N Australia
37 N11 **Joseph City** Arizona, SW USA 34°56′N 110°18′W
13 O9 **Joseph, Lake** ◎ Newfoundland and Labrador, E Canada
14 G13 **Joseph, Lake** ◎ Ontario, S Canada
186 C6 **Josephstaal** Madang, N Papua New Guinea 04°42′S 144°55′E
**José P.Varela** *see* José Pedro Varela
59 J14 **José Rodrigues** Pará, N Brazil 05°45′S 51°20′W
152 K9 **Joshimath** Uttarākhand, N India 30°33′N 79°35′E
25 T7 **Joshua** Texas, SW USA 32°27′N 97°23′W
35 V15 **Joshua Tree** California, W USA 34°07′N 116°18′W
77 V14 **Jos Plateau** *plateau* C Nigeria
102 H6 **Josselin** Morbihan, NW France 47°57′N 02°35′W
**Jos Sudarso** *see* Yos Sudarso, Pulau
94 E11 **Jostedalsbreen** *glacier* S Norway
94 F12 **Jotunheimen** ▲ S Norway
138 G7 **Joûnié** *var.* Juniyah. W Lebanon 33°54′N 35°36′E
25 R13 **Jourdanton** Texas, SW USA 28°55′N 98°34′W
98 L7 **Joure** *Fris.* De Jouwer. Fryslân, N Netherlands 52°58′N 05°48′E
93 M18 **Joutsa** Keski-Suomi, C Finland 61°46′N 26°09′E
93 N18 **Joutseno** Etelä-Karjala, SE Finland 61°06′N 28°30′E
92 M12 **Joutsijärvi** Lappi, NE Finland 66°40′N 28°00′E
108 A9 **Joux, Lac de** ◎ W Switzerland
**Jovakān** *see* Jowkān
44 D5 **Jovellanos** Matanzas, W Cuba 22°49′N 81°11′W
153 V13 **Jowai** Meghālaya, NE India 25°25′N 92°21′E
**Jōwat** *see* Jabwot
**Jowhar** *see* Jawhar
143 O12 **Jowkān** *var.* Jovakān. Fārs, S Iran
**Jowzam** *see* Javazm
149 N2 **Jowzjān** ◆ *province* N Afghanistan
**Joypurhat** *see* Jaipurhat
**Józseffalva** *see* Žabalj
**J.Storm Thurmond Reservoir** *see* Clark Hill Lake
45 T6 **Juana Díaz** C Puerto Rico 18°03′N 66°30′W
40 L9 **Juan Aldama** Zacatecas, C Mexico 24°20′N 103°23′W
0 E9 **Juan de Fuca Plate** *tectonic feature*
32 F7 **Juan de Fuca, Strait of** *strait* Canada/USA
**Juan Fernandez Islands** *see* Juan Fernández, Islas
193 S11 **Juan Fernández, Islas** *Eng.* Juan Fernandez Islands. *island group* W Chile
55 O4 **Juangriego** Nueva Esparta, NE Venezuela 11°06′N 63°59′W
56 D11 **Juanjuí** *var.* Juanjuy. San Martín, N Peru 07°10′S 76°44′W
**Juanjuy** *see* Juanjuí
93 N16 **Juankoski** Pohjois-Savo, C Finland 63°01′N 28°24′E
**Juan Lacaze** *see* Juan L. Lacaze
61 E20 **Juan L. Lacaze** *var.* Juan Lacaze, Puerto Sauce; *prev.* Sauce. Colonia, SW Uruguay 34°26′S 57°25′W
62 L5 **Juan Solá** Salta, N Argentina 23°30′S 62°42′W
63 F21 **Juan Stuven, Isla** *island* S Chile
59 H16 **Juará** Mato Grosso, W Brazil 11°10′S 57°28′W
41 N7 **Juárez** *var.* Villa Juárez. Coahuila, NE Mexico 27°39′N 100°43′W
40 C2 **Juárez, Sierra de** ▲▲ NW Mexico
59 O15 **Juazeiro** *prev.* Joazeiro. Bahia, E Brazil 09°25′S 40°30′W
59 P14 **Juazeiro do Norte** Ceará, E Brazil 07°10′S 39°18′W
81 F15 **Juba** *var.* Jūbā. ● Central Equatoria, S South Sudan 04°50′N 31°35′E
81 L17 **Juba** *Amh.* Genalē Wenz, *It.* Guiba, *Som.* Ganaane, Webi Jubba. ⇝ Ethiopia/Somalia
**Jubayl** *see* Jbail
81 L18 **Jubbada Dhexe** *off.* Gobolka Jubbada Dhexe. ◆ *region* SW Somalia
**Jubbada Dhexe, Gobolka** *see* Jubbada Dhexe
81 K18 **Jubbada Hoose** ◆ *region* SW Somalia
**Jubba, Webi** *see* Juba
**Jubbulpore** *see* Jabalpur
**Jubeil** *see* Jbail
74 B9 **Juby, Cap** *headland* SW Morocco 27°58′N 12°56′W
105 R10 **Júcar** *var.* Jucar. ⇝ C Spain
40 L12 **Juchipila** Zacatecas, C Mexico 21°25′N 103°06′W
41 S16 **Juchitán** *var.* Juchitán de Zaragosa. Oaxaca, SE Mexico 16°27′N 95°W
**Juchitán de Zaragosa** *see* Juchitán
138 G11 **Judaea** *cultural region* Israel/West Bank
138 F11 **Judaean Hills** *Heb.* Haré Yehuda. *hill range* E Israel
138 H8 **Judaydah** *Fr.* Jdaïdé. Rīf Dimashq, W Syria 33°17′N 36°15′E
139 P11 **Judayyidat Hāmir** Al Anbār, S Iraq 31°50′N 41°50′E
109 U8 **Judenburg** Steiermark, C Austria 47°09′N 14°43′E
33 T8 **Judith River** ⇝ Montana, NW USA
27 V11 **Judsonia** Arkansas, C USA 35°16′N 91°38′W
141 P14 **Jufrah, Wādī al** *dry watercourse* NW Yemen
**Jugar** *see* Sêrxü
**Jugoslavija** *see* Serbia
42 K10 **Juigalpa** Chontales, S Nicaragua 12°04′N 85°21′W
100 E9 **Juist** *island* NW Germany
**Juisui** *see* Ruisui
59 M21 **Juiz de Fora** Minas Gerais, SE Brazil 21°47′S 43°23′W
62 J5 **Jujuy** *off.* Provincia de Jujuy. ◆ *province* N Argentina
**Jujuy** *see* San Salvador de Jujuy
**Jujuy, Provincia de** *see* Jujuy
92 J11 **Jukkasjärvi** *Lapp.* Čohkkiras. Norrbotten, N Sweden 67°52′N 20°39′E
**Jula** *see* Gyula, Hungary
**Jūlā** *see* Jālū, Libya
37 W2 **Julesburg** Colorado, C USA 40°59′N 102°15′W
**Julia Beterrae** *see* Béziers
57 I17 **Juliaca** Puno, SE Peru 15°32′S 70°10′W
181 U6 **Julia Creek** Queensland, C Australia 20°40′S 141°49′E
35 V17 **Julian** California, W USA 33°04′N 116°36′W
98 H7 **Julianadorp** Noord-Holland, NW Netherlands 52°53′N 04°43′E
109 S11 **Julian Alps** *Ger.* Julische Alpen, *It.* Alpi Giulie, *Slvn.* Julijske Alpe. ▲▲ Italy/Slovenia
55 V11 **Juliana Top** ▲ C Suriname 03°39′N 56°36′W
**Julianehåb** *see* Qaqortoq
**Julijske Alpe** *see* Julian Alps
40 J6 **Julimes** Chihuahua, N Mexico 28°29′N 105°21′W
**Julio Briga** *see* Bragança
**Juliobriga** *see* Logroño
61 G15 **Júlio de Castilhos** Rio Grande do Sul, S Brazil 29°14′S 53°42′W
**Juliomagus** *see* Angers
**Julische Alpen** *see* Julian Alps
**Jullundur** *see* Jalandhar
147 N11 **Juma** *Rus.* Dzhuma. Samarqand Viloyati, C Uzbekistan 39°43′N 66°37′E
161 O3 **Juma He** ⇝ E China
81 L18 **Jumba** *prev.* Jumboo. Jubbada Hoose, S Somalia 0°12′S 42°34′E
**Jumboo** *see* Jumba
35 Y11 **Jumbo Peak** ▲ Nevada, W USA 36°12′N 114°09′W
105 R12 **Jumilla** Murcia, SE Spain 38°28′N 01°19′W
153 N10 **Jumla** Mid Western, NW Nepal 29°22′N 82°13′E
**Jummoo** *see* Jammu
**Jumna** *see* Yamuna
**Jumporn** *see* Chumphon
30 K5 **Jump River** ⇝ Wisconsin, N USA
154 B11 **Jūnāgadh** *var.* Junagarh. Gujarāt, W India 21°32′N 70°32′E
**Junagarh** *see* Jūnāgadh
161 Q6 **Junan** *var.* Shizilu. Shandong, E China 35°11′N 118°47′E
62 G11 **Juncal, Cerro** ▲ C Chile 33°03′S 70°02′W
25 Q10 **Junction** Texas, SW USA 30°31′N 99°48′W
36 K6 **Junction** Utah, W USA 38°14′N 112°13′W
27 O4 **Junction City** Kansas, C USA 39°02′N 96°51′W
32 F13 **Junction City** Oregon, NW USA 44°13′N 123°12′W
60 M10 **Jundiaí** São Paulo, S Brazil 23°10′S 46°54′W
39 X12 **Juneau** *state capital* Alaska, USA 58°13′N 134°11′W
30 M8 **Juneau** Wisconsin, N USA 43°23′N 88°42′W
105 U6 **Juneda** Cataluña, NE Spain 41°33′N 00°49′E
183 Q9 **Junee** New South Wales, SE Australia 34°51′S 147°33′E
35 R8 **June Lake** California, W USA 37°46′N 119°04′W
**Jungbunzlau** *see* Mladá Boleslav
158 L4 **Junggar Pendi** *Eng.* Dzungarian Basin. *basin* NW China
99 N24 **Junglinster** Grevenmacher, C Luxembourg 49°43′N 06°15′E
18 F14 **Juniata River** ⇝ Pennsylvania, NE USA
61 B20 **Junín** Buenos Aires, E Argentina 34°36′S 61°02′W
57 E14 **Junín** Junín, C Peru 11°11′S 76°00′W
57 F14 **Junín** *off.* Región de Junín. ◆ *region* C Peru
63 H15 **Junín de los Andes** Neuquén, W Argentina 39°57′S 71°05′W
57 D14 **Junín, Lago de** ◎ C Peru
**Junín, Región de** *see* Junín
**Juniyah** *see* Joûnié
**Junkseylon** *see* Phuket
160 I11 **Junlian** Sichuan, C China 28°11′N 104°31′E
25 O11 **Juno** Texas, SW USA 30°09′N 101°07′W
92 J11 **Junosuando** *Lapp.* Čunusavvon. Norrbotten, N Sweden 67°25′N 22°28′E
93 H16 **Junsele** Västernorrland, C Sweden 63°42′N 16°54′E
32 L14 **Juntura** Oregon, NW USA 43°43′N 118°05′W
93 N14 **Juntusranta** Kainuu, E Finland 65°12′N 29°30′E
118 H11 **Juodupė** Panevėžys, NE Lithuania 56°07′N 25°37′E
119 H14 **Juozapinės Kalnas** ▲ SE Lithuania 54°29′N 25°27′E
99 K19 **Juprelle** Liège, E Belgium 50°43′N 05°31′E
80 D13 **Jur** ⇝ W South Sudan
103 S9 **Jura** ◆ *department* E France
108 C7 **Jura** ◆ *canton* NW Switzerland
108 B8 **Jura** *var.* Jura Mountains. ▲▲ France/Switzerland
96 G12 **Jura** *island* SW Scotland, United Kingdom
**Juraciszki** *see* Yuratsishki
54 C8 **Juradó** Chocó, NW Colombia 07°07′N 77°45′W
**Jura Mountains** *see* Jura
96 G12 **Jura, Sound of** *strait* W Scotland, United Kingdom
139 V15 **Juraybīyāt, Bi'r** *well* S Iraq
118 E13 **Jurbarkas** *Ger.* Georgenburg, Jurburg. Tauragė, W Lithuania 55°04′N 22°45′E
99 F20 **Jurbise** Hainaut, SW Belgium 50°33′N 03°54′E
**Jurburg** *see* Jurbarkas
118 F9 **Jūrmala** C Latvia 56°57′N 23°42′E
58 D13 **Juruá** Amazonas, NW Brazil 03°08′S 65°59′W
48 F7 **Juruá, Rio** *var.* Río Yuruá. ⇝ Brazil/Peru
59 G16 **Juruena** Mato Grosso, W Brazil 10°32′S 58°38′W
59 G16 **Juruena, Rio** ⇝ W Brazil
165 Q6 **Jūsan-ko** ◎ Honshū, C Japan
25 O6 **Justiceburg** Texas, SW USA 32°57′N 101°07′W
**Justinianopolis** *see* Kirşehir
62 K11 **Justo Daract** San Luis, C Argentina 33°52′S 65°12′W
59 C14 **Jutaí** Amazonas, W Brazil 05°10′S 68°45′W
58 C13 **Jutaí, Rio** ⇝ NW Brazil
100 N13 **Jüterbog** Brandenburg, E Germany 51°58′N 13°06′E
42 E6 **Jutiapa** Jutiapa, S Guatemala 14°18′N 89°52′W
42 A3 **Jutiapa** *off.* Departamento de Jutiapa. ◆ *department* SE Guatemala
**Jutiapa, Departamento de** *see* Jutiapa
42 J6 **Juticalpa** Olancho, C Honduras 14°39′N 86°12′W
82 I13 **Jutila** North Western, NW Zambia 12°33′S 26°09′E
**Jutland** *see* Jylland
84 F8 **Jutland Bank** *undersea feature* SE North Sea 56°50′N 07°20′E
93 N16 **Juuka** Pohjois-Karjala, E Finland 63°12′N 29°17′E
93 N17 **Juva** Etelä-Savo, E Finland 61°55′N 27°54′E
**Juvavum** *see* Salzburg
44 C5 **Juventud, Isla de la** ◆ *special municipality* W Cuba
44 A6 **Juventud, Isla de la** *var.* Isla de Pinos, *Eng.* Isle of Youth; *prev.* The Isle of the Pines. *island* W Cuba
**Juwārtā** *see* Chwarta
**Juwārtā** *see* Chemchemal
161 Q5 **Juxian** *var.* Chengyang, Ju Xian. Shandong, E China 35°33′N 118°45′E
**Ju Xian** *see* Juxian
161 P6 **Juye** Shandong, E China 35°26′N 116°04′E
113 O15 **Južna Morava** *Ger.* Südliche Morava. ⇝ SE Serbia
83 H20 **Jwaneng** Southern, S Botswana 24°35′N 24°45′E
95 I23 **Jyderup** Sjælland, E Denmark 55°40′N 11°25′E
95 F22 **Jylland** *Eng.* Jutland. *peninsula* W Denmark
**Jyrgalan** *see* Dzhergalan
93 M17 **Jyväskylä** Keski-Suomi, C Finland 62°08′N 25°47′E


# K


38 D9 **Ka'a'awa** *var.* Kaaawa. O'ahu, Hawaii, USA, C Pacific Ocean 21°33′N 157°47′W
**Kaaawa** *see* Ka'a'awa
81 G16 **Kaabong** NE Uganda 03°30′N 34°08′E
**Kaaden** *see* Kadaň
**Kaafu Atoll** *see* Male' Atoll
55 V9 **Kaaimanston** Sipaliwini, N Suriname 05°06′N 56°04′W
**Kaakhka** *see* Kaka
**Kaala** *see* Caála
187 O16 **Kaala-Gomen** Province Nord, W New Caledonia 20°40′S 164°24′E
92 L9 **Kaamanen** *Lapp.* Gámas. Lappi, N Finland 69°05′N 27°16′E
**Kaapstad** *see* Cape Town
**Kaarasjoki** *see* Karasjok
**Kaaresuanto** *see* Karesuando
92 J10 **Kaaresuvanto** *N. Sami.* Gárassavon. Lappi, N Finland 68°28′N 22°29′E
93 K19 **Kaarina** Varsinais-Suomi, SW Finland 60°24′N 22°25′E
99 I14 **Kaatsheuvel** Noord-Brabant, S Netherlands 51°39′N 05°02′E
93 N16 **Kaavi** Pohjois-Savo, C Finland 62°58′N 28°30′E
**Kaba** *see* Habahe
171 O14 **Kabaena, Pulau** *island* C Indonesia
**Kabakly** *see* Gabakly
76 J14 **Kabala** N Sierra Leone 09°40′N 11°36′W
81 E19 **Kabale** SW Uganda 01°15′S 29°58′E
55 U10 **Kabalebo Rivier** ⇝ W Suriname
79 N22 **Kabalo** Katanga, SE Dem. Rep. Congo 06°02′S 26°55′E
79 O21 **Kabambare** Maniema, E Dem. Rep. Congo 04°40′S 27°41′E
145 W13 **Kabanbay** *Kaz.* Qabanbay; *prev.* Andreyevka, *Kaz.* Andreevka. Almaty, SE Kazakhstan 45°50′N 80°34′E
145 Q9 **Kabanbay Batyr** *prev.* Rozhdestvenka. Akmola, C Kazakhstan 50°51′N 71°25′E
187 Y15 **Kabara** *prev.* Kambara. *island* Lau Group, E Fiji
**Kabardino-Balkaria** *see* Kabardino-Balkarskaya Respublika
126 M15 **Kabardino-Balkarskaya Respublika** *Eng.* Kabardino-Balkaria. ◆ *autonomous republic* SW Russia
79 O19 **Kabare** Sud-Kivu, E Dem. Rep. Congo 02°13′S 28°40′E
171 T11 **Kabarei** Papua Barat, E Indonesia 0°01′S 130°58′E
171 P7 **Kabasalan** Mindanao, S Philippines 07°46′N 122°49′E
77 U15 **Kabba** Kogi, S Nigeria 07°48′N 06°07′E
92 I13 **Kåbdalis** *Lapp.* Goabddális. Norrbotten, N Sweden 66°08′N 20°03′E
138 M6 **Kabd aş Şārim** *hill range* E Syria
14 B7 **Kabenung Lake** ◎ Ontario, S Canada
29 W3 **Kabetogama Lake** ◎ Minnesota, N USA
**Kabia, Pulau** *see* Kabin, Pulau
79 M22 **Kabinda** Kasai-Oriental, SE Dem. Rep. Congo 06°09′S 24°29′E
**Kabinda** *see* Cabinda
171 O15 **Kabin, Pulau** *var.* Pulau Kabia. *island* W Indonesia
171 P16 **Kabir** Pulau Pantar, S Indonesia 08°15′S 124°12′E
149 T10 **Kabīrwala** Punjab, E Pakistan 30°24′N 71°51′E
114 M9 **Kableshkovo** Burgas, E Bulgaria 42°65′N 27°34′E
78 I13 **Kabo** Ouham, NW Central African Republic 07°43′N 18°38′E
**Kābol** *see* Kābul
83 H14 **Kabompo** North Western, W Zambia 13°36′S 24°10′E
83 H14 **Kabompo** ⇝ W Zambia
79 M22 **Kabongo** Katanga, SE Dem. Rep. Congo 07°20′S 25°34′E
120 K11 **Kaboudia, Rass** *headland* E Tunisia 35°13′N 11°09′E
124 J14 **Kabozha** Novgorodskaya Oblast', W Russia 58°48′N 35°00′E
**Kabūd Gonbad** *see* Kalāt
142 L5 **Kabūd Rāhang** Hamadān, W Iran 35°12′N 48°44′E
82 L12 **Kabuko** Muchinga, NE Zambia 11°31′S 31°16′E
149 Q5 **Kābul** *prev.* Kābol. ● (Afghanistan) Kābul, E Afghanistan 34°34′N 69°08′E
149 Q5 **Kābul** *prev.* Kābol. ◆ *province* E Afghanistan
149 R5 **Kabul** *var.* Daryā-ye Kābul. ⇝ Afghanistan/Pakistan *see also* Kābul, Daryā-ye
**Kabul** *see* Kābul, Daryā-ye
149 S5 **Kābul, Daryā-ye** *var.* Kabul. ⇝ Afghanistan/Pakistan *see also* Kabul
**Kābul, Daryā-ye** *see* Kabul
79 O25 **Kabunda** Katanga, SE Dem. Rep. Congo 12°21′S 29°14′E
171 R9 **Kaburuang, Pulau** *island* Kepulauan Talaud, N Indonesia
80 G8 **Kabushiya** River Nile, NE Sudan 16°54′N 33°41′E
83 J14 **Kabwe** Central, C Zambia 14°29′S 28°25′E
186 E7 **Kabwum** Morobe, C Papua New Guinea 06°04′S 147°09′E
113 N17 **Kačanik** *Serb.* Kačanik. S Kosovo 42°13′N 21°16′E
**Kačanik** *see* Kaçanik
118 F13 **Kačerginė** Kaunas, C Lithuania 54°55′N 23°40′E
117 S13 **Kacha** Avtonomna Respublika Krym, S Ukraine 44°46′N 33°33′E
154 A10 **Kachchh, Gulf of** *var.* Gulf of Cutch, Gulf of Kutch. *gulf* W India
154 I11 **Kachchhīdhāna** Madhya Pradesh, C India 21°33′N 78°54′E
149 Q11 **Kachchh, Rann of** *var.* Rann of Kachh, Rann of Kutch. *salt marsh* India/Pakistan
39 Q13 **Kachemak Bay** *bay* Alaska, USA
**Kachh, Rann of** *see* Kachchh, Rann of
77 V14 **Kachia** Kaduna, C Nigeria 09°52′N 08°00′E
167 N2 **Kachin State** ◆ *state* N Myanmar (Burma)
**Kachiry** *see* Kashyr
137 Q11 **Kaçkar Dağları** ▲▲ NE Turkey
155 C21 **Kadamatt Island** *island* Lakshadweep, India, N Indian Ocean
111 B15 **Kadaň** *Ger.* Kaaden. Ústecký Kraj, NW Czechia 50°24′N 13°16′E
1667 N11 **Kadan Kyun** *prev.* King Island. *island* Mergui Archipelago, S Myanmar (Burma)
155 I18 **Kadapa** *prev.* Cuddapah. Andhra Pradesh, S India 14°30′N 78°50′E
187 X15 **Kadavu** *prev.* Kandavu. *island* S Fiji
187 X15 **Kadavu Passage** *channel* S Fiji
79 G16 **Kadéï** ⇝ Cameroon/Central African Republic
**Kadhimain** *see* Al Kāẓimīyah
**Kadijica** *see* Kadiytsa
114 M13 **Kadiköy Barajı** ⊠ NW Turkey
182 I8 **Kadina** South Australia 33°59′S 137°43′E
136 H15 **Kadınhanı** Konya, C Turkey 38°15′N 32°14′E
76 M14 **Kadiolo** Sikasso, S Mali 10°30′N 05°43′W
136 L16 **Kadirli** Osmaniye, S Turkey 37°22′N 36°05′E
117 Y7 **Kadiyivka** *prev.* Stakhanov. Luhans'ka Oblast', E Ukraine 48°30′N 38°42′E
114 G11 **Kadiytsa** *Mac.* Kadijica. ▲ Bulgaria/North Macedonia 41°48′N 22°58′E
28 L10 **Kadoka** South Dakota, N USA 43°49′N 101°30′W
127 N5 **Kadom** Ryazanskaya Oblast', W Russia 54°35′N 42°27′E
83 K16 **Kadoma** *prev.* Gatooma. Mashonaland West, C Zimbabwe 18°22′S 29°55′E
80 E12 **Kadugli** Southern Kordofan, S Sudan 11°N 29°44′E
77 V14 **Kaduna** Kaduna, C Nigeria 10°32′N 07°26′E
77 V14 **Kaduna** ◆ *state* C Nigeria
77 V15 **Kaduna** ⇝ N Nigeria
124 K14 **Kaduy** Vologodskaya Oblast', NW Russia 59°10′N 37°11′E
154 E13 **Kadwa** ⇝ W India
123 S9 **Kadykchan** Magadanskaya Oblast', E Russia 62°54′N 146°53′E
**Kadzharan** *see* K'ajaran
125 T7 **Kadzherom** Respublika Komi, NW Russia 64°42′N 55°51′E
**Kadzhi-Say** *see* Bokonbayevo
76 I10 **Kaédi** Gorgol, S Mauritania 16°12′N 13°32′W
78 G12 **Kaélé** Extrême-Nord, N Cameroon 10°05′N 14°28′E
38 C9 **Ka'ena Point** *var.* Kaena Point. *headland* O'ahu, Hawai'i, USA 21°34′N 158°16′W
184 J2 **Kaeo** Northland, North Island, New Zealand 35°03′S 173°40′E
163 X14 **Kaesŏng** *var.* Kaesŏng-si. S North Korea 37°58′N 126°31′E
**Kaesŏng-si** *see* Kaesŏng
**Kaewieng** *see* Kavieng
79 L24 **Kafakumba** Shaba, S Dem. Rep. Congo 09°39′S 23°43′E
**Kafan** *see* Kapan
77 V14 **Kafanchan** Kaduna, C Nigeria 09°32′N 08°18′E
**Kaffa** *see* Feodosiya
76 G11 **Kaffrine** C Senegal 14°07′N 15°27′W
**Kafiréas, Akrotírio** *see* Ntóro, Kávo
115 I19 **Kafiréos, Stenó** *strait* Évvoia/Kykládes, Greece, Aegean Sea
**Kafirnigan** *see* Kofarnihon
**Kafo** *see* Kafu
75 W7 **Kafr ash Shaykh** *var.* Kafrel Sheik, Kafr el Sheikh. N Egypt 31°07′N 30°56′E
**Kafr el Sheikh** *see* Kafr ash Shaykh
81 F17 **Kafu** *var.* Kafo. ⇝ W Uganda
83 J15 **Kafue** Lusaka, SE Zambia 15°44′S 28°10′E
83 I14 **Kafue** ⇝ C Zambia
67 T13 **Kafue Flats** *plain* C Zambia
164 K12 **Kaga** Ishikawa, Honshū, SW Japan 36°18′N 136°19′E
79 J14 **Kaga Bandoro** *prev.* Fort-Crampel. Nana-Grébizi, C Central African Republic 06°54′N 19°10′E
81 E18 **Kagadi** W Uganda 0°57′N 30°52′E
38 H17 **Kagalaska Island** *island* Aleutian Islands, Alaska, USA
**Kagan** *see* Kogon
**Kaganovichabad** *see* Kolkhozobod
**Kagarlyk** *see* Kaharlyk
164 H14 **Kagawa** *off.* Kagawa-ken. ◆ *prefecture* Shikoku, SW Japan
**Kagawa-ken** *see* Kagawa
154 J13 **Kagaznagar** Telangana, C India 19°25′N 79°30′E
93 J14 **Kåge** Västerbotten, N Sweden 64°49′N 21°00′E
81 E19 **Kagera** *var.* Ziwa Magharibi, *Eng.* West Lake. ◆ *region* NW Tanzania
81 E19 **Kagera** *var.* Akagera. ⇝ Rwanda/Tanzania
**Kagera** *see* Akagera
76 L5 **Kâghet** *var.* Karet. *physical region* N Mauritania
**Kagi** *see* Chiayi
137 S12 **Kağızman** Kars, NE Turkey 40°08′N 43°07′E
188 I6 **Kagman Point** *headland* Saipan, S Northern Mariana Islands
164 C16 **Kagoshima** *var.* Kagosima. Kagoshima, Kyūshū, SW Japan 31°37′N 130°33′E
164 C16 **Kagoshima** *off.* Kagoshima-ken, *var.* Kagosima. ◆ *prefecture* Kyūshū, SW Japan
**Kagoshima-ken** *see* Kagoshima
**Kagosima** *see* Kagoshima
**Kagul** *see* Cahul
**Kagul, Ozero** *see* Kahul, Ozero
38 B8 **Kahala Point** *headland* Kaua'i, Hawai'i, USA 22°08′N 159°17′W
81 F21 **Kahama** Shinyanga, NW Tanzania 03°48′S 32°36′E
117 P5 **Kaharlyk** *Rus.* Kagarlyk. Kyivs'ka Oblast', N Ukraine 49°50′N 30°50′E
169 T13 **Kahayan, Sungai** ⇝ Borneo, C Indonesia
79 I22 **Kahemba** Bandundu, SW Dem. Rep. Congo 07°20′S 19°00′E
185 A23 **Kaherekoau Mountains** ▲▲ South Island, New Zealand
143 W14 **Kahīrī** *var.* Kūhīrī. Sīstān va Balūchestān, SE Iran 26°55′N 61°04′E
101 L16 **Kahla** Thüringen, C Germany 50°49′N 11°33′E
101 G15 **Kahler Asten** ▲ W Germany 51°11′N 08°32′E
**Kahmard, Daryā-ye** *see* Surkh Āb, Daryā-ye
143 T13 **Kahnūj** Kermān, SE Iran 28°N 57°41′E
27 V1 **Kahoka** Missouri, C USA 40°24′N 91°44′W
38 E10 **Kaho'olawe** *var.* Kahoolawe. *island* Hawai'i, USA, C Pacific Ocean
**Kahoolawe** *see* Kaho'olawe
136 M16 **Kahramanmaraş** *var.* Kahraman Maraş, Maraş, Marash. Kahramanmaraş, S Turkey 37°34′N 36°54′E
136 L15 **Kahramanmaraş** *var.* Kahraman Maraş, Maraş, Marash. ◆ *province* C Turkey
**Kahraman Maraş** *see* Kahramanmaraş
**Kahror/Kahror Pakka** *see* Kahror Pakka
149 T11 **Kahror Pakka** *var.* Kahror, Koror Pacca. Punjab, E Pakistan 29°38′N 71°59′E
137 N15 **Kâhta** Adıyaman, S Turkey 37°48′N 38°35′E
38 D8 **Kahuku** O'ahu, Hawaii, USA, C Pacific Ocean 21°40′N 157°57′W
38 D8 **Kahuku Point** *headland* O'ahu, Hawai'i, USA 21°42′N 157°59′W
116 M12 **Kahul, Ozero** *var.* Lacul Cahul, *Rus.* Ozero Kagul. ◎ Moldova/Ukraine
143 V11 **Kahūrak** Sīstān va Balūchestān, SE Iran 29°25′N 59°38′E
184 G13 **Kahurangi Point** *headland* South Island, New Zealand 40°41′S 171°57′E
149 V6 **Kahuta** Punjab, E Pakistan 33°38′N 73°27′E
77 S14 **Kaiama** Kwara, W Nigeria 09°37′N 03°58′E
186 D7 **Kaiapit** Morobe, C Papua New Guinea 06°12′S 146°09′E
185 I18 **Kaiapoi** Canterbury, South Island, New Zealand 43°23′S 172°40′E
36 K9 **Kaibab Plateau** *plain* Arizona, SW USA
171 U14 **Kai Besar, Pulau** *island* Kepulauan Kai, E Indonesia
36 L9 **Kaibito Plateau** *plain* Arizona, SW USA
158 K6 **Kaidu He** *var.* Karaxahar. ⇝ NW China
55 S10 **Kaieteur Falls** *waterfall* C Guyana
161 O6 **Kaifeng** Henan, C China 34°47′N 114°20′E
184 J3 **Kaihu** Northland, North Island, New Zealand 35°47′S 173°39′E
**Kaihua** *see* Wenshan
171 U14 **Kai Kecil, Pulau** *island* Kepulauan Kai, E Indonesia
169 U16 **Kai, Kepulauan** *prev.* Kei Islands. *island group* Maluku, SE Indonesia
184 J3 **Kaikohe** Northland, North Island, New Zealand 35°25′S 173°48′E
185 J16 **Kaikoura** Canterbury, South Island, New Zealand 42°22′S 173°40′E
185 J16 **Kaikoura Peninsula** *peninsula* South Island, New Zealand
**Kailas Range** *see* Gangdisê Shan
160 K12 **Kaili** Guizhou, S China 26°34′N 107°58′E
38 F10 **Kailua** Maui, Hawaii, USA, C Pacific Ocean 20°53′N 156°13′W
**Kailua** *see* Kalaoa
38 G11 **Kailua-Kona** *var.* Kona. Hawaii, USA, C Pacific Ocean 19°43′N 155°58′W
186 B7 **Kaim** ⇝ W Papua New Guinea
171 X14 **Kaima** Papua, E Indonesia 05°36′S 138°39′E
184 M7 **Kaimai Range** ▲▲ North Island, New Zealand
114 E13 **Kaïmaktsalán** *var.* Kajmakčalan. ▲ Greece/North Macedonia 40°57′N 21°48′E *see also* Kajmakčalan
**Kaïmaktsalán** *see* Kajmakčalan
185 C20 **Kaimanawa Mountains** ▲▲ North Island, New Zealand
118 E4 **Käina** *Ger.* Keinis; *prev.* Keina. Hiiumaa, W Estonia 58°50′N 22°49′E
109 V7 **Kainach** ⇝ SE Austria
164 I14 **Kainan** Tokushima, Shikoku, SW Japan 33°36′N 134°20′E
164 H15 **Kainan** Wakayama, Honshū, SW Japan 34°09′N 135°12′E
147 U7 **Kaindy** *Kyr.* Kayyngdy. Chuyskaya Oblast', N Kyrgyzstan 42°48′N 73°39′E
77 T14 **Kainji Dam** *dam* W Nigeria
**Kainji Lake** *see* Kainji Reservoir
77 T14 **Kainji Reservoir** *var.* Kainji Lake. ⊠ W Nigeria
186 D8 **Kaintiba** *var.* Kamina. Gulf, S Papua New Guinea 07°29′S 146°04′E
92 K12 **Kainulasjärvi** Norrbotten, N Sweden 67°00′N 22°31′E
184 K5 **Kaipara Harbour** *harbor* North Island, New Zealand
152 I10 **Kairāna** Uttar Pradesh, N India 29°24′N 77°10′E
74 M6 **Kairouan** *var.* Al Qayrawān. E Tunisia 35°46′N 10°11′E
**Kaisaria** *see* Kayseri
101 F20 **Kaiserslautern** Rheinland-Pfalz, SW Germany 49°27′N 07°46′E
118 G13 **Kaišiadorys** Kaunas, S Lithuania 54°51′N 24°27′E
184 I2 **Kaitaia** Northland, North Island, New Zealand 35°07′S 173°13′E
185 E24 **Kaitangata** Otago, South Island, New Zealand 46°18′S 169°52′E
152 I9 **Kaithal** Haryāna, NW India 29°47′N 76°26′E
**Kaitong** *see* Tongyu
169 N13 **Kait, Tanjung** *headland* Sumatera, W Indonesia 03°13′S 106°03′E
38 E9 **Kaiwi Channel** *channel* Hawai'i, USA, C Pacific Ocean
160 K9 **Kaixian** *var.* Hanfeng. Sichuan, C China 31°13′N 108°25′E
163 V11 **Kaiyuan** *var.* K'ai-yüan. Liaoning, NE China 42°33′N 124°04′E
160 H14 **Kaiyuan** Yunnan, SW China 23°42′N 103°14′E
**K'ai-yüan** *see* Kaiyuan
39 O9 **Kaiyuh Mountains** ▲▲ Alaska, USA
93 M15 **Kajaani** *Swe.* Kajana. Kainuu, C Finland 64°17′N 27°46′E
149 N7 **Kajakī, Band-e** ◎ C Afghanistan
**Kajan** *see* Kayan, Sungai
**Kajana** *see* Kajaani
137 V13 **K'ajaran** *Rus.* Kadzharan. SE Armenia 39°10′N 46°09′E
**Kajisay** *see* Bokonbayevo
113 O20 **Kajmakčalan** *var.* Kaïmaktsalán. ▲ S North Macedonia 40°57′N 21°48′E *see also* Kaïmaktsalán
**Kajmakčalan** *see* Kaïmaktsalán
**Kajnar** *see* Kaynar
149 N6 **Kajrān** Dāykundī, C Afghanistan 33°12′N 65°28′E
149 N5 **Kaj Rōd** ⇝ C Afghanistan
146 G14 **Kaka** *Rus.* Kaakhka. Ahal Welaýaty, S Turkmenistan 37°20′N 59°37′E
12 C12 **Kakabeka Falls** Ontario, S Canada 48°24′N 89°40′W
83 F23 **Kakamas** Northern Cape, W South Africa 28°45′S 20°33′E
81 H18 **Kakamega** Kakamega, W Kenya 0°17′N 34°47′E
112 H13 **Kakanj** Federacija Bosne I Hercegovine, C Bosnia and Herzegovina 44°06′N 18°07′E
185 F22 **Kakanui Mountains** ▲▲ South Island, New Zealand
184 K11 **Kakaramea** Taranaki, North Island, New Zealand 39°42′S 174°27′E
76 J16 **Kakata** C Liberia 06°35′N 10°19′W
184 M11 **Kakatahi** Manawatu-Wanganui, North Island, New Zealand 39°40′S 175°20′E
113 M23 **Kakavi** Gjirokastër, S Albania 39°55′N 20°19′E
147 O14 **Kakaydi** Surkhondaryo Viloyati, S Uzbekistan 37°37′N 67°30′E
164 F13 **Kake** Hiroshima, Honshū, SW Japan 34°37′N 132°17′E
39 X13 **Kake** Kupreanof Island, Alaska, USA 56°58′N 133°57′W
171 P14 **Kakea** Pulau Wowoni, C Indonesia 04°09′S 123°06′E
164 M14 **Kakegawa** Shizuoka, Honshū, S Japan 34°47′N 138°02′E
165 V16 **Kakeroma-jima** Kagoshima, SW Japan
143 T6 **Kākhak** Khorāsān-e Razavī, E Iran
118 L11 **Kakhanavichy** *Rus.* Kokhanovichi. Vitsyebskaya Voblasts', N Belarus 55°52′N 28°08′E
39 P13 **Kakhonak** Alaska, USA 59°26′N 154°48′W
117 S10 **Kakhovka** Khersons'ka Oblast', S Ukraine 46°40′N 33°30′E
117 U9 **Kakhovs'ke Vodoskhovyshche** *Rus.* Kakhovskoye Vodokhranilishche. ⊠ SE Ukraine
**Kakhovskoye Vodokhranilishche** *see* Kakhovs'ke Vodoskhovyshche
117 T11 **Kakhovs'kyy Kanal** *canal* S Ukraine
**Kakia** *see* Khakhea
155 L16 **Kākināda** *prev.* Cocanada. Andhra Pradesh, E India 16°56′N 82°13′E
**Käkisalmi** *see* Priozersk
164 I13 **Kakogawa** Hyōgo, Honshū, SW Japan 34°49′N 134°52′E
81 F18 **Kakoge** C Uganda 01°03′N 32°30′E
145 O7 **Kak, Ozero** ◎ N Kazakhstan
**Ka-Krem** *see* Malyy Yenisey
**Kakshaal-Too, Khrebet** *see* Kokshaal-Tau
39 S5 **Kaktovik** Alaska, USA 70°08′N 143°37′W
165 Q11 **Kakuda** Miyagi, Honshū, C Japan 37°59′N 140°48′E
165 Q8 **Kakunodate** Akita, Honshū, C Japan 39°37′N 140°35′E
**Kalaallit Nunaat** *see* Greenland
149 T7 **Kālābāgh** Punjab, E Pakistan 33°00′N 71°35′E
171 Q16 **Kalabahi** Pulau Alor, S Indonesia 08°14′S 124°32′E
188 I5 **Kalabera** Saipan, S Northern Mariana Islands
83 G14 **Kalabo** Western, W Zambia 15°00′S 22°37′E
155 G15 **Kalaburagi** *prev.* Gulbarga. Karnātaka, C India 17°22′N 76°47′E
126 M9 **Kalach** Voronezhskaya Oblast', W Russia 50°24′N 41°00′E
127 N10 **Kalach-na-Donu** Volgogradskaya Oblast', SW Russia 48°45′N 43°29′E
166 K5 **Kaladan** ⇝ W Myanmar (Burma)
14 K14 **Kaladar** Ontario, SE Canada 44°38′N 77°06′W
38 G13 **Ka Lae** *var.* South Cape, South Point. *headland* Hawai'i, USA, C Pacific Ocean 18°54′N 155°40′W
83 G19 **Kalahari Desert** *desert* Southern Africa
38 B8 **Kalāheo** *var.* Kalaheo. Kaua'i, Hawaii, USA, C Pacific Ocean 21°55′N 159°31′W
**Kalaheo** *see* Kalāheo
**Kalaikhum** *see* Qal'aikhum
**Kala-i-Mor** *see* Galaýmor
93 K15 **Kalajoki** Pohjois-Pohjanmaa, W Finland 64°15′N 24°E
**Kalak** *see* Eski Kaļak
**Kal al Sraghna** *see* El Keläa Srarhna
32 G10 **Kalama** Washington, NW USA 46°00′N 122°50′W
**Kalámai** *see* Kalámata
115 G14 **Kalamariá** Kentrikí Makedonía, N Greece 40°37′N 22°58′E
**Kalamás** *see* Thýamis
115 E21 **Kalámata** *prev.* Kalámai. Pelopónnisos, S Greece 37°02′N 22°07′E
148 L16 **Kalamat, Khor** *Eng.* Kalmat Lagoon. *lagoon* SW Pakistan
148 L16 **Kalamat, Khor** *Eng.* Kalmat Lagoon. *lagoon* SW Pakistan
31 P10 **Kalamazoo** Michigan, N USA 42°17′N 85°35′W
31 P9 **Kalamazoo River** ⇝ Michigan, N USA
**Kalambaka** *see* Kalampáka
117 S13 **Kalamits'ka Zatoka** *Rus.* Kalamitskiy Zaliv. *gulf* S Ukraine
**Kalamitskiy Zaliv** *see* Kalamits'ka Zatoka
115 H18 **Kálamos** Attikí, C Greece 38°16′N 23°51′E
115 C18 **Kálamos** *island* Iónioi Nísia, Greece, C Mediterranean Sea
115 D15 **Kalampáka** *var.* Kalambaka. Thessalía, C Greece 39°43′N 21°36′E
**Kalan** *see* Călan, Romania
**Kalan** *see* Tunceli, Turkey
117 S11 **Kalanchak** Khersons'ka Oblast', S Ukraine 46°14′N 33°19′E
38 G11 **Kalaoa** *var.* Kailua. Hawaii, USA, C Pacific Ocean 19°43′N 155°59′W
171 O15 **Kalaotoa, Pulau** *island* W Indonesia
155 J24 **Kala Oya** ⇝ NW Sri Lanka
**Kalarash** *see* Călăraşi
93 H17 **Kälarne** Jämtland, C Sweden 63°00′N 16°10′E
143 V15 **Kalar Rūd** ⇝ SE Iran
169 R9 **Kalasin** *var.* Muang Kalasin. Kalasin, E Thailand 16°29′N 103°31′E
143 U4 **Kalāt** *var.* Kabūd Gonbad. Khorāsān-e Razavī, NE Iran 37°02′N 59°46′E
149 O11 **Kalat** *var.* Kelat, Khelat. Baluchistan, SW Pakistan 29°01′N 66°38′E
**Kalāt** *see* Qalāt
115 J14 **Kalathriá, Ákrotírio** *headland* Samothráki, NE Greece 40°24′N 25°34′E
193 W17 **Kalau** *island* Tongatapu Group, SE Tonga
38 E9 **Kalaupapa** Moloka'i, Hawaii, USA, C Pacific Ocean 21°11′N 156°59′W
127 N13 **Kalaus** ⇝ SW Russia
**Kalávrita** *see* Kalávryta
115 E19 **Kalávryta** *var.* Kalávrita. Dytikí Elláda, S Greece 38°02′N 22°06′E
**Kalayaan, Kapuluan ng** *see* Spratly Islands
137 V12 **Kälbäcär** SW Azerbaijan 40°04′N 46°00′E
141 Y10 **Kalbān** W Oman 20°19′N 58°40′E
**Kalbar** *see* Kalimantan Barat
180 H11 **Kalbarri** Western Australia 27°43′S 114°08′E
**Kalbinskiy Khrebet** *see* Khrebet Kalba
144 G10 **Kaldygayty** ⇝ W Kazakhstan
166 L4 **Kale** Sagaing, W Myanmar (Burma) 23°11′N 94°03′E
136 I12 **Kalecik** Ankara, N Turkey 40°08′N 33°27′E
79 O19 **Kalehe** Sud-Kivu, E Dem. Rep. Congo 02°05′S 28°52′E
79 P22 **Kalemie** *prev.* Albertville. Katanga, SE Dem. Rep. Congo 05°55′S 29°09′E
**Kalemyo** *see* Kale
82 H12 **Kalene Hill** North Western, NW Zambia 11°10′S 24°12′E
167 T11 **Kaléng** *prev.* Phumī Kaléng. Stung Treng, NE Cambodia 13°57′N 106°17′E
**Kale Sultanie** *see* Çanakkale


◆ Country
● Country Capital
◇ Dependent Territory
○ Dependent Territory Capital
◆ Administrative Regions
✈ International Airport
▲ Mountain
▲▲ Mountain Range
⚠ Volcano
⇝ River
◎ Lake
⊠ Reservoir

KALEVALA – KARA-BOGAZ-GOL, ZALIV


124 I7 **Kalevala** Respublika Kareliya, NW Russia 65°12′N 31°16′E
166 L4 **Kalewa** Sagaing, C Myanmar (Burma) 23°15′N 94°19′E
**Kalgan** *see* Zhangjiakou
39 Q12 **Kalgin Island** *island* Alaska, USA
180 L12 **Kalgoorlie** Western Australia 30°51′S 121°27′E
**Kali** *see* Sārda
115 E17 **Kaliakoúda** ▲ C Greece 38°47′N 21°42′E
114 O8 **Kaliakra, Nos** *headland* NE Bulgaria 43°22′N 28°28′E
115 F19 **Kaliánoi** Pelopónnisos, S Greece 37°55′N 22°28′E
115 N24 **Kalí Límni** ▲ Kárpathos, SE Greece 35°34′N 27°08′E
79 N20 **Kalima** Maniema, E Dem. Rep. Congo 02°34′S 26°27′E
169 S11 **Kalimantan** *Eng.* Indonesian Borneo. ◆ *geopolitical region* Borneo, C Indonesia
169 Q11 **Kalimantan Barat** *off.* Propinsi Kalimantan Berat, *var.* Kalbar, *Eng.* West Borneo, West Kalimantan. ◆ *province* N Indonesia
**Kalimantan Barat, Propinsi** *see* Kalimantan Barat
169 T13 **Kalimantan Selatan** *off.* Propinsi Kalimantan Selatan, *var.* Kalsel, *Eng.* South Borneo, South Kalimantan. ◆ *province* N Indonesia
**Kalimantan Selatan, Propinsi** *see* Kalimantan Selatan
169 R12 **Kalimantan Tengah** *off.* Propinsi Kalimantan Tengah, *var.* Kalteng, *Eng.* Central Borneo, Central Kalimantan. ◆ *province* N Indonesia
**Kalimantan Tengah, Propinsi** *see* Kalimantan Tengah
169 U10 **Kalimantan Timur** *off.* Propinsi Kalimantan Timur, *var.* Kaltim, *Eng.* East Borneo, East Kalimantan. ◆ *province* N Indonesia
**Kalimantan Timur, Propinsi** *see* Kalimantan Timur
**Kálimnos** *see* Kálymnos
153 S12 **Kālimpang** West Bengal, NE India 27°02′N 88°34′E
**Kalinin** *see* Tver'
**Kalinin** *see* Boldumsaz
**Kalininabad** *see* Levakant
126 B3 **Kaliningrad** Kaliningradskaya Oblast', W Russia 54°48′N 21°33′E
**Kaliningrad** *see* Kaliningradskaya Oblast'
126 A3 **Kaliningradskaya Oblast'** *var.* Kaliningrad. ◆ *province and enclave* W Russia
**Kalinino** *see* Tashir
**Kalininobod** *see* Levakant
127 O8 **Kalininsk** Saratovskaya Oblast', W Russia 51°31′N 44°25′E
**Kalininsk** *see* Boldumsaz
**Kalinisk** *see* Cupcina
119 M19 **Kalinkavichy** *Rus.* Kalinkovichi. Homyel'skaya Voblasts', SE Belarus 52°08′N 29°19′E
**Kalinkovichi** *see* Kalinkavichy
81 G18 **Kaliro** SE Uganda 0°54′N 33°30′E
**Kalisch/Kalish** *see* Kalisz
33 O7 **Kalispell** Montana, NW USA 48°12′N 114°18′W
110 I13 **Kalisz** *Ger.* Kalisch, *Rus.* Kalish; *anc.* Calisia. Wielkopolskie, C Poland 51°46′N 18°04′E
110 F9 **Kalisz Pomorski** *Ger.* Kallies. Zachodnio-pomorskie, NW Poland 53°55′N 15°55′E
126 M10 **Kalitva** 🌊 SW Russia
81 F21 **Kaliua** Tabora, C Tanzania 05°03′S 31°48′E
92 K13 **Kalix** Norrbotten, N Sweden 65°51′N 23°14′E
92 K12 **Kalixälven** 🌊 N Sweden
92 J11 **Kalixfors** Norrbotten, N Sweden 67°45′N 20°20′E
145 T8 **Kalkaman** *Kaz.* Qalqaman. Pavlodar, NE Kazakhstan 51°57′N 75°58′E
**Kalkandelen** *see* Tetovo
181 O4 **Kalkarindji** Northern Territory, N Australia 17°32′S 130°40′E
31 P6 **Kalkaska** Michigan, N USA 44°44′N 85°11′W
93 F16 **Kall** Jämtland, C Sweden 63°31′N 13°16′E
189 X2 **Kallalen** *var.* Calalen. *island* Ratak Chain, SE Marshall Islands
118 J5 **Kallaste** *Ger.* Krasnogor. Tartumaa, SE Estonia 58°40′N 27°12′E
93 N16 **Kallavesi** ◎ SE Finland
115 F17 **Kallídromo** ▲▲ C Greece
**Kallies** *see* Kalisz Pomorski
95 M22 **Kallinge** Blekinge, S Sweden 56°14′N 15°17′E
115 L16 **Kalloní** Lésvos, E Greece 39°14′N 26°16′E
93 F16 **Kallsjön** ◎ C Sweden
95 N21 **Kalmar** *var.* Calmar. Kalmar, S Sweden 56°40′N 16°22′E
95 M19 **Kalmar** *var.* Calmar. ◆ *county* S Sweden
95 N20 **Kalmarsund** *strait* S Sweden
**Kalmat Lagoon** *see* Kalamat, Khor
117 X9 **Kal'mius** 🌊 E Ukraine
99 H15 **Kalmthout** Antwerpen, N Belgium 51°24′N 04°27′E
**Kalmykia/Kalmykiya-Khal'mg Tangch, Respublika** *see* Kalmykiya, Respublika
127 O12 **Kalmykiya, Respublika** *var.* Respublika Kalmykiya-Khal'mg Tangch, *Eng.* Kalmykia; *prev.* Kalmytskaya ASSR. ◆ *autonomous republic* SW Russia
**Kalmytskaya ASSR** *see* Kalmykiya, Respublika
118 F9 **Kalnciems** C Latvia 56°46′N 23°37′E
114 L10 **Kalnitsa** 🌊 SE Bulgaria
111 J24 **Kalocsa** Bács-Kiskun, S Hungary 46°31′N 19°00′E
114 J9 **Kalofer** Plovdiv, C Bulgaria 42°36′N 25°00′E
38 E10 **Kalohi Channel** *channel* C Pacific Ocean
33 I16 **Kalomo** Southern, S Zambia 17°02′S 26°29′E
29 X14 **Kalona** Iowa, C USA 41°28′N 91°42′W
115 K22 **Kalotási, Akrotírio** *cape* Amorgós, Kykládes, Greece, Aegean Sea
152 J8 **Kalpa** Himāchal Pradesh, N India 31°33′N 78°16′E
115 C15 **Kalpáki** Ípeiros, W Greece 39°53′N 20°38′E
155 C22 **Kalpeni Island** *island* Lakshadweep, India, N Indian Ocean
152 K13 **Kālpi** Uttar Pradesh, N India 26°07′N 79°44′E
158 G7 **Kalpin** Xinjiang Uygur Zizhiqu, NW China 40°35′N 78°52′E
149 P16 **Kalri Lake** ◎ SE Pakistan
**Kalsel** *see* Kalimantan Selatan
143 R5 **Kāl Shūr** 🌊 N Iran
39 N11 **Kalskag** Alaska, USA 61°32′N 160°15′W
**Kalsø** *see* Kalsoy
95 B18 **Kalsoy** *Dan.* Kalsø. *island* N Faroe Islands
39 O9 **Kaltag** Alaska, USA 64°19′N 158°43′W
108 H7 **Kaltbrunn** Sankt Gallen, NE Switzerland 47°11′N 09°00′E
**Kaltdorf** *see* Pruszków
**Kalteng** *see* Kalimantan Tengah
**Kaltim** *see* Kalimantan Timur
77 X14 **Kaltungo** Gombe, E Nigeria 09°49′N 11°22′E
126 K4 **Kaluga** Kaluzhskaya Oblast', W Russia 54°31′N 36°16′E
155 J26 **Kalu Ganga** 🌊 S Sri Lanka
82 J13 **Kalulushi** Copperbelt, C Zambia 12°50′S 28°03′E
180 M2 **Kalumburu** Western Australia 14°11′S 126°40′E
95 H23 **Kalundborg** Sjælland, E Denmark 55°42′N 11°06′E
82 K11 **Kalungwishi** 🌊 N Zambia
149 T8 **Kalur Kot** Punjab, E Pakistan 32°08′N 71°20′E
116 I6 **Kalush** *Pol.* Kałusz. Ivano-Frankivs'ka Oblast', W Ukraine 49°02′N 24°20′E
**Kałusz** *see* Kalush
110 N11 **Kałuszyn** Mazowieckie, C Poland 52°12′N 21°43′E
155 J26 **Kalutara** Western Province, SW Sri Lanka 06°35′N 79°59′E
**Kaluwawa** *see* Fergusson Island
126 J5 **Kaluzhskaya Oblast'** ◆ *province* W Russia
119 E14 **Kalvarija** *Pol.* Kalwaria. Marijampolė, S Lithuania 54°25′N 23°13′E
93 K15 **Kälviä** Keski-Pohjanmaa, W Finland 63°53′N 23°30′E
109 U6 **Kalwang** Steiermark, E Austria 47°25′N 14°48′E
**Kalwaria** *see* Kalvarija
154 D13 **Kalyān** Mahārāshtra, W India 19°17′N 73°11′E
124 K16 **Kalyazin** Tverskaya Oblast', W Russia 57°15′N 37°53′E
115 D18 **Kalydón** *anc.* Calydon. *site of ancient city* Dytikí Elláda, C Greece
115 M21 **Kálymnos** *var.* Kálimnos. Kálymnos, Dodekánisa, Greece, Aegean Sea 36°57′N 26°59′E
115 M21 **Kálymnos** *var.* Kálimnos. *island* Dodekánisa, Greece, Aegean Sea
117 O5 **Kalynivka** Kyivs'ka Oblast', N Ukraine 50°14′N 30°16′E
117 N6 **Kalynivka** Vinnyts'ka Oblast', C Ukraine 49°27′N 28°32′E
145 W15 **Kalzhat** *prev.* Kol'zhat. Almaty, SE Kazakhstan 43°29′N 80°37′E
42 M10 **Kama** *var.* Cama. Costa Caribe Sur, SE Nicaragua 12°06′N 83°55′W
165 R9 **Kamaishi** *var.* Kamaisi. Iwate, Honshū, C Japan 39°18′N 141°52′E
**Kamaisi** *see* Kamaishi
118 H13 **Kamajai** Utena, E Lithuania 55°49′N 25°30′E
**Kamajai** *see* Toliejai
149 U9 **Kamālia** Punjab, NE Pakistan 30°44′N 72°39′E
83 I14 **Kamalondo** North Western, NW Zambia 13°42′S 25°38′E
136 I13 **Kaman** Kirşehir, C Turkey 39°22′N 33°43′E
79 O20 **Kamanyola** Sud-Kivu, E Dem. Rep. Congo 02°54′S 29°04′E
141 N14 **Kamarān** *island* W Yemen
55 R9 **Kamarang** W Guyana 05°49′N 60°38′W
**Kāmāreddi/Kamareddy** *see* Rāmāreddi
**Kama Reservoir** *see* Kamskoye Vodokhranilishche
148 K13 **Kamarod** Baluchistān, SW Pakistan 27°34′N 63°36′E
171 P14 **Kamaru** Pulau Buton, C Indonesia 05°10′S 123°03′E
77 S13 **Kamba** Kebbi, NW Nigeria 11°50′N 03°44′E
**Kambaeng Petch** *see* Kamphaeng Phet
180 L12 **Kambalda** Western Australia 31°15′S 121°33′E
149 P13 **Kambar** *var.* Qambar. Sindh, SE Pakistan 27°35′N 68°03′E
**Kambara** *see* Kabara
76 I14 **Kambia** W Sierra Leone 09°09′N 12°53′W
**Kambos** *see* Kámpos
79 N25 **Kambove** Katanga, SE Dem. Rep. Congo 10°50′S 26°39′E
**Kambryk** *see* Cambrai
123 V10 **Kamchatka** 🌊 E Russia
**Kamchatka** *see* Kamchatka, Poluostrov
**Kamchatka Basin** *see* Komandorskaya Basin
123 U10 **Kamchatka, Poluostrov** *Eng.* Kamchatka. *peninsula* E Russia
123 V10 **Kamchatskiy Kray** ◆ *province* E Russia
123 V10 **Kamchatskiy Zaliv** *gulf* E Russia
114 N9 **Kamchia** *var.* Kamchiya. 🌊 E Bulgaria
114 L9 **Kamchia, Yazovir** *var.* Yazovir Kamchiya. ◎ E Bulgaria
**Kamchiya** *see* Kamchia
**Kamchiya, Yazovir** *see* Kamchia, Yazovir
149 T4 **Kāmdēsh** *var.* Kamdesh; *prev.* Kāmdeysh. Nūrestān, E Afghanistan 35°25′N 71°26′E
**Kamdesh** *see* Kāmdēsh
**Kāmdeysh** *see* Kāmdēsh
**Kamen'** *see* Kamyen'
**Kamenets** *see* Kamyanyets
**Kamenets-Podol'skaya Oblast'** *see* Khmel'nyts'ka Oblast'
**Kamenets-Podol'skiy** *see* Kam"yanets'-Podil's'kyy
113 Q18 **Kamenica** NE Macedonia 42°03′N 22°34′E
113 O16 **Kamenicë** *var.* Dardanë, *Serb.* Kosovska Kamenica. E Kosovo 42°37′N 21°33′E
112 A11 **Kamenjak, Rt** *headland* NW Croatia
125 O6 **Kamenka** Arkhangel'skaya Oblast', NW Russia 65°55′N 44°01′E
126 6 **Kamenka** Penzenskaya Oblast', W Russia 53°12′N 44°00′E
127 L8 **Kamenka** Voronezhskaya Oblast', W Russia 50°44′N 39°31′E
**Kamenka** *see* Taskala
**Kamenka** *see* Camenca
**Kamenka** *see* Kam"yanka
**Kamenka-Bugskaya** *see* Kam"yanka-Buz'ka
**Kamenka Dneprovskaya** *see* Kam"yanka-Dniprovs'ka
**Kamen Kashirskiy** *see* Kamin'-Kashyrs'kyy
**Kamenka-Strumilov** *see* Kam"yanka-Buz'ka
126 L15 **Kamennomostskiy** Respublika Adygeya, SW Russia 44°13′N 40°12′E
126 L11 **Kamenolomni** Rostovskaya Oblast, SW Russia 47°36′N 40°18′E
127 P8 **Kamenskiy** Saratovskaya Oblast', W Russia 50°56′N 45°32′E
126 L11 **Kamensk-Shakhtinskiy** Rostovskaya Oblast', SW Russia 48°18′N 40°16′E
101 P15 **Kamenz** Sachsen, E Germany 51°15′N 14°06′E
164 J13 **Kameoka** Kyōto, Honshū, SW Japan 35°02′N 135°35′E
126 M3 **Kameshkovo** Vladimirskaya Oblast', W Russia 56°21′N 41°01′E
164 C11 **Kami-Agata** Nagasaki, Tsushima, SW Japan 34°40′N 129°27′E
33 N10 **Kamiah** Idaho, NW USA 46°13′N 116°01′W
**Kamień Koszyrski** *see* Kamin'-Kashyrs'kyy
110 H9 **Kamień Krajeński** *Ger.* Kamin in Westpreussen. Kujawski-pomorskie, C Poland 53°31′N 17°31′E
111 F15 **Kamienna Góra** *Ger.* Landeshut, Landeshut in Schlesien. Dolnośląskie, SW Poland 50°48′N 16°00′E
110 D8 **Kamień Pomorski** *Ger.* Cummin in Pommern. Zachodnio-pomorskie, NW Poland 53°57′N 14°44′E
165 R5 **Kamiiso** Hokkaidō, NE Japan 41°50′N 140°38′E
79 L22 **Kamiji** Kasai-Oriental, S Dem. Rep. Congo 06°39′S 23°27′E
165 T3 **Kamikawa** Hokkaidō, NE Japan 43°51′N 142°47′E
164 B15 **Kami-Koshiki-jima** *island* SW Japan
79 M23 **Kamina** Katanga, S Dem. Rep. Congo 08°42′S 25°01′E
**Kamina** *see* Kaintiba
42 C6 **Kaminaljuyú** *ruins* Guatemala, C Guatemala
**Kamin in Westpreussen** *see* Kamień Krajeński
116 J2 **Kamin'-Kashyrs'kyy** *Pol.* Kamień Koszyrski, *Rus.* Kamen Kashirskiy. Volyns'ka Oblast', NW Ukraine 51°39′N 24°59′E
**Kaminka Strumiłowa** *see* Kam"yanka-Buz'ka
165 Q5 **Kaminokuni** Hokkaidō, NE Japan 41°48′N 140°05′E
165 P10 **Kaminoyama** Yamagata, Honshū, C Japan 38°10′N 140°16′E
39 Q13 **Kamishak Bay** *bay* Alaska, USA
165 U4 **Kamishihoro** Hokkaidō, NE Japan 43°14′N 143°18′E
**Kamishli** *see* Al Qāmishlī
**Kamissar** *see* Kamsar
164 C11 **Kami-Tsushima** Nagasaki, Tsushima, SW Japan 34°40′N 129°27′E
79 O20 **Kamituga** Sud-Kivu, E Dem. Rep. Congo 03°07′S 28°10′E
164 B17 **Kamiyaku** Kagoshima, Yaku-shima, SW Japan 30°24′N 130°32′E
11 N16 **Kamloops** British Columbia, SW Canada 50°39′N 120°24′W
107 G25 **Kamma** Sicilia, Italy, C Mediterranean Sea 36°46′N 12°03′E
192 K4 **Kammu Seamount** *undersea feature* N Pacific Ocean 32°09′N 173°00′E
109 U11 **Kamnik** *Ger.* Stein. C Slovenia 46°13′N 14°34′E
**Kamniške Alpe** *see* Kamniško-Savinjske Alpe
109 T10 **Kamniško-Savinjske Alpe** *var.* Kamniške Alpe, Sanntaler Alpen, *Ger.* Steiner Alpen. ▲▲ N Slovenia
**Kamo** *see* Gavarr
165 R3 **Kamoenai** *var.* Kamuenai. Hokkaidō, NE Japan 43°07′N 140°25′E
165 O14 **Kamogawa** Chiba, Honshū, S Japan 35°05′N 140°04′E
149 W8 **Kāmoke** Punjab, E Pakistan 31°54′N 74°15′E
82 L13 **Kamoto** Eastern, E Zambia 13°16′S 32°04′E
109 V3 **Kamp** 🌊 N Austria
81 F18 **Kampala** ● (Uganda) S Uganda 0°20′N 32°28′E
168 K11 **Kampar, Sungai** 🌊 Sumatera, W Indonesia
98 L9 **Kampen** Overijssel, E Netherlands 52°33′N 05°55′E
79 N20 **Kampene** Maniema, E Dem. Rep. Congo 03°35′S 26°40′E
29 Q9 **Kampeska, Lake** ◎ South Dakota, N USA
167 O9 **Kamphaeng Phet** *var.* Kambaeng Petch. Kamphaeng Phet, W Thailand 16°28′N 99°31′E
**Kampo** *see* Campo, Cameroon
**Kampo** *see* Ntem, Cameroon/Equatorial Guinea
167 S12 **Kampong Cham** *var.* Kâmpóng Cham. Kampong Cham, C Cambodia 12°N 105°27′E
167 R12 **Kampong Chhnang** *var.* Kâmpóng Chhnăng. Kampong Chhnang, C Cambodia 12°15′N 104°40′E
**Kâmpóng Chhnăng** *see* Kampong Chhnang
167 R12 **Kâmpóng Khleăng** *prev.* Kompong Kleang. Siem Reap, NW Cambodia 13°04′N 104°07′E
**Kâmpóng Saôm** *see* Sihanoukville
167 R13 **Kampong Speu** *var.* Kâmpóng Spœ. Kampong Speu, S Cambodia 11°28′N 104°29′E
167 S12 **Kampong Thom** *var.* Kâmpóng Thum, Trâpeăng Vêng. Kampong Thom, C Cambodia 12°37′N 104°58′E
**Kâmpóng Thum** *see* Kampong Thom
167 S12 **Kâmpóng Trâbêk** *prev.* Phumĭ Kâmpóng Trâbêk, Phum Kompong Trabek. Kampong Thom, C Cambodia 13°06′N 105°16′E
121 O2 **Kámpos** *var.* Kambos. NW Cyprus 35°03′N 32°44′E
167 R14 **Kampot** *var.* Kâmpôt. Kampot, SW Cambodia 10°37′N 104°11′E
**Kâmpôt** *see* Kampot
**Kamptee** *see* Kāmthi
77 O14 **Kampti** SW Burkina Faso 10°07′N 03°22′W
**Kampuchea** *see* Cambodia
**Kampuchea, Democratic** *see* Cambodia
**Kampuchea, People's Democratic Republic of** *see* Cambodia
169 Q9 **Kampung Sirik** Sarawak, East Malaysia 02°42′N 111°28′E
11 V15 **Kamsack** Saskatchewan, S Canada 51°34′N 101°51′W
76 H13 **Kamsar** *var.* Kamissar. Guinée-Maritime, W Guinea 10°33′N 14°34′W
127 R4 **Kamskoye Ust'ye** Respublika Tatarstan, W Russia 55°13′N 49°11′E
125 U14 **Kamskoye Vodokhranilishche** *var.* Kama Reservoir. ⊠ NW Russia
154 I12 **Kāmthi** *prev.* Kamptee. Mahārāshtra, C India 21°19′N 79°11′E
**Kamuela** *see* Waimea
**Kamuenai** *see* Kamoenai
165 T5 **Kamui-dake** ▲ Hokkaidō, NE Japan 42°24′N 142°57′E
165 R3 **Kamui-misaki** *headland* Hokkaidō, NE Japan 43°20′N 140°20′E
43 O15 **Kámuk, Cerro** ▲ SE Costa Rica 09°15′N 83°01′W
116 K7 **Kam"yanets'-Podil's'kyy** *Rus.* Kamenets-Podol'skiy. Khmel'nyts'ka Oblast', W Ukraine 48°43′N 26°36′E
117 Q6 **Kam"yanka** *Rus.* Kamenka. Cherkas'ka Oblast', C Ukraine 49°03′N 32°06′E
116 I5 **Kam"yanka-Buz'ka** *prev.* Kamenka-Strumilov, *Pol.* Kaminka Strumiłowa, *Rus.* Kamenka-Bugskaya. L'vivs'ka Oblast', NW Ukraine 50°04′N 24°21′E
117 T9 **Kam"yanka-Dniprovs'ka** *Rus.* Kamenka Dneprovskaya. Zaporiz'ka Oblast', SE Ukraine 47°28′N 34°24′E
117 T7 **Kam"yans'ke** *prev.* Dniprodzerzhyns'k. Dnipropetrovs'ka Oblast', E Ukraine 48°30′N 34°35′E
119 F19 **Kamyanyets** *Rus.* Kamenets. Brestskaya Voblasts', SW Belarus 52°24′N 23°49′E
118 M13 **Kamyen'** *Rus.* Kamen'. Vitsyebskaya Voblasts', N Belarus 55°01′N 28°53′E
127 P9 **Kamyshin** Volgogradskaya Oblast', SW Russia 50°07′N 45°20′E
127 Q13 **Kamyzyak** Astrakhanskaya Oblast', SW Russia 46°07′N 48°03′E
12 K8 **Kanaaupscow** 🌊 Québec, C Canada
36 K8 **Kanab** Utah, W USA 37°03′N 112°31′W
36 K9 **Kanab Creek** 🌊 Arizona/Utah, SW USA
187 Y14 **Kanacea** *prev.* Kanathea. Taveuni, N Fiji 16°59′S 179°54′E
38 G17 **Kanaga Island** *island* Aleutian Islands, Alaska, USA
38 G17 **Kanaga Volcano** ▲ Kanaga Island, Alaska, USA 51°55′N 177°09′W
164 N14 **Kanagawa** *off.* Kanagawa-ken. ◆ *prefecture* Honshū, S Japan
**Kanagawa-ken** *see* Kanagawa
13 Q8 **Kanairiktok** 🌊 Newfoundland and Labrador, E Canada
**Kanaky** *see* New Caledonia
79 K22 **Kananga** *prev.* Luluabourg. Kasai-Occidental, S Dem. Rep. Congo 05°51′S 22°22′E
**Kanara** *see* Karnātaka
36 J7 **Kanarraville** Utah, W USA 37°32′N 113°10′W
127 Q4 **Kanash** Chuvashskaya Respublika, W Russia 55°30′N 47°27′E
**Kanathea** *see* Kanacea
21 Q4 **Kanawha River** 🌊 West Virginia, NE USA
164 L13 **Kanayama** Gifu, Honshū, SW Japan 35°46′N 137°15′E
164 L11 **Kanazawa** Ishikawa, Honshū, SW Japan 36°35′N 136°40′E
166 M4 **Kanbalu** Sagaing, C Myanmar (Burma) 23°10′N 95°31′E
166 L8 **Kanbe** Yangon, SW Myanmar (Burma) 16°40′N 96°01′E
167 O11 **Kanchanaburi** Kanchanaburi, W Thailand 14°02′N 99°32′E
**Kanchanjańghā/Kānchenjunga** *see* Kangchenjunga
155 J19 **Kānchīpuram** *prev.* Conjeeveram. Tamil Nādu, SE India 12°50′N 79°44′E
149 N8 **Kandahār** *Per.* Qandahār. Kandahār, S Afghanistan 31°36′N 65°48′E
149 N9 **Kandahār** *Per.* Qandahār. ◆ *province* SE Afghanistan
**Kandalakša** *see* Kandalaksha
124 I5 **Kandalaksha** *var.* Kandalakša, *Fin.* Kantalahti. Murmanskaya Oblast', NW Russia 67°09′N 32°14′E
**Kandalaksha Gulf/Kandalakshskaya Guba** *see* Kandalakshskiy Zaliv
124 K6 **Kandalakshskiy Zaliv** *var.* Kandalakshskaya Guba, *Eng.* Kandalaksha Gulf. *bay* NW Russia
83 G17 **Kandalengoti** *var.* Kandalengoti. Ngamiland, NW Botswana 19°25′S 22°12′E
**Kandalengoti** *see* Kandalengoti
169 U13 **Kandangan** Borneo, C Indonesia 02°50′S 115°15′E
**Kandau** *see* Kandava
118 E8 **Kandava** *Ger.* Kandau. W Latvia 57°02′N 22°48′E
**Kandavu** *see* Kadavu
77 R14 **Kandé** *var.* Kanté. NE Togo 09°55′N 01°01′E
101 F23 **Kandel** ▲ SW Germany 48°03′N 08°00′E
186 C7 **Kandep** Enga, W Papua New Guinea 05°54′S 143°34′E
149 R12 **Kandh Kot** Sindh, SE Pakistan 28°15′N 69°18′E
77 S13 **Kandi** N Benin 11°05′N 02°59′E
149 P14 **Kandiaro** Sindh, SE Pakistan 27°02′N 68°16′E
136 F11 **Kandıra** Kocaeli, NW Turkey 41°05′N 30°08′E
183 S8 **Kandos** New South Wales, SE Australia 32°52′S 149°58′E
148 M16 **Kandrach** *var.* Kanrach. Baluchistan, SW Pakistan 25°26′N 65°28′E
172 I4 **Kandreho** Mahajanga, C Madagascar 17°27′S 46°06′E
186 F7 **Kandrian** New Britain, E Papua New Guinea 06°14′S 149°32′E
155 J17 **Kandukūr** *var.* Kandukur. Andhra Pradesh, E India 15°17′N 79°49′E
**Kandukur** *see* Kandukūr
155 K25 **Kandy** Central Province, C Sri Lanka 07°17′N 80°40′E
144 I10 **Kandyagash** *Kaz.* Qandyaghash; *prev.* Oktyab'rsk. Aktyubinsk, W Kazakhstan 49°25′N 57°24′E
18 D12 **Kane** Pennsylvania, NE USA 41°39′N 78°47′W
64 I11 **Kane Fracture Zone** *tectonic feature* NW Atlantic Ocean
**Kanëka** *see* Kanëvka
78 G9 **Kanem** *off.* Région du Kanem. ◆ *region* W Chad
**Kanem, Région du** *see* Kanem
38 D9 **Kāne'ohe** *var.* Kaneohe. O'ahu, Hawaii, USA, C Pacific Ocean 21°25′N 157°48′W
**Kanestron, Akrotírio** *see* Palioúri, Akrotírio
**Kanëv** *see* Kaniv
124 M5 **Kanëvka** *var.* Kanëka. Murmanskaya Oblast', NW Russia 67°07′N 39°43′E
126 K13 **Kanevskaya** Krasnodarskiy Kray, SW Russia 46°07′N 38°57′E
**Kanevskoye Vodokhranilishche** *see* Kanivs'ke Vodoskhovyshche
165 P9 **Kaneyama** Yamagata, Honshū, C Japan 38°54′N 140°20′E
83 G20 **Kang** Kgalagadi, C Botswana 23°41′S 22°50′E
76 L13 **Kangaba** Koulikoro, SW Mali 11°57′N 08°24′W
136 M13 **Kangal** Sivas, C Turkey 39°15′N 37°23′E
**Kangān** *see* Bandar-e Kangān
168 J6 **Kangar** Perlis, Peninsular Malaysia 06°28′N 100°10′E
76 L13 **Kangaré** Sikasso, S Mali 11°39′N 08°10′W
182 F10 **Kangaroo Island** *island* South Australia
93 M17 **Kangasniemi** Etelä-Savo, E Finland 61°58′N 26°37′E
142 K6 **Kangāvar** *var.* Kangāwar. Kermānshāhān, W Iran 34°29′N 47°55′E
**Kangāwar** *see* Kangāvar
153 S11 **Kangchenjunga** *var.* Kānchenjunga, *Nep.* Kanchanjańghā. ▲ NE India 27°36′N 88°06′E
160 G9 **Kangding** *var.* Lucheng, *Tib.* Dardo. Sichuan, C China 30°03′N 101°56′E
169 U16 **Kangean, Kepulauan** *island group* S Indonesia
169 T16 **Kangean, Pulau** *island* Kepulauan Kangean, S Indonesia
67 U8 **Kangen** *var.* Kengen. 🌊 E South Sudan
197 N14 **Kangerlussuaq** *Dan.* Søndre Strømfjord. ✈ Qeqqata, W Greenland 66°59′N 50°28′E
197 Q15 **Kangertittivaq** *Dan.* Scoresby Sund. *fjord* E Greenland
167 O2 **Kangfang** Kachin State, N Myanmar (Burma) 26°09′N 98°36′E
163 X12 **Kanggye** N North Korea 40°58′N 126°37′E
197 P15 **Kangikajik** *var.* Kap Brewster. *headland* E Greenland 70°10′N 22°00′W
13 N5 **Kangiqsualujjuaq** *prev.* George River, Port-Nouveau-Québec. Québec, E Canada 58°35′N 65°59′W
12 L2 **Kangiqsujuaq** *prev.* Maricourt, Wakeham Bay. Québec, NE Canada 61°35′N 72°00′W
12 M4 **Kangirsuk** *prev.* Bellin, Payne. Québec, E Canada 60°00′N 70°01′W
**Kangle** *see* Wanzai
158 M16 **Kangmar** Xizang Zizhiqu, W China 28°34′N 89°40′E
**Kangnŭng** *see* Gangneung
79 D18 **Kango** Estuaire, NW Gabon 0°17′N 10°00′E
152 I7 **Kāngra** Himāchal Pradesh, NW India 32°04′N 76°16′E
153 Q16 **Kangsabati Reservoir** ⊠ N India
159 O17 **Kangto** ▲ China/India 27°54′N 92°33′E
159 W12 **Kangxian** *var.* Kang Xian, Zuitai, Zuitaizi. Gansu, C China 33°21′N 105°40′E
**Kang Xian** *see* Kangxian
76 M15 **Kani** NW Ivory Coast 08°29′N 06°36′W
166 L4 **Kani** Sagaing, C Myanmar (Burma) 22°24′N 94°55′E
79 M23 **Kaniama** Katanga, S Dem. Rep. Congo 07°32′S 24°11′E
**Kanibadam** *see* Konibodom
169 V6 **Kanibongan** Sabah, East Malaysia 06°40′N 117°12′E
185 F17 **Kaniere** West Coast, South Island, New Zealand 42°45′S 171°00′E
185 G17 **Kaniere, Lake** ◎ South Island, New Zealand
188 E17 **Kanifaay** Yap, W Micronesia
125 O4 **Kanin Kamen'** ▲▲ NW Russia
125 N3 **Kanin Nos** Nenetskiy Avtonomnyy Okrug, NW Russia 68°38′N 43°19′E
125 N3 **Kanin Nos, Mys** *cape* NW Russia
125 O5 **Kanin, Poluostrov** *peninsula* NW Russia
139 V8 **Kānī Sakht** Wāsiţ, E Iraq 33°19′N 46°04′E
139 T3 **Kānī Slēman** *Ar.* Kānī Sulaymān. Arbīl, N Iraq 35°54′N 44°35′E
**Kānī Sulaymān** *see* Kānī Slēman
165 Q6 **Kanita** Aomori, Honshū, C Japan 41°04′N 140°36′E
117 Q5 **Kaniv** *Rus.* Kanëv. Cherkas'ka Oblast', C Ukraine 49°46′N 31°28′E
182 K11 **Kaniva** Victoria, SE Australia 36°25′S 141°13′E
117 Q5 **Kanivs'ke Vodoskhovyshche** *Rus.* Kanevskoye Vodokhranilishche. ⊠ C Ukraine
112 L8 **Kanjiža** *Ger.* Altkanischa, *Hung.* Magyarkanizsa, Ókanizsa; *prev.* Stara Kanjiža. Vojvodina, N Serbia 46°03′N 20°03′E
93 K18 **Kankaanpää** Satakunta, SW Finland 61°47′N 22°25′E
30 M12 **Kankakee** Illinois, N USA 41°07′N 87°51′W
31 O11 **Kankakee River** 🌊 Illinois/Indiana, N USA
76 K14 **Kankan** E Guinea 10°25′N 09°19′W
154 K13 **Kānker** Chhattīsgarh, C India 20°19′N 81°29′E
76 J10 **Kankossa** Assaba, S Mauritania 15°54′N 11°31′W
169 N12 **Kanmaw Kyun** *var.* Kisseraing, Kithareng. *island* Mergui Archipelago, S Myanmar (Burma)
164 F12 **Kanmuri-yama** ▲ Kyūshū, SW Japan 34°28′N 132°03′E
21 R10 **Kannapolis** North Carolina, SE USA 35°30′N 80°36′W
93 L16 **Kannonkoski** Keski-Suomi, C Finland 62°59′N 25°20′E
155 F20 **Kannur** *var.* Cannanore, Jagatsinghapur. Kerala, SW India 11°53′N 75°23′E *see also* Cannanore
93 K15 **Kannus** Keski-Pohjanmaa, W Finland 63°55′N 23°55′E
77 V13 **Kano** Kano, N Nigeria 11°56′N 08°31′E
77 V13 **Kano** ◆ *state* N Nigeria
77 V13 **Kano** ✈ Kano, N Nigeria 11°56′N 08°26′E
164 G14 **Kan'onji** *var.* Kanonzi. Kagawa, Shikoku, SW Japan 34°08′N 133°38′E
**Kanonzi** *see* Kan'onji
26 M5 **Kanopolis Lake** ⊠ Kansas, C USA
36 K5 **Kanosh** Utah, W USA 38°48′N 112°26′W
169 R9 **Kanowit** Sarawak, East Malaysia 02°03′N 112°15′E
164 C16 **Kanoya** Kagoshima, Kyūshū, SW Japan 31°22′N 130°50′E
152 L13 **Kānpur** *Eng.* Cawnpore. Uttar Pradesh, N India 26°28′N 80°21′E
**Kanrach** *see* Kandrach
164 I14 **Kansai** ✈ (Ōsaka) Ōsaka, Honshū, SW Japan 34°25′N 135°13′E
27 R9 **Kansas** Oklahoma, C USA 36°14′N 94°46′W
26 L5 **Kansas** *off.* State of Kansas, *also known as* Jayhawker State, Sunflower State. ◆ *state* C USA
27 R4 **Kansas City** Kansas, C USA 39°07′N 94°38′W
27 R4 **Kansas City** Missouri, C USA 39°06′N 94°35′W
27 R3 **Kansas City** ✈ Missouri, C USA 39°18′N 94°45′W
27 P4 **Kansas River** 🌊 Kansas, C USA
122 L14 **Kansk** Krasnoyarskiy Kray, S Russia 56°11′N 95°32′E
**Kansu** *see* Gansu
147 V7 **Kant** Chuyskaya Oblast', N Kyrgyzstan 42°54′N 74°47′E
**Kantalahti** *see* Kandalaksha
167 N16 **Kantang** *var.* Ban Kantang. Trang, SW Thailand 07°25′N 99°30′E
115 H25 **Kántanos** Kríti, Greece, E Mediterranean Sea 35°20′N 23°42′E
77 R12 **Kantchari** E Burkina Faso 12°47′N 01°37′E
**Kanté** *see* Kandé
**Kantemir** *see* Cantemir
126 L9 **Kantemirovka** Voronezhskaya Oblast', W Russia 49°44′N 39°53′E
167 R11 **Kantharalak** Si Sa Ket, E Thailand 14°32′N 104°37′E
**Kantipur** *see* Kathmandu
39 Q9 **Kantishna River** 🌊 Alaska, USA
191 S3 **Kanton** *var.* Abariringa, Canton Island; *prev.* Mary Island. *atoll* Phoenix Islands, C Kiribati
97 C20 **Kanturk** *Ir.* Ceann Toirc. Cork, SW Ireland 52°12′N 08°54′W
55 T11 **Kanuku Mountains** ▲▲ S Guyana
165 O12 **Kanuma** Tochigi, Honshū, S Japan 36°34′N 139°44′E
83 H20 **Kanye** Southern, SE Botswana 24°55′S 25°14′E
83 H17 **Kanyu** Ngamiland, C Botswana 20°04′S 24°36′E
166 M7 **Kanyutkwin** Bago, C Myanmar (Burma) 18°19′N 96°30′E
79 M24 **Kanzenze** Katanga, SE Dem. Rep. Congo 10°33′S 25°28′E
193 Y15 **Kao** *island* Kotu Group, W Tonga
**Kaôh Kŏng** *see* Koh Kong
161 S14 **Kaohsiung** *var.* Gaoxiong, *Jap.* Takao, Takow. S Taiwan 22°36′N 120°17′E
161 S14 **Kaohsiung** ✈ S Taiwan 22°26′N 120°32′E
**Kaokaona** *see* Kirakira
83 B17 **Kaoko Veld** ▲▲ N Namibia
76 G11 **Kaolack** *var.* Kaolak. W Senegal 14°09′N 16°08′W
**Kaolak** *see* Kaolack
**Kaolan** *see* Lanzhou
186 M8 **Kaolo** San Jorge, N Solomon Islands 08°24′S 159°35′E
83 H14 **Kaoma** Western, W Zambia 14°50′S 24°48′E
38 B8 **Kapa'a** *var.* Kapaa. Kaua'i, Hawaii, USA, C Pacific Ocean 22°04′N 159°19′W
**Kapaa** *see* Kapa'a
113 J16 **Kapa Moračka** ▲ C Montenegro 42°53′N 19°01′E
137 V13 **Kapan** *Rus.* Kafan; *prev.* Ghap'an. SE Armenia 39°13′N 46°25′E
82 L13 **Kapandashila** Muchinga, NE Zambia 12°43′S 31°00′E
79 L23 **Kapanga** Katanga, S Dem. Rep. Congo 08°22′S 22°37′E
**Kapchagay** *see* Kapshagay
**Kapchagayskoye Vodokhranilishche** *see* Vodokhranilishche Kapshagay
99 F15 **Kapelle** Zeeland, SW Netherlands 51°29′N 03°58′E
99 G16 **Kapellen** Antwerpen, N Belgium 51°19′N 04°25′E
95 P15 **Kapellskär** Stockholm, C Sweden 59°43′N 19°03′E
81 H18 **Kapenguria** West Pokit, W Kenya 01°14′N 35°08′E
109 V6 **Kapfenberg** Steiermark, C Austria 47°27′N 15°18′E
83 J14 **Kapiri Mposhi** Central, C Zambia 13°59′S 28°40′E
149 R4 **Kāpīsā** ◆ *province* E Afghanistan
12 G10 **Kapiskau** 🌊 Ontario, C Canada
184 K13 **Kapiti Island** *island* C New Zealand
78 K9 **Kapka, Massif du** ▲▲ E Chad
**Kaplamada** *see* Kaubalatmada, Gunung
22 H9 **Kaplan** Louisiana, S USA 30°00′N 92°16′W
**Kaplangky, Plato** *see* Gaplaňgyr Platosy
111 D19 **Kaplice** *Ger.* Kaplitz. Jihočeský Kraj, S Czechia 48°42′N 14°27′E
**Kaplitz** *see* Kaplice
**Kapoche** *see* Capoche
171 T12 **Kapocol** Papua Barat, E Indonesia 01°59′S 130°11′E
167 N14 **Kapoe** Ranong, SW Thailand 09°33′N 98°37′E
**Kapoeas** *see* Kapuas, Sungai
81 G15 **Kapoeta** Eastern Equatoria, SE South Sudan 04°50′N 33°35′E
111 I25 **Kapos** 🌊 S Hungary
111 H25 **Kaposvár** Somogy, SW Hungary 46°23′N 17°54′E
94 H13 **Kapp** Oppland, S Norway 60°42′N 10°49′E
100 I7 **Kappeln** Schleswig-Holstein, N Germany 54°41′N 09°56′E
**Kaproncza** *see* Koprivnica
109 P7 **Kaprun** Salzburg, C Austria 47°15′N 12°48′E
145 U15 **Kapshagay** *prev.* Kapchagay. Almaty, SE Kazakhstan 43°52′N 77°05′E
**Kapstad** *see* Cape Town
**Kapsukas** *see* Marijampolė
171 Y13 **Kaptiau** Papua, E Indonesia 02°23′S 139°51′E
119 L19 **Kaptsevichy** *Rus.* Koptsevichi. Homyel'skaya Voblasts', SE Belarus 52°14′N 28°19′E
**Kapuas Hulu, Banjaran/Kapuas Hulu, Pegunungan** *see* Kapuas Mountains
169 S10 **Kapuas Mountains** *Ind.* Banjaran Kapuas Hulu, Pegunungan Kapuas Hulu. ▲▲ Indonesia/Malaysia
169 P11 **Kapuas, Sungai** 🌊 Borneo, N Indonesia
169 T13 **Kapuas, Sungai** *prev.* Kapoeas. 🌊 Borneo, C Indonesia
182 J9 **Kapunda** South Australia 34°23′S 138°51′E
152 H8 **Kapūrthala** Punjab, N India 31°20′N 75°26′E
12 G12 **Kapuskasing** Ontario, S Canada 49°25′N 82°26′W
14 D6 **Kapuskasing** 🌊 Ontario, S Canada
127 P11 **Kapustin Yar** Astrakhanskaya Oblast', SW Russia 48°36′N 45°49′E
82 K11 **Kaputa** Northern, NE Zambia 08°28′S 29°41′E
111 G22 **Kapuvár** Győr-Moson-Sopron, NW Hungary 47°35′N 17°01′E
**Kapydzhik, Gora** *see* Qazangödağ
119 J17 **Kapyl'** *Rus.* Kopyl'. Minskaya Voblasts', C Belarus 53°09′N 27°05′E
43 N9 **Kara** *var.* Cara. Costa Caribe Sur, E Nicaragua 12°50′N 83°35′W
77 R14 **Kara** *var.* Lama-Kara. NE Togo 09°33′N 01°12′E
77 Q14 **Kara** 🌊 N Togo
147 U7 **Kara-Balta** Chuyskaya Oblast', N Kyrgyzstan 42°51′N 73°51′E
144 L7 **Karabalyk** *var.* Komsomolets, *Kaz.* Komsomol. Kostanay, N Kazakhstan 53°47′N 61°58′E
144 G11 **Karabau** *Kaz.* Qarabaū. Atyrau, W Kazakhstan 48°29′N 53°05′E
146 E7 **Karabaur', Uval** *Kaz.* Korabavur Pastligi, *Uzb.* Qorabowur Kirlari. *physical region* Kazakhstan/Uzbekistan
**Karabekaul** *see* Garabekewül
**Karabil', Vozvyshennost'** *see* Garabil Belentligi
**Kara-Bogaz-Gol** *see* Garabogazköl
**Kara-Bogaz-Gol, Zaliv** *see* Garabogaz Aylagy




◆ Country
● Country Capital
◇ Dependent Territory
○ Dependent Territory Capital
◆ Administrative Regions
✈ International Airport
▲ Mountain
▲▲ Mountain Range
Volcano
🌊 River
◎ Lake
⊠ Reservoir

**145 R15 Karaboget** *Kaz.* Qaraböget. Zhambyl, S Kazakhstan 44°36′N 72°03′E
**136 H11 Karabük** Karabük, NW Turkey 41°12′N 32°36′E
**136 H11 Karabük** ◆ *province* NW Turkey
**122 L12 Karabula** Krasnoyarskiy Kray, C Russia 58°01′N 97°17′E
**145 V14 Karabulak** *Kaz.* Qarabulaq. Taldykorgan, SE Kazakhstan 44°53′N 78°29′E
**145 Q17 Karabulak** *Kaz.* Qarabulaq. Turkestan, S Kazakhstan 42°31′N 69°47′E
**145 Y11 Karabulak** *Kaz.* Qarabulaq. Vostochnyy Kazakhstan, E Kazakhstan 47°34′N 84°40′E
**Karabura** *see* Yumin
**136 C17 Kara Burnu** *headland* SW Turkey 36°34′N 28°00′E
**144 K10 Karabutak** *Kaz.* Qarabutaq. Aktyubinsk, W Kazakhstan 49°55′N 60°05′E
**136 D12 Karacabey** Bursa, NW Turkey 40°14′N 28°22′E
**114 O12 Karacaköy** İstanbul, NW Turkey 41°24′N 28°21′E
**114 M12 Karacaoğlan** Kırklareli, NW Turkey 41°30′N 27°06′E
**Karachay-Cherkessia** *see* Karachayevo-Cherkesskaya Respublika
**126 L15 Karachayevo-Cherkesskaya Respublika** *Eng.* Karachay-Cherkessia. ◆ *autonomous republic* SW Russia
**126 M15 Karachayevsk** Karachayevo-Cherkesskaya Respublika, SW Russia 43°43′N 41°53′E
**126 J6 Karachev** Bryanskaya Oblast', W Russia 53°07′N 35°56′E
**149 O16 Karachi** Sindh, SE Pakistan 24°51′N 67°02′E
**149 O16 Karachi** Sindh, S Pakistan 24°51′N 67°02′E
**149 O16 Karachi** ✈ Sindh, S Pakistan 24°51′N 67°02′E
**Karácsonkő** *see* Piatra-Neamţ
**155 E15 Karād** Mahārāshtra, W India 17°19′N 74°15′E
**136 H16 Karadağ** ▲ S Turkey 37°00′N 33°00′E
**147 T10 Karadar'ya** *Uzb.* Qoradaryo. ⊘ Kyrgyzstan/Uzbekistan
**Karadeniz** *see* Black Sea
**Karadeniz Boğazı** *see* İstanbul Boğazı
**146 B13 Karadepe** Balkan Welaýaty, W Turkmenistan 38°04′N 54°01′E
**Karadzhar** *see* Qorajar
**Karaferiye** *see* Véroia
**Karagan** *see* Garagan
**Karaganda** *see* Karagandy
**Karaganda** *see* Karagandy
**Karagandinskaya Oblast'** *see* Karagandy
**145 R10 Karagandy** *Kaz.* Qaraghandy; *prev.* Karaganda. Karaganda, C Kazakhstan 49°53′N 73°07′E
**145 R10 Karagandy** *off.* Karagandinskaya Oblast', *Kaz.* Qaraghandy Oblysy; *prev.* Karaganda. ◆ *province* C Kazakhstan
**145 T10 Karagayly** *Kaz.* Qaraghayly. Karaganda, C Kazakhstan 49°25′N 75°31′E
**Karagel'** *see* Garagöl'
**123 U9 Karaginskiy, Ostrov** *island* E Russia
**197 T1 Karaginskiy Zaliv** *bay* E Russia
**137 P13 Karagöl Dağları** ▲ NE Turkey
**Karagumskiy Kanal** *see* Garagum Kanaly
**114 L13 Karahisar** Edirne, NW Turkey 40°47′N 26°34′E
**127 V3 Karaidel'** Respublika Bashkortostan, W Russia 55°50′N 56°55′E
**114 L13 Karaidemir Barajı** ▣
**155 J21 Käraikäl** Puducherry, SE India 10°58′N 79°50′E
**155 I22 Käraikkudi** Tamil Nādu, SE India 10°04′N 78°46′E
**Kara Irtysh** *see* Kara Yertis
**143 N5 Karaj** Alborz, N Iran 35°44′N 51°26′E
**168 K8 Karak** Pahang, Peninsular Malaysia 03°24′N 101°59′E
**Karak** *see* Al Karak
**147 T11 Kara-Kabak** Oshskaya Oblast', SW Kyrgyzstan 39°40′N 72°45′E
**Kara-Kala** *see* Magtymguly
**Karakala** *see* Oqqal'a
**Karakalpakstan, Respublika** *see* Qoraqalpog'iston Respublikasi
**Karakalpakya** *see* Qoraqalpog'iston
**158 G10 Karakax He** ⊘ NW China
**121 X8 Karakaya Barajı** ▣ C Turkey
**171 Q9 Karakelong, Pulau** *island* N Indonesia
**Karak, Muḥāfaẓat** *see* Al Karak
**147 X8 Karakol** *var.* Karakolka. Issyk-Kul'skaya Oblast', NE Kyrgyzstan 41°30′N 77°18′E
**147 Y7 Karakol** *prev.* Przheval'sk. Issyk-Kul'skaya Oblast', NE Kyrgyzstan 42°32′N 78°21′E
**Kara-Köl** *see* Kara-Kul'
**Karakolka** *see* Karakol
**149 W2 Karakoram Highway** *road* China/Pakistan
**149 Z3 Karakoram Pass** *Chin.* Karakoram Shankou. *pass* C Asia
**152 I3 Karakoram Range** ▲ C Asia
**Karakoram Shankou** *see* Karakoram Pass
**Karaköse** *see* Ağrı
**145 P14 Karakoyyn, Ozero** *Kaz.* Qarakoyyn. ⊘ C Kazakhstan
**83 F19 Karakubis** Ghanzi, W Botswana 22°03′S 20°36′E
**147 T9 Kara-Kul'** *Kyr.* Kara-Köl. Dzhalal-Abadskaya Oblast', W Kyrgyzstan 40°35′N 73°36′E
**Karakul'** *see* Qorakül,
**Karakul'** *see* Qorako'l, Uzbekistan
**147 U10 Kara-Kul'dzha** Oshskaya Oblast', SW Kyrgyzstan 40°32′N 73°50′E

**127 T3 Karakulino** Udmurtskaya Respublika, NW Russia 56°02′N 53°45′E
**Karakul', Ozero** *see* Qarokül
**Kara Kum** *see* Garagum
**Kara Kum Canal/ Karakumskiy Kanal** *see* Garagum Kanaly
**Karakumy, Peski** *see* Garagum
**83 E17 Karakuwisa** Kavango East, NE Namibia 18°56′S 19°40′E
**122 M13 Karam** Irkutskaya Oblast', S Russia 55°07′N 107°21′E
**169 T14 Karamain, Pulau** *island* N Indonesia
**136 I16 Karaman** Karaman, S Turkey 37°11′N 33°13′E
**136 H16 Karaman** ◆ *province* S Turkey
**114 M8 Karamandere** ▲ NE Bulgaria
**158 J4 Karamay** *var.* Karamai, Kelamayi; *prev. Chin.* K'o-la-ma-i. Xinjiang Uygur Zizhiqu, NW China 45°33′N 84°45′E
**169 U14 Karambu** Borneo, N Indonesia 03°48′S 116°06′E
**185 H14 Karamea** West Coast, South Island, New Zealand 41°15′S 172°07′E
**185 H14 Karamea** ⊘ South Island, New Zealand
**185 G15 Karamea Bight** *gulf* South Island, New Zealand
**Karamet-Niyaz** *see* Garamätnyýaz
**158 K10 Karamiran He** ⊘ NW China
**147 S11 Karamyk** Oshskaya Oblast', SW Kyrgyzstan 39°28′N 71°45′E
**169 U17 Karangasem** Bali, S Indonesia 08°24′S 115°40′E
**154 H12 Kāranja** Mahārāshtra, C India 20°30′N 77°26′E
**152 F9 Karanpura** *var.* Karanpura. Rajasthan, NW India 29°46′N 73°30′E
**Karänsebes/Karansebesch** *see* Caransebeş
**145 T14 Karaoy** *Kaz.* Qaraoy. Almaty, SE Kazakhstan 45°52′N 74°44′E
**144 E10 Karaozen** *Kaz.* Ülkenözen; *prev.* Bol'shoy Uzen'. ⊘ Kazakhstan/Russia
**114 N7 Karapelit** *Rom.* Stejarul. Dobrich, NE Bulgaria 43°40′N 27°33′E
**136 I15 Karapınar** Konya, C Turkey 37°43′N 33°34′E
**83 D22 //Karas** ◇ *region* S Namibia
**147 Y8 Kara-Say** Issyk-Kul'skaya Oblast', NE Kyrgyzstan 41°34′N 77°56′E
**83 E22 Karasburg** //Karas, S Namibia 27°59′S 18°48′E
**92 K9 Kárášjohka** *var.* Karasjok. ▲ N Norway
**92 L9 Karasjok** *Fin.* Kaarasjoki, *Lapp.* Kárášjohka. Finnmark, N Norway 69°27′N 25°28′E
**Kárášjokka** *see* Kárášjohka
**Kara Sea** *see* Karskoye More
**92 L9 Karasu** *Kaz.* Qarasū. Kostanay, N Kazakhstan 52°44′N 65°29′E
**136 F11 Karasu** Sakarya, NW Turkey 41°07′N 30°37′E
**Kara Su** *see* Mesta/Néstos
**Karasubazar** *see* Bilohirs'k
**122 I12 Karasuk** Novosibirskaya Oblast', C Russia 53°41′N 78°04′E
**145 U13 Karatal** *Kaz.* Qaratal. ⊘ SE Kazakhstan
**136 K17 Karataş** Adana, S Turkey 36°32′N 35°22′E
**145 Q16 Karatau** *Kaz.* Qarataū. Zhambyl, S Kazakhstan 43°09′N 70°28′E
**145 P16 Karatau, Khrebet** *var.* Karatau, *Kaz.* Qarataū. ▲ S Kazakhstan
**144 G13 Karaton** *Kaz.* Qaraton. Atyrau, W Kazakhstan 46°33′N 53°31′E
**164 C13 Karatsu** *var.* Karatu. Saga, Kyūshū, SW Japan 33°28′N 129°48′E
**Karatu** *see* Karatsu
**122 K8 Karaul** Krasnoyarskiy Kray, N Russia 70°07′N 83°12′E
**Karaulbazar** *see* Qorovulbozor
**184 D16 Kárává** ▲ C Greece 39°10′N 21°33′E
**Karawanke** *see* Karawanken
**115 F22 Karavás** Kýthira, S Greece 36°21′N 22°57′E
**113 J20 Karavastasë, Laguna e** *var.* Kënet' e Karavastas, Kravasta Lagoon. *lagoon* W Albania
**Karavastasë, Laguna e Karavastasë, Kënet' e** *see* Karavastasë, Laguna e
**118 I5 Kärävere** Tartumaa, E Estonia 58°25′N 26°29′E
**115 L23 Karavónisia** *island* Kykládes, Greece, Aegean Sea
**169 O15 Karawang** *prev.* Krawang. Jawa, C Indonesia 06°13′S 107°16′E
**109 T10 Karawanken** *Slvn.* ▲ Austria/Serbia
**Karaxanar** *see* Kaidu He
**137 R13 Karayazı** Erzurum, NE Turkey 39°42′N 42°08′E
**Kara Yertis** *Rus.* Chërnyy Irtysh *prev.* Kara Irtysh. ⊘ NE Kazakhstan
**145 Q12 Karazhal** *Kaz.* Qarazhal. Karaganda, C Kazakhstan 48°02′N 70°52′E
**139 S9 Karbalā'** *var.* Kerbala, Kerbela. Karbalā', S Iraq 32°37′N 44°03′E
**139 S9 Karbalā'** *off.* Muḥāfaẓat Karbalā'. ◆ *governorate* S Iraq
**Karbalā', Muḥāfaẓat** *see* Karbalā'
**94 L11 Kärböle** Gävleborg, C Sweden 61°59′N 15°16′E
**111 M23 Karcag** *Ger.* Kartzag. Jász-Nagykun-Szolnok, E Hungary 47°22′N 20°51′E
**Kardak** *see* Imia
**128 N7 Kardam** Dobrich, NE Bulgaria 43°45′N 28°06′E
**Kardamila** *see* Kardámyla

**115 L18 Kardámyla** *var.* Kardamila, Kardhámila. Chíos, E Greece 38°33′N 26°04′E
**Kardeljevo** *see* Ploče
**Kardh** *see* Qardho
**115 E16 Kardhámila** *see* Kardámyla
**Kardhítsa** *see* Karditsa
**118 E4 Kärdla** *Ger.* Kertel. Hiiumaa, W Estonia 59°00′N 22°42′E
**114 J11 Kärdžali** *var.* Kürdzhali, Kürdžali, Kirdzhali. Kardzhali, S Bulgaria 41°39′N 25°23′E
**114 K11 Kardzhali** *var* Kürdzhali. ◆ *province* S Bulgaria
**114 J11 Kardzhali, Yazovir** *var.* Yazovir Kürdzhali. ▣ S Bulgaria
**Karelia** *see* Kareliya, Respublika
**119 I16 Karelichy** *Pol.* Korelicze, *Rus.* Korelichi. Hrodzyenskaya Voblasts', W Belarus 53°34′N 26°08′E
**124 I10 Kareliya, Respublika** *prev.* Karel'skaya ASSR, *Eng.* Karelia. ◆ *autonomous republic* NW Russia
**Karel'skaya ASSR** *see* Kareliya, Respublika
**81 E22 Karema** Katavi, W Tanzania 06°50′S 30°25′E
**Karen** *see* Hualien
**83 I14 Karenda** Central, C Zambia 14°42′S 26°52′E
**Karen State** *see* Kayin State
**92 J10 Karesuando** *Fin.* Kaaresuanto, *Lapp.* Gárasavvon. Norrbotten, N Sweden 68°25′N 22°28′E
**Karet** *see* Kåghet
**Kareyz-e-Elyās/Kärez Iliäs** *see* Kärēz-e Elyās
**148 J4 Kärēz-e Ilyās** *var.* Kareyz-e-Elyās, Kärez Iliäs. Herät, NW Afghanistan 35°26′N 61°24′E
**122 J11 Kargasok** Tomskaya Oblast', C Russia 59°01′N 80°34′E
**122 I12 Kargat** Novosibirskaya Oblast', C Russia 55°07′N 80°09′E
**136 J11 Kargı** Çorum, N Turkey 41°09′N 34°32′E
**152 I5 Kargil** Jammu and Kashmir, NW India 34°34′N 76°06′E
**Kargilik** *see* Yecheng
**124 L11 Kargopol'** Arkhangel'skaya Oblast', NW Russia 61°30′N 38°53′E
**110 F12 Kargowa** *Ger.* Unruhstadt. Lubuskie, W Poland 52°05′N 15°50′E
**77 X13 Kari** Bauchi, E Nigeria 11°13′N 10°34′E
**83 J15 Kariba** Mashonaland West, N Zimbabwe 16°29′S 28°48′E
**83 J15 Kariba, Lake** ▣ Zambia/Zimbabwe
**165 Q4 Kariba-yama** ▲ Hokkaidō, NE Japan 42°36′N 139°55′E
**83 C19 Karibib** Erongo, C Namibia 21°56′S 15°51′E
**Karies** *see* Karyés
**92 L9 Karigasniemi** *N. Sami.* Garegasnjárga. Lappi, N Finland 69°24′N 25°52′E
**184 J2 Karikari, Cape** *headland* North Island, New Zealand 34°47′S 173°24′E
**149 W3 Karimabad** *prev.* Hunza. Jammu and Kashmir, NE Pakistan 36°23′N 74°43′E
**169 P12 Karimata, Kepulauan** *island group* N Indonesia
**169 P12 Karimata, Pulau** *island* Kepulauan Karimata, N Indonesia
**155 I14 Karimnagar** Telangana, C India 18°28′N 79°09′E
**186 C7 Karimui** Chimbu, C Papua New Guinea 06°19′S 144°48′E
**169 Q15 Karimunjawa, Pulau** *island* S Indonesia
**80 N12 Karin** Woqooyi Galbeed, N Somalia 10°48′N 45°46′E
**93 L20 Karis** *Fin.* Karjaa. Uusimaa, SW Finland 60°05′N 23°39′E
**Káristos** *see* Kárystos
**Karja** *see* Karis
**Karjaa** *see* Karis
**145 T10 Karkaraly** *prev.* Karkaralinsk. Karaganda, E Kazakhstan 49°31′N 75°53′E
**186 D6 Karkar Island** *island* N Papua New Guinea
**148 N7 Karkas, Kūh-e** ▲ C Iran
**142 K8 Karkheh, Rūd-e** ⊘ SW Iran
**115 L20 Karkinágri** *var.* Karkinagrio. Ikaría, Dodekánisa, Greece, Aegean Sea 37°31′N 26°01′E
**Karkinagrio** *see* Karkinágri
**117 R12 Karkinits'ka Zatoka** *Rus.* Karkinitskiy Zaliv. *gulf* S Ukraine
**Karkinitskiy Zaliv** *see* Karkinits'ka Zatoka
**93 L19 Karkkila** *Swe.* Högfors. Uusimaa, S Finland 60°32′N 24°10′E
**93 M19 Kärkölä** Päijät-Häme, S Finland 60°52′N 25°17′E
**182 G9 Karkoo** South Australia 34°03′S 135°45′E
**118 D5 Kärla** *Ger.* Kergel. Saaremaa, W Estonia 58°20′N 22°12′E
**110 F7 Karlino** *Ger.* Körlin an der Persante. Zachodnio-pomorskie, NW Poland 54°02′N 15°52′E
**137 Q13 Karlıova** Bingöl, E Turkey 39°16′N 41°01′E
**117 U6 Karlivka** Poltavs'ka Oblast', NE Ukraine 49°27′N 35°08′E
**Karl-Marx-Stadt** *see* Chemnitz
**Karlo** *see* Hailuoto
**112 C11 Karlobag** *It.* Carlopago. Lika-Senj, C Croatia 44°32′N 15°06′E
**112 D9 Karlovac** *Ger.* Karlstadt, *Hung.* Károlyváros. Karlovac, C Croatia 45°29′N 15°31′E
**112 C10 Karlovac** *off.* Karlovačka Županija. ◆ *province* C Croatia
**Karlovačka Županija** *see* Karlovac

**111 A16 Karlovarský Kraj** ◇ NW Czechia
**115 M19 Karlovasi** *var.* Néon Karlovásion, Néon Karlovasi. Sámos, Dodekánisa, Greece, Aegean Sea 37°47′N 26°40′E
**114 J9 Karlovo** *prev.* Levskigrad. Plovdiv, C Bulgaria 42°38′N 24°49′E
**111 A16 Karlovy Vary** *Ger.* Karlsbad; *prev. Eng.* Carlsbad. Karlovarský Kraj, W Czechia 50°13′N 12°51′E
**95 L17 Karlsborg** Västra Götaland, S Sweden 58°32′N 14°32′E
**95 L22 Karlshamn** Blekinge, S Sweden 56°10′N 14°50′E
**95 J15 Karlskoga** Örebro, C Sweden 59°19′N 14°33′E
**95 L22 Karlskrona** Blekinge, S Sweden 56°11′N 15°39′E
**101 G20 Karlsruhe** *var.* Carlsruhe. Baden-Württemberg, SW Germany 49°01′N 08°24′E
**95 K16 Karlstad** Värmland, C Sweden 59°22′N 13°36′E
**29 R3 Karlstad** Minnesota, N USA 48°34′N 96°31′W
**101 I18 Karlstadt** Bayern, C Germany 49°59′N 09°46′E
**Karlstadt** *see* Karlovac
**119 O17 Karma** *Rus.* Korma. Homyel'skaya Voblasts', SE Belarus 53°07′N 30°48′E
**155 F14 Karmala** Mahārāshtra, W India 18°26′N 75°18′E
**146 M11 Karmana** Navoiy Viloyati, C Uzbekistan 40°09′N 65°18′E
**138 G8 Karmi'el** *var.* Carmiel. Northern, N Israel 32°55′N 35°18′E
**95 B16 Karmøy** *island* S Norway
**152 I9 Karnāl** Haryāna, N India 29°41′N 76°58′E
**153 W15 Karnaphuli Reservoir** ☒ NE India
**155 F17 Karnātaka** *var.* Kanara; *prev.* Maisur, Mysore. ◆ *state* W India
**25 S13 Karnes City** Texas, SW USA 28°54′N 97°55′W
**109 P9 Karnische Alpen** *It.* Alpi Carniche. ▲ Austria/Italy
**114 M9 Karnobat** Burgas, E Bulgaria 42°39′N 26°59′E
**109 Q7 Kärnten** *off.* Land Kärten, *Eng.* Carinthia, *Slvn.* Koróška. ◆ *state* S Austria
**Karnul** *see* Kurnool
**83 K16 Karoi** Mashonaland West, N Zimbabwe 16°50′S 29°40′E
**Karol** *see* Carei
**Károly-Fehérvár** *see* Alba Iulia
**Károlyváros** *see* Karlovac
**82 M12 Karonga** Northern, N Malawi 09°54′S 33°55′E
**147 W10 Karool-Döbö** *Kas.* Karool-Döbö; *prev.* Karool-Tëbë. Narynskaya Oblast', C Kyrgyzstan 40°33′N 75°52′E
**Karool-Döbö** *see* Karool-Tëbë
**Karool-Tëbë** *see* Karool-Döbö
**182 J6 Karoonda** South Australia 35°04′S 139°58′E
**149 Sror** *var.* Koror Lal Esan. Punjab, E Pakistan 31°15′N 70°58′E
**81 I18 Karossa** W Uganda 0°10′N 30°06′E
**152 J11 Käsganj** Uttar Pradesh, N India 27°48′N 78°38′E
**143 N7 Käshän** Eşfahän, C Iran 33°57′N 51°31′E
**126 M10 Kashary** Rostovskaya Oblast', SW Russia 49°00′N 40°58′E
**39 O12 Kasegaluk** Alaska, USA
**81 E21 Kasese** Kigoma, W Tanzania 04°33′S 30°06′E
**152 J9 Käsganj** Uttar Pradesh, N India 27°48′N 78°38′E
**158 C8 Kashi** *Chin.* Kaxgar, K'o-shih, *Uigh.* Kashgar, *var.* Uygur Zizhiqu, NW China 39°32′N 75°58′E
**164 I12 Kashihara** *var.* Kasihara. Nara, Honshū, SW Japan 34°28′N 135°46′E
**149 W9 Kasur** Punjab, E Pakistan 31°07′N 74°30′E
**124 K15 Kasimov** Tverskaya Oblast', W Russia
**152 K10 Kāshīpur** Uttarākhand, N India 29°13′N 78°58′E
**126 L4 Kashira** Moskovskaya Oblast', W Russia 54°53′N 38°11′E
**165 N11 Kashiwazaki** Niigata, Honshū, C Japan 37°22′N 138°33′E
**Kashkadar'inskaya Oblast'** *see* Qashqadaryo Viloyati
**143 T5 Käshmar** *var.* Torshiz; *prev.* Solṭānābād, Torshiz, Khorāsān, NE Iran 35°13′N 58°25′E
**Kashmir** *see* Jammu and Kashmir
**149 N12 Kashmor** Sindh, SE Pakistan 28°24′N 69°42′E
**180 J13 Kanning** Western Australia 33°45′S 117°33′E
**81 P8 Kata Tjuta** *var.* Mount Olga. ▲ C Australia 25°20′S 30°47′E
**Katawaz** *see* Zarghün Shahr
**93 K17 Katanga** off. Région du Katanga; *prev. Rus.* Katanga. ◇ *region* SE Dem. Rep. Congo
**122 M11 Katanga, Région du** *var.* Katanga
**154 J11 Katängi** Madhya Pradesh, C India 21°46′N 79°50′E
**93 K16 Kaukonen** ...
**151 Q22 Katchall Island** *island* Nicobar Islands, India, NE Indian Ocean
**152 J9 Käsganj** Uttar Pradesh, N India
**115 F14 Katerini** Kentrikí Makedonía, N Greece 40°16′N 22°30′E
**117 P7 Katerynopil'** Cherkas'ka Oblast', C Ukraine
**166 M3 Katha** Sagaing, N Myanmar
**181 P2 Katherine** Northern Territory, N Australia 14°29′S 132°20′E
**154 B11 Käthiäwär Peninsula** *peninsula* W India
**153 P11 Kathmandu** *prev.* Kantipur. ● (Nepal) Central, C Nepal 27°42′N 85°19′E
**153 P12 Kathua** Jammu and Kashmir, NW India 32°23′N 75°31′E
**76 L12 Kati** Koulikoro, SW Mali 12°41′N 08°04′W
**153 R13 Katihär** Bihār, NE India 25°35′N 87°35′E
**184 N7 Katikati** Bay of Plenty, North Island, New Zealand 37°31′S 175°58′E
**83 H16 Katima Mulilo** Caprivi, NE Namibia 17°31′S 24°20′E

**165 R8 Karumai** Iwate, Honshū, C Japan 40°19′N 141°27′E
**181 U4 Karumba** Queensland, NE Australia 17°31′S 140°51′E
**142 L10 Kārūn** *var.* Rūd-e Kārūn. ⊘ SW Iran
**92 K13 Karungi** Norrbotten, N Sweden 66°03′N 23°55′E
**93 K13 Karunki** Lappi, N Finland 66°01′N 24°06′E
**155 H21 Karūr** Tamil Nādu, SE India 10°58′N 78°03′E
**93 K17 Karvia** Satakunta, SW Finland 62°07′N 22°34′E
**111 J17 Karviná** *Ger.* Karwin, *Pol.* Karwina; *prev.* Nová Karwina. Moravskoslezský Kraj, E Czechia 49°50′N 18°30′E
**155 E17 Kārwār** Karnātaka, W India 14°50′N 74°09′E
**108 M7 Karwendelgebirge** ▲ Austria/Germany
**Karwin/Karwina** *see* Karviná
**115 I14 Karyés** *var.* Karies. Ágion Óros, N Greece 40°15′N 24°15′E
**115 I19 Kárystos** *var.* Káristos. Évvoia, C Greece 38°01′N 24°25′E
**136 E17 Kaş** Antalya, SW Turkey 36°12′N 29°38′E
**39 Y14 Kasaan** Prince of Wales Island, Alaska, USA 55°32′N 132°24′W
**164 I13 Kasai** Hyōgo, Honshū, SW Japan 34°56′N 134°49′E
**79 K21 Kasai** *var.* Cassai, Kassai. ⊘ Angola/Dem. Rep. Congo
**79 K22 Kasai-Occidental** ◆ *région* S Dem. Rep. Congo
**Kasai Occidental, Région** *see* Kasai-Occidental
**79 L21 Kasai-Oriental** *off.* Région Kasai Oriental. ◆ *région* C Dem. Rep. Congo
**Kasai Oriental, Région** *see* Kasai-Oriental
**79 L24 Kasaji** Katanga, S Dem. Rep. Congo 10°22′S 23°29′E
**82 J12 Kasama** Northern, N Zambia 10°14′S 31°12′E
**Kasan** *see* Koson
**83 H16 Kasane** North-East, NE Botswana 17°48′S 25°09′E
**81 E23 Kasanga** Rukwa, W Tanzania 08°27′S 31°10′E
**79 G21 Kasangulu** Bas-Congo, W Dem. Rep. Congo 04°35′S 15°12′E
**Kasansay** *see* Kosonsoy
**155 E20 Kasaragod** Kerala, SW India 12°30′N 74°59′E
**118 P13 Kasari** *var.* Kasari Jõgi, *Ger.* Kasargen. ⊘ W Estonia
**Kasari Jõgi** *see* Kasari
**Kasargen** *see* Kasari
**8 L12 Kasba Lake** ⊘ Northwest Territories, Nunavut N Canada
**164 C13 Kaseda** *var.* Kaseta. Kagoshima, Kyūshū, SW Japan 31°25′N 130°19′E
**Kaseta** *see* Kaseda
**83 I14 Kasempa** North Western, NW Zambia 13°27′S 25°49′E
**79 O24 Kasenga** Katanga, SE Dem. Rep. Congo 10°22′S 28°37′E
**79 P17 Kasenye** *var.* Kasenyi. Orientale, NE Dem. Rep. Congo 01°23′N 30°27′E
**Kasenyi** *see* Kasenye
**95 J23 Kastrup** ✈ (København) København, E Denmark 55°36′N 12°39′E
**95 N21 Kastlösa** Kalmar, S Sweden 56°25′N 16°25′E
**115 D14 Kastoría** Dytikí Makedonía, N Greece 40°33′N 21°15′E
**126 K7 Kastornoye** Kurskaya Oblast', W Russia 51°49′N 38°07′E
**115 I21 Kástro** Sífnos, Kykládes, Greece, Aegean Sea 36°58′N 24°45′E
**115 I14 Kasumi** Hyōgo, Honshū, SW Japan 35°36′N 134°37′E
**82 M13 Kasungu** Central, C Malawi 13°04′S 33°29′E
**149 W9 Kasur** Punjab, E Pakistan 31°07′N 74°30′E
**83 I15 Kataba** Western, W Zambia 15°28′S 25°55′E
**19 R4 Katahdin, Mount** ▲ Maine, NE USA 45°54′N 68°55′W
**79 M20 Katako-Kombe** Kasai-Oriental, C Dem. Rep. Congo 03°24′S 24°25′E
**25 U7 Katalla** Alaska, USA 60°12′N 144°31′W
**39 T12 Katana** Jammu and Kashmir, NW India 32°23′N 74°36′E

**169 T12 Kasongan** Borneo, C Indonesia 02°01′S 113°21′E
**79 N21 Kasongo** Maniema, E Dem. Rep. Congo 04°32′S 26°42′E
**79 H22 Kasongo-Lunda** Bandundu, SW Dem. Rep. Congo 06°30′S 16°51′E
**115 M24 Kásos** *island* S Greece
**115 M25 Kásos, Stenó** *var.* Kasos Strait. *strait* Dodekánisos/ Kríti, Greece, Aegean Sea
**137 T10 K'asp'i** *prev.* Kaspi. C Georgia 41°54′N 44°25′E
**Kaspi** *see* K'asp'i
**114 M8 Kaspichan** Shumen, NE Bulgaria 43°18′N 27°09′E
**127 Q16 Kaspiyskiy** Respublika Dagestan, SW Russia 42°52′N 47°40′E
**Kaspiyskoye** *see* Lagan'
**Kaspiyskoye More/Kaspiy Tengizi** *see* Caspian Sea
**Kassa** *see* Košice
**80 I9 Kassala** Kassala. E Sudan 15°24′N 36°25′E
**80 H9 Kassala** ◆ *state* NE Sudan
**114 H12 Kassándra** *prev.* Pallíni; *anc.* Pallene. *peninsula* NE Greece
**Kassándra** *see* Kassandra
**115 G15 Kassándra** *headland* N Greece 39°58′N 23°22′E
**115 H15 Kassándras, Kólpos** *var.* Kólpos Toronaïkós. *gulf* N Greece
**139 Y11 Kassārah** Maysān, E Iraq 31°21′N 47°25′E
**101 I15 Kassel** *prev.* Cassel. Hessen, C Germany 51°19′N 09°30′E
**74 M6 Kasserine** *var.* Al Qasrayn. W Tunisia 35°11′N 08°48′E
**14 J14 Kasshabog Lake** ⊘ Ontario, SE Canada
**139 O5 Kassir, Sabkhat al** ☒ E Syria
**29 W10 Kasson** Minnesota, N USA 44°00′N 92°42′W
**115 C17 Kassópeia** *var.* Kassópi. *site of ancient city* Ípeiros, W Greece
**Kassópi** *see* Kassópeia
**136 I11 Kastamonu** *var.* Castamoni, Kastamuni. Kastamonu, N Turkey 41°22′N 33°47′E
**136 I10 Kastamonu** *var* Kastamuni. ◆ *province* N Turkey
**Kastamuni** *see* Kastamonu
**115 E14 Kastaneá** Kentrikí Makedonía, N Greece 40°25′N 22°09′E
**Kastéllí** *see* Kíssamos
**115 N24 Kástelo, Akrotírio** *prev.* Akrotírio Kastállou. *headland* Kárpathos, SE Greece 35°24′N 27°08′E
**Kastéllou, Akrotírio** *see* Kástelo, Akrotírio
**115 D14 Kastoría** Dytikí Makedonía, N Greece 40°33′N 21°15′E
**126 K7 Kastyukovichy** *Rus.* Kostyukovichi i. Mahilyowskaya Voblasts', E Belarus 53°20′N 32°03′E
**Kastowitz** *see* Košice
**Katun'** *var.* Katsura. ⊘ Katsura
**Katuura** *var.* Katsura
**Katuyama** *see* Katsuyama
**98 G11 Katwijk aan Zee** *var.* Katwijk. Zuid-Holland, W Netherlands 59°12′N 04°24′E
**Katwijk** *see* Katwijk aan Zee
**38 B8 Kaua'i** *var.* Kauai. *island* Hawaiian Islands, Hawai'i, USA, C Pacific Ocean
**38 C8 Kaua'i Channel** *var.* Kauai Channel. *channel* Hawai'i, USA, C Pacific Ocean
**Kauai Channel** *see* Kaua'i Channel
**171 R13 Kaubalatmada, Gunung** *var.* Kabalatmada. ▲ Pulau Buru, E Indonesia 03°16′S 126°17′E
**191 U10 Kauehi** *atoll* Îles Tuamotu, C French Polynesia
**101 K24 Kaufbeuren** Bayern, S Germany 47°53′N 10°37′E
**25 U7 Kaufman** Texas, SW USA 32°36′N 96°18′W
**101 I15 Kaufungen** Hessen, C Germany 51°16′N 09°39′E
**93 K17 Kauhajoki** Etelä-Pohjanmaa, W Finland 62°26′N 22°11′E
**93 K16 Kauhava** Etelä-Pohjanmaa, W Finland 63°10′N 23°07′E
**30 M7 Kaukauna** Wisconsin, N USA 44°18′N 88°18′W
**92 L11 Kaukonen** Lappi, N Finland 67°31′N 24°52′E
**38 A8 Kaulakahi Channel** *channel* Hawai'i, USA, C Pacific Ocean
**38 E9 Kaunakakai** Moloka'i, Hawai'i, USA, C Pacific Ocean 21°05′N 157°01′W
**38 F11 Kaunā Point** *var.* Kauna Point. *headland* Hawai'i, USA, C Pacific Ocean 19°02′N 155°52′W
**Kauna Point** *see* Kaunā Point
**118 F13 Kaunas** *Ger.* Kauen, *Pol.* Kowno; *prev.* Kovno. Kaunas, C Lithuania 54°54′N 23°57′E
**118 F13 Kaunas** ◆ *province* C Lithuania
**186 C6 Kaup** East Sepik, NW Papua New Guinea 03°50′S 144°01′E
**77 U12 Kaura Namoda** Zamfara, NW Nigeria 12°39′N 06°17′E
**93 K16 Kaustinen** Keski-Pohjanmaa, W Finland 63°33′N 23°40′E
**99 M23 Kautenbach** Diekirch, NE Luxembourg 49°58′N 06°01′E
**92 K10 Kautokeino** *Lapp.* Guovdageaidnu. Finnmark, N Norway 69°00′N 23°01′E
**113 P19 Kavadarci** *Turk.* Kavadar. C Macedonia 41°26′N 22°00′E
**Kavaja** *see* Kavajë
**113 K20 Kavajë** *It.* Kavaja. Kavajë. Tiranë, W Albania 41°11′N 19°33′E

---

◆ Country  ◇ Dependent Territory  ◈ Administrative Regions  ▲ Mountain  ☒ Volcano  ⊘ Lake
● Country Capital  ○ Dependent Territory Capital  ✈ International Airport  ▲ Mountain Range  ⊘ River  ▣ Reservoir

# Kavak Çayı – Khadzhiyska Reka



114 M13 **Kavak Çayı** NW Turkey
**Kavakli** *see* Topolovgrad
114 I13 **Kavála** *prev.* Kaválla. Anatolikí Makedonía kai Thráki, NE Greece *40°57′N 24°26′E*
114 I13 **Kavális, Kólpos** *gulf* Aegean Sea, NE Mediterranean Sea
155 J17 **Kāvali** Andhra Pradesh, E India *15°05′N 80°02′E*
**Kavála** *see* Kavála
**Kavango** *see* Cubango/ Okavango
83 F17 **Kavango East** ◆ *region* NE Namibia
83 E17 **Kavango West** ◆ *region* NE Namibia
155 C21 **Kavaratti** Lakshadweep, SW India *10°33′N 72°38′E*
114 O8 **Kavarna** Dobrich, NE Bulgaria *43°27′N 28°21′E*
118 G12 **Kavarskas** Utena, E Lithuania *55°27′N 24°55′E*
76 I13 **Kavendou** ▲ C Guinea *10°49′N 12°14′W*
**Kavengo** *see* Cubango/ Okavango
155 F20 **Kāveri** *var.* Cauvery. S India
186 G5 **Kavieng** *var.* Kaewieng. New Ireland, NE Papua New Guinea *04°13′S 152°11′E*
83 H16 **Kavimba** Chobe, NE Botswana *18°02′S 24°38′E*
83 I15 **Kavingu** Southern, S Zambia *15°39′S 26°03′E*
143 Q6 **Kavīr, Dasht-e** *var.* Great Salt Desert. *salt pan* N Iran
**Kavirondo Gulf** *see* Winam Gulf
**Kavkaz** *see* Caucasus
95 K23 **Kävlinge** Skåne, S Sweden *55°47′N 13°05′E*
82 G12 **Kavungo** Moxico, E Angola *11°31′S 22°59′E*
165 Q8 **Kawabe** Akita, Honshū, C Japan *39°39′N 140°14′E*
165 R9 **Kawai** Iwate, Honshū, C Japan *39°36′N 141°40′E*
38 A8 **Kawaihoa Point** *headland* Ni'ihau, Hawai'i, USA, C Pacific Ocean *21°47′N 160°12′W*
184 K3 **Kawakawa** Northland, North Island, New Zealand *35°23′S 174°06′E*
82 I13 **Kawama** North Western, NW Zambia *13°04′S 25°59′E*
82 K11 **Kawambwa** Luapula, N Zambia *09°45′S 29°10′E*
154 K11 **Kawardha** Chhattīsgarh, C India *21°59′N 81°12′E*
14 I14 **Kawartha Lakes** Ontario, SE Canada
165 O13 **Kawasaki** Kanagawa, Honshū, S Japan *35°32′N 139°41′E*
171 R12 **Kawassi** Pulau Obi, E Indonesia *01°32′S 127°25′E*
165 R6 **Kawauchi** Aomori, Honshū, C Japan *41°11′N 141°00′E*
184 L5 **Kawau Island** *island* N New Zealand
184 N10 **Kaweka Range** ▲▲ North Island, New Zealand
**Kawelecht** *see* Puhja
184 O8 **Kawerau** Bay of Plenty, North Island, New Zealand *38°06′S 176°43′E*
184 L8 **Kawhia** Waikato, North Island, New Zealand *38°04′S 174°49′E*
184 K8 **Kawhia Harbour** *inlet* North Island, New Zealand
35 V8 **Kawich Peak** ▲ Nevada, W USA *38°00′N 116°27′W*
35 V9 **Kawich Range** ▲▲ Nevada, W USA
14 G12 **Kawigamog Lake** Ontario, S Canada
171 P9 **Kawio, Kepulauan** *island group* N Indonesia
167 N9 **Kawkareik** Kayin State, S Myanmar (Burma) *16°33′N 98°18′E*
27 O8 **Kaw Lake** Oklahoma, C USA
166 M3 **Kawlin** Sagaing, N Myanmar (Burma) *23°48′N 95°41′E*
75 X11 **Kawm Umbū** *var.* Kom Ombo. SE Egypt *24°26′N 32°57′E*
**Kawthule State** *see* Kayin State
**Kaxgar** *see* Kashi
158 D7 **Kaxgar He** NW China
158 J5 **Kax He** NW China
77 P12 **Kaya** C Burkina Faso *13°04′N 01°09′W*
167 N6 **Kayah State** ◆ *state* C Myanmar (Burma)
39 T12 **Kayak Island** *island* Alaska, USA
114 M11 **Kayalıköy Barajı** NW Turkey
166 M8 **Kayan** Yangon, SW Myanmar (Burma) *16°54′N 96°35′E*
**Kayangel Islands** *see* Ngcheangel
155 G23 **Kāyankulam** Kerala, SW India *09°10′N 76°31′E*
169 V9 **Kayan, Sungai** *prev.* Kajan. Borneo, C Indonesia
144 F14 **Kaydak, Sor** *salt flat* SW Kazakhstan
**Kaydanovo** *see* Dzyarzhynsk
37 N9 **Kayenta** Arizona, SW USA *36°43′N 110°15′W*
76 J11 **Kayes** Kayes, W Mali *14°26′N 11°22′W*
76 J11 **Kayes** ◆ *region* SW Mali
167 N8 **Kayin State** *var.* Kawthule State, Karen State. ◆ *state* S Myanmar (Burma)
145 U10 **Kaynar** *Kaz.* Qaynar, *var.* Kajnar. Vostochnyy Kazakhstan, E Kazakhstan *49°13′N 77°27′E*
**Kaynary** *see* Căinari
83 H15 **Kayoya** Western, W Zambia *16°13′S 24°09′E*
**Kayrakkum** *see* Guliston
**Kayrakkumskoye Vodokhranilishche** *see* Qayroqqum, Obanbori
136 K14 **Kayseri** *var.* Kaisaria; *anc.* Caesarea Mazaca, Mazaca. Kayseri, C Turkey *38°42′N 35°28′E*
136 K14 **Kayseri** *var.* Kaisaria. ◆ *province* C Turkey
36 L2 **Kaysville** Utah, W USA *41°10′N 111°55′W*
**Kayyngdy** *see* Kaindy
14 L11 **Kazabazua** Québec, SE Canada *45°58′N 76°00′W*
14 L12 **Kazabazua** Québec, SE Canada
123 Q7 **Kazach'ye** Respublika Sakha (Yakutiya), NE Russia *70°38′N 135°54′E*
**Kazakdar'ya** *see* Qozoqdaryo
146 E9 **Kazakhlyshor, Solonchak** *var.* Solonchak Shorkazakhly. *salt marsh* NW Turkmenistan
**Kazakhskaya SSR/Kazakh Soviet Socialist Republic** *see* Kazakhstan
144 L12 **Kazakhstan** *off.* Republic of Kazakhstan, *var.* Kazakstan, *Kaz.* Qazaqstan, Qazaqstan Respūblīkasy; *prev.* Kazakh Soviet Socialist Republic, *Rus.* Kazakhskaya SSR, Respublika Kazakhstan. ◆ *republic* C Asia
**Kazakhstan, Republic of** *see* Kazakhstan
**Kazakhstan, Respublika** *see* Kazakhstan
129 Q6 **Kazakh Steppe** *grassland* C Kazakhstan
**Kazakh Uplands** *see* Saryarka
**Kazakstan** *see* Kazakhstan
**Kazalinsk** *see* Kazaly
144 L14 **Kazaly** *prev.* Kazalinsk. Kzyl-Orda, S Kazakhstan *45°45′N 62°01′E*
127 R4 **Kazan'** Respublika Tatarstan, W Russia *55°43′N 49°07′E*
8 M10 **Kazan** Nunavut, NW Canada
127 R4 **Kazan'** ✈ Respublika Tatarstan, W Russia *55°46′N 49°21′E*
**Kazandzhik** *see* Bereket
117 R8 **Kazanka** Mykolayivs'ka Oblast', S Ukraine *47°49′N 32°50′E*
**Kazanketken** *see* Qozonketkan
114 J9 **Kazanlak** *var.* Kazanlŭk; *prev.* Kazanlik. Stara Zagora, C Bulgaria *42°38′N 25°24′E*
**Kazanlik** *see* Kazanlak
**Kazanlŭk** *see* Kazanlak
165 Y16 **Kazan-rettō** *Eng.* Volcano Islands. *island group* SE Japan
**Kazantip, Mys** *see* Kazantyp, Mys
117 V12 **Kazantyp, Mys** *prev.* Mys Kazantip. *headland* S Ukraine *45°27′N 35°50′E*
147 U9 **Kazarman** Narynskaya Oblast', C Kyrgyzstan *41°21′N 74°03′E*
**Kazatin** *see* Kozyatyn
**Kazbegi** *see* Step'ants'minda
**Kazbegi** *see* Kazbek
137 T9 **Kazbek** *var.* Kazbegi, *Geor.* Mqinvartsveri. ▲ N Georgia *42°43′N 44°28′E*
82 M13 **Kazembe** Eastern, NE Zambia *12°06′S 32°45′E*
143 N11 **Kāzerūn** Fārs, S Iran *29°41′N 51°38′E*
125 R12 **Kazhym** Respublika Komi, NW Russia *60°19′N 51°26′E*
**Kazi Ahmad** *see* Qazi Ahmad
136 H16 **Kazımkarabekir** Karaman, S Turkey *37°13′N 32°58′E*
111 M20 **Kazincbarcika** Borsod-Abaúj-Zemplén, NE Hungary *48°15′N 20°40′E*
119 H17 **Kazlowshchyna** *Pol.* Kozlowszczyzna, *Rus.* Kozlovshchina. Hrodzyenskaya Voblasts', W Belarus *53°19′N 25°18′E*
119 E14 **Kazlų Rūda** Marijampolė, S Lithuania *54°45′N 23°28′E*
144 E9 **Kaztalovka** Zapadnyy Kazakhstan, W Kazakhstan *49°45′N 48°42′E*
79 K22 **Kazumba** Kasai-Occidental, S Dem. Rep. Congo *06°25′S 22°02′E*
165 Q8 **Kazuno** Akita, Honshū, C Japan *40°14′N 140°48′E*
**Kazvin** *see* Qazvīn
118 J12 **Kazyany** *Rus.* Koz'yany. Vitsyebskaya Voblasts', NW Belarus *55°18′N 26°52′E*
122 H9 **Kazym** N Russia
110 H10 **Kcynia** *Ger.* Exin. Kujawsko-pomorskie, C Poland *53°00′N 17°29′E*
115 I20 **Kéa** *var.* Tziá, Kéos; *anc.* Ceos. *island* Kykládes, Greece, Aegean Sea
38 H11 **Kea'au** *var.* Keaau. Hawaii, USA, C Pacific Ocean *19°36′N 155°01′W*
**Keaau** *see* Kea'au
38 F11 **Keāhole Point** *var.* Keahole Point. *headland* Hawai'i, USA, C Pacific Ocean *19°43′N 156°03′W*
38 G12 **Kealakekua** Hawaii, USA, C Pacific Ocean *19°31′N 155°56′W*
38 H11 **Kea, Mauna** ▲ Hawai'i, USA *19°50′N 155°30′W*
37 N10 **Keams** Arizona, SW USA *35°47′N 110°09′W*
**Kéamu** *see* Aneityum
29 O16 **Kearney** Nebraska, C USA *40°42′N 99°06′W*
36 L3 **Kearns** Utah, W USA *40°39′N 112°00′W*
115 H20 **Kéas, Stenó** *strait* SE Greece
137 O14 **Keban Barajı** *dam* C Turkey
137 O14 **Keban Barajı** C Turkey
77 S13 **Kebbi** ◆ *state* NW Nigeria
76 G10 **Kébémèr** NW Senegal *15°24′N 16°25′W*
74 M7 **Kebili** *var.* Qibilī. C Tunisia *33°42′N 09°06′E*
138 H4 **Kebir, Nahr el** NW Syria
80 A10 **Kebkabiya** Northern Darfur, W Sudan *13°39′N 24°05′E*
92 I11 **Kebnekaise** *Lapp.* Giebnegáisi. ▲ N Sweden *68°01′N 18°24′E*
81 M14 **K'ebrī Dehar** Sumalē, E Ethiopia *06°43′N 44°15′E*
148 K15 **Kech** SW Pakistan
10 K10 **Kechika** British Columbia, W Canada
111 K23 **Kecskemét** Bács-Kiskun, C Hungary *46°54′N 19°42′E*
168 J6 **Kedah** ◆ *state* Peninsular Malaysia
118 F12 **Kėdainiai** Kaunas, C Lithuania *55°19′N 24°00′E*
152 K8 **Kedārnāth** Uttarākhand, N India *30°44′N 79°03′E*
**Kedder** *see* Kehra
13 N13 **Kedgwick** New Brunswick, SE Canada *47°38′N 67°21′W*
169 R16 **Kediri** Jawa, C Indonesia *07°45′S 112°01′E*
171 Y13 **Kedir Sarmi** Papua, E Indonesia *02°00′S 139°01′E*
163 V7 **Kedong** Heilongjiang, NE China *48°00′N 126°15′E*
76 I12 **Kédougou** SE Senegal *12°35′N 12°09′W*
122 I11 **Kedrovyy** Tomskaya Oblast', C Russia *57°31′N 79°45′E*
111 H16 **Kędzierzyn-Kozle** *Ger.* Heydebrech. Opolskie, S Poland *50°20′N 18°12′E*
8 H8 **Keele** Northwest Territories, NW Canada
10 K6 **Keele Peak** ▲ Yukon, NW Canada *63°31′N 130°21′W*
161 T12 **Keelung** *prev.* Chilung, *var.* Jilong, *Jap.* Kirun, Kirun'; *prev. Sp.* Santissima Trinidad. N Taiwan *25°10′N 121°43′E*
19 N10 **Keene** New Hampshire, NE USA *42°56′N 72°14′W*
99 H17 **Keerbergen** Vlaams Brabant, C Belgium *51°01′N 04°39′E*
83 E21 **Keetmanshoop** //Karas, S Namibia *26°36′S 18°08′E*
12 A11 **Keewatin** Ontario, S Canada *49°47′N 94°30′W*
29 V4 **Keewatin** Minnesota, N USA *47°24′N 93°04′W*
**Kefallinía** *see* Kefalloniá
115 B18 **Kefalloniá** *var.* Kefallinía, Cephalonia. *island* Iónia Nisiá, Greece, C Mediterranean Sea
115 M22 **Kéfalos** Kos, Dodekánisa, Greece, Aegean Sea *36°44′N 26°58′E*
171 Q17 **Kefamenanu** Timor, C Indonesia *09°31′S 124°29′E*
**Kefar Sava** *see* Kfar Sava
**Kefe** *see* Feodosiya
77 V15 **Keffi** Nassarawa, C Nigeria *08°52′N 07°54′E*
92 H4 **Keflavík** Suðurnes, W Iceland *64°01′N 22°35′W*
92 H4 **Keflavik** ✈ (Reykjavík) Suðurnes, W Iceland *63°58′N 22°37′W*
**Kegalee** *see* Kegalla
155 J25 **Kegalla** *var.* Kegalee, Kegalle. Sabaragamuwa Province, C Sri Lanka *07°14′N 80°21′E*
**Kegalle** *see* Kegalla
**Kegayli** *see* Kegeyli
**Kegel** *see* Keila
145 W16 **Kegen** Almaty, SE Kazakhstan *42°58′N 79°12′E*
146 H7 **Kegeyli** *prev.* Kegayli. Qoraqalpog'iston Respublikasi, W Uzbekistan *42°46′N 59°49′E*
101 F22 **Kehl** Baden-Württemberg, SW Germany *48°34′N 07°49′E*
118 H3 **Kehra** *Ger.* Kedder. Harjumaa, NW Estonia *59°19′N 25°21′E*
117 U6 **Kehychivka** Kharkivs'ka Oblast', E Ukraine *49°18′N 35°46′E*
97 L17 **Keighley** N England, United Kingdom *53°51′N 01°58′W*
**Kei Islands** *see* Kai, Kepulauan
**Keijō** *see* Seoul
118 G3 **Keila** *Ger.* Kegel. Harjumaa, NW Estonia *59°18′N 24°29′E*
**Keilberg** *see* Klínovec
83 F23 **Keimoes** Northern Cape, W South Africa *28°41′S 20°59′E*
**Keina/Keinis** *see* Käina
**Keishū** *see* Gyeongju
77 T11 **Keïta** Tahoua, C Niger *14°45′N 05°40′E*
78 J12 **Kéita, Bahr** *var.* Doka. S Chad
182 K10 **Keith** South Australia *36°01′S 140°22′E*
96 K8 **Keith** NE Scotland, United Kingdom *57°33′N 02°57′W*
26 K3 **Keith Sebelius Lake** Kansas, C USA
32 G11 **Keizer** Oregon, NW USA *44°59′N 123°01′W*
38 A8 **Kekaha** Kaua'i, Hawaii, USA, C Pacific Ocean *21°58′N 159°43′W*
147 U10 **Këk-Art** *prev.* Alaykel', Alay-Kuu. Oshskaya Oblast', SW Kyrgyzstan *40°16′N 74°21′E*
147 W10 **Këk-Aygyr** *var.* Keyaygyr. Narynskaya Oblast', C Kyrgyzstan *40°42′N 75°37′E*
147 V9 **Këk-Dzhar** Narynskaya Oblast', C Kyrgyzstan *41°28′N 74°48′E*
14 L8 **Kekek** Québec, SE Canada
185 K15 **Kekerengu** Canterbury, South Island, New Zealand *41°55′S 174°05′E*
111 L21 **Kékes** ▲ N Hungary *47°53′N 19°59′E*
171 P17 **Kekneno, Gunung** ▲ Timor, S Indonesia
147 S9 **Këk-Tash** *Kyr.* Kök-Tash. Dzhalal-Abadskaya Oblast', W Kyrgyzstan *41°08′N 72°25′E*
81 M15 **K'elafo** Sumalē, E Ethiopia *05°36′N 44°12′E*
169 U10 **Kelai, Sungai** Borneo, N Indonesia
**Kelamayi** *see* Karamay
**Kelang** *see* Klang
168 K7 **Kelantan** ◆ *state* Peninsular Malaysia
**Kelantan** *see* Kelantan, Sungai
168 K7 **Kelantan, Sungai** *var.* Kelantan. Peninsular Malaysia
**Kelat** *see* Kalat
**Këlcyra** *see* Këlcyrë
113 L22 **Këlcyrë** *var.* Këlcyra. Gjirokastër, S Albania *40°19′N 20°10′E*
**Kelifskiy Uzboy** *see* Kelif Uzboýy
146 L14 **Kelif Uzboýy** *Rus.* Kelifskiy Uzboy. *salt marsh* E Turkmenistan
137 O12 **Kelkit** Gümüşhane, NE Turkey *40°07′N 39°28′E*
136 M12 **Kelkit Çayı** N Turkey
79 G18 **Kéllé** Cuvette-Ouest, W Congo *0°04′S 14°33′E*
77 W11 **Kellé** Zinder, S Niger *14°10′N 10°10′E*
145 P7 **Kellerovka** Severnyy Kazakhstan, N Kazakhstan *53°51′N 69°15′E*
8 I5 **Kellett, Cape** *headland* Banks Island, Northwest Territories, NW Canada *71°57′N 125°55′W*
31 S11 **Kelleys Island** *island* Ohio, N USA
33 N8 **Kellogg** Idaho, NW USA *47°30′N 116°07′W*
92 M12 **Kelloselkä** Lappi, N Finland *66°56′N 28°52′E*
97 F17 **Kells** *Ir.* Ceanannas. Meath, E Ireland *53°44′N 06°53′W*
118 E12 **Kelmė** Šiaulai, C Lithuania *55°39′N 22°57′E*
99 M19 **Kelmis** *var.* La Calamine. Liège, E Belgium *50°43′N 06°01′E*
78 H12 **Kélo** Tandjilé, SW Chad *09°21′N 15°50′E*
83 I14 **Kelongwa** North Western, NW Zambia *13°41′S 26°19′E*
11 N17 **Kelowna** British Columbia, SW Canada *49°50′N 119°29′W*
11 X12 **Kelsey** Manitoba, C Canada *56°02′N 96°31′W*
34 M6 **Kelseyville** California, W USA *38°58′N 122°51′W*
96 K13 **Kelso** SE Scotland, United Kingdom *55°36′N 02°27′W*
32 G10 **Kelso** Washington, NW USA *46°09′N 122°54′W*
195 W15 **Keltie, Cape** *headland* Antarctica
**Keltsy** *see* Kielce
168 L9 **Keluang** *var.* Kluang. Johor, Peninsular Malaysia *02°01′N 103°18′E*
168 M11 **Kelume** Pulau Lingga, W Indonesia *0°12′S 104°27′E*
11 U15 **Kelvington** Saskatchewan, S Canada *52°10′N 103°30′W*
124 J7 **Kem'** Respublika Kareliya, NW Russia *64°55′N 34°18′E*
124 I7 **Kem'** NW Russia
137 O13 **Kemah** Erzincan, E Turkey *39°35′N 39°02′E*
137 N13 **Kemaliye** Erzincan, C Turkey *39°16′N 38°29′E*
**Kemaman** *see* Cukai
**Kemanlar** *see* Isperih
10 K14 **Kemano** British Columbia, SW Canada *53°39′N 127°58′W*
**Kemarat** *see* Khemmarat
171 P12 **Kembani** Pulau Peleng, N Indonesia *01°32′S 122°57′E*
136 F17 **Kemer** Antalya, SW Turkey *36°39′N 30°33′E*
122 J12 **Kemerovo** *prev.* Shcheglovsk. Kemerovskaya Oblast', C Russia *55°25′N 86°05′E*
122 K12 **Kemerovskaya Oblast'** ◆ *province* S Russia
92 L13 **Kemi** Lappi, NW Finland *65°46′N 24°34′E*
92 M12 **Kemijärvi** *Swe.* Kemiträsk. Lappi, N Finland *66°41′N 27°24′E*
92 M12 **Kemijärvi** N Finland
92 L13 **Kemijoki** NW Finland
147 V7 **Kemin** *prev.* Bystrovka. Chuyskaya Oblast', N Kyrgyzstan
92 L13 **Keminmaa** Lappi, NW Finland *65°49′N 24°34′E*
**Kemins Island** *see* Nikumaroro
**Kemiö** *see* Kimito
**Kemiträsk** *see* Kemijärvi
127 P5 **Kemlya** Respublika Mordoviya, W Russia *54°42′N 45°16′E*
99 B18 **Kemmel** West-Vlaanderen, W Belgium *50°42′N 02°51′E*
33 S16 **Kemmerer** Wyoming, C USA *41°47′N 110°32′W*
121 O15 **Kemmuna** *var.* Comino. *island* C Malta
79 I14 **Kémo** ◆ *prefecture* S Central African Republic
25 U7 **Kemp** Texas, SW USA *32°26′N 96°13′W*
93 L14 **Kempele** Pohjois-Pohjanmaa, C Finland *64°56′N 25°26′E*
101 D15 **Kempen** Nordrhein-Westfalen, W Germany *51°22′N 06°25′E*
25 Q5 **Kemp, Lake** Texas, SW USA
195 W5 **Kemp Land** *physical region* Antarctica
25 S9 **Kempner** Texas, SW USA *31°03′N 98°01′W*
44 H3 **Kemp's Bay** Andros Island, W The Bahamas *24°02′N 77°32′W*
183 U6 **Kempsey** New South Wales, SE Australia *31°05′S 152°50′E*
101 J24 **Kempten** Bayern, S Germany *47°44′N 10°19′E*
15 N9 **Kempt, Lac** Québec, SE Canada
183 P17 **Kempton** Tasmania, SE Australia *42°34′S 147°13′E*
154 J9 **Ken** C India
39 R12 **Kenai** Alaska, USA *60°33′N 151°15′W*
0 D5 **Kenai Mountains** ▲▲ Alaska, USA
39 R12 **Kenai Peninsula** *peninsula* Alaska, USA
21 V11 **Kenansville** North Carolina, SE USA *34°57′N 77°54′W*
146 A10 **Kenar** *prev. Rus.* Ufra. Balkan Welaýaty, NW Turkmenistan *40°00′N 53°05′E*
97 K16 **Kendal** NW England, United Kingdom *54°20′N 02°45′W*
23 Y16 **Kendall** Florida, SE USA *25°39′N 80°18′W*
9 O8 **Kendall, Cape** *headland* Nunavut, E Canada *63°31′N 87°09′W*
18 J15 **Kendall Park** New Jersey, NE USA *40°25′N 74°33′W*
31 Q11 **Kendallville** Indiana, N USA *41°24′N 85°10′W*
171 P14 **Kendari** Sulawesi, C Indonesia *03°57′S 122°36′E*
169 Q13 **Kendawangan** Borneo, C Indonesia *02°32′S 110°13′E*
**Kendrāpāra** *see* Kendrāparha
154 O12 **Kendrāparha** *var.* Kendrāpāra. Odisha, E India *20°29′N 86°25′E*
154 O11 **Kendujhargarh** *prev.* Keonjihargarh. Odisha, E India *21°38′N 85°40′E*
25 S13 **Kenedy** Texas, SW USA *28°49′N 97°51′W*
76 J15 **Kenema** SE Sierra Leone *07°55′N 11°12′W*
29 P16 **Kenesaw** Nebraska, C USA *40°37′N 98°39′W*
**Këneurgench** *see* Köneürgenç
79 H21 **Kenge** Bandundu, SW Dem. Rep. Congo *04°52′S 16°59′E*
**Kengen** *see* Kangen
167 O5 **Kengtung** Shan State, E Myanmar (Burma) *21°18′N 99°36′E*
83 F23 **Kenhardt** Northern Cape, W South Africa *29°19′S 21°08′E*
76 J12 **Kéniéba** Kayes, W Mali *12°47′N 11°16′W*
**Kenimekh** *see* Konimex
169 U7 **Keningau** Sabah, East Malaysia *05°21′N 116°11′E*
74 F6 **Kénitra** *prev.* Port-Lyautey. NW Morocco *34°20′N 06°29′W*
21 V9 **Kenly** North Carolina, SE USA *35°39′N 78°16′W*
97 B21 **Kenmare** *Ir.* Neidín. S Ireland *51°53′N 09°35′W*
28 L2 **Kenmare** North Dakota, N USA *48°40′N 102°04′W*
97 A21 **Kenmare River** *Ir.* An Ribhéar. *inlet* NE Atlantic Ocean
18 D10 **Kenmore** New York, NE USA *42°58′N 78°52′W*
25 W8 **Kennard** Texas, SW USA *31°21′N 95°10′W*
29 N10 **Kennebec** South Dakota, N USA *43°53′N 99°51′W*
19 Q7 **Kennebec River** Maine, NE USA
19 P9 **Kennebunk** Maine, NE USA *43°22′N 70°33′W*
39 R13 **Kennedy Entrance** *strait* Alaska, USA
166 L3 **Kennedy Peak** ▲ W Myanmar (Burma) *23°18′N 93°52′E*
22 K9 **Kenner** Louisiana, S USA *29°57′N 90°15′W*
180 I8 **Kenneth Range** ▲▲ Western Australia
27 Y9 **Kennett** Missouri, C USA *36°15′N 90°04′W*
18 I16 **Kennett Square** Pennsylvania, NE USA *39°50′N 75°40′W*
32 K10 **Kennewick** Washington, NW USA *46°12′N 119°08′W*
12 E11 **Kenogami** Ontario, S Canada
15 Q7 **Kénogami, Lac** Québec, SE Canada
14 G8 **Kenogami Lake** Ontario, S Canada *48°04′N 80°10′W*
14 F7 **Kenogamissi Lake** Ontario, S Canada
10 I6 **Keno Hill** Yukon, NW Canada *63°54′N 135°18′W*
12 A11 **Kenora** Ontario, S Canada *49°47′N 94°26′W*
31 N9 **Kenosha** Wisconsin, N USA *42°34′N 87°50′W*
13 P14 **Kensington** Prince Edward Island, SE Canada *46°26′N 63°39′W*
26 L3 **Kensington** Kansas, C USA *39°46′N 99°01′W*
32 I11 **Kent** Oregon, NW USA *45°14′N 120°43′W*
24 J9 **Kent** Texas, SW USA *31°03′N 104°13′W*
32 H8 **Kent** Washington, NW USA *47°22′N 122°13′W*
97 P22 **Kent** *cultural region* SE England, United Kingdom
145 P16 **Kentau** Turkestan, S Kazakhstan *43°28′N 68°41′E*
183 P14 **Kent Group** *island group* Tasmania, SE Australia
31 N12 **Kentland** Indiana, N USA *40°46′N 87°26′W*
31 R12 **Kenton** Ohio, N USA *40°39′N 83°36′W*
8 K7 **Kent Peninsula** *peninsula* Nunavut, N Canada
115 F14 **Kentrikí Makedonía** *Eng.* Macedonia Central. ◆ *region* N Greece
20 J6 **Kentucky** *off.* Commonwealth of Kentucky, *also known as* Bluegrass State. ◆ *state* C USA
20 H8 **Kentucky Lake** Kentucky/Tennessee, S USA
13 P15 **Kentville** Nova Scotia, SE Canada *45°04′N 64°30′W*
22 K8 **Kentwood** Louisiana, S USA *30°56′N 90°30′W*
31 P9 **Kentwood** Michigan, N USA *42°52′N 85°33′W*
81 H17 **Kenya** *off.* Republic of Kenya. ◆ *republic* E Africa
**Kenya, Mount** *see* Kirinyaga
**Kenya, Republic of** *see* Kenya
168 L7 **Kenyir, Tasik** *var.* Tasek Kenyir. Peninsular Malaysia
29 W10 **Kenyon** Minnesota, N USA *44°16′N 92°59′W*
29 Y16 **Keokuk** Iowa, C USA *40°24′N 91°22′W*
**Keonjihargarh** *see* Kendujhargarh
**Kéos** *see* Kéa
29 X16 **Keosauqua** Iowa, C USA *40°43′N 91°58′W*
29 X15 **Keota** Iowa, C USA *41°21′N 91°57′W*
21 O11 **Keowee, Lake** South Carolina, SE USA
124 I7 **Kepa** *var.* Kepe. Respublika Kareliya, NW Russia *65°09′N 32°15′E*
**Kepe** *see* Kepa
189 O13 **Kepirohi Falls** *waterfall* Pohnpei, E Micronesia
185 B22 **Kepler Mountains** ▲▲ South Island, New Zealand
111 I14 **Kępno** Wielkopolskie, C Poland *51°17′N 17°57′E*
65 C24 **Keppel Island** *island* N Falkland Islands
**Keppel Island** *see* Niuatoputapu
65 C23 **Keppel Sound** *sound* N Falkland Islands
**Kepri** *see* Kepulauan Riau
136 D12 **Kepsut** Balıkesir, NW Turkey *39°41′N 28°09′E*
168 M11 **Kepulauan Riau** *off.* Propinsi Kepulauan Riau, *var.* Kepri. ◆ *province* NW Indonesia
**Kequ** *see* Gadê
171 V13 **Kerai** Papua Barat, E Indonesia *03°53′S 134°30′E*
**Kerak** *see* Al Karak
155 F22 **Kerala** ◆ *state* S India
165 R16 **Kerama-rettō** *island group* SW Japan
183 N10 **Kerang** Victoria, SE Australia *35°46′S 144°01′E*
**Kerasunt** *see* Giresun
115 H19 **Keratéa** *var.* Keratea. Attikí, C Greece *37°48′N 23°58′E*
**Keratea** *see* Keratéa
93 M19 **Kerava** *Swe.* Kervo. Uusimaa, S Finland *60°25′N 25°10′E*
**Kerbala/Kerbela** *see* Karbalā'
32 F15 **Kerby** Oregon, NW USA *42°10′N 123°39′W*
117 W12 **Kerch** *Rus.* Kerch'. Avtonomna Respublika Krym, SE Ukraine *45°22′N 36°30′E*
**Kerch'** *see* Kerch
**Kerchens'ka Protska/ Kerchenskiy Proliv** *see* Kerch Strait
117 V13 **Kerchens'kyy Pivostriv** *peninsula* S Ukraine
121 V4 **Kerch Strait** *var.* Bosporus Cimmerius, Enikale Strait, *Rus.* Kerchenskiy Proliv, *Ukr.* Kerchens'ka Protska. *strait* Black Sea/Sea of Azov
**Kerdilio** *see* Kerdýlio
114 H13 **Kerdýlio** *var.* Kerdilio. ▲ N Greece *40°46′N 23°37′E*
186 D8 **Kerema** Gulf, S Papua New Guinea *07°59′S 145°46′E*
**Keremitlik** *see* Lyulyakovo
136 I9 **Kerempe Burnu** *headland* N Turkey *42°01′N 33°20′E*
80 J9 **Keren** *var.* Cheren. C Eritrea *15°45′N 38°22′E*
25 U7 **Kerens** Texas, SW USA *32°07′N 96°13′W*
184 M6 **Kerepehi** Waikato, North Island, New Zealand *37°18′S 175°33′E*
145 P10 **Kerey, Ozero** C Kazakhstan
**Kergel** *see* Kärla
173 Q12 **Kerguelen** *island* C French Southern and Antarctic Lands
173 Q13 **Kerguelen Plateau** *undersea feature* S Indian Ocean
115 C20 **Kerí** Zákynthos, Iónia Nisiá, Greece, C Mediterranean Sea *37°40′N 20°48′E*
81 H19 **Kericho** Kericho, W Kenya *0°22′S 35°19′E*
184 K2 **Kerikeri** Northland, North Island, New Zealand *35°14′S 173°58′E*
93 O17 **Kerimäki** Etelä-Savo, E Finland *61°56′N 29°18′E*
168 K12 **Kerinci, Gunung** ▲ Sumatera, W Indonesia *02°00′S 101°40′E*
**Keriya** *see* Yutian
158 H9 **Keriya He** NW China
98 J9 **Kerkbuurt** Noord-Holland, C Netherlands *52°29′N 05°08′E*
98 J13 **Kerkdriel** Gelderland, C Netherlands *51°46′N 05°21′E*
75 N6 **Kerkennah, Îles** *var.* Kerkennah Islands, *Ar.* Juzur Qarqannah. *island group* E Tunisia
**Kerkennah Islands** *see* Kerkennah, Îles
115 M20 **Kerketévs** ▲ Sámos, Dodekánisa, Greece, Aegean Sea *37°44′N 26°39′E*
29 T8 **Kerkhoven** Minnesota, N USA *45°12′N 95°18′W*
**Kerki** *see* Atamyrat
**Kerkichi** *see* Kerkiçi
146 M14 **Kerkiçi** *Rus.* Kerkichi. Lebap Welaýaty, E Turkmenistan *37°46′N 65°18′E*
115 F16 **Kerkíneo** *prehistoric site* Thessalía, C Greece
114 G12 **Kerkíni, Límni** *var.* Límni Kerkinitis. N Greece
**Kerkinitis Límni** *see* Kerkíni, Límni
**Kérkira** *see* Kérkyra
99 M18 **Kerkrade** Limburg, SE Netherlands *50°53′N 06°04′E*
**Kerkuk** *see* Kirkūk
115 B16 **Kérkyra** *var.* Kérkira, *Eng.* Corfu. Kérkyra, Iónia Nisiá, Greece, C Mediterranean Sea *39°37′N 19°56′E*
115 B16 **Kerkyra** ✈ Kérkyra, Iónia Nisiá, Greece, C Mediterranean Sea *39°36′N 19°55′E*
115 A16 **Kérkyra** *var.* Kérkira, *Eng.* Corfu. *island* Iónia Nisiá, Greece, C Mediterranean Sea
192 K10 **Kermadec Islands** *island group* New Zealand, SW Pacific Ocean
175 R10 **Kermadec Ridge** *undersea feature* SW Pacific Ocean *30°30′S 178°30′W*
175 R11 **Kermadec Trench** *undersea feature* SW Pacific Ocean
143 S10 **Kermān** *var.* Kirman; *anc.* Carmana. Kermān, C Iran *30°18′N 57°05′E*
143 R11 **Kermān** *off.* Ostān-e Kermān, *var.* Kirman; *anc.* Carmania. ◆ *province* SE Iran
143 U12 **Kermān, Bīābān-e** *desert* SE Iran
**Kermān, Ostān-e** *see* Kermān
142 K6 **Kermānshāh** *var.* Qahremānshahr; *prev.* Bākhtarān. Kermānshāhān, W Iran *34°19′N 47°04′E*
143 Q9 **Kermānshāh** Yazd, C Iran *34°19′N 47°04′E*
142 J6 **Kermānshāh** *off.* Ostān-e Kermānshāh; *prev.* Bākhtarān. ◆ *province* W Iran
**Kermānshāh, Ostān-e** *see* Kermānshāh
114 L10 **Kermen** Sliven, C Bulgaria *42°30′N 26°12′E*
24 L8 **Kermit** Texas, SW USA *31°49′N 103°07′W*
21 P6 **Kermit** West Virginia, NE USA *37°51′N 82°24′W*
21 S9 **Kernersville** North Carolina, SE USA *36°12′N 80°13′W*
35 S12 **Kern River** California, W USA
35 S12 **Kernville** California, W USA *35°44′N 118°25′W*
115 K21 **Kéros** *island* Kykládes, Greece, Aegean Sea
76 K14 **Kérouané** SE Guinea *09°16′N 09°00′W*
101 D16 **Kerpen** Nordrhein-Westfalen, W Germany *50°51′N 06°40′E*
146 I11 **Kerpichli** Lebap Welaýaty, NE Turkmenistan *40°12′N 61°09′E*
24 M1 **Kerrick** Texas, SW USA *36°29′N 102°14′W*
**Kerr Lake** *see* John H. Kerr Reservoir
11 S15 **Kerrobert** Saskatchewan, S Canada *51°56′N 109°09′W*
25 Q11 **Kerrville** Texas, SW USA *30°03′N 99°09′W*
97 B20 **Kerry** *Ir.* Ciarraí. *cultural region* SW Ireland
21 S11 **Kershaw** South Carolina, SE USA *34°33′N 80°34′W*
**Kertel** *see* Kärdla
95 H23 **Kerteminde** Syddtjylland, C Denmark *55°27′N 10°40′E*
163 Q7 **Kerulen** *Chin.* Herlen He, *Mong.* Herlen Gol. China/ Mongolia
**Kervo** *see* Kerava
**Kerýneia** *see* Girne
12 H11 **Kesagami Lake** Ontario, SE Canada
93 O17 **Kesälahti** Pohjois-Karjala, SE Finland *61°54′N 29°49′E*
136 B11 **Keşan** Edirne, NW Turkey *40°52′N 26°37′E*
165 R9 **Kesennuma** Miyagi, Honshū, C Japan *38°55′N 141°35′E*
163 V7 **Keshan** Heilongjiang, NE China *48°00′N 125°46′E*
30 M6 **Keshena** Wisconsin, N USA *44°54′N 88°37′W*
136 I13 **Keskin** Kırıkkale, C Turkey *39°41′N 33°36′E*
**Késmárk** *see* Kežmarok
124 I6 **Kesten'ga** *var.* Kest Enga. Respublika Kareliya, NW Russia *65°53′N 31°47′E*
**Kest Enga** *see* Kesten'ga
98 K12 **Kesteren** Gelderland, C Netherlands *51°55′N 05°34′E*
14 H14 **Keswick** Ontario, S Canada *44°15′N 79°26′W*
97 K15 **Keswick** NW England, United Kingdom *54°30′N 03°04′W*
111 H24 **Keszthely** Zala, SW Hungary *46°47′N 17°16′E*
122 K11 **Ket'** C Russia
77 R17 **Keta** SE Ghana *05°55′N 00°59′E*
169 Q12 **Ketapang** Borneo, C Indonesia *01°50′S 109°59′E*
127 O12 **Ketchenery** *prev.* Sovetskoye. Respublika Kalmykiya, SW Russia *47°18′N 44°31′E*
39 Y14 **Ketchikan** Revillagigedo Island, Alaska, USA *55°21′N 131°39′W*
33 O14 **Ketchum** Idaho, NW USA *43°40′N 114°24′W*
**Kete/Kete Krakye** *see* Kete-Krachi
77 Q15 **Kete-Krachi** *var.* Kete, Kete Krakye. E Ghana *07°50′N 00°03′W*
98 L9 **Ketelmeer** *channel* E Netherlands
149 P17 **Keti Bandar** Sindh, SE Pakistan *23°55′N 67°31′E*
77 S16 **Kétou** SE Benin *07°25′N 02°36′E*
110 M7 **Kętrzyn** *Ger.* Rastenburg. Warmińsko-Mazurskie, NE Poland *54°05′N 21°24′E*
97 N20 **Kettering** C England, United Kingdom *52°24′N 00°44′W*
31 R14 **Kettering** Ohio, N USA *39°41′N 84°10′W*
18 F13 **Kettle Creek** Pennsylvania, NE USA
32 L7 **Kettle Falls** Washington, NW USA *48°36′N 118°03′W*
14 D16 **Kettle Point** *headland* Ontario, S Canada *43°12′N 82°01′W*
29 V6 **Kettle River** Minnesota, N USA
186 B7 **Ketu** W Papua New Guinea
18 G10 **Keuka Lake** New York, NE USA
**Keupriya** *see* Primorsko
93 L17 **Keuruu** Keski-Suomi, C Finland *62°15′N 24°34′E*
**Kevevára** *see* Kovin
92 L9 **Kevo** *Lapp.* Geavvú. Lappi, N Finland *69°42′N 27°08′E*
44 M6 **Kew** North Caicos, N Turks and Caicos Islands *21°52′N 71°57′W*
30 K11 **Kewanee** Illinois, N USA *41°15′N 89°55′W*
31 N7 **Kewaunee** Wisconsin, N USA *44°27′N 87°31′W*
30 M3 **Keweenaw Bay** Michigan, N USA
31 N2 **Keweenaw Peninsula** *peninsula* Michigan, N USA
31 N2 **Keweenaw Point** *peninsula* Michigan, N USA
29 N12 **Keya Paha River** Nebraska/South Dakota, N USA
**Keyaygyr** *see* Këk-Aygyr
23 Z16 **Key Biscayne** Florida, SE USA *25°41′N 80°09′W*
26 G8 **Keyes** Oklahoma, C USA *36°48′N 102°15′W*
23 Y17 **Key Largo** Key Largo, Florida, SE USA *25°06′N 80°25′W*
21 U3 **Keyser** West Virginia, NE USA *39°25′N 78°59′W*
27 O9 **Keystone Lake** Oklahoma, C USA
36 L16 **Keystone Peak** ▲ Arizona, SW USA *31°52′N 111°12′W*
**Keystone State** *see* Pennsylvania
21 U7 **Keysville** Virginia, NE USA *37°02′N 78°28′W*
27 T3 **Keytesville** Missouri, C USA *39°25′N 92°56′W*
23 W17 **Key West** Florida Keys, Florida, SE USA *24°34′N 81°48′W*
127 T1 **Kez** Udmurtskaya Respublika, NW Russia *57°55′N 53°42′E*
**Kezdivásárhely** *see* Târgu Secuiesc
122 M12 **Kezhma** Krasnoyarskiy Kray, C Russia *58°57′N 101°00′E*
111 L18 **Kežmarok** *Ger.* Käsmark, *Hung.* Késmárk. Prešovský Kraj, E Slovakia *49°09′N 20°25′E*
**Kfar Saba** *see* Kfar Sava
138 F10 **Kfar Sava** *var.* Kfar Saba; *prev.* Kefar Sava. Central, C Israel *32°11′N 34°58′E*
83 F20 **Kgalagadi** ◆ *district* SW Botswana
83 I20 **Kgatleng** ◆ *district* SE Botswana
188 F8 **Kgkeklau** Babeldaob, N Palau
125 R6 **Khabarikha** *var.* Chabaricha. Respublika Komi, NW Russia *65°52′N 52°19′E*
123 S14 **Khabarovsk** Khabarovskiy Kray, SE Russia *48°32′N 135°08′E*
123 R11 **Khabarovskiy Kray** ◆ *territory* E Russia
141 W7 **Khabb** Abū Ẓaby, E United Arab Emirates *24°39′N 55°43′E*
**Khabour, Nahr al** *see* Khābūr, Nahr al
**Khabura** *see* Al Khābūrah
139 N2 **Khābūr, Nahr al** *var.* Nahr al Khabour. Syria/Turkey
**Khachmas** *see* Xaçmaz
80 B12 **Khadari** W Sudan
**Khadera** *see* Hadera
141 X12 **Khādhil** *var.* Khudal. SE Oman *18°48′N 56°48′E*
155 E14 **Khadki** *prev.* Kirkee. Mahārāshtra, W India *18°34′N 73°52′E*
126 L14 **Khadyzhensk** Krasnodarskiy Kray, SW Russia *44°26′N 39°31′E*
**Khadzhiyska Reka** *see* Hadzhiyska Reka




◆ Country
● Country Capital
◇ Dependent Territory
○ Dependent Territory Capital
◆ Administrative Regions
✈ International Airport
▲ Mountain
▲▲ Mountain Range
Volcano
River
Lake
Reservoir

Khadzhybeys'kyy Lyman – King Salmon


117 P10 **Khadzhybeys'kyy Lyman** ◎ SW Ukraine

138 K3 **Khafsah** Ḩalab, N Syria 36°16′N 38°03′E

152 M13 **Khāga** Uttar Pradesh, N India 25°47′N 81°05′E

153 Q13 **Khagaria** Bihār, NE India 25°31′N 86°27′E

149 Q13 **Khairpur** Sindh, SE Pakistan 27°30′N 68°50′E

122 K13 **Khakasiya, Respublika** *prev.* Khakasskaya Avtonomnaya Oblast', *Eng.* Khakassia. ◈ *autonomous republic* C Russia

**Khakassia/Khakasskaya Avtonomnaya Oblast'** *see* Khakasiya, Respublika

167 N9 **Kha Khaeng, Khao** ▲ W Thailand 16°13′N 99°03′E

83 G20 **Khakhea** *var.* Kakia. Southern, S Botswana 24°41′S 23°29′E

**Khalach** *see* Halaç

**Khalándrion** *see* Chalándri

75 T7 **Khalīj as Sallūm** *Ar.* Gulf of Salûm. *gulf* Egypt/Libya

75 X8 **Khalīj as Suways** *var.* Suez, Gulf of. *gulf* NE Egypt

127 W7 **Khalilovo** Orenburgskaya Oblast', W Russia 51°25′N 58°13′E

**Khalkabad** *see* Xalqobod

142 L3 **Khalkhāl** *prev.* Herowābād. Ardabīl, NW Iran 37°36′N 48°36′E

**Khalkidhikí** *see* Chalkidikí

**Khalkís** *see* Chalkída

125 W3 **Khal'mer-Yu** Respublika Komi, NW Russia 68°00′N 64°45′E

119 M14 **Khalopyenichy** *Rus.* Kholopenichi. Minskaya Voblasts', NE Belarus 54°31′N 28°58′E

**Khalturin** *see* Orlov

141 Y10 **Khalūf** *var.* Al Khaluf. E Oman 20°27′N 57°59′E

154 K10 **Khamaria** Madhya Pradesh, C India 23°07′N 80°54′E

154 D11 **Khambhāt** Gujarāt, W India 22°19′N 72°39′E

154 C12 **Khambhāt, Gulf of** *Eng.* Gulf of Cambay. *gulf* W India

167 U10 **Khâm Đức** *var.* Phước Sơn. Quang Nam-Đa Năng, C Vietnam 15°28′N 107°49′E

154 G12 **Khāmgaon** Mahārāshtra, C India 20°41′N 76°34′E

141 O14 **Khamir** *var.* Khamr. W Yemen 16°N 43°56′E

141 N12 **Khamīs Mushayṭ** *var.* Hamīs Musait. 'Asīr, SW Saudi Arabia 18°19′N 42°41′E

123 P10 **Khampa** Respublika Sakha (Yakutiya), NE Russia 63°43′N 123°02′E

**Khamr** *see* Khamir

83 C19 **Khan** ≈ W Namibia

149 Q2 **Khānābād** Kunduz, NE Afghanistan 36°42′N 69°08′E

**Khân Abou Châmâte/Khan Abou Ech Cham** *see* Khān Abū Shāmāt

138 I7 **Khān Abū Shāmāt** *var.* Khân Abou Châmâte, Khan Abou Ech Cham. Rīf Dimashq, W Syria 33°43′N 36°56′E

**Khān al Baghdādī** *see* Al Baghdādī

**Khān al Maḩāwīl** *see* Al Maḩāwīl

139 T7 **Khān al Mashāhidah** Baghdād, C Iraq 33°40′N 44°15′E

139 T10 **Khān al Muşallá** An Najaf, S Iraq 32°09′N 44°20′E

139 U6 **Khānaqīn** Diyālá, E Iraq 34°22′N 45°22′E

139 T11 **Khān ar Ruḩbah** An Najaf, S Iraq 31°42′N 44°18′E

139 P2 **Khān as Sūr** Nīnawá, N Iraq 36°28′N 41°36′E

139 T8 **Khān Āzād** Baghdād, C Iraq 33°08′N 44°21′E

154 N13 **Khandaparha** *prev.* Khandpara. Odisha, E India 20°15′N 85°11′E

**Khandpara** *see* Khandaparha

149 T2 **Khandūd** *var.* Khandud, Wakhan. Badakhshān, NE Afghanistan 36°57′N 72°19′E

**Khandud** *see* Khandūd

154 G11 **Khandwa** Madhya Pradesh, C India 21°49′N 76°23′E

123 R10 **Khandyga** Respublika Sakha (Yakutiya), NE Russia 62°39′N 135°30′E

149 T10 **Khanewal** Punjab, NE Pakistan 30°18′N 71°56′E

149 S10 **Khangarh** Punjab, E Pakistan 29°57′N 71°14′E

**Khanh Hung** *see* Soc Trăng

**Khaniá** *see* Chaniá

**Khanka** *see* Xonqa

163 Z8 **Khanka, Lake** *var.* Hsing-K'ai Hu, Lake Hanka, *Chin.* Xingkai Hu, *Rus.* Ozero Khanka. ◎ China/Russia

**Khanka, Ozero** *see* Khanka, Lake

**Khankendi** *see* Xankändi

123 O9 **Khannya** ≈ NE Russia

144 D10 **Khan Ordasy** *prev.* Urda. Zapadnyy Kazakhstan, W Kazakhstan 48°52′N 47°31′E

149 S12 **Khanpur** Punjab, E Pakistan 28°31′N 70°30′E

138 I4 **Khān Shaykhūn** *var.* Khan Sheikhun. Idlib, NW Syria 35°27′N 36°38′E

**Khan Sheikhun** *see* Khān Shaykhūn

**Khanshyngghys** *see* Khrebet Khanshyngys

145 S15 **Khantau** Zhambyl, S Kazakhstan 44°13′N 73°47′E

145 W16 **Khan Tengri, Pik** ▲ SE Kazakhstan 42°17′N 80°11′E

**Khan-Tengri, Pik** *see* Hantengri Feng

**Khanthabouli** *see* Savannakhét

127 V8 **Khanty-Mansiysk** *prev.* Ostyako-Voguls'k. Khanty-Mansiyskiy Avtonomnyy Okrug-Yugra, C Russia 61°01′N 69°E

125 V8 **Khanty-Mansiyskiy Avtonomnyy Okrug-Yugra** ◈ *autonomous district* C Russia

139 R4 **Khānūqah** Nīnawýé, C Iraq 35°25′N 43°15′E

138 E11 **Khān Yūnis** *var.* Khān Yūnus. S Gaza Strip 31°21′N 34°18′E

**Khān Yūnus** *see* Khān Yūnis

**Khanzi** *see* Ghanzi

**Khān Zūr** *see* Xan Sûr

167 N10 **Khao Laem Reservoir** ⊞ W Thailand

123 O14 **Khapcheranga** Zabaykal'skiy Kray, S Russia 49°46′N 112°21′E

127 Q12 **Kharabali** Astrakhanskaya Oblast', SW Russia 47°28′N 47°14′E

153 R16 **Kharagpur** West Bengal, NE India 22°30′N 87°19′E

139 V11 **Kharā'ib 'Abd al Karīm** Al Muthanná, S Iraq 31°07′N 45°33′E

143 Q8 **Kharānaq** Yazd, C Iran 31°54′N 54°21′E

**Kharbin** *see* Harbin

**Kharchi** *see* Mārwār

146 H13 **Khardzhagaz** Ahal Welaýaty, C Turkmenistan 37°54′N 60°10′E

**Kharga** *see* Al Khārijah

154 F11 **Khargon** Madhya Pradesh, C India 21°49′N 75°39′E

149 V7 **Kharian** Punjab, NE Pakistan 32°52′N 73°52′E

117 V5 **Kharkiv** *Rus.* Khar'kov. Kharkivs'ka Oblast', NE Ukraine 50°N 36°14′E

117 V5 **Kharkiv** ✈ Kharkivs'ka Oblast', E Ukraine 49°54′N 36°20′E

**Kharkiv** *see* Kharkivs'ka Oblast'

117 U5 **Kharkivs'ka Oblast'** *var.* Kharkiv, *Rus.* Khar'kovskaya Oblast'. ◈ *province* E Ukraine

**Khar'kov** *see* Kharkiv

**Khar'kovskaya Oblast'** *see* Kharkivs'ka Oblast'

124 L3 **Kharlovka** Murmanskaya Oblast', NW Russia 68°47′N 37°09′E

**Kharmanli** *see* Harmanli

**Kharmanliyska Reka** *see* Harmanliyska Reka

124 M13 **Kharovsk** Vologodskaya Oblast', NW Russia 59°57′N 40°05′E

80 F9 **Khartoum** *var.* El Khartûm, Khartum. ● (Sudan) Khartoum, C Sudan 15°33′N 32°32′E

80 F9 **Khartoum** ◈ *state* NE Sudan

80 F9 **Khartoum** ✈ Khartoum, C Sudan 15°36′N 32°37′E

80 F9 **Khartoum North** Khartoum, C Sudan 15°38′N 32°33′E

117 X8 **Khartsyz'k** Donets'ka Oblast', E Ukraine 48°01′N 38°10′E

117 X8 **Khartsyz'k** *Rus.* Khartsyzsk. Donets'ka Oblast', SE Ukraine 48°01′N 38°10′E

**Khartsyzsk** *see* Khartsyz'k

**Khartum** *see* Khartoum

**Kharwazawk** *see* Xêrzok

**Khasab** *see* Al Khaşab

123 S15 **Khasan** Primorskiy Kray, SE Russia 42°24′N 130°45′E

127 P16 **Khasavyurt** Respublika Dagestan, SW Russia 43°16′N 46°33′E

143 W12 **Khāsh** *prev.* Vāsht. Sīstān va Balūchestān, SE Iran 28°15′N 61°11′E

148 K8 **Khāsh, Dasht-e** *Eng.* Khash Desert. *desert* SW Afghanistan

**Khash Desert** *see* Khāsh, Dasht-e

**Khashim Al Qirba/Khashm al Qirbah** *see* Khashm el Girba

80 H9 **Khashm el Girba** *var.* Khashim Al Qirba, Khashm al Qirbah. Kassala, E Sudan 15°00′N 35°59′E

138 G14 **Khashsh, Jabal al** ▲▲ S Jordan

137 S10 **Khashuri** C Georgia 41°59′N 43°36′E

153 V13 **Khāsi Hills** *hill range* NE India

**Khaskovo** *see* Haskovo

**Khaskovo** *see* Haskovo

122 M7 **Khatanga** ≈ N Russia

**Khatanga, Gulf of** *see* Khatangskiy Zaliv

123 N7 **Khatangskiy Zaliv** *var.* Gulf of Khatanga. *bay* N Russia

141 W7 **Khatmat al Malāḩah** N Oman 24°58′N 56°22′E

143 S16 **Khaṭmat al Malāḩah** Ash Shāriqah, E United Arab Emirates

123 V7 **Khatyrka** Chukotskiy Avtonomnyy Okrug, NE Russia 62°03′N 175°09′E

**Khauz-Khan** *see* Hanhowuz

**Khauzkhanskoye Vodoranilishche** *see* Hanhowuz Suw Howdany

**Khavaling** *see* Khovaling

**Khavast** *see* Xovos

139 W10 **Khawrah, Nahr al** ≈ S Iraq

**Khawr Barakah** *see* Barka

141 W7 **Khawr Fakkān** *var.* Khor Fakkan. Ash Shāriqah, NE United Arab Emirates 25°22′N 56°19′E

140 L6 **Khaybar** Al Madīnah al Munawwarah, NW Saudi Arabia 25°53′N 39°16′E

**Khaybar, Kowtal-e** *see* Khyber Pass

147 S11 **Khaydarkan** *var.* Khaydarken. Batkenskaya Oblast', SW Kyrgyzstan 39°56′N 71°17′E

**Khaydarken** *see* Khaydarkan

125 U2 **Khaypudyrskaya Guba** *bay* NW Russia

**Khayrūzuk** *see* Xêrzok

**Khazar, Baḩr-e/Khazar, Daryā-ye** *see* Caspian Sea

**Khazarosp** *see* Hazorasp

**Khazretishi, Khrebet** *see* Hazratishoh, Qatorkŭhi

75 X11 **Khazzān Aswān** *Eng.* Aswan Dam. *dam* SE Egypt

**Khelat** *see* Kalat

74 F6 **Khemisset** NW Morocco 33°52′N 06°04′W

167 R10 **Khemmarat** *var.* Kemarat. Ubon Ratchathani, E Thailand 16°03′N 105°11′E

74 L6 **Khenchela** *var.* Khenchla. NE Algeria 35°22′N 07°09′E

**Khenchla** *see* Khenchela

74 G7 **Khénifra** C Morocco 32°59′N 05°37′W

**Khersān, Rūd-e** *see* Garm, Āb-e

117 R10 **Kherson** Khersons'ka Oblast', S Ukraine 46°39′N 32°38′E

**Kherson** *see* Khersons'ka Oblast'

117 S14 **Khersones, Mys** *Rus.* Mys Khersonesskiy. *headland* S Ukraine 44°34′N 33°24′E

**Khersonesskiy, Mys** *see* Khersones, Mys

117 R10 **Khersons'ka Oblast'** *var.* Kherson, *Rus.* Khersonskaya Oblast'. ◈ *province* S Ukraine

**Khersonskaya Oblast'** *see* Khersons'ka Oblast'

122 L8 **Kheta** ≈ N Russia

149 U7 **Khewra** Punjab, E Pakistan 32°41′N 73°04′E

**Khiam** *see* El Khiyam

124 J4 **Khibiny** ▲▲ NW Russia

126 K3 **Khimki** Moskovskaya Oblast', W Russia 55°57′N 37°48′E

147 S12 **Khingov** *Rus.* Obi-Khingou. ≈ C Tajikistan

**Khíos** *see* Chíos

149 R15 **Khipro** Sindh, SE Pakistan 25°50′N 69°24′E

139 S10 **Khirr, Wādī al** *dry watercourse* S Iraq

**Khisarya** *see* Hisarya

**Khiva/Khiwa** *see* Xiva

167 N9 **Khlong Khlung** Kamphaeng Phet, W Thailand 16°15′N 99°41′E

167 N15 **Khlong Thom** Krabi, SW Thailand 07°55′N 99°09′E

167 P12 **Khlung** Chantaburi, S Thailand 12°25′N 102°12′E

**Khmel'nik** *see* Khmil'nyk

**Khmel'nitskaya Oblast'** *see* Khmel'nyts'ka Oblast'

**Khmel'nitskiy** *see* Khmel 'nyts'kyy

116 K5 **Khmel'nyts'ka Oblast'** *var.* Khmel'nyts'kyy, *Rus.* Khmel'nitskaya Oblast'; *prev.* Kamenets-Podol'skaya Oblast'. ◈ *province* NW Ukraine

116 L6 **Khmel 'nyts'kyy** *Rus.* Khmel'nitskiy; *prev.* Proskurov. Khmel'nyts'ka Oblast', W Ukraine 49°24′N 26°59′E

**Khmel'nyts'kyy** *see* Khmel'nyts'ka Oblast'

116 M6 **Khmil'nyk** *Rus.* Khmel'nik. Vinnyts'ka Oblast', C Ukraine 49°36′N 27°59′E

**Khobda** *see* Kobda

137 R9 **Khobi** W Georgia 42°20′N 41°54′E

119 P15 **Khodasy** *Rus.* Khodosy. Mahilyowskaya Voblasts', E Belarus 53°56′N 31°29′E

116 I6 **Khodoriv** *Pol.* Chodorów, *Rus.* Khodorov. L'vivs'ka Oblast', NW Ukraine 49°20′N 24°19′E

**Khodorov** *see* Khodoriv

**Khodosy** *see* Khodasy

**Khodzhakala** *see* Hojagala

**Khodzhambas** *see* Hojambaz

**Khodzhent** *see* Khujand

**Khodzheyli** *see* Xo'jayli

**Khoi** *see* Khvoy

**Khojend** *see* Khujand

**Khokand** *see* Qo'qon

126 L8 **Khokhol'skiy** Voronezhskaya Oblast', W Russia 51°33′N 38°43′E

167 P10 **Khok Samrong** Lop Buri, C Thailand 15°03′N 100°44′E

124 H15 **Kholm** Novgorodskaya Oblast', W Russia 57°10′N 31°06′E

**Kholm** *see* Khulm

**Kholm** *see* Chełm

**Kholmech'** *see* Kholmyech

123 T13 **Kholmsk** Ostrov Sakhalin, Sakhalinskaya Oblast', SE Russia 46°57′N 142°10′E

119 O19 **Kholmyech** *Rus.* Kholmech'. Homyel'skaya Voblasts', SE Belarus 52°09′N 30°37′E

**Kholon** *see* Holon

**Kholopenichi** *see* Khalopyenichy

83 D19 **Khomas** ◈ *region* C Namibia

83 D19 **Khomas Hochland** *var.* Khomasplato. *plateau* C Namibia

**Khomasplato** *see* Khomas Hochland

**Khomein** *see* Khomeyn

142 M7 **Khomeyn** *var.* Khomein, Khumain. Markazī, W Iran 33°38′N 50°03′E

143 N8 **Khomeynīshahr** *prev.* Homāyūnshahr. Eşfahān, C Iran 32°42′N 51°28′E

**Khoms** *see* Al Khums

**Khong Sedone** *see* Muang Khôngxédôn

167 Q9 **Khon Kaen** *var.* Muang Khon Kaen. Khon Kaen, E Thailand 16°25′N 102°50′E

**Khonqa** *see* Xonqa

167 Q9 **Khon San** Khon Kaen, E Thailand 16°40′N 101°51′E

123 R8 **Khonuu** Respublika Sakha (Yakutiya), NE Russia 66°24′N 143°15′E

127 N8 **Khopër** *var.* Khoper. ≈ SW Russia

**Khoper** *see* Khopër

123 S14 **Khor** Khabarovskiy Kray, SE Russia 47°44′N 134°48′E

143 U9 **Khorāsān-e Jonūbī** *off.* Ostan-e Khorāsān-e Jonūbī. ◈ *province* E Iran

143 S3 **Khorāsān-e Shomālī** *off.* Ostan-e Khorāsān-e Shomālī. ◈ *province* NE Iran

**Khorat** *see* Nakhon Ratchasima

154 O13 **Khordha** *prev.* Khurda. Odisha, E India 20°10′N 85°42′E

125 U4 **Khorey-Ver** Nenetskiy Avtonomnyy Okrug, NW Russia 67°25′N 58°05′E

**Khorezmskaya Oblast'** *see* Xorazm Viloyati

**Khor Fakkan** *see* Khawr Fakkān

**Khorgos** *see* Korgas

123 N13 **Khorinsk** Respublika Buryatiya, S Russia 52°13′N 109°52′E

83 C18 **Khorixas** Kunene, NW Namibia 20°23′S 14°55′E

141 O17 **Khormaksar** *var.* Aden. ✈ ('Adan) SW Yemen 12°56′N 45°00′E

**Khormal** *see* Xurmał

**Khormuj** *see* Khvormūj

**Khorog** *see* Khorugh

117 S5 **Khorol** Poltavs'ka Oblast', NE Ukraine 49°49′N 33°17′E

142 L7 **Khorramābād** *var.* Khurramabad. Lorestān, W Iran 33°29′N 48°21′E

143 R9 **Khorramdasht** Kermān, C Iran 31°41′N 56°10′E

142 K10 **Khorramshahr** *var.* Khurramshahr, Muhammerah; *prev.* Mohammerah. Khūzestān, SW Iran 30°30′N 48°09′E

147 S14 **Khorugh** *Rus.* Khorog. S Tajikistan 37°30′N 71°31′E

**Khorvot Khalutsa** *see* Horvot Halutsa

127 Q12 **Khosheutovo** Astrakhanskaya Oblast', SW Russia 47°04′N 47°49′E

149 R6 **Khōst** *prev.* Khowst. Khōst, E Afghanistan 33°22′N 69°57′E

149 S6 **Khōst** *prev.* Khowst. ◈ *province* E Afghanistan

**Khotan** *see* Hotan

**Khotimsk** *see* Khotsimsk

**Khotin** *see* Khotyn

119 R16 **Khotsimsk** *Rus.* Khotimsk. Mahilyowskaya Voblasts', E Belarus 53°24′N 32°35′E

116 K7 **Khotyn** *Rom.* Hotin, *Rus.* Khotin. Chernivets'ka Oblast', W Ukraine 48°29′N 26°30′E

74 F7 **Khouribga** C Morocco 32°55′N 06°51′W

147 Q13 **Khovaling** *Rus.* Khavaling. SW Tajikistan 38°22′N 69°54′E

**Khovd** *see* Hovd

**Khowst** *see* Khōst

**Khoy** *see* Khvoy

119 N20 **Khoyniki** Homyel'skaya Voblasts', SE Belarus 51°54′N 29°58′E

**Khozretishi, Khrebet** *see* Hazratishoh, Qatorkŭhi

145 V11 **Khrebet Khanshyngys** *Kas.* Khanshyngghys; *prev.* Khrebet Kanchingiz. ▲▲ E Kazakhstan

145 X10 **Khrebet Kalba** *Kaz.* Qalba Zhotasy; *prev.* Kalbinskiy Khrebet. ▲▲ E Kazakhstan

**Khrebet Kanchingiz** *see* Khrebet Khanshyngys

**Khrebet Ketmen** *see* Khrebet Uzynkara

145 Y10 **Khrebet Naryn** *Kaz.* Naryn Zhotasy; *prev.* Narymskiy Khrebet. ▲▲ E Kazakhstan

145 W16 **Khrebet Uzynkara** *prev.* Khrebet Ketmen. ▲▲ SE Kazakhstan

117 X8 **Khrestivka** *prev.* Kirovs'ke. Donets'ka Oblast', E Ukraine 48°12′N 38°20′E

**Khrisoúpolis** *see* Chrysoúpoli

144 J10 **Khromtau** *Kaz.* Khromtaū. Aktyubinsk, W Kazakhstan 50°14′N 58°22′E

**Khromtaū** *see* Khromtau

117 Y7 **Khrustal'nyy** *prev.* Krasnyy Luch, Krindachevka. Luhans'ka Oblast', E Ukraine 48°09′N 38°52′E

**Khrysokhou Bay** *see* Chrysochoús, Kólpos

117 O7 **Khrystynivka** Cherkas'ka Oblast', C Ukraine 48°49′N 29°55′E

167 R10 **Khuang Nai** Ubon Ratchathani, E Thailand 15°22′N 104°33′E

**Khudal** *see* Khādhil

**Khudat** *see* Xudat

149 W9 **Khudian** Punjab, E Pakistan 30°59′N 74°19′E

**Khudzhand** *see* Khujand

83 G21 **Khuis** Kgalagadi, SW Botswana 26°37′S 21°50′E

147 Q11 **Khujand** *var.* Khodzhent, Khojend, *Rus.* Khudzhand; *prev.* Leninabad, *Taj.* Leninobod. N Tajikistan 40°17′N 69°37′E

167 R11 **Khukhan** Si Sa Ket, E Thailand 14°38′N 104°12′E

149 P2 **Khulm** *var.* Tashqurghan; *prev.* Kholm. Balkh, N Afghanistan 36°42′N 67°41′E

153 T16 **Khulna** Khulna, SW Bangladesh 22°48′N 89°32′E

153 T16 **Khulna** ◈ *division* SW Bangladesh

**Khumain** *see* Khomeyn

**Khums** *see* Al Khums

149 W2 **Khunjerab Pass** *pass* China/Pakistan

**Khunjerab Pass** *see* Kunjirap Daban

153 P16 **Khunti** Jhārkhand, N India 23°02′N 85°19′E

167 N7 **Khun Yuam** Mae Hong Son, NW Thailand 18°54′N 97°54′E

**Khurais** *see* Khurayş

141 R7 **Khurayş** *var.* Khurais. Ash Sharqīyah, C Saudi Arabia 25°06′N 48°03′E

**Khurda** *see* Khordha

152 J11 **Khurja** Uttar Pradesh, N India 28°15′N 77°51′E

**Khūrmāl** *see* Xurmał

**Khurramabad** *see* Khorramābād

**Khurramshahr** *see* Khorramshahr

149 U7 **Khushab** Punjab, NE Pakistan 32°16′N 72°18′E

116 H8 **Khust** *var.* Husté, *Cz.* Chust, *Hung.* Huszt. Zakarpats'ka Oblast', W Ukraine 48°11′N 23°19′E

80 D11 **Khuwei** Western Kordofan, C Sudan 13°02′N 29°13′E

149 O13 **Khuzdar** Baluchistan, SW Pakistan 27°49′N 66°39′E

142 L9 **Khūzestān** *off.* Ostān-e Khūzestān, *var.* Khuzistan, *prev.* Arabistan; *anc.* Susiana. ◈ *province* SW Iran

**Khūzestān, Ostān-e** *see* Khūzestān

**Khuzistan** *see* Khūzestān

**Khvājeh Ghār** *see* Khwājeh Ghār

127 Q7 **Khvalynsk** Saratovskaya Oblast', W Russia 52°30′N 48°06′E

143 N12 **Khvormūj** *var.* Khormuj. Būshehr, S Iran 28°32′N 51°22′E

142 I2 **Khvoy** *var.* Khoi, Khoy. Āžarbāyjān-e Bākhtarī, NW Iran 38°36′N 45°04′E

**Khwajaghar/Khwaja-i-Ghar** *see* Khwājeh Ghār

149 R2 **Khwājeh Ghār** *var.* Khwajaghar, Khwaja-i-Ghar; *prev.* Khvājeh Ghār. Takhār, NE Afghanistan 37°08′N 69°24′E

149 U4 **Khyber Pakhtunkhwa** *prev.* North-West Frontier Province. ◈ *province* NW Pakistan

149 S5 **Khyber Pass** *var.* Kowtal-e Khaybar. *pass* Afghanistan/Pakistan

186 L8 **Kia** Santa Isabel, N Solomon Islands 07°34′S 158°31′E

183 S10 **Kiama** New South Wales, SE Australia 34°41′S 150°49′E

79 O22 **Kiambi** Katanga, SE Dem. Rep. Congo 07°15′S 28°01′E

81 I19 **Kiambu** ◈ *county* C Kenya

27 Q12 **Kiamichi Mountains** ▲▲ Oklahoma, C USA

27 Q12 **Kiamichi River** ≈ Oklahoma, C USA

14 M10 **Kiamika, Réservoir** ⊞ Québec, SE Canada

**Kiamusze** *see* Jiamusi

39 N7 **Kiana** Alaska, USA 66°58′N 160°25′W

**Kiangmai** *see* Chiang Mai

**Kiang-ning** *see* Nanjing

**Kiangsi** *see* Jiangxi

**Kiangsu** *see* Jiangsu

93 M14 **Kiantajärvi** ◎ E Finland

115 F19 **Kiáto** *prev.* Kiáton. Pelopónnisos, S Greece 38°01′N 22°45′E

**Kiáton** *see* Kiáto

**Kiayi** *see* Chiayi

95 F22 **Kibæk** Midtjylland, W Denmark 56°03′N 08°52′E

67 T9 **Kibali** *var.* Uele (upper course). ≈ NE Dem. Rep. Congo

79 E20 **Kibangou** Niari, SW Congo 03°27′S 12°21′E

**Kibarty** *see* Kybartai

92 M8 **Kiberg** Finnmark, N Norway 70°17′N 30°47′E

79 N20 **Kibombo** Maniema, E Dem. Rep. Congo 03°52′S 25°59′E

81 E20 **Kibondo** Kigoma, NW Tanzania 03°34′S 30°41′E

81 J15 **Kibre Mengist** *var.* Adola. Oromīya, C Ethiopia 05°50′N 39°06′E

**Kıbrıs** *see* Cyprus

**Kıbrıs/Kıbrıs Cumhuriyeti** *see* Cyprus

81 E20 **Kibungo** *var.* Kibungu. SE Rwanda 02°09′S 30°30′E

**Kibungu** *see* Kibungo

113 N19 **Kičevo** SW North Macedonia 41°31′N 20°57′E

125 P13 **Kichmengskiy Gorodok** Vologodskaya Oblast', NW Russia 60°00′N 45°52′E

30 J8 **Kickapoo River** ≈ Wisconsin, N USA

11 P16 **Kicking Horse Pass** *pass* Alberta/British Columbia, SW Canada

77 R9 **Kidal** Kidal, C Mali 18°22′N 01°21′E

77 Q8 **Kidal** ◈ *region* NE Mali

171 Q7 **Kidapawan** Mindanao, S Philippines 07°02′N 125°04′E

97 L20 **Kidderminster** C England, United Kingdom 52°23′N 02°14′W

76 I11 **Kidira** E Senegal 14°28′N 12°13′W

184 O11 **Kidnappers, Cape** *headland* North Island, New Zealand 41°13′S 175°15′E

100 J8 **Kiel** Schleswig-Holstein, N Germany 54°21′N 10°05′E

111 L15 **Kielce** *Rus.* Keltsy. Świętokrzyskie, C Poland 50°53′N 20°39′E

100 K7 **Kieler Bucht** *bay* N Germany

100 J7 **Kieler Förde** *inlet* N Germany

167 U13 **Kiên Đức** *var.* Đak Lap. Đăc Lăc, S Vietnam 11°59′N 107°30′E

79 N24 **Kienge** Katanga, SE Dem. Rep. Congo 10°33′S 27°33′E

100 Q12 **Kietz** Brandenburg, NE Germany 52°33′N 14°36′E

**Kiev** *see* Kyiv

**Kiev Reservoir** *see* Kyivs'ke Vodoskhovyshche

76 J10 **Kiffa** Assaba, S Mauritania 16°38′N 11°23′W

115 H19 **Kifisiá** Attikí, C Greece 38°04′N 23°49′E

115 F18 **Kifisós** ≈ C Greece

139 U5 **Kifrī** At Ta'mím, N Iraq 34°44′N 44°58′E

81 D20 **Kigali** ● (Rwanda) C Rwanda 01°59′S 30°02′E

81 E20 **Kigali** ✈ C Rwanda 01°43′S 30°01′E

137 P13 **Kiğı** Bingöl, E Turkey 39°19′N 40°20′E

81 E21 **Kigoma** Kigoma, W Tanzania 04°52′S 29°36′E

81 E21 **Kigoma** ◈ *region* W Tanzania

38 F10 **Kīhei** *var.* Kihei. Maui, Hawaii, USA, C Pacific Ocean 20°47′N 156°28′W

93 K17 **Kihniö** Pirkanmaa, W Finland 62°11′N 23°10′E

118 F6 **Kihnu** *var.* Kihnu Saar, *Ger.* Kühnö. *island* SW Estonia

**Kihnu Saar** *see* Kihnu

38 A8 **Kii Landing** Ni'ihau, Hawaii, USA, C Pacific Ocean 21°58′N 160°03′W

93 L14 **Kiiminki** Pohjois-Pohjanmaa, C Finland 65°05′N 25°47′E

164 J14 **Kii-Nagashima** *var.* Nagashima. Mie, Honshū, SW Japan 34°10′N 136°18′E

164 J14 **Kii-sanchi** ▲▲ Honshū, SW Japan

92 L11 **Kiistala** Lappi, N Finland 67°52′N 25°19′E

164 I15 **Kii-suidō** *strait* S Japan

165 V16 **Kikai-shima** *island* Nansei-shotō, SW Japan

112 M8 **Kikinda** *Ger.* Grosskikinda, *Hung.* Nagykikinda; *prev.* Velika Kikinda. Vojvodina, N Serbia 45°48′N 20°29′E

**Kikládhes** *see* Kykládes

165 Q5 **Kikonai** Hokkaidō, NE Japan 41°40′N 140°25′E

186 C8 **Kikori** Gulf, S Papua New Guinea 07°25′S 144°13′E

186 C8 **Kikori** ≈ W Papua New Guinea

165 O14 **Kikuchi** *var.* Kikuti. Kumamoto, Kyūshū, SW Japan 33°00′N 130°49′E

**Kikuti** *see* Kikuchi

127 N8 **Kikvidze** Volgogradskaya Oblast', SW Russia 50°47′N 42°58′E

14 I10 **Kikwissi, Lac** ◎ Québec, SE Canada

79 I21 **Kikwit** Bandundu, W Dem. Rep. Congo 05°S 18°53′E

95 K15 **Kil** Värmland, C Sweden 59°30′N 13°20′E

94 N12 **Kilafors** Gävleborg, C Sweden 61°13′N 16°34′E

38 B8 **Kīlauea** Kaua'i, Hawaii, USA, C Pacific Ocean 22°12′N 159°24′W

38 H12 **Kīlauea Caldera** *var.* Kilauea Caldera. *crater* Hawai'i, USA, C Pacific Ocean

**Kilauea Caldera** *see* Kīlauea Caldera

109 V4 **Kilb** Niederösterreich, C Austria 48°06′N 15°21′E

39 O12 **Kilbuck Mountains** ▲▲ Alaska, USA

163 Y12 **Kilchu** NE North Korea 40°58′N 129°22′E

97 F18 **Kilcock** *Ir.* Cill Choca. Kildare, E Ireland 53°25′N 06°40′W

183 V2 **Kilcoy** Queensland, E Australia 26°58′S 152°30′E

97 F18 **Kildare** *Ir.* Cill Dara. E Ireland 53°10′N 06°55′W

97 F18 **Kildare** *Ir.* Cill Dara. *cultural region* E Ireland

124 K2 **Kil'din, Ostrov** *island* NW Russia

25 W7 **Kilgore** Texas, SW USA 32°23′N 94°52′W

**Kilien Mountains** *see* Qilian Shan

114 K9 **Kilifarevo** Veliko Tŭrnovo, N Bulgaria 43°00′N 25°36′E

81 K20 **Kilifi** Kilifi, SE Kenya 03°37′S 39°50′E

189 U9 **Kili Island** *var.* Kōle. *island* Ralik Chain, S Marshall Islands

149 V2 **Kilik Pass** *pass* Afghanistan/China

**Kilimane** *see* Quelimane

81 I21 **Kilimanjaro** ◈ *region* E Tanzania

81 I20 **Kilimanjaro** *var.* Uhuru Peak. ⛰ NE Tanzania 03°01′S 37°14′E

**Kilimbangara** *see* Kolombangara

**Kilinailau Islands** *see* Tulun Islands

81 K23 **Kilindoni** Pwani, E Tanzania 07°56′S 39°40′E

118 H6 **Kilingi-Nõmme** *Ger.* Kurkund. Pärnumaa, SW Estonia 58°07′N 24°00′E

136 M17 **Kilis** Kilis, S Turkey 36°43′N 37°07′E

136 M16 **Kilis** ◈ *province* S Turkey

117 N12 **Kiliya** *Rom.* Chilia-Nouă. Odes'ka Oblast', SW Ukraine 45°30′N 29°16′E

97 B19 **Kilkee** *Ir.* Cill Chaoi. Clare, W Ireland 52°41′N 09°38′W

97 E19 **Kilkenny** *Ir.* Cill Chainnigh. Kilkenny, S Ireland 52°39′N 07°15′W

97 E19 **Kilkenny** *Ir.* Cill Chainnigh. *cultural region* S Ireland

97 B18 **Kilkieran Bay** *Ir.* Cuan Chill Chiaráin. *bay* W Ireland

114 G13 **Kilkís** Kentrikí Makedonía, N Greece 40°59′N 22°55′E

97 C15 **Killala Bay** *Ir.* Cuan Chill Ala. *inlet* NW Ireland

11 R15 **Killam** Alberta, SW Canada 52°45′N 111°46′W

183 U3 **Killarney** Queensland, E Australia 28°18′S 152°15′E

11 W17 **Killarney** Manitoba, S Canada 49°12′N 99°40′W

14 E11 **Killarney** Ontario, S Canada 45°58′N 81°27′W

97 B20 **Killarney** *Ir.* Cill Airne. Kerry, SW Ireland 52°03′N 09°30′W

28 K4 **Killdeer** North Dakota, N USA 47°21′N 102°45′W

28 J4 **Killdeer Mountains** ▲▲ North Dakota, N USA

45 V15 **Killdeer River** ≈ Trinidad, Trinidad and Tobago

25 S9 **Killeen** Texas, SW USA 31°07′N 97°44′W

39 P6 **Killik River** ≈ Alaska, USA

11 T7 **Killinek Island** *island* Nunavut, NE Canada

**Killini** *see* Kyllíni

115 C19 **Killínis, Akrotírio** *headland* S Greece 37°55′N 21°07′E

97 D15 **Killybegs** *Ir.* Na Cealla Beaga. NW Ireland 54°38′N 08°27′W

**Kilmain** *see* Quelimane

96 I13 **Kilmarnock** W Scotland, United Kingdom 55°37′N 04°30′W

21 X6 **Kilmarnock** Virginia, NE USA 37°42′N 76°22′W

125 S16 **Kil'mez'** Kirovskaya Oblast', NW Russia 56°55′N 51°03′E

127 S2 **Kil'mez'** Udmurtskaya Respublika, NW Russia 57°04′N 51°22′E

125 R16 **Kil'mez'** ≈ NW Russia

67 V11 **Kilombero** ≈ S Tanzania

92 J10 **Kilpisjärvi** *N. Sami* Gilbbesjávri. Lappi, N Finland 69°03′N 20°50′E

97 B19 **Kilrush** *Ir.* Cill Rois. Clare, W Ireland 52°39′N 09°29′W

79 O24 **Kilwa** Katanga, SE Dem. Rep. Congo 09°22′S 28°19′E

**Kilwa** *see* Kilwa Kivinje

81 J24 **Kilwa Kivinje** *var.* Kilwa. Lindi, SE Tanzania 08°45′S 39°21′E

81 J24 **Kilwa Masoko** Lindi, SE Tanzania 08°55′S 39°31′E

171 T13 **Kilwo** Pulau Seram, E Indonesia 03°36′S 130°48′E

114 P12 **Kilyos** İstanbul, NW Turkey 41°15′N 29°01′E

37 V8 **Kim** Colorado, C USA 37°12′N 103°22′W

145 O9 **Kima** *prev.* Kiyma. Akmola, C Kazakhstan 51°37′N 67°31′E

169 U7 **Kimanis, Teluk** *bay* Sabah, East Malaysia

182 H8 **Kimba** South Australia 33°09′S 136°26′E

28 I15 **Kimball** Nebraska, C USA 41°16′N 103°40′W

29 O11 **Kimball** South Dakota, N USA 43°45′N 98°57′W

79 I21 **Kimbao** Bandundu, SW Dem. Rep. Congo 05°27′S 17°40′E

186 F7 **Kimbe** New Britain, E Papua New Guinea 05°36′S 150°10′E

186 G7 **Kimbe Bay** *inlet* New Britain, E Papua New Guinea

11 P17 **Kimberley** British Columbia, SW Canada 49°40′N 115°58′W

83 H23 **Kimberley** Northern Cape, C South Africa 28°45′S 24°46′E

180 M4 **Kimberley Plateau** *plateau* Western Australia

33 P15 **Kimberly** Idaho, NW USA 42°31′N 114°21′W

163 Y12 **Kimch'aek** *prev.* Sŏngjin. E North Korea 40°42′N 129°13′E

**Kimch'ŏn** *see* Gimcheon

**Kim Hae** *see* Gimhae

**Kími** *see* Kými

93 K20 **Kimito** *Swe.* Kemiö. Varsinais-Suomi, SW Finland 60°10′N 22°45′E

9 R7 **Kimmirut** *prev.* Lake Harbour. Baffin Island, Nunavut, NE Canada 62°48′N 69°49′W

165 R4 **Kimobetsu** Hokkaidō, NE Japan 42°47′N 140°55′E

115 I21 **Kímolos** *island* Kykládes, Greece, Aegean Sea

115 I21 **Kímolou Sífnou, Stenó** *strait* Kykládes, Greece, Aegean Sea

126 L5 **Kimovsk** Tul'skaya Oblast', W Russia 53°59′N 38°34′E

**Kimpolung** *see* Câmpulung Moldovenesc

124 K16 **Kimry** Tverskaya Oblast', W Russia 56°52′N 37°21′E

79 H21 **Kimvula** Bas-Congo, SW Dem. Rep. Congo 05°44′S 15°58′E

169 U6 **Kinabalu, Gunung** ▲ East Malaysia 05°52′N 116°08′E

**Kinabatangan** *see* Kinabatangan, Sungai

169 V7 **Kinabatangan, Sungai** *var.* Kinabatangan. ≈ East Malaysia

115 L21 **Kínaros** *island* Kykládes, Greece, Aegean Sea

11 O15 **Kinbasket Lake** ⊞ British Columbia, SW Canada

96 I7 **Kinbrace** N Scotland, United Kingdom 58°16′N 02°59′W

14 E14 **Kincardine** Ontario, S Canada 44°11′N 81°38′W

96 K10 **Kincardine** *cultural region* E Scotland, United Kingdom

79 K21 **Kinda** Kasai-Occidental, SE Dem. Rep. Congo 04°48′S 21°50′E

79 M24 **Kinda** Katanga, SE Dem. Rep. Congo 09°20′S 25°06′E

166 L3 **Kindat** Sagaing, N Myanmar (Burma) 23°42′N 94°29′E

109 V6 **Kindberg** Steiermark, C Austria 47°31′N 15°27′E

22 H8 **Kinder** Louisiana, S USA 30°29′N 92°51′W

98 H13 **Kinderdijk** Zuid-Holland, SW Netherlands 51°52′N 04°37′E

97 M17 **Kinder Scout** ▲ C England, United Kingdom 53°25′N 01°52′W

11 S16 **Kindersley** Saskatchewan, S Canada 51°29′N 109°08′W

76 I14 **Kindia** Guinée-Maritime, SW Guinea 10°12′N 12°26′W

64 B11 **Kindley Field** *air base* E Bermuda

29 R6 **Kindred** North Dakota, N USA 46°39′N 97°01′W

79 N20 **Kindu** *prev.* Kindu-Port-Empain. Maniema, C Dem. Rep. Congo 02°57′S 25°54′E

**Kindu-Port-Empain** *see* Kindu

127 S6 **Kinel'** Samarskaya Oblast', W Russia 53°14′N 50°40′E

125 N15 **Kineshma** Ivanovskaya Oblast', W Russia 57°28′N 42°08′E

**King** *see* King William's Town

140 K10 **King Abdul Aziz** ✈ (Makkah al Mukarramah) Makkah al Mukarramah, W Saudi Arabia 21°44′N 39°08′E

**Kingait** *see* Cape Dorset

21 X6 **King and Queen Court House** Virginia, NE USA 37°40′N 76°49′W

**King Charles Islands** *see* Kong Karls Land

**King Christian IX Land** *see* Kong Christian IX Land

**King Christian X Land** *see* Kong Christian X Land

35 O11 **King City** California, W USA 36°12′N 121°09′W

27 R2 **King City** Missouri, C USA 40°03′N 94°31′W

38 M16 **King Cove** Alaska, USA 55°03′N 162°19′W

26 M10 **Kingfisher** Oklahoma, C USA 35°53′N 97°56′W

**King Frederik VI Coast** *see* Kong Frederik VI Kyst

**King Frederik VIII Land** *see* Kong Frederik VIII Land

65 B24 **King George Bay** *bay* West Falkland, Falkland Islands

194 G3 **King George Island** *var.* King George Land. *island* South Shetland Islands, Antarctica

12 I6 **King George Islands** *island group* Northwest Territories, C Canada

**King George Land** *see* King George Island

124 G13 **Kingisepp** Leningradskaya Oblast', NW Russia 59°23′N 28°37′E

183 N14 **King Island** *island* Tasmania, SE Australia

10 J15 **King Island** *island* British Columbia, SW Canada

**King Island** *see* Kadan Kyun

**Kingissepp** *see* Kuressaare

141 Q7 **King Khalid** ✈ (Ar Riyāḑ) Ar Riyāḑ, C Saudi Arabia 25°00′N 46°40′E

35 S2 **King Lear Peak** ▲ Nevada, W USA 41°13′N 118°30′W

195 Y8 **King Leopold and Queen Astrid Land** *physical region* Antarctica

180 M4 **King Leopold Ranges** ▲▲ Western Australia

36 I11 **Kingman** Arizona, SW USA 35°12′N 114°02′W

26 M6 **Kingman** Kansas, C USA 37°39′N 98°07′W

192 L7 **Kingman Reef** ◇ *US unincorporated territory* C Pacific Ocean

79 N20 **Kingombe** Maniema, E Dem. Rep. Congo 02°37′S 26°39′E

182 F5 **Kingoonya** South Australia 30°56′S 135°20′E

194 J10 **King Peninsula** *peninsula* Antarctica

39 P13 **King Salmon** Alaska, USA 58°41′N 156°39′W


◆ Country
● Country Capital
◇ Dependent Territory
○ Dependent Territory Capital
◈ Administrative Regions
✈ International Airport
▲ Mountain
▲▲ Mountain Range
⛰ Volcano
≈ River
◎ Lake
⊞ Reservoir

KINGS BEACH – KOFARNIKHON


35 Q6 **Kings Beach** California, W USA 39°13′N 120°02′W
35 R11 **Kingsburg** California, W USA 36°30′N 119°33′W
182 I10 **Kingscote** South Australia 35°41′S 137°36′E
**King's County** *see* Offaly
194 H2 **King Sejong** *research station (South Korea)* King George Island, Antarctica 61°57′S 58°23′W
183 T9 **Kingsford Smith** ✈ (Sydney) New South Wales, SE Australia 33°58′S 151°09′E
11 P17 **Kingsgate** British Columbia, SW Canada 48°58′N 116°09′W
23 W8 **Kingsland** Georgia, SE USA 30°48′N 81°41′W
29 S13 **Kingsley** Iowa, C USA 42°35′N 95°58′W
97 O19 **King's Lynn** *var.* Bishop's Lynn, Kings Lynn, Lynn, Lynn Regis. E England, United Kingdom 52°45′N 00°24′E
**Kings Lynn** *see* King's Lynn
21 Q10 **Kings Mountain** North Carolina, SE USA 35°15′N 81°20′W
180 K4 **King Sound** *sound* Western Australia
37 N2 **Kings Peak** ▲ Utah, W USA 40°43′N 110°27′W
21 O8 **Kingsport** Tennessee, S USA 36°32′N 82°33′W
35 R11 **Kings River** ⟿ California, W USA
183 P17 **Kingston** Tasmania, SE Australia 42°57′S 147°18′E
14 K14 **Kingston** Ontario, SE Canada 44°14′N 76°30′W
44 K13 **Kingston** ● (Jamaica) E Jamaica 17°58′N 76°48′W
185 C22 **Kingston** Otago, South Island, New Zealand 45°20′S 168°45′E
19 P12 **Kingston** Massachusetts, NE USA 41°59′N 70°43′W
27 S3 **Kingston** Missouri, C USA 39°36′N 94°02′W
18 K12 **Kingston** New York, NE USA 41°55′N 74°00′W
31 S14 **Kingston** Ohio, N USA 39°28′N 82°54′W
19 O13 **Kingston** Rhode Island, NE USA 41°28′N 71°31′W
20 M9 **Kingston** Tennessee, S USA 35°52′N 84°30′W
35 W12 **Kingston Peak** ▲ California, W USA 35°43′N 115°54′W
182 J11 **Kingston Southeast** South Australia 36°51′S 139°53′E
97 N17 **Kingston upon Hull** *var.* Hull. E England, United Kingdom 53°45′N 00°20′W
97 N22 **Kingston upon Thames** SE England, United Kingdom 51°26′N 00°18′W
45 P14 **Kingstown** ● (Saint Vincent and the Grenadines) Saint Vincent, Saint Vincent and the Grenadines 13°09′N 61°14′W
**Kingstown** *see* Dún Laoghaire
21 T13 **Kingstree** South Carolina, SE USA 33°40′N 79°50′W
64 L8 **Kings Trough** *undersea feature* E Atlantic Ocean 22°00′W 43°48′N
14 C18 **Kingsville** Ontario, S Canada 42°03′N 82°43′W
25 S15 **Kingsville** Texas, SW USA 27°32′N 97°53′W
21 W6 **King William** Virginia, NE USA 37°42′N 77°03′W
9 N7 **King William Island** *island* Nunavut, N Canada
83 I25 **King William's Town** *var.* King, Kingwilliamstown. Eastern Cape, S South Africa 32°53′S 27°24′E
**Kingwilliamstown** *see* King William's Town
21 T3 **Kingwood** West Virginia, NE USA 39°27′N 79°43′W
136 C13 **Kınık** İzmir, W Turkey 39°05′N 27°25′E
79 G21 **Kinkala** Pool, S Congo 04°18′S 14°49′E
165 R10 **Kinka-san** *headland* Honshū, C Japan 38°17′N 141°34′E
184 M8 **Kinleith** Waikato, North Island, New Zealand 38°16′S 175°53′E
161 R13 **Kinmen Island** *var.* Jinmen Dao, Chinmen Tao, Quemoy. *island* W Taiwan
19 J19 **Kinna** Västra Götaland, S Sweden 57°32′N 12°42′E
96 L8 **Kinnaird Head** *var.* Kinnairds Head. *headland* NE Scotland, United Kingdom 58°39′N 03°22′W
**Kinnairds Head** *see* Kinnaird Head
95 K20 **Kinnared** Halland, S Sweden 57°01′N 13°04′E
92 L7 **Kinnarodden** *headland* N Norway 71°07′N 27°40′E
138 G8 **Kinneret, Yam** *var.* Sea of Galilee, Lake Tiberias, Chinnereth, Sea of Bahr Tabariya, *Ar.* Buḩayrat Ţabarīyā. ◎ N Israel
155 K24 **Kinniyai** Eastern Province, NE Sri Lanka 08°30′N 81°11′E
93 L16 **Kinnula** Keski-Suomi, C Finland 63°24′N 25°E
14 I8 **Kinojévis** ⟿ Québec, SE Canada
164 I14 **Kino-kawa** ⟿ Honshū, SW Japan
11 U11 **Kinoosao** Saskatchewan, C Canada 57°06′N 101°02′W
99 L17 **Kinrooi** Limburg, NE Belgium 51°09′N 05°48′E
96 J11 **Kinross** C Scotland, United Kingdom 56°14′N 03°27′W
96 J11 **Kinross** *cultural region* C Scotland, United Kingdom
97 C21 **Kinsale** *Ir.* Cionn tSáile. Cork, SW Ireland 51°42′N 08°32′W
95 D14 **Kinsarvik** Hordaland, S Norway 60°22′N 06°43′E
79 G21 **Kinshasa** *prev.* Léopoldville. ● Kinshasa, W Dem. Rep. Congo 04°21′S 15°16′E
79 G21 **Kinshasa** *off.* Ville de Kinshasa, *var.* Kinshasa City. ◈ *region (Dem. Rep. Congo)* SW Dem. Rep. Congo
79 G21 **Kinshasa** ✈ Kinshasa, SW Dem. Rep. Congo 04°23′S 15°30′E
**Kinshasa City** *see* Kinshasa
117 U9 **Kins'ka** ⟿ SE Ukraine
26 K6 **Kinsley** Kansas, C USA 37°55′N 99°26′W
21 W10 **Kinston** North Carolina, SE USA 35°16′N 77°35′W
77 P15 **Kintampo** W Ghana 08°06′N 01°40′W
182 B1 **Kintore, Mount** ▲ South Australia 26°30′S 130°24′E
96 G13 **Kintyre** *peninsula* W Scotland, United Kingdom
96 G13 **Kintyre, Mull of** *headland* W Scotland, United Kingdom 55°16′N 05°46′W
166 M4 **Kin-u** Sagaing, C Myanmar (Burma) 22°47′N 95°36′E
12 G8 **Kinushseo** ⟿ Ontario, C Canada
11 P13 **Kinuso** Alberta, W Canada 55°19′N 115°23′W
154 I13 **Kinwat** Mahārāshtra, C India 19°37′N 78°12′E
81 F16 **Kinyeti** ▲ S South Sudan 03°56′N 32°52′E
101 I17 **Kinzig** ⟿ SW Germany
**Kioga, Lake** *see* Kyoga, Lake
26 M8 **Kiowa** Kansas, C USA 37°01′N 98°29′W
27 P12 **Kiowa** Oklahoma, C USA 34°43′N 95°54′W
**Kiparissía** *see* Kyparissía
14 H10 **Kipawa, Lac** ◎ Québec, SE Canada
81 G24 **Kipengere Range** ▲▲ SW Tanzania
81 E23 **Kipili** Rukwa, W Tanzania 07°30′S 30°39′E
81 K20 **Kipini** Tana River, SE Kenya 02°30′S 40°30′E
11 V16 **Kipling** Saskatchewan, S Canada 50°04′N 102°45′W
38 M13 **Kipnuk** Alaska, USA 59°56′N 164°02′W
97 F18 **Kippure** *Ir.* Cipiúr. ▲ E Ireland 53°10′N 06°22′W
79 N25 **Kipushi** Katanga, SE Dem. Rep. Congo 11°45′S 27°20′E
187 N10 **Kirakira** *var.* Kaokaona. Makira-Ulawa, SE Solomon Islands 10°28′S 161°54′E
155 K14 **Kirandul** *var.* Bailādila. Chhattīsgarh, C India 18°46′N 81°18′E
155 J21 **Kīranūr** Tamil Nādu, SE India 11°37′N 79°10′E
119 N21 **Kiraw** *Rus.* Kirovo. Homyel'skaya Voblasts', SE Belarus 51°30′N 29°25′E
119 M17 **Kirawsk** *Rus.* Kirovsk; *prev.* Startsy. Mahilyowskaya Voblasts', E Belarus 53°16′N 29°29′E
118 F5 **Kirbla** Läänemaa, W Estonia 58°45′N 23°57′E
25 Y9 **Kirbyville** Texas, SW USA 30°39′N 93°53′W
114 M12 **Kircasalih** Edirne, NW Turkey 41°24′N 26°48′E
109 W8 **Kirchbach** *var.* Kirchbach in Steiermark. Steiermark, SE Austria 46°55′N 15°40′E
**Kirchbach in Steiermark** *see* Kirchbach
108 H7 **Kirchberg** Sankt Gallen, NE Switzerland 47°24′N 09°03′E
109 S5 **Kirchdorf an der Krems** Oberösterreich, N Austria 47°55′N 14°08′E
**Kirchheim** *see* Kirchheim unter Teck
101 I22 **Kirchheim unter Teck** *var.* Kirchheim. Baden-Württemberg, SW Germany 48°39′N 09°28′E
139 T1 **Kirdī Kawrāw, Qimmat** *var.* Sar-i Kōrāwa. NE Iraq 37°08′N 44°39′E
**Kirdzhali** *see* Kardzhali
123 N13 **Kirenga** ⟿ S Russia
123 N12 **Kirensk** Irkutskaya Oblast', C Russia 57°37′N 107°54′E
**Kirghizia** *see* Kyrgyzstan
145 S16 **Kirghiz Range** *Rus.* Kirgizskiy Khrebet; *prev.* Alexander Range. ▲▲ Kazakhstan/Kyrgyzstan
**Kirghiz SSR** *see* Kyrgyzstan
**Kirghiz Steppe** *see* Saryarka
**Kirgizskaya SSR** *see* Kyrgyzstan
**Kirgizskiy Khrebet** *see* Kirghiz Range
79 I19 **Kiri** Bandundu, W Dem. Rep. Congo 01°29′S 19°00′E
**Kiriath-Arba** *see* Hebron
191 R3 **Kiribati** *off.* Republic of Kiribati. ◆ *republic* C Pacific Ocean
**Kiribati, Republic of** *see* Kiribati
136 L17 **Kırıkhan** Hatay, S Turkey 36°30′N 36°20′E
136 I13 **Kırıkkale** Kırıkkale, C Turkey 39°50′N 33°31′E
136 C10 **Kırıkkale** ◈ *province* C Turkey
124 L13 **Kirillov** Vologodskaya Oblast', NW Russia 59°52′N 38°24′E
**Kirin** *see* Jilin
81 I18 **Kirinyaga** *prev.* Mount Kenya. ✲ Kirinyaga, C Kenya 0°02′S 37°19′E
124 H13 **Kirishi** *var.* Kirisi. Leningradskaya Oblast', NW Russia 59°28′N 32°02′E
164 C16 **Kirishima-yama** ▲ Kyūshū, SW Japan 31°58′N 130°51′E
**Kirisi** *see* Kirishi
191 Y2 **Kiritimati** ✈ Kiritimati, E Kiribati 02°00′N 157°30′W
191 Y2 **Kiritimati** *prev.* Christmas Island. *atoll* Line Islands, E Kiribati
186 G9 **Kiriwina Island** *Eng.* Trobriand Island. *island* SE Papua New Guinea
186 G9 **Kiriwina Islands** *var.* Trobriand Islands. *island group* S Papua New Guinea
96 K12 **Kirkcaldy** E Scotland, United Kingdom 56°07′N 03°10′W
97 I14 **Kirkcudbright** S Scotland, United Kingdom 54°50′N 04°03′W
97 I14 **Kirkcudbright** *cultural region* S Scotland, United Kingdom
**Kirkee** *see* Khadki
95 I14 **Kirkenær** Hedmark, S Norway 60°27′N 12°04′E
92 M8 **Kirkenes** *Fin.* Kirkkoniemi. Finnmark, N Norway 69°43′N 30°02′E
92 J4 **Kirkjubæjarklaustur** Suðurland, S Iceland 63°46′N 18°03′W
**Kirk-Kilissa** *see* Kırklareli
**Kirkkoniemi** *see* Kirkenes
93 L20 **Kirkkonummi** *Swe.* Kyrkslätt. Uusimaa, S Finland 60°06′N 24°20′E
14 G7 **Kirkland Lake** Ontario, S Canada 48°10′N 80°02′W
136 C9 **Kırklareli** *prev.* Kirk-Kilissa. Kırklareli, NW Turkey 41°45′N 27°12′E
136 I13 **Kırklareli** ◈ *province* NW Turkey
185 F20 **Kirkliston Range** ▲▲ South Island, New Zealand
14 D10 **Kirkpatrick Lake** ◎ Ontario, S Canada
195 Q11 **Kirkpatrick, Mount** ▲ Antarctica 84°37′S 164°36′E
27 U2 **Kirksville** Missouri, C USA 40°12′N 92°35′W
139 T4 **Kirkūk** *var.* Karkūk, Kerkuk. Kirkūk, N Iraq 35°28′N 44°26′E
139 S4 **Kirkūk** *off.* Muḩāfa at at Kirkūk; *prev.* At Ta'mīm. ◈ *governorate* NE Iraq
**Kirkūk, Muḩāfa at at** *see* Kirkūk
139 U7 **Kir Kush** Diyālá, E Iraq 33°42′N 45°15′E
96 K5 **Kirkwall** NE Scotland, United Kingdom 58°59′N 02°58′W
83 H25 **Kirkwood** Eastern Cape, S South Africa 33°23′S 25°19′E
27 X5 **Kirkwood** Missouri, C USA 38°35′N 90°24′W
**Kirman** *see* Kermān
**Kir Moab/Kir of Moab** *see* Al Karak
126 I5 **Kirov** Kaluzhskaya Oblast', W Russia 54°02′N 34°17′E
125 R14 **Kirov** *prev.* Vyatka. Kirovskaya Oblast', NW Russia 58°35′N 49°39′E
**Kirov** *see* Balpyk Bi/ Ust'yevoye
**Kirovabad** *see* Gäncä
**Kirovabad** *see* Panj, Tajikistan
**Kirovakan** *see* Vanadzor
**Kirov/Kirova** *see* Kopbirlik, Kazakhstan
**Kirovo** *see* Kiraw, Belarus
**Kirovo** *see* Beshariq, Uzbekistan
125 R14 **Kirovo-Chepetsk** Kirovskaya Oblast', NW Russia 58°33′N 50°06′E
**Kirovogradskaya Oblast'/Kirovohrad** *see* Kirovohrads'ka Oblast'
117 P7 **Kirovohrads'ka Oblast'** *var.* Kirovohrad, *Rus.* Kirovogradskaya Oblast'. ◈ *province* C Ukraine
**Kirovo/Kirovograd** *see* Kropyvnyts'kyy
124 J4 **Kirovsk** Murmanskaya Oblast', NW Russia 67°37′N 33°38′E
**Kirovsk** *see* Kirawsk, Belarus
**Kirovsk** *see* Babadaýhan, Turkmenistan
**Kirovs'k** *see* Holubivka
122 E9 **Kirovskaya Oblast'** ◈ *province* NW Russia
**Kirovs'ke** *see* Islyam-Terek
**Kirovs'ke** *see* Khrestivka
**Kirovskiy** *see* Balpyk Bi
**Kirovskiy** *see* Ust'yevoye
**Kirovskoye** *see* Kyzyl-Adyr
121 R1 **Kırpaşa** *var.* Karpas Peninsula, *Gk.* Karpasía. *peninsula* NE Cyprus
146 E11 **Kirpili** Ahal Welaýaty, C Turkmenistan 39°31′N 57°13′E
96 K10 **Kirriemuir** E Scotland, United Kingdom 56°38′N 03°01′W
125 S13 **Kirs** Kirovskaya Oblast', NW Russia 59°22′N 52°20′E
127 N7 **Kirsanov** Tambovskaya Oblast', W Russia 52°40′N 42°48′E
136 J14 **Kırşehir** *anc.* Justinianopolis. Kırşehir, C Turkey 39°09′N 34°08′E
136 I13 **Kırşehir** ◈ *province* C Turkey
149 P4 **Kirthar Range** ▲▲ S Pakistan
37 P9 **Kirtland** New Mexico, SW USA 36°43′N 108°21′W
92 J11 **Kiruna** *Lapp.* Giron. Norrbotten, N Sweden 67°50′N 20°16′E
79 M18 **Kirundu** Orientale, NE Dem. Rep. Congo 0°45′S 25°28′E
**Kirun/Kirun'** *see* Keelung
26 L3 **Kirwin Reservoir** ⊠ Kansas, C USA
127 Q4 **Kirya** Chuvashskaya Respublika, W Russia 55°04′N 46°50′E
138 G8 **Kiryat Shmona** *prev.* Qiryat Shemona. Northern, N Israel 33°13′N 35°35′E
95 M18 **Kisa** Östergötland, S Sweden 58°N 15°39′E
165 P9 **Kisakata** Akita, Honshū, C Japan 39°12′N 139°55′E
**Kisalföld** *see* Little Alföld
79 L18 **Kisangani** *prev.* Stanleyville. Orientale, NE Dem. Rep. Congo 0°30′N 25°14′E
39 N12 **Kisaralik River** ⟿ Alaska, USA
165 O14 **Kisarazu** Chiba, Honshū, S Japan 35°23′N 139°57′E
111 I22 **Kisbér** Komárom-Esztergom, NW Hungary 47°30′N 18°00′E
11 V17 **Kisbey** Saskatchewan, S Canada 49°41′N 102°39′W
122 J13 **Kiselevsk** Kemerovskaya Oblast', S Russia 54°00′N 86°38′E
153 R13 **Kishanganj** Bihār, NE India 26°06′N 87°57′E
152 G12 **Kishangarh** Rājasthān, N India 26°33′N 74°52′E
**Kishegyes** *see* Mali Idoš
77 S15 **Kishi** Oyo, W Nigeria 09°01′N 03°53′E
**Kishinev** *see* Chişinău
**Kishiözen** *see* Saryozen
164 I14 **Kishiwada** *var.* Kisiwada. Ōsaka, Honshū, SW Japan 34°28′N 135°22′E
143 P14 **Kish, Jazīreh-ye** *var.* Qey. *island* S Iran
145 R7 **Kishkenekol'** *prev.* Kzyltu, *Kaz.* Qyzyltū. Kokshetau, N Kazakhstan 53°39′N 72°22′E
138 G9 **Kishon, Nahal** *prev.* Nahal Qishon. ⟿ N Israel
152 I6 **Kishtwār** Jammu and Kashmir, NW India 33°20′N 75°49′E
81 H19 **Kisii** Kisii, SW Kenya 0°40′S 34°47′E
81 J23 **Kisiju** Pwani, E Tanzania 07°25′S 39°20′E
**Kisiwada** *see* Kishiwada
**Kisjenő** *see* Chişineu-Criş
38 E17 **Kiska Island** *island* Aleutian Islands, Alaska, USA
**Kiskapus** *see* Copşa Mică
111 M22 **Kiskörei-víztároló** ⊠ E Hungary
**Kis-Küküllo** *see* Târnava Mică
111 L24 **Kiskunfélegyháza** *var.* Félegyháza. Bács-Kiskun, C Hungary 46°42′N 19°52′E
111 K25 **Kiskunhalas** *var.* Halas. Bács-Kiskun, S Hungary 46°26′N 19°29′E
111 K24 **Kiskunmajsa** Bács-Kiskun, S Hungary 46°30′N 19°46′E
127 N15 **Kislovodsk** Stavropol'skiy Kray, SW Russia 43°55′N 42°45′E
81 L18 **Kismaayo** *var.* Chisimayu, Kismayu, *It.* Chisimaio. Jubbada Hoose, S Somalia 0°05′S 42°35′E
**Kismayu** *see* Kismaayo
164 M13 **Kiso-sanmyaku** ▲▲ Honshū, S Japan
115 H24 **Kíssamos** *prev.* Kastélli. Kriti, Greece, E Mediterranean Sea 35°30′N 23°39′E
**Kisseraing** *see* Kanmaw Kyun
76 K14 **Kissidougou** Guinée-Forestière, S Guinea 09°15′N 10°08′W
23 X12 **Kissimmee** Florida, SE USA 28°17′N 81°24′W
23 X12 **Kissimmee, Lake** ◎ Florida, SE USA
23 X13 **Kissimmee River** ⟿ Florida, SE USA
11 V13 **Kississing Lake** ◎ Manitoba, C Canada
111 L24 **Kistelek** Csongrád, SE Hungary 46°27′N 19°58′E
**Kistna** *see* Krishna
111 M23 **Kisújszállás** Jász-Nagykun-Szolnok, E Hungary 47°14′N 20°45′E
164 G12 **Kisuki** *var.* Unnan. Shimane, Honshū, SW Japan 35°25′N 133°15′E
81 H18 **Kisumu** *prev.* Port Florence. Kisumu, W Kenya 0°02′N 34°42′E
**Kisutzaneustadtl** *see* Kysucké Nové Mesto
111 O20 **Kisvárda** *Ger.* Kleinwardein. Szabolcs-Szatmár-Bereg, E Hungary 48°13′N 22°03′E
81 J24 **Kiswere** Lindi, SE Tanzania 09°24′S 39°37′E
**Kiszucaújhely** *see* Kysucké Nové Mesto
76 K12 **Kita** Kayes, W Mali 13°00′N 09°28′W
**Kitaa** ◈ *province* W Greenland
**Kita-Akita** *see* Takanosu
**Kitab** *see* Kitob
165 Q4 **Kitahiyama** Hokkaidō, NE Japan 42°25′N 139°55′E
165 P12 **Kitaibaraki** Ibaraki, Honshū, S Japan 36°46′N 140°45′E
165 X16 **Kita-Iō-jima** *Eng.* San Alessandro. *island* SE Japan
165 Q9 **Kitakami** Iwate, Honshū, C Japan 39°18′N 141°05′E
165 P11 **Kitakata** Fukushima, Honshū, C Japan 37°38′N 139°52′E
164 D13 **Kitakyūshū** *var.* Kitakyûsyû. Fukuoka, Kyūshū, SW Japan 33°51′N 130°49′E
**Kitakyûsyû** *see* Kitakyūshū
81 H18 **Kitale** Trans Nzoia, W Kenya 01°01′N 35°01′E
165 U3 **Kitami** Hokkaidō, NE Japan 43°52′N 143°51′E
165 T2 **Kitami-sanchi** ▲▲ Hokkaidō, NE Japan
37 W5 **Kit Carson** Colorado, C USA 38°45′N 102°47′W
180 M12 **Kitchener** Western Australia 31°03′S 124°00′E
14 F16 **Kitchener** Ontario, S Canada 43°28′N 80°27′W
93 O17 **Kitee** Pohjois-Karjala, SE Finland 62°06′N 30°09′E
81 G16 **Kitgum** N Uganda 03°17′N 32°54′E
**Kithareng** *see* Kanmaw Kyun
**Kíthira** *see* Kýthira
**Kíthnos** *see* Kýthnos
8 L8 **Kitikmeot** ◈ *cultural region* Nunavut, N Canada
10 J13 **Kitimat** British Columbia, SW Canada 54°05′N 128°38′W
92 L11 **Kitinen** ⟿ N Finland
147 N12 **Kitob** *Rus.* Kitab. Qashqadaryo Viloyati, S Uzbekistan 39°06′N 66°47′E
116 K7 **Kitsman'** *Ger.* Kotzman, *Rom.* Cozmeni, *Rus.* Kitsman. Chernivets'ka Oblast', W Ukraine 48°30′N 25°50′E
164 E14 **Kitsuki** *var.* Kituki. Ōita, Kyūshū, SW Japan 33°24′N 131°36′E
18 C14 **Kittanning** Pennsylvania, NE USA 40°48′N 79°28′W
19 P10 **Kittery** Maine, NE USA 43°05′N 70°44′W
92 L11 **Kittilä** Lappi, N Finland 67°39′N 24°53′E
109 Z4 **Kittsee** Burgenland, E Austria 48°06′N 17°03′E
81 J19 **Kitui** Kitui, S Kenya 01°25′S 38°00′E
**Kituki** *see* Kitsuki
81 G22 **Kitunda** Tabora, C Tanzania 06°47′S 33°13′E
10 K13 **Kitwanga** British Columbia, SW Canada 55°07′N 128°03′W
82 J13 **Kitwe** *var.* Kitwe-Nkana. Copperbelt, C Zambia 12°48′S 28°13′E
**Kitwe-Nkana** *see* Kitwe
109 O7 **Kitzbühel** Tirol, W Austria 47°27′N 12°23′E
109 O7 **Kitzbüheler Alpen** ▲▲ W Austria
101 J19 **Kitzingen** Bayern, SE Germany 49°45′N 10°11′E
153 Q14 **Kiul** Bihār, NE India 25°10′N 86°06′E
186 A7 **Kiunga** Western, SW Papua New Guinea 06°10′S 141°15′E
93 M16 **Kiuruvesi** Pohjois-Savo, C Finland 63°38′N 26°40′E
38 M7 **Kivalina** Alaska, USA 67°44′N 164°32′W
9 O10 **Kivalliq** ◈ *cultural region* Nunavut, N Canada
92 L13 **Kivalo** *ridge* C Finland
116 J3 **Kivertsi** *Pol.* Kiwerce, *Rus.* Kivertsy. Volyns'ka Oblast', NW Ukraine 50°50′N 25°31′E
**Kivertsy** *see* Kivertsi
93 L16 **Kivijärvi** Keski-Suomi, C Finland 63°09′N 25°04′E
95 L23 **Kivik** Skåne, S Sweden 55°40′N 14°15′E
118 J3 **Kiviõli** Ida-Virumaa, NE Estonia 59°20′N 27°00′E
**Kivu, Lac** *see* Kivu, Lake
67 U10 **Kivu, Lake** *Fr.* Lac Kivu. ◎ Rwanda/Dem. Rep. Congo
186 C9 **Kiwai Island** *island* SW Papua New Guinea
39 N8 **Kiwalik** Alaska, USA 66°01′N 161°50′W
**Kiwerce** *see* Kivertsi
**Kiyev** *see* Kyiv
145 R10 **Kiyevka** Karaganda, C Kazakhstan 50°15′N 71°33′E
**Kiyevskaya Oblast'** *see* Kyivs'ka Oblast'
**Kiyevskoye Vodokhranilishche** *see* Kyivs'ke Vodoskhovyshche
136 D10 **Kıyıköy** Kırklareli, NW Turkey 41°37′N 28°07′E
**Kiyma** *see* Kima
125 V13 **Kizel** Permskiy Kray, NW Russia 58°59′N 57°37′E
125 O12 **Kizema** *var.* Kizëma. Arkhangel'skaya Oblast', NW Russia 61°06′N 44°51′E
**Kizëma** *see* Kizema
**Kizilagach** *see* Elhovo
136 H12 **Kızılcahamam** Ankara, N Turkey 40°28′N 32°37′E
136 J10 **Kızıl Irmak** ⟿ C Turkey
**Kizil Kum** *see* Kyzyl Kum
137 P16 **Kızıltepe** Mardin, SE Turkey 37°12′N 40°36′E
**Ki Zil Uzen** *see* Qezel Owzan, Rūd-e
127 Q16 **Kizilyurt** Respublika Dagestan, SW Russia 43°13′N 46°54′E
127 Q15 **Kizlyar** Respublika Dagestan, SW Russia 43°51′N 46°39′E
127 S3 **Kizner** Udmurtskaya Respublika, NW Russia 56°19′N 51°37′E
**Kizyl-Arvat** *see* Serdar
**Kizyl-Atrek** *see* Etrek
**Kizyl-Kaya** *see* Gyzylgaýa
**Kizyl-Su** *see* Gyzylsuw
95 H16 **Kjerkøy** *island* S Norway
**Kjølen** *see* Kölen
92 L7 **Kjøllefjord** Finnmark, N Norway 70°55′N 27°19′E
92 H11 **Kjøpsvik** *Lapp.* Gásluokta. Nordland, C Norway 68°06′N 16°21′E
169 N12 **Klabat, Teluk** *bay* Pulau Bangka, W Indonesia
112 I12 **Kladanj** ◈ Federacija Bosna I Hercegovine, E Bosnia and Herzegovina
171 X16 **Kladar** Papua, E Indonesia 08°14′S 137°46′E
111 C16 **Kladno** Středočeský, NW Czechia 50°10′N 14°05′E
112 P11 **Kladovo** Serbia, E Serbia 44°37′N 22°36′E
167 P12 **Klaeng** Rayong, S Thailand 12°48′N 101°41′E
109 T9 **Klagenfurt** *Slvn.* Celovec. Kärnten, S Austria 46°38′N 14°20′E
118 B11 **Klaipėda** *Ger.* Memel. Klaipeda, NW Lithuania 55°42′N 21°09′E
118 C11 **Klaipėda** ◈ *province* W Lithuania
**Klaksvig** *see* Klaksvík
95 B18 **Klaksvík** *Dan.* Klaksvig. Faroe Islands 62°13′N 06°34′W
34 L2 **Klamath** California, W USA 41°31′N 124°02′W
32 H16 **Klamath Falls** Oregon, NW USA 42°14′N 121°47′W
34 M1 **Klamath Mountains** ▲▲ California/Oregon, W USA
34 L2 **Klamath River** ⟿ California/Oregon, W USA
168 K9 **Klang** *var.* Kelang; *prev.* Port Swettenham. Selangor, Peninsular Malaysia 03°02′N 101°27′E
94 J13 **Klarälven** ⟿ Norway/ Sweden
111 B15 **Klášterec nad Ohří** *Ger.* Klösterle an der Eger. Ústecky Kraj, NW Czechia 50°24′N 13°10′E
111 B18 **Klatovy** *Ger.* Klattau. Plzeňský Kraj, W Czechia 49°24′N 13°16′E
**Klattau** *see* Klatovy
**Klausenburg** *see* Cluj-Napoca
39 Y14 **Klawock** Prince of Wales Island, Alaska, USA 55°33′N 133°06′W
98 P8 **Klazienaveen** Drenthe, NE Netherlands 52°43′N 07°00′E
**Kleck** *see* Klyetsk
110 H11 **Kłecko** Weilkopolskie, C Poland 52°37′N 17°27′E
110 I11 **Kleczew** Wielkopolskie, C Poland 52°22′N 18°12′E
10 L15 **Kleena Kleene** British Columbia, SW Canada 51°55′N 124°54′W
83 D20 **Klein Aub** Hardap, C Namibia 23°48′S 16°39′E
**Kleine Donau** *see* Mosoni-Duna
101 O14 **Kleine Elster** ⟿ E Germany
**Kleine Kokel** *see* Târnava Mică
99 I16 **Kleine Nete** ⟿ N Belgium
**Kleines Ungarisches Tiefland** *see* Little Alföld
83 E22 **Klein Karas** //Karas, S Namibia 27°36′S 18°05′E
**Kleinkopisch** *see* Copşa Mică
**Klein-Marien** *see* Väike-Maarja
**Kleinschlatten** *see* Zlatna
83 D23 **Kleinsee** Northern Cape, W South Africa 29°43′S 17°03′E
**Kleinwardein** *see* Kisvárda
115 C16 **Kleisoúra** Ípeiros, W Greece 39°21′N 20°52′E
95 C17 **Klepp** Rogaland, S Norway 58°46′N 05°39′E
83 I22 **Klerksdorp** North-West, N South Africa 26°52′S 26°39′E
126 I5 **Kletnya** Bryanskaya Oblast', W Russia 53°25′N 32°58′E
**Kletsk** *see* Klyetsk
101 D14 **Kleve** *Eng.* Cleves, *Fr.* Clèves; *prev.* Cleve. Nordrhein-Westfalen, W Germany 51°47′N 06°11′E
113 J16 **Kličevo** C Montenegro 42°45′N 18°58′E
119 M16 **Klichaw** *Rus.* Klichev. Mahilyowskaya Voblasts', E Belarus 53°29′N 29°21′E
**Klichev** *see* Klichaw
119 Q16 **Klimavichy** *Rus.* Klimovichi. Mahilyowskaya Voblasts', E Belarus 53°37′N 31°58′E
114 M7 **Kliment** Shumen, NE Bulgaria 43°37′N 27°00′E
**Klimovichi** *see* Klimavichy
93 G14 **Klimpfjäll** Västerbotten, N Sweden 65°05′N 14°50′E
126 K3 **Klin** Moskovskaya Oblast', W Russia 56°19′N 36°45′E
**Klina** *see* Klinë
113 M16 **Klinë** *Serb.* Klina. W Kosovo 42°38′N 20°35′E
111 B15 **Klínovec** *Ger.* Keilberg. ▲ NW Czechia 50°23′N 12°57′E
95 P19 **Klintehamn** Gotland, SE Sweden 57°22′N 18°15′E
127 R8 **Klintsovka** Saratovskaya Oblast', W Russia 51°42′N 49°17′E
126 H6 **Klintsy** Bryanskaya Oblast', W Russia 52°46′N 32°21′E
95 K22 **Klippan** Skåne, S Sweden 56°08′N 13°10′E
92 G13 **Klippen** Västerbotten, N Sweden 65°50′N 15°07′E
121 P2 **Klirou** W Cyprus 35°01′N 33°11′E
114 I9 **Klisura** Plovdiv, C Bulgaria 42°40′N 24°28′E
95 F20 **Klitmøller** Midtjylland, NW Denmark 57°01′N 08°29′E
112 F11 **Ključ** Federacija Bosne I Hercegovine, NW Bosnia and Herzegovina 44°32′N 16°46′E
111 J14 **Kłobuck** Śląskie, S Poland 50°56′N 18°55′E
110 J11 **Kłodawa** Wielkopolskie, C Poland 52°14′N 18°55′E
111 G16 **Kłodzko** *Ger.* Glatz. Dolnośląskie, SW Poland 50°27′N 16°37′E
95 I14 **Kløfta** Akershus, S Norway 60°04′N 11°06′E
112 P12 **Klokočevac** Serbia, E Serbia 44°19′N 22°11′E
118 G3 **Klooga** *Ger.* Lodensee. Harjumaa, NW Estonia 59°18′N 24°10′E
99 F15 **Kloosterzande** Zeeland, SW Netherlands 51°22′N 04°01′E
113 L19 **Klos** *var.* Klosi. Dibër, C Albania 41°30′N 20°07′E
**Klosi** *see* Klos
**Klösterle an der Eger** *see* Klášterec nad Ohří
109 X3 **Klosterneuburg** Niederösterreich, NE Austria 48°19′N 16°20′E
108 J9 **Klosters** Graubünden, SE Switzerland 46°54′N 09°52′E
108 G7 **Kloten** Zürich, N Switzerland 47°27′N 08°35′E
108 G7 **Kloten** ✈ (Zürich) Zürich, N Switzerland 47°25′N 08°36′E
100 K12 **Klötze** Sachsen-Anhalt, C Germany 52°37′N 11°09′E
12 K3 **Klotz, Lac** ◎ Québec, NE Canada
101 O15 **Klotzsche** ✈ (Dresden) Sachsen, E Germany 51°06′N 13°44′E
10 H7 **Kluane Lake** ◎ Yukon, W Canada
**Kluang** *see* Keluang
111 I14 **Kluczbork** *Ger.* Kreuzburg, Kreuzburg in Oberschlesien. Opolskie, S Poland 50°59′N 18°13′E
39 W12 **Klukwan** Alaska, USA 59°24′N 135°49′W
**Klyastitsy** *see* Klyastsitsy
118 L11 **Klyastsitsy** *Rus.* Klyastitsy. Vitsyebskaya Voblasts', N Belarus 55°53′N 28°36′E
127 T5 **Klyavlino** Samarskaya Oblast', W Russia 54°21′N 52°12′E
84 K9 **Klyaz'in** ⟿ W Russia
127 N3 **Klyaz'ma** ⟿ W Russia
119 J17 **Klyetsk** *Pol.* Kleck, *Rus.* Kletsk. Minskaya Voblasts', SW Belarus 53°04′N 26°38′E
147 S8 **Klyuchevka** Talasskaya Oblast', NW Kyrgyzstan 42°34′N 71°45′E
123 V10 **Klyuchevskaya Sopka, Vulkan** ✲ E Russia 56°03′N 160°38′E
95 D17 **Knaben** Vest-Agder, S Norway 58°46′N 07°04′E
95 K21 **Knäred** Halland, S Sweden 56°30′N 13°21′E
97 M16 **Knaresborough** N England, United Kingdom 54°01′N 01°35′W
114 H8 **Knezha** Vratsa, NW Bulgaria 43°29′N 24°04′E
25 O9 **Knickerbocker** Texas, SW USA 31°18′N 100°35′W
28 K5 **Knife River** ⟿ North Dakota, N USA
10 K16 **Knight Inlet** *inlet* British Columbia, W Canada
39 S12 **Knight Island** *island* Alaska, USA
97 K20 **Knighton** E Wales, United Kingdom 52°20′N 03°01′W
35 O7 **Knights Landing** California, W USA 38°47′N 121°43′W
112 E13 **Knin** Šibenik-Knin, S Croatia 44°03′N 16°12′E
25 Q12 **Knippal** Texas, SW USA 29°26′N 99°38′W
109 U7 **Knittelfeld** Steiermark, C Austria 47°14′N 14°50′E
95 O15 **Knivsta** Uppsala, C Sweden 59°43′N 17°49′E
113 P14 **Knjaževac** Serbia, E Serbia 43°34′N 22°16′E
27 S4 **Knob Noster** Missouri, C USA 38°47′N 93°33′W
99 D15 **Knokke-Heist** West-Vlaanderen, NW Belgium 51°21′N 03°19′E
95 H20 **Knøsen** *hill* N Denmark
**Knosós** *see* Knossos
115 J25 **Knossos** *Gk.* Knosós. *prehistoric site* Kriti, Greece, E Mediterranean Sea
25 N7 **Knott** Texas, SW USA 32°21′N 101°35′W
194 K5 **Knowles, Cape** *headland* Antarctica 71°45′S 60°20′W
31 O11 **Knox** Indiana, N USA 41°17′N 86°37′W
29 O3 **Knox** North Dakota, N USA 48°19′N 99°43′W
18 C13 **Knox** Pennsylvania, NE USA 41°13′N 79°33′W
189 X8 **Knox Atoll** *var.* Nadikdik, Narikrik. *atoll* Ratak Chain, SE Marshall Islands
10 H13 **Knox, Cape** *headland* Graham Island, British Columbia, SW Canada 54°05′N 133°02′W
25 P5 **Knox City** Texas, SW USA 33°25′N 99°49′W
195 Y11 **Knox Coast** *physical region* Antarctica
31 T12 **Knox Lake** ⊠ Ohio, N USA
23 T5 **Knoxville** Georgia, SE USA 32°44′N 83°58′W
30 K12 **Knoxville** Illinois, N USA 40°54′N 90°16′W
29 W15 **Knoxville** Iowa, C USA 41°19′N 93°06′W
21 N9 **Knoxville** Tennessee, S USA 35°58′N 83°55′W
197 P11 **Knud Rasmussen Land** *physical region* N Greenland
**Knüll** *see* Knüllgebirge
101 I16 **Knüllgebirge** *var.* Knüll. ▲▲ C Germany
124 I5 **Knyazhegubskoye Vodokhranilishche** ⊠ NW Russia
**Knyazhevo** *see* Sredishte
**Knyazhitsy** *see* Knyazhytsy
119 O15 **Knyazhytsy** *Rus.* Knyazhitsy. Mahilyowskaya Voblasts', E Belarus 54°10′N 30°28′E
83 G26 **Knysna** Western Cape, SW South Africa 34°03′S 23°03′E
**Koartac** *see* Quaqtaq
169 N13 **Koba** Pulau Bangka, W Indonesia 02°30′S 106°26′E
**Kobanê** *see* 'Ayn al 'Arab
**Kobani** *see* 'Ayn al 'Arab
164 D16 **Kobayashi** *var.* Kobayasi. Miyazaki, Kyūshū, SW Japan 32°00′N 130°58′E
**Kobayasi** *see* Kobayashi
144 I10 **Kobda** *prev.* Khobda, Novoalekseyevka. Aktyubinsk, W Kazakhstan 50°09′N 55°39′E
144 H9 **Kobda** *Kaz.* Ülkenqobda; *prev.* Bol'shaya Khobda. ⟿ Kazakhstan/Russia
**Kobdo** *see* Hovd
164 I13 **Kōbe** Hyōgo, Honshū, SW Japan 34°40′N 135°10′E
**Kobelyaki** *see* Kobelyaky
117 T6 **Kobelyaky** *Rus.* Kobelyaki. Poltavs'ka Oblast', NE Ukraine 49°10′N 34°13′E
95 J22 **København** *Eng.* Copenhagen; *anc.* Hafnia. ● (Denmark) Sjælland, København, E Denmark 55°43′N 12°34′E
76 K10 **Kobenni** Hodh el Gharbi, S Mauritania 15°58′N 09°24′W
171 T13 **Kobi** Pulau Seram, E Indonesia 02°56′S 129°53′E
101 F17 **Koblenz** *prev.* Coblenz, *Fr.* Coblence; *anc.* Confluentes. Rheinland-Pfalz, W Germany 50°21′N 07°36′E
108 F6 **Koblenz** Aargau, N Switzerland 47°34′N 08°16′E
**Kobrin** *see* Kobryn
171 V15 **Kobroor, Pulau** *island* Kepulauan Aru, E Indonesia
119 G19 **Kobryn** *Rus.* Kobrin. Brestskaya Voblasts', SW Belarus 52°13′N 24°21′E
39 O7 **Kobuk** Alaska, USA 66°54′N 156°52′W
39 O7 **Kobuk River** ⟿ Alaska, USA
137 Q10 **Kobuleti** *prev.* K'obulet'i. W Georgia 41°47′N 41°47′E
**K'obulet'i** *see* Kobuleti
123 P10 **Kobyay** Respublika Sakha (Yakutiya), NE Russia 63°36′N 126°33′E
136 E11 **Kocaeli** ◈ *province* NW Turkey
113 P18 **Kočani** NE North Macedonia 41°55′N 22°25′E
112 K12 **Koceljevo** Serbia, W Serbia 44°28′N 19°49′E
109 U12 **Kočevje** *Ger.* Gottschee. S Slovenia 45°41′N 14°48′E
153 T12 **Koch Bihār** West Bengal, NE India 26°19′N 89°26′E
**Kochchi** *see* Kochi
122 M9 **Kochechum** ⟿ N Russia
101 I20 **Kocher** ⟿ SW Germany
125 T13 **Kochevo** Komi-Permyatskiy Okrug, NW Russia 59°37′N 54°16′E
155 F23 **Kochi** *var.* Cochin, Kochchi. Kerala, SW India 09°56′N 76°15′E
164 G14 **Kōchi** *var.* Kôti. Kōchi, Shikoku, SW Japan 33°31′N 133°30′E
164 G14 **Kōchi** *off.* Kōchi-ken, *var.* Kôti. ◈ *prefecture* Shikoku, SW Japan
**Kōchi-ken** *see* Kōchi
**Kochiu** *see* Gejiu
**Kochkor** *see* Kochkorka
147 V8 **Kochkorka** *Kyr.* Kochkor. Narynskaya Oblast', C Kyrgyzstan 42°09′N 75°42′E
125 V5 **Kochmes** Respublika Komi, NW Russia 66°10′N 60°46′E
127 P15 **Kochubey** Respublika Dagestan, SW Russia 44°25′N 46°33′E
115 I17 **Kochylas** ▲ Skýros, Vóreies Sporádes, Greece, Aegean Sea 38°50′N 24°35′E
110 O13 **Kock** Lubelskie, E Poland 51°39′N 22°26′E
81 J19 **Kodacho** *spring/well* S Kenya 01°52′S 39°22′E
155 K24 **Koddiyar Bay** *bay* NE Sri Lanka
39 Q14 **Kodiak** Kodiak Island, Alaska, USA 57°47′N 152°24′W
39 Q14 **Kodiak Island** *island* Alaska, USA
154 B12 **Kodīnār** Gujarāt, W India 20°44′N 70°46′E
124 M9 **Kodino** Arkhangel'skaya Oblast', NW Russia 63°36′N 39°54′E
122 M12 **Kodinsk** Krasnoyarskiy Kray, C Russia 58°37′N 99°18′E
80 F12 **Kodok** Upper Nile, NE South Sudan 09°51′N 32°07′E
117 N8 **Kodyma** Odes'ka Oblast', SW Ukraine 48°05′N 29°09′E
**Koedoes** *see* Kudus
99 B17 **Koekelare** West-Vlaanderen, W Belgium 51°07′N 02°58′E
**Koeln** *see* Köln
**Koepang** *see* Kupang
**Ko-erh-mu** *see* Golmud
99 J17 **Koersel** Limburg, NE Belgium 51°04′N 05°17′E
83 E21 **Koës** //Karas, SE Namibia 25°59′S 19°08′E
**Koetai** *see* Mahakam, Sungai
**Koetaradja** *see* Banda Aceh
36 I14 **Kofa Mountains** ▲▲ Arizona, SW USA
171 Y15 **Kofarau** Papua, E Indonesia 07°29′S 140°28′E
147 P14 **Kofarnihon** *Rus.* Kafirnigan. ⟿ SW Tajikistan
**Kofarnihon** *see* Vahdat




◆ Country ● Country Capital ◇ Dependent Territory ○ Dependent Territory Capital ◈ Administrative Regions ✈ International Airport ▲ Mountain ▲▲ Mountain Range ✲ Volcano ⟿ River ◎ Lake ⊠ Reservoir

Kofçaz – Koshoba


114 M11 **Kofçaz** Kırklareli, NW Turkey 41°58′N 27°12′E
115 J25 **Kófinas** ▲ Kríti, Greece, E Mediterranean Sea 34°58′N 25°03′E
121 P3 **Kofínou** var. Kophinou. S Cyprus 34°49′N 33°24′E
109 V8 **Köflach** Steiermark, SE Austria 47°04′N 15°04′E
77 Q17 **Koforidua** SE Ghana 06°01′N 00°12′W
164 H12 **Kōfu** Tottori, Honshū, SW Japan 35°16′N 133°31′E
164 M13 **Kōfu** var. Kôhu. Yamanashi, Honshū, S Japan 35°41′N 138°33′E
81 F22 **Koga** Tabora, C Tanzania 06°08′S 32°20′E
**Kogălniceanu** see Mihail Kogălniceanu
13 P6 **Kogaluk** ≈ Newfoundland and Labrador, E Canada
12 J4 **Kogaluk, Riviére** ≈ Québec, NE Canada
145 V14 **Kogaly** Kaz. Qoghaly; prev. Kugaly. Almaty, SE Kazakhstan 44°30′N 78°40′E
122 I10 **Kogalym** Khanty-Mansiyskiy Avtonomnyy Okrug-Yugra, C Russia 62°13′N 74°34′E
95 J23 **Køge** Sjælland, E Denmark 55°28′N 12°12′E
95 J23 **Køge Bugt** bay E Denmark
77 U16 **Kogi** ◈ state C Nigeria
146 L11 **Kogon** Rus. Kagan. Buxoro Viloyati, C Uzbekistan 39°47′N 64°29′E
**Kŏgŭm-do** see Geogeum-do
**Kőhalom** see Rupea
149 T6 **Kohat** Khyber Pakhtunkhwa, NW Pakistan 33°37′N 71°30′E
142 L10 **Kohgīlūyeh va Bowyer Aḩmad** off. Ostān-e Kohgīlūyeh va Bowyer Aḩmad, var. Boyer Ahmadī va Kohkīlūyeh. ◈ province SW Iran
**Kohgīlūyeh va Bowyer Aḩmad, Ostān-e** see Kohgīlūyeh va Bowyer Aḩmad
118 G4 **Kohila** Ger. Koil. Raplamaa, NW Estonia 59°09′N 24°45′E
153 X13 **Kohīma** state capital Nāgāland, E India 25°40′N 94°08′E
167 Q13 **Koh Kong** var. Kaôh Kŏng. Koh Kong, SW Cambodia 11°37′N 102°59′E
**Kohsān** see Kuhsān
118 J3 **Kohtla-Järve** Ida-Virumaa, NE Estonia 59°22′N 27°21′E
**Kôhu** see Kōfu
**Kohyl'nyk** see Cogîlnic
165 N11 **Koide** Niigata, Honshū, C Japan 37°13′N 138°58′E
10 G7 **Koidern** Yukon, W Canada 61°55′N 140°22′W
76 J15 **Koidu** E Sierra Leone 08°40′N 11°01′W
118 I4 **Koigi** Järvamaa, C Estonia 58°51′N 25°45′E
**Koil** see Kohila
172 H13 **Koimbani** Grande Comore, NW Comoros 11°37′S 43°23′E
93 O16 **Koitere** ◎ E Finland
**Koivisto** see Primorsk
**Kŏje-do** see Geogeum-do
80 J13 **K'ok'a Hāyk'** ◎ C Ethiopia
**Kokand** see Qoʻqon
182 F6 **Kokatha** South Australia 31°17′S 135°16′E
146 M10 **Koʻkcha** Rus. Kokcha. Buxoro Viloyati, C Uzbekistan 40°30′N 64°58′E
**Kokcha** see Koʻkcha
**Kokchetav** see Kokshetau
93 K18 **Kokemäenjoki** ≈ SW Finland
171 W14 **Kokenau** var. Kokonau. Papua, E Indonesia 04°38′S 136°24′E
83 E22 **Kokerboom** //Karas, SE Namibia 28°11′S 19°25′E
119 N14 **Kokhanava** Rus. Kokhanovo. Vitsyebskaya Voblasts', NE Belarus 54°28′N 29°59′E
**Kokhanovichi** see Kakhanavichy
**Kokhanovo** see Kokhanava
**Kök-Janggak** see Kok-Yangak
93 K16 **Kokkola** Swe. Karleby; prev. Swe. Gamlakarleby. Keski-Pohjanmaa, W Finland 63°50′N 23°10′E
158 L3 **Kok Kuduk** spring/well N China 46°03′N 87°34′E
118 H9 **Koknese** C Latvia 56°38′N 25°27′E
77 T13 **Koko** Kebbi, W Nigeria 11°25′N 04°33′E
186 E9 **Kokoda** Northern, S Papua New Guinea 08°52′S 147°44′E
76 K12 **Kokofata** Kayes, W Mali 12°48′N 09°56′W
39 N6 **Kokolik River** ≈ Alaska, USA
31 O13 **Kokomo** Indiana, N USA 40°29′N 86°07′W
**Kokonau** see Kokenau
**Koko Nor** see Qinghai, China
**Koko Nor** see Qinghai Hu, China
186 H6 **Kokopo** var. Kopopo; prev. Herbertshöhe. New Britain, E Papua New Guinea 04°18′S 152°17′E
**Kokpekti** see Kokpekty
**Kokpekti** see Kokpekty
145 X10 **Kokpekty** prev. Kokpekti. Vostochnyy Kazakhstan, E Kazakhstan 48°47′N 82°28′E
145 X11 **Kokpekty** prev. Kokpekti. ≈ E Kazakhstan
39 P9 **Kokrines** Alaska, USA 64°58′N 154°42′W
39 P9 **Kokrines Hills** ▲▲ Alaska, USA
145 P17 **Koksaray** Turkestan, S Kazakhstan 42°34′N 68°06′E
147 X9 **Kokshaal-Tau** Rus. Khrebet Kakshaal-Too. ▲▲ China/Kyrgyzstan
145 P7 **Kokshetau** Kaz. Kökshetaū; prev. Kokchetav. Kokshetau, N Kazakhstan 53°18′N 69°25′E
**Kökshetaū** see Kokshetau
99 A17 **Koksijde** West-Vlaanderen, W Belgium 51°07′N 02°40′E
12 M5 **Koksoak** ≈ Québec, E Canada
83 K24 **Kokstad** KwaZulu/Natal, E South Africa 30°23′S 29°23′E
145 V14 **Koksu** Kaz. Rūdnīchnyy. Almaty, SE Kazakhstan 44°39′N 78°57′E
145 W15 **Koktal** Kaz. Köktal. Almaty, SE Kazakhstan 44°05′N 79°44′E
145 Q12 **Koktas** ≈ C Kazakhstan
**Kök-Tash** see Këk-Tash
**Koktokay** see Fuyun
147 T9 **Kok-Yangak** Kyr. Kök-Janggak. Dzhalal-Abadskaya Oblast', W Kyrgyzstan 41°02′N 73°11′E
158 F9 **Kokyar** Xinjiang Uygur Zizhiqu, W China 37°41′N 77°15′E
149 O13 **Kolachi** var. Kulachi. SW Pakistan
76 J15 **Kolahun** N Liberia 08°24′N 10°02′W
171 O14 **Kolaka** Sulawesi, C Indonesia 04°04′S 121°38′E
**K'o-la-ma-i** see Karamay
**Kola Peninsula** see Kol'skiy Poluostrov
155 H19 **Kolār** Karnātaka, E India 13°10′N 78°10′E
155 H19 **Kolār Gold Fields** Karnātaka, E India 12°56′N 78°16′E
92 K11 **Kolari** Lappi, NW Finland 67°20′N 23°51′E
111 I21 **Kolárovo** Ger. Gutta; prev. Guta, Hung. Gúta. Nitriansky Kraj, SW Slovakia 47°54′N 18°01′E
113 K16 **Kolašin** E Montenegro 42°49′N 19°32′E
**Kolāyat** see Shir Kolāyat
95 N15 **Kolbäck** Västmanland, C Sweden 59°33′N 16°15′E
**Kolbcha** see Kowbcha
197 Q15 **Kolbeinsey Ridge** undersea feature Denmark Strait/Norwegian Sea 69°00′N 17°30′W
**Kolberg** see Kołobrzeg
95 H15 **Kolbotn** Akershus, S Norway 62°15′N 10°24′E
111 N16 **Kolbuszowa** Podkarpackie, SE Poland 50°12′N 22°07′E
126 L3 **Kol'chugino** Vladimirskaya Oblast', W Russia 56°19′N 39°24′E
76 H12 **Kolda** S Senegal 12°58′N 14°58′W
95 G23 **Kolding** Syddanmark, C Denmark 55°29′N 09°30′E
79 K20 **Kole** Kasai-Oriental, SW Dem. Rep. Congo 03°30′S 22°28′E
79 M17 **Kole** Orientale, N Dem. Rep. Congo 02°08′N 25°25′E
**Kōle** see Kili Island
84 F6 **Kölen** Nor. Kjølen. ▲▲ Norway/Sweden
**Kolepom, Pulau** see Yos Sudarso, Pulau
118 H3 **Kolga Laht** Ger. Kolko-Wiek. bay N Estonia
125 Q3 **Kolguyev, Ostrov** island NW Russia
155 E16 **Kolhāpur** Mahārāshtra, SW India 16°42′N 74°13′E
151 K21 **Kolhumadulu** var. Thaa Atoll. atoll S Maldives
93 O16 **Koli** var. Kolinkylä. Pohjois-Karjala, E Finland 63°06′N 29°46′E
39 O13 **Koliganek** Alaska, USA 59°43′N 157°16′W
111 E16 **Kolín** Ger. Kolin. Střední Čechy, C Czechia 50°02′N 15°10′E
**Kolinkylä** see Koli
190 E12 **Koliu** Île Futuna, W Wallis and Futuna
118 E7 **Kolka** NW Latvia 57°44′N 22°34′E
118 E7 **Kolkasrags** prev. Eng. Cape Domesnes. headland NW Latvia 57°45′N 22°35′E
153 S16 **Kolkāta** prev. Calcutta. state capital West Bengal, NE India 22°30′N 88°20′E
**Kolkhozabad** see Kolkhozobod
147 P14 **Kolkhozobod** Rus. Kolkhozabad; prev. Kaganovichabad, Tugalan. SW Tajikistan 37°33′N 68°34′E
**Kolki/Kołki** see Kolky
**Kolko-Wiek** see Kolga Laht
116 K3 **Kolky** Pol. Kołki, Rus. Kolki. Volyns'ka Oblast', NW Ukraine 51°05′N 25°40′E
155 G24 **Kollam** var. Quilon. Kerala, SW India 08°57′N 76°37′E
155 G20 **Kollegāl** Karnātaka, W India 12°08′N 77°06′E
98 M5 **Kollum** Fryslân, N Netherlands 53°17′N 06°09′E
**Kolmar** see Colmar
101 E16 **Köln** var. Koeln, Eng./Fr. Cologne, prev. Cöln; anc. Colonia Agrippina, Oppidum Ubiorum. Nordrhein-Westfalen, W Germany 50°57′N 06°57′E
110 N9 **Kolno** Podlaskie, NE Poland 53°24′N 21°57′E
110 J12 **Koło** Wielkopolskie, C Poland 52°11′N 18°39′E
38 B8 **Kōloa** var. Koloa. Kaua'i, Hawaii, USA, C Pacific Ocean 21°54′N 159°28′W
**Koloa** see Kōloa
110 E7 **Kołobrzeg** Ger. Kolberg. Zachodnio-pomorskie, NW Poland 54°11′N 15°34′E
126 H4 **Kolodnya** Smolenskaya Oblast', W Russia 54°57′N 32°22′E
190 E13 **Kolofau, Mont** ⛰ Île Alofi, S Wallis and Futuna 14°21′S 178°02′W
125 O14 **Kologriv** Kostromskaya Oblast', NW Russia 58°49′N 44°22′E
76 L12 **Kolokani** Koulikoro, W Mali 13°35′N 08°01′W
77 N13 **Koloko** W Burkina Faso 11°06′N 05°18′W
186 K8 **Kolombangara** var. Kilimbangara, Nduke. island New Georgia Islands, NW Solomon Islands
**Kolomea** see Kolomyya
126 L4 **Kolomna** Moskovskaya Oblast', W Russia 55°03′N 38°52′E
116 J7 **Kolomyya** Ger. Kolomea. Ivano-Frankivs'ka Oblast', W Ukraine 48°31′N 25°00′E
76 M13 **Kolondiéba** Sikasso, SW Mali 11°04′N 06°55′W
193 V15 **Kolonga** Tongatapu, S Tonga 21°07′S 175°05′W
189 U16 **Kolonia** var. Colonia. Pohnpei, E Micronesia 06°57′N 158°12′E
**Kolonja** see Kolonjë
113 K21 **Kolonjë** var. Kolonja. Fier, C Albania 40°49′N 19°37′E
**Kolonjë** see Ersekë
**Kolosjoki** see Nikel'
**Kolotambu** see Avuavu
193 U15 **Kolovai** Tongatapu, S Tonga 21°05′S 175°20′W
**Kolozsvár** see Cluj-Napoca
112 C9 **Kolpa** Ger. Kulpa, SCr. Kupa. ≈ Croatia/Slovenia
122 J11 **Kolpashevo** Tomskaya Oblast', C Russia 58°21′N 82°44′E
124 H13 **Kolpino** Leningradskaya Oblast', NW Russia 59°44′N 30°39′E
100 M10 **Kölpinsee** ◎ NE Germany
**Kólpos Mórfu** see Güzelyurt
146 K8 **Koʻlquduq** Rus. Kulkuduk. Navoiy Viloyati, N Uzbekistan 42°36′N 63°24′E
124 K5 **Kol'skiy Poluostrov** Eng. Kola Peninsula. peninsula NW Russia
127 T6 **Koltubanovskiy** Orenburgskaya Oblast', W Russia 53°00′N 52°00′E
112 L11 **Kolubara** ≈ C Serbia
**Kolupchii** see Gurkovo
110 K13 **Koluszki** Łódźskie, C Poland 51°44′N 19°50′E
125 T6 **Kolva** ≈ NW Russia
93 E14 **Kolvereid** Nord-Trøndelag, W Norway 64°47′N 11°22′E
79 M24 **Kolwezi** Katanga, S Dem. Rep. Congo 10°43′S 25°29′E
123 S7 **Kolyma** ≈ NE Russia
**Kolyma Lowland** see Kolymskaya Nizmennost'
**Kolyma Range/Kolymskiy, Khrebet** see Kolymskoye Nagor'ye
123 S7 **Kolymskaya Nizmennost'** Eng. Kolyma Lowland. lowlands NE Russia
123 S7 **Kolymskoye** Respublika Sakha (Yakutiya), NE Russia 68°42′N 158°46′E
123 U8 **Kolymskoye Nagor'ye** var. Khrebet Kolymskiy, Eng. Kolyma Range. ▲▲ E Russia
123 V5 **Kolyuchinskaya Guba** bay NE Russia
**Kol'zhat** see Kalzhat
114 G8 **Kom** ▲ NW Bulgaria 43°10′N 23°02′E
80 I13 **Koma** Oromīya, C Ethiopia 08°19′N 36°48′E
77 X12 **Komadugu Gana** ≈ NE Nigeria
164 M13 **Komagane** Nagano, Honshū, S Japan 35°44′N 137°54′E
79 P17 **Komanda** Orientale, NE Dem. Rep. Congo 01°25′N 29°43′E
197 U1 **Komandorskaya Basin** var. Kamchatka Basin. undersea feature SW Bering Sea 57°00′N 168°00′E
125 Pp9 **Komandorskiye Ostrova** Eng. Commander Islands. island group E Russia
**Komándfalva** see Comănești
111 I22 **Komárno** Ger. Komorn, Hung. Komárom. Nitriansky Kraj, SW Slovakia 47°46′N 18°07′E
111 I22 **Komárom** Komárom-Esztergom, NW Hungary 47°43′N 18°06′E
**Komárom** see Komárno
111 I22 **Komárom-Esztergom** off. Komárom-Esztergom Megye. ◈ county N Hungary
**Komárom-Esztergom Megye** see Komárom-Esztergom
164 K11 **Komatsu** var. Komatu. Ishikawa, Honshū, SW Japan 36°25′N 136°27′E
**Komatu** see Komatsu
83 D17 **Kombat** Otjozondjupa, N Namibia 19°42′S 17°45′E
**Kombissiguiri** see Kombissiri
77 P13 **Kombissiri** var. Kombissiguiri. C Burkina Faso 12°01′N 01°27′W
188 E10 **Komebail Lagoon** lagoon N Palau
81 F20 **Kome Island** island N Tanzania
**Komeyo** see Wandai
117 P10 **Kominternivs'ke** Odes'ka Oblast', SW Ukraine 46°52′N 30°56′E
125 R8 **Komi, Respublika** ◈ autonomous republic NW Russia
111 I25 **Komló** Baranya, SW Hungary 46°11′N 18°15′E
**Kommunarsk** see Alchevs'k
**Kommunizm, Qullai** see Ismoili Somoní, Qullai
186 B7 **Komo** Hela, W Papua New Guinea 06°06′S 142°52′E
170 M16 **Komodo, Pulau** island Nusa Tenggara, S Indonesia
77 N15 **Komoé** var. Komoé Fleuve. ≈ E Ivory Coast
**Komoé Fleuve** see Komoé
79 F20 **Komono** Lékoumou, SW Congo 03°15′S 13°14′E
171 Y16 **Komoran** Papua, E Indonesia 08°14′S 138°51′E
171 Y16 **Komoran, Pulau** island E Indonesia
**Komori, Udzima wa** see Comoros
**Komorn** see Komárno
**Komornok** see Comorâște
**Komosolabad** see Darband
**Komotau** see Chomutov
114 K13 **Komotiní** var. Gümüljina, Turk. Gümülcine. Anatolikí Makedonía kai Thráki, NE Greece 41°07′N 25°27′E
113 K16 **Komovi** ▲▲ E Montenegro
117 R8 **Kompaniyivka** Kirovohrads'ka Oblast', C Ukraine 48°16′N 32°12′E
**Kâmpóng Cham** see Kampong Cham
**Kompong Kleang** see Kâmpóng Khleăng
**Kâmpóng Spœ** see Kampong Speu
**Komrat** see Comrat
144 G12 **Komsomol** prev. Komsomol'skiy. Atyrau, W Kazakhstan 47°18′N 53°37′E
125 W4 **Komsomol** prev. Komsomol'skiy. Respublika Komi, NW Russia 67°33′N 64°00′E
122 K14 **Komsomolets, Ostrov** island Severnaya Zemlya, N Russia
144 F13 **Komsomolets, Zaliv** lake gulf SW Kazakhstan
**Komsomol/Komsomolets** see Karabalyk, Kostanay, Kazakhstan
**Komsomolobod** see Darband
124 M16 **Komsomol'sk** Ivanovskaya Oblast', W Russia 56°58′N 40°15′E
146 M11 **Komsomol'sk** Navoiy Viloyati, N Uzbekistan 40°14′N 65°10′E
**Komsomol's'k** see Horishni Plavni
**Komsomol'skiy** see Komsomol
**Komsomol'skiy** see Komsomol
123 S13 **Komsomol'sk-na-Amure** Khabarovskiy Kray, SE Russia 50°32′N 136°59′E
**Komsomol'sk-na-Ustyurte** see Kubla-Ustyurt
144 K10 **Komsomol'skoye** Aktyubinsk, NW Kazakhstan
127 Q8 **Komsomol'skoye** Saratovskaya Oblast', W Russia 50°45′N 47°00′E
145 P10 **Kon** ≈ C Kazakhstan
**Kona** see Kailua-Kona
124 K16 **Konakovo** Tverskaya Oblast', W Russia 56°42′N 36°44′E
143 V15 **Konārak** Sīstān va Balūchestān, SE Iran 25°26′N 60°23′E
27 O11 **Konawa** Oklahoma, C USA 34°57′N 96°45′W
122 H10 **Konda** ≈ C Russia
154 L13 **Kondagaon** Chhattīsgarh, C India 19°38′N 81°41′E
14 K10 **Kondiaronk, Lac** ◎ Québec, SE Canada
180 J13 **Kondinin** Western Australia 32°31′S 118°15′E
81 H21 **Kondoa** Dodoma, C Tanzania 04°54′S 35°46′E
127 P6 **Kondol'** Penzenskaya Oblast', W Russia 52°49′N 45°03′E
114 N10 **Kondolovo** Burgas, E Bulgaria 42°07′N 27°43′E
171 Z16 **Kondomirat** Papua, E Indonesia 08°57′S 140°55′E
124 J10 **Kondopoga** Respublika Kareliya, NW Russia 62°13′N 34°17′E
**Kondoz** see Kunduz
**Kondūz** see Kunduz
187 P16 **Koné** Province Nord, W New Caledonia 21°04′S 164°51′E
146 E13 **Könekesir** Balkan Welaýaty, W Turkmenistan 38°16′N 56°51′E
146 G8 **Köneürgenç** var. Köneürgench, Rus. Këneurgench; prev. Kunya-Urgench. Daşoguz Welaýaty, N Turkmenistan 42°21′N 59°09′E
77 N15 **Kong** N Ivory Coast 09°10′N 04°33′W
39 S5 **Kongakut River** ≈ Alaska, USA
197 O14 **Kong Christian IX Land** Eng. King Christian IX Land. physical region SE Greenland
197 P13 **Kong Christian X Land** Eng. King Christian X Land. physical region E Greenland
197 N13 **Kong Frederik IX Land** physical region SW Greenland
197 Q12 **Kong Frederik VIII Land** Eng. King Frederik VIII Land. physical region NE Greenland
197 N15 **Kong Frederik VI Kyst** Eng. King Frederik VI Coast. physical region SE Greenland
167 P13 **Kŏng, Kaôh** prev. Kas Kong. island SW Cambodia
92 P2 **Kong Karls Land** Eng. King Charles Islands. island group SE Svalbard
81 G14 **Kong Kong** ≈ E South Sudan
**Kongo** see Congo (river)
83 G16 **Kongola** Zambezi, NE Namibia 17°47′S 23°24′E
79 N21 **Kongolo** Katanga, E Dem. Rep. Congo 05°20′S 26°58′E
81 F14 **Kongor** Jonglei, E South Sudan 07°09′N 31°44′E
197 Q14 **Kong Oscar Fjord** fjord E Greenland
77 P12 **Kongoussi** N Burkina Faso 13°19′N 01°31′W
95 G15 **Kongsberg** Buskerud, S Norway 59°39′N 09°38′E
92 Q2 **Kongsøya** island Kong Karls Land, E Svalbard
95 I14 **Kongsvinger** Hedmark, S Norway 60°10′N 12°00′E
**Kongtong** see Pingliang
167 T11 **Kŏng, Tônlé** var. Xê Kong. ≈ Cambodia/Laos
158 E8 **Kongur Shan** ▲ NW China 38°39′N 75°21′E
81 I22 **Kongwa** Dodoma, C Tanzania 06°13′S 36°28′E
**Kong, Xê** see Kŏng, Tônlé
**Konia** see Konya
147 R11 **Konibodom** Rus. Kanibadam. N Tajikistan 40°16′N 70°20′E
111 K15 **Koniecpol nad Pilicą** Śląskie, S Poland 50°47′N 19°45′E
**Konieh** see Konya
**Königgrätz** see Hradec Králové
**Königinhof an der Elbe** see Dvůr Králové nad Labem
101 K23 **Königsbrunn** Bayern, S Germany 48°16′N 10°52′E
101 O24 **Königssee** ◎ SE Germany
**Königshütte** see Chorzów
109 S8 **Königstuhl** ▲ S Austria 46°57′N 13°47′E
109 U3 **Königswiesen** Oberösterreich, N Austria 48°25′N 14°48′E
101 E17 **Königswinter** Nordrhein-Westfalen, W Germany 50°40′N 07°12′E
146 M11 **Konimex** Rus. Kenimekh. Navoiy Viloyati, N Uzbekistan 40°14′N 65°10′E
110 I12 **Konin** Ger. Kuhnau. Weilkopolskie, C Poland 52°13′N 18°17′E
**Koninkrijk der Nederlanden** see Netherlands
113 L24 **Konispol** var. Konispoli. Vlorë, S Albania 39°40′N 20°10′E
**Konispoli** see Konispol
115 C15 **Kónitsa** Ípeiros, W Greece 40°04′N 20°48′E
**Konitz** see Chojnice
108 D8 **Köniz** Bern, W Switzerland 46°56′N 07°25′E
113 H14 **Konjic** ◈ Federacija Bosne I Hercegovine, S Bosnia and Herzegovina
92 J10 **Könkämäälven** ≈ Finland/Sweden
155 D14 **Konkan** plain W India
83 D22 **Konkiep** ≈ S Namibia
76 I14 **Konkouré** ≈ W Guinea
77 O11 **Konna** Mopti, S Mali 14°58′N 03°49′W
186 H6 **Konogaiang, Mount** ▲ New Ireland, NE Papua New Guinea 04°05′S 152°43′E
186 H5 **Konogogo** New Ireland, NE Papua New Guinea 03°25′S 152°09′E
108 E9 **Konolfingen** Bern, W Switzerland 46°53′N 07°36′E
77 P16 **Konongo** C Ghana 06°39′N 01°06′W
186 H5 **Konos** New Ireland, NE Papua New Guinea 03°09′S 151°47′E
124 M12 **Konosha** Arkhangel'skaya Oblast', NW Russia 60°58′N 40°09′E
117 R3 **Konotop** Sums'ka Oblast', NE Ukraine 51°15′N 33°14′E
158 L7 **Konqi He** ≈ NW China
111 L14 **Końskie** Siętokrzyskie, C Poland 51°12′N 20°23′E
**Konstantinovka** see Kostyantynivka
126 M11 **Konstantinovsk** Rostovskaya Oblast', SW Russia 47°37′N 41°07′E
101 H24 **Konstanz** var. Constanz, Eng. Constance, hist. Kostnitz; anc. Constantia. Baden-Württemberg, S Germany 47°40′N 09°10′E
**Konstanza** see Constanța
77 T14 **Kontagora** Niger, W Nigeria 10°25′N 05°29′E
78 E13 **Kontcha** Nord, N Cameroon 08°00′N 12°13′E
99 G17 **Kontich** Antwerpen, N Belgium 51°08′N 04°27′E
93 O16 **Kontiolahti** Pohjois-Karjala, SE Finland 62°46′N 29°51′E
93 M15 **Kontiomäki** Kainuu, C Finland 64°20′N 28°09′E
167 U11 **Kon Tum** var. Kontum. Kon Tum, C Vietnam 14°23′N 108°00′E
**Kontum** see Kon Tum
**Konur** see Sulakyurt
136 H15 **Konya** var. Konieh, prev. Konia; anc. Iconium. Konya, C Turkey 37°51′N 32°30′E
136 H15 **Konya** var. Konia, Konieh. ◈ province C Turkey
151 E15 **Konya Reservoir** prev. Shivāji Sāgar. ▣ W India
145 T13 **Konyrat** var. Kounradskiy, Kaz. Qongyrat. Karaganda, SE Kazakhstan 46°57′N 75°01′E
145 W15 **Konyrolen** Almaty, SE Kazakhstan 44°16′N 79°18′E
81 I19 **Konza** Kajiado, S Kenya 01°44′S 37°07′E
98 I9 **Koog aan den Zaan** Noord-Holland, C Netherlands 52°28′N 04°49′E
182 E7 **Koonibba** South Australia 31°55′S 133°23′E
31 O11 **Koontz Lake** Indiana, N USA 41°25′N 86°24′W
171 U12 **Koor** Papua Barat, E Indonesia 0°21′S 132°28′E
183 R9 **Koorawatha** New South Wales, SE Australia 34°03′S 148°33′E
118 J5 **Koosa** Tartumaa, E Estonia 58°31′N 27°06′E
33 N7 **Kootenai** var. Kootenay. ≈ Canada/USA see also Kootenay
**Kootenai** see Kootenay
11 P17 **Kootenay** var. Kootenai. ≈ Canada/USA see also Kootenai
**Kootenay** see Kootenai
83 F24 **Kootjieskolk** Northern Cape, W South Africa 31°16′S 20°21′E
113 M15 **Kopaonik** ▲▲ S Serbia
**Kopar** see Koper
92 K1 **Kópasker** Norðurland Eystra, N Iceland 66°15′N 16°23′W
92 H4 **Kópavogur** Höfuðborgarsvæðið, W Iceland 64°06′N 21°47′W
145 U13 **Kopbirlik** prev. Kīrov, Kirova. Almaty, SE Kazakhstan 46°24′N 77°16′E
109 S13 **Koper** It. Capodistria; prev. Kopar. SW Slovenia 45°32′N 13°43′E
95 C16 **Kopervik** Rogaland, S Norway 59°17′N 05°20′E
**Köpetdag Gershi/Kopetdag, Khrebet** see Koppeh Dāgh
**Kophinou** see Kofínou
182 G8 **Kopi** South Australia 33°24′S 135°40′E
153 W12 **Kopili** ≈ NE India
95 M15 **Köping** Västmanland, C Sweden 59°31′N 16°00′E
113 K17 **Koplik** var. Kopliku. Shkodër, NW Albania 42°12′N 19°26′E
**Kopliku** see Koplik
**Kopopo** see Kokopo
94 I11 **Koppang** Hedmark, S Norway 61°34′N 11°04′E
**Kopparberg** see Dalarna
143 S3 **Koppeh Dāgh** Rus. Khrebet Kopetdag, Turkm. Köpetdag Gershi. ▲▲ Iran/Turkmenistan
**Koppename** see Coppename Rivier
95 J15 **Koppom** Värmland, C Sweden 59°42′N 12°07′E
**Kopreinitz** see Koprivnica
114 K9 **Koprinka, Yazovir** prev. Yazovir Georgi Dimitrov. ▣ C Bulgaria
112 F7 **Koprivnica** Ger. Kopreinitz, Hung. Kaproncza. Koprivnica-Križevci, N Croatia 46°10′N 16°49′E
112 F8 **Koprivnica-Križevci** off. Koprivničko-Križevačka Županija. ◈ province N Croatia
111 I17 **Kopřivnice** Ger. Nesselsdorf. Moravskoslezský Kraj, E Czechia 49°36′N 18°09′E
**Koprivničko-Križevačka Županija** see Koprivnica-Križevci
**Köprülü** see Veles
**Koptsevichi** see Kaptsevichy
**Kopyl'** see Kapyl'
119 O14 **Kopys'** Vitsyebskaya Voblasts', NE Belarus 54°19′N 30°18′E
113 M18 **Korab** ▲ Albania/North Macedonia 41°48′N 20°33′E
**Korabavur Pastligi** see Karabaur', Uval
124 M5 **Korabel'noye** Murmanskaya Oblast', NW Russia 67°00′N 41°10′E
81 M14 **K'orahē** Sumalē, E Ethiopia 06°36′N 44°21′E
115 L16 **Kórakas, Akrotírio** cape Lésvos, E Greece
112 D9 **Korana** ≈ C Croatia
155 L14 **Korāput** Odisha, E India 18°48′N 82°41′E
**Korat** see Nakhon Ratchasima
167 Q9 **Korat Plateau** plateau E Thailand
**Kōrāwa, Sar-I** see Kirdī Kawrāw, Qimmat
154 L11 **Korba** Chhattīsgarh, C India 22°25′N 82°43′E
101 H15 **Korbach** Hessen, C Germany 51°16′N 08°52′E
**Korça** see Korçë
113 M21 **Korçë** var. Korca, Gk. Korytsa, It. Corriza; prev. Koritsa. Korçë, SE Albania 40°38′N 20°47′E
113 M21 **Korçë** ◈ county SE Albania
113 G15 **Korčula** It. Curzola. Dubrovnik-Neretva, S Croatia 42°57′N 17°08′E
113 F15 **Korčula** It. Curzola; anc. Corcyra Nigra. island S Croatia
113 F15 **Korčulanski Kanal** channel S Croatia
145 T6 **Korday** prev. Georgiyevka. Zhambyl, SE Kazakhstan 43°03′N 74°43′E
142 J5 **Kordestān** off. Ostān-e Kordestān, var. Kurdestan. ◈ province W Iran
**Kordestān, Ostān-e** see Kordestān
143 P4 **Kord Kūy** var. Kurd Kui. Golestān, N Iran 36°49′N 54°05′E
163 V13 **Korea Bay** bay China/North Korea
**Korea, Democratic People's Republic of** see North Korea
171 T15 **Koreare** Pulau Yamdena, E Indonesia 07°33′S 131°13′E
**Korea, Republic of** see South Korea
163 Z17 **Korea Strait** Jap. Chōsen-kaikyō, Kor. Taehan-haehyŏp. channel Japan/South Korea
**Korelichi/Korelicze** see Karelichy
80 J11 **Korem** Tigrai, N Ethiopia 12°32′N 39°29′E
77 U11 **Korén Adoua** ≈ C Niger
126 I7 **Korenevo** Kurskaya Oblast', W Russia 51°21′N 34°53′E
126 L13 **Korenovsk** Krasnodarskiy Kray, SW Russia 45°28′N 39°25′E
116 L4 **Korets'** Pol. Korzec, Rus. Korets. Rivnens'ka Oblast', NW Ukraine 50°38′N 27°12′E
**Korets** see Korets'
194 L7 **Korff Ice Rise** ice cap Antarctica
145 Q10 **Korgalzhyn** var. Kurgal'dzhino, Kurgal'dzhinsky, Kaz. Qorghalzhyn. Akmola, C Kazakhstan 50°33′N 69°58′E
145 W15 **Korgas**; prev. Khorgos. Almaty, SE Kazakhstan 44°13′N 80°22′E
92 G13 **Korgen** Troms, N Norway 66°04′N 13°51′E
147 R9 **Korgon-Dëbë** Dzhalal-Abadskaya Oblast', W Kyrgyzstan 41°51′N 70°52′E
76 M14 **Korhogo** N Ivory Coast 09°29′N 05°39′W
115 F19 **Korinthiakós Kólpos** Eng. Gulf of Corinth; anc. Corinthiacus Sinus. gulf C Greece
115 F19 **Kórinthos** anc. Corinthus Eng. Corinth. Pelopónnisos, S Greece 37°56′N 22°55′E
115 G19 **Korínthou, Dióryga** Eng. Corinth Canal. canal S Greece
113 M18 **Koritnik** ▲ S Serbia 42°06′N 20°34′E
**Koritsa** see Korçë
165 P11 **Kōriyama** Fukushima, Honshū, C Japan 37°25′N 140°20′E
136 E16 **Korkuteli** Antalya, SW Turkey 37°07′N 30°11′E
158 K6 **Korla** Chin. K'u-erh-lo. Xinjiang Uygur Zizhiqu, NW China 41°48′N 36°10′E
122 J10 **Korliki** Khanty-Mansiyskiy Avtonomnyy Okrug-Yugra, C Russia 61°28′N 82°12′E
**Körlin an der Persante** see Karlino
**Korma** see Karma
14 D8 **Kormak** Ontario, S Canada 47°38′N 83°00′W
**Kormakítis, Akrotírio/Kormakiti, Cape/Kormakítis** see Koruçam Burnu
111 G23 **Körmend** Vas, W Hungary 47°02′N 16°35′E
**Kōrmōr** Şalāḩ ad Dīn, E Iraq 35°06′N 44°47′E
112 C13 **Kornat** It. Incoronata. island W Croatia
**Korneshty** see Cornești
109 X3 **Korneuburg** Niederösterreich, NE Austria 48°22′N 16°20′E
145 P7 **Korneyevka** Severnyy Kazakhstan, N Kazakhstan 54°01′N 68°30′E
95 I17 **Kornsjø** Østfold, S Norway 58°55′N 11°40′E
77 O11 **Koro** Mopti, S Mali 14°05′N 03°06′W
1873 Y14 **Koro** island C Fiji
186 B7 **Koroba** Hela, W Papua New Guinea 05°46′S 142°48′E
126 K8 **Korocha** Belgorodskaya Oblast', W Russia 50°49′N 37°08′E
136 H12 **Köroğlu Dağları** ▲▲ C Turkey
183 V6 **Korogoro Point** headland New South Wales, SE Australia 31°03′S 153°04′E
81 J21 **Korogwe** Tanga, E Tanzania 05°10′S 38°30′E
182 L13 **Koroit** Victoria, SE Australia 38°17′S 142°22′E
187 X15 **Korolevu** Viti Levu, W Fiji 18°12′S 177°44′E
190 I17 **Koromiri** island S Cook Islands
171 Q8 **Koronadal** Mindanao, S Philippines 06°23′N 124°54′E
114 G13 **Koróneia, Límni** var. Límni Korónia. ◎ N Greece
115 E22 **Koróni** Pelopónnisos, S Greece 36°47′N 21°57′E
**Korónia, Límni** see Koróneia, Límni
110 I9 **Koronowo** Ger. Krone an der Brahe. Kujawski-pomorskie, C Poland 53°18′N 17°56′E
117 R2 **Korop** Chernihivs'ka Oblast', N Ukraine 51°35′N 32°57′E
115 H19 **Koropí** Attikí, C Greece 37°54′N 23°52′E
188 C8 **Koror** Oreor, N Palau 07°21′N 134°28′E
**Koror** see Oreor
**Koror Lal Esan** see Karor
**Koror Pacca** see Kahror Pakka
111 L23 **Körös** ≈ E Hungary
**Kőrös** see Križevci
**Körösbánya** see Baia de Criș
187 Y14 **Koro Sea** sea C Fiji
**Koroška** see Kärnten
117 N3 **Korosten'** Zhytomyrs'ka Oblast', NW Ukraine 50°56′N 28°39′E
**Korostyshev** see Korostyshiv
117 N4 **Korostyshiv** Rus. Korostyshev. Zhytomyrs'ka Oblast', N Ukraine 50°18′N 29°05′E
125 V3 **Korotaikha** ≈ NW Russia
122 J9 **Korotchayevo** Yamalo-Nenetskiy Avtonomnyy Okrug, N Russia 66°00′N 78°11′E
78 I8 **Koro Toro** Borkou, N Chad 16°01′N 18°27′E
39 N16 **Korovin Island** island Shumagin Islands, Alaska, USA
187 X14 **Korovou** Viti Levu, W Fiji 17°48′S 178°32′E
93 M17 **Korpilahti** Keski-Suomi, C Finland 62°02′N 25°34′E
92 K12 **Korpilombolo** Lapp. Dállogilli. Norrbotten, N Sweden 66°51′N 23°00′E
123 T13 **Korsakov** Ostrov Sakhalin, Sakhalinskaya Oblast', SE Russia 46°41′N 142°45′E
93 J16 **Korsholm** Fin. Mustasaari. Österbotten, W Finland 63°05′N 21°43′E
95 I23 **Korsør** Sjælland, E Denmark 55°19′N 11°09′E
**Korsovka** see Kārsava
117 P6 **Korsun'-Shevchenkivs'kyy** Rus. Korsun'-Shevchenkovskiy. Cherkas'ka Oblast', C Ukraine 49°26′N 31°15′E
**Korsun'-Shevchenkovskiy** see Korsun'-Shevchenkivs'kyy
99 C17 **Kortemark** West-Vlaanderen, W Belgium 51°03′N 03°03′E
99 H18 **Kortenberg** Vlaams Brabant, C Belgium 50°53′N 04°33′E
99 K18 **Kortessem** Limburg, NE Belgium 50°52′N 05°22′E
99 E14 **Kortgene** Zeeland, SW Netherlands 51°34′N 03°48′E
80 F8 **Korti** Northern, N Sudan 18°06′N 31°33′E
99 C18 **Kortrijk** Fr. Courtrai. West-Vlaanderen, W Belgium 50°50′N 03°17′E
121 O2 **Koruçam Burnu** var. Cape Kormakiti, Kormakítis, Gk. Akrotírio Kormakítis. headland N Cyprus 35°24′N 32°55′E
183 O13 **Korumburra** Victoria, SE Australia 38°27′S 145°48′E
**Koryak Range** see Koryakskoye Nagor'ye
**Koryakskiy Khrebet** see Koryakskoye Nagor'ye
123 V8 **Koryakskiy Okrug** ◈ autonomous district E Russia
123 V7 **Koryakskoye Nagor'ye** var. Koryakskiy Khrebet, Eng. Koryak Range. ▲▲ NE Russia
125 P11 **Koryazhma** Arkhangel'skaya Oblast', NW Russia 61°16′N 47°07′E
**Kōryō** see Gangneung
**Korytsa** see Korçë
117 Q2 **Koryukivka** Chernihivs'ka Oblast', N Ukraine 51°45′N 32°16′E
**Korzec** see Korets'
115 N21 **Kos** Kos, Dodekánisa, Greece, Aegean Sea 36°53′N 27°19′E
115 M21 **Kos** It. Coo; anc. Cos. island Dodekánisa, Greece, Aegean Sea
125 T12 **Kosa** Komi-Permyatskiy Okrug, NW Russia 59°55′N 54°54′E
125 T13 **Kosa** ≈ NW Russia
164 B12 **Kō-saki** headland Nagasaki, Tsushima, SW Japan 34°06′N 129°13′E
163 X13 **Kosan** SE North Korea 38°50′N 127°26′E
119 H18 **Kosava** Rus. Kosovo. Brestskaya Voblasts', SW Belarus 52°45′N 25°16′E
**Kosch** see Kose
**Koschagyl** see Kosshagyl
110 G12 **Kościan** Ger. Kosten. Wielkopolskie, C Poland 52°05′N 16°38′E
110 I7 **Kościerzyna** Pomorskie, NW Poland 54°07′N 17°55′E
22 L4 **Kosciusko** Mississippi, S USA 33°03′N 89°35′W
**Kosciusko, Mount** see Kosciuszko, Mount
183 R11 **Kosciuszko, Mount** prev. Mount Kosciusko. ▲ New South Wales, SE Australia 36°28′S 148°15′E
118 H4 **Kose** Ger. Kosch. Harjumaa, NW Estonia 59°11′N 25°10′E
25 U9 **Kosse** Texas, SW USA 31°16′N 96°38′W
114 G6 **Koshava** Vidin, NW Bulgaria 44°03′N 23°00′E
147 U9 **Kosh-Dëbë** var. Koshtebë. Narynskaya Oblast', C Kyrgyzstan 41°03′N 74°08′E
**K'o-shih** see Kashi
164 B12 **Koshikijima-rettō** var. Kosikizima Rettô. island group SW Japan
145 W13 **Koshkarkol', Ozero** ◎ SE Kazakhstan
30 L9 **Koshkonong, Lake** ◎ Wisconsin, N USA
**Koshoba** see Goşabo
**Koshoba** see Goşoba


◆ Country
● Country Capital
◇ Dependent Territory
○ Dependent Territory Capital
◈ Administrative Regions
✈ International Airport
▲ Mountain
▲▲ Mountain Range
⛰ Volcano
≈ River
◎ Lake
▣ Reservoir

KŌSHOKU – KSAR EL BOUKHARI

164 M12 **Kōshoku** var. Kôsyoku. Nagano, Honshū, S Japan 36°33′N 138°09′E
**Koshtebë** see Kosh-Dëbë
**Kōshū** see Enzan
**Kōshū** see Gwangju
111 N19 **Košice** Ger. Kaschau, Hung. Kassa. Košický Kraj, E Slovakia 48°44′N 21°15′E
111 M20 **Košický Kraj** ⬖ region E Slovakia
**Kosikizima Rettô** see Koshikijima-rettō
153 R12 **Kosi Reservoir** ⊠ E Nepal
116 J8 **Kosiv** Ivano-Frankivs'ka Oblast', W Ukraine 48°19′N 25°04′E
145 O11 **Koskol'** Kaz. Qosköl. Karaganda, C Kazakhstan 49°32′N 67°08′E
125 Q9 **Koslan** Respublika Komi, NW Russia 63°27′N 48°52′E
**Köslin** see Koszalin
146 M12 **Koson** Rus. Kasan. Qashqadaryo Viloyati, S Uzbekistan 39°04′N 65°35′E
**Kosŏng** see Goseong
147 S9 **Kosonsoy** Rus. Kasansay. Namangan Viloyati, E Uzbekistan 41°15′N 71°28′E
**Kosova** see Kosovo
**Kosova, Republika** see Kosovo
**Kosovës, Republika e** see Kosovo
113 M16 **Kosovo** off. Republic of Kosovo; prev. Autonomous Province of Kosovo and Metohija, Alb. Kosova, Republika e Kosovës, Serb. Kosovo, Republika Kosova. ◆ republic (not recognised by the UN) SE Europe
**Kosovo** see Kosava
**Kosovo and Metohija, Autonomous Province of** see Kosovo
**Kosovo Polje** see Fushë Kosovë
**Kosovo, Republic of** see Kosovo
**Kosovska Kamenica** see Kamenicë
**Kosovska Mitrovica** see Mitrovicë
189 X17 **Kosrae** ⬖ state E Micronesia
189 Y14 **Kosrae** prev. Kusaie. island Caroline Islands, E Micronesia
109 P6 **Kössen** Tirol, W Austria 47°40′N 12°24′E
144 G12 **Kosshagyl** prev. Koschagyl, Kaz. Qosshaghyl. Atyrau, W Kazakhstan 46°52′N 53°46′E
76 M16 **Kossou, Lac de** ◎ C Ivory Coast
**Kossukavak** see Krumovgrad
**Kostajnica** see Hrvatska Kostanjnica
**Kostamus** see Kostomuksha
144 M7 **Kostanay** var. Kustanay, Kaz. Qostanay. Kostanay, N Kazakhstan 53°16′N 63°34′E
144 L8 **Kostanay** var. Kostanayskaya Oblast', Kaz. Qostanay Oblysy. ⬖ province N Kazakhstan
**Kostanayskaya Oblast'** see Kostanay
**Kosten** see Kościan
114 H10 **Kostenets** prev. Georgi Dimitrov. Sofia, W Bulgaria 42°15′N 23°48′E
80 F10 **Kosti** White Nile, C Sudan 13°11′N 32°38′E
**Kostnitz** see Konstanz
124 H7 **Kostomuksha** Fin. Kostamus. Respublika Kareliya, NW Russia 64°33′N 30°28′E
116 K3 **Kostopil'** Rus. Kostopol'. Rivnens'ka Oblast', NW Ukraine 50°20′N 26°29′E
**Kostopol'** see Kostopil'
124 M15 **Kostroma** Kostromskaya Oblast', NW Russia 57°46′N 41°E
125 N14 **Kostroma** ≈ NW Russia
125 N14 **Kostromskaya Oblast'** ⬖ province NW Russia
110 D11 **Kostrzyn** Ger. Cüstrin, Küstrin. Lubuskie, W Poland 52°35′N 14°40′E
110 H11 **Kostrzyn** Wielkopolskie, C Poland 52°23′N 17°13′E
117 X7 **Kostyantynivka** Rus. Konstantinovka. Donets'ka Oblast', SE Ukraine
**Kostyukovichi** see Kastsyukovichy
**Kostyukovka** see Kastsyukowka
**Kôsyoku** see Kōshoku
125 U6 **Kos'yu** Respublika Komi, NW Russia 65°39′N 59°01′E
125 U6 **Kos'yu** ≈ NW Russia
110 F7 **Koszalin** Ger. Köslin. Zachodnio-pomorskie, NW Poland 54°12′N 16°10′E
111 F22 **Kőszeg** Ger. Güns. Vas, W Hungary 47°23′N 16°33′E
152 H13 **Kota** prev. Kotah. Rājasthān, N India 25°14′N 75°52′E
**Kota Baharu** see Kota Bharu
**Kota Bahru** see Kota Bharu
169 U13 **Kotabaru** Pulau Laut, C Indonesia 03°15′S 116°15′E
168 K12 **Kota Baru** Sumatera, W Indonesia 01°07′S 101°43′E
**Kotabaru** see Jayapura
168 K6 **Kota Bharu** var. Kota Baharu, Kota Bahru. Kelantan, Peninsular Malaysia 06°07′N 102°15′E
**Kotaboemi** see Kotabumi
168 M14 **Kotabumi** prev. Kotaboemi. Sumatera, W Indonesia 04°50′S 104°54′E
149 S10 **Kot Addu** Punjab, E Pakistan 30°28′N 70°58′E
**Kotah** see Kota
169 U7 **Kota Kinabalu** prev. Jesselton. Sabah, East Malaysia 05°59′N 116°04′E
169 U7 **Kota Kinabalu** ✈ Sabah, East Malaysia 05°59′N 116°04′E
92 M12 **Kotala** Lappi, N Finland 67°01′N 29°00′E
**Kotamobagoe** see Kotamobagu
171 Q11 **Kotamobagu** prev. Kotamobagoe. Sulawesi, C Indonesia 0°46′N 124°21′E
155 L14 **Kotapad** var. Kotapārh. Odisha, E India 19°10′N 82°23′E
**Kotapārh** see Kotapad
166 N17 **Ko Ta Ru Tao** island SW Thailand
169 R13 **Kotawaringin, Teluk** bay Borneo, C Indonesia
149 Q13 **Kot Diji** Sindh, SE Pakistan 27°16′N 68°44′E
152 K9 **Kotdwāra** Uttarākhand, N India 29°44′N 78°33′E
125 Q14 **Kotel'nich** Kirovskaya Oblast', NW Russia 58°19′N 48°12′E
127 N12 **Kotel'nikovo** Volgogradskaya Oblast', SW Russia 47°37′N 43°07′E
123 Q6 **Kotel'nyy, Ostrov** island Novosibirskiye Ostrova, N Russia
117 T5 **Kotel'va** Poltavs'ka Oblast', C Ukraine 50°04′N 34°46′E
101 M14 **Köthen** var. Cöthen. Sachsen-Anhalt, C Germany 51°46′N 11°59′E
**Kôti** see Kōchi
81 G17 **Kotido** NE Uganda 03°03′N 34°07′E
93 N19 **Kotka** Kymenlaakso, S Finland 60°28′N 26°55′E
125 P11 **Kotlas** Arkhangel'skaya Oblast', NW Russia 61°14′N 46°43′E
38 M10 **Kotlik** Alaska, USA 63°01′N 163°33′W
77 Q17 **Kotoka** ✈ (Accra) S Ghana 05°41′N 00°10′W
**Kotonu** see Cotonou
113 J17 **Kotor** It. Cattaro. SW Montenegro 42°25′N 18°47′E
**Kotor** see Kotoriba
112 F7 **Kotoriba** Hung. Kotor. Medimurje, N Croatia 46°20′N 16°47′E
113 I17 **Kotorska, Boka** It. Bocche di Cattaro. bay SW Montenegro
112 H11 **Kotorsko** ⬖ Republika Srpska, N Bosnia and Herzegovina
112 G11 **Kotor Varoš** ⬖ Republika Srpska, N Bosnia and Herzegovina
**Koto Sho/Kotosho** see Lan Yu
126 M7 **Kotovsk** Tambovskaya Oblast', W Russia 52°39′N 41°31′E
**Kotovsk** see Hîncești
119 G16 **Kotra** ≈ W Belarus
149 P16 **Kotri** Sindh, SE Pakistan 25°22′N 68°18′E
109 Q9 **Kötschach** Kärnten, S Austria 46°41′N 12°57′E
155 K15 **Kottagūdem** Telangana, E India 17°36′N 80°40′E
155 F21 **Kottappadi** Kerala, SW India 11°38′N 76°03′E
155 G23 **Kottayam** Kerala, SW India 09°34′N 76°31′E
**Kottbus** see Cottbus
79 K15 **Kotto** ≈ Central African Republic/Dem. Rep. Congo
193 X15 **Kotu Group** island group W Tonga
**Koturdepe** see Goturdepe
122 M9 **Kotuy** ≈ N Russia
83 M16 **Kotwa** Mashonaland East, NE Zimbabwe 16°58′S 32°46′E
39 N7 **Kotzebue** Alaska, USA 66°54′N 162°36′W
38 M7 **Kotzebue Sound** inlet Alaska, USA
**Kotzenan** see Chocianów
**Kotzman** see Kitsman'
77 R14 **Kouandé** NW Benin 10°20′N 01°42′E
79 J15 **Kouango** Ouaka, S Central African Republic 05°00′N 20°01′E
77 O13 **Koudougou** C Burkina Faso 12°15′N 02°23′W
98 K7 **Koudum** Fryslân, N Netherlands 52°55′N 05°26′E
115 L25 **Koufonísi** island SE Greece
115 K21 **Koufonísi** island Kykládes, Greece, Aegean Sea
38 M8 **Kougarok Mountain** ▲ Alaska, USA 65°41′N 165°29′W
79 E21 **Kouilou** ⬖ department SW Congo
79 E20 **Kouilou** ≈ S Congo
167 Q11 **Koŭk Kduŏch** prev. Phumĭ Koŭk Kduŏch. Battambang, NW Cambodia 13°16′N 103°08′E
121 O3 **Koúklia** SW Cyprus 34°42′N 32°35′E
79 E19 **Koulamoutou** Ogooué-Lolo, C Gabon 01°07′S 12°27′E
76 L12 **Koulikoro** Koulikoro, SW Mali 12°55′N 07°31′W
76 L11 **Koulikoro** ⬖ region SW Mali
187 P16 **Koumac** Province Nord, W New Caledonia 20°34′S 164°18′E
165 N12 **Koumi** Nagano, Honshū, S Japan 36°06′N 138°27′E
78 I13 **Koumra** Mandoul, S Chad 08°56′N 17°32′E
**Kounadougou** see Koundougou
76 M15 **Kounahiri** C Ivory Coast 07°47′N 05°51′W
76 I12 **Koundâra** Moyenne-Guinée, NW Guinea 12°28′N 13°15′W
77 N13 **Koundougou** var. Kounadougou. C Burkina Faso 11°43′N 04°40′W
76 H11 **Koungheul** C Senegal 14°00′N 14°48′W
**Kounradskiy** see Konyrat
25 X10 **Kountze** Texas, SW USA 30°22′N 94°20′W
77 Q13 **Koupéla** C Burkina Faso 12°07′N 00°21′W
77 N13 **Kouri** Sikasso, SW Mali 12°09′N 04°46′W
55 Y9 **Kourou** N French Guiana 05°08′N 52°37′W
114 J12 **Kouroú** ≈ NE Greece
76 K14 **Kouroussa** C Guinea 10°40′N 09°50′W
**Kousseir** see Al Quşayr
78 G11 **Kousséri** prev. Fort-Foureau. Extrême-Nord, NE Cameroon 12°05′N 14°56′E
**Kouteifé** see Al Quţayfah
76 M13 **Koutiala** Sikasso, S Mali 12°20′N 05°23′W
76 M14 **Kouto** NW Ivory Coast 09°51′N 06°25′W
93 M19 **Kouvola** Kymenlaakso, S Finland 60°50′N 26°43′E
79 G18 **Kouyou** ≈ C Congo
112 M10 **Kovačica** Hung. Antafalva; prev. Kovacsicza. Vojvodina, N Serbia 45°08′N 20°36′E
**Kovacsicza** see Kovačica
**Kővárhosszúfalu** see Satulung
**Kovászna** see Covasna
124 I4 **Kovdor** Murmanskaya Oblast', NW Russia 67°32′N 30°27′E
116 J3 **Kovel'** Pol. Kowel. Volyns'ka Oblast', NW Ukraine 51°14′N 24°43′E
112 M11 **Kovin** Hung. Kevevára; prev. Temes-Kubin. Vojvodina, NE Serbia 44°45′N 20°59′E
**Kovno** see Kaunas
127 N3 **Kovrov** Vladimirskaya Oblast', W Russia 56°24′N 41°21′E
127 O5 **Kovylkino** Respublika Mordoviya, W Russia 54°03′N 43°52′E
110 J11 **Kowal** Kujawsko-pomorskie, C Poland 52°31′N 19°09′E
110 J9 **Kowalewo Pomorskie** Ger. Schönsee. Kujawsko-pomorskie, N Poland 53°07′N 18°48′E
**Kowasna** see Covasna
119 M16 **Kowbcha** Rus. Kolbcha. Mahilyowskaya Voblasts', E Belarus 53°39′N 29°14′E
**Koweit** see Kuwait
**Kowel** see Kovel'
185 F17 **Kowhitirangi** West Coast, South Island, New Zealand 42°54′S 171°01′E
161 O15 **Kowloon** Hong Kong, S China
**Kowno** see Kaunas
159 N7 **Kox Kuduk** well NW China
136 D16 **Köyceğiz** Muğla, SW Turkey 36°57′N 28°40′E
125 N6 **Koyda** Arkhangel'skaya Oblast', NW Russia 66°22′N 42°42′E
139 T3 **Koye** Ar. Küysanjaq, var. Koi Sanjaq. Arbīl, N Iraq 36°05′N 44°38′E
**Koymat** see Goymat
**Koymatdag, Gory** see Goymatdag, Gory
151 E15 **Koyna Reservoir** ⊠ W India
165 P9 **Koyoshi-gawa** ≈ Honshū, C Japan
**Koi Sanjaq** see Koye
**Koytash** see Qo'ytosh
146 M14 **Köýtendag** prev. Rus. Charshanga, Charshangy, Turkm. Charshangngy. Lebap Welaýaty, E Turkmenistan 37°31′N 65°58′E
39 N9 **Koyuk** Alaska, USA 64°55′N 161°09′W
39 N9 **Koyuk River** ≈ Alaska, USA
39 O9 **Koyukuk** Alaska, USA 64°52′N 157°42′W
39 O9 **Koyukuk River** ≈ Alaska, USA
136 J13 **Kozaklı** Nevşehir, C Turkey 39°12′N 34°48′E
136 K16 **Kozan** Adana, S Turkey 37°27′N 35°47′E
115 E14 **Kozáni** Dytikí Makedonía, N Greece 40°19′N 21°48′E
112 F10 **Kozara** ▲▲ NW Bosnia and Herzegovina
**Kozarska Dubica** see Bosanska Dubica
117 P3 **Kozelets'** Rus. Kozelets. Chernihivs'ka Oblast', NE Ukraine 50°54′N 31°09′E
**Kozelets** see Kozelets'
117 S6 **Kozel'shchyna** Poltavs'ka Oblast', C Ukraine 49°13′N 33°49′E
126 J5 **Kozel'sk** Kaluzhskaya Oblast', W Russia 54°04′N 35°51′E
155 F21 **Kozhikode** var. Calicut. Kerala, SW India 11°17′N 75°49′E
**Kozhimiz, Gora** see Kozhymiz, Gora
124 L9 **Kozhozero, Ozero** ◎ NW Russia
125 T7 **Kozhva** Respublika Komi, NW Russia 65°06′N 57°00′E
125 T7 **Kozhva** ≈ NW Russia
125 U6 **Kozhym** Respublika Komi, NW Russia 65°43′N 59°25′E
125 V9 **Kozhymiz, Gora** prev. Gora Kozhimiz. ▲ NW Russia 63°13′N 58°54′E
110 N13 **Kozienice** Mazowieckie, C Poland 51°35′N 21°31′E
109 S13 **Kozina** SW Slovenia 45°36′N 13°56′E
114 H7 **Kozloduy** Vratsa, NW Bulgaria 43°48′N 23°42′E
127 Q3 **Kozlovka** Chuvashskaya Respublika, W Russia 55°53′N 48°07′E
**Kozlovshchina/Kozlowszczyzna** see Kazlowshchyna
127 P3 **Koz'modem'yansk** Respublika Mariy El, W Russia 56°19′N 46°33′E
116 J6 **Kozova** Ternopil's'ka Oblast', W Ukraine 49°25′N 25°09′E
165 N15 **Kōzu-shima** island E Japan
**Koz'yany** see Kazyany
117 N5 **Kozyatyn** Rus. Kazatin. Vinnyts'ka Oblast', C Ukraine 49°41′N 28°49′E
77 Q16 **Kpalimé** var. Palimé. SW Togo 06°54′N 00°38′E
77 Q16 **Kpandu** E Ghana 07°00′N 00°18′E
99 F15 **Krabbendijke** Zeeland, SW Netherlands 51°25′N 04°07′E
167 N15 **Krabi** var. Muang Krabi. Krabi, SW Thailand 08°04′N 98°52′E
167 N13 **Kra Buri** Ranong, SW Thailand 10°25′N 98°48′E
**Krâchéh** see Kratie
95 G17 **Kragerø** Telemark, S Norway 58°54′N 09°25′E
112 M13 **Kragujevac** Serbia, C Serbia 44°01′N 20°55′E
**Krainburg** see Kranj
166 N13 **Kra, Isthmus of** isthmus Malaysia/Thailand
112 D12 **Krajina** cultural region SW Croatia
**Krakatau, Pulau** see Rakata, Pulau
**Krakau** see Kraków
111 L16 **Kraków** Eng. Cracow, Ger. Krakau; anc. Cracovia. Małopolskie, S Poland 50°03′N 19°58′E
100 L9 **Krakower See** ◎ NE Germany
167 Q11 **Krâlănh** Siem Reap, NW Cambodia 13°35′N 103°27′E
45 Q16 **Kralendijk** ○ Bonaire 12°07′N 68°13′W
112 B10 **Kraljevica** It. Porto Re. Primorje-Gorski Kotar, NW Croatia 45°15′N 14°36′E
112 M13 **Kraljevo** prev. Rankovićevo. Serbia, C Serbia 43°44′N 20°40′E
111 E16 **Královehradecký Kraj** prev. Hradecký Kraj. ⬖ region N Czechia
**Kralup an der Moldau** see Kralupy nad Vltavou
111 C16 **Kralupy nad Vltavou** Ger. Kralup an der Moldau. Středočeský Kraj, NW Czechia 50°15′N 14°20′E
117 W7 **Kramators'k** Rus. Kramatorsk. Donets'ka Oblast', SE Ukraine 48°43′N 37°34′E
**Kramatorsk** see Kramators'k
93 H17 **Kramfors** Västernorrland, C Sweden 62°55′N 17°50′E
**Kranéa** see Kraniá
108 M7 **Kranebitten** ✈ (Innsbruck) Tirol, W Austria 47°18′N 11°21′E
115 D15 **Kraniá** var. Kranéa. Dytikí Makedonía, N Greece 39°54′N 21°21′E
115 G20 **Kranídi** Pelopónnisos, S Greece 37°21′N 23°09′E
109 T11 **Kranj** Ger. Krainburg. NW Slovenia 46°17′N 14°16′E
115 F16 **Krannón** battleground Thessalía, C Greece
**Kranz** see Zelenogradsk
112 D7 **Krapina** Krapina-Zagorje, N Croatia 46°12′N 15°52′E
112 E8 **Krapina** ≈ N Croatia
112 D8 **Krapina-Zagorje** off. Krapinsko-Zagorska Županija. ⬖ province N Croatia
114 L7 **Krapinets** ≈ NE Bulgaria
**Krapinsko-Zagorska Županija** see Krapina-Zagorje
111 I15 **Krapkowice** Ger. Krappitz. Opolskie, SW Poland 50°29′N 17°56′E
**Krappitz** see Krapkowice
125 O12 **Krasavino** Vologodskaya Oblast', NW Russia 60°56′N 46°27′E
122 H6 **Krasino** Novaya Zemlya, Arkhangel'skaya Oblast', N Russia 70°45′N 54°16′E
123 S15 **Kraskino** Primorskiy Kray, SE Russia 42°40′N 130°51′E
118 J11 **Krāslava** SE Latvia 55°56′N 27°08′E
119 M14 **Krasnaluki** Rus. Krasnoluki. Vitsyebskaya Voblasts', N Belarus 54°37′N 28°50′E
119 P17 **Krasnapollye** Rus. Krasnopol'ye. Mahilyowskaya Voblasts', E Belarus 53°20′N 31°24′E
126 L15 **Krasnaya Polyana** Krasnodarskiy Kray, SW Russia 43°40′N 40°13′E
**Krasnaya Slabada / Krasnaya Sloboda** see Chyrvonaya Slabada
119 J15 **Krasnaye** Rus. Krasnoye. Minskaya Voblasts', C Belarus 54°14′N 27°05′E
111 O14 **Kraśnik** Ger. Kratznick. Lubelskie, E Poland 50°56′N 22°14′E
**Krasni Okny** see Okny
127 P8 **Krasnoarmeysk** Saratovskaya Oblast', W Russia 51°02′N 45°42′E
**Krasnoarmeysk** see Tayynsha
123 T6 **Krasnoarmeyskiy** Chukotskiy Avtonomnyy Okrug, NE Russia 69°30′N 171°44′E
**Krasnoarmiys'k** see Krasnoarmiys'k/Tayynsha
125 P11 **Krasnoborsk** Arkhangel'skaya Oblast', NW Russia 61°31′N 45°57′E
126 K14 **Krasnodar** prev. Ekaterinodar, Yekaterinodar. Krasnodarskiy Kray, SW Russia 45°06′N 39°01′E
126 K13 **Krasnodarskiy Kray** ⬖ territory SW Russia
**Krasnodon** see Sorokyne
**Krasnogor** see Kallaste
127 T2 **Krasnogorskoye** Udmurtskaya Respublika, NW Russia 57°42′N 52°29′E
**Krasnograd** see Krasnohrad
**Krasnogvardeysk** see Bulungh'ur
126 M13 **Krasnogvardeyskoye** Stavropol'skiy Kray, SW Russia 45°49′N 41°31′E
117 U6 **Krasnohrad** Rus. Krasnograd. Kharkivs'ka Oblast', E Ukraine 49°22′N 35°28′E
**Krasnohvardiys'ke** see Kurman
123 P14 **Krasnokamensk** Zabaykal'skiy Kray, S Russia 50°03′N 118°01′E
125 U14 **Krasnokamsk** Permskiy Kray, W Russia 58°08′N 55°48′E
127 U8 **Krasnokholm** Orenburgskaya Oblast', W Russia 51°34′N 54°11′E
117 U5 **Krasnokuts'k** Rus. Krasnokutsk. Kharkivs'ka Oblast', E Ukraine 50°01′N 35°03′E
**Krasnokutsk** see Krasnokuts'k
126 L7 **Krasnolesnyy** Voronezhskaya Oblast', W Russia 51°53′N 39°37′E
**Krasnoluki** see Krasnaluki
**Krasnoosol'skoye Vodokhranilishche** see Chervonooskil's'ke Vodoskhovyshche
**Krasnoperekops'k** see Yany Kapu
117 U4 **Krasnopillya** Sums'ka Oblast', NE Ukraine 50°46′N 35°17′E
**Krasnopol'ye** see Krasnapollye
124 L5 **Krasnoshchel'ye** Murmanskaya Oblast', NW Russia 67°22′N 37°03′E
127 O5 **Krasnoslobodsk** Respublika Mordoviya, W Russia 54°24′N 43°51′E
127 T2 **Krasnoslobodsk** Volgogradskaya Oblast', SW Russia 48°41′N 44°34′E
**Krasnostav** see Krasnystaw
127 V5 **Krasnousol'skiy** Respublika Bashkortostan, W Russia 53°55′N 56°22′E
125 U12 **Krasnovishersk** Permskiy Kray, NW Russia 60°22′N 57°04′E
**Krasnovodsk** see Türkmenbaşy
**Krasnovodskiy Zaliv** see Türkmenbasy Aylagy
146 B10 **Krasnovodskoye Plato** Turkm. Krasnowodsk Platosy. plateau NW Turkmenistan
**Krasnowodsk Aylagy** see Türkmenbasy Aylagy
**Krasnowodsk Platosy** see Krasnovodskoye Plato
122 K12 **Krasnoyarsk** Krasnoyarskiy Kray, S Russia 56°05′N 92°46′E
127 X7 **Krasnoyarskiy** Orenburgskaya Oblast', W Russia 51°56′N 59°54′E
122 K11 **Krasnoyarskiy Kray** ⬖ territory C Russia
**Krasnoye** see Krasnaye
**Krasnoye Znamya** see Gyzylbaydak
125 R11 **Krasnozatonskiy** Respublika Komi, NW Russia 61°39′N 51°00′E
118 D13 **Krasnoznamensk** prev. Lasdehnen, Ger. Haselberg. Kaliningradskaya Oblast', W Russia 54°57′N 22°28′E
126 K3 **Krasnoznamensk** Moskovskaya Oblast', W Russia 55°40′N 37°05′E
117 R11 **Krasnoznam"yans'kyy Kanal** canal S Ukraine
111 P14 **Krasnystaw** Rus. Krasnostav. Lubelskie, SE Poland 51°N 23°10′E
126 H4 **Krasnyy** Smolenskaya Oblast', W Russia 54°36′N 31°27′E
127 P2 **Krasnyye Baki** Nizhegorodskaya Oblast', W Russia 57°07′N 45°12′E
127 Q13 **Krasnyye Barrikady** Astrakhanskaya Oblast', SW Russia 46°14′N 47°48′E
124 K15 **Krasnyy Kholm** Tverskaya Oblast', W Russia 58°04′N 37°05′E
127 Q8 **Krasnyy Kut** Saratovskaya Oblast', W Russia 50°54′N 46°58′E
**Krasnyy Luch** see Khrustal'nyy
**Krasnyy Lyman** see Lyman
127 R3 **Krasnyy Steklovar** Respublika Mariy El, W Russia 56°14′N 48°49′E
127 P8 **Krasnyy Tekstil'shchik** Saratovskaya Oblast', W Russia 51°35′N 45°49′E
127 R13 **Krasnyy Yar** Astrakhanskaya Oblast', SW Russia 46°33′N 48°21′E
**Krassóvár** see Caraşova
116 L5 **Krasyliv** Khmel'nyts'ka Oblast', W Ukraine 49°38′N 26°59′E
111 O21 **Kraszna** Rom. Crasna. ≈ Hungary/Romania
167 S12 **Kratie** var. Krâchéh. Kratie, E Cambodia 12°29′N 106°01′E
113 P17 **Kratovo** NE North Macedonia 42°04′N 22°08′E
**Kratznick** see Kraśnik
171 Y13 **Krau** Papua, E Indonesia 03°15′S 140°07′E
167 Q13 **Krâvanh, Chuŏr Phnum** Eng. Cardamom Mountains, Fr. Chaîne des Cardamomes. ▲▲ W Cambodia
**Kravasta Lagoon** see Karavastasë, Laguna e
**Krawang** see Karawang
127 Q15 **Kraynovka** Respublika Dagestan, SW Russia 43°58′N 47°24′E
118 D12 **Kražiai** Šiaulai, C Lithuania 55°36′N 22°41′E
27 P11 **Krebs** Oklahoma, C USA 34°55′N 95°43′W
101 D15 **Krefeld** Nordrhein-Westfalen, W Germany 51°20′N 06°34′E
**Kreisstadt** see Krosno Odrzańskie
115 D17 **Kremastón, Technití Límni** ⊠ C Greece
**Kremenchug** see Kremenchuk
**Kremenchugskoye Vodokhranilishche/Kremenchuk Reservoir** see Kremenchuts'ke Vodoskhovyshche
117 S6 **Kremenchuk** Rus. Kremenchug. Poltavs'ka Oblast', NE Ukraine 49°04′N 33°27′E
117 R6 **Kremenchuts'ke Vodoskhovyshche** Eng. Kremenchuk Reservoir, Rus. Kremenchugskoye Vodokhranilishche. ⊠ C Ukraine
116 K5 **Kremenets'** Pol. Krzemieniec, Rus. Kremenets. Ternopil's'ka Oblast', W Ukraine 50°06′N 25°43′E
**Kremennaya** see Kreminna
117 X6 **Kreminna** Rus. Kremennaya. Luhans'ka Oblast', E Ukraine 49°03′N 38°15′E
37 R4 **Kremmling** Colorado, C USA 40°03′N 106°23′W
109 V3 **Krems** ≈ NE Austria
**Krems** see Krems an der Donau
109 W3 **Krems an der Donau** var. Krems. Niederösterreich, N Austria 48°25′N 15°36′E
**Kremsier** see Kroměříž
109 S4 **Kremsmünster** Oberösterreich, N Austria 48°04′N 14°08′E
38 M17 **Krenitzin Islands** island Aleutian Islands, Alaska, USA
**Kresena** see Kresna
114 G11 **Kresna** var. Kresena. Blagoevgrad, SW Bulgaria 41°43′N 23°10′E
112 O12 **Krespoljin** Serbia, E Serbia 44°22′N 21°36′E
25 N4 **Kress** Texas, SW USA 34°21′N 101°43′W
123 V6 **Kresta, Zaliv** bay E Russia
115 D20 **Kréstena** prev. Selinoús. Dytikí Elláda, S Greece 37°36′N 21°36′E
124 H14 **Kresttsy** Novgorodskaya Oblast', W Russia 58°15′N 32°28′E
**Kretikon Delagos** see Kritikó Pélagos
118 C11 **Kretinga** Ger. Krottingen. Klaipėda, NW Lithuania 55°53′N 21°13′E
**Kreutz** see Cristuru Secuiesc
**Kreuz** see Križevci, Croatia
**Kreuz** see Risti, Estonia
**Kreuzburg/Kreuzburg in Oberschlesien** see Kluczbork
**Kreuzingen** see Bol'shakovo
108 H6 **Kreuzlingen** Thurgau, NE Switzerland 47°38′N 09°12′E
101 K25 **Kreuzspitze** ▲ S Germany 47°30′N 10°55′E
101 F16 **Kreuztal** Nordrhein-Westfalen, W Germany 50°58′N 08°00′E
119 I15 **Kreva** Rus. Krevo. Hrodzyenskaya Voblasts', W Belarus 54°19′N 26°17′E
**Krevo** see Kreva
**Kría Vrísi** see Krýa Vrýsi
79 D16 **Kribi** Sud, SW Cameroon 02°53′N 09°57′E
**Krichëv** see Krychaw
**Krickerhäu/Kriegerhaj** see Handlová
109 W6 **Krieglach** Steiermark, E Austria 47°33′N 15°37′E
108 F8 **Kriens** Luzern, W Switzerland 47°03′N 08°17′E
**Krievija** see Russia
**Krimmitschau** see Crimmitschau
98 H12 **Krimpen aan den IJssel** Zuid-Holland, SW Netherlands 51°56′N 04°39′E
**Krindachevka** see Khrustal'nyy
115 G25 **Kríos, Akrotírio** headland Kríti, Greece, E Mediterranean Sea 35°17′N 23°31′E
155 J16 **Krishna** prev. Kistna. ≈ C India
155 H20 **Krishnagiri** Tamil Nādu, SE India 12°33′N 78°11′E
155 K17 **Krishna, Mouths of the** delta SE India
153 S15 **Krishnanagar** West Bengal, N India 23°22′N 88°32′E
155 G20 **Krishnarājāsāgara** var. Paradip. ⊠ W India
95 N19 **Kristdala** Kalmar, S Sweden 57°24′N 16°12′E
**Kristiania** see Oslo
95 E18 **Kristiansand** var. Christiansand. Vest-Agder, S Norway 58°08′N 07°52′E
95 L22 **Kristianstad** Skåne, S Sweden 56°02′N 14°10′E
94 F8 **Kristiansund** var. Christiansund. Møre og Romsdal, S Norway 63°07′N 07°45′E
**Kristiinankaupunki** see Kristinestad
93 I14 **Kristineberg** Västerbotten, N Sweden 65°07′N 18°36′E
95 L16 **Kristinehamn** Värmland, C Sweden 59°17′N 14°09′E
93 J17 **Kristinestad** Fin. Kristiinankaupunki. Österbotten, W Finland 62°15′N 21°24′E
**Kristyor** see Crişcior
115 J25 **Kríti** Eng. Crete. ⬖ region Greece, Aegean Sea
115 J24 **Kríti** Eng. Crete. island Greece, Aegean Sea
115 J23 **Kritikó Pélagos** var. Kretikon Delagos, Eng. Sea of Crete; anc. Mare Creticum. sea Greece, Aegean Sea
**Kriulyany** see Criuleni
112 I12 **Krivaja** ≈ NE Bosnia and Herzegovina
**Krivaja** see Mali Iđoš
113 P17 **Kriva Palanka** Turk. Eğri Palanka. NE Macedonia 42°13′N 22°19′E
**Krivichi** see Kryvichy
114 H8 **Krivodol** Vratsa, NW Bulgaria 43°23′N 23°30′E
126 M10 **Krivorozh'ye** Rostovskaya Oblast', SW Russia 48°51′N 40°49′E
**Krivoshin** see Kryvoshyn
**Krivoy Rog** see Kryvyy Rih
112 F7 **Križevci** Ger. Kreuz, Hung. Kőrös. Varaždin, NE Croatia 46°02′N 16°32′E
112 B10 **Krk** It. Veglia. Primorje-Gorski Kotar, NW Croatia 45°01′N 14°36′E
112 B10 **Krk** It. Veglia; anc. Curieta. island NW Croatia
109 V12 **Krka** ≈ SE Slovenia
**Krka** see Gurk
109 R11 **Krn** ▲ NW Slovenia 46°15′N 13°37′E
111 H16 **Krnov** Ger. Jägerndorf. Moravskoslezský Kraj, E Czechia 50°05′N 17°40′E
95 G14 **Krøderen** Buskerud, S Norway 60°06′N 09°48′E
95 G14 **Krøderen** ◎ S Norway
**Kroi** see Krui
95 N17 **Krokek** Östergötland, S Sweden 58°40′N 16°25′E
**Krokodil** see Crocodile
93 G16 **Krokom** Jämtland, C Sweden 63°20′N 14°30′E
117 S2 **Krolevets'** Rus. Krolevets. Sums'ka Oblast', NE Ukraine 51°34′N 33°24′E
**Krolevets** see Krolevets'
**Królewska Huta** see Chorzów
111 H18 **Kroměříž** Ger. Kremsier. Zlínský Kraj, E Czechia 49°18′N 17°24′E
98 I9 **Krommenie** Noord-Holland, C Netherlands 52°30′N 04°46′E
126 J6 **Kromy** Orlovskaya Oblast', W Russia 52°41′N 35°45′E
101 L18 **Kronach** Bayern, E Germany 50°14′N 11°19′E
**Krone an der Brahe** see Koronowo
**Krŏng Kêb** see Krong Kep
167 R14 **Krong Kep** var. Krŏng Kêb. Kep, S Cambodia 10°29′N 104°19′E
95 K21 **Kronoberg** ⬖ county S Sweden
123 V10 **Kronotskiy Zaliv** bay E Russia
195 O2 **Kronprinsesse Märtha Kyst** physical region Antarctica
195 V3 **Kronprins Olav Kyst** physical region Antarctica
124 G12 **Kronshtadt** Leningradskaya Oblast', NW Russia 60°01′N 29°42′E
**Kronstadt** see Braşov
83 I22 **Kroonstad** Free State, C South Africa 27°40′S 27°15′E
123 O12 **Kropotkin** Irkutskaya Oblast', C Russia 58°30′N 115°21′E
126 L14 **Kropotkin** Krasnodarskiy Kray, SW Russia 45°29′N 40°31′E
117 R7 **Kropyvnytskyy** prev. Kirovohrad, Kirovo, Yelizavetgrad, Zinov'yevsk. Kirovohrads'ka Oblast', C Ukraine 48°30′N 31°17′E
110 J11 **Krośniewice** Łódzskie, C Poland 52°14′N 19°10′E
111 N17 **Krosno** Ger. Krossen. Podkarpackie, SE Poland 49°40′N 21°46′E
110 E12 **Krosno Odrzańskie** Ger. Crossen, Kreisstadt. Lubuskie, W Poland 52°02′N 15°06′E
**Krossen** see Krosno
**Krotoschin** see Krotoszyn
110 H13 **Krotoszyn** Ger. Krotoschin. Wielkopolskie, C Poland 51°43′N 17°24′E
**Krottingen** see Kretinga
**Krousón** see Krousónas
115 J25 **Krousónas** prev. Krousón, Kroussón. Kríti, Greece, E Mediterranean Sea 35°14′N 24°59′E
**Kroussón** see Krousónas
**Krraba** see Krrabë
113 L20 **Krrabë** var. Krraba. Tiranë, C Albania 41°15′N 19°56′E
113 L17 **Krrabit, Mali i** ▲▲ N Albania
109 W12 **Krško** Ger. Gurkfeld; prev. Videm-Krško. E Slovenia 45°57′N 15°31′E
83 K19 **Kruger National Park** national park Northern, N South Africa
83 J21 **Krugersdorp** Gauteng, NE South Africa 26°06′S 27°46′E
38 D16 **Krugloi Point** headland Agattu Island, Alaska, USA 52°30′N 173°46′E
**Krugloye** see Kruhlaye
119 N15 **Kruhlaye** Rus. Krugloye. Mahilyowskaya Voblasts', E Belarus 54°15′N 29°48′E
168 L15 **Krui** var. Kroi. Sumatera, SW Indonesia 05°11′S 103°55′E
99 G16 **Kruibeke** Oost-Vlaanderen, N Belgium 51°10′N 04°18′E
83 G25 **Kruidfontein** Western Cape, SW South Africa 32°50′S 21°59′E
99 F15 **Kruiningen** Zeeland, SW Netherlands 51°28′N 04°01′E
**Kruja** see Krujë
113 L19 **Krujë** var. Kruja, It. Croia. Durrës, C Albania 41°30′N 19°48′E
**Krulevshchina/Krulewshchyna** see Krulyewshchyzna
118 K13 **Krulyewshchyzna** Rus. Krulevshchina, Krulewshchyna. Vitsyebskaya Voblasts', N Belarus 55°02′N 27°45′E
25 T6 **Krum** Texas, SW USA 33°15′N 97°14′W
101 J23 **Krumbach** Bayern, S Germany 48°12′N 10°21′E
113 M17 **Krumë** Kukës, NE Albania 42°11′N 20°25′E
**Krummau** see Český Krumlov
114 K12 **Krumovgrad** prev. Kossukavak. Yambol, E Bulgaria 41°27′N 25°40′E
114 K12 **Krumovitsa** ≈ S Bulgaria
114 L10 **Krumovo** Yambol, E Bulgaria 42°16′N 26°25′E
167 O11 **Krung Thep, Ao** var. Bight of Bangkok. bay S Thailand
**Krung Thep Mahanakhon** see Ao Krung Thep
**Krupa/Krupa na Uni** see Bosanska Krupa
119 M15 **Krupki** Minskaya Voblasts', C Belarus 54°19′N 29°08′E
95 G24 **Kruså** var. Krusaa. Syddanmark, SW Denmark 54°50′N 09°25′E
**Krusaa** see Kruså
113 N14 **Kruševac** Serbia, C Serbia 43°37′N 21°20′E
113 N19 **Kruševo** SW North Macedonia 41°22′N 21°15′E
111 A15 **Krušné Hory** Eng. Ore Mountains, Ger. Erzgebirge. ▲ Czechia/Germany see also Erzgebirge
**Krušné Hory** see Erzgebirge
39 W13 **Kruzof Island** island Alexander Archipelago, Alaska, USA
114 F13 **Krýa Vrýsi** var. Kría Vrísi. Kentrikí Makedonía, N Greece 40°41′N 22°18′E
119 P16 **Krychaw** Rus. Krichëv. Mahilyowskaya Voblasts', E Belarus 53°42′N 31°43′E
64 K11 **Krylov Seamount** undersea feature E Atlantic Ocean 17°35′N 30°07′W
**Krym** see Krym, Avtonomna Respublika
117 S13 **Krym, Avtonomna Respublika** var. Krym, Eng. Crimea, Crimean Oblast; prev. Rus. Krymskaya ASSR, Krymskaya Oblast'. ⬖ province SE Ukraine
126 K14 **Krymsk** Krasnodarskiy Kray, SW Russia 44°56′N 38°02′E
**Krymskaya ASSR/Krymskaya Oblast'** see Krym, Avtonomna Respublika
117 T13 **Krymś'ki Hory** ▲▲ S Ukraine
117 T13 **Kryms'kyy Pivostriv** peninsula S Ukraine
111 M18 **Krynica** Ger. Tannenhof. Małopolskie, S Poland 49°25′N 20°56′E
117 P8 **Kryve Ozero** Odes'ka Oblast', SW Ukraine 47°54′N 30°19′E
119 K14 **Kryvichy** Rus. Krivichi. Minskaya Voblasts', C Belarus 54°43′N 27°17′E
119 I18 **Kryvoshyn** Rus. Krivoshin. Brestskaya Voblasts', SW Belarus 52°52′N 26°08′E
117 S8 **Kryvyy Rih** Rus. Krivoy Rog. Dnipropetrovs'ka Oblast', SE Ukraine 47°53′N 33°24′E
117 N8 **Kryzhopil'** Vinnyts'ka Oblast', C Ukraine 48°22′N 28°51′E
**Krzemieniec** see Kremenets'
111 J14 **Krzepice** Śląskie, S Poland 50°58′N 18°42′E
110 F10 **Krzyż Wielkopolskie** Wielkopolskie, W Poland 52°52′N 16°03′E
**Ksar al Kabir** see Ksar-el-Kebir
**Ksar al Soule** see Er-Rachidia
74 J5 **Ksar El Boukhari** N Algeria 35°55′N 02°47′E



◆ Country
● Country Capital
◇ Dependent Territory
○ Dependent Territory Capital
⬖ Administrative Regions
✈ International Airport
▲ Mountain
▲▲ Mountain Range
Volcano
≈ River
◎ Lake
⊠ Reservoir

KSAR-EL-KEBIR – KYAUNKPYU


74 G5 **Ksar-el-Kebir** *var.* Alcázar, Ksar al Kabir, Ksar-el-Kébir, *Ar.* Al-Kasr al-Kebir, Al-Qsar al-Kbir, *Sp.* Alcazarquivir. NW Morocco *35°04′N 05°56′W*
**Ksar-el-Kébir** *see* Ksar-el-Kebir
110 H12 **Książ Wielkopolski** *Ger.* Xions. Weilkopolskie, W Poland *52°03′N 17°10′E*
127 O3 **Kstovo** Nizhegorodskaya Oblast', W Russia *56°07′N 44°12′E*
169 T8 **Kuala Belait** W Brunei *04°48′N 114°12′E*
**Kuala Dungun** *see* Dungun
169 S10 **Kualakeriau** Borneo, C Indonesia
169 S12 **Kualakuayan** Borneo, C Indonesia *02°01′S 112°35′E*
168 K8 **Kuala Lipis** Pahang, Peninsular Malaysia *04°11′N 102°00′E*
168 K9 **Kuala Lumpur** ● (Malaysia) Kuala Lumpur, Peninsular Malaysia *03°08′N 101°42′E*
168 K9 **Kuala Lumpur International** ✈ Selangor, Peninsular Malaysia *02°51′N 101°45′E*
**Kuala Pelabohan Kelang** *see* Pelabuhan Klang
169 U7 **Kuala Penyu** Sabah, East Malaysia *05°37′N 115°36′E*
38 E9 **Kualapu'u** *var.* Kualapuu. Moloka'i, Hawaii, USA, C Pacific Ocean *21°09′N 157°02′W*
**Kualapuu** *see* Kualapu'u
168 L7 **Kuala Terengganu** *var.* Kuala Trengganu. Terengganu, Peninsular Malaysia *05°20′N 103°07′E*
168 L11 **Kualatungkal** Sumatera, W Indonesia *0°49′S 103°22′E*
171 P11 **Kuandang** Sulawesi, N Indonesia *0°50′N 122°55′E*
163 V12 **Kuandian** *var.* Kuandian Manzu Zizhixian. Liaoning, NE China *40°41′N 124°46′E*
**Kuandian Manzu Zizhixian** *see* Kuandian
83 E15 **Kuando Kubango** *prev.* Cuando Cubango. ◈ *province* SE Angola
**Kuang-chou** *see* Guangzhou
**Kuang-hsi** *see* Guangxi Zhuangzu Zizhiqu
**Kuang-tung** *see* Guangdong
**Kuang-yuan** *see* Guangyuan
**Kuantan, Batang** *see* Indragiri, Sungai
**Kuanzhou** *see* Qingjian
**Kuba** *see* Quba
**Kubango** *see* Cubango/Okavango
141 X8 **Kubārah** NW Oman *23°03′N 56°52′E*
93 H16 **Kubbe** Västernorrland, C Sweden *63°31′N 18°04′E*
80 A11 **Kubbum** Southern Darfur, W Sudan *11°47′N 23°47′E*
124 L13 **Kubenskoye, Ozero** ◎ NW Russia
146 G6 **Kubla-Ustyurt** *Rus.* Komsomol'sk-na-Ustyurte. Qoraqalpog'iston Respublikasi, NW Uzbekistan *44°06′N 58°14′E*
164 G15 **Kubokawa** Kōchi, Shikoku, SW Japan *33°22′N 133°14′E*
114 L7 **Kubrat** *prev.* Balbunar. Razgrad, N Bulgaria *43°48′N 26°31′E*
112 O13 **Kučajske Planine** ▲ E Serbia
165 T1 **Kuccharo-ko** ◎ Hokkaidō, N Japan
112 O11 **Kučevo** Serbia, NE Serbia *44°29′N 21°42′E*
**Kuchan** *see* Qūchān
169 Q10 **Kuching** *prev.* Sarawak. Sarawak, East Malaysia *01°32′N 110°20′E*
169 Q10 **Kuching** ✈ Sarawak, East Malaysia *01°32′N 110°20′E*
164 B17 **Kuchinoerabu-jima** *island* Nansei-shotō, SW Japan
109 Q6 **Kuchl** Salzburg, NW Austria *47°37′N 13°12′E*
148 L9 **Kūchnay Darwēshān** *prev.* Kūchnay Darweyshān. Helmand, S Afghanistan *31°02′N 64°10′E*
**Kūchnay Darweyshān** *see* Kūchnay Darwēshān
**Kuchurgan** *see* Kuchurhan
117 O9 **Kuchurhan** *Rus.* Kuchurgan. ≈ NE Ukraine
**Kuçova** *see* Kuçovë
113 L21 **Kuçovë** *var.* Kuçova; *prev.* Qyteti Stalin. Berat, C Albania *40°48′N 19°55′E*
136 D11 **Küçük Çekmece** İstanbul, NW Turkey *41°01′N 28°47′E*
164 F14 **Kudamatsu** *var.* Kudamatu. Yamaguchi, Honshū, SW Japan *34°00′N 131°53′E*
**Kudamatu** *see* Kudamatsu
**Kudara** *see* Ghŭdara
169 V6 **Kudat** Sabah, East Malaysia *06°54′N 116°47′E*
**Küddow** *see* Gwda
155 G17 **Kūdligi** Karnātaka, W India *14°58′N 76°24′E*
**Kudowa** *see* Kudowa-Zdrój
111 F16 **Kudowa-Zdrój** *Ger.* Kudowa. Wałbrzych, SW Poland *50°27′N 16°20′E*
117 P9 **Kudryavtsivka** Mykolayivs'ka Oblast', S Ukraine *47°18′N 31°02′E*
169 R16 **Kudus** *prev.* Koedoes. Jawa, C Indonesia *06°46′S 110°48′E*
125 T13 **Kudymkar** Permskiy Kray, NW Russia *59°01′N 54°40′E*
**Kudzsir** *see* Cugir
**Kuei-chou** *see* Guizhou
**Kuei-lin** *see* Guilin
**Kuei-Yang/Kuei-yang** *see* Guiyang
**K'u-erh-lo** *see* Korla
**Kueyang** *see* Guiyang
**Kufa** *see* Al Kūfah
136 E14 **Küfiçayı** ≈ C Turkey
109 O6 **Kufstein** Tirol, W Austria *47°36′N 12°10′E*
9 N7 **Kugaaruk** *prev.* Pelly Bay. Nunavut, N Canada *68°38′N 89°45′W*
**Kugaly** *see* Kogaly
8 K8 **Kugluktuk** *var.* Qurlurtuuq; *prev.* Coppermine. Nunavut, NW Canada *67°49′N 115°12′W*
143 Y13 **Kūhak** Sīstān va Balūchestān, SE Iran *27°10′N 63°15′E*
143 R9 **Kūhbonān** Kermān, C Iran *31°23′N 56°16′E*
**Kūhestān** *see* Kuhsān
**Kūhīrī** *see* Kahīrī
93 N15 **Kuhmo** Kainuu, E Finland *64°04′N 29°34′E*
93 L18 **Kuhmoinen** Keski-Suomi, C Finland *61°32′N 25°09′E*
**Kuhnau** *see* Konin
**Kühnö** *see* Kihnu
143 O8 **Kūhpāyeh** Eşfahān, C Iran *32°42′N 52°25′E*
148 J5 **Kuhsān** *var.* Kohsān, Kūhestān. Herāt, W Afghanistan *34°40′N 61°11′E*
167 O12 **Kui Buri** *var.* Ban Kui Nua. Prachuap Khiri Khan, SW Thailand *12°10′N 99°49′E*
**Kuibyshev** *see* Kuybyshevskoye Vodokhranilishche
82 D13 **Kuito** *Port.* Silva Porto, *var.* Cuito. Bié, C Angola *12°21′S 16°55′E*
39 X14 **Kuiu Island** *island* Alexander Archipelago, Alaska, USA
92 L13 **Kuivaniemi** Pohjois-Pohjanmaa, C Finland *65°34′N 25°13′E*
**Kujalleo, Kommune** *see* Kujalleq
196 M15 **Kujalleq** *off.* Kommune Kujalleo. ◈ *municipality* S Greenland
77 V14 **Kujama** Kaduna, C Nigeria *10°27′N 07°39′E*
110 I10 **Kujawsko-pomorskie** ◈ *province* C Poland
165 R8 **Kuji** *var.* Kuzi. Iwate, Honshū, C Japan *40°12′N 141°47′E*
**Kujto, Ozero** *see* Yushkozerskoye Vodokhranilishche
**Kujū-renzan** *see* Kujū-san
164 D14 **Kujū-san** *var.* Kujū-renzan. ▲ Kyūshū, SW Japan *33°07′N 131°13′E*
43 N7 **Kukalaya, Rio** *var.* Rio Cuculaya, Rio Kukulaya. ≈ NE Nicaragua
113 O16 **Kukavica** *var.* Vlajna. ▲ SE Serbia *42°46′N 21°58′E*
113 M18 **Kukës** *var.* Kukësi. Kukës, NE Albania *42°03′N 20°25′E*
113 L18 **Kukës** ◈ *county* NE Albania
**Kukësi** *see* Kukës
186 D8 **Kukipi** Gulf, S Papua New Guinea *08°11′S 146°09′E*
127 S3 **Kukmor** Respublika Tatarstan, W Russia *56°11′N 50°56′E*
**Kukong** *see* Shaoguan
39 N6 **Kukpowruk River** ≈ Alaska, USA
38 M6 **Kukpuk River** ≈ Alaska, USA
**Kükürdağ** *see* Gogi, Mount
**Kukukhoto** *see* Hohhot
**Kukulaya, Rio** *see* Kukalaya, Rio
189 W12 **Kuku Point** *headland* NW Wake Island *19°19′N 166°36′E*
146 G11 **Kukurtli** Ahal Welaýaty, C Turkmenistan *39°58′N 58°47′E*
**Kül** *see* Kül, Rūd-e
114 F7 **Kula** Vidin, NW Bulgaria *43°55′N 22°32′E*
112 K9 **Kula** Vojvodina, NW Serbia *45°37′N 19°31′E*
136 D14 **Kula** Manisa, W Turkey *38°33′N 28°38′E*
149 S8 **Kulachi** Khyber Pakhtunkhwa, NW Pakistan *31°58′N 70°30′E*
**Kulachi** *see* Kolachi
**Kulagino** *see* Yesbol
168 L10 **Kulai** Johor, Peninsular Malaysia *01°41′N 103°33′E*
114 M7 **Kulak** ≈ NE Bulgaria
153 T11 **Kula Kangri** *var.* Kulhakangri. ▲ Bhutan/China *28°06′N 90°19′E*
144 E13 **Kulaly, Ostrov** *island* SW Kazakhstan
145 S16 **Kulan** *Kaz.* Qulan; *prev.* Lugovoy, Lugovoye. Zhambyl, S Kazakhstan *42°54′N 72°45′E*
147 V9 **Kulanak** Narynskaya Oblast', C Kyrgyzstan *41°18′N 75°38′E*
**Gory Kulandag** *see* Gulandag
153 V14 **Kulaura** Sylhet, NE Bangladesh *24°32′N 92°02′E*
118 D9 **Kuldīga** *Ger.* Goldingen. W Latvia *56°57′N 21°59′E*
**Kuldja** *see* Yining
**Kul'dzhuktau, Gory** *see* QuljuqtovTog'lari
127 N4 **Kulebaki** Nizhegorodskaya Oblast', W Russia *55°25′N 42°31′E*
112 E11 **Kulen Vakuf** *var.* Spasovo. ◈ Federacija Bosne I Hercegovine, NW Bosnia and Herzegovina
181 Q9 **Kulgera Roadhouse** Northern Territory, N Australia *25°49′S 133°30′E*
**Kulhakangri** *see* Kula Kangri
127 T1 **Kuliga** Udmurtskaya Respublika, NW Russia *58°14′N 53°49′E*
**Kulkuduk** *see* Ko'lquduq
118 G4 **Kullamaa** Läänemaa, W Estonia *58°52′N 24°05′E*
197 O12 **Kullorsuaq** *var.* Kuvdlorssuak. ◈ Avannaata, C Greenland
29 O6 **Kulm** North Dakota, N USA *46°18′N 98°57′W*
**Kulm** *see* Chełmno
126 D12 **Kul'mach** *prev. Turkm.* Isgender. Balkan Welaýaty, W Turkmenistan *39°04′N 55°49′E*
101 L18 **Kulmbach** Bayern, SE Germany *50°07′N 11°27′E*
**Kulmsee** *see* Chełmża
147 Q14 **Kŭlob** *Rus.* Kulyab. SW Tajikistan *37°55′N 68°46′E*
92 M13 **Kuloharju** Lappi, N Finland *65°51′N 28°10′E*
125 N7 **Kuloy** Arkhangel'skaya Oblast', NW Russia *64°55′N 43°35′E*
125 N7 **Kuloy** ≈ NW Russia
137 Q14 **Kulp** Dıyarbakır, SE Turkey *38°32′N 41°01′E*
**Kulpa** *see* Kolpa
77 P14 **Kulpawn** ≈ N Ghana
143 R13 **Kül, Rūd-e** *var.* Kül. ≈ S Iran
144 G12 **Kul'sary** *Kaz.* Qulsary. Atyrau, W Kazakhstan *46°59′N 54°02′E*
153 R15 **Kulti** West Bengal, NE India *23°45′N 86°50′E*
93 G14 **Kultsjön** *Lapp.* Gålto. ◎ N Sweden
136 I14 **Kulu** Konya, W Turkey *39°06′N 33°02′E*
123 S9 **Kulu** ≈ E Russia
122 I13 **Kulunda** Altayskiy Kray, S Russia *52°33′N 79°04′E*
**Kulunda Steppe** *see* Ravnina Kulyndy
**Kulundinskaya Ravnina** *see* Ravnina Kulyndy
182 M9 **Kulwin** Victoria, SE Australia *35°04′S 142°37′E*
**Kulyab** *see* Kŭlob
117 Q3 **Kulykivka** Chernihivs'ka Oblast', N Ukraine *51°23′N 31°39′E*
**Kum** *see* Qom
164 F14 **Kuma** Ehime, Shikoku, SW Japan *33°36′N 132°53′E*
127 P14 **Kuma** ≈ SW Russia
165 O12 **Kumagaya** Saitama, Honshū, S Japan *36°09′N 139°22′E*
165 Q5 **Kumaishi** Hokkaidō, NE Japan *42°08′N 139°57′E*
169 R13 **Kumai, Teluk** *bay* Borneo, C Indonesia
127 Y7 **Kumak** Orenburgskaya Oblast', W Russia *51°16′N 60°06′E*
164 C14 **Kumamoto** Kumamoto, Kyūshū, SW Japan *32°49′N 130°41′E*
164 D15 **Kumamoto** *off.* Kumamoto-ken. ◈ *prefecture* Kyūshū, SW Japan
**Kumamoto-ken** *see* Kumamoto
164 J15 **Kumano** Mie, Honshū, SW Japan *33°54′N 136°08′E*
**Kumanova** *see* Kumanovo
113 O17 **Kumanovo** *Turk.* Kumanova. N Macedonia *42°08′N 21°43′E*
185 G17 **Kumara** West Coast, South Island, New Zealand *42°39′S 171°12′E*
180 J8 **Kumarina Roadhouse** Western Australia *24°46′S 119°39′E*
153 T15 **Kumarkhali** Khulna, W Bangladesh *23°54′N 89°16′E*
77 P16 **Kumasi** *prev.* Coomassie. C Ghana *06°41′N 01°40′W*
**Kumayri** *see* Gyumri
79 D15 **Kumba** Sud-Ouest, W Cameroon *04°39′N 09°26′E*
114 N13 **Kumbağ** Tekirdağ, NW Turkey *40°51′N 27°26′E*
155 J21 **Kumbakonam** Tamil Nādu, SE India *10°59′N 79°24′E*
**Kum-Dag** *see* Gumdag
165 R16 **Kume-jima** *island* Nansei-shotō, SW Japan
127 V6 **Kumertau** Respublika Bashkortostan, W Russia *52°48′N 55°48′E*
**Kumillā** *see* Comilla
35 R4 **Kumiva Peak** ▲ Nevada, W USA *40°24′N 119°16′W*
159 N7 **Kum Kuduk** Xinjiang Uygur Zizhiqu, W China *40°15′N 91°55′E*
159 N8 **Kum Kuduk** *well* NW China
**Kumkurgan** *see* Qumqo'rg'on
95 M16 **Kumla** Örebro, C Sweden *59°08′N 15°09′E*
136 E17 **Kumluca** Antalya, SW Turkey *36°23′N 30°17′E*
100 N9 **Kummerower See** ◎ NE Germany
77 X14 **Kumo** Gombe, E Nigeria *10°03′N 11°14′E*
145 O13 **Kumola** ≈ C Kazakhstan
167 N1 **Kumon Range** ▲ N Myanmar (Burma)
83 F22 **Kums** //Karas, SE Namibia *28°07′S 19°40′E*
155 E18 **Kumta** Karnātaka, W India *14°25′N 74°24′E*
38 H12 **Kumukahi, Cape** *headland* Hawai'i, USA, C Pacific Ocean *19°31′N 154°48′W*
127 Q17 **Kumukh** Respublika Dagestan, SW Russia *42°10′N 47°07′E*
**Kumul** *see* Hami
158 L6 **Kümüx** Xinjiang Uygur Zizhiqu, W China
127 N9 **Kumylzhenskaya** Volgogradskaya Oblast', SW Russia *49°54′N 42°35′E*
141 W6 **Kumzār** N Oman *26°19′N 56°26′E*
43 N15 **Kuna de Wargandí** ◈ *special territory* NE Panama
149 S4 **Kunar** *prev.* Kunar, Kunarha. E Afghanistan
**Kunar** *see* Kunar
**Kunarha** *see* Kunar
**Kunashiri** *see* Kunashir, Ostrov
123 U14 **Kunashir, Ostrov** *var.* Kunashiri. *island* Kuril'skiye Ostrova, SE Russia
118 I3 **Kunda** Lääne-Virumaa, NE Estonia *59°31′N 26°33′E*
152 M13 **Kunda** Uttar Pradesh, N India *25°43′N 81°31′E*
155 E19 **Kundāpura** *var.* Coondapoor. Karnātaka, W India *13°39′N 74°41′E*
79 O24 **Kundelungu, Monts** ▲ S Dem. Rep. Congo
**Kundert** *see* Hernád
186 D7 **Kundiawa** Chimbu, W Papua New Guinea *06°00′S 144°57′E*
**Kundla** *see* Sāvarkundla
**Kunduk, Ozero** *see* Sasyk, Ozero
**Kunduk, Ozero Sasyk** *see* Sasyk, Ozero
168 L10 **Kundur, Pulau** *island* W Indonesia
149 Q2 **Kunduz** *var.* Kondūz, Qondūz; *prev.* Kondoz, Kundūz. Kunduz, NE Afghanistan *36°49′N 68°50′E*
149 Q2 **Kunduz** *prev.* Kondoz. ◈ *province* NE Afghanistan
**Kunduz/Kundūz** *see* Kunduz
**Kuneitra** *see* Al Qunayţirah
83 B18 **Kunene** ◈ *region* NE Namibia
83 A16 **Kunene** *var.* Cunene. ≈ Angola/Namibia *see also* Cunene
**Kunene** *see* Cunene
**Künes** *see* Xinyuan
158 J5 **Künes He** ≈ NW China
95 I19 **Kungälv** Västra Götaland, S Sweden *57°54′N 12°00′E*
147 W7 **Kungei Ala-Tau** *Rus.* Khrebet Kyungëy Ala-Too, *Kyr.* Küngöy Ala-Too. ▲ Kazakhstan/Kyrgyzstan
**Küngöy Ala-Too** *see* Kungei Ala-Tau
**Kungrad** *see* Qo'ng'irot
95 J19 **Kungsbacka** Halland, S Sweden *57°30′N 12°05′E*
95 I18 **Kungshamn** Västra Götaland, S Sweden *58°21′N 11°15′E*
95 M16 **Kungsör** Västmanland, C Sweden *59°25′N 16°05′E*
79 J16 **Kungu** Equateur, NW Dem. Rep. Congo *02°47′N 19°12′E*
125 V15 **Kungur** Permskiy Kray, NW Russia *57°24′N 56°56′E*
166 L9 **Kungyangon** Yangon, SW Myanmar (Burma) *16°27′N 96°00′E*
111 M22 **Kunhegyes** Jász-Nagykun-Szolnok, E Hungary *47°22′N 20°36′E*
167 O5 **Kunhing** Shan State, E Myanmar (Burma) *21°17′N 98°26′E*
158 D9 **Kunjirap Daban** *var.* Khunjerab Pass. *pass* China/Pakistan *see also* Khūnjerāb Pass
**Kunjirap Daban** *see* Khunjerab Pass
**Kunlun Mountains** *see* Kunlun Shan
158 H10 **Kunlun Shan** *Eng.* Kunlun Mountains. ▲ NW China
159 P11 **Kunlun Shankou** *pass* C China
160 G13 **Kunming** *var.* K'un-ming; *prev.* Yunnan. *province capital* Yunnan, SW China *25°04′N 102°41′E*
**K'un-ming** *see* Kunming
**Kunø** *see* Kunoy
95 B18 **Kunoy** *Dan.* Kunø. *island* N Faroe Islands
**Kunsan** *see* Gunsan
111 L24 **Kunszentmárton** Jász-Nagykun-Szolnok, E Hungary *46°50′N 20°19′E*
111 J23 **Kunszentmiklós** Bács-Kiskun, C Hungary *47°00′N 19°07′E*
181 N3 **Kununurra** Western Australia *15°50′S 128°44′E*
**Kunyang** *see* Pingyang
**Kunya-Urgench** *see* Köneürgenç
**Kunyé** *see* Pins, Île des
169 T11 **Kunyi** Borneo, C Indonesia *03°23′S 119°20′E*
101 I20 **Künzelsau** Baden-Württemberg, S Germany *49°22′N 09°43′E*
161 S10 **Kuocang Shan** ▲ SE China
**Kuolajärvi** *see* Kuoloyarvi
124 H5 **Kuoloyarvi** *Finn.* Kuolajärvi, *var.* Luolajarvi. Murmanskaya Oblast', NW Russia *66°58′N 29°13′E*
93 N16 **Kuopio** Pohjois-Savo, C Finland *62°54′N 27°41′E*
93 K17 **Kuortane** Etelä-Pohjanmaa, W Finland *62°48′N 23°30′E*
93 M18 **Kuortti** Etelä-Savo, E Finland *61°25′N 26°25′E*
**Kupa** *see* Kolpa
171 P17 **Kupang** *prev.* Koepang. Timor, C Indonesia *10°13′S 123°38′E*
39 Q5 **Kuparuk River** ≈ Alaska, USA
**Kupchino** *see* Cupcina
186 E9 **Kupiano** Central, S Papua New Guinea *10°06′S 148°12′E*
180 M4 **Kupingarri** Western Australia *16°46′S 125°57′E*
122 I12 **Kupino** Novosibirskaya Oblast', C Russia *54°22′N 77°09′E*
118 H11 **Kupiškis** Panevėžys, NE Lithuania *55°51′N 24°58′E*
114 L13 **Küplü** Edirne, NW Turkey *41°06′N 26°23′E*
39 X13 **Kupreanof Island** *island* Alexander Archipelago, Alaska, USA
39 O16 **Kupreanof Point** *headland* Alaska, USA *55°34′N 159°36′W*
112 G13 **Kupres** ◈ Federacija Bosne I Hercegovine, SW Bosnia and Herzegovina
117 W5 **Kup"yans'k** *Rus.* Kupyansk. Kharkivs'ka Oblast', E Ukraine *49°42′N 37°36′E*
**Kupyansk** *see* Kup"yans'k
117 W5 **Kup"yans'k-Vuzlovyy** Kharkivs'ka Oblast', E Ukraine *49°40′N 37°41′E*
158 I6 **Kuqa** Xinjiang Uygur Zizhiqu, NW China *41°43′N 82°58′E*
**Kür** *see* Kura
137 W11 **Kura** ≈ SW Asia
55 R8 **Kuracki** NW Guyana *06°52′N 60°13′W*
**Kura Kurk** *see* Irbe Strait
147 Q10 **Kurama Range** *Rus.* Kuraminskiy Khrebet. ▲ Tajikistan/Uzbekistan
**Kuraminskiy Khrebet** *see* Kurama Range
**Kura Nehri** *see* Kura
119 J14 **Kuranyets** *Rus.* Kurenets. Minskaya Voblasts', C Belarus *54°33′N 26°57′E*
164 H13 **Kurashiki** *var.* Kurasiki. Okayama, Honshū, SW Japan *34°35′N 133°44′E*
154 L10 **Kurasia** Chhattīsgarh, C India *23°11′N 82°16′E*
**Kurasiki** *see* Kurashiki
164 H12 **Kurayoshi** *var.* Kurayosi. Tottori, Honshū, SW Japan *35°27′N 133°52′E*
**Kurayosi** *see* Kurayoshi
163 X6 **Kurbin He** ≈ NE China
**Kurchum** *see* Kurshim
**Kurchum** *see* Kurshim
137 X11 **Kürdämir** *Rus.* Kyurdamir. C Azerbaijan *40°21′N 48°08′E*
**Kurdestan** *see* Kordestān
139 S1 **Kurdistan** *cultural region* SW Asia
**Kurd Kui** *see* Kord Küy
155 F15 **Kurduvādi** Mahārāshtra, W India *18°06′N 75°31′E*
**Kŭrdzhali** *see* Kardzhali
**Kŭrdzhali** *see* Kardzhali
**Kŭrdzhali, Yazovir** *see* Kardzhali, Yazovir
164 F13 **Kure** Hiroshima, Honshū, SW Japan *34°15′N 132°33′E*
192 K5 **Kure Atoll** *var.* Ocean Island. *atoll* Hawaiian Islands, Hawaii, USA
136 J10 **Küre Dağları** ▲ N Turkey
146 C11 **Kürendag** *Rus.* Gora Kyuren. ▲ W Turkmenistan *39°05′N 55°09′E*
**Kurenets** *see* Kuranyets
118 E6 **Kuressaare** *Ger.* Arensburg; *prev.* Kingissepp. Saaremaa, W Estonia *58°17′N 22°29′E*
122 K9 **Kureyka** Krasnoyarskiy Kray, N Russia *66°22′N 87°21′E*
122 K9 **Kureyka** ≈ N Russia
**Kurgal'dzhino/Kurgal'dzhinsky** *see* Korgalzhyn
122 G11 **Kurgan** Kurganskaya Oblast', C Russia *55°30′N 65°20′E*
126 L14 **Kurganinsk** Krasnodarskiy Kray, SW Russia *44°55′N 40°45′E*
122 G11 **Kurganskaya Oblast'** ◈ *province* C Russia
**Kurgan-Tyube** *see* Bokhtar
191 O2 **Kuria** *prev.* Woodle Island. *island* Tungaru, W Kiribati
**Kuria Muria Bay** *see* Ḩalānīyāt, Khalīj al
**Kuria Muria Islands** *see* Ḩalānīyāt, Juzur al
153 T13 **Kurigram** Rajshahi, N Bangladesh *25°49′N 89°39′E*
93 K17 **Kurikka** Etelä-Pohjanmaa, W Finland *62°36′N 22°25′E*
192 I3 **Kuril Basin** *var.* Kurile Basin. *undersea basin* NW Pacific Ocean
**Kurile Basin** *see* Kuril Basin
**Kurile Islands** *see* Kuril'skiye Ostrova
**Kurile-Kamchatka Depression** *see* Kuril-Kamchatka Trench
**Kurile Trench** *see* Kuril-Kamchatka Trench
**Kuril Islands** *see* Kuril'skiye Ostrova
192 J3 **Kuril-Kamchatka Trench** *var.* Kurile-Kamchatka Depression, Kurile Trench. *trench* NW Pacific Ocean
127 Q9 **Kurilovka** Saratovskaya Oblast', W Russia *50°39′N 48°02′E*
123 U13 **Kuril'sk** *Jap.* Shana. Kuril'skiye Ostrova, Sakhalinskaya Oblats', SE Russia *45°10′N 147°51′E*
122 G11 **Kuril'skiye Ostrova** *Eng.* Kuril Islands, Kurile Islands. *island group* SE Russia
42 M9 **Kurinwas, Río** ≈ E Nicaragua
**Kurisches Haff** *see* Courland Lagoon
**Kurkund** *see* Kilingi-Nõmme
126 M4 **Kurlovskiy** Vladimirskaya Oblast', W Russia *55°25′N 40°39′E*
117 S12 **Kurman** *prev.* Krasnohvardiys'ke. Avtonomna Respublika Krym, S Ukraine *45°30′N 34°19′E*
80 G12 **Kurmuk** Blue Nile, SE Sudan *10°36′N 34°16′E*
**Kurna** *see* Al Qurnah
155 H17 **Kurnool** *var.* Karnul. Andhra Pradesh, S India *15°51′N 78°01′E*
164 M11 **Kurobe** Toyama, Honshū, SW Japan *36°55′N 137°24′E*
165 Q7 **Kuroishi** *var.* Kuroisi. Aomori, Honshū, C Japan *40°37′N 140°34′E*
**Kuroisi** *see* Kuroishi
165 O12 **Kuroiso** Tochigi, Honshū, S Japan *36°58′N 140°02′E*
165 Q4 **Kuromatsunai** Hokkaidō, NE Japan *42°40′N 140°18′E*
164 B17 **Kuro-shima** *island* SW Japan
185 F21 **Kurow** Canterbury, South Island, New Zealand *44°44′S 170°29′E*
127 N15 **Kursavka** Stavropol'skiy Kray, SW Russia *44°28′N 42°31′E*
118 E11 **Kuršėnai** Šiauliai, N Lithuania *56°00′N 22°56′E*
145 X10 **Kurshim** *prev.* Kurchum. Vostochnyy Kazakhstan, E Kazakhstan *48°35′N 83°37′E*
145 Y10 **Kurshim** *prev.* Kurchum. ≈ E Kazakhstan
**Kurshskaya Kosa/Kuršių Nerija** *see* Courland Spit
126 J7 **Kursk** Kurskaya Oblast', W Russia *51°44′N 36°47′E*
126 I7 **Kurskaya Oblast'** ◈ *province* W Russia
**Kurskiy Zaliv** *see* Courland Lagoon
113 N15 **Kuršumlija** Serbia, S Serbia *43°09′N 21°16′E*
137 R15 **Kurtalan** Siirt, SE Turkey *37°58′N 41°36′E*
**Kurtbunar** *see* Tervel
**Kurt-Dere** *see* Valchi Dol
**Kurtitsch/Kürtös** *see* Curtici
145 U15 **Kurtty** ≈ SE Kazakhstan
93 L18 **Kuru** Pirkanmaa, W Finland *61°51′N 23°46′E*
80 C13 **Kuru** ≈ W South Sudan
114 M13 **Kuru Dağı** ▲ NW Turkey
158 L7 **Kuruktag** ▲ NW China
83 G22 **Kuruman** Northern Cape, N South Africa *27°28′S 23°27′E*
67 T14 **Kuruman** ≈ W South Africa
164 D14 **Kurume** Fukuoka, Kyūshū, SW Japan *33°15′N 130°27′E*
123 N13 **Kurumkan** Respublika Buryatiya, S Russia *54°13′N 110°21′E*
155 J25 **Kurunegala** North Western Province, C Sri Lanka *07°28′N 80°23′E*
55 T10 **Kurupukari** C Guyana *04°39′N 58°39′W*
125 U10 **Kur"ya** Respublika Komi, NW Russia *61°38′N 57°12′E*
144 E15 **Kuryk** *var.* Yeraliyev, *Kaz.* Quryq. Mangistau, SW Kazakhstan *43°12′N 51°43′E*
136 B15 **Kuşadası** Aydın, SW Turkey *37°50′N 27°16′E*
115 M19 **Kuşadası Körfezi** *gulf* SW Turkey
164 A17 **Kusagaki-guntō** *island* SW Japan
**Kusaie** *see* Kosrae
145 T12 **Kusak** ≈ C Kazakhstan
**Kusary** *see* Qusar
167 P7 **Ku Sathan, Doi** ▲ NW Thailand *18°22′N 100°31′E*
164 J13 **Kusatsu** *var.* Kusatu. Shiga, Honshū, SW Japan *35°02′N 136°00′E*
**Kusatu** *see* Kusatsu
138 F11 **Kuseifa** Southern, C Israel *31°15′N 35°01′E*
136 C12 **Kuş Gölü** ◎ NW Turkey
126 L12 **Kushchevskaya** Krasnodarskiy Kray, SW Russia *46°35′N 39°40′E*
164 D16 **Kushima** *var.* Kusima. Miyazaki, Kyūshū, SW Japan *31°28′N 131°14′E*
164 I15 **Kushimoto** Wakayama, Honshū, SW Japan *33°28′N 135°45′E*
165 V4 **Kushiro** *var.* Kusiro. Hokkaidō, NE Japan *42°58′N 144°24′E*
148 K4 **Kushk** *prev.* Kūshk. Herāt, W Afghanistan *34°55′N 62°20′E*
**Kushka** *see* Gushgy/Serhetabat
**Kushka** *see* Serhetabat
**Kushmurun** *see* Kusmuryn
**Kushmurun, Ozero** *see* Kusmuryn, Ozero
127 U4 **Kushnarenkovo** Respublika Bashkortostan, W Russia *55°07′N 55°24′E*
**Kushrabat** *see* Qo'shrabot
**Kushtia** *see* Kustia
**Kusima** *see* Kushima
**Kusiro** *see* Kushiro
38 M13 **Kuskokwim Bay** *bay* Alaska, USA
39 P11 **Kuskokwim Mountains** ▲ Alaska, USA
39 N12 **Kuskokwim River** ≈ Alaska, USA
145 N8 **Kusmuryn** *Kaz.* Qusmuryn; *prev.* Kushmurun. Kostanay, N Kazakhstan *52°27′N 64°31′E*
145 N8 **Kusmuryn, Ozero** *Kaz.* Qusmuryn; *prev.* Ozero Kushmurun. ◎ N Kazakhstan
108 G7 **Küsnacht** Zürich, N Switzerland *47°19′N 08°34′E*
165 V4 **Kussharo-ko** *var.* Kussyaro. ◎ Hokkaidō, NE Japan
**Küssnacht** *see* Küssnacht am Rigi
108 F8 **Küssnacht am Rigi** *var.* Küssnacht. Schwyz, C Switzerland *47°03′N 08°25′E*
**Kussyaro** *see* Kussharo-ko
**Kustanay** *see* Kostanay
**Küstence/Küstendje** *see* Constanța
100 F11 **Küstenkanal** *var.* Ems-Hunte Canal. *canal* NW Germany
153 T15 **Kustia** *var.* Kushtia. Khulna, W Bangladesh *23°54′N 89°07′E*
**Küstrin** *see* Kostrzyn
171 R11 **Kusu** Pulau Halmahera, E Indonesia *0°51′N 127°41′E*
170 L16 **Kuta** Pulau Lombok, S Indonesia *08°53′S 116°15′E*
139 T4 **Kutabān** Kirkūk, N Iraq *35°21′N 44°45′E*
136 E13 **Kütahya** *prev.* Kutaia. Kütahya, W Turkey *39°25′N 29°56′E*
136 E13 **Kütahya** *var.* Kutaia. ◈ *province* W Turkey
**Kutai** *see* Mahakam, Sungai
**Kutaia** *see* Kütahya
137 R9 **Kutaisi** W Georgia *42°16′N 42°42′E*
**Kūt al 'Amārah** *see* Al Kūt
**Kut al Hai/Kūt al Ḩayy** *see* Al Ḩayy
**Kut al Imara** *see* Al Kūt
123 Q11 **Kutana** Respublika Sakha (Yakutiya), NE Russia *59°05′N 131°43′E*
**Kutaradja/Kutaraja** *see* Banda Aceh
165 R4 **Kutchan** Hokkaidō, NE Japan *42°54′N 140°46′E*
**Kutch, Gulf of** *see* Kachchh, Gulf of
**Kutch, Rann of** *see* Kachchh, Rann of
112 F9 **Kutina** Sisak-Moslavina, NE Croatia *45°29′N 16°45′E*
112 H9 **Kutjevo** Požega-Slavonija, NE Croatia *45°26′N 17°54′E*
111 E17 **Kutná Hora** *Ger.* Kuttenberg. Střední Čechy, C Czechia *49°58′N 15°18′E*
110 K12 **Kutno** Łódzkie, C Poland *52°14′N 19°23′E*
**Kuttenberg** *see* Kutná Hora
79 I20 **Kutu** Bandundu, W Dem. Rep. Congo *02°42′S 18°10′E*
153 V17 **Kutubdia Island** *island* SE Bangladesh
80 B10 **Kutum** Northern Darfur, W Sudan *14°10′N 24°40′E*
147 Y7 **Kuturgu** Issyk-Kul'skaya Oblast', E Kyrgyzstan *42°45′N 78°04′E*
12 M5 **Kuujjuaq** *prev.* Fort-Chimo. Québec, E Canada *58°10′N 68°15′W*
12 I7 **Kuujjuarapik** *prev.* Poste-de-la-Baleine. Québec, NE Canada *55°13′N 77°54′W*
12 I7 **Kuujjuarapik** Québec, C Canada *55°07′N 78°09′W*
**Kuuli-Mayak** *see* Guwlumaýak
118 I6 **Kuulsemägi** ▲ S Estonia
92 N13 **Kuusamo** Pohjois-Pohjanmaa, E Finland *65°57′N 29°15′E*
93 M19 **Kuusankoski** Kymenlaakso, S Finland *60°51′N 26°40′E*
127 W7 **Kuvandyk** Orenburgskaya Oblast', W Russia *51°27′N 57°18′E*
**Kuvango** *see* Cubango
**Kuvasay** *see* Quvasoy
**Kuvdlorssuak** *see* Kullorsuaq
124 I16 **Kuvshinovo** Tverskaya Oblast', W Russia *57°03′N 34°09′E*
141 Q4 **Kuwait** *off.* State of Kuwait, *var.* Dawlat al Kuwait, Koweit, Kuweit. ◆ *monarchy* SW Asia
**Kuwait** *see* Al Kuwayt
**Kuwait Bay** *see* Kuwayt, Jūn al
**Kuwait City** *see* Al Kuwayt
**Kuwait, Dawlat al** *see* Kuwait
**Kuwait, State of** *see* Kuwait
**Kuwajleen** *see* Kwajalein Atoll
164 K13 **Kuwana** Mie, Honshū, SW Japan *35°04′N 136°40′E*
139 X9 **Kuwayt** Maysān, E Iraq *32°26′N 47°12′E*
142 K11 **Kuwayt, Jūn al** *var.* Kuwait Bay. *bay* E Kuwait
**Kuweit** *see* Kuwait
117 P10 **Kuyal'nyts'kyy Lyman** ◎ SW Ukraine
122 I12 **Kuybyshev** Novosibirskaya Oblast', C Russia *55°28′N 77°55′E*
**Kuybyshev** *see* Bolgar, Respublika Tatarstan, Russian Federation
**Kuybyshev** *see* Samara
**Kuybysheve** *see* Bilmak
**Kuybyshev Reservoir** *see* Kuybyshevskoye Vodokhranilishche
**Kuybyshevskaya Oblast'** *see* Samarskaya Oblast'
**Kuybyshevskiy** *see* Novoishimskiy
127 R4 **Kuybyshevskoye Vodokhranilishche** *var.* Kuibyshev, *Eng.* Kuybyshev Reservoir. ⊠ W Russia
123 S9 **Kuydusun** Respublika Sakha (Yakutiya), NE Russia *63°15′N 143°10′E*
125 U16 **Kuyeda** Permskiy Kray, NW Russia *56°23′N 55°19′E*
**Küysanjaq** *see* Koye
158 J4 **Kuytun** Xinjiang Uygur Zizhiqu, NW China *44°25′N 84°55′E*
122 M13 **Kuytun** Irkutskaya Oblast', S Russia *54°18′N 101°28′E*
55 S12 **Kuyuwini Landing** S Guyana *02°06′N 59°14′W*
**Kuzi** *see* Kuji
38 M9 **Kuzitrin River** ≈ Alaska, USA
127 P6 **Kuznetsk** Penzenskaya Oblast', W Russia *53°06′N 46°27′E*
**Kuznetsovs'k** *see* Varash
165 R8 **Kuzumaki** Iwate, Honshū, C Japan *40°04′N 141°26′E*
95 H24 **Kværndrup** Syddtjylland, C Denmark *55°10′N 10°31′E*
92 H9 **Kvaløya** *island* N Norway
92 K8 **Kvalsund** Finnmark, N Norway *70°30′N 23°56′E*
94 G11 **Kvam** Oppland, S Norway *61°42′N 09°43′E*
127 X7 **Kvarkeno** Orenburgskaya Oblast', W Russia *52°09′N 59°44′E*
93 G15 **Kvarnbergsvattnet** *var.* Frostviken. ◎ N Sweden
112 A11 **Kvarner** *var.* Carnaro, *It.* Quarnero. *gulf* W Croatia
112 B11 **Kvarnerić** *channel* W Croatia
39 O14 **Kvichak Bay** *bay* Alaska, USA
92 H12 **Kvikkjokk** *Lapp.* Huhttán. Norrbotten, N Sweden *66°58′N 17°45′E*
95 D17 **Kvina** ≈ S Norway
92 Q1 **Kvitøya** *island* NE Svalbard
95 F16 **Kvitseid** Telemark, S Norway *59°23′N 08°31′E*
79 H20 **Kwa** ≈ W Dem. Rep. Congo
77 Q15 **Kwadwokurom** C Ghana *07°49′N 00°15′W*
186 M8 **Kwailibesi** Malaita, N Solomon Islands *08°25′S 160°48′E*
189 S6 **Kwajalein Atoll** *var.* Kuwajleen. *atoll* Ralik Chain, C Marshall Islands
55 W9 **Kwakoegron** Brokopondo, N Suriname *05°14′N 55°20′W*
81 J21 **Kwale** Kwale, S Kenya *04°10′S 39°27′E*
77 U17 **Kwale** Delta, S Nigeria *05°51′N 06°29′E*
79 H20 **Kwamouth** Bandundu, W Dem. Rep. Congo *03°11′S 16°16′E*
**Kwando** *see* Cuando
**Kwangchow** *see* Guangzhou
**Kwangchu** *see* Gwangju
**Kwangju** *see* Gwangju
79 H20 **Kwango** *Port.* Cuango. ≈ Angola/Dem. Rep. Congo *see also* Cuango
**Kwango** *see* Cuango
**Kwangsi/Kwangsi Chuang Autonomous Region** *see* Guangxi Zhuangzu Zizhiqu
**Kwangtung** *see* Guangdong
**Kwangyuan** *see* Guangyuan
81 F17 **Kwania, Lake** ◎ C Uganda
**Kwanza** *see* Cuanza
82 B11 **Kwanza Norte** *prev.* Cuanza Norte. ◈ *province* NE Angola
82 B12 **Kwanza Sul** *prev.* Cuanza Sul. ◈ *province* NE Angola
77 S15 **Kwara** ◈ *state* SW Nigeria
83 K22 **KwaZulu/Natal** *off.* KwaZulu/Natal Province; *prev.* Natal. ◈ *province* E South Africa
**KwaZulu/Natal Province** *see* KwaZulu/Natal
**Kweichow** *see* Guizhou
**Kweichu** *see* Guiyang
**Kweilin** *see* Guilin
**Kweisui** *see* Hohhot
**Kweiyang** *see* Guiyang
83 K17 **Kwekwe** *prev.* Que Que. Midlands, C Zimbabwe *18°56′S 29°49′E*
83 G20 **Kweneng** ◈ *district* S Botswana
**Kwesui** *see* Hohhot
39 N12 **Kwethluk** Alaska, USA *60°48′N 161°26′W*
39 N12 **Kwethluk River** ≈ Alaska, USA
110 J8 **Kwidzyń** *Ger.* Marienwerder. Pomorskie, N Poland *53°44′N 18°55′E*
38 M13 **Kwigillingok** Alaska, USA *59°52′N 163°08′W*
186 E9 **Kwikila** Central, S Papua New Guinea *09°51′S 147°43′E*
79 I20 **Kwilu** ≈ W Dem. Rep. Congo
**Kwito** *see* Cuito
171 U12 **Kwoka, Gunung** ▲ Papua Barat, E Indonesia *0°34′S 132°25′E*
78 I12 **Kyabé** Moyen-Chari, S Chad *09°28′N 18°54′E*
183 O11 **Kyabram** Victoria, SE Australia *36°21′S 145°05′E*
166 M9 **Kyaikkami** *prev.* Amherst. Mon State, S Myanmar (Burma) *16°03′N 97°36′E*
166 L9 **Kyaiklat** Ayeyarwady, SW Myanmar (Burma) *16°25′N 95°42′E*
166 M8 **Kyaikto** Mon State, S Myanmar (Burma) *17°16′N 97°01′E*
123 N14 **Kyakhta** Respublika Buryatiya, S Russia *50°25′N 106°13′E*
182 G8 **Kyancutta** South Australia *33°10′S 135°33′E*
167 T8 **Ky Anh** Ha Tinh, N Vietnam *18°05′N 106°16′E*
166 L5 **Kyaukpadaung** Mandalay, C Myanmar (Burma) *20°50′N 95°08′E*
166 J6 **Kyaukpyu** *var.* Kyaukpyu. Rakhine State, W Myanmar (Burma) *19°27′N 93°33′E*
166 M5 **Kyaukse** Mandalay, C Myanmar (Burma) *21°33′N 96°06′E*
166 L8 **Kyaunggon** Ayeyarwady, SW Myanmar (Burma) *17°04′N 95°12′E*
**Kyaunkpyu** *see* Kyaukpyu


◆ Country
● Country Capital
◇ Dependent Territory
○ Dependent Territory Capital
◈ Administrative Regions
✈ International Airport
▲ Mountain
▲ Mountain Range
Volcano
≈ River
◎ Lake
⊠ Reservoir

KYBARTAI – LAK SAO


119 E14 **Kybartai** *Pol.* Kibarty. Marijampolė, S Lithuania 54°37′N 22°44′E
152 I7 **Kyelang** Himāchal Pradesh, NW India 32°33′N 77°03′E
117 P4 **Kyiv** *Eng.* Kiev, *Rus.* Kiyev, *var.* Kyyiv. ● (Ukraine) Kyivs'ka Oblast', N Ukraine 50°26′N 30°32′E
117 O4 **Kyivs'ka Oblast'** *var.* Kyyivs'ka Oblast', *Rus.* Kiyevskaya Oblast'. ◈ *province* N Ukraine
117 P3 **Kyivs'ke Vodoskhovyshche** *Eng.* Kiev Reservoir, *Rus.* Kiyevskoye Vodokhranilishche. ⊠ N Ukraine
111 G19 **Kyjov** *Ger.* Gaya. Jihomoravský Kraj, SE Czechia 49°00′N 17°07′E
115 J21 **Kykládes** *var.* Kikládhes, *Eng.* Cyclades. *island group* SE Greece
25 S11 **Kyle** Texas, SW USA 29°59′N 97°52′W
96 G9 **Kyle of Lochalsh** N Scotland, United Kingdom 57°18′N 05°39′W
101 D18 **Kyll** ∿ W Germany
115 F19 **Kyllíni** *var.* Killini. ▲▲ S Greece
115 H18 **Kými** *prev.* Kími. Évvoia, C Greece 38°38′N 24°06′E
93 M19 **Kymijoki** ∿ S Finland
115 H18 **Kýmis, Akrotírio** *headland* Évvoia, C Greece 38°39′N 24°08′E
125 W14 **Kyn** Permskiy Kray, NW Russia 57°48′N 58°38′E
183 N12 **Kyneton** Victoria, SE Australia 37°14′S 144°28′E
81 G17 **Kyoga, Lake** *var.* Lake Kioga. ◎ C Uganda
164 J12 **Kyōga-misaki** *headland* Honshū, SW Japan 35°46′N 135°13′E
183 V4 **Kyogle** New South Wales, SE Australia 28°37′S 153°00′E
**Kyŏnggi-man** *see* Gyeonggi-man
**Kyŏngju** *see* Gyeongju
**Kyŏngsŏng** *see* Seoul
**Kyōsai-tō** *see* Geogeum-do
81 F19 **Kyotera** S Uganda 0°38′S 31°34′E
164 J13 **Kyōto** Kyōto, Honshū, SW Japan 35°01′N 135°46′E
164 J13 **Kyōto** *off.* Kyōto-fu, *var.* Kyōto Hu. ◈ *urban prefecture* Honshū, SW Japan
**Kyōto-fu/Kyōto Hu** *see* Kyōto
115 D21 **Kyparissía** *var.* Kiparissía. Pelopónnisos, S Greece 37°15′N 21°40′E
115 D20 **Kyparissiakós Kólpos** *gulf* S Greece
**Kyperounda** *see* Kyperoúnta
121 P3 **Kyperoúnta** *var.* Kyperounda. C Cyprus 34°57′N 33°02′E
**Kypriakí Dimokratía** *see* Cyprus
**Kýpros** *see* Cyprus
115 H16 **Kyrá Panagía** *island* Vóreies Sporádes, Greece, Aegean Sea
**Kyrenia** *see* Girne
**Kyrenia Mountains** *see* Beşparmak Dağları
**Kyrgyz Republic** *see* Kyrgyzstan
**Kyrgyz Respublikasy** *see* Kyrgyzstan
**Kyrgyzskaya Respublika** *see* Kyrgyzstan
147 U9 **Kyrgyzstan** *off.* Kyrgyz Republic, *var.* Kirghizia, *Kyr.* Kyrgyz Respublikasy, *Rus.* Kyrgyzskaya Respublika; *prev.* Kirgizskaya SSR, Kirghiz SSR, Republic of Kyrgyzstan. ◆ *republic* C Asia
**Kyrgyzstan, Republic of** *see* Kyrgyzstan
138 F11 **Kyriat Gat** *prev.* Qiryat Gat. Southern, C Israel 31°37′N 34°47′E
100 M11 **Kyritz** Brandenburg, NE Germany 52°56′N 12°24′E
94 G8 **Kyrkseterøra** Sør-Trøndelag, S Norway 63°17′N 09°06′E
**Kyrkslätt** *see* Kirkkonummi
125 U8 **Kyrta** Respublika Komi, NW Russia 64°03′N 57°41′E
111 J18 **Kysucké Nové Mesto** *prev.* Horné Nové Mesto, *Ger.* Kisutzaneustadtl, Oberneustadtl, *Hung.* Kiszucaújhely. Zílinský Kraj, N Slovakia 49°18′N 18°48′E
117 N12 **Kytay, Ozero** ◎ SW Ukraine
115 F23 **Kýthira** *var.* Kíthira, *It.* Cerigo, *Lat.* Cythera. Kńythira, S Greece 41°39′N 26°30′E
115 F23 **Kýthira** *var.* Kíthira, *It.* Cerigo, *Lat.* Cythera. *island* S Greece
115 I20 **Kýthnos** Kńythnos, Kykládes, Greece, Aegean Sea 37°24′N 24°28′E
115 I20 **Kýthnos** *var.* Kíthnos, Thermiá, *It.* Termia; *anc.* Cythnos. *island* Kykládes, Greece, Aegean Sea
115 I20 **Kýthnou, Stenó** *strait* Kykládes, Greece, Aegean Sea
**Kyungëy Ala-Too, Khrebet** *see* Kungei Ala-Tau
**Kyurdamir** *see* Kürdämir
164 D15 **Kyūshū** *var.* Kyûsyû. *island* SW Japan
192 H6 **Kyushu-Palau Ridge** *var.* Kyusyu-Palau Ridge. *undersea feature* W Pacific Ocean 20°00′N 136°00′E
114 F10 **Kyustendil** *anc.* Pautalia. Kyustendil, W Bulgaria 42°17′N 22°42′E
114 G11 **Kyustendil** ◈ *province* W Bulgaria
**Kyûsyû** *see* Kyūshū
**Kyusyu-Palau Ridge** *see* Kyushu-Palau Ridge
123 P8 **Kyusyur** Respublika Sakha (Yakutiya), NE Russia 70°36′N 127°19′E
183 P10 **Kywong** New South Wales, SE Australia 34°59′S 146°42′E
**Kyyiv** *see* Kyiv
**Kyyivs'ka Oblast'** *see* Kyivs'ka Oblast'
93 L16 **Kyyjärvi** Keski-Suomi, C Finland 63°02′N 24°34′E
122 K14 **Kyzyl** Respublika Tyva, C Russia 51°45′N 94°28′E
147 S8 **Kyzyl-Adyr** *var.* Kirovskoye. Talasskaya Oblast', NW Kyrgyzstan 42°37′N 71°34′E
145 V14 **Kyzylagash** *Kaz.* Qyzylaghash. Almaty, SE Kazakhstan 45°20′N 78°45′E
146 C13 **Kyzylbair** Balkan Welaýaty, W Turkmenistan 38°13′N 55°38′E
**Kyzyl-Dzhiik, Pereval** *see* Uzbel Shankou
145 S7 **Kyzylkak, Ozero** ◎ NE Kazakhstan
145 X11 **Kyzylkesek** Vostochnyy Kazakhstan, E Kazakhstan 47°56′N 82°02′E
147 S10 **Kyzyl-Kiya** *Kyr.* Kyzyl-Kyya. Batkenskaya Oblast', SW Kyrgyzstan 40°15′N 72°07′E
144 L11 **Kyzylkol', Ozero** ◎ C Kazakhstan
122 K14 **Kyzyl Kum** *var.* Kizil Kum, Qizil Qum, *Uzb.* Qizilqum. *desert* Kazakhstan/Uzbekistan
**Kyzyl-Kyya** *see* Kyzyl-Kiya
145 N15 **Kyzylorda** *var.* Kzyl-Orda, Qizil Orda, Qyzylorda; *prev.* Kzylorda, Perovsk. Kyzylorda, S Kazakhstan 44°54′N 65°31′E
144 L14 **Kyzylorda** *off.* Kyzylordinskaya Oblast', *Kaz.* Qyzylorda Oblysy. ◈ *province* S Kazakhstan
**Kyzylordinskaya Oblast'** *see* Kyzylorda
**Kyzylrabat** *see* Qizilravote
**Kyzylrabot** *see* Qizilrabot
**Kyzylsu** *see* Kyzyl-Suu
147 X7 **Kyzyl-Suu** *prev.* Pokrovka. Issyk-Kul'skaya Oblast', NE Kyrgyzstan 42°20′N 77°55′E
147 S12 **Kyzyl-Suu** *var.* Kyzylsu. ∿ Kyrgyzstan/Tajikistan
147 X8 **Kyzyl-Tuu** Issyk-Kul'skaya Oblast', E Kyrgyzstan 42°06′N 76°54′E
145 Q12 **Kyzylzhar** *Kaz.* Qyzylzhar. Karaganda, C Kazakhstan 48°22′N 70°00′E
**Kzyl-Orda** *see* Kyzylorda
**Kzylorda** *see* Kyzylorda
**Kzyltu** *see* Kishkenekol'


# L


109 X2 **Laa an der Thaya** Niederösterreich, NE Austria 48°44′N 16°23′E
63 K15 **La Adela** La Pampa, SE Argentina 38°57′S 64°02′W
**Laagen** *see* Numedalslågen
109 S5 **Laakirchen** Oberösterreich, N Austria 47°59′N 13°49′E
**Laaland** *see* Lolland
104 I11 **La Albuera** Extremadura, W Spain 38°43′N 06°49′W
105 O7 **La Alcarria** *physical region* C Spain
104 K14 **La Algaba** Andalucía, S Spain 37°27′N 06°01′W
105 P9 **La Almarcha** Castilla-La Mancha, C Spain 39°41′N 02°23′W
105 R6 **La Almunia de Doña Godina** Aragón, NE Spain 41°28′N 01°23′W
41 N5 **La Amistad, Presa** ⊠ NW Mexico
118 F4 **Läänemaa** *var.* Lääne Maakond. ◈ *province* NW Estonia
**Lääne Maakond** *see* Läänemaa
118 I3 **Lääne-Virumaa** *off.* Lääne-Viru Maakond. ◈ *province* NE Estonia
**Lääne-Viru Maakond** *see* Lääne-Virumaa
62 J9 **La Antigua, Salina** *salt lake* W Argentina
99 E17 **Laarne** Oost-Vlaanderen, NW Belgium 51°03′N 03°50′E
80 O13 **Laas Caanood** Sool, N Somalia 08°33′N 47°44′E
41 O9 **La Ascensión** Nuevo León, NE Mexico 24°15′N 99°53′W
80 N12 **Laas Dhaareed** Togdheer, N Somalia 10°12′N 46°09′E
55 O4 **La Asunción** Nueva Esparta, NE Venezuela 11°06′N 63°53′W
**Laatokka** *see* Ladozhskoye, Ozero
100 I13 **Laatzen** Niedersachsen, NW Germany 52°19′N 09°46′E
38 E9 **La'au Point** *var.* Laau Point. *headland* Moloka'i, Hawai'i, USA 21°06′N 157°18′W
**Laau Point** *see* La'au Point
42 D6 **La Aurora** ✈ (Ciudad de Guatemala) Guatemala, C Guatemala 14°33′N 90°30′W
74 C9 **Laâyoune** *var.* Aaiún. ● (Western Sahara) NW Western Sahara 27°10′N 13°11′W
126 L14 **Laba** ∿ SW Russia
40 M6 **La Babia** Coahuila, NE Mexico 28°39′N 102°00′W
15 R7 **La Baie** Québec, SE Canada 48°20′N 70°54′W
171 P16 **Labala** Pulau Lomblen, S Indonesia 08°30′S 123°27′E
62 K8 **La Banda** Santiago del Estero, N Argentina 27°44′S 64°14′W
**La Banda Oriental** *see* Uruguay
104 K4 **La Bañeza** Castilla y León, N Spain 42°18′N 05°54′W
167 T11 **Labăng** *prev.* Phumĭ Labăng. Ratanakiri, NE Cambodia 13°51′N 107°01′E
40 M13 **La Barca** Jalisco, SW Mexico 20°20′N 102°33′W
40 K14 **La Barra de Navidad** Jalisco, C Mexico 19°12′N 104°38′W
187 Y13 **Labasa** *prev.* Lambasa. Vanua Levu, N Fiji 16°25′S 179°24′E
102 H8 **la Baule-Escoublac** Loire-Atlantique, NW France 47°17′N 02°24′W
76 I13 **Labé** NW Guinea 11°19′N 12°17′W
**Labe** *see* Elbe
15 N11 **Labelle** Québec, SE Canada 46°15′N 74°43′W
23 X14 **La Belle** Florida, SE USA 26°45′N 81°26′W
10 H7 **Laberge, Lake** ◎ Yukon, W Canada
**Labes** *see* Łobez
**Labiau** *see* Polessk
112 A10 **Labin** *It.* Albona. Istra, NW Croatia 45°05′N 14°10′E
126 L14 **Labinsk** Krasnodarskiy Kray, SW Russia 44°39′N 40°43′E
105 X5 **La Bisbal d'Empordà** Cataluña, NE Spain 41°58′N 03°02′E
119 P16 **Labkovichy** *Rus.* Lobkovichi. Mahilyowskaya Voblasts', E Belarus 53°50′N 31°45′E
15 S4 **La Blache, Lac de** ◎ Québec, SE Canada
171 P4 **Labo** Luzon, N Philippines 14°10′N 122°47′E
**Laboehanbadjo** *see* Labuhanbajo
**Laborca** *see* Laborec
111 N18 **Laborec** *Hung.* Laborca. ∿ E Slovakia
108 D11 **La Borgne** ∿ S Switzerland
45 T12 **Laborie** SW Saint Lucia 13°45′N 61°00′W
102 J14 **Labouheyre** Landes, SW France 44°12′N 00°55′W
62 L12 **Laboulaye** Córdoba, C Argentina 34°05′S 63°20′W
13 Q7 **Labrador** *cultural region* Newfoundland and Labrador, SW Canada
64 I6 **Labrador Basin** *var.* Labrador Sea Basin. *undersea feature* Labrador Sea 53°00′N 48°00′W
13 N9 **Labrador City** Newfoundland and Labrador, E Canada 52°56′N 66°52′W
13 Q5 **Labrador Sea** *sea* NW Atlantic Ocean
**Labrador Sea Basin** *see* Labrador Basin
**Labrang** *see* Xiahe
54 G9 **Labranzagrande** Boyacá, C Colombia 05°34′N 72°34′W
59 D14 **Lábrea** Amazonas, N Brazil 07°20′S 64°46′W
45 U15 **La Brea** Trinidad, Trinidad and Tobago 10°14′N 61°37′W
15 S6 **Labrieville** Québec, SE Canada 49°15′N 69°31′W
102 K14 **Labrit** Landes, SW France 44°03′N 00°29′W
108 C9 **La Broye** ∿ SW Switzerland
103 N15 **Labruguière** Tarn, S France 43°32′N 02°15′E
168 M11 **Labu** Pulau Singkep, W Indonesia 0°34′S 104°24′E
169 T7 **Labuan** *var.* Victoria. Labuan, East Malaysia 05°20′N 115°14′E
169 T7 **Labuan** ◈ *federal territory* East Malaysia
**Labuan** *see* Labuan, Pulau
169 T7 **Labuan, Pulau** *var.* Labuan. *island* East Malaysia
**Labudalin** *see* Ergun
171 N16 **Labuhanbajo** *prev.* Laboehanbadjo. Flores, S Indonesia 08°33′S 119°55′E
168 J9 **Labuhanbilik** Sumatera, N Indonesia 02°30′N 100°10′E
168 G8 **Labuhanhaji** Sumatera, W Indonesia 03°31′N 97°00′E
**Labuk** *see* Labuk, Sungai
**Labuk Bay** *see* Labuk, Teluk
169 V7 **Labuk, Sungai** *var.* Labuk. ∿ East Malaysia
169 W6 **Labuk, Teluk** *var.* Labuk Bay, Telukan Labuk. *bay* S Sulu Sea
**Labuk, Telukan** *see* Labuk, Teluk
166 K9 **Labutta** Ayeyarwady, SW Myanmar (Burma) 16°08′N 94°45′E
122 I8 **Labytnangi** Yamalo-Nenetskiy Avtonomnyy Okrug, N Russia 66°39′N 66°26′E
113 K19 **Laç** *var.* Laci. Lezhë, C Albania 41°37′N 19°37′E
78 F10 **Lac** *off.* Région du Lac. ◈ *region* W Chad
57 K19 **Lacajahuira, Rio** ∿ W Bolivia
**La Calamine** *see* Kelmis
62 G11 **La Calera** Valparaíso, C Chile 32°47′S 71°16′W
13 P11 **Lac-Allard** Québec, E Canada 50°37′N 63°26′W
104 L13 **La Campana** Andalucía, S Spain 37°35′N 05°24′W
102 J12 **Lacanau** Gironde, SW France 44°59′N 01°04′W
42 C2 **Lacandón, Sierra del** ▲▲ Guatemala/Mexico
**La Cañiza** *see* A Cañiza
41 W16 **Lacantún, Río** ∿ SE Mexico
103 Q3 **la Capelle** Aisne, N France 49°58′N 03°55′E
112 K10 **Laćarak** Vojvodina, NW Serbia 45°00′N 19°34′E
62 L11 **La Carlota** Córdoba, C Argentina 33°30′S 63°15′W
104 L13 **La Carlota** Andalucía, S Spain 37°40′N 04°56′W
105 N12 **La Carolina** Andalucía, S Spain 38°15′N 03°37′W
103 O15 **Lacaune** Tarn, S France 43°42′N 02°42′E
15 P7 **Lac-Bouchette** Québec, SE Canada 48°14′N 72°11′W
**Laccadive Islands/Laccadive Minicoy and Amindivi Islands, the** *see* Lakshadweep
11 Y16 **Lac du Bonnet** Manitoba, S Canada 50°13′N 96°04′W
30 L4 **Lac du Flambeau** Wisconsin, N USA 45°58′N 89°51′W
15 P8 **Lac-Édouard** Québec, SE Canada 47°39′N 72°16′W
42 I4 **La Ceiba** Atlántida, N Honduras 15°45′N 86°29′W
54 E9 **La Ceja** Antioquia, W Colombia 06°02′N 75°30′W
182 J11 **Lacepede Bay** *bay* South Australia
32 G9 **Lacey** Washington, NW USA 47°01′N 122°49′W
103 P12 **la Chaise-Dieu** Haute-Loire, C France 45°19′N 03°41′E
114 G13 **Lachanás** Kentrikí Makedonía, N Greece 40°57′N 23°15′E
124 L11 **Lacha, Ozero** ◎ NW Russia
103 O8 **la Charité-sur-Loire** Nièvre, C France 47°10′N 02°59′E
103 N9 **la Châtre** Indre, C France 46°35′N 01°59′E
108 C8 **La Chaux-de-Fonds** Neuchâtel, W Switzerland 47°07′N 06°51′E
**Lach Dera** *see* Dheere Laaq
108 G8 **Lachen** Schwyz, C Switzerland 47°12′N 08°51′E
183 Q8 **Lachlan River** ∿ New South Wales, SE Australia
43 T15 **La Chorrera** Panamá, C Panama 08°51′N 79°46′W
15 V7 **Lac-Humqui** Québec, SE Canada 48°21′N 67°32′W
15 N12 **Lachute** Québec, SE Canada 45°39′N 74°21′W
**Lachyn** *see* Laçın
**Laci** *see* Laç
137 W13 **Laçın** *Rus.* Lachyn. SW Azerbaijan 39°36′N 46°34′E
103 S16 **la Ciotat** *anc.* Citharista. Bouches-du-Rhône, SE France 43°10′N 05°36′E
18 D10 **Lackawanna** New York, NE USA 42°49′N 78°49′W
11 Q13 **Lac La Biche** Alberta, SW Canada 54°46′N 111°59′W
**Lac la Martre** *see* Wha Ti
15 R12 **Lac-Mégantic** *var.* Mégantic. Québec, SE Canada 45°35′N 70°53′W
**Lacobriga** *see* Lagos
40 G5 **La Colorada** Sonora, NW Mexico 28°49′N 110°32′W
11 Q15 **Lacombe** Alberta, SW Canada 52°30′N 113°42′W
30 L12 **Lacon** Illinois, N USA 41°01′N 89°24′W
43 P16 **La Concepción** *var.* Concepción. Chiriquí, W Panama 08°31′N 82°39′W
54 H5 **La Concepción** Zulia, NW Venezuela 10°48′N 71°46′W
107 C19 **Laconi** Sardegna, Italy, C Mediterranean Sea 39°52′N 09°02′E
19 O9 **Laconia** New Hampshire, NE USA 43°32′N 71°29′W
61 H19 **La Coronilla** Rocha, E Uruguay 33°44′S 53°31′W
**La Coruña** *see* A Coruña
103 O11 **la Courtine** Creuse, C France 45°42′N 02°18′E
102 J16 **Lacq** Pyrénées-Atlantiques, SW France 43°25′N 00°37′W
**Lac, Région du** *see* Lac
15 P9 **La Croche** Québec, SE Canada 47°38′N 72°42′W
29 X3 **la Croix, Lac** ◎ Canada/USA
26 K5 **La Crosse** Kansas, C USA 38°32′N 99°19′W
21 V7 **La Crosse** Virginia, NE USA 36°41′N 78°03′W
32 L9 **La Crosse** Washington, NW USA 46°48′N 117°51′W
30 J7 **La Crosse** Wisconsin, N USA 43°46′N 91°12′W
54 C13 **La Cruz** Nariño, SW Colombia 01°33′N 76°58′W
42 K12 **La Cruz** Guanacaste, NW Costa Rica 11°05′N 85°39′W
40 I10 **La Cruz** Sinaloa, W Mexico 23°53′N 106°53′W
61 F19 **La Cruz** Florida, S Uruguay 33°54′S 56°11′W
42 M9 **La Cruz de Río Grande** Costa Caribe Sur, E Nicaragua 13°04′N 84°12′W
54 J4 **La Cruz de Taratara** Falcón, N Venezuela 11°03′N 69°44′W
15 Q10 **Lac-St-Charles** Québec, SE Canada 46°56′N 71°24′W
40 M6 **La Cuesta** Coahuila, NE Mexico 28°45′N 102°26′W
57 A17 **La Cumbra, Volcán** ⛰ Galapagos Islands, Ecuador, E Pacific Ocean 0°21′S 91°30′W
152 J5 **Ladākh Range** ▲▲ NE India
26 I5 **Ladder Creek** ∿ Kansas, C USA
45 X10 **la Désirade** *atoll* E Guadeloupe
**Lādhiqīyah, Muḥāfaẓat al** *see* Al Lādhiqīyah
**Lådik** *see* Lødingen
83 F25 **Ladismith** Western Cape, SW South Africa 33°30′S 12°15′E
152 G11 **Lādnūn** Rājasthān, NW India 27°36′N 74°26′E
**Ladoga, Lake** *see* Ladozhskoye, Ozero
115 E19 **Ládon** ∿ S Greece
54 E9 **La Dorada** Caldas, C Colombia 05°28′N 74°41′W
124 H11 **Ladozhskoye, Ozero** *Eng.* Lake Ladoga, *Fin.* Laatokka. ◎ NW Russia
37 R12 **Ladron Peak** ▲ New Mexico, SW USA 34°25′N 107°04′W
124 J11 **Ladva-Vetka** Respublika Kareliya, NW Russia 61°18′N 34°24′E
183 Q15 **Lady Barron** Tasmania, SE Australia 40°12′S 148°12′E
14 G9 **Lady Evelyn Lake** ◎ Ontario, S Canada
23 W11 **Lady Lake** Florida, SE USA 28°55′N 81°55′W
10 L17 **Ladysmith** Vancouver Island, British Columbia, SW Canada 48°55′N 123°45′W
83 J22 **Ladysmith** KwaZulu/Natal, E South Africa 28°34′S 29°47′E
30 J5 **Ladysmith** Wisconsin, N USA 45°27′N 91°07′W
**Ladyzhenka** *see* Tilekey
186 E7 **Lae** Morobe, W Papua New Guinea 06°45′S 147°00′E
189 R6 **Lae Atoll** *atoll* Ralik Chain, W Marshall Islands
40 C3 **La Encantada, Cerro de** ▲ NW Mexico 31°03′N 115°25′W
55 N11 **La Esmeralda** Amazonas, S Venezuela 03°11′N 65°33′W
42 G7 **La Esperanza** Intibucá, SW Honduras 14°19′N 88°09′W
30 K8 **La Farge** Wisconsin, N USA 43°36′N 90°39′W
23 R5 **Lafayette** Alabama, S USA 32°54′N 85°24′W
37 T4 **Lafayette** Colorado, C USA 39°59′N 105°06′W
23 R2 **La Fayette** Georgia, SE USA 34°42′N 85°16′W
31 O13 **Lafayette** Indiana, N USA 40°25′N 86°52′W
22 I9 **Lafayette** Louisiana, S USA 30°13′N 92°01′W
20 K8 **Lafayette** Tennessee, S USA 36°31′N 86°01′W
19 N7 **Lafayette, Mount** ▲ New Hampshire, NE USA 44°09′N 71°37′W
**La Fe** *see* Santa Fé
103 P3 **la Fère** Aisne, N France 49°41′N 03°20′E
102 L6 **la Ferté-Bernard** Sarthe, NW France 48°13′N 00°40′E
102 K5 **la Ferté-Macé** Orne, N France 48°35′N 00°21′W
103 N7 **la Ferté-St-Aubin** Loiret, C France 47°42′N 01°57′E
103 P5 **la Ferté-sous-Jouarre** Seine-et-Marne, N France 48°57′N 03°08′E
77 V15 **Lafia** Nassarawa, C Nigeria 08°29′N 08°34′E
77 T15 **Lafiagi** Kwara, W Nigeria 08°52′N 05°25′E
11 T17 **Lafleche** Saskatchewan, S Canada 49°40′N 106°28′W
102 K7 **la Flèche** Sarthe, NW France 47°42′N 00°04′W
109 X7 **Lafnitz** *Hung.* Lapines. ∿ Austria/Hungary
187 P17 **La Foa** Province Sud, S New Caledonia 21°46′S 165°49′E
20 M8 **La Follette** Tennessee, S USA 36°22′N 84°07′W
15 N12 **Lafontaine** Québec, SE Canada 45°52′N 74°01′W
22 K10 **Lafourche, Bayou** ∿ Louisiana, S USA
62 K6 **La Fragua** Santiago del Estero, N Argentina 26°06′S 64°06′W
54 H7 **La Fría** Táchira, NW Venezuela 08°13′N 72°15′W
104 J7 **La Fuente de San Esteban** Castilla y León, N Spain 40°48′N 06°14′W
186 C7 **Lagaip** ∿ W Papua New Guinea
61 B15 **La Gallareta** Santa Fe, C Argentina 29°34′S 60°23′W
127 Q14 **Lagan'** *prev.* Kaspiyskiy. Respublika Kalmykiya, SW Russia 45°25′N 47°19′E
95 L20 **Lagan** Kronoberg, S Sweden 56°55′N 14°01′E
95 K21 **Lågan** ∿ S Sweden
92 L2 **Lagarfljót** *var.* Lögurinn. ◎ E Iceland
37 R7 **La Garita Mountains** ▲▲ Colorado, C USA
171 O2 **Lagawe** Luzon, N Philippines 16°46′N 121°06′E
78 F13 **Lagdo** Nord, N Cameroon 09°12′N 13°43′E
78 F13 **Lagdo, Lac de** ◎ N Cameroon
100 H13 **Lage** Nordrhein-Westfalen, W Germany 52°00′N 08°48′E
94 H12 **Lågen** ∿ S Norway
61 J14 **Lages** Santa Catarina, S Brazil 27°45′S 50°16′W
**Lágesvuotna** *see* Laksefjorden
149 R4 **Laghmān** ◈ *province* E Afghanistan
74 J6 **Laghouat** N Algeria 33°49′N 02°59′E
105 Q10 **La Gineta** Castilla-La Mancha, C Spain 39°08′N 02°00′W
115 E21 **Lagkáda** *var.* Langada. Pelopónnisos, S Greece 36°49′N 22°19′E
114 G13 **Lagkadás** *var.* Langades, Langadhás. Kentrikí Makedonía, N Greece 40°45′N 23°04′E
115 E20 **Lagkádia** *var.* Langádhia, *cont.* Langadia. Pelopónnisos, S Greece 37°40′N 22°01′E
54 F6 **La Gloria** Cesar, N Colombia 08°37′N 73°51′W
41 O7 **La Gloria** Nuevo León, NE Mexico
92 N3 **Lågneset** *headland* W Svalbard 77°46′N 13°44′E
104 G14 **Lagoa** Faro, S Portugal 37°07′N 08°27′W
**La Goagira** *see* La Guajira
**Lago Agrio** *see* Nueva Loja
61 I14 **Lagoa Vermelha** Rio Grande do Sul, S Brazil 28°13′S 51°32′W
137 V10 **Lagodekhi** SE Georgia 41°49′N 46°15′E
42 C7 **La Gomera** Escuintla, S Guatemala 14°05′N 91°03′W
**Lagone** *see* Logone
107 M19 **Lagonegro** Basilicata, S Italy 40°06′N 15°42′E
63 G16 **Lago Ranco** Los Ríos, S Chile 40°21′S 72°29′W
77 S16 **Lagos** Lagos, SW Nigeria 06°24′N 03°17′E
104 F14 **Lagos** *anc.* Lacobriga. Faro, S Portugal 37°05′N 08°40′W
77 S16 **Lagos** ◈ *state* SW Nigeria
40 M12 **Lagos de Moreno** Jalisco, SW Mexico 21°21′N 101°55′W
**Lagosta** *see* Lastovo
74 A12 **Lagouira** SW Western Sahara 20°55′N 17°05′W
92 O1 **Lågøya** *island* N Svalbard
32 L11 **La Grande** Oregon, NW USA 45°21′N 118°05′W
103 Q14 **la Grande-Combe** Gard, S France 44°13′N 04°01′E
12 K9 **La Grande Rivière** *var.* Fort George. ∿ Québec, SE Canada
23 R4 **La Grange** Georgia, SE USA 33°02′N 85°02′W
31 P11 **Lagrange** Indiana, N USA 41°38′N 85°25′W
20 L5 **La Grange** Kentucky, S USA 38°24′N 85°23′W
27 V2 **La Grange** Missouri, C USA 40°00′N 91°31′W
21 V10 **La Grange** North Carolina, SE USA 35°18′N 77°47′W
25 U11 **La Grange** Texas, SW USA 29°55′N 96°54′W
105 N7 **La Granja** Castilla y León, N Spain 40°53′N 04°01′W
55 Q9 **La Gran Sabana** *grassland* E Venezuela
54 H7 **La Grita** Táchira, NW Venezuela 08°09′N 71°58′W
**La Grulla** *see* Grulla
15 R11 **La Guadeloupe** Québec, SE Canada 45°57′N 70°56′W
65 L6 **La Guaira** Distrito Federal, N Venezuela 10°35′N 66°52′W
54 G4 **La Guajira** *off.* Departamento de La Guajira, *var.* Guajira, La Goagira. ◈ *province* NE Colombia
188 I4 **Lagua Lichan, Punta** *headland* Saipan, S Northern Mariana Islands
105 P4 **Laguardia** *Basq.* Biasteri. País Vasco, N Spain 42°32′N 02°31′W
18 K14 **La Guardia** ✈ (New York) Long Island, New York, NE USA 40°44′N 73°51′W
**La Guardia/Laguardia** *see* A Guarda
**La Gudiña** *see* A Gudiña
103 O9 **la Guerche-sur-l'Aubois** Cher, C France 46°55′N 03°00′E
103 O13 **Laguiole** Aveyron, S France 44°42′N 02°51′E
83 F26 **L'Agulhas** *var.* Agulhas. Western Cape, SW South Africa 34°49′S 20°01′E
61 K14 **Laguna** Santa Catarina, S Brazil 28°29′S 48°45′W
37 Q11 **Laguna** New Mexico, SW USA 35°03′N 107°30′W
35 T16 **Laguna Beach** California, W USA 33°32′N 117°46′W
35 Y17 **Laguna Dam** *dam* Arizona/California, W USA
40 L7 **Laguna El Rey** Coahuila, N Mexico
35 V17 **Laguna Mountains** ▲▲ California, W USA
61 B17 **Laguna Paiva** Santa Fe, C Argentina 31°21′S 60°40′W
62 H3 **Lagunas** Tarapacá, N Chile 21°01′S 69°36′W
56 E9 **Lagunas** Loreto, N Peru 05°15′S 75°24′W
57 M20 **Lagunillas** Santa Cruz, SE Bolivia 19°38′S 63°39′W
54 H6 **Lagunillas** Mérida, NW Venezuela 08°31′N 71°24′W
44 C4 **La Habana** *var.* Havana. ● (Cuba) Ciudad de La Habana, W Cuba 23°07′N 82°25′W
44 C4 **La Habana** ◈ *province* W Cuba
169 W7 **Lahad Datu** Sabah, East Malaysia 05°01′N 118°20′E
169 W7 **Lahad Datu, Teluk** *var.* Telukan Lahad Datu, Teluk Darvel, Teluk Datu; *prev.* Darvel Bay. *bay* Sabah, East Malaysia, C Pacific Ocean
**Lahad Datu, Telukan** *see* Lahad Datu, Teluk
38 F10 **Lahaina** Maui, Hawaii, USA, C Pacific Ocean 20°52′N 156°40′W
168 L14 **Lahat** Sumatera, W Indonesia 03°46′S 103°32′E
**La Haye** *see* 's-Gravenhage
**Lahej** *see* Laḥij
62 G9 **La Higuera** Coquimbo, N Chile 29°33′S 71°15′W
141 S13 **Lahī, Ḥisā' al** *spring/well* NE Yemen 17°28′N 50°05′E
141 O16 **Laḥij** *var.* Laḥj, *Eng.* Lahej. SW Yemen 13°04′N 44°55′E
142 M3 **Lāhījān** Gīlān, NW Iran 37°12′N 50°00′E
119 I19 **Lahishyn** *Pol.* Lohiszyn, *Rus.* Logishin. Brestskaya Voblasts', SW Belarus 52°20′N 25°59′E
**Laḥj** *see* Laḥij
101 F18 **Lahn** ∿ W Germany
**Lähn** *see* Wleń
95 J21 **Laholm** Halland, S Sweden 56°30′N 13°05′E
95 J21 **Laholmsbukten** *bay* S Sweden
35 R6 **Lahontan Reservoir** ⊠ Nevada, W USA
149 W8 **Lahore** Punjab, NE Pakistan 31°36′N 74°18′E
149 W8 **Lahore** ✈ Punjab, E Pakistan 31°34′N 74°22′E
55 Q6 **La Horqueta** Delta Amacuro, NE Venezuela 09°13′N 62°02′W
119 K15 **Lahoysk** *Rus.* Logoysk. Minskaya Voblasts', C Belarus 54°12′N 27°53′E
101 F22 **Lahr** Baden-Württemberg, S Germany 48°21′N 07°52′E
93 M19 **Lahti** *Swe.* Lahtis. Päijät-Häme, S Finland 61°N 25°40′E
**Lahtis** *see* Lahti
40 M14 **La Huacana** Michoacán, SW Mexico 18°56′N 101°52′W
40 K14 **La Huerta** Jalisco, SW Mexico 19°29′N 104°40′W
78 H12 **Laï** *prev.* Behagle, De Behagle. Tandjilé, S Chad 09°22′N 16°14′E
**Laibach** *see* Ljubljana
167 Q5 **Lai Châu** Lai Châu, N Vietnam 22°04′N 103°10′E
**Laichow Bay** *see* Laizhou Wan
38 D9 **Lā'ie** *var.* Laie. O'ahu, Hawaii, USA, C Pacific Ocean 21°39′N 157°55′W
**Laie** *see* Lā'ie
102 L5 **l'Aigle** Orne, N France 48°46′N 00°37′E
103 Q7 **Laignes** Côte d'Or, C France 47°51′N 04°24′E
93 K17 **Laihia** Österbotten, W Finland 62°58′N 22°00′E
**Laila** *see* Laylā
83 F25 **Laingsburg** Western Cape, SW South Africa 33°12′S 20°51′E
109 U2 **Lainsitz** *Cz.* Lužnice. ∿ Austria/Czechia
96 I7 **Lairg** N Scotland, United Kingdom 58°02′N 04°23′W
81 I17 **Laisamis** Marsabit, N Kenya 01°35′N 37°49′E
**Laisberg** *see* Leisi
127 R4 **Laishevo** Respublika Tatarstan, W Russia 55°26′N 49°27′E
**Laisholm** *see* Jõgeva
92 H13 **Laisvall** Norrbotten, N Sweden 66°07′N 17°10′E
93 K19 **Laitila** Varsinais-Suomi, SW Finland 60°52′N 21°40′E
161 P5 **Laiwu** Shandong, E China 36°14′N 117°40′E
161 R4 **Laixi** *var.* Shuiji. Shandong, E China 36°50′N 120°40′E
161 R4 **Laiyang** Shandong, E China 36°58′N 120°40′E
161 O3 **Laiyuan** Hebei, E China 39°19′N 114°44′E
161 R4 **Laizhou** *var.* Ye Xian. Shandong, E China 37°12′N 120°01′E
161 Q4 **Laizhou Wan** *var.* Laichow Bay. *bay* E China
37 S8 **La Jara** Colorado, C USA 37°16′N 105°57′W
61 I15 **Lajeado** Rio Grande do Sul, S Brazil 29°28′S 52°00′W
112 L12 **Lajkovac** Serbia, C Serbia 44°22′N 20°12′E
111 K23 **Lajosmizse** Bács-Kiskun, C Hungary 47°02′N 19°31′E
**Lajta** *see* Leitha
40 I6 **La Junta** Chihuahua, N Mexico 28°30′N 107°20′W
37 V7 **La Junta** Colorado, C USA 37°59′N 103°34′W
92 J13 **Lakaträsk** Norrbotten, N Sweden 66°16′N 21°10′E
**Lak Dera** *see* Dheere Laaq
**Lakeamu** *see* Lakekamu
29 P12 **Lake Andes** South Dakota, N USA 43°08′N 98°33′W
22 H9 **Lake Arthur** Louisiana, S USA 30°04′N 92°40′W
187 Z15 **Lakeba** *prev.* Lakemba. *island* Lau Group, E Fiji
187 Z14 **Lakeba Passage** *channel* E Fiji
29 S10 **Lake Benton** Minnesota, N USA 44°15′N 96°17′W
23 V9 **Lake Butler** Florida, SE USA 30°01′N 82°20′W
183 P8 **Lake Cargelligo** New South Wales, SE Australia 33°21′S 146°25′E
22 G9 **Lake Charles** Louisiana, S USA 30°14′N 93°13′W
27 X9 **Lake City** Arkansas, C USA 35°50′N 90°28′W
37 Q7 **Lake City** Colorado, C USA 38°01′N 107°18′W
23 V9 **Lake City** Florida, SE USA 30°12′N 82°39′W
29 U13 **Lake City** Iowa, C USA 42°16′N 94°43′W
31 P7 **Lake City** Michigan, N USA 44°22′N 85°12′W
29 W9 **Lake City** Minnesota, N USA 44°27′N 92°16′W
21 T13 **Lake City** South Carolina, SE USA 33°52′N 79°45′W
29 Q7 **Lake City** South Dakota, N USA 45°42′N 97°22′W
20 M8 **Lake City** Tennessee, S USA 36°13′N 84°09′W
10 L17 **Lake Cowichan** Vancouver Island, British Columbia, SW Canada 48°50′N 124°04′W
29 U10 **Lake Crystal** Minnesota, N USA 44°07′N 94°13′W
25 T6 **Lake Dallas** Texas, SW USA 33°06′N 97°01′W
97 K15 **Lake District** *physical region* NW England, United Kingdom
18 D10 **Lake Erie Beach** New York, NE USA 42°37′N 79°04′W
29 T11 **Lakefield** Minnesota, N USA 43°40′N 95°10′W
25 V6 **Lake Fork Reservoir** ◎ Texas, SW USA
30 M9 **Lake Geneva** Wisconsin, N USA 42°36′N 88°25′W
18 L9 **Lake George** New York, NE USA 43°25′N 73°45′W
**Lake Harbour** *see* Kimmirut
36 I12 **Lake Havasu City** Arizona, SW USA 34°26′N 114°20′W
25 W12 **Lake Jackson** Texas, SW USA 29°01′N 95°25′W
186 D8 **Lakekamu** *var.* Lakeamu. ∿ S Papua New Guinea
180 K13 **Lake King** Western Australia 33°09′S 119°46′E
23 V12 **Lakeland** Florida, SE USA 28°03′N 81°57′W
23 U7 **Lakeland** Georgia, SE USA 31°02′N 83°04′W
181 W4 **Lakeland Downs** Queensland, NE Australia 15°54′S 144°54′E
11 P16 **Lake Louise** Alberta, SW Canada 51°26′N 116°10′W
**Lakemba** *see* Lakeba
29 V11 **Lake Mills** Iowa, C USA 43°25′N 93°31′W
39 Q10 **Lake Minchumina** Alaska, USA 63°55′N 152°25′W
**Lakemti** *see* Nek'emtē
186 A7 **Lake Murray** Western, SW Papua New Guinea 06°35′S 141°28′E
31 R9 **Lake Orion** Michigan, N USA 42°46′N 83°14′W
190 B16 **Lakepa** NE Niue 18°59′S 169°48′E
29 T11 **Lake Park** Iowa, C USA 43°27′N 95°19′W
18 K7 **Lake Placid** New York, NE USA 44°16′N 73°57′W
18 K9 **Lake Pleasant** New York, NE USA 43°27′N 74°24′W
34 M6 **Lakeport** California, W USA 39°04′N 122°56′W
29 Q10 **Lake Preston** South Dakota, N USA 44°21′N 97°22′W
22 J5 **Lake Providence** Louisiana, S USA 32°48′N 91°10′W
185 E20 **Lake Pukaki** Canterbury, South Island, New Zealand 44°12′S 170°10′E
81 D14 **Lakes** *var.* El Buhayrat. ◈ *state* C South Sudan
183 Q12 **Lakes Entrance** Victoria, SE Australia 37°52′S 147°58′E
37 N12 **Lakeside** Arizona, SW USA 34°09′N 109°58′W
35 V17 **Lakeside** California, W USA 32°50′N 116°55′W
23 S9 **Lakeside** Florida, SE USA 30°22′N 84°18′W
28 K13 **Lakeside** Nebraska, C USA 42°01′N 102°27′W
32 E13 **Lakeside** Oregon, NW USA 43°34′N 124°10′W
21 W6 **Lakeside** Virginia, NE USA 37°36′N 77°28′W
**Lake State** *see* Michigan
185 F20 **Lake Tekapo** Canterbury, South Island, New Zealand 44°01′S 170°29′E
21 O10 **Lake Toxaway** North Carolina, SE USA 35°06′N 82°57′W
29 T13 **Lake View** Iowa, C USA 42°18′N 95°04′W
32 I16 **Lakeview** Oregon, NW USA 42°13′N 120°21′W
25 O3 **Lakeview** Texas, SW USA 34°38′N 100°36′W
27 W14 **Lake Village** Arkansas, C USA 33°20′N 91°19′W
23 W12 **Lake Wales** Florida, SE USA 27°54′N 81°35′W
37 T4 **Lakewood** Colorado, C USA 39°38′N 105°07′W
18 K15 **Lakewood** New Jersey, NE USA 40°04′N 74°11′W
18 C11 **Lakewood** New York, NE USA 42°03′N 79°19′W
31 T11 **Lakewood** Ohio, N USA 41°28′N 81°48′W
23 Y13 **Lakewood Park** Florida, SE USA 27°32′N 80°24′W
23 Z14 **Lake Worth** Florida, SE USA 26°37′N 80°03′W
124 H11 **Lakhdenpokh'ya** Respublika Kareliya, NW Russia 61°25′N 30°05′E
152 L11 **Lakhīmpur** Uttar Pradesh, N India 27°57′N 80°47′E
154 J11 **Lakhnādon** Madhya Pradesh, C India 22°34′N 79°38′E
**Lakhnau** *see* Lucknow
154 A9 **Lakhpat** Gujarāt, W India 23°49′N 68°54′E
119 K19 **Lakhva** Brestskaya Voblasts', SW Belarus 52°13′N 27°06′E
26 I6 **Lakin** Kansas, C USA 37°57′N 101°16′W
149 S7 **Lakki** *var.* Lakki Marwat. Khyber Pakhtunkhwa, NW Pakistan 32°35′N 70°58′E
**Lakki Marwat** *see* Lakki
115 F21 **Lakonía** *historical region* S Greece
115 F22 **Lakonikós Kólpos** *gulf* S Greece
76 M17 **Lakota** S Ivory Coast 05°50′N 05°40′W
29 U11 **Lakota** Iowa, C USA 43°22′N 94°04′W
29 P3 **Lakota** North Dakota, N USA 48°02′N 98°20′W
**Lak Sao** *see* Ban Lakxao




◆ Country
● Country Capital
◇ Dependent Territory
○ Dependent Territory Capital
◈ Administrative Regions
✈ International Airport
▲ Mountain
▲▲ Mountain Range
⛰ Volcano
∿ River
◎ Lake
⊠ Reservoir

Laksefjorden – La Souterraine


92 *L8* **Laksefjorden** *Lapp.* Lágesvuotna. *fjord* N Norway
92 *K8* **Lakselv** *Lapp.* Leavdnja. Finnmark, N Norway *70°02′N 24°57′E*
155 *B21* **Lakshadweep** *prev.* the Laccadive Minicoy and Amindivi Islands. ◆ *union territory* India, N Indian Ocean
155 *C22* **Lakshadweep** *Eng.* Laccadive Islands. *island group* India, N Indian Ocean
153 *S17* **Lakshmikāntapur** West Bengal, NE India *22°05′N 88°19′E*
112 *G11* **Laktaši** ◆ Republika Srpska, N Bosnia and Herzegovina
149 *V7* **Lala Musa** Punjab, NE Pakistan *32°41′N 74°01′E*
**la Laon** *see* Laon
114 *M11* **Lalapaşa** Edirne, NW Turkey *41°52′N 26°44′E*
83 *P14* **Lalaua** Nampula, N Mozambique *14°21′S 38°16′E*
105 *S9* **L'Alcora** *var.* Alcora. Comunitat Valenciana, E Spain *40°05′N 00°14′W*
105 *S10* **L'Alcúdia** *var.* L'Alcudia. Comunitat Valenciana, E Spain *39°10′N 00°30′W*
42 *E8* **La Libertad** La Libertad, SW El Salvador *13°28′N 89°20′W*
42 *E3* **La Libertad** Petén, N Guatemala *16°49′N 90°08′W*
42 *H6* **La Libertad** Comayagua, SW Honduras *14°43′N 87°36′W*
40 *E4* **La Libertad** *var.* Puerto Libertad. Sonora, NW Mexico *29°52′N 112°39′W*
42 *K10* **La Libertad** Chontales, S Nicaragua *12°12′N 85°10′W*
42 *A9* **La Libertad** ◆ *department* SW El Salvador
56 *B11* **La Libertad** *off.* Región de La Libertad. ◆ *region* W Peru
**La Libertad, Región de** *see* La Libertad
62 *G11* **La Ligua** Valparaíso, C Chile *31°30′S 71°16′W*
139 *U5* **La'li Khān** As Sulaymānīyah, E Iraq *34°58′N 45°36′E*
104 *H3* **Lalín** Galicia, NW Spain *42°40′N 08°06′W*
102 *L13* **Lalinde** Dordogne, SW France *44°52′N 00°42′E*
104 *K16* **La Línea de la Concepción** Andalucía, S Spain *36°10′N 05°21′W*
152 *J14* **Lalitpur** Uttar Pradesh, N India *24°42′N 78°24′E*
153 *P11* **Lalitpur** Central, C Nepal *27°45′N 85°18′E*
152 *K10* **Lālkua** Uttarachal, N India *29°04′N 79°31′E*
153 *T12* **Lalmanirhat** Rājshāhi, N Bangladesh *25°51′N 89°34′E*
11 *R12* **La Loche** Saskatchewan, C Canada *56°31′N 109°27′W*
102 *M6* **la Loupe** Eure-et-Loir, C France *48°30′N 01°04′E*
99 *G20* **La Louvière** Hainaut, S Belgium *50°29′N 04°15′E*
**L'Altissima** *see* Hochwilde
104 *L14* **La Luisiana** Andalucía, S Spain *37°30′N 05°14′W*
37 *S14* **La Luz** New Mexico, SW USA *32°58′N 105°56′W*
107 *D16* **la Maddalena** Sardegna, Italy, C Mediterranean Sea *41°13′N 09°25′E*
62 *J7* **La Madrid** Tucumán, N Argentina *27°37′S 65°16′W*
**Lama-Kara** *see* Kara
15 *S8* **La Malbaie** Québec, SE Canada *47°39′N 70°11′W*
**Lamam** *see* Xékong
105 *P10* **La Mancha** *physical region* C Spain
**la Manche** *see* English Channel
187 *R13* **Lamap** Malekula, C Vanuatu *16°26′S 167°47′E*
37 *W6* **Lamar** Colorado, C USA *38°40′N 102°37′W*
27 *S7* **Lamar** Missouri, C USA *37°30′N 94°18′W*
21 *S12* **Lamar** South Carolina, SE USA *34°10′N 80°03′W*
107 *C19* **La Marmora, Punta** ▲ Sardegna, Italy, C Mediterranean Sea *39°58′N 09°20′E*
8 *I9* **La Martre, Lac** ◎ Northwest Territories, NW Canada
56 *D10* **Lamas** San Martín, N Peru *06°28′S 76°31′W*
42 *I5* **La Masica** Atlántida, NW Honduras *15°38′N 87°08′W*
103 *R12* **Lamastre** Ardèche, E France *45°00′N 04°32′E*
**La Matepec** *see* Santa Ana, Volcán de
44 *I7* **La Maya** Santiago de Cuba, E Cuba *20°11′N 75°40′W*
109 *S5* **Lambach** Oberösterreich, N Austria *48°06′N 13°52′E*
168 *I11* **Lambak** Pulau Pini, W Indonesia *0°08′N 98°36′E*
102 *H5* **Lamballe** Côtes d'Armor, NW France *48°28′N 02°31′W*
79 *D18* **Lambaréné** Moyen-Ogooué, W Gabon *0°41′S 10°13′E*
**Lambasa** *see* Labasa
56 *B11* **Lambayeque** Lambayeque, W Peru *06°42′S 79°55′W*
56 *A10* **Lambayeque** *off.* Región de Lambayeque. ◆ *region* NW Peru
**Lambayeque, Región de** *see* Lambayeque
97 *G17* **Lambay Island** *Ir.* Reachrainn. *island* E Ireland
186 *G6* **Lambert, Cape** *headland* New Britain, E Papua New Guinea *04°15′S 151°31′E*
195 *W6* **Lambert Glacier** *glacier* Antarctica
29 *T10* **Lamberton** Minnesota, N USA *44°14′N 95°15′W*
27 *X4* **Lambert-Saint Louis** ✕ Missouri, C USA *38°43′N 90°19′W*
31 *R11* **Lambertville** Michigan, N USA *41°46′N 83°37′W*
18 *J15* **Lambertville** New Jersey, NE USA *40°20′N 74°55′W*
171 *N12* **Lambogo** Sulawesi, N Indonesia *0°57′S 120°23′E*
106 *D8* **Lambro** ⚞ N Italy
33 *W11* **Lame Deer** Montana, NW USA *45°37′N 106°37′W*
104 *H6* **Lamego** Viseu, N Portugal *41°05′N 07°49′W*
187 *Q14* **Lamen Bay** Épi, C Vanuatu *16°36′S 168°10′E*
45 *X6* **Lamentin** Basse Terre, N Guadeloupe *16°16′N 61°38′W*
**Lamentin** *see* le Lamentin
182 *K10* **Lameroo** South Australia *35°22′S 140°30′E*
54 *F10* **La Mesa** Cundinamarca, C Colombia *04°37′N 74°30′W*
35 *U17* **La Mesa** California, W USA *32°44′N 117°00′W*
37 *R16* **La Mesa** New Mexico, SW USA *32°03′N 106°41′W*
25 *N6* **Lamesa** Texas, SW USA *32°43′N 101°57′W*
107 *N21* **Lamezia Terme** Calabria, SE Italy *38°54′N 16°13′E*
115 *F17* **Lamía** Stereá Elláda, C Greece *38°54′N 22°27′E*
171 *O8* **Lamitan** Basilan Island, SW Philippines *06°40′N 122°07′E*
187 *Y14* **Lamiti** Gau, C Fiji *18°00′S 179°20′E*
171 *T11* **Lamlam** Papua Barat, E Indonesia *0°03′S 130°46′E*
188 *B16* **Lamlam, Mount** ▲ SW Guam *13°20′N 144°40′E*
109 *Q6* **Lammer** ⚞ E Austria
185 *E23* **Lammerlaw Range** ▲▲ South Island, New Zealand
95 *L20* **Lammhult** Kronoberg, S Sweden *57°09′N 14°35′E*
93 *L18* **Lammi** Kanta-Häme, S Finland *61°06′N 25°00′E*
189 *U11* **Lamoil** *island* Chuuk, C Micronesia
35 *W3* **Lamoille** Nevada, W USA *40°47′N 115°37′W*
18 *M7* **Lamoille River** ⚞ Vermont, NE USA
30 *J13* **La Moine River** ⚞ Illinois, N USA
171 *P4* **Lamon Bay** *bay* Luzon, N Philippines
29 *V16* **Lamoni** Iowa, C USA *40°37′N 93°56′W*
35 *R13* **Lamont** California, W USA *35°15′N 118°54′W*
27 *N8* **Lamont** Oklahoma, C USA *36°41′N 97°33′W*
54 *E13* **La Montañita** *var.* Montañita. Caquetá, S Colombia *01°22′N 75°25′W*
43 *N8* **La Mosquitia** *var.* Miskito Coast, *Eng.* Mosquito Coast. *coastal region* E Nicaragua
102 *I9* **la Mothe-Achard** Vendée, NW France *46°37′N 01°37′W*
188 *L15* **Lamotrek Atoll** *atoll* Caroline Islands, C Micronesia
29 *P6* **La Moure** North Dakota, N USA *46°21′N 98°17′W*
167 *O8* **Lampang** *var.* Muang Lampang. Lampang, NW Thailand *18°16′N 99°30′E*
167 *R9* **Lam Pao Reservoir** ⊠ E Thailand
25 *S9* **Lampasas** Texas, SW USA *31°04′N 98°12′W*
25 *S9* **Lampasas River** ⚞ Texas, SW USA
41 *N7* **Lampazos** *var.* Lampazos de Naranjo. Nuevo León, NE Mexico *27°00′N 100°28′W*
**Lampazos de Naranjo** *see* Lampazos
115 *E19* **Lámpeia** Dytikí Elláda, S Greece *37°51′N 21°48′E*
101 *G19* **Lampertheim** Hessen, W Germany *49°36′N 08°28′E*
97 *I20* **Lampeter** SW Wales, United Kingdom *52°08′N 04°04′W*
167 *O7* **Lamphun** *var.* Lampun, Muang Lamphun. Lamphun, NW Thailand *18°36′N 99°02′E*
11 *X10* **Lamprey** Manitoba, C Canada *58°18′N 94°06′W*
**Lampun** *see* Lamphun
168 *M15* **Lampung** *off.* Propinsi Lampung. ◆ *province* SW Indonesia
**Lampung, Propinsi** *see* Lampung
126 *K6* **Lamskoye** Lipetskaya Oblast', W Russia *52°57′N 38°04′E*
81 *K20* **Lamu** Lamu, SE Kenya *02°17′S 40°54′E*
81 *K20* **Lamu** ◆ *county* SE Kenya
43 *N14* **La Muerte, Cerro** ▲ C Costa Rica *09°33′N 83°47′W*
103 *S13* **la Mure** Isère, E France *44°54′N 05°48′E*
37 *S10* **Lamy** New Mexico, SW USA *35°27′N 105°52′W*
119 *J18* **Lan'** ⚞ C Belarus
38 *E10* **Lāna'i** *var.* Lanai. *island* Hawai'i, USA, C Pacific Ocean
38 *E10* **Lāna'i City** *var.* Lanai City. Lanai, Hawaii, USA, C Pacific Ocean *20°49′N 156°55′W*
**Lanai City** *see* Lāna'i City
99 *L18* **Lanaken** Limburg, NE Belgium *50°53′N 05°39′E*
171 *Q7* **Lanao, Lake** *var.* Lake Sultan Alonto. ◎ Mindanao, S Philippines
96 *J12* **Lanark** S Scotland, United Kingdom *55°38′N 04°25′W*
96 *I13* **Lanark** *cultural region* C Scotland, United Kingdom
104 *L9* **La Nava de Ricomalillo** Castilla-La Mancha, C Spain *39°40′N 04°59′W*
166 *M13* **Lanbi Kyun** *prev.* Sullivan Island. *island* Mergui Archipelago, S Myanmar (Burma)
**Lancang Jiang** *see* Mekong
97 *K17* **Lancashire** *cultural region* N England, United Kingdom
15 *N13* **Lancaster** Ontario, SE Canada *45°10′N 74°31′W*
97 *K16* **Lancaster** NW England, United Kingdom *54°03′N 02°48′W*
35 *T14* **Lancaster** California, W USA *34°42′N 118°08′W*
20 *M6* **Lancaster** Kentucky, S USA *37°35′N 84°34′W*
27 *U1* **Lancaster** Missouri, C USA *40°32′N 92°31′W*
19 *O7* **Lancaster** New Hampshire, NE USA *44°29′N 71°34′W*
18 *D10* **Lancaster** New York, NE USA *42°54′N 78°40′W*
31 *T14* **Lancaster** Ohio, N USA *39°42′N 82°36′W*
18 *H16* **Lancaster** Pennsylvania, NE USA *40°03′N 76°18′W*
21 *R11* **Lancaster** South Carolina, SE USA *34°43′N 80°47′W*
25 *U7* **Lancaster** Texas, SW USA *32°35′N 96°45′W*
21 *X5* **Lancaster** Virginia, NE USA *37°48′N 76°30′W*
30 *J9* **Lancaster** Wisconsin, N USA *42°52′N 90°43′W*
197 *N10* **Lancaster Sound** *sound* Nunavut, N Canada
**Lan-chou/Lan-chow/ Lanchow** *see* Lanzhou
107 *K14* **Lanciano** Abruzzo, C Italy *42°13′N 14°23′E*
111 *O16* **Łańcut** Podkarpackie, SE Poland *50°04′N 22°14′E*
169 *Q11* **Landak, Sungai** ⚞ Borneo, N Indonesia
**Landao** *see* Lantau Island
**Landau** *see* Landau an der Isar
**Landau** *see* Landau in der Pfalz
101 *N22* **Landau an der Isar** *var.* Landau. Bayern, SE Germany *48°40′N 12°41′E*
101 *F20* **Landau in der Pfalz** *var.* Landau. Rheinland-Pfalz, SW Germany *49°12′N 08°07′E*
**Land Burgenland** *see* Burgenland
108 *K8* **Landeck** Tirol, W Austria *47°09′N 10°35′E*
99 *J19* **Landen** Vlaams Brabant, C Belgium *50°45′N 05°05′E*
33 *U15* **Lander** Wyoming, C USA *42°49′N 108°43′W*
102 *F5* **Landerneau** Finistère, NW France *48°27′N 04°16′W*
95 *K20* **Landeryd** Halland, S Sweden *57°04′N 13°15′E*
102 *J15* **Landes** ◆ *department* SW France
**Landeshut/Landeshut in Schlesien** *see* Kamienna Góra
105 *R9* **Landete** Castilla-La Mancha, C Spain *39°54′N 01°22′W*
99 *M18* **Landgraaf** Limburg, SE Netherlands *50°55′N 06°04′E*
102 *F5* **Landivisiau** Finistère, NW France *48°31′N 04°03′W*
**Land Kärten** *see* Kärnten
**Land of Enchantment** *see* New Mexico
**The Land of Opportunity** *see* Arkansas
**Land of Steady Habits** *see* Connecticut
**Land of the Midnight Sun** *see* Alaska
108 *I8* **Landquart** Graubünden, SE Switzerland *46°58′N 09°35′E*
108 *J9* **Landquart** ⚞ Austria/Switzerland
21 *P10* **Landrum** South Carolina, SE USA *35°10′N 82°11′W*
**Landsberg** *see* Gorzów Wielkopolski, Lubuskie, Poland
**Landsberg** *see* Górowo Iławeckie, Warmińsko-Mazurskie, NE Poland
101 *K23* **Landsberg am Lech** Bayern, S Germany *48°03′N 10°52′E*
**Landsberg an der Warthe** *see* Gorzów Wielkopolski
97 *G25* **Land's End** *headland* SW England, United Kingdom *50°02′N 05°41′W*
101 *M22* **Landshut** Bayern, SE Germany *48°32′N 12°09′E*
**Landskron** *see* Lanškroun
95 *J22* **Landskrona** Skåne, S Sweden *55°52′N 12°52′E*
98 *I10* **Landsmeer** Noord-Holland, C Netherlands *52°26′N 04°55′E*
95 *J19* **Landvetter** ✕ (Göteborg) Västra Götaland, S Sweden *57°39′N 12°22′E*
**Landwarów** *see* Lentvaris
23 *R5* **Lanett** Alabama, S USA *32°52′N 85°11′W*
108 *C8* **La Neuveville** *var.* Neuveville, *Ger.* Neuenstadt. Neuchâtel, W Switzerland *47°05′N 07°03′E*
95 *G21* **Langå** *var.* Langaa. Midtjylland, C Denmark *56°23′N 09°55′E*
**Langaa** *see* Langå
158 *G14* **La'nga Co** ◎ W China
**Langada** *see* Lagkáda
**Langades/Langadhás** *see* Lagkadás
**Langádhia/** *see* Lagkádia
147 *T14* **Langar** *Rus.* Lyangar. SE Tajikistan *37°04′N 72°39′E*
146 *M10* **Langar** *Rus.* Lyangar. Navoiy Viloyati, C Uzbekistan *40°27′N 65°54′E*
142 *M3* **Langarūd** Gīlān, NW Iran *37°10′N 50°09′E*
11 *V16* **Langbank** Saskatchewan, S Canada *50°01′N 102°16′W*
29 *P2* **Langdon** North Dakota, N USA *48°45′N 98°22′W*
103 *P12* **Langeac** Haute-Loire, C France *45°06′N 03°31′E*
102 *L8* **Langeais** Indre-et-Loire, C France *47°22′N 00°27′E*
80 *I8* **Langeb, Wadi** ⚞ NE Sudan
**Långed** *see* Dals Långed
95 *G25* **Langeland** *island* S Denmark
99 *B18* **Langemark** West-Vlaanderen, W Belgium *50°55′N 02°55′E*
101 *G18* **Langen** Hessen, W Germany *49°58′N 08°40′E*
101 *J22* **Langenau** Baden-Württemberg, S Germany *48°30′N 10°08′E*
11 *V16* **Langenburg** Saskatchewan, S Canada *50°50′N 101°43′W*
108 *L8* **Längenfeld** Tirol, W Austria *47°04′N 10°59′E*
101 *E16* **Langenfeld** Nordrhein-Westfalen, W Germany *51°06′N 06°57′E*
100 *I12* **Langenhagen** Niedersachsen, N Germany *52°26′N 09°45′E*
100 *I12* **Langenhagen** ✕ (Hannover) Niedersachsen, NW Germany *52°28′N 09°40′E*
109 *W3* **Langenlois** Niederösterreich, NE Austria *48°29′N 15°42′E*
108 *E7* **Langenthal** Bern, NW Switzerland *47°13′N 07°48′E*
109 *W6* **Langenwang** Steiermark, E Austria *47°34′N 15°39′E*
109 *X3* **Langenzersdorf** Niederösterreich, E Austria *48°20′N 16°22′E*
100 *F9* **Langeoog** *island* NW Germany
95 *H23* **Langeskov** Syddtjylland, C Denmark *55°22′N 10°36′E*
95 *G16* **Langesund** Telemark, S Norway *59°00′N 09°43′E*
95 *G17* **Langesundsfjorden** *fjord* S Norway
94 *D10* **Langevågen** Møre og Romsdal, S Norway *62°26′N 06°15′E*
161 *P3* **Langfang** Hebei, E China *39°30′N 116°39′E*
94 *E9* **Langfjorden** *fjord* S Norway
29 *Q8* **Langford** South Dakota, N USA *45°36′N 97°48′W*
168 *I10* **Langgapayung** Sumatera, W Indonesia *01°42′N 99°57′E*
106 *E9* **Langhirano** Emilia-Romagna, C Italy *44°37′N 10°16′E*
97 *K14* **Langholm** S Scotland, United Kingdom *55°14′N 03°11′W*
92 *I3* **Langjökull** *glacier* C Iceland
168 *I6* **Langkawi, Pulau** *island* Peninsular Malaysia
166 *M14* **Langkha Tuk, Khao** ▲ SW Thailand *09°19′N 98°39′E*
14 *L8* **Langlade** Québec, SE Canada *48°13′N 75°58′W*
10 *M17* **Langley** British Columbia, SW Canada *49°07′N 122°39′W*
167 *S7* **Lang Mô** Thanh Hoa, N Vietnam *19°36′N 105°30′E*
**Langnau** *see* Langnau im Emmental
108 *E8* **Langnau im Emmental** *var.* Langnau. Bern, W Switzerland *46°57′N 07°47′E*
103 *Q13* **Langogne** Lozère, S France *44°40′N 03°52′E*
102 *K13* **Langon** Gironde, SW France *44°33′N 00°14′W*
**La Ngounié** *see* Ngounié
92 *G10* **Langøya** *island* C Norway
158 *G14* **Langqên Zangbo** ⚞ China/India
**Langreo** *see* Llangréu
103 *S7* **Langres** Haute-Marne, N France *47°53′N 05°20′E*
103 *R8* **Langres, Plateau de** *plateau* C France
168 *H8* **Langsa** Sumatera, W Indonesia *04°30′N 97°53′E*
93 *H16* **Långsele** Västernorrland, C Sweden *63°11′N 17°05′E*
162 *L12* **Lang Shan** ▲▲ N China
95 *M14* **Långshyttan** Dalarna, C Sweden *60°26′N 16°02′E*
167 *T5* **Lang Sơn** *var.* Langson. Lang Sơn, N Vietnam *21°50′N 106°45′E*
**Langson** *see* Lang Sơn
167 *N14* **Lang Suan** Chumphon, SW Thailand *09°55′N 99°07′E*
93 *J14* **Långträsk** Norrbotten, N Sweden *65°22′N 20°19′E*
25 *N11* **Langtry** Texas, SW USA *29°46′N 101°25′W*
103 *P16* **Languedoc** *cultural region* S France
27 *X10* **L'Anguille River** ⚞ Arkansas, C USA
93 *I16* **Långviksmon** Västernorrland, N Sweden *63°39′N 18°45′E*
101 *K22* **Langweid** Bayern, S Germany *48°29′N 10°50′E*
160 *J8* **Langzhong** Sichuan, C China *31°46′N 105°55′E*
**Lan Hsü** *see* Lan Yu
11 *U15* **Lanigan** Saskatchewan, S Canada *51°50′N 105°01′W*
116 *K5* **Lanivtsi** Ternopil's'ka Oblast', W Ukraine *49°52′N 26°05′E*
137 *Y13* **Länkäran** *Rus.* Lenkoran'. S Azerbaijan *38°46′N 48°51′E*
102 *L16* **Lannemezan** Hautes-Pyrénées, S France *43°08′N 00°22′E*
102 *G5* **Lannion** Côtes d'Armor, NW France *48°44′N 03°27′W*
14 *M11* **L'Annonciation** Québec, SE Canada *46°22′N 74°51′W*
105 *V5* **L'Anoia** ⚞ NE Spain
18 *I15* **Lansdale** Pennsylvania, NE USA *40°14′N 75°13′W*
14 *L14* **Lansdowne** Ontario, SE Canada *44°25′N 76°00′W*
152 *K9* **Lansdowne** Uttarākhand, N India *29°50′N 78°42′E*
30 *M3* **L'Anse** Michigan, N USA *46°45′N 88°27′W*
15 *S7* **L'Anse-St-Jean** Québec, SE Canada *48°14′N 70°13′W*
29 *Y11* **Lansing** Iowa, C USA *43°22′N 91°11′W*
27 *R4* **Lansing** Kansas, C USA *39°15′N 94°54′W*
31 *Q9* **Lansing** *state capital* Michigan, N USA *42°44′N 84°33′W*
**Länsi-Suomi** ◆ *province* W Finland
92 *J12* **Lansjärv** Norrbotten, N Sweden *66°39′N 22°10′E*
111 *G17* **Lanškroun** *Ger.* Landskron. Pardubický Kraj, E Czechia *49°55′N 16°38′E*
167 *N16* **Lanta, Ko** *island* S Thailand
161 *O15* **Lantau Island** *Cant.* Tai Yue Shan, *Chin.* Landao. *island* Hong Kong, S China
**Lantian** *see* Lianyuan
**Lantung, Gulf of** *see* Liaodong Wan
171 *O11* **Lanu** Sulawesi, N Indonesia *01°00′N 121°33′E*
107 *D19* **Lanusei** Sardegna, Italy, C Mediterranean Sea *39°55′N 09°31′E*
102 *H7* **Lanvaux, Landes de** *physical region* NW France
163 *W8* **Lanxi** Heilongjiang, NE China *46°18′N 126°15′E*
161 *R10* **Lanxi** Zhejiang, SE China *29°12′N 119°27′E*
**La Nyanga** *see* Nyanga
161 *T15* **Lan Yu** *var.* Huoshao Tao, Hungt'ou, Lan Hsü, Lanyü, *Eng.* Orchid Island; *prev.* Kotosho, Koto Sho, Lan Yü. *island* SE Taiwan
**Lanyü** *see* Lan Yu
64 *P11* **Lanzarote** *island* Islas Canarias, Spain, NE Atlantic Ocean
159 *V10* **Lanzhou** *var.* Lan-chou, Lanchow, Lan-chow; *prev.* Kaolan. *province capital* Gansu, C China *36°01′N 103°52′E*
106 *B8* **Lanzo Torinese** Piemonte, NE Italy *45°18′N 07°26′E*
171 *O11* **Laoag** Luzon, N Philippines *18°11′N 120°34′E*
171 *Q5* **Laoang** Samar, C Philippines *12°29′N 125°01′E*
167 *R5* **Lao Cai** Lao Cai, N Vietnam *22°29′N 104°00′E*
**Laodicea/Laodicea ad Mare** *see* Al Lādhiqīyah
**Laoet** *see* Laut, Pulau
163 *T11* **Laoha He** ⚞ NE China
160 *M8* **Laohekou** *var.* Guanghua. Hubei, C China *32°20′N 111°42′E*
**Laoi, An** *see* Lee
97 *E19* **Laois** *prev.* Leix, Queen's County. *cultural region* C Ireland
163 *W12* **Lao Ling** ▲▲ N China
64 *Q11* **La Oliva** *var.* Oliva. Fuerteventura, Islas Canarias, Spain, NE Atlantic Ocean *28°36′N 13°53′W*
**Lao, Loch** *see* Belfast Lough
**Laolong** *see* Longchuan
**Lao Mangnai** *see* Mangnai
103 *P3* **Laon** *var.* la Laon; *anc.* Laudunum. Aisne, N France *49°34′N 03°37′E*
**Lao People's Democratic Republic** *see* Laos
54 *M3* **La Orchila, Isla** *island* N Venezuela
64 *O11* **La Orotava** Tenerife, Islas Canarias, Spain, NE Atlantic Ocean *28°23′N 16°32′W*
57 *E14* **La Oroya** Junín, C Peru *11°36′S 75°54′W*
167 *Q7* **Laos** *off.* Lao People's Democratic Republic, *Lao.* Sathalanalat Paxathipatai Paxaxôn Lao. ◆ *republic* SE Asia
**Lao, Sathalanalat Paxathipatai Paxaxôn** *see* Laos
161 *R5* **Laoshan Wan** *bay* E China
163 *Y10* **Laoye Ling** ▲▲ NE China
60 *J12* **Lapa** Paraná, S Brazil *25°46′S 49°44′W*
103 *P10* **Lapalisse** Allier, C France *46°13′N 03°39′E*
54 *F9* **La Palma** Cundinamarca, C Colombia *05°23′N 74°24′W*
42 *F7* **La Palma** Chalatenango, N El Salvador *14°19′N 89°10′W*
43 *W16* **La Palma** Darién, SE Panama *08°24′N 78°09′W*
64 *N11* **La Palma** *island* Islas Canarias, Spain, NE Atlantic Ocean
104 *J14* **La Palma del Condado** Andalucía, S Spain *37°23′N 06°33′W*
61 *F18* **La Paloma** Durazno, C Uruguay *32°54′S 55°36′W*
61 *G20* **La Paloma** Rocha, E Uruguay *34°37′S 54°08′W*
61 *A21* **La Pampa** *off.* Provincia de La Pampa. ◆ *province* C Argentina
**La Pampa, Provincia de** *see* La Pampa
55 *P8* **La Paragua** Bolívar, E Venezuela *06°53′N 63°16′W*
119 *O16* **Lapatsichy** *Rus.* Lopatichi. Mahilyowskaya Voblasts', E Belarus *53°34′N 30°53′E*
61 *C16* **La Paz** Entre Ríos, E Argentina *30°45′S 59°36′W*
62 *I11* **La Paz** Mendoza, C Argentina *33°30′S 67°36′W*
57 *J18* **La Paz** *var.* La Paz de Ayacucho. ● (Bolivia-seat of government) La Paz, W Bolivia *16°30′S 68°13′W*
42 *H6* **La Paz** La Paz, SW Honduras *14°20′N 87°40′W*
40 *F9* **La Paz** Baja California Sur, NW Mexico *24°07′N 110°18′W*
61 *F20* **La Paz** Canelones, S Uruguay *34°46′S 56°13′W*
57 *J16* **La Paz** ◆ *department* W Bolivia
42 *B9* **La Paz** ◆ *department* S El Salvador
42 *G7* **La Paz** ◆ *department* SW Honduras
**La Paz** *see* El Alto, Bolivia
**La Paz** *see* Robles, Colombia
**La Paz** *see* La Paz Centro
40 *F9* **La Paz, Bahía de** *bay* NW Mexico
42 *I10* **La Paz Centro** *var.* La Paz. León, W Nicaragua *12°20′N 86°41′W*
**La Paz de Ayacucho** *see* La Paz
54 *J15* **La Pedrera** Amazonas, SE Colombia *01°19′S 69°31′W*
31 *S9* **Lapeer** Michigan, N USA *43°03′N 83°19′W*
40 *K6* **La Perla** Chihuahua, N Mexico *28°18′N 104°34′W*
165 *T1* **La Pérouse Strait** *Jap.* Sōya-kaikyō, *Rus.* Proliv Laperuza. *strait* Japan/Russia
63 *I14* **La Perra, Salitral de** *salt lake* C Argentina
**Laperuza, Proliv** *see* La Pérouse Strait
41 *Q10* **La Pesca** Tamaulipas, C Mexico *23°49′N 97°45′W*
40 *M13* **La Piedad Cavadas** Michoacán, C Mexico *20°20′N 102°01′W*
**Lapines** *see* Lafnitz
93 *M16* **Lapinlahti** Pohjois-Savo, C Finland *63°21′N 27°25′E*
**Lápithos** *see* Lapta
22 *K9* **Laplace** Louisiana, S USA *30°04′N 90°28′W*
45 *X12* **La Plaine** SE Dominica *15°20′N 61°15′W*
173 *P16* **La Plaine-des-Palmistes** C Réunion
92 *K11* **Lapland** *Fin.* Lappi, *Swe.* Lappland. *cultural region* N Europe
**Lapland** *see* Lappi
28 *M8* **La Plant** South Dakota, N USA *45°06′N 100°40′W*
61 *D20* **La Plata** Buenos Aires, E Argentina *34°56′S 57°55′W*
54 *D12* **La Plata** Huila, SW Colombia *02°33′N 75°55′W*
21 *W4* **La Plata** Maryland, NE USA *38°32′N 76°59′W*
**La Plata** *see* Sucre
45 *U6* **la Plata, Río de** ⚞ C Puerto Rico
105 *W4* **La Pobla de Lillet** Cataluña, NE Spain *42°15′N 01°57′E*
105 *U4* **La Pobla de Segur** Cataluña, NE Spain *42°15′N 00°58′E*
15 *S9* **La Pocatière** Québec, SE Canada *47°21′N 70°04′W*
104 *K2* **La Pola** *prev.* Pola de Lena. Asturias, N Spain *43°10′N 05°49′W*
104 *L3* **La Pola de Gordón** Castilla y León, N Spain *42°50′N 05°38′W*
104 *L2* **La Pola Siero** *prev.* Pola de Siero. Asturias, N Spain *43°24′N 05°39′W*
31 *O11* **La Porte** Indiana, N USA *41°36′N 86°43′W*
18 *H13* **Laporte** Pennsylvania, NE USA *41°25′N 76°29′W*
29 *X13* **La Porte City** Iowa, C USA *42°19′N 92°11′W*
62 *J8* **La Posta** Catamarca, C Argentina *27°59′S 65°32′W*
40 *E8* **La Poza Grande** Baja California Sur, NW Mexico *25°50′N 112°00′W*
93 *K16* **Lappajärvi** Etelä-Pohjanmaa, W Finland *63°13′N 23°40′E*
93 *L16* **Lappajärvi** ◎ W Finland
93 *N18* **Lappeenranta** *Swe.* Villmanstrand. Etelä-Karjala, SE Finland *61°04′N 28°15′E*
93 *J17* **Lappfjärd** *Fin.* Lapväärtti. Österbotten, W Finland *62°14′N 21°30′E*
92 *L12* **Lappi** *Swe.* Lappland, *Eng.* Lapland. ◆ *region* N Finland
**Lappi/Lappland** *see* Lapland
**Lappo** *see* Lapua
61 *C23* **Laprida** Buenos Aires, E Argentina *37°34′S 60°45′W*
25 *P13* **La Pryor** Texas, SW USA *28°56′N 99°51′W*
136 *B11* **Lâpseki** Çanakkale, NW Turkey *40°22′N 26°42′E*
121 *P2* **Lapta** *Gk.* Lápithos. NW Cyprus *35°20′N 33°11′E*
**Laptev Sea** *see* Laptevykh, More
122 *N6* **Laptevykh, More** *Eng.* Laptev Sea. *sea* Arctic Ocean
93 *K16* **Lapua** *Swe.* Lappo. Etelä-Pohjanmaa, W Finland *62°57′N 23°E*
105 *P3* **La Puebla de Arganzón** País Vasco, N Spain *42°45′N 02°49′W*
104 *L14* **La Puebla de Cazalla** Andalucía, S Spain *37°14′N 05°18′W*
104 *M9* **La Puebla de Montalbán** Castilla-La Mancha, C Spain *39°52′N 04°22′W*
54 *I6* **La Puerta** Trujillo, NW Venezuela *09°08′N 70°46′W*
**Lapurdum** *see* Bayonne
40 *E7* **La Purísima** Baja California Sur, NW Mexico *26°10′N 112°05′W*
**Lapväärtti** *see* Lappfjärd
110 *O10* **Łapy** Podlaskie, NE Poland *53°N 22°54′E*
80 *D6* **Laqiya Arba'in** Northern, NW Sudan *20°01′N 28°01′E*
62 *J4* **La Quiaca** Jujuy, N Argentina *22°12′S 65°36′W*
107 *J14* **L'Aquila** *var.* Aquila, Aquila degli Abruzzi. Abruzzo, C Italy *42°21′N 13°24′E*
143 *Q13* **Lār** Fārs, S Iran *27°42′N 54°19′E*
54 *J5* **Lara** *off.* Estado Lara. ◆ *state* NW Venezuela
104 *G2* **Laracha** Galicia, NW Spain *43°14′N 08°34′W*
74 *G5* **Larache** *var.* al Araïch, El Araïch, *prev.* El Araïche; *anc.* Lixus. NW Morocco *35°12′N 06°10′W*
**Lara, Estado** *see* Lara
103 *T14* **Laragne-Montéglin** Hautes-Alpes, SE France *44°21′N 05°46′E*
104 *M13* **La Rambla** Andalucía, S Spain *37°37′N 04°44′W*
33 *Y17* **Laramie** Wyoming, C USA *41°18′N 105°35′W*
33 *X15* **Laramie Mountains** ▲▲ Wyoming, C USA
33 *Y16* **Laramie River** ⚞ Wyoming, C USA
60 *H12* **Laranjeiras do Sul** Paraná, S Brazil *25°23′S 52°23′W*
**Larantoeka** *see* Larantuka
171 *P16* **Larantuka** *prev.* Larantoeka. Flores, C Indonesia *08°20′S 123°00′E*
171 *U15* **Larat** Pulau Larat, E Indonesia *07°07′S 131°46′E*
171 *U15* **Larat, Pulau** *island* Kepulauan Tanimbar, E Indonesia
95 *P19* **Lärbro** Gotland, SE Sweden *57°46′N 18°49′E*
106 *A9* **Larche, Col de** *pass* France/Italy
14 *H8* **Larder Lake** Ontario, S Canada *48°06′N 79°44′W*
105 *O2* **Laredo** Cantabria, N Spain *43°23′N 03°22′W*
25 *Q15* **Laredo** Texas, SW USA *27°30′N 99°30′W*
40 *H9* **La Reforma** Sinaloa, W Mexico *25°05′N 108°03′W*
98 *N11* **Laren** Gelderland, E Netherlands *52°12′N 06°22′E*
98 *J11* **Laren** Noord-Holland, C Netherlands *52°15′N 05°13′E*
102 *K13* **la Réole** Gironde, SW France *44°34′N 00°00′W*
**La Réunion** *see* Réunion
**Largeau** *see* Faya
103 *U13* **l'Argentière-la-Bessée** Hautes-Alpes, SE France *44°49′N 06°34′E*
**Lar Gerd** *see* Largird
**Largird** *see* Largird
23 *V12* **Largo** Florida, SE USA *27°55′N 82°47′W*
37 *Q9* **Largo, Canon** *valley* New Mexico, SW USA
44 *D6* **Largo, Cayo** *island* W Cuba
23 *Z17* **Largo, Key** *island* Florida Keys, Florida, SE USA
96 *H12* **Largs** W Scotland, United Kingdom *55°48′N 04°50′W*
102 *I16* **la Rhune** *var.* Larrún. ▲ France/Spain *43°19′N 01°36′W* *see also* Larrún
**la Rhune** *see* Larrún
**la Riège** *see* Ariège
29 *Q4* **Larimore** North Dakota, N USA *47°54′N 97°37′W*
107 *L15* **Larino** Molise, C Italy *41°46′N 14°50′E*
**Lario** *see* Como, Lago di
62 *J9* **La Rioja** La Rioja, NW Argentina *29°26′S 66°50′W*
62 *I9* **La Rioja** *off.* Provincia de La Rioja. ◆ *province* NW Argentina
105 *O4* **La Rioja** ◆ *autonomous community* N Spain
**La Rioja, Provincia de** *see* La Rioja
115 *F16* **Lárisa** *var.* Larissa. Thessalía, C Greece *39°38′N 22°27′E*
**Larissa** *see* Lárisa
149 *Q13* **Lārkāna** *var.* Larkhana. Sindh, SE Pakistan *27°32′N 68°18′E*
**Larkhana** *see* Lārkāna
149 *O4* **Larkird** *var.* Largird. Sar-e Pul, N Afghanistan *35°29′N 66°39′E*
**Larnaca** *see* Lárnaka
121 *Q3* **Lárnaka** *var.* Larnaca, Larnax. SE Cyprus *34°55′N 33°39′E*
121 *Q3* **Lárnaka** ✕ SE Cyprus *34°52′N 33°38′E*
**Larnax** *see* Lárnaka
97 *G14* **Larne** *Ir.* Latharna. E Northern Ireland United Kingdom *54°51′N 05°49′W*
26 *L5* **Larned** Kansas, C USA *38°12′N 99°05′W*
104 *L3* **La Robla** Castilla y León, N Spain *42°48′N 05°37′W*
104 *J10* **La Roca de la Sierra** Extremadura, W Spain *39°06′N 06°41′W*
99 *K22* **La Roche-en-Ardenne** Luxembourg, SE Belgium *50°11′N 05°35′E*
102 *L11* **la Rochefoucauld** Charente, W France *45°43′N 00°23′E*
102 *J10* **la Rochelle** *anc.* Rupella. Charente-Maritime, W France *46°09′N 01°07′W*
102 *I9* **la Roche-sur-Yon** *prev.* Bourbon Vendée, Napoléon-Vendée. Vendée, NW France *46°40′N 01°26′W*
105 *Q10* **La Roda** Castilla-La Mancha, C Spain *39°13′N 02°10′W*
104 *L14* **La Roda de Andalucía** Andalucía, S Spain *37°12′N 04°45′W*
45 *P9* **La Romana** E Dominican Republic *18°25′N 69°00′W*
11 *T13* **La Ronge** Saskatchewan, C Canada *55°07′N 105°18′W*
11 *U13* **La Ronge, Lac** ◎ Saskatchewan, C Canada
22 *K10* **Larose** Louisiana, S USA *29°34′N 90°22′W*
42 *M7* **La Rosita** Costa Caribe Norte, NE Nicaragua *13°55′N 84°23′W*
181 *Q3* **Larrimah** Northern Territory, N Australia *15°30′S 133°12′E*
62 *N11* **Larroque** Entre Ríos, E Argentina *33°05′S 59°06′W*
105 *Q2* **Larrún** *Fr.* la Rhune. ▲ France/Spain *43°18′N 01°35′W* *see also* la Rhune
**Larrún** *see* la Rhune
195 *X6* **Lars Christensen Coast** *physical region* Antarctica
39 *Q14* **Larsen Bay** Kodiak Island, Alaska, USA *57°32′N 153°58′W*
194 *I5* **Larsen Ice Shelf** *ice shelf* Antarctica
8 *M6* **Larsen Sound** *sound* Nunavut, N Canada
**La Rúa** *see* A Rúa de Valdeorras
102 *K16* **Laruns** Pyrénées-Atlantiques, SW France *43°00′N 00°25′W*
95 *G16* **Larvik** Vestfold, S Norway *59°04′N 10°02′E*
**La-sa** *see* Lhasa
171 *S13* **Lasahata** Pulau Seram, E Indonesia *02°52′S 128°27′E*
**Lasahau** *see* Lasihao
37 *O6* **La Sal** Utah, W USA *38°19′N 109°14′W*
14 *C17* **La Salle** Ontario, S Canada *42°13′N 83°05′W*
30 *L11* **La Salle** Illinois, N USA *41°19′N 89°06′W*
45 *O9* **Las Americas** ✕ (Santo Domingo) S Dominican Republic *18°24′N 69°38′W*
37 *V6* **Las Animas** Colorado, C USA *38°04′N 103°13′W*
108 *D10* **La Sarine** *var.* Sarine. ⚞ SW Switzerland
108 *B9* **La Sarraz** Vaud, W Switzerland *46°40′N 06°32′E*
12 *H12* **La Sarre** Québec, SE Canada *48°49′N 79°12′W*
54 *L3* **Las Aves, Islas** *var.* Islas de Aves. *island group* N Venezuela
55 *N7* **Las Bonitas** Bolívar, C Venezuela *07°50′N 65°40′W*
104 *K15* **Las Cabezas de San Juan** Andalucía, S Spain *36°59′N 05°56′W*
61 *G19* **Lascano** Rocha, E Uruguay *33°40′S 54°12′W*
62 *I5* **Lascar, Volcán** ⛰ N Chile *23°22′S 67°33′W*
41 *T15* **Las Choapas** *var.* Choapas. Veracruz, SE Mexico *17°51′N 94°00′W*
37 *R15* **Las Cruces** New Mexico, SW USA *32°19′N 106°49′W*
**Lasdehnen** *see* Krasnoznamensk
**La Selle** *see* Selle, Pic de la
62 *G9* **La Serena** Coquimbo, C Chile *29°54′S 71°18′W*
104 *K11* **La Serena** *physical region* W Spain
105 *V4* **La Seu d'Urgell** *var.* La Seo de Urgel, *prev.* Seo de Urgel. Cataluña, NE Spain *42°22′N 01°27′E*
**La Seu d'Urgell** *see* La Seu d'Urgell
103 *T16* **la Seyne-sur-Mer** Var, SE France *43°07′N 05°53′E*
61 *D21* **Las Flores** Buenos Aires, E Argentina *36°03′S 59°08′W*
62 *H9* **Las Flores** San Juan, W Argentina *30°14′S 69°10′W*
11 *S14* **Lashburn** Saskatchewan, S Canada *53°09′N 109°37′W*
62 *I11* **Las Heras** Mendoza, W Argentina *32°48′S 68°50′W*
148 *M8* **Lashkar Gāh** *var.* Lash-Kar-Gar'. Helmand, S Afghanistan *31°35′N 64°21′E*
**Lash-Kar-Gar'** *see* Lashkar Gāh
171 *P14* **Lasihao** *var.* Lasahau. Pulau Muna, C Indonesia *05°01′S 122°23′E*
107 *N21* **La Sila** ▲▲ SW Italy
63 *H23* **La Silueta, Cerro** ▲ S Chile *52°22′S 72°09′W*
42 *L9* **La Sirena** Costa Caribe Sur, E Nicaragua *12°59′N 84°35′W*
110 *J13* **Łask** Łódzkie, C Poland *51°36′N 19°06′E*
109 *V11* **Laško** *Ger.* Tüffer. C Slovenia *46°08′N 15°13′E*
63 *H14* **Las Lajas** Neuquén, W Argentina *38°31′S 70°22′W*
63 *H15* **Las Lajas, Cerro** ▲ W Argentina *38°49′S 70°42′W*
62 *M6* **Las Lomitas** Formosa, N Argentina *24°45′S 60°35′W*
41 *V16* **Las Margaritas** Chiapas, SE Mexico *16°15′N 91°58′W*
**Las Marismas** *see* Guadalquivir, Marismas del
54 *M6* **Las Mercedes** Guárico, N Venezuela *09°08′N 66°27′W*
42 *F6* **Las Minas, Cerro** ▲ W Honduras *14°33′N 88°41′W*
105 *O11* **La Solana** Castilla-La Mancha, C Spain *38°56′N 03°14′W*
45 *Q14* **La Soufrière** ⛰ Saint Vincent, Saint Vincent and the Grenadines *13°20′N 61°11′W*
102 *M10* **la Souterraine** Creuse, C France *46°15′N 01°28′E*


◆ Country ◇ Dependent Territory ◆ Administrative Regions ▲ Mountain ⛰ Volcano ◎ Lake
● Country Capital ○ Dependent Territory Capital ✕ International Airport ▲▲ Mountain Range ⚞ River ⊠ Reservoir

LAS PALMAS – LENNE


62 N7 **Las Palmas** Chaco, N Argentina 27°08′S 58°45′W
43 Q16 **Las Palmas** Veraguas, W Panama 08°09′N 81°28′W
64 P12 **Las Palmas** *var.* Las Palmas de Gran Canaria. Gran Canaria, Islas Canarias, Spain, NE Atlantic Ocean 28°08′N 15°27′W
64 P12 **Las Palmas** ◈ *province* Islas Canarias, Spain, NE Atlantic Ocean
64 Q12 **Las Palmas** ✈ Gran Canaria, Islas Canarias, Spain, NE Atlantic Ocean
**Las Palmas de Gran Canaria** *see* Las Palmas
40 D6 **Las Palomas** Baja California, W Mexico 31°44′N 107°37′W
105 P10 **Las Pedroñeras** Castilla-La Mancha, C Spain 39°27′N 02°41′W
106 E10 **La Spezia** Liguria, NW Italy 44°08′N 09°50′E
61 F20 **Las Piedras** Canelones, S Uruguay 34°42′S 56°14′W
63 J18 **Las Plumas** Chubut, S Argentina 43°46′S 67°15′W
61 B18 **Las Rosas** Santa Fe, C Argentina 32°27′S 61°30′W
**Lassa** *see* Lhasa
35 O4 **Lassen Peak** ▲ California, W USA 40°27′N 121°28′W
194 K6 **Lassiter Coast** *physical region* Antarctica
109 V9 **Lassnitz** ≋ SE Austria
15 O12 **L'Assomption** Québec, SE Canada 45°48′N 73°27′W
15 N11 **L'Assomption** ≋ Québec, SE Canada
43 S17 **Las Tablas** Los Santos, S Panama 07°45′N 80°17′W
**Lastarria, Volcán** *see* Azufre, Volcán
37 V4 **Last Chance** Colorado, C USA 39°41′N 103°34′W
**Last Frontier, The** *see* Alaska
11 U16 **Last Mountain Lake** ◎ Saskatchewan, S Canada
62 H9 **Las Tórtolas, Cerro** ▲ W Argentina 29°57′S 69°49′W
61 C14 **Las Toscas** Santa Fe, C Argentina 28°22′S 59°20′W
79 F19 **Lastoursville** Ogooué-Lolo, E Gabon 0°50′S 12°43′E
113 F16 **Lastovo** *It.* Lagosta. *island* SW Croatia
113 F16 **Lastovski Kanal** *channel* SW Croatia
40 E6 **Las Tres Vírgenes, Volcán** ⋏ NW Mexico 27°27′N 112°34′W
40 F4 **Las Trincheras** Sonora, NW Mexico 30°21′N 111°27′W
55 N8 **Las Trincheras** Bolívar, E Venezuela 06°57′N 64°49′W
44 H7 **Las Tunas** *var.* Victoria de las Tunas. Las Tunas, E Cuba 20°58′N 76°59′W
44 H7 **Las Tunas** ◈ *province* E Cuba
**La Suisse** *see* Switzerland
40 I5 **Las Varas** Chihuahua, N Mexico 29°35′N 108°01′W
40 J12 **Las Varas** Nayarit, C Mexico 21°12′N 105°10′W
62 L10 **Las Varillas** Córdoba, E Argentina 31°54′S 62°45′W
35 X11 **Las Vegas** Nevada, W USA 36°09′N 115°10′W
37 T10 **Las Vegas** New Mexico, SW USA 35°35′N 105°15′W
187 P10 **Lata** Nendö, Solomon Islands 10°45′S 165°43′E
13 R10 **La Tabatière** Québec, E Canada 50°51′N 58°59′W
56 C6 **Latacunga** Cotopaxi, C Ecuador 0°58′S 78°36′W
194 I7 **Latady Island** *island* Antarctica
54 E14 **La Tagua** Putumayo, S Colombia 0°05′S 74°39′W
**Latakia** *see* Al Lādhiqīyah
92 J10 **Lätäseno** ≋ NW Finland
14 H9 **Latchford** Ontario, S Canada 47°20′N 79°45′W
14 J13 **Latchford Bridge** Ontario, SE Canada 45°16′N 77°29′W
193 Y14 **Late** *island* Vava'u Group, N Tonga
153 P15 **Lātehār** Jhārkhand, N India 23°48′N 84°28′E
15 R7 **Laterrière** Québec, SE Canada 48°17′N 71°10′W
102 J13 **la Teste** Gironde, SW France 44°38′N 01°04′W
25 V8 **Latexo** Texas, SW USA 31°24′N 95°28′W
18 L10 **Latham** New York, NE USA 42°45′N 73°45′W
**Latharna** *see* Larne
108 B9 **La Thielle** *var.* Thièle. ≋ W Switzerland
27 R3 **Lathrop** Missouri, C USA 39°33′N 94°19′W
107 I16 **Latina** *prev.* Littoria. Lazio, C Italy 41°28′N 12°53′E
41 R14 **La Tinaja** Veracruz, S Mexico
106 J7 **Latisana** Friuli-Venezia Giulia, NE Italy 45°47′N 13°01′E
**Latium** *see* Lazio
115 K25 **Lató** *site of ancient city* Kríti, Greece, E Mediterranean Sea
187 Q17 **La Tontouta** ✈ (Noumea) Province Sud, S New Caledonia 22°06′S 166°12′E
55 N4 **La Tortuga, Isla** *var.* Isla Tortuga. *island* N Venezuela
108 C10 **La Tour-de-Peilz** *var.* La Tour de Peilz. Vaud, SW Switzerland 46°28′N 06°52′E
**La Tour de Peilz** *see* La Tour-de-Peilz
103 S11 **la Tour-du-Pin** Isère, E France 45°34′N 05°25′E
102 J11 **la Tremblade** Charente-Maritime, W France 45°45′N 01°07′W
102 L10 **la Trimouille** Vienne, W France 46°27′N 01°02′E
42 J9 **La Trinidad** Estelí, NW Nicaragua 12°57′N 86°15′W
41 V16 **La Trinitaria** Chiapas, SE Mexico 16°02′N 92°00′W
45 Q11 **la Trinité** E Martinique 14°44′N 60°58′W
15 U7 **La Trinité-des-Monts** Québec, SE Canada 48°07′N 68°31′W
18 C15 **Latrobe** Pennsylvania, NE USA 40°18′N 79°19′W
183 P13 **La Trobe River** ≋ Victoria, SE Australia
**Lattakia/Lattaquié** *see* Al Lādhiqīyah
171 S13 **Latu** Pulau Seram, E Indonesia 03°24′S 128°37′E
15 P9 **La Tuque** Québec, SE Canada 47°26′N 72°47′W
155 G14 **Lātūr** Mahārāshtra, C India 18°24′N 76°34′E
118 G8 **Latvia** *off.* Republic of Latvia, *Ger.* Lettland, *Latv.* Latvija, Latvijas Republika; *prev.* Latvian SSR, *Rus.* Latviyskaya SSR. ◆ *republic* NE Europe
**Latvian SSR/Latvija/Latvijas Republika/Latviyskaya SSR** *see* Latvia
**Latvia, Republic of** *see* Latvia
186 H7 **Lau** New Britain, E Papua New Guinea 05°46′S 151°21′E
175 R9 **Lau Basin** *undersea feature* S Pacific Ocean
101 O15 **Lauchhammer** Brandenburg, E Germany 51°30′N 13°48′E
105 O3 **Laudio** *var.* Llodio. País Vasco, N Spain 43°08′N 02°59′W
**Laudunum** *see* Laon
**Laudus** *see* St-Lô
**Lauenburg/Lauenburg in Pommern** *see* Lębork
101 L20 **Lauf an der Pegnitz** Bayern, SE Germany 49°31′N 11°16′E
108 D7 **Laufen** Basel, NW Switzerland 47°26′N 07°31′E
109 P5 **Lauffen** Salzburg, NW Austria 47°54′N 12°57′E
92 I2 **Laugarbakki** Norðurland Vestra, N Iceland 65°18′N 20°51′W
92 I4 **Laugarvatn** Suðurland, SW Iceland 64°09′N 20°43′W
31 O3 **Laughing Fish Point** *headland* Michigan, N USA 46°31′N 87°01′W
187 Z14 **Lau Group** *island group* E Fiji
**Lauis** *see* Lugano
93 M17 **Laukaa** Keski-Suomi, C Finland 62°27′N 25°58′E
118 D12 **Laukuva** Tauragė, W Lithuania 55°37′N 22°12′E
**Laun** *see* Louny
183 P16 **Launceston** Tasmania, SE Australia 41°25′S 147°07′E
97 I24 **Launceston** *anc.* Dunheved. SW England, United Kingdom 50°38′N 04°21′W
54 C13 **La Unión** Nariño, SW Colombia 01°35′N 77°09′W
42 H8 **La Unión** La Unión, SE El Salvador 13°20′N 87°50′W
42 I6 **La Unión** Olancho, C Honduras 15°02′N 86°40′W
40 M15 **La Unión** Guerrero, S Mexico 17°58′N 101°49′W
41 Y14 **La Unión** Quintana Roo, E Mexico 18°00′N 101°48′W
105 S13 **La Unión** Murcia, SE Spain 37°37′N 00°54′W
54 L7 **La Unión** Barinas, C Venezuela 08°15′N 67°46′W
42 B10 **La Unión** ◈ *department* E El Salvador
38 H11 **Laupāhoehoe** *var.* Laupahoehoe. Hawaii, USA, C Pacific Ocean 20°00′N 155°15′W
**Laupahoehoe** *see* Laupāhoehoe
101 I23 **Laupheim** Baden-Württemberg, S Germany 48°13′N 09°54′E
181 W3 **Laura** Queensland, NE Australia 15°37′S 144°34′E
189 X2 **Laura** *atoll* Majuro Atoll, SE Marshall Islands
**Laurana** *see* Lovran
54 L8 **La Urbana** Bolívar, C Venezuela 07°05′N 66°58′W
21 Y4 **Laurel** Delaware, NE USA 38°33′N 75°34′W
23 V14 **Laurel** Florida, SE USA 27°07′N 82°27′W
21 W3 **Laurel** Maryland, NE USA 39°06′N 76°51′W
22 M6 **Laurel** Mississippi, S USA 31°41′N 89°10′W
33 U11 **Laurel** Montana, NW USA 45°40′N 108°46′W
29 R13 **Laurel** Nebraska, C USA 42°25′N 97°04′W
18 H15 **Laureldale** Pennsylvania, NE USA 40°24′N 75°52′W
18 C16 **Laurel Hill** *ridge* Pennsylvania, NE USA
29 T12 **Laurens** Iowa, C USA 42°51′N 94°51′W
21 P11 **Laurens** South Carolina, SE USA 34°29′N 82°01′W
**Laurentian Highlands** *see* Laurentian Mountains
15 P10 **Laurentian Mountains** *var.* Laurentian Highlands, *Fr.* Les Laurentides. *plateau* Newfoundland and Labrador/Québec, Canada
15 O12 **Laurentides** Québec, SE Canada 45°51′N 73°49′W
**Laurentides, Les** *see* Laurentian Mountains
107 M19 **Lauria** Basilicata, S Italy 40°03′N 15°50′E
194 I1 **Laurie Island** *island* Antarctica
21 T11 **Laurinburg** North Carolina, SE USA 34°46′N 79°29′W
30 M2 **Laurium** Michigan, N USA 47°14′N 88°26′W
**Lauru** *see* Choiseul
108 B9 **Lausanne** *It.* Losanna. Vaud, SW Switzerland 46°32′N 06°39′E
101 Q16 **Lausche** *var.* Luže. ▲ Czechia/Germany 50°52′N 14°39′E *see also* Luže
**Lausche** *see* Luže
101 Q16 **Lausitzer Bergland** *var.* Lausitzer Gebirge, *Cz.* Gory Lużyckie, Lužické Hory', *Eng.* Lusatian Mountains. ▲▲ E Germany
**Lausitzer Gebirge** *see* Lausitzer Bergland
**Lausitzer Neisse** *see* Neisse
103 T12 **Lautaret, Col du** *pass* SE France
63 G15 **Lautaro** Araucanía, C Chile 38°30′S 71°30′W
101 F21 **Lauter** ≋ W Germany
108 I7 **Lauterach** Vorarlberg, NW Austria 47°29′N 09°44′E
101 I17 **Lauterbach** Hessen, C Germany 50°37′N 09°24′E
108 E9 **Lauterbrunnen** Bern, C Switzerland 46°36′N 07°52′E
169 U14 **Laut Kecil, Kepulauan** *island group* N Indonesia
187 X14 **Lautoka** Viti Levu, W Fiji 17°36′S 177°28′E
169 O8 **Laut, Pulau** *prev.* Laoet. *island* Borneo, C Indonesia
169 V14 **Laut, Pulau** *island* Kepulauan Natuna, W Indonesia
169 U13 **Laut, Selat** *strait* Borneo, C Indonesia
168 H8 **Laut Tawar, Danau** ◎ Sumatera, NW Indonesia
189 V14 **Lauvergne Island** *island* Chuuk, C Micronesia
98 M5 **Lauwers Meer** ◎ N Netherlands
98 M4 **Lauwersoog** Groningen, NE Netherlands 53°25′N 06°14′E
102 M14 **Lauzerte** Tarn-et-Garonne, S France 44°15′N 01°08′E
25 U13 **Lavaca Bay** *bay* Texas, SW USA
25 U12 **Lavaca River** ≋ Texas, SW USA
15 O12 **Laval** Québec, SE Canada 45°32′N 73°44′W
102 J6 **Laval** Mayenne, NW France 48°04′N 00°46′W
15 T6 **Laval** ≋ Québec, SE Canada
105 S9 **La Vall d'Uixó** *var.* Vall D'Uxó. Comunitat Valenciana, E Spain 39°49′N 00°15′W
61 F19 **Lavalleja** ◈ *department* S Uruguay
15 O12 **Lavaltrie** Québec, SE Canada 45°56′N 73°14′W
186 M10 **Lavanggu** Rennell, S Solomon Islands 11°39′S 160°13′E
143 O14 **Lāvān, Jazīreh-ye** *island* S Iran
109 U8 **Lavant** ≋ S Austria
118 G5 **Lavassaare** *Ger.* Lawassaar. Pärnumaa, SW Estonia 58°29′N 24°22′E
104 L3 **La Vecilla de Curueño** Castilla y León, N Spain 42°51′N 05°24′W
45 N8 **La Vega** *var.* Concepción de la Vega. C Dominican Republic 19°15′N 70°33′W
**La Vela** *see* La Vela de Coro
54 J4 **La Vela de Coro** *var.* La Vela. Falcón, N Venezuela 11°30′N 69°33′W
103 N17 **Lavelanet** Ariège, S France 42°56′N 01°50′E
107 M17 **Lavello** Basilicata, S Italy 41°03′N 15°48′E
36 J8 **La Verkin** Utah, W USA 37°12′N 113°16′W
26 J8 **Laverne** Oklahoma, C USA 36°42′N 99°53′W
25 S12 **La Vernia** Texas, SW USA 29°19′N 98°07′W
93 K18 **Lavia** Satakunta, SW Finland 61°36′N 22°34′E
14 I12 **Lavieille, Lake** ◎ Ontario, SE Canada
94 C12 **Lavik** Sogn Og Fjordane, S Norway 61°06′N 05°25′E
**La Vila Joíosa** *see* Villajoyosa
33 U10 **Lavina** Montana, NW USA 46°18′N 108°55′W
194 H5 **Lavoisier Island** *island* Antarctica
23 U2 **Lavonia** Georgia, SE USA 34°26′N 83°06′W
103 R13 **la Voulte-sur-Rhône** Ardèche, E France 44°49′N 04°46′E
123 W5 **Lavrentiya** Chukotskiy Avtonomnyy Okrug, NE Russia 65°33′N 171°12′W
115 H20 **Lávrio** *prev.* Lávrion. Attikí, C Greece 37°43′N 24°03′E
**Lávrion** *see* Lávrio
83 L22 **Lavumisa** *prev.* Gollel. SE Eswatini 27°18′S 31°55′E
149 T4 **Lawarai Pass** *pass* N Pakistan
**Lawassaar** *see* Lavassaare
141 P16 **Lawdar** SW Yemen 13°49′N 45°55′E
25 Q7 **Lawn** Texas, SW USA 32°07′N 99°45′W
195 Y4 **Law Promontory** *headland* Antarctica
77 O14 **Lawra** NW Ghana 10°40′N 02°49′W
185 E23 **Lawrence** Otago, South Island, New Zealand 45°53′S 169°43′E
31 P14 **Lawrence** Indiana, N USA 39°49′N 86°01′W
27 Q4 **Lawrence** Kansas, C USA 38°58′N 95°15′W
19 O10 **Lawrence** Massachusetts, NE USA 42°42′N 71°09′W
20 L5 **Lawrenceburg** Kentucky, S USA 38°02′N 84°53′W
20 I10 **Lawrenceburg** Tennessee, S USA 35°16′N 87°20′W
23 T3 **Lawrenceville** Georgia, SE USA 33°57′N 83°59′W
31 N15 **Lawrenceville** Illinois, N USA 38°43′N 87°40′W
21 V7 **Lawrenceville** Virginia, NE USA 36°45′N 77°50′W
27 S3 **Lawson** Missouri, C USA 39°26′N 94°12′W
26 L12 **Lawton** Oklahoma, C USA 34°35′N 98°20′W
140 I4 **Lawz, Jabal al** ▲ NW Saudi Arabia 28°45′N 35°20′E
95 L16 **Laxå** Örebro, C Sweden 59°00′N 14°37′E
125 T5 **Laya** ≋ NW Russia
57 I19 **La Yarada** Tacna, SW Peru 18°14′S 70°30′W
141 S15 **Layjūn** C Yemen 15°27′N 49°16′E
141 Q9 **Laylā** *var.* Laila. Ar Riyāḍ, C Saudi Arabia 22°14′N 46°40′E
23 P4 **Lay Lake** ▣ Alabama, S USA
45 P14 **Layou** Saint Vincent, Saint Vincent and the Grenadines 13°11′N 61°16′W
**La Youne** *see* El Ayoun
192 L5 **Laysan Island** *island* Hawaiian Islands, Hawai'i, USA
36 L2 **Layton** Utah, W USA 41°03′N 112°00′W
34 L5 **Laytonville** California, N USA 39°39′N 123°30′W
172 H17 **Lazare, Pointe** *headland* Mahé, NE Seychelles 04°46′S 55°28′E
123 T12 **Lazarev** Khabarovskiy Kray, SE Russia 52°11′N 141°18′E
112 L12 **Lazarevac** Serbia, C Serbia 44°25′N 20°17′E
65 N22 **Lazarev Sea** *sea* Antarctica
40 M15 **Lázaro Cárdenas** Michoacán, SW Mexico 17°56′N 102°13′W
119 F15 **Lazdijai** Alytus, S Lithuania 54°13′N 23°33′E
107 H15 **Lazio** *anc.* Latium. ◈ *region* C Italy
111 A16 **Lázně Kynžvart** *Ger.* Bad Königswart. Karlovarský Kraj, W Czechia 50°00′N 12°40′E
**Lazovsk** *see* Sîngerei
167 R12 **Léach** Pursat, W Cambodia 12°19′N 103°45′E
27 X9 **Leachville** Arkansas, C USA 35°56′N 90°15′W
28 I9 **Lead** South Dakota, N USA 44°21′N 103°45′W
11 S16 **Leader** Saskatchewan, S Canada 50°55′N 109°31′W
19 S6 **Lead Mountain** ▲ Maine, NE USA 44°53′N 68°07′W
37 R5 **Leadville** Colorado, C USA 39°15′N 106°17′W
11 V12 **Leaf Rapids** Manitoba, C Canada 56°30′N 100°02′W
22 M7 **Leaf River** ≋ Mississippi, S USA
25 W11 **League City** Texas, SW USA 29°30′N 95°05′W
92 K8 **Leaibevuotna** *Nor.* Olderfjord. Finnmark, N Norway 70°29′N 24°58′E
23 N7 **Leakesville** Mississippi, S USA 31°09′N 88°33′W
25 Q11 **Leakey** Texas, SW USA 29°44′N 99°48′W
**Leal** *see* Lihula
83 G15 **Lealui** Western, W Zambia 15°12′S 22°59′E
**Leamhcán** *see* Lucan
14 C18 **Leamington** Ontario, S Canada 42°03′N 82°35′W
**Leamington/Leamington Spa** *see* Royal Leamington Spa
**Leammi** *see* Lemmenjoki
25 S10 **Leander** Texas, SW USA 30°34′N 97°51′W
60 F13 **Leandro N. Alem** Misiones, NE Argentina 27°34′S 55°15′W
97 A20 **Leane, Lough** *Ir.* Loch Léin. ◎ SW Ireland
180 G8 **Learmonth** Western Australia 22°17′S 114°03′E
**Leau** *see* Zoutleeuw
**L'Eau d'Heure** *see* Plate Taille, Lac de la
190 D12 **Leava** Île Futuna, S Wallis and Futuna
**Leavdnja** *see* Lakselv
27 R3 **Leavenworth** Kansas, C USA 39°19′N 94°55′W
32 I8 **Leavenworth** Washington, NW USA 47°36′N 120°39′W
92 L8 **Leavvajohka** *var.* Levajok. Finnmark, N Norway 69°57′N 26°18′E
27 R4 **Leawood** Kansas, C USA 38°57′N 94°37′W
110 H6 **Łeba** *Ger.* Leba. Pomorskie, N Poland 54°45′N 17°32′E
110 I6 **Łeba** *Ger.* Leba. ≋ N Poland
**Leba** *see* Łeba
101 D20 **Lebach** Saarland, SW Germany 49°25′N 06°54′E
**Łeba, Jezioro** *see* Łebsko, Jezioro
171 P8 **Lebak** Mindanao, S Philippines 06°28′N 124°03′E
**Lebanese Republic** *see* Lebanon
31 O13 **Lebanon** Indiana, N USA 40°03′N 86°28′W
20 L6 **Lebanon** Kentucky, S USA 37°33′N 85°15′W
27 U6 **Lebanon** Missouri, C USA 37°40′N 92°40′W
19 N9 **Lebanon** New Hampshire, NE USA 43°40′N 72°15′W
32 G12 **Lebanon** Oregon, NW USA 44°32′N 122°54′W
18 H15 **Lebanon** Pennsylvania, NE USA 40°20′N 76°24′W
20 J8 **Lebanon** Tennessee, S USA 36°11′N 86°19′W
21 P7 **Lebanon** Virginia, NE USA 36°52′N 82°07′W
138 G6 **Lebanon** *off.* Lebanese Republic, *Ar.* Lubnān, *Fr.* Liban. ◆ *republic* SW Asia
20 K6 **Lebanon Junction** Kentucky, S USA 37°49′N 85°43′W
**Lebanon, Mount** *see* Liban, Jebel
146 J10 **Lebap** Lebapskiy Velayat, NE Turkmenistan 41°04′N 61°49′E
**Lebapskiy Velayat** *see* Lebap Welaýaty
146 J11 **Lebap Welaýaty** *Rus.* Lebapskiy Velayat; *prev.* *Rus.* Chardzhevskaya Oblast, *Turkm.* Chärjew Oblasty. ◈ *province* E Turkmenistan
**Lebasee** *see* Łebsko, Jezioro
99 F17 **Lebbeke** Oost-Vlaanderen, NW Belgium 51°00′N 04°08′E
35 S14 **Lebec** California, W USA 34°51′N 118°52′W
**Lebedin** *see* Lebedyn
123 Q11 **Lebedinyy** Respublika Sakha (Yakutiya), NE Russia 58°23′N 125°24′E
126 L6 **Lebedyan'** Lipetskaya Oblast', W Russia 53°00′N 39°11′E
117 T4 **Lebedyn** *Rus.* Lebedin. Sums'ka Oblast', NE Ukraine 50°36′N 34°30′E
12 I12 **Lebel-sur-Quévillon** Québec, SE Canada 49°01′N 76°56′W
92 L8 **Lebesby** *Lapp.* Davvesiida. Finnmark, N Norway 70°31′N 27°00′E
102 M9 **le Blanc** Indre, C France 46°38′N 01°04′E
79 L15 **Lebo** Orientale, N Dem. Rep. Congo 04°30′N 23°58′E
27 P5 **Lebo** Kansas, C USA 38°22′N 95°50′W
110 H6 **Lębork** *var.* Lębórk, *Ger.* Lauenburg, Lauenburg in Pommern. Pomorskie, N Poland 54°32′N 17°43′E
103 O17 **le Boulou** Pyrénées-Orientales, S France 42°32′N 02°50′E
108 A9 **Le Brassus** Vaud, W Switzerland 46°35′N 06°14′E
104 J15 **Lebrija** Andalucía, S Spain 36°55′N 06°04′W
110 G6 **Łebsko, Jezioro** *Ger.* Lebasee; *prev.* Jezioro Łeba. ◎ N Poland
63 F14 **Lebu** Bío Bío, C Chile 37°38′S 73°43′W
**Lebyazh'ye** *see* Akku
104 F6 **Leça da Palmeira** Porto, N Portugal 41°12′N 08°43′W
103 U15 **le Cannet** Alpes-Maritimes, SE France 43°35′N 07°E
**Le Cap** *see* Cap-Haïtien
103 P2 **le Cateau-Cambrésis** Nord, N France 50°05′N 03°32′E
107 Q18 **Lecce** Puglia, SE Italy 40°23′N 18°11′E
106 D7 **Lecco** Lombardia, N Italy 45°51′N 09°23′E
29 V10 **Le Center** Minnesota, N USA 44°23′N 93°43′W
108 J7 **Lech** Vorarlberg, W Austria 47°14′N 10°10′E
101 K22 **Lech** ≋ Austria/Germany
115 D19 **Lechainá** *var.* Lehena, Lekhainá. Dytikí Elláda, S Greece 37°57′N 21°16′E
102 J11 **le Château d'Oléron** Charente-Maritime, W France 45°53′N 01°12′W
103 R3 **le Chesne** Ardennes, N France 49°33′N 04°42′E
103 R13 **le Cheylard** Ardèche, E France 44°55′N 04°27′E
108 K7 **Lechtaler Alpen** ▲▲ W Austria
100 H6 **Leck** Schleswig-Holstein, N Germany 54°45′N 09°00′E
14 L9 **Lecointre, Lac** ◎ Québec, SE Canada
22 H7 **Lecompte** Louisiana, S USA 31°05′N 92°24′W
103 Q9 **le Creusot** Saône-et-Loire, C France 46°48′N 04°27′E
**Lecumberri** *see* Lekunberri
110 P13 **Łęczna** Lubelskie, E Poland 51°20′N 22°52′E
110 J12 **Łęczyca** *Ger.* Lentschiza, *Rus.* Lenchitsa. Łódzkie, C Poland 52°04′N 19°10′E
100 F10 **Leda** ≋ NW Germany
109 Y9 **Ledava** ≋ NE Slovenia
99 F17 **Lede** Oost-Vlaanderen, NW Belgium 50°58′N 03°59′E
104 K6 **Ledesma** Castilla y León, N Spain 41°05′N 06°00′W
45 Q12 **le Diamant** SW Martinique 14°29′N 61°02′W
172 J16 **Le Digue** *island* Inner Islands, NE Seychelles
103 Q10 **le Donjon** Allier, C France 46°19′N 03°50′E
102 M10 **le Dorat** Haute-Vienne, C France 46°14′N 01°05′E
**Ledo Salinarius** *see* Lons-le-Saunier
11 Q14 **Leduc** Alberta, SW Canada 53°17′N 113°30′W
123 V7 **Ledyanaya, Gora** ▲ E Russia 61°51′N 171°03′E
97 C21 **Lee** *Ir.* An Laoi. ≋ SW Ireland
29 U5 **Leech Lake** ◎ Minnesota, N USA
26 K10 **Leedey** Oklahoma, C USA 35°54′N 99°21′W
97 M17 **Leeds** N England, United Kingdom 53°50′N 01°35′W
23 P4 **Leeds** Alabama, S USA 33°33′N 86°32′W
29 O3 **Leeds** North Dakota, N USA 48°19′N 99°43′W
98 N6 **Leek** Groningen, NE Netherlands 53°10′N 06°24′E
99 K15 **Leende** Noord-Brabant, SE Netherlands 51°21′N 05°34′E
100 F10 **Leer** Niedersachsen, NW Germany 53°14′N 07°26′E
98 J13 **Leerdam** Zuid-Holland, C Netherlands 51°54′N 05°06′E
98 K12 **Leersum** Utrecht, C Netherlands 52°01′N 05°26′E
23 W11 **Leesburg** Florida, SE USA 28°48′N 81°52′W
21 V3 **Leesburg** Virginia, NE USA 39°09′N 77°34′W
27 R4 **Lees Summit** Missouri, C USA 38°55′N 94°21′W
22 G7 **Leesville** Louisiana, S USA 31°08′N 93°15′W
25 S12 **Leesville** Texas, SW USA 29°22′N 97°45′W
31 U13 **Leesville Lake** ▣ Ohio, N USA
**Leesville Lake** *see* Smith Mountain Lake
183 P9 **Leeton** New South Wales, SE Australia 34°33′S 146°24′E
98 L6 **Leeuwarden** *Fris.* Ljouwert. Fryslân, N Netherlands 53°15′N 05°48′E
180 I14 **Leeuwin, Cape** *headland* Western Australia 34°18′S 115°03′E
35 R8 **Lee Vining** California, W USA 37°57′N 119°07′W
45 V8 **Leeward Islands** *island group* E West Indies
**Leeward Islands** *see* Sotavento, Ilhas de
**Leeward Islands** *see* Vent, Îles Sous le
79 G20 **Léfini** ≋ SE Congo
115 C17 **Lefkáda** *prev.* Levkás. Lefkáda, Iónia Nisiá, Greece, C Mediterranean Sea 38°50′N 20°42′E
115 B17 **Lefkáda** *It.* Santa Maura, *prev.* Levkás; *anc.* Leucas. *island* Iónia Nisiá, Greece, C Mediterranean Sea
115 H25 **Lefká Óri** ▲▲ Kríti, Greece, E Mediterranean Sea
115 B16 **Lefkímmi** *var.* Levkímmi. Kérkyra, Iónia Nisiá, Greece, C Mediterranean Sea 39°26′N 20°05′E
**Lefkonico/Lefkónikon** *see* Geçitkale
**Lefkosía/Lefkoşa** *see* Nicosia
25 O2 **Lefors** Texas, SW USA 35°26′N 100°48′W
45 R12 **le François** E Martinique 14°36′N 60°59′W
180 L12 **Lefroy, Lake** *salt lake* Western Australia
**Legaceaster** *see* Chester
105 N8 **Leganés** Madrid, C Spain 40°20′N 03°46′W
**Legaspi** *see* Legazpi City
**Leghorn** *see* Livorno
110 M11 **Legionowo** Mazowieckie, C Poland 52°25′N 20°56′E
99 K24 **Léglise** Luxembourg, SE Belgium 49°48′N 05°31′E
106 G8 **Legnago** Lombardia, NE Italy 45°13′N 11°18′E
106 D7 **Legnano** Veneto, NE Italy 45°36′N 08°54′E
111 F14 **Legnica** *Ger.* Liegnitz. Dolnośląskie, SW Poland 51°12′N 16°11′E
35 Q9 **Le Grand** California, W USA 37°12′N 120°15′W
103 Q15 **le Grau-du-Roi** Gard, S France 43°32′N 04°10′E
183 U3 **Legume** New South Wales, SE Australia 28°24′S 152°20′E
102 L4 **le Havre** *Eng.* Havre; *prev.* le Havre-de-Grâce. Seine-Maritime, N France 49°30′N 00°06′E
**le Havre-de-Grâce** *see* le Havre
**Lehena** *see* Lechainá
36 L3 **Lehi** Utah, W USA 40°23′N 111°51′W
18 I14 **Lehighton** Pennsylvania, NE USA 40°49′N 75°42′W
29 O6 **Lehr** North Dakota, N USA 46°15′N 99°21′W
38 A8 **Lehua Island** *island* Hawaiian Islands, Hawai'i, USA
149 S9 **Leiah** Punjab, NE Pakistan 30°59′N 70°58′E
109 W9 **Leibnitz** Steiermark, SE Austria 46°48′N 15°33′E
97 M19 **Leicester** *Lat.* Batae Coritanorum. C England, United Kingdom 52°38′N 01°05′W
97 M19 **Leicestershire** *cultural region* C England, United Kingdom
**Leicheng** *see* Leizhou
98 H11 **Leiden** *prev.* Leyden; *anc.* Lugdunum Batavorum. Zuid-Holland, W Netherlands 52°09′N 04°30′E
98 H11 **Leiderdorp** Zuid-Holland, W Netherlands 52°08′N 04°32′E
98 G11 **Leidschendam** Zuid-Holland, W Netherlands 52°05′N 04°24′E
99 D18 **Leie** *Fr.* Lys. ≋ Belgium/France
**Leifear** *see* Lifford
184 L4 **Leigh** Auckland, North Island, New Zealand 36°17′S 174°48′E
97 K17 **Leigh** NW England, United Kingdom 53°30′N 02°33′W
182 I5 **Leigh Creek** South Australia 30°27′S 138°23′E
23 O2 **Leighton** Alabama, S USA 34°42′N 87°31′W
97 M21 **Leighton Buzzard** E England, United Kingdom 51°55′N 00°41′W
**Léim an Bhradáin** *see* Leixlip
**Léim An Mhadaidh** *see* Limavady
**Léime, Ceann** *see* Loop Head, Ireland
**Léime, Ceann** *see* Slyne Head, Ireland
101 G20 **Leimen** Baden-Württemberg, SW Germany 49°21′N 08°40′E
100 I13 **Leine** ≋ NW Germany
101 J15 **Leinefelde** Thüringen, C Germany 51°22′N 10°19′E
**Léin, Loch** *see* Leane, Lough
97 D19 **Leinster** *Ir.* Cúige Laighean. *cultural region* E Ireland
97 F19 **Leinster, Mount** *Ir.* Stua Laighean. ▲ SE Ireland 52°36′N 06°45′W
119 F15 **Leipalingis** Alytus, S Lithuania 54°05′N 23°52′E
92 J12 **Leipojärvi** Norrbotten, N Sweden 67°03′N 21°15′E
31 R12 **Leipsic** Ohio, N USA 41°06′N 83°58′W
**Leipsic** *see* Leipzig
115 M20 **Leipsoí** *island* Dodekánisa, Greece, Aegean Sea
101 M15 **Leipzig** *Pol.* Lipsk, *hist.* Leipsic; *anc.* Lipsia. Sachsen, E Germany 51°19′N 12°24′E
101 M15 **Leipzig Halle** ✈ Sachsen, E Germany 51°26′N 12°14′E
104 G9 **Leiria** *anc.* Collipo. Leiria, C Portugal 39°45′N 08°49′W
104 F9 **Leiria** ◈ *district* C Portugal
95 C15 **Leirvik** Hordaland, S Norway 59°49′N 05°27′E
118 E5 **Leisi** *Ger.* Laisberg. Saaremaa, W Estonia 58°33′N 22°41′E
104 J3 **Leitariegos, Puerto de** *pass* NW Spain
20 J6 **Leitchfield** Kentucky, S USA 37°28′N 86°19′W
109 Y5 **Leitha** *Hung.* Lajta. ≋ Austria/Hungary
**Leitir Ceanainn** *see* Letterkenny
**Leitmeritz** *see* Litoměřice
**Leitomischl** *see* Litomyšl
97 D16 **Leitrim** *Ir.* Liatroim. *cultural region* NW Ireland
**Leix** *see* Laois
97 F18 **Leixlip** *Eng.* Salmon Leap, *Ir.* Léim an Bhradáin. Kildare, E Ireland 53°23′N 06°32′W
64 N8 **Leixões** Porto, N Portugal 41°11′N 08°41′W
161 N12 **Leiyang** Hunan, S China 26°23′N 112°49′E
160 L16 **Leizhou** *var.* Haikang, Leicheng. Guangdong, S China 20°54′N 110°05′E
160 L16 **Leizhou Bandao** *var.* Luichow Peninsula. *peninsula* S China
98 H13 **Lek** ≋ SW Netherlands
114 I13 **Lekánis** ▲▲ NE Greece
172 H13 **Le Kartala** ▲ Grande Comore, NW Comoros
**Le Kef** *see* El Kef
79 G20 **Lékéti, Monts de la** ▲▲ S Congo
**Lekhainá** *see* Lechainá
92 G11 **Leknes** Nordland, C Norway 68°07′N 13°36′E
79 F20 **Lékoumou** ◈ *department* SW Congo
94 L13 **Leksand** Dalarna, C Sweden 60°44′N 15°E
124 H8 **Leksozero, Ozero** ◎ NW Russia
105 Q3 **Lekunberri** *var.* Lecumberri. Navarra, N Spain 43°00′N 01°54′W
171 S11 **Lelai, Tanjung** *headland* Pulau Halmahera, N Indonesia 01°32′N 128°43′E
45 Q12 **le Lamentin** *var.* Lamentin. C Martinique 14°37′N 61°01′W
31 P6 **Leland** Michigan, N USA 45°01′N 85°44′W
22 J4 **Leland** Mississippi, S USA 33°24′N 90°54′W
95 J16 **Lelång** *var.* Lelången. ◎ S Sweden
**Lelången** *see* Lelång
**Lel'chitsy** *see* Lyel'chytsy
**le Léman** *see* Geneva, Lake
**Leli** *see* Tianlin
25 O3 **Lelia Lake** Texas, SW USA 34°52′N 100°42′W
113 I14 **Lelija** ▲ SE Bosnia and Herzegovina 43°25′N 18°31′E
108 C8 **Le Locle** Neuchâtel, W Switzerland 47°04′N 06°45′E
189 Y14 **Lelu** Kosrae, E Micronesia
**Lelu** *see* Lelu Island
189 Y14 **Lelu Island** *var.* Lelu. *island* Kosrae, E Micronesia
55 W9 **Lelydorp** Wanica, N Suriname 05°36′N 55°04′W
98 K9 **Lelystad** Flevoland, C Netherlands 52°30′N 05°26′E
63 K25 **Le Maire, Estrecho de** *strait* S Argentina
168 L10 **Lemang** Pulau Rangsang, W Indonesia 01°04′N 102°44′E
186 I7 **Lemankoa** Buka Island, NE Papua New Guinea 05°06′S 154°23′E
**Léman, Lac** *see* Geneva, Lake
102 L6 **le Mans** Sarthe, NW France 48°N 00°12′E
29 S12 **Le Mars** Iowa, C USA 42°47′N 96°10′W
109 S3 **Lembach im Mühlkreis** Oberösterreich, N Austria 48°28′N 13°53′E
101 G23 **Lemberg** ▲ SW Germany 48°09′N 08°47′E
**Lemberg** *see* L'viv
**Lemdiyya** *see* Médéa
121 P3 **Lemesós** *var.* Limassol. SW Cyprus 34°41′N 33°02′E
100 H13 **Lemgo** Nordrhein-Westfalen, W Germany 52°02′N 08°54′E
33 P13 **Lemhi Range** ▲▲ Idaho, NW USA
9 S6 **Lemieux Islands** *island group* Nunavut, NE Canada
171 O11 **Lemito** Sulawesi, N Indonesia 0°34′N 121°31′E
92 L10 **Lemmenjoki** *Lapp.* Leammi. ≋ NE Finland
98 L7 **Lemmer** *Fris.* De Lemmer. Fryslân, N Netherlands 52°50′N 05°43′E
28 L7 **Lemmon** South Dakota, N USA 45°54′N 102°08′W
36 M15 **Lemmon, Mount** ▲ Arizona, SW USA 32°26′N 110°47′W
**Lemnos** *see* Límnos
31 O14 **Lemon, Lake** ◎ Indiana, N USA
102 J5 **le Mont St-Michel** *castle* Manche, N France
35 Q11 **Lemoore** California, W USA 36°16′N 119°48′W
189 T13 **Lemotol Bay** *bay* Chuuk Islands, C Micronesia
45 Y5 **le Moule** *var.* Moule. Grande Terre, NE Guadeloupe 16°20′N 61°21′W
**Lemovices** *see* Limoges
**Le Moyen-Ogooué** *see* Moyen-Ogooué
12 M6 **le Moyne, Lac** ◎ Québec, E Canada
93 L18 **Lempäälä** Pirkanmaa, W Finland 61°14′N 23°47′E
42 E7 **Lempa, Río** ≋ Central America
42 F7 **Lempira** *prev.* Gracias. ◈ *department* SW Honduras
**Lemsalu** *see* Limbaži
107 N17 **Le Murge** ▲▲ SE Italy
125 V6 **Lemva** ≋ NW Russia
95 F21 **Lemvig** Midtjylland, W Denmark 56°31′N 08°19′E
166 K8 **Lemyethna** Ayeyarwady, SW Myanmar (Burma) 17°36′N 95°08′E
30 K10 **Lena** Illinois, N USA 42°22′N 89°49′W
129 V4 **Lena** ≋ NE Russia
173 N13 **Lena Tablemount** *undersea feature* S Indian Ocean 51°06′S 56°54′E
**Lenchitsa** *see* Łęczyca
59 N17 **Lençóis** Bahia, E Brazil 12°36′S 41°24′W
60 K9 **Lençóis Paulista** São Paulo, S Brazil 22°35′S 48°51′W
109 Y9 **Lendava** *Hung.* Lendva, *Ger.* Unterlimbach; *prev.* Dolnja Lendava. NE Slovenia 46°33′N 16°27′E
83 F20 **Lendepas** Hardap, SE Namibia 24°41′S 19°58′E
124 H9 **Lendery** *Finn.* Lentiira. Respublika Kareliya, NW Russia 63°20′N 31°18′E
**Lendum** *see* Lens
**Lendva** *see* Lendava
27 R4 **Lenexa** Kansas, C USA 38°57′N 94°43′W
109 Q5 **Lengau** Oberösterreich, N Austria 48°01′N 13°17′E
145 Q17 **Lenger** Turkestan, S Kazakhstan 42°10′N 69°54′E
**Lenghu** *see* Lenghuzhen
159 O9 **Lenghuzhen** *var.* Lenghu. Qinghai, C China 38°50′N 93°25′E
159 T9 **Lenglong Ling** ▲ N China 37°40′N 102°13′E
108 D7 **Lengnau** Bern, W Switzerland 47°12′N 07°23′E
95 M20 **Lenhovda** Kronoberg, S Sweden 57°00′N 15°16′E
**Lenīn** *see* Uzynkol', Kazakhstan
**Lenin** *see* Akdepe, Turkmenistan
**Leninabad** *see* Khujand
**Leninakan** *see* Gyumri
**Lenina, Pik** *see* Lenin Peak
**Lenine** *see* Lenine, Ukraine
**Leningrad** *see* Sankt-Peterburg
**Leningrad** *see* Mu'minobod
126 L13 **Leningradskaya** Krasnodarskiy Kray, SW Russia 46°19′N 39°23′E
124 H12 **Leningradskaya Oblast'** ◈ *province* NW Russia
**Leningradskiy** *see* Mu'minobod
**Lenino** *see* Lyenina, Belarus
**Leninobod** *see* Khujand
**Leninogorsk** *see* Ridder
147 T12 **Lenin Peak** *Rus.* Pik Lenina, *Taj.* Qullai Lenin. ▲ Kyrgyzstan/Tajikistan 39°20′N 72°50′E
147 S8 **Leninpol'** Talasskaya Oblast', NW Kyrgyzstan 42°29′N 71°54′E
**Lenin, Qullai** *see* Lenin Peak
127 P11 **Leninsk** Volgogradskaya Oblast', SW Russia 48°41′N 45°18′E
**Leninsk** *see* Baykonyr, Kazakhstan
**Leninsk** *see* Akdepe, Turkmenistan
**Leninsk** *see* Asaka, Uzbekistan
145 T8 **Leninskiy** Pavlodar, E Kazakhstan 52°13′N 76°50′E
122 I13 **Leninsk-Kuznetskiy** Kemerovskaya Oblast', S Russia 54°42′N 86°16′E
125 P15 **Leninskoje** Kirovskaya Oblast', NW Russia 58°19′N 47°03′E
**Leninskoye** *see* Uzynkol'
**Lenin-Turkmenski** *see* Türkmenabat
**Leninváros** *see* Tiszaújváros
**Lenkoran'** *see* Länkäran
101 F15 **Lenne** ≋ W Germany




◆ Country
● Country Capital
◇ Dependent Territory
○ Dependent Territory Capital
◈ Administrative Regions
✈ International Airport
▲ Mountain
▲▲ Mountain Range
⋏ Volcano
≋ River
◎ Lake
▣ Reservoir

Lennestadt – Limín Vathéos


101 G16 **Lennestadt** Nordrhein-Westfalen, W Germany 51°07′N 08°04′E
29 R11 **Lennox** South Dakota, N USA 43°21′N 96°53′W
63 J25 **Lennox, Isla** *Eng.* Lennox Island. *island* S Chile
**Lennox Island** *see* Lennox, Isla
21 Q9 **Lenoir** North Carolina, SE USA 35°56′N 81°31′W
20 M9 **Lenoir City** Tennessee, S USA 35°48′N 84°15′W
108 C7 **Le Noirmont** Jura, NW Switzerland 47°14′N 06°57′E
14 L9 **Lenôtre, Lac** ◎ Québec, SE Canada
29 U15 **Lenox** Iowa, C USA 40°52′N 94°33′W
103 O2 **Lens** *anc.* Lendum, Lentium. Pas-de-Calais, N France 50°26′N 02°50′E
123 O11 **Lensk** Respublika Sakha (Yakutiya), NE Russia 60°43′N 115°16′E
111 F24 **Lenti** Zala, SW Hungary 46°38′N 16°30′E
**Lentia** *see* Linz
93 N14 **Lentiira** Kainuu, E Finland 64°22′N 29°52′E
**Lentiira** *see* Lendery
107 L25 **Lentini** *anc.* Leontini. Sicilia, Italy, C Mediterranean Sea 37°17′N 15°00′E
**Lentium** *see* Lens
**Lentschiza** *see* Łęczyca
93 N15 **Lentua** ◎ E Finland
119 H14 **Lentvaris** *Pol.* Landwarów. Vilnius, SE Lithuania 24°39′N 24°58′E
108 F7 **Lenzburg** Aargau, N Switzerland 47°23′N 08°11′E
109 R5 **Lenzing** Oberösterreich, N Austria 47°58′N 13°34′E
77 P13 **Léo** SW Burkina Faso 11°07′N 02°08′W
109 V7 **Leoben** Steiermark, C Austria 47°23′N 15°06′E
**Leobschütz** *see* Głubczyce
44 L9 **Léogâne** S Haiti 18°32′N 72°37′W
171 O11 **Leok** Sulawesi, N Indonesia 01°10′N 121°20′E
29 O7 **Leola** South Dakota, N USA 45°41′N 98°58′W
97 K20 **Leominster** W England, United Kingdom 52°09′N 02°18′W
19 N11 **Leominster** Massachusetts, NE USA 42°29′N 71°43′W
102 I15 **Léon** Landes, SW France 43°54′N 01°17′W
40 M12 **León** *var.* León de los Aldamas. Guanajuato, C Mexico 21°05′N 101°43′W
42 I10 **León** León, NW Nicaragua 12°24′N 86°52′W
104 L4 **León** Castilla y León, NW Spain 42°34′N 05°34′W
29 V16 **Leon** Iowa, C USA 40°44′N 93°45′W
42 I9 **León** ◆ *department* W Nicaragua
104 K4 **León** ◆ *province* Castilla y León, NW Spain
**León** *see* Cotopaxi
25 V9 **Leona** Texas, SW USA 31°09′N 95°58′W
25 U5 **Leonard** Texas, SW USA 33°22′N 96°15′W
107 H15 **Leonardo da Vinci** *prev.* Fiumicino. ✈ (Roma) Lazio, C Italy 41°48′N 12°15′E
21 X5 **Leonardtown** Maryland, NE USA 38°17′N 76°35′W
25 Q13 **Leona River** ⛐ Texas, SW USA
41 Z11 **Leona Vicario** Quintana Roo, SE Mexico 20°57′N 87°06′W
101 H21 **Leonberg** Baden-Württemberg, SW Germany 48°48′N 09°01′E
62 M3 **León, Cerro** ▲ NW Paraguay 20°21′S 60°16′W
**León de los Aldamas** *see* León
109 T4 **Leonding** Oberösterreich, N Austria 48°17′N 14°15′E
107 I14 **Leonessa** Lazio, C Italy 42°36′N 12°56′E
107 K24 **Leonforte** Sicilia, Italy, C Mediterranean Sea 37°38′N 14°23′E
183 O13 **Leongatha** Victoria, SE Australia 38°30′S 145°56′E
**Leonídi** *see* Leonídio
115 F21 **Leonídio** *var.* Leonídi. Pelopónnisos, S Greece 37°11′N 22°50′E
104 J4 **León, Montes de** ▲ NW Spain
180 K11 **Leonora** Western Australia 28°52′S 121°16′E
25 S8 **Leon River** ⛐ Texas, SW USA
**Leontini** *see* Lentini
**Léopold II, Lac** *see* Mai-Ndombe, Lac
99 J17 **Leopoldsburg** Limburg, NE Belgium 51°07′N 05°16′E
**Léopoldville** *see* Kinshasa
26 I5 **Leoti** Kansas, C USA 38°28′N 101°22′W
116 M11 **Leova** *Rus.* Leovo. SW Moldova 46°31′N 28°16′E
**Leovo** *see* Leova
102 G8 **le Palais** Morbihan, NW France 47°20′N 03°08′W
27 X10 **Lepanto** Arkansas, C USA 35°34′N 90°21′W
169 N13 **Lepar, Pulau** *island* W Indonesia
104 I14 **Lepe** Andalucía, S Spain 37°15′N 07°12′W
**Lepel'** *see* Lyepyel'
83 E25 **Lepelle** *var.* Elefantes; *prev.* Olifants. ⛐ SW South Africa
83 I20 **Lephepe** *var.* Lephephe. Kweneng, SE Botswana 23°20′S 25°50′E
**Lephephe** *see* Lephepe
161 Q10 **Leping** Jiangxi, S China 28°57′N 117°07′E
**Lépontiennes, Alpes/ Lepontine, Alpi** *see* Lepontine Alps
108 G10 **Lepontine Alps** *Fr.* Alpes Lépontiennes, *It.* Alpi Lepontine. ▲ Italy/ Switzerland
**Le Pool** *see* Pool
173 O16 **Le Port** NW Réunion
103 N1 **le Portel** Pas-de-Calais, N France 50°42′N 01°35′E
93 N17 **Leppävirta** Pohjois-Savo, C Finland 62°30′N 27°50′E
45 Q11 **le Prêcheur** NW Martinique 14°48′N 61°14′W
145 V13 **Lepsi** *prev.* Lepsy. Taldykorgan, SE Kazakhstan 46°14′N 78°56′E
145 V13 **Lepsi** *prev.* Lepsy. ⛐ SE Kazakhstan
**Lepsy** *see* Lepsi
**Le Puglie** *see* Puglia
103 Q12 **le Puy** *prev.* le Puy-en-Velay, *hist.* Anicium, Podium Anicensis. Haute-Loire, C France 45°03′N 03°53′E
**le Puy-en-Velay** *see* le Puy
45 X11 **le Raizet** *var.* Le Raizet. ✈ (Pointe-à-Pitre) Grande Terre, C Guadeloupe 16°16′N 61°31′W
107 J24 **Lercara Friddi** Sicilia, Italy, C Mediterranean Sea 37°45′N 13°37′E
78 G12 **Léré** Mayo-Kébbi Ouest, SW Chad 09°41′N 14°17′E
**Leribe** *see* Hlotse
106 E10 **Lerici** Liguria, NW Italy 44°06′N 09°53′E
54 I14 **Lérida** Vaupés, SE Colombia 0°01′S 70°28′W
105 U5 **Lérida** ◆ *province* Cataluña, NE Spain
**Lérida** *see* Lleida
105 N5 **Lerma** Castilla y León, N Spain 42°02′N 03°46′W
40 M13 **Lerma, Río** ⛐ C Mexico
**Lerna** *see* Lérni
**Lernayin Gharabagh** *see* Nagornyy Karabakh
115 F20 **Lérni** *var.* Lerna. *prehistoric site* Pelopónnisos, S Greece
45 R11 **le Robert** E Martinique 14°41′N 60°57′W
115 M21 **Léros** *island* Dodekánisa, Greece, Aegean Sea
30 L13 **Le Roy** Illinois, N USA 40°21′N 88°45′W
27 Q6 **Le Roy** Kansas, C USA 38°04′N 95°37′W
29 W11 **Le Roy** Minnesota, N USA 43°30′N 92°30′W
18 E10 **Le Roy** New York, NE USA 42°58′N 77°58′W
95 J19 **Lerum** Västra Götaland, S Sweden 57°46′N 12°12′E
96 M2 **Lerwick** NE Scotland, United Kingdom 60°09′N 01°09′W
45 Y6 **les Abymes** *var.* Abymes. Grande Terre, C Guadeloupe 16°16′N 61°31′W
**les Albères** *see* Albères, Chaîne des
102 M4 **les Andelys** Eure, N France 49°15′N 01°26′E
45 Q12 **les Anses-d'Arlets** SW Martinique 14°29′N 61°05′W
104 L2 **Les Arriondes** *prev.* Arriondas. Asturias, N Spain 43°23′N 05°11′W
105 U6 **Les Borges Blanques** *var.* Borjas Blancas. Cataluña, NE Spain 41°31′N 00°52′E
**Lesbos** *see* Lésvos
**Les Cayes** *see* Cayes
31 Q4 **Les Cheneaux Islands** *island* Michigan, N USA
105 S9 **Les Coves de Vinromá** *Cast.* Cuevas de Vinromá. Comunitat Valenciana, E Spain 40°18′N 00°07′E
103 T12 **les Écrins** ▲ E France 44°54′N 06°25′E
108 C10 **Le Sépey** Vaud, W Switzerland 46°21′N 07°04′E
15 T7 **Les Escoumins** Québec, SE Canada 48°21′N 69°26′W
**Les Gonaïves** *see* Gonaïves
160 H9 **Leshan** Sichuan, C China 29°42′N 103°43′E
108 D11 **Les Haudères** Valais, SW Switzerland 46°02′N 07°27′E
102 J9 **les Herbiers** Vendée, NW France 46°52′N 01°01′W
**Lesh/Leshi** *see* Lezhë
125 O8 **Leshukonskoye** Arkhangel'skaya Oblast', NW Russia 64°54′N 45°48′E
**Lesina** *see* Hvar
107 M15 **Lesina, Lago di** ◎ SE Italy
94 G10 **Lesja** Oppland, S Norway 62°07′N 08°56′E
95 L15 **Lesjöfors** Värmland, C Sweden 59°57′N 14°12′E
111 O18 **Lesko** Podkarpackie, SE Poland 49°28′N 22°19′E
113 O15 **Leskovac** Serbia, SE Serbia 43°00′N 21°58′E
113 M22 **Leskovik** *var.* Leskoviku. Korçë, S Albania 40°09′N 20°39′E
**Leskoviku** *see* Leskovik
33 P14 **Leslie** Idaho, NW USA 43°51′N 113°28′W
31 Q10 **Leslie** Michigan, N USA 42°27′N 84°25′W
**Lesna/Lesnaya** *see* Lyasnaya
**Lesnaya** *see* Lyasnaya
102 F5 **Lesneven** Finistère, NW France 48°35′N 04°19′W
112 J11 **Lešnica** Serbia, W Serbia 44°40′N 19°18′E
125 S13 **Lesnoy** Kirovskaya Oblast', NW Russia 59°49′N 52°07′E
122 G10 **Lesnoy** Sverdlovskaya Oblast', C Russia 58°40′N 59°48′E
122 K12 **Lesosibirsk** Krasnoyarskiy Kray, C Russia 58°13′N 92°23′E
83 J23 **Lesotho** *off.* Kingdom of Lesotho; *prev.* Basutoland. ◆ *monarchy* S Africa
**Lesotho, Kingdom of** *see* Lesotho
102 J12 **Lesparre-Médoc** Gironde, SW France 45°18′N 00°57′W
108 C8 **Les Ponts-de-Martel** Neuchâtel, W Switzerland 47°00′N 06°45′E
103 P1 **Lesquin** ✈ Nord, N France 50°34′N 3°07′E
102 I9 **les Sables-d'Olonne** Vendée, NW France 46°30′N 01°47′W
109 S7 **Lessach** *var.* Lessachbach. ⛐ E Austria
**Lessachbach** *see* Lessach
45 W11 **les Saintes** *var.* Îles des Saintes. *island group* S Guadeloupe
74 L5 **Les Salines** ✈ (Annaba) NE Algeria 36°45′N 07°57′E
99 J22 **Lesse** ⛐ SE Belgium
95 M21 **Lessebo** Kronoberg, S Sweden 56°45′N 15°19′E
**Lesser Antarctica** *see* West Antarctica
45 P15 **Lesser Antilles** *island group* E West Indies
137 T10 **Lesser Caucasus** *Rus.* Malyy Kavkaz. ▲ SW Asia
**Lesser Khingan Range** *see* Xiao Hinggan Ling
11 P13 **Lesser Slave Lake** ◎ Alberta, W Canada
99 E19 **Lessines** Hainaut, SW Belgium 50°43′N 05°50′E
103 R16 **les Stes-Maries-de-la-Mer** Bouches-du-Rhône, SE France 43°27′N 04°26′E
14 G15 **Lester B. Pearson** *var.* Toronto. ✈ (Toronto) Ontario, S Canada 43°59′N 81°30′W
29 U9 **Lester Prairie** Minnesota, N USA 44°52′N 94°02′W
93 L16 **Lestijärvi** Keski-Pohjanmaa, W Finland 63°29′N 24°41′E
**L'Estuaire** *see* Estuaire
29 U9 **Le Sueur** Minnesota, N USA 44°27′N 93°53′W
108 B8 **Les Verrières** Neuchâtel, W Switzerland 46°54′N 06°29′E
115 L17 **Lésvos** *anc.* Lesbos. *island* E Greece
110 G12 **Leszno** *Ger.* Lissa. Wielkopolskie, C Poland 51°51′N 16°35′E
83 L20 **Letaba** Northern, NE South Africa 23°44′S 31°29′E
173 P17 **Le Tampon** SW Réunion
97 O21 **Letchworth** E England, United Kingdom 51°58′N 00°14′W
111 G25 **Letenye** Zala, SW Hungary 46°25′N 16°44′E
11 Q17 **Lethbridge** Alberta, SW Canada 49°43′N 112°48′W
55 S11 **Lethem** S Guyana 03°24′N 59°45′W
83 H18 **Letiahau** ⛐ W Botswana
54 J18 **Leticia** Amazonas, S Colombia 04°09′S 69°57′W
171 S16 **Leti, Kepulauan** *island group* E Indonesia
83 I18 **Letlhakane** Central, C Botswana 21°26′S 25°36′E
83 H20 **Letlhakeng** Kweneng, SE Botswana 24°05′S 25°03′E
114 J8 **Letnitsa** Lovech, N Bulgaria 43°19′N 25°02′E
103 N1 **le Touquet-Paris-Plage** Pas-de-Calais, N France 50°31′N 01°36′E
166 L8 **Letpadan** Bago, SW Myanmar (Burma) 17°46′N 94°45′E
166 K6 **Letpan** Rakhine State, W Myanmar (Burma) 19°22′N 94°11′E
102 M2 **le Tréport** Seine-Maritime, N France 50°03′N 01°21′E
166 M12 **Letsôk-aw Kyun** *var.* Letsutan Island; *prev.* Domel Island. *island* Mergui Archipelago, S Myanmar (Burma)
**Letsutan Island** *see* Letsôk-aw Kyun
97 E14 **Letterkenny** *Ir.* Leitir Ceanainn. Donegal, NW Ireland 54°57′N 07°44′W
**Lettland** *see* Latvia
116 M6 **Letychiv** Khmel'nyts'ka Oblast', W Ukraine 49°24′N 27°39′E
**Lëtzebuerg** *see* Luxembourg
116 H14 **Leu** Dolj, SW Romania 44°10′N 24°01′E
**Leucas** *see* Lefkáda
103 P17 **Leucate** Aude, S France 42°55′N 03°03′E
103 P17 **Leucate, Étang de** ◎ S France
108 E10 **Leuk** Valais, SW Switzerland 46°18′N 07°46′E
108 E10 **Leukerbad** Valais, SW Switzerland 46°22′N 07°47′E
**Leusden** *see* Leusden-Centrum
98 K11 **Leusden-Centrum** *var.* Leusden. Utrecht, C Netherlands 52°08′N 05°25′E
**Leutensdorf** *see* Litvínov
**Leutschau** *see* Levoča
99 H18 **Leuven** *Fr.* Louvain, *Ger.* Löwen. Vlaams Brabant, C Belgium 50°53′N 04°42′E
99 I20 **Leuze** Namur, C Belgium 50°33′N 04°55′E
**Leuze** *see* Leuze-en-Hainaut
99 E19 **Leuze-en-Hainaut** *var.* Leuze. Hainaut, SW Belgium 50°36′N 03°37′E
**Léva** *see* Levice
**Levádia** *see* Liváddeia
**Levajok** *see* Leavvajohka
147 P14 **Levakant** *prev.* Kalininobod, *Rus.* Kalininabad. SW Tajikistan 37°49′N 68°55′E
36 L4 **Levan** Utah, W USA 39°33′N 111°51′W
93 E16 **Levanger** Nord-Trøndelag, C Norway 63°45′N 11°18′E
106 D10 **Levanto** Liguria, W Italy 44°12′N 09°33′E
107 H23 **Levanzo, Isola di** *island* Isole Egadi, S Italy
127 Q17 **Levashi** Respublika Dagestan, SW Russia 42°27′N 47°19′E
24 M5 **Levelland** Texas, SW USA 33°35′N 102°23′W
39 P13 **Levelock** Alaska, USA 59°07′N 156°51′W
101 E16 **Leverkusen** Nordrhein-Westfalen, W Germany 51°02′N 07°E
111 J21 **Levice** *Ger.* Lewentz, *Hung.* Léva, Lewenz. Nitriansky Kraj, SW Slovakia 48°14′N 18°38′E
106 G6 **Levico Terme** Trentino-Alto Adige, N Italy 46°02′N 11°19′E
115 E20 **Levídi** Pelopónnisos, S Greece 37°39′N 22°13′E
103 P14 **le Vigan** Gard, S France 43°00′N 03°36′E
184 L13 **Levin** Manawatu-Wanganui, North Island, New Zealand 40°38′S 175°17′E
15 R10 **Lévis** *var.* Levis. Québec, SE Canada 46°47′N 71°12′W
**Levis** *see* Lévis
21 P6 **Levisa Fork** ⛐ Kentucky/ Virginia, S USA
115 L21 **Levítha** *island* Kykládes, Greece, Aegean Sea
18 L14 **Levittown** Long Island, New York, NE USA 40°42′N 73°29′W
18 J15 **Levittown** Pennsylvania, NE USA 40°09′N 74°49′W
**Levkás** *see* Lefkáda
**Levkímmi** *see* Lefkímmi
111 L19 **Levoča** *Ger.* Leutschau, *Hung.* Locse. Prešovský Kraj, E Slovakia 49°01′N 20°34′E
**Lévrier, Baie du** *see* Nouâdhibou, Dakhlet
103 N9 **Levroux** Indre, C France 47°00′N 01°37′E
114 J8 **Levski** Pleven, N Bulgaria 43°21′N 25°11′E
**Levskigrad** *see* Karlovo
126 L6 **Lev Tolstoy** Lipetskaya Oblast', W Russia 53°12′N 39°28′E
187 X14 **Levuka** Ovalau, C Fiji 17°42′S 178°50′E
166 L6 **Lewe** Mandalay, C Myanmar (Burma) 19°40′N 96°04′E
**Lewentz/Lewenz** *see* Levice
97 O23 **Lewes** SE England, United Kingdom 50°52′N 00°01′E
21 Z4 **Lewes** Delaware, NE USA 38°46′N 75°08′W
29 Q12 **Lewis And Clark Lake** ▣ Nebraska/South Dakota, N USA
18 G14 **Lewisburg** Pennsylvania, NE USA 40°57′N 76°52′W
20 J10 **Lewisburg** Tennessee, S USA 35°29′N 86°49′W
21 S6 **Lewisburg** West Virginia, NE USA 37°49′N 80°28′W
96 F6 **Lewis, Butt of** *headland* NW Scotland, United Kingdom 58°31′N 06°18′W
96 F7 **Lewis, Isle of** *island* NW Scotland, United Kingdom
35 U4 **Lewis, Mount** ▲ Nevada, W USA 40°22′N 116°50′W
185 H16 **Lewis Pass** *pass* South Island, New Zealand
33 P7 **Lewis Range** ▲ Montana, NW USA
23 O3 **Lewis Smith Lake** ▣ Alabama, S USA
32 M10 **Lewiston** Idaho, NW USA 46°25′N 117°01′W
19 P7 **Lewiston** Maine, NE USA 44°08′N 70°14′W
29 X10 **Lewiston** Minnesota, N USA 43°58′N 91°52′W
18 D9 **Lewiston** New York, NE USA 43°10′N 79°02′W
36 L1 **Lewiston** Utah, W USA 41°58′N 111°52′W
30 K13 **Lewistown** Illinois, N USA 40°23′N 90°09′W
33 T9 **Lewistown** Montana, NW USA 47°04′N 109°26′W
27 T14 **Lewisville** Arkansas, C USA 33°21′N 93°38′W
25 T6 **Lewisville** Texas, SW USA 33°00′N 96°57′W
25 T6 **Lewisville, Lake** ▣ Texas, SW USA
**Le Woleu-Ntem** *see* Woleu-Ntem
23 U3 **Lexington** Georgia, SE USA 33°51′N 83°04′W
20 M5 **Lexington** Kentucky, S USA 38°03′N 84°30′W
22 L4 **Lexington** Mississippi, S USA 33°06′N 90°03′W
27 S4 **Lexington** Missouri, C USA 39°11′N 93°52′W
29 N16 **Lexington** Nebraska, C USA 40°46′N 99°44′W
20 S9 **Lexington** North Carolina, SE USA 35°49′N 80°15′W
27 N11 **Lexington** Oklahoma, C USA 35°00′N 97°20′W
21 R12 **Lexington** South Carolina, SE USA 33°59′N 81°11′W
20 G9 **Lexington** Tennessee, S USA 35°39′N 88°24′W
25 T10 **Lexington** Texas, SW USA 30°25′N 97°00′W
21 T6 **Lexington** Virginia, NE USA 37°47′N 79°27′W
21 X5 **Lexington Park** Maryland, NE USA 38°16′N 76°27′W
**Leyden** *see* Leiden
102 J14 **Leyre** ⛐ SW France
171 Q5 **Leyte** *island* C Philippines
171 Q6 **Leyte Gulf** *gulf* E Philippines
111 O16 **Leżajsk** Podkarpackie, SE Poland 50°15′N 22°25′E
**Lezha** *see* Lezhë
113 K18 **Lezhë** *var.* Lezha; *prev.* Lesh, Leshi. Lezhë, NW Albania 41°46′N 19°40′E
113 K18 **Lezhë** ◆ *county* NW Albania
103 O16 **Lézignan-Corbières** Aude, S France 43°12′N 02°46′E
126 J7 **L'gov** Kurskaya Oblast', W Russia 51°38′N 35°17′E
159 P15 **Lhari** Xizang Zizhiqu, W China 30°34′N 93°40′E
159 N16 **Lhasa** *var.* La-sa, Lassa. Xizang Zizhiqu, W China 29°41′N 91°10′E
159 O15 **Lhasa He** ⛐ W China
**Lhaviyani Atoll** *see* Faadhippolhu Atoll
158 K16 **Lhazê** *var.* Quxar. Xizang Zizhiqu, W China 29°07′N 87°32′E
158 K14 **Lhazhong** Xizang Zizhiqu, W China 31°58′N 86°43′E
168 H7 **Lhoksukon** Sumatera, W Indonesia 05°04′N 97°19′E
159 Q15 **Lhorong** *var.* Zito. Xizang Zizhiqu, W China 30°51′N 95°41′E
105 W6 **L'Hospitalet de Llobregat** *var.* Hospitalet. Cataluña, NE Spain 41°21′N 02°06′E
153 R11 **Lhotse** ▲ China/Nepal 28°00′N 86°55′E
159 N17 **Lhozhag** *var.* Garbo. Xizang Zizhiqu, W China 28°21′N 90°47′E
159 O16 **Lhünzê** *var.* Xingba. Xizang Zizhiqu, W China 28°25′N 92°30′E
159 N15 **Lhünzhub** *var.* Ganqu. Xizang Zizhiqu, W China 30°14′N 91°20′E
167 N8 **Li** Lamphun, NW Thailand 17°46′N 98°54′E
115 L21 **Liádi** *var.* Livádi. *island* Kykládes, Greece, Aegean Sea
161 P12 **Liancheng** *var.* Lianfeng. Fujian, SE China 25°47′N 116°42′E
**Liancheng** *see* Lianjiang, Guangdong, China
**Liancheng** *see* Qinglong, Guizhou, China
**Liancheng** *see* Guangnan, Yunnan, China
**Lianfeng** *see* Liancheng
160 K9 **Liangping** *var.* Liangshan. Sichuan, C China 30°40′N 107°46′E
**Liangshan** *see* Liangping
**Liangzhou** *see* Wuwei
161 O9 **Liangzi Hu** ◎ C China
161 R12 **Lianjiang** *var.* Fengcheng. Fujian, SE China 26°14′N 119°33′E
160 L15 **Lianjiang** *var.* Liancheng. Guangdong, S China 21°41′N 110°12′E
**Lianjiang** *see* Xingguo
161 O13 **Lianping** *var.* Yuanshan. Guangdong, S China 24°18′N 114°27′E
**Lianshan** *see* Huludao
**Lian Xian** *see* Lianzhou
160 M11 **Lianyuan** *prev.* Lantian. Hunan, S China 27°51′N 111°44′E
161 Q6 **Lianyungang** *var.* Xinpu. Jiangsu, E China 34°38′N 119°12′E
161 N13 **Lianzhou** *var.* Linxian; *prev.* Lian Xian. Guangdong, S China 24°48′N 112°26′E
**Lianzhou** *see* Hepu
**Liao** *see* Liaoning
161 P5 **Liaocheng** Shandong, E China 36°31′N 115°59′E
163 U13 **Liaodong Bandao** *var.* Liaotung Peninsula. *peninsula* NE China
163 T13 **Liaodong Wan** *Eng.* Gulf of Lantung, Gulf of Liaotung. *gulf* NE China
163 U11 **Liao He** ⛐ NE China
163 U12 **Liaoning** *var.* Liao, Liaoning Sheng, Shengking, *hist.* Fengtien, Shenking. ◆ *province* NE China
**Liaoning Sheng** *see* Liaoning
**Liaotung Peninsula** *see* Liaodong Bandao
163 V12 **Liaoyang** *var.* Liao-yang. Liaoning, NE China 41°16′N 123°12′E
**Liao-yang** *see* Liaoyang
163 V11 **Liaoyuan** *var.* Dongliao, Shuang-liao, *Jap.* Chengchiatun. Jilin, NE China 42°52′N 125°09′E
163 U12 **Liaozhong** Liaoning, NE China 41°33′N 122°54′E
**Liaqatabad** *see* Piplan
10 M10 **Liard** ⛐ W Canada
**Liard** *see* Fort Liard
10 L10 **Liard River** British Columbia, W Canada 59°23′N 126°05′W
149 O15 **Liari** Baluchistan, SW Pakistan 25°43′N 66°28′E
**Liatroim** *see* Leitrim
189 S6 **Lib** *var.* Ellep. *island* Ralik Chain, C Marshall Islands
**Liban** *see* Lebanon
138 H6 **Liban, Jebel** *Ar.* Jabal al Gharbī, Jabal Lubnān, *Eng.* Mount Lebanon. ▲ C Lebanon
**Libau** *see* Liepāja
33 N7 **Libby** Montana, NW USA 48°25′N 115°33′W
79 I16 **Libenge** Equateur, NW Dem. Rep. Congo 03°39′N 18°39′E
26 I7 **Liberal** Kansas, C USA 37°03′N 100°56′W
27 R7 **Liberal** Missouri, C USA 37°33′N 94°31′W
**Liberalitas Julia** *see* Évora
111 D15 **Liberec** *Ger.* Reichenberg. Liberecký Kraj, N Czechia 50°45′N 15°05′E
111 D15 **Liberecký Kraj** ◆ *region* N Czechia
42 K12 **Liberia** Guanacaste, NW Costa Rica 10°36′N 85°26′W
76 K17 **Liberia** *off.* Republic of Liberia. ◆ *republic* W Africa
**Liberia, Republic of** *see* Liberia
61 D16 **Libertad** Corrientes, NE Argentina 30°01′S 57°51′W
61 E20 **Libertad** San José, S Uruguay 34°38′S 56°39′W
54 I7 **Libertad** Barinas, NW Venezuela 08°21′N 69°39′W
54 K6 **Libertad** Cojedes, N Venezuela 09°15′N 68°30′W
**Libertador General Bernardo O'Higgins, Región del** *see* O'Higgins
**Libertador General San Martín** *see* Ciudad de Libertador General San Martín
20 L6 **Liberty** Kentucky, S USA 37°19′N 84°58′W
22 J7 **Liberty** Mississippi, S USA 31°09′N 90°49′W
27 R4 **Liberty** Missouri, C USA 39°15′N 94°22′W
18 J12 **Liberty** New York, NE USA 41°48′N 74°45′W
21 T9 **Liberty** North Carolina, SE USA 35°49′N 79°34′W
**Libian Desert** *see* Libyan Desert
99 J23 **Libin** Luxembourg, SE Belgium 50°01′N 05°13′E
**Libiyah, Dawlat** *see* Libya
**Libiyah, Aş Şahrā' al** *see* Libyan Desert
160 K13 **Libo** *var.* Yuping. Guizhou, S China 25°28′N 107°52′E
**Libohova** *see* Libohovë
113 L23 **Libohovë** *var.* Libohova. Gjirokastër, S Albania 40°03′N 20°13′E
81 K18 **Liboi** Wajir, E Kenya 0°23′N 40°55′E
102 K13 **Libourne** Gironde, SW France 44°55′N 00°14′W
99 K23 **Libramont** Luxembourg, SE Belgium 49°55′N 05°21′E
113 M20 **Librazhd** *var.* Librazhdi. Elbasan, E Albania 41°10′N 20°22′E
**Librazhdi** *see* Librazhd
79 C18 **Libreville** ● (Gabon) Estuaire, NW Gabon 0°25′N 09°29′E
75 P10 **Libya** *off.* State of Libya, *Ar.* Dawlat Libiyā; *prev.* Libyan Arab Republic, Great Socialist People's Libyan Arab Jamahiriya. ◆ *republic* N Africa
**Libyan Arab Republic** *see* Libya
75 T11 **Libyan Desert** *var.* Libian Desert, *Ar.* Aş Şahrā' al Lībīyah. *desert* N Africa
75 T8 **Libyan Plateau** *var.* Aḍ Diffah. *plateau* Egypt/Libya
**Libya, State of** *see* Libya
62 G12 **Licantén** Maule, C Chile 35°00′S 72°00′W
107 J25 **Licata** *anc.* Phintias. Sicilia, Italy, C Mediterranean Sea 37°07′N 13°57′E
137 P14 **Lice** Diyarbakır, SE Turkey 38°29′N 40°39′E
**Licheng** *see* Lipu
97 L19 **Lichfield** C England, United Kingdom 52°42′N 01°48′W
83 N14 **Lichinga** Niassa, N Mozambique 13°19′S 35°13′E
109 V3 **Lichtenau** Niederösterreich, N Austria 48°29′N 15°24′E
83 I21 **Lichtenburg** North-West, N South Africa 26°09′S 26°11′E
101 K18 **Lichtenfels** Bayern, SE Germany 50°09′N 11°04′E
98 O12 **Lichtenvoorde** Gelderland, E Netherlands 51°59′N 06°34′E
**Lichtenwald** *see* Sevnica
99 C17 **Lichtervelde** West-Vlaanderen, W Belgium 51°02′N 03°09′E
160 L9 **Lichuan** Hubei, C China 30°20′N 108°56′E
27 V7 **Licking** Missouri, C USA 37°30′N 91°51′W
20 M4 **Licking River** ⛐ Kentucky, S USA
112 C11 **Lički Osik** Lika-Senj, C Croatia 44°36′N 15°24′E
**Ličko-Senjska Županija** *see* Lika-Senj
107 K19 **Licosa, Punta** *headland* S Italy 40°15′N 14°54′E
119 H16 **Lida** Hrodzyenskaya Voblasts', W Belarus 53°53′N 25°20′E
93 H17 **Liden** Västernorrland, C Sweden 62°43′N 16°49′E
29 R7 **Lidgerwood** North Dakota, N USA 46°04′N 97°09′W
**Lidhorikíon** *see* Lidoríki
95 K21 **Lidhult** Kronoberg, S Sweden 56°49′N 13°25′E
95 P16 **Lidingö** Stockholm, C Sweden 59°22′N 18°10′E
95 K17 **Lidköping** Västra Götaland, S Sweden 58°30′N 13°10′E
**Lido di Iesolo** *see* Lido di Jesolo
106 I8 **Lido di Jesolo** *var.* Lido di Iesolo. Veneto, NE Italy 45°30′N 12°37′E
107 H15 **Lido di Ostia** Lazio, C Italy 41°42′N 12°19′E
**Lidokhorikion** *see* Lidoríki
115 E18 **Lidoríki** *prev.* Lidhorikíon, Lidokhorikion. Stereá Elláda, C Greece 38°32′N 22°12′E
110 K9 **Lidzbark** Warmińsko-Mazurskie, NE Poland 53°15′N 19°49′E
110 L7 **Lidzbark Warmiński** *Ger.* Heilsberg. Olsztyn, N Poland 54°08′N 20°35′E
109 U3 **Liebenau** Oberösterreich, N Austria 48°33′N 14°48′E
181 P7 **Liebig, Mount** ▲ Northern Territory, C Australia 23°19′S 131°30′E
109 V8 **Lieboch** Steiermark, SE Austria 47°00′N 15°21′E
108 I8 **Liechtenstein** *off.* Principality of Liechtenstein. ◆ *principality* C Europe
**Liechtenstein, Principality of** *see* Liechtenstein
99 F18 **Liedekerke** Vlaams Brabant, C Belgium 50°51′N 04°05′E
99 K19 **Liège** *Dut.* Luik, *Ger.* Lüttich. Liège, E Belgium 50°38′N 05°35′E
99 K20 **Liège** *Dut.* Luik. ◆ *province* E Belgium
**Liegnitz** *see* Legnica
93 O16 **Lieksa** Pohjois-Karjala, E Finland 63°20′N 30°E
118 F10 **Lielupe** ⛐ Latvia/Lithuania
118 G9 **Lielvārde** C Latvia 56°45′N 24°48′E
167 U13 **Liên Hương** *var.* Tuy Phong. Binh Thuân, S Vietnam 11°13′N 108°40′E
167 U13 **Liên Nghia** *var.* Đưc Trong *var.* Liên Nghia. Lâm Đông, S Vietnam 11°45′N 108°24′E
**Liên Nghia** *see* Liên Nghia
109 P9 **Lienz** Tirol, W Austria 46°50′N 12°45′E
118 B10 **Liepāja** *Ger.* Libau. W Latvia 56°32′N 21°02′E
99 H17 **Lier** *Fr.* Lierre. Antwerpen, N Belgium 51°08′N 04°35′E
95 H15 **Lierbyen** Buskerud, S Norway 59°57′N 10°14′E
99 L21 **Lierneux** Liège, E Belgium 50°12′N 05°51′E
**Lierre** *see* Lier
101 D18 **Lieser** ⛐ W Germany
109 U7 **Liesing** ⛐ E Austria
108 E6 **Liestal** Basel Landschaft, N Switzerland 47°29′N 07°43′E
**Lietuva** *see* Lithuania
**Lietuvos Respublika** *see* Lithuania
**Lievenhof** *see* Līvāni
103 O2 **Liévin** Pas-de-Calais, N France 50°25′N 02°48′E
14 M9 **Lièvre, Rivière du** ⛐ Québec, SE Canada
109 T6 **Liezen** Steiermark, C Austria 47°34′N 14°12′E
97 E14 **Lifford** *Ir.* Leifear. Donegal, NW Ireland 54°50′N 07°29′W
187 Q16 **Lifou** *island* Îles Loyauté, E New Caledonia
193 Y15 **Lifuka** *island* Ha'apai Group, C Tonga
171 P4 **Ligao** Luzon, N Philippines 13°16′N 123°30′E
**Liger** *see* Loire
42 H2 **Lighthouse Reef** *reef* E Belize
183 Q4 **Lightning Ridge** New South Wales, SE Australia 29°29′S 148°00′E
103 N9 **Lignières** Cher, C France 46°45′N 02°10′E
103 S5 **Ligny-en-Barrois** Meuse, NE France 48°42′N 05°22′E
83 P15 **Ligonha** ⛐ NE Mozambique
31 P11 **Ligonier** Indiana, N USA 41°25′N 85°33′W
81 I25 **Ligunga** Ruvuma, S Tanzania 10°51′S 37°10′E
106 D9 **Ligure, Appennino** *Eng.* Ligurian Mountains. ▲ NW Italy
**Ligure, Mar** *see* Ligurian Sea
106 C9 **Liguria** ◆ *region* NW Italy
**Ligurian Mountains** *see* Ligure, Appennino
120 K6 **Ligurian Sea** *Fr.* Mer Ligurienne, *It.* Mar Ligure. *sea* N Mediterranean Sea
**Ligurienne, Mer** *see* Ligurian Sea
186 H5 **Lihir Group** *island group* NE Papua New Guinea
38 B8 **Lihu'e** *var.* Lihue. Kaua'i, Hawaii, USA 21°59′N 159°23′W
**Lihue** *see* Lihu'e
118 F5 **Lihula** *Ger.* Leal. Läänemaa, W Estonia 58°44′N 23°49′E
124 I2 **Liinakhamari** *var.* Linacmamari. Murmanskaya Oblast', NW Russia 69°40′N 31°27′E
**Liivi Laht** *see* Riga, Gulf of
160 F11 **Lijiang** *var.* Dayan, Lijiang Naxizu Zizhixian. Yunnan, SW China 26°52′N 100°10′E
**Lijiang Naxizu Zizhixian** *see* Lijiang
112 C11 **Lika-Senj** *off.* Ličko-Senjska Županija. ◆ *province* W Croatia
79 N25 **Likasi** *prev.* Jadotville. Shaba, SE Dem. Rep. Congo 11°02′S 26°51′E
79 L16 **Likati** Orientale, N Dem. Rep. Congo 03°28′N 23°45′E
10 M15 **Likely** British Columbia, SW Canada 52°40′N 121°34′W
153 Y11 **Likhapāni** Assam, NE India 27°19′N 95°54′E
124 J16 **Likhoslavl'** Tverskaya Oblast', W Russia 57°08′N 35°27′E
189 U5 **Likiep Atoll** *atoll* Ratak Chain, C Marshall Islands
95 D18 **Liknes** Vest-Agder, S Norway 58°20′N 06°58′E
79 H16 **Likouala** ◆ *department* NE Congo
79 H18 **Likouala** ⛐ N Congo
79 H18 **Likouala aux Herbes** ⛐ E Congo
190 B16 **Liku** E Niue 19°02′S 169°47′E
**Likupang, Selat** *see* Bangka, Selat
27 Y8 **Lilbourn** Missouri, C USA 36°35′N 89°37′W
103 X14 **l'Île-Rousse** Corse, France, C Mediterranean Sea 42°39′N 08°59′E
109 W5 **Lilienfeld** Niederösterreich, NE Austria 48°01′N 15°36′E
161 N11 **Liling** Hunan, S China 27°42′N 113°49′E
95 J18 **Lilla Edet** Västra Götaland, S Sweden 58°08′N 12°08′E
103 P1 **Lille** *var.* l'Isle, *Dut.* Rijssel, *Flem.* Ryssel, *prev.* Lisle; *anc.* Insula. Nord, N France 50°38′N 03°04′E
95 G24 **Lillebælt** *var.* Lille Bælt, *Eng.* Little Belt. *strait* S Denmark
**Lille Bælt** *see* Lillebælt
102 L3 **Lillebonne** Seine-Maritime, N France 49°30′N 00°34′E
94 H12 **Lillehammer** Oppland, S Norway 61°07′N 10°28′E
103 O1 **Lillers** Pas-de-Calais, N France 50°34′N 02°26′E
95 F18 **Lillesand** Aust-Agder, S Norway 58°15′N 08°23′E
95 I15 **Lillestrøm** Akershus, S Norway 59°58′N 11°05′E
93 F18 **Lillhärdal** Jämtland, C Sweden 61°51′N 14°04′E
21 U10 **Lillington** North Carolina, SE USA 35°25′N 78°50′W
105 O9 **Lillo** Castilla-La Mancha, C Spain 39°43′N 03°19′W
10 M16 **Lillooet** British Columbia, SW Canada 50°41′N 121°59′W
83 M14 **Lilongwe** ● (Malawi) Central, W Malawi 13°58′S 33°48′E
83 M14 **Lilongwe** ✈ Central, W Malawi 13°46′S 33°44′E
83 M14 **Lilongwe** ⛐ W Malawi
171 P7 **Liloy** Mindanao, S Philippines 08°04′N 122°42′E
**Lilybaeum** *see* Marsala
182 J7 **Lilydale** South Australia 32°57′S 140°00′E
183 P16 **Lilydale** Tasmania, SE Australia 41°17′S 147°13′E
113 J14 **Lim** ⛐ SE Europe
57 D15 **Lima** ● (Peru) Provincia de Lima, W Peru 12°06′S 78°W
94 K13 **Lima** Dalarna, C Sweden 60°55′N 13°19′E
31 R12 **Lima** Ohio, NE USA 40°43′N 84°06′W
57 D14 **Lima** *off.* Región de Lima. ◆ *region* W Peru
**Lima** *see* Jorge Chávez Internacional
137 Y13 **Liman** *prev.* Port-Iliç. SE Azerbaijan 38°54′N 48°49′E
111 L17 **Limanowa** Małopolskie, S Poland 49°43′N 20°25′E
57 D15 **Lima, Provincia de** ◆ *province* W Peru
**Lima, Región de** *see* Lima
104 G5 **Lima, Rio** *Sp.* Limia. ⛐ Portugal/Spain *see also* Limia
**Lima, Rio** *see* Limia
168 M11 **Limas** Pulau Sebangka, W Indonesia 0°09′N 104°31′E
**Limassol** *see* Lemesós
97 F14 **Limavady** *Ir.* Léim An Mhadaidh. NW Northern Ireland, United Kingdom 55°03′N 06°57′W
63 J14 **Limay Mahuida** La Pampa, C Argentina 37°09′S 66°40′W
63 H15 **Limay, Río** ⛐ W Argentina
101 N16 **Limbach-Oberfrohna** Sachsen, E Germany 50°52′N 12°46′E
81 F22 **Limba Limba** ⛐ C Tanzania
107 C17 **Limbara, Monte** ▲ Sardegna, Italy, C Mediterranean Sea 40°50′N 09°10′E
118 G7 **Limbaži** *Est.* Lemsalu. N Latvia 57°33′N 24°46′E
44 M8 **Limbé** N Haiti 19°44′N 72°25′W
99 L19 **Limbourg** Liège, E Belgium 50°37′N 05°56′E
99 K17 **Limburg** ◆ *province* NE Belgium
99 L16 **Limburg** ◆ *province* SE Netherlands
101 F17 **Limburg an der Lahn** Hessen, W Germany 50°22′N 08°04′E
94 K13 **Limedsforsen** Dalarna, C Sweden 60°52′N 13°25′E
60 L9 **Limeira** São Paulo, S Brazil 22°34′S 47°25′W
97 C19 **Limerick** *Ir.* Luimneach. Limerick, SW Ireland 52°40′N 08°38′W
97 C20 **Limerick** *Ir.* Luimneach. *cultural region* SW Ireland
19 S2 **Limestone** Maine, NE USA 46°52′N 67°49′W
25 U9 **Limestone, Lake** ◎ Texas, SW USA
39 P12 **Lime Village** Alaska, USA 61°21′N 155°26′W
95 F20 **Limfjorden** *fjord* N Denmark
95 J23 **Limhamn** Skåne, S Sweden 55°34′N 12°57′E
104 H5 **Limia** *Port.* Rio Lima. ⛐ Portugal/Spain *see also* Lima, Rio
**Limia** *see* Lima, Rio
93 L14 **Liminka** Pohjois-Pohjanmaa, C Finland 64°48′N 25°19′E
**Limín Vathéos** *see* Sámos


◆ Country
● Country Capital
◇ Dependent Territory
○ Dependent Territory Capital
◆ Administrative Regions
✈ International Airport
▲ Mountain
▲ Mountain Range
⛰ Volcano
⛐ River
◎ Lake
▣ Reservoir

LÍMNI – LŌGAR


115 G17 Límni Évvoia, C Greece 38°46´N 23°20´E
115 J15 Límnos anc. Lemnos. island E Greece
102 M11 Limoges anc. Augustoritum Lemovicensium, Lemovices. Haute-Vienne, C France 45°51´N 01°16´E
43 O13 Limón var. Puerto Limón. Limón, E Costa Rica 09°59´N 83°02´W
42 K4 Limón Colón, NE Honduras 15°50´N 85°31´W
37 U5 Limon Colorado, C USA 39°15´N 103°41´W
43 N13 Limón off. Provincia de Limón. ◈ province E Costa Rica
106 A10 Limone Piemonte Piemonte, NE Italy 44°12´N 07°37´E
Limones see Valdéz
Limón, Provincia de see Limón
Limonum see Poitiers
103 N16 Limoux Aude, S France 43°03´N 02°13´E
83 J20 Limpopo off. Limpopo Province; prev. Northern, Northern Transvaal. ◈ province NE South Africa
83 L19 Limpopo var. Crocodile. ∽ S Africa
Limpopo Province see Limpopo
160 K17 Limu Ling ▲▲ S China
113 M20 Lin var. Lini. Elbasan, E Albania 41°03´N 20°37´E
Linacmamari see Liinakhamari
62 G13 Linares Maule, C Chile 35°50´S 71°37´W
54 C13 Linares Nariño, SW Colombia 01°24´N 77°30´W
41 O9 Linares Nuevo León, NE Mexico 24°54´N 99°38´W
105 N12 Linares Andalucía, S Spain 38°05´N 03°38´W
107 G15 Linaro, Capo headland C Italy 42°01´N 11°49´E
106 D8 Linate ✈ (Milano) Lombardia, N Italy 45°27´N 09°18´E
167 T8 Lin Camh prev. Đưc Tho. Ha Tinh, N Vietnam 18°30´N 105°36´E
160 F13 Lincang Yunnan, SW China 23°55´N 100°03´E
Lincheng see Lingao
Linchuan see Fuzhou
61 B20 Lincoln Buenos Aires, E Argentina 34°54´S 61°30´W
185 H19 Lincoln Canterbury, South Island, New Zealand 43°37´S 172°30´E
97 N18 Lincoln anc. Lindum, Lindum Colonia. E England, United Kingdom 53°14´N 00°33´W
35 O6 Lincoln California, W USA 38°52´N 121°18´W
30 L13 Lincoln Illinois, N USA 40°09´N 89°21´W
26 M4 Lincoln Kansas, C USA 39°03´N 98°09´W
19 S5 Lincoln Maine, NE USA 45°22´N 68°30´W
27 T5 Lincoln Missouri, C USA 38°23´N 93°19´W
29 R16 Lincoln state capital Nebraska, C USA 40°46´N 96°43´W
32 F11 Lincoln City Oregon, NW USA 44°57´N 124°01´W
167 X10 Lincoln Island Chin. Dong Dao, Viet. Đao Linh Côn. island E Paracel Islands
197 Q11 Lincoln Sea sea Arctic Ocean
97 N18 Lincolnshire cultural region E England, United Kingdom
21 R10 Lincolnton North Carolina, SE USA 35°27´N 81°16´W
25 V7 Lindale Texas, SW USA 32°31´N 95°24´W
101 I25 Lindau var. Lindau am Bodensee. Bayern, S Germany 47°33´N 09°41´E
Lindau am Bodensee see Lindau
123 P9 Linde ∽ NE Russia
55 T9 Linden E Guyana 05°58´N 58°12´W
23 O6 Linden Alabama, S USA 32°18´N 87°48´W
20 H9 Linden Tennessee, S USA 35°38´N 87°50´W
25 X6 Linden Texas, SW USA 33°01´N 94°22´W
44 H2 Linden Pindling ✈ New Providence, C The Bahamas 25°00´N 77°26´W
18 J16 Lindenwold New Jersey, NE USA 39°47´N 74°58´W
95 M15 Lindesberg Örebro, C Sweden 59°36´N 15°15´E
95 D18 Lindesnes headland S Norway 57°58´N 07°03´E
Líndhos see Líndos
81 K24 Lindi Lindi, SE Tanzania 10°S 39°41´E
81 J24 Lindi ◈ region SE Tanzania
79 N17 Lindi ∽ NE Dem. Rep. Congo
163 V7 Lindian Heilongjiang, NE China 47°15´N 124°51´E
185 E21 Lindis Pass pass South Island, New Zealand
83 J22 Lindley Free State, C South Africa 27°52´S 27°55´E
95 J19 Lindome Västra Götaland, S Sweden 57°34´N 12°05´E
163 S10 Lindong var. Bairin Zuoqi. Nei Mongol Zizhiqu, N China 43°59´N 119°24´E
115 O23 Líndos var. Líndhos. Ródos, Dodekánisa, Greece, Aegean Sea 36°05´N 28°05´E
14 I14 Lindsay Ontario, SE Canada 44°21´N 78°44´W
35 R11 Lindsay California, W USA 36°11´N 119°06´W
33 X8 Lindsay Montana, NW USA 47°13´N 105°10´W
27 N11 Lindsay Oklahoma, C USA 34°50´N 97°37´W
27 N5 Lindsborg Kansas, C USA 38°34´N 97°39´W
95 N21 Lindsdal Kalmar, S Sweden 56°44´N 16°18´E
Lindum/Lindum Colonia see Lincoln
191 W3 Line Islands island group E Kiribati
Linëvo see Linova
160 M5 Linfen var. Lin-fen. Shanxi, C China 36°08´N 111°34´E
Lin-fen see Linfen
104 L2 L'Infiestu prev. Infiesto. Asturias, N Spain 43°21´N 05°21´W
155 F18 Linganamakki Reservoir ⊞ SW India
160 L17 Lingao var. Lincheng. Hainan, S China 19°44´N 109°23´E
171 N3 Lingayen Luzon, N Philippines 16°00´N 120°12´E
160 M6 Lingbao var. Guolüezhen. Henan, C China 34°34´N 110°50´E
94 N12 Lingbo Gävleborg, C Sweden 61°04´N 16°45´E
Lingcheng see Beiliu,Guangxi, China
Lingcheng see Lingshan, Guangxi, China
Lingeh see Bandar-e Lengeh
100 E12 Lingen var. Lingen an der Ems. Niedersachsen, NW Germany 52°31´N 07°19´E
Lingen an der Ems see Lingen
168 M11 Lingga, Kepulauan island group W Indonesia
168 L11 Lingga, Pulau island Kepulauan Lingga, W Indonesia
14 J14 Lingham Lake ⊚ Ontario, SE Canada
94 M13 Linghed Dalarna, C Sweden 60°48´N 15°55´E
33 Z15 Lingle Wyoming, C USA 42°07´N 104°21´W
18 G15 Linglestown Pennsylvania, NE USA 40°20´N 76°46´W
160 M12 Lingling prev. Yongzhou, Zhishan. Hunan, S China 26°13´N 111°36´E
79 K18 Lingomo 11 Equateur, NW Dem. Rep. Congo 0°42´N 21°59´E
160 L15 Lingshan var. Lingcheng. Guangxi Zhuangzu Zizhiqu, S China 22°28´N 109°19´E
160 L17 Lingshui var. Lingshui Lizu Zizhixian. Hainan, S China 18°35´N 110°03´E
Lingshui Lizu Zizhixian see Lingshui
155 G16 Lingsugūr Karnātaka, C India 16°13´N 76°33´E
107 L23 Linguaglossa Sicilia, Italy, C Mediterranean Sea 37°51´N 15°06´E
76 H10 Linguère N Senegal 15°24´N 15°06´W
159 W8 Lingwu Ningxia, N China 38°04´N 106°21´E
Lingxi see Yongshun, Hunan, China
Lingxi see Cangnan, Zhejiang, China
Lingxian/Ling Xian see Yanling
163 S12 Lingyuan Liaoning, NE China 41°09´N 119°24´E
163 U4 Linhai Heilongjiang, NE China 51°30´N 124°18´E
161 S10 Linhai var. Taizhou. Zhejiang, SE China 28°54´N 121°08´E
59 O20 Linhares Espírito Santo, SE Brazil 19°22´S 40°04´W
Linh Côn, Đao see Lincoln Island
Linhe see Bayannur
Lini see Lin
Linik, Chiyā-ē see Linkī, Chiya-ī
Linjiang see Shanghang
139 S1 Linkī, Chiya-ī Ar. Jabal Linkī, var. Chiyā-ē Linik, Chiyā-ī Linkī Kurezūr. ▲▲ N Iraq
Linkī, Jabal see Linkī, Chiya-ī
95 M18 Linköping Östergötland, S Sweden 58°25´N 15°37´E
163 Y8 Linkou Heilongjiang, NE China 45°18´N 130°17´E
118 F11 Linkuva Šiaulai, N Lithuania 56°06´N 23°58´E
27 V5 Linn Missouri, C USA 38°29´N 91°51´W
25 S16 Linn Texas, SW USA 26°32´N 98°06´W
27 T2 Linneus Missouri, C USA 39°53´N 93°10´W
96 H10 Linnhe, Loch inlet W Scotland, United Kingdom
119 G19 Linova Rus. Linëvo. Brestskaya Voblasts', SW Belarus 52°29´N 24°30´E
161 O5 Linqing Shandong, E China 36°51´N 115°42´E
60 K8 Lins São Paulo, S Brazil 21°40´S 49°44´W
93 F17 Linsell Jämtland, C Sweden 62°10´N 14°E
160 J9 Linshui Sichuan, C China 30°24´N 106°54´E
44 K12 Linstead C Jamaica 18°08´N 77°02´W
159 U11 Lintan Gansu, N China 34°43´N 101°27´E
159 V11 Lintao var. Taoyang. Gansu, C China 35°23´N 103°54´E
15 S12 Lintère ∽ Québec, SE Canada
108 H8 Linth ∽ NW Switzerland
108 H8 Linthal Glarus, NE Switzerland 46°59´N 08°57´E
31 N15 Linton Indiana, N USA 39°01´N 87°10´W
29 N6 Linton North Dakota, N USA 46°16´N 100°13´W
163 R11 Linxi Nei Mongol Zizhiqu, N China 43°29´N 117°59´E
159 U11 Linxia var. Linxia Huizu Zizhizhou. Gansu, C China 35°34´N 103°08´E
Linxia Huizu Zizhizhou see Linxia
Linxian see Lianzhou
161 P4 Linyi var. Yishi. Shandong, E China 37°12´N 116°54´E
161 Q6 Linyi Shandong, S China 37°06´N 118°18´E
160 M6 Linyi Shanxi, C China 35°10´N 118°18´E
109 T4 Linz anc. Lentia. Oberösterreich, N Austria 48°19´N 14°18´E
159 S8 Linze var. Shahe; prev. Shahepu. Gansu, N China 39°06´N 100°03´E
44 J13 Lionel Town C Jamaica 17°49´N 77°14´W
103 Q16 Lion, Golfe du Eng. Gulf of Lion, Gulf of Lions; anc. Sinus Gallicus. gulf S France
Lion, Gulf of/Lions, Gulf of see Lion, Golfe du
83 K16 Lions Den Mashonaland West, N Zimbabwe 17°16´S 30°00´E
14 F13 Lion's Head Ontario S Canada 44°59´N 81°16´W
Lios Ceannúir, Bá see Liscannor Bay
Lios Mór see Lismore
Lios na gCearrbhach see Lisburn
Lios Tuathail see Listowel
79 G17 Liouesso Sangha, N Congo 01°02´N 15°43´E
Liozno see Lyozna
171 O4 Lipa off. Lipa City. Luzon, N Philippines 13°57´N 121°10´E
Lipa City see Lipa
25 S7 Lipan Texas, SW USA 32°31´N 98°03´W
Lipari Islands/Lipari, Isole see Eolie, Isole
107 L22 Lipari, Isola island Isole Eolie, S Italy
116 L8 Lipcani Rus. Lipkany. N Moldova 48°16´N 26°47´E
93 N17 Liperi Pohjois-Karjala, SE Finland 62°33´N 29°29´E
126 L7 Lipetsk Lipetskaya Oblast', W Russia 52°37´N 39°38´E
126 K6 Lipetskaya Oblast' ◈ province W Russia
57 K22 Lipez, Cordillera de ▲▲ SW Bolivia
110 E10 Lipiany Ger. Lippehne. Zachodnio-pomorskie, W Poland 53°00´N 14°58´E
112 G9 Lipik Požega-Slavonija, NE Croatia 45°24´N 17°08´E
124 L12 Lipin Bor Vologodskaya Oblast', NW Russia 60°12´N 38°04´E
160 L12 Liping var. Defeng. Guizhou, S China 26°16´N 109°08´E
Lipkany see Lipcani
119 H15 Lipnishki Hrodzyenskaya Voblasts', W Belarus 54°00´N 25°37´E
110 J10 Lipno Kujawsko-pomorskie, C Poland 52°52´N 19°11´E
116 F11 Lipova Hung. Lippa. Arad, W Romania 46°05´N 21°42´E
Lipovets see Lypovets'
Lippa see Lipova
101 E14 Lippe ∽ W Germany
Lippehne see Lipiany
101 G14 Lippstadt Nordrhein-Westfalen, W Germany 51°41´N 08°20´E
25 P1 Lipscomb Texas, SW USA 36°14´N 100°16´W
Lipsia/Lipsk see Leipzig
Liptau-Sankt-Nikolaus/Liptószentmiklós see Liptovský Mikuláš
111 K19 Liptovský Mikuláš Ger. Liptau-Sankt-Nikolaus, Hung. Liptószentmiklós. Žilinský Kraj, N Slovakia 49°06´N 19°36´E
183 O13 Liptrap, Cape headland Victoria, SE Australia 38°55´S 145°58´E
160 L13 Lipu var. Licheng. Guangxi Zhuangzu Zizhiqu, S China 24°25´N 110°15´E
81 G17 Lira N Uganda 02°15´N 32°55´E
57 F15 Lircay Huancavelica, C Peru 12°59´S 74°44´W
107 K17 Liri ∽ C Italy
144 M8 Lisakovsk Kostanay, NW Kazakhstan 52°32´N 62°32´E
79 K17 Lisala Equateur, N Dem. Rep. Congo 02°10´N 21°29´E
104 F11 Lisboa Eng. Lisbon; anc. Felicitas Julia, Olisipo. ● (Portugal) Lisboa, W Portugal 38°44´N 09°08´W
104 F10 Lisboa Eng. Lisbon. ◈ district C Portugal
19 N7 Lisbon New Hampshire, NE USA 44°11´N 71°52´W
29 Q6 Lisbon North Dakota, N USA 46°27´N 97°42´W
Lisbon see Lisboa
19 Q8 Lisbon Falls Maine, NE USA 44°00´N 70°03´W
97 G15 Lisburn Ir. Lios na gCearrbhach. E Northern Ireland, United Kingdom 54°31´N 06°03´W
38 L6 Lisburne, Cape headland Alaska, USA 68°52´N 166°13´W
97 B19 Liscannor Bay Ir. Bá Lios Ceannúir. inlet W Ireland
113 Q18 Lisec ▲ E North Macedonia 41°46´N 22°30´E
160 F13 Lishe Jiang ∽ SW China
Lishi see Lüliang
163 V10 Lishu Jilin, NE China 43°21´N 124°19´E
161 R10 Lishui Zhejiang, SE China 28°27´N 119°25´E
192 L5 Lisianski Island island Hawaiian Islands, Hawai'i, USA
Lisichansk see Lysychans'k
102 L4 Lisieux anc. Noviomagus. Calvados, N France 49°09´N 00°13´E
126 L8 Liski prev. Georgiu-Dezh. Voronezhskaya Oblast', W Russia 51°00´N 39°36´E
103 N4 l'Isle-Adam Val-d'Oise, N France 49°07´N 02°13´E
Lisle/l'Isle see Lille
103 R15 l'Isle-sur-la-Sorgue Vaucluse, SE France 43°55´N 05°03´E
15 S9 L'Islet Québec, SE Canada 47°07´N 70°18´W
182 M12 Lismore Victoria, SE Australia 37°59´S 143°18´E
97 D20 Lismore Ir. Lios Mór. S Ireland 52°10´N 07°10´W
Lissa see Vis, Croatia
Lissa see Leszno, Poland
98 H11 Lisse Zuid-Holland, W Netherlands 52°15´N 04°33´E
114 K13 Lissos var. Filiouri. ∽ NE Greece
95 D18 Lista peninsula S Norway
95 D18 Listafjorden fjord S Norway
195 R13 Lister, Mount ▲ Antarctica 78°12´S 161°46´E
126 M8 Listopadovka Voronezhskaya Oblast', W Russia 51°54´N 41°08´E
14 F15 Listowel Ontario, S Canada 43°44´N 80°57´W
97 B20 Listowel Ir. Lios Tuathail. Kerry, SW Ireland 52°27´N 09°29´W
160 L14 Litang Guangxi Zhuangzu Zizhiqu, S China 23°09´N 109°08´E
160 F9 Litang var. Gaocheng. Sichuan, C China 30°03´N 100°12´E
160 F10 Litang Qu ∽ C China
55 X12 Litani var. Itany. ∽ French Guiana/Suriname
138 G8 Lītani, Nahr el var. Nahr al Litant. ∽ C Lebanon
Litant, Nahr al see Lītani, Nahr el
Litauen see Lithuania
30 K14 Litchfield Illinois, N USA 39°17´N 89°52´W
29 U8 Litchfield Minnesota, N USA 45°09´N 94°31´W
36 K13 Litchfield Park Arizona, SW USA 33°29´N 112°21´W
183 S8 Lithgow New South Wales, SE Australia 33°30´S 150°09´E
115 I26 Líthino, Akrotírio headland Kríti, Greece, E Mediterranean Sea 34°55´N 24°43´E
118 D12 Lithuania off. Republic of Lithuania, Lith. Lietuva, Lietuvos Respublika, Ger. Litauen, Pol. Litwa, Rus. Litva; prev. Lithuanian SSR, Rus. Litovskaya SSR. ◆ republic NE Europe
Lithuanian SSR see Lithuania
Lithuania, Republic of see Lithuania
109 U11 Litija Ger. Littai. C Slovenia 46°03´N 14°50´E
18 H15 Lititz Pennsylvania, NE USA 40°09´N 76°18´W
115 F15 Litóchoro var. Litohoro, Litókhoron. Kentrikí Makedonía, N Greece 40°06´N 22°30´E
Litohoro/Litókhoron see Litóchoro
111 C15 Litoměřice Ger. Leitmeritz. Ústecký Kraj, NW Czechia 50°33´N 14°10´E
111 F17 Litomyšl Ger. Leitomischl. Pardubický Kraj, C Czechia 49°54´N 16°18´E
111 G17 Litovel Ger. Littau. Olomoucký Kraj, E Czechia 49°42´N 17°05´E
123 S13 Litovko Khabarovskiy Kray, SE Russia 49°22´N 135°10´E
Litovskaya SSR see Lithuania
Littai see Litija
Littau see Litovel
44 G1 Little Abaco var. Abaco Island. island N The Bahamas
111 I21 Little Alföld Ger. Kleines Ungarisches Tiefland, Hung. Kisalföld, Slvk. Podunajská Rovina. plain Hungary/Slovakia
151 Q20 Little Andaman island Andaman Islands, India, NE Indian Ocean
26 M5 Little Arkansas River ∽ Kansas, C USA
Little Barrier Island see Te Hauturu-o-Toi / Little Barrier Island
Little Belt see Lillebælt
38 M11 Little Black River ∽ Alaska, USA
27 O2 Little Blue River ∽ Kansas/Nebraska, C USA
44 D8 Little Cayman island E Cayman Islands
11 X11 Little Churchill ∽ Manitoba, C Canada
166 J10 Little Coco Island island SW Myanmar (Burma)
36 L10 Little Colorado River ∽ Arizona, SW USA
14 E11 Little Current Manitoulin Island, Ontario, S Canada 45°57´N 81°56´W
12 E11 Little Current ∽ Ontario, S Canada
38 L8 Little Diomede Island island Alaska, USA
44 I4 Little Exuma island C The Bahamas
29 U7 Little Falls Minnesota, N USA 45°59´N 94°21´W
18 J10 Little Falls New York, NE USA 43°02´N 74°51´W
24 M5 Littlefield Texas, SW USA 33°56´N 102°20´W
29 V3 Littlefork Minnesota, N USA 48°24´N 93°33´W
29 V3 Little Fork River ∽ Minnesota, N USA
11 N16 Little Fort British Columbia, SW Canada 51°27´N 120°15´W
11 Y14 Little Grand Rapids Manitoba, C Canada 52°06´N 95°29´W
97 N23 Littlehampton SE England, United Kingdom 50°48´N 00°33´W
35 T2 Little Humboldt River ∽ Nevada, W USA
44 K6 Little Inagua var. Inagua Islands. island S The Bahamas
21 Q4 Little Kanawha River ∽ West Virginia, NE USA
83 F25 Little Karoo plateau S South Africa
39 O16 Little Koniuji Island island Shumagin Islands, Alaska, USA
44 H12 Little London W Jamaica 18°15´N 78°13´W
13 R10 Little Mecatina Fr. Rivière du Petit Mécatina. ∽ Newfoundland and Labrador/Québec, E Canada
96 F8 Little Minch, The strait NW Scotland, United Kingdom
27 T13 Little Missouri River ∽ Arkansas, USA
28 J7 Little Missouri River ∽ NW USA
28 J3 Little Muddy River ∽ North Dakota, N USA
151 Q22 Little Nicobar island Nicobar Islands, India, NE Indian Ocean
27 R6 Little Osage River ∽ Missouri, C USA
97 P20 Little Ouse ∽ E England, United Kingdom
149 V2 Little Pamir Pash. Pāmīr-e Khord, Rus. Malyy Pamir. ▲▲ Afghanistan/Tajikistan
21 U12 Little Pee Dee River ∽ North Carolina/South Carolina, SE USA
27 V10 Little Red River ∽ Arkansas, C USA
Little Rhody see Rhode Island
185 I19 Little River Canterbury, South Island, New Zealand 43°45´S 172°49´E
21 U12 Little River South Carolina, SE USA 33°52´N 78°36´W
27 Y9 Little River ∽ Arkansas/Missouri, C USA
27 R13 Little River ∽ Arkansas/Oklahoma, USA
23 T7 Little River ∽ Georgia, SE USA
22 H6 Little River ∽ Louisiana, S USA
25 T10 Little River ∽ Texas, SW USA
27 V12 Little Rock state capital Arkansas, C USA 34°45´N 92°17´W
31 N8 Little Sable Point headland Michigan, N USA 43°38´N 86°32´W
103 U11 Little Saint Bernard Pass Fr. Col du Petit St-Bernard, It. Colle del Piccolo San Bernardo. pass France/Italy
36 K7 Little Salt Lake ⊚ Utah, W USA
180 K8 Little Sandy Desert desert Western Australia
29 S13 Little Sioux River ∽ Iowa, C USA
38 E17 Little Sitkin Island island Aleutian Islands, Alaska, USA
11 O13 Little Smoky Alberta, W Canada 54°35´N 117°06´W
11 O14 Little Smoky ∽ Alberta, W Canada
37 P3 Little Snake River ∽ Colorado, C USA
64 A12 Little Sound bay Bermuda, NW Atlantic Ocean
37 T4 Littleton Colorado, C USA 39°36´N 105°01´W
19 N7 Littleton New Hampshire, NE USA 44°18´N 71°46´W
18 D11 Little Valley New York, NE USA 42°15´N 78°47´W
30 M15 Little Wabash River ∽ Illinois, N USA
14 D10 Little White River ∽ Ontario, S Canada
28 M12 Little White River ∽ South Dakota, N USA
25 R5 Little Wichita River ∽ Texas, SW USA
142 I4 Little Zab Ar. Nahraz Zāb aş Şaghīr, Kurd. Zē-i Kōya, Per. Rūdkhāneh-ye Zāb-e Kūchek. ∽ Iran/Iraq
79 D15 Littoral ◈ region W Cameroon
Littoria see Latina
Litva/Litwa see Lithuania
111 B15 Litvínov Ger. Leutensdorf. Ústecký Kraj, NW Czechia 50°38´N 13°30´E
116 M6 Lityn Vinnyts'ka Oblast', C Ukraine 49°19´N 28°06´E
Liu-chou/Liuchow see Liuzhou
163 W11 Liuhe Jilin, NE China 42°15´N 125°49´E
Liujiaxia see Yongjing
Liulin see Jonê
Liupanshui see Lupanshui
83 Q15 Liúpo Nampula, NE Mozambique 15°36´S 39°57´E
83 G14 Liuwa Plain plain W Zambia
160 L13 Liuzhou var. Liu-chou, Liuchow. Guangxi Zhuangzu Zizhiqu, S China 24°09´N 108°55´E
116 H8 Livada Hung. Sárköz. Satu Mare, NW Romania 47°52´N 23°04´E
115 J20 Liváda, Akrotírio headland Tínos, Kykládes, Greece, Aegean Sea 37°36´N 25°15´E
115 F18 Livádeia prev. Levádia. Stereá Elláda, C Greece 38°24´N 22°51´E
Livádi see Liádi
Livanátai see Livanátes
115 G18 Livanátes prev. Livanátai. Stereá Elláda, C Greece 38°43´N 23°03´E
118 I10 Līvāni Ger. Lievenhof. SE Latvia 56°22´N 26°12´E
65 E25 Lively Island island SE Falkland Islands
65 D25 Lively Sound sound SE Falkland Islands
39 R8 Livengood Alaska, USA 65°31´N 148°32´W
106 I7 Livenza ∽ NE Italy
35 O6 Live Oak California, W USA 39°17´N 121°41´W
23 U9 Live Oak Florida, SE USA 30°18´N 82°59´W
35 O9 Livermore California, W USA 37°40´N 121°46´W
20 I6 Livermore Kentucky, S USA 37°31´N 87°08´W
19 Q7 Livermore Falls Maine, NE USA 44°30´N 70°09´W
24 J10 Livermore, Mount ▲ Texas, SW USA 30°37´N 104°10´W
13 P16 Liverpool Nova Scotia, SE Canada 44°03´N 64°43´W
97 K17 Liverpool NW England, United Kingdom 53°25´N 02°55´W
97 K18 Liverpool ✈ NW England, United Kingdom 53°20´N 02°51´W
183 S7 Liverpool Range ▲▲ New South Wales, SE Australia
42 F4 Livingston Izabal, E Guatemala 15°50´N 88°44´W
96 J12 Livingston C Scotland, United Kingdom 55°51´N 03°31´W
23 N5 Livingston Alabama, S USA 32°35´N 88°12´W
35 P9 Livingston California, W USA 37°22´N 120°45´W
22 J8 Livingston Louisiana, S USA 30°30´N 90°45´W
33 S11 Livingston Montana, NW USA 45°40´N 110°33´W
20 L8 Livingston Tennessee, S USA 36°22´N 85°20´W
25 W9 Livingston Texas, SW USA 30°42´N 94°58´W
83 I16 Livingstone var. Maramba. Southern, S Zambia 17°51´S 25°48´E
185 B22 Livingstone Mountains ▲▲ South Island, New Zealand
80 K13 Livingstone Mountains ▲▲ S Tanzania
82 N12 Livingstonia Northern, N Malawi 10°29´S 34°06´E
194 G4 Livingston Island island Antarctica
25 W9 Livingston, Lake ⊞ Texas, SW USA
112 F13 Livno ◈ Federicija Bosna I Hercegovina, SW Bosnia and Herzegovina
126 K7 Livny Orlovskaya Oblast', W Russia 52°25´N 37°42´E
93 M14 Livojoki ∽ C Finland
31 R10 Livonia Michigan, N USA 42°22´N 83°22´W
106 E11 Livorno Eng. Leghorn. Toscana, C Italy 43°32´N 10°18´E
Livramento see Santana do Livramento
141 U8 Liwā var. Al Liwā'. oasis region S United Arab Emirates
81 I24 Liwale Lindi, SE Tanzania 09°46´S 37°56´E
159 W9 Liwang Ningxia, N China 36°42´N 106°05´E
83 N15 Liwonde Southern, S Malawi 15°01´S 35°15´E
159 V11 Lixian var. Li Xian. Gansu, C China 34°15´N 105°07´E
160 H8 Lixian var. Li Xian. Zagunao. Sichuan, C China 31°27´N 103°06´E
Li Xian see Lixian
Lixian Jiang see Black River
115 B18 Lixoúri prev. Lixoúrion. Kefallinía, Iónia Nisiá, Greece, C Mediterranean Sea 38°14´N 20°24´E
Lixoúrion see Lixoúri
Lixus see Larache
33 U15 Lizard Head Peak ▲ Wyoming, C USA 42°47´N 109°12´W
97 H25 Lizard Point headland SW England, United Kingdom 49°57´N 05°12´W
Lizarra see Estella
112 L12 Ljig Serbia, C Serbia 44°14´N 20°16´E
Ljouwert see Leeuwarden
Ljubelj see Loibl Pass
109 U11 Ljubljana Ger. Laibach, It. Lubiana; anc. Aemona, Emona. ● (Slovenia) C Slovenia 46°03´N 14°29´E
109 T11 Ljubljana ✈ C Slovenia 46°14´N 14°26´E
113 N17 Ljuboten Alb. Luboten. ▲ S Serbia 42°12´N 21°06´E
95 P19 Ljugarn Gotland, SE Sweden 57°23´N 18°45´E
84 G7 Ljungan ∽ N Sweden
93 F17 Ljungan ∽ C Sweden
95 K21 Ljungby Kronoberg, S Sweden 56°49´N 13°55´E
95 M17 Ljungsbro Östergötland, S Sweden 58°31´N 15°30´E
95 I18 Ljungskile Västra Götaland, S Sweden 58°14´N 11°55´E
94 M11 Ljusdal Gävleborg, C Sweden 61°50´N 16°10´E
94 M11 Ljusnan ∽ C Sweden
94 N12 Ljusne Gävleborg, C Sweden 61°11´N 17°07´E
95 P15 Ljusterö Stockholm, C Sweden 59°31´N 18°40´E
109 X9 Ljutomer Ger. Luttenberg. NE Slovenia 46°31´N 16°12´E
63 G15 Llaima, Volcán ※ S Chile 39°01´S 71°38´W
105 X4 Llançà var. Llansá. Cataluña, NE Spain 42°23´N 03°08´E
97 J21 Llandovery C Wales, United Kingdom 52°01´N 03°47´W
97 J20 Llandrindod Wells E Wales, United Kingdom 52°15´N 03°23´W
97 J18 Llandudno N Wales, United Kingdom 53°19´N 03°49´W
97 I21 Llanelli prev. Llanelly. SW Wales, United Kingdom 51°41´N 04°12´W
Llanelly see Llanelli
104 M2 Llanes Asturias, N Spain 43°25´N 04°46´W
97 K19 Llangollen NE Wales, United Kingdom 52°58´N 03°10´W
104 K2 Llangréu var. Langreo, Sama de Langreo. Asturias, N Spain 43°18´N 05°40´W
25 R10 Llano Texas, SW USA 30°49´N 98°42´W
25 Q10 Llano River ∽ Texas, SW USA
54 I9 Llanos physical region Colombia/Venezuela
63 G16 Llanquihue, Lago ⊚ S Chile
Llansá see Llançà
105 U5 Lleida Cast. Lérida; anc. Ilerda. Cataluña, NE Spain 41°38´N 00°35´E
104 K12 Llerena Extremadura, W Spain 38°13´N 06°00´W
Linkī Kurezūr, Chiyā-ī see Linkī, Chiya-ī
105 S9 Llíria Comunitat Valenciana, E Spain 39°38´N 00°36´W
105 W4 Llívia Cataluña, NE Spain 42°27´N 02°00´E
Llodio see Laudio
105 X5 Lloret de Mar Cataluña, NE Spain 41°42´N 02°51´E
Llorri see Toretta de l'Orrí
10 L11 Lloyd George, Mount ▲ British Columbia, W Canada 57°46´N 124°57´W
11 R14 Lloydminster Alberta/Saskatchewan, SW Canada 53°18´N 110°00´W
104 K2 Lluanco var. Luanco. Asturias, N Spain 43°36´N 05°48´W
105 X9 Llucmajor Mallorca, Spain, W Mediterranean Sea 39°29´N 02°53´E
36 L6 Loa Utah, W USA 38°24´N 111°38´W
169 S8 Loagan Bunut ⊚ East Malaysia
38 G12 Loa, Mauna ▲ Hawai'i, USA 19°28´N 155°39´W
Loanda see Luanda
79 J22 Loange ∽ S Dem. Rep. Congo
79 E21 Loango Kouilou, S Congo 04°38´S 11°50´E
106 B10 Loano Liguria, NW Italy 44°07´N 08°15´E
62 H4 Loa, Río ∽ N Chile
83 L22 Lobamba ● (Eswatini-royal and legislative) NW Eswatini 26°25´S 31°10´E
83 I20 Lobatse var. Lobatsi. Kgatleng, SE Botswana 25°11´S 25°40´E
Lobatsi see Lobatse
101 Q15 Löbau Sachsen, E Germany 51°07´N 14°40´E
79 H16 Lobaye ◈ prefecture SW Central African Republic
79 I16 Lobaye ∽ SW Central African Republic
99 G21 Lobbes Hainaut, S Belgium 50°21´N 04°16´E
61 D23 Lobería Buenos Aires, E Argentina 38°08´S 58°48´W
110 F8 Łobez Ger. Labes. Zacodnio-pomorskie, NW Poland 53°38´N 15°39´E
82 A13 Lobito Benguela, W Angola 12°20´S 13°34´E
Lobkovichi see Labkovichy
Lob Nor see Lop Nur
171 V13 Lobo Papua Barat, E Indonesia 03°41´S 134°06´E
104 J11 Lobón Extremadura, W Spain 38°51´N 06°38´W
61 D20 Lobos Buenos Aires, E Argentina 35°11´S 59°08´W
40 E4 Lobos, Cabo headland NW Mexico 29°53´N 112°43´W
40 F6 Lobos, Isla island NW Mexico
Lobositz see Lovosice
Lobsens see Łobżenica
Loburi see Lop Buri
110 H9 Łobżenica Ger. Lobsens. Wielkopolskie, C Poland 53°19´N 17°11´E
108 G11 Locarno Ger. Luggarus. Ticino, S Switzerland 46°11´N 08°48´E
96 E9 Lochboisdale NW Scotland, United Kingdom 57°08´N 07°17´W
98 N11 Lochem Gelderland, E Netherlands 52°10´N 06°25´E
102 M8 Loches Indre-et-Loire, C France 47°08´N 01°00´E
Loch Garman see Wexford
96 H12 Lochgilphead W Scotland, United Kingdom 56°02´N 05°27´W
96 H7 Lochinver N Scotland, United Kingdom 58°10´N 05°15´W
96 F8 Lochmaddy NW Scotland, United Kingdom 57°35´N 07°10´W
96 J10 Lochnagar ▲ C Scotland, United Kingdom 56°58´N 03°09´W
99 E17 Lochristi Oost-Vlaanderen, NW Belgium 51°07´N 03°49´E
96 H9 Lochy, Loch ⊚ N Scotland, United Kingdom
182 G8 Lock South Australia 33°37´S 135°45´E
97 J14 Lockerbie S Scotland, United Kingdom 55°11´N 03°27´W
27 S13 Lockesburg Arkansas, C USA 33°58´N 94°10´W
183 P10 Lockhart New South Wales, SE Australia 35°15´S 146°43´E
25 S11 Lockhart Texas, SW USA 29°54´N 97°41´W
18 F13 Lock Haven Pennsylvania, NE USA 41°08´N 77°27´W
25 N4 Lockney Texas, SW USA 34°06´N 101°27´W
100 O12 Löcknitz ∽ NE Germany
18 E9 Lockport New York, NE USA 43°09´N 78°40´W
167 T13 Lộc Ninh Sông Be, S Vietnam 11°51´N 106°35´E
107 N23 Locri Calabria, SW Italy 38°16´N 16°16´E
Locse see Levoča
27 T2 Locust Creek ∽ Missouri, C USA
23 P3 Locust Fork ∽ Alabama, S USA
27 Q9 Locust Grove Oklahoma, C USA 36°12´N 95°10´W
94 E11 Lodalskåpa ▲ S Norway 61°47´N 07°10´E
183 N10 Loddon River ∽ Victoria, SE Australia
Lodensee see Klooga
103 P15 Lodève anc. Luteva. Hérault, S France 43°44´N 03°19´E
124 I12 Lodeynoye Pole Leningradskaya Oblast', NW Russia 60°41´N 33°29´E
33 V11 Lodge Grass Montana, NW USA 45°19´N 107°20´W
28 J15 Lodgepole Creek ∽ Nebraska/Wyoming, C USA
149 T11 Lodhran Punjab, E Pakistan 29°32´N 71°40´E
106 D8 Lodi Lombardia, NW Italy 45°19´N 09°30´E
35 O8 Lodi California, W USA 38°07´N 121°17´W
31 T12 Lodi Ohio, N USA 41°00´N 82°01´W
92 H10 Lødingen Lapp. Lådik. Nordland, C Norway 68°25´N 16°00´E
79 L20 Lodja Kasai-Oriental, C Dem. Rep. Congo 03°29´S 23°25´E
37 O3 Lodore, Canyon of canyon Colorado, C USA
105 Q4 Lodosa Navarra, N Spain 42°26´N 02°05´W
81 H16 Lodwar Turkana, NW Kenya 03°06´N 35°38´E
110 K13 Łódź Rus. Lodz. Łódź, C Poland 51°51´N 19°26´E
110 E12 Łódzkie ◈ province C Poland
167 P8 Loei var. Loey, Muang Loei. Loei, C Thailand 17°32´N 101°40´E
98 I11 Loenen Utrecht, C Netherlands 52°13´N 05°01´E
167 R9 Loeng Nok Tha Yasothon, E Thailand 16°12´N 104°31´E
83 F24 Loeriesfontein Northern Cape, W South Africa 30°59´S 19°29´E
Loewoek see Luwuk
Loey see Loei
76 J16 Lofa ∽ N Liberia
109 P6 Lofer Salzburg, C Austria 47°37´N 12°42´E
92 F11 Lofoten var. Lofoten Islands. island group C Norway
Lofoten Islands see Lofoten
95 N18 Loftahammar Kalmar, S Sweden 57°55´N 16°45´E
127 O10 Log Volgogradskaya Oblast', SW Russia 49°32´N 43°52´E
77 S12 Loga Dosso, SW Niger 13°40´N 03°15´E
29 S14 Logan Iowa, C USA 41°38´N 95°47´W
26 K3 Logan Kansas, C USA 39°39´N 99°34´W
31 T14 Logan Ohio, N USA 39°32´N 82°24´W
36 L1 Logan Utah, W USA 41°45´N 111°50´W
21 P6 Logan West Virginia, NE USA 37°52´N 82°00´W
35 Y10 Logandale Nevada, W USA 36°36´N 114°28´W
19 O11 Logan International ✈ (Boston) Massachusetts, NE USA 42°22´N 71°00´W
11 N16 Logan Lake British Columbia, SW Canada 50°28´N 120°42´W
23 Q4 Logan Martin Lake ⊞ Alabama, S USA
10 G8 Logan, Mount ▲ Yukon, W Canada 60°32´N 140°34´W
32 I7 Logan, Mount ▲ Washington, NW USA 48°32´N 120°57´W
33 P7 Logan Pass pass Montana, NW USA
31 O12 Logansport Indiana, N USA 40°44´N 86°25´W
22 F6 Logansport Louisiana, S USA 31°58´N 94°00´W
149 Q5 Lōgar prev. Lowgar. ◈ province E Afghanistan




◆ Country
● Country Capital
◇ Dependent Territory
○ Dependent Territory Capital
◈ Administrative Regions
✈ International Airport
▲ Mountain
▲▲ Mountain Range
※ Volcano
∽ River
⊚ Lake
⊞ Reservoir

LOGE – LÜBEN


67 R11 **Loge** ≈ NW Angola
**Logishin** see Lahishyn
**Log na Coille** see Lugnaquillia Mountain
78 G11 **Logone** var. Lagone. ≈ Cameroon/Chad
78 G13 **Logone-Occidental** off. Région du Logone-Occidental. ◈ region SW Chad
78 H13 **Logone Occidental** ≈ SW Chad
**Logone-Occidental, Région du** see Logone-Occidental
78 G13 **Logone-Oriental** off. Région du Logone-Oriental. ◈ region SW Chad
78 H13 **Logone Oriental** ≈ SW Chad
**Logone Oriental** see Pendé
**Logone-Oriental, Région du** see Logone-Oriental
**L'Ogooué-Ivindo** see Ogooué-Ivindo
**L'Ogooué-Lolo** see Ogooué-Lolo
**L'Ogooué-Maritime** see Ogooué-Maritime
**Logoysk** see Lahoysk
105 P4 **Logroño** anc. Vareia, Lat. Juliobriga. La Rioja, N Spain 42°28′N 02°26′W
104 L10 **Logrosán** Extremadura, W Spain 39°21′N 05°29′W
95 G20 **Løgstør** Nordjylland, N Denmark 56°57′N 09°19′E
95 H22 **Løgten** Midtjylland, C Denmark 56°17′N 10°20′E
95 F24 **Løgumkloster** Syddanmark, SW Denmark 55°04′N 08°58′E
**Lögurinn** see Lagarfljót
153 P15 **Lohārdaga** Jhārkhand, N India 23°27′N 84°42′E
152 H10 **Lohāru** Haryāna, N India 28°28′N 75°50′E
101 D15 **Lohausen** ✕ (Düsseldorf) Nordrhein-Westfalen, W Germany 51°18′N 06°51′E
189 O14 **Lohd** Pohnpei, E Micronesia
92 L12 **Lohiniva** Lappi, N Finland 67°09′N 25°04′E
**Lohiszyn** see Lahishyn
93 L20 **Lohja** var. Lojo. Uusimaa, S Finland 60°14′N 24°07′E
169 V11 **Lohjanan** Borneo, C Indonesia
25 Q9 **Lohn** Texas, SW USA 31°15′N 99°22′W
100 G12 **Löhne** Niedersachsen, NW Germany 52°40′N 08°13′E
**Lohr** see Lohr am Main
101 I18 **Lohr am Main** var. Lohr. Bayern, C Germany 50°00′N 09°30′E
109 T10 **Loibl Pass** Ger. Loiblpass, Slvn. Ljubelj. pass Austria/Slovenia
**Loiblpass** see Loibl Pass
167 N6 **Loikaw** Kayah State, C Myanmar (Burma) 19°40′N 97°17′E
93 K19 **Loimaa** Varsinais-Suomi, SW Finland 60°51′N 23°03′E
103 O6 **Loing** ≈ C France
167 R6 **Loi, Phou** ▲ N Laos 20°18′N 103°14′E
102 L7 **Loir** ≈ C France
103 Q11 **Loire** ◈ department E France
102 M7 **Loire** var. Liger. ≈ C France
102 I7 **Loire-Atlantique** ◈ department NW France
103 O7 **Loiret** ◈ department C France
102 M8 **Loir-et-Cher** ◈ department C France
101 L24 **Loisach** ≈ SE Germany
56 B9 **Loja** Loja, S Ecuador 03°59′S 79°16′W
104 M14 **Loja** Andalucía, S Spain 37°10′N 04°09′W
56 B9 **Loja** ◈ province S Ecuador
**Lojo** see Lohja
116 J4 **Lokachi** Volyns'ka Oblast', NW Ukraine 50°44′N 24°39′E
79 M20 **Lokandu** Maniema, C Dem. Rep. Congo 02°34′S 25°44′E
92 M11 **Lokan Tekojärvi** ◎ NE Finland
137 Z11 **Lökbatan** Rus. Lokbatan. E Azerbaijan 40°21′N 49°43′E
**Lokbatan** see Lökbatan
99 F17 **Lokeren** Oost-Vlaanderen, NW Belgium 51°06′N 03°59′E
**Lokhvitsa** see Lokhvytsya
117 S4 **Lokhvytsya** Rus. Lokhvitsa. Poltavs'ka Oblast', NE Ukraine 50°22′N 33°16′E
81 H17 **Lokichar** Turkana, NW Kenya 02°23′N 35°40′E
81 G16 **Lokichokio** Turkana, NW Kenya 04°16′N 34°22′E
81 H16 **Lokitaung** Turkana, NW Kenya 04°15′N 35°45′E
92 M11 **Lokka** Lappi, N Finland 67°48′N 27°41′E
94 G8 **Løkken Verk** Sør-Trøndelag, S Norway 63°06′N 09°43′E
124 G16 **Loknya** Pskovskaya Oblast', W Russia 56°48′N 30°08′E
77 V15 **Loko** Nassarawa, C Nigeria 08°00′N 07°48′E
77 U15 **Lokoja** Kogi, C Nigeria 07°48′N 06°45′E
81 H17 **Lokori** Turkana, W Kenya 01°56′N 36°03′E
77 R16 **Lokossa** S Benin 06°38′N 01°43′E
118 I3 **Loksa** Ger. Loxa. Harjumaa, NW Estonia 59°32′N 25°42′E
9 T7 **Loks Land** island Nunavut, NE Canada
80 C13 **Lol** ≈ NW South Sudan
76 K15 **Lola** SE Guinea 07°52′N 08°29′W
35 Q5 **Lola, Mount** ▲ California, W USA 39°27′N 120°20′W
81 H20 **Loliondo** Arusha, NE Tanzania 02°03′S 35°46′E
95 H25 **Lolland** prev. Laaland. island S Denmark
186 G6 **Lolobau Island** island E Papua New Guinea
79 E16 **Lolodorf** Sud, SW Cameroon 03°17′N 10°50′E
114 G7 **Lom** prev. Lom-Palanka. Montana, NW Bulgaria 43°49′N 23°16′E
114 G7 **Lom** ≈ NW Bulgaria
79 M19 **Lomami** ≈ C Dem. Rep. Congo
57 F17 **Lomas** Arequipa, SW Peru 15°29′S 74°54′W
63 I23 **Lomas, Bahía** bay S Chile
61 D20 **Lomas de Zamora** Buenos Aires, E Argentina 34°53′S 58°26′W
61 D20 **Loma Verde** Buenos Aires, E Argentina 35°16′S 58°24′W
180 K4 **Lombadina** Western Australia 16°39′S 122°54′E
106 E6 **Lombardia** Eng. Lombardy. ◈ region N Italy
**Lombardy** see Lombardia
102 M15 **Lombez** Gers, S France 43°29′N 00°54′E
171 Q16 **Lomblen, Pulau** island Nusa Tenggara, S Indonesia
173 W7 **Lombok Basin** undersea feature E Indian Ocean 09°50′S 116°00′E
170 L16 **Lombok, Pulau** island Nusa Tenggara, C Indonesia
77 Q16 **Lomé** ● (Togo) S Togo 06°08′N 01°13′E
77 Q16 **Lomé** ✕ S Togo 06°08′N 01°13′E
79 L19 **Lomela** Kasai-Oriental, C Dem. Rep. Congo 02°19′S 23°15′E
25 R9 **Lometa** Texas, SW USA 31°13′N 98°23′W
79 F16 **Lomié** Est, SE Cameroon 03°09′N 13°35′E
30 M8 **Lomira** Wisconsin, N USA 43°36′N 88°26′W
95 K23 **Lomma** Skåne, S Sweden 55°41′N 13°05′E
99 J16 **Lommel** Limburg, N Belgium 51°14′N 05°19′E
96 I11 **Lomond, Loch** ◎ C Scotland, United Kingdom
197 R9 **Lomonosov Ridge** var. Harris Ridge, Rus. Khrebet Homonsova. undersea feature Arctic Ocean 88°00′N 140°00′E
**Lomonsova, Khrebet** see Lomonosov Ridge
**Lom-Palanka** see Lom
**Lomphat** see Lumphăt
35 P14 **Lompoc** California, W USA 34°39′N 120°29′W
167 P9 **Lom Sak** var. Muang Lom Sak. Phetchabun, C Thailand 16°45′N 101°12′E
110 N9 **Łomża** Rus. Lomzha. Podlaskie, NE Poland 53°11′N 22°04′E
**Lomzha** see Łomża
**Lonaula** see Lonāvale
155 D14 **Lonāvale** prev. Lonaula. Mahārāshtra, W India 18°45′N 73°27′E
63 G15 **Loncoche** Araucanía, C Chile 39°22′S 72°34′W
63 H14 **Loncopue** Neuquén, W Argentina 38°04′S 70°43′W
99 G17 **Londerzeel** Vlaams Brabant, C Belgium 51°00′N 04°19′E
**Londinium** see London
14 E16 **London** Ontario, S Canada 42°59′N 81°13′W
191 Y2 **London** Kiritimati, E Kiribati 02°00′N 157°28′W
97 O22 **London** anc. Augusta, Lat. Londinium. ● (United Kingdom) SE England, United Kingdom 51°30′N 00°10′W
21 N7 **London** Kentucky, S USA 37°07′N 84°05′W
31 S13 **London** Ohio, NE USA 39°52′N 83°27′W
25 Q10 **London** Texas, SW USA 30°40′N 99°33′W
97 O22 **London City** ✕ SE England, United Kingdom 51°31′N 00°07′E
97 E14 **Londonderry** var. Derry, Ir. Doire. NW Northern Ireland, United Kingdom 55°N 07°19′W
97 F14 **Londonderry** cultural region NW Northern Ireland, United Kingdom
180 M2 **Londonderry, Cape** cape Western Australia
63 H25 **Londonderry, Isla** island S Chile
43 O7 **Londres, Cayos** reef NE Nicaragua
60 I10 **Londrina** Paraná, S Brazil 23°18′S 51°13′W
27 N13 **Lone Grove** Oklahoma, C USA 34°11′N 97°15′W
14 E12 **Lonely Island** island Ontario, S Canada
35 T8 **Lone Mountain** ▲ Nevada, W USA 38°01′N 117°28′W
25 V6 **Lone Oak** Texas, SW USA 33°02′N 95°58′W
35 T11 **Lone Pine** California, W USA 36°36′N 118°04′W
**Lone Star State** see Texas
**Lone Tree Islet** see Iku
83 D14 **Longa** Kuando Kubango, C Angola 14°44′S 18°36′E
82 B12 **Longa** ≈ W Angola
83 E15 **Longa** ≈ SE Angola
**Long'an** see Pingwu
163 W11 **Longang Shan** ▲▲ NE China
197 S4 **Longa, Proliv** Eng. Long Strait. strait NE Russia
44 J13 **Long Bay** bay W Jamaica
21 V13 **Long Bay** bay North Carolina/South Carolina, E USA
35 T16 **Long Beach** California, W USA 33°46′N 118°11′W
22 M9 **Long Beach** Mississippi, S USA 30°21′N 89°09′W
18 L14 **Long Beach** Long Island, New York, NE USA 40°34′N 73°38′W
32 F9 **Long Beach** Washington, NW USA 46°21′N 124°03′W
18 K16 **Long Beach Island** island New Jersey, NE USA
65 M25 **Longbluff** headland SW Tristan da Cunha
23 U13 **Longboat Key** island Florida, SE USA
18 K15 **Long Branch** New Jersey, NE USA 40°18′N 73°59′W
44 J5 **Long Cay** island SE The Bahamas
**Longcheng** see Xiaoxian
161 P14 **Longchuan** var. Laolong. Guangdong, S China 24°07′N 115°10′E
**Longchuan** see Nanhua
**Longchuan Jiang** see Shweli
32 K12 **Long Creek** Oregon, NW USA 44°40′N 119°07′W
159 W10 **Longde** Ningxia, N China 35°37′N 106°07′E
183 P16 **Longford** Tasmania, SE Australia 41°41′S 147°03′E
97 D17 **Longford** Ir. An Longfort. Longford, C Ireland 53°45′N 07°50′W
97 E17 **Longford** Ir. An Longfort. cultural region C Ireland
**Longgang** see Dazu
161 P1 **Longhua** Hebei, E China 41°18′N 117°44′E
169 U11 **Longiram** Borneo, C Indonesia 0°02′S 115°36′E
12 H8 **Long Island** island Nunavut, C Canada
186 D7 **Long Island** var. Arop Island. island N Papua New Guinea
44 J4 **Long Island** island C The Bahamas
18 L14 **Long Island** island New York, NE USA
**Long Island** see Bermuda
18 M14 **Long Island Sound** sound NE USA
163 U7 **Longjiang** Heilongjiang, NE China 47°20′N 123°09′E
160 K13 **Long Jiang** ≈ S China
163 Y10 **Longjing** var. Yanji. Jilin, NE China 42°48′N 129°26′E
161 R4 **Longkou** Shandong, E China 37°40′N 120°21′E
12 E11 **Longlac** Ontario, S Canada 49°47′N 86°34′W
19 S1 **Long Lake** ◎ Maine, NE USA
31 R5 **Long Lake** ◎ Michigan, N USA
31 O6 **Long Lake** ◎ Michigan, N USA
29 N6 **Long Lake** ◎ North Dakota, N USA
30 J4 **Long Lake** ⊠ Wisconsin, N USA
99 K23 **Longlier** Luxembourg, SE Belgium 49°51′N 05°27′E
160 I13 **Longlin** var. Longlin Gezu Zizhixian, Xinzhou. Guangxi Zhuangzu Zizhiqu, S China 24°46′N 105°19′E
**Longlin Gezu Zizhixian** see Longlin
37 T3 **Longmont** Colorado, C USA 40°09′N 105°07′W
157 P10 **Longnan** var. Wudu. Gansu, C China 33°27′N 104°57′E
29 N13 **Long Pine** Nebraska, C USA 42°32′N 99°42′W
**Longping** see Luodian
14 F17 **Long Point** headland Ontario, S Canada 42°33′N 80°15′W
14 K15 **Long Point** headland Ontario, SE Canada 43°56′N 76°53′W
184 P10 **Long Point** headland North Island, New Zealand 39°07′S 177°41′E
30 L2 **Long Point** headland Michigan, N USA 47°50′N 89°09′W
14 G17 **Long Point Bay** lake bay Ontario, S Canada
29 T7 **Long Prairie** Minnesota, N USA 45°58′N 94°52′W
**Longquan** see Fenggang
**Longquan** see Yanggao
13 S11 **Long Range Mountains** hill range Newfoundland and Labrador, E Canada
65 H25 **Long Range Point** headland SE Saint Helena 16°00′S 05°41′W
181 V8 **Longreach** Queensland, E Australia 23°31′S 144°18′E
160 H7 **Longriba** Sichuan, C China 32°32′N 102°20′E
160 L10 **Longshan** var. Min'an. Hunan, S China 29°25′N 109°28′E
37 S3 **Longs Peak** ▲ Colorado, C USA 40°15′N 105°37′W
**Long Strait** see Longa, Proliv
102 K8 **Longué** Maine-et-Loire, NW France 47°23′N 00°07′W
13 P11 **Longue-Pointe** Québec, E Canada 50°20′N 64°13′W
103 S4 **Longuyon** Meurthe-et-Moselle, NE France 49°25′N 05°37′E
25 W7 **Longview** Texas, SW USA 32°30′N 94°45′W
32 G10 **Longview** Washington, NW USA 46°08′N 122°56′W
65 H25 **Longwood** C Saint Helena
25 P7 **Longworth** Texas, SW USA 32°37′N 100°20′W
103 S3 **Longwy** Meurthe-et-Moselle, NE France 49°31′N 05°46′E
159 V11 **Longxi** var. Gongchang. Gansu, C China 35°00′N 104°34′E
**Longxian** see Wengyuan
167 S14 **Long Xuyên** var. Longxuyen. An Giang, S Vietnam 10°23′N 105°25′E
**Longxuyen** see Long Xuyên
161 Q13 **Longyan** Fujian, SE China 25°06′N 117°02′E
92 O3 **Longyearbyen** ○ (Svalbard) Spitsbergen, W Svalbard 78°12′N 15°39′E
160 J15 **Longzhou** Guangxi Zhuangzu Zizhiqu, S China 22°22′N 106°46′E
**Longzhouping** see Changyang
100 F12 **Löningen** Niedersachsen, NW Germany 52°43′N 07°42′E
27 V11 **Lonoke** Arkansas, C USA 34°46′N 91°56′W
95 L21 **Lönsboda** Skåne, S Sweden 56°24′N 14°19′E
103 S9 **Lons-le-Saunier** anc. Ledo Salinarius. Jura, E France 46°41′N 05°32′E
31 O15 **Loogootee** Indiana, N USA 38°40′N 86°54′W
31 Q9 **Looking Glass River** ≈ Michigan, N USA
21 X11 **Lookout, Cape** headland North Carolina, SE USA 34°36′N 76°31′W
39 O6 **Lookout Ridge** ridge Alaska, USA
**Lookransar** see Lūnkaransar
181 N11 **Loongana** Western Australia 30°53′S 127°15′E
99 I14 **Loon op Zand** Noord-Brabant, S Netherlands 51°38′N 05°05′E
97 A19 **Loop Head** Ir. Ceann Léime. promontory W Ireland
109 V4 **Loosdorf** Niederösterreich, NE Austria 48°13′N 15°25′E
158 G10 **Lop** Xinjiang Uygur Zizhiqu, NW China 37°06′N 80°12′E
112 J11 **Lopare** ◈ Republika Srpska, NE Bosnia and Herzegovina
**Lopatichi** see Lapatsichy
127 P7 **Lopatino** Penzenskaya Oblast', W Russia 52°38′N 45°46′E
167 P10 **Lop Buri** var. Loburi. Lop Buri, C Thailand 14°49′N 100°37′E
25 R16 **Lopeno** Texas, SW USA 26°42′N 99°06′W
79 C18 **Lopez, Cap** headland W Gabon 0°39′S 08°44′E
98 I12 **Lopik** Utrecht, C Netherlands 51°58′N 04°57′E
**Lop Nor** see Lop Nur
158 M7 **Lop Nur** var. Lob Nor, Lop Nor, Lo-pu Po. seasonal lake NW China
**Lopnur** see Yuli
79 K17 **Lopori** ≈ NW Dem. Rep. Congo
98 O5 **Loppersum** Groningen, NE Netherlands 53°20′N 06°45′E
92 I8 **Lopphavet** sound N Norway
**Lo-pu Po** see Lop Nur
**Lora** see Lwarah Rōd
182 F3 **Lora Creek** seasonal river South Australia
104 K13 **Lora del Río** Andalucía, S Spain 37°39′N 05°32′W
148 M11 **Lora, Hamun-i** wetland SW Pakistan
31 T11 **Lorain** Ohio, N USA 41°27′N 82°10′W
25 O7 **Loraine** Texas, SW USA 32°24′N 100°42′W
31 R13 **Loramie, Lake** ⊠ Ohio, N USA
105 Q13 **Lorca** Ar. Lurka; anc. Eliocroca, Lat. Illurco. Murcia, S Spain 37°40′N 01°41′W
192 I10 **Lord Howe Island** island E Australia
**Lord Howe Island** see Ontong Java Atoll
175 O10 **Lord Howe Rise** undersea feature SW Pacific Ocean
192 J10 **Lord Howe Seamounts** undersea feature W Pacific Ocean
37 P15 **Lordsburg** New Mexico, SW USA 32°19′N 108°42′W
186 E5 **Lorengau** var. Lorungau. Manus Island, N Papua New Guinea 02°01′S 147°15′E
25 N5 **Lorenzo** Texas, SW USA 33°40′N 101°31′W
142 K7 **Lorestān** off. Ostān-e Lorestān, var. Luristan. ◈ province W Iran
**Lorestān, Ostān-e** see Lorestān
57 M17 **Loreto** Beni, N Bolivia 15°13′S 64°44′W
106 J12 **Loreto** Marche, C Italy 43°25′N 13°37′E
40 F8 **Loreto** Baja California Sur, NW Mexico 25°59′N 111°22′W
40 M11 **Loreto** Zacatecas, C Mexico 22°15′N 102°00′W
56 E9 **Loreto** off. Región de Loreto. ◈ region NE Peru
**Loreto, Región de** see Loreto
81 K18 **Lorian Swamp** swamp E Kenya
54 E6 **Lorica** Córdoba, NW Colombia 09°14′N 75°50′W
102 G7 **Lorient** prev. l'Orient. Morbihan, NW France 47°45′N 03°22′W
**l'Orient** see Lorient
111 K22 **Lőrinci** Heves, NE Hungary 47°46′N 19°40′E
14 G11 **Loring** Ontario, S Canada 45°55′N 79°59′W
33 V6 **Loring** Montana, NW USA 48°49′N 107°48′W
103 R13 **Loriol-sur-Drôme** Drôme, E France 44°46′N 04°51′E
21 U12 **Loris** South Carolina, SE USA 34°03′N 78°53′W
57 I18 **Loriscota, Laguna** ◎ S Peru
183 N13 **Lorne** Victoria, SE Australia 38°33′S 143°57′E
96 G11 **Lorn, Firth of** inlet W Scotland, United Kingdom
**Loro Sae** see East Timor
101 F24 **Lörrach** Baden-Württemberg, S Germany 47°38′N 07°40′E
**Lorungau** see Lorengau
94 L11 **Los** Gävleborg, C Sweden 61°43′N 15°15′E
35 P14 **Los Alamos** California, W USA 34°44′N 120°16′W
37 S10 **Los Alamos** New Mexico, SW USA 35°52′N 106°17′W
42 F5 **Los Amates** Izabal, E Guatemala 15°14′N 89°06′W
63 G14 **Los Ángeles** Bío Bío, C Chile 37°30′S 72°18′W
35 S15 **Los Angeles** California, W USA 34°03′N 118°15′W
35 S15 **Los Angeles** ✕ California, W USA 33°54′N 118°24′W
35 T13 **Los Angeles Aqueduct** aqueduct California, W USA
**Losanna** see Lausanne
63 H20 **Los Antiguos** Santa Cruz, SW Argentina 46°36′S 71°31′W
189 Q16 **Losap Atoll** atoll C Micronesia
35 P10 **Los Banos** California, W USA 37°00′N 120°39′W
104 K16 **Los Barrios** Andalucía, S Spain 36°11′N 05°30′W
62 L5 **Los Blancos** Salta, N Argentina 23°36′S 62°35′W
42 L12 **Los Chiles** Alajuela, NW Costa Rica 11°00′N 84°42′W
105 O2 **Los Corrales de Buelna** Cantabria, N Spain 43°15′N 04°04′W
25 T17 **Los Fresnos** Texas, SW USA 26°03′N 97°28′W
35 N9 **Los Gatos** California, W USA 37°13′N 121°58′W
127 P10 **Loshchina** Volgogradskaya Oblast', SW Russia 48°58′N 46°14′E
110 O11 **Łosice** Mazowieckie, C Poland 52°13′N 22°42′E
112 B11 **Lošinj** Ger. Lussin, It. Lussino. island W Croatia
**Los Jardines** see Ngetik Atoll
63 G15 **Los Lagos** Los Ríos, C Chile 39°50′S 72°50′W
63 F17 **Los Lagos** off. Región de los Lagos. ◈ region C Chile
**los Lagos, Región de** see Los Lagos
**Loslau** see Wodzisław Śląski
64 N11 **Los Llanos de Aridane** var. Los Llanos de Aridane. La Palma, Islas Canarias, Spain, NE Atlantic Ocean 28°39′N 17°54′W
**Los Llanos de Aridane** see Los Llanos de Aridane
37 R11 **Los Lunas** New Mexico, SW USA 34°48′N 106°43′W
63 I16 **Los Menucos** Río Negro, C Argentina 40°52′S 68°07′W
40 H8 **Los Mochis** Sinaloa, C Mexico 25°48′N 108°58′W
35 N4 **Los Molinos** California, W USA 40°00′N 122°05′W
104 M9 **Los Navalmorales** Castilla-La Mancha, C Spain 39°43′N 04°38′W
25 S15 **Los Olmos Creek** ≈ Texas, SW USA
**Losonc/Losontz** see Lučenec
167 S5 **Lô, Sông** var. Panlong Jiang. ≈ China/Vietnam
44 B5 **Los Palacios** Pinar del Río, W Cuba 22°35′N 83°16′W
104 K14 **Los Palacios y Villafranca** Andalucía, S Spain 37°10′N 05°55′W
37 R12 **Los Pinos Mountains** ▲▲ New Mexico, SW USA
37 R11 **Los Ranchos de Albuquerque** New Mexico, SW USA 35°09′N 106°37′W
40 M14 **Los Reyes** Michoacán, SW Mexico 19°36′N 102°29′W
63 G15 **Los Ríos** ◈ region C Chile
56 B7 **Los Ríos** ◈ province C Ecuador
64 O11 **Los Rodeos** ✕ (Santa Cruz de Tenerife) Tenerife, Islas Canarias, Spain, NE Atlantic Ocean 28°27′N 16°20′W
54 L4 **Los Roques, Islas** island group N Venezuela
43 S17 **Los Santos** Los Santos, S Panama 07°56′N 80°23′W
43 S17 **Los Santos** off. Provincia de Los Santos. ◈ province S Panama
**Los Santos** see Los Santos de Maimona
104 J12 **Los Santos de Maimona** var. Los Santos. Extremadura, W Spain 38°27′N 06°22′W
**Los Santos, Provincia de** see Los Santos
98 P10 **Losser** Overijssel, E Netherlands 52°16′N 06°25′E
96 J8 **Lossiemouth** NE Scotland, United Kingdom 57°43′N 03°18′W
61 B14 **Los Tábanos** Santa Fe, C Argentina 28°27′S 59°57′W
54 J4 **Los Taques** Falcón, N Venezuela 11°50′N 70°16′W
14 G11 **Lost Channel** Ontario, S Canada 45°54′N 80°20′W
54 L5 **Los Teques** Miranda, N Venezuela 10°25′N 67°01′W
35 Q12 **Lost Hills** California, W USA 35°35′N 119°40′W
36 I7 **Lost Peak** ▲ Utah, W USA 37°30′N 113°57′W
33 P11 **Lost Trail Pass** pass Montana, NW USA
186 G9 **Losuia** Kiriwina Island, SE Papua New Guinea 08°29′S 151°03′E
62 G10 **Los Vilos** Coquimbo, C Chile 31°56′S 71°35′W
105 N10 **Los Yébenes** Castilla-La Mancha, C Spain 39°35′N 03°52′W
103 N13 **Lot** ◈ department S France
103 N13 **Lot** ≈ S France
63 F14 **Lota** Bío Bío, C Chile 37°07′S 73°10′W
81 G15 **Lotagipi Swamp** wetland Kenya/Sudan
102 K14 **Lot-et-Garonne** ◈ department SW France
83 K21 **Lothair** Mpumalanga, NE South Africa 26°23′S 30°26′E
33 R7 **Lothair** Montana, NW USA 48°28′N 111°15′W
79 L20 **Loto** Kasai-Oriental, C Dem. Rep. Congo 02°48′S 22°30′E
108 E10 **Lötschbergtunnel** tunnel Valais, SW Switzerland
25 T9 **Lott** Texas, SW USA 31°12′N 97°02′W
124 H3 **Lotta** var. Lutto. ≈ Finland/Russia
184 Q7 **Lottin Point** headland North Island, New Zealand 37°26′S 178°07′E
**Lötzen** see Giżycko
**Loualaba** see Lualaba
167 P6 **Louangnamtha** var. Luong Nam Tha. Louang Namtha, N Laos 20°55′N 101°24′E
167 Q7 **Louangphabang** var. Louangphrabang, Luang Prabang. Louangphabang, N Laos 19°51′N 102°08′E
**Louangphrabang** see Louangphabang
194 H5 **Loubet Coast** physical region Antarctica
**Loubomo** see Dolisie
**Louch** see Loukhi
102 H6 **Loudéac** Côtes d'Armor, NW France 48°11′N 02°45′W
160 M11 **Loudi** Hunan, S China 27°51′N 111°59′E
79 F21 **Loudima** Bouenza, S Congo 04°06′S 13°05′E
20 M9 **Loudon** Tennessee, S USA 35°43′N 84°19′W
31 T12 **Loudonville** Ohio, N USA 40°38′N 82°13′W
102 L8 **Loudun** Vienne, W France 47°01′N 00°05′E
102 K7 **Loué** Sarthe, NW France 48°00′N 00°14′W
76 G10 **Louga** NW Senegal 15°36′N 16°15′W
97 M19 **Loughborough** C England, United Kingdom 52°47′N 01°11′W
97 C18 **Loughrea** Ir. Baile Locha Riach. Galway, W Ireland 53°12′N 08°34′W
103 S9 **Louhans** Saône-et-Loire, C France 46°38′N 05°12′E
21 P5 **Louisa** Kentucky, S USA 38°06′N 82°37′W
21 V5 **Louisa** Virginia, NE USA 38°02′N 78°00′W
21 V9 **Louisburg** North Carolina, SE USA 36°05′N 78°18′W
25 U12 **Louise** Texas, SW USA 29°07′N 96°22′W
15 P11 **Louiseville** Québec, SE Canada 46°15′N 72°54′W
27 W3 **Louisiana** Missouri, C USA 39°25′N 91°03′W
22 G8 **Louisiana** off. State of Louisiana, also known as Creole State, Pelican State. ◈ state S USA
83 K19 **Louis Trichardt** prev. Makhado. Northern, NE South Africa 23°01′S 29°43′E
23 V4 **Louisville** Georgia, SE USA 33°00′N 82°24′W
30 M15 **Louisville** Illinois, N USA 38°46′N 88°32′W
20 K5 **Louisville** Kentucky, S USA 38°15′N 85°46′W
22 M4 **Louisville** Mississippi, S USA 33°07′N 89°03′W
29 S15 **Louisville** Nebraska, C USA 41°00′N 96°09′W
192 L11 **Louisville Ridge** undersea feature S Pacific Ocean
124 J6 **Loukhi** var. Louch. Respublika Kareliya, NW Russia 66°05′N 33°04′E
79 H19 **Loukoléla** Cuvette, E Congo 01°04′S 17°10′E
104 G14 **Loulé** Faro, S Portugal 37°08′N 08°02′W
111 C16 **Louny** Ger. Laun. Ústecký Kraj, NW Czechia 50°22′N 13°50′E
29 O15 **Loup City** Nebraska, C USA 41°16′N 98°58′W
29 P15 **Loup River** ≈ Nebraska, C USA
15 S9 **Loup, Rivière du** ≈ Québec, SE Canada
12 K7 **Loups Marins, Lacs des** ◎ Québec, NE Canada
102 K16 **Lourdes** Hautes-Pyrénées, S France 43°06′N 00°03′W
**Lourenço Marques** see Maputo
104 F11 **Loures** Lisboa, C Portugal 38°50′N 09°10′W
104 F10 **Lourinhã** Lisboa, C Portugal 39°14′N 09°19′W
115 C16 **Loúros** ≈ W Greece
104 G8 **Lousã** Coimbra, N Portugal 40°07′N 08°15′W
**Loushanguan** see Tongzi
160 M10 **Lou Shui** ≈ C China
183 O5 **Louth** New South Wales, SE Australia 30°34′S 145°07′E
97 O18 **Louth** E England, United Kingdom 53°19′N 00°00′E
97 F17 **Louth** Ir. Lú. cultural region NE Ireland
115 H15 **Loutrá** Kentrikí Makedonía, N Greece 39°55′N 23°37′E
115 G19 **Loutráki** Pelopónnisos, S Greece 37°55′N 22°55′E
**Louvain** see Leuven
99 H19 **Louvain-la Neuve** Walloon Brabant, C Belgium 50°39′N 04°36′E
14 J8 **Louvicourt** Québec, SE Canada 48°04′N 77°22′W
102 M4 **Louviers** Eure, N France 49°13′N 01°11′E
30 K14 **Lou Yaeger, Lake** ⊠ Illinois, N USA
93 J15 **Lövånger** Västerbotten, N Sweden 64°22′N 21°19′E
124 J14 **Lovat'** ≈ NW Russia
113 J17 **Lovćen** ▲ SW Montenegro 42°22′N 18°49′E
114 I8 **Lovech** Lovech, N Bulgaria 43°08′N 24°45′E
114 I9 **Lovech** ◈ province N Bulgaria
25 V9 **Lovelady** Texas, SW USA 31°07′N 95°27′W
37 T3 **Loveland** Colorado, C USA 40°24′N 105°04′W
33 U12 **Lovell** Wyoming, C USA 44°50′N 108°23′W
**Lovello, Monte** see Grosser Löffler
35 S4 **Lovelock** Nevada, W USA 40°11′N 118°30′W
106 E7 **Lovere** Lombardia, N Italy 45°51′N 10°06′E
30 L10 **Loves Park** Illinois, N USA 42°19′N 89°03′W
26 M2 **Lovewell Reservoir** ⊠ Kansas, C USA
93 M19 **Loviisa** Swe. Lovisa. Uusimaa, S Finland 60°27′N 26°15′E
37 V15 **Loving** New Mexico, SW USA 32°17′N 104°06′W
21 U6 **Lovingston** Virginia, NE USA 37°46′N 78°54′W
37 V14 **Lovington** New Mexico, SW USA 32°56′N 103°21′W
**Lovisa** see Loviisa
111 C15 **Lovosice** Ger. Lobositz. Ústecký Kraj, NW Czechia 50°30′N 14°02′E
124 K4 **Lovozero** Murmanskaya Oblast', NW Russia 68°00′N 35°03′E
124 K4 **Lovozero, Ozero** ◎ NW Russia
112 B9 **Lovran** It. Laurana. Primorje-Gorski Kotar, NW Croatia 45°16′N 14°15′E
116 E11 **Lovrin** Ger. Lowrin. Timiş, W Romania 45°58′N 20°49′E
82 E10 **Lóvua** Lunda Norte, NE Angola 07°21′S 20°09′E
82 G12 **Lóvua** Moxico, E Angola 11°33′S 23°35′E
65 D25 **Low Bay** bay East Falkland, Falkland Islands
9 P9 **Low, Cape** headland Nunavut, E Canada 63°05′N 85°27′W
33 N10 **Lowell** Idaho, NW USA 46°07′N 115°36′W
19 O10 **Lowell** Massachusetts, NE USA 42°38′N 71°19′W
**Löwen** see Leuven
**Löwenberg in Schlesien** see Lwówek Śląski
**Lower Austria** see Niederösterreich
**Lower Bann** see Bann
**Lower California** see Baja California
**Lower Danube** see Niederösterreich
185 L14 **Lower Hutt** Wellington, North Island, New Zealand 41°13′S 174°51′E
39 N11 **Lower Kalskag** Alaska, USA 61°30′N 160°28′W
35 O1 **Lower Klamath Lake** ◎ California, W USA
35 Q2 **Lower Lake** ◎ California/Nevada, W USA
97 E15 **Lower Lough Erne** ◎ SW Northern Ireland, United Kingdom
**Lower Lusatia** see Niederlausitz
10 K9 **Lower Post** British Columbia, W Canada 59°53′N 128°19′W
29 T4 **Lower Red Lake** ◎ Minnesota, N USA
**Lower Rhine** see Neder Rijn
**Lower Saxony** see Niedersachsen
97 Q19 **Lowestoft** E England, United Kingdom 52°29′N 01°45′E
**Lowgar** see Lōgar
182 H7 **Low Hill** South Australia 32°17′S 136°46′E
110 K12 **Łowicz** Łódzkie, C Poland 52°06′N 19°55′E
33 N13 **Lowman** Idaho, NW USA 44°04′N 115°37′W
**Lowrah** see Lwarah Rōd
**Lowrin** see Lovrin
183 N17 **Low Rocky Point** headland Tasmania, SE Australia 42°59′S 145°28′E
18 I8 **Lowville** New York, NE USA 43°47′N 75°29′W
**Loxa** see Loksa
182 K9 **Loxton** South Australia 34°30′S 140°36′E
81 G21 **Loya** Tabora, C Tanzania 04°57′S 33°53′E
30 K6 **Loyal** Wisconsin, N USA 44°45′N 90°30′W
18 G13 **Loyalsock Creek** ≈ Pennsylvania, NE USA
35 Q5 **Loyalton** California, W USA 39°39′N 120°16′W
**Lo-yang** see Luoyang
187 Q16 **Loyauté, Îles** island group S New Caledonia
**Loyev** see Loyew
119 O20 **Loyew** Rus. Loyev. Homyel'skaya Voblasts', SE Belarus 51°56′N 30°48′E
125 S13 **Loyno** Kirovskaya Oblast', NW Russia 59°44′N 52°42′E
103 P13 **Lozère** ◈ department S France
103 Q14 **Lozère, Mont** ▲ S France 44°27′N 03°44′E
112 J11 **Loznica** Serbia, W Serbia 44°32′N 19°13′E
117 V7 **Lozova** Rus. Lozovaya. Kharkivs'ka Oblast', E Ukraine 48°54′N 36°23′E
**Lozovaya** see Lozova
105 N7 **Lozoyuela** Madrid, C Spain 40°55′N 03°36′W
**Lu** see Shandong, China
**Lú** see Louth, Ireland
82 F12 **Luacano** Moxico, E Angola 11°19′S 21°30′E
79 N21 **Lualaba** Fr. Loualaba. ≈ SE Dem. Rep. Congo
83 H14 **Luampa** Western, NW Zambia 15°02′S 24°27′E
83 H15 **Luampa Kuta** Western, W Zambia 15°22′S 24°40′E
161 P8 **Lu'an** Anhui, E China 31°46′N 116°31′E
**Luanco** see Lluanco
82 A11 **Luanda** var. Loanda, Port. São Paulo de Loanda. ● Luanda, NW Angola 08°48′S 13°17′E
82 A11 **Luanda** ◈ province (Angola) NW Angola
82 A11 **Luanda** ✕ Luanda, NW Angola 08°49′S 13°16′E
82 D12 **Luando** ≈ C Angola
**Luang** see Tapi, Mae Nam
83 G14 **Luanginga** var. Luanguinga. ≈ Angola/Zambia
167 N15 **Luang, Khao** ▲ SW Thailand 08°21′N 99°46′E
**Luang Prabang** see Louangphabang
167 P8 **Luang Prabang Range** Th. Thiukhaoluang Phrahang. ▲▲ Laos/Thailand
167 N16 **Luang, Thale** lagoon S Thailand
**Luangua, Rio** see Luangwa
82 E11 **Luangue** ≈ NE Angola
**Luanguinga** see Luanginga
83 K15 **Luangwa** var. Aruângua. Lusaka, C Zambia 15°36′S 30°27′E
83 K14 **Luangwa** var. Aruângua, Rio Luangua. ≈ Mozambique/Zambia
161 Q2 **Luan He** ≈ E China
190 G11 **Luaniva, Île** island E Wallis and Futuna
161 P2 **Luanping** var. Anjiangying. Hebei, E China 40°55′N 117°19′E
82 J13 **Luanshya** Copperbelt, C Zambia 13°09′S 28°24′E
62 K13 **Luan Toro** La Pampa, C Argentina 36°14′S 64°15′W
161 Q2 **Luanxian** var. Luan Xian. Hebei, E China 39°46′N 118°46′E
**Luan Xian** see Luanxian
82 J12 **Luapula** ◈ province N Zambia
79 O25 **Luapula** ≈ Dem. Rep. Congo/Zambia
104 J2 **Luarca** Asturias, N Spain 43°33′N 06°31′W
169 R10 **Luar, Danau** ◎ Borneo, N Indonesia
79 L25 **Luashi** Katanga, S Dem. Rep. Congo 10°54′S 23°55′E
82 G12 **Luau** Port. Vila Teixeira de Sousa. Moxico, NE Angola 10°42′S 22°12′E
79 C16 **Luba** prev. San Carlos. Isla de Bioco, NW Equatorial Guinea 03°26′N 08°36′E
42 F4 **Lubaantun** ruins Toledo, S Belize
111 P16 **Lubaczów** var. Lúbaczów. Podkarpackie, SE Poland 50°10′N 23°08′E
**Lubale** see Lubalo
82 E11 **Lubalo** Lunda Norte, NE Angola 09°02′S 19°11′E
82 E11 **Lubalo** var. Lubale. ≈ Angola/Dem. Rep. Congo
118 J9 **Lubāna** E Latvia 56°55′N 29°43′E
**Lubānas Ezers** see Lubāns
171 N4 **Lubang Island** island N Philippines
83 B15 **Lubango** Port. Sá da Bandeira. Huíla, SW Angola 14°55′S 13°33′E
118 J9 **Lubāns** var. Lubānas Ezers. ◎ E Latvia
79 M21 **Lubao** Kasai-Oriental, C Dem. Rep. Congo 05°21′S 25°42′E
110 O13 **Lubartów** Ger. Qumälisch. Lublin, E Poland 51°29′N 22°38′E
100 G13 **Lübbecke** Nordrhein-Westfalen, NW Germany 52°18′N 08°37′E
100 O13 **Lübben** Brandenburg, E Germany 51°56′N 13°52′E
101 P14 **Lübbenau** Brandenburg, E Germany 51°52′N 13°57′E
25 N5 **Lubbock** Texas, SW USA 33°35′N 101°51′W
**Lubcz** see Lyubcha
19 U6 **Lubec** Maine, NE USA 44°49′N 67°00′W
100 K9 **Lübeck** Schleswig-Holstein, N Germany 53°52′N 10°41′E
100 K8 **Lübecker Bucht** bay N Germany
79 M21 **Lubefu** Kasai-Oriental, C Dem. Rep. Congo 04°43′S 24°25′E
163 T10 **Lubei** var. Jarud Qi. Nei Mongol Zizhiqu, N China 44°25′N 121°12′E
111 O14 **Lubelska, Wyżyna** plateau SE Poland
110 O13 **Lubelskie** ◈ province E Poland
**Lubembe** see Luembe
**Lüben** see Lubin


◆ Country ● Country Capital ◇ Dependent Territory ○ Dependent Territory Capital ◈ Administrative Regions ✕ International Airport ▲ Mountain ▲▲ Mountain Range Volcano ≈ River ◎ Lake ⊠ Reservoir

281

LUBENKA – MACÁ, CERRO

144 H9 **Lubenka** Zapadnyy Kazakhstan, W Kazakhstan *50°27′N 54°07′E*
79 P18 **Lubero** Nord-Kivu, E Dem. Rep. Congo *0°10′S 29°12′E*
79 L22 **Lubi** S Dem. Rep. Congo
**Lubiana** *see* Ljubljana
110 J11 **Lubień Kujawski** Kujawsko-pomorskie, C Poland *52°25′N 19°10′E*
67 T11 **Lubilandji** S Dem. Rep. Congo
110 F13 **Lubin** *Ger.* Lüben. Dolnośląskie, SW Poland *51°23′N 16°12′E*
111 O14 **Lublin** *Rus.* Lyublin. Lubelskie, E Poland *51°15′N 22°33′E*
111 J15 **Lubliniec** Śląskie, S Poland *50°41′N 18°41′E*
**Lubnān** *see* Lebanon
**Lubnān, Jabal** *see* Liban, Jebel
117 R5 **Lubny** Poltavs'ka Oblast', NE Ukraine *50°00′N 33°00′E*
**Luboml** *see* Lyuboml'
110 G11 **Luboń** *Ger.* Peterhof. Wielkolpolskie, C Poland *52°23′N 16°54′E*
**Luboten** *see* Ljuboten
110 D12 **Lubsko** *Ger.* Sommerfeld. Lubuskie, W Poland *51°47′N 14°57′E*
79 N24 **Lubudi** Katanga, SE Dem. Rep. Congo *09°57′S 25°59′E*
168 L13 **Lubuklinggau** Sumatera, W Indonesia *03°10′S 102°52′E*
79 N25 **Lubumbashi** *prev.* Élisabethville. Shaba, SE Dem. Rep. Congo *11°40′S 27°31′E*
83 I14 **Lubungu** Central, C Zambia *14°28′S 26°30′E*
110 E12 **Lubuskie** ◆ *province* W Poland
**Lubuskie** *see* Dobiegniew
79 N18 **Lubutu** Maniema, E Dem. Rep. Congo *0°48′S 26°39′E*
**Luca** *see* Lucca
82 C11 **Lucala** W Angola
14 E16 **Lucan** Ontario, S Canada *43°10′N 81°22′W*
97 F18 **Lucan** *Ir.* Leamhcán. Dublin, E Ireland *53°22′N 06°27′W*
**Lucanian Mountains** *see* Lucano, Appennino
107 M18 **Lucano, Appennino** *Eng.* Lucanian Mountains. ▲▲ S Italy
82 F11 **Lucapa** *var.* Lukapa. Lunda Norte, NE Angola *08°24′S 20°42′E*
29 V15 **Lucas** Iowa, C USA *41°01′N 93°26′W*
61 C18 **Lucas González** Entre Ríos, E Argentina *32°25′S 59°33′W*
65 C25 **Lucas Point** *headland* West Falkland, Falkland Islands *52°10′S 60°22′W*
31 S15 **Lucasville** Ohio, N USA *38°52′N 83°00′W*
106 F11 **Lucca** *anc.* Luca. Toscana, C Italy *43°50′N 10°30′E*
44 H12 **Lucea** W Jamaica *18°26′N 78°11′W*
97 H15 **Luce Bay** *inlet* SW Scotland, United Kingdom
22 M8 **Lucedale** Mississippi, S USA *30°55′N 88°35′W*
171 O4 **Lucena** *off.* Lucena City. Luzon, N Philippines *13°57′N 121°38′E*
104 M14 **Lucena** Andalucía, S Spain *37°25′N 04°29′W*
**Lucena City** *see* Lucena
105 S8 **Lucena del Cid** Comunitat Valenciana, E Spain *40°07′N 00°15′W*
111 D15 **Lučenec** *Ger.* Losontz, *Hung.* Losonc. Banskobystrický Kraj, C Slovakia *48°21′N 19°37′E*
**Lucentum** *see* Alicante
107 M16 **Lucera** Puglia, SE Italy *41°30′N 15°19′E*
**Lucerna/Lucerne** *see* Luzern
**Lucerne, Lake of** *see* Vierwaldstätter See
40 J4 **Lucero** Chihuahua, N Mexico *30°50′N 106°30′W*
123 S15 **Luchegorsk** Primorskiy Kray, SE Russia *46°26′N 134°10′E*
105 Q13 **Luchena** S Spain
**Lucheng** *see* Kangding
82 N13 **Lucheringo** *var.* Luchulingo. N Mozambique
**Luchesa** *see* Luchosa
**Luchin** *see* Luchyn
118 N13 **Luchosa** *Rus.* Luchesa. N Belarus
100 K11 **Lüchow** Mecklenburg-Vorpommern, N Germany *52°57′N 11°10′E*
**Luchow** *see* Hefei
**Luchulingo** *see* Lucheringo
119 N17 **Luchyn** *Rus.* Luchin. Homyel'skaya Voblasts', SE Belarus *53°01′N 30°01′E*
55 U11 **Lucie Rivier** W Suriname
182 K11 **Lucindale** South Australia *36°57′S 140°20′E*
83 A14 **Lucira** Namibe, SW Angola *13°51′S 12°35′E*
**Łuck** *see* Luts'k
101 O14 **Luckau** Brandenburg, E Germany *51°50′N 13°42′E*
100 N13 **Luckenwalde** Brandenburg, E Germany *52°05′N 13°11′E*
14 E15 **Lucknow** Ontario, S Canada *43°58′N 81°30′W*
152 L12 **Lucknow** *var.* Lakhnau. *state capital* Uttar Pradesh, N India *26°50′N 80°54′E*
102 J10 **Luçon** Vendée, NW France *46°27′N 01°10′W*
44 I7 **Lucrecia, Cabo** *headland* E Cuba *21°00′N 75°34′W*
82 F13 **Lucusse** Moxico, E Angola *12°32′S 20°46′E*
**Lüda** *see* Dalian
114 M9 **Luda Kamchia** *var.* Luda Kamchiya. E Bulgaria
**Luda Kamchiya** *see* Luda Kamchia
161 T14 **Lü Dao** *var.* Huoshao Dao, Lütao, *Eng.* Green Island; *prev.* Lü Tao. *island* SE Taiwan
**Ludasch** *see* Luduş
114 J10 **Luda Yana** C Bulgaria
112 F7 **Ludbreg** Varaždin, N Croatia *46°15′N 16°36′E*
29 P7 **Ludden** North Dakota, N USA *45°58′N 98°07′W*
101 F15 **Lüdenscheid** Nordrhein-Westfalen, W Germany *51°13′N 07°38′E*
83 C21 **Lüderitz** *prev.* Angra Pequena. //Karas, SW Namibia *26°38′S 15°10′E*
152 H8 **Ludhiāna** Punjab, N India *30°56′N 75°52′E*
31 O7 **Ludington** Michigan, N USA *43°58′N 86°27′W*
97 K20 **Ludlow** W England, United Kingdom *52°20′N 02°28′W*
35 W14 **Ludlow** California, W USA *34°43′N 116°07′W*
28 J7 **Ludlow** South Dakota, N USA *45°48′N 103°21′W*
18 M9 **Ludlow** Vermont, NE USA *43°24′N 72°39′W*
114 L7 **Ludogorie** *physical region* NE Bulgaria
23 W6 **Ludowici** Georgia, SE USA *31°42′N 81°44′W*
**Ludsan** *see* Ludza
116 I10 **Luduş** *Ger.* Ludasch, *Hung.* Marosludas. Mureş, C Romania *46°28′N 24°05′E*
95 M14 **Ludvika** Dalarna, C Sweden *60°08′N 15°14′E*
101 H21 **Ludwigsburg** Baden-Württemberg, SW Germany *48°54′N 09°12′E*
100 O13 **Ludwigsfelde** Brandenburg, NE Germany *52°17′N 13°15′E*
101 G20 **Ludwigshafen** *var.* Ludwigshafen am Rhein. Rheinland-Pfalz, W Germany *49°29′N 08°24′E*
**Ludwigshafen am Rhein** *see* Ludwigshafen
101 L20 **Ludwigskanal** *canal* SE Germany
100 L10 **Ludwigslust** Mecklenburg-Vorpommern, N Germany *53°19′N 11°29′E*
118 K10 **Ludza** *Ger.* Ludsan. E Latvia *56°32′N 27°41′E*
79 K21 **Luebo** Kasai-Occidental, SW Dem. Rep. Congo *05°19′S 21°21′E*
25 Q6 **Lueders** Texas, SW USA *32°46′N 99°38′W*
79 N20 **Lueki** Maniema, C Dem. Rep. Congo *03°25′S 25°50′E*
82 F10 **Luembe** *var.* Lubembe. Angola/Dem. Rep. Congo
82 E13 **Luena** *var.* Lwena, *Port.* Luso. Moxico, E Angola *11°47′S 19°52′E*
79 M24 **Luena** Katanga, SE Dem. Rep. Congo *09°28′S 25°45′E*
82 K12 **Luena** Northern, NE Zambia *10°40′S 30°21′E*
82 F13 **Luena** E Angola
83 F16 **Luenge** SE Angola
67 V13 **Luenha** W Mozambique
83 G15 **Lueti** Angola/Zambia
160 J7 **Lüeyang** *var.* Hejiayan. Shaanxi, C China *33°12′N 106°31′E*
161 P14 **Lufeng** Guangdong, S China *22°59′N 115°40′E*
79 N24 **Lufira** SE Dem. Rep. Congo
79 N25 **Lufira, Lac de Retenue de la** *var.* Lac Tshangalele. SE Dem. Rep. Congo
25 W8 **Lufkin** Texas, SW USA *31°21′N 94°47′W*
82 L11 **Lufubu** N Zambia
124 G14 **Luga** Leningradskaya Oblast', NW Russia *58°43′N 29°46′E*
124 G13 **Luga** NW Russia
**Luganer See** *see* Lugano, Lago di
108 H11 **Lugano** *Ger.* Lauis. Ticino, S Switzerland *46°01′N 08°57′E*
108 H12 **Lugano, Lago di** *var.* Ceresio, *Ger.* Luganer See. S Switzerland
**Lugansk** *see* Luhans'k
187 Q13 **Luganville** Espiritu Santo, C Vanuatu *15°31′S 167°12′E*
**Lugdunum** *see* Lyon
**Lugdunum Batavorum** *see* Leiden
83 O15 **Lugela** Zambézia, NE Mozambique *16°27′S 36°47′E*
83 O16 **Lugela** C Mozambique
82 P13 **Lugenda, Rio** N Mozambique
**Luggarus** *see* Locarno
**Lugh Ganana** *see* Luuq
97 G19 **Lugnaquillia Mountain** *Ir.* Log na Coille. ▲ E Ireland *52°58′N 06°27′W*
106 H10 **Lugo** Emilia-Romagna, N Italy *44°25′N 11°53′E*
104 I3 **Lugo** *anc.* Lugus Augusti. Galicia, NW Spain *43°N 07°33′W*
104 I3 **Lugo** ◆ *province* Galicia, NW Spain
21 R12 **Lugoff** South Carolina, SE USA *34°13′N 80°41′W*
116 F12 **Lugoj** *Ger.* Lugosch, *Hung.* Lugos. Timiş, W Romania *45°41′N 21°56′E*
**Lugos/Lugosch** *see* Lugoj
**Lugovoy/Lugovoye** *see* Kulan
158 I13 **Lugu** Xizang Zizhiqu, W China *33°26′N 84°10′E*
**Lugus Augusti** *see* Lugo
**Luguvallium/Luguvallum** *see* Carlisle
117 Y7 **Luhans'k** *Rus.* Lugansk; *prev.* Voroshilovgrad. Luhans'ka Oblast', E Ukraine *48°32′N 39°21′E*
117 Y7 **Luhans'k** ✈ Luhans'ka Oblast', E Ukraine *48°25′N 39°24′E*
**Luhans'k** *see* Luhans'ka Oblast'
117 X6 **Luhans'ka Oblast'** *var.* Luhans'k; *prev.* Voroshilovgrad, *Rus.* Voroshilovgradskaya Oblast'. ◆ *province* E Ukraine
161 Q7 **Luhe** Jiangsu, E China *32°20′N 118°52′E*
171 S13 **Luhu** Pulau Seram, E Indonesia *03°20′S 127°58′E*
**Luhua** *see* Heishui
160 G8 **Luhuo** *var.* Xindu, *Tib.* Zhaggo. Sichuan, C China *31°18′N 100°39′E*
116 M3 **Luhyny** Zhytomyrs'ka Oblast', N Ukraine *51°06′N 28°24′E*
83 G15 **Lui** W Zambia
83 G16 **Luiana** SE Angola
83 L15 **Luia, Rio** *var.* Ruya. Mozambique/Zimbabwe
**Luichow Peninsula** *see* Leizhou Bandao
**Luik** *see* Liège
82 C13 **Luimbale** Huambo, C Angola *12°15′S 15°19′E*
**Luimneach** *see* Limerick
106 D6 **Luino** Lombardia, N Italy *46°00′N 08°45′E*
82 E13 **Luio** E Angola
92 L11 **Luiro** NE Finland
79 N25 **Luishia** Katanga, SE Dem. Rep. Congo *11°18′S 27°08′E*
59 M19 **Luislândia do Oeste** Minas Gerais, SE Brazil *17°59′S 45°35′W*
40 K5 **Luis L. León, Presa** N Mexico
45 U5 **Luis Muñoz Marín** *var.* Luis Muñoz Marin. ✈ NE Puerto Rico *18°27′N 66°05′W*
**Luis Muñoz Marín** *see* Luis Muñoz Marín
195 N5 **Luitpold Coast** *physical region* Antarctica
79 K22 **Luiza** Kasai-Occidental, S Dem. Rep. Congo *07°11′S 22°27′E*
61 D20 **Luján** Buenos Aires, E Argentina *34°34′S 59°07′W*
79 N24 **Lukafu** Katanga, SE Dem. Rep. Congo *10°28′S 27°32′E*
**Lukapa** *see* Lucapa
112 I11 **Lukavac** ◆ Federacija Bosne I Hercegovine, NE Bosnia and Herzegovina
79 I20 **Lukenie** C Dem. Rep. Congo
79 H19 **Lukolela** Equateur, W Dem. Rep. Congo *01°10′S 17°11′E*
**Lukoml'skaye, Vozyera** *see* Lukomskaye, Vozyera
**Lukoml'skoye, Ozero** *see* Lukomskaye, Vozyera
119 M14 **Lukomskaye, Vozyera** *Rus.* Ozero Lukoml'skoye; *prev.* Vozyera Lukoml'skaye. N Belarus
114 I8 **Lukovit** Lovech, N Bulgaria *43°11′N 24°10′E*
110 O12 **Łuków** *Ger.* Bogendorf. Lubelskie, E Poland *51°57′N 22°22′E*
127 O4 **Lukoyanov** Nizhegorodskaya Oblast', W Russia *55°02′N 44°26′E*
**Lukransar** *see* Lūnkaransar
79 N22 **Lukuga** SE Dem. Rep. Congo
79 F21 **Lukula** Bas-Congo, SW Dem. Rep. Congo *05°23′S 12°57′E*
83 G14 **Lukulu** Western, NW Zambia *14°24′S 23°12′E*
189 R17 **Lukunor Atoll** *atoll* Mortlock Islands, C Micronesia
82 J12 **Lukwesa** Luapula, NE Zambia *10°03′S 28°42′E*
93 K14 **Luleå** Norrbotten, N Sweden *65°35′N 22°10′E*
92 J13 **Luleälven** N Sweden
136 C10 **Lüleburgaz** Kırklareli, NW Turkey *41°25′N 27°22′E*
160 M4 **Lüliang** *var.* Lishi. Shanxi, C China *37°27′N 111°05′E*
160 M4 **Lüliang Shan** ▲▲ C China
79 O21 **Lulimba** Maniema, E Dem. Rep. Congo *04°42′S 28°38′E*
22 K9 **Luling** Louisiana, S USA *29°55′N 90°22′W*
25 T11 **Luling** Texas, SW USA *29°40′N 97°39′W*
79 I18 **Lulonga** NW Dem. Rep. Congo
79 K22 **Lulua** S Dem. Rep. Congo
**Luluabourg** *see* Kananga
192 L17 **Luma** Ta'ū, E American Samoa *14°15′S 169°30′W*
169 S17 **Lumajang** Jawa, C Indonesia *08°06′S 113°13′E*
158 G12 **Lumajangdong Co** W China
82 G13 **Lumbala Kaquengue** Moxico, E Angola *12°40′S 22°34′E*
83 F14 **Lumbala N'Guimbo** *var.* Nguimbo, Gago Coutinho, *Port.* Vila Gago Coutinho. Moxico, E Angola *14°08′S 21°25′E*
21 T11 **Lumber River** North Carolina/South Carolina, SE USA
**Lumber State** *see* Maine
22 L8 **Lumberton** Mississippi, S USA *31°00′N 89°27′W*
21 U11 **Lumberton** North Carolina, SE USA *34°37′N 79°00′W*
105 R4 **Lumbier** Navarra, N Spain *42°39′N 01°19′W*
83 Q15 **Lumbo** Nampula, NE Mozambique *15°S 40°40′E*
124 M4 **Lumbovka** Murmanskaya Oblast', NW Russia *67°4[illegible]′N 40°31′E*
104 J7 **Lumbrales** Castilla y León, N Spain *40°57′N 06°43′W*
153 W13 **Lumding** Assam, NE India *25°46′N 93°10′E*
82 F12 **Lumege** *var.* Lumeje. Moxico, E Angola *11°30′S 20°57′E*
**Lumeje** *see* Lumege
99 J17 **Lummen** Limburg, NE Belgium *50°58′N 05°12′E*
93 J20 **Lumparland** Åland, SW Finland *60°06′N 20°15′E*
167 T11 **Lumphăt** *prev.* Lomphat. Ratanakiri, NE Cambodia *13°30′N*
11 U16 **Lumsden** Saskatchewan, S Canada *50°39′N 104°52′W*
185 C23 **Lumsden** Southland, South Island, New Zealand *45°43′S 168°26′E*
169 N14 **Lumut, Tanjung** *headland* Sumatera, W Indonesia *03°47′S 105°55′E*
157 P4 **Lün** Töv, C Mongolia *47°51′N 105°11′E*
116 I13 **Lunca Corbului** Argeş, S Romania *44°41′N 24°46′E*
95 K23 **Lund** Skåne, S Sweden *55°42′N 13°10′E*
35 X6 **Lund** Nevada, W USA *38°50′N 115°00′W*
82 D11 **Lunda Norte** ◆ *province* NE Angola
82 E12 **Lunda Sul** ◆ *province* NE Angola
82 M13 **Lundazi** Eastern, NE Zambia *12°19′S 33°11′E*
95 G16 **Lunde** Telemark, S Norway *61°31′N 06°38′E*
**Lundenburg** *see* Břeclav
95 C17 **Lundevatnet** S Norway
**Lundi** *see* Runde
97 I23 **Lundy** *island* SW England, United Kingdom
100 J10 **Lüneburg** Niedersachsen, N Germany *53°15′N 10°25′E*
100 J11 **Lüneburger Heide** *heathland* NW Germany
103 Q15 **Lunel** Hérault, S France *43°40′N 04°08′E*
101 F14 **Lünen** Nordrhein-Westfalen, W Germany *51°37′N 07°31′E*
13 P16 **Lunenburg** Nova Scotia, SE Canada *44°23′N 64°21′W*
21 V7 **Lunenburg** Virginia, NE USA *36°56′N 78°15′W*
103 T5 **Lunéville** Meurthe-et-Moselle, NE France *48°35′N 06°30′E*
83 I14 **Lunga** C Zambia
**Lunga, Isola** *see* Dugi Otok
158 H12 **Lungdo** Xizang Zizhiqu, W China *33°45′N 82°09′E*
158 I14 **Lunggar** Xizang Zizhiqu, W China *31°10′N 84°01′E*
76 I15 **Lungi** ✈ (Freetown) W Sierra Leone *08°36′N 13°10′W*
**Lungkiang** *see* Qiqihar
**Lungleh** *see* Lunglei
153 W15 **Lunglei** *prev.* Lungleh. Mizoram, NE India *22°55′N 92°49′E*
158 L15 **Lungsang** Xizang Zizhiqu, W China *29°50′N 88°27′E*
82 E13 **Lungué-Bungo** *var.* Lungwebungu. Angola/Zambia *see also* Lungwebungu
**Lungué-Bungo** *see* Lungwebungu
83 G14 **Lungwebungu** *var.* Lungué-Bungo. Angola/Zambia *see also* Lungué-Bungo
**Lungwebungu** *see* Lungué-Bungo
152 F12 **Lūni** Rājasthān, N India *26°03′N 73°00′E*
152 F12 **Lūni** N India
**Luninets** *see* Luninyets
35 S7 **Luning** Nevada, W USA *38°29′N 118°10′W*
**Łuniniec** *see* Luninyets
127 P6 **Lunino** Penzenskaya Oblast', W Russia *53°35′N 45°12′E*
119 J19 **Luninyets** *Pol.* Łuniniec, *Rus.* Luninets. Brestskaya Voblasts', SW Belarus *52°15′N 26°48′E*
152 F10 **Lūnkaransar** *var.* Lookransar, Lukransar. Rājasthān, NW India *28°32′N 73°50′E*
119 G17 **Lunna** *Pol.* Łunna, *Rus.* Lunno. Hrodzyenskaya Voblasts', W Belarus *53°27′N 24°16′E*
**Łunna** *see* Lunna
**Lunno** *see* Lunna
76 I15 **Lunsar** W Sierra Leone *08°41′N 12°32′W*
83 K14 **Lunsemfwa** C Zambia
158 J6 **Luntai** *var.* Bügür. Xinjiang Uygur Zizhiqu, NW China *41°48′N 84°14′E*
98 K11 **Lunteren** Gelderland, C Netherlands *52°05′N 05°38′E*
109 U5 **Lunz am See** Niederösterreich, C Austria *47°54′N 15°01′E*
163 Y7 **Luobei** *var.* Fengxiang. Heilongjiang, NE China *47°35′N 130°50′E*
**Luocheng** *see* Hui'an, Fujian, China
**Luocheng** *see* Luoding, Guangdong, China
160 J13 **Luodian** *var.* Longping. Guizhou, S China *25°25′N 106°49′E*
160 M15 **Luoding** *var.* Luocheng. Guangdong, S China *22°44′N 111°28′E*
161 N7 **Luohe** Henan, C China *33°37′N 114°00′E*
160 M6 **Luo He** C China
160 L5 **Luo He** C China
**L i Li m, Nhóm** *see* Crescent Group
**Luolajarvi** *see* Kuoloyarvi
**Luong Nam Tha** *see* Louangnamtha
160 L13 **Luoqing Jiang** S China
161 O8 **Luoshan** Henan, C China *32°12′N 114°30′E*
161 O12 **Luoxiao Shan** ▲▲ S China
161 N6 **Luoyang** *var.* Honan, Lo-yang. Henan, C China *34°41′N 112°25′E*
161 R12 **Luoyuan** *var.* Fengshan. Fujian, SE China *26°29′N 119°32′E*
79 F21 **Luozi** Bas-Congo, W Dem. Rep. Congo *04°57′S 14°08′E*
83 J17 **Lupane** Matabeleland North, W Zimbabwe *18°54′S 27°44′E*
160 I12 **Lupanshui** *var.* Liupanshui; *prev.* Shuicheng. Guizhou, S China *26°38′N 104°49′E*
169 R10 **Lupar, Batang** East Malaysia
**Lupatia** *see* Altamura
116 G12 **Lupeni** *Hung.* Lupény. Hunedoara, SW Romania *45°20′N 23°10′E*
**Lupény** *see* Lupeni
82 N13 **Lupiliche** Niassa, N Mozambique *11°36′S 35°15′E*
83 E14 **Lupire** Kuando Kubango, E Angola *14°39′S 19°39′E*
79 L22 **Luputa** Kasai-Oriental, S Dem. Rep. Congo *07°07′S 23°43′E*
121 P16 **Luqa** ✈ (Valletta) S Malta *35°53′N 14°27′E*
159 U11 **Luqu** *var.* Ma'ai. Gansu, C China *34°34′N 102°27′E*
45 U5 **Luquillo, Sierra de** ▲▲ E Puerto Rico
26 L4 **Luray** Kansas, C USA *39°06′N 98°41′W*
21 U4 **Luray** Virginia, NE USA *38°40′N 78°28′W*
103 T7 **Lure** Haute-Saône, E France *47°42′N 06°30′E*
82 D11 **Luremo** Lunda Norte, NE Angola *08°32′S 17°55′E*
97 F15 **Lurgan** *Ir.* An Lorgain. S Northern Ireland, United Kingdom *54°28′N 06°20′W*
57 K18 **Luribay** La Paz, W Bolivia *17°05′S 67°37′W*
**Luring** *see* Gêrzê
83 Q14 **Lúrio** Nampula, NE Mozambique *13°32′S 40°34′E*
83 P14 **Lúrio, Rio** NE Mozambique
**Luristan** *see* Lorestān
**Lurka** *see* Lorca
83 J15 **Lusaka** ● (Zambia) Lusaka, SE Zambia *15°24′S 28°17′E*
83 J15 **Lusaka** ◆ *province* C Zambia
83 J15 **Lusaka** ✈ Lusaka, C Zambia *15°10′S 28°22′E*
79 L21 **Lusambo** Kasai-Oriental, C Dem. Rep. Congo *04°59′S 23°26′E*
186 F8 **Lusancay Islands and Reefs** *island group* SE Papua New Guinea
79 I21 **Lusanga** Bandundu, SW Dem. Rep. Congo *04°55′S 18°40′E*
79 N21 **Lusangi** Maniema, E Dem. Rep. Congo *04°39′S 27°10′E*
**Lusatian Mountains** *see* Lausitzer Bergland
**Lushar** *see* Huangzhong
**Lushnja** *see* Lushnjë
113 K21 **Lushnjë** *var.* Lushnja. Fier, C Albania *40°54′N 19°43′E*
81 J21 **Lushoto** Tanga, E Tanzania *04°48′S 38°20′E*
102 L10 **Lusignan** Vienne, W France *46°25′N 00°06′E*
33 Z15 **Lusk** Wyoming, C USA *42°45′N 104°27′W*
**Luso** *see* Luena
102 L10 **Lussac-les-Châteaux** Vienne, W France *46°23′N 00°44′E*
**Lussin/Lussino** *see* Lošinj
**Lussinpiccolo** *see* Mali Lošinj
108 I7 **Lustenau** Vorarlberg, W Austria *47°26′N 09°42′E*
**Lü Tao** *see* Lü Dao
**Lütao** *see* Lü Dao
**Lūt, Baḩrat/Lut, Bahret** *see* Dead Sea
22 K9 **Lutcher** Louisiana, S USA *30°02′N 90°42′W*
143 T9 **Lūt, Dasht-e** *var.* Kavīr-e Lūt. *desert* E Iran
83 F14 **Lutembo** Moxico, E Angola *13°30′S 21°21′E*
**Lutetia/Lutetia Parisiorum** *see* Paris
**Luteva** *see* Lodève
14 G15 **Luther Lake** Ontario, S Canada
186 K8 **Luti** Choiseul, NW Solomon Islands *07°13′S 157°01′E*
**Lūt, Kavīr-e** *see* Lūt, Dasht-e
97 N21 **Luton** E England, United Kingdom *51°53′N 00°25′W*
97 N21 **Luton** ✈ (London) SE England, United Kingdom *51°54′N 00°24′W*
108 B10 **Lutry** Vaud, SW Switzerland *46°31′N 06°32′E*
8 K10 **Łutsel'k'e** *prev.* Snowdrift. Northwest Territories, W Canada *62°24′N 110°42′W*
8 K10 **Łutsel'k'e** *var.* Snowdrift. Northwest Territories, NW Canada
29 Y4 **Lutsen** Minnesota, N USA *47°39′N 90°37′W*
116 J4 **Luts'k** *Pol.* Łuck, *Rus.* Lutsk. Volyns'ka Oblast', NW Ukraine *50°45′N 25°23′E*
**Lutsk** *see* Luts'k
**Luttenberg** *see* Ljutomer
**Lüttich** *see* Liège
83 G25 **Luttig** Western Cape, SW South Africa *32°33′S 22°13′E*
**Lutto** *see* Lotta
82 E13 **Lutuai** Moxico, E Angola *12°38′S 20°06′E*
117 Y7 **Lutuhyne** Luhans'ka Oblast', E Ukraine *48°24′N 39°12′E*
171 V14 **Lutur, Pulau** *island* Kepulauan Aru, E Indonesia
23 V12 **Lutz** Florida, SE USA *28°09′N 82°27′W*
**Lutzow-Holm Bay** *see* Lützow Holmbukta
195 V2 **Lützow Holmbukta** *var.* Lutzow-Holm Bay. *bay* Antarctica
81 L16 **Luuq** *It.* Lugh Ganana. Gedo, SW Somalia *03°42′N 42°34′E*
92 M12 **Luusua** Lappi, NE Finland *66°28′N 27°16′E*
23 Q6 **Luverne** Alabama, S USA *31°43′N 86°15′W*
29 S11 **Luverne** Minnesota, N USA *43°39′N 96°12′W*
79 O22 **Luvua** SE Dem. Rep. Congo
82 F13 **Luvuei** Moxico, E Angola *13°08′S 21°09′E*
81 H24 **Luwego** S Tanzania
82 K12 **Luwingu** Northern, NE Zambia *10°13′S 29°58′E*
171 P12 **Luwuk** *prev.* Loewoek. Sulawesi, C Indonesia *0°56′S 122°47′E*
23 N3 **Luxapallila Creek** Alabama/Mississippi, S USA
99 M25 **Luxembourg** ● (Luxembourg) Luxembourg, S Luxembourg *49°37′N 06°08′E*
99 M25 **Luxembourg** *off.* Grand Duchy of Luxembourg, *var.* Lëtzebuerg, Luxemburg. ◆ *monarchy* NW Europe
99 J23 **Luxembourg** ◆ *province* SE Belgium
99 L24 **Luxembourg** ◆ *district* S Luxembourg
31 N6 **Luxemburg** Wisconsin, N USA *44°32′N 87°42′W*
**Luxemburg** *see* Luxembourg
103 U7 **Luxeuil-les-Bains** Haute-Saône, E France *47°49′N 06°22′E*
160 E13 **Luxi** *prev.* Mangshi. Yunnan, SW China *24°27′N 98°31′E*
82 E10 **Luxico** Angola/Dem. Rep. Congo
75 X10 **Luxor** ✈ C Egypt *25°39′N 32°48′E*
**Luxor** *see* Al Uqşur
160 M4 **Luya Shan** ▲▲ C China
102 J15 **Luy de Béarn** SW France
102 J15 **Luy de France** SW France
125 P12 **Luza** Kirovskaya Oblast', NW Russia *60°38′N 47°13′E*
125 Q12 **Luza** NW Russia
104 I16 **Luz, Costa de la** *coastal region* SW Spain
111 K20 **Luže** *var.* Lausche. ▲ Czechia/Germany *50°51′N 14°40′E* *see also* Lausche
**Luže** *see* Lausche
108 F8 **Luzern** *Fr.* Lucerne, *It.* Lucerna. Luzern, C Switzerland *47°03′N 08°17′E*
108 E8 **Luzern** *Fr.* Lucerne. ◆ *canton* C Switzerland
160 L13 **Luzhai** Guangxi Zhuangzu Zizhiqu, S China *24°31′N 109°46′E*
118 K12 **Luzhki** Vitsyebskaya Voblasts', N Belarus *55°21′N 27°52′E*
160 I10 **Luzhou** Sichuan, C China *28°55′N 105°25′E*
**Lužická Nisa** *see* Neisse
**Lužické Hory'** *see* Lausitzer Bergland
**Lužnice** *see* Lainsitz
171 O2 **Luzon** *island* N Philippines
171 N1 **Luzon Strait** *strait* Philippines/Taiwan
**Lužycke, Gory** *see* Lausitzer Bergland
116 I5 **L'viv** *Ger.* Lemberg, *Pol.* Lwów, *Rus.* L'vov. L'vivs'ka Oblast', W Ukraine *49°49′N 24°05′E*
**L'viv** *see* L'vivs'ka Oblast'
116 I4 **L'vivs'ka Oblast'** *var.* L'viv, *Rus.* L'vovskaya Oblast'. ◆ *province* NW Ukraine
**L'vov** *see* L'viv
**L'vovskaya Oblast'** *see* L'vivs'ka Oblast'
149 P8 **Lwarah Rōd** *var.* Lora, Lowrah. SE Afghanistan
**Lwena** *see* Luena
**Lwów** *see* L'viv
110 F11 **Lwówek** *Ger.* Neustadt bei Pinne. Wielkopolskie, C Poland *52°27′N 16°10′E*
111 E14 **Lwówek Śląski** *Ger.* Löwenberg in Schlesien. Jelenia Góra, SW Poland *51°06′N 15°35′E*
119 I18 **Lyakhavichy** *Rus.* Lyakhovichi. Brestskaya Voblasts', SW Belarus *53°02′N 26°16′E*
**Lyakhovichi** *see* Lyakhavichy
185 B22 **Lyall, Mount** ▲ South Island, New Zealand *45°14′S 167°31′E*
**Lyallpur** *see* Faisalabad
**Lyangar** *see* Langar
124 H11 **Lyaskelya** Respublika Kareliya, NW Russia *61°42′N 31°06′E*
119 I18 **Lyasnaya** *Rus.* Lesnaya. Brestskaya Voblasts', SW Belarus *52°59′N 25°46′E*
119 F19 **Lyasnaya** *Pol.* Leśna, *Rus.* Lesnaya. SW Belarus
124 H15 **Lychkovo** Novgorodskaya Oblast', W Russia *57°55′N 32°24′E*
**Lyck** *see* Ełk
93 I15 **Lycksele** Västerbotten, N Sweden *64°34′N 18°40′E*
18 G13 **Lycoming Creek** Pennsylvania, NE USA
**Lycopolis** *see* Asyūţ
195 N3 **Lyddan Island** *island* Antarctica
**Lydenburg** *see* Mashishing
**Lýðveldið Ísland** *see* Iceland
119 L20 **Lyel'chytsy** *Rus.* Lel'chitsy. Homyel'skaya Voblasts', SE Belarus *51°47′N 28°20′E*
119 P14 **Lyenina** *Rus.* Lenino. Mahilyowskaya Voblasts', E Belarus *54°25′N 31°08′E*
118 L13 **Lyepyel'** *Rus.* Lepel'. Vitsyebskaya Voblasts', N Belarus *54°54′N 28°44′E*
25 S17 **Lyford** Texas, SW USA *26°24′N 97°47′W*
95 E17 **Lygna** S Norway
18 G14 **Lykens** Pennsylvania, NE USA *40°33′N 76°42′W*
115 E21 **Lykódimo** ▲ S Greece *36°56′N 21°49′E*
117 X6 **Lyman** *prev.* Krasnyy Lyman. Donets'ka Oblast', SE Ukraine *49°00′N 37°50′E*
97 K24 **Lyme Bay** *bay* S England, United Kingdom
97 K24 **Lyme Regis** S England, United Kingdom *50°44′N 02°56′W*
110 L7 **Łyna** *Ger.* Alle. N Poland
29 P12 **Lynch** Nebraska, C USA *42°49′N 98°27′W*
20 J10 **Lynchburg** Tennessee, S USA *35°17′N 86°22′W*
21 T6 **Lynchburg** Virginia, NE USA *37°24′N 79°09′W*
21 T12 **Lynches River** South Carolina, SE USA
32 H6 **Lynden** Washington, NW USA *48°57′N 122°27′W*
182 I5 **Lyndhurst** South Australia *30°19′S 138°20′E*
27 Q5 **Lyndon** Kansas, C USA *38°37′N 95°40′W*
19 N7 **Lyndonville** Vermont, NE USA *44°31′N 71°58′W*
95 D18 **Lyngdal** Vest-Agder, S Norway *58°10′N 07°08′E*
92 I9 **Lyngen** *Lapp.* Ivgovuotna. *inlet* Arctic Ocean
95 G17 **Lyngør** Aust-Agder, S Norway *58°38′N 09°05′E*
92 I9 **Lyngseidet** Troms, N Norway *69°36′N 20°07′E*
19 P11 **Lynn** Massachusetts, NE USA *42°28′N 70°57′W*
**Lynn** *see* King's Lynn
23 R9 **Lynn Haven** Florida, SE USA *30°15′N 85°39′W*
11 V11 **Lynn Lake** Manitoba, C Canada *56°51′N 101°01′W*
**Lynn Regis** *see* King's Lynn
118 I13 **Lyntupy** Vitsyebskaya Voblasts', NW Belarus *55°03′N 26°19′E*
103 R11 **Lyon** *Eng.* Lyons; *anc.* Lugdunum. Rhône, E France *45°46′N 04°50′E*
8 I6 **Lyon, Cape** *headland* Northwest Territories, NW Canada *69°47′N 123°10′W*
18 K6 **Lyon Mountain** ▲ New York, NE USA *44°42′N 73°52′W*
103 Q11 **Lyonnais, Monts du** ▲▲ C France
65 N25 **Lyon Point** *headland* SE Tristan da Cunha *37°06′S 12°13′W*
182 E5 **Lyons** South Australia *30°40′S 133°50′E*
37 T3 **Lyons** Colorado, C USA *40°13′N 105°16′W*
23 V6 **Lyons** Georgia, SE USA *32°12′N 82°19′W*
26 M5 **Lyons** Kansas, C USA *38°22′N 98°13′W*
29 R14 **Lyons** Nebraska, C USA *41°56′N 96°28′W*
18 G10 **Lyons** New York, NE USA *43°03′N 76°58′W*
**Lyons** *see* Lyon
118 O13 **Lyozna** *Rus.* Liozno. Vitsyebskaya Voblasts', NE Belarus *55°02′N 30°48′E*
117 S4 **Lypova Dolyna** Sums'ka Oblast', NE Ukraine *50°36′N 33°50′E*
117 N6 **Lypovets'** *Rus.* Lipovets. Vinnyts'ka Oblast', C Ukraine *49°13′N 29°06′E*
**Lys** *see* Leie
111 I18 **Lysá Hora** ▲ E Czechia *49°31′N 18°27′E*
95 D16 **Lysefjorden** *fjord* S Norway
95 I18 **Lysekil** Västra Götaland, S Sweden *58°16′N 11°26′E*
**Lýsi** *see* Akdoğan
33 V14 **Lysite** Wyoming, C USA *43°16′N 107°42′W*
127 P3 **Lyskovo** Nizhegorodskaya Oblast', W Russia *56°04′N 45°01′E*
108 D8 **Lyss** Bern, W Switzerland *47°04′N 07°19′E*
95 H22 **Lystrup** Midtjylland, C Denmark *56°14′N 10°14′E*
125 V14 **Lys'va** Permskiy Kray, NW Russia *58°04′N 57°48′E*
117 P6 **Lysyanka** Cherkas'ka Oblast', C Ukraine *49°15′N 30°50′E*
117 X6 **Lysychans'k** *Rus.* Lisichansk. Luhans'ka Oblast', E Ukraine *48°52′N 38°27′E*
97 K17 **Lytham St Anne's** NW England, United Kingdom *53°45′N 03°01′W*
185 I19 **Lyttelton** South Island, New Zealand *43°35′S 172°44′E*
10 M17 **Lytton** British Columbia, SW Canada *50°12′N 121°34′W*
119 L18 **Lyuban'** Minskaya Voblasts', S Belarus *52°48′N 28°00′E*
119 L18 **Lyubanskaye Vodaskhovishcha** *Rus.* Lyubanskoye Vodokhranilishche. C Belarus
**Lyubanskoye Vodokhranilishche** *see* Lyubanskaye Vodaskhovishcha
116 M5 **Lyubar** Zhytomyrs'ka Oblast', N Ukraine *49°54′N 27°48′E*
**Lyubashëvka** *see* Lyubashivka
117 O8 **Lyubashivka** *Rus.* Lyubashëvka. Odes'ka Oblast', SW Ukraine *47°49′N 30°18′E*
119 I16 **Lyubcha** *Pol.* Lubcz. Hrodzyenskaya Voblasts', W Belarus *53°45′N 26°04′E*
126 L4 **Lyubertsy** Moskovskaya Oblast', W Russia *55°37′N 38°02′E*
116 K2 **Lyubeshiv** Volyns'ka Oblast', NW Ukraine *51°46′N 25°33′E*
124 M14 **Lyubim** Yaroslavskaya Oblast', NW Russia *58°21′N 40°46′E*
114 K11 **Lyubimets** Haskovo, S Bulgaria *41°51′N 26°03′E*
**Lyublin** *see* Lublin
116 I3 **Lyuboml'** *Pol.* Luboml. Volyns'ka Oblast', NW Ukraine *51°12′N 24°01′E*
**Lyubotin** *see* Lyubotyn
117 U5 **Lyubotyn** *Rus.* Lyubotin. Kharkivs'ka Oblast', E Ukraine *49°57′N 35°57′E*
126 I5 **Lyudinovo** Kaluzhskaya Oblast', W Russia *53°52′N 34°28′E*
127 T2 **Lyuk** Udmurtskaya Respublika, NW Russia *56°55′N 52°45′E*
114 M9 **Lyulyakovo** *prev.* Keremitlik. Burgas, E Bulgaria *42°53′N 27°05′E*
119 I18 **Lyusina** *Rus.* Lyusino. Brestskaya Voblasts', SW Belarus *52°38′N 26°31′E*
**Lyusino** *see* Lyusina

# M

138 G9 **Ma'ād** Irbid, N Jordan *32°37′N 35°36′E*
**Ma'ai** *see* Luqu
**Maalahti** *see* Malax
151 K19 **Maale** *var.* Male. ● (Maldives) Male' Atoll, C Maldives *04°10′N 73°29′E*
138 G13 **Ma'ān** Ma'ān, SW Jordan *30°11′N 35°45′E*
138 H13 **Ma'ān** *off.* Muḩāfaz̧at Ma'ān, *var.* Ma'an, Ma'ān. ◆ *governorate* S Jordan
93 M16 **Maaninka** Pohjois-Savo, C Finland *63°10′N 27°19′E*
**Maanīt** *see* Bayan, Töv, Mongolia
**Maanīt** *see* Hishig Öndör, Bulgan, Mongolia
**Ma'ān, Muḩāfaz̧at** *see* Ma'ān
93 N15 **Maanselkä** Kainuu, C Finland *63°54′N 28°28′E*
161 Q8 **Ma'anshan** Anhui, E China *31°45′N 118°32′E*
188 F16 **Maap** *island* Caroline Islands, W Micronesia
118 H3 **Maardu** *Ger.* Maart. Harjumaa, NW Estonia *59°28′N 24°56′E*
**Ma'aret-en-Nu'man** *see* Ma'arrat an Nu'mān
99 K16 **Maarheeze** Noord-Brabant, SE Netherlands *51°19′N 05°37′E*
**Maarianhamina** *see* Mariehamn
138 I4 **Ma'arrat an Nu'mān** *var.* Ma'aret-en-Nu'man, *Fr.* Maarret enn Naamâne. Idlib, NW Syria *35°40′N 36°40′E*
**Maarret enn Naamâne** *see* Ma'arrat an Nu'mān
98 I11 **Maarssen** Utrecht, C Netherlands *52°08′N 05°03′E*
**Maart** *see* Maardu
99 L17 **Maas** *Fr.* Meuse. W Europe *see also* Meuse
**Maas** *see* Meuse
99 M15 **Maasbree** Limburg, SE Netherlands *51°22′N 06°03′E*
99 L17 **Maaseik** *prev.* Maeseyck. Limburg, NE Belgium *51°05′N 05°48′E*
171 Q6 **Maasin** Leyte, C Philippines *10°10′N 124°55′E*
99 L17 **Maasmechelen** Limburg, NE Belgium *50°58′N 05°42′E*
98 G12 **Maassluis** Zuid-Holland, SW Netherlands *51°55′N 04°15′E*
99 L18 **Maastricht** *var.* Maestricht; *anc.* Traiectum ad Mosam, Traiectum Tungorum. Limburg, SE Netherlands *50°51′N 05°42′E*
183 N18 **Maatsuyker Group** *island group* Tasmania, SE Australia
**Maba** *see* Qujiang
83 L20 **Mabalane** Gaza, S Mozambique *23°43′S 32°37′E*
25 V7 **Mabank** Texas, SW USA *32°22′N 96°06′W*
97 O18 **Mablethorpe** E England, United Kingdom *53°21′N 00°14′E*
171 V12 **Maboi** Papua Barat, E Indonesia *01°00′S 134°02′E*
83 M19 **Mabote** Inhambane, S Mozambique *22°03′S 34°09′E*
32 J10 **Mabton** Washington, NW USA *46°13′N 120°00′W*
83 H20 **Mabutsane** Southern, S Botswana *24°24′S 23°34′E*
63 G19 **Macá, Cerro** ▲ S Chile *45°07′S 73°11′W*



◆ Country
● Country Capital
◇ Dependent Territory
○ Dependent Territory Capital
◆ Administrative Regions
✈ International Airport
▲ Mountain
▲▲ Mountain Range
Volcano
River
Lake
Reservoir

MACAÉ – MAISKHAL ISLAND


60 Q9 **Macaé** Rio de Janeiro, SE Brazil 22°21′S 41°48′W
82 N13 **Macaloge** Niassa, N Mozambique 12°27′S 35°25′E
**Macan** *see* Bonerate, Kepulauan
161 N15 **Macao** *off.* Macao Special Administrative Region, *var.* Macao S.A.R., *Chin.* Aomen Tebie Xingzhengqu, *Port.* Região Administrativa Especial de Macau. Guangdong, SE China 22°06′N 113°30′E
104 H9 **Mação** Santarém, C Portugal 39°33′N 08°00′W
**Macao S.A.R.** *see* Macao
**Macao Special Administrative Region** *see* Macao
58 J11 **Macapá** *state capital* Amapá, N Brazil 0°04′N 51°04′W
43 S17 **Macaracas** Los Santos, S Panama 07°46′N 80°31′W
55 P6 **Macare, Caño** NE Venezuela
55 Q6 **Macareo, Caño** NE Venezuela
**Macarsca** *see* Makarska
182 L12 **Macarthur** Victoria, SE Australia 38°04′S 142°02′E
**MacArthur** *see* Ormoc
56 C7 **Macas** Morona Santiago, SE Ecuador 02°22′S 78°08′W
**Macassar** *see* Makassar
59 Q14 **Macau** Rio Grande do Norte, E Brazil 05°05′S 36°37′W
**Macău** *see* Makó, Hungary
**Macau, Região Administrativa Especial de** *see* Macao
65 E24 **Macbride Head** *headland* East Falkland, Falkland Islands 51°25′S 57°55′W
23 V9 **Macclenny** Florida, SE USA 30°16′N 82°07′W
97 L18 **Macclesfield** C England, United Kingdom 53°16′N 02°07′W
192 F6 **Macclesfield Bank** *undersea feature* N South China Sea 15°50′N 114°20′E
**MacCluer Gulf** *see* Berau, Teluk
181 N7 **Macdonald, Lake** *salt lake* Western Australia
181 Q7 **Macdonnell Ranges** Northern Territory, C Australia
96 K8 **Macduff** NE Scotland, United Kingdom 57°40′N 02°29′W
104 I6 **Macedo de Cavaleiros** Bragança, N Portugal 41°31′N 06°57′W
**Macedonia Central** *see* Kentrikí Makedonía
**Macedonia East and Thrace** *see* Anatolikí Makedonía kai Thráki
**Macedonia West** *see* Dytikí Makedonía
59 Q16 **Maceió** *state capital* Alagoas, E Brazil 09°40′S 35°44′W
76 K15 **Macenta** SE Guinea 08°31′N 09°32′W
106 J12 **Macerata** Marche, C Italy 43°18′N 13°27′E
11 S11 **MacFarlane** Saskatchewan, C Canada
182 H7 **Macfarlane, Lake** *var.* Lake Mcfarlane. South Australia
**Macgillicuddy's Reeks Mountains** *see* Macgillycuddy's Reeks
97 B21 **Macgillycuddy's Reeks** *var.* Macgillicuddy's Reeks Mountains, *Ir.* Na Cruacha Dubha. SW Ireland
11 X16 **MacGregor** Manitoba, S Canada 49°58′N 98°49′W
149 O10 **Mach** Baluchistan, SW Pakistan 29°52′N 67°20′E
56 C6 **Machachi** Pichincha, C Ecuador 0°33′S 78°34′W
83 M19 **Machaila** Gaza, S Mozambique 22°15′S 32°57′E
**Machaire Fíolta** *see* Magherafelt
**Machaire Rátha** *see* Maghera
81 I19 **Machakos** Machakos, S Kenya 01°31′S 37°16′E
56 B8 **Machala** El Oro, SW Ecuador 03°20′S 79°57′W
83 J19 **Machaneng** Central, SE Botswana 23°12′S 27°30′E
83 M18 **Machanga** Sofala, E Mozambique 20°56′S 35°04′E
80 G13 **Machar Marshes** *wetland* SE Sudan
102 I8 **Machecoul** Loire-Atlantique, NW France 46°59′N 01°51′W
161 O8 **Macheng** Hubei, C China 31°10′N 115°00′E
155 J16 **Mācherla** Andhra Pradesh, C India 16°29′N 79°25′E
153 O11 **Māchhāpuchhre** ▲ C Nepal 28°30′N 83°57′E
19 T6 **Machias** Maine, NE USA 44°44′N 67°28′W
19 T6 **Machias River** Maine, NE USA
19 R3 **Machias River** Maine, NE USA
64 P5 **Machico** Madeira, Portugal, NE Atlantic Ocean 32°43′N 16°47′W
155 K16 **Machilīpatnam** *var.* Bandar Masulipatnam. Andhra Pradesh, E India 16°12′N 81°11′E
54 G5 **Machiques** Zulia, NW Venezuela 10°04′N 72°37′W
57 G15 **Machu Picchu** Cusco, C Peru 13°08′S 72°30′W
83 M20 **Macia** *var.* Vila de Macia. Gaza, S Mozambique 25°02′S 33°08′E
**Macías Nguema Biyogo** *see* Bioco, Isla de
116 M13 **Măcin** Tulcea, SE Romania 45°15′N 28°09′E
183 T4 **Macintyre River** New South Wales/Queensland, SE Australia
181 Y7 **Mackay** Queensland, NE Australia 21°10′S 149°10′E
181 O7 **Mackay, Lake** *salt lake* Northern Territory/Western Australia
10 M13 **Mackenzie** British Columbia, W Canada 55°18′N 123°09′W
8 I9 **Mackenzie** Northwest Territories, NW Canada
195 Y6 **Mackenzie Bay** *bay* Antarctica
10 J1 **Mackenzie Bay** *bay* NW Canada
2 D9 **Mackenzie Delta** *delta* Northwest Territories, NW Canada
197 P8 **Mackenzie King Island** *island* Queen Elizabeth Islands, Northwest Territories, N Canada
8 H8 **Mackenzie Mountains** Northwest Territories, NW Canada
31 Q5 **Mackinac, Straits of** Michigan, N USA
194 K5 **Mackintosh, Cape** *headland* Antarctica 72°52′S 60°00′W
11 R15 **Macklin** Saskatchewan, S Canada 52°19′N 109°51′W
183 V6 **Macksville** New South Wales, SE Australia 30°39′S 152°54′E
183 V5 **Maclean** New South Wales, SE Australia 29°30′S 153°15′E
83 J24 **Maclear** Eastern Cape, SE South Africa 31°05′S 28°22′E
183 U6 **Macleay River** New South Wales, SE Australia
**MacLeod** *see* Fort Macleod
180 G9 **Macleod, Lake** Western Australia
10 I6 **Macmillan** Yukon, NW Canada
30 J12 **Macomb** Illinois, N USA 40°27′N 90°40′W
107 B18 **Macomer** Sardegna, Italy, C Mediterranean Sea 40°15′N 08°47′E
82 Q13 **Macomia** Cabo Delgado, NE Mozambique 12°15′S 40°06′E
103 R10 **Mâcon** *anc.* Matisco, Matisco Ædourum. Saône-et-Loire, C France 46°19′N 04°49′E
23 T5 **Macon** Georgia, SE USA 32°49′N 83°41′W
23 N4 **Macon** Mississippi, S USA 33°06′N 88°33′W
27 U3 **Macon** Missouri, C USA 39°44′N 92°27′W
22 J6 **Macon, Bayou** Arkansas/Louisiana, S USA
82 G13 **Macondo** Moxico, E Angola 12°31′S 23°45′E
83 M16 **Macossa** Manica, C Mozambique 17°51′S 33°54′E
11 T12 **Macoun Lake** Saskatchewan, C Canada
30 K14 **Macoupin Creek** Illinois, N USA
**Macouria** *see* Tonate
83 N18 **Macovane** Inhambane, SE Mozambique 21°30′S 35°07′E
183 N17 **Macquarie Harbour** *inlet* Tasmania, SE Australia
192 J13 **Macquarie Island** *island* New Zealand, SW Pacific Ocean
183 T8 **Macquarie, Lake** *lagoon* New South Wales, SE Australia
183 Q6 **Macquarie Marshes** *wetland* New South Wales, SE Australia
175 O13 **Macquarie Ridge** *undersea feature* SW Pacific Ocean 57°00′S 159°00′E
183 Q6 **Macquarie River** New South Wales, SE Australia
183 P17 **Macquarie River** Tasmania, SE Australia
195 V5 **Mac. Robertson Land** *physical region* Antarctica
97 C21 **Macroom** *Ir.* Maigh Chromtha. Cork, SW Ireland 51°54′N 08°57′W
42 G5 **Macuelizo** Santa Bárbara, NW Honduras 15°21′N 88°31′W
182 G2 **Macumba River** South Australia
57 I16 **Macusani** Puno, S Peru 14°05′S 70°24′W
56 E8 **Macusarí, Río** N Peru
41 U15 **Macuspana** Tabasco, SE Mexico 17°43′N 92°36′W
138 G10 **Mādabā** *var.* Ma'dabā, Madeba; *anc.* Medeba. Mādabā, NW Jordan 31°44′N 35°48′E
138 G11 **Mādabā** *off.* Muḥāfa at Mādabā, *var.* Ma'dabā. ◆ *governorate* C Jordan
**Ma'dabā** *see* Mādabā
**Ma'dabā** *see* Mādabā
**Mādabā, Muḥāfa at** *see* Mādabā
172 G2 **Madagascar** *off.* Republic of Madagascar, *Malg.* Madagasikara, Repoblikan'i Madagasikara, *Fr.* République de Madagascar; *prev.* Malagasy Republic, Democratic Republic of Madagascar. ◆ *republic* W Indian Ocean
172 I5 **Madagascar** *island* W Indian Ocean
128 L17 **Madagascar Basin** *undersea feature* W Indian Ocean 27°00′S 53°00′E
**Madagascar, Democratic Republic of** *see* Madagascar
128 L16 **Madagascar Plain** *undersea feature* W Indian Ocean 19°00′S 52°00′E
67 Y14 **Madagascar Plateau** *var.* Madagascar Ridge, Madagascar Rise, *Rus.* Madagaskarskiy Khrebet. *undersea feature* W Indian Ocean 30°00′S 45°00′E
**Madagascar, Republic of** *see* Madagascar
**Madagascar, République de** *see* Madagascar
**Madagascar Rise/ Madagascar Ridge** *see* Madagascar Plateau
**Madagasikara** *see* Madagascar
**Madagasikara, Repoblikan'i** *see* Madagascar
**Madagaskarskiy Khrebet** *see* Madagascar Plateau
64 N2 **Madalena** Pico, Azores, Portugal, NE Atlantic Ocean 38°32′N 28°15′W
77 Y6 **Madama** Agadez, NE Niger 21°54′N 13°43′E
114 J12 **Madan** Smolyan, S Bulgaria 41°29′N 24°56′E
155 I19 **Madanapalle** Andhra Pradesh, E India 13°33′N 78°31′E
186 D7 **Madang** Madang, N Papua New Guinea 05°14′S 145°45′E
186 C6 **Madang** ◆ *province* N Papua New Guinea
146 G7 **Madaniyat** *Rus.* Madeniyet. Qoraqalpog'iston Respublikasi, W Uzbekistan 42°48′N 59°00′E
**Madaniyin** *see* Médenine
77 U11 **Madaoua** Tahoua, SW Niger 14°06′N 06°01′E
**Mađaras** *see* Vtáčnik
153 U15 **Madaripur** Dhaka, C Bangladesh 23°09′N 90°11′E
77 U12 **Madarounfa** Maradi, S Niger 13°16′N 07°07′E
**Mađarska** *see* Hungary
146 B13 **Madau** Balkan Welaýaty, W Turkmenistan 38°11′N 54°46′E
186 H9 **Madau Island** *island* SE Papua New Guinea
19 S1 **Madawaska** Maine, NE USA 47°19′N 68°19′W
14 J13 **Madawaska** Ontario, SE Canada
**Madawaska Highlands** *see* Haliburton Highlands
166 M4 **Madaya** Mandalay, C Myanmar (Burma) 22°12′N 96°05′E
107 K17 **Maddaloni** Campania, S Italy 41°03′N 14°23′E
29 O3 **Maddock** North Dakota, N USA 47°57′N 99°31′W
99 I14 **Made** Noord-Brabant, S Netherlands 51°41′N 04°48′E
**Madeba** *see* Mādabā
64 L9 **Madeira** *var.* Ilha de Madeira. *island* Madeira, Portugal, NE Atlantic Ocean
**Madeira, Ilha de** *see* Madeira
64 O5 **Madeira Islands** *Port.* Região Autónoma da Madeira. ◆ *autonomous region* Madeira, Portugal, NE Atlantic Ocean
64 L9 **Madeira Plain** *undersea feature* E Atlantic Ocean
**Madeira, Região Autónoma da** *see* Madeira Islands
64 L9 **Madeira Ridge** *undersea feature* E Atlantic Ocean 35°30′N 15°45′W
59 F14 **Madeira, Rio** *var.* Río Madera. Bolivia/Brazil *see also* Madera, Río
**Madeira, Rio** *see* Madera, Río
101 J25 **Mädelegabel** ▲ Austria/ Germany 47°18′N 10°19′E
15 X6 **Madeleine** Québec, SE Canada
15 X5 **Madeleine, Cap de la** *headland* Québec, SE Canada 49°13′N 65°20′W
13 Q13 **Madeleine, Îles de la** *Eng.* Magdalen Islands. *island group* Québec, E Canada
29 U10 **Madelia** Minnesota, N USA 44°03′N 94°26′W
35 P3 **Madeline** California, W USA 41°02′N 120°28′W
30 K3 **Madeline Island** *island* Apostle Islands, Wisconsin, N USA
137 O15 **Maden** Elazığ, SE Turkey 38°24′N 39°42′E
145 V12 **Madeniyet** Vostochnyy Kazakhstan, E Kazakhstan 47°51′N 78°37′E
**Madeniyet** *see* Madaniyat
40 H5 **Madera** Chihuahua, N Mexico 29°10′N 108°10′W
35 Q10 **Madera** California, W USA 36°57′N 120°02′W
56 L13 **Madera, Río** *Port.* Rio Madeira. Bolivia/Brazil *see also* Madeira, Rio
**Madera, Río** *see* Madeira, Rio
106 D6 **Madesimo** Lombardia, N Italy 46°20′N 09°26′E
141 O14 **Madhāb, Wādī** *dry watercourse* NW Yemen
153 R13 **Madhepura** *prev.* Madhipure. Bihār, NE India 25°56′N 86°48′E
**Madhipure** *see* Madhepura
153 Q13 **Madhubani** Bihār, N India 26°21′N 86°05′E
153 Q15 **Madhupur** Jhārkhand, NE India 24°17′N 86°38′E
154 I10 **Madhya Pradesh** *prev.* Central Provinces and Berar. ◆ *state* C India
57 K15 **Madidi, Río** W Bolivia
155 F20 **Madikeri** *prev.* Mercara. Karnātaka, W India 12°29′N 75°40′E
27 O13 **Madill** Oklahoma, C USA 34°06′N 96°46′W
79 G21 **Madimba** Bas-Congo, SW Dem. Rep. Congo 04°58′S 15°08′E
138 M4 **Ma'dīn** Ar Raqqah, C Syria 35°45′N 39°36′E
**Madīnah, Mintaqat al** *see* Al Madīnah al Munawwarah
76 M14 **Madinani** NW Ivory Coast 09°37′N 06°57′W
141 O17 **Madīnat ash Sha'b** *prev.* Al Ittiḥād. SW Yemen 12°52′N 44°55′E
173 O6 **Madingley Rise** *undersea feature* W Indian Ocean
79 E21 **Madingo-Kayes** Kouilou, S Congo 04°27′S 11°43′E
79 F21 **Madingou** Bouenza, S Congo 04°10′S 13°33′E
**Madioen** *see* Madiun
23 U8 **Madison** Florida, SE USA 30°27′N 83°24′W
23 T3 **Madison** Georgia, SE USA 33°37′N 83°28′W
31 P15 **Madison** Indiana, N USA 38°44′N 85°22′W
27 P5 **Madison** Kansas, C USA 38°08′N 96°07′W
19 Q6 **Madison** Maine, NE USA 44°48′N 69°52′W
29 S9 **Madison** Minnesota, N USA 45°00′N 96°12′W
22 K5 **Madison** Mississippi, S USA 32°27′N 90°07′W
29 Q14 **Madison** Nebraska, C USA 41°49′N 97°27′W
29 R10 **Madison** South Dakota, N USA 44°00′N 97°06′W
21 V5 **Madison** Virginia, NE USA 38°23′N 78°16′W
21 Q5 **Madison** West Virginia, NE USA 38°03′N 81°50′W
30 L9 **Madison** *state capital* Wisconsin, N USA 43°04′N 89°22′W
21 T6 **Madison Heights** Virginia, NE USA 37°25′N 79°07′W
20 I6 **Madisonville** Kentucky, S USA 37°20′N 87°30′W
20 M10 **Madisonville** Tennessee, S USA 35°31′N 84°21′W
25 V9 **Madisonville** Texas, SW USA 30°58′N 95°56′W
**Madisonville** *see* Taiohae
169 R16 **Madiun** *prev.* Madioen. Jawa, C Indonesia 07°37′S 111°33′E
**Madjene** *see* Majene
14 J14 **Madoc** Ontario, SE Canada 44°31′N 77°27′W
**Madoera** *see* Madura, Pulau
81 J18 **Mado Gashi** Garissa, E Kenya 0°40′N 39°09′E
159 R11 **Madoi** *var.* Huanghe; *prev.* Huangheyan. Qinghai, C China 34°53′N 98°07′E
189 O13 **Madolenihmw** Pohnpei, E Micronesia
118 I9 **Madona** *Ger.* Modohn. E Latvia 56°51′N 26°10′E
107 J23 **Madonie** Sicilia, Italy, C Mediterranean Sea
141 Y11 **Madrakah, Ra's** *headland* E Oman 18°56′N 57°54′E
32 I12 **Madras** Oregon, NW USA 44°39′N 121°08′W
**Madras** *see* Tamil Nādu
**Madras** *see* Chennai
57 H14 **Madre de Dios** *off.* Región de Madre de Dios. ◆ *region* E Peru
63 F22 **Madre de Dios, Isla** *island* S Chile
**Madre de Dios, Región de** *see* Madre de Dios
57 J14 **Madre de Dios, Río** Bolivia/Peru
0 H15 **Madre del Sur, Sierra** S Mexico
41 Q9 **Madre, Laguna** *lagoon* NE Mexico
25 T16 **Madre, Laguna** *lagoon* Texas, SW USA
37 Q12 **Madre Mount** ▲ New Mexico, SW USA 34°18′N 107°54′W
0 H13 **Madre Occidental, Sierra** *var.* Western Sierra Madre. C Mexico
0 H13 **Madre Oriental, Sierra** *var.* Eastern Sierra Madre. C Mexico
41 U17 **Madre, Sierra** *var.* Sierra de Soconusco. Guatemala/ Mexico
37 R2 **Madre, Sierra** Colorado/ Wyoming, C USA
105 N8 **Madrid** ● (Spain) Madrid, C Spain 40°25′N 03°43′W
29 V14 **Madrid** Iowa, C USA 41°52′N 93°49′W
105 N7 **Madrid** *var.* Comunidad de Madrid. ◆ *autonomous community* C Spain
**Madrid, Comunidad de** *see* Madrid
105 N10 **Madridejos** Castilla-La Mancha, C Spain 39°29′N 03°32′W
104 L7 **Madrigal de las Altas Torres** Castilla y León, N Spain 41°05′N 05°00′W
104 K10 **Madrigalejo** Extremadura, W Spain 39°08′N 05°36′W
34 L3 **Mad River** California, W USA
42 J8 **Madriz** ◆ *department* NW Nicaragua
104 K10 **Madroñera** Extremadura, W Spain 39°25′N 05°46′W
181 N12 **Madura** Western Australia 31°52′S 127°01′E
**Madura** *see* Madurai
155 H22 **Madurai** *prev.* Madura, Mathurai. Tamil Nādu, S India 09°55′N 78°07′E
169 S16 **Madura, Pulau** *prev.* Madoera. *island* C Indonesia
169 S16 **Madura, Selat** *strait* C Indonesia
127 Q17 **Madzhalis** Respublika Dagestan, SW Russia 42°12′N 47°46′E
114 K12 **Madzharovo** Haskovo, S Bulgaria 41°36′N 25°52′E
83 M14 **Madzimoyo** Eastern, E Zambia 13°42′S 32°34′E
165 O12 **Maebashi** *var.* Maebasi, Mayebashi. Gunma, Honshū, S Japan 36°24′N 139°02′E
**Maebasi** *see* Maebashi
167 O6 **Mae Chan** Chiang Rai, NW Thailand 20°13′N 99°52′E
167 N7 **Mae Hong Son** *var.* Maehongson, Muai To. Mae Hong Son, NW Thailand 19°16′N 97°56′E
**Maehongson** *see* Mae Hong Son
**Mae Nam Khong** *see* Mekong
167 Q7 **Mae Nam Nan** NW Thailand
167 O10 **Mae Nam Tha Chin** W Thailand
167 P7 **Mae Nam Yom** W Thailand
37 O3 **Maeser** Utah, W USA 40°28′N 109°35′W
**Maeseyck** *see* Maaseik
167 N9 **Mae Sot** *var.* Ban Mae Sot. Tak, W Thailand 16°44′N 98°32′E
44 H8 **Maestra, Sierra** E Cuba
**Maestricht** *see* Maastricht
167 O7 **Mae Suai** *var.* Ban Mae Suai. Chiang Rai, NW Thailand 19°43′N 99°30′E
167 O7 **Mae Tho, Doi** ▲ NW Thailand 18°56′N 99°20′E
172 I4 **Maevatanana** Mahajanga, C Madagascar 16°57′S 46°50′E
187 R13 **Maéwo** *prev.* Aurora. *island* C Vanuatu
171 S11 **Mafa** Pulau Halmahera, E Indonesia 0°01′N 127°50′E
83 I23 **Mafeteng** W Lesotho 29°48′S 27°15′E
99 J21 **Maffe** Namur, SE Belgium 50°21′N 05°19′E
183 P12 **Maffra** Victoria, SE Australia 37°59′S 147°03′E
81 K23 **Mafia** *island* E Tanzania
81 J23 **Mafia Channel** *sea waterway* E Tanzania
83 I21 **Mafikeng** *off.* Mahikeng. North-West, N South Africa 25°53′S 25°39′E
60 J12 **Mafra** Santa Catarina, S Brazil 26°08′S 49°47′W
104 F10 **Mafra** Lisboa, C Portugal 38°57′N 09°19′W
143 Q17 **Mafraq** Abū Ẓaby, C United Arab Emirates 24°21′N 54°33′E
**Mafraq/Muḥāfaẓat al Mafraq** *see* Al Mafraq
123 T10 **Magadan** Magadanskaya Oblast', E Russia 59°38′N 150°50′E
123 T9 **Magadanskaya Oblast'** ◆ *province* E Russia
108 G11 **Magadino** Ticino, S Switzerland 46°09′N 08°50′E
**Magallanes** *see* Punta Arenas
**Magallanes, Estrecho de** *see* Magellan, Strait of
63 G23 **Magallanes y de la Antártica Chilena** *var.* Región de Magallanes y de la Antártica Chilena. ◆ *region* S Chile
**Magallanes y de la Antártica Chilena, Región de** *see* Magallanes y de la Antártica Chilena
14 I10 **Maganasipi, Lac** Québec, SE Canada
54 F6 **Magangué** Bolívar, N Colombia 09°14′N 74°46′W
191 Y13 **Magareva** *var.* Mangareva. *island* Îles Tuamotu, SE French Polynesia
77 V12 **Magaria** Zinder, S Niger 13°00′N 08°55′E
186 F10 **Magarida** Central, SW Papua New Guinea 10°10′S 149°21′E
127 O16 **Magas** Respublika Ingushetiya, SW Russia 43°10′N 44°48′E
171 O2 **Magat** Luzon, N Philippines
27 T11 **Magazine Mountain** ▲ Arkansas, C USA 35°10′N 93°38′W
76 I15 **Magburaka** C Sierra Leone 08°44′N 11°57′W
123 Q13 **Magdagachi** Amurskaya Oblast', SE Russia 53°25′N 125°41′E
62 O12 **Magdalena** Buenos Aires, E Argentina 35°05′S 57°30′W
57 M15 **Magdalena** Beni, N Bolivia 13°22′S 64°07′W
40 F4 **Magdalena** Sonora, NW Mexico 30°38′N 110°59′W
37 Q13 **Magdalena** New Mexico, SW USA 34°07′N 107°14′W
54 F5 **Magdalena** *off.* Departamento del Magdalena. ◆ *province* N Colombia
40 E9 **Magdalena, Bahía** *bay* W Mexico
**Magdalena, Departamento del** *see* Magdalena
63 G19 **Magdalena, Isla** *island* Archipiélago de los Chonos, S Chile
40 D8 **Magdalena, Isla** *island* NW Mexico
47 P6 **Magdalena, Río** C Colombia
40 F4 **Magdalena, Río** NW Mexico
**Magdalen Islands** *see* Madeleine, Îles de la
147 N14 **Magdanly** *Rus.* Govurdak; *prev.* gowurdak, Guardak. Lebap Welaýaty, E Turkmenistan 37°50′N 66°06′E
100 L13 **Magdeburg** Sachsen-Anhalt, C Germany 52°08′N 11°39′E
22 L6 **Magee** Mississippi, S USA 31°52′N 89°43′W
169 Q16 **Magelang** Jawa, C Indonesia 07°28′S 110°11′E
192 K7 **Magellan Rise** *undersea feature* C Pacific Ocean
63 H24 **Magellan, Strait of** *Sp.* Estrecho de Magallanes. *strait* Argentina/Chile
106 D7 **Magenta** Lombardia, NW Italy 45°28′N 08°52′E
**Magerøy** *see* Magerøya
92 K7 **Magerøya** *var.* Magerøy, *Lapp.* Máhkarávju. *island* N Norway
164 C17 **Mage-shima** *island* Nansei-shotō, SW Japan
108 G11 **Maggia** Ticino, S Switzerland 46°15′N 08°42′E
108 G10 **Maggia** SW Switzerland
**Maggiore, Lago** *see* Maggiore, Lake
106 C6 **Maggiore, Lake** *It.* Lago Maggiore. Italy/ Switzerland
44 I12 **Maggotty** W Jamaica 18°09′N 77°46′W
76 I10 **Maghama** Gorgol, S Mauritania 15°31′N 12°50′W
97 F14 **Maghera** *Ir.* Machaire Rátha. C Northern Ireland, United Kingdom 54°51′N 06°40′W
97 F15 **Magherafelt** *Ir.* Machaire Fíolta. C Northern Ireland, United Kingdom 54°45′N 06°36′W
188 H6 **Magicienne Bay** *bay* Saipan, S Northern Mariana Islands
105 O13 **Magina** ▲ S Spain 37°43′N 03°24′W
81 H24 **Magingo** Ruvuma, S Tanzania 09°57′S 35°23′E
112 H11 **Maglaj** ◆ Federacija Bosne I Hercegovine, N Bosnia and Herzegovina
107 Q19 **Maglie** Puglia, SE Italy 40°07′N 18°18′E
36 L2 **Magna** Utah, W USA 40°42′N 112°06′W
**Magnesia** *see* Manisa
14 G12 **Magnetawan** Ontario, S Canada
27 T14 **Magnolia** Arkansas, C USA 33°17′N 93°16′W
22 K7 **Magnolia** Mississippi, S USA 31°08′N 90°27′W
25 V10 **Magnolia** Texas, SW USA 30°12′N 95°46′W
**Magnolia State** *see* Mississippi
95 J15 **Magnor** Hedmark, S Norway 59°57′N 12°14′E
187 Y14 **Mago** *prev.* Mango. *island* Lau Group, E Fiji
83 L15 **Màgoé** Tete, NW Mozambique 15°50′S 31°42′E
15 Q13 **Magog** Québec, SE Canada 45°16′N 72°09′W
161 R14 **Magong** *prev.* Mako, Makung. *county capital* W Taiwan
83 J15 **Magoye** Southern, S Zambia 16°00′S 27°34′E
41 Q12 **Magozal** Veracruz, C Mexico 21°33′N 97°57′W
14 B7 **Magpie** Ontario, S Canada
11 Q17 **Magrath** Alberta, SW Canada 49°27′N 112°52′W
105 R10 **Magre** Comunitat Valenciana, E Spain
76 I9 **Magta' Lahjar** *var.* Magta Lahjar, Magta' Lahjar, Magtá Lahjar. Brakna, SW Mauritania 17°27′N 13°07′W
146 D12 **Magtymguly** *prev.* Garrygala, *Rus.* Kara-Kala. Balkan Welaýaty, W Turkmenistan 38°27′N 56°15′E
83 L20 **Magude** Maputo, S Mozambique 25°02′S 32°40′E
77 Y12 **Magumeri** Borno, NE Nigeria 12°07′N 12°48′E
189 O14 **Magur Islands** *island group* Caroline Islands, C Micronesia
166 L6 **Magway** *var.* Magwe. Magway, W Myanmar (Burma) 20°08′N 94°55′E
166 L6 **Magway** *var.* Magwe. ◆ *region* C Myanmar (Burma)
**Magwe** *see* Magway
**Magyar-Becse** *see* Bečej
**Magyarkanizsa** *see* Kanjiža
**Magyarország** *see* Hungary
**Magyarzsombor** *see* Zimbor
142 J4 **Mahābād** *var.* Mehabad; *prev.* Sāūjbulāgh. Āžarbāyjān-e Gharbī, NW Iran 36°44′N 45°44′E
172 H5 **Mahabo** Toliara, W Madagascar 20°22′S 44°39′E
**Maha Chai** *see* Samut Sakhon
155 D14 **Mahād** Mahārāshtra, W India 18°04′N 73°21′E
81 N17 **Mahadday Weyne** Shabeellaha Dhexe, C Somalia 02°55′N 45°30′E
79 Q17 **Mahagi** Orientale, NE Dem. Rep. Congo 02°16′N 30°59′E
**Mahāil** *see* Muhāyil
172 I4 **Mahajamba** *seasonal river* NW Madagascar
152 G10 **Mahājan** Rājasthān, NW India 28°47′N 73°50′E
172 I3 **Mahajanga** *var.* Majunga. Mahajanga, NW Madagascar 15°40′S 46°20′E
172 I3 **Mahajanga** ◆ *province* W Madagascar
172 I3 **Mahajanga** ✕ Mahajanga, NW Madagascar 15°40′S 46°20′E
169 U10 **Mahakam, Sungai** *var.* Koetai, Kutai. Borneo, C Indonesia
83 I19 **Mahalapye** *var.* Mahalatswe. Central, SE Botswana 23°02′S 26°53′E
**Mahalatswe** *see* Mahalapye
**Mahalla el Kubra** *see* El Maḥalla el Kubra
171 O13 **Mahalona** Sulawesi, C Indonesia 02°37′S 121°26′E
**Mahameru** *see* Semeru, Gunung
143 S11 **Māhān** Kermān, E Iran 30°00′N 57°00′E
154 N12 **Mahanādi** E India
172 J5 **Mahanoro** Toamasina, E Madagascar 19°53′S 48°48′E
153 P13 **Mahārājganj** Bihār, N India 26°07′N 84°31′E
154 G13 **Mahārāshtra** ◆ *state* W India
172 I4 **Mahavavy** *seasonal river* N Madagascar
155 K24 **Mahaweli Ganga** C Sri Lanka
**Mahbés** *see* El Mahbas
155 J15 **Mahbūbābād** Telangana, E India 17°35′N 80°00′E
155 H16 **Mahbūbnagar** Telangana, C India 16°46′N 78°01′E
140 M8 **Mahd adh Dhahab** Al Madīnah al Munawwarah, W Saudi Arabia 23°33′N 40°56′E
55 S9 **Mahdia** C Guyana 05°16′N 59°08′W
75 N6 **Mahdia** *var.* Al Mahdīyah, Mehdia. NE Tunisia 35°14′N 11°06′E
155 F20 **Mahe** *Fr.* Mahé; *prev.* Mayyali. Puducherry, SW India 11°41′N 75°31′E
172 I16 **Mahé** ✕ Mahé, NE Seychelles 04°37′S 55°27′E
172 H16 **Mahé** *island* Inner Islands, NE Seychelles
**Mahé** *see* Mahe
173 Y17 **Mahebourg** SE Mauritius 20°24′S 57°42′E
152 I11 **Mahendragarh** *prev.* Mohendergarh. Haryāna, N India 28°17′N 76°14′E
152 L10 **Mahendranagar** Far Western, W Nepal 28°58′N 80°13′E
81 I23 **Mahenge** Morogoro, SE Tanzania 08°41′S 36°41′E
185 F22 **Maheno** Otago, South Island, New Zealand 45°10′S 170°51′E
154 D9 **Mahesāna** Gujarāt, W India 23°37′N 72°28′E
154 F11 **Maheshwar** Madhya Pradesh, C India 22°11′N 75°40′E
153 V17 **Maheskhali Island** *var.* Maiskhal Island. *island* SE Bangladesh
151 F14 **Mahi** N India
184 Q10 **Mahia Peninsula** *peninsula* North Island, New Zealand
**Mahikeng** *see* Mafikeng
119 O16 **Mahilyow** *Rus.* Mogilëv. Mahilyowskaya Voblasts', E Belarus 53°55′N 30°23′E
119 M16 **Mahilyowskaya Voblasts'** *Rus.* Mogilëvskaya Oblast'. ◆ *province* E Belarus
191 P7 **Mahina** Tahiti, W French Polynesia 17°29′S 149°27′W
185 E23 **Mahinerangi, Lake** South Island, New Zealand
**Máhkarávju** *see* Magerøya
83 L22 **Mahlabatini** KwaZulu/Natal, E South Africa 28°15′S 31°28′E
166 L5 **Mahlaing** Mandalay, C Myanmar (Burma) 21°03′N 95°44′E
109 X8 **Mahldorf** Steiermark, SE Austria 46°54′N 15°55′E
**Maḥmūd-e 'Erāqī** *see* Maḥmūd-e Rāqī
149 R4 **Maḥmūd-e Rāqī** *var.* Maḥmūd-e 'Erāqī. Kāpīsā, NE Afghanistan 35°01′N 69°20′E
**Mahmudiya** *see* Al Maḥmūdīyah
29 S5 **Mahnomen** Minnesota, N USA 47°19′N 95°58′W
152 K14 **Mahoba** Uttar Pradesh, N India 25°18′N 79°53′E
18 D14 **Mahoning Creek Lake** Pennsylvania, NE USA
105 Q10 **Mahora** Castilla-La Mancha, C Spain 39°13′N 01°44′W
**Mähren** *see* Moravia
**Mährisch-Budwitz** *see* Moravské Budějovice
**Mährisch-Kromau** *see* Moravský Krumlov
**Mährisch-Neustadt** *see* Uničov
**Mährisch-Schönberg** *see* Šumperk
**Mährisch-Trübau** *see* Moravská Třebová
**Mährisch-Weisskirchen** *see* Hranice
**Māh-Shahr** *see* Bandar-e Māhshahr
79 N19 **Mahulu** Maniema, E Dem. Rep. Congo 01°04′S 27°10′E
154 C12 **Mahuva** Gujarāt, W India 21°06′N 71°46′E
114 N11 **Mahya Dağı** ▲ NW Turkey 41°47′N 27°34′E
105 T6 **Maials** *var.* Mayals. Cataluña, NE Spain 41°22′N 00°30′E
191 O2 **Maiana** *prev.* Hall Island. *atoll* Tungaru, W Kiribati
191 S11 **Maiao** *var.* Tapuaemanu, Tubuai-Manu. *island* Îles du Vent, W French Polynesia
54 H4 **Maicao** La Guajira, N Colombia 11°23′N 72°16′W
**Mai Ceu/Mai Chio** *see* Maych'ew
103 U8 **Maîche** Doubs, E France 47°15′N 06°43′E
149 Q5 **Maīdān Shahr** *var.* Maydān Shahr; *prev.* Meydān Shahr. Wardak, E Afghanistan 34°27′N 68°48′E
97 N22 **Maidenhead** S England, United Kingdom 51°32′N 00°44′W
11 S15 **Maidstone** Saskatchewan, S Canada 53°06′N 109°21′W
97 P22 **Maidstone** SE England, United Kingdom 51°17′N 00°31′E
77 Y13 **Maiduguri** Borno, NE Nigeria 11°51′N 13°10′E
108 I8 **Maienfeld** Sankt Gallen, NE Switzerland 47°01′N 09°30′E
116 J12 **Măieruş** *Hung.* Szászmagyarós. Braşov, C Romania 45°55′N 25°30′E
**Maigh Chromtha** *see* Macroom
**Maigh Eo** *see* Mayo
55 N9 **Maigualida, Sierra** S Venezuela
154 K9 **Maihar** Madhya Pradesh, C India 24°18′N 80°46′E
154 K11 **Maikala Range** C India
67 T10 **Maiko** W Dem. Rep. Congo
**Mailand** *see* Milano
152 L11 **Mailāni** Uttar Pradesh, N India 28°17′N 80°20′E
149 U10 **Māilsi** Punjab, E Pakistan 29°46′N 72°15′E
147 R8 **Maimak** Talasskaya Oblast', NW Kyrgyzstan 42°40′N 71°12′E
**Maimāna** *see* Maīmanah
148 M3 **Maīmanah** *var.* Maimāna, Maymana; *prev.* Meymaneh. Fāryāb, NW Afghanistan 35°57′N 64°48′E
171 V13 **Maimawa** Papua Barat, E Indonesia 03°21′S 133°36′E
**Maimuna** *see* Al Maymūnah
101 G18 **Main** C Germany
115 F22 **Maïna** *ancient monument* Pelopónnisos, S Greece
115 E20 **Maïnalo** S Greece
101 L22 **Mainburg** Bayern, SE Germany 48°40′N 11°48′E
**Main Camp** *see* Banana
14 E12 **Main Channel** *lake channel* Ontario, S Canada
79 I20 **Mai-Ndombe, Lac** *prev.* Lac Léopold II. W Dem. Rep. Congo
101 K20 **Main-Donau-Kanal** *canal* SE Germany
19 R6 **Maine** *off.* State of Maine, *also known as* Lumber State, Pine Tree State. ◆ *state* NE USA
102 K6 **Maine** *cultural region* NW France
102 J7 **Maine-et-Loire** ◆ *department* NW France
19 Q9 **Maine, Gulf of** *gulf* NE USA
77 X12 **Maïné-Soroa** Diffa, SE Niger 13°14′N 12°00′E
167 N2 **Maingkwan** *var.* Mungkawn. Kachin State, N Myanmar (Burma) 26°20′N 96°37′E
**Main Island** *see* Bermuda
**Mainistir Fhear Maí** *see* Fermoy
**Mainistirna Búille** *see* Boyle
**Mainistir na Corann** *see* Midleton
**Mainistir na Féile** *see* Abbeyfeale
96 J5 **Mainland** *island* N Scotland, United Kingdom
96 L2 **Mainland** *island* NE Scotland, United Kingdom
159 P16 **Mainling** *var.* Tungdor. Xizang Zizhiqu, W China 29°12′N 94°06′E
152 K12 **Mainpuri** Uttar Pradesh, N India 27°14′N 79°01′E
103 N5 **Maintenon** Eure-et-Loir, C France 48°35′N 01°34′E
172 H4 **Maintirano** Mahajanga, W Madagascar 18°01′S 44°03′E
93 M15 **Mainua** Kainuu, C Finland 64°05′N 27°28′E
101 G18 **Mainz** *Fr.* Mayence. Rheinland-Pfalz, SW Germany 50°00′N 08°16′E
76 I9 **Maio** *var.* Vila do Maio. Maio, S Cape Verde 15°07′N 23°12′W
76 E10 **Maio** *var.* Mayo. *island* Ilhas de Sotavento, SE Cape Verde
62 G12 **Maipo, Río** C Chile
62 H12 **Maipo, Volcán** W Argentina 34°09′S 69°51′W
61 E22 **Maipú** Buenos Aires, E Argentina 36°52′S 57°52′W
62 I11 **Maipú** Mendoza, E Argentina 33°00′S 68°46′W
62 H11 **Maipú** Santiago, C Chile 33°30′S 70°52′W
106 A9 **Maira** NW Italy
108 I10 **Maira** *It.* Mera. Italy/ Switzerland
153 V12 **Mairābari** Assam, NE India 26°28′N 92°22′E
44 K7 **Maisí** Guantánamo, E Cuba 20°13′N 74°08′W
118 H13 **Maišiagala** Vilnius, SE Lithuania 54°52′N 25°03′E
**Maiskhal Island** *see* Maheskhali Island


◆ Country ● Country Capital ◇ Dependent Territory ○ Dependent Territory Capital ◆ Administrative Regions ✕ International Airport ▲ Mountain ▲ Mountain Range Volcano River Lake Reservoir

MAI SOMBUN – MANGAWĀN


167 N13 **Mai Sombun** Chumphon, SW Thailand 10°49′N 99°13′E
**Mai Son** *see* Hat Lot
**Maisur** *see* Mysore, India
**Maisur** *see* Karnātaka, India
183 T3 **Maitland** New South Wales, SE Australia 32°33′S 151°33′E
182 I9 **Maitland** South Australia 34°21′S 137°42′E
14 F15 **Maitland** ≈ Ontario, S Canada
195 R1 **Maitri** *research station (India)* Antarctica 70°03′S 08°59′E
159 N15 **Maizhokunggar** Xizang Zizhiqu, W China 29°50′N 91°40′E
43 C10 **Maíz, Islas del** *var.* Corn Islands. *island group* SE Nicaragua
164 J12 **Maizuru** Kyōto, Honshū, SW Japan 35°30′N 135°20′E
54 F5 **Majagual** Sucre, N Colombia 08°36′N 74°39′W
41 Z13 **Majahual** Quintana Roo, E Mexico 18°43′N 87°43′W
**Mājeej** *see* Mejit Island
171 N13 **Majene** *prev.* Madjene. Sulawesi, C Indonesia 03°33′S 118°59′E
43 V15 **Majé, Serranía de** ▲▲ E Panama
112 I11 **Majevica** ▲▲ NE Bosnia and Herzegovina
81 H15 **Majī** Southern Nationalities, S Ethiopia 06°11′N 35°32′E
141 X7 **Majīs** NW Oman 24°25′N 56°34′E
**Majorca** *see* Mallorca
105 X9 **Major, Puig** ▲ Mallorca, Spain, W Mediterranean Sea 39°50′N 2°50′E
**Mājro** *see* Majuro Atoll
**Majunga** *see* Mahajanga
189 Y3 **Majuro** ✈ Majuro Atoll, SE Marshall Islands 07°05′N 171°08′E
189 Y2 **Majuro Atoll** *var.* Mājro. ● (Marshall Islands) Ratak Chain, SE Marshall Islands
189 X2 **Majuro Lagoon** *lagoon* Majuro Atoll, SE Marshall Islands
76 H11 **Maka** C Senegal 13°40′N 14°12′W
79 F20 **Makabana** Niari, SW Congo 03°28′S 12°36′E
38 D9 **Mākaha** *var.* Makaha. O'ahu, Hawaii, USA, C Pacific Ocean 21°28′N 158°13′W
38 B8 **Makahū'ena Point** *var.* Makahuena Point. *headland* Kaua'i, Hawai'i, USA 21°52′N 159°28′W
38 D9 **Makakilo City** O'ahu, Hawaii, USA, C Pacific Ocean 21°21′N 158°05′W
83 H18 **Makalamabedi** Central, C Botswana 20°19′S 23°51′E
**Makale** *see* Mek'elē
158 K17 **Makalu** *Chin.* Makaru Shan. ▲ China/Nepal 27°53′N 87°09′E
81 G23 **Makampi** Mbeya, S Tanzania 08°00′S 33°17′E
**Makanchi** *see* Makanshy
145 X12 **Makanshy** *prev.* Makanchi. Vostochnyy Kazakhstan, E Kazakhstan 46°47′N 82°00′E
42 M8 **Makantaka** Costa Caribe Norte, NE Nicaragua 13°13′N 84°04′W
190 B16 **Makapu Point** *headland* W Niue 18°59′S 169°56′E
185 C24 **Makarewa** Southland, South Island, New Zealand 46°17′S 168°16′E
117 O4 **Makariv** Kyivs'ka Oblast', N Ukraine 50°28′N 29°49′E
185 D20 **Makarora** ≈ South Island, New Zealand
123 T13 **Makarov** Ostrov Sakhalin, Sakhalinskaya Oblast', SE Russia 48°24′N 142°37′E
197 R9 **Makarov Basin** *undersea feature* Arctic Ocean
192 I5 **Makarov Seamount** *undersea feature* W Pacific Ocean 29°30′N 153°30′E
113 F15 **Makarska** *It.* Macarsca. Split-Dalmacija, SE Croatia 43°18′N 17°00′E
**Makaru Shan** *see* Makalu
125 O15 **Makar'yev** Kostromskaya Oblast', NW Russia 57°52′N 43°46′E
82 L11 **Makasa** Northern, NE Zambia 09°42′S 31°54′E
**Makasar** *see* Makassar
**Makasar, Selat** *see* Makassar Straits
170 M14 **Makassar** *var.* Macassar, Makasar; *prev.* Ujungpandang. Sulawesi, C Indonesia 05°09′S 119°28′E
192 F7 **Makassar Straits** *Ind.* Makasar Selat. *strait* C Indonesia
144 G12 **Makat** *Kaz.* Maqat. Atyrau, SW Kazakhstan 47°40′N 53°28′E
191 T10 **Makatea** *island* Îles Tuamotu, C French Polynesia
139 U7 **Makātū** Diyālá, E Iraq 33°55′N 45°25′E
172 H6 **Makay** *var.* Massif du Makay. ▲▲ SW Madagascar
**Makay, Massif du** *see* Makay
114 J12 **Makaza** *pass* Bulgaria/Greece
**Makedonija, Republika Severna** *see* North Macedonia
190 B16 **Makefu** W Niue 18°59′S 169°55′W
191 V10 **Makemo** *atoll* Îles Tuamotu, C French Polynesia
76 I15 **Makeni** C Sierra Leone 08°57′N 12°02′W
**Makenzen** *see* Orlyak
**Makeyevka** *see* Makiyivka
127 Q16 **Makhachkala** *prev.* Petrovsk-Port. Respublika Dagestan, SW Russia 42°58′N 47°30′E
**Makhado** *see* Louis Trichardt
144 F11 **Makhambet** Atyrau, W Kazakhstan 47°35′N 51°35′E
**Makharadze** *see* Ozurgeti
139 W13 **Makhfar al Buşayyah** Al Muthanná, S Iraq 30°09′N 46°09′E
**Makhmūr** *see* Mexmûr
138 I11 **Makhrūq, Wadi al** *dry watercourse* E Jordan
139 R4 **Makḩūl, Jabal** ▲▲ C Iraq
141 R13 **Makhyah, Wādī** *dry watercourse* N Yemen
171 V13 **Maki** Papua Barat, E Indonesia 03°00′S 134°10′E
185 G21 **Makikihi** Canterbury, South Island, New Zealand 44°36′S 171°09′E
191 O2 **Makin** *prev.* Pitt Island. *atoll* Tungaru, W Kiribati
81 I20 **Makindu** Makueni, S Kenya 02°15′S 37°49′E
145 Q8 **Makinsk** Akmola, N Kazakhstan 52°40′N 70°28′E
**Makira** *see* Makira-Ulawa
**Makira** *see* San Cristobal
187 N10 **Makira-Ulawa** *prev.* Makira. ⬖ *province* SE Solomon Islands
117 X8 **Makiyivka** *Rus.* Makeyevka; *prev.* Dmitriyevsk. Donets'ka Oblast', E Ukraine 47°57′N 37°47′E
140 L10 **Makkah** *Eng.* Mecca. Makkah al Mukarramah, W Saudi Arabia 21°28′N 39°50′E
140 M10 **Makkah al Mukarramah** *var.* Minţaqat Makkah. ⬖ *region* W Saudi Arabia
**Makkah, Minţaqat** *see* Makkah al Mukarramah
13 R7 **Makkovik** Newfoundland and Labrador, NE Canada 55°06′N 59°07′W
98 K6 **Makkum** Fryslân, N Netherlands 53°03′N 05°25′E
111 M25 **Makó** *Rom.* Macău. Csongrád, SE Hungary 46°14′N 20°28′E
**Mako** *see* Magong
14 G9 **Makobe Lake** ◎ Ontario, S Canada
79 F18 **Makokou** Ogooué-Ivindo, NE Gabon 0°38′N 12°47′E
81 G23 **Makongolosi** Mbeya, S Tanzania 08°24′S 33°09′E
81 E19 **Makota** SW Uganda 0°37′S 30°12′E
79 G18 **Makoua** Cuvette, C Congo 0°01′S 15°40′E
110 M10 **Maków Mazowiecki** Mazowieckie, C Poland 52°51′N 21°06′E
111 K17 **Maków Podhalański** Małopolskie, S Poland 49°43′N 19°40′E
143 V14 **Makran** *cultural region* Iran/Pakistan
152 G12 **Makrāna** Rājasthān, N India 27°02′N 74°44′E
143 U15 **Makran Coast** *coastal region* SE Iran
119 F20 **Makrany** *Rus.* Mokrany. Brestskaya Voblasts', SW Belarus 51°50′N 24°15′E
**Makrinoros** *see* Makrynóros
115 H20 **Makrónisosi** *island* Kykládes, Greece, Aegean Sea
115 D17 **Makrynóros** *var.* Makrinoros. ▲▲ C Greece
115 G19 **Makryplági** ▲ C Greece 38°00′N 23°06′E
**Maksamaa** *see* Maxmo
**Maksatha** *see* Maksatikha
**Maksaticha** *see* Maksatikha
124 J15 **Maksatikha** *var.* Maksatha, Maksaticha. Tverskaya Oblast', W Russia 57°49′N 35°46′E
154 G10 **Maksi** Madhya Pradesh, C India 23°20′N 76°36′E
142 I1 **Mākū** Āžarbāyjān-e Gharbī, NW Iran 39°20′N 44°50′E
153 Y11 **Mākum** Assam, NE India 27°28′N 95°28′E
**Makung** *see* Magong
164 B16 **Makurazaki** Kagoshima, Kyūshū, SW Japan 31°16′N 130°18′E
77 V15 **Makurdi** Benue, C Nigeria 07°42′N 08°36′E
38 L17 **Makushin Volcano** ⛰ Unalaska Island, Alaska, USA 53°53′N 166°55′W
83 K16 **Makwiro** Mashonaland West, N Zimbabwe 17°58′S 30°25′E
57 D15 **Mala** Lima, W Peru 12°40′S 76°36′W
93 I14 **Malå** Västerbotten, N Sweden 65°12′N 18°45′E
**Mala** *see* Mallow, Ireland
**Mala** *see* Malaita, Solomon Islands
171 P8 **Malabang** Mindanao, S Philippines
155 E21 **Malabār Coast** *coast* SW India
79 C16 **Malabo** *prev.* Santa Isabel. ● (Equatorial Guinea) Isla de Bioco, NW Equatorial Guinea 03°43′N 08°52′E
79 C16 **Malabo** ✈ Isla de Bioco, N Equatorial Guinea 03°44′N 08°51′E
**Malaca** *see* Málaga
**Malacca** *see* Melaka
168 I7 **Malacca, Strait of** *Ind.* Selat Malaka. *strait* Indonesia/Malaysia
**Malacka** *see* Malacky
111 G20 **Malacky** *Hung.* Malacka. Bratislavský Kraj, W Slovakia 48°26′N 17°01′E
33 R16 **Malad City** Idaho, NW USA 42°10′N 112°16′W
117 Q4 **Mala Divytsya** Chernihivs'ka Oblast', N Ukraine 50°40′N 32°13′E
119 J15 **Maladzyechna** *Pol.* Molodeczno, *Rus.* Molodechno. Minskaya Voblasts', C Belarus 54°19′N 26°51′E
190 D12 **Malaee** Île Futuna, N Wallis and Futuna
190 G12 **Mala'etoli** Île Uvea, E Wallis and Futuna
54 G8 **Málaga** Santander, C Colombia 06°44′N 72°45′W
104 M15 **Málaga** *anc.* Malaca. Andalucía, S Spain 36°43′N 04°25′W
37 V15 **Malaga** New Mexico, SW USA 32°10′N 104°04′W
104 L15 **Málaga** ⬖ *province* Andalucía, S Spain
104 M15 **Málaga** ✈ Andalucía, S Spain 36°38′N 04°36′W
**Malagasy Republic** *see* Madagascar
105 N10 **Malagón** Castilla-La Mancha, C Spain 39°10′N 03°51′W
97 G18 **Malahide** *Ir.* Mullach Íde. Dublin, E Ireland 53°27′N 06°09′W
187 N9 **Malaita** *off.* Malaita Province. ⬖ *province* N Solomon Islands
187 N8 **Malaita** *var.* Mala. *island* N Solomon Islands
**Malaita Province** *see* Malaita
80 F13 **Malakal** Upper Nile, NE South Sudan 09°31′N 31°40′E
112 C10 **Mala Kapela** ▲▲ NW Croatia
25 V7 **Malakoff** Texas, SW USA 32°10′N 96°00′W
**Malakula** *see* Malekula
149 V7 **Malakwal** *var.* Malikwala. Punjab, E Pakistan 32°32′N 73°18′E
186 E7 **Malalamai** Madang, W Papua New Guinea 05°49′S 146°44′E
171 O13 **Malamala** Sulawesi, C Indonesia 03°21′S 120°58′E
169 S17 **Malang** Jawa, C Indonesia 07°59′S 112°45′E
83 O14 **Malanga** Niassa, N Mozambique 13°27′S 36°05′E
**Malange** *see* Malanje
92 I9 **Malangen** *sound* N Norway
82 C11 **Malanje** *var.* Malange. Malanje, NW Angola 09°34′S 16°25′E
82 C11 **Malanje** *var.* Malange. ⬖ *province* N Angola
148 M16 **Malan, Ras** *cape* SW Pakistan
77 S13 **Malanville** NE Benin 11°50′N 03°23′E
**Malapane** *see* Ozimek
155 F21 **Malappuram** Kerala, SW India 11°00′N 76°02′E
43 T17 **Mala, Punta** *headland* S Panama 07°28′N 79°58′W
148 L15 **Malar** Baluchistan, SW Pakistan 26°19′N 64°55′E
95 N16 **Mälaren** ◎ C Sweden
62 H13 **Malargüe** Mendoza, W Argentina 35°32′S 69°35′W
14 J8 **Malartic** Québec, SE Canada 48°09′N 78°09′W
119 F20 **Malaryta** *Pol.* Maloryta, *Rus.* Malorita. Brestskaya Voblasts', SW Belarus 51°47′N 24°05′E
63 J19 **Malaspina** Chubut, SE Argentina 44°56′S 66°52′W
10 G8 **Malaspina Glacier** *glacier* Yukon, W Canada
39 U12 **Malaspina Glacier** *glacier* Alaska, USA
137 N15 **Malatya** *anc.* Melitene. Malatya, SE Turkey 38°22′N 38°18′E
136 M14 **Malatya** ⬖ *province* C Turkey
**Malavate** *see* Pédima
117 Q7 **Mala Vyska** *Rus.* Malaya Viska. Kirovohrads'ka Oblast', S Ukraine 48°37′N 31°36′E
83 M14 **Malawi** *off.* Republic of Malawi; *prev.* Nyasaland, Nyasaland Protectorate. ◆ *republic* S Africa
**Malawi, Lake** *see* Nyasa, Lake
**Malawi, Republic of** *see* Malawi
93 J17 **Malax** *Fin.* Maalahti. Österbotten, W Finland 62°55′N 21°30′E
124 H14 **Malaya Vishera** Novgorodskaya Oblast', W Russia 58°52′N 32°12′E
**Malaya Viska** *see* Mala Vyska
171 Q7 **Malaybalay** Mindanao, S Philippines 08°10′N 125°08′E
142 L6 **Malāyer** *prev.* Daulatabad. Hamadān, W Iran 34°20′N 48°47′E
168 J7 **Malay Peninsula** *peninsula* Malaysia/Thailand
168 L7 **Malaysia** *off.* Malaysia, *var.* Federation of Malaysia; *prev.* the separate territories of Federation of Malaya, Sarawak and Sabah (North Borneo) and Singapore. ◆ *monarchy* SE Asia
**Malaysia, Federation of** *see* Malaysia
137 R14 **Malazgirt** Muş, E Turkey 39°09′N 42°30′E
15 R8 **Malbaie** ≈ Québec, SE Canada
77 T12 **Malbaza** Tahoua, S Niger 13°57′N 05°32′E
110 J7 **Malbork** *Ger.* Marienburg, Marienburg in Westpreussen. Pomorskie, N Poland 54°01′N 19°03′E
100 N9 **Malchin** Mecklenburg-Vorpommern, N Germany 53°43′N 12°46′E
100 M9 **Malchiner See** ◎ NE Germany
99 D16 **Maldegem** Oost-Vlaanderen, NW Belgium 51°12′N 03°27′E
98 L13 **Malden** Gelderland, SE Netherlands 51°47′N 05°51′E
19 O11 **Malden** Massachusetts, NE USA 42°25′N 71°04′W
27 Y8 **Malden** Missouri, C USA 36°33′N 89°58′W
191 X4 **Malden Island** *prev.* Independence Island. *atoll* E Kiribati
173 Q6 **Maldives** *off.* Republic of Maldives, *Div.* Dhivehi Raaje, Dhivehi Raajjeyge Jumhooriyyaa. ◆ *republic* N Indian Ocean
**Maldives, Republic of** *see* Maldives
97 P21 **Maldon** E England, United Kingdom 51°44′N 00°40′E
61 G20 **Maldonado** Maldonado, S Uruguay 34°57′S 54°59′W
61 G20 **Maldonado** ⬖ *department* S Uruguay
41 P17 **Maldonado, Punta** *headland* S Mexico 16°18′N 98°31′W
106 G6 **Malè** Trentino-Alto Adige, N Italy 46°21′N 10°51′E
**Male** *see* Maale
76 K13 **Malea** *var.* Maléya. NE Guinea 11°46′N 09°43′W
**Maleas, Ákra** *see* Agriliá, Akrotírio
115 G22 **Maleas, Akrotírio** *headland* S Greece 36°25′N 23°11′E
151 K19 **Male' Atoll** *var.* Kaafu Atoll. *atoll* C Maldives
**Malebo, Pool** *see* Stanley Pool
154 E12 **Mālegaon** Mahārāshtra, W India 20°33′N 74°32′E
81 F15 **Malek** Jonglei, E South Sudan 06°04′N 31°36′E
187 Q13 **Malekula** *var.* Malakula; *prev.* Mallicolo. *island* W Vanuatu
189 Y15 **Malem** Kosrae, E Micronesia 05°16′N 163°01′E
83 O15 **Malema** Nampula, N Mozambique 14°57′S 37°28′E
79 N23 **Malemba-Nkulu** Katanga, SE Dem. Rep. Congo 08°01′S 26°48′E
139 T1 **Male Mela** *Ar.* Marī Mīlā, *var.* Mārī Mīlah. Arbīl, E Iraq 36°58′N 44°42′E
124 K9 **Malen'ga** Respublika Kareliya, NW Russia 63°50′N 36°21′E
95 M20 **Målerås** Kalmar, S Sweden 56°55′N 15°34′E
103 O6 **Malesherbes** Loiret, C France 48°18′N 02°25′E
115 G18 **Malesína** Stereá Elláda, E Greece 38°37′N 23°15′E
**Maléya** *see* Maléa
127 O15 **Malgobek** Respublika Ingushetiya, SW Russia 43°34′N 44°34′E
105 X5 **Malgrat de Mar** Cataluña, NE Spain 41°39′N 02°45′E
80 C9 **Malha** Northern Darfur, W Sudan 15°07′N 26°00′E
139 Q5 **Malḩah** *var.* Malḩāt. Şalāḩ ad Dīn, C Iraq 34°44′N 42°41′E
**Malḩāt** *see* Malḩah
32 K14 **Malheur Lake** ◎ Oregon, NW USA
32 L14 **Malheur River** ≈ Oregon, NW USA
76 I13 **Mali** NW Guinea 12°08′N 12°29′W
77 O9 **Mali** *off.* Republic of Mali, *Fr.* République du Mali; *prev.* French Sudan, Sudanese Republic. ◆ *republic* W Africa
171 Q16 **Maliana** W East Timor 08°57′S 125°25′E
167 O2 **Mali Hka** ≈ N Myanmar (Burma)
**Mali Idjoš** *see* Mali Iđoš
112 K8 **Mali Iđoš** *var.* Mali Idjoš, *Hung.* Kishegyes; *prev.* Krivaja. Vojvodina, N Serbia 45°43′N 19°40′E
113 M18 **Mali i Sharrit** *Serb.* Šar Planina. ▲▲ North Macedonia/Serbia
**Mali i Zi** *see* Crna Gora
112 K9 **Mali Kanal** *canal* N Serbia
171 P12 **Maliku** Sulawesi, N Indonesia 0°36′S 123°13′E
**Malik, Wadi al** *see* Milk, Wadi el
**Malikwala** *see* Malakwal
167 N11 **Mali Kyun** *var.* Tavoy Island. *island* Mergui Archipelago, S Myanmar (Burma)
95 M19 **Målilla** Kalmar, S Sweden 57°24′N 15°49′E
112 B11 **Mali Lošinj** *It.* Lussinpiccolo. Primorje-Gorski Kotar, W Croatia 44°31′N 14°28′E
**Malin** *see* Malyn
171 P7 **Malindang, Mount** ▲ Mindanao, S Philippines 08°12′N 123°37′E
81 K20 **Malindi** Kilifi, SE Kenya 03°14′S 40°05′E
**Malines** *see* Mechelen
96 E13 **Malin Head** *Ir.* Cionn Mhálanna. *headland* NW Ireland 55°37′N 07°37′W
171 O11 **Malino, Gunung** ▲ Sulawesi, N Indonesia 0°44′N 120°45′E
113 M21 **Maliq** *var.* Maliqi. Korçë, SE Albania 40°45′N 20°45′E
**Maliqi** *see* Maliq
**Mali, Republic of** *see* Mali
**Mali, République du** *see* Mali
171 Q8 **Malita** Mindanao, S Philippines 06°13′N 125°39′E
**Maljovica** *see* Malyovitsa
154 G12 **Malkāpur** Mahārāshtra, C India 20°52′N 76°18′E
136 B10 **Malkara** Tekirdağ, NW Turkey 40°54′N 26°54′E
119 J19 **Mal'kavichy** *Rus.* Mal'kovichi. Brestskaya Voblasts', SW Belarus 52°31′N 26°36′E
**Malkiye** *see* Al Mālikīyah
114 L11 **Malko Sharkovo, Yazovir** ▣ SE Bulgaria
114 N11 **Malko Tarnovo** *var.* Malko Tŭrnovo. Burgas, E Bulgaria 42°00′N 27°33′E
**Malko Tŭrnovo** *see* Malko Tarnovo
**Mal'kovichi** *see* Mal'kavichy
183 R12 **Mallacoota** Victoria, SE Australia 37°34′S 149°45′E
96 G10 **Mallaig** N Scotland, United Kingdom 57°04′N 05°48′W
182 I9 **Mallala** South Australia 34°29′S 138°30′E
75 W9 **Mallawī** *var.* Mallawi. C Egypt 27°44′N 30°50′E
**Mallawi** *see* Mallawī
105 R5 **Mallén** Aragón, NE Spain 41°53′N 01°25′W
106 F5 **Malles Venosta** *Ger.* Mals im Vinschgau. Trentino-Alto Adige, N Italy 46°40′N 10°37′E
**Mallicolo** *see* Malekula
109 Q8 **Mallnitz** Salzburg, S Austria 46°58′N 13°09′E
105 W9 **Mallorca** *Eng.* Majorca; *anc.* Baleares Major. *island* Islas Baleares, Spain, W Mediterranean Sea
97 C20 **Mallow** *Ir.* Mala. SW Ireland 52°08′N 08°39′W
93 E15 **Malm** Nord-Trøndelag, C Norway 64°04′N 11°12′E
95 L19 **Malmbäck** Jönköping, S Sweden 57°34′N 14°30′E
92 J12 **Malmberget** *Lapp.* Malmivaara. Norrbotten, N Sweden 67°09′N 20°39′E
99 M20 **Malmédy** Liège, E Belgium 50°26′N 06°02′E
83 E25 **Malmesbury** Western Cape, SW South Africa 33°28′S 18°43′E
**Malmivaara** *see* Malmberget
95 N16 **Malmköping** Södermanland, C Sweden 59°08′N 16°49′E
95 K23 **Malmö** Skåne, S Sweden 55°36′N 13°E
95 K23 **Malmo** ✈ Skåne, S Sweden 55°33′N 13°23′E
45 Q16 **Malmok** *headland* N Bonaire 12°16′N 68°21′W
95 M18 **Malmslätt** Östergötland, S Sweden 58°25′N 15°30′E
125 R16 **Malmyzh** Kirovskaya Oblast', NW Russia 56°30′N 50°37′E
187 Q13 **Malo** *island* W Vanuatu
126 J7 **Maloarkhangel'sk** Orlovskaya Oblast', W Russia 52°25′N 36°37′E
**Maļoeļap** *see* Maloelap Atoll
189 V6 **Maloelap Atoll** *var.* Maļoeļap. *atoll* E Marshall Islands
**Maloenda** *see* Malunda
108 I10 **Maloja** Graubünden, S Switzerland 46°25′N 09°42′E
82 L12 **Malole** Northern, NE Zambia 10°05′S 31°37′E
171 O3 **Malolos** Luzon, N Philippines 14°51′N 120°49′E
18 K6 **Malone** New York, NE USA 44°51′N 74°18′W
79 K25 **Malonga** Katanga, S Dem. Rep. Congo 10°26′S 23°10′E
111 L17 **Małopolskie** ⬖ *province* SE Poland
**Malorita/Maloryta** *see* Malaryta
124 K9 **Maloshuyka** Arkhangel'skaya Oblast', NW Russia 63°43′N 37°20′E
**Mal'ovitsa** *see* Malyovitsa
145 V15 **Malovodnoye** Almaty, SE Kazakhstan 43°31′N 77°42′E
94 C10 **Måløy** Sogn Og Fjordane, S Norway 61°57′N 05°06′E
126 K4 **Maloyaroslavets** Kaluzhskaya Oblast', W Russia 55°03′N 36°31′E
122 G7 **Malozemel'skaya Tundra** *physical region* NW Russia
104 J10 **Malpartida de Cáceres** Extremadura, W Spain 39°26′N 06°30′W
104 K9 **Malpartida de Plasencia** Extremadura, W Spain 39°59′N 06°03′W
106 C7 **Malpensa** ✈ (Milano) Lombardia, N Italy 45°41′N 08°40′E
76 J6 **Malqteïr** *desert* N Mauritania
**Mals im Vinschgau** *see* Malles Venosta
118 J10 **Malta** SE Latvia 56°19′N 27°11′E
33 V7 **Malta** Montana, NW USA 48°21′N 107°52′W
120 M11 **Malta** ◆ *republic* C Mediterranean Sea
109 R8 **Malta** *var.* Maltabach. ≈ S Austria
120 M11 **Malta** *island* Malta, C Mediterranean Sea
**Maltabach** *see* Malta
**Malta, Canale di** *see* Malta Channel
120 M11 **Malta Channel** *It.* Canale di Malta. *strait* Italy/Malta
83 D20 **Maltahöhe** Hardap, SW Namibia 24°50′S 17°00′E
**Malta, Ir-Repubblika ta'** *see* Malta
**Malta, Republic of** *see* Malta
97 N16 **Malton** N England, United Kingdom 54°07′N 00°50′W
171 R13 **Maluku** *off.* Propinsi Maluku, *Dut.* Molukken, *Eng.* Moluccas. ⬖ *province* E Indonesia
171 R13 **Maluku** *Dut.* Molukken, *Eng.* Moluccas; *prev.* Spice Islands. *island group* E Indonesia
**Maluku, Laut** *see* Molucca Sea
**Maluku, Propinsi** *see* Maluku
171 R11 **Maluku Utara** *off.* Propinsi Maluku Utara. ⬖ *province* E Indonesia
**Maluku Utara, Propinsi** *see* Maluku Utara
77 V13 **Malumfashi** Katsina, N Nigeria 11°51′N 07°39′E
171 N13 **Malunda** *prev.* Maloenda. Sulawesi, C Indonesia 02°58′S 118°52′E
94 K13 **Malung** Dalarna, C Sweden 60°40′N 13°45′E
94 K13 **Malungsfors** Dalarna, C Sweden 60°43′N 13°34′E
186 M8 **Maluu** *var.* Malu'u. Malaita, N Solomon Islands 08°22′S 160°39′E
**Malu'u** *see* Maluu
155 D16 **Mālvan** Mahārāshtra, W India 16°05′N 73°28′E
**Malventum** *see* Benevento
27 U12 **Malvern** Arkansas, C USA 34°21′N 92°50′W
29 S15 **Malvern** Iowa, C USA 40°59′N 95°36′W
44 I13 **Malvern** ▲ W Jamaica 17°59′N 77°42′W
**Malvina, Isla Gran** *see* West Falkland
**Malvinas, Islas** *see* Falkland Islands
117 N4 **Malyn** *Rus.* Malin. Zhytomyrs'ka Oblast', N Ukraine 50°46′N 29°14′E
114 G10 **Malyovitsa** *var.* Maljovica, Mal'ovitsa. ▲ W Bulgaria 42°12′N 23°19′E
127 O11 **Malyye Derbety** Respublika Kalmykiya, SW Russia 47°57′N 44°39′E
**Malyy Kavkaz** *see* Lesser Caucasus
123 Q6 **Malyy Lyakhovskiy, Ostrov** *island* NE Russia
**Malyy Pamir** *see* Little Pamir
122 N5 **Malyy Taymyr, Ostrov** *island* Severnaya Zemlya, N Russia
**Malyy Uzen'** *see* Saryozen
122 L14 **Malyy Yenisey** *var.* Ka-Krem. ≈ S Russia
127 S3 **Mamadysh** Respublika Tatarstan, W Russia 55°46′N 51°22′E
117 N14 **Mamaia** Constanţa, E Romania 44°13′N 28°37′E
187 W14 **Mamanuca Group** *island group* Yasawa Group, W Fiji
146 L13 **Mamash** Lebap Welaýaty, E Turkmenistan 38°24′N 64°12′E
79 O17 **Mambasa** Orientale, NE Dem. Rep. Congo 01°20′N 29°05′E
171 X13 **Mamberamo, Sungai** ≈ Papua, E Indonesia
79 G15 **Mambéré** ≈ SW Central African Republic
79 G15 **Mambéré-Kadéï** ⬖ *prefecture* SW Central African Republic
**Mambij** *see* Manbij
79 H18 **Mambili** ≈ W Congo
83 N18 **Mambone** *var.* Nova Mambone. Inhambane, E Mozambique 20°59′S 35°04′E
171 O4 **Mamburao** Mindoro, N Philippines 13°16′N 120°36′E
172 I16 **Mamelles** *island* Inner Islands, NE Seychelles
99 M25 **Mamer** Luxembourg, SW Luxembourg 49°37′N 06°01′E
102 L6 **Mamers** Sarthe, NW France 48°21′N 00°22′E
79 D15 **Mamfe** Sud-Ouest, W Cameroon 05°46′N 09°18′E
145 P6 **Mamlyutka** Severnyy Kazakhstan, N Kazakhstan 54°54′N 68°36′E
36 M15 **Mammoth** Arizona, SW USA 32°43′N 110°38′W
33 S12 **Mammoth Hot Springs** Wyoming, C USA 44°57′N 110°40′W
**Mamoedjoe** *see* Mamuju
119 A14 **Mamonovo** *Ger.* Heiligenbeil. Kaliningradskaya Oblast', W Russia 54°28′N 19°57′E
57 L14 **Mamoré, Rio** ≈ Bolivia/Brazil
76 I14 **Mamou** W Guinea 10°24′N 12°05′W
22 H8 **Mamou** Louisiana, S USA 30°37′N 92°25′W
172 I14 **Mamoudzou** ○ (Mayotte) C Mayotte 12°48′S 45°E
172 I3 **Mampikony** Mahajanga, N Madagascar 16°03′S 47°39′E
77 P16 **Mampong** C Ghana 07°06′N 01°20′W
110 M7 **Mamry, Jezioro** *Ger.* Mauersee. ◎ NE Poland
171 N13 **Mamuju** *prev.* Mamoedjoe. Sulawesi, S Indonesia 02°41′S 118°55′E
83 F19 **Mamuno** Ghanzi, W Botswana 22°15′S 20°02′E
113 K19 **Mamuras** *var.* Mamurasi, Mamurras. Lezhë, C Albania 41°34′N 19°42′E
**Mamurasi/Mamurras** *see* Mamuras
76 L16 **Man** W Ivory Coast 07°24′N 07°33′W
55 X9 **Mana** NW French Guiana 05°40′N 53°49′W
56 A6 **Manabí** ⬖ *province* W Ecuador
42 G4 **Manabique, Punta** *var.* Cabo Tres Puntas. *headland* E Guatemala 15°57′N 88°37′W
54 G11 **Manacacías, Río** ≈ C Colombia
58 F13 **Manacapuru** Amazonas, N Brazil 03°16′S 60°37′W
105 Y9 **Manacor** Mallorca, Spain, W Mediterranean Sea 39°35′N 03°12′E
171 Q11 **Manado** *prev.* Menado. Sulawesi, C Indonesia 01°32′N 124°55′E
188 H5 **Managaha** *island* S Northern Mariana Islands
99 G20 **Manage** Hainaut, S Belgium 50°30′N 04°14′E
42 J10 **Managua** ● (Nicaragua) Managua, W Nicaragua 12°08′N 86°15′W
42 J10 **Managua** ⬖ *department* W Nicaragua
42 J10 **Managua** ✈ Managua, W Nicaragua 12°07′N 86°11′W
42 J10 **Managua, Lago de** *var.* Xolotlán. ◎ W Nicaragua
**Manaḩ** *see* Bilād Manaḩ
18 K16 **Manahawkin** New Jersey, NE USA 39°39′N 74°12′W
184 K11 **Manaia** Taranaki, North Island, New Zealand 39°33′S 174°07′E
172 J6 **Manakara** Fianarantsoa, SE Madagascar 22°09′S 48°E
152 J7 **Manāli** Himāchal Pradesh, NW India 32°12′N 77°06′E
**Ma, Nam** *see* Sông Ma
**Manama** *see* Al Manāmah
186 D6 **Manam Island** *island* N Papua New Guinea
67 Y13 **Mananara Avaratra** ≈ SE Madagascar
182 M9 **Manangatang** Victoria, SE Australia 35°04′S 142°53′E
172 J6 **Mananjary** Fianarantsoa, SE Madagascar 21°13′S 48°20′E
76 L14 **Manankoro** Sikasso, SW Mali 10°33′N 07°25′W
76 J12 **Manantali, Lac de** ▣ W Mali
**Manáos** *see* Manaus
185 B23 **Manapouri** Southland, South Island, New Zealand 45°33′S 167°38′E
185 B23 **Manapouri, Lake** ◎ South Island, New Zealand
58 F13 **Manaquiri** Amazonas, NW Brazil 03°27′S 60°37′W
**Manar** *see* Mannar
158 K5 **Manas** Xinjiang Uygur Zizhiqu, NW China 44°16′N 86°12′E
153 U12 **Manās** *var.* Dangme Chu. ≈ Bhutan/India
153 P10 **Manāsalu** *var.* Manaslu. ▲ C Nepal 28°33′N 84°33′E
147 R8 **Manas, Gora** ▲ Kyrgyzstan/Uzbekistan 42°17′N 71°04′E
158 K3 **Manas Hu** ◎ NW China
**Manaslu** *see* Manāsalu
37 S8 **Manassa** Colorado, C USA 37°10′N 105°56′W
21 W4 **Manassas** Virginia, NE USA 38°45′N 77°28′W
45 T5 **Manatí** C Puerto Rico 18°26′N 66°29′W
186 E8 **Manau** Northern, S Papua New Guinea 08°02′S 148°00′E
54 H4 **Manaure** La Guajira, N Colombia 11°46′N 72°28′W
58 F12 **Manaus** *prev.* Manáos. *state capital* Amazonas, NW Brazil 03°06′S 60°W
136 G17 **Manavgat** Antalya, SW Turkey 36°47′N 31°28′E
184 H1 **Manawatāwhi / Three Kings Islands** *var.* Three Kings Islands. *island group* N New Zealand
184 M13 **Manawatu** ≈ North Island, New Zealand
184 L11 **Manawatu-Wanganui** *off.* Manawatu-Wanganui Region. ⬖ *region* North Island, New Zealand
**Manawatu-Wanganui Region** *see* Manawatu-Wanganui
171 R7 **Manay** Mindanao, S Philippines 07°12′N 126°29′E
138 K2 **Manbij** *var.* Mambij, *Fr.* Membidj. Ḩalab, N Syria 36°32′N 37°55′E
105 N13 **Mancha Real** Andalucía, S Spain 37°47′N 03°37′W
102 I4 **Manche** ⬖ *department* N France
97 L17 **Manchester** *Lat.* Mancunium. NW England, United Kingdom 53°30′N 02°15′W
23 S5 **Manchester** Georgia, SE USA 32°51′N 84°37′W
29 Y13 **Manchester** Iowa, C USA 42°28′N 91°27′W
21 N7 **Manchester** Kentucky, S USA 37°09′N 83°46′W
19 O10 **Manchester** New Hampshire, NE USA 42°59′N 71°26′W
20 K10 **Manchester** Tennessee, S USA 35°28′N 86°05′W
18 M9 **Manchester** Vermont, NE USA 43°09′N 73°03′W
97 L18 **Manchester** ✈ NW England, United Kingdom 53°21′N 02°16′W
149 P15 **Manchhar Lake** ◎ SE Pakistan
**Man-chou-li** *see* Manzhouli
129 X7 **Manchurian Plain** *plain* NE China
**Máncio Lima** *see* Japiim
**Mancunium** *see* Manchester
148 J15 **Mand** Baluchistan, SW Pakistan 26°06′N 61°58′E
**Mand** *see* Mand, Rūd-e
81 H25 **Manda** Njombe, SW Tanzania 10°30′S 34°37′E
172 H6 **Mandabe** Toliara, W Madagascar 21°02′S 44°56′E
162 M10 **Mandah** *var.* Töhöm. Dornogovĭ, SE Mongolia 44°25′N 108°18′E
95 E18 **Mandal** Vest-Agder, S Norway 58°02′N 07°30′E
**Mandal** *see* Arbulag, Hövsgöl, Mongolia
**Mandal** *see* Batsümber, Töv, Mongolia
166 L5 **Mandalay** Mandalay, C Myanmar (Burma) 21°57′N 96°04′E
166 M6 **Mandalay** ⬖ *region* C Myanmar (Burma)
162 L9 **Mandalgovĭ** Dundgovĭ, C Mongolia 45°47′N 106°18′E
139 V7 **Mandalī** Diyālá, E Iraq 33°43′N 45°33′E
162 K10 **Mandal-Ovoo** *var.* Sharhulsan. Ömnögovĭ, S Mongolia 44°43′N 104°06′E
95 E18 **Mandalselva** ≈ S Norway
163 P11 **Mandalt** *var.* Sonid Zuoqi. Nei Mongol Zizhiqu, N China 43°49′N 113°36′E
28 M5 **Mandan** North Dakota, N USA 46°49′N 100°53′W
**Mandargiri Hill** *see* Mandār Hill
153 R14 **Mandār Hill** *prev.* Mandargiri Hill. Bihār, NE India 24°51′N 87°03′E
170 M13 **Mandar, Teluk** *bay* Sulawesi, C Indonesia
107 C19 **Mandas** Sardegna, Italy, C Mediterranean Sea 39°40′N 09°07′E
**Mandasor** *see* Mandsaur
81 L16 **Mandera** Mandera, NE Kenya 03°56′N 41°53′E
81 K17 **Mandera** ⬖ *county* NE Kenya
33 V13 **Manderson** Wyoming, C USA 44°13′N 107°55′W
44 J12 **Mandeville** C Jamaica 18°02′N 77°31′W
22 K9 **Mandeville** Louisiana, S USA 30°21′N 90°04′W
152 I7 **Mandi** Himāchal Pradesh, NW India 31°40′N 76°59′E
76 K14 **Mandiana** E Guinea 10°37′N 08°39′W
**Mandi Būrewāla** *see* Burewala
**Mandidzudzure** *see* Chimanimani
83 M15 **Mandié** Manica, NW Mozambique 16°27′S 33°28′E
83 N14 **Mandimba** Niassa, N Mozambique 14°21′S 35°40′E
57 Q19 **Mandioré, Laguna** ◎ E Bolivia
154 J10 **Mandla** Madhya Pradesh, C India 22°36′N 80°23′E
83 M20 **Mandlakazi** *var.* Manjacaze. Gaza, S Mozambique 24°47′S 33°50′E
95 E24 **Mandø** *var.* Manø. *island* W Denmark
**Mandoúdhion/Mandoudi** *see* Mantoúdi
115 G19 **Mándra** Attikí, C Greece 38°04′N 23°30′E
172 I7 **Mandrare** ≈ S Madagascar
114 M10 **Mandra, Yazovir** *salt lake* SE Bulgaria
107 L23 **Mandrazzi, Portella** *pass* Sicilia, Italy, C Mediterranean Sea
172 J3 **Mandritsara** Mahajanga, N Madagascar 15°49′S 48°50′E
143 O13 **Mand, Rūd-e** *var.* Mand. ≈ S Iran
154 F9 **Mandsaur** *prev.* Mandasor. Madhya Pradesh, C India 24°03′N 75°10′E
154 F11 **Māndu** Madhya Pradesh, C India 22°22′N 75°24′E
169 W8 **Mandul, Pulau** *island* N Indonesia
83 G15 **Mandundu** Western, W Zambia 16°34′S 22°18′E
180 I13 **Mandurah** Western Australia 32°31′S 115°41′E
107 P18 **Manduria** Puglia, SE Italy 40°24′N 17°38′E
155 G20 **Mandya** Karnātaka, C India 12°34′N 76°55′E
77 P12 **Mané** C Burkina Faso 12°59′N 01°21′W
106 E8 **Manerbio** Lombardia, NW Italy 45°22′N 10°09′E
**Manevichi** *see* Manevychi
116 K3 **Manevychi** *Pol.* Maniewicze, *Rus.* Manevichi. Volyns'ka Oblast', NW Ukraine 51°18′N 25°29′E
107 N16 **Manfredonia** Puglia, SE Italy 41°38′N 15°54′E
107 N16 **Manfredonia, Golfo di** *gulf* Adriatic Sea, N Mediterranean Sea
77 P13 **Manga** C Burkina Faso 11°41′N 01°04′W
59 L16 **Mangabeiras, Chapada das** ▲▲ E Brazil
79 J20 **Mangai** Bandundu, W Dem. Rep. Congo 03°58′S 19°32′E
190 L17 **Mangaia** *island group* S Cook Islands
184 M9 **Mangakino** Waikato, North Island, New Zealand 38°23′S 175°47′E
116 M15 **Mangalia** *anc.* Callatis. Constanţa, SE Romania 43°48′N 28°35′E
78 J11 **Mangalmé** Guéra, SE Chad 12°26′N 19°37′E
**Mangalore** *see* Mangalūru
155 E19 **Mangalūru** *prev.* Mangalore. Karnātaka, W India 12°54′N 74°51′E
**Mangareva** *see* Magareva
83 I23 **Mangaung** Free State, C South Africa 29°10′S 26°19′E
**Mangaung** *see* Bloemfontein
154 K9 **Mangawān** Madhya Pradesh, C India 24°39′N 81°33′E




◆ Country
● Country Capital
◇ Dependent Territory
○ Dependent Territory Capital
⬖ Administrative Regions
✈ International Airport
▲ Mountain
▲▲ Mountain Range
⛰ Volcano
≈ River
◎ Lake
▣ Reservoir

MANGAWEKA – MARION


184 M11 **Mangaweka** Manawatu-Wanganui, North Island, New Zealand 39°49'S 175°47'E
184 N11 **Mangaweka** ▲ North Island, New Zealand 39°51'S 176°06'E
79 P17 **Mangbwalu** Orientale, NE Dem. Rep. Congo 02°06'N 30°04'E
139 R1 **Mangêsh** *Ar.* Māngīsh, *var.* Mangish. Dahūk, N Iraq 37°03'N 43°04'E
101 L24 **Mangfall** ⚟ SE Germany
169 P13 **Manggar** Pulau Belitung, W Indonesia 02°52'S 108°13'E
**Mangghystaū Ūstirti'** *see* Mangystau, Plato
166 M2 **Mangin Range** ▲ N Myanmar (Burma)
**Mangish** *see* Mangêsh
**Māngīsh** *see* Mangêsh
**Mangistau** *see* Mangystau
146 H8 **Mang'it** *Rus.* Mangit. Qoraqalpog'iston Respublikasi, W Uzbekistan 42°06'N 60°02'E
**Mangit** *see* Mang'it
54 A13 **Manglares, Cabo** *headland* SW Colombia 01°36'N 79°02'W
149 V6 **Mangla Reservoir** ⊠ NE Pakistan
159 N9 **Mangnai** *var.* Lao Mangnai. Qinghai, C China 37°52'N 91°45'E
**Mango** *see* Mago, Fiji
**Mango** *see* Sansanné-Mango, Togo
**Mangoche** *see* Mangochi
83 N14 **Mangochi** *var.* Mangoche; *prev.* Fort Johnston. Southern, SE Malawi 14°30'S 35°15'E
77 N14 **Mangodara** SW Burkina Faso 09°49'N 04°22'W
172 H6 **Mangoky** ⚟ W Madagascar
171 Q12 **Mangole, Pulau** *island* Kepulauan Sula, E Indonesia
184 J2 **Mangonui** Northland, North Island, New Zealand 35°00'S 173°30'E
**Mangqystaū Oblysy** *see* Mangystau
**Mangqystaū Shyghanaghy** *see* Mangystau Zaliv
**Mangshi** *see* Luxi
104 H7 **Mangualde** Viseu, N Portugal 40°36'N 07°46'W
61 H18 **Mangueira, Lagoa** ◎ S Brazil
77 X6 **Manguéni, Plateau du** ▲ NE Niger
163 T4 **Mangui** Nei Mongol Zizhiqu, N China 52°02'N 122°13'E
26 K11 **Mangum** Oklahoma, C USA 34°52'N 99°30'W
79 O18 **Mangurdjipa** Nord-Kivu, E Dem. Rep. Congo 0°28'N 28°33'E
83 L16 **Mangwendi** Mashonaland East, E Zimbabwe 18°22'S 31°24'E
**Mangyshlak, Plato** *see* Mangystau, Plato
**Mangyshlakskiy Zaliv** *see* Mangystau Zaliv
**Mangyshlaskaya** *see* Mangystau
144 F15 **Mangystau** *Kaz.* Mangqystaū Oblysy *prev.* Mangistau; *prev.* Mangyshlakskaya. ◆ *province* SW Kazakhstan
144 F15 **Mangystau, Plato** *plateau* SW Kazakhstan
144 E14 **Mangystau Zaliv** *Kaz.* Mangqystaū Shyghanaghy; *prev.* Mangyshlakskiy Zaliv. *gulf* SW Kazakhstan
162 E7 **Manhan** *var.* Tögrög. Hovd, W Mongolia 47°24'N 92°06'E
**Manhan** *see* Alag-Erdene
27 O4 **Manhattan** Kansas, C USA 39°11'N 96°35'W
99 L21 **Manhay** Luxembourg, SE Belgium 50°13'N 05°43'E
83 L21 **Manhiça** *prev.* Vila de Manhiça. Maputo, S Mozambique 25°25'S 32°49'E
83 L21 **Manhoca** Maputo, S Mozambique 26°49'S 32°36'E
59 N20 **Manhuaçu** Minas Gerais, SE Brazil 20°16'S 42°01'W
117 W9 **Manhush** *prev.* Pershotravneve. Donets'ka Oblast', E Ukraine 47°03'N 37°20'E
54 H10 **Maní** Casanare, C Colombia 04°50'N 72°15'W
143 R11 **Mānī** Kermān, C Iran
83 M17 **Manica** *var.* Vila de Manica. Manica, W Mozambique 18°56'S 32°52'E
83 M17 **Manica** *off.* Província de Manica. ◆ *province* W Mozambique
83 L17 **Manicaland** ◆ *province* E Zimbabwe
**Manica, Província de** *see* Manica
15 U5 **Manic Deux, Réservoir** ⊠ Québec, SE Canada
**Manich** *see* Manych
59 F14 **Manicoré** Amazonas, N Brazil 05°48'S 61°16'W
13 N11 **Manicouagan** Québec, SE Canada 50°40'N 68°46'W
13 N11 **Manicouagan** ⚟ Québec, SE Canada
15 U6 **Manicouagan, Péninsule de** *peninsula* Québec, SE Canada
13 N11 **Manicouagan, Réservoir** ◎ Québec, E Canada
15 T4 **Manic Trois, Réservoir** ⊠ Québec, SE Canada
79 M20 **Maniema** *off.* Région du Maniema. ◆ *region* E Dem. Rep. Congo
**Maniema, Région du** *see* Maniema
**Maniewicze** *see* Manevychi
160 F8 **Maniganggo** Sichuan, C China 32°01'N 99°04'E
11 Y15 **Manigotagan** Manitoba, S Canada 51°06'N 96°18'W
153 R13 **Manihāri** Bihār, N India 25°21'N 87°37'E
191 U9 **Manihi** *island* Îles Tuamotu, C French Polynesia
190 L13 **Manihiki** *atoll* N Cook Islands
175 U8 **Manihiki Plateau** *undersea feature* C Pacific Ocean
196 M14 **Maniitsoq** *var.* Manitsoq, *Dan.* Sukkertoppen. ◆ Qeqqata, S Greenland
153 T15 **Manikganj** Dhaka, C Bangladesh 23°52'N 90°00'E
152 M14 **Mānikpur** Uttar Pradesh, N India 25°04'N 81°06'E
171 N4 **Manila** *off.* City of Manila, *Fil.* Maynila. Lungsod ng Maynila. ● (Philippines) Luzon, N Philippines 14°34'N 120°59'E
27 Y9 **Manila** Arkansas, C USA 35°52'N 90°10'W
**Manila, City of** *see* Manila
189 N16 **Manila Reef** *reef* W Micronesia
183 T6 **Manilla** New South Wales, SE Australia 30°44'S 150°43'E
192 P6 **Maniloa** *island* Tongatapu Group, S Tonga
123 U8 **Manily** Krasnoyarskiy Kray, E Russia 62°33'N 165°03'E
171 V12 **Manim, Pulau** *island* E Indonesia
168 I11 **Maninjau, Danau** ◎ Sumatera, W Indonesia
153 W13 **Manipur** ◆ *state* NE India
153 X14 **Manipur Hills** *hill range* E India
136 C14 **Manisa** *var.* Manissa, *prev.* Saruhan; *anc.* Magnesia. Manisa, W Turkey 38°36'N 27°29'E
136 C13 **Manisa** *var.* Manissa. ◆ *province* W Turkey
**Manissa** *see* Manisa
31 O7 **Manistee** Michigan, N USA 44°14'N 86°19'W
31 P7 **Manistee River** ⚟ Michigan, N USA
31 O4 **Manistique** Michigan, N USA 45°57'N 86°15'W
31 P4 **Manistique Lake** ◎ Michigan, N USA
11 W13 **Manitoba** ◆ *province* S Canada
11 X16 **Manitoba, Lake** ◎ Manitoba, S Canada
11 X17 **Manitou** Manitoba, S Canada 49°12'N 98°28'W
31 N2 **Manitou Island** *island* Michigan, N USA
14 H11 **Manitou Lake** ◎ Ontario, SE Canada
12 G15 **Manitoulin Island** *island* Ontario, S Canada
37 T5 **Manitou Springs** Colorado, C USA 38°51'N 104°56'W
14 G12 **Manitouwabing Lake** ◎ Ontario, S Canada
12 E12 **Manitouwadge** Ontario, S Canada 49°14'N 85°51'W
12 G15 **Manitowaning** Manitoulin Island, Ontario, S Canada 45°44'N 81°50'W
14 B7 **Manitowik Lake** ◎ Ontario, S Canada
31 N7 **Manitowoc** Wisconsin, N USA 44°04'N 87°40'W
**Manitsoq** *see* Maniitsoq
139 O7 **Mānī', Wādī al** *dry watercourse* W Iraq
12 J14 **Maniwaki** Québec, SE Canada 46°22'N 75°58'W
171 W13 **Maniwori** Papua, E Indonesia 02°49'S 136°00'E
54 E10 **Manizales** Caldas, W Colombia 05°03'N 73°52'W
112 F11 **Manjača** ▲ NW Bosnia and Herzegovina
**Manjacaze** *see* Mandlakazi
180 J14 **Manjimup** Western Australia 34°18'S 116°14'E
109 V4 **Mank** Niederösterreich, C Austria 48°06'N 15°13'E
79 I17 **Mankanza** Equateur, NW Dem. Rep. Congo 01°40'N 19°08'E
153 N12 **Mankāpur** Uttar Pradesh, N India 27°03'N 82°12'E
26 M3 **Mankato** Kansas, C USA 39°48'N 98°13'W
29 U10 **Mankato** Minnesota, N USA 44°10'N 94°00'W
117 O7 **Man'kivka** Cherkas'ka Oblast', C Ukraine 48°58'N 30°10'E
76 M15 **Mankono** C Ivory Coast 08°01'N 06°09'W
11 T17 **Mankota** Saskatchewan, S Canada 49°25'N 107°05'W
155 K23 **Mankulam** Northern Province, N Sri Lanka 09°07'N 80°27'E
162 L10 **Manlay** *var.* Üydzen. Ömnögovĭ, S Mongolia 44°08'N 106°48'E
39 Q9 **Manley Hot Springs** Alaska, USA 65°00'N 150°37'W
18 H10 **Manlius** New York, NE USA 43°00'N 75°58'W
105 W5 **Manlleu** Cataluña, NE Spain 41°59'N 02°17'E
29 V11 **Manly** Iowa, C USA 43°17'N 93°12'W
154 E13 **Manmād** Mahārāshtra, W India 20°15'N 74°29'E
182 J7 **Mannahill** South Australia 32°29'S 139°58'E
155 J23 **Mannar** *var.* Manar. Northern Province, NW Sri Lanka 09°01'N 79°53'E
155 I24 **Mannar, Gulf of** *gulf* India/Sri Lanka
155 J23 **Mannar Island** *island* N Sri Lanka
**Mannersdorf** *see* Mannersdorf am Leithagebirge
109 Y5 **Mannersdorf am Leithagebirge** *var.* Mannersdorf. Niederösterreich, E Austria 47°59'N 16°36'E
109 Y6 **Mannersdorf an der Rabnitz** Burgenland, E Austria 47°25'N 16°32'E
101 G20 **Mannheim** Baden-Württemberg, SW Germany 49°29'N 08°29'E
11 O12 **Manning** Alberta, W Canada 56°53'N 117°39'W
29 T14 **Manning** Iowa, C USA 41°54'N 95°03'W
28 K5 **Manning** North Dakota, N USA 47°15'N 102°48'W
21 S13 **Manning** South Carolina, SE USA 33°42'N 80°12'W
191 Y2 **Manning, Cape** *headland* Kiritimati, NE Kiribati 02°02'N 157°26'W
21 S3 **Mannington** West Virginia, NE USA 39°31'N 80°20'W
182 A1 **Mann Ranges** ▲ South Australia
107 C19 **Mannu** ⚟ Sardegna, Italy, C Mediterranean Sea
11 R14 **Mannville** Alberta, SW Canada 53°19'N 111°08'W
76 J15 **Mano** ⚟ Liberia/Sierra Leone
**Manø** *see* Mandø
61 F15 **Manoel Viana** Rio Grande do Sul, S Brazil 29°33'S 55°28'W
39 O13 **Manokotak** Alaska, USA 59°00'N 158°58'W
171 V12 **Manokwari** Papua Barat, E Indonesia 0°53'S 134°05'E
79 N22 **Manono** Shaba, SE Dem. Rep. Congo 07°18'S 27°25'E
25 T10 **Manor** Texas, SW USA 30°20'N 97°33'W
97 D16 **Manorhamilton** *Ir.* Cluainín. Leitrim, NW Ireland 54°18'N 08°10'W
103 S15 **Manosque** Alpes-de-Haute-Provence, SE France 43°50'N 05°47'E
12 L11 **Manouane, Lac** ◎ Québec, SE Canada
163 W12 **Manp'o** *var.* Manp'ojin. NW North Korea 41°10'N 126°24'E
**Manp'ojin** *see* Manp'o
191 T4 **Manra** *prev.* Sydney Island. *atoll* Phoenix Islands, C Kiribati
105 V5 **Manresa** Cataluña, NE Spain 41°43'N 01°50'E
152 H9 **Mānsa** Punjab, NW India 30°00'N 75°25'E
82 J12 **Mansa** *prev.* Fort Rosebery. Luapula, N Zambia 11°14'S 28°55'E
76 G12 **Mansa Konko** C The Gambia 13°26'N 15°29'W
15 Q11 **Mansau** Québec, SE Canada 46°23'N 71°59'W
149 U5 **Mansehra** Khyber Pakhtunkhwa, NW Pakistan 34°23'N 73°18'E
9 Q9 **Mansel Island** *island* Nunavut, NE Canada
183 O12 **Mansfield** Victoria, SE Australia 37°04'S 146°06'E
97 M18 **Mansfield** C England, United Kingdom 53°09'N 01°11'W
27 S11 **Mansfield** Arkansas, C USA 35°03'N 94°15'W
22 G6 **Mansfield** Louisiana, S USA 32°02'N 93°42'W
19 O12 **Mansfield** Massachusetts, NE USA 42°00'N 71°11'W
31 T12 **Mansfield** Ohio, N USA 40°45'N 82°31'W
18 G12 **Mansfield** Pennsylvania, NE USA 41°46'N 77°02'W
18 M7 **Mansfield, Mount** ▲ Vermont, NE USA 44°31'N 72°49'W
59 M16 **Mansidão** Bahia, E Brazil 10°46'S 44°04'W
102 L11 **Mansle** Charente, W France 45°52'N 00°11'E
76 G12 **Mansôa** C Guinea-Bissau 12°08'N 15°18'W
47 V8 **Manso, Rio** ⚟ C Brazil
**Manșūra** *see* Al Manșūrah
**Mansurabad** *see* Mehrān, Rūd-e
56 A6 **Manta** Manabí, W Ecuador 0°59'S 80°44'W
56 A6 **Manta, Bahía de** *bay* W Ecuador
57 F14 **Mantaro, Río** ⚟ C Peru
35 O8 **Manteca** California, W USA 37°48'N 121°13'W
54 J7 **Mantecal** Apure, C Venezuela 07°34'N 69°07'W
31 N11 **Manteno** Illinois, N USA 41°15'N 87°49'W
21 Y9 **Manteo** Roanoke Island, North Carolina, SE USA 35°54'N 75°42'W
**Mantes-Gassicourt** *see* Mantes-la-Jolie
103 N5 **Mantes-la-Jolie** *prev.* Mantes-Gassicourt, Mantes-sur-Seine; *anc.* Medunta. Yvelines, N France 48°59'N 01°43'E
**Mantes-sur-Seine** *see* Mantes-la-Jolie
36 L5 **Manti** Utah, W USA 39°16'N 111°38'W
**Mantinea** *see* Mantíneia
115 F20 **Mantíneia** *anc.* Mantinea. *site of ancient city* Pelopónnisos, S Greece
59 M21 **Mantiqueira, Serra da** ▲ S Brazil
29 W10 **Mantorville** Minnesota, N USA 44°04'N 92°45'W
115 G17 **Mantoúdi** *var.* Mandoudi; *prev.* Mandoúdhion. Évvoia, C Greece 38°47'N 23°29'E
**Mantoue** *see* Mantova
106 F8 **Mantova** *Eng.* Mantua, *Fr.* Mantoue. Lombardia, NW Italy 45°10'N 10°47'E
93 M19 **Mäntsälä** Uusimaa, S Finland 60°38'N 25°21'E
93 L17 **Mänttä** Pirkanmaa, W Finland 62°00'N 24°36'E
**Mantua** *see* Mantova
125 O14 **Manturovo** Kostromskaya Oblast', NW Russia 58°19'N 44°42'E
93 M18 **Mäntyharju** Etelä-Savo, SE Finland 61°25'N 26°53'E
92 M13 **Mäntyjärvi** Lappi, N Finland 66°00'N 27°35'E
190 L16 **Manuae** *island* S Cook Islands
191 Q10 **Manuae** *atoll* Îles Sous le Vent, W French Polynesia
192 L16 **Manu'a Islands** *island group* E American Samoa
40 L5 **Manuel Benavides** Chihuahua, N Mexico 29°07'N 103°52'W
61 D21 **Manuel J. Cobo** Buenos Aires, E Argentina 35°49'S 57°54'W
58 M12 **Manuel Luís, Recife** *reef* E Brazil
59 I14 **Manuel Zinho** Pará, N Brazil 07°21'S 54°47'W
191 V11 **Manuhagi** *prev.* Manuhangi. *atoll* Îles Tuamotu, C French Polynesia
**Manuhangi** *see* Manuhagi
185 E22 **Manuherikia** ⚟ South Island, New Zealand
171 P13 **Manui, Pulau** *island* N Indonesia
**Manukau** *see* Manurewa
184 L6 **Manukau Harbour** *harbor* North Island, New Zealand
191 Z2 **Manulu Lagoon** ◎ Kiritimati, E Kiribati
182 J7 **Manunda Creek** *seasonal river* South Australia
57 K15 **Manupari, Río** ⚟ N Bolivia
184 L6 **Manurewa** *var.* Manukau. Auckland, North Island, New Zealand 37°01'S 174°55'E
57 K15 **Manurimi, Río** ⚟ NW Bolivia
186 D5 **Manus** ◆ *province* N Papua New Guinea
186 D5 **Manus Island** *var.* Great Admiralty Island. *island* N Papua New Guinea
171 T16 **Manuwui** Pulau Babar, E Indonesia 07°47'S 129°39'E
29 Q3 **Manvel** North Dakota, N USA 48°07'N 97°15'W
33 Z14 **Manville** Wyoming, C USA 42°45'N 104°38'W
22 G6 **Many** Louisiana, S USA 31°34'N 93°28'W
81 H21 **Manyara, Lake** ◎ NE Tanzania
126 L12 **Manych** *var.* Manich. ⚟ SW Russia
83 H14 **Manyinga** North Western, NW Zambia 13°28'S 24°18'E
105 O11 **Manzanares** Castilla-La Mancha, C Spain 39°N 03°23'W
44 H7 **Manzanillo** Granma, E Cuba 20°21'N 77°07'W
40 K14 **Manzanillo** Colima, SW Mexico 19°00'N 104°19'W
40 K14 **Manzanillo, Bahía** *bay* SW Mexico
37 S11 **Manzano Mountains** ▲ New Mexico, SW USA
37 R12 **Manzano Peak** ▲ New Mexico, SW USA 34°35'N 106°27'W
163 R6 **Manzhouli** *var.* Man-chou-li. Nei Mongol Zizhiqu, N China 49°36'N 117°28'E
**Manzil Bū Ruqaybah** *see* Menzel Bourguiba
139 X9 **Manzilīyah** Maysān, E Iraq 32°26'N 47°01'E
83 L21 **Manzini** *prev.* Bremersdorp. C Eswatini 26°30'S 31°22'E
83 L21 **Manzini** ✈ (Mbabane) C Eswatini 26°36'S 31°25'E
78 G10 **Mao** Kanem, W Chad 14°06'N 15°17'E
45 N8 **Mao** NW Dominican Republic 19°37'N 71°04'W
**Maoemere** *see* Maumere
159 W9 **Maojing** Gansu, N China 36°26'N 106°36'E
171 Y14 **Maoke, Pegunungan** *Dut.* Sneeuw-gebergte, *Eng.* Snow Mountains. ▲ Papua, E Indonesia
**Maol Réidh, Caoc** *see* Mweelrea
105 Z9 **Maó-Mahón** , *Eng.* Port Mahon; *anc.* Portus Magonis. Menorca, Spain, W Mediterranean Sea 39°54'N 04°15'E
160 M15 **Maoming** Guangdong, S China 21°46'N 110°51'E
160 H8 **Maoxian** *var.* Mao Xian; *prev.* Fengyizhen. Sichuan, C China 31°42'N 103°48'E
**Mao Xian** *see* Maoxian
83 L19 **Mapai** Gaza, SW Mozambique 22°52'S 32°00'E
158 H15 **Mapam Yumco** ◎ W China
83 I15 **Mapanza** Southern, S Zambia 16°16'S 26°54'E
54 J4 **Mapararí** Falcón, N Venezuela 10°52'N 69°27'W
41 U17 **Mapastepec** Chiapas, SE Mexico 15°28'N 93°00'W
169 V9 **Mapat, Pulau** *island* N Indonesia
171 Y15 **Mapi** Papua, E Indonesia 07°02'S 139°24'E
171 V11 **Mapia, Kepulauan** *island group* E Indonesia
40 L8 **Mapimí** Durango, C Mexico 25°50'N 103°50'W
83 N19 **Mapinhane** Inhambane, SE Mozambique 22°14'S 35°07'E
55 N7 **Mapire** Monagas, NE Venezuela 07°48'N 64°40'W
11 S17 **Maple Creek** Saskatchewan, S Canada 49°55'N 109°28'W
31 Q9 **Maple River** ⚟ Michigan, N USA
29 P7 **Maple River** ⚟ North Dakota/South Dakota, N USA
29 S13 **Mapleton** Iowa, C USA 42°10'N 95°47'W
29 U10 **Mapleton** Minnesota, N USA 43°55'N 93°57'W
29 R5 **Mapleton** North Dakota, N USA 46°51'N 97°04'W
32 F13 **Mapleton** Oregon, NW USA 44°01'N 123°56'W
36 L3 **Mapleton** Utah, W USA 40°07'N 111°37'W
192 K5 **Mapmaker Seamounts** *undersea feature* N Pacific Ocean 25°00'N 165°00'E
186 B6 **Maprik** East Sepik, NW Papua New Guinea 03°38'S 143°02'E
83 L21 **Maputo** *prev.* Lourenço Marques. ● (Mozambique) Maputo, S Mozambique 25°58'S 32°35'E
83 L21 **Maputo** ◆ *province* S Mozambique
67 V14 **Maputo** ⚟ S Mozambique
83 L21 **Maputo** ✈ Maputo, S Mozambique 25°47'S 32°36'E
**Maqat** *see* Makat
113 M19 **Maqellarë** Dibër, C Albania 41°36'N 20°29'E
159 S12 **Maqên** *var.* Dawo; *prev.* Dawu. Qinghai, C China 34°32'N 100°17'E
159 R12 **Maqên Kangri** ▲ C China 34°44'N 99°25'E
141 X7 **Maqiz al Kurbā** N Oman 24°13'N 56°48'E
159 U12 **Maqu** *var.* Nyinma. Gansu, C China 34°02'N 102°00'E
104 M9 **Maqueda** Castilla-La Mancha, C Spain 40°04'N 04°22'W
82 B9 **Maquela do Zombo** Uíge, NW Angola 06°06'S 15°12'E
63 I16 **Maquinchao** Río Negro, C Argentina 41°19'S 68°47'W
29 Z13 **Maquoketa** Iowa, C USA 42°03'N 90°42'W
29 Y13 **Maquoketa River** ⚟ Iowa, C USA
14 F13 **Mar** Ontario, S Canada 44°48'N 81°12'W
95 F14 **Mår** ◎ S Norway
81 G19 **Mara** ◆ *region* N Tanzania
58 D12 **Maraā** Amazonas, NW Brazil 01°48'S 65°21'W
191 P8 **Maraa** Tahiti, W French Polynesia 17°44'S 149°34'W
191 O8 **Maraa, Pointe** *headland* Tahiti, W French Polynesia 17°44'S 149°34'W
59 K14 **Marabá** Pará, NE Brazil 05°23'S 49°10'W
54 H5 **Maracaibo** Zulia, NW Venezuela 10°40'N 71°39'W
**Maracaibo, Gulf of** *see* Venezuela, Golfo de
54 H5 **Maracaibo, Lago de** *var.* Lake Maracaibo. *inlet* NW Venezuela
**Maracaibo, Lake** *see* Maracaibo, Lago de
58 K10 **Maracá, Ilha de** *island* NE Brazil
59 H20 **Maracaju, Serra de** ▲ S Brazil
58 I11 **Maracanaquará, Planalto** ▲ NE Brazil
54 L5 **Maracay** Aragua, N Venezuela 10°15'N 67°36'W
**Marada** *see* Marādah
75 R9 **Marādah** *var.* Marada. N Libya 29°16'N 19°29'E
77 U12 **Maradi** Maradi, S Niger 13°30'N 07°05'E
77 U11 **Maradi** ◆ *region* S Niger
81 E21 **Maragarazi** *var.* Muragarazi. ⚟ Burundi/Tanzania
**Maragha** *see* Marāgheh
142 J3 **Marāgheh** *var.* Maragha. Āžarbāyjān-e Khāvarī, NW Iran 37°21'N 46°14'E
141 P7 **Marāh** *var.* Marrāt. Ar Riyāḑ, C Saudi Arabia 25°04'N 45°30'E
55 N11 **Marahuaca, Cerro** ▲ S Venezuela 03°37'N 65°25'W
27 R5 **Marais des Cygnes River** ⚟ Kansas/Missouri, C USA
58 L11 **Marajó, Baía de** *bay* N Brazil
59 K12 **Marajó, Ilha de** *island* N Brazil
191 O2 **Marakei** *atoll* Tungaru, W Kiribati
**Marakesh** *see* Marrakech
81 I18 **Maralal** Samburu, C Kenya 01°05'N 36°42'E
83 G21 **Maralaleng** Kgalagadi, S Botswana 25°42'S 22°39'E
145 U8 **Maraldy, Ozero** ◎ NE Kazakhstan
182 C5 **Maralinga** South Australia 30°16'S 131°35'E
**Máramarossziget** *see* Sighetu Marmației
187 N9 **Maramasike** *var.* Small Malaita. *island* N Solomon Islands
**Maramba** *see* Livingstone
194 H3 **Marambio** *research station* (Argentina) Antarctica 64°22'S 57°18'W
116 H9 **Maramureș** ◆ *county* NW Romania
36 L15 **Marana** Arizona, SW USA 32°24'N 111°12'W
105 P7 **Maranchón** Castilla-La Mancha, C Spain 41°02'N 02°11'W
142 J2 **Marand** *var.* Merend. Āžarbāyjān-e Sharqī, NW Iran 38°25'N 45°40'E
**Marandellas** *see* Marondera
58 L13 **Maranhão** *off.* Estado do Maranhão. ◆ *state* E Brazil
104 H10 **Maranhão, Barragem do** ⊠ C Portugal
**Maranhão, Estado do** *see* Maranhão
149 O11 **Maran, Koh-I** ▲ SW Pakistan 29°24'N 66°50'E
106 J7 **Marano, Laguna di** *lagoon* NE Italy
56 E9 **Marañón, Río** ⚟ N Peru
102 J10 **Marans** Charente-Maritime, W France 46°19'N 00°58'W
83 M20 **Marão** Inhambane, S Mozambique 24°15'S 34°09'E
185 B23 **Mararoa** ⚟ South Island, New Zealand
**Maraș/Marash** *see* Kahramanmaraș
107 M19 **Maratea** Basilicata, S Italy 39°57'N 15°44'E
104 G11 **Marateca** Setúbal, S Portugal 38°34'N 08°40'W
115 B20 **Marathiá, Akrotírio** *headland* Zákynthos, Iónia Nisiá, Greece, C Mediterranean Sea 37°39'N 20°49'E
12 E12 **Marathon** Ontario, S Canada 48°44'N 86°23'W
23 Y17 **Marathon** Florida Keys, Florida, SE USA 24°42'N 81°05'W
24 L10 **Marathon** Texas, SW USA 30°10'N 103°14'W
**Marathón** *see* Marathónas
115 H19 **Marathónas** *prev.* Marathón. Attikí, C Greece 38°09'N 23°57'E
169 W9 **Maratua, Pulau** *island* N Indonesia
59 O18 **Maraú** Bahia, SE Brazil 14°07'S 39°02'W
143 R3 **Marāveh Tappeh** Golestān, N Iran 37°53'N 55°57'E
24 L11 **Maravillas Creek** ⚟ Texas, SW USA
186 D8 **Marawaka** Eastern Highlands, C Papua New Guinea 06°56'S 145°54'E
171 Q7 **Marawi** Mindanao, S Philippines 07°59'N 124°16'E
**Mārāzā** *see* Qobustan
**Marbat** *see* Mirbāṭ
104 L16 **Marbella** Andalucía, S Spain 36°31'N 04°50'W
180 J7 **Marble Bar** Western Australia 21°13'S 119°48'E
36 L9 **Marble Canyon** *canyon* Arizona, SW USA
25 S10 **Marble Falls** Texas, SW USA 30°34'N 98°16'W
27 Y7 **Marble Hill** Missouri, C USA 37°18'N 89°58'W
33 T15 **Marbleton** Wyoming, C USA 42°31'N 110°06'W
**Marburg** *see* Marburg an der Lahn, Germany
**Marburg** *see* Maribor, Slovenia
101 H16 **Marburg an der Lahn** *hist.* Marburg. Hessen, W Germany 50°49'N 08°46'E
111 H23 **Marcal** ⚟ W Hungary
42 G7 **Marcala** La Paz, SW Honduras 14°11'N 88°00'W
111 H24 **Marcali** Somogy, SW Hungary 46°33'N 17°29'E
83 A16 **Marca, Ponta da** *headland* SW Angola 16°31'S 11°42'E
59 I16 **Marcelândia** Mato Grosso, W Brazil 11°18'S 54°49'W
27 T3 **Marceline** Missouri, C USA 39°42'N 92°57'W
60 I13 **Marcelino Ramos** Rio Grande do Sul, S Brazil 27°31'S 51°57'W
55 Y12 **Marcel, Mont** ▲ S French Guiana 02°32'N 53°00'W
97 O19 **March** E England, United Kingdom 52°37'N 00°13'E
109 Z3 **March** *var.* Morava. ⚟ C Europe *see also* Morava
**March** *see* Morava
106 I12 **Marche** *Eng.* Marches. ◆ *region* C Italy
103 N11 **Marche** *cultural region* C France
99 J21 **Marche-en-Famenne** Luxembourg, SE Belgium 50°13'N 05°21'E
104 K14 **Marchena** Andalucía, S Spain 37°20'N 05°24'W
57 B17 **Marchena, Isla** *var.* Bindloe Island. *island* Galapagos Islands, Ecuador, E Pacific Ocean
**Marches** *see* Marche
99 J20 **Marchin** Liège, E Belgium 50°30'N 05°17'E
181 S1 **Marchinbar Island** *island* Wessel Islands, Northern Territory, N Australia
62 L9 **Mar Chiquita, Laguna** ◎ C Argentina
103 Q10 **Marcigny** Saône-et-Loire, C France 46°16'N 04°04'E
23 W16 **Marco** Florida, SE USA 25°56'N 81°43'W
**Marcodurum** *see* Düren
59 O15 **Marcolândia** Pernambuco, E Brazil 07°21'S 40°40'W
106 I8 **Marco Polo** ✈ (Venezia) Veneto, NE Italy 45°30'N 12°21'E
**Marcounda** *see* Markounda
**Marcq** *see* Mark
116 M8 **Mărculești** *Rus.* Markuleshty. N Moldova 47°54'N 28°14'E
29 S12 **Marcus** Iowa, C USA 42°49'N 95°48'W
39 S11 **Marcus Baker, Mount** ▲ Alaska, USA 61°26'N 147°45'W
192 I5 **Marcus Island** *var.* Minami Tori Shima. *island* E Japan
18 K8 **Marcy, Mount** ▲ New York, NE USA 44°06'N 73°55'W
149 T5 **Mardan** Khyber Pakhtunkhwa, N Pakistan 34°14'N 71°59'E
63 N14 **Mar del Plata** Buenos Aires, E Argentina 38°S 57°32'W
137 Q16 **Mardin** Mardin, SE Turkey 37°19'N 40°43'E
137 Q16 **Mardin** ◆ *province* SE Turkey
137 Q16 **Mardin Dağları** ▲ SE Turkey
**Mardzad** *see* Hayrhandulaan
187 R17 **Maré** *island* Îles Loyauté, E New Caledonia
**Marea Neagră** *see* Black Sea
105 Z8 **Mare de Déu del Toro** *var.* El Toro. ▲ Menorca, Spain, W Mediterranean Sea 39°59'N 04°06'E
181 W4 **Mareeba** Queensland, NE Australia 17°03'S 145°30'E
96 G8 **Maree, Loch** ◎ N Scotland, United Kingdom
**Mareeq** *see* Mereeg
**Marek** *see* Dupnitsa
76 J11 **Maréna** Kayes, W Mali 14°36'N 10°57'W
190 I2 **Marenanuka** *atoll* Tungaru, W Kiribati
29 X14 **Marengo** Iowa, C USA 41°48'N 92°04'W
102 J11 **Marennes** Charente-Maritime, W France 45°47'N 01°04'W
107 G23 **Marettimo, Isola** *island* Isole Egadi, S Italy
24 K10 **Marfa** Texas, SW USA 30°19'N 104°03'W
57 P17 **Marfil, Laguna** ◎ E Bolivia
**Margarets** *see* Marhanets'
25 Q4 **Margaret** Texas, SW USA 34°00'N 99°38'W
180 I14 **Margaret River** Western Australia 33°58'S 115°10'E
186 C7 **Margarima** Hela, W Papua New Guinea 06°00'S 143°23'E
55 N4 **Margarita, Isla de** *island* N Venezuela
115 I25 **Margarítes** Kríti, Greece, E Mediterranean Sea 35°19'N 24°40'E
97 Q22 **Margate** *prev.* Mergate. SE England, United Kingdom 51°24'N 01°24'E
23 Z15 **Margate** Florida, SE USA 26°14'N 80°12'W
**Margelan** *see* Marg'ilon
103 P13 **Margeride, Montagnes de la** ▲ C France
**Margherita** *see* Jamaame
107 N16 **Margherita di Savoia** Puglia, SE Italy 41°23'N 16°09'E
**Margherita, Lake** *see* Ābaya Hāyk'
81 E18 **Margherita Peak** *Fr.* Pic Marguerite. ▲ Uganda/Dem. Rep. Congo 0°28'N 29°58'E
149 O4 **Marghī** Bāmyān, N Afghanistan 34°58'N 66°31'E
116 G9 **Marghita** *Hung.* Margitta. Bihor, NW Romania 47°20'N 22°20'E
**Margilan** *see* Marg'ilon
147 S10 **Marg'ilon** *var.* Margelan, *Rus.* Margilan. Farg'ona Viloyati, E Uzbekistan 40°29'N 71°43'E
116 K8 **Marginea** Suceava, NE Romania 47°49'N 25°47'E
**Margitta** *see* Marghita
148 K9 **Mārgō, Dasht-e** *desert* SW Afghanistan
99 L18 **Margraten** Limburg, SE Netherlands 50°49'N 05°49'E
10 M15 **Marguerite** British Columbia, SW Canada 52°17'N 122°10'W
15 V3 **Marguerite** ⚟ Québec, SE Canada
194 I6 **Marguerite Bay** *bay* Antarctica
**Marguerite, Pic** *see* Margherita Peak
117 T9 **Marhanets'** *Rus.* Marganets. Dnipropetrovs'ka Oblast', E Ukraine 47°35'N 34°37'E
186 B9 **Mari** Western, SW Papua New Guinea 09°10'S 141°39'E
191 Y12 **Maria** *atoll* Groupe Actéon, SE French Polynesia
191 R12 **Maria** *island* Îles Australes, SW French Polynesia
40 I12 **María Cleofas, Isla** *island* C Mexico
62 H4 **María Elena** *var.* Oficina María Elena. Antofagasta, N Chile 22°18'S 69°40'W
95 G21 **Mariager** Midtjylland, C Denmark 56°39'N 09°59'E
61 C22 **María Ignacia** Buenos Aires, E Argentina 37°24'S 59°30'W
183 P17 **Maria Island** *island* Tasmania, SE Australia
40 H12 **María Madre, Isla** *island* C Mexico
40 I12 **María Magdalena, Isla** *island* C Mexico
192 H6 **Mariana Islands** *island group* Guam/Northern Mariana Islands
175 N3 **Mariana Trench** *var.* Challenger Deep. *undersea feature* W Pacific Ocean 15°00'N 147°30'E
153 X12 **Mariāni** Assam, NE India 26°39'N 94°18'E
27 X11 **Marianna** Arkansas, C USA 34°46'N 90°49'W
23 R8 **Marianna** Florida, SE USA 30°46'N 85°13'W
172 J16 **Marianne** *island* Inner Islands, NE Seychelles
95 M19 **Mariannelund** Jönköping, S Sweden 57°37'N 15°33'E
61 D15 **Mariano I. Loza** Corrientes, NE Argentina 29°22'S 58°12'W
**Mariano Machado** *see* Ganda
111 A16 **Mariánské Lázně** *Ger.* Marienbad. Karlovarský Kraj, W Czechia 49°57'N 12°43'E
**Máriaradna** *see* Radna
33 S7 **Marias River** ⚟ Montana, NW USA
**Maria-Theresiopel** *see* Subotica
**Máriatölgyes** *see* Dubnica nad Váhom
184 H1 **Maria van Diemen, Cape** *headland* North Island, New Zealand 34°27'S 172°38'E
109 V5 **Mariazell** Steiermark, E Austria 47°47'N 15°20'E
141 P15 **Ma'rib** W Yemen 15°28'N 45°25'E
95 I25 **Maribo** Sjælland, S Denmark 54°47'N 11°30'E
109 W9 **Maribor** *Ger.* Marburg. NE Slovenia 46°34'N 15°40'E
**Marica** *see* Maritsa
35 R13 **Maricopa** California, W USA 35°03'N 119°24'W
**Maricourt** *see* Kangiqsujuaq
81 D15 **Maridi** Western Equatoria, SW South Sudan 04°55'N 29°30'E
194 M11 **Marie Byrd Land** *physical region* Antarctica
193 P14 **Marie Byrd Seamount** *undersea feature* N Amundsen Sea 70°00'S 118°00'W
45 X11 **Marie-Galante** *var.* Ceyre to the Caribs. *island* SE Guadeloupe
45 Y6 **Marie-Galante, Canal de** *channel* S Guadeloupe
93 J20 **Mariehamn** *Fin.* Maarianhamina. Åland, SW Finland 60°05'N 19°55'E
44 C4 **Mariel** ◆ Artemisa, W Cuba
99 H22 **Mariembourg** Namur, S Belgium 50°07'N 04°30'E
**Marienbad** *see* Mariánské Lázně
**Marienburg** *see* Alūksne, Latvia
**Marienburg** *see* Malbork, Poland
**Marienburg** *see* Feldioara, Romania
**Marienburg in Westpreussen** *see* Malbork
**Marienhausen** *see* Viļaka
83 D20 **Mariental** Hardap, SW Namibia 24°35'S 17°56'E
18 D13 **Marienville** Pennsylvania, NE USA 41°27'N 79°07'W
**Marienwerder** *see* Kwidzyń
58 C12 **Marié, Rio** ⚟ NW Brazil
95 K17 **Mariestad** Västra Götaland, S Sweden 58°42'N 13°50'E
23 S3 **Marietta** Georgia, SE USA 33°57'N 84°34'W
31 U14 **Marietta** Ohio, N USA 39°25'N 81°27'W
27 N13 **Marietta** Oklahoma, C USA 33°57'N 97°08'W
81 H18 **Marigat** Baringo, W Kenya 0°29'S 35°59'E
103 S16 **Marignane** Bouches-du-Rhône, SE France 43°25'N 05°12'E
**Marignano** *see* Melegnano
45 O11 **Marigot** NE Dominica 15°32'N 61°18'W
122 K12 **Mariinsk** Kemerovskaya Oblast', S Russia 56°13'N 87°27'E
127 Q3 **Mariinskiy Posad** Respublika Mariy El, W Russia 56°07'N 47°44'E
119 E14 **Marijampolė** *prev.* Kapsukas. Marijampolė, S Lithuania 54°33'N 23°21'E
**Marikostenovo** *see* Marikostinovo
114 G12 **Marikostinovo** *prev.* Marikostenovo. Blagoevgrad, SW Bulgaria 41°25'N 23°21'E
60 J9 **Marília** São Paulo, S Brazil 22°13'S 49°58'W
82 D11 **Marimba** Malanje, NW Angola 08°18'S 16°58'E
**Mārī Mīlā** *see* Mahe Mela
**Mārī Mīlah** *see* Mahe Mela
104 G4 **Marín** Galicia, NW Spain 42°23'N 08°43'W
35 N10 **Marina** California, W USA 36°40'N 121°48'W
**Mar"ina Gorka** *see* Mar"ina Horka
119 L17 **Mar"ina Horka** *Rus.* Mar'ina Gorka. Minskaya Voblasts', C Belarus 53°31'N 28°09'E
171 O4 **Marinduque** *island* C Philippines
31 S9 **Marine City** Michigan, N USA 42°43'N 82°29'W
31 N6 **Marinette** Wisconsin, N USA 45°06'N 87°38'W
60 I10 **Maringá** Paraná, S Brazil 23°26'S 51°55'W
83 N16 **Maringuè** Sofala, C Mozambique 17°57'S 34°23'E
104 F9 **Marinha Grande** Leiria, C Portugal 39°45'N 08°55'W
107 I15 **Marino** Lazio, C Italy 41°46'N 12°40'E
59 A15 **Mário Lobão** Acre, W Brazil 08°21'S 72°58'W
23 O5 **Marion** Alabama, S USA 32°37'N 87°19'W
27 Y11 **Marion** Arkansas, C USA 35°12'N 90°12'W
30 L17 **Marion** Illinois, N USA 37°43'N 88°55'W
31 P13 **Marion** Indiana, N USA 40°32'N 85°40'W
29 X13 **Marion** Iowa, C USA 42°01'N 91°36'W
27 O5 **Marion** Kansas, C USA 38°22'N 97°02'W
20 H6 **Marion** Kentucky, S USA 37°19'N 88°06'W


◆ Country
● Country Capital
◇ Dependent Territory
○ Dependent Territory Capital
◆ Administrative Regions
✈ International Airport
▲ Mountain
▲ Mountain Range
Volcano
⚟ River
◎ Lake
⊠ Reservoir

MARION – MATTERHORN


21 P9 **Marion** North Carolina, SE USA 35°43′N 82°00′W
31 S12 **Marion** Ohio, N USA 40°35′N 83°08′W
21 T12 **Marion** South Carolina, SE USA 34°11′N 79°23′W
21 Q7 **Marion** Virginia, NE USA 36°51′N 81°30′W
27 O5 **Marion Lake** ⊠ Kansas, C USA
21 S13 **Marion, Lake** ⊠ South Carolina, SE USA
27 S8 **Marionville** Missouri, C USA 37°00′N 93°38′W
55 N7 **Maripa** Bolívar, E Venezuela 07°27′N 65°10′W
55 X11 **Maripasoula** W French Guiana 03°43′N 54°04′W
35 Q9 **Mariposa** California, W USA 37°28′N 119°59′W
61 G19 **Mariscala** Lavalleja, S Uruguay 34°03′S 54°47′W
62 M4 **Mariscal Estigarribia** Boquerón, NW Paraguay 22°03′S 60°39′W
56 C6 **Mariscal Sucre** *var.* Quito. ✈ (Quito) Pichincha, C Ecuador 0°21′S 78°37′W
30 K16 **Marissa** Illinois, N USA 38°15′N 89°45′W
103 U14 **Maritime Alps** *Fr.* Alpes Maritimes, *It.* Alpi Marittime. ▲▲ France/Italy
**Maritimes, Alpes** *see* Maritime Alps
**Maritime Territory** *see* Primorskiy Kray
114 K11 **Maritsa** *var.* Marica, *Gk.* Évros, *Turk.* Meriç; *anc.* Hebrus. ≈ SW Europe *see also* Évros/Meriç
**Maritsa** *see* Simeonovgrad, Bulgaria
**Marittime, Alpi** *see* Maritime Alps
**Maritzburg** *see* Pietermaritzburg
117 X9 **Mariupol'** *prev.* Zhdanov. Donets'ka Oblast', SE Ukraine 47°06′N 37°34′E
55 Q6 **Mariusa, Caño** ≈ NE Venezuela
142 J5 **Marīvān** *prev.* Dezh Shāhpūr. Kordestān, W Iran 35°30′N 46°09′E
127 R3 **Mariyets** Respublika Mariy El, W Russia 56°31′N 49°48′E
118 G4 **Märjamaa** *Ger.* Merjama. Raplamaa, NW Estonia 58°54′N 24°21′E
99 I15 **Mark** *Fr.* Marcq. ≈ Belgium/Netherlands
81 N17 **Marka** *var.* Merca. Shabeellaha Hoose, S Somalia 01°43′N 44°45′E
145 Z10 **Markakol', Ozero** *Kaz.* Marqaköl. ◎ E Kazakhstan
76 M12 **Markala** Ségou, W Mali 13°38′N 06°07′W
159 S15 **Markam** *var.* Gartog. Xizang Zizhiqu, W China 29°40′N 98°33′E
95 K21 **Markaryd** Kronoberg, S Sweden 56°26′N 13°35′E
142 L7 **Markazī** *off.* Ostān-e Markazī. ◆ *province* W Iran
**Markazī, Ostān-e** *see* Markazī
14 F14 **Markdale** Ontario, S Canada 44°19′N 80°37′W
27 X10 **Marked Tree** Arkansas, C USA 35°31′N 90°25′W
98 N11 **Markelo** Overijssel, E Netherlands 52°15′N 06°30′E
98 J9 **Markermeer** ◎ C Netherlands
97 N20 **Market Harborough** C England, United Kingdom 52°30′N 00°57′W
97 N18 **Market Rasen** E England, United Kingdom 53°23′N 00°21′W
123 O10 **Markha** ≈ NE Russia
12 H16 **Markham** Ontario, S Canada 43°54′N 79°16′W
25 V12 **Markham** Texas, SW USA 28°57′N 96°04′W
186 E7 **Markham** ≈ C Papua New Guinea
195 Q11 **Markham, Mount** ▲ Antarctica 82°58′S 163°30′E
110 M11 **Marki** Mazowieckie, C Poland 52°20′N 21°07′E
158 F8 **Markit** Xinjiang Uygur Zizhiqu, NW China 38°55′N 77°40′E
117 Y5 **Markivka** *Rus.* Markovka. Luhans'ka Oblast', E Ukraine 49°34′N 39°35′E
35 Q7 **Markleeville** California, W USA 38°41′N 119°46′W
98 L8 **Marknesse** Flevoland, N Netherlands 52°44′N 05°54′E
79 H14 **Markounda** *var.* Marcounda. Ouham, NW Central African Republic 07°38′N 17°00′E
**Markovka** *see* Markivka
123 U7 **Markovo** Chukotskiy Avtonomnyy Okrug, NE Russia 64°43′N 170°13′E
127 P8 **Marks** Saratovskaya Oblast', W Russia 51°40′N 46°44′E
22 K2 **Marks** Mississippi, S USA 34°15′N 90°16′W
22 I7 **Marksville** Louisiana, S USA 31°07′N 92°04′W
101 I19 **Marktheidenfeld** Bayern, C Germany 49°50′N 09°36′E
101 J24 **Marktoberdorf** Bayern, S Germany 47°45′N 10°36′E
101 M18 **Marktredwitz** Bayern, E Germany 50°N 12°04′E
**Markt-Übelbach** *see* Übelbach
27 V3 **Mark Twain Lake** ⊠ Missouri, C USA
**Markuleshty** *see* Mărculeşti
101 E14 **Marl** Nordrhein-Westfalen, W Germany 51°38′N 07°06′E
182 E2 **Marla** South Australia 27°19′S 133°35′E
181 Y8 **Marlborough** Queensland, E Australia 22°55′S 150°07′E
97 M22 **Marlborough** S England, United Kingdom 51°25′N 01°45′W
185 I15 **Marlborough** *off.* Marlborough District. ◆ *unitary authority* South Island, New Zealand
**Marlborough District** *see* Marlborough
103 P3 **Marle** Aisne, N France 49°44′N 03°47′E
31 S8 **Marlette** Michigan, N USA 43°20′N 83°05′W
25 T9 **Marlin** Texas, SW USA 31°20′N 96°55′W
21 S5 **Marlinton** West Virginia, NE USA 38°14′N 80°06′W
26 M12 **Marlow** Oklahoma, C USA 34°39′N 97°57′W
155 E17 **Marmagao** Goa, W India 15°26′N 73°50′E
**Marmanda** *see* Marmande
102 L13 **Marmande** *anc.* Marmanda. Lot-et-Garonne, SW France 44°30′N 00°10′E
136 C11 **Marmara** Balıkesir, NW Turkey 40°36′N 27°34′E
136 D11 **Marmara Denizi** *Eng.* Sea of Marmara. *sea* NW Turkey
114 N13 **Marmaraereğlisi** Tekirdağ, NW Turkey 40°59′N 27°57′E
**Marmara, Sea of** *see* Marmara Denizi
136 C16 **Marmaris** Muğla, SW Turkey 36°52′N 28°17′E
28 J6 **Marmarth** North Dakota, N USA 46°17′N 103°55′W
21 Q5 **Marmet** West Virginia, NE USA 38°12′N 81°31′W
106 H5 **Marmolada, Monte** ▲ N Italy 46°36′N 11°58′E
104 M13 **Marmolejo** Andalucía, S Spain 38°03′N 04°10′W
14 J14 **Marmora** Ontario, SE Canada 44°29′N 77°40′W
39 Q14 **Marmot Bay** *bay* Alaska, USA
103 Q4 **Marne** ◆ *department* N France
103 Q4 **Marne** ≈ N France
137 U10 **Marneuli** *prev.* Borchalo, Sarvani. S Georgia 41°28′N 44°45′E
78 I13 **Maro** Moyen-Chari, S Chad 08°25′N 18°46′E
54 L12 **Maroa** Amazonas, S Venezuela 02°40′N 67°33′W
172 J3 **Maroantsetra** Toamasina, NE Madagascar 15°23′S 49°44′E
191 W11 **Marokau** *atoll* Îles Tuamotu, C French Polynesia
172 J5 **Marolambo** Toamasina, E Madagascar 20°03′S 48°08′E
172 J2 **Maromokotro** ▲ N Madagascar
83 L16 **Marondera** *prev.* Marandellas. Mashonaland East, NE Zimbabwe 18°11′S 31°33′E
55 X9 **Maroni** *Dut.* Marowijne. ≈ French Guiana/Suriname
183 V2 **Maroochydore-Mooloolaba** Queensland, E Australia 26°36′S 153°04′E
171 N14 **Maros** Sulawesi, C Indonesia 04°59′S 119°35′E
116 H11 **Maros** *var.* Mureş, Mureşul, *Ger.* Marosch, Mieresch. ≈ Hungary/Romania *see also* Mureş
**Marosch** *see* Maros/Mureş
**Maroshevíz** *see* Topliţa
**Marosillye** *see* Ilia
**Marosludas** *see* Luduş
**Marosújvár/ Marosújvárakna** *see* Ocna Mureş
**Marosvásárhely** *see* Târgu Mureş
191 V14 **Marotiri** *var.* Îlots de Bass, Morotiri. *island group* Îles Australes, SW French Polynesia
78 G12 **Maroua** Extrême-Nord, N Cameroon 10°35′N 14°20′E
55 X12 **Marouini River** ≈ SE Suriname
172 I3 **Marovoay** Mahajanga, NW Madagascar 16°05′S 46°40′E
55 W9 **Marowijne** ◆ *district* NE Suriname
**Marowijne** *see* Maroni
**Marqaköl** *see* Markakol', Ozero
193 P8 **Marquesas Fracture Zone** *tectonic feature* E Pacific Ocean
**Marquesas Islands** *see* Marquises, Îles
23 W17 **Marquesas Keys** *island group* Florida, SE USA
29 Y12 **Marquette** Iowa, C USA 43°02′N 91°10′W
31 N3 **Marquette** Michigan, N USA 46°32′N 87°24′W
103 N1 **Marquise** Pas-de-Calais, N France 50°49′N 01°42′E
191 X7 **Marquises, Îles** *Eng.* Marquesas Islands. *island group* N French Polynesia
183 Q6 **Marra Creek** ≈ New South Wales, SE Australia
80 B10 **Marra Hills** *plateau* W Sudan
80 B11 **Marra, Jebel** ▲ W Sudan 12°59′N 24°16′E
74 E7 **Marrakech** *var.* Marakesh, *Eng.* Marrakesh; *prev.* Morocco. W Morocco 31°39′N 07°58′W
**Marrakesh** *see* Marrakech
**Marrāt** *see* Marāh
183 N15 **Marrawah** Tasmania, SE Australia 40°56′S 144°41′E
182 I4 **Marree** South Australia 29°40′S 138°06′E
81 L17 **Marrehan** ▲▲ SW Somalia
83 N17 **Marromeu** Sofala, C Mozambique 18°18′S 35°58′E
104 J17 **Marroquí, Punta** *headland* SW Spain 36°01′N 05°39′W
183 N8 **Marrowie Creek** *seasonal river* New South Wales, SE Australia
83 O14 **Marrupa** Niassa, N Mozambique 13°10′S 37°30′E
182 D1 **Marryat** South Australia 26°22′S 133°22′E
75 Y10 **Marsá 'Alam** SE Egypt 25°03′N 33°44′E
75 R8 **Marsá al Burayqah** *var.* Al Burayqah. N Libya 30°21′N 19°37′E
81 J17 **Marsabit** Marsabit, N Kenya 02°20′N 37°59′E
81 J17 **Marsabit** ◆ *county* N Kenya
107 H23 **Marsala** *anc.* Lilybaeum. Sicilia, Italy, C Mediterranean Sea 37°48′N 12°26′E
75 U7 **Marsá Maṭrūḥ** *var.* Maṭrūḥ; *anc.* Paraetonium. NW Egypt 31°21′N 27°15′E
**Marsaxlokk Bay** *see* Il-Bajja ta' Marsaxlokk
65 G15 **Mars Bay** *bay* Ascension Island, C Atlantic Ocean
101 H15 **Marsberg** Nordrhein-Westfalen, W Germany 51°28′N 08°51′E
11 R15 **Marsden** Saskatchewan, S Canada 52°50′N 109°45′W
98 H7 **Marsdiep** *strait* NW Netherlands
103 R16 **Marseille** *Eng.* Marseilles; *anc.* Massilia. Bouches-du-Rhône, SE France 43°19′N 05°22′E
**Marseille-Marignane** *see* Provence
30 M11 **Marseilles** Illinois, N USA 41°19′N 88°42′W
**Marseilles** *see* Marseille
76 J16 **Marshall** W Liberia 06°10′N 10°23′W
39 N11 **Marshall** Alaska, USA 61°52′N 162°04′W
27 U9 **Marshall** Arkansas, C USA 35°54′N 92°40′W
31 N14 **Marshall** Illinois, N USA 39°23′N 87°41′W
31 Q10 **Marshall** Michigan, N USA 42°16′N 84°57′W
29 S9 **Marshall** Minnesota, N USA 44°26′N 95°48′W
27 T4 **Marshall** Missouri, C USA 39°07′N 93°12′W
21 O9 **Marshall** North Carolina, SE USA 35°48′N 82°43′W
25 X6 **Marshall** Texas, SW USA 32°33′N 94°22′W
189 S4 **Marshall Islands** *off.* Republic of the Marshall Islands, *Mar.* Aolepān Aorōkin M̧ajel. ◆ *republic* W Pacific Ocean
175 Q3 **Marshall Islands** *island group* W Pacific Ocean
**Marshall Islands, Republic of the** *see* Marshall Islands
192 K6 **Marshall Seamounts** *undersea feature* SW Pacific Ocean 10°00′N 165°00′E
29 W13 **Marshalltown** Iowa, C USA 42°01′N 92°54′W
19 P12 **Marshfield** Massachusetts, NE USA 42°04′N 70°40′W
27 T7 **Marshfield** Missouri, C USA 37°20′N 92°55′W
30 K6 **Marshfield** Wisconsin, N USA 44°41′N 90°12′W
44 H1 **Marsh Harbour** Great Abaco, W The Bahamas 26°31′N 77°03′W
19 S3 **Mars Hill** Maine, NE USA 46°31′N 67°51′W
21 P9 **Mars Hill** North Carolina, SE USA 35°49′N 82°33′W
22 H10 **Marsh Island** *island* Louisiana, S USA
21 S11 **Marshville** North Carolina, SE USA 34°59′N 80°22′W
15 W5 **Marsoui** Québec, SE Canada 49°12′N 65°58′W
15 R8 **Mars, Rivière à** ≈ Québec, SE Canada
95 O15 **Märsta** Stockholm, C Sweden 59°37′N 17°52′E
95 H24 **Marstal** Syddtjylland, C Denmark 54°52′N 10°32′E
95 I19 **Marstrand** Västra Götaland, S Sweden 57°54′N 11°31′E
25 U8 **Mart** Texas, SW USA 31°32′N 96°49′W
**Martaban** *see* Mottama
**Martaban, Gulf of** *see* Mottama, Gulf of
107 Q19 **Martano** Puglia, SE Italy 40°12′N 18°19′E
**Martapoera** *see* Martapura
169 T13 **Martapura** *prev.* Martapoera. Borneo, C Indonesia 03°25′S 114°51′E
99 L23 **Martelange** Luxembourg, SE Belgium 49°50′N 05°43′E
114 L7 **Marten** Ruse, N Bulgaria 43°57′N 26°08′E
14 H10 **Marten River** Ontario, S Canada 46°43′N 79°45′W
11 T15 **Martensville** Saskatchewan, S Canada 52°15′N 106°42′W
**Marteskirch** *see* Târnăveni
**Martes Tolosane** *see* Martres-Tolosane
115 K25 **Mártha** Kríti, Greece, E Mediterranean Sea 35°03′N 25°22′E
183 Q6 **Marthaguy Creek** ≈ New South Wales, SE Australia
19 P13 **Martha's Vineyard** *island* Massachusetts, NE USA
108 C11 **Martigny** Valais, SW Switzerland 46°06′N 07°04′E
103 R16 **Martigues** Bouches-du-Rhône, SE France 43°24′N 05°03′E
111 J19 **Martin** *Ger.* Sankt Martin, *Hung.* Turócszentmárton; *prev.* Turčiansky Svätý Martin. Žilinský Kraj, N Slovakia 49°03′N 18°54′E
28 L11 **Martin** South Dakota, N USA 43°10′N 101°43′W
20 G8 **Martin** Tennessee, S USA 36°26′N 88°51′W
105 S7 **Martín** ≈ E Spain
107 P18 **Martina Franca** Puglia, SE Italy 40°42′N 17°20′E
185 M14 **Martinborough** Wellington, North Island, New Zealand 41°12′S 175°28′E
25 S11 **Martindale** Texas, SW USA 29°45′N 97°49′W
35 N8 **Martinez** California, W USA 38°00′N 122°12′W
23 V3 **Martinez** Georgia, SE USA 33°31′N 82°04′W
41 Q13 **Martínez de La Torre** Veracruz, E Mexico 20°05′N 97°02′W
45 Y12 **Martinique** ◇ *French overseas department* E West Indies
1 O15 **Martinique** *island* E West Indies
**Martinique Channel** *see* Martinique Passage
45 X12 **Martinique Passage** *var.* Dominica Channel, Martinique Channel. *channel* Dominica/Martinique
23 Q5 **Martin Lake** ⊠ Alabama, S USA
115 G18 **Martíno** *prev.* Martínon. Stereá Elláda, C Greece 38°34′N 23°13′E
**Martínon** *see* Martíno
194 J11 **Martin Peninsula** *peninsula* Antarctica
39 S5 **Martin Point** *headland* Alaska, USA 70°06′N 143°04′W
109 V3 **Martinsberg** Niederösterreich, NE Austria 48°23′N 15°09′E
21 V3 **Martinsburg** West Virginia, NE USA 39°28′N 77°59′W
31 V13 **Martins Ferry** Ohio, N USA 40°06′N 80°43′W
**Martinskirch** *see* Târnăveni
31 O14 **Martinsville** Indiana, N USA 39°25′N 86°25′W
21 S8 **Martinsville** Virginia, NE USA 36°43′N 79°53′W
65 K16 **Martin Vaz, Ilhas** *island group* E Brazil
144 I9 **Martok** *prev.* Martuk. Aktyubinsk, NW Kazakhstan 50°45′N 56°30′E
184 M12 **Marton** Manawatu-Wanganui, North Island, New Zealand 40°05′S 175°22′E
105 N13 **Martos** Andalucía, S Spain 37°44′N 03°58′W
102 M16 **Martres-Tolosane** *var.* Martes Tolosane. Haute-Garonne, S France 43°13′N 01°00′E
92 M11 **Martti** Lappi, NE Finland 67°28′N 28°20′E
**Martuk** *see* Martok
137 U12 **Martuni** E Armenia 40°07′N 45°20′E
58 L11 **Marudá** Pará, E Brazil 05°25′S 49°04′W
169 V6 **Marudu, Teluk** *bay* East Malaysia
149 O8 **Ma'rūf** Kandahār, SE Afghanistan 31°34′N 67°06′E
164 H13 **Marugame** Kagawa, Shikoku, SW Japan 34°17′N 133°46′E
185 H16 **Maruia** ≈ South Island, New Zealand
98 M6 **Marum** Groningen, NE Netherlands 53°07′N 06°16′E
187 R13 **Marum, Mount** ▲ Ambrym, C Vanuatu 16°15′S 168°07′E
79 P23 **Marungu** ▲▲ SE Dem. Rep. Congo
191 Y12 **Marutea** *atoll* Groupe Actéon, C French Polynesia
143 O11 **Marv Dasht** *var.* Mervdasht. Fārs, S Iran 29°50′N 52°40′E
103 P13 **Marvejols** Lozère, S France 44°35′N 03°16′E
27 X12 **Marvell** Arkansas, C USA 34°33′N 90°52′W
36 L6 **Marvine, Mount** ▲ Utah, W USA 38°40′N 111°38′W
139 Q7 **Marwānīyah** Al Anbār, C Iraq 33°58′N 42°31′E
152 F13 **Mārwār** *var.* Kharchi, Marwar Junction. Rājasthān, N India 25°41′N 73°42′E
**Marwar Junction** *see* Mārwār
11 R14 **Marwayne** Alberta, SW Canada 53°30′N 110°25′W
146 I14 **Mary** *prev.* Merv. Mary Welaýaty, S Turkmenistan 37°25′N 61°48′E
**Mary** *see* Mary Welaýaty
181 Z9 **Maryborough** Queensland, E Australia 25°32′S 152°36′E
182 M11 **Maryborough** Victoria, SE Australia 37°05′S 143°47′E
**Maryborough** *see* Port Laoise
83 G23 **Marydale** Northern Cape, W South Africa 29°25′S 22°06′E
117 W8 **Mar"yinka** Donets'ka Oblast', E Ukraine 47°57′N 37°27′E
**Mary Island** *see* Kanton
21 W4 **Maryland** *off.* State of Maryland, *also known as* America in Miniature, Cockade State, Free State, Old Line State. ◆ *state* NE USA
**Maryland, State of** *see* Maryland
25 P7 **Maryneal** Texas, SW USA 32°12′N 100°25′W
97 J15 **Maryport** NW England, United Kingdom 54°45′N 03°28′W
13 U13 **Marystown** Newfoundland, Newfoundland and Labrador, SE Canada 47°10′N 55°10′W
36 K6 **Marysvale** Utah, W USA 38°26′N 112°14′W
35 O6 **Marysville** California, W USA 39°07′N 121°35′W
27 O3 **Marysville** Kansas, C USA 39°48′N 96°37′W
31 S9 **Marysville** Michigan, N USA 42°54′N 82°29′W
31 S13 **Marysville** Ohio, NE USA 40°13′N 83°22′W
32 H7 **Marysville** Washington, NW USA 48°03′N 122°10′W
27 R2 **Maryville** Missouri, C USA 40°20′N 94°53′W
21 N9 **Maryville** Tennessee, S USA 35°45′N 83°59′W
146 I15 **Mary Welaýaty** *var.* Mary, *Rus.* Maryyskiy Velayat. ◆ *province* S Turkmenistan
**Maryyskiy Velayat** *see* Mary Welaýaty
**Marzūq** *see* Murzuq
42 J11 **Masachapa** *var.* Puerto Masachapa. Managua, W Nicaragua 11°47′N 86°31′W
81 G19 **Masai Mara National Reserve** *reserve* SW Kenya
81 I21 **Masai Steppe** *grassland* NW Tanzania
81 F19 **Masaka** SW Uganda 0°20′S 31°46′E
169 T15 **Masalembo Besar, Pulau** *island* S Indonesia
137 Y13 **Masallı** *Rus.* Masally. S Azerbaijan 39°03′N 48°39′E
**Masally** *see* Masallı
171 N13 **Masamba** Sulawesi, C Indonesia 02°33′S 120°20′E
**Masampo** *see* Masan
163 Y16 **Masan** *prev.* Masampo. S South Korea 35°11′N 128°36′E
**Masandam Peninsula** *see* Musandam Peninsula
81 J25 **Masasi** Mtwara, SE Tanzania 10°43′S 38°48′E
**Masawa/Massawa** *see* Mits'iwa
42 J10 **Masaya** Masaya, W Nicaragua 11°59′N 86°06′W
42 J10 **Masaya** ◆ *department* W Nicaragua
171 P5 **Masbate** Masbate, N Philippines 12°21′N 123°34′E
171 P5 **Masbate** *island* C Philippines
74 I6 **Mascara** *var.* Mouaskar. NW Algeria 35°20′N 00°09′E
173 O7 **Mascarene Basin** *undersea feature* W Indian Ocean 15°00′S 56°00′E
173 O9 **Mascarene Islands** *island group* W Indian Ocean
173 N9 **Mascarene Plain** *undersea feature* W Indian Ocean 19°00′S 52°00′E
173 O7 **Mascarene Plateau** *undersea feature* W Indian Ocean 10°00′S 60°00′E
194 H5 **Mascart, Cape** *headland* Adelaide Island, Antarctica
62 J10 **Mascasín, Salinas de** *salt lake* C Argentina
40 K13 **Mascota** Jalisco, C Mexico 20°31′N 104°46′W
15 O12 **Mascouche** Québec, SE Canada 45°46′N 73°37′W
124 J9 **Masel'gskaya** Respublika Kareliya, NW Russia 63°09′N 34°22′E
83 J23 **Maseru** ● (Lesotho) W Lesotho 29°21′S 27°35′E
83 J23 **Maseru** ✈ W Lesotho 29°27′S 27°37′E
**Mashaba** *see* Mashava
160 K14 **Mashan** *var.* Baishan. Guangxi Zhuangzu Zizhiqu, S China 23°40′N 108°10′E
83 K17 **Mashava** *prev.* Mashaba. Masvingo, SE Zimbabwe 20°03′S 30°29′E
143 U4 **Mashhad** *var.* Meshed. Khorāsān-e Razavī, NE Iran 36°16′N 59°34′E
165 S3 **Mashike** Hokkaidō, NE Japan 43°51′N 141°30′E
83 K20 **Mashishing** *prev.* Lydenburg. Mpumalanga, NE South Africa 25°10′S 30°29′E
**Mashīz** *see* Bardsīr
149 N14 **Mashkai** ≈ SW Pakistan
143 X13 **Māshkel** *var.* Rūd-i Māshkel, Rūd-e Māshkīd. ≈ Iran/Pakistan
148 K12 **Māshkel, Hamun-i** *salt marsh* SW Pakistan
**Māshkel, Rūd-i/Māshkīd, Rūd-e** *see* Mashkel
83 K15 **Mashonaland Central** ◆ *province* N Zimbabwe
83 K16 **Mashonaland East** ◆ *province* NE Zimbabwe
83 J16 **Mashonaland West** ◆ *province* NW Zimbabwe
**Mashtagi** *see* Maştağa
141 S14 **Masīlah, Wādī al** *dry watercourse* SE Yemen
79 I21 **Masi-Manimba** Bandundu, SW Dem. Rep. Congo 04°47′S 17°54′E
81 F17 **Masindi** W Uganda 01°41′N 31°45′E
81 I19 **Masinga Reservoir** ⊠ S Kenya
**Masīra** *see* Maṣīrah, Jazīrat
**Masira, Gulf of** *see* Maṣīrah, Khalīj
141 Y10 **Maṣīrah, Jazīrat** *var.* Masīra. *island* E Oman
141 Y10 **Maṣīrah, Khalīj** *var.* Gulf of Masira. *bay* E Oman
**Masis** *see* Büyük Ağrı Dağı
79 O19 **Masisi** Nord-Kivu, E Dem. Rep. Congo 01°25′S 28°50′E
**Masjed-e Soleymān** *see* Masjed Soleymān
142 L9 **Masjed Soleymān** *var.* Masjed-e Soleymān, Masjid-i Sulaiman. Khūzestān, SW Iran 31°59′N 49°18′E
**Masjid-i Sulaiman** *see* Masjed Soleymān
138 K3 **Maskanah** *prev.* Bīrīn. Ḥalab, N Syria 36°01′N 38°03′E
**Maskat** *see* Masqaṭ
139 Q7 **Maskhān** Al Anbār, C Iraq 33°41′N 42°46′E
141 X8 **Maskin** *var.* Miskin. NW Oman 23°28′N 56°46′E
97 B17 **Mask, Lough** *Ir.* Loch Measca. ◎ W Ireland
114 N10 **Maslen Nos** *headland* E Bulgaria 42°19′N 27°47′E
172 K3 **Masoala, Tanjona** *headland* NE Madagascar 15°59′N 50°13′E
**Masohi** *see* Amahai
31 Q9 **Mason** Michigan, N USA 42°33′N 84°25′W
31 R14 **Mason** Ohio, N USA 39°21′N 84°18′W
25 Q10 **Mason** Texas, SW USA 30°45′N 99°15′W
21 P4 **Mason** West Virginia, NE USA 39°01′N 82°01′W
185 B25 **Mason Bay** *bay* Stewart Island, New Zealand
30 K13 **Mason City** Illinois, N USA 40°12′N 89°42′W
29 V12 **Mason City** Iowa, C USA 43°09′N 93°12′W
18 B16 **Masontown** Pennsylvania, NE USA 39°49′N 79°53′W
141 Y8 **Masqaṭ** *var.* Maskat, *Eng.* Muscat. ● (Oman) NE Oman 23°35′N 58°36′E
106 E10 **Massa** Toscana, C Italy 44°02′N 10°07′E
18 M11 **Massachusetts** *off.* Commonwealth of Massachusetts, *also known as* Bay State, Old Bay State, Old Colony State. ◆ *state* NE USA
19 P11 **Massachusetts Bay** *bay* Massachusetts, NE USA
35 R2 **Massacre Lake** ◎ Nevada, W USA
107 O18 **Massafra** Puglia, SE Italy 40°35′N 17°08′E
108 G11 **Massagno** Ticino, S Switzerland 46°01′N 08°55′E
78 G11 **Massaguet** Hadjer-Lamis, W Chad 12°28′N 15°26′E
**Massakori** *see* Massakory
78 G10 **Massakory** *var.* Massakori; *prev.* Dagana. Hadjer-Lamis, W Chad 13°02′N 15°43′E
78 H11 **Massalassef** Hadjer-Lamis, SW Chad 11°37′N 17°09′E
106 F13 **Massa Marittima** Toscana, C Italy 43°03′N 10°55′E
82 B11 **Massangano** Kwanza Norte, NW Angola 09°40′S 14°13′E
83 M18 **Massangena** Gaza, S Mozambique 21°34′S 32°57′E
80 K9 **Massawa Channel** *channel* E Eritrea
18 J6 **Massena** New York, NE USA 44°55′N 74°53′W
78 H11 **Massenya** Chari-Baguirmi, SW Chad 11°21′N 16°09′E
10 I13 **Masset** Graham Island, British Columbia, SW Canada 54°00′N 132°09′W
102 L16 **Masseube** Gers, S France 43°26′N 00°33′E
14 E11 **Massey** Ontario, S Canada 46°13′N 82°06′W
103 P12 **Massiac** Cantal, C France 45°16′N 03°13′E
103 P12 **Massif Central** *plateau* C France
**Massif de L'Isalo** *see* Isalo
**Massilia** *see* Marseille
31 U12 **Massillon** Ohio, N USA 40°48′N 81°31′W
77 N12 **Massina** Ségou, W Mali 13°58′N 05°24′W
83 N19 **Massinga** Inhambane, SE Mozambique 23°20′S 35°25′E
83 L20 **Massingir** Gaza, SW Mozambique 23°51′S 31°58′E
195 Z10 **Masson Island** *island* Antarctica
**Massoukou** *see* Franceville
137 Z11 **Maştağa** *Rus.* Mashtagi, Mastaga. E Azerbaijan 40°31′N 50°01′E
**Mastanli** *see* Momchilgrad
184 M13 **Masterton** Wellington, North Island, New Zealand 40°56′S 175°40′E
18 M14 **Mastic** Long Island, New York, NE USA 40°48′N 72°50′W
149 O10 **Mastung** Baluchistān, SW Pakistan 29°44′N 66°56′E
119 J20 **Mastva** *Rus.* Mostva. ≈ SW Belarus
119 G17 **Masty** *Rus.* Mosty. Hrodzyenskaya Voblasts', W Belarus 53°25′N 24°32′E
164 F12 **Masuda** Shimane, Honshū, SW Japan 34°40′N 131°50′E
92 J11 **Masugnsbyn** Norrbotten, N Sweden 67°28′N 22°01′E
**Masuku** *see* Franceville
83 K17 **Masvingo** *prev.* Fort Victoria, Nyanda, Victoria. Masvingo, SE Zimbabwe 20°05′S 30°50′E
83 K18 **Masvingo** *prev.* Victoria. ◆ *province* SE Zimbabwe
138 H5 **Maşyāf** *Fr.* Misiaf. Ḥamāh, C Syria 35°04′N 36°21′E
110 E9 **Maszewo** Zachodniopomorskie, NW Poland 53°29′N 15°01′E
**Mata-Au** *see* Clutha River / Mata-Au
83 I17 **Matabeleland North** ◆ *province* W Zimbabwe
83 J18 **Matabeleland South** ◆ *province* S Zimbabwe
82 O13 **Mataca** Niassa, N Mozambique 12°27′S 36°13′E
14 G8 **Matachewan** Ontario, S Canada 47°58′N 80°37′W
163 O8 **Matad** *var.* Dzüünbulag. Dornod, E Mongolia 46°48′N 115°21′E
79 F22 **Matadi** Bas-Congo, W Dem. Rep. Congo 05°49′S 13°31′E
25 O4 **Matador** Texas, SW USA 34°01′N 100°50′W
42 J9 **Matagalpa** Matagalpa, C Nicaragua 12°53′N 85°56′W
42 K9 **Matagalpa** ◆ *department* W Nicaragua
12 I12 **Matagami** Québec, S Canada 49°47′N 77°38′W
25 U13 **Matagorda** Texas, SW USA 28°40′N 96°57′W
25 U13 **Matagorda Bay** *inlet* Texas, SW USA
25 U14 **Matagorda Island** *island* Texas, SW USA
25 V13 **Matagorda Peninsula** *headland* Texas, SW USA 28°34′N 96°01′W
191 Q8 **Mataiea** Tahiti, W French Polynesia 17°46′S 149°25′W
191 T9 **Mataiva** *atoll* Îles Tuamotu, C French Polynesia
183 O7 **Matakana** New South Wales, SE Australia 32°59′S 145°53′E
184 N7 **Matakana Island** *island* NE New Zealand
83 C15 **Matala** Huíla, SW Angola 14°45′S 15°02′E
190 G12 **Matala'a Pointe** *headland* Île Uvea, N Wallis and Futuna 13°20′S 176°08′W
155 K25 **Matale** Central Province, C Sri Lanka 07°29′N 80°38′E
190 E12 **Matalesina, Pointe** *headland* Île Alofi, W Wallis and Futuna
76 I10 **Matam** NE Senegal 15°40′N 13°18′W
184 M8 **Matamata** Waikato, North Island, New Zealand 37°49′S 175°45′E
77 V12 **Matamey** Zinder, S Niger 13°27′N 08°27′E
40 L8 **Matamoros** Coahuila, NE Mexico 25°34′N 103°13′W
41 P15 **Matamoros** *var.* Izúcar de Matamoros. Puebla, S Mexico 18°38′N 98°30′W
41 Q8 **Matamoros** Tamaulipas, C Mexico 25°50′N 97°31′W
75 S13 **Ma'ṭan as Sārah** SE Libya 21°45′N 21°55′E
82 J12 **Matanda** Luapula, N Zambia 11°24′S 28°25′E
81 J24 **Matandu** ≈ S Tanzania
15 V6 **Matane** Québec, SE Canada 48°50′N 67°31′W
15 V6 **Matane** ≈ Québec, SE Canada
77 S12 **Matankari** Dosso, SW Niger 13°39′N 04°03′E
39 R11 **Matanuska River** ≈ Alaska, USA
54 G7 **Matanza** Santander, N Colombia 07°22′N 73°02′W
44 D4 **Matanzas** Matanzas, NW Cuba 23°N 81°32′W
44 D4 **Matanzas** ◆ *province* NW Cuba
15 V7 **Matapédia** ≈ Québec, SE Canada
15 V6 **Matapédia, Lac** ◎ Québec, SE Canada
190 B17 **Mata Point** *headland* SE Niue 19°07′S 169°51′E
190 D12 **Matapu, Pointe** *headland* Île Futuna, W Wallis and Futuna
62 G12 **Mataquito, Río** ≈ C Chile
155 K26 **Matara** Southern Province, S Sri Lanka 05°58′N 80°33′E
115 D18 **Matarágka** *var.* Mataránga. Dytikí Elláda, C Greece 38°32′N 21°28′E
171 K16 **Mataram** Pulau Lombok, C Indonesia 08°36′S 116°07′E
**Mataránga** *see* Matarágka
181 Q3 **Mataranka** Northern Territory, N Australia 14°55′S 133°03′E
105 W6 **Mataró** *anc.* Illuro. Cataluña, E Spain 41°32′N 02°27′E
184 O8 **Matata** Bay of Plenty, North Island, New Zealand 37°54′S 176°45′E
192 K16 **Matātula, Cape** *headland* Tutuila, W American Samoa 14°15′S 170°35′W
185 D24 **Mataura** Southland, South Island, New Zealand 46°12′S 168°53′E
185 D24 **Mataura** ≈ South Island, New Zealand
**Mata Uta** *see* Matā'utu
192 H16 **Matā'utu** Upolu, C Samoa 13°57′S 171°55′W
190 G11 **Matā'utu** *var.* Mata Uta. ○ (Wallis and Futuna) Île Uvea, Wallis and Futuna 13°22′S 176°12′W
190 G12 **Matā'utu, Baie de** *bay* Île Uvea, Wallis and Futuna
191 P7 **Matavai, Baie de** *bay* Tahiti, W French Polynesia
190 I16 **Matavera** Rarotonga, S Cook Islands 21°13′S 159°44′W
191 V16 **Mataveri** Easter Island, Chile, E Pacific Ocean 27°10′S 109°27′W
191 V17 **Mataveri** ✈ (Easter Island) Easter Island, Chile, E Pacific Ocean 27°10′S 109°27′W
184 P9 **Matawai** Gisborne, North Island, New Zealand 38°23′S 177°31′E
15 O10 **Matawin** ≈ Québec, SE Canada
145 V13 **Matay** Almaty, SE Kazakhstan 45°53′N 78°45′E
14 K8 **Matchi-Manitou, Lac** ◎ Québec, SE Canada
41 O10 **Matehuala** San Luis Potosí, C Mexico 23°40′N 100°40′W
45 V13 **Matelot** Trinidad, Trinidad and Tobago 10°48′N 61°06′W
83 M15 **Matenge** Tete, NW Mozambique 15°22′S 33°47′E
107 O18 **Matera** Basilicata, S Italy 40°39′N 16°35′E
111 O21 **Mátészalka** Szabolcs-Szatmár-Bereg, E Hungary 47°58′N 22°17′E
93 H17 **Matfors** Västernorrland, C Sweden 62°21′N 17°02′E
102 K11 **Matha** Charente-Maritime, W France 45°50′N 00°13′W
0 F15 **Mathematicians Seamounts** *undersea feature* E Pacific Ocean 15°00′N 111°00′W
21 X6 **Mathews** Virginia, NE USA 37°26′N 76°20′W
25 S14 **Mathis** Texas, SW USA 28°05′N 97°49′W
152 J11 **Mathura** *prev.* Muttra. Uttar Pradesh, N India 27°30′N 77°42′E
**Mathurai** *see* Madurai
171 R7 **Mati** Mindanao, S Philippines 06°58′N 126°11′E
**Matianus** *see* Orūmīyeh, Daryācheh-ye
**Matiara** *see* Matiari
149 Q15 **Matiari** *var.* Matiara. Sindh, SE Pakistan 25°38′N 68°29′E
41 S16 **Matías Romero** Oaxaca, SE Mexico 16°53′N 95°02′W
43 O13 **Matina** Limón, E Costa Rica 10°06′N 83°18′W
14 D10 **Matinenda Lake** ◎ Ontario, S Canada
19 R8 **Matinicus Island** *island* Maine, NE USA
**Matisco/Matisco Ædourum** *see* Mâcon
113 K19 **Matit, Lumi i** ≈ NW Albania
149 Q16 **Matli** Sindh, SE Pakistan 25°06′N 68°37′E
97 M18 **Matlock** C England, United Kingdom 53°08′N 01°32′W
59 F18 **Mato Grosso** *prev.* Vila Bela da Santissima Trindade. Mato Grosso, W Brazil 14°53′S 59°58′W
59 G17 **Mato Grosso** *off.* Estado de Mato Grosso; *prev.* Matto Grosso. ◆ *state* W Brazil
60 H8 **Mato Grosso do Sul** *off.* Estado de Mato Grosso do Sul. ◆ *state* S Brazil
**Mato Grosso do Sul, Estado de** *see* Mato Grosso do Sul
**Mato Grosso, Estado de** *see* Mato Grosso
59 I18 **Mato Grosso, Planalto de** *plateau* C Brazil
83 L21 **Matola** Maputo, S Mozambique 25°57′S 32°27′E
104 G6 **Matosinhos** *prev.* Matozinhos. Porto, NW Portugal 41°11′N 08°42′W
**Matou** *see* Pingguo
55 Z10 **Matoury** NE French Guiana 04°49′N 52°17′W
**Matozinhos** *see* Matosinhos
111 L21 **Mátra** ▲▲ N Hungary
141 Y8 **Maṭraḥ** *var.* Mutrah. NE Oman 23°35′N 58°31′E
116 L12 **Mătrașeşti** Vrancea, E Romania 45°53′N 27°14′E
108 M8 **Matrei am Brenner** Tirol, W Austria 47°09′N 11°28′E
109 P8 **Matrei in Osttirol** Tirol, W Austria 47°04′N 12°31′E
76 I15 **Matru** SW Sierra Leone 07°37′N 12°08′W
**Maṭrūḥ** *see* Marsá Maṭrūḥ
165 U16 **Matsubara** *var.* Matubara. Kagoshima, Tokuno-shima, SW Japan 32°58′N 129°56′E
164 G12 **Matsue** *var.* Matsuye, Matue. Shimane, Honshū, SW Japan 35°27′N 133°04′E
165 Q6 **Matsumae** Hokkaidō, NE Japan 41°27′N 140°04′E
164 M12 **Matsumoto** *var.* Matumoto. Nagano, Honshū, S Japan 36°18′N 137°58′E
164 K14 **Matsusaka** *var.* Matsuzaka, Matusaka. Mie, Honshū, SW Japan 34°33′N 136°31′E
**Matsu Tao** *see* Nangan Dao
**Matsutō** *see* Mattō
164 F14 **Matsuyama** *var.* Matuyama. Ehime, Shikoku, SW Japan 33°50′N 132°47′E
**Matsuye** *see* Matsue
**Matsuzaka** *see* Matsusaka
164 M14 **Matsuzaki** Shizuoka, Honshū, S Japan 34°43′N 138°45′E
14 F8 **Mattagami** ≈ Ontario, S Canada
14 F8 **Mattagami Lake** ◎ Ontario, S Canada
62 K12 **Mattaldi** Córdoba, C Argentina 34°26′S 64°14′W
21 Y9 **Mattamuskeet, Lake** ◎ North Carolina, SE USA
21 W6 **Mattaponi River** ≈ Virginia, NE USA
14 I11 **Mattawa** Ontario, SE Canada 46°19′N 78°42′W
14 I11 **Mattawa** ≈ Ontario, SE Canada
19 S5 **Mattawamkeag** Maine, NE USA 45°30′N 68°20′W
19 S4 **Mattawamkeag Lake** ◎ Maine, NE USA
108 D11 **Matterhorn** *It.* Monte Cervino. ▲ Italy/Switzerland 45°58′N 07°36′E *see also* Cervino, Monte
32 L12 **Matterhorn** *var.* Sacajawea Peak. ▲ Oregon, NW USA 45°12′N 117°18′W
35 W1 **Matterhorn** ▲ Nevada, W USA 41°48′N 115°22′W
**Matterhorn** *see* Cervino, Monte




◆ Country
● Country Capital
◇ Dependent Territory
○ Dependent Territory Capital
◆ Administrative Regions
✈ International Airport
▲ Mountain
▲▲ Mountain Range
Volcano
≈ River
◎ Lake
⊠ Reservoir

Matterhorn Peak – Mehrān


35 R8 Matterhorn Peak ▲ California, W USA 38°06′N 119°19′W
109 Y5 Mattersburg Burgenland, E Austria 47°45′N 16°24′E
108 E11 Matter Vispa ≈ S Switzerland
55 R7 Matthews Ridge N Guyana 07°30′N 60°07′W
44 K7 Matthew Town Great Inagua, S The Bahamas 20°56′N 73°41′W
109 Q4 Mattighofen Oberösterreich, NW Austria 48°07′N 13°09′E
107 N16 Mattinata Puglia, SE Italy 41°41′N 16°01′E
141 T9 Maṭṭī, Sabkhat salt flat Saudi Arabia/United Arab Emirates
18 M14 Mattituck Long Island, New York, NE USA 40°59′N 72°31′W
164 L11 Mattō var. Hakusan, Matsutō. Ishikawa, Honshū, SW Japan 36°31′N 136°34′E
Matto Grosso see Mato Grosso
30 M14 Mattoon Illinois, N USA 39°28′N 88°22′W
57 L16 Mattos, Río ≈ C Bolivia
Mattu see Metu
169 R9 Matu Sarawak, East Malaysia 02°39′N 111°31′E
Matubara see Matsubara
57 E14 Matucana Lima, W Peru 11°54′S 76°25′W
Matue see Matsue
187 Y15 Matuku island S Fiji
112 B9 Matulji Primorje-Gorski Kotar, NW Croatia 45°21′N 14°18′E
Matumoto see Matsumoto
55 P5 Maturín Monagas, NE Venezuela 09°45′N 63°10′W
Matusaka see Matsusaka
Matuyama see Matsuyama
126 K11 Matveyev Kurgan Rostovskaya Oblast', SW Russia 47°31′N 38°55′E
127 O8 Matyshevo Volgogradskaya Oblast', SW Russia 50°53′N 44°09′E
Mau see Maunath Bhanjan
83 O14 Maúa Niassa, N Mozambique 13°53′S 37°10′E
102 M17 Maubermé, Pic de var. Tuc de Moubermé, Sp. Pico Mauberme; prev. Tuc de Maubermé. ▲ France/Spain 42°48′N 00°54′E see also Moubermé, Tuc de
Maubermé, Pic de see Maubermé, Tuc de
Mauberme, Pico see Maubermé, Pic de/Moubermé, Tuc de
Maubermé, Tuc de see Maubermé, Pic de/Moubermé, Tuc de
103 Q2 Maubeuge Nord, N France 50°16′N 04°00′E
166 L8 Maubin Ayeyarwady, SW Myanmar (Burma) 16°44′N 95°37′E
152 L13 Maudaha Uttar Pradesh, N India 25°41′N 80°07′E
183 N9 Maude New South Wales, SE Australia 34°30′S 144°20′E
195 P3 Maudheimvidda physical region Antarctica
65 N22 Maud Rise undersea feature S Atlantic Ocean
109 Q4 Mauerkirchen Oberösterreich, NW Austria 48°11′N 13°08′E
Mauersee see Mamry, Jezioro
188 K2 Maug Islands island group N Northern Mariana Islands
103 Q15 Mauguio Hérault, S France 43°37′N 04°01′E
193 N5 Maui island Hawai'i, USA, C Pacific Ocean
190 M16 Mauke atoll S Cook Islands
62 G13 Maule var. Región del Maule. ◈ region C Chile
102 J9 Mauléon Deux-Sèvres, W France 46°55′N 00°45′W
102 J16 Mauléon-Licharre Pyrénées-Atlantiques, SW France 43°14′N 00°51′W
Maule, Región del see Maule
62 G13 Maule, Río ≈ C Chile
63 G17 Maullín Los Lagos, S Chile 41°38′S 73°35′W
31 R11 Maumee Ohio, N USA 41°34′N 83°40′W
31 Q12 Maumee River ≈ Indiana/Ohio, N USA
27 U11 Maumelle Arkansas, C USA 34°51′N 92°24′W
27 T11 Maumelle, Lake ▣ Arkansas, C USA
171 O16 Maumere prev. Maoemere. Flores, S Indonesia 08°35′S 122°13′E
83 G17 Maun Ngamiland, C Botswana 20°01′S 23°28′E
153 O13 Maunath Bhanjan var. Mau. Uttar Pradesh, N India 25°57′N 83°33′E
Maunawai see Waimea
190 H16 Maungaroa ▲ Rarotonga, S Cook Islands 21°13′S 159°48′W
184 K3 Maungatapere Northland, North Island, New Zealand 35°46′S 174°10′E
184 K4 Maungaturoto Northland, North Island, New Zealand 36°06′S 174°21′E
166 J5 Maungdaw var. Zullapara. Rakhine State, W Myanmar (Burma) 20°51′N 92°23′E
191 R10 Maupiti var. Maurua. island Îles Sous le Vent, W French Polynesia
152 K14 Mau Rānīpur Uttar Pradesh, N India 25°14′N 79°07′E
22 K9 Maurepas, Lake ◎ Louisiana, S USA
103 T16 Maures ▲▲ SE France
103 O12 Mauriac Cantal, C France 45°13′N 02°21′E
Maurice see Mauritius
65 J20 Maurice Ewing Bank undersea feature SW Atlantic Ocean 51°00′S 43°00′W
182 C4 Maurice, Lake salt lake South Australia
18 I17 Maurice River ≈ New Jersey, NE USA
25 Y10 Mauriceville Texas, SW USA 30°13′N 93°52′W
98 K12 Maurik Gelderland, C Netherlands 51°57′N 05°25′E
76 H8 Mauritania off. Islamic Republic of Mauritania, Ar. Mūrītānīyah, Al Jumhūrīyah al Islāmīyah al Mūrītānīyah. ◆ republic W Africa
Mauritania, Islamic Republic of see Mauritania
173 W15 Mauritius off. Republic of Mauritius, Fr. Maurice. ◆ republic W Indian Ocean
128 M17 Mauritius island W Indian Ocean
Mauritius, Republic of see Mauritius
173 N9 Mauritius Trench undersea feature W Indian Ocean
102 H6 Mauron Morbihan, NW France 48°06′N 02°16′W
103 N13 Maurs Cantal, C France 44°45′N 02°12′E
Maurua see Maupiti
Maury Mid-Ocean Channel see Maury Seachannel
64 L6 Maury Seachannel var. Maury Mid-Ocean Channel. undersea feature N Atlantic Ocean 56°33′N 24°00′W
30 K8 Mauston Wisconsin, N USA 43°46′N 90°06′W
109 R8 Mauterndorf Salzburg, NW Austria 47°09′N 13°39′E
109 T4 Mauthausen Oberösterreich, N Austria 48°13′N 14°30′E
109 Q9 Mauthen Kärnten, S Austria 46°39′N 12°58′E
83 F15 Mavinga Kuando Kubango, SE Angola 15°44′S 20°21′E
83 M17 Mavita Manica, W Mozambique 19°31′S 33°09′E
115 K22 Mavrópetra, Akrotírio headland Santoríni, Kykládes, Greece, Aegean Sea 36°28′N 25°22′E
115 F16 Mavrovoúni ▲ C Greece 39°37′N 22°45′E
184 Q8 Mawhai Point headland North Island, New Zealand 38°08′S 178°24′E
166 L3 Mawlaik Sagaing, C Myanmar (Burma) 23°40′N 94°26′E
Mawlamyaing see Mawlamyine
166 M9 Mawlamyine var. Mawlamyaing, Moulmein. Mon State, S Myanmar (Burma) 16°30′N 97°39′E
166 L8 Mawlamyinegyunn var. Moulmeingyun. Ayeyarwady, SW Myanmar (Burma) 16°24′N 95°15′E
141 N14 Mawr, Wādī dry watercourse NW Yemen
Mawşil, Al see Nīnawá
195 X5 Mawson research station (Australia) Antarctica 67°24′S 63°16′E
195 X5 Mawson Coast physical region Antarctica
28 M4 Max North Dakota, N USA 47°48′N 101°18′W
41 W12 Maxcanú Yucatán, SE Mexico 20°35′N 90°00′W
Maxesibebi see Mount Ayliff
109 Q5 Maxglan ✈ (Salzburg) Salzburg, W Austria 47°46′N 13°00′E
93 K16 Maxmo Fin. Maksamaa. Österbotten, W Finland 63°13′N 22°04′E
21 T11 Maxton North Carolina, SE USA 34°47′N 79°34′W
25 R8 May Texas, SW USA 31°58′N 98°54′W
186 B6 May ≈ NW Papua New Guinea
123 R10 Maya ≈ E Russia
151 Q19 Māyābandar Andaman and Nicobar Islands, India, E Indian Ocean 12°43′N 92°52′E
44 C5 Mayabeque ◈ province W Cuba
Mayadin see Al Mayādīn
44 L5 Mayaguana island SE The Bahamas
44 L5 Mayaguana Passage passage SE The Bahamas
45 S6 Mayagüez W Puerto Rico 18°12′N 67°08′W
45 R6 Mayagüez, Bahía de bay W Puerto Rico
Mayals see Maials
79 G20 Mayama Pool, SE Congo 03°50′S 14°52′E
37 V8 Maya, Mesa De ▲ Colorado, C USA 37°06′N 103°30′W
143 R4 Mayamey Semnān, N Iran 36°50′N 55°50′E
42 F3 Maya Mountains Sp. Montañas Mayas. ▲▲ Belize/Guatemala
44 I7 Mayarí Holguín, E Cuba 20°41′N 75°42′W
Mayas, Montañas see Maya Mountains
18 I17 May, Cape headland New Jersey, NE USA 38°55′N 74°57′W
80 J11 Maych'ew var. Mai Chio, It. Mai Ceu. Tigray, N Ethiopia 12°55′N 39°30′E
138 I2 Maydān Ikbiz Ḩalab, N Syria 36°51′N 36°40′E
Maydān Shahr see Maīdān Shahr
80 O12 Maydh Sanaag, N Somalia 10°57′N 47°07′E
Maydī see Mīdī
Mayebashi see Maebashi
Mayence see Mainz
102 K6 Mayenne Mayenne, NW France 48°18′N 00°37′W
102 J6 Mayenne ◈ department NW France
102 J7 Mayenne ≈ N France
36 K12 Mayer Arizona, SW USA 34°25′N 112°15′W
22 J4 Mayersville Mississippi, S USA 32°54′N 91°04′W
11 P14 Mayerthorpe Alberta, SW Canada 53°59′N 115°06′W
21 S12 Mayesville South Carolina, SE USA 34°00′N 80°10′W
185 G19 Mayfield Canterbury, South Island, New Zealand 43°50′S 171°24′E
33 N14 Mayfield Idaho, NW USA 43°24′N 115°56′W
20 G7 Mayfield Kentucky, S USA 36°45′N 88°40′W
36 L5 Mayfield Utah, W USA 39°06′N 111°42′W
Mayhan see Sant
37 T14 Mayhill New Mexico, SW USA 32°52′N 105°28′W
Maykain see Maykayyn
145 T9 Maykayyn Kaz. Mayqayyng prev. Maykain. Pavlodar, NE Kazakhstan 51°27′N 75°52′E
126 L14 Maykop Respublika Adygeya, SW Russia 44°36′N 40°07′E
Maylibash see Maylybas
Mayli-Say see Mayluu-Suu
147 T9 Mayluu-Suu prev. Mayli-Say, Kyr. Mayly-Say. Dzhalal-Abadskaya Oblast', W Kyrgyzstan 41°16′N 72°27′E
144 L14 Maylybas prev. Maylibash. Kzylorda, S Kazakhstan 45°51′N 62°37′E
Mayly-Say see Mayluu-Suu
Maymana see Maīmanah
Maymyo see Pyinoolwin
123 V7 Mayn ≈ NE Russia
127 Q5 Mayna Ul'yanovskaya Oblast', W Russia 54°04′N 47°20′E
21 N8 Maynardville Tennessee, S USA 36°15′N 83°48′W
Maynila see Manila
Maynila, Lungsod ng see Manila
14 J13 Maynooth Ontario, SE Canada 45°14′N 77°54′W
10 I6 Mayo Yukon, NW Canada 63°37′N 135°48′W
23 U9 Mayo Florida, SE USA 30°03′N 83°10′W
97 B16 Mayo Ir. Maigh Eo. cultural region W Ireland
Mayo see Maio
78 G12 Mayo-Kébbi Est off. Région du Mayo-Kébbi Est. ◈ region SW Chad
Mayo-Kébbi Est, Région du see Mayo-Kébbi Est
79 F19 Mayoko Niari, SW Congo 02°19′S 12°47′E
171 P4 Mayon Volcano ⛰ Luzon, N Philippines 13°15′N 123°41′E
61 A24 Mayor Buratovich Buenos Aires, E Argentina 39°15′S 62°35′W
104 L4 Mayorga Castilla y León, N Spain 42°10′N 05°16′W
184 N6 Mayor Island island NE New Zealand
Mayor Pablo Lagerenza see Capitán Pablo Lagerenza
173 I14 Mayotte ◇ French overseas department E Africa
Mayoumba see Mayumba
44 J13 May Pen C Jamaica 17°58′N 77°15′W
Mayqayyng see Maykayyn
171 O1 Mayraira Point headland Luzon, N Philippines 18°36′N 120°47′E
109 N8 Mayrhofen Tirol, W Austria 47°09′N 11°52′E
186 A6 May River East Sepik, NW Papua New Guinea 04°24′S 141°52′E
139 Y10 Maysān off. Muḩāfaz at Maysān, var. Al 'Amārah, Mīsān. ◈ governorate SE Iraq
Maysān, Muḩāfaz at see Maysān
123 R13 Mayskiy Amurskaya Oblast', SE Russia 52°13′N 129°30′E
127 O15 Mayskiy Kabardino-Balkarskaya Respublika, SW Russia 43°37′N 44°04′E
145 U9 Mayskoye Pavlodar, NE Kazakhstan 50°55′N 78°11′E
18 J17 Mays Landing New Jersey, NE USA 39°27′N 74°44′W
21 N4 Maysville Kentucky, S USA 38°38′N 83°46′W
27 R2 Maysville Missouri, C USA 39°53′N 94°21′W
79 D20 Mayumba var. Mayoumba. Nyanga, S Gabon 03°23′S 10°38′E
31 S8 Mayville Michigan, N USA 43°18′N 83°16′W
18 C11 Mayville New York, NE USA 42°15′N 79°32′W
29 Q4 Mayville North Dakota, N USA 47°27′N 97°17′W
Mayyali see Mahe
Mayyit, Al Baḩr al see Dead Sea
83 J15 Mazabuka Southern, S Zambia 15°52′S 27°46′E
Mazaca see Kayseri
Mazagan see El-Jadida
32 J7 Mazama Washington, NW USA 48°34′N 120°26′W
103 O15 Mazamet Tarn, S France 43°30′N 02°21′E
143 O4 Māzandarān off. Ostān-e Māzandarān. ◈ province N Iran
Māzandarān, Daryā-ye see Caspian Sea
Māzandarān, Ostān-e see Māzandarān
156 F7 Mazar Xinjiang Uygur Zizhiqu, NW China 36°28′N 77°00′E
107 H24 Mazara del Vallo Sicilia, Italy, C Mediterranean Sea 37°39′N 12°36′E
149 O2 Mazār-e Sharif var. Mazār-i Sharif. Balkh, N Afghanistan 36°44′N 67°06′E
Mazār-i Sharif see Mazār-e Sharif
105 R13 Mazarrón Murcia, SE Spain 37°36′N 01°19′W
105 R14 Mazarrón, Golfo de gulf SE Spain
55 S9 Mazaruni River ≈ N Guyana
42 B6 Mazatenango Suchitepéquez, SW Guatemala 14°31′N 91°30′W
40 I10 Mazatlán Sinaloa, C Mexico 23°15′N 106°24′W
36 L12 Mazatzal Mountains ▲▲ Arizona, SW USA
118 D10 Mažeikiai Telšiai, NW Lithuania 56°19′N 22°22′E
118 D7 Mazirbe NW Latvia 57°39′N 22°16′E
40 G5 Mazocahui Sonora, NW Mexico 29°32′N 110°09′W
57 I18 Mazocruz Puno, S Peru 16°41′S 69°42′W
Mazoe, Rio see Mazowe
79 N21 Mazomeno Maniema, E Dem. Rep. Congo 04°54′S 27°13′E
159 Q6 Mazong Shan ▲ N China 41°40′N 97°10′E
83 L16 Mazowe var. Rio Mazoe. ≈ Mozambique/Zimbabwe
110 M11 Mazowieckie ◈ province C Poland
Mazra'a see Al Mazra'ah
138 G6 Mazraat Kfar Debiâne C Lebanon 34°00′N 35°51′E
118 H7 Mazsalaca Est. Väike-Salatsi, Ger. Salisburg. N Latvia 57°52′N 25°03′E
Mazu Dao see Nangan Dao
110 L9 Mazury physical region NE Poland
Mazu Tao see Nangan Dao
119 M20 Mazyr Rus. Mozyr'. Homyel'skaya Voblasts', SE Belarus 52°04′N 29°15′E
107 K25 Mazzarino Sicilia, Italy, C Mediterranean Sea 37°18′N 14°13′E
Mba see Ba
83 L21 Mbabane ● (Eswatini-administrative capital) NW Eswatini 26°24′S 31°13′E
Mbacké see Mbaké
77 N16 Mbahiakro E Ivory Coast 07°33′N 04°19′W
79 I16 Mbaïki var. M'Baiki. Lobaye, SW Central African Republic 03°52′N 17°58′E
M'Baiki see Mbaïki
79 F14 Mbakaou, Lac de ◎ C Cameroon
76 G11 Mbaké var. Mbacké. W Senegal 14°47′N 15°54′W
82 L11 Mbala prev. Abercorn. Northern, NE Zambia 08°50′S 31°23′E
83 J18 Mbalabala prev. Balla Balla. Matabeleland South, SW Zimbabwe 20°27′S 29°03′E
81 G18 Mbale E Uganda 01°04′N 34°12′E
79 E16 Mbalmayo var. M'Balmayo. Centre, S Cameroon 03°30′N 11°31′E
M'Balmayo see Mbalmayo
81 H25 Mbamba Bay Ruvuma, S Tanzania 11°15′S 34°44′E
79 I18 Mbandaka prev. Coquilhatville. Equateur, NW Dem. Rep. Congo 0°07′N 18°12′E
82 B9 M'banza Kongo Zaire Province, NW Angola 06°11′S 14°16′E
79 G21 Mbanza-Ngungu Bas-Congo, W Dem. Rep. Congo 05°19′S 14°45′E
67 V11 Mbarangandu ≈ E Tanzania
81 E19 Mbarara SW Uganda 0°36′S 30°40′E
79 L15 Mbari ≈ SE Central African Republic
81 I24 Mbarika Mountains ▲▲ S Tanzania
78 F13 Mbé Nord, N Cameroon 07°51′N 13°36′E
81 J24 Mbemkuru var. Mbwemkuru. ≈ S Tanzania
Mbengga see Beqa
172 H13 Mbéni Grande Comore, NW Comoros
83 K18 Mberengwa Midlands, S Zimbabwe 20°29′S 29°55′E
81 G24 Mbeya Mbeya, SW Tanzania 08°54′S 33°29′E
81 G23 Mbeya ◈ region S Tanzania
83 J24 Mbhashe prev. Mbashe. ≈ S South Africa
79 E19 Mbigou Ngounié, C Gabon 01°54′S 12°00′E
Mbilua see Vella Lavella
79 F19 Mbinda Niari, SW Congo 02°07′S 12°52′E
79 D17 Mbini W Equatorial Guinea 01°34′N 09°39′E
Mbini see Uolo, Río
83 L18 Mbizi Masvingo, SE Zimbabwe 21°23′S 30°54′E
81 G23 Mbogo Mbeya, W Tanzania 07°24′S 33°26′E
79 N15 Mboki Haut-Mbomou, SE Central African Republic 05°18′N 25°52′E
79 G18 Mbomo Cuvette-Ouest, NW Congo 0°25′N 14°42′E
79 L15 Mbomou ◈ prefecture SE Central African Republic
Mbomou/M'Bomu/Mbomu see Bomu
76 F11 Mbour W Senegal 14°22′N 16°54′W
76 I10 Mbout Gorgol, S Mauritania 16°02′N 12°38′W
79 J14 Mbrès var. Mbrés. Nana-Grébizi, C Central African Republic 06°40′N 19°46′E
Mbrés see Mbrès
79 L22 Mbuji-Mayi prev. Bakwanga. Kasai-Oriental, S Dem. Rep. Congo 06°05′S 23°30′E
81 H21 Mbulu Manyara, N Tanzania 03°45′S 35°33′E
186 E5 M'bunai var. Bunai. Manus Island, N Papua New Guinea 02°08′S 147°13′E
62 N8 Mburucuyá Corrientes, NE Argentina 28°03′S 58°15′W
Mbutha see Buca
Mbwemkuru see Mbemkuru
81 G21 Mbwikwe Singida, C Tanzania 05°19′S 34°09′E
13 O15 McAdam New Brunswick, SE Canada 45°34′N 67°20′W
25 O5 McAdoo Texas, SW USA 33°41′N 100°58′W
35 V2 McAfee Peak ▲ Nevada, W USA 41°31′N 115°57′W
27 P11 McAlester Oklahoma, C USA 34°56′N 95°46′W
25 S17 McAllen Texas, SW USA 26°12′N 98°14′W
21 S11 McBee South Carolina, SE USA 34°30′N 80°12′W
11 N14 McBride British Columbia, SW Canada 53°21′N 120°19′W
24 M9 McCamey Texas, SW USA 31°08′N 102°13′W
33 R15 McCammon Idaho, NW USA 42°38′N 112°10′W
35 X11 McCarran ✈ (Las Vegas) Nevada, W USA 36°04′N 115°07′W
39 T11 McCarthy Alaska, USA 61°25′N 142°55′W
30 M5 McCaslin Mountain hill Wisconsin, N USA
25 O2 McClellan Creek ≈ Texas, SW USA
21 T14 McClellanville South Carolina, SE USA 33°07′N 79°27′W
195 R12 McClintock, Mount ▲ Antarctica 80°09′S 156°42′E
35 N2 McCloud California, W USA 41°15′N 122°09′W
35 N3 McCloud River ≈ California, W USA
35 Q9 McClure, Lake ▣ California, W USA
197 O8 McClure Strait strait Northwest Territories, N Canada
29 N4 McClusky North Dakota, N USA 47°27′N 100°25′W
21 T11 McColl South Carolina, SE USA 34°40′N 79°33′W
22 K7 McComb Mississippi, S USA 31°14′N 90°27′W
18 E16 McConnellsburg Pennsylvania, NE USA 39°56′N 78°00′W
31 T14 McConnelsville Ohio, N USA 39°39′N 81°51′W
28 M17 McCook Nebraska, C USA 40°12′N 100°38′W
21 P13 McCormick South Carolina, SE USA 33°55′N 82°19′W
11 W16 McCreary Manitoba, S Canada 50°48′N 99°34′W
27 W11 McCrory Arkansas, C USA 35°15′N 91°12′W
25 T10 McDade Texas, SW USA 30°15′N 97°15′W
23 O8 McDavid Florida, SE USA 30°51′N 87°18′W
35 T1 McDermitt Nevada, W USA 41°57′N 117°43′W
23 S4 McDonough Georgia, SE USA 33°27′N 84°09′W
36 L12 McDowell Mountains ▲▲ Arizona, SW USA
20 H8 McEwen Tennessee, S USA 36°06′N 87°37′W
35 R12 McFarland California, W USA 35°41′N 119°14′W
McFarlane, Lake see Macfarlane, Lake
27 P12 McGee Creek Lake ▣ Oklahoma, C USA
27 W13 McGehee Arkansas, C USA 33°37′N 91°24′W
35 X5 McGill Nevada, W USA 39°24′N 114°46′W
14 K11 McGillivray, Lac ◎ Québec, SE Canada
39 P10 McGrath Alaska, USA 62°57′N 155°36′W
25 T8 McGregor Texas, SW USA 31°26′N 97°24′W
33 O12 McGuire, Mount ▲ Idaho, NW USA 45°10′N 114°36′W
83 M14 Mchinji prev. Fort Manning. Central, W Malawi 13°48′S 32°55′E
28 M7 McIntosh South Dakota, N USA 45°56′N 101°21′W
9 S7 McKeand ≈ Baffin Island, Nunavut, NE Canada
191 R4 McKean Island island Phoenix Islands, C Kiribati
30 J13 McKee Creek ≈ Illinois, N USA
18 C15 Mckeesport Pennsylvania, NE USA 40°18′N 79°48′W
21 V7 McKenney Virginia, NE USA 36°57′N 77°42′W
20 G8 McKenzie Tennessee, S USA 36°07′N 88°31′W
185 B20 McKerrow, Lake ◎ South Island, New Zealand
McKinley, Mount see Denali
39 R10 McKinley Park Alaska, USA 63°42′N 149°01′W
34 K3 McKinleyville California, W USA 40°56′N 124°06′W
25 U6 McKinney Texas, SW USA 33°14′N 96°37′W
26 I5 McKinney, Lake ◎ Kansas, C USA
28 M7 McLaughlin South Dakota, N USA 45°48′N 100°48′W
25 O2 McLean Texas, SW USA 35°13′N 100°36′W
30 M16 Mcleansboro Illinois, N USA 38°05′N 88°32′W
11 O13 McLennan Alberta, W Canada 55°42′N 116°50′W
14 L9 McLennan, Lac ◎ Québec, SE Canada
10 M13 McLeod Lake British Columbia, W Canada 55°03′N 123°02′W
8 L6 M'Clintock Channel channel Nunavut, N Canada
27 N10 McLoud Oklahoma, C USA 35°26′N 97°05′W
32 G15 McLoughlin, Mount ▲ Oregon, NW USA 42°27′N 122°18′W
37 U15 McMillan, Lake ▣ New Mexico, SW USA
32 G11 McMinnville Oregon, NW USA 45°14′N 123°12′W
20 K9 McMinnville Tennessee, S USA 35°40′N 85°49′W
195 R13 McMurdo research station (US) Antarctica 77°40′S 167°16′E
37 N13 Mcnary Arizona, SW USA 34°04′N 109°51′W
24 H9 McNary Texas, SW USA 31°15′N 105°46′W
27 N5 McPherson Kansas, C USA 38°22′N 97°41′W
McPherson see Fort McPherson
23 U6 McRae Georgia, SE USA 32°04′N 82°54′W
29 P4 McVille North Dakota, N USA 47°45′N 98°10′W
83 J25 Mdantsane Eastern Cape, SE South Africa 32°55′S 27°39′E
167 T6 Me Ninh Binh, N Vietnam 20°21′N 105°49′E
26 J7 Meade Kansas, C USA 37°17′N 100°21′W
39 O5 Meade River ≈ Alaska, USA
35 Y11 Mead, Lake ▣ Arizona/Nevada, W USA
24 M5 Meadow Texas, SW USA 33°20′N 102°12′W
11 S14 Meadow Lake Saskatchewan, C Canada 54°90′N 108°30′W
35 Y10 Meadow Valley Wash ≈ Nevada, W USA
22 J7 Meadville Mississippi, S USA 31°28′N 90°51′W
18 B12 Meadville Pennsylvania, NE USA 41°38′N 80°09′W
14 F14 Meaford Ontario, S Canada 44°35′N 80°35′W
Meáin, Inis see Inishmaan
104 G8 Mealhada Aveiro, N Portugal 40°22′N 08°27′W
13 R8 Mealy Mountains ▲▲ Newfoundland and Labrador, E Canada
11 O10 Meander River Alberta, W Canada 59°02′N 117°42′W
32 E11 Meares, Cape headland Oregon, NW USA 45°29′N 123°59′W
47 V6 Mearim, Rio ≈ NE Brazil
Measca, Loch see Mask, Lough
97 F17 Meath Ir. An Mhí. cultural region E Ireland
11 T14 Meath Park Saskatchewan, S Canada 53°25′N 105°18′W
103 O5 Meaux Seine-et-Marne, N France 48°47′N 02°54′E
21 T9 Mebane North Carolina, SE USA 36°06′N 79°16′W
171 U12 Mebo, Gunung ▲ Papua Barat, E Indonesia 01°10′S 133°53′E
94 I8 Mebonden Sør-Trøndelag, S Norway 63°13′N 11°00′E
82 A10 Mebridege ≈ NW Angola
35 W16 Mecca California, W USA 33°34′N 116°04′W
Mecca see Makkah
29 Y14 Mechanicsville Iowa, C USA 41°54′N 91°15′W
18 L10 Mechanicville New York, NE USA 42°54′N 73°41′W
99 H17 Mechelen Eng. Mechlin, Fr. Malines. Antwerpen, C Belgium 51°02′N 04°29′E
188 C8 Mecherchar var. Eil Malk. island Palau Islands, Palau
101 D17 Mechernich Nordrhein-Westfalen, W Germany 50°36′N 06°39′E
126 L12 Mechetinskaya Rostovskaya Oblast', SW Russia 46°46′N 40°30′E
114 J11 Mechka ≈ S Bulgaria
Mechlin see Mechelen
61 D23 Mechongué Buenos Aires, E Argentina 38°09′S 58°13′W
115 L14 Mecidiye Edirne, NW Turkey 40°39′N 26°33′E
101 I24 Meckenbeuren Baden-Württemberg, S Germany 47°42′N 09°34′E
100 L8 Mecklenburger Bucht bay N Germany
100 M10 Mecklenburgische Seenplatte wetland NE Germany
100 L9 Mecklenburg-Vorpommern ◈ state NE Germany
83 Q15 Meconta Nampula, NE Mozambique 15°01′S 39°52′E
111 I25 Mecsek ▲▲ SW Hungary
83 P14 Mecubúri ≈ N Mozambique
83 Q14 Mecúfi Cabo Delgado, NE Mozambique 13°20′S 40°32′E
82 O13 Mecula Niassa, N Mozambique 12°03′S 37°37′E
168 I8 Medan Sumatera, E Indonesia 03°35′N 98°39′E
61 A24 Médanos var. Medanos. Buenos Aires, E Argentina 38°52′S 62°45′W
61 C19 Médanos Entre Ríos, E Argentina 33°28′S 59°07′W
155 K24 Medawachchiya North Central Province, N Sri Lanka 08°32′N 80°30′E
106 C8 Mede Lombardia, N Italy 45°06′N 08°43′E
74 J5 Médéa var. El Mediyya, Lemdiyya. N Algeria 36°15′N 02°48′E
Medeba see Mādabā
54 E8 Medellín Antioquia, NW Colombia 06°15′N 75°36′W
100 H9 Medem ≈ NW Germany
98 J8 Medemblik Noord-Holland, NW Netherlands 52°47′N 05°06′E
75 N7 Médenine var. Madanīyīn. SE Tunisia 33°23′N 10°30′E
76 G9 Mederdra Trarza, SW Mauritania 16°56′N 15°40′W
Medeshamstede see Peterborough
42 F4 Medesto Mendez Izabal, NE Guatemala 15°54′N 89°13′W
19 O11 Medford Massachusetts, NE USA 42°25′N 71°08′W
27 N8 Medford Oklahoma, C USA 36°48′N 97°45′W
32 G15 Medford Oregon, NW USA 42°20′N 122°52′W
30 K6 Medford Wisconsin, N USA 45°08′N 90°22′W
39 P10 Medfra Alaska, USA 63°06′N 154°42′W
116 M14 Medgidia Constanța, SE Romania 44°15′N 28°16′E
Medgyes see Mediaș
43 O5 Media Luna, Arrecifes de la reef E Honduras
60 G11 Medianeira Paraná, S Brazil 25°15′S 54°07′W
29 Y15 Mediapolis Iowa, C USA 41°00′N 91°09′W
116 I11 Mediaș Ger. Mediasch, Hung. Medgyes. Sibiu, C Romania 46°10′N 24°20′E
41 S15 Medias Aguas Veracruz, SE Mexico 17°40′N 95°02′W
Mediasch see Mediaș
106 G10 Medicina Emilia-Romagna, C Italy 44°29′N 11°41′E
33 X16 Medicine Bow Wyoming, C USA 41°52′N 106°11′W
37 S2 Medicine Bow Mountains ▲▲ Colorado/Wyoming, C USA
33 X16 Medicine Bow River ≈ Wyoming, C USA
11 R17 Medicine Hat Alberta, SW Canada 50°03′N 110°41′W
26 L7 Medicine Lodge Kansas, C USA 37°18′N 98°35′W
26 L7 Medicine Lodge River ≈ Kansas/Oklahoma, C USA
112 E7 Međimurje off. Međimurska Županija. ◈ province N Croatia
Međimurska Županija see Međimurje
54 G10 Medina Cundinamarca, C Colombia 04°31′N 73°21′W
18 E9 Medina New York, NE USA 43°13′N 78°23′W
29 O5 Medina North Dakota, N USA 46°53′N 99°18′W
31 T11 Medina Ohio, N USA 41°08′N 81°51′W
25 Q11 Medina Texas, SW USA 29°46′N 99°14′W
Medina see Al Madīnah
105 P6 Medinaceli Castilla y León, N Spain 41°10′N 02°26′W
104 L6 Medina del Campo Castilla y León, N Spain 41°18′N 04°55′W
104 L5 Medina de Ríoseco Castilla y León, N Spain 41°53′N 05°03′W
Médina Gonassé see Médina Gounas
76 H12 Médina Gounas var. Médina Gonassé. S Senegal 13°06′N 13°49′W
25 S12 Medina River ≈ Texas, SW USA
104 K16 Medina Sidonia Andalucía, S Spain 36°28′N 05°55′W
Medinat Israel see Israel
119 H14 Medininkai Vilnius, SE Lithuania 54°32′N 25°40′E
153 R16 Medinīpur West Bengal, NE India 22°25′N 87°24′E
Mediolanum see Saintes, France
Mediolanum see Milano, Italy
Mediomatrica see Metz
121 Q11 Mediterranean Ridge undersea feature C Mediterranean Sea 34°00′N 23°00′E
121 O16 Mediterranean Sea Fr. Mer Méditerranée. sea Africa/Asia/Europe
Méditerranée, Mer see Mediterranean Sea
79 N17 Medje Orientale, NE Dem. Rep. Congo 02°27′N 27°14′E
Medjerda, Oued see Mejerda
114 G7 Medkovets Montana, NW Bulgaria 43°39′N 23°22′E
93 J15 Medle Västerbotten, N Sweden 64°45′N 20°45′E
127 W7 Mednogorsk Orenburgskaya Oblast', W Russia 51°24′N 57°37′E
123 W9 Mednyy, Ostrov island E Russia
102 J12 Médoc cultural region SW France
159 Q16 Mêdog Xizang Zizhiqu, W China 29°26′N 95°26′E
28 J5 Medora North Dakota, N USA 46°56′N 103°40′W
79 E17 Médouneu Woleu-Ntem, N Gabon 0°58′N 10°50′E
106 I7 Meduna ≈ NE Italy
Medunta see Mantes-la-Jolie
Medvedica see Medveditsa
124 J16 Medveditsa var. Medvedica. ≈ W Russia
127 O9 Medveditsa ≈ SW Russia
112 E8 Medvednica ▲▲ NE Croatia
125 R15 Medvedok Kirovskaya Oblast', NW Russia 57°23′N 50°01′E
123 S6 Medvezh'i, Ostrova island group NE Russia
124 J9 Medvezh'yegorsk Respublika Kareliya, NW Russia 62°56′N 34°26′E
109 T11 Medvode Ger. Zwischenwässern. NW Slovenia 46°09′N 14°21′E
126 J4 Medyn' Kaluzhskaya Oblast', W Russia 54°59′N 35°52′E
180 J10 Meekatharra Western Australia 26°37′S 118°35′E
37 Q4 Meeker Colorado, C USA 40°02′N 107°54′W
13 T12 Meelpaeg Lake ◎ Newfoundland, Newfoundland and Labrador, E Canada
Meemu Atoll see Mulakatholhu
Meenen see Menen
101 M16 Meerane Sachsen, E Germany 50°50′N 12°28′E
101 D15 Meerbusch Nordrhein-Westfalen, W Germany 51°19′N 06°43′E
98 I12 Meerkerk Zuid-Holland, C Netherlands 51°55′N 05°00′E
99 L18 Meerssen var. Mersen. Limburg, SE Netherlands 50°53′N 05°45′E
152 J10 Meerut Uttar Pradesh, N India 29°01′N 77°41′E
33 U13 Meeteetse Wyoming, C USA 44°10′N 108°53′W
99 K17 Meeuwen Limburg, NE Belgium 51°04′N 05°36′E
81 J16 Mēga Oromīya, C Ethiopia 04°03′N 38°15′E
81 J16 Mēga Escarpment escarpment S Ethiopia
Megála Kalívia see Megála Kalývia
115 E16 Megála Kalývia var. Megála Kalívia. Thessalía, C Greece 39°30′N 21°48′E
115 H14 Megáli Panagiá var. Megáli Panayía. Kentrikí Makedonía, N Greece 40°24′N 23°42′E
Megáli Panayía see Megáli Panagiá
Megáli Préspa, Límni see Prespa, Lake
114 K12 Megálo Livádi ▲ Bulgaria/Greece 41°18′N 25°51′E
115 E20 Megalópoli prev. Megalópolis. Pelopónnisos, S Greece 37°24′N 22°08′E
Megalópolis see Megalópoli
171 U12 Megamo Papua Barat, E Indonesia 0°55′S 131°46′E
115 C18 Meganísi island Iónia Nisiá, Greece, C Mediterranean Sea
Meganom, Mys see Mehanom, Mys
Mégantic see Lac-Mégantic
15 R12 Mégantic, Mont ▲ Québec, SE Canada 45°27′N 71°09′W
115 G19 Mégara Attikí, C Greece 38°00′N 23°20′E
25 R5 Megargel Texas, SW USA 33°27′N 98°55′W
98 K13 Megen Noord-Brabant, S Netherlands 51°49′N 05°34′E
153 U13 Meghālaya ◈ state NE India
153 U16 Meghna Nadi ≈ S Bangladesh
137 V14 Meghri Rus. Megri. SE Armenia 38°57′N 46°15′E
115 Q23 Megísti var. Kastellórizo. island SE Greece
Megri see Meghri
Mehabad see Mahābād
116 F13 Mehadia Hung. Mehádia. Caraş-Severin, SW Romania 44°53′N 22°20′E
Mehádia see Mehadia
92 L7 Mehamn Finnmark, N Norway 71°01′N 27°46′E
117 U13 Mehanom, Mys Rus. Mys Meganom. headland S Ukraine 44°48′N 35°04′E
149 P14 Mehar Sindh, SE Pakistan 27°12′N 67°51′E
180 J8 Meharry, Mount ▲ Western Australia 23°17′S 118°48′E
Mehdia see Mahdia
116 G14 Mehedinți ◈ county SW Romania
153 S15 Meherpur Khulna, W Bangladesh 23°47′N 88°40′E
21 W8 Meherrin River ≈ North Carolina/Virginia, SE USA
Meheso see Mī'ēso
191 T11 Mehetia island Îles du Vent, W French Polynesia
118 K6 Mehikoorma Tartumaa, E Estonia 58°14′N 27°29′E
Me Hka see Nmai Hka
143 N5 Mehrabad ✈ (Tehrān) Tehrān, N Iran 35°46′N 51°07′E
142 J7 Mehrān Īlām, W Iran 33°07′N 46°10′E


◆ Country ● Country Capital ◇ Dependent Territory ○ Dependent Territory Capital ◈ Administrative Regions ✈ International Airport ▲ Mountain ▲▲ Mountain Range ⛰ Volcano ≈ River ◎ Lake ▣ Reservoir

Mehrān, Rūd-e – Miami


143 *Q14* **Mehrān, Rūd-e** *prev.* Mansurabad. W Iran
143 *Q9* **Mehrīz** Yazd, C Iran *31°32′N 54°28′E*
149 *R5* **Mehtar Lām** *var.* Mehtarlām, Meterlam, Methariam, Metharlam. Laghmān, E Afghanistan *34°39′N 70°10′E*
**Mehtarlām** *see* Mehtar Lām
103 *N8* **Mehun-sur-Yèvre** Cher, C France *47°09′N 02°15′E*
79 *G14* **Meiganga** Adamaoua, NE Cameroon *06°31′N 14°07′E*
160 *H10* **Meigu** *var.* Bapu. Sichuan, C China *28°16′N 103°20′E*
163 *W11* **Meihekou** *var.* Hailong. Jilin, NE China *42°31′N 125°40′E*
99 *L15* **Meijel** Limburg, SE Netherlands *51°22′N 05°52′E*
**Meijiang** *see* Ningdu
166 *M5* **Meiktila** Mandalay, C Myanmar (Burma) *20°53′N 95°54′E*
**Meilbhe, Loch** *see* Melvin, Lough
108 *G7* **Meilen** Zürich, N Switzerland *47°17′N 08°39′E*
**Meilu** *see* Wuchuan
101 *J17* **Meiningen** Thüringen, C Germany *50°34′N 10°25′E*
108 *F9* **Meiringen** Bern, S Switzerland *46°42′N 08°13′E*
**Meishan** *see* Jinzhai
101 *O15* **Meissen** *Ger.* Meißen. Sachsen, E Germany *51°10′N 13°28′E*
**Meißen** *see* Meissen
101 *I15* **Meissner** ▲ C Germany *51°13′N 09°52′E*
99 *K25* **Meix-devant-Virton** Luxembourg, SE Belgium *49°36′N 05°27′E*
**Meixian** *see* Meizhou
**Meixing** *see* Xinjin
161 *P13* **Meizhou** *var.* Meixian, Mei Xian. Guangdong, S China *24°21′N 116°05′E*
67 *P2* **Mejerda** *var.* Oued Medjerda, Wādī Majardah. Algeria/Tunisia *see also* Medjerda, Oued
42 *F7* **Mejicanos** San Salvador, C El Salvador *13°50′N 89°13′W*
**Méjico** *see* Mexico
62 *G5* **Mejillones** Antofagasta, N Chile *23°03′S 70°25′W*
189 *V5* **Mejit Island** *var.* Mājeej. *island* Ratak Chain, NE Marshall Islands
79 *F17* **Mékambo** Ogooué-Ivindo, NE Gabon *01°03′N 13°50′E*
80 *J10* **Mek'elē** *var.* Makale. Tigray, N Ethiopia *13°36′N 39°29′E*
74 *I10* **Mekerrhane, Sebkha** *var.* Sebkha Meqerghane, Sebkra Mekerrhane. *salt flat* C Algeria
**Mekerrhane, Sebkra** *see* Mekerrhane, Sebkha
76 *G10* **Mékhé** NW Senegal *15°02′N 16°40′W*
146 *G14* **Mekhinli** Ahal Welaýaty, C Turkmenistan *37°28′N 59°20′E*
15 *P9* **Mékinac, Lac** Québec, SE Canada
**Meklong** *see* Samut Songkhram
74 *G6* **Meknès** N Morocco *33°54′N 05°27′W*
129 *U12* **Mekong** *Cam.* Mékôngk, *Chin.* Lancang Jiang, *Lao.* Mènam Khong, Nam Khong, *Th.* Mae Nam Khong, *Tib.* Dza Chu, *Vtn.* Sông Tiên Giang. SE Asia
**Mékôngk** *see* Mekong
167 *T15* **Mekong, Mouths of the** *delta* S Vietnam
38 *L12* **Mekoryuk** Nunivak Island, Alaska, USA *60°23′N 166°11′W*
77 *R14* **Mékrou** N Benin
168 *K9* **Melaka** *var.* Malacca. Melaka, Peninsular Malaysia *02°14′N 102°14′E*
168 *L9* **Melaka** *var.* Malacca. ◐ *state* Peninsular Malaysia
**Melaka, Selat** *see* Malacca, Strait of
175 *O6* **Melanesia** *island group* W Pacific Ocean
175 *P5* **Melanesian Basin** *undersea feature* W Pacific Ocean *0°05′N 160°35′E*
171 *R9* **Melanguane** Pulau Karakelang, N Indonesia *04°02′N 126°43′E*
169 *R11* **Melawi, Sungai** Borneo, N Indonesia
183 *N12* **Melbourne** *state capital* Victoria, SE Australia *37°51′S 144°56′E*
27 *V9* **Melbourne** Arkansas, C USA *36°04′N 91°54′W*
23 *Y12* **Melbourne** Florida, SE USA *28°04′N 80°36′W*
29 *W14* **Melbourne** Iowa, C USA *41°57′N 93°07′W*
92 *G10* **Melbu** Nordland, C Norway *68°31′N 14°50′E*
**Melchor de Mencos** *see* Ciudad Melchor de Mencos
63 *F19* **Melchor, Isla** *island* Archipiélago de los Chonos, S Chile
40 *M9* **Melchor Ocampo** Zacatecas, C Mexico *24°45′N 101°38′W*
14 *C11* **Meldrum Bay** Manitoulin Island, Ontario, S Canada *45°55′N 83°06′W*
**Meleda** *see* Mljet
106 *D8* **Melegnano** *prev.* Marignano. Lombardia, N Italy *45°22′N 09°19′E*
188 *F9* **Melekeok** Babeldaob, N Palau *07°30′N 134°37′E*
112 *L9* **Melenci** *Hung.* Melencze. Vojvodina, N Serbia *45°32′N 20°18′E*
**Melencze** *see* Melenci
127 *N4* **Melenki** Vladimirskaya Oblast', W Russia *55°21′N 41°37′E*
127 *V6* **Meleuz** Respublika Bashkortostan, W Russia *52°55′N 55°54′E*
12 *L6* **Mélèzes, Rivière aux** Québec, C Canada
78 *I11* **Melfi** Guéra, S Chad *11°05′N 17°57′E*
107 *M17* **Melfi** Basilicata, S Italy *41°00′N 15°33′E*
11 *U14* **Melfort** Saskatchewan, S Canada *52°52′N 104°38′W*
104 *H4* **Melgaço** Viana do Castelo, N Portugal *42°07′N 08°15′W*
105 *N4* **Melgar de Fernamental** Castilla y León, N Spain *42°24′N 04°15′W*
74 *L6* **Melghir, Chott** *var.* Chott Melrhir. *salt lake* E Algeria
94 *H8* **Melhus** Sør-Trøndelag, S Norway *63°17′N 10°18′E*
104 *H3* **Melide** Galicia, NW Spain *42°54′N 08°01′W*
**Meligalá** *see* Meligalás
115 *E21* **Meligalás** *prev.* Meligalá. Pelopónnisos, S Greece *37°13′N 21°58′E*
60 *L12* **Mel, Ilha do** *island* S Brazil
120 *E10* **Melilla** *off.* Cuidad Autónoma de Melilla; *anc.* Rusaddir, Russadir. Melilla, N Africa *35°18′N 02°56′W*
71 *N1* **Melilla** *enclave* Spain, N Africa
**Melilla, Cuidad Autónoma de** *see* Melilla
63 *G18* **Melimoyu, Monte** ▲ S Chile *44°06′S 72°49′W*
169 *V11* **Melintang, Danau** Borneo, N Indonesia
117 *U7* **Melioratyvne** Dnipropetrovs'ka Oblast', E Ukraine *48°35′N 35°18′E*
62 *G11* **Melipilla** Santiago, C Chile *33°42′S 71°15′W*
115 *I25* **Mélissa, Akrotírio** *headland* Kríti, Greece, E Mediterranean Sea *35°06′N 24°33′E*
11 *W17* **Melita** Manitoba, S Canada *49°16′N 100°59′W*
**Melita** *see* Mljet
**Melitene** *see* Malatya
107 *M23* **Melito di Porto Salvo** Calabria, SW Italy *37°55′N 15°48′E*
117 *U10* **Melitopol'** Zaporiz'ka Oblast', SE Ukraine *46°49′N 35°23′E*
109 *V4* **Melk** Niederösterreich, NE Austria *48°14′N 15°21′E*
95 *K15* **Mellan-Fryken** C Sweden
99 *E17* **Melle** Oost-Vlaanderen, NW Belgium *51°N 03°48′E*
100 *G13* **Melle** Niedersachsen, NW Germany *52°12′N 08°19′E*
95 *J17* **Mellerud** Västra Götaland, S Sweden *58°42′N 12°27′E*
102 *K10* **Melle-sur-Bretonne** Deux-Sèvres, W France *46°13′N 00°07′W*
29 *P8* **Mellette** South Dakota, N USA *45°07′N 98°29′W*
121 *O15* **Mellieħa** E Malta *35°58′N 14°21′E*
80 *B10* **Mellit** Northern Darfur, W Sudan *14°07′N 25°34′E*
75 *N7* **Mellita** ✈ SE Tunisia *33°47′N 10°51′E*
63 *G21* **Mellizo Sur, Cerro** ▲ S Chile *48°27′S 73°10′W*
100 *G9* **Mellum** *island* NW Germany
83 *L22* **Melmoth** KwaZulu/Natal, E South Africa *28°35′S 31°25′E*
111 *D16* **Mělník** *Ger.* Melnik. Středočeský Kraj, NW Czechia *50°21′N 14°30′E*
122 *J12* **Mel'nikovo** Tomskaya Oblast', C Russia *56°35′N 84°11′E*
61 *G18* **Melo** Cerro Largo, NE Uruguay *32°22′S 54°10′W*
**Melodunum** *see* Melun
**Melrhir, Chott** *see* Melghir, Chott
183 *P7* **Melrose** New South Wales, SE Australia *32°41′S 146°58′E*
182 *I7* **Melrose** South Australia *32°52′S 138°16′E*
29 *T7* **Melrose** Minnesota, N USA *45°40′N 94°46′W*
33 *Q11* **Melrose** Montana, NW USA *45°33′N 112°41′W*
37 *V12* **Melrose** New Mexico, SW USA *34°25′N 103°37′W*
108 *I8* **Mels** Sankt Gallen, NE Switzerland *47°03′N 09°26′E*
**Melsetter** *see* Chimanimani
33 *V9* **Melstone** Montana, NW USA *46°37′N 107°49′W*
101 *I16* **Melsungen** Hessen, C Germany *51°08′N 09°33′E*
92 *L12* **Meltaus** Lappi, NW Finland *66°54′N 25°18′E*
97 *N19* **Melton Mowbray** C England, United Kingdom *52°46′N 01°04′W*
82 *Q13* **Meluco** Cabo Delgado, NE Mozambique *12°31′S 39°39′E*
103 *O5* **Melun** *anc.* Melodunum. Seine-et-Marne, N France *48°32′N 02°40′E*
80 *F12* **Melut** Upper Nile, NE South Sudan *10°27′N 32°13′E*
27 *P5* **Melvern Lake** Kansas, C USA
11 *V16* **Melville** Saskatchewan, S Canada *50°57′N 102°49′W*
**Melville Bay/Melville Bugt** *see* Qimusseriarsuaq
45 *O11* **Melville Hall** ✈ (Dominica) NE Dominica *15°33′N 61°19′W*
181 *O1* **Melville Island** *island* Northern Territory, N Australia
197 *O8* **Melville Island** *island* Parry Islands, Northwest Territories, NW Canada
11 *W9* **Melville, Lake** Newfoundland and Labrador, E Canada
9 *O7* **Melville Peninsula** *peninsula* Nunavut, NE Canada
**Melville Sound** *see* Viscount Melville Sound
25 *Q9* **Melvin** Texas, SW USA *31°12′N 99°34′W*
97 *D15* **Melvin, Lough** *Ir.* Loch Meilbhe. S Northern Ireland, United Kingdom/Ireland
169 *S12* **Memala** Borneo, C Indonesia *01°44′S 112°36′E*
113 *L22* **Memaliaj** Gjirokastër, S Albania *40°21′N 19°56′E*
83 *Q14* **Memba** Nampula, NE Mozambique *14°07′S 40°33′E*
83 *Q14* **Memba, Baia de** *inlet* NE Mozambique
**Membidj** *see* Manbij
**Memel** *see* Neman, NE Europe
**Memel** *see* Klaipeda, Lithuania
101 *J23* **Memmingen** Bayern, S Germany *47°59′N 10°11′E*
27 *U1* **Memphis** Missouri, C USA *40°28′N 92°11′W*
20 *E10* **Memphis** Tennessee, S USA *35°09′N 90°03′W*
25 *P3* **Memphis** Texas, SW USA *34°43′N 100°34′W*
20 *E10* **Memphis** ✈ Tennessee, S USA *35°02′N 89°57′W*
15 *Q13* **Memphrémagog, Lac** *var.* Lake Memphremagog. Canada/USA *see also* Lake Memphremagog
19 *N6* **Memphremagog, Lake** *var.* Lac Memphrémagog. Canada/USA *see also* Memphrémagog, Lac
117 *Q2* **Mena** Chernihivs'ka Oblast', NE Ukraine *51°30′N 32°15′E*
27 *S12* **Mena** Arkansas, C USA *34°40′N 94°15′W*
**Menaam** *see* Menaldum
**Menado** *see* Manado
106 *D6* **Menaggio** Lombardia, N Italy *46°03′N 09°14′E*
29 *T6* **Menahga** Minnesota, N USA *46°45′N 95°06′W*
77 *R10* **Ménaka** Goa, E Mali *15°55′N 02°25′E*
98 *K5* **Menaldum** *Fris.* Menaam. Fryslân, N Netherlands *53°14′N 05°38′E*
**Mènam Khong** *see* Mekong
74 *E7* **Menara** ✈ (Marrakech) C Morocco *31°36′N 08°00′W*
25 *Q9* **Menard** Texas, SW USA *30°56′N 99°48′W*
193 *Q12* **Menard Fracture Zone** *tectonic feature* E Pacific Ocean
30 *M7* **Menasha** Wisconsin, N USA *44°13′N 88°25′W*
**Mencezi Garagum** *see* Merkezi Garagumy
193 *U9* **Mendaña Fracture Zone** *tectonic feature* E Pacific Ocean
169 *S13* **Mendawai, Sungai** Borneo, C Indonesia
103 *P13* **Mende** *anc.* Mimatum. Lozère, S France *44°32′N 03°30′E*
81 *J14* **Mendebo** ▲▲ C Ethiopia
80 *J9* **Mendefera** *prev.* Adi Ugri. S Eritrea *14°53′N 38°51′E*
197 *S7* **Mendeleyev Ridge** *undersea feature* Arctic Ocean
127 *T3* **Mendeleyevsk** Respublika Tatarstan, W Russia *55°54′N 52°19′E*
101 *F15* **Menden** Nordrhein-Westfalen, W Germany *51°26′N 07°47′E*
22 *L6* **Mendenhall** Mississippi, S USA *31°57′N 89°52′W*
38 *L13* **Mendenhall, Cape** *headland* Nunivak Island, Alaska, USA *59°45′N 166°10′W*
41 *P9* **Méndez** *var.* Villa de Méndez. Tamaulipas, C Mexico *25°06′N 98°32′W*
80 *H13* **Mendī** Oromīya C Ethiopia *09°43′N 35°07′E*
186 *C7* **Mendi** Southern Highlands, W Papua New Guinea *06°13′S 143°39′E*
97 *K22* **Mendip Hills** *var.* Mendips. *hill range* S England, United Kingdom
**Mendips** *see* Mendip Hills
34 *L6* **Mendocino** California, W USA *39°18′N 123°48′W*
34 *J3* **Mendocino, Cape** *headland* California, W USA *40°26′N 124°24′W*
0 *B8* **Mendocino Fracture Zone** *tectonic feature* NE Pacific Ocean
35 *P10* **Mendota** California, W USA *36°44′N 120°24′W*
30 *L11* **Mendota** Illinois, N USA *41°32′N 89°04′W*
30 *K8* **Mendota, Lake** Wisconsin, N USA
62 *I11* **Mendoza** Mendoza, W Argentina *33°00′S 68°47′W*
62 *I12* **Mendoza** *off.* Provincia de Mendoza. ◐ *province* W Argentina
**Mendoza, Provincia de** *see* Mendoza
108 *H12* **Mendrisio** Ticino, S Switzerland *45°53′N 08°59′E*
168 *L10* **Mendung** Pulau Mendol, W Indonesia *0°33′N 103°09′E*
54 *I5* **Mene de Mauroa** Falcón, NW Venezuela *10°39′N 71°04′W*
54 *I5* **Mene Grande** Zulia, NW Venezuela *09°51′N 70°57′W*
136 *B14* **Menemen** İzmir, W Turkey *38°34′N 27°03′E*
99 *C18* **Menen** *var.* Meenen, *Fr.* Menin. West-Vlaanderen, W Belgium *50°48′N 03°07′E*
163 *Q8* **Menengiyn Tal** *plain* E Mongolia
189 *R9* **Meneng Point** *headland* SW Nauru *0°33′S 166°57′E*
92 *L10* **Menesjärvi** *Lapp.* Menešjávri. Lappi, N Finland *68°39′N 26°22′E*
**Menešjávri** *see* Menesjärvi
107 *I24* **Menfi** Sicilia, Italy, C Mediterranean Sea *37°36′N 12°59′E*
161 *P7* **Mengcheng** Anhui, E China *33°15′N 116°33′E*
160 *F15* **Menghai** Yunnan, SW China *22°02′N 100°18′E*
160 *F15* **Mengla** Yunnan, SW China *21°30′N 101°33′E*
65 *F24* **Menguera Point** *headland* East Falkland, Falkland Islands
160 *M13* **Mengzhu Ling** ▲▲ S China
160 *H14* **Mengzi** Yunnan, SW China *23°20′N 103°32′E*
114 *H13* **Meníkio** *var.* Menoíkio. ▲ NE Greece *40°50′N 12°40′E*
**Menin** *see* Menen
182 *L7* **Menindee** New South Wales, SE Australia *32°24′S 142°25′E*
182 *L7* **Menindee Lake** New South Wales, SE Australia
182 *J10* **Meningie** South Australia *35°43′S 139°20′E*
103 *O5* **Mennecy** Essonne, N France *48°34′N 02°25′E*
29 *Q12* **Menno** South Dakota, N USA *43°14′N 97°34′W*
114 *H13* **Menoíkio** ▲▲ NE Greece
**Menoíkio** *see* Meníkio
31 *N5* **Menominee** Michigan, N USA *45°06′N 87°36′W*
30 *M5* **Menominee River** Michigan/Wisconsin, N USA
30 *M8* **Menomonee Falls** Wisconsin, N USA *43°11′N 88°09′W*
30 *I6* **Menomonie** Wisconsin, N USA *44°52′N 91°55′W*
83 *D14* **Menongue** *var.* Vila Serpa Pinto, *Port.* Serpa Pinto. Kuando Kubango, C Angola *14°38′S 17°39′E*
120 *H8* **Menorca** *Eng.* Minorca; *anc.* Balearis Minor. *island* Islas Baleares, Spain, W Mediterranean Sea
105 *S13* **Menor, Mar** *lagoon* SE Spain
39 *S10* **Mentasta Lake** Alaska, USA
39 *S10* **Mentasta Mountains** ▲▲ Alaska, USA
168 *I13* **Mentawai, Kepulauan** *island group* W Indonesia
168 *I12* **Mentawai, Selat** *strait* W Indonesia
168 *M12* **Mentok** Pulau Bangka, W Indonesia *02°01′S 105°10′E*
103 *V15* **Menton** *It.* Mentone. Alpes-Maritimes, SE France *43°47′N 07°30′E*
24 *K8* **Mentone** Texas, SW USA *31°42′N 103°36′W*
**Mentone** *see* Menton
31 *U11* **Mentor** Ohio, N USA *41°40′N 81°20′W*
169 *U10* **Menyapa, Gunung** ▲ Borneo, N Indonesia *01°04′N 116°01′E*
159 *T9* **Menyuan** *var.* Menyuan Huizu Zizhixian. Qinghai, C China *37°27′N 101°33′E*
**Menyuan Huizu Zizhixian** *see* Menyuan
74 *M5* **Menzel Bourguiba** *var.* Manzil Bū Ruqaybah; *prev.* Ferryville. N Tunisia *37°09′N 09°51′E*
136 *M15* **Menzelet Barajı** C Turkey
127 *T4* **Menzelinsk** Respublika Tatarstan, W Russia *55°44′N 53°00′E*
180 *K11* **Menzies** Western Australia *29°42′S 121°04′E*
195 *V6* **Menzies, Mount** ▲ Antarctica *73°32′S 61°02′E*
40 *J6* **Meoqui** Chihuahua, N Mexico *28°18′N 105°30′W*
83 *N14* **Meponda** Niassa, NE Mozambique *13°20′S 34°53′E*
98 *M8* **Meppel** Drenthe, NE Netherlands *52°42′N 06°12′E*
100 *E12* **Meppen** Niedersachsen, NW Germany *52°42′N 07°18′E*
**Meqerghane, Sebkha** *see* Mekerrhane, Sebkha
105 *T6* **Mequinenza, Embalse de** NE Spain
30 *M8* **Mequon** Wisconsin, N USA *43°13′N 87°57′W*
**Mera** *see* Maira
182 *D3* **Meramangye, Lake** *salt lake* South Australia
27 *W5* **Meramec River** Missouri, C USA
**Meran** *see* Merano
168 *K13* **Merangin** Sumatera, W Indonesia
106 *G5* **Merano** *Ger.* Meran. Trentino-Alto Adige, N Italy *46°40′N 11°10′E*
168 *K8* **Merapuh Lama** Pahang, Peninsular Malaysia *04°37′N 101°58′E*
106 *D7* **Merate** Lombardia, N Italy *45°42′N 09°26′E*
169 *U13* **Meratus, Pegunungan** ▲▲ Borneo, N Indonesia
171 *Y16* **Merauke, Sungai** Papua, E Indonesia
182 *L9* **Merbein** Victoria, SE Australia *34°11′S 142°03′E*
99 *F21* **Merbes-le-Château** Hainaut, S Belgium *50°19′N 04°09′E*
**Merca** *see* Marka
54 *C13* **Mercaderes** Cauca, SW Colombia *01°46′N 77°09′W*
**Mercara** *see* Madikeri
35 *P9* **Merced** California, W USA *37°17′N 120°30′W*
61 *C20* **Mercedes** Buenos Aires, E Argentina *34°42′S 59°30′W*
61 *D15* **Mercedes** Corrientes, NE Argentina *29°09′S 58°05′W*
61 *D19* **Mercedes** Soriano, SW Uruguay *33°16′S 58°01′W*
25 *S17* **Mercedes** Texas, SW USA *26°09′N 97°54′W*
**Mercedes** *see* Villa Mercedes
35 *R9* **Merced Peak** ▲ California, W USA *37°34′N 119°30′W*
35 *P9* **Merced River** California, W USA
18 *B13* **Mercer** Pennsylvania, NE USA *41°14′N 80°14′W*
99 *G18* **Merchtem** Vlaams Brabant, C Belgium *50°57′N 04°14′E*
15 *O13* **Mercier** Québec, SE Canada *45°15′N 73°45′W*
25 *Q9* **Mercury** Texas, SW USA *31°23′N 99°09′W*
184 *M5* **Mercury Islands** *island group* N New Zealand
19 *O9* **Meredith** New Hampshire, NE USA *43°36′N 71°28′W*
65 *B25* **Meredith, Cape** *var.* Cabo Belgrano. *headland* West Falkland, Falkland Islands *52°15′S 60°40′W*
37 *V6* **Meredith, Lake** Colorado, C USA
25 *N2* **Meredith, Lake** Texas, SW USA
81 *O16* **Mereeg** *var.* Mareeq, *It.* Meregh. Galguduud, E Somalia *03°47′N 47°19′E*
117 *V5* **Merefa** Kharkivs'ka Oblast', E Ukraine *49°49′N 36°05′E*
**Meregh** *see* Mereeg
99 *E17* **Merelbeke** Oost-Vlaanderen, NW Belgium *51°00′N 03°45′E*
**Merend** *see* Marand
157 *T12* **Méreuch** Mondolkiri, E Cambodia *13°01′N 107°26′E*
**Mergate** *see* Margate
**Mergui** *see* Myeik
**Mergui Archipelago** *see* Myeik Archipelago
114 *L12* **Meriç** Edirne, NW Turkey *41°12′N 26°24′E*
114 *L12* **Meriç** *Bul.* Maritsa, *Gk.* Évros; *anc.* Hebrus. SE Europe *see also* Évros/Maritsa
41 *X12* **Mérida** Yucatán, SW Mexico *20°58′N 89°35′W*
104 *J11* **Mérida** *anc.* Augusta Emerita. Extremadura, W Spain *38°55′N 06°20′W*
54 *I6* **Mérida** Mérida, W Venezuela *08°36′N 71°08′W*
54 *H7* **Mérida** *off.* Estado Mérida. ◐ *state* W Venezuela
**Mérida, Estado** *see* Mérida
18 *M13* **Meriden** Connecticut, NE USA *41°32′N 72°48′W*
22 *M5* **Meridian** Mississippi, S USA *32°24′N 88°43′W*
25 *S8* **Meridian** Texas, SW USA *31°56′N 97°40′W*
102 *J13* **Mérignac** Gironde, SW France *44°50′N 00°40′W*
102 *J13* **Mérignac** ✈ (Bordeaux) Gironde, SW France *44°51′N 00°44′W*
93 *J18* **Merikarvia** Satakunta, SW Finland *61°51′N 21°30′E*
183 *R12* **Merimbula** New South Wales, SE Australia *36°52′S 149°51′E*
182 *L9* **Meringur** Victoria, SE Australia *34°26′S 141°19′E*
**Merín, Laguna** *see* Mirim Lagoon
97 *I19* **Merioneth** *cultural region* W Wales, United Kingdom
188 *A11* **Merir** *island* Palau Islands, N Palau
188 *B17* **Merizo** SW Guam *13°15′N 144°40′E*
**Merjama** *see* Märjamaa
**Merke** *see* Merki
25 *P7* **Merkel** Texas, SW USA *32°28′N 100°00′W*
146 *E12* **Merkezi Garagumy** *var.* Mencezi Garagum, *Rus.* Tsentral'nyye Nizmennyye Garagumy. *desert* C Turkmenistan
145 *S16* **Merki** *prev.* Merke. Zhambyl, S Kazakhstan *42°48′N 73°10′E*
119 *F15* **Merkinė** Alytus, S Lithuania *54°09′N 24°11′E*
99 *G16* **Merksem** Antwerpen, N Belgium *51°17′N 04°26′E*
99 *I15* **Merksplas** Antwerpen, N Belgium *51°22′N 04°54′E*
**Merkulovichi** *see* Myerkulavichy
119 *G15* **Merkys** S Lithuania
32 *F15* **Merlin** Oregon, NW USA *42°34′N 123°23′W*
61 *C20* **Merlo** Buenos Aires, E Argentina *34°39′S 58°45′W*
138 *G8* **Meron, Harei** *prev.* Haré Meron. ▲ N Israel *35°06′N 33°00′E*
74 *K6* **Merouane, Chott** *salt lake* NE Algeria
80 *F7* **Merowe** Northern, N Sudan *18°29′N 31°49′E*
180 *J12* **Merredin** Western Australia *31°31′S 118°18′E*
97 *I14* **Merrick** ▲ S Scotland, United Kingdom *55°09′N 04°28′W*
32 *H16* **Merrill** Oregon, NW USA *42°00′N 121°37′W*
30 *L5* **Merrill** Wisconsin, N USA *45°12′N 89°43′W*
31 *N11* **Merrillville** Indiana, N USA *41°28′N 87°19′W*
19 *O10* **Merrimack River** Massachusetts/New Hampshire, NE USA
28 *L12* **Merriman** Nebraska, C USA *42°54′N 101°42′W*
11 *N17* **Merritt** British Columbia, SW Canada *50°09′N 120°49′W*
23 *Y12* **Merritt Island** Florida, SE USA *28°21′N 80°42′W*
23 *Y11* **Merritt Island** *island* Florida, SE USA
28 *M12* **Merritt Reservoir** Nebraska, C USA
183 *S7* **Merriwa** New South Wales, SE Australia *32°09′S 150°24′E*
183 *O8* **Merriwagga** New South Wales, SE Australia *33°51′S 145°38′E*
22 *G8* **Merryville** Louisiana, S USA *30°45′N 93°32′W*
80 *K9* **Mersa Fat'ma** E Eritrea *14°52′N 40°16′E*
102 *M7* **Mer St-Aubin** Loir-et-Cher, C France *47°42′N 01°31′E*
99 *M24* **Mersch** Luxembourg, C Luxembourg *49°45′N 06°06′E*
101 *M15* **Merseburg** Sachsen-Anhalt, C Germany *51°22′N 12°00′E*
**Mersen** *see* Meerssen
97 *K18* **Mersey** NW England, United Kingdom
136 *J17* **Mersin** *var.* İçel. İçel, S Turkey *36°50′N 34°39′E*
**Mersin** *see* İçel
168 *L9* **Mersing** Johor, Peninsular Malaysia *02°25′N 103°50′E*
118 *E8* **Mērsrags** NW Latvia *57°21′N 23°05′E*
**Merta** *see* Merta City
152 *G12* **Merta City** *var.* Merta. Rājasthān, N India *26°40′N 74°04′E*
152 *F12* **Merta Road** Rājasthān, N India *26°42′N 73°54′E*
97 *J21* **Merthyr Tydfil** S Wales, United Kingdom *51°46′N 03°23′W*
104 *H13* **Mértola** Beja, S Portugal *37°38′N 07°40′W*
144 *G14* **Mertvyy Kultuk, Sor** *salt flat* SW Kazakhstan
195 *V16* **Mertz Glacier** *glacier* Antarctica
99 *M24* **Mertzig** Diekirch, C Luxembourg *49°50′N 06°00′E*
25 *O9* **Mertzon** Texas, SW USA *31°16′N 100°50′W*
103 *N4* **Méru** Oise, N France *49°15′N 02°07′E*
81 *I18* **Meru** Meru, C Kenya *0°03′N 37°38′E*
81 *I20* **Meru, Mount** ▲ NE Tanzania *03°12′S 36°45′E*
**Merv** *see* Mary
**Mervdasht** *see* Marv Dasht
136 *K11* **Merzifon** Amasya, N Turkey *40°52′N 35°28′E*
101 *D20* **Merzig** Saarland, SW Germany *49°27′N 06°39′E*
36 *L14* **Mesa** Arizona, SW USA *33°25′N 111°49′W*
29 *V4* **Mesabi Range** ▲▲ Minnesota, N USA
54 *H6* **Mesa Bolívar** Mérida, NW Venezuela *08°30′N 71°38′W*
107 *Q18* **Mesagne** Puglia, SE Italy *40°33′N 17°49′E*
39 *P12* **Mesa Mountain** ▲ Alaska, USA *60°26′N 155°14′W*
115 *J25* **Mesará** *lowland* Kríti, Greece, E Mediterranean Sea
37 *S14* **Mescalero** New Mexico, SW USA *33°09′N 105°46′W*
101 *G15* **Meschede** Nordrhein-Westfalen, W Germany *51°21′N 08°16′E*
137 *Q12* **Mescit Dağları** ▲▲ NE Turkey
189 *V13* **Mesegon** *island* Chuuk, C Micronesia
**Meseritz** *see* Międzyrzecz
54 *F11* **Mesetas** Meta, C Colombia *03°14′N 74°09′W*
**Meshchera Lowland** *see* Meshcherskaya Nizmennost'
**Meshcherskaya Nizina** *see* Meshcherskaya Nizmennost'
126 *M4* **Meshcherskaya Nizmennost'** *var.* Meshcherskaya Nizina, *Eng.* Meshchera Lowland. *basin* W Russia
126 *J5* **Meshchovsk** Kaluzhskaya Oblast', W Russia *54°21′N 35°23′E*
125 *R9* **Meshchura** Respublika Komi, NW Russia *63°18′N 50°56′E*
**Meshed** *see* Mashhad
**Meshed-i-Sar** *see* Bābolsar
80 *E13* **Meshra'er Req** Warap, W South Sudan *08°30′N 29°27′E*
37 *R15* **Mesilla** New Mexico, SW USA *32°15′N 106°49′W*
108 *H10* **Mesocco** *Ger.* Misox. Ticino, S Switzerland *46°18′N 09°13′E*
115 *D18* **Mesolóngi** *prev.* Mesolóngion. Dytikí Elláda, W Greece *38°21′N 21°26′E*
**Mesolóngion** *see* Mesolóngi
14 *E8* **Mesomikenda Lake** Ontario, S Canada
61 *D15* **Mesopotamia** *var.* Mesopotamia Argentina. *physical region* NE Argentina
**Mesopotamia Argentina** *see* Mesopotamia
35 *Y10* **Mesquite** Nevada, W USA *36°47′N 114°04′W*
82 *Q13* **Messalo, Rio** *var.* Mualo. NE Mozambique
**Messana/Messene** *see* Messina
99 *L25* **Messancy** Luxembourg, SE Belgium *49°36′N 05°49′E*
107 *M23* **Messina** *var.* Messana, Messene; *anc.* Zancle. Sicilia, Italy, C Mediterranean Sea *38°12′N 15°33′E*
**Messina** *see* Musina
**Messina, Strait of** *see* Messina, Stretto di
107 *M23* **Messina, Stretto di** *Eng.* Strait of Messina. *strait* SW Italy
115 *E21* **Messíni** Pelopónnisos, S Greece *37°03′N 22°00′E*
115 *E21* **Messinía** *peninsula* S Greece
115 *E22* **Messiniakós Kólpos** *gulf* S Greece
122 *J8* **Messoyakha** N Russia
114 *H11* **Mesta** *Gk.* Néstos, *Turk.* Kara Su. Bulgaria/Greece *see also* Néstos
**Mesta** *see* Néstos
**Mestghanem** *see* Mostaganem
137 *R8* **Mest'ia** *prev.* Mestia, *var.* Mestiya. N Georgia *43°03′N 42°50′E*
**Mestia** *see* Mest'ia
**Mestiya** *see* Mest'ia
115 *K18* **Mestón, Akrotírio** *cape* Chíos, E Greece
106 *H8* **Mestre** Veneto, NE Italy *45°30′N 12°14′E*
59 *M16* **Mestre, Espigão** ▲▲ E Brazil
169 *N14* **Mesuji** Sumatera, W Indonesia
**Mesule** *see* Grosser Möseler
10 *J10* **Meszah Peak** ▲ British Columbia, W Canada *58°31′N 131°28′W*
54 *G11* **Meta** *off.* Departamento del Meta. ◐ *province* C Colombia
15 *Q8* **Metabetchouane** Québec, SE Canada
**Meta, Departamento del** *see* Meta
9 *S7* **Meta Incognita Peninsula** *peninsula* Baffin Island, Nunavut, NE Canada
22 *K9* **Metairie** Louisiana, S USA *29°58′N 90°09′W*
32 *M6* **Metaline Falls** Washington, NW USA *48°51′N 117°21′W*
62 *K6* **Metán** Salta, N Argentina *25°29′S 64°57′W*
82 *N13* **Metangula** Niassa, N Mozambique *12°41′S 34°50′E*
42 *E7* **Metapán** Santa Ana, NW El Salvador *14°20′N 89°28′W*
54 *K9* **Meta, Río** Colombia/Venezuela
106 *I11* **Metauro** C Italy
80 *H11* **Metema** Āmara, N Ethiopia *12°53′N 36°10′E*
115 *D15* **Metéora** *religious building* Thessalía, C Greece
65 *O20* **Meteor Rise** *undersea feature* SW Indian Ocean *46°00′S 05°30′E*
186 *G5* **Meteran** New Hanover, NE Papua New Guinea *02°40′S 150°12′E*
**Meterlam** *see* Mehtar Lām
115 *G20* **Methanon** *peninsula* S Greece
**Methariam/Metharlam** *see* Mehtar Lām
32 *J6* **Methow River** Washington, NW USA
19 *O10* **Methuen** Massachusetts, NE USA *42°43′N 71°10′W*
185 *G19* **Methven** Canterbury, South Island, New Zealand *43°37′S 171°38′E*
**Metis** *see* Metz
113 *G15* **Metković** Dubrovnik-Neretva, SE Croatia *43°02′N 17°37′E*
39 *Y14* **Metlakatla** Annette Island, Alaska, USA *55°07′N 131°34′W*
109 *V13* **Metlika** *Ger.* Möttling. SE Slovenia *45°38′N 15°18′E*
109 *T8* **Metnitz** Kärnten, S Austria *46°58′N 14°09′E*
27 *W12* **Meto, Bayou** Arkansas, C USA
168 *M15* **Metro** Sumatera, W Indonesia *05°05′S 105°20′E*
30 *M17* **Metropolis** Illinois, N USA *37°09′N 88°43′W*
**Metropolitan** *see* Santiago
35 *N8* **Metropolitan Oakland** ✈ California, W USA *37°42′N 122°13′W*
115 *D15* **Métsovo** *prev.* Métsovon. Ípeiros, C Greece *39°47′N 21°12′E*
**Métsovon** *see* Métsovo
23 *V5* **Metter** Georgia, SE USA *32°24′N 82°03′W*
99 *H21* **Mettet** Namur, S Belgium *50°19′N 04°43′E*
101 *D20* **Mettlach** Saarland, SW Germany *49°28′N 06°37′E*
**Mettu** *see* Metu
80 *H13* **Metu** *var.* Mattu, Mettu. Oromīya, C Ethiopia *08°18′N 35°39′E*
138 *G8* **Metula** *prev.* Metulla. Northern, N Israel *33°16′N 35°35′E*
169 *T10* **Metulang** Borneo, N Indonesia *01°28′N 114°40′E*
**Metulla** *see* Metula
103 *T4* **Metz** *anc.* Divodurum Mediomatricum, Mediomatrica, Metis. Moselle, NE France *49°07′N 06°09′E*
101 *H22* **Metzingen** Baden-Württemberg, S Germany *48°31′N 09°16′E*
168 *G8* **Meulaboh** Sumatera, W Indonesia *04°10′N 96°09′E*
99 *D18* **Meulebeke** West-Vlaanderen, W Belgium *50°57′N 03°18′E*
103 *U6* **Meurthe** NE France
103 *S5* **Meurthe-et-Moselle** ◐ *department* NE France
103 *S4* **Meuse** ◐ *department* NE France
84 *F10* **Meuse** *Dut.* Maas. W Europe *see also* Maas
**Meuse** *see* Maas
**Mexcala, Río** *see* Balsas, Río
25 *U8* **Mexia** Texas, SW USA *31°40′N 96°28′W*
58 *K11* **Mexiana, Ilha** *island* NE Brazil
40 *C1* **Mexicali** Baja California, NW Mexico *32°34′N 115°26′W*
**Mexicanos, Estados Unidos** *see* Mexico
27 *V4* **Mexico** Missouri, C USA *19°10′N 99°04′W*
18 *H9* **Mexico** New York, NE USA *43°27′N 76°14′W*
40 *L7* **Mexico** *off.* United Mexican States, *var.* Méjico, México, *Sp.* Estados Unidos Mexicanos. ◆ *federal republic* N Central America
41 *O13* **México** ◐ *state* S Mexico
**México** *see* Mexico
0 *J13* **Mexico Basin** *var.* Sigsbee Deep. *undersea feature* C Gulf of Mexico *25°00′N 92°00′W*
**Mexico City** *see* México, Ciudad de
41 *O14* **México, Ciudad de** *Eng.* Mexico City. ● (Mexico) México, C Mexico *19°26′N 99°08′W*
**México, Golfo de** *see* Mexico, Gulf of
44 *B4* **Mexico, Gulf of** *Sp.* Golfo de México. *gulf* W Atlantic Ocean
139 *R4* **Mexmûr** *Ar.* Makhmūr. Arbīl, N Iraq *35°47′N 43°32′E*
**Meyadine** *see* Al Mayādīn
**Meydān Shahr** *see* Maīdān Shahr
39 *Y14* **Meyers Chuck** Etolin Island, Alaska, USA *55°44′N 132°15′W*
**Meymaneh** *see* Maīmanah
143 *N7* **Meymeh** Eşfahān, C Iran *33°29′N 51°09′E*
123 *V7* **Meynypil'gyno** Chukotskiy Avtonomnyy Okrug, NE Russia *62°33′N 177°00′E*
108 *A10* **Meyrin** Genève, SW Switzerland *46°14′N 06°05′E*
166 *L7* **Mezaligon** Ayeyarwady, SW Myanmar (Burma) *17°53′N 95°12′E*
41 *O15* **Mezcala** Guerrero, S Mexico *17°55′N 99°34′W*
114 *H8* **Mezdra** Vratsa, NW Bulgaria *43°08′N 23°42′E*
103 *P16* **Mèze** Hérault, S France *43°26′N 03°37′E*
125 *O6* **Mezen'** Arkhangel'skaya Oblast', NW Russia *65°54′N 44°10′E*
125 *P8* **Mezen'** NW Russia
**Mezen, Bay of** *see* Mezenskaya Guba
103 *Q13* **Mézenc, Mont** ▲ C France *44°57′N 04°15′E*
125 *O8* **Mezenskaya Guba** *var.* Bay of Mezen. *bay* NW Russia
**Mezha** *see* Myazha
122 *H6* **Mezhdusharskiy, Ostrov** *island* Novaya Zemlya, N Russia
**Mezhëvo** *see* Myezhava
**Mezhgor'ye** *see* Mizhhir"ya
117 *V8* **Mezhova** Dnipropetrovs'ka Oblast', E Ukraine *48°15′N 36°44′E*
10 *J12* **Meziadin Junction** British Columbia, W Canada *56°06′N 129°15′W*
111 *G16* **Mezileské Sedlo** *var.* Przełęcz Międzyleska. *pass* Czechia/Poland
102 *L14* **Mézin** Lot-et-Garonne, SW France *44°03′N 00°16′E*
111 *M24* **Mezőberény** Békés, SE Hungary *46°49′N 21°00′E*
111 *M25* **Mezőhegyes** Békés, SE Hungary *46°20′N 20°48′E*
111 *M25* **Mezőkovácsháza** Békés, SE Hungary *46°24′N 20°52′E*
111 *M21* **Mezőkövesd** Borsod-Abaúj-Zemplén, NE Hungary *47°49′N 20°32′E*
**Mezőtelegd** *see* Tileagd
111 *M23* **Mezőtúr** Jász-Nagykun-Szolnok, E Hungary *47°N 20°37′E*
40 *K10* **Mezquital** Durango, C Mexico *23°31′N 104°19′W*
106 *G6* **Mezzolombardo** Trentino-Alto Adige, N Italy *46°13′N 11°08′E*
82 *L13* **Mfuwe** Muchinga, N Zambia *13°00′S 31°45′E*
121 *O15* **Mġarr** Gozo, N Malta *36°01′N 14°18′E*
126 *H6* **Mglin** Bryanskaya Oblast', W Russia *53°01′N 32°54′E*
**Mhálanna, Cionn** *see* Malin Head
154 *G10* **Mhow** Madhya Pradesh, C India *22°32′N 75°49′E*
**Miadziel Nowy** *see* Myadzyel
171 *O6* **Miagao** Panay Island, C Philippines *10°40′N 122°15′E*
41 *R17* **Miahuatlán** *var.* Miahuatlán de Porfirio Díaz. Oaxaca, SE Mexico *16°21′N 96°36′W*
**Miahuatlán de Porfirio Díaz** *see* Miahuatlán
104 *K10* **Miajadas** Extremadura, W Spain *39°10′N 05°54′W*
**Miajlar** *see* Myājlār
36 *M14* **Miami** Arizona, SW USA *33°23′N 110°53′W*
23 *Z16* **Miami** Florida, SE USA *25°46′N 80°12′W*
27 *R8* **Miami** Oklahoma, C USA *36°53′N 94°54′W*




◆ Country
● Country Capital
◇ Dependent Territory
○ Dependent Territory Capital
◐ Administrative Regions
✈ International Airport
▲ Mountain
▲▲ Mountain Range
Volcano
River
Lake
Reservoir

MIAMI – MIRPUR


25 O2 **Miami** Texas, SW USA *35°42′N 100°37′W*
23 Z16 **Miami** ✈ Florida, SE USA *25°47′N 80°16′W*
23 Z16 **Miami Beach** Florida, SE USA *25°47′N 80°08′W*
23 Y15 **Miami Canal** *canal* Florida, SE USA
31 R14 **Miamisburg** Ohio, N USA *39°38′N 84°17′W*
149 U10 **Mian Channun** Punjab, E Pakistan *30°24′N 72°27′E*
142 J4 **Mīāndowāb** *var.* Mianduab, Miyāndoāb. Āżarbāyjān-e Gharbī, NW Iran *36°57′N 46°06′E*
172 H5 **Miandrivazo** Toliara, C Madagascar *19°31′S 45°29′E*
**Mianduab** *see* Mīāndowāb
142 K3 **Mīāneh** *var.* Miyāneh. Āżarbāyjān-e Sharqī, NW Iran *37°23′N 47°45′E*
161 T12 **Mianhua Yu** *prev.* Mienhua Yü. *island* N Taiwan
149 O16 **Miani Hor** *lagoon* S Pakistan
160 G10 **Mianning** Sichuan, C China *28°34′N 102°12′E*
149 T7 **Mianwali** Punjab, NE Pakistan *32°32′N 71°33′E*
160 J7 **Mianxian** *var.* Mian Xian. Shaanxi, C China *33°12′N 106°36′E*
**Mian Xian** *see* Mianxian
160 I8 **Mianyang** Sichuan, C China *31°29′N 104°43′E*
**Mianyang** *see* Xiantao
161 R3 **Miaodao Qundao** *island group* E China
161 S13 **Miaoli** N Taiwan *24°33′N 120°48′E*
122 F11 **Miass** Chelyabinskaya Oblast', C Russia *55°00′N 59°55′E*
110 G8 **Miastko** *Ger.* Rummelsburg in Pommern. Pomorskie, N Poland *54°N 16°58′E*
**Miava** *see* Myjava
11 O15 **Mica Creek** British Columbia, SW Canada *51°58′N 118°29′W*
160 J7 **Micang Shan** ▲▲ C China
**Mi Chai** *see* Nong Khai
111 O19 **Michalovce** *Ger.* Grossmichel, ***Hung.*** Nagymihály. Košický Kraj, E Slovakia *48°46′N 21°55′E*
99 M20 **Michel, Baraque** *hill* E Belgium
39 S5 **Michelson, Mount** ▲ Alaska, USA *69°19′N 144°16′W*
45 P9 **Miches** E Dominican Republic *18°59′N 69°03′W*
30 M4 **Michigamme, Lake** ◎ Michigan, N USA
30 M4 **Michigamme Reservoir** ⊠ Michigan, N USA
31 N4 **Michigamme River** ≈ Michigan, N USA
31 O7 **Michigan** *off.* State of Michigan, ***also known as*** Great Lakes State, Lake State, Wolverine State. ◈ *state* N USA
31 O11 **Michigan City** Indiana, N USA *41°43′N 86°52′W*
31 O8 **Michigan, Lake** ◎ N USA
31 P2 **Michipicoten Bay** *lake bay* Ontario, N Canada
14 A8 **Michipicoten Island** *island* Ontario, S Canada
14 B7 **Michipicoten River** Ontario, S Canada *47°56′N 84°48′W*
**Michurin** *see* Tsarevo
126 M6 **Michurinsk** Tambovskaya Oblast', W Russia *52°56′N 40°31′E*
**Mico, Punta/Mico, Punto** *see* Monkey Point
42 L10 **Mico, Río** ≈ SE Nicaragua
45 T12 **Micoud** SE Saint Lucia *13°49′N 60°54′W*
189 N16 **Micronesia** *off.* Federated States of Micronesia. ◆ *federation* W Pacific Ocean
175 P4 **Micronesia** *island group* W Pacific Ocean
**Micronesia, Federated States of** *see* Micronesia
169 O9 **Midai, Pulau** *island* Kepulauan Natuna, W Indonesia
**Mid-Atlantic Cordillera** *see* Mid-Atlantic Ridge
65 M17 **Mid-Atlantic Ridge** *var.* Mid-Atlantic Cordillera, Mid-Atlantic Rise, Mid-Atlantic Swell. *undersea feature* Atlantic Ocean *0°00′N 20°00′W*
**Mid-Atlantic Rise/ Mid-Atlantic Swell** *see* Mid-Atlantic Ridge
99 E15 **Middelburg** Zeeland, SW Netherlands *51°30′N 03°36′E*
83 H24 **Middelburg** Eastern Cape, S South Africa *31°28′S 25°01′E*
83 K21 **Middelburg** Mpumalanga, NE South Africa *25°47′S 29°28′E*
95 G23 **Middelfart** Syddtjylland, C Denmark *55°30′N 09°44′E*
98 G13 **Middelharnis** Zuid-Holland, SW Netherlands *51°45′N 04°10′E*
99 B16 **Middelkerke** West-Vlaanderen, W Belgium *51°12′N 02°51′E*
98 I9 **Middenbeemster** Noord-Holland, C Netherlands *52°33′N 04°55′E*
98 I8 **Middenmeer** Noord-Holland, NW Netherlands *52°48′N 04°58′E*
35 Q2 **Middle Alkali Lake** ◎ California, W USA
193 S6 **Middle America Trench** *undersea feature* E Pacific Ocean *15°00′N 95°00′W*
151 P19 **Middle Andaman** *island* Andaman Islands, India, NE Indian Ocean
**Middle Atlas** *see* Moyen Atlas
21 R3 **Middlebourne** West Virginia, NE USA *39°30′N 80°53′W*
23 W9 **Middleburg** Florida, SE USA *30°03′N 81°55′W*
**Middleburg Island** *see* 'Eua
**Middle Caicos** *see* Grand Caicos
25 N8 **Middle Concho River** ≈ Texas, SW USA
**Middle Congo** *see* Congo (Republic of)
39 R6 **Middle Fork Chandalar River** ≈ Alaska, USA
39 Q7 **Middle Fork Koyukuk River** ≈ Alaska, USA
33 O12 **Middle Fork Salmon River** ≈ Idaho, NW USA
11 T15 **Middle Lake** Saskatchewan, S Canada *52°31′N 105°16′W*
28 L13 **Middle Loup River** ≈ Nebraska, C USA
185 E22 **Middlemarch** Otago, South Island, New Zealand *45°30′S 170°07′E*
31 T15 **Middleport** Ohio, N USA *39°00′N 82°03′W*
29 U14 **Middle Raccoon River** ≈ Iowa, C USA
29 R3 **Middle River** ≈ Minnesota, N USA
21 N8 **Middlesboro** Kentucky, S USA *36°37′N 83°42′W*
97 M15 **Middlesbrough** N England, United Kingdom *54°35′N 01°14′W*
42 G3 **Middlesex** Stann Creek, C Belize *17°00′N 88°31′W*
97 N22 **Middlesex** *cultural region* SE England, United Kingdom
13 P15 **Middleton** Nova Scotia, SE Canada *44°56′N 65°04′W*
20 F10 **Middleton** Tennessee, S USA *35°05′N 88°57′W*
30 L9 **Middleton** Wisconsin, N USA *43°06′N 89°30′W*
39 S13 **Middleton Island** *island* Alaska, USA
34 M7 **Middletown** California, W USA *38°44′N 122°39′W*
21 Y2 **Middletown** Delaware, NE USA *39°25′N 75°39′W*
18 K15 **Middletown** New Jersey, NE USA *40°23′N 74°08′W*
18 K13 **Middletown** New York, NE USA *41°27′N 74°25′W*
31 R14 **Middletown** Ohio, N USA *39°33′N 84°19′W*
18 G15 **Middletown** Pennsylvania, NE USA *40°11′N 76°42′W*
141 N14 **Mīdī** *var.* Maydī. NW Yemen *16°18′N 42°51′E*
103 O16 **Midi, Canal du** *canal* S France
102 K17 **Midi de Bigorre, Pic du** ▲ S France *42°57′N 00°08′E*
102 K17 **Midi d'Ossau, Pic du** ▲ SW France *42°51′N 00°27′W*
173 R7 **Mid-Indian Basin** *undersea feature* N Indian Ocean *10°00′S 80°00′E*
173 P7 **Mid-Indian Ridge** *var.* Central Indian Ridge. *undersea feature* C Indian Ocean *12°00′S 66°00′E*
25 N8 **Midkiff** Texas, SW USA *31°35′N 101°51′W*
14 G13 **Midland** Ontario, S Canada *44°45′N 79°53′W*
31 R8 **Midland** Michigan, N USA *43°37′N 84°15′W*
28 M10 **Midland** South Dakota, N USA *44°04′N 101°07′W*
24 M8 **Midland** Texas, SW USA *32°N 102°05′W*
83 K17 **Midlands** ◈ *province* C Zimbabwe
97 D21 **Midleton** *Ir.* Mainistir na Corann. SW Ireland *51°55′N 08°10′W*
25 T7 **Midlothian** Texas, SW USA *32°28′N 96°59′W*
96 K12 **Midlothian** *cultural region* S Scotland, United Kingdom
172 I7 **Midongy Atsimo** Fianarantsoa, S Madagascar *21°58′S 47°47′E*
102 K15 **Midou** ≈ SW France
192 J6 **Mid-Pacific Mountains** *var.* Mid-Pacific Seamounts. *undersea feature* NW Pacific Ocean *20°00′N 178°00′W*
**Mid-Pacific Seamounts** *see* Mid-Pacific Mountains
171 Q7 **Midsayap** Mindanao, S Philippines *07°12′N 124°31′E*
95 F21 **Midtjylland** ◈ *county* NW Denmark
36 L3 **Midway** Utah, W USA *40°30′N 111°28′W*
192 L5 **Midway Islands** ◇ *US unincorporated territory* C Pacific Ocean
33 X14 **Midwest** Wyoming, C USA *43°24′N 106°15′W*
27 N10 **Midwest City** Oklahoma, C USA *35°28′N 98°24′W*
152 M10 **Mid Western** ◈ *zone* W Nepal
98 P5 **Midwolda** Groningen, NE Netherlands *53°12′N 07°00′E*
137 Q16 **Midyat** Mardin, SE Turkey *37°25′N 41°20′E*
114 F8 **Midzhur** *SCr.* Midžor. ▲ Bulgaria/Serbia *43°24′N 22°41′E* ***see also*** Midžor
**Midzhur** *see* Midžor
113 Q14 **Midžor** *Bul.* Midzhur. ▲ Bulgaria/Serbia *43°24′N 22°40′E* ***see also*** Midzhur
**Midžor** *see* Midzhur
164 K14 **Mie** *off.* Mie-ken. ◈ *prefecture* Honshū, SW Japan
111 L16 **Miechów** Małopolskie, S Poland *50°21′N 20°01′E*
110 F11 **Międzychód** *Ger.* Mitteldorf. Wielkopolskie, C Poland *52°36′N 15°53′E*
**Międzyleska, Przełęcz** *see* Mezileské Sedlo
110 O12 **Międzyrzec Podlaski** Lubelskie, E Poland *52°N 22°47′E*
110 E11 **Międzyrzecz** *Ger.* Meseritz. Lubuskie, W Poland *52°26′N 15°33′E*
**Mie-ken** *see* Mie
102 L16 **Miélan** Gers, S France *43°26′N 00°19′E*
111 N16 **Mielec** Podkarpackie, SE Poland *50°18′N 21°27′E*
95 L21 **Mien** ◎ S Sweden
**Mienhua Yü** *see* Mianhua Yu
41 O8 **Mier** Tamaulipas, C Mexico *26°28′N 99°10′W*
116 J11 **Miercurea-Ciuc** *Ger.* Szeklerburg, ***Hung.*** Csíkszereda. Harghita, C Romania *46°24′N 25°48′E*
**Mieresch** *see* Maros/Mureş
104 K2 **Mieres del Camín** *var.* Mieres del Camino. Asturias, NW Spain *43°15′N 05°46′W*
**Mieres del Camino** *see* Mieres del Camín
99 K15 **Mierlo** Noord-Brabant, SE Netherlands *51°27′N 05°37′E*
41 O10 **Mier y Noriega** Nuevo León, NE Mexico *23°24′N 100°06′W*
**Mies** *see* Stříbro
80 K13 **Mī'ēso** *var.* Meheso, Miesso. Oromīya, C Ethiopia *09°13′N 40°47′E*
**Miesso** *see* Mī'ēso
110 D10 **Mieszkowice** *Ger.* Bärwalde Neumark. Zachodnio-pomorskie, W Poland *52°45′N 14°24′E*
18 G14 **Mifflinburg** Pennsylvania, NE USA *40°55′N 77°03′W*
18 F14 **Mifflintown** Pennsylvania, NE USA *40°34′N 77°24′W*
138 F8 **Mifrats Hefa** *Eng.* Bay of Haifa; ***prev.*** MifrazḪefa. *bay* N Israel
81 G19 **Migori** ◈ *county* W Kenya
41 R15 **Miguel Alemán, Presa** ⊠ SE Mexico
40 L9 **Miguel Asua** *var.* Miguel Auza. Zacatecas, C Mexico *24°17′N 103°29′W*
**Miguel Auza** *see* Miguel Asua
43 S15 **Miguel de la Borda** *var.* Donoso. Colón, C Panama *09°09′N 80°20′W*
41 N13 **Miguel Hidalgo** ✈ (Guadalajara) Jalisco, SW Mexico *20°52′N 101°09′W*
40 H7 **Miguel Hidalgo, Presa** ⊠ W Mexico
116 J14 **Mihăileşti** Giurgiu, S Romania *44°20′N 25°54′E*
116 M14 **Mihail Kogălniceanu** *var.* Kogălniceanu; ***prev.*** Caramurat, Ferdinand. Constanţa, SE Romania *44°22′N 28°27′E*
117 N14 **Mihai Viteazu** Constanţa, SE Romania *44°37′N 28°41′E*
136 G12 **Mihalıççık** Eskişehir, NW Turkey *39°52′N 31°30′E*
164 G13 **Mihara** Hiroshima, Honshū, SW Japan *34°24′N 133°04′E*
165 N14 **Mihara-yama** ⛰ Miyako-jima, SE Japan *34°43′N 139°23′E*
105 S8 **Mijares** ≈ E Spain
98 I11 **Mijdrecht** Utrecht, C Netherlands *52°12′N 04°52′E*
165 S4 **Mikasa** Hokkaidō, NE Japan *43°15′N 141°57′E*
**Mikashevichi** *see* Mikashevichy
119 K19 **Mikashevichy** *Pol.* Mikaszewicze, ***Rus.*** Mikashevichi. Brestskaya Voblasts', SW Belarus *52°13′N 27°28′E*
**Mikaszewicze** *see* Mikashevichy
126 L5 **Mikhaylov** Ryazanskaya Oblast', W Russia *54°12′N 39°03′E*
**Mikhaylovgrad** *see* Montana
195 Z8 **Mikhaylov Island** *island* Antarctica
145 T6 **Mikhaylovka** Pavlodar, N Kazakhstan *53°49′N 76°31′E*
127 N9 **Mikhaylovka** Volgogradskaya Oblast', SW Russia *50°06′N 43°17′E*
**Mikhaylovka** *see* Mykhaylivka
81 K24 **Mikindani** Mtwara, SE Tanzania *10°16′S 40°05′E*
93 N18 **Mikkeli** *Swe.* Sankt Michel. Etelä-Savo, SE Finland *61°41′N 27°14′E*
110 M8 **Mikołajki** *Ger.* Nikolaiken. Warmińsko-Mazurskie, NE Poland *53°49′N 21°31′E*
**Míkonos** *see* Mýkonos
114 I9 **Mikre** Lovech, N Bulgaria *43°01′N 24°31′E*
114 C13 **Mikrí Préspa, Límni** ◎ N Greece
125 P4 **Mikulkin, Mys** *headland* NW Russia *67°50′N 46°36′E*
81 I23 **Mikumi** Morogoro, SE Tanzania *07°22′S 37°00′E*
125 R10 **Mikun'** Respublika Komi, NW Russia *62°20′N 50°02′E*
164 K13 **Mikuni** Fukui, Honshū, SW Japan *36°12′N 136°09′E*
165 X13 **Mikura-jima** *island* E Japan
29 V7 **Milaca** Minnesota, N USA *45°45′N 93°40′W*
62 J10 **Milagro** La Rioja, C Argentina *31°00′S 66°01′W*
56 B7 **Milagro** Guayas, SW Ecuador *02°11′S 79°36′W*
31 P4 **Milakokia Lake** ◎ Michigan, N USA
30 J1 **Milan** Illinois, N USA *41°27′N 90°33′W*
31 R10 **Milan** Michigan, N USA *42°05′N 83°40′W*
27 T2 **Milan** Missouri, C USA *40°12′N 93°08′W*
37 Q11 **Milan** New Mexico, SW USA *35°10′N 107°53′W*
20 G9 **Milan** Tennessee, S USA *35°55′N 88°45′W*
**Milan** *see* Milano
95 F15 **Miland** Telemark, S Norway *59°57′N 08°48′E*
83 N15 **Milange** Zambézia, NE Mozambique *16°09′S 35°44′E*
106 D8 **Milano** *Eng.* Milan, ***Ger.*** Mailand; ***anc.*** Mediolanum. Lombardia, N Italy *45°28′N 09°10′E*
25 U10 **Milano** Texas, SW USA *30°42′N 96°51′W*
136 C15 **Milas** Muğla, SW Turkey *37°17′N 27°46′E*
119 K21 **Milashavichy** *Rus.* Milashevichi. Homyel'skaya Voblasts', SE Belarus *51°39′N 27°56′E*
**Milashevichi** *see* Milashavichy
119 I18 **Milavidy** *Rus.* Milovidy. Brestskaya Voblasts', SW Belarus *52°54′N 25°51′E*
107 L23 **Milazzo** *anc.* Mylae. Sicilia, Italy, C Mediterranean Sea *38°13′N 15°15′E*
29 R8 **Milbank** South Dakota, N USA *45°12′N 96°36′W*
19 T7 **Milbridge** Maine, NE USA *44°31′N 67°55′W*
100 L11 **Milde** ≈ C Germany
14 F14 **Mildmay** Ontario, S Canada *44°03′N 81°07′W*
182 L9 **Mildura** Victoria, SE Australia *34°13′S 142°09′E*
137 X12 **Mil Düzü** *Rus.* Mil'skaya Ravnina, Mil'skaya Step'. *physical region* C Azerbaijan
160 H13 **Mile** *var.* Miyang. Yunnan, SW China *24°28′N 103°26′E*
**Mile** *see* Mili Atoll
181 Y10 **Miles** Queensland, E Australia *26°41′S 150°15′E*
25 P8 **Miles** Texas, SW USA *31°36′N 100°10′W*
33 X9 **Miles City** Montana, NW USA *46°24′N 105°48′W*
11 U17 **Milestone** Saskatchewan, S Canada *50°00′N 104°24′W*
107 N22 **Mileto** Calabria, SW Italy *38°35′N 16°03′E*
107 K16 **Miletto, Monte** ▲ C Italy *41°28′N 14°21′E*
18 M13 **Milford** Connecticut, NE USA *41°12′N 73°01′W*
21 Y3 **Milford** *var.* Milford City. Delaware, NE USA *38°54′N 75°25′W*
29 T11 **Milford** Iowa, C USA *43°19′N 95°09′W*
19 S6 **Milford** Maine, NE USA *44°57′N 68°37′W*
29 R16 **Milford** Nebraska, C USA *40°46′N 97°03′W*
19 O10 **Milford** New Hampshire, NE USA *42°49′N 71°38′W*
18 J13 **Milford** Pennsylvania, NE USA *41°20′N 74°48′W*
25 T7 **Milford** Texas, SW USA *32°07′N 96°57′W*
36 K6 **Milford** Utah, W USA *38°22′N 112°57′W*
**Milford** *see* Milford Haven
**Milford City** *see* Milford
97 H21 **Milford Haven** *prev.* Milford. SW Wales, United Kingdom *51°44′N 05°02′W*
27 O4 **Milford Lake** ⊠ Kansas, C USA
185 B21 **Milford Sound** Southland, South Island, New Zealand *44°41′S 167°57′E*
185 B21 **Milford Sound** *inlet* South Island, New Zealand
**Milhau** *see* Millau
**Milḩ, Baḩr al** *see* Razāzah, Buḩayrat ar
139 T10 **Milḩ, Wādī al** *dry watercourse* S Iraq
189 W8 **Mili Atoll** *var.* Mile. *atoll* Ratak Chain, SE Marshall Islands
110 H13 **Milicz** Dolnośląskie, SW Poland *51°32′N 17°15′E*
107 L25 **Militello in Val di Catania** Sicilia, Italy, C Mediterranean Sea *37°17′N 14°47′E*
11 R17 **Milk River** Alberta, SW Canada *49°10′N 112°06′W*
44 J13 **Milk River** ≈ C Jamaica
33 W7 **Milk River** ≈ Montana, NW USA
80 D9 **Milk, Wadi el** *var.* Wadi al Malik. ≈ C Sudan
99 L14 **Mill** Noord-Brabant, SE Netherlands *51°42′N 05°46′E*
103 P14 **Millau** *var.* Milhau; ***anc.*** Æmilianum. Aveyron, S France *44°06′N 03°05′E*
14 I14 **Millbrook** Ontario, SE Canada *44°09′N 78°26′W*
23 U4 **Milledgeville** Georgia, SE USA *33°04′N 83°13′W*
12 C12 **Mille Lacs, Lac des** ◎ Ontario, S Canada
29 V6 **Mille Lacs Lake** ◎ Minnesota, N USA
23 V4 **Millen** Georgia, SE USA *32°50′N 81°56′W*
191 Y5 **Millennium Island** *prev.* Caroline Island, Thornton Island. *atoll* Line Islands, E Kiribati
29 O9 **Miller** South Dakota, N USA *44°31′N 98°59′W*
30 K5 **Miller Dam Flowage** ◎ Wisconsin, N USA
39 U12 **Miller, Mount** ▲ Alaska, USA *60°29′N 142°16′W*
126 L10 **Millerovo** Rostovskaya Oblast', SW Russia *48°57′N 40°26′E*
37 N17 **Miller Peak** ▲ Arizona, SW USA *31°23′N 110°17′W*
31 T12 **Millersburg** Ohio, N USA *40°33′N 81°55′W*
18 G15 **Millersburg** Pennsylvania, NE USA *40°31′N 76°56′W*
185 D23 **Millers Flat** Otago, South Island, New Zealand *45°42′S 169°25′E*
25 Q8 **Millersview** Texas, SW USA *31°26′N 99°44′W*
106 B10 **Millesimo** Piemonte, NE Italy *44°24′N 08°09′E*
12 C12 **Milles Lacs, Lac des** ◎ Ontario, SW Canada
25 Q13 **Millett** Texas, SW USA *28°33′N 99°10′W*
103 N11 **Millevaches, Plateau de** *plateau* C France
182 K12 **Millicent** South Australia *37°29′S 140°01′E*
98 M13 **Millingen aan den Rijn** Gelderland, SE Netherlands *51°52′N 06°02′E*
20 E10 **Millington** Tennessee, S USA *35°20′N 89°54′W*
19 R4 **Millinocket** Maine, NE USA *45°38′N 68°45′W*
19 R4 **Millinocket Lake** ◎ Maine, NE USA
195 Z11 **Mill Island** *island* Antarctica
183 T3 **Millmerran** Queensland, E Australia *27°53′S 151°15′E*
109 R9 **Millstatt** Kärnten, S Austria *46°45′N 13°36′E*
97 B19 **Milltown Malbay** *Ir.* Sráid na Cathrach. W Ireland *52°51′N 09°23′W*
18 J17 **Millville** New Jersey, NE USA *39°24′N 75°01′W*
27 S13 **Millwood Lake** ⊠ Arkansas, C USA
**Milne Bank** *see* Milne Seamounts
186 G10 **Milne Bay** ◈ *province* SE Papua New Guinea
64 J8 **Milne Seamounts** *var.* Milne Bank. *undersea feature* N Atlantic Ocean
29 Q6 **Milnor** North Dakota, N USA *46°15′N 97°27′W*
19 R5 **Milo** Maine, NE USA *45°15′N 69°01′W*
115 I22 **Mílos** *island* Kykládes, Greece, Aegean Sea
**Mílos** *see* Pláka
110 H11 **Miłosław** Wielkopolskie, C Poland *52°13′N 17°28′E*
113 K19 **Milot** *var.* Miloti. Lezhë, C Albania *41°42′N 19°43′E*
**Miloti** *see* Milot
117 Z5 **Milove** Luhans'ka Oblast', E Ukraine *49°22′N 40°09′E*
**Milovidy** *see* Milavidy
182 L4 **Milparinka** New South Wales, SE Australia *29°48′S 141°57′E*
35 N9 **Milpitas** California, W USA *37°25′N 121°54′W*
**Mil'skaya Ravnina/ Mil'skaya Step'** *see* Mil Düzü
14 G15 **Milton** Ontario, S Canada *43°31′N 79°53′W*
185 E24 **Milton** Otago, South Island, New Zealand *46°08′S 169°59′E*
21 Y4 **Milton** Delaware, NE USA *38°48′N 75°21′W*
23 P8 **Milton** Florida, SE USA *30°37′N 87°02′W*
18 G14 **Milton** Pennsylvania, NE USA *41°01′N 76°49′W*
18 L7 **Milton** Vermont, NE USA *44°37′N 73°04′W*
32 K11 **Milton-Freewater** Oregon, NW USA *45°54′N 118°24′W*
97 N21 **Milton Keynes** SE England, United Kingdom *52°N 00°43′W*
27 N3 **Miltonvale** Kansas, C USA *39°21′N 97°27′W*
161 N10 **Miluo** Hunan, S China *28°52′N 113°00′E*
30 M9 **Milwaukee** Wisconsin, N USA *43°03′N 87°56′W*
**Milyang** *see* Miryang
**Mimatum** *see* Mende
37 Q15 **Mimbres Mountains** ▲▲ New Mexico, SW USA
182 D2 **Mimili** South Australia *27°01′S 132°33′E*
102 J14 **Mimizan** Landes, SW France *44°12′N 01°12′W*
**Mimmaya** *see* Minmaya
79 E19 **Mimongo** Ngounié, C Gabon *01°36′S 11°44′E*
**Min** *see* Fujian
35 T7 **Mina** Nevada, W USA *38°23′N 118°07′W*
143 S14 **Mīnāb** Hormozgān, SE Iran *27°08′N 57°02′E*
**Mînâ Baranîs** *see* Baranīs
149 R9 **Mina Bazar** Baluchistan, SW Pakistan *30°58′N 69°11′E*
**Minami-Awaji** *see* Nandan
165 X17 **Minami-Iō-jima** *Eng.* San Augustine. *island* SE Japan
165 R5 **Minami-Kayabe** Hokkaidō, NE Japan *41°54′N 140°58′E*
164 B16 **Minamisatsuma** *var.* Kaseda. Kagoshima, Kyūshū, SW Japan *31°25′N 130°17′E*
164 C14 **Minamishimabara** Nagasaki, Kyūshū, SW Japan *32°40′N 130°18′E*
164 C17 **Minamitane** Kagoshima, Tanega-shima, SW Japan *30°23′N 130°54′E*
**Minami Tori Shima** *see* Marcus Island
**Min'an** *see* Longshan
62 J4 **Mina Pirquitas** Jujuy, NW Argentina *22°48′S 66°24′W*
173 O3 **Mīnā' Qābūs** NE Oman
61 F19 **Minas** Lavalleja, S Uruguay *34°20′S 55°15′W*
13 P15 **Minas Basin** *bay* Nova Scotia, SE Canada
61 F17 **Minas de Corrales** Rivera, NE Uruguay *31°35′S 55°20′W*
44 A5 **Minas de Matahambre** Pinar del Río, W Cuba *22°34′N 83°57′W*
104 J13 **Minas de Ríotinto** Andalucía, S Spain *37°40′N 06°36′W*
60 K7 **Minas Gerais** *off.* Estado de Minas Gerais. ◈ *state* E Brazil
**Minas Gerais, Estado de** *see* Minas Gerais
42 E5 **Minas, Sierra de las** ▲▲ E Guatemala
41 T15 **Minatitlán** Veracruz, E Mexico *17°59′N 94°32′W*
166 L6 **Minbu** Magway, W Myanmar (Burma) *20°09′N 94°52′E*
149 V10 **Minchinabad** Punjab, E Pakistan *30°10′N 73°40′E*
63 G17 **Minchinmávida, Volcán** ⛰ S Chile *42°51′S 72°23′W*
96 G7 **Minch, The** *var.* North Minch. *strait* NW Scotland, United Kingdom
106 F8 **Mincio** *anc.* Mincius. ≈ N Italy
**Mincius** *see* Mincio
26 M11 **Minco** Oklahoma, C USA *35°18′N 97°56′W*
171 Q7 **Mindanao** *island* S Philippines
**Mindanao Sea** *see* Bohol Sea
101 J23 **Mindel** ≈ S Germany
101 J23 **Mindelheim** Bayern, S Germany *48°03′N 10°30′E*
**Mindello** *see* Mindelo
76 C9 **Mindelo** *var.* Mindello; ***prev.*** Porto Grande. São Vicente, N Cape Verde *16°54′N 25°01′W*
14 I13 **Minden** Ontario, SE Canada *44°54′N 78°41′W*
100 H13 **Minden** *anc.* Minthun. Nordrhein-Westfalen, NW Germany *52°18′N 08°55′E*
22 G5 **Minden** Louisiana, S USA *32°37′N 93°17′W*
29 O16 **Minden** Nebraska, C USA *40°30′N 98°57′W*
35 Q6 **Minden** Nevada, W USA *38°58′N 119°47′W*
182 L8 **Mindona Lake** *seasonal lake* New South Wales, SE Australia
171 O4 **Mindoro** *island* N Philippines
171 N5 **Mindoro Strait** *strait* W Philippines
97 J23 **Minehead** SW England, United Kingdom *51°13′N 03°29′W*
97 E21 **Mine Head** *Ir.* Mionn Ard. *headland* S Ireland *51°58′N 07°36′W*
59 J19 **Mineiros** Goiás, C Brazil *17°34′S 52°33′W*
25 V6 **Mineola** Texas, SW USA *32°39′N 95°29′W*
25 S13 **Mineral** Texas, SW USA *28°32′N 97°54′W*
127 N15 **Mineral'nyye Vody** Stavropol'skiy Kray, SW Russia *44°13′N 43°06′E*
30 K9 **Mineral Point** Wisconsin, N USA *42°54′N 90°09′W*
25 S6 **Mineral Wells** Texas, SW USA *32°48′N 98°06′W*
36 K6 **Minersville** Utah, W USA *38°12′N 112°56′W*
31 U12 **Minerva** Ohio, N USA *40°43′N 81°06′W*
107 N17 **Minervino Murge** Puglia, SE Italy *41°06′N 16°05′E*
103 O16 **Minervois** *physical region* S France
158 I10 **Minfeng** *var.* Niya. Xinjiang Uygur Zizhiqu, NW China *37°07′N 82°43′E*
79 O25 **Minga** Katanga, SE Dem. Rep. Congo *11°06′S 27°57′E*
137 W11 **Mingäçevir** *Rus.* Mingechaur, Mingechevir. C Azerbaijan *40°46′N 47°02′E*
137 W11 **Mingäçevir Su Anbarı** *Rus.* Mingechaurskoye Vodokhranilishche, Mingechevirskoye Vodokhranilishche. ⊠ NW Azerbaijan
166 L8 **Mingaladon** ✈ (Yangon) Yangon, SW Myanmar (Burma) *16°55′N 96°11′E*
13 P11 **Mingan** Québec, E Canada *50°19′N 64°02′W*
**Mingāora** *see* Saidu
146 K8 **Mingbuloq** *Rus.* Mynbulak. Navoiy Viloyati, N Uzbekistan *42°18′N 62°53′E*
146 K9 **Mingbuloq Botig'I** *Rus.* Vpadina Mynbulak. *depression* N Uzbekistan
**Mingechaur/Mingechevir** *see* Mingäçevir
**Mingechaurskoye Vodokhranilishche/ Mingechevirskoye Vodokhranilishche** *see* Mingäçevir Su Anbarı
161 Q7 **Mingguang** *prev.* Jiashan. Anhui, SE China *32°45′N 117°59′E*
166 L4 **Mingin** Sagaing, C Myanmar (Burma) *22°51′N 94°30′E*
105 Q10 **Minglanilla** Castilla-La Mancha, C Spain *39°32′N 01°36′W*
31 V13 **Mingo Junction** Ohio, N USA *40°19′N 80°36′W*
**Mingora** *see* Saidu
163 V7 **Mingshui** Heilongjiang, NE China *47°10′N 125°53′E*
**Mingtekl Daban** *see* Mintaka Pass
**Mingu** *see* Zhenfeng
83 Q14 **Minguri** Nampula, NE Mozambique *14°30′S 40°37′E*
**Mingzhou** *see* Suide
159 U10 **Minhe** *var.* Chuankou; ***prev.*** Minhe Huizu Tuzu Zizhixian, Shangchuankou. Qinghai, C China *36°21′N 102°40′E*
**Minhe Huizu Tuzu Zizhixian** *see* Minhe
166 L6 **Minhla** Magway, W Myanmar (Burma) *19°58′N 95°03′E*
167 S14 **Minh Lương** Kiên Giang, S Vietnam *09°52′N 105°10′E*
104 G5 **Minho** *former province* N Portugal
104 G5 **Minho, Rio** *Sp.* Miño. ≈ Portugal/Spain ***see also*** Miño
**Minho, Rio** *see* Miño
155 C24 **Minicoy Island** *island* SW India
33 P15 **Minidoka** Idaho, NW USA *42°45′N 113°29′W*
118 C11 **Minija** ≈ W Lithuania
180 G9 **Minilya** Western Australia *23°45′S 114°03′E*
14 E8 **Minisinakwa Lake** ◎ Ontario, S Canada
45 T12 **Ministre Point** *headland* S Saint Lucia *13°42′N 60°57′W*
11 V15 **Minitonas** Manitoba, S Canada *52°07′N 101°02′W*
**Minius** *see* Miño
161 R12 **Min Jiang** ≈ SE China
160 H10 **Min Jiang** ≈ C China
182 H9 **Minlaton** South Australia *34°52′S 137°33′E*
159 S9 **Minle** Gansu, N China
165 Q6 **Minmaya** *var.* Mimmaya. Aomori, Honshū, C Japan *41°10′N 140°24′E*
77 U14 **Minna** Niger, C Nigeria *09°33′N 06°33′E*
165 P16 **Minna-jima** *island* Sakishima-shotō, SW Japan
27 N4 **Minneapolis** Kansas, C USA *39°08′N 97°43′W*
29 U9 **Minneapolis** Minnesota, N USA *44°59′N 93°16′W*
29 V8 **Minneapolis-Saint Paul** ✈ Minnesota, N USA *44°53′N 93°13′W*
11 W16 **Minnedosa** Manitoba, S Canada *50°14′N 99°50′W*
26 J7 **Minneola** Kansas, C USA *37°26′N 100°00′W*
29 S7 **Minnesota** *off.* State of Minnesota, ***also known as*** Gopher State, New England of the West, North Star State. ◈ *state* N USA
29 S9 **Minnesota River** ≈ Minnesota/South Dakota, N USA
29 V9 **Minnetonka** Minnesota, N USA *44°55′N 93°28′W*
29 O3 **Minnewaukan** North Dakota, N USA *48°04′N 99°14′W*
182 F7 **Minnipa** South Australia *32°52′S 135°07′E*
104 G5 **Miño** *var.* Minho, Minius, ***Port.*** Rio Minho. ≈ Portugal/Spain ***see also*** Minho, Rio
**Miño** *see* Minho, Rio
30 L4 **Minocqua** Wisconsin, N USA *45°53′N 89°42′W*
30 L12 **Minonk** Illinois, N USA *40°54′N 89°01′W*
**Minorca** *see* Menorca
28 M3 **Minot** North Dakota, N USA *48°15′N 101°19′W*
159 U8 **Minqin** Gansu, N China *38°35′N 103°07′E*
119 J16 **Minsk** ● (Belarus) Horad Minsk, C Belarus *53°52′N 27°34′E*
**Minsk-2** *see* Minsk National
**Minskaya Oblast'** *see* Minskaya Voblasts'
119 K16 **Minskaya Voblasts'** *prev.* ***Rus.*** Minskaya Oblast'. ◈ *province* C Belarus
**Minskaya Vozvyshennost'** *see* Minskaye Wzvyshsha
119 J16 **Minskaye Wzvyshsha** *Rus.* Minskaya Vozvyshennost'. ▲▲ C Belarus
110 N12 **Mińsk Mazowiecki** *var.* Nowo-Minsk. Mazowieckie, C Poland *52°10′N 21°31′E*
119 L16 **Minsk National** *prev.* Minsk-2. ✈ Minskaya Voblasts', C Belarus *53°52′N 27°58′E*
31 Q13 **Minster** Ohio, N USA *40°23′N 84°22′W*
79 F15 **Minta** Centre, C Cameroon *04°34′N 12°54′E*
149 W2 **Mintaka Pass** *Chin.* Mingtekl Daban. *pass* China/Pakistan
115 D20 **Mínthi** ▲▲ S Greece
**Minthun** *see* Minden
13 O14 **Minto** New Brunswick, SE Canada *46°05′N 66°05′W*
10 H6 **Minto** Yukon, W Canada *62°33′N 136°45′W*
39 R9 **Minto** Alaska, USA *65°07′N 149°22′W*
29 Q3 **Minto** North Dakota, N USA *48°17′N 97°22′W*
12 K6 **Minto, Lac** ◎ Québec, C Canada
195 R16 **Minto, Mount** ▲ Antarctica *71°38′S 169°11′E*
11 U17 **Minton** Saskatchewan, S Canada *49°12′N 104°33′W*
189 R15 **Minto Reef** *atoll* Caroline Islands, C Micronesia
37 R4 **Minturn** Colorado, C USA *39°34′N 106°21′W*
107 J16 **Minturno** Lazio, C Italy *41°15′N 13°47′E*
122 K13 **Minusinsk** Krasnoyarskiy Kray, S Russia *53°37′N 91°49′E*
108 G11 **Minusio** Ticino, S Switzerland *46°11′N 08°47′E*
79 E17 **Minvoul** Woleu-Ntem, N Gabon *02°08′N 12°12′E*
141 R13 **Minwakh** N Yemen *16°55′N 48°04′E*
159 V11 **Minxian** *var.* Min Xian, Minyang. Gansu, C China *34°20′N 104°09′E*
**Min Xian** *see* Minxian
**Minya** *see* Al Minyā
**Minyang** *see* Minxian
31 R6 **Mio** Michigan, N USA *44°40′N 84°09′W*
**Mionn Ard** *see* Mine Head
**Miory** *see* Myory
158 L5 **Miquan** Xinjiang Uygur Zizhiqu, NW China *44°04′N 87°40′E*
119 I17 **Mir** Hrodzyenskaya Voblasts', W Belarus *53°25′N 26°28′E*
106 H8 **Mira** Veneto, NE Italy *45°25′N 12°07′E*
12 K15 **Mirabel** *var.* Montreal. ✈ (Montréal) Québec, SE Canada *45°27′N 73°47′W*
60 Q8 **Miracema** Rio de Janeiro, SE Brazil *21°24′S 42°10′W*
54 G9 **Miraflores** Boyacá, C Colombia *05°07′N 73°09′W*
40 G10 **Miraflores** Baja California Sur, NW Mexico *23°24′N 109°45′W*
44 L9 **Miragoâne** S Haiti *18°25′N 73°07′W*
155 E16 **Miraj** Mahārāshtra, W India *16°51′N 74°42′E*
61 E23 **Miramar** Buenos Aires, E Argentina *38°15′S 57°50′W*
103 R15 **Miramas** Bouches-du-Rhône, SE France *43°33′N 05°02′E*
102 K12 **Mirambeau** Charente-Maritime, W France *45°23′N 00°33′W*
102 L13 **Miramont-de-Guyenne** Lot-et-Garonne, SW France *44°34′N 00°20′E*
115 L25 **Mirampéllou Kólpos** *gulf* Kríti, Greece, E Mediterranean Sea
158 L8 **Miran** Xinjiang Uygur Zizhiqu, NW China *39°13′N 88°58′E*
54 M5 **Miranda** *off.* Estado Miranda. ◈ *state* N Venezuela
**Miranda de Corvo** *see* Miranda do Corvo
105 O3 **Miranda de Ebro** La Rioja, N Spain *42°41′N 02°57′W*
104 G8 **Miranda do Corvo** *var.* Miranda de Corvo. Coimbra, N Portugal *40°05′N 08°20′W*
104 J6 **Miranda do Douro** Bragança, N Portugal *41°30′N 06°16′W*
**Miranda, Estado** *see* Miranda
102 L15 **Mirande** Gers, S France *43°31′N 00°25′E*
104 I6 **Mirandela** Bragança, N Portugal *41°28′N 07°10′W*
25 R15 **Mirando City** Texas, SW USA *27°24′N 99°00′W*
106 G9 **Mirandola** Emilia-Romagna, N Italy *44°52′N 11°04′E*
60 I8 **Mirandópolis** São Paulo, S Brazil *21°10′S 51°03′W*
104 G13 **Mira, Rio** ≈ S Portugal
60 K8 **Mirassol** São Paulo, S Brazil *20°50′S 49°30′W*
104 J3 **Miravalles** ▲ NW Spain *42°52′N 06°45′W*
42 L12 **Miravalles, Volcán** ⛰ NW Costa Rica *10°43′N 85°07′W*
141 W13 **Mirbāṭ** *var.* Marbat. S Oman *17°03′N 54°44′E*
44 M9 **Mirebalais** C Haiti *18°51′N 72°08′W*
103 T6 **Mirecourt** Vosges, NE France *48°19′N 06°04′E*
103 N16 **Mirepoix** Ariège, S France *43°05′N 01°51′E*
**Mirgorod** *see* Myrhorod
139 W10 **Mīr Ḩājī Khalīl** Wāsiţ, E Iraq *32°11′N 46°19′E*
169 T8 **Miri** Sarawak, East Malaysia *04°23′N 113°59′E*
77 W12 **Miria** Zinder, S Niger *13°39′N 09°15′E*
182 F5 **Mirikata** South Australia *29°56′S 135°13′E*
54 K4 **Mirimire** Falcón, N Venezuela *11°14′N 68°39′W*
61 H18 **Mirim Lagoon** *var.* Lake Mirim, ***Sp.*** Laguna Merín. *lagoon* Brazil/Uruguay
**Mirim, Lake** *see* Mirim Lagoon
**Mírina** *see* Mýrina
172 H14 **Miringoni** Mohéli, S Comoros *12°17′S 93°39′E*
143 W11 **Mīrjāveh** Sīstān va Balūchestān, SE Iran *29°04′N 61°24′E*
195 Z9 **Mirny** *research station (Russia)* Antarctica *66°25′S 93°09′E*
124 M10 **Mirnyy** Arkhangel'skaya Oblast', NW Russia *62°50′N 40°20′E*
123 O10 **Mirnyy** Respublika Sakha (Yakutiya), NE Russia *62°30′N 113°58′E*
**Mironovka** *see* Myronivka
110 F9 **Mirosławiec** Zachodnio-pomorskie, NW Poland *53°21′N 16°04′E*
**Mirovo** *see* Vrattsa
100 N10 **Mirow** Mecklenburg-Vorpommern, N Germany *53°16′N 12°48′E*
152 G6 **Mīrpur** Jammu and Kashmir, NW India *33°06′N 73°49′E*
**Mirpur** *see* New Mirpur


◆ Country
● Country Capital
◇ Dependent Territory
○ Dependent Territory Capital
◈ Administrative Regions
✈ International Airport
▲ Mountain
▲▲ Mountain Range
⛰ Volcano
≈ River
◎ Lake
⊠ Reservoir

Mirpur Batoro – Mongol Uls


149 P17 **Mirpur Batoro** Sindh, SE Pakistan 24°40′N 68°15′E
149 Q16 **Mirpur Khas** Sindh, SE Pakistan 25°31′N 69°01′E
149 P17 **Mirpur Sakro** Sindh, SE Pakistan 24°32′N 67°38′E
143 T14 **Mīr Shahdād** Hormozgān, S Iran 26°15′N 58°29′E
115 G21 **Mirtóo Pélagos** *Eng.* Myrtoan Sea; *anc.* Myrtoum Mare. *sea* S Greece
163 Z16 **Miryang** *var.* Milyang, *Jap.* Mitsuō. SE South Korea 35°30′N 128°46′E
**Mirzachirla** *see* Murzechirla
164 E14 **Misaki** Ehime, Shikoku, SW Japan 33°22′N 132°04′E
**Misān** *see* Maysān
41 Q13 **Misantla** Veracruz, E Mexico 19°54′N 96°51′W
165 R7 **Misawa** Aomori, Honshū, C Japan 40°42′N 141°26′E
57 G14 **Mishagua, Río** C Peru
163 Z8 **Mishan** Heilongjiang, NE China 45°30′N 131°53′E
31 O11 **Mishawaka** Indiana, N USA 41°40′N 86°10′W
39 N6 **Misheguk Mountain** ▲ Alaska, USA 68°13′N 161°11′W
165 N14 **Mishima** *var.* Misima. Shizuoka, Honshū, S Japan 35°08′N 138°54′E
164 E12 **Mi-shima** *island* SW Japan
127 V4 **Mishkino** Respublika Bashkortostan, W Russia 55°31′N 55°57′E
153 Y10 **Mishmi Hills** *hill range* NE India
161 N11 **Mi Shui** S China
**Misiaf** *see* Maşyāf
107 J23 **Misilmeri** Sicilia, Italy, C Mediterranean Sea 38°03′N 13°27′E
**Misima** *see* Mishima
14 C7 **Missinaibi Lake** ◎ Ontario, S Canada
**Misión de Guana** *see* Guana
60 F13 **Misiones** *off.* Provincia de Misiones. ⬥ *province* NE Argentina
62 P8 **Misiones** *off.* Departamento de las Misiones. ⬥ *department* S Paraguay
**Misiones, Departamento de las** *see* Misiones
**Misiones, Provincia de** *see* Misiones
**Misión San Fernando** *see* San Fernando
**Miskin** *see* Maskin
**Miskito Coast** *see* La Mosquitia
43 O7 **Miskitos, Cayos** *island group* NE Nicaragua
111 M21 **Miskolc** Borsod-Abaúj-Zemplén, NE Hungary 48°05′N 20°46′E
171 T12 **Misool, Pulau** *island* Papua Barat, E Indonesia
**Misox** *see* Mesocco
29 Y3 **Misquah Hills** *hill range* Minnesota, N USA
**Mişr** *see* Egypt
**Mişr al ʻArabīyah, Jumhūrīyat** *see* Egypt
75 P7 **Mişrātah** *var.* Misurata. NW Libya 32°23′N 15°06′E
75 P7 **Mişrātah, Râs** *headland* N Libya 32°22′N 15°16′E
14 C7 **Missanabie** Ontario, S Canada 48°18′N 84°04′W
58 E10 **Missão Catrimani** Roraima, N Brazil 01°26′N 62°05′W
14 D6 **Missinaibi** Ontario, S Canada
11 T13 **Missinipe** Saskatchewan, C Canada 55°36′N 104°45′W
28 M11 **Mission** South Dakota, N USA 43°16′N 100°38′W
25 S17 **Mission** Texas, SW USA 26°13′N 98°19′W
12 F10 **Missisa Lake** ◎ Ontario, C Canada
18 M6 **Missisquoi Bay** *lake bay* Canada/USA
14 C10 **Mississagi** Ontario, S Canada
14 G15 **Mississauga** Ontario, S Canada 43°38′N 79°36′W
31 P12 **Mississinewa Lake** ⊠ Indiana, N USA
31 P12 **Mississinewa River** Indiana/Ohio, N USA
22 K4 **Mississippi** *off.* State of Mississippi, *also known as* Bayou State, Magnolia State. ⬥ *state* SE USA
14 K13 **Mississippi** Ontario, SE Canada
47 N1 **Mississippi Fan** *undersea feature* N Gulf of Mexico 26°45′N 88°30′W
14 L13 **Mississippi Lake** ◎ Ontario, SE Canada
22 M10 **Mississippi Delta** *delta* Louisiana, S USA
0 J11 **Mississippi River** C USA
22 M9 **Mississippi Sound** *sound* Alabama/Mississippi, S USA
33 P9 **Missoula** Montana, NW USA 46°54′N 114°03′W
27 T5 **Missouri** *off.* State of Missouri, *also known as* Bullion State, Show Me State. ⬥ *state* C USA
25 V11 **Missouri City** Texas, SW USA 29°37′N 95°32′W
0 J10 **Missouri River** C USA
15 Q6 **Mistassibi** Québec, SE Canada
15 P6 **Mistassini** Québec, SE Canada
12 J11 **Mistassini, Lac** ◎ Québec, SE Canada
109 Y3 **Mistelbach an der Zaya** Niederösterreich, NE Austria 48°34′N 16°33′E
107 L24 **Misterbianco** Sicilia, Italy, C Mediterranean Sea 37°31′N 15°01′E
95 N19 **Misterhult** Kalmar, S Sweden 57°28′N 16°34′E
12 K11 **Mistissini** *var.* Baie-du-Poste. Québec, SE Canada 50°20′N 73°50′W
57 H17 **Misti, Volcán** S Peru 16°20′S 71°22′W
**Mistras** *see* Mystrás
107 K23 **Mistretta** *anc.* Amestratus. Sicilia, Italy, C Mediterranean Sea 37°56′N 14°22′E
164 F12 **Misumi** Shimane, Honshū, SW Japan 34°47′N 132°00′E
**Misurata** *see* Mişrātah
83 O14 **Mitande** Niassa, N Mozambique 14°06′S 36°03′E
40 J13 **Mita, Punta de** *headland* C Mexico 20°46′N 105°31′W
55 W12 **Mitaraka, Massif du** ▲ NE South America 02°18′N 54°31′W
**Mitau** *see* Jelgava
181 X9 **Mitchell** Queensland, E Australia 26°29′S 148°00′E
14 E15 **Mitchell** Ontario, S Canada 43°28′N 81°11′W
28 I13 **Mitchell** Nebraska, C USA 41°56′N 103°48′W
32 J12 **Mitchell** Oregon, NW USA 44°34′N 120°09′W
29 P11 **Mitchell** South Dakota, N USA 43°42′N 98°01′W
23 P5 **Mitchell Lake** ⊠ Alabama, S USA
31 P7 **Mitchell, Lake** ◎ Michigan, N USA
21 P9 **Mitchell, Mount** ▲ North Carolina, SE USA 35°46′N 82°16′W
181 V3 **Mitchell River** Queensland, NE Australia
97 D20 **Mitchelstown** *Ir.* Baile Mhistéala. SW Ireland 52°20′N 08°16′W
14 M9 **Mitchinamécus, Lac** ◎ Québec, SE Canada
**Mitèmboni** *see* Mitemele, Río
79 D17 **Mitemele, Río** *var.* Mitèmboni, Temboni, Utamboni. S Equatorial Guinea
149 S12 **Mithan Kot** Punjab, E Pakistan 28°53′N 70°25′E
149 T7 **Mitha Tiwana** Punjab, E Pakistan 32°18′N 72°08′E
149 R17 **Mithi** Sindh, SE Pakistan 24°43′N 69°53′E
**Míthimna** *see* Míthymna
**Mi Tho** *see* My Tho
115 L16 **Míthymna** *var.* Míthimna. Lésvos, E Greece 39°20′N 26°12′E
190 L16 **Mitiaro** *island* S Cook Islands
**Mitilíni** *see* Mytilíni
15 U7 **Mitis** Québec, SE Canada
41 R16 **Mitla** Oaxaca, SE Mexico 16°56′N 96°19′W
165 P13 **Mito** Ibaraki, Honshū, S Japan 36°21′N 140°26′E
92 N2 **Mitra, Kapp** *headland* W Svalbard 79°07′N 11°11′E
184 M13 **Mitre** ▲ North Island, New Zealand 40°46′S 175°27′E
185 B21 **Mitre Peak** ▲ South Island, New Zealand 44°37′S 167°45′E
39 O15 **Mitrofania Island** *island* Alaska, USA
**Mitrovica/Mitrovicë** *see* Kosovska Mitrovica, Serbia
**Mitrovica/Mitrowitz** *see* Sremska Mitrovica, Serbia
113 M16 **Mitrovicë** *Serb.* Mitrovica, Kosovska Mitrovica, Titova Mitrovica. N Kosovo 42°54′N 20°52′E
172 H12 **Mitsamiouli** Grande Comore, NW Comoros 11°22′S 43°19′E
172 I13 **Mitsinjo** Mahajanga, NW Madagascar 16°00′S 45°52′E
80 J9 **Mits'iwa** *var.* Masawa, Massawa. E Eritrea 15°37′N 39°27′E
172 H13 **Mitsoudjé** Grande Comore, NW Comoros
138 F12 **Mitspe Ramon** *prev.* Mizpe Ramon. Southern, S Israel 30°38′N 34°47′E
165 T5 **Mitsuishi** Hokkaidō, NE Japan 42°12′N 142°40′E
165 O11 **Mitsuke** *var.* Mituke. Niigata, Honshū, C Japan 37°30′N 138°54′E
**Mitsuō** *see* Miryang
164 C12 **Mitsushima** Nagasaki, Tsushima, SW Japan 34°16′N 129°18′E
100 G12 **Mittelandkanal** *canal* NW Germany
108 J7 **Mittelberg** Vorarlberg, NW Austria 47°19′N 10°09′E
**Mitteldorf** *see* Międzychód
**Mittelstadt** *see* Baia Sprie
**Mitterburg** *see* Pazin
109 P7 **Mittersill** Salzburg, NW Austria 47°16′N 12°27′E
**Mittimatalik** *see* Pond Inlet
101 N16 **Mittweida** Sachsen, E Germany 50°59′N 12°57′E
54 J13 **Mitú** Vaupés, SE Colombia 01°07′N 70°05′W
**Mituke** *see* Mitsuke
**Mitumba, Chaîne des/Mitumba Range** *see* Mitumba, Monts
79 O22 **Mitumba, Monts** *var.* Chaîne des Mitumba, Mitumba Range. ▲▲ E Dem. Rep. Congo
79 N23 **Mitwaba** Katanga, SE Dem. Rep. Congo 08°37′S 27°20′E
79 E18 **Mitzic** Woleu-Ntem, N Gabon 0°48′N 11°30′E
82 K11 **Miueru Wantipa, Lake** ◎ N Zambia
165 N14 **Miura** Kanagawa, Honshū, S Japan 35°08′N 139°37′E
165 Q10 **Miyagi** *off.* Miyagi-ken. ⬥ *prefecture* Honshū, C Japan
**Miyagi-ken** *see* Miyagi
138 M7 **Miyāh, Wādī al** *dry watercourse* E Syria
165 X13 **Miyake** Tōkyō, Miyako-jima, SE Japan 34°35′N 135°33′E
165 Q16 **Miyake-jima** *island* Sakishima-shotō, SW Japan
165 R8 **Miyako** Iwate, Honshū, C Japan 39°39′N 141°57′E
164 D16 **Miyakonojō** *var.* Miyakonzyō. Miyazaki, Kyūshū, SW Japan 31°42′N 131°04′E
**Miyakonzyô** *see* Miyakonojō
165 Q16 **Miyako-shotō** *island group* SW Japan
144 G11 **Miyaly** Atyrau, W Kazakhstan 48°52′N 53°55′E
**Miyāndoāb** *see* Miāndowāb
**Miyāneh** *see* Miāneh
**Miyang** *see* Mile
164 D16 **Miyazaki** Miyazaki, Kyūshū, SW Japan 31°55′N 131°24′E
164 D16 **Miyazaki** *off.* Miyazaki-ken. ⬥ *prefecture* Kyūshū, SW Japan
**Miyazaki-ken** *see* Miyazaki
164 J12 **Miyazu** Kyōto, Honshū, SW Japan 35°33′N 135°12′E
**Miyory** *see* Myory
164 G12 **Miyoshi** *var.* Miyosi. Hiroshima, Honshū, SW Japan 34°48′N 132°51′E
**Miyosi** *see* Miyoshi
**Miza** *see* Mizë
81 H14 **Mīzan Teferī** Southern Nationalities, S Ethiopia 06°57′N 35°30′E
**Mizda** *see* Mizdah
75 O8 **Mizdah** *var.* Mizda. NW Libya 31°26′N 12°59′E
113 K20 **Mizë** *var.* Miza. Fier, W Albania 40°58′N 19°32′E
97 A22 **Mizen Head** *Ir.* Carn Uí Néid. *headland* SW Ireland 51°26′N 09°50′W
116 H7 **Mizhhir"ya** *Rus.* Mezhgor'ye. Zakarpats'ka Oblast', W Ukraine 48°30′N 23°30′E
160 L4 **Mizhi** Shaanxi, C China 37°50′N 110°03′E
114 H7 **Mizia** *var.* Miziya. Vratsa, NW Bulgaria 43°42′N 23°52′E
116 K13 **Mizil** Prahova, SE Romania 45°00′N 26°29′E
**Miziya** *see* Mizia
153 W15 **Mizo Hills** *hill range* E India
153 W15 **Mizoram** ⬥ *state* NE India
**Mizpe Ramon** *see* Mitspe Ramon
57 L19 **Mizque** Cochabamba, C Bolivia 17°57′S 65°10′W
57 M19 **Mizque, Río** C Bolivia
165 Q9 **Mizusawa** *var.* Ōshū. Iwate, Honshū, C Japan 39°10′N 141°07′E
95 M18 **Mjölby** Östergötland, S Sweden 58°19′N 15°10′E
95 G15 **Mjøndalen** Buskerud, S Norway 59°45′N 09°58′E
95 J19 **Mjörn** ◎ S Sweden
94 I13 **Mjøsa** *var.* Mjøsen. ◎ S Norway
**Mjøsen** *see* Mjøsa
81 G21 **Mkalama** Singida, C Tanzania 04°09′S 34°35′E
80 K13 **Mkata** C Tanzania
83 K14 **Mkushi** Central, C Zambia 13°40′S 29°26′E
83 L22 **Mkuze** KwaZulu/Natal, E South Africa 27°37′S 32°03′E
81 J22 **Mkwaja** Tanga, E Tanzania 05°42′S 38°48′E
111 D16 **Mladá Boleslav** *Ger.* Jungbunzlau. Středočeský Kraj, N Czechia 50°26′N 14°55′E
112 M12 **Mladenovac** Serbia, C Serbia 44°27′N 20°42′E
114 L11 **Mladinovo** Haskovo, S Bulgaria 41°57′N 26°13′E
113 O17 **Mlado Nagoričane** N North Macedonia 42°11′N 21°49′E
**Mlanje** *see* Mulanje
112 N12 **Mlava** E Serbia
110 L9 **Mława** Mazowieckie, C Poland 53°07′N 20°23′E
113 G16 **Mljet** *It.* Meleda; *anc.* Melita. *island* S Croatia
167 S11 **Mlu Prey** *prev.* Phumĭ Mlu Prey. Preah Vihear, N Cambodia 13°48′N 105°16′E
116 K4 **Mlyniv** Rivnens'ka Oblast', NW Ukraine 50°31′N 25°36′E
83 I21 **Mmabatho** North-West, N South Africa 25°51′S 25°37′E
83 I19 **Mmashoro** Central, E Botswana 21°56′S 26°39′E
44 J7 **Moa** Holguín, E Cuba 20°42′N 74°57′W
76 J15 **Moa** Guinea/Sierra Leone
37 O6 **Moab** Utah, W USA 38°35′N 109°34′W
181 V1 **Moa Island** *island* Queensland, NE Australia
187 Y15 **Moala** *island* S Fiji
83 L21 **Moamba** Maputo, SW Mozambique 25°35′S 32°13′E
79 F19 **Moanda** *var.* Mouanda. Haut-Ogooué, SE Gabon 01°31′S 13°07′E
83 M15 **Moatize** Tete, NW Mozambique 16°04′S 33°43′E
79 P22 **Moba** Katanga, E Dem. Rep. Congo 07°03′S 29°52′E
**Mobay** *see* Montego Bay
79 K15 **Mobaye** Basse-Kotto, S Central African Republic 04°19′N 21°17′E
79 K15 **Mobayi-Mbongo** Equateur, NW Dem. Rep. Congo 04°21′N 21°10′E
25 P2 **Mobeetie** Texas, SW USA 35°33′N 100°25′W
27 U3 **Moberly** Missouri, C USA 39°25′N 92°26′W
23 N8 **Mobile** Alabama, S USA 30°42′N 88°03′W
23 N9 **Mobile Bay** *bay* Alabama, S USA
23 N8 **Mobile River** Alabama, S USA
29 N8 **Mobridge** South Dakota, N USA 45°32′N 100°25′W
**Mobutu Sese Seko, Lac** *see* Albert, Lake
45 N8 **Moca** N Dominican Republic 19°26′N 70°33′W
83 Q15 **Moçambique** Nampula, NE Mozambique 15°00′S 40°44′E
**Moçambique** *see* Mozambique
**Moçambique, República de** *see* Mozambique
**Moçâmedes** *see* Namibe
167 S6 **Môc Châu** Son La, N Vietnam 20°49′N 104°38′E
187 Z15 **Moce** *island* Lau Group, E Fiji
**Mocha** *see* Al Mukhā
193 T11 **Mocha Fracture Zone** *tectonic feature* SE Pacific Ocean
63 F14 **Mocha, Isla** *island* C Chile
56 C12 **Moche, Río** W Peru
167 S14 **Môc Hoa** Long An, S Vietnam 10°46′N 105°56′E
83 I20 **Mochudi** Kgatleng, SE Botswana 24°25′S 26°07′E
82 Q13 **Mocímboa da Praia** *var.* Vila de Mocímboa da Praia. Cabo Delgado, N Mozambique 11°17′S 40°21′E
94 L13 **Mockfjärd** Dalarna, C Sweden 60°30′N 14°57′E
21 R9 **Mocksville** North Carolina, SE USA 35°53′N 80°33′W
32 F8 **Moclips** Washington, NW USA 47°11′N 124°13′W
82 C13 **Môco** *var.* Morro de Môco. ▲ W Angola 12°36′S 15°09′E
54 D13 **Mocoa** Putumayo, SW Colombia 01°07′N 76°38′W
60 M8 **Mococa** São Paulo, S Brazil 21°30′S 47°00′W
**Môco, Morro de** *see* Môco
40 H8 **Mocorito** Sinaloa, C Mexico 25°24′N 107°55′W
40 J4 **Moctezuma** Chihuahua, N Mexico 30°10′N 106°28′W
41 N11 **Moctezuma** San Luis Potosí, C Mexico 22°46′N 101°06′W
40 G4 **Moctezuma** Sonora, NW Mexico 29°50′N 109°40′W
41 P12 **Moctezuma, Río** C Mexico
**Mó, Cuan** *see* Clew Bay
83 O16 **Mocuba** Zambézia, NE Mozambique 16°50′S 37°02′E
103 U12 **Modane** Savoie, E France 45°14′N 06°41′E
106 F9 **Modena** *anc.* Mutina. Emilia-Romagna, N Italy 44°39′N 10°55′E
36 I7 **Modena** Utah, W USA 37°46′N 113°54′W
35 O9 **Modesto** California, W USA 37°38′N 121°02′W
107 L25 **Modica** *anc.* Motyca. Sicilia, Italy, C Mediterranean Sea 36°52′N 14°45′E
83 J20 **Modimolle** *prev.* Nylstroom. Limpopo, NE South Africa 24°39′S 28°23′E
79 K17 **Modjamboli** Equateur, N Dem. Rep. Congo 02°27′N 22°03′E
109 X4 **Mödling** Niederösterreich, NE Austria 48°06′N 16°18′E
**Modohn** *see* Madona
**Modot** *see* Tsenhermandal
171 V14 **Modowi** Papua Barat, E Indonesia 04°05′S 134°39′E
112 I12 **Modračko Jezero** ⊠ NE Bosnia and Herzegovina
112 I10 **Modriča** Republika Srpska, N Bosnia and Herzegovina 44°57′N 18°17′E
183 O13 **Moe** Victoria, SE Australia 38°11′S 146°18′E
**Moearatewe** *see* Muaratewe
**Moei, Mae Nam** *see* Thaungyin
94 H13 **Moely** Hedmark, S Norway 60°55′N 10°47′E
92 I10 **Moen** Troms, N Norway 69°08′N 18°35′E
**Möen** *see* Møn, Denmark
**Moen** *see* Weno, Micronesia
**Moena** *see* Muna, Pulau
36 M10 **Moenkopi Wash** Arizona, SW USA
185 F22 **Moeraki Point** *headland* South Island, New Zealand 45°23′S 170°52′E
99 F16 **Moerbeke** Oost-Vlaanderen, NW Belgium 51°11′N 03°57′E
99 H14 **Moerdijk** Noord-Brabant, S Netherlands 51°42′N 04°37′E
**Moero, Lac** *see* Mweru, Lake
101 D15 **Moers** *var.* Mörs. Nordrhein-Westfalen, W Germany 51°27′N 06°36′E
**Moesi** *see* Musi, Air
**Moeskroen** *see* Mouscron
96 J13 **Moffat** S Scotland, United Kingdom 55°29′N 03°36′W
185 C22 **Moffat Peak** ▲ South Island, New Zealand 44°57′S 168°10′E
79 N19 **Moga** Sud-Kivu, E Dem. Rep. Congo 02°16′S 26°54′E
152 H8 **Moga** Punjab, N India 30°49′N 75°13′E
**Mogadiscio/Mogadishu** *see* Muqdisho
**Mogador** *see* Essaouira
104 J6 **Mogadouro** Bragança, N Portugal 41°20′N 06°43′W
167 N2 **Mogaung** Kachin State, N Myanmar (Burma) 25°20′N 96°54′E
110 L13 **Mogielnica** Mazowieckie, C Poland 51°40′N 20°42′E
**Mogilëv** *see* Mahilyow
**Mogilev-Podol'skiy** *see* Mohyliv-Podil's'kyy
**Mogilëvskaya Oblast'** *see* Mahilyowskaya Voblasts'
110 I11 **Mogilno** Kujawsko-pomorskie, C Poland 52°39′N 17°58′E
83 Q15 **Mogincual** Nampula, NE Mozambique 15°33′S 40°28′E
114 E13 **Moglenítsas** N Greece
106 H8 **Mogliano Veneto** Veneto, NE Italy 45°34′N 12°14′E
113 M21 **Mogliçë** Korçë, SE Albania 40°43′N 20°22′E
123 O13 **Mogocha** Zabaykal'skiy Kray, S Russia 53°39′N 119°47′E
122 J11 **Mogochin** Tomskaya Oblast', C Russia 57°42′N 83°24′E
80 E13 **Mogogh** Jonglei, E South Sudan 08°26′N 31°19′E
171 U12 **Mogoi** Papua Barat, E Indonesia 01°44′S 133°13′E
166 M4 **Mogok** Mandalay, C Myanmar (Burma) 22°55′N 96°29′E
37 P14 **Mogollon Mountains** ▲▲ New Mexico, SW USA
36 M12 **Mogollon Rim** *cliff* Arizona, SW USA
61 E23 **Mogotes, Punta** *headland* E Argentina 38°03′S 57°31′W
42 J8 **Mogotón** ▲ NW Nicaragua 13°45′N 86°22′W
104 I14 **Moguer** Andalucía, S Spain 37°15′N 06°52′W
111 I26 **Mohács** Baranya, SW Hungary 46°N 18°40′E
185 C20 **Mohaka** North Island, New Zealand
28 M2 **Mohall** North Dakota, N USA 48°45′N 101°30′W
**Moḩammadābād** *see* Dargaz
143 U12 **Moḩammadābād-e Rīgān** Kermān, SE Iran 28°39′N 59°01′E
74 F6 **Mohammedia** *prev.* Fédala. NW Morocco 33°46′N 07°16′W
74 F6 **Mohammed V** ✕ (Casablanca) W Morocco 33°07′N 08°28′W
**Mohammerah** *see* Khorramshahr
36 H10 **Mohave, Lake** ⊠ Arizona/Nevada, W USA
36 I12 **Mohave Mountains** ▲▲ Arizona, SW USA
36 I15 **Mohawk Mountains** ▲▲ Arizona, SW USA
18 J10 **Mohawk River** New York, NE USA
163 T3 **Mohe** *var.* Xilinji. Heilongjiang, NE China 53°01′N 122°26′E
95 L20 **Moheda** Kronoberg, S Sweden 57°00′N 14°34′E
**Mohéli** *see* Mwali
**Mohendergarh** *see* Mahendragarh
38 K12 **Mohican, Cape** *headland* Nunivak Island, Alaska, USA 60°12′N 167°25′W
**Mohn** *see* Muhu
101 G15 **Möhne** W Germany
101 G15 **Möhne-Stausee** ⊠ W Germany
92 P2 **Mohn, Kapp** *headland* NW Svalbard 79°26′N 25°44′E
197 S14 **Mohns Ridge** *undersea feature* Greenland Sea/Norwegian Sea 72°30′N 05°00′E
57 I17 **Moho** Puno, SE Peru 15°21′S 69°32′W
**Mohokare** *see* Caledon
95 L17 **Moholm** Västra Götaland, S Sweden 58°37′N 14°04′E
36 I11 **Mohon Peak** ▲ Arizona, SW USA 34°55′N 113°07′W
81 J23 **Mohoro** Pwani, E Tanzania 08°09′S 39°10′E
**Mohra** *see* Moravice
**Mohrungen** *see* Morąg
116 M7 **Mohyliv-Podil's'kyy** *Rus.* Mogilev-Podol'skiy. Vinnyts'ka Oblast', C Ukraine 48°29′N 27°49′E
95 D17 **Moi** Rogaland, S Norway 58°27′N 06°32′E
**Moili** *see* Mwali
116 K11 **Moinești** *Hung.* Mojnest. Bacău, E Romania 46°27′N 26°31′E
**Móinteach Mílic** *see* Mountmellick
14 J14 **Moira** Ontario, SE Canada
92 G13 **Mo i Rana** Nordland, C Norway 66°19′N 14°10′E
153 X14 **Moirāng** Manipur, NE India 24°29′N 93°45′E
115 J25 **Moíres** Kríti, Greece, E Mediterranean Sea 35°03′N 24°51′E
118 H6 **Mõisaküla** *Ger.* Moiseküll. Viljandimaa, S Estonia 58°05′N 25°12′E
**Moisekull** *see* Mõisaküla
15 W4 **Moisie** Québec, E Canada 50°12′N 66°06′W
15 W3 **Moisie** Québec, SE Canada
102 M14 **Moissac** Tarn-et-Garonne, S France 44°07′N 01°05′E
78 I13 **Moïssala** Mandoul, S Chad 08°21′N 17°46′E
55 O7 **Moitaco** Bolívar, E Venezuela 08°00′N 64°22′W
95 P15 **Möja** Stockholm, C Sweden 59°25′N 18°55′E
105 Q14 **Mojácar** Andalucía, S Spain 37°09′N 01°50′W
35 T13 **Mojave** California, W USA 35°03′N 118°10′W
35 V13 **Mojave Desert** *plain* California, W USA
35 V13 **Mojave River** California, W USA
60 L9 **Moji-Mirim** *var.* Moji-Mirim. São Paulo, S Brazil 22°26′S 46°55′W
**Moji-Mirim** *see* Moji-Mirim
113 K15 **Mojkovac** E Montenegro 42°57′N 19°34′E
**Mojnest** *see* Moinești
**Mōka** *see* Mooka
153 Q13 **Mokāma** *prev.* Mokameh, Mukama. Bihār, N India 25°24′N 85°55′E
**Mokameh** *see* Mokāma
79 O25 **Mokambo** Katanga, SE Dem. Rep. Congo 12°23′S 28°21′E
38 D9 **Mōkapu Point** *var.* Mokapu Point. *headland* Oʻahu, Hawaiʻi, USA 21°27′N 157°43′W
184 L9 **Mokau** Waikato, North Island, New Zealand 38°42′S 174°37′E
184 L9 **Mokau** North Island, New Zealand
35 P7 **Mokelumne River** California, W USA
83 J23 **Mokhotlong** NE Lesotho 29°19′S 29°06′E
**Mokil Atoll** *see* Mwokil Atoll
95 N14 **Möklinta** Västmanland, C Sweden 60°04′N 16°34′E
**Mokna** *see* Mokra Gora
184 L4 **Mokohinau Islands** *island group* N New Zealand
153 X12 **Mokokchūng** Nāgāland, NE India 26°20′N 94°30′E
78 F12 **Mokolo** Extrême-Nord, N Cameroon 10°49′N 13°54′E
83 J20 **Mokopane** *prev.* Potgietersrus. Limpopo, NE South Africa 24°09′S 28°58′E
185 D24 **Mokoreta** South Island, New Zealand
163 X17 **Mokpo** *Jap.* Moppo; *prev.* Mokp'o. SW South Korea 34°50′N 126°26′E
**Mokp'o** *see* Mokpo
113 L16 **Mokra Gora** *Alb.* Mokna. ▲▲ S Serbia
**Mokrany** *see* Makrany
127 O5 **Moksha** W Russia
143 X12 **Mok Sukhteh-ye Pāyīn** Sīstān va Balūchestān, SE Iran
**Moktama** *see* Mottama
77 T14 **Mokwa** Niger, W Nigeria 09°19′N 05°01′E
99 J16 **Mol** *prev.* Moll. Antwerpen, N Belgium 51°11′N 05°07′E
107 O17 **Mola di Bari** Puglia, SE Italy 41°03′N 17°05′E
**Molai** *see* Moláoi
41 P13 **Molango** Hidalgo, C Mexico 20°48′N 98°44′W
115 F22 **Moláoi** *var.* Molai. Pelopónnisos, S Greece 36°48′N 22°51′E
41 Z12 **Molas del Norte, Punta** *var.* Punta Molas. *headland* SE Mexico 20°34′N 86°43′W
**Molas, Punta** *see* Molas del Norte, Punta
105 R11 **Molatón** ▲ C Spain 38°58′N 01°19′W
97 K18 **Mold** NE Wales, United Kingdom 53°10′N 03°08′W
**Moldau** *see* Vltava, Czech Republic
**Moldau** *see* Moldova
**Moldavia** *see* Moldova
**Moldavian SSR/Moldavskaya SSR** *see* Moldova
94 E9 **Molde** Møre og Romsdal, S Norway 62°44′N 07°08′E
**Moldotau, Khrebet** *see* Moldo-Too, Khrebet
147 V9 **Moldo-Too, Khrebet** *prev.* Khrebet Moldotau. ▲▲ C Kyrgyzstan
116 L9 **Moldova** *off.* Republic of Moldova, *var.* Moldavia; *prev.* Moldavian SSR, *Rus.* Moldavskaya SSR. ◆ *republic* SE Europe
116 K9 **Moldova** *Eng.* Moldavia, *Ger.* Moldau. *former province* NE Romania
116 K9 **Moldova** N Romania
116 F13 **Moldova Nouă** *Ger.* Neumoldowa, *Hung.* Újmoldova. Caraş-Severin, SW Romania 44°45′N 21°39′E
**Moldova, Republic of** *see* Moldova
116 F13 **Moldova Veche** *Ger.* Altmoldowa, *Hung.* Ómoldova. Caraş-Severin, SW Romania 44°45′N 21°13′E
**Moldoveanul** *see* Vârful Moldoveanu
83 I20 **Molepolole** Kweneng, SE Botswana 24°25′S 25°30′E
44 L8 **Môle-St-Nicolas** NW Haiti 19°46′N 73°19′W
118 H13 **Molėtai** Utena, E Lithuania 55°14′N 25°25′E
107 O17 **Molfetta** Puglia, SE Italy 41°12′N 16°35′E
171 P11 **Molibagu** Sulawesi, N Indonesia 0°25′N 123°57′E
62 G12 **Molina** Maule, C Chile 35°06′S 71°18′W
105 Q7 **Molina de Aragón** Castilla-La Mancha, C Spain 40°50′N 01°54′W
105 R13 **Molina de Segura** Murcia, SE Spain 38°03′N 01°11′W
30 J11 **Moline** Illinois, N USA 41°30′N 90°31′W
27 P7 **Moline** Kansas, C USA 37°21′N 96°18′W
79 P23 **Moliro** Katanga, SE Dem. Rep. Congo 08°11′S 30°31′E
107 K16 **Molise** ⬥ *region* S Italy
95 K15 **Molkom** Värmland, C Sweden 59°36′N 13°43′E
109 Q9 **Möll** S Austria
**Moll** *see* Mol
146 I14 **Mollanepes Adyndaky** *Rus.* Imeni Mollanepesa. Mary Welaýaty, S Turkmenistan 37°36′N 61°54′E
95 J22 **Mölle** Skåne, S Sweden 56°15′N 12°19′E
57 H18 **Mollendo** Arequipa, SW Peru 17°02′S 72°01′W
105 U5 **Mollerussa** Cataluña, NE Spain 41°37′N 00°53′E
108 H8 **Mollis** Glarus, NE Switzerland 47°05′N 09°03′E
95 J19 **Mölndal** Västra Götaland, S Sweden 57°39′N 12°05′E
95 J19 **Mölnlycke** Västra Götaland, S Sweden 57°39′N 12°09′E
117 U9 **Molochans'k** *Rus.* Molochansk. Zaporiz'ka Oblast', SE Ukraine 47°10′N 35°38′E
117 U10 **Molochna** *Rus.* Molochnaya. S Ukraine
**Molochnaya** *see* Molochna
117 U10 **Molochnyy Lyman** *bay* N Black Sea
**Molodechno/Molodeczno** *see* Maladzyechna
124 J14 **Mologa** NW Russia
38 E9 **Molokaʻi** *var.* Molokai. *island* Hawaiian Islands, Hawaiʻi, USA
175 X3 **Molokai Fracture Zone** *tectonic feature* NE Pacific Ocean
124 K15 **Molokovo** Tverskaya Oblast', W Russia 58°10′N 36°43′E
125 Q14 **Moloma** NW Russia
183 R8 **Molong** New South Wales, SE Australia 33°07′S 148°52′E
83 H21 **Molopo** *seasonal river* Botswana/South Africa
115 F17 **Mólos** Stereá Elláda, C Greece 38°48′N 22°39′E
171 O11 **Molosipat** Sulawesi, N Indonesia 0°28′N 121°08′E
**Molotov** *see* Severodvinsk, Arkhangel'skaya Oblast', Russian Federation
**Molotov** *see* Perm', Permskaya Oblast', Russian Federation
79 G17 **Moloundou** Est, SE Cameroon 02°03′N 15°14′E
103 U5 **Molsheim** Bas-Rhin, NE France 48°33′N 07°30′E
11 X13 **Molson Lake** ◎ Manitoba, C Canada
**Moluccas** *see* Maluku
171 Q12 **Molucca Sea** *Ind.* Laut Maluku. *sea* E Indonesia
**Molukken** *see* Maluku
83 O15 **Molumbo** Zambézia, N Mozambique 15°33′S 36°19′E
171 T15 **Molu, Pulau** *island* Maluku, E Indonesia
83 P16 **Moma** Nampula, NE Mozambique 16°42′S 39°12′E
171 X14 **Momats** Papua, E Indonesia
42 J11 **Mombacho, Volcán** SW Nicaragua 11°49′N 85°58′W
81 K21 **Mombasa** Mombasa, SE Kenya 04°04′S 39°40′E
81 J21 **Mombasa** ✕ Mombasa, SE Kenya 04°01′S 39°31′E
**Mombetsu** *see* Monbetsu
114 J12 **Momchilgrad** *prev.* Mastanli. Kardzhali, S Bulgaria 41°33′N 25°25′E
99 F23 **Momignies** Hainaut, S Belgium 50°02′N 04°10′E
54 E6 **Momil** Córdoba, NW Colombia 09°15′N 75°40′W
42 I10 **Momotombo, Volcán** W Nicaragua 12°25′N 86°33′W
56 B5 **Mompiche, Ensenada de** *bay* NW Ecuador
79 K18 **Mompono** Equateur, NW Dem. Rep. Congo 0°11′N 21°31′E
54 F6 **Mompós** Bolívar, NW Colombia 09°15′N 74°29′W
95 J24 **Møn** *prev.* Möen. *island* SE Denmark
36 L4 **Mona** Utah, W USA 39°49′N 111°52′W
**Mona, Canal de la** *see* Mona Passage
96 E8 **Monach Islands** *island group* NW Scotland, United Kingdom
103 V14 **Monaco** *var.* Monaco-Ville; *anc.* Monoecus. ● (Monaco) S Monaco 43°46′N 07°23′E
103 V14 **Monaco** *off.* Principality of Monaco. ◆ *monarchy* W Europe
**Monaco** *see* München
**Monaco Basin** *see* Canary Basin
**Monaco, Principality of** *see* Monaco
**Monaco, Principauté de** *see* Monaco
**Monaco-Ville** *see* Monaco
96 I9 **Monadhliath Mountains** ▲▲ N Scotland, United Kingdom
55 O6 **Monagas** *off.* Estado Monagas. ⬥ *state* NE Venezuela
**Monagas, Estado** *see* Monagas
97 F16 **Monaghan** *Ir.* Muineachán. Monaghan, N Ireland 54°15′N 06°58′W
97 E16 **Monaghan** *Ir.* Muineachán. *cultural region* N Ireland
43 S16 **Monagrillo** Herrera, S Panama 08°00′N 80°28′W
24 L8 **Monahans** Texas, SW USA 31°35′N 102°54′W
45 Q9 **Mona, Isla** *island* W Puerto Rico
45 Q9 **Mona Passage** *Sp.* Canal de la Mona. *channel* Dominican Republic/Puerto Rico
43 O14 **Mona, Punta** *headland* E Costa Rica 09°44′N 82°48′W
155 K25 **Monaragala** Uva Province, SE Sri Lanka 06°52′N 81°22′E
33 S9 **Monarch** Montana, NW USA 47°04′N 110°51′W
10 H14 **Monarch Mountain** ▲ British Columbia, SW Canada 51°59′N 125°56′W
**Monasterio** *see* Monesterio
**Monasterzyska** *see* Monastyrys'ka
**Monastir** *see* Bitola
**Monastyriska** *see* Monastyrys'ka
117 O7 **Monastyryshche** Cherkas'ka Oblast', C Ukraine 48°59′N 29°47′E
116 J6 **Monastyrys'ka** *Pol.* Monasterzyska, *Rus.* Monastyriska. Ternopil's'ka Oblast', W Ukraine 49°05′N 25°10′E
79 E15 **Monatélé** Centre, SW Cameroon 04°16′N 11°12′E
165 U2 **Monbetsu** *var.* Mombetsu, Monbetu. Hokkaidō, NE Japan 44°23′N 143°22′E
**Monbetu** *see* Monbetsu
106 B8 **Moncalieri** Piemonte, NW Italy 45°N 07°41′E
104 G4 **Monção** Viana do Castelo, N Portugal 42°03′N 08°29′W
105 Q5 **Moncayo** ▲ N Spain 41°43′N 01°51′W
105 Q5 **Moncayo, Sierra del** ▲▲ N Spain
124 J4 **Monchegorsk** Murmanskaya Oblast', NW Russia 67°56′N 32°47′E
101 D15 **Mönchengladbach** *prev.* München-Gladbach. Nordrhein-Westfalen, W Germany 51°12′N 06°35′E
104 F14 **Monchique** Faro, S Portugal 37°19′N 08°33′W
104 G14 **Monchique, Serra de** ▲▲ S Portugal
21 S14 **Moncks Corner** South Carolina, SE USA 33°12′N 80°00′W
41 N7 **Monclova** Coahuila, NE Mexico 26°55′N 101°25′W
**Moncorvo** *see* Torre de Moncorvo
13 P14 **Moncton** New Brunswick, SE Canada 46°04′N 64°50′W
104 F8 **Mondego, Cabo** *headland* N Portugal 40°10′N 08°58′W
104 G8 **Mondego, Rio** N Portugal
104 I2 **Mondoñedo** Galicia, NW Spain 43°25′N 07°22′W
99 N25 **Mondorf-les-Bains** Grevenmacher, SE Luxembourg 49°30′N 06°16′E
102 M7 **Mondoubleau** Loir-et-Cher, C France 48°00′N 00°49′E
106 B9 **Mondovì** Piemonte, NW Italy 44°23′N 07°56′E
30 J6 **Mondovi** Wisconsin, N USA 44°34′N 91°40′W
**Mondragón** *see* Arrasate
107 J17 **Mondragone** Campania, S Italy 41°07′N 13°53′E
109 R5 **Mondsee** ◎ N Austria
115 G22 **Monemvasiá** *var.* Monemvasía. Pelopónnisos, S Greece 36°22′N 23°03′E
18 B15 **Monessen** Pennsylvania, NE USA 40°07′N 79°51′W
104 J12 **Monesterio** *var.* Monasterio. Extremadura, W Spain 38°05′N 06°16′W
14 L8 **Monet** Québec, SE Canada 48°09′N 75°37′W
27 S8 **Monett** Missouri, C USA 36°55′N 93°55′W
27 X9 **Monette** Arkansas, C USA 35°53′N 90°20′W
14 G11 **Monetville** Ontario, S Canada 46°08′N 80°24′W
106 J7 **Monfalcone** Friuli-Venezia Giulia, NE Italy 45°49′N 13°32′E
104 H10 **Monforte** Portalegre, C Portugal 39°03′N 07°26′W
104 I4 **Monforte de Lemos** Galicia, NW Spain 42°32′N 07°30′W
79 L16 **Monga** Orientale, N Dem. Rep. Congo 04°12′N 22°49′E
81 I24 **Monga** Lindi, SE Tanzania 09°05′S 37°51′E
81 F15 **Mongalla** Central Equatoria, S South Sudan 05°12′N 31°42′E
153 U11 **Mongar** E Bhutan 27°16′N 91°07′E
167 U6 **Mong Cai** *var.* Hai Ninh. Quang Ninh, N Vietnam 21°33′N 107°56′E
180 I11 **Mongers Lake** *salt lake* Western Australia
186 K8 **Mongga** Kolombangara, NW Solomon Islands 07°51′S 157°00′E
167 O6 **Monghpyak** Shan State, E Myanmar (Burma) 20°56′N 100°00′E
**Monghyr** *see* Munger
106 B10 **Mongioie** ▲ NW Italy 44°13′N 07°46′E
153 T16 **Mongla** *var.* Mungla. Khulna, S Bangladesh 22°18′N 89°34′E
188 C15 **Mongmong** C Guam
167 N6 **Möng Nai** Shan State, E Myanmar (Burma) 20°28′N 97°51′E
78 I11 **Mongo** Guéra, C Chad 12°12′N 18°40′E
76 I14 **Mongo** N Sierra Leone
163 I8 **Mongolia** *Mong.* Mongol Uls. ◆ *republic* E Asia
129 V8 **Mongolia, Plateau of** *plateau* E Mongolia
**Mongolküre** *see* Zhaosu
**Mongol Uls** *see* Mongolia




◆ Country
● Country Capital
◇ Dependent Territory
○ Dependent Territory Capital
⬥ Administrative Regions
✕ International Airport
▲ Mountain
▲▲ Mountain Range
Volcano
River
◎ Lake
⊠ Reservoir

MONGOMO – MORUYA


79 E17 **Mongomo** E Equatorial Guinea 01°39′N 11°18′E
162 M7 **Möngönmorït** *var.* Bulag. Töv, C Mongolia 48°09′N 108°33′E
77 Y12 **Mongonu** *var.* Monguno. Borno, NE Nigeria 12°42′N 13°37′E
**Mongora** *see* Saidu
78 K11 **Mongororo** Sila, SE Chad 12°03′N 22°26′E
**Mongos, Chaîne des** *see* Bongo, Massif des
79 I16 **Mongoumba** Lobaye, SW Central African Republic 03°39′N 18°30′E
**Mongrove, Punta** *see* Cayacal, Punta
83 G15 **Mongu** Western, W Zambia 15°13′S 23°09′E
76 I10 **Mônguel** Gorgol, SW Mauritania 16°25′N 13°08′W
**Monguno** *see* Mongonu
167 N4 **Mongyai** Shan State, E Myanmar (Burma) 22°25′N 98°02′E
167 O5 **Mong Yang** Shan State, E Myanmar (Burma) 21°52′N 99°31′E
167 N3 **Mŏng Yu** Shan State, E Myanmar (Burma) 24°00′N 97°57′E
**Mönhbulag** *see* Yösöndzüyl
163 O8 **Mönhhaan** *var.* Bayasgalant. Sühbaatar, E Mongolia 46°55′N 112°11′E
162 E7 **Mönhhayrhan** *var.* Tsenher. Hovd, W Mongolia 47°07′N 92°04′E
**Mönh Sarĭdag** *see* Munku-Sardyk, Gora
186 P9 **Moni** ⚘ S Papau New Guinea
115 I15 **Moní Megístis Lávras** *monastery* Kentrikí Makedonía, N Greece
115 F18 **Moní Osíou Loúkas** *monastery* Stereá Elláda, C Greece
54 F9 **Moniquirá** Boyacá, C Colombia 05°54′N 73°35′W
103 Q12 **Monistrol-sur-Loire** Haute-Loire, C France 45°19′N 04°12′E
35 V7 **Monitor Range** ▲▲ Nevada, W USA
115 I14 **Moní Vatopedíou** *monastery* Kentrikí Makedonía, N Greece
**Monkchester** *see* Newcastle upon Tyne
83 N14 **Monkey Bay** Southern, SE Malawi 14°09′S 34°53′E
43 N11 **Monkey Point** *var.* Punta Mico, Punte Mono, Punto Mico. *headland* SE Nicaragua 11°37′N 83°39′W
**Monkey River** *see* Monkey River Town
42 G3 **Monkey River Town** *var.* Monkey River. Toledo, SE Belize 16°22′N 88°29′W
14 M13 **Monkland** Ontario, SE Canada 45°11′N 74°51′W
79 J19 **Monkoto** Equateur, NW Dem. Rep. Congo 01°39′S 20°41′E
97 K21 **Monmouth** *Wel.* Trefynwy. SE Wales, United Kingdom 51°50′N 02°43′W
30 J12 **Monmouth** Illinois, N USA 40°54′N 90°39′W
32 F12 **Monmouth** Oregon, NW USA 44°51′N 123°13′W
97 K21 **Monmouth** *cultural region* SE Wales, United Kingdom
98 I10 **Monnickendam** Noord-Holland, C Netherlands 52°28′N 05°02′E
77 R15 **Mono** ⚘ C Togo
**Monoecus** *see* Monaco
35 R8 **Mono Lake** ◎ California, W USA
115 O23 **Monólithos** Ródos, Dodekánisa, Greece, Aegean Sea 36°08′N 27°45′E
19 Q12 **Monomoy Island** *island* Massachusetts, NE USA
31 O12 **Monon** Indiana, N USA 40°52′N 86°54′W
29 Y12 **Monona** Iowa, C USA 43°03′N 91°23′W
30 L9 **Monona** Wisconsin, N USA 43°03′N 89°18′W
18 B15 **Monongahela** Pennsylvania, NE USA 40°10′N 79°54′W
18 B16 **Monongahela River** ⚘ NE USA
107 P17 **Monopoli** Puglia, SE Italy 40°57′N 17°18′E
**Mono, Punte** *see* Monkey Point
111 K23 **Monor** Pest, C Hungary 47°21′N 18°27′E
**Monostor** *see* Beli Manastir
78 K8 **Monou** Ennedi-Ouest, NE Chad 16°22′N 22°15′E
105 S12 **Monóvar** *Cat.* Monòver. Comunitat Valenciana, E Spain 38°26′N 00°50′W
**Monòver** *see* Monóvar
105 R7 **Monreal del Campo** Aragón, NE Spain 40°47′N 01°20′W
107 I23 **Monreale** Sicilia, Italy, C Mediterranean Sea 38°05′N 13°17′E
23 T3 **Monroe** Georgia, SE USA 33°47′N 83°42′W
29 W14 **Monroe** Iowa, C USA 41°31′N 93°06′W
22 I5 **Monroe** Louisiana, S USA 32°32′N 92°06′W
31 S10 **Monroe** Michigan, N USA 41°55′N 83°24′W
18 K13 **Monroe** New York, NE USA 41°18′N 74°09′W
21 S11 **Monroe** North Carolina, SE USA 35°00′N 80°35′W
36 L6 **Monroe** Utah, W USA 38°37′N 112°07′W
32 H7 **Monroe** Washington, NW USA 47°51′N 121°58′W
30 L9 **Monroe** Wisconsin, N USA 42°35′N 89°39′W
27 V3 **Monroe City** Missouri, C USA 39°39′N 91°43′W
31 O15 **Monroe Lake** ▣ Indiana, N USA
23 O7 **Monroeville** Alabama, S USA 31°31′N 87°19′W
18 C15 **Monroeville** Pennsylvania, NE USA 40°24′N 79°44′W
76 J16 **Monrovia** ● (Liberia) W Liberia 06°18′N 10°48′W
76 J16 **Monrovia** ✈ W Liberia 06°22′N 10°50′W
105 T7 **Monroyo** Aragón, NE Spain 40°47′N 00°03′W
99 F20 **Mons** *Dut.* Bergen. Hainaut, S Belgium 50°28′N 03°58′E
104 I8 **Monsanto** Castelo Branco, C Portugal 40°02′N 07°07′W
106 H8 **Monselice** Veneto, NE Italy 45°15′N 11°47′E
166 M9 **Mon State** ◆ *state* S Myanmar (Burma)
98 G12 **Monster** Zuid-Holland, W Netherlands 52°01′N 04°10′E
95 N20 **Mönsterås** Kalmar, S Sweden 57°03′N 16°27′E
101 F17 **Montabaur** Rheinland-Pfalz, W Germany 50°25′N 07°48′E
106 G8 **Montagnana** Veneto, NE Italy 45°14′N 11°31′E
35 N1 **Montague** California, W USA 41°43′N 122°31′W
25 S5 **Montague** Texas, SW USA 33°40′N 97°44′W
183 S11 **Montague Island** *island* New South Wales, SE Australia
39 S12 **Montague Island** *island* Alaska, USA
39 S13 **Montague Strait** *strait* N Gulf of Alaska
102 J8 **Montaigu** Vendée, NW France 46°58′N 01°18′W
**Montaigu** *see* Scherpenheuvel
105 S7 **Montalbán** Aragón, NE Spain 40°49′N 00°48′W
106 G13 **Montalcino** Toscana, C Italy 43°01′N 11°34′E
104 H5 **Montalegre** Vila Real, N Portugal 41°49′N 07°48′W
114 G8 **Montana** *prev.* Ferdinand, Mikhaylovgrad. Montana, NW Bulgaria 43°25′N 23°14′E
108 D10 **Montana** Valais, SW Switzerland 46°23′N 07°29′E
39 R11 **Montana** Alaska, USA 62°06′N 150°03′W
114 G8 **Montana** ◆ *province* NW Bulgaria
33 T9 **Montana** *off.* State of Montana, *also known as* Mountain State, Treasure State. ◆ *state* NW USA
104 J10 **Montánchez** Extremadura, W Spain 39°15′N 06°07′W
**Montañita** *see* La Montañita
15 Q8 **Mont-Apica** Québec, SE Canada 47°57′N 71°24′W
104 G10 **Montargil** Portalegre, C Portugal 39°05′N 08°10′W
104 G10 **Montargil, Barragem de** ▣ C Portugal
103 O7 **Montargis** Loiret, C France 48°N 02°44′E
103 O4 **Montataire** Oise, N France 49°16′N 02°24′E
102 M14 **Montauban** Tarn-et-Garonne, S France 44°01′N 01°20′E
19 N14 **Montauk** Long Island, New York, NE USA 41°01′N 71°58′W
19 N14 **Montauk Point** *headland* Long Island, New York, NE USA 41°04′N 71°51′W
103 Q7 **Montbard** Côte d'Or, C France 47°35′N 04°25′E
103 U7 **Montbéliard** Doubs, E France 47°31′N 06°49′E
25 W11 **Mont Belvieu** Texas, SW USA 29°51′N 94°53′W
105 U6 **Montblanc** *prev.* Montblanch. Cataluña, NE Spain 41°23′N 01°10′E
**Montblanch** *see* Montblanc
103 Q11 **Montbrison** Loire, E France 45°37′N 04°04′E
**Montcalm, Lake** *see* Dogai Coring
103 Q9 **Montceau-les-Mines** Saône-et-Loire, C France 46°40′N 04°19′E
103 U12 **Mont Cenis, Col du** *pass* E France
102 K15 **Mont-de-Marsan** Landes, SW France 43°54′N 00°30′W
103 O3 **Montdidier** Somme, N France 49°39′N 02°35′E
187 Q17 **Mont-Dore** Province Sud, S New Caledonia 22°18′S 166°34′E
20 K10 **Monteagle** Tennessee, S USA 35°15′N 85°47′W
57 M20 **Monteagudo** Chuquisaca, S Bolivia 19°48′S 63°57′W
41 R16 **Monte Albán** *ruins* Oaxaca, S Mexico
105 R11 **Montealegre del Castillo** Castilla-La Mancha, C Spain 38°48′N 01°18′W
59 N18 **Monte Azul** Minas Gerais, SE Brazil 15°13′S 42°53′W
14 M12 **Montebello** Québec, SE Canada 45°40′N 74°56′W
106 H7 **Montebelluna** Veneto, NE Italy 45°46′N 12°03′E
60 G13 **Montecarlo** Misiones, NE Argentina 26°38′S 54°45′W
61 D16 **Monte Caseros** Corrientes, NE Argentina 30°15′S 57°39′W
60 J13 **Monte Castelo** Santa Catarina, S Brazil 26°34′S 50°12′W
106 F11 **Montecatini Terme** Toscana, C Italy 43°53′N 10°46′E
42 H7 **Montecillos, Cordillera de** ▲▲ W Honduras
62 I12 **Monte Comén** Mendoza, W Argentina 34°35′S 67°53′W
44 M8 **Monte Cristi** *var.* San Fernando de Monte Cristi. NW Dominican Republic 19°52′N 71°39′W
58 C13 **Monte Cristo** Amazonas, W Brazil 03°14′S 68°00′W
107 E14 **Montecristo, Isola di** *island* Archipelago Toscano, C Italy
**Monte Croce Carnico, Passo di** *see* Plöcken Pass
58 J12 **Monte Dourado** Pará, NE Brazil 0°48′S 52°32′W
40 L11 **Monte Escobedo** Zacatecas, C Mexico 22°19′N 103°30′W
106 I13 **Montefalco** Umbria, C Italy 42°54′N 12°40′E
107 H14 **Montefiascone** Lazio, C Italy 42°33′N 12°01′E
105 N14 **Montefrío** Andalucía, S Spain 37°19′N 04°00′W
44 I11 **Montego Bay** *var.* Mobay. W Jamaica 18°28′N 77°55′W
**Montego Bay** *see* Sangster
104 J8 **Montehermoso** Extremadura, W Spain 40°05′N 06°20′W
104 F10 **Montejunto, Serra de** ▲ C Portugal 39°10′N 09°01′W
**Monteleone di Calabria** *see* Vibo Valentia
54 E7 **Montelíbano** Córdoba, NW Colombia 08°02′N 75°29′W
103 R13 **Montélimar** *anc.* Acunum Acusio, Montilium Adhemari. Drôme, E France 44°33′N 04°45′E
104 K15 **Montellano** Andalucía, S Spain 37°00′N 05°34′W
35 Y2 **Montello** Nevada, W USA 41°18′N 114°10′W
30 L8 **Montello** Wisconsin, N USA 43°47′N 89°20′W
63 J18 **Montemayor, Meseta de** *plain* SE Argentina
41 O9 **Montemorelos** Nuevo León, NE Mexico 25°10′N 99°52′W
104 G11 **Montemor-o-Novo** Évora, S Portugal 38°38′N 08°13′W
104 G8 **Montemor-o-Velho** *var.* Montemor-o-Vélho. Coimbra, N Portugal 40°11′N 08°41′W
**Montemor-o-Vélho** *see* Montemor-o-Velho
104 H7 **Montemuro, Serra de** ▲ N Portugal 40°59′N 07°59′W
102 K12 **Montendre** Charente-Maritime, W France 45°17′N 00°24′W
61 I15 **Montenegro** Rio Grande do Sul, S Brazil 29°40′S 51°32′W
113 J16 **Montenegro** *Serb.* Crna Gora. ◆ *republic* SW Europe
62 G10 **Monte Patria** Coquimbo, N Chile 30°40′S 71°00′W
45 O9 **Monte Plata** E Dominican Republic 18°50′N 69°47′W
83 P14 **Montepuez** Cabo Delgado, N Mozambique 13°09′S 39°00′E
83 P14 **Montepuez** ⚘ N Mozambique
106 G13 **Montepulciano** Toscana, C Italy 43°02′N 11°51′E
62 L6 **Monte Quemado** Santiago del Estero, N Argentina 25°48′S 62°52′W
103 O6 **Montereau-Faut-Yonne** *anc.* Condate. Seine-St-Denis, N France 48°23′N 02°57′E
35 N11 **Monterey** California, W USA 36°36′N 121°53′W
20 L9 **Monterey** Tennessee, S USA 36°09′N 85°16′W
21 T5 **Monterey** Virginia, NE USA 38°24′N 79°36′W
**Monterey** *see* Monterrey
35 N10 **Monterey Bay** *bay* California, W USA
54 D6 **Montería** Córdoba, NW Colombia 08°45′N 75°54′W
57 N18 **Montero** Santa Cruz, C Bolivia 17°20′S 63°15′W
62 J7 **Monteros** Tucumán, C Argentina 27°12′S 65°30′W
104 I5 **Monterrei** Galicia, NW Spain 41°56′N 07°27′W
41 O8 **Monterrey** *var.* Monterey. Nuevo León, NE Mexico 25°41′N 100°16′W
32 F9 **Montesano** Washington, NW USA 46°58′N 123°37′W
107 M19 **Montesano sulla Marcellana** Campania, S Italy 40°15′N 15°41′E
107 N16 **Monte Sant' Angelo** Puglia, SE Italy 41°43′N 15°58′E
59 O16 **Monte Santo** Bahia, E Brazil 10°25′S 39°18′W
107 D18 **Monte Santu, Capo di** *headland* Sardegna, Italy, C Mediterranean Sea 40°05′N 09°43′E
59 M19 **Montes Claros** Minas Gerais, SE Brazil 16°45′S 43°52′W
107 K14 **Montesilvano Marina** Abruzzo, C Italy 42°28′N 14°07′E
23 P4 **Montevallo** Alabama, S USA 33°06′N 86°51′W
106 G12 **Montevarchi** Toscana, C Italy 43°32′N 11°34′E
61 F20 **Montevideo** ● (Uruguay) Montevideo, S Uruguay 34°55′S 56°10′W
29 S9 **Montevideo** Minnesota, N USA 44°56′N 95°43′W
37 S7 **Monte Vista** Colorado, C USA 37°33′N 106°08′W
23 T5 **Montezuma** Georgia, SE USA 32°18′N 84°01′W
29 W14 **Montezuma** Iowa, C USA 41°35′N 92°31′W
26 J6 **Montezuma** Kansas, C USA 37°33′N 100°25′W
103 U12 **Montgenèvre, Col de** *pass* France/Italy
97 K20 **Montgomery** E Wales, United Kingdom 52°38′N 03°05′W
23 Q5 **Montgomery** *state capital* Alabama, S USA 32°22′N 86°18′W
29 V9 **Montgomery** Minnesota, N USA 44°26′N 93°34′W
18 G13 **Montgomery** Pennsylvania, NE USA 41°08′N 76°52′W
21 Q5 **Montgomery** West Virginia, NE USA 38°07′N 81°19′W
97 K19 **Montgomery** *cultural region* E Wales, United Kingdom
**Montgomery** *see* Sahiwal
27 V4 **Montgomery City** Missouri, C USA 38°57′N 91°27′W
35 S8 **Montgomery Pass** *pass* Nevada, W USA
102 K12 **Montguyon** Charente-Maritime, W France 45°12′N 00°13′W
108 C10 **Monthey** Valais, SW Switzerland 46°15′N 06°56′E
27 V13 **Monticello** Arkansas, C USA 33°38′N 91°49′W
23 T4 **Monticello** Florida, SE USA 30°33′N 83°52′W
23 T8 **Monticello** Georgia, SE USA 33°18′N 83°40′W
30 M13 **Monticello** Illinois, N USA 40°01′N 88°34′W
31 O12 **Monticello** Indiana, N USA 40°45′N 86°46′W
29 Y13 **Monticello** Iowa, C USA 42°14′N 91°11′W
20 L7 **Monticello** Kentucky, S USA 36°50′N 84°50′W
29 V8 **Monticello** Minnesota, N USA 45°19′N 93°45′W
22 K7 **Monticello** Mississippi, S USA 31°33′N 90°06′W
27 V2 **Monticello** Missouri, C USA 40°07′N 91°42′W
18 J12 **Monticello** New York, NE USA 41°39′N 74°41′W
37 O7 **Monticello** Utah, W USA 37°52′N 109°20′W
106 F8 **Montichiari** Lombardia, N Italy 45°24′N 10°27′E
102 M12 **Montignac** Dordogne, SW France 45°24′N 00°54′E
99 G21 **Montignies-le-Tilleul** *var.* Montigny-le-Tilleul. Hainaut, S Belgium 50°22′N 04°23′E
14 J8 **Montigny, Lac de** ◎ Québec, SE Canada
103 S6 **Montigny-le-Roi** Haute-Marne, N France 48°02′N 05°28′E
**Montigny-le-Tilleul** *see* Montignies-le-Tilleul
43 R16 **Montijo** Veraguas, S Panama 07°59′N 80°58′W
104 F11 **Montijo** Setúbal, W Portugal 38°42′N 08°59′W
104 J11 **Montijo** Extremadura, W Spain 38°55′N 06°38′W
**Montilium Adhemari** *see* Montélimar
104 M13 **Montilla** Andalucía, S Spain 37°36′N 04°39′W
102 L3 **Montivilliers** Seine-Maritime, N France 49°31′N 00°10′E
15 U7 **Mont-Joli** Québec, SE Canada 48°36′N 68°14′W
14 M10 **Mont-Laurier** Québec, SE Canada 46°33′N 75°31′W
15 X5 **Mont-Louis** Québec, SE Canada 49°15′N 65°46′W
103 N17 **Mont-Louis** *var.* Mont Louis. Pyrénées-Orientales, S France 42°30′N 02°08′E
103 O10 **Montluçon** Allier, C France 46°21′N 02°37′E
15 R10 **Montmagny** Québec, SE Canada 47°00′N 70°31′W
103 S3 **Montmédy** Meuse, NE France 49°31′N 05°21′E
103 P5 **Montmirail** Marne, N France 48°53′N 03°31′E
15 R9 **Montmorency** ⚘ Québec, SE Canada
102 M10 **Montmorillon** Vienne, W France 46°26′N 00°52′E
107 J14 **Montorio al Vomano** Abruzzo, C Italy 42°31′N 13°39′E
104 M13 **Montoro** Andalucía, S Spain 38°00′N 04°21′W
33 S16 **Montpelier** Idaho, NW USA 42°19′N 111°18′W
29 P6 **Montpelier** North Dakota, N USA 46°40′N 98°34′W
18 M7 **Montpelier** *state capital* Vermont, NE USA 44°16′N 72°32′W
103 Q15 **Montpellier** Hérault, S France 43°37′N 03°52′E
102 L12 **Montpon-Ménestérol** Dordogne, SW France 45°01′N 00°10′E
12 K15 **Montréal** *Eng.* Montreal. Québec, SE Canada 45°30′N 73°36′W
14 G8 **Montreal** ⚘ Ontario, S Canada
**Montreal** *see* Mirabel
11 T14 **Montreal Lake** ◎ Saskatchewan, C Canada
14 B9 **Montreal River** Ontario, S Canada 47°13′N 84°36′W
103 N2 **Montreuil** Pas-de-Calais, N France 50°28′N 01°46′E
102 K8 **Montreuil-Bellay** Maine-et-Loire, NW France 47°07′N 00°10′W
108 C10 **Montreux** Vaud, SW Switzerland 46°27′N 06°55′E
108 B9 **Montricher** Vaud, W Switzerland 46°37′N 06°24′E
96 K10 **Montrose** E Scotland, United Kingdom 56°43′N 02°29′W
27 W14 **Montrose** Arkansas, C USA 33°18′N 91°29′W
37 Q6 **Montrose** Colorado, C USA 38°29′N 107°53′W
29 Y16 **Montrose** Iowa, C USA 40°31′N 91°24′W
18 H12 **Montrose** Pennsylvania, NE USA 41°49′N 75°53′W
21 X5 **Montross** Virginia, NE USA 38°04′N 76°51′W
15 O12 **Mont-St-Hilaire** Québec, SE Canada 45°34′N 73°10′W
103 S3 **Mont-St-Martin** Meurthe-et-Moselle, NE France 49°31′N 05°51′E
45 V10 **Montserrat** *var.* Emerald Isle. ◇ *UK Overseas Territory* E West Indies
105 V5 **Montserrat** ▲ NE Spain 41°39′N 01°44′E
104 M7 **Montuenga** Castilla y León, N Spain 41°04′N 04°38′W
99 M19 **Montzen** Liège, E Belgium 50°42′N 05°59′E
37 N8 **Monument Valley** *valley* Arizona/Utah, SW USA
166 L4 **Monywa** Sagaing, C Myanmar (Burma) 22°05′N 95°12′E
106 D7 **Monza** Lombardia, N Italy 45°35′N 09°16′E
83 J15 **Monze** Southern, S Zambia 16°20′S 27°29′E
105 T5 **Monzón** Aragón, NE Spain 41°54′N 00°12′E
25 T9 **Moody** Texas, SW USA 31°18′N 97°21′W
98 L13 **Mook** Limburg, SE Netherlands 51°45′N 05°52′E
165 O12 **Mooka** *var.* Môka. Tochigi, Honshū, S Japan 36°27′N 139°59′E
182 K3 **Moomba** South Australia 28°07′S 140°12′E
14 G13 **Moon** ⚘ Ontario, S Canada
**Moon** *see* Muhu
181 Y10 **Moonie** Queensland, E Australia 27°46′S 150°22′E
193 O5 **Moonless Mountains** *undersea feature* E Pacific Ocean 30°40′N 140°00′W
182 L13 **Moonlight Head** *headland* Victoria, SE Australia 38°47′S 143°12′E
**Moon-Sund** *see* Väinameri
182 H8 **Moonta** South Australia 34°03′S 137°36′E
**Moor** *see* Mór
180 I12 **Moora** Western Australia 30°23′S 116°05′E
98 H12 **Moordrecht** Zuid-Holland, C Netherlands 51°59′N 04°40′E
33 T9 **Moore** Montana, NW USA 47°00′N 109°40′W
27 N11 **Moore** Oklahoma, C USA 35°21′N 97°30′W
25 R12 **Moore** Texas, SW USA 29°03′N 99°01′W
191 S10 **Moorea** *island* Îles du Vent, W French Polynesia
21 U3 **Moorefield** West Virginia, NE USA 39°04′N 78°59′W
23 X14 **Moore Haven** Florida, SE USA 26°49′N 81°05′W
180 J11 **Moore, Lake** ◎ Western Australia
19 N7 **Moore Reservoir** ▣ New Hampshire/Vermont, NE USA
44 G1 **Moores Island** *island* N The Bahamas
21 R10 **Mooresville** North Carolina, SE USA 35°34′N 80°48′W
29 R5 **Moorhead** Minnesota, N USA 46°51′N 96°44′W
22 K4 **Moorhead** Mississippi, S USA 33°27′N 90°30′W
99 F18 **Moorsel** Oost-Vlaanderen, C Belgium 50°58′N 04°06′E
99 C18 **Moorslede** West-Vlaanderen, W Belgium 50°53′N 03°03′E
18 L8 **Moosalamoo, Mount** ▲ Vermont, NE USA 43°55′N 73°03′W
101 M22 **Moosburg in der Isar** Bayern, SE Germany 48°28′N 11°55′E
33 S14 **Moose** Wyoming, C USA 43°38′N 110°42′W
12 H11 **Moose** ⚘ Ontario, S Canada
12 H10 **Moose Factory** Ontario, S Canada 51°16′N 80°32′W
19 Q4 **Moosehead Lake** ◎ Maine, NE USA
11 U16 **Moose Jaw** Saskatchewan, S Canada 50°23′N 105°35′W
11 V14 **Moose Lake** Manitoba, C Canada 53°42′N 100°22′W
29 W6 **Moose Lake** Minnesota, N USA 46°28′N 92°46′W
19 P6 **Mooselookmeguntic Lake** ◎ Maine, NE USA
39 R12 **Moose Pass** Alaska, USA 60°28′N 149°21′W
19 P5 **Moose River** ⚘ Maine, NE USA
18 J9 **Moose River** ⚘ New York, NE USA
11 V16 **Moosomin** Saskatchewan, S Canada 50°09′N 101°41′W
12 H10 **Moosonee** Ontario, SE Canada 51°18′N 80°40′W
19 N12 **Moosup** Connecticut, NE USA 41°42′N 71°51′W
83 N16 **Mopeia** Zambézia, NE Mozambique 17°59′S 35°43′E
83 H18 **Mopipi** Central, C Botswana 21°07′S 24°55′E
**Moppo** *see* Mokpo
77 N11 **Mopti** Mopti, C Mali 14°30′N 04°15′W
77 O11 **Mopti** ◆ *region* S Mali
57 H18 **Moquegua** Moquegua, SE Peru 17°07′S 70°55′W
57 H18 **Moquegua** *off.* Región de Moquegua. ◆ *region* S Peru
**Moquegua, Región de** *see* Moquegua
111 I23 **Mór** *Ger.* Moor. Fejér, C Hungary 47°21′N 18°12′E
78 G11 **Mora** Extrême-Nord, N Cameroon 11°02′N 14°07′E
104 G11 **Mora** Évora, S Portugal 38°56′N 08°10′W
105 N9 **Mora** Castilla-La Mancha, C Spain 39°40′N 03°46′W
94 L12 **Mora** Dalarna, C Sweden 61°N 14°30′E
29 V7 **Mora** Minnesota, N USA 45°52′N 93°18′W
37 T10 **Mora** New Mexico, SW USA 35°56′N 105°16′W
113 J17 **Morača** ⚘ S Montenegro
152 K10 **Morādābād** Uttar Pradesh, N India 28°50′N 78°45′E
105 U6 **Móra d'Ebre** *var.* Mora de Ebro. Cataluña, NE Spain 41°05′N 00°38′E
**Mora de Ebro** *see* Móra d'Ebre
105 S8 **Mora de Rubielos** Aragón, NE Spain 40°15′N 00°45′W
172 H4 **Morafenobe** Mahajanga, W Madagascar 17°49′S 44°54′E
110 K8 **Morąg** *Ger.* Mohrungen. Warmińsko-Mazurskie, N Poland 53°55′N 19°56′E
111 L25 **Mórahalom** Csongrád, S Hungary 46°14′N 19°52′E
105 N11 **Moral de Calatrava** Castilla-La Mancha, C Spain 38°50′N 03°34′W
63 G19 **Moraleda, Canal** *strait* SE Pacific Ocean
54 J3 **Morales** Bolívar, N Colombia 08°17′N 73°52′W
54 D12 **Morales** Cauca, SW Colombia 02°46′N 76°44′W
42 F5 **Morales** Izabal, E Guatemala 15°28′N 88°46′W
172 J5 **Moramanga** Toamasina, E Madagascar 18°57′S 48°13′E
27 Q6 **Moran** Kansas, C USA 37°55′N 95°10′W
25 Q7 **Moran** Texas, SW USA 32°33′N 99°10′W
181 X7 **Moranbah** Queensland, NE Australia 22°01′S 148°08′E
44 L13 **Morant Bay** E Jamaica 17°53′N 76°25′W
96 G10 **Morar, Loch** ◎ N Scotland, United Kingdom
**Morata** *see* Goodenough Island
105 Q12 **Moratalla** Murcia, SE Spain 38°11′N 01°53′W
108 C8 **Morat, Lac de** *Ger.* Murtensee. ◎ W Switzerland
84 I11 **Morava** *var.* March. ⚘ C Europe *see also* March
**Morava** *see* March
**Morava** *see* Moravia, Czech Republic
**Morava** *see* Velika Morava, Serbia
29 W15 **Moravia** Iowa, C USA 40°53′N 92°49′W
111 F18 **Moravia** *Cz.* Morava, *Ger.* Mähren. *cultural region* E Czechia
111 H17 **Moravice** *Ger.* Mohra. ⚘ NE Czechia
116 E12 **Moravița** Timiș, SW Romania 45°15′N 21°17′E
111 G17 **Moravská Třebová** *Ger.* Mährisch-Trübau. Pardubický Kraj, C Czechia 49°47′N 16°40′E
111 E19 **Moravské Budějovice** *Ger.* Mährisch-Budwitz. Vysočina, C Czechia 49°03′N 15°48′E
111 H17 **Moravskoslezský Kraj** *prev.* Ostravský Kraj. ◆ *region* E Czechia
111 F19 **Moravský Krumlov** *Ger.* Mährisch-Kromau. Jihomoravský Kraj, SE Czechia 48°58′N 16°30′E
96 J8 **Moray** *cultural region* N Scotland, United Kingdom
96 J8 **Moray Firth** *inlet* N Scotland, United Kingdom
42 B10 **Morazán** ◆ *department* NE El Salvador
154 C10 **Morbi** Gujarāt, W India 22°51′N 70°49′E
102 G7 **Morbihan** ◆ *department* NW France
**Mörbisch** *see* Mörbisch am See
109 Y5 **Mörbisch am See** *var.* Mörbisch. Burgenland, E Austria 47°43′N 16°40′E
95 N21 **Mörbylånga** Kalmar, S Sweden 56°31′N 16°25′E
102 J14 **Morcenx** Landes, SW France 44°04′N 00°55′W
**Morcheh Khort** *see* Mürcheh Khvort
163 T5 **Mordaga** Nei Mongol Zizhiqu, N China 51°15′N 120°47′E
11 X17 **Morden** Manitoba, S Canada 49°12′N 98°05′W
**Mordovia** *see* Mordoviya, Respublika
127 N5 **Mordoviya, Respublika** *prev.* Mordovskaya ASSR, *Eng.* Mordovia, Mordvinia. ◆ *autonomous republic* W Russia
126 M7 **Mordovo** Tambovskaya Oblast', W Russia 52°05′N 40°49′E
**Mordovskaya ASSR/ Mordvinia** *see* Mordoviya, Respublika
**Morea** *see* Pelopónnisos
28 K8 **Moreau River** ⚘ South Dakota, N USA
97 K16 **Morecambe** NW England, United Kingdom 54°04′N 02°53′W
97 K16 **Morecambe Bay** *inlet* NW England, United Kingdom
183 S4 **Moree** New South Wales, SE Australia 29°29′S 149°53′E
21 N5 **Morehead** Kentucky, S USA 38°11′N 83°27′W
21 X11 **Morehead City** North Carolina, SE USA 34°43′N 76°43′W
27 Y8 **Morehouse** Missouri, C USA 36°51′N 89°41′W
108 E10 **Mörel** Valais, SW Switzerland 46°22′N 08°03′E
54 D13 **Morelia** Caquetá, S Colombia 01°30′N 75°43′W
41 N14 **Morelia** Michoacán, S Mexico 19°40′N 101°11′W
105 T7 **Morella** Comunitat Valenciana, E Spain 40°37′N 00°06′W
40 I7 **Morelos** Chihuahua, N Mexico 26°37′N 107°37′W
41 O15 **Morelos** ◆ *state* S Mexico
154 H7 **Morena** Madhya Pradesh, C India 26°30′N 78°04′E
104 L12 **Morena, Sierra** ▲▲ S Spain
37 O14 **Morenci** Arizona, SW USA 33°05′N 109°21′W
31 R11 **Morenci** Michigan, N USA 41°43′N 84°13′W
116 J13 **Moreni** Dâmbovița, S Romania 44°59′N 25°39′E
94 D9 **Møre og Romsdal** ◆ *county* S Norway
10 I14 **Moresby Island** *island* Queen Charlotte Islands, British Columbia, SW Canada
183 W2 **Moreton Island** *island* Queensland, E Australia
103 O3 **Moreuil** Somme, N France 49°47′N 02°28′E
35 V7 **Morey Peak** ▲ Nevada, W USA 38°40′N 116°16′W
125 U4 **More-Yu** ⚘ NW Russia
103 T9 **Morez** Jura, E France 46°33′N 06°01′E
**Morfou Bay/Mórfou, Kólpos** *see* Güzelyurt Körfezi
182 J8 **Morgan** South Australia 34°02′S 139°39′E
23 S7 **Morgan** Georgia, SE USA 31°31′N 84°34′W
25 S8 **Morgan** Texas, SW USA 32°01′N 97°36′W
22 J10 **Morgan City** Louisiana, S USA 29°42′N 91°12′W
20 H6 **Morganfield** Kentucky, S USA 37°41′N 87°55′W
35 O10 **Morgan Hill** California, W USA 37°05′N 121°38′W
21 Q9 **Morganton** North Carolina, SE USA 35°44′N 81°43′W
20 J7 **Morgantown** Kentucky, S USA 37°12′N 86°42′W
21 S2 **Morgantown** West Virginia, NE USA 39°38′N 79°57′W
108 B10 **Morges** Vaud, SW Switzerland 46°31′N 06°30′E
**Morghāb, Daryā-ye** *see* Murgap
**Morghāb, Daryā-ye** *see* Murghāb, Daryā-ye
96 I9 **Mor, Glen** *var.* Glen Albyn, Great Glen. *valley* N Scotland, United Kingdom
103 T5 **Morhange** Moselle, NE France 48°56′N 06°37′E
158 M5 **Mori** *var.* Mori Kazak Zizhixian. Xinjiang Uygur Zizhiqu, NW China 43°48′N 90°21′E
165 R5 **Mori** Hokkaidō, NE Japan 42°04′N 140°36′E
35 Y6 **Moriah, Mount** ▲ Nevada, W USA 39°16′N 114°10′W
37 S11 **Moriarty** New Mexico, SW USA 34°59′N 106°03′W
54 J12 **Morichal** Guaviare, E Colombia 02°09′N 70°35′W
**Mori Kazak Zizhixian** *see* Mori
**Morin Dawa Daurzu Zizhiqi** *see* Nirji
11 Q14 **Morinville** Alberta, SW Canada 53°48′N 113°38′W
165 R8 **Morioka** Iwate, Honshū, C Japan 39°42′N 141°08′E
183 T8 **Morisset** New South Wales, SE Australia 33°07′S 151°32′E
165 Q8 **Moriyoshi-zan** ▲ Honshū, C Japan 39°58′N 140°32′E
92 K13 **Morjärv** Norrbotten, N Sweden 66°03′N 22°45′E
127 R3 **Morki** Respublika Mariy El, W Russia 56°27′N 49°01′E
123 N10 **Morkoka** ⚘ NE Russia
102 F5 **Morlaix** Finistère, NW France 48°35′N 03°50′W
95 M20 **Mörlunda** Kalmar, S Sweden 57°19′N 15°52′E
107 N19 **Mormanno** Calabria, SW Italy 39°54′N 15°58′E
36 L11 **Mormon Lake** ◎ Arizona, SW USA
35 Y10 **Mormon Peak** ▲ Nevada, W USA 36°59′N 114°25′W
**Mormon State** *see* Utah
45 Y5 **Morne-à-l'Eau** Grande Terre, N Guadeloupe 16°20′N 61°31′W
29 Y15 **Morning Sun** Iowa, C USA 41°06′N 91°15′W
193 S12 **Mornington Abyssal Plain** *undersea feature* SE Pacific Ocean 50°00′S 90°00′W
63 F22 **Mornington, Isla** *island* S Chile
181 T4 **Mornington Island** *island* Wellesley Islands, Queensland, N Australia
115 E18 **Mórnos** ⚘ C Greece
149 P14 **Moro** Sindh, SE Pakistan 26°36′N 67°59′E
32 I11 **Moro** Oregon, NW USA 45°30′N 120°46′W
186 E8 **Morobe** Morobe, C Papua New Guinea 07°46′S 147°35′E
186 E8 **Morobe** ◆ *province* C Papua New Guinea
31 N12 **Morocco** Indiana, N USA 40°57′N 87°27′W
74 E8 **Morocco** *off.* Kingdom of Morocco, *Ar.* Al Maghrib, Al Mamlakah al Maghribīyah. ◆ *monarchy* N Africa
**Morocco** *see* Marrakech
**Morocco, Kingdom of** *see* Morocco
81 I22 **Morogoro** Morogoro, E Tanzania 06°49′S 37°40′E
81 H24 **Morogoro** ◆ *region* SE Tanzania
171 Q7 **Moro Gulf** *gulf* S Philippines
41 N13 **Moroleón** Guanajuato, C Mexico 20°00′N 101°13′W
172 H6 **Morombe** Toliara, W Madagascar 21°47′S 43°21′E
44 G5 **Morón** Ciego de Ávila, C Cuba 22°08′N 78°39′W
163 N8 **Mörön** Hentiy, C Mongolia 47°21′N 110°21′E
162 I6 **Mörön** Hövsgöl, N Mongolia 49°39′N 100°08′E
54 K5 **Morón** Carabobo, N Venezuela 10°29′N 68°11′W
**Morón** *see* Morón de la Frontera
56 D8 **Morona, Río** ⚘ N Peru
56 C8 **Morona Santiago** ◆ *province* E Ecuador
172 H5 **Morondava** Toliara, W Madagascar 20°19′S 44°17′E
104 K14 **Morón de la Frontera** *var.* Morón. Andalucía, S Spain 37°07′N 05°27′W
172 G13 **Moroni** ● (Comoros) Grande Comore, NW Comoros 11°41′S 43°16′E
171 S10 **Morotai, Pulau** *island* Maluku, E Indonesia
**Morotiri** *see* Marotiri
81 H17 **Moroto** NE Uganda 02°32′N 34°41′E
**Morozov** *see* Bratan
126 M11 **Morozovsk** Rostovskaya Oblast', SW Russia 48°21′N 41°54′E
97 L14 **Morpeth** N England, United Kingdom 55°10′N 01°41′W
**Morphou** *see* Güzelyurt
**Morphou Bay** *see* Güzelyurt Körfezi
28 I13 **Morrill** Nebraska, C USA 41°57′N 103°55′W
27 U11 **Morrilton** Arkansas, C USA 35°09′N 92°45′W
11 Q16 **Morrin** Alberta, SW Canada 51°40′N 112°45′W
184 M7 **Morrinsville** Waikato, North Island, New Zealand 37°41′S 175°32′E
11 X16 **Morris** Manitoba, S Canada 49°22′N 97°21′W
30 M11 **Morris** Illinois, N USA 41°21′N 88°25′W
29 S8 **Morris** Minnesota, N USA 45°32′N 95°53′W
14 M13 **Morrisburg** Ontario, SE Canada 44°55′N 75°07′W
197 R11 **Morris Jesup, Kap** *headland* N Greenland 83°33′N 32°40′W
182 B1 **Morris, Mount** ▲ South Australia 26°04′S 131°03′E
30 K10 **Morrison** Illinois, N USA 41°48′N 89°58′W
36 K13 **Morristown** Arizona, SW USA 33°48′N 112°34′W
18 J14 **Morristown** New Jersey, NE USA 40°48′N 74°29′W
21 O8 **Morristown** Tennessee, S USA 36°13′N 83°18′W
42 L11 **Morrito** Río San Juan, SW Nicaragua 11°37′N 85°05′W
35 P13 **Morro Bay** California, W USA 35°21′N 120°51′W
95 L22 **Mörrum** Blekinge, S Sweden 56°11′N 14°45′E
83 N16 **Morrumbala** Zambézia, NE Mozambique 17°17′S 35°35′E
83 N20 **Morrumbene** Inhambane, SE Mozambique 23°41′S 35°25′E
95 F21 **Mors** *island* NW Denmark
**Mors** *see* Moers
25 N1 **Morse** Texas, SW USA 36°03′N 101°28′W
127 N6 **Morshansk** Tambovskaya Oblast', W Russia 53°27′N 41°46′E
102 L5 **Mortagne-au-Perche** Orne, N France 48°32′N 00°31′E
102 J8 **Mortagne-sur-Sèvre** Vendée, NW France 47°00′N 00°57′W
104 G8 **Mortágua** Viseu, N Portugal 40°24′N 08°14′W
102 J5 **Mortain** Manche, N France 48°39′N 00°51′W
106 C8 **Mortara** Lombardia, N Italy 45°15′N 08°44′E
59 J17 **Mortes, Rio das** ⚘ C Brazil
182 M12 **Mortlake** Victoria, SE Australia 38°06′S 142°48′E
**Mortlock Group** *see* Takuu Islands
189 Q17 **Mortlock Islands** *prev.* Nomoi Islands. *island group* C Micronesia
29 T9 **Morton** Minnesota, N USA 44°33′N 94°58′W
22 L5 **Morton** Mississippi, S USA 32°21′N 89°39′W
24 M5 **Morton** Texas, SW USA 33°40′N 102°45′W
32 H9 **Morton** Washington, NW USA 46°33′N 122°16′W
0 D7 **Morton Seamount** *undersea feature* NE Pacific Ocean 50°15′N 142°45′W
45 U15 **Moruga** Trinidad, Trinidad and Tobago 10°04′N 61°16′W
183 P9 **Morundah** New South Wales, SE Australia 34°57′S 146°18′E
191 X12 **Mururoa** *var.* Mururoa. *atoll* Îles Tuamotu, SE French Polynesia
183 S11 **Moruya** New South Wales, SE Australia 35°55′S 150°04′E


◆ Country
● Country Capital
◇ Dependent Territory
○ Dependent Territory Capital
◆ Administrative Regions
✈ International Airport
▲ Mountain
▲▲ Mountain Range
⚘ Volcano
⚘ River
◎ Lake
▣ Reservoir

Morvan – Mülig-Hofmann Mountains

103 Q8 **Morvan** *physical region* C France
185 G21 **Morven** Canterbury, South Island, New Zealand 44°51′S 171°07′E
183 O13 **Morwell** Victoria, SE Australia 38°14′S 146°25′E
125 N6 **Morzhovets, Ostrov** *island* NW Russia
126 J4 **Mosal'sk** Kaluzhskaya Oblast', W Russia 54°30′N 34°55′E
101 H20 **Mosbach** Baden-Württemberg, SW Germany 49°21′N 09°06′E
95 E18 **Mosby** Vest-Agder, S Norway 58°12′N 07°55′E
33 V9 **Mosby** Montana, NW USA 46°58′N 107°53′W
32 M9 **Moscow** Idaho, NW USA 46°43′N 117°00′W
20 F10 **Moscow** Tennessee, S USA 35°04′N 89°27′W
**Moscow** *see* Moskva
101 D19 **Mosel** *Fr.* Moselle. ≈ W Europe *see also* Moselle
**Mosel** *see* Moselle
103 T4 **Moselle** ◈ *department* NE France
103 T6 **Moselle** *Ger.* Mosel. ≈ W Europe *see also* Mosel
**Moselle** *see* Mosel
32 K9 **Moses Lake** ◎ Washington, NW USA
83 I18 **Mosetse** Central, E Botswana 20°40′S 26°38′E
92 H4 **Mosfellsbær** Höfuðborgarsvæðið, SW Iceland 65°09′N 21°43′W
183 N8 **Mossgiel** New South Wales, SE Australia 33°16′S 144°34′E
185 F23 **Mosgiel** Otago, South Island, New Zealand 45°51′S 170°22′E
124 M11 **Mosha** ≈ NW Russia
81 I20 **Moshi** Kilimanjaro, NE Tanzania 03°21′S 37°19′E
110 G12 **Mosina** Wielkolpolskie, C Poland 52°15′N 16°50′E
30 L6 **Mosinee** Wisconsin, N USA 44°45′N 89°39′W
92 F13 **Mosjøen** Nordland, C Norway 65°49′N 13°12′E
123 S12 **Moskal'vo** Ostrov Sakhalin, Sakhalinskaya Oblast', SE Russia 53°36′N 142°31′E
92 I13 **Moskosel** Norrbotten, N Sweden 65°52′N 19°30′E
126 K4 **Moskovskaya Oblast'** ◈ *province* W Russia
**Moskovskiy** *see* Moskva
126 J3 **Moskva** *Eng.* Moscow. ● (Russia) Gorod Moskva, W Russia 55°45′N 37°42′E
147 Q14 **Moskva** *Rus.* Moskovskiy; *prev.* Chubek. SW Tajikistan 37°41′N 69°33′E
126 L4 **Moskva** ≈ W Russia
83 I20 **Mosomane** Kgatleng, SE Botswana 24°04′S 26°15′E
**Moson and Magyaróvár** *see* Mosonmagyaróvár
111 H21 **Mosoni-Duna** *Ger.* Kleine Donau. ≈ NW Hungary
111 H21 **Mosonmagyaróvár** *Ger.* Wieselburg-Ungarisch-Altenburg; *prev.* Moson and Magyaróvár, *Ger.* Wieselburg and Ungarisch-Altenburg. Győr-Moson-Sopron, NW Hungary 47°52′N 17°15′E
**Mospino** *see* Mospyne
117 X8 **Mospyne** *Rus.* Mospino. Donets'ka Oblast', E Ukraine 47°53′N 38°03′E
54 B12 **Mosquera** Nariño, SW Colombia 02°32′N 78°24′W
37 U10 **Mosquero** New Mexico, SW USA 35°46′N 103°57′W
**Mosquito Coast** *see* La Mosquitia
31 U11 **Mosquito Creek Lake** ⊠ Ohio, N USA
**Mosquito Gulf** *see* Mosquitos, Golfo de los
23 X11 **Mosquito Lagoon** *wetland* Florida, SE USA
43 N10 **Mosquito, Punta** *headland* E Nicaragua 12°18′N 83°38′W
43 W14 **Mosquito, Punta** *headland* NE Panama 09°06′N 77°52′W
43 Q15 **Mosquitos, Golfo de los** *Eng.* Mosquito Gulf. *gulf* N Panama
95 H16 **Moss** Østfold, S Norway 59°25′N 10°40′E
**Mossâmedes** *see* Namibe
22 G8 **Moss Bluff** Louisiana, S USA 30°18′N 93°11′W
185 C23 **Mossburn** Southland, South Island, New Zealand 45°40′S 168°15′E
83 G26 **Mosselbaai** *var.* Mosselbai, *Eng.* Mossel Bay. Western Cape, SW South Africa 34°11′S 22°08′E
**Mosselbai/Mossel Bay** *see* Mosselbaai
79 F20 **Mossendjo** Niari, SW Congo 02°57′S 12°40′E
101 H22 **Mössingen** Baden-Württemberg, S Germany 48°22′N 09°01′E
181 W4 **Mossman** Queensland, NE Australia 16°34′S 145°27′E
59 P14 **Mossoró** Rio Grande do Norte, NE Brazil 05°11′S 37°20′W
23 N9 **Moss Point** Mississippi, S USA 30°24′N 88°31′W
183 S9 **Moss Vale** New South Wales, SE Australia 34°33′S 150°20′E
32 G9 **Mossyrock** Washington, NW USA 46°32′N 122°30′W
111 B15 **Most** *Ger.* Brüx. Ústecký Kraj, NW Czechia 50°30′N 13°37′E
162 E7 **Möst** *var.* Ulaantolgoy. Hovd, W Mongolia 46°39′N 92°50′E
121 P16 **Mosta** *var.* Musta. C Malta 35°54′N 14°25′E
74 I5 **Mostaganem** *var.* Mestghanem. NW Algeria 35°54′N 00°05′E
113 H14 **Mostar** Federacija Bosne I Hercegovine, S Bosnia and Herzegovina 43°21′N 17°47′E
61 J17 **Mostardas** Rio Grande do Sul, S Brazil 31°02′S 50°51′W
116 K14 **Mostiştea** ≈ S Romania
**Mostva** *see* Mastva
**Mosty** *see* Masty
116 H5 **Mostys'ka** L'vivs'ka Oblast', W Ukraine 49°47′N 23°09′E
**Mosul** *see* Al Mawşil
95 F15 **Møsvatnet** ◎ S Norway
80 J12 **Mot'a** Āmara, N Ethiopia 11°03′N 38°03′E
79 H16 **Motaba** ≈ N Congo
105 O10 **Mota del Cuervo** Castilla-La Mancha, C Spain 39°30′N 02°52′W
104 L5 **Mota del Marqués** Castilla y León, N Spain 41°38′N 05°11′W
42 F5 **Motagua, Río** ≈ Guatemala/Honduras
119 H19 **Motal'** Brestskaya Voblasts', SW Belarus 52°13′N 25°34′E
95 L17 **Motala** Östergötland, S Sweden 58°34′N 15°05′E
191 X7 **Motane** *island* Îles Marquises, NE French Polynesia
152 K13 **Moth** Uttar Pradesh, N India 25°44′N 78°56′E
**Mother of Presidents/ Mother of States** *see* Virginia
96 I12 **Motherwell** C Scotland, United Kingdom 55°48′N 04°W
153 P12 **Motīhāri** Bihār, N India 26°40′N 84°55′E
105 Q10 **Motilla del Palancar** Castilla-La Mancha, C Spain 39°34′N 01°55′W
184 N7 **Motiti Island** *island* NE New Zealand
65 E25 **Motley Island** *island* SE Falkland Islands
33 J19 **Motloutse** ≈ E Botswana
41 V17 **Motozintla de Mendoza** Chiapas, SE Mexico 15°21′N 92°14′W
105 N15 **Motril** Andalucía, S Spain 36°45′N 03°30′W
116 G13 **Motru** Gorj, SW Romania 44°49′N 22°56′E
165 Q4 **Motsuta-misaki** *headland* Hokkaidō, NE Japan 42°36′N 139°48′E
28 L6 **Mott** North Dakota, N USA 46°21′N 102°17′W
166 M9 **Mottama** *var.* Martaban, Moktama. Mon State, S Myanmar (Burma) 16°32′N 97°35′E
166 L9 **Mottama, Gulf of** *var.* Gulf of Martaban. *gulf* S Myanmar (Burma)
**Möttling** *see* Metlika
107 O18 **Mottola** Puglia, SE Italy 40°38′N 17°02′E
184 P8 **Motu** ≈ North Island, New Zealand
185 I14 **Motueka** Tasman, South Island, New Zealand 41°08′S 173°00′E
185 I14 **Motueka** ≈ South Island, New Zealand
**Motu Iti** *see* Tupai
41 X12 **Motul** *var.* Motul de Felipe Carrillo Puerto. Yucatán, SE Mexico 21°06′N 89°17′W
**Motul de Felipe Carrillo Puerto** *see* Motul
191 U17 **Motu Nui** *island* Easter Island, Chile, E Pacific Ocean
191 Q10 **Motu One** *var.* Bellingshausen. *atoll* Îles Sous le Vent, W French Polynesia
190 I16 **Motutapu** *island* E Cook Islands
193 V15 **Motu Tapu** *island* Tongatapu Group, S Tonga
184 L5 **Motutapu Island** *island* N New Zealand
**Motyca** *see* Modica
**Mouanda** *see* Moanda
**Mouaskar** *see* Mascara
105 U3 **Moubermé, Tuc de** *Fr.* Pic de Maubermé, *Sp.* Pico Mauberme; *prev.* Tuc de Maubermé. ▲ France/ Spain 42°48′N 00°57′E *see also* Maubermé, Pic de
**Moubermé, Tuc de** *see* Maubermé, Pic de
45 N7 **Mouchoir Passage** *passage* SE Turks and Caicos Islands
76 I9 **Moudjéria** Tagant, SW Mauritania 17°52′N 12°20′W
108 C9 **Moudon** Vaud, W Switzerland 46°41′N 06°49′E
**Mouhoun** *see* Black Volta
79 E19 **Mouila** Ngounié, C Gabon 01°50′S 11°02′E
79 K14 **Mouka** Haute-Kotto, C Central African Republic 07°12′N 21°52′E
**Moukden** *see* Shenyang
183 N10 **Moulamein** New South Wales, SE Australia 35°06′S 144°03′E
**Moulamein Creek** *see* Billabong Creek
74 F6 **Moulay-Bousselham** NW Morocco 35°00′N 06°22′W
**Moule** *see* le Moule
80 M11 **Moulhoulé** N Djibouti 12°34′N 43°06′E
103 P9 **Moulins** Allier, C France 46°34′N 03°20′E
**Moulmein** *see* Mawlamyine
**Moulmeingyun** *see* Mawlamyinegyunn
74 G6 **Moulouya** *var.* Mulucha, Muluya, Mulwiya. *seasonal river* NE Morocco
23 O2 **Moulton** Alabama, S USA 34°28′N 87°18′W
29 W16 **Moulton** Iowa, C USA 40°41′N 92°40′W
25 T11 **Moulton** Texas, SW USA 29°34′N 97°08′W
23 T7 **Moultrie** Georgia, SE USA 31°10′N 83°47′W
21 S14 **Moultrie, Lake** ⊠ South Carolina, SE USA
22 K3 **Mound Bayou** Mississippi, S USA 33°52′N 90°43′W
30 L17 **Mound City** Illinois, N USA 37°06′N 89°09′W
27 R6 **Mound City** Kansas, C USA 38°07′N 94°49′W
27 Q2 **Mound City** Missouri, C USA 40°07′N 95°13′W
29 N7 **Mound City** South Dakota, N USA 45°44′N 100°03′W
78 H13 **Moundou** Logone-Occidental, SW Chad 08°35′N 16°01′E
27 P10 **Mounds** Oklahoma, C USA 35°52′N 96°03′W
21 R2 **Moundsville** West Virginia, NE USA 39°54′N 80°44′W
167 R11 **Moŭng** *prev.* Phumĭ Moŭng. Siem Reap, NW Cambodia 13°45′N 103°35′E
167 Q12 **Moŭng Roessei** Battambang, W Cambodia 12°47′N 103°28′E
**Moun Hou** *see* Black Volta
8 H8 **Mountain** ≈ Northwest Territories, NW Canada
37 S12 **Mountainair** New Mexico, SW USA 34°31′N 106°14′W
35 V1 **Mountain City** Nevada, W USA 41°48′N 115°58′W
21 Q8 **Mountain City** Tennessee, S USA 36°28′N 81°48′W
27 U7 **Mountain Grove** Missouri, C USA 37°07′N 92°15′W
27 U9 **Mountain Home** Arkansas, C USA 35°19′N 92°24′W
33 N15 **Mountain Home** Idaho, NW USA 43°07′N 115°42′W
25 Q11 **Mountain Home** Texas, SW USA 30°11′N 99°19′W
29 W4 **Mountain Iron** Minnesota, N USA 47°31′N 92°37′W
29 T10 **Mountain Lake** Minnesota, N USA 43°57′N 94°54′W
23 S3 **Mountain Park** Georgia, SE USA 34°04′N 84°24′W
35 W12 **Mountain Pass** *pass* California, W USA
27 T12 **Mountain Pine** Arkansas, C USA 34°34′N 93°10′W
39 Y14 **Mountain Point** Annette Island, Alaska, USA 55°17′N 131°31′W
**Mountain State** *see* Montana
**Mountain State** *see* West Virginia
27 V7 **Mountain View** Arkansas, C USA 35°52′N 92°07′W
38 H12 **Mountain View** Hawaii, USA, C Pacific Ocean 19°32′N 155°03′W
27 V10 **Mountain View** Missouri, C USA 37°00′N 91°42′W
38 M11 **Mountain Village** Alaska, USA 62°06′N 163°42′W
21 R8 **Mount Airy** North Carolina, SE USA 36°30′N 80°36′W
83 K24 **Mount Ayliff** *Xh.* Maxesibebi. Eastern Cape, SE South Africa 30°48′S 29°23′E
29 U16 **Mount Ayr** Iowa, C USA 40°42′N 94°14′W
182 J9 **Mount Barker** South Australia 35°06′S 138°52′E
180 J14 **Mount Barker** Western Australia 34°42′S 117°40′E
183 P11 **Mount Beauty** Victoria, SE Australia 36°47′S 147°12′E
14 E16 **Mount Brydges** Ontario, S Canada 42°54′N 81°29′W
31 N16 **Mount Carmel** Illinois, N USA 38°23′N 87°46′W
30 K10 **Mount Carroll** Illinois, N USA 42°05′N 89°59′W
31 S9 **Mount Clemens** Michigan, N USA 42°36′N 82°52′W
83 L16 **Mount Darwin** Mashonaland Central, NE Zimbabwe 16°45′S 31°39′E
19 S7 **Mount Desert Island** *island* Maine, NE USA
23 W11 **Mount Dora** Florida, SE USA 28°48′N 81°38′W
182 G5 **Mount Eba** South Australia 30°11′S 135°40′E
25 W8 **Mount Enterprise** Texas, SW USA 31°53′N 94°40′W
182 J4 **Mount Fitton** South Australia 29°55′S 139°26′E
83 J24 **Mount Fletcher** Eastern Cape, SE South Africa 30°41′S 28°30′E
14 F15 **Mount Forest** Ontario, S Canada 43°58′N 80°44′W
182 K12 **Mount Gambier** South Australia 37°47′S 140°49′E
181 W5 **Mount Garnet** Queensland, NE Australia 17°41′S 145°07′E
21 P6 **Mount Gay** West Virginia, NE USA 37°49′N 82°00′W
31 S12 **Mount Gilead** Ohio, N USA 40°33′N 82°49′W
186 C7 **Mount Hagen** Western Highlands, C Papua New Guinea 05°54′S 144°13′E
18 J16 **Mount Holly** New Jersey, NE USA 39°59′N 74°46′W
21 R10 **Mount Holly** North Carolina, SE USA 35°18′N 81°01′W
27 T12 **Mount Ida** Arkansas, C USA 34°32′N 93°38′W
181 T6 **Mount Isa** Queensland, C Australia 20°48′S 139°32′E
21 U4 **Mount Jackson** Virginia, NE USA 38°45′N 78°38′W
18 D12 **Mount Jewett** Pennsylvania, NE USA 41°43′N 78°37′W
18 L13 **Mount Kisco** New York, NE USA 41°12′N 73°42′W
18 B15 **Mount Lebanon** Pennsylvania, NE USA 40°21′N 80°03′W
182 J8 **Mount Lofty Ranges** ▲▲ South Australia
180 J10 **Mount Magnet** Western Australia 28°09′S 117°52′E
184 N7 **Mount Maunganui** Bay of Plenty, North Island, New Zealand 37°39′S 176°11′E
97 E18 **Mountmellick** *Ir.* Móinteach Mílic. Laois, C Ireland 53°07′N 07°20′W
30 L10 **Mount Morris** Illinois, N USA 42°03′N 89°25′W
31 R9 **Mount Morris** Michigan, N USA 43°07′N 83°42′W
18 F10 **Mount Morris** New York, NE USA 42°43′N 77°51′W
18 B16 **Mount Morris** Pennsylvania, NE USA 39°43′N 80°06′W
30 K15 **Mount Olive** Illinois, N USA 39°04′N 89°43′W
21 V10 **Mount Olive** North Carolina, SE USA 35°12′N 78°03′W
21 N4 **Mount Olivet** Kentucky, S USA 38°32′N 84°01′W
29 Y15 **Mount Pleasant** Iowa, C USA 40°57′N 91°33′W
31 Q8 **Mount Pleasant** Michigan, N USA 43°36′N 84°46′W
18 C15 **Mount Pleasant** Pennsylvania, NE USA 40°07′N 79°33′W
21 T14 **Mount Pleasant** South Carolina, SE USA 32°47′N 79°51′W
20 I9 **Mount Pleasant** Tennessee, S USA 35°32′N 87°11′W
25 W6 **Mount Pleasant** Texas, SW USA 33°10′N 94°49′W
36 L4 **Mount Pleasant** Utah, W USA 39°33′N 111°27′W
63 N23 **Mount Pleasant** ✈ (Stanley) East Falkland, Falkland Islands
97 G25 **Mount's Bay** *inlet* SW England, United Kingdom
35 N2 **Mount Shasta** California, W USA 41°18′N 122°19′W
30 J13 **Mount Sterling** Illinois, N USA 39°59′N 90°44′W
21 N5 **Mount Sterling** Kentucky, S USA 38°03′N 83°56′W
18 E15 **Mount Union** Pennsylvania, NE USA 40°21′N 77°51′W
23 V6 **Mount Vernon** Georgia, SE USA 32°10′N 82°35′W
30 L16 **Mount Vernon** Illinois, N USA 38°19′N 88°54′W
20 M6 **Mount Vernon** Kentucky, S USA 37°20′N 84°20′W
27 S7 **Mount Vernon** Missouri, C USA 37°05′N 93°49′W
31 T13 **Mount Vernon** Ohio, N USA 40°23′N 82°29′W
32 K13 **Mount Vernon** Oregon, NW USA 44°22′N 119°07′W
25 W6 **Mount Vernon** Texas, SW USA 33°11′N 95°13′W
32 H7 **Mount Vernon** Washington, NW USA 48°25′N 122°19′W
20 L5 **Mount Washington** Kentucky, S USA 38°03′N 85°33′W
182 F8 **Mount Wedge** South Australia 33°29′S 135°08′E
30 L14 **Mount Zion** Illinois, N USA 39°46′N 88°52′W
181 Y9 **Moura** Queensland, NE Australia 24°34′S 149°57′E
58 F12 **Moura** Amazonas, NW Brazil 01°32′S 61°43′W
104 H12 **Moura** Beja, S Portugal 38°08′N 07°27′W
104 I12 **Mourão** Évora, S Portugal 38°22′N 07°20′W
76 L11 **Mourdiah** Koulikoro, W Mali 14°28′N 07°31′W
78 K7 **Mourdi, Dépression du** *desert lowland* Chad/Sudan
102 J16 **Mourenx** Pyrénées-Atlantiques, SW France 43°24′N 00°37′W
**Mourgana** *see* Mourgkána
115 C15 **Mourgkána** *var.* Mourgana. ▲ Albania/Greece 39°48′N 20°24′E
97 G16 **Mourne Mountains** *Ir.* Beanna Boirche. ▲▲ SE Northern Ireland, United Kingdom
115 I15 **Moúrtzeflos, Akrotírio** *headland* Límnos, E Greece 40°00′N 25°02′E
99 C19 **Mouscron** *Dut.* Moeskroen. Hainaut, W Belgium 50°44′N 03°14′E
**Mouse River** *see* Souris River
78 H10 **Moussoro** Bahr el Gazel, W Chad 13°41′N 16°31′E
103 T11 **Moûtiers** Savoie, E France 45°28′N 06°31′E
172 J14 **Moutsamoudou** *var.* Moutsamudou. Anjouan, SE Comoros 12°10′S 44°25′E
**Moutsamudou** *see* Moutsamoudou
74 K11 **Mouydir, Monts de** ▲▲ S Algeria
79 F20 **Mouyondzi** Bouenza, S Congo 03°58′S 13°57′E
115 E16 **Mouzáki** *prev.* Mouzákion. Thessalía, C Greece 39°25′N 21°40′E
**Mouzákion** *see* Mouzáki
29 S13 **Moville** Iowa, C USA 42°30′N 96°04′W
82 E13 **Moxico** ◈ *province* E Angola
172 I14 **Moya** Anjouan, SE Comoros 12°18′S 44°27′E
40 L12 **Moyahua** Zacatecas, C Mexico 21°18′N 103°09′W
81 J16 **Moyalē** Oromīya, C Ethiopia 03°34′N 38°58′E
76 I15 **Moyamba** W Sierra Leone 08°04′N 12°30′W
74 G7 **Moyen Atlas** *Eng.* Middle Atlas. ▲▲ N Morocco
78 H13 **Moyen-Chari** *off.* Région du Moyen-Chari. ◈ *region* S Chad
**Moyen-Chari, Région du** *see* Moyen-Chari
83 J24 **Moyeni** *var.* Quthing. SW Lesotho 30°25′S 27°43′E
79 D18 **Moyen-Ogooué** *off.* Province du Moyen-Ogooué, *var.* Le Moyen-Ogooué. ◈ *province* C Gabon
**Moyen-Ogooué, Province du** *see* Moyen-Ogooué
103 S4 **Moyeuvre-Grande** Moselle, NE France 49°15′N 06°03′E
33 N7 **Moyie Springs** Idaho, NW USA 48°43′N 116°15′W
146 G6 **Mo'ynoq** *Rus.* Muynak. Qoraqalpog'iston Respublikasi, NW Uzbekistan 43°45′N 59°03′E
81 F16 **Moyo** NW Uganda 03°38′N 31°43′E
56 D10 **Moyobamba** San Martín, NW Peru 06°04′S 76°56′W
78 H10 **Moyto** Hadjer-Lamis, W Chad 12°35′N 16°33′E
158 G9 **Moyu** *var.* Karakax. Xinjiang Uygur Zizhiqu, NW China 37°16′N 79°39′E
122 M9 **Moyyero** ≈ N Russia
145 S15 **Moyynkum** *var.* Furmanovka, *Kaz.* Fūrmanov. Zhambyl, S Kazakhstan 44°15′N 72°55′E
145 Q15 **Moyynkum, Peski** *Kaz.* Moyynqum. *desert* S Kazakhstan
**Moyynqum** *see* Moyynkum, Peski
145 S12 **Moyynty** Karaganda, C Kazakhstan 47°10′N 73°24′E
145 S12 **Moyynty** ≈ Karaganda, C Kazakhstan
**Mozambika, Lakandranon' i** *see* Mozambique Channel
83 M18 **Mozambique** *off.* Republic of Mozambique, *Port.* Moçambique, República de Moçambique; *prev.* People's Republic of Mozambique, Portuguese East Africa. ◆ *republic* S Africa
**Mozambique Basin** *see* Natal Basin
**Mozambique, Canal de** *see* Mozambique Channel
83 P17 **Mozambique Channel** *Fr.* Canal de Mozambique, *Mal.* Lakandranon' i Mozambika. *strait* W Indian Ocean
172 L11 **Mozambique Escarpment** *var.* Mozambique Scarp. *undersea feature* SW Indian Ocean 33°00′S 36°30′E
**Mozambique, People's Republic of** *see* Mozambique
172 L10 **Mozambique Plateau** *var.* Mozambique Rise. *undersea feature* SW Indian Ocean 32°00′S 35°00′E
**Mozambique, Republic of** *see* Mozambique
**Mozambique Rise** *see* Mozambique Plateau
**Mozambique Scarp** *see* Mozambique Escarpment
127 O15 **Mozdok** Respublika Severnaya Osetiya, SW Russia 43°48′N 44°42′E
57 K17 **Mozetenes, Serranías de** ▲▲ C Bolivia
126 J4 **Mozhaysk** Moskovskaya Oblast', W Russia 55°31′N 36°01′E
127 T3 **Mozhga** Udmurtskaya Respublika, NW Russia 56°24′N 52°13′E
**Mozyr'** *see* Mazyr
79 P22 **Mpala** Katanga, E Dem. Rep. Congo 06°43′S 29°28′E
79 G19 **Mpama** ≈ C Congo
81 E22 **Mpanda** Katavi, W Tanzania 06°21′S 31°01′E
82 L11 **Mpande** Northern, NE Zambia 09°13′S 31°42′E
83 J18 **Mphoengs** Matabeleland South, SW Zimbabwe 21°04′S 27°56′E
81 F18 **Mpigi** S Uganda 0°14′N 32°19′E
82 L13 **Mpika** Muchinga, NE Zambia 11°50′S 31°30′E
83 J14 **Mpima** Central, C Zambia 14°25′S 28°34′E
82 J13 **Mpongwe** Copperbelt, C Zambia 13°25′S 28°13′E
82 K11 **Mporokoso** Northern, N Zambia 09°22′S 30°06′E
79 H20 **Mpouya** Plateaux, SE Congo 02°38′S 16°13′E
77 P16 **Mpraeso** C Ghana 06°36′N 00°43′W
82 L11 **Mpulungu** Northern, N Zambia 08°50′S 31°06′E
83 K21 **Mpumalanga** *prev.* Eastern Transvaal, *Afr.* Oos-Transvaal. ◈ *province* NE South Africa
83 D16 **Mpungu** Kavango West, N Namibia 17°36′S 18°16′E
81 I22 **Mpwapwa** Dodoma, C Tanzania 06°21′S 36°29′E
**Mqinvartsveri** *see* Kazbek
110 M8 **Mrągowo** *Ger.* Sensburg. Warmińsko-Mazurskie, NE Poland 53°53′N 21°19′E
127 V6 **Mrakovo** Respublika Bashkortostan, W Russia 52°43′N 56°36′E
172 I13 **Mramani** Anjouan, E Comoros 12°18′N 44°39′E
**Mrauk-oo** *see* Mrauk-U
166 K5 **Mrauk-U** *var.* Mrauk-oo, Myohaung. Rakhine State, W Myanmar (Burma) 20°35′N 93°12′E
112 F12 **Mrkonjić Grad** ◈ Republika Srpska, W Bosnia and Herzegovina
110 H9 **Mrocza** Kujawsko-pomorskie, C Poland 53°15′N 17°38′E
124 I14 **Msta** ≈ NW Russia
**Mstislavl'** *see* Mstsislaw
119 P15 **Mstsislaw** *Rus.* Mstislavl'. Mahilyowskaya Voblasts', E Belarus 54°01′N 31°43′E
83 J24 **Mthatha** *prev.* Umtata. Eastern Cape, SE South Africa 31°33′S 28°47′E *see also* Umtata
**Mt'k'vari** *see* Kura
**Mtoko** *see* Mutoko
126 K6 **Mtsensk** Orlovskaya Oblast', W Russia 53°17′N 36°34′E
81 K24 **Mtwara** Mtwara, SE Tanzania 10°17′S 40°11′E
81 J25 **Mtwara** ◈ *region* SE Tanzania
104 G14 **Mu** ▲ S Portugal 37°24′N 08°04′W
193 V15 **Mu'a** Tongatapu, S Tonga 21°11′S 175°07′W
**Muai To** *see* Mae Hong Son
83 P16 **Mualama** Zambézia, NE Mozambique 16°51′S 38°21′E
**Mualo** *see* Messalo, Rio
79 E22 **Muanda** Bas-Congo, SW Dem. Rep. Congo 05°53′S 12°17′E
**Muang Chiang Rai** *see* Chiang Rai
167 R6 **Muang Ham** Houaphan, N Laos 20°19′N 104°00′E
167 S8 **Muang Hinboun** Khammouan, C Laos 17°37′N 104°37′E
**Muang Kalasin** *see* Kalasin
**Muang Khammouan** *see* Thakhèk
167 S11 **Muang Không** Champasak, S Laos 14°08′N 105°48′E
167 S10 **Muang Khôngxédôn** *var.* Khong Sedone. Salavan, S Laos 15°34′N 105°46′E
**Muang Khon Kaen** *see* Khon Kaen
167 Q6 **Muang Khoua** Phôngsali, N Laos 21°07′N 102°31′E
**Muang Krabi** *see* Krabi
**Muang Lampang** *see* Lampang
**Muang Lamphun** *see* Lamphun
**Muang Loei** *see* Loei
**Muang Lom Sak** *see* Lom Sak
**Muang Nakhon Sawan** *see* Nakhon Sawan
167 Q6 **Muang Namo** Oudômxai, N Laos 20°58′N 101°46′E
**Muang Nan** *see* Nan
167 Q6 **Muang Ngoy** Louangphabang, N Laos 20°43′N 102°42′E
167 Q5 **Muang Ou Tai** Phôngsali, N Laos 22°06′N 101°59′E
**Muang Pak Lay** *see* Pak Lay
**Muang Pakxan** *see* Pakxan
167 T10 **Muang Pakxong** Champasak, S Laos 15°10′N 106°17′E
167 S9 **Muang Phalan** *var.* Muang Phalane. Savannakhét, S Laos 16°40′N 105°33′E
**Muang Phalane** *see* Muang Phalan
**Muang Phan** *see* Phan
**Muang Phayao** *see* Phayao
**Muang Phichit** *see* Phichit
167 T9 **Muang Phin** Savannakhét, S Laos 16°31′N 106°01′E
**Muang Phitsanulok** *see* Phitsanulok
**Muang Phrae** *see* Phrae
**Muang Roi Et** *see* Roi Et
**Muang Sakon Nakhon** *see* Sakon Nakhon
**Muang Samut Prakan** *see* Samut Prakan
167 P6 **Muang Sing** Louang Namtha, N Laos 21°12′N 101°09′E
**Muang Ubon** *see* Ubon Ratchathani
**Muang Uthai Thani** *see* Uthai Thani
167 P7 **Muang Vangviang** Viangchan, C Laos 18°53′N 102°27′E
**Muang Xaignabouri** *see* Xaignabouli
**Muang Xay** *see* Oudômxai
167 S9 **Muang Xépôn** *var.* Sepone. Savannakhét, S Laos 16°40′N 106°15′E
168 K10 **Muar** *var.* Bandar Maharani. Johor, Peninsular Malaysia 02°01′N 102°35′E
168 J9 **Muara** Sumatera, W Indonesia 02°18′N 98°54′E
168 L13 **Muarabeliti** Sumatera, W Indonesia 03°13′S 103°00′E
168 K12 **Muarabungo** Sumatera, W Indonesia 01°28′S 102°06′E
168 L13 **Muaraenim** Sumatera, W Indonesia 03°40′S 103°48′E
169 T11 **Muarajuloi** Borneo, C Indonesia 0°12′S 114°03′E
169 U12 **Muarakaman** Borneo, C Indonesia 0°09′S 116°43′E
168 H12 **Muarasigep** Pulau Siberut, W Indonesia 01°01′S 98°48′E
168 L12 **Muaratembesi** Sumatera, W Indonesia 01°40′S 103°08′E
169 T12 **Muaratewe** *var.* Muarateweh; *prev.* Moearatewe. Borneo, C Indonesia 0°58′S 114°52′E
**Muarateweh** *see* Muaratewe
169 U10 **Muarawahau** Borneo, N Indonesia 01°03′N 116°48′E
138 G13 **Mubārak, Jabal** ▲ S Jordan 29°19′N 35°13′E
153 N13 **Mubārakpur** Uttar Pradesh, N India 26°05′N 83°19′E
**Mubarek** *see* Muborak
81 F18 **Mubende** SW Uganda 0°35′N 31°24′E
77 Y14 **Mubi** Adamawa, NE Nigeria 10°15′N 13°18′E
146 M12 **Muborak** *Rus.* Mubarek. Qashqadaryo Viloyati, S Uzbekistan 39°17′N 65°10′E
171 U12 **Mubrani** Papua Barat, E Indonesia 0°42′S 133°25′E
67 U12 **Muchinga Escarpment** *escarpment* NE Zambia
127 N7 **Muchkapskiy** Tambovskaya Oblast', W Russia 51°51′N 42°25′E
96 G10 **Muck** *island* W Scotland, United Kingdom
82 Q13 **Mucojo** Cabo Delgado, N Mozambique 12°05′S 40°30′E
82 F12 **Muconda** Lunda Sul, NE Angola 10°37′S 21°19′E
54 I10 **Muco, Río** ≈ E Colombia
83 O16 **Mucubela** Zambézia, NE Mozambique 16°51′S 37°48′E
42 J5 **Mucupina, Monte** ▲ N Honduras 15°07′N 86°36′W
136 J14 **Mucur** Kirşehir, C Turkey 39°05′N 34°25′E
143 U8 **Mūd** Khorāsān-e Janūbī, E Iran 32°41′N 59°30′E
163 Y9 **Mudanjiang** *var.* Mu-tan-chiang. Heilongjiang, NE China 44°33′N 129°40′E
163 Y9 **Mudan Jiang** ≈ NE China
136 D11 **Mudanya** Bursa, NW Turkey 40°23′N 28°53′E
28 K8 **Mud Butte** South Dakota, N USA 45°00′N 102°51′W
155 G16 **Muddebihāl** Karnātaka, C India 16°26′N 76°07′E
27 P12 **Muddy Boggy Creek** ≈ Oklahoma, C USA
36 M6 **Muddy Creek** ≈ Utah, W USA
37 V7 **Muddy Creek Reservoir** ⊠ Colorado, C USA
33 W15 **Muddy Gap** Wyoming, C USA 42°21′N 107°27′W
35 Y11 **Muddy Peak** ▲ Nevada, W USA 36°17′N 114°40′W
183 R7 **Mudgee** New South Wales, SE Australia 32°37′S 149°36′E
29 S3 **Mud Lake** ◎ Minnesota, N USA
29 P7 **Mud Lake Reservoir** ⊠ South Dakota, N USA
167 N9 **Mudon** Mon State, S Myanmar (Burma) 16°17′N 97°40′E
81 O14 **Mudug** *off.* Gobolka Mudug. ◈ *region* NE Somalia
81 O14 **Mudug** *var.* Mudugh. *plain* N Somalia
**Mudug, Gobolka** *see* Mudug
**Mudugh** *see* Mudug
83 Q15 **Muecate** Nampula, NE Mozambique 14°56′S 39°38′E
82 Q13 **Mueda** Cabo Delgado, NE Mozambique 11°40′S 39°31′E
42 L10 **Muelle de los Bueyes** Costa Caribe Sur, SE Nicaragua 12°03′N 84°34′W
**Muenchen** *see* München
83 M14 **Muende** Tete, NW Mozambique 14°22′S 33°00′E
25 T5 **Muenster** Texas, SW USA 33°39′N 97°22′W
**Muenster** *see* Münster
43 O6 **Muerto, Cayo** *reef* NE Nicaragua
41 T17 **Muerto, Mar** *lagoon* SE Mexico
64 F11 **Muertos Trough** *undersea feature* N Caribbean Sea
83 H14 **Mufaya Kuta** Western, NW Zambia 14°30′S 24°18′E
82 J13 **Mufulira** Copperbelt, C Zambia 12°33′S 28°16′E
161 O10 **Mufu Shan** ▲▲ C China
**Mugalla** *see* Yutian
**Mugalzhar Taūlary** *see* Mugodzhary, Gory
137 Y12 **Muğan Düzü** *Rus.* Muganskaya Ravnina, Muganskaya Step'. *physical region* S Azerbaijan
**Muganskaya Ravnina/ Muganskaya Step'** *see* Muğan Düzü
106 K8 **Múggia** Friuli-Venezia Giulia, NE Italy 45°36′N 13°48′E
153 N14 **Mughal Sarāi** Uttar Pradesh, N India 25°18′N 83°07′E
**Mughla** *see* Muğla
141 W11 **Mughshin** *var.* Muqshin. S Oman 19°26′N 54°38′E
147 S12 **Mughsu** *Rus.* Muksu. ≈ C Tajikistan
164 H14 **Mugi** Tokushima, Shikoku, SW Japan 33°39′N 134°24′E
136 C16 **Muğla** *var.* Mughla. Muğla, SW Turkey 37°13′N 28°22′E
136 C16 **Muğla** *var.* Mughla. ◈ *province* SW Turkey
144 J11 **Mugodzhary, Gory** *Kaz.* Mugalzhar Taūlary. ▲▲ W Kazakhstan
83 O15 **Mugulama** Zambézia, NE Mozambique 16°01′S 37°33′E
**Muḥāfazat Hims** *see* Ḩimş
139 U9 **Muḩammad** Wāsiţ, E Iraq 32°46′N 45°14′E
139 R8 **Muḩammadīyah** Al Anbār, C Iraq 33°22′N 42°48′E
80 I6 **Muhammad Qol** Red Sea, NE Sudan 20°53′N 37°09′E
**Muhammerah** *see* Khorramshahr
140 M12 **Muhāyil** *var.* Mahāil. 'Asīr, SW Saudi Arabia 18°34′N 42°01′E
139 O7 **Muḩaywīr** Al Anbār, W Iraq 33°35′N 41°06′E
101 H21 **Mühlacker** Baden-Württemberg, SW Germany 48°57′N 08°51′E
**Mühlbach** *see* Sebeş
**Mühldorf** *see* Mühldorf am Inn
101 N23 **Mühldorf am Inn** *var.* Mühldorf. Bayern, SE Germany 48°14′N 12°32′E
101 J15 **Mühlhausen** *var.* Mühlhausen in Thüringen. Thüringen, C Germany 51°13′N 10°28′E
**Mühlhausen in Thüringen** *see* Mühlhausen
195 Q2 **Mühlig-Hofmanfjella** *Eng.* Mülig-Hofmann Mountains. ▲▲ Antarctica
93 L14 **Muhos** Pohjois-Pohjanmaa, C Finland 64°48′N 26°00′E
138 K6 **Mūḩ, Sabkhat al** ◎ C Syria
118 E5 **Muhu** *Ger.* Mohn, Moon. *island* W Estonia
81 F19 **Muhutwe** Kagera, NW Tanzania 01°31′S 31°41′E
**Muhu Väin** *see* Väinameri
98 J10 **Muiden** Noord-Holland, C Netherlands 52°19′N 05°04′E
193 W15 **Mui Hopohoponga** *headland* Tongatapu, S Tonga 21°09′S 175°02′W
**Muinchille** *see* Cootehill
**Muineachán** *see* Monaghan
97 F19 **Muine Bheag** *Eng.* Bagenalstown. Carlow, SE Ireland 52°42′N 06°57′W
56 B5 **Muisne** Esmeraldas, NW Ecuador 0°35′N 79°58′W
83 P14 **Muite** Nampula, NE Mozambique 14°02′S 39°06′E
41 Z11 **Mujeres, Isla** *island* E Mexico
116 G7 **Mukacheve** *Hung.* Munkács, *Rus.* Mukachevo. Zakarpats'ka Oblast', W Ukraine 48°27′N 22°45′E
**Mukachevo** *see* Mukacheve
169 R9 **Mukah** Sarawak, East Malaysia 02°56′N 112°02′E
**Mukalla** *see* Al Mukallā
**Mukama** *see* Mokāma
**Mukāshafa/Mukashshafah** *see* Mukayshīfah
139 S6 **Mukayshīfah** *var.* Mukāshafa, Mukashshafah. Şalāḩ ad Dīn, N Iraq 34°24′N 43°44′E
167 R9 **Mukdahan** Mukdahan, E Thailand 16°31′N 104°43′E
**Mukden** *see* Shenyang
165 Y15 **Mukojima-rettō** *Eng.* Parry group. *island group* SE Japan
146 M14 **Mukry** Lebap Welaýaty, E Turkmenistan 37°39′N 65°37′E
**Muksu** *see* Mughsu
**Muktagacha** *see* Muktagachha
153 U14 **Muktagachha** *var.* Muktagacha. N Bangladesh 24°46′N 90°16′E
82 K13 **Mukuku** Central, C Zambia 12°10′S 29°50′E
82 K11 **Mukupa Kaoma** Northern, NE Zambia 09°55′S 30°19′E
81 I18 **Mukutan** Baringo, W Kenya 01°06′N 36°16′E
83 F16 **Mukwe** Kavango East, NE Namibia 18°01′S 21°24′E
105 R13 **Mula** Murcia, SE Spain 38°02′N 01°29′W
151 K20 **Mulakatholhu** *var.* Meemu Atoll, Mulaku Atoll. *atoll* C Maldives
**Mulaku Atoll** *see* Mulakatholhu
83 J15 **Mulalika** Lusaka, C Zambia 15°37′S 28°48′E
163 X8 **Mulan** Heilongjiang, NE China 45°57′N 128°00′E
83 N15 **Mulanje** *var.* Mlanje. Southern, S Malawi 16°05′S 35°29′E
40 H5 **Mulatos** Sonora, NW Mexico 28°42′N 108°44′W
23 P3 **Mulberry Fork** ≈ Alabama, S USA
39 P12 **Mulchatna River** ≈ Alaska, USA
125 W4 **Mul'da** Respublika Komi, NW Russia 67°29′N 63°55′E
101 M14 **Mulde** ≈ E Germany
27 R10 **Muldrow** Oklahoma, C USA 35°25′N 94°34′W
40 E7 **Mulegé** Baja California Sur, NW Mexico 26°54′N 112°00′W
108 I10 **Mulegns** Graubünden, S Switzerland 46°30′N 09°36′E
79 M21 **Mulenda** Kasai-Oriental, C Dem. Rep. Congo 04°19′S 24°55′E
24 M4 **Muleshoe** Texas, SW USA 34°13′N 102°43′W
83 O15 **Mulevala** Zambézia, NE Mozambique 16°25′S 37°35′E
183 P5 **Mulgoa Creek** *seasonal river* New South Wales, SE Australia
105 O15 **Mulhacén** *var.* Cerro de Mulhacén. ▲ S Spain 37°07′N 03°11′W
**Mulhacén, Cerro de** *see* Mulhacén
**Mülhausen** *see* Mulhouse
101 E24 **Müllheim** Baden-Württemberg, SW Germany 47°50′N 07°37′E
101 E15 **Mülheim** *var.* Mulheim an der Ruhr. Nordrhein-Westfalen, W Germany 51°25′N 06°50′E
**Mulheim an der Ruhr** *see* Mülheim
103 U7 **Mulhouse** *Ger.* Mülhausen. Haut-Rhin, NE France 47°45′N 07°20′E
160 G11 **Muli** *var.* Qiaowa, Muli Zangzu Zizhixian. Sichuan, C China 27°49′N 101°10′E
171 X15 **Muli** *channel* Papua, E Indonesia
**Mülig-Hofmann Mountains** *see* Mühlig-Hofmanfjella



◆ Country
● Country Capital
◇ Dependent Territory
○ Dependent Territory Capital
◈ Administrative Regions
✈ International Airport
▲ Mountain
▲▲ Mountain Range
Volcano
≈ River
◎ Lake
⊠ Reservoir

MULING – NÅDENDAL


163 Y9 **Muling** Heilongjiang, NE China *44°54′N 130°35′E*
**Muli Zangzu Zizhixian** *see* Muli
**Mullach Íde** *see* Malahide
**Mullaitivu** *see* Mullaittivu
155 K23 **Mullaittivu** *var.* Mullaitivu. Northern Province, N Sri Lanka *09°15′N 80°48′E*
33 N8 **Mullan** Idaho, NW USA *47°28′N 115°48′W*
28 M13 **Mullen** Nebraska, C USA *42°02′N 101°01′W*
183 Q6 **Mullengudgery** New South Wales, SE Australia *31°42′S 147°24′E*
21 Q6 **Mullens** West Virginia, NE USA *37°34′N 81°22′W*
**Müller-gerbergte** *see* Muller, Pegunungan
169 T10 **Muller, Pegunungan** *Dut.* Müller-gerbergte. ▲▲ Borneo, C Indonesia
31 Q5 **Mullett Lake** ◎ Michigan, N USA
18 J16 **Mullica River** ≈ New Jersey, NE USA
25 R8 **Mullin** Texas, SW USA *31°33′N 98°40′W*
97 E17 **Mullingar** *Ir.* An Muileann gCearr. C Ireland *53°32′N 07°20′W*
21 T12 **Mullins** South Carolina, SE USA *34°12′N 79°15′W*
96 G11 **Mull, Isle of** *island* W Scotland, United Kingdom
127 R5 **Mullovka** Ul'yanovskaya Oblast', W Russia *54°13′N 49°19′E*
95 K19 **Mullsjö** Västra Götaland, S Sweden *57°56′N 13°55′E*
183 V4 **Mullumbimby** New South Wales, SE Australia *28°34′S 153°28′E*
83 H15 **Mulobezi** Western, SW Zambia *16°48′S 25°11′E*
83 C15 **Mulondo** Huíla, SW Angola *15°41′S 15°09′E*
83 G15 **Mulonga Plain** *plain* W Zambia
79 N23 **Mulongo** Katanga, SE Dem. Rep. Congo *07°44′S 26°57′E*
149 T10 **Multan** Punjab, E Pakistan *30°12′N 71°30′E*
93 L17 **Multia** Keski-Suomi, C Finland *62°27′N 24°49′E*
**Mulucha** *see* Moulouya
83 J14 **Mulungushi** Central, C Zambia *14°15′S 28°27′E*
83 K14 **Mulungwe** Central, C Zambia *13°57′S 29°51′E*
**Muluya** *see* Moulouya
27 N7 **Mulvane** Kansas, C USA *37°28′N 97°14′W*
183 O10 **Mulwala** New South Wales, SE Australia *35°59′S 146°00′E*
**Mulwiya** *see* Moulouya
182 K6 **Mulyungarie** South Australia *31°29′S 140°45′E*
154 D13 **Mumbai** *prev.* Bombay. *state capital* Mahārāshtra, W India *18°56′N 72°51′E*
154 D13 **Mumbai** ✈ Mahārāshtra, W India *19°10′N 72°51′E*
83 D14 **Mumbué** Bié, C Angola *13°52′S 17°15′E*
186 E8 **Mumeng** Morobe, C Papua New Guinea *06°57′S 146°34′E*
171 V12 **Mumi** Papua Barat, E Indonesia *01°33′S 134°09′E*
**Muminabad/Mŭ'minobod** *see* Mu'minobod
147 Q13 **Mu'minobod** *Rus.* Leningradskiy, Muminabad; *prev.* Leningrad. SW Tajikistan *38°03′N 69°50′E*
127 Q13 **Mumra** Astrakhanskaya Oblast', SW Russia *45°46′N 47°46′E*
41 X12 **Muna** Yucatán, SE Mexico *20°29′N 89°41′W*
123 O9 **Muna** ≈ NE Russia
152 C12 **Munābāo** Rājasthān, NW India *25°46′N 70°19′E*
**Munamägi** *see* Suur Munamägi
171 O14 **Muna, Pulau** *prev.* Moena. *island* C Indonesia
166 J7 **Munaung Island** *island* W Myanmar (Burma)
101 L18 **Münchberg** Bayern, E Germany *50°10′N 11°50′E*
101 L23 **München** *var.* Muenchen, *Eng.* Munich, *It.* Monaco. Bayern, SE Germany *48°09′N 11°34′E*
**München-Gladbach** *see* Mönchengladbach
108 E6 **Münchenstein** Basel Landschaft, NW Switzerland *47°31′N 07°38′E*
10 L10 **Muncho Lake** British Columbia, W Canada *58°52′N 125°40′W*
31 P13 **Muncie** Indiana, N USA *40°11′N 85°22′W*
18 G13 **Muncy** Pennsylvania, NE USA *41°10′N 76°46′W*
11 Q14 **Mundare** Alberta, SW Canada *53°34′N 112°20′W*
25 Q5 **Munday** Texas, SW USA *33°27′N 99°37′W*
31 N10 **Mundelein** Illinois, N USA *42°15′N 88°00′W*
101 I15 **Münden** Niedersachsen, C Germany *52°16′N 08°54′E*
105 Q12 **Mundo** ≈ S Spain
82 B12 **Munenga** Kwanza Sul, NW Angola *10°03′S 14°40′E*
105 P11 **Munera** Castilla-La Mancha, C Spain *39°03′N 02°29′W*
20 E9 **Munford** Tennessee, S USA *35°27′N 89°49′W*
20 K7 **Munfordville** Kentucky, S USA *37°17′N 85°55′W*
182 D5 **Mungala** South Australia *30°36′S 132°57′E*
83 M16 **Mungári** Manica, C Mozambique *17°09′S 33°33′E*
79 O16 **Mungbere** Orientale, NE Dem. Rep. Congo *02°38′N 28°30′E*
153 Q13 **Munger** *prev.* Monghyr. Bihār, NE India *25°23′N 86°28′E*
182 I2 **Mungeranie** South Australia *28°02′S 138°42′E*
**Mu Nggava** *see* Rennell
169 O10 **Mungguresak, Tanjung** *headland* Borneo, N Indonesia *01°57′N 109°19′E*
**Mungiki** *see* Bellona
183 R4 **Mungindi** New South Wales, SE Australia *28°59′S 149°00′E*
**Mungkawn** *see* Maingkwan
**Mungla** *see* Mongla
82 C13 **Mungo** Huambo, W Angola *11°49′S 16°16′E*
188 F16 **Munguuy Bay** *bay* Yap, W Micronesia
82 E13 **Munhango** Bié, C Angola *12°12′S 18°34′E*
**Munich** *see* München
105 S7 **Muniesa** Aragón, NE Spain *41°02′N 00°49′W*
31 O4 **Munising** Michigan, N USA *46°24′N 86°39′W*
**Munkács** *see* Mukacheve
95 I17 **Munkedal** Västra Götaland, S Sweden *58°28′N 11°38′E*
95 K15 **Munkfors** Värmland, C Sweden *59°50′N 13°35′E*
122 M14 **Munku-Sardyk, Gora** *var.* Mönh Sarĭdag. ▲ Mongolia/Russia *51°45′N 100°22′E*
99 E18 **Munkzwalm** Oost-Vlaanderen, NW Belgium *50°53′N 03°44′E*
167 R10 **Mun, Mae Nam** ≈ E Thailand
153 U15 **Munshiganj** Dhaka, C Bangladesh *23°32′N 90°32′E*
108 D8 **Münsingen** Bern, W Switzerland *46°53′N 07°34′E*
103 U6 **Munster** Haut-Rhin, NE France *48°03′N 07°09′E*
100 J11 **Münster** Niedersachsen, NW Germany *52°59′N 10°07′E*
100 F13 **Münster** *var.* Muenster, Münster in Westfalen. Nordrhein-Westfalen, W Germany *51°58′N 07°38′E*
108 F10 **Münster** Valais, S Switzerland *46°31′N 08°18′E*
97 B20 **Munster** *Ir.* Cúige Mumhan. *cultural region* S Ireland
**Münsterberg in Schlesien** *see* Ziębice
**Münster in Westfalen** *see* Münster
100 E13 **Münsterland** *cultural region* NW Germany
100 F13 **Münster-Osnabruck** ✈ Nordrhein-Westfalen, NW Germany *52°08′N 07°41′E*
**Muntafiq, Al** *see* Dhī Qār
31 R4 **Munuscong Lake** ◎ Michigan, N USA
83 K17 **Munyati** ≈ C Zimbabwe
109 R3 **Münzkirchen** Oberösterreich, N Austria *48°29′N 13°37′E*
92 K11 **Muodoslompolo** Norrbotten, N Sweden *67°57′N 23°31′E*
92 M13 **Muojärvi** ◎ NE Finland
167 S6 **Mương Khên** Hoa Binh, N Vietnam *20°34′N 105°18′E*
**Muong Sai** *see* Oudômxai
167 Q7 **Muong Xiang Ngeun** *var.* Xieng Ngeun. Louangphabang, N Laos *19°43′N 102°09′E*
92 K11 **Muonio** Lappi, N Finland *67°58′N 23°40′E*
**Muonioälv/Muoniojoki** *see* Muonionjoki
92 K11 **Muonionjoki** *var.* Muoniojoki, *Swe.* Muonioälv. ≈ Finland/Sweden
**Muorjek** *see* Murjek
83 N17 **Mupa** ≈ C Mozambique
83 E16 **Mupini** Kavango West, NE Namibia *17°55′S 19°34′E*
80 F8 **Muqaddam, Wadi** ≈ N Sudan
138 K9 **Muqāṭ** Al Mafraq, E Jordan *32°28′N 38°04′E*
81 N17 **Muqdisho** *Eng.* Mogadishu, *It.* Mogadiscio. ● (Somalia) Banaadir, S Somalia *02°06′N 45°27′E*
81 N17 **Muqdisho** ✈ Banaadir, E Somalia *01°58′N 45°18′E*
**Muqshin** *see* Mughshin
109 T8 **Mur** *SCr.* Mura. ≈ C Europe
109 X9 **Mura** ≈ NE Slovenia
**Mura** *see* Mur
137 T14 **Muradiye** Van, E Turkey *39°N 43°44′E*
**Muragarazi** *see* Maragarazi
165 O10 **Murakami** Niigata, Honshū, C Japan *38°13′N 139°28′E*
63 G22 **Murallón, Cerro** ▲ S Argentina *49°49′S 73°25′W*
81 E20 **Muramvya** C Burundi *03°18′S 29°41′E*
81 I19 **Murang'a** *prev.* Fort Hall. Murang'a, SW Kenya *0°43′S 37°10′E*
81 H16 **Murangering** Turkana, NW Kenya *03°48′N 35°29′E*
**Murapara** *see* Murupara
140 M5 **Murār, Bi'r al** *well* NW Saudi Arabia
125 Q13 **Murashi** Kirovskaya Oblast', NW Russia *59°27′N 48°02′E*
103 O12 **Murat** Cantal, C France *45°07′N 02°52′E*
114 N12 **Muratlı** Tekirdağ, NW Turkey *41°12′N 27°30′E*
137 R14 **Murat Nehri** *var.* Eastern Euphrates; *anc.* Arsanias. ≈ NE Turkey
107 D20 **Muravera** Sardegna, Italy, C Mediterranean Sea *39°24′N 09°34′E*
165 P10 **Murayama** Yamagata, Honshū, C Japan *38°29′N 140°21′E*
121 R13 **Muraysah, Ra's al** *headland* N Libya *31°58′N 25°00′E*
104 I6 **Murça** Vila Real, N Portugal *41°24′N 07°28′W*
80 Q11 **Murcanyo** Bari, NE Somalia *11°39′N 50°27′E*
143 N8 **Mūrcheh Khvort** *var.* Morcheh Khort. Eşfahān, C Iran *33°07′N 51°26′E*
185 H15 **Murchison** Tasman, South Island, New Zealand *41°48′S 172°19′E*
185 B22 **Murchison Mountains** ▲▲ South Island, New Zealand
180 I10 **Murchison River** ≈ Western Australia
105 R13 **Murcia** Murcia, SE Spain *37°59′N 01°08′W*
105 Q13 **Murcia** *var.* Región de Murcia. ◈ *autonomous community* SE Spain
**Murcia, Región de** *see* Murcia
103 O13 **Mur-de-Barrez** Aveyron, S France *44°48′N 02°39′E*
182 G8 **Murdinga** South Australia *33°46′S 135°46′E*
28 M10 **Murdo** South Dakota, N USA *43°53′N 100°42′W*
15 X6 **Murdochville** Québec, SE Canada *48°57′N 65°30′W*
109 W9 **Mureck** Steiermark, SE Austria *46°42′N 15°46′E*
114 M13 **Mürefte** Tekirdağ, NW Turkey *40°40′N 27°15′E*
116 I10 **Mureş** ◈ *county* N Romania
84 J11 **Mureş** ≈ Hungary/Romania
**Mureş** *see* Maros
**Mureşul** *see* Maros/Mureş
102 M16 **Muret** Haute-Garonne, S France *43°28′N 01°19′E*
27 T13 **Murfreesboro** Arkansas, C USA *34°04′N 93°42′W*
21 W8 **Murfreesboro** North Carolina, SE USA *36°26′N 77°06′W*
20 J9 **Murfreesboro** Tennessee, S USA *35°50′N 86°25′W*
**Murgab** *see* Morghāb, Daryā-ye/Murgap
**Murgab** *see* Murghob
146 I14 **Murgap** Mary Welaýaty, S Turkmenistan *37°19′N 61°48′E*
146 J16 **Murgap** *var.* Deryasy Murgap, Murghab, *Pash.* Daryā-ye Morghāb, *Rus.* Murgab. ≈ Afghanistan/Turkmenistan *see also* Morghāb, Daryā-ye
**Murgap** *see* Murghāb, Daryā-ye
**Murgap, Deryasy** *see* Morghāb, Daryā-ye/Murgap
114 H9 **Murgash** ▲ W Bulgaria *42°51′N 23°58′E*
**Murghab** *see* Morghāb, Daryā-ye/Murgap
148 M4 **Murghāb, Daryā-ye** *Rus.* Murgab, Murghab, *Turk.* Murgap, Deryasy Murgap; *prev.* Morghāb, Daryā-ye. ≈ Afghanistan/Turkmenistan *see also* Murgap
147 U13 **Murghob** *Rus.* Murgab. SE Tajikistan *38°11′N 74°E*
147 U13 **Murghob** *Rus.* Murgab. ≈ SE Tajikistan
181 Z10 **Murgon** Queensland, E Australia *26°08′S 152°04′E*
190 I16 **Muri** Rarotonga, S Cook Islands *21°15′S 159°44′W*
108 F7 **Muri** Aargau, W Switzerland *47°16′N 08°21′E*
108 D8 **Muri** *var.* Muri bei Bern. Bern, W Switzerland *46°55′N 07°30′E*
104 K3 **Murias de Paredes** Castilla y León, N Spain *42°51′N 06°11′W*
**Muri bei Bern** *see* Muri
82 F11 **Muriege** Lunda Sul, NE Angola *09°55′S 21°12′E*
189 P14 **Murilo Atoll** *atoll* Hall Islands, C Micronesia
**Mūrītānīyah** *see* Mauritania
**Mūrītānīyah, Al Jumhūrīyah al Islāmīyah al** *see* Mauritania
100 N10 **Müritz** *var.* Müritzee. ◎ NE Germany
**Müritzee** *see* Müritz
100 L10 **Müritz-Elde-Wasserstrasse** *canal* N Germany
184 K6 **Muriwai Beach** Auckland, North Island, New Zealand *36°56′S 174°28′E*
92 J13 **Murjek** *Lapp.* Muorjek. Norrbotten, N Sweden *66°27′N 20°54′E*
124 J3 **Murmansk** Murmanskaya Oblast', NW Russia *68°59′N 33°08′E*
124 I4 **Murmanskaya Oblast'** ◈ *province* NW Russia
197 V14 **Murmansk Rise** *undersea feature* SW Barents Sea *71°00′N 37°00′E*
124 J3 **Murmashi** Murmanskaya Oblast', NW Russia *68°49′N 32°43′E*
126 M5 **Murmino** Ryazanskaya Oblast', W Russia *54°31′N 40°01′E*
101 K24 **Murnau** Bayern, SE Germany *47°41′N 11°12′E*
103 X16 **Muro, Capo di** *headland* Corse, France, C Mediterranean Sea *41°45′N 08°40′E*
107 M18 **Muro Lucano** Basilicata, S Italy *40°48′N 15°33′E*
127 N4 **Murom** Vladimirskaya Oblast', W Russia *55°33′N 42°03′E*
122 I11 **Muromtsevo** Omskaya Oblast', C Russia *56°18′N 75°15′E*
165 R5 **Muroran** Hokkaidō, NE Japan *42°20′N 140°58′E*
104 G3 **Muros** Galicia, NW Spain *42°47′N 09°04′W*
104 F3 **Muros e Noia, Ría de** *estuary* NW Spain
164 H15 **Muroto** Kōchi, Shikoku, SW Japan *33°16′N 134°10′E*
164 H15 **Muroto-zaki** Shikoku, SW Japan
116 L7 **Murovani Kurylivtsi** Vinnyts'ka Oblast', C Ukraine *48°43′N 27°31′E*
110 G11 **Murowana Goślina** Wielkolpolskie, W Poland *52°33′N 16°59′E*
32 M14 **Murphy** Idaho, NW USA *43°14′N 116°36′W*
21 N10 **Murphy** North Carolina, SE USA *35°05′N 84°02′W*
35 P8 **Murphys** California, W USA *38°07′N 120°27′W*
30 L17 **Murphysboro** Illinois, N USA *37°45′N 89°20′W*
29 V15 **Murray** Iowa, C USA *41°03′N 93°56′W*
20 H8 **Murray** Kentucky, S USA *36°35′N 88°20′W*
182 J10 **Murray Bridge** South Australia *35°10′S 139°17′E*
175 X2 **Murray Fracture Zone** *tectonic feature* NE Pacific Ocean
192 H11 **Murray, Lake** ◎ SW Papua New Guinea
21 P12 **Murray, Lake** ▣ South Carolina, SE USA
10 K8 **Murray, Mount** ▲ Yukon, NW Canada *60°49′N 128°57′W*
**Murray Range** *see* Murray Ridge
173 O3 **Murray Ridge** *var.* Murray Range. *undersea feature* N Arabian Sea *21°45′N 61°50′E*
183 N10 **Murray River** ≈ SE Australia
182 K10 **Murrayville** Victoria, SE Australia *35°17′S 141°12′E*
149 U5 **Murree** Punjab, E Pakistan *33°55′N 73°26′E*
101 I21 **Murrhardt** Baden-Württemberg, S Germany *49°00′N 09°34′E*
183 O9 **Murrumbidgee River** ≈ New South Wales, SE Australia
83 P15 **Murrupula** Nampula, NE Mozambique *15°26′S 38°46′E*
183 T7 **Murrurundi** New South Wales, SE Australia *31°47′S 150°51′E*
109 X9 **Murska Sobota** *Ger.* Olsnitz. NE Slovenia *46°41′N 16°09′E*
154 G12 **Murtajāpur** *prev.* Murtazapur. Mahārāshtra, C India *20°43′N 77°28′E*
77 S16 **Murtala Muhammed** ✈ (Lagos) Ogun, SW Nigeria *06°31′N 03°12′E*
**Murtazapur** *see* Murtajāpur
108 C8 **Murten** Neuchâtel, W Switzerland *46°55′N 07°06′E*
**Murtensee** *see* Morat, Lac de
182 L11 **Murtoa** Victoria, SE Australia *36°39′S 142°27′E*
92 N13 **Murtovaara** Pohjois-Pohjanmaa, E Finland *65°40′N 29°25′E*
**Murua Island** *see* Woodlark Island
155 D14 **Murud** Mahārāshtra, W India *18°27′N 72°56′E*
184 O9 **Murupara** *var.* Murapara. Bay of Plenty, North Island, New Zealand *38°27′S 176°41′E*
**Mururoa** *see* Moruroa
**Murviedro** *see* Sagunto
154 J9 **Murwāra** Madhya Pradesh, N India *23°50′N 80°23′E*
183 V4 **Murwillumbah** New South Wales, SE Australia *28°20′S 153°24′E*
146 H11 **Murzechirla** *prev.* Mirzachirla. Ahal Welaýaty, C Turkmenistan *39°33′N 60°02′E*
**Murzuk** *see* Murzuq
75 O11 **Murzuq** *var.* Marzūq, Murzuk. SW Libya *25°55′N 13°55′E*
**Murzuq, Edeyin** *see* Murzuq, Idhān
75 N11 **Murzuq, Ḥammādat** *plateau* W Libya
75 O11 **Murzuq, Idhān** *var.* Edeyin Murzuq. *desert* SW Libya
109 W6 **Mürzzuschlag** Steiermark, E Austria *47°35′N 15°41′E*
137 Q14 **Muş** *var.* Mush. Muş, E Turkey *38°45′N 41°30′E*
137 Q14 **Muş** *var.* Mush. ◈ *province* E Turkey
118 G11 **Mūša** ≈ Latvia/Lithuania
186 F9 **Musa** ≈ S Papua New Guinea
**Musaad** *see* Umm Sā'd
**Mûsa, Gebel** *see* Mūsá, Jabal
**Musā'id** *see* Umm Sā'd
**Musaiyib** *see* Al Musayyib
75 X8 **Mūsá, Jabal** *var.* Gebel Mûsa, *Eng.* Mount Sinai. ▲ NE Egypt *28°33′N 33°51′E*
149 R9 **Musa Khel** *var.* Mūsa Khel Bāzār. Baluchistan, SW Pakistan *30°53′N 69°52′E*
**Mūsa Khel Bāzār** *see* Musa Khel
139 Z13 **Mūsá, Khowr-e** *bay* Iraq/Kuwait
114 H10 **Musala** ▲ W Bulgaria *42°12′N 23°36′E*
168 H10 **Musala, Pulau** *island* W Indonesia
83 I15 **Musale** Southern, S Zambia *15°27′S 26°50′E*
141 Y9 **Muşalla** NE Oman *22°20′N 58°03′E*
141 W6 **Musandam Peninsula** *Ar.* Masandam Peninsula. *peninsula* N Oman
**Musay'īd** *see* Umm Sa'īd
**Muscat** *see* Masqaţ
**Muscat and Oman** *see* Oman
29 Y14 **Muscatine** Iowa, C USA *41°25′N 91°03′W*
**Muscat Sīb Airport** *see* Seeb
31 O15 **Muscatuck River** ≈ Indiana, N USA
30 K8 **Muscoda** Wisconsin, N USA *43°11′N 90°27′W*
185 F19 **Musgrave, Mount** ▲ South Island, New Zealand *43°48′S 170°43′E*
181 P9 **Musgrave Ranges** ▲▲ South Australia
**Mush** *see* Muş
138 H12 **Mushayyish, Qaşr al** *castle* Ma'ān, C Jordan
79 H20 **Mushie** Bandundu, W Dem. Rep. Congo *03°00′S 16°55′E*
168 M13 **Musi, Air** *prev.* Moesi. ≈ Sumatera, W Indonesia
192 M4 **Musicians Seamounts** *undersea feature* N Pacific Ocean
83 K19 **Musina** *prev.* Messina. Limpopo, NE South Africa *22°18′S 30°02′E*
54 D8 **Musinga, Alto** ▲ NW Colombia *06°49′N 76°24′W*
29 T2 **Muskeg Bay** *lake bay* Minnesota, N USA
31 O8 **Muskegon** Michigan, N USA *43°13′N 86°15′W*
31 O8 **Muskegon Heights** Michigan, N USA *43°12′N 86°14′W*
31 P8 **Muskegon River** ≈ Michigan, N USA
31 T14 **Muskingum River** ≈ Ohio, N USA
95 P16 **Muskö** Stockholm, C Sweden *58°58′N 18°10′E*
**Muskogean** *see* Tallahassee
27 Q10 **Muskogee** Oklahoma, C USA *35°45′N 95°21′W*
14 H13 **Muskoka, Lake** ◎ Ontario, S Canada
80 H8 **Musmar** Red Sea, NE Sudan *18°13′N 35°40′E*
83 K14 **Musofu** Central, C Zambia *13°31′S 29°02′E*
81 G19 **Musoma** Mara, N Tanzania *01°31′S 33°49′E*
82 L13 **Musoro** Central, C Zambia *13°21′S 31°04′E*
186 F4 **Mussau Island** *island* NE Papua New Guinea
98 P7 **Musselkanaal** Groningen, NE Netherlands *52°55′N 07°01′E*
33 V9 **Musselshell River** ≈ Montana, NW USA
82 C12 **Mussende** Kwanza Sul, NW Angola *10°33′S 16°02′E*
102 L12 **Mussidan** Dordogne, SW France *45°03′N 00°22′E*
99 L25 **Musson** Luxembourg, SE Belgium *49°33′N 05°42′E*
152 J9 **Mussoorie** Uttarākhand, N India *30°26′N 78°04′E*
**Musta** *see* Mosta
152 M13 **Mustafābād** Uttar Pradesh, N India *25°54′N 81°17′E*
136 D12 **Mustafakemalpaşa** Bursa, NW Turkey *40°03′N 28°25′E*
**Mustafa-Pasha** *see* Svilengrad
81 M15 **Mustahīl** Sumalē, E Ethiopia *05°18′N 44°34′E*
24 M7 **Mustang Draw** *valley* Texas, SW USA
25 T14 **Mustang Island** *island* Texas, SW USA
**Mustasaari** *see* Korsholm
**Mustér** *see* Disentis
63 I19 **Musters, Lago** ◎ S Argentina
45 Y14 **Mustique** *island* C Saint Vincent and the Grenadines
118 I6 **Mustla** Viljandimaa, S Estonia *58°12′N 25°50′E*
118 J4 **Mustvee** *Ger.* Tschorna. Jõgevamaa, E Estonia *58°51′N 26°59′E*
42 L9 **Musún, Cerro** ▲ NE Nicaragua *13°01′N 85°02′W*
183 T7 **Muswellbrook** New South Wales, SE Australia *32°17′S 150°55′E*
111 M18 **Muszyna** Małopolskie, SE Poland *49°21′N 20°54′E*
75 V10 **Mūţ** *var.* Mut. C Egypt *25°28′N 28°58′E*
136 I17 **Mut** İçel, S Turkey *36°38′N 33°27′E*
109 V9 **Muta** N Slovenia *46°37′N 15°09′E*
190 B15 **Mutalau** N Niue *18°56′S 169°50′E*
**Mu-tan-chiang** *see* Mudanjiang
82 I13 **Mutanda** North Western, NW Zambia *12°24′S 26°13′E*
59 O17 **Mutá, Ponta do** *headland* E Brazil *13°54′S 38°54′W*
83 L17 **Mutare** *var.* Mutari; *prev.* Umtali. Manicaland, E Zimbabwe *18°55′S 32°36′E*
**Mutari** *see* Mutare
54 D8 **Mutatá** Antioquia, NW Colombia *07°16′N 76°32′W*
**Muthannār, Muḩāfaz at al** *see* Al Muthannā
**Mutina** *see* Modena
83 L16 **Mutoko** *prev.* Mtoko. Mashonaland East, NE Zimbabwe *17°24′S 32°13′E*
81 J20 **Mutomo** Kitui, S Kenya *01°50′S 38°13′E*
**Mutrah** *see* Maţraḩ
79 M24 **Mutshatsha** Katanga, S Dem. Rep. Congo *10°40′S 24°26′E*
165 R6 **Mutsu** *var.* Mutu. Aomori, Honshū, N Japan *41°18′N 141°11′E*
165 R6 **Mutsu-wan** *bay* N Japan
108 E6 **Muttenz** Basel Landschaft, NW Switzerland *47°31′N 07°39′E*
185 A26 **Muttonbird Islands** *island group* SW New Zealand
**Muttra** *see* Mathura
**Mutu** *see* Mutsu
83 O15 **Mutuáli** Nampula, N Mozambique *14°51′S 37°01′E*
82 D13 **Mutumbo** Bié, C Angola *13°10′S 17°22′E*
189 Y14 **Mutunte, Mount** *var.* Mount Buache. ▲ Kosrae, E Micronesia *05°21′N 163°00′E*
155 K24 **Mutur** Eastern Province, E Sri Lanka *08°27′N 81°15′E*
92 L13 **Muurola** Lappi, NW Finland *66°22′N 25°20′E*
162 M14 **Mu Us Shadi** *var.* Ordos Desert; *prev.* Mu Us Shamo. *desert* N China
**Mu Us Shamo** *see* Mu Us Shadi
82 B11 **Muxima** Bengo, NW Angola *09°33′S 13°58′E*
124 I8 **Muyezerskiy** Respublika Kareliya, NW Russia *63°54′N 32°00′E*
81 E20 **Muyinga** NE Burundi *02°54′S 30°19′E*
42 K9 **Muy Muy** Matagalpa, C Nicaragua *12°43′N 85°35′W*
**Muynak** *see* Mo'ynoq
79 N22 **Muyumba** Katanga, SE Dem. Rep. Congo *07°13′S 27°02′E*
149 V5 **Muzaffarabad** Jammu and Kashmir, NE Pakistan *34°23′N 73°34′E*
149 S10 **Muzaffargarh** Punjab, E Pakistan *30°04′N 71°15′E*
152 J9 **Muzaffarnagar** Uttar Pradesh, N India *29°28′N 77°42′E*
153 P13 **Muzaffarpur** Bihār, N India *26°07′N 85°23′E*
158 H6 **Muzat He** ≈ W China
83 L15 **Muze** Tete, NW Mozambique *15°05′S 31°16′E*
122 H8 **Muzhi** Yamalo-Nenetskiy Avtonomnyy Okrug, N Russia *65°25′N 64°28′E*
102 H7 **Muzillac** Morbihan, NW France *47°34′N 02°30′W*
**Muzkol, Khrebet** *see* Muzqŭl, Qatorkŭhi
112 L9 **Mužlja** *Hung.* Felsőmuzslya; *prev.* Gornja Mužlja. Vojvodina, N Serbia *45°21′N 20°25′E*
54 F9 **Muzo** Boyacá, C Colombia *05°34′N 74°07′W*
83 J15 **Muzoka** Southern, S Zambia *16°39′S 27°18′E*
39 Y15 **Muzon, Cape** *headland* Dall Island, Alaska, USA *54°39′N 132°41′W*
40 M6 **Múzquiz** Coahuila, NE Mexico *27°54′N 101°30′W*
147 U13 **Muzqŭl, Qatorkŭhi** *Rus.* Khrebet Muzkol. ▲▲ SE Tajikistan
**Muztag** *see* Muztag Feng
158 D8 **Muztagata** ▲ NW China *38°16′N 75°03′E*
158 K10 **Muztag Feng** *var.* Muztag. ▲ W China *36°26′N 87°15′E*
83 K17 **Mvuma** *prev.* Umvuma. Midlands, C Zimbabwe *19°17′S 30°32′E*
172 H13 **Mwali** *var.* Moili, *Fr.* Mohéli. *island* S Comoros
82 L13 **Mwanya** Eastern, E Zambia *12°40′S 32°15′E*
79 N23 **Mwanza** Katanga, SE Dem. Rep. Congo *07°49′S 26°49′E*
81 F20 **Mwanza** ◈ *region* N Tanzania
81 G20 **Mwanza** ◈ *state capital* Mwanza, NW Tanzania
82 M13 **Mwase Lundazi** Eastern, E Zambia *12°26′S 33°20′E*
97 B17 **Mweelrea** *Ir.* Caoc Maol Réidh. ▲ W Ireland *53°37′N 09°47′W*
79 K21 **Mweka** Kasai-Occidental, C Dem. Rep. Congo *04°52′S 21°38′E*
82 K12 **Mwenda** Luapula, N Zambia *10°30′S 30°21′E*
79 L22 **Mwene-Ditu** Kasai-Oriental, S Dem. Rep. Congo *07°06′S 23°34′E*
83 L18 **Mwenezi** ≈ S Zimbabwe
79 O20 **Mwenga** Sud-Kivu, E Dem. Rep. Congo *03°00′S 28°28′E*
82 K11 **Mweru, Lake** *var.* Lac Moero. ◎ Dem. Rep. Congo/Zambia
82 H13 **Mwinilunga** North Western, NW Zambia *11°44′S 24°24′E*
189 V16 **Mwokil Atoll** *prev.* Mokil Atoll. *atoll* Caroline Islands, E Micronesia
**Myadel'** *see* Myadzyel
118 J13 **Myadzyel** *Pol.* Miadzioł Nowy, *Rus.* Myadel'. Minskaya Voblasts', N Belarus *54°51′N 26°51′E*
152 C12 **Myājlār** *var.* Miajlar. Rājasthān, NW India *26°16′N 70°21′E*
123 T9 **Myakit** Magadanskaya Oblast', E Russia *61°23′N 151°58′E*
23 W13 **Myakka River** ≈ Florida, SE USA
124 L14 **Myaksa** Vologodskaya Oblast', NW Russia *58°54′N 38°15′E*
183 U8 **Myall Lake** ◎ New South Wales, SE Australia
166 L7 **Myanaung** Ayeyarwady, SW Myanmar (Burma) *18°17′N 95°19′E*
166 M4 **Myanmar (Burma)** *off.* Republic of the Union of Myanmar, *Bur.* Pyidaungzu Thammada Myanma Naingngandaw; *prev.* Union of Myanmar, *var.* Burma. ◆ *republic* SE Asia
**Myanmar, Republic of the Union of** *see* Myanmar (Burma)
**Myanmar, Union of** *see* Myanmar (Burma)
166 K8 **Myaungmya** Ayeyarwady, SW Myanmar (Burma) *16°33′N 94°55′E*
**Myaydo** *see* Aunglan
118 N11 **Myazha** *Rus.* Mezha. Vitsyebskaya Voblasts', NE Belarus *55°41′N 30°25′E*
167 N12 **Myeik** *var.* Mergui. Taninthayi, S Myanmar (Burma) *12°26′N 98°34′E*
166 M12 **Myeik Archipelago** *var.* Mergui Archipelago. *island group* S Myanmar (Burma)
119 O18 **Myerkulavichy** *Rus.* Merkulovichi. Homyel'skaya Voblasts', SE Belarus *52°58′N 30°36′E*
119 N14 **Myezhava** *Rus.* Mezhëvo. Vitsyebskaya Voblasts', NE Belarus *54°38′N 30°20′E*
**Myggenaes** *see* Mykines
166 L5 **Myingyan** Mandalay, C Myanmar (Burma) *21°25′N 95°20′E*
167 N12 **Myitkyina** Kachin State, N Myanmar (Burma) *25°24′N 97°25′E*
166 M5 **Myittha** Mandalay, C Myanmar (Burma) *21°21′N 96°06′E*
111 H19 **Myjava** *Hung.* Miava. Trenčiansky Kraj, W Slovakia *48°45′N 17°35′E*
**Myjeldino** *see* Myyëldino
117 U9 **Mykhaylivka** *Rus.* Mikhaylovka. Zaporiz'ka Oblast', SE Ukraine *47°16′N 35°14′E*
95 A18 **Mykines** *Dan.* Myggenaes. *island* W Faroe Islands
116 I5 **Mykolayiv** L'vivs'ka Oblast', W Ukraine *49°34′N 23°58′E*
117 Q10 **Mykolayiv** *Rus.* Nikolayev. Mykolayivs'ka Oblast', S Ukraine *46°58′N 31°59′E*
117 Q10 **Mykolayiv** ✈ Mykolayivs'ka Oblast', S Ukraine *47°02′N 31°54′E*
**Mykolayiv** *see* Mykolayivs'ka Oblast'
117 S13 **Mykolayivka** Avtonomna Respublika Krym, S Ukraine *44°58′N 33°37′E*
117 P9 **Mykolayivka** Odes'ka Oblast', SW Ukraine *47°34′N 30°48′E*
117 P9 **Mykolayivs'ka Oblast'** *var.* Mykolayiv, *Rus.* Nikolayevskaya Oblast'. ◈ *province* S Ukraine
115 J20 **Mýkonos** Mýkonos, Kykládes, Greece, Aegean Sea *37°27′N 25°20′E*
115 K20 **Mýkonos** *var.* Míkonos. *island* Kykládes, Greece, Aegean Sea
125 R7 **Myla** Respublika Komi, NW Russia *65°24′N 50°51′E*
**Mylae** *see* Milazzo
93 M19 **Myllykoski** Kymenlaakso, S Finland *60°45′N 26°52′E*
153 U14 **Mymensing** *var.* Mymensingh. Dhaka, N Bangladesh *24°45′N 90°23′E*
**Mymensingh** *see* Mymensing
93 K19 **Mynämäki** Varsinais-Suomi, SW Finland *60°41′N 22°00′E*
145 S14 **Mynaral** *Kaz.* Myngaral. Zhambyl, S Kazakhstan *45°25′N 73°37′E*
**Mynbulak** *see* Mingbuloq
**Mynbulak, Vpadina** *see* Mingbuloq Botig'I
**Myngaral** *see* Mynaral
**Myohaung** *see* Mrauk-U
163 W13 **Myohyang-sanmaek** ▲▲ C North Korea
164 M11 **Myōkō-san** ▲ Honshū, S Japan *36°54′N 138°05′E*
83 J15 **Myooye** Central, C Zambia *15°11′S 27°10′E*
118 K12 **Myory** *prev.* Miyory, *Rus.* Miory. Vitsyebskaya Voblasts', N Belarus *55°39′N 27°39′E*
92 J4 **Mýrdalsjökull** *glacier* S Iceland
92 G10 **Myre** Nordland, C Norway *68°54′N 15°04′E*
117 S5 **Myrhorod** *Rus.* Mirgorod. Poltavs'ka Oblast', NE Ukraine *49°58′N 33°37′E*
115 J15 **Mýrina** *var.* Mírina. Límnos, SE Greece *39°52′N 25°04′E*
117 W7 **Myrnohrad** *prev.* Dymytrov. Donets'ka Oblast', SE Ukraine *48°18′N 37°19′E*
117 P5 **Myronivka** *Rus.* Mironovka. Kyivs'ka Oblast', N Ukraine *49°40′N 30°59′E*
21 U13 **Myrtle Beach** South Carolina, SE USA *33°41′N 78°53′W*
32 F14 **Myrtle Creek** Oregon, NW USA *43°01′N 123°19′W*
183 P11 **Myrtleford** Victoria, SE Australia *36°34′S 146°45′E*
32 E14 **Myrtle Point** Oregon, NW USA *43°04′N 124°08′W*
**Myrtoan Sea** *see* Mirtóo Pélagos
115 K25 **Mýrtos** Kríti, Greece, E Mediterranean Sea *35°00′N 25°34′E*
**Myrtoum Mare** *see* Mirtóo Pélagos
93 G17 **Myrviken** Jämtland, C Sweden *62°59′N 14°19′E*
95 I15 **Mysen** Østfold, S Norway *59°33′N 11°20′E*
124 L15 **Myshkin** Yaroslavskaya Oblast', NW Russia *57°47′N 38°28′E*
111 K17 **Myślenice** Malopolskie, S Poland *49°50′N 19°55′E*
110 D10 **Myślibórz** Zachodnio-pomorskie, NW Poland *52°55′N 14°51′E*
**Mysore** *see* Karnātaka
**Mysore** *see* Mysūru
115 F21 **Mystrás** *var.* Mistras. Pelopónnisos, S Greece *37°03′N 22°22′E*
155 G20 **Mysūru** *prev.* Mysore, *var.* Maisur. Karnātaka, W India *12°18′N 76°37′E*
111 K15 **Myszków** Śląskie, S Poland *50°36′N 19°20′E*
167 T14 **My Tho** *var.* Mi Tho. Tiền Giang, S Vietnam *10°21′N 106°21′E*
**Mytilene** *see* Mytilíni
115 L17 **Mytilíni** *var.* Mitilíni; *anc.* Mytilene. Lésvos, E Greece *39°06′N 26°33′E*
126 K3 **Mytishchi** Moskovskaya Oblast', W Russia *56°00′N 37°51′E*
37 N3 **Myton** Utah, W USA *40°11′N 110°03′W*
92 K2 **Mývatn** ◎ C Iceland
125 T11 **Myyëldino** *var.* Myjeldino. Respublika Komi, NW Russia *61°46′N 54°48′E*
82 M13 **Mzimba** Northern, NW Malawi *11°56′S 33°36′E*
82 M12 **Mzuzu** Northern, N Malawi *11°23′S 34°03′E*


# N


101 M19 **Naab** ≈ SE Germany
98 G12 **Naaldwijk** Zuid-Holland, W Netherlands *52°00′N 04°13′E*
38 G12 **Nā'ālehu** *var.* Naalehu. Hawaii, USA, C Pacific Ocean *19°04′N 155°36′W*
93 K19 **Naantali** *Swe.* Nådendal. Varsinais-Suomi, SW Finland *60°28′N 22°05′E*
98 J10 **Naarden** Noord-Holland, C Netherlands *52°18′N 05°10′E*
109 U4 **Naarn** ≈ N Austria
97 F18 **Naas** *Ir.* An Nás, Nás na Ríogh. Kildare, C Ireland *53°13′N 06°39′W*
92 M9 **Näätämöjoki** *Lapp.* Njávdám. ≈ NE Finland
83 E23 **Nababeep** *var.* Nababiep. Northern Cape, W South Africa *29°36′S 17°46′E*
**Nababiep** *see* Nababeep
**Nabadwip** *see* Navadwīp
164 J14 **Nabari** Mie, Honshū, SW Japan *34°37′N 136°05′E*
**Nabatié** *see* Nabatîyé
138 G8 **Nabatîyé** *var.* An Nabatīyah at Taḩtā, Nabatié, Nabatiyet et Tahta. SW Lebanon *33°18′N 35°36′E*
**Nabatiyet et Tahta** *see* Nabatîyé
187 X14 **Nabavatu** Vanua Levu, N Fiji *16°35′S 178°55′E*
190 I2 **Nabeina** *island* Tungaru, W Kiribati
127 T4 **Naberezhnyye Chelny** *prev.* Brezhnev. Respublika Tatarstan, W Russia *55°43′N 52°21′E*
39 T10 **Nabesna** Alaska, USA *62°22′N 143°00′W*
39 T10 **Nabesna River** ≈ Alaska, USA
75 N5 **Nabeul** *var.* Nābul. NE Tunisia *36°32′N 10°45′E*
152 I9 **Nābha** Punjab, NW India *30°22′N 76°12′E*
171 W13 **Nabire** Papua, E Indonesia *03°23′S 135°31′E*
141 O15 **Nabī Shu'ayb, Jabal an** ▲ W Yemen *15°24′N 44°04′E*
138 F10 **Nablus** *var.* Nābulus, *Heb.* Shekhem; *anc.* Neapolis, *Bibl.* Shechem. N West Bank *32°13′N 35°16′E*
187 X14 **Nabouwalu** Vanua Levu, N Fiji *17°00′S 178°43′E*
**Nābul** *see* Nabeul
**Nābulus** *see* Nablus
187 Y13 **Nabuna** Vanua Levu, N Fiji *16°13′S 179°46′E*
83 Q14 **Nacala** Nampula, NE Mozambique *14°30′S 40°37′E*
42 H8 **Nacaome** Valle, S Honduras *13°30′N 87°31′W*
**Na Cealla Beaga** *see* Killybegs
**Na-Ch'ii** *see* Nagqu
164 J15 **Nachikatsuura** *var.* Nachi-Katsuura. Wakayama, Honshū, SE Japan *33°37′N 135°54′E*
**Nachi-Katsuura** *see* Nachikatsuura
81 J24 **Nachingwea** Lindi, SE Tanzania *10°21′S 38°46′E*
111 F16 **Náchod** Královéhradecký Kraj, N Czechia *50°26′N 16°10′E*
**Na Clocha Liatha** *see* Greystones
40 G3 **Naco** Sonora, NW Mexico *31°16′N 109°56′W*
25 X8 **Nacogdoches** Texas, SW USA *31°36′N 94°40′W*
40 G4 **Nacozari de García** Sonora, NW Mexico *30°27′N 109°43′W*
**Nada** *see* Danzhou
77 O14 **Nadawli** NW Ghana *10°30′N 02°40′W*
104 I3 **Nadela** Galicia, NW Spain *42°58′N 07°33′W*
**Nådendal** *see* Naantali


◆ Country ● Country Capital ◇ Dependent Territory ○ Dependent Territory Capital ◈ Administrative Regions ✈ International Airport ▲ Mountain ▲▲ Mountain Range Volcano ≈ River ◎ Lake ▣ Reservoir

NADEZHDINKA – NASE


144 M7 **Nadezhdinka** *prev.* Nadezhdinskiy. Kostanay, N Kazakhstan 53°46'N 63°44'E
**Nadezhdinskiy** *see* Nadezhdinka
**Nadgan** *see* Nadqān, Qalamat
187 W14 **Nadi** *prev.* Nandi. Viti Levu, W Fiji 17°47'S 177°32'E
187 X14 **Nadi** *prev.* Nandi. ✈ Viti Levu, W Fiji 17°46'S 177°28'E
154 D10 **Nadiād** Gujarāt, W India 22°42'N 72°55'E
**Nadikdik** *see* Knox Atoll
116 E11 **Nădlac** *Ger.* Nadlak, *Hung.* Nagylak. Arad, W Romania 46°10'N 20°47'E
**Nadlak** *see* Nădlac
74 H6 **Nador** *prev.* Villa Nador. NE Morocco 35°10'N 05°22'W
141 S9 **Nadqān, Qalamat** *var.* Nadgan. *well* E Saudi Arabia
111 N22 **Nádudvar** Hajdú-Bihar, E Hungary 47°36'N 21°09'E
121 O15 **Nadur** Gozo, N Malta 36°03'N 14°18'E
187 X13 **Naduri** *prev.* Nanduri. Vanua Levu, N Fiji 16°26'S 179°08'E
116 I7 **Nadvirna** *Pol.* Nadwórna, *Rus.* Nadvornaya. Ivano-Frankivs'ka Oblast', W Ukraine 48°27'N 24°30'E
124 J8 **Nadvoitsy** Respublika Kareliya, NW Russia 63°53'N 34°17'E
**Nadvornaya/Nadwórna** *see* Nadvirna
122 I9 **Nadym** Yamalo-Nenetskiy Avtonomnyy Okrug, N Russia 65°25'N 72°40'E
122 I9 **Nadym** ↝ C Russia
186 E7 **Nadzab** Morobe, C Papua New Guinea 06°36'S 146°46'E
95 C17 **Nærbø** Rogaland, S Norway 58°40'N 05°39'E
95 I24 **Næstved** Sjælland, SE Denmark 55°12'N 11°47'E
77 X13 **Nafada** Gombe, E Nigeria 11°02'N 11°18'E
108 H8 **Näfels** Glarus, NE Switzerland 47°06'N 09°04'E
115 E18 **Náfpaktos** *var.* Návpaktos. Dytikí Elláda, C Greece 38°23'N 21°50'E
115 F20 **Náfplio** *prev.* Návplion. Pelopónnisos, S Greece 37°34'N 22°50'E
139 U6 **Naft Khāneh** Diyālá, E Iraq 34°01'N 45°26'E
149 N13 **Nāg** Baluchistān, SW Pakistan 27°43'N 65°31'E
171 P4 **Naga** *off.* Naga City; *prev.* Nueva Caceres. Luzon, N Philippines 13°36'N 123°10'E
**Nagaarzê** *see* Nagarzê
**Naga City** *see* Naga
12 F11 **Nagagami** ↝ Ontario, S Canada
164 F14 **Nagahama** Ehime, Shikoku, SW Japan 33°36'N 132°29'E
153 X12 **Nāga Hills** ▲▲ NE India
165 P10 **Nagai** Yamagata, Honshū, C Japan 38°08'N 140°00'E
**Na Gaibhlte** *see* Galty Mountains
39 N16 **Nagai Island** *island* Shumagin Islands, Alaska, USA
153 X12 **Nāgāland** ◈ *state* NE India
164 M11 **Nagano** Nagano, Honshū, S Japan 36°39'N 138°11'E
164 M12 **Nagano** *off.* Nagano-ken. ◈ *prefecture* Honshū, S Japan
**Nagano-ken** *see* Nagano
165 N11 **Nagaoka** Niigata, Honshū, C Japan 37°26'N 138°48'E
153 W12 **Nagaon** *prev.* Nowgong. Assam, NE India 26°21'N 92°41'E
155 J21 **Nāgappattinam** *var.* Negapatam, Negapattinam. Tamil Nādu, SE India 10°45'N 79°50'E
**Nagara Nayok** *see* Nakhon Nayok
**Nagara Panom** *see* Nakhon Phanom
**Nagara Pathom** *see* Nakhon Pathom
**Nagara Sridharmaraj** *see* Nakhon Si Thammarat
**Nagara Svarga** *see* Nakhon Sawan
155 H16 **Nāgārjuna Sāgar** ⊠ E India
42 I10 **Nagarote** León, SW Nicaragua 12°15'N 86°35'W
158 M16 **Nagarzê** *var.* Nagaarzê. Xizang Zizhiqu, W China 28°57'N 90°26'E
164 C14 **Nagasaki** Nagasaki, Kyūshū, SW Japan 32°45'N 129°52'E
164 C14 **Nagasaki** *off.* Nagasaki-ken. ◈ *prefecture* Kyūshū, SW Japan
**Nagasaki-ken** *see* Nagasaki
**Nagashima** *see* Kii-Nagashima
164 E12 **Nagato** Yamaguchi, Honshū, SW Japan 34°22'N 131°10'E
152 F11 **Nāgaur** Rājasthān, NW India 27°12'N 73°48'E
154 F10 **Nāgda** Madhya Pradesh, C India 23°30'N 75°29'E
98 L8 **Nagele** Flevoland, N Netherlands 52°39'N 05°43'E
155 H24 **Nāgercoil** Tamil Nādu, SE India 08°11'N 77°30'E
153 X12 **Nāginimāra** Nāgāland, NE India 26°44'N 94°51'E
**Na Gleannta** *see* Glenties
165 T16 **Nago** Okinawa, Okinawa, SW Japan 26°36'N 127°59'E
154 K9 **Nāgod** Madhya Pradesh, C India 24°34'N 80°34'E
155 J26 **Nagoda** Southern Province, S Sri Lanka 06°13'N 80°13'E
101 G22 **Nagold** Baden-Württemberg, SW Germany 48°33'N 08°43'E
**Nagorno Karabakh** *see* Nagornyy Karabakh
**Nagorno- Karabakhskaya Avtonomnaya Oblast** *see* Nagornyy Karabakh
123 Q12 **Nagornyy** Respublika Sakha (Yakutiya), NE Russia 55°53'N 124°58'E
137 V12 **Nagornyy Karabakh** *var.* Nagorno-Karabakh; *prev.* Nagorno- Karabakhskaya Avtonomnaya Oblast, *Az.* Dağlıq Qarabağ, *Arm.* Lernayin Gharabagh. ◈ *former autonomous region* SW Azerbaijan
125 R13 **Nagorsk** Kirovskaya Oblast', NW Russia 59°18'N 50°49'E
164 K13 **Nagoya** Aichi, Honshū, SW Japan 35°10'N 136°53'E
154 I12 **Nāgpur** Mahārāshtra, C India 21°09'N 79°06'E
156 K10 **Nagqu** *Chin.* Na-Ch'ii; *prev.* Hei-ho. Xizang Zizhiqu, W China 31°30'N 91°57'E
152 J8 **Nāg Tibba Range** ▲▲ N India
45 O8 **Nagua** NE Dominican Republic 19°25'N 69°49'W
111 H25 **Nagyatád** Somogy, SW Hungary 46°15'N 17°25'E
**Nagybánya** *see* Baia Mare
**Nagybecskerek** *see* Zrenjanin
**Nagydisznód** *see* Cisnădie
**Nagyenyed** *see* Aiud
111 N21 **Nagykálló** Szabolcs-Szatmár-Bereg, E Hungary 47°50'N 21°47'E
111 G25 **Nagykanizsa** *Ger.* Grosskanizsa. Zala, SW Hungary 46°27'N 17°E
**Nagykároly** *see* Carei
111 K22 **Nagykáta** Pest, C Hungary 47°25'N 19°45'E
111 K23 **Nagykőrös** Pest, C Hungary 47°01'N 19°46'E
**Nagy-Küküllő** *see* Târnava Mare
**Nagylak** *see* Nădlac
**Nagymihály** *see* Michalovce
**Nagyrőce** *see* Revúca
**Nagysomkút** *see* Şomcuta Mare
**Nagysurány** *see* Šurany
**Nagyszalonta** *see* Salonta
**Nagyszeben** *see* Sibiu
**Nagyszentmiklós** *see* Sânnicolau Mare
**Nagyszöllös** *see* Vynohradiv
**Nagyszombat** *see* Trnava
**Nagytapolcsány** *see* Topoľčany
**Nagyvárad** *see* Oradea
165 S17 **Naha** Okinawa, Okinawa, SW Japan 26°10'N 127°40'E
152 J8 **Nāhan** Himāchal Pradesh, NW India 30°33'N 77°18'E
**Nahang, Rūd-e** *see* Nihing
138 F8 **Nahariya** *prev.* Nahariyya. Northern, N Israel 33°01'N 35°05'E
**Nahariyya** *see* Nahariya
142 L6 **Nahāvand** *var.* Nehavend. Hamadān, W Iran 34°13'N 48°21'E
101 F19 **Nahe** ↝ SW Germany
**Na H-Iarmhidhe** *see* Westmeath
189 O13 **Nahnalaud** ▲ Pohnpei, E Micronesia
**Nahoi, Cape** *see* Cumberland, Cape
**Nahtavárr** *see* Nattavaara
63 H16 **Nahuel Huapí, Lago** ◎ W Argentina
23 W7 **Nahunta** Georgia, SE USA 31°11'N 81°58'W
40 J6 **Naica** Chihuahua, N Mexico 27°53'N 105°30'W
11 U15 **Naicam** Saskatchewan, S Canada 52°26'N 104°30'W
**Naiman Qi** *see* Daqin Tal
158 M4 **Naimin Bulak** *spring* NW China
13 P6 **Nain** Newfoundland and Labrador, NE Canada 56°33'N 61°46'W
143 P8 **Nā'īn** Eşfahān, C Iran 32°52'N 53°05'E
152 K10 **Naini Tāl** Uttarākhand, N India 29°22'N 79°26'E
154 J11 **Nainpur** Madhya Pradesh, C India 22°26'N 80°10'E
96 J8 **Nairn** N Scotland, United Kingdom 57°36'N 03°51'W
96 I8 **Nairn** *cultural region* NE Scotland, United Kingdom
81 I19 **Nairobi** ● (Kenya) Nairobi City, S Kenya 01°17'S 36°50'E
81 I19 **Nairobi** ✈ Nairobi City, S Kenya 01°21'S 37°01'E
82 P13 **Nairoto** Cabo Delgado, NE Mozambique 12°22'S 39°05'E
118 G3 **Naissaar** *island* N Estonia
**Naissus** *see* Niš
187 Z14 **Naitaba** *var.* Naitauba; *prev.* Naitamba. *island* Lau Group, E Fiji
**Naitamba/Naitauba** *see* Naitaba
81 I19 **Naivasha** Nakuru, SW Kenya 0°44'S 36°26'E
81 H19 **Naivasha, Lake** ◎ SW Kenya
**Najaf** *see* An Najaf
143 N8 **Najafābād** *var.* Nejafabad. Eşfahān, C Iran 32°38'N 51°23'E
**Najaf, Muḩāfa at an** *see* An Najaf
**Najaf, Muḩāfaz at an** *see* An Najaf
141 N7 **Najd** *var.* Nejd. *cultural region* C Saudi Arabia
105 O4 **Nájera** La Rioja, N Spain 42°25'N 02°45'W
105 P4 **Najerilla** ↝ N Spain
163 U7 **Naji** *var.* Arun Qi. Nei Mongol Zizhiqu, N China 48°05'N 123°28'E
152 J9 **Najībābād** Uttar Pradesh, N India 29°37'N 78°19'E
**Najima** *see* Fukuoka
**Najin** *see* Rajin
139 T9 **Najm al Ḩassūn** Bābil, C Iraq 32°24'N 44°13'E
141 O13 **Najrān** *var.* Abā as Su'ūd. Najrān, S Saudi Arabia 17°31'N 44°09'E
141 P12 **Najrān** *var.* Minţaqat al Najrān. ◈ *region* S Saudi Arabia
**Najrān, Minţaqat al** *see* Najrān
165 T2 **Nakagawa** Hokkaidō, NE Japan 44°49'N 142°04'E
38 F9 **Nākālele Point** *var.* Nakalele Point. *headland* Maui, Hawai'i, USA 21°01'N 156°35'W
164 D13 **Nakama** Fukuoka, Kyūshū, SW Japan 33°53'N 130°48'E
**Nakambé** *see* White Volta
**Nakamti** *see* Nek'emtē
164 F15 **Nakamura** *var.* Shimanto. Kōchi, Shikoku, SW Japan 33°00'N 132°55'E
186 H7 **Nakanai Mountains** ▲▲ New Britain, E Papua New Guinea
164 H11 **Nakano-shima** *island* Okishotō, SW Japan
165 Q6 **Nakasato** Aomori, Honshū, C Japan 40°58'N 140°26'E
165 T5 **Nakasatsunai** Hokkaidō, NE Japan 42°42'N 143°09'E
165 W4 **Nakashibetsu** Hokkaidō, NE Japan 43°31'N 144°58'E
81 F18 **Nakasongola** C Uganda 01°19'N 32°28'E
165 T1 **Nakatonbetsu** Hokkaidō, NE Japan 44°58'N 142°18'E
164 L13 **Nakatsugawa** *var.* Nakatugawa. Gifu, Honshū, SW Japan 35°30'N 137°29'E
**Nakatugawa** *see* Nakatsugawa
**Nakdong** *see* Nakdong-gang
163 Y15 **Nakdong-gang** *var.* Nakdong, *Jap.* Rakutō-kō; *prev.* Naktong-gang. ↝ C South Korea
**Nakel** *see* Nakło nad Notecią
**Nakfa** *see* Nak'fa
80 J8 **Nak'fa** *var.* Nakfa. N Eritrea 16°38'N 38°26'E
**Nakhichevan'** *see* Naxçıvan
123 S15 **Nakhodka** Primorskiy Kray, SE Russia 42°46'N 132°48'E
122 J8 **Nakhodka** Yamalo-Nenetskiy Avtonomnyy Okrug, N Russia 67°48'N 77°48'E
**Nakhon Navok** *see* Nakhon Nayok
167 P11 **Nakhon Nayok** *var.* Nagara Nayok, Nakhon Navok. Nakhon Nayok, C Thailand 14°15'N 101°12'E
167 O11 **Nakhon Pathom** *var.* Nagara Pathom, Nakorn Pathom. Nakhon Pathom, W Thailand 13°49'N 100°06'E
167 R8 **Nakhon Phanom** *var.* Nagara Panom. Nakhon Phanom, E Thailand 17°22'N 104°46'E
167 Q10 **Nakhon Ratchasima** *var.* Khorat, Korat. Nakhon Ratchasima, E Thailand 15°N 102°06'E
167 O9 **Nakhon Sawan** *var.* Muang Nakhon Sawan, Nagara Svarga. Nakhon Sawan, W Thailand 15°42'N 100°06'E
167 N15 **Nakhon Si Thammarat** *var.* Nagara Sridharmaraj, Nakhon Sithammaraj. Nakhon Si Thammarat, SW Thailand 08°24'N 99°58'E
**Nakhon Sithammaraj** *see* Nakhon Si Thammarat
139 Y11 **Nakhrash** Al Başrah, SE Iraq 31°13'N 47°24'E
10 I9 **Nakina** British Columbia, W Canada 59°12'N 132°48'W
110 H9 **Nakło nad Notecią** *Ger.* Nakel. Kujawsko-pomorskie, C Poland 53°08'N 17°35'E
39 P13 **Naknek** Alaska, USA 58°45'N 157°01'W
152 H8 **Nakodar** Punjab, NW India 31°06'N 75°31'E
82 M11 **Nakonde** Muchinga, NE Zambia 09°22'S 32°47'E
**Nakorn Pathom** *see* Nakhon Pathom
95 H24 **Nakskov** Sjælland, SE Denmark 54°50'N 11°10'E
**Naktong-gang** *see* Nakdong-gang
81 H18 **Nakuru** Nakuru, SW Kenya 0°16'S 36°04'E
81 H19 **Nakuru, Lake** ◎ Nakuru, C Kenya
11 O17 **Nakusp** British Columbia, SW Canada 50°14'N 117°48'W
149 N15 **Nal** ↝ W Pakistan
162 M7 **Nalayh** Töv, C Mongolia 47°48'N 107°17'E
153 V12 **Nalbāri** Assam, NE India 26°36'N 91°49'E
63 G19 **Nalcayec, Isla** *island* Archipiélago de los Chonos, S Chile
127 N15 **Nal'chik** Kabardino-Balkarskaya Respublika, SW Russia 43°30'N 43°39'E
155 I16 **Nalgonda** Telangana, C India 17°04'N 79°15'E
153 S14 **Nalhāti** West Bengal, NE India 24°19'N 87°53'E
153 U14 **Nalitabari** Dhaka, N Bangladesh 25°06'N 90°11'E
155 I17 **Nallamala Hills** ▲▲ E India
136 G12 **Nallıhan** Ankara, NW Turkey 40°12'N 31°22'E
104 K2 **Nalón** ↝ NW Spain
167 N3 **Nalong** Kachin State, N Myanmar (Burma) 24°42'N 97°27'E
75 N8 **Nālūt** NW Libya 31°52'N 10°59'E
171 T14 **Nama** Pulau Manawoka, E Indonesia 04°07'S 131°22'E
189 Q16 **Nama** *island* C Micronesia
83 O16 **Namacurra** Zambézia, NE Mozambique 17°31'S 37°03'E
188 F9 **Namai Bay** *bay* Babeldaob, N Palau
29 W2 **Namakan Lake** ◎ Canada/USA
143 O6 **Namak, Daryācheh-ye** *marsh* N Iran
143 T6 **Namak, Kavīr-e** *salt pan* NE Iran
167 O6 **Namaklwe** Shan State, E Myanmar (Burma) 19°45'N 99°01'E
**Namaksār, Kowl-e/ Namakzar, Daryācheh-ye** *see* Namakzar
148 I5 **Namakzar** *Pash.* Daryācheh-ye Namakzār, Kowl-e Namaksār. *marsh* Afghanistan/Iran
171 V15 **Namalau** Pulau Jursian, E Indonesia 05°50'S 134°43'E
81 I20 **Namanga** Kajiado, S Kenya 02°33'S 36°48'E
147 S10 **Namangan** Namangan Viloyati, E Uzbekistan 40°59'N 71°34'E
**Namanganskaya Oblast'** *see* Namangan Viloyati
147 R10 **Namangan Viloyati** *Rus.* Namanganskaya Oblast'. ◈ *province* E Uzbekistan
83 Q14 **Namapa** Nampula, NE Mozambique 13°43'S 39°48'E
83 C21 **Namaqualand** *physical region* S Namibia
81 G18 **Namasagali** C Uganda 01°02'N 32°58'E
186 H6 **Namatanai** New Ireland, NE Papua New Guinea 03°40'S 152°26'E
83 I14 **Nambala** Central, C Zambia 15°04'S 26°56'E
81 J23 **Nambanje** Lindi, SE Tanzania 08°37'S 38°21'E
183 V2 **Nambour** Queensland, E Australia 26°40'S 152°52'E
183 V6 **Nambucca Heads** New South Wales, SE Australia 30°37'S 153°00'E
159 N15 **Nam Co** ◎ W China
167 R5 **Nam Cum** Lai Châu, N Vietnam 22°37'N 103°12'E
**Namdik** *see* Namorik Atoll
167 T6 **Nam Định** Nam Ha, N Vietnam 20°25'N 106°12'E
99 I20 **Namêche** Namur, SE Belgium 50°29'N 05°02'E
30 I4 **Namekagon Lake** ◎ Wisconsin, N USA
188 F10 **Namekakl Passage** *passage* Babeldaob, N Palau
**Namen** *see* Namur
83 P15 **Nametil** Nampula, NE Mozambique 15°46'S 39°21'E
163 X14 **Nam-gang** ↝ C North Korea
163 Y16 **Nam-gang** ↝ S South Korea
163 Y17 **Namhae-do** *Jap.* Nankai-tō. *island* S South Korea
**Namhoi** *see* Foshan
83 C19 **Namib Desert** *desert* W Namibia
83 A15 **Namibe** *Port.* Moçâmedes, Mossâmedes. Namibe, SW Angola 15°10'S 12°09'E
83 A15 **Namibe** ◈ *province* SE Angola
83 C18 **Namibia** *off.* Republic of Namibia, *var.* South West Africa, *Afr.* Suidwes-Afrika, *Ger.* Deutsch-Südwestafrika; *prev.* German Southwest Africa, South-West Africa. ◆ *republic* S Africa
65 O17 **Namibia Plain** *undersea feature* S Atlantic Ocean
**Namibia, Republic of** *see* Namibia
165 Q11 **Namie** Fukushima, Honshū, C Japan 37°29'N 140°58'E
165 Q7 **Namioka** Aomori, Honshū, C Japan 40°43'N 140°34'E
40 I5 **Namiquipa** Chihuahua, N Mexico 29°15'N 107°25'W
159 P15 **Namjagbarwa Feng** ▲ W China 29°39'N 95°00'E
**Namka** *see* Doilungdêqên
**Nam Khong** *see* Mekong
171 R13 **Namlea** Pulau Buru, E Indonesia 03°12'S 127°06'E
158 L16 **Namling** Xizang Zizhiqu, W China 29°40'N 88°58'E
**Namnetes** *see* Nantes
167 R8 **Nam Ngum** ↝ C Laos
**Namo** *see* Namu Atoll
183 R5 **Namoi River** ↝ New South Wales, SE Australia
189 Q17 **Namoluk Atoll** *atoll* Mortlock Islands, C Micronesia
189 O15 **Namonuito Atoll** *atoll* Caroline Islands, C Micronesia
189 T9 **Namorik Atoll** *var.* Namdik. *atoll* Ralik Chain, S Marshall Islands
167 Q6 **Nam Ou** ↝ N Laos
32 M14 **Nampa** Idaho, NW USA 43°32'N 116°33'W
76 M11 **Nampala** Ségou, W Mali 15°21'N 05°32'W
163 W14 **Namp'o** SW North Korea 38°46'N 125°25'E
83 P15 **Nampula** Nampula, NE Mozambique 15°09'S 39°14'E
83 P15 **Nampula** *off.* Província de Nampula. ◈ *province* NE Mozambique
**Nampula, Província de** *see* Nampula
163 W13 **Namsan-ni** NW North Korea 40°25'N 125°01'E
**Namslau** *see* Namysłów
93 E15 **Namsos** Nord-Trøndelag, C Norway 64°28'N 11°31'E
93 F14 **Namsskogan** Nord-Trøndelag, C Norway 64°57'N 13°04'E
167 O6 **Nam Teng** ↝ E Myanmar (Burma)
167 P6 **Nam Tha** ↝ N Laos
123 Q10 **Namtsy** Respublika Sakha (Yakutiya), NE Russia 62°42'N 129°30'E
167 N4 **Namtu** Shan State, E Myanmar (Burma) 23°04'N 97°26'E
10 J15 **Namu** British Columbia, SW Canada 51°46'N 127°49'W
185 T7 **Namu Atoll** *var.* Namo. *atoll* Ralik Chain, C Marshall Islands
187 Y15 **Namuka-i-lau** *island* Lau Group, E Fiji
83 O15 **Namuli, Mont** ▲ NE Mozambique 15°15'S 37°33'E
83 P14 **Namuno** Cabo Delgado, N Mozambique 13°39'S 38°50'E
99 I20 **Namur** *Dut.* Namen. Namur, SE Belgium 50°28'N 04°52'E
99 H21 **Namur** *Dut.* Namen. ◈ *province* S Belgium
83 D17 **Namutoni** Kunene, N Namibia 18°49'S 16°55'E
163 Y16 **Namwon** *Jap.* Nangen; *prev.* Namwŏn. S South Korea 35°24'N 127°20'E
**Namwŏn** *see* Namwon
111 H14 **Namysłów** *Ger.* Namslau. Opole, SW Poland 51°03'N 17°41'E
167 P7 **Nan** *var.* Muang Nan. Nan, NW Thailand 18°47'N 100°50'E
79 G15 **Nana** ↝ W Central African Republic
165 R5 **Nanae** Hokkaidō, NE Japan 41°55'N 140°40'E
79 I14 **Nana-Grébizi** ◈ *prefecture* N Central African Republic
10 L17 **Nanaimo** Vancouver Island, British Columbia, SW Canada 49°08'N 123°58'W
38 C9 **Nānākuli** *var.* Nanakuli. O'ahu, Hawaii, USA, C Pacific Ocean 21°23'N 158°09'W
79 G15 **Nana-Mambéré** ◈ *prefecture* W Central African Republic
161 R13 **Nan'an** Fujian, SE China 24°59'N 118°22'E
183 U2 **Nanango** Queensland, E Australia 26°42'S 151°58'E
164 L11 **Nanao** Ishikawa, Honshū, SW Japan 37°03'N 136°58'E
161 T13 **Nan'ao** N Taiwan 24°28'N 121°49'E
161 Q14 **Nan'ao Dao** *island* S China
164 L10 **Nanatsu-shima** *island* SW Japan
56 F8 **Nanay, Río** ↝ NE Peru
160 J8 **Nanbu** Sichuan, C China 31°19'N 106°02'E
163 X7 **Nancha** Heilongjiang, NE China 47°09'N 129°17'E
161 P10 **Nanchang** *var.* Nan-ch'ang, Nanch'ang-hsien. *province capital* Jiangxi, S China 28°38'N 115°58'E
**Nan-ch'ang** *see* Nanchang
**Nanch'ang-hsien** *see* Nanchang
161 P11 **Nancheng** *var.* Jianchang. Jiangxi, S China 27°37'N 116°37'E
**Nan-ching** *see* Nanjing
160 J9 **Nanchong** Sichuan, C China 30°47'N 106°03'E
160 J10 **Nanchuan** Chongqing Shi, C China 29°06'N 107°13'E
103 T5 **Nancy** Meurthe-et-Moselle, NE France 48°40'N 06°11'E
185 A22 **Nancy Sound** *sound* South Island, New Zealand
152 L9 **Nanda Devi** ▲ NW India 30°27'N 80°00'E
42 J11 **Nandaime** Granada, SW Nicaragua 11°45'N 86°02'W
160 K13 **Nandan** *var.* Minami-Awaji. Guangxi Zhuangzu Zizhiqu, S China 25°03'N 107°31'E
155 H14 **Nānded** Mahārāshtra, C India 19°11'N 77°21'E
183 S5 **Nandewar Range** ▲▲ New South Wales, SE Australia
**Nandi** *see* Nadi
160 E13 **Nanding He** ↝ China/ Vietnam
**Nándorhgy** *see* Oţelu Roşu
154 E11 **Nandurbār** Mahārāshtra, W India 21°22'N 74°18'E
**Nanduri** *see* Naduri
155 I17 **Nandyāl** Andhra Pradesh, E India 15°30'N 78°28'E
161 P11 **Nanfeng** *var.* Qincheng. Jiangxi, S China 27°15'N 116°16'E
**Nang** *see* Nangxian
79 E15 **Nanga Eboko** Centre, C Cameroon 04°38'N 12°21'E
**Nangah Serawai** *see* Nangaserawai
161 S12 **Nangan Dao** *var.* Mazu Dao, Mazu Tao, Matsu Tao. *island* NW Taiwan
149 W4 **Nanga Parbat** ▲ India/ Pakistan 35°15'N 74°36'E
169 R11 **Nangapinoh** Borneo, C Indonesia 0°21'S 111°44'E
149 R5 **Nangarhār** ◈ *province* E Afghanistan
169 S11 **Nangaserawai** *var.* Nangah Serawai. Borneo, C Indonesia 0°20'S 112°26'E
169 Q12 **Nangatayap** Borneo, C Indonesia 01°30'S 110°33'E
**Nangen** *see* Namwon
103 P5 **Nangis** Seine-et-Marne, N France 48°36'N 03°02'E
163 X13 **Nangnim-sanmaek** ▲▲ C North Korea
161 O4 **Nangong** Hebei, E China 37°22'N 115°20'E
159 Q14 **Nangqên** *var.* Xangda. Qinghai, C China 32°05'N 96°28'E
167 Q10 **Nang Rong** Buri Ram, E Thailand 14°37'N 102°48'E
159 O16 **Nangxian** *var.* Nang. Xizang Zizhiqu, W China 29°04'N 93°03'E
160 L8 **Nan He** ↝ C China
160 F12 **Nanhua** *var.* Longchuan. Yunnan, SW China 25°15'N 101°15'E
**Naniwa** *see* Ōsaka
155 G20 **Nanjangūd** Karnātaka, W India 12°07'N 76°40'E
161 Q8 **Nanjing** *var.* Nan-ching, Nanking; *prev.* Chianning, Chian-ning, Kiang-ning. Jiangsu. *province capital* Jiangsu, E China 32°03'N 118°47'E
**Nankai-tō** *see* Namhae-do
161 O12 **Nankang** *var.* Rongjiang. Jiangxi, S China 25°42'N 114°45'E
**Nanking** *see* Nanjing
161 N13 **Nan Ling** ▲▲ S China
160 L15 **Nanliu Jiang** ↝ S China
189 P13 **Nan Madol** *ruins* Temwen Island, E Micronesia
160 K15 **Nanning** *var.* Nan-ning; *prev.* Yung-ning. Guangxi Zhuangzu Zizhiqu, S China 22°50'N 108°19'E
**Nan-ning** *see* Nanning
196 M15 **Nanortalik** Kujalleq, S Greenland 60°08'M 45°14'W
**Nanouki** *see* Aranuka
160 H13 **Nanpan Jiang** ↝ S China
152 M11 **Nānpāra** Uttar Pradesh, N India 27°51'N 81°30'E
161 Q12 **Nanping** *var.* Nan-p'ing; *prev.* Yenping. Fujian, SE China 26°40'N 118°07'E
**Nan-p'ing** *see* Nanping
**Nanping** *see* Jiuzhaigou
**Nanqiao** *see* Fengxian
161 R12 **Nanri Dao** *island* SE China
165 S16 **Nansei-shotō** *Eng.* Ryukyu Islands. *island group* SW Japan
**Nansei Syotō Trench** *see* Ryukyu Trench
197 T10 **Nansen Basin** *undersea feature* Arctic Ocean
**Nansen Cordillera** *see* Gakkel Ridge
129 T9 **Nan Shan** ▲▲ C China
**Nansha Qundao** *see* Spratly Islands
12 K3 **Nantais, Lac** ◎ Québec, NE Canada
103 N5 **Nanterre** Hauts-de-Seine, N France 48°53'N 02°13'E
102 I8 **Nantes** *Bret.* Naoned; *anc.* Condivincum, Namnetes. Loire-Atlantique, NW France 47°12'N 01°32'W
14 G17 **Nanticoke** Ontario, S Canada 42°49'N 80°04'W
18 H13 **Nanticoke** Pennsylvania, NE USA 41°12'N 76°00'W
21 Y4 **Nanticoke River** ↝ Delaware/Maryland, NE USA
11 Q17 **Nanton** Alberta, SW Canada 50°21'N 113°47'W
161 S8 **Nantong** Jiangsu, E China 32°00'N 120°52'E
161 S13 **Nantou** *prev.* Nant'ou. W Taiwan 23°54'N 120°51'E
**Nant'ou** *see* Nantou
103 S10 **Nantua** Ain, E France 46°10'N 05°34'E
19 Q13 **Nantucket** Nantucket Island, Massachusetts, NE USA 41°15'N 70°05'W
19 Q13 **Nantucket Island** *island* Massachusetts, NE USA
19 Q13 **Nantucket Sound** *sound* Massachusetts, NE USA
82 P13 **Nantulo** Cabo Delgado, N Mozambique 12°30'S 39°03'E
189 O12 **Nanuh** Pohnpei, E Micronesia
190 D6 **Nanumaga** *var.* Nanumanga. *atoll* NW Tuvalu
**Nanumanga** *see* Nanumaga
190 D5 **Nanumea Atoll** *atoll* NW Tuvalu
59 O19 **Nanuque** Minas Gerais, SE Brazil 17°49'S 40°21'W
171 R10 **Nanusa, Kepulauan** *island group* N Indonesia
**Nanwei Dao** *see* Spratly Island
163 U4 **Nanweng He** ↝ NE China
160 I10 **Nanxi** Sichuan, C China 28°54'N 104°59'E
161 N10 **Nanxian** *var.* Nan Xian, Nanzhou. Hunan, S China 29°23'N 112°18'E
**Nan Xian** *see* Nanxian
161 N7 **Nanyang** *var.* Nan-yang. Henan, C China 32°59'N 112°29'E
**Nan-yang** *see* Nanyang
161 P6 **Nanyang Hu** ◎ E China
165 P10 **Nan'yō** Yamagata, Honshū, C Japan 38°04'N 140°06'E
81 I18 **Nanyuki** Laikipia, C Kenya 0°01'N 37°05'E
160 M8 **Nanzhang** Hubei, C China 31°47'N 111°48'E
**Nanzhou** *see* Nanxian
105 T11 **Nao, Cabo de La** *headland* E Spain 38°43'N 00°13'E
12 M9 **Naococane, Lac** ◎ Québec, E Canada
153 S14 **Naogaon** Rajshahi, NW Bangladesh 24°49'N 88°59'E
**Naokot** *see* Naukot
187 R13 **Naone** Maewo, C Vanuatu 15°03'S 168°06'E
**Naoned** *see* Nantes
115 E14 **Náousa** Kentrikí Makedonía, N Greece 40°38'N 22°04'E
35 N8 **Napa** California, W USA 38°15'N 122°17'W
39 O11 **Napaimiut** Alaska, USA 61°32'N 158°46'W
39 N12 **Napakiak** Alaska, USA 60°42'N 161°57'W
122 J7 **Napalkovo** Yamalo-Nenetskiy Avtonomnyy Okrug, N Russia 70°06'N 73°43'E
12 I16 **Napanee** Ontario, SE Canada 44°13'N 76°57'W
39 N12 **Napaskiak** Alaska, USA 60°42'N 161°46'W
167 S5 **Na Phác** Cao Bằng, N Vietnam 22°24'N 105°54'E
184 O11 **Napier** Hawke's Bay, North Island, New Zealand 39°30'S 176°55'E
195 X3 **Napier Mountains** ▲▲ Antarctica
15 O13 **Napierville** Québec, SE Canada 45°12'N 73°25'W
23 W15 **Naples** Florida, SE USA 26°08'N 81°48'W
25 W5 **Naples** Texas, SW USA 33°12'N 94°40'W
**Naples** *see* Napoli
160 I14 **Napo** Guangxi Zhuangzu Zizhiqu, S China 23°21'N 105°47'E
56 C6 **Napo** ◈ *province* NE Ecuador
29 O6 **Napoleon** North Dakota, N USA 46°30'N 99°46'W
31 R11 **Napoleon** Ohio, N USA 41°23'N 84°07'W
**Napoléon-Vendée** *see* la Roche-sur-Yon
22 J9 **Napoleonville** Louisiana, S USA 29°55'N 91°01'W
107 K17 **Napoli** *Eng.* Naples, *Ger.* Neapel; *anc.* Neapolis. Campania, S Italy 40°52'N 14°15'E
107 J18 **Napoli, Golfo di** *gulf* S Italy
57 F7 **Napo, Río** ↝ Ecuador/Peru
191 W9 **Napuka** *island* Îles Tuamotu, C French Polynesia
142 J3 **Naqadeh** Āžarbāyjān-e Bākhtarī, NW Iran 36°57'N 45°24'E
139 U6 **Naqnah** Diyālá, E Iraq 34°13'N 45°33'E
**Nar** *see* Nera
164 J14 **Nara** Nara, Honshū, SW Japan 34°41'N 135°49'E
76 L11 **Nara** Koulikoro, W Mali 15°04'N 07°19'W
149 R14 **Nara Canal** *irrigation canal* S Pakistan
182 K11 **Naracoorte** South Australia 37°02'S 140°45'E
183 P8 **Naradhan** New South Wales, SE Australia 33°37'S 146°19'E
**Naradhivas** *see* Narathiwat
56 B8 **Naranjal** Guayas, W Ecuador 02°43'S 79°38'W
57 Q19 **Naranjos** Santa Cruz, E Bolivia
41 Q12 **Naranjos** Veracruz, E Mexico 21°21'N 97°41'W
159 Q6 **Naran Sebstein Bulag** *spring* NW China
164 B14 **Narao** Nagasaki, Nakadōri-jima, SW Japan 32°40'N 129°03'E
155 J16 **Narasaraopet** Andhra Pradesh, E India 16°16'N 80°06'E
158 J5 **Narat** Xinjiang Uygur Zizhiqu, W China 43°20'N 84°02'E
167 P17 **Narathiwat** *var.* Naradhivas. Narathiwat, SW Thailand 06°25'N 101°48'E
37 V10 **Nara Visa** New Mexico, SW USA 35°35'N 103°06'W
**Nārāyāni** *see* Gandak
**Narbada** *see* Narmada
**Narbo Martius** *see* Narbonne
103 P16 **Narbonne** *anc.* Narbo Martius. Aude, S France 43°11'N 03°E
**Narborough Island** *see* Fernandina, Isla
104 J2 **Narcea** ↝ NW Spain
152 J9 **Narendranagar** Uttarākhand, N India 30°10'N 78°21'E
**Nares Abyssal Plain** *see* Nares Plain
64 G11 **Nares Plain** *var.* Nares Abyssal Plain. *undersea feature* NW Atlantic Ocean 23°30'N 63°00'W
**Nares Stræde** *see* Nares Strait
197 P10 **Nares Strait** *Dan.* Nares Stræde. *strait* Canada/ Greenland
110 O9 **Narew** ↝ E Poland
155 F17 **Nargund** Karnātaka, W India 15°43'N 75°23'E
83 D20 **Narib** Hardap, S Namibia 24°11'S 17°46'E
**Narikrik** *see* Knox Atoll
**Narin Gol** *see* Omon Gol
54 B13 **Nariño** *off.* Departamento de Nariño. ◈ *province* SW Colombia
165 P13 **Narita** Chiba, Honshū, S Japan 35°46'N 140°20'E
165 P13 **Narita** ✈ (Tōkyō) Chiba, Honshū, S Japan 35°45'N 140°23'E
**Nariya** *see* An Nu'ayrīyah
162 F5 **Nariyn Gol** ↝ Mongolia/ Russia
162 J8 **Nariynteel** *var.* Tsagaan-Ovoo. Övörhangay, C Mongolia 45°57'N 101°25'E
152 J8 **Narkanda** Himāchal Pradesh, NW India 31°14'N 77°27'E
92 L13 **Narkaus** Lappi, NW Finland 66°13'N 26°09'E
154 E11 **Narmada** *var.* Narbada. ↝ C India
152 H11 **Narnaul** *var.* Nārnaul. Haryāna, N India 28°04'N 76°10'E
107 I14 **Narni** Umbria, C Italy 42°31'N 12°31'E
107 J24 **Naro** Sicilia, Italy, C Mediterranean Sea 37°18'N 13°48'E
**Narodichi** *see* Narodychi
125 V7 **Narodnaya, Gora** ▲ NW Russia 65°04'N 60°12'E
117 N3 **Narodychi** *Rus.* Narodichi. Zhytomyrs'ka Oblast', N Ukraine 51°11'N 29°01'E
126 J4 **Naro-Fominsk** Moskovskaya Oblast', W Russia 55°25'N 36°41'E
81 H19 **Narok** Narok, SW Kenya 01°04'S 35°54'E
104 H2 **Narón** Galicia, NW Spain 43°31'N 08°08'W
183 S11 **Narooma** New South Wales, SE Australia 36°16'S 150°08'E
**Narova** *see* Narva
**Narovlya** *see* Narowlya
149 W8 **Narowal** Punjab, E Pakistan 32°04'N 74°54'E
119 N20 **Narowlya** *Rus.* Narovlya. Homyel'skaya Voblasts', SE Belarus 51°48'N 29°30'E
93 J17 **Närpes** *Fin.* Närpiö. Österbotten, W Finland 62°28'N 21°19'E
**Närpiö** *see* Närpes
183 S5 **Narrabri** New South Wales, SE Australia 30°21'S 149°48'E
183 P9 **Narrandera** New South Wales, SE Australia 34°46'S 146°32'E
183 Q4 **Narran Lake** ◎ New South Wales, SE Australia
183 Q4 **Narran River** ↝ New South Wales/Queensland, SE Australia
180 J13 **Narrogin** Western Australia 32°53'S 117°17'E
183 Q7 **Narromine** New South Wales, SE Australia 32°16'S 148°15'E
21 R6 **Narrows** Virginia, NE USA 37°19'N 80°48'W
196 M15 **Narsarsuaq** ✈ Kujalleq, S Greenland 61°07'N 45°03'W
154 I10 **Narsimhapur** Madhya Pradesh, C India 22°58'N 79°15'E
153 U15 **Narsingdi** *var.* Narsinghdi. Dhaka, C Bangladesh 23°56'N 90°40'E
**Narsinghdi** *see* Narsingdi
154 H9 **Narsinghgarh** Madhya Pradesh, C India 23°42'N 77°08'E
163 Q11 **Nart** Nei Mongol Zizhiqu, N China 42°54'N 115°55'E
**Nartës, Gjol i/Nartës, Laguna e** *see* Nartës, Liqeni i
113 J22 **Nartës, Liqeni i** *var.* Gjol i Nartës, Laguna e Nartës. ◎ SW Albania
115 F17 **Narthákio** ▲ C Greece 39°12'N 22°24'E
127 O15 **Nartkala** Kabardino-Balkarskaya Respublika, SW Russia 43°34'N 43°55'E
118 K3 **Narva** Ida-Virumaa, NE Estonia 59°23'N 28°12'E
118 K4 **Narva** *prev.* Narova. ↝ Estonia/Russia
118 J3 **Narva Bay** *Est.* Narva Laht, *Ger.* Narwa-Bucht, *Rus.* Narvskiy Zaliv. *bay* Estonia/ Russia
**Narva Laht** *see* Narva Bay
124 F13 **Narva Reservoir** *Est.* Narva Veehoidla, *Rus.* Narvskoye Vodokhranilishche. ⊠ Estonia/Russia
**Narva Veehoidla** *see* Narva Reservoir
92 H10 **Narvik** Nordland, C Norway 68°26'N 17°24'E
**Narvskiy Zaliv** *see* Narva Bay
**Narvskoye Vodokhranilishche** *see* Narva Reservoir
**Narwa-Bucht** *see* Narva Bay
152 I9 **Narwāna** Haryāna, NW India 29°36'N 76°11'E
125 R4 **Nar'yan-Mar** *prev.* Beloshchel'ye, Dzerzhinskiy. Nenetskiy Avtonomnyy Okrug, NW Russia 67°38'N 53°E
122 J12 **Narym** Tomskaya Oblast', C Russia 58°59'N 81°20'E
**Narymskiy Khrebet** *see* Khrebet Naryn
147 W9 **Naryn** Narynskaya Oblast', C Kyrgyzstan 41°24'N 76°E
147 U8 **Naryn** ↝ Kyrgyzstan/ Uzbekistan
145 W16 **Narynkol** *Kaz.* Narynqol. Almaty, SE Kazakhstan 42°45'N 80°12'E
**Naryn Oblasty** *see* Narynskaya Oblast'
**Narynqol** *see* Narynkol
147 V9 **Narynskaya Oblast'** *Kyr.* Naryn Oblasty. ◈ *province* C Kyrgyzstan
**Naryn Zhotasy** *see* Khrebet Naryn
126 J6 **Naryshkino** Orlovskaya Oblast', W Russia 53°00'N 35°41'E
95 L14 **Nås** Dalarna, C Sweden 60°28'N 14°30'E
10 J11 **Nass** ↝ British Columbia, SW Canada
92 G13 **Nasafjellet** *Lapp.* Násávárre. ▲ C Norway 66°29'N 15°23'E
93 H16 **Näsåker** Västernorrland, C Sweden 63°27'N 16°55'E
187 Y14 **Nasau** Koro, C Fiji 17°20'S 179°26'E
190 J13 **Nasau** *island* N Cook Islands
116 I9 **Năsăud** *Ger.* Nussdorf, *Hung.* Naszód. Bistriţa-Năsăud, N Romania 47°16'N 24°24'E
**Násávárre** *see* Nasafjellet
103 P13 **Nasbinals** Lozère, S France 44°40'N 03°03'E
**Na Sceirí** *see* Skerries
**Nase** *see* Naze




◆ Country ● Country Capital ◇ Dependent Territory ○ Dependent Territory Capital ◈ Administrative Regions ✈ International Airport ▲ Mountain ▲▲ Mountain Range Ѫ Volcano ↝ River ◎ Lake ⊠ Reservoir

NASEBY – NEUSOHL

185 E22 Naseby Otago, South Island, New Zealand 45°02′S 170°09′E
143 R10 Nāşerīyeh Kermān, C Iran
25 X5 Nash Texas, SW USA 33°26′N 94°04′W
154 E13 Nāshik prev. Nāsik. Mahārāshtra, W India 20°05′N 73°48′E
56 E7 Nashiño, Río ⇝ Ecuador/Peru
29 W12 Nashua Iowa, C USA 42°57′N 92°32′W
33 W7 Nashua Montana, NW USA 48°06′N 106°16′W
19 O10 Nashua New Hampshire, NE USA 42°45′N 71°26′W
27 S13 Nashville Arkansas, C USA 33°57′N 93°50′W
23 U7 Nashville Georgia, SE USA 31°12′N 83°15′W
30 L16 Nashville Illinois, N USA 38°20′N 89°22′W
31 O14 Nashville Indiana, N USA 39°13′N 86°15′W
21 V9 Nashville North Carolina, SE USA 35°58′N 78°00′W
20 J8 Nashville state capital Tennessee, S USA 36°11′N 86°48′W
20 J9 Nashville ✈ Tennessee, S USA 36°06′N 86°44′W
64 H10 Nashville Seamount undersea feature NW Atlantic Ocean 30°00′N 57°20′W
112 H9 Našice Osijek-Baranja, E Croatia 45°29′N 18°05′E
110 M11 Nasielsk Mazowieckie, C Poland 52°33′N 20°46′E
93 K18 Näsijärvi ◎ SW Finland
Nāsik see Nāshik
80 G13 Nasir Upper Nile, NE South Sudan 08°37′N 33°06′E
148 K15 Nasīrābad Baluchistān, SW Pakistan 26°15′N 62°32′E
Nasir, Buhayrat/Nâşir,Buḩeiret see Nasser, Lake
Nāsiri see Ahvāz
Nasiriya see An Nāşirīyah
Nāşirīyah, An see Dhī Qār
Nás na Ríogh see Naas
107 L23 Naso Sicilia, Italy, C Mediterranean Sea 38°07′N 14°46′E
Nasratabad see Zābol
77 V15 Nassarawa Nassarawa, C Nigeria 08°33′N 07°42′E
44 H2 Nassau ● (The Bahamas) New Providence, N The Bahamas 25°03′N 77°21′W
23 W8 Nassau Sound sound Florida, SE USA
108 L7 Nassereith Tirol, W Austria 47°19′N 10°51′E
80 F5 Nasser, Lake var. Buhayrat Nasir, Buḩayrat Nāşir, Buḩeiret Nâşir. ◎ Egypt/Sudan
95 L19 Nässjö Jönköping, S Sweden 57°39′N 14°40′E
99 K22 Nassogne Luxembourg, SE Belgium 50°08′N 05°19′E
12 J6 Nastapoka Islands island group Northwest Territories, C Canada
93 M19 Nastola Päijät-Häme, S Finland 60°57′N 25°56′E
171 O4 Nasugbu Luzon, N Philippines 14°03′N 120°39′E
94 N11 Näsviken Gävleborg, C Sweden 61°46′N 16°55′E
Naszód see Năsăud
83 I17 Nata Central, NE Botswana 20°11′S 26°10′E
54 E11 Natagaima Tolima, C Colombia 03°38′N 75°07′W
59 Q14 Natal state capital Rio Grande do Norte, E Brazil 05°46′S 35°15′W
168 I11 Natal Sumatera, N Indonesia 0°32′N 99°07′E
Natal see KwaZulu/Natal
173 L10 Natal Basin var. Mozambique Basin. undersea feature W Indian Ocean 30°00′S 40°00′E
25 R12 Natalia Texas, SW USA 29°11′N 98°51′W
67 W15 Natal Valley undersea feature SW Indian Ocean 31°00′S 33°15′E
Natanya see Netanya
143 O7 Naţanz Eşfahān, C Iran 33°31′N 51°55′E
13 Q11 Natashquan Québec, E Canada 50°10′N 61°50′W
13 Q10 Natashquan ⇝ Newfoundland and Labrador/Québec, E Canada
22 J7 Natchez Mississippi, S USA 31°34′N 91°24′W
22 G6 Natchitoches Louisiana, S USA 31°45′N 93°05′W
108 E10 Naters Valais, S Switzerland 46°22′N 08°00′E
Nathanya see Netanya
92 O3 Nathorst Land physical region W Svalbard
186 E9 National Capital District ◈ province S Papua New Guinea
35 U17 National City California, W USA 32°40′N 117°06′W
184 M10 National Park Manawatu-Wanganui, North Island, New Zealand 39°11′S 175°22′E
77 R14 Natitingou NW Benin 10°21′N 01°26′E
40 B5 Natividad, Isla island NW Mexico
165 Q10 Natori Miyagi, Honshū, C Japan 38°12′N 140°51′E
18 C14 Natrona Heights Pennsylvania, NE USA 40°37′N 79°42′W
81 H20 Natron, Lake ◎ Kenya/Tanzania
Natsrat see Natzrat
166 L7 Nattalin Bago, C Myanmar (Burma) 18°25′N 95°34′E
92 J12 Nattavaara Lapp. Nahtavárr. Norrbotten, N Sweden 66°45′N 20°58′E
109 S3 Natternbach Oberösterreich, N Austria 48°26′N 13°44′E
95 M22 Nättraby Blekinge, S Sweden 56°12′N 15°30′E
169 P10 Natuna Besar, Pulau island Kepulauan Natuna, W Indonesia
Natuna Islands see Natuna, Kepulauan
169 O9 Natuna, Kepulauan var. Natuna Islands. island group W Indonesia
21 N6 Natural Bridge tourist site Kentucky, C USA
173 V11 Naturaliste Fracture Zone tectonic feature E Indian Ocean
174 J10 Naturaliste Plateau undersea feature E Indian Ocean
138 G9 Natzrat var. Natsrat, Ar. En Nazira, Eng. Nazareth; prev. Nazerat. Northern, N Israel 32°42′N 35°18′E
Nau see Nov
103 O14 Naucelle Aveyron, S France 44°10′N 02°19′E
83 D20 Nauchas Hardap, C Namibia 23°40′S 16°19′E
108 K9 Nauders Tirol, W Austria 46°52′N 10°31′E
Naugard see Nowogard
9 O7 Naujaat prev. Repulse Bay. Nunavut, N Canada 66°35′N 86°20′W
118 F12 Naujamiestis Panevėžys, C Lithuania 55°42′N 24°10′E
118 E10 Naujoji Akmenė Šiaulai, NW Lithuania 56°20′N 22°57′E
149 R16 Naukot var. Naokot. Sindh, SE Pakistan 24°52′N 69°27′E
101 L16 Naumburg var. Naumburg an der Saale. Sachsen-Anhalt, C Germany 51°09′N 11°48′E
Naumburg am Queis see Nowogrodziec
Naumburg an der Saale see Naumburg
191 W15 Naunau ancient monument Easter Island, Chile, E Pacific Ocean
138 G10 Nā'ūr 'Ammān, W Jordan 31°52′N 35°50′E
189 Q8 Nauru off. Republic of Nauru; prev. Pleasant Island. ◆ republic W Pacific Ocean
175 P5 Nauru island W Pacific Ocean
189 Q9 Nauru International ✈ S Nauru
Nauru, Republic of see Nauru
Nausari see Navsāri
19 Q12 Nauset Beach beach Massachusetts, NE USA
Naushahra see Nowshera
149 P14 Naushahro Firoz Sindh, SE Pakistan 26°51′N 68°11′E
Naushara see Nowshera
187 X14 Nausori Viti Levu, W Fiji 18°01′S 178°31′E
56 F9 Nauta Loreto, N Peru 04°31′S 73°36′W
153 O12 Nautanwa Uttar Pradesh, N India 27°26′N 83°25′E
41 R13 Nautla Veracruz, E Mexico 20°15′N 96°45′W
Nauzad see Now Zād
41 N6 Nava Coahuila, NE Mexico 28°28′N 100°45′W
Navabad see Navobod
104 L6 Nava del Rey Castilla y León, N Spain 41°19′N 05°04′W
153 S15 Navadwīp prev. Nabadwip. West Bengal, NE India 23°24′N 88°23′E
104 M9 Navahermosa Castilla-La Mancha, C Spain 39°39′N 04°25′W
119 I16 Navahrudak Pol. Nowogródek, Rus. Novogrudok. Hrodzyenskaya Voblasts', W Belarus 53°36′N 25°50′E
119 I16 Navahrudskaye Wzvyshsha Rus. Novogrudskaya Vozvyshennost'. ▲ W Belarus
36 M8 Navajo Mount ▲ Utah, W USA 37°00′N 110°52′W
37 Q9 Navajo Reservoir ▣ New Mexico, SW USA
104 K9 Navalmoral de la Mata Extremadura, W Spain 39°54′N 05°33′W
104 K10 Navalvillar de Pelea Extremadura, W Spain 39°05′N 05°27′W
97 F17 Navan Ir. An Uaimh. E Ireland 53°39′N 06°41′W
Navanagar see Jāmnagar
118 L12 Navapolatsk Rus. Novopolotsk. Vitsyebskaya Voblasts', N Belarus 55°34′N 28°35′E
123 W6 Navarin, Mys headland NE Russia 62°18′N 179°06′E
63 I25 Navarino, Isla island S Chile
105 Q4 Navarra var. Comunidad Foral de Navarra, Eng./Fr. Navarre. ◈ autonomous community N Spain
Navarra, Comunidad Foral de see Navarra
Navarre see Navarra
105 P4 Navarrete La Rioja, N Spain 42°26′N 02°34′W
61 C20 Navarro Buenos Aires, E Argentina 35°00′S 59°15′W
105 O12 Navas de San Juan Andalucía, S Spain 38°11′N 03°19′W
25 V10 Navasota Texas, SW USA 30°23′N 96°05′W
25 U9 Navasota River ⇝ Texas, SW USA
44 I9 Navassa Island ◇ US unincorporated territory C West Indies
119 L19 Navasyolki Rus. Novosëlki. Homyel'skaya Voblasts', SE Belarus 52°24′N 28°33′E
119 H17 Navayel'nya Pol. Nowojelnia, Rus. Novoyel'nya. Hrodzyenskaya Voblasts', W Belarus 53°28′N 25°35′E
171 Y13 Naver Papua, E Indonesia 03°27′S 139°45′E
118 H5 Navesti ⇝ C Estonia
104 J2 Navia Asturias, N Spain 43°33′N 06°43′W
104 J2 Navia ⇝ NW Spain
59 I21 Naviraí Mato Grosso do Sul, SW Brazil 23°01′S 54°09′W
126 I6 Navlya Bryanskaya Oblast', W Russia 52°47′N 34°28′E
187 X13 Navoalevu Vanua Levu, N Fiji 16°22′S 179°28′E
147 R12 Navobod Rus. Navabad, Novabad. C Tajikistan 39°00′N 70°06′E
147 P13 Navobod Rus. Navabad. W Tajikistan 38°37′N 68°42′E
Navoi see Navoiy
146 M11 Navoiy Rus. Navoi. Navoiy Viloyati, C Uzbekistan 40°05′N 65°23′E
Navoiyskaya Oblast' see Navoiy Viloyati
146 K8 Navoiy Viloyati Rus. Navoiyskaya Oblast'. ◈ province N Uzbekistan
40 G7 Navojoa Sonora, NW Mexico 27°04′N 109°28′W
Navolat see Navolato
40 H9 Navolato var. Navolat. Sinaloa, C Mexico 24°46′N 107°42′W
187 Q13 Navonda Ambae, C Vanuatu 15°21′S 167°58′E
Návpaktos see Náfpaktos
Návplion see Náfplio
77 P14 Navrongo N Ghana 10°51′N 01°03′W
154 D12 Navsāri var. Nausari. Gujarāt, W India 20°55′N 72°55′E
187 X15 Navua Viti Levu, W Fiji 18°15′S 178°10′E
138 H8 Nawá Dar'ā, S Syria 32°53′N 36°03′E
Nawabashah see Nawābshāh
153 S14 Nawabganj Rajshahi, NW Bangladesh 24°35′N 88°21′E
153 S14 Nawābganj Uttar Pradesh, N India 26°52′N 82°09′E
149 Q15 Nawābshāh var. Nawabashah. Sindh, S Pakistan 26°15′N 68°26′E
153 P14 Nawāda Bihār, N India 24°54′N 85°33′E
152 H11 Nawalgarh Rājasthān, N India 27°48′N 75°21′E
Nawāl, Sabkhat an see Noual, Sebkhet en
149 P6 Nāwēr, Dasht-e desert C Afghanistan
167 N4 Nawnghkio var. Nawngkio. Shan State, C Myanmar (Burma) 22°17′N 96°50′E
Nawngkio see Nawnghkio
137 U13 Naxçıvan Rus. Nakhichevan'. SW Azerbaijan 39°14′N 45°24′E
160 I10 Naxi Sichuan, C China 28°50′N 105°20′E
115 K21 Náxos var. Naxos. Náxos, Kykládes, Greece, Aegean Sea 37°06′N 25°24′E
115 K21 Náxos island Kykládes, Greece, Aegean Sea
40 J11 Nayarit ◈ state C Mexico
187 Y14 Nayau island Lau Group, E Fiji
143 S8 Nāy Band Khorāsān-e Janūbī, E Iran 32°26′N 57°30′E
165 T2 Nayoro Hokkaidō, NE Japan 44°22′N 142°27′E
104 F9 Nazaré var. Nazare. Leiria, C Portugal 39°36′N 09°04′W
Nazare see Nazaré
24 M4 Nazareth Texas, SW USA 34°32′N 102°06′W
Nazareth see Natzrat
173 O8 Nazareth Bank undersea feature W Indian Ocean
40 K9 Nazas Durango, C Mexico 25°15′N 104°06′W
57 F16 Nazca Ica, S Peru 14°53′S 74°54′W
0 L17 Nazca Plate tectonic feature
193 U9 Nazca Ridge undersea feature E Pacific Ocean 22°00′S 82°00′W
165 V15 Naze var. Nase. Kagoshima, Amami-ōshima, SW Japan 28°21′N 129°30′E
Nazerat see Natzrat
137 R14 Nazik Gölü ◎ E Turkey
136 C15 Nazilli Aydın, SW Turkey 37°55′N 28°20′E
137 P14 Nazımiye Tunceli, E Turkey 39°12′N 39°51′E
Nazinon see Red Volta
10 L15 Nazko British Columbia, SW Canada 52°57′N 123°44′W
80 J13 Nazrēt var. Adama, Hadama. Oromīya, C Ethiopia 08°31′N 39°20′E
Nazwāh see Nizwa
82 J13 Nchanga Copperbelt, C Zambia 12°30′S 27°53′E
82 J11 Nchelenge Luapula, N Zambia 09°20′S 28°50′E
Ncheu see Ntcheu
83 J25 Nciba Eng. Great Kei; prev. Groot-Kei. ⇝ S South Africa
Ndaghamcha, Sebkra de see Te-n-Dghâmcha, Sebkhet
81 G21 Ndala Tabora, C Tanzania 04°45′S 33°15′E
82 B11 N'Dalatando Port. Salazar, Vila Salazar. Kwanza Norte, NW Angola 09°19′S 14°48′E
77 S14 Ndali C Benin 09°50′N 02°46′E
81 E18 Ndeke SW Uganda 0°11′S 30°04′E
78 J13 Ndélé Bamingui-Bangoran, N Central African Republic 08°24′N 20°41′E
79 E19 Ndendé Ngounié, S Gabon 02°21′S 11°20′E
79 E20 Ndindi Nyanga, S Gabon 03°47′S 11°06′E
78 G11 N'Djaména var. Ndjamena; prev. Fort-Lamy. ● (Chad) Ville de N'Djaména, W Chad 12°08′N 15°02′E
78 G11 N'Djaména ✈ Ville de N'Djaména, W Chad 12°09′N 15°00′E
Ndjamena see N'Djaména
79 D18 Ndjolé Moyen-Ogooué, W Gabon 0°07′S 10°45′E
82 J13 Ndola Copperbelt, C Zambia 12°59′S 28°35′E
Ndrhamcha, Sebkha de see Te-n-Dghâmcha, Sebkhet
79 L15 Ndu Orientale, N Dem. Rep. Congo 04°36′N 22°49′E
81 H21 Nduguti Singida, C Tanzania 04°19′S 34°40′E
186 M9 Nduindui Guadalcanal, C Solomon Islands 09°46′S 159°54′E
Nduke see Kolombangara
Ndzouani see Nzwani
115 F16 Néa Anchíalos var. Nea Anhialos, Néa Ankhíalos. Thessalía, C Greece 39°16′N 22°49′E
Nea Anhialos/Néa Ankhíalos see Néa Anchíalos
115 H18 Néa Artáki Évvoia, C Greece 38°31′N 23°39′E
97 F15 Neagh, Lough ◎ E Northern Ireland, United Kingdom
32 F7 Neah Bay Washington, NW USA 48°21′N 124°39′W
115 J22 Nea Kaméni island Kykládes, Greece, Aegean Sea
181 O8 Neale, Lake ◎ Northern Territory, C Australia
182 G2 Neales River seasonal river South Australia
115 G14 Néa Moudaniá var. Néa Moudhaniá. Kentrikí Makedonía, N Greece 40°14′N 23°17′E
Néa Moudhaniá see Néa Moudaniá
116 K10 Neamț ◈ county NE Romania
Neapel see Napoli
115 D14 Neápoli prev. Neápolis. Dytikí Makedonía, N Greece 40°19′N 21°23′E
115 K25 Neápoli Kríti, Greece, E Mediterranean Sea 35°15′N 25°37′E
115 G22 Neápoli Pelopónnisos, S Greece 36°29′N 23°05′E
Neápolis see Neápoli, Greece
Neapolis see Napoli, Italy
Neapolis see Nablus, West Bank
38 D16 Near Islands island group Aleutian Islands, Alaska, USA
97 J21 Neath S Wales, United Kingdom 51°40′N 03°48′W
114 H13 Néa Zíchni var. Néa Zíkhni; prev. Néa Zíkhna. Kentrikí Makedonía, NE Greece 41°02′N 23°50′E
Néa Zíkhna/Néa Zíkhni see Néa Zíchni
42 C5 Nebaj Quiché, W Guatemala 15°25′N 91°05′W
77 P13 Nebbou S Burkina Faso 11°22′N 01°49′W
Nebitdag see Balkanabat
54 M13 Neblina, Pico da ▲ NW Brazil 0°49′N 66°31′W
124 I13 Nebolchi Novgorodskaya Oblast', W Russia 59°08′N 33°19′E
36 L4 Nebo, Mount ▲ Utah, W USA 39°47′N 111°46′W
28 L14 Nebraska off. State of Nebraska, also known as Blackwater State, Cornhusker State, Tree Planters State. ◈ state C USA
29 S16 Nebraska City Nebraska, C USA 40°38′N 95°52′W
107 K23 Nebrodi, Monti var. Monti Caronie. ▲▲ Sicilia, Italy, C Mediterranean Sea
10 L14 Nechako ⇝ British Columbia, SW Canada
29 Q2 Neche North Dakota, N USA 48°57′N 97°33′W
25 V8 Neches Texas, SW USA 31°51′N 95°28′W
25 W8 Neches River ⇝ Texas, SW USA
101 H20 Neckar ⇝ SW Germany
101 H20 Neckarsulm Baden-Württemberg, SW Germany 49°12′N 09°13′E
192 L5 Necker Island island C British Virgin Islands
175 U3 Necker Ridge undersea feature N Pacific Ocean
61 D23 Necochea Buenos Aires, E Argentina 38°34′S 58°42′W
104 H2 Neda Galicia, NW Spain 43°29′N 08°09′W
115 E20 Néda var. Nédas. ⇝ S Greece
Nédas see Néda
25 Y11 Nederland Texas, SW USA 29°58′N 93°59′W
Nederland see Netherlands
98 K12 Neder Rijn Eng. Lower Rhine. ⇝ C Netherlands
99 L16 Nederweert Limburg, SE Netherlands 51°17′N 05°45′E
95 G16 Nedre Tokke ◎ S Norway
Nedrigaylov see Nedryhayliv
117 S3 Nedryhayliv Rus. Nedrigaylov. Sums'ka Oblast', NE Ukraine 50°51′N 33°54′E
98 O11 Neede Gelderland, E Netherlands 52°08′N 06°36′E
33 T13 Needle Mountain ▲ Wyoming, C USA 44°03′N 109°33′W
35 Y14 Needles California, W USA 34°50′N 114°37′W
97 M24 Needles, The rocks S England, United Kingdom
62 O7 Ñeembucú off. Departamento de Ñeembucú. ◈ department SW Paraguay
Ñeembucú, Departamento de see Ñeembucú
30 M7 Neenah Wisconsin, N USA 44°09′N 88°26′W
11 W16 Neepawa Manitoba, S Canada 50°14′N 99°29′W
99 K16 Neerpelt Limburg, NE Belgium 51°13′N 05°26′E
74 M6 Nefta ✈ W Tunisia 34°03′N 08°05′E
126 L15 Neftegorsk Krasnodarskiy Kray, SW Russia 44°21′N 39°40′E
127 U3 Neftekamsk Respublika Bashkortostan, W Russia 56°07′N 54°13′E
127 O14 Neftekumsk Stavropol'skiy Kray, SW Russia 44°45′N 45°00′E
Neftezavodsk see Seýdi
82 C10 Negage var. N'Gage. Uíge, NW Angola 07°47′S 15°27′E
Negapatam/Negapattinam see Nāgappattinam
169 T17 Negara Bali, Indonesia 08°21′S 114°35′E
169 T13 Negara Borneo, C Indonesia 02°40′S 115°05′E
Negara Brunei Darussalam see Brunei
31 N4 Negaunee Michigan, N USA 46°30′N 87°36′W
81 J15 Negēlē var. Negelli, It. Neghelli. Oromīya, C Ethiopia 05°13′N 39°43′E
Negelli see Negēlē
Negeri Pahang Darul Makmur see Pahang
Negeri Selangor Darul Ehsan see Selangor
168 K9 Negeri Sembilan var. Negri Sembilan. ◈ state Peninsular Malaysia
92 P3 Negerpynten headland S Svalbard 77°15′N 22°40′E
Negev see HaNegev
Neghelli see Negēlē
116 I12 Negoiu var. Negoiul. ▲ S Romania 45°34′N 24°34′E
Negoiul see Negoiu
82 P13 Negomane var. Negomano. Cabo Delgado, N Mozambique 11°22′S 38°32′E
Negomano see Negomane
155 J25 Negombo Western Province, SW Sri Lanka 07°13′N 79°51′E
191 W11 Negonego prev. Nengonengo. atoll Îles Tuamotu, C French Polynesia
Negoreloye see Nyeharelaye
112 P12 Negotin Serbia, E Serbia 44°14′N 22°31′E
113 P19 Negotino C Macedonia 41°29′N 22°04′E
56 A10 Negra, Punta headland NW Peru 06°03′S 81°08′W
104 G3 Negreira Galicia, NW Spain 42°54′N 08°46′W
116 L10 Negreşti Vaslui, E Romania 46°50′N 27°28′E
Negreşti see Negreşti-Oaş
116 H8 Negreşti-Oaş Hung. Avasfelsőfalu; prev. Negreşti. Satu Mare, NE Romania 47°56′N 23°22′E
44 H12 Negril W Jamaica 18°16′N 78°21′W
Negri Sembilan see Negeri Sembilan
63 K15 Negro, Río ⇝ E Argentina
62 N7 Negro, Río ⇝ NE Argentina
57 N17 Negro, Río ⇝ E Bolivia
48 F6 Negro, Río ⇝ N South America
61 E18 Negro, Río ⇝ Brazil/Uruguay
62 O5 Negro, Río ⇝ C Paraguay
Negro, Río see Chixoy, Río, Guatemala/Mexico
Negro, Río see Sico Tinto, Río, Honduras
171 P6 Negros island C Philippines
116 M15 Negru Vodă Constanţa, SE Romania 43°49′N 28°12′E
13 P13 Neguac New Brunswick, SE Canada 47°16′N 65°04′W
14 B7 Negwazu, Lake ◎ Ontario, S Canada
Négyfalu see Săcele
32 F10 Nehalem Oregon, NW USA 45°42′N 123°55′W
32 F10 Nehalem River ⇝ Oregon, NW USA
Nehavend see Nahāvand
143 V9 Nehbandān Khorāsān-e Jonūbī, E Iran 31°00′N 60°00′E
163 V6 Nehe Heilongjiang, NE China 48°28′N 124°52′E
193 Y14 Neiafu 'Uta Vava'u, N Tonga 18°36′S 173°58′W
45 N9 Neiba var. Neyba. SW Dominican Republic 18°31′N 71°25′W
Néid, Carn Uí see Mizen Head
92 M9 Neiden Finnmark, N Norway 69°41′N 29°23′E
Neidín see Kenmare
Néifinn see Nephin
103 S10 Neige, Crêt de la ▲ E France 46°18′N 05°58′E
173 O16 Neiges, Piton des ▲ C Réunion 21°05′S 55°28′E
15 R9 Neiges, Rivière des ⇝ Québec, SE Canada
160 I10 Neijiang Sichuan, C China 29°32′N 105°03′E
30 K6 Neillsville Wisconsin, N USA 44°34′N 90°36′W
Nei Monggol Zizhiqu/Nei Mongol see Nei Mongol Zizhiqu
163 Q10 Nei Mongol Gaoyuan plateau NE China
163 O12 Nei Mongol Zizhiqu var. Nei Mongol, Eng. Inner Mongolia, Inner Mongolian Autonomous Region; prev. Nei Monggol Zizhiqu. ◈ autonomous region N China
161 O4 Neiqiu Hebei, E China 37°22′N 114°34′E
Neiriz see Neyrīz
101 Q16 Neisse Pol. Nisa Cz. Lužická Nisa, Ger. Lausitzer Neisse, Nysa Łużycka. ⇝ C Europe
Neisse see Nysa
54 E11 Neiva Huila, S Colombia 02°58′N 75°15′W
160 M7 Neixiang Henan, C China 33°08′N 111°50′E
Nejafabad see Najafābād
11 V9 Nejanilini Lake ◎ Manitoba, C Canada
Nejd see Najd
80 I13 Nek'emtē var. Lakemti, Nakamti. Oromīya, C Ethiopia 09°06′N 36°31′E
126 M9 Nekhayevskaya Volgogradskaya Oblast', SW Russia 50°25′N 41°44′E
30 K7 Nekoosa Wisconsin, N USA 44°19′N 89°54′W
Neksø Bornholm see Nexø
104 H7 Nelas Viseu, N Portugal 40°32′N 07°52′W
124 H16 Nelidovo Tverskaya Oblast', W Russia 56°13′N 32°45′E
29 P13 Neligh Nebraska, C USA 42°07′N 98°01′W
123 R11 Nel'kan Khabarovskiy Kray, E Russia 57°44′N 136°09′E
92 M10 Nellim var. Nellimö, Lapp. Njellim. Lappi, N Finland 68°49′N 28°18′E
Nellimö see Nellim
155 J18 Nellore Andhra Pradesh, E India 14°29′N 80°E
61 B17 Nelson Santa Fe, C Argentina 31°16′S 60°45′W
11 O17 Nelson British Columbia, SW Canada 49°29′N 117°17′W
185 I14 Nelson Nelson, South Island, New Zealand 41°17′S 173°17′E
97 L17 Nelson NW England, United Kingdom 53°51′N 02°13′W
29 P17 Nelson Nebraska, C USA 40°12′N 98°04′W
185 J14 Nelson ◈ unitary authority South Island, New Zealand
11 X12 Nelson ⇝ Manitoba, C Canada
183 U8 Nelson Bay New South Wales, SE Australia 32°48′S 152°10′E
182 K13 Nelson, Cape headland Victoria, SE Australia 38°25′S 141°33′E
63 G23 Nelson, Estrecho strait SE Pacific Ocean
11 W12 Nelson House Manitoba, C Canada 55°49′N 98°51′W
30 J4 Nelson Lake ◎ Wisconsin, N USA
31 T14 Nelsonville Ohio, N USA 39°27′N 82°13′W
27 S2 Nelsoon River ⇝ Iowa/Missouri, C USA
83 K21 Nelspruit province capital Mpumalanga, NE South Africa 25°28′S 30°58′E
76 L10 Néma Hodh ech Chargui, SE Mauritania 16°32′N 07°12′W
118 D13 Neman Ger. Ragnit. Kaliningradskaya Oblast', W Russia 55°01′N 22°00′E
84 I9 Neman Bel. Nyoman, Ger. Memel, Lith. Nemunas, Pol. Niemen. ⇝ NE Europe
Nemausus see Nîmes
115 F19 Neméa Pelopónnisos, S Greece 37°49′N 22°40′E
Německý Brod see Havlíčkův Brod
14 D7 Nemegosenda ⇝ Ontario, S Canada
14 D8 Nemegosenda Lake ◎ Ontario, S Canada
119 H14 Nemenčinė Vilnius, SE Lithuania 54°50′N 25°29′E
Nemetocenna see Arras
Nemirov see Nemyriv
103 O6 Nemours Seine-et-Marne, N France 48°16′N 02°41′E
Nemunas see Neman
165 W4 Nemuro Hokkaidō, NE Japan 43°20′N 145°35′E
165 W4 Nemuro-hantō peninsula Hokkaidō, NE Japan
165 W3 Nemuro-kaikyō strait Japan/Russia
165 W4 Nemuro-wan bay N Japan
116 H5 Nemyriv Rus. Nemirov. L'vivs'ka Oblast', NW Ukraine 50°08′N 23°28′E
117 N7 Nemyriv Rus. Nemirov. Vinnyts'ka Oblast', C Ukraine 48°58′N 28°50′E
97 D19 Nenagh Ir. An tAonach. Tipperary, C Ireland 52°52′N 08°12′W
39 R9 Nenana Alaska, USA 64°33′N 149°05′W
39 R9 Nenana River ⇝ Alaska, USA
187 P10 Nendö var. Swallow Island. island Santa Cruz Islands, E Solomon Islands
97 O19 Nene ⇝ E England, United Kingdom
125 R4 Nenetskiy Avtonomnyy Okrug ◈ autonomous district Arkhangel'skaya Oblast', NW Russia
Nengonengo see Negonego
163 V6 Nenjiang Heilongjiang, NE China 49°11′N 125°18′E
163 U6 Nen Jiang var. Nonni. ⇝ NE China
189 P16 Neoch atoll Caroline Islands, C Micronesia
115 D18 Neochóri Dytikí Elláda, C Greece 38°23′N 21°14′E
27 Q7 Neodesha Kansas, C USA 37°25′N 95°40′W
29 S14 Neola Iowa, C USA 41°27′N 95°40′W
115 E16 Néo Monastíri var. Néon Monastiri. Thessalía, C Greece 39°22′N 21°55′E
Néon Karlovasi/Néon Karlovásion see Karlovási
Néon Monastiri see Néo Monastíri
27 R8 Neosho Missouri, C USA 36°53′N 94°24′W
27 Q7 Neosho River ⇝ Kansas/Oklahoma, C USA
123 N12 Nepa ⇝ C Russia
153 N10 Nepal off. Federal Democratic Republic of Nepal, Nep. Sanghīya Loktāntrik Ganatantra Nepāl. ◆ monarchy S Asia
Nepal, Federal Democratic Republic of see Nepal
152 M11 Nepālganj Mid Western, SW Nepal 28°04′N 81°37′E
Nepāl, Sanghīya Loktāntrik Ganatantra see Nepal
14 L13 Nepean Ontario, SE Canada 45°19′N 75°54′W
36 L4 Nephi Utah, W USA 39°43′N 111°50′W
97 B16 Nephin Ir. Néifinn. ▲ W Ireland 54°00′N 09°21′W
67 T9 Nepoko ⇝ NE Dem. Rep. Congo
18 K15 Neptune New Jersey, NE USA 40°10′N 74°03′W
182 G10 Neptune Islands island group South Australia
107 I14 Nera anc. Nar. ⇝ C Italy
102 L14 Nérac Lot-et-Garonne, SW France 44°08′N 00°21′E
111 D16 Neratovice Ger. Neratowitz. Středočeský Kraj, C Czechia 50°16′N 14°31′E
Neratowitz see Neratovice
123 O13 Nercha ⇝ S Russia
123 O13 Nerchinsk Zabaykal'skiy Kray, S Russia 52°01′N 116°25′E
123 P14 Nerchinskiy Zavod Zabaykal'skiy Kray, S Russia 51°13′N 119°25′E
124 M15 Nerekhta Kostromskaya Oblast', NW Russia 57°27′N 40°33′E
118 H10 Nereta S Latvia 56°12′N 25°18′E
106 K13 Nereto Abruzzo, C Italy 42°49′N 13°50′E
113 H15 Neretva ⇝ Bosnia and Herzegovina/Croatia
115 C17 Nerikós ruins Lefkáda, Iónia Nisiá, Greece, C Mediterranean Sea
83 F15 Neriquinha Kuando Kubango, SE Angola 15°44′S 21°34′E
118 I13 Neris Bel. Viliya, Pol. Wilia; prev. Pol. Wilja. ⇝ Belarus/Lithuania
Neris see Viliya
105 N15 Nerja Andalucía, S Spain 36°45′N 03°35′W
124 L16 Nerl' ⇝ W Russia
105 P12 Nerpio Castilla-La Mancha, C Spain 38°08′N 02°18′W
104 J13 Nerva Andalucía, S Spain 37°40′N 06°31′W
98 L4 Nes Fryslân, N Netherlands 53°28′N 05°46′E
94 G13 Nesbyen Buskerud, S Norway 60°36′N 09°35′E
Neshcherdo, Ozero see Nyeshcharda, Vozyera
92 L2 Neskaupstadur Austurland, E Iceland 65°08′N 13°45′W
92 F13 Nesna Nordland, C Norway 66°11′N 12°54′E
26 K5 Ness City Kansas, C USA 38°27′N 99°54′W
Nesselsdorf see Kopřivnice
108 H7 Nesslau Sankt Gallen, NE Switzerland 47°13′N 09°12′E
96 I9 Ness, Loch ◎ N Scotland, United Kingdom
Nesterov see Zhovkva
114 I12 Néstos Bul. Mesta, Turk. Kara Su. ⇝ Bulgaria/Greece see also Mesta
Néstos see Mesta
95 C14 Nesttun Hordaland, S Norway 60°19′N 05°16′E
Nesvizh see Nyasvizh
138 F9 Netanya var. Natanya, Nathanya. Central, C Israel 32°20′N 34°51′E
98 I9 Netherlands off. Kingdom of the Netherlands, var. Holland, Dut. Koninkrijk der Nederlanden, Nederland. ◆ monarchy NW Europe
Netherlands East Indies see Indonesia
Netherlands Guiana see Suriname
Netherlands, Kingdom of the see Netherlands
Netherlands New Guinea see Papua
116 L4 Netishyn Khmel'nyts'ka Oblast', W Ukraine 50°20′N 26°38′E
138 E11 Netivot Southern, S Israel 31°26′N 34°36′E
107 O21 Neto ⇝ S Italy
9 Q6 Nettilling Lake ◎ Baffin Island, Nunavut, N Canada
29 V3 Nett Lake ◎ Minnesota, N USA
107 I16 Nettuno Lazio, C Italy 41°27′N 12°40′E
Netum see Noto
41 U16 Netzahualcóyotl, Presa ▣ SE Mexico
Netze see Noteć
Neu Amerika see Puławy
Neubetsche see Novi Bečej
Neubidschow see Nový Bydžov
Neubistritz see Nová Bystřice
100 N9 Neubrandenburg Mecklenburg-Vorpommern, NE Germany 53°33′N 13°16′E
101 K22 Neuburg an der Donau Bayern, S Germany 48°43′N 11°10′E
108 C8 Neuchâtel Ger. Neuenburg. Neuchâtel, W Switzerland 46°59′N 06°55′E
108 C8 Neuchâtel Ger. Neuenburg. ◈ canton W Switzerland
108 C8 Neuchâtel, Lac de Ger. Neuenburger See. ◎ W Switzerland
Neudorf see Spišská Nová Ves
100 L10 Neue Elde canal N Germany
Neuenburg see Neuchâtel
Neuenburg an der Elbe see Nymburk
Neuenburger See see Neuchâtel, Lac de
108 F7 Neuenhof Aargau, N Switzerland 47°27′N 08°17′E
100 H11 Neuenland ✈ (Bremen) Bremen, NW Germany 53°03′N 08°46′E
Neuenstadt see La Neuveville
101 C18 Neuerburg Rheinland-Pfalz, W Germany 50°01′N 06°13′E
99 K24 Neufchâteau Luxembourg, SE Belgium 49°50′N 05°26′E
103 S6 Neufchâteau Vosges, NE France 48°21′N 05°42′E
102 M3 Neufchâtel-en-Bray Seine-Maritime, N France 49°44′N 01°26′E
109 S3 Neufelden Oberösterreich, N Austria 48°27′N 14°01′E
Neugradisk see Nova Gradiška
Neuhaus see Jindřichův Hradec
Neuhäusel see Nové Zámky
108 G6 Neuhausen var. Neuhausen am Rheinfall. Schaffhausen, N Switzerland 47°24′N 08°37′E
Neuhausen am Rheinfall see Neuhausen
101 I17 Neuhof Hessen, C Germany 50°26′N 09°34′E
Neuhof see Zgierz
Neukuhren see Pionerskiy
Neu-Langenburg see Tukuyu
109 W4 Neulengbach Niederösterreich, NE Austria 48°10′N 15°53′E
113 G15 Neum Federacija Bosne I Hercegovine, S Bosnia and Herzegovina 42°57′N 17°33′E
Neumark see Nowy Targ, Małopolskie, Poland
Neumark see Nowe Miasto Lubawskie, Warmińsko-Mazurskie, Poland
Neumarkt see Neumarkt im Hausruckkreis, Oberösterreich, Austria
Neumarkt see Neumarkt am Wallersee, Salzburg, Austria
Neumarkt see Środa Śląska, Dolnośląskie, Poland
Neumarkt see Târgu Secuiesc, Covasna, Romania
Neumarkt see Târgu Mureş
109 Q5 Neumarkt am Wallersee var. Neumarkt. Salzburg, NW Austria 47°55′N 13°16′E
109 R4 Neumarkt im Hausruckkreis var. Neumarkt. Oberösterreich, N Austria 48°16′N 13°40′E
101 L20 Neumarkt in der Oberpfalz Bayern, SE Germany 49°16′N 11°28′E
Neumarktl see Tržič
195 O1 Neumayer III research station (Germany) Antarctica 70°41′S 08°18′W
Neumoldowa see Moldova Nouă
100 J8 Neumünster Schleswig-Holstein, N Germany 54°04′N 09°59′E
109 X5 Neunkirchen var. Neunkirchen am Steinfeld. Niederösterreich, E Austria 47°44′N 16°05′E
101 E20 Neunkirchen Saarland, SW Germany 49°21′N 07°11′E
Neunkirchen am Steinfeld see Neunkirchen
Neuoderberg see Bohumín
63 I15 Neuquén Neuquén, SE Argentina 39°03′S 68°36′W
63 H14 Neuquén off. Provincia de Neuquén. ◈ province W Argentina
Neuquén, Provincia de see Neuquén
63 H14 Neuquén, Río ⇝ W Argentina
Neurode see Nowa Ruda
100 N11 Neuruppin Brandenburg, NE Germany 52°56′N 12°49′E
Neusalz an der Oder see Nowa Sól
Neu Sandec see Nowy Sącz
101 K22 Neusäss Bayern, S Germany 48°24′N 10°49′E
Neusatz see Novi Sad
Neuschliss see Gherla
21 N8 Neuse River ⇝ North Carolina, SE USA
109 Z5 Neusiedl am See Burgenland, E Austria 47°58′N 16°51′E
111 G22 Neusiedler See Hung. Fertő. ◎ Austria/Hungary
Neusohl see Banská Bystrica

◆ Country ● Country Capital ◇ Dependent Territory ○ Dependent Territory Capital ◈ Administrative Regions ✈ International Airport ▲ Mountain ▲▲ Mountain Range Volcano ⇝ River ◎ Lake ▣ Reservoir

NEUSS – NIKOPOL

101 D15 **Neuss** *anc.* Novaesium, Novesium. Nordrhein-Westfalen, W Germany 51°12′N 06°42′E
**Neuss** *see* Nyon
**Neustadt** *see* Neustadt an der Aisch, Bayern, Germany
**Neustadt** *see* Neustadt bei Coburg, Bayern, Germany
**Neustadt** *see* Prudnik, Opole, Poland
**Neustadt** *see* Baia Mare, Maramureș, Romania
100 I12 **Neustadt am Rübenberge** Niedersachsen, N Germany 52°30′N 09°28′E
101 J19 **Neustadt an der Aisch** *var.* Neustadt. Bayern, C Germany 49°34′N 10°36′E
**Neustadt an der Haardt** *see* Neustadt an der Weinstrasse
101 F20 **Neustadt an der Weinstrasse** *prev.* Neustadt an der Haardt, *hist.* Niewenstat; *anc.* Nova Civitas. Rheinland-Pfalz, SW Germany 49°21′N 08°09′E
101 K18 **Neustadt bei Coburg** *var.* Neustadt. Bayern, C Germany 50°19′N 11°06′E
**Neustadt bei Pinne** *see* Lwówek
**Neustadt in Oberschlesien** *see* Prudnik
**Neustadtl** *see* Novo mesto
**Neustadtl in Mähren** *see* Nové Město na Moravě
**Neustettin** *see* Szczecinek
108 M8 **Neustift im Stubaital** *var.* Stubaital. Tirol, W Austria 47°07′N 11°26′E
100 N10 **Neustrelitz** Mecklenburg-Vorpommern, NE Germany 53°22′N 13°05′E
**Neutitschein** *see* Nový Jičín
**Neutra** *see* Nitra
101 J22 **Neu-Ulm** Bayern, S Germany 48°23′N 10°02′E
**Neuveville** *see* La Neuveville
103 N12 **Neuvic** Corrèze, C France 45°23′N 02°16′E
**Neuwarp** *see* Nowe Warpno
100 G9 **Neuwerk** *island* NW Germany
101 E17 **Neuwied** Rheinland-Pfalz, W Germany 50°26′N 07°28′E
**Neuzen** *see* Terneuzen
124 H12 **Neva** ≈ NW Russia
29 V14 **Nevada** Iowa, C USA 42°01′N 93°27′W
27 R6 **Nevada** Missouri, C USA 37°51′N 94°22′W
35 R5 **Nevada** *off.* State of Nevada, *also known as* Battle Born State, Sagebrush State, Silver State. ◈ *state* W USA
35 P6 **Nevada City** California, W USA 39°15′N 121°02′W
105 O14 **NevadaSierra** ▲▲ S Spain
35 P6 **Nevada, Sierra** ▲▲ W USA
62 I13 **Nevado, Sierra del** ▲▲ W Argentina
124 G16 **Nevel'** Pskovskaya Oblast', W Russia 56°01′N 29°54′E
123 T14 **Nevel'sk** Ostrov Sakhalin, Sakhalinskaya Oblast', SE Russia 46°41′N 141°54′E
123 Q13 **Never** Amurskaya Oblast', SE Russia 53°58′N 124°04′E
127 Q6 **Neverkino** Penzenskaya Oblast', W Russia 52°53′N 46°46′E
103 P9 **Nevers** *anc.* Noviodunum. Nièvre, C France 47°N 03°09′E
18 J12 **Neversink River** ≈ New York, NE USA
183 Q6 **Nevertire** New South Wales, SE Australia 31°52′S 147°42′E
113 H15 **Nevesinje** ◈ Republika Srpska, S Bosnia and Herzegovina
118 G12 **Nevėžis** ≈ C Lithuania
138 F11 **Neve Zohar** *prev.* Newé Zohar. Southern, E Israel 31°07′N 35°23′E
126 M14 **Nevinnomyssk** Stavropol'skiy Kray, SW Russia 44°39′N 41°57′E
45 W10 **Nevis** *island* Saint Kitts and Nevis
**Nevoso, Monte** *see* Veliki Snežnik
**Nevrokop** *see* Gotse Delchev
136 J14 **Nevşehir** *var.* Nevshehr. Nevşehir, C Turkey 38°38′N 34°43′E
136 J14 **Nevşehir** *var.* Nevshehr. ◈ *province* C Turkey
**Nevshehr** *see* Nevşehir
122 G10 **Nev'yansk** Sverdlovskaya Oblast', C Russia 57°26′N 60°15′E
81 J25 **Newala** Mtwara, SE Tanzania 10°59′S 39°18′E
31 P16 **New Albany** Indiana, N USA 38°17′N 85°50′W
22 M2 **New Albany** Mississippi, S USA 34°29′N 89°00′W
29 Y11 **New Albin** Iowa, C USA 43°30′N 91°17′W
55 U8 **New Amsterdam** E Guyana 06°17′N 57°31′W
183 Q4 **New Angledool** New South Wales, SE Australia 29°06′S 147°54′E
21 Y2 **Newark** Delaware, NE USA 39°42′N 75°45′W
18 K14 **Newark** New Jersey, NE USA 40°42′N 74°12′W
18 G10 **Newark** New York, NE USA 43°01′N 77°04′W
31 T13 **Newark** Ohio, N USA 40°03′N 82°24′W
**Newark** *see* Newark-on-Trent
35 W5 **Newark Lake** ◎ Nevada, W USA
97 N18 **Newark-on-Trent** *var.* Newark. C England, United Kingdom 53°05′N 00°49′W
22 M7 **New Augusta** Mississippi, S USA 31°12′N 89°03′W
19 P12 **New Bedford** Massachusetts, NE USA 41°38′N 70°55′W
32 G11 **Newberg** Oregon, NW USA 45°18′N 122°58′W
21 X10 **New Bern** North Carolina, SE USA 35°05′N 77°04′W
20 F8 **Newbern** Tennessee, S USA 36°06′N 89°15′W
31 P4 **Newberry** Michigan, N USA 46°21′N 85°30′W
21 Q12 **Newberry** South Carolina, SE USA 34°17′N 81°39′W
18 F15 **New Bloomfield** Pennsylvania, NE USA 40°24′N 77°08′W
25 X5 **New Boston** Texas, SW USA 33°27′N 94°25′W
25 S11 **New Braunfels** Texas, SW USA 29°43′N 98°09′W
31 Q13 **New Bremen** Ohio, N USA 40°26′N 84°22′W
97 F18 **Newbridge** *Ir.* An Droichead Nua. Kildare, C Ireland 53°11′N 06°48′W
18 B14 **New Brighton** Pennsylvania, NE USA 40°44′N 80°18′W
18 M12 **New Britain** Connecticut, NE USA 41°37′N 72°45′W
186 G7 **New Britain** *island* E Papua New Guinea
192 I8 **New Britain Trench** *undersea feature* W Pacific Ocean
18 J15 **New Brunswick** New Jersey, NE USA 40°29′N 74°27′W
15 V8 **New Brunswick** *Fr.* Nouveau-Brunswick. ◈ *province* SE Canada
18 K13 **Newburgh** New York, NE USA 41°30′N 74°00′W
97 M22 **Newbury** S England, United Kingdom 51°25′N 01°20′W
19 P10 **Newburyport** Massachusetts, NE USA 42°49′N 70°53′W
77 T14 **New Bussa** Niger, W Nigeria 09°50′N 04°32′E
187 O17 **New Caledonia** *var.* Kanaky, *Fr.* Nouvelle-Calédonie. ◇ *French self-governing territory of special status* SW Pacific Ocean
187 O15 **New Caledonia** *island* SW Pacific Ocean
175 O10 **New Caledonia Basin** *undersea feature* W Pacific Ocean
183 T8 **Newcastle** New South Wales, SE Australia 32°55′S 151°46′E
13 O14 **Newcastle** New Brunswick, SE Canada 47°01′N 65°36′W
14 I15 **Newcastle** Ontario, SE Canada 43°55′N 78°35′W
83 K22 **Newcastle** KwaZulu/Natal, E South Africa 27°45′S 29°55′E
97 G16 **Newcastle** *Ir.* An Caisleán Nua. SE Northern Ireland, United Kingdom 54°12′N 05°54′W
31 P13 **New Castle** Indiana, N USA 39°56′N 85°21′W
20 L5 **New Castle** Kentucky, S USA 38°28′N 85°10′W
27 N11 **Newcastle** Oklahoma, C USA 35°15′N 97°36′W
18 B13 **New Castle** Pennsylvania, NE USA 41°00′N 80°22′W
25 R6 **Newcastle** Texas, SW USA 33°11′N 98°44′W
36 J7 **Newcastle** Utah, W USA 37°40′N 113°31′W
21 S6 **New Castle** Virginia, NE USA 37°31′N 80°09′W
33 Z13 **Newcastle** Wyoming, C USA 43°52′N 104°14′W
97 L14 **Newcastle** ✈ NE England, United Kingdom 55°03′N 01°42′W
**Newcastle** *see* Newcastle upon Tyne
97 L18 **Newcastle-under-Lyme** C England, United Kingdom 53°N 02°14′W
97 M14 **Newcastle upon Tyne** *var.* Newcastle, *hist.* Monkchester, *Lat.* Pons Aelii. NE England, United Kingdom 54°59′N 01°35′W
181 Q4 **Newcastle Waters** Northern Territory, N Australia 17°20′S 133°26′E
**Newchwang** *see* Yingkou
18 K13 **New City** New York, NE USA 41°08′N 73°57′W
31 U13 **Newcomerstown** Ohio, N USA 40°16′N 81°36′W
18 G15 **New Cumberland** Pennsylvania, NE USA 40°13′N 76°52′W
21 R1 **New Cumberland** West Virginia, NE USA 40°30′N 80°35′W
152 I10 **New Delhi** ● (India) Delhi, N India 28°35′N 77°15′E
11 O17 **New Denver** British Columbia, SW Canada 49°58′N 117°21′W
28 J9 **Newell** South Dakota, N USA 44°42′N 103°25′W
21 Q13 **New Ellenton** South Carolina, SE USA 33°25′N 81°41′W
22 J6 **Newellton** Louisiana, S USA 32°04′N 91°14′W
28 K6 **New England** North Dakota, N USA 46°32′N 102°52′W
19 P8 **New England** *cultural region* NE USA
**New England of the West** *see* Minnesota
183 U5 **New England Range** ▲▲ New South Wales, SE Australia
64 G9 **New England Seamounts** *var.* Bermuda-New England Seamount Arc. *undersea feature* W Atlantic Ocean 38°00′N 61°00′W
38 M14 **Newenham, Cape** *headland* Alaska, USA 58°39′N 162°10′W
**Newé Zohar** *see* Neve Zohar
18 D9 **Newfane** New York, NE USA 43°16′N 78°40′W
97 M23 **New Forest** *physical region* S England, United Kingdom
13 T12 **Newfoundland** *Fr.* Terre-Neuve. *island* Newfoundland and Labrador, SE Canada
13 R9 **Newfoundland and Labrador** *Fr.* Terre Neuve. ◈ *province* E Canada
65 J8 **Newfoundland Basin** *undersea feature* NW Atlantic Ocean 45°00′N 40°00′W
64 I8 **Newfoundland Ridge** *undersea feature* NW Atlantic Ocean
64 J8 **Newfoundland Seamounts** *undersea feature* N Sargasso Sea
18 G16 **New Freedom** Pennsylvania, NE USA 39°43′N 76°41′W
186 K9 **New Georgia** *island* New Georgia Islands, NW Solomon Islands
186 K8 **New Georgia Islands** *island group* NW Solomon Islands
186 L8 **New Georgia Sound** *var.* The Slot. *sound* E Solomon Sea
30 L9 **New Glarus** Wisconsin, N USA 42°50′N 89°38′W
13 Q15 **New Glasgow** Nova Scotia, SE Canada 45°36′N 62°38′W
**New Goa** *see* Panaji
186 A6 **New Guinea** *Dut.* Nieuw Guinea, *Ind.* Irian. *island* Indonesia/Papua New Guinea
192 H8 **New Guinea Trench** *undersea feature* SW Pacific Ocean
32 I6 **Newhalem** Washington, NW USA 48°40′N 121°18′W
39 P13 **Newhalen** Alaska, USA 59°43′N 154°54′W
29 X13 **Newhall** Iowa, C USA 42°00′N 91°58′W
14 F16 **New Hamburg** Ontario, S Canada 43°24′N 80°37′W
19 N9 **New Hampshire** *off.* State of New Hampshire, *also known as* Granite State. ◈ *state* NE USA
29 W12 **New Hampton** Iowa, C USA 43°03′N 92°19′W
186 G5 **New Hanover** *island* NE Papua New Guinea
97 P23 **Newhaven** SE England, United Kingdom 50°48′N 00°00′E
18 M13 **New Haven** Connecticut, NE USA 41°18′N 72°55′W
31 Q12 **New Haven** Indiana, N USA 41°02′N 84°59′W
27 W5 **New Haven** Missouri, C USA 38°34′N 91°15′W
10 K13 **New Hazelton** British Columbia, SW Canada 55°15′N 127°30′W
**New Hebrides** *see* Vanuatu
175 P9 **New Hebrides Trench** *undersea feature* N Coral Sea
18 H15 **New Holland** Pennsylvania, NE USA 40°06′N 76°05′W
22 I9 **New Iberia** Louisiana, S USA 30°00′N 91°51′W
186 G5 **New Ireland** ◈ *province* NE Papua New Guinea
186 G5 **New Ireland** *island* NE Papua New Guinea
65 A24 **New Island** *island* W Falkland Islands
18 J15 **New Jersey** *off.* State of New Jersey, *also known as* The Garden State. ◈ *state* NE USA
18 C14 **New Kensington** Pennsylvania, NE USA 40°33′N 79°45′W
21 W6 **New Kent** Virginia, NE USA 37°32′N 76°59′W
27 O8 **Newkirk** Oklahoma, C USA 36°54′N 97°03′W
21 Q9 **Newland** North Carolina, SE USA 36°04′N 81°50′W
28 L6 **New Leipzig** North Dakota, N USA 46°21′N 101°54′W
14 H9 **New Liskeard** Ontario, S Canada 47°31′N 79°41′W
22 G7 **Newllano** Louisiana, S USA 31°06′N 93°16′W
19 N13 **New London** Connecticut, NE USA 41°21′N 72°04′W
29 Y15 **New London** Iowa, C USA 40°55′N 91°24′W
29 T8 **New London** Minnesota, N USA 45°18′N 94°56′W
27 V3 **New London** Missouri, C USA 39°34′N 91°24′W
30 M7 **New London** Wisconsin, N USA 44°25′N 88°44′W
27 Y8 **New Madrid** Missouri, C USA 36°34′N 89°32′W
180 J8 **Newman** Western Australia 23°18′S 119°45′E
194 M13 **Newman Island** *island* Antarctica
14 H15 **Newmarket** Ontario, S Canada 44°03′N 79°27′W
97 P20 **Newmarket** E England, United Kingdom 52°18′N 00°28′E
19 P10 **Newmarket** New Hampshire, NE USA 43°04′N 70°53′W
21 U4 **New Market** Virginia, NE USA 38°39′N 78°40′W
21 R2 **New Martinsville** West Virginia, NE USA 39°39′N 80°52′W
31 U14 **New Matamoras** Ohio, N USA 39°32′N 81°04′W
32 M12 **New Meadows** Idaho, NW USA 44°57′N 116°16′W
26 R12 **New Mexico** *off.* State of New Mexico, *also known as* Land of Enchantment, Sunshine State. ◈ *state* SW USA
149 V6 **New Mirpur** *var.* Mirpur. Sindh, SE Pakistan 33°11′N 73°46′E
151 N15 **New Moore Island** *Island* E India
23 S4 **Newnan** Georgia, SE USA 33°22′N 84°48′W
183 P17 **New Norfolk** Tasmania, SE Australia 42°46′S 147°02′E
22 K9 **New Orleans** Louisiana, S USA 30°00′N 90°01′W
22 K9 **New Orleans** ✈ Louisiana, S USA 29°59′N 90°17′W
18 K12 **New Paltz** New York, NE USA 41°44′N 74°04′W
31 U12 **New Philadelphia** Ohio, N USA 40°29′N 81°27′W
184 K10 **New Plymouth** Taranaki, North Island, New Zealand 39°04′S 174°06′E
97 M24 **Newport** S England, United Kingdom 50°42′N 01°18′W
97 K22 **Newport** SE Wales, United Kingdom 51°35′N 03°W
27 W10 **Newport** Arkansas, C USA 35°36′N 91°16′W
31 N13 **Newport** Indiana, N USA 39°52′N 87°24′W
20 M3 **Newport** Kentucky, S USA 39°05′N 84°27′W
29 W9 **Newport** Minnesota, N USA 44°52′N 93°00′W
32 F12 **Newport** Oregon, NW USA 44°39′N 124°04′W
19 O13 **Newport** Rhode Island, NE USA 41°29′N 71°17′W
21 O9 **Newport** Tennessee, S USA 35°58′N 83°13′W
19 N6 **Newport** Vermont, NE USA 44°56′N 72°13′W
32 M7 **Newport** Washington, NW USA 48°08′N 117°05′W
21 X7 **Newport News** Virginia, NE USA 36°59′N 76°26′W
97 N20 **Newport Pagnell** SE England, United Kingdom 52°05′N 00°44′W
23 U12 **New Port Richey** Florida, SE USA 28°14′N 82°42′W
29 V9 **New Prague** Minnesota, N USA 44°32′N 93°34′W
44 H3 **New Providence** *island* N The Bahamas
97 I20 **New Quay** SW Wales, United Kingdom 52°13′N 04°22′W
97 H24 **Newquay** SW England, United Kingdom 50°27′N 05°03′W
29 V10 **New Richland** Minnesota, N USA 43°53′N 93°29′W
15 X7 **New-Richmond** Québec, SE Canada 48°12′N 65°52′W
31 R15 **New Richmond** Ohio, N USA 38°57′N 84°16′W
30 I5 **New Richmond** Wisconsin, N USA 45°09′N 92°31′W
42 G1 **New River** ≈ N Belize
55 T12 **New River** ≈ SE Guyana
21 R6 **New River** ≈ West Virginia, NE USA
42 G1 **New River Lagoon** ◎ N Belize
22 J8 **New Roads** Louisiana, S USA 30°42′N 91°26′W
18 L14 **New Rochelle** New York, NE USA 40°55′N 73°44′W
29 O4 **New Rockford** North Dakota, N USA 47°40′N 99°08′W
97 P23 **New Romney** SE England, United Kingdom 50°58′N 00°56′E
97 F20 **New Ross** *Ir.* Ros Mhic Thriúin. Wexford, SE Ireland 52°24′N 06°56′W
97 F16 **Newry** *Ir.* An tIúr. SE Northern Ireland, United Kingdom 54°11′N 06°20′W
28 M5 **New Salem** North Dakota, N USA 46°51′N 101°24′W
**New Sarum** *see* Salisbury
29 W14 **New Sharon** Iowa, C USA 41°28′N 92°39′W
**New Siberian Islands** *see* Novosibirskiye Ostrova
23 X11 **New Smyrna Beach** Florida, SE USA 29°01′N 80°55′W
183 O7 **New South Wales** ◈ *state* SE Australia
39 O13 **New Stuyahok** Alaska, USA 59°27′N 157°18′W
21 N8 **New Tazewell** Tennessee, S USA 36°26′N 83°36′W
152 K9 **New Tehri** *prev.* Tehri. Uttarākhand, N India 30°12′N 78°29′E
38 M12 **Newtok** Alaska, USA 60°56′N 164°37′W
23 S7 **Newton** Georgia, SE USA 31°18′N 84°20′W
29 W14 **Newton** Iowa, C USA 41°42′N 93°03′W
27 N6 **Newton** Kansas, C USA 38°02′N 97°22′W
19 O11 **Newton** Massachusetts, NE USA 42°19′N 71°10′W
22 M5 **Newton** Mississippi, S USA 32°19′N 89°09′W
18 J14 **Newton** New Jersey, NE USA 41°03′N 74°45′W
21 R9 **Newton** North Carolina, SE USA 35°42′N 81°14′W
25 Y9 **Newton** Texas, SW USA 30°51′N 93°45′W
97 J24 **Newton Abbot** SW England, United Kingdom 50°33′N 03°34′W
96 K13 **Newton St Boswells** SE Scotland, United Kingdom 55°34′N 02°40′W
97 I14 **Newton Stewart** S Scotland, United Kingdom 54°58′N 04°30′W
92 O2 **Newtontoppen** ▲ C Svalbard 78°57′N 17°34′E
97 J20 **Newtown** E Wales, United Kingdom 52°32′N 03°19′W
28 K3 **New Town** North Dakota, N USA 47°58′N 102°30′W
97 G15 **Newtownabbey** *Ir.* Baile na Mainistreach. E Northern Ireland, United Kingdom 54°40′N 05°57′W
97 G15 **Newtownards** *Ir.* Baile Nua na hArda. SE Northern Ireland, United Kingdom 54°36′N 05°41′W
29 U10 **New Ulm** Minnesota, N USA 44°20′N 94°28′W
28 K10 **New Underwood** South Dakota, N USA 44°05′N 102°46′W
25 V10 **New Waverly** Texas, SW USA 30°32′N 95°28′W
18 K14 **New York** New York, NE USA 40°45′N 73°57′W
18 G10 **New York** ◈ *state* NE USA
35 X13 **New York Mountains** ▲▲ California, W USA
184 K12 **New Zealand** ◆ *commonwealth republic* SW Pacific Ocean
95 M24 **Nexø** *var.* Neksø Bornholm. E Denmark 55°04′N 15°09′E
125 O15 **Neya** Kostromskaya Oblast', NW Russia 58°19′N 43°51′E
**Neyba** *see* Neiba
143 Q12 **Neyrīz** *var.* Neiriz, Niriz. Fārs, S Iran 29°14′N 54°18′E
143 T4 **Neyshābūr** *var.* Nishapur. Khorāsān-Razavī, NE Iran 36°15′N 58°47′E
155 J21 **Neyveli** Tamil Nādu, SE India 11°36′N 79°26′E
**Nezhin** *see* Nizhyn
33 N10 **Nezperce** Idaho, NW USA 46°14′N 116°15′W
22 H8 **Nezpique, Bayou** ≈ Louisiana, S USA
77 Y13 **Ngadda** ≈ NE Nigeria
**N'Gage** *see* Negage
185 G16 **Ngahere** West Coast, South Island, New Zealand 42°22′S 171°29′E
77 Z12 **Ngala** Borno, NE Nigeria 12°19′N 14°11′E
83 G17 **Ngamiland** ◈ *district* NW Botswana
158 K16 **Ngamring** Xizang Zizhiqu, W China 29°16′N 87°10′E
81 K19 **Ngangerabeli Plain** *plain* SE Kenya
158 I14 **Ngangla Ringco** ◎ W China
158 H13 **Nganglong Kangri** ▲ W China 32°55′N 81°00′E
158 K15 **Ngangzê Co** ◎ W China
79 F14 **Ngaoundéré** *var.* N'Gaoundéré. Adamaoua, N Cameroon 07°20′N 13°35′E
**N'Gaoundéré** *see* Ngaoundéré
81 E20 **Ngara** Kagera, NW Tanzania 02°30′S 30°40′E
188 F8 **Ngardmau Bay** *bay* Babeldaob, N Palau
188 F7 **Ngaregur** *island* Palau Islands, N Palau
**Ngarrab** *see* Gyaca
184 L7 **Ngaruawahia** Waikato, North Island, New Zealand 37°41′S 175°10′E
184 N11 **Ngaruroro** ≈ North Island, New Zealand
190 I16 **Ngatangiia** Rarotonga, S Cook Islands 21°14′S 159°44′W
184 M6 **Ngatea** Waikato, North Island, New Zealand 37°16′S 175°29′E
166 L8 **Ngathainggyaung** Ayeyarwady, SW Myanmar (Burma) 17°22′N 95°04′E
**Ngatik** *see* Ngetik Atoll
**Ngau** *see* Gau
**Ngawa** *see* Aba
172 G12 **Ngazidja** *Fr.* Grande Comore, *var.* Njazidja. *island* NW Comoros
188 C7 **Ngcheangel** *var.* Kayangel Islands. *island* Palau Islands, N Palau
188 E10 **Ngchemiangel** Babeldaob, N Palau
188 C8 **Ngeaur** *var.* Angaur. *island* Palau Islands, S Palau
188 E10 **Ngerkeai** Babeldaob, N Palau
188 F9 **Ngermechau** Babeldaob, N Palau 07°35′N 134°39′E
188 C8 **Ngeruktabel** *prev.* Urukthapel. *island* Palau Islands, S Palau
188 C8 **Ngerulmud** ● (Palau) Babeldaob, N Palau 07°30′N 134°35′E
188 F8 **Ngetbong** Babeldaob, N Palau 07°37′N 134°35′E
189 T17 **Ngetik Atoll** *var.* Ngatik; *prev.* Los Jardines. *atoll* Caroline Islands, E Micronesia
188 E10 **Ngetkip** Babeldaob, N Palau
**Nghia Dan** *see* Thai Hoa
**N'Giva** *see* Ondjiva
79 G20 **Ngo** Plateaux, SE Congo 02°28′S 15°43′E
167 S7 **Ngoc Lặc** Thanh Hoa, N Vietnam 20°06′N 105°21′E
79 G17 **Ngoko** ≈ Cameroon/Congo
81 H19 **Ngorengore** Narok, SW Kenya 01°01′S 35°26′E
159 Q11 **Ngoring Hu** ◎ C China
**Ngorolaka** *see* Banifing
81 H20 **Ngorongoro Crater** *crater* N Tanzania
79 D19 **Ngounié** *off.* Province de la Ngounié, *var.* La Ngounié. ◈ *province* S Gabon
79 D19 **Ngounié** ≈ Congo/Gabon
**Ngounié, Province de la** *see* Ngounié
78 H10 **Ngoura** *var.* NGoura. Hadjer-Lamis, W Chad 12°52′N 16°27′E
**NGoura** *see* Ngoura
78 G10 **Ngouri** *var.* NGouri; *prev.* Fort-Millot. Lac, W Chad 13°42′N 15°19′E
**NGouri** *see* Ngouri
77 Y10 **Ngourti** Diffa, E Niger 15°22′N 13°13′E
77 Y11 **Nguigmi** *var.* N'Guigmi. Diffa, SE Niger 14°17′N 13°07′E
**N'Guigmi** *see* Nguigmi
**Nguimbo** *see* Lumbala N'Guimbo
188 F15 **Ngulu Atoll** *atoll* Caroline Islands, W Micronesia
187 R14 **Nguna** *island* C Vanuatu
**N'Gunza** *see* Sumbe
169 U17 **Ngurah Rai** ✈ (Bali) Bali, S Indonesia 8°40′S 115°14′E
77 W12 **Nguru** Yobe, NE Nigeria 12°55′N 10°31′E
**Ngwaketze** *see* Southern
83 I16 **Ngweze** ≈ S Zambia
83 M17 **Nhamatanda** Sofala, C Mozambique 19°16′S 34°10′E
58 G12 **Nhamundá, Rio** *var.* Jamundá, Yamundá. ≈ N Brazil
60 J7 **Nhandeara** São Paulo, S Brazil 20°40′S 50°03′W
82 D12 **Nharêa** *var.* N'Harea, Nhareia. Bié, W Angola 11°38′S 16°58′E
**N'Harea** *see* Nharêa
**Nhareia** *see* Nharêa
167 V12 **Nha Trang** Khanh Hoa, S Vietnam 12°15′N 109°10′E
182 L11 **Nhill** Victoria, SE Australia 36°21′S 141°38′E
83 L22 **Nhlangano** *prev.* Goedgegun. SW Eswatini 27°06′S 31°12′E
181 S1 **Nhulunbuy** Northern Territory, N Australia 12°16′S 136°46′E
77 N10 **Niafounké** Tombouctou, W Mali 15°54′N 03°58′W
31 N5 **Niagara** Wisconsin, N USA 45°45′N 87°57′W
14 H16 **Niagara** ≈ Ontario, S Canada
14 G15 **Niagara Escarpment** *hill range* Ontario, S Canada
14 H16 **Niagara Falls** Ontario, S Canada 43°05′N 79°06′W
18 D9 **Niagara Falls** New York, NE USA 43°06′N 79°04′W
14 H16 **Niagara Falls** *waterfall* Canada/USA
76 K12 **Niagassola** *var.* Nyagassola. Haute-Guinée, NE Guinea 12°24′N 09°03′W
77 R12 **Niamey** ● (Niger) Niamey, SW Niger 13°28′N 02°03′E
77 R12 **Niamey** ✈ Niamey, SW Niger 13°28′N 02°14′E
77 R14 **Niamtougou** N Togo 09°50′N 01°08′E
79 O16 **Niangara** Orientale, NE Dem. Rep. Congo 03°45′N 27°54′E
77 O10 **Niangay, Lac** ◎ E Mali
77 N14 **Niangoloko** SW Burkina Faso 10°15′N 04°53′W
27 U6 **Niangua River** ≈ Missouri, C USA
79 O17 **Nia-Nia** Orientale, NE Dem. Rep. Congo 01°26′N 27°38′E
19 N13 **Niantic** Connecticut, NE USA 41°19′N 72°11′W
163 U7 **Nianzishan** Heilongjiang, NE China 47°31′N 122°53′E
79 E20 **Niari** ◈ *department* SW Congo
168 H10 **Nias, Pulau** *island* W Indonesia
82 O13 **Niassa** *off.* Província do Niassa. ◈ *province* N Mozambique
**Niassa, Província do** *see* Niassa
191 U10 **Niau** *island* Îles Tuamotu, C French Polynesia
95 G20 **Nibe** Nordjylland, N Denmark 56°59′N 09°39′E
189 Q8 **Nibok** N Nauru 0°31′S 166°55′E
118 C10 **Nica** W Latvia 56°21′N 21°03′E
**Nicaea** *see* Nice
42 J9 **Nicaragua** *off.* Republic of Nicaragua. ◆ *republic* Central America
42 K11 **Nicaragua, Lago de** *var.* Cocibolca, Gran Lago, *Eng.* Lake Nicaragua. ◎ S Nicaragua
**Nicaragua, Lake** *see* Nicaragua, Lago de
64 D11 **Nicaraguan Rise** *undersea feature* NW Caribbean Sea 16°00′N 80°00′W
**Nicaragua, Republic of** *see* Nicaragua
**Nicaria** *see* Ikaría
107 N21 **Nicastro** Calabria, SW Italy 38°59′N 16°20′E
103 V15 **Nice** *It.* Nizza; *anc.* Nicaea. Alpes-Maritimes, SE France 43°43′N 07°13′E
**Nice** *see* Côte d'Azur
**Nicephorium** *see* Ar Raqqah
12 M9 **Nichicun, Lac** ◎ Québec, E Canada
164 D16 **Nichinan** *var.* Nitinan. Miyazaki, Kyūshū, SW Japan 31°36′N 131°23′E
44 E4 **Nicholas Channel** *channel* N Cuba
**Nicholas II Land** *see* Severnaya Zemlya
149 U2 **Nicholas Range** *Pash.* Selselehye Kuhe Vākhān, *Taj.* Qatorkŭhi Vakhon. ▲▲ Afghanistan/Tajikistan
20 M6 **Nicholasville** Kentucky, S USA 37°52′N 84°34′W
44 G2 **Nicholls Town** Andros Island, NW The Bahamas 25°07′N 78°01′W
21 U12 **Nichols** South Carolina, SE USA 34°13′N 79°09′W
55 U9 **Nickerie** ◈ *district* NW Suriname
55 V9 **Nickerie Rivier** ≈ NW Suriname
151 P22 **Nicobar Islands** *island group* India, E Indian Ocean
116 L9 **Nicolae Bălcescu** Botoşani, NE Romania 47°33′N 26°52′E
15 P11 **Nicolet** Québec, SE Canada 46°13′N 72°37′W
15 Q12 **Nicolet** ≈ Québec, SE Canada
31 Q4 **Nicolet, Lake** ◎ Michigan, N USA
29 U10 **Nicollet** Minnesota, N USA 44°16′N 94°11′W
61 F19 **Nico Pérez** Florida, S Uruguay 33°30′S 55°10′W
**Nicopolis** *see* Nikopol, Bulgaria
**Nicopolis** *see* Nikópoli, Greece
121 P2 **Nicosia** *Gk.* Lefkosía, *Turk.* Lefkoşa. ● (Cyprus) C Cyprus 35°10′N 33°23′E
107 K24 **Nicosia** Sicilia, Italy, C Mediterranean Sea 37°45′N 14°24′E
107 N22 **Nicotera** Calabria, SW Italy 38°33′N 15°55′E
42 K13 **Nicoya** Guanacaste, W Costa Rica 10°09′N 85°26′W
42 L14 **Nicoya, Golfo de** *gulf* W Costa Rica
42 L14 **Nicoya, Península de** *peninsula* NW Costa Rica
**Nictheroy** *see* Niterói
118 B12 **Nida** *Ger.* Nidden. Klaipėda, SW Lithuania 55°20′N 21°00′E
111 L15 **Nida** ≈ S Poland
**Nidaros** *see* Trondheim
108 D8 **Nidau** Bern, W Switzerland 47°07′N 07°15′E
101 H17 **Nidda** ≈ W Germany
**Nidden** *see* Nida
95 F17 **Nidelva** ≈ S Norway
108 F9 **Nidwalden** ◈ *canton* C Switzerland
110 L9 **Nidzica** *Ger.* Niedenburg. Warmińsko-Mazurskie, NE Poland 53°22′N 20°27′E
100 H6 **Niebüll** Schleswig-Holstein, N Germany 54°47′N 08°51′E
**Niedenburg** *see* Nidzica
99 N25 **Niederanven** Luxembourg, C Luxembourg 49°39′N 06°15′E
103 V4 **Niederbronn-les-Bains** Bas-Rhin, NE France 48°57′N 07°37′E
**Niederdonau** *see* Niederösterreich
109 S7 **Niedere Tauern** ▲▲ C Austria
101 P14 **Niederlausitz** *Eng.* Lower Lusatia, *Lus.* Donja Łužica. *physical region* E Germany
109 U5 **Niederösterreich** *off.* Land Niederösterreich, *Eng.* Lower Austria, *Ger.* Niederdonau; *prev.* Lower Danube. ◈ *state* NE Austria
**Niederösterreich, Land** *see* Niederösterreich
100 G12 **Niedersachsen** *Eng.* Lower Saxony, *Fr.* Basse-Saxe. ◈ *state* NW Germany
79 D17 **Niefang** *var.* Sevilla de Niefang. Río Muni, NW Equatorial Guinea 01°52′N 10°12′E
83 G23 **Niekerkshoop** Northern Cape, W South Africa 29°21′S 22°49′E
99 G17 **Niel** Antwerpen, N Belgium 51°07′N 04°20′E
**Niélé** *see* Niellé
76 M14 **Niellé** *var.* Niélé. N Ivory Coast 10°12′N 05°38′W
79 O22 **Niemba** Katanga, E Dem. Rep. Congo 05°58′S 28°24′E
111 G15 **Niemcza** *Ger.* Nimptsch. Dolnośląskie, SW Poland 50°45′N 16°52′E
**Niemen** *see* Neman
92 J13 **Niemisel** Norrbotten, N Sweden 66°00′N 22°00′E
111 H15 **Niemodlin** *Ger.* Falkenberg. Opolskie, SW Poland 50°37′N 17°45′E
76 M13 **Niéna** Sikasso, SW Mali 11°24′N 06°20′W
100 H12 **Nienburg** Niedersachsen, N Germany 52°37′N 09°12′E
100 N13 **Nieplitz** ≈ NE Germany
111 L16 **Niepołomice** Małopolskie, S Poland 50°02′N 20°12′E
101 D14 **Niers** ≈ Germany/Netherlands
101 Q15 **Niesky** *Lus.* Niska. Sachsen, E Germany 51°16′N 14°49′E
**Nieśwież** *see* Nyasvizh
**Nieuport** *see* Nieuwpoort
98 O8 **Nieuw-Amsterdam** Drenthe, NE Netherlands 52°43′N 06°52′E
55 W9 **Nieuw Amsterdam** Commewijne, NE Suriname 05°53′N 55°05′W
99 M14 **Nieuw-Bergen** Limburg, SE Netherlands 51°36′N 06°04′E
98 O7 **Nieuw-Buinen** Drenthe, NE Netherlands 52°57′N 06°55′E
98 J12 **Nieuwegein** Utrecht, C Netherlands 52°03′N 05°06′E
98 P6 **Nieuwe Pekela** Groningen, NE Netherlands 53°04′N 06°58′E
98 P5 **Nieuweschans** Groningen, NE Netherlands 53°10′N 07°10′E
**Nieuw Guinea** *see* New Guinea
98 I11 **Nieuwkoop** Zuid-Holland, C Netherlands 52°09′N 04°46′E
98 M9 **Nieuwleusen** Overijssel, S Netherlands 52°34′N 06°16′E
98 J11 **Nieuw-Loosdrecht** Noord-Holland, C Netherlands 52°12′N 05°08′E
55 U9 **Nieuw Nickerie** Nickerie, NW Suriname 05°56′N 57°W
98 P5 **Nieuwolda** Groningen, NE Netherlands 53°15′N 06°58′E
99 B17 **Nieuwpoort** *var.* Nieuport. West-Vlaanderen , W Belgium 51°08′N 02°45′E
99 G14 **Nieuw-Vossemeer** Noord-Brabant, S Netherlands 51°34′N 04°13′E
98 P7 **Nieuw-Weerdinge** Drenthe, NE Netherlands 52°51′N 07°00′E
40 L10 **Nieves** Zacatecas, C Mexico 24°00′N 102°57′W
64 O11 **Nieves, Pico de las** ▲ Gran Canaria, Islas Canarias, Spain, NE Atlantic Ocean 27°58′N 15°34′W
103 P8 **Nièvre** ◈ *department* C France
**Niewenstat** *see* Neustadt an der Weinstrasse
136 J15 **Niğde** Niğde, C Turkey 37°58′N 34°42′E
136 J15 **Niğde** ◈ *province* C Turkey
83 J21 **Nigel** Gauteng, NE South Africa 26°25′S 28°28′E
77 V10 **Niger** *off.* Republic of Niger, *Fr.* République du Niger. ◆ *republic* W Africa
77 T14 **Niger** ◈ *state* C Nigeria
67 P8 **Niger** ≈ W Africa
**Niger Cone** *see* Niger Fan
67 P9 **Niger Delta** *delta* S Nigeria
67 P9 **Niger Fan** *var.* Niger Cone. *undersea feature* E Atlantic Ocean 04°15′N 05°00′E
77 T13 **Nigeria** *off.* Federal Republic of Nigeria. ◆ *federal republic* W Africa
**Nigeria, Federal Republic of** *see* Nigeria
77 T17 **Niger, Mouths of the** *delta* S Nigeria
**Niger, Republic of** *see* Niger
**Niger, République du** *see* Niger
185 C24 **Nightcaps** Southland, South Island, New Zealand 45°58′S 168°03′E
14 F7 **Night Hawk Lake** ◎ Ontario, S Canada
65 M19 **Nightingale Island** *island* S Tristan da Cunha, S Atlantic Ocean
38 M12 **Nightmute** Alaska, USA 60°28′N 164°43′W
114 G13 **Nigríta** Kentrikí Makedonía, NE Greece 40°54′N 23°29′E
148 J15 **Nihing** *Per.* Rūd-e Nahang. ≈ Iran/Pakistan
191 V10 **Nihiru** *atoll* Îles Tuamotu, C French Polynesia
**Nihommatsu** *see* Nihonmatsu
**Nihon** *see* Japan
165 P11 **Nihonmatsu** *var.* Nihommatsu, Nihonmatu. Fukushima, Honshū, C Japan 37°34′N 140°25′E
**Nihonmatu** *see* Nihonmatsu
62 I12 **Nihuil, Embalse del** ◎ W Argentina
165 O10 **Niigata** Niigata, Honshū, C Japan 37°55′N 139°01′E
165 O11 **Niigata** *off.* Niigata-ken. ◈ *prefecture* Honshū, C Japan
**Niigata-ken** *see* Niigata
165 G14 **Niihama** Ehime, Shikoku, SW Japan 33°57′N 133°15′E
38 A8 **Ni'ihau** *var.* Niihau. *island* Hawai'i, USA, C Pacific Ocean
165 X12 **Nii-jima** *island* E Japan
165 H12 **Niimi** Okayama, Honshū, SW Japan 35°00′N 133°27′E
165 O10 **Niitsu** *var.* Niitu. Niigata, Honshū, C Japan 37°48′N 139°09′E
**Niitu** *see* Niitsu
105 P15 **Níjar** Andalucía, S Spain 36°57′N 02°13′W
98 K11 **Nijkerk** Gelderland, C Netherlands 52°13′N 05°30′E
99 H16 **Nijlen** Antwerpen, N Belgium 51°10′N 04°40′E
98 L13 **Nijmegen** *Ger.* Nimwegen; *anc.* Noviomagus. Gelderland, SE Netherlands 51°50′N 05°52′E
98 N10 **Nijverdal** Overijssel, E Netherlands 52°22′N 06°28′E
190 G16 **Nikao** Rarotonga, S Cook Islands
**Nikaria** *see* Ikaría
124 I2 **Nikel'** *Finn.* Kolosjoki. Murmanskaya Oblast', NW Russia 69°25′N 30°12′E
171 Q17 **Nikiniki** Timor, S Indonesia 10°S 124°30′E
129 Q15 **Nikitin Seamount** *undersea feature* E Indian Ocean 05°48′S 84°48′E
77 S14 **Nikki** E Benin 09°55′N 03°12′E
**Niklasmarkt** *see* Gheorgheni
39 P10 **Nikolai** Alaska, USA 63°00′N 154°22′W
**Nikolaiken** *see* Mikołajki
**Nikolainkaupunki** *see* Vaasa
**Nikolayev** *see* Mykolayiv
145 O6 **Nikolayevka** Severnyy Kazakhstan, N Kazakhstan
**Nikolayevka** *see* Zhetigen
127 P9 **Nikolayevsk** Volgogradskaya Oblast', SW Russia 50°03′N 45°30′E
**Nikolayevskaya Oblast'** *see* Mykolayivs'ka Oblast'
123 S12 **Nikolayevsk-na-Amure** Khabarovskiy Kray, SE Russia 53°04′N 140°39′E
127 P6 **Nikol'sk** Penzenskaya Oblast', W Russia 53°46′N 46°03′E
125 O13 **Nikol'sk** Vologodskaya Oblast', NW Russia 59°35′N 45°31′E
**Nikol'sk** *see* Ussuriysk
117 W9 **Nikol's'ke** *prev.* Volodars'ke. Donets'ka Oblast', E Ukraine 47°11′N 37°19′E
38 K17 **Nikolski** Umnak Island, Alaska, USA 52°56′N 168°52′W
**Nikol'skiy** *see* Satpayev
127 V7 **Nikol'skoye** Orenburgskaya Oblast', W Russia 52°01′N 55°48′E
**Nikol'sk-Ussuriyskiy** *see* Ussuriysk
114 J7 **Nikopol** *anc.* Nicopolis. Pleven, N Bulgaria 43°43′N 24°55′E



◆ Country ● Country Capital ◇ Dependent Territory ○ Dependent Territory Capital ◈ Administrative Regions ✈ International Airport ▲ Mountain ▲▲ Mountain Range ⋀ Volcano ≈ River ◎ Lake ▣ Reservoir

NIKOPOL' – NORTHERN COOK ISLANDS


117 S9 Nikopol' Dnipropetrovs'ka Oblast', SE Ukraine 47°34'N 34°23'E
115 C17 Nikópoli anc. Nicopolis. site of ancient city Ípeiros, W Greece
136 M12 Niksar Tokat, N Turkey 40°35'N 36°59'E
143 V14 Nikshahr Sīstān va Balūchestān, SE Iran 26°15'N 60°10'E
113 J16 Nikšić C Montenegro 42°47'N 18°56'E
191 R4 Nikumaroro; prev. Gardner Island. atoll Phoenix Islands, C Kiribati
191 P3 Nikunau var. Nukunau; prev. Byron Island. atoll Tungaru, W Kiribati
155 G21 Nilambūr Kerala, SW India 11°17'N 76°15'E
35 X16 Niland California, W USA 33°14'N 115°31'W
80 G8 Nile former province NW Uganda
67 T3 Nile Ar. Nahr an Nil. ≈ N Africa
75 W7 Nile Delta delta N Egypt
67 T3 Nile Fan undersea feature E Mediterranean Sea 33°00'N 31°00'E
31 O11 Niles Michigan, N USA 41°49'N 86°15'W
31 V11 Niles Ohio, N USA 41°10'N 80°46'W
155 F20 Nileswaram Kerala, SW India 12°18'N 75°07'E
14 K10 Nilgaut, Lac ◎ Québec, SE Canada
149 O6 Nīlī Dāykundī, C Afghanistan 33°43'N 66°07'E
158 I5 Nilka Xinjiang Uygur Zizhiqu, NW China 43°46'N 82°33'E
Nīl, Nahr an see Nile
93 N16 Nilsiä Pohjois-Savo, C Finland 63°13'N 28°00'E
154 F9 Nīmach Madhya Pradesh, C India 24°27'N 74°56'E
152 G14 Nimbāhera Rājasthān, N India 24°38'N 74°45'E
76 L15 Nimba, Monts var. Nimba Mountains. ▲ W Africa
Nimba Mountains see Nimba, Monts
Nimburg see Nymburk
103 Q15 Nîmes anc. Nemausus, Nismes. Gard, S France 43°49'N 04°20'E
152 H11 Nīm ka Thāna Rājasthān, N India 27°42'N 75°50'E
183 R11 Nimmitabel New South Wales, SE Australia 36°34'S 149°18'E
Nimptsch see Niemcza
195 R11 Nimrod Glacier glacier Antarctica
148 K8 Nīmrōz var. Nimroze; prev. Chakhānsūr, Nīmrūz. ◆ province SW Afghanistan
Nimroze see Nīmrōz
Nīmrūz see Nīmrōz
81 F16 Nimule Eastern Equatoria, S South Sudan 03°35'N 32°03'E
Nimwegen see Nijmegen
139 Q3 Nīnawá off. Muḩāfaz at Nīnawá, var. Al Mawşil, Nineveh. ◆ governorate NW Iraq
Nīnawá, Muḩāfaz at see Nīnawá
155 C23 Nine Degree Channel channel India/Maldives
18 G9 Ninemile Point headland New York, NE USA 43°31'N 76°22'W
173 S8 Ninetyeast Ridge undersea feature E Indian Ocean 04°00'S 90°00'E
183 P13 Ninety Mile Beach beach Victoria, SE Australia
184 I2 Ninety Mile Beach beach North Island, New Zealand
21 P12 Ninety Six South Carolina, SE USA 34°10'N 82°01'W
Nineveh see Nīnawá
163 Y9 Ning'an Heilongjiang, NE China 44°20'N 129°28'E
161 S9 Ningbo var. Ning-po, Yin-hsien; prev. Ninghsien. Zhejiang, SE China 29°54'N 121°33'E
161 U12 Ningde Fujian, SE China 26°48'N 119°33'E
161 P12 Ningdu var. Meijiang. Jiangxi, S China 26°28'N 115°53'E
Ning'er see Pu'er
186 A7 Ningerum Western, SW Papua New Guinea 05°40'S 141°10'E
161 R9 Ningguo Anhui, E China 30°33'N 118°58'E
161 S9 Ninghai Zhejiang, SE China 29°18'N 121°26'E
Ning-hsia see Ningxia
Ninghsien see Ningbo
160 J15 Ningming var. Chengzhong. Guangxi Zhuangzu Zizhiqu, S China 22°07'N 106°43'E
160 H11 Ningnan var. Pisha. Sichuan, C China 26°59'N 102°49'E
Ning-po see Ningbo
Ningsia/Ningsia Hui/Ningsia Hui Autonomous Region see Ningxia
160 J5 Ningxia off. Ningxia Huizu Zizhiqu, var. Ning-hsia, Ningsia, Eng. Ningsia Hui, Ningsia Hui Autonomous Region. ◆ autonomous region N China
Ningxia Huizu Zizhiqu see Ningxia
159 X10 Ningxian var. Xinning. Gansu, N China 35°30'N 108°05'E
167 T7 Ninh Binh Ninh Bình, N Vietnam 20°14'N 106°00'E
167 V12 Ninh Hoa Khanh Hoa, S Vietnam 12°28'N 109°07'E
186 C4 Ninigo Group island group N Papua New Guinea
39 Q12 Ninilchik Alaska, USA 60°03'N 151°40'W
27 N7 Ninnescah River ≈ Kansas, C USA
195 U16 Ninnis Glacier glacier Antarctica
165 R8 Ninohe Iwate, Honshū, C Japan 40°16'N 141°18'E
99 F18 Ninove Oost-Vlaanderen, C Belgium 50°50'N 04°02'E
171 O4 Ninoy Aquino ✈ (Manila) Luzon, N Philippines 14°26'N 121°00'E
Nio see Íos
29 P12 Niobrara Nebraska, C USA 42°43'N 97°59'W
28 M12 Niobrara River ≈ Nebraska/Wyoming, C USA
79 I20 Nioki Bandundu, W Dem. Rep. Congo 02°44'S 17°42'E
76 M11 Niono Ségou, C Mali 14°18'N 05°59'W
76 K11 Nioro var. Nioro du Sahel. Kayes, W Mali 15°13'N 09°39'W
76 G11 Nioro du Rip SW Senegal 13°44'N 15°48'W
Nioro du Sahel see Nioro
102 K10 Niort Deux-Sèvres, W France 46°21'N 00°25'W
172 H14 Nioumachoua Mohéli, S Comoros 12°21'S 43°43'E
186 C7 Nipa Southern Highlands, W Papua New Guinea 06°11'S 143°27'E
11 U14 Nipawin Saskatchewan, S Canada 52°23'N 104°01'W
12 D12 Nipigon Ontario, S Canada 49°02'N 88°15'W
12 D11 Nipigon, Lake ◎ Ontario, S Canada
11 S13 Nipin ≈ Saskatchewan, C Canada
14 G11 Nipissing, Lake ◎ Ontario, S Canada
35 P13 Nipomo California, W USA 35°02'N 120°28'W
Nippon see Japan
138 K6 Niqniqīyah, Jabal an ▲ C Syria
62 I9 Niquivil San Juan, W Argentina 30°25'S 68°42'W
171 Y13 Nirabotong Papua, E Indonesia 02°35'S 140°08'E
Niriz see Neyrīz
163 U7 Nirji var. Morin Dawa Daurzu Zizhiqi. Nei Mongol Zizhiqu, N China 48°21'N 124°32'E
155 I14 Nirmal Telangana, C India 19°04'N 78°21'E
153 Q13 Nirmāli Bihār, NE India 26°18'N 86°35'E
113 O14 Niš Eng. Nish, Ger. Nisch; anc. Naissus. Serbia, SE Serbia 43°21'N 21°53'E
104 H9 Nisa Portalegre, C Portugal 39°31'N 07°39'W
Nisa see Neisse
141 P4 Nişab Al Ḩudūd ash Shamālīyah, N Saudi Arabia 29°11'N 44°43'E
141 Q15 Nişāb var. Anşāb. SW Yemen 14°24'N 46°47'E
113 P14 Nišava Bul. Nishava. ≈ Bulgaria/Serbia see also Nishava
Nišava see Nishava
107 K25 Niscemi Sicilia, Italy, C Mediterranean Sea 37°09'N 14°23'E
Nisch/Nish see Niš
165 R4 Niseko Hokkaidō, NE Japan 42°50'N 140°43'E
Nishapur see Neyshābūr
114 G9 Nishava var. Nišava. ≈ Bulgaria/Serbia see also Nišava
Nishava see Nišava
118 L11 Nishcha ≈ N Belarus
165 C17 Nishinoomote Kagoshima, Tanega-shima, SW Japan 30°42'N 130°59'E
165 X15 Nishino-shima Eng. Rosario. island Ogasawara-shotō, SE Japan
165 I13 Nishiwaki var. Nisiwaki. Hyōgo, Honshū, SW Japan 34°59'N 134°58'E
141 U14 Nishtūn SE Yemen 15°47'N 52°08'E
Nisibin see Nusaybin
Nisiros see Nísyros
Nisiwaki see Nishiwaki
Niska see Niesky
113 O14 Niška Banja Serbia, SE Serbia 43°18'N 22°01'E
12 D6 Niskibi ≈ Ontario, C Canada
111 O15 Nisko Podkrapackie, SE Poland 50°31'N 22°09'E
10 H7 Nisling ≈ Yukon, W Canada
99 H22 Nismes Namur, S Belgium 50°04'N 04°31'E
Nismes see Nîmes
116 M10 Nisporeni Rus. Nisporeny. W Moldova 47°04'N 28°10'E
Nisporeny see Nisporeni
95 K20 Nissan ≈ S Sweden
Nissan Islands see Green Islands
95 F16 Nisser ◎ S Norway
95 E21 Nissum Bredning inlet NW Denmark
29 U6 Nisswa Minnesota, N USA 46°31'N 94°17'W
Nistru see Dniester
115 M22 Nísyros var. Nisiros. island Dodekánisa, Greece, Aegean Sea
118 H8 Nītaure C Latvia 57°05'N 25°12'E
60 P10 Niterói prev. Nictheroy. Rio de Janeiro, SE Brazil 22°54'S 43°06'W
14 F16 Nith ≈ Ontario, S Canada
96 J13 Nith ≈ S Scotland, United Kingdom
Nitinan see Nichinan
111 I21 Nitra Ger. Neutra, Hung. Nyitra. Nitriansky Kraj, SW Slovakia 48°20'N 18°05'E
111 I20 Nitra Ger. Neutra, Hung. Nyitra. ≈ W Slovakia
111 I21 Nitriansky Kraj ◆ region SW Slovakia
21 Q5 Nitro West Virginia, NE USA 38°24'N 81°50'W
Niuatobutabu see Niuatoputapu
193 X13 Niuatoputapu var. Niuatobutabu; prev. Keppel Island. island N Tonga
193 U15 Niu'Aunofa headland Tongatapu, S Tonga 21°03'S 175°19'W
Niuchwang see Yingkou
190 B16 Niue ◇ self-governing entity in free association with New Zealand S Pacific Ocean
190 F10 Niulakita var. Nurakita. atoll S Tuvalu
190 E6 Niutao atoll NW Tuvalu
93 L15 Nivala Pohjois-Pohjanmaa, C Finland 63°56'N 25°00'E
102 I15 Nive ≈ SW France
99 G19 Nivelles Walloon Brabant, C Belgium 50°36'N 04°04'E
103 P8 Nivernais cultural region C France
15 N8 Niverville, Lac ◎ Québec, SE Canada
27 T7 Nixa Missouri, C USA 37°02'N 93°17'W
35 R5 Nixon Nevada, W USA 39°48'N 119°24'W
25 S12 Nixon Texas, SW USA 29°16'N 97°45'W
Niya see Minfeng
Niyazov see Nyýazow
155 H14 Nizāmābād Telangana, C India 18°40'N 78°05'E
155 H15 Nizām Sāgar ◎ C India
125 N16 Nizhegorodskaya Oblast' ◆ province W Russia
Nizhnegorskiy see Nyzhn'ohirs'kyy
127 S4 Nizhnekamsk Respublika Tatarstan, W Russia 55°36'N 51°45'E
127 U3 Nizhnekamskoye Vodokhranilishche ⊠ W Russia
123 S14 Nizhneleninskoye Yevreyskaya Avtonomnaya Oblast', SE Russia 47°50'N 132°30'E
122 L13 Nizhneudinsk Irkutskaya Oblast', S Russia 54°48'N 98°51'E
122 I10 Nizhnevartovsk Khanty-Mansiyskiy Avtonomnyy Okrug-Yugra, C Russia 60°57'N 76°40'E
123 Q7 Nizhneyansk Respublika Sakha (Yakutiya), NE Russia 71°25'N 135°59'E
127 Q11 Nizhniy Baskunchak Astrakhanskaya Oblast', SW Russia 48°15'N 46°49'E
127 O6 Nizhniy Lomov Penzenskaya Oblast', W Russia 53°32'N 43°39'E
127 P3 Nizhniy Novgorod prev. Gor'kiy. Nizhegorodskaya Oblast', W Russia 56°17'N 44°E
125 T8 Nizhniy Odes Respublika Komi, NW Russia 63°42'N 54°59'E
Nizhniy Pyandzh see Panji Poyon
122 G10 Nizhniy Tagil Sverdlovskaya Oblast', C Russia 57°57'N 59°51'E
125 T9 Nizhnyaya-Omra Respublika Komi, NW Russia 62°46'N 55°54'E
125 P5 Nizhnyaya Pësha Nenetskiy Avtonomnyy Okrug, NW Russia 66°54'N 47°37'E
117 Q3 Nizhyn Rus. Nezhin. Chernihivs'ka Oblast', NE Ukraine 51°03'N 31°54'E
136 M17 Nizip Gaziantep, S Turkey 37°02'N 37°47'E
141 X8 Nizwa var. Nazwāh. NE Oman 23°00'N 57°50'E
Nizza see Nice
106 C9 Nizza Monferrato Piemonte, NE Italy 44°47'N 08°22'E
Njávdám see Näätämöjoki
Njazidja see Ngazidja
Njellim see Nellim
81 H24 Njombe Njombe, S Tanzania 09°20'S 34°47'E
81 G23 Njombe ≈ C Tanzania
Njuk, Ozero see Nyuk, Ozero
Njuksenica see Nyuksenitsa
92 I10 Njunis ▲ N Norway 68°47'N 19°24'E
Njurunda see Njurundabommen
93 H17 Njurundabommen prev. Njurunda. Västernorrland, C Sweden 62°15'N 17°24'E
94 N11 Njutånger Gävleborg, C Sweden 61°37'N 17°04'E
79 D14 Nkambe Nord-Ouest, NW Cameroon 06°35'N 10°44'E
Nkata Bay see Nkhata Bay
79 F21 Nkayi prev. Jacob. Bouenza, S Congo 04°11'S 13°17'E
83 J17 Nkayi Matabeleland North, W Zimbabwe 19°00'S 28°54'E
82 N13 Nkhata Bay var. Nkata Bay. Northern, N Malawi 11°37'S 34°20'E
81 E22 Nkonde Kigoma, N Tanzania 06°16'S 30°17'E
79 D15 Nkongsamba var. N'Kongsamba. Littoral, W Cameroon 04°59'N 09°53'E
N'Kongsamba see Nkongsamba
83 E16 Nkurenkuru Kavango West, N Namibia 17°38'S 18°39'E
77 Q15 Nkwanta E Ghana 08°18'N 00°27'E
167 O2 Nmai Hka var. Me Hka. ≈ N Myanmar (Burma)
Noardwâlde see Noordwolde
39 N7 Noatak Alaska, USA 67°34'N 162°58'W
39 N7 Noatak River ≈ Alaska, USA
164 E15 Nobeoka Miyazaki, Kyūshū, SW Japan 32°34'N 131°37'E
27 N11 Noble Oklahoma, C USA 35°08'N 97°23'W
31 P13 Noblesville Indiana, N USA 40°03'N 86°00'W
165 R5 Noboribetsu var. Noboribetu. Hokkaidō, NE Japan 42°27'N 141°08'E
Noboribetu see Noboribetsu
59 H18 Nobres Mato Grosso, W Brazil 14°44'S 56°15'W
107 N21 Nocera Terinese Calabria, S Italy 39°03'N 16°10'E
41 Q16 Nochixtlán var. Asunción Nochixtlán. Oaxaca, SE Mexico 17°29'N 97°17'W
25 S5 Nocona Texas, SW USA 33°47'N 97°43'W
63 K21 Nodales, Bahía de los bay S Argentina
27 Q2 Nodaway River ≈ Iowa/Missouri, C USA
27 R8 Noel Missouri, C USA 36°33'N 94°29'W
40 H3 Nogales Chihuahua, NW Mexico 18°50'N 97°12'W
40 F3 Nogales Sonora, NW Mexico 31°17'N 110°53'W
36 M17 Nogales Arizona, SW USA 31°20'N 110°55'W
Nogal Valley see Dooxo Nugaaleed
102 K15 Nogaro Gers, S France 43°46'N 00°01'W
110 J7 Nogat ≈ N Poland
164 D12 Nōgata Fukuoka, Kyūshū, SW Japan 33°46'N 130°42'E
127 P15 Nogayskaya Step' steppe SW Russia
102 M6 Nogent-le-Rotrou Eure-et-Loir, C France 48°19'N 00°50'E
103 O4 Nogent-sur-Oise Oise, N France 49°16'N 02°28'E
103 P6 Nogent-sur-Seine Aube, N France 48°30'N 03°31'E
122 L10 Noginsk Krasnoyarskiy Kray, N Russia 64°28'N 91°09'E
126 L3 Noginsk Moskovskaya Oblast', W Russia 55°51'N 38°23'E
123 T12 Nogliki Ostrov Sakhalin, Sakhalinskaya Oblast', SE Russia 51°44'N 143°14'E
164 K12 Nōgōhaku-san ▲ Honshū, SW Japan 35°46'N 136°30'E
162 D5 Nogoonnuur Bayan-Ölgiy, NW Mongolia 49°31'N 89°48'E
61 C18 Nogoyá Entre Ríos, E Argentina 32°25'S 59°50'W
111 K21 Nógrád off. Nógrád Megye. ◆ county N Hungary
Nógrád Megye see Nógrád
105 U5 Noguera Pallaresa ≈ NE Spain
105 U4 Noguera Ribagorçana ≈ NE Spain
101 E19 Nohfelden Saarland, SW Germany 49°35'N 07°08'E
38 A8 Nohili Point headland Kaua'i, Hawai'i, USA 22°03'N 159°48'W
104 G3 Noia Galicia, NW Spain 42°48'N 08°52'W
103 N16 Noire, Montagne ▲ S France
15 P12 Noire, Rivière ≈ Québec, SE Canada
14 J10 Noire, Rivière ≈ Québec, SE Canada
Noire, Rivi`ere see Black River
102 G6 Noires, Montagnes ▲ NW France
102 H8 Noirmoutier-en-l'Île Vendée, NW France 47°00'N 02°15'W
102 H8 Noirmoutier, Île de island NW France
187 Q10 Noka Nendö, E Solomon Islands 10°42'S 165°57'E
83 G17 Nokaneng Ngamiland, NW Botswana 19°40'S 22°12'E
93 L18 Nokia Pirkanmaa, W Finland 61°29'N 23°30'E
148 K11 Nok Kundi Baluchistān, SW Pakistan 28°49'N 62°39'E
30 L14 Nokomis Illinois, N USA 39°18'N 89°17'W
30 K5 Nokomis, Lake ⊠ Wisconsin, N USA
78 G9 Nokou Kanem, W Chad 14°36'N 14°45'E
187 Q12 Nokuku Espiritu Santo, W Vanuatu 14°56'S 166°34'E
95 J18 Nol Västra Götaland, S Sweden 57°55'N 12°03'E
79 H16 Nola Sangha-Mbaéré, SW Central African Republic 03°29'N 16°05'E
25 P7 Nolan Texas, SW USA 32°15'N 100°15'W
125 R15 Nolinsk Kirovskaya Oblast', NW Russia 57°35'N 49°54'E
Nolsø see Nólsoy
95 B19 Nólsoy Dan. Nolsø. island E Faeroe Islands
186 B7 Nomad Western, SW Papua New Guinea 06°11'S 142°13'E
164 B16 Noma-zaki Kyūshū, SW Japan
40 K10 Nombre de Dios Durango, C Mexico 23°51'N 104°14'W
42 I5 Nombre de Dios, Cordillera ▲▲ N Honduras
38 M9 Nome Alaska, USA 64°30'N 165°24'W
29 Q6 Nome North Dakota, N USA 46°39'N 97°49'W
38 M9 Nome, Cape headland Alaska, USA 64°25'N 165°00'W
162 K11 Nomgon var. Sangiyn Dalay. Ömnögovĭ, S Mongolia 42°50'N 105°04'E
14 M11 Nominingue, Lac ◎ Québec, SE Canada
Nomoi Islands see Mortlock Islands
164 B16 Nomo-zaki headland Kyūshū, SW Japan 32°34'N 129°45'E
162 G6 Nömrög var. Hödrögö. Dzavhan, N Mongolia 48°51'N 96°48'E
193 X15 Nomuka island Nomuka Group, C Tonga
193 X15 Nomuka Group island group W Tonga
189 Q15 Nomwin Atoll atoll Hall Islands, C Micronesia
8 L10 Nonacho Lake ◎ Northwest Territories, NW Canada
Nondaburi see Nonthaburi
39 P12 Nondalton Alaska, USA 59°58'N 154°51'W
163 V10 Nong'an Jilin, NE China 44°25'N 125°10'E
169 P10 Nong Bua Khok Nakhon Ratchasima, C Thailand 15°23'N 101°51'E
167 Q9 Nong Bua Lamphu Udon Thani, E Thailand 17°11'N 102°27'E
167 R7 Nông Hèt Xiangkhoang, N Laos 19°27'N 104°02'E
Nongkaya see Nong Khai
167 Q8 Nong Khai var. Mi Chai, Nongkaya. Nong Khai, E Thailand 17°52'N 102°44'E
Nongle see Jiuzhaigou
167 N14 Nong Met Surat Thani, SW Thailand 09°27'N 99°09'E
83 L22 Nongoma KwaZulu/Natal, E South Africa 27°54'S 31°40'E
167 P9 Nong Phai Phetchabun, C Thailand 15°58'N 101°02'E
153 U13 Nongstoin Meghālaya, NE India 25°24'N 91°19'E
83 C19 Nonidas Erongo, N Namibia 22°36'S 14°40'E
Nonni see Nen Jiang
40 I7 Nonoava Chihuahua, N Mexico 27°24'N 106°18'W
191 O3 Nonouti prev. Sydenham Island. atoll Tungaru, W Kiribati
167 O11 Nonthaburi var. Nondaburi, Nontha Buri. Nonthaburi, C Thailand 13°48'N 100°11'E
Nontha Buri see Nonthaburi
102 L11 Nontron Dordogne, SW France 45°34'N 00°41'E
147 T10 Nookat var. Iski-Naukat; prev. Eski-Nookat. Oshskaya Oblast', SW Kyrgyzstan 40°18'N 72°29'E
181 P1 Noonamah Northern Territory, N Australia 12°46'S 131°08'E
28 K2 Noonan North Dakota, N USA 48°51'N 102°57'W
Noonu see South Miladhunmadulu Atoll
99 E14 Noord-Beveland var. North Beveland. island SW Netherlands
99 J14 Noord-Brabant Eng. North Brabant. ◆ province S Netherlands
98 H7 Noorder Haaks spit NW Netherlands
98 H9 Noord-Holland Eng. North Holland. ◆ province NW Netherlands
Noordhollandsch Kanaal see Noordhollands Kanaal
98 H8 Noordhollands Kanaal var. Noordhollandsch Kanaal. canal NW Netherlands
Noord-Kaap see Northern Cape
98 L8 Noordoostpolder island N Netherlands
45 P16 Noordpunt headland N Curaçao 12°21'N 69°08'W
98 I8 Noord-Scharwoude Noord-Holland, NW Netherlands 52°42'N 04°48'E
Noordwes see North-West
98 G11 Noordwijk aan Zee Zuid-Holland, W Netherlands 52°15'N 04°25'E
98 H11 Noordwijkerhout Zuid-Holland, W Netherlands 52°16'N 04°30'E
98 M7 Noordwolde Fris. Noardwâlde. Fryslân, N Netherlands 52°54'N 06°10'E
Noordzee see North Sea
98 H10 Noordzee-Kanaal canal NW Netherlands
93 K18 Noormarkku Swe. Normark. Satakunta, SW Finland 61°35'N 21°54'E
39 N8 Noorvik Alaska, USA 66°50'N 161°01'W
10 J17 Nootka Sound inlet British Columbia, W Canada
82 A9 Nóqui Zaire Province, NW Angola 05°54'S 13°30'E
95 L15 Nora Örebro, C Sweden 59°31'N 15°02'E
147 Q13 Norak Rus. Nurek. W Tajikistan 38°23'N 69°14'E
13 I13 Noranda Québec, SE Canada 48°16'N 79°03'W
29 W12 Nora Springs Iowa, C USA 43°08'N 93°00'W
95 M14 Norberg Västmanland, C Sweden 60°04'N 15°56'E
14 K13 Norcan Lake ◎ Ontario, SE Canada
197 R12 Nord N Greenland 81°38'N 12°51'W
78 F13 Nord Eng. North. ◆ region N Cameroon
103 P2 Nord ◆ department N France
92 P1 Nordaustlandet island NE Svalbard
95 G24 Nordborg Ger. Nordburg. Syddanmark, SW Denmark 55°04'N 09°41'E
Nordburg see Nordborg
95 F23 Nordby Syddtjylland, W Denmark 55°27'N 08°25'E
11 P15 Nordegg Alberta, SW Canada 52°27'N 116°06'W
100 E9 Norden Niedersachsen, NW Germany 53°36'N 07°12'E
100 G10 Nordenham Niedersachsen, NW Germany 53°30'N 08°29'E
122 M6 Nordenshel'da, Arkhipelag island group N Russia
92 O3 Nordenskiold Land physical region W Svalbard
100 E9 Norderney island NW Germany
100 J9 Norderstedt Schleswig-Holstein, N Germany 53°42'N 09°59'E
94 D11 Nordfjord fjord S Norway
94 C11 Nordfjord physical region S Norway
94 D11 Nordfjordeid Sogn og Fjordane, S Norway 61°54'N 06°E
92 G11 Nordfold Nordland, C Norway 67°48'N 15°16'E
Nordfriesische Inseln see North Frisian Islands
100 H7 Nordfriesland cultural region N Germany
101 K15 Nordhausen Thüringen, C Germany 51°31'N 10°48'E
25 T13 Nordheim Texas, SW USA 28°55'N 97°36'W
94 C13 Nordhordland physical region S Norway
100 E12 Nordhorn Niedersachsen, NW Germany 52°26'N 07°04'E
172 H16 Nord, Île du island Inner Islands, NE Seychelles
95 F20 Nordjylland ◆ county N Denmark
92 K7 Nordkapp Eng. North Cape. headland N Norway 25°47'E 71°10'N
92 O1 Nordkapp headland N Svalbard 80°31'N 19°58'E
Nordkinn see Kinnarodden
79 N19 Nord-Kivu off. Région du Nord Kivu. ◆ region E Dem. Rep. Congo
Nord-Kivu, Région du see Nord-Kivu
92 G12 Nordland ◆ county C Norway
101 J21 Nördlingen Bayern, S Germany 48°49'N 10°28'E
93 I16 Nordmaling Västerbotten, N Sweden 63°35'N 19°30'E
95 K15 Nordmark Värmland, C Sweden 59°52'N 14°04'E
Nord, Mer du see North Sea
94 F8 Nordmøre physical region S Norway
100 I8 Nord-Ostee-Kanal canal N Germany
0 J3 Nordøstrundingen cape NE Greenland
Nord-Ouest see North-West
Nord-Ouest, Territoires du see Northwest Territories
101 F19 Nordpfälzer Bergland ▲ W Germany
Nord, Pointe see Fatua, Pointe
187 P16 Nord, Province ◆ province C New Caledonia
101 D14 Nordrhein-Westfalen Eng. North Rhine-Westphalia, Fr. Rhénanie du Nord-Westphalie. ◆ state W Germany
Nordsee/Nordsjøen/Nordsøen see North Sea
100 H9 Nordstrand island N Germany
93 E15 Nord-Trøndelag ◆ county C Norway
92 I1 Norðurfjörður Vestfirðir, NW Iceland 66°01'N 21°33'W
92 J1 Norðurland Eystra ◆ region N Iceland
92 I2 Norðurland Vestra ◆ region N Iceland
97 E19 Nore Ir. An Fheoir. ≈ S Ireland
29 Q14 Norfolk Nebraska, C USA 42°01'N 97°25'W
21 X7 Norfolk Virginia, NE USA 36°51'N 76°17'W
97 P19 Norfolk cultural region E England, United Kingdom
192 K10 Norfolk Island ◇ Australian self-governing territory SW Pacific Ocean
175 P9 Norfolk Ridge undersea feature W Pacific Ocean
27 U8 Norfork Lake ⊠ Arkansas/Missouri, C USA
98 N6 Norg Drenthe, NE Netherlands 53°04'N 06°28'E
Norge see Norway
Norge, Kongeriket see Norway
95 D14 Norheimsund Hordaland, S Norway 60°22'N 06°09'E
25 S16 Norias Texas, SW USA 26°47'N 97°45'W
164 L12 Norikura-dake ▲ Honshū, S Japan 36°06'N 137°33'E
122 K8 Noril'sk Krasnoyarskiy Kray, N Russia 69°21'N 88°02'E
14 I13 Norland Ontario, SE Canada 44°46'N 78°48'W
21 V8 Norlina North Carolina, SE USA 36°26'N 78°11'W
30 L13 Normal Illinois, N USA 40°30'N 88°59'W
27 N11 Norman Oklahoma, C USA 35°13'N 97°27'W
Norman see Tulita
186 G9 Normanby Island island SE Papua New Guinea
Normandes, Îles see Channel Islands
58 G9 Normandia Roraima, N Brazil 03°57'N 59°39'W
102 K5 Normandie ◆ region N France
102 L5 Normandie Eng. Normandy. cultural region N France
102 J5 Normandie, Collines de hill range NW France
Normandy see Normandie
25 V9 Normangee Texas, SW USA 31°01'N 96°06'W
21 Q10 Norman, Lake ⊠ North Carolina, SE USA
44 K13 Norman Manley ✈ (Kingston) E Jamaica 17°55'N 76°46'W
181 U5 Norman River ≈ Queensland, NE Australia
181 U4 Normanton Queensland, NE Australia 17°49'S 141°08'E
8 I8 Norman Wells Northwest Territories, NW Canada 65°18'N 126°42'W
12 H12 Normétal Québec, S Canada 48°59'N 79°23'W
163 O7 Norovlin var. Uldz. Hentiy, NE Mongolia 48°47'N 112°01'E
11 V15 Norquay Saskatchewan, S Canada 51°51'N 102°04'W
93 G15 Norråker Jämtland, C Sweden 64°25'N 15°40'E
94 N12 Norrala Gävleborg, C Sweden 61°22'N 17°04'E
Norra Ny see Stöllet
92 G13 Norra Storfjället ▲ N Sweden 65°57'N 15°15'E
92 I13 Norrbotten ◆ county N Sweden
94 N11 Norrdellen ◎ C Sweden
95 G23 Nørre Aaby var. Nørre Åby. Syddtjylland, C Denmark 55°28'N 09°53'E
Nørre Åby see Nørre Aaby
95 I24 Nørre Alslev Sjælland, SE Denmark 54°54'N 11°53'E
95 E23 Nørre Nebel Syddtjylland, W Denmark 55°45'N 08°16'E
95 G20 Nørresundby Nordjylland, N Denmark 57°05'N 09°55'E
21 N8 Norris Lake ⊠ Tennessee, S USA
18 I15 Norristown Pennsylvania, NE USA 40°07'N 75°20'W
95 N17 Norrköping Östergötland, S Sweden 58°35'N 16°10'E
Norrmark see Noormarkku
94 N13 Norrsundet Gävleborg, C Sweden 60°55'N 17°09'E
95 P15 Norrtälje Stockholm, C Sweden 59°46'N 18°42'E
180 L12 Norseman Western Australia 32°16'S 121°46'E
93 I14 Norsjö Västerbotten, N Sweden 64°55'N 19°30'E
95 G16 Norsjø ◎ S Norway
123 R13 Norsk Amurskaya Oblast', SE Russia 52°20'N 129°57'E
Norske Havet see Norwegian Sea
187 Q13 Norsup Malekula, C Vanuatu 16°05'S 167°24'E
191 V15 Norte, Cabo headland Easter Island, Chile, E Pacific Ocean 27°03'S 109°24'W
54 F7 Norte de Santander off. Departamento de Norte de Santander. ◆ province N Colombia
Norte de Santander, Departamento de see Norte de Santander
61 E21 Norte, Punta headland E Argentina 36°17'S 56°46'W
21 R13 North South Carolina, SE USA 33°37'N 81°06'W
North see Nord
18 L10 North Adams Massachusetts, NE USA 42°40'N 73°06'W
113 L17 North Albanian Alps Alb. Bjeshkët e Namuna, SCr. Prokletije. ▲ SE Europe
97 M15 Northallerton N England, United Kingdom 54°20'N 01°26'W
180 J12 Northam Western Australia 31°40'S 116°40'E
83 J20 Northam Northern, N South Africa 24°56'S 27°18'E
1 North America continent
1 N12 North American Basin undersea feature W Sargasso Sea 30°00'N 60°00'W
0 C5 North American Plate tectonic feature
18 M11 North Amherst Massachusetts, NE USA 42°24'N 72°31'W
97 N20 Northampton C England, United Kingdom 52°14'N 00°54'W
97 M20 Northamptonshire cultural region C England, United Kingdom
151 P18 North Andaman island Andaman Islands, India, NE Indian Ocean
65 D25 North Arm East Falkland, Falkland Islands 52°06'S 59°21'W
21 Q13 North Augusta South Carolina, SE USA 33°30'N 81°58'W
173 W8 North Australian Basin Fr. Bassin Nord de l' Australie. undersea feature E Indian Ocean
31 R11 North Baltimore Ohio, N USA 41°10'N 83°40'W
11 T15 North Battleford Saskatchewan, S Canada 52°47'N 108°19'W
14 H11 North Bay Ontario, S Canada 46°20'N 79°28'W
12 H6 North Belcher Islands island group Belcher Islands, Nunavut, C Canada
29 R15 North Bend Nebraska, C USA 41°27'N 96°46'W
32 E14 North Bend Oregon, NW USA 43°24'N 124°13'W
96 K12 North Berwick SE Scotland, United Kingdom 56°04'N 02°44'W
North Beveland see Noord-Beveland
North Borneo see Sabah
183 P5 North Bourke New South Wales, SE Australia 30°03'S 145°56'E
North Brabant see Noord-Brabant
182 F2 North Branch Neales seasonal river South Australia
44 M6 North Caicos island NW Turks and Caicos Islands
26 L10 North Canadian River ≈ Oklahoma, C USA
31 U12 North Canton Ohio, N USA 40°52'N 81°24'W
13 R13 North, Cape headland Cape Breton Island, Nova Scotia, SE Canada 47°06'N 60°24'W
184 I1 North Cape headland North Island, New Zealand 34°23'S 173°02'E
186 G5 North Cape headland New Ireland, NE Papua New Guinea 02°33'S 150°48'E
North Cape see Nordkapp
18 J17 North Cape May New Jersey, NE USA 38°59'N 74°55'W
12 C9 North Caribou Lake ◎ Ontario, C Canada
21 U10 North Carolina off. State of North Carolina, also known as Old North State, Tar Heel State, Turpentine State. ◆ state SE USA
North Celebes see Sulawesi Utara
155 J24 North Central ◆ province N Sri Lanka
31 S4 North Channel lake channel Canada/USA
97 G14 North Channel strait Northern Ireland/Scotland, United Kingdom
21 S14 North Charleston South Carolina, SE USA 32°53'N 79°59'W
31 N10 North Chicago Illinois, N USA 42°19'N 87°50'W
195 Y10 Northcliffe Glacier glacier Antarctica
31 Q14 North College Hill Ohio, N USA 39°13'N 84°33'W
25 O8 North Concho River ≈ Texas, SW USA
19 O8 North Conway New Hampshire, NE USA 44°03'N 71°06'W
27 V14 North Crossett Arkansas, C USA 33°10'N 91°56'W
28 L4 North Dakota off. State of North Dakota, also known as Flickertail State, Peace Garden State, Sioux State. ◆ state N USA
North Devon Island see Devon Island
97 O22 North Downs hill range SE England, United Kingdom
18 C11 North East Pennsylvania, NE USA 42°13'N 79°49'W
83 I18 North East ◆ district NE Botswana
65 G15 North East Bay bay Ascension Island, C Atlantic Ocean
38 L10 Northeast Cape headland Saint Lawrence Island, Alaska, USA 63°16'N 168°50'W
North East Frontier Agency/North East Frontier Agency of Assam see Arunāchal Pradesh
Northeast Greenland National Park see Avannaarsuani Tunumilu Nuna Allanngutsaaliugaq
65 E25 North East Island island E Falkland Islands
189 V11 Northeast Island island Chuuk, C Micronesia
44 L12 North East Point headland E Jamaica 18°09'N 76°19'W
191 Z2 Northeast Point headland Kiritimati, E Kiribati 10°23'S 105°45'E
44 K5 Northeast Point headland Acklins Island, SE The Bahamas 22°43'N 73°50'W
44 L6 Northeast Point headland Great Inagua, S The Bahamas 21°18'N 73°01'W
44 H2 Northeast Providence Channel channel N The Bahamas
101 J14 Northeim Niedersachsen, C Germany 51°42'N 10°E
29 X14 North English Iowa, C USA 41°30'N 92°04'W
138 G8 Northern ◆ district N Israel
82 M12 Northern ◆ region N Malawi
186 F8 Northern var. Oro. ◆ province S Papua New Guinea
155 J23 Northern ◆ province N Sri Lanka
80 D7 Northern ◆ state N Sudan
82 K12 Northern ◆ province NE Zambia
Northern see Limpopo
80 B13 Northern Bahr el Ghazal ◆ state NW South Sudan
Northern Border Region see Al Ḩudūd ash Shamālīyah
83 F24 Northern Cape off. Northern Cape Province, Afr. Noord-Kaap. ◆ province W South Africa
Northern Cape Province see Northern Cape
190 K14 Northern Cook Islands island group N Cook Islands


◆ Country
● Country Capital
◇ Dependent Territory
○ Dependent Territory Capital
◆ Administrative Regions
✈ International Airports
▲ Mountain
▲▲ Mountain Range
Volcano
≈ River
◎ Lake
⊠ Reservoir

NORTHERN DARFUR – NSANJE


80 B8 **Northern Darfur** ◈ *state* NW Sudan
**Northern Dvina** *see* Severnaya Dvina
97 F14 **Northern Ireland** *var.* The Six Counties. ◈ *political division* Northern Ireland, United Kingdom
97 F14 **Northern Ireland** *var.* The Six Counties. *cultural region* Northern Ireland, United Kingdom
80 D9 **Northern Kordofan** ◈ *state* C Sudan
187 Z14 **Northern Lau Group** *island group* Lau Group, NE Fiji
188 K3 **Northern Mariana Islands** ◇ *commonwealth in political union with the US* W Pacific Ocean
**Northern Rhodesia** *see* Zambia
**Northern Sporades** *see* Vóreies Sporádes
182 D1 **Northern Territory** ◈ *territory* N Australia
**Northern Transvaal** *see* Limpopo
**Northern Ural Hills** *see* Severnyye Uvaly
84 I9 **North European Plain** *plain* N Europe
27 V2 **North Fabius River** ≈ Missouri, C USA
65 D24 **North Falkland Sound** *sound* N Falkland Islands
29 V9 **Northfield** Minnesota, N USA 44°27′N 93°10′W
19 O9 **Northfield** New Hampshire, NE USA 43°26′N 71°34′W
175 Q8 **North Fiji Basin** *undersea feature* N Coral Sea
97 Q22 **North Foreland** *headland* SE England, United Kingdom 51°22′N 01°26′E
35 P6 **North Fork American River** ≈ California, W USA
39 R7 **North Fork Chandalar River** ≈ Alaska, USA
28 K7 **North Fork Grand River** ≈ North Dakota/South Dakota, N USA
21 O6 **North Fork Kentucky River** ≈ Kentucky, S USA
39 Q7 **North Fork Koyukuk River** ≈ Alaska, USA
39 Q10 **North Fork Kuskokwim River** ≈ Alaska, USA
26 K11 **North Fork Red River** ≈ Oklahoma/Texas, SW USA
26 K3 **North Fork Solomon River** ≈ Kansas, C USA
23 W14 **North Fort Myers** Florida, SE USA 26°40′N 81°52′W
31 P5 **North Fox Island** *island* Michigan, N USA
100 G6 **North Frisian Islands** *var.* Nordfriesische Inseln. *island group* N Germany
197 N9 **North Geomagnetic Pole** *pole* Arctic Ocean
18 M13 **North Haven** Connecticut, NE USA 41°25′N 72°51′W
184 J5 **North Head** *headland* North Island, New Zealand 36°23′S 174°01′E
18 L6 **North Hero** Vermont, NE USA 44°49′N 73°14′W
35 O7 **North Highlands** California, W USA 38°40′N 121°25′W
**North Holland** *see* Noord-Holland
81 I16 **North Horr** Marsabit, N Kenya 03°17′N 37°08′E
151 K21 **North Huvadhu Atoll** *var.* Gaafu Alifu Atoll. *atoll* S Maldives
65 A24 **North Island** *island* W Falkland Islands
21 U14 **North Island** *island* South Carolina, SE USA
184 N9 **North Island / Te Ika-a-Māui** *var.* Te Ika-a-Māui. *island* N New Zealand
31 O11 **North Judson** Indiana, N USA 41°12′N 86°44′W
**North Kazakhstan** *see* Severnyy Kazakhstan
31 V10 **North Kingsville** Ohio, N USA 41°54′N 80°41′W
163 Y13 **North Korea** *off.* Democratic People's Republic of Korea, *Kor.* Chosŏn-minjujuŭi-inmin-konghwaguk. ◆ *republic* E Asia
153 X11 **North Lakhimpur** Assam, NE India 27°10′N 94°00′E
184 J3 **Northland** *off.* Northland Region. ◈ *region* North Island, New Zealand
192 K11 **Northland Plateau** *undersea feature* S Pacific Ocean
**Northland Region** *see* Northland
35 X11 **North Las Vegas** Nevada, W USA 36°12′N 115°07′W
31 O11 **North Liberty** Indiana, N USA 41°36′N 86°22′W
29 X14 **North Liberty** Iowa, C USA 41°45′N 91°36′W
27 V12 **North Little Rock** Arkansas, C USA 34°46′N 92°15′W
28 M13 **North Loup River** ≈ Nebraska, C USA
151 K18 **North Maalhosmadulu Atoll** *var.* North Malosmadulu Atoll, Raa Atoll. *atoll* N Maldives
113 O19 **North Macedonia** *off.* Republic of North Macedonia, *Mac.* Severna Makedonija, Republika Severna Makedonija. ◆ *republic* SE Europe
**North Macedonia, Republic of** *see* North Macedonia
31 U10 **North Madison** Ohio, N USA 41°48′N 81°03′W
**North Malosmadulu Atoll** *see* North Maalhosmadulu Atoll
31 P12 **North Manchester** Indiana, N USA 41°00′N 85°45′W
31 P6 **North Manitou Island** *island* Michigan, N USA
29 U10 **North Mankato** Minnesota, N USA 44°11′N 94°03′W
23 Z15 **North Miami** Florida, SE USA 25°54′N 80°11′W
151 K18 **North Miladhunmadulu Atoll** *var.* Shaviyani Atoll. *atoll* N Maldives
**North Minch** *see* Minch, The
23 W15 **North Naples** Florida, SE USA 26°13′N 81°47′W
175 P8 **North New Hebrides Trench** *undersea feature* N Coral Sea
23 Y15 **North New River Canal** ≈ Florida, SE USA
151 K20 **North Nilandhe Atoll** *atoll* C Maldives
36 L2 **North Ogden** Utah, W USA 41°18′N 111°57′W
**North Ossetia** *see* Severnaya Osetiya-Alaniya, Respublika
35 S10 **North Palisade** ▲ California, W USA 37°06′N 118°31′W
189 U11 **North Pass** *passage* Chuuk Islands, C Micronesia
28 M15 **North Platte** Nebraska, C USA 41°07′N 100°46′W
33 X17 **North Platte River** ≈ C USA
65 G14 **North Point** *headland* Ascension Island, C Atlantic Ocean
172 I16 **North Point** *headland* Mahé, NE Seychelles 04°23′S 55°28′E
31 S6 **North Point** *headland* Michigan, N USA
31 R5 **North Point** *headland* Michigan, N USA 45°21′N 83°30′W
39 S9 **North Pole** Alaska, USA 64°42′N 147°09′W
197 R9 **North Pole** *pole* Arctic Ocean
23 O4 **Northport** Alabama, S USA 33°13′N 87°34′W
23 W14 **North Port** Florida, SE USA 27°03′N 82°15′W
32 L6 **Northport** Washington, NW USA 48°54′N 117°48′W
32 L12 **North Powder** Oregon, NW USA 45°00′N 117°56′W
29 U13 **North Raccoon River** ≈ Iowa, C USA
**North Rhine-Westphalia** *see* Nordrhein-Westfalen
97 M16 **North Riding** *cultural region* N England, United Kingdom
96 G5 **North Rona** *island* NW Scotland, United Kingdom
96 K4 **North Ronaldsay** *island* NE Scotland, United Kingdom
36 L2 **North Salt Lake** Utah, W USA 40°51′N 111°54′W
11 P15 **North Saskatchewan** ≈ Alberta/Saskatchewan, S Canada
35 X5 **North Schell Peak** ▲ Nevada, W USA 39°25′N 114°34′W
**North Scotia Ridge** *see* South Georgia Ridge
86 D10 **North Sea** *Dan.* Nordsøen, *Dut.* Noordzee, *Fr.* Mer du Nord, *Ger.* Nordsee, *Nor.* Nordsjøen; *prev.* German Ocean, *Lat.* Mare Germanicum. *sea* NW Europe
35 T6 **North Shoshone Peak** ▲ Nevada, W USA 39°08′N 117°28′W
**North Siberian Lowland/ North Siberian Plain** *see* Severo-Sibirskaya Nizmennost'
29 R13 **North Sioux City** South Dakota, N USA 42°31′N 96°28′W
96 K4 **North Sound, The** *sound* N Scotland, United Kingdom
183 T4 **North Star** New South Wales, SE Australia 28°55′S 150°25′E
**North Star State** *see* Minnesota
183 V3 **North Stradbroke Island** *island* Queensland, E Australia
**North Sulawesi** *see* Sulawesi Utara
**North Sumatra** *see* Sumatera Utara
14 D17 **North Sydenham** ≈ Ontario, S Canada
18 H9 **North Syracuse** New York, NE USA 43°07′N 76°07′W
184 K9 **North Taranaki Bight** *gulf* North Island, New Zealand
12 H9 **North Twin Island** *island* Nunavut, C Canada
96 E8 **North Uist** *island* NW Scotland, United Kingdom
97 L14 **Northumberland** *cultural region* N England, United Kingdom
181 Y7 **Northumberland Isles** *island group* Queensland, NE Australia
13 Q14 **Northumberland Strait** *strait* SE Canada
32 G14 **North Umpqua River** ≈ Oregon, NW USA
45 Q13 **North Union** Saint Vincent, Saint Vincent and the Grenadines 13°15′N 61°07′W
10 L17 **North Vancouver** British Columbia, SW Canada 49°21′N 123°05′W
18 K9 **Northville** New York, NE USA 43°13′N 74°08′W
97 Q19 **North Walsham** E England, United Kingdom 52°49′N 01°22′E
39 T10 **Northway** Alaska, USA 62°57′N 141°56′W
79 D14 **North-West** *Fr.* Nord-Ouest. ◈ *region* NW Cameroon
83 G21 **North-West** *off.* North-West Province, *Afr.* Noordwes. ◈ *province* N South Africa
64 I6 **Northwest Atlantic Mid-Ocean Canyon** *undersea feature* N Atlantic Ocean
180 G8 **North West Cape** *cape* Western Australia
38 J9 **Northwest Cape** *headland* Saint Lawrence Island, Alaska, USA 63°46′N 171°45′W
155 J24 **North Western** ◈ *province* W Sri Lanka
82 H13 **North Western** ◈ *province* W Zambia
**North-West Frontier Province** *see* Khyber Pakhtunkhwa
96 H8 **North West Highlands** ▲▲ N Scotland, United Kingdom
192 J4 **Northwest Pacific Basin** *undersea feature* NW Pacific Ocean 40°00′N 150°00′E
191 Y2 **Northwest Point** *headland* Kiritimati, E Kiribati 10°25′S 105°35′E
44 G1 **Northwest Providence Channel** *channel* N The Bahamas
**North-West Province** *see* North-West
13 Q8 **North West River** Newfoundland and Labrador, E Canada 53°30′N 60°10′W
8 J9 **Northwest Territories** *Fr.* Territoires du Nord-Ouest. ◈ *territory* NW Canada
97 K18 **Northwich** C England, United Kingdom 53°16′N 02°32′W
25 Q5 **North Wichita River** ≈ Texas, SW USA
18 J17 **North Wildwood** New Jersey, NE USA 39°00′N 74°45′W
21 R9 **North Wilkesboro** North Carolina, SE USA 36°09′N 81°09′W
19 P8 **North Windham** Maine, NE USA 43°51′N 70°25′W
197 Q6 **Northwind Plain** *undersea feature* Arctic Ocean
29 V11 **Northwood** Iowa, C USA 43°26′N 93°13′W
29 Q4 **Northwood** North Dakota, N USA 47°43′N 97°34′W
97 M15 **North York Moors** *moorland* N England, United Kingdom
25 V9 **North Zulch** Texas, SW USA 30°54′N 96°06′W
26 K2 **Norton** Kansas, C USA 39°51′N 99°53′W
31 S13 **Norton** Ohio, N USA 40°25′N 83°04′W
21 P7 **Norton** Virginia, NE USA 36°56′N 82°37′W
39 N9 **Norton Bay** *bay* Alaska, USA
**Norton de Matos** *see* Balombo
31 O9 **Norton Shores** Michigan, N USA 43°10′N 86°15′W
38 M10 **Norton Sound** *inlet* Alaska, USA
27 Q3 **Nortonville** Kansas, C USA 39°25′N 95°19′W
102 I8 **Nort-sur-Erdre** Loire-Atlantique, NW France 47°27′N 01°30′W
195 N2 **Norvegia, Cape** *headland* Antarctica 71°16′S 12°25′W
18 L13 **Norwalk** Connecticut, NE USA 41°08′N 73°28′W
29 V14 **Norwalk** Iowa, C USA 41°28′N 93°40′W
31 S11 **Norwalk** Ohio, N USA 41°14′N 82°37′W
19 P7 **Norway** Maine, NE USA 44°13′N 70°30′W
31 N5 **Norway** Michigan, N USA 45°47′N 87°54′W
93 E17 **Norway** *off.* Kingdom of Norway, *Nor.* Norge. Kongeriket Norge. ◆ *monarchy* N Europe
11 X13 **Norway House** Manitoba, C Canada 53°59′N 97°50′W
**Norway, Kingdom of** *see* Norway
197 R16 **Norwegian Basin** *undersea feature* NW Norwegian Sea 68°00′N 02°00′W
84 D6 **Norwegian Sea** *var.* Norske Havet. *sea* NE Atlantic Ocean
197 S17 **Norwegian Trench** *undersea feature* NE North Sea 59°00′N 04°30′E
14 F16 **Norwich** Ontario, S Canada 42°57′N 80°37′W
97 Q19 **Norwich** E England, United Kingdom 52°38′N 01°18′E
19 N13 **Norwich** Connecticut, NE USA 41°30′N 72°02′W
18 I11 **Norwich** New York, NE USA 42°31′N 75°31′W
29 U9 **Norwood** Minnesota, N USA 44°46′N 93°55′W
31 Q15 **Norwood** Ohio, N USA 39°07′N 84°27′W
14 H11 **Nosbonsing, Lake** ◎ Ontario, S Canada
**Nösen** *see* Bistrița
165 T1 **Noshappu-misaki** *headland* Hokkaidō, NE Japan 45°26′N 141°38′E
165 P7 **Noshiro** *var.* Nosiro; *prev.* Noshirominato. Akita, Honshū, C Japan 40°11′N 140°02′E
**Noshirominato/Nosiro** *see* Noshiro
117 Q3 **Nosivka** *Rus.* Nosovka. Chernihivs'ka Oblast', NE Ukraine 50°55′N 31°37′E
67 T14 **Nosop** *var.* Nossob, Nossop. ≈ Botswana/Namibia
83 E20 **Nossop** ≈ E Namibia
125 S4 **Nosovaya** Nenetskiy Avtonomnyy Okrug, NW Russia 68°12′N 54°33′E
**Nosovka** *see* Nosivka
143 V11 **Nosratābād** Sīstān va Balūchestān, E Iran 29°53′N 59°57′E
95 J18 **Nossebro** Västra Götaland, S Sweden 58°12′N 12°42′E
96 K6 **Noss Head** *headland* N Scotland, United Kingdom 58°29′N 03°03′W
**Nossi-Bé** *see* Be, Nosy
**Nossob/Nossop** *see* Nosop
172 J2 **Nosy Be** ✈ Antsirāṇana, N Madagascar 23°36′S 47°36′E
172 J6 **Nosy Varika** Fianarantsoa, SE Madagascar 20°36′S 48°31′E
14 L10 **Notawassi** ≈ Québec, SE Canada
14 M9 **Notawassi, Lac** ◎ Québec, SE Canada
36 J5 **Notch Peak** ▲ Utah, W USA 39°08′N 113°24′W
110 G10 **Noteć** *Ger.* Netze. ≈ NW Poland
**Nóties Sporádes** *see* Dodekánisa
115 J22 **Nótio Aigaío** *Eng.* Aegean South. ◈ *region* E Greece
115 H18 **Nótios Evvoïkós Kólpos** *gulf* E Greece
115 B16 **Nótio Stenó Kérkyras** *strait* W Greece
107 L25 **Noto** *anc.* Netum. Sicilia, Italy, C Mediterranean Sea 36°53′N 15°05′E
164 M10 **Noto** Ishikawa, Honshū, SW Japan 37°18′N 137°11′E
95 G15 **Notodden** Telemark, S Norway 59°35′N 09°18′E
107 L25 **Noto, Golfo di** *gulf* Sicilia, Italy, C Mediterranean Sea
164 L10 **Noto-hantō** *peninsula* Honshū, SW Japan
164 L11 **Noto-jima** *island* SW Japan
13 T11 **Notre Dame Bay** *bay* Newfoundland, Newfoundland and Labrador, E Canada
15 P6 **Notre-Dame-de-Lorette** Québec, SE Canada 49°05′N 72°24′W
14 L11 **Notre-Dame-de-Pontmain** Québec, SE Canada 46°18′N 75°37′W
15 T8 **Notre-Dame-du-Lac** Québec, SE Canada 47°36′N 68°48′W
15 Q6 **Notre-Dame-du-Rosaire** Québec, SE Canada 48°48′N 71°27′W
15 U8 **Notre-Dame, Monts** ▲▲ Québec, S Canada
77 R16 **Notsé** S Togo 06°59′N 01°12′E
14 G14 **Nottawasaga** ≈ Ontario, S Canada
14 G14 **Nottawasaga Bay** *lake bay* Ontario, S Canada
12 I11 **Nottaway** ≈ Québec, SE Canada
23 S1 **Nottely Lake** ⊠ Georgia, SE USA
95 H16 **Nøtterøy** *island* S Norway
97 M19 **Nottingham** C England, United Kingdom 52°58′N 01°10′W
9 E14 **Nottingham Island** *island* Nunavut, NE Canada
97 N18 **Nottinghamshire** *cultural region* C England, United Kingdom
21 V7 **Nottoway** Virginia, NE USA 37°07′N 78°03′W
21 V7 **Nottoway River** ≈ Virginia, NE USA
76 G7 **Nouâdhibou** *prev.* Port-Étienne. Dakhlet Nouâdhibou, W Mauritania 20°54′N 17°01′W
76 G7 **Nouâdhibou** ✈ Dakhlet Nouâdhibou, W Mauritania 20°59′N 17°02′W
76 F7 **Nouâdhibou, Dakhlet** *prev.* Baie du Lévrier. *bay* W Mauritania
76 F7 **Nouâdhibou, Râs** *prev.* Cap Blanc. *headland* NW Mauritania 20°48′N 17°03′W
76 G9 **Nouakchott** ● (Mauritania) Nouakchott District, SW Mauritania 18°09′N 15°58′W
76 G9 **Nouakchott** ✈ Trarza, SW Mauritania 18°18′N 15°54′W
120 J11 **Noual, Sebkhet en** *var.* Sabkhat an Nawāl. *salt flat* C Tunisia
76 G8 **Nouâmghâr** *var.* Nouamrhar. Dakhlet Nouâdhibou, W Mauritania 19°22′N 16°31′W
**Nouamrhar** *see* Nouâmghâr
**Nouă Sulița** *see* Novoselytsya
187 Q17 **Nouméa** ○ (New Caledonia) Province Sud, S New Caledonia 22°13′S 166°29′E
79 E15 **Noun** ≈ C Cameroon
77 N12 **Nouna** W Burkina Faso 12°44′N 03°54′W
83 H24 **Noupoort** Northern Cape, C South Africa 31°11′S 24°57′E
**Nouveau-Brunswick** *see* New Brunswick
**Nouveau-Comptoir** *see* Wemindji
15 T4 **Nouvel, Lacs** ◎ Québec, SE Canada
15 W7 **Nouvelle** Québec, SE Canada 48°07′N 66°16′W
15 W7 **Nouvelle** ≈ Québec, SE Canada
103 K11 **Nouvelle-Aquitaine** ◈ *region* C France
**Nouvelle-Calédonie** *see* New Caledonia
**Nouvelle Écosse** *see* Nova Scotia
103 R3 **Nouzonville** Ardennes, N France 49°49′N 04°45′E
147 Q11 **Nov** *Rus.* Nau. NW Tajikistan 40°10′N 69°16′E
59 I21 **Nova Alvorada** Mato Grosso do Sul, SW Brazil 21°25′S 54°19′W
**Novabad** *see* Navobod
111 D19 **Nová Bystřice** *Ger.* Neubistritz. Jihočeský Kraj, S Czechia 49°N 15°05′E
116 H13 **Novaci** Gorj, SW Romania 45°07′N 23°37′E
**Nova Civitas** *see* Neustadt an der Weinstrasse
**Novaesium** *see* Neuss
60 H10 **Nova Esperança** Paraná, S Brazil 23°09′S 52°13′W
106 H11 **Novafeltria** Marche, C Italy 43°54′N 12°18′E
60 Q9 **Nova Friburgo** Rio de Janeiro, SE Brazil 22°16′S 42°34′W
82 D12 **Nova Gaia** *var.* Cambundi-Catembo. Malanje, NE Angola 10°09′S 17°31′E
109 S12 **Nova Gorica** W Slovenia 45°57′N 13°40′E
112 G10 **Nova Gradiška** *Ger.* Neugradisk, *Hung.* Újgradiska. Brod-Posavina, NE Croatia 45°15′N 17°23′E
60 K7 **Nova Granada** São Paulo, S Brazil 20°33′S 49°19′W
60 O10 **Nova Iguaçu** Rio de Janeiro, SE Brazil 22°31′S 44°05′W
117 S10 **Nova Kakhovka** *Rus.* Novaya Kakhovka. Khersons'ka Oblast', SE Ukraine 46°45′N 33°20′E
**Nová Karvinná** *see* Karviná
**Nova Lamego** *see* Gabú
**Nova Lisboa** *see* Huambo
112 C11 **Novalja** Lika-Senj, W Croatia 44°33′N 14°53′E
119 M14 **Novalukoml'** *Rus.* Novolukoml'. Vitsyebskaya Voblasts', N Belarus 54°40′N 29°09′E
**Nova Mambone** *see* Mambone
83 P16 **Nova Nabúri** Zambézia, NE Mozambique 16°47′S 38°55′E
117 Q9 **Nova Odesa** *var.* Novaya Odessa. Mykolayivs'ka Oblast', S Ukraine 47°19′N 31°45′E
60 H10 **Nova Olímpia** Paraná, S Brazil 23°28′S 53°12′W
61 I15 **Nova Prata** Rio Grande do Sul, S Brazil 28°45′S 51°37′W
14 H12 **Novar** Ontario, S Canada 45°26′N 79°14′W
106 C7 **Novara** *anc.* Novaria. Piemonte, NW Italy 45°27′N 08°36′E
**Novaria** *see* Novara
13 P15 **Nova Scotia** *Fr.* Nouvelle Écosse. ◈ *province* SE Canada
0 M9 **Nova Scotia** *physical region* SE Canada
34 M8 **Novato** California, W USA 38°06′N 122°35′W
192 M7 **Nova Trough** *undersea feature* W Pacific Ocean
116 L7 **Nova Ushytsya** Khmel'nyts'ka Oblast', W Ukraine 48°50′N 27°16′E
83 M17 **Nova Vanduzi** Manica, C Mozambique 18°54′S 33°18′E
117 U5 **Nova Vodolaha** *Rus.* Novaya Vodolaga. Kharkivs'ka Oblast', E Ukraine 49°43′N 35°49′E
123 O12 **Novaya Chara** Zabaykal'skiy Kray, S Russia 56°45′N 117°58′E
122 M12 **Novaya Igirma** Irkutskaya Oblast', C Russia 57°08′N 103°52′E
**Novaya Kakhovka** *see* Nova Kakhovka
**Novaya Kazanka** *see* Zhanakazan
124 I12 **Novaya Ladoga** Leningradskaya Oblast', NW Russia 60°03′N 32°15′E
127 R5 **Novaya Malykla** Ul'yanovskaya Oblast', W Russia 54°13′N 49°55′E
**Novaya Odessa** *see* Nova Odesa
123 Q5 **Novaya Sibir', Ostrov** *island* Novosibirskiye Ostrova, NE Russia
**Novaya Vodolaga** *see* Nova Vodolaha
122 I6 **Novaya Zemlya** *island group* N Russia
**Novaya Zemlya Trough** *see* East Novaya Zemlya Trough
114 K10 **Nova Zagora** Sliven, C Bulgaria 42°29′N 26°00′E
105 S12 **Novelda** Comunitat Valenciana, E Spain 38°24′N 00°45′W
111 H19 **Nové Mesto nad Váhom** *Ger.* Waagneustadtl, *Hung.* Vágújhely. Trenčiansky Kraj, W Slovakia 48°46′N 17°50′E
111 F17 **Nové Město na Moravě** *Ger.* Neustadtl in Mähren. Vysočina, C Czechia 49°34′N 16°05′E
**Novesium** *see* Neuss
111 I21 **Nové Zámky** *Ger.* Neuhäusel, *Hung.* Érsekújvár. Nitriansky Kraj, SW Slovakia 49°00′N 18°10′E
**Novgorod** *see* Velikiy Novgorod
**Novgorod-Severskiy** *see* Novhorod-Sivers'kyy
122 C7 **Novgorodskaya Oblast'** ◈ *province* W Russia
117 R8 **Novhorodka** Kirovohrads'ka Oblast', C Ukraine 48°21′N 32°38′E
117 R2 **Novhorod-Sivers'kyy** *Rus.* Novgorod-Severskiy. Chernihivs'ka Oblast', NE Ukraine 52°00′N 33°15′E
31 R10 **Novi** Michigan, N USA 42°28′N 83°28′W
**Novi** *see* Novi Vinodolski
112 L9 **Novi Bečej** *prev.* Új-Becse, Vološinovo, *Ger.* Neubetsche, *Hung.* Törökbecse. Vojvodina, N Serbia 45°36′N 20°09′E
116 M3 **Novi Bilokorovychi** *Rus.* Belokorovichi; *prev.* Bilokorovychi. Zhytomyrs'ka Oblast', N Ukraine 51°07′N 28°02′E
25 Q8 **Novice** Texas, SW USA 32°00′N 99°38′W
112 A9 **Novigrad** Istra, NW Croatia 45°19′N 13°33′E
**Novi Grad** *see* Bosanski Novi
114 G9 **Novi Iskar** Sofia Grad, W Bulgaria 42°46′N 23°19′E
106 C9 **Novi Ligure** Piemonte, NW Italy 44°46′N 08°47′E
99 L22 **Noville** Luxembourg, SE Belgium 50°04′N 05°46′E
194 I10 **Noville Peninsula** *peninsula* Thurston Island, Antarctica
**Noviodunum** *see* Soissons, Aisne, France
**Noviodunum** *see* Nevers, Nièvre, France
**Noviodunum** *see* Nyon, Vaud, Switzerland
**Noviomagus** *see* Lisieux, Calvados, France
**Noviomagus** *see* Nijmegen, Netherlands
114 M8 **Novi Pazar** Shumen, NE Bulgaria 43°20′N 27°12′E
113 M15 **Novi Pazar** *Turk.* Yenipazar. Serbia, S Serbia 43°09′N 20°31′E
112 K10 **Novi Sad** *Ger.* Neusatz, *Hung.* Újvidék. Vojvodina, N Serbia 45°16′N 19°49′E
117 T6 **Novi Sanzhary** Poltavs'ka Oblast', C Ukraine 49°21′N 34°18′E
112 H12 **Novi Travnik** *prev.* Pučarevo. Federacija Bosne I Hercegovine, C Bosnia and Herzegovina 44°12′N 17°39′E
112 B10 **Novi Vinodolski** *var.* Novi. Primorje-Gorski Kotar, NW Croatia 45°08′N 14°46′E
58 F12 **Novo Airão** Amazonas, N Brazil 02°06′S 61°20′W
**Novoalekseyevka** *see* Kobda
127 N9 **Novoanninskiy** Volgogradskaya Oblast', SW Russia 50°31′N 42°43′E
58 F13 **Novo Aripuanã** Amazonas, N Brazil 05°05′S 60°20′W
117 P7 **Novoarkhangel's'k** Kirovohrads'ka Oblast', C Ukraine 48°39′N 30°48′E
117 Y6 **Novoaydar** Luhans'ka Oblast', E Ukraine 49°00′N 39°00′E
117 X9 **Novoazovs'k** *Rus.* Novoazovsk. Donets'ka Oblast', E Ukraine 47°07′N 38°06′E
123 R14 **Novobureyskiy** Amurskaya Oblast', SE Russia 49°42′N 129°46′E
127 Q3 **Novocheboksarsk** Chuvashskaya Respublika, W Russia 56°07′N 47°33′E
127 R5 **Novocheremshansk** Ul'yanovskaya Oblast', W Russia 54°23′N 50°08′E
126 L12 **Novocherkassk** Rostovskaya Oblast', SW Russia 47°23′N 40°00′E
127 R6 **Novodevich'ye** Samarskaya Oblast', W Russia 53°33′N 48°51′E
124 M8 **Novodvinsk** Arkhangel'skaya Oblast', NW Russia 64°22′N 40°49′E
**Novograd-Volynskiy** *see* Novohrad-Volyns'kyy
**Novogrudok** *see* Navahrudak
**Novogrudskaya Vozvyshennost'** *see* Navahrudskaye Wzvyshsha
61 I15 **Novo Hamburgo** Rio Grande do Sul, S Brazil 29°42′S 51°07′W
59 H16 **Novo Horizonte** Mato Grosso, W Brazil 11°19′S 57°11′W
60 K8 **Novo Horizonte** São Paulo, S Brazil 21°27′S 49°14′W
116 M4 **Novohrad-Volyns'kyy** *Rus.* Novograd-Volynskiy. Zhytomyrs'ka Oblast', N Ukraine 50°34′N 27°32′E
145 O7 **Novoishimskiy** *prev.* Kuybyshevskiy. Severnyy Kazakhstan, N Kazakhstan 53°15′N 66°51′E
**Novokazalinsk** *see* Ayteke Bi
126 M8 **Novokhopersk** Voronezhskaya Oblast', W Russia 51°09′N 41°34′E
127 R6 **Novokuybyshevsk** Samarskaya Oblast', W Russia 53°06′N 49°56′E
122 J13 **Novokuznetsk** *prev.* Stalinsk. Kemerovskaya Oblast', S Russia 53°45′N 87°12′E
195 R1 **Novolazarevskaya** *research station (Russia)* Antarctica 70°42′S 11°31′E
**Novolukoml'** *see* Novalukoml'
109 V12 **Novo mesto** *Ger.* Rudolfswert; *prev. Ger.* Neustadtl. SE Slovenia 45°49′N 15°09′E
126 K15 **Novomikhaylovskiy** Krasnodarskiy Kray, SW Russia 44°18′N 38°49′E
112 L8 **Novo Miloševo** Vojvodina, N Serbia 45°43′N 20°20′E
**Novomirgorod** *see* Novomyrhorod
126 L5 **Novomoskovsk** Tul'skaya Oblast', W Russia 54°05′N 38°23′E
117 U7 **Novomoskovs'k** *Rus.* Novomoskovsk. Dnipropetrovs'ka Oblast', E Ukraine 48°38′N 35°15′E
117 V8 **Novomykolayivka** Zaporiz'ka Oblast', SE Ukraine 47°58′N 35°54′E
117 Q7 **Novomyrhorod** *Rus.* Novomirgorod. Kirovohrads'ka Oblast', S Ukraine 48°46′N 31°39′E
127 N8 **Novonikolayevskiy** Volgogradskaya Oblast', SW Russia 50°55′N 42°24′E
127 P10 **Novonikol'skoye** Volgogradskaya Oblast', SW Russia 49°23′N 45°06′E
127 X7 **Novoorsk** Orenburgskaya Oblast', W Russia 51°21′N 59°03′E
126 M13 **Novopokrovskaya** Krasnodarskiy Kray, SW Russia 45°58′N 40°43′E
**Novopolotsk** *see* Navapolatsk
117 Y5 **Novopskov** Luhans'ka Oblast', E Ukraine 49°33′N 39°07′E
**Novoradomsk** *see* Radomsko
**Novo Redondo** *see* Sumbe
127 R8 **Novorepnoye** Saratovskaya Oblast', W Russia 51°04′N 48°34′E
126 K14 **Novorossiysk** Krasnodarskiy Kray, SW Russia 44°50′N 37°38′E
**Novorossiyskiy/ Novorossiyskoye** *see* Akzhar
124 F15 **Novorzhev** Pskovskaya Oblast', W Russia 57°01′N 29°19′E
**Novoselitsa** *see* Novoselytsya
117 S12 **Novoselivs'ke** Avtonomna Respublika Krym, S Ukraine 45°26′N 33°37′E
**Novosëlki** *see* Navasyolki
114 G6 **Novo Selo** Vidin, NW Bulgaria 44°08′N 22°48′E
113 M14 **Novo Selo** Serbia, C Serbia 43°39′N 20°54′E
116 K8 **Novoselytsya** *Rom.* Nouă Sulița, *Rus.* Novoselitsa. Chernivets'ka Oblast', W Ukraine 48°14′N 26°18′E
127 U7 **Novosergiyevka** Orenburgskaya Oblast', W Russia 52°04′N 53°40′E
126 L11 **Novoshakhtinsk** Rostovskaya Oblast', SW Russia 47°48′N 39°51′E
122 J12 **Novosibirsk** Novosibirskaya Oblast', C Russia 55°04′N 83°05′E
122 J12 **Novosibirskaya Oblast'** ◈ *province* C Russia
122 M4 **Novosibirskiye Ostrova** *Eng.* New Siberian Islands. *island group* N Russia
126 K6 **Novosil'** Orlovskaya Oblast', W Russia 53°00′N 37°59′E
124 G16 **Novosokol'niki** Pskovskaya Oblast', W Russia 56°21′N 30°07′E
127 Q6 **Novospasskoye** Ul'yanovskaya Oblast', W Russia 53°08′N 47°48′E
**Novotroickoje** *see* Birlik
127 X8 **Novotroitsk** Orenburgskaya Oblast', W Russia 51°10′N 58°18′E
**Novotroitskoye** *see* Brlik, Kazakhstan
**Novotroitskoye** *see* Novotroyits'ke, Ukraine
117 T11 **Novotroyits'ke** *Rus.* Novotroitskoye. Khersons'ka Oblast', S Ukraine 46°21′N 34°21′E
**Novoukrainka** *see* Novoukrayinka
117 Q8 **Novoukrayinka** *Rus.* Novoukrainka. Kirovohrads'ka Oblast', C Ukraine 48°19′N 31°33′E
127 Q5 **Novoul'yanovsk** Ul'yanovskaya Oblast', W Russia 54°10′N 48°19′E
127 W8 **Novoural'sk** Orenburgskaya Oblast', W Russia 51°19′N 56°57′E
**Novo-Urgench** *see* Urganch
116 I4 **Novovolyns'k** *Rus.* Novovolynsk. Volyns'ka Oblast', NW Ukraine 50°46′N 24°09′E
117 S9 **Novovorontsovka** Khersons'ka Oblast', S Ukraine 47°28′N 33°55′E
147 Y7 **Novovoznesenovka** Issyk-Kul'skaya Oblast', E Kyrgyzstan 42°36′N 78°44′E
125 R14 **Novovyatsk** Kirovskaya Oblast', NW Russia 58°30′N 49°42′E
**Novoyel'nya** *see* Navayel'nya
117 O6 **Novozhyvotiv** Vinnyts'ka Oblast', C Ukraine 49°16′N 29°31′E
126 H6 **Novozybkov** Bryanskaya Oblast', W Russia 52°36′N 31°58′E
112 F9 **Novska** Sisak-Moslavina, NE Croatia 45°20′N 16°58′E
**Nový Bohumín** *see* Bohumín
111 D15 **Nový Bor** *Ger.* Haida; *prev.* Bor u České Lípy, Hajda. Liberecký Kraj, N Czechia 50°46′N 14°32′E
111 E16 **Nový Bydžov** *Ger.* Neubidschow. Královéhradecký Kraj, N Czechia 50°15′N 15°27′E
119 G18 **Novy Dvor** *Rus.* Novyy Dvor. Hrodzyenskaya Voblasts', W Belarus 53°48′N 24°34′E
111 I17 **Nový Jičín** *Ger.* Neutitschein. Moravskoslezský Kraj, E Czechia 49°36′N 18°00′E
118 K12 **Novy Pahost** *Rus.* Novyy Pogost. Vitsyebskaya Voblasts', NW Belarus 55°30′N 27°29′E
**Novyy Bug** *see* Novyy Buh
117 R9 **Novyy Buh** *Rus.* Novyy Bug. Mykolayivs'ka Oblast', S Ukraine 47°40′N 32°30′E
117 Q4 **Novyy Bykiv** Chernihivs'ka Oblast', N Ukraine 50°36′N 31°39′E
**Novyy Dvor** *see* Novy Dvor
**Novyye Aneny** *see* Anenii Noi
127 P7 **Novyye Burasy** Saratovskaya Oblast', W Russia 52°10′N 46°00′E
**Novyy Margilan** *see* Farg'ona
126 K8 **Novyy Oskol** Belgorodskaya Oblast', W Russia 50°43′N 37°55′E
**Novyy Pogost** *see* Novy Pahost
127 R2 **Novyy Tor"yal** Respublika Mariy El, W Russia 56°59′N 48°53′E
123 N12 **Novyy Uoyan** Respublika Buryatiya, S Russia 56°06′N 111°27′E
122 J9 **Novyy Urengoy** Yamalo-Nenetskiy Avtonomnyy Okrug, N Russia 66°06′N 76°25′E
**Novyy Uzen'** *see* Zhanaozen
111 N16 **Nowa Dęba** Podkarpackie, SE Poland 50°31′N 21°53′E
111 G15 **Nowa Ruda** *Ger.* Neurode. Dolnośląskie, SW Poland 50°34′N 16°30′E
110 F12 **Nowa Sól** *var.* Nowasól, *Ger.* Neusalz an der Oder. Lubuskie, W Poland 51°47′N 15°43′E
**Nowasól** *see* Nowa Sól
27 Q8 **Nowata** Oklahoma, C USA 36°42′N 95°36′W
142 M6 **Nowbarān** Markazī, W Iran 35°07′N 49°51′E
110 J8 **Nowe** Kujawsko-pomorskie, N Poland 53°40′N 18°44′E
110 K9 **Nowe Miasto Lubawskie** *Ger.* Neumark. Warmińsko-Mazurskie, NE Poland 53°24′N 19°36′E
110 L13 **Nowe Miasto nad Pilicą** Mazowieckie, C Poland 51°37′N 20°34′E
110 D8 **Nowe Warpno** *Ger.* Neuwarp. Zachodnio-pomorskie, NW Poland 53°52′N 14°12′E
**Nowgong** *see* Nagaon
110 E8 **Nowogard** *var.* Nowógard, *Ger.* Naugard. Zachodnio-pomorskie, NW Poland 53°41′N 15°09′E
110 N9 **Nowogród** Podlaskie, NE Poland 53°14′N 21°52′E
**Nowogródek** *see* Navahrudak
111 E14 **Nowogrodziec** *Ger.* Naumburg am Queis. Dolnośląskie, SW Poland 51°12′N 15°24′E
**Nowojelnia** *see* Navayel'nya
**Nowo-Minsk** *see* Mińsk Mazowiecki
33 V13 **Nowood River** ≈ Wyoming, C USA
**Nowo-Święciany** *see* Švenčionėliai
183 S10 **Nowra-Bomaderry** New South Wales, SE Australia 34°51′S 150°41′E
149 T5 **Nowshera** *var.* Naushahra, Naushara. Khyber Pakhtunkhwa, NE Pakistan 34°00′N 72°00′E
110 J7 **Nowy Dwór Gdański** *Ger.* Tiegenhof. Pomorskie, N Poland 54°12′N 19°03′E
110 L11 **Nowy Dwór Mazowiecki** Mazowieckie, C Poland 52°26′N 20°43′E
111 M17 **Nowy Sącz** *Ger.* Neu Sandec. Małopolskie, S Poland 49°36′N 20°42′E
111 L18 **Nowy Targ** *Ger.* Neumarkt. Małopolskie, S Poland 49°28′N 20°00′E
110 F11 **Nowy Tomyśl** *var.* Nowy Tomysl. Wielkopolskie, C Poland 52°18′N 16°07′E
**Nowy Tomysl** *see* Nowy Tomyśl
148 M7 **Now Zād** *var.* Nauzad. Helmand, S Afghanistan 32°22′N 64°32′E
23 N4 **Noxubee River** ≈ Alabama/Mississippi, S USA
122 I10 **Noyabr'sk** Yamalo-Nenetskiy Avtonomnyy Okrug, N Russia 63°08′N 75°19′E
102 L8 **Noyant** Maine-et-Loire, NW France 47°28′N 00°08′W
39 X14 **Noyes Island** *island* Alexander Archipelago, Alaska, USA
103 O3 **Noyon** Oise, N France 49°35′N 03°E
102 I7 **Nozay** Loire-Atlantique, NW France 47°34′N 01°36′W
82 L12 **Nsando** Northern, NE Zambia 10°22′S 31°14′E
83 N16 **Nsanje** Southern, S Malawi 16°57′S 35°10′E


◆ Country
● Country Capital
◇ Dependent Territory
○ Dependent Territory Capital
◈ Administrative Regions
✈ International Airport
▲ Mountain
▲▲ Mountain Range
⩘ Volcano
≈ River
◎ Lake
⊠ Reservoir

NSAWAM – OGAADEEN


77 Q17 **Nsawam** SE Ghana 05°47′N 00°19′W
79 E16 **Nsimalen** ✈ Centre, C Cameroon 19°15′N 81°22′E
82 K12 **Nsombo** Northern, NE Zambia 10°35′S 29°58′E
82 H13 **Ntambu** North Western, NW Zambia 12°21′S 25°03′E
83 N14 **Ntcheu** *var.* Ncheu. Central, S Malawi 14°49′S 34°37′E
79 D17 **Ntem** *prev.* Campo, Kampo. ⇝ Cameroon/Equatorial Guinea
83 I14 **Ntemwa** North Western, NW Zambia 14°03′S 26°13′E
**Ntlenyana, Mount** *see* Thabana Ntlenyana
79 I19 **Ntomba, Lac** *var.* Lac Tumba. ◎ NW Dem. Rep. Congo
115 I19 **Ntóro, Kávo** *prev.* Akrotírio Kafiréas. *cape* Évvoia, C Greece
81 E19 **Ntungamo** SW Uganda 0°54′S 30°16′E
81 E18 **Ntusi** SW Uganda 0°05′N 31°13′E
83 H18 **Ntwetwe Pan** *salt lake* NE Botswana
93 M15 **Nuasjärvi** ◎ C Finland
80 F11 **Nuba Mountains** ▲ C Sudan
68 J9 **Nubian Desert** *desert* NE Sudan
63 G14 **Ñuble** *region* C Chile
116 G10 **Nucet** *Hung.* Diófás. Bihor, W Romania 46°28′N 22°35′E
**Nu Chiang** *see* Thanlwin
145 U9 **Nuclear Testing Ground** *nuclear site* Pavlodar, E Kazakhstan
56 E9 **Nucuray, Río** ⇝ N Peru
25 R14 **Nueces River** ⇝ Texas, SW USA
9 V9 **Nueltin Lake** ◎ Manitoba/Northwest Territories, C Canada
99 K15 **Nuenen** Noord-Brabant, S Netherlands 51°29′N 05°36′E
62 G6 **Nueva Señora, Bahía** *bay* N Chile
61 D14 **Nuestra Señora Rosario de Caa Catí** Corrientes, NE Argentina 27°48′S 57°42′W
54 J9 **Nueva Antioquia** Vichada, E Colombia 06°04′N 69°30′W
**Nueva Caceres** *see* Naga
41 O7 **Nueva Ciudad Guerrera** Tamaulipas, C Mexico 26°32′N 99°13′W
55 N4 **Nueva Esparta** *off.* Estado Nueva Esparta. ◆ *state* NE Venezuela
**Nueva Esparta, Estado** *see* Nueva Esparta
44 C5 **Nueva Gerona** Isla de la Juventud, S Cuba 21°49′N 82°49′W
42 H8 **Nueva Guadalupe** San Miguel, E El Salvador 13°30′N 88°21′W
42 M11 **Nueva Guinea** Costa Caribe Sur, SE Nicaragua 11°40′N 84°22′W
61 D19 **Nueva Helvecia** Colonia, SW Uruguay 34°16′S 57°53′W
63 J25 **Nueva, Isla** *island* S Chile
40 M14 **Nueva Italia** Michoacán, SW Mexico 19°01′N 102°06′W
56 D6 **Nueva Loja** *var.* Lago Agrio. Sucumbíos, NE Ecuador
42 F6 **Nueva Ocotepeque** *prev.* Ocotepeque. Ocotepeque, W Honduras 14°25′N 89°10′W
61 D19 **Nueva Palmira** Colonia, SW Uruguay 33°53′S 58°25′W
41 N6 **Nueva Rosita** Coahuila, NE Mexico 27°58′N 101°11′W
42 E7 **Nueva San Salvador** *prev.* Santa Tecla. La Libertad, SW El Salvador 13°40′N 89°18′W
42 J8 **Nueva Segovia** ◆ *department* NW Nicaragua
**Nueva Tabarca** *see* Plana, Isla
**Nueva Villa de Padilla** *see* Nuevo Padilla
61 B21 **Nueve de Julio** Buenos Aires, E Argentina 35°29′S 60°52′W
44 H6 **Nuevitas** Camagüey, E Cuba 21°34′N 77°18′W
61 D18 **Nuevo Berlín** Río Negro, W Uruguay 32°59′S 58°03′W
40 I4 **Nuevo Casas Grandes** Chihuahua, N Mexico 30°23′N 107°54′W
43 T14 **Nuevo Chagres** Colón, C Panama 09°14′N 80°05′W
41 W15 **Nuevo Coahuila** Campeche, E Mexico 17°53′N 90°46′W
63 K17 **Nuevo, Golfo** *gulf* S Argentina
41 O7 **Nuevo Laredo** Tamaulipas, NE Mexico 27°28′N 99°32′W
41 N8 **Nuevo León** ◆ *state* NE Mexico
41 P10 **Nuevo Padilla** *var.* Nueva Villa de Padilla. Tamaulipas, C Mexico 24°01′N 98°48′W
56 E6 **Nuevo Rocafuerte** Orellana, E Ecuador 0°59′S 75°27′W
**Nuga** *see* Dzavhanmandal
80 O13 **Nugaal** *off.* Gobolka Nugaal. ◆ *region* N Somalia
**Nugaal, Gobolka** *see* Nugaal
185 E24 **Nugget Point** *headland* South Island, New Zealand 46°26′S 169°49′E
186 J5 **Nuguria Islands** *island group* E Papua New Guinea
184 P10 **Nuhaka** Hawke's Bay, North Island, New Zealand 39°03′S 177°43′E
138 M10 **Nuhaydayn, Wādī an** *dry watercourse* W Iraq
190 E7 **Nui Atoll** *atoll* W Tuvalu
**Nu Jiang** *see* Thanlwin
**Nûk** *see* Nuuk
182 G7 **Nukey Bluff** *hill* South Australia
**Nukha** *see* Şäki
123 T9 **Nukh Yablonevyy, Gora** ▲ E Russia 60°26′N 151°45′E
186 K7 **Nukiki** Choiseul, NW Solomon Islands 06°45′S 156°30′E
186 B6 **Nuku** West Sepik, NW Papua New Guinea 03°48′S 142°23′E
193 W15 **Nukuʻalofa** Tongatapu Group, NE Tonga
193 U15 **Nukuʻalofa** Tongatapu, S Tonga 21°09′S 175°14′W
193 Y16 **Nukuʻalofa** ● (Tonga) Tongatapu, S Tonga 21°08′S 175°13′W
190 G12 **Nukuatea** *island* N Wallis and Futuna
190 F7 **Nukufetau Atoll** *atoll* C Tuvalu
190 G12 **Nukuhifala** *island* E Wallis and Futuna
191 W7 **Nuku Hiva** *island* Îles Marquises, NE French Polynesia
191 W7 **Nuku Hiva Island** *island* Îles Marquises, N French Polynesia
190 F9 **Nukulaelae Atoll** *var.* Nukulailai. *atoll* E Tuvalu
**Nukulailai** *see* Nukulaelae Atoll
190 G11 **Nukuloa** *island* N Wallis and Futuna
186 L6 **Nukumanu Islands** *prev.* Tasman Group. *island group* NE Papua New Guinea
**Nukunau** *see* Nikunau
190 J9 **Nukunonu Atoll** *island* C Tokelau
190 J9 **Nukunonu Village** Nukunonu Atoll, C Tokelau
189 S18 **Nukuoro Atoll** *atoll* Caroline Islands, S Micronesia
146 H8 **Nukus** Qoraqalpog'iston Respublikasi, W Uzbekistan 42°29′N 59°32′E
190 G11 **Nukutapu** *island* N Wallis and Futuna
39 O9 **Nulato** Alaska, USA 64°43′N 158°06′W
39 O10 **Nulato Hills** ▲ Alaska, USA
105 T9 **Nules** Comunitat Valenciana, E Spain 39°52′N 00°10′W
**Nuling** *see* Sultan Kudarat
182 C6 **Nullarbor** South Australia 31°28′S 130°57′E
180 M11 **Nullarbor Plain** *plateau* South Australia/Western Australia
163 S12 **Nulu'erhu Shan** ▲ N China
77 X14 **Numan** Adamawa, E Nigeria 09°26′N 11°58′E
165 S3 **Numata** Hokkaidō, NE Japan 43°48′N 141°55′E
81 C15 **Numatinna** ⇝ W South Sudan
95 F14 **Numedalen** *valley* S Norway
95 G14 **Numedalslågen** *var.* Laagen. ⇝ S Norway
93 L19 **Nummela** Uusimaa, S Finland 60°21′N 24°20′E
183 O11 **Numurkah** Victoria, SE Australia 36°04′S 145°28′E
196 L16 **Nunap Isua** *var.* Uummannarsuaq, *Dan.* Kap Farvel, *Eng.* Cape Farewell. *cape* S Greenland
9 N8 **Nunavut** ◇ *territory* N Canada
54 H9 **Nunchia** Casanare, C Colombia 05°37′N 72°13′W
97 M20 **Nuneaton** C England, United Kingdom 52°32′N 01°28′W
153 W14 **Nungba** Manipur, NE India 24°46′N 93°25′E
38 L12 **Nunivak Island** *island* Alaska, USA
152 I5 **Nun Kun** ▲ NW India 34°01′N 76°04′E
98 L10 **Nunspeet** Gelderland, E Netherlands 52°21′N 05°45′E
107 C18 **Nuoro** Sardegna, Italy, C Mediterranean Sea 40°20′N 09°20′E
75 R12 **Nuqayy, Jabal** *hill range* S Libya
54 C9 **Nuquí** Chocó, W Colombia 05°44′N 77°16′W
143 O4 **Nūr** Māzandarān, N Iran 36°32′N 52°00′E
145 Q9 **Nura** ⇝ N Kazakhstan
143 N11 **Nūrābād** Fārs, C Iran 30°08′N 51°30′E
**Nurakita** *see* Niulakita
**Nurata** *see* Nurota
**Nuratau, Khrebet** *see* Nurota Tizmasi
136 L17 **Nur Dağları** ▲ S Turkey
**Nurek** *see* Norak
**Nuremberg** *see* Nürnberg
**Nürestān** *see* Nüristān
136 M15 **Nurhak** Kahramanmaraş, S Turkey 37°57′N 37°21′E
182 J9 **Nuriootpa** South Australia 34°28′S 139°00′E
149 S4 **Nūristān** *prev.* Nūrestān. ◆ *province* C Afghanistan
127 S5 **Nurlat** Respublika Tatarstan, W Russia 54°26′N 50°48′E
93 N15 **Nurmes** Pohjois-Karjala, E Finland 63°31′N 29°10′E
101 K20 **Nürnberg** *Eng.* Nuremberg. Bayern, S Germany 49°27′N 11°05′E
101 K20 **Nürnberg** ✈ Bayern, SE Germany 49°29′N 11°04′E
146 M10 **Nurota** *Rus.* Nurata. Navoiy Viloyati, C Uzbekistan 40°41′N 65°43′E
147 N10 **Nurota Tizmasi** *Rus.* Khrebet Nuratau. ▲ C Uzbekistan
149 T8 **Nurpur** Punjab, E Pakistan 31°54′N 71°55′E
183 P6 **Nurri, Mount** *hill* New South Wales, SE Australia
25 T13 **Nursery** Texas, SW USA 28°55′N 97°05′W
145 Q9 **Nur-Sultan** *prev.* Astana, Akmola, Akmolinsk, Tselinograd, Aqmola. ● (Kazakhstan) Akmola, N Kazakhstan 51°13′N 71°25′E
169 V17 **Nusa Tenggara Barat** *off.* Propinsi Nusa Tenggara Barat, *Eng.* West Nusa Tenggara. ◆ *province* S Indonesia
**Nusa Tenggara Barat, Propinsi** *see* Nusa Tenggara Barat
171 O16 **Nusa Tenggara Timur** *off.* Propinsi Nusa Tenggara Timur, *Eng.* East Nusa Tenggara. ◆ *province* S Indonesia
**Nusa Tenggara Timur, Propinsi** *see* Nusa Tenggara Timur
171 U14 **Nusawulan** Papua Barat, E Indonesia 04°03′S 132°56′E
137 Q16 **Nusaybin** *var.* Nisibin. Manisa, SE Turkey 37°08′N 41°11′E
39 O14 **Nushagak Bay** *bay* Alaska, USA
39 O13 **Nushagak Peninsula** *headland* Alaska, USA 58°39′N 159°03′W
39 O13 **Nushagak River** ⇝ Alaska, USA
160 E11 **Nu Shan** ▲ SW China
149 N11 **Nushki** Baluchistan, SW Pakistan 29°33′N 66°01′E
**Nussdorf** *see* Năsăud
112 J9 **Nuštar** Vukovar-Srijem, E Croatia 45°20′N 18°48′E
99 L18 **Nuth** Limburg, SE Netherlands 50°55′N 05°52′E
100 N13 **Nuthe** ⇝ NE Germany
**Nutmeg State** *see* Connecticut
39 T10 **Nutzotin Mountains** ▲ Alaska, USA
64 I5 **Nuuk** *var.* Nûk, *Dan.* Godthaab, Godthåb. ○ (Greenland) Sermersooq, SW Greenland 64°15′N 51°35′W
92 L13 **Nuupas** Lappi, NW Finland 66°01′N 26°19′E
191 O7 **Nuupere, Pointe** *headland* Moorea, W French Polynesia 17°35′S 149°47′W
191 O7 **Nuuroa, Pointe** *headland* Tahiti, W French Polynesia
**Nüürst** *see* Baganuur
**Nuwara** *see* Nuwara Eliya
155 K25 **Nuwara Eliya** *var.* Nuwara. Central Province, S Sri Lanka 06°58′N 80°46′E
182 E7 **Nuyts Archipelago** *island group* South Australia
83 F17 **Nxaunxau** Ngamiland, NW Botswana 18°57′S 21°18′E
39 N12 **Nyac** Alaska, USA 61°00′N 159°56′W
122 H9 **Nyagan'** Khanty-Mansiyskiy Avtonomnyy Okrug-Yugra, N Russia 62°10′N 65°32′E
**Nyagassola** *see* Niagassola
**Nyagquka** *see* Yajiang
81 I18 **Nyahururu** Nyandarua, C Kenya 0°04′N 36°22′E
182 M10 **Nyah West** Victoria, SE Australia 35°14′S 143°18′E
158 M15 **Nyainqêntanglha Feng** ▲ W China 30°20′N 90°28′E
159 N15 **Nyainqêntanglha Shan** ▲ W China
80 B11 **Nyala** Southern Darfur, W Sudan 12°01′N 24°50′E
83 M16 **Nyamapanda** Mashonaland East, NE Zimbabwe 16°59′S 32°52′E
81 H25 **Nyamtumbo** Ruvuma, S Tanzania 10°33′S 36°08′E
**Nyanda** *see* Masvingo
124 M11 **Nyandoma** Arkhangel'skaya Oblast', NW Russia 61°39′N 40°10′E
83 M16 **Nyanga** *prev.* Inyanga. Manicaland, E Zimbabwe 18°13′S 32°46′E
79 D20 **Nyanga** *off.* Province de la Nyanga, *var.* La Nyanga. ◆ *province* SW Gabon
79 E20 **Nyanga** ⇝ Congo/Gabon
83 M16 **Nyangani** ▲ NE Zimbabwe 18°22′S 32°57′E
**Nyanga, Province de la** *see* Nyanga
81 F20 **Nyantakara** Kagera, NW Tanzania 03°05′S 31°23′E
81 E21 **Nyanza-Lac** S Burundi 04°16′S 29°38′E
68 J14 **Nyasa, Lake** *var.* Lake Malawi; *prev.* Lago Nyassa. ◎ E Africa
**Nyasaland/Nyasaland Protectorate** *see* Malawi
**Nyassa, Lago** *see* Nyasa, Lake
119 J17 **Nyasvizh** *Pol.* Nieśwież, *Rus.* Nesvizh. Minskaya Voblasts', C Belarus 53°13′N 26°40′E
166 M8 **Nyaunglebin** Bago, SW Myanmar (Burma) 17°59′N 96°44′E
166 M5 **Nyaung-U** Magway, C Myanmar (Burma) 21°03′N 95°44′E
95 H24 **Nyborg** Syddtjylland, C Denmark 55°19′N 10°48′E
95 N21 **Nybro** Kalmar, S Sweden 56°45′N 15°54′E
119 J16 **Nyeharelaye** *Rus.* Negoreloye. Minskaya Voblasts', C Belarus 53°36′N 27°04′E
195 W3 **Nye Mountains** ▲ Antarctica
81 I19 **Nyeri** Nyeri, C Kenya 0°25′S 36°56′E
118 M11 **Nyeshcharda, Vozyera** *Rus.* Ozero Neshcherdo. ◎ N Belarus
92 O2 **Ny-Friesland** *physical region* N Svalbard
95 L14 **Nyhammar** Dalarna, C Sweden 60°19′N 14°55′E
160 F7 **Nyikog Qu** ⇝ C China
83 L14 **Nyimba** Eastern, E Zambia 14°33′S 30°49′E
159 P15 **Nyingchi** *var.* Pula. Xizang Zizhiqu, W China 29°34′N 94°33′E
**Nyinma** *see* Maqu
111 O21 **Nyírbátor** Szabolcs-Szatmár-Bereg, E Hungary 47°50′N 22°09′E
111 N21 **Nyíregyháza** Szabolcs-Szatmár-Bereg, NE Hungary 47°57′N 21°43′E
**Nyiro** *see* Ewaso Ng'iro
**Nyitra** *see* Nitra
**Nyitrabánya** *see* Handlová
93 K16 **Nykarleby** *Fin.* Uusikaarlepyy. Österbotten, W Finland 63°22′N 22°30′E
95 F21 **Nykøbing** Midtjylland, NW Denmark 56°48′N 08°52′E
95 I22 **Nykøbing** Sjælland, C Denmark 55°56′N 11°41′E
95 I25 **Nykøbing** Sjælland, SE Denmark 54°47′N 11°53′E
95 N17 **Nyköping** Södermanland, S Sweden 58°45′N 17°03′E
95 L15 **Nykroppa** Värmland, C Sweden 59°37′N 14°18′E
**Nylstroom** *see* Modimolle
183 P7 **Nymagee** New South Wales, SE Australia 32°06′S 146°19′E
183 V5 **Nymboida** New South Wales, SE Australia 29°57′S 152°45′E
183 U5 **Nymboida River** ⇝ New South Wales, SE Australia
111 D16 **Nymburk** *var.* Neuenburg an der Elbe, *Ger.* Nimburg. Středočeský Kraj, C Czechia 50°12′N 15°00′E
95 O16 **Nynäshamn** Stockholm, C Sweden 58°54′N 17°55′E
183 Q6 **Nyngan** New South Wales, SE Australia 31°36′S 147°07′E
**Nyoman** *see* Neman
108 A10 **Nyon** *Ger.* Neuss; *anc.* Noviodunum. Vaud, SW Switzerland 46°23′N 06°15′E
79 D16 **Nyong** ⇝ SW Cameroon
103 S14 **Nyons** Drôme, E France 44°22′N 05°06′E
79 D14 **Nyos, Lac** *Eng.* Lake Nyos. ◎ NW Cameroon
**Nyos, Lake** *see* Nyos, Lac
125 U11 **Nyrob** *var.* Nyrov. Permskiy Kray, NW Russia 60°41′N 56°42′E
**Nyrov** *see* Nyrob
111 H15 **Nysa** *Ger.* Neisse. Opolskie, S Poland 50°28′N 17°20′E
32 M13 **Nyssa** Oregon, NW USA 43°52′N 116°59′W
**Nysa Łużycka** *see* Neisse
**Nyslott** *see* Savonlinna
**Nystad** *see* Uusikaupunki
95 I25 **Nysted** Sjælland, SE Denmark 54°40′N 11°41′E
125 U14 **Nytva** Permskiy Kray, NW Russia 57°56′N 55°22′E
165 P8 **Nyūdō-zaki** *headland* Honshū, C Japan 39°59′N 139°40′E
125 P9 **Nyukhcha** Arkhangel'skaya Oblast', NW Russia 63°24′N 46°34′E
124 H8 **Nyuk, Ozero** *var.* Ozero Njuk. ◎ NW Russia
125 O12 **Nyuksenitsa** *var.* Njuksenica. Vologodskaya Oblast', NW Russia 60°25′N 44°12′E
79 O22 **Nyunzu** Katanga, SE Dem. Rep. Congo 05°55′S 28°00′E
123 O10 **Nyurba** Respublika Sakha (Yakutiya), NE Russia 63°17′N 118°15′E
123 O11 **Nyuya** Respublika Sakha (Yakutiya), NE Russia 60°33′N 116°10′E
146 K12 **Nyýazow** *Rus.* Niyazov. Lebap Welaýaty, NE Turkmenistan 39°13′N 63°16′E
117 T10 **Nyzhni Sirohozy** Khersons'ka Oblast', S Ukraine 46°49′N 34°21′E
117 U12 **Nyzhn'ohirs'kyy** *Rus.* Nizhnegorskiy. Avtonomna Respublika Krym, S Ukraine 45°26′N 34°42′E
**NZ** *see* New Zealand
81 G21 **Nzega** Tabora, C Tanzania 04°13′S 33°11′E
76 K15 **Nzérékoré** SE Guinea 07°45′N 08°49′W
82 A10 **N'Zeto** *prev.* Ambrizete. Zaire Province, NW Angola 07°14′S 12°52′E
79 M24 **Nzilo, Lac** *prev.* Lac Delcommune. ◎ SE Dem. Rep. Congo
172 I13 **Nzwani** *Fr.* Anjouan, *var.* Ndzouani. *island* SE Comoros

# O

29 O11 **Oacoma** South Dakota, N USA 43°49′N 99°25′W
29 N9 **Oahe Dam** *dam* South Dakota, N USA
28 M9 **Oahe, Lake** ▣ North Dakota/South Dakota, N USA
38 C9 **Oaʻhu** *var.* Oahu. *island* Hawai'ian Islands, Hawai'i, USA
165 V4 **O-Akan-dake** ▲ Hokkaidō, NE Japan 43°26′N 144°09′E
182 K8 **Oakbank** South Australia 33°07′S 140°36′E
19 P13 **Oak Bluffs** Martha's Vineyard, New York, NE USA 41°25′N 70°32′W
36 K4 **Oak City** Utah, W USA 39°22′N 112°19′W
37 R3 **Oak Creek** Colorado, C USA 40°16′N 106°57′W
35 P8 **Oakdale** California, W USA 37°46′N 120°51′W
22 H8 **Oakdale** Louisiana, S USA 30°49′N 92°39′W
29 P7 **Oakes** North Dakota, N USA 46°08′N 98°05′W
22 J4 **Oak Grove** Louisiana, S USA 32°51′N 91°25′W
97 N19 **Oakham** C England, United Kingdom 52°41′N 00°45′W
32 H7 **Oak Harbor** Washington, NW USA 48°17′N 122°38′W
21 R5 **Oak Hill** West Virginia, NE USA 37°59′N 81°09′W
35 N8 **Oakland** California, W USA 37°48′N 122°16′W
29 S15 **Oakland** Iowa, C USA 41°18′N 95°22′W
19 Q7 **Oakland** Maine, NE USA 44°32′N 69°43′W
21 T3 **Oakland** Maryland, NE USA 39°24′N 79°25′W
29 R14 **Oakland** Nebraska, C USA 41°50′N 96°28′W
31 N11 **Oak Lawn** Illinois, N USA 41°43′N 87°45′W
33 P16 **Oakley** Idaho, NW USA 42°13′N 113°54′W
26 I4 **Oakley** Kansas, C USA 39°08′N 100°53′W
31 N10 **Oak Park** Illinois, N USA 41°53′N 87°46′W
11 X16 **Oak Point** Manitoba, S Canada 50°23′N 97°00′W
32 G13 **Oakridge** Oregon, NW USA 43°45′N 122°27′W
20 M9 **Oak Ridge** Tennessee, S USA 36°02′N 84°12′W
184 K10 **Oakura** Taranaki, North Island, New Zealand 39°07′S 173°58′E
22 L7 **Oak Vale** Mississippi, S USA 31°26′N 89°57′W
14 G16 **Oakville** Ontario, S Canada 43°27′N 79°41′W
25 V8 **Oakwood** Texas, SW USA 31°34′N 95°51′W
185 F22 **Oamaru** Otago, South Island, New Zealand 45°10′S 170°51′E
96 F13 **Oa, Mull of** *headland* W Scotland, United Kingdom 55°35′N 06°20′W
171 O11 **Oan** Sulawesi, N Indonesia 01°16′N 121°25′E
185 J17 **Oaro** Canterbury, South Island, New Zealand 42°29′S 173°30′E
35 X2 **Oasis** Nevada, W USA 41°01′N 114°29′W
195 S15 **Oates Land** *physical region* Antarctica
183 P17 **Oatlands** Tasmania, SE Australia 42°21′S 147°23′E
36 I11 **Oatman** Arizona, SW USA 35°03′N 114°19′W
41 R16 **Oaxaca** *var.* Oaxaca de Juárez; *prev.* Antequera. Oaxaca, SE Mexico 17°04′N 96°41′W
41 Q16 **Oaxaca** ◆ *state* SE Mexico
**Oaxaca de Juárez** *see* Oaxaca
122 I19 **Ob'** ⇝ C Russia
145 X9 **Oba** *prev.* Uba. ⇝ E Kazakhstan
14 G9 **Obabika Lake** ◎ Ontario, S Canada
**Obagan** *see* Ubagan
118 M12 **Obal'** *Rus.* Obol'. Vitsyebskaya Voblasts', N Belarus 55°22′N 29°17′E
79 E16 **Obala** Centre, SW Cameroon 04°09′N 11°32′E
14 C6 **Oba Lake** ◎ Ontario, S Canada
164 J12 **Obama** Fukui, Honshū, SW Japan 35°32′N 135°45′E
96 H11 **Oban** W Scotland, United Kingdom 56°25′N 05°29′W
**Oban** *see* Halfmoon Bay
**Obando** *see* Puerto Inírida
104 I4 **O Barco** *var.* El Barco, El Barco de Valdeorras, O Barco de Valdeorras. Galicia, NW Spain 42°24′N 07°00′W
**O Barco de Valdeorras** *see* O Barco
**Obbia** *see* Hobyo
93 J16 **Obbola** Västerbotten, N Sweden 63°41′N 20°16′E
**Obbrovazzo** *see* Obrovac
**Obchuga** *see* Abchuha
**Obdorsk** *see* Salekhard
**Óbecse** *see* Bečej
118 I11 **Obeliai** Panevėžys, NE Lithuania 55°57′N 25°47′E
60 F13 **Oberá** Misiones, NE Argentina 27°29′S 55°08′W
108 E8 **Oberburg** Bern, W Switzerland 47°00′N 07°37′E
109 Q9 **Oberdrauburg** Salzburg, S Austria 46°45′N 12°59′E
**Oberglogau** *see* Głogówek
109 W4 **Ober Grafendorf** Niederösterreich, NE Austria 48°09′N 15°33′E
101 E15 **Oberhausen** Nordrhein-Westfalen, W Germany 51°27′N 06°50′E
**Oberhollabrunn** *see* Tulln
**Oberlaibach** *see* Vrhnika
101 Q15 **Oberlausitz** *var.* Hornja Łužica. *physical region* E Germany
26 J2 **Oberlin** Kansas, C USA 39°49′N 100°33′W
22 H8 **Oberlin** Louisiana, S USA 30°37′N 92°45′W
31 T11 **Oberlin** Ohio, N USA 41°17′N 82°13′W
103 U5 **Obernai** Bas-Rhin, NE France 48°28′N 07°30′E
109 R4 **Obernberg am Inn** Oberösterreich, N Austria 48°19′N 13°20′E
**Oberndorf** *see* Oberndorf am Neckar
101 G23 **Oberndorf am Neckar** *var.* Oberndorf. Baden-Württemberg, SW Germany 48°18′N 08°32′E
109 Q5 **Oberndorf bei Salzburg** Salzburg, W Austria 47°57′N 12°57′E
**Obernneustadtl** *see* Kysucké Nové Mesto
183 S8 **Oberon** New South Wales, SE Australia 33°42′S 149°50′E
109 Q4 **Oberösterreich** *off.* Land Oberösterreich, *Eng.* Upper Austria. ◆ *state* NW Austria
**Oberösterreich, Land** *see* Oberösterreich
**Oberpahlen** *see* Põltsamaa
101 M19 **Oberpfälzer Wald** ▲ SE Germany
109 Y6 **Oberpullendorf** Burgenland, E Austria 47°32′N 16°30′E
**Oberradkersburg** *see* Gornja Radgona
101 G18 **Oberursel** Hessen, W Germany 50°12′N 08°34′E
109 Q8 **Obervellach** Salzburg, S Austria 46°56′N 13°10′E
109 X7 **Oberwart** Burgenland, SE Austria 47°18′N 16°12′E
**Oberwischau** *see* Vişeu de Sus
109 T7 **Oberwölz** *var.* Oberwölz-Stadt. Steiermark, SE Austria 47°12′N 14°20′E
**Oberwölz-Stadt** *see* Oberwölz
31 S13 **Obetz** Ohio, N USA 39°52′N 82°57′W
**Ob', Gulf of** *see* Obskaya Guba
58 H12 **Óbidos** Pará, NE Brazil 01°52′S 55°30′W
104 F10 **Óbidos** Leiria, C Portugal 39°21′N 09°09′W
**Obidovichi** *see* Abidavichy
147 Q13 **Obigarm** W Tajikistan 38°42′N 69°34′E
165 T2 **Obihiro** Hokkaidō, NE Japan 42°56′N 143°10′E
**Obi-Khingou** *see* Khingov
147 P13 **Obikiik** SW Tajikistan 38°07′N 68°36′E
**Obilić** *see* Obiliq
113 N16 **Obiliq** *Serb.* Obilić. N Kosovo 42°50′N 20°57′E
127 O12 **Obil'noye** Respublika Kalmykiya, SW Russia 47°31′N 44°24′E
20 F8 **Obion** Tennessee, S USA 36°15′N 89°11′W
20 F8 **Obion River** ⇝ Tennessee, S USA
171 S12 **Obi, Pulau** *island* Maluku, E Indonesia
165 S2 **Obira** Hokkaidō, NE Japan 44°01′N 141°39′E
127 N11 **Oblivskaya** Rostovskaya Oblast', SW Russia 48°34′N 42°31′E
123 R14 **Obluch'ye** Yevreyskaya Avtonomnaya Oblast', SE Russia 48°59′N 131°18′E
126 K4 **Obninsk** Kaluzhskaya Oblast', W Russia 55°06′N 36°40′E
114 J8 **Obnova** Pleven, N Bulgaria 43°26′N 25°04′E
79 N15 **Obo** Haut-Mbomou, E Central African Republic 05°20′N 26°29′E
159 T9 **Obo** Qinghai, C China 37°57′N 101°03′E
80 M11 **Obock** E Djibouti 11°57′N 43°09′E
**Obol'** *see* Obal'
**Obolyanka** *see* Abalyanka
171 V13 **Obome** Papua Barat, E Indonesia 03°42′S 133°21′E
110 G11 **Oborniki** Wielkolpolskie, W Poland 52°38′N 16°48′E
79 G19 **Obouya** Cuvette, C Congo 0°56′S 15°41′E
126 J8 **Oboyan'** Kurskaya Oblast', W Russia 51°12′N 36°15′E
124 M9 **Obozerskiy** Arkhangel'skaya Oblast', NW Russia 63°26′N 40°20′E
112 L11 **Obrenovac** Serbia, N Serbia 44°39′N 20°12′E
112 D12 **Obrovac** *It.* Obbrovazzo. Zadar, SW Croatia 44°12′N 15°40′E
**Obrovo** *see* Abrova
35 Q3 **Observation Peak** ▲ California, W USA 40°48′N 120°07′W
122 J8 **Obskaya Guba** *Eng.* Gulf of Ob. *gulf* N Russia
173 N13 **Ob' Tablemount** *undersea feature* S Indian Ocean 50°16′S 51°59′E
173 T10 **Ob' Trench** *undersea feature* E Indian Ocean
77 P16 **Obuasi** S Ghana 06°15′N 01°36′W
117 P5 **Obukhiv** *Rus.* Obukhov. Kyivs'ka Oblast', N Ukraine 50°05′N 30°37′E
**Obukhov** *see* Obukhiv
125 U14 **Obva** ⇝ NW Russia
108 F8 **Obwalden** ◆ *canton* C Switzerland
117 V10 **Obytichna Kosa** *spit* SE Ukraine
117 V10 **Obytichna Zatoka** *gulf* SE Ukraine
105 O3 **Oca** ⇝ N Spain
23 W10 **Ocala** Florida, SE USA 29°11′N 82°08′W
40 M7 **Ocampo** Coahuila, NE Mexico 27°18′N 102°24′W
54 G7 **Ocaña** Norte de Santander, N Colombia 08°15′N 73°21′W
105 N9 **Ocaña** Castilla-La Mancha, C Spain 39°57′N 03°30′W
104 H4 **O Carballiño** *Cast.* Carballiño. Galicia, NW Spain 42°26′N 08°05′W
37 T9 **Ocate** New Mexico, SW USA 36°09′N 105°03′W
**Ocavango** *see* Okavango
57 D14 **Occidental, Cordillera** ▲ W South America
103 O14 **Occitanie** ◆ *region* S France
21 Q6 **Oceana** West Virginia, NE USA 37°41′N 81°37′W
21 Z4 **Ocean City** Maryland, NE USA 38°20′N 75°05′W
18 J17 **Ocean City** New Jersey, NE USA 39°15′N 74°33′W
10 K15 **Ocean Falls** British Columbia, SW Canada 52°24′N 127°42′W
**Ocean Island** *see* Banaba
**Ocean Island** *see* Kure Atoll
64 J9 **Oceanographer Fracture Zone** *tectonic feature* NW Atlantic Ocean
35 U17 **Oceanside** California, W USA 33°12′N 117°23′W
22 M9 **Ocean Springs** Mississippi, S USA 30°24′N 88°49′W
**Ocean State** *see* Rhode Island
25 O9 **O C Fisher Lake** ▣ Texas, SW USA
117 Q10 **Ochakiv** *Rus.* Ochakov. Mykolayivs'ka Oblast', S Ukraine 46°36′N 31°33′E
**Ochakov** *see* Ochakiv
**Ochamchira** *see* Ochamchire
137 Q9 **Ochamchire** *Rus.* Ochamchira; *prev.* Och'amch'ire. W Georgia 42°45′N 41°30′E
**Och'amch'ire** *see* Ochamchire
**Ochansk** *see* Okhansk
125 T15 **Ochër** Permskiy Kray, NW Russia 57°54′N 54°40′E
115 I19 **Óchi** ▲ Évvoia, C Greece 38°03′N 24°27′E
165 W4 **Ochiishi-misaki** *headland* Hokkaidō, NE Japan 43°10′N 145°29′E
23 S9 **Ochlockonee River** ⇝ Florida/Georgia, SE USA
44 K12 **Ocho Rios** C Jamaica 18°24′N 77°06′W
**Ochrida** *see* Ohrid
**Ochrida, Lake** *see* Ohrid, Lake
101 J19 **Ochsenfurt** Bayern, C Germany 49°39′N 10°03′E
23 U7 **Ocilla** Georgia, SE USA 31°35′N 83°15′W
94 N13 **Ockelbo** Gävleborg, C Sweden 60°51′N 16°46′E
**Ocker** *see* Oker
95 I19 **Öckerö** Västra Götaland, S Sweden 57°43′N 11°39′E
23 U6 **Ocmulgee River** ⇝ Georgia, SE USA
116 H11 **Ocna Mureş** *Hung.* Marosújvár; *prev.* Ocna Mureşului, *prev. Hung.* Marosújvárakna. Alba, C Romania 46°25′N 23°53′E
**Ocna Mureşului** *see* Ocna Mureş
116 H11 **Ocna Sibiului** *Ger.* Salzburg, *Hung.* Vizakna. Sibiu, C Romania 45°52′N 23°59′E
116 H13 **Ocnele Mari** *prev.* Vioara. Vâlcea, S Romania 45°03′N 24°18′E
116 L7 **Ocniţa** *Rus.* Oknitsa. N Moldova 48°25′N 27°30′E
23 U4 **Oconee, Lake** ▣ Georgia, SE USA
23 U5 **Oconee River** ⇝ Georgia, SE USA
30 M9 **Oconomowoc** Wisconsin, N USA 43°06′N 88°29′W
30 M6 **Oconto** Wisconsin, N USA 44°55′N 87°52′W
30 M6 **Oconto Falls** Wisconsin, N USA 44°52′N 88°06′W
30 M6 **Oconto River** ⇝ Wisconsin, N USA
104 I3 **O Corgo** Galicia, NW Spain 42°56′N 07°25′W
41 V16 **Ocosingo** Chiapas, SE Mexico 17°04′N 92°15′W
42 J8 **Ocotal** Nueva Segovia, NW Nicaragua 13°38′N 86°28′W
42 F6 **Ocotepeque** ◆ *department* W Honduras
**Ocotepeque** *see* Nueva Ocotepeque
40 L13 **Ocotlán** Jalisco, SW Mexico 20°21′N 102°42′W
41 R16 **Ocotlán** *var.* Ocotlán de Morelos. Oaxaca, SE Mexico 16°49′N 96°49′W
**Ocotlán de Morelos** *see* Ocotlán
41 U16 **Ocozocuautla** Chiapas, SE Mexico 16°46′N 93°22′W
21 Y10 **Ocracoke Island** *island* North Carolina, SE USA
102 I3 **Octeville** Manche, N France 49°37′N 01°39′W
**October Revolution Island** *see* Oktyabr'skoy Revolyutsii, Ostrov
43 R17 **Ocú** Herrera, S Panama 07°55′N 80°43′W
83 Q14 **Ocua** Cabo Delgado, NE Mozambique 13°37′S 39°44′E
**Ocumare** *see* Ocumare del Tuy
54 M5 **Ocumare del Tuy** *var.* Ocumare. Miranda, N Venezuela 10°07′N 66°47′W
77 P17 **Oda** SE Ghana 05°55′N 00°56′W
165 G12 **Ōda** *var.* Oda. Shimane, Honshū, SW Japan 35°10′N 132°29′E
92 K3 **Ódaðahraun** *lava flow* C Iceland
165 Q7 **Ōdate** Akita, Honshū, C Japan 40°18′N 140°34′E
165 N14 **Odawara** Kanagawa, Honshū, S Japan 35°15′N 139°08′E
95 D14 **Odda** Hordaland, S Norway 60°03′N 06°34′E
95 G22 **Odder** Midtjylland, C Denmark 55°59′N 10°10′E
**Oddur** *see* Xuddur
29 T13 **Odebolt** Iowa, C USA 42°18′N 95°15′W
104 H14 **Odeleite** Faro, S Portugal 37°02′N 07°29′W
25 Q4 **Odell** Texas, SW USA 34°19′N 99°24′W
25 T14 **Odem** Texas, SW USA 27°57′N 97°34′W
104 F13 **Odemira** Beja, S Portugal 37°35′N 08°38′W
136 C14 **Ödemiş** İzmir, SW Turkey 38°11′N 27°58′E
**Ödenburg** *see* Sopron
83 I22 **Odendaalsrus** Free State, C South Africa 27°52′S 26°42′E
**Odenpäh** *see* Otepää
95 H23 **Odense** Syddtjylland, C Denmark 55°24′N 10°23′E
101 H19 **Odenwald** ▲ W Germany
84 H10 **Oder** *Cz./Pol.* Odra. ⇝ C Europe
**Oderberg** *see* Bohumín
100 P11 **Oderbruch** *wetland* Germany/Poland
**Oderhaff** *see* Szczeciński, Zalew
100 O11 **Oder-Havel-Kanal** *canal* NE Germany
**Oderhellen** *see* Odorheiu Secuiesc
100 P13 **Oder-Spree-Kanal** *canal* NE Germany
**Odertal** *see* Zdzieszowice
106 I7 **Oderzo** Veneto, NE Italy 45°48′N 12°33′E
177 P10 **Odesa** *Rus.* Odessa. Odes'ka Oblast', SW Ukraine 46°29′N 30°44′E
24 M8 **Odessa** Texas, SW USA 31°51′N 102°22′W
32 K8 **Odessa** Washington, NW USA 47°19′N 118°41′W
**Odessa** *see* Odes'ka Oblast'
95 L18 **Ödeshög** Östergötland, S Sweden 58°13′N 14°40′E
117 O9 **Odes'ka Oblast'** *var.* Odesa, *Rus.* Odesskaya Oblast'. ◆ *province* SW Ukraine
**Odessa** *see* Odesa
**Odesskaya Oblast'** *see* Odes'ka Oblast'
122 H12 **Odesskoye** Omskaya Oblast', C Russia 54°15′N 72°45′E
**Odessus** *see* Varna
102 F6 **Odet** ⇝ NW France
104 I14 **Odiel** ⇝ SW Spain
76 L14 **Odienné** NW Ivory Coast 09°32′N 07°35′W
171 O4 **Odiongan** Tablas Island, C Philippines 12°23′N 122°01′E
153 P17 **Odisha** *prev.* Orissa. ◆ *state* NE India
116 L12 **Odobeşti** Vrancea, E Romania 45°46′N 27°06′E
110 H13 **Odolanów** *Ger.* Adelnau. Wielkopolskie, C Poland 51°35′N 17°42′E
167 R13 **Ŏdôngk** Kampong Speu, S Cambodia 11°48′N 104°45′E
25 N6 **O'donnell** Texas, SW USA 32°57′N 101°49′W
98 O7 **Odoorn** Drenthe, NE Netherlands 52°52′N 06°49′E
**Odorhei** *see* Odorheiu Secuiesc
116 J11 **Odorheiu Secuiesc** *Ger.* Oderhellen, *Hung.* Vámosudvarhely; *prev.* Odorhei, *Ger.* Hofmarkt. Harghita, C Romania 46°18′N 25°19′E
**Odra** *see* Oder
112 J9 **Odžaci** *Ger.* Hodschag, *Hung.* Hodság. Vojvodina, NW Serbia 45°31′N 19°15′E
59 N14 **Oeiras** Piauí, E Brazil 07°00′S 42°07′W
104 F11 **Oeiras** Lisboa, C Portugal 38°41′N 09°18′W
101 G14 **Oelde** Nordrhein-Westfalen, W Germany 51°49′N 08°09′E
28 J11 **Oelrichs** South Dakota, N USA 43°08′N 103°13′W
101 M17 **Oelsnitz** Sachsen, E Germany 50°22′N 12°12′E
**Oels/Oels in Schlesien** *see* Oleśnica
29 X12 **Oelwein** Iowa, C USA 42°40′N 91°54′W
**Oeniadae** *see* Oiniádes
191 N17 **Oeno Island** *atoll* Pitcairn Group of Islands, C Pacific Ocean
**Oesel** *see* Saaremaa
108 L7 **Oetz** *var.* Ötz. Tirol, W Austria 47°15′N 10°56′E
137 P11 **Of** Trabzon, NE Turkey 40°57′N 40°17′E
30 K15 **O'Fallon** Illinois, N USA 38°35′N 89°54′W
27 W4 **O'Fallon** Missouri, C USA 38°54′N 90°31′W
107 N16 **Ofanto** ⇝ S Italy
97 D18 **Offaly** *Ir.* Ua Uíbh Fhailí; *prev.* King's County. *cultural region* C Ireland
101 H18 **Offenbach** *var.* Offenbach am Main. Hessen, W Germany 50°06′N 08°46′E
**Offenbach am Main** *see* Offenbach
101 F22 **Offenburg** Baden-Württemberg, SW Germany 48°28′N 07°57′E
182 C2 **Officer Creek** *seasonal river* South Australia
**Oficina María Elena** *see* María Elena
**Oficina Pedro de Valdivia** *see* Pedro de Valdivia
115 K22 **Ofidoússa** *island* Kykládes, Greece, Aegean Sea
**Ofiral** *see* Sharm ash Shaykh
92 H10 **Ofotfjorden** *fjord* N Norway
192 L16 **Ofu** *island* Manua Islands, E American Samoa
165 R9 **Ōfunato** Iwate, Honshū, C Japan 39°04′N 141°43′E
165 P8 **Oga** Akita, Honshū, C Japan 39°56′N 139°47′E
**Ogaadeen** *see* Ogaden


◆ Country
● Country Capital
◇ Dependent Territory
○ Dependent Territory Capital
◆ Administrative Regions
✈ International Airport
▲ Mountain
▲ Mountain Range
Volcano
⇝ River
◎ Lake
▣ Reservoir

OGACHI – ON-TAKE


165 Q9 **Ogachi** Akita, Honshū, C Japan 39°03′N 140°26′E
165 P9 **Ogachi-tōge** pass Honshū, C Japan
81 N14 **Ogaden** Som. Ogaadeen. plateau Ethiopia/Somalia
165 P8 **Oga-hantō** peninsula Honshū, C Japan
165 K13 **Ōgaki** Gifu, Honshū, SW Japan 35°22′N 136°35′E
28 L15 **Ogallala** Nebraska, C USA 41°09′N 101°44′W
168 M14 **Ogan, Air** ≈ Sumatera, W Indonesia
165 Y15 **Ogasawara-shotō** Eng. Bonin Islands. island group SE Japan
14 I9 **Ogascanane, Lac** ◎ Québec, SE Canada
165 R7 **Ogawara-ko** ◎ Honshū, C Japan
77 T15 **Ogbomosho** var. Ogmoboso. Oyo, W Nigeria 08°10′N 04°16′E
29 U13 **Ogden** Iowa, C USA 42°03′N 94°01′W
36 L2 **Ogden** Utah, W USA 41°09′N 111°58′W
18 I6 **Ogdensburg** New York, NE USA 44°42′N 75°25′W
23 W5 **Ogeechee River** ≈ Georgia, SE USA
**Oger** see Ogre
165 N10 **Ogi** Niigata, Sado, C Japan 37°49′N 138°16′E
10 H5 **Ogilvie** Yukon, NW Canada 63°34′N 139°44′W
10 H4 **Ogilvie** ≈ Yukon, NW Canada
10 H5 **Ogilvie Mountains** ▲▲ Yukon, NW Canada
**Oginskiy Kanal** see Ahinski Kanal
162 J7 **Ögiynuur** var. Dzegstey. Arhangay, C Mongolia 47°38′N 102°31′E
146 F6 **Og'iyon Sho'rxogi** wetland NW Uzbekistan
146 B10 **Oglanly** Balkan Welaýaty, W Turkmenistan 39°56′N 54°25′E
23 T5 **Oglethorpe** Georgia, SE USA 32°17′N 84°03′W
23 T2 **Oglethorpe, Mount** ▲ Georgia, SE USA 34°29′N 84°19′W
106 F7 **Oglio** anc. Ollius. ≈ N Italy
**Ogmoboso** see Ogbomosho
103 T8 **Ognon** ≈ E France
123 R13 **Ogodzha** Amurskaya Oblast', S Russia 52°51′N 132°49′E
77 W16 **Ogoja** Cross River, S Nigeria 06°37′N 08°48′E
12 C10 **Ogoki** ≈ Ontario, S Canada
12 D11 **Ogoki Lake** ◎ Ontario, C Canada
**Ögöömör** see Hanhongor
79 F19 **Ogooué** ≈ Congo/Gabon
79 E18 **Ogooué-Ivindo** off. Province de l'Ogooué-Ivindo, var. L'Ogooué-Ivindo. ◈ province N Gabon
**Ogooué-Ivindo, Province de l'** see Ogooué-Ivindo
79 E19 **Ogooué-Lolo** off. Province de l'Ogooué-Lolo, var. L'Ogooué-Lolo. ◈ province C Gabon
**Ogooué-Lolo, Province de l'** see Ogooué-Lolo
79 C19 **Ogooué-Maritime** off. Province de l'Ogooué-Maritime, var. L'Ogooué-Maritime. ◈ province W Gabon
**Ogooué-Maritime, Province de l'** see Ogooué-Maritime
165 D14 **Ogōri** Fukuoka, Kyūshū, SW Japan 33°24′N 130°34′E
114 H7 **Ogosta** ≈ NW Bulgaria
112 Q9 **Ogražden** Bul. Ograzhden. ▲ Bulgaria/North Macedonia see also Ograzhden
114 G12 **Ograzhden** Mac. Orgraždеn. ▲ Bulgaria/North Macedonia see also Orgraždеn
**Ograzhden** see Ogražden
118 G9 **Ogre** Ger. Oger. C Latvia 56°49′N 24°36′E
118 H9 **Ogre** ≈ C Latvia
**Oguaa** see Cape Coast
112 C10 **Ogulin** Karlovac, NW Croatia 45°15′N 15°13′E
77 S16 **Ogun** ◈ state SW Nigeria
**Ogurdzhaly, Ostrov** see OgurjalyAdasy
146 A12 **OgurjalyAdasy** Rus. Ogurdzhaly, Ostrov. island W Turkmenistan
77 U16 **Ogwashi-Uku** Delta, S Nigeria 06°08′N 06°38′E
185 B23 **Ohai** Southland, South Island, New Zealand 45°56′S 167°59′E
74 M11 **Ohanet** prev. Fort Charlet, Djanet. SE Algeria 24°34′N 09°33′E
147 Q10 **Ohangaron** Rus. Akhangaran. Toshkent Viloyati, E Uzbekistan 40°56′N 69°37′E
147 Q10 **Ohangaron** Rus. Akhangaran. ≈ E Uzbekistan
83 C16 **Ohangwena** ◈ region N Namibia
30 M10 **O'Hare** ✈ (Chicago) Illinois, N USA 41°59′N 87°56′W
165 R6 **Ōhata** Aomori, Honshū, C Japan 41°23′N 141°09′E
184 L13 **Ohau** Manawatu-Wanganui, North Island, New Zealand 40°40′S 175°15′E
185 E20 **Ohau, Lake** ◎ South Island, New Zealand
**Ohcejohka** see Utsjoki
99 J20 **Ohey** Namur, SE Belgium 50°26′N 05°07′E
62 G12 **O'Higgins** off. Región del Libertador General Bernardo O'Higgins. ◈ region C Chile
194 H3 **O'Higgins** research station (Chile) Antarctica 63°09′S 57°13′W
191 X15 **O'Higgins, Cabo** headland Easter Island, Chile, E Pacific Ocean 27°05′S 109°15′W
**O'Higgins, Lago** see San Martín, Lago
31 S12 **Ohio** off. State of Ohio, also known as Buckeye State. ◈ state N USA
0 L10 **Ohio River** ≈ N USA
**Ohlau** see Oława
101 H16 **Ohm** ≈ C Germany
193 W16 **Ohonua** 'Eua, E Tonga 21°20′S 174°57′W
23 V5 **Ohoopee River** ≈ Georgia, SE USA
100 L12 **Ohre** Ger. Eger. ≈ Czechia/Germany
**Ohri** see Ohrid
113 M20 **Ohrid** Turk. Ochrida, Ohri. SW North Macedonia 41°07′N 20°48′E
113 M20 **Ohrid, Lake** var. Lake Ochrida, Alb. Liqeni i Ohrit, Mac. Ohridsko Ezero. ◎ Albania/North Macedonia
**Ohridsko Ezero/Ohrit, Liqeni i** see Ohrid, Lake
184 L9 **Ohura** Manawatu-Wanganui, North Island, New Zealand 38°51′S 174°58′E
58 J9 **Oiapoque** Amapá, E Brazil 03°54′N 51°46′W
58 J10 **Oiapoque, Rio** var. Fleuve l'Oyapok, Oyapock. ≈ Brazil/French Guiana see also Oyapok, Fleuve l'
**Oiapoque, Rio** see Oyapok, Fleuve l'
54 G8 **Oiba** Santander, C Colombia 06°16′N 73°18′W
15 O9 **Oies, Île aux** island Québec, SE Canada
92 L13 **Oijärvi** Pohjois-Pohjanmaa, C Finland 65°38′N 26°05′E
92 L12 **Oikarainen** Lappi, N Finland 66°30′N 25°46′E
188 F10 **Oikuul** Babeldaob, N Palau
18 C13 **Oil City** Pennsylvania, NE USA 41°25′N 79°42′W
18 C12 **Oil Creek** ≈ Pennsylvania, NE USA
35 R13 **Oildale** California, W USA 35°25′N 119°01′W
**Oileán Ciarral** see Castleisland
**Oil Islands** see Chagos Archipelago
115 D18 **Oiniádes** anc. Oeniadae. site of ancient city Dytikí Elláda, W Greece
115 L18 **Oinoússes** island E Greece
**Oírr, Inis** see Inisheer
99 J15 **Oirschot** Noord-Brabant, S Netherlands 51°30′N 05°18′E
103 N4 **Oise** ◈ department N France
103 P3 **Oise** ≈ N France
99 J14 **Oisterwijk** Noord-Brabant, S Netherlands 51°35′N 05°12′E
45 O14 **Oistins** S Barbados 13°04′N 59°33′W
165 E4 **Ōita** Ōita, Kyūshū, SW Japan 33°15′N 131°35′E
165 D14 **Ōita** off. Ōita-ken. ◈ prefecture Kyūshū, SW Japan
**Ōita-ken** see Ōita
115 E17 **Oíti** ▲ C Greece 38°48′N 22°12′E
165 S4 **Oiwake** Hokkaidō, NE Japan 42°54′N 141°49′E
35 R14 **Ojai** California, W USA 34°25′N 119°15′W
94 K13 **Öje** Dalarna, C Sweden 60°49′N 13°54′E
93 J14 **Öjebyn** Norrbotten, N Sweden 65°20′N 21°26′E
165 B13 **Ojika-jima** island SW Japan
40 K5 **Ojinaga** Chihuahua, N Mexico 29°31′N 104°26′W
40 M11 **Ojo Caliente** var. Ojocaliente. Zacatecas, C Mexico 22°35′N 102°18′W
**Ojocaliente** see Ojo Caliente
40 D6 **Ojo de Liebre, Laguna** var. Laguna Scammon, Scammon Lagoon. lagoon NW Mexico
62 I7 **Ojos del Salado, Cerro** ▲ W Argentina 27°04′S 68°34′W
105 R7 **Ojos Negros** Aragón, NE Spain 40°43′N 01°30′W
40 M12 **Ojuelos de Jalisco** Aguascalientes, C Mexico 21°52′N 101°40′W
127 N4 **Oka** ≈ W Russia
83 D19 **Okahandja** Otjozondjupa, C Namibia 21°58′S 16°55′E
184 L9 **Okahukura** Manawatu-Wanganui, North Island, New Zealand 38°48′S 175°13′E
184 J3 **Okaihau** Northland, North Island, New Zealand 35°19′S 173°45′E
83 D18 **Okakarara** Otjozondjupa, N Namibia 20°33′S 17°20′E
13 P5 **Okak Islands** island group Newfoundland and Labrador, E Canada
10 M17 **Okanagan** ≈ British Columbia, SW Canada
11 N17 **Okanagan Lake** ◎ British Columbia, SW Canada
**Ókanizsa** see Kanjiža
83 C16 **Okankolo** Oshikoto, N Namibia 17°57′S 16°28′E
32 K6 **Okanogan River** ≈ Washington, NW USA
83 D18 **Okaputa** Otjozondjupa, N Namibia 20°09′S 16°56′E
149 V9 **Okara** Punjab, E Pakistan 30°49′N 73°31′E
26 M10 **Okarche** Oklahoma, C USA 35°43′N 97°58′W
**Okarem** see Ekerem
189 X14 **Okat Harbor** harbor Kosrae, E Micronesia
22 M5 **Okatibbee Creek** ≈ Mississippi, S USA
83 C17 **Okaukuejo** Kunene, N Namibia 19°10′S 15°23′E
**Okavanggo** see Cubango/Okavango
83 G17 **Okavango** var. Cubango, Kavango, Kavengo, Kubango, Okavanggo, Port. Ocavango. ≈ S Africa see also Cubango
**Okavango** see Cubango
83 G17 **Okavango Delta** wetland N Botswana
164 M12 **Okaya** Nagano, Honshū, S Japan 36°03′N 138°00′E
164 H13 **Okayama** Okayama, Honshū, SW Japan 34°40′N 133°54′E
164 H13 **Okayama** off. Okayama-ken. ◈ prefecture Honshū, SW Japan
**Okayama-ken** see Okayama
164 L14 **Okazaki** Aichi, Honshū, C Japan 34°58′N 137°10′E
110 M12 **Okęcie** ✈ (Warszawa) Mazowieckie, C Poland 52°08′N 20°57′E
23 Y13 **Okeechobee** Florida, SE USA 27°14′N 80°49′W
23 Y14 **Okeechobee, Lake** ◎ Florida, SE USA
26 M9 **Okeene** Oklahoma, C USA 36°07′N 98°19′W
23 V8 **Okefenokee Swamp** wetland Georgia, SE USA
97 J24 **Okehampton** SW England, United Kingdom 50°44′N 04°W
27 P10 **Okemah** Oklahoma, C USA 35°25′N 96°20′W
77 U16 **Okene** Kogi, S Nigeria 07°31′N 06°15′E
100 K13 **Oker** var. Ocker. ≈ NW Germany
101 J14 **Oker-Stausee** ◎ C Germany
123 T12 **Okha** Ostrov Sakhalin, Sakhalinskaya Oblast', SE Russia 53°33′N 142°55′E
125 U15 **Okhansk** var. Ochansk. Permskiy Kray, NW Russia 57°44′N 55°20′E
123 S10 **Okhotsk** Khabarovskiy Kray, E Russia 59°21′N 143°15′E
192 J2 **Okhotsk, Sea of** sea NW Pacific Ocean
117 T4 **Okhtyrka** Rus. Akhtyrka. Sums'ka Oblast', NE Ukraine 50°19′N 34°54′E
83 E23 **Okiep** Northern Cape, W South Africa 29°39′S 17°53′E
**Oki-guntō** see Oki-shotō
164 H11 **Oki-kaikyō** strait SW Japan
165 P16 **Okinawa** Okinawa, SW Japan 26°20′N 127°47′E
165 S16 **Okinawa** off. Okinawa-ken. ◈ prefecture Okinawa, SW Japan
165 S16 **Okinawa** island SW Japan
**Okinawa-ken** see Okinawa
165 U16 **Okinoerabu-jima** island Nansei-shotō, SW Japan
164 F15 **Okino-shima** island SW Japan
164 H11 **Oki-shotō** var. Oki-guntō. island group SW Japan
77 T16 **Okitipupa** Ondo, SW Nigeria 06°33′N 04°43′E
166 L8 **Okkan** Bago, SW Myanmar (Burma) 17°30′N 95°52′E
27 N10 **Oklahoma** off. State of Oklahoma, also known as The Sooner State. ◈ state C USA
27 N11 **Oklahoma City** state capital Oklahoma, C USA 35°28′N 97°31′W
25 Q4 **Oklaunion** Texas, SW USA 34°07′N 99°07′W
23 W10 **Oklawaha River** ≈ Florida, SE USA
27 P10 **Okmulgee** Oklahoma, C USA 35°38′N 95°59′W
**Oknitsa** see Ocniţa
117 O9 **Okny** prev. Krasni Okny. Odes'ka Oblast', SW Ukraine 47°33′N 29°28′E
22 M3 **Okolona** Mississippi, S USA 34°00′N 88°45′W
165 U2 **Okoppe** Hokkaidō, NE Japan 44°27′N 143°06′E
11 Q16 **Okotoks** Alberta, SW Canada 50°46′N 113°57′W
80 H6 **Oko, Wadi** ≈ NE Sudan
79 G19 **Okoyo** Cuvette, W Congo 01°28′S 15°04′E
77 S15 **Okpara** ≈ Benin/Nigeria
92 J8 **Øksfjord** Finnmark, N Norway 70°13′N 22°22′E
125 R4 **Oksino** Nenetskiy Avtonomnyy Okrug, NW Russia 67°33′N 52°15′E
92 G13 **Oksskolten** ▲ C Norway 66°00′N 14°18′E
**Oksu** see Oqsu
144 M8 **Oktaybr'skiy** Kostanay, N Kazakhstan
186 B7 **Ok Tedi** Western, W Papua New Guinea
**Oktemberyan** see Armavir
166 M7 **Oktwin** Bago, C Myanmar (Burma) 18°47′N 96°21′E
127 R6 **Oktyabr'sk** Samarskaya Oblast', W Russia 53°13′N 48°36′E
**Oktyab'rsk** see Kandyagash
125 N12 **Oktyabr'skiy** Arkhangel'skaya Oblast', NW Russia 61°03′N 43°16′E
122 E10 **Oktyabr'skiy** Kamchatskiy Kray, E Russia 52°35′N 156°18′E
127 T5 **Oktyabr'skiy** Respublika Bashkortostan, W Russia 54°28′N 53°29′E
127 O11 **Oktyabr'skiy** Volgogradskaya Oblast', SW Russia 48°00′N 43°35′E
**Oktyabr'skiy** see Aktsyabrski
127 V7 **Oktyabr'skoye** Orenburgskaya Oblast', W Russia 52°22′N 55°39′E
122 M5 **Oktyabr'skoy Revolyutsii, Ostrov** Eng. October Revolution Island. island Severnaya Zemlya, N Russia
**Ōkuchi** see Isa
124 I14 **Okulovka** var. Okulovka. Novgorodskaya Oblast', W Russia 58°24′N 33°16′E
**Okulovka** see Okulovka
165 Q4 **Okushiri-tō** var. Okusiri Tô. island NE Japan
**Okusiri Tô** see Okushiri-tō
77 S15 **Okuta** Kwara, W Nigeria 09°18′N 03°09′E
**Ôkuti** see Isa
83 F19 **Okwa** var. Chapman's. ≈ Botswana/Namibia
123 T10 **Ola** Magadanskaya Oblast', E Russia 59°36′N 151°18′E
27 T11 **Ola** Arkansas, C USA 35°01′N 93°13′W
**Ola** see Ala
35 T11 **Olacha Peak** ▲ California, W USA 36°15′N 118°07′W
92 J1 **Ólafsfjörður** Norðurland Eystra, N Iceland 66°04′N 18°36′W
92 H3 **Ólafsvík** Vesturland, W Iceland 64°52′N 23°45′W
**Oláhbrettye** see Bretea-Română
**Oláhszentgyőrgy** see Sângeorz-Băi
**Oláh-Toplicza** see Toplița
118 F9 **Olaine** C Latvia 56°47′N 23°56′E
35 T11 **Olancha** California, W USA 36°16′N 118°00′W
42 J5 **Olanchito** Yoro, C Honduras 15°30′N 86°34′W
42 J6 **Olancho** ◈ department E Honduras
95 O20 **Öland** island S Sweden
95 O19 **Ölands norra udde** headland S Sweden 57°21′N 17°06′E
95 N22 **Ölands södra udde** headland S Sweden 56°12′N 16°26′E
182 K7 **Olary** South Australia 32°18′S 140°16′E
27 R4 **Olathe** Kansas, C USA 38°52′N 94°50′W
61 C22 **Olavarría** Buenos Aires, E Argentina 36°57′S 60°20′W
92 O2 **Olav V Land** physical region C Svalbard
111 H14 **Oława** Ger. Ohlau. Dolnośląskie, SW Poland 50°57′N 17°18′E
107 D17 **Olbia** prev. Terranova Pausania. Sardegna, Italy, C Mediterranean Sea 40°55′N 09°30′E
44 G5 **Old Bahama Channel** channel The Bahamas/Cuba
**Old Bay State/Old Colony State** see Massachusetts
10 H2 **Old Crow** Yukon, NW Canada 67°34′N 139°55′W
**Old Dominion** see Virginia
**Oldeberkeap** see Oldeberkoop
98 M7 **Oldeberkoop** Fris. Oldeberkeap. Fryslân, N Netherlands 52°55′N 06°07′E
98 L10 **Oldebroek** Gelderland, E Netherlands 52°27′N 05°54′E
98 L8 **Oldemarkt** Overijssel, N Netherlands 52°49′N 05°58′E
94 E11 **Olden** Sogn Og Fjordane, C Norway 61°52′N 06°44′E
100 G10 **Oldenburg** Niedersachsen, NW Germany 53°09′N 08°13′E
100 K8 **Oldenburg** var. Oldenburg in Holstein. Schleswig-Holstein, N Germany 54°17′N 10°55′E
**Oldenburg in Holstein** see Oldenburg
98 P10 **Oldenzaal** Overijssel, E Netherlands 52°19′N 06°53′E
**Olderfjord** see Leaibevuotna
18 J8 **Old Forge** New York, NE USA 43°42′N 74°59′W
**Old Goa** see Goa
97 L17 **Oldham** NW England, United Kingdom 53°36′N 02°W
39 Q14 **Old Harbor** Kodiak Island, Alaska, USA 57°12′N 153°18′W
44 J13 **Old Harbour** C Jamaica 17°56′N 77°06′W
97 C22 **Old Head of Kinsale** Ir. An Seancheann. headland SW Ireland 51°37′N 08°33′W
20 J8 **Old Hickory Lake** ⊠ Tennessee, S USA
**Old Line State** see Maryland
**Old North State** see North Carolina
81 I17 **Ol Doinyo Lengeyo** ▲▲ C Kenya
11 Q16 **Olds** Alberta, SW Canada 51°50′N 114°06′W
19 O7 **Old Speck Mountain** ▲ Maine, NE USA 44°34′N 70°55′W
19 S6 **Old Town** Maine, NE USA 44°55′N 68°39′W
11 T17 **Old Wives Lake** ◎ Saskatchewan, S Canada
162 J7 **Öldziyt** var. Höshööt. Arhangay, C Mongolia 48°06′N 102°34′E
162 I8 **Öldziyt** var. Ulaan-Uul. Bayanhongor, C Mongolia 46°03′N 100°52′E
162 L10 **Öldziyt** var. Rashaant. Dundgovĭ, C Mongolia 44°54′N 106°32′E
162 K8 **Öldziyt** var. Sangiyn Dalay. Övörhangay, C Mongolia 46°35′N 103°18′E
**Öldziyt** see Erdenemandal, Arhangay, Mongolia
**Öldziyt** see Sayhandulaan, Dornogovĭ, Mongolia
188 H6 **Oleai** var. San Jose. Saipan, S Northern Mariana Islands
18 E11 **Olean** New York, NE USA 42°04′N 78°24′W
110 O7 **Olecko** Ger. Treuburg. Warmińsko-Mazurskie, NE Poland 54°02′N 22°29′E
106 C7 **Oleggio** Piemonte, NE Italy 45°36′N 08°37′E
123 P11 **Olëkma** Amurskaya Oblast', SE Russia 57°00′N 120°27′E
123 P12 **Olëkma** ≈ C Russia
123 P11 **Olëkminsk** Respublika Sakha (Yakutiya), NE Russia 60°25′N 120°25′E
117 W7 **Oleksandrivka** Donets'ka Oblast', E Ukraine 48°42′N 36°56′E
117 R7 **Oleksandrivka** Rus. Aleksandrovka. Kirovohrads'ka Oblast', C Ukraine 48°59′N 32°14′E
117 Q9 **Oleksandrivka** Mykolayivs'ka Oblast', S Ukraine 47°42′N 31°17′E
117 S7 **Oleksandriya** Rus. Aleksandriya. Kirovohrads'ka Oblast', C Ukraine 48°42′N 33°07′E
93 B20 **Ølen** Hordaland, S Norway 59°36′N 05°48′E
124 J4 **Olenegorsk** Murmanskaya Oblast', NW Russia 68°06′N 33°15′E
123 N9 **Olenëk** Respublika Sakha (Yakutiya), NE Russia 68°28′N 112°18′E
123 N9 **Olenëk** ≈ NE Russia
123 O7 **Olenëkskiy Zaliv** bay N Russia
124 K6 **Olenitsa** Murmanskaya Oblast', NW Russia 66°27′N 35°21′E
102 I11 **Oléron, Île d'** island W France
117 R10 **Oleshky** prev. Tsyurupyns'k. Khersons'ka Oblast', S Ukraine 46°35′N 32°43′E
111 H14 **Oleśnica** Ger. Oels, Oels in Schlesien. Dolnośląskie, SW Poland 51°13′N 17°20′E
111 I15 **Olesno** Ger. Rosenberg. Opolskie, S Poland 50°53′N 18°23′E
116 M3 **Olevs'k** Rus. Olevsk. Zhytomyrs'ka Oblast', N Ukraine 51°12′N 27°38′E
**Olevsk** see Olevs'k
123 S15 **Ol'ga** Primorskiy Kray, SE Russia 43°41′N 135°06′E
**Olga, Mount** see Kata Tjuṯa
92 P2 **Olgastretet** strait E Svalbard
162 D5 **Ölgiy** Bayan-Ölgiy, W Mongolia 48°57′N 89°59′E
95 F23 **Ølgod** Syddtjylland, W Denmark 55°44′N 08°37′E
104 H14 **Olhão** Faro, S Portugal 37°01′N 07°50′W
93 L14 **Olhava** Pohjois-Pohjanmaa, C Finland 65°28′N 25°25′E
105 V5 **Oliana** Cataluña, NE Spain 42°04′N 01°19′E
112 B12 **Olib** It. Ulbo. island W Croatia
83 B16 **Olifa** Kunene, NW Namibia 17°25′S 14°27′E
83 E20 **Olifants** var. Elephant River. ≈ E Namibia
**Olifants** see Lepelle
83 I20 **Olifants Drift** var. Oliphants Drift. Kgatleng, SE Botswana 24°13′S 26°52′E
83 G22 **Olifantshoek** Northern Cape, N South Africa 27°56′S 22°45′E
188 L15 **Olimarao Atoll** atoll Caroline Islands, C Micronesia
**Ólimbos** see Ólympos
**Olimpo** see Fuerte Olimpo
59 Q15 **Olinda** Pernambuco, E Brazil 08°S 34°51′W
**Olinthos** see Ólynthos
**Oliphants Drift** see Olifants Drift
**Olisipo** see Lisboa
**Olita** see Alytus
105 Q4 **Olite** Navarra, N Spain 42°29′N 01°40′W
62 K10 **Oliva** Córdoba, C Argentina 32°03′S 63°34′W
105 T11 **Oliva** Comunitat Valenciana, E Spain 38°55′N 00°09′W
**Oliva** see La Oliva
104 I12 **Oliva de la Frontera** Extremadura, W Spain 38°17′N 06°54′W
**Olivares** see Olivares de Júcar
62 H9 **Olivares, Cerro de** ▲ N Chile 30°25′S 69°52′W
105 P9 **Olivares de Júcar** var. Olivares. Castilla-La Mancha, C Spain 39°45′N 02°21′W
22 L1 **Olive Branch** Mississippi, S USA 34°58′N 89°49′W
21 O5 **Olive Hill** Kentucky, S USA 38°18′N 83°10′W
35 O6 **Olivehurst** California, W USA 39°05′N 121°33′W
104 G7 **Oliveira de Azeméis** Aveiro, N Portugal 40°49′N 08°29′W
104 I11 **Olivenza** Extremadura, W Spain 38°41′N 07°06′W
11 N17 **Oliver** British Columbia, SW Canada 49°10′N 119°37′W
103 N7 **Olivet** Loiret, C France 47°53′N 01°53′E
29 Q12 **Olivet** South Dakota, N USA 43°14′N 97°40′W
29 T9 **Olivia** Minnesota, N USA 44°46′N 94°59′W
185 C20 **Olivine Range** ▲▲ South Island, New Zealand
108 H10 **Olivone** Ticino, S Switzerland 46°32′N 08°55′E
**Ölkeyek** see Ol'keyyek
144 L11 **Ol'keyyek** Kaz. Ölkeyek; prev. Ul'kayak. ≈ C Kazakhstan
127 O9 **Ol'khovka** Volgogradskaya Oblast', SW Russia 49°54′N 44°36′E
111 K16 **Olkusz** Małopolskie, S Poland 50°18′N 19°33′E
22 I6 **Olla** Louisiana, S USA 31°54′N 92°14′W
62 I4 **Ollagüe, Volcán** var. Oyahue, Volcán Oyahue. ⛰ N Chile 21°25′S 68°10′W
189 U13 **Ollan** island Chuuk, C Micronesia
188 F7 **Ollei** Babeldaob, N Palau 07°43′N 134°37′E
**Ollius** see Oglio
108 C10 **Ollon** Vaud, W Switzerland 46°19′N 07°00′E
147 Q10 **Olmaliq** Rus. Almalyk. Toshkent Viloyati, E Uzbekistan 40°51′N 69°39′E
104 M6 **Olmedo** Castilla y León, N Spain 41°17′N 04°41′W
56 B10 **Olmos** Lambayeque, W Peru 06°00′S 79°43′W
**Olmütz** see Olomouc
30 M15 **Olney** Illinois, N USA 38°43′N 88°05′W
25 R5 **Olney** Texas, SW USA 33°22′N 98°45′W
95 L22 **Olofström** Blekinge, S Sweden 56°16′N 14°33′E
187 N9 **Olomburi** Malaita, N Solomon Islands 09°00′S 161°09′E
111 H17 **Olomouc** Ger. Olmütz, Pol. Ołomuniec. Olomoucký Kraj, E Czechia 49°36′N 17°13′E
111 H18 **Olomoucký Kraj** ◈ region E Czechia
**Ołomuniec** see Olomouc
122 D7 **Olonets** Respublika Kareliya, NW Russia 60°58′N 33°01′E
171 N3 **Olongapo** off. Olongapo City. Luzon, N Philippines 14°52′N 120°16′E
**Olongapo City** see Olongapo
102 J16 **Oloron-Ste-Marie** Pyrénées-Atlantiques, SW France 43°12′N 00°35′W
192 L16 **Olosega** island Manua Islands, E American Samoa
105 W4 **Olot** Cataluña, NE Spain 42°11′N 02°30′E
146 K12 **Olot** Rus. Alat. Buxoro Viloyati, C Uzbekistan 39°22′N 63°42′E
112 I12 **Olovo** Federacija Bosne I Hercegovine, E Bosnia and Herzegovina 44°08′N 18°35′E
123 O14 **Olovyannaya** Zabaykal'skiy Kray, S Russia 50°59′N 115°24′E
123 T7 **Oloy** ≈ NE Russia
101 F16 **Olpe** Nordrhein-Westfalen, W Germany 51°02′N 07°51′E
109 N8 **Olperer** ▲ SW Austria 47°03′N 11°36′E
**Olshanka** see Vil'shanka
**Ol'shany** see Al'shany
**Olsnitz** see Murska Sobota
98 M10 **Olst** Overijssel, E Netherlands 52°19′N 06°06′E
110 L8 **Olsztyn** Ger. Allenstein. Warmińsko-Mazurskie, N Poland 53°46′N 20°28′E
110 L8 **Olsztynek** Ger. Hohenstein in Ostpreussen. Warmińsko-Mazurskie, N Poland 53°35′N 20°17′E
116 I14 **Olt** ◈ county SW Romania
116 I14 **Olt** var. Oltul, Ger. Alt. ≈ S Romania
108 E7 **Olten** Solothurn, NW Switzerland 47°22′N 07°55′E
116 K14 **Oltenița** prev. Eng. Oltenitsa; anc. Constantiola. Călărași, SE Romania 44°05′N 26°40′E
**Oltenitsa** see Oltenița
116 H14 **Olteț** ≈ S Romania
24 M4 **Olton** Texas, SW USA 34°10′N 102°07′W
137 R12 **Oltu** Erzurum, NE Turkey 40°34′N 41°59′E
**Oltul** see Olt
146 G7 **Oltynko'l** Qoraqalpog'iston Respublikasi, NW Uzbekistan 43°04′N 58°51′E
161 S15 **Oluan Bi** Eng. Cape Olwanpi, var. Eluan Pi. headland S Taiwan 21°57′N 120°48′E
**Ólubló** see Stará L'ubovňa
137 R11 **Olur** Erzurum, NE Turkey 40°49′N 42°08′E
104 L15 **Olvera** Andalucía, S Spain 36°56′N 05°15′W
**Ol'viopol'** see Pervomays'k
**Olwanpi, Cape** see Oluan Bi
115 D20 **Olympía** Dytikí Elláda, S Greece 37°39′N 21°36′E
32 G9 **Olympia** state capital Washington, NW USA 47°02′N 122°54′W
182 H5 **Olympic Dam** South Australia 30°25′S 136°56′E
32 F7 **Olympic Mountains** ▲▲ Washington, NW USA
121 O3 **Ólympos** var. Troodos, Eng. Mount Olympus. ▲ C Cyprus 34°55′N 32°49′E
115 F15 **Ólympos** var. Ólimbos, Eng. Mount Olympus. ▲ N Greece 40°04′N 22°24′E
115 L17 **Ólympos** ▲ Lésvos, E Greece 39°03′N 26°20′E
16 C5 **Olympus, Mount** ▲ Washington, NW USA 47°48′N 123°42′W
**Olympus, Mount** see Ólympos
115 G14 **Ólynthos** var. Olinthos; anc. Olynthus. site of ancient city Kentrikí Makedonía, N Greece
**Olynthus** see Ólynthos
117 Q3 **Olyshivka** Chernihivs'ka Oblast', N Ukraine 51°13′N 31°19′E
123 W8 **Olyutorskiy, Mys** headland E Russia 59°56′N 170°22′E
123 V8 **Olyutorskiy Zaliv** bay E Russia
186 M10 **Om** ≈ W Papua New Guinea
129 S6 **Om'** ≈ N Russia
158 I13 **Oma** Xizang Zizhiqu, W China 32°30′N 83°14′E
165 R6 **Ōma** Aomori, Honshū, C Japan 41°31′N 140°54′E
125 P6 **Oma** ≈ NW Russia
164 M12 **Ōmachi** var. Ōmati. Nagano, Honshū, S Japan 36°30′N 137°51′E
165 Q8 **Ōmagari** Akita, Honshū, C Japan 39°29′N 140°29′E
97 E15 **Omagh** Ir. An Ómaigh. W Northern Ireland, United Kingdom 54°36′N 07°18′W
29 S15 **Omaha** Nebraska, C USA 41°14′N 95°57′W
83 E19 **Omaheke** ◈ region W Namibia
141 W10 **Oman** off. Sultanate of Oman, Ar. 'Umān, Salṭanat 'Umān; prev. Muscat and Oman. ◆ monarchy SW Asia
129 O10 **Oman Basin** var. Bassin d'Oman. undersea feature N Indian Ocean 23°20′N 63°00′E
**Oman, Bassin d'** see Oman Basin
129 N10 **Oman, Gulf of** Ar. Khalīj 'Umān. gulf N Arabian Sea
**Oman, Sultanate of** see Oman
184 J3 **Omapere** Northland, North Island, New Zealand 35°32′S 173°24′E
185 E20 **Omarama** Canterbury, South Island, New Zealand 44°29′S 169°57′E
112 F11 **Omarska** ◈ Republika Srpska, NW Bosnia and Herzegovina
83 C18 **Omaruru** Erongo, NW Namibia 21°28′S 15°56′E
83 C19 **Omaruru** ≈ W Namibia
83 E17 **Omatako** ≈ NE Namibia
**Ōmati** see Ōmachi
83 E18 **Omawewozonyanda** Omaheke, E Namibia 21°30′S 19°34′E
165 R6 **Ōma-zaki** headland Honshū, C Japan 41°32′N 140°53′E
**Omba** see Ambae
**Ombai** see Alor, Pulau
83 C16 **Ombalantu** Omusati, N Namibia 17°33′S 14°58′E
79 H15 **Ombella-Mpoko** ◈ prefecture S Central African Republic
**Ombetsu** see Onbetsu
83 B17 **Ombombo** Kunene, NW Namibia 18°43′S 13°53′E
79 D19 **Omboué** Ogooué-Maritime, W Gabon 01°38′S 09°20′E
106 G13 **Ombrone** ≈ C Italy
80 F9 **Omdurman** var. Umm Durmān. Khartoum, C Sudan 15°37′N 32°29′E
165 N13 **Ōme** Tōkyō, Honshū, S Japan 35°48′N 139°17′E
106 C6 **Omegna** Piemonte, NE Italy 45°54′N 08°25′E
183 P12 **Omeo** Victoria, SE Australia 37°09′S 147°36′E
138 F11 **Omer** Southern, C Israel 31°16′N 34°51′E
41 P16 **Ometepec** Guerrero, S Mexico 16°39′N 98°23′W
42 K11 **Ometepe, Isla de** island S Nicaragua
**Om Hager** see Om Ḥajer
80 I10 **Om Ḥajer** var. Om Hager. SW Eritrea 14°19′N 36°46′E
165 J13 **Ōmihachiman** Shiga, Honshū, SW Japan 35°08′N 136°04′E
10 L12 **Omineca Mountains** ▲▲ British Columbia, W Canada
113 F14 **Omiš** It. Almissa. Split-Dalmacija, S Croatia 43°27′N 16°41′E
112 B10 **Omišalj** Primorje-Gorski Kotar, NW Croatia 45°10′N 14°33′E
83 D19 **Omitara** Khomas, C Namibia 22°18′S 18°01′E
41 O16 **Omitlán, Río** ≈ S Mexico
39 X14 **Ommaney, Cape** headland Baranof Island, Alaska, USA 56°10′N 134°40′W
98 N9 **Ommen** Overijssel, E Netherlands 52°31′N 06°25′E
163 N7 **Ömnödelger** var. Bayanbulag. Hentiy, C Mongolia 47°54′N 109°51′E
162 K11 **Ömnögovĭ** ◈ province S Mongolia
191 X7 **Omoa** Fatu Hira, NE French Polynesia 10°30′S 138°41′E
**Omo Botego** see Omo Wenz
**Ómoldova** see Moldova Veche
123 T7 **Omolon** Chukotskiy Avtonomnyy Okrug, NE Russia 65°11′N 160°33′E
123 T7 **Omolon** ≈ NE Russia
123 Q8 **Omoloy** ≈ NE Russia
162 I12 **Omon Gol** Chin. Dong He, var. Narin Gol. ≈ N China
165 P8 **Omono-gawa** ≈ Honshū, C Japan
81 I14 **Omo Wenz** var. Omo Botego. ≈ Ethiopia/Kenya
122 H12 **Omsk** Omskaya Oblast', C Russia 55°N 73°22′E
122 H11 **Omskaya Oblast'** ◈ province C Russia
165 U2 **Ōmu** Hokkaidō, NE Japan 44°36′N 142°55′E
110 M9 **Omulew** ≈ NE Poland
116 J12 **Omul, Vârful** prev. Vîrful Omu. ▲ C Romania 45°24′N 25°26′E
83 D16 **Omundaungilo** Ohangwena, N Namibia 17°28′S 16°39′E
164 C14 **Ōmura** Nagasaki, Kyūshū, SW Japan 32°56′N 129°58′E
83 B17 **Omusati** ◈ region N Namibia
164 C14 **Ōmuta** Fukuoka, Kyūshū, SW Japan 33°01′N 130°27′E
125 S14 **Omutninsk** Kirovskaya Oblast', NW Russia 58°37′N 52°08′E
**Omu, Vîrful** see Omul, Vârful
29 V7 **Onamia** Minnesota, N USA 46°04′N 93°40′W
21 Y5 **Onancock** Virginia, NE USA 37°42′N 75°45′W
14 E10 **Onaping Lake** ◎ Ontario, S Canada
30 M12 **Onarga** Illinois, N USA 40°39′N 88°00′W
15 R6 **Onatchiway, Lac** ◎ Québec, SE Canada
29 S14 **Onawa** Iowa, C USA 42°01′N 96°06′W
165 U5 **Onbetsu** var. Ombetsu. Hokkaidō, NE Japan 42°52′N 143°54′E
83 B16 **Oncócua** Cunene, SW Angola 16°37′S 13°23′E
105 S9 **Onda** Comunitat Valenciana, E Spain 39°58′N 00°17′W
111 N18 **Ondava** ≈ NE Slovakia
83 C16 **Ondjiva** Cunene, S Angola 17°02′S 15°42′E
77 T16 **Ondo** Ondo, SW Nigeria 07°07′N 04°50′E
77 T16 **Ondo** ◈ state SW Nigeria
163 N8 **Öndörhaan** var. Undur Khan; prev. Tsetsen Khan. Hentiy, E Mongolia 47°21′N 110°42′E
162 M9 **Öndörshil** var. Böhöt. Dundgovĭ, C Mongolia 45°13′N 108°12′E
162 L8 **Öndörshireet** var. Bayshint. Töv, C Mongolia 47°22′N 105°04′E
162 I7 **Öndör-Ulaan** var. Teel. Arhangay, C Mongolia 48°01′N 100°30′E
83 D18 **Ondundazongonda** Otjozondjupa, N Namibia 20°28′S 18°00′E
151 K21 **One and Half Degree Channel** channel S Maldives
187 Z15 **Oneata** island Lau Group, E Fiji
124 L9 **Onega** Arkhangel'skaya Oblast', NW Russia 63°54′N 37°59′E
124 L9 **Onega** ≈ NW Russia
**Onega Bay** see Onezhskaya Guba
**Onega, Lake** see Onezhskoye Ozero
18 I10 **Oneida** New York, NE USA 43°05′N 75°39′W
20 M8 **Oneida** Tennessee, S USA 36°30′N 84°30′W
18 H9 **Oneida Lake** ◎ New York, NE USA
29 P13 **O'Neill** Nebraska, C USA 42°28′N 98°38′W
123 V12 **Onekotan, Ostrov** island Kuril'skiye Ostrova, SE Russia
23 P3 **Oneonta** Alabama, S USA 33°57′N 86°28′W
18 J11 **Oneonta** New York, NE USA 42°27′N 75°03′W
190 I16 **Oneroa** island S Cook Islands
116 K11 **Onești** Hung. Onyest; prev. Gheorghe Gheorghiu-Dej. Bacău, E Romania 46°14′N 26°46′E
193 V15 **Onevai** island Tongatapu Group, S Tonga
108 A11 **Onex** Genève, SW Switzerland 46°12′N 06°04′E
124 K8 **Onezhskaya Guba** Eng. Onega Bay. bay NW Russia
122 D7 **Onezhskoye Ozero** Eng. Lake Onega. ◎ NW Russia
83 C16 **Ongandjera** Omusati, N Namibia 17°49′S 15°06′E
184 N12 **Ongaonga** Hawke's Bay, North Island, New Zealand 39°57′S 176°21′E
**Ongi** see Sayhan-Ovoo, Dundgovĭ, Mongolia
**Ongi** see Uyanga
163 W14 **Ongjin** SW North Korea 37°56′N 125°22′E
155 J17 **Ongole** Andhra Pradesh, E India 15°33′N 80°03′E
**Ongon** see Bürd
99 I21 **Onhaye** Namur, S Belgium 50°15′N 04°51′E
166 M8 **Onhne** Bago, SW Myanmar (Burma) 17°02′N 96°28′E
137 S9 **Oni** N Georgia 42°36′N 43°13′E
29 N9 **Onida** South Dakota, N USA 44°42′N 100°03′W
164 F15 **Onigajō-yama** ▲ Shikoku, SW Japan 33°10′N 132°37′E
172 H7 **Onilahy** ≈ S Madagascar
77 U16 **Onitsha** Anambra, S Nigeria 06°09′N 06°48′E
164 K12 **Ōno** Fukui, Honshū, SW Japan 35°59′N 136°30′E
164 I13 **Ono** Hyōgo, Honshū, SW Japan 34°52′N 134°55′E
187 K15 **Ono** island SW Fiji
164 E13 **Onoda** Yamaguchi, Honshū, SW Japan 34°00′N 131°11′E
187 Z16 **Ono-i-lau** island SE Fiji
164 D13 **Ōnojō** var. Ônozyô. Fukuoka, Kyūshū, SW Japan 33°34′N 130°29′E
163 O7 **Onon Gol** ≈ N Mongolia
**Ononte** see Orontes
55 N6 **Onoto** Anzoátegui, NE Venezuela 09°36′N 65°12′W
191 O3 **Onotoa** prev. Clerk Island. atoll Tungaru, W Kiribati
**Ônozyô** see Ōnojō
83 E23 **Onseepkans** Northern Cape, W South Africa 28°44′S 19°18′E
104 F4 **Ons, Illa de** island NW Spain
180 H7 **Onslow** Western Australia 21°42′S 115°08′E
21 W11 **Onslow Bay** bay North Carolina, E USA
98 P6 **Onstwedde** Groningen, NE Netherlands 53°01′N 07°04′E
164 C16 **On-take** ▲ Kyūshū, SW Japan 31°35′N 130°39′E




◆ Country
● Country Capital
◇ Dependent Territory
○ Dependent Territory Capital
◈ Administrative Regions
✈ International Airport
▲ Mountain
▲▲ Mountain Range
⛰ Volcano
≈ River
◎ Lake
⊠ Reservoir

ONTARIO – ØSTREHOGNA


35 T15 **Ontario** California, W USA 34°03′N 117°39′W
32 M13 **Ontario** Oregon, NW USA 44°01′N 116°57′W
12 D10 **Ontario** ◆ *province* S Canada
11 P14 **Ontario, Lake** ◎ Canada/ USA
0 L9 **Ontario Peninsula** *peninsula* Canada/USA
**Onteniente** *see* Ontinyent
105 S11 **Ontinyent** *var.* Onteniente. Comunitat Valenciana, E Spain 38°49′N 00°37′W
93 N15 **Ontojärvi** ◎ E Finland
30 L3 **Ontonagon** Michigan, N USA 46°52′N 89°18′W
30 L3 **Ontonagon River** ⁓ Michigan, N USA
186 M7 **Ontong Java Atoll** *prev.* Lord Howe Island. *atoll* N Solomon Islands
175 N5 **Ontong Java Rise** *undersea feature* W Pacific Ocean 01°00′N 157°00′E
**Onuba** *see* Huelva
55 W9 **Onverwacht** Para, N Suriname 05°36′N 55°12′W
**Onyest** *see* Onești
**Oodeypore** *see* Udaipur
182 J7 **Oodla Wirra** South Australia 32°52′S 139°05′E
182 F2 **Oodnadatta** South Australia 27°34′S 135°27′E
182 C5 **Ooldea** South Australia 30°29′S 131°50′E
27 Q8 **Oologah Lake** ▣ Oklahoma, C USA
**Oos-Kaap** *see* Eastern Cape
**Oos-Londen** *see* East London
99 E17 **Oostakker** Oost-Vlaanderen, NW Belgium 51°06′N 03°46′E
99 D15 **Oostburg** Zeeland, SW Netherlands 51°20′N 03°30′E
98 K9 **Oostelijk-Flevoland** *polder* C Netherlands
99 B16 **Oostende** *Eng.* Ostend, *Fr.* Ostende. West-Vlaanderen, NW Belgium 51°13′N 02°55′E
99 B16 **Oostende** ✈ West-Vlaanderen, NW Belgium 51°12′N 02°55′E
98 L12 **Oosterbeek** Gelderland, SE Netherlands 51°59′N 05°51′E
99 I14 **Oosterhout** Noord-Brabant, S Netherlands 51°38′N 04°51′E
98 O6 **Oostermoers Vaart** *var.* Hunze. ⁓ NE Netherlands
99 F14 **Oosterschelde** *Eng.* Eastern Scheldt. *inlet* SW Netherlands
99 E14 **Oosterscheldedam** *dam* SW Netherlands
98 M7 **Oosterwolde** *Fris.* Easterwâlde. Fryslân, N Netherlands 53°01′N 06°15′E
98 I9 **Oosthuizen** Noord-Holland, NW Netherlands 52°34′N 05°00′E
99 H16 **Oostmalle** Antwerpen, N Belgium 51°18′N 04°44′E
**Oos-Transvaal** *see* Mpumalanga
99 E15 **Oost-Souburg** Zeeland, SW Netherlands 51°28′N 03°36′E
99 E17 **Oost-Vlaanderen** *Eng.* East Flanders. ◆ *province* NW Belgium
98 J5 **Oost-Vlieland** Fryslân, N Netherlands 53°19′N 05°02′E
98 F12 **Oostvoorne** Zuid-Holland, SW Netherlands 51°55′N 04°06′E
**Ootacamund** *see* Udagamandalam
98 O10 **Ootmarsum** Overijssel, E Netherlands 52°25′N 06°55′E
10 K14 **Ootsa Lake** ▣ British Columbia, SW Canada
**Ooty** *see* Udagamandalam
114 L8 **Opaka** Targovishte, N Bulgaria 43°26′N 26°12′E
79 M18 **Opala** Orientale, C Dem. Rep. Congo 0°40′S 24°20′E
125 Q13 **Oparino** Kirovskaya Oblast′, NW Russia 59°52′N 48°14′E
14 H8 **Opasatica, Lac** ◎ Québec, SE Canada
112 B9 **Opatija** *It.* Abbazia. Primorje-Gorski Kotar, NW Croatia 45°18′N 14°15′E
111 N15 **Opatów** Świętokrzyskie, C Poland 50°45′N 21°27′E
111 I17 **Opava** *Ger.* Troppau. Moravskoslezský Kraj, E Czechia 49°56′N 17°53′E
111 H16 **Opava** *Ger.* Oppa. ⁓ NE Czechia
**Ópazova** *see* Stara Pazova
**Ópécska** *see* Pecica
14 E8 **Opeepeesway Lake** ◎ Ontario, S Canada
23 R5 **Opelika** Alabama, S USA 32°39′N 85°22′W
22 I8 **Opelousas** Louisiana, S USA 30°31′N 92°04′W
186 G6 **Open Bay** *bay* New Britain, E Papua New Guinea
14 I12 **Opeongo Lake** ◎ Ontario, SE Canada
99 K17 **Opglabbeek** Limburg, NE Belgium 51°04′N 05°39′E
33 W6 **Opheim** Montana, NW USA 48°50′N 106°24′W
39 P10 **Ophir** Alaska, USA 63°08′N 156°31′W
**Ophiusa** *see* Formentera
79 N18 **Opienge** Orientale, E Dem. Rep. Congo 0°15′N 27°25′E
185 G20 **Opihi** ⁓ South Island, New Zealand
12 J9 **Opinaca** ⁓ Québec, C Canada
12 J10 **Opinaca, Réservoir** ▣ Québec, E Canada
117 T5 **Opishnya** *Rus.* Oposhnya. Poltavs′ka Oblast′, NE Ukraine 49°58′N 34°37′E
98 I8 **Opmeer** Noord-Holland, NW Netherlands 52°43′N 04°56′E
77 V17 **Opobo** Akwa Ibom, S Nigeria 04°36′N 07°37′E
124 F16 **Opochka** Pskovskaya Oblast′, W Russia 56°42′N 28°40′E
110 L13 **Opoczno** Łodzkie, C Poland 51°24′N 20°18′E
111 I15 **Opole** *Ger.* Oppeln. Opolskie, S Poland 50°40′N 17°56′E
111 H15 **Opolskie** ◆ *province* S Poland
**Oporny** *see* Borankul
104 G4 **O Porriño** *var.* Porriño. Galicia, NW Spain 42°10′N 08°38′W
**Oporto** *see* Porto
**Oposhnya** *see* Opishnya
184 P8 **Opotiki** Bay of Plenty, North Island, New Zealand 38°02′S 177°18′E
23 Q7 **Opp** Alabama, S USA 31°16′N 86°14′W
**Oppa** *see* Opava
94 G9 **Oppdal** Sør-Trøndelag, S Norway 62°36′N 09°41′E
**Oppeln** *see* Opole
107 N23 **Oppido Mamertina** Calabria, SW Italy 38°17′N 15°58′E
**Oppidum Ubiorum** *see* Köln
94 F12 **Oppland** ◆ *county* S Norway
118 J12 **Opsa** Vitsyebskaya Voblasts′, NW Belarus 55°32′N 26°50′E
26 I8 **Optima Lake** ▣ Oklahoma, C USA
184 J11 **Opunake** Taranaki, North Island, New Zealand 39°27′S 173°52′E
191 N6 **Opunohu, Baie d′** *bay* Moorea, W French Polynesia
83 B17 **Opuwo** Kunene, NW Namibia 18°03′S 13°54′E
146 H6 **Oqqal′a** *var.* Akkala, *Rus.* Karakala. Qoraqalpog′iston Respublikasi, NW Uzbekistan 43°43′N 59°25′E
147 V13 **Oqsu** *Rus.* Oksu. ⁓ SE Tajikistan
147 P14 **Oqtogh, Qatorkŭhi** *Rus.* Khrebet Aktau. ▲▲ SW Tajikistan
146 M11 **Oqtosh** *Rus.* Aktash. Samarqand Viloyati, C Uzbekistan 39°23′N 65°46′E
147 N11 **Oqtov Tizmasi** *var.* Khrebet Aktau. ▲▲ C Uzbekistan
30 J12 **Oquawka** Illinois, N USA 40°56′N 90°56′W
144 J10 **Or′** *Kaz.* Or. ⁓ Kazakhstan/Russia
36 M15 **Oracle** Arizona, SW USA 32°36′N 110°46′W
147 N13 **O′radaryo** *Rus.* Uradar′ya. ⁓ S Uzbekistan
116 F9 **Oradea** *prev.* Oradea Mare, *Ger.* Grosswardein, *Hung.* Nagyvárad. Bihor, NW Romania 47°03′N 21°56′E
**Oradea Mare** *see* Oradea
**Orahovac** *see* Rahovec
112 H9 **Orahovica** Virovitica-Podravina, NE Croatia 45°33′N 17°54′E
152 K13 **Orai** Uttar Pradesh, N India 26°00′N 79°26′E
92 K12 **Orajärvi** Lappi, NW Finland 66°54′N 24°04′E
138 F9 **Or′Akiva** *prev.* Or ′Aqiva. Haifa, N Israel 32°40′N 34°58′E
**Oral** *see* Ural′sk
74 I5 **Oran** *var.* Ouahran, Wahran. NW Algeria 35°42′N 00°37′W
183 R8 **Orange** New South Wales, SE Australia 33°16′S 149°06′E
103 R14 **Orange** *anc.* Arausio. Vaucluse, SE France 44°06′N 04°52′E
25 Y10 **Orange** Texas, SW USA 30°05′N 93°43′W
21 V5 **Orange** Virginia, NE USA 38°14′N 78°07′W
21 R13 **Orangeburg** South Carolina, SE USA 33°28′N 80°53′W
58 J9 **Orange, Cabo** *headland* NE Brazil 04°24′N 51°33′W
29 S12 **Orange City** Iowa, C USA 43°00′N 96°03′W
**Orange Cone** *see* Orange Fan
172 J10 **Orange Fan** *var.* Orange Cone. *undersea feature* SW Indian Ocean 32°00′S 12°00′E
**Orange Free State** *see* Free State
25 S14 **Orange Grove** Texas, SW USA 27°57′N 97°56′W
18 K13 **Orange Lake** New York, NE USA 41°32′N 74°06′W
23 V10 **Orange Lake** ◎ Florida, SE USA
**Orange Mouth/ Orangemund** *see* Oranjemund
23 W9 **Orange Park** Florida, SE USA 30°10′N 81°42′W
83 E23 **Orange River** *Afr.* Oranjerivier. ⁓ S Africa
14 G15 **Orangeville** Ontario, S Canada 43°55′N 80°06′W
36 M5 **Orangeville** Utah, W USA 39°14′N 111°03′W
42 G1 **Orange Walk** Orange Walk, N Belize 18°06′N 88°30′W
42 F1 **Orange Walk** ◆ *district* NW Belize
100 N11 **Oranienburg** Brandenburg, NE Germany 52°46′N 13°15′E
98 O7 **Oranjekanaal** *canal* NE Netherlands
83 D23 **Oranjemund** *var.* Orangemund; *prev.* Orange Mouth. //Karas, SW Namibia 28°33′S 16°28′E
**Oranjerivier** *see* Orange River
45 N16 **Oranjestad** ○ (Aruba) W Aruba 12°31′N 70°W
**Oranje Vrystaat** *see* Free State
**Orany** *see* Varėna
83 H18 **Orapa** Central, C Botswana 21°16′S 25°22′E
**Or ′Aqiva** *see* Or′Akiva
112 I10 **Orašje** ◆ Federacija Bosna I Hercegovina, N Bosnia and Herzegovina
116 G11 **Orăștie** *Ger.* Broos, *Hung.* Szászváros. Hunedoara, W Romania 45°50′N 23°11′E
**Orașul Stalin** *see* Brașov
111 K18 **Orava** *Hung.* Árva, *Pol.* Orawa. ⁓ N Slovakia
**Oravainen** *see* Oravais
93 K16 **Oravais** *Fin.* Oravainen. Österbotten, W Finland 63°18′N 22°25′E
**Oravicabánya** *see* Oravița
116 F13 **Oravița** *Ger.* Orawitza, *Hung.* Oravicabánya. Caraș-Severin, SW Romania 45°02′N 21°43′E
**Orawa** *see* Orava
185 B24 **Orawia** Southland, South Island, New Zealand 46°03′S 167°49′E
**Orawitza** *see* Oravița
103 P16 **Orb** ⁓ S France
106 C9 **Orba** ⁓ NW Italy
158 H12 **Orba Co** ◎ W China
108 B9 **Orbe** Vaud, W Switzerland 46°42′N 06°28′E
107 G14 **Orbetello** Toscana, C Italy 42°28′N 11°15′E
104 K3 **Orbigo** ⁓ NW Spain
183 Q12 **Orbost** Victoria, SE Australia 37°44′S 148°28′E
95 O14 **Örbyhus** Uppsala, C Sweden 60°15′N 17°43′E
194 I1 **Orcadas** *research station (Argentina)* South Orkney Islands, Antarctica 60°37′S 44°48′W
105 P12 **Orcera** Andalucía, S Spain 38°20′N 02°36′W
33 P9 **Orchard Homes** Montana, NW USA 46°52′N 114°01′W
37 P5 **Orchard Mesa** Colorado, C USA 39°02′N 108°33′W
18 D10 **Orchard Park** New York, NE USA 42°46′N 78°44′W
**Orchid Island** *see* Lan Yu
115 G18 **Orchómenos** *var.* Orhomenos, Orkhómenos, *prev.* Skripón; *anc.* Orchomenus. Stereá Elláda, C Greece 38°29′N 22°58′E
**Orchomenus** *see* Orchómenos
106 B7 **Orco** ⁓ NW Italy
103 R8 **Or, Côte d′** *physical region* C France
29 O14 **Ord** Nebraska, C USA 41°36′N 98°55′W
119 O15 **Ordats′** *Rus.* Ordat′. Mahilyowskaya Voblasts′, E Belarus 54°10′N 30°42′E
36 K8 **Orderville** Utah, W USA 37°16′N 112°38′W
104 H2 **Ordes** Galicia, NW Spain 43°04′N 08°25′W
35 V14 **Ord Mountain** ▲ California, W USA 34°41′N 116°46′W
163 N14 **Ordos** *prev.* Dongsheng. Nei Mongol Zizhiqu, N China 39°51′N 110°00′E
**Ordos Desert** *see* Mu Us Shadi
188 B16 **Ordot** C Guam
137 N11 **Ordu** *anc.* Cotyora. Ordu, N Turkey 41°N 37°52′E
136 M11 **Ordu** ◆ *province* N Turkey
137 V14 **Ordubad** SW Azerbaijan 38°55′N 46°00′E
**Orduña** *see* Urduña
37 U6 **Ordway** Colorado, C USA 38°13′N 103°45′W
**Ordzhonikidze** *see* Denisovka, Kazakhstan
**Ordzhonikidze** *see* Vladikavkaz, Russian Federation
**Ordzhonikidze** *see* Pokrov
**Ordzhonikidze** *see* Yenakiyeve, Ukraine
**Ordzhonikidzeabad** *see* Vahdat
55 U9 **Orealla** E Guyana 05°13′N 57°17′W
113 G15 **Orebić** *It.* Sabbioncello. Dubrovnik-Neretva, S Croatia 42°58′N 17°12′E
95 M16 **Örebro** Örebro, C Sweden 59°18′N 15°12′E
95 L16 **Örebro** ◆ *county* C Sweden
25 W6 **Ore City** Texas, SW USA 32°48′N 94°43′W
30 L10 **Oregon** Illinois, N USA 42°00′N 89°19′W
27 Q2 **Oregon** Missouri, C USA 39°59′N 95°08′W
31 R11 **Oregon** Ohio, N USA 41°38′N 83°29′W
32 H13 **Oregon** *off.* State of Oregon, *also known as* Beaver State, Sunset State, Valentine State, Webfoot State. ◆ *state* NW USA
32 G11 **Oregon City** Oregon, NW USA 45°21′N 122°36′W
**Oregon, State of** *see* Oregon
95 P14 **Öregrund** Uppsala, C Sweden 60°19′N 18°30′E
**Orekhov** *see* Orikhiv
126 L3 **Orekhovo-Zuyevo** Moskovskaya Oblast′, W Russia 55°46′N 39°01′E
**Orekhovsk** *see* Arekhawsk
126 J6 **Orël** Orlovskaya Oblast′, W Russia 52°57′N 36°06′E
**Orel** *see* Oril′
56 E11 **Orellana** Loreto, N Peru 06°53′S 75°10′W
56 E6 **Orellana** ◆ *province* NE Ecuador
104 L11 **Orellana, Embalse de** ▣ W Spain
36 L3 **Orem** Utah, W USA 40°18′N 111°42′W
**Ore Mountains** *see* Erzgebirge/Krušné Hory
127 V7 **Orenburg** *prev.* Chkalov. Orenburgskaya Oblast′, W Russia 51°46′N 55°12′E
127 V7 **Orenburg** ✈ Orenburgskaya Oblast′, W Russia 51°54′N 55°15′E
127 T7 **Orenburgskaya Oblast′** ◆ *province* W Russia
**Orense** *see* Ourense
188 C8 **Oreor** *var.* Koror. *island* N Palau
185 B24 **Orepuki** Southland, South Island, New Zealand 46°17′S 167°45′E
114 L12 **Orestiáda** *prev.* Orestiás. Anatolikí Makedonía kai Thráki, NE Greece 41°30′N 26°31′E
**Orestiás** *see* Orestiáda
**Øresund/Oresund** *see* Sound, The
185 C23 **Oreti** ⁓ South Island, New Zealand
184 L5 **Orewa** Auckland, North Island, New Zealand 36°34′S 174°43′E
65 A25 **Orford, Cape** *headland* West Falkland, Falkland Islands 52°00′S 61°04′W
44 B5 **Órganos, Sierra de los** ▲▲ W Cuba
37 R15 **Organ Peak** ▲ New Mexico, SW USA 32°17′N 106°35′W
105 N9 **Orgaz** Castilla-La Mancha, C Spain 39°39′N 03°52′W
**Orgeyev** *see* Orhei
**Orgil** *see* Jargalant
105 O15 **Orgiva** *var.* Orjiva. Andalucía, S Spain 36°54′N 03°25′W
163 O10 **Örgön** *var.* Senj. Dornogovĭ, SE Mongolia 44°34′N 110°58′E
**Örgön** *see* Bayangovĭ
**Orgražden** *see* Ograzhden
117 N9 **Orhei** *var.* Orheiu, *Rus.* Orgeyev. N Moldova 47°25′N 28°48′E
**Orheiu** *see* Orhei
105 R3 **Orhi** *var.* Orhy, Pico de Orhy, Pic d′Orhy. ▲ France/ Spain 42°55′N 01°01′W *see also* Orhy
**Orhi** *see* Orhy
**Orhomenos** *see* Orchómenos
162 K6 **Orhon** ◆ *province* N Mongolia
162 L6 **Orhon Gol** ⁓ N Mongolia
102 J16 **Orhy** *var.* Orhi, Pico de Orhy, Pic d′Orhy. ▲ France/ Spain 43°00′N 01°00′W *see also* Orhi
**Orhy** *see* Orhi
**Orhy, Pic d′/Orhy, Pico de** *see* Orhi/Orhy
34 L2 **Orick** California, W USA 41°16′N 124°03′W
32 L6 **Orient** Washington, NW USA 48°51′N 118°14′W
48 D6 **Oriental, Cordillera** ▲▲ Bolivia/Peru
48 D6 **Oriental, Cordillera** ▲▲ C Colombia
57 H16 **Oriental, Cordillera** ▲▲ C Peru
63 M15 **Oriente** Buenos Aires, E Argentina 38°45′S 60°37′W
105 R12 **Orihuela** Comunitat Valenciana, E Spain 38°05′N 00°56′W
117 V9 **Orikhiv** *Rus.* Orekhov. Zaporiz′ka Oblast′, SE Ukraine 47°32′N 35°48′E
113 K22 **Orikum** *var.* Orikumi. Vlorë, SW Albania 40°20′N 19°28′E
**Orikumi** *see* Orikum
117 V6 **Oril′** *Rus.* Orel. ⁓ E Ukraine
14 H14 **Orillia** Ontario, S Canada 44°36′N 79°26′W
93 M19 **Orimattila** Päijät-Häme, S Finland 60°48′N 25°40′E
33 Y15 **Orin** Wyoming, C USA 42°39′N 105°10′W
47 R4 **Orinoco, Río** ⁓ Colombia/ Venezuela
54 I11 **Orinoquía** *physical region* W Colombia
186 C9 **Oriomo** Western, SW Papua New Guinea 08°53′S 143°13′E
30 K11 **Orion** Illinois, N USA 41°21′N 90°22′W
29 Q5 **Oriska** North Dakota, N USA 46°54′N 97°46′W
**Orissa** *see* Odisha
**Orissaar** *see* Orissaare
118 E5 **Orissaare** *Ger.* Orissaar. Saaremaa, W Estonia 58°34′N 23°05′E
107 B19 **Oristano** Sardegna, Italy, C Mediterranean Sea 39°54′N 08°35′E
107 A19 **Oristano, Golfo di** *gulf* Sardegna, Italy, C Mediterranean Sea
54 D13 **Orito** Putumayo, SW Colombia 0°49′N 76°57′W
93 L18 **Orivesi** Häme, W Finland 61°39′N 24°21′E
93 N17 **Orivesi** ◎ Etelä-Savo, SE Finland
58 H12 **Oriximiná** Pará, NE Brazil 01°45′S 55°50′W
41 Q14 **Orizaba** Veracruz, E Mexico 18°51′N 97°08′W
41 Q14 **Orizaba, Volcán Pico de** *var.* Citlaltépetl. ▲ S Mexico 19°00′N 97°15′W
95 I16 **Ørje** Østfold, S Norway 59°28′N 11°40′E
113 I16 **Orjen** ▲▲ Bosnia and Herzegovina/Montenegro
**Orjiva** *see* Orgiva
**Orjonikidzeobod** *see* Vahdat
94 G8 **Orkanger** Sør-Trøndelag, S Norway 63°17′N 09°52′E
94 G8 **Orkdalen** *valley* S Norway
95 K22 **Örkelljunga** Skåne, S Sweden 56°17′N 13°20′E
**Orkhaniye** *see* Botevgrad
**Orkhómenos** *see* Orchómenos
94 H9 **Orkla** ⁓ S Norway
**Orkney** *see* Orkney Islands
65 J22 **Orkney Deep** *undersea feature* Scotia Sea/Weddell Sea
96 J4 **Orkney Islands** *var.* Orkney, Orkneys. *island group* N Scotland, United Kingdom
**Orkneys** *see* Orkney Islands
24 K8 **Orla** Texas, SW USA 31°48′N 103°55′W
35 N5 **Orland** California, W USA 39°43′N 122°12′W
23 X11 **Orlando** Florida, SE USA 28°32′N 81°23′W
23 X12 **Orlando** ✈ Florida, SE USA 28°24′N 81°16′W
107 K23 **Orlando, Capo d′** *headland* Sicilia, Italy, C Mediterranean Sea 38°10′N 14°44′E
**Orlau** *see* Orlová
103 N6 **Orléanais** *cultural region* C France
103 N7 **Orléans** *anc.* Aurelianum. Loiret, C France 47°54′N 01°53′E
34 L2 **Orleans** California, W USA 41°16′N 123°36′W
19 Q12 **Orleans** Massachusetts, NE USA 41°48′N 69°57′W
15 R10 **Orléans, Île d′** *island* Québec, SE Canada
**Orléansville** *see* Chlef
111 F16 **Orlice** *Ger.* Adler. ⁓ NE Czechia
122 L13 **Orlik** Respublika Buryatiya, S Russia 52°32′N 99°36′E
125 Q14 **Orlov** *prev.* Khalturin. Kirovskaya Oblast′, NW Russia 58°34′N 48°57′E
111 I17 **Orlová** *Ger.* Orlau, *Pol.* Orłowa. Moravskoslezský Kraj, E Czechia 49°50′N 18°21′E
**Orlov, Mys** *see* Orlovskiy, Mys
126 I6 **Orlovskaya Oblast′** ◆ *province* W Russia
124 M5 **Orlovskiy, Mys** *var.* Mys Orlov. *headland* NW Russia 67°14′N 41°17′E
**Orłowa** *see* Orlová
103 O5 **Orly** ✈ (Paris) Essonne, N France 48°43′N 02°24′E
119 G16 **Orlya** Hrodzyenskaya Voblasts′, W Belarus 53°30′N 24°59′E
114 M7 **Orlyak** *prev.* Makenzen, Trubchular, *Rom.* Trupcilar. Dobrich, NE Bulgaria 43°39′N 27°21′E
148 L16 **Ormara** Baluchistan, SW Pakistan 25°14′N 64°36′E
171 P5 **Ormoc** *off.* Ormoc City, *var.* MacArthur. Leyte, C Philippines 11°02′N 124°35′E
**Ormoc City** *see* Ormoc
23 X10 **Ormond Beach** Florida, SE USA 29°16′N 81°04′W
109 X10 **Ormož** *Ger.* Friedau. NE Slovenia 46°24′N 16°09′E
14 J13 **Ormsby** Ontario, SE Canada 44°52′N 77°45′W
97 K17 **Ormskirk** NW England, United Kingdom 53°35′N 02°54′W
**Ormsö** *see* Vormsi
15 N13 **Ormstown** Québec, SE Canada 45°08′N 73°57′W
**Ormuz, Strait of** *see* Hormuz, Strait of
103 T8 **Ornans** Doubs, E France 47°06′N 06°06′E
102 K5 **Orne** ◆ *department* N France
102 K5 **Orne** ⁓ N France
92 G12 **Ørnes** Nordland, C Norway 66°51′N 13°43′E
110 L7 **Orneta** Warmińsko-Mazurskie, NE Poland 54°07′N 20°10′E
95 P16 **Ornö** Stockholm, C Sweden 59°03′N 18°28′E
37 Q3 **Orno Peak** ▲ Colorado, C USA 40°06′N 107°06′W
93 I16 **Örnsköldsvik** Västernorrland, C Sweden 63°16′N 18°45′E
163 X13 **Oro** E North Korea 39°59′N 127°27′E
**Oro** *see* Northern
45 T6 **Orocovis** C Puerto Rico 18°13′N 66°22′W
54 H10 **Orocué** Casanare, E Colombia 04°51′N 71°21′W
77 N13 **Orodara** SW Burkina Faso 11°00′N 04°54′W
105 S4 **Oroel, Peña de** ▲ N Spain 42°30′N 00°31′W
33 N10 **Orofino** Idaho, NW USA 46°28′N 116°15′W
162 I9 **Orog Nuur** ◎ S Mongolia
35 U14 **Oro Grande** California, W USA 34°36′N 117°19′W
37 S15 **Orogrande** New Mexico, SW USA 32°24′N 106°04′W
191 Q7 **Orohena, Mont** ⛰ Tahiti, W French Polynesia 17°37′S 149°27′W
**Orolaunum** *see* Arlon
**Orol Dengizi** *see* Aral Sea
189 S15 **Oroluk Atoll** *atoll* Caroline Islands, C Micronesia
80 J13 **Oromīya** *var.* Oromo. ◆ C Ethiopia
**Oromo** *see* Oromīya
13 O15 **Oromocto** New Brunswick, SE Canada 45°50′N 66°28′W
191 S4 **Orona** *prev.* Hull Island. *atoll* Phoenix Islands, C Kiribati
191 V17 **Orongo** *ancient monument* Easter Island, Chile, E Pacific Ocean
138 I3 **Orontes** *var.* Ononte, Nahr el Aassi, *Ar.* Nahr al ′Aṣī. ⁓ SW Asia
104 L9 **Oropesa** Castilla-La Mancha, C Spain 39°55′N 05°10′W
**Oropesa** *see* Oropesa del Mar
105 T8 **Oropesa del Mar** *var.* Oropesa, *Cat.* Orpes. Comunitat Valenciana, E Spain 40°06′N 00°07′E
**Oropeza** *see* Cochabamba
**Oroqen Zizhiqi** *see* Alihe
171 P7 **Oroquieta** *var.* Oroquieta City. Mindanao, S Philippines 08°27′N 123°46′E
**Oroquieta City** *see* Oroquieta
40 J8 **Oro, Río del** ⁓ C Mexico
59 O14 **Orós, Açude** ▣ E Brazil
107 D18 **Orosei, Golfo di** *gulf* Tyrrhenian Sea, C Mediterranean Sea
**Oroszlány Rodópis** *see* Rhodope Mountains
111 M24 **Orosháza** Békés, SE Hungary 46°33′N 20°40′E
111 I22 **Oroszlány** Komárom-Esztergom, W Hungary 47°28′N 18°16′E
188 B16 **Orote Peninsula** *peninsula* W Guam
123 T9 **Orotukan** Magadanskaya Oblast′, E Russia 62°18′N 150°46′E
35 O5 **Oroville** California, W USA 39°29′N 121°35′W
32 K6 **Oroville** Washington, NW USA 48°56′N 119°25′W
35 O5 **Oroville, Lake** ▣ California, W USA
0 G15 **Orozco Fracture Zone** *tectonic feature* E Pacific Ocean
**Orpes** *see* Oropesa del Mar
**Orpesa** *see* Oropesa del Mar
64 I7 **Orphan Knoll** *undersea feature* NW Atlantic Ocean 51°00′N 47°00′W
29 V3 **Orr** Minnesota, N USA 48°03′N 92°48′W
95 M21 **Orrefors** Kalmar, S Sweden 56°48′N 15°45′E
182 I7 **Orroroo** South Australia 32°46′S 138°38′E
31 T12 **Orrville** Ohio, N USA 40°50′N 81°45′W
94 L12 **Orsa** Dalarna, C Sweden 61°07′N 14°40′E
**Orschowa** *see* Orșova
**Orschütz** *see* Orzyc
119 O14 **Orsha** Vitsyebskaya Voblasts′, NE Belarus 54°30′N 30°26′E
127 Q2 **Orshanka** Respublika Mariy El, W Russia 56°54′N 47°54′E
108 C11 **Orsières** Valais, SW Switzerland 46°00′N 07°09′E
127 X8 **Orsk** Orenburgskaya Oblast′, W Russia 51°13′N 58°35′E
116 F13 **Orșova** *Ger.* Orschowa, *Hung.* Orsova. Mehedinți, SW Romania 44°42′N 22°22′E
94 D10 **Ørsta** Møre og Romsdal, S Norway 62°12′N 06°09′E
95 O15 **Örsundsbro** Uppsala, C Sweden 59°45′N 17°19′E
136 D16 **Ortaca** Muğla, SW Turkey 36°49′N 28°43′E
136 G10 **Ortakarya Burnu** *headland* NW Turkey 41°18′N 31°24′E
83 I21 **O.R. Tambo** ✈ (Johannesburg) Gauteng, NE South Africa 26°08′S 28°01′E
107 M16 **Orta Nova** Puglia, SE Italy 41°20′N 15°43′E
136 I17 **Orta Toroslar** ▲ S Turkey
54 E11 **Ortega** Tolima, W Colombia 03°57′N 75°11′W
104 H1 **Ortegal, Cabo** *headland* NW Spain 43°46′N 07°54′W
**Ortelsburg** *see* Szczytno
102 J15 **Orthez** Pyrénées-Atlantiques, SW France 43°29′N 00°46′W
60 J10 **Ortigueira** Paraná, S Brazil 24°10′S 50°55′W
104 H1 **Ortigueira** Galicia, NW Spain 43°40′N 07°50′W
106 H5 **Ortisei** *Ger.* Sankt-Ulrich. Trentino-Alto Adige, N Italy 46°35′N 11°42′E
40 F6 **Ortiz** Sonora, NW Mexico 28°18′N 110°40′W
54 L5 **Ortiz** Guárico, N Venezuela 09°37′N 67°20′W
**Ortler** *see* Ortles
106 F5 **Ortles** *Ger.* Ortler. ▲ N Italy 46°29′N 10°33′E
107 K14 **Ortona** Abruzzo, C Italy 42°21′N 14°24′E
57 K14 **Ortón, Río** ⁓ N Bolivia
29 R8 **Ortonville** Minnesota, N USA 45°18′N 96°26′W
147 W8 **Orto-Tokoy** Issyk-Kul′skaya Oblast′, NE Kyrgyzstan 42°20′N 76°03′E
93 I15 **Örträsk** Västerbotten, N Sweden 64°10′N 19°00′E
100 J12 **Örtze** ⁓ NW Germany
**Oruba** *see* Aruba
142 I3 **Orūmīyeh** *var.* Rizaiyeh, Urmia, Urmiyeh; *prev.* Reẕā′īyeh. Āżarbāyjān-e Gharbī, NW Iran 37°33′N 45°06′E
142 J3 **Orūmīyeh, Daryācheh-ye** *var.* Matianus, Sha Hi, Urumi Yeh, *Eng.* Lake Urmia; *prev.* Daryācheh-ye Reẕā′īyeh. ◎ NW Iran
57 K19 **Oruro** Oruro, W Bolivia 17°58′S 67°06′W
57 J19 **Oruro** ◆ *department* W Bolivia
95 I18 **Orust** *island* S Sweden
**Orūzgān** *see* Uruzgān
106 H13 **Orvieto** *anc.* Velsuna. Umbria, C Italy 42°43′N 12°06′E
194 K7 **Orville Coast** *physical region* Antarctica
114 H7 **Oryahovo** *var.* Oryakhovo. Vratsa, NW Bulgaria 43°44′N 23°58′E
**Oryakhovo** *see* Oryahovo
**Oryokko** *see* Yalu
117 R5 **Orzhytsya** Poltavs′ka Oblast′, C Ukraine 49°48′N 32°40′E
110 M9 **Orzyc** *Ger.* Orschütz. ⁓ NE Poland
110 N8 **Orzysz** *Ger.* Arys. Warmińsko-Mazurskie, NE Poland 53°49′N 21°54′E
98 K13 **Oss** Noord-Brabant, S Netherlands 51°46′N 05°32′E
94 I10 **Os** Hedmark, S Norway 62°29′N 11°14′E
125 U15 **Osa** Permskiy Kray, NW Russia 57°16′N 55°22′E
115 F15 **Óssa** ▲▲ C Greece
104 H11 **Ossa** ▲ S Portugal 38°43′N 07°33′W
29 W11 **Osage** Iowa, C USA 43°16′N 92°48′W
27 U5 **Osage Beach** Missouri, C USA 38°09′N 92°37′W
27 P5 **Osage City** Kansas, C USA 38°37′N 95°49′W
27 U7 **Osage Fork River** ⁓ Missouri, C USA
27 U5 **Osage River** ⁓ Missouri, C USA
164 J13 **Ōsaka** *hist.* Naniwa. Ōsaka, Honshū, SW Japan 34°38′N 135°28′E
164 I13 **Ōsaka** *off.* Ōsaka-fu, *var.* Ōsaka Hu. ◆ *urban prefecture* Honshū, SW Japan
**Ōsaka-fu/Ōsaka Hu** *see* Ōsaka
145 R10 **Osakarovka** Karaganda, C Kazakhstan 50°32′N 72°39′E
**Ōsaki** *see* Furukawa
29 T7 **Osakis** Minnesota, N USA 45°51′N 95°08′W
114 I9 **Osam** *var.* Osŭm. ⁓ N Bulgaria
43 N16 **Osa, Península de** *peninsula* S Costa Rica
60 M10 **Osasco** São Paulo, S Brazil 23°32′S 46°46′W
27 R5 **Osawatomie** Kansas, C USA 38°30′N 94°57′W
26 L3 **Osborne** Kansas, C USA 39°26′N 98°42′W
173 S8 **Osborn Plateau** *undersea feature* E Indian Ocean
95 L21 **Osby** Skåne, S Sweden 56°24′N 14°00′E
**Osca** *see* Huesca
92 N2 **Oscar II Land** *physical region* W Svalbard
27 Y10 **Osceola** Arkansas, C USA 35°43′N 89°58′W
29 V15 **Osceola** Iowa, C USA 41°01′N 93°45′W
27 S6 **Osceola** Missouri, C USA 38°01′N 93°41′W
29 Q15 **Osceola** Nebraska, C USA 41°09′N 97°28′W
101 N15 **Oschatz** Sachsen, E Germany 51°17′N 13°10′E
100 K13 **Oschersleben** Sachsen-Anhalt, C Germany 52°02′N 11°14′E
31 R7 **Oscoda** Michigan, N USA 44°25′N 83°19′W
**Ösel** *see* Saaremaa
94 H6 **Osen** Sør-Trøndelag, S Norway 64°17′N 10°29′E
94 I12 **Osensjøen** ◎ S Norway
164 A14 **Ōse-zaki** Fukue-jima, SW Japan
147 T10 **Osh** Oshskaya Oblast′, SW Kyrgyzstan 40°34′N 72°46′E
83 C16 **Oshakati** Oshana, N Namibia 17°46′S 15°43′E
83 C16 **Oshana** ◆ *region* N Namibia
14 H15 **Oshawa** Ontario, SE Canada 43°54′N 78°50′W
165 R10 **Oshika-hantō** *peninsula* Honshū, C Japan
83 C16 **Oshikango** Ohangwena, N Namibia 17°29′S 15°54′E
83 C17 **Oshikoto** *var.* Otjikoto. ◆ *region* N Namibia
165 P5 **Ō-shima** *island* NE Japan
165 N14 **Ō-shima** *island* S Japan
165 Q5 **Oshima-hantō** ▲▲ Hokkaidō, NE Japan
83 D17 **Oshivelo** Oshikoto, N Namibia 18°37′S 17°10′E
28 K14 **Oshkosh** Nebraska, C USA 41°25′N 102°21′W
30 M7 **Oshkosh** Wisconsin, N USA 44°01′N 88°32′W
**Oshmyany** *see* Ashmyany
**Osh Oblasty** *see* Oshskaya Oblast′
77 T16 **Oshogbo** *var.* Osogbo. Osun, W Nigeria 07°42′N 04°31′E
147 S11 **Oshskaya Oblast′** *Kyr.* Osh Oblasty. ◆ *province* SW Kyrgyzstan
**Öshū** *see* Mizusawa
**Oshun** *see* Osun
79 J20 **Oshwe** Bandundu, C Dem. Rep. Congo 03°24′S 19°32′E
**Osiek** *see* Osijek
112 I9 **Osijek** *prev.* Osiek, Osijek, *Ger.* Esseg, *Hung.* Eszék. Osijek-Baranja, E Croatia 45°33′N 18°41′E
112 I9 **Osijek-Baranja** *off.* Osječko-Baranjska Županija. ◆ *province* E Croatia
106 J12 **Osimo** Marche, C Italy 43°28′N 13°29′E
122 M12 **Osinovka** Irkutskaya Oblast′, C Russia 56°19′N 101°55′E
**Osintorf** *see* Asintorf
112 N11 **Osipaonica** Serbia, NE Serbia 44°34′N 21°00′E
**Osipenko** *see* Berdyans′k
**Osipovichi** *see* Asipovichy
**Osječko-Baranjska Županija** *see* Osijek-Baranja
**Osjek** *see* Osijek
29 W15 **Oskaloosa** Iowa, C USA 41°17′N 92°38′W
27 Q4 **Oskaloosa** Kansas, C USA 39°14′N 95°21′W
95 N20 **Oskarshamn** Kalmar, S Sweden 57°16′N 16°25′E
95 J21 **Oskarström** Halland, S Sweden 56°48′N 13°00′E
14 M8 **Oskélanéo** Québec, SE Canada 48°06′N 75°12′W
**Öskemen** *see* Ust′-Kamenogorsk
117 W5 **Oskil** *Rus.* Oskol. ⁓ Russia/ Ukraine
**Oskil** *see* Oskil
93 D20 **Oslo** *prev.* Christiania, Kristiania. ● (Norway) Oslo, S Norway 59°54′N 10°44′E
93 D20 **Oslo** ◆ *county* S Norway
93 D21 **Oslofjorden** *fjord* S Norway
155 G15 **Osmānābād** Mahārāshtra, C India 18°09′N 76°06′E
136 J11 **Osmancık** Çorum, N Turkey 40°58′N 34°50′E
136 L16 **Osmaniye** Osmaniye, S Turkey 37°04′N 36°15′E
136 L16 **Osmaniye** ◆ *province* S Turkey
95 O16 **Ösmo** Stockholm, C Sweden 58°58′N 17°55′E
118 E3 **Osmussaar** *island* W Estonia
100 G13 **Osnabrück** Niedersachsen, NW Germany 52°09′N 07°42′E
110 D11 **Ośno Lubuskie** *Ger.* Drossen. Lubuskie, W Poland 52°28′N 14°51′E
**Osogbo** *see* Oshogbo
113 P19 **Osogov Mountains** *var.* Osogovske Planine, Osogovski Planina, *Mac.* Osogovski Planini. ▲▲ Bulgaria/North Macedonia
**Osogovske Planine/ Osogovski Planina/ Osogovski Planini** *see* Osogov Mountains
165 R6 **Osore-zan** ▲ Honshū, C Japan 41°18′N 141°06′E
**Oșorhei** *see* Târgu Mureș
61 J16 **Osório** Rio Grande do Sul, S Brazil 29°53′S 50°17′W
63 G16 **Osorno** Los Lagos, C Chile 40°39′S 73°05′W
104 M4 **Osorno** Castilla y León, N Spain 42°24′N 04°22′W
11 N17 **Osoyoos** British Columbia, SW Canada 49°02′N 119°31′W
95 C14 **Osøyro** Hordaland, S Norway 60°11′N 05°30′E
54 J6 **Ospino** Portuguesa, N Venezuela 09°17′N 69°26′W
23 X6 **Ossabaw Island** *island* Georgia, SE USA
23 X6 **Ossabaw Sound** *sound* Georgia, SE USA
183 O16 **Ossa, Mount** ▲ Tasmania, SE Australia 41°55′S 146°03′E
104 H11 **Ossa, Serra d′** ▲▲ SE Portugal
77 U16 **Osse** ⁓ S Nigeria
30 J6 **Osseo** Wisconsin, N USA 44°33′N 91°13′W
109 S9 **Ossiacher See** ◎ S Austria
18 K13 **Ossining** New York, NE USA 41°10′N 73°50′W
123 V9 **Ossora** Krasnoyarskiy Kray, E Russia 59°16′N 163°02′E
124 I15 **Ostashkov** Tverskaya Oblast′, W Russia 57°08′N 33°10′E
100 H9 **Oste** ⁓ NW Germany
**Ostee** *see* Baltic Sea
**Ostend/Ostende** *see* Oostende
117 P3 **Oster** Chernihivs′ka Oblast′, N Ukraine 50°57′N 30°55′E
95 O14 **Österbybruk** Uppsala, C Sweden 60°13′N 17°55′E
95 M19 **Österbymo** Östergötland, S Sweden 57°49′N 15°15′E
94 K12 **Österdalälven** ⁓ C Sweden
94 I12 **Østerdalen** *valley* S Norway
95 L18 **Östergötland** ◆ *county* S Sweden
100 H10 **Osterholz-Scharmbeck** Niedersachsen, NW Germany 53°13′N 08°46′E
**Östermark** *see* Teuva
**Östermyra** *see* Seinäjoki
**Østerø** *see* Eysturoy
101 J14 **Osterode am Harz** Niedersachsen, C Germany 51°43′N 10°15′E
**Osterode/Osterode in Ostpreussen** *see* Ostróda
**Osterøy** *see* Osterøyni
94 C13 **Osterøyni** *prev.* Osterøy. *island* S Norway
**Österreich** *see* Austria
93 G16 **Östersund** Jämtland, C Sweden 63°10′N 14°44′E
95 N14 **Östervåla** Västmanland, C Sweden 60°10′N 17°13′E
101 H22 **Ostfildern** Baden-Württemberg, SW Germany 48°43′N 09°16′E
95 H16 **Østfold** ◆ *county* S Norway
100 E9 **Ostfriesische Inseln** *Eng.* East Frisian Islands. *island group* NW Germany
100 F10 **Ostfriesland** *historical region* NW Germany
95 P14 **Östhammar** Uppsala, C Sweden 60°15′N 18°25′E
**Ostia Aterni** *see* Pescara
106 G8 **Ostiglia** Lombardia, N Italy 45°04′N 11°09′E
95 J14 **Östmark** Värmland, C Sweden 60°15′N 12°45′E
95 K22 **Östra Ringsjön** ◎ S Sweden
111 I17 **Ostrava** Moravskoslezský Kraj, E Czechia 49°50′N 18°15′E
**Ostravský Kraj** *see* Moravskoslezský Kraj
94 J11 **Østrehogna** *Swe.* Härjahågnen, Härjehågna. ▲ Norway/Sweden 61°43′N 12°07′E


◆ Country
● Country Capital
◇ Dependent Territory
○ Dependent Territory Capital
◆ Administrative Regions
✈ International Airport
▲ Mountain
▲▲ Mountain Range
⛰ Volcano
⁓ River
◎ Lake
▣ Reservoir

OSTRÓDA – PAINT RIVER


110 K8 **Ostróda** *Ger.* Osterode, Osterode in Ostpreussen. Warmińsko-Mazurskie, NE Poland 53°42'N 19°59'E
**Ostrog/Ostróg** *see* Ostroh
126 L8 **Ostrogozhsk** Voronezhskaya Oblast', W Russia 50°52'N 39°00'E
116 L4 **Ostroh** *Pol.* Ostróg, *Rus.* Ostrog. Rivnens'ka Oblast', NW Ukraine 50°20'N 26°29'E
110 N9 **Ostrołęka** *Ger.* Wiesenhof, *Rus.* Ostrolenka. Mazowieckie, C Poland 53°06'N 21°34'E
**Ostrolenka** *see* Ostrołęka
111 A16 **Ostrov** *Ger.* Schlackenwerth. Karlovarský Kraj, W Czechia 50°18'N 12°56'E
124 F15 **Ostrov** *Latv.* Austrava. Pskovskaya Oblast', W Russia 57°21'N 28°18'E
**Ostrovets** *see* Ostrowiec Świętokrzyski
113 M21 **Ostrovicës, Mali i** ▲ SE Albania 40°36'N 20°25'E
165 Z2 **Ostrov Iturup** *island* NE Russia
124 M4 **Ostrovnoy** Murmanskaya Oblast', NW Russia 68°00'N 39°40'E
114 L7 **Ostrovo** *prev.* Golema Ada. Razgrad, N Bulgaria 43°40'N 26°37'E
125 N15 **Ostrovskoye** Kostromskaya Oblast', NW Russia 57°46'N 42°18'E
**Ostrów** *see* Ostrów Wielkopolski
**Ostrowiec** *see* Ostrowiec Świętokrzyski
111 M14 **Ostrowiec Świętokrzyski** *var.* Ostrowiec, *Rus.* Ostrovets. Świętokrzyskie, C Poland 50°55'N 21°23'E
110 P13 **Ostrów Lubelski** Lubelskie, E Poland 51°29'N 22°57'E
110 N10 **Ostrów Mazowiecka** *var.* Ostrów Mazowiecki. Mazowieckie, NE Poland 52°49'N 21°53'E
**Ostrów Mazowiecki** *see* Ostrów Mazowiecka
**Ostrowo** *see* Ostrów Wielkopolski
110 H13 **Ostrów Wielkopolski** *var.* Ostrów, *Ger.* Ostrowo. Wielkopolskie, C Poland 51°40'N 17°47'E
**Ostryna** *see* Astryna
110 I13 **Ostrzeszów** Wielkopolskie, C Poland 51°25'N 17°55'E
107 P18 **Ostuni** Puglia, SE Italy 40°44'N 17°35'E
**Ostyako-Voguls'k** *see* Khanty-Mansiysk
**Osum** *see* Osumit, Lumi i
**Osŭm** *see* Osam
164 C17 **Ōsumi-hantō** ▲▲ Kyūshū, SW Japan
164 C17 **Ōsumi-kaikyō** *strait* SW Japan
113 L22 **Osumit, Lumi i** *var.* Osum. ~ SE Albania
77 T16 **Osun** *var.* Oshun. ◈ *state* SW Nigeria
104 L14 **Osuna** Andalucía, S Spain 37°14'N 05°06'W
60 J8 **Osvaldo Cruz** São Paulo, S Brazil 21°49'S 50°52'W
**Osveya** *see* Asvyeya
18 J7 **Oswegatchie River** ~ New York, NE USA
27 Q7 **Oswego** Kansas, C USA 37°11'N 95°10'W
18 H9 **Oswego** New York, NE USA 43°27'N 76°13'W
97 K19 **Oswestry** W England, United Kingdom 52°51'N 03°06'W
111 J16 **Oświęcim** *Ger.* Auschwitz. Małopolskie, S Poland 50°02'N 19°11'E
185 E22 **Otago** *off.* Otago Region. ◈ *region* South Island, New Zealand
185 F23 **Otago Peninsula** *peninsula* South Island, New Zealand
**Otago Region** *see* Otago
165 F13 **Ōtake** Hiroshima, Honshū, SW Japan 34°13'N 132°12'E
184 L13 **Otaki** Wellington, North Island, New Zealand 40°46'S 175°08'E
93 M15 **Otanmäki** Kainuu, C Finland 64°07'N 27°04'E
145 T15 **Otar** Zhambyl, SE Kazakhstan 43°30'N 75°13'E
165 R4 **Otaru** Hokkaidō, NE Japan 43°14'N 140°59'E
185 C24 **Otatara** Southland, South Island, New Zealand 46°26'S 168°18'E
185 C24 **Otautau** Southland, South Island, New Zealand 46°10'S 168°01'E
93 M18 **Otava** Etelä-Savo, E Finland 61°37'N 27°07'E
111 B18 **Otava** *Ger.* Wottawa. ~ SW Czechia
56 C6 **Otavalo** Imbabura, N Ecuador 0°13'N 78°15'W
83 D17 **Otavi** Otjozondjupa, N Namibia 19°35'S 17°25'E
165 P12 **Ōtawara** Tochigi, Honshū, S Japan 36°52'N 140°01'E
83 B16 **Otchinjau** Cunene, SW Angola 16°31'S 13°54'E
116 F12 **Oţelu Roşu** *Ger.* Ferdinandsberg, *Hung.* Nándorhgy. Caras-Severin, SW Romania 45°30'N 22°22'E
185 E21 **Otematata** Canterbury, South Island, New Zealand 44°37'S 170°12'E
118 I6 **Otepää** *Ger.* Odenpäh. Valgamaa, SE Estonia 58°01'N 26°30'E
144 G14 **Otes** *Kaz.* Say-Ötesh; *prev.* Say-Utës. Mangistau, SW Kazakhstan 44°20'N 53°32'E
162 H7 **Otgon** *var.* Buyant. Dzavhan, C Mongolia 47°14'N 97°14'E
32 K9 **Othello** Washington, NW USA 46°49'N 119°10'W
83 K23 **oThongathi** *prev.* Tongaat, *var.* uThongathi. KwaZulu/Natal, E South Africa 29°35'S 31°07'E *see also*
115 A15 **Othonoí** *island* Iónia Nisiá, Greece, C Mediterranean Sea
**Othris** *see* Óthrys
115 F17 **Óthrys** *var.* Othris. ▲ C Greece
77 Q14 **Oti** ~ N Togo
40 K10 **Otinapa** Durango, C Mexico 24°01'N 104°58'W
185 G17 **Otira** West Coast, South Island, New Zealand 42°52'S 171°33'E
37 V3 **Otis** Colorado, C USA 40°09'N 102°57'W
12 L10 **Otish, Monts** ▲▲ Québec, E Canada
33 C17 **Otjikondo** Kunene, N Namibia 19°50'S 15°23'E
**Otjikoto** *see* Oshikoto
33 E18 **Otjinene** Omaheke, NE Namibia 21°10'S 18°43'E
33 D18 **Otjiwarongo** Otjozondjupa, N Namibia 20°29'S 16°36'E
33 D18 **Otjosondu** *var.* Otjosundu. Otjozondjupa, C Namibia 21°19'S 17°51'E
**Otjosundu** *see* Otjosondu
33 D18 **Otjozondjupa** ◈ *region* C Namibia
112 C11 **Otočac** Lika-Senj, W Croatia 44°52'N 15°13'E
**Otog Qi** *see* Ulan
112 J10 **Otok** Vukovar-Srijem, E Croatia 45°10'N 18°52'E
116 K14 **Otopeni** ✕ (Bucureşti) Ilfov, S Romania 44°34'N 26°09'E
184 L8 **Otorohanga** Waikato, North Island, New Zealand 38°10'S 175°14'E
12 D9 **Otoskwin** ~ Ontario, C Canada
165 G14 **Ōtoyo** Kōchi, Shikoku, SW Japan 33°45'N 133°42'E
95 E16 **Otra** ~ S Norway
107 R19 **Otranto** Puglia, SE Italy 40°08'N 18°28'E
**Otranto, Canale d'** *see* Otranto, Strait of
107 Q18 **Otranto, Strait of** *It.* Canale d'Otranto. *strait* Albania/Italy
111 H18 **Otrokovice** *Ger.* Otrokowitz. Zlínský Kraj, E Czechia 49°13'N 17°33'E
**Otrokowitz** *see* Otrokovice
31 P10 **Otsego** Michigan, N USA 42°27'N 85°42'W
31 Q6 **Otsego Lake** ◎ Michigan, N USA
18 I11 **Otselic River** ~ New York, NE USA
164 J14 **Ōtsu** *var.* Ōtu. Shiga, Honshū, SW Japan 35°03'N 135°49'E
94 G11 **Otta** Oppland, S Norway 61°46'N 09°33'E
189 U13 **Otta** *island* Chuuk, C Micronesia
94 F11 **Otta** ~ S Norway
189 U13 **Otta Pass** *passage* Chuuk Islands, C Micronesia
95 J22 **Ottarp** Skåne, S Sweden 55°55'N 12°55'E
14 L12 **Ottawa** ● (Canada) Ontario, SE Canada 45°24'N 75°41'W
30 L11 **Ottawa** Illinois, N USA 41°21'N 88°50'W
27 Q5 **Ottawa** Kansas, C USA 38°35'N 95°16'W
31 R12 **Ottawa** Ohio, N USA 41°01'N 84°03'W
14 L12 **Ottawa** *var.* Uplands. ✕ Ontario, SE Canada 45°19'N 75°39'W
14 M12 **Ottawa** *Fr.* Outaouais. ~ Ontario/Québec, SE Canada
9 R10 **Ottawa Islands** *island group* Nunavut, C Canada
18 L8 **Otter Creek** ~ Vermont, NE USA
36 L6 **Otter Creek Reservoir** ⊠ Utah, W USA
98 L11 **Otterlo** Gelderland, E Netherlands 52°06'N 05°46'E
94 D9 **Otterøya** *island* S Norway
29 S6 **Otter Tail Lake** ◎ Minnesota, N USA
29 R7 **Otter Tail River** ~ Minnesota, C USA
95 H23 **Otterup** Syddtjylland, C Denmark 55°31'N 10°25'E
99 H19 **Ottignies** Wallon Brabant, C Belgium 50°40'N 04°34'E
101 L23 **Ottobrunn** Bayern, SE Germany 48°02'N 11°40'E
29 X15 **Ottumwa** Iowa, C USA 41°00'N 92°24'W
**Ōtu** *see* Ōtsu
83 B16 **Otuazuma** Kunene, NW Namibia 17°52'S 13°16'E
77 V16 **Oturkpo** Benue, S Nigeria 07°12'N 08°06'E
193 Y15 **Otu Tolu Group** *island group* SE Tonga
182 M13 **Otway, Cape** *headland* Victoria, SE Australia 38°52'S 143°31'E
63 H24 **Otway, Seno** *inlet* S Chile
**Ötz** *see* Oetz
108 L8 **Ötztaler Ache** ~ W Austria
108 L9 **Ötztaler Alpen** *It.* Alpi Venoste. ▲▲ SW Austria
27 T12 **Ouachita, Lake** ⊠ Arkansas, C USA
27 R11 **Ouachita Mountains** ▲▲ Arkansas/Oklahoma, C USA
27 U13 **Ouachita River** ~ Arkansas/Louisiana, C USA
**Ouadaï** *see* Ouaddaï
76 J7 **Ouadâne** *var.* Ouadane. Adrar, C Mauritania 20°57'N 11°35'W
78 K13 **Ouadda** Haute-Kotto, N Central African Republic 08°02'N 22°22'E
78 J10 **Ouaddaï** *off.* Région du Ouaddaï, *var.* Ouadaï, Wadai. ◈ *region* SE Chad
**Ouaddaï, Région du** *see* Ouaddaï
77 P13 **Ouagadougou** *var.* Wagadugu. ● (Burkina Faso) C Burkina 12°20'N 01°32'W
77 P13 **Ouagadougou** ✕ C Burkina Faso 12°21'N 01°27'W
77 O12 **Ouahigouya** NW Burkina Faso 13°31'N 02°20'W
**Ouahran** *see* Oran
79 J14 **Ouaka** ◈ *prefecture* C Central African Republic
79 J15 **Ouaka** ~ S Central African Republic
**Oualam** *see* Ouallam
76 M9 **Oualâta** *var.* Oualata. Hodh ech Chargui, SE Mauritania 17°18'N 07°00'W
77 R11 **Ouallam** *var.* Oualam. Tillabéri, W Niger 14°23'N 02°09'E
172 H14 **Ouanani** Mohéli, S Comoros 12°19'S 93°98'E
55 Z10 **Ouanary** E French Guiana 04°11'N 51°40'W
78 L13 **Ouanda Djallé** Vakaga, NE Central African Republic 08°53'N 22°47'E
79 N14 **Ouando** Haut-Mbomou, SE Central African Republic 05°57'N 25°57'E
79 L15 **Ouango** Mbomou, S Central African Republic 04°19'N 22°30'E
77 N14 **Ouangolodougou** *var.* Wangolodougou. N Ivory Coast 09°58'N 05°09'W
172 I13 **Ouani** Anjouan, SE Comoros
79 M15 **Ouara** ~ E Central African Republic
76 K7 **Ouarâne** *desert* C Mauritania
15 O11 **Ouareau** ~ Québec, SE Canada
74 K7 **Ouargla** *var.* Wargla. NE Algeria 32°N 05°16'E
74 F8 **Ouarzazate** S Morocco 30°54'N 06°55'W
77 Q11 **Ouatagouna** Gao, E Mali 15°06'N 00°41'E
74 G6 **Ouazzane** *var.* Ouezzane, *Ar.* Wazan, Wazzan. N Morocco 34°52'N 05°35'W
**Oubangui** *see* Ubangi
**Oubangui-Chari** *see* Central African Republic
**Oubangui-Chari, Territoire de l'** *see* Central African Republic
**Oubari, Edeyen d'** *see* Awbāri, Idhān
98 G13 **Oud-Beijerland** Zuid-Hollanc, SW Netherlands 51°50'N 04°25'E
98 F13 **Ouddorp** Zuid-Holland, SW Netherlands 51°49'N 03°55'E
77 P9 **Oudeïka** *oasis* C Mali
98 G13 **Oude Maas** ~ SW Netherlands
99 E18 **Oudenaarde** *Fr.* Audenarde. Oost-Vlaanderen, SW Belgium 50°50'N 03°37'E
99 H14 **Oudenbosch** Noord-Brabant, S Netherlands 51°35'N 04°32'E
98 P6 **Oude Pekela** Groningen, NE Netherlands 53°06'N 07°00'E
**Ouderkerk** *see* Ouderkerk aan den Amstel
98 I10 **Ouderkerk aan den Amstel** *var.* Ouderkerk. Noord-Hollanc, C Netherlands 52°18'N 04°54'E
98 I6 **Oudeschild** Noord-Hollanc, NW Netherlands 53°01'N 04°51'E
99 G14 **Oude-Tonge** Zuid-Hollanc, SW Netherlands 51°40'N 04°13'E
98 I12 **Oudewater** Utrecht, C Netherlands 52°02'N 04°54'E
**Oudjda** *see* Oujda
**Oudkerk** *see* Aldtsjerk
167 Q6 **Oudômxai** *var.* Muang Xay, Muong Sai, Xai. Oudômxai, N Laos 20°41'N 102°00'E
102 J7 **Oudon** ~ NW France
98 I9 **Oudorp** Noord-Holland, NW Netherlands 52°39'N 04°47'E
83 G25 **Oudtshoorn** Western Cape, SW South Africa 33°35'S 22°14'E
99 I16 **Oud-Turnhout** Antwerpen, N Belgium 51°19'N 05°01'E
74 F7 **Oued-Zem** C Morocco 32°53'N 06°30'W
187 P16 **Ouégoa** Province Nord, C New Caledonia 20°22'S 164°25'E
76 L13 **Ouéléssébougou** *var.* Ouolossébougou. Koulikoro, SW Mali 11°58'N 07°51'W
77 N16 **Ouellé** E Ivory Coast 07°18'N 04°01'W
77 R16 **Ouémé** ~ C Benin
77 O13 **Ouessa** S Burkina Faso 11°02'N 02°44'W
102 D5 **Ouessant, Île d'** *Eng.* Ushant. *island* NW France
79 H17 **Ouésso** Sangha, NW Congo 01°38'N 16°03'E
79 D15 **Ouest** *Eng.* West. ◈ *province* W Cameroon
190 G11 **Ouest, Baie del'** *bay* Îles Wallis, E Wallis and Futuna
15 Y7 **Ouest, Pointe de l'** *headland* Québec, SE Canada 48°08'N 64°57'W
**Ouezzane** *see* Ouazzane
99 K20 **Ouffet** Liège, E Belgium 50°30'N 05°31'E
79 H14 **Ouham** ◈ *prefecture* NW Central African Republic
78 I13 **Ouham** ~ Central African Republic/Chad
79 G14 **Ouham-Pendé** ◈ *prefecture* W Central African Republic
77 R16 **Ouidah** *Eng.* Whydah, Wida. S Benin 06°23'N 02°08'E
74 H6 **Oujda** *Ar.* Oudjda, Ujda. NE Morocco 34°45'N 01°53'W
76 I7 **Oujeft** Adrar, C Mauritania 20°05'N 13°00'W
93 L15 **Oulainen** Pohjois-Pohjanmaa, C Finland 64°14'N 24°50'E
**Ould Yanja** *see* Ould Yenjé
76 J10 **Ould Yenjé** *var.* Ould Yanja. Guidimaka, S Mauritania 15°33'N 11°43'W
93 L14 **Oulu** *Swe.* Uleåborg. Pohjois-Pohjanmaa, C Finland 65°01'N 25°28'E
**Oulu** *Swe.* Uleåborg. ◈ *province* N Finland
93 L15 **Oulujärvi** *Swe.* Uleträsk. ◎ C Finland
93 M14 **Oulujoki** *Swe.* Uleälv. ~ C Finland
93 L14 **Oulunsalo** Pohjois-Pohjanmaa, C Finland 64°55'N 25°19'E
106 A8 **Oulx** Piemonte, NE Italy 45°05'N 06°41'E
78 J9 **Oum-Chalouba** Ennedi-Ouest, NE Chad 15°48'N 20°46'E
76 M16 **Oumé** C Ivory Coast 06°25'N 05°23'W
74 F7 **Oum er Rbia** ~ C Morocco
78 J10 **Oum-Hadjer** Batha, E Chad 13°18'N 19°41'E
92 K10 **Ounasjoki** ~ N Finland
78 J7 **Ounianga Kébir** Ennedi-Ouest, N Chad 19°06'N 20°29'E
**Ouolossébougou** *see* Ouéléssébougou
**Oup** *see* Auob
99 K19 **Oupeye** Liège, E Belgium 50°42'N 05°38'E
99 N21 **Our** ~ NW Europe
37 Q7 **Ouray** Colorado, C USA 38°01'N 107°40'W
103 R7 **Ource** ~ C France
104 G9 **Ourém** Santarém, C Portugal 39°40'N 08°32'W
104 H4 **Ourense** *Cast.* Orense, *Lat.* Aurium. Galicia, NW Spain 42°20'N 07°52'W
104 I4 **Ourense** *Cast.* Orense. ◈ *province* Galicia, NW Spain
59 O15 **Ouricuri** Pernambuco, E Brazil 07°51'S 40°05'W
60 J9 **Ourinhos** São Paulo, S Brazil 22°59'S 49°52'W
104 G13 **Ourique** Beja, S Portugal 37°38'N 08°13'W
59 M20 **Ouro Preto** Minas Gerais, NE Brazil 20°25'S 43°30'W
**Ours, Grand Lac de l'** *see* Great Bear Lake
99 K20 **Ourthe** ~ E Belgium
165 Q9 **Ou-sanmyaku** ▲▲ Honshū, C Japan
97 M17 **Ouse** ~ N England, United Kingdom
**Ouse** *see* Great Ouse
102 H7 **Oust** ~ NW France
**Outaouais** *see* Ottawa
15 T4 **Outardes Quatre, Réservoir** ⊠ Québec, SE Canada
15 T5 **Outardes, Rivière aux** ~ Québec, SE Canada
96 E8 **Outer Hebrides** *var.* Western Isles. *island group* NW Scotland, United Kingdom
30 K3 **Outer Island** *island* Apostle Islands, Wisconsin, N USA
35 S16 **Outer Santa Barbara Passage** *passage* California, SW USA
83 C18 **Outjo** Kunene, N Namibia 20°08'S 16°08'E
11 T16 **Outlook** Saskatchewan, S Canada 51°30'N 107°03'W
93 N16 **Outokumpu** Pohjois-Karjala, E Finland 62°43'N 29°05'E
96 M2 **Out Skerries** *island group* NE Scotland, United Kingdom
187 Q16 **Ouvéa** *island* Îles Loyauté, NE New Caledonia
103 S14 **Ouvèze** ~ SE France
182 L9 **Ouyen** Victoria, SE Australia 35°07'S 142°19'E
39 Q14 **Ouzinkie** Kodiak Island, Alaska, USA 57°54'N 152°27'W
137 O13 **Ovacık** Tunceli, E Turkey 39°23'N 39°13'E
106 C9 **Ovada** Piemonte, NE Italy 44°41'N 08°39'E
187 X14 **Ovalau** *island* C Fiji
62 G9 **Ovalle** Coquimbo, N Chile 30°33'S 71°16'W
83 C17 **Ovamboland** *physical region* N Namibia
54 L10 **Ovana, Cerro** ▲ S Venezuela 04°41'N 66°54'W
104 G7 **Ovar** Aveiro, N Portugal 40°52'N 08°38'W
114 L10 **Ovcharitsa, Yazovir** ⊠ SE Bulgaria
54 E6 **Ovejas** Sucre, NW Colombia 09°32'N 75°14'W
101 E16 **Overath** Nordrhein-Westfalen, W Germany 50°55'N 07°16'E
98 F13 **Overflakkee** *island* SW Netherlands
99 H19 **Overijse** Vlaams Brabant, C Belgium 50°46'N 04°32'E
98 N10 **Overijssel** ◈ *province* E Netherlands
98 M9 **Overijssels Kanaal** *canal* E Netherlands
92 K13 **Överkalix** Norrbotten, N Sweden 66°19'N 22°49'E
27 R4 **Overland Park** Kansas, C USA 38°57'N 94°41'W
99 L14 **Overloon** Noord-Brabant, SE Netherlands 51°35'N 05°54'E
99 K16 **Overpelt** Limburg, NE Belgium 51°13'N 05°24'E
35 Y10 **Overton** Nevada, W USA 36°32'N 114°25'W
25 W7 **Overton** Texas, SW USA 32°16'N 94°58'W
92 K13 **Övertorneå** Norrbotten, N Sweden 66°22'N 23°40'E
95 N18 **Överum** Kalmar, S Sweden 57°58'N 16°20'E
92 G13 **Överuman** ◎ N Sweden
117 P11 **Ovidiopol'** Odes'ka Oblast', SW Ukraine 46°15'N 30°27'E
116 M14 **Ovidiu** Constanţa, SE Romania 44°16'N 28°34'E
45 N10 **Oviedo** SW Dominican Republic 17°47'N 71°22'W
104 K2 **Oviedo** *anc.* Asturias. Asturias, NW Spain 43°21'N 05°50'W
104 K2 **Oviedo** ✕ Asturias, N Spain 43°21'N 05°50'W
**Ovilava** *see* Wels
118 D7 **Oviši** W Latvia 57°34'N 21°43'E
146 K10 **Ovminzatovo Tog'lari** *Rus.* Gory Auminzatau. ▲▲ N Uzbekistan
**Ovögdiy** *see* Telmen
**Ovoot** *see* Dariganga
157 O4 **Övörhangay** ◈ *province* C Mongolia
94 E12 **Øvre Årdal** Sogn Og Fjordane, S Norway 61°18'N 07°48'E
95 J14 **Övre Fryken** ◎ C Sweden
92 J11 **Övre Soppero** *Lapp.* Badje-Sohppar. Norrbotten, N Sweden 68°07'N 21°40'E
117 N3 **Ovruch** Zhytomyrs'ka Oblast', N Ukraine 51°20'N 28°50'E
**Övt** *see* Bat-Öldziy
185 E24 **Owaka** Otago, South Island, New Zealand 46°27'S 169°42'E
79 H18 **Owando** *prev.* Fort Rousset. Cuvette, C Congo 0°29'S 15°55'E
164 J14 **Owase** Mie, Honshū, SW Japan 34°04'N 136°11'E
27 P9 **Owasso** Oklahoma, C USA 36°16'N 95°51'W
29 V10 **Owatonna** Minnesota, N USA 44°04'N 93°13'W
173 O4 **Owen Fracture Zone** *tectonic feature* W Arabian Sea
185 H15 **Owen, Mount** ▲ South Island, New Zealand 41°32'S 172°33'E
185 H15 **Owen River** Tasman, South Island, New Zealand 41°40'S 172°28'E
44 D8 **Owen Roberts** ✕ Grand Cayman, Cayman Islands 19°15'N 81°22'W
20 I6 **Owensboro** Kentucky, S USA 37°46'N 87°07'W
35 T11 **Owens Lake** *salt flat* California, W USA
14 F14 **Owen Sound** Ontario, S Canada 44°34'N 80°56'W
14 F13 **Owen Sound** ◎ Ontario, S Canada
35 T10 **Owens River** ~ California, W USA
186 F9 **Owen Stanley Range** ▲▲ S Papua New Guinea
27 V5 **Owensville** Missouri, C USA 38°21'N 91°30'W
20 M4 **Owenton** Kentucky, S USA 38°33'N 84°50'W
77 U17 **Owerri** Imo, S Nigeria 05°19'N 07°07'E
184 M10 **Owhango** Manawatu-Wanganui, North Island, New Zealand 39°01'S 175°22'E
21 N5 **Owingsville** Kentucky, S USA 38°09'N 83°46'W
77 T16 **Owo** Ondo, SW Nigeria 07°10'N 05°31'E
31 R9 **Owosso** Michigan, N USA 43°00'N 84°10'W
35 V1 **Owyhee** Nevada, W USA 41°57'N 116°07'W
32 L14 **Owyhee, Lake** ◎ Oregon, NW USA
32 L15 **Owyhee River** ~ Idaho/Oregon, NW USA
92 K1 **Öxarfjörður** *var.* Axarfjördhur. *fjord* N Iceland
94 K12 **Oxberg** Dalarna, C Sweden 61°07'N 14°10'E
11 V17 **Oxbow** Saskatchewan, S Canada 49°16'N 102°12'W
95 O17 **Oxelösund** Södermanland, S Sweden 58°40'N 17°10'E
185 H18 **Oxford** Canterbury, South Island, New Zealand 43°18'S 172°10'E
97 M21 **Oxford** *Lat.* Oxonia. S England, United Kingdom 51°46'N 01°15'W
23 Q3 **Oxford** Alabama, S USA 33°36'N 85°50'W
22 L2 **Oxford** Mississippi, S USA 34°23'N 89°30'W
29 N16 **Oxford** Nebraska, C USA 40°15'N 99°37'W
18 I11 **Oxford** New York, NE USA 42°21'N 75°39'W
21 U8 **Oxford** North Carolina, SE USA 36°22'N 78°37'W
31 Q14 **Oxford** Ohio, N USA 39°30'N 84°45'W
18 H16 **Oxford** Pennsylvania, NE USA 39°46'N 75°57'W
11 X12 **Oxford House** Manitoba, C Canada 54°55'N 95°13'W
29 Y13 **Oxford Junction** Iowa, C USA 41°58'N 90°57'W
11 X12 **Oxford Lake** ◎ Manitoba, C Canada
97 M21 **Oxfordshire** *cultural region* S England, United Kingdom
**Oxia** *see* Oxyá
41 X12 **Oxkutzcab** Yucatán, SE Mexico 20°18'N 89°26'W
35 R15 **Oxnard** California, W USA 34°12'N 119°10'W
**Oxonia** *see* Oxford
14 I12 **Oxtongue** ~ Ontario, SE Canada
**Oxus** *see* Amu Darya
115 E15 **Oxyá** *var.* Oxia. ▲ C Greece 39°46'N 21°56'E
164 L11 **Oyabe** Toyama, Honshū, SW Japan 36°42'N 136°52'E
**Oyahue/Oyahue, Volcán** *see* Ollagüe, Volcán
165 O12 **Oyama** Tochigi, Honshū, S Japan 36°19'N 139°46'E
47 U5 **Oyapock** ~ E French Guiana
**Oyapock** *see* Oiapoque, Rio/Oyapok, Fleuve l'
55 Z10 **Oyapok, Baie de L'** *bay* Brazil/French Guiana South America W Atlantic Ocean
55 Z11 **Oyapok, Fleuve l'** *var.* Rio Oiapoque, Oyapock. ~ Brazil/French Guiana *see also* Oiapoque, Rio
**Oyapok, Fleuve l'** *see* Oiapoque, Rio
79 E17 **Oyem** Woleu-Ntem, N Gabon 01°34'N 11°31'E
11 R16 **Oyen** Alberta, SW Canada 51°20'N 110°28'W
95 I15 **Øyeren** ◎ S Norway
**Oygon** *see* Tüdevtey
96 I7 **Oykel** ~ N Scotland, United Kingdom
123 R9 **Oymyakon** Respublika Sakha (Yakutiya), NE Russia 63°28'N 142°22'E
79 H19 **Oyo** Cuvette, C Congo 01°17'S 16°00'E
77 S15 **Oyo** Oyo, W Nigeria 07°51'N 03°57'E
77 S15 **Oyo** ◈ *state* SW Nigeria
56 D13 **Oyón** Lima, C Peru 10°39'S 76°44'W
103 S10 **Oyonnax** Ain, E France 46°16'N 05°39'E
146 L10 **Oyoqog'itma** *Rus.* Ayakagytma. Buxoro Viloyati, C Uzbekistan 40°37'N 64°26'E
146 M9 **Oyoqquduq** *Rus.* Ayakkuduk. Navoiy Viloyati, N Uzbekistan 41°16'N 65°12'E
32 F9 **Oysterville** Washington, NW USA 46°33'N 124°03'W
95 D14 **Øystese** Hordaland, S Norway 60°23'N 06°13'E
145 S16 **Oytal** Zhambyl, S Kazakhstan 42°54'N 73°21'E
147 U10 **Oy-Tal** Osh Oblast', SW Kyrgyzstan 40°23'N 74°04'E
147 T10 **Oy-Tal** ~ SW Kyrgyzstan
145 Q15 **Oyyk** *prev.* Uyuk. Zhambyl, S Kazakhstan 43°46'N 70°55'E
144 H10 **Oyyl** *prev.* Uil. Aktyubinsk, W Kazakhstan 49°06'N 54°41'E
144 H10 **Oyyl** *prev.* Uil. ~ W Kazakhstan
**Ozarichi** *see* Azarychy
23 R7 **Ozark** Alabama, S USA 31°27'N 85°38'W
27 S10 **Ozark** Arkansas, C USA 35°30'N 93°50'W
27 T8 **Ozark** Missouri, C USA 37°01'N 93°12'W
27 T8 **Ozark Plateau** *plain* Arkansas/Missouri, C USA
27 T6 **Ozarks, Lake of the** ⊠ Missouri, C USA
**O'zbekiston** *see* Uzbekistan
**O'zbekiston Respublikasi** *see* Uzbekistan
192 L10 **Ozbourn Seamount** *undersea feature* W Pacific Ocean 26°00'S 174°49'W
111 L20 **Ózd** Borsod-Abaúj-Zemplén, NE Hungary 48°15'N 20°18'E
112 D11 **Ozeblin** ▲ C Croatia 44°37'N 15°52'E
123 V11 **Ozernovskiy** Kamchatskiy Kray, E Russia 51°28'N 156°32'E
144 M7 **Ozërnoye** *var.* Ozërnyy. Kostanay, N Kazakhstan 53°29'N 63°14'E
124 J15 **Ozërnyy** Tverskaya Oblast', W Russia 57°55'N 33°43'E
**Ozërnyy** *see* Ozërnoye
**Ozero Azhbulat** *see* Ozero Ul'ken Azhibolat
**Ozero Segozero** *see* Segozerskoye Vodokhranilishche
115 D18 **Ozerós, Límni** ◎ W Greece
145 T7 **Ozero Ul'ken Azhibolat** *prev.* Ozero Azhbulat. ◎ NE Kazakhstan
119 D14 **Ozersk** *prev.* Darkehnen, *Ger.* Angerapp. Kaliningradskaya Oblast', W Russia 54°23'N 21°59'E
126 L4 **Ozery** Moskovskaya Oblast', W Russia 54°51'N 38°37'E
**Özgön** *see* Uzgen
107 C17 **Ozieri** Sardegna, Italy, C Mediterranean Sea 40°35'N 09°01'E
111 I15 **Ozimek** *Ger.* Malapane. Opolskie, SW Poland 50°41'N 18°16'E
127 R8 **Ozinki** Saratovskaya Oblast', W Russia 51°16'N 49°45'E
25 O10 **Ozona** Texas, SW USA 30°43'N 101°13'W
**Ozorkov** *see* Ozorków
110 J12 **Ozorków** *Rus.* Ozorkov. Łódźy, C Poland 51°58'N 19°17'E
164 F14 **Ōzu** Ehime, Shikoku, SW Japan 33°30'N 132°33'E
137 R10 **Ozurgeti** *prev.* Makharadze, Ozurget'i. W Georgia 41°57'N 42°01'E
**Ozurget'i** *see* Ozurgeti


# P


99 J17 **Paal** Limburg, NE Belgium 51°03'N 05°08'E
196 M14 **Paamiut** *var.* Pâmiut, *Dan.* Frederikshåb. Sermersooq, S Greenland 61°59'N 49°40'W
**Pa-an** *see* Hpa-An
101 L22 **Paar** ~ SE Germany
83 E26 **Paarl** Western Cape, SW South Africa 33°45'S 18°58'E
93 L15 **Paavola** Pohjois-Pohjanmaa, C Finland 64°34'N 25°15'E
96 E8 **Pabbay** *island* NW Scotland, United Kingdom
153 T15 **Pabna** Rajshahi, W Bangladesh 24°02'N 89°15'E
109 U4 **Pabneukirchen** Oberösterreich, N Austria 48°19'N 14°49'E
118 H13 **Pabradė** *Pol.* Podbrodzie. Vilnius, SE Lithuania 54°58'N 25°43'E
56 L13 **Pacahuaras, Río** ~ N Bolivia
**Pacaraima, Sierra/Pacaraim, Serra** *see* Pakaraima Mountains
56 B11 **Pacasmayo** La Libertad, W Peru 07°27'S 79°33'W
42 D6 **Pacaya, Volcán de** ▲ S Guatemala 14°19'N 90°36'W
115 K23 **Pacheía** *var.* Pachía. *island* Kykládes, Greece, Aegean Sea
**Pachía** *see* Pacheía
107 L26 **Pachino** Sicilia, Italy, C Mediterranean Sea 36°43'N 15°06'E
56 F12 **Pachitea, Río** ~ C Peru
154 I11 **Pachmarhi** Madhya Pradesh, C India 22°36'N 78°18'E
121 P3 **Páchna** *var.* Pakhna. SW Cyprus 34°47'N 32°48'E
115 H25 **Páchnes** ▲ Kríti, Greece, E Mediterranean Sea 35°19'N 24°00'E
54 F9 **Pacho** Cundinamarca, C Colombia 05°09'N 74°08'W
154 F12 **Pāchora** Mahārāshtra, C India 20°52'N 75°28'E
41 P13 **Pachuca** *var.* Pachuca de Soto. Hidalgo, C Mexico 20°05'N 98°46'W
**Pachuca de Soto** *see* Pachuca
27 W5 **Pacific** Missouri, C USA 38°28'N 90°44'W
192 L14 **Pacific-Antarctic Ridge** *undersea feature* S Pacific Ocean 62°00'S 157°00'W
32 F8 **Pacific Beach** Washington, NW USA 47°09'N 124°12'W
35 N10 **Pacific Grove** California, W USA 36°35'N 121°54'W
29 S15 **Pacific Junction** Iowa, C USA 41°01'N 95°48'W
192-193 **Pacific Ocean** *ocean*
129 Z10 **Pacific Plate** *tectonic feature*
113 J15 **Pačir** ▲ N Montenegro 43°19'N 19°07'E
182 L5 **Packsaddle** New South Wales, SE Australia 30°42'S 141°55'E
32 H9 **Packwood** Washington, NW USA 46°37'N 121°38'W
**Padalung** *see* Phatthalung
168 J12 **Padang** Sumatera, W Indonesia 01°S 100°21'E
168 L9 **Padang Endau** Pahang, Peninsular Malaysia 02°38'N 103°37'E
**Padangpandjang** *see* Padangpanjang
168 I11 **Padangpanjang** *prev.* Padangpandjang. Sumatera, W Indonesia 0°30'S 100°26'E
168 I10 **Padangsidempuan** *prev.* Padangsidimpoean. Sumatera, W Indonesia 01°23'N 99°15'E
**Padangsidimpoean** *see* Padangsidempuan
124 I9 **Padany** Respublika Kareliya, NW Russia 63°18'N 33°20'E
93 M18 **Padasjoki** Päijät-Häme, S Finland 61°20'N 25°21'E
57 M22 **Padcaya** Tarija, S Bolivia 21°52'S 64°46'W
101 H14 **Paderborn** Nordrhein-Westfalen, NW Germany 51°43'N 08°45'E
**Padeşul/Padeş, Vîrful** *see* Padeş, Vârful
116 F12 **Padeş, Vârful** *var.* Padeşul; *prev.* Vîrful Padeş. ▲ W Romania 45°39'N 22°19'E
112 L10 **Padinska Skela** Serbia, N Serbia 44°58'N 20°25'E
153 S14 **Padma** *var.* Ganges. ~ Bangladesh/India *see also* Ganges
**Padma** *see* Brahmaputra
**Padma** *see* Ganges
106 H8 **Padova** *Eng.* Padua; *anc.* Patavium. Veneto, NE Italy 45°24'N 11°52'E
82 A10 **Padrão, Ponta do** *headland* NW Angola 06°06'S 12°18'E
25 T16 **Padre Island** *island* Texas, SW USA
104 G3 **Padrón** Galicia, NW Spain 42°44'N 08°40'W
118 K13 **Padsvillye** *Rus.* Podsvil'ye. Vitsyebskaya Voblasts', N Belarus 55°09'N 27°58'E
182 K11 **Padthaway** South Australia 36°39'S 140°30'E
**Padua** *see* Padova
20 G7 **Paducah** Kentucky, S USA 37°03'N 88°36'W
25 P4 **Paducah** Texas, SW USA 34°01'N 100°18'W
105 N15 **Padul** Andalucía, S Spain 37°02'N 03°37'W
191 P8 **Paea** Tahiti, W French Polynesia 17°41'S 149°35'W
185 L14 **Paekakariki** Wellington, North Island, New Zealand 41°00'S 174°58'E
163 X11 **Paektu-san** *var.* Baitou Shan. ▲ China/North Korea 42°00'N 128°03'W
**Paengnyŏng** *see* Baengnyeong-do
184 M7 **Paeroa** Waikato, North Island, New Zealand 37°23'S 175°40'E
54 D12 **Páez** Cauca, SW Colombia 02°37'N 76°00'W
121 O3 **Páfos** *var.* Paphos. W Cyprus 34°46'N 32°26'E
121 O3 **Páfos** ✕ SW Cyprus 34°46'N 32°25'E
83 L19 **Pafúri** Gaza, SW Mozambique 22°27'S 31°21'E
112 C12 **Pag** *It.* Pago. Lika-Senj, SW Croatia 44°26'N 15°01'E
112 B11 **Pag** *It.* Pago. *island* Zadar, C Croatia
171 P7 **Pagadian** Mindanao, S Philippines 07°47'N 123°22'E
168 J13 **Pagai Selatan, Pulau** *island* Kepulauan Mentawai, W Indonesia
168 J13 **Pagai Utara, Pulau** *island* Kepulauan Mentawai, W Indonesia
188 K4 **Pagan** *island* C Northern Mariana Islands
115 G16 **Pagasitikós Kólpos** *gulf* E Greece
36 L8 **Page** Arizona, SW USA 36°54'N 111°23'W
29 Q5 **Page** North Dakota, N USA 47°09'N 97°33'W
118 D13 **Pagėgiai** *Ger.* Pogegen. Tauragė, SW Lithuania 55°08'N 21°54'E
21 S11 **Pageland** South Carolina, SE USA 34°46'N 80°23'W
81 G16 **Pager** ~ NE Uganda
149 Q5 **Paghmān** Kābul, E Afghanistan 34°33'N 68°55'E
**Pago** *see* Pag
188 C16 **Pago Bay** *bay* E Guam, W Pacific Ocean
115 M20 **Pagóndas** *var.* Pagondhas. Sámos, Dodekánisa, Greece, Aegean Sea 37°41'N 26°50'E
**Pagóndhas** *see* Pagóndas
192 J16 **Pago Pago** ○ (American Samoa) Tutuila, W American Samoa 14°16'S 170°43'W
37 R8 **Pagosa Springs** Colorado, C USA 37°13'N 107°01'W
**Pagqên** *see* Gadê
38 H12 **Pāhala** *var.* Pahala. Hawaii, USA, C Pacific Ocean 19°12'N 155°28'W
168 K8 **Pahang** *var.* Negeri Pahang Darul Makmur. ◈ *state* Peninsular Malaysia
**Pahang** *see* Pahang, Sungai
168 L8 **Pahang, Sungai** *var.* Pahang, Sungei Pahang. ~ Peninsular Malaysia
149 S8 **Paharpur** Khyber Pakhtunkhwa, NW Pakistan 32°06'N 71°00'E
185 B24 **Pahia Point** *headland* South Island, New Zealand 46°19'S 167°42'E
184 M13 **Pahiatua** Manawatu-Wanganui, North Island, New Zealand 40°30'S 175°49'E
38 H12 **Pāhoa** *var.* Pahoa. Hawaii, USA, C Pacific Ocean 19°29'N 154°56'W
23 Y14 **Pahokee** Florida, SE USA 26°49'N 80°40'W
35 X9 **Pahranagat Range** ▲▲ Nevada, W USA
35 W11 **Pahrump** Nevada, W USA 36°11'N 115°58'W
**Pahsien** *see* Chongqing
35 V9 **Pahute Mesa** ▲ Nevada, W USA
167 N7 **Pai** Mae Hong Son, NW Thailand 19°24'N 98°26'E
38 F10 **Pa'ia** *var.* Paia. Maui, Hawaii, USA, C Pacific Ocean 20°54'N 156°22'W
**Paia** *see* Pa'ia
**Pai-ch'eng** *see* Baicheng
118 H4 **Paide** *Ger.* Weissenstein. Järvamaa, N Estonia 58°55'N 25°36'E
97 J24 **Paignton** SW England, United Kingdom 50°26'N 03°34'W
184 K3 **Paihia** Northland, North Island, New Zealand 35°18'S 174°06'E
93 M18 **Päijänne** ◎ C Finland
114 F13 **Páiko** ▲ N Greece
57 M17 **Paila, Río** ~ C Bolivia
167 Q12 **Pailin** *var.* Pailin. Pailin, W Cambodia 12°51'N 102°34'E
**Pailin** *see* Pailin
**Pailing** *see* Chun'an
54 F6 **Pailitas** Cesar, N Colombia 08°58'N 73°38'W
38 F9 **Pailolo Channel** *channel* Hawai'i, USA, C Pacific Ocean
93 K19 **Paimio** *Swe.* Pemar. Varsinais-Suomi, SW Finland 60°27'N 22°42'E
165 O16 **Paimi-saki** *var.* Yaeme-saki. *headland* Iriomote-jima, SW Japan 24°18'N 123°40'E
102 G5 **Paimpol** Côtes d'Armor, NW France 43°47'N 03°03'W
168 J12 **Painan** Sumatera, W Indonesia 01°22'S 100°33'E
63 G23 **Paine, Cerro** ▲ S Chile 51°01'S 72°57'W
31 U11 **Painesville** Ohio, N USA 41°43'N 81°15'W
31 S14 **Paint Creek** ~ Ohio, N USA
36 L10 **Painted Desert** *desert* Arizona, SW USA
**Paint Hills** *see* Wemindji
30 M4 **Paint River** ~ Michigan, N USA




◆ Country
● Country Capital
◇ Dependent Territory
○ Dependent Territory Capital
◈ Administrative Regions
✕ International Airport
▲ Mountain
▲▲ Mountain Range
Volcano
~ River
◎ Lake
⊠ Reservoir

PAINT ROCK – PARIA, GOLFO DE


25 P8 **Paint Rock** Texas, SW USA 31°32′N 99°56′W
21 O6 **Paintsville** Kentucky, S USA 37°48′N 82°48′W
**Paisance** see Piacenza
96 I12 **Paisley** W Scotland, United Kingdom 55°50′N 04°26′W
32 I15 **Paisley** Oregon, NW USA 42°40′N 120°31′W
105 O3 **País Vasco** Basq. Euskadi, Eng. The Basque Country. ◈ autonomous community N Spain
56 A9 **Paita** Piura, NW Peru 05°11′S 81°09′W
169 V6 **Paitan, Teluk** bay Sabah, East Malaysia
104 H7 **Paiva, Rio** ≈ N Portugal
92 K12 **Pajala** Norrbotten, N Sweden 67°12′N 23°19′E
104 K3 **Pajares, Puerto de** pass NW Spain
54 G9 **Pajarito** Boyacá, C Colombia 05°18′N 72°43′W
54 G4 **Pajaro** La Guajira, S Colombia 11°41′N 72°37′W
**Pakanbaru** see Pekanbaru
55 Q10 **Pakaraima Mountains** var. Serra Pacaraim, Sierra Pacaraima. ▲▲ N South America
**Pākaur** see Pākur
167 P10 **Pak Chong** Nakhon Ratchasima, C Thailand 14°38′N 101°22′E
123 V8 **Pakhachi** Krasnoyarskiy Kray, E Russia 60°36′N 168°59′E
**Pakhna** see Páchna
189 U16 **Pakin Atoll** atoll Caroline Islands, E Micronesia
149 Q12 **Pakistan** off. Islamic Republic of Pakistan, var. Islāmī Jumhūrīyah Pākistān. ◆ republic S Asia
**Pakistan, Islamic Republic of** see Pakistan
**Pākistān, Islāmī Jumhūrīyah** see Pakistan
167 P8 **Pak Lay** var. Muang Pak Lay. Xaignabouli, C Laos 18°06′N 101°21′E
**Paknam** see Samut Prakan
166 L5 **Pakokku** Magway, C Myanmar (Burma) 21°20′N 95°05′E
110 I10 **Pakość** Ger. Pakosch. Kujawski-pomorskie, C Poland 52°47′N 18°03′E
**Pakosch** see Pakość
149 V10 **Pakpattan** Punjab, E Pakistan 30°20′N 73°27′E
167 O15 **Pak Phanang** var. Ban Pak Phanang. Nakhon Si Thammarat, SW Thailand 08°20′N 100°10′E
112 G9 **Pakrac** Hung. Pakrácz. Požega-Slavonija, NE Croatia 45°26′N 17°09′E
**Pakrácz** see Pakrac
118 F11 **Pakruojis** Šiaulai, N Lithuania 56°N 23°51′E
111 J24 **Paks** Tolna, S Hungary 46°38′N 18°51′E
**Pak Sane** see Pakxan
**Paksé** see Pakxé
167 Q10 **Pak Thong Chai** Nakhon Ratchasima, C Thailand 14°43′N 102°01′E
**Paktīā** see Paktiyā
149 Q7 **Paktīkā** ◈ province SE Afghanistan
149 R6 **Paktiyā** prev. Paktīā. ◈ province SE Afghanistan
171 N12 **Pakuli** Sulawesi, C Indonesia 01°14′S 119°55′E
153 S14 **Pākur** var. Pākaur. Jharkhand, N India 24°48′N 87°14′E
81 F17 **Pakwach** NW Uganda 02°28′N 31°28′E
167 R8 **Pakxan** var. Muang Pakxan, Pak Sane. Bolikhamxai, C Laos 18°27′N 103°38′E
167 S10 **Pakxé** var. Paksé. Champasak, S Laos 15°09′N 105°49′E
78 G12 **Pala** Mayo-Kébbi Ouest, SW Chad 09°22′N 14°54′E
61 A17 **Palacios** Santa Fe, C Argentina 30°43′S 61°37′W
25 V13 **Palacios** Texas, SW USA 28°42′N 96°13′W
105 X5 **Palafrugell** Cataluña, NE Spain 41°55′N 03°10′E
107 L24 **Palagonia** Sicilia, Italy, C Mediterranean Sea 37°20′N 14°45′E
113 E17 **Palagruža** It. Pelagosa. island SW Croatia
115 G20 **Palaiá Epídavros** Pelopónnisos, S Greece 37°38′N 23°09′E
121 P3 **Palaichóri** var. Palekhori. C Cyprus 34°55′N 33°06′E
115 H25 **Palaiochóra** Kríti, Greece, E Mediterranean Sea 35°14′N 23°37′E
115 A15 **Palaiolastrítsa** religious building Kérkyra, Iónia Nisiá, Greece, C Mediterranean Sea
115 J19 **Palaiópoli** Ándros, Kykládes, Greece, Aegean Sea 37°49′N 24°49′E
103 N5 **Palaiseau** Essonne, N France 48°41′N 02°14′E
155 G22 **Palakkad** var. Pālghāt. Kerala, SW India 10°46′N 76°42′E
154 N11 **Pāla Laharha** Odisha, E India 21°25′N 85°18′E
83 G19 **Palamakoloi** Ghanzi, C Botswana 23°10′S 22°22′E
115 E16 **Palamás** Thessalía, C Greece 39°28′N 22°05′E
105 X5 **Palamós** Cataluña, NE Spain 41°51′N 03°06′E
118 J5 **Palamuse** Ger. Sankt-Bartholomäi. Jõgevamaa, E Estonia 58°41′N 26°35′E
183 Q14 **Palana** Tasmania, SE Australia 39°48′S 147°54′E
123 U9 **Palana** Krasnoyarskiy Kray, E Russia 59°05′N 159°59′E
118 C11 **Palanga** Ger. Polangen. Klaipėda, NW Lithuania 05°54′N 21°05′E
143 V10 **Palangān, Kūh-e** ▲▲ E Iran
**Palangkaraja** see Palangkaraya
169 T12 **Palangkaraya** prev. Palangkaraja. Borneo, C Indonesia 02°16′S 113°55′E
155 H22 **Palani** Tamil Nādu, SE India 10°30′N 77°24′E
**Palanka** see Bačka Palanka
154 D9 **Pālanpur** Gujarāt, W India 24°12′N 72°29′E
**Palantia** see Palencia
83 I19 **Palapye** Central, SE Botswana 22°37′S 27°06′E
155 J19 **Pālār** ≈ SE India
104 H3 **Palas de Rei** Galicia, NW Spain 42°52′N 07°51′W
123 T9 **Palatka** Magadanskaya Oblast', E Russia 60°09′N 150°33′E
23 W10 **Palatka** Florida, SE USA 29°39′N 81°38′W
188 B9 **Palau** off. Republic of Palau, var. Belau. ◆ republic W Pacific Ocean
**Palau** see Palau Islands
129 Y14 **Palau Islands** var. Palau. island group N Palau
192 G16 **Palauli Bay** bay Savai'i, C Samoa, C Pacific Ocean
**Palau, Republic of** see Palau
167 N11 **Palaw** Tanintharyi, S Myanmar (Burma) 12°57′N 98°39′E
170 M6 **Palawan** island W Philippines
171 N6 **Palawan Passage** passage W Philippines
192 E7 **Palawan Trough** undersea feature S South China Sea 07°00′N 115°00′E
155 H23 **Pālayankottai** Tamil Nādu, SE India 08°42′N 77°46′E
107 L25 **Palazzola Acreide** anc. Acrae. Sicilia, Italy, C Mediterranean Sea 37°04′N 14°54′E
118 G3 **Paldiski** prev. Baltiski, Eng. Baltic Port, Ger. Baltischport. Harjumaa, NW Estonia 59°22′N 24°08′E
112 I13 **Pale** Republika Srpska, SE Bosnia and Herzegovina 43°49′N 18°35′E
**Palekhori** see Palaichóri
168 L13 **Palembang** Sumatera, W Indonesia 02°59′S 104°45′E
63 G18 **Palena** Los Lagos, S Chile 43°40′S 71°50′W
63 G18 **Palena, Río** ≈ S Chile
104 M5 **Palencia** anc. Palantia, Pallantia. Castilla y León, NW Spain 42°23′N 04°32′W
104 M3 **Palencia** ◈ province Castilla y León, N Spain
35 X15 **Palen Dry Lake** ◎ California, W USA
41 V15 **Palenque** Chiapas, SE Mexico 17°32′N 91°59′W
41 V15 **Palenque** var. Ruinas de Palenque. ruins Chiapas, SE Mexico
45 O9 **Palenque, Punta** headland S Dominican Republic 18°13′N 70°08′W
**Palenque, Ruinas de** see Palenque
**Palerme** see Palermo
107 I23 **Palermo** Fr. Palerme; anc. Panhormus, Panormus. Sicilia, Italy, C Mediterranean Sea 38°08′N 13°23′E
25 V8 **Palestine** Texas, SW USA 31°45′N 93°39′W
25 V7 **Palestine, Lake** ⊠ Texas, SW USA
107 I15 **Palestrina** Lazio, C Italy 41°49′N 12°53′E
166 K5 **Paletwa** Chin State, W Myanmar (Burma) 21°25′N 92°49′E
**Pālghāt** see Palakkad
152 F13 **Pāli** Rājasthān, N India 25°48′N 73°21′E
167 N16 **Palian** Trang, SW Thailand
189 O12 **Palikir** ● (Micronesia) Pohnpei, E Micronesia 06°58′N 158°13′E
**Palimé** see Kpalimé
107 L19 **Palinuro, Capo** headland S Italy 40°02′N 15°16′E
115 H15 **Palioúri, Akrotírio** var. Akrotírio Kanestron. headland N Greece 39°55′N 23°45′E
33 R14 **Palisades Reservoir** ⊠ Idaho, NW USA
99 J23 **Paliseul** Luxembourg, SE Belgium 49°55′N 05°09′E
154 C11 **Pālitāna** Gujarāt, W India 21°30′N 71°50′E
118 F4 **Palivere** Läänemaa, W Estonia 58°59′N 23°58′E
41 V14 **Palizada** Campeche, SE Mexico 18°15′N 92°03′W
93 L18 **Pälkäne** Pirkanmaa, W Finland 61°22′N 24°16′E
155 J22 **Palk Strait** strait India/Sri Lanka
155 J23 **Pallai** Northern Province, NW Sri Lanka 09°35′N 80°20′E
**Pallantia** see Palencia
106 C6 **Pallanza** Piemonte, NE Italy 45°57′N 08°32′E
127 Q9 **Pallasovka** Volgogradskaya Oblast', SW Russia 50°06′N 46°52′E
**Pallene/Pallíni** see Kassándra
185 L15 **Palliser Bay** bay North Island, New Zealand
185 L15 **Palliser, Cape** headland North Island, New Zealand 41°37′S 175°16′E
191 U9 **Palliser, Îles** island group Îles Tuamotu, C French Polynesia
82 Q12 **Palma** Cabo Delgado, N Mozambique 10°46′S 40°30′E
105 X9 **Palma** var. Palma de Mallorca. Mallorca, Spain, W Mediterranean Sea 39°35′N 02°39′E
105 X9 **Palma** ✈ Mallorca, Spain, W Mediterranean Sea
105 X10 **Palma, Badia de** bay Mallorca, Spain, W Mediterranean Sea
104 L13 **Palma del Río** Andalucía, S Spain 37°42′N 05°16′W
**Palma de Mallorca** see Palma
107 J25 **Palma di Montechiaro** Sicilia, Italy, C Mediterranean Sea 37°12′N 13°46′E
106 J7 **Palmanova** Friuli-Venezia Giulia, NE Italy 45°54′N 13°20′E
54 J7 **Palmarito** Apure, C Venezuela 07°36′N 70°08′W
43 N15 **Palmar Sur** Puntarenas, SE Costa Rica 08°54′N 83°27′W
60 I12 **Palmas** Paraná, S Brazil 26°29′S 52°00′W
59 K16 **Palmas** var. Palmas do Tocantins. Tocantins, C Brazil 10°24′S 48°19′W
76 L18 **Palmas, Cape** Fr. Cap des Palmès. headland SW Ivory Coast 04°18′N 07°31′W
**Palmas do Tocantins** see Palmas
54 D11 **Palmaseca** ✈ (Cali) Valle del Cauca, SW Colombia 03°31′N 76°27′W
107 B21 **Palmas, Golfo di** gulf Sardegna, Italy, C Mediterranean Sea
44 I7 **Palma Soriano** Santiago de Cuba, E Cuba 20°10′N 76°00′W
23 Y12 **Palm Bay** Florida, SE USA 28°01′N 80°35′W
35 T14 **Palmdale** California, W USA 34°34′N 118°07′W
61 H14 **Palmeira das Missões** Rio Grande do Sul, S Brazil 27°54′S 53°20′W
82 A11 **Palmeirinhas, Ponta das** headland NW Angola 09°04′S 13°02′E
39 R11 **Palmer** Alaska, USA 61°36′N 149°06′W
19 N11 **Palmer** Massachusetts, NE USA 42°09′N 72°19′W
25 U7 **Palmer** Texas, SW USA 32°25′N 96°40′W
194 H4 **Palmer** research station (US) Antarctica 64°37′S 64°01′W
15 R11 **Palmer** ≈ Québec, SE Canada
37 T5 **Palmer Lake** Colorado, C USA 39°07′N 104°55′W
194 J6 **Palmer Land** physical region Antarctica
14 F15 **Palmerston** Ontario, SE Canada 43°51′N 80°49′W
185 F22 **Palmerston** Otago, South Island, New Zealand 45°27′S 170°42′E
190 K15 **Palmerston** island S Cook Islands
**Palmerston** see Darwin
184 M12 **Palmerston North** Manawatu-Wanganui, North Island, New Zealand 40°20′S 175°52′E
23 V13 **Palmetto** Florida, SE USA 27°31′N 82°34′W
**The Palmetto State** see South Carolina
107 M22 **Palmi** Calabria, SW Italy 38°21′N 15°51′E
54 D11 **Palmira** Valle del Cauca, W Colombia 03°33′N 76°17′W
56 F8 **Palmira, Río** ≈ N Peru
61 D19 **Palmitas** Soriano, SW Uruguay 33°27′S 57°48′W
**Palmnicken** see Yantarnyy
35 V15 **Palm Springs** California, W USA 33°48′N 116°33′W
27 V2 **Palmyra** Missouri, C USA 39°48′N 91°31′W
18 G10 **Palmyra** New York, NE USA 43°02′N 77°13′W
18 G15 **Palmyra** Pennsylvania, NE USA 40°18′N 76°35′W
21 V5 **Palmyra** Virginia, NE USA 37°53′N 78°17′W
**Palmyra** see Tadmur
192 L7 **Palmyra Atoll** ◇ US incorporated territory C Pacific Ocean
154 P12 **Palmyras Point** headland E India 20°46′N 87°00′E
35 N9 **Palo Alto** California, W USA 37°26′N 122°08′W
25 O1 **Palo Duro Creek** ≈ Texas, SW USA
**Paloe** see Denpasar, Bali, C Indonesia
**Paloe** see Palu
168 L9 **Paloh** Johor, Peninsular Malaysia 02°10′N 103°11′E
80 F12 **Paloich** Upper Nile, NE South Sudan 10°29′N 32°31′E
40 I3 **Palomas** Chihuahua, N Mexico 31°45′N 107°38′W
107 I15 **Palombara Sabina** Lazio, C Italy 42°04′N 12°45′E
105 S13 **Palos, Cabo de** headland SE Spain 37°38′N 00°42′W
104 I14 **Palos de la Frontera** Andalucía, S Spain 37°14′N 06°53′W
60 G11 **Palotina** Paraná, S Brazil 24°16′S 53°49′W
32 M9 **Palouse** Washington, NW USA 46°54′N 117°04′W
32 L9 **Palouse River** ≈ Washington, NW USA
35 Y16 **Palo Verde** California, W USA 33°25′N 114°43′W
57 E16 **Palpa** Ica, W Peru 14°35′S 75°09′W
95 M16 **Pålsboda** Örebro, C Sweden 59°04′N 15°21′E
93 M15 **Paltamo** Kainuu, C Finland 64°25′N 27°50′E
171 N12 **Palu** prev. Paloe. Sulawesi, C Indonesia 0°54′S 119°52′E
137 P14 **Palu** Elazığ, E Turkey 38°43′N 39°56′E
152 I11 **Palwal** Haryāna, N India 28°15′N 77°18′E
123 U6 **Palyavaam** ≈ NE Russia
77 Q13 **Pama** SE Burkina Faso 11°13′N 00°46′E
172 J14 **Pamandzi** ✈ (Mamoudzou) Petite-Terre, E Mayotte
**Pamangkat** see Pemangkat
143 R11 **Pā Mazār** Kermān, C Iran
83 N19 **Pambarra** Inhambane, SE Mozambique 21°57′S 35°06′E
171 X12 **Pamdai** Papua, E Indonesia 01°58′S 137°19′E
103 N16 **Pamiers** Ariège, S France 43°07′N 01°37′E
147 T14 **Pamir** var. Daryā-ye Pāmīr, Taj. Dar"yoi Pomir. ≈ Afghanistan/Tajikistan see also Pāmīr, Daryā-ye
**Pamir** see Pāmīr, Daryā-ye
149 U1 **Pāmīr, Daryā-ye** var. Pamir, Taj. Dar"yoi Pomir. ≈ Afghanistan/Tajikistan see also Pamir
**Pāmīr, Daryā-ye** see Pamir
**Pāmīr-e Khord** see Little Pamir
**Pamir/Pāmīr, Daryā-ye** see Pamirs
129 Q8 **Pamirs** Pash. Daryā-ye Pāmīr, Rus. Pamir. ▲▲ C Asia
**Pâmiut** see Paamiut
21 X10 **Pamlico River** ≈ North Carolina, SE USA
21 Y10 **Pamlico Sound** sound North Carolina, SE USA
25 O2 **Pampa** Texas, SW USA 35°32′N 100°58′W
**Pampa Aullagas, Lago** see Poopó, Lago
61 B21 **Pampa Húmeda** grassland E Argentina
56 A10 **Pampa las Salinas** salt lake NW Peru
57 F15 **Pampas** Huancavelica, C Peru 12°22′S 74°53′W
62 K13 **Pampas** plain C Argentina
55 O4 **Pampatar** Nueva Esparta, NE Venezuela 11°03′N 63°51′W
**Pampeluna** see Pamplona
104 H8 **Pampilhosa da Serra** var. Pampilhosa de Serra. Coimbra, N Portugal 40°03′N 07°58′W
173 Y15 **Pamplemousses** N Mauritius 20°06′S 57°34′E
54 G7 **Pamplona** Norte de Santander, N Colombia 07°24′N 72°38′W
105 Q3 **Pamplona** var. Iruña, prev. Pampeluna; anc. Pompaelo. Navarra, N Spain 42°49′N 01°39′W
114 I11 **Pamporovo** prev. Vasil Kolarov. Smolyan, S Bulgaria 41°39′N 24°45′E
136 D15 **Pamukkale** Denizli, W Turkey 37°51′N 29°13′E
21 W5 **Pamunkey River** ≈ Virginia, NE USA
152 K5 **Pamzal** Jammu and Kashmir, NW India 34°17′N 78°50′E
30 L14 **Pana** Illinois, N USA 39°23′N 89°04′W
41 Y11 **Panabá** Yucatán, SE Mexico 21°20′N 88°16′W
35 Y8 **Panaca** Nevada, W USA 37°47′N 114°24′W
115 E19 **Panachaikó** ▲▲ S Greece
14 F11 **Panache Lake** ◎ Ontario, S Canada
114 I10 **Panagyurishte** Pazardzhik, C Bulgaria 42°30′N 24°11′E
168 M16 **Panaitan, Pulau** island S Indonesia
115 D18 **Panaitolikó** ▲▲ C Greece
155 E17 **Panaji** var. Pangim, Panjim, New Goa. state capital Goa, W India 15°31′N 73°52′E
43 T15 **Panamá** var. Ciudad de Panama, Eng. Panama City. ● (Panama) Panamá, C Panama 08°57′N 79°33′W
43 T14 **Panama** off. Republic of Panama. ◆ republic Central America
43 U14 **Panamá** off. Provincia de Panamá. ◈ province E Panama
43 U15 **Panamá, Bahía de** bay N Gulf of Panama
193 T7 **Panama Basin** undersea feature E Pacific Ocean 05°00′N 83°30′W
43 T15 **Panama Canal** canal E Panama
23 R9 **Panama City** Florida, SE USA 30°09′N 85°39′W
43 T14 **Panama City** ✈ Panamá, C Panama 09°02′N 79°24′W
**Panama City** see Panamá
23 Q9 **Panama City Beach** Florida, SE USA 30°10′N 85°48′W
43 T17 **Panamá, Golfo de** var. Gulf of Panama. gulf S Panama
**Panama, Gulf of** see Panamá, Golfo de
**Panama, Isthmus of** see Panama, Istmo de
43 T15 **Panama, Istmo de** Eng. Isthmus of Panama; prev. Isthmus of Darien. isthmus E Panama
43 T15 **Panamá Oeste** var. West Panamá. ◈ province C Panama
**Panamá, Provincia de** see Panamá
**Panama, Republic of** see Panama
35 U11 **Panamint Range** ▲▲ California, W USA
107 L22 **Panarea, Isola** island Isole Eolie, S Italy
106 G9 **Panaro** ≈ N Italy
171 P5 **Panay Island** island C Philippines
35 W7 **Pancake Range** ▲▲ Nevada, W USA
112 M11 **Pančevo** Ger. Pantschowa, Hung. Pancsova. Vojvodina, N Serbia 44°53′N 20°40′E
113 M15 **Pančićev Vrh** ▲ SW Serbia 43°16′N 20°49′E
116 L12 **Panciu** Vrancea, E Romania 45°54′N 27°08′E
116 F10 **Pâncota** Hung. Pankota; prev. Pîncota. Arad, W Romania 46°20′N 21°45′E
**Pancsova** see Pančevo
83 N20 **Panda** Inhambane, SE Mozambique 24°02′S 34°45′E
171 X12 **Pandaidori, Kepulauan** island group E Indonesia
25 N11 **Pandale** Texas, SW USA 30°09′N 101°34′W
169 P12 **Pandang Tikar, Pulau** island N Indonesia
61 F20 **Pan de Azúcar** Maldonado, S Uruguay 34°45′S 55°14′W
118 H11 **Pandėlys** Panevėžys, NE Lithuania 56°04′N 25°18′E
155 F15 **Pandharpur** Mahārāshtra, W India 17°42′N 75°24′E
182 J1 **Pandie Pandie** South Australia 26°06′S 139°26′E
171 O12 **Pandiri** Sulawesi, C Indonesia 01°32′S 120°47′E
61 F20 **Pando** Canelones, S Uruguay 34°44′S 55°58′W
57 J14 **Pando** ◈ department N Bolivia
192 K9 **Pandora Bank** undersea feature W Pacific Ocean
95 G20 **Pandrup** Nordjylland, N Denmark 57°14′N 09°42′E
79 J15 **Pandu** Equateur, NW Dem. Rep. Congo 05°03′N 19°14′E
153 V12 **Pandu** Assam, NE India 26°08′N 91°37′E
**Paneas** see Bāniyās
59 F15 **Panelas** Mato Grosso, W Brazil 09°06′S 60°41′W
118 G12 **Panevėžys** Panevėžys, C Lithuania 55°44′N 24°21′E
118 G11 **Panevėžys** ◈ province NW Lithuania
**Panfilov** see Zharkent
127 N9 **Panfilovo** Volgogradskaya Oblast', SW Russia 50°25′N 42°55′E
79 N17 **Panga** Orientale, N Dem. Rep. Congo 01°52′N 26°18′E
193 Y15 **Pangai** Lifuka, C Tonga 19°50′S 174°23′W
114 H13 **Pangaío** ▲▲ N Greece
79 G20 **Pangala** Pool, S Congo 03°26′S 14°38′E
81 J22 **Pangani** Tanga, E Tanzania 05°27′S 39°00′E
81 I21 **Pangani** ≈ NE Tanzania
186 K8 **Panggoe** Choiseul, NW Solomon Islands 07°00′S 157°05′E
79 N20 **Pangi** Maniema, E Dem. Rep. Congo 03°12′S 26°39′E
**Pangim** see Panaji
168 H8 **Pangkalanbrandan** Sumatera, W Indonesia 04°00′N 98°15′E
**Pangkalanbun** see Pangkalanbuun
169 R13 **Pangkalanbuun** var. Pangkalanbun. Borneo, C Indonesia 02°43′S 111°38′E
169 N12 **Pangkalpinang** Pulau Bangka, W Indonesia 02°05′S 106°09′E
11 U17 **Pangman** Saskatchewan, S Canada 49°37′N 104°33′W
**Pang-Nga** see Phang-Nga
9 S6 **Pangnirtung** Baffin Island, Nunavut, NE Canada 66°05′N 65°45′W
152 K6 **Pangong Tso** var. Bangong Co. ◎ China/India see also Bangong Co
**Pangong Tso** see Banggong Co
36 K7 **Panguitch** Utah, W USA 37°49′N 112°26′W
186 J7 **Panguna** Bougainville Island, NE Papua New Guinea 06°22′S 155°20′E
171 N8 **Pangutaran Group** island group Sulu Archipelago, SW Philippines
25 N2 **Panhandle** Texas, SW USA 35°21′N 101°24′W
**Panhormus** see Palermo
171 W14 **Paniai, Danau** ◎ Papua, E Indonesia
79 L21 **Pania-Mutombo** Kasai-Oriental, C Dem. Rep. Congo 05°09′S 23°49′E
187 P16 **Panié, Mont** ▲ C New Caledonia 20°33′S 164°41′E
**Panikoilli** see Jājapur
152 I10 **Pānīpat** Haryāna, N India 29°18′N 77°00′E
147 Q14 **Panj** Rus. Pyandzh; prev. Kirovabad. SW Tajikistan 37°39′N 69°55′E
147 P15 **Panj** Rus. Pyandzh. ≈ Afghanistan/Tajikistan
149 O5 **Panjāb** Bāmyān, C Afghanistan 34°21′N 67°00′E
147 O12 **Panjakent** Rus. Pendzhikent. W Tajikistan 39°28′N 67°33′E
148 L14 **Panjgur** Baluchistan, SW Pakistan 26°58′N 64°05′E
**Panjim** see Panaji
163 U12 **Panjin** Liaoning, NE China 41°11′N 122°05′E
147 P14 **Panji Poyon** Rus. Nizhniy Pyandzh. SW Tajikistan 37°14′N 68°32′E
149 S4 **Panjshayr** var. Panjshīr. ◈ province NE Afghanistan
149 Q4 **Panjshayr** prev. Panjshīr. ≈ E Afghanistan
**Panjshīr** see Panjshayr
**Panjshīr** see Panjshayr
**Pankota** see Pâncota
77 W14 **Pankshin** Plateau, C Nigeria 09°21′N 09°27′E
163 Y10 **Pan Ling** ▲▲ N China
**Panlong Jiang** see Lô, Sông
154 J9 **Panna** Madhya Pradesh, C India 24°43′N 80°11′E
99 M16 **Panningen** Limburg, SE Netherlands 51°20′N 05°59′E
149 R13 **Pano Aqil** Sindh, SE Pakistan 27°55′N 69°18′E
121 P3 **Páno Léfkara** S Cyprus 34°52′N 33°18′E
121 O3 **Páno Panagiá** var. Pano Panayia. W Cyprus 34°55′N 32°38′E
**Pano Panayia** see Páno Panagiá
**Panopolis** see Akhmīm
29 U14 **Panora** Iowa, C USA 41°41′N 94°21′W
60 I8 **Panorama** São Paulo, S Brazil 21°22′S 51°51′W
115 I24 **Pánormos** Kríti, Greece, E Mediterranean Sea 35°24′N 24°42′E
**Panormus** see Palermo
163 W11 **Panshi** Jilin, NE China 42°56′N 126°02′E
**Panshi Yu** see Passu Keah
59 H19 **Pantanal** var. Pantanalmato-Grossense. swamp SW Brazil
**Pantanalmato-Grossense** see Pantanal
61 H16 **Pântano Grande** Rio Grande do Sul, S Brazil 30°12′S 52°24′W
171 Q16 **Pantar, Pulau** island Kepulauan Alor, S Indonesia
21 X9 **Pantego** North Carolina, SE USA 35°34′N 76°39′E
107 G25 **Pantelleria** anc. Cossyra, Cosyra. Sicilia, Italy, C Mediterranean Sea 36°47′N 12°00′E
107 G25 **Pantelleria, Isola di** island SW Italy
**Pante Makasar/Pante Macassar/Pante Makassar** see Ponte Macassar
152 K10 **Pantnagar** Uttarākhand, N India 29°00′N 79°28′E
115 A15 **Pantokrátoras** ▲ Kérkyra, Iónia Nisiá, Greece, C Mediterranean Sea 39°45′N 19°51′E
**Pantschowa** see Pančevo
41 P11 **Pánuco** Veracruz, E Mexico 22°01′N 98°13′W
41 P11 **Pánuco, Río** ≈ C Mexico
160 I12 **Panxian** Guizhou, S China 25°45′N 104°39′E
168 I10 **Panyabungan** Sumatera, N Indonesia 0°55′N 99°30′E
77 W14 **Panyam** Plateau, C Nigeria 09°28′N 09°13′E
157 N13 **Panzhihua** prev. Dukou, Tu-k'ou. Sichuan, C China 26°35′N 101°41′E
79 I22 **Panzi** Bandundu, SW Dem. Rep. Congo 07°10′S 17°55′E
42 E5 **Panzós** Alta Verapaz, E Guatemala 15°21′N 89°40′W
**Pao-chi/Paoki** see Baoji
**Pao-king** see Shaoyang
107 N20 **Paola** Calabria, SW Italy 39°21′N 16°03′E
121 P16 **Paola** E Malta 35°52′N 14°30′E
27 R5 **Paola** Kansas, C USA 38°34′N 94°54′W
31 O15 **Paoli** Indiana, N USA 38°35′N 86°25′W
187 R14 **Paonangisu** Éfaté, C Vanuatu 17°33′S 168°23′E
171 S13 **Paoni** var. Pauni. Pulau Seram, E Indonesia 02°48′S 129°03′E
37 Q5 **Paonia** Colorado, C USA 38°52′N 107°35′W
191 O7 **Paopao** Moorea, W French Polynesia 17°28′S 149°48′W
**Pao-shan** see Baoshan
**Pao-ting** see Baoding
**Pao-t'ou/Paotow** see Baotou
79 H14 **Paoua** Ouham-Pendé, W Central African Republic 07°22′N 16°25′E
**Pap** see Pop
111 H23 **Pápa** Veszprém, W Hungary 47°20′N 17°29′E
42 J12 **Papagayo, Golfo de** gulf NW Costa Rica
38 H11 **Pāpa'ikou** var. Papaikou. Hawaii, USA, C Pacific Ocean 19°45′N 155°06′W
41 R15 **Papaloapan, Río** ≈ S Mexico
184 L6 **Papakura** Auckland, North Island, New Zealand 37°03′S 174°57′E
41 Q13 **Papantla** var. Papantla de Olarte. Veracruz, E Mexico 20°30′N 97°21′W
**Papantla de Olarte** see Papantla
191 P8 **Papara** Tahiti, W French Polynesia 17°45′S 149°33′W
184 K4 **Paparoa** Northland, North Island, New Zealand 36°06′S 174°12′E
185 G16 **Paparoa Range** ▲▲ South Island, New Zealand
115 K20 **Pápas, Akrotírio** headland Ikaría, Dodekánisa, Greece, Aegean Sea 37°31′N 25°58′E
96 L2 **Papa Stour** island NE Scotland, United Kingdom
184 L6 **Papatoetoe** Auckland, North Island, New Zealand 36°58′S 174°52′E
185 E25 **Papatowai** Otago, South Island, New Zealand 46°33′S 169°33′E
96 K4 **Papa Westray** island NE Scotland, United Kingdom
191 T10 **Papeete** ○ (French Polynesia) Tahiti, W French Polynesia 17°32′S 149°34′W
100 F11 **Papenburg** Niedersachsen, NW Germany 53°04′N 07°24′E
98 H13 **Papendrecht** Zuid-Holland, SW Netherlands 51°50′N 04°42′E
191 Q7 **Papenoo** Tahiti, W French Polynesia 17°29′S 149°25′W
191 Q7 **Papenoo Rivière** ≈ Tahiti, W French Polynesia
191 N7 **Papetoai** Moorea, W French Polynesia 17°29′S 149°52′W
92 L3 **Papey** island E Iceland
**Paphos** see Páfos
40 H5 **Papigochic, Río** ≈ NW Mexico
118 E10 **Papilė** Šiaulai, NW Lithuania 56°08′N 22°51′E
29 S15 **Papillion** Nebraska, C USA 41°09′N 96°02′W
15 T5 **Papinachois** ≈ Québec, SE Canada
171 X13 **Papua** var. Irian Barat, West Irian, West New Guinea, West Papua; prev. Dutch New Guinea, Irian Jaya, Netherlands New Guinea. ◈ province E Indonesia
**Papua and New Guinea, Territory of** see Papua New Guinea
171 V10 **Papua Barat** off. Propinsi Papua Barat; prev. Irian Jaya Barat, Eng. West Papua. ◈ province E Indonesia
186 C9 **Papua, Gulf of** gulf S Papua New Guinea
186 C8 **Papua New Guinea** off. Independent State of Papua New Guinea; prev. Territory of Papua and New Guinea. ◆ commonwealth republic NW Melanesia
**Papua New Guinea, Independent State of** see Papua New Guinea
192 H8 **Papua Plateau** undersea feature N Coral Sea
112 G9 **Papuk** ▲▲ NE Croatia
**Papun** see Hpapun
42 L14 **Paquera** Puntarenas, W Costa Rica 09°52′N 84°56′W
58 I13 **Pará** off. Estado do Pará. ◈ state NE Brazil
55 V9 **Para** ◈ district N Suriname
**Pará** see Belém
180 I8 **Paraburdoo** Western Australia 23°07′S 117°40′E
57 E16 **Paracas, Península de** peninsula W Peru
59 L19 **Paracatu** Minas Gerais, NE Brazil 17°14′S 46°52′W
192 E6 **Paracel Islands** Chin. Xisha Qundao, Viet. Quần Đảo Hoàng Sa. ◇ disputed territory SE Asia
182 I6 **Parachilna** South Australia 31°09′S 138°23′E
149 R6 **Parachinar** Khyber Pakhtunkhwa, NW Pakistan 33°56′N 70°04′E
112 N13 **Paraćin** Serbia, C Serbia 43°51′N 21°25′E
**Paradip** see Krishnarājāsāgara
14 K8 **Paradis** Québec, SE Canada 48°13′N 76°36′W
39 N11 **Paradise** var. Paradise Hill. Alaska, USA 62°28′N 160°09′W
35 O5 **Paradise** California, W USA 39°42′N 121°39′W
35 X11 **Paradise** Nevada, W USA 36°05′N 115°10′W
**Paradise Hill** see Paradise
37 R11 **Paradise Hills** New Mexico, SW USA 35°12′N 106°42′W
**Paradise of the Pacific** see Hawaii
36 L13 **Paradise Valley** Arizona, SW USA 33°31′N 111°56′W
35 T2 **Paradise Valley** Nevada, W USA 41°30′N 117°30′W
115 O22 **Paradisi** ✈ (Ródos) Ródos, Dodekánisa, Greece, Aegean Sea 36°24′N 28°08′E
154 P12 **Pārādwīp** Odisha, E India 20°17′N 86°42′E
**Pará, Estado do** see Pará
**Paraetonium** see Marsá Maţrūḩ
117 R4 **Parafiyivka** Chernihivs'ka Oblast', N Ukraine 50°53′N 32°40′E
36 K7 **Paragonah** Utah, W USA 37°53′N 112°46′W
27 X9 **Paragould** Arkansas, C USA 36°02′N 90°30′W
47 X8 **Paraguaçu** var. Paraguassú. ≈ E Brazil
60 J9 **Paraguaçu Paulista** São Paulo, S Brazil 22°22′S 50°35′W
54 H4 **Paraguaipoa** Zulia, NW Venezuela 11°21′N 71°58′W
62 O6 **Paraguarí** Paraguarí, S Paraguay 25°36′S 57°06′W
62 O7 **Paraguarí** off. Departamento de Paraguarí. ◈ department S Paraguay
**Paraguarí, Departamento de** see Paraguarí
57 O16 **Paraguá, Río** ≈ NE Bolivia
55 O8 **Paragua, Río** ≈ SE Venezuela
**Paraguassú** see Paraguaçu
62 N5 **Paraguay** off. Republic of Paraguay. ◆ republic C South America
47 U10 **Paraguay** var. Río Paraguay. ≈ C South America
**Paraguay, Republic of** see Paraguay
**Paraguay, Río** see Paraguay
**Parahiba/Parahyba** see Paraíba
59 P15 **Paraíba** off. Estado da Paraíba; prev. Parahiba, Parahyba. ◈ state E Brazil
**Paraíba** see João Pessoa
60 P9 **Paraíba do Sul, Rio** ≈ SE Brazil
**Paraíba, Estado da** see Paraíba
**Parainen** see Pargas
43 N14 **Paraíso** Cartago, C Costa Rica 09°51′N 83°50′W
41 U14 **Paraíso** Tabasco, SE Mexico 18°26′N 93°10′W
57 O17 **Paraíso, Río** ≈ E Bolivia
**Parajd** see Praid
77 S14 **Parakou** C Benin 09°23′N 02°40′E
115 F20 **Paralía Tyrou** Pelopónnisos, S Greece 37°17′N 22°50′E
121 Q2 **Paralímni** E Cyprus 35°02′N 34°00′E
115 G18 **Paralímni, Límni** ◎ C Greece
55 W8 **Paramaribo** ● (Suriname) Paramaribo, N Suriname 05°52′N 55°14′W
55 W9 **Paramaribo** ◈ district N Suriname
55 W9 **Paramaribo** ✈ Paramaribo, N Suriname 05°52′N 55°14′W
**Paramithiá** see Paramythiá
56 C13 **Paramonga** Lima, W Peru 10°42′S 77°50′W
123 V12 **Paramushir, Ostrov** island SE Russia
115 C16 **Paramythiá** var. Paramithiá. Ípeiros, W Greece 39°28′N 20°31′E
62 M10 **Paraná** Entre Ríos, E Argentina 31°48′S 60°29′W
60 H11 **Paraná** off. Estado do Paraná. ◈ state S Brazil
47 U11 **Paraná** var. Alto Paraná. ≈ C South America
**Paraná, Estado do** see Paraná
60 K12 **Paranaguá** Paraná, S Brazil 25°32′S 48°36′W
59 J20 **Paranaíba, Rio** ≈ E Brazil
61 C19 **Paraná Ibicuy, Río** ≈ E Argentina
59 H15 **Paranaíta** Mato Grosso, W Brazil 09°35′S 57°01′W
60 H9 **Paranapanema, Rio** ≈ S Brazil
60 K11 **Paranapiacaba, Serra do** ▲▲ S Brazil
60 H9 **Paranavaí** Paraná, S Brazil 23°02′S 52°36′W
143 N5 **Parandak** Markazī, W Iran 35°19′N 50°40′E
114 I12 **Paranéstio** var. Paranestio. Anatolikí Makedonía kai Thráki, NE Greece 41°16′N 24°31′E
**Paranestio** see Paranéstio
191 W11 **Paraoa** atoll Îles Tuamotu, C French Polynesia
184 L13 **Paraparaumu** Wellington, North Island, New Zealand 40°55′S 175°01′E
57 N20 **Parapetí, Río** ≈ SE Bolivia
54 L10 **Paraque, Cerro** ▲ W Venezuela 06°00′S 67°00′W
154 I11 **Parāsiya** Madhya Pradesh, C India 22°11′N 78°50′E
115 M23 **Paraspóri, Akrotírio** headland Kárpathos, SE Greece 35°54′N 27°15′E
60 O10 **Parati** Rio de Janeiro, SE Brazil 23°15′S 44°42′W
59 K14 **Parauapebas** Pará, N Brazil 06°03′S 49°48′W
103 Q10 **Paray-le-Monial** Saône-et-Loire, C France 46°27′N 04°07′E
**Parbatsar** see Parvatsar
154 G13 **Parbhani** Mahārāshtra, C India 19°16′N 76°51′E
100 L10 **Parchim** Mecklenburg-Vorpommern, N Germany 53°26′N 11°51′E
**Parchwitz** see Prochowice
110 P13 **Parczew** Lubelskie, E Poland 51°40′N 23°E
60 L8 **Pardo, Rio** ≈ S Brazil
111 E16 **Pardubice** Ger. Pardubitz. Pardubický Kraj, C Czechia 50°01′N 15°47′E
111 E17 **Pardubický Kraj** ◈ region N Czechia
**Pardubitz** see Pardubice
119 F16 **Parechcha** Pol. Porzecze, Rus. Porech'ye. Hrodzyenskaya Voblasts', W Belarus 53°53′N 24°08′E
59 F17 **Parecis, Chapada dos** var. Serra dos Parecis. ▲▲ W Brazil
**Parecis, Serra dos** see Parecis, Chapada dos
104 M4 **Paredes de Nava** Castilla y León, N Spain 42°09′N 04°42′W
189 U12 **Parem** island Chuuk, C Micronesia
189 O12 **Parem Island** island E Micronesia
184 I1 **Parengarenga Harbour** inlet North Island, New Zealand
15 N8 **Parent** Québec, SE Canada 47°55′N 74°36′W
102 J14 **Parentis-en-Born** Landes, SW France 44°22′N 01°04′W
**Parenzo** see Poreč
185 G20 **Pareora** Canterbury, South Island, New Zealand 44°28′S 171°12′E
171 N14 **Parepare** Sulawesi, C Indonesia 04°S 119°40′E
115 B16 **Párga** Ípeiros, W Greece 39°18′N 20°19′E
93 K20 **Pargas** Swe. Parainen. Varsinais-Suomi, SW Finland 60°18′N 22°20′E
64 O5 **Pargo, Ponta do** headland Madeira, Portugal, NE Atlantic Ocean 32°48′N 17°17′W
**Paria, Golfo de** see Paria, Gulf of


◆ Country
● Country Capital
◇ Dependent Territory
○ Dependent Territory Capital
◈ Administrative Regions
✈ International Airport
▲ Mountain
▲▲ Mountain Range
⋀ Volcano
≈ River
◎ Lake
⊠ Reservoir

PARIAGUÁN – PEMAR


55 N6 **Pariaguán** Anzoátegui, NE Venezuela 08°51′N 64°43′W
45 X17 **Paria, Gulf of** *var.* Golfo de Paria. *gulf* Trinidad and Tobago/Venezuela
57 I15 **Pariamanu, Río** ≈ E Peru
36 L8 **Paria River** ≈ Utah, W USA
**Parichi** *see* Parychy
40 M14 **Paricutín, Volcán** ⛰ C Mexico 19°25′N 102°20′W
43 P16 **Parida, Isla** *island* SW Panama
55 T8 **Parika** NE Guyana 06°51′N 58°25′W
93 O18 **Parikkala** Etelä-Karjala, SE Finland 61°33′N 29°34′E
58 E10 **Parima, Serra** *var.* Sierra Parima. ▲ Brazil/Venezuela *see also* Parima, Sierra
55 N11 **Parima, Sierra** *var.* Serra Parima. ▲ Brazil/Venezuela *see also* Parima, Serra
57 F17 **Parinacochas, Laguna** ◎ SW Peru
56 A9 **Pariñas, Punta** *headland* NW Peru 04°45′S 81°22′W
58 H12 **Parintins** Amazonas, N Brazil 02°38′S 56°45′W
103 O5 **Paris** *anc.* Lutetia, Lutetia Parisiorum, Parisii. ● (France) Paris, N France 48°52′N 02°19′E
191 Y2 **Paris** Kiritimati, E Kiribati 01°55′N 157°30′W
27 S11 **Paris** Arkansas, C USA 35°17′N 93°46′W
33 S16 **Paris** Idaho, NW USA 42°14′N 111°24′W
31 N14 **Paris** Illinois, N USA 39°36′N 87°42′W
20 M5 **Paris** Kentucky, S USA 38°13′N 84°15′W
27 V3 **Paris** Missouri, C USA 39°28′N 92°00′W
20 H8 **Paris** Tennessee, S USA 36°19′N 88°20′W
25 V5 **Paris** Texas, SW USA 33°41′N 95°33′W
**Parisii** *see* Paris
43 S16 **Parita** Herrera, S Panama 08°01′N 80°30′W
43 S16 **Parita, Bahía de** *bay* S Panama
93 K18 **Parkano** Pirkanmaa, W Finland 62°03′N 23°E
**Parkan/Párkány** *see* Štúrovo
27 N6 **Park City** Kansas, C USA 37°48′N 97°19′W
36 L3 **Park City** Utah, W USA 40°39′N 111°30′W
36 I12 **Parker** Arizona, SW USA 34°07′N 114°16′W
23 R9 **Parker** Florida, SE USA 30°07′N 85°36′W
29 R11 **Parker** South Dakota, N USA 43°24′N 97°08′W
35 Z14 **Parker Dam** California, W USA 34°17′N 114°08′W
29 W13 **Parkersburg** Iowa, C USA 42°34′N 92°47′W
21 Q3 **Parkersburg** West Virginia, NE USA 39°17′N 81°33′W
29 T7 **Parkers Prairie** Minnesota, N USA 46°09′N 95°19′W
171 P8 **Parker Volcano** ⛰ Mindanao, S Philippines 06°09′N 124°52′E
181 W13 **Parkes** New South Wales, SE Australia 33°10′S 148°10′E
30 K4 **Park Falls** Wisconsin, N USA 45°57′N 90°25′W
**Parkhar** *see* Farkhor
14 E16 **Parkhill** Ontario, S Canada 43°11′N 81°39′W
29 T5 **Park Rapids** Minnesota, N USA 46°55′N 95°03′W
29 Q3 **Park River** North Dakota, N USA 48°24′N 97°44′W
29 Q11 **Parkston** South Dakota, N USA 43°24′N 97°58′W
10 L17 **Parksville** Vancouver Island, British Columbia, SW Canada 49°13′N 124°13′W
37 S3 **Parkview Mountain** ▲ Colorado, C USA 40°19′N 106°08′W
105 N8 **Parla** Madrid, C Spain 40°13′N 03°48′W
29 S8 **Parle, Lac qui** ⊠ Minnesota, N USA
155 G14 **Parli Vaijnāth** Mahārāshtra, C India 18°53′N 76°36′E
106 F9 **Parma** Emilia-Romagna, N Italy 44°50′N 10°20′E
31 T11 **Parma** Ohio, N USA 41°24′N 81°43′W
**Parnahyba** *see* Parnaíba
58 N13 **Parnaíba** *var.* Parnahyba. Piauí, E Brazil 02°58′S 41°46′W
65 J14 **Parnaíba Ridge** *undersea feature* C Atlantic Ocean
58 N13 **Parnaíba, Rio** ≈ NE Brazil
115 F18 **Parnassós** ▲▲ C Greece
185 J17 **Parnassus** Canterbury, South Island, New Zealand 42°41′S 173°18′E
182 H10 **Parndana** South Australia 35°48′S 137°13′E
115 H19 **Párnitha** ▲▲ C Greece
**Parnon** *see* Párnonas
115 F21 **Párnonas** *var.* Parnon. ▲▲ S Greece
118 G5 **Pärnu** *Ger.* Pernau, *Latv.* Pērnava; *prev. Rus.* Pernov. Pärnumaa, SW Estonia 58°24′N 24°32′E
118 G6 **Pärnu** *var.* Parnu Jōgi, *Ger.* Pernau. ≈ SW Estonia
118 G5 **Pärnu-Jaagupi** *Ger.* Sankt-Jakobi. Pärnumaa, SW Estonia 58°36′N 24°30′E
**Parnu Jōgi** *see* Pärnu
118 G5 **Pärnu Laht** *Ger.* Pernauer Bucht. *bay* SW Estonia
118 F5 **Pärnumaa** *var.* Pärnu Maakond. ◈ *province* SW Estonia
**Pärnu Maakond** *see* Pärnumaa
153 T11 **Paro** W Bhutan 27°23′N 89°31′E
153 T11 **Paro** ✈ (Thimphu) W Bhutan 27°23′N 89°31′E
185 G17 **Paroa** West Coast, South Island, New Zealand 42°31′S 171°10′E
163 X14 **Paro-ho** *var.* Hwach'ŏn-chŏsuji; *prev.* P'aro-ho. ⊠ N South Korea
**P'aro-ho** *see* Paro-ho
115 J21 **Pároikiá** *prev.* Páros. Páros, Kykládes, Greece, Aegean Sea 37°04′N 25°06′E
183 N6 **Paroo River** *seasonal river* New South Wales/Queensland, SE Australia
**Paropamisus Range** *see* Safēd Kōh, Silsilah-ye
115 J21 **Páros** *island* Kykládes, Greece, Aegean Sea
**Páros** *see* Pároikiá
36 K7 **Parowan** Utah, W USA 37°50′N 112°49′W
103 U13 **Parpaillon** ▲▲ SE France
108 I9 **Parpan** Graubünden, S Switzerland 46°46′N 09°32′E
62 G13 **Parral** Maule, C Chile 36°08′S 71°52′W
**Parral** *see* Hidalgo del Parral
183 T9 **Parramatta** New South Wales, SE Australia 33°49′S 150°59′E
21 Y6 **Parramore Island** *island* Virginia, NE USA
40 M8 **Parras** *var.* Parras de la Fuente. Coahuila, NE Mexico 25°26′N 102°07′W
**Parras de la Fuente** *see* Parras
42 M14 **Parrita** Puntarenas, S Costa Rica 09°30′N 84°20′W
**Parry group** *see* Mukojima-rettō
14 G13 **Parry Island** *island* Ontario, S Canada
197 O9 **Parry Islands** *island group* Nunavut, NW Canada
14 G12 **Parry Sound** Ontario, S Canada 45°21′N 80°03′W
110 F7 **Parsęta** *Ger.* Persante. ≈ NW Poland
28 L3 **Parshall** North Dakota, N USA 47°57′N 102°07′W
27 Q7 **Parsons** Kansas, C USA 37°20′N 95°15′W
20 H9 **Parsons** Tennessee, S USA 35°39′N 88°07′W
21 T3 **Parsons** West Virginia, NE USA 39°06′N 79°43′W
**Parsonstown** *see* Birr
100 P11 **Parsteiner See** ◎ NE Germany
107 I24 **Partanna** Sicilia, Italy, C Mediterranean Sea 37°43′N 12°54′E
108 J8 **Partenen** Graubünden, E Switzerland 46°58′N 10°01′E
102 K9 **Parthenay** Deux-Sèvres, W France 46°39′N 00°13′W
95 J19 **Partille** Västra Götaland, S Sweden 57°43′N 12°12′E
107 I23 **Partinico** Sicilia, Italy, C Mediterranean Sea 38°03′N 13°07′E
111 I20 **Partizánske** *prev.* Šimonovany, *Hung.* Simony. Trenčiansky Kraj, W Slovakia 48°35′N 18°23′E
58 H11 **Paru de Oeste, Rio** ≈ N Brazil
149 T4 **Pārūn** Nūristān NE Afghanistan 35°25′N 70°55′E
182 K9 **Paruna** South Australia 34°45′S 140°43′E
58 I11 **Paru, Rio** ≈ N Brazil
**Parvān** *see* Parwān
155 M14 **Pārvatipuram** Andhra Pradesh, E India 17°01′N 81°47′E
152 G12 **Parvatsar** *prev.* Parbatsar. Rājasthān, N India 26°52′N 74°49′E
114 J11 **Parvomay**, Pŭrvomay; *prev.* Borisovgrad. Plovdiv, C Bulgaria 42°06′N 25°13′E
149 Q5 **Parwān** *prev.* Parvān. E Afghanistan
158 I15 **Paryang** Xizang Zizhiqu, W China 30°04′N 83°28′E
119 M18 **Parychy** *Rus.* Parichi. Homyel'skaya Voblasts', SE Belarus 52°48′N 29°25′E
83 J21 **Parys** Free State, C South Africa 26°55′S 27°28′E
35 T15 **Pasadena** California, W USA 34°09′N 118°09′W
25 W11 **Pasadena** Texas, SW USA 29°41′N 95°13′W
56 B8 **Pasaje** El Oro, SW Ecuador 03°23′S 79°50′W
137 T9 **Pasanauri** *prev.* P'asanauri. N Georgia 42°21′N 44°40′E
**P'asanauri** *see* Pasanauri
168 I13 **Pasapuat** Pulau Pagai Utara, W Indonesia 02°36′S 99°58′E
**Pasawng** *see* Hpasawng
114 L13 **Paşayiğit** Edirne, NW Turkey 40°58′N 26°38′E
23 N9 **Pascagoula** Mississippi, S USA 30°21′N 88°32′W
22 M8 **Pascagoula River** ≈ Mississippi, S USA
116 F12 **Paşcani** *Hung.* Páskán. Iași, NE Romania 47°14′N 26°46′E
109 T4 **Pasching** Oberösterreich, N Austria 48°16′N 14°10′E
32 K10 **Pasco** Washington, NW USA 46°13′N 119°06′W
56 E13 **Pasco** *off.* Región de Pasco. ◈ *region* C Peru
**Pasco, Región de** *see* Pasco
191 N11 **Pascua, Isla de** *var.* Rapa Nui, Easter Island. *island* E Pacific Ocean
63 G21 **Pascua, Río** ≈ S Chile
103 N1 **Pas-de-Calais** ◈ *department* N France
100 P10 **Pasewalk** Mecklenburg-Vorpommern, NE Germany 53°31′N 13°59′E
11 T10 **Pasfield Lake** ◎ Saskatchewan, C Canada
**Pa-shih Hai-hsia** *see* Bashi Channel
**Pashkeni** *see* Bolyarovo
**Pashmakli** *see* Smolyan
153 X10 **Pāsighāt** Arunāchel Pradesh, NE India 28°08′N 95°13′E
137 Q12 **Pasinler** Erzurum, NE Turkey 39°59′N 41°41′E
**Pasi Oloy, Qatorkŭhi** *see* Zaalayskiy Khrebet
42 E3 **Pasión, Río de la** ≈ N Guatemala
168 J12 **Pasirganting** Sumatera, W Indonesia 02°04′S 100°51′E
**Pasirpangarayan** *see* Bagansiapiapi
168 K6 **Pasir Puteh** *var.* Pasir Putih. Kelantan, Peninsular Malaysia 05°50′N 102°24′E
**Pasir Putih** *see* Pasir Puteh
169 R9 **Pasir, Tanjung** *headland* East Malaysia 02°24′N 111°12′E
95 N20 **Påskallavik** Kalmar, S Sweden 57°10′N 16°25′E
**Páskán** *see* Paşcani
**Paskevicha, Zaliv** *see* Tushchybas, Zaliv
110 K7 **Pasłęk** *Ger.* Preußisch Holland. Warmińsko-Mazurskie, NE Poland 54°03′N 19°40′E
110 K7 **Pasłęka** *Ger.* Passarge. ≈ N Poland
148 K16 **Pasni** Baluchistan, SW Pakistan 25°13′N 63°30′E
63 I18 **Paso de Indios** Chubut, S Argentina 43°52′S 69°06′W
54 L7 **Paso del Caballo** Guárico, N Venezuela 08°19′N 67°08′W
61 E15 **Paso de los Libres** Corrientes, NE Argentina 29°43′S 57°09′W
61 E18 **Paso de los Toros** Tacuarembó, C Uruguay 32°45′S 56°30′W
**Pasoeroean** *see* Pasuruan
35 P12 **Paso Robles** California, W USA 35°37′N 120°42′W
15 Y7 **Paspébiac** Québec, SE Canada 48°03′N 65°10′W
11 U14 **Pasquia Hills** ▲▲ Saskatchewan, S Canada
149 W7 **Pasrur** Punjab, E Pakistan 32°12′N 74°42′E
30 M1 **Passage Island** *island* Michigan, N USA
65 B24 **Passage Islands** *island group* W Falkland Islands
8 K5 **Passage Point** *headland* Banks Island, Northwest Territories, NW Canada 73°31′N 115°12′W
**Passarge** *see* Pasłęka
115 C15 **Passarón** *ancient monument* Ípeiros, W Greece
**Passarowitz** *see* Požarevac
101 O22 **Passau** Bayern, SE Germany 48°34′N 13°28′E
22 M9 **Pass Christian** Mississippi, S USA 30°19′N 89°15′W
107 L26 **Passero, Capo** *headland* Sicilia, Italy, C Mediterranean Sea 36°40′N 15°09′E
171 P5 **Passi** Panay Island, C Philippines 11°05′N 122°37′E
61 H14 **Passo Fundo** Rio Grande do Sul, S Brazil 28°16′S 52°20′W
60 H13 **Passo Fundo, Barragem de** ⊠ S Brazil
61 H15 **Passo Real, Barragem de** ⊠ S Brazil
59 L20 **Passos** Minas Gerais, NE Brazil 20°45′S 46°38′W
167 X10 **Passu Keah** *Chin.* Panshi Yu, *Viet.* Đảo Bắc Quy. *island* S Paracel Islands
118 J13 **Pastavy** *Pol.* Postawy, *Rus.* Postavy. Vitsyebskaya Voblasts', NW Belarus 55°07′N 26°50′E
56 D7 **Pastaza** ◈ *province* E Ecuador
56 D9 **Pastaza, Río** ≈ Ecuador/Peru
61 A21 **Pasteur** Buenos Aires, E Argentina 35°10′S 62°14′W
15 V3 **Pasteur** ≈ Québec, SE Canada
147 Q12 **Pastigav** *Rus.* Pastigov. W Tajikistan 39°27′N 69°16′E
**Pastigov** *see* Pastigav
54 C13 **Pasto** Nariño, SW Colombia 01°12′N 77°17′W
38 M10 **Pastol Bay** *bay* Alaska, USA
37 O8 **Pastora Peak** ▲ Arizona, SW USA 36°48′N 109°10′W
105 O8 **Pastrana** Castilla-La Mancha, C Spain 40°24′N 02°55′W
169 S16 **Pasuruan** *prev.* Pasoeroean. Jawa, C Indonesia 07°38′S 112°44′E
118 F11 **Pasvalys** Panevėžys, N Lithuania 56°03′N 24°24′E
111 K21 **Pásztó** Nógrád, N Hungary 47°57′N 19°41′E
189 U12 **Pata** *var.* Patta. *atoll* Chuuk Islands, C Micronesia
36 M16 **Patagonia** Arizona, SW USA 31°32′N 110°45′W
63 H20 **Patagonia** *physical region* Argentina/Chile
**Patalung** *see* Phatthalung
154 D9 **Pātan** Gujarāt, W India 23°51′N 72°11′E
154 J10 **Pātan** Madhya Pradesh, C India 23°19′N 79°41′E
171 S11 **Patani** Pulau Halmahera, E Indonesia 0°19′N 128°46′E
**Patani** *see* Pattani
15 V7 **Patapédia Est** ≈ Québec, SE Canada
116 K13 **Pătâriagele** *prev.* Pătîriagele. Buzău, SE Romania 45°19′N 26°21′E
**Patavium** *see* Padova
182 I5 **Patawarta Hill** ▲ South Australia 30°57′S 138°42′E
182 L10 **Patchewollock** Victoria, SE Australia 35°24′S 142°11′E
184 K11 **Patea** Taranaki, North Island, New Zealand 39°48′S 174°35′E
184 K11 **Patea** ≈ North Island, New Zealand
77 U15 **Pategi** Kwara, C Nigeria 08°39′N 05°46′E
81 K20 **Pate Island** *var.* Patta Island. *island* SE Kenya
105 S10 **Paterna** Comunitat Valenciana, E Spain 39°30′N 00°24′W
109 R9 **Paternion** *Slvn.* Špatrjan. Kärnten, S Austria 46°40′N 13°43′E
107 L24 **Paternò** *anc.* Hybla, Hybla Major. Sicilia, Italy, C Mediterranean Sea 37°34′N 14°55′E
32 J7 **Pateros** Washington, NW USA 48°01′N 119°55′W
18 J14 **Paterson** New Jersey, NE USA 40°55′N 74°12′W
32 J10 **Paterson** Washington, NW USA 45°56′N 119°37′W
185 C25 **Paterson Inlet** *inlet* Stewart Island, New Zealand
98 N6 **Paterswolde** Drenthe, NE Netherlands 53°07′N 06°32′E
152 H7 **Pathānkot** Himāchal Pradesh, N India 32°16′N 75°43′E
166 K8 **Pathein** *var.* Bassein. Ayeyarwady, SW Myanmar (Burma) 16°46′N 94°45′E
33 W15 **Pathfinder Reservoir** ⊠ Wyoming, C USA
167 O11 **Pathum Thani** *var.* Patumdhani, Prathum Thani. Pathum Thani, C Thailand 14°03′N 100°29′E
54 C12 **Patía** *var.* El Bordo. Cauca, SW Colombia 02°07′N 76°57′W
152 I9 **Patiāla** *var.* Puttiala. Punjab, NW India 30°21′N 76°27′E
54 B12 **Patía, Río** ≈ SW Colombia
188 D15 **Pati Point** *headland* NE Guam 13°36′N 144°39′E
**Pătîriagele** *see* Pătâriagele
56 C13 **Pativilca** Lima, W Peru 10°44′S 77°45′W
166 M1 **Patkai Bum** *var.* Patkai Range. ▲▲ Myanmar (Burma)/India
**Patkai Range** *see* Patkai Bum
115 L20 **Pátmos** Pátmos, Dodekánisa, Greece, Aegean Sea 37°18′N 26°32′E
115 L20 **Pátmos** *island* Dodekánisa, Greece, Aegean Sea
153 P13 **Patna** *var.* Azimabad. *state capital* Bihār, N India 25°36′N 85°11′E
154 M12 **Patnāgarh** Odisha, E India 20°42′N 83°12′E
171 O5 **Patnongon** Panay Island, C Philippines 10°56′N 122°03′E
137 S13 **Patnos** Ağrı, E Turkey 39°14′N 42°52′E
60 H12 **Pato Branco** Paraná, S Brazil 26°20′S 52°40′W
31 O16 **Patoka Lake** ◎ Indiana, N USA
92 L9 **Patoniva** *Lapp.* Buoddobohki. Lappi, N Finland 69°44′N 27°01′E
113 K21 **Patos** *var.* Patosi. Fier, SW Albania 40°40′N 19°37′E
**Patos** *see* Patos de Minas
59 K19 **Patos de Minas** *var.* Patos. Minas Gerais, NE Brazil 18°35′S 46°32′W
**Patosi** *see* Patos
61 I17 **Patos, Lagoa dos** *lagoon* S Brazil
62 J9 **Patquía** La Rioja, C Argentina 30°02′S 66°54′W
115 E19 **Pátra** *Eng.* Patras; *prev.* Pátrai. Dytikí Elláda, S Greece 38°14′N 21°45′E
115 D18 **Patraïkós Kólpos** *gulf* S Greece
**Pátrai/Patras** *see* Pátra
92 G2 **Patreksfjörður** Vestfirðir, W Iceland 65°33′N 23°54′W
24 M7 **Patricia** Texas, SW USA 32°34′N 102°00′W
63 F21 **Patricio Lynch, Isla** *island* S Chile
**Patta** *see* Pata
**Patta Island** *see* Pate Island
167 O16 **Pattani** *var.* Patani. Pattani, SW Thailand 06°50′N 101°20′E
167 P12 **Pattaya** Chon Buri, S Thailand 12°57′N 100°53′E
19 S4 **Patten** Maine, NE USA 45°58′N 68°27′W
35 O9 **Patterson** California, W USA 37°27′N 121°07′W
22 J10 **Patterson** Louisiana, S USA 29°41′N 91°18′W
35 R7 **Patterson, Mount** ▲ California, W USA 38°27′N 119°16′W
31 P4 **Patterson, Point** *headland* Michigan, N USA 45°58′N 85°39′W
107 L23 **Patti** Sicilia, Italy, C Mediterranean Sea 38°08′N 14°58′E
107 L23 **Patti, Golfo di** *gulf* Sicilia, Italy
93 L14 **Pattijoki** Pohjois-Pohjanmaa, W Finland 64°41′N 24°40′E
193 Q4 **Patton Escarpment** *undersea feature* E Pacific Ocean
27 S2 **Pattonsburg** Missouri, C USA 40°03′N 94°08′W
0 D6 **Patton Seamount** *undersea feature* NE Pacific Ocean 54°40′N 150°30′W
10 J12 **Pattullo, Mount** ▲ British Columbia, W Canada 56°18′N 129°43′W
153 U16 **Patuakhali** *var.* Patukhali. Barisal, S Bangladesh 22°20′N 90°20′E
42 M5 **Patuca, Río** ≈ E Honduras
**Patukhali** *see* Patuakhali
**Patumdhani** *see* Pathum Thani
40 M14 **Pátzcuaro** Michoacán, SW Mexico 19°30′N 101°38′W
42 C6 **Patzicía** Chimaltenango, S Guatemala 14°38′N 90°52′W
102 K16 **Pau** Pyrénées-Atlantiques, SW France 43°18′N 00°22′W
102 J12 **Pauillac** Gironde, SW France 45°12′N 00°44′W
166 L5 **Pauk** Magway, W Myanmar (Burma) 21°25′N 94°30′E
8 I6 **Paulatuk** Northwest Territories, NW Canada 69°23′N 124°W
42 K5 **Paulayá, Río** ≈ NE Honduras
22 M6 **Paulding** Mississippi, S USA 32°01′N 89°01′W
31 Q12 **Paulding** Ohio, N USA 41°08′N 84°34′W
29 S12 **Paullina** Iowa, C USA 42°58′N 95°41′W
59 P15 **Paulo Afonso** Bahia, E Brazil 09°21′S 38°14′W
38 M16 **Pauloff Harbor** *var.* Pavlor Harbour. Sanak Island, Alaska, USA 54°26′N 162°43′W
27 N12 **Pauls Valley** Oklahoma, C USA 34°46′N 97°14′W
166 L7 **Paungde** Bago, C Myanmar (Burma) 18°30′N 95°30′E
**Pauni** *see* Paoni
152 K9 **Pauri** Uttaranchal, N India 30°08′N 78°48′E
**Pautalia** *see* Kyustendil
142 J5 **Pāveh** Kermānshāhān, NW Iran 35°02′N 46°15′E
126 L5 **Pavelets** Ryazanskaya Oblast', W Russia 53°47′N 39°22′E
106 D8 **Pavia** *anc.* Ticinum. Lombardia, N Italy 45°10′N 09°10′E
118 C9 **Pāvilosta** W Latvia 56°52′N 21°12′E
125 P14 **Pavino** Kostromskaya Oblast', NW Russia 59°10′N 46°09′E
114 J8 **Pavlikeni** Veliko Tarnovo, N Bulgaria 43°14′N 25°20′E
145 T8 **Pavlodar** Pavlodar, NE Kazakhstan 52°21′N 76°59′E
145 S9 **Pavlodar** *off.* Pavlodarskaya Oblast', *Kaz.* Pavlodar Oblysy. ◈ *province* NE Kazakhstan
**Pavlodar Oblysy/Pavlodarskaya Oblast'** *see* Pavlodar
**Pavlograd** *see* Pavlohrad
117 U7 **Pavlohrad** *Rus.* Pavlograd. Dnipropetrovs'ka Oblast', E Ukraine 48°32′N 35°50′E
**Pavlor Harbour** *see* Pauloff Harbor
145 R9 **Pavlovka** Akmola, C Kazakhstan 51°22′N 72°35′E
127 V4 **Pavlovka** Respublika Bashkortostan, W Russia 55°28′N 56°36′E
127 Q7 **Pavlovka** Ul'yanovskaya Oblast', W Russia 52°40′N 47°08′E
127 N3 **Pavlovo** Nizhegorodskaya Oblast', W Russia 55°59′N 43°03′E
126 L9 **Pavlovsk** Voronezhskaya Oblast', W Russia 50°26′N 40°08′E
126 L13 **Pavlovskaya** Krasnodarskiy Kray, SW Russia 46°06′N 39°52′E
117 S7 **Pavlysh** Kirovohrads'ka Oblast', C Ukraine 48°54′N 33°20′E
106 F10 **Pavullo nel Frignano** Emilia-Romagna, C Italy 44°19′N 10°52′E
27 P8 **Pawhuska** Oklahoma, C USA 36°42′N 96°21′W
21 U13 **Pawleys Island** South Carolina, SE USA 33°27′N 79°07′W
30 K14 **Pawnee** Illinois, N USA 39°35′N 89°34′W
27 O9 **Pawnee** Oklahoma, C USA 36°21′N 96°50′W
37 U2 **Pawnee Buttes** ▲ Colorado, C USA 40°49′N 103°58′W
29 S17 **Pawnee City** Nebraska, C USA 40°06′N 96°09′W
26 K5 **Pawnee River** ≈ Kansas, C USA
167 N6 **Pawn, Nam** ≈ C Myanmar (Burma)
31 O10 **Paw Paw** Michigan, N USA 42°12′N 86°09′W
31 O10 **Paw Paw Lake** Michigan, N USA 42°12′N 86°16′W
19 O12 **Pawtucket** Rhode Island, NE USA 41°52′N 71°22′W
**Pax Augusta** *see* Badajoz
115 I25 **Paximádia** *island* SE Greece
**Pax Julia** *see* Beja
115 B16 **Paxoí** *island* Iónia Nisiá, Greece, C Mediterranean Sea
39 S10 **Paxson** Alaska, USA 62°58′N 145°27′W
147 O11 **Paxtakor** Jizzax Viloyati, C Uzbekistan 40°21′N 67°54′E
30 M13 **Paxton** Illinois, N USA 40°27′N 88°06′W
124 J11 **Pay** Respublika Kareliya, NW Russia 61°10′N 34°24′E
166 M8 **Payagyi** Bago, SW Myanmar (Burma) 17°28′N 96°32′E
108 C9 **Payerne** *Ger.* Peterlingen. Vaud, W Switzerland 46°49′N 06°57′E
32 M13 **Payette** Idaho, NW USA 44°04′N 116°55′W
32 M13 **Payette River** ≈ Idaho, NW USA
125 V2 **Pay-Khoy, Khrebet** ▲▲ NW Russia
**Payne** *see* Kangirsuk
12 K4 **Payne, Lac** ◎ Québec, NE Canada
29 T8 **Paynesville** Minnesota, N USA 45°22′N 94°42′W
169 S8 **Payong, Tanjung** *cape* East Malaysia
**Payo Obispo** *see* Chetumal
61 D18 **Paysandú** Paysandú, W Uruguay 32°21′S 58°05′W
61 D17 **Paysandú** ◈ *department* W Uruguay
102 I7 **Pays de la Loire** ◈ *region* NW France
36 L12 **Payson** Arizona, SW USA 34°13′N 111°19′W
36 L4 **Payson** Utah, W USA 40°02′N 111°43′W
125 W4 **Payyer, Gora** ▲ NW Russia 66°49′N 64°33′E
**Payzawat** *see* Jiashi
137 Q11 **Pazar** Rize, NE Turkey 41°10′N 40°53′E
136 F10 **Pazarbaşı Burnu** *headland* NW Turkey 41°12′N 30°18′E
136 M16 **Pazarcık** Kahramanmaraş, S Turkey 37°31′N 37°19′E
114 I10 **Pazardzhik** *prev.* Tatar Pazardzhik. Pazardzhik, SW Bulgaria 42°11′N 24°21′E
64 H11 **Pazardzhik** ◈ *province* C Bulgaria
54 H9 **Paz de Ariporo** Casanare, E Colombia 05°54′N 71°52′W
112 A10 **Pazin** *Ger.* Mitterburg, *It.* Pisino. Istra, NW Croatia 45°14′N 13°56′E
42 D7 **Paz, Río** ≈ El Salvador/Guatemala
113 O18 **Pčinja** ≈ N Macedonia
193 V15 **Pea** Tongatapu, S Tonga 21°10′S 175°14′W
27 O6 **Peabody** Kansas, C USA 38°10′N 97°06′W
11 O12 **Peace** ≈ Alberta/British Columbia, W Canada
**Peace Garden State** *see* North Dakota
11 Q10 **Peace Point** Alberta, C Canada 59°11′N 112°12′W
11 O12 **Peace River** Alberta, W Canada 56°15′N 117°18′W
23 W13 **Peace River** ≈ Florida, SE USA
11 N17 **Peachland** British Columbia, SW Canada 49°49′N 119°48′W
36 J10 **Peach Springs** Arizona, SW USA 35°33′N 113°27′W
**Peach State** *see* Georgia
23 S4 **Peachtree City** Georgia, SE USA 33°24′N 84°36′W
189 Y13 **Peacock Point** *point* SE Wake Island
97 M18 **Peak District** *physical region* C England, United Kingdom
183 Q7 **Peak Hill** New South Wales, SE Australia 32°39′S 148°12′E
65 G15 **Peak, The** ▲ C Ascension Island
105 O13 **Peal de Becerro** Andalucía, S Spain 37°55′N 03°08′W
189 X11 **Peale Island** *island* N Wake Island
37 O6 **Peale, Mount** ▲ Utah, W USA 38°26′N 109°13′W
39 O4 **Peard Bay** *bay* Alaska, USA
23 Q7 **Pea River** ≈ Alabama/Florida, S USA
25 W11 **Pearland** Texas, SW USA 29°33′N 95°17′W
38 D9 **Pearl City** O'ahu, Hawaii, USA, C Pacific Ocean 21°24′N 157°58′W
38 D9 **Pearl Harbor** *inlet* O'ahu, Hawai'i, USA, C Pacific Ocean
**Pearl Islands** *see* Perlas, Archipiélago de las
**Pearl Lagoon** *see* Perlas, Laguna de
22 M5 **Pearl River** ≈ Louisiana/Mississippi, S USA
25 Q13 **Pearsall** Texas, SW USA 28°54′N 99°07′W
23 U7 **Pearson** Georgia, SE USA 31°18′N 82°51′W
25 P4 **Pease River** ≈ Texas, SW USA
12 F7 **Peawanuck** Ontario, C Canada 54°55′N 85°31′W
12 E8 **Peawanuk** ≈ Ontario, S Canada
83 P16 **Pebane** Zambézia, NE Mozambique 17°14′S 38°10′E
65 C23 **Pebble Island** *island* N Falkland Islands
65 C23 **Pebble Island Settlement** Pebble Island, N Falkland Islands 51°20′S 59°40′W
**Peć** *see* Pejë
25 R8 **Pecan Bayou** ≈ Texas, SW USA
22 H10 **Pecan Island** Louisiana, S USA 29°39′N 92°26′W
60 L12 **Peças, Ilha das** *island* S Brazil
30 L10 **Pecatonica River** ≈ Illinois/Wisconsin, N USA
108 G10 **Peccia** Ticino, S Switzerland 46°24′N 08°39′E
**Pechenegi** *see* Pechenihy
**Pechenezhskoye Vodokhranilishche** *see* Pecheniz'ke Vodoskhovyshche
124 I2 **Pechenga** *Fin.* Petsamo. Murmanskaya Oblast', NW Russia 69°34′N 31°14′E
117 V5 **Pechenihy** *Rus.* Pechenegi. Kharkivs'ka Oblast', E Ukraine 49°49′N 36°57′E
117 V5 **Pecheniz'ke Vodoskhovyshche** *Rus.* Pechenezhskoye Vodokhranilishche. ⊠ E Ukraine
125 U7 **Pechora** Respublika Komi, NW Russia 65°09′N 57°09′E
125 R6 **Pechora** ≈ NW Russia
**Pechora Bay** *see* Pechorskaya Guba
**Pechora Sea** *see* Pechorskoye More
125 S3 **Pechorskaya Guba** *Eng.* Pechora Bay. *bay* NW Russia
122 H7 **Pechorskoye More** *Eng.* Pechora Sea. *sea* NW Russia
116 E11 **Pecica** *Ger.* Petschka, *Hung.* Ópécska. Arad, W Romania 46°09′N 21°06′E
24 K8 **Pecos** Texas, SW USA 31°25′N 103°30′W
25 N11 **Pecos River** ≈ New Mexico/Texas, SW USA
111 I25 **Pécs** *Ger.* Fünfkirchen, *Lat.* Sopianae. Baranya, SW Hungary 46°05′N 18°11′E
43 T17 **Pedasí** Los Santos, S Panama 07°36′N 80°04′W
**Pedde** *see* Pedja
183 O17 **Pedder, Lake** ◎ Tasmania, SE Australia
44 M10 **Pedernales** SW Dominican Republic 18°02′N 71°41′W
55 Q5 **Pedernales** Delta Amacuro, NE Venezuela 09°58′N 62°15′W
25 R10 **Pedernales River** ≈ Texas, SW USA
62 H6 **Pedernales, Salar de** *salt lake* N Chile
**Pedhoulas** *see* Pedoulás
55 X11 **Pédima** *var.* Malavate. SW French Guiana 03°15′N 54°08′W
182 F1 **Pedirka** South Australia 26°41′S 135°11′E
171 S11 **Pediwang** Pulau Halmahera, E Indonesia 01°29′N 127°57′E
118 I5 **Pedja** *var.* Pedja Jōgi, *Ger.* Pedde. ≈ E Estonia
**Pedja Jōgi** *see* Pedja
121 O3 **Pedoulás** *var.* Pedhoulas. W Cyprus 34°58′N 32°51′E
59 N18 **Pedra Azul** Minas Gerais, NE Brazil 16°02′S 41°17′W
104 I3 **Pedrafita, Porto de** *var.* Puerto de Piedrafita. *pass* NW Spain
76 E9 **Pedra Lume** Sal, NE Cape Verde 16°47′N 22°54′W
43 P16 **Pedregal** Chiriquí, W Panama 09°04′N 79°25′W
54 J4 **Pedregal** Falcón, N Venezuela 11°04′N 70°08′W
40 L9 **Pedriceña** Durango, C Mexico 25°08′N 103°46′W
60 L11 **Pedro Barros** São Paulo, S Brazil 24°12′S 47°22′W
39 Q13 **Pedro Bay** Alaska, USA 59°47′N 154°06′W
62 H4 **Pedro de Valdivia** *var.* Oficina Pedro de Valdivia. Antofagasta, N Chile 22°33′S 69°38′W
62 P4 **Pedro Juan Caballero** Amambay, E Paraguay 22°34′S 55°41′W
63 L15 **Pedro Luro** Buenos Aires, E Argentina 39°30′S 62°38′W
105 O10 **Pedro Muñoz** Castilla-La Mancha, C Spain 39°25′N 02°56′W
155 J22 **Pedro, Point** *headland* NW Sri Lanka 09°54′N 80°08′E
182 K9 **Peebinga** South Australia 34°56′S 140°56′E
96 J13 **Peebles** SE Scotland, United Kingdom 55°40′N 03°15′W
31 S15 **Peebles** Ohio, N USA 38°57′N 83°23′W
96 J12 **Peebles** *cultural region* SE Scotland, United Kingdom
18 K13 **Peekskill** New York, NE USA 41°17′N 73°54′W
97 I16 **Peel** W Isle of Man 54°13′N 04°04′W
8 G7 **Peel** ≈ Northwest Territories/Yukon, NW Canada
8 K5 **Peel Point** *headland* Victoria Island, Northwest Territories, NW Canada 73°22′N 114°33′W
8 M5 **Peel Sound** *passage* Nunavut, N Canada
100 N9 **Peene** ≈ NE Germany
99 K17 **Peer** Limburg, NE Belgium 51°08′N 05°29′E
14 H14 **Pefferlaw** Ontario, S Canada 44°18′N 79°11′W
185 I18 **Pegasus Bay** *bay* South Island, New Zealand
121 O3 **Pégeia** *var.* Peyia. SW Cyprus 34°52′N 32°24′E
109 V7 **Peggau** Steiermark, SE Austria 47°10′N 15°20′E
101 L19 **Pegnitz** Bayern, SE Germany 49°45′N 11°33′E
101 L19 **Pegnitz** ≈ SE Germany
105 T11 **Pego** Comunitat Valenciana, E Spain 38°51′N 00°08′W
**Pegu** *see* Bago
**Pegu** *see* Bago
189 N13 **Pehleng** Pohnpei, E Micronesia
114 M12 **Pehlivanköy** Kırklareli, NW Turkey 41°21′N 26°55′E
77 R14 **Péhonko** C Benin 10°14′N 01°57′E
61 B21 **Pehuajó** Buenos Aires, E Argentina 35°48′S 61°53′W
**Pei-ching** *see* Beijing/Beijing Shi
100 J13 **Peine** Niedersachsen, C Germany 52°19′N 10°14′E
**Pei-p'ing** *see* Beijing/Beijing Shi
**Peipsi Järv/Peipus-See** *see* Peipus, Lake
118 J5 **Peipus, Lake** *Est.* Peipsi Järv, *Ger.* Peipus-See, *Rus.* Chudskoye Ozero. ◎ Estonia/Russia
115 H19 **Peiraiás** *prev.* Piraiévs, *Eng.* Piraeus. Attikí, C Greece 37°57′N 23°42′E
**Peisern** *see* Pyzdry
60 I8 **Peixe, Rio do** ≈ S Brazil
59 I16 **Peixoto de Azevedo** Mato Grosso, W Brazil 10°18′S 55°03′W
168 O11 **Pejantan, Pulau** *island* W Indonesia
113 L16 **Pejë** *Serb.* Peć. W Kosovo 42°40′N 20°19′E
112 N11 **Pek** ≈ E Serbia
**Pèk** *see* Phônsaven
169 Q16 **Pekalongan** Jawa, C Indonesia 06°54′S 109°37′E
168 K11 **Pekanbaru** *var.* Pakanbaru. Sumatera, W Indonesia 0°31′N 101°27′E
30 L12 **Pekin** Illinois, N USA 40°34′N 89°38′W
**Peking** *see* Beijing/Beijing Shi
**Pelabohan Kelang/Pelabuhan Kelang** *see* Pelabuhan Klang
168 J9 **Pelabuhan Klang** *var.* Kuala Pelabohan Kelang, Pelabohan Kelang, Pelabuhan Kelang, Port Klang, Port Swettenham. Selangor, Peninsular Malaysia 02°57′N 101°24′E
120 L11 **Pelagie, Isole** *island group* SW Italy
**Pelagosa** *see* Palagruža
22 L5 **Pelahatchie** Mississippi, S USA 32°19′N 89°48′W
169 T14 **Pelaihari** *var.* Pleihari. Borneo, C Indonesia 03°48′S 114°45′E
103 U14 **Pelat, Mont** ▲ SE France 44°16′N 06°46′E
116 F12 **Peleaga, Vârful** *prev.* Vîrful Peleaga. ▲ W Romania 45°23′N 22°52′E
**Peleaga, Vîrful** *see* Peleaga, Vârful
123 O11 **Peleduy** Respublika Sakha (Yakutiya), NE Russia 59°39′N 112°36′E
14 C18 **Pelee Island** *island* Ontario, S Canada
45 Q11 **Pelée, Montagne** ▲ N Martinique 14°47′N 61°10′W
14 D18 **Pelee, Point** *headland* Ontario, S Canada 41°56′N 82°30′W
171 P12 **Pelei** Pulau Peleng, N Indonesia 01°26′S 123°27′E
**Peleliu** *see* Beliliou
171 P12 **Peleng, Pulau** *island* Kepulauan Banggai, N Indonesia
23 T7 **Pelham** Georgia, SE USA 31°07′N 84°09′W
111 E18 **Pelhřimov** *Ger.* Pilgram. Vysočina, C Czechia 49°26′N 15°14′E
39 W13 **Pelican** Chichagof Island, Alaska, USA 57°52′N 136°05′W
191 Z3 **Pelican Lagoon** ◎ Kiritimati, E Kiribati
29 U6 **Pelican Lake** ◎ Minnesota, N USA
29 V3 **Pelican Lake** ◎ Minnesota, N USA
30 L5 **Pelican Lake** ◎ Wisconsin, N USA
44 G1 **Pelican Point** Grand Bahama Island, N The Bahamas 26°39′N 78°09′W
83 B19 **Pelican Point** *headland* W Namibia 22°55′S 14°25′E
29 S6 **Pelican Rapids** Minnesota, N USA 46°34′N 96°04′W
**Pelican State** *see* Louisiana
11 U13 **Pelikan Narrows** Saskatchewan, C Canada 55°11′N 102°51′W
115 L18 **Pelinaío** ▲ Chíos, E Greece 38°31′N 26°01′E
**Pelinnaeum** *see* Pelinnaío
115 E16 **Pelinnaío** *anc.* Pelinnaeum. *ruins* Thessalía, C Greece
113 N20 **Pelister** ▲ SW North Macedonia 41°00′N 21°12′E
113 G15 **Pelješac** *peninsula* S Croatia
92 M12 **Pelkosenniemi** Lappi, NE Finland 67°06′N 27°30′E
29 W15 **Pella** Iowa, C USA 41°24′N 92°55′W
114 F13 **Pélla** *site of ancient city* Kentrikí Makedonía, N Greece
23 Q3 **Pell City** Alabama, S USA 33°35′N 86°17′W
61 A22 **Pellegrini** Buenos Aires, E Argentina 36°16′S 63°07′W
92 K12 **Pello** Lappi, NW Finland 66°47′N 24°E
100 G7 **Pellworm** *island* N Germany
10 H6 **Pelly** ≈ Yukon, NW Canada
**Pelly Bay** *see* Kugaaruk
10 I8 **Pelly Mountains** ▲▲ Yukon, W Canada
**Pélmonostor** *see* Beli Manastir
37 P13 **Pelona Mountain** ▲ New Mexico, SW USA 33°40′N 108°06′W
**Peloponnese/Peloponnesus** *see* Pelopónnisos
115 E20 **Pelopónnisos** *Eng.* Peloponnese. ◈ *region* S Greece
115 E20 **Pelopónnisos** *var.* Morea, *Eng.* Peloponnese; *anc.* Peloponnesus. *peninsula* S Greece
107 L23 **Peloritani, Monti** *anc.* Pelorus and Neptunius. ▲▲ Sicilia, Italy, C Mediterranean Sea
107 M22 **Peloro, Capo** *var.* Punta del Faro. *headland* S Italy 38°15′N 15°39′E
**Pelorus and Neptunius** *see* Peloritani, Monti
61 H17 **Pelotas** Rio Grande do Sul, S Brazil 31°45′S 52°20′W
61 I14 **Pelotas, Rio** ≈ S Brazil
92 K10 **Peltovuoma** *Lapp.* Bealdovuopmi. Lappi, N Finland 68°23′N 24°12′E
19 R4 **Pemadumcook Lake** ◎ Maine, NE USA
169 Q16 **Pemalang** Jawa, C Indonesia 06°53′S 109°07′E
169 P10 **Pemangkat** *var.* Pamangkat. Borneo, C Indonesia 01°11′N 109°00′E
**Pemar** *see* Paimio




◆ Country
● Country Capital
◇ Dependent Territory
○ Dependent Territory Capital
◈ Administrative Regions
✈ International Airport
▲ Mountain
▲▲ Mountain Range
⛰ Volcano
≈ River
◎ Lake
⊠ Reservoir

Pematangsiantar – Phuket


168 I9 **Pematangsiantar** Sumatera, W Indonesia 02°59′N 99°01′E
83 Q14 **Pemba** *prev.* Port Amelia, Porto Amélia. Cabo Delgado, NE Mozambique 13°S 40°35′E
81 J22 **Pemba** ◈ *region* E Tanzania
81 K21 **Pemba** *island* E Tanzania
83 Q14 **Pemba, Baia de** *inlet* NE Mozambique
81 J21 **Pemba Channel** *channel* E Tanzania
180 J14 **Pemberton** Western Australia 34°27′S 116°09′E
10 M16 **Pemberton** British Columbia, SW Canada 50°19′N 122°49′W
29 Q2 **Pembina** North Dakota, N USA 48°58′N 97°14′W
11 P15 **Pembina** ≈ Alberta, SW Canada
29 Q2 **Pembina** ≈ Canada/USA
171 X16 **Pembre** Papua, E Indonesia 07°49′S 138°01′E
14 K12 **Pembroke** Ontario, SE Canada 45°49′N 77°08′W
97 H21 **Pembroke** SW Wales, United Kingdom 51°41′N 04°55′W
23 W6 **Pembroke** Georgia, SE USA 32°09′N 81°35′W
21 U11 **Pembroke** North Carolina, SE USA 34°40′N 79°12′W
21 R7 **Pembroke** Virginia, NE USA 37°19′N 80°38′W
97 H21 **Pembroke** *cultural region* SW Wales, United Kingdom
**Pembuang, Sungai** *see* Seruyan, Sungai
43 S15 **Peña Blanca, Cerro** ▲ C Panama 08°39′N 80°39′W
104 K8 **Peña de Francia, Sierra de la** ▲▲ W Spain
104 G6 **Penafiel** *var.* Peñafiel. Porto, N Portugal 41°12′N 08°17′W
105 N6 **Peñafiel** Castilla y León, N Spain 41°36′N 04°07′W
**Peñafiel** *see* Penafiel
**Peñagolosa** *see* Penyagolosa
105 N7 **Peñalara, Pico de** ▲ C Spain 40°52′N 03°55′W
171 X16 **Penambo, Banjaran** *var.* Banjaran Tama Abu, Penambo Range. ▲▲ Indonesia/Malaysia
**Penambo Range** *see* Penambo, Banjaran
41 O10 **Peña Nevada, Cerro** ▲ C Mexico 23°46′N 99°52′W
**Penang** *see* Pinang, Pulau, Peninsular Malaysia
**Penang** *see* Pinang
**Penang** *see* George Town
60 J8 **Penápolis** São Paulo, S Brazil 21°23′S 50°02′W
104 L7 **Peñaranda de Bracamonte** Castilla y León, N Spain 40°54′N 05°13′W
105 S8 **Peñarroya** ▲ E Spain 40°24′N 00°42′W
104 L12 **Peñarroya-Pueblonuevo** Andalucía, S Spain 38°21′N 05°18′W
97 K22 **Penarth** S Wales, United Kingdom 51°27′N 03°11′W
104 K1 **Peñas, Cabo de** *headland* N Spain 43°39′N 05°52′W
63 F20 **Penas, Golfo de** *gulf* S Chile
**Pen-ch'i** *see* Benxi
79 H14 **Pendé** *var.* Logone Oriental. ≈ Central African Republic/Chad
76 I14 **Pendembu** E Sierra Leone 09°06′N 12°12′W
29 R13 **Pender** Nebraska, C USA 42°06′N 96°42′W
**Penderma** *see* Bandırma
32 K11 **Pendleton** Oregon, NW USA 45°40′N 118°47′W
32 M7 **Pend Oreille, Lake** ◎ Idaho, NW USA
32 M7 **Pend Oreille River** ≈ Idaho/Washington, NW USA
**Pendzhikent** *see* Panjakent
**Peneius** *see* Pineiós
104 G8 **Penela** Coimbra, N Portugal 40°02′N 08°23′W
14 G13 **Penetanguishene** Ontario, S Canada 44°45′N 79°55′W
151 H15 **Penganga** ≈ C India
**P'engchia Yu** *see* Pengjia Yu
79 M21 **Penge** Kasai-Oriental, C Dem. Rep. Congo 05°29′S 24°38′E
**Penghu Archipelago/P'enghu Ch'üntao/Penghu Islands** *see* Penghu Qundao
161 S14 **Penghu Gangdao** *var.* Pescadores Channel. *channel* W Taiwan
**P'enghu Liehtao** *see* Penghu Qundao
161 R14 **Penghu Qundao** *var.* P'enghu Ch'üntao, Penghu Islands, P'enghu Liehtao, Penghu Archipelago, *Eng.* Pescadores, *Jap.* Hoko-guntō, Hoko-shotō. *island group* W Taiwan
161 T12 **Pengjia Yu** *prev.* P'engchia Yu. *island* N Taiwan
161 R4 **Penglai** *var.* Dengzhou. Shandong, E China 37°50′N 120°45′E
**Peng-pu** *see* Bengbu
**Penhsihu** *see* Benxi
**Penibético, Sistema** *see* Béticos, Sistemas
104 F10 **Peniche** Leiria, W Portugal 39°21′N 09°23′W
169 U17 **Penida, Nusa** *island* S Indonesia
**Peninsular State** *see* Florida
105 T8 **Peníscola** *var.* Peñíscola. Comunitat Valenciana, E Spain 40°22′N 00°24′E
40 M13 **Pénjamo** Guanajuato, C Mexico 20°26′N 101°44′W
**Penki** *see* Benxi
102 F7 **Penmarch, Pointe de** *headland* NW France 47°46′N 04°34′W
107 L15 **Penna, Punta della** *headland* C Italy 42°10′N 14°43′E
107 K14 **Penne** Abruzzo, C Italy 42°28′N 13°57′E
**Penner** *see* Penneru
155 J18 **Penneru** *var.* Penner. ≈ C India
182 I10 **Penneshaw** South Australia 35°45′S 137°57′E
18 C14 **Penn Hills** Pennsylvania, NE USA 40°28′N 79°53′W
**Penninae, Alpes/Pennine, Alpi** *see* Pennine Alps
108 D11 **Pennine Alps** *Fr.* Alpes Pennines, *It.* Alpi Pennine, *Lat.* Alpes Penninae. ▲▲ Italy/Switzerland
**Pennine Chain** *see* Pennines
97 L15 **Pennines** *var.* Pennine Chain. ▲▲ N England, United Kingdom
**Pennines, Alpes** *see* Pennine Alps
21 O8 **Pennington Gap** Virginia, NE USA 36°45′N 83°01′W
18 I16 **Penns Grove** New Jersey, NE USA 39°42′N 75°27′W
18 I16 **Pennsville** New Jersey, NE USA 39°37′N 75°29′W
18 E14 **Pennsylvania** *off.* Commonwealth of Pennsylvania, ***also known as*** Keystone State. ◈ *state* NE USA
18 G10 **Penn Yan** New York, NE USA 42°39′N 77°02′W
124 H16 **Peno** Tverskaya Oblast', W Russia 56°55′N 32°44′E
19 R7 **Penobscot Bay** *bay* Maine, NE USA
19 S5 **Penobscot River** ≈ Maine, NE USA
182 K12 **Penola** South Australia 37°24′S 140°50′E
40 K9 **Peñón Blanco** Durango, C Mexico 25°12′N 100°50′W
182 E7 **Penong** South Australia 31°57′S 133°01′E
43 S16 **Penonomé** Coclé, C Panama 08°29′N 80°22′W
190 L13 **Penrhyn** *atoll* N Cook Islands
192 M9 **Penrhyn Basin** *undersea feature* C Pacific Ocean
183 S9 **Penrith** New South Wales, SE Australia 33°45′S 150°48′E
97 K15 **Penrith** NW England, United Kingdom 54°40′N 02°44′W
23 O9 **Pensacola** Florida, SE USA 30°25′N 87°13′W
23 O9 **Pensacola Bay** *bay* Florida, SE USA
195 N7 **Pensacola Mountains** ▲▲ Antarctica
182 L12 **Penshurst** Victoria, SE Australia 37°54′S 142°19′E
**Pentadáktylos** *see* Beşparmak Dağları
187 R13 **Pentecost** *Fr.* Pentecôte. *island* C Vanuatu
15 V4 **Pentecôte** ≈ Québec, SE Canada
**Pentecôte** *see* Pentecost
15 V4 **Pentecôte, Lac** ◎ Québec, SE Canada
8 H15 **Penticton** British Columbia, SW Canada 49°29′N 119°38′W
96 J6 **Pentland Firth** *strait* N Scotland, United Kingdom
96 J12 **Pentland Hills** *hill range* S Scotland, United Kingdom
171 Q12 **Penu** Pulau Taliabu, E Indonesia 01°43′S 125°09′E
155 H18 **Penukonda** Andhra Pradesh, E India 14°04′N 77°38′E
166 L7 **Penwegon** Bago, C Myanmar (Burma) 18°14′N 96°34′E
24 M8 **Penwell** Texas, SW USA 31°45′N 102°32′W
105 S8 **Penyagolosa** *var.* Peñagolosa. ▲ E Spain 40°10′N 00°15′W
97 J21 **Pen y Fan** ▲ SE Wales, United Kingdom 51°52′N 03°25′W
97 L16 **Pen-y-ghent** ▲ N England, United Kingdom 54°11′N 02°15′W
127 O6 **Penza** Penzenskaya Oblast', W Russia 53°11′N 45°E
97 G25 **Penzance** SW England, United Kingdom 50°08′N 05°33′W
127 N6 **Penzenskaya Oblast'** ◈ *province* W Russia
123 U7 **Penzhina** ≈ E Russia
123 U9 **Penzhinskaya Guba** *bay* E Russia
**Penzig** *see* Pieńsk
36 K13 **Peoria** Arizona, SW USA 33°34′N 112°14′W
30 L12 **Peoria** Illinois, N USA 40°42′N 89°35′W
30 L12 **Peoria Heights** Illinois, N USA 40°45′N 89°34′W
31 N11 **Peotone** Illinois, N USA 41°19′N 87°47′W
18 J11 **Pepacton Reservoir** ▣ New York, NE USA
76 I15 **Pepel** W Sierra Leone 08°39′N 13°04′W
30 I6 **Pepin, Lake** ▣ Minnesota/Wisconsin, N USA
99 L20 **Pepinster** Liège, E Belgium 50°34′N 05°49′E
113 L20 **Peqin** *var.* Peqini. Elbasan, C Albania 41°03′N 19°46′E
**Peqini** *see* Peqin
40 D7 **Pequeña, Punta** *headland* NW Mexico 26°13′N 112°34′W
168 J8 **Perak** ◈ *state* Peninsular Malaysia
105 R7 **Perales del Alfambra** Aragón, NE Spain 40°38′N 01°00′W
115 C15 **Pérama** *var.* Perama. Ípeiros, W Greece 39°42′N 20°51′E
**Perama** *see* Pérama
92 M13 **Perä-Posio** Lappi, NE Finland 66°10′N 27°56′E
15 Z6 **Percé** Québec, SE Canada 48°32′N 64°14′W
15 Z6 **Percé, Rocher** *island* Québec, S Canada
102 L5 **Perche, Collines de** ▲▲ N France
109 X4 **Perchtoldsdorf** Niederösterreich, NE Austria 48°06′N 16°16′E
180 L6 **Percival Lakes** *lakes* Western Australia
105 T3 **Perdido, Monte** ▲ NE Spain 42°41′N 00°01′E
23 O8 **Perdido River** ≈ Alabama/Florida, S USA
**Perece Vela Basin** *see* West Mariana Basin
116 G7 **Perechyn** Zakarpats'ka Oblast', W Ukraine 48°45′N 22°28′E
54 E10 **Pereira** Risaralda, W Colombia 04°47′N 75°46′W
60 I7 **Pereira Barreto** São Paulo, S Brazil 20°37′S 51°07′W
59 G15 **Pereirinha** Pará, N Brazil 08°18′S 57°30′W
127 N10 **Perelazovskiy** Volgogradskaya Oblast', SW Russia 49°10′N 42°30′E
127 S7 **Perelyub** Saratovskaya Oblast', W Russia 51°52′N 50°19′E
31 P7 **Pere Marquette River** ≈ Michigan, N USA
**Peremyshl** *see* Przemyśl
116 I5 **Peremyshlyany** L'vivs'ka Oblast', W Ukraine 49°42′N 24°33′E
**Pereshchepino** *see* Pereshchepyne
116 L9 **Pereshchepyne** *Rus.* Pereshchepino. Dnipropetrovs'ka Oblast', E Ukraine 48°59′N 35°22′E
124 L16 **Pereslavl'-Zalesskiy** Yaroslavskaya Oblast', W Russia 56°42′N 38°45′E
117 Y7 **Pereval's'k** Luhans'ka Oblast', E Ukraine 48°28′N 38°54′E
127 U7 **Perevolotskiy** Orenburgskaya Oblast', W Russia 51°54′N 54°05′E
**Pereyaslav-Khmel'nitskiy** *see* Pereyaslav-Khmel'nyts'kyy
117 Q5 **Pereyaslav-Khmel'nyts'kyy** *Rus.* Pereyaslav-Khmel'nitskiy. Kyivs'ka Oblast', N Ukraine 50°05′N 31°28′E
109 U4 **Perg** Oberösterreich, N Austria 48°15′N 14°38′E
61 B19 **Pergamino** Buenos Aires, E Argentina 33°56′S 60°38′W
106 G6 **Pergine Valsugana** *Ger.* Persen. Trentino-Alto Adige, N Italy 46°04′N 11°13′E
29 S6 **Perham** Minnesota, N USA 46°35′N 95°34′W
93 L16 **Perho** Keski-Pohjanmaa, W Finland 63°15′N 24°25′E
116 E11 **Periam** *Ger.* Perjamosch, *Hung.* Perjámos. Timiş, W Romania 46°02′N 20°54′E
15 Q6 **Péribonca** ≈ Québec, SE Canada
12 L11 **Péribonca, Lac** ◎ Québec, SE Canada
15 Q6 **Péribonca, Petite Rivière** ≈ Québec, SE Canada
15 Q7 **Péribonka** Québec, SE Canada 48°45′N 72°01′W
40 I9 **Pericos** Sinaloa, C Mexico 25°03′N 107°42′W
169 Q10 **Perigi** Borneo, C Indonesia
102 L12 **Périgueux** *anc.* Vesuna. Dordogne, SW France 45°12′N 00°41′E
54 G5 **Perijá, Serranía de** ▲▲ Columbia/Venezuela
115 H17 **Peristéra** *island* Vóreies Sporádes, Greece, Aegean Sea
63 H20 **Perito Moreno** Santa Cruz, S Argentina 46°35′S 71°W
155 G22 **Periyāl** *var.* Periyār. ≈ SW India
**Periyār** *see* Periyāl
155 G23 **Periyār Lake** ◎ S India
**Perjámos/Perjamosch** *see* Periam
27 O9 **Perkins** Oklahoma, C USA 35°58′N 97°01′W
116 L7 **Perkivtsi** Chernivets'ka Oblast', W Ukraine 48°28′N 26°48′E
43 U15 **Perlas, Archipiélago de las** *Eng.* Pearl Islands. *island group* SE Panama
43 O10 **Perlas, Cayos de** *reef* SE Nicaragua
43 N9 **Perlas, Laguna de** *Eng.* Pearl Lagoon. *lagoon* E Nicaragua
43 N10 **Perlas, Punta de** *headland* E Nicaragua 12°22′N 83°30′W
100 L11 **Perleberg** Brandenburg, N Germany 53°04′N 11°52′E
**Perlepe** *see* Prilep
168 I6 **Perlis** ◈ *state* Peninsular Malaysia
125 U14 **Perm'** *prev.* Molotov. Permskiy Kray, NW Russia 58°01′N 56°10′E
113 M22 **Përmet** *var.* Përmeti, Prëmet. Gjirokastër, S Albania 40°12′N 20°24′E
**Përmeti** *see* Përmet
125 U15 **Permskiy Kray** ◈ *province* NW Russia
59 P15 **Pernambuco** *off.* Estado de Pernambuco. ◈ *state* E Brazil
**Pernambuco** *see* Recife
**Pernambuco Abyssal Plain** *see* Pernambuco Plain
**Pernambuco, Estado de** *see* Pernambuco
47 Y6 **Pernambuco Plain** *var.* Pernambuco Abyssal Plain. *undersea feature* E Atlantic Ocean 07°30′S 27°00′W
65 K15 **Pernambuco Seamounts** *undersea feature* C Atlantic Ocean
182 H6 **Pernatty Lagoon** *salt lake* South Australia
**Pernau** *see* Pärnu
**Pernauer Bucht** *see* Pärnu Laht
**Pērnava** *see* Pärnu
114 G9 **Pernik** *prev.* Dimitrovo. Pernik, W Bulgaria 42°36′N 23°02′E
114 G10 **Pernik** ◈ *province* W Bulgaria
93 K20 **Perniö** *Swe.* Bjärnå. Varsinais-Suomi, SW Finland 60°13′N 23°10′E
109 X5 **Pernitz** Niederösterreich, E Austria 47°54′N 15°58′E
**Pernov** *see* Pärnu
103 O3 **Péronne** Somme, N France 49°56′N 02°57′E
14 L8 **Péronne, Lac** ◎ Québec, SE Canada
106 A8 **Perosa Argentina** Piemonte, NE Italy 45°02′N 07°10′E
41 Q14 **Perote** Veracruz, E Mexico 19°32′N 97°16′W
**Pérouse** *see* Perugia
191 W15 **Pérouse, Bahía de la** *bay* Easter Island, Chile, E Pacific Ocean
**Perovsk** *see* Kyzylorda
103 O17 **Perpignan** Pyrénées-Orientales, S France 42°41′N 02°53′E
113 M20 **Përrenjas** *var.* Përrenjasi, Prenjas, Prenjasi. Elbasan, E Albania 41°04′N 20°34′E
**Përrenjasi** *see* Përrenjas
92 O2 **Perriertoppen** ▲ C Svalbard 79°10′N 17°01′E
25 S6 **Perrin** Texas, SW USA 32°59′N 98°03′W
23 Y16 **Perrine** Florida, SE USA 25°36′N 80°21′W
37 S12 **Perro, Laguna del** ◎ New Mexico, SW USA
102 G5 **Perros-Guirec** Côtes d'Armor, NW France 48°49′N 03°28′W
23 T9 **Perry** Florida, SE USA 30°07′N 83°34′W
23 T5 **Perry** Georgia, SE USA 32°27′N 83°43′W
29 U14 **Perry** Iowa, C USA 41°50′N 94°06′W
18 E10 **Perry** New York, NE USA 42°43′N 78°00′W
27 N9 **Perry** Oklahoma, C USA 36°17′N 97°18′W
27 Q3 **Perry Lake** ▣ Kansas, C USA
31 R11 **Perrysburg** Ohio, N USA 41°33′N 83°37′W
25 O1 **Perryton** Texas, SW USA 36°23′N 100°48′W
39 O15 **Perryville** Alaska, USA 55°55′N 159°08′W
27 U11 **Perryville** Arkansas, C USA 35°00′N 92°48′W
27 Y6 **Perryville** Missouri, C USA 37°43′N 89°51′W
**Persante** *see* Parsęta
**Persen** *see* Pergine Valsugana
**Pershay** *see* Pyarshai
117 V7 **Pershotravens'k** Dnipropetrovs'ka Oblast', E Ukraine 48°19′N 36°22′E
**Pershotravneve** *see* Manhush
**Persia** *see* Iran
141 T5 **Persian Gulf** *var.* The Gulf, *Ar.* Khalīj al 'Arabī, *Per.* Khalīj-e Fars. *gulf* SW Asia
**Persis** *see* Fārs
95 K22 **Perstorp** Skåne, S Sweden 56°08′N 13°23′E
137 O14 **Pertek** Tunceli, C Turkey 38°53′N 39°19′E
183 P16 **Perth** Tasmania, SE Australia 41°39′S 147°11′E
180 I13 **Perth** *state capital* Western Australia 31°58′S 115°49′E
14 L13 **Perth** Ontario, SE Canada 44°54′N 76°15′W
96 J11 **Perth** C Scotland, United Kingdom 56°24′N 03°28′W
96 J10 **Perth** *cultural region* C Scotland, United Kingdom
180 I12 **Perth** ✈ Western Australia 31°51′S 116°06′E
173 V10 **Perth Basin** *undersea feature* SE Indian Ocean 28°30′S 110°00′E
103 S15 **Pertuis** Vaucluse, SE France 43°42′N 05°30′E
103 Y16 **Pertusato, Capo** *headland* Corse, France, C Mediterranean Sea 41°22′N 09°10′E
30 L11 **Peru** Illinois, N USA 41°18′N 89°09′W
31 P12 **Peru** Indiana, N USA 40°45′N 86°04′W
57 E13 **Peru** *off.* Republic of Peru. ◆ *republic* W South America
**Peru** *see* Beru
193 T9 **Peru Basin** *undersea feature* E Pacific Ocean 15°00′S 85°00′W
193 U8 **Peru-Chile Trench** *undersea feature* E Pacific Ocean 20°00′S 73°00′W
112 F13 **Perućko Jezero** ◎ S Croatia
106 H13 **Perugia** *Fr.* Pérouse; *anc.* Perusia. Umbria, C Italy 43°06′N 12°24′E
**Perugia, Lake of** *see* Trasimeno, Lago
61 D15 **Perugorría** Corrientes, NE Argentina 29°21′S 58°35′W
60 M11 **Peruíbe** São Paulo, S Brazil 24°18′S 47°01′W
155 B21 **Perumalpār** *reef* India, N Indian Ocean
**Peru, Republic of** *see* Peru
**Perusia** *see* Perugia
99 D20 **Péruwelz** Hainaut, SW Belgium 50°30′N 03°35′E
137 R15 **Pervari** Siirt, SE Turkey 37°55′N 42°32′E
127 O4 **Pervomaysk** Nizhegorodskaya Oblast', W Russia 54°52′N 43°49′E
117 X7 **Pervomays'k** Luhans'ka Oblast', E Ukraine 48°38′N 38°36′E
117 P8 **Pervomays'k** *prev.* Ol'viopol'. Mykolayivs'ka Oblast', S Ukraine 48°02′N 30°51′E
117 S12 **Pervomays'ke** Avtonomna Respublika Krym, S Ukraine 45°43′N 33°49′E
127 V7 **Pervomayskiy** Orenburgskaya Oblast', W Russia 51°32′N 54°58′E
126 M6 **Pervomayskiy** Tambovskaya Oblast', W Russia 53°15′N 40°20′E
117 V6 **Pervomays'kyy** Kharkivs'ka Oblast', E Ukraine 49°24′N 36°12′E
122 F10 **Pervoural'sk** Sverdlovskaya Oblast', C Russia 56°58′N 59°50′E
123 V11 **Pervyy Kuril'skiy Proliv** *strait* E Russia
99 I19 **Perwez** Walloon Brabant, C Belgium 50°39′N 04°49′E
106 I11 **Pesaro** *anc.* Pisaurum. Marche, C Italy 43°55′N 12°53′E
35 N9 **Pescadero** California, W USA 37°15′N 122°23′W
**Pescadores** *see* Penghu Qundao
**Pescadores Channel** *see* Penghu Gangdao
107 K14 **Pescara** *anc.* Aternum, Ostia Aterni. Abruzzo, C Italy 42°28′N 14°13′E
107 K15 **Pescara** ≈ C Italy
106 F11 **Pescia** Toscana, C Italy 43°54′N 10°41′E
108 C8 **Peseux** Neuchâtel, W Switzerland 46°59′N 06°53′E
125 P6 **Pësha** ≈ NW Russia
149 T5 **Peshawar** Khyber Pakhtunkhwa, N Pakistan 34°01′N 71°33′E
149 T6 **Peshawar** ✈ Khyber Pakhtunkhwa, N Pakistan 34°01′N 71°40′E
113 M19 **Peshkopi** *var.* Peshkopia, Peshkopija. Dibër, NE Albania 41°40′N 20°25′E
**Peshkopia/Peshkopija** *see* Peshkopi
114 I11 **Peshtera** Pazardzhik, C Bulgaria 42°02′N 24°18′E
31 N6 **Peshtigo** Wisconsin, N USA 45°04′N 87°43′W
31 N6 **Peshtigo River** ≈ Wisconsin, N USA
**Peski** *see* Pyaski
125 S13 **Peskovka** Kirovskaya Oblast', NW Russia 59°04′N 52°17′E
103 S8 **Pesmes** Haute-Saône, E France 47°17′N 05°33′E
104 H6 **Peso da Régua** *var.* Pêso da Regua. Vila Real, N Portugal 41°10′N 07°47′W
40 F5 **Pesqueira** Sonora, NW Mexico 29°22′N 110°58′W
102 J13 **Pessac** Gironde, SW France 44°46′N 00°42′W
111 J23 **Pest** *off.* Pest Megye. ◈ *county* C Hungary
**Pest Megye** *see* Pest
124 J14 **Pestovo** Novgorodskaya Oblast', W Russia 58°37′N 35°48′E
40 M15 **Petacalco, Bahía** *bay* W Mexico
**Petach-Tikva** *see* Petah Tikva
138 F10 **Petah Tikva** *var.* Petach-Tikva, Petah Tiqva, Petakh Tikva; *prev.* Petah Tiqwa. Tel Aviv, C Israel 32°05′N 34°53′E
**Petah Tiqwa** *see* Petah Tikva
93 L17 **Petäjävesi** Keski-Suomi, C Finland 62°17′N 25°10′E
**Petakh Tikva/Petah Tiqva** *see* Petah Tikva
22 M7 **Petal** Mississippi, S USA 31°21′N 89°15′W
115 I19 **Petalioí** *island* C Greece
115 H19 **Petalión, Kólpos** *gulf* E Greece
115 J19 **Pétalo** ▲ Ándros, Kykládes, Greece, Aegean Sea 37°51′N 24°50′E
34 M8 **Petaluma** California, W USA 38°15′N 122°37′W
99 L25 **Pétange** Luxembourg, SW Luxembourg 49°33′N 05°53′E
54 M5 **Petare** Miranda, N Venezuela 10°31′N 66°50′W
41 N16 **Petatlán** Guerrero, S Mexico 17°31′N 101°16′W
83 L14 **Petauke** Eastern, E Zambia 14°12′S 31°16′E
14 J12 **Petawawa** Ontario, SE Canada 45°54′N 77°18′W
14 J11 **Petawawa** ≈ Ontario, SE Canada
**Petchaburi** *see* Phetchaburi
42 D2 **Petén** *off.* Departamento del Petén. ◈ *department* N Guatemala
**Petén, Departamento del** *see* Petén
42 D2 **Petén Itzá, Lago** *var.* Lago de Flores. ◎ N Guatemala
30 K7 **Petenwell Lake** ▣ Wisconsin, N USA
14 D6 **Peterbell** Ontario, S Canada 48°34′N 83°19′W
182 I7 **Peterborough** South Australia 32°59′S 138°51′E
14 I14 **Peterborough** Ontario, SE Canada 44°19′N 78°20′W
97 N20 **Peterborough** *prev.* Medeshamstede. E England, United Kingdom 52°35′N 00°15′W
19 N10 **Peterborough** New Hampshire, NE USA 42°51′N 71°54′W
96 L8 **Peterhead** NE Scotland, United Kingdom 57°30′N 01°46′W
**Peterhof** *see* Luboń
**Peter I øy** *see* Peter I Øy
193 Q14 **Peter I Øy** ◈ *Norwegian dependency* Antarctica
194 H9 **Peter I Øy** *var.* Peter I øy. *island* Antarctica
97 M14 **Peterlee** N England, United Kingdom 54°45′N 01°18′W
**Peterlingen** *see* Payerne
197 P14 **Petermann Bjerg** ▲ C Greenland 73°16′N 27°59′W
11 S12 **Peter Pond Lake** ◎ Saskatchewan, C Canada
39 X13 **Petersburg** Mytkof Island, Alaska, USA 56°43′N 132°51′W
30 K13 **Petersburg** Illinois, N USA 40°01′N 89°52′W
31 N16 **Petersburg** Indiana, N USA 38°30′N 87°16′W
29 Q3 **Petersburg** North Dakota, N USA 47°59′N 97°59′W
25 N5 **Petersburg** Texas, SW USA 33°52′N 101°36′W
21 V7 **Petersburg** Virginia, NE USA 37°14′N 77°24′W
21 T4 **Petersburg** West Virginia, NE USA 39°01′N 79°09′W
100 H12 **Petershagen** Nordrhein-Westfalen, NW Germany 52°22′N 08°58′E
55 S9 **Peters Mine** *var.* Peter's Mine. N Guyana 06°13′N 59°18′W
107 O21 **Petilia Policastro** Calabria, SW Italy 39°07′N 16°48′E
44 M9 **Pétionville** S Haiti 18°29′N 72°16′W
45 X6 **Petit-Bourg** Basse Terre, C Guadeloupe 16°12′N 61°36′W
15 Y5 **Petit-Cap** Québec, SE Canada 49°00′N 64°26′W
45 Y6 **Petit Cul-de-Sac Marin** *bay* C Guadeloupe
44 M9 **Petite-Rivière-de-l'Artibonite** C Haiti 19°10′N 72°30′W
173 X16 **Petite Rivière Noire, Piton de la** ▲ C Mauritius
15 R9 **Petite-Rivière-St-François** Québec, SE Canada 47°18′N 70°34′W
44 L9 **Petit-Goâve** S Haiti 18°27′N 72°51′W
**Petitjean** *see* Sidi-Kacem
13 N10 **Petit Lac Manicouagan** ◎ Québec, E Canada
19 T7 **Petit Manan Point** *headland* Maine, NE USA 44°23′N 67°54′W
**Petit Mécatina, Rivière du** *see* Little Mecatina
11 N10 **Petitot** ≈ Alberta/British Columbia, W Canada
45 S12 **Petit Piton** ▲ SW Saint Lucia 13°49′N 61°03′W
**Petit-Popo** *see* Aného
**Petit St-Bernard, Col du** *see* Little Saint Bernard Pass
13 O8 **Petitsikapau Lake** ◎ Newfoundland and Labrador, E Canada
92 L11 **Petkula** Lappi, N Finland 67°41′N 26°44′E
41 X12 **Peto** Yucatán, SE Mexico 20°09′N 88°55′W
62 G10 **Petorca** Valparaíso, C Chile 32°18′S 70°49′W
31 Q5 **Petoskey** Michigan, N USA 45°51′N 88°03′W
138 G14 **Petra** *archaeological site* Ma'ān, W Jordan
**Petra** *see* Wādī Mūsā
115 F14 **Pétras, Sténa** *pass* N Greece
123 S16 **Petra Velikogo, Zaliv** *bay* SE Russia
**Petrel** *see* Petrer
14 K15 **Petre, Point** *headland* Ontario, SE Canada 43°49′N 77°07′W
105 S12 **Petrer** *var.* Petrel. Comunitat Valenciana, E Spain 38°28′N 00°46′W
125 U11 **Petretsovo** Permskiy Kray, NW Russia 61°22′N 57°21′E
114 G12 **Petrich** Blagoevgrad, SW Bulgaria 41°25′N 23°12′E
187 P15 **Petrie, Récif** *reef* N New Caledonia
37 N11 **Petrified Forest** *prehistoric site* Arizona, SW USA
**Petrikau** *see* Piotrków Trybunalski
**Petrikov** *see* Pyetrykaw
116 H12 **Petrila** *Hung.* Petrilla. Hunedoara, W Romania 45°27′N 23°25′E
**Petrilla** *see* Petrila
112 E9 **Petrinja** Sisak-Moslavina, C Croatia 45°27′N 16°14′E
**Petroaleksandrovsk** *see* To'rtkok'l
**Petrőcz** *see* Bački Petrovac
124 G12 **Petrodvorets** *Fin.* Pietarhovi. Leningradskaya Oblast', NW Russia 59°53′N 29°52′E
**Petrograd** *see* Sankt-Peterburg
**Petrokov** *see* Piotrków Trybunalski
54 G6 **Petrólea** Norte de Santander, NE Colombia 08°30′N 72°35′W
14 D16 **Petrolia** Ontario, S Canada 42°54′N 82°07′W
25 S4 **Petrolia** Texas, SW USA 34°00′N 98°13′W
59 O15 **Petrolina** Pernambuco, E Brazil 09°22′S 40°30′W
45 T6 **Petrona, Punta** *headland* C Puerto Rico 17°57′N 66°23′W
**Petropavl** *see* Petropavlovsk
117 V7 **Petropavlivka** Dnipropetrovs'ka Oblast', E Ukraine 48°28′N 36°28′E
145 P6 **Petropavlovsk** *Kaz.* Petropavl. Severnyy Kazakhstan, N Kazakhstan 54°47′N 69°06′E
123 V11 **Petropavlovsk-Kamchatskiy** Kamchatskiy Kray, E Russia 53°03′N 158°43′E
60 P9 **Petrópolis** Rio de Janeiro, SE Brazil 22°30′S 43°28′W
116 H12 **Petroşani** *var.* Petroşeni, *Ger.* Petroschen, *Hung.* Petrozsény. Hunedoara, W Romania 45°25′N 23°22′E
**Petroschen/Petroşeni** *see* Petroşani
**Petroskoi** *see* Petrozavodsk
112 N12 **Petrovac** Serbia, E Serbia 42°22′N 21°25′E
**Petrovac** *see* Bosanski Petrovac
113 J17 **Petrovac na Moru** S Montenegro 42°11′N 19°00′E
**Petrovac/Petrovácz** *see* Bački Petrovac
117 S8 **Petrove** Kirovohrads'ka Oblast', C Ukraine 48°22′N 33°12′E
113 O18 **Petrovec** C North Macedonia 41°57′N 21°37′E
**Petrovgrad** *see* Zrenjanin
127 P7 **Petrovsk** Saratovskaya Oblast', W Russia 52°20′N 45°23′E
**Petrovsk-Port** *see* Makhachkala
127 P9 **Petrov Val** Volgogradskaya Oblast', SW Russia 50°10′N 45°16′E
124 J11 **Petrozavodsk** *Fin.* Petroskoi. Respublika Kareliya, NW Russia 61°46′N 34°19′E
**Petrozsény** *see* Petroşani
83 D20 **Petrusdal** Hardap, C Namibia 23°42′S 17°23′E
117 T7 **Petrykivka** Dnipropetrovs'ka Oblast', E Ukraine 48°44′N 34°42′E
**Petsamo** *see* Pechenga
**Petschka** *see* Pecica
**Pettau** *see* Ptuj
109 S5 **Pettenbach** Oberösterreich, C Austria 47°58′N 14°03′E
25 S13 **Pettus** Texas, SW USA 28°34′N 97°49′W
122 G12 **Petukhovo** Kurganskaya Oblast', C Russia 55°04′N 67°49′E
**Petuna** *see* Songyuan
109 R4 **Peuerbach** Oberösterreich, N Austria 48°19′N 13°45′E
62 G12 **Peumo** O'Higgins, C Chile 34°20′S 71°12′W
123 T6 **Pevek** Chukotskiy Avtonomnyy Okrug, NE Russia 69°41′N 170°19′E
27 X5 **Pevely** Missouri, C USA 38°16′N 90°24′W
**Peyia** *see* Pégeia
102 J15 **Peyrehorade** Landes, SW France 43°33′N 01°05′W
124 J14 **Peza** ≈ NW Russia
103 P16 **Pézenas** Hérault, S France 43°28′N 03°25′E
111 H20 **Pezinok** *Ger.* Bösing, *Hung.* Bazin. Bratislavský Kraj, W Slovakia 48°17′N 17°15′E
101 L22 **Pfaffenhofen an der Ilm** Bayern, SE Germany 48°31′N 11°30′E
108 G7 **Pfäffikon** Schwyz, C Switzerland 47°11′N 08°46′E
101 F20 **Pfälzer Wald** *hill range* W Germany
101 N22 **Pfarrkirchen** Bayern, SE Germany 48°25′N 12°56′E
101 G21 **Pforzheim** Baden-Württemberg, SW Germany 48°53′N 08°42′E
101 H24 **Pfullendorf** Baden-Württemberg, S Germany 47°55′N 09°16′E
108 K8 **Pfunds** Tirol, W Austria 46°56′N 10°30′E
101 G19 **Pfungstadt** Hessen, W Germany 49°48′N 08°36′E
83 L20 **Phalaborwa** *var.* Ba-Pahalaborwa. Limpopo, NE South Africa 23°59′S 31°04′E
152 E11 **Phalodi** Rājasthān, NW India 27°06′N 72°22′E
152 E12 **Phalsund** Rājasthān, NW India 26°22′N 71°56′E
155 E15 **Phaltan** Mahārāshtra, W India 18°01′N 74°31′E
167 O7 **Phan** *var.* Muang Phan. Chiang Rai, NW Thailand 19°34′N 99°44′E
167 O14 **Phangan, Ko** *island* SW Thailand
166 M15 **Phang-Nga** *var.* Pang-Nga, Phangnga. Phangnga, SW Thailand 08°29′N 98°31′E
**Phangnga** *see* Phang-Nga
**Phan Rang/Phanrang** *see* Phan Rang-Thap Cham
167 V13 **Phan Rang-Thap Cham** *var.* Phanrang, Phan Rang, Phan Rang Thap Cham. Ninh Thuân, S Vietnam 11°34′N 109°00′E
167 U13 **Phan Ri** Binh Thuân, S Vietnam 11°11′N 108°31′E
167 U13 **Phan Thiêt** Binh Thuân, S Vietnam 10°56′N 108°06′E
**Pharnacia** *see* Giresun
25 S17 **Pharr** Texas, SW USA 26°11′N 98°10′W
**Pharus** *see* Hvar
167 N16 **Phatthalung** *var.* Padalung, Patalung. Phatthalung, SW Thailand 07°38′N 100°04′E
167 O7 **Phayao** *var.* Muang Phayao. Phayao, NW Thailand 19°10′N 99°55′E
11 U10 **Phelps Lake** ◎ Saskatchewan, C Canada
21 X9 **Phelps Lake** ◎ North Carolina, SE USA
23 R5 **Phenix City** Alabama, S USA 32°28′N 85°00′W
**Phet Buri** *see* Phetchaburi
167 O11 **Phetchaburi** *var.* Bejraburi, Petchaburi, Phet Buri. Phetchaburi, SW Thailand 13°05′N 99°58′E
167 O9 **Phichit** *var.* Bichitra, Muang Phichit, Pichit. Phichit, C Thailand 16°29′N 100°21′E
22 M5 **Philadelphia** Mississippi, S USA 32°45′N 89°06′W
18 I7 **Philadelphia** New York, NE USA 44°10′N 75°40′W
18 I16 **Philadelphia** Pennsylvania, NE USA 40°N 75°10′W
18 I16 **Philadelphia** ✈ Pennsylvania, NE USA 39°51′N 75°13′W
**Philadelphia** *see* 'Amman
28 L10 **Philip** South Dakota, N USA 44°02′N 101°39′W
99 H22 **Philippeville** Namur, S Belgium 50°12′N 04°33′E
**Philippeville** *see* Skikda
21 S3 **Philippi** West Virginia, NE USA 39°08′N 80°03′W
**Philippi** *see* Fílippoi
195 Y9 **Philippi Glacier** *glacier* Antarctica
192 G6 **Philippine Basin** *undersea feature* W Pacific Ocean 17°00′N 132°00′E
129 X12 **Philippine Plate** *tectonic feature*
171 O5 **Philippines** *off.* Republic of the Philippines, *Fil.* Pilipinas, Republika ng Pilipinas. ◆ *republic* SE Asia
129 X13 **Philippines** *island group* W Pacific Ocean
171 P3 **Philippine Sea** *sea* W Pacific Ocean
**Philippines, Republic of the** *see* Philippines
192 F6 **Philippine Trench** *undersea feature* W Philippine Sea
83 H23 **Philippolis** Free State, C South Africa 30°16′S 25°16′E
**Philippopolis** *see* Plovdiv
**Philippopolis** *see* Shahbā', Syria
45 V9 **Philipsburg** ○ Sint Maarten 17°58′N 63°02′W
33 P10 **Philipsburg** Montana, NW USA 46°19′N 113°17′W
39 R6 **Philip Smith Mountains** ▲▲ Alaska, USA
152 H8 **Phillaur** Punjab, N India 31°02′N 75°50′E
183 N13 **Phillip Island** *island* Victoria, SE Australia
25 N2 **Phillips** Texas, SW USA 35°39′N 101°21′W
30 K5 **Phillips** Wisconsin, N USA 45°42′N 90°23′W
26 K3 **Phillipsburg** Kansas, C USA 39°45′N 99°19′W
18 I14 **Phillipsburg** New Jersey, NE USA 40°39′N 75°09′W
21 S7 **Philpott Lake** ▣ Virginia, NE USA
**Phintias** *see* Licata
167 P9 **Phitsanulok** *var.* Bisnulok, Muang Phitsanulok, Pitsanulok. Phitsanulok, C Thailand 16°49′N 100°15′E
**Phlórina** *see* Flórina
167 S13 **Phnom Penh** *Khm.* Phnum Pénh. ● (Cambodia) Phnum Penh, S Cambodia 11°35′N 104°55′E
**Phnum Pénh** *see* Phnom Penh
36 K13 **Phoenix** *state capital* Arizona, SW USA 33°27′N 112°04′W
**Phoenix Island** *see* Rawaki
191 R3 **Phoenix Islands** *island group* C Kiribati
18 I15 **Phoenixville** Pennsylvania, NE USA 40°07′N 75°31′W
83 K22 **Phofung** *var.* Mont-aux-Sources. ▲ N Lesotho 28°47′S 28°52′E
167 Q10 **Phon** Khon Kaen, E Thailand 15°47′N 102°35′E
167 Q5 **Phôngsali** *var.* Phong Saly. Phôngsali, N Laos 21°40′N 102°04′E
**Phong Saly** *see* Phôngsali
**Phônhông** *see* Ban Phônhông
167 R7 **Phônsaven** *var.* Pèk, Xieng Khouang; *prev.* Xiangkhoang. Xiangkhoang, N Laos 19°19′N 103°23′E
167 R5 **Phô Rang** *var.* Bao Yèn. Lao Cai, N Vietnam 22°12′N 104°27′E
**Phort Láirge, Cuan** *see* Waterford Harbour
**Phou Louang** *see* Annamite Mountains
167 N10 **Phra Chedi Sam Ong** Kanchanaburi, W Thailand 15°18′N 98°26′E
167 O8 **Phrae** *var.* Muang Phrae, Prae. Phrae, NW Thailand 18°07′N 100°09′E
**Phra Nakhon Si Ayutthaya** *see* Ayutthaya
167 M14 **Phra Thong, Ko** *island* SW Thailand
**Phu Cường** *see* Thu Dâu Một
166 M15 **Phuket** *var.* Bhuket, Puket, *Mal.* Ujung Salang; *prev.* Junkseylon, Salang. Phuket, SW Thailand 07°52′N 98°22′E


◆ Country ● Country Capital ◇ Dependent Territory ○ Dependent Territory Capital ◈ Administrative Regions ✈ International Airport ▲ Mountain ▲▲ Mountain Range Volcano ≈ River ◎ Lake ▣ Reservoir

◆ Country  ● Country Capital  ◇ Dependent Territory  ○ Dependent Territory Capital  ✦ Administrative Regions  ✕ International Airport  ▲ Mountain  ▲ Mountain Range  ♒ River  ⌖ Volcano  ☒ Lake  ☒ Reservoir

PLECHÝ – PORTALEGRE


111 *B19* **Plechý** *var.* Plöckenstein. ▲ Austria/Czechia *48°45′N 13°50′E*
**Pleebo** *see* Plibo
**Pleihari** *see* Pelaihari
167 *U11* **Plei Ku** *prev.* Plây Cu. Gia Lai, C Vietnam *13°57′N 108°01′E*
101 *M16* **Pleisse** ≈ E Germany
**Plencia** *see* Plentzia
184 *O7* **Plenty, Bay of** *bay* North Island, New Zealand
33 *Y6* **Plentywood** Montana, NW USA *48°46′N 104°33′W*
105 *O2* **Plentzia** *var.* Plencia. País Vasco, N Spain *43°25′N 02°56′W*
102 *H5* **Plérin** Côtes d'Armor, NW France *48°33′N 02°46′W*
124 *M10* **Plesetsk** Arkhangel'skaya Oblast', NW Russia *62°41′N 40°14′E*
**Pleshchenitsy** *see* Plyeshchanitsy
**Pleskau** *see* Pskov
**Pleskauer See** *see* Pskov, Lake
**Pleskava** *see* Pskov
112 *E8* **Pleso International** ✈ (Zagreb) Zagreb, NW Croatia *45°45′N 16°00′E*
**Pless** *see* Pszczyna
15 *Q11* **Plessisville** Québec, SE Canada *46°14′N 71°46′W*
110 *H12* **Pleszew** Wielkopolskie, C Poland *51°54′N 17°47′E*
12 *L10* **Plétipi, Lac** ◎ Québec, SE Canada
101 *F15* **Plettenberg** Nordrhein-Westfalen, W Germany *51°13′N 07°52′E*
114 *I8* **Pleven** *prev.* Plevna. Pleven, N Bulgaria *43°25′N 24°36′E*
114 *I8* **Pleven** ◈ *province* N Bulgaria
**Plevlja/Plevlje** *see* Pljevlja
**Plevna** *see* Pleven
**Plezzo** *see* Bovec
**Pliberk** *see* Bleiburg
76 *L17* **Plibo** *var.* Pleebo. SE Liberia *04°38′N 07°41′W*
121 *R11* **Pliny Trench** *undersea feature* C Mediterranean Sea
118 *K13* **Plisa** *Rus.* Plissa. Vitsyebskaya Voblasts', N Belarus *55°13′N 27°57′E*
**Plissa** *see* Plisa
112 *D11* **Plitvica Selo** Lika-Senj, W Croatia *44°53′N 15°36′E*
112 *D11* **Plješevica** ▲▲ C Croatia
113 *K14* **Pljevlja** *prev.* Plevlja, Plevlje. N Montenegro *43°21′N 19°21′E*
**Ploça** *see* Ploçë
**Plocce** *see* Ploče
113 *K22* **Ploçë** *var.* Ploça. Vlorë, SW Albania *40°24′N 19°41′E*
113 *G15* **Ploče** *It.* Plocce; *prev.* Kardeljevo. Dubrovnik-Neretva, SE Croatia *43°02′N 17°25′E*
110 *K11* **Płock** *Ger.* Plozk. Mazowieckie, C Poland *52°32′N 19°40′E*
109 *Q10* **Plöcken Pass** *Ger.* Plöckenpass, *It.* Passo di Monte Croce Carnico. *pass* SW Austria
**Plöckenpass** *see* Plöcken Pass
**Plöckenstein** *see* Plechý
99 *B19* **Ploegsteert** Hainaut, W Belgium *50°45′N 02°52′E*
102 *H6* **Ploërmel** Morbihan, NW France *47°57′N 02°24′W*
**Ploeşti** *see* Ploieşti
116 *K13* **Ploieşti** *prev.* Ploeşti. Prahova, SE Romania *44°56′N 26°03′E*
115 *L17* **Plomári** *prev.* Plomárion. Lésvos, E Greece *38°58′N 26°24′E*
**Plomárion** *see* Plomári
103 *O12* **Plomb du Cantal** ▲ C France *45°03′N 02°48′E*
183 *V6* **Plomer, Point** *headland* New South Wales, SE Australia *31°19′S 153°00′E*
100 *J8* **Plön** Schleswig-Holstein, N Germany *54°10′N 10°25′E*
110 *L11* **Płońsk** Mazowieckie, C Poland *52°38′N 20°23′E*
119 *J20* **Plotnitsa** Brestskaya Voblasts', SW Belarus *52°03′N 26°39′E*
110 *E8* **Płoty** *Ger.* Plathe. Zachodnio-pomorskie, NW Poland *53°48′N 15°16′E*
102 *G7* **Plouay** Morbihan, NW France *47°54′N 03°14′W*
111 *D15* **Ploučnice** *Ger.* Polzen. ≈ NE Czechia
114 *I10* **Plovdiv** *prev.* Eumolpias; *anc.* Evmolpia, Philippopolis, *Lat.* Trimontium. Plovdiv, C Bulgaria *42°09′N 24°47′E*
114 *I11* **Plovdiv** ◈ *province* C Bulgaria
30 *L6* **Plover** Wisconsin, N USA *44°30′N 89°33′W*
**Plozk** *see* Płock
27 *U11* **Plumerville** Arkansas, C USA *35°09′N 92°38′W*
19 *P10* **Plum Island** *island* Massachusetts, NE USA
32 *M9* **Plummer** Idaho, NW USA *47°19′N 116°54′W*
83 *J18* **Plumtree** Matabeleland South, SW Zimbabwe *20°30′S 27°50′E*
118 *D11* **Plungė** Telšiai, W Lithuania *55°55′N 21°53′E*
113 *J15* **Plužine** NW Montenegro *43°08′N 18°49′E*
119 *K14* **Plyeshchanitsy** *Rus.* Pleshchenitsy. Minskaya Voblasts', N Belarus *54°25′N 27°50′E*
97 *I24* **Plymouth** SW England, United Kingdom *50°23′N 04°10′W*
31 *O11* **Plymouth** Indiana, N USA *41°20′N 86°19′W*
19 *P12* **Plymouth** Massachusetts, NE USA *41°57′N 70°40′W*
19 *N8* **Plymouth** New Hampshire, NE USA *43°43′N 71°39′W*
21 *X9* **Plymouth** North Carolina, SE USA *35°53′N 76°46′W*
30 *M8* **Plymouth** Wisconsin, N USA *43°48′N 87°58′W*
**Plymouth** *see* Brades
97 *J20* **Plynlimon** ▲ C Wales, United Kingdom *52°27′N 03°48′W*
124 *G14* **Plyussa** Pskovskaya Oblast', W Russia *58°27′N 29°21′E*
111 *B17* **Plzeň** *Ger.* Pilsen, *Pol.* Pilzno. Plzeňský Kraj, W Czechia *49°45′N 13°23′E*
111 *B17* **Plzeňský Kraj** ◈ *region* W Czechia
110 *F11* **Pniewy** *Ger.* Pinne. Wielkolpolskie, W Poland *52°31′N 16°14′E*
77 *P13* **Pô** S Burkina Faso *11°11′N 01°10′W*
106 *D8* **Po** ≈ N Italy
42 *M13* **Poás, Volcán** ⛰ NW Costa Rica *10°12′N 84°12′W*
77 *S16* **Pobè** S Benin *07°00′N 02°41′E*
123 *S8* **Pobeda, Gora** ▲ NE Russia *65°28′N 145°44′E*
**Pobeda Peak** *see* Pobedy, Pik/Tomur Feng
147 *Z7* **Pobedy, Pik** *Chin.* Tomür Feng. ▲ China/Kyrgyzstan *42°02′N 80°02′E* ***see also*** Tomür Feng
**Pobedy, Pik** *see* Tomür Feng
110 *H11* **Pobiedziska** *Ger.* Pudewitz. Wielkolpolskie, C Poland *52°30′N 17°19′E*
**Po, Bocche del** *see* Po, Foci del
27 *W9* **Pocahontas** Arkansas, C USA *36°15′N 91°00′W*
29 *U12* **Pocahontas** Iowa, C USA *42°44′N 94°40′W*
33 *Q15* **Pocatello** Idaho, NW USA *42°52′N 112°27′W*
167 *S13* **Pochentong** ✈ (Phnum Penh) Phnum Penh, S Cambodia *11°24′N 104°52′E*
126 *I6* **Pochep** Bryanskaya Oblast', W Russia *52°56′N 33°20′E*
126 *H4* **Pochinok** Smolenskaya Oblast', W Russia *54°21′N 32°29′E*
41 *R17* **Pochutla** *var.* San Pedro Pochutla. Oaxaca, SE Mexico *15°45′N 96°30′W*
62 *I6* **Pocitos, Salar** *var.* Salar Quiróm. *salt lake* NW Argentina
101 *O22* **Pocking** Bayern, SE Germany *48°22′N 13°17′E*
186 *I10* **Pocklington Reef** *reef* SE Papua New Guinea
59 *P15* **Poço da Cruz, Açude** ⊞ E Brazil
27 *R11* **Pocola** Oklahoma, C USA *35°13′N 94°28′W*
21 *Y5* **Pocomoke City** Maryland, NE USA *38°04′N 75°34′W*
59 *L21* **Poços de Caldas** Minas Gerais, NE Brazil *21°48′S 46°33′W*
124 *H14* **Podberez'ye** Novgorodskaya Oblast', NW Russia *58°42′N 31°22′E*
**Podbrodzie** *see* Pabradė
125 *U8* **Podcher'ye** Respublika Komi, NW Russia *63°55′N 57°34′E*
111 *E16* **Poděbrady** *Ger.* Podiebrad. Středočeský Kraj, C Czechia *50°10′N 15°06′E*
126 *L9* **Podgorenskiy** Voronezhskaya Oblast', W Russia *50°22′N 39°43′E*
113 *J17* **Podgorica** *prev.* Titograd. ● S Montenegro *42°25′N 19°16′E*
113 *K17* **Podgorica** ✈ S Montenegro *42°22′N 19°16′E*
109 *T13* **Podgrad** SW Slovenia *45°31′N 14°09′E*
**Podiebrad** *see* Poděbrady
117 *O9* **Podil's'k** *prev.* Kotovs'k. Odes'ka Oblast', SW Ukraine *47°42′N 29°30′E*
116 *M5* **Podil's'ka Vysochina** *plateau* W Ukraine
**Podium Anicensis** *see* le Puy
122 *L11* **Podkamennaya Tunguska** *Eng.* Stony Tunguska. ≈ C Russia
111 *N17* **Podkarpackie** ◈ *province* SW Poland
**Pod Klošter** *see* Arnoldstein
110 *P9* **Podlaskie** ◈ *province* Mazowieckie, C Poland
127 *Q8* **Podlesnoye** Saratovskaya Oblast', W Russia *51°51′N 47°03′E*
126 *K4* **Podol'sk** Moskovskaya Oblast', W Russia *55°24′N 37°30′E*
76 *H10* **Podor** N Senegal *16°40′N 14°57′W*
125 *P12* **Podosinovets** Kirovskaya Oblast', NW Russia *60°15′N 47°06′E*
124 *I12* **Podporozh'ye** Leningradskaya Oblast', NW Russia *60°52′N 34°00′E*
**Podravska Slatina** *see* Slatina
112 *J13* **Podromanlja** Republika Srpska, SE Bosnia and Herzegovina *43°55′N 18°46′E*
**Podsvil'ye** *see* Padsvillye
116 *L9* **Podu Iloaiei** *prev.* Podul Iloaiei. Iaşi, NE Romania *47°13′N 27°16′E*
113 *N15* **Podujevë** *Serb.* Podujevo. N Kosovo *42°56′N 21°13′E*
**Podujevo** *see* Podujevë
**Podul Iloaiei** *see* Podu Iloaiei
**Podunajská Rovina** *see* Little Alföld
124 *M12* **Podyuga** Arkhangel'skaya Oblast', NW Russia *61°04′N 40°46′E*
56 *A9* **Poechos, Embalse** ◎ NW Peru
55 *W10* **Poeketi** Sipaliwini, E Suriname
100 *L8* **Poel** *island* N Germany
83 *M20* **Poelela, Lagoa** ◎ S Mozambique
**Poerwodadi** *see* Purwodadi
**Poerwokerto** *see* Purwokerto
**Poerworedjo** *see* Purworejo
**Poetovio** *see* Ptuj
83 *E23* **Pofadder** Northern Cape, W South Africa *29°09′S 19°25′E*
106 *I9* **Po, Foci del** *var.* Bocche del Po. ≈ NE Italy
116 *E12* **Pogăniş** ≈ W Romania
**Pogegen** *see* Pagėgiai
106 *G12* **Poggibonsi** Toscana, C Italy *43°28′N 11°09′E*
107 *I14* **Poggio Mirteto** Lazio, C Italy *42°17′N 12°42′E*
109 *V4* **Pöggstall** Niederösterreich, N Austria *48°19′N 15°10′E*
116 *L13* **Pogoanele** Buzău, SE Romania *44°55′N 27°00′E*
**Pogónion** *see* Delvináki
113 *M21* **Pogradec** *var.* Pogradeci. Korçë, SE Albania *40°54′N 20°40′E*
**Pogradeci** *see* Pogradec
123 *S15* **Pogranichnyy** Primorskiy Kray, SE Russia *44°18′N 131°33′E*
38 *M16* **Pogromni Volcano** ▲ Unimak Island, Alaska, USA *54°34′N 164°41′W*
163 *Z15* **Pohang** *Jap.* Hokō; *prev.* P'ohang. E South Korea *36°02′N 129°20′E*
**P'ohang** *see* Pohang
15 *T9* **Pohénégamook, Lac** ◎ Québec, SE Canada
93 *L20* **Pohja** *Swe.* Pojo. Uusimaa, SW Finland *60°07′N 23°30′E*
**Pohjanlahti** *see* Bothnia, Gulf of
189 *U16* **Pohnpei** ◈ *state* E Micronesia
189 *O12* **Pohnpei** ✈ Pohnpei, E Micronesia
189 *O12* **Pohnpei** *prev.* Ponape Ascension Island. *island* E Micronesia
111 *F19* **Pohořelice** *Ger.* Pohrlitz. Jihomoravský Kraj, SE Czechia *48°58′N 16°30′E*
109 *V10* **Pohorje** *Ger.* Bacher. ▲▲ N Slovenia
117 *N6* **Pohrebyshche** Vinnyts'ka Oblast', C Ukraine *49°31′N 29°16′E*
**Pohrlitz** *see* Pohořelice
161 *P9* **Po Hu** ⊞ E China
116 *G15* **Poiana Mare** Dolj, S Romania *43°55′N 23°02′E*
**Poictiers** *see* Poitiers
127 *N6* **Poim** Penzenskaya Oblast', W Russia *53°03′N 43°11′E*
159 *N15* **Poindo** Xigzang Zizhiqu, W China *29°58′N 91°20′E*
195 *Y13* **Poinsett, Cape** *headland* Antarctica *65°35′S 113°00′E*
29 *R9* **Poinsett, Lake** ◎ South Dakota, N USA
22 *I10* **Point Au Fer Island** *island* Louisiana, S USA
39 *X14* **Point Baker** Prince of Wales Island, Alaska, USA *56°19′N 133°31′W*
25 *U13* **Point Comfort** Texas, SW USA *28°40′N 96°33′W*
**Point de Galle** *see* Galle
44 *K10* **Pointe à Gravois** *headland* SW Haiti *18°00′N 73°53′W*
22 *L10* **Pointe a la Hache** Louisiana, S USA *29°34′N 89°48′W*
45 *Y6* **Pointe-à-Pitre** Grande Terre, C Guadeloupe *16°14′N 61°32′W*
15 *U7* **Pointe-au-Père** Québec, SE Canada *48°31′N 68°27′W*
15 *V5* **Pointe-aux-Anglais** Québec, SE Canada *49°40′N 67°09′W*
45 *T10* **Pointe Du Cap** *headland* N Saint Lucia *14°06′N 60°56′W*
79 *E21* **Pointe-Noire** Pointe-Noire, S Congo *04°46′S 11°53′E*
45 *X6* **Pointe Noire** Basse Terre, W Guadeloupe *16°14′N 61°47′W*
79 *E21* **Pointe Noire** ◈ *department* SW Congo
79 *E21* **Pointe-Noire** ✈ Pointe-Noire, S Congo *04°45′S 11°55′E*
45 *U15* **Point Fortin** Trinidad, Trinidad and Tobago *10°12′N 61°41′W*
38 *M6* **Point Hope** Alaska, USA *68°21′N 166°48′W*
39 *N5* **Point Lay** Alaska, USA *69°42′N 162°57′W*
18 *B16* **Point Marion** Pennsylvania, NE USA *39°44′N 79°53′W*
18 *K16* **Point Pleasant** New Jersey, NE USA *40°04′N 74°00′W*
21 *P4* **Point Pleasant** West Virginia, NE USA *38°53′N 82°07′W*
45 *R14* **Point Salines** ✈ (St. George's) SW Grenada *12°00′N 61°47′W*
102 *L9* **Poitiers** *prev.* Poictiers; *anc.* Limonum. Vienne, W France *46°35′N 00°19′E*
102 *K9* **Poitou** *cultural region* W France
103 *N3* **Poix-de-Picardie** Somme, N France *49°47′N 01°58′E*
**Pojo** *see* Pohja
37 *S10* **Pojoaque** New Mexico, SW USA *35°52′N 106°01′W*
152 *E11* **Pokaran** Rājasthān, NW India *26°55′N 71°55′E*
183 *R4* **Pokataroo** New South Wales, SE Australia *29°37′S 148°43′E*
119 *P18* **Pokats'** *Rus.* Pokot'. ≈ SE Belarus
29 *V5* **Pokegama Lake** ◎ Minnesota, N USA
184 *L6* **Pokeno** Waikato, North Island, New Zealand *37°15′S 175°01′E*
153 *O11* **Pokharā** Western, C Nepal *28°14′N 84°E*
127 *T6* **Pokhvistnevo** Samarskaya Oblast', W Russia *53°38′N 52°07′E*
55 *W10* **Pokigron** Sipaliwini, C Suriname *04°31′N 55°23′W*
92 *L10* **Pokka** *Lapp.* Bohkká. Lappi, N Finland *68°11′N 25°45′E*
79 *N16* **Poko** Orientale, NE Dem. Rep. Congo *03°08′N 26°52′E*
**Pokot'** *see* Pokats'
**Po-ko-to Shan** *see* Bogda Shan
117 *T9* **Pokrov** *prev.* Ordzhonikidze. Dnipropetrovs'ka Oblast', E Ukraine *47°39′N 34°08′E*
147 *S7* **Pokrovka** Talasskaya Oblast', NW Kyrgyzstan *42°45′N 71°33′E*
**Pokrovka** *see* Kyzyl-Suu
117 *W7* **Pokrovs'k** *prev.* Krasnoarmiys'k. Donets'ka Oblast', SE Ukraine *48°17′N 37°14′E*
117 *V8* **Pokrovs'ke** *Rus.* Pokrovskoye. Dnipropetrovs'ka Oblast', E Ukraine *47°58′N 36°15′E*
**Pokrovskoye** *see* Pokrovs'ke
**Pola** *see* Pula
37 *N10* **Polacca** Arizona, SW USA *35°49′N 110°21′W*
**Pola de Laviana** *see* Pola de Llaviana
**Pola de Lena** *see* La Pola
104 *L2* **Pola de Llaviana** *var.* Pola de Laviana. Asturias, N Spain *43°15′N 05°33′W*
**Pola de Siero** *see* La Pola Siero
191 *Y3* **Poland** Kiritimati, E Kiribati *01°52′N 157°33′W*
110 *H12* **Poland** *off.* Republic of Poland, *var.* Polish Republic, *Pol.* Polska, Rzeczpospolita Polska; *prev. Pol.* Polska Rzeczpospolita Ludowa, The Polish People's Republic. ◆ *republic* C Europe
**Poland, Republic of** *see* Poland
**Polangen** *see* Palanga
110 *G7* **Polanów** *Ger.* Pollnow. Zachodnio-pomorskie, NW Poland *54°07′N 16°38′E*
136 *H13* **Polatlı** Ankara, C Turkey *39°34′N 32°08′E*
118 *L12* **Polatsk** *Rus.* Polotsk. Vitsyebskaya Voblasts', N Belarus *55°29′N 28°47′E*
110 *F8* **Połczyn-Zdrój** *Ger.* Bad Polzin. Zachodnio-pomorskie, NW Poland *53°44′N 16°02′E*
**Pol-e-'Alam** *see* Pul-e-'Alam
**Polekhatum** *see* Pulhatyn
**Pol-e Khomrī** *see* Pul-e Khumrī
197 *S10* **Pole Plain** *undersea feature* Arctic Ocean
**Pol-e-Safid** *see* Pol-e Sefīd
143 *P5* **Pol-e Sefīd** *var.* Pol-e-Safid, Pul-i-Sefid. Māzandarān, N Iran *36°05′N 53°01′E*
118 *B13* **Polessk** *Ger.* Labiau. Kaliningradskaya Oblast', W Russia *54°52′N 21°06′E*
**Polesskoye** *see* Polis'ke
171 *N13* **Polewali** Sulawesi, C Indonesia *03°26′S 119°23′E*
114 *G11* **Polezhan** ▲ SW Bulgaria *41°42′N 23°28′E*
78 *F13* **Poli** Nord, N Cameroon *09°31′N 13°10′E*
**Poli** *see* Pólis
107 *M19* **Policastro, Golfo di** *gulf* S Italy
110 *D8* **Police** *Ger.* Politz. Zachodnio-pomorskie, NW Poland *53°34′N 14°34′E*
172 *I17* **Police, Pointe** *headland* Mahé, NE Seychelles *04°48′S 55°31′E*
115 *L17* **Polichnítos** *var.* Polihnitos, Políkhnitos. Lésvos, E Greece *39°04′N 26°10′E*
**Poligiros** *see* Polýgyros
107 *P17* **Polignano a Mare** Puglia, SE Italy *40°59′N 17°13′E*
103 *S9* **Poligny** Jura, E France *46°51′N 05°42′E*
**Polihnitos** *see* Polichnítos
**Polikastro/Políkastron** *see* Polýkastro
**Políkhnitos** *see* Polichnítos
171 *O3* **Polillo Islands** *island group* N Philippines
109 *Q9* **Polinik** ▲ SW Austria *46°54′N 13°10′E*
115 *J15* **Políochni** *var.* Polýochni. *site of ancient city* Límnos, E Greece
121 *O2* **Pólis** *var.* Poli. W Cyprus *35°02′N 32°27′E*
**Polish People's Republic, The** *see* Poland
**Polish Republic** *see* Poland
117 *O3* **Polis'ke** *Rus.* Polesskoye. Kyivs'ka Oblast', N Ukraine *51°16′N 29°27′E*
107 *N22* **Polistena** Calabria, SW Italy *38°25′N 16°05′E*
**Politz** *see* Police
**Políyiros** *see* Polýgyros
29 *V14* **Polk City** Iowa, C USA *41°46′N 93°42′W*
110 *F13* **Polkowice** *Ger.* Heerwegen. Dolnośląskie, W Poland *51°32′N 16°06′E*
155 *G22* **Pollāchi** Tamil Nādu, SE India *10°38′N 77°00′E*
109 *W7* **Pöllau** Steiermark, SE Austria *47°18′N 15°46′E*
189 *T13* **Polle** *atoll* Chuuk Islands, C Micronesia
105 *X9* **Pollença** Mallorca, Spain, W Mediterranean Sea *39°52′N 03°01′E*
**Pollnow** *see* Polanów
29 *N7* **Pollock** South Dakota, N USA *45°53′N 100°15′W*
92 *L8* **Polmak** Finnmark, N Norway *70°01′N 28°04′E*
30 *L10* **Polo** Illinois, N USA *41°59′N 89°34′W*
193 *V15* **Poloa** *island* Tongatapu Group, N Tonga
42 *E5* **Polochic, Río** ≈ C Guatemala
**Pologi** *see* Polohy
117 *V9* **Polohy** *Rus.* Pologi. Zaporiz'ka Oblast', SE Ukraine *47°30′N 36°18′E*
83 *K20* **Polokwane** *prev.* Pietersburg. Limpopo, NE South Africa *23°54′S 29°23′E*
14 *M10* **Polonais, Lac des** ◎ Québec, SE Canada
61 *G20* **Polonio, Cabo** *headland* E Uruguay *34°22′S 53°46′W*
155 *K24* **Polonnaruwa** North Central Province, C Sri Lanka *07°56′N 81°02′E*
116 *L5* **Polonne** *Rus.* Polonnoye. Khmel'nyts'ka Oblast', NW Ukraine *50°10′N 27°30′E*
**Polonnoye** *see* Polonne
**Polotsk** *see* Polatsk
**Polovinka** *see* Ugleural'skiy
109 *T7* **Pöls** *var.* Pölsbach. ≈ E Austria
**Pölsbach** *see* Pöls
**Polska/Polska, Rzeczpospolita/Polska Rzeczpospolita Ludowa** *see* Poland
114 *L10* **Polski Gradets** Stara Zagora, C Bulgaria *42°12′N 26°06′E*
114 *K8* **Polski Trambesh** *var.* Polski Trŭmbesh. Veliko Tarnovo, N Bulgaria *43°22′N 25°38′E*
**Polski Trŭmbesh** *see* Polski Trambesh
33 *P8* **Polson** Montana, NW USA *47°41′N 114°09′W*
117 *T6* **Poltava** Poltavs'ka Oblast', NE Ukraine *49°33′N 34°32′E*
**Poltava** *see* Poltavs'ka Oblast'
117 *R5* **Poltavs'ka Oblast'** *var.* Poltava, *Rus.* Poltavskaya Oblast'. ◈ *province* NE Ukraine
**Poltavskaya Oblast'** *see* Poltavs'ka Oblast'
**Poltoratsk** *see* Aşgabat
118 *I5* **Põltsamaa** *Ger.* Oberpahlen. Jõgevamaa, E Estonia *58°40′N 26°00′E*
118 *I4* **Põltsamaa** *var.* Põltsamaa Jõgi. ≈ C Estonia
**Põltsamaa Jõgi** *see* Põltsamaa
122 *I8* **Poluy** ≈ N Russia
118 *J6* **Põlva** *Ger.* Pölwe. Põlvamaa, SE Estonia *58°04′N 27°06′E*
93 *N16* **Polvijärvi** Pohjois-Karjala, SE Finland *62°53′N 29°20′E*
**Pölwe** *see* Põlva
115 *I22* **Polýaigos** *island* Kykládes, Greece, Aegean Sea
115 *I22* **Polyaígou Folégandrou, Stenó** *strait* Kykládes, Greece, Aegean Sea
124 *J3* **Polyarnyy** Murmanskaya Oblast', NW Russia *69°10′N 33°21′E*
125 *W5* **Polyarnyy Ural** ▲▲ NW Russia
115 *G14* **Polýgyros** *var.* Poligiros, Políyiros. Kentrikí Makedonía, N Greece *40°21′N 23°27′E*
114 *F13* **Polýkastro** *var.* Polikastro; *prev.* Políkastron. Kentrikí Makedonía, N Greece *41°01′N 22°33′E*
193 *O9* **Polynesia** *island group* C Pacific Ocean
**Polýochni** *see* Políochni
41 *Y13* **Polyuc** Quintana Roo, E Mexico
109 *V10* **Polzela** C Slovenia *46°18′N 15°04′E*
**Polzen** *see* Ploučnice
56 *D12* **Pomabamba** Ancash, C Peru *08°48′S 77°30′W*
185 *D23* **Pomahaka** ≈ South Island, New Zealand
106 *F12* **Pomarance** Toscana, C Italy *43°19′N 10°53′E*
104 *G9* **Pombal** Leiria, C Portugal *39°55′N 08°38′W*
76 *D9* **Pombas** Santo Antão, NW Cape Verde *17°09′N 25°02′W*
83 *N19* **Pomene** Inhambane, SE Mozambique *22°57′S 35°34′E*
110 *G8* **Pomerania** *cultural region* Germany/Poland
110 *D7* **Pomeranian Bay** *Ger.* Pommersche Bucht, *Pol.* Zatoka Pomorska. *bay* Germany/Poland
31 *T15* **Pomeroy** Ohio, N USA *39°01′N 82°01′W*
32 *L10* **Pomeroy** Washington, NW USA *46°28′N 117°36′W*
117 *Q8* **Pomichna** Kirovohrads'ka Oblast', C Ukraine *48°07′N 31°25′E*
186 *H7* **Pomio** New Britain, E Papua New Guinea *05°31′S 151°30′E*
**Pomir, Dar''yoi** *see* Pamir/Pāmīr, Daryā-ye
27 *T6* **Pomme de Terre Lake** ⊞ Missouri, C USA
29 *S8* **Pomme de Terre River** ≈ Minnesota, N USA
**Pommersche Bucht** *see* Pomeranian Bay
35 *T15* **Pomona** California, W USA *34°03′N 117°45′W*
114 *N9* **Pomorie** Burgas, E Bulgaria *42°32′N 27°39′E*
**Pomorska, Zatoka** *see* Pomeranian Bay
110 *H8* **Pomorskie** ◈ *province* N Poland
125 *Q4* **Pomorskiy Proliv** *strait* NW Russia
125 *T10* **Pomozdino** Respublika Komi, NW Russia *62°11′N 54°13′E*
**Pompaelo** *see* Pamplona
23 *Z15* **Pompano Beach** Florida, SE USA *26°14′N 80°06′W*
107 *K18* **Pompei** Campania, S Italy *40°45′N 14°27′E*
33 *V10* **Pompeys Pillar** Montana, NW USA *45°58′N 107°55′W*
**Ponape Ascension Island** *see* Pohnpei
29 *R13* **Ponca** Nebraska, C USA *42°35′N 96°42′W*
27 *O8* **Ponca City** Oklahoma, C USA *36°41′N 97°04′W*
45 *T6* **Ponce** C Puerto Rico *18°01′N 66°36′W*
23 *X10* **Ponce de Leon Inlet** *inlet* Florida, SE USA
22 *K8* **Ponchatoula** Louisiana, S USA *30°26′N 90°26′W*
26 *M8* **Pond Creek** Oklahoma, C USA *36°40′N 97°48′W*
155 *J20* **Pondicherry** *var.* Puduchcheri, *Fr.* Pondichéry. Puducherry, SE India *11°59′N 79°50′E*
**Pondicherry** *see* Puducherry
**Pondichéry** *see* Puducherry
197 *N11* **Pond Inlet** *var.* Mittimatalik. Baffin Island, Nunavut, NE Canada *72°37′N 77°56′W*
187 *P16* **Ponérihouen** Province Nord, C New Caledonia *21°04′S 165°24′E*
104 *J4* **Ponferrada** Castilla y León, NW Spain *42°33′N 06°35′W*
184 *N13* **Pongaroa** Manawatu-Wanganui, North Island, New Zealand *40°36′S 176°08′E*
167 *Q12* **Pong Nam Ron** Chantaburi, S Thailand *12°55′N 102°15′E*
81 *C14* **Pongo** ≈ W South Sudan
152 *I7* **Pong Reservoir** ⊞ N India
111 *N14* **Poniatowa** Lubelskie, E Poland *51°11′N 22°05′E*
167 *R12* **Pônley** Kampong Chhnang, C Cambodia *12°26′N 104°25′E*
155 *I20* **Ponnaiyār** ≈ SE India
11 *Q15* **Ponoka** Alberta, SW Canada *52°42′N 113°33′W*
127 *U6* **Ponomarevka** Orenburgskaya Oblast', W Russia *53°16′N 54°10′E*
169 *Q17* **Ponorogo** Jawa, C Indonesia *07°51′S 111°30′E*
122 *F6* **Ponoy** ≈ NW Russia
102 *K11* **Pons** Charente-Maritime, W France *45°31′N 00°31′W*
**Pons** *see* Ponts
**Pons Aelii** *see* Newcastle upon Tyne
**Pons Vetus** *see* Pontevedra
99 *G20* **Pont-à-Celles** Hainaut, S Belgium *50°31′N 04°21′E*
102 *K16* **Pontacq** Pyrénées-Atlantiques, SW France *43°11′N 00°06′W*
64 *P3* **Ponta Delgada** São Miguel, Azores, Portugal, NE Atlantic Ocean *37°29′N 25°40′W*
64 *P3* **Ponta Delgado** ✈ São Miguel, Azores, Portugal, NE Atlantic Ocean *37°28′N 25°40′W*
64 *N2* **Ponta do Pico** ▲ Pico, Azores, Portugal, NE Atlantic Ocean *38°28′N 28°25′W*
60 *J11* **Ponta Grossa** Paraná, S Brazil *25°07′S 50°09′W*
103 *S5* **Pont-à-Mousson** Meurthe-et-Moselle, NE France *48°55′N 06°03′E*
103 *T9* **Pontarlier** Doubs, E France *46°54′N 06°20′E*
106 *G11* **Pontassieve** Toscana, C Italy *43°46′N 11°28′E*
102 *L4* **Pont-Audemer** Eure, N France *49°22′N 00°31′E*
22 *K9* **Pontchartrain, Lake** ◎ Louisiana, S USA
102 *I8* **Pontchâteau** Loire-Atlantique, NW France *47°26′N 02°04′W*
103 *R10* **Pont-de-Vaux** Ain, E France *46°25′N 04°57′E*
104 *G4* **Ponteareas** Galicia, NW Spain *42°11′N 08°29′W*
106 *J6* **Pontebba** Friuli-Venezia Giulia, NE Italy *46°32′N 13°18′E*
104 *G4* **Ponte Caldelas** Galicia, NW Spain *42°23′N 08°30′W*
107 *J16* **Pontecorvo** Lazio, C Italy *41°27′N 13°40′E*
104 *G5* **Ponte da Barca** Viana do Castelo, N Portugal *41°48′N 08°25′W*
104 *G5* **Ponte de Lima** Viana do Castelo, N Portugal *41°46′N 08°35′W*
106 *F11* **Pontedera** Toscana, C Italy *43°40′N 10°38′E*
104 *H10* **Ponte de Sor** Portalegre, C Portugal *39°15′N 08°01′W*
104 *H2* **Pontedeume** Galicia, NW Spain *43°22′N 08°09′W*
106 *F6* **Ponte di Legno** Lombardia, N Italy *46°16′N 10°31′E*
11 *T17* **Ponteix** Saskatchewan, S Canada *49°43′N 107°22′W*
171 *Q16* **Ponte Macassar** *var.* Pante Macassar, Pante Makasar, Pante Makassar. W East Timor *09°11′S 124°27′E*
59 *N20* **Ponte Nova** Minas Gerais, NE Brazil *20°25′S 42°54′W*
59 *G18* **Pontes e Lacerda** Mato Grosso, W Brazil *15°14′S 59°21′W*
104 *G4* **Pontevedra** *anc.* Pons Vetus. Galicia, NW Spain *42°25′N 08°39′W*
104 *G3* **Pontevedra** ◈ *province* Galicia, NW Spain
104 *G4* **Pontevedra, Ría de** *estuary* NW Spain
30 *M12* **Pontiac** Illinois, N USA *40°54′N 88°36′W*
31 *R9* **Pontiac** Michigan, N USA *42°38′N 83°17′W*
169 *P11* **Pontianak** Borneo, C Indonesia *0°05′S 109°16′E*
107 *I16* **Pontino, Agro** *plain* C Italy
**Pontisarae** *see* Pontoise
102 *H6* **Pontivy** Morbihan, NW France *48°04′N 02°58′W*
102 *F6* **Pont-l'Abbé** Finistère, NW France *47°52′N 04°14′W*
103 *N4* **Pontoise** *anc.* Briva Isarae, Cergy-Pontoise, Pontisarae. Val-d'Oise, N France *49°03′N 02°05′E*
11 *W13* **Ponton** Manitoba, C Canada *54°36′N 99°02′W*
102 *J5* **Pontorson** Manche, N France *48°33′N 01°31′W*
22 *M2* **Pontotoc** Mississippi, S USA *34°15′N 89°00′W*
25 *R9* **Pontotoc** Texas, SW USA *30°52′N 98°57′W*
106 *E10* **Pontremoli** Toscana, C Italy *44°24′N 09°55′E*
108 *J10* **Pontresina** Graubünden, S Switzerland *46°29′N 09°52′E*
105 *U5* **Ponts** *var.* Pons. Cataluña, NE Spain *41°55′N 01°12′E*
103 *R14* **Pont-St-Esprit** Gard, S France *44°15′N 04°37′E*
97 *K21* **Pontypool** *Wel.* Pontypŵl. SE Wales, United Kingdom *51°43′N 03°02′W*
97 *J22* **Pontypridd** S Wales, United Kingdom *51°37′N 03°22′W*
**Pontypŵl** *see* Pontypool
43 *R17* **Ponuga** Veraguas, SE Panama *07°50′N 80°58′W*
184 *L6* **Ponui Island** *island* N New Zealand
119 *K14* **Ponya** ≈ N Belarus
107 *I17* **Ponza, Isola di** *Island* Isole Ponziane, S Italy
107 *I17* **Ponziane, Isole** *island* C Italy
182 *F7* **Poochera** South Australia *32°45′S 134°51′E*
79 *G20* **Pool** *var.* Le Pool. ◈ *department* S Congo
97 *L24* **Poole** S England, United Kingdom *50°43′N 01°59′W*
25 *S6* **Poolville** Texas, SW USA *33°00′N 97°55′W*
**Poona** *see* Pune
182 *M8* **Pooncarie** New South Wales, SE Australia *33°26′S 142°37′E*
183 *N6* **Poopelloe Lake** *seasonal lake* New South Wales, SE Australia
57 *K19* **Poopó** Oruro, C Bolivia *18°23′S 66°58′W*
57 *K19* **Poopó, Lago** *var.* Lago Pampa Aullagas. ◎ W Bolivia
184 *L3* **Poor Knights Islands** *island* N New Zealand
39 *P10* **Poorman** Alaska, USA *64°05′N 155°34′W*
182 *E3* **Pootnoura** South Australia *28°31′S 134°09′E*
147 *R10* **Pop** *Rus.* Pap. Namangan Viloyati, E Uzbekistan *40°49′N 71°06′E*
117 *X7* **Popasna** *Rus.* Popasnaya. Luhans'ka Oblast', E Ukraine *48°38′N 38°24′E*
**Popasnaya** *see* Popasna
54 *D12* **Popayán** Cauca, SW Colombia *02°27′N 76°32′W*
99 *B18* **Poperinge** West-Vlaanderen, W Belgium *50°52′N 02°44′E*
123 *N7* **Popigay** Krasnoyarskiy Kray, N Russia *71°54′N 110°45′E*
123 *N7* **Popigay** ≈ N Russia
117 *O5* **Popil'nya** Zhytomyrs'ka Oblast', N Ukraine *49°57′N 29°24′E*
182 *K8* **Popiltah Lake** *seasonal lake* New South Wales, SE Australia
33 *X7* **Poplar** Montana, NW USA *48°06′N 105°12′W*
11 *Y14* **Poplar** ≈ Manitoba, C Canada
27 *X8* **Poplar Bluff** Missouri, C USA *36°45′N 90°23′W*
33 *X6* **Poplar River** ≈ Montana, NW USA
41 *P14* **Popocatépetl** ⛰ S Mexico *18°59′N 98°37′W*
79 *H21* **Popokabaka** Bandundu, SW Dem. Rep. Congo *05°42′S 16°35′E*
107 *J15* **Popoli** Abruzzo, C Italy *42°09′N 13°51′E*
186 *F9* **Popondetta** Northern, S Papua New Guinea *08°45′S 148°15′E*
112 *F9* **Popovača** Sisak-Moslavina, NE Croatia *45°35′N 16°37′E*
114 *L8* **Popovo** Targovishte, N Bulgaria *43°20′N 26°14′E*
**Popovo** *see* Iskra
**Popper** *see* Poprad
30 *M5* **Popple River** ≈ Wisconsin, N USA
111 *L19* **Poprad** *Ger.* Deutschendorf, *Hung.* Poprád. Prešovský Kraj, E Slovakia *49°04′N 20°16′E*
111 *L18* **Poprad** *Ger.* Popper, *Hung.* Poprád. ≈ Poland/Slovakia
111 *L19* **Poprad-Tatry** ✈ (Poprad) Prešovský Kraj, E Slovakia *49°04′N 20°21′E*
21 *X7* **Poquoson** Virginia, NE USA *37°08′N 76°21′W*
149 *O15* **Porali** SW Pakistan
184 *N12* **Porangahau** Hawke's Bay, North Island, New Zealand *40°19′S 176°36′E*
59 *K17* **Porangatu** Goiás, C Brazil *13°28′S 49°14′W*
119 *G18* **Porazava** *Pol.* Porozow, *Rus.* Porozovo. Hrodzyenskaya Voblasts', W Belarus *52°56′N 24°22′E*
154 *A11* **Porbandar** Gujarāt, W India *21°40′N 69°40′E*
10 *I13* **Porcher Island** *island* British Columbia, SW Canada
104 *M13* **Porcuna** Andalucía, S Spain *37°52′N 04°12′W*
14 *F7* **Porcupine** Ontario, S Canada *48°31′N 81°07′W*
64 *M6* **Porcupine Bank** *undersea feature* N Atlantic Ocean
11 *V15* **Porcupine Hills** ▲▲ Manitoba/Saskatchewan, S Canada
30 *L3* **Porcupine Mountains** *hill range* Michigan, N USA
64 *M7* **Porcupine Plain** *undersea feature* E Atlantic Ocean *16°00′W 49°00′N*
8 *G7* **Porcupine River** ≈ Canada/USA
106 *I7* **Pordenone** *anc.* Portenau. Friuli-Venezia Giulia, NE Italy *45°58′N 12°39′E*
54 *H9* **Pore** Casanare, E Colombia *05°42′N 71°59′W*
112 *A9* **Poreč** *It.* Parenzo. Istra, NW Croatia *45°16′N 13°36′E*
60 *I9* **Porecatu** Paraná, S Brazil *22°46′S 51°22′W*
**Porech'ye** *see* Parechcha
127 *P4* **Poretskoye** Chuvashskaya Respublika, W Russia *55°12′N 46°20′E*
77 *Q13* **Porga** N Benin *11°04′N 00°58′E*
186 *B7* **Porgera** Enga, W Papua New Guinea *05°32′S 143°08′E*
93 *K18* **Pori** *Swe.* Björneborg. Satakunta, SW Finland *61°28′N 21°50′E*
185 *L14* **Porirua** Wellington, North Island, New Zealand *41°08′S 174°51′E*
92 *I12* **Porjus** *Lapp.* Bårjås. Norrbotten, N Sweden *66°55′N 19°55′E*
124 *G14* **Porkhov** Pskovskaya Oblast', W Russia *57°46′N 29°27′E*
55 *O4* **Porlamar** Nueva Esparta, NE Venezuela *10°57′N 63°51′W*
102 *I8* **Pornic** Loire-Atlantique, NW France *47°07′N 02°07′W*
186 *B7* **Poroma** Southern Highlands, W Papua New Guinea *06°15′S 143°34′E*
123 *T13* **Poronaysk** Ostrov Sakhalin, Sakhalinskaya Oblast', SE Russia *49°15′N 143°00′E*
115 *G20* **Póros** Póros, S Greece *37°30′N 23°27′E*
115 *C19* **Póros** Kefallinía, Iónia Nisiá, Greece, C Mediterranean Sea *38°09′N 20°46′E*
115 *G20* **Póros** *island* S Greece
81 *G24* **Poroto Mountains** ▲▲ SW Tanzania
112 *B10* **Porozina** Primorje-Gorski Kotar, NW Croatia *45°07′N 14°17′E*
**Porozovo/Porozow** *see* Porazava
195 *X15* **Porpoise Bay** *bay* Antarctica
65 *G15* **Porpoise Point** *headland* NE Ascension Island *07°54′S 14°22′W*
65 *C25* **Porpoise Point** *headland* East Falkland, Falkland Islands *52°20′S 59°18′W*
108 *C6* **Porrentruy** Jura, NW Switzerland *47°25′N 07°06′E*
106 *F10* **Porretta Terme** Emilia-Romagna, C Italy *44°10′N 11°01′E*
**Porriño** *see* O Porriño
92 *L7* **Porsangenfjorden** *Lapp.* Porsáŋgguvuotna. *fjord* N Norway
92 *K8* **Porsangerhalvøya** *peninsula* N Norway
**Porsáŋgguvuotna** *see* Porsangenfjorden
95 *G16* **Porsgrunn** Telemark, S Norway *59°08′N 09°38′E*
136 *E13* **Porsuk Çayı** ≈ C Turkey
**Porsy** *see* Boldumsaz
57 *N18* **Portachuelo** Santa Cruz, C Bolivia *17°21′S 63°24′W*
182 *I9* **Port Adelaide** South Australia *34°49′S 138°31′E*
97 *F15* **Portadown** *Ir.* Port An Dúnáin. S Northern Ireland, United Kingdom *54°26′N 06°27′W*
31 *P10* **Portage** Michigan, N USA *42°12′N 85°34′W*
18 *D15* **Portage** Pennsylvania, NE USA *40°23′N 78°40′W*
30 *K8* **Portage** Wisconsin, N USA *43°33′N 89°29′W*
30 *M3* **Portage Lake** ◎ Michigan, N USA
11 *X16* **Portage la Prairie** Manitoba, S Canada *49°58′N 98°20′W*
31 *R11* **Portage River** ≈ Ohio, N USA
27 *Y8* **Portageville** Missouri, C USA *36°25′N 89°42′W*
28 *L2* **Portal** North Dakota, N USA *48°57′N 102°33′W*
10 *L17* **Port Alberni** Vancouver Island, British Columbia, SW Canada *49°11′N 124°49′W*
14 *E15* **Port Albert** Ontario, S Canada *43°51′N 81°42′W*
104 *I10* **Portalegre** *anc.* Ammaia, Amoea. Portalegre, E Portugal *39°17′N 07°25′W*
104 *H10* **Portalegre** ◈ *district* C Portugal


◆ Country
● Country Capital
◇ Dependent Territory
○ Dependent Territory Capital
◈ Administrative Regions
✈ International Airport
▲ Mountain
▲▲ Mountain Range
⛰ Volcano
≈ River
◎ Lake
⊞ Reservoir

37 V12 **Portales** New Mexico, SW USA 34°11´N 103°19´W

39 X14 **Port Alexander** Baranof Island, Alaska, USA 56°15´N 134°39´W

83 I25 **Port Alfred** Eastern Cape, S South Africa 33°31´S 26°55´E

10 J16 **Port Alice** Vancouver Island, British Columbia, SW Canada 50°23´N 127°24´W

22 J8 **Port Allen** Louisiana, S USA 30°27´N 91°12´W

**Port Amelia** see Pemba
**Port An Dúnáin** see Portadown

32 G7 **Port Angeles** Washington, NW USA 48°06´N 123°26´W

44 L12 **Port Antonio** NE Jamaica 18°10´N 76°27´W

115 D16 **Pórta Panagía** religious building Thessalía, C Greece

25 T14 **Port Aransas** Texas, SW USA 27°49´N 97°03´W

97 E18 **Portarlington** Ir. Cúil an tSúdaire. Laois/Offaly, C Ireland 53°10´N 07°11´W

183 P17 **Port Arthur** Tasmania, SE Australia 43°09´S 147°51´E

25 Y11 **Port Arthur** Texas, SW USA 29°55´N 93°56´W

96 G12 **Port Askaig** W Scotland, United Kingdom 55°51´N 06°06´W

182 I7 **Port Augusta** South Australia 32°29´S 137°44´E

44 M9 **Port-au-Prince** haiti. Pòtoprens. ● (Haiti) C Haiti 18°33´N 72°20´W

22 I8 **Port Barre** Louisiana, S USA 30°33´N 91°57´W

**Port-Bergé** see Borzjiny

151 Q19 **Port Blair** Andaman and Nicobar Islands, SE India 11°40´N 92°44´E

25 X12 **Port Bolivar** Texas, SW USA 29°21´N 94°45´W

105 X4 **Portbou** Cataluña, NE Spain 42°26´N 03°10´E

77 N17 **Port Bouet** ✈ (Abidjan) SE Ivory Coast 05°17´N 03°55´W

182 I8 **Port Broughton** South Australia 33°39´S 137°55´E

14 F17 **Port Burwell** Ontario, S Canada 42°39´N 80°47´W

12 G17 **Port Burwell** Québec, NE Canada 60°25´N 64°49´W

182 M13 **Port Campbell** Victoria, SE Australia 38°37´S 143°00´E

15 V4 **Port-Cartier** Québec, SE Canada 50°00´N 66°55´W

185 F23 **Port Chalmers** Otago, South Island, New Zealand 45°46´S 170°37´E

23 W14 **Port Charlotte** Florida, SE USA 27°00´N 82°07´W

38 L9 **Port Clarence** Alaska, USA 65°15´N 166°51´W

10 I13 **Port Clements** Graham Island, British Columbia, SW Canada 53°37´N 132°12´W

31 S11 **Port Clinton** Ohio, N USA 41°30´N 82°56´W

14 H17 **Port Colborne** Ontario, S Canada 42°51´N 79°16´W

15 Y7 **Port-Daniel** Québec, SE Canada 48°10´N 64°58´W

183 O17 **Port Davey** headland Tasmania, SE Australia 43°19´S 145°54´E

44 K8 **Port-de-Paix** NW Haiti 19°56´N 72°52´W

181 W4 **Port Douglas** Queensland, NE Australia 16°33´S 145°27´E

10 J13 **Port Edward** British Columbia, SW Canada 54°11´N 130°16´W

83 K24 **Port Edward** KwaZulu/Natal, SE South Africa 31°03´S 30°14´E

58 I12 **Portel** Pará, NE Brazil 01°58´S 50°45´W

104 H12 **Portel** Évora, S Portugal 38°18´N 07°42´W

14 E14 **Port Elgin** Ontario, S Canada 44°26´N 81°22´W

45 Y14 **Port Elizabeth** Bequia, Saint Vincent and the Grenadines 13°01´N 61°15´W

83 I26 **Port Elizabeth** Eastern Cape, S South Africa 33°58´S 25°36´E

96 G13 **Port Ellen** W Scotland, United Kingdom 55°37´N 06°12´W

**Portenau** see Pordenone

97 H16 **Port Erin** SW Isle of Man 54°05´N 04°42´W

45 U14 **Porter Point** headland Saint Vincent, Saint Vincent and the Grenadines 13°22´N 61°10´W

185 G18 **Porters Pass** pass South Island, New Zealand

83 E25 **Porterville** Western Cape, SW South Africa 33°01´S 18°59´E

35 R12 **Porterville** California, W USA 36°03´N 119°03´W

**Port-Étienne** see Nouâdhibou

182 L13 **Port Fairy** Victoria, SE Australia 38°24´S 142°13´E

184 M4 **Port Fitzroy** Great Barrier Island, Auckland, NE New Zealand 36°10´S 175°21´E

**Port Florence** see Kisumu
**Port-Francqui** see Ilebo
**Port-Gentil** Ogooué-Maritime, W Gabon 0°40´S 08°50´E

182 I7 **Port Germein** South Australia 33°03´S 138°01´E

22 J6 **Port Gibson** Mississippi, S USA 31°57´N 90°58´W

29 Q13 **Port Graham** Alaska, USA 59°21´N 151°49´W

77 U17 **Port Harcourt** Rivers, S Nigeria 04°43´N 07°02´E

10 J16 **Port Hardy** Vancouver Island, British Columbia, SW Canada 50°41´N 127°30´W

**Port Harrison** see Inukjuak

13 R14 **Port Hawkesbury** Cape Breton Island, Nova Scotia, SE Canada 45°36´N 61°22´W

180 I6 **Port Hedland** Western Australia 20°23´S 118°40´E

39 O15 **Port Heiden** Alaska, USA 56°54´N 158°40´W

97 I19 **Porthmadog** var. Portmadoc. NW Wales, United Kingdom 52°55´N 04°08´W

31 T9 **Port Huron** Michigan, N USA 42°58´N 82°25´W

107 K17 **Portici** Campania, S Italy 40°48´N 14°20´E

**Port-Iliç** see Liman

104 G14 **Portimão** var. Vila Nova de Portimão. Faro, S Portugal 37°08´N 08°32´W

25 T17 **Port Isabel** Texas, SW USA 26°04´N 97°13´W

18 J13 **Port Jervis** New York, NE USA 41°22´N 74°39´W

55 S7 **Port Kaituma** NW Guyana 07°42´N 59°52´W

126 K12 **Port Katon** Rostovskaya Oblast´, SW Russia 46°52´N 38°46´E

83 S9 **Port Kembla** New South Wales, SE Australia 34°30´S 150°54´E

182 F8 **Port Kenny** South Australia 33°09´S 134°38´E

**Port Klang** see Pelabuhan Klang

**Port Láirge** see Waterford

103 X15 **Porto, Golfe de** gulf Corse, France, C Mediterranean Sea

106 I7 **Portogruaro** Veneto, NE Italy 45°46´N 12°50´E

35 P5 **Portola** California, W USA 39°48´N 120°28´W

187 Q13 **Port-Olry** Espiritu Santo, C Vanuatu 15°03´S 167°04´E

93 J17 **Pörtom** Fin. Pirttikylä. Österbotten, W Finland 62°42´N 21°40´E

**Port Omna** see Portumna

59 G21 **Porto Murtinho** Mato Grosso do Sul, SW Brazil 21°42´S 57°52´W

59 K16 **Porto Nacional** Tocantins, C Brazil 10°41´S 48°20´W

77 S16 **Porto-Novo** ● (Benin-official capital) S Benin 06°29´N 02°37´E

23 X10 **Port Orange** Florida, SE USA 29°06´N 80°59´W

32 G8 **Port Orchard** Washington, NW USA 47°32´N 122°38´W

**Porto Re** see Kraljevica

32 E15 **Port Orford** Oregon, NW USA 42°45´N 124°30´W

106 J13 **Porto Rico** see Puerto Rico

107 F14 **Porto San Giorgio** Marche, C Italy 43°10´N 13°31´E

64 P5 **Porto San Stefano** Toscana, C Italy 42°26´N 11°06´E

64 Q5 **Porto Santo** var. Vila Baleira. Porto Santo, Madeira, Portugal, NE Atlantic Ocean 33°04´N 16°20´W

64 P5 **Porto Santo** ✈ Porto Santo, Madeira, Portugal, NE Atlantic Ocean 33°04´N 16°20´W

**Porto Santo** var. Ilha de Porto Santo. island Madeira, Portugal, NE Atlantic Ocean
**Porto Santo, Ilha do** see Porto Santo

60 H9 **Porto São José** Paraná, S Brazil 22°43´S 53°10´W

59 O19 **Porto Seguro** Bahia, E Brazil 16°25´S 39°07´W

107 B17 **Porto Torres** Sardegna, Italy, C Mediterranean Sea 40°50´N 08°23´E

59 J23 **Porto União** Santa Catarina, S Brazil 26°15´S 51°02´W

103 Y16 **Porto-Vecchio** Corse, France, C Mediterranean Sea 41°35´N 09°17´E

57 G14 **Porto Velho** var. Velho. state capital Rondônia, W Brazil 08°45´S 63°54´W

56 A6 **Portoviejo** var. Puertoviejo. Manabí, W Ecuador 01°03´S 80°31´W

185 B26 **Port Pegasus** bay Stewart Island, New Zealand

14 H15 **Port Perry** Ontario, SE Canada 44°08´N 78°57´W

183 N12 **Port Phillip Bay** harbor Victoria, SE Australia

182 I8 **Port Pirie** South Australia 33°11´S 138°01´E

96 G9 **Portree** N Scotland, United Kingdom 57°26´N 06°12´W

**Port Rex** see East London
**Port Roís** see Portrush

44 K13 **Port Royal** E Jamaica 18°22´N 76°54´W

21 R15 **Port Royal** South Carolina, SE USA 32°22´N 80°41´W

21 R15 **Port Royal Sound** inlet South Carolina, SE USA

97 F14 **Portrush** Ir. Port Roís. N Northern Ireland, United Kingdom 55°12´N 06°40´W

**Port Said** see Būr Sa'īd

59 I16 **Pôsto Jacaré** Mato Grosso, W Brazil

23 R9 **Port Saint Joe** Florida, SE USA 29°49´N 85°18´W

23 Y11 **Port Saint John** Florida, SE USA 28°30´N 80°46´W

103 R16 **Port-St-Louis-du-Rhône** Bouches-du-Rhône, SE France 43°22´N 04°48´E

44 K10 **Port Sakut** SW Haiti 18°04´N 73°55´W

65 E24 **Port Salvador** inlet East Falkland, Falkland Islands

65 D24 **Port San Carlos** East Falkland, Falkland Islands 51°30´S 58°59´W

13 S10 **Port Saunders** Newfoundland, Newfoundland and Labrador, SE Canada 50°40´N 57°17´W

83 K24 **Port Shepstone** KwaZulu/Natal, SE South Africa 30°44´S 30°28´E

45 O11 **Portsmouth** var. Grand-Anse. N Dominica 15°34´N 61°27´W

97 N24 **Portsmouth** S England, United Kingdom 50°48´N 01°05´W

31 P10 **Portsmouth** New Hampshire, NE USA 43°04´N 70°45´W

31 S15 **Portsmouth** Ohio, N USA 38°43´N 83°00´W

21 X7 **Portsmouth** Virginia, NE USA 36°50´N 76°18´W

14 E17 **Port Stanley** Ontario, S Canada 42°39´N 81°12´W

**Port Stanley** see Stanley

59 B25 **Porto Amboim** Kwanza Sul, NW Angola 10°47´S 13°43´E

**Porto Amélia** see Pemba

43 T14 **Portobelo** var. Porto Bello, Puerto Bello. Colón, N Panama 09°31´N 79°37´W

**Port Stóbhaird** see Portstewart

51 G10 **Pôrto Camargo** Paraná, S Brazil 23°23´S 53°47´W

97 F14 **Portstewart** Ir. Port Stíobhaird. N Northern Ireland, United Kingdom 55°11´N 06°43´W

33 N9 **Pot Mountain** ▲ Idaho, NW USA 46°55´N 116°51´W

79 U13 **Port O'Connor** Texas, SW USA 28°26´N 96°26´W

113 H14 **Potoci** Federacija Bosni i Hercegovina ◊ Bosnia and Herzegovina 43°24´N 17°52´E

**Pôrto de Mós** see Porto de Moz

65 K24 **Port St. Johns** Eastern Cape, S South Africa 31°37´N 29°32´E

58 J12 **Porto de Moz** var. Pôrto de Mós. Pará, NE Brazil 01°45´S 52°15´W

64 O5 **Porto do Moniz** Madeira, Portugal, NE Atlantic Ocean

59 H16 **Porto dos Gaúchos** Mato Grosso, W Brazil 11°32´S 57°16´W

107 J24 **Porto Empedocle** Sicilia, Italy, C Mediterranean Sea 37°18´N 13°32´E

59 H20 **Porto Esperança** Mato Grosso do Sul, SW Brazil 19°36´S 57°24´W

106 E13 **Portoferraio** Toscana, C Italy 42°49´N 10°18´E

96 G6 **Port of Ness** NW Scotland, United Kingdom 58°29´N 06°15´W

45 U14 **Port of Spain** ● (Trinidad and Tobago) Trinidad, Trinidad and Tobago 10°39´N 61°30´W

**Port of Spain** see Piarco

80 I7 **Port Sudan** Red Sea, NE Sudan 19°37´N 37°14´E

22 L10 **Port Sulphur** Louisiana, S USA 29°28´N 89°41´W

**Port Swettenham** see Klang/Pelabuhan Klang

97 J22 **Port Talbot** S Wales, United Kingdom 51°36´N 03°47´W

92 L11 **Porttipahdan Tekojärvi** ◊ N Finland

32 G7 **Port Townsend** Washington, NW USA 48°06´N 122°45´W

104 H9 **Portugal** off. Portuguese Republic, Port. República Portuguesa. ● republic SW Europe

105 O2 **Portugalete** País Vasco, N Spain 43°19´N 03°01´W

54 L7 **Portuguesa** off. Estado Portuguesa. ◊ state N Venezuela

**Portuguesa, Estado** see Portuguesa

**Portuguesa, República** see Portugal

**Portuguese East Africa** see Mozambique

**Portuguese Guinea** see Guinea-Bissau

**Portuguese Republic** see Portugal

**Portuguese Timor** see East Timor

**Portuguese West Africa** see Angola

97 D18 **Portumna** Ir. Port Omna. Galway, W Ireland 53°06´N 08°13´W

**Portus Cale** see Porto

**Portus Magnus** see Almería

**Portus Magonis** see Maó-Mahón

103 P17 **Port-Vendres** var. Port Vendres. Pyrénées-Orientales, S France 42°31´N 03°06´E

182 H9 **Port Victoria** South Australia 34°34´S 137°31´E

187 Q14 **Port-Vila** var. Vila. ● (Vanuatu) Éfaté, C Vanuatu 17°45´S 168°21´E

**Port Vila** see Bauer Field

182 I9 **Port Wakefield** South Australia 34°13´S 138°10´E

31 N8 **Port Washington** Wisconsin, N USA 43°23´N 87°54´W

57 O18 **Porvenir** Pando, NW Bolivia 11°15´S 68°43´W

63 H25 **Porvenir** Magallanes y de la Antártica Chilena, S Chile 53°18´S 70°22´W

93 N19 **Porvoo** Swe. Borgå. Uusimaa, S Finland 60°25´N 25°40´E

93 M19 **Porvoo** Swe. Borgå. Uusimaa, S Finland 60°25´N 25°40´E

104 M10 **Porzuna** Castilla-La Mancha, C Spain 39°10´N 04°10´W

61 E14 **Posadas** Misiones, NE Argentina 27°27´S 55°52´W

104 L13 **Posadas** Andalucía, S Spain 37°48´N 05°06´W

108 J11 **Poschiavino** Italy/Switzerland

108 J10 **Poschiavo** Ger. Puschlav. Graubünden, S Switzerland 46°19´N 10°02´E

112 C12 **Posedarje** Zadar, SW Croatia 44°12´N 15°27´E

29 U17 **Posen** see Poznań

**Posen** see Poznań

52 Y10 **Posio** Lappi, NE Finland 66°06´N 28°15´E

184 M10 **Posjet** see Pos'yet

**Poskam** see Zepu

**Posnania** see Poznań

171 O12 **Poso** Sulawesi, C Indonesia 01°23´S 120°45´E

171 O12 **Poso, Danau** ◊ Sulawesi, C Indonesia

137 R10 **Posof** Ardahan, NE Turkey 41°30´N 42°43´E

25 T14 **Post** Texas, SW USA 33°11´N 101°24´W

25 N6 **Post** Texas, SW USA 33°14´N 101°24´W

**Postavy/Postawy** see Pastavy

**Poste-de-la-Baleine** see Kuujjuarapik

99 M17 **Posterholt** Limburg, SE Netherlands 51°07´N 06°02´E

83 G22 **Postmasburg** Northern Cape, N South Africa 28°20´S 23°05´E

111 O12 **Postojna** Ger. Adelsberg, It. Postumia. SW Slovenia 45°48´N 14°12´E

29 X12 **Postville** Iowa, C USA 43°04´N 91°34´W

113 G14 **Posušje** Federacija Bosni i Hercegovine, SW Bosnia and Herzegovina 43°28´N 17°20´E

171 O16 **Pota** Flores, C Indonesia 08°21´S 120°52´E

115 G23 **Potamós** Kýthira, S Greece 35°53´N 23°17´E

55 S9 **Potaro River** ← C Guyana

83 I21 **Potchefstroom** North-West, N South Africa 26°42´S 27°06´E

27 Q11 **Poteau** Oklahoma, C USA 35°03´N 94°36´W

25 S12 **Poteet** Texas, SW USA 29°02´N 98°34´W

115 O22 **Potídaia** site of ancient city Kentrikí Makedonía, N Greece

107 M18 **Potenza** anc. Potentia. Basilicata, S Italy

185 A24 **Poteriteri, Lake** ◊ South Island, New Zealand

104 M2 **Potes** Cantabria, N Spain 43°10´N 04°40´W

62 J9 **Potgietersrus** see Mokopane

25 O11 **Poth** Texas, SW USA 29°02´N 98°04´W

62 H7 **Pozo Almonte** Tarapacá, N Chile 20°16´S 69°50´W

62 I7 **Pozoblanco** Andalucía, S Spain 38°23´N 04°48´W

105 Q11 **Pozo Cañada** Castilla-La Mancha, C Spain 38°49´N 01°45´E

62 J20 **Pozo Colorado** Presidente Hayes, C Paraguay 23°26´S 58°51´W

113 J20 **Pozos, Punta** headland S Argentina 47°55´S 65°46´W

113 H14 **Potoci** Federacija Bosni i Hercegovine ◊ Bosnia and Herzegovina 43°24´N 17°52´E

77 X13 **Potiskum** Yobe, NE Nigeria 11°40´N 11°07´E

137 Q9 **Poti** prev. P'ot'i. W Georgia 42°11´N 41°41´E

**P'ot'i** see Poti

21 V3 **Potomac River** ← NE USA

57 L20 **Potosí** Potosí, S Bolivia 19°35´S 65°51´W

42 H9 **Potosí** Chinandega, NW Nicaragua 12°58´N 87°30´W

27 W6 **Potosí** Missouri, C USA 37°57´N 90°49´W

57 K21 **Potosí ◊** department SW Bolivia

62 H7 **Potrerillos** Atacama, N Chile 26°30´S 69°25´W

42 H5 **Potrerillos** Cortés, NW Honduras 15°10´N 87°58´W

62 H8 **Potro, Cerro del** ▲ N Chile 28°22´S 69°34´W

100 N12 **Potsdam** Brandenburg, NE Germany 52°24´N 13°04´E

18 J7 **Potsdam** New York, NE USA 44°40´N 74°58´W

109 X6 **Pottendorf** Niederösterreich, E Austria 47°55´N 16°23´E

109 X5 **Pottenstein** Niederösterreich, E Austria 47°58´N 16°07´E

18 I15 **Pottstown** Pennsylvania, NE USA 40°15´N 75°39´W

18 H14 **Pottsville** Pennsylvania, NE USA 40°40´N 76°12´W

155 L25 **Pottuvil** Eastern Province, SE Sri Lanka 06°53´N 81°50´E

149 U6 **Potwar Plateau** plateau NE Pakistan

102 J7 **Pouancé** Maine-et-Loire, W France 47°46´N 01°11´W

18 M12 **Poughkeepsie** New York, NE USA 41°42´N 73°55´W

15 R6 **Poulin de Courval, Lac** ◊ Québec, SE Canada

18 L9 **Poultney** Vermont, NE USA 43°31´N 73°12´W

187 O16 **Poum** Province Nord, W New Caledonia 20°15´S 164°03´E

59 L21 **Pouso Alegre** Minas Gerais, NE Brazil 22°13´S 45°56´W

192 I16 **Poutasi** Upolu, SE Samoa 14°00´S 171°43´W

187 R12 **Poûthisât, Stœ̆ng** prev. Pursat. ← W Cambodia

102 J9 **Pouzauges** Vendée, NW France 46°47´N 00°54´W

187 R12 **Po, Valle del** see Po Valley

**Po Valley** It. Valle del Po. valley N Italy

111 I19 **Považská Bystrica** Ger. Waagbistritz, Hung. Vágbeszterce. Trenčiansky Kraj, W Slovakia 49°07´N 18°26´E

124 J10 **Povenets** Respublika Kareliya, NW Russia 62°50´N 34°47´E

184 Q9 **Poverty Bay** inlet North Island, New Zealand

112 K12 **Povlen** ▲ W Serbia

104 G6 **Póvoa de Varzim** Porto, NW Portugal 41°22´N 08°46´W

127 N8 **Povorino** Voronezhskaya Oblast´, W Russia 51°09´N 42°16´E

14 H11 **Povungnituq** see Puvirnituq

**Povungnituk, Rivière de** see Puvirnituq, Riviere de

14 H11 **Powassan** Ontario, S Canada 46°05´N 79°21´W

33 U17 **Poway** California, W USA 32°57´N 117°02´W

33 W14 **Powder River** Wyoming, C USA 43°01´N 106°57´W

35 Y10 **Powder River** ← Montana/Wyoming, NW USA

32 L12 **Powder River** ← Oregon, NW USA

33 W13 **Powder River Pass** pass Wyoming, C USA

33 U11 **Powell** Wyoming, C USA 44°45´N 108°45´W

194 L7 **Powell Basin** undersea feature NW Weddell Sea

36 M8 **Powell, Lake** ◊ Utah, W USA

9 R4 **Powell, Mount** ▲ Colorado, C USA 39°25´N 106°20´W

10 L17 **Powell River** British Columbia, SW Canada 49°54´N 124°34´W

31 N5 **Powers** Michigan, N USA 45°40´N 87°29´W

28 K4 **Powers Lake** North Dakota, N USA 48°33´N 102°37´W

21 V6 **Powhatan** Virginia, NE USA 37°33´N 77°56´W

31 V13 **Powhatan Point** Ohio, N USA 39°49´N 80°49´W

97 J20 **Powys** cultural region E Wales, United Kingdom

187 P17 **Poya** Province Nord, C New Caledonia 21°19´S 165°07´E

161 P10 **Poyang Hu** ◊ S China 29°00´N 116°20´E

30 L7 **Poygan, Lake** ◊ Wisconsin, N USA

109 Y2 **Poysdorf** Niederösterreich, NE Austria 48°40´N 16°38´E

112 N11 **Požarevac** Ger. Passarowitz. Serbia, NE Serbia 44°37´N 21°11´E

41 Q13 **Poza Rica** var. Poza Rica de Hidalgo. Veracruz, E Mexico 20°34´N 97°26´W

**Poza Rica de Hidalgo** see Poza Rica

112 L13 **Požega** prev. Slavonska Požega, Ger. Poschega, Hung. Pozsega. Požega-Slavonija, NE Croatia 45°20´N 17°41´E

112 L13 **Požega-Slavonija** off. Požeško-Slavonska Županija. ◊ province NE Croatia

**Požeško-Slavonska Županija** see Požega-Slavonija

125 V13 **Pozhva** Komi-Permyatskiy Okrug, NW Russia 59°07´N 56°04´E

110 H11 **Poznań** Ger. Posen, Posnania. Wielkopolskie, C Poland 52°24´N 16°56´E

104 L13 **Pozo Alcón** Andalucía, S Spain 37°43´N 02°55´W

22 L7 **Prentiss** Mississippi, S USA 31°36´N 89°52´W

100 O10 **Prenzlau** Brandenburg, NE Germany 53°19´N 13°52´E

123 N11 **Preobrazhenka** Irkutskaya Oblast´, C Russia 60°01´N 108°00´E

166 J9 **Preparis Island** island SW Myanmar (Burma)

111 C19 **Prachatice** Ger. Prachatitz. Jihočeský Kraj, S Czechia 49°01´N 14°02´E

167 P11 **Prachin Buri** var. Prachinburi. Prachin Buri, C Thailand 14°05´N 101°23´E

**Prachinburi** see Prachin Buri

167 O12 **Prachuap Khiri Khan** var. Prachuap Girikhand. Prachuap Khiri Khan, SW Thailand 11°50´N 99°49´E

**Prachuap Girikhand** see Prachuap Khiri Khan

111 H16 **Praděd Ger.** Altvater. ▲ NE Czechia 50°06´N 17°14´E

54 D11 **Pradera** Valle del Cauca, SW Colombia 03°23´N 76°11´W

104 I5 **Prades** Pyrénées-Orientales, S France 42°37´N 02°25´E

59 O17 **Prado** Bahia, SE Brazil 17°13´S 39°15´W

54 E11 **Prado** Tolima, C Colombia 03°45´N 74°55´W

**Prado del Ganso** see Goose Green

**Prae** see Phrae
**Praga/Prague** see Praha

95 I24 **Præsto** Sjælland, SE Denmark 55°08´N 12°03´E

111 D16 **Praha** Eng. Prague, Ger. Prag, Pol. Praga. ● (Czech Republic) Středočeský Kraj, NW Czechia 50°06´N 14°26´E

116 J13 **Prahova ◊** county SE Romania

116 J13 **Prahova ◊** S Romania

76 E10 **Praia** ● (Cape Verde) Santiago, S Cape Verde 14°55´N 23°31´W

83 M21 **Praia do Bilene** Gaza, S Mozambique 25°18´S 33°10´E

83 M20 **Praia do Xai-Xai** Gaza, S Mozambique 25°33´S 33°43´E

116 J10 **Praid** Hung. Parajd. Harghita, C Romania 46°33´N 25°06´E

111 J19 **Prakovce** Košice, E Slovakia 48°52´N 20°37´E

30 J9 **Prairie du Chien** Wisconsin, N USA 43°03´N 91°09´W

27 S9 **Prairie Grove** Arkansas, C USA 35°58´N 94°19´W

31 P10 **Prairie River** ← Michigan, N USA

**Prairie State** see Illinois

25 V11 **Prairie View** Texas, SW USA 30°05´N 95°59´W

167 Q10 **Prakhon Chai** Buri Ram, E Thailand 14°36´N 103°04´E

167 Q12 **Prâmaôy** prev. Phumi Prâmaôy. Pursat, W Cambodia 12°13´N 103°05´E

192 S4 **Prambachkirchen** Oberösterreich, N Austria 48°18´N 13°50´E

118 H2 **Prangli** island N Estonia

154 J13 **Prānhita** ← C India

172 I15 **Praslin** island Inner Islands, NE Seychelles

115 O23 **Prasonísi, Akrotírio** cape Ródos, Dodekánisa, Greece, Aegean Sea

110 I13 **Praszka** Opolskie, S Poland 51°05´N 18°29´E

119 M18 **Pratasy** Rus. Protasy. Homyel'skaya Voblasts´, SE Belarus 52°47´N 29°05´E

167 Q10 **Prathai** Nakhon Ratchasima, E Thailand 15°31´N 102°42´E

**Prathet Thai** see Thailand

**Prathum Thani** see Pathum Thani

63 F21 **Prat, Isla** island S Chile

106 G11 **Prato** Toscana, C Italy 43°53´N 11°05´E

103 O17 **Prats-de-Mollo-la-Preste** Pyrénées-Orientales, S France 42°25´N 02°28´E

26 L6 **Pratt** Kansas, C USA 37°40´N 98°45´W

108 E6 **Prattein** Basel Landschaft, NW Switzerland 47°30´N 07°42´E

193 O2 **Pratt Seamount** undersea feature N Pacific Ocean

23 P4 **Prattville** Alabama, S USA 32°27´N 86°27´W

119 B14 **Praust** see Pruszcz Gdański

119 B14 **Pravdinsk** Ger. Friedland. Kaliningradskaya Oblast´, W Russia 54°26´N 21°01´E

104 K2 **Pravia** Asturias, N Spain 43°30´N 06°06´W

152 M13 **Prayagraj** prev. Allāhābād. Uttar Pradesh, N India 25°27´N 81°50´E

112 N11 **Prazaroki** Rus. Prozoroki. Vitsyebskaya Voblasts´, N Belarus 55°17´N 27°49´E

109 W2 **Prázsmár** see Prejmer

**Prásmár** see Prejmer

112 L12 **Požega** prev. Slavonska Požega, Ger. Poschega, Hung. Pozsega. Požega-Slavonija, NE Croatia

167 S11 **Preăh Vihéar** Preah Vihear, N Cambodia 13°57´N 104°48´E

116 J12 **Predeal** Hung. Predeál. Brașov, C Romania 45°30´N 25°31´E

109 S8 **Predlitz** Steiermark, SE Austria 47°13´N 13°54´E

1 V15 **Preeceville** Saskatchewan, S Canada 51°58´N 102°40´W

125 O13 **Pré-en-Pail** Mayenne, NW France 48°27´N 00°15´W

109 T4 **Pregarten** Oberösterreich, N Austria 48°21´N 14°31´E

54 H7 **Pregonero** Táchira, NW Venezuela 08°02´N 71°35´W

118 I11 **Preiļi** Ger. Preli. SE Latvia 56°18´N 26°43´E

116 M13 **Prejmer** Ger. Tartlau, Hung. Prázsmár. Brașov, C Romania 45°42´N 25°49´E

113 J16 **Prekornica** ▲ C Montenegro

**Preli** see Preiļi
**Prëmet** see Përmet

100 M12 **Premnitz** Brandenburg, NE Germany 52°33´N 12°22´E

25 S15 **Premont** Texas, SW USA 27°21´N 98°07´W

113 H14 **Prenj** ▲ S Bosnia and Herzegovina 43°34´N 17°53´E

**Prenjas/Prenjasi** see Përrenjas

100 O10 **Prenzlau** Brandenburg, NE Germany

**Preny** see Prienai

100 O10 **Prenzlau** Brandenburg, NE Germany 53°19´N 13°52´E

77 P17 **Pra** ← S Ghana

111 C19 **Prachatice** Jihočeský Kraj, S Czechia 49°01´N 14°02´E

166 J9 **Preparis Island** island SW Myanmar (Burma)

**Prerau** see Přerov

111 H18 **Přerov** Ger. Prerau. Olomoucký Kraj, E Czechia 49°27´N 17°27´E

14 M14 **Prescott** Ontario, SE Canada 44°43´N 75°33´W

36 K12 **Prescott** Arizona, SW USA 34°33´N 112°26´W

27 T13 **Prescott** Arkansas, C USA 33°49´N 93°25´W

32 L10 **Prescott** Washington, NW USA 46°17´N 118°21´W

185 A24 **Preservation Inlet** inlet South Island, New Zealand

112 O7 **Preševo** Serbia, SE Serbia 42°20´N 21°38´E

29 N10 **Presho** South Dakota, N USA 43°54´N 100°03´W

58 M13 **Presidente Dutra** Maranhão, E Brazil 05°17´S 44°30´W

60 I8 **Presidente Epitácio** São Paulo, S Brazil 21°45´S 52°07´W

62 N5 **Presidente Hayes** off. Departamento de Presidente Hayes. ◊ department C Paraguay

**Presidente Hayes, Departamento de** see Presidente Hayes

60 I9 **Presidente Prudente** São Paulo, S Brazil 22°09´S 51°24´W

**Presidente Stroessner** see Ciudad del Este
**Presidente Vargas** see Itabira

60 I8 **Presidente Venceslau** São Paulo, S Brazil 21°51´S 51°51´W

193 O10 **President Thiers Seamount** undersea feature C Pacific Ocean 24°35´S 145°50´W

24 J11 **Presidio** Texas, SW USA 29°33´N 104°22´W

111 M19 **Prešov** var. Preschau, Ger. Eperies, Hung. Eperjes. Prešovský Kraj, E Slovakia 49°00´N 21°14´E

111 M19 **Prešovský Kraj ◊** region E Slovakia

113 N20 **Prespa, Lake** Alb. Liqeni i Prespës, Gk. Límni Megáli Préspa, Límni Prespa, Mac. Prespansko Ezero, Serb. Prespansko Jezero. ◊ SE Europe

**Prespa, Limni/Prespansko Ezero/Prespansko Jezero/Prespës, Liqen i see** Prespa, Lake

19 S2 **Presque Isle** Maine, NE USA 46°40´N 168°01´W

18 B11 **Presque Isle** Pennsylvania, NE USA 42°09´N 80°06´W

77 P17 **Prestea** SW Ghana 05°22´N 02°07´W

97 K17 **Preston** NW England, United Kingdom 53°46´N 02°42´W

23 S6 **Preston** Georgia, SE USA 32°03´N 84°32´W

33 R16 **Preston** Idaho, NW USA 42°06´N 111°52´W

29 Z13 **Preston** Iowa, C USA 42°03´N 90°24´W

29 X11 **Preston** Minnesota, N USA 43°41´N 92°06´W

21 O6 **Prestonsburg** Kentucky, S USA 37°40´N 82°47´W

96 I13 **Prestwick** W Scotland, United Kingdom 55°31´N 04°39´W

**Pretoria** see Tshwane

**Pretoria-Witwatersrand-Vereeniging** see Gauteng

113 M21 **Pretushë** var. Pretusha. Korçë, SE Albania 40°50´N 20°45´E

**Pretusha** see Pretushë

193 O2 **Pratt Seamount** undersea feature N Pacific Ocean 56°09´N 142°30´W

115 C17 **Préveza** Ípeiros, W Greece 38°59´N 20°44´E

37 V3 **Prewitt Reservoir** ◊ Colorado, C USA

167 S13 **Prey Vêng** S Cambodia 11°30´N 105°20´E

**Prey Vêng** see Prey Vêng

144 M12 **Priaral'skiy Karakum** prev. Priaral'skiye Karakumy, Peski. desert SW Kazakhstan

123 P14 **Priargunsk** Zabaykal'skiy Kray, S Russia 50°25´N 119°12´E

38 K14 **Pribilof Islands** island group Alaska, USA

113 K14 **Priboj** Serbia, W Serbia 43°34´N 19°30´E

111 C17 **Příbram** Ger. Pibrans. Středočeský Kraj, W Czechia 49°41´N 14°01´E

37 N5 **Price** Utah, W USA 39°35´N 110°49´W

37 N5 **Price River** ← Utah, W USA

23 N8 **Prichard** Alabama, S USA 30°44´N 88°04´W

25 R8 **Priddy** Texas, SW USA 31°39´N 98°30´W

105 P8 **Priego** Castilla-La Mancha, C Spain 40°26´N 02°19´W

104 M14 **Priego de Córdoba** Andalucía, S Spain 37°27´N 04°12´W

118 C10 **Priekule** Ger. Preenkuln. W Latvia 56°26´N 21°35´E

118 C12 **Priekule** Ger. Prökuls. W Lithuania 55°33´N 21°19´E

118 F12 **Prienai** Pol. Preny. S Lithuania 54°38´N 23°57´E

83 G23 **Prieska** Northern Cape, C South Africa 29°40´S 22°45´E

32 M7 **Priest Lake** ◊ Idaho, NW USA

32 M7 **Priest River** Idaho, NW USA 48°10´N 117°02´W

◆ Country ● Country Capital ◇ Dependent Territory ○ Dependent Territory Capital ◈ Administrative Regions ✈ International Airport ▲ Mountain ▲▲ Mountain Range ← River ✖ Volcano ◊ Lake ◈ Reservoir

Prieta, Peña – Purwodadi


104 M3 **Prieta, Peña** ▲ N Spain 43°01′N 04°42′W
40 J10 **Prieto, Cerro** ▲ C Mexico 24°10′N 105°21′W
111 J19 **Prievidza** *var.* Priewitz, *Ger.* Priwitz, *Hung.* Privigye. Trenčiansky Kraj, W Slovakia 48°47′N 18°35′E
**Priewitz** *see* Prievidza
112 F10 **Prijedor** ◆ Republika Srpska, NW Bosnia and Herzegovina
113 K14 **Prijepolje** Serbia, W Serbia 43°24′N 19°39′E
**Prikaspiyskaya Nizmennost'** *see* Caspian Depression
113 O19 **Prilep** *Turk.* Perlepe. S North Macedonia 41°21′N 21°34′E
108 B9 **Prilly** Vaud, SW Switzerland 46°32′N 06°38′E
**Priluki** *see* Pryluky
62 L10 **Primero, Río** ⇝ C Argentina
29 S12 **Primghar** Iowa, C USA 43°05′N 95°37′W
112 B9 **Primorje-Gorski Kotar** *off.* Primorsko-Goranska Županija. ◆ *province* NW Croatia
118 A13 **Primorsk** *Ger.* Fischhausen. Kaliningradskaya Oblast', W Russia 54°45′N 20°00′E
124 G12 **Primorsk** *Fin.* Koivisto. Leningradskaya Oblast', NW Russia 60°20′N 28°39′E
123 S14 **Primorskiy Kray** *prev. Eng.* Maritime Territory. ◆ *territory* SE Russia
114 N10 **Primorsko** *prev.* Keupriya. Burgas, E Bulgaria 42°15′N 27°45′E
126 K13 **Primorsko-Akhtarsk** Krasnodarskiy Kray, SW Russia 46°03′N 38°44′E
**Primorsko-Goranska Županija** *see* Primorje-Gorski Kotar
**Primorsk/Primorskoye** *see* Prymors'k
113 D14 **Primošten** Šibenik-Knin, S Croatia 43°34′N 15°57′E
11 R13 **Primrose Lake** ◎ Saskatchewan, C Canada
11 T14 **Prince Albert** Saskatchewan, S Canada 53°09′N 105°43′W
83 G25 **Prince Albert** Western Cape, SW South Africa 33°13′S 22°03′E
8 J5 **Prince Albert Peninsula** *peninsula* Victoria Island, Northwest Territories, NW Canada
8 J6 **Prince Albert Sound** *inlet* Northwest Territories, N Canada
J5 8 **Prince Alfred, Cape** *headland* Northwest Territories, NW Canada
9 P6 **Prince Charles Island** *island* Nunavut, NE Canada
195 W6 **Prince Charles Mountains** ▲▲ Antarctica
**Prince-Édouard, Île-du** *see* Prince Edward Island
172 M13 **Prince Edward Fracture Zone** *tectonic feature* SW Indian Ocean
13 P14 **Prince Edward Island** *Fr.* Île-du Prince-Édouard. ◆ *province* SE Canada
13 Q14 **Prince Edward Island** *Fr.* Île-du Prince-Édouard. *island* SE Canada
173 M12 **Prince Edward Islands** *island group* S South Africa
21 X4 **Prince Frederick** Maryland, NE USA 38°32′N 76°35′W
10 M14 **Prince George** British Columbia, SW Canada 53°55′N 122°49′W
21 W6 **Prince George** Virginia, NE USA 37°13′N 77°13′W
197 O8 **Prince Gustaf Adolf Sea** *sea* Nunavut, N Canada
197 Q3 **Prince of Wales, Cape** *headland* Alaska, USA 65°39′N 168°12′W
181 V1 **Prince of Wales Island** *island* Queensland, E Australia
8 L5 **Prince of Wales Island** *island* Queen Elizabeth Islands, Nunavut, NW Canada
39 Y14 **Prince of Wales Island** *island* Alexander Archipelago, Alaska, USA
**Prince of Wales Island** *see* Pinang, Pulau
8 J5 **Prince of Wales Strait** *strait* Northwest Territories, N Canada
197 O8 **Prince Patrick Island** *island* Parry Islands, Northwest Territories, NW Canada
9 N5 **Prince Regent Inlet** *channel* Nunavut, N Canada
10 J13 **Prince Rupert** British Columbia, SW Canada 54°18′N 130°17′W
**Prince's Island** *see* Príncipe
21 Y5 **Princess Anne** Maryland, NE USA 38°12′N 75°42′W
**Princess Astrid Coast** *see* Prinsesse Astrid Kyst
181 W2 **Princess Charlotte Bay** *bay* Queensland, NE Australia
195 W7 **Princess Elizabeth Land** *physical region* Antarctica
10 J14 **Princess Royal Island** *island* British Columbia, SW Canada
45 U15 **Princes Town** Trinidad, Trinidad and Tobago 10°16′N 61°23′W
11 N17 **Princeton** British Columbia, SW Canada 49°25′N 120°35′W
30 L11 **Princeton** Illinois, N USA 41°22′N 89°27′W
31 N16 **Princeton** Indiana, N USA 38°21′N 87°33′W
29 Z14 **Princeton** Iowa, C USA 41°40′N 90°21′W
20 H7 **Princeton** Kentucky, S USA 37°06′N 87°52′W
29 V8 **Princeton** Minnesota, N USA 45°34′N 93°34′W
27 S1 **Princeton** Missouri, C USA 40°22′N 93°37′W
18 J15 **Princeton** New Jersey, NE USA 40°21′N 74°39′W
21 R6 **Princeton** West Virginia, NE USA 37°23′N 81°06′W
39 S12 **Prince William Sound** *inlet* Alaska, USA
67 P9 **Príncipe** *var.* Príncipe Island, *Eng.* Prince's Island. *island* N Sao Tome and Principe
**Príncipe Island** *see* Príncipe
32 I13 **Prineville** Oregon, NW USA 44°19′N 120°50′W
28 J11 **Pringle** South Dakota, N USA 43°34′N 103°34′W
25 N1 **Pringle** Texas, SW USA 35°55′N 101°28′W
99 H14 **Prinsenbeek** Noord-Brabant, S Netherlands 51°36′N 04°42′E
98 L6 **Prinses Margriet Kanaal** *canal* N Netherlands
195 R1 **Prinsesse Astrid Kyst** *Eng.* Princess Astrid Coast. *physical region* Antarctica
195 T2 **Prinsesse Ragnhild Kyst** *physical region* Antarctica
195 U2 **Prins Harald Kyst** *physical region* Antarctica
92 N2 **Prins Karls Forland** *island* W Svalbard
43 N8 **Prinzapolka** Costa Caribe Norte, NE Nicaragua 13°19′N 83°35′W
42 L8 **Prinzapolka, Río** ⇝ NE Nicaragua
122 H9 **Priob'ye** Khanty-Mansiyskiy Avtonomnyy Okrug-Yugra, N Russia 62°25′N 65°36′E
104 H1 **Prior, Cabo** *headland* NW Spain 43°33′N 08°21′W
29 V9 **Prior Lake** Minnesota, N USA 44°42′N 93°25′W
124 H11 **Priozersk** *Fin.* Käkisalmi. Leningradskaya Oblast', NW Russia 61°02′N 30°07′E
119 J20 **Pripet** *Bel.* Prypyats', *Ukr.* Pryp"yat'. ⇝ Belarus/Ukraine
119 J20 **Pripet Marshes** *wetland* Belarus/Ukraine
113 N16 **Prishtinë** *var.* Pristina, *Serb.* Priština. ● (Kosovo) C Kosovo 42°40′N 21°10′E
126 J8 **Pristen'** Kurskaya Oblast', W Russia 51°15′N 36°47′E
**Pristina** *see* Prishtinë
**Priština** *see* Prishtinë
100 M10 **Pritzwalk** Brandenburg, NE Germany 53°10′N 12°11′E
103 R13 **Privas** Ardèche, E France 44°45′N 04°35′E
107 I16 **Priverno** Lazio, C Italy 41°28′N 13°11′E
**Privigye** *see* Prievidza
112 C12 **Privlaka** Zadar, SW Croatia 44°15′N 15°07′E
124 M15 **Privolzhsk** Ivanovskaya Oblast', NW Russia 57°24′N 41°16′E
127 P7 **Privolzhskaya Vozvyshennost'** *var.* Volga Uplands. ▲▲ W Russia
127 P8 **Privolzhskoye** Saratovskaya Oblast', W Russia 51°08′N 45°57′E
**Priwitz** *see* Prievidza
127 N13 **Priyutnoye** Respublika Kalmykiya, SW Russia 46°08′N 43°33′E
113 M17 **Prizren** S Kosovo 42°14′N 20°46′E
107 I24 **Prizzi** Sicilia, Italy, C Mediterranean Sea 37°44′N 13°26′E
113 P18 **Probištip** NE North Macedonia 42°00′N 22°06′E
169 S16 **Probolinggo** Jawa, C Indonesia 07°45′S 113°12′E
**Probstberg** *see* Wyszków
111 F14 **Prochowice** *Ger.* Parchwitz. Dolnośląskie, SW Poland 51°15′N 16°22′E
29 W5 **Proctor** Minnesota, N USA 46°46′N 92°13′W
25 R8 **Proctor** Texas, SW USA 31°57′N 98°25′W
25 R8 **Proctor Lake** ⊠ Texas, SW USA
155 I18 **Proddatūr** Andhra Pradesh, E India 14°45′N 78°34′E
104 H9 **Proença-a-Nova** *var.* Proença a Nova. Castelo Branco, C Portugal 39°45′N 07°56′W
**Proença a Nova** *see* Proença-a-Nova
99 I21 **Profondeville** Namur, SE Belgium 50°22′N 04°52′E
41 W11 **Progreso** Yucatán, SE Mexico 21°14′N 89°41′W
123 R14 **Progress** Amurskaya Oblast', SE Russia 49°40′N 129°30′E
127 O15 **Prokhladnyy** Kabardino-Balkarskaya Respublika, SW Russia 43°48′N 44°02′E
**Prokletije** *see* North Albanian Alps
**Prökuls** *see* Priekulė
113 O15 **Prokuplje** Serbia, SE Serbia 43°15′N 21°35′E
124 H14 **Proletariy** Novgorodskaya Oblast', W Russia 58°24′N 31°40′E
126 M12 **Proletarsk** Rostovskaya Oblast', SW Russia 46°42′N 41°48′E
127 N13 **Proletarskoye Vodokhranilishche** *salt lake* SW Russia
**Prome** *see* Pyay
60 J8 **Promissão** São Paulo, S Brazil 21°33′S 49°51′W
60 J8 **Promissão, Represa de** ⊠ S Brazil
125 V4 **Promyshlennyy** Respublika Komi, NW Russia 67°36′N 64°E
119 O16 **Pronya** ⇝ E Belarus
10 M11 **Prophet River** British Columbia, W Canada 58°07′N 122°39′W
30 K11 **Prophetstown** Illinois, N USA 41°40′N 89°56′W
**Propinsi Kepulauan Riau** *see* Kepulauan Riau
**Propinsi Papua Barat** *see* Papua Barat
59 P16 **Propriá** Sergipe, E Brazil 10°15′S 36°51′W
103 X16 **Propriano** Corse, France, C Mediterranean Sea 41°41′N 08°54′E
**Prościejów** *see* Prostějov
**Proskurov** *see* Khmel 'nyts'kyy
114 H12 **Prosotsáni** Anatolikí Makedonía kai Thráki, NE Greece 41°11′N 23°59′E
171 Q7 **Prosperidad** Mindanao, S Philippines 08°36′N 125°54′E
32 J10 **Prosser** Washington, NW USA 46°12′N 119°46′W
**Prossnitz** *see* Prostějov
111 G18 **Prostějov** *Ger.* Prossnitz, *Pol.* Prościejów. Olomoucký Kraj, E Czechia 49°29′N 17°08′E
117 V8 **Prosyana** Dnipropetrovs'ka Oblast', E Ukraine 48°07′N 36°22′E
111 L16 **Proszowice** Małopolskie, S Poland 50°12′N 20°15′E
**Protasy** *see* Pratasy
172 J11 **Protea Seamount** *undersea feature* SW Indian Ocean 36°50′S 18°05′E
115 D21 **Próti** *island* S Greece
114 N8 **Provadia** , Provadiya. Varna, E Bulgaria 43°10′N 27°29′E
**Provadiya** *see* Provadia
103 T14 **Provence** *cultural region* SE France
103 S15 **Provence** *prev.* Marseille-Marigrane. ✈ (Marseille) Bouches-du-Rhône, SE France 43°25′N 05°15′E
103 T14 **Provence-Alpes-Côte d'Azur** ◆ *region* SE France
20 H6 **Providence** Kentucky, S USA 37°23′N 87°47′W
19 N12 **Providence** *state capital* Rhode Island, NE USA 41°50′N 71°26′W
36 L1 **Providence** Utah, W USA 41°42′N 111°49′W
**Providence** *see* Fort Providence
**Providence** *see* Providence Atoll
67 X10 **Providence Atoll** *var.* Providence. *atoll* S Seychelles
14 D12 **Providence Bay** Manitoulin Island, Ontario, S Canada 45°39′N 82°16′W
23 R6 **Providence Canyon** *valley* Alabama/Georgia, S USA
22 I5 **Providence, Lake** ◎ Louisiana, S USA
35 X13 **Providence Mountains** ▲▲ California, W USA
44 L6 **Providenciales** *island* W Turks and Caicos Islands
19 Q12 **Provincetown** Massachusetts, NE USA 42°01′N 70°10′W
103 P5 **Provins** Seine-et-Marne, N France 48°34′N 03°18′E
36 L3 **Provo** Utah, W USA 40°14′N 111°39′W
11 R15 **Provost** Alberta, SW Canada 52°24′N 110°16′W
112 G13 **Prozor** Federacija Bosne I Hercegovine, SW Bosnia and Herzegovina 43°46′N 17°38′E
**Prozoroki** *see* Prazaroki
60 I11 **Prudentópolis** Paraná, S Brazil 25°12′S 50°58′W
39 R5 **Prudhoe Bay** Alaska, USA 70°16′N 148°18′W
39 R4 **Prudhoe Bay** *bay* Alaska, USA
111 H16 **Prudnik** *Ger.* Neustadt, Neustadt in Oberschlesien. Opole, SW Poland 50°20′N 17°34′E
119 J16 **Prudy** Minskaya Voblasts', C Belarus 53°47′N 26°32′E
101 D18 **Prüm** Rheinland-Pfalz, W Germany 50°15′N 06°27′E
101 D18 **Prüm** ⇝ W Germany
**Prusa** *see* Bursa
110 J7 **Pruszcz Gdański** *Ger.* Praust. Pomorskie, N Poland 54°16′N 18°36′E
110 M12 **Pruszków** *Ger.* Kaltdorf. Mazowieckie, C Poland 52°09′N 20°49′E
116 K8 **Prut** *Ger.* Pruth. ⇝ E Europe
**Pruth** *see* Prut
108 L8 **Prutz** Tirol, W Austria 47°07′N 10°42′E
**Pružana** *see* Pruzhany
119 G19 **Pruzhany** *Pol.* Prużana. Brestskaya Voblasts', SW Belarus 52°33′N 24°28′E
124 I11 **Pryazha** Respublika Kareliya, NW Russia 61°42′N 33°39′E
117 U10 **Pryazovs'ke** Zaporiz'ka Oblast', SE Ukraine 46°43′N 35°39′E
**Prychornomor'ska Nyzovyna** *see* Black Sea Lowland
**Prydniprovs'ka Nyzovyna/ Prydnyaprowskaya Nizina** *see* Dnieper Lowland
195 Y7 **Prydz Bay** *bay* Antarctica
117 R4 **Pryluky** *Rus.* Priluki. Chernihivs'ka Oblast', NE Ukraine 50°35′N 32°23′E
117 V10 **Prymors'k** *Rus.* Primorsk; *prev.* Primorskoye. Zaporiz'ka Oblast', SE Ukraine 46°44′N 36°19′E
117 U13 **Prymors'kyy** Avtonomna Respublika Krym, S Ukraine 45°09′N 35°33′E
27 Q9 **Pryor** Oklahoma, C USA 36°19′N 95°19′W
33 U11 **Pryor Creek** ⇝ Montana, NW USA
**Pryp"yat'/Prypyats'** *see* Pripet
110 M10 **Przasnysz** Mazowieckie, C Poland 53°01′N 20°51′E
111 K14 **Przedbórz** Łodzkie, S Poland 51°04′N 19°51′E
111 P17 **Przemyśl** *Rus.* Peremyshl. Podkarpackie, C Poland 49°47′N 22°47′E
111 O16 **Przeworsk** Podkarpackie, SE Poland 50°04′N 22°30′E
**Przheval'sk** *see* Karakol
110 L13 **Przysucha** Mazowieckie, SE Poland 51°22′N 20°36′E
115 H18 **Psachná** *var.* Psahna, Psakhná. Évvoia, C Greece 38°35′N 23°39′E
**Psahna/Psakhná** *see* Psachná
115 K18 **Psará** *island* E Greece
115 I16 **Psathoúra** *island* Vóreies Sporádes, Greece, Aegean Sea
**Pschestitz** *see* Přeštice
**Psein Lora** *see* Pishin Lora
117 S5 **Psel** *Rus.* Psël. ⇝ Russia/Ukraine
**Psël** *see* Psel
115 M21 **Psérimos** *island* Dodekánisa, Greece, Aegean Sea
**Pseyn Bowr** *see* Pishin Lora
**Pskem** *see* Piskom
147 R8 **Pskemskiy Khrebet** *Uzb.* Piskom Tizmasi. ▲▲ Kyrgyzstan/Uzbekistan
124 F14 **Pskov** *Ger.* Pleskau, *Latv.* Pleskava. Pskovskaya Oblast', W Russia 58°32′N 31°15′E
118 K6 **Pskov, Lake** *Est.* Pihkva Järv, *Ger.* Pleskauer See, *Rus.* Pskovskoye Ozero. ◎ Estonia/Russia
124 F15 **Pskovskaya Oblast'** ◆ *province* W Russia
**Pskovskoye Ozero** *see* Pskov, Lake
112 G9 **Psunj** ▲▲ NE Croatia
111 J17 **Pszczyna** *Ger.* Pless. Śląskie, S Poland 49°59′N 18°54′E
**Ptačnik/Ptacsnik** *see* Vtáčnik
115 D17 **Ptéri** ▲ C Greece 39°08′N 21°32′E
**Ptich'** *see* Ptsich
115 E14 **Ptolemaïda** *prev.* Ptolemaïs. Dytikí Makedonía, N Greece 40°34′N 21°42′E
**Ptolemaïs** *see* Ptolemaïda, Greece
**Ptolemaïs** *see* 'Akko, Israel
119 M19 **Ptsich** *Rus.* Ptich'. Homyel'skaya Voblasts', SE Belarus 52°11′N 28°49′E
119 M18 **Ptsich** *Rus.* Ptich'. ⇝ SE Belarus
109 X10 **Ptuj** *Ger.* Pettau; *anc.* Poetovio. NE Slovenia 46°26′N 15°54′E
61 A23 **Puán** Buenos Aires, E Argentina 37°35′S 62°45′W
192 H15 **Pu'apu'a** Savai'i, C Samoa 13°32′S 172°09′W
192 G15 **Puava, Cape** *headland* Savai'i, NW Samoa
**Pubao** *see* Baingoin
56 F12 **Pucallpa** Ucayali, C Peru 08°21′S 74°33′W
57 J17 **Pucarani** La Paz, NW Bolivia 16°25′S 68°29′W
**Pučarevo** *see* Novi Travnik
157 U12 **Pucheng** Shaanxi, SE China 35°00′N 109°34′E
160 L6 **Pucheng** *var.* Nanpu. Fujian, C China 27°59′N 118°31′E
125 N16 **Puchezh** Ivanovskaya Oblast', W Russia 56°58′N 41°08′E
111 I19 **Púchov** *Hung.* Puhó. Trenčiansky Kraj, W Slovakia 49°08′N 18°15′E
116 J13 **Pucioasa** Dâmbovița, S Romania 45°04′N 25°23′E
110 I6 **Puck** Pomorskie, N Poland 54°43′N 18°24′E
30 L8 **Puckaway Lake** ◎ Wisconsin, N USA
63 G15 **Pucón** Araucanía, S Chile 39°18′S 71°52′W
148 L8 **Pūdah Tal, Shēlah-ye** ⇝ SW Afghanistan
93 M14 **Pudasjärvi** Pohjois-Pohjanmaa, C Finland 65°20′N 27°02′E
127 S1 **Pudem** Udmurtskaya Respublika, NW Russia 58°18′N 52°08′E
**Pudewitz** *see* Pobiedziska
124 K11 **Pudozh** Respublika Kareliya, NW Russia 61°48′N 36°30′E
97 M17 **Pudsey** N England, United Kingdom 53°48′N 01°40′W
**Puduchcheri** *see* Puducherry
151 I20 **Puducherry** *prev.* Pondicherry, *var.* Puduchcheri, *Fr.* Pondichéry. ◆ *union territory* India
151 H21 **Pudukkottai** Tamil Nādu, SE India 10°23′N 78°47′E
171 Z13 **Pue** Papua, E Indonesia 02°42′S 140°36′E
41 P14 **Puebla** *var.* Puebla de Zaragoza. Puebla, S Mexico 19°02′N 98°13′W
41 P15 **Puebla** ◆ *state* S Mexico
104 L11 **Puebla de Alcocer** Extremadura, W Spain 38°59′N 05°14′W
**Puebla de Don Fabrique** *see* Puebla de Don Fadrique
105 P13 **Puebla de Don Fadrique** *var.* Puebla de Don Fabrique. Andalucía, S Spain 37°58′N 02°25′W
104 J11 **Puebla de la Calzada** Extremadura, W Spain 38°54′N 06°38′W
104 J5 **Puebla de Sanabria** Castilla y León, N Spain 42°04′N 06°38′W
**Puebla de Trives** *see* A Pobla de Trives
**Puebla de Zaragoza** *see* Puebla
37 T6 **Pueblo** Colorado, C USA 38°15′N 104°37′W
37 N10 **Pueblo Colorado Wash** *valley* Arizona, SW USA
61 C16 **Pueblo Libertador** Corrientes, NE Argentina 30°13′S 59°23′W
40 J10 **Pueblo Nuevo** Durango, C Mexico 23°24′N 105°21′W
42 J8 **Pueblo Nuevo** Estelí, NW Nicaragua 13°21′N 86°30′W
54 J3 **Pueblo Nuevo** Falcón, N Venezuela 11°59′N 69°57′W
42 B6 **Pueblo Nuevo Tiquisate** *var.* Tiquisate. Escuintla, SW Guatemala 14°16′N 91°21′W
41 Q11 **Pueblo Viejo, Laguna de** *lagoon* E Mexico
63 J14 **Puelches** La Pampa, C Argentina 38°08′S 65°56′W
104 L14 **Puente-Genil** Andalucía, S Spain 37°23′N 04°45′W
105 Q3 **Puente la Reina** *Bas.* Gares. Navarra, N Spain 42°40′N 01°49′W
104 L12 **Puente Nuevo, Embalse de** ⊠ S Spain
57 D14 **Puente Piedra** Provincia de Lima, W Peru 11°49′S 77°01′W
160 F14 **Pu'er** *var.* Ning'er. Yunnan, SW China 23°09′N 100°58′E
45 V6 **Puerca, Punta** *headland* E Puerto Rico 18°13′N 65°36′W
37 R12 **Puerco, Rio** ⇝ New Mexico, SW USA
57 J17 **Puerto Acosta** La Paz, W Bolivia 15°33′S 69°15′W
63 G19 **Puerto Aisén** Aysén, S Chile 45°24′S 72°42′W
41 R17 **Puerto Ángel** Oaxaca, SE Mexico 15°39′N 96°29′W
**Puerto Argentino** *see* Stanley
41 T17 **Puerto Arista** Chiapas, SE Mexico 15°55′N 93°47′W
43 O16 **Puerto Armuelles** Chiriquí, SW Panama 08°19′N 82°51′W
**Puerto Arrecife** *see* Arrecife
54 D14 **Puerto Asís** Putumayo, SW Colombia 0°31′N 76°31′W
54 L9 **Puerto Ayacucho** Amazonas, SW Venezuela 05°45′N 67°37′W
57 C18 **Puerto Ayora** Galapagos Islands, Ecuador, E Pacific Ocean 0°45′S 90°19′W
57 C18 **Puerto Baquerizo Moreno** *var.* Baquerizo Moreno. Galapagos Islands, Ecuador, E Pacific Ocean 0°54′S 89°37′W
42 G4 **Puerto Barrios** Izabal, E Guatemala 15°42′N 88°34′W
**Puerto Bello** *see* Portobelo
54 F8 **Puerto Berrío** Antioquia, C Colombia 06°28′N 74°28′W
54 F9 **Puerto Boyaca** Boyacá, C Colombia 05°58′N 74°36′W
54 K4 **Puerto Cabello** Carabobo, N Venezuela 10°29′N 68°02′W
43 N7 **Puerto Cabezas** *var.* Bilwi. Costa Caribe Norte, NE Nicaragua 14°05′N 83°22′W
54 L9 **Puerto Carreño** Vichada, E Colombia 06°08′N 67°30′W
54 E4 **Puerto Colombia** Atlántico, N Colombia 10°59′N 74°57′W
42 H4 **Puerto Cortés** Cortés, NW Honduras 15°50′N 87°55′W
54 J4 **Puerto Cumarebo** Falcón, N Venezuela 11°29′N 69°21′W
**Puerto de Cabras** *see* Puerto del Rosario
55 Q5 **Puerto de Hierro** Sucre, NE Venezuela 10°40′N 62°03′W
64 O11 **Puerto de la Cruz** Tenerife, Islas Canarias, Spain, NE Atlantic Ocean 28°24′N 16°33′W
64 Q11 **Puerto del Rosario** *var.* Puerto de Cabras. Fuerteventura, Islas Canarias, Spain, NE Atlantic Ocean 28°29′N 13°52′W
63 J20 **Puerto Deseado** Santa Cruz, SE Argentina 47°46′S 65°53′W
40 F8 **Puerto Escondido** Baja California Sur, NW Mexico 25°48′N 111°20′W
41 R17 **Puerto Escondido** Oaxaca, SE Mexico 15°48′N 96°57′W
60 G12 **Puerto Esperanza** Misiones, NE Argentina 26°01′S 54°39′W
54 H10 **Puerto Gaitán** Meta, C Colombia 04°20′N 72°10′W
**Puerto Gallegos** *see* Río Gallegos
60 G12 **Puerto Iguazú** Misiones, NE Argentina 25°39′S 54°35′W
56 F12 **Puerto Inca** Huánuco, N Peru 09°22′S 74°54′W
54 L11 **Puerto Inírida** *var.* Obando. Guainía, E Colombia 03°48′N 67°54′W
42 K13 **Puerto Jesús** Guanacaste, NW Costa Rica 10°08′N 85°26′W
41 Z11 **Puerto Juárez** Quintana Roo, SE Mexico 21°06′N 86°46′W
55 N5 **Puerto La Cruz** Anzoátegui, NE Venezuela 10°14′N 64°40′W
54 E14 **Puerto Leguízamo** Putumayo, S Colombia 0°14′S 74°45′W
43 N5 **Puerto Lempira** Gracias a Dios, E Honduras 15°14′N 83°48′W
**Puerto Libertad** *see* La Libertad
54 I11 **Puerto Limón** Meta, E Colombia 04°00′N 71°09′W
54 D13 **Puerto Limón** Putumayo, SW Colombia 01°02′N 76°30′W
**Puerto Limón** *see* Limón
105 N11 **Puertollano** Castilla-La Mancha, C Spain 38°41′N 04°07′W
63 K17 **Puerto Lobos** Chubut, SE Argentina 42°00′S 64°58′W
54 I3 **Puerto López** La Guajira, N Colombia 11°54′N 71°21′W
105 Q14 **Puerto Lumbreras** Murcia, SE Spain 37°35′N 01°49′W
41 V17 **Puerto Madero** Chiapas, SE Mexico 14°44′N 92°25′W
63 K17 **Puerto Madryn** Chubut, S Argentina 42°45′S 65°02′W
**Puerto Magdalena** *see* Bahía Magdalena
57 J15 **Puerto Maldonado** Madre de Dios, E Peru 12°37′S 69°11′W
**Puerto Masachapa** *see* Masachapa
**Puerto México** *see* Coatzacoalcos
63 G17 **Puerto Montt** Los Lagos, C Chile 41°28′S 72°57′W
41 Z12 **Puerto Morelos** Quintana Roo, SE Mexico 20°47′N 86°54′W
54 L10 **Puerto Nariño** Vichada, E Colombia 04°57′N 67°51′W
63 H23 **Puerto Natales** Magallanes y de la Antártica Chilena, S Chile 51°42′S 72°28′W
43 X15 **Puerto Obaldía** Guna Yala, NE Panama 08°38′N 77°26′W
44 H6 **Puerto Padre** Las Tunas, E Cuba 21°13′N 76°35′W
54 L9 **Puerto Páez** Apure, C Venezuela 06°10′N 67°30′W
40 E3 **Puerto Peñasco** Sonora, NW Mexico 31°20′N 113°35′W
55 N5 **Puerto Píritu** Anzoátegui, NE Venezuela 10°04′N 65°00′W
45 N8 **Puerto Plata** *var.* San Felipe de Puerto Plata. N Dominican Republic 19°46′N 70°42′W
**Puerto Presidente Stroessner** *see* Ciudad del Este
171 N6 **Puerto Princesa** *off.* Puerto Princesa City. Palawan, W Philippines 09°48′N 118°43′E
**Puerto Princesa City** *see* Puerto Princesa
**Puerto Príncipe** *see* Camagüey
**Puerto Quellón** *see* Quellón
60 F13 **Puerto Rico** Misiones, NE Argentina 26°48′S 54°59′W
57 K14 **Puerto Rico** Pando, N Bolivia 11°07′S 67°32′W
54 E12 **Puerto Rico** Caquetá, S Colombia 01°54′N 75°13′W
45 U5 **Puerto Rico** *off.* Commonwealth of Puerto Rico; *prev.* Porto Rico. ◇ *unincorporated territory of the US with commonwealth status* C West Indies
64 F11 **Puerto Rico** *island* C West Indies
**Puerto Rico, Commonwealth of** *see* Puerto Rico
64 G11 **Puerto Rico Trench** *undersea feature* NE Caribbean Sea
54 I8 **Puerto Rondón** Arauca, E Colombia 06°16′N 71°05′W
**Puerto San José** *see* San José
63 J21 **Puerto San Julián** *var.* San Julián. Santa Cruz, SE Argentina 49°14′S 67°41′W
63 I22 **Puerto Santa Cruz** *var.* Santa Cruz. Santa Cruz, SE Argentina 50°05′S 68°31′W
**Puerto Sauce** *see* Juan L. Lacaze
57 Q20 **Puerto Suárez** Santa Cruz, E Bolivia 18°59′S 57°47′W
54 D13 **Puerto Umbría** Putumayo, SW Colombia 0°52′N 76°36′W
40 J13 **Puerto Vallarta** Jalisco, SW Mexico 20°35′N 105°15′W
63 G16 **Puerto Varas** Los Lagos, C Chile 41°20′S 73°00′W
42 M13 **Puerto Viejo** Heredia, NE Costa Rica 10°27′N 84°00′W
**Puertoviejo** *see* Portoviejo
57 B18 **Puerto Villamil** *var.* Villamil. Galapagos Islands, Ecuador, E Pacific Ocean 0°57′S 91°00′W
54 F8 **Puerto Wilches** Santander, N Colombia 07°22′N 73°53′W
63 H20 **Pueyrredón, Lago** *var.* Lago Cochrane. ◎ S Argentina
127 R7 **Pugachëv** Saratovskaya Oblast', W Russia 52°06′N 48°50′E
127 T3 **Pugachëvo** Udmurtskaya Respublika, NW Russia 56°38′N 53°03′E
32 H8 **Puget Sound** *sound* Washington, NW USA
107 O17 **Puglia** *var.* Le Puglie, *Eng.* Apulia. ◆ *region* SE Italy
107 N17 **Puglia, Canosa di** *anc.* Canusium. Puglia, SE Italy 41°13′N 16°04′E
118 I6 **Puhja** *Ger.* Kawelecht. Tartumaa, SE Estonia 58°20′N 26°19′E
**Puhó** *see* Púchov
105 V4 **Puigcerdà** Cataluña, NE Spain 42°25′N 01°53′E
**Puigmal** *see* Puigmal d'Err
103 N17 **Puigmal d'Err** *var.* Puigmal. ▲ S France 42°24′N 02°07′E
76 I16 **Pujehun** Sierra Leone 07°23′N 11°44′W
**Puka** *see* Pukë
185 E20 **Pukaki, Lake** ◎ South Island, New Zealand
38 F10 **Pukalani** Maui, Hawaii, USA, C Pacific Ocean 20°50′N 156°20′W
190 J13 **Pukapuka** *atoll* N Cook Islands
191 X9 **Pukapuka** *atoll* Îles Tuamotu, E French Polynesia
**Pukari Neem** *see* Purekkari Neem
191 X11 **Pukarua** *var.* Pukaruha. *atoll* Îles Tuamotu, E French Polynesia
**Pukaruha** *see* Pukarua
14 A7 **Pukaskwa** ⇝ Ontario, S Canada
11 V12 **Pukatawagan** Manitoba, C Canada 55°46′N 101°14′W
191 X16 **Pukatikei, Maunga** ▲ Easter Island, Chile, E Pacific Ocean
182 C1 **Pukatja** *var.* Ernabella. South Australia 26°18′S 132°13′E
163 Y12 **Pukch'ŏng** E North Korea 40°13′N 128°20′E
113 L18 **Pukë** *var.* Puka. Shkodër, N Albania 42°03′N 19°53′E
184 L6 **Pukekohe** Auckland, North Island, New Zealand 37°12′S 174°54′E
184 L7 **Pukemiro** Waikato, North Island, New Zealand 37°37′S 175°02′E
190 D12 **Puke, Mont** ▲ Île Futuna, W Wallis and Futuna
**Puket** *see* Phuket
185 C20 **Puketeraki Range** ▲▲ South Island, New Zealand
184 N13 **Puketoi Range** ▲▲ North Island, New Zealand
185 F21 **Pukeuri Junction** Otago, South Island, New Zealand 45°01′S 171°01′E
119 L16 **Pukhavichy** *Rus.* Pukhovichi. Minskaya Voblasts', C Belarus 53°32′N 28°15′E
**Pukhovichi** *see* Pukhavichy
124 M10 **Puksoozero** Arkhangel'skaya Oblast', NW Russia 62°37′N 40°29′E
112 A10 **Pula** *It.* Pola; *prev.* Pulj. Istra, NW Croatia 44°53′N 13°51′E
**Pula** *see* Nyingchi
163 U14 **Pulandian** *var.* Xinjin. Liaoning, NE China 39°25′N 121°58′E
163 T14 **Pulandian Wan** *bay* NE China
189 O15 **Pulap Atoll** *atoll* Caroline Islands, C Micronesia
18 H9 **Pulaski** New York, NE USA 43°34′N 76°06′W
20 I10 **Pulaski** Tennessee, S USA 35°11′N 87°00′W
21 R7 **Pulaski** Virginia, NE USA 37°03′N 80°47′W
171 Y14 **Pulau, Sungai** ⇝ Papua, E Indonesia
110 N13 **Puławy** *Ger.* Neu Amerika. Lubelskie, E Poland 51°25′N 21°57′E
149 R5 **Pul-e-'Alam** *prev.* Pol-e-'Alam. Lōgar, E Afghanistan 33°59′N 69°02′E
149 Q3 **Pul-e Khumrī** *prev.* Pol-e Khomrī. Baghlān, NE Afghanistan 35°55′N 68°45′E
146 I16 **Pulhatyn** *Rus.* Polekhatum; *prev.* Pul'-I-Khatum. Ahal Welaýaty, S Turkmenistan 36°01′N 61°08′E
101 E16 **Pulheim** Nordrhein-Westfalen, W Germany 51°00′N 06°48′E
155 J19 **Pulicat Lake** *lagoon* SE India
**Pul'-I-Khatum** *see* Pulhatyn
**Pul-i-Sefid** *see* Pol-e Sefid
**Pulj** *see* Pula
109 W2 **Pulkau** ⇝ NE Austria
93 L15 **Pulkkila** Pohjois-Pohjanmaa, C Finland 64°15′N 25°53′E
122 C7 **Pulkovo** ✈ (Sankt-Peterburg) Leningradskaya Oblast', NW Russia 60°06′N 30°23′E
32 M9 **Pullman** Washington, NW USA 46°43′N 117°10′W
108 B10 **Pully** Vaud, SW Switzerland 46°31′N 06°40′E
40 F7 **Púlpita, Punta** *headland* NW Mexico 26°30′N 111°28′W
110 M10 **Pułtusk** Mazowieckie, C Poland 52°41′N 21°04′E
158 H10 **Pulu** Xinjiang Uygur Zizhiqu, W China 36°10′N 81°29′E
137 P13 **Pülümür** Tunceli, E Turkey 39°30′N 39°54′E
189 N16 **Pulusuk** *island* Caroline Islands, C Micronesia
189 N16 **Puluwat Atoll** *atoll* Caroline Islands, C Micronesia
116 M4 **Pulyny** *prev.* Chervonoarmiys'k. Zhytomyrs'ka Oblast', N Ukraine 50°27′N 28°15′E
25 N11 **Pumpville** Texas, SW USA 29°55′N 101°43′W
191 P7 **Punaauia** *var.* Hakapehi. Tahiti, W French Polynesia 17°38′S 149°37′W
56 B8 **Puná, Isla** *island* SW Ecuador
185 G16 **Punakaiki** West Coast, South Island, New Zealand 42°07′S 171°21′E
153 T11 **Punakha** C Bhutan 27°38′N 89°50′E
57 L18 **Punata** Cochabamba, C Bolivia 17°32′S 65°50′W
155 E14 **Pune** *prev.* Poona. Mahārāshtra, W India 18°32′N 73°52′E
83 M17 **Pungoè, Rio** *var.* Púnguè, Pungwe. ⇝ C Mozambique
21 X10 **Pungo River** ⇝ North Carolina, SE USA
**Púnguè/Pungwe** *see* Pungoè, Rio
79 N19 **Punia** Maniema, E Dem. Rep. Congo 01°28′S 26°25′E
62 H8 **Punilla, Sierra de la** ▲▲ W Argentina
161 P14 **Puning** Guangdong, S China 23°24′N 116°14′E
62 G10 **Punitaqui** Coquimbo, C Chile 30°50′S 71°29′W
149 T9 **Punjab** *prev.* West Punjab, Western Punjab. ◆ *province* E Pakistan
152 H8 **Punjab** *state* NW India
129 Q9 **Punjab Plains** *plain* N India
93 O17 **Punkaharju** *var.* Punkasalmi. Etelä-Savo, E Finland 61°45′N 29°21′E
**Punkasalmi** *see* Punkaharju
57 I17 **Puno** Puno, SE Peru 15°53′S 70°03′W
57 H17 **Puno** *off.* Región de Puno. ◆ *region* S Peru
**Puno, Región de** *see* Puno
61 B24 **Punta Alta** Buenos Aires, E Argentina 38°54′S 62°01′W
63 H24 **Punta Arenas** *prev.* Magallanes. Magallanes y de la Antártica Chilena, S Chile 53°10′S 70°56′W
45 T6 **Punta, Cerro de** ▲ C Puerto Rico 18°10′N 66°36′W
43 T15 **Punta Chame** West Panamá, C Panama 08°39′N 79°42′W
57 G17 **Punta Colorada** Arequipa, SW Peru 16°17′S 72°31′W
40 F9 **Punta Coyote** Baja California Sur, NW Mexico
62 G8 **Punta de Díaz** Atacama, N Chile 28°03′S 70°36′W
61 G20 **Punta del Este** Maldonado, S Uruguay 34°59′S 54°58′W
63 K17 **Punta Delgada** Chubut, SE Argentina 42°46′S 63°40′W
55 O5 **Punta de Mata** Monagas, NE Venezuela 09°48′N 63°38′W
55 O4 **Punta de Piedras** Nueva Esparta, NE Venezuela 10°57′N 64°06′W
42 F4 **Punta Gorda** Toledo, SE Belize 16°07′N 88°47′W
43 N11 **Punta Gorda** Costa Caribe Sur, SE Nicaragua 11°31′N 83°46′W
23 W14 **Punta Gorda** Florida, SE USA 26°55′N 82°03′W
42 M11 **Punta Gorda, Río** ⇝ SE Nicaragua
62 H6 **Punta Negra, Salar de** *salt lake* N Chile
40 D5 **Punta Prieta** Baja California, NW Mexico 28°56′N 114°11′W
42 L13 **Puntarenas** Puntarenas, W Costa Rica 09°58′N 84°50′W
42 L13 **Puntarenas** *off.* Provincia de Puntarenas. ◆ *province* W Costa Rica
**Puntarenas, Provincia de** *see* Puntarenas
80 P13 **Puntland** *cultural region* NE Somalia
54 J4 **Punto Fijo** Falcón, N Venezuela 11°42′N 70°13′W
105 S4 **Puntón de Guara** ▲ N Spain 42°18′N 00°13′W
18 D14 **Punxsutawney** Pennsylvania, NE USA 40°55′N 78°57′W
93 M14 **Puolanka** Kainuu, C Finland 64°51′N 27°42′E
57 J17 **Pupuya, Nevado** ▲ W Bolivia 15°04′S 69°01′W
**Puqi** *see* Chibi
57 F16 **Puquio** Ayacucho, S Peru 14°44′S 74°07′W
122 J9 **Pur** ⇝ N Russia
186 D7 **Purari** ⇝ S Papua New Guinea
27 N11 **Purcell** Oklahoma, C USA 35°00′N 97°21′W
11 O16 **Purcell Mountains** ▲▲ British Columbia, SW Canada
105 P14 **Purchena** Andalucía, S Spain 37°21′N 02°21′W
27 S8 **Purdy** Missouri, C USA 36°49′N 93°55′W
118 I2 **Purekkari Neem** *prev.* Pukari Neem. *headland* N Estonia 59°33′N 24°49′E
37 U7 **Purgatoire River** ⇝ Colorado, C USA
**Purgstall** *see* Purgstall an der Erlauf
109 V5 **Purgstall an der Erlauf** *var.* Purgstall. Niederösterreich, NE Austria 48°01′N 15°08′E
154 O13 **Puri** *var.* Jagannath. Odisha, E India 19°52′N 85°49′E
**Puriramya** *see* Buriram
109 X4 **Purkersdorf** Niederösterreich, NE Austria 48°13′N 16°12′E
98 I9 **Purmerend** Noord-Holland, C Netherlands 52°30′N 04°56′E
151 G16 **Pūrna** ⇝ C India
153 R13 **Purnia** *prev.* Purnea. Bihār, NE India 25°47′N 87°28′E
167 R12 **Pursat** *var.* Poŭthĭsăt. Pursat, W Cambodia 12°32′N 103°55′E
**Pursat** *see* Poŭthĭsăt, Stœng, W Cambodia
**Purulia** *see* Puruliya
153 Q15 **Puruliya** *prev.* Purulia. West Bengal, NE India 23°20′N 86°24′E
47 G7 **Purus, Rio** *var.* Río Purús. ⇝ Brazil/Peru
186 C9 **Purutu Island** *island* SW Papua New Guinea
93 N17 **Puruvesi** ◎ SE Finland
22 L7 **Purvis** Mississippi, S USA 31°08′N 89°24′W
**Pŭrvomay** *see* Parvomay
169 R16 **Purwodadi** *prev.* Poerwodadi. Jawa, C Indonesia 07°05′S 110°53′E


◆ Country ● Country Capital ◇ Dependent Territory ○ Dependent Territory Capital ◆ Administrative Regions ✈ International Airport ▲ Mountain ▲▲ Mountain Range 🌋 Volcano ⇝ River ◎ Lake ⊠ Reservoir

Purwokerto – Quila

169 P16 **Purwokerto** *prev.* Poerwokerto. Jawa, C Indonesia *07°25′S 109°14′E*
169 P16 **Purworejo** *prev.* Poerworedjo. Jawa, C Indonesia *07°45′S 110°04′E*
20 H8 **Puryear** Tennessee, S USA *36°25′N 88°21′W*
154 H13 **Pusad** Mahārāshtra, C India *19°56′N 77°40′E*
**Pusan** *see* Busan
168 H7 **Pusatgajo, Pegunungan** ▲▲ Sumatera, NW Indonesia
**Puschlav** *see* Poschiavo
124 G13 **Pushkin** *prev.* Tsarskoye Selo. Leningradskaya Oblast', NW Russia *59°42′N 30°24′E*
126 L3 **Pushkino** Moskovskaya Oblast', W Russia *55°57′N 37°45′E*
127 Q8 **Pushkino** Saratovskaya Oblast', W Russia *51°09′N 47°00′E*
**Pushkino** *see* Biläsuvar
111 M22 **Püspökladány** Hajdú-Bihar, E Hungary *47°20′N 21°05′E*
118 J3 **Püssi** *Ger.* Isenhof. Ida-Virumaa, NE Estonia *59°22′N 27°04′E*
116 I5 **Pustomyty** L'vivs'ka Oblast', W Ukraine *49°43′N 23°55′E*
124 F16 **Pustoshka** Pskovskaya Oblast', W Russia *56°21′N 29°16′E*
**Pusztakalán** *see* Călan
167 N1 **Puta-O** *prev.* Fort Hertz. Kachin State, N Myanmar (Burma) *27°22′N 97°24′E*
184 M8 **Putaruru** Waikato, North Island, New Zealand *38°03′S 175°48′E*
**Puteoli** *see* Pozzuoli
161 R12 **Putian** Fujian, SE China *25°32′N 119°02′E*
107 O17 **Putignano** Puglia, SE Italy *40°51′N 17°08′E*
**Puting** *see* De'an
**Putivl'** *see* Putyvl'
41 Q16 **Putla** *var.* Putla de Guerrero. Oaxaca, SE Mexico *17°01′N 97°56′W*
**Putla de Guerrero** *see* Putla
19 N12 **Putnam** Connecticut, NE USA *41°56′N 71°52′W*
25 Q7 **Putnam** Texas, SW USA *32°22′N 99°11′W*
18 M10 **Putney** Vermont, NE USA *42°59′N 72°30′W*
111 L20 **Putnok** Borsod-Abaúj-Zemplén, NE Hungary *48°18′N 20°25′E*
**Putorana, Gory/Putorana Mountains** *see* Putorana, Plato
122 L8 **Putorana, Plato** *var.* Gory Putorana, *Eng.* Putorana Mountains. ▲▲ N Russia
168 K9 **Putrajaya** ● (Malaysia) Kuala Lumpur, Peninsular Malaysia *02°57′N 101°42′E*
62 H2 **Putre** Arica y Parinacota, N Chile *18°11′S 69°30′W*
155 J24 **Puttalam** North Western Province, W Sri Lanka *08°02′N 79°55′E*
155 J24 **Puttalam Lagoon** *lagoon* W Sri Lanka
99 H17 **Putte** Antwerpen, C Belgium *51°04′N 04°39′E*
94 E10 **Puttegga** ▲ S Norway *62°13′N 07°40′E*
98 K11 **Putten** Gelderland, C Netherlands *52°15′N 05°36′E*
100 K7 **Puttgarden** Schleswig-Holstein, N Germany *54°30′N 11°13′E*
**Puttiala** *see* Patiāla
101 D20 **Püttlingen** Saarland, SW Germany *49°16′N 06°52′E*
54 D14 **Putumayo** *off.* Intendencia del Putumayo. ◈ *province* S Colombia
**Putumayo, Intendencia del** *see* Putumayo
48 E7 **Putumayo, Río** *var.* Içá, Rio. ≈ NW South America *see also* Içá, Rio
**Putumayo, Río** *see* Içá, Rio
169 P11 **Putus, Tanjung** *headland* Borneo, N Indonesia *0°27′S 109°04′E*
116 J8 **Putyla** Chernivets'ka Oblast', W Ukraine *47°59′N 25°04′E*
117 S3 **Putyvl'** *Rus.* Putivl'. Sums'ka Oblast', NE Ukraine *51°21′N 33°53′E*
93 M18 **Puula** ◎ SE Finland
93 N18 **Puumala** Etelä-Savo, E Finland *61°31′N 28°12′E*
118 I5 **Puurmani** *Ger.* Talkhof. Jõgevamaa, E Estonia *58°36′N 26°17′E*
99 G17 **Puurs** Antwerpen, N Belgium *51°05′N 04°17′E*
38 F10 **Pu'u 'Ula'ula** *var.* Red Hill. ▲ Maui, Hawai'i, USA *20°42′N 156°16′W*
38 A8 **Pu'uwai** *var.* Puuwai. Ni'ihau, Hawaii, USA, C Pacific Ocean *21°54′N 160°11′W*
12 J4 **Puvirnituq** *prev.* Povungnituk. Québec, NE Canada *60°10′N 77°20′W*
12 J3 **Puvirnituq, Riviere de** *prev.* Rivière de Povungnituk. ≈ Québec, NE Canada
32 H8 **Puyallup** Washington, NW USA *47°11′N 122°17′W*
161 O5 **Puyang** Henan, C China *35°40′N 115°00′E*
103 O11 **Puy-de-Dôme** ◈ *department* C France
103 N15 **Puylaurens** Tarn, S France *43°33′N 02°01′E*
102 M13 **Puy-l'Evêque** Lot, S France *44°31′N 01°10′E*
103 N17 **Puymorens, Col de** *pass* S France
56 C7 **Puyo** Pastaza, C Ecuador *01°30′S 77°58′W*
185 A24 **Puysegur Point** *headland* South Island, New Zealand *46°09′S 166°38′E*
148 J8 **Pūzak, Jahīl-e** ◎ SW Afghanistan
81 J23 **Pwani** *Eng.* Coast. ◈ *region* E Tanzania
79 O23 **Pweto** Katanga, SE Dem. Rep. Congo *08°28′S 28°52′E*
97 I19 **Pwllheli** NW Wales, United Kingdom *52°54′N 04°23′W*
189 O14 **Pwok** Pohnpei, E Micronesia
122 I9 **Pyakupur** ≈ N Russia
124 M6 **Pyalitsa** Murmanskaya Oblast', NW Russia *66°17′N 39°56′E*
124 K10 **Pyal'ma** Respublika Kareliya, NW Russia *62°24′N 35°56′E*
**Pyandzh** *see* Panj
166 L9 **Pyapon** Ayeyarwady, SW Myanmar (Burma) *16°15′N 95°40′E*
119 J15 **Pyarshai** *Rus.* Pershay. Minskaya Voblasts', C Belarus *54°02′N 26°41′E*
114 I10 **Pyasachnik, Yazovir** *var.* Yazovir Pyasŭchnik. ⊠ C Bulgaria
122 K8 **Pyasina** ≈ N Russia
119 G17 **Pyaski** *Rus.* Peski; *prev.* Pyeski. Hrodzyenskaya Voblasts', W Belarus *53°21′N 24°38′E*
**Pyasŭchnik, Yazovir** *see* Pyasachnik, Yazovir
**Pyatikhatki** *see* P"yatykhatky
117 S7 **P"yatykhatky** *Rus.* Pyatikhatki. Dnipropetrovs'ka Oblast', E Ukraine *48°23′N 33°43′E*
166 M6 **Pyawbwe** Mandalay, C Myanmar (Burma) *20°39′N 96°04′E*
166 L7 **Pyay** *var.* Prome, Pye. Bago, C Myanmar (Burma) *18°50′N 95°14′E*
127 T3 **Pychas** Udmurtskaya Respublika, NW Russia *56°30′N 52°33′E*
**Pye** *see* Pyay
166 K6 **Pyechin** Chin State, W Myanmar (Burma) *20°01′N 93°36′E*
163 X15 **Pyeongtaek** *prev.* P'yŏngt'aek. NW South Korea *37°00′N 127°04′E*
**Pyeski** *see* Pyaski
119 L19 **Pyetrykaw** *Rus.* Petrikov. Homyel'skaya Voblasts', SE Belarus *52°08′N 28°30′E*
93 O17 **Pyhäjärvi** ◎ SE Finland
93 M16 **Pyhäjärvi** ◎ C Finland
93 L15 **Pyhäjoki** Pohjois-Pohjanmaa, W Finland *64°28′N 24°15′E*
93 L15 **Pyhäjoki** ≈ W Finland
93 M15 **Pyhäntä** Pohjois-Pohjanmaa, C Finland *64°07′N 26°19′E*
93 M16 **Pyhäsalmi** Pohjois-Pohjanmaa, C Finland *63°38′N 26°E*
93 O17 **Pyhäselkä** ◎ SE Finland
93 M19 **Pyhtää** *Swe.* Pyttis. Kymenlaakso, S Finland *60°29′N 26°40′E*
166 M5 **Pyinoolwin** *var.* Maymyo. Mandalay, C Myanmar (Burma) *22°03′N 96°30′E*
115 N24 **Pylés** *var.* Piles. Kárpathos, SE Greece *35°31′N 27°08′E*
115 D21 **Pýlos** *var.* Pilos. Pelopónnisos, S Greece *36°55′N 21°42′E*
18 B12 **Pymatuning Reservoir** ⊠ Ohio/Pennsylvania, NE USA
**P'yŏngt'aek** *see* Pyeongtaek
163 V14 **P'yŏngyang** *var.* P'yŏngyang-si, *Eng.* Pyongyang. ● (North Korea) SW North Korea *39°04′N 125°46′E*
**P'yŏngyang-si** *see* P'yŏngyang
35 Q4 **Pyramid Lake** ◎ Nevada, W USA
37 P15 **Pyramid Mountains** ▲▲ New Mexico, SW USA
37 R5 **Pyramid Peak** ▲ Colorado, C USA *39°04′N 106°57′W*
115 D17 **Pyramíva** *var.* Piramiva. ▲ C Greece *39°08′N 21°18′E*
**Pyrenaei Montes** *see* Pyrenees
86 B12 **Pyrenees** *Fr.* Pyrénées, *Sp.* Pirineos; *anc.* Pyrenaei Montes. ▲▲ SW Europe
102 J16 **Pyrénées-Atlantiques** ◈ *department* SW France
103 N17 **Pyrénées-Orientales** ◈ *department* S France
115 L19 **Pyrgí** *var.* Pirgi. Chíos, E Greece *38°13′N 26°01′E*
115 D20 **Pýrgos** *var.* Pírgos. Dytikí Elláda, S Greece *37°40′N 21°27′E*
**Pyritz** *see* Pyrzyce
115 E19 **Pýrros** ≈ S Greece
117 R4 **Pyryatyn** *Rus.* Piryatin. Poltavs'ka Oblast', NE Ukraine *50°14′N 32°31′E*
110 D9 **Pyrzyce** *Ger.* Pyritz. Zachodnio-pomorskie, NW Poland *53°09′N 14°53′E*
124 F15 **Pytalovo** *Latv.* Abrene; *prev.* Jaunlatgale. Pskovskaya Oblast', W Russia *57°06′N 27°55′E*
115 M20 **Pythagóreio** *var.* Pithagorio. Sámos, Dodekánisa, Greece, Aegean Sea *37°42′N 26°57′E*
14 L11 **Pythonga, Lac** ◎ Québec, SE Canada
**Pyttis** *see* Pyhtää
**Pyu** *see* Phyu
166 M8 **Pyuntaza** Bago, SW Myanmar (Burma) *17°51′N 96°44′E*
153 N11 **Pyuthān** Mid Western, W Nepal *28°09′N 82°50′E*
110 H12 **Pyzdry** *Ger.* Peisern. Wielkopolskie, C Poland *52°10′N 17°42′E*

## Q

138 H13 **Qā' al Jafr** ◎ S Jordan
197 O11 **Qaanaaq** *var.* Qânâq, *Dan.* Thule. ◈ Avannaata, N Greenland
**Qabanbay** *see* Kabanbay
138 G7 **Qabb Eliâs** E Lebanon *33°46′N 35°49′E*
**Qabil** *see* Al Qābil
**Qabırrı** *see* Iori
**Qābis** *see* Gabès
**Qābis, Khalīj** *see* Gabès, Golfe de
**Qabqa** *see* Gonghe
141 S14 **Qabr Hūd** C Yemen *16°02′N 49°36′E*
**Qacentina** *see* Constantine
**Qādes** *see* Qādis
148 L4 **Qādis** *prev.* Qādes. Bādghīs, NW Afghanistan *34°48′N 63°26′E*
139 T11 **Qādisīyah** Al Qādisīyah, S Iraq *31°43′N 44°28′E*
**Qādisīyah, Muḩāfaz at al** *see* Al Qādisīyah
143 O4 **Qā'emshahr** *prev.* 'Alīābad, Shāhī. Māzandarān, N Iran *36°31′N 52°49′E*
143 U7 **Qā'en** *var.* Qain, Qāyen. Khorāsān-e Jonūbī, E Iran *33°43′N 59°07′E*
141 U13 **Qafa** *spring/well* SW Oman *17°46′N 52°55′E*
**Qafṣah** *see* Gafsa
163 Q12 **Qagan Nur** *var.* Xulun Hobot Qagan, Zhengxiangbai Qi. Nei Mongol Zizhiqu, N China *42°10′N 114°57′E*
163 V9 **Qagan Nur** ◎ NE China
163 Q11 **Qagan Nur** ◎ N China
**Qagan Us** *see* Dulan
158 H13 **Qagcaka** Xizang Zizhiqu, W China *32°32′N 81°52′E*
**Qagchêng** *see* Xiangcheng
**Qahremānshahr** *see* Kermānshāh
159 Q10 **Qaidam He** ≈ C China
156 L8 **Qaidam Pendi** *basin* C China
**Qain** *see* Qā'en
**Qala Āhangarān** *see* Chaghcharān
**Qal̄ā Diza** *see* Qeładize
**Qal'ah Sālih** *see* Qal'at Şāliḩ
149 N4 **Qal'ah Shahr** *Pash.* Qala Shāhar; *prev.* Qal'eh Shahr. Sar-e Pul, N Afghanistan *35°34′N 65°38′E*
148 L4 **Qal'ah-ye Now** *var.* Qala Nau; *prev.* Qal'eh-ye Now. Bādghīs, NW Afghanistan *35°N 63°08′E*
149 T2 **Qal'ah-ye Panjah** *var.* Qala Panja. Badakhshān, NE Afghanistan *36°56′N 72°15′E*
147 R13 **Qal'aikhum** *Rus.* Kalaikhum. S Tajikistan *38°28′N 70°49′E*
**Qala Nau** *see* Qal'ah-ye Now
141 V17 **Qalansīyah** Suquṭrā, W Yemen *12°40′N 53°30′E*
**Qala Panja** *see* Qal'ah-ye Panjah
**Qala Shāhar** *see* Qal'ah Shahr
149 O8 **Qalāt** *Per.* Kalāt. Zābul, S Afghanistan *32°10′N 66°54′E*
139 W9 **Qal'at Aḩmad** Maysān, E Iraq *32°24′N 46°46′E*
141 N11 **Qal'at Bīshah** 'Asīr, SW Saudi Arabia *19°59′N 42°38′E*
138 H4 **Qal'at Burzay** Ḩamāh, W Syria *35°37′N 36°16′E*
**Qal 'at Dīzah** *see* Qeładize
139 W9 **Qal'at Ḩuşayn** Maysān, E Iraq *32°19′N 46°46′E*
139 V10 **Qal'at Majnūnah** Al Qādisīyah, S Iraq *31°39′N 45°44′E*
139 X11 **Qal'at Şāliḩ** *var.* Qal'ah Sālih. Maysān, E Iraq *31°30′N 47°24′E*
139 V10 **Qal'at Sukkar** Dhī Qār, SE Iraq *31°52′N 46°05′E*
**Qalba Zhotasy** *see* Khrebet Kalba
143 Q12 **Qal'eh Biābān** Fārs, S Iran
**Qal'eh Shahr** *see* Qal'ah Shahr
**Qal'eh-ye Now** *see* Qal'ah-ye Now
**Qalqaman** *see* Kalkaman
**Qamanittuaq** *see* Baker Lake
**Qamar al Muttaḩidah, Jumhūrīyat al** *see* Comoros
**Qamar Bay** *see* Qamar, Ghubbat al
141 U14 **Qamar, Ghubbat al** *Eng.* Qamar Bay. *bay* Oman/Yemen
141 V13 **Qamar, Jabal al** ▲▲ SW Oman
147 N12 **Qamashi** Qashqadaryo Viloyati, S Uzbekistan *38°52′N 66°30′E*
**Qambar** *see* Kambar
159 R14 **Qamdo** Xizang Zizhiqu, W China *31°09′N 97°09′E*
75 R7 **Qamīnis** NE Libya *31°48′N 20°04′E*
**Qamishly** *see* Al Qāmishlī
**Qânâq** *see* Qaanaaq
75 W7 **Qanāt as Suways** *Eng.* Suez Canal. *canal* NE Egypt
**Qandahār** *see* Kandahār
80 Q11 **Qandala** Bari, NE Somalia *11°30′N 50°00′E*
**Qandyaghash** *see* Kandyagash
138 L2 **Qanṭārī** Ar Raqqah, N Syria *36°24′N 39°16′E*
**Qapiciğ Dağı** *see* Qazangöldağ
158 H5 **Qapqal** *var.* Qapqal Xibe Zizhixian. Xinjiang Uygur Zizhiqu, NW China *43°46′N 81°09′E*
**Qapqal Xibe Zizhixian** *see* Qapqal
**Qapshagay Böyeni** *see* Vodokhranilishche Kapshagay
**Qapugtang** *see* Zadoi
196 M15 **Qaqortoq** *Dan.* Julianehåb. ◈ Kujalleq, S Greenland
139 T4 **Qara Anjīr** Kirkūk, N Iraq *35°30′N 44°37′E*
**Qarabāgh** *see* Qarah Bāgh
**Qarabaū** *see* Karabau
**Qaraböget** *see* Karaboget
**Qarabulaq** *see* Karabulak
**Qarabutaq** *see* Karabutak
**Qaraghandy/Qaraghandy Oblysy** *see* Karagandy
**Qaraghayly** *see* Karagayly
**Qara Gol** *see* Qere Gol
75 U8 **Qārah** *var.* Qâra. NW Egypt *29°34′N 26°28′E*
**Qārah** *see* Qārah
148 J4 **Qarah Bāgh** *var.* Qarabāgh. Herāt, NW Afghanistan *35°06′N 61°33′E*
**Qarah Gawl** *see* Qere Gol
138 G7 **Qaraoun, Lac de** *var.* Buḩayrat al Qir'awn. ◎ S Lebanon
**Qaraoy** *see* Karaoy
**Qaraqoyyn** *see* Karakoyyn, Ozero
**Qara Qum** *see* Garagum
**Qarasū** *see* Karasu
**Qaratal** *see* Karatal
**Qarataū** *see* Karatau, Khrebet, Kazakhstan
**Qarataū** *see* Karatau, Zhambyl, Kazakhstan
**Qaraton** *see* Karaton
**Qarazhal** *see* Karazhal
80 P13 **Qardho** *var.* Kardh, *It.* Gardo. Bari, N Somalia *09°34′N 49°30′E*
142 M6 **Qareh Chāy** ≈ N Iran
142 K2 **Qareh Sū** ≈ NW Iran
**Qariateïne** *see* Al Qaryatayn
**Qarkilik** *see* Ruoqiang
147 O13 **Qarluq** *Rus.* Karluk. Surkhondaryo Viloyati, S Uzbekistan *38°17′N 67°39′E*
147 U12 **Qarokŭl** *Rus.* Karakul'. E Tajikistan *39°07′N 73°33′E*
147 T12 **Qarokŭl** *Rus.* Ozero Karakul'. ◎ E Tajikistan
**Qarqan** *see* Qiemo
158 K9 **Qarqan He** ≈ NW China
**Qarqannah, Juzur** *see* Kerkennah, Îles
149 O1 **Qarqīn** Jowzjān, N Afghanistan *37°25′N 66°03′E*
**Qars** *see* Kars
**Qarsaqbay** *see* Karsakpay
146 M12 **Qarshi** *Rus.* Karshi; *prev.* Bek-Budi. Qashqadaryo Viloyati, S Uzbekistan *38°54′N 65°48′E*
146 L12 **Qarshi Cho'li** *Rus.* Karshinskaya Step. *grassland* S Uzbekistan
146 M13 **Qarshi Kanali** *Rus.* Karshinskiy Kanal. *canal* Turkmenistan/Uzbekistan
**Qaryatayn** *see* Al Qaryatayn
**Qāsh, Nahr al** *see* Gash
146 M12 **Qashqadaryo Viloyati** *Rus.* Kashkadar'inskaya Oblast'. ◈ *province* S Uzbekistan
**Qasigianguit** *see* Qasigiannguit
197 N13 **Qasigiannguit** *var.* Qasigianguit, *Dan.* Christianshåb. ◈ Qeqertalik, C Greenland
**Qaşīm, Minṭaqat** *see* Al Qaşīm
75 V10 **Qaşr al Farāfirah** *var.* Qasr Farâfra. W Egypt *27°00′N 27°59′E*
139 P8 **Qaşr 'Amīj** Al Anbār, C Iraq *33°30′N 41°52′E*
139 R9 **Qaşr Darwīshāh** Karbalā', C Iraq *32°36′N 43°27′E*
142 J6 **Qaşr-e Shīrīn** Kermānshāhān, W Iran *34°32′N 45°36′E*
**Qasr Farâfra** *see* Qaşr al Farāfirah
**Qassim** *see* Al Qaşīm
141 O16 **Qa'ṭabah** SW Yemen *13°51′N 44°42′E*
138 H7 **Qaṭanā** *var.* Katana. Rīf Dimashq, S Syria *33°27′N 36°04′E*
143 N15 **Qatar** *off.* State of Qatar, *Ar.* Dawlat Qaṭar. ◆ *monarchy* SW Asia
**Qatar, State of** *see* Qatar
**Qatrana** *see* Al Qaṭrānah
143 Q12 **Qaṭrūyeh** Fārs, S Iran *29°08′N 54°42′E*
**Qattara Depression/ Qaṭṭārah, Munkhafaḑ al** *see* Qaṭṭārah, Munkhafaḑ al
75 U8 **Qaṭṭārah, Munkhafaḑ al** *var.* Monkhafad el Qaṭṭâra, *Eng.* Qattara Depression. *desert* NW Egypt
**Qaṭṭâra, Monkhafad el** *see* Qaṭṭārah, Munkhafaḑ al
**Qattinah, Buhayrat** *see* Ḩimş, Buḩayrat
**Qausuittuq** *see* Resolute
**Qaydār** *see* Qeydār
**Qāyen** *see* Qā'en
**Qaynar** *see* Kaynar
**Qayroqqum** *see* Guliston
147 Q10 **Qayroqqum, Obanbori** *Rus.* Kayrakkumskoye Vodokhranilishche. ⊠ NW Tajikistan
137 V13 **Qazangöldağ** *Rus.* Gora Kapydzhik, *Turk.* Qapiciğ Dağı. ▲ SW Azerbaijan *39°18′N 46°00′E*
139 U7 **Qazānīyah** *var.* Dhū Shaykh. Diyālá, E Iraq *33°39′N 45°33′E*
**Qazaqstan/Qazaqstan Respublikasy** *see* Kazakhstan
**Q'azbegi** *see* Step'ants'minda
149 P15 **Qazi Ahmad** *var.* Kazi Ahmad. Sindh, SE Pakistan *26°19′N 68°08′E*
**Qazimämmäd** *see* Hacıqabul
**Qazris** *see* Cáceres
142 M4 **Qazvīn** *var.* Kazvin. Qazvīn, N Iran *36°16′N 50°E*
142 M5 **Qazvīn** *off.* Ostān-e Qazvīn. ◈ *province* N Iran
**Qazvīn, Ostān-e** *see* Qazvīn
139 U3 **Qeładize** *Ar.* Qal 'at Dīzah, *var.* Qal̄ā Diza. As Sulaymānīyah, NE Iraq *36°11′N 45°07′E*
187 Z13 **Qelelevu Lagoon** *lagoon* NE Fiji
**Qena** *see* Qīna
113 L23 **Qeparo** Vlorë, S Albania *40°04′N 19°49′E*
197 N13 **Qeqertalik** ◈ *municipality* W Greenland
**Qeqertarssuaq** *see* Qeqertarsuaq
197 N13 **Qeqertarsuaq** *var.* Qeqertarssuaq, *Dan.* Godhavn. Qeqertalik, S Greenland *69°27′N 52°54′W*
196 M13 **Qeqertarsuaq** *island* W Greenland
197 N13 **Qeqertarsuup Tunua** *Dan.* Disko Bugt. *inlet* W Greenland
197 N14 **Qeqqata** *off.* Qeqqata Kommunia. ◈ *municipality* W Greenland
**Qeqqata Kommunia** *see* Qeqqata
139 U4 **Qere Gol** *Ar.* Qarah Gawl, *var.* Qara Gol. As Sulaymānīyah, NE Iraq *35°21′N 45°38′E*
**Qerveh** *see* Qorveh
143 S14 **Qeshm** Hormozgān, S Iran *26°58′N 56°17′E*
143 R14 **Qeshm** *var.* Jazīreh-ye Qeshm, Qeshm Island. *island* S Iran
**Qeshm Island/Qeshm, Jazīreh-ye** *see* Qeshm
**Qey** *see* Kīsh, Jazīreh-ye
142 L4 **Qeydār** *var.* Qaydār. Zanjān, NW Iran *36°50′N 47°40′E*
142 K5 **Qezel Owzan, Rūd-e** *var.* Ki Zil Uzen, Qi Zil Uzun. ≈ NW Iran
**Qian** *see* Guizhou
161 Q2 **Qian'an** Heilongjiang, E China *45°00′N 124°00′E*
161 R10 **Qiandao Hu** *prev.* Xin'anjiang Shuiku. ⊠ SE China
**Qiandaohu** *see* Chun'an
**Qian Gorlo/Qian Gorlos/ Qian Gorlos Mongolzu Zizhixian/Quianguozhen** *see* Qianguo
163 V9 **Qianguo** *var.* Qian Gorlo, Qian Gorlos, Qian Gorlos Mongolzu Zizhixian, Quianguozhen. Jilin, NE China *45°08′N 124°48′E*
161 N9 **Qianjiang** Hubei, C China *30°23′N 112°58′E*
160 K10 **Qianjiang** Sichuan, C China *29°30′N 108°45′E*
160 L14 **Qian Jiang** ≈ S China
160 G9 **Qianning** *var.* Gartar. Sichuan, C China *30°27′N 101°24′E*
163 U13 **Qian Shan** ▲▲ NE China
160 H10 **Qianwei** *var.* Yujin. Sichuan, C China *29°15′N 103°52′E*
160 J11 **Qianxi** Guizhou, S China *27°00′N 106°01′E*
**Qiaotou** *see* Datong
**Qiaowa** *see* Muli
159 Q7 **Qiaowan** Gansu, N China *40°37′N 96°40′E*
**Qibilī** *see* Kebili
158 K9 **Qiemo** *var.* Qarqan. Xinjiang Uygur Zizhiqu, NW China *38°09′N 85°30′E*
160 J10 **Qijiang** *var.* Gunan. Chongqing Shi, C China *29°01′N 106°40′E*
159 N5 **Qijiaojing** Xinjiang Uygur Zizhiqu, NW China *43°29′N 91°35′E*
**Qike** *see* Xunke
9 N5 **Qikiqtaaluk** ◈ *cultural region* Nunavut, N Canada
9 R5 **Qikiqtarjuaq** *prev.* Broughton Island. Nunavut, NE Canada *67°35′N 63°55′W*
149 P9 **Qila Saifullah** Baluchistan, SW Pakistan *30°45′N 68°08′E*
159 S9 **Qilian** *var.* Babao. Qinghai, C China *38°09′N 100°08′E*
159 N8 **Qilian Shan** *var.* Kilien Mountains. ▲▲ N China
197 O11 **Qimusseriarsuaq** *Dan.* Melville Bugt, *Eng.* Melville Bay. *bay* NW Greenland
75 X10 **Qīna** *var.* Qena; *anc.* Caene, Caenepolis. E Egypt *26°12′N 32°49′E*
159 W11 **Qin'an** Gansu, C China *34°49′N 105°50′E*
**Qincheng** *see* Nanfeng
**Qing** *see* Qinghai
163 W7 **Qing'an** Heilongjiang, NE China *46°53′N 127°29′E*
159 X10 **Qingcheng** *var.* Xifeng. Gansu, C China *35°46′N 107°35′E*
161 R5 **Qingdao** *var.* Ching-Tao, Ch'ing-tao, Tsingtao, Tsintao, *Ger.* Tsingtau. Shandong, E China *36°31′N 120°55′E*
163 V8 **Qinggang** Heilongjiang, NE China *46°41′N 126°05′E*
**Qinggil** *see* Qinghe
159 P11 **Qinghai** *var.* Chinghai, Koko Nor, Qing, Qinghai Sheng, Tsinghai. ◈ *province* C China
159 S10 **Qinghai Hu** *var.* Ch'ing Hai, Tsing Hai, *Mong.* Koko Nor. ◎ C China
**Qinghai Sheng** *see* Qinghai
158 M3 **Qinghe** *var.* Qinggil. Xinjiang Uygur Zizhiqu, NW China *46°42′N 90°19′E*
160 L4 **Qingjian** *var.* Kuanzhou; *prev.* Xiuyan. Shaanxi, C China *37°10′N 110°09′E*
160 L9 **Qing Jiang** ≈ C China
**Qingjiang** *see* Huai'an
**Qingkou** *see* Ganyu
160 I12 **Qinglong** *var.* Liancheng. Guizhou, S China *25°49′N 105°10′E*
161 Q2 **Qinglong** Hebei, E China *40°24′N 118°57′E*
**Qingshan** *see* Wudalianchi
159 R12 **Qingshuihe** Qinghai, C China *33°47′N 97°10′E*
**Qingyang** *see* Jinjiang
161 N14 **Qingyuan** Guangdong, S China *23°42′N 113°02′E*
163 V11 **Qingyuan** *var.* Qingyuan Manzu Zizhixian. Liaoning, NE China *42°08′N 124°55′E*
**Qingyuan** *see* Shandan
**Qingyuan** *see* Weiyuan
**Qingyuan Manzu Zizhixian** *see* Qingyuan
158 L13 **Qingzang Gaoyuan** *var.* Xizang Gaoyuan, *Eng.* Plateau of Tibet. *plateau* W China
161 Q4 **Qingzhou** *prev.* Yidu. Shandong, E China *36°41′N 118°29′E*
157 R9 **Qin He** ≈ C China
161 Q2 **Qinhuangdao** Hebei, E China *39°57′N 119°31′E*
160 K7 **Qin Ling** ▲▲ C China
161 N5 **Qinxian** *var.* Dingchang, Qin Xian. Shanxi, C China *36°46′N 112°42′E*
**Qin Xian** *see* Qinxian
161 N6 **Qinyang** Henan, C China *35°05′N 112°56′E*
160 K15 **Qinzhou** Guangxi Zhuangzu Zizhiqu, S China *22°09′N 108°36′E*
**Qiong** *see* Hainan
160 L17 **Qionghai** *prev.* Jiaji. Hainan, S China *19°12′N 110°26′E*
160 H9 **Qionglai** Sichuan, C China *30°24′N 103°28′E*
160 H8 **Qionglai Shan** ▲▲ C China
**Qiongxi** *see* Hongyuan
160 L17 **Qiongzhou Haixia** *var.* Hainan Strait. *strait* S China
163 U7 **Qiqihar** *var.* Ch'i-ch'i-ha-erh, Tsitsihar; *prev.* Lungkiang. Heilongjiang, NE China *47°23′N 124°E*
**Qir** *see* Qīr-va-Kārzīn
158 H10 **Qira** Xinjiang Uygur Zizhiqu, NW China *37°05′N 80°45′E*
**Qir'awn, Buḩayrat al** *see* Qaraoun, Lac de
143 P12 **Qīr-va-Kārzīn** *var.* Qir. Fārs, S Iran *28°27′N 53°04′E*
**Qiryat Gat** *see* Kyriat Gat
**Qiryat Shemona** *see* Kiryat Shmona
**Qishlaq** *see* Garmsār
141 U14 **Qishn** SE Yemen *15°29′N 51°44′E*
**Qishon, Naẖal** *see* Kishon, Nahal
**Qiṭā' Ghazzah** *see* Gaza Strip
156 K5 **Qitai** Xinjiang Uygur Zizhiqu, NW China *44°N 89°34′E*
163 Y8 **Qitaihe** Heilongjiang, NE China *45°45′N 130°53′E*
141 W12 **Qitbīt, Wādī** *dry watercourse* S Oman
161 O5 **Qixian** *var.* Qi Xian, Zhaoge. Henan, C China *35°35′N 114°10′E*
**Qi Xian** *see* Qixian
**Qīzān** *see* Jāzān
**Qizil Orda** *see* Kyzylorda
**Qizil Qum/Qizilqum** *see* Kyzyl Kum
147 V14 **Qizilrabot** *Rus.* Kyzylrabot. SE Tajikistan *37°29′N 74°44′E*
146 J10 **Qizilravote** *Rus.* Kyzylrabat. Buxoro Viloyati, C Uzbekistan *40°35′N 62°09′E*
**Qi Zil Uzun** *see* Qezel Owzan, Rūd-e
139 S4 **Qizil Yār** Kirkūk, N Iraq *35°26′N 44°12′E*
164 J12 **Qkutango-hantō** *peninsula* Honshū, SW Japan
137 Y11 **Qobustan** *prev.* Märäzä. E Azerbaijan *40°32′N 48°56′E*
**Qoghaly** *see* Kogaly
**Qogir Feng** *see* K2
143 N6 **Qom** *var.* Kum, Qum. Qom, N Iran *34°43′N 50°54′E*
143 N6 **Qom** *off.* Ostān-e Qom. ◈ *province* N Iran
**Qomisheh** *see* Shahreẕā
**Qomolangma Feng** *see* Everest, Mount
**Qom, Ostān-e** *see* Qom
142 M7 **Qom, Rūd-e** ≈ C Iran
**Qomsheh** *see* Shahreẕā
**Qomul** *see* Hami
**Qondūz** *see* Kunduz
146 G7 **Qo'ng'irot** *Rus.* Kungrad. Qoraqalpog'iston Respublikasi, NW Uzbekistan *43°01′N 58°49′E*
**Qongyrat** *see* Konyrat
**Qoqek** *see* Tacheng
147 R10 **Qo'qon** *var.* Khokand, *Rus.* Kokand. Far'gona Viloyati, E Uzbekistan *40°34′N 70°55′E*
**Qorabowur Kirlari** *see* Karabaur', Uval
**Qoradaryo** *see* Karadar'ya
146 G6 **Qorajar** *Rus.* Karadzhar. Qoraqalpog'iston Respublikasi, NW Uzbekistan *43°34′N 58°35′E*
146 K12 **Qorako'l** *Rus.* Karakul'. Buxoro Viloyati, C Uzbekistan *39°27′N 63°45′E*
146 H7 **Qorao'zak** *Rus.* Karauzyak. Qoraqalpog'iston Respublikasi, NW Uzbekistan *43°07′N 60°03′E*
146 E5 **Qoraqalpog'iston** *Rus.* Karakalpakya. Qoraqalpog'iston Respublikasi, NW Uzbekistan *44°45′N 56°06′E*
146 G7 **Qoraqalpog'iston Respublikasi** *Rus.* Respublika Karakalpakstan. ◈ *autonomous republic* NW Uzbekistan
**Qorghalzhyn** *see* Korgalzhyn
138 H6 **Qornet es Saouda** ▲ NE Lebanon *36°06′N 34°06′E*
146 L12 **Qorowulbozor** *Rus.* Karaulbazar. Buxoro Viloyati, C Uzbekistan *39°28′N 64°49′E*
142 K5 **Qorveh** *var.* Qerveh, Qurveh. Kordestān, W Iran *35°09′N 47°48′E*
147 N11 **Qo'shrabot** *Rus.* Kushrabat. Samarqand Viloyati, C Uzbekistan *40°15′N 66°40′E*
**Qosköl** *see* Koskol'
**Qosshaghyl** *see* Kosshagyl
**Qostanay/Qostanay Oblysy** *see* Kostanay
143 P12 **Qoṭbābād** Fārs, S Iran *28°52′N 53°40′E*
143 R13 **Qoṭbābād** Hormozgān, S Iran *27°49′N 56°00′E*
138 H6 **Qoubaïyât** *var.* Al Qubayyāt. N Lebanon *37°00′N 34°30′E*
**Qoussantîna** *see* Constantine
**Qowowuyag** *see* Cho Oyu
147 O11 **Qo'ytosh** *Rus.* Koytash. Jizzax Viloyati, C Uzbekistan *40°13′N 67°19′E*
146 G7 **Qozonketkan** *Rus.* Kazanketken. Qoraqalpog'iston Respublikasi, W Uzbekistan *42°59′N 59°21′E*
146 H6 **Qozoqdaryo** *Rus.* Kazakdar'ya. Qoraqalpog'iston Respublikasi, NW Uzbekistan *43°26′N 59°47′E*
19 N11 **Quabbin Reservoir** ⊠ Massachusetts, NE USA
100 F12 **Quakenbrück** Niedersachsen, NW Germany *52°41′N 07°57′E*
18 I15 **Quakertown** Pennsylvania, NE USA *40°26′N 75°17′W*
182 M10 **Quambatook** Victoria, SE Australia *35°52′S 143°28′E*
25 Q4 **Quanah** Texas, SW USA *34°17′N 99°46′W*
167 V10 **Quang Ngai** *var.* Quangngai, Quang Nghia. Quang Ngai, C Vietnam *15°09′N 108°50′E*
**Quangngai** *see* Quang Ngai
**Quang Nghia** *see* Quang Ngai
167 T9 **Quang Tri** *var.* Triêu Hai. Quang Tri, C Vietnam *16°46′N 107°11′E*
**Quanjiang** *see* Suichuan
**Quan Long** *see* Ca Mau
152 L4 **Quanshuigou** China/India *35°40′N 79°28′E*
161 R13 **Quanzhou** *var.* Ch'uan-chou, Tsinkiang; *prev.* Chin-chiang. Fujian, SE China *24°56′N 118°31′E*
160 M12 **Quanzhou** Guangxi Zhuangzu Zizhiqu, S China *25°59′N 111°02′E*
11 V16 **Qu'Appelle** ≈ Saskatchewan, S Canada
12 M3 **Quaqtaq** *prev.* Koartac. Québec, NE Canada *60°50′N 69°30′W*
61 E16 **Quaraí** Rio Grande do Sul, S Brazil *30°38′S 56°25′W*
59 H24 **Quaraí, Rio** *Sp.* Río Cuareim. ≈ Brazil/Uruguay *see also* Cuareim, Río
**Quaraí, Rio** *see* Cuareim, Río
171 N13 **Quarles, Pegunungan** ▲▲ Sulawesi, C Indonesia
**Quarnero** *see* Kvarner
107 C20 **Quartu Sant' Elena** Sardegna, Italy, C Mediterranean Sea *39°15′N 09°12′E*
29 X13 **Quasqueton** Iowa, C USA *42°23′N 91°45′W*
173 X16 **Quatre Bornes** W Mauritius *20°15′S 57°28′E*
172 I17 **Quatre Bornes** Mahé, NE Seychelles
137 X10 **Quba** *Rus.* Kuba. N Azerbaijan *41°22′N 48°30′E*
**Qubba** *see* Ba'qūbah
143 T3 **Qūchān** *var.* Kuchan. Khorāsān-e Razavī, NE Iran *37°12′N 58°28′E*
183 R10 **Queanbeyan** New South Wales, SE Australia *35°24′S 149°17′E*
15 Q10 **Québec** *var.* Quebec. *province capital* Québec, SE Canada *46°50′N 71°15′W*
14 K10 **Québec** *var.* Quebec. ◈ *province* SE Canada
61 D17 **Quebracho** Paysandú, W Uruguay *31°58′S 57°53′W*
101 K14 **Quedlinburg** Sachsen-Anhalt, C Germany *51°48′N 11°09′E*
138 H10 **Queen Alia** ✕ ('Ammān) 'Ammān, C Jordan
10 L16 **Queen Bess, Mount** ▲ British Columbia, SW Canada *51°15′N 124°29′W*
10 I14 **Queen Charlotte** British Columbia, SW Canada *53°18′N 132°04′W*
65 B24 **Queen Charlotte Bay** *bay* West Falkland, W Falkland Islands
**Queen Charlotte Islands** *see* Haida Gwaii
10 I15 **Queen Charlotte Sound** *sea area* British Columbia, W Canada
10 J16 **Queen Charlotte Strait** *strait* British Columbia, W Canada
27 U1 **Queen City** Missouri, C USA *40°24′N 92°34′W*
25 X5 **Queen City** Texas, SW USA *33°09′N 94°09′W*
197 O9 **Queen Elizabeth Islands** *Fr.* Îles de la Reine-Élisabeth. *island group* Nunavut, N Canada
195 Y10 **Queen Mary Coast** *physical region* Antarctica
65 N24 **Queen Mary's Peak** ▲ C Tristan da Cunha
196 M8 **Queen Maud Gulf** *gulf* Arctic Ocean
195 P11 **Queen Maud Mountains** ▲▲ Antarctica
**Queen's County** *see* Laois
181 U7 **Queensland** ◈ *state* N Australia
192 I9 **Queensland Plateau** *undersea feature* N Coral Sea
183 O16 **Queenstown** Tasmania, SE Australia *42°06′S 145°33′E*
185 C22 **Queenstown** Otago, South Island, New Zealand *45°01′S 168°44′E*
83 I24 **Queenstown** Eastern Cape, S South Africa *31°52′S 26°50′E*
**Queenstown** *see* Cobh
32 F8 **Queets** Washington, NW USA *47°31′N 124°19′W*
61 D18 **Queguay Grande, Río** ≈ W Uruguay
59 O16 **Queimadas** Bahia, E Brazil *10°59′S 39°38′W*
82 D11 **Quela** Malanje, NW Angola *09°18′S 17°07′E*
83 O16 **Quelimane** *var.* Kilimane, Kilmain, Quilimane. Zambézia, NE Mozambique *17°53′S 36°51′E*
63 G18 **Quellón** *var.* Puerto Quellón. Los Lagos, S Chile *43°05′S 73°38′W*
**Quelpart** *see* Jeju-do
37 P12 **Quemado** New Mexico, SW USA *34°18′N 108°29′W*
25 O12 **Quemado** Texas, SW USA *28°58′N 100°36′W*
44 K7 **Quemado, Punta de** *headland* E Cuba *20°13′N 74°07′W*
**Quemoy** *see* Kinmen Island
62 K13 **Quemú Quemú** La Pampa, E Argentina *36°03′S 63°36′W*
155 E17 **Quepem** Goa, W India *15°13′N 74°03′E*
42 M14 **Quepos** Puntarenas, S Costa Rica *09°28′N 84°10′W*
**Que Que** *see* Kwekwe
61 D23 **Quequén** Buenos Aires, E Argentina *38°30′S 58°44′W*
61 D23 **Quequén Grande, Río** ≈ E Argentina
61 C23 **Quequén Salado, Río** ≈ E Argentina
**Quera** *see* Chur
41 N13 **Querétaro** Querétaro de Arteaga, C Mexico *20°36′N 100°24′W*
40 F4 **Querobabi** Sonora, NW Mexico *30°02′N 111°02′W*
42 M13 **Quesada** *var.* Ciudad Quesada, San Carlos. Alajuela, N Costa Rica *10°19′N 84°26′W*
105 O13 **Quesada** Andalucía, S Spain *37°52′N 03°05′W*
161 O7 **Queshan** Henan, C China *32°48′N 114°03′E*
10 M15 **Quesnel** British Columbia, SW Canada *52°59′N 122°30′W*
37 S9 **Questa** New Mexico, SW USA *36°41′N 105°37′W*
102 H7 **Questembert** Morbihan, NW France *47°39′N 02°24′W*
57 K22 **Quetena, Río** ≈ SW Bolivia
149 O10 **Quetta** Baluchistan, SW Pakistan *30°15′N 67°E*
**Quetzalcoalco** *see* Coatzacoalcos
42 B6 **Quetzaltenango** Quetzaltenango, W Guatemala *14°50′N 91°30′W*
42 A2 **Quetzaltenango** *off.* Departamento de Quezaltenango. ◈ *department* SW Guatemala
56 B6 **Quevedo** Los Ríos, C Ecuador *01°02′S 79°27′W*
**Quezaltenango, Departamento de** *see* Quetzaltenango
42 E6 **Quezaltepeque** Chiquimula, SE Guatemala *14°38′N 89°25′W*
170 M6 **Quezon** Palawan, W Philippines *09°13′N 118°01′E*
161 P5 **Qufu** Shandong, E China *35°37′N 117°05′E*
82 B12 **Quibala** Kwanza Sul, NW Angola *10°44′S 14°58′E*
82 B11 **Quibaxe** *var.* Quibaxi. Kwanza Norte, NW Angola *08°30′S 14°36′E*
**Quibaxi** *see* Quibaxe
54 D9 **Quibdó** Chocó, W Colombia *05°40′N 76°38′W*
102 G7 **Quiberon** Morbihan, NW France *47°30′N 03°07′W*
102 G7 **Quiberon, Baie de** *bay* NW France
54 J5 **Quíbor** Lara, N Venezuela *09°55′N 69°35′W*
42 C4 **Quiché** *off.* Departamento del Quiché. ◈ *department* W Guatemala
**Quiché, Departamento del** *see* Quiché
99 E21 **Quiévrain** Hainaut, S Belgium *50°25′N 03°41′E*
40 I9 **Quila** Sinaloa, C Mexico *24°24′N 107°11′W*

◆ Country
● Country Capital
◇ Dependent Territory
○ Dependent Territory Capital
◈ Administrative Regions
✕ International Airport
▲ Mountain
▲▲ Mountain Range
⛰ Volcano
≈ River
◎ Lake
⊠ Reservoir

QUILENGUES – RATAK CHAIN


83 B14 **Quilengues** Huíla, SW Angola 14°09′S 14°04′E
**Quilimane** see Quelimane
57 G15 **Quillabamba** Cusco, C Peru 12°49′S 72°41′W
57 L18 **Quillacollo** Cochabamba, C Bolivia 17°26′S 66°16′W
62 H4 **Quillagua** Antofagasta, N Chile 21°33′S 69°32′W
103 N17 **Quillan** Aude, S France 42°52′N 02°11′E
11 U15 **Quill Lakes** ◎ Saskatchewan, S Canada
62 G11 **Quillota** Valparaíso, C Chile 32°54′S 71°16′W
**Quilon** see Kollam
181 V9 **Quilpie** Queensland, C Australia 26°39′S 144°15′E
149 O4 **Quil-Qala** Bāmyān, N Afghanistan 35°13′N 67°02′E
62 L7 **Quimilí** Santiago del Estero, C Argentina 27°35′S 62°25′W
57 O19 **Quimome** Santa Cruz, E Bolivia 17°45′S 61°15′W
102 F6 **Quimper** anc. Quimper Corentin. Finistère, NW France 48°00′N 04°05′W
**Quimper Corentin** see Quimper
102 G7 **Quimperlé** Finistère, NW France 47°52′N 03°33′W
32 F8 **Quinault** Washington, NW USA 47°27′N 123°53′W
32 F8 **Quinault River** ≈ Washington, NW USA
35 P5 **Quincy** California, W USA 39°56′N 120°56′W
23 S8 **Quincy** Florida, SE USA 30°35′N 84°34′W
30 I13 **Quincy** Illinois, N USA 39°56′N 91°24′W
19 O11 **Quincy** Massachusetts, NE USA 42°15′N 71°00′W
32 J9 **Quincy** Washington, NW USA 47°13′N 119°51′W
54 E10 **Quindío** off. Departamento del Quindío. ◈ province C Colombia
54 E10 **Quindío, Nevado del** ▲ C Colombia 04°42′N 75°25′W
62 J10 **Quines** San Luis, C Argentina 32°15′S 65°46′W
39 N13 **Quinhagak** Alaska, USA 59°45′N 161°55′W
76 G13 **Quinhámel** W Guinea-Bissau 11°52′N 15°52′W
**Qui Nhon/Quinhon** see Quy Nhơn
**Quinindé** see Rosa Zárate
25 U6 **Quinlan** Texas, SW USA 32°54′N 96°08′W
61 H17 **Quinta** Rio Grande do Sul, S Brazil 32°05′S 52°18′W
105 O10 **Quintanar de la Orden** Castilla-La Mancha, C Spain 39°36′N 03°03′W
41 X13 **Quintana Roo** ◈ state SE Mexico
105 S6 **Quinto** Aragón, NE Spain 41°25′N 00°31′W
108 G10 **Quinto** Ticino, S Switzerland 46°32′N 08°44′E
27 Q11 **Quinton** Oklahoma, C USA 35°07′N 95°22′W
62 K12 **Quinto, Río** ≈ C Argentina
82 A10 **Quinzau** Zaire Province, NW Angola 06°50′S 12°48′E
14 H8 **Quinze, Lac des** ◎ Québec, SE Canada
83 B15 **Quipungo** Huíla, C Angola 14°49′S 14°29′E
62 G13 **Quirihue** Ñuble, C Chile 36°15′S 72°35′W
82 D12 **Quirima** Malanje, NW Angola 10°51′S 18°06′E
183 T6 **Quirindi** New South Wales, SE Australia 31°29′S 150°40′E
55 P5 **Quiriquire** Monagas, NE Venezuela 09°59′N 63°14′W
14 D10 **Quirke Lake** ◎ Ontario, S Canada
61 B21 **Quiroga** Buenos Aires, E Argentina 35°18′S 61°22′W
104 I4 **Quiroga** Galicia, NW Spain 42°28′N 07°15′W
**Quirón, Salar** see Pocitos, Salar
56 B9 **Quiroz, Río** ≈ NW Peru
82 Q13 **Quissanga** Cabo Delgado, NE Mozambique 12°24′S 40°33′E
83 M20 **Quissico** Inhambane, S Mozambique 24°42′S 34°44′E
25 O4 **Quitaque** Texas, SW USA 34°22′N 101°03′W
82 Q13 **Quiterajo** Cabo Delgado, NE Mozambique 11°37′S 40°22′E
23 T6 **Quitman** Georgia, SE USA 30°46′N 83°33′W
22 M6 **Quitman** Mississippi, S USA 32°02′N 88°43′W
25 V6 **Quitman** Texas, SW USA 32°37′N 95°26′W
56 C6 **Quito** ● (Ecuador) Pichincha, N Ecuador 0°14′S 78°30′W
**Quito** see Mariscal Sucre
58 P13 **Quixadá** Ceará, E Brazil 04°57′S 39°04′W
83 Q15 **Quixaxe** Nampula, NE Mozambique 15°15′S 40°07′E
161 N13 **Qujiang** var. Maba. Guangdong, S China 24°47′N 113°34′E
160 J9 **Qu Jiang** ≈ C China
161 R10 **Qu Jiang** ≈ SE China
160 H12 **Qujing** Yunnan, SW China 25°39′N 103°52′E
**Qulan** see Kulan
**Qulin Gol** see Chaor Hol
146 L10 **Quljuqtov Tog'lari** Rus. Gory Kul'dzhuktau. ▲▲ C Uzbekistan
**Qulsary** see Kul'sary
**Qulyndy Zhazyghy** see Ravnina Kulyndy
**Qum** see Qom
**Qumälisch** see Lubartów
159 P11 **Qumar He** ≈ C China
159 Q12 **Qumarlêb** var. Yuegai; prev. Yuegaitan. Qinghai, C China 34°06′N 95°54′E
**Qumisheh** see Shahrezā
147 O14 **Qumqo'rg'on** Rus. Kumkurgan. Surkhondaryo Viloyati, S Uzbekistan 37°54′N 67°31′E
**Qunaytirah/Qunaytirah, Muḩāfaẓat al** see Al Qunayṭirah
189 V12 **Quoi** island Chuuk, C Micronesia
9 N8 **Quoich** ≈ Nunavut, NE Canada
83 E26 **Quoin Point** headland SW South Africa 34°48′S 19°39′E
182 F7 **Quorn** South Australia 32°22′S 138°03′E
**Qurein** see Al Kuwayt
**Qŭrghonteppa** see Bokhtar
**Qurlurtuuq** see Kugluktuk
**Qurveh** see Qorveh
**Quryq** see Kuryk
137 X10 **Qusar** Rus. Kusary. NE Azerbaijan 41°26′N 48°27′E
**Quşayr** see Al Quşayr
**Quseir** see Al Quşayr
142 I2 **Qūshchī** Āżarbāyjān-e Gharbī, N Iran 37°59′N 45°05′E
**Qusmuryn** see Kushmurun, Kostanay, Kazakhstan
**Qusmuryn** see Kusmuryn, Ozero
**Quṭayfah/Qutayfe/Quteife** see Al Quṭayfah
**Quthing** see Moyeni
147 S10 **Quvasoy** Rus. Kuvasay. Farg'ona Viloyati, E Uzbekistan 40°17′N 71°53′E
**Quwair** see Guwēr
**Quxar** see Lhazê
**Qu Xian** see Quzhou
159 N16 **Qūxü** var. Xoi. Xizang Zizhiqu, W China 29°25′N 90°48′E
**Quyang** see Jingzhou
167 V11 **Quy Nhơn** var. Quinhon, Qui Nhon. Binh Định, C Vietnam 13°47′N 109°11′E
161 R10 **Quzhou** var. Qu Xian. Zhejiang, SE China 28°55′N 118°54′E
**Qyteti Stalin** see Kuçovë
**Qyzylaghash** see Kyzylagash
**Qyzylorda** see Kyzylorda
**Qyzyltū** see Kishkenekol'
**Qyzylzhar** see Kyzylzhar


# R


**Raa Atoll** see North Maalhosmadulu Atoll
109 R4 **Raab** Oberösterreich, N Austria 48°19′N 13°40′E
109 X8 **Raab** Hung. Rába. ≈ Austria/Hungary see also Rába
**Raab** see Rába
**Raab** see Győr
109 V2 **Raabs an der Thaya** Niederösterreich, E Austria 48°51′N 15°28′E
93 L14 **Raahe** Swe. Brahestad. Pohjois-Pohjanmaa, W Finland 64°42′N 24°31′E
98 M10 **Raalte** Overijssel, E Netherlands 52°23′N 06°16′E
99 I14 **Raamsdonksveer** Noord-Brabant, S Netherlands 51°42′N 04°54′E
92 L12 **Raanujärvi** Lappi, NW Finland 66°39′N 24°40′E
96 G9 **Raasay** island NW Scotland, United Kingdom
118 H3 **Raasiku** Ger. Rasik. Harjumaa, NW Estonia 59°22′N 25°11′E
112 B11 **Rab** It. Arbe. Primorje-Gorski Kotar, NW Croatia 44°46′N 14°46′E
112 B11 **Rab** It. Arbe. island NW Croatia
171 N16 **Raba** Sumbawa, S Indonesia 08°27′S 118°45′E
111 G22 **Rába** Ger. Raab. ≈ Austria/Hungary see also Raab
**Rába** see Raab
112 A10 **Rabac** Istra, NW Croatia 45°03′N 14°09′E
104 I2 **Rábade** Galicia, NW Spain 43°07′N 07°37′W
80 F10 **Rabak** White Nile, C Sudan 13°12′N 32°44′E
186 G9 **Rabaraba** Milne Bay, SE Papua New Guinea 10°00′S 149°50′E
102 K16 **Rabastens-de-Bigorre** Hautes-Pyrénées, S France 43°23′N 00°10′E
121 O16 **Rabat** W Malta 35°51′N 14°25′E
74 F6 **Rabat** var. al Dar al Baida. ● (Morocco) NW Morocco 34°02′N 06°51′W
**Rabat** see Victoria
186 H6 **Rabaul** New Britain, E Papua New Guinea 04°13′S 152°11′E
**Rabbah Ammon/Rabbath Ammon** see 'Amman
28 K8 **Rabbit Creek** ≈ South Dakota, N USA
14 H10 **Rabbit Lake** ◎ Ontario, S Canada
187 Y14 **Rabi** prev. Rambi. island N Fiji
140 K9 **Rābigh** Makkah al Mukarramah, W Saudi Arabia 22°51′N 39°E
42 D5 **Rabinal** Baja Verapaz, C Guatemala 15°05′N 90°26′W
168 G9 **Rabi, Pulau** island NW Indonesia, East Indies
111 L17 **Rabka** Małopolskie, S Poland 49°38′N 20°E
155 F16 **Rabkavi** Karnātaka, W India 16°40′N 75°03′E
**Râbniţa** see Ribniţa
109 Y6 **Rabnitz** ≈ E Austria
124 J7 **Rabocheostrovsk** Respublika Kareliya, NW Russia 64°58′N 34°46′E
23 U1 **Rabun Bald** ▲ Georgia, SE USA 34°58′N 83°18′W
75 S11 **Rabyānah** SE Libya 24°07′N 21°58′E
75 S11 **Rabyānah, Ramlat** var. Rebiana Sand Sea, Şahrā' Rabyānah. desert SE Libya
**Rabyānah, Şahrā'** see Rabyānah, Ramlat
116 L11 **Răcăciuni** Bacău, E Romania 46°20′N 27°00′E
**Racaka** see Riwoqê
107 J24 **Racalmuto** Sicilia, Italy, C Mediterranean Sea 37°25′N 13°44′E
116 J14 **Răcari** Dâmbovița, SE Romania 44°37′N 25°43′E
**Răcari** see Durankulak
116 F13 **Răcăşdia** Hung. Rakasd. Caraş-Severin, SW Romania 44°58′N 21°36′E
106 B9 **Racconigi** Piemonte, NE Italy 44°45′N 07°41′E
31 T15 **Raccoon Creek** ≈ Ohio, N USA
13 V13 **Race, Cape** headland Newfoundland, Newfoundland and Labrador, E Canada 46°40′N 53°05′W
22 K10 **Raceland** Louisiana, S USA 29°43′N 90°36′W
19 Q12 **Race Point** headland Massachusetts, NE USA 42°03′N 70°14′W
167 S14 **Rach Gia** Kiên Giang, S Vietnam 10°01′N 105°05′E
167 S14 **Rach Gia, Vinh** bay S Vietnam
76 J8 **Rachid** Tagant, C Mauritania 18°48′N 11°41′W
110 L10 **Raciąż** Mazowieckie, C Poland 52°46′N 20°04′E
111 I16 **Racibórz** Ger. Ratibor. Śląskie, S Poland 50°05′N 18°10′E
31 N9 **Racine** Wisconsin, N USA 42°42′N 87°50′W
14 D7 **Racine Lake** ◎ Ontario, S Canada
111 J23 **Ráckeve** Pest, C Hungary 47°10′N 18°58′E
**Rácz-Becse** see Bečej
141 O15 **Radā'** var. Ridā'. W Yemen 14°24′N 44°49′E
113 O15 **Radan** ▲ SE Serbia 42°59′N 21°31′E
63 J19 **Rada Tilly** Chubut, SE Argentina 45°54′S 67°33′W
116 K8 **Rădăuţi** Ger. Radautz, Hung. Rádóc. Suceava, N Romania 47°49′N 25°58′E
116 L8 **Rădăuţi-Prut** Botoşani, NE Romania 48°14′N 26°47′E
**Radautz** see Rădăuţi
**Radbusa** see Radbuza
111 A17 **Radbuza** Ger. Radbusa. ≈ SE Czechia
20 K6 **Radcliff** Kentucky, S USA 37°50′N 85°57′W
139 O2 **Radd, Wādī ar** dry watercourse N Syria
95 H16 **Råde** Østfold, S Norway 59°21′N 10°53′E
109 V11 **Radeče** Ger. Ratschach. C Slovenia 46°01′N 15°10′E
**Radein** see Radenci
116 J4 **Radekhiv** Pol. Radziechów, Rus. Radekhov. L'vivs'ka Oblast', W Ukraine 50°17′N 24°39′E
**Radekhov** see Radekhiv
109 X9 **Radenci** Ger. Radein; prev. Radinci. NE Slovenia 46°36′N 16°02′E
109 S9 **Radenthein** Kärnten, S Austria 46°48′N 13°42′E
**Rádeyilikóé** see Fort Good Hope
21 R7 **Radford** Virginia, NE USA 37°07′N 80°34′W
154 C9 **Rādhanpur** Gujarāt, W India 23°52′N 71°49′E
**Radinci** see Radenci
127 Q6 **Radishchevo** Ul'yanovskaya Oblast', W Russia 52°49′N 47°54′E
12 I9 **Radisson** Québec, E Canada 53°47′N 77°35′W
11 P16 **Radium Hot Springs** British Columbia, SW Canada 50°39′N 116°09′W
116 F11 **Radna** Hung. Máriaradna. Arad, W Romania 46°05′N 21°41′E
**Rádnávrre** see Randijaure
114 K10 **Radnevo** Stara Zagora, C Bulgaria 42°17′N 25°58′E
97 J20 **Radnor** cultural region E Wales, United Kingdom
**Radnót** see Iernut
**Radóc** see Rădăuţi
101 H24 **Radolfzell am Bodensee** Baden-Württemberg, S Germany 47°43′N 08°58′E
110 M13 **Radom** Mazowieckie, C Poland 51°23′N 21°08′E
116 I14 **Radomireşti** Olt, S Romania 44°06′N 25°00′E
111 K14 **Radomsko** Rus. Novoradomsk. Łódzkie, C Poland 51°04′N 19°25′E
117 N4 **Radomyshl'** Zhytomyrs'ka Oblast', N Ukraine 50°30′N 29°16′E
113 P19 **Radoviš** prev. Radovište. E Macedonia 41°39′N 22°26′E
**Radovište** see Radoviš
**Radøy** see Radøyni
94 B13 **Radøyni** prev. Radøy. island S Norway
109 R7 **Radstadt** Salzburg, NW Austria 47°24′N 13°31′E
182 E8 **Radstock, Cape** headland South Australia 33°11′S 134°18′E
109 U10 **Raduha** ▲ N Slovenia 46°24′N 14°46′E
119 G15 **Radun'** Hrodzyenskaya Voblasts', W Belarus 54°03′N 25°00′E
126 M3 **Raduzhnyy** Vladimirskaya Oblast', W Russia 55°59′N 40°15′E
118 F11 **Radviliškis** Šiaulai, N Lithuania 55°48′N 23°32′E
11 U17 **Radville** Saskatchewan, S Canada 49°28′N 104°19′W
140 K7 **Raḑwá, Jabal** ▲ W Saudi Arabia 24°31′N 38°21′E
111 P16 **Radymno** Podkarpackie, SE Poland 49°57′N 22°49′E
116 J5 **Radyvyliv** Rivnens'ka Oblast', NW Ukraine 50°07′N 25°12′E
**Radziechów** see Radekhiv
110 I11 **Radziejów** Kujawsko-pomorskie, C Poland 52°36′N 18°33′E
110 O12 **Radzyń Podlaski** Lubelskie, E Poland 51°48′N 22°37′E
8 J7 **Rae** ≈ Nunavut, NW Canada
152 M13 **Rāe Bareli** Uttar Pradesh, N India 26°14′N 81°14′E
**Rae-Edzo** see Edzo
21 T11 **Raeford** North Carolina, SE USA 34°59′N 79°15′W
99 M19 **Raeren** Liège, E Belgium 50°42′N 06°06′E
9 N7 **Rae Strait** strait Nunavut, N Canada
184 L11 **Raetihi** Manawatu-Wanganui, North Island, New Zealand 39°29′S 175°16′E
**Raevavae** see Raivavae
**Rafa** see Rafah
62 M10 **Rafaela** Santa Fe, E Argentina 31°16′S 61°25′W
54 E5 **Rafael Núñez** ✈ (Cartagena) Bolívar, NW Colombia 10°27′N 75°31′W
138 E11 **Rafah** var. Rafa, Rafaḩ, Heb. Rafiaḩ, Raphiah. SW Gaza Strip 31°18′N 34°15′E
79 L15 **Rafaï** Mbomou, SE Central African Republic 05°01′N 23°51′E
141 O4 **Rafḩah** Al Ḩudūd ash Shamālīyah, N Saudi Arabia 29°41′N 43°29′E
**Rafiaḩ** see Rafah
143 R10 **Rafsanjān** Kermān, C Iran 30°25′N 56°E
80 B13 **Raga** Western Bahr el Ghazal, W South Sudan 08°28′N 25°41′E
19 S8 **Ragged Island** island Maine, NE USA
44 I5 **Ragged Island Range** island group S The Bahamas
184 L7 **Raglan** Waikato, North Island, New Zealand 37°48′S 174°54′E
22 G8 **Ragley** Louisiana, S USA 30°31′N 93°13′W
**Ragnit** see Neman
107 K25 **Ragusa** Sicilia, Italy, C Mediterranean Sea 36°56′N 14°42′E
**Ragusa** see Dubrovnik
**Ragusavecchia** see Cavtat
171 P14 **Raha** Pulau Muna, C Indonesia 04°50′S 122°43′E
119 N17 **Rahachow** Rus. Rogachëv. Homyel'skaya Voblasts', SE Belarus 53°03′N 30°03′E
67 U6 **Rahad** var. Nahr ar Rahad. ≈ W Sudan
**Rahad, Nahr ar** see Rahad
**Rahaeng** see Tak
138 F11 **Rahat** Southern, C Israel 31°20′N 34°43′E
140 L8 **Rahat, Ḩarrat** lava flow W Saudi Arabia
149 S12 **Rahimyar Khan** Punjab, SE Pakistan 28°27′N 70°21′E
95 I14 **Råholt** Akershus, S Norway 60°16′N 11°10′E
113 M17 **Rahovec** Serb. Orahovac. W Kosovo 42°24′N 20°40′E
191 S10 **Raiatea** island Îles Sous le Vent, W French Polynesia
155 H16 **Rāichūr** Karnātaka, C India 16°15′N 77°20′E
**Raidestos** see Tekirdağ
153 S13 **Rāiganj** West Bengal, NE India 25°38′N 88°11′E
154 M11 **Raigarh** Chhattīsgarh, C India 21°53′N 83°28′E
183 O16 **Railton** Tasmania, SE Australia 41°24′S 146°28′E
36 L8 **Rainbow Bridge** natural arch Utah, W USA
23 Q3 **Rainbow City** Alabama, S USA 33°57′N 86°02′W
11 N11 **Rainbow Lake** Alberta, W Canada 58°30′N 119°24′W
21 R5 **Rainelle** West Virginia, NE USA 37°57′N 80°46′W
32 G10 **Rainier** Oregon, NW USA 46°05′N 122°55′W
32 H9 **Rainier, Mount** ⛰ Washington, NW USA 46°51′N 121°45′W
23 Q2 **Rainsville** Alabama, S USA 34°29′N 85°51′W
12 B11 **Rainy Lake** ◎ Canada/USA
12 A11 **Rainy River** Ontario, C Canada 48°44′N 94°33′W
**Raippaluoto** see Replot
154 K12 **Raipur** Chhattīsgarh, C India 21°16′N 81°42′E
154 H10 **Raisen** Madhya Pradesh, C India 23°21′N 77°49′E
15 N13 **Raisin** ≈ Ontario, SE Canada
31 R11 **Raisin, River** ≈ Michigan, N USA
191 U13 **Raivavae** var. Raevavae. Îles Australes, SW French Polynesia
149 W9 **Raiwind** Punjab, E Pakistan 31°14′N 74°10′E
171 T12 **Raja Ampat, Kepulauan** island group E Indonesia
155 L16 **Rājahmundry** Andhra Pradesh, E India 17°05′N 81°42′E
155 I18 **Rājampet** Andhra Pradesh, E India 14°09′N 79°10′E
**Rajang** see Rajang, Batang
169 S9 **Rajang, Batang** var. Rajang. ≈ East Malaysia
149 S11 **Rajanpur** Punjab, E Pakistan 29°05′N 70°25′E
155 H23 **Rājapālaiyam** Tamil Nādu, SE India 09°26′N 77°36′E
152 E12 **Rājasthān** ◈ state NW India
153 T15 **Rajbari** Dhaka, C Bangladesh 23°47′N 89°39′E
153 R12 **Rajbiraj** Eastern, E Nepal 26°34′N 86°52′E
154 G9 **Rājgarh** Madhya Pradesh, C India 24°01′N 76°42′E
152 H10 **Rājgarh** Rājasthān, NW India 28°38′N 75°21′E
153 P14 **Rājgīr** Bihār, N India 25°01′N 85°26′E
110 O8 **Rajgród** Podlaskie, NE Poland 53°43′N 22°40′E
154 L12 **Rājim** Chhattīsgarh, C India 20°57′N 81°58′E
163 Y11 **Rajin** var. Najin. NE North Korea 42°13′N 130°16′E
112 C11 **Rajinac, Mali** ▲ W Croatia 44°47′N 15°04′E
154 B10 **Rājkot** Gujarāt, W India 22°18′N 70°47′E
153 R14 **Rājmahal** Jhārkhand, NE India 25°03′N 87°49′E
153 Q14 **Rājmahāl Hills** hill range N India
154 K12 **Rāj Nāndgaon** Chhattīsgarh, C India 21°06′N 81°02′E
152 I8 **Rājpura** Punjab, NW India 30°29′N 76°40′E
153 S14 **Rajshahi** prev. Rampur Boalia. Rajshahi, W Bangladesh 24°24′N 88°40′E
153 S13 **Rajshahi** ◈ division NW Bangladesh
190 K13 **Rakahanga** atoll N Cook Islands
185 H19 **Rakaia** Canterbury, South Island, New Zealand 43°45′S 172°02′E
185 G19 **Rakaia** ≈ South Island, New Zealand
152 H3 **Rakaposhi** ▲ N India 36°06′N 74°31′E
**Rakasd** see Răcăşdia
169 N15 **Rakata, Pulau** var. Pulau Krakatau. island S Indonesia
141 U10 **Rakbah, Qalamat ar** well SE Saudi Arabia
166 K6 **Rakhine State** var. Arakan State. ◈ state W Myanmar (Burma)
166 K5 **Rakhine Yoma** var. Arakan Yoma. ▲▲ W Myanmar (Burma)
116 I8 **Rakhiv** Zakarpats'ka Oblast', W Ukraine 48°05′N 24°15′E
141 V13 **Rakhyūt** SW Oman 16°41′N 53°09′E
192 K9 **Rakiraki** Viti Levu, W Fiji 17°22′S 178°10′E
126 J8 **Rakitnoye** Belgorodskaya Oblast', W Russia 50°50′N 35°51′E
**Rakiura** see Stewart Island / Rakiura
**Rakka** see Ar Raqqah
118 I4 **Rakke** Lääne-Virumaa, NE Estonia 58°58′N 26°14′E
95 I16 **Rakkestad** Østfold, S Norway 59°25′N 11°17′E
110 F12 **Rakoniewice** Ger. Rakwitz. Wielkopolskie, C Poland 52°09′N 16°10′E
**Rakonitz** see Rakovník
83 H18 **Rakops** Central, C Botswana 21°01′S 24°20′E
111 C16 **Rakovník** Ger. Rakonitz. Středočeský Kraj, W Czechia 50°07′N 13°44′E
114 J10 **Rakovski** Plovdiv, C Bulgaria 42°16′N 24°58′E
**Rakutō-kō** see Nakdong-gang
118 I3 **Rakvere** Ger. Wesenberg. Lääne-Virumaa, N Estonia 59°21′N 26°20′E
**Rakwitz** see Rakoniewice
22 L6 **Raleigh** Mississippi, S USA 32°01′N 89°30′W
21 U9 **Raleigh** state capital North Carolina, SE USA 35°46′N 78°38′W
21 Y11 **Raleigh Bay** bay North Carolina, SE USA
21 U9 **Raleigh-Durham** ✈ North Carolina, SE USA 35°54′N 78°45′W
189 S6 **Ralik Chain** island group Ralik Chain, W Marshall Islands
25 N5 **Ralls** Texas, SW USA 33°40′N 101°23′W
18 G13 **Ralston** Pennsylvania, NE USA 41°29′N 76°57′W
141 O16 **Ramādah** W Yemen 13°35′N 43°50′E
**Ramadi** see Ar Ramādī
155 I14 **Ramagundam** Telangana, C India 18°45′N 79°28′E
105 N2 **Ramales de la Victoria** Cantabria, N Spain 43°15′N 03°28′W
138 F10 **Ramallah** C West Bank 31°55′N 35°12′E
61 C19 **Ramallo** Buenos Aires, E Argentina 33°30′S 60°01′W
155 H20 **Rāmanagaram** Karnātaka, E India 12°45′N 77°16′E
155 I23 **Rāmanāthapuram** Tamil Nādu, SE India 09°23′N 78°53′E
154 N12 **Rāmapur** Odisha, E India 21°48′N 84°00′E
155 I14 **Rāmāreddi** var. Kāmāreddi, Kamareddy. Telangana, C India 18°19′N 78°23′E
138 F10 **Ramat Gan** Tel Aviv, W Israel 32°04′N 34°48′E
103 T6 **Rambervillers** Vosges, NE France 48°15′N 06°50′E
**Rambi** see Rabi
103 N5 **Rambouillet** Yvelines, N France 48°39′N 01°50′E
186 E5 **Rambutyo Island** island N Papua New Guinea
153 Q12 **Ramechhāp** Central, C Nepal 27°20′N 86°05′E
183 R12 **Rame Head** headland Victoria, SE Australia 37°48′S 149°30′E
126 L4 **Ramenskoye** Moskovskaya Oblast', W Russia 55°31′N 38°24′E
124 J15 **Rameshki** Tverskaya Oblast', W Russia 57°21′N 36°05′E
153 P14 **Rāmgarh** Jhārkhand, N India 23°37′N 85°32′E
152 D11 **Rāmgarh** Rājasthān, NW India 27°29′N 70°38′E
142 M9 **Rāmhormoz** var. Ram Hormuz, Ramuz. Khūzestān, SW Iran 31°15′N 49°38′E
**Ram Hormuz** see Rāmhormoz
**Ram, Jebel** see Ramm, Jabal
138 F10 **Ramla** var. Ramle, Ramleh, Ar. Er Ramle. Central, C Israel 31°56′N 34°52′E
**Ramle/Ramleh** see Ramla
138 F14 **Ramm, Jabal** var. Jebel Ram. ▲ SW Jordan 29°34′N 35°24′E
152 K10 **Rāmnagar** Uttarākhand, N India 29°23′N 79°07′E
95 N15 **Ramnäs** Västmanland, C Sweden 59°46′N 16°16′E
**Râmnicul-Sărat** see Râmnicu Sărat
116 L12 **Râmnicu Sărat** prev. Râmnicul-Sărat, Rîmnicu-Sărat. Buzău, E Romania 45°24′N 27°06′E
116 I13 **Râmnicu Vâlcea** prev. Rîmnicu Vîlcea. Vâlcea, C Romania 45°04′N 24°32′E
**Ramokgwebana** see Ramokgwebane
83 J18 **Ramokgwebane** var. Ramokgwebana. Central, NE Botswana 20°38′S 27°40′E
126 L7 **Ramon'** Voronezhskaya Oblast', W Russia 51°51′N 39°18′E
35 V17 **Ramona** California, W USA 33°02′N 116°52′W
56 A10 **Ramón, Laguna** ◎ NW Peru
14 G7 **Ramore** Ontario, S Canada 48°26′N 80°19′W
40 M11 **Ramos** San Luis Potosí, C Mexico 22°48′N 101°55′W
40 M8 **Ramos Arizpe** Coahuila, NE Mexico 25°35′N 100°59′W
41 J9 **Ramos, Río de** ≈ C Mexico
83 J21 **Ramotswa** South East, S Botswana 24°56′S 25°50′E
39 R8 **Rampart** Alaska, USA 65°30′N 150°10′W
8 H8 **Ramparts** ≈ Northwest Territories, NW Canada
152 K10 **Rāmpur** Uttar Pradesh, N India 28°48′N 79°03′E
154 F9 **Rāmpura** Madhya Pradesh, C India 24°30′N 75°32′E
**Rampur Boalia** see Rajshahi
166 K6 **Ramree Island** island W Myanmar (Burma)
141 W6 **Rams** var. Ar Rams. Ra's al Khaymah, NE United Arab Emirates 25°52′N 56°01′E
143 N4 **Rāmsar** prev. Sakhtsar. Māzandarān, N Iran 36°55′N 50°39′E
93 H16 **Ramsele** Västernorrland, N Sweden 63°33′N 16°35′E
21 T9 **Ramseur** North Carolina, SE USA 35°43′N 79°39′W
97 I16 **Ramsey** NE Isle of Man 54°19′N 04°24′W
97 I16 **Ramsey Bay** bay NE Isle of Man
14 E9 **Ramsey Lake** ◎ Ontario, S Canada
97 Q22 **Ramsgate** SE England, United Kingdom 51°20′N 01°25′E
94 M10 **Ramsjö** Gävleborg, C Sweden 62°10′N 15°40′E
154 I12 **Rāmtek** Mahārāshtra, C India 21°28′N 79°28′E
**Ramtha** see Ar Ramthā
**Ramuz** see Rāmhormoz
118 G12 **Ramygala** Panevėžys, C Lithuania 55°30′N 24°18′E
152 H14 **Rāna Pratāp Sāgar** ◎ N India
169 V7 **Ranau** Sabah, East Malaysia 05°56′N 116°43′E
168 L14 **Ranau, Danau** ◎ Sumatera, W Indonesia
62 H12 **Rancagua** O'Higgins, C Chile 34°10′S 70°45′W
99 G22 **Rance** Hainaut, S Belgium 50°09′N 04°16′E
102 H6 **Rance** ≈ NW France
60 J9 **Rancharia** São Paulo, S Brazil 22°13′S 50°53′W
153 P15 **Rānchi** Jhārkhand, N India 23°22′N 85°20′E
61 D21 **Ranchos** Buenos Aires, E Argentina 35°32′S 58°22′W
37 S9 **Ranchos De Taos** New Mexico, SW USA 36°21′N 105°36′W
63 G16 **Ranco, Lago** ◎ C Chile
95 C16 **Randaberg** Rogaland, S Norway 59°00′N 05°38′E
29 U7 **Randall** Minnesota, N USA 46°05′N 94°30′W
107 L23 **Randazzo** Sicilia, Italy, C Mediterranean Sea 37°52′N 14°57′E
95 G21 **Randers** Midtjylland, C Denmark 56°28′N 10°03′E
92 I12 **Randijaure** Lapp. Rádnávrre. ◎ N Sweden
21 T9 **Randleman** North Carolina, SE USA 35°49′N 79°48′W
19 O11 **Randolph** Massachusetts, NE USA 42°09′N 71°02′W
29 Q13 **Randolph** Nebraska, C USA 42°25′N 97°05′W
36 M1 **Randolph** Utah, W USA 41°40′N 111°10′W
100 P9 **Randow** ≈ NE Germany
95 H14 **Randsfjorden** ◎ S Norway
92 K13 **Råneå** Norrbotten, N Sweden 65°52′N 22°17′E
92 G12 **Ranelva** ≈ C Norway
93 F15 **Ranemsletta** Nord-Trøndelag, C Norway 64°36′N 11°55′E
76 H10 **Ranérou** C Senegal 15°17′N 14°00′W
**Råneš** see Ringvassøya
185 E22 **Ranfurly** Otago, South Island, New Zealand 45°07′S 170°06′E
167 P17 **Rangae** Narathiwat, SW Thailand 06°15′N 101°45′E
153 V16 **Rangamati** Chittagong, SE Bangladesh 22°40′N 92°10′E
184 J2 **Rangaunu Bay** bay North Island, New Zealand
19 P6 **Rangeley** Maine, NE USA 44°58′N 70°37′W
37 O4 **Rangely** Colorado, C USA 40°05′N 108°48′W
25 R7 **Ranger** Texas, SW USA 32°28′N 98°40′W
14 C9 **Ranger Lake** Ontario, S Canada 46°51′N 83°34′W
14 C9 **Ranger Lake** ◎ Ontario, S Canada
153 V12 **Rangia** Assam, NE India 26°26′N 91°38′E
185 I18 **Rangiora** Canterbury, South Island, New Zealand 43°19′S 172°34′E
191 T9 **Rangiroa** atoll Îles Tuamotu, W French Polynesia
184 N9 **Rangitaiki** ≈ North Island, New Zealand
185 F19 **Rangitata** ≈ South Island, New Zealand
184 M12 **Rangitikei** ≈ North Island, New Zealand
184 L6 **Rangitoto Island** island N New Zealand
184 K13 **Rangitoto ki te Tonga / D'Urville Island** var. D'Urville Island. island C New Zealand
**Rangkasbitoeng** see Rangkasbitung
169 N16 **Rangkasbitung** prev. Rangkasbitoeng. Jawa, SW Indonesia 06°21′S 106°12′E
167 P9 **Rang, Khao** ▲ C Thailand 16°13′N 99°03′E
147 V13 **Rangkŭl** Rus. Rangkul'. SE Tajikistan 38°30′N 74°24′E
**Rangkul'** see Rangkŭl
**Rangoon** see Yangon
153 T13 **Rangpur** Rajshahi, N Bangladesh 25°46′N 89°20′E
155 F18 **Rānībennur** Karnātaka, W India 14°36′N 75°39′E
153 R15 **Rāniganj** West Bengal, NE India 23°34′N 87°13′E
149 Q13 **Rānīpur** Sindh, SE Pakistan 27°17′N 68°34′E
**Rānīyah** see Ranye
25 N9 **Rankin** Texas, SW USA 31°14′N 101°56′W
9 O9 **Rankin Inlet** Nunavut, C Canada 62°52′N 92°14′W
183 P8 **Rankins Springs** New South Wales, SE Australia 33°51′S 146°16′E
**Rankovićevo** see Kraljevo
108 I7 **Rankweil** Vorarlberg, W Austria 47°17′N 09°40′E
**Rann** see Brežice
127 T8 **Ranneye** Orenburgskaya Oblast', W Russia 51°28′N 52°29′E
96 I10 **Rannoch, Loch** ◎ C Scotland, United Kingdom
191 U17 **Rano Kau** var. Rano Kao. crater Easter Island, Chile, E Pacific Ocean
167 N14 **Ranong** Ranong, SW Thailand 05°59′N 98°40′E
186 J8 **Ranongga** var. Ghanongga. island NW Solomon Islands
191 W16 **Rano Raraku** ancient monument Easter Island, Chile, E Pacific Ocean
171 V12 **Ransiki** Papua Barat, E Indonesia 01°27′S 134°12′E
92 K12 **Rantajärvi** Norrbotten, N Sweden 66°45′N 23°39′E
93 N17 **Rantasalmi** Etelä-Savo, SE Finland 62°02′N 28°22′E
169 U13 **Rantau** Borneo, C Indonesia 02°56′S 115°09′E
168 L10 **Rantau, Pulau** var. Pulau Tebingtinggi. island W Indonesia
171 N13 **Rantepao** Sulawesi, C Indonesia 02°58′S 119°58′E
30 M13 **Rantoul** Illinois, N USA 40°19′N 88°08′W
93 L15 **Rantsila** Pohjois-Pohjanmaa, C Finland 64°31′N 25°40′E
92 L13 **Ranua** Lappi, NW Finland 65°55′N 26°34′E
**Rānya** see Ranye
139 T3 **Ranye** Ar. Rānīyah, var. Rānya. As Sulaymānīyah, NE Iraq 36°15′N 44°53′E
157 X3 **Raohe** Heilongjiang, NE China 46°49′N 134°00′E
74 H9 **Raoui, Erg er** desert W Algeria
193 O10 **Rapa** island Îles Australes, S French Polynesia
191 V14 **Rapa Iti** island Îles Australes, SW French Polynesia
106 D10 **Rapallo** Liguria, NW Italy 44°21′N 09°13′E
**Rapa Nui** see Pascua, Isla de
**Raphiah** see Rafah
21 V5 **Rapidan River** ≈ Virginia, NE USA
28 J10 **Rapid City** South Dakota, N USA 44°05′N 103°14′W
15 P8 **Rapide-Blanc** Québec, SE Canada 47°48′N 72°57′W
14 I8 **Rapide-Deux** Québec, SE Canada 47°56′N 78°33′W
118 K6 **Räpina** Ger. Rappin. Põlvamaa, SE Estonia 58°06′N 27°27′E
118 G4 **Rapla** Ger. Rappel. Raplamaa, NW Estonia 59°00′N 24°46′E
118 G4 **Raplamaa** var. Rapla Maakond. ◈ province NW Estonia
**Rapla Maakond** see Raplamaa
21 X6 **Rappahannock River** ≈ Virginia, NE USA
**Rappel** see Rapla
108 G7 **Rapperswil** Sankt Gallen, NE Switzerland 47°14′N 08°50′E
**Rappin** see Räpina
153 N12 **Rāpti** ≈ N India
57 K16 **Rápulo, Río** ≈ E Bolivia
**Raqqa** see Ar Raqqah
**Raqqah/Raqqah, Muḩāfaẓat al** see Ar Raqqah
18 J8 **Raquette Lake** ◎ New York, NE USA
18 J6 **Raquette River** ≈ New York, NE USA
191 V10 **Raraka** atoll Îles Tuamotu, C French Polynesia
191 V10 **Raroia** atoll Îles Tuamotu, C French Polynesia
190 H15 **Rarotonga** ✈ Rarotonga, S Cook Islands, C Pacific Ocean 21°15′S 159°45′W
190 H16 **Rarotonga** island S Cook Islands, C Pacific Ocean
147 P12 **Rarz** W Tajikistan 39°23′N 68°43′E
**Ras al'Ain** see Ra's al 'Ayn
139 N2 **Ra's al 'Ayn** var. Ras al'Ain. Al Ḩasakah, N Syria 36°52′N 40°05′E
138 H3 **Ra's al Basīṭ** Al Lādhiqīyah, W Syria 35°57′N 35°55′E
**Ra's al-Hafğī** see Ra's al Khafjī
141 R5 **Ra's al Khafjī** var. Ra's al-Hafğī. Ash Sharqīyah, NE Saudi Arabia 28°22′N 48°30′E
**Ras al-Khaimah/Ras al Khaimah** see Ra's al Khaymah
143 R15 **Ra's al Khaymah** var. Ras al Khaimah. Ra's al Khaymah, NE United Arab Emirates 25°44′N 55°55′E
143 R15 **Ra's al Khaymah** var. Ras al-Khaimah. ✈ Ra's al Khaymah, NE United Arab Emirates 25°37′N 55°51′E
138 G13 **Ra's an Naqb** Ma'ān, S Jordan 30°00′N 35°29′E
61 B26 **Rasa, Punta** headland E Argentina 40°50′S 62°15′W
171 V12 **Rasawi** Papua Barat, E Indonesia 02°04′S 134°02′E
**Râşcani** see Rîşcani
80 J10 **Ras Dashen Terara** ▲ N Ethiopia 13°12′N 38°09′E
**Rasdhoo Atoll** see Rasdu Atoll
151 K19 **Rasdu Atoll** var. Rasdhoo Atoll. atoll C Maldives
118 E12 **Raseiniai** Kaunas, C Lithuania 55°23′N 23°06′E
75 X8 **Ra's Ghārib** var. Râs Ghârib. E Egypt 28°16′N 33°01′E
**Râs Ghârib** see Ra's Ghārib
162 J6 **Rashaant** Hövsgöl, N Mongolia 49°08′N 101°27′E
**Rashaant** see Delüün, Bayan-Ölgiy, Mongolia
**Rashaant** see Öldziyt, Dundgovĭ, Mongolia
75 V7 **Rashîd** Eng. Rosetta. N Egypt 31°25′N 30°25′E
139 Y11 **Rashīd** Al Başrah, E Iraq 31°15′N 47°31′E
142 M3 **Rasht** var. Resht. Gīlān, NW Iran 37°18′N 49°38′E
**Rashwān** see Reshwan
**Rashwan** see Reshwan
**Rasik** see Raasiku
113 M15 **Raška** Serbia, C Serbia 43°18′N 20°37′E
75 Y9 **Muḩammad, Ra's** headland E Egypt 27°45′N 34°18′E
119 P15 **Rasna** Rus. Ryasna. Mahilyowskaya Voblasts', E Belarus 54°01′N 31°12′E
116 J12 **Râşnov** prev. Rîşno, Rozsnyó, Hung. Barcarozsnyó. Braşov, C Romania 45°35′N 25°27′E
118 L11 **Rasony** Rus. Rossony. Vitsyebskaya Voblasts', N Belarus 55°53′N 28°50′E
**Ra's Shamrah** see Ugarit
127 N7 **Rasskazovo** Tambovskaya Oblast', W Russia 52°42′N 41°45′E
119 O16 **Rasta** Rus. Resta. ≈ E Belarus
**Rastadt** see Rastatt
**Rastâne** see Ar Rastān
141 S6 **Ra's Tannūrah** Eng. Ras Tanura. Ash Sharqīyah, NE Saudi Arabia 26°44′N 50°04′E
**Ras Tanura** see Ra's Tannūrah
101 G21 **Rastatt** var. Rastadt. Baden-Württemberg, SW Germany 48°51′N 08°13′E
**Rastenburg** see Kętrzyn
149 V7 **Rasulnagar** Punjab, E Pakistan 32°20′N 73°51′E
189 U6 **Ratak Chain** island group Ratak Chain, E Marshall Islands


◆ Country
● Country Capital
◇ Dependent Territory
○ Dependent Territory Capital
◈ Administrative Regions
✈ International Airport
▲ Mountain
▲▲ Mountain Range
⛰ Volcano
≈ River
◎ Lake
⊠ Reservoir

# RATAMKA – RHOON



119 K15 **Ratamka** *Rus.* Ratomka. Minskaya Voblasts', C Belarus *53°56′N 27°21′E*
93 G17 **Ratän** Jämtland, C Sweden *62°28′N 14°35′E*
152 G11 **Ratangarh** Rājasthān, NW India *28°02′N 74°39′E*
**Rat Buri** *see* Ratchaburi
167 O11 **Ratchaburi** *var.* Rat Buri. Ratchaburi, W Thailand *13°30′N 99°50′E*
29 W15 **Rathbun Lake** ⊠ Iowa, C USA
**Ráth Caola** *see* Rathkeale
166 K5 **Rathedaung** Rakhine State, W Myanmar (Burma) *20°30′N 92°48′E*
100 M12 **Rathenow** Brandenburg, NE Germany *52°37′N 12°21′E*
97 C19 **Rathkeale** *Ir.* Ráth Caola. Limerick, SW Ireland *52°32′N 08°56′W*
96 F13 **Rathlin Island** *Ir.* Reachlainn. *island* N Northern Ireland, United Kingdom
97 C20 **Ráth Luirc** *Ir.* An Ráth. Cork, SW Ireland *52°22′N 08°44′W*
**Ratibor** *see* Racibórz
**Ratisbon/Ratisbona/ Ratisbonne** *see* Regensburg
**Rätische Alpen** *see* Rhaetian Alps
38 E17 **Rat Island** *island* Aleutian Islands, Alaska, USA
38 E17 **Rat Islands** *island group* Aleutian Islands, Alaska, USA
154 F10 **Ratlām** *prev.* Rutlam. Madhya Pradesh, C India *23°23′N 75°04′E*
155 D15 **Ratnāgiri** Mahārāshtra, W India *17°00′N 73°20′E*
155 K26 **Ratnapura** Sabaragamuwa Province, S Sri Lanka *06°41′N 80°25′E*
**Ratne** *see* Ratno
116 J2 **Ratno** *var.* Ratne. Volyns'ka Oblast', NW Ukraine *51°40′N 24°33′E*
**Ratomka** *see* Ratamka
37 U8 **Raton** New Mexico, SW USA *36°54′N 104°27′W*
139 O7 **Ratqah, Wādī ar** *dry watercourse* W Iraq
**Ratschach** *see* Radeče
167 O16 **Rattaphum** Songkhla, SW Thailand *07°07′N 100°16′E*
26 L6 **Rattlesnake Creek** ≈ Kansas, C USA
94 L13 **Rättvik** Dalarna, C Sweden *60°53′N 15°12′E*
100 K9 **Ratzeburg** Mecklenburg-Vorpommern, N Germany *53°41′N 10°48′E*
100 K9 **Ratzeburger See** ◎ N Germany
10 J10 **Ratz, Mount** ▲ British Columbia, SW Canada *57°22′N 132°17′W*
61 D22 **Rauch** Buenos Aires, E Argentina *36°45′S 59°05′W*
41 U16 **Raudales** Chiapas, SE Mexico
**Raudhatain** *see* Ar Rawḑatayn
**Raudnitz an der Elbe** *see* Roudnice nad Labem
92 K1 **Raufarhöfn** Norðurland Eystra, NE Iceland *66°27′N 15°58′W*
94 H13 **Raufoss** Oppland, S Norway *60°44′N 10°39′E*
**Raukawa** *see* Cook Strait
184 Q8 **Raukumara** ▲ North Island, New Zealand *37°46′S 178°07′E*
192 K11 **Raukumara Plain** *undersea feature* N Coral Sea
184 P8 **Raukumara Range** ▲▲ North Island, New Zealand
**Rāulakela** *see* Rāurkela
95 F15 **Rauland** Telemark, S Norway *59°41′N 07°57′E*
93 J19 **Rauma** *Swe.* Raumo. Satakunta, SW Finland *61°09′N 21°30′E*
94 F10 **Rauma** ≈ S Norway
**Raumo** *see* Rauma
118 H8 **Rauna** C Latvia *57°19′N 25°34′E*
169 T17 **Raung, Gunung** ▲ Jawa, S Indonesia *08°00′S 114°07′E*
154 N11 **Rāurkela** *var.* Rāulakela, Rourkela. Odisha, E India *22°13′N 84°53′E*
95 J22 **Raus** Skåne, S Sweden *56°01′N 12°48′E*
165 W3 **Rausu** Hokkaidō, NE Japan *44°00′N 145°06′E*
165 W3 **Rausu-dake** ▲ Hokkaidō, NE Japan *44°06′N 145°04′E*
116 M9 **Răut** *var.* Răuţel. ≈ C Moldova
93 M17 **Rautalampi** Pohjois-Savo, C Finland *62°37′N 26°48′E*
93 N16 **Rautavaara** Pohjois-Savo, C Finland *63°30′N 28°19′E*
**Răuţel** *see* Răut
93 O18 **Rautjärvi** Etelä-Karjala, SE Finland *61°21′N 29°20′E*
**Rautu** *see* Sosnovo
191 V11 **Ravahere** *atoll* Îles Tuamotu, C French Polynesia
107 J25 **Ravanusa** Sicilia, Italy, C Mediterranean Sea *37°16′N 13°59′E*
143 S9 **Rāvar** Kermān, C Iran *31°15′N 56°51′E*
147 Q11 **Ravat** Batkenskaya Oblast', SW Kyrgyzstan *39°54′N 70°06′E*
18 K11 **Ravena** New York, NE USA *42°28′N 73°49′W*
106 H10 **Ravenna** Emilia-Romagna, N Italy *44°28′N 12°15′E*
29 O15 **Ravenna** Nebraska, C USA *41°01′N 98°54′W*
31 U11 **Ravenna** Ohio, N USA *41°09′N 81°14′W*
101 I24 **Ravensburg** Baden-Württemberg, S Germany *47°47′N 09°37′E*
181 W4 **Ravenshoe** Queensland, NE Australia *17°29′S 145°28′E*
180 K13 **Ravensthorpe** Western Australia *33°37′S 120°03′E*
21 Q4 **Ravenswood** West Virginia, NE USA *38°57′N 81°45′W*
149 U9 **Ravi** ≈ India/Pakistan
112 C9 **Ravna Gora** Primorje-Gorski Kotar, NW Croatia *45°20′N 14°54′E*
109 U10 **Ravne na Koroškem** *Ger.* Gutenstein. N Slovenia *46°33′N 14°57′E*
145 T7 **Ravnina Kulyndy** *prev.* Kulunda Steppe, *Kaz.* Qulyndy Zhazyghy, *Rus.* Kulundinskaya Ravnina. *grassland* Kazakhstan/Russia
139 P6 **Rāwah** Al Anbār, W Iraq *34°32′N 41°54′E*
191 T4 **Rawaki** *prev.* Phoenix Island. *atoll* Phoenix Islands, C Kiribati
149 U6 **Rawalpindi** Punjab, NE Pakistan *33°38′N 73°06′E*
110 L13 **Rawa Mazowiecka** Łódzkie, C Poland *51°47′N 20°16′E*
**Rawāndiz** *see* Rewanduz
171 U12 **Rawas** Papua Barat, E Indonesia *01°07′S 132°12′E*
139 O4 **Rawḑah** ◎ E Syria
110 G13 **Rawicz** *Ger.* Rawitsch. Wielkopolskie, C Poland *51°37′N 16°51′E*
**Rawitsch** *see* Rawicz
180 M11 **Rawlinna** Western Australia *31°01′S 125°36′E*
33 W16 **Rawlins** Wyoming, C USA *41°47′N 107°14′W*
63 K17 **Rawson** Chubut, SE Argentina *43°22′S 65°01′W*
159 R16 **Rawu** Xizang Zizhiqu, W China *29°30′N 96°42′E*
153 P12 **Raxaul** Bihār, N India *26°58′N 84°51′E*
28 K3 **Ray** North Dakota, N USA *48°19′N 103°11′W*
169 S11 **Raya, Bukit** ▲ Borneo, C Indonesia *0°40′S 112°40′E*
155 I18 **Rāyachoti** Andhra Pradesh, E India *14°03′N 78°43′E*
**Rāyadrug** *see* Rāyagarha
**Rāyagada** *see* Rāyagarha
155 M14 **Rāyagarha** *prev.* Rāyadrug, *var.* Rāyagada. Odisha, E India *19°10′N 83°28′E*
138 H7 **Rayak** *var.* Rayaq, Riyāq. E Lebanon *33°51′N 36°03′E*
**Rayaq** *see* Rayak
139 T2 **Rayat** *Ar.* Rāyāt, *var.* Rāyat. Arbīl, E Iraq *36°39′N 44°56′E*
**Rāyāt** *see* Rayat
**Rāyat** *see* Rayat
169 N12 **Raya, Tanjung** *cape* Pulau Bangka, W Indonesia
13 R13 **Ray, Cape** *headland* Newfoundland, Newfoundland and Labrador, E Canada *47°38′N 59°15′W*
123 Q13 **Raychikhinsk** Amurskaya Oblast', SE Russia *49°47′N 129°19′E*
127 U5 **Rayevskiy** Respublika Bashkortostan, W Russia *54°04′N 54°58′E*
11 Q17 **Raymond** Alberta, SW Canada *49°30′N 112°41′W*
22 K6 **Raymond** Mississippi, S USA *32°15′N 90°25′W*
32 F9 **Raymond** Washington, NW USA *46°41′N 123°43′W*
183 T8 **Raymond Terrace** New South Wales, SE Australia *32°47′S 151°45′E*
25 T17 **Raymondville** Texas, SW USA *26°30′N 97°48′W*
11 U16 **Raymore** Saskatchewan, S Canada *51°24′N 104°34′W*
39 Q8 **Ray Mountains** ▲▲ Alaska, USA
22 H9 **Rayne** Louisiana, S USA *30°13′N 92°15′W*
41 O12 **Rayón** San Luis Potosí, C Mexico *21°54′N 99°33′W*
40 G4 **Rayón** Sonora, NW Mexico *29°45′N 110°33′W*
167 P12 **Rayong** Rayong, S Thailand *12°42′N 101°17′E*
25 T5 **Ray Roberts, Lake** ◎ Texas, SW USA
18 E15 **Raystown Lake** ⊠ Pennsylvania, NE USA
141 V13 **Raysūt** SW Oman *16°58′N 54°02′E*
27 R4 **Raytown** Missouri, C USA *39°00′N 94°27′W*
22 I5 **Rayville** Louisiana, S USA *32°29′N 91°45′W*
142 L5 **Razan** Hamadān, W Iran *35°22′N 48°58′E*
139 S9 **Razāzah, Buḩayrat ar** *var.* Baḩr al Milḩ. ◎ C Iraq
114 L9 **Razboyna** ▲ E Bulgaria *42°54′N 26°31′E*
**Razdan** *see* Hrazdan
**Razdolnoye** *see* Rozdol'ne
**Razelm, Lacul** *see* Razim, Lacul
**Razga** *see* Rezge
114 L8 **Razgrad** Razgrad, N Bulgaria *43°33′N 26°31′E*
114 L8 **Razgrad** ◈ *province* NE Bulgaria
114 I10 **Razhevo Konare** *var.* Rŭzhevo Konare. Plovdiv, C Bulgaria *42°16′N 24°58′E*
117 N13 **Razim, Lacul** *prev.* Lacul Razelm. *lagoon* NW Black Sea
**Razkah** *see* Rezge
114 G11 **Razlog** Blagoevgrad, SW Bulgaria *41°53′N 23°28′E*
118 K10 **Rāznas Ezers** ◎ SE Latvia
102 E6 **Raz, Pointe du** *headland* NW France *48°06′N 04°52′W*
**Reachlainn** *see* Rathlin Island
**Reachrainn** *see* Lambay Island
97 N22 **Reading** S England, United Kingdom *51°28′N 00°59′W*
18 H15 **Reading** Pennsylvania, NE USA *40°20′N 75°55′W*
48 C7 **Real, Cordillera** ▲▲ C Ecuador
62 K12 **Realicó** La Pampa, C Argentina *35°02′S 64°14′W*
25 R15 **Realitos** Texas, SW USA *27°26′N 98°31′W*
108 G9 **Realp** Uri, C Switzerland *46°36′N 08°32′E*
167 Q12 **Reăng Kesei** Battambang, W Cambodia *12°57′N 103°15′E*
191 Y11 **Reao** *atoll* Îles Tuamotu, E French Polynesia
**Reate** *see* Rieti
**Greater Antarctica** *see* East Antarctica
180 L11 **Rebecca, Lake** ◎ Western Australia
**Rebiana Sand Sea** *see* Rabyānah, Ramlat
124 H8 **Reboly** *Finn.* Repola. Respublika Kareliya, NW Russia *63°51′N 30°49′E*
165 S1 **Rebun** Rebun-tō, NE Japan *45°19′N 141°02′E*
165 S1 **Rebun-tō** *island* NE Japan
106 J12 **Recanati** Marche, C Italy *43°23′N 13°34′E*
**Rechitsa** *see* Rechytsa
109 Y7 **Rechnitz** Burgenland, SE Austria *47°19′N 16°26′E*
119 J20 **Rechytsa** *Rus.* Rechitsa. Brestskaya Voblasts', SW Belarus *51°51′N 26°48′E*
119 O19 **Rechytsa** *Rus.* Rechitsa. Homyel'skaya Voblasts', SE Belarus *52°22′N 30°23′E*
59 Q15 **Recife** *prev.* Pernambuco. *state capital* Pernambuco, E Brazil *08°06′S 34°53′W*
83 I26 **Recife, Cape** *Afr.* Kaap Recife. *headland* S South Africa *34°03′S 25°37′E*
**Recife, Kaap** *see* Recife, Cape
172 I16 **Récifs, Îles aux** *island* Inner Islands, NE Seychelles
101 E14 **Recklinghausen** Nordrhein-Westfalen, W Germany *51°37′N 07°12′E*
100 M8 **Recknitz** ≈ NE Germany
99 K23 **Recogne** Luxembourg, SE Belgium *49°56′N 05°20′E*
61 C15 **Reconquista** Santa Fe, C Argentina *29°08′S 59°38′W*
195 O6 **Recovery Glacier** *glacier* Antarctica
59 G15 **Recreio** Mato Grosso, W Brazil *08°13′S 58°15′W*
27 X9 **Rector** Arkansas, C USA *36°15′N 90°17′W*
110 E9 **Recz** *Ger.* Reetz Neumark. Zachodnio-pomorskie, NW Poland *53°16′N 15°32′E*
99 L24 **Redange** *var.* Redange-sur-Attert. Diekirch, W Luxembourg *49°46′N 05°53′E*
**Redange-sur-Attert** *see* Redange
18 C13 **Redbank Creek** ≈ Pennsylvania, NE USA
13 S9 **Red Bay** Québec, E Canada *51°40′N 56°37′W*
23 N2 **Red Bay** Alabama, S USA *34°26′N 88°08′W*
35 N4 **Red Bluff** California, W USA *40°09′N 122°14′W*
24 J8 **Red Bluff Reservoir** ◎ New Mexico/Texas, SW USA
30 K16 **Red Bud** Illinois, N USA *38°12′N 89°59′W*
30 J5 **Red Cedar River** ≈ Wisconsin, N USA
11 R17 **Redcliff** Alberta, SW Canada *50°06′N 110°48′W*
83 K17 **Redcliff** Midlands, C Zimbabwe *19°00′S 29°49′E*
182 L9 **Red Cliffs** Victoria, SE Australia *34°21′S 142°12′E*
29 P17 **Red Cloud** Nebraska, C USA *40°05′N 98°31′W*
22 L8 **Red Creek** ≈ Mississippi, S USA
11 P15 **Red Deer** Alberta, SW Canada *52°15′N 113°48′W*
11 Q16 **Red Deer** ≈ Alberta, SW Canada
39 O11 **Red Devil** Alaska, USA *61°45′N 157°18′W*
35 N3 **Redding** California, W USA *40°33′N 122°26′W*
97 L20 **Redditch** W England, United Kingdom *52°19′N 01°56′W*
29 P9 **Redfield** South Dakota, N USA *44°51′N 98°31′W*
24 J12 **Redford** Texas, SW USA *29°31′N 104°19′W*
45 V13 **Redhead** Trinidad, Trinidad and Tobago *10°44′N 60°58′W*
182 I8 **Red Hill** South Australia *33°34′S 138°13′E*
**Red Hill** *see* Pu'u 'Ula'ula
26 K7 **Red Hills** *hill range* Kansas, C USA
13 T12 **Red Indian Lake** ◎ Newfoundland, Newfoundland and Labrador, E Canada
124 J16 **Redkino** Tverskaya Oblast', W Russia *56°41′N 36°07′E*
12 A10 **Red Lake** Ontario, C Canada *51°00′N 93°55′W*
36 I10 **Red Lake** *salt flat* Arizona, SW USA
29 S4 **Red Lake Falls** Minnesota, N USA *47°52′N 96°16′W*
29 R4 **Red Lake River** ≈ Minnesota, N USA
35 U15 **Redlands** California, W USA *34°03′N 117°10′W*
18 G16 **Red Lion** Pennsylvania, NE USA *39°53′N 76°36′W*
33 U11 **Red Lodge** Montana, NW USA *45°11′N 109°15′W*
32 H13 **Redmond** Oregon, NW USA *44°16′N 121°10′W*
36 L5 **Redmond** Utah, W USA *39°00′N 111°51′W*
32 H8 **Redmond** Washington, NW USA *47°40′N 122°07′W*
**Rednitz** *see* Regnitz
29 T15 **Red Oak** Iowa, C USA *41°00′N 95°10′W*
18 K12 **Red Oaks Mill** New York, NE USA *41°39′N 73°52′W*
102 I7 **Redon** Ille-et-Vilaine, NW France *47°39′N 02°05′W*
45 W10 **Redonda** *island* SW Antigua and Barbuda
104 G4 **Redondela** Galicia, NW Spain *42°17′N 08°36′W*
104 H11 **Redondo** Évora, S Portugal *38°38′N 07°32′W*
39 Q12 **Redoubt Volcano** ▲ Alaska, USA *60°29′N 152°44′W*
11 Y16 **Red River** ≈ Canada/USA
129 U12 **Red River** *var.* Yuan, *Chin.* Yuan Jiang, *Vtn.* Sông Hông Hà. ≈ China/Vietnam
25 W4 **Red River** ≈ S USA
22 H7 **Red River** ≈ Louisiana, S USA
30 M6 **Red River** ≈ Wisconsin, N USA
**Red Rock, Lake** *see* Red Rock Reservoir
29 W14 **Red Rock Reservoir** *var.* Lake Red Rock. ⊠ Iowa, C USA
80 H7 **Red Sea** ◈ *state* NE Sudan
75 Y9 **Red Sea** *var.* Sinus Arabicus. *sea* Africa/Asia
21 T11 **Red Springs** North Carolina, SE USA *34°49′N 79°10′W*
8 I9 **Redstone** ≈ Northwest Territories, NW Canada
11 V17 **Redvers** Saskatchewan, S Canada *49°31′N 101°33′W*
77 P13 **Red Volta** *var.* Nazinon, *Fr.* Volta Rouge. ≈ Burkina Faso/Ghana
11 Q14 **Redwater** Alberta, SW Canada *53°57′N 113°06′W*
28 M16 **Red Willow Creek** ≈ Nebraska, C USA
29 W9 **Red Wing** Minnesota, N USA *44°33′N 92°31′W*
35 N9 **Redwood City** California, W USA *37°29′N 122°13′W*
29 T9 **Redwood Falls** Minnesota, N USA *44°33′N 95°07′W*
31 P7 **Reed City** Michigan, N USA *43°52′N 85°30′W*
28 K6 **Reeder** North Dakota, N USA *46°03′N 102°55′W*
35 R11 **Reedley** California, W USA *36°35′N 119°27′W*
33 T11 **Reedpoint** Montana, NW USA *45°41′N 109°33′W*
30 K8 **Reedsburg** Wisconsin, N USA *43°33′N 90°03′W*
32 E13 **Reedsport** Oregon, NW USA *43°42′N 124°06′W*
187 Q9 **Reef Islands** *island group* Santa Cruz Islands, E Solomon Islands
185 H16 **Reefton** West Coast, South Island, New Zealand *42°07′S 171°53′E*
20 F8 **Reelfoot Lake** ◎ Tennessee, S USA
97 D17 **Ree, Lough** *Ir.* Loch Rí. ◎ C Ireland
**Reengus** *see* Rīngas
35 U4 **Reese River** ≈ Nevada, W USA
98 M8 **Reest** ≈ E Netherlands
**Reetz Neumark** *see* Recz
**Reevhtse** *see* Røssvatnet
137 N13 **Refahiye** Erzincan, C Turkey *39°54′N 38°45′E*
23 N4 **Reform** Alabama, S USA *33°22′N 88°01′W*
95 K20 **Reftele** Jönköping, S Sweden *57°10′N 13°34′E*
25 T14 **Refugio** Texas, SW USA *28°19′N 97°18′W*
110 E8 **Rega** ≈ NW Poland
**Regar** *see* Tursunzoda
101 O21 **Regen** Bayern, SE Germany *48°57′N 13°10′E*
101 M20 **Regen** ≈ SE Germany
101 M21 **Regensburg** *Eng.* Ratisbon, *Fr.* Ratisbonne, *hist.* Ratisbona; *anc.* Castra Regina, Reginum. Bayern, SE Germany *49°01′N 12°06′E*
101 M21 **Regenstauf** Bayern, SE Germany *49°06′N 12°07′E*
**Rēgestān** *see* Rēgistān
74 I10 **Reggane** C Algeria *26°46′N 00°09′E*
98 N9 **Regge** ≈ E Netherlands
**Reggio** *see* Reggio nell'Emilia
**Reggio Calabria** *see* Reggio di Calabria
107 M23 **Reggio di Calabria** *var.* Reggio Calabria, *Gk.* Rhegion; *anc.* Regium, Rhegium. Calabria, SW Italy *38°06′N 15°39′E*
**Reggio Emilia** *see* Reggio nell'Emilia
106 F9 **Reggio nell'Emilia** *var.* Reggio Emilia, *abbrev.* Reggio; *anc.* Regium Lepidum. Emilia-Romagna, N Italy *44°42′N 10°37′E*
116 I10 **Reghin** *Ger.* Sächsisch-Reen, *Hung.* Szászrégen; *prev.* Reghinul Săsesc, *Ger.* Sächsisch-Regen. Mureş, C Romania *46°46′N 24°41′E*
**Reghinul Săsesc** *see* Reghin
11 U16 **Regina** *province capital* Saskatchewan, S Canada *50°25′N 104°39′W*
55 Z10 **Régina** E French Guiana *04°20′N 52°07′W*
11 U16 **Regina** ✈ Saskatchewan, S Canada *50°21′N 104°43′W*
11 U16 **Regina Beach** Saskatchewan, S Canada *50°44′N 105°03′W*
**Reginum** *see* Regensburg
**Région du Haut-Congo** *see* Haut-Congo
148 M10 **Rēgistān** *var.* Rēgestān. *desert region* S Afghanistan
60 L11 **Registro** São Paulo, S Brazil *24°30′S 47°50′W*
**Regium** *see* Reggio di Calabria
**Regium Lepidum** *see* Reggio nell'Emilia
101 K19 **Regnitz** *var.* Rednitz. ≈ SE Germany
40 K10 **Regocijo** Durango, W Mexico *23°35′N 105°11′W*
104 H12 **Reguengos de Monsaraz** Évora, S Portugal *38°25′N 07°32′W*
101 M18 **Rehau** Bayern, E Germany *50°15′N 12°03′E*
83 D19 **Rehoboth** Hardap, C Namibia *23°18′S 17°03′E*
21 Z4 **Rehoboth Beach** Delaware, NE USA *38°42′N 75°03′W*
138 F10 **Rehovot** ; *prev.* Rehovot. Central, C Israel *31°54′N 34°49′E*
**Rehovot** *see* Rehovot
81 J20 **Rei** *spring/well* S Kenya *03°24′S 39°18′E*
**Reichenau** *see* Rychnov nad Kněžnou
**Reichenau** *see* Bogatynia, Poland
101 M17 **Reichenbach** *var.* Reichenbach im Vogtland. Sachsen, E Germany *50°36′N 12°18′E*
**Reichenbach** *see* Dzierżoniów
**Reichenbach im Vogtland** *see* Reichenbach
**Reichenberg** *see* Liberec
181 O11 **Reid** Western Australia *30°49′S 128°24′E*
23 V6 **Reidsville** Georgia, SE USA *32°05′N 82°07′W*
21 T8 **Reidsville** North Carolina, SE USA *36°21′N 79°39′W*
**Reifnitz** *see* Ribnica
97 O22 **Reigate** SE England, United Kingdom *51°14′N 00°13′W*
**Reikjavik** *see* Reykjavík
102 I10 **Ré, Île de** *island* W France
37 N15 **Reiley Peak** ▲ Arizona, SW USA *32°24′N 110°09′W*
103 Q4 **Reims** *Eng.* Rheims; *anc.* Durocortorum, Remi. Marne, N France *49°16′N 04°01′E*
63 G23 **Reina Adelaida, Archipiélago** *island group* S Chile
45 O16 **Reina Beatrix** ✈ (Oranjestad) C Aruba *12°30′N 69°57′W*
108 F7 **Reinach** Aargau, W Switzerland *47°16′N 08°12′E*
108 E6 **Reinach** Basel Landschaft, NW Switzerland *47°30′N 07°36′E*
64 O11 **Reina Sofía** ✈ (Tenerife) Tenerife, Islas Canarias, Spain, NE Atlantic Ocean
29 W13 **Reinbeck** Iowa, C USA *42°19′N 92°36′W*
100 J10 **Reinbek** Schleswig-Holstein, N Germany *53°31′N 10°15′E*
11 U12 **Reindeer** ≈ Saskatchewan, C Canada
11 U11 **Reindeer Lake** ◎ Manitoba/ Saskatchewan, C Canada
**Reine-Charlotte, Îles de la** *see* Haida Gwaii
**Reine-Élisabeth, Îles de la** *see* Queen Elizabeth Islands
94 F13 **Reineskarvet** ▲ S Norway *60°38′N 07°48′E*
184 H1 **Reinga, Cape** *headland* North Island, New Zealand *34°24′S 172°40′E*
105 N3 **Reinosa** Cantabria, N Spain *43°01′N 04°09′W*
109 R8 **Reisseck** ▲ S Austria *46°57′N 13°21′E*
21 W3 **Reisterstown** Maryland, NE USA *39°27′N 76°46′W*
**Reisui** *see* Yeosu
98 N5 **Reitdiep** ≈ NE Netherlands
191 V10 **Reitoru** *atoll* Îles Tuamotu, C French Polynesia
95 M17 **Rejmyre** Östergötland, S Sweden *58°49′N 15°55′E*
**Reka** *see* Rijeka
**Reka Ili** *see* Ile/Ili He
**Rekarne** *see* Tumbo
**Rekhovot** *see* Rehovot
8 K9 **Reliance** Northwest Territories, C Canada *62°45′N 109°08′W*
33 U16 **Reliance** Wyoming, C USA *41°42′N 109°13′W*
74 I5 **Relizane** *var.* Ghelîzâne, Ghilizane. NW Algeria *35°45′N 00°33′E*
182 I7 **Remarkable, Mount** ▲ South Australia *32°46′S 138°08′E*
54 E8 **Remedios** Antioquia, N Colombia *07°02′N 74°42′W*
43 Q16 **Remedios** Veraguas, W Panama *08°13′N 81°48′W*
42 D8 **Remedios, Punta** *headland* SW El Salvador *13°31′N 89°48′W*
**Remi** *see* Reims
99 N25 **Remich** Grevenmacher, SE Luxembourg *49°33′N 06°23′E*
99 J19 **Remicourt** Liège, E Belgium *50°40′N 05°19′E*
14 H8 **Rémigny, Lac** ◎ Québec, SE Canada
55 Z10 **Rémire** NE French Guiana *04°52′N 52°16′W*
127 N13 **Remontnoye** Rostovskaya Oblast', SW Russia *46°35′N 43°38′E*
171 U14 **Remoon** Pulau Kur, E Indonesia *05°18′S 131°59′E*
99 L20 **Remouchamps** Liège, E Belgium *50°29′N 05°43′E*
103 R15 **Remoulins** Gard, S France *43°56′N 04°34′E*
173 X16 **Rempart, Mont du** *hill* W Mauritius
101 E15 **Remscheid** Nordrhein-Westfalen, W Germany *51°10′N 07°11′E*
29 S12 **Remsen** Iowa, C USA *42°48′N 95°58′W*
94 I12 **Rena** Hedmark, S Norway *61°08′N 11°21′E*
94 I11 **Renåa** ≈ S Norway
**Renaix** *see* Ronse
118 H7 **Rencēni** N Latvia *57°43′N 25°25′E*
118 D9 **Renda** W Latvia *57°04′N 22°18′E*
107 N20 **Rende** Calabria, SW Italy *39°19′N 16°10′E*
99 K21 **Rendeux** Luxembourg, SE Belgium *50°15′N 05°28′E*
**Rendina** *see* Rentína
30 L16 **Rend Lake** ⊠ Illinois, N USA
186 K9 **Rendova** *island* New Georgia Islands, NW Solomon Islands
100 I8 **Rendsburg** Schleswig-Holstein, N Germany *54°18′N 09°40′E*
108 B9 **Renens** Vaud, SW Switzerland *46°32′N 06°36′E*
14 K12 **Renfrew** Ontario, SE Canada *45°28′N 76°44′W*
96 I12 **Renfrew** *cultural region* SW Scotland, United Kingdom
168 L11 **Rengat** Sumatera, W Indonesia *0°26′S 102°38′E*
153 W12 **Rengma Hills** ▲▲ NE India
62 H12 **Rengo** O'Higgins, C Chile *34°24′S 70°50′W*
116 M12 **Reni** Odes'ka Oblast', SW Ukraine *45°30′N 28°18′E*
80 F11 **Renk** Upper Nile, NE South Sudan *11°48′N 32°49′E*
93 L19 **Renko** Kanta-Häme, S Finland *60°52′N 24°16′E*
98 L12 **Renkum** Gelderland, SE Netherlands *51°58′N 05°43′E*
182 K9 **Renmark** South Australia *34°12′S 140°43′E*
186 L10 **Rennell** *var.* Mu Nggava. *island* S Solomon Islands
186 M9 **Rennell and Bellona** *prev.* Central. ◈ *province* S Solomon Islands
181 Q4 **Renner Springs Roadhouse** Northern Territory, N Australia *18°12′S 133°48′E*
102 I6 **Rennes** *Bret.* Roazon; *anc.* Condate. Ille-et-Vilaine, NW France *48°08′N 01°40′W*
195 S16 **Rennick Glacier** *glacier* Antarctica
11 Y16 **Rennie** Manitoba, S Canada *49°51′N 95°28′W*
35 Q5 **Reno** Nevada, W USA *39°32′N 119°49′W*
106 H10 **Reno** ≈ N Italy
35 Q5 **Reno-Cannon** ✈ Nevada, W USA *39°26′N 119°42′W*
83 F24 **Renoster** ≈ SW South Africa
15 T5 **Renouard, Lac** ◎ Québec, SE Canada
18 F13 **Renovo** Pennsylvania, NE USA *41°19′N 77°42′W*
161 O3 **Renqiu** Hebei, E China *38°49′N 116°02′E*
160 I9 **Renshou** Sichuan, C China *30°02′N 104°09′E*
31 N12 **Rensselaer** Indiana, N USA *40°57′N 87°09′W*
18 L11 **Rensselaer** New York, NE USA *42°38′N 73°44′W*
**Rentería** *see* Errenteria
115 E17 **Rentína** *var.* Rendina. Thessalía, C Greece *39°04′N 21°58′E*
29 T9 **Renville** Minnesota, N USA *44°48′N 95°13′W*
77 O13 **Réo** W Burkina Faso *12°20′N 02°28′W*
15 O12 **Repentigny** Québec, SE Canada *45°42′N 73°28′W*
146 K13 **Repetek** Lebap Welaýaty, E Turkmenistan *38°40′N 63°12′E*
93 J16 **Replot** *Fin.* Raippaluoto. *island* W Finland
**Repola** *see* Reboly
**Reppen** *see* Rzepin
**Reps** *see* Rupea
27 T7 **Republic** Missouri, C USA *37°07′N 93°28′W*
32 K7 **Republic** Washington, NW USA *48°39′N 118°44′W*
27 N3 **Republican River** ≈ Kansas/Nebraska, C USA
**Repulse Bay** *see* Naujaat
56 F9 **Requena** Loreto, NE Peru *05°05′S 73°52′W*
105 R10 **Requena** Comunitat Valenciana, E Spain *39°29′N 01°08′W*
103 O14 **Réquista** Aveyron, S France *44°00′N 02°31′E*
136 M12 **Reşadiye** Tokat, N Turkey *40°24′N 37°19′E*
**Reschenpass** *see* Resia, Passo di
**Reschitza** *see* Reşiţa
113 N20 **Resen** *Turk.* Resne. SW North Macedonia *41°07′N 21°00′E*
60 J11 **Reserva** Paraná, S Brazil *24°40′S 50°52′W*
11 V15 **Reserve** Saskatchewan, S Canada *52°24′N 102°37′W*
37 P13 **Reserve** New Mexico, SW USA *33°42′N 108°45′W*
**Reshetilovka** *see* Reshetylivka
117 S6 **Reshetylivka** *Rus.* Reshetilovka. Poltavs'ka Oblast', NE Ukraine *49°34′N 34°05′E*
**Resht** *see* Rasht
139 S2 **Reshwan** *Ar.* Rashwān, *var.* Rashwan. Arbīl, N Iraq *36°28′N 43°54′E*
106 F5 **Resia, Passo di** *Ger.* Reschenpass. *pass* Austria/ Italy
**Resicabánya** *see* Reşiţa
62 N7 **Resistencia** Chaco, NE Argentina *27°27′S 58°56′W*
116 F12 **Reşiţa** *Ger.* Reschitza, *Hung.* Resicabánya. Caraş-Severin, W Romania *45°14′N 21°58′E*
**Resne** *see* Resen
197 N9 **Resolute** *Inuit* Qausuittuq. Cornwallis Island, Nunavut, N Canada *74°41′N 94°54′W*
**Resolution** *see* Fort Resolution
9 T7 **Resolution Island** *island* Nunavut, NE Canada
185 A23 **Resolution Island** *island* SW New Zealand
**Resta** *see* Rasta
15 W7 **Restigouche** Québec, SE Canada *48°02′N 66°42′W*
11 W17 **Reston** Manitoba, S Canada *49°33′N 101°03′W*
14 H11 **Restoule Lake** ◎ Ontario, S Canada
54 F10 **Restrepo** Meta, C Colombia *04°20′N 73°29′W*
42 B6 **Retalhuleu** Retalhuleu, SW Guatemala *14°31′N 91°40′W*
42 A1 **Retalhuleu** *off.* Departamento de Retalhuleu. ◈ *department* SW Guatemala
**Retalhuleu, Departamento de** *see* Retalhuleu
97 N18 **Retford** C England, United Kingdom *53°18′N 00°52′W*
103 Q3 **Rethel** Ardennes, N France *49°31′N 04°22′E*
**Rethimno/Réthimnon** *see* Réthymno
115 I25 **Réthymno** *prev.* Rethimno, Réthimnon. Kríti, Greece, E Mediterranean Sea *35°21′N 24°29′E*
**Retiche, Alpi** *see* Rhaetian Alps
99 J16 **Retie** Antwerpen, N Belgium *51°18′N 05°05′E*
111 J21 **Rétság** Nógrád, N Hungary *47°57′N 19°08′E*
109 W2 **Retz** Niederösterreich, NE Austria *48°46′N 15°58′E*
173 N15 **Réunion** *off.* La Réunion. ◇ *French overseas department* W Indian Ocean
128 L17 **Réunion** *island* W Indian Ocean
105 U6 **Reus** Cataluña, E Spain *41°10′N 01°06′E*
108 F7 **Reuss** ≈ NW Switzerland
99 J15 **Reusel** Noord-Brabant, S Netherlands *51°21′N 05°10′E*
**Reuţel** *see* Ciuhuru
101 H22 **Reutlingen** Baden-Württemberg, S Germany *48°30′N 09°13′E*
108 L7 **Reutte** Tirol, W Austria *47°30′N 10°44′E*
99 M16 **Reuver** Limburg, SE Netherlands *51°17′N 06°05′E*
28 K7 **Reva** South Dakota, N USA *45°30′N 103°03′W*
**Reval/Revel** *see* Tallinn
124 J4 **Revda** Murmanskaya Oblast', NW Russia *67°57′N 34°29′E*
122 F6 **Revda** Sverdlovskaya Oblast', C Russia *56°48′N 59°42′E*
103 N16 **Revel** Haute-Garonne, S France *43°27′N 01°59′E*
11 O16 **Revelstoke** British Columbia, SW Canada *51°02′N 118°12′W*
43 N13 **Reventazón, Río** ≈ E Costa Rica
106 G9 **Revere** Lombardia, N Italy *45°03′N 11°07′E*
39 Y14 **Revillagigedo Island** *island* Alexander Archipelago, Alaska, USA
103 R3 **Revin** Ardennes, N France *49°57′N 04°39′E*
92 O3 **Revnosa** *headland* C Svalbard *78°03′N 18°52′E*
**Revolyutsii, Pik** *see* Revolyutsiya, Qullai
147 T13 **Revolyutsiya, Qullai** *Rus.* Pik Revolyutsii. ▲ SE Tajikistan *38°40′N 72°26′E*
111 L19 **Revúca** *Ger.* Grossrauschenbach, *Hung.* Nagyrőce. Banskobystrický Kraj, C Slovakia *48°40′N 20°10′E*
154 K9 **Rewa** Madhya Pradesh, C India *24°32′N 81°18′E*
139 T2 **Rewanduz** *Ar.* Rawāndūz, *var.* Rawāndiz. Arbīl, N Iraq *36°38′N 44°32′E*
152 I11 **Rewāri** Haryāna, N India *28°14′N 76°38′E*
33 R14 **Rexburg** Idaho, NW USA *43°49′N 111°47′W*
78 G13 **Rey Bouba** Nord, NE Cameroon *08°40′N 14°11′E*
92 L3 **Reyðarfjörður** Austurland, E Iceland *65°02′N 14°12′W*
57 K16 **Reyes** Beni, NW Bolivia *14°17′S 67°18′W*
34 L8 **Reyes, Point** *headland* California, W USA *37°59′N 123°01′W*
54 B12 **Reyes, Punta** *headland* SW Colombia *02°44′N 78°08′W*
136 L17 **Reyhanlı** Hatay, S Turkey *36°16′N 36°35′E*
43 U16 **Rey, Isla del** *island* Archipiélago de las Perlas, SE Panama
92 H2 **Reykhólar** Vestfirðir, W Iceland *65°28′N 22°12′W*
92 K2 **Reykjahlíð** Norðurland Eystra, NE Iceland *65°37′N 16°54′W*
197 O16 **Reykjanes Basin** *var.* Irminger Basin. *undersea feature* N Atlantic Ocean *62°30′N 33°30′W*
197 N17 **Reykjanes Ridge** *undersea feature* N Atlantic Ocean *62°00′N 27°00′W*
92 H4 **Reykjavík** *var.* Reikjavik. ● (Iceland) Höfudhborgarsvaedhi, W Iceland *64°08′N 21°54′W*
18 D13 **Reynoldsville** Pennsylvania, NE USA *41°04′N 78°51′W*
41 P8 **Reynosa** Tamaulipas, C Mexico *26°03′N 98°19′W*
**Reẕā'īyeh** *see* Orūmīyeh
**Reẕā'īyeh, Daryācheh-ye** *see* Orūmīyeh, Daryācheh-ye
102 I8 **Rezé** Loire-Atlantique, NW France *47°10′N 01°36′W*
118 K10 **Rēzekne** *Ger.* Rositten; *prev. Rus.* Rezhitsa. SE Latvia *56°31′N 27°22′E*
139 U2 **Rezge** *Ar.* Razkah, *var.* Razga. As Sulaymānīyah, E Iraq *36°25′N 45°06′E*
**Rezhitsa** *see* Rēzekne
117 N9 **Rezina** NE Moldova *47°44′N 28°58′E*
114 N11 **Rezovo** *Turk.* Rezve. Burgas, E Bulgaria *42°00′N 28°00′E*
114 N11 **Rezovska Reka** *Turk.* Rezve Deresi. ≈ Bulgaria/Turkey *see also* Rezve Deresi
**Rezovska Reka** *see* Rezve Deresi
**Rezve** *see* Rezovo
114 N11 **Rezve Deresi** *Bul.* Rezovska Reka. ≈ Bulgaria/Turkey *see also* Rezovska Reka
**Rezve Deresi** *see* Rezovska Reka
**Rhadames** *see* Ghadāmis
**Rhaedestus** *see* Tekirdağ
108 J10 **Rhaetian Alps** *Fr.* Alpes Rhétiques, *Ger.* Rätische Alpen, *It.* Alpi Retiche. ▲▲ C Europe
108 I8 **Rhätikon** ▲▲ C Europe
101 G14 **Rheda-Wiedenbrück** Nordrhein-Westfalen, W Germany *51°51′N 08°17′E*
98 M12 **Rheden** Gelderland, E Netherlands *52°01′N 06°03′E*
**Rhegion/Rhegium** *see* Reggio di Calabria
**Rheims** *see* Reims
**Rhein** *see* Rhine
101 E17 **Rheinbach** Nordrhein-Westfalen, W Germany *50°37′N 06°57′E*
100 F13 **Rheine** *var.* Rheine in Westfalen. Nordrhein-Westfalen, NW Germany *52°17′N 07°27′E*
**Rheine in Westfalen** *see* Rheine
**Rheinfeld** *see* Rheinfelden
101 F24 **Rheinfelden** Baden-Württemberg, S Germany *47°34′N 07°46′E*
108 E6 **Rheinfelden** *var.* Rheinfeld. Aargau, N Switzerland *47°33′N 07°47′E*
101 E17 **Rheinisches Schiefergebirge** *var.* Rhine State Uplands, *Eng.* Rhenish Slate Mountains. ▲▲ W Germany
101 D18 **Rheinland-Pfalz** *Eng.* Rhineland-Palatinate, *Fr.* Rhénanie-Palatinat. ◈ *state* W Germany
101 G18 **Rhein Main** ✈ (Frankfurt am Main) Hessen, W Germany *50°03′N 08°33′E*
**Rhénanie du Nord-Westphalie** *see* Nordrhein-Westfalen
**Rhénanie-Palatinat** *see* Rheinland-Pfalz
98 K12 **Rhenen** Utrecht, C Netherlands *52°01′N 06°02′E*
**Rhenish Slate Mountains** *see* Rheinisches Schiefergebirge
**Rhétiques, Alpes** *see* Rhaetian Alps
100 N10 **Rhin** ≈ NE Germany
**Rhin** *see* Rhine
84 F10 **Rhine** *Dut.* Rijn, *Fr.* Rhin, *Ger.* Rhein. ≈ W Europe
30 L5 **Rhinelander** Wisconsin, N USA *45°39′N 89°23′W*
**Rhineland-Palatinate** *see* Rheinland-Pfalz
**Rhine State Uplands** *see* Rheinisches Schiefergebirge
100 N11 **Rhinkanal** *canal* NE Germany
81 F17 **Rhino Camp** NW Uganda *02°58′N 31°24′E*
74 D7 **Rhir, Cap** *headland* W Morocco *30°40′N 09°54′W*
106 D7 **Rho** Lombardia, N Italy *45°32′N 09°02′E*
19 N12 **Rhode Island** *off.* State of Rhode Island and Providence Plantations, *also known as* Little Rhody, Ocean State. ◈ *state* NE USA
19 O13 **Rhode Island** *island* Rhode Island, NE USA
19 O13 **Rhode Island Sound** *sound* Maine/Rhode Island, NE USA
**Rhodes** *see* Ródos
**Rhode-Saint-Genèse** *see* Sint-Genesius-Rode
84 L14 **Rhodes Basin** *undersea feature* E Mediterranean Sea *35°55′N 28°30′E*
**Rhodesia** *see* Zimbabwe
114 I12 **Rhodope Mountains** *var.* Rodópi Óri, *Bul.* Rodopi Planina, Rodopi, *Gk.* Oroseirá Rodópis, *Turk.* Dospad Dagh, Rodoplar. ▲▲ Bulgaria/Greece
101 I18 **Rhön** ▲▲ C Germany
103 Q10 **Rhône** ◈ *department* E France
86 C12 **Rhône** ≈ France/ Switzerland
98 G13 **Rhoon** Zuid-Holland, SW Netherlands *51°52′N 04°25′E*



312

◆ Country
● Country Capital
◇ Dependent Territory
○ Dependent Territory Capital
◈ Administrative Regions
✈ International Airport
▲ Mountain
▲▲ Mountain Range
Volcano
≈ River
◎ Lake
⊠ Reservoir

RHUM – RODOSTO


96 G9 **Rhum** *var.* Rum. *island* W Scotland, United Kingdom
**Rhuthun** *see* Ruthin
97 J18 **Rhyl** NE Wales, United Kingdom 53°19´N 03°28´W
59 K18 **Rialma** Goiás, S Brazil 15°22´S 49°35´W
104 L3 **Riaño** Castilla y León, N Spain 42°59´N 05°00´W
105 O9 **Riansáres** ⁓ C Spain
152 H6 **Riāsi** Jammu and Kashmir, NW India 33°03´N 74°51´E
168 K10 **Riau** *off.* Propinsi Riau. ◆ *province* W Indonesia
**Riau Archipelago** *see* Riau, Kepulauan
168 M11 **Riau, Kepulauan** *var.* Riau Archipelago, *Dut.* Riouw-Archipel. *island group* W Indonesia
**Riau, Propinsi** *see* Riau
105 O6 **Riaza** Castilla y León, N Spain 41°17´N 03°29´W
105 N6 **Riaza** ⁓ N Spain
81 K17 **Riba** *spring/well* NE Kenya 01°56´N 40°38´E
104 H4 **Ribadavia** Galicia, NW Spain 42°17´N 08°08´W
104 J2 **Ribadeo** Galicia, NW Spain 43°32´N 07°04´W
104 L2 **Ribadesella** *var.* Ribeseya. Asturias, N Spain 43°27´N 05°04´W
104 G10 **Ribatejo** *former province* C Portugal
83 P15 **Ribáuè** Nampula, N Mozambique 14°56´S 38°19´E
97 K17 **Ribble** ⁓ NW England, United Kingdom
95 F23 **Ribe** Syddtjylland, W Denmark 55°20´N 08°47´E
**Ribeira** *see* Sanata Uxía de Ribeira
64 O5 **Ribeira Brava** Madeira, Portugal, NE Atlantic Ocean 32°39´N 17°04´W
64 P3 **Ribeira Grande** São Miguel, Azores, Portugal, NE Atlantic Ocean 37°34´N 25°32´W
60 L8 **Ribeirão Preto** São Paulo, S Brazil 21°09´S 47°48´W
60 L11 **Ribeira, Rio** ⁓ S Brazil
107 I24 **Ribera** Sicilia, Italy, C Mediterranean Sea 37°31´N 13°16´E
57 L14 **Riberalta** Beni, N Bolivia 11°01´S 66°04´W
105 W4 **Ribes de Freser** Cataluña, NE Spain 42°18´N 02°11´E
**Ribeseya** *see* Ribadesella
30 L6 **Rib Mountain** ▲ Wisconsin, N USA 44°55´N 89°41´W
109 U12 **Ribnica** *Ger.* Reifnitz. S Slovenia 45°46´N 14°40´E
117 N9 **Rîbniţa** *var.* Râbniţa, *Rus.* Rybnitsa. NE Moldova 47°46´N 29°01´E
100 M8 **Ribnitz-Damgarten** Mecklenburg-Vorpommern, NE Germany 54°14´N 12°25´E
111 D16 **Říčany** *Ger.* Ritschan. Středočeský Kraj, W Czechia 49°59´N 14°40´E
29 U7 **Rice** Minnesota, N USA 45°42´N 94°10´W
30 J5 **Rice Lake** Wisconsin, N USA 45°33´N 91°43´W
14 E8 **Rice Lake** ⊗ Ontario, S Canada
14 I15 **Rice Lake** ⊗ Ontario, SE Canada
23 V3 **Richard B. Russell Lake** ⊠ Georgia, SE USA
25 U6 **Richardson** Texas, SW USA 32°55´N 96°44´W
11 R11 **Richardson** ⁓ Alberta, C Canada
10 I3 **Richardson Mountains** ▲▲ Yukon, NW Canada
185 C21 **Richardson Mountains** ▲▲ South Island, New Zealand
42 F3 **Richardson Peak** ▲ SE Belize 16°34´N 88°46´W
76 G10 **Richard Toll** N Senegal 16°28´N 15°44´W
28 L5 **Richardton** North Dakota, N USA 46°52´N 102°19´W
14 F13 **Rich, Cape** *headland* Ontario, S Canada 44°42´N 80°37´W
102 L8 **Richelieu** Indre-et-Loire, C France 47°01´N 00°18´E
33 P15 **Richfield** Idaho, NW USA 43°03´N 114°11´W
36 K5 **Richfield** Utah, W USA 38°45´N 112°05´W
18 J10 **Richfield Springs** New York, NE USA 42°52´N 74°57´W
18 M6 **Richford** Vermont, NE USA 44°59´N 72°37´W
27 R6 **Rich Hill** Missouri, C USA 38°06´N 94°22´W
13 P14 **Richibucto** New Brunswick, SE Canada 46°42´N 64°54´W
108 G8 **Richisau** Glarus, NE Switzerland 47°00´N 08°54´E
23 S6 **Richland** Georgia, SE USA 32°05´N 84°40´W
27 U6 **Richland** Missouri, C USA 37°51´N 92°24´W
25 U8 **Richland** Texas, SW USA 31°55´N 96°25´W
32 K10 **Richland** Washington, NW USA 46°17´N 119°16´W
30 K8 **Richland Center** Wisconsin, N USA 43°22´N 90°24´W
21 W11 **Richlands** North Carolina, SE USA 34°52´N 77°33´W
21 Q7 **Richlands** Virginia, NE USA 37°05´N 81°47´W
25 R9 **Richland Springs** Texas, SW USA 31°16´N 98°56´W
183 S8 **Richmond** New South Wales, SE Australia 33°36´S 150°44´E
10 L17 **Richmond** British Columbia, SW Canada 49°07´N 123°09´W
14 L13 **Richmond** Ontario, SE Canada 45°12´N 75°49´W
15 Q12 **Richmond** Québec, SE Canada 45°39´N 72°07´W
185 I14 **Richmond** Tasman, South Island, New Zealand 41°25´S 173°04´E
35 N8 **Richmond** California, W USA 37°57´N 122°22´W
31 Q14 **Richmond** Indiana, N USA 39°50´N 84°51´W
20 M6 **Richmond** Kentucky, S USA 37°45´N 84°19´W
27 S4 **Richmond** Missouri, C USA 39°15´N 93°59´W
25 V11 **Richmond** Texas, SW USA 29°36´N 95°48´W
36 L1 **Richmond** Utah, W USA 41°55´N 111°51´W
21 W6 **Richmond** *state capital* Virginia, NE USA 37°33´N 77°28´W
14 H15 **Richmond Hill** Ontario, S Canada 43°51´N 79°24´W
185 J15 **Richmond Range** ▲▲ South Island, New Zealand
27 S12 **Rich Mountain** ▲ Arkansas, C USA 34°37´N 94°17´W
31 S13 **Richwood** Ohio, N USA 40°25´N 83°18´W
21 R5 **Richwood** West Virginia, NE USA 38°13´N 80°31´W
104 K5 **Ricobayo, Embalse de** ⊠ NW Spain
**Ricomagus** *see* Riom
**Ridà'** *see* Radā'
145 X9 **Ridder** *prev.* Leninogorsk. Vostochnyy Kazakhstan, E Kazakhstan 50°20´N 83°34´E
127 T5 **Ridder** Respublika Tatarstan, W Russia 54°34´N 52°27´E
98 H13 **Ridderkerk** Zuid-Holland, SW Netherlands 51°52´N 04°35´E
33 N16 **Riddle** Idaho, NW USA 42°07´N 116°09´W
32 F14 **Riddle** Oregon, NW USA 42°57´N 123°21´W
14 L13 **Rideau** ⁓ Ontario, SE Canada
35 T12 **Ridgecrest** California, W USA 35°37´N 117°40´W
18 L13 **Ridgefield** Connecticut, NE USA 41°16´N 73°30´W
22 K5 **Ridgeland** Mississippi, S USA 32°25´N 90°07´W
21 R15 **Ridgeland** South Carolina, SE USA 32°30´N 80°59´W
20 F8 **Ridgely** Tennessee, S USA 36°15´N 89°29´W
14 D17 **Ridgetown** Ontario, S Canada 42°27´N 81°52´W
21 R12 **Ridgeway** South Carolina, SE USA 34°17´N 80°56´W
**Ridgeway** *see* Ridgway
18 D13 **Ridgway** *var.* Ridgeway. Pennsylvania, NE USA 41°24´N 78°40´W
11 W16 **Riding Mountain** ▲▲ Manitoba, S Canada
**Ried** *see* Ried im Innkreis
109 R4 **Ried im Innkreis** *var.* Ried. Oberösterreich, NW Austria 48°13´N 13°29´E
109 X8 **Riegersburg** Steiermark, SE Austria 47°03´N 15°52´E
108 E6 **Riehen** Basel-Stadt, NW Switzerland 47°35´N 07°39´E
**Riehppegáisá** *var.* Rieppe. ▲ N Norway 69°38´N 21°31´E
92 J9
99 K18 **Riemst** Limburg, NE Belgium 50°49´N 05°36´E
**Rieppe** *see* Riehppegáisá
101 O15 **Riesa** Sachsen, E Germany 51°18´N 13°18´E
63 H24 **Riesco, Isla** *island* S Chile
107 K25 **Riesi** Sicilia, Italy, C Mediterranean Sea 37°17´N 14°05´E
83 I23 **Riet** ⁓ SW South Africa
83 F25 **Riet** ⁓ SW South Africa
118 D11 **Rietavas** Telšiai, W Lithuania 55°43´N 21°56´E
83 F19 **Rietfontein** Omaheke, E Namibia 21°58´S 20°58´E
107 I14 **Rieti** *anc.* Reate. Lazio, C Italy 42°24´N 12°51´E
84 D14 **Rif** *var.* Riff, Er Rif, Er Riff. ▲▲ N Morocco
138 I8 **Rif Dimashq** *off.* Muḩāfaẓat Dimashq, *var.* Damascus, *Ar.* Ash Sham, Ash Shām, Damasco, Esh Sham, *Fr.* Damas. ◆ *governorate* S Syria
**Riff** *see* Rif
37 Q4 **Rifle** Colorado, C USA 39°30´N 107°46´W
31 R7 **Rifle River** ⁓ Michigan, N USA
**Rift Valley** *see* Great Rift Valley
118 F9 **Riga** *Eng.* Riga. ● C Latvia 56°57´N 24°08´E
**Rigaer Bucht** *see* Riga, Gulf of
118 F6 **Riga, Gulf of** *Est.* Liivi Laht, *Ger.* Rigaer Bucht, *Latv.* Rigas Jūras Līcis, *Rus.* Rizhskiy Zaliv; *prev. Est.* Riia Laht. *gulf* Estonia/Latvia
**Rigas Jūras Līcis** *see* Riga, Gulf of
15 N12 **Rigaud** ⁓ Ontario/Québec, SE Canada
33 R14 **Rigby** Idaho, NW USA 43°40´N 111°54´W
32 M11 **Riggins** Idaho, NW USA 45°24´N 116°18´W
13 R8 **Rigolet** Newfoundland and Labrador, NE Canada 54°10´N 58°25´W
78 G9 **Rig-Rig** Kanem, W Chad 14°16´N 14°21´E
118 F4 **Riguldi** Läänemaa, W Estonia 59°07´N 23°34´E
**Riia Laht** *see* Riga, Gulf of
93 L19 **Riihimäki** Kanta-Häme, S Finland 60°45´N 24°45´E
195 U2 **Riiser-Larsen Peninsula** *peninsula* Antarctica
65 P22 **Riiser-Larsen Sea** *sea* Antarctica
**Riisser Larsen Ice Shelf** *see* Riiser-Larsenisen
40 D2 **Riíto** Sonora, NW Mexico 32°06´N 114°57´W
112 B9 **Rijeka** *Ger.* Sankt Veit am Flaum, *It.* Fiume, *Slvn.* Reka; *anc.* Tarsatica. Primorje-Gorski Kotar, NW Croatia 45°20´N 14°26´E
99 I14 **Rijen** Noord-Brabant, S Netherlands 51°35´N 04°55´E
99 H15 **Rijkevorsel** Antwerpen, N Belgium 51°23´N 04°43´E
**Rijn** *see* Rhine
98 G11 **Rijnsburg** Zuid-Holland, W Netherlands 52°12´N 04°27´E
**Rijssel** *see* Lille
98 N10 **Rijssen** Overijssel, E Netherlands 52°19´N 06°30´E
98 G12 **Rijswijk** *Eng.* Ryswick. Zuid-Holland, W Netherlands 52°03´N 04°20´E
92 I10 **Riksgränsen** Norrbotten, N Sweden 68°24´N 18°15´E
165 U4 **Rikubetsu** Hokkaidō, NE Japan 43°30´N 143°43´E
165 R9 **Rikuzen-Takata** Iwate, Honshū, C Japan 39°03´N 141°38´E
27 O4 **Riley** Kansas, C USA 39°18´N 96°49´W
99 I17 **Rillaar** Vlaams Brabant, C Belgium 50°58´N 04°58´E
**Ril, Loch** *see* Ree, Lough
114 G11 **Rilska Reka** ⁓ W Bulgaria
77 T12 **Rima** ⁓ N Nigeria
141 N7 **Rimah, Wādī ar** *var.* Wādī ar Rummah. *dry watercourse* C Saudi Arabia
**Rimaszombat** *see* Rimavská Sobota
191 R12 **Rimatara** *island* Îles Australes, SW French Polynesia
111 L20 **Rimavská Sobota** *Ger.* Gross-Steffelsdorf, *Hung.* Rimaszombat. Bankobystrický Kraj, C Slovakia 48°24´N 20°01´E
11 Q15 **Rimbey** Alberta, SW Canada 52°39´N 114°10´W
95 P15 **Rimbo** Stockholm, C Sweden 59°44´N 18°21´E
95 M18 **Rimforsa** Östergötland, S Sweden 58°06´N 15°40´E
106 I11 **Rimini** *anc.* Ariminum. Emilia-Romagna, N Italy 44°03´N 12°33´E
**Rîmnicu-Sărat** *see* Râmnicu Sărat
**Rîmnicu Vîlcea** *see* Râmnicu Vâlcea
149 Y3 **Rimo Muztagh** ▲▲ India/Pakistan
15 U7 **Rimouski** Québec, SE Canada 48°26´N 68°32´W
158 M16 **Rinbung** Xizang Zizhiqu, W China 29°15´N 89°40´E
**Rinchinlhumbe** *see* Dzöölön
62 I5 **Rincón, Cerro** ▲ N Chile 24°01´S 67°19´W
104 M15 **Rincón de la Victoria** Andalucía, S Spain 36°43´N 04°18´W
**Rincón del Bonete, Lago Artificial de** *see* Río Negro, Embalse del
105 Q4 **Rincón de Soto** La Rioja, N Spain 42°15´N 01°50´W
94 G8 **Rindal** Møre og Romsdal, S Norway 63°02´N 09°09´E
115 J20 **Ríneia** *island* Kykládes, Greece, Aegean Sea
152 H11 **Ringas** *prev.* Reengus, Ringus. Rājasthān, N India 27°18´N 75°27´E
95 H24 **Ringe** Syddtjylland, C Denmark 55°14´N 10°30´E
94 H11 **Ringebu** Oppland, S Norway 61°31´N 10°09´E
**Ringen** *see* Rõngu
186 K8 **Ringgi** Kolombangara, NW Solomon Islands 08°03´S 157°08´E
23 R1 **Ringgold** Georgia, SE USA 34°55´N 85°06´W
22 G5 **Ringgold** Louisiana, S USA 32°19´N 93°16´W
25 S5 **Ringgold** Texas, SW USA 33°47´N 97°56´W
155 E22 **Ringkøbing** Midtjylland, W Denmark 56°04´N 08°22´E
95 E22 **Ringkøbing Fjord** *fjord* W Denmark
33 S10 **Ringling** Montana, NW USA 46°15´N 110°48´W
27 N13 **Ringling** Oklahoma, C USA 34°12´N 97°35´W
94 H13 **Ringsaker** Hedmark, S Norway 60°54´N 10°45´E
95 I23 **Ringsted** Sjælland, E Denmark 55°28´N 11°48´E
**Ringus** *see* Ringas
92 I9 **Ringvassøya** *Lapp.* Ráneš. *island* N Norway
18 K13 **Ringwood** New Jersey, NE USA 41°06´N 74°15´W
**Rinn Duáin** *see* Hook Head
100 H13 **Rinteln** Niedersachsen, NW Germany 52°10´N 09°04´E
115 E18 **Río** Dytikí Elláda, S Greece 38°18´N 21°48´E
**Rio** *see* Rio de Janeiro
56 C7 **Riobamba** Chimborazo, C Ecuador 01°44´S 78°40´W
60 P9 **Rio Bonito** Rio de Janeiro, SE Brazil 22°42´S 42°38´W
59 C16 **Rio Branco** *state capital* Acre, W Brazil 09°59´S 67°49´W
61 H18 **Río Branco** Cerro Largo, NE Uruguay 32°32´S 53°28´W
**Rio Branco, Território de** *see* Roraima
41 P8 **Río Bravo** Tamaulipas, C Mexico 25°57´N 98°03´W
63 G16 **Río Bueno** Los Ríos, C Chile 40°20´S 72°55´W
55 P5 **Río Caribe** Sucre, NE Venezuela 10°43´N 63°06´W
54 M5 **Río Chico** Miranda, N Venezuela 10°18´N 66°00´W
63 H18 **Río Cisnes** Aysén, S Chile 44°29´S 71°15´W
60 L9 **Rio Claro** São Paulo, S Brazil 22°19´S 47°35´W
45 V14 **Rio Claro** Trinidad, Trinidad and Tobago 10°18´N 61°11´W
54 J5 **Río Claro** Lara, N Venezuela 09°54´N 69°23´W
63 K15 **Río Colorado** Río Negro, E Argentina 39°01´S 64°05´W
62 K11 **Río Cuarto** Córdoba, C Argentina 33°06´S 64°20´W
60 P10 **Rio de Janeiro** *var.* Rio. *state capital* Rio de Janeiro, SE Brazil 22°53´S 43°17´W
60 P9 **Rio de Janeiro** *off.* Estado do Rio de Janeiro. ◆ *state* SE Brazil
**Rio de Janeiro, Estado do** *see* Rio de Janeiro
43 R17 **Río de Jesús** Veraguas, S Panama 07°58´N 81°01´W
34 K3 **Rio Dell** California, W USA 40°30´N 124°07´W
60 K13 **Rio do Sul** Santa Catarina, S Brazil 27°15´S 49°37´W
63 I23 **Río Gallegos** *var.* Gallegos, Puerto Gallegos. Santa Cruz, S Argentina 51°40´S 69°21´W
63 J24 **Río Grande** Tierra del Fuego, S Argentina 53°45´S 67°46´W
61 I18 **Rio Grande** *var.* São Pedro do Rio Grande do Sul. Rio Grande do Sul, S Brazil 32°03´S 52°08´W
40 L10 **Río Grande** Zacatecas, C Mexico 23°50´N 103°20´W
42 J9 **Río Grande** León, NW Nicaragua 12°59´N 86°34´W
45 V5 **Río Grande** E Puerto Rico 18°23´N 65°51´W
24 I9 **Rio Grande** ⁓ Texas, SW USA
25 R17 **Rio Grande City** Texas, SW USA 26°24´N 98°50´W
59 P14 **Rio Grande do Norte** *off.* Estado do Rio Grande do Norte. ◆ *state* E Brazil
**Rio Grande do Norte, Estado do** *see* Rio Grande do Norte
61 G15 **Rio Grande do Sul** *off.* Estado do Rio Grande do Sul. ◆ *state* S Brazil
**Rio Grande do Sul, Estado do** *see* Rio Grande do Sul
65 M17 **Rio Grande Fracture Zone** *tectonic feature* C Atlantic Ocean
65 J18 **Rio Grande Gap** *undersea feature* S Atlantic Ocean
**Rio Grande Plateau** *see* Rio Grande Rise
65 J18 **Rio Grande Rise** *var.* Rio Grande Plateau. *undersea feature* SW Atlantic Ocean 31°00´S 35°00´W
54 G4 **Ríohacha** La Guajira, N Colombia 11°23´N 72°47´W
43 S16 **Río Hato** Coclé, C Panama 08°21´N 80°10´W
25 T17 **Rio Hondo** Texas, SW USA 26°14´N 97°34´W
56 D10 **Rioja** San Martín, N Peru 06°02´S 77°10´W
41 Y11 **Río Lagartos** Yucatán, SE Mexico 21°35´N 88°08´W
103 P11 **Riom** *anc.* Ricomagus. Puy-de-Dôme, C France 45°54´N 03°06´E
104 F10 **Rio Maior** Santarém, C Portugal 39°20´N 08°55´W
103 O12 **Riom-ès-Montagnes** Cantal, C France 45°15´N 02°39´E
60 J12 **Rio Negro** Paraná, S Brazil 26°06´S 49°46´W
63 I15 **Río Negro** *off.* Provincia de Río Negro. ◆ *province* C Argentina
61 D18 **Río Negro** ◆ *department* W Uruguay
47 V12 **Río Negro, Embalse del** *var.* Lago Artificial de Rincón del Bonete. ⊠ C Uruguay
**Río Negro, Provincia de** *see* Río Negro
107 M17 **Rionero in Vulture** Basilicata, S Italy 40°55´N 15°40´E
137 S9 **Rioni** ⁓ W Georgia
105 P12 **Riópar** Castilla-La Mancha, C Spain 38°31´N 02°27´W
61 H16 **Rio Pardo** Rio Grande do Sul, S Brazil 29°41´S 52°25´W
37 R11 **Rio Rancho Estates** New Mexico, SW USA 35°14´N 106°40´W
42 L11 **Río San Juan** ◆ *department* S Nicaragua
54 E9 **Riosucio** Caldas, W Colombia 05°26´N 75°44´W
54 C7 **Riosucio** Chocó, NW Colombia 07°25´N 77°05´W
62 K10 **Río Tercero** Córdoba, C Argentina 32°15´S 64°08´W
42 K5 **Río Tinto, Sierra** ▲▲ NE Honduras
54 J5 **Río Tocuyo** Lara, N Venezuela 10°18´N 70°00´W
**Riouw-Archipel** *see* Riau, Kepulauan
59 J19 **Rio Verde** Goiás, C Brazil 17°50´S 50°55´W
41 O12 **Río Verde** *var.* Rioverde. San Luis Potosí, C Mexico 21°58´N 100°00´W
**Rioverde** *see* Río Verde
35 O8 **Rio Vista** California, W USA 38°09´N 121°42´W
112 M11 **Ripanj** Serbia, N Serbia 44°37´N 20°30´E
106 J13 **Ripatransone** Marche, C Italy 43°00´N 13°45´E
22 M2 **Ripley** Mississippi, S USA 34°43´N 88°57´W
31 R15 **Ripley** Ohio, N USA 38°45´N 83°51´W
20 F9 **Ripley** Tennessee, S USA 35°43´N 89°30´W
21 Q4 **Ripley** West Virginia, NE USA 38°49´N 81°44´W
105 W4 **Ripoll** Cataluña, NE Spain 42°12´N 02°12´E
97 M16 **Ripon** N England, United Kingdom 54°07´N 01°31´W
30 M7 **Ripon** Wisconsin, N USA 43°52´N 88°48´W
107 L24 **Riposto** Sicilia, Italy, C Mediterranean Sea 37°44´N 15°13´E
99 L14 **Rips** Noord-Brabant, SE Netherlands 51°31´N 05°49´E
54 D9 **Risaralda** *off.* Departamento de Risaralda. ◆ *province* C Colombia
**Risaralda, Departamento de** *see* Risaralda
116 L8 **Rîşcani** *var.* Râşcani, *Rus.* Ryshkany. NW Moldova 47°55´N 27°31´E
152 J9 **Rishikesh** Uttarākhand, N India 30°06´N 78°16´E
165 S1 **Rishiri-tō** *var.* Risiri Tô. *island* NE Japan
165 S1 **Rishiri-yama** ⛰ Rishiri-tō, NE Japan 45°11´N 141°11´E
25 R7 **Rising Star** Texas, SW USA 32°06´N 98°57´W
31 Q15 **Rising Sun** Indiana, N USA 38°58´N 84°53´W
**Risiri Tô** *see* Rishiri-tō
102 L4 **Risle** ⁓ N France
**Rîşno** *see* Râşnov
27 V13 **Rison** Arkansas, C USA 33°58´N 92°11´W
95 G17 **Risør** Aust-Agder, S Norway 58°44´N 09°15´E
92 H10 **Risøyhamn** Nordland, C Norway 69°00´N 15°37´E
101 I23 **Riss** ⁓ S Germany
118 G4 **Risti** *Ger.* Kreuz. Läänemaa, W Estonia 59°01´N 24°01´E
15 V8 **Ristigouche** ⁓ Québec, SE Canada
93 N18 **Ristiina** Etelä-Savo, E Finland 61°32´N 27°15´E
93 N14 **Ristijärvi** Kainuu, C Finland 64°30´N 28°15´E
188 C14 **Ritidian Point** *headland* N Guam 13°39´N 144°51´E
**Ritschan** *see* Říčany
35 R9 **Ritter, Mount** ▲ California, W USA 37°40´N 119°10´W
31 T12 **Rittman** Ohio, N USA 40°58´N 81°46´W
32 L9 **Ritzville** Washington, NW USA 47°07´N 118°22´W
**Riva** *see* Riva del Garda
61 A21 **Rivadavia** Buenos Aires, E Argentina 35°29´S 62°59´W
106 F7 **Riva del Garda** *var.* Riva. Trentino-Alto Adige, N Italy 45°54´N 10°50´E
106 B8 **Rivarolo Canavese** Piemonte, W Italy 45°21´N 07°42´E
42 K11 **Rivas** Rivas, SW Nicaragua 11°26´N 85°50´W
42 J11 **Rivas** ◆ *department* SW Nicaragua
103 R11 **Rive-de-Gier** Loire, E France 45°31´N 04°36´E
61 A22 **Rivera** Buenos Aires, E Argentina 37°13´S 63°14´W
61 F16 **Rivera** Rivera, NE Uruguay 30°54´S 55°31´W
61 F17 **Rivera** ◆ *department* NE Uruguay
35 P9 **Riverbank** California, W USA 37°43´N 120°59´W
76 K17 **River Cess** SW Liberia 05°28´N 09°32´W
28 M4 **Riverdale** North Dakota, N USA 47°29´N 101°22´W
30 I6 **River Falls** Wisconsin, N USA 44°52´N 92°38´W
11 T16 **Riverhurst** Saskatchewan, S Canada 50°52´N 106°49´W
183 O10 **Riverina** *physical region* New South Wales, SE Australia
80 G8 **River Nile** ◆ *state* NE Sudan
63 F19 **Rivero, Isla** *island* Archipiélago de los Chonos, S Chile
11 W16 **Rivers** Manitoba, S Canada 50°02´N 100°14´W
77 U17 **Rivers** ◆ *state* S Nigeria
185 D23 **Riversdale** Southland, South Island, New Zealand 45°54´S 168°44´E
83 F26 **Riversdale** Western Cape, SW South Africa 34°05´S 21°15´E
35 U15 **Riverside** California, W USA 33°58´N 117°25´W
25 W9 **Riverside** Texas, SW USA 30°51´N 95°24´W
37 U3 **Riverside Reservoir** ⊠ Colorado, C USA
10 K15 **Rivers Inlet** British Columbia, SW Canada 51°43´N 127°19´W
10 K15 **Rivers Inlet** *inlet* British Columbia, SW Canada
11 X15 **Riverton** Manitoba, S Canada 51°00´N 97°00´W
185 C24 **Riverton** Southland, South Island, New Zealand 46°20´S 168°02´E
30 L13 **Riverton** Illinois, N USA 39°50´N 89°31´W
36 L3 **Riverton** Utah, W USA 40°32´N 111°57´W
33 V15 **Riverton** Wyoming, C USA 43°01´N 108°22´W
14 G10 **River Valley** Ontario, S Canada 46°36´N 80°09´W
13 P14 **Riverview** New Brunswick, SE Canada 46°03´N 64°47´W
103 O17 **Rivesaltes** Pyrénées-Orientales, S France 42°46´N 02°48´E
36 H11 **Riviera** Arizona, SW USA 35°06´N 114°36´W
25 S15 **Riviera** Texas, SW USA 27°15´N 97°48´W
23 Z14 **Riviera Beach** Florida, SE USA 26°46´N 80°03´W
15 Q10 **Rivière-à-Pierre** Québec, SE Canada 46°59´N 72°12´W
15 T9 **Rivière-Bleue** Québec, SE Canada 47°26´N 69°02´W
15 T8 **Rivière-du-Loup** Québec, SE Canada 47°49´N 69°32´W
173 Y15 **Rivière du Rempart** NE Mauritius 20°06´S 57°41´E
45 R12 **Rivière-Pilote** S Martinique 14°29´N 60°54´W
173 O17 **Rivière St-Etienne, Pointe de la** *headland* SW Réunion
13 S10 **Rivière-St-Paul** Québec, E Canada 51°26´N 57°52´W
**Rivière Sèche** *see* Bel Air
116 K4 **Rivne** *Pol.* Równe, *Rus.* Rovno. Rivnens'ka Oblast', NW Ukraine 50°37´N 26°16´E
**Rivne** *see* Rivnens'ka Oblast'
116 K3 **Rivnens'ka Oblast'** *var.* Rivne, *Rus.* Rovenskaya Oblast'. ◆ *province* NW Ukraine
106 B8 **Rivoli** Piemonte, NW Italy 45°04´N 07°31´E
159 Q14 **Riwoqê** *var.* Racaka. Xizang Zizhiqu, W China 31°10´N 96°25´E
99 H19 **Rixensart** Walloon Brabant, C Belgium 50°43´N 04°32´E
**Riyadh/Riyāḑ, Minţaqat ar** *see* Ar Riyāḑ
**Riyāq** *see* Rayak
**Rizaiyeh** *see* Orūmīyeh
137 P11 **Rize** Rize, NE Turkey 41°03´N 40°33´E
137 P11 **Rize** *prev.* Çoruh. ◆ *province* NE Turkey
161 R5 **Rizhao** Shandong, E China 35°23´N 119°32´E
**Rizhskiy Zaliv** *see* Riga, Gulf of
**Rizokarpaso** *see* Dipkarpaz
107 O21 **Rizzuto, Capo** *headland* S Italy 38°54´N 17°05´E
95 F15 **Rjukan** Telemark, S Norway 59°54´N 08°33´E
95 D16 **Rjuven** ▲ S Norway
76 H9 **Rkîz** Trarza, W Mauritania 16°50´N 15°20´W
115 Q23 **Ro** *prev.* Ágios Geórgios. *island* SE Greece
95 H14 **Roa** Oppland, S Norway 60°16´N 10°38´E
105 N5 **Roa** Castilla y León, N Spain 41°42´N 03°55´W
45 T9 **Road Town** ○ (British Virgin Islands) Tortola, C British Virgin Islands 18°28´N 64°39´W
96 F6 **Roag, Loch** *inlet* NW Scotland, United Kingdom
37 O5 **Roan Cliffs** *cliff* Colorado/Utah, W USA
21 P9 **Roan High Knob** *var.* Roan Mountain. ▲ North Carolina/Tennessee, SE USA 36°09´N 82°07´W
**Roan Mountain** *see* Roan High Knob
103 Q10 **Roanne** *anc.* Rodunma. Loire, E France 46°03´N 04°04´E
23 R4 **Roanoke** Alabama, S USA 33°09´N 85°22´W
21 S7 **Roanoke** Virginia, NE USA 37°16´N 79°57´W
21 Z9 **Roanoke Island** *island* North Carolina, SE USA
21 W8 **Roanoke Rapids** North Carolina, SE USA 36°27´N 77°39´W
21 X9 **Roanoke River** ⁓ North Carolina/Virginia, SE USA
37 O4 **Roan Plateau** *plain* Utah, W USA
37 R5 **Roaring Fork River** ⁓ Colorado, C USA
25 O5 **Roaring Springs** Texas, SW USA 33°54´N 100°51´W
42 J4 **Roatán** *var.* Coxen Hole, Coxin Hole. Islas de la Bahía, N Honduras 16°19´N 86°33´W
42 I4 **Roatán, Isla de** *island* Islas de la Bahía, N Honduras
**Roat Kampuchea** *see* Cambodia
**Roazon** *see* Rennes
143 T7 **Robāţ-e Chāh Gonbad** Khorāsān-e Janūbī, E Iran 33°24´N 57°43´E
143 R7 **Robāţ-e Khān** Khorāsān-e Janūbī, C Iran 33°24´N 56°04´E
143 T7 **Robāţ-e Khvosh Āb** Khorāsān-e Janūbī, E Iran
143 R8 **Robāţ-e Posht-e Bādām** Yazd, NE Iran 33°01´N 55°34´E
143 Q8 **Robāţ-e Rizāb** Yazd, C Iran
175 S8 **Robbie Ridge** *undersea feature* W Pacific Ocean
21 T10 **Robbins** North Carolina, SE USA 35°25´N 79°35´W
183 N15 **Robbins Island** *island* Tasmania, SE Australia
21 N10 **Robbinsville** North Carolina, SE USA 35°18´N 83°49´W
182 J12 **Robe** South Australia 37°11´S 139°48´E
21 W9 **Robersonville** North Carolina, SE USA 35°49´N 77°15´W
45 V10 **Robert L. Bradshaw** ✈ (Basseterre) Saint Kitts, Saint Kitts and Nevis 17°16´N 62°43´W
25 P8 **Robert Lee** Texas, SW USA 31°50´N 100°30´W
35 V5 **Roberts Creek Mountain** ▲ Nevada, W USA 39°52´N 116°16´W
93 J15 **Robertsfors** Västerbotten, N Sweden 64°12´N 20°50´E
27 R11 **Robert S. Kerr Reservoir** ⊠ Oklahoma, C USA
38 L12 **Roberts Mountain** ▲ Nunivak Island, Alaska, USA 60°01´N 166°15´W
83 F26 **Robertson** Western Cape, SW South Africa 33°48´S 19°53´E
194 H4 **Robertson Island** *island* Antarctica
76 J16 **Robertsport** W Liberia 06°45´N 11°15´W
182 J8 **Robertstown** South Australia 34°00´S 139°04´E
**Robert Williams** *see* Caála
15 P7 **Roberval** Québec, SE Canada 48°31´N 72°16´W
31 N15 **Robinson** Illinois, N USA 39°00´N 87°44´W
193 U11 **Róbinson Crusoe, Isla** *island* Islas Juan Fernández, Chile, E Pacific Ocean
180 J9 **Robinson Range** ▲▲ Western Australia
182 M9 **Robinvale** Victoria, SE Australia 34°37´S 142°45´E
105 P11 **Robledo** Castilla-La Mancha, C Spain 38°45´N 02°27´W
54 G5 **Robles** *var.* La Paz, Robles La Paz. Cesar, N Colombia 10°24´N 73°11´W
**Robles La Paz** *see* Robles
11 V15 **Roblin** Manitoba, S Canada 51°15´N 101°20´W
11 S17 **Robsart** Saskatchewan, S Canada 49°22´N 109°15´W
11 N15 **Robson, Mount** ▲ British Columbia, SW Canada 53°09´N 119°16´W
25 T14 **Robstown** Texas, SW USA 27°47´N 97°40´W
25 P6 **Roby** Texas, SW USA 32°42´N 100°23´W
104 E11 **Roca, Cabo da** *cape* C Portugal
**Rocadas** *see* Xangongo
41 S14 **Roca Partida, Punta** *headland* C Mexico 18°43´N 95°11´W
47 X6 **Rocas, Atol das** *island* E Brazil
107 L18 **Roccadaspide** *var.* Rocca d'Aspide. Campania, S Italy 40°25´N 15°12´E
**Rocca d'Aspide** *see* Roccadaspide
107 K15 **Roccaraso** Abruzzo, C Italy 41°49´N 14°01´E
106 H10 **Rocca San Casciano** Emilia-Romagna, C Italy 44°06´N 11°51´E
106 G13 **Roccastrada** Toscana, C Italy 43°00´N 11°09´E
61 G20 **Rocha** Rocha, E Uruguay 34°30´S 54°22´W
61 G19 **Rocha** ◆ *department* E Uruguay
97 L17 **Rochdale** NW England, United Kingdom 53°38´N 02°09´W
102 L11 **Rochechouart** Haute-Vienne, C France 45°49´N 00°49´E
99 J22 **Rochefort** Namur, SE Belgium 50°10´N 05°13´E
102 J11 **Rochefort** *var.* Rochefort sur Mer. Charente-Maritime, W France 45°57´N 00°58´W
**Rochefort sur Mer** *see* Rochefort
125 N10 **Rochegda** Arkhangel'skaya Oblast', NW Russia 62°37´N 43°21´E
30 L10 **Rochelle** Illinois, N USA 41°54´N 89°03´W
25 Q9 **Rochelle** Texas, SW USA 31°13´N 99°10´W
15 V3 **Rochers Ouest, Rivière aux** ⁓ Québec, SE Canada
97 O22 **Rochester** *anc.* Durobrivae. SE England, United Kingdom 51°24´N 00°30´E
31 O12 **Rochester** Indiana, N USA 41°03´N 86°13´W
29 W10 **Rochester** Minnesota, N USA 44°01´N 92°28´W
19 O9 **Rochester** New Hampshire, NE USA 43°18´N 70°58´W
18 F9 **Rochester** New York, NE USA 43°09´N 77°37´W
25 P5 **Rochester** Texas, SW USA 33°19´N 99°51´W
31 S9 **Rochester Hills** Michigan, N USA 42°39´N 83°04´W
**Rocheuses, Montagnes/Rockies** *see* Rocky Mountains
64 M6 **Rockall** *island* N Atlantic Ocean, United Kingdom
64 L6 **Rockall Bank** *undersea feature* N Atlantic Ocean
84 B8 **Rockall Rise** *undersea feature* N Atlantic Ocean 59°00´N 14°00´W
84 C9 **Rockall Trough** *undersea feature* N Atlantic Ocean 57°00´N 12°00´W
35 U2 **Rock Creek** ⁓ Nevada, W USA
25 T10 **Rockdale** Texas, SW USA 30°39´N 96°58´W
195 N12 **Rockefeller Plateau** *plateau* Antarctica
30 K11 **Rock Falls** Illinois, N USA 41°46´N 89°41´W
23 Q5 **Rockford** Alabama, S USA 32°53´N 86°11´W
30 L10 **Rockford** Illinois, N USA 42°16´N 89°06´W
15 Q12 **Rock Forest** Québec, SE Canada 45°21´N 71°58´W
11 T17 **Rockglen** Saskatchewan, S Canada 49°11´N 105°57´W
181 Y8 **Rockhampton** Queensland, E Australia 23°31´S 150°31´E
21 R11 **Rock Hill** South Carolina, SE USA 34°55´N 81°01´W
180 I13 **Rockingham** Western Australia 32°16´S 115°21´E
21 T11 **Rockingham** North Carolina, SE USA 34°56´N 79°47´W
30 J11 **Rock Island** Illinois, N USA 41°30´N 90°34´W
25 U12 **Rock Island** Texas, SW USA 29°31´N 96°33´W
14 C10 **Rock Lake** Ontario, S Canada 46°25´N 83°49´W
29 O2 **Rock Lake** North Dakota, N USA 48°45´N 99°12´W
14 I12 **Rock Lake** ⊗ Ontario, SE Canada
14 M12 **Rockland** Ontario, SE Canada 45°33´N 75°16´W
19 R7 **Rockland** Maine, NE USA 44°08´N 69°06´W
182 L11 **Rocklands Reservoir** ⊠ Victoria, SE Australia
35 O7 **Rocklin** California, W USA 38°48´N 121°13´W
23 R3 **Rockmart** Georgia, SE USA 34°00´N 85°02´W
31 N16 **Rockport** Indiana, N USA 37°53´N 87°04´W
27 Q1 **Rock Port** Missouri, C USA 40°26´N 95°30´W
25 T14 **Rockport** Texas, SW USA 28°02´N 99°04´W
32 I7 **Rockport** Washington, NW USA 48°28´N 121°36´W
29 S11 **Rock Rapids** Iowa, C USA 43°25´N 96°10´W
30 K11 **Rock River** ⁓ Illinois/Wisconsin, N USA
44 I3 **Rock Sound** Eleuthera Island, C The Bahamas 24°52´N 76°10´W
25 P11 **Rocksprings** Texas, SW USA 30°02´N 100°14´W
33 U17 **Rock Springs** Wyoming, C USA 41°35´N 109°12´W
55 T9 **Rockstone** C Guyana 05°58´N 58°33´W
29 S12 **Rock Valley** Iowa, C USA 43°12´N 96°17´W
31 N14 **Rockville** Indiana, N USA 39°45´N 87°15´W
21 W3 **Rockville** Maryland, NE USA 39°05´N 77°10´W
25 U6 **Rockwall** Texas, SW USA 32°56´N 96°27´W
29 U13 **Rockwell City** Iowa, C USA 42°24´N 94°37´W
31 S10 **Rockwood** Michigan, N USA 42°04´N 83°15´W
20 M9 **Rockwood** Tennessee, S USA 35°52´N 84°41´W
25 Q8 **Rockwood** Texas, SW USA 31°29´N 99°23´W
37 U6 **Rocky Ford** Colorado, C USA 38°03´N 103°45´W
14 D9 **Rocky Island Lake** ⊗ Ontario, S Canada
21 V9 **Rocky Mount** North Carolina, SE USA 35°56´N 77°48´W
21 S7 **Rocky Mount** Virginia, NE USA 37°00´N 79°53´W
33 Q8 **Rocky Mountain** ▲ Montana, NW USA 47°45´N 112°46´W
11 P15 **Rocky Mountain House** Alberta, SW Canada 52°24´N 114°52´W
37 T3 **Rocky Mountain National Park** *national park* Colorado, C USA
2 E12 **Rocky Mountains** *var.* Rockies, *Fr.* Montagnes Rocheuses. ▲▲ Canada/USA
42 H1 **Rocky Point** *headland* NE Belize 18°21´N 88°04´W
83 A17 **Rocky Point** *headland* NW Namibia 19°01´S 12°27´E
95 F14 **Rødberg** Buskerud, S Norway 60°16´N 09°00´E
95 I25 **Rødbyhavn** Sjælland, SE Denmark 54°42´N 11°24´E
95 I25 **Rødbyhavn** Sjælland, SE Denmark 54°39´N 11°24´E
13 T10 **Roddickton** Newfoundland, Newfoundland and Labrador, SE Canada 50°51´N 56°03´W
95 F23 **Rødding** Syddanmark, SW Denmark 55°22´N 09°04´E
95 M22 **Rödeby** Blekinge, S Sweden 56°16´N 15°35´E
98 N6 **Roden** Drenthe, NE Netherlands 53°08´N 06°26´E
62 H9 **Rodeo** San Juan, W Argentina 30°12´S 69°06´W
103 O14 **Rodez** *anc.* Segodunum. Aveyron, S France 44°21´N 02°34´E
**Rodholívos** *see* Rodolívos
**Ródhos/Rodi** *see* Ródos
107 N15 **Rodi Garganico** Puglia, SE Italy 41°54´N 15°51´E
101 N20 **Roding** Bayern, SE Germany 49°12´N 12°30´E
113 J19 **Rodinit, Kepi i** *headland* W Albania 41°35´N 19°27´E
116 I9 **Rodnei, Munţii** ▲▲ N Romania
184 L4 **Rodney, Cape** *headland* North Island, New Zealand 36°16´S 174°48´E
38 L9 **Rodney, Cape** *headland* Alaska, USA 64°39´N 166°24´W
124 M16 **Rodniki** Ivanovskaya Oblast', W Russia 57°04´N 41°45´E
119 Q16 **Rodnya** Mahilyowskaya Voblasts', E Belarus 53°31´N 32°07´E
**Rodó** *see* José Enrique Rodó
114 H13 **Rodolívos** *var.* Rodholívos. Kentrikí Makedonía, NE Greece 40°55´N 24°00´E
**Rodopi** *see* Rhodope Mountains
**Rodópi Óri** *see* Rhodope Mountains
**Rodopi Planina** *see* Rhodope Mountains
**Rodoplar** *see* Rhodope Mountains
115 O22 **Ródos** *var.* Ródhos, *Eng.* Rhodes, *It.* Rodi. Ródos, Dodekánisa, Greece, Aegean Sea 36°26´N 28°14´E
115 O22 **Ródos** *var.* Ródhos, *Eng.* Rhodes, *It.* Rodi; *anc.* Rhodos. *island* Dodekánisa, Greece, Aegean Sea
**Rodosto** *see* Tekirdağ


◆ Country
● Country Capital
◇ Dependent Territory
○ Dependent Territory Capital
◆ Administrative Regions
✈ International Airport
▲ Mountain
▲▲ Mountain Range
⛰ Volcano
⁓ River
⊗ Lake
⊠ Reservoir

RODRIGUES – RUIVO DE SANTANA, PICO


59 A14 **Rodrigues** Amazonas, W Brazil 06°50′S 73°45′W
173 P8 **Rodrigues** var. Rodriquez. island E Mauritius
**Rodriquez** see Rodrigues
**Rodunma** see Roanne
180 I7 **Roebourne** Western Australia 20°49′S 117°04′E
83 J20 **Roedtan** Limpopo, NE South Africa 24°37′S 29°05′E
98 H11 **Roelofarendsveen** Zuid-Holland, W Netherlands 52°12′N 04°37′E
**Roepat** see Rupat, Pulau
**Roer** see Rur
99 M16 **Roermond** Limburg, SE Netherlands 51°12′N 06°E
99 C18 **Roeselare** Fr. Roulers; prev. Rousselaere. West-Vlaanderen, W Belgium 50°57′N 03°08′E
9 P8 **Roes Welcome Sound** strait Nunavut, N Canada
**Roeteng** see Ruteng
**Rofreit** see Rovereto
**Rogachëv** see Rahachow
57 L15 **Rogagua, Laguna** ◎ NW Bolivia
95 C16 **Rogaland** ⬖ county S Norway
25 Y9 **Roganville** Texas, SW USA 30°49′N 93°54′W
109 W11 **Rogaška Slatina** Ger. Rohitsch-Sauerbrunn; prev. Rogatec-Slatina. E Slovenia 46°13′N 15°38′E
**Rogatec-Slatina** see Rogaška Slatina
112 J13 **Rogatica** Republika Srpska, SE Bosnia and Herzegovina 43°50′N 18°55′E
**Rogatin** see Rohatyn
93 F17 **Rogen** ◎ C Sweden
27 S9 **Rogers** Arkansas, C USA 36°19′N 94°07′W
29 P5 **Rogers** North Dakota, N USA 47°03′N 98°12′W
25 T9 **Rogers** Texas, SW USA 30°53′N 97°10′W
31 R5 **Rogers City** Michigan, N USA 45°25′N 83°49′W
**Roger Simpson Island** see Abemama
35 T14 **Rogers Lake** salt flat California, W USA
21 Q8 **Rogers, Mount** ▲ Virginia, NE USA 36°39′N 81°32′W
33 O16 **Rogerson** Idaho, NW USA 42°11′N 114°36′W
11 O16 **Rogers Pass** pass British Columbia, SW Canada
21 O8 **Rogersville** Tennessee, S USA 36°26′N 83°01′W
99 L16 **Roggel** Limburg, SE Netherlands 51°16′N 05°55′E
**Roggeveen** see Roggewein, Cabo
193 R10 **Roggeveen Basin** undersea feature E Pacific Ocean 31°30′S 95°30′W
191 X16 **Roggewein, Cabo** var. Roggeveen. headland Easter Island, Chile, E Pacific Ocean 27°07′S 109°15′W
103 Y13 **Rogliano** Corse, France, C Mediterranean Sea 42°58′N 09°25′E
107 N21 **Rogliano** Calabria, SW Italy 39°09′N 16°18′E
92 G12 **Rognan** Nordland, C Norway 67°04′N 15°21′E
100 K10 **Rögnitz** ≈ N Germany
**Rogozhina/Rogozhinë** see Rrogozhinë
110 G10 **Rogoźno** Wielkopolskie, C Poland 52°46′N 16°58′E
32 E15 **Rogue River** ≈ Oregon, NW USA
116 I6 **Rohatyn** Rus. Rogatin. Ivano-Frankivs'ka Oblast', W Ukraine 49°25′N 24°35′E
189 O14 **Rohi** Pohnpei, E Micronesia
**Rohitsch-Sauerbrunn** see Rogaška Slatina
149 Q13 **Rohri** Sindh, SE Pakistan 27°39′N 68°57′E
152 I10 **Rohtak** Haryāna, N India 28°57′N 76°38′E
**Roi Ed** see Roi Et
167 R9 **Roi Et** var. Muang Roi Et, Roi Ed. Roi Et, E Thailand 16°05′N 103°38′E
191 U9 **Roi Georges, Îles du** island group Îles Tuamotu, C French Polynesia
153 Y10 **Roing** Arunāchal Pradesh, NE India 28°06′N 95°46′E
118 E7 **Roja** NW Latvia 57°31′N 22°44′E
61 B20 **Rojas** Buenos Aires, E Argentina 34°10′S 60°45′W
149 R12 **Rojhan** Punjab, E Pakistan 28°39′N 70°00′E
41 Q12 **Rojo, Cabo** headland C Mexico 21°33′N 97°19′W
45 Q10 **Rojo, Cabo** headland W Puerto Rico 17°57′N 67°10′W
168 K10 **Rokan Kiri, Sungai** ≈ Sumatera, W Indonesia
118 I11 **Rokiškis** Panevėžys, NE Lithuania 55°58′N 25°35′E
165 R7 **Rokkasho** Aomori, Honshū, C Japan 40°59′N 141°22′E
111 B17 **Rokycany** Ger. Rokytzan. Plzeňský Kraj, W Czechia 49°45′N 13°36′E
117 P6 **Rokytne** Kyivs'ka Oblast', N Ukraine 49°40′N 30°29′E
116 L3 **Rokytne** Rivnens'ka Oblast', NW Ukraine 51°19′N 27°09′E
**Rokytzan** see Rokycany
158 L11 **Rola Co** ◎ W China
29 V13 **Roland** Iowa, C USA 42°10′N 93°30′W
95 D15 **Røldal** Hordaland, S Norway 59°52′N 06°49′E
98 O7 **Rolde** Drenthe, NE Netherlands 52°58′N 06°39′E
29 O2 **Rolette** North Dakota, N USA 48°39′N 99°50′W
27 V6 **Rolla** Missouri, C USA 37°56′N 91°47′W
29 O2 **Rolla** North Dakota, N USA 48°51′N 99°37′W
108 A10 **Rolle** Vaud, W Switzerland 46°27′N 06°19′E
181 X8 **Rolleston** Queensland, E Australia 24°30′S 148°36′E
185 H19 **Rolleston** Canterbury, South Island, New Zealand 43°34′S 172°24′E
185 G18 **Rolleston Range** ▲▲ South Island, New Zealand
14 H8 **Rollet** Québec, SE Canada 47°56′N 79°14′W
22 J4 **Rolling Fork** Mississippi, S USA 32°54′N 90°52′W
20 L6 **Rolling Fork** ≈ Kentucky, S USA
14 J11 **Rolphton** Ontario, SE Canada 46°09′N 77°43′W
**Röm** see Rømø
181 X10 **Roma** Queensland, E Australia 26°37′S 148°54′E
107 I15 **Roma** Eng. Rome. ● (Italy) Lazio, C Italy 41°53′N 12°30′E
95 P19 **Roma** Gotland, SE Sweden 57°31′N 18°28′E
21 T14 **Romain, Cape** headland South Carolina, SE USA 33°00′N 79°21′W
13 P11 **Romaine** ≈ Newfoundland and Labrador/Québec, E Canada
25 R17 **Roma Los Saenz** Texas, SW USA 26°24′N 99°01′W
114 H8 **Roman** Vratsa, NW Bulgaria 43°09′N 23°56′E
116 L10 **Roman** Hung. Románvásár. Neamț, NE Romania 46°46′N 26°56′E
64 M13 **Romanche Fracture Zone** tectonic feature E Atlantic Ocean
61 C15 **Romang** Santa Fe, C Argentina 29°30′S 59°46′W
171 R15 **Romang, Pulau** var. Pulau Roma. island Kepulauan Damar, E Indonesia
171 R15 **Romang, Selat** strait Nusa Tenggara, S Indonesia
116 J11 **Romania** Bul. Rumŭniya, Ger. Rumänien, Hung. Románia, Rom. România, SCr. Rumunjska, Ukr. Rumuniya, prev. Republica Socialistă România, Roumania, Rumania, Socialist Republic of Romania, prev.Rom. Romînia. ◆ republic SE Europe
**România, Republica Socialistă** see Romania
**Romania, Socialist Republic of** see Romania
116 M5 **Romaniv** prev. Dzerzhyns'k. Zhytomyrs'ka Oblast', N Ukraine 50°07′N 27°56′E
23 W16 **Romano, Cape** headland Florida, SE USA 25°51′N 81°40′W
44 G5 **Romano, Cayo** island C Cuba
123 O13 **Romanovka** Respublika Buryatiya, S Russia 53°10′N 112°34′E
127 N8 **Romanovka** Saratovskaya Oblast', W Russia 51°45′N 42°45′E
108 I6 **Romanshorn** Thurgau, NE Switzerland 47°34′N 09°23′E
103 R12 **Romans-sur-Isère** Drôme, E France 45°03′N 05°03′E
189 U12 **Romanum** island Chuuk, C Micronesia
**Románvásár** see Roman
39 S5 **Romanzof Mountains** ▲▲ Alaska, USA
**Roma, Pulau** see Romang, Pulau
103 S4 **Rombas** Moselle, NE France 49°15′N 06°04′E
23 R2 **Rome** Georgia, SE USA 34°01′N 85°02′W
18 I9 **Rome** New York, NE USA 43°13′N 75°28′W
**Rome** see Roma
31 S9 **Romeo** Michigan, N USA 42°48′N 83°00′W
**Römerstadt** see Rýmařov
**Rometan** see Romiton
103 P5 **Romilly-sur-Seine** Aube, N France 48°31′N 03°44′E
**Romînia** see Romania
146 L11 **Romiton** Rus. Rometan. Buxoro Viloyati, C Uzbekistan 39°56′N 64°21′E
21 U3 **Romney** West Virginia, NE USA 39°21′N 78°44′W
117 S4 **Romny** Sums'ka Oblast', NE Ukraine 50°45′N 33°30′E
95 E24 **Rømø** Ger. Röm. island SW Denmark
117 S5 **Romodan** Poltavs'ka Oblast', NE Ukraine 50°00′N 33°20′E
127 P5 **Romodanovo** Respublika Mordoviya, W Russia 54°25′N 45°24′E
**Romorantin** see Romorantin-Lanthenay
103 N8 **Romorantin-Lanthenay** var. Romorantin. Loir-et-Cher, C France 47°22′N 01°44′E
94 F9 **Romsdal** physical region S Norway
94 F10 **Romsdalen** valley S Norway
94 E9 **Romsdalsfjorden** fjord S Norway
33 P8 **Ronan** Montana, NW USA 47°31′N 114°06′W
59 M14 **Roncador** Maranhão, E Brazil 05°48′S 45°08′W
186 M7 **Roncador Reef** reef N Solomon Islands
59 J17 **Roncador, Serra do** ▲▲ C Brazil
21 S6 **Ronceverte** West Virginia, NE USA 37°45′N 80°27′W
107 H14 **Ronciglione** Lazio, C Italy 42°16′N 12°15′E
104 L15 **Ronda** Andalucía, S Spain 36°45′N 05°10′W
94 G11 **Rondane** ▲▲ S Norway
104 L15 **Ronda, Serranía de** ▲▲ S Spain
95 H22 **Rønde** Midtjylland, C Denmark 56°18′N 10°28′E
**Ronde, Île** see Round Island
**Rondo** see Rongrik Atoll
59 E16 **Rondônia** off. Estado de Rondônia; prev. Território de Rondônia. ⬖ state W Brazil
**Rondônia, Estado de** see Rondônia
**Rondônia, Território de** see Rondônia
59 I18 **Rondonópolis** Mato Grosso, W Brazil 16°29′S 54°37′W
94 G11 **Rondslottet** ▲ S Norway 61°54′N 09°48′E
95 P20 **Ronehamn** Gotland, SE Sweden 57°10′N 18°30′E
160 L13 **Rong'an** var. Chang'an, Rongan. Guangxi Zhuangzu Zizhiqu, S China 25°14′N 109°20′E
**Rongan** see Rong'an
**Rongcheng** see Rongxian, Guangxi, China
**Rongcheng** see Jianli, Hubei, China
189 R4 **Rongelap Atoll** var. Rönlap. atoll Ralik Chain, NW Marshall Islands
**Rongerik** see Rongrik Atoll
160 K12 **Rongjiang** var. Guzhou. Guizhou, S China 25°59′N 108°27′E
160 L13 **Rong Jiang** ≈ S China
**Rongjiang** see Nankang
**Rong, Kas** see Rŭng, Kaôh
167 P8 **Rong Kwang** Phrae, NW Thailand 18°19′N 100°18′E
189 T4 **Rongrik Atoll** var. Röndik, Rongerik. atoll Ralik Chain, N Marshall Islands
189 X2 **Rongrong** island SE Marshall Islands
160 L13 **Rongshui** var. Rongshui Miaozu Zizhixian. Guangxi Zhuangzu Zizhiqu, S China 25°05′N 109°09′E
**Rongshui Miaozu Zizhixian** see Rongshui
118 I6 **Rõngu** Ger. Ringen. Tartumaa, SE Estonia 58°10′N 26°17′E
**Rongwo** see Tongren
160 L15 **Rongxian** var. Rongzhou; prev. Rongcheng. Guangxi Zhuangzu Zizhiqu, S China 22°52′N 110°33′E
**Rongzhag** see Danba
**Rongzhou** see Rongxian
**Roniu, Mont** see Rooniu, Mont
189 N13 **Ronkiti** Pohnpei, E Micronesia 06°48′N 158°10′E
**Rönlap** see Rongelap Atoll
95 L24 **Rønne** Bornholm, E Denmark 55°07′N 14°43′E
95 M22 **Ronneby** Blekinge, S Sweden 56°12′N 15°18′E
194 J7 **Ronne Entrance** inlet Antarctica
194 L6 **Ronne Ice Shelf** ice shelf Antarctica
99 E19 **Ronse** Fr. Renaix. Oost-Vlaanderen, SW Belgium 50°45′N 03°36′E
30 K14 **Roodhouse** Illinois, N USA 39°28′N 90°22′W
83 C19 **Rooibank** Erongo, W Namibia 23°04′S 14°34′E
**Rooke Island** see Umboi Island
65 N24 **Rookery Point** headland NE Tristan da Cunha 37°03′S 12°15′W
191 R8 **Rooniu, Mont** prev. Mont Roniu. ⛰ Tahiti, W French Polynesia 17°49′S 149°12′W
171 V13 **Roon, Pulau** island E Indonesia
173 V7 **Roo Rise** undersea feature E Indian Ocean
152 J9 **Roorkee** Uttarākhand, N India 29°51′N 77°54′E
99 H15 **Roosendaal** Noord-Brabant, S Netherlands 51°32′N 04°29′E
25 P10 **Roosevelt** Texas, SW USA 30°28′N 100°06′W
37 N3 **Roosevelt** Utah, W USA 40°18′N 109°59′W
47 T8 **Roosevelt** ≈ W Brazil
195 O13 **Roosevelt Island** island Antarctica
10 L10 **Roosevelt, Mount** ▲ British Columbia, W Canada 58°28′N 125°22′W
11 P17 **Roosville** British Columbia, SW Canada 48°59′N 115°03′W
29 X10 **Root River** ≈ Minnesota, N USA
111 N16 **Ropczyce** Podkarpackie, SE Poland 50°04′N 21°31′E
181 Q3 **Roper Bar** Northern Territory, N Australia 14°45′S 134°30′E
24 M5 **Ropesville** Texas, SW USA 33°24′N 102°09′W
102 K14 **Roquefort** Landes, SW France 44°01′N 00°18′W
61 C21 **Roque Pérez** Buenos Aires, E Argentina 35°25′S 59°24′W
58 E10 **Roraima** off. Estado de Roraima; prev. Território de Rio Branco, Território de Roraima. ⬖ state N Brazil
**Roraima, Estado de** see Roraima
58 F9 **Roraima, Mount** ▲ N South America 05°10′N 60°36′W
**Roraima, Território de** see Roraima
94 I9 **Røros** Sør-Trøndelag, S Norway 62°37′N 11°25′E
108 I7 **Rorschach** Sankt Gallen, NE Switzerland 47°28′N 09°30′E
93 E14 **Rørvik** Nord-Trøndelag, C Norway 64°54′N 11°15′E
119 G17 **Ros'** Rus. Ross'. Hrodzyenskaya Voblasts', W Belarus 53°25′N 24°24′E
185 F17 **Ross** West Coast, South Island, New Zealand 42°54′S 170°52′E
119 G17 **Ros'** Rus. Ross'. ≈ W Belarus
10 J7 **Ross** ≈ Yukon, W Canada
117 O6 **Ros'** ≈ N Ukraine
44 K7 **Rosa, Lake** ◎ Great Inagua, S The Bahamas
32 M9 **Rosalia** Washington, NW USA 47°14′N 117°22′W
191 W15 **Rosalia, Punta** headland Easter Island, Chile, E Pacific Ocean 27°04′S 109°19′W
45 P12 **Rosalie** E Dominica 15°22′N 61°15′W
35 T14 **Rosamond** California, W USA 34°51′N 118°09′W
35 S14 **Rosamond Lake** salt flat California, W USA
96 H8 **Ross and Cromarty** cultural region N Scotland, United Kingdom
61 B18 **Rosario** Santa Fe, C Argentina 32°56′S 60°39′W
40 J11 **Rosario** Sinaloa, C Mexico 23°00′N 105°51′W
40 G6 **Rosario** Sonora, NW Mexico 27°53′N 109°18′W
62 O6 **Rosario** San Pedro, C Paraguay 24°26′S 57°06′W
61 E20 **Rosario** Colonia, SW Uruguay 34°20′S 57°26′W
54 H5 **Rosario** Zulia, NW Venezuela 10°18′N 72°19′W
**Rosario** see Nishino-shima
**Rosario** see Rosarito
40 B4 **Rosario, Bahía del** bay NW Mexico
62 K6 **Rosario de la Frontera** Salta, N Argentina 25°50′S 65°00′W
61 C18 **Rosario del Tala** Entre Ríos, E Argentina 32°20′S 59°10′W
61 F16 **Rosário do Sul** Rio Grande do Sul, S Brazil 30°15′S 54°55′W
59 H18 **Rosário Oeste** Mato Grosso, W Brazil 14°50′S 56°25′W
40 B1 **Rosarito** var. Rosario. Baja California, NW Mexico 32°25′N 117°04′W
40 F7 **Rosarito** Baja California Sur, NW Mexico 26°28′N 111°41′W
104 L9 **Rosarito, Embalse del** ⊠ W Spain
107 N22 **Rosarno** Calabria, SW Italy 38°29′N 15°59′E
56 B5 **Rosa Zárate** var. Quinindé. Esmeraldas, SW Ecuador 0°14′N 79°28′W
**Roscianum** see Rossano
29 O8 **Roscoe** South Dakota, N USA 45°24′N 99°19′W
25 P7 **Roscoe** Texas, SW USA 32°27′N 100°32′W
102 F5 **Roscoff** Finistère, NW France 48°43′N 04°00′W
**Ros Comáin** see Roscommon
97 C17 **Roscommon** Ir. Ros Comáin. C Ireland 53°38′N 08°11′W
31 Q7 **Roscommon** Michigan, N USA 44°30′N 84°35′W
97 C17 **Roscommon** Ir. Ros Comáin. cultural region C Ireland
**Ros. Cré** see Roscrea
97 D19 **Roscrea** Ir. Ros. Cré. C Ireland 52°57′N 07°47′W
14 H13 **Rosseau** Ontario, S Canada 45°15′N 79°38′W
45 X12 **Roseau** prev. Charlotte Town. ● (Dominica) SW Dominica 15°17′N 61°23′W
29 S2 **Roseau** Minnesota, N USA 48°51′N 95°45′W
173 Y16 **Rose Belle** SE Mauritius 20°24′S 57°36′E
183 O16 **Rosebery** Tasmania, SE Australia 41°51′S 145°33′E
21 U11 **Roseboro** North Carolina, SE USA 34°58′N 78°31′W
25 T9 **Rosebud** Texas, SW USA 31°04′N 96°58′W
33 W10 **Rosebud Creek** ≈ Montana, NW USA
32 F14 **Roseburg** Oregon, NW USA 43°13′N 123°21′W
22 J3 **Rosedale** Mississippi, S USA 33°51′N 91°01′W
99 H21 **Rosée** Namur, S Belgium 50°15′N 04°43′E
55 U8 **Rose Hall** E Guyana 06°14′N 57°30′W
173 X16 **Rose Hill** W Mauritius 20°14′S 57°29′E
80 H12 **Roseires, Reservoir** var. Lake Rusayris. ⊠ E Sudan
**Rosenau** see Rožnov pod Radhoštěm
**Rosenau** see Rožňava
25 V11 **Rosenberg** Texas, SW USA 29°33′N 95°48′W
**Rosenberg** see Olesno, Poland
**Rosenberg** see Ružomberok, Slovakia
100 I10 **Rosengarten** Niedersachsen, N Germany 53°24′N 09°54′E
101 M24 **Rosenheim** Bayern, S Germany 47°51′N 12°08′E
**Rosenhof** see Zilupe
105 X4 **Roses** Cataluña, NE Spain 42°15′N 03°11′E
105 X4 **Roses, Golf de** gulf NE Spain
107 K14 **Roseto degli Abruzzi** Abruzzo, C Italy 42°39′N 14°01′E
11 S16 **Rosetown** Saskatchewan, S Canada 51°34′N 107°59′W
**Rosetta** see Rashīd
35 O7 **Roseville** California, W USA 38°44′N 121°16′W
30 J12 **Roseville** Illinois, N USA 40°42′N 90°40′W
29 V8 **Roseville** Minnesota, N USA 45°00′N 93°09′W
29 R7 **Rosholt** South Dakota, N USA 45°51′N 96°42′W
106 F12 **Rosignano Marittimo** Toscana, C Italy 43°24′N 10°28′E
116 I14 **Roșiori de Vede** Teleorman, S Romania 44°06′N 25°00′E
114 K8 **Rositsa** ≈ N Bulgaria
**Rositten** see Rēzekne
95 J23 **Roskilde** Sjælland, E Denmark 55°39′N 12°07′E
**Ros Láir** see Rosslare
126 H5 **Roslavl'** Smolenskaya Oblast', W Russia 54°N 32°57′E
32 I8 **Roslyn** Washington, NW USA 47°13′N 120°52′W
99 K14 **Rosmalen** Noord-Brabant, S Netherlands 51°43′N 05°21′E
**Ros Mhic Thriúin** see New Ross
113 P19 **Rosoman** C North Macedonia 41°31′N 21°55′E
102 F6 **Rosporden** Finistère, NW France 47°58′N 03°54′W
**Ross'** see Ros'
107 O20 **Rossano** anc. Roscianum. Calabria, SW Italy 39°35′N 16°38′E
22 L5 **Ross Barnett Reservoir** ⊠ Mississippi, S USA
11 W16 **Rossburn** Manitoba, S Canada 50°42′N 100°49′W
14 H13 **Rosseau, Lake** ◎ Ontario, S Canada
186 I10 **Rossel Island** prev. Yela Island. island SE Papua New Guinea
195 P12 **Ross Ice Shelf** ice shelf Antarctica
13 P16 **Rossignol, Lake** ◎ Nova Scotia, SE Canada
83 C19 **Rössing** Erongo, W Namibia 22°31′S 14°52′E
195 Q14 **Ross Island** island Antarctica
**Rossitten** see Rybachiy
**Rossiyskaya Federatsiya** see Russia
11 N17 **Rossland** British Columbia, SW Canada 49°03′N 117°49′W
97 F20 **Rosslare** Ir. Ros Láir. Wexford, SE Ireland 52°16′N 06°23′W
97 F20 **Rosslare Harbour** Wexford, SE Ireland 52°15′N 06°20′W
101 M14 **Rosslau** Sachsen-Anhalt, E Germany 51°52′N 12°15′E
76 G10 **Rosso** Trarza, SW Mauritania 16°36′N 15°50′W
103 X14 **Rosso, Cap** headland Corse, France, C Mediterranean Sea 42°25′N 08°22′E
93 H16 **Rossön** Jämtland, C Sweden 63°54′N 16°21′E
97 K21 **Ross-on-Wye** W England, United Kingdom 51°55′N 02°34′W
**Rossony** see Rasony
126 L9 **Rossosh'** Voronezhskaya Oblast', W Russia 50°10′N 39°34′E
181 Q7 **Ross River** Northern Territory, N Australia 23°36′S 134°30′E
10 J7 **Ross River** Yukon, W Canada 61°57′N 132°26′W
195 O15 **Ross Sea** sea Antarctica
92 G13 **Røssvatnet** Lapp. Reevhtse. ◎ C Norway
23 R1 **Rossville** Georgia, SE USA 34°59′N 85°22′W
**Rostak** see Ar Rustāq
143 P14 **Rostāq** Hormozgān, S Iran 26°48′N 53°50′E
117 N5 **Rostavytsya** ≈ N Ukraine
11 T15 **Rosthern** Saskatchewan, S Canada 52°40′N 106°20′W
100 M8 **Rostock** Mecklenburg-Vorpommern, NE Germany 54°05′N 12°08′E
124 L16 **Rostov** Yaroslavskaya Oblast', W Russia 57°11′N 39°19′E
**Rostov** see Rostov-na-Donu
126 L12 **Rostov-na-Donu** var. Rostov, Eng. Rostov-on-Don. Rostovskaya Oblast', SW Russia 47°16′N 39°45′E
**Rostov-on-Don** see Rostov-na-Donu
126 L10 **Rostovskaya Oblast'** ⬖ province SW Russia
93 J14 **Rosvik** Norrbotten, N Sweden 65°26′N 21°48′E
23 S3 **Roswell** Georgia, SE USA 34°01′N 84°21′W
37 U14 **Roswell** New Mexico, SW USA 33°23′N 104°31′W
94 K12 **Rot** Dalarna, C Sweden 61°16′N 14°04′E
101 I23 **Rot** ≈ S Germany
104 J15 **Rota** Andalucía, S Spain 36°39′N 06°20′W
188 K9 **Rota** island S Northern Mariana Islands
25 P6 **Rotan** Texas, SW USA 32°51′N 100°28′W
**Rotcher Island** see Tamana
100 I11 **Rotenburg** Niedersachsen, NW Germany 53°06′N 09°25′E
**Rotenburg** see Rotenburg an der Fulda
101 I16 **Rotenburg an der Fulda** var. Rotenburg. Thüringen, C Germany 51°00′N 09°43′E
101 L18 **Roter Main** ≈ E Germany
101 K20 **Roth** Bayern, SE Germany 49°15′N 11°06′E
101 G16 **Rothaargebirge** ▲▲ W Germany
**Rothenburg** see Rothenburg ob der Tauber
101 J20 **Rothenburg ob der Tauber** var. Rothenburg. Bayern, S Germany 49°23′N 10°10′E
194 H6 **Rothera** research station (UK) Antarctica 67°28′S 68°31′W
185 I17 **Rotherham** Canterbury, South Island, New Zealand 42°42′S 172°56′E
97 M17 **Rotherham** N England, United Kingdom 53°26′N 01°20′W
96 H12 **Rothesay** W Scotland, United Kingdom 55°49′N 05°03′W
108 E7 **Rothrist** Aargau, N Switzerland 47°18′N 07°54′E
194 H6 **Rothschild Island** island Antarctica
171 P17 **Roti, Pulau** island S Indonesia
95 H14 **Rotnes** Akershus, S Norway 60°08′N 10°45′E
183 O8 **Roto** New South Wales, SE Australia 33°04′S 145°27′E
184 N8 **Rotoiti, Lake** ◎ North Island, New Zealand
**Rotomagus** see Rouen
107 N19 **Rotondella** Basilicata, S Italy 40°12′N 16°30′E
103 X15 **Rotondo, Monte** ▲ Corse, France, C Mediterranean Sea 42°15′N 09°03′E
185 I15 **Rotoroa, Lake** ◎ South Island, New Zealand
184 N8 **Rotorua** Bay of Plenty, North Island, New Zealand 38°10′S 176°14′E
184 N8 **Rotorua, Lake** ◎ North Island, New Zealand
101 N22 **Rott** ≈ SE Germany
108 F10 **Rotten** ≈ S Switzerland
109 T6 **Rottenmann** Steiermark, E Austria 47°31′N 14°18′E
98 H12 **Rotterdam** Zuid-Holland, SW Netherlands 51°55′N 04°30′E
18 K10 **Rotterdam** New York, NE USA 42°46′N 73°57′W
95 M21 **Rottnen** ◎ S Sweden
98 N4 **Rottumeroog** island Waddeneilanden, NE Netherlands
98 N4 **Rottumerplaat** island Waddeneilanden, NE Netherlands
101 G23 **Rottweil** Baden-Württemberg, S Germany 48°10′N 08°38′E
191 O7 **Rotui, Mont** ▲ Moorea, W French Polynesia 17°30′S 149°50′W
103 P1 **Roubaix** Nord, N France 50°42′N 03°10′E
111 C15 **Roudnice nad Labem** Ger. Raudnitz an der Elbe. Ústecký Kraj, NW Czechia 50°25′N 14°14′E
102 M4 **Rouen** anc. Rotomagus. Seine-Maritime, N France 49°26′N 01°05′E
171 X13 **Rouffaer Reserves** reserve Papua, E Indonesia
15 N10 **Rouge, Rivière** ≈ Québec, SE Canada
20 J6 **Rough River** ≈ Kentucky, S USA
20 J6 **Rough River Lake** ⊠ Kentucky, S USA
**Rouhaïbé** see Ar Ruḩaybah
102 K11 **Rouillac** Charente, W France 45°46′N 00°04′W
**Roulers** see Roeselare
**Roumania** see Romania
173 Y15 **Round Island** var. Île Ronde. island NE Mauritius
14 J12 **Round Lake** ◎ Ontario, SE Canada
35 U7 **Round Mountain** Nevada, W USA 38°42′N 117°04′W
25 R10 **Round Mountain** Texas, SW USA 30°25′N 98°20′W
183 U5 **Round Mountain** ▲ New South Wales, SE Australia 30°22′S 152°13′E
25 S10 **Round Rock** Texas, SW USA 30°30′N 97°40′W
33 U10 **Roundup** Montana, NW USA 46°27′N 108°32′W
55 Y10 **Roura** NE French Guiana 04°44′N 52°16′W
**Rourkela** see Rāurkela
96 J4 **Rousay** island N Scotland, United Kingdom
**Rousselaere** see Roeselare
103 O17 **Roussillon** cultural region S France
15 V7 **Routhierville** Québec, SE Canada 48°09′N 67°07′W
99 K25 **Rouvroy** Luxembourg, SE Belgium 49°33′N 05°28′E
14 I7 **Rouyn-Noranda** Québec, SE Canada 48°16′N 79°03′W
**Rouyuan** see Huachi
**Rouyuanchengzi** see Huachi
92 L12 **Rovaniemi** Lappi, N Finland 66°29′N 25°40′E
106 E7 **Rovato** Lombardia, N Italy 45°34′N 10°03′E
125 N11 **Rovdino** Arkhangel'skaya Oblast', NW Russia 61°36′N 42°28′E
**Roven'ki** see Roven'ky
117 Y8 **Roven'ky** var. Roven'ki. Luhans'ka Oblast', E Ukraine 48°05′N 39°20′E
**Rovenskaya Oblast'** see Rivnens'ka Oblast'
**Rovenskaya Sloboda** see Rovyenskaya Slabada
106 G7 **Rovereto** Ger. Rofreit. Trentino-Alto Adige, N Italy 45°53′N 11°03′E
167 S12 **Rôviěng Tbong** Preah Vihear, N Cambodia 13°18′N 105°06′E
**Rovigno** see Rovinj
106 H8 **Rovigo** Veneto, NE Italy 45°04′N 11°48′E
112 A10 **Rovinj** It. Rovigno. Istra, NW Croatia 45°06′N 13°39′E
54 E10 **Rovira** Tolima, C Colombia 04°15′N 75°15′W
**Rovno** see Rivne
127 P9 **Rovnoye** Saratovskaya Oblast', W Russia 50°43′N 46°03′E
82 Q12 **Rovuma, Rio** var. Ruvuma. ≈ Mozambique/Tanzania see also Ruvuma
**Rovuma, Rio** see Ruvuma
119 O19 **Rovyenskaya Slabada** Rus. Rovenskaya Sloboda. Homyel'skaya Voblasts', SE Belarus 52°13′N 30°19′E
183 R5 **Rowena** New South Wales, SE Australia 29°51′S 148°55′E
21 T11 **Rowland** North Carolina, SE USA 34°32′N 79°17′W
9 P5 **Rowley** ≈ Baffin Island, Nunavut, NE Canada
9 P6 **Rowley Island** island Nunavut, NE Canada
173 W8 **Rowley Shoals** reef NW Australia
**Równe** see Rivne
171 O4 **Roxas** Mindoro, N Philippines 12°36′N 121°29′E
171 P5 **Roxas City** Panay Island, C Philippines 11°33′N 122°43′E
21 U8 **Roxboro** North Carolina, SE USA 36°24′N 79°00′W
185 D23 **Roxburgh** Otago, South Island, New Zealand 45°32′S 169°18′E
96 K13 **Roxburgh** cultural region SE Scotland, United Kingdom
182 H5 **Roxby Downs** South Australia 30°29′S 136°56′E
95 M17 **Roxen** ◎ S Sweden
25 V5 **Roxton** Texas, SW USA 33°33′N 95°43′W
15 P12 **Roxton-Sud** Québec, SE Canada 45°30′N 72°35′W
33 U8 **Roy** Montana, NW USA 47°19′N 108°55′W
37 U10 **Roy** New Mexico, SW USA 35°56′N 104°12′W
97 E17 **Royal Canal** Ir. An Chanáil Ríoga. canal C Ireland
30 L1 **Royale, Isle** island Michigan, N USA
37 S6 **Royal Gorge** valley Colorado, C USA
97 M20 **Royal Leamington Spa** var. Leamington, Leamington Spa. C England, United Kingdom 52°18′N 01°31′W
97 O23 **Royal Tunbridge Wells** var. Tunbridge Wells. SE England, United Kingdom 51°08′N 00°16′E
24 L9 **Royalty** Texas, SW USA 31°21′N 102°51′W
102 J11 **Royan** Charente-Maritime, W France 45°37′N 01°01′W
65 B24 **Roy Cove Settlement** West Falkland, Falkland Islands 51°32′S 60°23′W
103 O3 **Roye** Somme, N France 49°42′N 02°46′E
95 H15 **Røyken** Buskerud, S Norway 59°47′N 10°21′E
93 F14 **Røyrvik** Nord-Trøndelag, C Norway 64°53′N 13°30′E
25 U6 **Royse City** Texas, SW USA 32°58′N 96°19′W
97 O21 **Royston** E England, United Kingdom 52°05′N 00°01′W
23 U2 **Royston** Georgia, SE USA 34°17′N 83°06′W
114 L10 **Roza** prev. Gyulovo. Yambol, E Bulgaria 42°29′N 26°30′E
113 L16 **Rožaje** E Montenegro 42°51′N 20°11′E
110 M10 **Różan** Mazowieckie, C Poland 52°36′N 21°27′E
117 O10 **Rozdil'na** Odes'ka Oblast', SW Ukraine 46°51′N 30°03′E
117 S12 **Rozdol'ne** Rus. Razdolnoye. Avtonomna Respublika Krym, S Ukraine 45°45′N 33°27′E
**Rozhdestvenka** see Kabanbay Batyr
116 I6 **Rozhnyativ** Ivano-Frankivs'ka Oblast', W Ukraine 48°58′N 24°07′E
116 J3 **Rozhyshche** Volyns'ka Oblast', NW Ukraine 50°54′N 25°16′E
**Roznau am Radhost** see Rožnov pod Radhoštěm
111 L19 **Rožňava** Ger. Rosenau, Hung. Rozsnyó. Košický Kraj, E Slovakia 48°41′N 20°32′E
116 K10 **Roznov** Neamț, NE Romania 46°47′N 26°33′E
111 I18 **Rožnov pod Radhoštěm** Ger. Rosenau, Roznau am Radhost. Zlínský Kraj, E Czechia 49°28′N 18°09′E
**Rózsahegy** see Ružomberok
**Rozsnyó** see Râșnov, Romania
**Rozsnyó** see Rožňava, Slovakia
113 K18 **Rranxë** Shkodër, NW Albania 41°58′N 19°27′E
113 L18 **Rrëshen** var. Rresheni, Rrshen. Lezhë, C Albania 41°46′N 19°54′E
**Rresheni** see Rrëshen
**Rrogozhina** see Rrogozhinë
113 K20 **Rrogozhinë** var. Rogozhina, Rogozhinë, Rrogozhina. Tiranë, W Albania 41°04′N 19°40′E
**Rrshen** see Rrëshen
112 O13 **Rtanj** ▲ E Serbia 43°45′N 21°54′E
127 O7 **Rtishchevo** Saratovskaya Oblast', W Russia 52°16′N 43°46′E
184 N12 **Ruahine Range** var. Ruarine. ▲▲ North Island, New Zealand
185 L14 **Ruamahanga** ≈ North Island, New Zealand
**Ruanda** see Rwanda
184 M10 **Ruapehu, Mount** ⛰ North Island, New Zealand 39°15′S 175°33′E
185 C25 **Ruapuke Island** island SW New Zealand
**Ruarine** see Ruahine Range
184 O9 **Ruatahuna** Bay of Plenty, North Island, New Zealand 38°38′S 176°56′E
184 Q8 **Ruatoria** Gisborne, North Island, New Zealand 37°54′S 178°18′E
184 K4 **Ruawai** Northland, North Island, New Zealand 36°08′S 174°04′E
15 N8 **Ruban** ≈ Québec, SE Canada
81 I22 **Rubeho Mountains** ▲▲ C Tanzania
165 U3 **Rubeshibe** Hokkaidō, NE Japan 43°49′N 143°37′E
**Rubezhnoye** see Rubizhne
113 L18 **Rubik** Lezhë, C Albania 41°46′N 19°48′E
54 H7 **Rubio** Táchira, W Venezuela 07°42′N 72°23′W
117 X6 **Rubizhne** Rus. Rubezhnoye. Luhans'ka Oblast', E Ukraine 49°01′N 38°22′E
81 F20 **Rubondo Island** island N Tanzania
122 I13 **Rubtsovsk** Altayskiy Kray, S Russia 51°34′N 81°11′E
39 P9 **Ruby** Alaska, USA 64°44′N 155°29′W
35 W3 **Ruby Dome** ▲ Nevada, W USA 40°35′N 115°25′W
35 W4 **Ruby Lake** ◎ Nevada, W USA
35 W4 **Ruby Mountains** ▲▲ Nevada, W USA
33 Q12 **Ruby Range** ▲▲ Montana, NW USA
118 C10 **Rucava** SW Latvia 56°09′N 21°10′E
143 S13 **Rūdān** var. Dehbārez. Hormozgān, S Iran 27°30′N 57°10′E
**Rudelstadt** see Ciechanowiec
**Rudensk** see Rudzyensk
119 G14 **Rūdiškės** Vilnius, S Lithuania 54°31′N 24°49′E
95 H24 **Rudkøbing** Syddanmark, C Denmark 54°57′N 10°43′E
125 S13 **Rudnichnyy** Kirovskaya Oblast', NW Russia 59°37′N 52°28′E
**Rūdnichnyy** see Koksu
**Rudny** see Rudnyy
126 H4 **Rudnya** Smolenskaya Oblast', W Russia 54°55′N 31°10′E
127 O8 **Rudnya** Volgogradskaya Oblast', SW Russia 50°54′N 44°27′E
144 M7 **Rudnyy** var. Rudny. Kostanay, N Kazakhstan 53°N 63°05′E
122 K3 **Rudol'fa, Ostrov** island Zemlya Frantsa-Iosifa, NW Russia
**Rudolf, Lake** see Turkana, Lake
**Rudolfswert** see Novo mesto
101 L17 **Rudolstadt** Thüringen, C Germany 50°44′N 11°20′E
31 Q4 **Rudyard** Michigan, N USA 46°15′N 84°36′W
33 S7 **Rudyard** Montana, NW USA 48°33′N 110°37′W
119 K16 **Rudzyensk** Rus. Rudensk. Minskaya Voblasts', C Belarus 53°36′N 27°52′E
104 L6 **Rueda** Castilla y León, N Spain 41°24′N 04°58′W
114 F10 **Ruen** ▲ Bulgaria/North Macedonia 42°10′N 22°31′E
80 G10 **Rufa'a** Gezira, C Sudan 14°49′N 33°21′E
102 L10 **Ruffec** Charente, W France 46°01′N 00°10′E
21 R14 **Ruffin** South Carolina, SE USA 33°00′N 80°48′W
81 J23 **Rufiji** ≈ E Tanzania
61 A20 **Rufino** Santa Fe, C Argentina 34°16′S 62°45′W
76 F11 **Rufisque** W Senegal 14°44′N 17°18′W
83 K14 **Rufunsa** Lusaka, C Zambia 15°02′S 29°35′E
118 J9 **Rugāji** E Latvia 57°01′N 27°07′E
161 R7 **Rugao** Jiangsu, E China 32°27′N 120°35′E
97 M20 **Rugby** C England, United Kingdom 52°22′N 01°18′W
29 N3 **Rugby** North Dakota, N USA 48°24′N 100°00′W
100 N7 **Rügen** headland NE Germany 54°25′N 13°21′E
**Ruhaybah** see Ar Ruḩaybah
81 E19 **Ruhengeri** NW Rwanda 01°39′S 29°16′E
**Ruhja** see Rūjiena
100 M10 **Ruhner Berg** hill N Germany
118 F7 **Ruhnu** var. Ruhnu Saar, Swe. Runö. island SW Estonia
**Ruhnu Saar** see Ruhnu
101 G15 **Ruhr** ≈ W Germany
91 W6 **Ruhr Valley** industrial region W Germany
161 S11 **Rui'an** var. Rui an. Zhejiang, SE China 27°51′N 120°39′E
**Rui an** see Rui'an
161 P10 **Ruichang** Jiangxi, S China 29°46′N 115°37′E
24 J11 **Ruidosa** Texas, SW USA 30°00′N 104°40′W
37 S14 **Ruidoso** New Mexico, SW USA 33°19′N 105°40′W
161 P12 **Ruijin** Jiangxi, S China 25°52′N 116°01′E
160 D13 **Ruili** Yunnan, SW China 24°04′N 97°49′E
98 N8 **Ruinen** Drenthe, NE Netherlands 52°46′N 06°19′E
99 D17 **Ruiselede** West-Vlaanderen, W Belgium 51°03′N 03°21′E
161 T13 **Ruisui** prev. Juisui. C Taiwan 23°43′N 121°28′E
64 P5 **Ruivo de Santana, Pico** ▲ Madeira, Portugal, NE Atlantic Ocean 32°46′N 16°57′W



◆ Country ● Country Capital ◇ Dependent Territory ○ Dependent Territory Capital ⬖ Administrative Regions ✈ International Airport ▲ Mountain ▲▲ Mountain Range ⛰ Volcano ≈ River ◎ Lake ⊠ Reservoir

Ruiz – St-Chamond


40 J12 Ruiz Nayarit, SW Mexico 22°00′N 105°09′W
54 E10 Ruiz, Nevado del ⛰ W Colombia 04°53′N 75°22′W
138 J9 Rujaylah, Ḩarrat ar salt lake N Jordan
Rujen see Rūjiena
118 H7 Rūjiena Est. Ruhja, Ger. Rujen. N Latvia 57°54′N 25°22′E
79 I18 Ruki ≈ W Dem. Rep. Congo
81 E22 Rukwa ◈ region SW Tanzania
81 E23 Rukwa, Lake ◎ SE Tanzania
25 P6 Rule Texas, SW USA 33°10′N 99°53′W
22 K3 Ruleville Mississippi, S USA 33°43′N 90°33′W
Rum see Rhum
112 K10 Ruma Vojvodina, N Serbia 45°02′N 19°51′E
Rumadiya see Ar Ramādī
141 Q7 Rumāḩ Ar Riyāḑ, C Saudi Arabia 25°35′N 47°09′E
Rumaitha see Ar Rumaythah
Rumania/Rumänien see Romania
Rumänisch-Sankt-Georgen see Sângeorz-Băi
139 Y13 Rumaylah Al Başrah, SE Iraq 30°16′N 47°22′E
139 P2 Rumaylah, Wādī dry watercourse NE Syria
171 U13 Rumbati Papua Barat, E Indonesia 02°44′S 132°04′E
81 E14 Rumbek Lakes, C South Sudan 06°50′N 29°42′E
Rumburg see Rumburk
111 D14 Rumburk Ger. Rumburg. Ústecký Kraj, NW Czechia 50°58′N 14°35′E
44 J4 Rum Cay island C The Bahamas
99 M26 Rumelange Luxembourg, S Luxembourg 49°28′N 06°02′E
99 D20 Rumes Hainaut, SW Belgium 50°33′N 03°19′E
19 P7 Rumford Maine, NE USA 44°31′N 70°31′W
110 I6 Rumia Pomorskie, N Poland 54°36′N 18°21′E
113 J17 Rumija ▲▲ S Montenegro
103 T11 Rumilly Haute-Savoie, E France 45°52′N 05°57′E
139 O6 Rūmiyah Al Anbār, W Iraq 34°28′N 41°17′E
Rummah, Wādī ar see Rimah, Wādī ar
Rummelsburg in Pommern see Miastko
165 S3 Rumoi Hokkaidō, NE Japan 43°57′N 141°40′E
82 M12 Rumphi var. Rumpi. Northern, N Malawi 11°00′S 33°51′E
Rumpi see Rumphi
29 V7 Rum River ≈ Minnesota, N USA
188 F16 Rumung island Caroline Islands, W Micronesia
Rumuniya/Rumŭniya/Rumunjska see Romania
185 G16 Runanga West Coast, South Island, New Zealand 42°25′S 171°15′E
184 P7 Runaway, Cape headland North Island, New Zealand 37°33′S 177°59′E
97 K18 Runcorn C England, United Kingdom 53°20′N 02°44′W
118 K10 Rundāni var. Rundāni. E Latvia 56°19′N 27°51′E
Rundāni see Rundāni
83 L18 Runde var. Lundi. ≈ SE Zimbabwe
83 E16 Rundu var. Runtu. Kavango East, NE Namibia 17°55′S 19°45′E
93 I16 Rundvik Västerbotten, N Sweden 63°31′N 19°22′E
81 G20 Runere Mwanza, N Tanzania 03°06′S 33°18′E
25 S13 Runge Texas, SW USA 28°52′N 97°42′W
167 Q13 Rŭng, Kaôh prev. Kas Rong. island SW Cambodia
79 O16 Rungu Orientale, NE Dem. Rep. Congo 03°11′N 27°52′E
81 F23 Rungwa Katavi, W Tanzania 07°18′S 31°40′E
81 G22 Rungwa Singida, C Tanzania 06°54′S 33°33′E
94 M14 Runn ◎ C Sweden
24 M4 Running Water Draw valley New Mexico/Texas, SW USA
Runō see Ruhnu
Runtu see Rundu
189 V12 Ruo island Caroline Islands, C Micronesia
158 L9 Ruoqiang var. Jo-ch'iang, Uigh. Charkhlik, Charkhliq, Qarkilik. Xinjiang Uygur Zizhiqu, NW China 38°59′N 88°08′E
159 S7 Ruo Shui ≈ N China
92 L8 Ruostekfielbmá var. Rustefjelbma Finnmark. Finnmark, N Norway 70°25′N 28°10′E
93 L18 Ruovesi Pirkanmaa, W Finland 61°59′N 24°05′E
112 B9 Rupa Primorje-Gorski Kotar, NW Croatia 45°29′N 14°15′E
182 M11 Rupanyup Victoria, SE Australia 36°38′S 142°37′E
168 K9 Rupat, Pulau prev. Roepat. island W Indonesia
168 K10 Rupat, Selat strait Sumatera, W Indonesia
116 J11 Rupea Ger. Reps, Hung. Kőhalom; prev. Cohalm. Brașov, C Romania 46°02′N 25°13′E
99 G17 Rupel ≈ N Belgium
Rupella see la Rochelle
33 P15 Rupert Idaho, NW USA 42°37′N 113°40′W
21 R5 Rupert West Virginia, NE USA 37°57′N 80°40′W
Rupert House see Waskaganish
12 J10 Rupert, Rivière de ≈ Québec, C Canada
194 M13 Ruppert Coast physical region Antarctica
100 N11 Ruppiner Kanal canal NE Germany
55 S11 Rupununi River ≈ S Guyana
101 D16 Rur Dut. Roer. ≈ Germany/Netherlands
58 H13 Rurópolis Presidente Medici Pará, N Brazil 04°05′S 55°26′W
191 S12 Rurutu island Îles Australes, SW French Polynesia
Rusaddir see Melilla
83 L17 Rusape Manicaland, E Zimbabwe 18°32′S 32°07′E
Rusayris, Lake see Roseires, Reservoir
Ruschuk/Rusçuk see Ruse
114 K7 Ruse var. Ruschuk, Rustchuk, Turk. Rusçuk. Ruse, N Bulgaria 43°50′N 25°59′E
109 W10 Ruše NE Slovenia 46°31′N 15°30′E
114 L7 Ruse ◈ province N Bulgaria
114 K7 Rusenski Lom ≈ N Bulgaria
97 G17 Rush Ir. An Ros. Dublin, E Ireland 53°32′N 06°06′W
161 S4 Rushan var. Xiacun. Shandong, E China 36°55′N 121°26′E
Rushan see Rŭshon
Rushanskiy Khrebet see Rushon, Qatorkŭhi
29 V7 Rush City Minnesota, N USA 45°41′N 92°56′W
37 V5 Rush Creek ≈ Colorado, C USA
29 X10 Rushford Minnesota, N USA 43°48′N 91°45′W
154 N13 Rushikulya ≈ E India
14 D8 Rush Lake ◎ Ontario, S Canada
30 M7 Rush Lake ◎ Wisconsin, N USA
28 J10 Rushmore, Mount ▲ South Dakota, N USA 43°52′N 103°27′W
147 S13 Rŭshon Rus. Rushan. S Tajikistan 37°58′N 71°31′E
147 S14 Rushon, Qatorkŭhi Rus. Rushanskiy Khrebet. ▲▲ SE Tajikistan
26 M12 Rush Springs Oklahoma, C USA 34°46′N 97°57′W
45 V15 Rushville Trinidad, Trinidad and Tobago 10°07′N 61°03′W
30 J13 Rushville Illinois, N USA 40°07′N 90°33′W
28 K12 Rushville Nebraska, C USA 42°41′N 102°28′W
183 O11 Rushworth Victoria, SE Australia 36°36′S 145°03′E
25 W8 Rusk Texas, SW USA 31°49′N 95°11′W
93 I14 Rusksele Västerbotten, N Sweden 64°49′N 18°55′E
118 C12 Rusnė Klaipėda, W Lithuania 55°18′N 21°19′E
114 M10 Rusokastrenska Reka ≈ E Bulgaria
Russadir see Melilla
109 X3 Russbach ≈ NE Austria
11 V16 Russell Manitoba, S Canada 50°47′N 101°17′W
184 K2 Russell Northland, North Island, New Zealand 35°17′S 174°07′E
26 L4 Russell Kansas, C USA 38°54′N 98°51′W
21 O4 Russell Kentucky, S USA 38°30′N 82°43′W
20 L7 Russell Springs Kentucky, S USA 37°02′N 85°03′W
23 O2 Russellville Alabama, S USA 34°30′N 87°43′W
27 T11 Russellville Arkansas, C USA 35°17′N 93°06′W
20 J7 Russellville Kentucky, S USA 36°50′N 86°54′W
101 G18 Rüsselsheim Hessen, W Germany 50°00′N 08°25′E
122 J11 Russia off. Russian Federation, Latv. Krievija, Rus. Rossiyskaya Federatsiya. ◆ republic Asia/Europe
Russian America see Alaska
Russian Federation see Russia
39 N11 Russian Mission Alaska, USA 61°48′N 161°23′W
34 M7 Russian River ≈ California, W USA
122 J5 Russkaya Gavan' Novaya Zemlya, Arkhangel'skaya Oblast', N Russia 76°13′N 62°48′E
122 J5 Russkiy, Ostrov island N Russia
109 Y5 Rust Burgenland, E Austria 47°48′N 16°42′E
Rustaq see Ar Rustāq
137 U10 Rustavi prev. Rust'avi. SE Georgia 41°36′N 45°00′E
Rust'avi see Rustavi
21 T7 Rustburg Virginia, NE USA 37°17′N 79°07′W
Rustchuk see Ruse
Rustefjelbma Finnmark see Ruostekfielbmá
83 I21 Rustenburg North-West, N South Africa 25°40′S 27°15′E
22 H5 Ruston Louisiana, S USA 32°31′N 92°38′W
81 E21 Rutana SE Burundi 04°01′S 30°01′E
62 I4 Rutana, Volcán ⛰ N Chile 22°43′S 67°52′W
Rutanzige, Lake see Edward, Lake
Rutba see Ar Rutbah
104 M14 Rute Andalucía, S Spain 37°20′N 04°23′W
171 N16 Ruteng prev. Roeteng. Flores, C Indonesia 08°35′S 120°28′E
194 L8 Rutford Ice Stream ice feature Antarctica
35 X6 Ruth Nevada, W USA 39°15′N 115°00′W
101 G15 Rüthen Nordrhein-Westfalen, W Germany 51°30′N 08°28′E
14 D17 Rutherford Ontario, S Canada 42°39′N 82°06′W
21 Q10 Rutherfordton North Carolina, SE USA 35°23′N 81°57′W
97 J18 Ruthin Wel. Rhuthun. NE Wales, United Kingdom 53°05′N 03°18′W
108 G7 Rüti Zürich, N Switzerland 47°16′N 08°51′E
Rutlam see Ratlām
18 M9 Rutland Vermont, NE USA 43°37′N 72°59′W
97 N19 Rutland cultural region C England, United Kingdom
21 N8 Rutledge Tennessee, S USA 36°16′N 83°31′W
158 G12 Rutog var. Rutög, Rutok. Xizang Zizhiqu, W China 33°27′N 79°43′E
Rutok see Rutog
79 P19 Rutshuru Nord-Kivu, E Dem. Rep. Congo 01°11′S 29°28′E
98 L8 Rutten Flevoland, N Netherlands 52°49′N 05°44′E
127 Q17 Rutul Respublika Dagestan, SW Russia 41°35′N 47°30′E
93 L14 Ruukki Pohjois-Pohjanmaa, C Finland 64°40′N 25°35′E
98 N11 Ruurlo Gelderland, E Netherlands 52°04′N 06°27′E
143 S15 Ru'ūs al Jibāl cape Oman/United Arab Emirates
138 I7 Ru'ūs at Ţiwāl, Jabal ▲▲ W Syria
81 H23 Ruvuma ◈ region SE Tanzania
81 I25 Ruvuma var. Rio Rovuma. ≈ Mozambique/Tanzania see also Rovuma, Rio
Ruvuma see Rovuma, Rio
Ruwais see Ar Ruways
138 L9 Ruwayshid, Wadi ar dry watercourse NE Jordan
141 Z10 Ruways, Ra's ar headland E Oman 20°58′N 59°00′E
79 P18 Ruwenzori ▲▲ Dem. Rep. Congo/Uganda
141 Y8 Ruwī NE Oman 23°33′N 58°31′E
114 F9 Ruy ▲ Bulgaria/Serbia 42°52′N 22°35′E
Ruya see Luia, Rio
81 E20 Ruyigi E Burundi 03°28′S 30°19′E
127 P5 Ruzayevka Respublika Mordoviya, W Russia 54°04′N 44°56′E
119 G18 Ruzhany Brestskaya Voblasts', SW Belarus 52°52′N 24°53′E
Rŭzhevo Konare see Razhevo Konare
Ruzhin see Ruzhyn
114 G7 Ruzhintsi Vidin, NW Bulgaria 43°38′N 22°50′E
161 N6 Ruzhou Henan, C China 34°10′N 112°51′E
117 N5 Ruzhyn Rus. Ruzhin. Zhytomyrs'ka Oblast', N Ukraine 49°42′N 29°01′E
111 K19 Ružomberok Ger. Rosenberg, Hung. Rózsahegy. Žilinský Kraj, N Slovakia 49°04′N 19°19′E
111 C16 Ruzyně ✈ (Praha) Praha, C Czechia
81 D19 Rwanda off. Republic of Rwanda; prev. Rwandese Republic, Ruanda. ◆ republic C Africa
Rwanda, Republic of see Rwanda
Rwandese Republic see Rwanda
95 G22 Ry Midtjylland, C Denmark 56°06′N 09°46′E
Ryasna see Rasna
126 L5 Ryazan' Ryazanskaya Oblast', W Russia 54°37′N 39°37′E
126 L5 Ryazanskaya Oblast' ◈ province W Russia
126 M6 Ryazhsk Ryazanskaya Oblast', W Russia 53°42′N 40°09′E
118 B13 Rybachiy Ger. Rossitten. Kaliningradskaya Oblast', W Russia 55°09′N 20°49′E
124 J2 Rybachiy, Poluostrov peninsula NW Russia
Rybach'ye see Balykchy
124 L15 Rybinsk prev. Andropov. Yaroslavskaya Oblast', W Russia 58°03′N 38°53′E
124 K14 Rybinskoye Vodokhranilishche Eng. Rybinsk Reservoir, Rybinsk Sea. ⊠ W Russia
Rybinsk Reservoir/Rybinsk Sea see Rybinskoye Vodokhranilishche
111 I16 Rybnik Śląskie, S Poland 50°05′N 18°31′E
Rybnitsa see Rîbnița
111 F16 Rychnov nad Kněžnou Ger. Reichenau. Královéhradecký Kraj, N Czechia 50°10′N 16°17′E
110 I12 Rychwał Wielkopolskie, C Poland 52°04′N 18°10′E
11 O13 Rycroft Alberta, W Canada 55°45′N 118°42′W
95 L21 Ryd Kronoberg, S Sweden 56°27′N 14°44′E
95 L20 Rydaholm Jönköping, S Sweden 56°57′N 14°19′E
194 I8 Rydberg Peninsula peninsula Antarctica
97 P23 Rye SE England, United Kingdom 50°57′N 00°42′E
33 T10 Ryegate Montana, NW USA 46°21′N 109°12′W
35 S3 Rye Patch Reservoir ⊠ Nevada, W USA
95 D15 Ryfylke physical region S Norway
95 H16 Rygge Østfold, S Norway 59°22′N 10°45′E
110 N13 Ryki Lubelskie, E Poland 51°38′N 21°57′E
Rykovo see Yenakiyeve
126 J7 Ryl'sk Kurskaya Oblast', W Russia 51°34′N 34°41′E
183 S8 Rylstone New South Wales, SE Australia 32°48′S 149°58′E
111 H17 Rýmařov Ger. Römerstadt. Moravskoslezský Kraj, E Czechia 49°56′N 17°15′E
144 E11 Ryn-Peski desert W Kazakhstan
165 N10 Ryōtsu var. Ryôtu. Niigata, Sado, C Japan 38°06′N 138°28′E
Ryôtu see Ryōtsu
110 K10 Rypin Kujawsko-pomorskie, C Poland 53°03′N 19°25′E
Ryshkany see Rîșcani
Ryssel see Lille
Ryswick see Rijswijk
95 M24 Rytterknægten hill E Denmark
Ryukyu Islands see Nansei-shotō
192 G5 Ryukyu Trench var. Nansei Syotō Trench. undersea feature S East China Sea 24°45′N 128°00′E
110 D10 Rzepin Ger. Reppen. Lubuskie, W Poland 52°20′N 14°48′E
111 N16 Rzeszów Podkarpackie, SE Poland 50°03′N 22°01′E
124 I16 Rzhev Tverskaya Oblast', W Russia 56°17′N 34°22′E
Rzhishchev see Rzhyshchiv
117 P5 Rzhyshchiv Rus. Rzhishchev. Kyivs'ka Oblast', N Ukraine 49°58′N 31°02′E


# S


138 E11 Sa'ad Southern, W Israel 31°27′N 34°31′E
109 P7 Saalach ≈ W Austria
101 L14 Saale ≈ C Germany
101 L17 Saalfeld var. Saalfeld an der Saale. Thüringen, C Germany 50°39′N 11°22′E
Saalfeld see Zalewo
Saalfeld an der Saale see Saalfeld
108 C8 Saane ≈ W Switzerland
101 D19 Saar Fr. Sarre. ≈ France/Germany
101 E20 Saarbrücken Fr. Sarrebruck. Saarland, SW Germany 49°13′N 07°01′E
Saarburg see Sarrebourg
118 D6 Sääre var. Sjar. Saaremaa, W Estonia 57°57′N 21°53′E
Saare see Saaremaa
118 D5 Saaremaa off. Saare Maakond. ◈ province W Estonia
118 E6 Saaremaa Ger. Oesel, Ösel; prev. Saare. island W Estonia
Saare Maakond see Saaremaa
92 L12 Saarenkylä Lappi, N Finland 66°31′N 25°51′E
Saargemund see Sarreguemines
93 L17 Saarijärvi Keski-Suomi, C Finland 62°42′N 25°16′E
Saar in Mähren see Žďár nad Sázavou
92 M10 Saariselkä N. Sami. Suoločielgi. Lappi, N Finland 68°27′N 27°29′E
92 L10 Saariselkä hill range NE Finland
101 D20 Saarland Fr. Sarre. ◈ state SW Germany
Saarlautern see Saarlouis
101 D20 Saarlouis prev. Saarlautern. Saarland, SW Germany 49°19′N 06°45′E
108 E11 Saaser Vispa ≈ S Switzerland
137 X12 Saatlı Rus. Saatly. C Azerbaijan 39°57′N 48°24′E
Saatly see Saatlı
Saaz see Žatec
45 V9 Saba ◇ special Municipality of the Netherlands Sint Maarten
138 J7 Sab' Ābār var. Sab'a Biyar, Sa'b Bi'ār. Ḩimş, C Syria 33°46′N 37°41′E
Sab'a Biyar see Sab' Ābār
112 K11 Šabac Serbia, W Serbia 44°45′N 19°42′E
105 W5 Sabadell Cataluña, E Spain 41°33′N 02°07′E
164 K12 Sabae Fukui, Honshū, SW Japan 36°00′N 136°12′E
169 V7 Sabah prev. British North Borneo, North Borneo. ◈ state East Malaysia
168 J8 Sabak var. Sabak Bernam. Selangor, Peninsular Malaysia 03°45′N 100°59′E
Sabak Bernam see Sabak
38 D16 Sabak, Cape headland Agattu Island, Alaska, USA 52°21′N 173°43′E
81 J20 Sabaki ≈ S Kenya
142 L2 Sabalān, Kuhhā-ye ▲ NW Iran 38°21′N 47°47′E
154 H7 Sabalgarh Madhya Pradesh, C India 26°18′N 77°28′E
44 E4 Sabana, Archipiélago de island group C Cuba
42 H7 Sabanagrande var. Sabana Grande. Francisco Morazán, S Honduras 13°48′N 87°15′W
Sabana Grande see Sabanagrande
54 E5 Sabanalarga Atlántico, N Colombia 10°38′N 74°55′W
41 W14 Sabancuy Campeche, SE Mexico 18°58′N 91°11′W
45 N8 Sabaneta NW Dominican Republic 19°30′N 71°21′W
54 J4 Sabaneta Falcón, N Venezuela 11°17′N 70°00′W
188 H4 Sabaneta, Puntan prev. Ushi Point. headland Saipan, S Northern Mariana Islands 15°17′N 145°49′E
171 X14 Sabang Papua, E Indonesia 04°33′S 138°42′E
116 L10 Săbăoani Neamț, NE Romania 47°01′N 26°51′E
155 J26 Sabaragamuwa ◈ province C Sri Lanka
Sabaria see Szombathely
154 D10 Sābarmati ≈ NW India
171 S10 Sabatai Pulau Morotai, E Indonesia 02°04′N 128°23′E
141 Q15 Sab'atayn, Ramlat as desert C Yemen
107 I16 Sabaudia Lazio, C Italy 41°17′N 13°02′E
57 J19 Sabaya Oruro, S Bolivia 19°09′S 68°21′W
Sa'b Bi'ār see Sab' Ābār
Sabbioncello see Orebić
148 I8 Şāberī, Hāmūn-e var. Daryācheh-ye Hāmun, Daryācheh-ye Sīstān. ◎ Afghanistan/Iran see also Sīstān, Daryācheh-ye
Şāberī, Hāmūn-e see Sīstān, Daryācheh-ye
27 P2 Sabetha Kansas, C USA 39°54′N 95°48′W
75 P10 Sabhā C Libya 27°02′N 14°26′E
67 V13 Sabi var. Save. ≈ Mozambique/Zimbabwe see also Save
Sabi see Save
118 E8 Sabile Ger. Zabeln. NW Latvia 57°03′N 22°33′E
31 R14 Sabina Ohio, N USA 39°29′N 83°38′W
40 I3 Sabinal Chihuahua, N Mexico 30°59′N 107°29′W
25 Q12 Sabinal Texas, SW USA 29°19′N 99°28′W
25 Q11 Sabinal River ≈ Texas, SW USA
105 S4 Sabiñánigo Aragón, NE Spain 42°31′N 00°22′W
41 N6 Sabinas Coahuila, NE Mexico 27°52′N 101°04′W
41 O8 Sabinas Hidalgo Nuevo León, NE Mexico 26°29′N 100°09′W
41 N6 Sabinas, Río ≈ NE Mexico
22 F9 Sabine Lake ◎ Louisiana/Texas, S USA
92 O3 Sabine Land physical region C Svalbard
25 W7 Sabine River ≈ Louisiana/Texas, SW USA
137 X12 Sabirabad C Azerbaijan 40°00′N 48°27′E
148 I8 Şābīrī, Hāmūn-e var. Daryācheh-ye Hāmūn. salt pan Afghanistan Asia
Sabkha see As Sabkhah
171 O4 Sablayan Mindoro, N Philippines 12°48′N 120°48′E
13 P16 Sable, Cape headland Newfoundland and Labrador, SE Canada 43°21′N 65°40′W
23 X17 Sable, Cape headland Florida, SE USA 25°12′N 81°06′W
13 R16 Sable Island island Nova Scotia, SE Canada
14 L11 Sables, Lac des ◎ Québec, SE Canada
14 E10 Sables, Rivière aux ≈ Ontario, S Canada
102 K7 Sable-sur-Sarthe Sarthe, NW France 47°49′N 00°19′W
125 U7 Sablya, Gora ▲ NW Russia 64°46′N 58°52′E
77 U14 Sabon Birnin Gwari Kaduna, C Nigeria 10°43′N 06°39′E
77 V11 Sabon Kafi Zinder, C Niger 14°37′N 08°46′E
104 I6 Sabor, Rio ≈ N Portugal
14 J8 Sabourin, Lac ◎ Québec, SE Canada
137 Y10 Şabran prev. Dəvəçi. NE Azerbaijan 41°15′N 48°58′E
102 J14 Sabres Landes, SW France 44°07′N 00°46′W
195 X13 Sabrina Coast physical region Antarctica
140 M11 Sabt al Ulāyā 'Asīr, SW Saudi Arabia 19°33′N 41°58′E
104 I8 Sabugal Guarda, N Portugal 40°20′N 07°05′W
29 Z13 Sabula Iowa, C USA 42°04′N 90°10′W
141 N13 Şabyā Jāzān, SW Saudi Arabia 17°50′N 42°50′E
Sabzawar see Sabzevār
Sabzawaran see Jīroft
143 S4 Sabzevār var. Sabzawar. Khorāsān-e Razavī, NE Iran 36°13′N 57°38′E
Sabzvārān see Jīroft
Sacajawea Peak see Matterhorn
82 C9 Sacandica Uíge, NW Angola 06°01′S 15°57′E
42 A2 Sacatepéquez off. Departamento de Sacatepéquez. ◈ department S Guatemala
Sacatepéquez, Departamento de see Sacatepéquez
104 F11 Sacavém Lisboa, W Portugal 38°47′N 09°06′W
29 T13 Sac City Iowa, C USA 42°25′N 94°59′W
105 P8 Sacedón Castilla-La Mancha, C Spain 40°29′N 02°44′W
116 J12 Săcele Ger. Vierdörfer, Hung. Négyfalu; prev. Ger. Sieben Dörfer, Hung. Hétfalu. Brașov, C Romania 45°36′N 25°40′E
163 Y16 Sacheon Jap. Sansenhō; prev. Sach'ŏn, Samch'ŏnpŏ. S South Korea 34°55′N 128°07′E
12 C7 Sachigo ≈ Ontario, C Canada
12 C8 Sachigo Lake Ontario, C Canada 53°52′N 92°16′W
12 C8 Sachigo Lake ◎ Ontario, C Canada
Sach'ŏn see Sacheon
101 O15 Sachsen Eng. Saxony, Fr. Saxe. ◈ state E Germany
101 K14 Sachsen-Anhalt Eng. Saxony-Anhalt. ◈ state C Germany
109 R9 Sachsenburg Salzburg, S Austria 46°49′N 13°23′E
Sachsenfeld see Žalec
8 I5 Sachs Harbour var. Ikaahuk. Banks Island, Northwest Territories, N Canada 72°N 125°14′W
Sächsisch-Reen/Sächsisch-Regen see Reghin
18 H8 Sackets Harbor New York, NE USA 43°57′N 76°06′W
13 P14 Sackville New Brunswick, SE Canada 45°54′N 64°23′W
19 P9 Saco Maine, NE USA 43°32′N 70°25′W
19 P8 Saco River ≈ Maine/New Hampshire, NE USA
35 O7 Sacramento state capital California, W USA 38°35′N 121°30′W
37 T14 Sacramento Mountains ▲▲ New Mexico, SW USA
35 N6 Sacramento River ≈ California, W USA
35 N5 Sacramento Valley valley California, W USA
36 I10 Sacramento Wash valley Arizona, SW USA
105 N15 Sacratif, Cabo headland S Spain 36°41′N 03°30′W
116 F9 Săcueni prev. Săcueni, Hung. Székelyhíd. Bihor, W Romania 47°20′N 22°05′E
Săcueni see Săcueni
105 R4 Sádaba Aragón, NE Spain 42°15′N 01°16′W
Sá da Bandeira see Lubango
138 I6 Şadad Ḩimş, W Syria 34°19′N 36°52′E
141 O13 Şa'dah NW Yemen 16°59′N 43°45′E
167 O16 Sadao Songkhla, SW Thailand 06°39′N 100°30′E
142 L8 Sadd-e Dez, Daryācheh-ye ◎ W Iran
19 S3 Saddleback Mountain hill Maine, NE USA
19 P6 Saddleback Mountain ▲ Maine, NE USA 44°57′N 70°27′W
141 W13 Sadḩ S Oman 17°11′N 55°08′E
76 J11 Sadiola Kayes, W Mali 13°48′N 11°47′W
149 R12 Sadiqabad Punjab, E Pakistan 28°16′N 70°10′E
153 Y10 Sadiya Assam, NE India 27°49′N 95°38′E
139 W9 Sa'dīyah, Hawr as ◎ E Iraq
Sado see Sadoga-shima
165 N9 Sadoga-shima var. Sado. island C Japan
104 F12 Sado, Rio ≈ S Portugal
114 I8 Sadovets Pleven, N Bulgaria 43°19′N 24°21′E
127 O11 Sadovoye Respublika Kalmykiya, SW Russia 47°51′N 44°34′E
105 W9 Sa Dragonera var. Isla Dragonera. island Islas Baleares, Spain, W Mediterranean Sea
114 I10 Saedinenie var. Săedinenie, Sŭedinenie. Plovdiv, C Bulgaria 42°14′N 24°36′E
Săedinenie see Saedinenie
105 P8 Saelices Castilla-La Mancha, C Spain 39°55′N 02°49′W
Saena Julia see Siena
Saetabicula see Alzira
114 O12 Safaalan Tekirdağ, NW Turkey 41°26′N 28°07′E
Safad see Tsefat
Safaga see Būr Safājah
Şafāqis see Sfax
143 P10 Şafāshahr var. Deh Bīd. Fārs, C Iran 30°50′N 53°50′E
192 I16 Safata Bay bay Upolu, Samoa, C Pacific Ocean
149 N3 Safēd, Darya-ye var. Āb-i-safed, Darya-ye Sefīd. ≈ N Afghanistan
148 K5 Safēd Kōh, Silsilah-ye Eng. Paropamisus Range. ▲▲ W Afghanistan
139 X11 Şaffāf, Ḩawr aş marshy lake S Iraq
95 J16 Säffle Värmland, C Sweden 59°08′N 12°55′E
37 N15 Safford Arizona, SW USA 32°46′N 109°41′W
74 E7 Safi W Morocco 32°19′N 09°14′W
126 I4 Safonovo Smolenskaya Oblast', W Russia 55°05′N 33°12′E
136 H11 Safranbolu Karabük, NW Turkey 41°16′N 32°41′E
139 Y13 Safwān Al Başrah, SE Iraq 30°06′N 47°44′E
158 J16 Saga var. Gya'gya. Xizang Zizhiqu, W China 29°22′N 85°19′E
164 C14 Saga Saga, Kyūshū, SW Japan 33°14′N 130°16′E
164 C13 Saga off. Saga-ken. ◈ prefecture Kyūshū, SW Japan
165 P10 Sagae Yamagata, Honshū, C Japan 38°22′N 140°12′E
166 L3 Sagaing Sagaing, C Myanmar (Burma) 21°55′N 95°56′E
166 L5 Sagaing ◈ region N Myanmar (Burma)
Saga-ken see Saga
165 N13 Sagamihara Kanagawa, Honshū, S Japan 35°34′N 139°22′E
165 N14 Sagami-nada inlet SW Japan
Sagan see Żagań
29 Y3 Saganaga Lake ◎ Minnesota, N USA
155 F18 Sāgar Karnātaka, W India 14°09′N 75°02′E
154 I9 Sāgar prev. Saugor. Madhya Pradesh, C India 23°53′N 78°46′E
15 S8 Sagard Québec, SE Canada 48°01′N 70°03′W
Sagarmāthā see Everest, Mount
Sagebrush State see Nevada
143 V11 Sāghand Yazd, C Iran 32°33′N 55°12′E
19 N14 Sag Harbor Long Island, New York, NE USA 40°59′N 72°15′W
Saghez see Saqqez
31 R8 Saginaw Michigan, N USA 43°25′N 83°57′W
31 R8 Saginaw Bay lake bay Michigan, N USA
Sagiz see Sagyz
64 H6 Saglek Bank undersea feature W Labrador Sea
13 P5 Saglek Bay bay SW Labrador Sea
Saglouc/Sagluk see Salluit
103 X15 Sagonne, Golfe de gulf Corse, France, C Mediterranean Sea
105 P13 Sagra ▲ S Spain 37°59′N 02°33′W
104 F14 Sagres Faro, S Portugal 37°01′N 08°56′W
37 S7 Saguache Colorado, C USA 38°05′N 106°05′W
44 J7 Sagua de Tánamo Holguín, E Cuba 20°38′N 75°14′W
44 E5 Sagua la Grande Villa Clara, C Cuba 22°48′N 80°06′W
15 R7 Saguenay ≈ Québec, SE Canada
74 C9 Saguia al Hamra var. As Saquia al Hamra. ≈ N Western Sahara
105 S9 Sagunto var. Sagunt, Ar. Murviedro; anc. Saguntum. Comunitat Valenciana, E Spain 39°40′N 00°17′W
Sagunt/Saguntum see Sagunto
144 H11 Sagyz prev. Sagiz. Atyrau, W Kazakhstan 48°12′N 54°56′E
138 H10 Saḩāb 'Ammān, NW Jordan 31°52′N 36°00′E
54 E6 Sahagún Córdoba, NW Colombia 08°58′N 75°30′W
104 L4 Sahagún Castilla y León, N Spain 42°23′N 05°02′W
141 X8 Saḩam N Oman 24°06′N 56°52′E
68 F9 Sahara desert Libya/Algeria
Sahara el Gharbiya see Aş Şaḩrā' al Gharbīyah
Saharan Atlas see Atlas Saharien
152 J9 Sahāranpur Uttar Pradesh, N India 29°58′N 77°33′E
64 L10 Saharan Seamounts var. Saharian Seamounts. undersea feature E Atlantic Ocean 25°00′N 20°00′W
Saharian Seamounts see Saharan Seamounts
153 Q13 Saharsa Bihār, NE India 25°54′N 86°36′E
67 O7 Sahel physical region C Africa
153 R14 Sāhibganj Jhārkhand, NE India 25°15′N 87°40′E
139 Q7 Sahīliyah Al Anbār, C Iraq 33°43′N 42°42′E
138 H4 Sāḩilīyah, Jibāl as ▲▲ NW Syria
114 M13 Şahin Tekirdağ, NW Turkey 41°01′N 26°51′E
149 U8 Sāhīwāl Punjab, E Pakistan 31°57′N 72°22′E
149 U9 Sāhīwāl prev. Montgomery. Punjab, E Pakistan 30°40′N 73°05′E
141 W11 Şaḩmah, Ramlat as desert C Oman
139 T13 Şaḩrā' al Ḩijārah desert S Iraq
40 H5 Sahuaripa Sonora, NW Mexico 29°02′N 109°14′W
36 M16 Sahuarita Arizona, SW USA 31°24′N 110°55′W
40 L13 Sahuayo var. Sahuayo de José María Morelos; prev. Sahuayo de Porfirio Díaz. Michoacán, SW Mexico 20°05′N 102°42′W
Sahuayo de Díaz/Sahuayo de José María Morelos/Sahuayo de Porfirio Díaz see Sahuayo
173 W8 Sahul Shelf undersea feature N Timor Sea
167 P17 Sai Buri Pattani, SW Thailand 06°42′N 101°37′E
74 I6 Saïda NW Algeria 34°50′N 00°10′E
138 G7 Saïda var. Şaydā, Sayida; anc. Sidon. W Lebanon 33°20′N 35°24′E
Sa'īdābād see Sīrjān
80 B13 Sa'id Bundas Western Bahr el Ghazal, W South Sudan 08°24′N 24°53′E
186 E7 Saidor Madang, N Papua New Guinea 05°38′S 146°28′E
153 S13 Saidpur var. Syedpur. Rajshahi, NW Bangladesh 25°48′N 89°E
149 U5 Saidu var. Mingora, Mongora; prev. Mingäora. Khyber Pakhtunkhwa, N Pakistan 34°45′N 72°21′E
108 C7 Saignelégier Jura, NW Switzerland 47°18′N 07°03′E
164 H11 Saigō Shimane, Dōgo, SW Japan 36°12′N 133°18′E
Saigon see Hô Chi Minh
163 P11 Saihan Tal var. Sonid Youqi. Nei Mongol Zizhiqu, N China 42°45′N 112°36′E
162 I12 Saihan Toroi Nei Mongol Zizhiqu, N China 41°44′N 100°29′E
Sai Hun see Syr Darya
92 M11 Saija Lappi, NE Finland 67°07′N 28°46′E
164 G14 Saijō Ehime, Shikoku, SW Japan 33°55′N 133°10′E
164 E15 Saiki Ōita, Kyūshū, SW Japan 32°57′N 131°52′E
93 N18 Saimaa ◎ SE Finland
93 N18 Saimaa Canal Fin. Saimaan Kanava, Rus. Saymenskiy Kanal. canal Finland/Russia
Saimaan Kanava see Saimaa Canal
40 L10 Saín Alto Zacatecas, C Mexico 23°36′N 103°14′W
96 L12 St Abb's Head headland SE Scotland, United Kingdom 55°54′N 02°07′W
11 Y16 St. Adolphe Manitoba, S Canada 49°39′N 96°55′W
103 O15 St-Affrique Aveyron, S France 43°57′N 02°52′E
15 Q10 St-Agapit Québec, SE Canada 46°22′N 71°37′W
97 O21 St Albans anc. Verulamium. E England, United Kingdom 51°46′N 00°21′W
18 L6 Saint Albans Vermont, NE USA 44°49′N 73°07′W
21 Q5 Saint Albans West Virginia, NE USA 38°21′N 81°47′W
St. Alban's Head see St Aldhelm's Head
11 Q14 St. Albert Alberta, SW Canada 53°38′N 113°38′W
97 M24 St Aldhelm's Head var. St. Alban's Head. headland S England, United Kingdom 50°34′N 02°04′W
15 O11 St-Alexis-des-Monts Québec, SE Canada 46°30′N 73°08′W
103 P2 St-Amand-les-Eaux Nord, N France 50°27′N 03°25′E
103 O9 St-Amand-Montrond var. St-Amand-Mont-Rond. Cher, C France 46°43′N 02°29′E
173 P16 St-André NE Réunion
14 M12 St-André-Avellin Québec, SE Canada 45°45′N 75°04′W
Saint-André, Cap see Vilanandro, Tanjona
102 K12 St-André-de-Cubzac Gironde, SW France 45°01′N 00°26′W
96 K11 St Andrews E Scotland, United Kingdom 56°20′N 02°49′W
23 Q9 Saint Andrews Bay bay Florida, SE USA
23 W7 Saint Andrew Sound sound Georgia, SE USA
Saint Anna Trough see Svyataya Anna Trough
44 J11 St. Ann's Bay C Jamaica 18°26′N 77°12′W
13 T10 St. Anthony Newfoundland and Labrador, SE Canada 51°22′N 55°34′W
33 R13 Saint Anthony Idaho, NW USA 43°56′N 111°38′W
182 M11 Saint Arnaud Victoria, SE Australia 36°39′S 143°15′E
185 I15 St.Arnaud Range ▲▲ South Island, New Zealand
13 R10 St-Augustin Québec, E Canada 51°13′N 58°39′W
23 X9 Saint Augustine Florida, SE USA 29°54′N 81°19′W
97 H24 St Austell SW England, United Kingdom 50°21′N 04°47′W
103 T4 St-Avold Moselle, NE France 49°06′N 06°43′E
103 N17 St-Barthélemy ▲ S France
45 V9 St Barthélemy French overseas collectivity E Caribbean Sea
102 L17 St-Béat Haute-Garonne, S France 42°55′N 00°39′E
97 I15 St Bees Head headland NW England, United Kingdom 54°30′N 03°39′W
173 P16 St-Benoit E Réunion
103 T13 St-Bonnet Hautes-Alpes, SE France 44°41′N 06°04′E
St.Botolph's Town see Boston
97 G21 St Brides Bay inlet SW Wales, United Kingdom
102 H5 St-Brieuc Côtes d'Armor, NW France 48°31′N 02°45′W
102 H5 St-Brieuc, Baie de bay NW France
102 L7 St-Calais Sarthe, NW France 47°55′N 00°48′E
15 Q10 St-Casimir Québec, SE Canada 46°40′N 72°05′W
14 H16 St. Catharines Ontario, S Canada 43°10′N 79°15′W
45 S14 St. Catherine, Mount ▲ N Grenada 12°10′N 61°41′W
64 C11 St Catherine Point headland E Bermuda
23 X6 Saint Catherines Island island Georgia, SE USA
97 M24 St Catherine's Point headland S England, United Kingdom 50°34′N 01°17′W
103 N13 St-Céré Lot, S France 44°52′N 01°53′E
108 A10 St. Cergue Vaud, W Switzerland 46°25′N 06°10′E
103 R11 St-Chamond Loire, E France 45°29′N 04°32′E


◆ Country
● Country Capital
◇ Dependent Territory
○ Dependent Territory Capital
◈ Administrative Regions
✈ International Airport
▲ Mountain
▲▲ Mountain Range
⛰ Volcano
≈ River
◎ Lake
⊠ Reservoir

SAINT CHARLES – SALIN


33 S16 **Saint Charles** Idaho, NW USA 42°05′N 111°23′W
27 X4 **Saint Charles** Missouri, C USA 38°48′N 90°29′W
103 P13 **St-Chély-d'Apcher** Lozère, S France 44°51′N 03°16′E
**Saint Christopher and Nevis, Federation of** see Saint Kitts and Nevis
**Saint Christopher-Nevis** see Saint Kitts and Nevis
31 S9 **Saint Clair** Michigan, N USA 42°49′N 82°29′W
183 O17 **St. Clair, Lake** ◎ Tasmania, SE Australia
14 C17 **St. Clair, Lake** var. Lac à L'Eau Claire. ◎ Canada/USA
31 S10 **Saint Clair Shores** Michigan, N USA 42°30′N 82°53′W
103 S10 **St-Claude** anc. Condate. Jura, E France 46°23′N 05°52′E
45 X6 **St-Claude** Basse Terre, SW Guadeloupe 16°02′N 61°42′W
23 X12 **Saint Cloud** Florida, SE USA 28°15′N 81°15′W
29 U8 **Saint Cloud** Minnesota, N USA 45°34′N 94°10′W
45 T9 **Saint Croix** island S Virgin Islands (US)
30 J4 **Saint Croix Flowage** ⊠ Wisconsin, N USA
19 T5 **Saint Croix River** ≈ Canada/USA
29 W7 **Saint Croix River** ≈ Minnesota/Wisconsin, N USA
45 S14 **St.David's** SE Grenada 12°01′N 61°40′W
97 H21 **St David's** SW Wales, United Kingdom 51°53′N 05°16′W
97 G21 **St David's Head** headland SW Wales, United Kingdom 51°54′N 05°19′W
64 C12 **St David's Island** island E Bermuda
173 O16 **St-Denis** ○ (Réunion) NW Réunion 20°55′S 14°34′E
103 U6 **St-Dié** Vosges, NE France 48°17′N 06°57′E
103 R5 **St-Dizier** anc. Desiderii Fanum. Haute-Marne, N France 48°39′N 05°00′E
15 N11 **St-Donat** Québec, SE Canada 46°19′N 74°15′W
15 N11 **Ste-Adèle** Québec, SE Canada 45°58′N 74°10′W
15 N11 **Ste-Agathe-des-Monts** Québec, SE Canada 46°03′N 74°19′W
11 Y16 **Ste. Anne** Manitoba, S Canada 49°40′N 96°40′W
45 R12 **Ste-Anne** Grande Terre, E Guadeloupe 16°13′N 61°23′W
45 Y6 **Ste-Anne** SE Martinique 14°26′N 60°53′W
15 Q10 **Ste-Anne** ≈ Québec, SE Canada
172 I16 **Sainte Anne** island Inner Islands, NE Seychelles
15 W6 **Ste-Anne-des-Monts** Québec, SE Canada 49°07′N 66°29′W
14 M10 **Ste-Anne-du-Lac** Québec, SE Canada 46°51′N 75°20′W
15 S10 **Ste-Apolline** Québec, SE Canada 46°47′N 70°15′W
15 R10 **Ste-Claire** Québec, SE Canada 46°30′N 70°40′W
15 Q10 **Ste-Croix** Québec, SE Canada 46°36′N 71°42′W
108 B8 **Ste. Croix** Vaud, SW Switzerland 46°50′N 06°31′E
103 P14 **St-Énimie** Lozère, S France 44°21′N 03°26′E
27 Y6 **Sainte Genevieve** Missouri, C USA 37°57′N 90°01′W
103 S12 **St-Egrève** Isère, E France 45°15′N 05°41′E
39 T12 **Saint Elias, Cape** headland Kayak Island, Alaska, USA 59°48′N 144°36′W
39 U11 **St Elias, Mount** ▲ Alaska, USA 60°18′N 140°57′W
10 G8 **Saint Elias Mountains** ▲ Canada/USA
55 Y10 **St-Élie** N French Guiana 04°50′N 53°21′W
103 O10 **St-Eloy-les-Mines** Puy-de-Dôme, C France 46°07′N 02°50′E
15 R10 **Ste-Marie** Québec, SE Canada 46°28′N 71°00′W
45 Q11 **Ste-Marie** NE Martinique 14°47′N 61°00′W
173 P16 **Ste-Marie** NE Réunion
103 U6 **Ste-Marie-aux-Mines** Haut-Rhin, NE France 48°16′N 07°12′E
**Sainte Marie, Cap** see Vohimena, Tanjona
102 L8 **Ste-Maure-de-Touraine** Indre-et-Loire, C France 47°06′N 00°38′E
103 R4 **Ste-Menehould** Marne, NE France 49°06′N 04°54′E
**Ste-Perpétue** see Ste-Perpétue-de-l'Islet
15 S9 **Ste-Perpétue-de-l'Islet** var. Ste-Perpétue. Québec, SE Canada 47°02′N 69°58′W
45 X11 **Ste-Rose** Basse Terre, N Guadeloupe 16°20′N 61°42′W
173 P16 **Ste-Rose** E Réunion
11 W15 **Ste. Rose du Lac** Manitoba, S Canada 51°04′N 99°31′W
102 J11 **Saintes** anc. Mediolanum. Charente-Maritime, W France 45°45′N 00°37′W
45 X7 **Saintes, Canal des** channel SW Guadeloupe
**Saintes, Îles des** see les Saintes
173 P16 **Ste-Suzanne** N Réunion
15 P10 **Ste-Thècle** Québec, SE Canada 46°48′N 72°31′W
103 Q12 **St-Étienne** Loire, E France 45°26′N 04°23′E
102 M4 **St-Étienne-du-Rouvray** Seine-Maritime, N France 49°22′N 01°07′E
**Saint Eustatius** see Sint Eustatius
14 M11 **Ste-Véronique** Québec, SE Canada 46°30′N 74°58′W
15 P7 **St-Félicien** Québec, SE Canada 48°38′N 72°29′W
15 O11 **St-Félix-de-Valois** Québec, SE Canada 46°10′N 73°26′W
103 Y14 **St-Florent** Corse, France, C Mediterranean Sea 42°41′N 09°19′E
103 Y14 **St-Florent, Golfe de** gulf Corse, France, C Mediterranean Sea
103 P6 **St-Florentin** Yonne, C France 48°00′N 03°46′E
103 N9 **St-Florent-sur-Cher** Cher, C France 47°00′N 02°13′E
103 P12 **St-Flour** Cantal, C France 45°02′N 03°05′E
26 H2 **Saint Francis** Kansas, C USA 39°45′N 101°31′W
83 H26 **St. Francis, Cape** headland S South Africa 34°11′S 24°45′E
27 X10 **Saint Francis River** ≈ Arkansas/Missouri, C USA
22 J8 **Saint Francisville** Louisiana, S USA 30°46′N 91°22′W
45 Y6 **St-François** Grande Terre, E Guadeloupe 16°15′N 61°17′W
15 Q12 **St-François** ≈ Québec, SE Canada
27 X7 **Saint Francois Mountains** ▲ Missouri, C USA
**St-Gall/Saint Gall/St. Gallen** see Sankt Gallen
**St-Gall** see St-Gall/Saint Gall/St.Gallen
102 L16 **St-Gaudens** Haute-Garonne, S France 43°07′N 00°43′E
15 R12 **St-Gédéon** Québec, SE Canada 45°51′N 70°36′W
181 X10 **Saint George** Queensland, E Australia 28°05′S 148°40′E
64 B12 **St George** N Bermuda 32°24′N 64°42′W
38 K15 **Saint George** Saint George Island, Alaska, USA 56°34′N 169°30′W
21 S14 **Saint George** South Carolina, SE USA 33°12′N 80°34′W
36 J8 **Saint George** Utah, W USA 37°06′N 113°35′W
13 R12 **St. George, Cape** headland Newfoundland and Labrador, E Canada 48°26′N 59°17′W
186 I6 **St. George, Cape** headland New Ireland, NE Papua New Guinea 04°49′S 152°52′E
38 J15 **Saint George Island** island Pribilof Islands, Alaska, USA
23 S10 **Saint George Island** island Florida, SE USA
99 J19 **Saint-Georges** Liège, E Belgium 50°36′N 05°20′E
15 R11 **St-Georges** Québec, SE Canada 46°08′N 70°40′W
55 Z11 **St-Georges** E French Guiana 03°55′N 51°49′W
45 R14 **St. George's** ● (Grenada) SW Grenada 12°04′N 61°45′W
13 R12 **St. George's Bay** inlet Newfoundland and Labrador, E Canada
97 G21 **St. George's Channel** channel Ireland/Wales, United Kingdom
186 H6 **St. George's Channel** channel NE Papua New Guinea
64 B11 **St George's Island** island E Bermuda
99 I21 **Saint-Gérard** Namur, S Belgium 50°20′N 04°47′E
**St-Germain** see St-Germain-en-Laye
15 P12 **St-Germain-de-Grantham** Québec, SE Canada 45°49′N 72°32′W
103 N5 **St-Germain-en-Laye** var. St-Germain. Yvelines, N France 48°53′N 02°04′E
102 H8 **St-Gildas, Pointe du** headland NW France 47°09′N 02°25′W
103 R15 **St-Gilles** Gard, S France 43°41′N 04°24′E
102 I9 **St-Gilles-Croix-de-Vie** Vendée, NW France 46°41′N 01°55′W
173 O16 **St-Gilles-les-Bains** W Réunion 21°02′S 55°14′E
102 M16 **St-Girons** Ariège, S France 42°58′N 01°07′E
**Saint Gotthard** see Szentgotthárd
108 G9 **St. Gotthard Tunnel** tunnel Ticino, S Switzerland
97 H22 **St Govan's Head** headland SW Wales, United Kingdom 51°35′N 04°55′W
34 M7 **Saint Helena** California, W USA 38°29′N 122°30′W
67 O12 **Saint Helena** island C Atlantic Ocean
**Saint Helena** see Saint Helena, Ascension and Tristan da Cunha
65 F24 **Saint Helena, Ascension and Tristan da Cunha** terr. Saint Helena, Ascension, Tristan da Cunha. ◇ UK Overseas Territory C Atlantic Ocean
65 M16 **Saint Helena Fracture Zone** tectonic feature C Atlantic Ocean
34 M7 **Saint Helena, Mount** ▲ California, W USA 38°40′N 122°39′W
21 S15 **Saint Helena Sound** inlet South Carolina, SE USA
31 Q7 **Saint Helen, Lake** ◎ Michigan, N USA
183 Q16 **Saint Helens** Tasmania, SE Australia 41°21′S 148°15′E
97 K18 **St Helens** NW England, United Kingdom 53°28′N 02°44′W
32 G10 **Saint Helens** Oregon, NW USA 45°54′N 122°50′W
32 H10 **Saint Helens, Mount** ⛰ Washington, NW USA 46°24′N 121°49′W
97 L26 **St Helier** ○ (Jersey) S Jersey, Channel Islands 49°12′N 02°07′W
15 S9 **St-Hilarion** Québec, SE Canada 47°34′N 70°24′W
99 K22 **Saint-Hubert** Luxembourg, SE Belgium 50°02′N 05°23′E
15 P12 **St-Hyacinthe** Québec, SE Canada 45°38′N 72°57′W
**St.Iago de la Vega** see Spanish Town
31 Q4 **Saint Ignace** Michigan, N USA 45°53′N 84°44′W
15 O10 **St-Ignace-du-Lac** Québec, SE Canada 46°43′N 73°49′W
12 D12 **St. Ignace Island** island Ontario, S Canada
108 C7 **St. Imier** Bern, W Switzerland 47°09′N 06°55′E
97 G25 **St Ives** SW England, United Kingdom 50°12′N 05°29′W
29 U10 **Saint James** Minnesota, N USA 44°00′N 94°36′W
10 I15 **St. James, Cape** headland Graham Island, British Columbia, SW Canada 51°57′N 131°04′W
15 O13 **St-Jean** var. St-Jean-sur-Richelieu. Québec, SE Canada 45°15′N 73°16′W
55 X9 **St-Jean** NW French Guiana 05°25′N 54°05′W
**Saint-Jean-d'Acre** see Akko
102 K11 **St-Jean-d'Angély** Charente-Maritime, W France 45°57′N 00°31′W
103 N7 **St-Jean-de-Braye** Loiret, C France 47°54′N 01°58′E
102 I16 **St-Jean-de-Luz** Pyrénées-Atlantiques, SW France 43°24′N 01°40′W
103 T12 **St-Jean-de-Maurienne** Savoie, E France 45°17′N 06°21′E
102 I9 **St-Jean-de-Monts** Vendée, NW France 46°45′N 02°00′W
103 Q14 **St-Jean-du-Gard** Gard, S France 44°06′N 03°49′E
15 Q7 **St-Jean, Lac** ◎ Québec, SE Canada
102 I16 **St-Jean-Pied-de-Port** Pyrénées-Atlantiques, SW France 43°10′N 01°14′W
15 S9 **St-Jean-Port-Joli** Québec, SE Canada 47°13′N 70°16′W
**St-Jean-sur-Richelieu** see St-Jean
15 N12 **St-Jérôme** Québec, SE Canada 45°47′N 74°01′W
25 T5 **Saint Jo** Texas, SW USA 33°42′N 97°33′W
13 O15 **St. John** New Brunswick, SE Canada 45°16′N 66°03′W
26 L6 **Saint John** Kansas, C USA 37°59′N 98°44′W
19 Q2 **Saint John** Fr. Saint-John. ≈ Canada/USA
76 K16 **Saint John** ≈ C Liberia
45 T9 **Saint John** island C Virgin Islands (US)
**Saint-John** see Saint John
22 I6 **Saint John, Lake** ◎ Louisiana, S USA
45 W10 **St John's** ● (Antigua and Barbuda) Antigua, Antigua and Barbuda 17°06′N 61°50′W
13 V12 **St. John's** province capital Newfoundland and Labrador, E Canada 47°34′N 52°41′W
37 O12 **Saint Johns** Arizona, SW USA 34°28′N 109°22′W
31 Q9 **Saint Johns** Michigan, N USA 43°01′N 84°31′W
13 V12 **St. John's** ✈ Newfoundland and Labrador, E Canada 47°22′N 52°45′W
23 X11 **Saint Johns River** ≈ Florida, SE USA
103 Q11 **St-Jost-St-Rambert** Loire, E France 45°30′N 04°13′E
45 N12 **St. Joseph** W Dominica 15°24′N 61°26′W
173 P17 **St-Joseph** S Réunion
22 J6 **Saint Joseph** Louisiana, S USA 31°56′N 91°14′W
31 O10 **Saint Joseph** Michigan, N USA 42°05′N 86°30′W
27 R3 **Saint Joseph** Missouri, C USA 39°46′N 94°49′W
20 I10 **Saint Joseph** Tennessee, S USA 35°02′N 87°29′W
22 R9 **Saint Joseph Bay** bay Florida, SE USA
15 R11 **St-Joseph-de-Beauce** Québec, SE Canada 46°20′N 70°52′W
12 C10 **St. Joseph, Lake** ◎ Ontario, C Canada
31 Q11 **Saint Joseph River** ≈ N USA
14 C11 **Saint Joseph's Island** island Ontario, S Canada
15 N11 **St-Jovite** Québec, SE Canada 46°07′N 74°35′W
**St. Julian's** see San Ġiljan
**St-Julien** see St-Julien-en-Genevois
103 T10 **St-Julien-en-Genevois** var. St-Julien. Haute-Savoie, E France 46°07′N 06°06′E
102 M11 **St-Junien** Haute-Vienne, C France 45°52′N 00°54′E
96 D8 **St Kilda** island NW Scotland, United Kingdom
45 V10 **Saint Kitts** island Saint Kitts and Nevis
45 U10 **Saint Kitts and Nevis** off. Federation of Saint Christopher and Nevis, var. Saint Christopher-Nevis. ◆ commonwealth republic E West Indies
11 X16 **St. Laurent** Manitoba, S Canada 50°20′N 97°55′W
**St-Laurent** see St-Laurent-du-Maroni
55 X9 **St-Laurent-du-Maroni** var. St-Laurent. NW French Guiana 05°29′N 54°03′W
**St-Laurent, Fleuve** see St. Lawrence
102 J12 **St-Laurent-Médoc** Gironde, SW France 45°11′N 00°50′W
13 N12 **St. Lawrence** Fr. Fleuve St-Laurent. ≈ Canada/USA
13 Q12 **St. Lawrence, Gulf of** gulf NW Atlantic Ocean
38 K10 **Saint Lawrence Island** island Alaska, USA
14 M14 **Saint Lawrence River** ≈ Canada/USA
99 L25 **Saint-Léger** Luxembourg, SE Belgium 49°36′N 05°39′E
13 N14 **St. Léonard** New Brunswick, SE Canada 47°10′N 67°55′W
15 P11 **St-Léonard** Québec, SE Canada 46°06′N 72°18′W
173 O17 **St-Leu** W Réunion 21°09′S 55°17′E
102 J4 **St-Lô** anc. Briovera, Laudus. Manche, N France 49°07′N 01°08′W
11 T15 **St. Louis** Saskatchewan, S Canada 52°50′N 105°43′W
103 V7 **St-Louis** Haut-Rhin, NE France 47°35′N 07°34′E
173 O17 **St-Louis** S Réunion
76 G10 **Saint Louis** NW Senegal 15°59′N 16°30′W
27 X4 **Saint Louis** Missouri, C USA 38°38′N 90°15′W
29 W5 **Saint Louis River** ≈ Minnesota, N USA
103 T7 **St-Loup-sur-Semouse** Haute-Saône, E France 47°53′N 06°15′E
15 O12 **St-Luc** Québec, SE Canada 45°19′N 73°18′W
45 X13 **Saint Lucia** ◆ commonwealth republic SE West Indies
47 S3 **Saint Lucia** island SE West Indies
83 L22 **St. Lucia, Cape** headland E South Africa 28°29′S 32°26′E
45 Y13 **Saint Lucia Channel** channel Martinique/Saint Lucia
23 Y14 **Saint Lucie Canal** canal Florida, SE USA
23 Z13 **Saint Lucie Inlet** inlet Florida, SE USA
96 L2 **St Magnus Bay** bay N Scotland, United Kingdom
102 K10 **St-Maixent-l'École** Deux-Sèvres, W France 46°24′N 00°13′W
11 Y16 **St. Malo** Manitoba, S Canada 49°16′N 96°58′W
102 I5 **St-Malo** Ille-et-Vilaine, NW France 48°39′N 02°00′W
102 H4 **St-Malo, Golfe de** gulf NW France
44 L9 **St-Marc** C Haiti 19°08′N 72°41′W
44 L9 **St-Marc, Canal de** channel W Haiti
103 S12 **St-Marcellin-le-Mollard** Isère, E France 45°12′N 05°18′E
55 Y12 **Saint-Marcel, Mont** ▲ S French Guiana 2°32′N 53°00′W
96 K5 **St Margaret's Hope** NE Scotland, United Kingdom 58°50′N 02°57′W
32 M9 **Saint Maries** Idaho, NW USA 47°19′N 116°37′W
23 T9 **Saint Marks** Florida, SE USA 30°09′N 84°12′W
108 D11 **St. Martin** Valais, SW Switzerland 46°09′N 07°27′E
45 V9 **St Martin** French overseas collectivity E Caribbean Sea
**Saint Martin** see Sint Maarten
31 O5 **Saint Martin Island** island Michigan, N USA
22 I9 **Saint Martinville** Louisiana, S USA 30°09′N 91°51′W
185 E20 **St. Mary, Mount** ▲ South Island, New Zealand 44°16′S 169°42′E
186 E8 **St. Mary, Mount** ▲ S Papua New Guinea 08°06′S 147°00′E
182 I6 **Saint Mary Peak** ▲ South Australia 31°25′S 138°39′E
183 Q16 **Saint Marys** Tasmania, SE Australia 41°34′S 148°13′E
14 E16 **St. Marys** Ontario, S Canada 43°15′N 81°08′W
38 M11 **Saint Marys** Alaska, USA 62°03′N 163°10′W
23 W8 **Saint Marys** Georgia, SE USA 30°44′N 81°30′W
27 P4 **Saint Marys** Kansas, C USA 39°09′N 96°00′W
31 Q4 **Saint Marys** Ohio, N USA 40°31′N 84°22′W
21 R3 **Saint Marys** West Virginia, NE USA 39°24′N 81°13′W
23 W8 **Saint Marys River** ≈ Florida/Georgia, SE USA
31 Q4 **Saint Marys River** ≈ Michigan, N USA
102 D6 **St-Mathieu, Pointe** headland NW France 48°17′N 04°56′W
38 J12 **Saint Matthew Island** island Alaska, USA
21 R13 **Saint Matthews** South Carolina, SE USA 33°40′N 80°44′W
**St.Matthew's Island** see Zadetkyi Kyun
186 G4 **St.Matthias Group** island group NE Papua New Guinea
108 C11 **St. Maurice** Valais, SW Switzerland 46°09′N 07°28′E
15 P9 **St-Maurice** ≈ Québec, SE Canada
102 J13 **St-Médard-en-Jalles** Gironde, SW France 44°54′N 00°43′W
39 N10 **Saint Michael** Alaska, USA 63°28′N 162°02′W
15 N10 **St-Michel-des-Saints** Québec, SE Canada 46°39′N 73°54′W
103 S5 **St-Mihiel** Meuse, NE France 48°57′N 05°33′E
108 J10 **St. Moritz** Ger. Sankt Moritz, Rmsch. San Murezzan. Graubünden, SE Switzerland 46°30′N 09°51′E
102 H8 **St-Nazaire** Loire-Atlantique, NW France 47°17′N 02°12′W
**Saint Nicholas** see São Nicolau
**Saint-Nicolas** see Sint-Niklaas
103 N1 **St-Omer** Pas-de-Calais, N France 50°45′N 02°15′E
102 J11 **Saintonge** cultural region W France
15 S9 **St-Pacôme** Québec, SE Canada 47°22′N 69°56′W
15 S10 **St-Pamphile** Québec, SE Canada 46°57′N 69°46′W
15 S9 **St-Pascal** Québec, SE Canada 47°32N 69°48′W
14 J11 **St-Patrice, Lac** ◎ Québec, SE Canada
11 R14 **St. Paul** Alberta, SW Canada 54°00′N 111°18′W
173 O16 **St-Paul** NW Réunion
38 K14 **Saint Paul** Saint Paul Island, Alaska, USA 57°08′N 170°13′W
29 V8 **Saint Paul** state capital Minnesota, N USA 45°N 93°10′W
29 P15 **Saint Paul** Nebraska, C USA 41°13′N 98°26′W
21 P7 **Saint Paul** Virginia, NE USA 36°53′N 82°18′W
77 Q17 **Saint Paul, Cape** headland S Ghana 05°44′N 00°55′E
103 O17 **St-Paul-de-Fenouillet** Pyrénées-Orientales, S France 42°49′N 02°29′E
65 K14 **Saint Paul Fracture Zone** tectonic feature E Atlantic Ocean
38 J14 **Saint Paul Island** island Pribilof Islands, Alaska, USA
102 J15 **St-Paul-les-Dax** Landes, SW France 43°45′N 01°01′W
21 U11 **Saint Pauls** North Carolina, SE USA 34°45′N 78°56′W
**Saint Paul's Bay** see San Pawl il Bahar
191 R16 **St Paul's Point** headland Pitcairn Island, Pitcairn Islands
29 U10 **Saint Peter** Minnesota, N USA 44°21′N 93°58′W
97 L26 **St Peter Port** ○ (Guernsey) C Guernsey, Channel Islands 49°28′N 02°33′W
23 V13 **Saint Petersburg** Florida, SE USA 27°47′N 82°37′W
**Saint Petersburg** see Sankt-Peterburg
23 V13 **Saint Petersburg Beach** Florida, SE USA 27°43′N 82°43′W
173 P17 **St-Philippe** SE Réunion 21°21′S 55°46′E
45 Q11 **St-Pierre** NW Martinique 14°44′N 61°11′W
173 O17 **St-Pierre** SW Réunion
13 S13 **St-Pierre and Miquelon** Fr. Îles St-Pierre et Miquelon. ◇ French overseas collectivity NE North America
15 P11 **St-Pierre, Lac** ◎ Québec, SE Canada
102 F5 **St-Pol-de-Léon** Finistère, NW France 48°42′N 04°00′W
103 O2 **St-Pol-sur-Ternoise** Pas-de-Calais, N France 50°22′N 02°21′E
**St. Pons** see St-Pons-de-Thomières
103 O16 **St-Pons-de-Thomières** var. St. Pons. Hérault, S France 43°28′N 02°48′E
103 P10 **St-Pourçain-sur-Sioule** Allier, C France 46°19′N 03°16′E
15 S11 **St-Prosper** Québec, SE Canada 46°14′N 70°28′W
103 P3 **St-Quentin** Aisne, N France 49°51′N 03°17′E
15 R10 **St-Raphaël** Québec, SE Canada 46°47′N 70°46′W
103 U15 **St-Raphaël** Var, SE France 43°26′N 06°46′E
15 Q10 **St-Raymond** Québec, SE Canada 46°53′N 71°49′W
33 O9 **Saint Regis** Montana, NW USA 47°18′N 115°06′W
18 J7 **Saint Regis River** ≈ New York, NE USA
103 R15 **St-Rémy-de-Provence** Bouches-du-Rhône, SE France 43°48′N 04°49′E
102 M9 **St-Savin** Vienne, W France 46°34′N 00°53′E
**Saint-Sébastien, Cap** see Anorontany, Tanjona
23 X7 **Saint Simons Island** island Georgia, SE USA
191 Y2 **Saint Stanislas Bay** bay Kiritimati, E Kiribati
13 O15 **St. Stephen** New Brunswick, SE Canada 45°12′N 67°18′W
39 X12 **Saint Terese** Alaska, USA 58°28′N 134°46′W
14 E17 **St. Thomas** Ontario, S Canada 42°46′N 81°12′W
29 Q2 **Saint Thomas** North Dakota, N USA 48°37′N 97°28′W
45 T9 **Saint Thomas** island W Virgin Islands (US)
**Saint Thomas** see São Tomé, Sao Tome and Principe
**Saint Thomas** see Charlotte Amalie, Virgin Islands (US)
15 P10 **St-Tite** Québec, SE Canada 46°42′N 72°32′W
**Saint-Trond** see Sint-Truiden
103 U16 **St-Tropez** Var, SE France 43°16′N 06°39′E
**Saint Ubes** see Setúbal
102 L3 **St-Valéry-en-Caux** Seine-Maritime, N France 49°53′N 00°42′E
103 Q9 **St-Vallier** Saône-et-Loire, C France 46°39′N 04°19′E
106 B7 **St-Vincent** Valle d'Aosta, NW Italy 45°47′N 07°42′E
45 Q14 **Saint Vincent** island N Saint Vincent and the Grenadines
**Saint Vincent** see São Vicente
45 W14 **Saint Vincent and the Grenadines** ◆ commonwealth republic SE West Indies
**Saint-Vincent, Cap** see Ankaboa, Tanjona
**Saint Vincent, Cape** see São Vicente, Cabo de
102 I15 **St-Vincent-de-Tyrosse** Landes, SW France 43°39′N 01°16′W
182 I9 **Saint Vincent, Gulf** gulf South Australia
23 R10 **Saint Vincent Island** island Florida, SE USA
45 T12 **Saint Vincent Passage** passage Saint Lucia/Saint Vincent and the Grenadines
183 N18 **Saint Vincent, Point** headland Tasmania, SE Australia 43°19′S 145°50′E
**Saint-Vith** see Sankt-Vith
11 S14 **St. Walburg** Saskatchewan, S Canada 53°38′N 109°12′W
**St Wolfgangsee** see Wolfgangsee
102 M11 **St-Yrieix-la-Perche** Haute-Vienne, C France 45°31′N 01°12′E
**Saint Yves** see Setúbal
188 H5 **Saipan** island ● (Northern Mariana Islands) S Northern Mariana Islands
188 H6 **Saipan Channel** channel S Northern Mariana Islands
188 H6 **Saipan International** ✈ Saipan, S Northern Mariana Islands
74 G6 **Saïs** ✈ (Fès) C Morocco 33°58′N 04°48′W
**Saishū** see Jeju-do
**Saishū** see Jeju
102 J16 **Saison** ≈ SW France
169 R10 **Sai, Sungai** ≈ Borneo, N Indonesia
165 N13 **Saitama** off. Saitama-ken. ◆ prefecture Honshū, S Japan
**Saitama** see Urawa
**Saitama-ken** see Saitama
**Saiyid Abid** see Sayyid 'Abid
57 J19 **Sajama, Nevado** ▲ W Bolivia 17°57′S 68°51′W
141 V13 **Sājir, Ras** headland S Oman 16°42′N 53°40′E
111 M20 **Sajószentpéter** Borsod-Abaúj-Zemplén, NE Hungary 48°13′N 20°43′E
83 F24 **Sak** ≈ SW South Africa
81 J18 **Saka** Tana River, E Kenya 0°11′S 39°27′E
167 P11 **Sa Kaeo** Prachin Buri, C Thailand 13°47′N 102°03′E
164 J14 **Sakai** Ōsaka, Honshū, SW Japan 34°35′N 135°28′E
164 H14 **Sakaide** Kagawa, Shikoku, SW Japan 34°19′N 133°50′E
164 H12 **Sakaiminato** Tottori, Honshū, SW Japan 35°34′N 133°12′E
140 M3 **Sakākah** Al Jawf, NW Saudi Arabia 29°56′N 40°10′E
28 L4 **Sakakawea, Lake** ◎ North Dakota, N USA
12 J9 **Sakami, Lac** ◎ Québec, C Canada
79 O26 **Sakania** Katanga, SE Dem. Rep. Congo 12°44′S 28°34′E
146 K12 **Sakar** Lebap Welaýaty, E Turkmenistan 38°57′N 63°46′E
172 H7 **Sakaraha** Toliara, SW Madagascar 22°54′S 44°31′E
146 I14 **Sakarçäge** var. Sakarchäge, Rus. Sakar-Chaga. Mary Welaýaty, C Turkmenistan 37°40′N 61°33′E
**Sakar-Chaga/Sakarchäge** see Sakarçäge
**Sakartvelo** see Georgia
136 F11 **Sakarya** ◆ province NW Turkey
136 F12 **Sakarya Nehri** ≈ NW Turkey
165 P9 **Sakata** Yamagata, Honshū, C Japan 38°54′N 139°51′E
123 P9 **Sakha (Yakutiya), Respublika** var. Respublika Yakutiya, Eng. Yakutia. ◆ autonomous republic NE Russia
**Sakhalin** see Sakhalin, Ostrov
192 I3 **Sakhalin, Ostrov** var. Sakhalin. island SE Russia
123 U12 **Sakhalinskaya Oblast'** ◆ province SE Russia
123 T12 **Sakhalinskiy Zaliv** gulf E Russia
**Sakhnovshchina** see Sakhnovshchyna
117 U6 **Sakhnovshchyna** Rus. Sakhnovshchina. Kharkivs'ka Oblast', E Ukraine 49°08′N 35°52′E
**Sakhon Nakhon** see Sakon Nakhon
**Sakhtsar** see Rāmsar
137 W10 **Şäki** Rus. Sheki; prev. Nukha. NW Azerbaijan 41°09′N 47°10′E
**Saki** see Saky
118 E13 **Šakiai** Ger. Schaken. Marijampolė, S Lithuania 54°57′N 23°04′E
165 O16 **Sakishima-shotō** var. Sakisima Syotō. island group SW Japan
**Sakisima Syotō** see Sakishima-shotō
**Sakiz** see Saqqez
**Sakiz-Adasi** see Chíos
155 F19 **Sakleshpur** Karnātaka, E India 12°58′N 75°45′E
167 S9 **Sakon Nakhon** var. Muang Sakon Nakhon, Sakhon Nakhon. Sakon Nakhon, E Thailand 17°10′N 104°08′E
149 P15 **Sakrand** Sindh, SE Pakistan 26°06′N 68°20′E
83 F24 **Sak River** Afr. Sakrivier. Northern Cape, W South Africa 30°49′S 20°24′E
**Sakrivier** see Sak River
**Saksaul'skiy** see Saksaul'skoye
144 K13 **Saksaul'skoye** var. Saksaul'skiy, Kaz. Sekseüil. Kzylorda, S Kazakhstan 47°07′N 61°06′E
95 I25 **Sakskøbing** Sjælland, SE Denmark 54°48′N 11°39′E
165 N12 **Saku** Nagano, Honshū, S Japan 36°17′N 138°29′E
117 S13 **Saky** Rus. Saki. Avtonomna Respublika Krym, S Ukraine 45°09′N 33°36′E
76 E9 **Sal** island Ilhas de Barlavento, NE Cape Verde
127 N12 **Sal** ≈ SW Russia
111 I21 **Sal'a** Hung. Sellye, Vágsellye. Nitriansky Kraj, SW Slovakia 48°09′N 17°51′E
95 N15 **Sala** Västmanland, C Sweden 59°55′N 16°38′E
15 N13 **Salaberry-de-Valleyfield** var. Valleyfield. Québec, SE Canada 45°15′N 74°07′W
118 G7 **Salacgrīva** Est. Salatsi. N Latvia 57°45′N 24°21′E
107 M18 **Sala Consilina** Campania, S Italy 40°23′N 15°35′E
40 C2 **Salada, Laguna** ◎ NW Mexico
61 D14 **Saladas** Corrientes, NE Argentina 28°15′S 58°40′W
61 C21 **Saladillo** Buenos Aires, E Argentina 35°40′S 59°50′W
61 B16 **Saladillo, Río** ≈ C Argentina
25 T9 **Salado** Texas, SW USA 30°57′N 97°32′W
63 J16 **Salado, Arroyo** ≈ SE Argentina
61 D21 **Salado, Río** ≈ E Argentina
62 J12 **Salado, Río** ≈ C Argentina
41 N7 **Salado, Río** ≈ NE Mexico
37 Q12 **Salado, Río** ≈ New Mexico, SW USA
143 N6 **Salafchegān** var. Sarafjagān. Quom, N Iran 34°28′N 50°28′E
77 Q15 **Salaga** C Ghana 08°31′N 00°37′W
139 S6 **Şalāḩ ad Dīn** off. Muḩāfaz̧at Şalāḩ ad Dīn, var. Salahuddin. ◆ governorate C Iraq
**Şalāḩ ad Dīn, Muḩāfaz̧at** see Şalāḩ ad Dīn
**Salahuddin** see Şalāḩ ad Dīn
192 G5 **Sala'ilua** Savai'i, W Samoa 13°39′S 172°33′W
116 G9 **Sălaj** ◆ county NW Romania
83 H20 **Salajwe** Kweneng, SE Botswana 23°40′S 24°46′E
78 H9 **Salal** Bahr el Gazel, W Chad 14°48′N 17°12′E
80 I6 **Salala** Red Sea, NE Sudan 21°17′N 36°16′E
141 V13 **Şalālah** SW Oman 17°01′N 54°04′E
42 D5 **Salamá** Baja Verapaz, C Guatemala 15°06′N 90°18′W
42 J6 **Salamá** Olancho, C Honduras 14°48′N 86°34′W
62 G10 **Salamanca** Coquimbo, C Chile 31°47′S 70°58′W
41 N13 **Salamanca** Guanajuato, C Mexico 20°34′N 101°12′W
104 K7 **Salamanca** anc. Helmantica, Salmantica. Castilla y León, NW Spain 40°58′N 05°40′W
18 D11 **Salamanca** New York, NE USA 42°09′N 78°43′W
104 J7 **Salamanca** ◆ province Castilla y León, W Spain
63 J19 **Salamanca, Pampa de** plain S Argentina
78 J12 **Salamat** off. Région du Salamat. ◆ region SE Chad
78 I12 **Salamat, Bahr** ≈ S Chad
**Salamat, Région du** see Salamat
54 F5 **Salamina** Magdalena, N Colombia 10°30′N 74°48′W
115 G19 **Salamína** var. Salamís. Salamína, C Greece 37°58′N 23°29′E
115 G19 **Salamína** island C Greece
**Salamís** see Salamína
138 I5 **Salamīyah** var. As Salamīyah. Ḩamāh, W Syria 35°01′N 37°02′E
31 P12 **Salamonie Lake** ⊠ Indiana, N USA
31 P12 **Salamonie River** ≈ Indiana, N USA
**Salang** see Phuket
192 I16 **Salani** Upolu, SE Samoa 14°00′S 171°35′W
118 C11 **Salantai** Klaipėda, NW Lithuania 56°05′N 21°36′E
104 K2 **Salas** Asturias, N Spain 43°25′N 06°15′W
105 O5 **Salas de los Infantes** Castilla y León, N Spain 42°02′N 03°17′W
102 M16 **Salat** ≈ S France
189 V13 **Salat** island Chuuk, C Micronesia
169 Q16 **Salatiga** Jawa, C Indonesia 07°15′S 110°34′E
189 V13 **Salat Pass** passage W Pacific Ocean
**Salatsi** see Salacgrīva
167 T10 **Salavan** var. Saravan, Saravane. Salavan, S Laos 15°43′N 106°26′E
127 V6 **Salavat** Respublika Bashkortostan, W Russia 53°20′N 55°54′E
56 C12 **Salaverry** La Libertad, N Peru 08°14′S 78°55′W
171 T12 **Salawati, Pulau** island E Indonesia
193 R10 **Sala y Gomez** island Chile, E Pacific Ocean
**Sala y Gomez Fracture Zone** see Sala y Gomez Ridge
193 S10 **Sala y Gomez Ridge** var. Sala y Gomez Fracture Zone. tectonic feature SE Pacific Ocean
61 A22 **Salazar** Buenos Aires, E Argentina 36°20′S 62°11′W
54 G7 **Salazar** Norte de Santander, N Colombia 07°46′N 72°46′W
**Salazar** see N'Dalatando
173 P16 **Salazie** C Réunion 21°02′S 55°33′E
103 N8 **Salbris** Loir-et-Cher, C France 47°25′N 02°02′E
57 G15 **Salcantay, Nevado** ▲ C Peru 13°21′S 72°31′W
45 O8 **Salcedo** N Dominican Republic 19°26′N 70°25′W
39 S9 **Salcha River** ≈ Alaska, USA
119 H15 **Šalčininkai** Vilnius, SE Lithuania 54°20′N 25°26′E
**Saldae** see Béjaïa
54 E11 **Saldaña** Tolima, C Colombia 03°57′N 75°01′W
104 M4 **Saldaña** Castilla y León, N Spain 42°31′N 04°44′W
83 E25 **Saldanha** Western Cape, SW South Africa 33°00′S 17°56′E
**Salduba** see Zaragoza
61 B23 **Saldungaray** Buenos Aires, E Argentina 38°15′S 61°45′W
118 D9 **Saldus** Ger. Frauenburg. W Latvia 56°40′N 22°29′E
183 P13 **Sale** Victoria, SE Australia 38°06′S 147°06′E
74 F6 **Salé** NW Morocco 34°07′N 06°40′W
74 F6 **Salé** ✈ (Rabat) W Morocco 34°09′N 06°30′W
**Salehābād** see Andīmeshk
170 M16 **Saleh, Teluk** bay Nusa Tenggara, S Indonesia
122 H8 **Salekhard** prev. Obdorsk. Yamalo-Nenetskiy Avtonomnyy Okrug, N Russia 66°33′N 66°35′E
192 H16 **Sālelologa** Savai'i, C Samoa 13°42′S 172°10′W
155 H21 **Salem** Tamil Nādu, SE India 11°38′N 78°08′E
27 V9 **Salem** Arkansas, C USA 36°21′N 91°49′W
30 L15 **Salem** Illinois, N USA 38°37′N 88°57′W
31 P15 **Salem** Indiana, N USA 38°38′N 86°06′W
19 P11 **Salem** Massachusetts, NE USA 42°30′N 70°51′W
27 V6 **Salem** Missouri, C USA 37°39′N 91°32′W
18 I16 **Salem** New Jersey, NE USA 39°33′N 75°26′W
31 U12 **Salem** Ohio, N USA 40°52′N 80°51′W
32 G12 **Salem** state capital Oregon, NW USA 44°57′N 123°01′W
29 Q11 **Salem** South Dakota, N USA 43°43′N 97°23′W
36 L4 **Salem** Utah, W USA 40°03′N 111°40′W
21 S7 **Salem** Virginia, NE USA 37°16′N 80°00′W
21 R3 **Salem** West Virginia, NE USA 39°15′N 80°32′W
107 H23 **Salemi** Sicilia, Italy, C Mediterranean Sea 37°48′N 12°48′E
**Salemy** see As Sālimī
94 K12 **Sälen** Dalarna, C Sweden 61°11′N 13°14′E
107 Q18 **Salentina, Campi** Puglia, SE Italy 40°23′N 18°01′E
107 Q18 **Salentina, Penisola** peninsula SE Italy
107 L18 **Salerno** anc. Salernum. Campania, S Italy 40°40′N 14°44′E
107 L18 **Salerno, Golfo di** Eng. Gulf of Salerno. gulf S Italy
**Salerno, Gulf of** see Salerno, Golfo di
**Salernum** see Salerno
97 K17 **Salford** NW England, United Kingdom 53°30′N 02°16′W
**Salgir** see Salhyr
111 K21 **Salgótarján** Nógrád, N Hungary 48°07′N 19°47′E
59 O15 **Salgueiro** Pernambuco, E Brazil 08°04′S 39°05′W
94 C13 **Salhus** Hordaland, S Norway 60°30′N 05°15′E
117 T12 **Salhyr** Rus. Salgir. ≈ S Ukraine
171 Q9 **Salibabu, Pulau** island N Indonesia
37 S6 **Salida** Colorado, C USA 38°29′N 105°57′W
102 J15 **Salies-de-Béarn** Pyrénées-Atlantiques, SW France 43°28′N 00°55′W
136 C14 **Salihli** Manisa, W Turkey 38°29′N 28°08′E
119 K18 **Salihorsk** Rus. Soligorsk. Minskaya Voblasts', S Belarus 52°48′N 27°32′E
119 K18 **Salihorskaye Vodaskhovishcha** Rus. Soligorskoye Vodokhranilishche. ⊠ C Belarus
83 N14 **Salima** Central, C Malawi 13°44′S 34°21′E
166 L5 **Salin** Magway, W Myanmar (Burma) 20°30′N 94°40′E




◆ Country ● Country Capital ◇ Dependent Territory ○ Dependent Territory Capital ◆ Administrative Regions ✈ International Airport ▲ Mountain ▲ Mountain Range ⛰ Volcano ≈ River ◎ Lake ⊠ Reservoir

SALINA – SAN FRANCISCO DEL RINCÓN


27 N4 **Salina** Kansas, C USA 38°53′N 97°36′W
36 L5 **Salina** Utah, W USA 38°57′N 111°54′W
41 S17 **Salina Cruz** Oaxaca, SE Mexico 16°11′N 95°12′W
107 L22 **Salina, Isola** *island* Isole Eolie, S Italy
44 J5 **Salina Point** *headland* Acklins Island, SE The Bahamas 22°10′N 74°16′W
56 A7 **Salinas** Santa Elena, W Ecuador 02°15′S 80°58′W
40 M11 **Salinas** *var.* Salinas de Hidalgo. San Luis Potosí, C Mexico 22°36′N 101°41′W
45 T6 **Salinas** C Puerto Rico 17°57′N 66°18′W
35 O10 **Salinas** California, W USA 36°41′N 121°40′W
**Salinas, Cabo de** *see* Salines, Cap de ses
**Salinas de Hidalgo** *see* Salinas
82 A13 **Salinas, Ponta das** *headland* W Angola 12°50′S 12°57′E
45 O10 **Salinas, Punta** *headland* S Dominican Republic 18°11′N 70°32′W
**Salinas, Río** *see* Chixoy, Río
35 O11 **Salinas River** California, W USA
22 H6 **Saline Lake** ◎ Louisiana, S USA
25 R17 **Salineno** Texas, SW USA 26°29′N 99°06′W
27 V14 **Saline River** Arkansas, C USA
30 M17 **Saline River** Illinois, N USA
105 X10 **Salines, Cap de ses** *var.* Cabo de Salinas. *headland* Mallorca, Spain, W Mediterranean Sea 39°15′N 03°03′E
**Salisburg** *see* Mazsalaca
45 O12 **Salisbury** *var.* Barouï. W Dominica 15°26′N 61°27′W
97 M23 **Salisbury** *var.* New Sarum. S England, United Kingdom 51°05′N 01°48′W
21 Y4 **Salisbury** Maryland, NE USA 38°22′N 75°37′W
27 T3 **Salisbury** Missouri, C USA 39°25′N 92°48′W
21 S9 **Salisbury** North Carolina, SE USA 35°40′N 80°28′W
**Salisbury** *see* Harare
9 Q7 **Salisbury Island** *island* Nunavut, NE Canada
**Salisbury, Lake** *see* Bisina, Lake
97 L23 **Salisbury Plain** *plain* S England, United Kingdom
21 R14 **Salkehatchie River** South Carolina, SE USA
138 I9 **Şalkhad** As Suwaydā', SW Syria 32°29′N 36°42′E
92 M12 **Salla** Lappi, NE Finland 66°50′N 28°40′E
**Sállan** *see* Sørøya
103 U11 **Sallanches** Haute-Savoie, E France 45°55′N 06°37′E
105 V5 **Sallent** Cataluña, NE Spain 41°48′N 01°52′E
**Salliq** *see* Coral Harbour
61 A22 **Salliqueló** Buenos Aires, E Argentina 36°45′S 62°55′W
27 R10 **Sallisaw** Oklahoma, C USA 35°27′N 94°49′W
80 I7 **Sallom** Red Sea, NE Sudan 19°17′N 37°02′E
12 J2 **Salluit** *prev.* Saglouc, Sagluk. Québec, NE Canada 62°10′N 75°40′W
**Sallyana** *see* Şalyān
13 S11 **Sally's Cove** Newfoundland and Labrador, E Canada 49°43′N 58°00′W
139 W9 **Salmān Bin 'Arāzah** Maysān, E Iraq 32°33′N 46°36′E
**Salmantica** *see* Salamanca
142 I2 **Salmās** *prev.* Dilman, Shāpūr. Āzarbāyjān-e Gharbī, NW Iran 38°13′N 44°50′E
124 I11 **Salmi** Respublika Kareliya, NW Russia 61°21′N 31°55′E
33 P12 **Salmon** Idaho, NW USA 45°10′N 113°54′W
11 N16 **Salmon Arm** British Columbia, SW Canada 50°41′N 119°18′W
192 L5 **Salmon Bank** *undersea feature* N Pacific Ocean 26°55′N 176°28′W
**Salmon Leap** *see* Leixlip
34 L2 **Salmon Mountains** ▲▲ California, W USA
14 J15 **Salmon Point** *headland* Ontario, SE Canada 43°51′N 77°15′W
33 N11 **Salmon River** Idaho, NW USA
18 K6 **Salmon River** New York, NE USA
33 N12 **Salmon River Mountains** ▲▲ Idaho, NW USA
18 I9 **Salmon River Reservoir** ⊠ New York, NE USA
93 K19 **Salo** Varsinais-Suomi, SW Finland 60°23′N 23°10′E
106 F7 **Salò** Lombardia, N Italy 45°37′N 10°30′E
**Salona/Salonae** *see* Solin
103 S15 **Salon-de-Provence** Bouches-du-Rhône, SE France 43°39′N 05°05′E
**Salonica/Salonika** *see* Thessaloníki
115 I14 **Salonikiós, Akrotírio** *var.* Akrotírio Salonikós. *headland* Thásos, E Greece 40°34′N 24°39′E
**Salonikós, Akrotírio** *see* Salonikiós, Akrotírio
116 F10 **Salonta** *Hung.* Nagyszalonta. Bihor, W Romania 46°49′N 21°40′E
104 I9 **Salor** W Spain
105 U6 **Salou** Cataluña, NE Spain 41°05′N 01°08′E
76 H11 **Saloum** C Senegal
42 H4 **Sal, Punta** *headland* NW Honduras 15°55′N 87°36′W
92 N3 **Salpynten** *headland* W Svalbard 78°12′N 12°11′E
138 I3 **Salqīn** Idlib, W Syria 36°09′N 36°27′E
93 F14 **Salsbruket** Nord-Trøndelag, C Norway 64°49′N 11°48′E
126 M13 **Sal'sk** Rostovskaya Oblast', SW Russia 46°30′N 41°31′E
107 K25 **Salso** Sicilia, Italy, C Mediterranean Sea
107 J25 **Salso** Sicilia, Italy, C Mediterranean Sea
106 E9 **Salsomaggiore Terme** Emilia-Romagna, N Italy 44°49′N 09°58′E
**Salt** *see* As Salṭ
62 J6 **Salta** Salta, NW Argentina 24°47′S 65°23′W
62 K6 **Salta** *off.* Provincia de Salta. ◈ *province* N Argentina
**Salta, Provincia de** *see* Salta
97 I24 **Saltash** SW England, United Kingdom 50°26′N 04°14′W
24 I8 **Salt Basin** *basin* Texas, SW USA
11 V16 **Saltcoats** Saskatchewan, S Canada 51°06′N 102°12′W
30 L13 **Salt Creek** Illinois, N USA
24 J9 **Salt Draw** Texas, SW USA
97 F21 **Saltee Islands** *island group* SE Ireland
92 G12 **Saltfjorden** *inlet* C Norway
24 I8 **Salt Flat** Texas, SW USA 31°43′N 105°05′W
27 N8 **Salt Fork Arkansas River** Oklahoma, C USA
31 T13 **Salt Fork Lake** ⊠ Ohio, N USA
26 J11 **Salt Fork Red River** Oklahoma/Texas, C USA
95 J23 **Saltholm** *island* E Denmark
41 N8 **Saltillo** Coahuila, NE Mexico 25°30′N 101°W
182 L5 **Salt Lake** *salt lake* New South Wales, SE Australia
37 V15 **Salt Lake** ◎ New Mexico, SW USA
36 K2 **Salt Lake City** *state capital* Utah, W USA 40°45′N 111°54′W
61 C20 **Salto** Buenos Aires, E Argentina 34°18′S 60°17′W
61 D17 **Salto** Salto, N Uruguay 31°23′S 57°58′W
61 E17 **Salto** ◈ *department* N Uruguay
107 I14 **Salto** C Italy
62 Q6 **Salto del Guairá** Canindeyú, E Paraguay 24°06′S 54°22′W
61 D17 **Salto Grande, Embalse de** *var.* Lago de Salto Grande. ⊠ Argentina/Uruguay
**Salto Grande, Lago de** *see* Salto Grande, Embalse de
35 W16 **Salton Sea** ◎ California, W USA
60 I12 **Salto Santiago, Represa de** ⊠ S Brazil
149 U7 **Salt Range** ▲▲ E Pakistan
36 M13 **Salt River** Arizona, SW USA
20 L5 **Salt River** Kentucky, S USA
27 V3 **Salt River** Missouri, C USA
95 F17 **Saltrød** Aust-Agder, S Norway 58°28′N 08°49′E
95 P16 **Saltsjöbaden** Stockholm, C Sweden 59°15′N 18°20′E
92 G12 **Saltstraumen** Nordland, C Norway 67°16′N 14°42′E
21 Q7 **Saltville** Virginia, NE USA 36°52′N 81°48′W
**Saluces/Saluciae** *see* Saluzzo
21 Q12 **Saluda** South Carolina, SE USA 34°00′N 81°47′W
21 X6 **Saluda** Virginia, NE USA 37°36′N 76°36′W
21 Q12 **Saluda River** South Carolina, SE USA
**Salûm** *see* As Sallūm
152 F14 **Sālūmbar** Rājasthān, N India 24°16′N 74°04′E
**Salûm, Gulf of** *see* Khalīj as Sallūm
171 O11 **Salumpaga** Sulawesi, N Indonesia 01°18′N 120°58′E
155 M14 **Sālūr** Andhra Pradesh, E India 18°31′N 83°16′E
55 Y9 **Salut, Îles du** *island group* N French Guiana
106 A9 **Saluzzo** *Fr.* Saluces; *anc.* Saluciae. Piemonte, NW Italy 44°39′N 07°29′E
63 F23 **Salvación, Bahía** *bay* S Chile
59 P17 **Salvador** *prev.* São Salvador. *state capital* Bahia, E Brazil 12°58′S 38°29′W
65 E24 **Salvador** East Falkland, Falkland Islands 51°28′S 58°22′W
22 K10 **Salvador, Lake** ◎ Louisiana, S USA
**Salvaleón de Higüey** *see* Higüey
104 F10 **Salvaterra de Magos** Santarém, C Portugal 39°01′N 08°47′W
41 N13 **Salvatierra** Guanajuato, C Mexico 20°14′N 100°52′W
105 P3 **Salvatierra** *Basq.* Agurain. País Vasco, N Spain 42°52′N 02°23′W
**Salween** *see* Thanlwin
137 Y12 **Salyan** *Rus.* Sal'yany. SE Azerbaijan 39°36′N 48°57′E
153 N11 **Salyan** *var.* Sallyana. Mid Western, W Nepal 28°22′N 82°10′E
**Sal'yany** *see* Salyan
21 O6 **Salyersville** Kentucky, S USA 37°43′N 83°06′W
109 V6 **Salza** E Austria
109 Q7 **Salzach** Austria/Germany
109 Q6 **Salzburg** *anc.* Juvavum. Salzburg, N Austria 47°48′N 13°03′E
109 O8 **Salzburg** *off.* Land Salzburg. ◈ *state* C Austria
**Salzburg** *see* Ocna Sibiului
**Salzburg Alps** *see* Salzburger Kalkalpen
109 Q7 **Salzburger Kalkalpen** *Eng.* Salzburg Alps. ▲▲ C Austria
**Salzburg, Land** *see* Salzburg
100 J13 **Salzgitter** *prev.* Watenstedt-Salzgitter. Niedersachsen, C Germany 52°07′N 10°24′E
101 G14 **Salzkotten** Nordrhein-Westfalen, W Germany 51°40′N 08°36′E
100 K11 **Salzwedel** Sachsen-Anhalt, N Germany 52°51′N 11°10′E
152 D11 **Sām** Rājasthān, NW India 26°50′N 70°30′E
**Samac** *see* Bosanski Šamac
54 G9 **Samacá** Boyacá, C Colombia 05°28′N 73°33′W
40 I7 **Samachique** Chihuahua, N Mexico 27°17′N 107°28′W
141 Y8 **Şamad** NE Oman 22°47′N 58°12′E
**Sama de Langreo** *see* Sama, Spain
**Samaden** *see* Samedan
57 M19 **Samaipata** Santa Cruz, C Bolivia 18°08′S 63°53′W
**Samakhixai** *see* Attapu
**Samakov** *see* Samokov
42 B6 **Samalá, Río** SW Guatemala
40 J3 **Samalayuca** Chihuahua, N Mexico 31°25′N 106°30′W
155 L16 **Sāmalkot** Andhra Pradesh, E India 17°03′N 82°15′E
45 P8 **Samaná** *var.* Santa Bárbara de Samaná. E Dominican Republic 19°14′N 69°20′W
45 P8 **Samaná, Bahía de** *bay* E Dominican Republic
44 K4 **Samana Cay** *island* SE The Bahamas
136 K17 **Samandağı** Hatay, S Turkey 36°07′N 35°55′E
149 P3 **Samangān** ◈ *province* N Afghanistan
**Samangān** *see* Aibak
165 T5 **Samani** Hokkaidō, NE Japan 42°07′N 142°57′E
54 C13 **Samaniego** Nariño, SW Colombia 01°22′N 77°35′W
171 Q5 **Samar** *island* C Philippines
127 S6 **Samara** *prev.* Kuybyshev. Samarskaya Oblast', W Russia 53°15′N 50°15′E
127 T7 **Samara** W Russia
127 S6 **Samara** ✈ Samarskaya Oblast', W Russia 53°11′N 50°27′E
117 V7 **Samara** E Ukraine
186 G10 **Samarai** Milne Bay, SE Papua New Guinea 10°36′S 150°39′E
**Samarang** *see* Semarang
123 T14 **Samarga** Khabarovskiy Kray, SE Russia 47°43′N 139°08′E
138 G9 **Samarian Hills** *hill range* N Israel
54 L9 **Samariapo** Amazonas, C Venezuela 05°16′N 67°43′W
169 V11 **Samarinda** Borneo, C Indonesia 0°30′S 117°09′E
**Samarkand** *see* Samarqand
**Samarkandskaya Oblast'** *see* Samarqand Viloyati
**Samarkandski/Samarkandskoye** *see* Temirtau
**Samarobriva** *see* Amiens
147 N11 **Samarqand** *Rus.* Samarkand. Samarqand Viloyati, C Uzbekistan 39°40′N 66°56′E
146 M11 **Samarqand Viloyati** *Rus.* Samarkandskaya Oblast'. ◈ *province* C Uzbekistan
139 S6 **Sāmarrā'** Şalāḩ ad Dīn, C Iraq 34°13′N 43°52′E
127 R7 **Samarskaya Oblast'** *prev.* Kuybyshevskaya Oblast'. ◈ *province* W Russia
153 Q13 **Samastīpur** Bihār, N India 25°52′N 85°47′E
76 L14 **Samatiguila** NW Ivory Coast 09°51′N 07°36′W
**Samawa** *see* As Samāwah
137 Y11 **Şamaxı** *Rus.* Shemakha. E Azerbaijan 40°38′N 48°34′E
79 K18 **Samba** Equateur, NW Dem. Rep. Congo 0°13′N 21°17′E
79 N21 **Samba** Maniema, E Dem. Rep. Congo 04°41′S 26°23′E
152 H6 **Samba** Jammu and Kashmir, NW India 32°32′N 75°08′E
169 W10 **Sambaliung, Pegunungan** ▲▲ Borneo, N Indonesia
154 M11 **Sambalpur** Odisha, E India 21°28′N 84°04′E
67 X12 **Sambao** W Madagascar
169 Q10 **Sambas, Sungai** Borneo, N Indonesia
172 K2 **Sambava** Antsiranana, NE Madagascar 14°16′S 50°10′E
152 J10 **Sambhal** Uttar Pradesh, N India 28°35′N 78°34′E
152 H12 **Sāmbhar Salt Lake** ◎ N India
107 N21 **Sambiase** Calabria, SW Italy 38°58′N 16°16′E
116 H5 **Sambir** *Rus.* Sambor. L'vivs'ka Oblast', NW Ukraine 49°31′N 23°10′E
82 C13 **Sambo** Huambo, C Angola 13°07′S 16°06′E
**Sambor** *see* Sambir
61 E21 **Samborombón, Bahía** *bay* NE Argentina
99 H20 **Sambre** Belgium/France
43 V16 **Sambú, Río** SE Panama
163 Z14 **Samcheok** *Jap.* Sanchoku; *prev.* Samch'ŏk. NE South Korea 37°21′N 129°12′E
**Samch'ŏk** *see* Samcheok
**Samch'ŏnp'o** *see* Sacheon
81 I21 **Same** Kilimanjaro, NE Tanzania 04°04′S 37°41′E
108 J10 **Samedan** *Ger.* Samaden. Graubünden, S Switzerland 46°31′N 09°51′E
82 K12 **Samfya** Luapula, N Zambia 11°22′S 29°34′E
141 W13 **Samḩān, Jabal** ▲▲ SW Oman
115 C18 **Sámi** Kefallonía, Iónia Nisiá, Greece, C Mediterranean Sea 38°15′N 20°39′E
56 F10 **Samiria, Río** N Peru
**Samirum** *see* Semīrom
167 Q13 **Samit** *prev.* Phumĭ Samĭt. Koh Kong, SW Cambodia 10°54′N 103°09′E
137 V11 **Şämkir** *Rus.* Shamkhor. NW Azerbaijan 40°51′N 46°03′E
167 S7 **Sam, Nam** *Vtn.* Sông Chu. Laos/Vietnam
**Samnān** *see* Semnān
**Sam Neua** *see* Xam Nua
75 P10 **Samnū** C Libya 27°19′N 15°01′E
192 H15 **Samoa** *off.* Independent State of Samoa, *var.* Sāmoa, Malo Sa'oloto Tuto'atasi o Samoa; *prev.* Western Samoa. ◆ *monarchy* W Polynesia
192 L9 **Sāmoa** *island group* C Pacific Ocean
**Sāmoa** *see* Samoa
175 T9 **Samoa Basin** *undersea feature* W Pacific Ocean
**Samoa, Independent State of** *see* Samoa
**Samoa, Malo Sa'oloto Tuto'atasi o** *see* Samoa
112 D8 **Samobor** Zagreb, N Croatia 45°48′N 15°38′E
114 H10 **Samokov** *var.* Samakov. Sofia, W Bulgaria 42°19′N 23°34′E
111 H21 **Šamorín** *Ger.* Sommerein, *Hung.* Somorja. Trnavský Kraj, W Slovakia 48°01′N 17°18′E
115 M19 **Sámos** *prev.* Limín Vathéos. Sámos, Dodekánisa, Greece, Aegean Sea 37°45′N 26°58′E
115 M20 **Sámos** *island* Dodekánisa, Greece, Aegean Sea
**Samosch** *see* Szamos
168 I9 **Samosir, Pulau** *island* W Indonesia
**Samothrace** *see* Samothráki
115 K14 **Samothráki** Samothráki, NE Greece 40°28′N 25°31′E
115 J14 **Samothráki** *anc.* Samothrace. *island* NE Greece
115 A15 **Samothráki** *island* Iónia Nisiá, Greece, C Mediterranean Sea
**Samotschin** *see* Szamocin
**Sampê** *see* Xiangcheng
169 S13 **Sampit** Borneo, C Indonesia 02°30′S 112°30′E
169 S12 **Sampit, Sungai** Borneo, N Indonesia
**Sampoku** *see* Sanpoku
186 H7 **Sampun** New Britain, E Papua New Guinea 05°19′S 152°06′E
79 N24 **Sampwe** Katanga, SE Dem. Rep. Congo 09°17′S 27°22′E
167 R11 **Samraong** *var.* Sâmraông. Oddar Meanchey, NW Cambodia 14°11′N 103°31′E
**Sâmraông** *see* Samraong
25 X8 **Sam Rayburn Reservoir** ⊠ Texas, SW USA
167 Q6 **Sam Sao, Phou** ▲▲ Laos/Thailand
95 H22 **Samsø** *island* E Denmark
95 H23 **Samsø Bælt** *channel* E Denmark
167 T7 **Sâm Sơn** Thanh Hoa, N Vietnam 19°44′N 105°53′E
136 L11 **Samsun** *anc.* Amisus. Samsun, N Turkey 41°17′N 36°22′E
136 K11 **Samsun** ◈ *province* N Turkey
137 R9 **Samt'redia** *prev.* Samtredia. W Georgia 42°09′N 42°20′E
**Samtredia** *see* Samt'redia
59 E15 **Samuel, Represa de** ⊠ W Brazil
167 O14 **Samui, Ko** *island* SW Thailand
**Samundari** *see* Samundri
149 U9 **Samundri** *var.* Samundari. Punjab, E Pakistan 31°04′N 72°58′E
137 X10 **Samur** Azerbaijan/Russia
137 Y11 **Samur-Abşeron Kanalı** *Rus.* Sam ur-Apsheronskiy Kanal. *canal* E Azerbaijan
**Sam ur-Apsheronskiy Kanal** *see* Samur-Abşeron Kanalı
167 O11 **Samut Prakan** *var.* Muang Samut Prakan, Paknam. Samut Prakan, C Thailand 13°36′N 100°36′E
167 O11 **Samut Sakhon** *var.* Maha Chai, Samut Sakorn, Tha Chin. Samut Sakhon, C Thailand 13°31′N 100°15′E
**Samut Sakorn** *see* Samut Sakhon
167 O11 **Samut Songkhram** *prev.* Meklong. Samut Songkhram, SW Thailand 13°25′N 100°01′E
77 N12 **San** Ségou, C Mali 13°21′N 04°57′W
111 O15 **San** SE Poland
**sanaebastian** *see* Donostia
141 O15 **Şan'ā'** *Eng.* Sanaa. ● (Yemen) W Yemen 15°24′N 44°14′E
112 F11 **Sana** NW Bosnia and Herzegovina
80 O12 **Sanaag** *off.* Gobolka Sanaag. ◈ *region* N Somalia
**Sanaag, Gobolka** *see* Sanaag
114 J8 **Sanadinovo** Pleven, N Bulgaria 43°33′N 25°00′E
195 P1 **Sanae IV** *research station* (South Africa) Antarctica 70°19′S 01°31′W
139 Y10 **Sanāf, Hawr as** ◎ S Iraq
79 E15 **Sanaga** C Cameroon
54 D12 **San Agustín** Huila, SW Colombia 01°53′N 76°14′W
171 R8 **San Agustin, Cape** *headland* Mindanao, S Philippines 06°17′N 126°12′E
37 Q13 **San Agustin, Plains of** *plain* New Mexico, SW USA
38 M16 **Sanak Islands** *island* Aleutian Islands, Alaska, USA
**San Alessandro** *see* Kita-Iō-jima
193 U10 **San Ambrosio, Isla** *Eng.* San Ambrosio Island. *island* W Chile
**San Ambrosio Island** *see* San Ambrosio, Isla
171 Q12 **Sanana** Pulau Sanana, E Indonesia 02°04′S 125°58′E
171 Q12 **Sanana, Pulau** *island* Maluku, E Indonesia
142 K5 **Sanandaj** *prev.* Sinneh. Kordestān, W Iran 35°18′N 47°01′E
35 P8 **San Andreas** California, W USA 38°10′N 120°40′W
2 C13 **San Andreas Fault** *fault* W USA
54 G8 **San Andrés** Santander, C Colombia 06°52′N 72°53′W
61 C20 **San Andrés de Giles** Buenos Aires, E Argentina 34°27′S 59°27′W
37 R14 **San Andres Mountains** ▲▲ New Mexico, SW USA
41 S15 **San Andrés Tuxtla** *var.* Tuxtla. Veracruz, E Mexico 18°28′N 95°15′W
25 P8 **San Angelo** Texas, SW USA 31°28′N 100°26′W
107 A20 **San Antioco, Isola di** *island* W Italy
42 F4 **San Antonio** Toledo, S Belize 16°13′N 89°02′W
62 G11 **San Antonio** Valparaíso, C Chile 33°35′S 71°38′W
188 H6 **San Antonio** Saipan, S Northern Mariana Islands
37 R13 **San Antonio** New Mexico, SW USA 33°53′N 106°52′W
25 R12 **San Antonio** Texas, SW USA 29°25′N 98°30′W
54 M11 **San Antonio** Amazonas, S Venezuela 03°31′N 66°47′W
54 I7 **San Antonio** Barinas, C Venezuela 07°24′N 71°28′W
55 O5 **San Antonio** Monagas, NE Venezuela 10°03′N 63°45′W
25 S12 **San Antonio** ✈ Texas, SW USA 29°31′N 98°11′W
**San Antonio** *see* San Antonio del Táchira
**San Antonio Abad** *see* Sant Antoni de Portmany
25 U13 **San Antonio Bay** *inlet* Texas, SW USA
61 E22 **San Antonio, Cabo** *headland* E Argentina 36°45′S 56°40′W
44 A5 **San Antonio, Cabo de** *headland* W Cuba 21°51′N 84°58′W
105 T11 **San Antonio, Cabo de** *headland* E Spain 38°50′N 00°09′E
54 H7 **San Antonio de Caparo** Táchira, W Venezuela 07°34′N 71°28′W
62 J5 **San Antonio de los Cobres** Salta, NE Argentina 24°10′S 66°17′W
54 H7 **San Antonio del Táchira** *var.* San Antonio. Táchira, W Venezuela 07°48′N 72°28′W
35 T15 **San Antonio, Mount** ▲ California, W USA 34°18′N 117°37′W
63 K16 **San Antonio Oeste** Río Negro, E Argentina 40°45′S 64°58′W
25 T13 **San Antonio River** Texas, SW USA
54 J5 **Sanare** Lara, N Venezuela 09°45′N 69°39′W
103 T16 **Sanary-sur-Mer** Var, SE France 43°07′N 05°48′E
104 G3 **Sanata Uxía de Ribeira** *var.* Ribeira. Galicia, NW Spain 42°33′N 09°01′W
25 X8 **San Augustine** Texas, SW USA 31°32′N 94°09′W
**San Augustine** *see* Minami-Iō-jima
141 T13 **Sanāw** *var.* Sanaw. NE Yemen 18°N 51°E
41 O11 **San Bartolo** San Luis Potosí, C Mexico 22°20′N 100°05′W
107 L16 **San Bartolomeo in Galdo** Campania, S Italy 41°24′N 15°01′E
106 K13 **San Benedetto del Tronto** Marche, C Italy 42°57′N 13°53′E
42 E3 **San Benito** Petén, N Guatemala 16°56′N 89°53′W
25 T17 **San Benito** Texas, SW USA 26°07′N 97°37′W
54 E6 **San Benito Abad** Sucre, N Colombia 08°56′N 75°02′W
35 P11 **San Benito Mountain** ▲ California, W USA 36°21′N 120°37′W
35 O10 **San Benito River** California, W USA
108 H10 **San Bernardino** Graubünden, S Switzerland 46°21′N 09°13′E
35 U15 **San Bernardino** California, W USA 34°06′N 117°15′W
35 U15 **San Bernardino Mountains** ▲▲ California, W USA
62 H11 **San Bernardo** Santiago, C Chile 33°37′S 70°45′W
40 J8 **San Bernardo** Durango, C Mexico 25°58′N 105°27′W
164 G12 **Sanbe-san** ▲ Kyūshū, SW Japan 35°09′N 132°36′E
**San Bizenti-Barakaldo** *see* San Vicente de Barakaldo
40 J12 **San Blas** Nayarit, C Mexico 21°35′N 105°20′W
40 H8 **San Blas** Sinaloa, C Mexico 26°05′N 108°44′W
**San Blas** *see* Guna Yala
43 U14 **San Blas, Archipiélago de** *island group* NE Panama
23 Q10 **San Blas, Cape** *headland* Florida, SE USA 29°39′N 85°21′W
43 V14 **San Blas, Cordillera de** ▲▲ NE Panama
62 J8 **San Blas de los Sauces** Catamarca, NW Argentina 28°18′S 67°12′W
106 G8 **San Bonifacio** Veneto, NE Italy 45°22′N 11°14′E
29 S12 **Sanborn** Iowa, C USA 43°10′N 95°39′W
40 M7 **San Buenaventura** Coahuila, NE Mexico 27°04′N 101°32′W
105 S5 **San Caprasio** ▲ N Spain 41°45′N 00°26′W
62 G13 **San Carlos** Ñuble, C Chile 36°25′S 71°58′W
40 E9 **San Carlos** Baja California Sur, NW Mexico 24°52′N 112°15′W
41 N5 **San Carlos** Coahuila, NE Mexico 29°00′N 100°51′W
41 P9 **San Carlos** Tamaulipas, C Mexico 24°36′N 98°42′W
42 L12 **San Carlos** Río San Juan, S Nicaragua 11°06′N 84°46′W
43 T16 **San Carlos** West Panamá, C Panama 08°29′N 79°58′W
171 N3 **San Carlos** *off.* San Carlos City. Luzon, N Philippines 15°57′N 120°18′E
61 G20 **San Carlos** Maldonado, S Uruguay 34°46′S 54°58′W
36 M14 **San Carlos** Arizona, SW USA 33°21′N 110°27′W
54 K5 **San Carlos** Cojedes, N Venezuela 09°39′N 68°35′W
**San Carlos** *see* Quesada, Costa Rica
**San Carlos** *see* Luba, Equatorial Guinea
61 B17 **San Carlos Centro** Santa Fe, C Argentina 31°45′S 61°05′W
171 P6 **San Carlos City** Negros, C Philippines 10°34′N 123°24′E
**San Carlos City** *see* San Carlos
**San Carlos de Ancud** *see* Ancud
63 H16 **San Carlos de Bariloche** Río Negro, SW Argentina 41°08′S 71°15′W
61 B21 **San Carlos de Bolívar** Buenos Aires, E Argentina 36°15′S 61°06′W
54 H6 **San Carlos del Zulia** Zulia, W Venezuela 09°01′N 71°58′W
54 L12 **San Carlos de Río Negro** Amazonas, S Venezuela 01°54′N 67°54′W
**San Carlos, Estrecho de** *see* Falkland Sound
36 M14 **San Carlos Reservoir** ⊠ Arizona, SW USA
42 M12 **San Carlos, Río** N Costa Rica
65 D24 **San Carlos Settlement** East Falkland, Falkland Islands
61 C23 **San Cayetano** Buenos Aires, E Argentina 38°20′S 59°37′W
103 O8 **Sancerre** Cher, C France 47°19′N 02°53′E
158 G7 **Sanchakou** Xinjiang Uygur Zizhiqu, NW China 39°56′N 78°28′E
**Sanchoku** *see* Samcheok
41 O12 **San Ciro** San Luis Potosí, C Mexico 21°40′N 99°50′W
105 P10 **San Clemente** Castilla-La Mancha, C Spain 39°24′N 02°25′W
35 T16 **San Clemente** California, W USA 33°25′N 117°36′W
61 E21 **San Clemente del Tuyú** Buenos Aires, E Argentina 36°22′S 56°43′W
35 S17 **San Clemente Island** *island* Channel Islands, California, W USA
103 O9 **Sancoins** Cher, C France 46°49′N 03°00′E
61 B16 **San Cristóbal** Santa Fe, C Argentina 30°20′S 61°14′W
44 B4 **San Cristóbal** Artemisa, W Cuba 22°43′N 83°03′W
45 O9 **San Cristóbal** *var.* Benemérita de San Cristóbal. S Dominican Republic 18°27′N 70°07′W
54 H7 **San Cristóbal** Táchira, W Venezuela 07°46′N 72°15′W
187 N10 **San Cristobal** *var.* Makira. *island* SE Solomon Islands
**San Cristóbal** *see* San Cristóbal de Las Casas
41 U16 **San Cristóbal de Las Casas** *var.* San Cristóbal. Chiapas, SE Mexico 16°44′N 92°40′W
187 N10 **San Cristóbal, Isla** *var.* Chatham Island. *island* Galapagos Islands, Ecuador, E Pacific Ocean
42 D5 **San Cristóbal Verapaz** Alta Verapaz, C Guatemala 15°21′N 90°22′W
44 F6 **Sancti Spíritus** Sancti Spíritus, C Cuba 21°54′N 79°27′W
44 F6 **Sancti Spíritus** ◈ *province* C Cuba
103 O11 **Sancy, Puy de** ▲ C France 45°33′N 02°48′E
95 D15 **Sand** Rogaland, S Norway 59°28′N 06°16′E
169 W7 **Sandakan** Sabah, East Malaysia 05°52′N 118°04′E
182 K9 **Sandalwood** South Australia 34°51′S 140°13′E
**Sandalwood Island** *see* Sumba, Pulau
94 D11 **Sandane** Sogn Og Fjordane, S Norway 61°47′N 06°14′E
114 G12 **Sandanski** *prev.* Sveti Vrach. Blagoevgrad, SW Bulgaria 41°36′N 23°19′E
**Sandaohezi** *see* Shawan
76 J11 **Sandaré** Kayes, W Mali 14°36′N 10°22′W
95 J19 **Sandared** Västra Götaland, S Sweden 57°43′N 12°47′E
94 N12 **Sandarne** Gävleborg, C Sweden 61°15′N 17°10′E
**Sandaun** *see* West Sepik
96 K4 **Sanday** *island* NE Scotland, United Kingdom
31 P15 **Sand Creek** Indiana, N USA
95 H15 **Sande** Vestfold, S Norway 59°34′N 10°13′E
95 H16 **Sandefjord** Vestfold, S Norway 59°10′N 10°15′E
77 O15 **Sandégué** E Ivory Coast 07°59′N 03°33′W
77 P14 **Sandema** N Ghana 10°42′N 01°17′W
37 O11 **Sanders** Arizona, SW USA 35°13′N 109°21′W
24 M11 **Sanderson** Texas, SW USA 30°08′N 102°25′W
23 U4 **Sandersville** Georgia, SE USA 32°58′N 82°48′W
92 H4 **Sandgerði** Suðurnes, SW Iceland 64°01′N 22°42′W
28 K14 **Sand Hills** ▲▲ Nebraska, C USA
25 S14 **Sandia** Texas, SW USA 27°59′N 97°52′W
35 T17 **San Diego** California, W USA 32°43′N 117°09′W
25 S14 **San Diego** Texas, SW USA 27°47′N 98°15′W
136 F14 **Sandıklı** Afyon, W Turkey 38°28′N 30°17′E
152 L12 **Sandīla** Uttar Pradesh, N India 27°05′N 80°37′E
**San Dimitri Point** *see* Il-Ponta ta' San Dimitri
**San Dimitri, Ras** *see* Il-Ponta ta' San Dimitri
168 J13 **Sanding, Selat** *strait* W Indonesia
30 J3 **Sand Island** *island* Apostle Islands, Wisconsin, N USA
95 C16 **Sandnes** Rogaland, S Norway 58°51′N 05°45′E
92 F13 **Sandnessjøen** Nordland, C Norway 66°00′N 12°37′E
**Sandø** *see* Sandoy
79 L24 **Sandoa** Katanga, S Dem. Rep. Congo 09°41′S 22°56′E
111 N15 **Sandomierz** *Rus.* Sandomir. Świętokrzyskie, C Poland 50°42′N 21°45′E
**Sandomir** *see* Sandomierz
54 C13 **Sandoná** Nariño, SW Colombia 01°18′N 77°28′W
106 I7 **San Donà di Piave** Veneto, NE Italy 45°38′N 12°34′E
124 K14 **Sandovo** Tverskaya Oblast', W Russia 58°26′N 36°30′E
**Sandoway** *see* Thandwe
97 M24 **Sandown** S England, United Kingdom 50°40′N 01°11′W
95 B19 **Sandoy** *Dan.* Sandø. *island* C Faroe Islands
39 N16 **Sand Point** Popof Island, Alaska, USA 55°20′N 160°30′W
32 M7 **Sandpoint** Idaho, NW USA 48°16′N 116°33′W
65 N24 **Sand Point** *headland* E Tristan da Cunha
31 R7 **Sand Point** *headland* Michigan, N USA 43°54′N 83°24′W
93 H14 **Sandsele** Västerbotten, N Sweden 65°16′N 17°40′E
10 I14 **Sandspit** Moresby Island, British Columbia, SW Canada 53°14′N 131°50′W
27 P9 **Sand Springs** Oklahoma, C USA 36°08′N 96°06′W
29 W7 **Sandstone** Minnesota, N USA 46°07′N 92°51′W
36 K15 **Sand Tank Mountains** ▲▲ Arizona, SW USA
31 S8 **Sandusky** Michigan, N USA 43°26′N 82°50′W
31 S11 **Sandusky** Ohio, N USA 41°27′N 82°42′W
31 S12 **Sandusky River** Ohio, N USA
83 D22 **Sandverhaar** //Karas, S Namibia 26°50′S 17°25′E
95 L24 **Sandvig** Bornholm, E Denmark 55°15′N 14°45′E
95 H15 **Sandvika** Akershus, S Norway 59°54′N 10°29′E
94 N13 **Sandviken** Gävleborg, C Sweden 60°38′N 16°50′E
30 M11 **Sandwich** Illinois, N USA 41°39′N 88°37′W
**Sandwich Island** *see* Efate
**Sandwich Islands** *see* Hawaiian Islands
153 V16 **Sandwip** *island* SE Bangladesh
11 U12 **Sandy Bay** Saskatchewan, C Canada 55°31′N 102°14′W
183 N16 **Sandy Cape** *headland* Tasmania, SE Australia 41°27′S 144°43′E
36 L3 **Sandy City** Utah, W USA 40°36′N 111°53′W
31 U12 **Sandy Creek** Ohio, N USA
21 O5 **Sandy Hook** Kentucky, S USA 38°05′N 83°09′W
18 K15 **Sandy Hook** *headland* New Jersey, NE USA 40°27′N 73°59′W
**Sandykachi/Sandykgachy** *see* Sandykgaçy
146 J15 **Sandykaçy** *var.* Sandykgachy. Maryyskiy Velayat, S Turkmenistan 36°34′N 62°28′E
**Sandykgachy** *see* Sandykaçy
146 J15 **Sandykgaçy** *var.* Sandykgachy, *Rus.* Sandykachi. Mary Welaýaty, S Turkmenistan 36°34′N 62°28′E
146 L13 **Sandykly Gumy** *Rus.* Peski Sandykly. *desert* E Turkmenistan
**Sandykly, Peski** *see* Sandykly Gumy
11 Q13 **Sandy Lake** Alberta, W Canada 55°50′N 113°30′W
12 B8 **Sandy Lake** Ontario, C Canada 53°00′N 93°25′W
12 B8 **Sandy Lake** ◎ Ontario, C Canada
23 S3 **Sandy Springs** Georgia, SE USA 33°57′N 84°23′W
24 H8 **San Elizario** Texas, SW USA 31°35′N 106°16′W
99 L25 **Sanem** Luxembourg, SW Luxembourg 49°33′N 05°56′E
42 K5 **San Esteban** Olancho, C Honduras 15°19′N 85°52′W
105 O6 **San Esteban de Gormaz** Castilla y León, N Spain 41°34′N 03°13′W
40 E5 **San Esteban, Isla** *island* NW Mexico
**San Eugenio/San Eugenio del Cuareim** *see* Artigas
62 H11 **San Felipe** *var.* San Felipe de Aconcagua. Valparaíso, C Chile 32°45′S 70°42′W
40 D3 **San Felipe** Baja California, NW Mexico 31°03′N 114°52′W
40 N12 **San Felipe** Guanajuato, C Mexico 21°30′N 101°15′W
54 K5 **San Felipe** Yaracuy, NW Venezuela 10°25′N 68°40′W
44 B5 **San Felipe, Cayos de** *island group* W Cuba
**San Felipe de Aconcagua** *see* San Felipe
**San Felipe de Puerto Plata** *see* Puerto Plata
37 R11 **San Felipe Pueblo** New Mexico, SW USA 35°25′N 106°27′W
**San Feliú de Guixols** *see* Sant Feliu de Guíxols
193 T10 **San Félix, Isla** *Eng.* San Felix Island. *island* W Chile
**San Felix Island** *see* San Félix, Isla
40 C4 **San Fernando** *var.* Misión San Fernando. Baja California, NW Mexico 29°58′N 115°14′W
41 P9 **San Fernando** Tamaulipas, C Mexico 24°50′N 98°10′W
171 N2 **San Fernando** Luzon, N Philippines 16°45′N 120°21′E
171 O3 **San Fernando** Luzon, N Philippines 15°01′N 120°41′E
104 J16 **San Fernando** *prev.* Isla de León. Andalucía, S Spain 36°28′N 06°12′W
45 U14 **San Fernando** Trinidad, Trinidad and Tobago 10°17′N 61°27′W
35 S15 **San Fernando** California, W USA 34°16′N 118°26′W
54 L7 **San Fernando** *var.* San Fernando de Apure. Apure, C Venezuela 07°54′N 67°28′W
**San Fernando de Apure** *see* San Fernando
54 L11 **San Fernando de Atabapo** Amazonas, S Venezuela 04°00′N 67°42′W
62 L8 **San Fernando del Valle de Catamarca** *var.* Catamarca. Catamarca, NW Argentina 28°28′S 65°46′W
**San Fernando de Monte Cristi** *see* Monte Cristi
41 P9 **San Fernando, Río** C Mexico
23 X11 **Sanford** Florida, SE USA 28°48′N 81°16′W
19 P9 **Sanford** Maine, NE USA 43°26′N 70°46′W
21 T10 **Sanford** North Carolina, SE USA 35°29′N 79°10′W
25 N2 **Sanford** Texas, SW USA 35°42′N 101°31′W
39 T10 **Sanford, Mount** ▲ Alaska, USA 62°21′N 144°12′W
42 G8 **San Francisco** *var.* Gotera, San Francisco Gotera. Morazán, E El Salvador 13°41′N 88°06′W
43 R16 **San Francisco** Veraguas, C Panama 08°19′N 80°59′W
171 N2 **San Francisco** *var.* Aurora. Luzon, N Philippines 13°22′N 122°31′E
35 L8 **San Francisco** California, W USA 37°47′N 122°25′W
54 H5 **San Francisco** Zulia, NW Venezuela 10°36′N 71°39′W
34 M8 **San Francisco** ✈ California, W USA 37°37′N 122°23′W
35 N9 **San Francisco Bay** *bay* California, W USA
61 C24 **San Francisco de Bellocq** Buenos Aires, E Argentina 38°42′S 60°01′W
40 I6 **San Francisco de Borja** Chihuahua, N Mexico 27°57′N 106°42′W
42 J6 **San Francisco de la Paz** Olancho, C Honduras 14°55′N 86°14′W
40 J7 **San Francisco del Oro** Chihuahua, N Mexico 26°52′N 105°50′W
40 M12 **San Francisco del Rincón** Jalisco, SW Mexico 21°00′N 101°51′W


◆ Country
● Country Capital
◇ Dependent Territory
○ Dependent Territory Capital
◈ Administrative Regions
✈ International Airport
▲ Mountain
▲▲ Mountain Range
Volcano
River
◎ Lake
⊠ Reservoir

San Francisco de Macorís – Santa Coloma de Gramanet


45 O8 **San Francisco de Macorís** C Dominican Republic 19°19′N 70°15′W
**San Francisco de Satipo** see Satipo
**San Francisco Gotera** see San Francisco
**San Francisco Telixtlahuaca** see Telixtlahuaca
107 K23 **San Fratello** Sicilia, Italy, C Mediterranean Sea 38°00′N 14°35′E
**San Fructuoso** see Tacuarembó
82 C12 **Sanga** Kwanza Sul, NW Angola 11°10′S 15°27′E
56 C5 **San Gabriel** Carchi, N Ecuador 0°35′N 77°48′W
159 S15 **Sa'ngain** Xizang Zizhiqu, W China 30°47′N 98°45′E
154 E13 **Sangamner** Mahārāshtra, W India 19°37′N 74°18′E
152 H12 **Sāngāner** Rājasthān, N India 26°48′N 75°48′E
149 N6 **Sangān, Kōh-e** Pash. Koh-i-Sangan. ▲ C Afghanistan
**Sangan, Koh-i-** see Sangān, Kōh-e
123 P10 **Sangar** Respublika Sakha (Yakutiya), NE Russia 63°48′N 127°37′E
169 V11 **Sangasanga** Borneo, C Indonesia 0°36′S 117°12′E
103 N1 **Sangatte** Pas-de-Calais, N France 50°56′N 01°41′E
107 B19 **San Gavino Monreale** Sardegna, Italy, C Mediterranean Sea 39°33′N 08°47′E
57 D16 **Sangayan, Isla** island W Peru
30 L14 **Sangchris Lake** ⊠ Illinois, N USA
171 N16 **Sangeang, Pulau** island S Indonesia
116 I10 **Sângeorgiu de Pădure** prev. Erdăt-Sângeorz, Sîngeorgiu de Pădure, Hung. Erdőszentgyörgy. Mureş, C Romania 46°27′N 24°50′E
116 I9 **Sângeorz-Băi** var. Singeroz Băi, Ger. Rumänisch-Sankt-Georgen, Hung. Oláhszentgyőrgy; prev. Sîngeorz-Băi. Bistriţa-Năsăud, N Romania 47°24′N 24°40′E
35 R10 **Sanger** California, W USA 36°42′N 119°33′W
25 T5 **Sanger** Texas, SW USA 33°21′N 97°10′W
**Sângerei** see Sîngerei
101 L15 **Sangerhausen** Sachsen-Anhalt, C Germany 51°29′N 11°18′E
45 S6 **San Germán** W Puerto Rico 18°05′N 67°02′W
**San Germano** see Cassino
161 N2 **Sanggan He** ∿ E China
169 Q11 **Sanggau** Borneo, C Indonesia 0°08′N 110°35′E
79 G17 **Sangha** ⬖ department N Congo
79 H16 **Sangha** ∿ Central African Republic/Congo
79 G16 **Sangha-Mbaéré** ⬖ prefecture SW Central African Republic
149 Q15 **Sanghar** Sindh, SE Pakistan 26°10′N 68°59′E
115 F22 **Sangiás** ▲ S Greece 36°39′N 22°24′E
**Sangihe, Kepulauan** see Sangir, Kepulauan
171 Q9 **Sangihe, Pulau** var. Sangir. island N Indonesia
54 G8 **San Gil** Santander, C Colombia 06°35′N 73°08′W
121 P16 **San Ġiljan** var. St Julian's. N Malta 35°55′N 14°29′E
106 F12 **San Gimignano** Toscana, C Italy 43°30′N 11°00′E
148 M8 **Sangin** var. Sangin. Helmand, S Afghanistan 32°03′N 64°50′E
**Sangin** see Sangīn
107 O21 **San Giovanni in Fiore** Calabria, SW Italy 39°15′N 16°42′E
107 M16 **San Giovanni Rotondo** Puglia, SE Italy 41°43′N 15°44′E
106 G12 **San Giovanni Valdarno** Toscana, C Italy 43°34′N 11°31′E
**Sangir** see Sangihe, Pulau
171 Q10 **Sangir, Kepulauan** var. Kepulauan Sangihe. island group N Indonesia
**Sangiyn Dalay** see Erdenedalay, Dundgovĭ, Mongolia
**Sangiyn Dalay** see Erdene, Govĭ-Altay, Mongolia
**Sangiyn Dalay** see Nomgon, Ömnögovĭ, Mongolia
**Sangiyn Dalay** see Öldziyt, Övörhangay, Mongolia
163 Y15 **Sangju** Jap. Shōshū. C South Korea 36°26′N 128°09′E
167 R11 **Sangkha** Surin, E Thailand 14°36′N 103°43′E
169 W10 **Sangkulirang** Borneo, N Indonesia 01°00′N 117°56′E
169 W10 **Sangkulirang, Teluk** bay Borneo, N Indonesia
155 E16 **Sāngli** Mahārāshtra, W India 16°55′N 74°37′E
79 E16 **Sangmélima** Sud, S Cameroon 02°57′N 11°56′E
35 V15 **San Gorgonio Mountain** ▲ California, W USA 34°06′N 116°50′W
37 T8 **Sangre de Cristo Mountains** ▲▲ Colorado/New Mexico, C USA
61 A20 **San Gregorio** Santa Fe, C Argentina 34°18′S 62°02′W
61 F18 **San Gregorio de Polanco** Tacuarembó, C Uruguay 32°37′S 55°50′W
45 V14 **Sangre Grande** Trinidad, Trinidad and Tobago 10°35′N 61°08′W
159 N16 **Sangri** Xizang Zizhiqu, W China 29°17′N 92°01′E
152 H9 **Sangrūr** Punjab, NW India 30°16′N 75°52′E
44 I11 **Sangster** off. Sir Donald Sangster International Airport, var. Montego Bay. ✈ (Montego Bay) W Jamaica 18°30′N 77°54′W
59 G17 **Sangue, Rio do** ∿ W Brazil
105 R4 **Sangüesa** Bas. Zangoza. Navarra, N Spain 42°34′N 01°17′W
61 C16 **San Gustavo** Entre Ríos, E Argentina 30°41′S 59°23′W
**Sangyuan** see Wuqiao
40 C6 **San Hipólito, Punta** headland NW Mexico 26°57′N 114°00′W
23 W15 **Sanibel** Sanibel Island, Florida, SE USA 26°27′N 82°01′W
23 V15 **Sanibel Island** island Florida, SE USA
60 F13 **San Ignacio** Misiones, NE Argentina 27°15′S 55°32′W
42 F2 **San Ignacio** prev. Cayo, El Cayo. Cayo, W Belize 17°09′N 89°02′W
57 L16 **San Ignacio** Beni, N Bolivia 14°54′S 65°35′W
57 O18 **San Ignacio** Santa Cruz, E Bolivia 16°23′S 60°59′W
42 M14 **San Ignacio** var. San Ignacio de Acosta. San José, W Costa Rica 09°46′N 84°10′W
40 E6 **San Ignacio** Baja California Sur, NW Mexico 27°18′N 112°51′W
40 J10 **San Ignacio** Sinaloa, W Mexico 23°55′N 106°25′W
56 B9 **San Ignacio** Cajamarca, N Peru 05°09′S 79°00′W
**San Ignacio de Acosta** see San Ignacio
40 D7 **San Ignacio, Laguna** lagoon W Mexico
12 I6 **Sanikiluaq** Belcher Islands, Nunavut, C Canada 55°20′N 77°50′W
171 O3 **San Ildefonso Peninsula** peninsula Luzon, N Philippines
**Saniquillie** see Sanniquellie
**Sanirajak** see Hall Beach
61 D20 **San Isidro** Buenos Aires, E Argentina 34°28′S 58°31′W
43 N14 **San Isidro** var. San Isidro de El General. San José, SE Costa Rica 09°28′N 83°42′W
**San Isidro de El General** see San Isidro
54 E5 **San Jacinto** Bolívar, N Colombia 09°53′N 75°06′W
35 U16 **San Jacinto** California, W USA 33°47′N 116°58′W
35 V15 **San Jacinto Peak** ▲ California, W USA 33°48′N 116°40′W
61 F14 **San Javier** Misiones, NE Argentina 27°50′S 55°06′W
61 C16 **San Javier** Santa Fe, C Argentina 30°35′S 59°59′W
105 S13 **San Javier** Murcia, SE Spain 37°49′N 00°50′W
61 D18 **San Javier** Río Negro, W Uruguay 32°41′S 58°08′W
61 C16 **San Javier, Río** ∿ C Argentina
160 L12 **Sanjiang** var. Guyi, Sanjiang Dongzu Zizhixian. Guangxi Zhuangzu Zizhiqu, S China 25°46′N 109°26′E
**Sanjiang** see Jinping, Guizhou
**Sanjiang Dongzu Zizhixian** see Sanjiang
**Sanjiaocheng** see Haiyan
165 N11 **Sanjō** var. Sanzyô. Niigata, Honshū, C Japan 37°39′N 139°00′E
57 M15 **San Joaquín** Beni, N Bolivia 13°06′S 64°46′W
55 O6 **San Joaquín** Anzoátegui, NE Venezuela 09°21′N 64°30′W
35 O9 **San Joaquin River** ∿ California, W USA
35 P10 **San Joaquin Valley** valley California, W USA
61 A18 **San Jorge** Santa Fe, C Argentina 31°50′S 61°50′W
40 D3 **San Jorge, Bahía de** bay NW Mexico
63 J19 **San Jorge, Golfo** var. Gulf of San Jorge. gulf S Argentina
**San Jorge, Gulf of** see San Jorge, Golfo
**San Jorge, Isla de** see Weddell Island
61 F14 **San José** Misiones, NE Argentina 27°46′S 55°47′W
57 P19 **San José** var. San José de Chiquitos. Santa Cruz, E Bolivia 14°13′S 68°05′W
42 M14 **San José** ● (Costa Rica) San José, C Costa Rica 09°55′N 84°05′W
42 C7 **San José** var. Puerto San José. Escuintla, S Guatemala 14°00′N 90°50′W
40 G6 **San José** Sonora, NW Mexico 27°32′N 110°09′W
188 K8 **San Jose** Tinian, S Northern Mariana Islands 15°00′S 145°38′E
105 U11 **San José** Eivissa, Spain, W Mediterranean Sea 38°55′N 01°18′E
35 N9 **San Jose** California, W USA 37°18′N 121°53′W
54 H5 **San José** Zulia, NW Venezuela 10°02′N 72°24′W
42 M14 **San José** off. Provincia de San José. ⬖ province W Costa Rica
61 E19 **San José** ⬖ department S Uruguay
42 M13 **San José** ✈ Alajuela, C Costa Rica 10°03′N 84°12′W
**San José** see San José del Guaviare, Colombia
**San Jose** see Oleai
**San Jose** see San Josep de sa Talaia, Ibiza, Spain
**San José** see San José de Mayo, Uruguay
171 O3 **San Jose City** Luzon, N Philippines 15°49′N 120°57′E
**San José de Chiquitos** see San José
**San José de Cúcuta** see Cúcuta
61 D16 **San José de Feliciano** Entre Ríos, E Argentina 30°26′S 58°46′W
55 O6 **San José de Guanipa** var. El Tigrito. Anzoátegui, NE Venezuela 08°54′N 64°10′W
62 I9 **San José de Jáchal** San Juan, W Argentina 30°15′S 68°46′W
40 G10 **San José del Cabo** Baja California Sur, NW Mexico 23°01′N 109°40′W
54 G12 **San José del Guaviare** var. San José. Guaviare, S Colombia 02°34′N 72°38′W
61 E20 **San José de Mayo** var. San José. San José, S Uruguay 34°20′S 56°42′W
54 I10 **San José de Ocuné** Vichada, E Colombia 04°10′N 70°21′W
41 O9 **San José de Raíces** Nuevo León, NE Mexico 24°32′N 100°15′W
63 K17 **San José, Golfo** gulf E Argentina
40 F9 **San José, Isla** island NW Mexico
43 U16 **San José, Isla** island SE Panama
25 U14 **San Jose Island** island Texas, SW USA
**San José, Provincia de** see San José
62 I10 **San Juan** San Juan, W Argentina 31°37′S 68°27′W
45 N9 **San Juan** var. San Juan de la Maguana. C Dominican Republic 18°49′N 71°12′W
57 E17 **San Juan** Ica, S Peru 15°22′S 75°07′W
45 U5 **San Juan** ○ (Puerto Rico) NE Puerto Rico 18°28′N 66°06′W
62 H10 **San Juan** off. Provincia de San Juan. ⬖ province W Argentina
**San Juan** see San Juan de los Morros
62 O7 **San Juan Bautista** Misiones, S Paraguay 26°40′S 57°08′W
35 O10 **San Juan Bautista** California, W USA 36°50′N 121°34′W
**San Juan Bautista** see Villahermosa
**San Juan Bautista Cuicatlán** see Cuicatlán
**San Juan Bautista Tuxtepec** see Tuxtepec
79 C17 **San Juan, Cabo** headland S Equatorial Guinea 01°09′N 09°25′E
**San Juan de Alicante** see Sant Joan d'Alacant
54 H7 **San Juan de Colón** Táchira, NW Venezuela 08°02′N 72°17′W
40 L9 **San Juan de Guadalupe** Durango, C Mexico 25°12′N 100°50′W
**San Juan de la Maguana** see San Juan
54 G4 **San Juan del Cesar** La Guajira, N Colombia 10°45′N 73°00′W
40 L15 **San Juan de Lima, Punta** headland SW Mexico 18°34′N 103°40′W
42 I8 **San Juan de Limay** Estelí, NW Nicaragua 13°10′N 86°36′W
43 N12 **San Juan del Norte** var. Greytown. Río San Juan, SE Nicaragua 10°58′N 83°40′W
54 K4 **San Juan de los Cayos** Falcón, N Venezuela 11°11′N 68°27′W
40 M12 **San Juan de los Lagos** Jalisco, C Mexico 21°15′N 102°15′W
54 L5 **San Juan de los Morros** var. San Juan. Guárico, N Venezuela 09°53′N 67°23′W
40 K9 **San Juan del Río** Durango, C Mexico 25°12′N 100°50′W
41 O13 **San Juan del Río** Querétaro de Arteaga, C Mexico 20°24′N 100°00′W
42 J11 **San Juan del Sur** Rivas, SW Nicaragua 11°16′N 85°51′W
54 M9 **San Juan de Manapiare** Amazonas, S Venezuela 05°15′N 66°05′W
40 E7 **San Juanico** Baja California Sur, NW Mexico
40 D7 **San Juanico, Punta** headland NW Mexico 26°01′N 112°17′W
32 G6 **San Juan Islands** island group Washington, NW USA
40 I6 **San Juanito** Chihuahua, N Mexico
40 I12 **San Juanito, Isla** island C Mexico
37 R8 **San Juan Mountains** ▲▲ Colorado, C USA
54 E5 **San Juan Nepomuceno** Bolívar, NW Colombia 09°57′N 75°06′W
44 E5 **San Juan, Pico** ▲ C Cuba 21°58′N 80°10′W
**San Juan, Provincia de** see San Juan
191 W15 **San Juan, Punta** headland Easter Island, Chile, E Pacific Ocean 27°03′S 109°22′W
42 M12 **San Juan, Río** ∿ Costa Rica/Nicaragua
41 S15 **San Juan, Río** ∿ SE Mexico
37 O8 **San Juan River** ∿ Colorado/Utah, W USA
**San Julián** see Puerto San Julián
61 B17 **San Justo** Santa Fe, C Argentina 30°47′S 60°32′W
109 W5 **Sankt Aegyd am Neuwalde** Niederösterreich, E Austria 47°51′N 15°34′E
109 U9 **Sankt Andrä** Slvn. Šent Andraž. Kärnten, S Austria 46°46′N 14°49′E
**Sankt Andrä** see Szentendre
**Sankt Anna** see Sântana
108 K8 **Sankt Anton-am-Arlberg** Vorarlberg, W Austria 47°08′N 10°11′E
101 E16 **Sankt Augustin** Nordrhein-Westfalen, W Germany 50°46′N 07°10′E
**Sankt-Eartholomäi** see Palamuse
101 F24 **Sankt Blasien** Baden-Württemberg, SW Germany 47°43′N 08°09′E
109 R3 **Sankt Florian am Inn** Oberösterreich, N Austria 48°24′N 13°27′E
108 I7 **Sankt Gallen** var. St. Gallen, Eng. Saint Gall, Fr. St-Gall. Sankt Gallen, NE Switzerland 47°25′N 09°23′E
108 H8 **Sankt Gallen** var. St.Gallen, Eng. Saint Gall, Fr. St-Gall. ⬖ canton NE Switzerland
108 J8 **Sankt Gallenkirch** Vorarlberg, W Austria 47°00′N 10°59′E
109 Q5 **Sankt Georgen** Salzburg, N Austria 47°59′N 12°57′E
**Sankt-Georgen** see Đurđevac
**Sankt-Georgen** see Sfântu Gheorghe
109 R6 **Sankt Gilgen** Salzburg, NW Austria 47°46′N 13°21′E
**Sankt Gotthard** see Szentgotthárd
101 E20 **Sankt Ingbert** Saarland, SW Germany 49°17′N 07°07′E
**Sankt-Jakobi** see Viru-Jaagupi, Lääne-Virumaa, Estonia
**Sankt-Jakobi** see Pärnu-Jaagupi, Pärnumaa, Estonia
**Sankt Johann** see Sankt Johann in Tirol
109 T7 **Sankt Johann am Tauern** Steiermark, E Austria 47°20′N 14°27′E
109 Q7 **Sankt Johann im Pongau** Salzburg, NW Austria 47°22′N 13°13′E
109 P6 **Sankt Johann in Tirol** var. Sankt Johann. Tirol, W Austria 47°32′N 12°26′E
**Sankt-Johannis** see Järva-Jaani
108 L8 **Sankt Leonhard** Tirol, W Austria 47°05′N 10°53′E
**Sankt Margarethen** see Sankt Margarethen im Burgenland
109 Y5 **Sankt Margarethen im Burgenland** var. Sankt Margarethen. Burgenland, E Austria 47°49′N 16°38′E
**Sankt Martin** see Martin
109 X8 **Sankt Martin an der Raab** Burgenland, SE Austria 46°59′N 16°12′E
109 U7 **Sankt Michael in Obersteiermark** Steiermark, SE Austria 47°21′N 14°59′E
**Sankt Michel** see Mikkeli
**Sankt Moritz** see St. Moritz
108 E11 **Sankt Niklaus** Valais, S Switzerland 46°09′N 07°48′E
109 S7 **Sankt Nikolai** var. Sankt Nikolai im Sölktal. Steiermark, SE Austria 47°18′N 14°04′E
**Sankt Nikolai im Sölktal** see Sankt Nikolai
109 U9 **Sankt Paul** var. Sankt Paul im Lavanttal. Kärnten, S Austria 46°42′N 14°53′E
**Sankt Paul im Lavanttal** see Sankt Paul
**Sankt Peter** see Pivka
109 W9 **Sankt Peter am Ottersbach** Steiermark, SE Austria 46°49′N 15°48′E
124 J13 **Sankt-Peterburg** prev. Leningrad, Petrograd, Eng. Saint Petersburg, Fin. Pietari. Leningradskaya Oblast', NW Russia 59°55′N 30°25′E
100 H8 **Sankt Peter-Ording** Schleswig-Holstein, N Germany 54°18′N 08°37′E
109 V4 **Sankt Pölten** Niederösterreich, N Austria 48°14′N 15°38′E
109 W7 **Sankt Ruprecht** var. Sankt Ruprecht an der Raab. Steiermark, SE Austria 47°10′N 15°41′E
**Sankt Ruprecht an der Raab** see Sankt Ruprecht
**Sankt-Ulrich** see Ortisei
109 T4 **Sankt Valentin** Niederösterreich, C Austria 48°11′N 14°33′E
**Sankt Veit am Flaum** see Rijeka
109 T9 **Sankt Veit an der Glan** Slvn. Št. Vid. Kärnten, S Austria 46°47′N 14°22′E
99 M21 **Sankt-Vith** var. Saint-Vith. Liège, E Belgium 50°17′N 06°07′E
101 E20 **Sankt Wendel** Saarland, SW Germany 49°28′N 07°10′E
109 R6 **Sankt Wolfgang** Salzburg, NW Austria 47°43′N 13°30′E
79 K21 **Sankuru** ∿ C Dem. Rep. Congo
40 D8 **San Lázaro, Cabo** headland NW Mexico 24°46′N 112°15′W
137 O16 **Şanlıurfa** prev. Sanli Urfa, Urfa; anc. Edessa. Şanlıurfa, S Turkey 37°08′N 38°45′E
137 O16 **Şanlıurfa** prev. Urfa. ⬖ province SE Turkey
**Sanli Urfa** see Şanlıurfa
137 O16 **Şanlıurfa Yaylası** plateau SE Turkey
61 B18 **San Lorenzo** Santa Fe, C Argentina 32°45′S 60°45′W
57 M21 **San Lorenzo** Tarija, S Bolivia 21°25′S 64°45′W
56 C5 **San Lorenzo** Esmeraldas, N Ecuador 01°15′N 78°51′W
42 H8 **San Lorenzo** Valle, S Honduras 13°24′N 87°27′W
56 A6 **San Lorenzo, Cabo** headland W Ecuador 0°57′S 80°49′W
105 N8 **San Lorenzo de El Escorial** var. El Escorial. Madrid, C Spain 40°36′N 04°07′W
40 E5 **San Lorenzo, Isla** island NW Mexico
57 C14 **San Lorenzo, Isla** island W Peru
63 G20 **San Lorenzo, Monte** ▲ S Argentina 47°40′S 72°12′W
40 I9 **San Lorenzo, Río** ∿ C Mexico
104 J15 **Sanlúcar de Barrameda** Andalucía, S Spain 36°46′N 06°21′W
104 J14 **Sanlúcar la Mayor** Andalucía, S Spain 37°24′N 06°13′W
40 F11 **San Lucas** Baja California Sur, NW Mexico 22°50′N 109°52′W
40 E6 **San Lucas** var. Cabo San Lucas. Baja California Sur, NW Mexico 27°14′N 112°15′W
40 G11 **San Lucas, Cabo** var. San Lucas Cape. headland NW Mexico 22°52′N 109°53′W
**San Lucas Cape** see San Lucas, Cabo
62 J11 **San Luis** San Luis, C Argentina 33°18′S 66°18′W
42 E4 **San Luis** Petén, NE Guatemala 16°16′N 89°27′W
42 M7 **San Luis** Costa Caribe Norte, NE Nicaragua 13°59′N 84°10′W
36 H15 **San Luis** Arizona, SW USA 32°27′N 114°45′W
37 T8 **San Luis** Colorado, C USA 37°09′N 105°24′W
54 J4 **San Luis** Falcón, N Venezuela 11°09′N 69°39′W
62 J11 **San Luis** off. Provincia de San Luis. ⬖ province C Argentina
41 N12 **San Luis de la Paz** Guanajuato, C Mexico 21°15′N 100°33′W
40 K8 **San Luis del Cordero** Durango, C Mexico 25°25′N 104°09′W
40 D4 **San Luis, Isla** island NW Mexico
42 E6 **San Luis Jilotepeque** Jalapa, SE Guatemala 14°40′N 89°42′W
57 M16 **San Luis, Laguna de** ◎ NW Bolivia
35 P13 **San Luis Obispo** California, W USA 35°17′N 120°40′W
37 R7 **San Luis Peak** ▲ Colorado, C USA 37°59′N 106°55′W
41 N11 **San Luis Potosí** San Luis Potosí, C Mexico 22°10′N 100°57′W
41 N11 **San Luis Potosí** ⬖ state C Mexico
**San Luis, Provincia de** see San Luis
35 O10 **San Luis Reservoir** ⊠ California, W USA
40 D2 **San Luis Río Colorado** var. San Luis Río Colorado. Sonora, NW Mexico 32°26′N 114°48′W
**San Luis Río Colorado** see San Luis Río Colorado
37 S8 **San Luis Valley** basin Colorado, C USA
107 C19 **Sanluri** Sardegna, Italy, C Mediterranean Sea 39°34′N 08°54′E
61 D23 **San Manuel** Buenos Aires, E Argentina 37°47′S 58°50′W
36 M15 **San Manuel** Arizona, SW USA 32°36′N 110°37′W
106 F11 **San Marcello Pistoiese** Toscana, C Italy 44°03′N 10°46′E
107 N20 **San Marco Argentano** Calabria, SW Italy 39°31′N 16°07′E
54 E6 **San Marcos** Sucre, N Colombia 08°38′N 75°10′W
42 M14 **San Marcos** San José, C Costa Rica 09°39′N 84°00′W
42 B5 **San Marcos** San Marcos, W Guatemala 14°58′N 91°48′W
42 F6 **San Marcos** Ocotepeque, SW Honduras 14°23′N 88°57′W
41 O16 **San Marcos** Guerrero, S Mexico 16°45′N 99°22′W
25 S11 **San Marcos** Texas, SW USA 29°54′N 97°57′W
42 A5 **San Marcos** off. Departamento de San Marcos. ⬖ department W Guatemala
**San Marcos de Arica** see Arica
**San Marcos, Departamento de** see San Marcos
40 E6 **San Marcos, Isla** island NW Mexico
106 H11 **San Marino** ● (San Marino) C San Marino 43°54′N 12°27′E
106 I11 **San Marino** off. Republic of San Marino, It. Repubblica di San Marino. ◆ republic S Europe
**San Marino, Repubblica di** see San Marino
**San Marino, Republic of** see San Marino
62 I11 **San Martín** Mendoza, C Argentina 33°05′S 68°28′W
54 F11 **San Martín** Meta, C Colombia 03°43′N 73°42′W
56 D11 **San Martín** off. Región de San Martín. ⬖ region C Peru
194 I5 **San Martín** research station (Argentina) Antarctica 68°18′S 67°03′W
63 H16 **San Martín de los Andes** Neuquén, W Argentina 40°11′S 71°22′W
104 M8 **San Martín de Valdeiglesias** Madrid, C Spain 40°21′N 04°24′W
63 G21 **San Martín, Lago** var. Lago O'Higgins. ◎ S Argentina
106 H6 **San Martino di Castrozza** Trentino-Alto Adige, N Italy 46°16′N 11°50′E
**San Martín, Región de** see San Martín
57 N16 **San Martín, Río** ∿ N Bolivia
**San Martín Texmelucan** see Texmelucan
35 N9 **San Mateo** California, W USA 37°33′N 122°19′W
55 O6 **San Mateo** Anzoátegui, NE Venezuela 09°48′N 64°36′W
42 B4 **San Mateo Ixtatán** Huehuetenango, W Guatemala 15°50′N 91°30′W
57 Q18 **San Matías** Santa Cruz, E Bolivia 16°20′S 58°24′W
63 K16 **San Matías, Golfo** var. Gulf of San Matías. gulf E Argentina
**San Matías, Gulf of** see San Matías, Golfo
15 O8 **Sanmaur** Québec, SE Canada 47°52′N 73°47′W
161 T10 **Sanmen Wan** bay E China
160 M6 **Sanmenxia** var. Shan Xian. Henan, C China 34°46′N 111°17′E
**Sânmiclăuş Mare** see Sânnicolau Mare
61 D14 **San Miguel** Corrientes, NE Argentina 28°02′S 57°41′W
57 L16 **San Miguel** Beni, N Bolivia 16°43′S 61°06′W
42 G8 **San Miguel** San Miguel, SE El Salvador 13°27′N 88°11′W
40 L6 **San Miguel** Coahuila, N Mexico 29°10′N 101°28′W
40 J9 **San Miguel** var. San Miguel de Cruces. Durango, C Mexico 24°25′N 105°55′W
43 U16 **San Miguel** Panamá, SE Panama 08°27′N 78°51′W
35 P12 **San Miguel** California, W USA 35°45′N 120°42′W
42 B9 **San Miguel** ⬖ department E El Salvador
41 N13 **San Miguel de Allende** Guanajuato, C Mexico 20°56′N 100°48′W
**San Miguel de Cruces** see San Miguel
**San Miguel de Ibarra** see Ibarra
61 D21 **San Miguel del Monte** Buenos Aires, E Argentina 35°26′S 58°50′W
62 J7 **San Miguel de Tucumán** var. Tucumán. Tucumán, N Argentina 26°47′S 65°15′W
43 V16 **San Miguel, Golfo de** gulf S Panama
35 P15 **San Miguel Island** island California, W USA
42 L11 **San Miguelito** Río San Juan, S Nicaragua 11°22′N 84°54′W
43 T15 **San Miguelito** Panamá, C Panama 08°58′N 79°31′W
57 N18 **San Miguel, Río** ∿ E Bolivia
56 D6 **San Miguel, Río** ∿ Colombia/Ecuador
40 I7 **San Miguel, Río** ∿ N Mexico
42 G8 **San Miguel, Volcán de** ⛰ SE El Salvador 13°27′N 88°18′W
161 Q12 **Sanming** Fujian, SE China 26°11′N 117°37′E
106 F11 **San Miniato** Toscana, C Italy 43°40′N 10°53′E
**San Murezzan** see St. Moritz
**Sannār** see Sennar
107 M15 **Sannicandro Garganico** Puglia, SE Italy 41°50′N 15°32′E
40 H6 **San Nicolás** Sonora, NW Mexico 28°31′N 109°24′W
61 C19 **San Nicolás de los Arroyos** Buenos Aires, E Argentina 33°20′S 60°13′W
35 R16 **San Nicolas Island** island Channel Islands, California, W USA
**Sânnicolaul-Mare** see Sânnicolau Mare
116 E11 **Sânnicolau Mare** var. Sânnicolaul-Mare, Hung. Nagyszentmiklós; prev. Sânmiclăuş Mare, Sînnicolau Mare. Timiş, W Romania 46°05′N 20°38′E
123 Q6 **Sannikova, Proliv** strait NE Russia
76 K16 **Sanniquellie** var. Saniquillie. NE Liberia 07°24′N 08°45′W
165 R7 **Sannohe** Aomori, Honshū, C Japan 40°23′N 141°16′E
**Sanntaler Alpen** see Kamniško-Savinjske Alpe
111 O17 **Sanok** Podkarpackie, SE Poland 49°31′N 22°14′E
54 E5 **San Onofre** Sucre, NW Colombia 09°45′N 75°33′W
57 K21 **San Pablo** Potosí, S Bolivia 21°43′S 66°38′W
171 O4 **San Pablo** off. San Pablo City. Luzon, N Philippines 14°04′N 121°16′E
**San Pablo Balleza** see Balleza
35 N8 **San Pablo Bay** bay California, W USA
**San Pablo City** see San Pablo
40 C6 **San Pablo, Punta** headland NW Mexico 27°12′N 114°30′W
43 R16 **San Pablo, Río** ∿ C Panama
171 P4 **San Pascual** Burias Island, C Philippines 13°06′N 122°59′E
121 Q16 **San Pawl il Baħar** Eng. Saint Paul's Bay. E Malta 35°57′N 14°24′E
61 C19 **San Pedro** Buenos Aires, E Argentina 33°43′S 59°45′W
62 K5 **San Pedro** Jujuy, N Argentina 24°12′S 64°55′W
60 G13 **San Pedro** Misiones, NE Argentina 26°38′S 54°12′W
42 H1 **San Pedro** Corozal, NE Belize 17°58′N 87°55′W
76 M17 **San-Pédro** S Ivory Coast 04°45′N 06°37′W
40 L8 **San Pedro** var. San Pedro de las Colonias. Coahuila, NE Mexico 25°47′N 102°57′W
62 O5 **San Pedro** San Pedro, SE Paraguay 24°08′S 57°08′W
62 O6 **San Pedro** off. Departamento de San Pedro. ⬖ department C Paraguay
44 G6 **San Pedro** ∿ C Cuba
77 N16 **San Pedro** ✈ (Yamoussoukro) C Ivory Coast 06°49′N 05°14′W
**San Pedro** see San Pedro del Pinatar
42 D5 **San Pedro Carchá** Alta Verapaz, C Guatemala 15°30′N 90°12′W
35 S16 **San Pedro Channel** channel California, W USA
62 I5 **San Pedro de Atacama** Antofagasta, N Chile 22°52′S 68°10′W
**San Pedro de Durazno** see Durazno
40 G5 **San Pedro de la Cueva** Sonora, NW Mexico 29°17′N 109°47′W
**San Pedro de las Colonias** see San Pedro
56 B11 **San Pedro de Lloc** La Libertad, NW Peru 07°26′S 79°31′W
105 S13 **San Pedro del Pinatar** var. San Pedro. Murcia, SE Spain 37°50′N 00°47′W
45 P9 **San Pedro de Macorís** SE Dominican Republic 18°30′N 69°18′W
**San Pedro, Departamento de** see San Pedro
40 C3 **San Pedro Mártir, Sierra** ▲▲ NW Mexico
**San Pedro Pochutla** see Pochutla
42 D2 **San Pedro, Río** ∿ Guatemala/Mexico
40 K10 **San Pedro, Río** ∿ C Mexico
104 J10 **San Pedro, Sierra de** ▲▲ W Spain
42 G5 **San Pedro Sula** Cortés, NW Honduras 15°26′N 88°01′W
**San Pedro Tapanatepec** see Tapanatepec
62 I4 **San Pedro, Volcán** ⛰ N Chile 21°46′S 68°13′W
106 E7 **San Pellegrino Terme** Lombardia, N Italy 45°53′N 09°42′E
25 T16 **San Perlita** Texas, SW USA 26°30′N 97°38′W
**San Pietro** see Supetar
**San Pietro del Carso** see Pivka
107 A20 **San Pietro, Isola di** island W Italy
32 K7 **Sanpoil River** ∿ Washington, NW USA
165 O9 **Sanpoku** var. Sampoku. Niigata, Honshū, C Japan 38°32′N 139°33′E
40 C3 **San Quintín** Baja California, NW Mexico 30°28′N 115°58′W
40 B3 **San Quintín, Bahía de** bay NW Mexico
40 B3 **San Quintín, Cabo** headland NW Mexico 30°22′N 116°01′W
62 I12 **San Rafael** Mendoza, W Argentina 34°44′S 68°15′W
41 N9 **San Rafael** Nuevo León, NE Mexico 25°01′N 100°33′W
34 M8 **San Rafael** California, W USA 37°58′N 122°31′W
37 Q11 **San Rafael** New Mexico, SW USA 35°03′N 107°52′W
54 H4 **San Rafael** var. El Moján. Zulia, NW Venezuela 10°58′N 71°45′W
42 J8 **San Rafael del Norte** Jinotega, NW Nicaragua 13°12′N 86°06′W
42 J10 **San Rafael del Sur** Managua, SW Nicaragua 11°51′N 86°24′W
36 M5 **San Rafael Knob** ▲ Utah, W USA 38°46′N 110°45′W
35 Q14 **San Rafael Mountains** ▲▲ California, W USA
42 M13 **San Ramón** Alajuela, C Costa Rica 10°04′N 84°31′W
57 E14 **San Ramón** Junín, C Peru 11°08′S 75°18′W
61 F19 **San Ramón** Canelones, S Uruguay 34°18′S 55°55′W
62 K5 **San Ramón de la Nueva Orán** Salta, N Argentina 23°08′S 64°20′W
57 O16 **San Ramón, Río** ∿ E Bolivia
106 B11 **San Remo** Liguria, NW Italy 43°48′N 07°47′E
54 J3 **San Román, Cabo** headland NW Venezuela 12°10′N 70°01′W
61 C15 **San Roque** Corrientes, NE Argentina 28°35′S 58°45′W
188 I4 **San Roque** Saipan, S Northern Mariana Islands 15°15′S 145°47′E
104 K16 **San Roque** Andalucía, S Spain 36°13′N 05°23′W
25 R9 **San Saba** Texas, SW USA 31°13′N 98°44′W
25 Q9 **San Saba River** ∿ Texas, SW USA
61 D17 **San Salvador** Entre Ríos, E Argentina 31°38′S 58°30′W
42 F7 **San Salvador** ● (El Salvador) San Salvador, SW El Salvador 13°42′N 89°12′W
42 A10 **San Salvador** ⬖ department C El Salvador
42 F8 **San Salvador** ✈ La Paz, S El Salvador 13°27′N 89°04′W
44 K4 **San Salvador** prev. Watlings Island. island E The Bahamas
62 J5 **San Salvador de Jujuy** var. Jujuy. Jujuy, N Argentina 24°10′S 65°20′W
42 F7 **San Salvador, Volcán de** ⛰ C El Salvador 13°58′N 89°14′W
77 Q14 **Sansanné-Mango** var. Mango. N Togo 10°21′N 00°28′E
45 S5 **San Sebastián** W Puerto Rico 18°21′N 67°00′W
63 J24 **San Sebastián, Bahía** bay S Argentina
**Sansenhō** see Sacheon
106 H12 **Sansepolcro** Toscana, C Italy 43°35′N 12°12′E
107 M16 **San Severo** Puglia, SE Italy 41°41′N 15°23′E
112 F11 **Sanski Most** ⬖ Federacija Bosne I Hercegovine, NW Bosnia and Herzegovina
171 W12 **Sansundi** Papua, E Indonesia 0°42′S 135°48′E
162 K9 **Sant** var. Mayhan. Övörhangay, C Mongolia 46°02′N 104°00′E
104 K11 **Santa Amalia** Extremadura, W Spain 39°00′N 06°01′W
60 F13 **Santa Ana** Misiones, NE Argentina 27°22′S 55°34′W
57 L16 **Santa Ana** Beni, N Bolivia 13°43′S 65°37′W
42 E7 **Santa Ana** Santa Ana, NW El Salvador 13°59′N 89°34′W
40 F4 **Santa Ana** Sonora, NW Mexico 30°31′N 111°08′W
35 T16 **Santa Ana** California, W USA 33°45′N 117°52′W
55 N6 **Santa Ana** Nueva Esparta, NE Venezuela 09°15′N 64°39′W
42 A9 **Santa Ana** ⬖ department NW El Salvador
**Santa Ana de Coro** see Coro
35 U16 **Santa Ana Mountains** ▲▲ California, W USA
42 E7 **Santa Ana, Volcán de** var. La Matepec. ⛰ W El Salvador 13°49′N 89°36′W
42 G6 **Santa Bárbara** Santa Bárbara, W Honduras 14°56′N 88°11′W
40 J7 **Santa Barbara** Chihuahua, N Mexico 26°46′N 105°46′W
35 Q14 **Santa Barbara** California, W USA 34°24′N 119°40′W
54 L11 **Santa Bárbara** Amazonas, S Venezuela 03°55′N 67°06′W
54 I7 **Santa Bárbara** Barinas, W Venezuela 07°48′N 71°10′W
42 F5 **Santa Bárbara** ⬖ department NW Honduras
**Santa Bárbara** see Iscuandé
35 Q15 **Santa Barbara Channel** channel California, W USA
**Santa Bárbara de Samaná** see Samaná
35 R16 **Santa Barbara Island** island Channel Islands, California, W USA
54 E5 **Santa Catalina** Bolívar, N Colombia 10°36′N 75°17′W
43 R15 **Santa Catalina** Ngöbe Bugle, W Panama 08°46′N 81°18′W
104 G2 **Santa Catalina de Armada** Galicia, NW Spain 43°02′N 08°49′W
35 T17 **Santa Catalina, Gulf of** gulf California, W USA
40 F8 **Santa Catalina, Isla** island NW Mexico
35 S16 **Santa Catalina Island** island Channel Islands, California, W USA
41 N8 **Santa Catarina** Nuevo León, NE Mexico 25°39′N 100°30′W
60 H13 **Santa Catarina** off. Estado de Santa Catarina. ⬖ state S Brazil
**Santa Catarina de Tepehuanes** see Tepehuanes
**Santa Catarina, Estado de** see Santa Catarina
60 L13 **Santa Catarina, Ilha de** island S Brazil
45 Q16 **Santa Catherina** Curaçao 12°07′N 68°46′W
44 E5 **Santa Clara** Villa Clara, C Cuba 22°25′N 78°01′W
35 N9 **Santa Clara** California, W USA 37°20′N 121°57′W
36 J8 **Santa Clara** Utah, W USA 37°07′N 113°36′W
**Santa Clara** see Santa Clara de Olimar
61 F18 **Santa Clara de Olimar** var. Santa Clara. Cerro Largo, NE Uruguay 32°50′S 54°54′W
61 A17 **Santa Clara de Saguier** Santa Fe, C Argentina 31°21′S 61°50′W
**Santa Coloma** see Santa Coloma de Gramenet
105 X5 **Santa Coloma de Farners** var. Santa Coloma de Farnés. Cataluña, NE Spain 41°52′N 02°39′E
**Santa Coloma de Farnés** see Santa Coloma de Farners
**Santa Coloma de Gramenet** see Santa Coloma de Gramenet


318
◆ Country
● Country Capital
◇ Dependent Territory
○ Dependent Territory Capital
⬖ Administrative Regions
✈ International Airport
▲ Mountain
▲▲ Mountain Range
⛰ Volcano
∿ River
◎ Lake
⊠ Reservoir

SANTA COLOMA DE GRAMENET – SAREZSKOYE OZERO

105 W6 Santa Coloma de Gramenet var. Santa Coloma; prev. Santa Coloma de Gramanet. Cataluña, NE Spain 41°28′N 02°14′E
Santa Comba see Uaco Cungo
104 H8 Santa Comba Dão Viseu, N Portugal 40°23′N 08°07′W
82 C10 Santa Cruz Uíge, NW Angola 06°56′S 16°25′E
57 N19 Santa Cruz var. Santa Cruz de la Sierra. Santa Cruz, C Bolivia 17°49′S 63°11′W
62 G12 Santa Cruz O'Higgins, C Chile 34°38′S 71°27′W
42 K13 Santa Cruz Guanacaste, W Costa Rica 10°15′N 85°35′W
44 I12 Santa Cruz W Jamaica 18°03′N 77°43′W
64 P6 Santa Cruz Madeira, Portugal, NE Atlantic Ocean 32°43′N 16°47′W
35 N10 Santa Cruz California, W USA 36°58′N 122°01′W
63 H20 Santa Cruz off. Provincia de Santa Cruz. ◆ province S Argentina
57 O18 Santa Cruz ◆ department E Bolivia
Santa Cruz see Puerto Santa Cruz
Santa Cruz see Viru-Viru
Santa Cruz Barillas see Barillas
59 O18 Santa Cruz Cabrália Bahia, E Brazil 16°17′S 39°03′W
Santa Cruz de El Seibo see El Seibo
64 N11 Santa Cruz de la Palma La Palma, Islas Canarias, Spain, NE Atlantic Ocean 28°41′N 17°46′W
Santa Cruz de la Sierra see Santa Cruz
105 O9 Santa Cruz de la Zarza Castilla-La Mancha, C Spain 39°59′N 03°10′W
42 C5 Santa Cruz del Quiché Quiché, W Guatemala 15°02′N 91°06′W
105 N8 Santa Cruz del Retamar Castilla-La Mancha, C Spain 40°08′N 04°14′W
Santa Cruz del Seibo see El Seibo
44 G7 Santa Cruz del Sur Camagüey, C Cuba 20°44′N 78°00′W
105 O11 Santa Cruz de Mudela Castilla-La Mancha, C Spain 38°37′N 03°27′W
64 Q11 Santa Cruz de Tenerife Tenerife, Islas Canarias, Spain, NE Atlantic Ocean 28°28′N 16°15′W
64 P11 Santa Cruz de Tenerife ◆ province Islas Canarias, Spain, NE Atlantic Ocean
60 K9 Santa Cruz do Rio Pardo São Paulo, S Brazil 22°52′S 49°37′W
61 H15 Santa Cruz do Sul Rio Grande do Sul, S Brazil 29°42′S 52°25′W
57 C17 Santa Cruz, Isla var. Indefatigable Island, Isla Chávez. island Galapagos Islands, Ecuador, E Pacific Ocean
40 F8 Santa Cruz, Isla island NW Mexico
35 Q15 Santa Cruz Island island California, W USA
187 Q10 Santa Cruz Islands island group E Solomon Islands
Santa Cruz, Provincia de see Santa Cruz
63 I22 Santa Cruz, Río ≈ S Argentina
36 L15 Santa Cruz River ≈ Arizona, SW USA
61 C17 Santa Elena Entre Ríos, E Argentina 30°58′S 59°47′W
42 F2 Santa Elena Cayo, W Belize 17°08′N 89°04′W
56 A8 Santa Elena Santa Elena, W Ecuador 02°13′S 80°51′W
25 R16 Santa Elena Texas, SW USA 26°43′N 98°30′W
56 A8 Santa Elena ◆ province W Ecuador
56 A7 Santa Elena, Bahía de bay W Ecuador
55 R10 Santa Elena de Uairén Bolívar, E Venezuela 04°40′N 61°03′W
42 K12 Santa Elena, Península peninsula NW Costa Rica
56 A7 Santa Elena, Punta headland W Ecuador 02°11′S 81°00′W
104 L11 Santa Eufemia Andalucía, S Spain 38°36′N 04°54′W
107 N21 Santa Eufemia, Golfo di gulf S Italy
105 S4 Santa Eulalia de Gállego Aragón, NE Spain 42°16′N 00°46′W
105 V11 Santa Eulalia del Río Ibiza, Spain, W Mediterranean Sea 39°00′N 01°33′E
61 B17 Santa Fe Santa Fe, C Argentina 31°36′S 60°47′W
44 C6 Santa Fé var. La Fe. Isla de la Juventud, W Cuba 21°45′N 82°45′W
43 R16 Santa Fé Veraguas, C Panama 08°29′N 80°50′W
105 N14 Santa Fe Andalucía, S Spain 37°11′N 03°43′W
37 S10 Santa Fe state capital New Mexico, SW USA 35°41′N 105°56′W
61 B15 Santa Fe off. Provincia de Santa Fe. ◆ province C Argentina
Santa Fe see Bogotá
Santa Fe de Bogotá see Bogotá
60 J7 Santa Fé do Sul São Paulo, S Brazil 20°13′S 50°56′W
57 B18 Santa Fe, Isla var. Barrington Island. island Galapagos Islands, Ecuador, E Pacific Ocean
Santa Fe, Provincia de see Santa Fe
23 V9 Santa Fe River ≈ Florida, SE USA
59 M15 Santa Filomena Piauí, E Brazil 09°06′S 45°52′W
40 G10 Santa Genoveva ▲ NW Mexico 23°07′N 109°56′W
153 S14 Santahar Rajshahi, NW Bangladesh 24°45′N 89°03′E
60 G11 Santa Helena Paraná, S Brazil 24°53′S 54°19′W
54 J5 Santa Inés Lara, N Venezuela 10°37′N 69°18′W
63 G24 Santa Inés, Isla island S Chile
62 J13 Santa Isabel La Pampa, C Argentina 36°11′S 66°59′W
43 U14 Santa Isabel Colón, N Panama 09°31′N 79°12′W
186 L8 Santa Isabel var. Bughotu. island N Solomon Islands
Santa Isabel see Malabo
58 D11 Santa Isabel do Rio Negro Amazonas, NW Brazil 0°40′S 64°56′W
61 C15 Santa Lucia Corrientes, NE Argentina 28°58′S 59°05′W
57 I17 Santa Lucía Puno, S Peru 15°45′S 70°34′W
61 F20 Santa Lucía var. Santa Lucia. Canelones, S Uruguay 34°26′S 56°25′W
42 B6 Santa Lucía Cotzumalguapa Escuintla, SW Guatemala 14°20′N 91°00′W
107 L23 Santa Lucia del Mela Sicilia, Italy, C Mediterranean Sea 38°08′N 15°17′E
35 O11 Santa Lucia Range ▲ California, W USA
40 D9 Santa Margarita, Isla island NW Mexico
62 J7 Santa María Catamarca, N Argentina 26°51′S 66°02′W
61 G15 Santa Maria Rio Grande do Sul, S Brazil 29°41′S 53°48′W
35 P13 Santa Maria California, W USA 34°56′N 120°25′W
64 Q4 Santa Maria ✈ Santa Maria, Azores, Portugal, NE Atlantic Ocean
64 P3 Santa Maria island Azores, Portugal, NE Atlantic Ocean
Santa Maria see Gaua
Santa María Asunción Tlaxiaco see Tlaxiaco
40 G9 Santa María, Bahía bay W Mexico
83 L21 Santa Maria, Cabo de headland S Mozambique 26°05′S 32°58′E
104 G15 Santa Maria, Cabo de headland S Portugal 36°57′N 07°55′W
44 J4 Santa Maria, Cape headland Long Island, C The Bahamas 23°40′N 75°20′W
107 J17 Santa Maria Capua Vetere Campania, S Italy 41°05′N 14°15′E
104 G7 Santa Maria da Feira Aveiro, N Portugal 40°55′N 08°32′W
59 M17 Santa Maria da Vitória Bahia, E Brazil 13°26′S 44°09′W
55 N9 Santa Maria de Erebato Bolívar, SE Venezuela 05°09′N 64°50′W
55 N6 Santa María de Ipire Guárico, C Venezuela 08°51′N 65°21′W
Santa María del Buen Aire see Buenos Aires
40 J8 Santa María del Oro Durango, C Mexico 25°57′N 105°22′W
41 N12 Santa María del Río San Luis Potosí, C Mexico 21°48′N 100°42′W
Santa Maria di Castellabate see Castellabate
107 Q20 Santa Maria di Leuca, Capo headland SE Italy 39°48′N 18°21′E
108 K10 Santa Maria-im-Munstertal Graubünden, SE Switzerland 46°36′N 10°25′E
57 B18 Santa María, Isla var. Isla Floreana, Charles Island. island Galapagos Islands, Ecuador, E Pacific Ocean
40 J3 Santa María, Laguna de ◎ N Mexico
61 G16 Santa Maria, Rio ≈ S Brazil
43 R16 Santa María, Río ≈ C Panama
36 J12 Santa Maria River ≈ Arizona, SW USA
107 G15 Santa Marinella Lazio, C Italy 42°01′N 11°51′E
54 F4 Santa Marta Magdalena, N Colombia 11°14′N 74°13′W
104 J11 Santa Marta Extremadura, W Spain 38°37′N 06°39′W
54 F4 Santa Marta, Sierra Nevada de ▲ NE Colombia
Santa Maura see Lefkáda
35 S15 Santa Monica California, W USA 34°01′N 118°29′W
116 F10 Săntana Ger. Sankt Anna, Hung. Újszentanna; prev. Sîntana. Arad, W Romania 46°20′N 21°30′E
61 F16 Santana, Coxilha de hill range S Brazil
61 H16 Santana da Boa Vista Rio Grande do Sul, S Brazil 30°52′S 53°03′W
61 F16 Santana do Livramento prev. Livramento. Rio Grande do Sul, S Brazil 30°52′S 55°30′W
105 N2 Santander Cantabria, N Spain 43°28′N 03°48′W
54 F8 Santander off. Departamento de Santander. ◆ province C Colombia
Santander, Departamento de see Santander
Santander Jiménez see Jiménez
Sant'Andrea see Svetac
107 B20 Sant'Antioco Sardegna, Italy, C Mediterranean Sea 39°03′N 08°28′E
105 V11 Sant Antoni de Portmany Cas. San Antonio Abad. Ibiza, Spain, W Mediterranean Sea 38°58′N 01°18′E
105 Y10 Santanyí Mallorca, Spain, W Mediterranean Sea 39°22′N 03°07′E
104 J13 Santa Olalla del Cala Andalucía, S Spain 37°54′N 06°13′W
35 R15 Santa Paula California, W USA 34°21′N 119°03′W
36 L4 Santaquin Utah, W USA 39°58′N 111°46′W
58 I12 Santarém Pará, N Brazil 02°26′S 54°41′W
104 G10 Santarém anc. Scalabis. Santarém, W Portugal 39°14′N 08°40′W
104 G10 Santarém ◆ district C Portugal
44 F4 Santaren Channel channel W The Bahamas
54 K10 Santa Rita Vichada, E Colombia 04°51′N 68°27′W
188 B16 Santa Rita SW Guam
42 H5 Santa Rita Cortés, NW Honduras 15°10′N 87°54′W
40 E9 Santa Rita Baja California Sur, NW Mexico 27°29′N 100°33′W
54 H5 Santa Rita Zulia, NW Venezuela 10°35′N 71°30′W
59 I19 Santa Rita de Araguaia Goiás, S Brazil 17°17′S 53°13′W
59 M16 Santa Rita de Cassia var. Cássia. Bahia, E Brazil 11°03′S 44°16′W
61 D14 Santa Rosa Corrientes, NE Argentina 28°18′S 58°04′W
62 K13 Santa Rosa La Pampa, C Argentina 36°38′S 64°15′W
61 G14 Santa Rosa Rio Grande do Sul, S Brazil 27°50′S 54°29′W
58 E10 Santa Rosa Roraima, N Brazil 03°41′N 62°29′W
56 B8 Santa Rosa El Oro, SW Ecuador 03°29′S 79°57′W
57 I16 Santa Rosa Puno, S Peru 14°38′S 70°45′W
34 M7 Santa Rosa California, W USA 38°27′N 122°42′W
37 U11 Santa Rosa New Mexico, SW USA 34°54′N 104°43′W
55 O6 Santa Rosa Anzoátegui, NE Venezuela 09°37′N 64°20′W
42 A3 Santa Rosa off. Departamento de Santa Rosa. ◆ department SE Guatemala
Santa Rosa see Santa Rosa de Copán
63 J15 Santa Rosa, Bajo de basin E Argentina
42 F6 Santa Rosa de Copán var. Santa Rosa. Copán, W Honduras 14°48′N 88°43′W
54 E8 Santa Rosa de Osos Antioquia, C Colombia 06°40′N 75°27′W
Santa Rosa, Departamento de see Santa Rosa
35 Q15 Santa Rosa Island island California, W USA
23 O9 Santa Rosa Island island Florida, SE USA
40 E6 Santa Rosalía Baja California Sur, NW Mexico 27°20′N 112°20′W
54 K6 Santa Rosalía Portuguesa, NW Venezuela 09°02′N 69°01′W
188 C15 Santa Rosa, Mount ▲ NE Guam
35 V16 Santa Rosa Mountains ▲ California, W USA
35 T2 Santa Rosa Range ▲ Nevada, W USA
62 M8 Santa Sylvina Chaco, N Argentina 27°49′S 61°09′W
Santa Tecla see Nueva San Salvador
61 B19 Santa Teresa Santa Fe, C Argentina 33°30′S 60°45′W
59 O20 Santa Teresa Espírito Santo, SE Brazil 19°51′S 40°49′W
61 E21 Santa Teresita Buenos Aires, E Argentina 36°32′S 56°41′W
61 H19 Santa Vitória do Palmar Rio Grande do Sul, S Brazil 33°32′S 53°25′W
35 Q14 Santa Ynez River ≈ California, W USA
Sant Carles de la Rápida see Sant Carles de la Ràpita
105 U7 Sant Carles de la Ràpita var. Sant Carles de la Rápida. Cataluña, NE Spain 40°37′N 00°36′E
105 W5 Sant Celoni Cataluña, NE Spain 41°39′N 02°25′E
35 U17 Santee California, W USA 32°50′N 116°58′W
21 T13 Santee River ≈ South Carolina, SE USA
40 K15 San Telmo, Punta headland SW Mexico 18°19′N 103°30′W
107 O17 Santeramo in Colle Puglia, SE Italy 40°47′N 16°45′E
107 M23 San Teresa di Riva Sicilia, Italy, C Mediterranean Sea 38°00′N 15°25′E
105 X5 Sant Feliu de Guíxols var. San Feliú de Guixols. Cataluña, NE Spain 41°47′N 03°02′E
105 W6 Sant Feliu de Llobregat Cataluña, NE Spain 41°22′N 02°00′E
106 C7 Santhià Piemonte, NE Italy 45°21′N 08°11′E
61 F15 Santiago Rio Grande do Sul, S Brazil 29°11′S 54°52′W
62 H11 Santiago var. Gran Santiago. ● (Chile) Santiago, C Chile 33°30′S 70°40′W
45 N8 Santiago var. Santiago de los Caballeros. N Dominican Republic 19°27′N 70°42′W
40 G10 Santiago Baja California Sur, NW Mexico 23°32′N 109°47′W
41 O8 Santiago Nuevo León, NE Mexico 25°22′N 100°09′W
43 R16 Santiago Veraguas, S Panama 08°06′N 80°59′W
57 E16 Santiago Ica, SW Peru 14°14′S 75°44′W
62 H11 Santiago off. Región Metropolitana de Santiago, var. Metropolitan. ◆ region C Chile
76 D10 Santiago var. São Tiago. island Ilhas de Sotavento, S Cape Verde
62 H11 Santiago ✈ Santiago, C Chile 33°27′S 70°40′W
104 G3 Santiago ✈ Galicia, NW Spain
Santiago see Santiago de Cuba, Cuba
Santiago see Grande de Santiago, Río, Mexico
Santiago see Santiago de Compostela
42 B6 Santiago Atitlán Solalá, SW Guatemala 14°39′N 91°12′W
43 Q16 Santiago, Cerro ▲ W Panama 08°27′N 81°42′W
104 G3 Santiago de Compostela var. Santiago, Eng. Compostella; anc. Campus Stellae. Galicia, NW Spain 42°52′N 08°33′W
44 I8 Santiago de Cuba var. Santiago. Santiago de Cuba, E Cuba 20°01′N 75°51′W
44 I7 Santiago de Cuba ◆ province SE Cuba
Santiago de Guayaquil see Guayaquil
62 K8 Santiago del Estero Santiago del Estero, C Argentina 27°51′S 64°16′W
61 A15 Santiago del Estero off. Provincia de Santiago del Estero. ◆ province N Argentina
Santiago del Estero, Provincia de see Santiago del Estero
40 I8 Santiago de los Caballeros Sinaloa, W Mexico 25°33′N 107°22′W
Santiago de los Caballeros see Santiago, Dominican Republic
Santiago de los Caballeros see Ciudad de Guatemala, Guatemala
42 F8 Santiago de María Usulután, SE El Salvador 13°28′N 88°28′W
104 F12 Santiago do Cacém Setúbal, S Portugal 38°01′N 08°42′W
40 J12 Santiago Ixcuintla Nayarit, C Mexico 21°50′N 105°11′W
Santiago Jamiltepec see Jamiltepec
24 L11 Santiago Mountains ▲ Texas, SW USA
40 J9 Santiago Papasquiaro Durango, C Mexico 25°00′N 105°27′W
Santiago Pinotepa Nacional see Pinotepa Nacional
Santiago, Región Metropolitana de see Santiago
56 C8 Santiago, Río ≈ N Peru
40 M10 San Tiburcio Zacatecas, C Mexico 24°08′N 101°29′W
105 N2 Santillana Cantabria, N Spain 43°24′N 04°06′W
54 I5 San Timoteo Zulia, NW Venezuela 09°50′N 71°05′W
Santi Quaranta see Sarandë
Santissima Trinidad see Keelung
105 O12 Santisteban del Puerto Andalucía, S Spain 38°15′N 03°11′W
105 S12 Sant Joan d'Alacant Cast. San Juan de Alicante. Comunitat Valenciana, E Spain 38°26′N 00°27′W
105 U7 Sant Jordi, Golf de gulf NE Spain
105 U11 Sant Josep de sa Talaia var. San Jose. Ibiza, Spain, W Mediterranean Sea 38°55′N 1°18′E
162 G6 Santmargats var. Holboo. Dzavhan, W Mongolia 48°35′N 95°25′E
105 T8 Sant Mateu Comunitat Valenciana, E Spain 40°28′N 00°10′E
25 S7 Santo Texas, SW USA 32°35′N 98°06′W
Santo see Espiritu Santo
60 M10 Santo Amaro, Ilha de island SE Brazil
61 G14 Santo Ângelo Rio Grande do Sul, S Brazil 28°17′S 54°15′W
76 C9 Santo Antão island Ilhas de Barlavento, N Cape Verde
60 J10 Santo Antônio da Platina Paraná, S Brazil 23°20′S 50°05′W
58 C13 Santo Antônio do Içá Amazonas, N Brazil 03°05′S 67°56′W
57 Q18 Santo Corazón, Río ≈ E Bolivia
44 E5 Santo Domingo Villa Clara, C Cuba 22°35′N 80°15′W
45 O9 Santo Domingo prev. Ciudad Trujillo. ● (Dominican Republic) SE Dominican Republic 18°30′N 69°57′W
40 E8 Santo Domingo Baja California Sur, NW Mexico 25°34′N 112°00′W
40 M10 Santo Domingo San Luis Potosí, C Mexico 23°18′N 101°42′W
42 L10 Santo Domingo Chontales, S Nicaragua 12°15′N 84°59′W
105 P4 Santo Domingo de la Calzada La Rioja, N Spain 42°26′N 02°57′W
56 B6 Santo Domingo de los Colorados Santo Domingo de los Tsáchilas, NW Ecuador 0°13′S 79°09′W
56 C6 Santo Domingo de los Tsáchilas ◆ province NW Ecuador
Santo Domingo Tehuantepec see Tehuantepec
55 O6 San Tomé Anzoátegui, NE Venezuela 08°58′N 64°08′W
San Tomé de Guayana see Ciudad Guayana
105 R13 Santomera Murcia, SE Spain 38°03′N 01°05′W
105 O2 Santoña Cantabria, N Spain 43°27′N 03°28′W
Santorin see Santoríni
115 K22 Santoríni var. Santorin, prev. Thíra; anc. Thera. island Kykládes, Greece, Aegean Sea
60 M10 Santos São Paulo, S Brazil 23°56′S 46°22′W
65 J17 Santos Plateau undersea feature SW Atlantic Ocean 25°00′S 43°00′W
104 G6 Santo Tirso Porto, N Portugal 41°20′N 08°25′W
40 B2 Santo Tomás Baja California, NW Mexico 31°32′N 116°26′W
42 L10 Santo Tomás Chontales, S Nicaragua 12°04′N 85°02′W
42 G5 Santo Tomás de Castilla Izabal, E Guatemala 15°40′N 88°36′W
40 B2 Santo Tomás, Punta headland NW Mexico 31°30′N 116°40′W
57 H16 Santo Tomás, Río ≈ C Peru
57 B18 Santo Tomás, Volcán Galapagos Islands, Ecuador, E Pacific Ocean 0°46′S 91°01′W
61 F14 Santo Tomé Corrientes, NE Argentina 28°31′S 56°03′W
Santo Tomé de Guayana see Ciudad Guayana
98 H10 Santpoort Noord-Holland, W Netherlands 52°26′N 04°38′E
Santurce see Santurtzi
105 O2 Santurtzi var. Santurce, Santurzi. País Vasco, N Spain 43°20′N 03°03′W
Santurzi see Santurtzi
63 G20 San Valentín, Cerro ▲ S Chile 46°36′S 73°17′W
42 F8 San Vicente San Vicente, C El Salvador 13°38′N 88°42′W*
40 C2 San Vicente Baja California, NW Mexico 31°20′N 116°15′W
188 H6 San Vicente Saipan, S Northern Mariana Islands
42 B9 San Vicente ◆ department E El Salvador
104 I10 San Vicente de Alcántara Extremadura, W Spain 39°21′N 07°07′W
105 N2 San Vicente de Barakaldo var. Baracaldo, Basq. San Bizenti-Barakaldo. País Vasco, N Spain 43°17′N 02°59′W
57 E15 San Vicente de Cañete var. Cañete. Lima, W Peru 13°06′S 76°23′W
104 M2 San Vicente de la Barquera Cantabria, N Spain 43°23′N 04°24′W
54 E12 San Vicente del Caguán Caquetá, S Colombia 02°07′N 74°47′W
42 F8 San Vicente, Volcán de C El Salvador 13°34′N 88°50′W
43 O15 San Vito Puntarenas, SE Costa Rica 08°49′N 82°58′W
106 I7 San Vito al Tagliamento Friuli-Venezia Giulia, NE Italy 45°54′N 12°55′E
107 H23 San Vito, Capo headland Sicilia, Italy, C Mediterranean Sea 38°11′N 12°41′E
107 P18 San Vito dei Normanni Puglia, SE Italy 40°40′N 17°42′E
160 L17 Sanya var. Ya Xian. Hainan, S China 18°25′N 109°27′E
83 J16 Sanyati ≈ N Zimbabwe
25 Q16 San Ygnacio Texas, SW USA 27°04′N 99°26′W
160 L6 Sanyuan Shaanxi, C China 34°40′N 108°56′E
123 P11 Sanyyakhtakh Respublika Sakha (Yakutiya), NE Russia 60°34′N 124°09′E
146 J15 S. A.Nyýazow Adyndaky Rus. Imeni S. A. Niyazova. Maryyskiy Velayat, S Turkmenistan 36°44′N 62°23′E
82 C10 Sanza Pombo Uíge, NW Angola 07°20′S 16°00′E
Sanzyô see Sanjō
104 G14 São Bartolomeu de Messines Faro, S Portugal 37°12′N 08°16′W
60 M10 São Bernardo do Campo São Paulo, S Brazil 23°45′S 46°34′W
61 F15 São Borja Rio Grande do Sul, S Brazil 28°35′S 56°01′W
104 H14 São Brás de Alportel Faro, S Portugal 37°09′N 07°55′W
60 M10 São Caetano do Sul São Paulo, S Brazil 23°37′S 46°34′W
60 L9 São Carlos São Paulo, S Brazil 22°02′S 47°53′W
59 P16 São Cristóvão Sergipe, E Brazil 10°59′S 37°10′W
61 F15 São Fancisco de Assis Rio Grande do Sul, S Brazil 29°32′S 55°07′W
58 K13 São Félix Pará, NE Brazil 06°43′S 51°56′W
São Félix see São Félix do Araguaia
59 J16 São Félix do Araguaia var. São Félix. Mato Grosso, W Brazil 11°36′S 50°40′W
59 J14 São Félix do Xingu Pará, NE Brazil 06°38′S 51°59′W
60 Q9 São Fidélis Rio de Janeiro, SE Brazil 21°37′S 41°40′W
76 D10 São Filipe Fogo, S Cape Verde 14°52′N 24°29′W
60 K12 São Francisco do Sul Santa Catarina, S Brazil 26°17′S 48°39′W
60 K12 São Francisco, Ilha de island S Brazil
59 P16 São Francisco, Rio ≈ E Brazil
61 G16 São Gabriel Rio Grande do Sul, S Brazil 30°17′S 54°17′W
60 P10 São Gonçalo Rio de Janeiro, SE Brazil 22°48′S 43°03′W
81 H23 Sao Hill Iringa, S Tanzania 08°19′S 35°11′E
60 R9 São João da Barra Rio de Janeiro, SE Brazil 21°39′S 41°04′W
104 G7 São João da Madeira Aveiro, N Portugal 40°52′N 08°28′W
58 M12 São João de Cortes Maranhão, E Brazil 02°30′S 44°27′W
59 M21 São João del Rei Minas Gerais, NE Brazil 21°08′S 44°15′W
59 N15 São João do Piauí Piauí, E Brazil 08°21′S 42°14′W
59 N14 São João dos Patos Maranhão, E Brazil 06°29′S 43°44′W
58 C11 São Joaquim Amazonas, NW Brazil 0°08′S 67°10′W
61 J14 São Joaquim Santa Catarina, S Brazil 28°20′S 49°55′W
60 L7 São Joaquim da Barra São Paulo, S Brazil 20°36′S 47°50′W
64 N2 São Jorge island Azores, Portugal, NE Atlantic Ocean
61 K14 São José Santa Catarina, S Brazil 27°34′S 48°39′W
60 M8 São José do Rio Pardo São Paulo, S Brazil 21°37′S 46°52′W
60 K8 São José do Rio Preto São Paulo, S Brazil 20°50′S 49°20′W
60 N10 São Jose dos Campos São Paulo, S Brazil 23°07′S 45°52′W
61 I17 São Lourenço do Sul Rio Grande do Sul, S Brazil 31°25′S 52°00′W
58 M12 São Luís state capital Maranhão, NE Brazil 02°34′S 44°16′W
58 F11 São Luís Roraima, N Brazil 01°11′N 60°15′W
58 M12 São Luís, Ilha de island NE Brazil
61 F14 São Luiz Gonzaga Rio Grande do Sul, S Brazil 28°24′S 54°58′W
São Mandol see São Manuel, Rio
47 U8 São Manuel ≈ C Brazil
59 H15 São Manuel, Rio var. São Mandol, Teles Pirés. ≈ C Brazil
58 C11 São Marcelino Amazonas, NW Brazil 0°53′N 67°16′W
58 N12 São Marcos, Baía de bay N Brazil
59 O20 São Mateus Espírito Santo, SE Brazil 18°44′S 39°53′W
60 J12 São Mateus do Sul Paraná, S Brazil 25°58′S 50°29′W
64 P3 São Miguel island Azores, Portugal, NE Atlantic Ocean
60 G13 São Miguel d'Oeste Santa Catarina, S Brazil 26°45′S 53°34′W
45 P9 Saona, Isla island SE Dominican Republic
172 H12 Saondzou ▲ Grande Comore, NW Comoros
103 R10 Saône ≈ E France
103 Q9 Saône-et-Loire ◆ department C France
76 D9 São Nicolau Eng. Saint Nicholas. island Ilhas de Barlavento, N Cape Verde
60 M10 São Paulo state capital São Paulo, S Brazil 23°33′S 46°39′W
60 K9 São Paulo off. Estado de São Paulo. ◆ state S Brazil
São Paulo de Loanda see Luanda
São Paulo, Estado de see São Paulo
São Pedro do Rio Grande do Sul see Rio Grande
104 H7 São Pedro do Sul Viseu, N Portugal 40°46′N 07°58′W
64 K13 São Pedro e São Paulo undersea feature C Atlantic Ocean 01°25′N 28°54′W
59 M14 São Raimundo das Mangabeiras Maranhão, E Brazil 07°00′S 45°30′W
59 Q14 São Roque, Cabo de headland E Brazil 05°29′S 35°16′W
São Salvador see Salvador, Brazil
São Salvador/São Salvador do Congo see M'Banza Congo, Angola
60 N10 São Sebastião, Ilha de island S Brazil
83 N19 São Sebastião, Ponta headland C Mozambique 22°09′S 35°33′E
104 F13 São Teotónio Beja, S Portugal 37°30′N 08°41′W
São Tiago see Santiago
79 B18 São Tomé ● (Sao Tome and Principe) São Tomé, S Sao Tome and Principe 0°22′N 06°41′E
79 B18 São Tomé ✈ São Tomé, S Sao Tome and Principe 0°24′N 06°39′E
79 B18 São Tomé Eng. Saint Thomas. island S Sao Tome and Principe
79 B17 Sao Tome and Principe off. Democratic Republic of Sao Tome and Principe, Port. República Democrática de São Tomé e Príncipe. ◆ republic E Atlantic Ocean
Sao Tome and Principe, Democratic Republic of see Sao Tome and Principe
São Tomé e Príncipe, República Democrática de see Sao Tome and Principe
74 H9 Saoura, Oued ≈ NW Algeria
60 M10 São Vicente Eng. Saint Vincent. São Paulo, S Brazil 23°55′S 46°25′W
64 O5 São Vicente Madeira, Portugal, NE Atlantic Ocean 32°48′N 17°03′W
76 C9 São Vicente Eng. Saint Vincent. island Ilhas de Barlavento, N Cape Verde
104 F14 São Vicente, Cabo de Eng. Cape Saint Vincent, Port. Cabode São Vicente. cape S Portugal
São Vicente, Cabo de see São Vicente, Cabo de
Sápai see Sápes
Sapaleri, Cerro see Zapaleri, Cerro
Saparoea see Saparua
171 S13 Saparua prev. Saparoea. Pulau Saparua, C Indonesia 03°35′S 128°37′E
168 L11 Sapat Sumatera, W Indonesia 0°18′S 103°18′E
77 U17 Sapele Delta, S Nigeria 05°54′N 05°43′E
23 X7 Sapelo Island island Georgia, SE USA
23 X7 Sapelo Sound sound Georgia, SE USA
114 K13 Sápes var. Sápai. Anatolikí Makedonía kai Thráki, NE Greece 41°02′N 25°44′E
Sapiéntza see Sapiénza
115 D22 Sapiénza var. Sapiéntza. island S Greece
138 F12 Sapir prev. Sappir. Southern, S Israel 30°43′N 35°11′E
61 I15 Sapiranga Rio Grande do Sul, S Brazil 29°39′S 50°58′W
114 K13 Sápka ▲ NE Greece
105 X9 Sa Pobla Mallorca, Spain, W Mediterranean Sea 39°46′N 03°03′E
56 D11 Saposoa San Martín, N Peru 06°53′S 76°45′W
119 F16 Sapotskin Pol. Sopockinie, Rus. Sapotskino, Sopotskin. Hrodzyenskaya Voblasts', W Belarus 53°50′N 23°39′E
77 P13 Sapoui var. Sapouy. S Burkina Faso 11°34′N 01°44′W
Sapouy see Sapoui
Sappir see Sapir
165 S4 Sapporo Hokkaidō, NE Japan 43°05′N 141°21′E
107 M19 Sapri Campania, S Italy 40°05′N 15°36′E
169 T16 Sapudi, Pulau island S Indonesia
27 P9 Sapulpa Oklahoma, C USA 36°00′N 96°06′W
142 J4 Saqqez var. Saghez, Sakiz, Saqqiz. Kordestān, NW Iran 36°31′N 46°16′E
Saqqiz see Saqqez
139 U8 Sarābādī Wāsiţ, E Iraq 33°00′N 44°52′E
167 P10 Sara Buri var. Saraburi. Saraburi, C Thailand 14°32′N 100°53′E
Saraburi see Sara Buri
Sarafjagān see Salafchegān
24 K9 Saragosa Texas, SW USA 31°03′N 103°39′W
Saragossa see Zaragoza
Saragt see Sarahs
56 B8 Saraguro Loja, S Ecuador 03°42′S 79°18′W
146 I15 Sarahs var. Saragt, Rus. Serakhs. Ahal Welaýaty, S Turkmenistan 36°33′N 61°10′E
126 M6 Sarai Ryazanskaya Oblast', W Russia 53°43′N 39°59′E
Sarāi see Sarāy
154 M12 Saraipāli Chhattīsgarh, C India 21°21′N 83°01′E
149 T9 Sarai Sidhu Punjab, E Pakistan 30°35′N 72°02′E
93 M15 Säräisniemi Kainuu, C Finland 64°25′N 26°50′E
113 I14 Sarajevo ● (Bosnia and Herzegovina) Federacija Bosne I Hercegovine, SE Bosnia and Herzegovina 43°53′N 18°24′E
112 I13 Sarajevo ✈ Federacija Bosne I Hercegovine, C Bosnia and Herzegovina 43°49′N 18°21′E
143 V4 Sarakhs Khorāsān-e Razavī, NE Iran 36°50′N 61°00′E
115 H17 Sarakíniko, Akrotírio headland Évvoia, C Greece 38°46′N 23°43′E
115 I18 Sarakinó island Vóreies Sporádes, Greece, Aegean Sea
127 V7 Saraktash Orenburgskaya Oblast', W Russia 51°46′N 56°23′E
30 L15 Sara, Lake ⊠ Illinois, N USA
23 N8 Saraland Alabama, S USA 30°49′N 88°04′W
55 V9 Saramacca ◆ district N Suriname
55 V10 Saramacca Rivier ≈ C Suriname
166 M2 Saramati ▲ N Myanmar (Burma) 25°46′N 95°01′E
145 R10 Saran' Kaz. Saran. Karaganda, C Kazakhstan 49°47′N 73°02′E
18 K7 Saranac Lake New York, NE USA 44°18′N 74°06′W
18 K7 Saranac River ≈ New York, NE USA
Saranda see Sarandë
113 L23 Sarandë var. Saranda, It. Porto Edda; prev. Santi Quaranta. Vlorë, S Albania 39°53′N 20°E
61 H14 Sarandi Rio Grande do Sul, S Brazil 27°57′S 52°58′W
61 F19 Sarandí del Yí Durazno, C Uruguay 33°18′S 55°38′W
61 F19 Sarandí Grande Florida, S Uruguay 33°43′S 56°19′W
171 Q8 Sarangani Islands island group S Philippines
127 P5 Saransk Respublika Mordoviya, W Russia 54°11′N 45°10′E
115 C14 Sarantáporos ≈ N Greece
114 H9 Sarantsi Sofia, W Bulgaria 42°43′N 23°46′E
127 T3 Sarapul Udmurtskaya Respublika, NW Russia 56°26′N 53°52′E
Sarāqeb see Sarāqib
138 I3 Sarāqib Fr. Saraqeb. Idlib, N Syria 35°52′N 36°48′E
54 J5 Sarare Lara, N Venezuela 09°47′N 69°10′W
55 O10 Sarariña Amazonas, S Venezuela 04°10′N 64°31′W
145 S10 Sar Ashk Kermān, C Iran
23 V13 Sarasota Florida, SE USA 27°20′N 82°31′W
117 O11 Sarata Odes'ka Oblast', SW Ukraine 46°01′N 29°40′E
116 I10 Sărăţel Hung. Szeretfalva. Bistriţa-Năsăud, N Romania 47°02′N 24°24′E
25 X10 Saratoga Texas, SW USA 30°15′N 94°31′W
18 K10 Saratoga Springs New York, NE USA 43°04′N 73°47′W
127 P8 Saratov Saratovskaya Oblast', W Russia 51°33′N 45°58′E
127 P8 Saratovskaya Oblast' ◆ province W Russia
127 Q7 Saratovskoye Vodokhranilishche ⊠ W Russia
143 X13 Sarāvān Sīstān va Balūchestān, SE Iran 27°11′N 62°35′E
Saravan/Saravane see Salavan
169 S9 Sarawak ◆ state East Malaysia
Sarawak see Kuching
139 U6 Sarāy var. Sarāi. Diyālá, E Iraq 34°06′N 45°06′E
136 D10 Saray Tekirdağ, NW Turkey 41°27′N 27°56′E
76 J12 Saraya SE Senegal 12°50′N 11°45′W
143 W14 Sarbāz Sīstān va Balūchestān, SE Iran 26°38′N 61°13′E
143 U8 Sarbīsheh Khorāsān-e Janūbī, E Iran 32°35′N 59°50′E
111 J24 Sárbogárd Fejér, C Hungary 46°54′N 18°36′E
Şarcad see Sarkad
27 S7 Sarcoxie Missouri, C USA 37°04′N 94°07′W
152 L11 Sārda Nep. Kali. ≈ India/Nepal
152 G10 Sardārshahr Rājasthān, NW India 28°30′N 74°30′E
107 C18 Sardegna Eng. Sardinia. ◆ region Italy, C Mediterranean Sea
107 A18 Sardegna Eng. Sardinia. island Italy, C Mediterranean Sea
42 K13 Sardinal Guanacaste, NW Costa Rica 10°30′N 85°38′W
54 G7 Sardinata Norte de Santander, N Colombia 08°07′N 72°47′W
Sardinia see Sardegna
120 K8 Sardinia-Corsica Trough undersea feature Tyrrhenian Sea, C Mediterranean Sea
22 L2 Sardis Mississippi, S USA 34°25′N 89°55′W
22 L2 Sardis Lake ⊠ Mississippi, S USA
27 P12 Sardis Lake ⊠ Oklahoma, C USA
92 H12 Sarek ▲ N Sweden
92 H11 Sarektjåhkkå ▲ N Sweden 67°28′N 17°56′E
Sar-e Pol see Sar-e Pul
Sar-e Pol see Sar-e Pol-e Žahāb
142 J6 Sar-e Pol-e Žahāb var. Sar-e Pol, Sar-i Pul. Kermānshāhān, W Iran 34°28′N 45°52′E
149 N3 Sar-e Pul var. Sar-i-Pul; prev. Sar-e Pol. Sar-e Pul, N Afghanistan 36°16′N 65°55′E
149 O3 Sar-e Pul ◆ province N Afghanistan
Sarera, Teluk see Cenderawasih, Teluk
147 T13 Sarez, Kŭli Rus. Sarezskoye Ozero. ◎ SE Tajikistan
Sarezskoye Ozero see Sarez, Kŭli

◆ Country ● Country Capital ◇ Dependent Territory ○ Dependent Territory Capital ◆ Administrative Regions ✈ International Airport ▲ Mountain ▲ Mountain Range Volcano ≈ River ◎ Lake ⊠ Reservoir

SARGASSO SEA – SCOTT RIVER


64 G10 **Sargasso Sea** *sea* W Atlantic Ocean
149 U8 **Sargodha** Punjab, NE Pakistan 32°06′N 72°48′E
78 I13 **Sarh** *prev.* Fort-Archambault. Moyen-Chari, S Chad 09°08′N 18°22′E
143 P4 **Sārī** *var.* Sari, Sāri. Māzandarān, N Iran 36°37′N 53°05′E
115 N23 **Saría** *island* SE Greece
**Sariasiya** *see* Sariosiyo
40 F3 **Saric** Sonora, NW Mexico 31°08′N 111°22′W
188 K6 **Sarigan** *island* C Northern Mariana Islands
136 D14 **Sarıgöl** Manisa, SW Turkey 38°16′N 28°41′E
139 T6 **Sārihah** At Ta'mím, E Iraq 34°34′N 44°38′E
137 R12 **Sarıkamış** Kars, NE Turkey 40°18′N 42°36′E
169 R9 **Sarikei** Sarawak, East Malaysia 02°07′N 111°30′E
147 U12 **Sarikol Range** *Rus.* Sarykol'skiy Khrebet. ▲ China/Tajikistan
181 Y7 **Sarina** Queensland, NE Australia 21°34′S 149°12′E
**Sarine** *see* La Sarine
105 S5 **Sariñena** Aragón, NE Spain 41°47′N 00°10′W
147 O13 **Sariosiyo** *Rus.* Sariasiya. Surkhondaryo Viloyati, S Uzbekistan 38°25′N 67°51′E
**Sar-i-Pul** *see* Sar-e Pol, Afghanistan
**Sar-i Pul** *see* Sar-e Pol-e Ẕahāb, Iran
**Sariqamish Kŭli** *see* Sarygamyş Köli
149 V1 **Sarī Qūl** *Rus.* Ozero Zurkul', *Taj.* Zŭrkŭl. ◎ Afghanistan/ Tajikistan *see also* Zŭrkŭl
**Sarī Qūl** *see* Zŭrkŭl
75 Q12 **Sarīr Tibistī** *var.* Serir Tibesti. *desert* S Libya
25 S15 **Sarita** Texas, SW USA 27°14′N 97°48′W
163 W14 **Sariwŏn** SW North Korea 38°30′N 125°52′E
114 P12 **Sarıyer** İstanbul, NW Turkey 41°11′N 29°03′E
97 L26 **Sark** *Fr.* Sercq. *island* Channel Islands
111 N24 **Sarkad** *Rom.* Şărcad. Békés, SE Hungary 46°44′N 21°25′E
145 W14 **Sarkand** *Kaz.* Sarqan. Almaty, SW Kazakhstan 45°24′N 79°55′E
152 D11 **Sarkāri Tala** Rājasthān, NW India 27°39′N 70°52′E
136 G15 **Şarkikaraağaç** *var.* Şarki Karaağaç. Isparta, SW Turkey 38°04′N 31°22′E
**Şarki Karaağaç** *see* Şarkikaraağaç
136 L13 **Şarkışla** Sivas, C Turkey 39°21′N 36°27′E
136 C11 **Şarköy** Tekirdağ, NW Turkey 40°37′N 27°07′E
**Sárköz** *see* Livada
**Sarlat** *see* Sarlat-la-Canéda
102 M13 **Sarlat-la-Canéda** *var.* Sarlat. Dordogne, SW France 44°54′N 01°12′E
109 S3 **Sarleinsbach** Oberösterreich, N Austria 48°33′N 13°55′E
**Šarma** *see* Ash Sharmah
171 Y12 **Sarmi** Papua, E Indonesia 01°51′S 138°45′E
63 I19 **Sarmiento** Chubut, S Argentina 45°38′S 69°07′W
63 H25 **Sarmiento, Monte** ▲ S Chile 54°28′S 70°49′W
94 J11 **Särna** Dalarna, C Sweden 61°40′N 13°10′E
108 F8 **Sarnen** Obwalden, C Switzerland 46°54′N 08°15′E
108 F9 **Sarner See** ◎ C Switzerland
14 D16 **Sarnia** Ontario, S Canada 42°58′N 82°23′W
116 L3 **Sarny** Rivnens'ka Oblast', NW Ukraine 51°20′N 26°35′E
171 O13 **Saroako** Sulawesi, C Indonesia 02°31′S 121°18′E
118 L13 **Sarochyna** *Rus.* Sorochino. Vitsyebskaya Voblasts', N Belarus 55°12′N 28°45′E
168 L12 **Sarolangun** Sumatera, W Indonesia 02°17′S 102°39′E
165 U3 **Saroma** Hokkaidō, NE Japan 44°01′N 143°43′E
165 V3 **Saroma-ko** ◎ Hokkaidō, NE Japan
**Saronic Gulf** *see* Saronikós Kólpos
115 H20 **Saronikós Kólpos** *Eng.* Saronic Gulf. *gulf* S Greece
106 D7 **Saronno** Lombardia, N Italy 45°38′N 09°02′E
136 B11 **Saros Körfezi** *gulf* NW Turkey
111 N20 **Sárospatak** Borsod-Abaúj-Zemplén, NE Hungary 48°18′N 21°30′E
127 O4 **Sarov** *prev.* Sarova. Respublika Mordoviya, SW Russia 54°39′N 43°09′E
**Sarova** *see* Sarov
127 P12 **Sarpa** Respublika Kalmykiya, SW Russia 47°00′N 45°42′E
127 P12 **Sarpa, Ozero** ◎ SW Russia
**Šar Planina** *see* Mali i Sharrit
95 I16 **Sarpsborg** Østfold, S Norway 59°16′N 11°07′E
139 U5 **Sarqalā** At Ta'mím, N Iraq
**Sarqan** *see* Sarkand
103 U4 **Sarralbe** Moselle, NE France 49°02′N 07°01′E
**Sarre** *see* Saar, France/ Germany
**Sarre** *see* Saarland, Germany
103 U5 **Sarrebourg** *Ger.* Saarburg. Moselle, NE France 48°43′N 07°03′E
**Sarrebruck** *see* Saarbrücken
103 U4 **Sarreguemines** *prev.* Saargemund. Moselle, NE France 49°06′N 07°04′E
104 I3 **Sarria** Galicia, NW Spain 42°47′N 07°25′W
105 S8 **Sarrión** Aragón, NE Spain 40°09′N 00°49′W
42 F4 **Sarstoon** *Sp.* Río Sarstún. ⚡ Belize/Guatemala
**Sarstún, Río** *see* Sarstoon
123 Q9 **Sartang** ⚡ NE Russia
103 X16 **Sartène** Corse, France, C Mediterranean Sea 41°38′N 08°58′E
102 K7 **Sarthe** ◆ *department* NW France
102 K7 **Sarthe** ⚡ N France
115 H15 **Sárti** Kentrikí Makedonía, N Greece 40°05′N 24°E
**Sartu** *see* Daqing
165 T1 **Sarufutsu** Hokkaidō, NE Japan 45°20′N 142°03′E
**Saruhan** *see* Manisa
152 G9 **Sarūpsar** Rājasthān, NW India 29°25′N 73°50′E
137 U13 **Şärur** *prev.* Il'ichevsk. SW Azerbaijan 39°30′N 44°59′E
**Sarvani** *see* Marneuli
111 G23 **Sárvár** Vas, W Hungary 47°15′N 16°59′E
143 P11 **Sarvestān** Fārs, S Iran 29°16′N 53°13′E
171 W12 **Sarwon** Papua, E Indonesia 0°58′S 136°08′E
145 P17 **Saryagash** *Kaz.* Saryaghash. Yuzhnyy Kazakhstan, S Kazakhstan 41°29′N 69°10′E
**Saryaghash** *see* Saryagash
145 R9 **Saryarka** *Eng.* Kazakh Uplands, Kirghiz Steppe. *uplands* C Kazakhstan
147 W8 **Sary-Bulak** Narynskaya Oblast', C Kyrgyzstan 41°56′N 75°44′E
147 U10 **Sary-Bulak** Oshskaya Oblast', SW Kyrgyzstan 40°49′N 73°44′E
117 S14 **Sarych, Mys** *headland* S Ukraine 44°23′N 33°44′E
**Sary-Dzhaz** *see* Aksu He
146 F8 **Sarygamyş Köli** *Rus.* Sarykamyshkoye Ozero, *Uzb.* Sariqamish Kŭli. *salt lake* Kazakhstan/Uzbekistan
144 G13 **Sarykamys** *Kaz.* Saryqamys. Mangistau, SW Kazakhstan 45°58′N 53°30′E
**Sarykamyshkoye Ozero** *see* Sarygamyş Köli
145 N7 **Sarykol'** *prev.* Uritskiy. Kustanay, N Kazakhstan 53°19′N 65°34′E
**Sarykol'skiy Khrebet** *see* Sarikol Range
144 M10 **Sarykopa, Ozero** ◎ C Kazakhstan
145 V15 **Saryozek** *Kaz.* Saryözek. Almaty, SE Kazakhstan 44°22′N 77°57′E
144 E10 **Saryozen** *Kaz.* Kishiözen; *prev.* Malyy Uzen'. ⚡ Kazakhstan/Russia
**Saryqamys** *see* Sarykamys
145 S13 **Saryshagan** *Kaz.* Saryshahan. Karaganda, SE Kazakhstan 46°05′N 73°38′E
**Saryshaghan** *see* Saryshagan
145 O13 **Sarysu** ⚡ S Kazakhstan
147 T11 **Sary-Tash** Oshskaya Oblast', SW Kyrgyzstan 39°44′N 73°14′E
145 T12 **Saryterek** Karaganda, C Kazakhstan 47°46′N 74°06′E
**Saryyazynskoye Vodokhranilishche** *see* Saryýazy Suw Howdany
146 J15 **Saryýazy Suw Howdany** *Rus.* Saryyazynskoye Vodokhranilishche. ⊠ S Turkmenistan
145 T14 **Saryyesik-Atyrau, Peski** *desert* E Kazakhstan
106 E10 **Sarzana** Liguria, NW Italy 44°07′N 09°59′E
188 B17 **Sasalaguan, Mount** ▲ S Guam
153 O14 **Sasarām** Bihār, N India 24°58′N 84°01′E
186 M8 **Sasari, Mount** ▲ Santa Isabel, N Solomon Islands 08°09′S 159°32′E
164 C13 **Sasebo** Nagasaki, Kyūshū, SW Japan 33°10′N 129°42′E
14 I9 **Saseginaga, Lac** ◎ Québec, SE Canada
**Saseno** *see* Sazan
11 R13 **Saskatchewan** ◆ *province* SW Canada
11 U14 **Saskatchewan** ⚡ Manitoba/Saskatchewan, C Canada
11 T15 **Saskatoon** Saskatchewan, S Canada 52°10′N 106°40′W
11 T15 **Saskatoon** ✕ Saskatchewan, S Canada 52°15′N 107°05′W
123 N7 **Saskylakh** Respublika Sakha (Yakutiya), NE Russia 71°56′N 114°07′E
42 L7 **Saslaya, Cerro** ▲ N Nicaragua 13°52′N 85°06′W
38 G17 **Sasmik, Cape** *headland* Tanaga Island, Alaska, USA 51°36′N 177°55′W
119 N19 **Sasnovy Bor** *Rus.* Sosnovyy Bor. Homyel'skaya Voblasts', SE Belarus 52°32′N 29°35′E
127 N5 **Sasovo** Ryazanskaya Oblast', W Russia 54°19′N 41°54′E
25 S12 **Saspamco** Texas, SW USA 29°13′N 98°18′W
109 W9 **Sass** *var.* Sassbach. ⚡ SE Austria
76 M17 **Sassandra** S Ivory Coast 04°58′N 06°08′W
76 M17 **Sassandra** *var.* Ibo, Sassandra Fleuve. ⚡ S Ivory Coast
**Sassandra Fleuve** *see* Sassandra
107 B17 **Sassari** Sardegna, Italy, C Mediterranean Sea 40°44′N 08°33′E
**Sassbach** *see* Sass
98 H11 **Sassenheim** Zuid-Holland, W Netherlands 52°14′N 04°31′E
**Sassmacken** *see* Valdemārpils
100 O7 **Sassnitz** Mecklenburg-Vorpommern, NE Germany 54°32′N 13°39′E
99 E16 **Sas van Gent** Zeeland, SW Netherlands 51°13′N 03°48′E
145 W12 **Sasykkol', Ozero** ◎ E Kazakhstan
117 O12 **Sasyk, Ozero** *Rus.* Ozero Sasyk Kunduk, *var.* Ozero Kunduk. ◎ SW Ukraine
76 J12 **Satadougou** Kayes, SW Mali 12°40′N 11°25′W
164 C17 **Sata-misaki** Kyūshū, SW Japan
26 I7 **Satanta** Kansas, C USA 37°23′N 102°00′W
155 E15 **Sātāra** Mahārāshtra, W India 17°41′N 73°59′E
192 G15 **Sātaua** Savai'i, NW Samoa 13°26′S 172°40′W
188 M16 **Satawal** *island* Caroline Islands, C Micronesia
189 R17 **Satawan Atoll** *atoll* Mortlock Islands, C Micronesia
**Sátbaev** *see* Satpayev
23 Y12 **Satellite Beach** Florida, SE USA 28°10′N 80°35′W
95 M14 **Säter** Dalarna, C Sweden 60°21′N 15°45′E
**Sathmar** *see* Satu Mare
23 V7 **Satilla River** ⚡ Georgia, SE USA
57 F14 **Satipo** *var.* San Francisco de Satipo. Junín, C Peru 11°19′S 74°37′W
122 F11 **Satka** Chelyabinskaya Oblast', C Russia 55°08′N 58°54′E
153 T16 **Satkhira** Khulna, SW Bangladesh 22°43′N 89°06′E
146 J13 **Şatlyk** *Rus.* Shatlyk. Mary Welaýaty, C Turkmenistan 37°55′N 61°00′E
154 K9 **Satna** *prev.* Sutna. Madhya Pradesh, C India 24°33′N 80°50′E
103 R11 **Satolas** ✕ (Lyon) Rhône, E France 45°44′N 05°01′E
111 N20 **Sátoraljaújhely** Borsod-Abaúj-Zemplén, NE Hungary 48°24′N 21°39′E
145 O12 **Satpayev** *Kaz.* Sätbaev; *prev.* Nikol'skiy. Karaganda, C Kazakhstan 47°59′N 67°27′E
154 G11 **Sātpura Range** ▲ C India
165 Q10 **Satsuma-Sendai** Miyagi, Honshū, C Japan 38°16′N 140°52′E
**Satsuma-Sendai** *see* Sendai
167 P12 **Sattahip** *var.* Ban Sattahip, Ban Sattahipp. Chon Buri, S Thailand 12°36′N 100°56′E
92 L11 **Sattanen** Lappi, NE Finland 67°31′N 26°35′E
**Satul** *see* Satun
116 H9 **Satulung** *Hung.* Kővárhosszúfalu. Maramureş, N Romania 47°34′N 23°26′E
**Satul-Vechi** *see* Staro Selo
116 G8 **Satu Mare** *Ger.* Sathmar, *Hung.* Szatmárrnémeti. Satu Mare, NW Romania 47°46′N 22°55′E
116 G8 **Satu Mare** ◆ *county* NW Romania
167 N16 **Satun** *var.* Satul, Setul. Satun, SW Thailand 06°40′N 100°01′E
192 G16 **Satupa'itea** Savai'i, W Samoa 13°46′S 172°26′W
**Sau** *see* Sava
14 F14 **Sauble** ⚡ Ontario, S Canada
14 F13 **Sauble Beach** Ontario, S Canada 44°36′N 81°15′W
61 C16 **Sauce** Corrientes, NE Argentina 30°05′S 58°46′W
**Sauce** *see* Juan L. Lacaze
36 K15 **Sauceda Mountains** ▲ Arizona, SW USA
61 C17 **Sauce de Luna** Entre Ríos, E Argentina 31°15′S 59°09′W
63 L15 **Sauce Grande, Río** ⚡ E Argentina
40 K6 **Saucillo** Chihuahua, N Mexico 28°01′N 105°17′W
95 D15 **Sauda** Rogaland, S Norway 59°38′N 06°23′E
145 Q16 **Saudakent** *Kaz.* Saūdakent; *prev.* Baykadam, *Kaz.* Bayqadam. Zhambyl, S Kazakhstan 43°49′N 69°56′E
92 J2 **Sauðárkrókur** Norðurland Vestra, N Iceland 65°45′N 19°39′W
141 P9 **Saudi Arabia** *off.* Kingdom of Saudi Arabia, Al 'Arabiyah as Su'ūdīyah, *Ar.* Al Mamlakah al 'Arabīyah as Su'ūdīyah. ◆ *monarchy* SW Asia
**Saudi Arabia, Kingdom of** *see* Saudi Arabia
101 D19 **Sauer** *var.* Sûre. ⚡ NW Europe *see also* Sûre
**Sauer** *see* Sûre
101 F15 **Sauerland** *forest* W Germany
14 F14 **Saugeen** ⚡ Ontario, S Canada
18 K12 **Saugerties** New York, NE USA 42°04′N 73°55′W
**Saugor** *see* Sāgar
10 K15 **Saugstad, Mount** ▲ British Columbia, SW Canada 52°12′N 126°35′W
**Sāūjbulāgh** *see* Mahābād
102 J11 **Saujon** Charente-Maritime, W France 45°40′N 00°54′W
29 T7 **Sauk Centre** Minnesota, N USA 45°44′N 94°57′W
30 L8 **Sauk City** Wisconsin, N USA 43°16′N 89°43′W
29 U7 **Sauk Rapids** Minnesota, N USA 45°35′N 94°09′W
55 Y11 **Saül** C French Guiana 03°37′N 53°12′W
103 O7 **Sauldre** ⚡ C France
101 I23 **Saulgau** Baden-Württemberg, SW Germany 48°03′N 09°28′E
103 Q8 **Saulieu** Côte d'Or, C France 47°15′N 04°15′E
118 G8 **Saulkrasti** C Latvia 57°14′N 24°25′E
15 S6 **Sault-aux-Cochons, Rivière du** ⚡ Québec, SE Canada
31 Q4 **Sault Sainte Marie** Michigan, N USA 46°29′N 84°22′W
12 F14 **Sault Ste. Marie** Ontario, S Canada 46°30′N 84°17′W
145 P7 **Saumalkol'** *prev.* Volodarskoye. Severnyy Kazakhstan, N Kazakhstan 53°19′N 68°05′E
190 E13 **Sauma, Pointe** *headland* Île Alofi, W Wallis and Futuna 14°21′S 177°58′W
171 T16 **Saumlaki** *var.* Saumlakki. Pulau Yamdena, E Indonesia 07°53′S 131°18′E
**Saumlakki** *see* Saumlaki
15 R12 **Saumon, Rivière au** ⚡ Québec, SE Canada
102 K8 **Saumur** Maine-et-Loire, NW France 47°16′N 00°04′W
185 F23 **Saunders, Cape** *headland* South Island, New Zealand 45°53′S 170°40′E
195 N13 **Saunders Coast** *physical region* Antarctica
65 B23 **Saunders Island** *island* NW Falkland Islands
65 C24 **Saunders Island Settlement** Saunders Island, NW Falkland Islands 51°22′S 60°05′W
82 F11 **Saurimo** *Port.* Henrique de Carvalho, Vila Henrique de Carvalho. Lunda Sul, NE Angola 09°39′S 20°24′E
55 S11 **Sauriwaunawa** S Guyana 03°10′N 59°51′W
82 D12 **Sautar** Malanje, NW Angola 11°10′S 18°26′E
45 S13 **Sauteurs** N Grenada 12°14′N 61°38′W
102 K13 **Sauveterre-de-Guyenne** Gironde, SW France 44°43′N 00°02′W
119 O14 **Sava** Mahilyowskaya Voblasts', E Belarus 54°22′N 30°49′E
42 J5 **Savá** Colón, N Honduras 15°30′N 86°16′W
84 H11 **Sava** *Eng.* Save, *Ger.* Sau, *Hung.* Száva. ⚡ SE Europe
33 Y8 **Savage** Montana, NW USA 47°28′N 104°17′W
183 N16 **Savage River** Tasmania, SE Australia 41°34′S 145°15′E
77 R15 **Savalou** S Benin 07°59′N 01°58′E
30 K10 **Savanna** Illinois, N USA 42°05′N 90°09′W
23 X6 **Savannah** Georgia, SE USA 32°02′N 81°01′W
27 R2 **Savannah** Missouri, C USA 39°57′N 94°49′W
20 H10 **Savannah** Tennessee, S USA 35°12′N 88°15′W
21 O12 **Savannah River** ⚡ Georgia/South Carolina, SE USA
167 S9 **Savannakhét** *var.* Khanthabouli. Savannakhét, S Laos 16°38′N 104°49′E
44 H12 **Savanna-La-Mar** W Jamaica 18°13′N 78°08′W
12 B10 **Savant Lake** ◎ Ontario, S Canada
155 F17 **Savanūr** Karnātaka, W India 14°58′N 75°19′E
93 J16 **Sävar** Västerbotten, N Sweden 63°52′N 20°33′E
**Savaria** *see* Szombathely
154 C11 **Sāvarkundla** *var.* Kundla. Gujarāt, W India 21°21′N 71°20′E
116 F11 **Săvârşin** *Hung.* Soborsin; *prev.* Săvirşin. Arad, W Romania 46°00′N 22°15′E
136 C13 **Savaştepe** Balıkesir, W Turkey 39°20′N 27°38′E
147 P11 **Savat** *Rus.* Savat. Sirdaryo Viloyati, E Uzbekistan 40°03′N 68°35′E
**Savat** *see* Savat
**Sávdijári** *see* Skaulo
77 R15 **Savè** SE Benin 08°04′N 02°29′E
83 N18 **Save** Inhambane, E Mozambique 21°07′S 34°35′E
102 L16 **Save** ⚡ S France
83 L17 **Save** *var.* Sabi. ⚡ Mozambique/Zimbabwe *see also* Sabi
**Save** *see* Sava
**Save** *see* Sabi
142 M6 **Sāveh** Markazī, W Iran 35°00′N 50°22′E
116 L8 **Săveni** Botoşani, NE Romania 47°57′N 26°52′E
103 N16 **Saverdun** Ariège, S France 43°15′N 01°34′E
103 U5 **Saverne** *var.* Zabern; *anc.* Tres Tabernae. Bas-Rhin, NE France 48°45′N 07°22′E
106 B9 **Savigliano** Piemonte, NW Italy 44°39′N 07°39′E
**Savigsivik** *see* Savissivik
109 U10 **Savinja** ⚡ N Slovenia
106 H11 **Savio** ⚡ C Italy
**Săvirşin** *see* Săvârşin
197 O11 **Savissivik** *var.* Savigsivik. ◆ Avannaata, N Greenland
93 N18 **Savitaipale** Etelä-Karjala, SE Finland 61°12′N 27°43′E
113 J15 **Šavnik** C Montenegro 42°57′N 19°04′E
108 I9 **Savognin** Graubünden, S Switzerland 46°34′N 09°35′E
103 T12 **Savoie** ◆ *department* E France
106 C10 **Savona** Liguria, NW Italy 44°18′N 08°29′E
93 N17 **Savonlinna** *Swe.* Nyslott. Etelä-Savo, E Finland 61°51′N 28°56′E
93 N17 **Savonranta** Etelä-Savo, E Finland 62°10′N 29°10′E
38 K10 **Savoonga** Saint Lawrence Island, Alaska, USA 63°40′N 170°29′W
30 M13 **Savoy** Illinois, N USA 40°03′N 88°15′W
117 O8 **Savran'** Odes'ka Oblast', SW Ukraine 48°07′N 30°00′E
137 R11 **Şavşat** Artvin, NE Turkey 41°15′N 42°30′E
95 L19 **Sävsjö** Jönköping, S Sweden 57°25′N 14°40′E
**Savu, Kepulauan** *see* Sawu, Kepulauan
92 M11 **Savukoski** Lappi, NE Finland 67°17′N 28°14′E
**Savu, Pulau** *see* Sawu, Pulau
187 Y14 **Savusavu** Vanua Levu, N Fiji 16°48′S 179°20′E
171 O17 **Savu Sea** *Ind.* Laut Sawu. *sea* S Indonesia
83 H17 **Savute** Chobe, N Botswana 18°33′S 24°06′E
139 N7 **Şawāb Uqlat** *well* W Iraq
138 M7 **Şawāb, Wādī aş** *dry watercourse* W Iraq
152 H13 **Sawāi Mādhopur** Rājasthān, N India 26°00′N 76°22′E
**Sawakin** *see* Suakin
167 R8 **Sawang Daen Din** Sakon Nakhon, E Thailand 17°28′N 103°27′E
167 O8 **Sawankhalok** *var.* Swankalok. Sukhothai, NW Thailand 17°19′N 99°50′E
165 P13 **Sawara** Chiba, Honshū, S Japan 35°52′N 140°31′E
37 R5 **Sawatch Range** ▲ Colorado, C USA
141 N12 **Sawdā', Jabal** ▲ SW Saudi Arabia 18°15′N 42°26′E
75 P9 **Sawdā', Jabal as** ▲ C Libya
**Sawdirī** *see* Sodiri
97 F14 **Sawel Mountain** ▲ C Northern Ireland, United Kingdom 54°49′N 07°04′W
**Sawhāj** *see* Sūhāj
77 O15 **Sawla** N Ghana 09°14′N 02°26′W
141 X12 **Şawqirah** *var.* Suqrah. S Oman 18°16′N 56°34′E
141 X12 **Şawqirah, Dawhat** *var.* Ghubbat Sawqirah, Sukra Bay, Suqrah Bay. *bay* S Oman
**Sawqirah, Ghubbat** *see* Şawqirah, Dawhat
183 V5 **Sawtell** New South Wales, SE Australia 30°22′S 153°04′E
138 K7 **Şawt, Wādī aş** *dry watercourse* S Syria
171 O17 **Sawu, Kepulauan** *var.* Kepulauan Savu. *island group* S Indonesia
**Sawu, Laut** *see* Savu Sea
171 O17 **Sawu, Pulau** *var.* Pulau Savu. *island* Kepulauan Sawu, S Indonesia
105 S12 **Sax** Comunitat Valenciana, E Spain 38°33′N 00°49′W
**Saxe** *see* Sachsen
108 C11 **Saxon** Valais, SW Switzerland 46°07′N 07°09′E
**Saxony** *see* Sachsen
**Saxony-Anhalt** *see* Sachsen-Anhalt
77 R12 **Say** Niamey, SW Niger 13°08′N 02°20′E
15 V7 **Sayabec** Québec, SE Canada 48°33′N 67°42′W
**Sayaboury** *see* Xaignabouli
145 U12 **Sayak** *Kaz.* Sayaq. Karaganda, E Kazakhstan 46°54′N 77°17′E
57 D14 **Sayán** Lima, W Peru 11°10′S 77°08′W
129 T6 **Sayanskiy Khrebet** ▲ S Russia
**Sayaq** *see* Sayak
146 K13 **Saýat** *Rus.* Sayat. Lebap Welaýaty, E Turkmenistan 38°44′N 63°51′E
42 D3 **Sayaxché** Petén, N Guatemala 16°34′N 90°14′W
**Şaydā/Sayida** *see* Saïda
162 J7 **Sayhan** *var.* Hüremt. Bulgan, C Mongolia 48°40′N 102°33′E
163 N10 **Sayhandulaan** *var.* Öldziyt. Dornogovĭ, SE Mongolia 44°42′N 109°10′E
162 K9 **Sayhan-Ovoo** *var.* Ongi. Dundgovĭ, C Mongolia 45°27′N 103°58′E
141 T15 **Sayḩūt** E Yemen 15°18′N 51°16′E
29 U14 **Saylorville Lake** ⊠ Iowa, C USA
**Saymenskiy Kanal** *see* Saimaa Canal
163 N10 **Saynshand** Dornogovĭ, SE Mongolia 44°51′N 110°07′E
**Saynshand** *see* Sevrey
**Sayn-Ust** *see* Hohmorït
**Say-Ötesh** *see* Otes
138 J7 **Şayqal, Baḩr** ◎ S Syria
**Sayrab** *see* Sayrob
158 H4 **Sayram Hu** ◎ NW China
26 K11 **Sayre** Oklahoma, C USA 35°18′N 99°38′W
18 H12 **Sayre** Pennsylvania, NE USA 41°57′N 76°30′W
18 K15 **Sayreville** New Jersey, NE USA 40°27′N 74°19′W
147 N13 **Sayrob** *Rus.* Sayrab. Surkhondaryo Viloyati, S Uzbekistan 38°03′N 66°54′E
40 L13 **Sayula** Jalisco, SW Mexico 19°52′N 103°36′W
141 R14 **Say'ūn** *var.* Saywūn. C Yemen 15°53′N 48°32′E
**Say-Utës** *see* Otes
10 K16 **Sayward** Vancouver Island, British Columbia, SW Canada 50°20′N 126°01′W
**Saywūn** *see* Say'ūn
**Sayyāl** *see* As Sayyāl
139 U8 **Sayyid 'Abīd** *var.* Saiyid Abid. Wāsiţ, E Iraq 32°51′N 45°07′E
113 J22 **Sazan** *var.* Ishulli i Sazanit, *It.* Saseno. *island* SW Albania
**Sazanit, Ishulli i** *see* Sazan
**Sazau/Sazawa** *see* Sázava
111 E17 **Sázava** *var.* Sazau, *Ger.* Sazawa. ⚡ C Czechia
114 K10 **Sazliyka** ⚡ C Bulgaria
124 J14 **Sazonovo** Vologodskaya Oblast', NW Russia 59°04′N 35°10′E
102 G6 **Scaër** Finistère, NW France 48°00′N 03°40′W
97 J15 **Scafell Pike** ▲ NW England, United Kingdom 54°26′N 03°10′W
**Scalabis** *see* Santarém
96 M2 **Scalloway** N Scotland, United Kingdom 60°10′N 01°17′W
38 M11 **Scammon Bay** Alaska, USA 61°50′N 165°34′W
**Scammon Lagoon/ Scammon, Laguna** *see* Ojo de Liebre, Laguna
84 F7 **Scandinavia** *geophysical region* NW Europe
**Scania** *see* Skåne
96 K5 **Scapa Flow** *sea basin* N Scotland, United Kingdom
107 K26 **Scaramia, Capo** *headland* Sicilia, Italy, C Mediterranean Sea 36°46′N 14°29′E
14 H15 **Scarborough** Ontario, SE Canada 43°46′N 79°14′W
45 Z16 **Scarborough** *prev.* Port Louis. Tobago, Trinidad and Tobago 11°11′N 60°45′W
97 N16 **Scarborough** N England, United Kingdom 54°17′N 00°24′W
185 I17 **Scargill** Canterbury, South Island, New Zealand 42°57′S 172°57′E
96 E7 **Scarp** *island* NW Scotland, United Kingdom
**Scarpanto** *see* Kárpathos
**Scarpanto Strait** *see* Karpathou, Stenó
107 G25 **Scauri** Sicilia, Italy, C Mediterranean Sea 36°45′N 12°06′E
**Scealg, Bá na** *see* Ballinskelligs Bay
**Scebeli** *see* Shebeli
100 K10 **Schaale** ⚡ N Germany
100 K9 **Schaalsee** ◎ N Germany
99 G18 **Schaerbeek** Brussels, C Belgium 50°52′N 04°21′E
108 G6 **Schaffhausen** *Fr.* Schaffhouse. Schaffhausen, N Switzerland 47°42′N 08°38′E
108 G6 **Schaffhausen** *Fr.* Schaffhouse. ◆ *canton* N Switzerland
**Schaffhouse** *see* Schaffhausen
98 I8 **Schagen** Noord-Holland, NW Netherlands 52°47′N 04°47′E
**Schaken** *see* Šakiai
98 M10 **Schalkhaar** Overijssel, E Netherlands 52°16′N 06°10′E
109 R3 **Schärding** Oberösterreich, N Austria 48°27′N 13°26′E
100 G9 **Scharhörn** *island* NW Germany
**Schässburg** *see* Sighişoara
**Schaulen** *see* Šiauliai
30 M10 **Schaumburg** Illinois, N USA 42°01′N 88°04′W
**Schebschi Mountains** *see* Shebshi Mountains
98 P6 **Scheemda** Groningen, NE Netherlands 53°10′N 06°58′E
100 I10 **Scheessel** Niedersachsen, NW Germany 53°11′N 09°33′E
13 N8 **Schefferville** Québec, E Canada 54°50′N 67°W
**Schelde** *see* Scheldt
99 D18 **Scheldt** *Dut.* Schelde, *Fr.* Escaut. ⚡ W Europe
35 X5 **Schell Creek Range** ▲ Nevada, W USA
18 K10 **Schenectady** New York, NE USA 42°48′N 73°57′W
99 I17 **Scherpenheuvel** *Fr.* Montaigu. Vlaams Brabant, C Belgium 51°00′N 04°57′E
98 K11 **Scherpenzeel** Gelderland, C Netherlands 52°07′N 05°30′E
25 S12 **Schertz** Texas, SW USA 29°33′N 98°16′W
98 G11 **Scheveningen** Zuid-Holland, W Netherlands 52°07′N 04°18′E
98 G12 **Schiedam** Zuid-Holland, SW Netherlands 51°55′N 04°25′E
99 M24 **Schieren** Diekirch, NE Luxembourg 49°50′N 06°06′E
98 M4 **Schiermonnikoog** *Fris.* Skiermûntseach. Fryslân, N Netherlands 53°28′N 06°09′E
98 M4 **Schiermonnikoog** *Fris.* Skiermûntseach. *island* Waddeneilanden, N Netherlands
99 K14 **Schijndel** Noord-Brabant, S Netherlands 51°37′N 05°27′E
**Schil** *see* Jiu
99 H16 **Schilde** Antwerpen, N Belgium 51°14′N 04°35′E
**Schillen** *see* Zhilino
103 V5 **Schiltigheim** Bas-Rhin, NE France 48°38′N 07°47′E
106 G7 **Schio** Veneto, NE Italy 45°42′N 11°21′E
98 H10 **Schiphol** ✕ (Amsterdam) Noord-Holland, C Netherlands 52°18′N 04°48′E
**Schippenbeil** *see* Sępopol
**Schiria** *see* Şiria
**Schivelbein** *see* Świdwin
115 D22 **Schiza** *island* S Greece
175 U3 **Schjetman Reef** *reef* Antarctica
**Schlackenwerth** *see* Ostrov
109 R7 **Schladming** Steiermark, SE Austria 47°24′N 13°42′E
**Schlan** *see* Slaný
**Schlanders** *see* Silandro
100 I7 **Schlei** *inlet* N Germany
101 D17 **Schleiden** Nordrhein-Westfalen, W Germany 50°31′N 06°30′E
**Schlelau** *see* Szydłowiec
100 I7 **Schleswig** Schleswig-Holstein, N Germany 54°31′N 09°34′E
29 T13 **Schleswig** Iowa, C USA 42°10′N 95°27′W
100 H8 **Schleswig-Holstein** ◆ *state* N Germany
**Schlettstadt** *see* Sélestat
108 F7 **Schlieren** Zürich, N Switzerland 47°23′N 08°27′E
**Schlochau** *see* Człuchów
**Schloppe** *see* Człopa
101 I18 **Schlüchtern** Hessen, C Germany 50°19′N 09°27′E
101 J17 **Schmalkalden** Thüringen, C Germany 50°42′N 10°26′E
109 W2 **Schmida** ⚡ NE Austria
65 P19 **Schmidt-Ott Seamount** *var.* Schmitt-Ott Seamount, Schmitt-Ott Tablemount. *undersea feature* SW Indian Ocean 39°37′S 13°00′E
**Schmiegel** *see* Śmigiel
**Schmitt-Ott Seamount/ Schmitt-Ott Tablemount** *see* Schmidt-Ott Seamount
15 V3 **Schmon** ⚡ Québec, SE Canada
101 M18 **Schneeberg** ▲ W Germany 50°03′N 11°51′E
**Schneeberg** *see* Veliki Snežnik
**Schnee-Eifel** *see* Schneifel
**Schneekoppe** *see* Sněžka
**Schneidemühl** *see* Piła
101 D18 **Schneifel** *var.* Schnee-Eifel. *plateau* W Germany
**Schnelle Körös/Schnelle Kreisch** *see* Crişul Repede
100 I11 **Schneverdingen** *var.* Schneverdingen (Wümme). Niedersachsen, NW Germany 53°07′N 09°48′E
**Schneverdingen (Wümme)** *see* Schneverdingen
**Schoden** *see* Skuodas
45 Q12 **Schœlcher** W Martinique 14°37′N 61°08′W
18 K10 **Schoharie** New York, NE USA 42°40′N 74°20′W
18 K11 **Schoharie Creek** ⚡ New York, NE USA
115 J21 **Schoinoússa** *island* Kykládes, Greece, Aegean Sea
100 L13 **Schönebeck** Sachsen-Anhalt, C Germany 52°01′N 11°45′E
**Schöneck** *see* Skarszewy
100 O12 **Schönefeld** ✕ (Berlin) Berlin, NE Germany 52°23′N 13°29′E
101 K24 **Schongau** Bayern, S Germany 47°49′N 10°54′E
100 K13 **Schöningen** Niedersachsen, C Germany 52°07′N 10°58′E
**Schönlanke** *see* Trzcianka
**Schönsee** *see* Kowalewo Pomorskie
31 P10 **Schoolcraft** Michigan, N USA 42°05′N 85°39′W
98 O8 **Schoonebeek** Drenthe, NE Netherlands 52°39′N 06°57′E
98 I12 **Schoonhoven** Zuid-Holland, C Netherlands 51°57′N 04°51′E
98 H8 **Schoorl** Noord-Holland, NW Netherlands 52°42′N 04°40′E
**Schooten** *see* Schoten
101 F24 **Schopfheim** Baden-Württemberg, SW Germany 47°39′N 07°49′E
101 I21 **Schorndorf** Baden-Württemberg, S Germany 48°48′N 09°31′E
100 F10 **Schortens** Niedersachsen, NW Germany 53°31′N 07°57′E
99 H16 **Schoten** *var.* Schooten. Antwerpen, N Belgium 51°15′N 04°30′E
183 Q17 **Schouten Island** *island* Tasmania, SE Australia
186 C5 **Schouten Islands** *island group* NW Papua New Guinea
98 E13 **Schouwen** *island* SW Netherlands
**Schreiberhau** *see* Szklarska Poręba
109 U2 **Schrems** Niederösterreich, E Austria 48°48′N 15°05′E
101 L22 **Schrobenhausen** Bayern, SE Germany 48°33′N 11°14′E
18 L8 **Schroon Lake** ◎ New York, NE USA
108 J8 **Schruns** Vorarlberg, W Austria 47°04′N 09°54′E
**Schubin** *see* Szubin
25 U11 **Schulenburg** Texas, SW USA 29°40′N 96°54′W
**Schuls** *see* Scuol
108 E8 **Schüpfheim** Luzern, C Switzerland 47°02′N 07°23′E
35 S6 **Schurz** Nevada, W USA 38°55′N 118°48′W
101 I24 **Schussen** ⚡ S Germany
**Schüttenhofen** *see* Sušice
29 R15 **Schuyler** Nebraska, C USA 41°25′N 97°04′W
18 L10 **Schuylerville** New York, NE USA 43°05′N 73°34′W
101 K20 **Schwabach** Bayern, SE Germany 49°20′N 11°02′E
**Schwabenalb** *see* Schwäbische Alb
101 I23 **Schwäbische Alb** *var.* Schwabenalb, *Eng.* Swabian Jura. ▲ S Germany
101 I22 **Schwäbisch Gmünd** *var.* Gmünd. Baden-Württemberg, SW Germany 48°49′N 09°48′E
101 I21 **Schwäbisch Hall** *var.* Hall. Baden-Württemberg, SW Germany 49°07′N 09°45′E
101 H16 **Schwalm** ⚡ C Germany
109 V9 **Schwanberg** Steiermark, SE Austria 46°46′N 15°12′E
108 H8 **Schwanden** Glarus, E Switzerland 47°02′N 09°04′E
101 M20 **Schwandorf** Bayern, SE Germany 49°20′N 12°07′E
109 S5 **Schwanenstadt** Oberösterreich, NW Austria 48°03′N 13°47′E
169 S11 **Schwaner, Pegunungan** ▲ Borneo, N Indonesia
109 W5 **Schwarza** ⚡ E Austria
109 P9 **Schwarzach** ⚡ S Austria
101 M20 **Schwarzach** *Cz.* Černice. ⚡ Czechia/Germany
**Schwarzach** *see* Schwarzach im Pongau
109 Q7 **Schwarzach im Pongau** *var.* Schwarzach. Salzburg, NW Austria 47°19′N 13°09′E
**Schwarzawa** *see* Svratka
101 N14 **Schwarze Elster** ⚡ E Germany
**Schwarze Körös** *see* Crişul Negru
108 D9 **Schwarzenburg** Bern, W Switzerland 46°51′N 07°28′E
83 D21 **Schwarzrand** ▲ S Namibia
101 G23 **Schwarzwald** *Eng.* Black Forest. ▲ SW Germany
**Schwarzwasser** *see* Wda
39 P7 **Schwatka Mountains** ▲ Alaska, USA
109 N7 **Schwaz** Tirol, W Austria 47°21′N 11°44′E
109 Y4 **Schwechat** Niederösterreich, NE Austria 48°09′N 16°29′E
109 Y4 **Schwechat** ✕ (Wien) Wien, E Austria 48°04′N 16°31′E
100 P11 **Schwedt** Brandenburg, NE Germany 53°04′N 14°16′E
101 D19 **Schweich** Rheinland-Pfalz, SW Germany 49°49′N 06°44′E
**Schweidnitz** *see* Świdnica
101 J18 **Schweinfurt** Bayern, SE Germany 50°03′N 10°13′E
**Schweiz** *see* Switzerland
100 L9 **Schwerin** Mecklenburg-Vorpommern, N Germany 53°38′N 11°25′E
**Schwerin** *see* Skwierzyna
100 L9 **Schweriner See** ◎ N Germany
**Schwertberg** *see* Świecie
101 F15 **Schwerte** Nordrhein-Westfalen, W Germany 51°27′N 07°34′E
**Schwiebus** *see* Świebodzin
100 P13 **Schwielochsee** ◎ NE Germany
**Schwihau** *see* Švihov
**Schwiz** *see* Schwyz
108 G8 **Schwyz** *var.* Schwiz. Schwyz, C Switzerland 47°02′N 08°39′E
108 G8 **Schwyz** *var.* Schwiz. ◆ *canton* C Switzerland
14 J11 **Schyan** ⚡ Québec, SE Canada
**Schyl** *see* Jiu
107 I24 **Sciacca** Sicilia, Italy, C Mediterranean Sea 37°31′N 13°05′E
**Sciasciamana** *see* Shashemenē
107 L26 **Scicli** Sicilia, Italy, C Mediterranean Sea 36°48′N 14°43′E
97 F25 **Scilly, Isles of** *island group* SW England, United Kingdom
111 H17 **Ščinawa** *Ger.* Steinau an der Elbe. Dolnośląskie, SW Poland 51°22′N 16°27′E
**Scio** *see* Chíos
31 S14 **Scioto River** ⚡ Ohio, N USA
36 L5 **Scipio** Utah, W USA 39°15′N 112°06′W
33 X6 **Scobey** Montana, NW USA 48°47′N 105°25′W
183 T7 **Scone** New South Wales, SE Australia 32°02′S 150°51′E
**Scoresby Sound/ Scoresbysund** *see* Ittoqqortoormiit
**Scoresby Sund** *see* Kangertittivaq
**Scorno, Punta dello** *see* Caprara, Punta
34 K3 **Scotia** California, W USA 40°34′N 124°07′W
47 Y14 **Scotia Plate** *tectonic feature*
47 V15 **Scotia Ridge** *undersea feature* S Atlantic Ocean
194 H2 **Scotia Sea** *sea* SW Atlantic Ocean
29 Q12 **Scotland** South Dakota, N USA 43°09′N 97°43′W
25 R5 **Scotland** Texas, SW USA 33°37′N 98°27′W
96 H11 **Scotland** ◆ *national region* Scotland, U K
21 W8 **Scotland Neck** North Carolina, SE USA 36°07′N 77°25′W
195 R13 **Scott Base** *research station (NZ)* Antarctica 77°52′S 167°18′E
10 J16 **Scott, Cape** *headland* Vancouver Island, British Columbia, SW Canada 50°43′N 128°24′W
26 I5 **Scott City** Kansas, C USA 38°28′N 100°55′W
27 Y7 **Scott City** Missouri, C USA 37°13′N 89°31′W
195 R14 **Scott Coast** *physical region* Antarctica
18 C15 **Scottdale** Pennsylvania, NE USA 40°05′N 79°35′W
195 Y11 **Scott Glacier** *glacier* Antarctica
195 Q17 **Scott Island** *island* Antarctica
26 L11 **Scott, Mount** ▲ Oklahoma, USA 34°52′N 98°34′W
32 G15 **Scott, Mount** ▲ Oregon, NW USA 42°53′N 122°06′W
34 M1 **Scott River** ⚡ California, W USA




◆ Country
● Country Capital
◇ Dependent Territory
○ Dependent Territory Capital
◆ Administrative Regions
✕ International Airport
▲ Mountain
▲ Mountain Range
⚠ Volcano
⚡ River
◎ Lake
⊠ Reservoir

Scottsbluff – Severo-Alichurskiy Khrebet


28 I13 **Scottsbluff** Nebraska, C USA 41°52′N 103°40′W
23 Q2 **Scottsboro** Alabama, S USA 34°40′N 86°01′W
31 P15 **Scottsburg** Indiana, N USA 38°42′N 85°47′W
183 P16 **Scottsdale** Tasmania, SE Australia 41°13′S 147°30′E
36 L13 **Scottsdale** Arizona, SW USA 33°31′N 111°54′W
45 O12 **Scotts Head Village** var. Cachacrou. S Dominica 15°12′N 61°22′W
192 L14 **Scott Shoal** undersea feature S Pacific Ocean
20 K7 **Scottsville** Kentucky, S USA 36°45′N 86°11′W
29 U14 **Scranton** Iowa, C USA 42°01′N 94°33′W
18 I13 **Scranton** Pennsylvania, NE USA 41°25′N 75°40′W
186 B6 **Screw** ≈ NW Papua New Guinea
29 R14 **Scribner** Nebraska, C USA 41°40′N 96°40′W
**Scrobesbyrig'** see Shrewsbury
14 I14 **Scugog** ≈ Ontario, SE Canada
14 I14 **Scugog, Lake** ⊚ Ontario, SE Canada
97 N17 **Scunthorpe** E England, United Kingdom 53°35′N 00°39′W
108 K9 **Scuol** Ger. Schuls. Graubünden, E Switzerland 46°51′N 10°21′E
**Scupi** see Skopje
**Scutari** see Shkodër
113 K17 **Scutari, Lake** Alb. Liqeni i Shkodrës, SCr. Skadarsko Jezero. ⊚ Albania/ Montenegro
**Scyros** see Skýros
**Scythopolis** see Beit She'an
138 E11 **Sderot** prev. Sederot. Southern, S Israel 31°31′N 34°35′E
25 U13 **Seadrift** Texas, SW USA 28°25′N 96°42′W
21 Y4 **Seaford** var. Seaford City. Delaware, NE USA 38°39′N 75°35′W
**Seaford City** see Seaford
14 E15 **Seaforth** Ontario, S Canada 43°33′N 81°25′W
24 M6 **Seagraves** Texas, SW USA 32°56′N 102°33′W
11 X9 **Seal** ≈ Manitoba, C Canada
182 M10 **Sea Lake** Victoria, SE Australia 35°34′S 142°51′E
83 G26 **Seal, Cape** headland S South Africa 34°06′S 23°18′E
65 D26 **Sea Lion Islands** island group SE Falkland Islands
19 S8 **Seal Island** island Maine, NE USA
25 V11 **Sealy** Texas, SW USA 29°46′N 96°09′W
35 X12 **Searchlight** Nevada, W USA 35°27′N 114°54′W
27 V11 **Searcy** Arkansas, C USA 35°14′N 91°43′W
19 R7 **Searsport** Maine, NE USA 44°28′N 68°54′W
35 N10 **Seaside** California, W USA 36°36′N 121°51′W
32 F10 **Seaside** Oregon, NW USA 45°57′N 123°55′W
18 K16 **Seaside Heights** New Jersey, NE USA 39°56′N 74°03′W
32 H8 **Seattle** Washington, NW USA 47°35′N 122°20′W
32 H9 **Seattle-Tacoma** ✈ Washington, NW USA 47°04′N 122°27′W
185 J16 **Seaward Kaikoura Range** ▲▲ South Island, New Zealand
42 J9 **Sébaco** Matagalpa, W Nicaragua 12°51′N 86°08′W
19 P8 **Sebago Lake** ⊚ Maine, NE USA
169 S13 **Sebangan, Teluk** bay Borneo, C Indonesia
**Sebaste/Sebastia** see Sivas
23 Y12 **Sebastian** Florida, SE USA 27°55′N 80°31′W
40 C5 **Sebastián Vizcaíno, Bahía** bay NW Mexico
19 R6 **Sebasticook Lake** ⊚ Maine, NE USA
34 M7 **Sebastopol** California, W USA 38°22′N 122°50′W
**Sebastopol** see Sevastopol'
169 W8 **Sebatik, Pulau** island N Indonesia
19 R5 **Sebec Lake** ⊚ Maine, NE USA
76 K12 **Sébékoro** Kayes, W Mali 13°00′N 09°03′W
**Sebenico** see Šibenik
40 G6 **Seberi, Cerro** ▲ NW Mexico 27°49′N 110°18′W
116 H11 **Sebeş** Ger. Mühlbach, Hung. Szászsebes; prev. Sebeşu Săsesc. Alba, W Romania 45°58′N 23°34′E
**Sebes-Körös** see Crişul Repede
**Sebeşu Săsesc** see Sebeş
31 R8 **Sebewaing** Michigan, N USA 43°43′N 83°27′W
124 F16 **Sebezh** Pskovskaya Oblast', W Russia 56°19′N 28°31′E
137 N12 **Şebinkarahisar** Giresun, N Turkey 40°19′N 38°25′E
116 F11 **Sebiş** Hung. Borossebes. Arad, W Romania 46°21′N 22°09′E
**Sebkra Azz el Matti** see Azzel Matti, Sebkha
19 Q4 **Seboomook Lake** ⊚ Maine, NE USA
74 G6 **Sebou** var. Sebu. ≈ N Morocco
20 I6 **Sebree** Kentucky, S USA 37°34′N 87°30′W
23 X13 **Sebring** Florida, SE USA 27°30′N 81°26′W
**Sebta** see Ceuta
**Sebu** see Sebou
169 U13 **Sebuku, Pulau** island N Indonesia
169 W8 **Sebuku, Teluk** bay Borneo, N Indonesia
106 F10 **Secchia** ≈ N Italy
10 L17 **Sechelt** British Columbia, SW Canada 49°25′N 123°37′W
56 C12 **Sechin, Río** ≈ W Peru
56 A10 **Sechura, Bahía de** bay NW Peru
185 A22 **Secretary Island** island SW New Zealand
155 I15 **Secunderābād** var. Sikandarabad. Telangana, C India 17°30′N 78°33′E
57 L17 **Sécure, Río** ≈ C Bolivia
118 D10 **Seda** Telšiai, NW Lithuania 56°10′N 22°04′E
27 T5 **Sedalia** Missouri, C USA 38°42′N 93°15′W
103 R3 **Sedan** Ardennes, N France 49°42′N 04°56′E
27 P7 **Sedan** Kansas, C USA 37°07′N 96°11′W
105 N3 **Sedano** Castilla y León, N Spain 42°43′N 03°43′W
104 H10 **Seda, Ribeira de** stream C Portugal
185 K15 **Seddon** Marlborough, South Island, New Zealand 41°42′S 174°05′E
185 H15 **Seddonville** West Coast, South Island, New Zealand 41°35′S 171°59′E
143 U7 **Sedeh** Khorāsān-e Janūbī, E Iran 33°18′N 59°12′E
**Sederot** see Sderot
65 B23 **Sedge Island** island NW Falkland Islands
76 G12 **Sédhiou** SW Senegal 12°39′N 15°33′W
11 U16 **Sedley** Saskatchewan, S Canada 50°06′N 103°51′W
**Sedlez** see Siedlce
117 Q2 **Sedniv** Chernihivs'ka Oblast', N Ukraine 51°39′N 31°34′E
36 L11 **Sedona** Arizona, SW USA 34°52′N 111°45′W
**Sedunum** see Sion
118 F12 **Šeduva** Šiauliai, N Lithuania 55°45′N 23°46′E
141 Y8 **Seeb** var. Muscat Sīb Airport. ✈ (Masqaṭ) NE Oman 23°36′N 58°27′E
**Seeb** see As Sīb
108 M7 **Seefeld-in-Tirol** Tirol, W Austria 47°19′N 11°16′E
83 E22 **Seeheim Noord** //Karas, S Namibia 26°50′S 17°45′E
**Seeland** see Sjælland
195 N9 **Seelig, Mount** ▲ Antarctica 81°45′S 102°15′W
**Seenu Atoll** see Addu Atoll
**Seeonee** see Seoni
**Seer** see Dörgön
102 L5 **Sées** Orne, N France 48°36′N 00°11′E
101 J14 **Seesen** Niedersachsen, C Germany 51°54′N 10°11′E
**Seesker Höhe** see Szeska Góra
100 J10 **Seevetal** Niedersachsen, N Germany 53°24′N 10°01′E
109 V6 **Seewiesen** Steiermark, E Austria 47°37′N 15°16′E
136 J13 **Şefaatli** var. Kızılkoca. Yozgat, C Turkey 39°32′N 34°45′E
143 V9 **Sefidābeh** Khorāsān-e Janūbī, E Iran 31°05′N 60°30′E
**Sefid, Darya-ye** see Safēd, Darya-ye
142 M4 **Sefid, Rūd-e** ≈ NW Iran
74 G6 **Sefrou** N Morocco 33°51′N 04°49′W
185 E19 **Sefton, Mount** ▲ South Island, New Zealand 43°43′S 169°58′E
171 S13 **Segaf, Kepulauan** island group E Indonesia
169 W7 **Segama, Sungai** ≈ East Malaysia
168 L9 **Segamat** Johor, Peninsular Malaysia 02°30′N 102°48′E
77 S13 **Ségbana** NE Benin 10°56′N 03°42′E
**Segestica** see Sisak
**Segesvár** see Sighişoara
171 T12 **Seget** Papua Barat, E Indonesia 01°21′S 131°04′E
**Segewold** see Sigulda
124 J9 **Segezha** Respublika Kareliya, NW Russia 63°39′N 34°24′E
**Seghedin** see Szeged
**Segna** see Senj
107 I16 **Segni** Lazio, C Italy 41°41′N 13°02′E
**Segodunum** see Rodez
105 S9 **Segorbe** Comunitat Valenciana, E Spain 39°51′N 00°30′W
76 M12 **Ségou** var. Segu. Ségou, C Mali 13°26′N 06°12′W
76 M12 **Ségou** ◆ region SW Mali
54 E8 **Segovia** Antioquia, N Colombia 07°08′N 74°39′W
105 N7 **Segovia** Castilla y León, C Spain 40°57′N 04°07′W
104 M6 **Segovia** ◆ province Castilla y León, N Spain
**Segoviao Wangkí** see Coco, Río
124 J9 **Segozerskoye Vodokhranilishche** prev. Ozero Segozero. ⊠ NW Russia
102 J7 **Segré** Maine-et-Loire, NW France 47°41′N 00°51′W
105 U5 **Segre** ≈ NE Spain
**Segu** see Ségou
38 I17 **Seguam Island** island Aleutian Islands, Alaska, USA
38 I17 **Seguam Pass** strait Aleutian Islands, Alaska, USA
77 Y7 **Séguédine** Agadez, NE Niger 20°12′N 13°03′E
76 M15 **Séguéla** W Ivory Coast 07°58′N 06°44′W
25 S11 **Seguin** Texas, SW USA 29°34′N 97°58′W
38 E17 **Segula Island** island Aleutian Islands, Alaska, USA
62 K10 **Segundo, Río** ≈ C Argentina
105 Q12 **Segura** ≈ S Spain
105 P13 **Segura, Sierra de** ▲▲ S Spain
83 G18 **Sehithwa** Ngamiland, N Botswana 20°28′S 22°43′E
154 H10 **Sehore** Madhya Pradesh, C India 23°12′N 77°08′E
186 G9 **Sehulea** Normanby Island, S Papua New Guinea 09°55′S 151°10′E
149 P15 **Sehwan** Sindh, SE Pakistan 26°26′N 67°52′E
109 V8 **Seiersberg** Steiermark, SE Austria 47°01′N 15°22′E
26 L9 **Seiling** Oklahoma, C USA 36°09′N 98°55′W
103 S9 **Seille** ≈ E France
99 J20 **Seilles** Namur, SE Belgium 50°31′N 05°12′E
93 K17 **Seinäjoki** Swe. Östermyra. Etelä-Pohjanmaa, W Finland 62°45′N 22°55′E
12 B12 **Seine** ≈ Ontario, S Canada
102 M4 **Seine** ≈ N France
102 K4 **Seine, Baie de la** bay N France
**Seine, Banc de la** see Seine Seamount
103 O5 **Seine-et-Marne** ◆ department N France
102 L3 **Seine-Maritime** ◆ department N France
84 B14 **Seine Plain** undersea feature E Atlantic Ocean 34°00′N 12°15′W
84 B15 **Seine Seamount** var. Banc de la Seine. undersea feature E Atlantic Ocean 33°45′N 14°25′W
102 E6 **Sein, Île de** island NW France
171 Y14 **Seinma** Papua, E Indonesia 04°10′S 138°54′E
**Seisbierrum** see Sexbierum
109 U5 **Seitenstetten Markt** Niederösterreich, C Austria 48°03′N 14°41′E
**Seiyo** see Uwa
**Seiyu** see Chŏnju
95 H22 **Sejerø** island E Denmark
110 P7 **Sejny** Podlaskie, NE Poland 54°09′N 23°21′E
163 X15 **Sejong City** ● (South Korea - administrative) E South Korea 36°29′N 127°16′E
81 G20 **Seke** Simiyu, N Tanzania 03°16′S 33°31′E
164 L13 **Seki** Gifu, Honshū, SW Japan 35°30′N 136°54′E
161 U12 **Sekibi-sho** Chin. Chiwei Yu. island (disputed) China/ Japan/Taiwan
165 U3 **Sekihoku-tōge** pass Hokkaidō, NE Japan
**Sekondi** see Sekondi-Takoradi
77 P17 **Sekondi-Takoradi** var. Sekondi. S Ghana 04°55′N 01°45′W
80 J11 **Sek'ot'a** Āmara, N Ethiopia 12°41′N 39°05′E
**Sekseūil** see Saksaul'skoye
32 I9 **Selah** Washington, NW USA 46°39′N 120°31′W
168 J8 **Selangor** var. Negeri Selangor Darul Ehsan. ◆ state Peninsular Malaysia
**Selânik** see Thessaloníki
167 R10 **Selaphum** Roi Et, E Thailand 16°00′N 103°54′E
171 T16 **Selaru, Pulau** island Kepulauan Tanimbar, E Indonesia
171 U13 **Selassi** Papua Barat, E Indonesia 03°16′S 132°50′E
168 J7 **Selatan, Selat** strait Peninsular Malaysia
168 K10 **Selatpanjang** Pulau Rantau, W Indonesia 01°00′N 102°44′E
39 N8 **Selawik** Alaska, USA 66°36′N 160°00′W
39 N8 **Selawik Lake** ⊚ Alaska, USA
171 N14 **Selayar, Selat** strait Sulawesi, C Indonesia
95 C14 **Selbjørnsfjorden** fjord S Norway
94 H8 **Selbusjøen** ⊚ S Norway
97 M17 **Selby** N England, United Kingdom 53°49′N 01°06′W
29 N8 **Selby** South Dakota, N USA 45°30′N 100°01′W
21 Z4 **Selbyville** Delaware, NE USA 38°28′N 75°12′W
136 B15 **Selçuk** var. Akıncılar. İzmir, SW Turkey 37°56′N 27°25′E
39 Q13 **Seldovia** Alaska, USA 59°26′N 151°42′W
107 M18 **Sele** anc. Silarius. ≈ S Italy
83 J19 **Selebi-Phikwe** Central, E Botswana 21°58′S 27°48′E
42 B5 **Selegua, Río** ≈ W Guatemala
129 X7 **Selemdzha** ≈ SE Russia
129 U7 **Selenga** Mong. Selenge Mörön. ≈ Mongolia/Russia
79 I19 **Selenge** Bandundu, W Dem. Rep. Congo 01°58′S 18°11′E
162 K6 **Selenge** var. Ingettolgoy. Bulgan, N Mongolia 49°27′N 103°59′E
162 L6 **Selenge** ◆ province N Mongolia
**Selenge** see Hyalganat, Bulgan, Mongolia
**Selenge** see Ih-Uul, Hövsgöl, Mongolia
**Selenge Mörön** see Selenga
123 N14 **Selenginsk** Respublika Buryatiya, S Russia 52°00′N 106°40′E
**Selenica** see Selenicë
113 K22 **Selenicë** var. Selenica. Vlorë, SW Albania 40°32′N 19°38′E
123 Q8 **Selennyakh** ≈ NE Russia
100 J8 **Selenter See** ⊚ N Germany
**Sele Sound** see Soela Väin
103 U6 **Sélestat** Ger. Schlettstadt. Bas-Rhin, NE France 48°16′N 07°28′E
**Seleucia** see Silifke
92 I4 **Selfoss** Suðurland, SW Iceland 63°56′N 20°59′W
28 M7 **Selfridge** North Dakota, N USA 46°01′N 100°52′W
76 I15 **Seli** ≈ N Sierra Leone
76 I11 **Sélibabi** var. Sélibaby. Guidimaka, S Mauritania 15°14′N 12°11′W
**Sélibaby** see Sélibabi
**Selidovka/Selidovo** see Selydove
124 I15 **Seliger, Ozero** ⊚ W Russia
36 J11 **Seligman** Arizona, SW USA 35°20′N 112°56′W
27 S8 **Seligman** Missouri, C USA 36°31′N 93°56′W
80 E6 **Selima Oasis** oasis N Sudan
76 K13 **Sélingué, Lac de** ⊠ S Mali
**Selinoús** see Kréstena
18 G14 **Selinsgrove** Pennsylvania, NE USA 40°47′N 76°51′W
**Selishche** see Syelishcha
124 I16 **Selizharovo** Tverskaya Oblast', W Russia 56°50′N 33°24′E
94 C10 **Selje** Sogn Og Fjordane, S Norway 62°02′N 05°22′E
11 X16 **Selkirk** Manitoba, S Canada 50°10′N 96°52′W
96 K13 **Selkirk** SE Scotland, United Kingdom 55°36′N 02°48′W
96 K13 **Selkirk** cultural region SE Scotland, United Kingdom
11 O16 **Selkirk Mountains** ▲▲ British Columbia, SW Canada
193 T11 **Selkirk Rise** undersea feature SE Pacific Ocean
115 F21 **Sellasía** Pelopónnisos, S Greece 37°14′N 22°24′E
44 M9 **Selle, Pic de la** var. La Selle. ▲ SE Haiti 18°18′N 71°55′W
102 M8 **Selles-sur-Cher** Loir-et-Cher, C France 47°16′N 01°31′E
36 K16 **Sells** Arizona, SW USA 31°54′N 111°52′W
**Sellye** see Sal'a
23 P5 **Selma** Alabama, S USA 32°24′N 87°01′W
35 Q11 **Selma** California, W USA 36°33′N 119°37′W
20 G10 **Selmer** Tennessee, S USA 35°10′N 88°34′W
173 N17 **Sel, Pointe au** headland W Réunion
**Selselehye Kuhe Vākhān** see Nicholas Range
127 S2 **Selty** Udmurtskaya Respublika, NW Russia 57°19′N 52°09′E
**Selukwe** see Shurugwi
62 L9 **Selva** Santiago del Estero, N Argentina 29°46′S 62°02′W
11 T9 **Selwyn Lake** ⊚ Northwest Territories/Saskatchewan, C Canada
10 K6 **Selwyn Mountains** ▲▲ Yukon, NW Canada
181 T6 **Selwyn Range** ▲▲ Queensland, C Australia
117 W8 **Selydove** var. Selidovka, Rus. Selidovo. Donets'ka Oblast', SE Ukraine 48°06′N 37°16′E
**Selzaete** see Zelzate
**Seman** see Semanit, Lumi i
168 M15 **Semangka, Teluk** bay Sumatera, SW Indonesia
113 D22 **Semanit, Lumi i** var. Seman. ≈ W Albania
169 Q16 **Semarang** var. Samarang. Jawa, C Indonesia 06°58′S 110°29′E
169 Q10 **Sematan** Sarawak, East Malaysia 01°50′N 109°44′E
171 P17 **Semau, Pulau** island S Indonesia
169 V8 **Sembakung, Sungai** ≈ Borneo, N Indonesia
79 G17 **Sembé** Sangha, NW Congo 01°38′N 14°35′E
169 S13 **Sembulu, Danau** ⊚ Borneo, N Indonesia
139 Q2 **Sēmēl** Ar. Sumayl, var. Summēl. Dahūk, N Iraq 36°52′N 42°51′E
**Semendria** see Smederevo
117 R1 **Semenivka** Chernihivs'ka Oblast', N Ukraine 52°10′N 32°37′E
117 S6 **Semenivka** Rus. Semenovka. Poltavs'ka Oblast', NE Ukraine 49°36′N 33°10′E
127 O3 **Semenov** Nizhegorodskaya Oblast', W Russia 56°47′N 44°27′E
**Semenovka** see Semenivka
169 S17 **Semeru, Gunung** var. Mahameru. ▲ Jawa, S Indonesia 08°01′S 112°53′E
145 V9 **Semey** prev. Semipalatinsk. Vostochnyy Kazakhstan, E Kazakhstan 50°26′N 80°16′E
**Semezhevo** see Syemyezhava
126 L7 **Semiluki** Voronezhskaya Oblast', W Russia 51°46′N 39°00′E
33 W16 **Seminoe Reservoir** ⊠ Wyoming, C USA
27 O11 **Seminole** Oklahoma, C USA 35°13′N 96°40′W
24 M6 **Seminole** Texas, SW USA 32°43′N 102°39′W
23 S8 **Seminole, Lake** ⊠ Florida/ Georgia, SE USA
**Semiozernoye** see Auliyekol'
**Semipalatinsk** see Semey
143 O9 **Semīrom** var. Samirum. Eşfahān, C Iran 31°20′N 51°50′E
38 F17 **Semisopochnoi Island** island Aleutian Islands, Alaska, USA
169 R11 **Semitau** Borneo, C Indonesia 0°30′N 111°59′E
81 E18 **Semliki** ≈ Uganda/Dem. Rep. Congo
143 P5 **Semnān** var. Samnān. Semnān, N Iran 35°37′N 53°21′E
143 Q5 **Semnān** off. Ostān-e Semnān. ◆ province N Iran
**Semnān, Ostān-e** see Semnān
99 K24 **Semois** ≈ SE Belgium
108 E8 **Sempacher See** ⊚ C Switzerland
**Sena** see Vila de Sena
30 L12 **Senachwine Lake** ⊚ Illinois, N USA
59 O14 **Senador Pompeu** Ceará, E Brazil 05°30′S 39°25′W
**Sena Gallica** see Senigallia
59 C15 **Sena Madureira** Acre, W Brazil 09°05′S 68°41′W
155 L25 **Senanayake Samudra** ⊚ E Sri Lanka
83 G15 **Senanga** Western, SW Zambia 16°09′S 23°16′E
27 Y9 **Senath** Missouri, C USA 36°07′N 90°09′W
22 L2 **Senatobia** Mississippi, S USA 34°37′N 89°58′W
164 C16 **Sendai** var. Satsuma-Sendai. Kagoshima, Kyūshū, SW Japan 31°49′N 130°17′E
165 Q11 **Sendai-wan** bay E Japan
101 J23 **Senden** Bayern, S Germany 48°18′N 10°04′E
154 F11 **Sendhwa** Madhya Pradesh, C India 21°38′N 75°04′E
111 H21 **Senec** Ger. Wartberg, Hung. Szenc; prev. Szempcz. Bratislavský Kraj, W Slovakia 48°14′N 17°24′E
27 P3 **Seneca** Kansas, C USA 39°50′N 96°04′W
27 R8 **Seneca** Missouri, C USA 36°50′N 94°36′W
32 K13 **Seneca** Oregon, NW USA 44°06′N 118°57′W
21 O11 **Seneca** South Carolina, SE USA 34°41′N 82°57′W
18 G11 **Seneca Lake** ⊚ New York, NE USA
31 U13 **Senecaville Lake** ⊚ Ohio, N USA
76 G11 **Senegal** off. Republic of Senegal, Fr. Sénégal, République du Sénégal. ♦ republic W Africa
76 H9 **Senegal** Fr. Sénégal. ≈ W Africa
**Senegal, Republic of** see Senegal
**Sénégal, République du** see Senegal
31 O4 **Seney Marsh** wetland Michigan, N USA
101 P14 **Senftenberg** Brandenburg, E Germany 51°31′N 14°01′E
82 L11 **Senga Hill** Northern, NE Zambia 09°26′S 31°12′E
158 G13 **Sênggê Zangbo** ≈ W China
171 Z13 **Senggi** Papua, E Indonesia 03°26′S 140°46′E
127 R5 **Sengiley** Ul'yanovskaya Oblast', W Russia 53°54′N 48°51′E
63 I19 **Senguerr, Río** ≈ S Argentina
83 J16 **Sengwa** ≈ C Zimbabwe
**Senia** see Senj
111 H19 **Senica** Ger. Senitz, Hung. Szenice. Trnavský Kraj, W Slovakia 48°40′N 17°22′E
**Senica** see Sjenica
106 J11 **Senigallia** anc. Sena Gallica. Marche, C Italy 43°43′N 13°13′E
136 F15 **Senirkent** Isparta, SW Turkey 38°07′N 30°34′E
**Senitz** see Senica
112 C10 **Senj** Ger. Zengg, It. Segna; anc. Senia. Lika-Senj, NW Croatia 44°58′N 14°55′E
**Senj** see Örgön
92 H9 **Senja** prev. Senjen. island N Norway
**Senjen** see Senja
161 U12 **Senkaku-shotō** Chin. Diaoyutai. island group (disputed) SW Japan
137 R12 **Şenkaya** Erzurum, NE Turkey 40°33′N 42°17′E
83 I16 **Senkobo** Southern, S Zambia 17°38′S 25°58′E
103 O4 **Senlis** Oise, N France 49°13′N 02°33′E
167 T12 **Sen Monorom** var. Sênmônoŭrôm. Mondolkiri, E Cambodia 12°27′N 107°12′E
**Sênmônoŭrôm** see Sen Monorom
80 G10 **Sennar** var. Sannār. Sinnar, C Sudan 13°31′N 33°38′E
**Senno** see Syanno
**Senones** see Sens
109 W11 **Senovo** E Slovenia 46°01′N 15°24′E
103 P6 **Sens** anc. Agendicum, Senones. Yonne, C France 48°12′N 03°17′E
**Sensburg** see Mrągowo
167 S11 **Sên, Stœng** ≈ C Cambodia
42 F7 **Sensuntepeque** Cabañas, NE El Salvador 13°52′N 88°38′W
112 L8 **Senta** Hung. Zenta. Vojvodina, N Serbia 45°57′N 20°04′E
**Šent Andraž** see Sankt Andrä
171 Y13 **Sentani, Danau** ⊚ Papua, E Indonesia
28 J5 **Sentinel Butte** ▲ North Dakota, N USA 46°52′N 103°50′W
10 M13 **Sentinel Peak** ▲ British Columbia, W Canada 54°51′N 122°02′W
59 N16 **Sento Sé** Bahia, E Brazil 09°51′S 41°56′W
**Šent Peter** see Pivka
**Št. Vid** see Sankt Veit an der Glan
**Seo de Urgel** see La Seu d'Urgell
163 X17 **Seogwipo** prev. Sŏgwip'o. S South Korea 33°14′N 126°33′E
154 I7 **Seondha** Madhya Pradesh, C India 26°09′N 78°47′E
163 Y17 **Seongsan** prev. Sŏngsan. S South Korea
154 J11 **Seoni** prev. Seeonee. Madhya Pradesh, C India 22°06′N 79°36′E
163 X14 **Seoul**, Jap. Keijō; prev. Kyŏngsŏng, Sŏul. ● (South Korea) NW South Korea 37°30′N 126°58′E
83 I17 **Sepako** Central, NE Botswana 19°50′S 26°29′E
184 I13 **Separation Point / Te Matau** var. Te Matau. headland South Island, New Zealand 40°46′S 172°58′E
169 V10 **Sepasu** Borneo, N Indonesia 0°44′N 117°38′E
186 B6 **Sepik** ≈ Indonesia/Papua New Guinea
**Sepone** see Muang Xépôn
110 M7 **Sępopol** Ger. Schippenbeil. Warmińsko-Mazurskie, N Poland 54°16′N 21°09′E
116 F10 **Şepreuş** Hung. Seprős. Arad, W Romania 46°34′N 21°44′E
**Seprős** see Şepreuş
**Şepşi-Sângeorz/ Sepsiszentgyörgy** see Sfântu Gheorghe
15 W4 **Sept-Îles** Québec, SE Canada 50°11′N 66°19′W
105 N6 **Sepúlveda** Castilla y León, N Spain 41°18′N 03°45′W
104 K8 **Sequeros** Castilla y León, N Spain 40°31′N 06°04′W
104 L5 **Sequillo** ≈ NW Spain
32 G7 **Sequim** Washington, NW USA 48°04′N 123°06′W
35 S11 **Sequoia National Park** national park California, W USA
137 Q14 **Şerafettin Dağları** ▲▲ E Turkey
127 N10 **Serafimovich** Volgogradskaya Oblast', SW Russia 49°34′N 42°43′E
171 Q10 **Serai** Sulawesi, N Indonesia 01°45′N 124°58′E
99 K19 **Seraing** Liège, E Belgium 50°37′N 05°31′E
**Sêraitang** see Baima
**Serakhs** see Sarahs
171 W13 **Serami** Papua, E Indonesia 02°11′S 136°46′E
**Seram, Laut** see Ceram Sea
**Serampore/Serampur** see Shrirāmpur
171 S13 **Seram, Pulau** var. Serang, Eng. Ceram. island Maluku, E Indonesia
169 N15 **Serang** Jawa, C Indonesia 06°07′S 106°09′E
**Serang** see Seram, Pulau
169 P9 **Serasan, Pulau** island Kepulauan Natuna, W Indonesia
169 P9 **Serasan, Selat** strait Indonesia/Malaysia
112 M13 **Serbia** off. Republic of Serbia; prev. Yugoslavia, SCr. Jugoslavija. ♦ republic SE Europe
112 M12 **Serbia** Ger. Serbien, Serb. Srbija. ◆ republic Serbia
**Serbia, Republic of** see Serbia
**Serbien** see Serbia
**Sercq** see Sark
146 D12 **Serdar** prev. Rus. Gyzyrlabat, Kizyl-Arvat. Balkan Welaýaty, W Turkmenistan 39°02′N 56°15′E
**Serdica** see Sofia
**Serdobol'** see Sortavala
127 O7 **Serdobsk** Penzenskaya Oblast', W Russia 52°30′N 44°16′E
145 X9 **Serebryansk** Vostochnyy Kazakhstan, E Kazakhstan 49°44′N 83°16′E
123 Q12 **Serebryanyy Bor** Respublika Sakha (Yakutiya), NE Russia 56°40′N 124°46′E
111 H20 **Sered'** Hung. Szered. Trnavský Kraj, W Slovakia 48°19′N 17°45′E
117 S1 **Seredyna-Buda** Sums'ka Oblast', NE Ukraine 52°09′N 34°00′E
118 E13 **Seredžius** Tauragė, C Lithuania 55°04′N 23°24′E
136 I14 **Şereflikoçhisar** Ankara, C Turkey 38°56′N 33°31′E
106 D7 **Seregno** Lombardia, N Italy 45°39′N 09°12′E
103 P7 **Serein** ≈ C France
**Sêrei Saôphoăn** see Sisophon
168 K9 **Seremban** Negeri Sembilan, Peninsular Malaysia 02°42′N 101°54′E
81 H20 **Serengeti Plain** plain N Tanzania
82 K13 **Serenje** Central, E Zambia 13°12′S 30°15′E
**Seres** see Sérres
116 J5 **Seret** ≈ W Ukraine
**Seret/Sereth** see Siret
115 I21 **Serfopoúla** island Kykládes, Greece, Aegean Sea
127 P4 **Sergach** Nizhegorodskaya Oblast', W Russia 55°31′N 45°29′E
29 S13 **Sergeant Bluff** Iowa, C USA 42°24′N 96°19′W
163 P7 **Sergelen** Dornod, NE Mongolia 48°31′N 114°01′E
**Sergelen** see Tüvshinshiree
168 H8 **Sergeulangit, Pegunungan** ▲▲ Sumatera, NW Indonesia
122 L5 **Sergeya Kirova, Ostrova** island N Russia
**Sergeyevichi** see Syarhyeyevichy
145 O7 **Sergeyevka** Severnyy Kazakhstan, N Kazakhstan 53°53′N 67°25′E
**Sergiopol** see Ayagoz
59 P16 **Sergipe** off. Estado de Sergipe. ◆ state E Brazil
**Sergipe, Estado de** see Sergipe
126 L3 **Sergiyev Posad** Moskovskaya Oblast', W Russia 56°21′N 38°10′E
124 K5 **Sergozero, Ozero** ⊚ NW Russia
146 J17 **Serhetabat** prev. Rus. Gushgy, Kushka. Mary Welaýaty, S Turkmenistan 35°19′N 62°17′E
169 Q10 **Serian** Sarawak, East Malaysia 01°10′N 110°35′E
115 I21 **Sérifos** anc. Seriphos. island Kykládes, Greece, Aegean Sea
115 I21 **Sérifou, Stenó** strait SE Greece
136 F16 **Serik** Antalya, SW Turkey 36°55′N 31°06′E
106 E7 **Serio** ≈ N Italy
**Seriphos** see Sérifos
**Serir Tibesti** see Sarīr Tībistī
**Sêrkog** see Sêrtar
197 O14 **Sermersooq** off. Kommuneqarfik Sermersooq. ◇ municipality S Greenland
**Sermersooq, Kommuneqarfik** see Sermersooq
127 S5 **Sernovodsk** Samarskaya Oblast', W Russia 53°56′N 51°16′E
127 R2 **Sernur** Respublika Mariy El, W Russia 56°55′N 49°09′E
110 M11 **Serock** Mazowieckie, C Poland 52°30′N 21°03′E
61 B18 **Serodino** Santa Fe, C Argentina 32°33′S 60°52′W
**Seroei** see Serui
105 P14 **Serón** Andalucía, S Spain 37°20′N 02°28′W
99 E14 **Serooskerke** Zeeland, SW Netherlands 51°42′N 03°52′E
105 T6 **Serós** Cataluña, NE Spain 41°27′N 00°24′E
122 G10 **Serov** Sverdlovskaya Oblast', C Russia 59°42′N 60°32′E
83 I19 **Serowe** Central, SE Botswana 22°26′S 26°44′E
104 H13 **Serpa** Beja, S Portugal 37°56′N 07°36′W
**Serpa Pinto** see Menongue
182 A4 **Serpentine Lakes** salt lake South Australia
45 T15 **Serpent's Mouth, The** Sp. Boca de la Serpiente. strait Trinidad and Tobago/ Venezuela
**Serpiente, Boca de la** see Serpent's Mouth, The
126 K4 **Serpukhov** Moskovskaya Oblast', W Russia 54°54′N 37°26′E
104 I10 **Serra de São Mamede** ▲ C Portugal 39°18′N 07°19′W
60 K13 **Serra do Mar** ▲▲ S Brazil
**Sérrai** see Sérres
107 N22 **Serra San Bruno** Calabria, SW Italy 38°32′N 16°18′E
103 S14 **Serres** Hautes-Alpes, SE France 44°26′N 05°42′E
114 H13 **Sérres** var. Seres; prev. Sérrai. Kentrikí Makedonía, NE Greece 41°03′N 23°33′E
62 J9 **Serrezuela** Córdoba, C Argentina 30°38′S 65°26′W
59 O16 **Serrinha** Bahia, E Brazil 11°38′S 38°56′W
59 M19 **Serro** var. Sêrro. Minas Gerais, NE Brazil 18°38′S 43°22′W
**Sêrro** see Serro
**Sert** see Siirt
104 H9 **Sertã** var. Sertá. Castelo Branco, C Portugal 39°48′N 08°05′W
**Sertá** see Sertã
60 L8 **Sertãozinho** São Paulo, S Brazil 21°04′S 47°55′W
160 F7 **Sêrtar** var. Sêrkog. Sichuan, C China 32°18′N 100°18′E
124 G12 **Sertolovo** Leningradskaya Oblast', NW Russia 60°08′N 30°06′E
171 W13 **Serui** prev. Seroei. Papua, E Indonesia 01°53′S 136°15′E
83 J19 **Serule** Central, E Botswana 21°58′S 27°20′E
169 S12 **Seruyan, Sungai** var. Sungai Pembuang. ≈ Borneo, N Indonesia
115 E14 **Sérvia** Dytikí Makedonía, N Greece 40°12′N 22°01′E
160 E7 **Sêrxü** var. Jugar. Sichuan, C China 32°54′N 98°06′E
123 R13 **Seryshevo** Amurskaya Oblast', SE Russia 51°03′N 128°16′E
**Sesana** see Sežana
169 V8 **Sesayap, Sungai** ≈ Borneo, N Indonesia
**Sesdlets** see Siedlce
79 N17 **Sese** Orientale, N Dem. Rep. Congo 02°13′N 25°52′E
81 F18 **Sese Islands** island group S Uganda
83 H16 **Sesheke** var. Sesheko. Western, SE Zambia 17°28′S 24°20′E
**Sesheko** see Sesheke
106 C8 **Sesia** anc. Sessites. ≈ NW Italy
104 F11 **Sesimbra** Setúbal, S Portugal 38°26′N 09°06′W
115 N22 **Seskliό** island Dodekánisa, Greece, Aegean Sea
30 L16 **Sesser** Illinois, N USA 38°05′N 89°03′W
**Sessites** see Sesia
106 G11 **Sesto Fiorentino** Toscana, C Italy 43°50′N 11°12′E
106 E7 **Sesto San Giovanni** Lombardia, N Italy 45°32′N 09°14′E
106 A8 **Sestriere** Piemonte, NE Italy 45°00′N 06°54′E
106 D10 **Sestri Levante** Liguria, NW Italy 44°16′N 09°22′E
107 C20 **Sestu** Sardegna, Italy, C Mediterranean Sea 39°15′N 09°06′E
112 E8 **Sesvete** Zagreb, N Croatia 45°50′N 16°03′E
118 G12 **Šeta** Kaunas, C Lithuania 55°17′N 24°16′E
**Setabis** see Xàtiva
165 Q4 **Setana** Hokkaidō, NE Japan 42°27′N 139°52′E
103 Q16 **Sète** prev. Cette. Hérault, S France 43°24′N 03°42′E
58 J11 **Sete Ilhas** Amapá, NE Brazil 01°06′N 52°06′W
59 L20 **Sete Lagoas** Minas Gerais, NE Brazil 19°29′S 44°15′W
60 G10 **Sete Quedas, Ilha das** island S Brazil
92 I10 **Setermoen** Troms, N Norway 68°51′N 18°20′E
95 E17 **Setesdal** valley S Norway
43 W16 **Setetule, Cerro** ▲ SE Panama 07°51′N 77°37′W
21 Q5 **Seth** West Virginia, NE USA 38°06′N 81°40′W
**Setia** see Sezze
74 K5 **Sétif** var. Stif. N Algeria 36°11′N 05°24′E
164 L5 **Seto** Aichi, Honshū, SW Japan 35°14′N 137°06′E
164 G13 **Seto-naikai** Eng. Inland Sea. sea S Japan
165 V16 **Setouchi** var. Setoushi. Kagoshima, Amami-Ō-shima, SW Japan 44°19′N 142°58′E
**Setoushi** see Setouchi
74 F6 **Settat** W Morocco 33°03′N 07°37′W
79 D20 **Setté Cama** Ogooué-Maritime, SW Gabon 02°32′S 09°46′E
11 W13 **Setting Lake** ⊚ Manitoba, C Canada
97 L16 **Settle** N England, United Kingdom 54°04′N 02°17′W
189 Y12 **Settlement** E Wake Island 19°17′N 166°38′E
104 F11 **Setúbal** Eng. Saint Ubes, Saint Yves. Setúbal, W Portugal 38°31′N 08°54′W
104 F11 **Setúbal** ◆ district S Portugal
104 F12 **Setúbal, Baía de** bay W Portugal
**Setul** see Satun
12 B10 **Seul, Lac** ⊚ Ontario, S Canada
103 R8 **Seurre** Côte d'Or, C France 47°00′N 05°09′E
137 U11 **Sevan** C Armenia 40°32′N 44°56′E
137 V12 **Sevana Lich** Eng. Lake Sevan, Rus. Ozero Sevan. ⊚ E Armenia
**Sevan, Lake/Sevan, Ozero** see Sevana Lich
77 N11 **Sévaré** Mopti, C Mali 14°32′N 04°06′W
117 S14 **Sevastopol'** Eng. Sebastopol. Avtonomna Respublika Krym, S Ukraine 44°36′N 33°33′E
25 R14 **Seven Sisters** Texas, SW USA 27°57′N 98°34′W
10 K13 **Seven Sisters Peaks** ▲ British Columbia, SW Canada 54°57′N 128°10′W
99 M15 **Sevenum** Limburg, SE Netherlands 51°25′N 06°01′E
103 P14 **Séverac-le-Château** Aveyron, S France 44°18′N 03°03′E
14 H13 **Severn** ≈ Ontario, S Canada
97 L21 **Severn** Wel. Hafren. ≈ England/Wales, United Kingdom
**Severna Makedonija** see North Macedonia
125 O11 **Severnaya Dvina** var. Northern Dvina. ≈ NW Russia
127 N16 **Severnaya Osetiya-Alaniya, Respublika** Eng. North Ossetia; prev. Respublika Severnaya Osetiya, Severo-Osetinskaya SSR. ◆ autonomous republic SW Russia
**Severnaya Osetiya, Respublika** see Severnaya Osetiya-Alaniya, Respublika
122 M5 **Severnaya Zemlya** var. Nicholas II Land. island group N Russia
127 T5 **Severnoye** Orenburgskaya Oblast', W Russia 54°03′N 52°31′E
35 S3 **Severn Troughs Range** ▲▲ Nevada, W USA
125 W3 **Severnyy** Respublika Komi, NW Russia 67°38′N 64°13′E
144 I13 **Severnyy Chink Ustyurta** ▲ W Kazakhstan
125 Q13 **Severnyye Uvaly** var. Northern Ural Hills. hill range NW Russia
145 O6 **Severnyy Kazakhstan** off. Severo-Kazakhstanskaya Oblast', var. North Kazakhstan, Kaz. Soltüstik Qazaqstan Oblysy. ◆ province N Kazakhstan
122 I6 **Severnyy, Ostrov** NW Russia
125 V9 **Severnyy Ural** ▲▲ NW Russia
**Severo-Alichurskiy Khrebet** see Alichuri Shimolí, Qatorkŭhi


♦ Country
● Country Capital
◇ Dependent Territory
○ Dependent Territory Capital
◆ Administrative Regions
✈ International Airport
▲ Mountain
▲▲ Mountain Range
Volcano
≈ River
⊚ Lake
⊠ Reservoir

SEVEROBAYKAL'SK – SHIKOTAN-TŌ


123 N12 **Severobaykal'sk** Respublika Buryatiya, S Russia 55°39'N 109°17'E
**Severodonetsk** *see* Syeverodonets'k
124 M8 **Severodvinsk** *prev.* Molotov, Sudostroy. Arkhangel'skaya Oblast', NW Russia 64°32'N 39°50'E
**Severo-Kazakhstanskaya Oblast'** *see* Severnyy Kazakhstan
123 U11 **Severo-Kuril'sk** Sakhalinskaya Oblast', SE Russia 50°38'N 155°57'E
124 J3 **Severomorsk** Murmanskaya Oblast', NW Russia 69°00'N 33°16'E
**Severo-Osetinskaya SSR** *see* Severnaya Osetiya-Alaniya, Respublika
122 M7 **Severo-Sibirskaya Nizmennost'** *var.* North Siberian Plain, *Eng.* North Siberian Lowland. *lowlands* N Russia
122 G10 **Severoural'sk** Sverdlovskaya Oblast', C Russia 60°09'N 59°58'E
122 L11 **Severo-Yeniseyskiy** Krasnoyarskiy Kray, C Russia 60°29'N 93°13'E
122 J12 **Seversk** Tomskaya Oblast', C Russia 53°37'N 84°47'E
126 M11 **Severskiy Donets** *Ukr.* Sivers'kyy Donets'. Russia/Ukraine *see also* Sivers'kyy Donets'
**Severskiy Donets** *see* Sivers'kyy Donets'
92 M9 **Sevettijärvi** Lappi, N Finland 69°31'N 28°40'E
36 M5 **Sevier Bridge Reservoir** Utah, W USA
36 J4 **Sevier Desert** *plain* Utah, W USA
36 J5 **Sevier Lake** Utah, W USA
21 N9 **Sevierville** Tennessee, S USA 35°53'N 83°34'W
104 J14 **Sevilla** *Eng.* Seville; *anc.* Hispalis. Andalucía, SW Spain 37°24'N 05°59'W
104 J13 **Sevilla** *province* Andalucía, SW Spain
**Sevilla de Niefang** *see* Niefang
43 O16 **Sevilla, Isla** *island* SW Panama
**Seville** *see* Sevilla
114 J9 **Sevlievo** Gabrovo, N Bulgaria 43°01'N 25°06'E
**Sevluš/Sevlyush** *see* Vynohradiv
109 V11 **Sevnica** *Ger.* Lichtenwald. E Slovenia 46°00'N 15°20'E
162 J11 **Sevrey** *var.* Saynshand. Ömnögovĭ, S Mongolia 43°30'N 102°08'E
126 I7 **Sevsk** Bryanskaya Oblast', W Russia 52°03'N 34°31'E
76 J15 **Sewa** E Sierra Leone
39 R12 **Seward** Alaska, USA 60°06'N 149°26'W
29 R15 **Seward** Nebraska, C USA 40°52'N 97°06'W
197 Q3 **Seward Peninsula** *peninsula* Alaska, USA
**Seward's Folly** *see* Alaska
62 H12 **Sewell** O'Higgins, C Chile 34°05'S 70°25'W
98 K5 **Sexbierum** *Fris.* Seisbierrum. Fryslân, N Netherlands 53°13'N 05°28'E
11 O13 **Sexsmith** Alberta, W Canada 55°18'N 118°45'W
41 W13 **Seybaplaya** Campeche, SE Mexico 19°39'N 90°36'W
173 N6 **Seychelles** *off.* Republic of Seychelles. ◆ *republic* W Indian Ocean
67 Z9 **Seychelles** *island group* NE Seychelles
173 N6 **Seychelles Bank** *var.* Le Banc des Seychelles. *undersea feature* W Indian Ocean 04°45'S 55°30'E
**Seychelles, Le Banc des** *see* Seychelles Bank
**Seychelles, Republic of** *see* Seychelles
172 H17 **Seychellois, Morne** ▲ Mahé, NE Seychelles
146 J12 **Seýdi** *Rus.* Seydi; *prev.* Neftezavodsk. Lebap Welaýaty, E Turkmenistan 39°31'N 62°53'E
136 G16 **Seydişehir** Konya, SW Turkey 37°25'N 31°51'E
92 I2 **Seyðisfjörður** Austurland, E Iceland 65°15'N 14°00'W
136 J13 **Seyfe Gölü** C Turkey
**Seyhan** *see* Adana
136 K16 **Seyhan Barajı** S Turkey
136 K17 **Seyhan Nehri** S Turkey
136 F13 **Seyitgazi** Eskişehir, W Turkey 39°27'N 30°42'E
126 J7 **Seym** W Russia
117 S3 **Seym** N Ukraine
123 T9 **Seymchan** Magadanskaya Oblast', E Russia 62°54'N 152°27'E
114 N12 **Seymen** Tekirdağ, NW Turkey 41°06'N 27°56'E
183 O11 **Seymour** Victoria, SE Australia 37°01'S 145°10'E
83 I25 **Seymour** Eastern Cape, S South Africa 32°33'S 26°46'E
29 W16 **Seymour** Iowa, C USA 40°40'N 93°07'W
27 U7 **Seymour** Missouri, C USA 37°09'N 92°46'W
25 Q5 **Seymour** Texas, SW USA 33°36'N 99°16'W
114 M12 **Şeytan Deresi** NW Turkey
109 S12 **Sežana** *It.* Sesana. SW Slovenia 45°42'N 13°52'E
103 P5 **Sézanne** Marne, N France 48°43'N 03°41'E
107 I16 **Sezze** *anc.* Setia. Lazio, C Italy 41°29'N 13°04'E
**Sfákia** *see* Chóra Sfakíon
115 D21 **Sfaktiría** *island* S Greece
116 J11 **Sfântu Gheorghe** *Ger.* Sankt-Georgen, *Hung.* Sepsiszentgyőrgy; *prev.* Şepşi-Sângeorz, Sfintu Gheorghe. Covasna, C Romania 45°52'N 25°49'E
117 N13 **Sfântu Gheorghe, Braţul** *var.* Gheorghe Braţul. E Romania
75 N6 **Sfax** *Ar.* Şafāqis. E Tunisia 34°45'N 10°45'E
75 N6 **Sfax** ✈ E Tunisia 34°43'N 10°37'E
**Sfintu Gheorghe** *see* Sfântu Gheorghe
98 H13 **'s-Gravendeel** Zuid-Holland, SW Netherlands 51°48'N 04°36'E
98 F11 **'s-Gravenhage** *var.* Den Haag, *Eng.* The Hague, *Fr.* La Haye. ● (Netherlands-seat of government) Zuid-Holland, W Netherlands 52°07'N 04°17'E
98 G12 **'s-Gravenzande** Zuid-Holland, W Netherlands 52°00'N 04°10'E
**Shaan/Shaanxi Sheng** *see* Shaanxi
159 X11 **Shaanxi** *var.* Shaan, Shaanxi Sheng, Shan-hsi, Shenshi, Shensi. ◆ *province* C China
**Shaartuz** *see* Shahritus
**Shaba** *see* Katanga
**Shabani** *see* Zvishavane
81 N17 **Shabeellaha Dhexe** *off.* Gobolka Shabeellaha Dhexe. ◆ *region* E Somalia
**Shabeellaha Dhexe, Gobolka** *see* Shabeellaha Dhexe
81 L17 **Shabeellaha Hoose** *off.* Gobolka Shabeellaha Hoose. ◆ *region* S Somalia
**Shabeellaha Hoose, Gobolka** *see* Shabeellaha Hoose
**Shabeelle, Webi** *see* Shebeli
114 O7 **Shabla** Dobrich, NE Bulgaria 43°33'N 28°31'E
114 O7 **Shabla, Nos** *headland* NE Bulgaria 43°30'N 28°36'E
13 N9 **Shabogama Lake** Newfoundland and Labrador, E Canada
79 N20 **Shabunda** Sud-Kivu, E Dem. Rep. Congo 02°42'S 27°20'E
141 Q15 **Shabwah** C Yemen 15°09'N 46°46'E
158 F8 **Shache** *var.* Yarkant. Xinjiang Uygur Zizhiqu, NW China 38°27'N 77°16'E
**Shacheng** *see* Huailai
195 R12 **Shackleton Coast** *physical region* Antarctica
195 Z10 **Shackleton Ice Shelf** *ice shelf* Antarctica
**Shaddādī** *see* Ash Shadādah
28 K7 **Shadehill Reservoir** South Dakota, N USA
122 G11 **Shadrinsk** Kurganskaya Oblast', C Russia 56°08'N 63°18'E
31 O12 **Shafer, Lake** Indiana, N USA
35 R13 **Shafter** California, W USA 35°27'N 119°15'W
24 J11 **Shafter** Texas, SW USA 29°49'N 104°18'W
97 L23 **Shaftesbury** S England, United Kingdom 51°01'N 02°12'W
185 F22 **Shag** South Island, New Zealand
145 V9 **Shagan** E Kazakhstan
39 O11 **Shageluk** Alaska, USA 62°40'N 159°33'W
122 K14 **Shagonar** Respublika Tyva, S Russia 51°31'N 93°06'E
185 F22 **Shag Point** *headland* South Island, New Zealand 45°28'S 170°50'E
144 J12 **Shagyray, Plato** *plain* SW Kazakhstan
**Shāhābād** *see* Eslāmābād-e Gharb
168 K9 **Shah Alam** Selangor, Peninsular Malaysia 03°02'N 101°31'E
117 O12 **Shahany, Ozero** SW Ukraine
138 H9 **Shahbā'** *anc.* Philippopolis. As Suwaydā', S Syria 32°50'N 36°38'E
**Shahbān** *see* Ad Dayr
149 P17 **Shah Bandar** Sindh, SE Pakistan 23°59'N 67°54'E
149 P13 **Shahdad Kot** Sindh, SW Pakistan 27°49'N 67°45'E
143 T10 **Shahdād, Namakzār-e** *salt pan* E Iran
149 Q15 **Shahdadpur** Sindh, SE Pakistan 25°56'N 68°40'E
154 K10 **Shahdol** Madhya Pradesh, C India 23°19'N 81°26'E
161 N7 **Sha He** C China
**Shahe** *see* Linze
**Shahepu** *see* Linze
153 N13 **Shāhganj** Uttar Pradesh, N India 26°03'N 82°41'E
152 C11 **Shāhgarh** Rājasthān, NW India 27°08'N 69°56'E
**Sha Hi** *see* Orūmīyeh, Daryācheh-ye
**Shāhī** *see* Qā'emshahr
**Shahjahanabad** *see* Delhi
152 L11 **Shāhjahānpur** Uttar Pradesh, N India 27°53'N 79°55'E
149 U7 **Shāhpur** Punjab, E Pakistan 32°15'N 72°32'E
**Shāhpur** *see* Shahpur Chakar
152 G13 **Shāhpura** Rājasthān, N India 25°38'N 75°01'E
149 Q15 **Shahpur Chakar** *var.* Shāhpur. Sindh, SE Pakistan 26°11'N 68°44'E
148 M5 **Shahrak** Ghōr, C Afghanistan 34°09'N 64°16'E
143 Q11 **Shahr-e Bābak** Kermān, C Iran 30°08'N 55°04'E
143 N8 **Shahr-e Kord** *var.* Shahr Kord. Chahār Maḩall va Bakhtīārī, C Iran 32°20'N 50°52'E
143 O9 **Shahreẓā** *var.* Qomisheh, Qumisheh, Shahriza; *prev.* Qomsheh. Eşfahān, C Iran 32°01'N 51°51'E
147 S10 **Shahrikhon** *Rus.* Shakhrikhan. Andijon Viloyati, E Uzbekistan 40°42'N 72°03'E
147 P11 **Shahriston** *Rus.* Shakhristan. NW Tajikistan 39°45'N 68°47'E
147 P14 **Shahritus** *prev.* Shahrtuz, *Rus.* Shaartuz. SW Tajikistan 37°13'N 68°05'E
**Shahriza** *see* Shahreẓā
**Shahr-i-Zabul** *see* Zābol
**Shahr Kord** *see* Shahr-e Kord
**Shahrtuz** *see* Shahritus
143 Q4 **Shāhrūd** *prev.* Emāmrūd, Emāmshahr. Semnān, N Iran 36°30'N 55°E
**Shahsavār/Shahsawar** *see* Tonekābon
**Shaikh Ābid** *see* Shaykh 'Abid
**Shaikh Fāris** *see* Shaykh Fāris
**Shaikh Najm** *see* Shaykh Najm
138 K5 **Shā'ir, Jabal** ▲ C Syria 34°51'N 37°49'E
154 G10 **Shājāpur** Madhya Pradesh, C India 23°27'N 76°21'E
80 J8 **Shakal, Ras** *headland* NE Sudan 18°04'N 38°34'E
83 G17 **Shakawe** Ngamiland, NW Botswana 18°25'S 21°53'E
**Shakhdarinskiy Khrebet** *see* Shokhdara, Qatorkŭhi
**Shakhrikhan** *see* Shahrikhon
**Shakhrisabz** *see* Sharixon
**Shakhristan** *see* Shahriston
**Shakhtërsk** *see* Zuhres
145 R10 **Shakhtinsk** Karaganda, C Kazakhstan 49°40'N 72°37'E
126 L11 **Shakhty** Rostovskaya Oblast', SW Russia 47°45'N 40°14'E
127 P2 **Shakhun'ya** Nizhegorodskaya Oblast', W Russia 57°42'N 46°36'E
77 S15 **Shaki** Oyo, W Nigeria 08°37'N 03°25'E
81 J15 **Shakiso** Oromīya, C Ethiopia 05°33'N 38°48'E
29 V9 **Shakopee** Minnesota, N USA 44°48'N 93°31'W
165 R3 **Shakotan-misaki** *headland* Hokkaidō, NE Japan 43°22'N 140°28'E
39 N9 **Shaktoolik** Alaska, USA 64°19'N 161°05'W
81 J14 **Shala Hāyk'** C Ethiopia
124 M10 **Shalakusha** Arkhangel'skaya Oblast', NW Russia 62°16'N 40°16'E
145 U8 **Shalday** Pavlodar, NE Kazakhstan 51°57'N 78°51'E
127 P16 **Shali** Chechenskaya Respublika, SW Russia 43°03'N 45°55'E
141 W12 **Shalim** *var.* Shelim. S Oman 18°07'N 55°39'E
**Shalīr, Āveh-ye** *see* Shilayr, Wādī
**Shaliuhe** *see* Gangca
144 K12 **Shalkar** *var.* Chelkar. Aktyubinsk, W Kazakhstan 47°50'N 59°29'E
144 F9 **Shalkar, Ozero** *prev.* Chelkar Ozero. W Kazakhstan
21 V12 **Shallotte** North Carolina, SE USA 33°58'N 78°21'W
25 N5 **Shallowater** Texas, SW USA 33°41'N 102°00'W
124 K11 **Shal'skiy** Respublika Kareliya, NW Russia 61°45'N 36°02'E
160 F9 **Shaluli Shan** ▲ C China
81 F22 **Shama** C Tanzania
11 Z11 **Shamattawa** Manitoba, C Canada 55°52'N 92°05'W
12 F8 **Shamattawa** Ontario, C Canada
**Shām, Bādiyat ash** *see* Syrian Desert
**Shamiya** *see* Ash Shāmīyah
141 X8 **Shām, Jabal ash** *var.* Jebel Sham. ▲ NW Oman 23°21'N 57°08'E
**Shām, Jebel** *see* Shām, Jabal ash
**Shamkhor** *see* Şämkir
18 G14 **Shamokin** Pennsylvania, NE USA 40°47'N 76°33'W
25 P2 **Shamrock** Texas, SW USA 35°12'N 100°15'W
**Shana** *see* Kuril'sk
**Sha'nabī, Jabal ash** *see* Chambi, Jebel
139 Y12 **Shanāwah** Al Başrah, E Iraq 30°57'N 47°25'E
**Shancheng** *see* Taining
159 T8 **Shandan** *var.* Qingyuan. Gansu, N China 38°50'N 101°08'E
**Shandi** *see* Shendi
161 Q5 **Shandong** *var.* Lu, Shandong Sheng, Shantung. ◆ *province* E China
161 R4 **Shandong Bandao** *var.* Shantung Peninsula. *peninsula* E China
**Shandong Sheng** *see* Shandong
139 U8 **Shandrūkh** Diyālá, E Iraq 33°20'N 45°19'E
83 J17 **Shangani** W Zimbabwe
161 O15 **Shangchuan Dao** *island* S China
**Shangchuankou** *see* Minhe
163 P12 **Shangdu** Nei Mongol Zizhiqu, N China 41°32'N 113°33'E
161 O11 **Shanggao** *var.* Aoyang. Jiangxi, S China 28°16'N 114°55'E
**Shangguan** *see* Daixian
161 S8 **Shanghai** *var.* Shang-hai. Shanghai Shi, E China 31°14'N 121°28'E
161 S8 **Shanghai Shi** *var.* Hu, Shanghai. ◆ *municipality* E China
161 P13 **Shanghang** *var.* Linjiang. Fujian, SE China 25°03'N 116°25'E
160 K14 **Shanglin** *var.* Dafeng. Guangxi Zhuangzu Zizhiqu, S China 23°26'N 108°32'E
160 L7 **Shangluo** *prev.* Shangxian, Shangzhou. Shaanxi, C China 33°51'N 109°55'E
83 G15 **Shangombo** Western, W Zambia 16°28'S 22°10'E
**Shangpai/Shangpaihe** *see* Feixi
161 O6 **Shangqiu** *var.* Zhuji. Henan, C China 34°24'N 115°37'E
161 Q10 **Shangrao** Jiangxi, S China 28°27'N 117°57'E
**Shangxian** *see* Shangluo
161 S9 **Shangyu** *var.* Baiguan. Zhejiang, SE China 30°03'N 120°52'E
163 X9 **Shangzhi** Heilongjiang, NE China 45°13'N 127°59'E
**Shangzhou** *see* Shangluo
**Shanhe** *see* Zhengning
163 W9 **Shanhetun** Heilongjiang, NE China 44°42'N 127°12'E
**Shan-hsi** *see* Shaanxi, China
**Shan-hsi** *see* Shanxi, China
159 O6 **Shankou** Xinjiang Uygur Zizhiqu, W China 42°02'N 94°08'E
184 M13 **Shannon** Manawatu-Wanganui, North Island, New Zealand 40°32'S 175°24'E
97 C17 **Shannon** *Ir.* An tSionainn. W Ireland
97 B19 **Shannon** ✈ W Ireland 52°42'N 08°57'W
167 N6 **Shan Plateau** *plateau* E Myanmar (Burma)
158 M6 **Shanshan** *var.* Piqan. Xinjiang Uygur Zizhiqu, NW China 42°53'N 90°18'E
**Shansi** *see* Shanxi
167 N5 **Shan State** ◆ *state* E Myanmar (Burma)
**Shantar Islands** *see* Shantarskiye Ostrova
123 S12 **Shantarskiye Ostrova** *Eng.* Shantar Islands. *island group* E Russia
161 Q14 **Shantou** *var.* Shan-t'ou, Swatow. Guangdong, S China 23°23'N 116°39'E
**Shan-t'ou** *see* Shantou
**Shantung** *see* Shandong
**Shantung Peninsula** *see* Shandong Bandao
163 O14 **Shanxi** *var.* Jin, Shan-hsi, Shansi, Shanxi Sheng. ◆ *province* C China
161 P6 **Shanxian** *var.* Shan Xian. Shandong, E China 34°51'N 116°09'E
**Shan Xian** *see* Sanmenxia
**Shan Xian** *see* Shanxian
**Shanxi Sheng** *see* Shanxi
160 L7 **Shanyang** Shaanxi, C China 33°35'N 109°48'E
161 N13 **Shanyin** *var.* Daiyue. Shanxi, C China E Asia 39°30'N 112°56'E
161 O13 **Shaoguan** *var.* Shao-kuan, *Cant.* Kukong; *prev.* Ch'u-chiang. Guangdong, S China 24°57'N 113°38'E
**Shao-kuan** *see* Shaoguan
161 Q11 **Shaowu** Fujian, SE China 27°24'N 117°26'E
161 S9 **Shaoxing** Zhejiang, SE China 30°02'N 120°35'E
160 M12 **Shaoyang** *var.* Tangdukou. Hunan, S China 26°54'N 111°14'E
160 M11 **Shaoyang** *var.* Baoqing, Shao-yang; *prev.* Pao-king. Hunan, S China 27°13'N 111°31'E
**Shao-yang** *see* Shaoyang
96 K5 **Shapinsay** *island* NE Scotland, United Kingdom
125 S4 **Shapkina** NW Russia
**Shāpūr** *see* Salmās
158 M4 **Shaqiuhe** Xinjiang Uygur Zizhiqu, W China 45°00'N 88°52'E
**Shaqlāwa** *see* Sheqlawe
**Shaqlāwah** *see* Sheqlawe
138 I8 **Shaqqā** As Suwaydā', S Syria 32°53'N 36°42'E
141 P7 **Shaqrā'** Ar Riyāḑ, C Saudi Arabia 25°11'N 45°08'E
**Shaqrā** *see* Shuqrah
145 W10 **Shar** *var.* Charsk. Vostochnyy Kazakhstan, E Kazakhstan 49°33'N 81°03'E
149 Q7 **Sharan** *var.* Zareh Sharan. Paktīkā, E Afghanistan 33°08'N 68°47'E
**Sharaqpur** *see* Sharqpur
145 U8 **Sharbakty** *Kaz.* Sharbaqty; *prev.* Shcherbakty. Pavlodar, E Kazakhstan 52°28'N 78°00'E
**Sharbaqty** *see* Sharbakty
141 X12 **Sharbatāt** S Oman 17°57'N 56°14'E
**Sharbatāt, Ra's** *see* Sharbithāt, Ras
141 X12 **Sharbithāt, Ras** *var.* Ra's Sharbatāt. *headland* S Oman 17°55'N 56°30'E
14 K14 **Sharbot Lake** Ontario, SE Canada 44°45'N 76°46'W
145 P17 **Shardara** *var.* Chardara. Turkestan, S Kazakhstan 41°15'N 68°01'E
**Shardara Dalasy** *see* Step' Shardara
145 P17 **Shardarinskoye Vodokhranilishche** *prev.* Chardarinskoye Vodokhranilishche. S Kazakhstan
162 F8 **Sharga** Govĭ-Altay, W Mongolia 46°16'N 95°32'E
**Sharga** *see* Tsagaan-Uul
116 M7 **Sharhorod** Vinnyts'ka Oblast', C Ukraine 48°46'N 28°05'E
**Sharhulsan** *see* Mandal-Ovoo
165 V3 **Shari** Hokkaidō, NE Japan 43°54'N 144°42'E
**Shari** *see* Chari
139 T6 **Shārī, Buḩayrat** C Iraq
147 N12 **Sharixon** *Rus.* Shakhrisabz. Qashqadaryo Viloyati, S Uzbekistan 39°01'N 66°45'E
**Sharjah** *see* Ash Shāriqah
118 K12 **Sharkawshchyna** *var.* Sharkowshchyna, *Pol.* Szarkowszczyzna, *Rus.* Sharkovshchina. Vitsyebskaya Voblasts', NW Belarus 55°27'N 27°28'E
180 G9 **Shark Bay** *bay* Western Australia
141 Y9 **Sharkh** E Oman 21°20'N 59°04'E
**Sharkovshchina/Sharkowshchyna** *see* Sharkawshchyna
127 U6 **Sharlyk** Orenburgskaya Oblast', W Russia 52°52'N 54°45'E
75 Y9 **Sharm ash Shaykh** *var.* Ofiral, Sharm el Sheikh. E Egypt 27°51'N 34°16'E
**Sharm el Sheikh** *see* Sharm ash Shaykh
18 B13 **Sharon** Pennsylvania, NE USA 41°12'N 80°28'W
26 H4 **Sharon Springs** Kansas, C USA 38°54'N 101°46'W
31 Q14 **Sharonville** Ohio, N USA 39°16'N 84°24'W
**Sharourah** *see* Sharūrah
29 O10 **Sharpe, Lake** South Dakota, N USA
**Sharqī, Al Jabal ash/Sharqi, Jebel esh** *see* Anti-Lebanon
**Sharqiyah, Al Minṭaqah ash** *see* Ash Sharqīyah
138 I6 **Sharqīyat an Nabk, Jabal** W Syria
149 W8 **Sharqpur** *var.* Sharaqpur. Punjab, E Pakistan 31°29'N 74°08'E
141 Q13 **Sharūrah** *var.* Sharourah. Najrān, S Saudi Arabia 17°29'N 47°05'E
125 O14 **Shar'ya** Kostromskaya Oblast', NW Russia 58°22'N 45°30'E
145 W15 **Sharyn** *prev.* Charyn. Almaty, SE Kazakhstan 43°48'N 79°22'E
145 V15 **Sharyn** *var.* Charyn. SE Kazakhstan
122 K13 **Sharypovo** Krasnoyarskiy Kray, C Russia 55°33'N 89°12'E
83 J18 **Shashe** Central, NE Botswana 21°25'S 27°28'E
83 J18 **Shashe** *var.* Shashi. Botswana/Zimbabwe
81 J14 **Shashemenē** *var.* Shashemenne, Shashhamana, *It.* Sciasciamana. Oromīya, C Ethiopia 07°16'N 38°38'E
**Shashemenne/Shashhamana** *see* Shashemenē
**Shashi** *see* Shashe
**Shashi/Sha-shih/Shasi** *see* Jingzhou, Hubei
35 N3 **Shasta Lake** California, W USA
35 N2 **Shasta, Mount** ▲ California, W USA 41°24'N 122°11'W
127 O4 **Shatki** Nizhegorodskaya Oblast', W Russia 55°09'N 44°04'E
**Shatlyk** *see* Şatlyk
**Shatra** *see* Ash Shaṭrah
119 K17 **Shatsk** Minskaya Voblasts', C Belarus 53°25'N 27°41'E
127 N5 **Shatsk** Ryazanskaya Oblast', W Russia 54°02'N 41°38'E
26 J9 **Shattuck** Oklahoma, C USA 36°16'N 99°52'W
145 P16 **Shaul'dir** *prev.* Shaul'der. Turkestan, S Kazakhstan 42°45'N 68°21'E
**Shaul'der** *see* Shaul'dir
11 S17 **Shaunavon** Saskatchewan, S Canada 49°49'N 108°25'W
**Shavat** *see* Shovot
**Shaviyani Atoll** *see* North Miladhunmadulu Atoll
158 K4 **Shawan** *var.* Sandaohezi. Xinjiang Uygur Zizhiqu, NW China 44°21'N 85°37'E
14 G12 **Shawanaga** Ontario, S Canada 45°29'N 80°16'W
30 M6 **Shawano** Wisconsin, N USA 44°46'N 88°38'W
30 M6 **Shawano Lake** Wisconsin, N USA
15 P10 **Shawinigan** *prev.* Shawinigan Falls. Québec, SE Canada 46°33'N 72°45'W
**Shawinigan Falls** *see* Shawinigan
15 P10 **Shawinigan-Sud** Québec, SE Canada 46°30'N 72°43'W
138 J5 **Shawmarīyah, Jabal ash** ▲ C Syria
27 O11 **Shawnee** Oklahoma, C USA 35°20'N 96°55'W
14 K12 **Shawville** Québec, SE Canada 45°37'N 76°31'W
145 Q16 **Shayan** *var.* Chayan. Turkestan, S Kazakhstan 42°59'N 69°22'E
**Shaykh** *see* Ash Shakk
139 W9 **Shaykh 'Ābid** *var.* Shaikh Ābid. Wāsiţ, E Iraq 32°40'N 46°09'E
139 Y10 **Shaykh Fāris** *var.* Shaikh Fāris. Maysān, E Iraq 32°06'N 47°39'E
139 T7 **Shaykh Ḩātim** Baghdād, E Iraq 33°29'N 44°15'E
**Shaykh, Jabal ash** *see* Hermon, Mount
139 X10 **Shaykh Najm** *var.* Shaikh Najm. Maysān, E Iraq 32°04'N 46°54'E
139 W9 **Shaykh Sa'd** Maysān, E Iraq 32°35'N 46°16'E
147 T14 **Shazud** SE Tajikistan 37°45'N 72°22'E
119 N18 **Shchadryn** *Rus.* Shchedrin. Homyel'skaya Voblasts', SE Belarus 52°53'N 29°33'E
119 H18 **Shchara** SW Belarus
**Shchedrin** *see* Shchadryn
**Shcheglovsk** *see* Kemerovo
126 K5 **Shchëkino** Tul'skaya Oblast', W Russia 53°57'N 37°33'E
125 S7 **Shchel'yayur** Respublika Komi, NW Russia 65°19'N 53°27'E
**Shcherbakty** *see* Sharbakty
126 K7 **Shchigry** Kurskaya Oblast', W Russia 51°53'N 36°49'E
**Shchitkovichi** *see* Shchytkavichy
**Shchors** *see* Snovs'k
117 T8 **Shchors'k** Dnipropetrovs'ka Oblast', E Ukraine 48°20'N 34°07'E
**Shchuchin** *see* Shchuchyn
145 Q7 **Shchuchinsk** *prev.* Shchuchye. Akmola, N Kazakhstan 52°57'N 70°10'E
**Shchuchye** *see* Shchuchinsk
119 G16 **Shchuchyn** *Pol.* Szczuczyn Nowogródzki, *Rus.* Shchuchin. Hrodzyenskaya Voblasts', W Belarus 53°36'N 24°45'E
119 K17 **Shchytkavichy** *Rus.* Shchitkovichi. Minskaya Voblasts', C Belarus 53°13'N 27°59'E
122 J13 **Shebalino** Respublika Altay, S Russia 51°16'N 85°41'E
126 J9 **Shebekino** Belgorodskaya Oblast', W Russia 50°25'N 36°55'E
**Shebelē Wenz, Wabē** *see* Shebeli
81 L14 **Shebeli** *Amh.* Wabē Shebelē Wenz, *It.* Scebeli, *Som.* Webi Shabeelle. Ethiopia/Somalia
113 M20 **Shebenikut, Maja e** ▲ E Albania 41°13'N 20°27'E
**Sheberghān** *see* Shibirghān
144 F14 **Shebir** Mangistau, SW Kazakhstan 44°52'N 52°01'E
31 N8 **Sheboygan** Wisconsin, N USA 43°46'N 87°44'W
77 X15 **Shebshi Mountains** *var.* Schebschi Mountains. ▲ E Nigeria
**Shechem** *see* Nablus
**Shedadi** *see* Ash Shadādah
13 P14 **Shediac** New Brunswick, SE Canada 46°13'N 64°35'W
126 L15 **Shedok** Krasnodarskiy Kray, SW Russia 44°12'N 40°49'E
**Sheekh** *see* Shiikh
38 M11 **Sheenjek River** Alaska, USA
96 D13 **Sheep Haven** *Ir.* Cuan na gCaorach. *inlet* N Ireland
35 X10 **Sheep Range** ▲ Nevada, W USA
98 M13 **'s-Heerenberg** Gelderland, E Netherlands 51°52'N 06°15'E
97 P22 **Sheerness** SE England, United Kingdom 51°27'N 00°45'E
13 Q15 **Sheet Harbour** Nova Scotia, SE Canada 44°56'N 62°31'W
185 H18 **Sheffield** Canterbury, South Island, New Zealand 43°22'S 172°01'E
97 M18 **Sheffield** N England, United Kingdom 53°23'N 01°30'W
23 O2 **Sheffield** Alabama, S USA 34°46'N 87°42'W
29 V12 **Sheffield** Iowa, C USA 42°53'N 93°13'W
25 N10 **Sheffield** Texas, SW USA 30°42'N 101°49'W
63 H22 **Shehuen, Río** S Argentina
**Shekhem** *see* Nablus
149 V8 **Shekhupura** Punjab, NE Pakistan 31°42'N 74°08'E
**Sheki** *see* Şäki
124 L14 **Sheksna** Vologodskaya Oblast', NW Russia 59°11'N 38°32'E
123 T5 **Shelagskiy, Mys** *headland* NE Russia 70°04'N 170°39'E
27 V3 **Shelbina** Missouri, C USA 39°41'N 92°02'W
13 P16 **Shelburne** Nova Scotia, SE Canada 43°47'N 65°20'W
14 G14 **Shelburne** Ontario, S Canada 44°04'N 80°12'W
33 R7 **Shelby** Montana, NW USA 48°30'N 111°52'W
21 Q10 **Shelby** North Carolina, SE USA 35°15'N 81°34'W
31 S12 **Shelby** Ohio, N USA 40°52'N 82°39'W
30 L14 **Shelbyville** Illinois, N USA 39°24'N 88°47'W
31 P14 **Shelbyville** Indiana, N USA 39°31'N 85°46'W
20 L5 **Shelbyville** Kentucky, S USA 38°13'N 85°12'W
27 V2 **Shelbyville** Missouri, C USA 39°48'N 92°01'W
20 J10 **Shelbyville** Tennessee, S USA 35°29'N 86°30'W
25 X8 **Shelbyville** Texas, SW USA 31°42'N 94°03'W
30 L14 **Shelbyville, Lake** Illinois, N USA
29 S12 **Sheldon** Iowa, C USA 43°10'N 95°51'W
38 M11 **Sheldons Point** Alaska, USA 62°31'N 165°03'W
145 V15 **Shelek** *prev.* Chilik. Almaty, SE Kazakhstan 43°35'N 78°12'E
145 V15 **Shelek** *prev.* Chilik. SE Kazakhstan
**Shelekhov Gulf** *see* Shelikhova, Zaliv
123 U9 **Shelikhova, Zaliv** *Eng.* Shelekhov Gulf. *gulf* E Russia
39 P14 **Shelikof Strait** *strait* Alaska, USA
**Shelim** *see* Shalim
11 T14 **Shellbrook** Saskatchewan, S Canada 53°14'N 106°24'W
28 L3 **Shell Creek** North Dakota, N USA
**Shellif** *see* Chelif, Oued
22 I10 **Shell Keys** *island group* Louisiana, S USA
30 J4 **Shell Lake** Wisconsin, N USA 45°44'N 91°56'W
29 W12 **Shell Rock** Iowa, C USA 42°42'N 92°34'W
185 C26 **Shelter Point** *headland* Stewart Island, New Zealand 47°04'S 168°13'E
18 L13 **Shelton** Connecticut, NE USA 41°19'N 73°06'W
32 G8 **Shelton** Washington, NW USA 47°13'N 123°06'W
**Shemakha** *see* Şamaxı
145 W9 **Shemonaikha** Vostochnyy Kazakhstan, E Kazakhstan 50°38'N 81°55'E
127 Q4 **Shemursha** Chuvashskaya Respublika, W Russia 54°57'N 47°27'E
38 D16 **Shemya Island** *island* Aleutian Islands, Alaska, USA
29 T16 **Shenandoah** Iowa, C USA 40°46'N 95°23'W
21 U4 **Shenandoah** Virginia, NE USA 38°26'N 78°34'W
21 U4 **Shenandoah Mountains** *ridge* West Virginia, NE USA
21 V3 **Shenandoah River** West Virginia, NE USA
77 W15 **Shendam** Plateau, C Nigeria 08°52'N 09°30'E
80 G8 **Shendi** *var.* Shandi. River Nile, NE Sudan 16°41'N 33°22'E
76 I15 **Shenge** SW Sierra Leone 07°54'N 12°54'W
146 L10 **Shengeldi** *Rus.* Chingildi. Navoiy Viloyati, N Uzbekistan 40°59'N 64°13'E
145 U15 **Shengel'dy** Almaty, SE Kazakhstan 44°04'N 77°31'E
113 K18 **Shëngjin** *var.* Shëngjini. Lezhë, NW Albania 41°49'N 19°34'E
**Shëngjini** *see* Shëngjin
**Shengking** *see* Liaoning
**Sheng Xian/Shengxian** *see* Shengzhou
161 S9 **Shengzhou** *var.* Shengxian, Sheng Xian. Zhejiang, SE China 29°36'N 120°42'E
**Shenking** *see* Liaoning
125 N11 **Shenkursk** Arkhangel'skaya Oblast', NW Russia 62°10'N 42°58'E
160 L3 **Shenmu** Shaanxi, C China 38°49'N 110°27'E
113 L19 **Shën Noj i Madh** ▲ C Albania 41°23'N 20°07'E
160 L8 **Shennong Ding** ▲ C China 31°24'N 110°16'E
**Shenshi/Shensi** *see* Shaanxi
163 V12 **Shenyang** *Chin.* Shen-yang, *Eng.* Moukden, Mukden; *prev.* Fengtien. *province capital* Liaoning, NE China 41°50'N 123°26'E
**Shen-yang** *see* Shenyang
161 O15 **Shenzhen** Guangdong, S China 22°39'N 114°02'E
154 G8 **Sheopur** Madhya Pradesh, C India 25°41'N 76°42'E
116 L5 **Shepetivka** *Rus.* Shepetovka. Khmel'nyts'ka Oblast', NW Ukraine 50°12'N 27°01'E
**Shepetovka** *see* Shepetivka
25 W10 **Shepherd** Texas, SW USA 30°30'N 95°00'W
187 R14 **Shepherd Islands** *island group* C Vanuatu
20 K5 **Shepherdsville** Kentucky, S USA 38°00'N 85°42'W
183 O11 **Shepparton** Victoria, SE Australia 36°25'S 145°26'E
97 P22 **Sheppey, Isle of** *island* SE England, United Kingdom
139 T2 **Sheqlawe** *Ar.* Shaqlāwah, *var.* Shaqlāwa. Arbil, E Iraq 36°24'N 44°21'E
**Sherabad** *see* Sherobod
9 O4 **Sherard, Cape** *headland* Nunavut, N Canada 74°36'N 80°10'W
97 L23 **Sherborne** S England, United Kingdom 50°58'N 02°30'W
76 H16 **Sherbro Island** *island* SW Sierra Leone
15 Q12 **Sherbrooke** Québec, SE Canada 45°23'N 71°55'W
29 T11 **Sherburn** Minnesota, N USA 43°39'N 94°43'W
78 H6 **Sherda** Tibesti, N Chad 20°04'N 16°48'E
80 G7 **Shereik** River Nile, N Sudan 18°44'N 33°37'E
126 K3 **Sheremet'yevo** ✈ (Moskva) Moskovskaya Oblast', W Russia 56°05'N 37°10'E
153 P14 **Sherghāti** Bihār, N India 24°35'N 84°51'E
27 U12 **Sheridan** Arkansas, C USA 34°18'N 92°22'W
33 W12 **Sheridan** Wyoming, C USA 44°47'N 106°59'W
182 G8 **Sheringa** South Australia 33°51'S 135°13'E
25 U5 **Sherman** Texas, SW USA 33°39'N 96°35'W
194 J10 **Sherman Island** *island* Antarctica
19 S4 **Sherman Mills** Maine, NE USA 45°51'N 68°23'W
29 O15 **Sherman Reservoir** Nebraska, C USA
147 N14 **Sherobod** *Rus.* Sherabad. Surkhondaryo Viloyati, S Uzbekistan 37°43'N 66°59'E
147 O13 **Sherobod** *Rus.* Sherabad. S Uzbekistan
153 T14 **Sherpur** Dhaka, N Bangladesh 25°00'N 90°01'E
37 T4 **Sherrelwood** Colorado, C USA 39°49'N 105°00'W
99 J14 **'s-Hertogenbosch** *Fr.* Bois-le-Duc, *Ger.* Herzogenbusch. Noord-Brabant, S Netherlands 51°41'N 05°19'E
28 M2 **Sherwood** North Dakota, N USA 48°55'N 101°36'W
11 Q14 **Sherwood Park** Alberta, SW Canada 53°34'N 113°04'W
56 F13 **Sheshea, Río** E Peru
143 T5 **Sheshtamad** Khorāsān-e Raẕavī, NE Iran 36°03'N 57°45'E
29 S10 **Shetek, Lake** Minnesota, N USA
96 M2 **Shetland Islands** *island group* NE Scotland, United Kingdom
144 F14 **Shetpe** Mangistau, SW Kazakhstan 44°06'N 52°03'E
154 C11 **Shetrunji** W India
**Shevchenko** *see* Aktau
117 W5 **Shevchenkove** Kharkivs'ka Oblast', E Ukraine 49°40'N 37°13'E
81 H14 **Shewa Gīmīra** Southern Nationalities, S Ethiopia 07°12'N 35°49'E
161 Q9 **Shexian** *var.* Huicheng, She Xian. Anhui, E China 29°53'N 118°27'E
**She Xian** *see* Shexian
161 R6 **Sheyang** *prev.* Hede. Jiangsu, E China 33°49'N 120°13'E
29 O4 **Sheyenne** North Dakota, N USA 47°49'N 99°08'W
29 P4 **Sheyenne River** North Dakota, N USA
96 G7 **Shiant Islands** *island group* NW Scotland, United Kingdom
123 U12 **Shiashkotan, Ostrov** *island* Kuril'skiye Ostrova, SE Russia
31 R9 **Shiawassee River** Michigan, N USA
141 R14 **Shibām** C Yemen 15°49'N 48°24'E
**Shibarghān** *see* Shibirghān
165 O10 **Shibata** *var.* Sibata. Niigata, Honshū, C Japan 37°57'N 139°20'E
**Shiberghan/Shiberghān** *see* Shibirghān
75 X8 **Shibh Jazīrat Sīnā'** *var.* Sinai Peninsula, Sinai, Sīnā. *physical region* NE Egypt
75 W8 **Shibīn al Kawm** *var.* Shibīn el Kôm. N Egypt 30°33'N 31°00'E
**Shibīn el Kôm** *see* Shibīn al Kawm
149 N2 **Shibirghān** *var.* Shibarghān, Shiberghan, Shiberghān; *prev.* Sheberghān. Jowzjān, N Afghanistan 36°41'N 65°45'E
143 O13 **Shīb, Kūh-e** S Iran
12 D8 **Shibogama Lake** Ontario, C Canada
**Shibotsu-jima** *see* Zelënyy, Ostrov
164 B16 **Shibushi** Kagoshima, Kyūshū, SW Japan 31°27'N 130°05'E
189 U13 **Shichiyo Islands** *island group* Chuuk, C Micronesia
**Shickshock Mountains** *see* Chic-Chocs, Monts
**shiderti** *see* Shiderty
**Shiderti** *see* Shiderty
145 S8 **Shiderty** *prev.* Shiderti. Pavlodar, NE Kazakhstan 51°40'N 74°50'E
145 S9 **Shiderty** *prev.* Shiderti. N Kazakhstan
96 G10 **Shiel, Loch** N Scotland, United Kingdom
164 J13 **Shiga** *off.* Shiga-ken, *var.* Siga. ◆ *prefecture* Honshū, SW Japan
**Shiga-ken** *see* Shiga
**Shigatse** *see* Xigazê
141 U13 **Shiḩan** *oasis* NE Yemen
**Shih-chia-chuang/Shihmen** *see* Shijiazhuang
158 K4 **Shihezi** Xinjiang Uygur Zizhiqu, NW China 44°21'N 85°59'E
**Shiichi** *see* Shyichy
80 N12 **Shiikh** *prev.* Sheekh. Togdheer, N Somalia 10°01'N 45°21'E
113 K19 **Shijak** *var.* Shijaku. Durrës, W Albania 41°21'N 19°34'E
**Shijaku** *see* Shijak
161 O4 **Shijiazhuang** *var.* Shih-chia-chuang; *prev.* Shihmen. *province capital* Hebei, E China 38°04'N 114°28'E
165 R5 **Shikabe** Hokkaidō, NE Japan 42°03'N 140°45'E
149 Q13 **Shikārpur** Sindh, S Pakistan 27°59'N 68°39'E
127 Q7 **Shikhany** Saratovskaya Oblast', W Russia 52°07'N 47°13'E
189 V12 **Shiki Islands** *island group* Chuuk, C Micronesia
164 G14 **Shikoku** *var.* Sikoku. *island* SW Japan
192 H5 **Shikoku Basin** *var.* Sikoku Basin. *undersea feature* N Philippine Sea 28°00'N 137°00'E
164 G14 **Shikoku-sanchi** ▲ Shikoku, SW Japan
165 X4 **Shikotan, Ostrov** *Jap.* Shikotan-tō. *island* NE Russia
**Shikotan-tō** *see* Shikotan, Ostrov




◆ Country
● Country Capital
◇ Dependent Territory
○ Dependent Territory Capital
◆ Administrative Regions
✈ International Airport
▲ Mountain
▲ Mountain Range
Volcano
River
Lake
Reservoir

SHIKOTSU-KO – SIMIKOT


165 R4 **Shikotsu-ko** *var.* Sikotu Ko. ◎ Hokkaidō, NE Japan
81 N15 **Shilabo** Sumalē, E Ethiopia 06°05′N 44°48′E
139 V3 **Shilayr, Wādī** *var.* Āw-e Shilēr, Āveh-ye Shalīr. ≈ E Iraq
127 X7 **Shil'da** Orenburgskaya Oblast', W Russia 51°46′N 59°48′E
**Shilēr, Āw-e** *see* Shilayr, Wādī
153 S12 **Shiliguri** *var.* Siliguri. West Bengal, NE India 26°46′N 88°24′E
**Shiliu** *see* Changjiang
129 V7 **Shilka** ≈ S Russia
18 H15 **Shillington** Pennsylvania, NE USA 40°18′N 75°57′W
153 V13 **Shillong** *state capital* Meghālaya, NE India 25°37′N 91°54′E
126 M5 **Shilovo** Ryazanskaya Oblast', W Russia 54°18′N 40°53′E
164 C14 **Shimabara** *var.* Simabara. Nagasaki, Kyūshū, SW Japan 32°48′N 130°20′E
164 C14 **Shimabara-wan** *bay* SW Japan
164 F12 **Shimane** *off.* Shimane-ken, *var.* Simane. ◈ *prefecture* Honshū, SW Japan
164 G11 **Shimane-hantō** *peninsula* Honshū, SW Japan
**Shimane-ken** *see* Shimane
123 Q13 **Shimanovsk** Amurskaya Oblast', SE Russia 52°00′N 127°36′E
**Shimanto** *see* Nakamura
**Shimbir Berris** *see* Shimbiris
80 O12 **Shimbiris** *var.* Shimbir Berris. ▲ N Somalia 10°43′N 47°10′E
165 T4 **Shimizu** Hokkaidō, NE Japan 42°58′N 142°54′E
164 M14 **Shimizu** *var.* Simizu. Shizuoka, Honshū, S Japan 35°01′N 138°29′E
152 I8 **Shimla** *prev.* Simla. *state capital* Himāchal Pradesh, N India 31°07′N 77°09′E
165 N14 **Shimoda** *var.* Simoda. Shizuoka, Honshū, S Japan 34°40′N 138°55′E
165 O13 **Shimodate** *var.* Simodate. Ibaraki, Honshū, S Japan 36°20′N 140°00′E
**Shimoga** *see* Shivamogga
164 C15 **Shimo-jima** *island* SW Japan
164 B15 **Shimo-Koshiki-jima** *island* SW Japan
81 J21 **Shimoni** Kwale, S Kenya 04°40′S 39°22′E
164 D13 **Shimonoseki** *var.* Simonoseki, *hist.* Akamagaseki, Bakan. Yamaguchi, Honshū, SW Japan 33°57′N 130°54′E
124 G14 **Shimsk** Novgorodskaya Oblast', NW Russia 58°12′N 30°43′E
141 W7 **Shināş** N Oman 24°45′N 56°24′E
148 J6 **Shīndand** *prev.* Shīndand. Herāt, W Afghanistan 33°19′N 62°09′E
**Shīndand** *see* Shīndand
**Shinei** *see* Xinying
162 H10 **Shinejinst** *var.* Dzalaa. Bayanhongor, C Mongolia 44°29′N 99°19′E
25 T12 **Shiner** Texas, SW USA 29°25′N 97°10′W
167 N1 **Shingbwiyang** Kachin State, N Myanmar (Burma) 26°40′N 96°14′E
**Shingozha** *see* Shynkozha
164 J15 **Shingū** *var.* Singû. Wakayama, Honshū, SW Japan 33°41′N 135°57′E
14 F8 **Shining Tree** Ontario, S Canada 47°36′N 81°12′W
165 P9 **Shinjō** *var.* Sinzyô. Yamagata, Honshū, C Japan 38°47′N 140°17′E
96 I7 **Shin, Loch** ◎ N Scotland, United Kingdom
21 S3 **Shinnston** West Virginia, NE USA 39°22′N 80°19′W
138 I6 **Shinshār** *Fr.* Chinnchâr. Ḩimş, W Syria 34°36′N 36°45′E
**Shinshū** *see* Jinju
165 T4 **Shintoku** Hokkaidō, NE Japan 43°03′N 142°50′E
81 G20 **Shinyanga** Shinyanga, NW Tanzania 03°40′S 33°25′E
81 G20 **Shinyanga** ◈ *region* N Tanzania
165 Q10 **Shiogama** *var.* Siogama. Miyagi, Honshū, C Japan 38°19′N 141°00′E
164 M12 **Shiojiri** *var.* Sioziri. Nagano, Honshū, S Japan 36°08′N 137°58′E
164 I15 **Shiono-misaki** *headland* Honshū, SW Japan 33°25′N 135°45′E
165 Q12 **Shioya-zaki** *headland* Honshū, C Japan 37°00′N 140°57′E
114 J9 **Shipchenski Prohod** , Shipchenski Prokhod. *pass* C Bulgaria
**Shipchenski Prokhod** *see* Shipchenski Prohod
160 G14 **Shiping** Yunnan, SW China 23°45′N 102°23′E
13 P13 **Shippagan** *var.* Shippegan. New Brunswick, SE Canada 47°45′N 64°44′W
**Shippegan** *see* Shippagan
18 F15 **Shippensburg** Pennsylvania, NE USA 40°03′N 77°31′W
37 P9 **Shiprock** New Mexico, SW USA 36°47′N 108°41′W
37 O9 **Ship Rock** ▲ New Mexico, SW USA 36°41′N 108°50′W
15 R6 **Shipshaw** ≈ Québec, SE Canada
123 V10 **Shipunskiy, Mys** *headland* E Russia 53°04′N 159°57′E
160 K7 **Shiquan** Shaanxi, C China 33°05′N 108°15′E
**Shiquanhe** *see* Gar
122 K13 **Shira** Respublika Khakasiya, S Russia 54°35′N 89°58′E
**Shirajganj Ghat** *see* Sirajganj
165 P12 **Shirakawa** *var.* Sirakawa. Fukushima, Honshū, C Japan 37°07′N 140°11′E
164 M13 **Shirane-san** ▲ Honshū, S Japan 35°39′N 138°13′E
165 U14 **Shiranuka** Hokkaidō, NE Japan 42°57′N 144°01′E
195 N12 **Shirase Coast** *physical region* Antarctica
165 U3 **Shirataki** Hokkaidō, NE Japan 43°55′N 143°14′E
143 O11 **Shīrāz** *var.* Shīrāz. Fārs, S Iran 29°38′N 52°34′E
83 N15 **Shire** *var.* Chire. ≈ Malawi/Mozambique
**Shiree** *see* Tsagaanhayrhan
**Shireet** *see* Bayandelger
165 W3 **Shiretoko-hantō** *headland* Hokkaidō, NE Japan 44°06′N 145°07′E
165 W3 **Shiretoko-misaki** *headland* Hokkaidō, NE Japan 44°20′N 145°19′E
127 N5 **Shiringushi** Respublika Mordoviya, W Russia 53°50′N 42°49′E
148 M3 **Shīrīn Tagāb** Fāryāb, N Afghanistan 36°49′N 65°01′E
149 N2 **Shīrīn Tagāb** ≈ N Afghanistan
165 R6 **Shiriya-zaki** *headland* Honshū, C Japan 41°24′N 141°27′E
144 I12 **Shirkala, Gryada** *plain* W Kazakhstan
152 F11 **Shir Kolāyat** *var.* Kolāyat. Rājasthān, NW India 27°56′N 73°02′E
165 P10 **Shiroishi** *var.* Siroisi. Miyagi, Honshū, C Japan 38°00′N 140°38′E
**Shirokoye** *see* Shyroke
165 O10 **Shirone** *var.* Sirone. Niigata, Honshū, C Japan 37°46′N 139°00′E
164 L12 **Shirotori** Gifu, Honshū, SW Japan 35°53′N 136°52′E
197 T1 **Shirshov Ridge** *undersea feature* W Bering Sea
**Shirshūtūr/Shirshyutyur, Peski** *see* Şirşütür Gumy
143 T3 **Shīrvān** *var.* Shirwān. Khorāsān-e Shomālī, NE Iran 37°25′N 57°55′E
**Shirwa, Lake** *see* Chilwa, Lake
**Shirwān** *see* Shīrvān
159 N5 **Shisanjianfang** Xinjiang Uygur Zizhiqu, W China 43°10′N 91°15′E
38 M16 **Shishaldin Volcano** ▲ Unimak Island, Alaska, USA 54°45′N 163°58′W
**Shishchitsy** *see* Shyshchytsy
83 G16 **Shishikola** North West, N Botswana 18°09′S 23°08′E
38 M8 **Shishmaref** Alaska, USA 66°15′N 166°04′W
**Shisur** *see* Ash Shişar
164 L13 **Shitara** Aichi, Honshū, SW Japan 35°06′N 137°33′E
152 D12 **Shiv** Rājasthān, NW India 26°11′N 71°14′E
**Shivāji Sāgar** *see* Konya Reservoir
155 F18 **Shivamogga** *prev.* Shimoga. Karnātaka, W India 13°56′N 75°31′E
154 H8 **Shivpuri** Madhya Pradesh, C India 25°28′N 77°41′E
36 J9 **Shivwits Plateau** *plain* Arizona, SW USA
**Shiwalik Range** *see* Siwalik Range
160 M8 **Shiyan** Hubei, C China 32°31′N 110°45′E
145 O15 **Shiyeli** *prev.* Chiili. Kzylorda, S Kazakhstan 44°13′N 66°46′E
**Shizilu** *see* Junan
160 H13 **Shizong** *var.* Danfeng. Yunnan, SW China 24°53′N 104′E
165 R10 **Shizugawa** Miyagi, Honshū, NE Japan 38°40′N 141°26′E
165 T5 **Shizunai** Hokkaidō, NE Japan 42°20′N 142°24′E
165 M14 **Shizuoka** *var.* Sizuoka. Shizuoka, Honshū, S Japan 34°59′N 138°20′E
164 M13 **Shizuoka** *off.* Shizuoka-ken, *var.* Sizuoka. ◈ *prefecture* Honshū, S Japan
**Shizuoka-ken** *see* Shizuoka
**Shklov** *see* Shklow
119 N15 **Shklow** *Rus.* Shklov. Mahilyowskaya Voblasts', E Belarus 54°13′N 30°18′E
113 K18 **Shkodër** *var.* Shkodra, *It.* Scutari, *SCr.* Skadar. Shkodër, NW Albania 42°03′N 19°31′E
113 K17 **Shkodër** ◈ *county* NW Albania
**Shkodra** *see* Shkodër
**Shkodrës, Liqeni i** *see* Scutari, Lake
113 L20 **Shkumbinit, Lumi i** *var.* Shkumbî, Shkumbin. ≈ C Albania
**Shkumbî/Shkumbin** *see* Shkumbinit, Lumi i
**Shligigh, Cuan** *see* Sligo Bay
122 L4 **Shmidta, Ostrov** *island* Severnaya Zemlya, N Russia
183 S10 **Shoalhaven River** ≈ New South Wales, SE Australia
11 W16 **Shoal Lake** Manitoba, S Canada 50°28′N 100°36′W
31 O15 **Shoals** Indiana, N USA 38°40′N 86°47′W
164 I13 **Shōdo-shima** *island* SW Japan
**Shōka** *see* Changhua
122 M5 **Shokal'skogo, Proliv** *strait* N Russia
147 T14 **Shokhdara, Qatorkŭhi** *Rus.* Shakhdarinskiy Khrebet. ▲▲ SE Tajikistan
145 T15 **Shokpar** *Kaz.* Shoqpar; *prev.* Chokpar. Zhambyl, S Kazakhstan 43°49′N 74°25′E
145 P15 **Sholakkorgan** *var.* Chulakkurgan. Turkestan, S Kazakhstan 43°45′N 69°10′E
145 N9 **Sholaksay** Kostanay, N Kazakhstan 51°45′N 64°45′E
**Sholāpur** *see* Solāpur
**Sholdaneshty** *see* Şoldăneşti
145 W15 **Shonzhy** *prev.* Chundzha. Almaty, SE Kazakhstan 43°32′N 79°28′E
**Shoqpar** *see* Shokpar
155 G21 **Shoranūr** Kerala, SW India 10°53′N 76°06′E
155 G16 **Shorāpur** Karnātaka, C India 16°34′N 76°48′E
147 O14 **Sho'rchi** *Rus.* Shurchi. Surkhondaryo Viloyati, S Uzbekistan 37°58′N 67°40′E
30 M11 **Shorewood** Illinois, N USA 41°31′N 88°12′W
**Shorkazakhly, Solonchak** *see* Kazakhlyshor, Solonchak
145 Q9 **Shortandy** Akmola, C Kazakhstan 51°45′N 71°01′E
149 O2 **Shōr Tepah** *var.* Shortepa, Shor Tepe; *prev.* Shūr Tappeh. Balkh, N Afghanistan 37°22′N 66°49′E
**Shortepa/Shor Tepe** *see* Shōr Tepah
186 J7 **Shortland Island** *var.* Alu. *island* Shortland Islands, NW Solomon Islands
**Shosambetsu** *see* Shosanbetsu
165 S2 **Shosanbetsu** *var.* Shosambetsu. Hokkaidō, NE Japan 44°31′N 141°47′E
33 O15 **Shoshone** Idaho, NW USA 42°56′N 114°24′W
35 T6 **Shoshone Mountains** ▲▲ Nevada, W USA
33 U12 **Shoshone River** ≈ Wyoming, C USA
83 I19 **Shoshong** Central, SE Botswana 23°02′S 26°31′E
33 V14 **Shoshoni** Wyoming, C USA 43°13′N 108°06′W
**Shōshū** *see* Sangju
117 S2 **Shostka** Sums'ka Oblast', NE Ukraine 51°52′N 33°30′E
185 C21 **Shotover** ≈ South Island, New Zealand
146 H9 **Shovot** *Rus.* Shavat. Xorazm Viloyati, W Uzbekistan 41°41′N 60°13′E
37 N12 **Show Low** Arizona, SW USA 34°15′N 110°01′W
**Show Me State** *see* Missouri
125 O4 **Shoyna** Nenetskiy Avtonomnyy Okrug, NW Russia 67°50′N 44°09′E
124 M11 **Shozhma** Arkhangel'skaya Oblast', NW Russia 61°57′N 40°10′E
117 Q7 **Shpola** Cherkas'ka Oblast', N Ukraine 49°00′N 31°27′E
**Shqipëria/Shqipërisë, Republika e** *see* Albania
22 G5 **Shreveport** Louisiana, S USA 32°32′N 93°45′W
97 K19 **Shrewsbury** *hist.* Scrobesbyrig'. W England, United Kingdom 52°43′N 02°45′W
152 D11 **Shri Mohangarh** *prev.* Sri Mohangorh. Rājasthān, NW India 27°17′N 71°18′E
153 S16 **Shrīrāmpur** *prev.* Serampore, Serampur. West Bengal, NE India 22°44′N 88°20′E
97 K19 **Shropshire** *cultural region* W England, United Kingdom
113 N17 **Shtime** *Serb.* Štimlje. C Kosovo 42°27′N 21°03′E
145 S16 **Shu** *Kaz.* Shū. Zhambyl, SE Kazakhstan 43°34′N 73°41′E
129 Q7 **Shu** *Kaz.* Shū; *prev.* Chu. ≈ Kazakhstan/Kyrgyzstan
160 G13 **Shuangbai** *var.* Tuodian. Yunnan, SW China 24°45′N 101°38′E
163 W9 **Shuangcheng** Heilongjiang, NE China 45°20′N 126°21′E
**Shuangcheng** *see* Zherong
160 E14 **Shuangjiang** *var.* Weiyuan. Yunnan, SW China 23°28′N 99°43′E
**Shuangjiang** *see* Jiangkou
**Shuangjiang** *see* Tongdao
163 U10 **Shuangliao** *var.* Zhengjiatun. Jilin, NE China 43°31′N 123°32′E
**Shuang-liao** *see* Liaoyuan
**Shuangshipu** *see* Fengxian
163 Y7 **Shuangyashan** *var.* Shuang-ya-shan. Heilongjiang, NE China 46°37′N 131°10′E
**Shuang-ya-shan** *see* Shuangyashan
**Shu'aymiah** *see* Shu'aymīyah
141 W12 **Shu'aymīyah** *var.* Shu'aymiah. S Oman 17°55′N 55°39′E
**Shubarkuduk** *see* Shubarkudyk
144 I10 **Shubarkudyk** *prev.* Shubarkuduk, *Kaz.* Shubarqudyq. Aktyubinsk, W Kazakhstan 49°09′N 56°31′E
**Shubarqudyq** *see* Shubarkudyk
145 N12 **Shubar-Tengiz, Ozero** ◎ C Kazakhstan
39 S5 **Shublik Mountains** ▲▲ Alaska, USA
**Shubrā al Khaymah** *see* Shubrâ el Kheima
121 U13 **Shubrâ el Kheima** *var.* Shubrā al Khaymah. N Egypt 30°06′N 31°15′E
158 E8 **Shufu** *var.* Tuokezhake. Xinjiang Uygur Zizhiqu, NW China 39°18′N 75°43′E
147 S14 **Shughnon, Qatorkŭhi** *Rus.* Shugnanskiy Khrebet. ▲▲ SE Tajikistan
**Shugnanskiy Khrebet** *see* Shughnon, Qatorkŭhi
161 Q6 **Shu He** ≈ E China
**Shuicheng** *see* Lupanshui
**Shuiding** *see* Huocheng
**Shuidong** *see* Dianbai
**Shuiji** *see* Laixi
**Shū-Ile Taūlary** *see* Gory Shu-Ile
**Shuilocheng** *see* Zhuanglang
**Shuiluo** *see* Zhuanglang
149 T10 **Shujaabad** Punjab, E Pakistan 29°53′N 71°23′E
**Shū, Kazakhstan** *see* Shu
**Shū, Kazakhstan/Kyrgyzstan** *see* Shu
163 W9 **Shulan** Jilin, NE China 44°28′N 126°57′E
158 E8 **Shule** Xinjiang Uygur Zizhiqu, NW China 39°19′N 76°06′E
**Shuleh** *see* Shule He
159 Q8 **Shule He** *var.* Shuleh, Sulo. ≈ C China
30 K9 **Shullsburg** Wisconsin, N USA 42°37′N 90°12′W
**Shulu** *see* Xinji
39 N16 **Shumagin Islands** *island group* Alaska, USA
146 G7 **Shumanay** Qoraqalpog'iston Respublikasi, W Uzbekistan 42°42′N 58°56′E
114 M8 **Shumen** Shumen, NE Bulgaria 43°17′N 26°57′E
114 M8 **Shumen** ◈ *province* NE Bulgaria
127 P4 **Shumerlya** Chuvashskaya Respublika, W Russia 55°31′N 46°24′E
122 G11 **Shumikha** Kurganskaya Oblast', C Russia 55°12′N 63°09′E
118 M12 **Shumilina** *Rus.* Shumilino. Vitsyebskaya Voblasts', NE Belarus 55°18′N 29°37′E
**Shumilino** *see* Shumilina
123 V11 **Shumshu, Ostrov** *island* SE Russia
116 K5 **Shums'k** Ternopil's'ka Oblast', W Ukraine 50°06′N 26°04′E
**Shūnan** *see* Tokuyama
39 O7 **Shungnak** Alaska, USA 66°53′N 157°08′W
**Shunsen** *see* Chuncheon
**Shuoxian** *see* Shuozhou
161 N3 **Shuozhou** *var.* Shuoxian. Shanxi, C China 39°20′N 112°25′E
141 P16 **Shuqrah** *var.* Shaqrā. SW Yemen 13°26′N 45°44′E
**Shurab** *see* Shŭrob
**Shurchi** *see* Sho'rchi
147 R11 **Shŭrob** *Rus.* Shurab. NW Tajikistan 40°02′N 70°31′E
143 T10 **Shūr, Rūd-e** ≈ E Iran
**Shūr Tappeh** *see* Shōr Tepah
83 K17 **Shurugwi** *prev.* Selukwe. Midlands, C Zimbabwe 19°40′S 30°00′E
142 L8 **Shūsh** *anc.* Susa, *Bibl.* Shushan. Khūzestān, SW Iran 32°12′N 48°20′E
**Shushan** *see* Shūsh
142 L9 **Shūshtar** *var.* Shustar, Shushter. Khūzestān, SW Iran 32°03′N 48°51′E
**Shushter/Shustar** *see* Shūshtar
141 T9 **Shuţfah, Qalamat** *well* E Saudi Arabia
139 V9 **Shuwayjah, Hawr ash** *var.* Hawr as Suwayqiyah. ◎ E Iraq
124 M16 **Shuya** Ivanovskaya Oblast', W Russia 56°51′N 41°24′E
39 Q14 **Shuyak Island** *island* Alaska, USA
166 M4 **Shwebo** Sagaing, C Myanmar (Burma) 22°35′N 95°42′E
166 L7 **Shwedaung** Bago, W Myanmar (Burma) 18°44′N 95°12′E
166 M7 **Shwegyin** Bago, SW Myanmar (Burma) 17°56′N 96°59′E
167 N4 **Shweli** *Chin.* Longchuan Jiang. ≈ Myanmar (Burma)/China
166 M6 **Shwemyo** Mandalay, C Myanmar (Burma) 20°04′N 96°13′E
145 S14 **Shyganak** *var.* Čiganak, Chiganak, *Kaz.* Shyghanaq. Zhambyl, SE Kazakhstan 45°10′N 73°55′E
**Shyghanaq** *see* Shyganak
**Shyghys Qazagastan Oblysy** *see* Vostochnyy Kazakhstan
**Shyghys Qongyrat** *see* Shygys Konyrat
145 T12 **Shygys Konyrat** , *Kaz.* Shyghys Qongyrat. Karaganda, C Kazakhstan 47°01′N 75°05′E
119 M19 **Shyichy** *Rus.* Shiichi. Homyel'skaya Voblasts', SE Belarus 52°15′N 29°14′E
145 Q17 **Shymkent** *prev.* Chimkent. Shymkent, S Kazakhstan 42°19′N 69°36′E
144 H9 **Shyngghyrlau** *prev.* Chingirlau. Zapadnyy Kazakhstan, W Kazakhstan 51°10′N 53°44′E
144 G9 **Shyngyrlau** *prev.* Utva. ≈ NW Kazakhstan
145 W11 **Shynkozha** *prev.* Shingozha. Vostochnyy Kazakhstan, E Kazakhstan 47°46′N 80°38′E
152 J5 **Shyok** Jammu and Kashmir, NW India 34°13′N 78°12′E
117 S9 **Shyroke** *Rus.* Shirokoye. Dnipropetrovs'ka Oblast', E Ukraine 47°41′N 33°16′E
117 O9 **Shyryayeve** Odes'ka Oblast', SW Ukraine 47°21′N 30°11′E
117 S5 **Shyshaky** Poltavs'ka Oblast', C Ukraine 49°54′N 34°00′E
119 K17 **Shyshchytsy** *Rus.* Shishchitsy. Minskaya Voblasts', C Belarus 53°13′N 27°33′E
149 Y3 **Siachen Muztagh** ▲▲ NE Pakistan
**Siadehan** *see* Tākestān
148 M13 **Siahan Range** ▲▲ W Pakistan
142 I1 **Sīāh Chashmeh** *var.* Chālderān. Āžarbāyjān-e Gharbī, N Iran 39°02′N 44°22′E
149 W7 **Sialkot** Punjab, NE Pakistan 32°29′N 74°35′E
186 E7 **Sialum** Morobe, C Papua New Guinea 06°02′S 147°37′E
**Siam** *see* Thailand
**Siam, Gulf of** *see* Thailand, Gulf of
**Sian** *see* Xi'an
**Siang** *see* Brahmaputra
**Siangtan** *see* Xiangtan
169 N8 **Siantan, Pulau** *island* Kepulauan Anambas, W Indonesia
54 H11 **Siare, Río** ≈ C Colombia
171 R6 **Siargao Island** *island* S Philippines
186 F72 **Siassi** Umboi Island, C Papua New Guinea 05°34′S 147°50′E
115 D14 **Siátista** Dytikí Makedonía, N Greece 40°16′N 21°34′E
166 K4 **Siatlai** Chin State, W Myanmar (Burma) 22°05′N 93°36′E
171 P6 **Siaton** Negros, C Philippines 09°03′N 123°03′E
171 P6 **Siaton Point** *headland* Negros, C Philippines 09°03′N 123°00′E
118 F11 **Šiauliai** *Ger.* Schaulen. Šiauliai, N Lithuania 55°55′N 23°21′E
118 E11 **Šiauliai** ◈ *province* N Lithuania
171 Q10 **Siau, Pulau** *island* N Indonesia
83 J15 **Siavonga** Southern, SE Zambia 16°33′S 28°42′E
**Siazan'** *see* Siyäzän
**Sibah** *see* As Sībah
107 N20 **Sibari** Calabria, S Italy 39°45′N 16°26′E
**Sibata** *see* Shibata
127 X6 **Sibay** Respublika Bashkortostan, W Russia 52°40′N 58°39′E
93 M19 **Sibbo** *Fin.* Sipoo. Uusimaa, S Finland 60°22′N 25°20′E
112 D13 **Šibenik** *It.* Sebenico. Šibenik-Knin, S Croatia 43°43′N 15°54′E
**Sibenik** *see* Šibenik-Knin
112 E13 **Šibenik-Knin** *off.* Šibenska Županija, *var.* Sibenik. ◈ *province* S Croatia
**Šibenik-Knin** *see* Drniš
**Šibenska Županija** *see* Šibenik-Knin
**Siberia** *see* Sibir'
**Siberoet** *see* Siberut, Pulau
168 H12 **Siberut, Pulau** *prev.* Siberoet. *island* Kepulauan Mentawai, W Indonesia
168 I12 **Siberut, Selat** *strait* W Indonesia
149 P11 **Sibi** Baluchistan, SW Pakistan 29°31′N 67°54′E
186 B9 **Sibidiri** Western, SW Papua New Guinea 08°58′S 142°14′E
123 N10 **Sibir'** *var.* Siberia. *physical region* NE Russia
79 F20 **Sibiti** Lékoumou, S Congo 03°41′S 13°20′E
81 G21 **Sibiti** ≈ C Tanzania
116 I12 **Sibiu** *Ger.* Hermannstadt, *Hung.* Nagyszeben. Sibiu, C Romania 45°48′N 24°09′E
116 I11 **Sibiu** ◈ *county* C Romania
29 S11 **Sibley** Iowa, C USA 43°24′N 95°45′W
169 R9 **Sibu** Sarawak, East Malaysia 02°18′N 111°49′E
42 G2 **Sibun** ≈ E Belize
79 I15 **Sibut** *prev.* Fort-Sibut. Kémo, S Central African Republic 05°44′N 19°07′E
171 P4 **Sibuyan Island** *island* C Philippines
189 U1 **Sibylla Island** *island* N Marshall Islands
11 N16 **Sicamous** British Columbia, SW Canada 50°49′N 118°52′W
**Sichelburger Gerbirge** *see* Gorjanci
167 N14 **Sichon** *var.* Ban Sichon, Si Chon. Nakhon Si Thammarat, SW Thailand 09°03′N 99°51′E
**Si Chon** *see* Sichon
160 H9 **Sichuan** *var.* Chuan, Sichuan Sheng, Ssu-ch'uan, Szechuan, Szechwan. ◈ *province* C China
160 I9 **Sichuan Pendi** *basin* C China
**Sichuan Sheng** *see* Sichuan
103 S16 **Sicie, Cap** *headland* SE France 43°03′N 05°50′E
107 J24 **Sicilia** *Eng.* Sicily; *anc.* Trinacria. ◈ *region* Italy, C Mediterranean Sea
107 M24 **Sicilia** *Eng.* Sicily; *anc.* Trinacria. *island* Italy, C Mediterranean Sea
**Sicilian Channel** *see* Sicily, Strait of
107 H24 **Sicily, Strait of** *var.* Sicilian Channel. *strait* C Mediterranean Sea
42 K5 **Sico Tinto, Río** *var.* Río Negro. ≈ NE Honduras
57 H16 **Sicuani** Cusco, S Peru 14°21′S 71°13′W
112 J10 **Šid** Vojvodina, NW Serbia 45°07′N 19°13′E
115 A15 **Sidári** Kérkyra, Iónia Nisiá, Greece, C Mediterranean Sea 39°47′N 19°43′E
169 Q11 **Sidas** Borneo, C Indonesia 0°24′N 109°46′E
98 O5 **Siddeburen** Groningen, NE Netherlands 53°15′N 06°52′E
154 D9 **Siddhapur** *prev.* Siddhpur, Sidhpur. Gujarāt, W India 23°57′N 72°28′E
**Siddhpur** *see* Siddhapur
155 I15 **Siddipet** Telangana, C India 18°10′N 78°54′E
77 N14 **Sidéradougou** SW Burkina Faso 10°39′N 04°16′W
107 N23 **Siderno** Calabria, SW Italy 38°18′N 16°19′E
**Siders** *see* Sierre
154 L9 **Sidhi** Madhya Pradesh, C India 24°24′N 81°54′E
**Sidhirókastron** *see* Sidirókastro
**Sidhpur** *see* Siddhapur
75 U7 **Sīdī Barrānī** NW Egypt 31°38′N 25°58′E
74 I6 **Sidi Bel Abbès** *var.* Sidi bel Abbès, Sidi-Bel-Abbès. NW Algeria 35°12′N 00°43′W
74 E7 **Sidi-Bennour** W Morocco 32°39′N 08°28′W
74 M6 **Sidi Bouzid** *var.* Gammouda, Sīdī Bu Zayd. C Tunisia 35°05′N 09°20′E
**Sīdī Bu Zayd** *see* Sidi Bouzid
74 D8 **Sidi-Ifni** SW Morocco 29°33′N 10°04′W
74 G6 **Sidi-Kacem** *prev.* Petitjean. N Morocco 34°21′N 05°46′W
114 G12 **Sidirókastro** *prev.* Sidhirókastron. Kentrikí Makedonía, NE Greece 41°14′N 23°23′E
194 L12 **Sidley, Mount** ▲ Antarctica 76°39′S 124°48′W
29 S16 **Sidney** Iowa, C USA 40°45′N 95°39′W
33 Y7 **Sidney** Montana, NW USA 47°42′N 104°10′W
28 J15 **Sidney** Nebraska, C USA 41°09′N 102°57′W
18 I11 **Sidney** New York, NE USA 42°18′N 75°21′W
31 R13 **Sidney** Ohio, N USA 40°16′N 84°09′W
23 T2 **Sidney Lanier, Lake** ⊠ Georgia, SE USA
**Sidon** *see* Saïda
122 J9 **Sidorovsk** Yamalo-Nenetskiy Avtonomnyy Okrug, N Russia 66°34′N 82°12′E
**Sidra** *see* Surt
**Sidra/Sidra, Gulf of** *see* Surt, Khalīj, N Libya
**Siebenbürgen** *see* Transylvania
**Sieben Dörfer** *see* Săcele
110 O12 **Siedlce** *Ger.* Sedlez, *Rus.* Sesdlets. Mazowieckie, C Poland 52°10′N 22°18′E
101 E16 **Sieg** ≈ W Germany
101 F16 **Siegen** Nordrhein-Westfalen, W Germany 50°53′N 08°02′E
109 X4 **Sieghartskirchen** Niederösterreich, E Austria 48°13′N 16°01′E
167 S12 **Siĕmbok** *prev.* Phumĭ Siĕmbok. Stung Treng, N Cambodia 13°28′N 105°59′E
110 O11 **Siemiatycze** Podlaskie, NE Poland 52°27′N 22°52′E
167 T11 **Siĕmpang** Stung Treng, NE Cambodia 14°07′N 106°24′E
**Siĕmréab** *see* Siem Reap
167 R11 **Siem Reap** *prev.* Siĕmréab. Siem Reap, NW Cambodia 13°21′N 103°50′E
106 G12 **Siena** *Fr.* Sienne; *anc.* Saena Julia. Toscana, C Italy 43°20′N 11°20′E
**Sienne** *see* Siena
92 K12 **Sieppijärvi** Lappi, NW Finland 67°09′N 23°58′E
110 J13 **Sieradz** Sieradz, C Poland 51°36′N 18°42′E
110 K10 **Sierpc** Mazowieckie, C Poland 52°51′N 19°44′E
24 I9 **Sierra Blanca** Texas, SW USA 31°10′N 105°22′W
37 S14 **Sierra Blanca Peak** ▲ New Mexico, SW USA 33°22′N 105°48′W
35 P5 **Sierra City** California, W USA 39°34′N 120°35′W
63 I16 **Sierra Colorada** Río Negro, S Argentina 40°37′S 67°48′W
63 J16 **Sierra Grande** Río Negro, E Argentina 41°34′S 65°21′W
76 G15 **Sierra Leone** *off.* Republic of Sierra Leone. ◆ *republic* W Africa
64 M13 **Sierra Leone Basin** *undersea feature* E Atlantic Ocean 05°00′N 17°00′W
66 K8 **Sierra Leone Fracture Zone** *tectonic feature* E Atlantic Ocean
**Sierra Leone, Republic of** *see* Sierra Leone
**Sierra Leone Ridge** *see* Sierra Leone Rise
64 L13 **Sierra Leone Rise** *var.* Sierra Leone Ridge, Sierra Leone Schwelle. *undersea feature* E Atlantic Ocean 05°30′N 21°00′W
**Sierra Leone Schwelle** *see* Sierra Leone Rise
40 L7 **Sierra Mojada** Coahuila, NE Mexico 27°13′N 103°42′W
37 N16 **Sierra Vista** Arizona, SW USA 31°33′N 110°18′W
108 D10 **Sierre** *Ger.* Siders. Valais, SW Switzerland 46°18′N 07°33′E
36 L16 **Sierrita Mountains** ▲▲ Arizona, SW USA
**Siete Moai** *see* Ahu Akivi
76 M15 **Sifié** W Ivory Coast 07°59′N 06°55′W
115 I21 **Sífnos** *anc.* Siphnos. *island* Kykládes, Greece, Aegean Sea
115 I21 **Sífnou, Stenó** *strait* SE Greece
**Siga** *see* Shiga
103 P16 **Sigean** Aude, S France 43°02′N 02°58′E
**Sighet** *see* Sighetu Marmaţiei
**Sighetul Marmaţiei** *see* Sighetu Marmaţiei
116 I8 **Sighetu Marmaţiei** *var.* Sighet, Sighetul Marmaţiei, *Hung.* Máramarossziget. Maramureş, N Romania 47°56′N 23°53′E
116 I11 **Sighişoara** *Ger.* Schässburg, *Hung.* Segesvár. Mureş, C Romania 46°12′N 24°48′E
168 G7 **Sigli** Sumatera, W Indonesia 05°21′N 95°56′E
92 J1 **Siglufjörður** Norðurland Vestra, N Iceland 66°09′N 18°56′W
101 H23 **Sigmaringen** Baden-Württemberg, S Germany 48°04′N 09°12′E
101 N20 **Signalberg** ▲ SE Germany 49°30′N 12°34′E
36 I13 **Signal Peak** ▲ Arizona, SW USA 33°20′N 114°03′W
**Signan** *see* Xi'an
29 X15 **Sigourney** Iowa, C USA 41°19′N 92°12′W
115 K17 **Sígri, Akrotírio** *headland* Lésvos, E Greece 39°12′N 25°49′E
**Sigsbee Deep** *see* Mexico Basin
47 N2 **Sigsbee Escarpment** *undersea feature* N Gulf of Mexico 26°00′N 92°30′W
56 C8 **Sigsig** Azuay, S Ecuador 03°04′S 78°50′W
95 O15 **Sigtuna** Stockholm, C Sweden 59°36′N 17°44′E
42 H6 **Siguatepeque** Comayagua, W Honduras 14°39′N 87°48′W
105 P7 **Sigüenza** Castilla-La Mancha, C Spain 41°04′N 02°38′W
105 R4 **Sigües** Aragón, NE Spain 42°39′N 01°00′W
76 K13 **Siguiri** NE Guinea 11°26′N 09°08′W
118 G8 **Sigulda** *Ger.* Segewold. C Latvia 57°08′N 24°51′E
167 Q14 **Sihanoukville** *var.* Preăh Seihânŭ, Kâmpóng Saôm. Sihanoukville, SW Cambodia 10°38′N 103°30′E
108 G8 **Sihlsee** ◎ NW Switzerland
93 K18 **Siikainen** Satakunta, SW Finland 61°52′N 21°49′E
93 M16 **Siilinjärvi** Pohjois-Savo, C Finland 63°05′N 27°40′E
137 R15 **Siirt** *var.* Sert; *anc.* Tigranocerta. Siirt, SE Turkey 37°56′N 41°56′E
137 R15 **Siirt** *var.* Sert. ◈ *province* SE Turkey
187 N8 **Sikaiana** *var.* Stewart Islands. *island group* W Solomon Islands
**Sikandarabad** *see* Secunderābād
152 J11 **Sikandra Rao** Uttar Pradesh, N India 27°42′N 78°21′E
10 M11 **Sikanni Chief** British Columbia, W Canada 57°16′N 122°44′W
10 M11 **Sikanni Chief** ≈ British Columbia, W Canada
152 H11 **Sīkar** Rājasthān, N India 27°33′N 75°12′E
76 M13 **Sikasso** Sikasso, S Mali 11°21′N 05°43′W
76 L13 **Sikasso** ◈ *region* SW Mali
167 N3 **Sikaw** Kachin State, C Myanmar (Burma) 23°50′N 97°04′E
83 H14 **Sikelenge** Western, W Zambia 14°51′S 24°13′E
27 Y7 **Sikeston** Missouri, C USA 36°52′N 89°35′W
93 J14 **Sikfors** Norrbotten, N Sweden 65°29′N 21°17′E
123 T14 **Sikhote-Alin', Khrebet** ▲▲ SE Russia
**Siking** *see* Xi'an
115 J22 **Síkinos** *island* Kykládes, Greece, Aegean Sea
153 S11 **Sikkim** *Tib.* Denjong. ◈ *state* N India
111 I26 **Siklós** Baranya, SW Hungary 45°51′N 18°18′E
**Sikoku** *see* Shikoku
**Sikoku Basin** *see* Shikoku Basin
83 G14 **Sikongo** Western, W Zambia 15°03′S 22°07′E
**Sikotu Ko** *see* Shikotsu-ko
**Sikouri/Sikoúrion** *see* Sykoúrio
123 P8 **Siktyakh** Respublika Sakha (Yakutiya), NE Russia 69°45′N 124°42′E
118 D12 **Šilalė** Tauragė, W Lithuania 55°29′N 22°10′E
106 G5 **Silandro** *Ger.* Schlanders. Trentino-Alto Adige, N Italy 46°39′N 10°55′E
41 N12 **Silao** Guanajuato, C Mexico 20°56′N 101°28′W
**Silarius** *see* Sele
153 W14 **Silchar** Assam, NE India 24°49′N 92°48′E
108 G9 **Silenen** Uri, C Switzerland 46°49′N 08°39′E
21 T9 **Siler City** North Carolina, SE USA 35°43′N 79°27′W
33 U11 **Silesia** Montana, NW USA 45°32′N 108°52′W
110 F13 **Silesia** *physical region* SW Poland
74 K12 **Silet** S Algeria 22°45′N 04°51′E
**Sileti** *see* Silety
**Siletitengiz** *see* Siletyteniz, Ozero
145 R8 **Silety** *prev.* Sileti. ≈ N Kazakhstan
145 R7 **Siletyteniz, Ozero** *Kaz.* Siletitengiz. ◎ N Kazakhstan
172 H16 **Silhouette** *island* Inner Islands, SE Seychelles
136 I17 **Silifke** *anc.* Seleucia. İçel, S Turkey 36°22′N 33°57′E
**Siliguri** *see* Shiliguri
156 J10 **Siling Co** ◎ W China
**Silinhot** *see* Xilinhot
192 G14 **Silisili, Mauga** ▲ Savai'i, C Samoa 13°37′S 172°26′W
114 M6 **Silistra** *var.* Silistria; *anc.* Durostorum. Silistra, NE Bulgaria 44°06′N 27°17′E
114 M7 **Silistra** ◈ *province* NE Bulgaria
**Silistria** *see* Silistra
136 D10 **Silivri** İstanbul, NW Turkey 41°05′N 28°15′E
94 L13 **Siljan** ◎ C Sweden
95 G22 **Silkeborg** Midtjylland, C Denmark 56°10′N 09°34′E
108 M8 **Sill** ≈ W Austria
105 S10 **Silla** Comunitat Valenciana, E Spain 39°22′N 00°25′W
62 H3 **Sillajguay, Cordillera** ▲ N Chile 19°45′S 68°39′W
118 K3 **Sillamäe** *Ger.* Sillamäggi. Ida-Virumaa, NE Estonia 59°23′N 27°45′E
**Sillamäggi** *see* Sillamäe
**Sillein** *see* Žilina
109 P9 **Sillian** Tirol, W Austria 46°45′N 12°25′E
112 B10 **Šilo** Primorje-Gorski Kotar, NW Croatia 45°09′N 14°39′E
27 R9 **Siloam Springs** Arkansas, C USA 36°11′N 94°32′W
25 X10 **Silsbee** Texas, SW USA 30°21′N 94°10′W
143 W15 **Sīlūp, Rūd-e** ≈ SE Iran
118 C12 **Šilutė** *Ger.* Heydekrug. Klaipėda, W Lithuania 55°20′N 21°30′E
137 Q15 **Silvan** Dıyarbakır, SE Turkey 38°08′N 41°E
108 J10 **Silvaplana** Graubünden, S Switzerland 46°27′N 09°45′E
**Silva Porto** *see* Kuito
58 M12 **Silva, Recife do** *reef* E Brazil
154 D12 **Silvassa** Dādra and Nagar Haveli, W India 20°13′N 73°03′E
29 X4 **Silver Bay** Minnesota, N USA 47°17′N 91°15′W
37 P15 **Silver City** New Mexico, SW USA 32°47′N 108°16′W
18 D10 **Silver Creek** New York, NE USA 42°32′N 79°10′W
37 N12 **Silver Creek** ≈ Arizona, SW USA
27 P4 **Silver Lake** Kansas, C USA 39°06′N 95°51′W
32 I14 **Silver Lake** Oregon, NW USA 43°07′N 121°04′W
35 T9 **Silver Peak Range** ▲▲ Nevada, W USA
21 W3 **Silver Spring** Maryland, NE USA 39°00′N 77°01′W
**Silver State** *see* Colorado
**Silver State** *see* Nevada
37 Q7 **Silverton** Colorado, C USA 37°48′N 107°39′W
18 K16 **Silverton** New Jersey, NE USA 40°00′N 74°09′W
32 G11 **Silverton** Oregon, NW USA 45°00′N 122°46′W
25 N4 **Silverton** Texas, SW USA 34°28′N 101°18′W
104 G14 **Silves** Faro, S Portugal 37°11′N 08°26′W
54 D12 **Silvia** Cauca, SW Colombia 02°37′N 76°24′W
108 J9 **Silvrettagruppe** ▲▲ Austria/Switzerland
**Sily-Vajdej** *see* Vulcan
108 L7 **Silz** Tirol, W Austria 47°17′N 11°00′E
172 I13 **Sima** Anjouan, SE Comoros 12°11′S 44°18′E
**Simabara** *see* Shimabara
83 H15 **Simakando** Western, W Zambia 16°43′S 24°46′E
**Simane** *see* Shimane
119 L20 **Simanichy** *Rus.* Simonichi. Homyel'skaya Voblasts', SE Belarus 51°53′N 28°05′E
160 F14 **Simao** Yunnan, SW China 22°30′N 101°06′E
153 P12 **Simarā** Central, C Nepal 27°14′N 85°00′E
14 I8 **Simard, Lac** ◎ Québec, SE Canada
136 D13 **Simav** Kütahya, W Turkey 39°05′N 28°59′E
136 D13 **Simav Çayı** ≈ NW Turkey
79 L18 **Simba** Orientale, N Dem. Rep. Congo 0°46′N 22°54′E
186 C7 **Simbai** Madang, N Papua New Guinea 05°12′S 144°33′E
**Simbirsk** *see* Ul'yanovsk
**Simbu** *see* Chimbu
14 F17 **Simcoe** Ontario, S Canada 42°50′N 80°19′W
14 H14 **Simcoe, Lake** ◎ Ontario, S Canada
80 J11 **Sīmēn** ▲▲ N Ethiopia
114 K11 **Simeonovgrad** *prev.* Maritsa. Haskovo, S Bulgaria 42°03′N 25°36′E
116 G11 **Simeria** *Ger.* Pischk, *Hung.* Piski. Hunedoara, W Romania 45°51′N 23°00′E
107 L24 **Simeto** ≈ Sicilia, Italy, C Mediterranean Sea
168 G9 **Simeulue, Pulau** *island* NW Indonesia
117 T13 **Simferopol'** Avtonomna Respublika Krym, S Ukraine 44°55′N 33°06′E
117 T13 **Simferopol'** ✈ Avtonomna Respublika Krym, S Ukraine 44°55′N 34°04′E
**Simi** *see* Sými
152 M9 **Simikot** Far Western, NW Nepal 30°02′N 81°49′E


◆ Country ● Country Capital ◇ Dependent Territory ○ Dependent Territory Capital ◈ Administrative Regions ✈ International Airport ▲ Mountain ▲▲ Mountain Range Volcano ≈ River ◎ Lake ⊠ Reservoir

Simití – Sliven


54 F7 **Simití** Bolívar, N Colombia *07°57′N 73°57′W*
114 G11 **Simitla** Blagoevgrad, SW Bulgaria *41°57′N 23°06′E*
35 S15 **Simi Valley** California, W USA *34°16′N 118°47′W*
**Simizu** *see* Shimizu
**Simla** *see* Shimla
**Şimlăul Silvaniei/Şimleul Silvaniei** *see* Şimleu Silvaniei
116 G9 **Şimleu Silvaniei** *Hung.* Szilágysomlyó; *prev.* Şimlăul Silvaniei, Şimleul Silvaniei. Sălaj, NW Romania *47°12′N 22°49′E*
**Simmer** *see* Simmerbach
101 E19 **Simmerbach** *var.* Simmer. ≈ W Germany
101 F18 **Simmern** Rheinland-Pfalz, W Germany *50°00′N 07°30′E*
22 I7 **Simmesport** Louisiana, S USA *30°58′N 91°48′W*
119 F14 **Simnas** Alytus, S Lithuania *54°23′N 23°40′E*
92 L13 **Simo** Lappi, NW Finland *65°40′N 25°04′E*
**Simoda** *see* Shimoda
**Simodate** *see* Shimodate
92 M13 **Simojärvi** ◎ N Finland
92 L13 **Simojoki** ≈ NW Finland
41 U15 **Simojovel** *var.* Simojovel de Allende. Chiapas, SE Mexico *17°14′N 92°40′W*
**Simojovel de Allende** *see* Simojovel
56 B7 **Simon Bolivar** *var.* Guayaquil. ✕ (Quayaquil) Guayas, W Ecuador *02°16′S 79°54′W*
54 L5 **Simon Bolívar** ✕ (Caracas) Vargas, N Venezuela *10°33′N 66°54′W*
**Simonichi** *see* Simanichy
14 M12 **Simon, Lac** ◎ Québec, SE Canada
**Simonoseki** *see* Shimonoseki
**Šimonovany** *see* Partizánske
**Simonstad** *see* Simon's Town
83 E26 **Simon's Town** *var.* Simonstad. Western Cape, SW South Africa *34°12′S 18°26′E*
**Simony** *see* Partizánske
**Simpeln** *see* Simplon
99 M18 **Simpelveld** Limburg, SE Netherlands *50°50′N 05°59′E*
108 E11 **Simplon** *var.* Simpeln. Valais, SW Switzerland *46°13′N 08°01′E*
108 E11 **Simplon Pass** *pass* S Switzerland
106 C6 **Simplon Tunnel** *tunnel* Italy/Switzerland
**Simpson** *see* Fort Simpson
182 G1 **Simpson Desert** *desert* Northern Territory/South Australia
10 J9 **Simpson Peak** ▲ British Columbia, W Canada *59°43′N 131°29′W*
9 N7 **Simpson Peninsula** *peninsula* Nunavut, NE Canada
21 P11 **Simpsonville** South Carolina, SE USA *34°44′N 82°15′W*
95 L23 **Simrishamn** Skåne, S Sweden *55°34′N 14°20′E*
123 U13 **Simushir, Ostrov** *island* Kuril'skiye Ostrova, SE Russia
168 G9 **Sinabang** Sumatera, W Indonesia *02°27′N 96°24′E*
81 N15 **Sina Dhaqa** Galguduud, C Somalia *05°21′N 46°21′E*
**sinai** *see* Shibh Jazīrat Sīnā'
116 J12 **Sinaia** Prahova, SE Romania *45°20′N 25°33′E*
**Sinai, Mount** *see* Mūsá, Jabal
188 B16 **Sinajana** C Guam *13°28′N 144°45′E*
40 H8 **Sinaloa** ◈ *state* C Mexico
54 H4 **Sinamaica** Zulia, NW Venezuela *11°06′N 71°52′W*
163 X14 **Sinan-ni** SE North Korea *38°37′N 127°43′E*
**Sīnā/Sinai Peninsula** *see* Shibh Jazīrat Sīnā'
**Sīnāwan** *see* Sīnāwin
75 N8 **Sīnāwin** *var.* Sīnāwan. NW Libya *31°00′N 10°37′E*
83 J16 **Sinazongwe** Southern, S Zambia *17°14′S 27°27′E*
166 L6 **Sinbaungwe** Magway, W Myanmar (Burma) *19°44′N 95°10′E*
166 L5 **Sinbyugyun** Magway, W Myanmar (Burma) *20°38′N 94°40′E*
54 E6 **Since** Sucre, NW Colombia *09°14′N 75°08′W*
54 E6 **Sincelejo** Sucre, NW Colombia *09°17′N 75°23′W*
23 U4 **Sinclair, Lake** ▣ Georgia, SE USA
10 M14 **Sinclair Mills** British Columbia, SW Canada *54°03′N 121°37′W*
154 I8 **Sind** ≈ N India
**Sind** *see* Sindh
95 H19 **Sindal** Nordjylland, N Denmark *57°29′N 10°13′E*
171 P7 **Sindañgan** Mindanao, S Philippines *08°09′N 122°59′E*
79 D19 **Sindara** Ngounié, W Gabon *01°07′S 10°41′E*
152 E13 **Sindari** *prev.* Sindri. Rājasthān, N India *25°32′N 71°58′E*
114 N8 **Sindel** Varna, E Bulgaria *43°07′N 27°35′E*
101 H22 **Sindelfingen** Baden-Württemberg, SW Germany *48°43′N 09°E*
155 G16 **Sindgi** Karnātaka, C India *17°01′N 76°22′E*
149 Q14 **Sindh** *prev.* Sind. ◈ *province* SE Pakistan
118 G5 **Sindi** *Ger.* Zintenhof. Pärnumaa, SW Estonia *58°28′N 24°41′E*
136 C13 **Sındırgı** Balıkesir, W Turkey *39°13′N 28°10′E*
77 N14 **Sindou** SW Burkina Faso *10°35′N 05°04′W*
**Sindri** *see* Sindari
149 T9 **Sind Sagar Doab** *desert* E Pakistan
126 M11 **Sinegorskiy** Rostovskaya Oblast', SW Russia *48°01′N 40°52′E*
123 S9 **Sinegor'ye** Magadanskaya Oblast', E Russia *62°04′N 150°33′E*
114 O12 **Sinekli** İstanbul, NW Turkey *41°13′N 28°13′E*
104 F12 **Sines** Setúbal, S Portugal *37°58′N 08°52′W*
104 F12 **Sines, Cabo de** *headland* S Portugal *37°57′N 08°55′W*
92 L12 **Sinettä** Lappi, NW Finland *66°39′N 25°25′E*
186 H6 **Sinewit, Mount** ▲ New Britain, C Papua New Guinea *04°42′S 151°58′E*
80 G11 **Singa** *var.* Sinja, Sinjah. Sinnar, E Sudan *13°11′N 33°55′E*
78 J12 **Singako** Moyen-Chari, S Chad *09°52′N 19°31′E*
**Singan** *see* Xi'an
168 K10 **Singapore** ● (Singapore) S Singapore *01°17′N 103°48′E*
168 L10 **Singapore** *off.* Republic of Singapore. ◆ *republic* SE Asia
**Singapore, Republic of** *see* Singapore
169 U17 **Singaraja** Bali, C Indonesia *08°06′S 115°04′E*
167 O10 **Sing Buri** *var.* Singhaburi. Sing Buri, C Thailand *14°56′N 100°21′E*
101 H24 **Singen** Baden-Württemberg, S Germany *47°46′N 08°50′E*
**Sîngeorgiu de Pădure** *see* Sângeorgiu de Pădure
**Sîngeorz-Băi/Singeroz Băi** *see* Sângeorz-Băi
116 M9 **Sîngerei** *var.* Sângerei; *prev.* Lazovsk. N Moldova *47°38′N 28°08′E*
**Singhaburi** *see* Sing Buri
81 H21 **Singida** Singida, C Tanzania *04°45′S 34°48′E*
81 G22 **Singida** ◈ *region* C Tanzania
**Singidunum** *see* Beograd
**Singkaling Hkamti** *see* Hkamti
171 N14 **Singkang** Sulawesi, C Indonesia *04°09′S 119°58′E*
168 J11 **Singkarak, Danau** ◎ Sumatera, W Indonesia
169 N10 **Singkawang** Borneo, C Indonesia *0°57′N 108°57′E*
168 M11 **Singkep, Pulau** *island* Kepulauan Lingga, W Indonesia
168 H9 **Singkilbaru** Sumatera, W Indonesia *02°18′N 97°47′E*
183 T7 **Singleton** New South Wales, SE Australia *32°38′S 151°00′E*
**Singora** *see* Songkhla
**Singû** *see* Shingū
**Sining** *see* Xining
107 D17 **Siniscola** Sardegna, Italy, C Mediterranean Sea *40°34′N 09°42′E*
113 F14 **Sinj** Split-Dalmacija, SE Croatia *43°41′N 16°37′E*
**Sinjajevina** *see* Sinjavina
139 P3 **Sinjār** Nīnawýa, NW Iraq *36°20′N 41°51′E*
139 P2 **Sinjār, Jabal** ▲▲ N Iraq
**Sinja/Sinjah** *see* Singa
113 K15 **Sinjavina** *var.* Sinjajevina. ▲▲ C Montenegro
80 I7 **Sinkat** Red Sea, NE Sudan *18°52′N 36°51′E*
**Sinkiang/Sinkiang Uighur Autonomous Region** *see* Xinjiang Uygur Zizhiqu
**Sînmartin** *see* Târnăveni
163 V13 **Sinmi-do** *island* NW North Korea
101 I18 **Sinn** ≈ C Germany
**Sinnamarie** *see* Sinnamary
55 Y9 **Sinnamary** *var.* Sinnamarie. N French Guiana *05°23′N 53°00′W*
80 G11 **Sinnar** ◈ *state* E Sudan
**Sinneh** *see* Sanandaj
18 E13 **Sinnemahoning Creek** ≈ Pennsylvania, NE USA
**Sînnicolau Mare** *see* Sânnicolau Mare
**Sinoe, Lacul** *see* Sinoie, Lacul
**Sinoia** *see* Chinhoyi
117 N14 **Sinoie, Lacul** *prev.* Lacul Sinoe. *lagoon* SE Romania
59 H16 **Sinop** Mato Grosso, W Brazil *11°38′S 55°27′W*
136 K10 **Sinop** *anc.* Sinope. Sinop, N Turkey *42°02′N 35°09′E*
136 J10 **Sinop** ◈ *province* N Turkey
136 K10 **Sinop Burnu** *headland* N Turkey *42°02′N 35°12′E*
**Sinope** *see* Sinop
**Sino/Sinoe** *see* Greenville
163 Y12 **Sinp'o** E North Korea *40°01′N 128°10′E*
101 H20 **Sinsheim** Baden-Württemberg, SW Germany *49°15′N 08°53′E*
**Sîntana** *see* Sântana
169 R11 **Sintang** Borneo, C Indonesia *0°03′N 111°31′E*
99 F14 **Sint Annaland** Zeeland, SW Netherlands *51°36′N 04°07′E*
98 L5 **Sint Annaparochie** *Fris.* Sint Anne. Fryslân, N Netherlands *53°20′N 05°46′E*
**Sint Anne** *see* Sint Annaparochie
45 V9 **Sint Eustatius** *var.* Statia, *Eng.* Saint Eustatius. ◇ *special Municipality of the Netherlands* NE Caribbean Sesa
99 G19 **Sint-Genesius-Rode** *Fr.* Rhode-Saint-Genèse. Vlaams Brabant, C Belgium *50°45′N 04°21′E*
99 F16 **Sint-Gillis-Waas** Oost-Vlaanderen, N Belgium *51°14′N 04°08′E*
99 H17 **Sint-Katelijne-Waver** Antwerpen, C Belgium *51°05′N 04°31′E*
99 E18 **Sint-Lievens-Houtem** Oost-Vlaanderen, NW Belgium *50°55′N 03°52′E*
45 V9 **Sint Maarten** *Eng.* Saint Martin. ◇ *self-governing country of the Kingdom of the Netherlands* NE Caribbean Sea
99 F14 **Sint Maartensdijk** Zeeland, SW Netherlands *51°33′N 04°05′E*
99 L19 **Sint-Martens-Voeren** *Fr.* Fouron-Saint-Martin. Limburg, NE Belgium *50°46′N 05°49′E*
99 J14 **Sint-Michielsgestel** Noord-Brabant, S Netherlands *51°38′N 05°21′E*
**Sîn-Miclăuş** *see* Gheorgheni
45 O16 **Sint Nicholaas** S Aruba *12°25′N 69°52′W*
99 F16 **Sint-Niklaas** *Fr.* Saint-Nicolas. Oost-Vlaanderen, N Belgium *51°10′N 04°09′E*
99 K14 **Sint-Oedenrode** Noord-Brabant, S Netherlands *51°34′N 05°28′E*
25 T14 **Sinton** Texas, SW USA *28°02′N 97°33′W*
99 G14 **Sint Philipsland** Zeeland, SW Netherlands *51°37′N 04°11′E*
99 G19 **Sint-Pieters-Leeuw** Vlaams Brabant, C Belgium *50°47′N 04°16′E*
104 E11 **Sintra** *prev.* Cintra. Lisboa, W Portugal *38°48′N 09°22′W*
99 J18 **Sint-Truiden** *Fr.* Saint-Trond. Limburg, NE Belgium *50°48′N 05°13′E*
99 H14 **Sint Willebrord** Noord-Brabant, S Netherlands *51°33′N 04°35′E*
163 V13 **Sinŭiju** W North Korea *40°08′N 124°33′E*
80 P13 **Sinujiif** Nugaal, NE Somalia *08°33′N 49°05′E*
**Sinus Aelaniticus** *see* Aqaba, Gulf of
**Sinus Gallicus** *see* Lion, Golfe du
**Sinyang** *see* Xinyang
**Sinyavka** *see* Sinyawka
119 I18 **Sinyawka** *Rus.* Sinyavka. Minskaya Voblasts', SW Belarus *52°57′N 26°29′E*
**Sinying** *see* Xinying
**Sinyukha** *see* Synyukha
**Sinzyô** *see* Shinjō
111 I24 **Sió** ≈ W Hungary
171 O7 **Siocon** Mindanao, S Philippines *07°37′N 122°09′E*
111 I24 **Siófok** Somogy, Hungary *46°54′N 18°03′E*
**Siogama** *see* Shiogama
83 G15 **Sioma** Western, SW Zambia *16°39′S 23°36′E*
108 D11 **Sion** *Ger.* Sitten; *anc.* Sedunum. Valais, SW Switzerland *46°15′N 07°23′E*
103 O11 **Sioule** ≈ C France
29 S12 **Sioux Center** Iowa, C USA *43°04′N 96°10′W*
29 R13 **Sioux City** Iowa, C USA *42°30′N 96°24′W*
29 R11 **Sioux Falls** South Dakota, N USA *43°33′N 96°45′W*
12 B11 **Sioux Lookout** Ontario, S Canada *49°27′N 94°06′W*
29 T12 **Sioux Rapids** Iowa, C USA *42°53′N 95°09′W*
**Sioux State** *see* North Dakota
**Sioziri** *see* Shiojiri
171 P6 **Sipalay** Negros, C Philippines *09°46′N 122°25′E*
55 V11 **Sipaliwini** ◈ *district* S Suriname
45 U15 **Siparia** Trinidad, Trinidad and Tobago *10°08′N 61°31′W*
**Siphnos** *see* Sífnos
163 V11 **Siping** *var.* Ssu-p'ing, Szeping; *prev.* Ssu-p'ing-chieh. Jilin, NE China *43°09′N 124°22′E*
11 X12 **Sipiwesk** Manitoba, C Canada *55°28′N 97°16′W*
11 W13 **Sipiwesk Lake** ◎ Manitoba, C Canada
195 O11 **Siple Coast** *physical region* Antarctica
194 K12 **Siple Island** *island* Antarctica
194 K13 **Siple, Mount** ▲ Siple Island, Antarctica *73°25′S 126°24′W*
**Sipoo** *see* Sibbo
112 G12 **Šipovo** Republika Srpska, W Bosnia and Herzegovina *44°16′N 17°05′E*
23 O4 **Sipsey River** ≈ Alabama, S USA
168 I13 **Sipura, Pulau** *island* W Indonesia
0 G16 **Siqueiros Fracture Zone** *tectonic feature* E Pacific Ocean
42 L10 **Siquia, Río** ≈ SE Nicaragua
43 N13 **Siquirres** Limón, E Costa Rica *10°05′N 83°30′W*
54 J5 **Siquisique** Lara, N Venezuela *10°36′N 69°45′W*
155 G19 **Sīra** Karnātaka, W India *13°46′N 76°54′E*
95 D16 **Sira** ≈ S Norway
167 P12 **Si Racha** *var.* Ban Si Racha, Si Racha. Chon Buri, S Thailand *13°10′N 100°57′E*
**Si Racha** *see* Si Racha
107 L25 **Siracusa** *Eng.* Syracuse. Sicilia, Italy, C Mediterranean Sea *37°04′N 15°17′E*
153 T14 **Sirajganj** *var.* Shirajganj Ghat. Rajshahi, C Bangladesh *24°27′N 89°42′E*
**Sirakawa** *see* Shirakawa
11 N14 **Sir Alexander, Mount** ▲ British Columbia, W Canada *54°00′N 120°33′W*
137 O12 **Şiran** Gümüşhane, NE Turkey *40°12′N 39°07′E*
77 Q12 **Sirba** ≈ E Burkina Faso
143 O17 **Şīr Banī Yās** *island* W United Arab Emirates
95 D17 **Sirdalsvatnet** ◎ S Norway
**Sir Darya/Sirdaryo** *see* Syr Darya
147 P10 **Sirdaryo** Sirdaryo Viloyati, E Uzbekistan *40°46′N 68°34′E*
147 O11 **Sirdaryo Viloyati** *Rus.* Syrdar'inskaya Oblast'. ◈ *province* E Uzbekistan
**Sir Donald Sangster International Airport** *see* Sangster
181 S3 **Sir Edward Pellew Group** *island group* Northern Territory, NE Australia
116 K8 **Siret** *Ger.* Sereth, *Hung.* Szeret. Suceava, N Romania *47°55′N 26°05′E*
116 K8 **Siret** *var.* Siretul, *Ger.* Sereth, *Rus.* Seret. ≈ Romania/Ukraine
**Siretul** *see* Siret
140 K3 **Sirḩān, Wādī as** *dry watercourse* Jordan/Saudi Arabia
152 I8 **Sirhind** Punjab, N India *30°39′N 75°28′E*
116 F11 **Şiria** *Ger.* Schiria. Arad, W Romania *46°16′N 21°38′E*
**Siria** *see* Syria
143 S14 **Sīrīk** Hormozgān, SE Iran *26°32′N 57°07′E*
167 P8 **Sirikit Reservoir** ◎ N Thailand
58 K12 **Sirituba, Ilha** *island* NE Brazil
143 R11 **Sīrjān** *prev.* Sa'īdābād. Kermān, S Iran *29°29′N 55°39′E*
182 H9 **Sir Joseph Banks Group** *island group* South Australia
92 K11 **Sirkka** Lappi, N Finland *67°49′N 24°48′E*
**Sirna** *see* Sýrna
137 R16 **Şırnak** Şırnak, SE Turkey *37°33′N 42°27′E*
137 S16 **Şırnak** ◈ *province* SE Turkey
**Siroisi** *see* Shiroishi
155 J14 **Sironcha** Mahārāshtra, C India *18°51′N 80°03′E*
**Sirone** *see* Shirone
**Síros** *see* Sýros
**Sirotino** *see* Sirotsina
118 M12 **Sirotsina** *Rus.* Sirotino. Vitsyebskaya Voblasts', N Belarus *55°23′N 29°37′E*
152 H9 **Sirsa** Haryāna, NW India *29°32′N 75°04′E*
173 Y17 **Sir Seewoosagur Ramgoolam** ✕ (port Louis) SE Mauritius
155 E18 **Sirsi** Karnātaka, W India *14°46′N 74°49′E*
146 K12 **Şirşütür Gumy** *var.* Shirshütür, *Rus.* Peski Shirshyutyur. *desert* E Turkmenistan
**Sirte** *see* Surt
182 A2 **Sir Thomas, Mount** ▲ South Australia *27°09′S 129°49′E*
**Sirti, Gulf of** *see* Surt, Khalīj
137 Y12 **Şirvan** *prev.* Äli-Bayramli. SE Azerbaijan *39°57′N 48°54′E*
142 J5 **Sīrvān, Rūdkhāneh-ye** *var.* Nahr Diyālá, Sirwan. ≈ Iran/Iraq *see also* Diyālá, Nahr
**Sīrvān, Rudkhaneh-ye** *see* Diyālá, Sirwan Nahr
118 H13 **Širvintos** Vilnius, SE Lithuania *55°01′N 24°58′E*
**Sīrwān** *see* Diyālá, Nahr/Sīrvān, Rudkhaneh-ye
11 N15 **Sir Wilfrid Laurier, Mount** ▲ British Columbia, SW Canada *52°45′N 119°51′W*
14 M10 **Sir-Wilfrid, Mont** ▲ Québec, SE Canada *46°57′N 75°33′W*
**Sisačko-Moslavačka Županija** *see* Sisak-Moslavina
112 E9 **Sisak** *var.* Siscia, *Ger.* Sissek, *Hung.* Sziszek; *anc.* Segestica. Sisak-Moslavina, C Croatia *45°28′N 16°21′E*
167 R10 **Si Sa Ket** *var.* Sisaket, Sri Saket. Si Sa Ket, E Thailand *15°08′N 104°18′E*
**Sisaket** *see* Si Sa Ket
112 E9 **Sisak-Moslavina** *off.* Sisačko-Moslavačka Županija. ◈ *province* C Croatia
167 O8 **Si Satchanalai** Sukhothai, NW Thailand
**Siscia** *see* Sisak
83 G22 **Sishen** Northern Cape, NW South Africa *27°47′S 22°59′E*
137 V13 **Sisian** SE Armenia *39°31′N 46°03′E*
197 N13 **Sisimiut** *var.* Holsteinborg, Holsteinsborg, Holstenborg, Holstensborg. Qeqqata, S Greenland *67°07′N 53°42′W*
30 M1 **Siskiwit Bay** *lake bay* Michigan, N USA
34 L1 **Siskiyou Mountains** ▲▲ California/Oregon, W USA
167 Q11 **Sisophon** *var.* Sěrei Saôphoăn. Banteay Meanchey, NW Cambodia *13°37′N 102°58′E*
108 E7 **Sissach** Basel Landschaft, NW Switzerland *47°28′N 07°48′E*
186 B5 **Sissano** West Sepik, NW Papua New Guinea *03°02′S 142°01′E*
**Sissek** *see* Sisak
29 R7 **Sisseton** South Dakota, N USA *45°39′N 97°03′W*
143 W9 **Sīstān, Daryācheh-ye** *var.* Daryācheh-ye Hāmūn, Hāmūn-e Şāberī. ◎ Afghanistan/Iran *see also* Şāberī, Hāmūn-e
**Sīstān, Daryācheh-ye** *see* Şāberī, Hāmūn-e
143 V12 **Sīstān va Balūchestān** *off.* Ostān-e Sīstān va Balūchestān, *var.* Balūchestān va Sīstān. ◈ *province* SE Iran
**Sīstān va Balūchestān, Ostān-e** *see* Sīstān va Balūchestān
103 T14 **Sisteron** Alpes-de-Haute-Provence, SE France *44°12′N 05°55′E*
32 H13 **Sisters** Oregon, NW USA *44°17′N 121°33′W*
65 G15 **Sisters Peak** ▲ N Ascension Island *07°56′S 14°23′W*
21 R3 **Sistersville** West Virginia, NE USA *39°33′N 81°00′W*
**Sistova** *see* Svishtov
**Sitakund** *see* Sitakunda
153 V16 **Sitakunda** *var.* Sitakund. Chittagong, SE Bangladesh *22°35′N 91°40′E*
153 P12 **Sītāmarhi** Bihār, N India *26°36′N 85°30′E*
152 L11 **Sītāpur** Uttar Pradesh, N India *27°33′N 80°40′E*
**Sitaş Cristuru** *see* Cristuru Secuiesc
115 L25 **Siteía** *var.* Sitía. Kríti, Greece, E Mediterranean Sea *35°13′N 26°06′E*
105 V6 **Sitges** Cataluña, NE Spain *41°14′N 01°49′E*
115 H15 **Sithonía** *var.* Chersónisos Sithonías. *peninsula* NE Greece
**Sithonías, Chersónisos** *see* Sithonía
**Sitía** *see* Siteía
54 F4 **Sitionuevo** Magdalena, N Colombia *10°46′N 74°43′W*
39 X13 **Sitka** Baranof Island, Alaska, USA *57°03′N 135°19′W*
39 Q15 **Sitkinak Island** *island* Trinity Islands, Alaska, USA
166 M7 **Sittang** *var.* Sittoung. ≈ S Myanmar (Burma)
99 L17 **Sittard** Limburg, SE Netherlands *51°N 05°52′E*
**Sitten** *see* Sion
108 H7 **Sitter** ≈ NW Switzerland
109 U10 **Sittersdorf** Kärnten, S Austria *46°31′N 14°34′E*
**Sittoung** *see* Sittang
166 K6 **Sittwe** *var.* Akyab. Rakhine State, W Myanmar (Burma) *22°09′N 92°51′E*
42 L8 **Siuna** Costa Caribe Norte, NE Nicaragua *13°44′N 84°46′W*
153 R15 **Siuri** West Bengal, NE India *23°54′N 87°32′E*
**Siut** *see* Asyūţ
123 Q13 **Sivaki** Amurskaya Oblast', SE Russia *52°39′N 126°43′E*
136 M13 **Sivas** *anc.* Sebastia, Sebaste. Sivas, C Turkey *39°44′N 37°01′E*
136 M13 **Sivas** ◈ *province* C Turkey
137 O15 **Siverek** Şanlıurfa, S Turkey *37°46′N 39°19′E*
117 X6 **Sivers'k** Donets'ka Oblast', E Ukraine *48°52′N 38°07′E*
124 G13 **Siverskiy** Leningradskaya Oblast', NW Russia *59°21′N 30°01′E*
117 X6 **Sivers'kyy Donets'** *Rus.* Severskiy Donets. ≈ Russia/Ukraine *see also* Severskiy Donets
**Sivers'kyy Donets'** *see* Severskiy Donets
125 W5 **Sivomaskinskiy** Respublika Komi, NW Russia *66°42′N 62°33′E*
136 G13 **Sivrihisar** Eskişehir, W Turkey *39°29′N 31°32′E*
99 F22 **Sivry** Hainaut, S Belgium *50°10′N 04°11′E*
123 V9 **Sivuchiy, Mys** *headland* E Russia *56°45′N 163°13′E*
**Siwa** *see* Sīwah
75 U9 **Sīwah** *var.* Siwa. NW Egypt *29°11′N 25°32′E*
152 J9 **Siwalik Range** *var.* Shiwalik Range. ▲▲ India/Nepal
153 O13 **Siwān** Bihār, N India *26°14′N 84°21′E*
43 O14 **Sixaola, Río** ≈ Costa Rica/Panama
**Six Counties, The** *see* Northern Ireland
103 T16 **Six-Fours-les-Plages** Var, SE France *43°05′N 05°50′E*
161 Q7 **Sixian** *var.* Si Xian. Anhui, E China *33°29′N 117°53′E*
**Si Xian** *see* Sixian
22 J9 **Six Mile Lake** ◎ Louisiana, S USA
**Siyāh Gūz** *see* Syagwêz
155 L25 **Siyambalanduwa** Uva Province, SE Sri Lanka *06°54′N 81°32′E*
137 Y10 **Siyäzän** *Rus.* Siazan'. NE Azerbaijan *41°05′N 49°05′E*
**Sizebolu** *see* Sozopol
**Sizuoka** *see* Shizuoka
95 I24 **Sjælland** ◈ *county* SE Denmark
95 I24 **Sjælland** *Eng.* Zealand, *Ger.* Seeland. *island* E Denmark
**Sjar** *see* Sääre
113 L15 **Sjenica** *Turk.* Seniça. Serbia, SW Serbia *43°16′N 20°01′E*
94 G11 **Sjoa** ≈ S Norway
95 K23 **Sjöbo** Skåne, S Sweden *55°37′N 13°45′E*
94 E9 **Sjøholt** Møre og Romsdal, S Norway *62°29′N 06°50′E*
92 O1 **Sjuøyane** *island group* N Svalbard
**Skadar** *see* Shkodër
**Skadarsko Jezero** *see* Scutari, Lake
117 R11 **Skadovs'k** Khersons'ka Oblast', S Ukraine *46°07′N 32°53′E*
95 I24 **Skælskør** Sjælland, E Denmark *55°16′N 11°18′E*
92 I2 **Skagaströnd** *prev.* Höfdhakaupstadhur. Norðurland Vestra, N Iceland *65°49′N 20°18′W*
95 H19 **Skagen** Nordjylland, N Denmark *57°44′N 10°37′E*
**Skagerak** *see* Skagerrak
95 L16 **Skagern** ◎ C Sweden
197 T17 **Skagerrak** *var.* Skagerak. *channel* N Europe
94 G12 **Skaget** ▲ S Norway *61°19′N 09°07′E*
32 H7 **Skagit River** ≈ Washington, NW USA
39 W12 **Skagway** Alaska, USA *59°27′N 135°18′W*
92 K8 **Skaidi** Finnmark, N Norway *70°26′N 24°31′E*
115 F21 **Skála** Pelopónnisos, S Greece *36°51′N 22°39′E*
116 K6 **Skalat** *Pol.* Skałat. Ternopil's'ka Oblast', W Ukraine *49°27′N 25°59′E*
95 J22 **Skälderviken** *inlet* Denmark/Sweden
92 I12 **Skalka** *Lapp.* Skalkká. ◎ N Sweden
**Skalkká** *see* Skalka
114 I12 **Skalotí** Anatolikí Makedonía kai Thráki, NE Greece *41°24′N 24°16′E*
95 G22 **Skanderborg** Midtjylland, C Denmark *56°02′N 09°57′E*
95 K22 **Skåne** *prev. Eng.* Scania. ◈ *county* S Sweden
75 N6 **Skanès** ✕ (Sousse) E Tunisia *35°36′N 10°56′E*
95 C15 **Skånevik** Hordaland, S Norway *59°43′N 06°35′E*
95 M18 **Skänninge** Östergötland, S Sweden *58°24′N 15°05′E*
95 J23 **Skanör med Falsterbo** Skåne, S Sweden *55°24′N 12°48′E*
115 H17 **Skantzoúra** *island* Vóreies Sporádes, Greece, Aegean Sea
95 K18 **Skara** Västra Götaland, S Sweden *58°23′N 13°25′E*
95 M17 **Skärblacka** Östergötland, S Sweden *58°34′N 15°54′E*
95 I18 **Skärhamn** Västra Götaland, S Sweden *57°59′N 11°33′E*
95 I14 **Skarnes** Hedmark, S Norway *60°14′N 11°41′E*
119 M21 **Skarodnaye** *Rus.* Skorodnoye. Homyel'skaya Voblasts', SE Belarus *51°38′N 28°50′E*
110 I8 **Skarszewy** *Ger.* Schöneck. Pomorskie, NW Poland *54°04′N 18°25′E*
111 M14 **Skarżysko-Kamienna** Świętokrzyskie, C Poland *51°07′N 20°52′E*
114 H8 **Skat** *var.* Skŭt. NW Bulgaria
95 K16 **Skattkärr** Värmland, C Sweden *59°25′N 13°42′E*
118 D12 **Skaudvilė** Tauragė, SW Lithuania *55°25′N 22°33′E*
92 J12 **Skaulo** *Lapp.* Sávdijári. Norrbotten, N Sweden *67°21′N 21°03′E*
111 K17 **Skawina** Małopolskie, S Poland *49°59′N 19°49′E*
10 K12 **Skeena** ≈ British Columbia, SW Canada
10 J11 **Skeena Mountains** ▲▲ British Columbia, W Canada
97 O18 **Skegness** E England, United Kingdom *53°10′N 00°21′E*
92 J4 **Skeiðarársandur** *coast* S Iceland
93 J15 **Skellefteå** Västerbotten, N Sweden *64°45′N 20°58′E*
93 I14 **Skellefteälven** ≈ N Sweden
93 J15 **Skelleftehamn** Västerbotten, N Sweden *64°41′N 21°13′E*
25 O2 **Skellytown** Texas, SW USA *35°34′N 101°10′W*
95 J19 **Skene** Västra Götaland, S Sweden *57°30′N 12°34′E*
97 G17 **Skerries** *Ir.* Na Sceirí. Dublin, E Ireland *53°35′N 06°07′W*
95 H15 **Ski** Akershus, S Norway *59°43′N 10°50′E*
115 G17 **Skiáthos** Skiáthos, Vóreies Sporádes, Greece, Aegean Sea *39°10′N 23°30′E*
115 G17 **Skiáthos** *island* Vóreies Sporádes, Greece, Aegean Sea
27 P9 **Skiatook** Oklahoma, C USA *36°22′N 96°00′W*
27 P9 **Skiatook Lake** ▣ Oklahoma, C USA
97 B22 **Skibbereen** *Ir.* An Sciobairín. Cork, SW Ireland *51°33′N 09°15′W*
92 I9 **Skibotn** Troms, N Norway *69°22′N 20°18′E*
119 F16 **Skidal'** *Rus.* Skidel'. Hrodzyenskaya Voblasts', W Belarus *53°35′N 24°15′E*
97 K15 **Skiddaw** ▲ NW England, United Kingdom *54°37′N 03°07′W*
**Skidel'** *see* Skidal'
25 T14 **Skidmore** Texas, SW USA *28°13′N 97°40′W*
95 G16 **Skien** Telemark, S Norway *59°14′N 09°37′E*
**Skiermûntseach** *see* Schiermonnikoog
110 L12 **Skierniewice** Łódzkie, C Poland *51°58′N 20°10′E*
74 L5 **Skikda** *prev.* Philippeville. NE Algeria *36°51′N 07°E*
30 M16 **Skillet Fork** ≈ Illinois, N USA
95 L19 **Skillingaryd** Jönköping, S Sweden *57°27′N 14°05′E*
115 B19 **Skinári, Akrotírio** *headland* Iónia Nisiá, Greece *37°55′N 20°57′E*
95 M15 **Skinnskatteberg** Västmanland, C Sweden *59°50′N 15°41′E*
182 M12 **Skipton** Victoria, SE Australia *37°44′S 143°21′E*
97 L16 **Skipton** N England, United Kingdom *53°57′N 02°W*
**Skiropoula** *see* Skyropoúla
**Skíros** *see* Skýros
95 F21 **Skive** Midtjylland, NW Denmark *56°34′N 09°02′E*
94 F11 **Skjåk** Oppland, S Norway *61°52′N 08°21′E*
95 F22 **Skjern** Midtjylland, W Denmark *55°57′N 08°30′E*
95 F22 **Skjern Å** *var.* Skjern Aa. ≈ W Denmark
**Skjern Aa** *see* Skjern Å
92 G12 **Skjerstad** Nordland, C Norway *67°14′N 15°00′E*
92 J8 **Skjervøy** Troms, N Norway *70°03′N 20°56′E*
92 I10 **Skjold** Troms, N Norway *69°03′N 19°18′E*
111 I17 **Skoczów** Śląskie, S Poland *49°49′N 18°45′E*
109 T11 **Škofja Loka** *Ger.* Bischoflack. NW Slovenia *46°12′N 14°16′E*
94 N12 **Skog** Gävleborg, C Sweden *61°10′N 16°49′E*
95 K16 **Skoghall** Värmland, C Sweden *59°20′N 13°30′E*
31 N10 **Skokie** Illinois, N USA *42°01′N 87°43′W*
116 H6 **Skole** L'vivs'ka Oblast', W Ukraine *49°04′N 23°29′E*
115 D19 **Skóllis** ▲ S Greece *37°58′N 21°33′E*
167 S13 **Skon** Kampong Cham, C Cambodia *12°56′N 104°36′E*
115 H17 **Skópelos** Skópelos, Vóreies Sporádes, Greece, Aegean Sea *39°07′N 23°43′E*
115 H17 **Skópelos** *island* Vóreies Sporádes, Greece, Aegean Sea
126 L5 **Skopin** Ryazanskaya Oblast', W Russia *53°46′N 39°37′E*
113 N18 **Skopje** *var.* Üsküb, *Turk.* Üsküp, *prev.* Skoplje; *anc.* Scupi. ● (North Macedonia) N North Macedonia *42°N 21°28′E*
113 O18 **Skopje** ✕ N North Macedonia *41°58′N 21°35′E*
**Skoplje** *see* Skopje
110 I8 **Skórcz** *Ger.* Skurz. Pomorskie, N Poland *53°46′N 18°43′E*
**Skorodnoye** *see* Skarodnaye
93 H16 **Skorped** Västernorrland, C Sweden *63°23′N 17°55′E*
95 G21 **Skørping** Nordjylland, N Denmark *56°50′N 09°55′E*
95 K18 **Skövde** Västra Götaland, S Sweden *58°24′N 13°52′E*
123 Q13 **Skovorodino** Amurskaya Oblast', SE Russia *54°03′N 123°47′E*
19 Q6 **Skowhegan** Maine, NE USA *44°46′N 69°41′W*
11 W15 **Skownan** Manitoba, S Canada *51°55′N 99°34′W*
94 H13 **Skreia** Oppland, S Norway *60°37′N 11°00′E*
**Skripón** *see* Orchómenos
118 H9 **Skrīveri** S Latvia *56°39′N 25°08′E*
118 J11 **Skrudaliena** SE Latvia *55°50′N 26°42′E*
118 D9 **Skrunda** W Latvia *56°39′N 22°01′E*
95 C16 **Skudeneshavn** Rogaland, S Norway *59°10′N 05°16′E*
95 C16 **Skudnesfjorden** S Norway
83 L20 **Skukuza** Mpumalanga, NE South Africa *25°01′S 31°35′E*
97 B22 **Skull** *Ir.* An Scoil. SW Ireland *51°32′N 09°34′W*
22 L3 **Skuna River** ≈ Mississippi, S USA
29 X15 **Skunk River** ≈ Iowa, C USA
**Skuø** *see* Skúvoy
118 C10 **Skuodas** *Ger.* Schoden, *Pol.* Szkudy. Klaipėda, NW Lithuania *56°16′N 21°30′E*
95 K23 **Skurup** Skåne, S Sweden *55°28′N 13°30′E*
**Skurz** *see* Skórcz
**Skŭt** *see* Skat
94 O13 **Skutskär** Uppsala, C Sweden *60°39′N 17°25′E*
95 B19 **Skúvoy** *Dan.* Skuø. *island* C Faroe Islands
**Skvira** *see* Skvyra
117 O5 **Skvyra** *Rus.* Skvira. Kyivs'ka Oblast', N Ukraine *49°44′N 29°42′E*
39 Q11 **Skwentna** Alaska, USA *61°56′N 151°03′W*
110 E11 **Skwierzyna** *Ger.* Schwerin. Lubuskie, W Poland *52°37′N 15°27′E*
96 G9 **Skye, Isle of** *island* NW Scotland, United Kingdom
36 K13 **Sky Harbor** ✕ (Phoenix) Arizona, SW USA *32°26′N 112°00′W*
32 I8 **Skykomish** Washington, NW USA *47°40′N 121°20′W*
**Skylge** *see* Terschelling
63 F19 **Skyring, Peninsula** *peninsula* S Chile
63 H24 **Skyring, Seno** *inlet* S Chile
115 H17 **Skyropoúla** *var.* Skiropoula. *island* Vóreies Sporádes, Greece, Aegean Sea
115 I17 **Skýros** *var.* Skíros. Skńyros, Vóreies Sporádes, Greece, Aegean Sea *38°55′N 24°34′E*
115 I17 **Skýros** *var.* Skíros; *anc.* Scyros. *island* Vóreies Sporádes, Greece, Aegean Sea
118 J12 **Slabodka** *Rus.* Slobodka. Vitsyebskaya Voblasts', NW Belarus *55°41′N 27°11′E*
95 I23 **Slagelse** Sjælland, E Denmark *55°25′N 11°22′E*
93 I14 **Slagnäs** Norrbotten, N Sweden *65°36′N 18°10′E*
39 T10 **Slana** Alaska, USA *62°46′N 144°00′W*
97 F20 **Slaney** *Ir.* An tSláine. ≈ SE Ireland
116 J13 **Slănic** Prahova, SE Romania *45°14′N 25°58′E*
116 K11 **Slănic Moldova** Bacău, E Romania *46°12′N 26°23′E*
113 H16 **Slano** Dubrovnik-Neretva, SE Croatia *42°47′N 17°54′E*
124 F13 **Slantsy** Leningradskaya Oblast', NW Russia *59°06′N 28°00′E*
111 C16 **Slaný** *Ger.* Schlan. Střední Čechy, NW Czechia *50°14′N 14°05′E*
111 K16 **Śląskie** ◈ *province* S Poland
12 C10 **Slate Falls** Ontario, S Canada *51°11′N 91°32′W*
27 T4 **Slater** Missouri, C USA *39°13′N 93°04′W*
112 H9 **Slatina** *Hung.* Szlatina; *prev.* Podravska Slatina. Virovitica-Podravina, NE Croatia *45°40′N 17°46′E*
116 I14 **Slatina** Olt, S Romania *45°27′N 24°21′E*
25 N5 **Slaton** Texas, SW USA *33°26′N 101°38′W*
95 H14 **Slattum** Akershus, S Norway *60°00′N 10°55′E*
11 R10 **Slave** ≈ Alberta/Northwest Territories, C Canada
68 E12 **Slave Coast** *coastal region* W Africa
11 P13 **Slave Lake** Alberta, SW Canada *55°17′N 114°46′W*
122 I13 **Slavgorod** Altayskiy Kray, S Russia *52°55′N 78°46′E*
**Slavgorod** *see* Slawharad
**Slavonia** *see* Slavonija
112 G9 **Slavonija** *Eng.* Slavonia, *Ger.* Slawonien, *Hung.* Szlavonia, Szlavonország. *cultural region* NE Croatia
112 H10 **Slavonski Brod** *Ger.* Brod, *Hung.* Bród; *prev.* Brod, Brod na Savi. Brod-Posavina, NE Croatia *45°09′N 18°00′E*
112 G10 **Slavonski Brod-Posavina** *off.* Brodsko-Posavska Županija, *var.* Brod-Posavina. ◈ *province* NE Croatia
116 L4 **Slavuta** Khmel'nyts'ka Oblast', NW Ukraine *50°18′N 26°52′E*
117 P2 **Slavutych** Chernihivs'ka Oblast', N Ukraine *51°31′N 30°47′E*
123 R15 **Slavyanka** Primorskiy Kray, SE Russia *42°46′N 131°19′E*
114 J8 **Slavyanovo** Pleven, N Bulgaria *43°28′N 24°52′E*
**Slavyansk** *see* Slov"yans'k
126 K14 **Slavyansk-na-Kubani** Krasnodarskiy Kray, SW Russia *45°16′N 38°09′E*
119 N20 **Slavyechna** *Rus.* Slovechna. ≈ Belarus/Ukraine
119 O16 **Slawharad** *Rus.* Slavgorod. Mahilyowskaya Voblasts', E Belarus *53°27′N 31°00′E*
110 G7 **Sławno** Zachodnio-pomorskie, NW Poland *54°23′N 16°43′E*
**Slawonien** *see* Slavonija
29 S10 **Slayton** Minnesota, N USA *43°59′N 95°45′W*
97 N18 **Sleaford** E England, United Kingdom *52°59′N 00°28′W*
97 A20 **Slea Head** *Ir.* Ceann Sléibhe. *headland* SW Ireland *52°05′N 10°25′W*
96 G9 **Sleat, Sound of** *strait* NW Scotland, United Kingdom
**Sledyuki** *see* Slyedzyuki
12 I5 **Sleeper Islands** *island group* Nunavut, C Canada
31 O6 **Sleeping Bear Point** *headland* Michigan, N USA *44°54′N 86°02′W*
29 T10 **Sleepy Eye** Minnesota, N USA *44°18′N 94°43′W*
39 O11 **Sleetmute** Alaska, USA *61°42′N 157°10′W*
**Sléibhe, Ceann** *see* Slea Head
**Slêmanî** *see* As Sulaymānīyah
**Slêmanî** *see* As Sulaymānīyah
**Slêmanî, Parêzga-î** *see* As Sulaymānīyah
195 O5 **Slessor Glacier** *glacier* Antarctica
22 L9 **Slidell** Louisiana, S USA *30°16′N 89°46′W*
18 K12 **Slide Mountain** ▲ New York, NE USA *42°00′N 74°23′W*
98 I13 **Sliedrecht** Zuid-Holland, C Netherlands *51°50′N 04°46′E*
121 P16 **Sliema** N Malta *35°54′N 14°31′E*
97 G16 **Slieve Donard** ▲ SE Northern Ireland, United Kingdom *54°10′N 05°57′W*
**Sligeach** *see* Sligo
97 D16 **Sligo** *Ir.* Sligeach. Sligo, NW Ireland *54°17′N 08°28′W*
97 C16 **Sligo** *Ir.* Sligeach. *cultural region* NW Ireland
97 C15 **Sligo Bay** *Ir.* Cuan Shligigh. *inlet* NW Ireland
18 B13 **Slippery Rock** Pennsylvania, NE USA *41°02′N 80°02′W*
95 P19 **Slite** Gotland, SE Sweden *57°37′N 18°46′E*
114 M8 **Slivak** Shumen, NE Bulgaria *43°27′N 26°56′E*
114 L9 **Sliven** *var.* Slivno. Sliven, C Bulgaria *42°42′N 26°21′E*


◆ Country
● Country Capital
◇ Dependent Territory
○ Dependent Territory Capital
◈ Administrative Regions
✕ International Airport
▲ Mountain
▲▲ Mountain Range
Volcano
≈ River
◎ Lake
▣ Reservoir

114 L10 **Sliven ◇** province C Bulgaria
114 G9 **Slivnitsa** Sofia, W Bulgaria 42°51´N 23°01´E
114 L7 **Slivo Pole** Ruse, N Bulgaria 43°57´N 26°15´E
29 S13 **Sloan** Iowa, C USA 42°13´N 96°13´W
35 X12 **Sloan** Nevada, W USA 35°56´N 115°13´W
**Slobodka** see Slabodka
125 R14 **Slobodskoy** Kirovskaya Oblast´, NW Russia 58°43´N 50°12´E
**Slobodzeya** see Slobozia
117 O10 **Slobozia** Rus. Slobodzeya. E Moldova 46°45´N 29°42´E
116 L14 **Slobozia** Ialomiţa, SE Romania 44°34´N 27°23´E
98 O5 **Slochteren** Groningen, NE Netherlands 53°13´N 06°48´E
119 H17 **Slonim** Pol. Słonim. Hrodzyenskaya Voblasts´, W Belarus 53°06´N 25°19´E
**Słonim** see Slonim
98 K7 **Sloter Meer** ☒ N Netherlands
**Slot, The** see New Georgia Sound
97 N22 **Slough** S England, United Kingdom 51°31´N 00°36´W
111 J20 **Slovakia** off. Slovak Republic, Slvk. Slovensko, Slovenská republika, Hung. Szlovákia, Ger. Slowakei. ◆ republic C Europe
**Slovak Ore Mountains** see Slovenské rudohorie
**Slovak Republic** see Slovakia
**Slovechna** see Slavyechna
109 S12 **Slovenia** off. Republic of Slovenia, Slvn. Slovenija, Republika Slovenija, Ger. Slowenien. ◆ republic SE Europe
**Slovenia, Republic of** see Slovenia
**Slovenija** see Slovenia
**Slovenija, Republika** see Slovenia
109 V10 **Slovenj Gradec** Ger. Windischgraz. N Slovenia 46°29´N 15°05´E
109 W10 **Slovenska Bistrica** Ger. Windischfeistritz. NE Slovenia 46°21´N 15°27´E
109 W10 **Slovenske Konjice** E Slovenia 46°21´N 15°28´E
111 K20 **Slovenské rudohorie** Eng. Slovak Ore Mountains, Ger. Slowakisches Erzgebirge, Ungarisches Erzgebirge. ▲▲ C Slovakia
**Slovensko** see Slovakia
117 Y7 **Slov”yanoserbs´k** Luhans´ka Oblast´, E Ukraine 48°41´N 39°00´E
117 W6 **Slov”yans´k** Rus. Slavyansk. Donets´ka Oblast´, E Ukraine 48°51´N 37°38´E
**Slowakei** see Slovakia
**Slowakisches Erzgebirge** see Slovenské rudohorie
**Slowenien** see Slovenia
110 D11 **Słubice** Ger. Frankfurt. Lubuskie, W Poland 52°20´N 14°35´E
119 K19 **Sluch** Rus. Sluch´. ☒ C Belarus
116 L4 **Sluch** ☒ N Ukraine
99 D16 **Sluis** Zeeland, SW Netherlands 51°18´N 03°22´E
112 D10 **Slunj** Hung. Szluin. Karlovac, C Croatia 45°06´N 15°35´E
110 I11 **Słupca** Wielkopolskie, C Poland 52°17´N 17°52´E
110 G6 **Słupia** Ger. Stolpe. ☒ NW Poland
110 G6 **Słupsk** Ger. Stolp. Pomorskie, N Poland 54°28´N 17°01´E
119 K18 **Slutsk** Minskaya Voblasts´, S Belarus 53°01´N 27°32´E
119 O16 **Slyedzyuki** Rus. Sledyuki. Mahilyowskaya Voblasts´, E Belarus 53°35´N 30°22´E
97 A17 **Slyne Head** Ir. Ceann Léime. headland W Ireland 53°25´N 10°11´W
27 U14 **Smackover** Arkansas, C USA 33°21´N 92°43´W
95 L20 **Småland** cultural region S Sweden
95 K20 **Smålandsstenar** Jönköping, S Sweden 57°10´N 13°24´E
**Small Malaita** see Maramasike
13 O8 **Smallwood Reservoir** ☒ Newfoundland and Labrador, E Canada
119 N14 **Smalyany** Rus. Smolyany. Vitsyebskaya Voblasts´, NE Belarus 54°36´N 30°04´E
119 L15 **Smalyavichy** Rus. Smolevichi. Minskaya Voblasts´, C Belarus 54°02´N 28°05´E
74 C9 **Smara** var. Es Semara. N Western Sahara 26°45´N 11°44´W
119 I14 **Smarhon´** Pol. Smorgonie, Rus. Smorgon´. Hrodzyenskaya Voblasts´, W Belarus 54°28´N 26°24´E
112 M11 **Smederevo** Ger. Semendria. Serbia, N Serbia 44°41´N 20°56´E
112 M12 **Smederevska Palanka** Serbia, C Serbia 44°24´N 20°56´E
95 M14 **Smedjebacken** Dalarna, C Sweden 60°08´N 15°25´E
116 L13 **Smeeni** Buzău, SE Romania 45°00´N 26°52´E
**Smela** see Smila
107 D16 **Smeralda, Costa** cultural region Sardegna, Italy, C Mediterranean Sea
111 J22 **Šmigiel** Ger. Schmiegel. Wielkopolskie, C Poland 52°02´N 16°13´E
117 Q6 **Smila** Rus. Smela. Cherkas´ka Oblast´, C Ukraine 49°15´N 31°51´E
98 N7 **Smilde** Drenthe, NE Netherlands 52°57´N 06°28´E
11 S16 **Smiley** Texas, SW USA 29°16´N 97°38´W
25 T12 **Smiley** Texas, SW USA 29°16´N 97°38´W
118 I8 **Smiltene** Ger. Smilten. N Latvia 57°25´N 25°53´E

123 T13 **Smirnykh** Ostrov Sakhalin, Sakhalinskaya Oblast´, SE Russia 49°43´N 142°48´E
11 Q13 **Smith** Alberta, W Canada 55°06´N 113°57´W
39 P4 **Smith Bay** bay Alaska, NW USA
12 I3 **Smith, Cape** headland Québec, C Canada 60°50´N 78°06´W
26 L3 **Smith Center** Kansas, C USA 39°46´N 98°46´W
10 K13 **Smithers** British Columbia, SW Canada 54°45´N 127°10´W
21 V10 **Smithfield** North Carolina, SE USA 35°30´N 78°21´W
36 L1 **Smithfield** Utah, W USA 41°50´N 111°49´W
21 X7 **Smithfield** Virginia, NE USA 36°41´N 76°38´W
12 I3 **Smith Island** island Nunavut, C Canada
**Smith Island** see Sumisu-jima
20 H7 **Smithland** Kentucky, S USA 37°07´N 88°24´W
21 T7 **Smith Mountain Lake** var. Leesville Lake. ☒ Virginia, NE USA
34 L3 **Smith River** California, W USA 41°54´N 124°09´W
33 R9 **Smith River** ☒ Montana, NW USA
14 L13 **Smiths Falls** Ontario, SE Canada 44°54´N 76°01´W
33 N13 **Smiths Ferry** Idaho, NW USA 44°19´N 116°04´W
20 K7 **Smiths Grove** Kentucky, S USA 37°01´N 86°14´W
183 N15 **Smithton** Tasmania, SE Australia 40°45´S 145°06´E
18 L14 **Smithtown** Long Island, New York, NE USA 40°52´N 73°13´W
20 K9 **Smithville** Tennessee, S USA 35°59´N 85°49´W
25 T11 **Smithville** Texas, SW USA 30°04´N 97°32´W
**Šmohor** see Hermagor
35 I4 **Smoke Creek Desert** desert Nevada, W USA
11 O14 **Smoky** ☒ Alberta, W Canada
182 E7 **Smoky Bay** South Australia 32°22´S 133°57´E
183 V6 **Smoky Cape** headland New South Wales, SE Australia 30°54´S 153°06´E
26 L4 **Smoky Hill River** ☒ Kansas, C USA
26 L4 **Smoky Hills** hill range Kansas, C USA
11 O14 **Smoky Lake** Alberta, SW Canada 54°08´N 112°26´W
94 H4 **Smøla** island N Norway
126 H4 **Smolensk** Smolenskaya Oblast´, W Russia 54°48´N 32°08´E
126 H4 **Smolenskaya Oblast´** ◇ province W Russia
**Smolensk-Moscow Upland** see Smolensko-Moskovskaya Vozvyshennost´
126 J2 **Smolensko-Moskovskaya Vozvyshennost´** var. Smolensk-Moscow Upland. ▲▲ W Russia
**Smolevichi** see Smalyavichy
115 C15 **Smólikas** var. Smolikás. ▲ W Greece 40°06´N 20°54´E
114 I12 **Smolyan** prev. Pashmakli. Smolyan, S Bulgaria 41°34´N 24°42´E
114 I12 **Smolyan** ◇ province S Bulgaria
**Smolyany** see Smalyany
33 S15 **Smoot** Wyoming, C USA 42°37´N 110°55´W
12 G12 **Smooth Rock Falls** Ontario, S Canada 49°17´N 81°37´W
**Smorgon´/Smorgonie** see Smarhon´
95 K23 **Smygehamn** Skåne, S Sweden 55°19´N 13°25´E
194 I7 **Smyley Island** island Antarctica
21 Y3 **Smyrna** Delaware, NE USA 39°18´N 75°36´W
21 S3 **Smyrna** Georgia, SE USA 33°52´N 84°30´W
20 J9 **Smyrna** Tennessee, S USA 36°00´N 86°30´W
**Smyrna** see İzmir
97 I16 **Snaefell** ▲ C Isle of Man 54°15´N 04°29´W
92 H3 **Snæfellsjökull** ▲ W Iceland 64°51´N 23°51´W
92 H3 **Snækollur** ▲ C Iceland 64°38´N 19°18´W
10 J4 **Snake** ☒ Yukon, NW Canada
29 O8 **Snake Creek** ☒ South Dakota, N USA
183 P13 **Snake Island** island Victoria, SE Australia
33 Y6 **Snake Range** ▲▲ Nevada, W USA
32 K10 **Snake River** ☒ NW USA
29 V6 **Snake River** ☒ Minnesota, N USA
28 L12 **Snake River** ☒ Nebraska, C USA
33 Q14 **Snake River Plain** plain Idaho, NW USA
93 F15 **Snåsa** Nord-Trøndelag, C Norway 64°16´N 12°25´E
21 O8 **Sneedville** Tennessee, S USA 36°31´N 83°13´W
98 K6 **Sneek** Fris. Snits. Fryslân, N Netherlands 53°02´N 05°40´E
**Sneeuw-gebergte** see Maoke, Pegunungan
95 F22 **Snejbjerg** Midtjylland, C Denmark 56°08´N 08°55´E
122 K9 **Snezhnogorsk** Krasnoyarskiy Kray, N Russia 68°06´N 87°37´E
124 J3 **Snezhnogorsk** Murmanskaya Oblast´, NW Russia 69°12´N 33°20´E
111 G15 **Sněžka** Ger. Schneekoppe, Pol. Śnieżka. ▲ N Czechia/ Poland 50°42´N 15°55´E
110 N8 **Śniardwy, Jezioro** Ger. Spirdingsee. ☒ NE Poland
**Śnieckus** see Visaginas
117 R10 **Snihurivka** Mykolayivs´ka Oblast´, S Ukraine 47°05´N 32°48´E
116 I5 **Snilov** ✈ (L´viv) L´vivs´ka Oblast´, W Ukraine 49°45´N 23°59´E
111 O19 **Snina** Hung. Szinna. Prešovský Kraj, E Slovakia 49°N 22°10´E

117 Y8 **Snizhne** Rus. Snezhnoye. Donets´ka Oblast´, SE Ukraine 48°01´N 38°46´E
94 G10 **Snøhetta** var. Snohetta. ▲ S Norway 62°22´N 09°08´E
92 G12 **Snøtinden** ▲ C Norway 66°39´N 13°50´E
117 Q2 **Snovs´k** prev. Shchors. Chernihivs´ka Oblast´, N Ukraine 51°49´N 31°58´E
117 U8 **Snowdon** ▲ NW Wales, United Kingdom 53°04´N 04°04´W
117 U8 **Snowdonia** ▲ NW Wales, United Kingdom 53°04´N 04°04´W
37 N12 **Snowflake** Arizona, SW USA 34°30´N 110°04´W
37 V3 **Snow Hill** Maryland, NE USA 38°11´N 75°23´W
21 W10 **Snow Hill** North Carolina, SE USA 35°26´N 77°39´W
194 H3 **Snowhill Island** island Antarctica
11 V13 **Snow Lake** Manitoba, C Canada 54°54´N 100°02´W
37 R5 **Snowmass Mountain** ▲ Colorado, C USA 39°07´N 107°04´W
18 M10 **Snow, Mount** ▲ Vermont, NE USA 42°56´N 72°52´W
34 M5 **Snow Mountain** ▲ California, W USA 39°44´N 123°01´W
**Snow Mountains** see Maoke, Pegunungan
33 N7 **Snowshoe Peak** ▲ Montana, NW USA 48°15´N 115°44´W
182 I8 **Snowtown** South Australia 33°49´S 138°13´E
36 K1 **Snowville** Utah, W USA 41°59´N 112°42´W
35 X3 **Snow Water Lake** ☒ Nevada, W USA
183 Q11 **Snowy Mountains** ▲▲ New South Wales/Victoria, SE Australia
183 Q12 **Snowy River** ☒ New South Wales/Victoria, SE Australia
44 K5 **Snug Corner** Acklins Island, SE The Bahamas 22°31´N 73°51´W
167 T13 **Snuŏl** Krâtié, E Cambodia 12°04´N 106°26´E
116 J7 **Snyatyn** Ivano-Frankivs´ka Oblast´, W Ukraine 48°30´N 25°50´E
26 L12 **Snyder** Oklahoma, C USA 34°37´N 98°56´W
25 O6 **Snyder** Texas, SW USA 32°43´N 100°54´W
172 H3 **Soalala** Mahajanga, W Madagascar 16°05´S 45°21´E
172 J4 **Soanierana-Ivongo** Toamasina, E Madagascar 16°53´S 49°35´E
171 R11 **Soasiu** var. Tidore. Pulau Tidore, E Indonesia 0°40´N 127°25´E
54 G8 **Soatá** Boyacá, C Colombia 06°23´N 72°40´W
172 I5 **Soavinandriana** Antananarivo, C Madagascar 19°09´S 46°43´E
77 V13 **Soba** Kaduna, C Nigeria
163 Y16 **Sobaek-sanmaek** ▲▲ S South Korea
80 F13 **Sobat** ☒ NE South Sudan
124 Z14 **Sobger, Sungai** ☒ Papua, E Indonesia
171 V13 **Sobiei** Papua Barat, E Indonesia 02°31´S 134°30´E
126 M3 **Sobinka** Vladimirskaya Oblast´, W Russia 56°00´N 39°55´E
122 S7 **Sobolevo** Orenburgskaya Oblast´, W Russia 51°57´N 51°42´E
124 D15 **Sobo-san** ▲ Kyūshū, SW Japan 32°50´N 131°16´E
114 G14 **Sobótka** Dolnośląskie, SW Poland 50°53´N 16°48´E
59 O15 **Sobradinho** Bahia, E Brazil 09°33´S 40°56´W
59 O16 **Sobradinho, Barragem de** see Sobradinho, Represa de
59 O16 **Sobradinho, Represa de** var. Barragem de Sobradinho. ☒ E Brazil
59 O13 **Sobral** Ceará, E Brazil 03°45´S 40°20´W
105 T4 **Sobrarbe** physical region NE Spain
109 R10 **Soča** It. Isonzo. ☒ Italy/ Slovenia
110 L11 **Sochaczew** Mazowieckie, C Poland 52°15´N 20°15´E
126 L15 **Sochi** Krasnodarskiy Kray, SW Russia 43°35´N 39°46´E
114 I5 **Sochós** var. Sohós, Sokhós. Kentrikí Makedonía, N Greece 40°49´N 23°23´E
191 R11 **Société, Archipel de la** var. Archipel de Tahiti, Îles de la Société, Eng. Society Islands. island group W French Polynesia
**Société, Îles de la/Society Islands** see Société, Archipel de la
21 T11 **Society Hill** South Carolina, SE USA 34°28´N 79°54´W
175 W9 **Society Ridge** undersea feature C Pacific Ocean
42 I5 **Socompa, Volcán** ▲ N Chile 24°18´S 68°03´W
**Soconusco, Sierra de** see Madre, Sierra
54 F8 **Socorro** Santander, C Colombia 06°30´N 73°17´W
37 R13 **Socorro** New Mexico, SW USA 33°58´N 106°55´W
40 C9 **Socorro, Isla** island W Mexico 18°42´N 110°58´W
189 N12 **Socorro Island** ☒ E Micronesia
88 S14 **Soc Trăng** var. Khanh Hung. Soc Trăng, S Vietnam 09°36´N 105°58´E
105 P10 **Socuéllamos** Castilla-La Mancha, C Spain 39°18´N 02°48´W
35 W13 **Soda Lake** salt flat California, W USA
92 L11 **Sodankylä** Lappi, N Finland 67°26´N 26°35´E
33 R15 **Soda Springs** Idaho, NW USA 42°39´N 111°36´W
**Sodari/Soddu** see Sodo
20 L10 **Soddy Daisy** Tennessee, S USA 35°14´N 85°11´W
95 L16 **Söderfors** Uppsala, C Sweden 60°23´N 17°14´E
94 N13 **Söderhamn** Gävleborg, C Sweden 61°19´N 17°10´E
95 N17 **Södermanland** ◇ county C Sweden

95 O16 **Södertälje** Stockholm, C Sweden 59°11´N 17°39´E
80 D10 **Sodiri** var. Sawdiri, Sodari. Northern Kordofan, C Sudan 14°23´N 29°06´E
81 I14 **Sodo** var. Soddo, Soddu. Southern Nationalities, S Ethiopia 06°49´N 37°43´E
95 M19 **Södra Vi** Kalmar, S Sweden 57°45´N 15°45´E
18 G9 **Sodus Point** headland New York, NE USA 43°16´N 76°59´W
171 Q17 **Soë** prev. Soö. Timor, C Indonesia 09°51´S 124°29´E
**Soebang** see Subang
**Soekaboemi** see Sukabumi
169 N15 **Soekarno-Hatta** ✈ (Jakarta) Jawa, S Indonesia
118 E5 **Soela Väin** prev. Eng. Sele Sound, Ger. Dagden-Sund, Soëla-Sund. strait W Estonia
**Soemba** see Sumba, Pulau
**Soembawa** see Sumbawa
**Soemenep** see Sumenep
**Soengaipenoeh** see Sungaipenuh
**Soerabaja** see Surabaya
**Soerakarta** see Surakarta
**Soö** see Soë
101 G14 **Soest** Nordrhein-Westfalen, W Germany 51°34´N 08°06´E
98 J11 **Soest** Utrecht, C Netherlands 52°10´N 05°20´E
100 F11 **Soeste** ☒ NW Germany
98 J11 **Soesterberg** Utrecht, C Netherlands 52°07´N 05°17´E
115 E16 **Sofádes** var. Sofádhes. Thessalía, C Greece 39°20´N 22°06´E
83 N18 **Sofala** Sofala, C Mozambique 20°04´S 34°43´E
83 N17 **Sofala** ◇ province C Mozambique
83 N18 **Sofala, Baia de** bay C Mozambique
114 G10 **Sofia** var. Sophia, Sofiya, Eng. Sofia, Lat. Serdica. ● (Bulgaria) Sofia Grad, W Bulgaria 42°42´N 23°20´E
114 G9 **Sofia** ◇ province W Bulgaria
114 G9 **Sofia** ✈ Sofia Grad, W Bulgaria 42°42´N 23°26´E
172 J3 **Sofia** seasonal river NW Madagascar
114 G9 **Sofia Grad** ◇ municipality W Bulgaria
115 G19 **Sofikó** Pelopónnisos, S Greece 37°46´N 23°04´E
**Sofi-Kurgan** see Sopu-Korgon
**Sofiya** see Sofia
117 S8 **Sofiyivka** Rus. Sofiyevka. Dnipropetrovs´ka Oblast´, E Ukraine 48°04´N 33°55´E
123 R12 **Sofiysk** Khabarovskiy Kray, SE Russia 51°32´N 139°46´E
123 R13 **Sofiysk** Khabarovskiy Kray, SE Russia 52°20´N 133°37´E
124 I6 **Sofporog** Respublika Kareliya, NW Russia 59°05´N 42°15´E
115 L23 **Sofraná** prev. Záfora. island Kyklades, Greece, Aegean Sea
165 Y14 **Sōfu-gan** island Izu-shotō, SE Japan
156 K10 **Sog** Xizang Zizhiqu, W China 31°52´N 93°40´E
54 G9 **Sogamoso** Boyacá, C Colombia 05°43´N 72°56´W
136 I11 **Soğanlı Çayı** ☒ N Turkey
94 E12 **Sogn** physical region S Norway
**Sogndal** see Sogndalsfjøra
94 D12 **Sogndalsfjøra** var. Sogndal. Sogn Og Fjordane, S Norway 61°13´N 07°05´E
95 E18 **Søgne** Vest-Agder, S Norway 58°05´N 07°49´E
94 D12 **Sognefjorden** fjord NE North Sea
94 C12 **Sogn Og Fjordane** ◇ county S Norway
162 I11 **Sogo Nur** ☒ N China
159 T12 **Soguma** Qinghai, W China 32°32´N 100°52´E
**Sögwip'o** see Seogwipo
64 H9 **Sohm Plain** undersea feature NW Atlantic Ocean
100 H7 **Soholmer Au** ☒ N Germany
**Sohos** see Sochós
**Sohrau** see Żory
99 F20 **Soignies** Hainaut, SW Belgium 50°35´N 04°04´E
159 R15 **Soila** Xizang Zizhiqu, W China 30°40´N 99°07´E
103 P4 **Soissons** anc. Augusta Suessionum, Noviodunum. Aisne, N France 49°23´N 03°20´E
164 N13 **Sōja** Okayama, Honshū, SW Japan 34°40´N 133°42´E
152 F13 **Sojat** Rājasthān, N India 25°53´N 73°45´E
163 W13 **Sŏjosŏn-man** inlet W North Korea
116 I4 **Sokal´** Rus. Sokal. L´vivs´ka Oblast´, W Ukraine 50°29´N 24°17´E
**Sŏkch'o** see Sokcho
163 Y14 **Sokcho** prev. Sokch'o. N South Korea 38°07´N 128°34´E
136 B15 **Söke** Aydın, SW Turkey 37°46´N 27°26´E
79 M24 **Sokele** Katanga, SE Dem. Rep. Congo 09°54´S 24°38´E
147 R11 **Sokh** Uzb. Sükh. ◇ Kyrgyzstan/Uzbekistan
**Sokh** see So'x
**Sokhós** see Sochós
137 Q8 **Sokhumi** Rus. Sukhumi. NW Georgia 43°02´N 41°01´E
77 R15 **Sokodé** C Togo 08°58´N 01°10´E
**Sokodu/Soddu** see Sodo
124 M13 **Sokol** Vologodskaya Oblast´, NW Russia 59°26´N 40°09´E
110 P9 **Sokółka** Podlaskie, NE Poland 53°24´N 23°31´E
76 M11 **Sokolo** Ségou, W Mali 14°43´N 06°02´W
111 A16 **Sokolov** Ger. Falkenau an der Eger; prev. Falknov nad Ohří. Karlovarský Kraj, W Czechia 50°10´N 12°38´E

111 O16 **Sokołów Małopolski** Podkarpackie, SE Poland 50°12´N 22°07´E
110 O11 **Sokołów Podlaski** Mazowieckie, C Poland 52°26´N 22°14´E
76 G12 **Sokone** W Senegal 13°53´N 16°22´W
77 S13 **Sokoto** Sokoto, NW Nigeria 13°05´N 05°16´E
77 S13 **Sokoto** ◇ state NW Nigeria
77 S12 **Sokoto** ☒ NW Nigeria
**Sokotra** see Suquṭrā
147 U7 **Solakli** Chuyskaya Oblast´, N Kyrgyzstan 42°53´N 74°19´E
116 L7 **Sokyryany** Chernivets´ka Oblast´, W Ukraine 48°28´N 27°25´E
95 C16 **Sola** Rogaland, S Norway 58°53´N 05°36´E
187 R12 **Sola** Vanua Lava, N Vanuatu 13°51´S 167°34´E
95 C17 **Sola** ✈ (Stavanger) Rogaland, S Norway 58°54´N 05°36´E
81 H18 **Solai** Nakuru, W Kenya 0°02´N 36°03´E
152 I8 **Solan** Himáchal Pradesh, N India 30°54´N 77°06´E
185 A25 **Solander Island** island SW New Zealand
155 F16 **Solāpur** var. Sholāpur. Mahārāshtra, W India 17°43´N 75°54´E
93 H16 **Solberg** Västernorrland, C Sweden 63°48´N 17°40´E
116 K9 **Solca** Ger. Solka. Suceava, N Romania 47°40´N 25°50´E
105 O16 **Sol, Costa del** coastal region S Spain
106 F5 **Solda** Ger. Sulden. Trentino-Alto Adige, N Italy 46°33´N 10°35´E
117 N9 **Soldănești** Rus. Sholdaneshty. N Moldova 47°49´N 28°45´E
108 L8 **Sölden** Tirol, W Austria 46°58´N 11°01´E
27 P3 **Soldier Creek** ☒ Kansas, C USA
39 R12 **Soldotna** Alaska, USA 60°29´N 151°03´W
110 I10 **Solec Kujawski** Kujawsko-pomorskie, C Poland 53°04´N 18°09´E
61 D14 **Soledad** Santa Fe, C Argentina 30°38´S 60°52´W
55 S4 **Soledad** Atlántico, N Colombia 10°54´N 74°48´W
35 O11 **Soledad** California, W USA 36°25´N 121°19´W
55 O7 **Soledad** Anzoátegui, NE Venezuela 08°10´N 63°36´W
61 H15 **Soledade** Rio Grande do Sul, S Brazil 28°50´S 52°30´W
**Isla Soledad** see East Falkland
103 Y15 **Solenzara** Corse, France, C Mediterranean Sea 41°55´N 09°24´E
**Soleure** see Solothurn
94 C12 **Solheim** Hordaland, S Norway 64°N 05°30´E
125 N14 **Soligalich** Kostromskaya Oblast´, NW Russia 59°05´N 42°15´E
**Soligorsk** see Salihorsk
97 M19 **Solihull** C England, United Kingdom 52°25´N 01°45´W
125 U13 **Solikamsk** Permskiy Kray, NW Russia 59°37´N 56°46´E
127 V8 **Sol'-Iletsk** Orenburgskaya Oblast´, W Russia 51°09´N 55°05´E
57 G17 **Solimana, Nevado** ▲ S Peru 15°24´S 72°49´W
58 E13 **Solimões, Rio** ☒ C Brazil
113 E14 **Solin** It. Salona; anc. Salonae. Split-Dalmacija, S Croatia 43°33´N 16°29´E
101 E15 **Solingen** Nordrhein-Westfalen, W Germany 51°10´N 07°05´E
93 G16 **Sollefteå** Västernorrland, C Sweden 63°09´N 17°15´E
105 X9 **Sóller** Mallorca, Spain, W Mediterranean Sea 39°46´N 02°42´E
101 I14 **Sollerön** Dalarna, C Sweden 60°55´N 14°34´E
101 L13 **Solling** hill range C Germany
95 O15 **Solna** Stockholm, C Sweden 59°22´N 18°01´E
126 M3 **Solnechnogorsk** Moskovskaya Oblast´, W Russia 56°07´N 37°04´E
123 R10 **Solnechnyy** Khabarovskiy Kray, SE Russia 50°41´N 136°42´E
123 S13 **Solnechnyy** Respublika Sakha (Yakutiya), NE Russia 60°13´N 137°42´E
**Solo** see Surakarta
171 Q8 **Solok** Sumatera, W Indonesia 0°45´S 100°42´E
42 C6 **Sololá** Sololá, W Guatemala 14°46´N 91°09´W
42 C6 **Sololá** ◇ department SW Guatemala
**Sololá, Departamento de** see Sololá
81 J16 **Soloma** Marsabit, N Kenya 03°31´N 38°39´E
42 C4 **Soloma** Huehuetenango, W Guatemala 15°38´N 91°25´W
38 M9 **Solomon** Alaska, USA 64°33´N 164°26´W
27 N4 **Solomon** Kansas, C USA 38°55´N 97°22´W
187 N9 **Solomon Islands** prev. British Solomon Islands Protectorate. ◆ commonwealth republic W Solomon Islands
186 M7 **Solomon Islands** island group Papua New Guinea/ Solomon Islands
26 M3 **Solomon River** ☒ Kansas, C USA
186 H8 **Solomon Sea** sea W Pacific Ocean
31 U11 **Solon** Ohio, N USA 41°23´N 81°26´W
117 T8 **Solone** Dnipropetrovs´ka Oblast´, E Ukraine 48°12´N 34°50´E
171 P16 **Solor, Kepulauan** island group S Indonesia

126 M4 **Solotcha** Ryazanskaya Oblast´, W Russia 54°47´N 39°45´E
108 D7 **Solothurn** Fr. Soleure. Solothurn, NW Switzerland 47°13´N 07°32´E
108 D7 **Solothurn** Fr. Soleure. ◇ canton NW Switzerland
124 J7 **Solovetskiye Ostrova** island group NW Russia
105 V5 **Solsona** Cataluña, NE Spain 42°00´N 01°31´E
113 E14 **Šolta** It. Solta. island S Croatia
**Solṭānābād** see Kāshmar
142 L4 **Solṭānīyeh** Zanjān, NW Iran 36°24´N 48°50´E
100 I11 **Soltau** Niedersachsen, NW Germany 52°59´N 09°50´E
124 G14 **Sol'tsy** Novgorodskaya Oblast´, W Russia 58°09´N 30°23´E
**Soltústik Qazaqstan Oblysy** see Severnyy Kazakhstan
**Solun** see Thessaloníki
113 O19 **Solunska Glava** ▲ N North Macedonia 41°43´N 21°24´E
95 L22 **Sölvesborg** Blekinge, S Sweden 56°04´N 14°35´E
97 J15 **Solway Firth** inlet England/ Scotland, United Kingdom
82 I13 **Solwezi** North Western, NW Zambia 12°11´S 26°23´E
165 Q11 **Sōma** Fukushima, Honshū, C Japan 37°49´N 140°52´E
136 C13 **Soma** Manisa, W Turkey 39°10´N 27°36´E
**Somali** see Sumalē
81 O15 **Somalia** off. Federal Republic of Somalia, Som. Soomaaliya, Jamhuuriyadda Federaalka Soomaaliya; prev. Italian Somaliland, Somaliland Prctectorate, Somali Democratic Republic. ◆ republic E Africa
**Somalia, Federal Republic of** see Somalia
173 N6 **Somali Basin** undersea feature W Indian Ocean 0°00´N 52°00´E
**Somali Democratic Republic** see Somalia
80 N12 **Somaliland** ◇ disputed territory N Somalia
**Somaliland Protectorate** see Somalia
67 Y8 **Somali Plain** undersea feature W Indian Ocean 01°00´N 51°30´E
112 J8 **Sombor** Hung. Zombor. Vojvodina, NW Serbia 45°46´N 19°07´E
99 H20 **Sombreffe** Namur, S Belgium 50°32´N 04°39´E
40 L10 **Sombrerete** Zacatecas, C Mexico 23°38´N 103°40´W
45 V8 **Sombrero** island N Anguilla
151 Q21 **Sombrero Channel** channel Nicobar Islands, India
116 H9 **Somcuţa Mare** Hung. Nagysomkút; prev. Somcuţa Mare. Maramureş, N Romania 47°29´N 23°29´E
**Somcuţa Mare** see Şomcuta Mare
167 R9 **Somdet** Kalasin, E Thailand 16°41´N 103°44´E
99 L15 **Someren** Noord-Brabant, SE Netherlands 51°23´N 05°42´E
93 L19 **Somero** Varsinais-Suomi, SW Finland 60°37´N 23°30´E
33 P7 **Somers** Montana, NW USA 48°04´N 114°16´W
6 A12 **Somerset** var. Somerset Village. W Bermuda 32°18´N 64°53´W
21 N5 **Somerset** Kentucky, S USA 37°05´N 84°36´W
19 O12 **Somerset** Massachusetts, NE USA 41°46´N 71°07´W
97 K23 **Somerset** cultural region SW England, United Kingdom
**Somerset East** see Somerset-Oos
6 A12 **Somerset Island** island Queen Elizabeth Islands, Nunavut, NW Canada
**Somerset Nile** see Victoria Nile
83 I25 **Somerset-Oos** var. Somerset East. Eastern Cape, South Africa 32°44´S 25°35´E
**Somerset West** see Somerset-Wes
83 E26 **Somerset-Wes** var. Somerset West. Western Cape, SW South Africa 34°05´S 18°51´E
19 P11 **Somersworth** New Hampshire, NE USA 43°15´N 70°52´W
36 H5 **Somerton** Arizona, SW USA 32°36´N 114°42´W
18 J14 **Somerville** New Jersey, NE USA 40°34´N 74°34´W
25 U10 **Somerville** Texas, SW USA 30°21´N 96°31´W
25 T10 **Somerville Lake** ☒ Texas, SW USA
**Someş/Somesch/Someşul** see Szamos
103 N4 **Somme** ◇ department N France
95 K18 **Sommen** Jönköping, S Sweden 58°N 15°15´E
95 M18 **Sommen** ☒ S Sweden
101 K16 **Sommerein** Thüringen, C Germany 50°N 11°07´E
**Sommerfeld** see Lubsko
101 L14 **Sömmerda** Thüringen, C Germany 51°10´N 11°07´E
55 Y11 **Sommet Tabulaire** ▲ Nord Itoupé. ▲ S French Guiana
111 H23 **Somogy** off. Somogy Megye. ◇ county SW Hungary
**Somogy Megye** see Somogy
113 K17 **Somorja** see Šamorín
167 S6 **Son Hao** Houaphan, N Laos 20°33´N 104°02´E

42 I8 **Somoto** Madriz, NW Nicaragua 13°29´N 86°36´W
110 I11 **Sompolno** Wielkopolskie, C Poland 52°24´N 18°30´E
102 J17 **Somport, Col du** var. Puerto de Somport, Sp. Somport; anc. Summus Portus. pass France/Spain see also Somport
99 K15 **Son** Noord-Brabant, S Netherlands 51°32´N 05°34´E
95 H15 **Son** Akershus, S Norway 59°32´N 10°42´E
154 L9 **Son** var. Sone. ☒ C India
43 R16 **Soná** Veraguas, W Panama 08°00´N 81°20´W
**Sonag** see Zêkog
95 G24 **Sønderborg** Ger. Sonderburg. Syddanmark, SW Denmark 54°55´N 09°48´E
**Sonderburg** see Sønderborg
101 K15 **Sondershausen** Thüringen, C Germany 51°22´N 10°52´E
106 E6 **Sondrio** Lombardia, N Italy 46°11´N 09°52´E
**Sone** see Son
**Sonepur** see Subarnapur
57 V12 **Sóng Câu** Phú Yên, C Vietnam 13°26´N 109°12´E
167 R15 **Sông Đốc** Minh Hai, S Vietnam 09°03´N 104°51´E
81 H25 **Songea** Ruvuma, S Tanzania 10°42´S 35°39´E
163 X10 **Songhua Hu** ☒ NE China
163 Y7 **Songhua Jiang** var. Sungari. ☒ NE China
161 S8 **Songjiang** Shanghai Shi, E China 31°01´N 121°14´E
**Söngjin** see Kimch'aek
167 O16 **Songkhla** var. Songkla, Mal. Singora. Songkhla, SW Thailand 07°12´N 100°35´E
**Songkla** see Songkhla
163 T13 **Song Ling** ▲▲ NE China
129 U12 **Sông Ma** Laos Nam, ▲▲ Laos/Vietnam
163 W14 **Songnim** N North Korea 38°43´N 125°40´E
82 B10 **Songo** Uíge, NW Angola 07°30´S 14°56´E
83 M15 **Songo** Tete, NW Mozambique 15°36´S 32°45´E
79 F21 **Songololo** Bas-Congo, SW Dem. Rep. Congo 05°40´S 14°05´E
160 H7 **Songpan** var. Jin'an, Tib. Sungpu. Sichuan, C China 32°49´N 103°39´E
161 R11 **Songxi** Fujian, SE China 27°33´N 118°46´E
160 M6 **Songxian** var. Song Xian. Henan, C China 34°11´N 112°04´E
161 R10 **Songyang** var. Xiping; prev. Songyin. Zhejiang, SE China 28°29´N 119°27´E
**Song Xian** see Songxian
163 V9 **Songyuan** var. Fu-yü, Petuna; prev. Fuyu. Jilin, NE China 45°11´N 124°49´E
152 I10 **Sonipat** Haryāna, N India 29°00´N 77°01´E
93 M15 **Sonkajärvi** Pohjois-Savo, C Finland 63°40´N 27°31´E
167 R6 **Son La** Son La, N Vietnam 21°20´N 103°55´E
149 O16 **Sonmiani** Baluchistan, S Pakistan 25°24´N 66°37´E
149 O16 **Sonmiani Bay** bay S Pakistan
101 K18 **Sonneberg** Thüringen, C Germany 50°22´N 11°10´E
111 N24 **Sonntagshorn** ▲ Austria/ Germany 47°40´N 12°43´E
**Sonoita, Rio** var. Río Sonoyta. ☒ Mexico/USA
35 N7 **Sonoma** California, W USA 38°16´N 122°28´W
35 T3 **Sonoma Peak** ▲ Nevada, W USA 40°31´N 117°34´W
35 P8 **Sonora** California, W USA 37°58´N 120°22´W
25 O10 **Sonora** Texas, SW USA 30°34´N 100°39´W
40 F5 **Sonora** ◇ state NW Mexico
35 X17 **Sonoran Desert** var. Desierto de Altar. desert Mexico/USA see also Altar, Desierto de
40 G5 **Sonora, Río** ☒ NW Mexico
40 E3 **Sonoyta** var. Sonoita. Sonora, NW Mexico 31°49´N 112°50´W
**Sonoyta, Río** see Sonoita, Río
142 K6 **Sonqor** var. Sunqur. Kermānshāhān, W Iran 34°45´N 47°39´E
105 N9 **Sonseca** var. Sonseca con Casalgordo. Castilla-La Mancha, C Spain 39°40´N 03°56´W
**Sonseca con Casalgordo** see Sonseca
54 E7 **Sonsón** Antioquia, W Colombia 05°45´N 75°18´W
42 A9 **Sonsonate** Sonsonate, SW El Salvador 13°44´N 89°43´W
42 A9 **Sonsonate** ◇ department SW El Salvador
188 A10 **Sonsorol Islands** island group S Palau
112 J9 **Sonta** Hung. Szonta. prev. Szonta. Vojvodina, NW Serbia
167 S6 **Sơn Tây** var. Sontay. Ha Tây, N Vietnam 21°06´N 105°32´E
101 J25 **Sonthofen** Bayern, S Germany 47°31´N 10°16´E
80 O13 **Sool** off. Gobolka Sool. ◇ region N Somalia
**Soomaaliya/Soomaaliyeed, Jamuuriyada Demuqraadiga ee** see Somalia
**Soome Laht** see Finland, Gulf of
23 V5 **Soperton** Georgia, SE USA 32°22´N 82°35´W
167 S6 **Sop Hao** Houaphan, N Laos 20°33´N 104°02´E
**Sophia** see Sofia
171 S10 **Sopi** Pulau Morotai, E Indonesia 02°36´N 128°32´E
**Sopianae** see Pécs
171 U13 **Sopinusa** Papua Barat, E Indonesia 03°31´S 133°31´E

SOPO – SPRUCE KNOB


81 B14 **Sopo** ≈ W South Sudan
**Sopockinie/Sopotskin/Sopotskino** *see* Sapotskin
114 I9 **Sopot** Plovdiv, C Bulgaria *42°39′N 24°43′E*
110 I7 **Sopot** *Ger.* Zoppot. Pomorskie, N Poland *54°26′N 18°33′E*
167 O8 **Sop Prap** *var.* Ban Sop Prap. Lampang, NW Thailand *17°55′N 99°20′E*
111 G22 **Sopron** *Ger.* Ödenburg. Győr-Moson-Sopron, NW Hungary *47°40′N 16°35′E*
147 U11 **Sopu-Korgon** *var.* Sofi-Kurgan. Oshskaya Oblast', SW Kyrgyzstan *40°03′N 73°30′E*
152 H5 **Sopur** Jammu and Kashmir, NW India *34°19′N 74°30′E*
107 J15 **Sora** Lazio, C Italy *41°43′N 13°37′E*
154 N13 **Sorada** Odisha, E India *19°46′N 84°29′E*
93 H17 **Söråker** Västernorrland, C Sweden *62°32′N 17°32′E*
57 J17 **Sorata** La Paz, W Bolivia *15°47′S 68°38′W*
**Sorau/Sorau in der Niederlausitz** *see* Żary
105 Q14 **Sorbas** Andalucía, S Spain *37°06′N 02°06′W*
94 N11 **Sördellen** ◎ C Sweden
**Sord/Sórd Choluim Chille** *see* Swords
15 O11 **Sorel** Québec, SE Canada *46°03′N 73°06′W*
183 P17 **Sorell** Tasmania, SE Australia *42°49′S 147°34′E*
183 O17 **Sorell, Lake** ◎ Tasmania, SE Australia
106 E8 **Soresina** Lombardia, N Italy *45°17′N 09°51′E*
95 D14 **Sørfjorden** *fjord* S Norway
94 N11 **Sörforsa** Gävleborg, C Sweden *61°45′N 17°00′E*
103 R14 **Sorgues** Vaucluse, SE France *44°N 04°52′E*
136 K13 **Sorgun** Yozgat, C Turkey *39°49′N 35°10′E*
105 P5 **Soria** Castilla y León, N Spain *41°47′N 02°26′W*
105 P6 **Soria** ◈ *province* Castilla y León, N Spain
61 D19 **Soriano** Soriano, SW Uruguay *33°25′S 58°21′W*
61 D19 **Soriano** ◈ *department* SW Uruguay
92 O4 **Sørkapp** *headland* SW Svalbard *76°34′N 16°33′E*
143 T5 **Sorkh, Kūh-e** ▲▲ NE Iran
95 I23 **Sorø** Sjælland, E Denmark *55°26′N 11°34′E*
**Soro** *see* Ghazal, Bahr el
116 M8 **Soroca** *Rus.* Soroki. N Moldova *48°10′N 28°18′E*
60 L10 **Sorocaba** São Paulo, S Brazil *23°29′S 47°27′W*
**Sorochino** *see* Sarochyna
127 T7 **Sorochinsk** Orenburgskaya Oblast', W Russia *52°26′N 53°10′E*
**Soroki** *see* Soroca
117 Z7 **Sorokyne** *prev.* Krasnodon. Luhans'ka Oblast', E Ukraine *48°17′N 39°44′E*
188 H15 **Sorol** *atoll* Caroline Islands, W Micronesia
171 T12 **Sorong** Papua Barat, E Indonesia *0°49′S 131°16′E*
81 G17 **Soroti** C Uganda *01°42′N 33°37′E*
**Sørøy** *see* Sørøya
92 J8 **Sørøya** *var.* Sørøy, *Lapp.* Sállan. *island* N Norway
104 G11 **Sorraia, Rio** ≈ C Portugal
92 I10 **Sørreisa** Troms, N Norway *69°08′N 18°09′E*
107 K18 **Sorrento** *anc.* Surrentum. Campania, S Italy *40°37′N 14°23′E*
104 H10 **Sor, Ribeira de** *stream* C Portugal
195 T3 **Sør Rondane** *Eng.* Sor Rondane Mountains. ▲▲ Antarctica
**Sor Rondane Mountains** *see* Sør Rondane
93 H14 **Sorsele** Västerbotten, N Sweden *65°31′N 17°34′E*
107 B17 **Sorso** Sardegna, Italy, C Mediterranean Sea *40°46′N 08°33′E*
171 P4 **Sorsogon** Luzon, N Philippines *12°57′N 124°04′E*
105 U4 **Sort** Cataluña, NE Spain *42°25′N 01°07′E*
124 H11 **Sortavala** *prev.* Serdobol'. Respublika Kareliya, NW Russia *61°45′N 30°37′E*
107 L25 **Sortino** Sicilia, Italy, C Mediterranean Sea *37°10′N 15°02′E*
92 G10 **Sortland** Nordland, C Norway *68°44′N 15°25′E*
94 G9 **Sør-Trøndelag** ◈ *county* S Norway
95 I15 **Sørumsand** Akershus, S Norway *59°58′N 11°13′E*
118 D6 **Sörve Säär** *headland* SW Estonia *57°54′N 22°02′E*
95 K22 **Sösdala** Skåne, S Sweden *56°00′N 13°36′E*
105 R4 **Sos del Rey Católico** Aragón, NE Spain *42°30′N 01°13′W*
93 F15 **Sösjöfjällen** ▲ C Sweden *63°51′N 13°15′E*
126 K7 **Sosna** ≈ W Russia
62 H12 **Sosneado, Cerro** ▲ W Argentina *34°44′S 69°52′W*
125 S9 **Sosnogorsk** Respublika Komi, NW Russia *63°33′N 53°55′E*
124 J8 **Sosnovets** Respublika Kareliya, NW Russia *64°25′N 34°23′E*
**Sosnovets** *see* Sosnowiec
127 Q3 **Sosnovka** Chuvashskaya Respublika, W Russia *56°18′N 47°14′E*
125 S16 **Sosnovka** Kirovskaya Oblast', NW Russia *56°15′N 51°20′E*
124 M6 **Sosnovka** Murmanskaya Oblast', NW Russia *66°28′N 40°31′E*
126 M6 **Sosnovka** Tambovskaya Oblast', W Russia *53°14′N 41°19′E*
124 H12 **Sosnovo** *Fin.* Rautu. Leningradskaya Oblast', NW Russia *60°30′N 30°13′E*
127 V3 **Sosnovyy Bor** Respublika Bashkortostan, W Russia *55°51′N 57°09′E*
**Sosnovyy Bor** *see* Sasnovy Bor
111 J16 **Sosnowiec** *Ger.* Sosnowitz, *Rus.* Sosnovets. Śląskie, S Poland *50°16′N 19°07′E*
**Sosnowitz** *see* Sosnowiec
117 R2 **Sosnytsya** Chernihivs'ka Oblast', N Ukraine *51°31′N 32°30′E*
109 V10 **Šoštanj** N Slovenia *46°23′N 15°03′E*
122 G10 **Sos'va** Sverdlovskaya Oblast', C Russia *59°13′N 61°58′E*
54 D12 **Sotará, Volcán** ⛰ S Colombia *02°04′N 76°40′W*
76 D10 **Sotavento, Ilhas de** *var.* Leeward Islands. *island group* S Cape Verde
93 N15 **Sotkamo** Kainuu, C Finland *64°06′N 28°30′E*
109 W11 **Sotla** ≈ E Slovenia
41 P10 **Soto la Marina** Tamaulipas, C Mexico *23°44′N 98°10′W*
41 P10 **Soto la Marina, Río** ≈ C Mexico
95 B14 **Sotra** *island* S Norway
41 X12 **Sotuta** Yucatán, SE Mexico *20°34′N 89°00′W*
79 F17 **Souanké** Sangha, NW Congo *02°03′N 14°02′E*
76 M17 **Soubré** S Ivory Coast *05°50′N 06°35′W*
115 H24 **Soúda** *var.* Soúdha, *Eng.* Suda. Kríti, Greece, E Mediterranean Sea *35°29′N 24°04′E*
**Soúdha** *see* Soúda
**Soueida** *see* As Suwaydā'
114 L12 **Souflí** *prev.* Souflíon. Anatolikí Makedonía kai Thráki, NE Greece *41°12′N 26°18′E*
**Souflíon** *see* Souflí
45 S11 **Soufrière** W Saint Lucia *13°51′N 61°03′W*
45 X6 **Soufrière** ⛰ Basse Terre, S Guadeloupe *16°03′N 61°39′W*
102 M13 **Souillac** Lot, S France *44°53′N 01°29′E*
173 Y17 **Souillac** S Mauritius *20°31′S 57°31′E*
74 M5 **Souk Ahras** NE Algeria *36°14′N 08°00′E*
**Souk el Arba du Rharb/Souk-el-Arba-du-Rharb/Souk-el-Arba-el-Rhab** *see* Souk-el-Arba-Rharb
74 E6 **Souk-el-Arba-Rharb** *var.* Souk el Arba du Rharb, Souk-el-Arba-du-Rharb, Souk-el-Arba-el-Rhab. NW Morocco *34°38′N 06°00′W*
**Soukhné** *see* As Sukhnah
**Sŏul** *see* Seoul
102 J11 **Soulac-sur-Mer** Gironde, SW France *45°31′N 01°06′W*
99 L19 **Soumagne** Liège, E Belgium *50°36′N 05°48′E*
18 M14 **Sound Beach** Long Island, New York, NE USA *40°56′N 72°58′W*
95 J22 **Sound, The** *Dan.* Øresund, *Swe.* Öresund. *strait* Denmark/Sweden
115 H20 **Soúnio, Akrotírio** *headland* C Greece *37°39′N 24°01′E*
138 F8 **Soûr** *var.* Şūr; *anc.* Tyre. SW Lebanon *33°18′N 35°30′E*
**Sources, Mont-aux-** *see* Phofung
104 G8 **Soure** Coimbra, N Portugal *40°04′N 08°38′W*
11 W17 **Souris** Manitoba, S Canada *49°38′N 100°17′W*
13 Q14 **Souris** Prince Edward Island, SE Canada *46°22′N 62°16′W*
28 L2 **Souris River** *var.* Mouse River. ≈ Canada/USA
25 X10 **Sour Lake** Texas, SW USA *30°08′N 94°24′W*
115 F17 **Soúrpi** Thessalía, C Greece *39°07′N 22°55′E*
104 H11 **Sousel** Portalegre, C Portugal *38°57′N 07°40′W*
75 N6 **Sousse** *var.* Sūsah. NE Tunisia *35°46′N 10°38′E*
14 H11 **South** ≈ Ontario, S Canada
**South** *see* Sud
83 G23 **South Africa** *off.* Republic of South Africa, *Afr.* Suid-Afrika, Republiek van Suid-Afrika. ◆ *republic* S Africa
**South Africa, Republic of** *see* South Africa
46-47 **South America** *continent*
2 J17 **South American Plate** *tectonic feature*
97 M23 **Southampton** *hist.* Hamwih, *Lat.* Clausentum. S England, United Kingdom *50°54′N 01°23′W*
19 N14 **Southampton** Long Island, New York, NE USA *40°52′N 72°22′W*
9 P8 **Southampton Island** *island* Nunavut, NE Canada
151 P20 **South Andaman** *island* Andaman Islands, India, NE Indian Ocean
13 Q6 **South Aulatsivik Island** *island* Newfoundland and Labrador, E Canada
182 E4 **South Australia** ◈ *state* S Australia
**South Australian Abyssal Plain** *see* South Australian Plain
192 G11 **South Australian Basin** *undersea feature* SW Indian Ocean *38°00′S 126°00′E*
173 X12 **South Australian Plain** *var.* South Australian Abyssal Plain. *undersea feature* SE Indian Ocean
37 R13 **South Baldy** ▲ New Mexico, SW USA *33°59′N 107°11′W*
23 Y14 **South Bay** Florida, SE USA *26°39′N 80°43′W*
14 E12 **South Baymouth** Manitoulin Island, Ontario, S Canada *45°33′N 82°01′W*
30 L10 **South Beloit** Illinois, N USA *42°29′N 89°02′W*
31 O11 **South Bend** Indiana, N USA *41°40′N 86°15′W*
25 R6 **South Bend** Texas, SW USA *32°58′N 98°39′W*
32 F9 **South Bend** Washington, NW USA *46°38′N 123°48′W*
**South Beveland** *see* Zuid-Beveland
**South Borneo** *see* Kalimantan Selatan
21 U7 **South Boston** Virginia, NE USA *36°42′N 78°58′W*
182 F2 **South Branch Neales** *seasonal river* South Australia
21 U3 **South Branch Potomac River** ≈ West Virginia, NE USA
185 H19 **Southbridge** Canterbury, South Island, New Zealand *43°49′S 172°17′E*
19 N12 **Southbridge** Massachusetts, NE USA *42°03′N 72°00′W*
183 P17 **South Bruny Island** *island* Tasmania, SE Australia
18 L7 **South Burlington** Vermont, NE USA *44°27′N 73°08′W*
44 M6 **South Caicos** *island* S Turks and Caicos Islands
**South Cape** *see* Ka Lae
23 V3 **South Carolina** *off.* State of South Carolina, *also known as* The Palmetto State. ◈ *state* SE USA
**South Carpathians** *see* Carpații Meridionali
**South Celebes** *see* Sulawesi Selatan
21 Q5 **South Charleston** West Virginia, NE USA *38°22′N 81°42′W*
192 D7 **South China Basin** *undersea feature* SE South China Sea *15°00′N 115°00′E*
169 R8 **South China Sea** *sea* SE Asia
33 Z10 **South Dakota** *off.* State of South Dakota, *also known as* The Coyote State, Sunshine State. ◈ *state* N USA
23 X10 **South Daytona** Florida, SE USA *29°09′N 81°01′W*
37 R10 **South Domingo Pueblo** New Mexico, SW USA *35°28′N 106°24′W*
97 N23 **South Downs** *hill range* SE England, United Kingdom
83 I21 **South East** ◈ *district* SE Botswana
65 H15 **South East Bay** *bay* Ascension Island, C Atlantic Ocean
183 O17 **South East Cape** *headland* Tasmania, SE Australia *43°36′S 146°52′E*
38 K10 **Southeast Cape** *headland* Saint Lawrence Island, Alaska, USA *62°56′N 169°39′W*
**South-East Celebes** *see* Sulawesi Tenggara
192 G12 **Southeast Indian Ridge** *undersea feature* Indian Ocean/Pacific Ocean *50°00′S 110°00′E*
**Southeast Island** *see* Tagula Island
193 P13 **Southeast Pacific Basin** *var.* Belling Hausen Mulde. *undersea feature* SE Pacific Ocean *60°00′S 115°00′W*
65 H15 **South East Point** *headland* SE Ascension Island
183 O14 **South East Point** *headland* Victoria, S Australia *39°10′S 146°21′E*
191 Z3 **South East Point** *headland* Kiritimati, NE Kiribati *01°42′N 157°10′W*
44 L5 **Southeast Point** *headland* Mayaguana, SE The Bahamas *22°15′N 72°44′W*
**South-East Sulawesi** *see* Sulawesi Tenggara
11 U12 **Southend** Saskatchewan, C Canada *56°20′N 103°14′W*
97 P22 **Southend-on-Sea** E England, United Kingdom *51°33′N 00°43′E*
83 H20 **Southern** *var.* Bangwaketse, Ngwaketze. ◈ *district* SE Botswana
138 E13 **Southern** ◈ *district* S Israel
83 N15 **Southern** ◈ *region* S Malawi
155 J26 **Southern** ◈ *province* S Sri Lanka
83 I15 **Southern** ◈ *province* S Zambia
185 E19 **Southern Alps / Kā Tiritiri o Te Moana** *var.* Kā Tiritiri o Te Moana. ▲▲ South Island, New Zealand
190 K15 **Southern Cook Islands** *island group* S Cook Islands
180 K12 **Southern Cross** Western Australia *31°17′S 119°15′E*
80 A12 **Southern Darfur** ◈ *state* W Sudan
186 B7 **Southern Highlands** ◈ *province* W Papua New Guinea
11 V11 **Southern Indian Lake** ◎ Manitoba, C Canada
80 E11 **Southern Kordofan** ◈ *state* C Sudan
187 Z15 **Southern Lau Group** *island group* Lau Group, SE Fiji
81 I15 **Southern Nationalities** ◈ *region* S Ethiopia
173 S13 **Southern Ocean** *ocean*
21 T10 **Southern Pines** North Carolina, SE USA *35°10′N 79°23′W*
96 I13 **Southern Uplands** ▲▲ S Scotland, United Kingdom
**Southern Urals** *see* Yuzhnyy Ural
183 P16 **South Esk River** ≈ Tasmania, SE Australia
11 U16 **Southey** Saskatchewan, S Canada *50°53′N 104°27′W*
27 V2 **South Fabius River** ≈ Missouri, C USA
31 S10 **Southfield** Michigan, N USA *42°28′N 83°12′W*
192 K10 **South Fiji Basin** *undersea feature* S Pacific Ocean *26°00′S 175°00′E*
97 Q22 **South Foreland** *headland* SE England, United Kingdom *51°08′N 01°22′E*
35 P7 **South Fork American River** ≈ California, W USA
28 K7 **South Fork Grand River** ≈ South Dakota, N USA
35 T12 **South Fork Kern River** ≈ California, W USA
39 Q7 **South Fork Koyukuk River** ≈ Alaska, USA
39 Q11 **South Fork Kuskokwim River** ≈ Alaska, USA
26 H2 **South Fork Republican River** ≈ C USA
26 L3 **South Fork Solomon River** ≈ Kansas, C USA
31 P5 **South Fox Island** *island* Michigan, N USA
20 G8 **South Fulton** Tennessee, S USA *36°28′N 88°53′W*
195 U10 **South Geomagnetic Pole** *pole* Antarctica
65 J20 **South Georgia** *island* South Georgia and the South Sandwich Islands, SW Atlantic Ocean
65 K21 **South Georgia and the South Sandwich Islands** ◇ *UK Overseas Territory* SW Atlantic Ocean
47 Y14 **South Georgia Ridge** *var.* North Scotia Ridge. *undersea feature* SW Atlantic Ocean *54°00′S 40°00′W*
181 Q1 **South Goulburn Island** *island* Northern Territory, N Australia
153 U16 **South Hatia Island** *island* SE Bangladesh
31 O10 **South Haven** Michigan, N USA *42°24′N 86°16′W*
21 V7 **South Hill** Virginia, NE USA *36°43′N 78°07′W*
**South Holland** *see* Zuid-Holland
21 P8 **South Holston Lake** ▦ Tennessee/Virginia, S USA
175 N1 **South Honshu Ridge** *undersea feature* W Pacific Ocean
26 M6 **South Hutchinson** Kansas, C USA *38°01′N 97°56′W*
151 K21 **South Huvadhu Atoll** *atoll* S Maldives
173 U14 **South Indian Basin** *undersea feature* Indian Ocean/Pacific Ocean *60°00′S 120°00′E*
11 W11 **South Indian Lake** Manitoba, C Canada *56°48′N 98°56′W*
81 I17 **South Island** *island* NW Kenya
185 C20 **South Island / Te Waipounamu** *var.* Te Waipounamu. *island* S New Zealand
65 B23 **South Jason** *island* Jason Islands, NW Falkland Islands
**South Kalimantan** *see* Kalimantan Selatan
**South Karelia** *see* Etelä-Karjala
163 X15 **South Korea** *off.* Republic of Korea, *Kor.* Taehan Min'guk. ◆ *republic* E Asia
35 Q6 **South Lake Tahoe** California, W USA *38°56′N 119°57′W*
25 N6 **Southland** Texas, SW USA *33°16′N 101°31′W*
185 B23 **Southland** *off.* Southland Region. ◈ *region* South Island, New Zealand
**Southland Region** *see* Southland
29 N15 **South Loup River** ≈ Nebraska, C USA
151 K19 **South Maalhosmadulu Atoll** *atoll* N Maldives
14 E15 **South Maitland** ≈ Ontario, S Canada
192 E8 **South Makassar Basin** *undersea feature* E Java Sea
31 O6 **South Manitou Island** *island* Michigan, N USA
151 K18 **South Miladhunmadulu Atoll** *var.* Noonu. *atoll* N Maldives
21 X8 **South Mills** North Carolina, SE USA *36°28′N 76°18′W*
8 H9 **South Nahanni** ≈ Northwest Territories, NW Canada
39 P13 **South Naknek** Alaska, USA *58°39′N 157°01′W*
14 M13 **South Nation** ≈ Ontario, SE Canada
44 F9 **South Negril Point** *headland* W Jamaica *18°14′N 78°21′W*
151 K20 **South Nilandhe Atoll** *var.* Dhaalu Atoll. *atoll* C Maldives
36 L2 **South Ogden** Utah, W USA *41°09′N 111°58′W*
18 M14 **Southold** Long Island, New York, NE USA *41°03′N 72°24′W*
194 H1 **South Orkney Islands** *island group* Antarctica
137 S9 **South Ossetia** *former autonomous region* SW Georgia
137 T9 **South Ossetia** ◈ *former autonomous area* C Georgia
**South Pacific Basin** *see* Southwest Pacific Basin
19 P7 **South Paris** Maine, NE USA *44°14′N 70°33′W*
189 U13 **South Pass** *passage* Chuuk Islands, C Micronesia
33 U15 **South Pass** *pass* Wyoming, C USA
20 K10 **South Pittsburg** Tennessee, S USA *35°00′N 85°42′W*
28 K15 **South Platte River** ≈ Colorado/Nebraska, C USA
31 T16 **South Point** Ohio, N USA *38°25′N 82°35′W*
65 G15 **South Point** *headland* S Ascension Island
31 R6 **South Point** *headland* Michigan, N USA *44°51′N 83°17′W*
**South Point** *see* Ka Lae
195 Q9 **South Pole** *pole* Antarctica
183 P17 **Southport** Tasmania, SE Australia *43°26′S 146°57′E*
97 K17 **Southport** NW England, United Kingdom *53°39′N 03°01′W*
21 V12 **Southport** North Carolina, SE USA *33°55′N 78°00′W*
19 P8 **South Portland** Maine, NE USA *43°38′N 70°14′W*
14 H12 **South River** Ontario, S Canada *45°50′N 79°23′W*
21 U11 **South River** ≈ North Carolina, SE USA
96 K5 **South Ronaldsay** *island* NE Scotland, United Kingdom
36 L2 **South Salt Lake** Utah, W USA *40°42′N 111°52′W*
65 L21 **South Sandwich Islands** *island group* SW Atlantic Ocean
65 K21 **South Sandwich Trench** *undersea feature* SW Atlantic Ocean *56°30′S 25°00′W*
11 S16 **South Saskatchewan** ≈ Alberta/Saskatchewan, S Canada
65 I21 **South Scotia Ridge** *undersea feature* S Scotia Sea
11 V10 **South Seal** ≈ Manitoba, C Canada
194 G4 **South Shetland Islands** *island group* Antarctica
65 H22 **South Shetland Trough** *undersea feature* Atlantic Ocean/Pacific Ocean *61°00′S 59°30′W*
97 M14 **South Shields** NE England, United Kingdom *55°N 01°25′W*
29 R13 **South Sioux City** Nebraska, C USA *42°28′N 96°24′W*
192 J9 **South Solomon Trench** *undersea feature* W Pacific Ocean
183 V3 **South Stradbroke Island** *island* Queensland, E Australia
81 E15 **South Sudan** *off.* Republic of South Sudan. ◆ E Africa
**South Sulawesi** *see* Sulawesi Selatan
**South Sumatra** *see* Sumatera Selatan
184 K11 **South Taranaki Bight** *bight* SE Tasman Sea
**South Tasmania Plateau** *see* Tasman Plateau
36 M15 **South Tucson** Arizona, SW USA *32°11′N 110°56′W*
12 H9 **South Twin Island** *island* Nunavut, C Canada
**South Tyrol** *see* Trentino-Alto Adige
96 E9 **South Uist** *island* NW Scotland, United Kingdom
79 C15 **South-West** *Fr.* Sud-Ouest. ◈ *region* W Cameroon
**South-West Africa/South West Africa** *see* Namibia
65 F15 **South West Bay** *bay* Ascension Island, C Atlantic Ocean
183 N18 **South West Cape** *headland* Tasmania, SE Australia *43°34′S 146°01′E*
185 B26 **South West Cape** *headland* Stewart Island, New Zealand *47°15′S 167°28′E*
38 J10 **Southwest Cape** *headland* Saint Lawrence Island, Alaska, USA *63°19′N 171°27′W*
**Southwest Indian Ocean Ridge** *see* Southwest Indian Ridge
173 N11 **Southwest Indian Ridge** *var.* Southwest Indian Ocean Ridge. *undersea feature* SW Indian Ocean *43°00′S 40°00′E*
192 L10 **Southwest Pacific Basin** *var.* South Pacific Basin. *undersea feature* SE Pacific Ocean *40°00′S 150°00′W*
191 X3 **South West Point** *headland* Kiritimati, NE Kiribati *01°53′N 157°34′E*
65 G25 **South West Point** *headland* SW Saint Helena *16°00′S 05°48′W*
44 H2 **Southwest Point** *headland* Great Abaco, N The Bahamas *25°50′N 77°12′W*
25 P5 **South Wichita River** ≈ Texas, SW USA
97 Q20 **Southwold** E England, United Kingdom *52°15′N 01°36′E*
19 Q12 **South Yarmouth** Massachusetts, NE USA *41°38′N 70°09′W*
116 J10 **Sovata** *Hung.* Szováta. Mureș, C Romania *46°36′N 25°04′E*
107 N22 **Soverato** Calabria, SW Italy *38°40′N 16°31′E*
121 O4 **Sovereign Base Area** *uk military installation* S Cyprus
**Sovetabad** *see* Ghafurov
126 C2 **Sovetsk** *Ger.* Tilsit. Kaliningradskaya Oblast', W Russia *53°04′N 21°52′E*
125 Q15 **Sovetsk** Kirovskaya Oblast', NW Russia *57°37′N 49°02′E*
127 N10 **Sovetskaya** Rostovskaya Oblast', SW Russia *49°00′N 42°09′E*
**Sovetskoye** *see* Ketchenery
146 I15 **Sovet"yab** *prev.* Sovet"yap. Ahal Welaýaty, S Turkmenistan *36°29′N 61°13′E*
**Sovet"yap** *see* Sovet"yab
**Sovyets'kyy** *see* Ichki
83 I18 **Sowa** *var.* Sua. Central, NE Botswana *20°33′S 26°18′E*
83 I18 **Sowa Pan** *var.* Sua Pan. *salt lake* NE Botswana
83 J21 **Soweto** Gauteng, NE South Africa *26°08′S 27°54′E*
147 R11 **So'x** *Rus.* Sokh. Far'gona Viloyati, E Uzbekistan *39°56′N 71°10′E*
**Sōya-kaikyō** *see* La Pérouse Strait
165 T1 **Sōya-misaki** *headland* Hokkaidō, NE Japan *45°31′N 141°55′E*
125 N7 **Soyana** ≈ NW Russia
146 A8 **Soye, Mys** *var.* Mys Suz. *headland* NW Turkmenistan *41°47′N 52°27′E*
82 A10 **Soyo** Zaire Province, NW Angola *06°07′S 12°18′E*
80 J10 **Soyra** ▲ C Eritrea *14°46′N 39°29′E*
145 P15 **Sozak** *Kaz.* Sozaq; *prev.* Suzak. Turkestan, S Kazakhstan *44°09′N 68°28′E*
**Sozaq** *see* Sozak
119 P16 **Sozh** ≈ NE Europe
114 N10 **Sozopol** *prev.* Sizebolu; *anc.* Apollonia. Burgas, E Bulgaria *42°25′N 27°42′E*
99 L20 **Spa** Liège, E Belgium *50°29′N 05°52′E*
194 I7 **Spaatz Island** *island* Antarctica
144 M14 **Space Launching Centre** *space station* Kzylorda, S Kazakhstan
105 O7 **Spain** *off.* Kingdom of Spain, *Sp.* España, Reino de España; *anc.* Hispania, Iberia, *Lat.* Hispana. ◆ *monarchy* SW Europe
**Spain, Kingdom of** *see* Spain
**Spalato** *see* Split
97 O19 **Spalding** E England, United Kingdom *52°49′N 00°06′W*
14 D11 **Spanish** Ontario, S Canada *46°12′N 82°21′W*
36 L3 **Spanish Fork** Utah, W USA *40°09′N 111°40′W*
64 B12 **Spanish Point** *headland* C Bermuda *32°18′N 64°49′W*
14 E9 **Spanish River** ≈ Ontario, S Canada
44 K13 **Spanish Town** *hist.* St.Iago de la Vega. C Jamaica *18°N 76°57′W*
**Spánta, Akrotírio** *see* Spátha, Akrotírio
35 Q5 **Sparks** Nevada, W USA *39°32′N 119°45′W*
**Sparnacum** *see* Épernay
95 N16 **Sparreholm** Södermanland, C Sweden *59°04′N 16°51′E*
23 U4 **Sparta** Georgia, SE USA *33°16′N 82°58′W*
30 K16 **Sparta** Illinois, N USA *38°07′N 89°42′W*
31 P9 **Sparta** Michigan, N USA *43°09′N 85°42′W*
21 R8 **Sparta** North Carolina, SE USA *36°30′N 81°07′W*
20 L9 **Sparta** Tennessee, S USA *35°55′N 85°30′W*
30 I7 **Sparta** Wisconsin, N USA *43°57′N 90°50′W*
**Sparta** *see* Spárti
21 Q11 **Spartanburg** South Carolina, SE USA *34°56′N 81°57′W*
115 F21 **Spárti** *Eng.* Sparta. Pelopónnisos, S Greece *37°05′N 22°25′E*
107 B21 **Spartivento, Capo** *headland* Sardegna, Italy, C Mediterranean Sea *38°52′N 08°50′E*
11 P17 **Sparwood** British Columbia, SW Canada *49°45′N 114°45′W*
126 I4 **Spas-Demensk** Kaluzhskaya Oblast', W Russia *54°22′N 34°16′E*
126 M4 **Spas-Klepiki** Ryazanskaya Oblast', W Russia *55°08′N 40°15′E*
**Spasovo** *see* Kulen Vakuf
123 R15 **Spassk-Dal'niy** Primorskiy Kray, SE Russia *44°34′N 132°52′E*
126 M5 **Spassk-Ryazanskiy** Ryazanskaya Oblast', W Russia *54°25′N 40°21′E*
115 H19 **Spáta** Attikí, C Greece *37°58′N 23°55′E*
121 Q11 **Spátha, Akrotírio** *var.* Akrotírio Spánta. *headland* Kríti, Greece, E Mediterranean Sea *35°42′N 23°44′E*
**Špatrjan** *see* Paternion
28 I9 **Spearfish** South Dakota, N USA *44°29′N 103°51′W*
25 O1 **Spearman** Texas, SW USA *36°12′N 101°13′W*
65 C25 **Speedwell Island** *island* S Falkland Islands
65 C25 **Speedwell Island Settlement** S Falkland Islands *52°13′S 59°41′W*
65 G25 **Speery Island** *island* S Saint Helena
45 N14 **Speightstown** NW Barbados *13°15′N 59°39′W*
106 I13 **Spello** Umbria, C Italy *43°00′N 12°41′E*
39 R12 **Spenard** Alaska, USA *61°09′N 150°03′W*
**Spence Bay** *see* Taloyoak
31 O14 **Spencer** Indiana, N USA *39°18′N 86°46′W*
29 T12 **Spencer** Iowa, C USA *43°09′N 95°07′W*
29 P12 **Spencer** Nebraska, C USA *42°52′N 98°42′W*
21 S9 **Spencer** North Carolina, SE USA *35°41′N 80°26′W*
20 L9 **Spencer** Tennessee, S USA *35°46′N 85°27′W*
21 Q4 **Spencer** West Virginia, NE USA *38°48′N 81°22′W*
30 K6 **Spencer** Wisconsin, N USA *44°46′N 90°17′W*
182 G10 **Spencer, Cape** *headland* South Australia *35°17′S 136°52′E*
39 V13 **Spencer, Cape** *headland* Alaska, USA *58°12′N 136°39′W*
182 H9 **Spencer Gulf** *gulf* South Australia
18 F9 **Spencerport** New York, NE USA *43°11′N 77°48′W*
31 Q12 **Spencerville** Ohio, N USA *40°42′N 84°21′W*
115 E17 **Spercheiáda** *var.* Sperhiada, Sperkhiás. Stereá Elláda, C Greece *38°54′N 22°07′E*
115 E17 **Spercheiós** ≈ C Greece
**Sperhiada** *see* Spercheiáda
95 G14 **Sperillen** ◎ S Norway
**Sperkhiás** *see* Spercheiáda
101 I18 **Spessart** *hill range* C Germany
**Spétsai** *see* Spétses
115 G21 **Spétses** *prev.* Spétsai. Spétses, S Greece *37°16′N 23°09′E*
115 G21 **Spétses** *island* S Greece
96 J8 **Spey** ≈ NE Scotland, United Kingdom
101 G20 **Speyer** *Eng.* Spires; *anc.* Civitas Nemetum, Spira. Rheinland-Pfalz, SW Germany *49°18′N 08°26′E*
101 G20 **Speyerbach** ≈ W Germany
107 N20 **Spezzano Albanese** Calabria, SW Italy *39°40′N 16°17′E*
**Spice Islands** *see* Maluku
100 F9 **Spiekeroog** *island* NW Germany
109 W9 **Spielfeld** Steiermark, SE Austria *46°43′N 15°36′E*
65 N21 **Spiess Seamount** *undersea feature* S Atlantic Ocean *53°00′S 02°00′W*
108 E9 **Spiez** Bern, W Switzerland *46°42′N 07°41′E*
98 G13 **Spijkenisse** Zuid-Holland, SW Netherlands *51°52′N 04°19′E*
39 T6 **Spike Mountain** ▲ Alaska, USA *67°42′N 141°39′W*
115 I25 **Spíli** Kríti, Greece, E Mediterranean Sea *35°12′N 24°33′E*
108 D10 **Spillgerten** ▲ W Switzerland *46°34′N 07°25′E*
118 F9 **Spilve** ✈ (Rīga) C Latvia *56°55′N 24°03′E*
107 N17 **Spinazzola** Puglia, SE Italy *40°58′N 16°06′E*
149 O9 **Spīn Bōldak** *prev.* Spīn Būldak. Kandahār, S Afghanistan *31°01′N 66°23′E*
**Spīn Būldak** *see* Spīn Bōldak
**Spira** *see* Speyer
**Spirdingsee** *see* Śniardwy, Jezioro
**Spires** *see* Speyer
29 T11 **Spirit Lake** Iowa, C USA *43°25′N 95°06′W*
29 T11 **Spirit Lake** ◎ Iowa, C USA
11 N13 **Spirit River** Alberta, W Canada *55°46′N 118°51′W*
11 S14 **Spiritwood** Saskatchewan, S Canada *53°18′N 107°33′W*
27 R11 **Spiro** Oklahoma, C USA *35°14′N 94°37′W*
111 L19 **Spišská Nová Ves** *Ger.* Neudorf, Zipser Neudorf, *Hung.* Igló. Košický Kraj, E Slovakia *48°58′N 20°35′E*
137 T11 **Spitak** NW Armenia *40°51′N 44°17′E*
92 O2 **Spitsbergen** *island* NW Svalbard
**Spittal** *see* Spittal an der Drau
109 R9 **Spittal an der Drau** *var.* Spittal. Kärnten, S Austria *46°48′N 13°30′E*
109 V3 **Spitz** Niederösterreich, NE Austria *48°24′N 15°22′E*
94 D9 **Spjelkavik** Møre og Romsdal, S Norway *62°28′N 06°22′E*
25 W10 **Splendora** Texas, SW USA *30°13′N 95°09′W*
113 E14 **Split** *It.* Spalato. Split-Dalmacija, S Croatia *43°31′N 16°27′E*
113 E14 **Split** ✈ Split-Dalmacija, S Croatia *43°33′N 16°19′E*
113 E14 **Split-Dalmacija** *off.* Splitsko-Dalmatinska Županija. ◈ *province* S Croatia
11 X12 **Split Lake** ◎ Manitoba, C Canada
**Splitsko-Dalmatinska Županija** *see* Split-Dalmacija
108 H10 **Splügen** Graubünden, S Switzerland *46°33′N 09°18′E*
**Spodnji Dravograd** *see* Dravograd
25 P12 **Spofford** Texas, SW USA *29°10′N 100°24′W*
118 J11 **Špoģi** SE Latvia *56°03′N 26°47′E*
32 L8 **Spokane** Washington, NW USA *47°40′N 117°26′W*
32 L8 **Spokane River** ≈ Washington, NW USA
106 I13 **Spoleto** Umbria, C Italy *42°44′N 12°44′E*
30 I4 **Spooner** Wisconsin, N USA *45°51′N 91°49′W*
30 K12 **Spoon River** ≈ Illinois, N USA
21 W5 **Spotsylvania** Virginia, NE USA *38°12′N 77°35′W*
32 L8 **Sprague** Washington, NW USA *47°19′N 117°55′W*
170 J5 **Spratly Island** *Chin.* Nanwei Dao, *Viet.* Đao Trương Sa Lơn. *island* SW Spratly Islands
192 E6 **Spratly Islands** *Chin.* Nansha Qundao, *Viet.* Quân Đao Trương Sa, *Fil.* Kapuluan ng Kalayaan, *Mal.* Kepulauan Spratly. ◇ *disputed territory* SE Asia
**Spratly, Kepulauan** *see* Spratly Islands
32 J12 **Spray** Oregon, NW USA *44°30′N 119°38′W*
112 I11 **Spreča** ≈ N Bosnia and Herzegovina
100 P13 **Spree** ≈ E Germany
100 P13 **Spreewald** *wetland* NE Germany
101 P14 **Spremberg** Brandenburg, E Germany *51°34′N 14°22′E*
25 W11 **Spring** Texas, SW USA *30°03′N 95°24′W*
31 Q10 **Spring Arbor** Michigan, N USA *42°12′N 84°33′W*
83 E23 **Springbok** Northern Cape, W South Africa *29°44′S 17°56′E*
18 I15 **Spring City** Pennsylvania, NE USA *40°10′N 75°33′W*
20 L9 **Spring City** Tennessee, S USA *35°41′N 84°51′W*
36 L4 **Spring City** Utah, W USA *39°28′N 111°30′W*
35 W3 **Spring Creek** Nevada, W USA *40°45′N 115°40′W*
27 S9 **Springdale** Arkansas, C USA *36°11′N 94°07′W*
31 Q14 **Springdale** Ohio, N USA *39°17′N 84°29′W*
100 I13 **Springe** Niedersachsen, N Germany *52°13′N 09°33′E*
37 U9 **Springer** New Mexico, SW USA *36°21′N 104°35′W*
37 W7 **Springfield** Colorado, C USA *37°24′N 102°36′W*
23 W5 **Springfield** Georgia, SE USA *32°21′N 81°20′W*
30 K14 **Springfield** *state capital* Illinois, N USA *39°48′N 89°39′W*
20 L6 **Springfield** Kentucky, S USA *37°42′N 85°18′W*
18 M12 **Springfield** Massachusetts, NE USA *42°06′N 72°32′W*
29 T10 **Springfield** Minnesota, N USA *44°15′N 94°58′W*
27 T7 **Springfield** Missouri, C USA *37°13′N 93°18′W*
31 R13 **Springfield** Ohio, N USA *39°55′N 83°49′W*
32 G13 **Springfield** Oregon, NW USA *44°03′N 123°01′W*
29 Q12 **Springfield** South Dakota, N USA *42°51′N 97°54′W*
20 J8 **Springfield** Tennessee, S USA *36°30′N 86°54′W*
18 M9 **Springfield** Vermont, NE USA *43°18′N 72°27′W*
30 K14 **Springfield, Lake** ▦ Illinois, N USA
55 T8 **Spring Garden** NE Guyana *06°58′N 58°34′W*
30 K8 **Spring Green** Wisconsin, N USA *43°10′N 90°02′W*
29 X11 **Spring Grove** Minnesota, N USA *43°33′N 91°38′W*
13 P15 **Springhill** Nova Scotia, SE Canada *45°40′N 64°04′W*
23 V12 **Spring Hill** Florida, SE USA *28°28′N 82°36′W*
27 R4 **Spring Hill** Kansas, C USA *38°44′N 94°49′W*
22 G4 **Springhill** Louisiana, S USA *33°01′N 93°27′W*
20 I9 **Spring Hill** Tennessee, S USA *35°46′N 86°55′W*
21 U10 **Spring Lake** North Carolina, SE USA *35°10′N 78°58′W*
24 M4 **Springlake** Texas, SW USA *34°13′N 102°18′W*
35 W11 **Spring Mountains** ▲▲ Nevada, W USA
65 B24 **Spring Point** West Falkland, Falkland Islands *51°49′S 60°27′W*
27 W9 **Spring River** ≈ Arkansas/Missouri, C USA
27 S7 **Spring River** ≈ Missouri/Oklahoma, C USA
83 J21 **Springs** Gauteng, NE South Africa *26°16′S 28°26′E*
185 H16 **Springs Junction** West Coast, South Island, New Zealand *42°21′S 172°11′E*
181 X8 **Springsure** Queensland, E Australia *24°09′S 148°06′E*
29 W11 **Spring Valley** Minnesota, N USA *43°41′N 92°23′W*
18 K13 **Spring Valley** New York, NE USA *41°10′N 73°58′W*
29 N12 **Springview** Nebraska, C USA *42°49′N 99°45′W*
18 D11 **Springville** New York, NE USA *42°27′N 78°52′W*
36 L3 **Springville** Utah, W USA *40°10′N 111°36′W*
**Sprottau** *see* Szprotawa
15 V4 **Sproule, Pointe** *headland* Québec, SE Canada *49°47′N 67°02′W*
11 Q14 **Spruce Grove** Alberta, SW Canada *53°36′N 113°55′W*
21 T4 **Spruce Knob** ▲ West Virginia, NE USA *38°40′N 79°37′W*




◆ Country
● Country Capital
◇ Dependent Territory
◗ Dependent Territory Capital
◈ Administrative Regions
✈ International Airport
▲ Mountain
▲▲ Mountain Range
⛰ Volcano
≈ River
◎ Lake
▦ Reservoir

SPRUCE MOUNTAIN – STOWMARKET


35 *X3* **Spruce Mountain** ▲ Nevada, W USA 40°33′N 114°46′W
21 *P9* **Spruce Pine** North Carolina, SE USA 35°55′N 82°03′W
98 *G13* **Spui** ≈ SW Netherlands
107 *O19* **Spulico, Capo** *headland* S Italy 39°57′N 16°38′E
25 *O5* **Spur** Texas, SW USA 33°28′N 100°51′W
97 *O17* **Spurn Head** *headland* E England, United Kingdom 53°34′N 00°06′E
99 *H20* **Spy** Namur, S Belgium 50°29′N 04°43′E
95 *I15* **Spydeberg** Østfold, S Norway 59°36′N 11°04′E
185 *J17* **Spy Glass Point** *var.* Piripaua. *headland* South Island, New Zealand 42°33′S 173°31′E
10 *L17* **Squamish** British Columbia, SW Canada 49°41′N 123°11′W
19 *O8* **Squam Lake** ◎ New Hampshire, NE USA
19 *S2* **Squa Pan Mountain** ▲ Maine, NE USA 46°36′N 68°09′W
39 *N16* **Squaw Harbor** Unga Island, Alaska, USA 55°12′N 160°41′W
14 *E11* **Squaw Island** *island* Ontario, S Canada
107 *O22* **Squillace, Golfo di** *gulf* S Italy
107 *Q18* **Squinzano** Puglia, SE Italy 40°26′N 18°03′E
**Sráid na Cathrach** *see* Milltown Malbay
167 *S11* **Srâlau** Stung Treng, N Cambodia 14°03′N 105°46′E
**Srath an Urláir** *see* Stranorlar
112 *G10* **Srbac** ◈ Republika Srpska, N Bosnia and Herzegovina
**Srbija** *see* Serbia
**Srbinje** *see* Foča
112 *K9* **Srbobran** *var.* Bácsszenttamás, ***Hung.*** Szenttamás. Vojvodina, N Serbia 45°33′N 19°46′E
**Srbobran** *see* Donji Vakuf
167 *R13* **Srê Âmběl** Koh Kong, SW Cambodia 11°07′N 103°46′E
112 *K13* **Srebrenica** Republika Srpska, E Bosnia and Herzegovina 44°04′N 19°18′E
112 *I11* **Srebrenik** Federacija Bosne I Hercegovine, NE Bosnia and Herzegovina 44°42′N 18°30′E
114 *K10* **Sredets** *prev.* Syulemeshlii. Stara Zagora, C Bulgaria 42°16′N 25°40′E
114 *M10* **Sredets** *prev.* Grudovo. ◈ Burgas, E Bulgaria
114 *M10* **Sredetska Reka** ≈ SE Bulgaria
123 *U9* **Sredinnyy Khrebet** ▲▲ E Russia
114 *N7* **Sredishte** ***Rom.*** Beibunar; ***prev.*** Knyazhevo. Dobrich, NE Bulgaria 43°51′N 27°30′E
114 *I10* **Sredna Gora** ▲▲ C Bulgaria
123 *R7* **Srednekolymsk** Respublika Sakha (Yakutiya), NE Russia 67°28′N 153°52′E
126 *K7* **Srednerusskaya Vozvyshennost'** ***Eng.*** Central Russian Upland. ▲▲ W Russia
122 *L9* **Srednesibirskoye Ploskogor'ye** *var.* Central Siberian Uplands, ***Eng.*** Central Siberian Plateau. ▲▲ N Russia
125 *V13* **Sredniy Ural** ▲▲ NW Russia
167 *T12* **Srê Khtŭm** Mondolkiri, E Cambodia 12°10′N 106°52′E
110 *G12* **Śrem** Wielkopolskie, C Poland 52°07′N 17°00′E
112 *K10* **Sremska Mitrovica** *prev.* Mitrovica, ***Ger.*** Mitrowitz. Vojvodina, NW Serbia 44°58′N 19°37′E
167 *R11* **Srêng, Stœ̆ng** ≈ NW Cambodia
167 *R11* **Srê Noy** Siem Reap, NW Cambodia 13°47′N 104°03′E
**Srepok, Sông** *see* Srêpôk, Tônle
167 *T12* **Srêpôk, Tônle** *var.* Sông Srepok. ≈ Cambodia/Vietnam
123 *P13* **Sretensk** Zabaykal'skiy Kray, S Russia 52°14′N 117°33′E
169 *R10* **Sri Aman** Sarawak, East Malaysia 01°13′N 111°25′E
117 *R4* **Sribne** Chernihivs'ka Oblast', N Ukraine 50°40′N 32°55′E
**Sri Jayawardanapura** *see* Sri Jayewardenepura Kotte
155 *I25* **Sri Jayewardenepura Kotte** *var.* Sri Jayawardanapura. ● (Sri Lanka - administrative and legislative) Western Province, W Sri Lanka 06°54′N 79°58′E
155 *M14* **Srīkākulam** Andhra Pradesh, E India 18°18′N 83°54′E
155 *I25* **Sri Lanka** *off.* Democratic Socialist Republic of Sri Lanka; ***prev.*** Ceylon. ◆ *republic* S Asia
130 *F14* **Sri Lanka** *island* S Asia
**Sri Lanka, Democratic Socialist Republic of** *see* Sri Lanka
153 *V14* **Srimangal** Sylhet, E Bangladesh 24°19′N 91°40′E
**Sri Mohangorh** *see* Shri Mohangarh
152 *H5* **Srīnagar** *state capital* Jammu and Kashmir, N India 34°07′N 74°50′E
167 *N10* **Srinagarind Reservoir** ◎ W Thailand
155 *F19* **Sringeri** Karnātaka, W India 13°26′N 75°13′E
155 *K25* **Sri Pada** ***Eng.*** Adam's Peak. ▲ S Sri Lanka 06°49′N 80°25′E
**Sri Saket** *see* Si Sa Ket
111 *G14* **Środa Śląska** ***Ger.*** Neumarkt. Dolnośląskie, SW Poland 51°10′N 16°30′E
110 *H12* **Środa Wielkopolska** Wielkopolskie, C Poland 52°13′N 17°17′E
**Srpska Kostajnica** *see* Bosanska Kostajnica
113 *G14* **Srpska, Republika** ◈ *republic* Bosnia and Herzegovina
**Srpski Brod** *see* Bosanski Brod
**Ssu-ch'uan** *see* Sichuan
**Ssu-p'ing/Ssu-p'ing-chieh** *see* Siping
**Stablo** *see* Stavelot
99 *G15* **Stabroek** Antwerpen, N Belgium 51°21′N 04°22′E
**Stackeln** *see* Strenči
96 *I5* **Stack Skerry** *island* N Scotland, United Kingdom
100 *I9* **Stade** Niedersachsen, NW Germany 53°36′N 09°29′E
94 *C10* **Stadlandet** *peninsula* S Norway
109 *R5* **Stadl-Paura** Oberösterreich, NW Austria 48°05′N 13°52′E
119 *L20* **Stadolichy** ***Rus.*** Stodolichi. Homyel'skaya Voblasts', SE Belarus 51°44′N 28°30′E
98 *P7* **Stadskanaal** Groningen, NE Netherlands 53°N 06°55′E
101 *H16* **Stadtallendorf** Hessen, C Germany 50°49′N 09°01′E
101 *K23* **Stadtbergen** Bayern, S Germany 48°21′N 10°50′E
108 *G7* **Stäfa** Zürich, NE Switzerland 47°14′N 08°45′E
95 *K23* **Staffanstorp** Skåne, S Sweden 55°38′N 13°13′E
101 *K18* **Staffelstein** Bayern, C Germany 50°05′N 11°00′E
97 *L19* **Stafford** C England, United Kingdom 52°48′N 02°07′W
26 *L6* **Stafford** Kansas, C USA 37°57′N 98°36′W
21 *W4* **Stafford** Virginia, NE USA 38°26′N 77°27′W
97 *L19* **Staffordshire** *cultural region* C England, United Kingdom
19 *N12* **Stafford Springs** Connecticut, NE USA 41°57′N 72°18′W
115 *H14* **Stágira** Kentrikí Makedonía, N Greece 40°31′N 23°46′E
118 *G7* **Staicele** N Latvia 57°52′N 24°48′E
**Ştaierdorf-Anina** *see* Anina
109 *V8* **Stainz** Steiermark, SE Austria 46°55′N 15°18′E
**Stájerlakanina** *see* Anina
**Stakhanov** *see* Kadiyivka
108 *E11* **Stalden** Valais, SW Switzerland 46°12′N 07°55′E
15 *S8* **St-Alexandre** Québec, SE Canada 47°39′N 69°36′W
**Stalin** *see* Varna
**Stalinabad** *see* Dushanbe
**Stalingrad** *see* Volgograd
**Staliniri** *see* Tskhinvali
**Stalino** *see* Donets'k
**Stalinobod** *see* Dushanbe
**Stalinov Štít** *see* Gerlachovský štít
**Stalinsk** *see* Novokuznetsk
**Stalins'kaya Oblast'** *see* Donets'ka Oblast'
**Stalinski Zaliv** *see* Varnenski Zaliv
**Stalin, Yazovir** *see* Iskar, Yazovir
111 *N15* **Stalowa Wola** Podkarpackie, SE Poland 50°35′N 22°02′E
114 *I11* **Stamboliyski** Plovdiv, C Bulgaria 42°09′N 24°32′E
15 *Q7* **St-Ambroise** Québec, SE Canada 48°35′N 71°19′W
97 *N19* **Stamford** E England, United Kingdom 52°39′N 00°32′W
18 *L14* **Stamford** Connecticut, NE USA 41°03′N 73°32′W
25 *P6* **Stamford** Texas, SW USA 32°55′N 99°49′W
25 *Q6* **Stamford, Lake** ▣ Texas, SW USA
108 *I10* **Stampa** Graubünden, SE Switzerland 46°21′N 09°35′E
**Stampalia** *see* Astypálaia
27 *T14* **Stamps** Arkansas, C USA 33°22′N 93°30′W
92 *G11* **Stamsund** Nordland, C Norway 68°07′N 13°50′E
27 *R2* **Stanberry** Missouri, C USA 40°12′N 94°33′W
195 *O3* **Stancomb-Wills Glacier** *glacier* Antarctica
83 *K21* **Standerton** Mpumalanga, E South Africa 26°57′S 29°14′E
31 *R7* **Standish** Michigan, N USA 43°59′N 83°58′W
20 *M6* **Stanford** Kentucky, S USA 37°30′N 84°40′W
33 *S9* **Stanford** Montana, NW USA 47°08′N 110°15′W
95 *P19* **Stånga** Gotland, SE Sweden 57°16′N 18°30′E
94 *I13* **Stange** Hedmark, S Norway 60°40′N 11°05′E
83 *L23* **Stanger** KwaZulu/Natal, E South Africa 29°20′S 31°18′E
**Stanimaka** *see* Asenovgrad
**Stanislau** *see* Ivano-Frankivs'k
35 *P8* **Stanislaus River** ≈ California, W USA
**Stanislav** *see* Ivano-Frankivs'k
**Stanislavskaya Oblast'** *see* Ivano-Frankivs'ka Oblast'
**Stanisławów** *see* Ivano-Frankivs'k
**Stanke Dimitrov** *see* Dupnitsa
183 *O15* **Stanley** Tasmania, SE Australia 40°48′S 145°18′E
65 *E24* **Stanley** *var.* Port Stanley, Puerto Argentino. ○ (Falkland Islands) East Falkland, Falkland Islands 51°45′S 57°56′W
33 *O13* **Stanley** Idaho, NW USA 44°12′N 114°58′W
28 *L3* **Stanley** North Dakota, N USA 48°19′N 102°23′W
21 *U4* **Stanley** Virginia, NE USA 38°34′N 78°30′W
30 *J6* **Stanley** Wisconsin, N USA 44°58′N 90°54′W
79 *G21* **Stanley Pool** *var.* Pool Malebo. ◎ Congo/Dem. Rep. Congo
155 *H20* **Stanley Reservoir** ▣ S India
**Stanleyville** *see* Kisangani
42 *G3* **Stann Creek** ◈ *district* SE Belize
**Stann Creek** *see* Dangriga
123 *Q12* **Stanovoy Khrebet** ▲▲ SE Russia
108 *F8* **Stans** Nidwalden, C Switzerland 46°57′N 08°23′E
97 *O21* **Stansted** ✈ (London) Essex, E England, United Kingdom 51°53′N 00°16′E
183 *U4* **Stanthorpe** Queensland, E Australia 28°35′S 151°52′E
21 *N6* **Stanton** Kentucky, S USA 37°51′N 83°51′W
31 *Q8* **Stanton** Michigan, N USA 43°19′N 85°04′W
29 *Q14* **Stanton** Nebraska, C USA 41°57′N 97°13′W
28 *L5* **Stanton** North Dakota, N USA 47°19′N 101°22′W
25 *N7* **Stanton** Texas, SW USA 32°07′N 101°47′W
32 *H7* **Stanwood** Washington, NW USA 48°14′N 122°22′W
117 *Y7* **Stanychno-Luhans'ke** Luhans'ka Oblast', E Ukraine 48°39′N 39°30′E
108 *K7* **Stanzach** Tirol, W Austria 47°24′N 10°36′E
98 *M9* **Staphorst** Overijssel, E Netherlands 52°38′N 06°12′E
14 *D18* **Staples** Ontario, S Canada 42°09′N 82°34′W
29 *T6* **Staples** Minnesota, N USA 46°21′N 94°47′W
28 *M14* **Stapleton** Nebraska, C USA 41°29′N 100°40′W
25 *S8* **Star** Texas, SW USA 31°27′N 98°16′W
111 *M14* **Starachowice** Świętokrzyskie, C Poland 51°04′N 21°02′E
**Stara Kanjiža** *see* Kanjiža
111 *M18* **Stará L'ubovňa** ***Ger.*** Altlublau, ***Hung.*** Ólubló. Prešovský Kraj, E Slovakia 49°19′N 20°40′E
112 *L10* **Stara Pazova** ***Ger.*** Altpasua, ***Hung.*** Ópazova. Vojvodina, N Serbia 44°59′N 20°10′E
**Stara Planina** *see* Balkan Mountains
114 *L9* **Stara Reka** ≈ C Bulgaria
116 *M5* **Stara Synyava** Khmel'nyts'ka Oblast', W Ukraine 49°39′N 27°39′E
116 *I2* **Stara Vyzhivka** Volyns'ka Oblast', NW Ukraine 51°27′N 24°25′E
**Staraya Belitsa** *see* Staraya Byelitsa
119 *M14* **Staraya Byelitsa** ***Rus.*** Staraya Belitsa. Vitsyebskaya Voblasts', NE Belarus 54°42′N 29°38′E
127 *R5* **Staraya Mayna** Ul'yanovskaya Oblast', W Russia 54°36′N 48°57′E
119 *O18* **Staraya Rudnya** Homyel'skaya Voblasts', SE Belarus 52°50′N 30°17′E
124 *H14* **Staraya Russa** Novgorodskaya Oblast', W Russia 57°59′N 31°18′E
114 *K10* **Stara Zagora** ***Lat.*** Augusta Trajana. Stara Zagora, C Bulgaria 42°26′N 25°39′E
114 *K10* **Stara Zagora** ◈ *province* C Bulgaria
29 *S8* **Starbuck** Minnesota, N USA 45°36′N 95°31′W
191 *W4* **Starbuck Island** *prev.* Volunteer Island. *island* E Kiribati
27 *V13* **Star City** Arkansas, C USA 33°56′N 91°52′W
112 *F13* **Staretina** ▲▲ W Bosnia and Herzegovina
**Stargard in Pommern** *see* Stargard Szczeciński
110 *E9* **Stargard Szczeciński** ***Ger.*** Stargard in Pommern. Zachodnio-pomorskie, NW Poland 53°20′N 15°02′E
187 *N10* **Star Harbour** *harbor* San Cristobal, SE Solomon Islands
**Stari Bečej** *see* Bečej
113 *F15* **Stari Grad** ***It.*** Cittavecchia. Split-Dalmacija, S Croatia 43°11′N 16°36′E
124 *J16* **Staritsa** Tverskaya Oblast', W Russia 56°28′N 34°51′E
23 *V9* **Starke** Florida, SE USA 29°56′N 82°07′W
22 *M4* **Starkville** Mississippi, S USA 33°27′N 88°49′W
186 *B7* **Star Mountains** ***Ind.*** Pegunungan Sterren. ▲▲ Indonesia/Papua New Guinea
101 *L23* **Starnberg** Bayern, SE Germany 48°00′N 11°19′E
101 *L24* **Starnberger See** ◎ SE Germany
**Starobel'sk** *see* Starobil's'k
117 *X8* **Starobesheve** Donets'ka Oblast', E Ukraine 47°45′N 38°01′E
117 *Y6* **Starobil's'k** ***Rus.*** Starobel'sk. Luhans'ka Oblast', E Ukraine 49°16′N 38°56′E
119 *K18* **Starobin** *var.* Starobyn. Minskaya Voblasts', S Belarus 52°44′N 27°28′E
**Starobyn** *see* Starobin
126 *H6* **Starodub** Bryanskaya Oblast', W Russia 52°30′N 32°56′E
110 *I8* **Starogard Gdański** ***Ger.*** Preussisch-Stargard. Pomorskie, N Poland 53°57′N 18°29′E
**Staroikan** *see* Ikan
**Starokonstantinov** *see* Starokostyantyniv
116 *L5* **Starokostyantyniv** ***Rus.*** Starokonstantinov. Khmel'nyts'ka Oblast', NW Ukraine 49°43′N 27°13′E
126 *K12* **Starominskaya** Krasnodarskiy Kray, SW Russia 46°31′N 39°03′E
114 *L7* **Staro Selo** ***Rom.*** Satul-Vechi; ***prev.*** Star-Smil. Silistra, NE Bulgaria 43°58′N 26°32′E
126 *K12* **Staroshcherbinovskaya** Krasnodarskiy Kray, SW Russia 46°36′N 38°42′E
127 *V6* **Starosubkhangulovo** Respublika Bashkortostan, W Russia 53°05′N 57°22′E
35 *S4* **Star Peak** ▲ Nevada, W USA 40°31′N 118°09′W
15 *T8* **St-Arsène** Québec, SE Canada 47°55′N 69°21′W
**Star-Smil** *see* Staro Selo
97 *J25* **Start Point** *headland* SW England, United Kingdom 50°13′N 03°38′W
**Startsy** *see* Kirawsk
**Starum** *see* Stavoren
119 *L18* **Staryya Darohi** ***Rus.*** Staryye Dorogi. Minskaya Voblasts', S Belarus 53°02′N 28°16′E
**Staryye Dorogi** *see* Staryya Darohi
127 *T2* **Staryye Zyattsy** Udmurtskaya Respublika, NW Russia 57°22′N 52°42′E
117 *U13* **Staryy Krym** Avtonomna Respublika Krym, S Ukraine 45°03′N 35°06′E
126 *K8* **Staryy Oskol** Belgorodskaya Oblast', W Russia 51°21′N 37°52′E
116 *H6* **Staryy Sambir** L'vivs'ka Oblast', W Ukraine 49°27′N 23°00′E
101 *L14* **Stassfurt** *var.* Staßfurt. Sachsen-Anhalt, C Germany 51°51′N 11°35′E
**Staßfurt** *see* Stassfurt
111 *M15* **Staszów** Świętokrzyskie, C Poland 50°33′N 21°07′E
29 *W13* **State Center** Iowa, C USA 42°01′N 93°09′W
18 *E14* **State College** Pennsylvania, NE USA 40°48′N 77°52′W
18 *K15* **Staten Island** *island* New York, NE USA
**Staten Island** *see* Estados, Isla de los
23 *U8* **Statenville** Georgia, SE USA 30°42′N 83°00′W
23 *W5* **Statesboro** Georgia, SE USA 32°28′N 81°47′W
**States, The** *see* United States of America
21 *R9* **Statesville** North Carolina, SE USA 35°46′N 80°54′W
95 *G16* **Stathelle** Telemark, S Norway 59°01′N 09°40′E
**Statia** *see* Sint Eustatius
30 *K15* **Staunton** Illinois, N USA 39°00′N 89°47′W
21 *T5* **Staunton** Virginia, NE USA 38°10′N 79°05′W
95 *C16* **Stavanger** Rogaland, S Norway 58°58′N 05°43′E
99 *L21* **Stavelot** ***Dut.*** Stablo. Liège, E Belgium 50°24′N 05°56′E
95 *G16* **Stavern** Vestfold, S Norway 58°58′N 10°01′E
**Stavers Island** *see* Vostok Island
98 *J7* **Stavoren** ***Fris.*** Starum. Fryslân, N Netherlands 52°52′N 05°22′E
115 *K21* **Stavrí, Akrotírio** *var.* Akrotírio Stavrós. *headland* Naxos, Kykládes, Greece, Aegean Sea 37°12′N 25°32′E
126 *M14* **Stavropol'** *prev.* Voroshilovsk. Stavropol'skiy Kray, SW Russia 45°02′N 41°58′E
**Stavropol'** *see* Tol'yatti
126 *M14* **Stavropol'skaya Vozvyshennost'** ▲▲ SW Russia
126 *M14* **Stavropol'skiy Kray** ◈ *territory* SW Russia
115 *H14* **Stavrós** Kentrikí Makedonía, N Greece 40°39′N 23°43′E
115 *J24* **Stavrós, Akrotírio** *headland* Kríti, Greece, E Mediterranean Sea 35°25′N 24°57′E
**Stavrós, Akrotírio** *see* Stavrí, Akrotírio
114 *I12* **Stavroúpoli** *prev.* Stavroúpolis. Anatolikí Makedonía kai Thráki, NE Greece 41°12′N 24°45′E
**Stavroúpolis** *see* Stavroúpoli
117 *O6* **Stavyshche** Kyivs'ka Oblast', N Ukraine 49°23′N 30°10′E
182 *M11* **Stawell** Victoria, SE Australia 37°06′S 142°52′E
110 *N9* **Stawiski** Podlaskie, NE Poland 53°22′N 22°08′E
14 *G14* **Stayner** Ontario, S Canada 44°25′N 80°05′W
14 *D17* **St. Clair** ≈ Canada/USA
37 *R3* **Steamboat Springs** Colorado, C USA 40°28′N 106°51′W
15 *U4* **Ste-Anne, Lac** ◎ Québec, SE Canada
20 *M8* **Stearns** Kentucky, S USA 36°39′N 84°27′W
39 *N10* **Stebbins** Alaska, USA 63°30′N 162°15′W
15 *U7* **Ste-Blandine** Québec, SE Canada 48°22′N 68°27′W
108 *K7* **Steeg** Tirol, W Austria 47°15′N 10°18′E
27 *Y9* **Steele** Missouri, C USA 36°04′N 89°49′W
29 *N5* **Steele** North Dakota, N USA 46°51′N 99°55′W
194 *J5* **Steele Island** *island* Antarctica
30 *K16* **Steeleville** Illinois, N USA 38°00′N 89°39′W
27 *W6* **Steelville** Missouri, C USA 37°57′N 91°21′W
99 *G14* **Steenbergen** Noord-Brabant, S Netherlands 51°35′N 04°19′E
**Steenkool** *see* Bintuni
11 *O10* **Steen River** Alberta, W Canada 59°37′N 117°17′W
98 *M8* **Steenwijk** Overijssel, N Netherlands 52°47′N 06°07′E
65 *A23* **Steeple Jason** *island* Jason Islands, NW Falkland Islands
174 *J8* **Steep Point** *headland* Western Australia 26°09′S 113°11′E
116 *L9* **Ştefăneşti** Botoşani, NE Romania 47°44′N 27°15′E
**Stefanie, Lake** *see* Ch'ew Bahir
8 *L5* **Stefansson Island** *island* Nunavut, N Canada
117 *O10* **Ştefan Vodă** ***Rus.*** Suvorovo. SE Moldova 46°33′N 29°39′E
63 *H18* **Steffen, Cerro** ▲ S Chile 44°27′S 71°42′W
108 *D9* **Steffisburg** Bern, C Switzerland 46°47′N 07°38′E
95 *J24* **Stege** Sjælland, SE Denmark 54°59′N 12°18′E
116 *G10* **Ştei** ***Hung.*** Vaskohsziklás. Bihor, W Romania 46°34′N 22°28′E
**Steier** *see* Steyr
**Steierdorf/Steierdorf-Anina** *see* Anina
109 *T7* **Steiermark** *off.* Land Steiermark, ***Eng.*** Styria. ◈ *state* C Austria
**Steiermark, Land** *see* Steiermark
101 *J19* **Steigerwald** *hill range* C Germany
99 *L17* **Stein** Limburg, SE Netherlands 50°58′N 05°45′E
**Stein** *see* Stein an der Donau
**Stein** *see* Kamnik, Slovenia
108 *M8* **Steinach** Tirol, W Austria 47°07′N 11°30′E
**Steinamanger** *see* Szombathely
109 *W3* **Stein an der Donau** *var.* Stein. Niederösterreich, NE Austria 48°25′N 15°35′E
**Steinau an der Elbe** *see* Ścinawa
11 *Y16* **Steinbach** Manitoba, S Canada 49°32′N 96°40′W
**Steiner Alpen** *see* Kamniško-Savinjske Alpe
99 *L24* **Steinfort** Luxembourg, W Luxembourg 49°39′N 05°55′E
100 *H12* **Steinhuder Meer** ◎ NW Germany
93 *E15* **Steinkjer** Nord-Trøndelag, C Norway 64°01′N 11°29′E
**Stejarul** *see* Karapelit
99 *F16* **Stekene** Oost-Vlaanderen, NW Belgium 51°13′N 04°04′E
83 *E26* **Stellenbosch** Western Cape, SW South Africa 33°56′S 18°51′E
98 *F13* **Stellendam** Zuid-Holland, SW Netherlands 51°48′N 04°01′E
39 *T12* **Steller, Mount** ▲ Alaska, USA 60°36′N 142°49′W
103 *Y14* **Stello, Monte** ▲ Corse, France, C Mediterranean Sea 42°49′N 09°24′E
106 *F5* **Stelvio, Passo dello** *pass* Italy/Switzerland
15 *S7* **Ste-Maguerite Nord-Est** ≈ Québec, SE Canada
15 *V4* **Ste-Marguerite, Pointe** *headland* Québec, SE Canada 50°01′N 66°43′W
12 *J14* **Ste-Marie, Lac** ▣ Québec, S Canada
103 *R3* **Stenay** Meuse, NE France 49°29′N 05°12′E
100 *L12* **Stendal** Sachsen-Anhalt, C Germany 52°36′N 11°52′E
118 *E8* **Stende** NW Latvia 57°09′N 22°33′E
182 *H10* **Stenhouse Bay** South Australia 35°15′S 136°58′E
95 *J23* **Stenløse** Hovedstaden, E Denmark 55°47′N 12°13′E
95 *L19* **Stensjön** Jönköping, S Sweden 57°36′N 14°42′E
95 *K18* **Stenstorp** Västra Götaland, S Sweden 58°15′N 13°45′E
95 *I18* **Stenungsund** Västra Götaland, S Sweden 58°05′N 11°49′E
**Stepanakert** *see* Xankändi
137 *T11* **Step'anavan** N Armenia 41°00′N 44°27′E
137 *T9* **Step'ants'minda** *prev.* Q'azbegi, ***Rus.*** Kazbegi. NE Georgia 42°39′N 44°36′E
100 *K9* **Stepenitz** ≈ N Germany
29 *O10* **Stephan** South Dakota, N USA 44°12′N 99°25′W
29 *R3* **Stephen** Minnesota, N USA 48°27′N 96°54′W
27 *T14* **Stephens** Arkansas, C USA 33°25′N 93°04′W
184 *J13* **Stephens, Cape** *headland* D'Urville Island, Marlborough, SW New Zealand 40°42′S 173°56′E
21 *V3* **Stephens City** Virginia, NE USA 39°03′N 78°10′W
182 *L6* **Stephens Creek** New South Wales, SE Australia 31°51′S 141°30′E
184 *K13* **Stephens Island** *island* C New Zealand
31 *N5* **Stephenson** Michigan, N USA 45°27′N 87°36′W
13 *S12* **Stephenville** Newfoundland, Newfoundland and Labrador, SE Canada 48°33′N 58°34′W
25 *S7* **Stephenville** Texas, SW USA 32°12′N 98°13′W
**Step' Nardara** *see* Step' Shardara
145 *R8* **Stepnogorsk** Akmola, C Kazakhstan 52°04′N 72°18′E
127 *O15* **Stepnoye** Stavropol'skiy Kray, SW Russia 44°18′N 44°34′E
145 *Q8* **Stepnyak** Akmola, N Kazakhstan 52°52′N 70°49′E
145 *P17* **Step' Shardara** ***Kaz.*** Shardara Dalasy; ***prev.*** Step' Nardara. *grassland* S Kazakhstan
192 *J17* **Steps Point** *headland* Tutuila, W American Samoa 14°23′S 170°46′W
115 *F17* **Stereá Elláda** *var.* Stereá Ellás ***Eng.*** Greece Central. ◈ *region* C Greece
**Stereá Ellás** *see* Stereá Elláda
83 *J24* **Sterkspruit** Eastern Cape, SE South Africa 30°31′S 27°22′E
127 *U6* **Sterlibashevo** Respublika Bashkortostan, W Russia 53°19′N 55°12′E
39 *R12* **Sterling** Alaska, USA 60°32′N 150°51′W
37 *V3* **Sterling** Colorado, C USA 40°37′N 103°12′W
30 *K11* **Sterling** Illinois, N USA 41°47′N 89°42′W
26 *M5* **Sterling** Kansas, C USA 38°12′N 98°12′W
25 *O8* **Sterling City** Texas, SW USA 31°50′N 101°00′W
31 *S9* **Sterling Heights** Michigan, N USA 42°34′N 83°01′W
21 *W3* **Sterling Park** Virginia, NE USA 39°00′N 77°24′W
37 *V2* **Sterling Reservoir** ▣ Colorado, C USA
22 *I5* **Sterlington** Louisiana, S USA 32°42′N 92°05′W
127 *U6* **Sterlitamak** Respublika Bashkortostan, W Russia 53°39′N 56°00′E
**Sternberg** *see* Šternberk
111 *H17* **Šternberk** ***Ger.*** Sternberg. Olomoucký Kraj, E Czechia 49°45′N 17°20′E
141 *V17* **Stēroh** Suquṭrā, S Yemen 12°21′N 53°50′E
**Sterren, Pegunungan** *see* Star Mountains
110 *G11* **Stęszew** Wielkopolskie, C Poland 52°16′N 16°41′E
**Stettin** *see* Szczecin
**Stettiner Haff** *see* Szczeciński, Zalew
11 *Q15* **Stettler** Alberta, SW Canada 52°21′N 112°40′W
31 *V13* **Steubenville** Ohio, N USA 40°21′N 80°37′W
97 *O21* **Stevenage** E England, United Kingdom 51°55′N 00°14′W
23 *Q1* **Stevenson** Alabama, S USA 34°52′N 85°50′W
32 *H11* **Stevenson** Washington, NW USA 45°43′N 121°54′W
182 *E1* **Stevenson Creek** *seasonal river* South Australia
39 *Q13* **Stevenson Entrance** *strait* Alaska, USA
30 *L6* **Stevens Point** Wisconsin, N USA 44°32′N 89°33′W
39 *R8* **Stevens Village** Alaska, USA 66°01′N 149°02′W
33 *P10* **Stevensville** Montana, NW USA 46°30′N 114°05′W
93 *E25* **Stevns Klint** *headland* E Denmark 55°15′N 12°25′E
10 *J12* **Stewart** British Columbia, W Canada 55°58′N 129°52′W
10 *J6* **Stewart** ≈ Yukon, NW Canada
10 *I6* **Stewart Crossing** Yukon, NW Canada 63°22′N 136°37′W
63 *H25* **Stewart, Isla** *island* S Chile
185 *B25* **Stewart Island / Rakiura** *var.* Rakiura. *island* S New Zealand
**Stewart Islands** *see* Sikaiana
181 *W6* **Stewart, Mount** ▲ Queensland, E Australia 20°11′S 145°29′E
10 *H6* **Stewart River** Yukon, NW Canada 63°17′N 139°24′W
27 *R3* **Stewartsville** Missouri, C USA 39°45′N 94°30′W
11 *S16* **Stewart Valley** Saskatchewan, S Canada 50°34′N 107°47′W
29 *W10* **Stewartville** Minnesota, N USA 43°51′N 92°29′W
**Steyerlak-Anina** *see* Anina
109 *T5* **Steyr** *var.* Steier. Oberösterreich, N Austria 48°02′N 14°26′E
109 *T5* **Steyr** ≈ NW Austria
15 *T7* **St-Fabien** Québec, SE Canada 48°19′N 68°51′W
15 *R11* **St-François, Lac** ◎ Québec, SE Canada
83 *E25* **St. Helena Bay** *bay* SW South Africa
15 *T8* **St-Hubert** Québec, SE Canada 47°46′N 69°15′W
29 *P11* **Stickney** South Dakota, N USA 43°24′N 98°23′W
98 *L5* **Stiens** Fryslân, N Netherlands 53°15′N 05°45′E
**Stif** *see* Sétif
27 *Q11* **Stigler** Oklahoma, C USA 35°16′N 95°08′W
107 *N18* **Stigliano** Basilicata, S Italy 40°24′N 16°13′E
95 *N17* **Stigtomta** Södermanland, C Sweden 58°48′N 16°47′E
10 *I11* **Stikine** ≈ British Columbia, W Canada
**Stilida/Stilís** *see* Stylída
95 *G22* **Stilling** Midtjylland, C Denmark 56°04′N 10°00′E
29 *W8* **Stillwater** Minnesota, N USA 45°03′N 92°48′W
27 *O9* **Stillwater** Oklahoma, C USA 36°07′N 97°03′W
35 *S5* **Stillwater Range** ▲▲ Nevada, W USA
18 *I8* **Stillwater Reservoir** ▣ New York, NE USA
107 *O22* **Stilo, Punta** *headland* S Italy 38°27′N 16°36′E
27 *R10* **Stilwell** Oklahoma, C USA 35°48′N 94°37′W
**Štimlje** *see* Shtime
25 *N1* **Stinnett** Texas, SW USA 35°49′N 101°27′W
113 *P18* **Štip** E North Macedonia 41°45′N 22°10′E
**Stira** *see* Stýra
96 *J12* **Stirling** C Scotland, United Kingdom 56°07′N 03°57′W
96 *I12* **Stirling** *cultural region* C Scotland, United Kingdom
180 *J14* **Stirling Range** ▲▲ Western Australia
15 *R8* **St-Jean** ≈ Québec, SE Canada
93 *E16* **Stjørdalshalsen** Nord-Trøndelag, C Norway 63°27′N 10°57′E
83 *L22* **St. Lucia** KwaZulu/Natal, E South Africa 28°22′N 32°25′E
45 *V9* **St Martin** ◇ *French overseas collectivity* NE Caribbean Sea
**Stochód** *see* Stokhid
101 *H24* **Stockach** Baden-Württemberg, S Germany 47°51′N 09°01′E
25 *S12* **Stockdale** Texas, SW USA 29°14′N 97°57′W
109 *X3* **Stockerau** Niederösterreich, NE Austria 48°24′N 16°13′E
93 *H20* **Stockholm** ● (Sweden) Stockholm, C Sweden 59°17′N 18°03′E
95 *O15* **Stockholm** ◈ *county* C Sweden
**Stockmannshof** *see* Pļaviņas
97 *L18* **Stockport** NW England, United Kingdom 53°25′N 02°10′W
65 *K15* **Stocks Seamount** *undersea feature* C Atlantic Ocean 11°42′S 33°48′W
35 *O8* **Stockton** California, W USA 37°56′N 121°19′W
26 *L3* **Stockton** Kansas, C USA 39°27′N 99°17′W
27 *S6* **Stockton** Missouri, C USA 37°43′N 93°49′W
30 *K3* **Stockton Island** *island* Apostle Islands, Wisconsin, N USA
27 *S7* **Stockton Lake** ▣ Missouri, C USA
97 *M15* **Stockton-on-Tees** *var.* Stockton on Tees. N England, United Kingdom 54°34′N 01°19′W
**Stockton on Tees** *see* Stockton-on-Tees
24 *M10* **Stockton Plateau** *plain* Texas, SW USA
28 *M16* **Stockville** Nebraska, C USA 40°33′N 100°20′W
93 *H17* **Stöde** Västernorrland, C Sweden 62°27′N 16°34′E
**Stodolichi** *see* Stadolichy
**Stœ̆ng Trĕng** *see* Stung Treng
113 *M19* **Stogovo Karaorman** ▲▲ W North Macedonia
**Stoke** *see* Stoke-on-Trent
97 *L19* **Stoke-on-Trent** *var.* Stoke. C England, United Kingdom 53°N 02°10′W
182 *M15* **Stokes Point** *headland* Tasmania, SE Australia 40°09′S 143°55′E
116 *J2* **Stokhid** ***Pol.*** Stochód, ***Rus.*** Stokhod. ≈ NW Ukraine
**Stokhod** *see* Stokhid
92 *I4* **Stokkseyri** Suðurland, SW Iceland 63°49′N 21°00′W
92 *G10* **Stokmarknes** Nordland, C Norway 68°34′N 14°55′E
**Stol** *see* Veliki Krš
113 *H15* **Stolac** Federacija Bosne I Hercegovine, S Bosnia and Herzegovina 43°04′N 17°58′E
**Stolbce** *see* Stowbtsy
101 *D16* **Stolberg** *var.* Stolberg im Rheinland. Nordrhein-Westfalen, W Germany 50°45′N 06°15′E
**Stolberg im Rheinland** *see* Stolberg
123 *P6* **Stolbovoy, Ostrov** *island* NE Russia
**Stolbtsy** *see* Stowbtsy
119 *J20* **Stolin** Brestskaya Voblasts', SW Belarus 51°53′N 26°51′E
95 *K14* **Stöllet** *var.* Norra Ny. Värmland, C Sweden 60°24′N 13°15′E
**Stolp** *see* Słupsk
**Stolpe** *see* Słupia
**Stolpmünde** *see* Ustka
115 *F15* **Stómio** Thessalía, C Greece 39°51′N 22°45′E
14 *J11* **Stonecliffe** Ontario, SE Canada 46°12′N 77°58′W
96 *L10* **Stonehaven** NE Scotland, United Kingdom 56°59′N 02°14′W
97 *M23* **Stonehenge** *ancient monument* Wiltshire, S England, United Kingdom
23 *T3* **Stone Mountain** ▲ Georgia, SE USA 33°48′N 84°10′W
11 *X16* **Stonewall** Manitoba, S Canada 50°08′N 97°20′W
21 *S3* **Stonewood** West Virginia, NE USA 39°15′N 80°18′W
14 *D17* **Stoney Point** Ontario, S Canada 42°18′N 82°32′W
92 *H10* **Stonglandseidet** Troms, N Norway 69°03′N 17°06′E
65 *N25* **Stonybeach Bay** *bay* Tristan da Cunha, SE Atlantic Ocean
35 *N5* **Stony Creek** ≈ California, W USA
65 *N25* **Stonyhill Point** *headland* S Tristan da Cunha
14 *I14* **Stony Lake** ◎ Ontario, SE Canada
11 *Q14* **Stony Plain** Alberta, SW Canada 53°31′N 114°04′W
21 *R9* **Stony Point** North Carolina, SE USA 35°51′N 81°04′W
18 *G8* **Stony Point** *headland* New York, NE USA 43°50′N 76°18′W
11 *T10* **Stony Rapids** Saskatchewan, C Canada 59°14′N 105°48′W
39 *P11* **Stony River** Alaska, USA 61°48′N 156°37′W
**Stony Tunguska** *see* Podkamennaya Tunguska
12 *G10* **Stooping** ≈ Ontario, C Canada
100 *I9* **Stör** ≈ N Germany
95 *M15* **Storå** Örebro, S Sweden 59°44′N 15°10′E
95 *J16* **Stora Gla** ◎ C Sweden
95 *I16* **Stora Le** ***Nor.*** Store Le. ◎ Norway/Sweden
92 *I12* **Stora Lulevatten** ◎ N Sweden
92 *H13* **Storavan** ◎ N Sweden
93 *I20* **Storby** Åland, SW Finland 60°12′N 19°33′E
94 *E10* **Stordalen** Møre og Romsdal, S Norway 62°22′N 07°00′E
95 *H23* **Storebælt** *var.* Store Bælt, ***Eng.*** Great Belt, Storebelt. *channel* Baltic Sea/Kattegat
**Store Bælt** *see* Storebælt
**Storebelt** *see* Storebælt
95 *M19* **Storebro** Kalmar, S Sweden 57°36′N 15°30′E
95 *J24* **Store Heddinge** Sjælland, SE Denmark 55°19′N 12°24′E
**Store Le** *see* Stora Le
93 *E16* **Støren** Sør-Trøndelag, S Norway 63°02′N 10°16′E
92 *O4* **Storfjorden** *fjord* S Norway
95 *L15* **Storfors** Värmland, C Sweden 59°33′N 14°16′E
92 *G13* **Storforshei** Nordland, C Norway 66°25′N 14°25′E
**Storhammer** *see* Hamar
93 *F16* **Storlien** Jämtland, C Sweden 63°18′N 12°10′E
183 *P17* **Storm Bay** *inlet* Tasmania, SE Australia
29 *T12* **Storm Lake** Iowa, C USA 42°38′N 95°12′W
29 *S13* **Storm Lake** ◎ Iowa, C USA
96 *G7* **Stornoway** NW Scotland, United Kingdom 58°13′N 06°23′W
**Storojineţ** *see* Storozhynets'
92 *P1* **Storøya** *island* NE Svalbard
125 *S10* **Storozhevsk** Respublika Komi, NW Russia 61°56′N 52°18′E
**Storozhinets** *see* Storozhynets'
116 *K8* **Storozhynets'** ***Ger.*** Storozynetz, ***Rom.*** Storojineţ, ***Rus.*** Storozhinets. Chernivets'ka Oblast', W Ukraine 48°11′N 25°42′E
**Storozynetz** *see* Storozhynets'
92 *H11* **Storriten** ***Lapp.*** Stuorrarijjda. ▲ C Norway 68°09′N 17°12′E
19 *N12* **Storrs** Connecticut, NE USA 41°48′N 72°15′W
94 *I11* **Storsjøen** ◎ S Norway
94 *N13* **Storsjön** ◎ C Sweden
93 *F16* **Storsjön** ◎ C Sweden
92 *J9* **Storslett** Troms, N Norway 69°45′N 21°03′E
94 *H11* **Storsølnkletten** ▲ S Norway 61°52′N 11°32′E
92 *I9* **Storsteinnes** Troms, N Norway 69°13′N 19°14′E
93 *J14* **Storsund** Norrbotten, N Sweden 65°36′N 20°40′E
94 *J9* **Storsylen** ***Swe.*** Sylarna. ▲ Norway/Sweden 63°00′N 12°14′E
92 *H11* **Stortoppen** ▲ N Sweden 67°33′N 17°27′E
93 *H14* **Storuman** Västerbotten, N Sweden 65°05′N 17°10′E
93 *H14* **Storuman** ◎ N Sweden
94 *N13* **Storvik** Gävleborg, C Sweden 60°37′N 16°30′E
95 *O14* **Storvreta** Uppsala, C Sweden 59°58′N 17°42′E
100 *L10* **Störwasserstrasse** *canal* N Germany
29 *V13* **Story City** Iowa, C USA 42°10′N 93°36′W
11 *V17* **Stoughton** Saskatchewan, S Canada 49°40′N 103°01′W
19 *O11* **Stoughton** Massachusetts, NE USA 42°07′N 71°06′W
30 *L9* **Stoughton** Wisconsin, N USA 42°56′N 89°12′W
97 *L23* **Stour** ≈ E England, United Kingdom
97 *P21* **Stour** ≈ S England, United Kingdom
27 *T5* **Stover** Missouri, C USA 38°26′N 92°59′W
95 *G21* **Støvring** Nordjylland, N Denmark 56°53′N 09°52′E
119 *J17* **Stowbtsy** ***Pol.*** Stolbce, ***Rus.*** Stolbtsy. Minskaya Voblasts', C Belarus 53°29′N 26°44′E
25 *X11* **Stowell** Texas, SW USA 29°47′N 94°22′W
97 *P20* **Stowmarket** E England, United Kingdom 52°05′N 00°54′E


◆ Country
● Country Capital
◇ Dependent Territory
○ Dependent Territory Capital
◈ Administrative Regions
✈ International Airport
▲ Mountain
▲▲ Mountain Range
Volcano
≈ River
◎ Lake
▣ Reservoir

STOZHER – SUNSET STATE


114 N8 **Stozher** Dobrich, NE Bulgaria 43°27′N 27°49′E
97 E14 **Strabane** *Ir.* An Srath Bán. W Northern Ireland, United Kingdom 54°49′N 07°27′W
121 S11 **Strabo Trench** *undersea feature* C Mediterranean Sea
27 T7 **Strafford** Missouri, C USA 37°16′N 93°07′W
183 N17 **Strahan** Tasmania, SE Australia 42°10′S 145°18′E
111 C18 **Strakonice** *Ger.* Strakonitz. Jihočeský Kraj, S Czechia 49°14′N 13°55′E
**Strakonitz** *see* Strakonice
100 N8 **Stralsund** Mecklenburg-Vorpommern, NE Germany 54°18′N 13°06′E
99 L16 **Stramproy** Limburg, SE Netherlands 51°12′N 05°43′E
83 E26 **Strand** Western Cape, SW South Africa 34°06′S 18°50′E
94 E10 **Stranda** Møre og Romsdal, S Norway 62°18′N 06°56′E
97 G15 **Strangford Lough** *Ir.* Loch Cuan. *inlet* E Northern Ireland, United Kingdom
95 N16 **Strängnäs** Södermanland, C Sweden 59°22′N 17°02′E
97 E14 **Stranorlar** *Ir.* Srath an Urláir. NW Ireland 54°48′N 07°46′W
97 H14 **Stranraer** S Scotland, United Kingdom 54°54′N 05°02′W
11 U16 **Strasbourg** Saskatchewan, S Canada 51°05′N 104°58′W
103 V5 **Strasbourg** *Ger.* Strassburg; *anc.* Argentoratum. Bas-Rhin, NE France 48°35′N 07°45′E
109 T8 **Strassburg** Kärnten, S Austria 46°54′N 14°21′E
37 U4 **Strasburg** Colorado, C USA 39°42′N 104°13′W
29 N7 **Strasburg** North Dakota, N USA 46°07′N 100°10′W
31 U12 **Strasburg** Ohio, N USA 40°35′N 81°31′W
21 U3 **Strasburg** Virginia, NE USA 38°59′N 78°21′W
117 N10 **Străşeni** *var.* Strasheny. C Moldova 47°07′N 28°37′E
**Strasheny** *see* Străşeni
**Strassburg** *see* Strasbourg, France
**Strassburg** *see* Aiud, Romania
99 M25 **Strassen** Luxembourg, S Luxembourg 49°37′N 06°05′E
109 R5 **Strasswalchen** Salzburg, C Austria 47°59′N 13°19′E
14 F16 **Stratford** Ontario, S Canada 43°22′N 81°00′W
184 K10 **Stratford** Taranaki, North Island, New Zealand 39°20′S 174°16′E
35 Q11 **Stratford** California, W USA 36°10′N 119°47′W
29 V13 **Stratford** Iowa, C USA 42°16′N 93°55′W
27 O12 **Stratford** Oklahoma, C USA 34°48′N 96°57′W
25 N1 **Stratford** Texas, SW USA 36°21′N 102°05′W
30 K6 **Stratford** Wisconsin, N USA 44°53′N 90°13′W
**Stratford** *see* Stratford-upon-Avon
97 M20 **Stratford-upon-Avon** *var.* Stratford. C England, United Kingdom 52°12′N 01°41′W
183 O17 **Strathgordon** Tasmania, SE Australia 42°49′S 146°04′E
11 Q16 **Strathmore** Alberta, SW Canada 51°05′N 113°20′W
35 R11 **Strathmore** California, W USA 36°07′N 119°04′W
14 E16 **Strathroy** Ontario, S Canada 42°57′N 81°40′W
96 I6 **Strathy Point** *headland* N Scotland, United Kingdom 58°36′N 04°04′W
37 W4 **Stratton** Colorado, C USA 39°16′N 102°34′W
19 P6 **Stratton** Maine, NE USA 45°08′N 70°25′W
18 M10 **Stratton Mountain** ▲ Vermont, NE USA 43°05′N 72°55′W
101 N21 **Straubing** Bayern, SE Germany 48°53′N 12°35′E
100 O12 **Strausberg** Brandenburg, E Germany 52°34′N 13°52′E
32 K13 **Strawberry Mountain** ▲ Oregon, NW USA 44°18′N 118°43′W
29 X12 **Strawberry Point** Iowa, C USA 42°40′N 91°31′W
36 M3 **Strawberry Reservoir** ⊠ Utah, W USA
36 M4 **Strawberry River** ⟿ Utah, W USA
25 R7 **Strawn** Texas, SW USA 32°33′N 98°30′W
113 P17 **Straža** ▲ Bulgaria/North Macedonia 42°16′N 22°13′E
111 I19 **Strážov** *Hung.* Sztrazsó. ▲ NW Slovakia 48°59′N 18°29′E
182 F7 **Streaky Bay** South Australia 32°49′S 134°13′E
182 E7 **Streaky Bay** *bay* South Australia
30 L12 **Streator** Illinois, N USA 41°07′N 88°50′W
**Streckenbach** *see* Świdnik
**Strednogorie** *see* Pirdop
111 C17 **Středočeský Kraj** ◆ *region* C Czechia
29 O6 **Streeter** North Dakota, N USA 46°37′N 99°23′W
25 U8 **Streetman** Texas, SW USA 31°52′N 96°19′W
116 G13 **Strehaia** Mehedinţi, SW Romania 44°37′N 23°10′E
**Strehlen** *see* Strzelin
114 I10 **Strelcha** Pazardzhik, C Bulgaria 42°28′N 24°21′E
122 L12 **Strelka** Krasnoyarskiy Kray, C Russia 58°05′N 92°54′E
124 L6 **Strel'na** ⟿ NW Russia
118 H7 **Strenči** *Ger.* Stackeln. N Latvia 57°38′N 25°42′E
15 V6 **St-René-de-Matane** Québec, SE Canada 48°42′N 67°22′W
108 K8 **Strengen** Tirol, W Austria 47°07′N 10°25′E
106 C6 **Stresa** Piemonte, NE Italy 45°52′N 08°32′E
**Streshin** *see* Streshyn
119 N18 **Streshyn** *Rus.* Streshin. Homyel'skaya Voblasts', SE Belarus 52°43′N 30°07′E
95 B18 **Streymoy** *Dan.* Strømø. *island* N Faroe Islands
95 G23 **Strib** Syddtjylland, C Denmark 55°33′N 09°47′E
111 A17 **Stříbro** *Ger.* Mies. Plzeňský Kraj, W Czechia 49°44′N 12°55′E
136 B7 **Strickland** ⟿ SW Papua New Guinea
**Striegau** *see* Strzegom
**Strigonium** *see* Esztergom
98 H13 **Strijen** Zuid-Holland, SW Netherlands 51°45′N 04°34′E
63 H21 **Strobel, Lago** ⊚ S Argentina
61 B25 **Stroeder** Buenos Aires, E Argentina 40°11′S 62°35′W
115 C20 **Strofádes** *island* Iónia Nisiá, Greece, C Mediterranean Sea
**Strofilia** *see* Strofyliá
115 G17 **Strofyliá** *var.* Strofilia. Évvoia, C Greece 38°49′N 23°25′E
100 O10 **Strom** ⟿ NE Germany
107 L22 **Stromboli** ☒ Isola Stromboli, SW Italy 38°48′N 15°13′E
107 L22 **Stromboli, Isola** *island* Isole Eolie, S Italy
96 H9 **Stromeferry** N Scotland, United Kingdom 57°20′N 05°35′W
96 J5 **Stromness** N Scotland, United Kingdom 58°57′N 03°18′W
**Strømø** *see* Streymoy
94 N11 **Strömsbruk** Gävleborg, C Sweden 61°52′N 17°19′E
29 Q15 **Stromsburg** Nebraska, C USA 41°06′N 97°36′W
95 K21 **Strömsnäsbruk** Kronoberg, S Sweden 56°35′N 13°45′E
95 I17 **Strömstad** Västra Götaland, S Sweden 58°56′N 11°11′E
93 G16 **Strömsund** Jämtland, C Sweden 63°51′N 15°35′E
93 G15 **Ströms Vattudal** *valley* N Sweden
27 V14 **Strong** Arkansas, C USA 33°06′N 92°19′W
**Strongilí** *see* Strongylí
107 O21 **Strongoli** Calabria, SW Italy 39°17′N 17°03′E
31 T11 **Strongsville** Ohio, N USA 41°18′N 81°50′W
115 Q23 **Strongylí** *var.* Strongilí. *island* SE Greece
96 K5 **Stronsay** *island* NE Scotland, United Kingdom
97 L21 **Stroud** C England, United Kingdom 51°46′N 02°15′W
27 O10 **Stroud** Oklahoma, C USA 35°45′N 96°39′W
18 I14 **Stroudsburg** Pennsylvania, NE USA 40°59′N 75°12′W
95 F21 **Struer** Midtjylland, W Denmark 56°29′N 08°37′E
113 M20 **Struga** SW North Macedonia 41°11′N 20°40′E
**Strugi-Kranyse** *see* Strugi-Krasnyye
124 G14 **Strugi-Krasnyye** *var.* Strugi-Kranyse. Pskovskaya Oblast', W Russia 58°19′N 29°09′E
114 G11 **Struma** *Gk.* Strymónas. ⟿ Bulgaria/Greece *see also* Strymónas
**Struma** *see* Strymónas
97 G21 **Strumble Head** *headland* SW Wales, United Kingdom 52°01′N 05°05′W
**Strumeshnitsa** *see* Strumica
113 Q19 **Strumica** E North Macedonia 41°27′N 22°39′E
113 Q19 **Strumica** *Bulg.* Strumeshnitsa. ⟿ Bulgaria/North Macedonia
114 G11 **Strumyani** Blagoevgrad, SW Bulgaria 41°41′N 23°13′E
31 V12 **Struthers** Ohio, N USA 41°03′N 80°36′W
114 I10 **Stryama** ⟿ C Bulgaria
114 G13 **Strymónas** *Bul.* Struma. ⟿ Bulgaria/Greece *see also* Struma
**Strymónas** *see* Struma
115 H14 **Strymonikós Kólpos** *gulf* N Greece
116 I6 **Stryy** L'vivs'ka Oblast', NW Ukraine 49°16′N 23°51′E
116 H6 **Stryy** ⟿ W Ukraine
111 F14 **Strzegom** *Ger.* Striegau. Wałbrzych, SW Poland 50°59′N 16°20′E
110 E10 **Strzelce Krajeńskie** *Ger.* Friedeberg Neumark. Lubuskie, W Poland 52°52′N 15°30′E
111 I15 **Strzelce Opolskie** *Ger.* Gross Strehlitz. Opolskie, SW Poland 50°31′N 18°19′E
182 K3 **Strzelecki Creek** *seasonal river* South Australia
182 J3 **Strzelecki Desert** *desert* South Australia
111 G15 **Strzelin** *Ger.* Strehlen. Dolnośląskie, SW Poland 50°48′N 17°03′E
110 I11 **Strzelno** Kujawsko-pomorski, C Poland 52°38′N 18°11′E
111 N17 **Strzyżów** Podkarpackie, SE Poland 49°52′N 21°46′E
15 S8 **St-Siméon** Québec, SE Canada 47°50′N 69°55′W
**Stua Laighean** *see* Leinster, Mount
23 Y13 **Stuart** Florida, SE USA 27°12′N 80°15′W
29 U14 **Stuart** Iowa, C USA 41°30′N 94°19′W
29 O13 **Stuart** Nebraska, C USA 42°36′N 99°08′W
21 S8 **Stuart** Virginia, NE USA 36°38′N 80°19′W
10 L13 **Stuart** ⟿ British Columbia, SW Canada
35 N10 **Stuart Island** *island* Alaska, USA
10 L13 **Stuart Lake** ⊚ British Columbia, SW Canada
185 B22 **Stuart Mountains** ▲▲ South Island, New Zealand
182 F3 **Stuart Range** *hill range* South Australia
**Stubaital** *see* Neustift im Stubaital
95 I24 **Stubbekøbing** Sjælland, SE Denmark 54°53′N 12°04′E
45 P14 **Stubbs** Saint Vincent, Saint Vincent and the Grenadines 13°08′N 61°09′W
109 V6 **Stübming** ⟿ E Austria
114 J11 **Studen Kladenets, Yazovir** ⊠ S Bulgaria
185 G21 **Studholme** Canterbury, South Island, New Zealand 44°44′S 171°08′E
**Stuhlweissenberg** *see* Székesfehérvár
**Stuhm** *see* Sztum
12 C7 **Stull Lake** ⊚ Ontario, C Canada
167 S11 **Stung Treng** *prev.* Stœng Trêng. Stung Treng, NE Cambodia 13°31′N 105°58′E
**Stuorrarijjda** *see* Storriten
126 L4 **Stupino** Moskovskaya Oblast', W Russia 54°54′N 38°06′E
27 U4 **Sturgeon** Missouri, C USA 39°13′N 92°16′W
14 G10 **Sturgeon** ⟿ Ontario, S Canada
31 N6 **Sturgeon Bay** Wisconsin, N USA 44°51′N 87°21′W
14 G11 **Sturgeon Falls** Ontario, S Canada 46°22′N 79°57′W
12 C11 **Sturgeon Lake** ⊚ Ontario, S Canada
30 M3 **Sturgeon River** ⟿ Michigan, N USA
20 H6 **Sturgis** Kentucky, S USA 37°33′N 87°58′W
31 P11 **Sturgis** Michigan, N USA 41°48′N 85°25′W
28 J9 **Sturgis** South Dakota, N USA 44°24′N 103°30′W
112 D10 **Šturlić** ◆ Federacija Bosne I Hercegovine, NW Bosnia and Herzegovina
111 J22 **Štúrovo** *Hung.* Párkány; *prev.* Parkan. Nitriansky Kraj, SW Slovakia 47°49′N 18°40′E
182 L4 **Sturt, Mount** *hill* New South Wales, SE Australia
181 P4 **Sturt Plain** *plain* Northern Territory, N Australia
181 T9 **Sturt Stony Desert** *desert* South Australia
83 J25 **Stutterheim** Eastern Cape, S South Africa 32°35′S 27°26′E
101 H21 **Stuttgart** Baden-Württemberg, SW Germany 48°47′N 09°12′E
27 W12 **Stuttgart** Arkansas, C USA 34°30′N 91°32′W
92 H2 **Stykkishólmur** Vesturland, W Iceland 65°04′N 22°43′W
115 F17 **Stylída** *var.* Stilida, Stilís. Stereá Elláda, C Greece 38°55′N 22°37′E
116 K2 **Styr** *Rus.* Styr'. ⟿ Belarus/Ukraine
115 I19 **Stýra** *var.* Stira. Évvoia, C Greece 38°10′N 24°13′E
**Styria** *see* Steiermark
15 Y5 **St-Yvon** Québec, SE Canada 49°09′N 64°51′W
**Su** *see* Jiangsu
**Sua** *see* Sowa
171 Q17 **Suai** W East Timor 09°19′S 125°16′E
54 G9 **Suaita** Santander, C Colombia 06°07′N 73°30′W
80 I7 **Suakin** *var.* Sawakin. Red Sea, NE Sudan 19°06′N 37°17′E
161 T13 **Su'ao** *Jap.* Suō. N Taiwan 24°33′N 121°48′E
**Suao** *see* Suau
**Sua Pan** *see* Sowa Pan
40 G6 **Suaqui Grande** Sonora, NW Mexico 28°22′N 109°52′W
61 A16 **Suardi** Santa Fe, C Argentina 30°32′S 61°58′W
54 D11 **Suárez** Cauca, SW Colombia 02°55′N 76°41′W
186 G10 **Suau** *var.* Suao. Suaul Island, SE Papua New Guinea 10°39′S 150°03′E
118 G12 **Subačius** Panevėžys, NE Lithuania 55°46′N 24°45′E
168 K9 **Subang** *prev.* Soebang. Jawa, C Indonesia 06°32′S 107°45′E
169 O16 **Subang** ✈ (Kuala Lumpur) Pahang, Peninsular Malaysia
129 S10 **Subansiri** ⟿ NE India
154 M12 **Subarnapur** *prev.* Sonapur, Sonepur. Odisha, E India 20°50′N 83°58′E
118 I11 **Subate** SE Latvia 56°00′N 25°54′E
139 N5 **Subaykhān** Dayr az Zawr, E Syria 34°52′N 40°35′E
**Subei/Subei Mongolzu Zizhixian** *see* Dangchengwan
169 P9 **Subi Besar, Pulau** *island* Kepulauan Natuna, W Indonesia
**Subiyah** *see* Aş Şubayhīyah
26 I7 **Sublette** Kansas, C USA 37°28′N 100°52′W
112 K8 **Subotica** *Ger.* Maria-Theresiopel, *Hung.* Szabadka. Vojvodina, N Serbia 46°06′N 19°41′E
116 K9 **Suceava** *Ger.* Suczawa, *Hung.* Szucsava. Suceava, NE Romania 47°41′N 26°16′E
116 J9 **Suceava** ◆ *county* NE Romania
116 K9 **Suceava** ⟿ N Romania
112 E12 **Sučevići** Zadar, SW Croatia 44°13′N 16°04′E
111 K17 **Sucha Beskidzka** Małopolskie, S Poland 49°44′N 19°36′E
111 M14 **Suchedniów** Świętokrzyskie, C Poland 51°01′N 20°49′E
42 A2 **Suchitepéquez** *off.* Departamento de Suchitepéquez. ◆ *department* SW Guatemala
**Suchitepéquez, Departamento de** *see* Suchitepéquez
**Su-chou** *see* Suzhou
**Suchow** *see* Suzhou, Jiangsu, China
**Suchow** *see* Xuzhou, Jiangsu, China
97 D17 **Suck** ⟿ C Ireland
**Sucker State** *see* Illinois
186 F9 **Suckling, Mount** ▲ S Papua New Guinea 09°36′S 149°00′E
57 L19 **Sucre** *hist.* Chuquisaca, La Plata. ● (Bolivia-official capital) Chuquisaca, S Bolivia 18°53′S 65°25′W
54 E6 **Sucre** Santander, N Colombia 08°50′N 74°22′W
56 A7 **Sucre** Manabí, W Ecuador 01°21′S 80°27′W
54 E6 **Sucre** *off.* Departamento de Sucre. ◆ *province* N Colombia
55 O5 **Sucre** *off.* Estado Sucre. ◆ *state* NE Venezuela
**Sucre, Departamento de** *see* Sucre
**Sucre, Estado** *see* Sucre
56 D6 **Sucumbíos** ◆ *province* NE Ecuador
113 G15 **Sućuraj** Split-Dalmacija, S Croatia 43°07′N 17°10′E
58 K10 **Sucuriju** Amapá, NE Brazil 01°31′N 50°W
**Suczawa** *see* Suceava
79 E16 **Sud** *Eng.* South. ◆ *province* S Cameroon
124 K13 **Suda** ⟿ NW Russia
**Suda** *see* Sóuda
117 U13 **Sudak** Avtonomna Respublika Krym, S Ukraine 44°52′N 34°57′E
24 M4 **Sudan** Texas, SW USA 34°04′N 102°32′W
80 C10 **Sudan** *off.* Republic of Sudan, *Ar.* As Sūdān, Jumhūrīyat as Sūdān; *prev.* Anglo-Egyptian Sudan. ◆ *republic* N Africa
**Sūdān, As** *see* Sudan
**Sudanese Republic** *see* Mali
**Sūdān, Jumhūrīyat as** *see* Sudan
**Sudan, Republic of** *see* Sudan
14 F10 **Sudbury** Ontario, S Canada 46°29′N 81°W
97 P20 **Sudbury** E England, United Kingdom 52°04′N 00°43′E
**Sud, Canal de** *see* Gonâve, Canal de la
80 E13 **Sudd** *swamp region* C South Sudan
100 K10 **Sude** ⟿ N Germany
**Suderø** *see* Suðuroy
**Sudest Island** *see* Tagula Island
111 E15 **Sudeten** *var.* Sudetes, Sudetic Mountains, *Cz./Pol.* Sudety. ▲▲ Czechia/Poland
**Sudetes/Sudetic Mountains/Sudety** *see* Sudeten
95 B19 **Suðuroy** *Dan.* Suderø. *island* S Faroe Islands
124 M15 **Sudislavl'** Kostromskaya Oblast', NW Russia 57°55′N 41°45′E
**Südkarpaten** *see* Carpaţii Meridionali
79 N20 **Sud-Kivu** *off.* Région Sud Kivu. ◆ *region* E Dem. Rep. Congo
**Sud Kivu, Région** *see* Sud-Kivu
**Südliche Morava** *see* Južna Morava
100 E12 **Süd-Nord-Kanal** *canal* NW Germany
126 M3 **Sudogda** Vladimirskaya Oblast', W Russia 55°58′N 40°57′E
**Sudostroy** *see* Severodvinsk
**Sud-Ouest** *see* South-West
173 X17 **Sud Ouest, Pointe** *headland* SW Mauritius 20°27′S 57°18′E
187 P17 **Sud, Province** ◆ *province* S New Caledonia
92 G1 **Suðureyri** Vestfirðir, NW Iceland 66°08′N 23°31′W
92 J4 **Suðurland** ◆ *region* S Iceland
92 H4 **Suðurnes** ◆ *region* SW Iceland
126 J8 **Sudzha** Kurskaya Oblast', W Russia 51°12′N 35°19′E
81 D15 **Sue** ⟿ W South Sudan
105 S10 **Sueca** Comunitat Valenciana, E Spain 39°13′N 00°19′W
**Süedinenie** *see* Saedinenie
**Suero** *see* Alzira
**Suez** *see* As Suways
**Suez Canal** *see* Qanāt as Suways
**Suez, Gulf of** *see* Khalīj as Suways
11 R17 **Suffield** Alberta, SW Canada 50°15′N 111°05′W
21 X7 **Suffolk** Virginia, NE USA 36°44′N 76°37′W
97 P20 **Suffolk** *cultural region* E England, United Kingdom
142 J2 **Şūfiān** Āzarbāyjān-e Sharqī, N Iran 38°15′N 45°59′E
30 L13 **Sugar Creek** ⟿ Illinois, N USA
31 N12 **Sugar Creek** ⟿ Illinois, N USA
31 R3 **Sugar Island** *island* Michigan, N USA
25 V11 **Sugar Land** Texas, SW USA 29°37′N 95°37′W
19 P6 **Sugarloaf Mountain** ▲ Maine, NE USA 45°01′N 70°18′W
65 G24 **Sugar Loaf Point** *headland* N Saint Helena 15°54′S 05°43′W
136 G16 **Suğla Gölü** ⊚ SW Turkey
123 T8 **Sugoy** ⟿ E Russia
158 F7 **Sugun** Xinjiang Uygur Zizhiqu, W China 39°46′N 76°45′E
147 U11 **Sugut, Gora** ▲ SW Kyrgyzstan 39°52′N 73°36′E
169 V6 **Sugut, Sungai** ⟿ East Malaysia
159 O9 **Suhai Hu** ⊚ C China
162 K14 **Suhait** Nei Mongol Zizhiqu, N China 39°29′N 105°11′E
75 X10 **Sūhāj** *var.* Sohag, Sawhāj, Suliag. C Egypt 26°28′N 31°44′E
141 X7 **Şuḩār** *var.* Sohar. N Oman 24°20′N 56°43′E
114 N8 **Suha Reka** ⟿ NE Bulgaria
113 M17 **Suharekë** *Serb.* Suva Reka. S Kosovo 42°23′N 20°50′E
162 L6 **Sühbaatar** Selenge, N Mongolia 50°12′N 106°14′E
163 P8 **Sühbaatar** *var.* Haylaastay. Sühbaatar, E Mongolia 46°44′N 113°51′E
163 P9 **Sühbaatar** ◆ *province* E Mongolia
114 J8 **Suhindol** *var.* Sukhindol. Veliko Turnovo, N Bulgaria 43°11′N 24°10′E
101 K17 **Suhl** Thüringen, C Germany 50°37′N 10°43′E
108 F7 **Suhr** Aargau, N Switzerland 47°23′N 08°05′E
**Sui'an** *see* Zhangpu
**Suicheng** *see* Suixi
161 O12 **Suichuan** *var.* Quanjiang. Jiangxi, S China 26°26′N 114°34′E
**Suid-Afrika** *see* South Africa
**Suid-Afrika, Republiek van** *see* South Africa
160 L4 **Suide** *var.* Mingzhou. Shaanxi, C China 37°30′N 110°10′E
**Suidwes-Afrika** *see* Namibia
163 Y9 **Suifenhe** Heilongjiang, NE China 44°22′N 131°12′E
**Suigen** *see* Suwon
163 W8 **Suihua** Heilongjiang, NE China 46°40′N 127°00′E
**Súilí, Loch** *see* Swilly, Lough
161 Q6 **Suining** Jiangsu, E China 33°54′N 117°58′E
160 I9 **Suining** Sichuan, C China 30°31′N 105°33′E
103 Q4 **Suippes** Marne, N France 49°08′N 04°31′E
97 E20 **Suir** *Ir.* An tSiúir. ⟿ S Ireland
165 J13 **Suita** Ōsaka, Honshū, SW Japan 34°39′N 135°27′E
160 L16 **Suixi** *var.* Suicheng. Guangdong, S China 21°23′N 110°14′E
**Sui Xian** *see* Suizhou
163 T13 **Suizhong** Liaoning, NE China 40°19′N 120°22′E
161 N8 **Suizhou** *prev.* Sui Xian. Hubei, C China 31°46′N 113°20′E
149 P17 **Sujawal** Sindh, SE Pakistan 24°36′N 68°06′E
169 O16 **Sukabumi** *prev.* Soekaboemi. Jawa, C Indonesia 06°55′S 106°56′E
169 Q12 **Sukadana, Teluk** *bay* Borneo, W Indonesia
165 P11 **Sukagawa** Fukushima, Honshū, C Japan 37°16′N 140°20′E
**Sukarnapura** *see* Jayapura
**Sukarno, Puntjak** *see* Jaya, Puncak
**Sŭkh** *see* Sokh
**Sukhindol** *see* Suhindol
126 J5 **Sukhinichi** Kaluzhskaya Oblast', W Russia 54°06′N 35°22′E
**Sukhne** *see* As Sukhnah
129 Q4 **Sukhona** *var.* Tot'ma. ⟿ NW Russia
167 O8 **Sukhothai** *var.* Sukotai. Sukhothai, W Thailand 17°00′N 99°51′E
**Sukhumi** *see* Sokhumi
**Sukkertoppen** *see* Maniitsoq
149 Q13 **Sukkur** Sindh, SE Pakistan 27°45′N 68°46′E
**Sukotai** *see* Sukhothai
**Sukra Bay** *see* Şawqirah, Dawḩat
125 V15 **Suksun** Permskiy Kray, NW Russia 57°10′N 57°27′E
165 F15 **Sukumo** Kōchi, Shikoku, SW Japan 32°55′N 132°42′E
94 B12 **Sula** *island* S Norway
125 Q5 **Sula** ⟿ NW Russia
117 R5 **Sula** ⟿ N Ukraine
42 H6 **Sulaco, Río** ⟿ NW Honduras
**Sulaimaniya** *see* As Sulaymānīyah
149 S10 **Sulaiman Range** ▲▲ C Pakistan
127 Q16 **Sulak** Respublika Dagestan, SW Russia 43°19′N 47°28′E
127 Q16 **Sulak** ⟿ SW Russia
171 Q13 **Sula, Kepulauan** *island group* C Indonesia
136 I12 **Sulakyurt** *var.* Konur. Kırıkkale, N Turkey 40°10′N 33°42′E
171 P17 **Sulamu** Timor, S Indonesia 09°57′S 123°33′E
96 F5 **Sula Sgeir** *island* NW Scotland, United Kingdom
171 N13 **Sulawesi** *Eng.* Celebes. *island* C Indonesia
**Sulawesi, Laut** *see* Celebes Sea
171 N14 **Sulawesi Selatan** *off.* Propinsi Sulawesi Selatan, *var.* Sulsel, *Eng.* South Celebes, South Sulawesi. ◆ *province* C Indonesia
**Sulawesi Selatan, Propinsi** *see* Sulawesi Selatan
171 P12 **Sulawesi Tengah** *off.* Propinsi Sulawesi Tengah, *var.* Sulteng, *Eng.* Central Celebes, Central Sulawesi. ◆ *province* N Indonesia
**Sulawesi Tengah, Propinsi** *see* Sulawesi Tengah
171 O14 **Sulawesi Tenggara** *off.* Propinsi Sulawesi Tenggara, *var.* Sultenggara, *Eng.* South-East Celebes, South-East Sulawesi. ◆ *province* C Indonesia
**Sulawesi Tenggara, Propinsi** *see* Sulawesi Tenggara
171 P11 **Sulawesi Utara** *off.* Propinsi Sulawesi Utara, *var.* Sulut, *Eng.* North Celebes, North Sulawesi. ◆ *province* N Indonesia
**Sulawesi Utara, Propinsi** *see* Sulawesi Utara
139 T5 **Sulaymān Beg** At Ta'mím, N Iraq
95 D15 **Suldalsvatnet** ⊚ S Norway
**Sulden** *see* Solda
110 E12 **Sulechów** *Ger.* Züllichau. Lubuskie, W Poland 52°05′N 15°37′E
110 E11 **Sulęcin** Lubuskie, W Poland 52°29′N 15°06′E
77 U14 **Suleja** Niger, C Nigeria 09°15′N 07°10′E
111 K14 **Sulejów** Łodzkie, S Poland 51°21′N 19°57′E
96 I5 **Sule Skerry** *island* N Scotland, United Kingdom
**Suliag** *see* Sūhāj
76 J16 **Sulima** S Sierra Leone 06°59′N 11°34′W
117 O13 **Sulina** Tulcea, SE Romania 45°07′N 29°40′E
117 N13 **Sulina, Braţul** ⟿ SE Romania
100 H12 **Sulingen** Niedersachsen, NW Germany 52°40′N 08°48′E
**Sulisjielmmá** *see* Sulitjelma
92 H12 **Suliskongen** ▲ C Norway 67°10′N 16°16′E
92 H12 **Sulitjelma** *Lapp.* Sulisjielmmá. Nordland, C Norway 67°10′N 16°05′E
56 A9 **Sullana** Piura, NW Peru 04°54′S 80°42′W
23 N3 **Sulligent** Alabama, S USA 33°54′N 88°07′W
30 M14 **Sullivan** Illinois, N USA 39°36′N 88°36′W
31 N15 **Sullivan** Indiana, N USA 39°05′N 87°24′W
27 W5 **Sullivan** Missouri, C USA 38°12′N 91°09′W
**Sullivan Island** *see* Lanbi Kyun
96 M1 **Sullom Voe** NE Scotland, United Kingdom 60°24′N 01°09′W
103 O7 **Sully-sur-Loire** Loiret, C France 47°46′N 02°21′E
**Sulmo** *see* Sulmona
107 K15 **Sulmona** *anc.* Sulmo. Abruzzo, C Italy 42°03′N 13°56′E
**Sulo** *see* Shule He
114 M11 **Süloğlu** Edirne, NW Turkey 41°46′N 26°55′E
22 G9 **Sulphur** Louisiana, S USA 30°14′N 93°22′W
27 O12 **Sulphur** Oklahoma, C USA 34°31′N 96°58′W
28 K9 **Sulphur Creek** ⟿ South Dakota, N USA
24 M5 **Sulphur Draw** ⟿ Texas, SW USA
25 W5 **Sulphur River** ⟿ Arkansas/Texas, SW USA
25 V6 **Sulphur Springs** Texas, SW USA 33°09′N 95°36′W
24 M6 **Sulphur Springs Draw** ⟿ Texas, SW USA
**Sulsel** *see* Sulawesi Selatan
14 D8 **Sultan** Ontario, S Canada 47°34′N 82°45′W
**Sultānābād** *see* Arāk
**Sultan Alonto, Lake** *see* Lanao, Lake
136 G15 **Sultan Dağları** ▲▲ C Turkey
114 N13 **Sultanköy** Tekirdağ, NW Turkey 41°01′N 27°58′E
171 Q7 **Sultan Kudarat** *var.* Nuling. Mindanao, S Philippines 07°20′N 124°16′E
152 M13 **Sultānpur** Uttar Pradesh, N India 26°15′N 82°04′E
**Sulteng** *see* Sulawesi Tengah
**Sultenggara** *see* Sulawesi Tenggara
171 O9 **Sulu Archipelago** *island group* SW Philippines
192 F7 **Sulu Basin** *undersea feature* SE South China Sea 08°00′N 121°30′E
**Sülüktü** *see* Sulyukta
**Sulu, Laut** *see* Sulu Sea
169 X6 **Sulu Sea** *var.* Laut Sulu. *sea* SW Philippines
**Sulut** *see* Sulawesi Utara
145 O15 **Sulutobe** *Kaz.* Sulütöbe. Kzylorda, S Kazakhstan 44°31′N 66°17′E
**Sulütöbe** *see* Sulutobe
147 Q11 **Sulyukta** *Kyr.* Sülüktü. Batkenskaya Oblast', SW Kyrgyzstan 39°57′N 69°31′E
**Sulz** *see* Sulz am Neckar
101 G22 **Sulz am Neckar** *var.* Sulz. Baden-Württemberg, SW Germany 48°22′N 08°37′E
101 L20 **Sulzbach-Rosenberg** Bayern, SE Germany 49°30′N 11°43′E
195 N13 **Sulzberger Bay** *bay* Antarctica
81 M14 **Sumalē** *var.* Somali. ◆ E Ethiopia
113 F15 **Šumartin** Split-Dalmacija, S Croatia 43°17′N 16°52′E
32 H6 **Sumas** Washington, NW USA 49°00′N 122°15′W
168 J10 **Sumatera** *Eng.* Sumatra. *island* W Indonesia
168 J12 **Sumatera Barat** *off.* Propinsi Sumatera Barat, *var.* Sumbar, *Eng.* West Sumatra. ◆ *province* W Indonesia
**Sumatera Barat, Propinsi** *see* Sumatera Barat
168 L13 **Sumatera Selatan** *off.* Propinsi Sumatera Selatan, *var.* Sumsel, *Eng.* South Sumatra. ◆ *province* W Indonesia
**Sumatera Selatan, Propinsi** *see* Sumatera Selatan
168 H10 **Sumatera Utara** *off.* Propinsi Sumatera Utara, *var.* Sumut, *Eng.* North Sumatra. ◆ *province* W Indonesia
**Sumatera Utara, Propinsi** *see* Sumatera Utara
**Sumatra** *see* Sumatera
**Šumava** *see* Bohemian Forest
**Sumayl** *see* Sêmêl
139 U7 **Sumayr al Muḩammad** Diyālá, E Iraq 33°34′N 45°06′E
171 N17 **Sumba, Pulau** *Eng.* Sandalwood Island; *prev.* Soemba. *island* Nusa Tenggara, C Indonesia
146 D12 **Sumbar** ⟿ W Turkmenistan
**Sumbar** *see* Sumatera Barat
192 E9 **Sumbawa** *prev.* Soembawa. *island* Nusa Tenggara, C Indonesia
170 L16 **Sumbawabesar** Sumbawa, S Indonesia 08°30′S 117°25′E
81 F23 **Sumbawanga** Rukwa, W Tanzania 07°57′S 31°37′E
82 B12 **Sumbe** *var.* N'Gunza, *Port.* Novo Redondo. Kwanza Sul, W Angola 11°13′S 13°53′E
96 M3 **Sumburgh Head** *headland* NE Scotland, United Kingdom 59°51′N 01°16′W
111 H23 **Sümeg** Veszprém, W Hungary 47°01′N 17°13′E
80 C12 **Sumeih** Eastern Darfur, S Sudan 09°50′N 27°39′E
169 T16 **Sumenep** *prev.* Soemenep. Pulau Madura, C Indonesia 07°01′S 113°51′E
**Sumgait** *see* Sumqayıt, Azerbaijan
**Sumgait** *see* Sumqayıtçay, Azerbaijan
165 Y14 **Sumisu-jima** *Eng.* Smith Island. *island* SE Japan
**Summël** *see* Sêmêl
31 O5 **Summer Island** *island* Michigan, N USA
32 H15 **Summer Lake** ⊚ Oregon, NW USA
11 N17 **Summerland** British Columbia, SW Canada 49°35′N 119°45′W
13 P14 **Summerside** Prince Edward Island, SE Canada 46°24′N 63°46′W
21 R5 **Summersville** West Virginia, NE USA 38°17′N 80°52′W
21 R5 **Summersville Lake** ⊠ West Virginia, NE USA
21 S13 **Summerton** South Carolina, SE USA 33°36′N 80°21′W
23 R2 **Summerville** Georgia, SE USA 34°28′N 85°21′W
21 S14 **Summerville** South Carolina, SE USA 33°01′N 80°10′W
39 R10 **Summit** Alaska, USA 63°21′N 148°50′W
35 V6 **Summit Mountain** ▲ Nevada, W USA 39°23′N 116°25′W
37 R8 **Summit Peak** ▲ Colorado, C USA 37°21′N 106°42′W
**Summus Portus** *see* Somport, Col du
29 X12 **Sumner** Iowa, C USA 42°51′N 92°05′W
22 K3 **Sumner** Mississippi, S USA 33°58′N 90°22′W
185 H17 **Sumner, Lake** ⊚ South Island, New Zealand
37 U12 **Sumner, Lake** ⊠ New Mexico, SW USA
111 G17 **Šumperk** *Ger.* Mährisch-Schönberg. Olomoucký Kraj, E Czechia 49°58′N 17°00′E
42 F7 **Sumpul, Río** ⟿ El Salvador/Honduras
137 Z11 **Sumqayıt** *Rus.* Sumgait. E Azerbaijan 40°33′N 49°41′E
137 Y11 **Sumqayıtçay** *Rus.* Sumgait. ⟿ E Azerbaijan
147 R9 **Sumsar** Dzhalal-Abadskaya Oblast', W Kyrgyzstan 41°12′N 71°16′E
**Sumsel** *see* Sumatera Selatan
117 S3 **Sums'ka Oblast'** *var.* Sumy, *Rus.* Sumskaya Oblast'. ◆ *province* NE Ukraine
**Sumskaya Oblast'** *see* Sums'ka Oblast'
124 J8 **Sumskiy Posad** Respublika Kareliya, NW Russia 64°12′N 35°22′E
21 S12 **Sumter** South Carolina, SE USA 33°54′N 80°22′W
**Sumut** *see* Sumatera Utara
117 T3 **Sumy** Sums'ka Oblast', NE Ukraine 50°54′N 34°49′E
**Sumy** *see* Sums'ka Oblast'
159 Q15 **Sumzom** Xizang Zizhiqu, W China 29°45′N 96°14′E
125 R15 **Suna** Kirovskaya Oblast', NW Russia 57°53′N 50°04′E
124 I10 **Suna** ⟿ NW Russia
165 S3 **Sunagawa** Hokkaidō, NE Japan 43°30′N 141°55′E
153 V13 **Sunamganj** Sylhet, NE Bangladesh 25°04′N 91°24′E
163 W14 **Sunan** ✈ (P'yŏngyang) SW North Korea 39°12′N 125°40′E
**Sunan/Sunan Yugurzu Zizhixian** *see* Hongwansi
19 N9 **Sunapee Lake** ⊚ New Hampshire, NE USA
139 P4 **Sunaysilah** *salt marsh* N Iraq
20 M8 **Sunbright** Tennessee, S USA 36°12′N 84°39′W
33 R6 **Sunburst** Montana, NW USA 48°51′N 111°54′W
183 N12 **Sunbury** Victoria, SE Australia 37°36′S 144°45′E
21 X8 **Sunbury** North Carolina, SE USA 36°27′N 76°34′W
18 G14 **Sunbury** Pennsylvania, NE USA 40°51′N 76°47′W
61 A17 **Sunchales** Santa Fe, C Argentina 30°58′S 61°35′W
163 Y16 **Suncheon** *prev.* Sunch'ŏn. South Korea 34°56′N 127°29′E
**Sunch'ŏn** *see* Suncheon
36 K13 **Sun City** Arizona, SW USA 33°36′N 112°16′W
19 O9 **Suncook** New Hampshire, NE USA 43°07′N 71°25′W
161 P5 **Suncun** *prev.* Xinwen. Shandong, E China 35°49′N 117°36′E
**Sunda Islands** *see* Greater Sunda Islands
33 Z12 **Sundance** Wyoming, C USA 44°24′N 104°22′W
153 T17 **Sundarbans** *wetland* Bangladesh/India
154 M11 **Sundargarh** Odisha, E India 22°07′N 84°02′E
129 U15 **Sunda Shelf** *undersea feature* S South China Sea 05°00′N 107°00′E
**Sunda Trench** *see* Java Trench
129 U17 **Sunda Trough** *undersea feature* E Indian Ocean 08°50′S 109°30′E
95 O16 **Sundbyberg** Stockholm, C Sweden 59°22′N 17°58′E
97 M14 **Sunderland** *var.* Wearmouth. NE England, United Kingdom 54°55′N 01°23′W
101 F15 **Sundern** Nordrhein-Westfalen, W Germany 51°19′N 08°00′E
136 F12 **Sündiken Dağları** ▲▲ C Turkey
24 M5 **Sundown** Texas, SW USA 33°27′N 102°29′W
11 P16 **Sundre** Alberta, SW Canada 51°49′N 114°46′W
14 H12 **Sundridge** Ontario, S Canada 45°45′N 79°25′W
93 H17 **Sundsvall** Västernorrland, C Sweden 62°22′N 17°20′E
26 H4 **Sunflower, Mount** ▲ Kansas, C USA 39°01′N 102°02′W
**Sunflower State** *see* Kansas
169 N14 **Sungaibuntu** Sumatera, SW Indonesia 04°04′S 105°37′E
168 K12 **Sungaidareh** Sumatera, W Indonesia 0°58′S 101°30′E
167 P17 **Sungai Kolok** *var.* Sungai Ko-Lok. Narathiwat, SW Thailand 06°02′N 101°58′E
**Sungai Ko-Lok** *see* Sungai Kolok
168 K12 **Sungaipenuh** *prev.* Soengaipenoeh. Sumatera, W Indonesia 02°S 101°28′E
169 P11 **Sungaipinyuh** Borneo, C Indonesia 0°16′N 109°06′E
**Sungari** *see* Songhua Jiang
**Sungaria** *see* Dzungaria
**Sungei Pahang** *see* Pahang, Sungai
167 O8 **Sung Men** Phrae, NW Thailand 17°59′N 100°07′E
83 M15 **Sungo** Tete, NW Mozambique 16°31′S 33°58′E
**Sungpu** *see* Songpan
168 M13 **Sungsang** Sumatera, W Indonesia 02°22′S 104°50′E
114 M9 **Sungurlare** Burgas, E Bulgaria 42°47′N 26°46′E
136 J12 **Sungurlu** Çorum, N Turkey 40°10′N 34°23′E
112 F9 **Sunja** Sisak-Moslavina, C Croatia 45°21′N 16°33′E
153 Q12 **Sun Koshī** ⟿ E Nepal
94 F9 **Sunndalen** *valley* S Norway
94 F9 **Sunndalsøra** Møre og Romsdal, S Norway 62°39′N 08°37′E
95 K15 **Sunne** Värmland, C Sweden 59°52′N 13°05′E
95 O15 **Sunnersta** Uppsala, C Sweden 59°46′N 17°40′E
94 C11 **Sunnfjord** *physical region* S Norway
95 C15 **Sunnhordland** *physical region* S Norway
94 D10 **Sunnmøre** *physical region* S Norway
37 N4 **Sunnyside** Utah, W USA 39°33′N 110°23′W
32 J10 **Sunnyside** Washington, NW USA 46°01′N 119°58′W
35 N9 **Sunnyvale** California, W USA 37°22′N 122°02′W
30 L8 **Sun Prairie** Wisconsin, N USA 43°12′N 89°12′W
**Sunqur** *see* Sonqor
25 N1 **Sunray** Texas, SW USA 36°01′N 101°49′W
22 I8 **Sunset** Louisiana, S USA 30°24′N 92°04′W
25 S5 **Sunset** Texas, SW USA 33°24′N 97°45′W
**Sunset State** *see* Oregon




◆ Country
● Country Capital
◇ Dependent Territory
○ Dependent Territory Capital
◆ Administrative Regions
✈ International Airport
▲ Mountain
▲▲ Mountain Range
☒ Volcano
⟿ River
⊚ Lake
⊠ Reservoir

SUNSHINE COAST – TABOR


181 Z10 **Sunshine Coast** *cultural region* Queensland, E Australia

**Sunshine State** *see* Florida

**Sunshine State** *see* New Mexico

**Sunshine State** *see* South Dakota

123 O10 **Suntar** Respublika Sakha (Yakutiya), NE Russia 62°10′N 117°34′E

39 R10 **Suntrana** Alaska, USA 63°51′N 148°51′W

148 J15 **Suntsar** Baluchistan, SW Pakistan 25°30′N 62°03′E

163 W15 **Sunwi-do** *island* SW North Korea

163 W6 **Sunwu** Heilongjiang, NE China 49°29′N 127°15′E

77 O16 **Sunyani** W Ghana 07°22′N 02°18′W

**Suō** *see* Su'ao

93 M17 **Suolahti** Keski-Suomi, C Finland 62°32′N 25°51′E

**Suoločielgi** *see* Saariselkä

**Suomenlahti** *see* Finland, Gulf of

**Suomen Tasavalta/Suomi** *see* Finland

93 N14 **Suomussalmi** Kainuu, E Finland 64°54′N 29°05′E

165 E13 **Suō-nada** *sea* SW Japan

93 M17 **Suonenjoki** Pohjois-Savo, C Finland 62°36′N 27°07′E

167 S13 **Suong** *var.* Suŏng. Tbong Khmum, S Cambodia 11°55′N 105°39′E

**Suŏng** *see* Suong

124 I10 **Suoyarvi** Respublika Kareliya, NW Russia 62°02′N 32°24′E

**Supanburi** *see* Suphan Buri

57 D14 **Supe** Lima, W Peru 10°49′S 77°40′W

15 V7 **Supérieur, Lac** ◎ Québec, SE Canada

**Supérieur, Lac** *see* Superior, Lake

36 M14 **Superior** Arizona, SW USA 33°17′N 111°06′W

33 O9 **Superior** Montana, NW USA 47°11′N 114°53′W

29 P17 **Superior** Nebraska, C USA 40°01′N 98°04′W

30 I3 **Superior** Wisconsin, N USA 46°42′N 92°04′W

41 S17 **Superior, Laguna** *lagoon* S Mexico

31 N2 **Superior, Lake** *Fr.* Lac Supérieur. ◎ Canada/USA

36 L13 **Superstition Mountains** ▲▲ Arizona, SW USA

113 F14 **Supetar** *It.* San Pietro. Split-Dalmacija, S Croatia 43°22′N 16°34′E

167 O10 **Suphan Buri** *var.* Supanburi. Suphan Buri, W Thailand 14°29′N 100°10′E

171 V12 **Supiori, Pulau** *island* E Indonesia

188 K2 **Supply Reef** *reef* N Northern Mariana Islands

195 O7 **Support Force Glacier** *glacier* Antarctica

137 R10 **Supsa** *prev.* Sup'sa. ≈ W Georgia

**Sup'sa** *see* Supsa

**Sūq 'Abs** *see* 'Abs

139 W12 **Sūq ash Shuyūkh** Dhī Qār, SE Iraq 30°53′N 46°28′E

138 H4 **Şuqaylibīyah** Ḩamāh, W Syria 35°21′N 36°24′E

161 Q6 **Suqian** Jiangsu, E China 33°57′N 118°18′E

**Suqrah** *see* Şawqirah

**Suqrah Bay** *see* Şawqirah, Dawḩat

141 V16 **Suquṭrā** *var.* Sokotra, *Eng.* Socotra. *island* SE Yemen

141 Z8 **Şūr** NE Oman 22°32′N 59°33′E

**Şūr** *see* Soûr

127 P5 **Sura** Penzenskaya Oblast', W Russia 53°23′N 45°03′E

127 P4 **Sura** ≈ W Russia

149 N12 **Surab** Baluchistan, SW Pakistan 28°28′N 66°15′E

**Surabaja** *see* Surabaya

192 E8 **Surabaya** *prev.* Surabaja, Soerabaja. Jawa, C Indonesia 07°14′S 112°45′E

95 N15 **Surahammar** Västmanland, C Sweden 59°43′N 16°13′E

169 Q16 **Surakarta** *Eng.* Solo; *prev.* Soerakarta. Jawa, S Indonesia 07°32′S 110°50′E

**Surakhany** *see* Suraxanı

137 S10 **Surami** C Georgia 41°59′N 43°36′E

143 X13 **Sūrān** Sīstān va Balūchestān, SE Iran 27°18′N 61°58′E

111 I21 **Šurany** *Hung.* Nagysurány. Nitriansky Kraj, SW Slovakia 48°05′N 18°10′E

154 D12 **Sūrat** Gujarāt, W India 21°10′N 72°54′E

**Suratdhani** *see* Surat Thani

152 G9 **Sūratgarh** Rājasthān, NW India 29°20′N 73°59′E

167 N14 **Surat Thani** *var.* Suratdhani. Surat Thani, SW Thailand 09°09′N 99°20′E

119 Q16 **Suraw** *Rus.* Surov. ≈ E Belarus

137 Z11 **Suraxanı** *Rus.* Surakhany. E Azerbaijan 40°25′N 49°59′E

141 Y11 **Surayr** E Oman 19°56′N 57°47′E

138 K2 **Suraysāt** Ḩalab, N Syria 36°42′N 38°01′E

118 O12 **Surazh** Vitsyebskaya Voblasts', NE Belarus 55°25′N 30°44′E

126 H6 **Surazh** Bryanskaya Oblast', W Russia 53°04′N 32°29′E

191 V17 **Sur, Cabo** *headland* Easter Island, Chile, E Pacific Ocean 27°11′S 109°26′W

112 L11 **Surčin** Serbia, N Serbia 44°48′N 20°19′E

116 H9 **Surduc** *Hung.* Szurduk. Sălaj, NW Romania 47°13′N 23°20′E

113 P16 **Surdulica** Serbia, SE Serbia 42°43′N 22°10′E

99 L24 **Sûre** *var.* Sauer. ≈ W Europe *see also* Sauer

**Sûre** *see* Sauer

154 C10 **Surendranagar** Gujarāt, W India 22°44′N 71°43′E

18 K16 **Surf City** New Jersey, NE USA 39°21′N 74°24′W

183 V3 **Surfers Paradise** Queensland, E Australia 27°54′S 153°18′E

21 U13 **Surfside Beach** South Carolina, SE USA 33°36′N 78°58′W

102 J10 **Surgères** Charente-Maritime, W France 46°07′N 00°44′W

122 H10 **Surgut** Khanty-Mansiyskiy Avtonomnyy Okrug-Yugra, C Russia 61°13′N 73°28′E

122 K10 **Surgutikha** Krasnoyarskiy Kray, N Russia 64°44′N 87°13′E

98 M6 **Surhuisterveen** *Fris.* Surhusterfean. Fryslân, N Netherlands 53°11′N 06°10′E

**Surhusterfean** *see* Surhuisterveen

105 V5 **Súria** Cataluña, NE Spain 41°50′N 01°45′E

143 P10 **Sūrīān** Fārs, S Iran

155 J15 **Suriāpet** Telangana, C India 17°10′N 79°42′E

171 Q6 **Surigao** Mindanao, S Philippines 09°43′N 125°31′E

167 R10 **Surin** Surin, E Thailand 14°53′N 103°29′E

**Surinam** *see* Suriname

55 U11 **Suriname** *off.* Republic of Suriname, *Dut.* Republiek Suriname, *var.* Surinam; *prev.* Dutch Guiana, Netherlands Guiana. ◆ *republic* N South America

**Suriname, Republic of** *see* Suriname

**Suriname, Republiek** *see* Suriname

**Sūrīyah** *see* Syria

**Surkhab, Darya-i-** *see* Surkh Āb, Daryā-ye

149 Q4 **Surkh Āb, Daryā-ye** *prev.* Darya-i-surkhab, Daryā-ye Kahmard. ≈ NE Afghanistan

**Surkhandar'inskaya Oblast'** *see* Surxondaryo Viloyati

**Surkhandar'ya** *see* Surxondaryo

**Surkhet** *see* Birendranagar

147 R12 **Surkhob** ≈ C Tajikistan

137 P11 **Sürmene** Trabzon, NE Turkey 40°56′N 40°03′E

**Surov** *see* Suraw

127 N11 **Surovikino** Volgogradskaya Oblast', SW Russia 48°39′N 42°46′E

35 N11 **Sur, Point** *headland* California, W USA 36°18′N 121°54′W

187 N15 **Surprise, Île** *island* N New Caledonia

61 E22 **Sur, Punta** *headland* E Argentina 50°59′S 69°10′W

**Surrentum** *see* Sorrento

28 M3 **Surrey** North Dakota, N USA 48°13′N 101°05′W

97 O22 **Surrey** *cultural region* SE England, United Kingdom

21 X7 **Surry** Virginia, NE USA 37°08′N 81°34′W

108 F8 **Sursee** Luzern, W Switzerland 47°11′N 08°07′E

127 P6 **Sursk** Penzenskaya Oblast', W Russia 53°06′N 45°46′E

127 P5 **Surskoye** Ul'yanovskaya Oblast', W Russia 54°28′N 46°47′E

75 P8 **Surt** *var.* Sidra, Sirte. N Libya 31°13′N 16°35′E

95 I19 **Surte** Västra Götaland, S Sweden 57°49′N 12°01′E

75 Q8 **Surt, Khalīj** *Eng.* Gulf of Sidra, Gulf of Sirti, Sidra. *gulf* N Libya

92 I5 **Surtsey** *island* S Iceland

137 N17 **Suruç** Şanlıurfa, S Turkey 36°58′N 38°24′E

168 L13 **Surulangun** Sumatera, W Indonesia 02°35′S 102°47′E

147 P13 **Surxondaryo** *Rus.* Surkhandar'ya. ≈ Tajikistan/Uzbekistan

147 N13 **Surxondaryo Viloyati** *Rus.* Surkhandar'inskaya Oblast'. ◐ *province* S Uzbekistan

**Süs** *see* Susch

106 A8 **Susa** Piemonte, NE Italy 45°10′N 07°01′E

165 E12 **Susa** Yamaguchi, Honshū, SW Japan 34°35′N 131°34′E

**Susa** *see* Shūsh

113 E16 **Sušac** *It.* Cazza. *island* SW Croatia

**Sūsah** *see* Sousse

164 G14 **Susaki** Kōchi, Shikoku, SW Japan 33°22′N 133°13′E

165 I15 **Susami** Wakayama, Honshū, SW Japan 33°32′N 135°32′E

142 K9 **Sūsangerd** *var.* Susangird. Khūzestān, SW Iran 31°40′N 48°06′E

**Susangird** *see* Sūsangerd

35 P4 **Susanville** California, W USA 40°25′N 120°39′W

108 J9 **Susch** *var.* Süs. Graubünden, SE Switzerland 46°45′N 10°04′E

137 N12 **Suşehri** Sivas, N Turkey 40°11′N 38°06′E

**Susiana** *see* Khūzestān

111 B18 **Sušice** *Ger.* Schüttenhofen. Plzeňský Kraj, W Czechia 49°14′N 13°32′E

39 R11 **Susitna** Alaska, USA 61°32′N 150°30′W

39 R11 **Susitna River** ≈ Alaska, USA

127 Q3 **Suslonger** Respublika Mariy El, W Russia 56°18′N 48°16′E

105 N14 **Suspiro del Moro, Puerto del** *pass* S Spain

18 H16 **Susquehanna River** ≈ New York/Pennsylvania, NE USA

13 O15 **Sussex** New Brunswick, SE Canada 45°43′N 65°32′W

18 J13 **Sussex** New Jersey, NE USA 41°12′N 74°34′W

21 W7 **Sussex** Virginia, NE USA 36°54′N 77°16′W

97 O23 **Sussex** *cultural region* S England, United Kingdom

183 S10 **Sussex Inlet** New South Wales, SE Australia 35°10′S 150°35′E

99 L17 **Susteren** Limburg, SE Netherlands 51°04′N 05°50′E

10 K12 **Sustut Peak** ▲ British Columbia, W Canada 56°25′N 126°34′W

123 S9 **Susuman** Magadanskaya Oblast', E Russia 62°46′N 148°08′E

188 H6 **Susupe** ● (Northern Mariana Islands-judicial capital) Saipan, S Northern Mariana Islands

136 D12 **Susurluk** Balıkesir, NW Turkey 39°55′N 28°10′E

114 M13 **Susuzmüsellim** Tekirdağ, NW Turkey 41°04′N 27°03′E

136 F15 **Sütçüler** Isparta, SW Turkey 37°31′N 31°00′E

116 L13 **Şuţeşti** Brăila, SE Romania 45°13′N 27°27′E

83 F25 **Sutherland** Western Cape, SW South Africa 32°24′S 20°40′E

28 L15 **Sutherland** Nebraska, C USA 41°09′N 101°07′W

96 I7 **Sutherland** *cultural region* N Scotland, United Kingdom

185 B21 **Sutherland Falls** *waterfall* South Island, New Zealand

32 F14 **Sutherlin** Oregon, NW USA 43°23′N 123°18′W

149 V10 **Sutlej** ≈ India/Pakistan

**Sutna** *see* Satna

35 P7 **Sutter Creek** California, W USA 38°22′N 120°49′W

39 R11 **Sutton** Alaska, USA 61°42′N 148°53′W

29 Q16 **Sutton** Nebraska, C USA 40°36′N 97°52′W

21 R4 **Sutton** West Virginia, NE USA 38°41′N 80°43′W

12 F8 **Sutton** ≈ Ontario, C Canada

97 M19 **Sutton Coldfield** C England, United Kingdom 52°34′N 01°48′W

21 R4 **Sutton Lake** ▣ West Virginia, NE USA

15 P13 **Sutton, Monts** *hill range* Québec, SE Canada

12 F8 **Sutton Ridges** ▲▲ Ontario, C Canada

165 Q4 **Suttsu** Hokkaidō, NE Japan 42°46′N 140°12′E

39 P15 **Sutwik Island** *island* Alaska, USA

**Süüj** *see* Dashinchilen

118 H5 **Suure-Jaani** *Ger.* Gross-Sankt-Johannis. Viljandimaa, S Estonia 58°34′N 25°28′E

118 J7 **Suur Munamägi** *var.* Munamägi, *Ger.* Eier-Berg. ▲ SE Estonia 57°42′N 27°03′E

118 F5 **Suur Väin** *Ger.* Grosser Sund. *strait* W Estonia

147 U8 **Suusamyr** Chuyskaya Oblast', C Kyrgyzstan 42°07′N 73°55′E

187 X14 **Suva** ● (Fiji) Viti Levu, W Fiji 18°08′S 178°27′E

187 X15 **Suva** ✈ Viti Levu, C Fiji 18°01′S 178°30′E

113 N18 **Suva Gora** ▲▲ W North Macedonia

118 H11 **Suvainiškis** Panevėžys, NE Lithuania 56°09′N 25°15′E

**Suvalkai/Suvalki** *see* Suwałki

113 P15 **Suva Planina** ▲▲ SE Serbia

**Suva Reka** *see* Suharekë

126 K5 **Suvorov** Tul'skaya Oblast', W Russia 54°08′N 36°33′E

117 N12 **Suvorove** Odes'ka Oblast', SW Ukraine 45°35′N 28°58′E

114 M8 **Suvorovo** Varna, E Bulgaria 43°19′N 27°26′E

**Suvorovo** *see* Ştefan Vodă

**Suwaik** *see* As Suwayq

**Suwaira** *see* Aş Şuwayrah

110 O7 **Suwałki** *Lith.* Suvalkai, *Rus.* Suvalki. Podlaskie, NE Poland 54°06′N 22°56′E

167 R10 **Suwannaphum** Roi Et, E Thailand 15°36′N 103°46′E

23 V8 **Suwannee River** ≈ Florida/Georgia, SE USA

**Şuwār** *see* Aş Şuwār

190 K14 **Suwarrow** *atoll* N Cook Islands

143 R16 **Suwaydān** *var.* Sweiham. Abū Ẓaby, E United Arab Emirates 24°30′N 55°19′E

**Suwaydá/Suwaydā', Muḩāfaẓat as** *see* As Suwaydā'

**Suwayqiyah, Hawr as** *see* Shuwayjah, Hawr ash

**Suweida** *see* As Suwaydā'

**Suweon** *see* Suwon

163 X15 **Suwon** *var.* Suweon; *prev.* Suwŏn, *Jap.* Suigen. NW South Korea 37°17′N 127°03′E

**Suwŏn** *see* Suwon

**Su Xian** *see* Suzhou

143 R14 **Sūzā** Hormozgān, S Iran 26°50′N 56°05′E

**Suzak** *see* Sozak

165 K14 **Suzaka** Mie, Honshū, SW Japan 34°52′N 136°37′E

165 N12 **Suzaka** Nagano, Honshū, S Japan 36°38′N 138°20′E

126 M3 **Suzdal'** Vladimirskaya Oblast', W Russia 56°27′N 40°29′E

161 P7 **Suzhou** *var.* Su Xian. Anhui, E China 33°38′N 117°02′E

161 R8 **Suzhou** *var.* Soochow, Su-chou, Suchow; *prev.* Wuhsien. Jiangsu, E China 31°23′N 120°34′E

**Suzhou** *see* Jiuquan

163 V12 **Suzi He** ≈ NE China

**Suz, Mys** *see* Soye, Mys

165 M10 **Suzu** Ishikawa, Honshū, SW Japan 37°24′N 137°12′E

165 M10 **Suzu-misaki** *headland* Honshū, SW Japan 37°31′N 137°19′E

**Svågälv** *see* Svågan

94 M10 **Svågan** *var.* Svågälv. ≈ C Sweden

**Svalava/Svaljava** *see* Svalyava

92 O2 **Svalbard** ◇ *constituent part of Norway* Arctic Ocean

92 J2 **Svalbarðseyri** Norðurland Eystra, N Iceland 65°43′N 18°03′W

95 K22 **Svalöv** Skåne, S Sweden 55°55′N 13°06′E

116 H7 **Svalyava** *Cz.* Svalava, Svaljava, *Hung.* Szolyva. Zakarpats'ka Oblast', W Ukraine 48°33′N 23°00′E

92 O2 **Svanbergfjellet** ▲ C Svalbard 78°40′N 18°10′E

95 M24 **Svaneke** Bornholm, E Denmark 55°07′N 15°08′E

95 L22 **Svängsta** Blekinge, S Sweden 56°16′N 14°46′E

95 J16 **Svanskog** Värmland, C Sweden 59°10′N 12°34′E

95 L16 **Svartå** Örebro, C Sweden 59°13′N 14°07′E

95 L15 **Svartälven** ≈ C Sweden

92 G12 **Svartisen** *glacier* C Norway

117 X6 **Svatove** *Rus.* Svatovo. Luhans'ka Oblast', E Ukraine 49°24′N 38°11′E

**Svatovo** *see* Svatove

**Sväty Kríž nad Hronom** *see* Žiar nad Hronom

167 Q11 **Svay Chék, Stœng** ≈ Cambodia/Thailand

167 S13 **Svay Rieng** *var.* Svay Riĕng. Svay Rieng, S Cambodia 11°05′N 105°48′E

**Svay Riĕng** *see* Svay Rieng

92 O3 **Sveagruva** Spitsbergen, W Svalbard 77°53′N 16°42′E

95 K23 **Svedala** Skåne, S Sweden 55°30′N 13°15′E

118 H12 **Svėdesai** Utena, NE Lithuania 55°42′N 25°22′E

93 G18 **Sveg** Jämtland, C Sweden 62°02′N 14°20′E

118 C12 **Švėkšna** Klaipėda, W Lithuania 55°31′N 21°37′E

94 C11 **Svelgen** Sogn Og Fjordane, S Norway 61°47′N 05°18′E

95 H15 **Svelvik** Vestfold, S Norway 59°37′N 10°24′E

118 I13 **Švenčionėliai** *Pol.* Nowo-Święciany. Vilnius, SE Lithuania 55°10′N 26°00′E

118 I13 **Švenčionys** *Pol.* Swięciany. Vilnius, SE Lithuania 55°08′N 26°08′E

95 H24 **Svendborg** Syddtjylland, C Denmark 55°04′N 10°38′E

95 K19 **Svenljunga** Västra Götaland, S Sweden 57°30′N 13°05′E

92 P2 **Svenskøya** *island* E Svalbard

93 G17 **Svenstavik** Jämtland, C Sweden 62°40′N 14°24′E

95 G20 **Svenstrup** Nordjylland, N Denmark 56°58′N 09°52′E

118 H12 **Šventoji** ≈ C Lithuania

**Sverdlovsk** *see* Yekaterinburg

127 W2 **Sverdlovskaya Oblast'** ◐ *province* C Russia

122 K6 **Sverdrupa, Ostrov** *island* N Russia

**Sverige** *see* Sweden

**Sverige, Konungariket** *see* Sweden

113 D15 **Svetac** *prev.* Sveti Andrea, *It.* Sant'Andrea. *island* SW Croatia

**Sveti Andrea** *see* Svetac

**Sveti Nikola** *see* Sveti Nikole

113 O18 **Sveti Nikole** *prev.* Sveti Nikola. C North Macedonia 41°54′N 21°55′E

**Sveti Vrach** *see* Sandanski

123 T14 **Svetlaya** Primorskiy Kray, SE Russia 46°33′N 138°20′E

126 B2 **Svetlogorsk** Kaliningradskaya Oblast', W Russia 54°56′N 20°09′E

122 K9 **Svetlogorsk** Krasnoyarskiy Kray, N Russia 66°51′N 88°29′E

**Svetlogorsk** *see* Svyetlahorsk

127 N14 **Svetlograd** Stavropol'skiy Kray, SW Russia 45°20′N 42°53′E

**Svetlovodsk** *see* Svitlovods'k

119 A14 **Svetlyy** *Ger.* Zimmerbude. Kaliningradskaya Oblast', W Russia 54°42′N 20°07′E

127 Y8 **Svetlyy** Orenburgskaya Oblast', W Russia 50°34′N 60°42′E

127 P7 **Svetlyy** Saratovskaya Oblast', W Russia 51°42′N 45°40′E

124 G11 **Svetogorsk** *Fin.* Enso. Leningradskaya Oblast', NW Russia 61°06′N 28°52′E

**Svetozarevo** *see* Jagodina

111 B18 **Švihov** *Ger.* Schwihau. Plzeňský Kraj, W Czechia 49°31′N 13°18′E

112 E13 **Svilaja** ▲▲ SE Croatia

112 N12 **Svilajnac** Serbia, C Serbia 44°15′N 21°12′E

114 L11 **Svilengrad** *prev.* Mustafa-Pasha. Haskovo, S Bulgaria 41°45′N 26°14′E

**Svinecea Mare, Munte** *see* Svinecea Mare, Vârful

116 F13 **Svinecea Mare, Vârful** *var.* Munte Svinecea Mare. ▲ SW Romania 44°47′N 22°10′E

**Svinø** *see* Svínoy

95 B18 **Svínoy** *Dan.* Svinø. *island* NE Faroe Islands

147 N14 **Svintsovyy Rudnik** *Turkm.* Swintsowyy Rudnik. Lebap Welaýaty, E Turkmenistan 37°54′N 66°25′E

118 I13 **Svir** *Rus.* Svir'. Minskaya Voblasts', NW Belarus 54°51′N 26°24′E

124 I12 **Svir'** *canal* NW Russia

**Svir', Ozero** *see* Svir, Vozyera

119 I14 **Svir, Vozyera** *Rus.* Ozero Svir'. ◎ C Belarus

114 J7 **Svishtov** *prev.* Sistova. Veliko Tarnovo, N Bulgaria 43°37′N 25°20′E

119 F18 **Svislach** *Pol.* Świsłocz, *Rus.* Svisloch'. Hrodzyenskaya Voblasts', W Belarus 53°02′N 24°06′E

119 M17 **Svislach** *Rus.* Svisloch'. Mahilyowskaya Voblasts', E Belarus 53°26′N 28°59′E

119 L17 **Svislach** *Rus.* Svisloch'. ≈ E Belarus

**Svisloch'** *see* Svislach

111 F17 **Svitavy** *Ger.* Zwittau. Pardubický Kraj, C Czechia 49°45′N 16°27′E

117 S6 **Svitlovods'k** *Rus.* Svetlovodsk. Kirovohrads'ka Oblast', C Ukraine 49°05′N 33°15′E

**Svizzera** *see* Switzerland

123 Q13 **Svobodnyy** Amurskaya Oblast', SE Russia 51°24′N 128°05′E

114 G9 **Svoge** Sofia, W Bulgaria 42°58′N 23°20′E

92 G11 **Svolvær** Nordland, C Norway 68°15′N 14°40′E

111 F18 **Svratka** *Ger.* Schwarzawa. ≈ SE Czechia

113 P14 **Svrljig** Serbia, E Serbia 43°26′N 22°07′E

197 U10 **Svyataya Anna Trough** *var.* Saint Anna Trough. *undersea feature* N Kara Sea

124 M4 **Svyatoy Nos, Mys** *headland* NW Russia 68°07′N 39°49′E

119 N18 **Svyetlahorsk** *Rus.* Svetlogorsk. Homyel'skaya Voblasts', SE Belarus 52°38′N 29°46′E

**Swabian Jura** *see* Schwäbische Alb

97 P19 **Swaffham** E England, United Kingdom 52°39′N 00°40′E

23 V5 **Swainsboro** Georgia, SE USA 32°36′N 82°19′W

83 C19 **Swakop** ≈ W Namibia

83 C19 **Swakopmund** Erongo, W Namibia 22°40′S 14°34′E

97 M15 **Swale** ≈ N England, United Kingdom

**Swallow Island** *see* Nendö

99 M16 **Swalmen** Limburg, SE Netherlands 51°13′N 06°02′E

12 G8 **Swan** ≈ Ontario, C Canada

97 L24 **Swanage** S England, United Kingdom 50°37′N 01°59′W

182 M10 **Swan Hill** Victoria, SE Australia 35°23′S 143°37′E

11 P13 **Swan Hills** Alberta, W Canada 54°41′N 116°20′W

65 D24 **Swan Island** *island* C Falkland Islands

**Swankalok** *see* Sawankhalok

29 U10 **Swan Lake** ◎ Minnesota, N USA

21 Y10 **Swanquarter** North Carolina, SE USA 35°24′N 76°20′W

182 J9 **Swan Reach** South Australia 34°39′S 139°35′E

11 V15 **Swan River** Manitoba, S Canada 52°06′N 101°17′W

183 P17 **Swansea** Tasmania, SE Australia 42°09′S 148°03′E

97 J22 **Swansea** *Wel.* Abertawe. S Wales, United Kingdom 51°38′N 03°57′W

21 R13 **Swansea** South Carolina, SE USA 33°47′N 81°06′W

19 S7 **Swans Island** *island* Maine, NE USA

28 L17 **Swanson Lake** ▣ Nebraska, C USA

31 R11 **Swanton** Ohio, N USA 41°35′N 83°53′W

110 G11 **Swarzędz** Poznań, W Poland 52°24′N 17°05′E

**Swatow** *see* Shantou

**Swaziland** *see* Eswatini

93 G18 **Sweden** *off.* Kingdom of Sweden, *Swe.* Sverige, Konungariket Sverige. ◆ *monarchy* N Europe

**Sweden, Kingdom of** *see* Sweden

**Swedru** *see* Agona Swedru

25 V12 **Sweeny** Texas, SW USA 29°02′N 95°42′W

33 R6 **Sweetgrass** Montana, NW USA 48°58′N 111°58′W

32 G12 **Sweet Home** Oregon, NW USA 44°24′N 122°44′W

25 T12 **Sweet Home** Texas, SW USA 29°21′N 97°04′W

27 T4 **Sweet Springs** Missouri, C USA 38°57′N 93°24′W

20 M10 **Sweetwater** Tennessee, S USA 35°36′N 84°27′W

25 P7 **Sweetwater** Texas, SW USA 32°27′N 100°25′W

33 V15 **Sweetwater River** ≈ Wyoming, C USA

**Sweiham** *see* Suwaydān

83 F26 **Swellendam** Western Cape, SW South Africa 34°01′S 20°26′E

111 G15 **Świdnica** *Ger.* Schweidnitz. Wałbrzych, SW Poland 50°51′N 16°29′E

111 O14 **Świdnik** *Ger.* Streckenbach. Lubelskie, E Poland 51°14′N 22°41′E

110 F8 **Świdwin** *Ger.* Schivelbein. Zachodnio-pomorskie, NW Poland 53°47′N 15°44′E

111 F15 **Świebodzice** *Ger.* Freiburg in Schlesien, Swiebodzice. Walbrzych, SW Poland 50°54′N 16°23′E

110 E11 **Świebodzin** *Ger.* Schwiebus. Lubuskie, W Poland 52°15′N 15°31′E

**Święciany** *see* Švenčionys

110 I9 **Świecie** *Ger.* Schwertberg. Kujawsko-pomorskie, C Poland 53°24′N 18°24′E

111 L15 **Świętokrzyskie** ◐ *province* S Poland

11 T16 **Swift Current** Saskatchewan, S Canada 50°17′N 107°49′W

98 K9 **Swifterbant** Flevoland, C Netherlands 52°36′N 05°33′E

183 Q12 **Swifts Creek** Victoria, SE Australia 37°17′S 147°41′E

96 E13 **Swilly, Lough** *Ir.* Loch Súilí. *inlet* N Ireland

97 M22 **Swindon** S England, United Kingdom 51°34′N 01°47′W

**Swinemünde** *see* Świnoujście

110 D8 **Świnoujście** *Ger.* Swinemünde. Zachodnio-pomorskie, NW Poland 53°54′N 14°13′E

**Swintsowyy Rudnik** *see* Svintsovyy Rudnik

**Świsłocz** *see* Svislach

**Swiss Confederation** *see* Switzerland

108 E9 **Switzerland** *off.* Swiss Confederation, *Fr.* La Suisse, *Ger.* Schweiz, *It.* Svizzera; *anc.* Helvetia. ◆ *federal republic* C Europe

97 F17 **Swords** *Ir.* Sord, Sórd Choluim Chille. Dublin, E Ireland 53°28′N 06°13′W

18 H13 **Swoyersville** Pennsylvania, NE USA 41°18′N 75°48′W

139 V3 **Syagwêz** *Ar.* Siyāh Gūz. As Sulaymānīyah, E Iraq 35°49′N 45°45′E

124 I10 **Syamozero, Ozero** ◎ NW Russia

124 M13 **Syamzha** Vologodskaya Oblast', NW Russia 60°02′N 41°09′E

118 N13 **Syanno** *Rus.* Senno. Vitsyebskaya Voblasts', NE Belarus 54°49′N 29°43′E

119 K16 **Syarhyeyevichy** *Rus.* Sergeyevichi. Minskaya Voblasts', C Belarus 53°30′N 27°45′E

124 I12 **Syas'stroy** Leningradskaya Oblast', NW Russia 60°05′N 32°37′E

**Sycaminum** *see* Hefa

30 M10 **Sycamore** Illinois, N USA 41°59′N 88°41′W

126 J3 **Sychëvka** Smolenskaya Oblast', W Russia 55°52′N 34°19′E

111 H14 **Syców** *Ger.* Gross Wartenberg. Dolnośląskie, SW Poland 51°18′N 17°42′E

95 F24 **Syddanmark** ◐ *county* SW Denmark

14 E17 **Sydenham** ≈ Ontario, S Canada

**Sydenham Island** *see* Nonouti

183 T9 **Sydney** *state capital* New South Wales, SE Australia 33°55′S 151°10′E

13 R14 **Sydney** Cape Breton Island, Nova Scotia, SE Canada 46°10′N 60°10′W

**Sydney Island** *see* Manra

13 R14 **Sydney Mines** Cape Breton Island, Nova Scotia, SE Canada 46°14′N 60°19′W

**Syedpur** *see* Saidpur

119 K18 **Syelishcha** *Rus.* Selishche. Minskaya Voblasts', C Belarus 53°01′N 27°25′E

119 J18 **Syemyezhava** *Rus.* Semezhevo. Minskaya Voblasts', C Belarus 52°58′N 27°00′E

**Syene** *see* Aswān

117 X6 **Syeverodonets'k** *Rus.* Severodonetsk. Luhans'ka Oblast', E Ukraine 48°59′N 38°28′E

161 T6 **Sÿiao Shan** *island* SE China

100 H11 **Syke** Niedersachsen, NW Germany 52°55′N 08°49′E

94 D10 **Sykkylven** Møre og Romsdal, S Norway 62°23′N 06°35′E

**Sykoúri** *see* Sykoúrio

115 F15 **Sykoúrio** *var.* Sikouri, Sykoúri; *prev.* Sikoúrion. Thessalía, C Greece 39°46′N 22°35′E

125 R11 **Syktyvkar** *prev.* Ust'-Sysol'sk. Respublika Komi, NW Russia 61°42′N 50°45′E

23 Q4 **Sylacauga** Alabama, S USA 33°10′N 86°15′W

**Sylarna** *see* Storsylen

153 V14 **Sylhet** Sylhet, NE Bangladesh 24°53′N 91°51′E

153 V13 **Sylhet** ◐ *division* NE Bangladesh

100 G6 **Sylt** *island* NW Germany

21 O10 **Sylva** North Carolina, SE USA 35°23′N 83°13′W

125 V15 **Sylva** ≈ NW Russia

23 W5 **Sylvania** Georgia, SE USA 32°45′N 81°38′W

31 R11 **Sylvania** Ohio, N USA 41°43′N 83°42′W

11 Q15 **Sylvan Lake** Alberta, SW Canada 52°18′N 114°02′W

33 T13 **Sylvan Pass** *pass* Wyoming, C USA

23 T7 **Sylvester** Georgia, SE USA 31°31′N 83°50′W

25 P6 **Sylvester** Texas, SW USA 32°42′N 100°15′W

10 L11 **Sylvia, Mount** ▲ British Columbia, W Canada 58°03′N 124°26′W

122 K11 **Sym** ≈ C Russia

115 N22 **Sými** *var.* Simi. *island* Dodekánisa, Greece, Aegean Sea

117 U8 **Synel'nykove** Dnipropetrovs'ka Oblast', E Ukraine 48°19′N 35°32′E

125 U6 **Synya** Respublika Komi, NW Russia 65°21′N 58°01′E

117 P7 **Synyukha** *Rus.* Sinyukha. ≈ S Ukraine

195 V2 **Syowa** *research station (Japan)* Antarctica 68°58′S 40°07′E

26 H6 **Syracuse** Kansas, C USA 38°00′N 101°43′W

29 S16 **Syracuse** Nebraska, C USA 40°39′N 96°11′W

18 H10 **Syracuse** New York, NE USA 43°03′N 76°09′W

**Syracuse** *see* Siracusa

**Syrdar'inskaya Oblast'** *see* Sirdaryo Viloyati

**Syrdariya** *see* Syr Darya

144 L14 **Syr Darya** *var.* Sai Hun, Sir Darya, Syrdarya, *Kaz.* Syrdariya, *Rus.* Syrdar'ya, *Uzb.* Sirdaryo; *anc.* Jaxartes. ≈ C Asia

**Syrdarya** *see* Syr Darya

138 J6 **Syria** *off.* Syrian Arab Republic, *var.* Siria, Syrie, *Ar.* Sūrīyah, Al-Jumhūrīyah al-'Arabīyah as-Sūrīyah. ◆ *republic* SW Asia

**Syrian Arab Republic** *see* Syria

138 L9 **Syrian Desert** *Ar.* Al Hamad, Bādiyat ash Shām. *desert* SW Asia

**Syrie** *see* Syria

115 L22 **Sýrna** *var.* Sirna. *island* Kykládes, Greece, Aegean Sea

115 I20 **Sýros** *var.* Síros. *island* Kykládes, Greece, Aegean Sea

93 M18 **Sysmä** Päijät-Häme, S Finland 61°28′N 25°37′E

125 R12 **Sysola** ≈ NW Russia

**Syulemeshlii** *see* Sredets

127 S2 **Syumsi** Udmurtskaya Respublika, NW Russia 57°07′N 51°35′E

**Syvash, Zaliv** *see* Syvash, Zatoka

117 U12 **Syvash, Zatoka** *Rus.* Zaliv Syvash. *inlet* S Ukraine

127 Q6 **Syzran'** Samarskaya Oblast', W Russia 53°10′N 48°23′E

**Szabadka** *see* Subotica

111 N21 **Szabolcs-Szatmár-Bereg** *off.* Szabolcs-Szatmár-Bereg Megye. ◐ *county* E Hungary

**Szabolcs-Szatmár-Bereg Megye** *see* Szabolcs-Szatmár-Bereg

110 G10 **Szamocin** *Ger.* Samotschin. Wielkopolskie, C Poland 53°02′N 17°04′E

116 H8 **Szamos** *var.* Someş, Someşul, *Ger.* Samosch, Somesch. ≈ Hungary/Romania

**Szamosújvár** *see* Gherla

110 G11 **Szamotuły** Poznań, W Poland 52°35′N 16°36′E

**Szarkowszczyzna** *see* Sharkawshchyna

111 M24 **Szarvas** Békés, SE Hungary 46°51′N 20°35′E

**Szászmagyarós** *see* Măieruş

**Szászrégen** *see* Reghin

**Szászsebes** *see* Sebeş

**Szászváros** *see* Orăştie

**Szatmárrnémeti** *see* Satu Mare

**Száva** *see* Sava

111 P15 **Szczebrzeszyn** Lubelskie, E Poland 50°43′N 23°00′E

110 D9 **Szczecin** *Eng./Ger.* Stettin. Zachodnio-pomorskie, NW Poland 53°25′N 14°32′E

110 G8 **Szczecinek** *Ger.* Neustettin. Zachodnio-pomorskie, NW Poland 53°43′N 16°40′E

110 D8 **Szczeciński, Zalew** *var.* Stettiner Haff, *Ger.* Oderhaff. *bay* Germany/Poland

111 K15 **Szczekociny** Śląskie, S Poland 50°38′N 19°46′E

110 N8 **Szczuczyn** Podlaskie, NE Poland 53°34′N 22°17′E

**Szczuczyn Nowogródzki** *see* Shchuchyn

110 M8 **Szczytno** *Ger.* Ortelsburg. Warmińsko-Mazurskie, NE Poland 53°34′N 21°E

**Szechuan/Szechwan** *see* Sichuan

111 K21 **Szécsény** Nógrád, N Hungary 48°07′N 19°30′E

111 L25 **Szeged** *Ger.* Szegedin, *Rom.* Seghedin. Csongrád, SE Hungary 46°17′N 20°06′E

**Szegedin** *see* Szeged

111 N23 **Szeghalom** Békés, SE Hungary 47°01′N 21°09′E

**Székelyhid** *see* Săcueni

**Székelykeresztúr** *see* Cristuru Secuiesc

111 I23 **Székesfehérvár** *Ger.* Stuhlweissenberg; *anc.* Alba Regia. Fejér, W Hungary 47°13′N 18°24′E

**Szeklerburg** *see* Miercurea-Ciuc

**Szekler Neumarkt** *see* Târgu Secuiesc

111 J25 **Szekszárd** Tolna, S Hungary 46°21′N 18°41′E

**Szempcz/Szenc** *see* Senec

**Szenice** *see* Senica

**Szentágota** *see* Agnita

111 J22 **Szentendre** *Ger.* Sankt Andrä. Pest, N Hungary 47°40′N 19°02′E

111 L24 **Szentes** Csongrád, SE Hungary 46°40′N 20°17′E

111 F23 **Szentgotthárd** *Eng.* Saint Gotthard, *Ger.* Sankt Gotthard. Vas, W Hungary 46°57′N 16°18′E

**Szentgyörgy** *see* Đurđevac

**Szenttamás** *see* Srbobran

**Széphely** *see* Jebel

**Szeping** *see* Siping

**Szered** *see* Sered'

111 N21 **Szerencs** Borsod-Abaúj-Zemplén, NE Hungary 48°10′N 21°11′E

**Szeret** *see* Siret

**Szeretfalva** *see* Sărăţel

110 N7 **Szeska Góra** *var.* Szeskie Wygórza, *Ger.* Seesker Höhe. *hill* NE Poland

**Szeskie Wygórza** *see* Szeska Góra

111 H25 **Szigetvár** Baranya, SW Hungary 46°01′N 17°50′E

**Szilágysomlyó** *see* Şimleu Silvaniei

**Szinna** *see* Snina

**Sziszek** *see* Sisak

**Szitás-Keresztúr** *see* Cristuru Secuiesc

111 E15 **Szklarska Poręba** *Ger.* Schreiberhau. Dolnośląskie, SW Poland 50°50′N 15°30′E

**Szkudy** *see* Skuodas

**Szlatina** *see* Slatina

**Szlavonia/Szlavonország** *see* Slavonija

**Szlovákia** *see* Slovakia

**Szluin** *see* Slunj

111 L23 **Szolnok** Jász-Nagykun-Szolnok, C Hungary 47°11′N 20°12′E

**Szolyva** *see* Svalyava

111 G23 **Szombathely** *Ger.* Steinamanger; *anc.* Sabaria, Savaria. Vas, W Hungary 47°14′N 16°38′E

**Szond/Szonta** *see* Sonta

**Szováta** *see* Sovata

110 F13 **Szprotawa** *Ger.* Sprottau. Lubuskie, W Poland 51°33′N 15°32′E

**Sztálinváros** *see* Dunaújváros

**Sztrazsó** *see* Strážov

110 J8 **Sztum** *Ger.* Stuhm. Pomorskie, N Poland 53°54′N 19°01′E

110 H10 **Szubin** *Ger.* Schubin. Kujawsko-pomorskie, C Poland 53°04′N 17°49′E

**Szucsava** *see* Suceava

**Szurduk** *see* Surduc

111 M14 **Szydłowiec** *Ger.* Schlelau. Mazowieckie, C Poland 51°14′N 20°50′E


# T


**Taalintehdas** *see* Dalsbruk

171 O4 **Taal, Lake** ◎ Luzon, NW Philippines

95 J23 **Taastrup** *var.* Tåstrup. Sjælland, E Denmark 55°39′N 12°19′E

111 I24 **Tab** Somogy, W Hungary 46°45′N 18°01′E

171 P4 **Tabaco** Luzon, N Philippines 13°22′N 123°42′E

186 G4 **Tabalo** Mussau Island, NE Papua New Guinea 01°22′S 149°37′E

104 K5 **Tábara** Castilla y León, N Spain 41°49′N 05°57′W

186 H5 **Tabar Islands** *island group* NE Papua New Guinea

**Ţabarīyā, Buḩayrat** *see* Kinneret, Yam

143 S7 **Ţabas** *var.* Golshan. Khorāsān-e Janūbī, C Iran 33°37′N 56°54′E

43 P15 **Tabasará, Serranía de** ▲▲ W Panama

41 U15 **Tabasco** ◐ *state* SE Mexico

**Tabasco** *see* Grijalva, Río

127 Q2 **Tabashino** Respublika Mariy El, W Russia 57°00′N 47°47′E

58 B13 **Tabatinga** Amazonas, N Brazil 04°14′S 69°44′W

74 G9 **Tabelbala** W Algeria 29°22′N 03°01′W

11 Q17 **Taber** Alberta, SW Canada 49°48′N 112°09′W

171 V15 **Taberfane** Pulau Trangan, E Indonesia 06°14′S 134°08′E

95 L19 **Taberg** Jönköping, S Sweden 57°42′N 14°05′E

191 O3 **Tabiteuea** *prev.* Drummond Island. *atoll* Tungaru, W Kiribati

171 O5 **Tablas Island** *island* C Philippines

184 Q10 **Table Cape** *headland* North Island, New Zealand 39°07′S 178°00′E

13 S13 **Table Mountain** ▲ Newfoundland, Newfoundland and Labrador, E Canada 47°39′N 59°15′W

173 P17 **Table, Pointe de la** *headland* SE Réunion 21°19′S 55°49′E

27 S8 **Table Rock Lake** ▣ Arkansas/Missouri, C USA

36 K14 **Table Top** ▲ Arizona, SW USA 32°45′N 112°07′W

186 D8 **Tabletop, Mount** ▲ C Papua New Guinea 06°51′S 146°00′E

111 D18 **Tábor** Jihočeský Kraj, S Czechia 49°25′N 14°41′E

123 R7 **Tabor** Respublika Sakha (Yakutiya), NE Russia 71°14′N 150°23′E


◆ Country
● Country Capital
◇ Dependent Territory
○ Dependent Territory Capital
◐ Administrative Regions
✈ International Airport
▲ Mountain
▲▲ Mountain Range
Volcano
≈ River
◎ Lake
▣ Reservoir

29 S15 **Tabor** Iowa, C USA 40°54′N 95°40′W
81 F21 **Tabora** Tabora, W Tanzania 05°04′S 32°49′E
81 F21 **Tabora** ◈ *region* C Tanzania
21 U12 **Tabor City** North Carolina, SE USA 34°09′N 78°52′W
147 Q10 **Taboshar** NW Tajikistan 40°37′N 69°33′E
76 L18 **Tabou** *var.* Tabu. S Ivory Coast 04°28′N 07°20′W
142 J2 **Tabrīz** *var.* Tebriz; *anc.* Tauris. Āžarbāyjān-e Sharqī, NW Iran 38°05′N 46°18′E
**Tabu** *see* Tabou
191 W1 **Tabuaeran** *prev.* Fanning Island. *atoll* Line Islands, E Kiribati
171 O2 **Tabuk** Luzon, N Philippines 17°26′N 121°25′E
140 J4 **Tabūk** Tabūk, NW Saudi Arabia 28°25′N 36°34′E
140 J5 **Tabūk** *off.* Minṭaqat Tabūk. ◈ *region* NW Saudi Arabia
**Tabūk, Minṭaqat** *see* Tabūk
187 Q13 **Tabwemasana, Mount** ▲ Espiritu Santo, W Vanuatu 15°22′S 166°44′E
95 O15 **Täby** Stockholm, C Sweden 59°29′N 18°04′E
41 N14 **Tacámbaro** Michoacán, SW Mexico 19°12′N 101°27′W
42 A5 **Tacaná, Volcán** ⛰ Guatemala/Mexico 15°07′N 92°06′W
43 X16 **Tacarcuna, Cerro** ▲ SE Panama 08°08′N 77°15′W
**Tachau** *see* Tachov
158 J3 **Tacheng** *var.* Qoqek. Xinjiang Uygur Zizhiqu, NW China 46°45′N 82°55′E
54 H7 **Táchira** *off.* Estado Táchira. ◈ *state* W Venezuela
**Táchira, Estado** *see* Táchira
111 A17 **Tachov** *Ger.* Tachau. Plveňský Kraj, W Czechia 49°48′N 12°38′E
171 Q5 **Tacloban** *off.* Tacloban City. Leyte, C Philippines 11°15′N 125°E
**Tacloban City** *see* Tacloban
57 I19 **Tacna** Tacna, SE Peru 18°S 70°15′W
57 H18 **Tacna** *off.* Región de Tacna. ◈ *region* S Peru
**Tacna, Región de** *see* Tacna
32 H8 **Tacoma** Washington, NW USA 47°15′N 122°27′W
18 L11 **Taconic Range** ▲▲ NE USA
62 L6 **Taco Pozo** Formosa, N Argentina 25°35′S 63°15′W
57 M20 **Tacsara, Cordillera de** ▲▲ S Bolivia
61 F17 **Tacuarembó** *prev.* San Fructuoso. Tacuarembó, C Uruguay 31°42′S 56°W
61 E18 **Tacuarembó** ◈ *department* C Uruguay
61 F17 **Tacuarembó, Río** ≈ C Uruguay
83 I14 **Taculi** North Western, NW Zambia 14°17′S 26°51′E
171 Q8 **Tacurong** Mindanao, S Philippines 06°42′N 124°40′E
77 V8 **Tadek** ≈ NW Niger
74 J9 **Tademaït, Plateau du** *plateau* C Algeria
187 R17 **Tadine** Province des Îles Loyauté, E New Caledonia 21°33′S 167°54′E
80 M11 **Tadjoura, Golfe de** *Eng.* Gulf of Tajura. *inlet* E Djibouti
80 L11 **Tadjourah** E Djibouti 11°47′N 42°51′E
**Tadmor/Tadmur** *see* Tadmur
138 K6 **Tadmur** *var.* Tudmur, Tamar, *Gk.* Palmyra, *Bibl.* Tadmor. Ḥimṣ, C Syria 34°36′N 38°15′E
11 W10 **Tadoule Lake** ◎ Manitoba, C Canada
15 S8 **Tadoussac** Québec, SE Canada 48°09′N 69°43′W
155 H18 **Tādpatri** Andhra Pradesh, E India 14°55′N 77°59′E
**Tadzhikabad** *see* Tojikobod
**Tadzhikistan** *see* Tajikistan
163 Y14 **Taebaek-sanmaek** *prev.* T'aebaek-sanmaek. ▲▲ E South Korea
**T'aebaek-sanmaek** *see* Taebaek-sanmaek
**Taechŏng-do** *see* Daecheong-do
163 X13 **Taedong-gang** ≈ C North Korea
**Taegu** *see* Daegu
**Taehan-haehyŏp** *see* Korea Strait
**Taehan Min'guk** *see* South Korea
**Taejŏn** *see* Daejeon
193 Z13 **Tafahi** *island* N Tonga
105 Q4 **Tafalla** Navarra, N Spain 42°32′N 01°41′W
77 W7 **Tafassâsset, Ténéré du** *desert* N Niger
75 M12 **Tafassâsset, Oued** ≈ SE Algeria
55 U11 **Tafelberg** ▲ S Suriname 03°55′N 56°09′W
97 J21 **Taff** ≈ SE Wales, United Kingdom
**Tafila/Ṭafīlah, Muḥāfaẓat aṭ** *see* Aṭ Ṭafīlah
77 N15 **Tafiré** N Ivory Coast 09°04′N 05°10′W
142 M6 **Tafresh** Markazī, W Iran 34°40′N 50°00′E
143 Q9 **Taft** Yazd, C Iran 31°45′N 54°14′E
35 R13 **Taft** California, W USA 35°08′N 119°27′W
25 T14 **Taft** Texas, SW USA 27°58′N 97°24′W
143 W12 **Taftān, Kūh-e** ▲ SE Iran 28°38′N 61°06′E
35 R13 **Taft Heights** California, W USA 35°06′N 119°29′W
189 Y14 **Tafunsak** Kosrae, E Micronesia 05°21′N 162°58′E
192 G16 **Tāga** Savai'i, SW Samoa 13°46′S 172°31′W
149 O6 **Tagāb** Dāikondī, E Afghanistan 33°53′N 66°23′E
39 O8 **Tagagawik River** ≈ Alaska, USA
165 Q10 **Tagajō** *var.* Tagazyô. Miyagi, Honshū, C Japan 38°18′N 140°58′E
126 K12 **Taganrog** Rostovskaya Oblast', SW Russia 47°10′N 38°55′E
126 K12 **Taganrog, Gulf of** *Rus.* Taganrogskiy Zaliv, *Ukr.* Tahanroz'ka Zatoka. *gulf* Russia/Ukraine
**Taganrogskiy Zaliv** *see* Taganrog, Gulf of
76 J8 **Tagant** ◈ *region* C Mauritania
148 M14 **Tagas** Baluchistan, SW Pakistan 27°09′N 64°36′E
149 N3 **Tagāw-Bāy** *var.* Bai, Tagow Bāy. Sar-e Pul, N Afghanistan 35°41′N 66°01′E
171 O4 **Tagaytay** Luzon, N Philippines 14°04′N 120°55′E
**Tagazyô** *see* Tagajō
171 P6 **Tagbilaran** *var.* Tagbilaran City. Bohol, C Philippines 09°41′N 123°54′E
**Tagbilaran City** *see* Tagbilaran
106 B10 **Taggia** Liguria, NW Italy 43°51′N 07°48′E
77 V9 **Taghouaji, Massif de** ▲ C Niger 17°13′N 08°37′E
107 J15 **Tagliacozzo** Lazio, C Italy 42°03′N 13°15′E
106 J7 **Tagliamento** ≈ NE Italy
**Tagow Bāy** *see* Tagāw-Bāy
146 H9 **Tagta** *var.* Tahta, *Rus.* Takhta. Daşoguz Welaýaty, N Turkmenistan 41°40′N 59°51′E
146 J16 **Tagtabazar** *var.* Takhtabazar. Mary Welaýaty, S Turkmenistan 35°57′N 62°49′E
59 L17 **Taguatinga** Tocantins, C Brazil 12°16′S 46°25′W
186 I10 **Tagula** Tagula Island, SE Papua New Guinea 11°21′S 153°11′E
186 I11 **Tagula Island** *prev.* Southeast Island, Sudest Island. *island* SE Papua New Guinea
171 Q7 **Tagum** Mindanao, S Philippines 07°22′N 125°51′E
54 C7 **Tagún, Cerro** *elevation* Colombia/Panama
105 P7 **Tagus** *Port.* Rio Tejo, *Sp.* Río Tajo. ≈ Portugal/Spain
64 M9 **Tagus Plain** *undersea feature* E Atlantic Ocean 37°30′N 12°00′W
191 S10 **Tahaa** *island* Îles Sous le Vent, W French Polynesia
191 U10 **Tahanea** *atoll* Îles Tuamotu, C French Polynesia
**Tahanroz'ka Zatoka** *see* Taganrog, Gulf of
74 K12 **Tahat** ▲ SE Algeria 23°15′N 05°34′E
163 U4 **Tahe** Heilongjiang, NE China 52°21′N 124°42′E
**Tahilt** *see* Tsogt
191 T10 **Tahiti** *island* Îles du Vent, W French Polynesia
**Tahiti, Archipel de** *see* Société, Archipel de la
118 E4 **Tahkuna Nina** *headland* W Estonia 59°06′N 22°35′E
148 K12 **Tahlab** ≈ W Pakistan
148 K12 **Tahlab, Dasht-I** *desert* SW Pakistan
27 R10 **Tahlequah** Oklahoma, C USA 35°57′N 94°58′W
35 Q6 **Tahoe City** California, W USA 39°09′N 120°09′W
35 P6 **Tahoe, Lake** ◎ California/Nevada, W USA
25 N6 **Tahoka** Texas, SW USA 33°10′N 101°47′W
32 F8 **Taholah** Washington, NW USA 47°19′N 124°17′W
77 T11 **Tahoua** Tahoua, W Niger 14°53′N 05°18′E
77 T11 **Tahoua** ◈ *region* W Niger
31 P3 **Tahquamenon Falls** *waterfall* Michigan, N USA
31 P4 **Tahquamenon River** ≈ Michigan, N USA
139 V10 **Ṭahrīr** Al Qādisīyah, S Iraq 31°58′N 45°34′E
10 K17 **Tahsis** Vancouver Island, British Columbia, SW Canada 49°42′N 126°31′W
75 W9 **Ṭahṭā** *var.* Ṭahta. C Egypt 26°47′N 31°31′E
**Tahta** *see* Tagta
136 L15 **Tahtalı Dağları** ▲▲ C Turkey
57 I14 **Tahuamanu, Río** ≈ Bolivia/Peru
56 F13 **Tahuanía, Río** ≈ E Peru
191 X7 **Tahuata** *island* Îles Marquises, NE French Polynesia
75 L17 **Taï** SW Ivory Coast 05°52′N 07°28′W
151 P5 **Tai'an** Shandong, E China 36°13′N 117°12′E
191 R8 **Taiarapu, Presqu'île de** *peninsula* Tahiti, W French Polynesia
**Taibad** *see* Tāybād
150 K7 **Taibai Shan** ▲ C China 33°57′N 107°31′E
**Taibei** *see* Taipei
105 Q12 **Taibilla, Sierra de** ▲ S Spain
**Taibus Qi** *see* Baochang
**Taichū** *see* Taichung
161 S13 **Taichung** *Jap.* Taichū; *prev.* Taizhong, Taiwan. C Taiwan 24°09′N 120°40′E
**Taiden** *see* Daejeon
**Taidong** *see* Taitung
185 E23 **Taieri** ≈ South Island, New Zealand
161 N4 **Taihang Shan** ▲▲ C China
184 M11 **Taihape** Manawatu-Wanganui, North Island, New Zealand 39°41′S 175°47′E
161 O7 **Taihe** Anhui, E China 33°14′N 115°35′E
161 O12 **Taihe** *var.* Chengjiang. Jiangxi, S China 26°47′N 114°52′E
**Taihoku** *see* Taipei
161 P9 **Taihu** Anhui, E China 30°22′N 116°20′E
161 R8 **Tai Hu** ◎ E China
159 O9 **Taikang** *var.* Dorbod, Dorbod Mongolzu Zizhixian. Heilongjiang, NE China 46°50′N 124°25′E
161 O6 **Taikang** Henan, C China 34°01′N 114°59′E
165 T5 **Taiki** Hokkaidō, NE Japan 42°29′N 143°15′E
166 L8 **Taikkyi** Yangon, SW Myanmar (Burma) 17°16′N 95°55′E
**Taikyū** *see* Daegu
163 U8 **Tailai** Heilongjiang, NE China 46°25′N 123°25′E
168 I12 **Taileleo** Pulau Siberut, W Indonesia 01°45′S 99°06′E
182 J10 **Tailem Bend** South Australia 35°20′S 139°34′E
96 I8 **Tain** N Scotland, United Kingdom 57°49′N 04°04′W
161 S14 **Tainan** *prev.* Dainan, T'ainan. S Taiwan 23°01′N 120°05′E
115 E22 **Taínaro, Akrotírio** *cape* S Greece
161 Q11 **Taining** *var.* Shancheng. Fujian, SE China 26°55′N 117°13′E
191 W7 **Taiohae** *prev.* Madisonville. Nuku Hiva, NE French Polynesia 08°55′S 140°04′W
161 T13 **Taipei** *var.* Taibei, Daihoku, *Jap.* Taihoku. ● (Taiwan) N Taiwan 25°02′N 121°28′E
168 J7 **Taiping** Perak, Peninsular Malaysia 04°54′N 100°42′E
**Taiping** *see* Chongzuo
163 S8 **Taiping Ling** ▲ NE China 47°27′N 120°27′E
165 Q4 **Taisei** Hokkaidō, NE Japan 42°13′N 139°52′E
165 G12 **Taisha** Shimane, Honshū, SW Japan 35°23′N 132°40′E
**Taishō-tō** *see* Sekibi-sho
109 R4 **Taiskirchen** Oberösterreich, NW Austria 48°15′N 13°33′E
63 F20 **Taitao, Peninsula de** *peninsula* S Chile
**Taitō** *see* Taitung
161 T14 **Taitung** *Jap.* Taitō; *prev.* Taidong. S Taiwan 22°43′N 121°10′E
92 M13 **Taivalkoski** Pohjois-Pohjanmaa, E Finland 65°35′N 28°20′E
93 K19 **Taivassalo** Varsinais-Suomi, SW Finland 60°35′N 21°36′E
161 T14 **Taiwan** *off.* Republic of China, *var.* Formosa, Formo'sa. ◆ *republic* E Asia
192 F5 **Taiwan** *var.* Formosa. *island* E Asia
**Taiwan** *see* Taichung
**T'aiwan Haihsia/Taiwan Haixia** *see* Taiwan Strait
**Taiwan Shan** *see* Zhongyang Shanmo
161 R13 **Taiwan Strait** *var.* Formosa Strait, *Chin.* T'aiwan Haihsia, Taiwan Haixia. *strait* China/Taiwan
161 S12 **Taiwan Taoyuan** *prev.* Chiang Kai-shek. ✈ (T'aibei) N Taiwan 25°09′N 121°20′E
161 N4 **Taiyuan** *var.* T'ai-yuan, T'ai-yüan; *prev.* Yangku. *province capital* Shanxi, C China 37°48′N 112°33′E
**T'ai-yuan/T'ai-yüan** *see* Taiyuan
**Taizhong** *see* Taichung
161 R7 **Taizhou** Jiangsu, E China 32°36′N 119°52′E
161 S10 **Taizhou** *var.* Jiaojiang; *prev.* Haimen. Zhejiang, SE China 28°36′N 121°19′E
**Taizhou** *see* Linhai
141 O16 **Ta'izz** SW Yemen 13°36′N 44°04′E
141 O16 **Ta'izz** ✈ SW Yemen 13°40′N 44°10′E
75 P12 **Tajarhī** SW Libya 24°21′N 14°28′E
147 P13 **Tajikistan** *off.* Republic of Tajikistan, *Taj.* Tojikiston, Jumhurii Tojikiston, *Rus.* Tadzhikistan; *prev.* Tajik S.S.R. ◆ *republic* C Asia
**Tajikistan, Republic of** *see* Tajikistan
**Tajik S.S.R** *see* Tajikistan
165 O11 **Tajima** Fukushima, Honshū, C Japan 37°10′N 139°46′E
**Tajoe** *see* Tayu
**Tajo, Río** *see* Tagus
42 B5 **Tajumulco, Volcán** ⛰ W Guatemala 15°04′N 91°50′W
105 P7 **Tajuña** ≈ C Spain
**Tajura, Gulf of** *see* Tadjoura, Golfe de
167 O9 **Tak** *var.* Rahaeng. Tak, W Thailand 16°51′N 99°08′E
189 U4 **Taka Atoll** *var.* Tōke. *atoll* Ratak Chain, N Marshall Islands
165 P12 **Takahagi** Ibaraki, Honshū, S Japan 36°42′N 140°42′E
165 H13 **Takahashi** *var.* Takahasi. Okayama, Honshū, SW Japan 34°48′N 133°38′E
**Takahasi** *see* Takahashi
189 P12 **Takaieu Island** *island* E Micronesia
184 I13 **Takaka** Tasman, South Island, New Zealand 40°52′S 172°49′E
170 M14 **Takalar** Sulawesi, C Indonesia 05°28′S 119°24′E
165 H13 **Takamatsu** *var.* Takamatu. Kagawa, Shikoku, SW Japan 34°19′N 133°59′E
**Takamatu** *see* Takamatsu
165 D14 **Takamori** Kumamoto, Kyūshū, SW Japan 32°50′N 131°08′E
165 D16 **Takanabe** Miyazaki, Kyūshū, SW Japan 32°13′N 131°31′E
170 M16 **Takan, Gunung** ▲ Pulau Sumba, S Indonesia 08°52′S 117°32′E
165 Q7 **Takanosu** *var.* Kita-Akita. Akita, Honshū, C Japan 40°13′N 140°23′E
**Takao** *see* Kaohsiung
165 L11 **Takaoka** Toyama, Honshū, SW Japan 36°44′N 137°02′E
184 N12 **Takapau** Hawke's Bay, North Island, New Zealand 40°01′S 176°21′E
191 U9 **Takapoto** *atoll* Îles Tuamotu, C French Polynesia
184 L5 **Takapuna** Auckland, North Island, New Zealand 36°48′S 174°46′E
165 J3 **Takarazuka** Hyōgo, Honshū, SW Japan 34°49′N 135°21′E
191 U9 **Takaroa** *atoll* Îles Tuamotu, C French Polynesia
165 N12 **Takasaki** Gunma, Honshū, S Japan 36°20′N 139°00′E
164 L12 **Takayama** Gifu, Honshū, SW Japan 36°09′N 137°16′E
164 K12 **Takefu** *var.* Echizen, Takehu. Fukui, Honshū, SW Japan 35°55′N 136°11′E
**Takehu** *see* Takefu
167 R13 **Takeo** *prev.* Takêv. Takeo, S Cambodia 10°59′N 104°47′E
164 C14 **Takeo** Saga, Kyūshū, SW Japan 33°13′N 130°00′E
164 C17 **Take-shima** *island* Nansei-shotō, SW Japan
142 M5 **Tākestān** *var.* Takistan; *prev.* Siadehan. Qazvīn, N Iran 36°02′N 49°40′E
164 D14 **Taketa** Ōita, Kyūshū, SW Japan 33°00′N 131°23′E
**Takêv** *see* Takeo
167 O10 **Tak Fah** Nakhon Sawan, C Thailand
139 T13 **Takhādīd** *well* S Iraq
149 R3 **Takhār** ◈ *province* NE Afghanistan
**Takhiatash** *see* Taxiatosh
167 S13 **Ta Khmau** Kandal, S Cambodia 11°30′N 104°59′E
**Takhta** *see* Tagta
**Takhtabazar** *see* Tagtabazar
145 O8 **Takhtabrod** Severnyy Kazakhstan, N Kazakhstan 52°35′N 67°37′E
**Takhtakupyr** *see* Taxtako'pir
142 M8 **Takht-e Shāh, Kūh-e** ▲ C Iran
77 V12 **Takiéta** Zinder, S Niger 13°43′N 08°33′E
8 J8 **Takijuq Lake** ◎ Nunavut, NW Canada
165 S3 **Takikawa** Hokkaidō, NE Japan 43°35′N 141°54′E
165 U3 **Takinoue** Hokkaidō, NE Japan 44°10′N 143°09′E
**Takistan** *see* Tākestān
185 B23 **Takitimu Mountains** ▲▲ South Island, New Zealand
**Takkaze** *see* Tekezē
165 R7 **Takko** Aomori, Honshū, C Japan 40°19′N 141°11′E
10 L13 **Takla Lake** ◎ British Columbia, SW Canada
**Takla Makan Desert** *see* Taklimakan Shamo
158 H9 **Taklimakan Shamo** *Eng.* Takla Makan Desert. *desert* NW China
167 T12 **Takôk** Mondolkiri, E Cambodia 12°37′N 106°30′E
39 P10 **Takotna** Alaska, USA 62°59′N 156°03′W
**Takow** *see* Kaohsiung
123 O12 **Taksimo** Respublika Buryatiya, S Russia 56°18′N 114°53′E
164 C13 **Taku** Saga, Kyūshū, SW Japan 33°19′N 130°06′E
10 I10 **Taku** ≈ British Columbia, W Canada
166 M15 **Takua Pa** *var.* Ban Takua Pa. Phangnga, SW Thailand 08°55′N 98°20′E
77 W16 **Takum** Taraba, E Nigeria 07°16′N 10°00′E
191 V10 **Takume** *atoll* Îles Tuamotu, C French Polynesia
190 L16 **Takutea** *island* S Cook Islands
186 K6 **Takuu Islands** *prev.* Mortlock Group. *island group* NE Papua New Guinea
119 L18 **Tal'** Minskaya Voblasts', S Belarus 52°52′N 27°58′E
40 L13 **Tala** Jalisco, C Mexico 20°39′N 103°45′W
61 F19 **Tala** Canelones, S Uruguay 34°24′S 55°45′W
**Talabriga** *see* Aveiro, Portugal
**Talabriga** *see* Talavera de la Reina, Spain
119 N14 **Talachyn** *Rus.* Tolochin. Vitsyebskaya Voblasts', NE Belarus 54°25′N 29°42′E
149 U7 **Talagang** Punjab, E Pakistan 32°55′N 72°29′E
105 V11 **Talaiassa** ▲ Ibiza, Spain, W Mediterranean Sea 38°55′N 01°17′E
155 J23 **Talaimannar** Northern Province, NW Sri Lanka 09°05′N 79°43′E
117 R3 **Talalayivka** Chernihivs'ka Oblast', N Ukraine 50°51′N 33°09′E
43 O15 **Talamanca, Cordillera de** ▲▲ S Costa Rica
56 A9 **Talara** Piura, NW Peru 04°31′S 81°17′W
104 L11 **Talarrubias** Extremadura, W Spain 39°03′N 05°14′W
147 S8 **Talas** Talasskaya Oblast', NW Kyrgyzstan 42°29′N 72°21′E
147 S8 **Talas** ≈ NW Kyrgyzstan
186 G7 **Talasea** New Britain, E Papua New Guinea 05°20′S 150°01′E
**Talas Oblasty** *see* Talasskaya Oblast'
147 S8 **Talasskaya Oblast'** *Kyr.* Talas Oblasty. ◈ *province* NW Kyrgyzstan
147 S8 **Talasskiy Alatau, Khrebet** ▲▲ Kazakhstan/Kyrgyzstan
77 U12 **Talata Mafara** Zamfara, NW Nigeria 12°33′N 06°01′E
171 R9 **Talaud, Kepulauan** *island group* E Indonesia
104 M9 **Talavera de la Reina** *anc.* Caesarobriga, Talabriga. Castilla-La Mancha, C Spain 39°58′N 04°50′W
104 J11 **Talavera la Real** Extremadura, W Spain 38°53′N 06°46′W
186 F7 **Talawe, Mount** ▲ New Britain, C Papua New Guinea 05°30′S 148°24′E
23 S5 **Talbotton** Georgia, SE USA 32°40′N 84°32′W
183 R7 **Talbragar River** ≈ New South Wales, SE Australia
62 G13 **Talca** Maule, C Chile 35°28′S 71°42′W
62 F13 **Talcahuano** Bío Bío, C Chile 36°43′S 73°07′W
154 O12 **Tālcher** Odisha, E India 20°57′N 85°13′E
25 W5 **Talco** Texas, SW USA 33°21′N 95°06′W
145 V14 **Taldykorgan** *Kaz.* Taldyqorghan; *prev.* Taldy-Kurgan. Taldykorgan, SE Kazakhstan 45°N 78°23′E
**Taldy-Kurgan/Taldyqorghan** *see* Taldykorgan
147 Y7 **Taldy-Suu** Issyk-Kul'skaya Oblast', E Kyrgyzstan 42°49′N 78°33′E
147 U10 **Taldy-Suu** Oshskaya Oblast', SW Kyrgyzstan 40°33′N 73°52′E
**Tal-e Khosravī** *see* Yāsūj
193 Y15 **Taleki Tonga** *island* Otu Tolu Group, C Tonga
193 Y15 **Taleki Vavu'u** *island* Otu Tolu Group, C Tonga
102 J13 **Talence** Gironde, SW France 44°49′N 00°35′W
145 U16 **Talgar** *Kaz.* Talghar. Almaty, SE Kazakhstan 43°17′N 77°15′E
**Talghar** *see* Talgar
171 Q12 **Taliabu, Pulau** *island* Kepulauan Sula, C Indonesia
115 L22 **Taliarós, Akrotírio** *headland* Astypálaia, Kykládes, Greece, Aegean Sea 36°31′N 26°18′E
**Ta-lien** *see* Dalian
27 Q12 **Talihina** Oklahoma, C USA 34°45′N 95°03′W
**Talimardzhan** *see* Tollimarjon
137 T12 **T'alin** *Rus.* Talin; *prev.* Verin T'alin. W Armenia 40°23′N 43°51′E
**Talin** *see* T'alin
81 E15 **Tali Post** Central Equatoria, S South Sudan 05°55′N 30°44′E
**Taliq-an** *see* Tāluqān
**Taliş Dağları** *see* Talish Mountains
142 L2 **Talish Mountains** *Az.* Taliş Dağları, *Per.* Kūhhā-ye Ṭavālesh, *Rus.* Talyshskiye Gory. ▲▲ Azerbaijan/Iran
170 M16 **Taliwang** Sumbawa, C Indonesia 08°45′S 116°55′E
119 L17 **Tal'ka** Minskaya Voblasts', C Belarus 53°22′N 28°21′E
39 R11 **Talkeetna** Alaska, USA 62°19′N 150°06′W
39 R11 **Talkeetna Mountains** ▲▲ Alaska, USA
**Talkhof** *see* Puurmani
92 H2 **Tálknafjörður** Vestfirðir, W Iceland 65°38′N 23°51′W
139 Q3 **Tall 'Abṭah** Nīnawá, N Iraq 35°52′N 42°40′E
138 M2 **Tall Abyaḍ** *var.* Tell Abiad. Ar Raqqah, N Syria 36°41′N 38°57′E
23 Q4 **Talladega** Alabama, S USA 33°26′N 86°06′W
139 Q2 **Tall 'Afar** Nīnawá, N Iraq 36°22′N 42°27′E
23 S8 **Tallahassee** *prev.* Muskogean. *state capital* Florida, SE USA 30°26′N 84°17′W
22 L2 **Tallahatchie River** ≈ Mississippi, S USA
**Tall al Abyaḍ** *see* At Tall al Abyaḍ
139 W12 **Tall al Laḥm** Dhī Qār, S Iraq 30°46′N 46°22′E
183 P11 **Tallangatta** Victoria, SE Australia 36°15′S 147°13′E
23 R4 **Tallapoosa River** ≈ Alabama/Georgia, S USA
103 T13 **Tallard** Hautes-Alpes, SE France 44°30′N 06°04′E
139 Q3 **Tall ash Sha'ir** Nīnawá, N Iraq 36°11′N 42°26′E
23 Q5 **Tallassee** Alabama, S USA 32°32′N 85°53′W
139 R4 **Tall 'Azbah** Nīnawá, NW Iraq 35°47′N 43°13′E
138 I5 **Tall Bīsah** Ḥimṣ, W Syria 34°50′N 36°44′E
139 R3 **Tall Ḥassūnah** Al Anbār, N Iraq 36°05′N 43°10′E
139 Q2 **Tall Ḥuqnah** *var.* Tell Huqnah. Nīnawá, N Iraq 36°33′N 42°34′E
**Tallin** *see* Tallinn
118 G3 **Tallinn** *Ger.* Reval, *Rus.* Tallin; *prev.* Revel. ● (Estonia) Harjumaa, NW Estonia 59°26′N 24°42′E
118 H3 **Tallinn** ✈ Harjumaa, NW Estonia 59°23′N 24°52′E
138 H5 **Tall Kalakh** *var.* Tell Kalakh. Ḥimṣ, C Syria 34°40′N 36°18′E
139 R2 **Tall Kayf** Nīnawá, NW Iraq 36°30′N 43°08′E
**Tall Kūchak** *see* Al Ya'rubīyah
31 U12 **Tallmadge** Ohio, N USA 41°06′N 81°26′W
22 J5 **Tallulah** Louisiana, S USA 32°22′N 91°12′W
139 Q2 **Tall 'Uwaynāt** Nīnawá, NW Iraq 36°43′N 42°18′E
139 Q2 **Tall Ẕāhir** Nīnawá, N Iraq 36°51′N 42°29′E
122 J13 **Tal'menka** Altayskiy Kray, S Russia 53°55′N 83°26′E
122 K8 **Talnakh** Krasnoyarskiy Kray, N Russia 69°26′N 88°27′E
117 P7 **Tal'ne** *Rus.* Tal'noye. Cherkas'ka Oblast', C Ukraine 48°55′N 30°40′E
**Tal'noye** *see* Tal'ne
80 E12 **Talodi** Southern Kordofan, C Sudan 10°40′N 30°25′E
188 B16 **Talofofo** SE Guam 13°21′N 144°45′E
188 B16 **Talofofo Bay** *bay* SE Guam
26 L9 **Taloga** Oklahoma, C USA 36°02′N 98°58′W
123 T10 **Talon** Magadanskaya Oblast', E Russia 59°47′N 148°46′E
14 H11 **Talon, Lake** ◎ Ontario, S Canada
126 M8 **Talovaya** Voronezhskaya Oblast', W Russia 51°07′N 40°46′E
9 N6 **Taloyoak** *prev.* Spence Bay. Nunavut, N Canada 69°30′N 93°25′W
25 Q8 **Talpa** Texas, SW USA 31°46′N 99°42′W
40 K13 **Talpa de Allende** Jalisco, C Mexico 20°22′N 104°51′W
23 S9 **Talquin, Lake** ◎ Florida, SE USA
**Talsen** *see* Talsi
**Talshand** *see* Chandmanī
118 E8 **Talsi** *Ger.* Talsen. NW Latvia 57°14′N 22°35′E
143 V11 **Tal Sīāh** Sīstān va Balūchestān, SE Iran 28°19′N 57°43′E
62 G6 **Taltal** Antofagasta, N Chile 25°22′S 70°27′W
8 K10 **Taltson** ≈ Northwest Territories, NW Canada
168 K11 **Taluk** Sumatera, W Indonesia 0°32′S 101°35′E
149 R2 **Tāluqān** *var.* Taliq-an. Takhār, NE Afghanistan 36°44′N 69°33′E
92 J8 **Talvik** Finnmark, N Norway 70°02′N 22°59′E
182 M7 **Talyawalka Creek** ≈ New South Wales, SE Australia
**Talyshskiye Gory** *see* Talish Mountains
29 W14 **Tama** Iowa, C USA 41°58′N 92°34′W
**Tama Abu, Banjaran** *see* Penambo, Banjaran
169 U9 **Tamabo, Banjaran** ▲▲ East Malaysia
190 B16 **Tamakautoga** SW Niue 19°05′S 169°55′W
127 N7 **Tamala** Penzenskaya Oblast', W Russia 52°32′N 43°18′E
77 P15 **Tamale** C Ghana 09°21′N 00°54′W
191 P3 **Tamana** *prev.* Rotcher Island. *atoll* Tungaru, W Kiribati
74 K12 **Tamanrasset** *var.* Tamenghest. S Algeria 22°49′N 05°32′E
74 J13 **Tamanrasset** *wadi* Algeria/Mali
166 M2 **Tamanthi** Sagaing, N Myanmar (Burma) 25°17′N 95°18′E
97 I24 **Tamar** ≈ SW England, United Kingdom
**Tamar** *see* Tadmur
54 H9 **Támara** Casanare, C Colombia 05°51′N 72°09′W
54 F7 **Tamar, Alto de** ▲ C Colombia 07°25′N 74°28′W
173 X16 **Tamarin** E Mauritius 20°20′S 57°22′E
105 T5 **Tamarite de Litera** *var.* Tararite de Llitera. Aragón, NE Spain 41°52′N 00°25′E
111 I24 **Tamási** Tolna, S Hungary 46°39′N 18°17′E
**Tamatave** *see* Toamasina
41 O9 **Tamaulipas** ◈ *state* C Mexico
41 P10 **Tamaulipas, Sierra de** ▲ C Mexico
56 F12 **Tamaya, Río** ≈ E Peru
40 I9 **Tamazula** Durango, C Mexico 24°43′N 106°33′W
40 L14 **Tamazula** Jalisco, C Mexico 19°41′N 103°18′W
**Tamazulápam** *see* Tamazulapán
41 Q15 **Tamazulapán** *var.* Tamazulápam. Oaxaca, SE Mexico 17°41′N 97°33′W
41 P12 **Tamazunchale** San Luis Potosí, C Mexico 21°17′N 98°46′W
76 H11 **Tambacounda** SE Senegal 13°44′N 13°43′W
83 M16 **Tambara** Manica, C Mozambique 16°42′S 34°14′E
77 T13 **Tambawel** Sokoto, NW Nigeria 12°24′N 04°42′E
186 M9 **Tambea** Guadalcanal, C Solomon Islands 09°19′S 159°42′E
169 N10 **Tambelan, Kepulauan** *island group* W Indonesia
57 E15 **Tambo de Mora** Ica, W Peru 13°30′S 76°08′W
170 L16 **Tambora, Gunung** ⛰ Sumbawa, S Indonesia 08°16′S 117°59′E
61 E17 **Tambores** Paysandú, W Uruguay 31°50′S 56°17′W
57 F14 **Tambo, Río** ≈ C Peru
56 F7 **Tamboryacu, Río** ≈ N Peru
126 M7 **Tambov** Tambovskaya Oblast', W Russia 52°43′N 41°28′E
126 L6 **Tambovskaya Oblast'** ◈ *province* W Russia
104 H3 **Tambre** ≈ NW Spain
169 V7 **Tambunan** Sabah, East Malaysia 05°40′N 116°22′E
81 C15 **Tambura** Western Equatoria, SW South Sudan 05°38′N 27°30′E
**Tâmchaket** *see* Tâmchekkeṭ
76 J9 **Tâmchekkeṭ** *var.* Tâmchaket. Hodh el Gharbi, S Mauritania 17°23′N 10°37′W
167 T7 **Tam Điêp** Ninh Binh, N Vietnam 20°09′N 105°54′E
**Tamdybulak** *see* Tomdibuloq
54 H8 **Tame** Arauca, C Colombia 06°27′N 71°42′W
104 H6 **Tâmega, Rio** *Sp.* Río Támega. ≈ Portugal/Spain
**Támega, Río** *see* Tâmega, Rio
115 H20 **Tamélos, Akrotírio** *headland* Tziá, Kykládes, Greece, Aegean Sea 37°31′N 24°16′E
**Tamenghest** *see* Tamanrasset
77 V8 **Tamgak, Adrar** ▲ C Niger 19°10′N 08°39′E
76 I13 **Tamgue** ▲ NW Guinea 12°14′N 12°18′W
41 Q12 **Tamiahua** Veracruz, E Mexico 21°15′N 97°27′W
41 Q12 **Tamiahua, Laguna de** *lagoon* E Mexico
23 Y16 **Tamiami Canal** *canal* Florida, SE USA
188 F17 **Tamil Harbor** *harbor* Yap, W Micronesia
155 H21 **Tamil Nādu** *prev.* Madras. ◈ *state* SE India
99 H20 **Tamines** Namur, S Belgium 50°27′N 04°37′E
116 E12 **Tamiš** *Ger.* Temesch, *Hung.* Temes. ≈ Romania/Serbia
167 U10 **Tam Ky** Quang Nam-Đa Năng, C Vietnam 15°32′N 108°30′E
**Tammerfors** *see* Tampere
**Tammisaari** *see* Ekenäs
95 N14 **Tämnaren** ◎ C Sweden
191 Q7 **Tamotoe, Passe** *passage* Tahiti, W French Polynesia
23 V12 **Tampa** Florida, SE USA 27°57′N 82°27′W
23 V12 **Tampa** ✈ Florida, SE USA 27°57′N 82°29′W
23 V13 **Tampa Bay** *bay* Florida, SE USA
93 L18 **Tampere** *Swe.* Tammerfors. Pirkanmaa, W Finland 61°30′N 23°45′E
41 Q11 **Tampico** Tamaulipas, C Mexico 22°18′N 97°52′W
171 P14 **Tampo** Pulau Muna, C Indonesia 04°38′S 122°40′E
167 V11 **Tam Quan** Binh Đinh, C Vietnam 14°34′N 109°00′E
162 J13 **Tamsag Muchang** Nei Mongol Zizhiqu, N China 40°28′N 102°34′E
**Tamsal** *see* Tamsalu
118 I4 **Tamsalu** *Ger.* Tamsal. Lääne-Virumaa, NE Estonia 59°10′N 26°07′E
109 S8 **Tamsweg** Salzburg, SW Austria 47°08′N 13°49′E
188 C15 **Tamuning** NW Guam 13°29′N 144°47′E
183 T6 **Tamworth** New South Wales, SE Australia 31°07′S 150°54′E
97 M19 **Tamworth** C England, United Kingdom 52°39′N 01°40′W
81 K19 **Tana** *Finn.* Tenojoki, *Lapp.* Deatnu. ≈ SE Kenya *see also* Deatnu, Tenojoki
**Tana** *see* Deatnu/Tana
164 I15 **Tanabe** Wakayama, Honshū, SW Japan 33°43′N 135°22′E
92 L8 **Tana Bru** Finnmark, N Norway 70°11′N 28°06′E
39 T10 **Tanacross** Alaska, USA 63°30′N 143°21′W
92 L7 **Tanafjorden** *Lapp.* Deanuvuotna. *fjord* N Norway
38 G17 **Tanaga Island** *island* Aleutian Islands, Alaska, USA
38 G17 **Tanaga Volcano** ▲ Tanaga Island, Alaska, USA 51°53′N 178°08′W
107 M18 **Tanagro** ≈ S Italy
80 I11 **T'ana Hāyk'** *var.* Lake Tana. ◎ NW Ethiopia
168 H11 **Tanahbela, Pulau** *island* Kepulauan Batu, W Indonesia
171 H15 **Tanahjampea, Pulau** *island* W Indonesia
168 H11 **Tanahmasa, Pulau** *island* Kepulauan Batu, W Indonesia
**Tanais** *see* Don
152 L10 **Tanakpur** Uttarākhand, N India 29°04′N 80°06′E
**Tana, Lake** *see* T'ana Hāyk'
181 P5 **Tanami Desert** *desert* Northern Territory, N Australia
167 T14 **Tân An** Long An, S Vietnam 10°32′N 106°24′E
39 Q9 **Tanana** Alaska, USA 65°12′N 152°00′W
**Tananarive** *see* Antananarivo
39 Q9 **Tanana River** ≈ Alaska, USA
95 C16 **Tananger** Rogaland, S Norway 58°55′N 05°34′E
188 H5 **Tanapag** Saipan, S Northern Mariana Islands 15°14′S 145°45′E
188 H5 **Tanapag, Puetton** *bay* Saipan, S Northern Mariana Islands
106 C9 **Tanaro** ≈ N Italy
163 Y12 **Tanch'ŏn** E North Korea 40°22′N 128°49′E
40 M14 **Tancítaro, Cerro** ▲ C Mexico 19°16′N 102°25′W
153 N12 **Tānda** Uttar Pradesh, N India 26°33′N 82°39′E
77 O15 **Tanda** E Ivory Coast 07°48′N 03°10′W
116 L14 **Țăndărei** Ialomița, SE Romania 44°39′N 27°40′E
63 N14 **Tandil** Buenos Aires, E Argentina 37°18′S 59°10′W
78 H12 **Tandjilé** *off.* Région du Tandjilé. ◈ *region* SW Chad
**Tandjilé, Région du** *see* Tandjilé
**Tandjoeng** *see* Tanjung
**Tandjoengkarang** *see* Bandar Lampung
**Tandjoengpandan** *see* Tanjungpandan
**Tandjoengpinang** *see* Tanjungpinang
**Tandjoengredeb** *see* Tanjungredeb
149 Q16 **Tando Allahyar** Sindh, SE Pakistan 25°28′N 68°44′E
149 Q17 **Tando Bago** Sindh, SE Pakistan 24°48′N 68°59′E
149 Q16 **Tando Muhammad Khan** Sindh, SE Pakistan 25°07′N 68°35′E
182 L7 **Tandou Lake** *seasonal lake* New South Wales, SE Australia
94 L11 **Tandsjöborg** Gävleborg, C Sweden 61°40′N 14°40′E
155 H15 **Tāndūr** Telangana, C India 17°16′N 77°37′E
164 C17 **Tanega-shima** *island* Nansei-shotō, SW Japan
165 R7 **Taneichi** Iwate, Honshū, C Japan 40°23′N 141°42′E
**Tanen Taunggyi** *see* Tane Range
167 N8 **Tane Range** *Bur.* Tanen Taunggyi. ▲ W Thailand
111 P15 **Tanew** ≈ SE Poland
21 W2 **Taneytown** Maryland, NE USA 39°39′N 77°10′W
74 H12 **Tanezrouft** *desert* Algeria/Mali
138 L7 **Ṭanf, Jabal aṭ** ▲ SE Syria 33°32′N 38°43′E
81 J21 **Tanga** Tanga, E Tanzania 05°07′S 39°05′E
81 I22 **Tanga** ◈ *region* E Tanzania
153 T14 **Tangail** Dhaka, C Bangladesh 24°15′N 89°55′E
186 I5 **Tanga Islands** *island group* NE Papua New Guinea
155 K26 **Tangalla** Southern Province, S Sri Lanka 06°02′N 80°47′E
**Tanganyika and Zanzibar** *see* Tanzania
68 J13 **Tanganyika, Lake** ◎ E Africa
56 E7 **Tangarana, Río** ≈ N Peru
191 V16 **Tangaroa, Maunga** ⛰ Easter Island, Chile, E Pacific Ocean
**Tangdukou** *see* Shaoyang
74 G5 **Tanger** *var.* Tangiers, Tangier, *Fr./Ger.* Tangerk, *Sp.* Tánger; *anc.* Tingis. NW Morocco 35°49′N 05°49′W
169 N15 **Tangerang** Jawa, C Indonesia 06°14′S 106°36′E
**Tangerk** *see* Tanger
100 M12 **Tangermünde** Sachsen-Anhalt, C Germany 52°35′N 11°57′E
159 O12 **Tanggulashan** *var.* Togton Heyan, Tuotuoheyan. Qinghai, C China 34°13′N 92°25′E
156 K10 **Tanggula Shan** *var.* Dangla, Tangla Range. ▲▲ W China
159 N13 **Tanggula Shan** ▲ W China 33°18′N 91°10′E
156 K10 **Tanggula Shankou** *Tib.* Dang La. *pass* W China
161 N7 **Tanghe** Henan, C China 32°40′N 112°53′E
149 T5 **Tangi** Khyber Pakhtunkhwa, NW Pakistan 34°18′N 71°42′E
**Tangier** *see* Tanger
21 Y5 **Tangier Island** *island* Virginia, NE USA
**Tangiers** *see* Tanger
22 K8 **Tangipahoa River** ≈ Louisiana, S USA
**Tangla Range** *see* Tanggula Shan
156 I10 **Tangra Yumco** *var.* Tangro Tso. ◎ W China
**Tangro Tso** *see* Tangra Yumco
157 T7 **Tangshan** *var.* T'ang-shan. Hebei, E China 39°39′N 118°15′E
**T'ang-shan** *see* Tangshan
77 R14 **Tanguiéta** NW Benin 10°35′N 01°19′E
163 X7 **Tangwang He** ≈ NE China
163 X7 **Tangyuan** Heilongjiang, NE China 46°45′N 129°52′E
167 S14 **Tân Hiệp** *var.* Phung Hiêp. Cân Thơ, S Vietnam 09°50′N 105°48′E
92 M11 **Tanhua** Lappi, N Finland 67°31′N 27°30′E
171 U16 **Tanimbar, Kepulauan** *island group* Maluku, E Indonesia
167 N11 **Tanintharyi** *var.* Tenasserim, Tanithayi. ◈ *region* S Myanmar (Burma)
**Tanintharyi** *see* Taninthayi



◆ Country
● Country Capital
◇ Dependent Territory
○ Dependent Territory Capital
◈ Administrative Regions
✈ International Airport
▲ Mountain
▲▲ Mountain Range
⛰ Volcano
≈ River
◎ Lake
⊠ Reservoir

Taninthayi – Te Awamutu


167 N12 **Taninthayi** *var.* Tenasserim. Taninthayi, S Myanmar (Burma) 12°05′N 99°00′E
**Tanithayi** *see* Tanintharyi
**Tānjarō** *see* Tancero
**Tānjarū** *see* Tancero
129 T15 **Tanjong Piai** *headland* Peninsular Malaysia
**Tanjore** *see* Thanjāvūr
169 U12 **Tanjung** *prev.* Tandjoeng. Borneo, C Indonesia 02°08′S 115°23′E
169 W9 **Tanjungbatu** Borneo, N Indonesia 02°19′N 118°03′E
**Tanjungkarang/Tanjungkarang-Telukbetung** *see* Bandar Lampung
169 N13 **Tanjungpandan** *prev.* Tandjoengpandan. Pulau Belitung, W Indonesia 02°44′S 107°36′E
168 M10 **Tanjungpinang** *prev.* Tandjoengpinang. Pulau Bintan, W Indonesia 0°55′N 104°28′E
169 V9 **Tanjungredeb** *var.* Tanjungredep; *prev.* Tandjoengredeb. Borneo, C Indonesia 02°09′N 117°29′E
**Tanjungredep** *see* Tanjungredeb
149 S8 **Tank** Khyber Pakhtunkhwa, NW Pakistan 32°14′N 70°29′E
187 S15 **Tanna** *island* S Vanuatu
93 F17 **Tännäs** Jämtland, C Sweden 62°27′N 12°40′E
**Tannenhof** *see* Krynica
108 K7 **Tannheim** Tirol, W Austria 47°30′N 10°32′E
**Tannu-Tuva** *see* Tyva, Respublika
171 Q12 **Tano** Pulau Taliabu, E Indonesia 01°51′S 124°55′E
77 O17 **Tano** ≈ S Ghana
152 D10 **Tanot** Rājasthān, NW India 27°44′N 70°17′E
77 V11 **Tanout** Zinder, C Niger 14°58′N 08°54′E
**Tân Phu** *see* Đinh Quan
41 P12 **Tanquián** San Luis Potosí, C Mexico 21°38′N 98°39′W
77 R13 **Tansarga** E Burkina Faso 11°51′N 01°51′E
167 T13 **Tan Son Nhat** ✈ (Hô Chi Minh) Tây Ninh, S Vietnam 10°52′N 106°38′E
75 V8 **Ṭanṭā** *var.* Tanta, Tantā. N Egypt 30°42′N 31°00′E
74 D9 **Tan-Tan** SW Morocco 28°30′N 11°11′W
41 P12 **Tantoyuca** Veracruz, E Mexico 21°21′N 98°12′W
152 J12 **Tāntpur** Uttar Pradesh, N India 26°51′N 77°29′E
**Tan-tung** *see* Dandong
38 M12 **Tanunak** Alaska, USA 60°35′N 165°15′W
166 L5 **Ta-nyaung** Magway, W Myanmar (Burma) 20°49′N 94°40′E
167 S5 **Tân Yên** Tuyên Quang, N Vietnam 22°08′N 104°58′E
81 F22 **Tanzania** *off.* United Republic of Tanzania, *Swa.* Jamhuri ya Muungano wa Tanzania; *prev.* German East Africa, Tanganyika and Zanzibar. ◆ *republic* E Africa
**Tanzania, Jamhuri ya Muungano wa** *see* Tanzania
**Tanzania, United Republic of** *see* Tanzania
**Tao'an** *see* Taonan
163 T8 **Tao'er He** ≈ NE China
159 U11 **Tao He** ≈ C China
163 U9 **Taonan** *var.* Tao'an. Jilin, NE China 45°20′N 122°46′E
**T'aon-an** *see* Baicheng
**Taongi** *see* Bokaak Atoll
107 M23 **Taormina** *anc.* Tauromenium. Sicilia, Italy, C Mediterranean Sea 37°54′N 15°18′E
37 S9 **Taos** New Mexico, SW USA 36°24′N 105°35′W
**Taoudenit** *see* Taoudenni
77 O6 **Taoudenni** *var.* Taoudenit. Tombouctou, N Mali 22°46′N 03°54′W
74 G6 **Taounate** N Morocco 34°33′N 04°39′N
**Taoyang** *see* Lintao
161 S13 **Taoyuan** *Jap.* Tōen; *prev.* T'aoyüan. N Taiwan 25°00′N 121°15′E
118 I3 **Tapa** *Ger.* Taps. Lääne-Virumaa, NE Estonia 59°15′N 26°E
41 V17 **Tapachula** Chiapas, SE Mexico 14°53′N 92°18′W
**Tapaiu** *see* Gvardeysk
59 H14 **Tapajós, Rio** *var.* Tapajóz. ≈ NW Brazil
**Tapajóz** *see* Tapajós, Rio
61 C21 **Tapalqué** *var.* Tapalquén. Buenos Aires, E Argentina 36°21′S 60°01′W
**Tapalquén** *see* Tapalqué
**Tapanahoni** *see* Tapanahony Rivier
55 W11 **Tapanahony Rivier** *var.* Tapanahoni. ≈ E Suriname
41 T16 **Tapanatepec** *var.* San Pedro Tapanatepec. Oaxaca, SE Mexico 16°23′N 94°09′W
185 D23 **Tapanui** Otago, South Island, New Zealand 45°55′S 169°16′E
59 E14 **Tapauá** Amazonas, N Brazil 05°42′S 64°15′W
47 R7 **Tapauá, Rio** ≈ W Brazil
185 I14 **Tapawera** Tasman, South Island, New Zealand 41°24′S 172°50′E
61 I16 **Tapes** Rio Grande do Sul, S Brazil 30°40′S 51°25′W
76 K16 **Tapeta** C Liberia 06°36′N 08°52′W
154 H11 **Tāpi** *prev.* Tāpti. ≈ W India
104 J2 **Tapia de Casariego** Asturias, N Spain 43°34′N 06°56′W
56 F10 **Tapiche, Río** ≈ N Peru
167 N15 **Tapi, Mae Nam** *var.* Luang. ≈ SW Thailand
186 E8 **Tapini** Central, S Papua New Guinea 08°16′S 146°09′E
**Tapirapecó, Serra** *see* Tapirapecó, Sierra
55 N13 **Tapirapecó, Sierra** *Port.* Serra Tapirapecó. ▲▲ Brazil/Venezuela
77 R13 **Tapoa** ≈ Benin/Niger
188 H5 **Tapochau, Mount** ▲ Saipan, S Northern Mariana Islands
111 H24 **Tapolca** Veszprém, W Hungary 46°54′N 17°29′E
21 X5 **Tappahannock** Virginia, NE USA 37°55′N 76°54′W
31 U13 **Tappan Lake** ⊠ Ohio, N USA
165 Q6 **Tappi-zaki** *headland* Honshū, C Japan 41°15′N 140°19′E
**Taps** *see* Tapa
**Tāpti** *see* Tāpi
**Tapuaemanu** *see* Maiao
185 J16 **Tapuaenuku** ▲ South Island, New Zealand 42°00′S 173°39′E
171 N8 **Tapul Group** *island group* Sulu Archipelago, SW Philippines
58 E11 **Tapurmcuará** *var.* Tapuruquara. Amazonas, NW Brazil 0°17′S 65°00′W
**Tapuruquara** *see* Tapurmcuará
192 J17 **Taputapu, Cape** *headland* Tutuila, W American Samoa 14°20′S 170°51′W
141 W13 **Ṭāqah** S Oman 17°02′N 54°23′E
139 T3 **Taqtaq** *Ar.* Ṭaqṭaq. Arbīl, N Iraq 35°54′N 44°36′E
**Ṭaqṭaq** *see* Taqtaq
61 J15 **Taquara** Rio Grande do Sul, S Brazil 29°36′S 50°46′W
59 H19 **Taquari, Rio** ≈ C Brazil
60 L8 **Taquaritinga** São Paulo, S Brazil 21°22′S 48°29′W
122 I11 **Tara** Omskaya Oblast', C Russia 56°54′N 74°17′E
83 I16 **Tara** Southern, S Zambia 16°56′S 26°50′E
113 J15 **Tara** ≈ Montenegro
112 K13 **Tara** ▲▲ W Serbia
77 W15 **Taraba** ◈ *state* E Nigeria
77 X15 **Taraba** ≈ E Nigeria
75 O7 **Ṭarābulus** *var.* Ṭarābulus al Gharb, *Eng.* Tripoli. ● (Libya) NW Libya 32°54′N 13°11′E
75 O7 **Ṭarābulus** ✈ NW Libya 32°37′N 13°07′E
**Ṭarābulus al Gharb** *see* Ṭarābulus
**Ṭarābulus/Ṭarābulus ash Shām** *see* Tripoli
105 O7 **Taracena** Castilla-La Mancha, C Spain 40°39′N 03°08′W
117 N12 **Taraclia** *Rus.* Tarakilya. S Moldova 45°55′N 28°40′E
139 V10 **Tarād al Kahf** Dhī Qār, SE Iraq 31°58′N 45°58′E
183 R10 **Tarago** New South Wales, SE Australia 35°04′S 149°40′E
162 J8 **Taragt** *var.* Hüremt. Övörhangay, C Mongolia 46°18′N 102°27′E
169 V8 **Tarakan** Borneo, C Indonesia 03°20′N 117°38′E
169 V9 **Tarakan, Pulau** *island* N Indonesia
**Tarakilya** *see* Taraclia
165 P16 **Tarama-jima** *island* Sakishima-shotō, SW Japan
184 K10 **Taranaki** *off.* Taranaki Region. ◈ *region* North Island, New Zealand
184 K10 **Taranaki, Mount** *var.* Egmont. ⛰ North Island, New Zealand 39°16′S 174°04′E
**Taranaki Region** *see* Taranaki
105 O9 **Tarancón** Castilla-La Mancha, C Spain 40°01′N 03°01′W
188 M15 **Tarang Reef** *reef* C Micronesia
96 E7 **Taransay** *island* NW Scotland, United Kingdom
107 P18 **Taranto** *var.* Tarentum. Puglia, SE Italy 40°30′N 17°11′E
107 O19 **Taranto, Golfo di** *Eng.* Gulf of Taranto. *gulf* S Italy
**Taranto, Gulf of** *see* Taranto, Golfo di
62 G3 **Tarapacá** *off.* Región de Tarapacá. ◈ *region* N Chile
**Tarapacá, Región de** *see* Tarapacá
187 N9 **Tarapaina** Maramasike Island, N Solomon Islands 09°28′S 161°24′E
56 D10 **Tarapoto** San Martín, N Peru 06°31′S 76°23′W
138 M6 **Ṭaraq an Na'jah** *hill range* E Syria
138 M6 **Ṭaraq Sidāwī** *hill range* E Syria
103 Q11 **Tarare** Rhône, E France 45°54′N 04°26′E
**Tararite de Llitera** *see* Tamarite de Litera
184 M13 **Tararua Range** ▲▲ North Island, New Zealand
151 Q22 **Tarāsa Dwīp** *island* Nicobar Islands, India, NE Indian Ocean
103 Q15 **Tarascon** Bouches-du-Rhône, SE France 43°48′N 04°39′E
102 M17 **Tarascon-sur-Ariège** Ariège, S France 42°51′N 01°35′E
117 P6 **Tarashcha** Kyivs'ka Oblast', N Ukraine 49°34′N 30°31′E
57 L18 **Tarata** Cochabamba, C Bolivia 17°35′S 66°04′W
57 I18 **Tarata** Tacna, SW Peru 17°30′S 70°00′W
190 H2 **Taratai** *atoll* Tungaru, W Kiribati
59 B15 **Tarauacá** Acre, W Brazil 08°06′S 70°45′W
59 B15 **Tarauacá, Rio** ≈ NW Brazil
191 Q8 **Taravao** Tahiti, W French Polynesia 17°44′S 149°19′W
191 R8 **Taravao, Baie de** *bay* Tahiti, W French Polynesia
191 Q8 **Taravao, Isthme de** *isthmus* Tahiti, W French Polynesia
103 X16 **Taravo** ≈ Corse, France, C Mediterranean Sea
190 J3 **Tarawa** ✈ Tarawa, W Kiribati 0°53′S 169°32′E
190 H2 **Tarawa Atoll** ● (Kiribati) Tungaru, W Kiribati
184 N10 **Tarawera** Hawke's Bay, North Island, New Zealand 39°03′S 176°34′E
184 N8 **Tarawera, Lake** ◎ North Island, New Zealand
184 N8 **Tarawera, Mount** ▲ North Island, New Zealand 38°13′S 176°29′E
105 S8 **Tarayuela** ▲ N Spain 40°28′N 00°22′W
145 R16 **Taraz** *prev.* Aulie Ata, Auliye-Ata, Dzhambul, Zhambyl. Zhambyl, S Kazakhstan 42°55′N 71°27′E
105 Q5 **Tarazona** Aragón, NE Spain 41°54′N 01°44′W
105 Q10 **Tarazona de la Mancha** Castilla-La Mancha, C Spain 39°16′N 01°55′W
145 X12 **Tarbagatay, Khrebet** ▲▲ China/Kazakhstan
96 J8 **Tarbat Ness** *headland* N Scotland, United Kingdom 57°51′N 03°48′W
149 U5 **Tarbela Reservoir** ⊠ N Pakistan
96 H12 **Tarbert** W Scotland, United Kingdom 55°52′N 05°26′W
96 F7 **Tarbert** NW Scotland, United Kingdom 57°54′N 06°48′W
102 K16 **Tarbes** *anc.* Bigorra. Hautes-Pyrénées, S France 43°14′N 00°04′E
21 W9 **Tarboro** North Carolina, SE USA 35°54′N 77°34′W
**Tarca** *see* Torysa
106 J6 **Tarcento** Friuli-Venezia Giulia, NE Italy 46°13′N 13°13′E
182 F5 **Tarcoola** South Australia 30°44′S 134°34′E
105 S5 **Tardienta** Aragón, NE Spain 41°58′N 00°31′W
102 L11 **Tardoire** ≈ W France
183 U7 **Taree** New South Wales, SE Australia 31°56′S 152°29′E
92 K12 **Tärendö** *Lapp.* Deargget. Norrbotten, N Sweden 67°10′N 22°40′E
**Tarentum** *see* Taranto
74 C9 **Tarfaya** SW Morocco 27°56′N 12°55′W
114 L8 **Targovishte**, Târgovište; *prev.* Eski Dzhumaya. Targovishte, N Bulgaria 43°15′N 26°34′E
114 L8 **Targovishte** *var.* Tŭrgovishte. ◈ *province* N Bulgaria
116 J13 **Târgovişte** *prev.* Tîrgovişte. Dâmboviţa, S Romania 44°54′N 25°29′E
**Tărgovište** *see* Targovishte
116 M12 **Târgu Bujor** *prev.* Tîrgu Bujor. Galaţi, E Romania 45°52′N 27°55′E
116 H13 **Târgu Cărbuneşti** *prev.* Tîrgu. Gorj, SW Romania 44°57′N 23°32′E
116 L9 **Târgu Frumos** *prev.* Tîrgu Frumos. Iaşi, NE Romania 47°12′N 27°00′E
116 H13 **Targu Jiu** *prev.* Tîrgu Jiu. Gorj, W Romania 45°03′N 23°20′E
116 H9 **Târgu Lăpuş** *prev.* Tîrgu Lăpuş. Maramureş, N Romania 47°28′N 23°54′E
**Târgul-Neamţ** *see* Târgu-Neamţ
**Târgul-Săcuiesc** *see* Târgu Secuiesc
116 I10 **Târgu Mureş** *prev.* Oşorhei, Tîrgu Mures, *Ger.* Neumarkt, *Hung.* Marosvásárhely. Mureş, C Romania 46°33′N 24°36′E
116 K9 **Târgu-Neamţ** *var.* Târgul-Neamţ; *prev.* Tîrgu-Neamţ. Neamţ, NE Romania 47°12′N 26°25′E
116 K11 **Târgu Ocna** *Hung.* Aknavásár; *prev.* Tîrgu Ocna. Bacău, E Romania 46°17′N 26°37′E
116 K11 **Târgu Secuiesc** *Ger.* Neumarkt, Szekler Neumarkt, *Hung.* Kezdivásárhely; *prev.* Chezdi-Oşorheiu, Târgul-Săcuiesc, Tîrgu Secuiesc. Covasna, E Romania 46°00′N 26°08′E
145 X10 **Targyn** Vostochnyy Kazakhstan, E Kazakhstan 49°32′N 82°47′E
**Tar Heel State** *see* North Carolina
186 C7 **Tari** Hela, W Papua New Guinea 05°52′S 142°58′E
162 J6 **Tarialan** *var.* Badrah. Hövsgöl, N Mongolia 49°33′N 101°58′E
162 I7 **Tariat** *var.* Horgo. Arhangay, C Mongolia 48°06′N 99°52′E
143 P17 **Ṭarīf** Abū Ẓaby, C United Arab Emirates 24°02′N 53°47′E
104 K16 **Tarifa** Andalucía, S Spain 36°01′N 05°36′W
84 C14 **Tarifa, Punta de** *headland* SW Spain 36°01′N 05°39′W
57 M21 **Tarija** Tarija, S Bolivia 21°33′S 64°42′W
57 M21 **Tarija** ◈ *department* S Bolivia
141 R14 **Tarīm** C Yemen 16°N 48°50′E
**Tarim Basin** *see* Tarim Pendi
81 G19 **Tarime** Mara, N Tanzania 01°20′S 34°24′E
129 S8 **Tarim He** ≈ NW China
159 H8 **Tarim Pendi** *Eng.* Tarim Basin. *basin* NW China
149 N7 **Tarīn Kōt** *var.* Terinkot; *prev.* Tarīn Kowt. Uruzgān, C Afghanistan 32°38′N 65°52′E
**Tarīn Kowt** *see* Tarīn Kōt
171 O12 **Taripa** Sulawesi, C Indonesia 01°51′S 120°46′E
117 Q12 **Tarkhankut, Mys** *headland* S Ukraine 45°20′N 32°32′E
27 Q1 **Tarkio** Missouri, C USA 40°25′N 95°24′W
122 J9 **Tarko-Sale** Yamalo-Nenetskiy Avtonomnyy Okrug, N Russia 64°55′N 77°34′E
77 P17 **Tarkwa** S Ghana 05°16′N 01°59′W
171 O3 **Tarlac** Luzon, N Philippines 15°29′N 120°34′E
95 F22 **Tarm** Midtjylland, W Denmark 55°55′N 08°32′E
57 E14 **Tarma** Junín, C Peru 11°28′S 75°41′W
103 N15 **Tarn** ◈ *department* S France
102 M15 **Tarn** ≈ S France
111 L22 **Tarna** ≈ C Hungary
92 G13 **Tärnaby** Västerbotten, N Sweden 65°44′N 15°20′E
149 P8 **Tarnak Rōd** ≈ SE Afghanistan
116 J11 **Târnava Mare** *Ger.* Grosse Kokel, *Hung.* Nagy-Küküllő; *prev.* Tîrnava Mare. ≈ S Romania
116 I11 **Târnava Mică** *Ger.* Kleine Kokel, *Hung.* Kis-Küküllo; *prev.* Tîrnava Mică. ≈ C Romania
116 I11 **Târnăveni** *Ger.* Marteskirch, Martinskirch, *Hung.* Dicsőszentmárton; *prev.* Sînmartin, Tîrnăveni. Mureş, C Romania 46°20′N 24°17′E
102 L14 **Tarn-et-Garonne** ◈ *department* S France
111 P18 **Tarnica** ▲ SE Poland 49°05′N 22°43′E
111 N15 **Tarnobrzeg** Podkarpackie, SE Poland 50°35′N 21°40′E
125 N12 **Tarnogskiy Gorodok** Vologodskaya Oblast', NW Russia 60°28′N 43°45′E
**Tarnopol** *see* Ternopil'
111 M16 **Tarnów** Małopolskie, S Poland 50°01′N 20°59′E
**Tarnowice/Tarnowitz** *see* Tarnowskie Góry
111 J16 **Tarnowskie Góry** *var.* Tarnowice, Tarnowskie Gory, *Ger.* Tarnowitz. Śląskie, S Poland 50°27′N 18°52′E
95 N14 **Tärnsjö** Västmanland, C Sweden 60°10′N 16°57′E
186 K7 **Taro** Choiseul, NW Solomon Islands 07°00′S 156°57′E
106 E9 **Taro** ≈ NW Italy
186 I6 **Taron** New Ireland, NE Papua New Guinea 04°22′S 153°04′E
74 E8 **Taroudannt** *var.* Taroudant. SW Morocco 30°31′N 08°50′W
**Taroudant** *see* Taroudannt
23 V12 **Tarpon, Lake** ◎ Florida, SE USA
23 V12 **Tarpon Springs** Florida, SE USA 28°09′N 82°45′W
107 G14 **Tarquinia** *anc.* Tarquinii, *hist.* Corneto. Lazio, C Italy 42°23′N 11°45′E
**Tarquinii** *see* Tarquinia
**Tarraco** *see* Tarragona
76 D10 **Tarrafal** Santiago, S Cape Verde 15°16′N 23°45′W
105 V6 **Tarragona** *anc.* Tarraco. Cataluña, E Spain 41°07′N 01°15′E
105 T7 **Tarragona** ◈ *province* Cataluña, NE Spain
183 O17 **Tarraleah** Tasmania, SE Australia 42°11′S 146°29′E
23 P3 **Tarrant City** Alabama, S USA 33°34′N 86°45′W
185 D21 **Tarras** Otago, South Island, New Zealand 44°48′S 169°25′E
**Tarrasa** *see* Terrassa
105 U5 **Tàrrega** *var.* Tarrega. Cataluña, NE Spain 41°39′N 01°09′E
21 W9 **Tar River** ≈ North Carolina, SE USA
**Tarsatica** *see* Rijeka
136 J17 **Tarsus** İçel, S Turkey 36°52′N 34°52′E
62 K4 **Tartagal** Salta, N Argentina 22°32′S 63°50′W
137 V12 **Tärtär** *Rus.* Terter. ≈ SW Azerbaijan
102 J15 **Tartas** Landes, SW France 43°52′N 00°45′W
**Tartlau** *see* Prejmer
**Tartous/Tartouss** *see* Ṭarṭūs
118 J5 **Tartu** *Ger.* Dorpat; *prev. Rus.* Yurev, Yury'ev. Tartumaa, SE Estonia 58°20′N 26°44′E
118 I5 **Tartumaa** *off.* Tartu Maakond. ◈ *province* E Estonia
**Tartu Maakond** *see* Tartumaa
138 H5 **Ṭarṭūs** *Fr.* Tartouss; *anc.* Tortosa. Ṭarṭūs, W Syria 34°55′N 35°52′E
138 H5 **Ṭarṭūs** *off.* Muḥāfaẓat Ṭarṭūs, *var.* Tartous, Tartus. ◈ *governorate* W Syria
**Ṭarṭūs, Muḥāfaẓat** *see* Ṭarṭūs
164 C16 **Tarumizu** Kagoshima, Kyūshū, SW Japan 31°30′N 130°40′E
126 K4 **Tarusa** Kaluzhskaya Oblast', W Russia 54°45′N 37°10′E
117 N11 **Tarutyne** Odes'ka Oblast', SW Ukraine 46°11′N 29°09′E
162 I7 **Tarvagatyn Nuruu** ▲▲ N Mongolia
106 J6 **Tarvisio** Friuli-Venezia Giulia, NE Italy 46°31′N 13°33′E
**Tarvisium** *see* Treviso
57 O16 **Tarvo, Río** ≈ E Bolivia
14 G8 **Tarzwell** Ontario, S Canada 48°00′N 79°58′W
40 K5 **Tasajera, Sierra de la** ▲▲ N Mexico
145 S13 **Tasaral** Karaganda, C Kazakhstan 46°17′N 73°54′E
145 N15 **Tasboget** *Kaz.* Tasböget; *prev.* Tasbuget. Kzylorda, S Kazakhstan 44°46′N 65°38′E
**Tasböget** *see* Tasboget
**Tasbuget** *see* Tasboget
108 E11 **Tasch** Valais, SW Switzerland 46°04′N 07°43′E
**Tasek Kenyir** *see* Kenyir, Tasik
122 J14 **Tashanta** Respublika Altay, S Russia 49°42′N 89°15′E
**Tashauz** *see* Daşoguz
**Tashi Chho Dzong** *see* Thimphu
153 U11 **Tashigang** E Bhutan 27°19′N 91°33′E
137 T11 **Tashir** *prev.* Kalinino. N Armenia 41°07′N 44°16′E
143 Q11 **Ṭashk, Daryācheh-ye** ◎ C Iran
**Tashkent** *see* Toshkent
**Tashkentskaya Oblast'** *see* Toshkent Viloyati
**Tashkepri** *see* Daşköpri
**Tash-Kömür** *see* Tash-Kumyr
147 S9 **Tash-Kumyr** *Kyr.* Tash-Kömür. Dzhalal-Abadskaya Oblast', W Kyrgyzstan 41°22′N 72°09′E
127 T7 **Tashla** Orenburgskaya Oblast', W Russia 51°42′N 52°33′E
**Tashqurghan** *see* Khulm
122 J13 **Tashtagol** Kemerovskaya Oblast', S Russia 52°49′N 88°00′E
95 H24 **Tåsinge** *island* C Denmark
12 M5 **Tasiujaq** Québec, E Canada 58°43′N 69°58′W
144 F8 **Taskala** *prev.* Kamenka. Zapadnyy Kazakhstan, NW Kazakhstan 51°06′N 51°16′E
77 W11 **Tasker** Zinder, C Niger 15°06′N 10°42′E
145 W12 **Taskesken** Vostochnyy Kazakhstan, E Kazakhstan 47°15′N 80°45′E
136 J10 **Taşköprü** Kastamonu, N Turkey 41°30′N 34°12′E
**Taskuduk, Peski** *see* Tosquduq Qumlari
186 G5 **Taskul** New Ireland, NE Papua New Guinea 02°34′S 150°25′E
137 S13 **Taşlıçay** Ağrı, E Turkey 39°37′N 43°23′E
185 H14 **Tasman** *off.* Tasman District. ◈ *unitary authority* South Island, New Zealand
192 J12 **Tasman Basin** *var.* East Australian Basin. *undersea feature* S Tasman Sea
185 I14 **Tasman Bay** *inlet* South Island, New Zealand
**Tasman District** *see* Tasman
192 I13 **Tasman Fracture Zone** *tectonic feature* S Indian Ocean
185 E19 **Tasman Glacier** *glacier* South Island, New Zealand
**Tasman Group** *see* Nukumanu Islands
183 N15 **Tasmania** *prev.* Van Diemen's Land. ◈ *state* SE Australia
183 Q16 **Tasmania** *island* SE Australia
185 H14 **Tasman Mountains** ▲▲ South Island, New Zealand
183 P17 **Tasman Peninsula** *peninsula* Tasmania, SE Australia
192 I11 **Tasman Plain** *undersea feature* W Tasman Sea
192 I12 **Tasman Plateau** *var.* South Tasmania Plateau. *undersea feature* SW Tasman Sea
192 I11 **Tasman Sea** *sea* SW Pacific Ocean
116 G9 **Tăşnad** *Ger.* Trestenberg, Trestendorf, *Hung.* Tasnád. Satu Mare, NW Romania 47°30′N 22°33′E
136 L11 **Taşova** Amasya, N Turkey 40°45′N 36°20′E
77 T10 **Tassara** Tahoua, W Niger 16°40′N 05°34′E
12 K4 **Tassialouc, Lac** ◎ Québec, C Canada
59 M15 **Tasso Fragoso** Maranhão, E Brazil 08°22′S 45°53′W
**Tåstrup** *see* Taastrup
145 O9 **Tasty-Taldy** Akmola, C Kazakhstan 50°47′N 66°31′E
143 W10 **Tāsūkī** Sīstān va Balūchestān, SE Iran
111 I22 **Tata** *Ger.* Totis. Komárom-Esztergom, NW Hungary 47°39′N 18°19′E
74 E8 **Tata** SW Morocco 29°38′N 08°04′W
**Tataaihoa, Pointe** *see* Vénus, Pointe
111 I22 **Tatabánya** Komárom-Esztergom, NW Hungary 47°33′N 18°23′E
191 X10 **Tatakoto** *atoll* Îles Tuamotu, E French Polynesia
75 N7 **Tataouine** *var.* Taṭāwīn. SE Tunisia 32°48′N 10°27′E
55 O5 **Tataracual, Cerro** ▲ NE Venezuela 10°13′N 64°20′W
117 O12 **Tatarbunary** Odes'ka Oblast', SW Ukraine 45°50′N 29°37′E
119 M17 **Tatarka** Mahilyowskaya Voblasts', E Belarus 53°15′N 28°50′E
**Tatar Pazardzhik** *see* Pazardzhik
122 I12 **Tatarsk** Novosibirskaya Oblast', C Russia 55°08′N 75°58′E
**Tatarskaya ASSR** *see* Tatarstan, Respublika
123 T13 **Tatarskiy Proliv** *Eng.* Tatar Strait. *strait* SE Russia
127 R4 **Tatarstan, Respublika** *prev.* Tatarskaya ASSR. ◈ *autonomous republic* W Russia
**Tatar Strait** *see* Tatarskiy Proliv
**Taṭāwīn** *see* Tataouine
171 N12 **Tate** Sulawesi, N Indonesia 0°12′S 119°44′E
141 N11 **Tathlīth** 'Asīr, S Saudi Arabia 19°38′N 43°32′E
141 O11 **Tathlīth, Wādī** *dry watercourse* S Saudi Arabia
183 R11 **Tathra** New South Wales, SE Australia 36°46′S 149°58′E
127 P8 **Tatishchevo** Saratovskaya Oblast', W Russia 51°43′N 45°35′E
39 S12 **Tatitlek** Alaska, USA 60°49′N 146°29′W
10 L15 **Tatla Lake** British Columbia, SW Canada 51°54′N 124°39′W
121 Q2 **Tatlısu** *Gk.* Akanthoú. N Cyprus 35°21′N 33°45′E
11 Z10 **Tatnam, Cape** *headland* Manitoba, C Canada 57°16′N 91°03′W
111 K18 **Tatra Mountains** *Ger.* Tatra, *Hung.* Tátra, *Pol./Slvk.* Tatry. ▲▲ Poland/Slovakia
**Tatra/Tátra** *see* Tatra Mountains
**Tatry** *see* Tatra Mountains
164 I13 **Tatsuno** *var.* Tatuno. Hyōgo, Honshū, SW Japan 34°54′N 134°30′E
**Tatti** *see* Tatty
145 S16 **Tatty** *prev.* Tatti. Zhambyl, S Kazakhstan 43°11′N 73°22′E
60 L10 **Tatuí** São Paulo, S Brazil 23°21′S 47°49′W
37 V14 **Tatum** New Mexico, SW USA 33°15′N 103°19′W
25 X7 **Tatum** Texas, SW USA 32°19′N 94°31′W
**Ta-t'ung/Tatung** *see* Datong
**Tatuno** *see* Tatsuno
137 R14 **Tatvan** Bitlis, SE Turkey 38°31′N 42°15′E
95 C16 **Tau** Rogaland, S Norway 59°04′N 05°55′E
192 L17 **Ta'ū** *var.* Tau. *island* Manua Islands, E American Samoa
193 W15 **Tau** *island* Tongatapu Group, N Tonga
59 O14 **Tauá** Ceará, E Brazil 06°04′S 40°26′W
60 N10 **Taubaté** São Paulo, S Brazil 23°S 45°36′W
101 I19 **Tauber** ≈ SW Germany
101 I19 **Tauberbiscofsheim** Baden-Württemberg, C Germany 49°37′N 09°39′E
**Tauchik** *see* Taushyk
191 W10 **Tauere** *atoll* Îles Tuamotu, C French Polynesia
101 H17 **Taufstein** ▲ C Germany 50°31′N 09°18′E
190 I17 **Taukoka** *island* SE Cook Islands
145 T15 **Taukum, Peski** *desert* SE Kazakhstan
184 L10 **Taumarunui** Manawatu-Wanganui, North Island, New Zealand 38°52′S 175°14′E
59 A15 **Taumaturgo** Acre, W Brazil 08°54′S 72°48′W
27 X6 **Taum Sauk Mountain** ▲ Missouri, C USA 37°34′N 90°43′W
83 H22 **Taung** North-West, N South Africa 27°32′S 24°48′E
166 L6 **Taungdwingyi** Magway, C Myanmar (Burma) 20°01′N 95°20′E
166 M6 **Taunggyi** Shan State, C Myanmar (Burma) 20°47′N 97°00′E
166 M7 **Taungoo** Bago, C Myanmar (Burma) 18°57′N 96°26′E
166 L5 **Taungtha** Mandalay, C Myanmar (Burma) 21°16′N 95°25′E
**Taungup** *see* Toungup
149 S9 **Taunsa** Punjab, E Pakistan 30°43′N 70°41′E
97 K23 **Taunton** SW England, United Kingdom 51°01′N 03°06′W
19 O12 **Taunton** Massachusetts, NE USA 41°54′N 71°03′W
101 F18 **Taunus** ▲▲ W Germany
101 G18 **Taunusstein** Hessen, W Germany 50°09′N 08°09′E
184 N9 **Taupo** Waikato, North Island, New Zealand 38°42′S 176°05′E
184 M9 **Taupo, Lake** ◎ North Island, New Zealand
109 R8 **Taurach** *var.* Taurachbach. ≈ E Austria
**Taurachbach** *see* Taurach
118 D12 **Tauragė** *Ger.* Tauroggen. Tauragė, SW Lithuania 55°16′N 22°17′E
118 D13 **Tauragė** ◈ *province* Lithuania
54 G10 **Tauramena** Casanare, C Colombia 05°02′N 72°43′W
184 N7 **Tauranga** Bay of Plenty, North Island, New Zealand 37°42′S 176°09′E
15 O10 **Taureau, Réservoir** ⊠ Québec, SE Canada
107 N22 **Taurianova** Calabria, SW Italy 38°22′N 16°01′E
**Tauris** *see* Tabrīz
184 I2 **Tauroa Point** *headland* North Island, New Zealand 35°09′S 173°02′E
**Tauroggen** *see* Tauragė
**Tauromenium** *see* Taormina
**Taurus Mountains** *see* Toros Dağları
**Taus** *see* Domažlice
144 E14 **Taushyk** *Kaz.* Taūshyq; *prev.* Tauchik. Mangistau, SW Kazakhstan 44°17′N 51°22′E
**Taūshyq** *see* Taushyk
105 R5 **Tauste** Aragón, NE Spain 41°55′N 01°15′W
191 V16 **Tautara, Motu** *island* Easter Island, Chile, E Pacific Ocean
191 R8 **Tautira** Tahiti, W French Polynesia 17°45′S 149°10′W
**Tauz** *see* Tovuz
**Ṭavālesh, Kūhhā-ye** *see* Talish Mountains
136 D15 **Tavas** Denizli, SW Turkey 37°33′N 29°04′E
**Tavastehus** *see* Hämeenlinna
**Tavau** *see* Davos
122 G10 **Tavda** Sverdlovskaya Oblast', C Russia 58°01′N 65°07′E
122 G10 **Tavda** ≈ C Russia
105 T11 **Tavernes de la Valldigna** Comunitat Valenciana, E Spain 39°03′N 00°13′W
81 I20 **Taveta** Taita/Taveta, S Kenya 03°23′S 37°40′E
187 Y14 **Taveuni** *island* N Fiji
147 R13 **Tavildara** *Rus.* Tavil'dara, Tovil'-Dora. C Tajikistan 38°42′N 70°27′E
**Tavin** *see* Adaatsag
104 H14 **Tavira** Faro, S Portugal 37°07′N 07°39′W
97 I24 **Tavistock** SW England, United Kingdom 50°33′N 04°08′W
**Tavoy** *see* Dawei
**Tavoy Island** *see* Mali Kyun
115 E16 **Tavropoú, Techníti Límni** ⊠ C Greece
136 E13 **Tavşanlı** Kütahya, NW Turkey 39°34′N 29°28′E
187 X14 **Tavua** Viti Levu, W Fiji 17°27′S 177°51′E
97 J23 **Taw** ≈ SW England, United Kingdom
185 L14 **Tawa** Wellington, North Island, New Zealand 41°10′S 174°50′E
25 V6 **Tawakoni, Lake** ⊠ Texas, SW USA
153 V11 **Tawang** Arunāchal Pradesh, NE India 27°34′N 91°54′E
169 R17 **Tawang, Teluk** *bay* Jawa, S Indonesia
31 R7 **Tawas Bay** ◎ Michigan, N USA
31 R7 **Tawas City** Michigan, N USA 44°16′N 83°33′W
169 V8 **Tawau** Sabah, East Malaysia 04°16′N 117°54′E
141 U10 **Ṭawīl, Qalamat aṭ** *well* SE Saudi Arabia
171 N9 **Tawitawi** *island* Tawitawi Group, SW Philippines
**Ṭawkar** *see* Tokar
**Tāwūq** *see* Dāqūq
**Tawzar** *see* Tozeur
41 O15 **Taxco** *var.* Taxco de Alarcón. Guerrero, S Mexico 18°32′N 99°37′W
**Taxco de Alarcón** *see* Taxco
146 H8 **Taxiatosh** *Rus.* Takhiatash. Qoraqalpog'iston Respublikasi, W Uzbekistan 42°27′N 59°27′E
158 D9 **Taxkorgan** *var.* Taxkorgan Tajik Zizhixian. Xinjiang Uygur Zizhiqu, NW China 37°43′N 75°13′E
**Taxkorgan Tajik Zizhixian** *see* Taxkorgan
146 H7 **Taxtako'pir** *Rus.* Takhtakupyr. Qoraqalpog'iston Respublikasi, NW Uzbekistan 43°04′N 60°23′E
96 J10 **Tay** ≈ C Scotland, United Kingdom
143 V6 **Tāybād** *var.* Taibad, Tāyybād, Tayyebāt. Khorāsān-e Razavī, NE Iran 34°48′N 60°46′E
**Taybert at Turkz** *see* Ṭayyibat at Turkī
124 J3 **Taybola** Murmanskaya Oblast', NW Russia 68°30′N 33°18′E
81 M16 **Tayeeglow** Bakool, C Somalia 04°01′N 44°25′E
96 K11 **Tay, Firth of** *inlet* E Scotland, United Kingdom
122 J12 **Tayga** Kemerovskaya Oblast', S Russia 56°02′N 85°26′E
**Taygan** *see* Delger
115 E21 **Taÿgetos** ▲▲ S Greece
123 T9 **Taygonos, Mys** *headland* E Russia 60°36′N 160°09′E
96 I11 **Tay, Loch** ◎ C Scotland, United Kingdom
11 N12 **Taylor** British Columbia, W Canada 56°09′N 120°43′W
29 O14 **Taylor** Nebraska, C USA 41°47′N 99°23′W
18 I13 **Taylor** Pennsylvania, NE USA 41°22′N 75°41′W
25 T10 **Taylor** Texas, SW USA 30°34′N 97°24′W
37 Q11 **Taylor, Mount** ▲ New Mexico, SW USA 35°14′N 107°36′W
37 R5 **Taylor Park Reservoir** ⊠ Colorado, C USA
37 R6 **Taylor River** ≈ Colorado, C USA
21 P11 **Taylors** South Carolina, SE USA 34°55′N 82°18′W
20 L5 **Taylorsville** Kentucky, S USA 38°01′N 85°21′W
21 R6 **Taylorsville** North Carolina, SE USA 35°56′N 81°10′W
30 L14 **Taylorville** Illinois, N USA 39°33′N 89°17′W
140 K5 **Taymā'** Tabūk, NW Saudi Arabia 27°39′N 38°32′E
122 M10 **Taymura** ≈ C Russia
123 O7 **Taymylyr** Respublika Sakha (Yakutiya), NE Russia 72°32′N 121°54′E
122 L7 **Taymyr, Ozero** ◎ N Russia
122 M6 **Taymyr, Poluostrov** *peninsula* N Russia
122 L8 **Taymyrskiy (Dolgano-Nenetskiy) Avtonomnyy Okrug** ◈ *autonomous district* Krasnoyarskiy Kray, N Russia
167 S13 **Tây Ninh** Tây Ninh, S Vietnam 11°21′N 106°07′E
122 L12 **Tayshet** Irkutskaya Oblast', S Russia 55°51′N 98°04′E
162 G8 **Tayshir** *var.* Tsagaan-Olom. Govĭ-Altay, C Mongolia 46°42′N 96°30′E
171 N5 **Taytay** Palawan, W Philippines 10°49′N 119°30′E
169 Q16 **Tayu** *prev.* Tajoe. Jawa, C Indonesia 06°32′S 111°02′E
**Tāyybād/Tayyebāt** *see* Tāybād
138 L5 **Ṭayyibah** *var.* At Taybé. Ḥimṣ, C Syria 35°13′N 38°51′E
138 I4 **Ṭayyibat at Turkī** *var.* Taybert at Turkz. Ḥamāh, W Syria 35°16′N 36°55′E
145 P7 **Tayynsha** *prev.* Krasnoarmeysk. Severnyy Kazakhstan, N Kazakhstan 53°52′N 69°51′E
122 J10 **Taz** ≈ N Russia
74 G6 **Taza** NE Morocco 34°13′N 04°06′W
139 T4 **Tāza Khurmātū** Kirkūk, E Iraq 35°18′N 44°22′E
165 Q8 **Tazawa-ko** ◎ Honshū, C Japan
21 N8 **Tazewell** Tennessee, S USA 36°27′N 83°34′W
21 Q7 **Tazewell** Virginia, NE USA 37°08′N 81°34′W
75 S11 **Tāzirbū** SE Libya 25°43′N 21°16′E
39 S11 **Tazlina Lake** ◎ Alaska, USA
122 J8 **Tazovskiy** Yamalo-Nenetskiy Avtonomnyy Okrug, N Russia 67°33′N 78°21′E
167 S11 **Tbeng Meanchey** *var.* Tbêng Méanchey. Preah Vihear, N Cambodia 13°45′N 104°58′E
**Tbêng Méanchey** *see* Tbeng Meanchey
137 U10 **Tbilisi** *Eng.* Tiflis. ● (Georgia) SE Georgia 41°41′N 44°55′E
137 T10 **Tbilisi** ✈ S Georgia 41°43′N 44°49′E
79 E14 **Tchabal Mbabo** ▲ NW Cameroon 07°12′N 12°16′E
**Tchad** *see* Chad
**Tchad, Lac** *see* Chad, Lake
77 S15 **Tchaourou** E Benin 08°58′N 02°40′E
79 E20 **Tchibanga** Nyanga, S Gabon 02°49′S 11°00′E
**Tchien** *see* Zwedru
77 Z6 **Tchigaï, Plateau du** ▲▲ NE Niger
77 V9 **Tchighozérine** Agadez, C Niger 17°15′N 07°48′E
77 T10 **Tchin-Tabaradene** Tahoua, W Niger 15°57′N 05°49′E
78 G13 **Tcholliré** Nord, NE Cameroon 08°48′N 14°00′E
**Tchongking** *see* Chongqing
22 K4 **Tchula** Mississippi, S USA 33°10′N 90°13′W
110 I7 **Tczew** *Ger.* Dirschau. Pomorskie, N Poland 54°05′N 18°46′E
116 I10 **Teaca** *Ger.* Tekendorf, *Hung.* Teke; *prev. Ger.* Teckendorf. Bistriţa-Năsăud, N Romania 46°55′N 24°30′E
40 J11 **Teacapán** Sinaloa, C Mexico 22°33′N 105°44′W
190 A10 **Teafuafou** *island* Funafuti Atoll, C Tuvalu
25 U8 **Teague** Texas, SW USA 31°37′N 96°16′W
191 R9 **Teahupoo** Tahiti, W French Polynesia 17°51′S 149°15′W
190 H15 **Te Aiti Point** *headland* Rarotonga, S Cook Islands 21°11′S 59°47′W
65 D24 **Teal Inlet** East Falkland, Falkland Islands 51°34′S 58°25′W
185 B22 **Te Anau** Southland, South Island, New Zealand 45°25′S 167°45′E
185 B22 **Te Anau, Lake** ◎ South Island, New Zealand
41 U15 **Teapa** Tabasco, SE Mexico 17°36′N 92°57′W
184 Q7 **Te Araroa** Gisborne, North Island, New Zealand 37°37′S 178°21′E
184 M7 **Te Aroha** Waikato, North Island, New Zealand 37°32′S 175°58′E
**Teate** *see* Chieti
190 A9 **Te Ava Fuagea** *channel* Funafuti Atoll, SE Tuvalu
190 B8 **Te Ava I Te Lape** *channel* Funafuti Atoll, SE Tuvalu
190 B9 **Te Ava Pua Pua** *channel* Funafuti Atoll, SE Tuvalu
184 M8 **Te Awamutu** Waikato, North Island, New Zealand 38°00′S 177°18′E


◆ Country ● Country Capital ◇ Dependent Territory ○ Dependent Territory Capital ◈ Administrative Regions ✈ International Airport ▲ Mountain ▲▲ Mountain Range ⛰ Volcano ≈ River ◎ Lake ⊠ Reservoir

TEBA – THALABÂRĬVĂT


171 X12 **Teba** Papua, E Indonesia 01°27′S 137°54′E
104 L15 **Teba** Andalucía, S Spain 36°59′N 04°54′W
126 M15 **Teberda** Karachayevo-Cherkesskaya Respublika, SW Russia 43°28′N 41°45′E
74 M6 **Tébessa** NE Algeria 35°21′N 08°06′E
62 O7 **Tebicuary, Río** ∿ S Paraguay
168 L13 **Tebingtinggi** Sumatera, W Indonesia 03°33′S 103°00′E
168 I8 **Tebingtinggi** Sumatera, N Indonesia 03°20′N 99°08′E
**Tebingtinggi, Pulau** see Rantau, Pulau
**Tebriz** see Tabrīz
137 U9 **T'ebulos Mta** Rus. Gora Tebulosmta; prev. Tebulos Mta. ▲ Georgia/Russia 42°33′N 45°21′E
**Tebulos Mta** see T'ebulos Mta
**Tebulosmta, Gora** see T'ebulos Mta
41 Q14 **Tecamachalco** Puebla, S Mexico 18°52′N 97°44′W
40 B1 **Tecate** Baja California, NW Mexico 32°33′N 116°38′W
136 M13 **Tecer Dağları** ▲▲ C Turkey
103 O17 **Tech** ∿ S France
77 P16 **Techiman** W Ghana 07°35′N 01°56′W
117 N15 **Techirghiol** Constanța, SE Romania 44°03′N 28°37′E
74 A12 **Techla** var. Techlé. SW Western Sahara 21°39′N 14°57′W
**Techlé** see Techla
63 H18 **Tecka, Sierra de** ▲▲ SW Argentina
**Teckendorf** see Teaca
40 K13 **Tecolotlán** Jalisco, SW Mexico 20°10′N 104°07′W
40 K14 **Tecomán** Colima, SW Mexico 18°53′N 103°54′W
35 V12 **Tecopa** California, W USA 35°51′N 116°14′W
40 G5 **Tecoripa** Sonora, NW Mexico 28°38′N 109°58′W
41 N16 **Tecpan** var. Tecpan de Galeana. Guerrero, S Mexico 17°12′N 100°39′W
**Tecpan de Galeana** see Tecpan
40 J11 **Tecuala** Nayarit, C Mexico 22°24′N 105°30′W
116 L12 **Tecuci** Galați, E Romania 45°50′N 27°27′E
31 R10 **Tecumseh** Michigan, N USA 42°00′N 83°57′W
29 S16 **Tecumseh** Nebraska, C USA 40°22′N 96°12′W
27 O11 **Tecumseh** Oklahoma, C USA 35°15′N 96°56′W
**Tedzhen** see Harīrūd/Tejen
**Tedzhen** see Tejen
146 H15 **Tedzhenstroy** Turkm. Tejenstroy. Ahal Welaýaty, S Turkmenistan 36°57′N 60°49′E
**Teel** see Öndör-Ulaan
97 L15 **Tees** ∿ N England, United Kingdom
14 E15 **Teeswater** Ontario, S Canada 44°00′N 81°17′W
190 A10 **Tefala** island Funafuti Atoll, C Tuvalu
58 D13 **Tefé** Amazonas, N Brazil 03°24′S 64°45′W
74 K11 **Tefedest** ▲ S Algeria
136 E16 **Tefenni** Burdur, SW Turkey 37°19′N 29°45′E
58 D13 **Tefé, Rio** ∿ NW Brazil
169 P16 **Tegal** Jawa, C Indonesia 06°52′S 109°07′E
100 O12 **Tegel** ✈ (Berlin) Berlin, NE Germany 52°33′N 13°16′E
99 M15 **Tegelen** Limburg, SE Netherlands 51°20′N 06°09′E
101 L24 **Tegernsee** ◎ SE Germany
107 M18 **Teggiano** Campania, S Italy 40°25′N 15°28′E
77 U14 **Tegina** Niger, C Nigeria 10°06′N 06°10′E
**Tegucigalpa** see Central District
**Tegucigalpa** see Toncontín
**Tegucigalpa** see Francisco Morazán
77 U9 **Teguidda-n-Tessoumt** Agadez, C Niger 17°27′N 06°40′E
64 Q11 **Teguise** Lanzarote, Islas Canarias, Spain, NE Atlantic Ocean 29°04′N 13°38′W
122 K12 **Tegul'det** Tomskaya Oblast', C Russia 57°16′N 87°58′E
35 S13 **Tehachapi** California, W USA 35°07′N 118°27′W
35 S13 **Tehachapi Mountains** ▲▲ California, W USA
**Tehama** see Tihāmah
184 L4 **Te Hauturu-o-Toi / Little Barrier Island** var. Little Barrier Island. island N New Zealand
**Teheran** see Tehrān
77 O14 **Téhini** NE Ivory Coast 09°36′N 03°40′W
143 N5 **Tehrān** var. Teheran. ● (Iran) Tehrān, N Iran 35°44′N 51°27′E
143 N6 **Tehrān** off. Ostān-e Tehrān, var. Tehran. ◈ province N Iran
**Tehrān, Ostān-e** see Tehrān
**Tehri** see Tīkamgarh
**Tehri** see New Tehri
41 Q15 **Tehuacán** Puebla, S Mexico 18°29′N 97°24′W
41 S17 **Tehuantepec** var. Santo Domingo Tehuantepec. Oaxaca, SE Mexico 16°18′N 95°14′W
41 S17 **Tehuantepec, Golfo de** var. Gulf of Tehuantepec. gulf S Mexico
**Tehuantepec, Gulf of** see Tehuantepec, Golfo de
**Tehuantepec, Isthmus of** see Tehuantepec, Istmo de
41 T16 **Tehuantepec, Istmo de** var. Isthmus of Tehuantepec. isthmus SE Mexico
0 I16 **Tehuantepec Ridge** undersea feature E Pacific Ocean 13°30′N 98°00′W
41 S16 **Tehuantepec, Río** ∿ SE Mexico
191 W10 **Tehuata** atoll Îles Tuamotu, C French Polynesia
64 O11 **Teide, Pico del** ▲ Gran Canaria, Islas Canarias, Spain, NE Atlantic Ocean 28°16′N 16°39′W
97 I21 **Teifi** ∿ SW Wales, United Kingdom
80 B9 **Teiga Plateau** plateau W Sudan
97 J24 **Teignmouth** SW England, United Kingdom 50°34′N 03°29′W
**Te Ika-a-Māui** see North Island / Te Ika-a-Māui
**Teisen** see Jecheon
116 H1 **Teiuș** Ger. Dreikirchen, Hung. Tövis. Alba, C Romania 46°12′N 23°40′E
169 U17 **Tejakula** Bali, C Indonesia 08°09′S 115°19′E
146 H14 **Tejen** Rus. Tedzhen. Ahal Welaýaty, S Turkmenistan 37°24′N 60°29′E
146 I15 **Tejen** Per. Harīrūd, Rus. Tedzhen. ∿ Afghanistan/Iran see also Harīrūd
**Tejen** see Harī Rōd
**Tejenstroy** see Tedzhenstroy
35 S14 **Tejon Pass** pass California, W USA
**Tejo, Rio** see Tagus
41 O14 **Tejupilco** var. Tejupilco de Hidalgo. México, S Mexico 18°55′N 100°10′W
**Tejupilco de Hidalgo** see Tejupilco
184 P7 **Te Kaha** Bay of Plenty, North Island, New Zealand 37°45′S 177°42′E
29 S14 **Tekamah** Nebraska, C USA 41°46′N 96°13′W
184 I1 **Te Kao** Northland, North Island, New Zealand 34°40′S 172°57′E
185 F20 **Tekapo** ∿ South Island, New Zealand
185 F19 **Tekapo, Lake** ◎ South Island, New Zealand
184 P9 **Te Karaka** Gisborne, North Island, New Zealand 38°30′S 177°52′E
184 L7 **Te Kauwhata** Waikato, North Island, New Zealand 37°22′S 175°07′E
41 X12 **Tekax** var. Tekax de Álvaro Obregón. Yucatán, SE Mexico 20°07′N 89°10′W
**Tekax de Álvaro Obregón** see Tekax
136 A14 **Teke Burnu** headland W Turkey 38°06′N 26°35′E
114 M12 **Teke Deresi** ∿ NW Turkey
146 D10 **Tekedzhik, Gory** hill range NW Turkmenistan
145 V14 **Tekeli** Almaty, SE Kazakhstan 44°50′N 78°47′E
145 R7 **Teke, Ozero** ◎ N Kazakhstan
158 I5 **Tekes** Xinjiang Uygur Zizhiqu, NW China 43°15′N 81°43′E
145 W16 **Tekes** Almaty, SE Kazakhstan 42°40′N 80°01′E
**Tekes** see Tekes He
158 H5 **Tekes He** Rus. Tekes. ∿ China/Kazakhstan
**Teke/Tekendorf** see Teaca
80 I10 **Tekezē** var. Takkaze. ∿ Eritrea/Ethiopia
**Tekhtin** see Tsyakhtsin
136 C10 **Tekirdağ** It. Rodosto; anc. Bisanthe, Raidestos, Rhaedestus. Tekirdağ, NW Turkey 40°59′N 27°31′E
136 C10 **Tekirdağ** ◈ province NW Turkey
155 N14 **Tekkali** Andhra Pradesh, E India 18°37′N 84°15′E
115 K15 **Tekke Burnu** Turk. İlyasbaba Burnu. headland NW Turkey 40°03′N 26°12′E
137 Q13 **Tekman** Erzurum, NE Turkey 39°39′N 41°31′E
32 M9 **Tekoa** Washington, NW USA 47°13′N 117°05′W
190 H16 **Te Kou** ▲ Rarotonga, S Cook Islands 21°14′S 159°46′W
**Tekrit** see Tikrīt
171 P12 **Teku** Sulawesi, N Indonesia 0°46′S 123°25′E
184 L9 **Te Kuiti** Waikato, North Island, New Zealand 38°21′S 175°10′E
42 H4 **Tela** Atlántida, NW Honduras 15°46′N 87°25′W
138 F12 **Telalim** Southern, S Israel 30°58′N 34°47′E
**Telanaipura** see Jambi
137 U10 **Telavi** prev. T'elavi. E Georgia 41°55′N 45°29′E
**T'elavi** see Telavi
138 F10 **Tel Aviv** ◈ district W Israel
**Tel Aviv-Jaffa** see Tel Aviv-Yafo
138 F10 **Tel Aviv-Yafo** var. Tel Aviv-Jaffa. Tel Aviv, C Israel 32°05′N 34°46′E
111 E18 **Telč** Ger. Teltsch. Vysočina, C Czechia 49°10′N 15°28′E
186 B6 **Telefomin** West Sepik, NW Papua New Guinea 05°08′S 141°31′E
10 J10 **Telegraph Creek** British Columbia, W Canada 57°56′N 131°10′W
190 B10 **Telele** island Funafuti Atoll, C Tuvalu
60 J11 **Telêmaco Borba** Paraná, S Brazil 24°20′S 50°44′W
95 E15 **Telemark** ◈ county S Norway
62 J13 **Telén** La Pampa, C Argentina 36°20′S 65°31′W
**Teleneshty** see Telenești
117 N9 **Telenești** Rus. Teleneshty. C Moldova 47°35′N 28°20′E
104 J4 **Teleno, El** ▲ NW Spain 42°19′N 06°21′W
116 I15 **Teleorman** ◈ county S Romania
116 I14 **Teleorman** ∿ S Romania
25 V5 **Telephone** Texas, SW USA 33°48′N 96°00′W
35 U11 **Telescope Peak** ▲ California, W USA 36°09′N 117°03′W
**Teles Pirés** see São Manuel, Rio
97 L19 **Telford** W England, United Kingdom 52°42′N 02°28′W
108 L7 **Telfs** Tirol, W Austria 47°19′N 11°05′E
42 I9 **Telica** León, NW Nicaragua 12°30′N 86°52′W
42 J6 **Telica, Río** ∿ C Honduras
76 I13 **Télimélé** W Guinea 10°45′N 13°02′W
43 O14 **Telire, Río** ∿ Costa Rica/Panama
114 I8 **Telish** prev. Azizie. Pleven, N Bulgaria 43°20′N 24°15′E
41 R16 **Telixtlahuaca** var. San Francisco Telixtlahuaca. Oaxaca, SE Mexico 17°18′N 96°54′W
10 K13 **Telkwa** British Columbia, SW Canada 54°39′N 126°51′W
25 P4 **Tell** Texas, SW USA 34°18′N 100°20′W
**Tell Abiad** see Tall Abyaḍ
**Tell Abiad/Tell Abyad** see At Tall al Abyaḍ
31 O16 **Tell City** Indiana, N USA 37°56′N 86°47′W
38 M9 **Teller** Alaska, USA 65°15′N 166°21′W
**Tell Huqnah** see Tall Ḥuqnah
**Tellicherry** see Thalassery
20 M10 **Tellico Plains** Tennessee, S USA 35°19′N 84°18′W
**Tell Kalakh** see Tall Kalakh
**Tell Mardīkh** see Ebla
54 E11 **Tello** Huila, C Colombia 03°06′N 75°08′W
**Tell Shedadi** see Ash Shadādah
37 Q7 **Telluride** Colorado, C USA 37°56′N 107°48′W
**Tel'manove** see Boykivs'ke
**Tel'man/Tel'mansk** see Gubadag
162 H6 **Telmen** var. Övögdiy. Dzavhan, C Mongolia 48°38′N 97°39′E
162 H6 **Telmen Nuur** ◎ NW Mongolia
**Teloekbetoeng** see Bandar Lampung
41 O15 **Teloloapán** Guerrero, S Mexico 18°21′N 99°52′W
**Telo Martius** see Toulon
**Telposiz, Gora** see Telpoziz, Gora
125 V8 **Telpoziz, Gora** prev. Gora Telposiz. ▲ NW Russia 63°52′N 59°15′E
**Telschen** see Telšiai
63 J17 **Telsen** Chubut, S Argentina 42°27′S 66°59′W
118 D11 **Telšiai** Ger. Telschen. Telšiai, NW Lithuania 55°59′N 22°21′E
118 D11 **Telšiai** ◈ province NW Lithuania
**Teltsch** see Telč
**Telukbetung** see Bandar Lampung
168 H10 **Telukdalam** Pulau Nias, W Indonesia 0°34′N 97°47′E
14 H9 **Temagami** Ontario, S Canada 47°03′N 79°47′W
14 G9 **Temagami, Lake** ◎ Ontario, S Canada
190 H16 **Te Manga** ▲ Rarotonga, S Cook Islands 21°13′S 159°45′W
191 W12 **Tematagi** prev. Tematangi. atoll Îles Tuamotu, S French Polynesia
**Tematangi** see Tematagi
**Te Matau** see Separation Point / Te Matau
41 X11 **Temax** Yucatán, SE Mexico 21°10′N 88°53′W
171 E14 **Tembagapura** Papua, E Indonesia 04°10′S 137°19′E
129 U5 **Tembenchi** ∿ N Russia
55 P6 **Temblador** Monagas, NE Venezuela 08°59′N 62°44′W
105 N9 **Tembleque** Castilla-La Mancha, C Spain 39°41′N 03°30′W
**Temboni** see Mitemele, Río
35 U16 **Temecula** California, W USA 33°29′N 117°09′W
168 K7 **Temengor, Tasik** ◎ Peninsular Malaysia
112 L9 **Temerin** Vojvodina, N Serbia 45°25′N 19°54′E
**Temeschburg/Temeschwar** see Timișoara
**Temes-Kubin** see Kovin
**Temes/Temesch** see Tamiš
**Temesvár/Temeswar** see Timișoara
**Teminaboean** see Teminabuan
171 U12 **Teminabuan** prev. Teminaboean. Papua Barat, E Indonesia 01°30′S 131°59′E
145 P17 **Temirlan** prev. Temirlanovka. Turkestan, S Kazakhstan 42°36′N 69°17′E
**Temirlanovka** see Temirlan
145 R10 **Temirtau** prev. Samarkandski, Samarkandskoye. Karaganda, C Kazakhstan 50°05′N 72°55′E
14 H10 **Témiscaming** Québec, SE Canada 46°40′N 79°04′W
**Témiscamingue, Lac** see Timiskaming, Lake
15 T8 **Témiscouata, Lac** ◎ Québec, SE Canada
127 N5 **Temnikov** Respublika Mordoviya, W Russia 54°39′N 43°09′E
191 Y13 **Temoe** island Îles Gambier, E French Polynesia
183 Q9 **Temora** New South Wales, SE Australia 34°28′S 147°33′E
40 H7 **Témoris** Chihuahua, W Mexico 27°16′N 108°15′W
40 I5 **Temósachic** Chihuahua, N Mexico 28°55′N 107°42′W
187 Q10 **Temotu** var. Temotu Province. ◈ province E Solomon Islands
**Temotu Province** see Temotu
36 L14 **Tempe** Arizona, SW USA 33°24′N 111°54′W
**Tempelburg** see Czaplinek
107 C17 **Tempio Pausania** Sardegna, Italy, C Mediterranean Sea 40°55′N 09°07′E
42 K12 **Tempisque, Río** ∿ NW Costa Rica
25 T9 **Temple** Texas, SW USA 31°06′N 97°22′W
100 O12 **Tempelhof** ✈ (Berlin) Berlin, NE Germany 52°28′N 13°24′E
97 D19 **Templemore** Ir. An Teampall Mór. Tipperary, C Ireland 52°48′N 07°50′W
100 O11 **Templin** Brandenburg, NE Germany 53°07′N 13°31′E
41 P12 **Tempoal** var. Tempoal de Sánchez. Veracruz, E Mexico 21°32′N 98°23′W
**Tempoal de Sánchez** see Tempoal
41 P13 **Tempoal, Río** ∿ C Mexico
83 E14 **Tempué** Moxico, C Angola 13°36′S 18°56′E
126 J14 **Temryuk** Krasnodarskiy Kray, SW Russia 45°15′N 37°26′E
99 G17 **Temse** Oost-Vlaanderen, N Belgium 51°08′N 04°13′E
63 F15 **Temuco** Araucanía, C Chile 38°45′S 72°37′W
185 G20 **Temuka** Canterbury, South Island, New Zealand 44°14′S 171°17′E
189 P13 **Temwen Island** island E Micronesia
56 C6 **Tena** Napo, C Ecuador 01°00′S 77°48′W
41 W13 **Tenabo** Campeche, E Mexico 20°02′N 90°12′W
**Tenaghau** see Aola
25 X7 **Tenaha** Texas, SW USA 31°56′N 94°14′W
39 X13 **Tenake** Chichagof Island, Alaska, USA 57°46′N 135°13′W
155 K16 **Tenāli** Andhra Pradesh, E India 16°13′N 80°36′E
**Tenan** see Cheonan
41 O14 **Tenancingo** var. Tenencingo de Degollado. México, S Mexico 18°57′N 99°39′W
191 X12 **Tenararo** island Groupe Actéon, SE French Polynesia
**Tenasserim** see Tanintharyi
**Tenasserim** see Tanintharyi
98 O5 **Ten Boer** Groningen, NE Netherlands 53°16′N 06°42′E
97 I21 **Tenby** SW Wales, United Kingdom 51°41′N 04°43′W
80 K11 **Tendaho** Āfar, NE Ethiopia 11°39′N 40°59′E
103 V14 **Tende** Alpes Maritimes, SE France 44°04′N 07°34′E
151 Q20 **Ten Degree Channel** strait Andaman and Nicobar Islands, India, E Indian Ocean
80 F11 **Tendelti** White Nile, E Sudan 13°01′N 31°55′E
76 G8 **Te-n-Dghâmcha, Sebkhet** var. Sebkha de Ndrhamcha, Sebkra de Ndaghamcha. salt lake W Mauritania
165 P10 **Tendō** Yamagata, Honshū, C Japan 38°22′N 140°22′E
74 H7 **Tendrara** NE Morocco 33°06′N 01°58′W
117 Q11 **Tendrivs'ka Kosa** spit S Ukraine
117 Q11 **Tendrivs'ka Zatoka** gulf S Ukraine
**Tenencingo de Degollado** see Tenancingo
77 N11 **Ténenkou** Mopti, C Mali 14°28′N 04°55′W
77 W9 **Ténéré** physical region C Niger
77 W9 **Ténére, Erg du** desert C Niger
64 O11 **Tenerife** island Islas Canarias, Spain, NE Atlantic Ocean
74 J5 **Ténès** NW Algeria 36°35′N 01°18′E
170 M15 **Tengah, Kepulauan** island group C Indonesia
**Tengcheng** see Tengxian
169 V11 **Tenggarong** Borneo, C Indonesia 0°23′S 117°00′E
162 J15 **Tengger Shamo** desert N China
168 L8 **Tenggul, Pulau** island Peninsular Malaysia
**Tengiz Köl** see Teniz, Ozero
76 M14 **Tengréla** var. Tingréla. N Ivory Coast 10°26′N 06°20′W
160 M14 **Tengxian** var. Tengcheng, Tengxian, Teng Xian. Guangxi Zhuangzu Zizhiqu, S China 23°24′N 110°49′E
**Tengxian** see Tengxian
**Teng Xian** see Tengxian
32 G9 **Tenino** Washington, NW USA 46°51′N 122°51′W
145 P9 **Teniz, Ozero** Kaz. Tengiz Köl. salt lake C Kazakhstan
112 I9 **Tenja** Osijek-Baranja, E Croatia 45°30′N 18°45′E
188 B16 **Tenjo, Mount** ▲ W Guam
155 H23 **Tenkāsi** Tamil Nādu, SE India 08°58′N 77°22′E
79 N24 **Tenke** Katanga, SE Dem. Rep. Congo 10°34′S 26°12′E
**Tenke** see Tinca
123 Q7 **Tenkeli** Respublika Sakha (Yakutiya), NE Russia 70°09′N 140°39′E
27 R10 **Tenkiller Ferry Lake** ⊠ Oklahoma, C USA
77 Q13 **Tenkodogo** S Burkina Faso 11°54′N 00°19′W
181 Q5 **Tennant Creek** Northern Territory, C Australia 19°40′S 134°16′E
20 G9 **Tennessee** off. State of Tennessee, also known as The Volunteer State. ◈ state SE USA
37 R5 **Tennessee Pass** pass Colorado, C USA
20 H10 **Tennessee River** ∿ S USA
23 N2 **Tennessee Tombigbee Waterway** canal Alabama/Mississippi, S USA
99 K22 **Tenneville** Luxembourg, SE Belgium 50°05′N 05°31′E
92 M11 **Tenniöjoki** ∿ NE Finland
92 L9 **Tenojoki** Lapp. Deatnu, Nor. Tana. ∿ Finland/Norway see also Deatnu, Tana
**Tenojoki** see Tana
169 U7 **Tenom** Sabah, East Malaysia 05°07′N 115°57′E
**Tenos** see Tínos
41 V15 **Tenosique** var. Tenosique de Pino Suárez. Tabasco, SE Mexico 17°30′N 91°24′W
**Tenosique de Pino Suárez** see Tenosique
22 I6 **Tensas River** ∿ Louisiana, S USA
23 O8 **Tensaw River** ∿ Alabama, S USA
74 E7 **Tensift** seasonal river W Morocco
171 O12 **Tentena** var. Tenteno. Sulawesi, C Indonesia 01°46′S 120°40′E
**Tenteno** see Tentena
183 U4 **Tenterfield** New South Wales, SE Australia 29°04′S 152°02′E
23 X16 **Ten Thousand Islands** island group Florida, SE USA
60 H9 **Teodoro Sampaio** São Paulo, S Brazil 22°30′S 52°13′W
59 N19 **Teófilo Otoni** var. Theophilo Ottoni. Minas Gerais, NE Brazil 17°52′S 41°31′W
116 K5 **Teofipol'** Khmel'nyts'ka Oblast', W Ukraine 50°00′N 26°22′E
**Teohatu** see Toahotu
41 P14 **Teotihuacán** ruins México, S Mexico
**Teotilán** see Teotitlán del Camino
41 Q15 **Teotitlán del Camino** var. Teotilán. Oaxaca, S Mexico 18°10′N 97°08′W
190 G12 **Tepa** Île Uvea, E Wallis and Futuna 13°19′S 176°09′W
191 P8 **Tepaee, Récif** reef Tahiti, W French Polynesia
40 L14 **Tepalcatepec** Michoacán, SW Mexico 19°11′N 102°50′W
190 A16 **Tepa Point** headland SW Niue 19°07′S 169°56′E
40 L13 **Tepatitlán** var. Tepatitlán de Morelos. Jalisco, SW Mexico 20°50′N 102°46′W
**Tepatitlán de Morelos** see Tepatitlán
40 J9 **Tepehuanes** var. Santa Catarina de Tepehuanes. Durango, C Mexico 25°22′N 105°42′W
**Tepelena** see Tepelenë
113 L22 **Tepelenë** var. Tepelena, It. Tepeleni. Gjirokastër, S Albania 40°18′N 20°00′E
**Tepeleni** see Tepelenë
40 K12 **Tepic** Nayarit, C Mexico 21°30′N 104°55′W
111 C15 **Teplice** Ger. Teplitz; prev. Teplice-Šanov, Teplitz-Schönau. Ústecký Kraj, NW Czechia 50°38′N 13°49′E
**Teplice-Šanov/Teplitz/Teplitz-Schönau** see Teplice
117 O7 **Teplyk** Vinnyts'ka Oblast', C Ukraine 48°40′N 29°46′E
123 R10 **Teplyy Klyuch** Respublika Sakha (Yakutiya), NE Russia 62°46′N 137°01′E
40 E5 **Tepoca, Cabo** headland NW Mexico 29°19′N 112°24′W
191 W9 **Tepoto** island Îles du Désappointement, C French Polynesia
92 L11 **Tepsa** Lappi, N Finland 67°34′N 25°36′E
190 B8 **Tepuka** atoll Funafuti Atoll, C Tuvalu
184 N7 **Te Puke** Bay of Plenty, North Island, New Zealand 37°48′S 176°19′E
40 L13 **Tequila** Jalisco, SW Mexico 20°52′N 103°48′W
41 O13 **Tequisquiapan** Querétaro de Arteaga, C Mexico 20°34′N 99°52′W
77 Q12 **Téra** Tillabéri, W Niger 14°01′N 00°45′E
104 J5 **Tera** ∿ NW Spain
191 V1 **Teraina** prev. Washington Island. atoll Line Islands, E Kiribati
81 F15 **Terakeka** Central Equatoria, S South Sudan 05°26′N 31°45′E
107 J14 **Teramo** anc. Interamna. Abruzzi, C Italy 42°40′N 13°43′E
98 P7 **Ter Apel** Groningen, NE Netherlands 52°52′N 07°05′E
104 H11 **Tera, Ribeira de** ∿ S Portugal
185 K14 **Terawhiti, Cape** headland North Island, New Zealand 41°17′S 174°36′E
98 N12 **Terborg** Gelderland, E Netherlands 51°55′N 06°22′E
137 P13 **Tercan** Erzincan, NE Turkey 39°47′N 40°23′E
64 O2 **Terceira** ✈ Terceira, Azores, Portugal, NE Atlantic Ocean 38°43′N 27°13′W
64 O2 **Terceira** var. Ilha Terceira. island Azores, Portugal, NE Atlantic Ocean
**Terceira, Ilha** see Terceira
116 K6 **Terebovlya** Ternopil's'ka Oblast', W Ukraine 49°18′N 25°44′E
127 O15 **Terek** ∿ SW Russia
**Terekhovka** see Tsyerakhowka
147 R9 **Terek-Say** Dzhalal-Abadskaya Oblast', W Kyrgyzstan 41°28′N 71°06′E
145 Z10 **Terekty** prev. Alekseevka, Alekseyevka. Vostochnyy Kazakhstan, E Kazakhstan 48°25′N 85°38′E
168 L7 **Terengganu** var. Trengganu. ◈ state Peninsular Malaysia
127 X7 **Terensay** Orenburgskaya Oblast', W Russia 51°35′N 59°28′E
58 N13 **Teresina** var. Therezina. state capital Piauí, NE Brazil 05°09′S 42°46′W
60 P9 **Teresópolis** Rio de Janeiro, SE Brazil 22°25′S 42°59′W
110 P12 **Terespol** Lubelskie, E Poland 52°05′N 23°37′E
191 V16 **Terevaka, Maunga** Ѫ Easter Island, Chile, E Pacific Ocean 27°05′S 109°23′W
103 P3 **Tergnier** Aisne, N France 49°39′N 03°18′E
43 O14 **Teribe, Río** ∿ NW Panama
124 K3 **Teriberka** Murmanskaya Oblast', NW Russia 69°10′N 35°18′E
**Terinkot** see Tarīn Kōt
**Terisaqqan** see Tersakkan
24 K12 **Terlingua** Texas, SW USA 29°18′N 103°36′W
24 K11 **Terlingua Creek** ∿ Texas, SW USA
62 K7 **Termas de Río Hondo** Santiago del Estero, N Argentina 27°29′S 64°52′W
136 M11 **Terme** Samsun, N Turkey 41°12′N 37°00′E
**Termez** see Termiz
**Termia** see Kýthnos
107 J23 **Termini Imerese** anc. Thermae Himerenses. Sicilia, Italy, C Mediterranean Sea 37°59′N 13°42′E
41 V14 **Términos, Laguna de** lagoon SE Mexico
77 X10 **Termit-Kaoboul** Zinder, C Niger 15°34′N 11°31′E
147 O14 **Termiz** Rus. Termez. Surkhondaryo Viloyati, S Uzbekistan 37°17′N 67°12′E
107 L15 **Termoli** Molise, C Italy 42°00′N 14°58′E
**Termonde** see Dendermonde
98 P5 **Termunten** Groningen, NE Netherlands 53°18′N 07°02′E
171 R11 **Ternate** Pulau Ternate, E Indonesia 0°48′N 127°23′E
109 T5 **Ternberg** Oberösterreich, N Austria 47°57′N 14°22′E
99 E15 **Terneuzen** var. Neuzen. Zeeland, SW Netherlands 51°20′N 03°50′E
123 T14 **Terney** Primorskiy Kray, SE Russia 45°03′N 136°43′E
107 I14 **Terni** anc. Interamna Nahars. Umbria, C Italy 42°34′N 12°38′E
109 X6 **Ternitz** Niederösterreich, E Austria 47°43′N 16°02′E
117 V7 **Ternivka** Dnipropetrovs'ka Oblast', E Ukraine 48°30′N 36°05′E
116 K6 **Ternopil'** Pol. Tarnopol, Rus. Ternopol'. Ternopil's'ka Oblast', W Ukraine 49°32′N 25°38′E
**Ternopil'** see Ternopil's'ka Oblast'
116 I6 **Ternopil's'ka Oblast'** var. Ternopil', Rus. Ternopol'skaya Oblast'. ◈ province NW Ukraine
**Ternopol'** see Ternopil'
**Ternopol'skaya Oblast'** see Ternopil's'ka Oblast'
123 U13 **Terpeniya, Mys** headland Ostrov Sakhalin, SE Russia 48°37′N 144°40′E
**Térraba, Río** see Grande de Térraba, Río
10 J13 **Terrace** British Columbia, W Canada 54°31′N 128°32′W
12 D12 **Terrace Bay** Ontario, S Canada 48°47′N 87°06′W
107 I16 **Terracina** Lazio, C Italy 41°18′N 13°13′E
93 F14 **Terråk** Troms, N Norway 65°03′N 12°22′E
26 M13 **Terral** Oklahoma, C USA 33°55′N 97°54′W
107 B19 **Terralba** Sardegna, Italy, C Mediterranean Sea 39°47′N 08°35′E
**Terranova di Sicilia** see Gela
**Terranova Pausania** see Olbia
105 W5 **Terrassa** Cast. Tarrasa. Cataluña, E Spain 41°34′N 02°01′E
15 O12 **Terrebonne** Québec, SE Canada 45°42′N 73°37′W
22 J11 **Terrebonne Bay** bay Louisiana, SE USA
31 N14 **Terre Haute** Indiana, N USA 39°27′N 87°24′W
25 U6 **Terrell** Texas, SW USA 32°44′N 96°16′W
**Terre Neuve** see Newfoundland and Labrador
33 Q14 **Terreton** Idaho, NW USA 43°49′N 112°25′W
103 T7 **Territoire-de-Belfort** ◈ department E France
33 X9 **Terry** Montana, NW USA 46°46′N 105°16′W
28 I9 **Terry Peak** ▲ South Dakota, N USA 44°19′N 103°49′W
136 H14 **Tersakan Gölü** ◎ C Turkey
145 O10 **Tersakkan** Kaz. Terisaqqan. ∿ C Kazakhstan
98 J4 **Terschelling** Fris. Skylge. island Waddeneilanden, N Netherlands
78 H10 **Tersef** Hadjer-Lamis, C Chad 12°55′N 16°49′E
147 X8 **Terskey Ala-Too, Khrebet** ▲▲ Kazakhstan/Kyrgyzstan
**Terter** see Tärtär
105 R8 **Teruel** anc. Turba. Aragón, E Spain 40°21′N 01°06′W
105 R7 **Teruel** ◈ province Aragón, E Spain
114 M7 **Tervel** prev. Kurtbunar, Rom. Curtbunar. Dobrich, NE Bulgaria 43°45′N 27°25′E
93 M16 **Tervo** Pohjois-Savo, C Finland 62°57′N 26°48′E
92 L13 **Tervola** Lappi, NW Finland 66°04′N 24°49′E
**Tervueren** see Tervuren
99 H18 **Tervuren** var. Tervueren. Vlaams Brabant, C Belgium 50°48′N 04°28′E
162 G5 **Tes** var. Dzür. Dzavhan, W Mongolia 49°37′N 95°46′E
112 H11 **Tešanj** Federacija Bosne I Hercegovine, N Bosnia and Herzegovina 44°37′N 18°00′E
**Teschen** see Cieszyn
83 M19 **Tesenane** Inhambane, S Mozambique 22°48′S 34°02′E
80 I9 **Teseney** var. Tessenei. W Eritrea 15°05′N 36°42′E
39 P5 **Teshekpuk Lake** ◎ Alaska, USA
**Teshevle** see Tsyeshawlya
162 K6 **Teshig** Bulgan, N Mongolia 49°51′N 102°45′E
165 T2 **Teshio** Hokkaidō, NE Japan 44°49′N 141°46′E
165 T2 **Teshio-sanchi** ▲▲ Hokkaidō, NE Japan
14 L7 **Tessier, Lac** ◎ Québec, SE Canada
**Těšín** see Cieszyn
**Tesiyn Gol** see Tes-Khem
129 T7 **Tes-Khem** var. Tesiyn Gol. ∿ Mongolia/Russia
112 H11 **Teslić** Republika Srpska, N Bosnia and Herzegovina 44°35′N 17°50′E
10 I9 **Teslin** Yukon, W Canada 60°12′N 132°44′W
10 I8 **Teslin** ∿ British Columbia/Yukon, W Canada
77 Q8 **Tessalit** Kidal, NE Mali 20°12′N 00°58′E
77 V12 **Tessaoua** Maradi, S Niger 13°46′N 07°55′E
99 J17 **Tessenderlo** Limburg, NE Belgium 51°05′N 05°04′E
**Tessenei** see Teseney
**Tessin** see Ticino
97 M23 **Test** ∿ S England, United Kingdom
**Testama** see Tõstamaa
55 P4 **Testigos, Islas los** island group N Venezuela
37 S10 **Tesuque** New Mexico, SW USA 35°45′N 105°55′W
103 O17 **Têt** var. Tet. ∿ S France
**Tet** see Têt
54 G5 **Tetas, Cerro de las** ▲ NW Venezuela 09°58′N 73°00′W
83 M15 **Tete** Tete, NW Mozambique 16°14′S 33°34′E
83 M15 **Tete** off. Província de Tete. ◈ province NW Mozambique
11 N15 **Tête Jaune Cache** British Columbia, SW Canada 52°52′N 119°22′W
184 O8 **Te Teko** Bay of Plenty, North Island, New Zealand 38°03′S 176°48′E
186 K9 **Tetepare** island New Georgia Islands, NW Solomon Islands
**Tete, Província de** see Tete
**Teterev** see Teteriv
116 M5 **Teteriv** Rus. Teterev. ∿ N Ukraine
100 M9 **Teterow** Mecklenburg-Vorpommern, NE Germany 53°47′N 12°34′E
114 I9 **Teteven** Lovech, N Bulgaria 42°54′N 24°18′E
191 T10 **Tetiaroa** atoll Îles du Vent, W French Polynesia
105 P14 **Tetica de Bacares** ▲ S Spain 37°15′N 02°24′W
**Tetiyev** see Tetiyiv
117 O6 **Tetiyiv** Rus. Tetiyev. Kyivs'ka Oblast', N Ukraine 49°21′N 29°40′E
39 T10 **Tetlin** Alaska, USA 63°08′N 142°31′W
33 R8 **Teton River** ∿ Montana, NW USA
74 G5 **Tétouan** var. Tetouan, Tetuán. N Morocco 35°33′N 05°22′W
**Tetova/Tetovë** see Tetovo
114 L7 **Tetovo** Razgrad, N Bulgaria 43°49′N 26°21′E
113 N18 **Tetovo** Alb. Tetova, Tetovë, Turk. Kalkandelen. NW North Macedonia 42°01′N 20°58′E
115 E20 **Tetrázio** ▲▲ S Greece
**Tetschen** see Děčín
**Tetuán** see Tétouan
191 Q8 **Tetufera, Mont** ▲ Tahiti, W French Polynesia 17°40′S 149°26′W
127 R4 **Tetyushi** Respublika Tatarstan, W Russia 54°55′N 48°46′E
108 I7 **Teufen** Ausser Rhoden, NE Switzerland 47°24′N 09°24′E
40 L12 **Teul** var. Teul de Gonzáles Ortega. Zacatecas, C Mexico 21°30′N 103°28′W
107 B21 **Teulada** Sardegna, Italy, C Mediterranean Sea 38°58′N 08°46′E
**Teul de Gonzáles Ortega** see Teul
11 X16 **Teulon** Manitoba, S Canada 50°20′N 97°14′W
42 I7 **Teupasenti** El Paraíso, S Honduras 14°13′N 86°42′W
165 S2 **Teuri-tō** island NE Japan
100 G13 **Teutoburger Wald** Eng. Teutoburg Forest. hill range NW Germany
**Teutoburg Forest** see Teutoburger Wald
93 K17 **Teuva** Swe. Östermark. Etelä-Pohjanmaa, W Finland 62°29′N 21°45′E
107 H15 **Tevere** Eng. Tiber. ∿ C Italy
**Teverya** see Tverya
96 K13 **Teviot** ∿ SE Scotland, United Kingdom
**Tevli** see Tewli
122 H11 **Tevriz** Omskaya Oblast', C Russia 57°30′N 72°13′E
185 B24 **Te Waewae Bay** bay South Island, New Zealand
**Te Waipounamu** see South Island / Te Waipounamu
97 L21 **Tewkesbury** C England, United Kingdom 51°59′N 02°09′W
119 F19 **Tewli** Rus. Tevli. Brestskaya Voblasts', SW Belarus 52°20′N 24°15′E
159 U12 **Têwo** var. Dêngka; prev. Dêngkagoin. Gansu, C China 34°05′N 103°15′E
**Tewulike** see Hoxud
25 U12 **Texana, Lake** ◎ Texas, SW USA
27 S14 **Texarkana** Arkansas, C USA 33°26′N 94°02′W
25 X5 **Texarkana** Texas, SW USA 33°26′N 94°03′W
25 N9 **Texas** off. State of Texas, also known as Lone Star State. ◈ state S USA
25 W12 **Texas City** Texas, SW USA 29°23′N 94°55′W
41 P14 **Texcoco** México, C Mexico 19°32′N 98°52′W
98 I6 **Texel** island Waddeneilanden, NW Netherlands
26 H8 **Texhoma** Oklahoma, C USA 36°30′N 101°46′W
25 N1 **Texhoma** Texas, SW USA 36°30′N 101°46′W
37 W12 **Texico** New Mexico, SW USA 34°23′N 103°03′W
24 L1 **Texline** Texas, SW USA 36°22′N 103°01′W
41 P14 **Texmelucan** var. San Martín Texmelucan. Puebla, S Mexico 19°46′N 98°53′W
27 O13 **Texoma, Lake** ⊠ Oklahoma/Texas, C USA
25 N9 **Texon** Texas, SW USA 31°13′N 101°42′W
83 J23 **Teyateyaneng** NW Lesotho 29°04′S 27°51′E
124 M16 **Teykovo** Ivanovskaya Oblast', W Russia 56°49′N 40°31′E
124 M16 **Teza** ∿ W Russia
41 Q13 **Teziutlán** Puebla, S Mexico 19°49′N 97°22′W
153 W12 **Tezpur** Assam, NE India 26°39′N 92°47′E
**Thaa Atoll** see Kolhumadulu
9 N10 **Tha-Anne** ∿ Nunavut, NE Canada
83 K23 **Thabana Ntlenyana** var. Thabantshonyana, Mount Ntlenyana. ▲ E Lesotho 29°26′S 29°16′E
**Thabantshonyana** see Thabana Ntlenyana
83 J23 **Thaba Putsoa** ▲ C Lesotho 29°48′S 27°46′E
167 Q8 **Tha Bo** Nong Khai, E Thailand 17°52′N 102°34′E
103 T12 **Thabor, Pic du** ▲ E France 45°07′N 06°34′E
**Tha Chin** see Samut Sakhon
166 M7 **Thagaya** Bago, C Myanmar (Burma) 19°19′N 96°16′E
**Thai, Ao** see Thailand, Gulf of
167 T6 **Thai Binh** Thai Binh, N Vietnam 20°27′N 106°20′E
167 S7 **Thai Hoa** var. Nghia Dan. Nghê An, N Vietnam 19°21′N 105°26′E
167 P9 **Thailand** off. Kingdom of Thailand, Th. Prathet Thai, Ratcha Anachak Thai; prev. Siam. ◆ monarchy SE Asia
167 P13 **Thailand, Gulf of** var. Gulf of Siam, Th. Ao Thai, Vtn. Vinh Thai Lan. gulf SE Asia
**Thailand, Kingdom of** see Thailand
**Thai Lan, Vinh** see Thailand, Gulf of
167 T6 **Thai Nguyên** Bắc Thai, N Vietnam 21°36′N 105°50′E
**Thai, Ratcha Anachak** see Thailand
167 S8 **Thakhèk** var. Muang Khammouan. Khammouan, C Laos 17°25′N 104°51′E
153 S13 **Thakurgaon** Rajshahi, NW Bangladesh 26°05′N 88°34′E
149 S6 **Thal** Khyber Pakhtunkhwa, NW Pakistan 33°24′N 70°32′E
167 S11 **Thalabârĭvăt** prev. Phumĭ Thalabârĭvăt. Stung Treng, N Cambodia 13°34′N 105°57′E




◆ Country
● Country Capital
◇ Dependent Territory
○ Dependent Territory Capital
◈ Administrative Regions
✈ International Airport
▲ Mountain
▲▲ Mountain Range
Ѫ Volcano
∿ River
◎ Lake
⊠ Reservoir

THALANG – TIPTON

166 M15 **Thalang** Phuket, SW Thailand 08°00′N 98°21′E
**Thalashsheri** see Thalassery
155 F21 **Thalassery** var. Tellicherry, Thalashsheri. Kerala, SW India 11°44′N 75°29′E
167 Q10 **Thalat Khae** Nakhon Ratchasima, C Thailand 15°15′N 102°24′E
109 Q5 **Thalgau** Salzburg, NW Austria 47°49′N 13°19′E
108 G7 **Thalwil** Zürich, NW Switzerland 47°17′N 08°35′E
83 I20 **Thamaga** Kweneng, SE Botswana 24°41′S 25°31′E
**Thamarid** see Thamarīt
141 V13 **Thamarīt** var. Thamarid, Thumrayt. SW Oman 17°39′N 54°02′E
141 P16 **Thamar, Jabal** ▲ SW Yemen 13°46′N 45°32′E
184 M6 **Thames** Waikato, North Island, New Zealand 37°10′S 175°33′E
14 D17 **Thames** Ontario, S Canada
97 O22 **Thames** S England, United Kingdom
184 M6 **Thames, Firth of** gulf North Island, New Zealand
14 D17 **Thamesville** Ontario, S Canada 42°33′N 81°58′W
141 S13 **Thamūd** N Yemen 17°18′N 49°57′E
167 N9 **Thanbyuzayat** Mon State, S Myanmar (Burma) 15°58′N 97°44′E
166 K7 **Thandwe** var. Sandoway. Rakhine State, W Myanmar (Burma) 18°28′N 94°20′E
152 I9 **Thānesar** Haryāna, NW India 29°58′N 76°48′E
167 T7 **Thanh Hoa** Thanh Hoa, N Vietnam 19°49′N 105°48′E
**Thanintari Taungdan** see Bilauktaung Range
155 I21 **Thanjāvūr** prev. Tanjore. Tamil Nādu, SE India 10°46′N 79°09′E
166 M7 **Thanlwin** Eng. Salween, Chin. Nu Chiang, Nu Jiang. SE Asia
103 U7 **Thann** Haut-Rhin, NE France 47°51′N 07°04′E
167 O16 **Tha Nong Phrom** Phatthalung, SW Thailand 07°24′N 100°04′E
167 N13 **Thap Sakae** var. Thap Sakau. Prachuap Khiri Khan, SW Thailand 11°30′N 99°35′E
**Thap Sakau** see Thap Sakae
98 L10 **'t Harde** Gelderland, E Netherlands 52°25′N 05°53′E
152 D11 **Thar Desert** var. Great Indian Desert, Indian Desert. desert India/Pakistan
181 V10 **Thargomindah** Queensland, C Australia 28°00′S 143°47′E
150 D11 **Thar Parkar** desert SE Pakistan
139 S7 **Tharthār al Furāt, Qanāt ath** canal C Iraq
139 R7 **Tharthār, Buḩayrat ath** ◎ C Iraq
139 R5 **Tharthār, Wādī ath** dry watercourse N Iraq
167 N13 **Tha Sae** Chumphon, SW Thailand
167 N15 **Tha Sala** Nakhon Si Thammarat, SW Thailand 08°43′N 99°54′E
114 I13 **Thásos** Thásos, E Greece 40°47′N 24°43′E
115 I14 **Thásos** island E Greece
37 N14 **Thatcher** Arizona, SW USA 32°47′N 109°46′W
167 T5 **Thât Khê** var. Trâng Dinh. Lang Sơn, N Vietnam 22°15′N 106°26′E
166 M8 **Thaton** Mon State, S Myanmar (Burma) 16°56′N 97°20′E
167 S9 **That Phanom** Nakhon Phanom, E Thailand 16°52′N 104°41′E
167 R10 **Tha Tum** Surin, E Thailand 15°18′N 103°39′E
103 P16 **Thau, Bassin de** var. Étang de Thau. ◎ S France
**Thau, Étang de** see Thau, Bassin de
166 L3 **Thaungdut** Sagaing, N Myanmar (Burma) 24°26′N 94°45′E
167 O8 **Thaungyin** Th. Mae Nam Moei. Myanmar (Burma)/Thailand
167 R8 **Tha Uthen** Nakhon Phanom, E Thailand 17°32′N 104°34′E
109 W2 **Thaya** var. Dyje. Austria/Czechia see also Dyje
**Thaya** see Dyje
27 V8 **Thayer** Missouri, C USA 36°31′N 91°34′W
166 L6 **Thayet** var. Thayetmyo. Magway, C Myanmar (Burma) 19°20′N 95°10′E
**Thayetmyo** see Thayet
33 S15 **Thayne** Wyoming, C USA 42°54′N 111°01′W
166 M5 **Thazi** Mandalay, C Myanmar (Burma) 20°50′N 96°04′E
**Thebes** see Thíva
44 L5 **The Carlton** var. Abraham Bay. Mayaguana, SE The Bahamas 22°21′N 72°56′W
45 O14 **The Crane** var. Crane. S Barbados 13°06′N 59°27′W
32 I11 **The Dalles** Oregon, NW USA 45°36′N 121°10′W
28 M14 **Thedford** Nebraska, C USA 41°59′N 100°32′W
**The Flatts Village** see Flatts Village
**The Hague** see 's-Gravenhage
**Theiss** see Tisa/Tisza
8 M9 **Thelon** Northwest Territories, N Canada
11 V15 **Theodore** Saskatchewan, S Canada 51°25′N 103°01′W
23 N8 **Theodore** Alabama, S USA 30°33′N 88°10′W
36 L13 **Theodore Roosevelt Lake** ⊠ Arizona, SW USA
**Theodosia** see Feodosiya
**Theophilo Ottoni** see Teófilo Otoni
11 V13 **The Pas** Manitoba, C Canada 53°49′N 101°09′W
31 T14 **The Plains** Ohio, N USA 39°22′N 82°07′W
**Thera** see Santoríni
172 H17 **Thérèse, Île** island Inner Islands, NE Seychelles
**Therezina** see Teresina
115 L20 **Thérma** Ikaría, Dodekánisa, Greece, Aegean Sea 37°37′N 26°18′E
**Thermae Himerenses** see Termini Imerese
**Thermae Pannonicae** see Baden
**Thermaic Gulf/Thermaicus Sinus** see Thermaïkós Kólpos
121 Q8 **Thermaïkós Kólpos** Eng. Thermaic Gulf; anc. Thermaicus Sinus. gulf N Greece
**Thermiá** see Kýthnos
115 L17 **Thermís** Lésvos, E Greece 39°08′N 26°32′E
115 E18 **Thérmo** Dytikí Elláda, C Greece 38°32′N 21°42′E
33 V14 **Thermopolis** Wyoming, C USA 43°39′N 108°12′W
183 P10 **The Rock** New South Wales, SE Australia 35°18′S 147°07′E
195 O5 **Theron Mountains** ▲▲ Antarctica
**The Sooner State** see Oklahoma
115 G18 **Thespiés** Stereá Elláda, C Greece 38°18′N 23°08′E
115 E16 **Thessalía** Eng. Thessaly. ◆ region C Greece
14 C10 **Thessalon** Ontario, S Canada 46°15′N 83°34′W
115 G14 **Thessaloníki** Eng. Salonica, Salonika, SCr. Solun, Turk. Selânik. Kentrikí Makedonía, N Greece 40°38′N 22°58′E
115 G14 **Thessaloníki** ✈ Kentrikí Makedonía, N Greece 40°30′N 22°58′E
**Thessaly** see Thessalía
84 B12 **Theta Gap** undersea feature E Atlantic Ocean 12°40′W 43°30′N
97 P20 **Thetford** E England, United Kingdom 52°25′N 00°45′E
15 R11 **Thetford-Mines** Québec, SE Canada 46°07′N 71°16′W
113 K17 **Theth** var. Thethi. Shkodër, N Albania 42°25′N 19°45′E
**Thethi** see Theth
99 L20 **Theux** Liège, E Belgium 50°33′N 05°48′E
45 V9 **The Valley** ○ (Anguilla) E Anguilla 18°13′N 63°00′W
27 N10 **The Village** Oklahoma, C USA 35°33′N 97°33′W
**The Volunteer State** see Tennessee
25 W10 **The Woodlands** Texas, SW USA 30°09′N 95°27′E
**Thiamis** see Thýamis
**Thian Shan** see Tien Shan
**Thibet** see Xizang Zizhiqu
22 J9 **Thibodaux** Louisiana, S USA 29°48′N 90°49′W
29 S3 **Thief Lake** ◎ Minnesota, N USA
29 S3 **Thief River** Minnesota, C USA
29 S3 **Thief River Falls** Minnesota, N USA 48°07′N 96°10′W
**Thièle** see La Thielle
32 G14 **Thielsen, Mount** ▲ Oregon, NW USA 43°09′N 122°04′W
**Thielt** see Tielt
106 G7 **Thiene** Veneto, NE Italy 45°43′N 11°29′E
**Thienen** see Tienen
103 P11 **Thiers** Puy-de-Dôme, C France 45°51′N 03°33′E
76 F11 **Thiès** W Senegal 14°49′N 16°52′W
81 I19 **Thika** Kiambu, S Kenya 01°03′S 37°05′E
**Thikombia** see Cikobia
151 K18 **Thiladhunmathi Atoll** var. Tiladummati Atoll. atoll N Maldives
**Thimbu** see Thimphu
153 T11 **Thimphu** var. Thimbu; prev. Tashi Chho Dzong. ● (Bhutan) W Bhutan 27°28′N 89°37′E
92 H2 **Þingeyri** Vestfirðir, NW Iceland 65°52′N 23°28′W
92 I3 **Þingvellir** Suðurland, SW Iceland 64°15′N 21°06′W
187 Q17 **Thio** Province Sud, C New Caledonia 21°37′S 166°13′E
103 T4 **Thionville** Ger. Diedenhofen. Moselle, NE France 49°22′N 06°11′E
77 O12 **Thiou** NW Burkina Faso 13°42′N 02°34′W
115 K22 **Thíra** Santoríni, Kykládes, Greece, Aegean Sea 36°25′N 25°26′E
**Thíra** see Santoríni
140 I5 **Thīrān, Jazīrat** island Saudi Arabia
115 J22 **Thirasía** island Kykládes, Greece, Aegean Sea
97 M16 **Thirsk** N England, United Kingdom 54°07′N 01°17′W
14 F12 **Thirty Thousand Islands** island group Ontario, S Canada
155 G24 **Thiruvanathapuram** var. Trivandrum, Tiruvantapuram. state capital Kerala, SW India 08°30′N 76°57′E
95 F20 **Thisted** Midtjylland, NW Denmark 56°58′N 08°42′E
**Thistil Fjord** see Þistilfjörður
92 L1 **Þistilfjörður** var. Thistil Fjord. fjord NE Iceland
182 G9 **Thistle Island** island South Australia
**Thithia** see Cicia
**Thiukhaoluang Phrahang** see Luang Prabang Range
115 G18 **Thíva** Eng. Thebes; prev. Thívai. Stereá Elláda, C Greece 38°19′N 23°19′E
**Thívai** see Thíva
102 M12 **Thiviers** Dordogne, SW France 45°24′N 00°54′E
92 J4 **Þjórsá** C Iceland
9 N10 **Thlewiaza** Nunavut, NE Canada
8 L10 **Thoa** Northwest Territories, NW Canada
99 G14 **Tholen** Zeeland, SW Netherlands 51°31′N 04°13′E
99 F14 **Tholen** island SW Netherlands
26 L10 **Thomas** Oklahoma, C USA 35°44′N 98°45′W
21 T3 **Thomas** West Virginia, NE USA 39°09′N 79°28′W
27 U3 **Thomas Hill Reservoir** ⊠ Missouri, C USA
23 S5 **Thomaston** Georgia, SE USA 32°53′N 84°19′W
19 R7 **Thomaston** Maine, NE USA 44°06′N 69°10′W
25 T12 **Thomaston** Texas, SW USA 28°56′N 97°07′W
23 O6 **Thomasville** Alabama, S USA 31°54′N 87°42′W
23 T8 **Thomasville** Georgia, SE USA 30°49′N 83°57′W
21 S9 **Thomasville** North Carolina, SE USA 35°52′N 80°04′W
35 N5 **Thomes Creek** California, W USA
11 W12 **Thompson** Manitoba, C Canada 55°45′N 97°54′W
29 R4 **Thompson** North Dakota, N USA 47°45′N 97°07′W
0 F8 **Thompson** Alberta/British Columbia, SW Canada
33 O8 **Thompson Falls** Montana, NW USA 47°36′N 115°20′W
29 Q10 **Thompson, Lake** ◎ South Dakota, N USA
34 M3 **Thompson Peak** ▲ California, W USA 41°00′N 123°01′W
27 S2 **Thompson River** Missouri, C USA
185 A22 **Thompson Sound** sound South Island, New Zealand
8 J5 **Thomsen** Banks Island, Northwest Territories, NW Canada
23 V4 **Thomson** Georgia, SE USA 33°28′N 82°30′W
103 T10 **Thonon-les-Bains** Haute-Savoie, E France 46°22′N 06°30′E
**Thoothukudi** see Tuticorin
103 O15 **Thoré** var. Thore. S France
**Thore** see Thoré
37 P11 **Thoreau** New Mexico, SW USA 35°24′N 108°13′W
**Thorenburg** see Turda
92 J3 **Þórisvatn** ◎ C Iceland
92 P4 **Thor, Kapp** headland S Svalbard 76°25′N 25°01′E
92 I4 **Þorlákshöfn** Suðurland, SW Iceland 63°52′N 21°24′W
**Thorn** see Toruń
25 T10 **Thorndale** Texas, SW USA 30°36′N 97°12′W
14 H10 **Thorne** Ontario, S Canada 46°38′N 79°04′W
97 J14 **Thornhill** S Scotland, United Kingdom 55°13′N 03°46′W
25 U8 **Thornton** Texas, SW USA 31°24′N 96°34′W
**Thornton Island** see Millennium Island
14 H16 **Thorold** Ontario, S Canada 43°07′N 79°15′W
32 J9 **Thorp** Washington, NW USA 47°03′N 120°40′W
**Thorshavn** see Tórshavn
195 S3 **Thorshavnheiane** physical region Antarctica
92 L1 **Þórshöfn** Norðurland Eystra, NE Iceland 66°09′N 15°18′W
**Thospitis** see Van Gölü
167 S14 **Thôt Nôt** Cân Thơ, S Vietnam 10°17′N 105°31′E
102 K8 **Thouars** Deux-Sèvres, W France 46°59′N 00°13′W
153 X14 **Thoubal** Manipur, NE India 24°40′N 94°00′E
102 K9 **Thouet** W France
**Thoune** see Thun
18 H7 **Thousand Islands** island Canada/USA
35 S15 **Thousand Oaks** California, W USA 34°10′N 118°50′W
114 L12 **Thrace** cultural region SE Europe
114 J13 **Thracian Sea** Gk. Thrakikó Pélagos; anc. Thracium Mare. sea Greece/Turkey
**Thracium Mare/Thrakikó Pélagos** see Thracian Sea
**Thrá Lí, Bá** see Tralee Bay
33 R11 **Three Forks** Montana, NW USA 45°53′N 111°34′W
162 M8 **Three Gorges Dam** dam Hubei, C China
160 L9 **Three Gorges Reservoir** ⊠ C China
11 Q16 **Three Hills** Alberta, SW Canada 51°43′N 113°15′W
183 N15 **Three Hummock Island** island Tasmania, SE Australia
**Three Kings Islands** see Manawatāwhi / Three Kings Islands
175 P10 **Three Kings Rise** undersea feature W Pacific Ocean
77 O18 **Three Points, Cape** headland S Ghana 04°43′N 02°03′W
31 P10 **Three Rivers** Michigan, N USA 41°56′N 85°37′W
25 S13 **Three Rivers** Texas, SW USA 28°27′N 98°10′W
83 G24 **Three Sisters** Northern Cape, SW South Africa 31°51′S 23°04′E
32 H13 **Three Sisters** ▲ Oregon, NW USA 44°08′N 121°46′W
187 N10 **Three Sisters Islands** island group SE Solomon Islands
155 G22 **Thrissur** var. Trichūr. Kerala, SW India 10°32′N 76°14′E
25 Q6 **Throckmorton** Texas, SW USA 33°11′N 99°12′W
180 M10 **Throssell, Lake** salt lake Western Australia
115 K25 **Thryptís** var. Thrýptis. ▲ Kríti, Greece, E Mediterranean Sea 35°06′N 25°51′E
167 U14 **Thuận Nam** prev. Ham Thuân Nam. Bình Thuận, S Vietnam 10°49′N 107°49′E
167 T13 **Thu Dâu Môt** var. Phu Cuong. Sông Be, S Vietnam 10°58′N 106°40′E
167 S6 **Thu Do** ✈ (Ha Nôi) Ha Nôi, N Vietnam 21°13′N 105°46′E
99 G21 **Thuin** Hainaut, S Belgium 50°21′N 04°18′E
149 Q12 **Thul** Sindh, SE Pakistan 28°14′N 68°50′E
**Thule** see Qaanaaq
83 J18 **Thuli** var. Tuli. S Zimbabwe
**Thumrayt** see Thamarīt
108 D9 **Thun** Fr. Thoune. Bern, W Switzerland 46°46′N 07°38′E
12 C12 **Thunder Bay** Ontario, S Canada 48°27′N 89°12′W
30 M1 **Thunder Bay** lake bay S Canada
31 R6 **Thunder Bay** lake bay Michigan, N USA
31 R6 **Thunder Bay River** Michigan, N USA
27 N11 **Thunderbird, Lake** ⊠ Oklahoma, C USA
28 L8 **Thunder Butte Creek** South Dakota, N USA
108 E9 **Thuner See** ◎ C Switzerland
167 N15 **Thung Song** var. Cha Mai. Nakhon Si Thammarat, SW Thailand 08°10′N 99°41′E
108 H7 **Thur** N Switzerland
108 G6 **Thurgau** Fr. Thurgovie. ◆ canton NE Switzerland
**Thurgovie** see Thurgau
**Thuringe** see Thüringen
108 J7 **Thüringen** Vorarlberg, W Austria 47°12′N 09°48′E
101 J17 **Thüringen** Eng. Thuringia, Fr. Thuringe. ◆ state C Germany
101 J17 **Thüringer Wald** Eng. Thuringian Forest. ▲▲ C Germany
**Thuringia** see Thüringen
**Thuringian Forest** see Thüringer Wald
97 D19 **Thurles** Ir. Durlas. S Ireland 52°41′N 07°49′W
21 W2 **Thurmont** Maryland, NE USA 39°36′N 77°22′W
**Thurø** see Thurø By
95 H24 **Thurø By** var. Thurø. Syddtjylland, C Denmark 55°03′N 10°43′E
14 M12 **Thurso** Québec, SE Canada 45°36′N 75°13′W
96 J6 **Thurso** N Scotland, United Kingdom 58°35′N 03°32′W
194 I10 **Thurston Island** island Antarctica
108 I9 **Thusis** Graubünden, S Switzerland 46°40′N 09°27′E
115 C15 **Thýamis** var. Thiamis, Kalamás. W Greece
95 E21 **Thyborøn** var. Tyborøn. Midtjylland, W Denmark 56°40′N 08°12′E
195 U3 **Thyer Glacier** glacier Antarctica
115 L20 **Thýmaina** island Dodekánisa, Greece, Aegean Sea
83 N15 **Thyolo** var. Cholo. Southern, S Malawi 16°03′S 35°11′E
183 U6 **Tia** New South Wales, SE Australia 31°14′S 151°51′E
54 H5 **Tía Juana** Zulia, NW Venezuela 10°18′N 71°24′W
**Tiancheng** see Chongyang
160 J14 **Tiandong** var. Pingma. Guangxi Zhuangzu Zizhiqu, S China 23°37′N 107°06′E
161 O3 **Tianjin** var. Tientsin. Tianjin Shi, E China 39°13′N 117°06′E
**Tianjin** see Tianjin Shi
161 P3 **Tianjin Shi** var. Jin, Tianjin, T'ien-ching, Tientsin. ◆ municipality E China
159 S10 **Tianjun** var. Xinyuan. Qinghai, C China 37°16′N 99°03′E
160 J13 **Tianlin** var. Leli. Guangxi Zhuangzu Zizhiqu, S China 24°27′N 106°03′E
**Tian Shan** see Tien Shan
159 W11 **Tianshui** Gansu, C China 34°33′N 105°51′E
150 I7 **Tianshuihai** Xinjiang Uygur Zizhiqu, W China 35°17′N 79°30′E
161 S10 **Tiantai** Zhejiang, SE China 29°11′N 121°01′E
160 J14 **Tianyang** var. Tianzhou. Guangxi Zhuangzu Zizhiqu, S China 23°50′N 106°52′E
**Tianzhou** see Tianyang
159 U9 **Tianzhu** var. Huazangsi, Tianzhu Zangzu Zizhixian. Gansu, C China 37°01′N 103°04′E
**Tianzhu Zangzu Zizhixian** see Tianzhu
191 Q7 **Tiarei** Tahiti, W French Polynesia 17°32′S 149°20′W
74 J6 **Tiaret** var. Tihert. NW Algeria 35°20′N 01°20′E
77 N17 **Tiassalé** S Ivory Coast 05°54′N 04°50′W
192 I16 **Ti'avea** Upolu, SE Samoa 13°58′S 171°30′W
**Tiba** see Chiba
60 J11 **Tibagi** var. Tibají. Paraná, S Brazil 24°29′S 50°29′W
60 J10 **Tibagi, Rio** var. Rio Tibají. S Brazil
**Tibaji** see Tibagi
**Tibají, Rio** see Tibagi, Rio
139 Q9 **Tibal, Wādī** dry watercourse S Iraq
54 G9 **Tibaná** Boyacá, C Colombia 05°19′N 73°25′W
79 F14 **Tibati** Adamaoua, N Cameroon 06°25′N 12°33′E
76 K15 **Tibé, Pic de** ▲ SE Guinea 08°39′N 08°58′W
**Tiber** see Tevere, Italy
**Tiber** see Tivoli, Italy
**Tiberias** see Tverya
**Tiberias, Lake** see Kinneret, Yam
78 H6 **Tibesti** var. Tibesti Massif, Ar. Tibistī. ▲▲ N Africa
**Tibesti Massif** see Tibesti
**Tibet** see Xizang Zizhiqu
**Tibetan Autonomous Region** see Xizang Zizhiqu
**Tibet, Plateau of** see Qingzang Gaoyuan
**Tibistī** see Tibesti
14 K7 **Tiblemont, Lac** ◎ Québec, SE Canada
139 X9 **Ţīb, Nahr aţ** S Iraq
**Tibnī** see At Tibnī
182 L4 **Tibooburra** New South Wales, SE Australia 29°24′S 142°01′E
95 L18 **Tibro** Västra Götaland, S Sweden 58°25′N 14°11′E
40 E5 **Tiburón, Isla** var. Isla del Tiburón. island NW Mexico
**Tiburón, Isla del** see Tiburón, Isla
23 W14 **Tice** Florida, SE USA 26°40′N 81°49′W
**Tichau** see Tychy
114 L8 **Ticha, Yazovir** ◎ NE Bulgaria
76 K9 **Tichît** var. Tichitt. Tagant, C Mauritania 18°26′N 09°31′W
**Tichitt** see Tichît
108 G11 **Ticino** Fr./Ger. Tessin. ◆ canton S Switzerland
106 D8 **Ticino** Italy/Switzerland
108 H11 **Ticino** Ger. Tessin. SW Switzerland
**Ticinum** see Pavia
41 X12 **Ticul** Yucatán, SE Mexico 20°22′N 89°30′W
95 K18 **Tidaholm** Västra Götaland, S Sweden 58°12′N 13°55′E
**Tidjikdja** see Tidjikja
76 J8 **Tidjikja** var. Tidjikdja; prev. Fort-Cappolani. Tagant, C Mauritania 18°31′N 11°24′W
**Tidore** see Soasiu
171 R11 **Tidore, Pulau** island E Indonesia
**Tidra, Île** see Et Tîdra
77 N16 **Tiébissou** var. Tiebissou. C Ivory Coast 07°10′N 05°10′W
**Tiebissou** see Tiébissou
**Tiefa** see Diaobingshan
108 I9 **Tiefencastel** Graubünden, S Switzerland 46°40′N 09°33′E
**Tiegenhof** see Nowy Dwór Gdański
**T'ieh-ling** see Tieling
98 K13 **Tiel** Gelderland, C Netherlands 51°53′N 05°26′E
163 W7 **Tieli** Heilongjiang, NE China 46°57′N 128°01′E
163 V11 **Tieling** var. T'ieh-ling. Liaoning, NE China 42°19′N 123°52′E
152 L4 **Tielongtan** China/India 35°10′N 79°32′E
99 D17 **Tielt** var. Thielt. West-Vlaanderen, W Belgium 51°00′N 03°20′E
**T'ien-ching** see Tianjin Shi
99 I18 **Tienen** var. Thienen, Fr. Tirlemont. Vlaams Brabant, C Belgium 50°48′N 04°56′E
**Tiên Giang, Sông** see Mekong
147 X9 **Tien Shan** Chin. Thian Shan, Tian Shan, T'ien Shan, Rus. Tyan'-Shan'. ▲▲ C Asia
**Tientsin** see Tianjin
167 U6 **Tiên Yên** Quang Ninh, N Vietnam 21°19′N 107°24′E
95 O14 **Tierp** Uppsala, C Sweden 60°20′N 17°30′E
62 H7 **Tierra Amarilla** Atacama, N Chile 27°28′S 70°17′W
37 R9 **Tierra Amarilla** New Mexico, SW USA 36°42′N 106°31′W
41 R15 **Tierra Blanca** Veracruz, E Mexico 18°28′N 96°21′W
41 O16 **Tierra Colorada** Guerrero, S Mexico 17°10′N 99°30′W
63 J17 **Tierra Colorada, Bajo de la** basin SE Argentina
63 I25 **Tierra del Fuego** off. Provincia de la Tierra del Fuego. ◆ province S Argentina
63 J24 **Tierra del Fuego** island Argentina/Chile
**Tierra del Fuego, Provincia de la** see Tierra del Fuego
54 D7 **Tierralta** Córdoba, NW Colombia 08°10′N 76°04′W
104 K9 **Tiétar** W Spain
60 L10 **Tietê** São Paulo, S Brazil 23°04′S 47°41′W
60 J8 **Tietê, Rio** S Brazil
32 I9 **Tieton** Washington, NW USA 46°41′N 120°43′W
32 J6 **Tiffany Mountain** ▲ Washington, NW USA 48°40′N 119°55′W
31 S12 **Tiffin** Ohio, N USA 41°06′N 83°10′W
31 Q11 **Tiffin River** Ohio, N USA
**Tiflis** see Tbilisi
23 U7 **Tifton** Georgia, SE USA 31°27′N 83°31′W
171 R13 **Tifu** Pulau Buru, E Indonesia 03°46′S 126°36′E
38 L17 **Tigalda Island** island Aleutian Islands, Alaska, USA
115 I15 **Tigáni, Akrotírio** headland Límnos, E Greece 39°50′N 25°03′E
169 V6 **Tiga Tarok** Sabah, East Malaysia 06°57′N 117°07′E
**Tighina** see Bender
145 X9 **Tigiretskiy Khrebet** ▲▲ E Kazakhstan
79 F14 **Tignère** Adamaoua, N Cameroon 07°24′N 12°35′E
13 P14 **Tignish** Prince Edward Island, SE Canada 46°58′N 64°03′W
186 M10 **Tigoa** var. Tinggoa. Rennell, S Solomon Islands 11°39′S 160°13′E
**Tigranocerta** see Siirt
80 I11 **Tigray** ◆ federal region N Ethiopia
41 O11 **Tigre, Cerro del** ▲ C Mexico 23°06′N 99°13′W
56 F8 **Tigre, Río** N Peru
139 X10 **Tigris** Ar. Dijlah, Turk. Dicle. Iraq/Syria/Turkey
76 G9 **Tiguent** Trarza, SW Mauritania 17°15′N 16°00′W
74 M10 **Tiguentourine** E Algeria 27°59′N 09°16′E
77 V10 **Tiguidit, Falaise de** ridge C Niger
141 N13 **Tihāmah** var. Tehama. plain Saudi Arabia/Yemen
**Tihert** see Tiaret
**Ti-hua/Tihwa** see Ürümqi
41 Q13 **Tihuatlán** Veracruz, E Mexico 20°44′N 97°30′W
40 B1 **Tijuana** Baja California, NW Mexico 32°32′N 117°01′W
42 E2 **Tikal** Petén, N Guatemala 17°11′N 89°36′W
154 I9 **Tīkamgarh** prev. Tehri. Madhya Pradesh, C India 24°44′N 78°50′E
158 L7 **Tikanlik** Xinjiang Uygur Zizhiqu, NW China 40°34′N 87°37′E
**Tikapa Moana** see Hauraki Gulf / Tīkapa Moana
77 P12 **Tikaré** N Burkina Faso 13°16′N 01°39′W
39 O12 **Tikchik Lakes** lakes Alaska, USA
191 T9 **Tikehau** atoll Îles Tuamotu, C French Polynesia
191 V9 **Tikei** island Îles Tuamotu, C French Polynesia
126 L13 **Tikhoretsk** Krasnodarskiy Kray, SW Russia 45°51′N 40°07′E
124 I13 **Tikhvin** Leningradskaya Oblast', NW Russia 59°37′N 33°30′E
193 P9 **Tiki Basin** undersea feature S Pacific Ocean
76 K13 **Tikinsso** NE Guinea
**Tikirarjuaq** see Whale Cove
184 Q8 **Tikitiki** Gisborne, North Island, New Zealand 37°49′S 178°23′E
79 D16 **Tiko** Sud-Ouest, SW Cameroon 04°02′N 09°19′E
139 S6 **Tikrīt** var. Tekrit. Şalāḩ ad Dīn, N Iraq 34°36′N 43°42′E
124 I8 **Tiksha** Respublika Kareliya, NW Russia 64°07′N 32°31′E
124 I6 **Tikshozero, Ozero** ◎ NW Russia
123 P7 **Tiksi** Respublika Sakha (Yakutiya), NE Russia 71°40′N 128°47′E
**Tiladummati Atoll** see Thiladhunmathi Atoll
42 A6 **Tilapa** San Marcos, SW Guatemala 14°31′N 92°11′W
42 L13 **Tilarán** Guanacaste, NW Costa Rica 10°28′N 84°57′W
99 J14 **Tilburg** Noord-Brabant, S Netherlands 51°34′N 05°05′E
14 D17 **Tilbury** Ontario, S Canada 42°15′N 82°26′W
182 K4 **Tilcha** South Australia 29°37′S 140°52′E
**Tilcha Creek** see Callabonna Creek
29 Q14 **Tilden** Nebraska, C USA 42°03′N 97°49′W
25 R13 **Tilden** Texas, SW USA 28°27′N 98°43′W
14 H10 **Tilden Lake** Ontario, S Canada 46°35′N 79°36′W
116 G9 **Tileagd** Hung. Mezőtelegd. Bihor, W Romania 47°03′N 22°11′E
145 P9 **Tilekey** prev. Ladyzhenka. Akmola, C Kazakhstan 50°58′N 68°44′E
77 Q8 **Tilemsi, Vallée de** C Mali
123 V8 **Tilichiki** Krasnoyarskiy Kray, E Russia 60°25′N 165°55′E
**Tiligul** see Tilihul
**Tiligul'skiy Liman** see Tilihul's'kyy Lyman
117 P9 **Tilihul** Rus. Tiligul. SW Ukraine
117 P10 **Tilihul's'kyy Lyman** Rus. Tiligul'skiy Liman. ◎ S Ukraine
**Tilimsen** see Tlemcen
**Tilio Martius** see Toulon
77 R11 **Tillabéri** var. Tillabéry. Tillabéri, W Niger 14°13′N 01°27′E
77 R11 **Tillabéri** ◆ region SW Niger
**Tillabéry** see Tillabéri
32 F11 **Tillamook** Oregon, NW USA 45°28′N 123°50′W
32 E11 **Tillamook Bay** inlet Oregon, NW USA
151 Q22 **Tillanchāng Dwīp** island Nicobar Islands, India, NE Indian Ocean
95 N15 **Tillberga** Västmanland, C Sweden 59°41′N 16°37′E
**Tillenberg** see Dyleň
21 S10 **Tillery, Lake** ⊠ North Carolina, SE USA
77 T10 **Tillia** Tahoua, W Niger 16°13′N 04°51′E
23 N8 **Tillmans Corner** Alabama, S USA 30°35′N 88°10′W
14 F17 **Tillsonburg** Ontario, S Canada 42°53′N 80°44′W
115 N22 **Tílos** island Dodekánisa, Greece, Aegean Sea
183 N5 **Tilpa** New South Wales, SE Australia 30°56′S 144°24′E
**Tilsit** see Sovetsk
31 N13 **Tilton** Illinois, N USA 40°06′N 87°39′W
126 K7 **Tim** Kurskaya Oblast', W Russia 51°39′N 37°11′E
54 D12 **Timaná** Huila, S Colombia 01°58′N 75°55′W
**Timan Ridge** see Timanskiy Kryazh
125 Q6 **Timanskiy Kryazh** Eng. Timan Ridge. ridge NW Russia
185 G20 **Timaru** Canterbury, South Island, New Zealand 44°23′S 171°15′E
127 S6 **Timashevo** Samarskaya Oblast', W Russia 53°22′N 51°13′E
126 K13 **Timashevsk** Krasnodarskiy Kray, SW Russia 45°37′N 38°57′E
**Timbaki/Timbákion** see Tympáki
22 K10 **Timbalier Bay** bay Louisiana, S USA
22 K11 **Timbalier Island** island Louisiana, S USA
76 L10 **Timbedgha** var. Timbédra. Hodh ech Chargui, SE Mauritania 15°17′N 08°14′W
**Timbédra** see Timbedgha
32 G10 **Timber** Oregon, NW USA 45°42′N 123°19′W
181 O3 **Timber Creek** Northern Territory, N Australia 15°35′S 130°21′E
28 M8 **Timber Lake** South Dakota, N USA 45°25′N 101°01′W
54 D12 **Timbío** Cauca, SW Colombia 02°20′N 76°40′W
54 C12 **Timbiquí** Cauca, SW Colombia 02°43′N 77°45′W
83 O17 **Timbue, Ponta** headland C Mozambique 18°49′S 36°22′E
**Timbuktu** see Tombouctou
169 W8 **Timbun Mata, Pulau** island E Malaysia
77 P8 **Timétrine** var. Ti-n-Kâr. oasis C Mali
**Timfi** see Týmfi
**Timfristos** see Tymfristós
77 V9 **Timia** Agadez, C Niger 18°07′N 08°49′E
171 X14 **Timika** Papua, E Indonesia 04°39′S 137°15′E
74 I9 **Timimoun** C Algeria 29°18′N 00°21′E
**Timiris, Cap** see Timirist, Râs
76 F8 **Timirist, Râs** var. Cap Timiris. headland NW Mauritania 19°18′N 16°28′W
145 O7 **Timiryazevo** Severnyy Kazakhstan, N Kazakhstan 53°45′N 66°33′E
116 E11 **Timiş** ◆ county SW Romania
14 H9 **Timiskaming, Lake** Fr. Lac Témiscamingue. ◎ Ontario/Québec, SE Canada
116 E11 **Timişoara** Ger. Temeschwar, Temeswar, Hung. Temesvár; prev. Temeschburg. Timiş, W Romania 45°46′N 21°17′E
116 E11 **Timişoara** ✈ Timiş, SW Romania 45°50′N 21°21′E
**Timkovichi** see Tsimkavichy
77 U8 **Ti-m-Meghsoï** NW Niger
100 K8 **Timmerdorfer Strand** Schleswig-Holstein, N Germany 53°59′N 10°50′E
14 F7 **Timmins** Ontario, S Canada 48°09′N 80°01′W
21 S12 **Timmonsville** South Carolina, SE USA 34°07′N 79°56′W
30 K5 **Timms Hill** ▲ Wisconsin, N USA 45°27′N 90°12′W
112 P12 **Timok** E Serbia
58 N13 **Timon** Maranhão, E Brazil 05°08′S 42°52′W
**Timor-Leste** see East Timor
**Timor-Leste, Democratic Republic of** see East Timor
**Timor-Leste, República Democrática de** see East Timor
**Timor Lorosa'e** see East Timor
**Timor Lorosa'e, República Demokrátika** see East Timor
171 Q17 **Timor Sea** sea E Indian Ocean
**Timor Timur** see East Timor
**Timor Trench** see Timor Trough
192 G8 **Timor Trough** var. Timor Trench. undersea feature NE Timor Sea
61 A21 **Timote** Buenos Aires, E Argentina 35°22′S 62°13′W
54 I6 **Timotes** Mérida, NW Venezuela 08°57′N 70°46′W
25 X8 **Timpson** Texas, SW USA 31°54′N 94°24′W
123 Q11 **Timpton** NE Russia
93 H17 **Timrå** Västernorrland, C Sweden 62°29′N 17°20′E
20 J10 **Tims Ford Lake** ⊠ Tennessee, S USA
168 L7 **Timur, Banjaran** ▲▲ Peninsular Malaysia
171 Q8 **Tinaca Point** headland Mindanao, S Philippines 05°35′N 125°18′E
54 K5 **Tinaco** Cojedes, N Venezuela 09°44′N 68°28′W
64 Q11 **Tinajo** Lanzarote, Islas Canarias, Spain, NE Atlantic Ocean 29°03′N 13°41′W
187 P10 **Tinakula** island Santa Cruz Islands, E Solomon Islands
54 K5 **Tinaquillo** Cojedes, N Venezuela 09°57′N 68°20′W
116 F10 **Tinca** Hung. Tenke. Bihor, W Romania 46°46′N 21°58′E
155 J20 **Tindivanam** Tamil Nādu, SE India 12°15′N 79°41′E
74 E9 **Tindouf** W Algeria 27°43′N 08°09′W
74 E9 **Tindouf, Sebkha de** salt lake W Algeria
104 J2 **Tineo** Asturias, N Spain 43°20′N 06°25′W
77 R9 **Ti-n-Essako** Kidal, E Mali 18°30′N 02°27′E
**Tinggoa** see Tigoa
183 T5 **Tingha** New South Wales, SE Australia 29°56′S 151°13′E
**Tingis** see Tanger
**Tinglett** see Tinglev
95 F24 **Tinglev** Ger. Tinglett. Syddanmark, SW Denmark 54°57′N 09°15′E
56 E12 **Tingo María** Huánuco, C Peru 09°10′S 76°00′W
**Tingréla** see Tengréla
158 K16 **Tingri** var. Xêgar. Xizang Zizhiqu, W China 28°40′N 87°04′E
95 M21 **Tingsryd** Kronoberg, S Sweden 56°30′N 15°E
95 P19 **Tingstäde** Gotland, SE Sweden 57°45′N 18°36′E
62 H12 **Tinguiririca, Volcán** (volcano) C Chile 34°52′S 70°24′W
94 F9 **Tingvoll** Møre og Romsdal, S Norway 62°55′N 08°13′E
188 K8 **Tinian** island S Northern Mariana Islands
**Ti-n-Kâr** see Timétrine
**Tinnevelly** see Tirunelveli
95 G15 **Tinnoset** Telemark, S Norway 59°43′N 09°03′E
95 F15 **Tinnsjå** prev. Tinnsjø, var. Tinnsjö. ◎ S Norway see also Tinnsjø
**Tinnsjø** see Tinnsjå
**Tinnsjö** see Tinnsjå
**Tino** see Chino
115 J20 **Tínos** Tínos, Kykládes, Greece, Aegean Sea 37°33′N 25°08′E
115 J20 **Tínos** anc. Tenos. island Kykládes, Greece, Aegean Sea
153 R14 **Tinpahar** Jhārkhand, NE India 25°00′N 87°43′E
153 X11 **Tinsukia** Assam, NE India 27°28′N 95°20′E
76 K10 **Tîntâne** Hodh el Gharbi, S Mauritania 16°25′N 10°08′W
62 L7 **Tintina** Santiago del Estero, N Argentina 27°00′S 62°45′W
182 K10 **Tintinara** South Australia 35°54′S 140°04′E
104 I14 **Tinto** SW Spain
77 S8 **Ti-n-Zaouâtene** Kidal, NE Mali 19°56′N 02°45′E
**Tiobraid Árann** see Tipperary
28 K3 **Tioga** North Dakota, N USA 48°24′N 102°56′W
18 G12 **Tioga** Pennsylvania, NE USA 41°54′N 77°07′W
25 T5 **Tioga** Texas, SW USA 33°28′N 96°55′W
35 Q8 **Tioga Pass** pass California, W USA
18 G12 **Tioga River** New York/Pennsylvania, NE USA
**Tioman Island** see Tioman, Pulau
168 M9 **Tioman, Pulau** var. Tioman Island. island Peninsular Malaysia
18 C12 **Tionesta** Pennsylvania, NE USA 41°31′N 79°30′W
18 D12 **Tionesta Creek** Pennsylvania, NE USA
168 J13 **Tiop** Pulau Pagai Selatan, W Indonesia 03°12′S 100°21′E
18 H11 **Tioughnioga River** New York, NE USA
74 J5 **Tipasa** var. Tipaza. N Algeria 36°35′N 02°27′E
**Tipaza** see Tipasa
42 J10 **Tipitapa** Managua, W Nicaragua 12°08′N 86°04′W
31 R13 **Tipp City** Ohio, N USA 39°57′N 84°10′W
31 O12 **Tippecanoe River** Indiana, N USA
97 D20 **Tipperary** Ir. Tiobraid Árann. S Ireland 52°29′N 08°10′W
97 D19 **Tipperary** Ir. Tiobraid Árann. cultural region S Ireland
35 R12 **Tipton** California, W USA 36°02′N 119°19′W
31 P13 **Tipton** Indiana, N USA 40°19′N 86°00′W
29 Y14 **Tipton** Iowa, C USA 41°46′N 91°07′W

◆ Country ● Country Capital ◇ Dependent Territory ○ Dependent Territory Capital ◆ Administrative Regions ✈ International Airport ▲ Mountain ▲▲ Mountain Range Volcano River ◎ Lake ⊠ Reservoir

TIPTON – TÖRÖKSZENTMIKLÓS


27 U5 **Tipton** Missouri, C USA 38°39′N 92°46′W
36 I10 **Tipton, Mount** ▲ Arizona, SW USA 35°32′N 114°11′W
20 F8 **Tiptonville** Tennessee, S USA 36°21′N 89°30′W
12 E12 **Tip Top Mountain** ▲ Ontario, S Canada 48°18′N 86°06′W
155 G19 **Tiptūr** Karnātaka, W India 13°17′N 76°31′E
**Tiquisate** *see* Pueblo Nuevo Tiquisate
58 L13 **Tiracambu, Serra do** ▲▲ E Brazil
**Tirana** *see* Tiranë
113 K19 **Tirana Rinas** ✈ Durrës, W Albania 41°25′N 19°41′E
113 L20 **Tiranë** *var.* Tirana. ● (Albania) Tiranë, C Albania 41°20′N 19°50′E
113 K20 **Tiranë** ◈ *county* W Albania
106 F6 **Tirano** Lombardia, N Italy 46°13′N 10°10′E
182 I2 **Tirari Desert** *desert* South Australia
117 O10 **Tiraspol** *Rus.* Tiraspol′. E Moldova 46°50′N 29°35′E
**Tiraspol′** *see* Tiraspol
184 M8 **Tirau** Waikato, North Island, New Zealand 37°59′S 175°44′E
136 C14 **Tire** İzmir, SW Turkey 38°04′N 27°45′E
137 O11 **Tirebolu** Giresun, N Turkey 41°01′N 38°49′E
96 F11 **Tiree** *island* W Scotland, United Kingdom
**Tîrgovişte** *see* Târgovişte
**Tîrgu** *see* Târgu Cărbuneşti
**Tîrgu Bujor** *see* Târgu Bujor
**Tîrgu Frumos** *see* Târgu Frumos
**Tîrgu Jiu** *see* Targu Jiu
**Tîrgu Lăpuş** *see* Târgu Lăpuş
**Tîrgu Mures** *see* Târgu Mureş
**Tîrgu-Neamţ** *see* Târgu-Neamţ
**Tîrgu Ocna** *see* Târgu Ocna
**Tîrgu Secuiesc** *see* Târgu Secuiesc
149 T3 **Tirich Mir** ▲ NW Pakistan 36°12′N 71°51′E
76 J5 **Tiris Zemmour** ◈ *region* N Mauritania
**Tirlemont** *see* Tienen
127 W5 **Tirlyanskiy** Respublika Bashkortostan, W Russia 54°09′N 58°32′E
**Tîrnava Mare** *see* Târnava Mare
**Tîrnava Mică** *see* Târnava Mică
**Tîrnăveni** *see* Târnăveni
**Tírnavos** *see* Týrnavos
**Tirnovo** *see* Veliko Tarnovo
154 J11 **Tirodi** Madhya Pradesh, C India 21°40′N 79°44′E
108 K8 **Tirol** *off.* Land Tirol, *var.* Tyrol, *It.* Tirolo. ◈ *state* W Austria
**Tirol, Land** *see* Tirol
**Tirolo** *see* Tirol
**Tirreno, Mare** *see* Tyrrhenian Sea
107 B19 **Tirso** ≈ Sardegna, Italy, C Mediterranean Sea
95 H22 **Tirstrup** ✈ (Århus) Århus, C Denmark 56°17′N 10°36′E
155 I21 **Tiruchchirāppalli** *prev.* Trichinopoly. Tamil Nādu, SE India 10°50′N 78°43′E
155 H23 **Tirunelveli** *var.* Tinnevelly. Tamil Nādu, SE India 08°45′N 77°43′E
155 J19 **Tirupati** Andhra Pradesh, E India 13°39′N 79°25′E
155 I20 **Tiruppattūr** Tamil Nādu, SE India 12°28′N 78°31′E
155 H21 **Tiruppur** Tamil Nādu, SW India 11°05′N 77°20′E
**Tiruvantapuram** *see* Thiruvanathapuram
155 I20 **Tiruyannāmalai** Tamil Nādu, SE India 12°13′N 79°07′E
112 L10 **Tisa** *Ger.* Theiss, *Hung.* Tisza, *Rus.* Tissa, *Ukr.* Tysa. ≈ SE Europe *see also* Tisza
**Tisa** *see* Tisza
**Tischnowitz** *see* Tišnov
11 U14 **Tisdale** Saskatchewan, S Canada 52°51′N 104°01′W
27 O13 **Tishomingo** Oklahoma, C USA 34°15′N 96°41′W
95 M17 **Tisnaren** ◎ S Sweden
111 F18 **Tišnov** *Ger.* Tischnowitz. Jihomoravský Kraj, SE Czechia 49°22′N 16°24′E
**Tissa** *see* Tisa/Tisza
74 J6 **Tissemsilt** N Algeria 35°37′N 01°48′E
153 S12 **Tista** ≈ NE India
112 L8 **Tisza** *Ger.* Theiss, *Rom./Slvn./SCr.* Tisa, *Rus.* Tissa, *Ukr.* Tysa. ≈ SE Europe *see also* Tisa
**Tisza** *see* Tisa
111 L23 **Tiszaföldvár** Jász-Nagykun-Szolnok, E Hungary 47°00′N 20°16′E
111 M22 **Tiszafüred** Jász-Nagykun-Szolnok, E Hungary 47°38′N 20°45′E
111 L23 **Tiszakécske** Bács-Kiskun, C Hungary 46°56′N 20°04′E
111 M21 **Tiszaújváros** *prev.* Leninváros. Borsod-Abaúj-Zemplén, NE Hungary 47°56′N 21°03′E
111 N21 **Tiszavasvári** Szabolcs-Szatmár-Bereg, NE Hungary 47°56′N 21°21′E
57 I17 **Titicaca, Lake** ◎ Bolivia/Peru
190 H17 **Titikaveka** Rarotonga, S Cook Islands 21°16′S 159°45′W
154 M13 **Titilāgarh** *var.* Titlagarh. Odisha, E India 20°18′N 83°09′E
168 K8 **Titiwangsa, Banjaran** ▲▲ Peninsular Malaysia
**Titlagarh** *see* Titilāgarh
**Titograd** *see* Podgorica
**Titose** *see* Chitose
**Titova Mitrovica** *see* Mitrovicë
**Titovo Užice** *see* Užice
113 M18 **Titov Vrv** ▲ NW North Macedonia 41°58′N 20°49′E
94 F7 **Titran** Sør-Trøndelag, S Norway 63°40′N 08°20′E
31 Q8 **Tittabawassee River** ≈ Michigan, N USA
116 J13 **Titu** Dâmboviţa, S Romania 44°40′N 25°32′E
79 M16 **Titule** Orientale, N Dem. Rep. Congo 03°20′N 25°23′E
23 X11 **Titusville** Florida, SE USA 28°37′N 80°50′W
18 C12 **Titusville** Pennsylvania, NE USA 41°36′N 79°39′W
76 G11 **Tivaouane** W Senegal 14°59′N 16°50′W
113 I17 **Tivat** SW Montenegro 42°25′N 18°43′E
14 E14 **Tiverton** Ontario, S Canada 44°15′N 81°31′W
97 J23 **Tiverton** SW England, United Kingdom 50°54′N 03°30′W
19 O12 **Tiverton** Rhode Island, NE USA 41°38′N 71°10′W
107 I15 **Tivoli** *anc.* Tiber. Lazio, C Italy 41°58′N 12°45′E
25 U13 **Tivoli** Texas, SW USA 28°26′N 96°54′W
141 Z8 **Ţīwī** NE Oman 22°43′N 59°20′E
41 Y11 **Tizimín** Yucatán, SE Mexico 21°10′N 88°09′W
74 K5 **Tizi Ouzou** *var.* Tizi-Ouzou. N Algeria 36°44′N 04°06′E
**Tizi-Ouzou** *see* Tizi Ouzou
74 D8 **Tiznit** SW Morocco 29°43′N 09°39′W
95 F23 **Tjæreborg** Syddtjylland, W Denmark 55°28′N 08°35′E
113 I14 **Tjentište** Republika Srpska, SE Bosnia and Herzegovina 43°23′N 18°42′E
98 L7 **Tjeukemeer** ◎ N Netherlands
**Tjiamis** *see* Ciamis
**Tjiandjoer** *see* Cianjur
**Tjilatjap** *see* Cilacap
**Tjirebon** *see* Cirebon
95 I18 **Tjörn** *island* S Sweden
92 O3 **Tjuvfjorden** *fjord* S Svalbard
**Tkvarcheli** *see* T′q′varcheli
40 L8 **Tlahualillo** Durango, N Mexico 26°06′N 103°25′W
41 P14 **Tlalnepantla** México, C Mexico 19°34′N 99°12′W
41 Q13 **Tlapacoyán** Veracruz, E Mexico 19°58′N 97°13′W
41 P16 **Tlapa de Comonfort** Guerrero, S Mexico 17°33′N 98°33′W
40 L13 **Tlaquepaque** Jalisco, C Mexico 20°36′N 103°19′W
**Tlascala** *see* Tlaxcala
41 P14 **Tlaxcala** *var.* Tlascala, Tlaxcala de Xicohténcatl. Tlaxcala, C Mexico 19°17′N 98°16′W
41 P14 **Tlaxcala** ◈ *state* S Mexico
**Tlaxcala de Xicohténcatl** *see* Tlaxcala
41 P14 **Tlaxco** *var.* Tlaxco de Morelos. Tlaxcala, S Mexico 19°38′N 98°06′W
**Tlaxco de Morelos** *see* Tlaxco
41 Q16 **Tlaxiaco** *var.* Santa María Asunción Tlaxiaco. Oaxaca, S Mexico 17°18′N 97°42′W
74 I6 **Tlemcen** *var.* Tilimsen, Tlemsen. NW Algeria 34°53′N 01°21′W
**Tlemsen** *see* Tlemcen
138 L4 **Tlété Ouâte Rharbi, Jebel** ▲ N Syria
116 J7 **Tlumach** Ivano-Frankivs′ka Oblast′, W Ukraine 48°53′N 25°00′E
127 P17 **Tlyarata** Respublika Dagestan, SW Russia 42°10′N 46°30′E
116 K10 **Toaca, Vârful** *prev.* Vîrful Toaca. ▲ NE Romania 46°58′N 25°55′E
**Toaca, Vîrful** *see* Toaca, Vârful
191 Q8 **Toahotu** *prev.* Teohatu. Tahiti, W French Polynesia
187 R13 **Toak** Ambrym, C Vanuatu 16°21′S 168°16′E
172 J4 **Toamasina** *prev./Fr.* Tamatave. Toamasina, E Madagascar 18°10′S 49°23′E
172 J4 **Toamasina** ◈ *province* E Madagascar
172 J4 **Toamasina** ✈ Toamasina, E Madagascar 18°10′S 49°23′E
21 X6 **Toano** Virginia, NE USA 37°22′N 76°46′W
191 U10 **Toau** *atoll* Îles Tuamotu, C French Polynesia
45 T6 **Toa Vaca, Embalse** ⊠ C Puerto Rico
62 K13 **Toay** La Pampa, C Argentina 36°43′S 64°22′W
159 R14 **Toba** Xizang Zizhiqu, W China 31°17′N 97°37′E
164 K14 **Toba** Mie, Honshū, SW Japan 34°29′N 136°51′E
168 I9 **Toba, Danau** ◎ Sumatera, W Indonesia
45 Y16 **Tobago** *island* NE Trinidad and Tobago
149 Q9 **Toba Kakar Range** ▲▲ NW Pakistan
105 Q12 **Tobarra** Castilla-La Mancha, C Spain 38°36′N 01°41′W
149 U9 **Toba Tek Singh** Punjab, E Pakistan 30°54′N 72°30′E
171 R11 **Tobelo** Pulau Halmahera, E Indonesia 01°45′N 127°59′E
14 E12 **Tobermory** Ontario, S Canada 45°15′N 81°39′W
96 G10 **Tobermory** W Scotland, United Kingdom 56°37′N 06°12′W
165 S4 **Tōbetsu** Hokkaidō, NE Japan 43°12′N 141°28′E
180 M6 **Tobin Lake** ◎ Western Australia
11 U14 **Tobin Lake** ◎ Saskatchewan, C Canada
35 T4 **Tobin, Mount** ▲ Nevada, W USA 40°25′N 117°28′W
165 O9 **Tobi-shima** *island* C Japan
169 N13 **Toboali** Pulau Bangka, W Indonesia 03°00′S 106°30′E
**Tobol** *see* Tobyl
122 H11 **Tobol′sk** Tyumenskaya Oblast′, C Russia 58°15′N 68°12′E
**Tobruch/Tobruk** *see* Ţubruq
125 R3 **Tobseda** Nenetskiy Avtonomnyy Okrug, NW Russia 68°37′N 52°24′E
144 M8 **Tobyl** *prev.* Tobol. Kustanay, N Kazakhstan 52°42′N 62°36′E
144 L8 **Tobyl** *prev.* Tobol. ≈ Kazakhstan/Russia
125 Q6 **Tobysh** ≈ NW Russia
54 F10 **Tocaima** Cundinamarca, C Colombia 04°30′N 74°38′W
59 K16 **Tocantins** *off.* Estado do Tocantins. ◈ *state* C Brazil
**Tocantins, Estado do** *see* Tocantins
59 K15 **Tocantins, Rio** ≈ N Brazil
23 T2 **Toccoa** Georgia, SE USA 34°34′N 83°19′W
165 O12 **Tochigi** *off.* Tochigi-ken, *var.* Totigi. ◈ *prefecture* Honshū, S Japan
**Tochigi-ken** *see* Tochigi
165 O11 **Tochio** *var.* Totio. Niigata, Honshū, C Japan 37°27′N 139°00′E
95 I15 **Töcksfors** Värmland, C Sweden 59°30′N 11°49′E
42 J5 **Tocoa** Colón, N Honduras 15°40′N 86°01′W
62 H4 **Tocopilla** Antofagasta, N Chile 22°06′S 70°08′W
62 I4 **Tocorpuri, Cerro de** ▲ Bolivia/Chile 22°26′S 67°53′W
183 O10 **Tocumwal** New South Wales, SE Australia 35°53′S 145°35′E
54 K4 **Tocuyo de la Costa** Falcón, NW Venezuela 11°04′N 68°23′W
152 H13 **Toda Rāisingh** Rājasthān, N India 26°02′N 75°35′E
106 H13 **Todi** Umbria, C Italy 42°47′N 12°25′E
108 G9 **Tödi** ▲ NE Switzerland 46°52′N 08°53′E
171 T12 **Todlo** Papua Barat, E Indonesia 0°46′S 130°50′E
165 S9 **Todoga-saki** *headland* Honshū, C Japan 39°33′N 142°02′E
59 P17 **Todos os Santos, Baía de** *bay* E Brazil
40 F10 **Todos Santos** Baja California Sur, NW Mexico 23°28′N 110°14′W
40 B2 **Todos Santos, Bahía de** *bay* NW Mexico
**Toeban** *see* Tuban
**Toekang Besi Eilanden** *see* Tukangbesi, Kepulauan
**Toeloengagoeng** *see* Tulungagung
**Tōen** *see* Taoyuan
185 D25 **Toetoes Bay** *bay* South Island, New Zealand
11 Q14 **Tofield** Alberta, SW Canada 53°22′N 112°39′W
10 K17 **Tofino** Vancouver Island, British Columbia, SW Canada 49°05′N 125°51′W
189 X17 **Tofol** Kosrae, E Micronesia
95 J20 **Tofta** Halland, S Sweden 57°10′N 12°19′E
95 H15 **Tofte** Buskerud, S Norway 59°31′N 10°33′E
95 F24 **Toftlund** Syddanmark, SW Denmark 55°12′N 09°04′E
193 X15 **Tofua** *island* Ha′apai Group, C Tonga
187 Q12 **Toga** *island* Torres Islands, N Vanuatu
80 N13 **Togdheer** *off.* Gobolka Togdheer. ◈ *region* NW Somalia
**Togdheer, Gobolka** *see* Togdheer
164 L11 **Togi** Ishikawa, Honshū, SW Japan 37°06′N 136°44′E
39 N13 **Togiak** Alaska, USA 59°03′N 160°31′W
171 O11 **Togian, Kepulauan** *island group* C Indonesia
77 Q15 **Togo** *off.* Togolese Republic, *Fr.* République Togolaise; *prev.* French Togoland. ◆ *republic* W Africa
**Togolaise, République** *see* Togo
**Togolese Republic** *see* Togo
162 F8 **Tögrög** Govĭ-Altay, SW Mongolia 45°51′N 95°04′E
162 F8 **Tögrög** *var.* Hoolt. Övörhangay, C Mongolia 45°31′N 103°06′E
**Tögrög** *see* Manhan
159 N12 **Togton He** *var.* Tuotuo He. ≈ C China
**Togton Heyan** *see* Tanggulashan
**Toguzak** *see* Togyzak
144 L7 **Togyzak** *prev.* Toguzak. ≈ Kazakhstan/Russia
37 P10 **Tohatchi** New Mexico, SW USA 35°51′N 108°45′W
191 O7 **Tohiea, Mont** ⛰ Moorea, W French Polynesia 17°33′S 149°48′W
137 N14 **Tohma Çayı** ≈ C Turkey
93 O17 **Tohmajärvi** Pohjois-Karjala, SE Finland 62°12′N 30°19′E
93 L16 **Toholampi** Keski-Pohjanmaa, W Finland 63°46′N 24°15′E
**Töhöm** *see* Mandah
23 X12 **Tohopekaliga, Lake** ◎ Florida, SE USA
164 M14 **Toi** Shizuoka, Honshū, S Japan 34°55′N 138°45′E
190 B15 **Toi** N Niue 18°57′S 169°51′W
93 L19 **Toijala** Pirkanmaa, SW Finland 61°09′N 23°51′E
171 P12 **Toima** Sulawesi, N Indonesia 0°48′S 122°21′E
164 D17 **Toi-misaki** Kyūshū, SW Japan
171 Q17 **Toineke** Timor, S Indonesia 10°06′S 124°22′E
**Toirc, Inis** *see* Inishturk
35 U6 **Toiyabe Range** ▲▲ Nevada, W USA
**Tojikiston** *see* Tajikistan
**Tojikiston, Jumhurii** *see* Tajikistan
147 R12 **Tojikobod** *Rus.* Tadzhikabad. C Tajikistan 39°08′N 70°54′E
164 G12 **Tōjō** Hiroshima, Honshū, SW Japan 34°54′N 133°15′E
39 T10 **Tok** Alaska, USA 63°20′N 142°59′W
164 K13 **Tōkai** Aichi, Honshū, SW Japan 35°01′N 136°51′E
111 N21 **Tokaj** Borsod-Abaúj-Zemplén, NE Hungary 48°08′N 21°25′E
165 N11 **Tōkamachi** Niigata, Honshū, C Japan 37°08′N 138°44′E
185 D25 **Tokanui** Southland, South Island, New Zealand 46°33′S 169°02′E
80 I7 **Tokar** *var.* Ţawkar. Red Sea, NE Sudan 18°27′N 37°41′E
136 L12 **Tokat** Tokat, N Turkey 40°20′N 36°35′E
136 L12 **Tokat** ◈ *province* N Turkey
**Tŏkchŏk-kundo** *see* Deokjeok-gundo
**Tōke** *see* Taka Atoll
190 J9 **Tokelau** ◇ *NZ overseas territory* W Polynesia
**Tőketerebes** *see* Trebišov
**Tokhtamyshbek** *see* Tŭkhtamish
24 M6 **Tokio** Texas, SW USA 33°09′N 102°31′W
**Tokio** *see* Tōkyō
189 W11 **Toki Point** *point* NW Wake Island
**Tokkuztara** *see* Gongliu
117 V9 **Tokmak** *var.* Velykyy Tokmak. Zaporiz′ka Oblast′, SE Ukraine 47°13′N 35°43′E
**Tokmak** *see* Tomok
184 Q8 **Tokomaru Bay** Gisborne, North Island, New Zealand 38°10′S 178°18′E
184 M8 **Tokoroa** Waikato, North Island, New Zealand 38°14′S 175°52′E
76 K14 **Tokounou** C Guinea 09°43′N 09°46′W
38 M12 **Toksook Bay** Alaska, USA 60°33′N 165°01′W
**Toksu** *see* Xinhe
**Toksum** *see* Toksun
158 L6 **Toksun** *var.* Toksum. Xinjiang Uygur Zizhiqu, NW China 42°47′N 88°38′E
147 T8 **Toktogul** Talasskaya Oblast′, NW Kyrgyzstan 41°51′N 72°56′E
147 T9 **Toktogul′skoye Vodokhranilishche** ⊠ W Kyrgyzstan
**Toktomush** *see* Tŭkhtamish
193 Y14 **Toku** *island* Vava′u Group, N Tonga
165 U16 **Tokunoshima** Kagoshima, Tokuno-shima, SW Japan
165 U16 **Tokuno-shima** *island* Nansei-shotō, SW Japan
164 I14 **Tokushima** *var.* Tokusima. Tokushima, Shikoku, SW Japan 34°04′N 134°28′E
164 H14 **Tokushima** *off.* Tokushima-ken, *var.* Tokusima. ◈ *prefecture* Shikoku, SW Japan
**Tokushima-ken** *see* Tokushima
**Tokusima** *see* Tokushima
164 E13 **Tokuyama** *var.* Shūnan. Yamaguchi, Honshū, SW Japan 34°04′N 131°48′E
165 N13 **Tōkyō** *var.* Tokio. ● (Japan) Tōkyō, Honshū, S Japan 35°40′N 139°45′E
165 O13 **Tōkyō** *off.* Tōkyō-to. ◈ *capital district* Honshū, S Japan
**Tōkyō-to** *see* Tōkyō
145 T12 **Tokyrau** ≈ C Kazakhstan
145 W13 **Tokzhaylau** *prev.* Dzerzhinskoye. Almaty, SE Kazakhstan 45°49′N 81°04′E
145 W13 **Tokzhaylau** *var.* Dzerzhinskoye. Taldykorgan, SE Kazakhstan 45°49′N 81°04′E
189 U12 **Tol** *atoll* Chuuk Islands, C Micronesia
184 Q9 **Tolaga Bay** Gisborne, North Island, New Zealand 38°22′S 178°17′E
172 I7 **Tôlañaro** *prev.* Faradofay, Fort-Dauphin. Toliara, SE Madagascar
162 D6 **Tolbo** Bayan-Ölgiy, W Mongolia 48°22′N 90°22′E
**Tolbukhin** *see* Dobrich
60 G11 **Toledo** Paraná, S Brazil 24°45′S 53°41′W
54 G8 **Toledo** Norte de Santander, N Colombia 07°16′N 72°28′W
105 N9 **Toledo** *anc.* Toletum. Castilla-La Mancha, C Spain 39°52′N 04°02′W
30 M14 **Toledo** Illinois, N USA 39°16′N 88°15′W
29 W13 **Toledo** Iowa, C USA 42°00′N 92°34′W
31 R11 **Toledo** Ohio, N USA 41°40′N 83°33′W
32 F12 **Toledo** Oregon, NW USA 44°37′N 123°56′W
32 G9 **Toledo** Washington, NW USA 46°27′N 122°49′W
42 F3 **Toledo** ◈ *district* S Belize
104 M9 **Toledo** ◈ *province* Castilla-La Mancha, C Spain
25 Y7 **Toledo Bend Reservoir** ⊠ Louisiana/Texas, SW USA
104 M10 **Toledo, Montes de** ▲▲ C Spain
106 J12 **Tolentino** Marche, C Italy 43°08′N 13°17′E
**Toletum** *see* Toledo
94 H10 **Tolga** Hedmark, S Norway 62°25′N 11°00′E
158 J3 **Toli** Xinjiang Uygur Zizhiqu, NW China 45°55′N 83°33′E
172 H7 **Toliara** *var.* Toliary; *prev.* Tuléar. Toliara, SW Madagascar 23°20′S 43°41′E
172 H7 **Toliara** ◈ *province* SW Madagascar
**Toliary** *see* Toliara
118 H11 **Toliejai** *prev.* Kamajai. Panevėžys, NE Lithuania 55°16′N 25°30′E
54 D11 **Tolima** *off.* Departamento del Tolima. ◈ *province* C Colombia
**Tolima, Departamento del** *see* Tolima
171 N11 **Tolitoli** Sulawesi, C Indonesia 01°05′N 120°50′E
95 K22 **Tollarp** Skåne, S Sweden 55°55′N 14°00′E
100 N9 **Tollense** ≈ NE Germany
100 N10 **Tollensesee** ◎ NE Germany
36 K13 **Tolleson** Arizona, SW USA 33°25′N 112°15′W
146 M13 **Tollimarjon** *Rus.* Talimardzhan. Qashqadaryo Viloyati, S Uzbekistan 38°22′N 65°31′E
**Tolmein** *see* Tolmin
106 J6 **Tolmezzo** Friuli-Venezia Giulia, NE Italy 46°27′N 13°01′E
109 S11 **Tolmin** *Ger.* Tolmein, *It.* Tolmino. W Slovenia 46°12′N 13°39′E
**Tolmino** *see* Tolmin
111 J25 **Tolna** *Ger.* Tolnau. Tolna, S Hungary 46°26′N 18°47′E
111 I24 **Tolna** *off.* Tolna Megye. ◈ *county* SW Hungary
**Tolna Megye** *see* Tolna
**Tolnau** *see* Tolna
79 I20 **Tolo** Bandundu, W Dem. Rep. Congo 02°57′S 18°35′E
**Tolochin** *see* Talachyn
190 D12 **Toloke** Île Futuna, W Wallis and Futuna
30 M13 **Tolono** Illinois, N USA 39°59′N 88°16′W
105 Q3 **Tolosa** País Vasco, N Spain 43°09′N 02°04′W
**Tolosa** *see* Toulouse
171 O13 **Tolo, Teluk** *bay* Sulawesi, C Indonesia
39 R9 **Tolovana River** ≈ Alaska, USA
123 U10 **Tolstoy, Mys** *headland* E Russia 59°12′N 155°04′E
63 G15 **Toltén** Araucanía, C Chile 39°13′S 73°15′W
63 G15 **Toltén, Río** ≈ S Chile
54 E6 **Tolú** Sucre, NW Colombia 09°32′N 75°34′W
41 O14 **Toluca** *var.* Toluca de Lerdo. México, S Mexico 19°20′N 99°40′W
**Toluca de Lerdo** *see* Toluca
41 O14 **Toluca, Nevado de** ⛰ C Mexico 19°05′N 99°45′W
127 R6 **Tol′yatti** *prev.* Stavropol′. Samarskaya Oblast′, W Russia 53°32′N 49°27′E
77 O12 **Toma** NW Burkina Faso 12°46′N 02°51′W
30 K7 **Tomah** Wisconsin, N USA 43°59′N 90°31′W
30 L5 **Tomahawk** Wisconsin, N USA 45°27′N 89°40′W
117 T8 **Tomakivka** Dnipropetrovs′ka Oblast′, E Ukraine 47°47′N 34°45′E
165 S4 **Tomakomai** Hokkaidō, NE Japan 42°38′N 141°32′E
165 S2 **Tomamae** Hokkaidō, NE Japan 44°18′N 141°38′E
104 G9 **Tomar** Santarém, W Portugal 39°36′N 08°25′W
123 T13 **Tomari** Ostrov Sakhalin, Sakhalinskaya Oblast′, SE Russia 47°47′N 142°09′E
115 C16 **Tómaros** ▲ W Greece 39°31′N 20°45′E
**Tomaschow** *see* Tomaszów Mazowiecki
**Tomaschow** *see* Tomaszów Lubelski
61 E16 **Tomás Gomensoro** Artigas, N Uruguay 30°28′S 57°28′W
117 N7 **Tomashpil′** Vinnyts′ka Oblast′, C Ukraine 48°32′N 28°31′E
**Tomaszów** *see* Tomaszów Mazowiecki
111 P15 **Tomaszów Lubelski** *Ger.* Tomaschow. Lubelskie, E Poland 50°29′N 23°23′E
**Tomaszów Mazowiecka** *see* Tomaszów Mazowiecki
110 L13 **Tomaszów Mazowiecki** *var.* Tomaszów Mazowiecka; *prev.* Tomaszów, *Ger.* Tomaschow. Łódzkie, C Poland 51°33′N 20°E
40 J13 **Tomatlán** Jalisco, C Mexico 19°53′N 105°18′W
81 F15 **Tombe** Jonglei, E South Sudan 05°52′N 31°40′E
23 N4 **Tombigbee River** ≈ Alabama/Mississippi, S USA
82 A10 **Tomboco** Zaire Province, NW Angola 06°50′S 13°20′E
77 O10 **Tombouctou** *Eng.* Timbuktu. Tombouctou, N Mali 16°47′N 03°03′W
77 N9 **Tombouctou** ◈ *region* W Mali
37 N16 **Tombstone** Arizona, SW USA 31°42′N 110°04′W
83 A15 **Tombua** *Port.* Porto Alexandre. Namibe, SW Angola 15°49′S 11°53′E
83 J19 **Tom Burke** Limpopo, NE South Africa 23°07′S 28°01′E
146 L9 **Tomdibuloq** *Rus.* Tamdybulak. Navoiy Viloyati, N Uzbekistan 41°48′N 64°33′E
146 L9 **Tomditov-Tog′lari** ▲▲ N Uzbekistan
62 G13 **Tomé** Bío Bío, C Chile 36°38′S 72°57′W
58 L12 **Tomé-Açu** Pará, NE Brazil 02°25′S 48°09′W
95 L23 **Tomelilla** Skåne, S Sweden 55°33′N 14°00′E
105 O10 **Tomelloso** Castilla-La Mancha, C Spain 39°09′N 03°01′W
14 H10 **Tomiko Lake** ◎ Ontario, S Canada
77 N12 **Tominian** Ségou, C Mali 13°18′N 04°39′W
**Tomini, Gulf of** *see* Tomini, Teluk
171 N12 **Tomini, Teluk** *var.* Gulf of Tomini; *prev.* Teluk Gorontalo. *bay* Sulawesi, C Indonesia
165 Q11 **Tomioka** Fukushima, Honshū, C Japan 37°19′N 140°57′E
113 G14 **Tomislavgrad** Federacija Bosne I Hercegovine, SW Bosnia and Herzegovina 43°43′N 17°15′E
181 O9 **Tomkinson Ranges** ▲▲ South Australia/Western Australia
123 Q11 **Tommot** Respublika Sakha (Yakutiya), NE Russia 58°57′N 126°24′E
171 Q11 **Tomohon** Sulawesi, N Indonesia 01°19′N 124°49′E
147 V7 **Tomok** *prev.* Tokmak. Chuyskaya Oblast′, N Kyrgyzstan 42°50′N 75°18′E
54 K9 **Tomo, Río** ≈ E Colombia
113 L21 **Tomorrit, Mali i** ▲ S Albania 40°43′N 20°12′E
11 S17 **Tompkins** Saskatchewan, S Canada 50°03′N 108°49′W
20 K8 **Tompkinsville** Kentucky, S USA 36°43′N 85°41′W
171 N11 **Tompo** Sulawesi, N Indonesia 0°56′N 120°16′E
180 I8 **Tom Price** Western Australia 22°48′S 117°49′E
122 J12 **Tomsk** Tomskaya Oblast′, C Russia 56°30′N 85°05′E
122 I11 **Tomskaya Oblast′** ◈ *province* C Russia
18 K16 **Toms River** New Jersey, NE USA 39°56′N 74°09′W
**Tom Steed Lake** *see* Tom Steed Reservoir
26 L12 **Tom Steed Reservoir** *var.* Tom Steed Lake. ⊠ Oklahoma, C USA
171 U13 **Tomu** Papua Barat, E Indonesia 02°07′S 133°01′E
158 H6 **Tomür Feng** *var.* Pobeda Peak, *Rus.* Pik Pobedy. ▲ China/Kyrgyzstan 42°02′N 80°07′E *see also* Pobedy, Pik
**Tomür Feng** *see* Pobedy, Pik
189 N13 **Tomworoahlang** Pohnpei, E Micronesia
41 U17 **Tonalá** Chiapas, SE Mexico 16°08′N 93°41′W
106 F6 **Tonale, Passo del** *pass* N Italy
164 I11 **Tonami** Toyama, Honshū, SW Japan 36°40′N 136°55′E
58 C12 **Tonantins** Amazonas, W Brazil 02°58′S 67°30′W
32 K6 **Tonasket** Washington, NW USA 48°41′N 119°27′W
55 Y9 **Tonate** *var.* Macouria. N French Guiana 05°00′N 52°28′W
18 D10 **Tonawanda** New York, NE USA 43°00′N 78°51′W
42 I7 **Toncontín** *prev.* Tegucigalpa. ● (Honduras) Francisco Morazán, SW Honduras 14°04′N 87°11′W
42 H7 **Toncontín** ✈ Central District, C Honduras 14°03′N 87°20′W
171 Q11 **Tondano** Sulawesi, C Indonesia 01°19′N 124°56′E
104 H7 **Tondela** Viseu, N Portugal 40°31′N 08°05′W
95 F24 **Tønder** *Ger.* Tondern. Syddanmark, SW Denmark 54°57′N 08°53′E
**Tondern** *see* Tønder
143 N4 **Tonekābon** *var.* Shahsawar, Tonkābon; *prev.* Shahsavār. Māzandarān, N Iran 36°40′N 51°25′E
**Tonezh** *see* Tonyezh
193 Y14 **Tonga** *off.* Kingdom of Tonga, *Tong.* Pule′anga Fakatu′i ′o Tonga, *var.* Friendly Islands. ◆ *monarchy* SW Pacific Ocean
175 R9 **Tonga** *island group* SW Pacific Ocean
**Tongaat** *see* oThongathi
**Tonga, Kingdom of** *see* Tonga
161 Q13 **Tong′an** *var.* Datong, Tong an. Fujian, SE China 24°43′N 118°07′E
**Tong an** *see* Tong′an
27 Q4 **Tonganoxie** Kansas, C USA 39°06′N 95°05′W
**Tonga, Pule′anga Fakatu′i ′o** *see* Tonga
39 Y13 **Tongass National Forest** *reserve* Alaska, USA
193 Y16 **Tongatapu** ✈ Tongatapu, S Tonga 21°10′S 175°10′W
193 Y16 **Tongatapu** *island* Tongatapu Group, S Tonga
193 Y16 **Tongatapu Group** *island group* S Tonga
175 S9 **Tonga Trench** *undersea feature* S Pacific Ocean
161 N8 **Tongbai Shan** ▲▲ C China
161 P8 **Tongcheng** Anhui, E China 31°16′N 117°00′E
160 L6 **Tongchuan** Shaanxi, C China 35°10′N 109°03′E
160 L12 **Tongdao** *var.* Tongdao Dongzu Zizhixian; *prev.* Shuangjiang. Hunan, S China 26°06′N 109°46′E
**Tongdao Dongzu Zizhixian** *see* Tongdao
159 T11 **Tongde** *var.* Gabasumdo. Qinghai, C China 35°13′N 100°39′E
99 K19 **Tongeren** *Fr.* Tongres. Limburg, NE Belgium 50°47′N 05°28′E
**Tonghae** *see* Donghae
160 G13 **Tonghai** *var.* Xiushan. Yunnan, SW China 24°06′N 102°45′E
163 X8 **Tonghe** Heilongjiang, NE China 46°00′N 128°45′E
163 W11 **Tonghua** Jilin, NE China 41°45′N 125°50′E
163 Z6 **Tongjiang** Heilongjiang, NE China 47°39′N 132°29′E
163 Y13 **Tongjosŏn-man** *prev.* Broughton Bay. *bay* E North Korea
163 V7 **Tongken He** ≈ NE China
**Tongking, Gulf of** *see* Tonkin, Gulf of
163 U10 **Tongliao** Nei Mongol Zizhiqu, N China 43°37′N 122°15′E
161 Q9 **Tongling** Anhui, E China 30°55′N 117°50′E
161 R9 **Tonglu** Zhejiang, SE China 29°50′N 119°38′E
187 R14 **Tongoa** *island* Shepherd Islands, S Vanuatu
62 G9 **Tongoy** Coquimbo, C Chile 30°16′S 71°31′W
160 L11 **Tongren** *var.* Rongwo. Guizhou, S China 27°44′N 109°10′E
159 T11 **Tongren** *var.* Rongwo. Qinghai, C China 35°31′N 101°58′E
**Tongres** *see* Tongeren
153 U11 **Tongsa** *var.* Tongsa Dzong. C Bhutan 27°33′N 90°30′E
**Tongsa Dzong** *see* Tongsa
**Tongshan** *see* Fuding, Fujian, China
**Tongshan** *see* Xuzhou, Jiangsu, China
**Tongshi** *see* Wuzhishan
159 P12 **Tongtian He** *var.* Zhi Qu. ≈ C China
96 I6 **Tongue** N Scotland, United Kingdom 58°30′N 04°25′W
44 H3 **Tongue of the Ocean** *strait* C The Bahamas
33 X10 **Tongue River** ≈ Montana, NW USA
33 W11 **Tongue River Resevoir** ⊠ Montana, NW USA
159 V11 **Tongwei** *var.* Pingxiang. Gansu, C China 35°09′N 105°15′E
159 W9 **Tongxin** Ningxia, N China 37°00′N 105°41′E
163 U9 **Tongyu** *var.* Kaitong. Jilin, NE China 44°49′N 123°08′E
160 J11 **Tongzi** *var.* Loushanguan. Guizhou, S China 28°08′N 106°49′E
162 F8 **Tonhil** *var.* Dzüyl. Govĭ-Altay, SW Mongolia 46°09′N 93°55′E
40 G5 **Tónichi** Sonora, NW Mexico 28°37′N 109°34′W
81 D14 **Tonj** Warap, W South Sudan 07°18′N 28°41′E
152 H13 **Tonk** Rājasthān, N India 26°10′N 75°50′E
**Tonkābon** *see* Tonekābon
27 N8 **Tonkawa** Oklahoma, C USA 36°40′N 97°18′W
167 T7 **Tonkin, Gulf of** *var.* Gulf of Tongking, *Chin.* Beibu Wan, *Vtn.* Vinh Băc Bô. *gulf* China/Vietnam
167 Q12 **Tonle Sap** *Eng.* Great Lake. ◎ W Cambodia
102 L14 **Tonneins** Lot-et-Garonne, SW France 44°21′N 00°21′E
103 Q7 **Tonnerre** Yonne, C France 47°50′N 04°00′E
**Tonoas** *see* Dublon
35 U8 **Tonopah** Nevada, W USA 38°04′N 117°13′W
164 H13 **Tonoshō** Okayama, Shōdo-shima, SW Japan 34°29′N 134°10′E
43 S17 **Tonosí** Los Santos, S Panama 07°23′N 80°26′W
95 H16 **Tønsberg** Vestfold, S Norway 59°16′N 10°25′E
39 T11 **Tonsina** Alaska, USA 61°39′N 145°10′W
95 D17 **Tonstad** Vest-Agder, S Norway 58°40′N 06°42′E
193 X15 **Tonumea** *island* Nomuka Group, W Tonga
137 O11 **Tonya** Trabzon, NE Turkey 40°52′N 39°17′E
119 K20 **Tonyezh** *Rus.* Tonezh. Homyel′skaya Voblasts′, SE Belarus 51°50′N 27°48′E
36 L3 **Tooele** Utah, W USA 40°32′N 112°18′W
122 L13 **Toora-Khem** Respublika Tyva, S Russia 52°25′N 96°01′E
183 O5 **Toorale East** New South Wales, SE Australia 30°29′S 145°25′E
83 H25 **Toorberg** ▲ S South Africa 32°02′S 24°02′E
118 G5 **Tootsi** Pärnumaa, SW Estonia 58°34′N 24°43′E
183 U3 **Toowoomba** Queensland, E Australia 27°35′S 151°54′E
27 Q4 **Topeka** *state capital* Kansas, C USA 39°03′N 95°41′W
122 J12 **Topki** Kemerovskaya Oblast′, S Russia 55°12′N 85°40′E
111 M18 **Topľa** *Hung.* Toplya. ≈ NE Slovakia
**Toplicza** *see* Topliţa
116 J10 **Topliţa** *Ger.* Töplitz, *Hung.* Maroshevíz; *prev.* Topliţa Română, *Hung.* Oláh-Toplicza, Toplicza. Harghita, C Romania 45°56′N 25°20′E
**Topliţa Română/Töplitz** *see* Topliţa
**Toplya** *see* Topľa
111 I20 **Topoľčany** *Hung.* Nagytapolcsány. Nitriansky Kraj, W Slovakia 48°33′N 18°10′E
40 G8 **Topolobampo** Sinaloa, C Mexico 25°36′N 109°04′W
116 I13 **Topoloveni** Argeş, S Romania 44°49′N 25°02′E
114 L11 **Topolovgrad** *prev.* Kavakli. Haskovo, S Bulgaria 42°06′N 26°20′E
**Topolya** *see* Bačka Topola
32 J10 **Toppenish** Washington, NW USA 46°22′N 120°18′W
181 P4 **Top Springs Roadhouse** Northern Territory, N Australia 16°37′S 131°49′E
189 U11 **Tora** *island* Chuuk, C Micronesia
148 K4 **Tōraghūndī** Herāt, NW Afghanistan 35°13′N 62°19′E
**Toraigh** *see* Tory Island
189 U11 **Tora Island Pass** *passage* Chuuk Islands, C Micronesia
144 M14 **Toratam** *var.* Töretam. Kyzylorda, S Kazakhstan 45°38′N 63°20′E
143 U5 **Torbat-e Ḩeydarīyeh** *var.* Turbat-i-Haidari. Khorāsān-e Razavī, NE Iran 35°18′N 59°12′E
143 V5 **Torbat-e Jām** *var.* Turbat-i-Jam. Khorāsān-e Razavī, NE Iran 35°16′N 60°36′E
39 Q11 **Torbert, Mount** ▲ Alaska, USA 61°30′N 152°15′W
31 P6 **Torch Lake** ◎ Michigan, N USA
**Törcsvár** *see* Bran
**Torda** *see* Turda
104 L6 **Tordesillas** Castilla y León, N Spain 41°30′N 05°00′W
92 K13 **Töre** Norrbotten, N Sweden 65°55′N 22°40′E
95 L17 **Töreboda** Västra Götaland, S Sweden 58°41′N 14°07′E
95 J21 **Torekov** Skåne, S Sweden 56°25′N 12°39′E
92 O3 **Torell Land** *physical region* SW Svalbard
**Töretam** *see* Toratam
117 X7 **Torets′k** *prev.* Dzerzhyns′k. Donets′ka Oblast′, SE Ukraine 48°21′N 37°50′E
105 U4 **Toretta de l′Orrí** *var.* Llorri; *prev.* Tossal de l′Orrí. ▲ NE Spain 42°24′N 01°15′E
**Torez** *see* Chystyakove
101 N14 **Torgau** Sachsen, E Germany 51°34′N 13°01′E
145 R8 **Torgay** *Kaz.* Torghay; *prev.* Turgay. Akmola, W Kazakhstan 51°46′N 72°45′E
145 N10 **Torgay** *prev.* Turgay. ≈ C Kazakhstan
**Torgay Üstirti** *see* Turgayskaya Stolovaya Strana
**Torghay** *see* Torgay
95 N22 **Torhamn** Blekinge, S Sweden 56°04′N 15°49′E
99 C17 **Torhout** West-Vlaanderen, W Belgium 51°04′N 03°06′E
106 B8 **Torino** *Eng.* Turin. Piemonte, NW Italy 45°03′N 07°39′E
**Tori-shima** *see* Io-Tori-shima
81 F16 **Torit** Eastern Equatoria, S South Sudan 04°27′N 32°31′E
186 H6 **Toriu** New Britain, E Papua New Guinea 04°39′S 151°42′E
104 L7 **Tormes** ≈ W Spain
**Tornacum** *see* Tournai
**Torneå** *see* Tornio
92 K12 **Torneälven** *var.* Torniojoki, *Fin.* Tornionjoki. ≈ Finland/Sweden
92 I11 **Torneträsk** ◎ N Sweden
13 O4 **Torngat Mountains** ▲▲ Newfoundland and Labrador, NE Canada
24 H8 **Tornillo** Texas, SW USA 31°26′N 106°06′W
92 K13 **Tornio** *Swe.* Torneå. Lappi, NW Finland 65°50′N 24°18′E
**Torniojoki/Tornionjoki** *see* Torneälven
61 B23 **Tornquist** Buenos Aires, E Argentina 38°08′S 62°15′W
104 L6 **Toro** Castilla y León, N Spain 41°31′N 05°24′W
62 H9 **Toro, Cerro del** ▲ N Chile 29°10′S 69°43′W
77 R12 **Torodi** Tillabéri, SW Niger 13°05′N 01°46′E
**Törökbecse** *see* Novi Bečej
186 J7 **Torokina** Bougainville, NE Papua New Guinea 06°12′S 155°04′E
111 L23 **Törökszentmiklós** Jász-Nagykun-Szolnok, E Hungary 47°11′N 20°26′E




◆ Country
● Country Capital
◇ Dependent Territory
○ Dependent Territory Capital
◈ Administrative Regions
✈ International Airport
▲ Mountain
▲▲ Mountain Range
⛰ Volcano
≈ River
◎ Lake
⊠ Reservoir

TOROLA, RÍO – TROPIC


42 G7 **Torola, Río** ≈ El Salvador/Honduras
**Toronaíos, Kólpos** *see* Kassándras, Kólpos
14 H15 **Toronto** *province capital* Ontario, S Canada *43°42′N 79°25′W*
31 V12 **Toronto** Ohio, N USA *40°27′N 80°36′W*
**Toronto** *see* Lester B. Pearson
27 P6 **Toronto Lake** ⊠ Kansas, C USA
35 V16 **Toro Peak** ▲ California, W USA *33°31′N 116°25′W*
124 H16 **Toropets** Tverskaya Oblast', W Russia *56°29′N 31°37′E*
81 G18 **Tororo** E Uganda *0°42′N 34°12′E*
136 H16 **Toros Dağları** *Eng.* Taurus Mountains. ▲ S Turkey
183 N13 **Torquay** Victoria, SE Australia *38°21′S 144°18′E*
97 J24 **Torquay** SW England, United Kingdom *50°28′N 03°30′W*
104 M5 **Torquemada** Castilla y León, N Spain *42°02′N 04°17′W*
35 S16 **Torrance** California, W USA *33°50′N 118°20′W*
104 G12 **Torrão** Setúbal, S Portugal *38°18′N 08°13′W*
104 H8 **Torre, Alto da** ▲ C Portugal *40°21′N 07°31′W*
107 K18 **Torre Annunziata** Campania, S Italy *40°45′N 14°27′E*
105 T8 **Torreblanca** Comunitat Valenciana, E Spain *40°14′N 00°12′E*
104 L15 **Torrecilla** ▲ S Spain *36°38′N 04°54′W*
105 P4 **Torrecilla en Cameros** La Rioja, N Spain *42°18′N 02°33′W*
105 N13 **Torredelcampo** Andalucía, S Spain *37°45′N 03°52′W*
107 K17 **Torre del Greco** Campania, S Italy *40°46′N 14°22′E*
104 I6 **Torre de Moncorvo** *var.* Moncorvo, Tôrre de Moncorvo. Bragança, N Portugal *41°10′N 07°03′W*
104 J9 **Torrejoncillo** Extremadura, W Spain *39°54′N 06°28′W*
105 O8 **Torrejón de Ardoz** Madrid, C Spain *40°27′N 03°29′W*
105 N7 **Torrelaguna** Madrid, C Spain *40°50′N 03°33′W*
105 N2 **Torrelavega** Cantabria, N Spain *43°21′N 04°03′W*
107 M16 **Torremaggiore** Puglia, SE Italy *41°42′N 15°17′E*
104 M15 **Torremolinos** Andalucía, S Spain *36°38′N 04°30′W*
182 I6 **Torrens, Lake** *salt lake* South Australia
105 S10 **Torrent** *Cas.* Torrente, *var.* Torrent de l'Horta. Comunitat Valenciana, E Spain *39°27′N 00°28′W*
**Torrent de l'Horta/Torrente** *see* Torrent
40 L8 **Torreón** Coahuila, NE Mexico *25°47′N 103°21′W*
105 R13 **Torre-Pacheco** Murcia, SE Spain *37°43′N 00°57′W*
106 A8 **Torre Pellice** Piemonte, NE Italy *44°49′N 07°12′E*
105 O13 **Torreperogil** Andalucía, S Spain *38°02′N 03°17′W*
61 J15 **Torres** Rio Grande do Sul, S Brazil *29°20′S 49°43′W*
**Torrès, Îles** *see* Torres Islands
187 Q11 **Torres Islands** *Fr.* Îles Torrès. *island group* N Vanuatu
104 G9 **Torres Novas** Santarém, C Portugal *39°28′N 08°32′W*
181 V1 **Torres Strait** *strait* Australia/Papua New Guinea
104 F10 **Torres Vedras** Lisboa, C Portugal *39°05′N 09°15′W*
105 S13 **Torrevieja** Comunitat Valenciana, S Spain *37°59′N 00°40′W*
186 B6 **Torricelli Mountains** ▲ NW Papua New Guinea
96 G8 **Torridon, Loch** *inlet* NW Scotland, United Kingdom
106 D9 **Torriglia** Liguria, NW Italy *44°31′N 09°08′E*
104 M9 **Torrijos** Castilla-La Mancha, C Spain *39°59′N 04°18′W*
18 L12 **Torrington** Connecticut, NE USA *41°48′N 73°07′W*
33 Z15 **Torrington** Wyoming, C USA *42°04′N 104°10′W*
**Torröjen** *see* Torrön
94 F16 **Torrön** *prev.* Torröjen. ◎ C Sweden
105 N15 **Torrox** Andalucía, S Spain *36°45′N 03°58′W*
94 N13 **Torsåker** Gävleborg, C Sweden *60°31′N 16°30′E*
95 N21 **Torsås** Kalmar, S Sweden *56°24′N 16°00′E*
95 J14 **Torsby** Värmland, C Sweden *60°07′N 13°E*
95 N16 **Torshälla** Södermanland, C Sweden *59°25′N 16°28′E*
95 B19 **Tórshavn** *Dan.* Thorshavn. ○ Faroe Islands *62°02′N 06°47′W*
**Torshiz** *see* Kāshmar
146 I9 **To'rtko'l** *var.* Türtkül, *Rus.* Turtkul'; *prev.* Petroaleksandrovsk. Qoraqalpog'iston Respublikasi, W Uzbekistan *41°35′N 61°E*
**Tortoise Islands** *see* Colón, Archipiélago de
45 T9 **Tortola** *island* C British Virgin Islands
106 D9 **Tortona** *anc.* Dertona. Piemonte, NW Italy *44°54′N 08°52′E*
107 L23 **Tortorici** Sicilia, Italy, C Mediterranean Sea *38°02′N 14°49′E*
105 U7 **Tortosa** *anc.* Dertosa. Cataluña, E Spain *40°49′N 00°31′E*
**Tortosa** *see* Ţarţūs
105 U7 **Tortosa, Cap** *cape* E Spain
44 L8 **Tortue, Île de la** *var.* Tortuga Island. *island* N Haiti
55 Y10 **Tortue, Montagne** ▲ C French Guiana
**Tortuga, Isla** *see* La Tortuga, Isla
**Tortuga Island** *see* Tortue, Île de la
54 C11 **Tortugas, Golfo** *gulf* W Colombia
45 T5 **Tortuguero, Laguna** *lagoon* N Puerto Rico
137 Q12 **Tortum** Erzurum, NE Turkey *40°20′N 41°36′E*
**Torugart, Pereval** *see* Turugart Shankou
137 O12 **Torul** Gümüşhane, NE Turkey *40°35′N 39°18′E*
110 J10 **Toruń** *Ger.* Thorn. Toruń, Kujawsko-pomorskie, C Poland *53°02′N 18°36′E*
95 K20 **Torup** Halland, S Sweden *56°57′N 13°04′E*
118 I6 **Tõrva** *Ger.* Törwa. Valgamaa, S Estonia *58°00′N 25°54′E*
**Törwa** *see* Tõrva
96 D13 **Tory Island** *Ir.* Toraigh. *island* NW Ireland
111 N19 **Torysa** *Hung.* Tarca. ≈ NE Slovakia
**Törzburg** *see* Bran
124 J16 **Torzhok** Tverskaya Oblast', W Russia *57°04′N 34°55′E*
164 F15 **Tosa-Shimizu** *var.* Tosasimizu. Kōchi, Shikoku, SW Japan *32°47′N 132°58′E*
**Tosasimizu** *see* Tosa-Shimizu
164 G15 **Tosa-wan** *bay* SW Japan
83 H21 **Tosca** North-West, N South Africa *25°51′S 23°56′E*
106 F12 **Toscana** *Eng.* Tuscany. ◈ *region* C Italy
107 E14 **Toscano, Archipelago** *Eng.* Tuscan Archipelago. *island group* C Italy
106 G10 **Tosco-Emiliano, Appennino** *Eng.* Tuscan-Emilian Mountains. ▲ C Italy
**Tösei** *see* Dongshi
165 N15 **To-shima** *island* Izu-shotō, SE Japan
147 Q9 **Toshkent** *Eng./Rus.* Tashkent. ● Toshkent Viloyati, E Uzbekistan *41°19′N 69°17′E*
147 Q9 **Toshkent** ✈ Toshkent Viloyati, E Uzbekistan *41°13′N 69°15′E*
147 P9 **Toshkent Viloyati** *Rus.* Tashkentskaya Oblast'. ◈ *province* E Uzbekistan
124 H13 **Tosno** Leningradskaya Oblast', NW Russia *59°34′N 30°48′E*
159 Q10 **Toson Hu** ◎ C China
162 H6 **Tosontsengel** Dzavhan, NW Mongolia *48°42′N 98°14′E*
162 J6 **Tosontsengel** *var.* Tsengel. Hövsgöl, N Mongolia *49°29′N 101°09′E*
146 I8 **Tosquduq Qumlari** *var.* Goshquduq Qum, Taskuduk, Peski. *desert* W Uzbekistan
**Tossal de l'Orrí** *see* Toretta de l'Orrí
61 A15 **Tostado** Santa Fe, C Argentina *29°15′S 61°45′W*
118 F6 **Tõstamaa** *Ger.* Testama. Pärnumaa, SW Estonia *58°20′N 23°59′E*
100 I10 **Tostedt** Niedersachsen, NW Germany *53°16′N 09°42′E*
136 J11 **Tosya** Kastamonu, N Turkey *41°02′N 34°02′E*
95 F15 **Totak** ◎ S Norway
105 R13 **Totana** Murcia, SE Spain *37°45′N 01°30′W*
94 H13 **Toten** *physical region* S Norway
83 G18 **Toteng** Ngamiland, C Botswana *20°25′S 23°00′E*
102 M3 **Tôtes** Seine-Maritime, N France *49°40′N 01°02′E*
**Totigi** *see* Tochigi
**Totio** *see* Tochio
**Totis** *see* Tata
189 U13 **Totiw** *island* Chuuk, C Micronesia
125 N13 **Tot'ma** *var.* Totma. Vologodskaya Oblast', NW Russia *59°58′N 42°42′E*
**Tot'ma** *see* Sukhona
55 V9 **Totness** Coronie, N Suriname *05°53′N 56°19′W*
42 C5 **Totonicapán** Totonicapán, W Guatemala *14°58′N 91°12′W*
42 A2 **Totonicapán** *off.* Departamento de Totonicapán. ◈ *department* W Guatemala
**Totonicapán, Departamento de** *see* Totonicapán
61 B18 **Totoras** Santa Fe, C Argentina *32°35′S 61°11′W*
187 Y15 **Totoya** *island* S Fiji
183 Q7 **Tottenham** New South Wales, SE Australia *32°16′S 147°23′E*
164 I12 **Tottori** Tottori, Honshū, SW Japan *35°29′N 134°14′E*
164 H12 **Tottori** *off.* Tottori-ken. ◈ *prefecture* Honshū, SW Japan
**Tottori-ken** *see* Tottori
76 I6 **Touâjîl** Tiris Zemmour, N Mauritania *22°03′N 12°40′W*
76 L15 **Touba** W Ivory Coast *08°17′N 07°41′W*
76 G11 **Touba** W Senegal *14°55′N 15°53′W*
74 E7 **Toubkal, Jbel** ▲ W Morocco *31°00′N 07°50′W*
32 K10 **Touchet** Washington, NW USA *46°03′N 118°40′W*
103 P7 **Toucy** Yonne, C France *47°45′N 03°18′E*
77 O12 **Tougan** W Burkina Faso *13°06′N 03°03′W*
74 L7 **Touggourt** NE Algeria *33°08′N 06°04′E*
77 Q12 **Tougouri** N Burkina Faso *13°22′N 00°25′W*
76 J13 **Tougué** NW Guinea *11°29′N 11°48′W*
76 K12 **Toukoto** Kayes, W Mali *13°27′N 09°52′W*
103 S5 **Toul** Meurthe-et-Moselle, NE France *48°41′N 05°54′E*
76 L16 **Toulépleu** *var.* Toulobli. W Ivory Coast *06°37′N 08°27′W*
**Touliu** *see* Douliu
15 U3 **Toulnustouc** ≈ Québec, SE Canada
**Toulobli** *see* Toulépleu
103 T16 **Toulon** *anc.* Telo Martius, Tilio Martius. Var, SE France *43°07′N 05°56′E*
30 K12 **Toulon** Illinois, N USA *41°05′N 89°54′W*
102 M15 **Toulouse** *anc.* Tolosa. Haute-Garonne, S France *43°37′N 01°25′E*
102 M15 **Toulouse** ✈ Haute-Garonne, S France *43°38′N 01°19′E*
77 N16 **Toumodi** C Ivory Coast *06°34′N 05°01′W*
74 G9 **Tounassine, Hamada** *hill range* W Algeria
**Toungoo** *see* Taungoo
166 K7 **Toungup** *var.* Taungup. Rakhine State, W Myanmar (Burma) *18°50′N 94°14′E*
102 L8 **Touraine** *cultural region* C France
**Tourane** *see* Đa Nâng
103 P1 **Tourcoing** Nord, N France *50°44′N 03°10′E*
104 F2 **Touriñán, Cabo** *headland* NW Spain *43°02′N 09°20′W*
76 J6 **Tourine** Tiris Zemmour, N Mauritania *22°23′N 11°50′W*
102 J3 **Tourlaville** Manche, N France *49°38′N 01°34′W*
99 D19 **Tournai** *var.* Tournay, *Dut.* Doornik; *anc.* Tornacum. Hainaut, SW Belgium *50°36′N 03°24′E*
102 L16 **Tournay** Hautes-Pyrénées, S France *43°10′N 00°16′E*
**Tournay** *see* Tournai
103 R12 **Tournon** Ardèche, E France *45°05′N 04°49′E*
103 R9 **Tournus** Saône-et-Loire, C France *46°33′N 04°53′E*
59 Q14 **Touros** Rio Grande do Norte, E Brazil *05°10′S 35°29′W*
102 L8 **Tours** *anc.* Caesarodunum, Turoni. Indre-et-Loire, C France *47°22′N 00°40′E*
183 Q17 **Tourville, Cape** *headland* Tasmania, SE Australia *42°09′S 148°20′E*
44 M9 **Toussaint Louverture** ✈ E Haiti *18°38′N 72°13′W*
162 L8 **Töv** ◈ *province* C Mongolia
54 H7 **Tovar** Mérida, NW Venezuela *08°22′N 71°50′W*
126 L5 **Tovarkovskiy** Tul'skaya Oblast', W Russia *53°41′N 38°18′E*
**Tovil'-Dora** *see* Tavildara
**Tövis** *see* Teiuş
137 V11 **Tovuz** *Rus.* Tauz. W Azerbaijan *40°58′N 45°41′E*
165 R7 **Towada** Aomori, Honshū, C Japan *40°35′N 141°13′E*
184 K3 **Towai** Northland, North Island, New Zealand *35°29′S 174°06′E*
18 H12 **Towanda** Pennsylvania, NE USA *41°45′N 76°25′W*
29 W4 **Tower** Minnesota, N USA *47°48′N 92°16′W*
171 N12 **Towera** Sulawesi, N Indonesia *0°29′S 120°01′E*
**Tower Island** *see* Genovesa, Isla
180 M13 **Tower Peak** ▲ Western Australia *33°23′S 123°27′E*
35 U11 **Towne Pass** *pass* California, W USA
29 N3 **Towner** North Dakota, N USA *48°20′N 100°27′W*
33 R10 **Townsend** Montana, NW USA *46°19′N 111°31′W*
181 X6 **Townsville** Queensland, NE Australia *19°24′S 146°53′E*
**Towoeti Meer** *see* Towuti, Danau
21 X3 **Towson** Maryland, NE USA *39°25′N 76°36′W*
171 O13 **Towuti, Danau** *Dut.* Towoeti Meer. ◎ Sulawesi, C Indonesia
**Toxkan He** *see* Ak-say
24 K9 **Toyah** Texas, SW USA *31°18′N 103°47′W*
165 R4 **Tōya-ko** ◎ Hokkaidō, NE Japan
164 L11 **Toyama** Toyama, Honshū, SW Japan *36°41′N 137°13′E*
164 L11 **Toyama** *off.* Toyama-ken. ◈ *prefecture* Honshū, SW Japan
**Toyama-ken** *see* Toyama
164 L11 **Toyama-wan** *bay* W Japan
164 H15 **Tōyo** Kōchi, Shikoku, SW Japan *33°22′N 134°18′E*
**Toyohara** *see* Yuzhno-Sakhalinsk
164 L14 **Toyohashi** *var.* Toyohasi. Aichi, Honshū, SW Japan *34°46′N 137°22′E*
**Toyohasi** *see* Toyohashi
164 L14 **Toyokawa** Aichi, Honshū, SW Japan *34°47′N 137°24′E*
164 I14 **Toyooka** Hyōgo, Honshū, SW Japan *35°35′N 134°48′E*
164 L13 **Toyota** Aichi, Honshū, SW Japan *35°04′N 137°09′E*
165 T1 **Toyotomi** Hokkaidō, NE Japan *45°07′N 141°45′E*
147 Q10 **To'ytepa** *Rus.* Toytepa. Toshkent Viloyati, E Uzbekistan *41°04′N 69°22′E*
**Toytepa** *see* To'ytepa
74 M6 **Tozeur** *var.* Tawzar. W Tunisia *34°00′N 08°09′E*
39 Q8 **Tozi, Mount** ▲ Alaska, USA *65°45′N 151°01′W*
137 Q9 **T'q'varcheli** *Rus.* Tkvarcheli; *prev.* Tqvarch'eli. NW Georgia *42°51′N 41°42′E*
**Tqvarch'eli** *see* T'q'varcheli
**Trâblous** *see* Tripoli
137 O11 **Trabzon** *Eng.* Trebizond; *anc.* Trapezus. Trabzon, NE Turkey *41°N 39°43′E*
137 O11 **Trabzon** *Eng.* Trebizond. ◈ *province* NE Turkey
13 P13 **Tracadie** New Brunswick, SE Canada *47°32′N 64°57′W*
**Trachenberg** *see* Żmigród
15 O11 **Tracy** Québec, SE Canada *45°59′N 73°07′W*
35 O8 **Tracy** California, W USA *37°43′N 121°27′W*
29 S10 **Tracy** Minnesota, N USA *44°14′N 95°37′W*
20 K10 **Tracy City** Tennessee, S USA *35°15′N 85°44′W*
106 D7 **Tradate** Lombardia, N Italy *45°43′N 08°57′E*
84 F6 **Traena Bank** *undersea feature* E Norwegian Sea *66°15′N 09°45′E*
29 W13 **Traer** Iowa, C USA *42°11′N 92°28′W*
104 J16 **Trafalgar, Cabo de** *headland* SW Spain *36°10′N 06°03′W*
**Traiectum ad Mosam/Traiectum Tungorum** *see* Maastricht
**Tráigh Mhór** *see* Tramore
11 O17 **Trail** British Columbia, SW Canada *49°94′N 117°39′W*
58 B11 **Traíra, Serra do** ▲ NW Brazil
109 V5 **Traisen** Niederösterreich, NE Austria *48°03′N 15°37′E*
109 X4 **Traisen** ≈ NE Austria
109 X4 **Traiskirchen** Niederösterreich, NE Austria *48°01′N 16°18′E*
**Trajani Portus** *see* Civitavecchia
**Trajectum ad Rhenum** *see* Utrecht
119 H14 **Trakai** *Ger.* Traken, *Pol.* Troki. Vilnius, SE Lithuania *54°39′N 24°58′E*
**Traken** *see* Trakai
97 B20 **Tralee** *Ir.* Trá Lí. SW Ireland *52°16′N 09°42′W*
97 A20 **Tralee Bay** *Ir.* Bá Thrá Lí. *bay* SW Ireland
**Trá Li** *see* Tralee
**Trälleborg** *see* Trelleborg
**Tralles Aydin** *see* Aydın
61 J16 **Tramandaí** Rio Grande do Sul, S Brazil *30°01′S 50°11′W*
108 C7 **Tramelan** Bern, W Switzerland *47°13′N 07°07′E*
**Trá Mhór** *see* Tramore
97 E20 **Tramore** *Ir.* Tráigh Mhór, Trá Mhór. Waterford, S Ireland *52°10′N 07°10′W*
114 F9 **Tran** *var.* Trŭn. Pernik, W Bulgaria *42°51′N 22°37′E*
95 L18 **Tranås** Jönköping, S Sweden *58°03′N 15°00′E*
62 J7 **Trancas** Tucumán, N Argentina *26°11′S 65°20′W*
104 I7 **Trancoso** Guarda, N Portugal *40°46′N 07°21′W*
95 H22 **Tranebjerg** Midtjylland, C Denmark *55°51′N 10°36′E*
95 K19 **Tranemo** Västra Götaland, S Sweden *57°30′N 13°20′E*
167 N16 **Trang** Trang, S Thailand *07°33′N 99°36′E*
171 V15 **Trangan, Pulau** *island* Kepulauan Aru, E Indonesia
**Trang Dinh** *see* Thất Khê
183 Q7 **Trangie** New South Wales, SE Australia *32°01′S 147°58′E*
94 K12 **Trängslet** Dalarna, C Sweden *61°22′N 13°43′E*
107 N16 **Trani** Puglia, SE Italy *41°17′N 16°25′E*
61 F17 **Tranqueras** Rivera, NE Uruguay *31°13′S 55°45′W*
63 G17 **Tranqui, Isla** *island* S Chile
39 V6 **Trans-Alaska pipeline** *oil pipeline* Alaska, USA
195 Q10 **Transantarctic Mountains** ▲ Antarctica
**Transcarpathian Oblast** *see* Zakarpats'ka Oblast'
122 E9 **Trans-Siberian Railway** *Railroad* Russia
**Transilvania** *see* Transylvania
**Transilvaniei, Alpi** *see* Carpaţii Meridionali
**Transjordan** *see* Jordan
172 L11 **Transkei Basin** *undersea feature* SW Indian Ocean *35°30′S 29°00′E*
117 O10 **Transnistria** *cultural region* E Moldova
**Transsylvanische Alpen/Transylvanian Alps** *see* Carpaţii Meridionali
94 K12 **Transtrand** Dalarna, C Sweden *61°06′N 13°19′E*
116 G10 **Transylvania** *Eng.* Ardeal, Transilvania, *Ger.* Siebenbürgen, *Hung.* Erdély. *cultural region* NW Romania
167 S14 **Tra Ôn** Vinh Long, S Vietnam *09°58′N 105°58′E*
107 H23 **Trapani** *anc.* Drepanum. Sicilia, Italy, C Mediterranean Sea *38°02′N 12°32′E*
**Trâpeăng Vêng** *see* Kampong Thom
**Trapezus** *see* Trabzon
114 L9 **Trapoklovo** Sliven, C Bulgaria *42°40′N 26°36′E*
183 P13 **Traralgon** Victoria, SE Australia *38°15′S 146°36′E*
76 H9 **Trarza** ◈ *region* SW Mauritania
**Trasimenischersee** *see* Trasimeno, Lago
106 H12 **Trasimeno, Lago** *Eng.* Lake of Perugia, *Ger.* Trasimenischersee. ◎ C Italy
95 J20 **Träslövsläge** Halland, S Sweden *57°02′N 12°18′E*
**Trás-os-Montes** *see* Cucumbi
104 I6 **Trás-os-Montes e Alto Douro** *former province* N Portugal
167 Q12 **Trat** *var.* Bang Phra. Trat, S Thailand *12°16′N 102°30′E*
**Trá Tholl, Inis** *see* Inishtrahull
**Traù** *see* Trogir
109 T4 **Traun** Oberösterreich, N Austria *48°14′N 14°15′E*
109 S5 **Traun** ≈ N Austria
**Traun, Lake** *see* Traunsee
101 N23 **Traunreut** Bayern, SE Germany *47°58′N 12°36′E*
109 S5 **Traunsee** *var.* Gmundner See, *Eng.* Lake Traun. ◎ N Austria
**Trautenau** *see* Trutnov
21 P11 **Travelers Rest** South Carolina, SE USA *34°58′N 82°26′W*
182 L8 **Travellers Lake** *seasonal lake* New South Wales, SE Australia
31 P6 **Traverse City** Michigan, N USA *44°45′N 85°37′W*
29 R7 **Traverse, Lake** ◎ Minnesota/South Dakota, N USA
185 I16 **Travers, Mount** ▲ South Island, New Zealand *42°01′S 172°46′E*
11 P17 **Travers Reservoir** ⊠ Alberta, SW Canada
167 T14 **Tra Vinh** *var.* Phu Vinh. Tra Vinh, S Vietnam *09°57′N 106°20′E*
25 S10 **Travis, Lake** ⊠ Texas, SW USA
112 H12 **Travnik** Federacija Bosne I Hercegovine, C Bosnia and Herzegovina *44°14′N 17°40′E*
109 V11 **Trbovlje** *Ger.* Trifail. C Slovenia *46°10′N 15°03′E*
23 V13 **Treasure Island** Florida, SE USA *27°46′N 82°46′W*
**Treasure State** *see* Montana
186 I8 **Treasury Islands** *island group* NW Solomon Islands
106 D9 **Trebbia** *anc.* Trebia. ≈ NW Italy
100 N8 **Trebel** ≈ NE Germany
103 O16 **Trèbes** Aude, S France *43°12′N 02°26′E*
**Trebia** *see* Trebbia
111 F18 **Třebíč** *Ger.* Trebitsch. Vysočina, C Czechia *49°13′N 15°52′E*
113 I16 **Trebinje** Republika Srpska, S Bosnia and Herzegovina *42°42′N 18°19′E*
**Trebišnica** *see* Trebišnjica
113 H16 **Trebišnjica** *var.* Trebišnica. ≈ S Bosnia and Herzegovina
111 N20 **Trebišov** *Hung.* Tőketerebes. Košický Kraj, E Slovakia *48°37′N 21°44′E*
**Trebitsch** *see* Třebíč
**Trebizond** *see* Trabzon
**Trebnitz** *see* Trzebnica
109 V12 **Trebnje** SE Slovenia *45°54′N 15°01′E*
111 D19 **Třeboň** *Ger.* Wittingau. Jihočeský Kraj, S Czechia *49°00′N 14°46′E*
104 J15 **Trebujena** Andalucía, S Spain *36°52′N 06°11′W*
100 I7 **Treene** ≈ N Germany
**Tree Planters State** *see* Nebraska
109 S9 **Treffen** Kärnten, S Austria *46°40′N 13°51′E*
**Trefynwy** *see* Monmouth
102 G5 **Tréguier** Côtes d'Armor, NW France *48°50′N 03°12′W*
61 G18 **Treinta y Tres** Treinta y Tres, E Uruguay *33°16′S 54°17′W*
61 F18 **Treinta y Tres** ◈ *department* E Uruguay
122 F11 **Trëkhgornyy** Chelyabinskaya Oblast', C Russia *54°42′N 58°25′E*
114 F9 **Treklyanska Reka** ≈ W Bulgaria
102 K8 **Trélazé** Maine-et-Loire, NW France *47°27′N 00°28′W*
63 K17 **Trelew** Chubut, SE Argentina *43°13′S 65°15′W*
95 K23 **Trelleborg** *var.* Trälleborg. Skåne, S Sweden *55°22′N 13°10′E*
113 P15 **Trem** ▲ SE Serbia *43°10′N 22°12′E*
15 N11 **Tremblant, Mont** ▲ Québec, SE Canada *46°13′N 74°34′W*
99 H17 **Tremelo** Vlaams Brabant, C Belgium *51°N 04°34′E*
107 M15 **Tremiti, Isole** *island group* SE Italy
30 K12 **Tremont** Illinois, N USA *40°30′N 89°31′W*
36 L1 **Tremonton** Utah, W USA *41°42′N 112°09′W*
105 U4 **Tremp** Cataluña, NE Spain *42°09′N 00°53′E*
30 J7 **Trempealeau** Wisconsin, N USA *44°00′N 91°25′W*
15 P8 **Trenche** ≈ Québec, SE Canada
15 O7 **Trenche, Lac** ◎ Québec, SE Canada
111 I20 **Trenčiansky Kraj** ◈ *region* W Slovakia
111 I19 **Trenčín** *Ger.* Trentschin, *Hung.* Trencsén. Trenčiansky Kraj, W Slovakia *48°54′N 18°03′E*
**Trencsén** *see* Trenčín
**Trengganu** *see* Terengganu
**Trengganu, Kuala** *see* Kuala Terengganu
61 A21 **Trenque Lauquen** Buenos Aires, E Argentina *36°01′S 62°47′W*
14 J14 **Trent** ≈ Ontario, SE Canada
97 N18 **Trent** ≈ C England, United Kingdom
**Trent** *see* Trento
106 F5 **Trentino-Alto Adige** *Eng.* South Tyrol, *Ger.* Trentino-Südtirol; *prev.* Venezia Tridentina. ◈ *region* N Italy
**Trentino-Südtirol** *see* Trentino-Alto Adige
106 G6 **Trento** *Eng.* Trent, *Ger.* Trient; *anc.* Tridentum. Trentino-Alto Adige, N Italy *46°05′N 11°08′E*
14 J15 **Trenton** Ontario, SE Canada *44°07′N 77°34′W*
23 V10 **Trenton** Florida, SE USA *29°36′N 82°49′W*
23 R1 **Trenton** Georgia, SE USA *34°52′N 85°27′W*
31 S10 **Trenton** Michigan, N USA *42°08′N 83°10′W*
27 S2 **Trenton** Missouri, C USA *40°04′N 93°37′W*
28 M17 **Trenton** Nebraska, C USA *40°10′N 101°00′W*
18 J15 **Trenton** *state capital* New Jersey, NE USA *40°13′N 74°45′W*
21 W10 **Trenton** North Carolina, SE USA *35°03′N 77°20′W*
20 G9 **Trenton** Tennessee, S USA *35°59′N 88°59′W*
36 L1 **Trenton** Utah, W USA *41°53′N 111°57′W*
**Trentschin** *see* Trenčín
**Treptow an der Rega** *see* Trzebiatów
61 C23 **Tres Arroyos** Buenos Aires, E Argentina *38°22′S 60°17′W*
61 J15 **Três Cachoeiras** Rio Grande do Sul, S Brazil *29°21′S 49°48′W*
106 E7 **Trescore Balneario** Lombardia, N Italy *45°43′N 09°52′E*
41 V17 **Tres Cruces, Cerro** ▲ SE Mexico *15°28′N 92°27′W*
57 K18 **Tres Cruces, Cordillera** ▲ W Bolivia
113 N18 **Treska** ≈ NW North Macedonia
113 I14 **Treskavica** ▲ SE Bosnia and Herzegovina
59 J20 **Três Lagoas** Mato Grosso do Sul, SW Brazil *20°46′S 51°43′W*
40 H12 **Tres Marías, Islas** *island group* C Mexico
59 M19 **Três Marias, Represa** ⊠ SE Brazil
63 F20 **Tres Montes, Península** *headland* S Chile *46°49′S 75°29′W*
105 O3 **Trespaderne** Castilla y León, N Spain *42°47′N 03°24′W*
60 G13 **Três Passos** Rio Grande do Sul, S Brazil *27°33′S 53°55′W*
61 A23 **Tres Picos, Cerro** ▲ E Argentina *38°10′S 61°54′W*
63 G17 **Tres Picos, Cerro** ▲ SW Argentina *42°22′S 71°51′W*
60 I12 **Três Pinheiros** Paraná, S Brazil *25°25′S 51°57′W*
59 M21 **Três Pontas** Minas Gerais, SE Brazil *21°33′S 45°18′W*
**Tres Puntas, Cabo** *see* Manabique, Punta
60 P9 **Três Rios** Rio de Janeiro, SE Brazil *22°06′S 43°15′W*
**Tres Tabernae** *see* Saverne
**Trestenberg/Trestendorf** *see* Tăşnad
41 R15 **Tres Valles** Veracruz, SE Mexico *18°14′N 96°03′W*
94 H12 **Tretten** Oppland, S Norway *61°19′N 10°19′E*
**Treuburg** *see* Olecko
101 K21 **Treuchtlingen** Bayern, S Germany *48°57′N 10°55′E*
100 N13 **Treuenbrietzen** Brandenburg, E Germany *52°06′N 12°52′E*
63 H17 **Trevelín** Chubut, SW Argentina *43°02′S 71°27′W*
**Treves/Trèves** *see* Trier
106 I13 **Trevi** Umbria, C Italy *42°52′N 12°46′E*
106 E7 **Treviglio** Lombardia, N Italy *45°32′N 09°35′E*
104 J4 **Trevinca, Peña** ▲ NW Spain *42°10′N 06°49′W*
105 P3 **Treviño** Castilla y León, N Spain *42°45′N 02°41′W*
106 I7 **Treviso** *anc.* Tarvisium. Veneto, NE Italy *45°40′N 12°15′E*
97 G24 **Trevose Head** *headland* SW England, United Kingdom *50°33′N 05°03′W*
**Trg** *see* Feldkirchen in Kärnten
183 P17 **Triabunna** Tasmania, SE Australia *42°33′S 147°55′E*
21 W4 **Triangle** Virginia, NE USA *38°30′N 77°17′W*
83 L18 **Triangle** Masvingo, SE Zimbabwe *20°58′S 31°28′E*
115 L23 **Tría Nisía** *island* Kykládes, Greece, Aegean Sea
**Triberg** *see* Triberg im Schwarzwald
101 G23 **Triberg im Schwarzwald** *var.* Triberg. Baden-Württemberg, SW Germany *48°07′N 08°13′E*
153 P11 **Tribhuvan** ✈ (Kathmandu) Central, C Nepal
54 C9 **Tribugá, Golfo de** *gulf* W Colombia
181 W4 **Tribulation, Cape** *headland* Queensland, NE Australia *16°14′S 145°48′E*
108 M8 **Tribulaun** ▲ SW Austria *46°59′N 11°18′E*
11 U17 **Tribune** Saskatchewan, S Canada *49°16′N 103°50′W*
26 H5 **Tribune** Kansas, C USA *38°27′N 101°46′W*
107 N18 **Tricarico** Basilicata, S Italy *40°37′N 16°09′E*
107 Q19 **Tricase** Puglia, SE Italy *39°56′N 18°21′E*
**Trichinopoly** *see* Tiruchchirappalli
115 D18 **Trichonída, Límni** ◎ C Greece
**Trichūr** *see* Thrissur
**Tricorno** *see* Triglav
183 O8 **Trida** New South Wales, SE Australia *33°02′S 145°03′E*
35 S1 **Trident Peak** ▲ Nevada, W USA *41°52′N 118°22′W*
**Tridentum/Trient** *see* Trento
109 T6 **Trieben** Steiermark, SE Austria *47°29′N 14°30′E*
101 D19 **Trier** *Eng.* Treves, *Fr.* Trèves; *anc.* Augusta Treverorum. Rheinland-Pfalz, SW Germany *49°45′N 06°39′E*
106 K7 **Trieste** *Slvn.* Trst. Friuli-Venezia Giulia, NE Italy *45°39′N 13°45′E*
**Trieste, Golfo di/Triest, Golf von** *see* Trieste, Gulf of
106 J8 **Trieste, Gulf of** *Cro.* Tršćanski Zaljev, *Ger.* Golf von Triest, *It.* Golfo di Trieste, *Slvn.* Tržaški Zaliv. *gulf* S Europe
109 W4 **Triesting** ≈ W Austria
**Triều Hai** *see* Quang Tri
**Trifail** *see* Trbovlje
116 L9 **Trifeşti** Iaşi, NE Romania *47°30′N 27°31′E*
109 S10 **Triglav** *It.* Tricorno. ▲ NW Slovenia *46°22′N 13°40′E*
104 I14 **Trigueros** Andalucía, S Spain *37°24′N 06°50′W*
115 E16 **Tríkala** *prev.* Trikkala. Thessalía, C Greece *39°33′N 21°46′E*
115 E17 **Trikeriótis** ≈ C Greece
**Trikkala** *see* Tríkala
97 F17 **Trim** *Ir.* Baile Átha Troim. Meath, E Ireland *53°34′N 06°47′W*
108 E7 **Trimbach** Solothurn, NW Switzerland *47°22′N 07°53′E*
109 Q5 **Trimmelkam** Oberösterreich, N Austria *48°02′N 12°55′E*
29 U11 **Trimont** Minnesota, N USA *43°45′N 94°42′W*
**Trimontium** *see* Plovdiv
**Trinacria** *see* Sicilia
155 K24 **Trincomalee** *var.* Trinkomali. Eastern Province, NE Sri Lanka *08°34′N 81°13′E*
65 K16 **Trindade, Ilha da** *island* Brazil, W Atlantic Ocean
47 Y9 **Trindade Spur** *undersea feature* SW Atlantic Ocean *21°00′S 35°00′W*
111 J17 **Třinec** *Ger.* Trzynietz. Moravskoslezský Kraj, E Czechia *49°41′N 18°39′E*
57 M16 **Trinidad** Beni, N Bolivia *14°52′S 64°54′W*
54 H9 **Trinidad** Casanare, E Colombia *05°25′N 71°39′W*
44 E6 **Trinidad** Sancti Spíritus, C Cuba *21°48′N 80°00′W*
61 E19 **Trinidad** Flores, S Uruguay *33°35′S 56°54′W*
37 U8 **Trinidad** Colorado, C USA *37°11′N 104°31′W*
45 Y17 **Trinidad** *island* C Trinidad and Tobago
**Trinidad** *see* Jose Abad Santos
45 Y16 **Trinidad and Tobago** *off.* Republic of Trinidad and Tobago. ◆ *republic* SE West Indies
**Trinidad and Tobago, Republic of** *see* Trinidad and Tobago
63 F22 **Trinidad, Golfo** *gulf* S Chile
61 B24 **Trinidad, Isla** *island* E Argentina
107 N16 **Trinitapoli** Puglia, SE Italy *41°22′N 16°06′E*
55 X10 **Trinité, Montagnes de la** ▲ C French Guiana
25 W9 **Trinity** Texas, SW USA *30°57′N 95°22′W*
13 U12 **Trinity Bay** *inlet* Newfoundland, Newfoundland and Labrador, E Canada
39 P15 **Trinity Islands** *island group* Alaska, USA
35 N2 **Trinity Mountains** ▲ California, W USA
35 S4 **Trinity Peak** ▲ Nevada, W USA *40°13′N 118°43′W*
35 S5 **Trinity Range** ▲ Nevada, W USA
35 N2 **Trinity River** ≈ California, W USA
25 V8 **Trinity River** ≈ Texas, SW USA
**Trinkomali** *see* Trincomalee
173 Y15 **Triolet** NW Mauritius *20°05′S 57°32′E*
107 O20 **Trionto, Capo** *headland* S Italy *39°37′N 16°46′E*
**Tripiti, Ákra** *see* Trypití, Akrotírio
115 F20 **Trípoli** *prev.* Trípolis. Pelopónnisos, S Greece *37°31′N 22°22′E*
138 G6 **Tripoli** *var.* Tarābulus, Ţarābulus ash Shām, Trâblous; *anc.* Tripolis. N Lebanon *34°30′N 35°42′E*
29 X12 **Tripoli** Iowa, C USA *42°48′N 92°15′W*
**Tripoli** *see* Ţarābulus
**Trípolis** *see* Trípoli, Greece
**Tripolis** *see* Tripoli, Lebanon
75 N8 **Tripolitania** ◈ *cultural region* NW Libya
29 Q12 **Tripp** South Dakota, N USA *43°12′N 97°57′W*
153 V15 **Tripura** *var.* Hill Tippera. ◈ *state* NE India
108 K8 **Trisanna** ≈ W Austria
100 H8 **Trischen** *island* NW Germany
**Tristan da Cunha** ◇ *dependency of Saint Helena* SE Atlantic Ocean
67 P15 **Tristan da Cunha** *island* SE Atlantic Ocean
**Tristan da Cunha** *see* Saint Helena, Ascension and Tristan da Cunha
65 L18 **Tristan da Cunha Fracture Zone** *tectonic feature* S Atlantic Ocean
167 S14 **Tri Tôn** An Giang, S Vietnam *10°26′N 105°01′E*
**Tri Tôn, Đao** *see* Triton Island
167 W10 **Triton Island** *Chin.* Zhongjian Dao, *Viet.* Đao Tri Tôn. *island* S Paracel Islands
**Trivandrum** *see* Thiruvananthapuram
111 H20 **Trnava** *Ger.* Tyrnau, *Hung.* Nagyszombat. Trnavský Kraj, W Slovakia *48°22′N 17°36′E*
111 H20 **Trnavský Kraj** ◈ *region* W Slovakia
**Trnovo** *see* Veliko Tarnovo
**Trobriand Island** *see* Kiriwina Island
**Trobriand Islands** *see* Kiriwina Islands
11 Q16 **Trochu** Alberta, SW Canada *51°48′N 113°12′W*
109 U7 **Trofaiach** Steiermark, SE Austria *47°25′N 15°01′E*
93 F14 **Trofors** Troms, N Norway *65°31′N 13°19′E*
113 E14 **Trogir** *It.* Traù. Split-Dalmacija, S Croatia *43°32′N 16°13′E*
112 F13 **Troglav** ▲ Bosnia and Herzegovina/Croatia *44°00′N 16°36′E*
107 M16 **Troia** Puglia, SE Italy *41°21′N 15°19′E*
107 K24 **Troina** Sicilia, Italy, C Mediterranean Sea *37°47′N 14°37′E*
173 O16 **Trois-Bassins** W Réunion *21°05′S 55°18′E*
101 E17 **Troisdorf** Nordrhein-Westfalen, W Germany *50°49′N 07°09′E*
74 H5 **Trois Fourches, Cap des** *headland* NE Morocco *35°27′N 02°58′W*
15 T8 **Trois-Pistoles** Québec, SE Canada *48°08′N 69°10′W*
99 L21 **Trois-Ponts** Liège, E Belgium *50°22′N 05°52′E*
15 P11 **Trois-Rivières** Québec, SE Canada *46°21′N 72°34′W*
55 Y12 **Trois Sauts** S French Guiana *02°15′N 52°52′W*
99 M22 **Troisvierges** Diekirch, N Luxembourg *50°07′N 06°00′E*
122 F11 **Troitsk** Chelyabinskaya Oblast', S Russia *54°04′N 61°31′E*
125 T9 **Troitsko-Pechorsk** Respublika Komi, NW Russia *62°39′N 56°06′E*
127 V7 **Troitskoye** Orenburgskaya Oblast', W Russia *52°23′N 56°24′E*
**Troki** *see* Trakai
195 Q2 **Troll** *research station (Norway)* Antarctica *70°00′S 02°32′E*
94 F9 **Trolla** ▲ S Norway *62°41′N 09°47′E*
95 J18 **Trollhättan** Västra Götaland, S Sweden *58°17′N 12°20′E*
94 G9 **Trollheimen** ▲ S Norway
94 E9 **Trolltindane** ▲ S Norway *62°30′N 07°43′E*
58 H11 **Trombetas, Rio** ≈ NE Brazil
128 L16 **Tromelin, Île** *island* W Indian Ocean
92 I9 **Troms** ◇ *county* N Norway
92 I9 **Tromsø** *Fin.* Tromssa. Troms, N Norway *69°39′N 19°01′E*
84 F5 **Tromsøflaket** *undersea feature* W Barents Sea *18°30′E 71°30′N*
**Tromssa** *see* Tromsø
94 H10 **Tron** ▲ S Norway *62°12′N 10°46′E*
35 U12 **Trona** California, W USA *35°46′N 117°21′W*
63 G16 **Tronador, Cerro** ▲ S Chile *41°12′S 71°51′W*
94 H8 **Trondheim** *Ger.* Drontheim; *prev.* Nidaros, Trondhjem. Sør-Trøndelag, S Norway *63°25′N 10°24′E*
94 H7 **Trondheimsfjorden** *fjord* S Norway
**Trondhjem** *see* Trondheim
107 J14 **Tronto** ≈ C Italy
121 P3 **Troódos** *var.* Troodos Mountains. ▲ C Cyprus
**Troodos** *see* Ólympos
**Troodos Mountains** *see* Troódos
96 I13 **Troon** W Scotland, United Kingdom *55°32′N 04°41′W*
107 M22 **Tropea** Calabria, SW Italy *38°40′N 15°52′E*
36 L7 **Tropic** Utah, W USA *37°37′N 112°04′W*


◆ Country ● Country Capital ◇ Dependent Territory ○ Dependent Territory Capital ◈ Administrative Regions ✈ International Airport ▲ Mountain ▲ Mountain Range Volcano ≈ River ◎ Lake ⊠ Reservoir

TROPIC SEAMOUNT – TURKS AND CAICOS ISLANDS

64 L10 **Tropic Seamount** *var.* Banc du Tropique. *undersea feature* E Atlantic Ocean *23°50′N 20°40′W*
**Tropique, Banc du** *see* Tropic Seamount
**Tropoja** *see* Tropojë
113 L17 **Tropojë** *var.* Tropoja. Kukës, N Albania *42°25′N 20°09′E*
**Troppau** *see* Opava
95 O16 **Trosa** Södermanland, C Sweden *58°54′N 17°35′E*
118 H12 **Troškūnai** Utena, E Lithuania *55°36′N 24°55′E*
101 G23 **Trossingen** Baden-Württemberg, SW Germany *48°04′N 08°37′E*
117 T4 **Trostyanets'** *Rus.* Trostyanets. Sums'ka Oblast', NE Ukraine *50°30′N 34°59′E*
117 N7 **Trostyanets'** *Rus.* Trostyanets. Vinnyts'ka Oblast', C Ukraine *48°35′N 29°10′E*
**Trostyanets** *see* Trostyanets'
116 L11 **Trotuș** ≈ E Romania
44 M8 **Trou-du-Nord** N Haiti *19°34′N 71°57′W*
25 W7 **Troup** Texas, SW USA *32°08′N 95°07′W*
8 I10 **Trout** ≈ Northwest Territories, NW Canada
33 N8 **Trout Creek** Montana, NW USA *47°51′N 115°40′W*
32 H10 **Trout Lake** Washington, NW USA *45°59′N 121°33′W*
12 B9 **Trout Lake** ◎ Ontario, S Canada
33 T12 **Trout Peak** ▲ Wyoming, C USA *44°36′N 109°33′W*
102 L4 **Trouville** Calvados, N France *49°21′N 00°07′E*
97 L22 **Trowbridge** S England, United Kingdom *51°20′N 02°13′W*
23 Q6 **Troy** Alabama, S USA *31°48′N 85°58′W*
27 Q3 **Troy** Kansas, C USA *39°45′N 95°06′W*
27 W4 **Troy** Missouri, C USA *38°59′N 90°59′W*
18 L10 **Troy** New York, NE USA *42°43′N 73°37′W*
21 S10 **Troy** North Carolina, SE USA *35°23′N 79°54′W*
31 R13 **Troy** Ohio, N USA *40°02′N 84°12′W*
25 T9 **Troy** Texas, SW USA *31°12′N 97°18′W*
114 I9 **Troyan** Lovech, N Bulgaria *42°52′N 24°42′E*
114 I9 **Troyanski Prohod** *var.* Troyanski Prokhod. *pass* N Bulgaria
**Troyanski Prokhod** *see* Troyanski Prohod
145 N6 **Troyebratskiy** Severnyy Kazakhstan, N Kazakhstan *54°25′N 66°03′E*
103 Q6 **Troyes** *anc.* Augustobona Tricassium. Aube, N France *48°18′N 04°04′E*
117 X5 **Troyits'ke** Luhans'ka Oblast', E Ukraine *49°55′N 38°18′E*
35 W7 **Troy Peak** ▲ Nevada, W USA *38°18′N 115°27′W*
113 G15 **Trpanj** Dubrovnik-Neretva, S Croatia *43°00′N 17°18′E*
**Tršćanski Zaljev** *see* Trieste, Gulf of
**Trst** *see* Trieste
113 N14 **Trstenik** Serbia, C Serbia *43°38′N 21°01′E*
126 I6 **Trubchevsk** Bryanskaya Oblast', W Russia *52°33′N 33°45′E*
**Trubchular** *see* Orlyak
37 S10 **Truchas Peak** ▲ New Mexico, SW USA *35°57′N 105°38′W*
143 P16 **Trucial Coast** *physical region* C United Arab Emirates
**Trucial States** *see* United Arab Emirates
35 Q6 **Truckee** California, W USA *39°18′N 120°10′W*
35 R5 **Truckee River** ≈ Nevada, W USA
127 Q13 **Trudfront** Astrakhanskaya Oblast', SW Russia *45°56′N 47°42′E*
14 I9 **Truite, Lac à la** ◎ Québec, SE Canada
42 K4 **Trujillo** Colón, NE Honduras *15°59′N 85°54′W*
56 C12 **Trujillo** La Libertad, NW Peru *08°04′S 79°02′W*
104 K10 **Trujillo** Extremadura, W Spain *39°28′N 05°53′W*
54 I6 **Trujillo** Trujillo, NW Venezuela *09°20′N 70°38′W*
54 I6 **Trujillo** *off.* Estado Trujillo. ◈ *state* W Venezuela
**Trujillo, Estado** *see* Trujillo
**Truk** *see* Chuuk
**Truk Islands** *see* Chuuk Islands
29 U10 **Truman** Minnesota, N USA *43°49′N 94°26′W*
27 X10 **Trumann** Arkansas, C USA *35°40′N 90°30′W*
36 J9 **Trumbull, Mount** ▲ Arizona, SW USA *36°22′N 113°09′W*
**Trŭn** *see* Tran
183 Q8 **Trundle** New South Wales, SE Australia *32°55′S 147°43′E*
129 U13 **Trung Phân** *physical region* S Vietnam
**Tr ng Sa L n, Đao** *see* Spratly Island
**Tr ng Sa, Qu n Đ o** *see* Spratly Islands
**Trupcilar** *see* Orlyak
13 Q15 **Truro** Nova Scotia, SE Canada *45°24′N 63°18′W*
97 H25 **Truro** SW England, United Kingdom *50°16′N 05°03′W*
25 P5 **Truscott** Texas, SW USA *33°43′N 99°48′W*
116 K9 **Trușești** Botoșani, NE Romania *47°45′N 27°01′E*
116 H6 **Truskavets'** L'vivs'ka Oblast', W Ukraine *49°15′N 23°30′E*
95 H22 **Trustrup** Midtjylland, C Denmark *56°20′N 10°46′E*
10 M11 **Trutch** British Columbia, W Canada *57°42′N 123°00′W*
37 Q14 **Truth Or Consequences** New Mexico, SW USA *33°07′N 107°15′W*
111 F15 **Trutnov** *Ger.* Trautenau. Královéhradecký Kraj, N Czechia *50°34′N 15°55′E*
103 P13 **Truyère** ≈ C France
114 K9 **Tryavna** Lovech, N Bulgaria *42°52′N 25°30′E*
28 M14 **Tryon** Nebraska, C USA *41°33′N 100°57′W*
115 J16 **Trypiti, Akrotírio** *var.* Ákra Tripití. *headland* Ágios Efstrátios, E Greece *39°28′N 24°58′E*
94 J12 **Trysil** Hedmark, S Norway *61°18′N 12°16′E*
94 I11 **Trysilelva** ≈ S Norway
112 D10 **Tržac** Federacija Bosne I Hercegovine, NW Bosnia and Herzegovina *44°58′N 15°48′E*
**Tržaški Zaliv** *see* Trieste, Gulf of
110 G10 **Trzcianka** *Ger.* Schönlanke. Pila, Wielkopolskie, C Poland *53°02′N 16°24′E*
110 E7 **Trzebiatów** *Ger.* Treptow an der Rega. Zachodnio-pomorskie, NW Poland *54°04′N 15°14′E*
111 G14 **Trzebnica** *Ger.* Trebnitz. Dolnośląskie, SW Poland *51°19′N 17°03′E*
109 T10 **Tržič** *Ger.* Neumarktl. NW Slovenia *46°22′N 14°17′E*
**Trzynietz** *see* Třinec
83 G21 **Tsabong** *var.* Tshabong. Kgalagadi, SW Botswana *26°03′S 22°27′E*
162 G7 **Tsagaanchuluut** Dzavhan, C Mongolia *47°06′N 96°40′E*
162 M8 **Tsagaandelger** *var.* Haraat. Dundgovĭ, C Mongolia *46°30′N 107°39′E*
**Tsagaanders** *see* Bayantümen
162 G7 **Tsagaanhayrhan** *var.* Shiree. Dzavhan, W Mongolia *47°30′N 96°48′E*
**Tsagaannuur** *see* Halhgol
**Tsagaan-Olom** *see* Tayshir
**Tsagaan-Ovoo** *see* Nariynteel
**Tsagaantüngi** *see* Altantsögts
162 H6 **Tsagaan-Uul** *var.* Sharga. Hövsgöl, N Mongolia *49°33′N 98°36′E*
162 J5 **Tsagaan-Üür** *var.* Bulgan. Hövsgöl, N Mongolia *50°30′N 101°28′E*
127 P12 **Tsagan Aman** Respublika Kalmykiya, SW Russia *47°37′N 46°43′E*
23 V11 **Tsala Apopka Lake** ◎ Florida, SE USA
**Tsamkong** *see* Zhanjiang
**Tsangpo** *see* Brahmaputra
**Tsant** *see* Deren
**Tsao** *see* Tsau
172 I4 **Tsaratanana** Mahajanga, C Madagascar *16°46′S 47°40′E*
114 N10 **Tsarevo** *prev.* Michurin. Burgas, E Bulgaria *42°10′N 27°51′E*
**Tsarigrad** *see* Istanbul
**Tsaritsyn** *see* Volgograd
114 K7 **Tsar Kaloyan** Ruse, N Bulgaria *43°36′N 26°14′E*
**Tsarskoye Selo** *see* Pushkin
117 T7 **Tsarychanka** Dnipropetrovs'ka Oblast', E Ukraine *48°56′N 34°29′E*
83 H21 **Tsatsu** Southern, S Botswana *25°21′S 24°45′E*
83 G17 **Tsau** *var.* Tsao. Ngamiland, NW Botswana *20°08′S 22°29′E*
81 J20 **Tsavo** Taita/Taveta, S Kenya *02°59′S 38°28′E*
83 E21 **Tsawisis** //Karas, S Namibia *26°18′S 18°09′E*
**Tschakathurn** *see* Čakovec
**Tschaslau** *see* Čáslav
**Tschenstochau** *see* Częstochowa
**Tschernembl** *see* Črnomelj
28 K6 **Tschida, Lake** ⊠ North Dakota, N USA
**Tschorna** *see* Mustvee
162 G8 **Tseel** Govĭ-Altay, SW Mongolia *45°45′N 95°54′E*
138 G8 **Tsefat** *var.* Safed, *Ar.* Safad; *prev.* Zefat. Northern, N Israel *32°57′N 35°27′E*
126 M13 **Tselina** Rostovskaya Oblast', SW Russia *46°31′N 41°01′E*
**Tselinograd** *see* Nur-Sultan
**Tselinogradskaya Oblast** *see* Akmola
**Tsengel** *see* Tosontsengel
162 J8 **Tsenher** *var.* Altan-Ovoo. Arhangay, C Mongolia *47°24′N 101°51′E*
**Tsenher** *see* Mönhhayrhan
163 N8 **Tsenhermandal** *var.* Modot. Hentiy, C Mongolia *47°45′N 109°03′E*
**Tsentral'nyye Nizmennyye Garagumy** *see* Merkezi Garagumy
83 E21 **Tses** //Karas, S Namibia *25°58′S 18°08′E*
**Tseshevlya** *see* Tsyeshawlya
162 E7 **Tsetseg** *var.* Tsetsegnuur. Hovd, W Mongolia *46°30′N 93°16′E*
**Tsetsegnuur** *see* Tsetseg
**Tsetsen Khan** *see* Öndörhaan
162 J8 **Tsetserleg** Arhangay, C Mongolia *47°29′N 101°19′E*
162 H6 **Tsetserleg** *var.* Halban. Hövsgöl, N Mongolia *49°30′N 97°33′E*
162 J8 **Tsetserleg** *var.* Hujirt. Övörhangay, C Mongolia *46°50′N 102°38′E*
77 R16 **Tsévié** S Togo *06°25′N 01°13′E*
**Tshabong** *see* Tsabong
83 G20 **Tshane** Kgalagadi, SW Botswana *24°05′S 21°54′E*
**Tshangalele, Lac** *see* Lufira, Lac de Retenue de la
83 H17 **Tshauxaba** Central, C Botswana *19°56′S 25°09′E*
79 F21 **Tshela** Bas-Congo, W Dem. Rep. Congo *04°56′S 13°02′E*
79 K22 **Tshibala** Kasai-Occidental, S Dem. Rep. Congo *06°53′S 22°01′E*
79 J22 **Tshikapa** Kasai-Occidental, SW Dem. Rep. Congo *06°23′S 20°47′E*
79 L22 **Tshilenge** Kasai Oriental , S Dem. Rep. Congo *06°17′S 23°48′E*
79 L24 **Tshimbalanga** Katanga. S Dem. Rep. Congo *09°42′S 23°04′E*
79 L22 **Tshimbulu** Kasai-Occidental, S Dem. Rep. Congo *06°27′S 22°54′E*
**Tshiumbe** *see* Chiumbe
79 M21 **Tshofa** Kasai-Oriental, C Dem. Rep. Congo *05°13′S 25°13′E*
79 K18 **Tshuapa** ≈ C Dem. Rep. Congo
114 G7 **Tsibritsa** ≈ NW Bulgaria
**Tsien Tang** *see* Fuchun Jiang
114 I12 **Tsiganško Gradishte** *Gr.* Giftokastro. ▲ Bulgaria/Greece *41°24′N 24°41′E*
**Tsihombe** *see* Tsiombe
8 H7 **Tsiigehtchic** *prev.* Arctic Red River. Northwest Territories, NW Canada *67°24′N 133°40′W*
125 Q7 **Tsil'ma** ≈ NW Russia
119 J17 **Tsimkavichy** *Rus.* Timkovichi. Minskaya Voblasts', C Belarus *53°04′N 26°59′E*
126 M11 **Tsimlyansk** Rostovskaya Oblast', SW Russia *47°39′N 42°05′E*
127 N11 **Tsimlyanskoye Vodokhranilishche** *var.* Tsimlyansk Vodoskhovshche, *Eng.* Tsimlyansk Reservoir. ⊠ SW Russia
**Tsimlyansk Reservoir** *see* Tsimlyanskoye Vodokhranilishche
**Tsimlyansk Vodoskhovshche** *see* Tsimlyanskoye Vodokhranilishche
**Tsinan** *see* Jinan
**Tsing Hai** *see* Qinghai Hu, China
**Tsinghai** *see* Qinghai, China
**Tsingtao/Tsingtau** *see* Qingdao
**Tsingyuan** *see* Baoding
**Tsinkiang** *see* Quanzhou
**Tsintao** *see* Qingdao
83 D17 **Tsintsabis** Oshikoto, N Namibia *18°45′S 17°51′E*
172 H8 **Tsiombe** *var.* Tsihombe. Toliara, S Madagascar
123 O13 **Tsipa** ≈ S Russia
172 H5 **Tsiribihina** ≈ W Madagascar
172 I5 **Tsiroanomandidy** Antananarivo, C Madagascar *18°44′S 46°02′E*
189 U13 **Tsis** *island* Chuuk, C Micronesia
**Tsitsihar** *see* Qiqihar
127 Q3 **Tsivil'sk** Chuvashskaya Respublika, W Russia *55°51′N 47°30′E*
137 T9 **Tskhinvali** *prev.* Staliniri, Ts'khinvali. C Georgia *42°12′N 43°58′E*
119 J19 **Tsna** ≈ SW Belarus
124 M15 **Tsna** *var.* Zna. ≈ W Russia
162 G9 **Tsogt** *var.* Tahilt. Govĭ-Altay, W Mongolia *45°20′N 96°42′E*
162 K10 **Tsogt-Ovoo** *var.* Doloon. Ömnögovĭ, S Mongolia *44°28′N 105°22′E*
162 L10 **Tsogttsetsiy** *var.* Baruunsuu. Ömnögovĭ, S Mongolia *43°46′N 105°28′E*
114 M9 **Tsonevo, Yazovir** *prev.* Yazovir Georgi Traykov. ⊠ NE Bulgaria
**Tsoohor** *see* Hürmen
164 K14 **Tsu** *var.* Tu. Mie, Honshū, SW Japan *34°41′N 136°30′E*
165 O10 **Tsubame** *var.* Tubame. Niigata, Honshū, C Japan *37°40′N 138°56′E*
165 V3 **Tsubetsu** Hokkaidō, NE Japan *43°43′N 144°01′E*
165 O13 **Tsuchiura** *var.* Tutiura. Ibaraki, Honshū, S Japan *36°05′N 140°11′E*
165 Q6 **Tsugaru-kaikyō** *strait* N Japan
164 E14 **Tsukumi** *var.* Tukumi. Ōita, Kyūshū, SW Japan *33°00′N 131°51′E*
**Tsul-Ulaan** *see* Bayannuur
**Tsul-Ulaan** *see* Bayanuur
83 D17 **Tsumeb** Oshikoto, N Namibia *19°13′S 17°42′E*
83 F17 **Tsumkwe** Otjozondjupa, NE Namibia *19°37′S 20°30′E*
164 D15 **Tsuno** Miyazaki, Kyūshū, SW Japan *32°43′N 131°32′E*
164 D12 **Tsuno-shima** *island* SW Japan
164 K12 **Tsuruga** *var.* Turuga. Fukui, Honshū, SW Japan *35°38′N 136°01′E*
164 H12 **Tsurugi-san** ▲ Shikoku, SW Japan *33°50′N 134°04′E*
165 P9 **Tsuruoka** *var.* Turuoka. Yamagata, Honshū, C Japan *38°44′N 139°48′E*
164 C12 **Tsushima** *prev.* Izuhara. Nagasaki, Tsushima, SW Japan *34°11′N 129°16′E*
164 C12 **Tsushima** *var.* Tsusima. *island group* SW Japan
**Tsushima-tō** *see* Tsushima
164 H12 **Tsuyama** *var.* Tuyama. Okayama, Honshū, SW Japan *35°04′N 134°01′E*
83 G19 **Tswaane** Ghanzi, W Botswana *22°21′S 21°52′E*
119 N16 **Tsyakhtsin** *Rus.* Tekhtin. Mahilyowskaya Voblasts', E Belarus *53°51′N 29°44′E*
119 P19 **Tsyerakhowka** *Rus.* Terekhovka. Homyel'skaya Voblasts', SE Belarus *52°13′N 31°24′E*
119 I17 **Tsyeshawlya** *prev.* Cheshevlya, Tseshevlya, *Rus.* Teshevle. Brestskaya Voblasts', SW Belarus *53°14′N 25°49′E*
**Tsyurupyns'k** *see* Oleshky
**Tu** *see* Tsu
186 C7 **Tua** ≈ C Papua New Guinea
**Tuaim** *see* Tuam
184 L6 **Tuakau** Waikato, North Island, New Zealand *37°16′S 174°56′E*
97 C17 **Tuam** *Ir.* Tuaim. Galway, W Ireland *53°31′N 08°50′W*
185 K14 **Tuamarina** Marlborough, South Island, New Zealand *41°27′S 174°00′E*
**Tuamotu, Archipel des** *see* Tuamotu, Îles
193 Q9 **Tuamotu Fracture Zone** *tectonic feature* E Pacific Ocean
191 W9 **Tuamotu, Îles** *var.* Archipel des Tuamotu, Dangerous Archipelago, Tuamotu Islands. *island group* N French Polynesia
**Tuamotu Islands** *see* Tuamotu, Îles
175 X10 **Tuamotu Ridge** *undersea feature* C Pacific Ocean
167 R5 **Tuân Giao** Lai Châu, N Vietnam *21°34′N 103°24′E*
171 O2 **Tuao** Luzon, N Philippines *17°42′N 121°25′E*
190 B15 **Tuapa** NW Niue *18°57′S 169°59′W*
43 N7 **Tuapí** Costa Caribe Norte, NE Nicaragua *14°10′N 83°20′W*
126 K15 **Tuapse** Krasnodarskiy Kray, SW Russia *44°08′N 39°07′E*
169 U6 **Tuaran** Sabah, East Malaysia *06°12′N 116°12′E*
104 I6 **Tua, Rio** ≈ N Portugal
192 H15 **Tuasivi** Savai'i, C Samoa *13°38′S 172°08′W*
185 B24 **Tuatapere** Southland, South Island, New Zealand *46°09′S 167°43′E*
36 M9 **Tuba City** Arizona, SW USA *36°08′N 111°14′W*
138 H11 **Ţubah, Qaşr aţ** *castle* 'Ammān, C Jordan
**Tubame** *see* Tsubame
169 R16 **Tuban** *prev.* Toeban. Jawa, C Indonesia *06°55′S 112°01′E*
141 O16 **Tuban, Wādī** *dry watercourse* SW Yemen
61 K14 **Tubarão** Santa Catarina, S Brazil *28°29′S 49°00′W*
98 O10 **Tubbergen** Overijssel, E Netherlands *52°25′N 06°46′E*
**Tubeke** *see* Tubize
101 H22 **Tübingen** *var.* Tuebingen. Baden-Württemberg, SW Germany *48°32′N 09°04′E*
127 W6 **Tubinskiy** Respublika Bashkortostan, W Russia *52°48′N 58°18′E*
99 G19 **Tubize** *Dut.* Tubeke. Walloon Brabant, C Belgium *50°43′N 04°14′E*
76 J16 **Tubmanburg** NW Liberia *06°50′N 10°53′W*
75 T7 **Ţubruq** *Eng.* Tobruk, *It.* Tobruch. NE Libya *32°05′N 23°59′E*
191 T13 **Tubuai** *island* Îles Australes, SW French Polynesia
**Tubuai, Îles/Tubuai Islands** *see* Australes, Îles
**Tubuai-Manu** *see* Maiao
40 F3 **Tubutama** Sonora, NW Mexico *30°51′N 111°31′W*
54 K4 **Tucacas** Falcón, N Venezuela *10°50′N 68°22′W*
59 P16 **Tucano** Bahia, E Brazil *10°52′S 38°48′W*
57 P19 **Tucavaca, Río** ≈ E Bolivia
110 H8 **Tuchola** Kujawsko-pomorskie, C Poland *53°36′N 17°50′E*
111 M17 **Tuchów** Małopolskie, S Poland *49°53′N 21°04′E*
23 S3 **Tucker** Georgia, SE USA *33°53′N 84°10′W*
27 W10 **Tuckerman** Arkansas, C USA *35°43′N 91°12′W*
64 B12 **Tucker's Town** E Bermuda *32°20′N 64°42′W*
**Tuckum** *see* Tukums
36 M15 **Tucson** Arizona, SW USA *32°14′N 111°01′W*
62 J7 **Tucumán** *off.* Provincia de Tucumán. ◈ *province* N Argentina
**Tucumán** *see* San Miguel de Tucumán
**Tucumán, Provincia de** *see* Tucumán
37 V11 **Tucumcari** New Mexico, SW USA *35°10′N 103°43′W*
58 H13 **Tucunaré** Pará, N Brazil *05°15′S 55°49′W*
55 Q6 **Tucupita** Delta Amacuro, NE Venezuela *09°02′N 62°04′W*
58 K13 **Tucuruí, Represa de** ⊠ NE Brazil
110 F9 **Tuczno** Zachodnio-pomorskie, NW Poland *53°12′N 16°08′E*
**Tuddo** *see* Tudu
105 Q5 **Tudela** *Basq.* Tutera; *anc.* Tutela. Navarra, N Spain *42°04′N 01°37′W*
104 M6 **Tudela de Duero** Castilla y León, N Spain *41°35′N 04°34′W*
162 G6 **Tüdevtey** *var.* Oygon. Dzavhan, N Mongolia *48°57′N 96°33′E*
118 J4 **Tudu** *Ger.* Tuddo. Lääne-Virumaa, NE Estonia *59°12′N 26°52′E*
**Tuebingen** *see* Tübingen
122 J14 **Tuekta** Respublika Altay, S Russia *50°51′N 85°52′E*
104 I5 **Tuela, Rio** ≈ N Portugal
153 X12 **Tuensang** Nāgāland, NE India *26°16′N 94°45′E*
136 L15 **Tufanbeyli** Adana, C Turkey *38°15′N 36°13′E*
**Tüffer** *see* Laško
186 F9 **Tufi** Northern, S Papua New Guinea *09°08′S 149°20′E*
193 O3 **Tufts Plain** *undersea feature* N Pacific Ocean
**Tugalan** *see* Kolkhozobod
67 V14 **Tugela** ≈ SE South Africa
21 P6 **Tug Fork** ≈ S USA
39 P15 **Tugidak Island** *island* Trinity Islands, Alaska, USA
171 O2 **Tuguegarao** Luzon, N Philippines *17°37′N 121°48′E*
123 S12 **Tugur** Khabarovskiy Kray, SE Russia *53°43′N 137°00′E*
161 P4 **Tuhai He** ≈ E China
104 G4 **Tui** Galicia, NW Spain *42°02′N 08°37′W*
77 O13 **Tui** *var.* Grand Balé. ≈ W Burkina Faso
57 J16 **Tuichi, Río** ≈ W Bolivia
64 Q11 **Tuineje** Fuerteventura, Islas Canarias, Spain, NE Atlantic Ocean *28°18′N 14°03′W*
43 X16 **Tuira, Río** ≈ SE Panama
**Tuisarkan** *see* Tūysarkān
**Tujiabu** *see* Yongxiu
127 W5 **Tukan** Respublika Bashkortostan, W Russia *53°58′N 57°29′E*
171 P14 **Tukangbesi, Kepulauan** *Dut.* Toekang Besi Eilanden. *island group* C Indonesia
147 V13 **Tŭkhtamish** *Rus.* Toktomush; *prev.* Tokhtamyshbek. SE Tajikistan *37°51′N 74°41′E*
184 O12 **Tukituki** ≈ North Island, New Zealand
**Tu-k'ou** *see* Panzhihua
121 P12 **Tūkrah** NE Libya *32°32′N 20°35′E*
8 H6 **Tuktoyaktuk** Northwest Territories, NW Canada *69°27′N 133°W*
168 I9 **Tuktuk** Pulau Samosir, W Indonesia *02°32′N 98°43′E*
**Tukumi** *see* Tsukumi
118 E9 **Tukums** *Ger.* Tuckum. W Latvia *56°58′N 23°12′E*
81 G24 **Tukuyu** *prev.* Neu-Langenburg. Mbeya, S Tanzania *09°14′S 33°39′E*
149 O3 **Tukzār** Sar-e Pul, N Afghanistan *35°47′N 66°28′E*
41 O13 **Tula** *var.* Tula de Allende. Hidalgo, C Mexico *20°01′N 99°21′W*
41 O11 **Tula** Tamaulipas, C Mexico *22°59′N 99°43′W*
126 K5 **Tula** Tul'skaya Oblast', W Russia *54°11′N 37°39′E*
**Tulach Mhór** *see* Tullamore
**Tula de Allende** *see* Tula
186 M9 **Tulaghi** *var.* Tulagi. Florida Islands, C Solomon Islands *09°04′S 160°09′E*
**Tulagi** *see* Tulaghi
159 N10 **Tulagt Ar Gol** ≈ W China
41 P13 **Tulancingo** Hidalgo, C Mexico *20°34′N 98°25′W*
35 R11 **Tulare** California, W USA *36°12′N 119°21′W*
29 P9 **Tulare** South Dakota, N USA *44°43′N 98°29′W*
35 Q12 **Tulare Lake Bed** *salt flat* California, W USA
37 S14 **Tularosa** New Mexico, SW USA *33°04′N 106°01′W*
37 P13 **Tularosa Mountains** ▲▲ New Mexico, SW USA
37 S15 **Tularosa Valley** *basin* New Mexico, SW USA
83 E25 **Tulbagh** Western Cape, SW South Africa *33°17′S 19°09′E*
56 C5 **Tulcán** Carchi, N Ecuador *0°44′N 77°43′W*
117 N13 **Tulcea** Tulcea, E Romania *45°11′N 28°49′E*
117 N13 **Tulcea** ◈ *county* SE Romania
**Tul'chin** *see* Tul'chyn
117 N7 **Tul'chyn** *Rus.* Tul'chin. Vinnyts'ka Oblast', C Ukraine *48°40′N 28°49′E*
**Tuléar** *see* Toliara
35 O1 **Tulelake** California, W USA *41°57′N 121°30′W*
116 J10 **Tulgheș** *Hung.* Gyergyótölgyes. Harghita, C Romania *46°57′N 25°46′E*
**Tuli** *see* Thuli
25 N4 **Tulia** Texas, SW USA *34°32′N 101°46′W*
8 I9 **Tulita** *prev.* Fort Norman, Norman. Northwest Territories, NW Canada *64°55′N 125°29′W*
20 J10 **Tullahoma** Tennessee, S USA *35°21′N 86°12′W*
183 N12 **Tullamarine** ✈ (Melbourne) Victoria, SE Australia *37°40′S 144°46′E*
183 Q7 **Tullamore** New South Wales, SE Australia *32°39′S 147°35′E*
97 E18 **Tullamore** *Ir.* Tulach Mhór. Offaly, C Ireland *53°16′N 07°30′W*
103 N12 **Tulle** *anc.* Tutela. Corrèze, C France *45°16′N 01°46′E*
109 X3 **Tulln** *var.* Oberhollabrunn. Niederösterreich, NE Austria *48°20′N 16°02′E*
109 W4 **Tulln** ≈ NE Austria
22 H6 **Tullos** Louisiana, S USA *31°48′N 92°19′W*
97 F19 **Tullow** *Ir.* An Tullach. Carlow, SE Ireland *52°48′N 06°44′W*
181 W5 **Tully** Queensland, NE Australia *18°03′S 145°56′E*
124 J3 **Tuloma** ≈ NW Russia
27 P9 **Tulsa** Oklahoma, C USA *36°09′N 96°W*
153 N11 **Tulsipur** Mid Western, W Nepal *28°01′N 82°22′E*
126 L15 **Tul'skaya Oblast'** ◈ *province* W Russia
126 L14 **Tul'skiy** Respublika Adygeya, SW Russia *44°26′N 40°12′E*
186 E5 **Tulu** Manus Island, N Papua New Guinea *01°58′S 146°50′E*
54 D10 **Tuluá** Valle del Cauca, W Colombia *04°01′N 76°16′W*
116 M12 **Tulucești** Galați, E Romania *45°35′N 28°01′E*
39 N12 **Tuluksak** Alaska, USA *61°06′N 160°57′W*
41 Z12 **Tulum, Ruinas de** *ruins* Quintana Roo, SE Mexico
169 R17 **Tulungagung** *prev.* Toeloengagoeng. Jawa, C Indonesia *08°03′S 111°54′E*
186 J6 **Tulun Islands** *var.* Kilinailau Islands; *prev.* Carteret Islands. *island group* NE Papua New Guinea
126 M4 **Tuma** Ryazanskaya Oblast', W Russia *55°09′N 40°27′E*
54 B12 **Tumaco** Nariño, SW Colombia *01°51′N 78°46′W*
54 B12 **Tumaco, Bahía de** *bay* SW Colombia
155 G19 **Tumakuru** *prev.* Tumkūr. Karnātaka, W India *13°20′N 77°06′E*
**Tuman-gang** *see* Tumen
42 L8 **Tuma, Río** ≈ N Nicaragua
95 O16 **Tumba** Stockholm, C Sweden *59°12′N 17°49′E*
**Tumba, Lac** *see* Ntomba, Lac
169 S12 **Tumbangsenamang** Borneo, C Indonesia *01°17′S 112°21′E*
183 Q10 **Tumbarumba** New South Wales, SE Australia *35°47′S 148°03′E*
56 A8 **Tumbes** Tumbes, NW Peru *03°33′S 80°27′W*
56 A9 **Tumbes** *off.* Región de Tumbes. ◈ *region* NW Peru
**Tumbes, Región de** *see* Tumbes
19 P5 **Tumbledown Mountain** ▲ Maine, NE USA *45°27′N 70°28′W*
11 N13 **Tumbler Ridge** British Columbia, W Canada *55°06′N 120°51′W*
95 N16 **Tumbo** *prev.* Rekarne. Västmanland, C Sweden *59°25′N 16°04′E*
167 Q12 **Tumbŏt, Phnum** ▲ W Cambodia *12°23′N 102°57′E*
182 G9 **Tumby Bay** South Australia *34°22′S 136°05′E*
163 Y10 **Tumen** Jilin, NE China *42°56′N 129°47′E*
163 Y11 **Tumen** *Chin.* Tumen Jiang, *Kor.* Tuman-gang, *Rus.* Tumyn'tszyan. ≈ E Asia
**Tumen Jiang** *see* Tumen
55 Q8 **Tumeremo** Bolívar, E Venezuela *07°17′N 61°30′W*
**Tumkūr** *see* Tumakuru
96 I10 **Tummel** ≈ C Scotland, United Kingdom
188 B15 **Tumon Bay** *bay* W Guam
77 P14 **Tumu** NW Ghana *10°55′N 01°59′W*
58 I10 **Tumuc-Humac Mountains** *var.* Serra Tumucumaque. ▲▲ N South America
**Tumucumaque, Serra** *see* Tumuc-Humac Mountains
183 Q10 **Tumut** New South Wales, SE Australia *35°20′S 148°14′E*
**Tumyn'tszyan** *see* Tumen
**Tün** *see* Ferdows
45 U14 **Tunapuna** Trinidad, Trinidad and Tobago *10°38′N 61°23′W*
60 K11 **Tunas** Paraná, S Brazil *24°57′S 49°05′W*
**Tunbridge Wells** *see* Royal Tunbridge Wells
114 L11 **Tunca Nehri** *Bul.* Tundzha. ≈ Bulgaria/Turkey *see also* Tundzha
**Tunca Nehri** *see* Tundzha
137 O14 **Tunceli** *var.* Kalan. Tunceli, E Turkey *39°07′N 39°34′E*
137 O14 **Tunceli** ◈ *province* C Turkey
152 J12 **Tūndla** Uttar Pradesh, N India *27°13′N 78°14′E*
81 I25 **Tunduru** Ruvuma, S Tanzania *11°08′S 37°21′E*
114 L10 **Tundzha** *Turk.* Tunca Nehri. ≈ Bulgaria/Turkey *see also* Tunca Nehri
**Tundzha** *see* Tunca Nehri
162 I6 **Tünel** *var.* Bulag. Hövsgöl, N Mongolia *49°51′N 100°41′E*
155 H17 **Tungabhadra** ≈ S India
155 F17 **Tungabhadra Reservoir** ◎ S India
191 P2 **Tungaru** *prev.* Gilbert Islands. *island group* W Kiribati
171 P7 **Tungawan** Mindanao, S Philippines *07°33′N 122°22′E*
**Tungdor** *see* Mainling
**T'ung-shan** *see* Xuzhou
**Tungshih** *see* Dongshi
8 H9 **Tungsten** Northwest Territories, W Canada *62°N 128°09′W*
**Tung-t'ing Hu** *see* Dongting Hu
56 A13 **Tungurahua** ◈ *province* C Ecuador
95 F14 **Tunhovdfjorden** ◎ S Norway
22 K2 **Tunica** Mississippi, S USA *34°40′N 90°22′W*
75 N5 **Tunis** *var.* Tūnis. ● (Tunisia) NE Tunisia *36°53′N 10°10′E*
**Tūnis** *see* Tunis
75 N5 **Tunis, Golfe de** *Ar.* Khalīj Tūnis. *gulf* NE Tunisia
75 N6 **Tunisia** *off.* Republic of Tunisia, *Ar.* Al Jumhūrīyah at Tūnisīyah, *Fr.* République Tunisienne. ◆ *republic* N Africa
**Tunisia, Republic of** *see* Tunisia
**Tunisienne, République** *see* Tunisia
**Tūnisīyah, Al Jumhūrīyah at** *see* Tunisia
**Tūnis, Khalīj** *see* Tunis, Golfe de
54 G9 **Tunja** Boyacá, C Colombia *05°33′N 73°23′W*
93 F14 **Tunnsjøen** *Lapp.* Dātnejaevrie. ◎ C Norway
39 N12 **Tuntutuliak** Alaska, USA *60°21′N 162°40′W*
197 P14 **Tunu** ◈ *province* E Greenland
147 U8 **Tunuk** Chuyskaya Oblast', C Kyrgyzstan *42°11′N 73°55′E*
13 Q6 **Tunungayualok Island** *island* Newfoundland and Labrador, E Canada
62 H11 **Tunuyán** Mendoza, W Argentina *33°35′S 69°00′W*
62 I11 **Tunuyán, Río** ≈ W Argentina
**Tunxi** *see* Huangshan
**Tuodian** *see* Shuangbai
**Tuoji** *see* Zhongba
**Tuokezhake** *see* Shufu
35 P9 **Tuolumne River** ≈ California, W USA
**Tuong Buong** *see* Tương Đương
167 R7 **Tương Đương** *var.* Tuong Buong. Nghê An, N Vietnam *19°15′N 104°30′E*
160 I13 **Tuoniang Jiang** ≈ S China
**Tuotiereke** *see* Jeminay
**Tuotuo He** *see* Togton He
**Tuotuoheyan** *see* Tanggulashan
**Tüp** *see* Tyup
60 J9 **Tupã** São Paulo, S Brazil *21°57′S 50°28′W*
191 S10 **Tupai** *var.* Motu Iti. *atoll* Îles Sous le Vent, W French Polynesia
61 G15 **Tupanciretã** Rio Grande do Sul, S Brazil *29°06′S 53°48′W*
22 M2 **Tupelo** Mississippi, S USA *34°15′N 88°42′W*
59 K18 **Tupiraçaba** Goiás, S Brazil *14°33′S 48°40′W*
57 L21 **Tupiza** Potosí, S Bolivia *21°27′S 65°45′W*
144 D14 **Tupkaragan, Mys** *prev.* Mys Tyub-Karagan. *headland* SW Kazakhstan *44°40′N 50°19′E*
11 N13 **Tupper** British Columbia, W Canada *55°30′N 119°59′W*
18 J8 **Tupper Lake** ◎ New York, NE USA
146 J10 **Tuproqqal'a** Khorazm Viloyati, W Uzbekistan *40°52′N 62°00′E*
146 J10 **Tuproqqal'a** *Rus.* Turpakkla. Xorazm Viloyati, W Uzbekistan *40°52′N 62°00′E*
62 H11 **Tupungato, Volcán** ⛰ W Argentina *33°27′S 69°42′W*
163 T9 **Tuquan** Nei Mongol Zizhiqu, N China *45°21′N 121°36′E*
54 C13 **Túquerres** Nariño, SW Colombia *01°06′N 77°37′W*
153 U13 **Tura** Meghālaya, NE India *25°33′N 90°14′E*
122 M10 **Tura** Krasnoyarskiy Kray, N Russia *64°20′N 100°17′E*
122 G10 **Tura** ≈ C Russia
140 M10 **Turabah** Makkah al Mukarramah, W Saudi Arabia *22°00′N 42°00′E*
55 O8 **Turagua, Cerro** ▲ C Venezuela *06°59′N 64°34′W*
184 L12 **Turakina** Manawatu-Wanganui, North Island, New Zealand *40°03′S 175°13′E*
185 K15 **Turakirae Head** *headland* North Island, New Zealand *41°26′S 174°54′E*
186 B8 **Turama** ≈ S Papua New Guinea
122 K13 **Turan** Respublika Tyva, S Russia *52°11′N 93°40′E*
184 M10 **Turangi** Waikato, North Island, New Zealand *39°01′S 175°47′E*
146 F11 **Turan Lowland** *var.* Turan Plain, *Kaz.* Turan Oypaty, *Rus.* Turanskaya Nizmennost', *Turk.* Turan Pesligi, *Uzb.* Turan Pasttekisligi. *plain* C Asia
**Turan Oypaty/Turan Pesligi/Turan Plain/Turanskaya Nizmennost'** *see* Turan Lowland
**Turan Pasttekisligi** *see* Turan Lowland
138 K7 **Ţurāq al 'Ilab** *hill range* S Syria
119 K20 **Turaw** *Rus.* Turov. Homyel'skaya Voblasts', SE Belarus *52°04′N 27°44′E*
140 L2 **Ţurayf** Al Ḩudūd ash Shamālīyah, NW Saudi Arabia *31°43′N 38°40′E*
**Turba** *see* Teruel
54 E5 **Turbaco** Bolívar, N Colombia *10°20′N 75°25′W*
148 K15 **Turbat** Baluchistan, SW Pakistan *26°02′N 62°56′E*
**Turbat-i-Haidari** *see* Torbat-e Ḩeydarīyeh
**Turbat-i-Jam** *see* Torbat-e Jām
54 D7 **Turbo** Antioquia, NW Colombia *08°06′N 76°44′W*
**Turčianský Svätý Martin** *see* Martin
116 H10 **Turda** *Ger.* Thorenburg, *Hung.* Torda. Cluj, NW Romania *46°35′N 23°50′E*
142 M7 **Ţūreh** Markazī, W Iran
191 X12 **Tureia** *atoll* Îles Tuamotu, SE French Polynesia
110 I12 **Turek** Wielkopolskie, C Poland *52°01′N 18°30′E*
93 L19 **Turenki** Kanta-Häme, SW Finland *60°55′N 24°38′E*
**Turfan** *see* Turpan
**Turgay** *see* Torgay
**Turgay** *see* Torgay
144 M8 **Turgayskaya Stolovaya Strana** *Kaz.* Torgay Üstirti. *plateau* Kazakhstan/Russia
**Turgel** *see* Türi
**Türgovishte** *see* Targovishte
**Türgovishte** *see* Targovishte
136 C14 **Turgutlu** Manisa, W Turkey *38°30′N 27°43′E*
136 L12 **Turhal** Tokat, N Turkey *40°23′N 36°05′E*
118 H4 **Türi** *Ger.* Turgel. Järvamaa, N Estonia *58°48′N 25°28′E*
105 S9 **Túria** ≈ E Spain
58 M12 **Turiaçu** Maranhão, E Brazil *01°40′S 45°22′W*
**Turin** *see* Torino
116 J2 **Turiya** *Pol.* Turja, *Rus.* Tur'ya; *prev.* Tur''ya. ≈ NW Ukraine
116 I3 **Turiys'k** Volyns'ka Oblast', NW Ukraine *51°05′N 24°31′E*
**Turja** *see* Turiya
116 H6 **Turka** L'vivs'ka Oblast', W Ukraine *49°07′N 23°01′E*
81 H16 **Turkana** ◈ *county* Kenya
81 H16 **Turkana, Lake** *var.* Lake Rudolf. ◎ N Kenya
145 P16 **Turkestan** *Kaz.* Türkistan. Türkistan, S Kazakhstan *43°18′N 68°18′E*
145 O15 **Turkestan** ◈ *province* S Kazakhstan
147 Q12 **Turkestan Range** *Rus.* Turkestanskiy Khrebet. ▲▲ C Asia
**Turkestanskiy Khrebet** *see* Turkestan Range
**Turkestanskya Oblast'** *see* Turkestan
111 M23 **Túrkeve** Jász-Nagykun-Szolnok, E Hungary *47°06′N 20°42′E*
25 O4 **Turkey** Texas, SW USA *34°23′N 100°54′W*
136 H14 **Turkey** *off.* Republic of Turkey, *Turk.* Türkiye Cumhuriyeti. ◆ *republic* SW Asia
181 N4 **Turkey Creek** Western Australia *16°54′S 128°12′E*
26 M9 **Turkey Creek** ≈ Oklahoma, C USA
37 T9 **Turkey Mountains** ▲▲ New Mexico, SW USA
**Turkey, Republic of** *see* Turkey
29 X11 **Turkey River** ≈ Iowa, C USA
127 N7 **Turki** Saratovskaya Oblast', W Russia *52°00′N 43°16′E*
121 O1 **Turkish Republic of Northern Cyprus** ◇ *disputed territory* Cyprus
**Turkistan** *see* Turkestan
**Turkistan Oblysy** *see* Turkestan
148 M4 **Turkistān, Silsilah-ye Band-e** ▲▲ NW Afghanistan
**Türkiye Cumhuriyeti** *see* Turkey
146 K12 **Türkmenabat** *prev.* *Rus.* Chardzhev, Chardzhou, Chardzhui, Lenin-Turkmenski, *Turkm.* Chärjew. Lebap Welaýaty, E Turkmenistan *39°07′N 63°30′E*
146 A11 **Türkmen Aylagy** *Rus.* Turkmenskiy Zaliv. *lake gulf* W Turkmenistan
**Turkmenbashi** *see* Türkmenbaşy
146 A10 **Türkmenbaşy** *Rus.* Turkmenbashi; *prev.* Krasnovodsk. Balkan Welaýaty, W Turkmenistan *40°N 53°04′E*
146 A10 **Türkmenbaşy Aylagy** *prev.* *Rus.* Krasnovodskiy Zaliv, *Turkm.* Krasnowodsk Aylagy. *lake Gulf* W Turkmenistan
146 J14 **Türkmengala** *Rus.* Turkmen-kala; *prev.* Turkmen-Kala. Mary Welaýaty, S Turkmenistan *37°25′N 62°19′E*
146 G13 **Turkmenistan**; *prev.* Turkmenskaya Soviet Socialist Republic. ◆ *republic* C Asia
**Turkmen-kala/Turkmen-Kala** *see* Türkmengala
**Turkmenskaya Soviet Socialist Republic** *see* Turkmenistan
**Turkmenskiy Zaliv** *see* Türkmen Aylagy
136 L16 **Türkoğlu** Kahramanmaraş, S Turkey *37°24′N 36°49′E*
44 L6 **Turks and Caicos Islands** ◇ *UK Overseas Territory* N West Indies

◆ Country
● Country Capital
◇ Dependent Territory
○ Dependent Territory Capital
◈ Administrative Regions
✈ International Airport
▲ Mountain
▲▲ Mountain Range
⛰ Volcano
≈ River
◎ Lake
⊠ Reservoir

Turks and Caicos Islands – Umm al Qaywayn


64 G10 **Turks and Caicos Islands** *UK dependant territory* N West Indies
45 N6 **Turks Islands** *island group* SE Turks and Caicos Islands
93 K19 **Turku** *Swe.* Åbo. Varsinais-Suomi, SW Finland 60°27′N 22°17′E
81 H17 **Turkwel** *seasonal river* NW Kenya
27 P9 **Turley** Oklahoma, C USA 36°14′N 95°58′W
35 P9 **Turlock** California, W USA 37°29′N 120°52′W
118 I12 **Turmantas** Utena, NE Lithuania 55°41′N 26°27′E
**Turmberg** *see* Wieżyca
54 L5 **Turmero** Aragua, N Venezuela South America 10°14′N 66°40′W
184 N13 **Turnagain, Cape** *headland* North Island, New Zealand 40°30′S 176°36′E
**Turnau** *see* Turnov
42 H2 **Turneffe Islands** *island group* E Belize
18 M11 **Turners Falls** Massachusetts, NE USA 42°36′N 72°31′W
11 P16 **Turner Valley** Alberta, SW Canada 50°43′N 114°19′W
99 I16 **Turnhout** Antwerpen, N Belgium 51°19′N 04°57′E
109 V5 **Türnitz** Niederösterreich, E Austria 47°56′N 15°26′E
11 S12 **Turnor Lake** ◎ Saskatchewan, C Canada
111 E15 **Turnov** *Ger.* Turnau. Liberecký Kraj, N Czechia 50°36′N 15°10′E
**Tŭrnovo** *see* Veliko Tarnovo
116 I15 **Turnu Măgurele** *var.* Turnu-Măgurele. Teleorman, S Romania 43°44′N 24°53′E
**Turnu Severin** *see* Drobeta-Turnu Severin
**Turócszentmárton** *see* Martin
**Turoni** *see* Tours
**Turov** *see* Turaw
**Turpakkla** *see* Tuproqqal'a
158 M6 **Turpan** *var.* Turfan. Xinjiang Uygur Zizhiqu, NW China 42°55′N 89°06′E
**Turpan Depression** *see* Turpan Pendi
158 M6 **Turpan Pendi** *Eng.* Turpan Depression. *depression* NW China
158 M5 **Turpan Zhan** Xinjiang Uygur Zizhiqu, W China 43°10′N 89°06′E
**Turpentine State** *see* North Carolina
44 H8 **Turquino, Pico** ▲ E Cuba 19°54′N 76°55′W
27 Y10 **Turrell** Arkansas, C USA 35°22′N 90°13′W
43 N14 **Turrialba** Cartago, E Costa Rica 09°56′N 83°40′W
96 K8 **Turriff** NE Scotland, United Kingdom 57°32′N 02°28′W
139 V7 **Tursāq** Diyālá, E Iraq 33°27′N 45°47′E
**Turshiz** *see* Kāshmar
**Tursunzade** *see* Tursunzoda
147 P13 **Tursunzoda** *Rus.* Tursunzade; *prev.* Regar. W Tajikistan 38°30′N 68°10′E
**Turt** *see* Hanh
**Tŭrtkŭl/Turtkul'** *see* To'rtkok'l
29 O9 **Turtle Creek** ≈ South Dakota, N USA
30 K4 **Turtle Flambeau Flowage** ⊠ Wisconsin, N USA
11 S14 **Turtleford** Saskatchewan, S Canada 53°21′N 108°48′W
28 M4 **Turtle Lake** North Dakota, N USA 47°31′N 100°53′W
92 K12 **Turtola** Lappi, NW Finland 66°39′N 23°55′E
122 M10 **Turu** ≈ N Russia
**Turuga** *see* Tsuruga
147 V10 **Turugart Pass** *pass* China/Kyrgyzstan
158 E7 **Turugart Shankou** *var.* Pereval Torugart. *pass* China/Kyrgyzstan
122 K9 **Turukhan** ≈ N Russia
122 K9 **Turukhansk** Krasnoyarskiy Kray, N Russia 65°50′N 87°48′E
139 N3 **Ţurumbah** *well* NE Syria
**Turuoka** *see* Tsuruoka
**Turush** *see* Turysh
60 K7 **Turvo, Rio** ≈ S Brazil
**Tur"ya** *see* Turiya
144 H14 **Turysh** *prev.* Turush. Mangistau, SW Kazakhstan 45°24′N 56°02′E
23 O4 **Tuscaloosa** Alabama, S USA 33°13′N 87°34′W
23 O4 **Tuscaloosa, Lake** ◎ Alabama, S USA
**Tuscan Archipelago** *see* Toscano, Archipelago
**Tuscan-Emilian Mountains** *see* Tosco-Emiliano, Appennino
**Tuscany** *see* Toscana
35 V2 **Tuscarora** Nevada, W USA 41°16′N 116°13′W
18 F15 **Tuscarora Mountain** *ridge* Pennsylvania, NE USA
30 M14 **Tuscola** Illinois, N USA 39°46′N 88°19′W
25 P7 **Tuscola** Texas, SW USA 32°12′N 99°48′W
23 O2 **Tuscumbia** Alabama, S USA 34°43′N 87°42′W
92 O4 **Tusenøyane** *island group* S Svalbard
144 K13 **Tushchybas, Zaliv** *prev.* Zaliv Paskevicha. *lake gulf* SW Kazakhstan
**Tusima** *see* Tsushima
171 Y15 **Tusirah** Papua, E Indonesia 06°46′S 140°19′E
23 Q5 **Tuskegee** Alabama, S USA 32°25′N 85°41′W
94 E8 **Tustna** *island* S Norway
39 R12 **Tustumena Lake** ◎ Alaska, USA
110 K13 **Tuszyn** Łódzkie, C Poland 51°36′N 19°31′E
137 S13 **Tutak** Ağrı, E Turkey 39°34′N 42°48′E
185 C20 **Tutamoe Range** ▲▲ North Island, New Zealand
**Tutasev** *see* Tutayev
124 L15 **Tutayev** *var.* Tutasev. Yaroslavskaya Oblast', W Russia 57°51′N 39°29′E
**Tutela** *see* Tulle, France
**Tutela** *see* Tudela, Spain
**Tutera** *see* Tudela
155 H23 **Tuticorin** *var.* Thoothukudi. Tamil Nādu, SE India 08°48′N 78°10′E
113 L15 **Tutin** Serbia, S Serbia 43°00′N 20°20′E
184 O10 **Tutira** Hawke's Bay, North Island, New Zealand 39°14′S 176°53′E
**Tutiura** *see* Tsuchiura
122 K10 **Tutonchny** Krasnoyarskiy Kray, N Russia 64°12′N 93°52′E
114 L6 **Tutrakan** Silistra, NE Bulgaria 44°03′N 26°38′E
29 N5 **Tuttle** North Dakota, N USA 47°07′N 99°58′W
26 M11 **Tuttle** Oklahoma, C USA 35°17′N 97°48′W
27 O3 **Tuttle Creek Lake** ⊠ Kansas, C USA
101 H23 **Tuttlingen** Baden-Württemberg, S Germany 47°59′N 08°49′E
171 R16 **Tutuala** East Timor 08°23′S 127°12′E
192 K17 **Tutuila** *island* W American Samoa
83 I18 **Tutume** Central, E Botswana 20°26′S 27°02′E
39 N7 **Tututalak Mountain** ▲ Alaska, USA 67°51′N 161°27′W
22 K3 **Tutwiler** Mississippi, S USA 34°00′N 90°25′W
162 L8 **Tuul Gol** ≈ N Mongolia
93 O16 **Tuupovaara** Pohjois-Karjala, E Finland 62°30′N 30°40′E
**Tuva** *see* Tyva, Respublika
190 E7 **Tuvalu** *prev.* Ellice Islands. ◆ *commonwealth republic* SW Pacific Ocean
**Tuvinskaya ASSR** *see* Tyva, Respublika
163 O9 **Tuvshinshiree** *var.* Sergelen. Sühbaatar, E Mongolia 46°12′N 111°48′E
141 P9 **Ţuwayq, Jabal** ▲▲ C Saudi Arabia
138 H13 **Ţuwayyil ash Shihāq** *desert* S Jordan
11 U16 **Tuxford** Saskatchewan, S Canada 50°33′N 105°32′W
167 U12 **Tu Xoay** Đắc Lắc, S Vietnam 12°18′N 107°33′E
40 L14 **Tuxpan** Jalisco, C Mexico 19°33′N 103°21′W
40 J12 **Tuxpan** Nayarit, C Mexico 21°57′N 105°12′W
41 Q12 **Tuxpán** *var.* Tuxpán de Rodríguez Cano. Veracruz, E Mexico 20°58′N 97°23′W
**Tuxpán de Rodríguez Cano** *see* Tuxpán
41 R15 **Tuxtepec** *var.* San Juan Bautista Tuxtepec. Oaxaca, S Mexico 18°02′N 96°05′W
41 U16 **Tuxtla** *var.* Tuxtla Gutiérrez. Chiapas, SE Mexico 16°44′N 93°03′W
**Tuxtla** *see* San Andrés Tuxtla
**Tuxtla Gutiérrez** *see* Tuxtla
**Tuyama** *see* Tsuyama
167 T5 **Tuyên Quang** Tuyên Quang, N Vietnam 21°48′N 105°18′E
167 U13 **Tuy Hoa** Binh Thuân, S Vietnam 11°03′N 108°12′E
167 V12 **Tuy Hoa** Phu Yên, S Vietnam 13°02′N 109°15′E
127 U5 **Tuymazy** Respublika Bashkortostan, W Russia 54°36′N 53°40′E
**Tuy Phong** *see* Liên Hương
142 L6 **Tūysarkān** *var.* Tuisarkan, Tuyserkān. Hamadān, W Iran 34°31′N 48°30′E
**Tuyserkān** *see* Tūysarkān
**Tuyuk** *see* Tuyyk
145 W16 **Tuyyk** *Kaz.* Tuyyq; *prev.* Tuyuk. Taldykorgan, SE Kazakhstan 43°07′N 79°24′E
**Tuyyq** *see* Tuyyk
136 I14 **Tuz Gölü** ◎ C Turkey
125 Q15 **Tuzha** Kirovskaya Oblast', NW Russia 57°37′N 48°02′E
113 K17 **Tuzi** S Montenegro 42°22′N 19°21′E
139 T5 **Tūz Khurmātū** At Ta'mím, N Iraq 34°56′N 44°38′E
112 I11 **Tuzla** Federacija Bosne I Hercegovine, NE Bosnia and Herzegovina 44°33′N 18°40′E
117 N15 **Tuzla** Constanţa, SE Romania 43°58′N 28°38′E
137 T12 **Tuzluca** İgdır, E Turkey 40°02′N 43°39′E
95 J20 **Tvååker** Halland, S Sweden 57°04′N 12°25′E
95 F17 **Tvedestrand** Aust-Agder, S Norway 58°36′N 08°55′E
124 J16 **Tver'** *prev.* Kalinin. Tverskaya Oblast', W Russia 56°53′N 35°52′E
126 I15 **Tverskaya Oblast'** ◈ *province* W Russia
124 I15 **Tvertsa** ≈ W Russia
138 G9 **Tverya** *var.* Tiberias; *prev.* Teverya. Northern, N Israel 32°48′N 35°32′E
95 F16 **Tvietsund** Telemark, S Norway 59°00′N 08°34′E
110 H13 **Twardogóra** *Ger.* Festenberg. Dolnośląskie, SW Poland 51°21′N 17°27′E
14 J14 **Tweed** Ontario, SE Canada 44°29′N 77°19′W
96 K13 **Tweed** ≈ England/Scotland, United Kingdom
98 O7 **Tweede-Exloërmond** Drenthe, NE Netherlands 52°55′N 06°55′E
183 V3 **Tweed Heads** New South Wales, SE Australia 28°10′S 153°32′E
98 M11 **Twello** Gelderland, E Netherlands 52°14′N 06°07′E
35 W15 **Twentynine Palms** California, W USA 34°08′N 116°03′W
25 P9 **Twin Buttes Reservoir** ⊠ Texas, SW USA
33 O15 **Twin Falls** Idaho, NW USA 42°34′N 114°28′W
39 N13 **Twin Hills** Alaska, USA 59°06′N 160°21′W
11 O11 **Twin Lakes** Alberta, W Canada 57°47′N 117°30′W
33 O12 **Twin Peaks** ▲ Idaho, NW USA 44°37′N 114°24′W
185 I14 **Twins, The** ▲ South Island, New Zealand 41°14′S 172°38′E
29 S5 **Twin Valley** Minnesota, N USA 47°15′N 96°15′W
100 G11 **Twistringen** Niedersachsen, NW Germany 52°48′N 08°39′E
185 E20 **Twizel** Canterbury, South Island, New Zealand 44°04′S 171°12′E
29 X5 **Two Harbors** Minnesota, N USA 47°01′N 91°40′W
11 R14 **Two Hills** Alberta, SW Canada 53°40′N 111°43′W
31 N7 **Two Rivers** Wisconsin, N USA 44°10′N 87°33′W
116 H8 **Tyachiv** Zakarpats'ka Oblast', W Ukraine 48°02′N 23°35′E
**Tyan'-Shan'** *see* Tien Shan
166 L3 **Tyao** ≈ Myanmar (Burma)/India
117 R6 **Tyasmyn** ≈ N Ukraine
23 X6 **Tybee Island** Georgia, SE USA 32°00′N 80°51′W
**Tyborøn** *see* Thyborøn
111 J16 **Tychy** *Ger.* Tichau. Śląskie, S Poland 50°12′N 19°01′E
111 O16 **Tyczyn** Podkarpackie, SE Poland 49°58′N 22°03′E
94 I8 **Tydal** Sør-Trøndelag, S Norway 63°01′N 11°36′E
115 H24 **Tyflós** ≈ Kríti, Greece, E Mediterranean Sea
21 S3 **Tygart Lake** ⊠ West Virginia, NE USA
123 Q13 **Tygda** Amurskaya Oblast', SE Russia 53°07′N 126°12′E
21 Q11 **Tyger River** ≈ South Carolina, SE USA
32 I11 **Tygh Valley** Oregon, NW USA 45°15′N 121°12′W
94 F12 **Tyin** ◎ S Norway
29 S10 **Tyler** Minnesota, N USA 44°16′N 96°07′W
25 W7 **Tyler** Texas, SW USA 32°21′N 95°18′W
25 W7 **Tyler, Lake** ⊠ Texas, SW USA
22 K7 **Tylertown** Mississippi, S USA 31°07′N 90°08′W
117 P10 **Tylihuls'kyy Lyman** ◎ SW Ukraine
**Tylos** *see* Bahrain
115 C15 **Týmfi** *var.* Timfi. ▲ W Greece 39°58′N 20°51′E
115 E17 **Tymfristós** *var.* Timfristos. ▲ C Greece 38°57′N 21°49′E
115 J25 **Tympáki** *var.* Timbaki; *prev.* Timbákion. Kríti, Greece, E Mediterranean Sea 35°04′N 24°47′E
123 Q12 **Tynda** Amurskaya Oblast', SE Russia 55°09′N 124°44′E
29 Q12 **Tyndall** South Dakota, N USA 42°57′N 97°52′W
97 L14 **Tyne** ≈ N England, United Kingdom
97 M14 **Tynemouth** NE England, United Kingdom 55°01′N 01°24′W
97 L14 **Tyneside** *cultural region* NE England, United Kingdom
94 H10 **Tynset** Hedmark, S Norway 61°45′N 10°49′E
39 Q12 **Tyonek** Alaska, USA 61°04′N 151°08′W
**Tyôsi** *see* Chōshi
**Tyras** *see* Dniester
**Tyras** *see* Bilhorod-Dnistrovs'kyy
**Tyre** *see* Soûr
95 G14 **Tyrifjorden** ◎ S Norway
95 K22 **Tyringe** Skåne, S Sweden 56°09′N 13°35′E
123 R13 **Tyrma** Khabarovskiy Kray, SE Russia 50°00′N 132°04′E
**Tyrnau** *see* Trnava
115 F15 **Týrnavos** *var.* Tírnavos. Thessalía, C Greece 39°45′N 22°18′E
127 N16 **Tyrnyauz** Kabardino-Balkarskaya Respublika, SW Russia 43°19′N 42°55′E
**Tyrol** *see* Tirol
18 E14 **Tyrone** Pennsylvania, NE USA 40°41′N 78°12′W
97 E15 **Tyrone** *cultural region* W Northern Ireland, United Kingdom
**Tyros** *see* Bahrain
182 M10 **Tyrrell, Lake** *salt lake* Victoria, SE Australia
84 H14 **Tyrrhenian Basin** *undersea feature* Tyrrhenian Sea, C Mediterranean Sea 39°30′N 13°00′E
120 L8 **Tyrrhenian Sea** *It.* Mare Tirreno. *sea* N Mediterranean Sea
94 J12 **Tyrsil** ≈ Hedmark, S Norway
**Tysa** *see* Tisa/Tisza
116 J7 **Tysmenytsya** Ivano-Frankivs'ka Oblast', W Ukraine 48°54′N 24°50′E
95 C14 **Tysnesøya** *island* S Norway
95 C14 **Tysse** Hordaland, S Norway 60°23′N 05°46′E
95 D14 **Tyssedal** Hordaland, S Norway 60°07′N 06°36′E
95 O17 **Tystberga** Södermanland, C Sweden 58°51′N 17°15′E
118 E12 **Tytuvėnai** Šiaulai, C Lithuania 55°36′N 23°14′E
**Tyub-Karagan, Mys** *see* Tupkaragan, Mys
147 V8 **Tyugel'-Say** Narynskaya Oblast', C Kyrgyzstan 41°57′N 74°40′E
122 H11 **Tyukalinsk** Omskaya Oblast', C Russia 55°56′N 72°02′E
127 V7 **Tyul'gan** Orenburgskaya Oblast', W Russia 52°27′N 56°08′E
122 G11 **Tyumen'** Tyumenskaya Oblast', C Russia 57°11′N 65°29′E
122 H11 **Tyumenskaya Oblast'** ◈ *province* C Russia
147 Y7 **Tyup** *Kyr.* Tüp. Issyk-Kul'skaya Oblast', NE Kyrgyzstan 42°44′N 78°18′E
122 L14 **Tyva, Respublika** *prev.* Tannu-Tuva, Tuva, Tuvinskaya ASSR. ◈ *autonomous republic* C Russia
117 N7 **Tyvriv** Vinnyts'ka Oblast', C Ukraine 49°01′N 28°28′E
97 J21 **Tywi** ≈ S Wales, United Kingdom
97 I19 **Tywyn** W Wales, United Kingdom 52°35′N 04°06′W
83 K20 **Tzaneen** Limpopo, NE South Africa 23°50′S 30°09′E
**Tzekung** *see* Zigong
**Tziá** *see* Kéa
41 X12 **Tzucacab** Yucatán, SE Mexico 20°04′N 89°03′W


# U


82 B12 **Uaco Cungo** *var.* Waku Kungo, *Port.* Santa Comba. Kwanza Sul, C Angola 11°21′S 15°04′E
**UAE** *see* United Arab Emirates
191 X7 **Ua Huka** *island* Îles Marquises, NE French Polynesia
58 E10 **Uaiacás** Roraima, N Brazil 03°28′N 63°13′W
**Uamba** *see* Wamba
**Uanle Uen** *see* Wanlaweyn
191 W7 **Ua Pu** *island* Îles Marquises, NE French Polynesia
81 L17 **Uar Garas** *spring/well* SW Somalia 01°19′N 41°22′E
58 G12 **Uatumã, Rio** ≈ C Brazil
**Ua Uíbh Fhailí** *see* Offaly
58 C11 **Uaupés, Rio** *var.* Río Vaupés. ≈ Brazil/Colombia *see also* Vaupés, Río
**Uaupés, Rio** *see* Vaupés, Río
**Uba** *see* Oba
145 N6 **Ubagan** *Kaz.* Obagan. ≈ Kazakhstan/Russia
186 G7 **Ubai** New Britain, E Papua New Guinea 05°38′S 150°45′E
79 J15 **Ubangi** *Fr.* Oubangui. ≈ C Africa
**Ubangi-Shari** *see* Central African Republic
119 L20 **Ubarts'** *Rus.,Ukr.* Ubort'. ≈ Belarus/Ukraine *see also* Ubort'
**Ubarts'** *see* Ubort'
54 F9 **Ubaté** Cundinamarca, C Colombia 05°20′N 73°50′W
60 N10 **Ubatuba** São Paulo, S Brazil 23°26′S 45°04′W
149 R12 **Ubauro** Sindh, SE Pakistan 28°08′N 69°43′E
171 Q6 **Ubay** Bohol, C Philippines 10°02′N 124°29′E
103 U14 **Ubaye** ≈ SE France
**Ubayid, Wadi al** *see* Ubayyiḍ, Wādī al
139 N8 **Ubaylah** Al Anbār, W Iraq 33°06′N 40°13′E
139 O10 **Ubayyiḍ, Wādī al** *var.* Wadi al Ubayid. *dry watercourse* SW Iraq
98 L13 **Ubbergen** Gelderland, E Netherlands 51°49′N 05°54′E
164 E13 **Ube** Yamaguchi, Honshū, SW Japan 33°57′N 131°15′E
105 O13 **Ubeda** Andalucía, S Spain 38°01′N 03°22′W
109 V7 **Übelbach** *var.* Markt-Übelbach. Steiermark, SE Austria 47°13′N 15°15′E
59 L20 **Uberaba** Minas Gerais, SE Brazil 19°47′S 47°57′W
57 Q19 **Uberaba, Laguna** ◎ E Bolivia
59 K19 **Uberlândia** Minas Gerais, SE Brazil 18°17′S 48°17′W
101 H24 **Überlingen** Baden-Württemberg, S Germany 47°46′N 09°10′E
77 U16 **Ubiaja** Edo, S Nigeria 06°39′N 06°23′E
104 K3 **Ubiña, Peña** ▲ NW Spain 43°01′N 05°58′W
57 H17 **Ubinas, Volcán** ⛰ S Peru 16°16′S 70°49′W
**Ubol Rajadhani/Ubol Ratchathani** *see* Ubon Ratchathani
167 P9 **Ubolratna Reservoir** ⊠ C Thailand
167 S10 **Ubon Ratchathani** *var.* Muang Ubon, Ubol Rajadhani, Ubol Ratchathani, Udon Ratchathani. Ubon Ratchathani, E Thailand 15°15′N 104°50′E
116 M3 **Ubort'** *Bel.* Ubarts'. ≈ Belarus/Ukraine *see also* Ubarts'
**Ubort'** *see* Ubarts'
104 K15 **Ubrique** Andalucía, S Spain 36°42′N 05°27′W
**Ubsu-Nur, Ozero** *see* Uvs Nuur
79 M18 **Ubundu** Orientale, C Dem. Rep. Congo 0°24′S 25°30′E
146 J13 **Üçajy** *var.* Üchajy, *Rus.* Uch-Adzhi. Mary Welaýaty, C Turkmenistan 38°06′N 62°44′E
137 X11 **Ucar** *Rus.* Udzhary. C Azerbaijan 40°31′N 47°40′E
56 G13 **Ucayali** *off.* Región de Ucayali. ◈ *region* E Peru
**Ucayali, Región de** *see* Ucayali
56 F10 **Ucayali, Río** ≈ C Peru
**Uccle** *see* Ukkel
**Uch-Adzhi/Üchajy** *see* Üçajy
127 X4 **Uchaly** Respublika Bashkortostan, W Russia 54°19′N 59°33′E
**Ucharal** *see* Usharal
164 C17 **Uchinoura** Kagoshima, Kyūshū, SW Japan 31°16′N 131°04′E
165 R5 **Uchiura-wan** *bay* NW Pacific Ocean
**Uchkuduk** *see* Uchquduq
147 S9 **Uchqo'rg'on** *Rus.* Uchkurghan. Namangan Viloyati, E Uzbekistan 41°06′N 72°04′E
146 K8 **Uchquduq** *Rus.* Uchkuduk. Navoiy Viloyati, N Uzbekistan 42°12′N 63°27′E
**Uchsay** *see* Uchsoy
146 G6 **Uchsoy** *Rus.* Uchsay. Qoraqalpog'iston Respublikasi, NW Uzbekistan 43°51′N 58°51′E
**Uchtagan Gumy/Uchtagan, Peski** *see* Uçtagan Gumy
123 R11 **Uchur** ≈ E Russia
100 O10 **Uckermark** *cultural region* E Germany
10 K17 **Ucluelet** Vancouver Island, British Columbia, SW Canada 48°55′N 123°34′W
146 D10 **Uçtagan Gumy** *var.* Uchtagan Gumy, *Rus.* Peski Uchtagan. *desert* NW Turkmenistan
122 M13 **Uda** ≈ S Russia
123 R12 **Uda** ≈ E Russia
123 N6 **Udachnyy** Respublika Sakha (Yakutiya), NE Russia 66°27′N 112°18′E
155 G21 **Udagamandalam** *var.* Ooty, Udhagamandalam; *prev.* Ootacamund. Tamil Nādu, SW India 11°28′N 76°42′E
152 F14 **Udaipur** *prev.* Oodeypore. Rājasthān, N India 24°35′N 73°41′E
**Udayadhani** *see* Uthai Thani
143 N16 **'Udayd, Khawr al** *var.* Khor al Udeid. *inlet* Qatar/Saudi Arabia
112 D11 **Udbina** Lika-Senj, W Croatia 44°33′N 15°46′E
95 I18 **Uddevalla** Västra Götaland, S Sweden 58°20′N 11°56′E
**Uddjaur** *see* Uddjaure
92 H13 **Uddjaure** *var.* Uddjaur. ◎ N Sweden
**Udeid, Khor al** *see* 'Udayd, Khawr al
99 K14 **Uden** Noord-Brabant, SE Netherlands 51°40′N 05°37′E
**Uden** *see* Udenhout
99 J14 **Udenhout** *var.* Uden. Noord-Brabant, S Netherlands 51°37′N 05°09′E
155 H14 **Udgīr** Mahārāshtra, C India 18°23′N 77°06′E
**Udhagamandalam** *see* Udagamandalam
152 H6 **Udhampur** Jammu and Kashmir, NW India 32°55′N 75°07′E
139 X14 **'Udhaybah, 'Uqlat al** *well* S Iraq
106 J7 **Udine** *anc.* Utina. Friuli-Venezia Giulia, NE Italy 46°05′N 13°10′E
175 T14 **Udintsev Fracture Zone** *tectonic feature* S Pacific Ocean
**Udipi** *see* Udupi
**Udmurtia** *see* Udmurtskaya Respublika
127 S2 **Udmurtskaya Respublika** *Eng.* Udmurtia. ◈ *autonomous republic* NW Russia
124 J15 **Udomlya** Tverskaya Oblast', W Russia 57°53′N 34°59′E
**Udon Ratchathani** *see* Ubon Ratchathani
167 Q8 **Udon Thani** *var.* Ban Mak Khaeng, Udorndhani. Udon Thani, N Thailand 17°25′N 102°45′E
**Udorndhani** *see* Udon Thani
189 U12 **Udot** *atoll* Chuuk Islands, C Micronesia
123 S12 **Udskaya Guba** *bay* E Russia
123 R12 **Udskoye** Khabarovskiy Kray, SE Russia 54°32′N 134°26′E
155 E19 **Udupi** *var.* Udipi. Karnātaka, SW India 13°18′N 74°46′E
**Udzhary** *see* Ucar
100 O9 **Uecker** ≈ NE Germany
100 P9 **Ueckermünde** Mecklenburg-Vorpommern, NE Germany 53°43′N 14°03′E
164 M12 **Ueda** *var.* Uyeda. Nagano, Honshū, S Japan 36°27′N 138°13′E
79 L16 **Uele** *var.* Welle. ≈ NE Dem. Rep. Congo
123 W5 **Uelen** Chukotskiy Avtonomnyy Okrug, NE Russia 66°01′N 169°52′W
**Uele (upper course)** *see* Kibali, Dem. Rep. Congo
**Uele (upper course)** *see* Uolo, Río, Equatorial Guinea/Gabon
100 J11 **Uelzen** Niedersachsen, N Germany 52°58′N 10°34′E
164 J14 **Ueno** Mie, Honshū, SW Japan 34°45′N 136°08′E
127 V4 **Ufa** Respublika Bashkortostan, W Russia 54°46′N 56°02′E
127 V4 **Ufa** ≈ W Russia
**Ufra** *see* Kenar
83 C18 **Ugab** ≈ C Namibia
118 D8 **Ugāle** NW Latvia 57°16′N 21°58′E
81 F17 **Uganda** *off.* Republic of Uganda. ◆ *republic* E Africa
**Uganda, Republic of** *see* Uganda
138 G4 **Ugarit** *Ar.* Ra's Shamrah. *site of ancient city* Al Lādhiqīyah, NW Syria
39 O14 **Ugashik** Alaska, USA 57°30′N 157°24′W
107 Q19 **Ugento** Puglia, SE Italy 39°53′N 18°09′E
105 O15 **Ugíjar** Andalucía, S Spain 36°58′N 03°03′W
103 T11 **Ugine** Savoie, E France 45°45′N 06°25′E
123 R13 **Uglegorsk** Amurskaya Oblast', S Russia 51°40′N 128°05′E
**Ugleural'sk** *see* Ugleural'skiy
125 V13 **Ugleural'skiy** *prev.* Polovinka, Ugleural'sk. Permskiy Kray, NW Russia 58°57′N 57°37′E
124 L15 **Uglich** Yaroslavskaya Oblast', W Russia 57°33′N 38°23′E
126 I4 **Ugra** ≈ W Russia
147 V9 **Ugyut** Narynskaya Oblast', C Kyrgyzstan 41°22′N 74°49′E
111 H19 **Uherské Hradiště** *Ger.* Ungarisch-Hradisch. Zlínský Kraj, E Czechia 49°05′N 17°26′E
111 H19 **Uherský Brod** *Ger.* Ungarisch-Brod. Zlínský Kraj, E Czechia 49°01′N 17°40′E
111 B17 **Úhlava** *Ger.* Angel. ≈ W Czechia
**Uhorshchyna** *see* Hungary
31 T13 **Uhrichsville** Ohio, N USA 40°23′N 81°21′W
**Uhuru Peak** *see* Kilimanjaro
96 G8 **Uig** N Scotland, United Kingdom 57°35′N 06°22′W
82 B10 **Uíge** *Port.* Carmona, Vila Marechal Carmona. Uíge, NW Angola 07°37′S 15°02′E
82 B10 **Uíge** ◈ *province* N Angola
193 Y15 **Uiha** *island* Ha'apai Group, C Tonga
189 U13 **Uijec** *island* Chuuk, C Micronesia
163 X14 **Uijeongbu** *Jap.* Giseifu; *prev.* Ŭijŏngbu. NW South Korea 37°42′N 127°02′E
**Ŭijŏngbu** *see* Uijeongbu
**Uil** *see* Oyyl
36 M3 **Uinta Mountains** ▲▲ Utah, W USA
83 C18 **Uis** Erongo, NW Namibia 21°08′S 14°49′E
83 I25 **Uitenhage** Eastern Cape, S South Africa 33°44′S 25°27′E
98 H9 **Uitgeest** Noord-Holland, W Netherlands 52°32′N 04°43′E
98 I11 **Uithoorn** Noord-Holland, C Netherlands 52°14′N 04°50′E
98 O4 **Uithuizen** Groningen, NE Netherlands 53°24′N 06°40′E
98 O4 **Uithuizermeeden** Groningen, NE Netherlands 53°25′N 06°43′E
189 R6 **Ujae Atoll** *var.* Wūjae. *atoll* Ralik Chain, W Marshall Islands
**Ujain** *see* Ujjain
111 I16 **Ujazd** Opolskie, S Poland 50°22′N 18°20′E
**Új-Becse** *see* Novi Bečej
**Ujda** *see* Oujda
189 N5 **Ujelang Atoll** *var.* Wujlān. *atoll* Ralik Chain, W Marshall Islands
111 N21 **Újfehértó** Szabolcs-Szatmár-Bereg, E Hungary 47°48′N 21°40′E
**Újgradiska** *see* Nova Gradiška
164 J13 **Uji** *var.* Uzi. Kyōto, Honshū, SW Japan 34°54′N 135°48′E
81 E21 **Ujiji** Kigoma, W Tanzania 04°55′S 29°39′E
154 G10 **Ujjain** *prev.* Ujain. Madhya Pradesh, C India 23°11′N 75°50′E
**Újlak** *see* Ilok
**'Ujmān** *see* 'Ajmān
**Újmoldova** *see* Moldova Nouă
**Újszentanna** *see* Sântana
**Ujungpandang** *see* Makassar
**Ujung Salang** *see* Phuket
**Újvidék** *see* Novi Sad
**UK** *see* United Kingdom
154 E11 **Ukāi Reservoir** ⊠ W India
81 G19 **Ukara Island** *island* N Tanzania
**'Ukash, Wādī** *see* 'Akāsh, Wādī
81 F19 **Ukerewe Island** *island* N Tanzania
139 S9 **Ukhayḍir** Al Anbār, C Iraq 32°28′N 43°36′E
153 X13 **Ukhrul** Manipur, NE India 25°08′N 94°24′E
125 S9 **Ukhta** Respublika Komi, NW Russia 63°31′N 53°48′E
34 L6 **Ukiah** California, W USA 39°07′N 123°14′W
32 K12 **Ukiah** Oregon, NW USA 45°06′N 118°57′W
99 G18 **Ukkel** *Fr.* Uccle. Brussels, C Belgium 50°47′N 04°19′E
118 G13 **Ukmergė** *Pol.* Wiłkomierz. Vilnius, C Lithuania 55°16′N 24°46′E
**Ukraina** *see* Ukraine
116 L6 **Ukraine** *off.* Ukraine, *Rus.* Ukraina, *Ukr.* Ukrayina; *prev.* Ukrainian Soviet Socialist Republic, Ukrainskay S.S.R. ◆ *republic* SE Europe
**Ukraine** *see* Ukraine
**Ukrainian Soviet Socialist Republic** *see* Ukraine
**Ukrainskay S.S.R/ Ukrayina** *see* Ukraine
82 B13 **Uku** Kwanza Sul, NW Angola 11°25′S 14°18′E
164 B13 **Uku-jima** *island* Gotō-rettō, SW Japan
83 F20 **Ukwi** Kgalagadi, SW Botswana 23°41′S 20°26′E
118 M13 **Ula** *Rus.* Ulla. Vitsyebskaya Voblasts', N Belarus 55°14′N 29°15′E
136 C16 **Ula** Muğla, SW Turkey 37°08′N 28°25′E
118 M13 **Ula** *Rus.* Ulla. ≈ N Belarus
162 L7 **Ulaanbaatar** *var.* Ulan Bator; *prev.* Urga. ● (Mongolia) Töv, C Mongolia 47°55′N 106°57′E
**Ulaan-Ereg** *see* Bayanmönh
162 E5 **Ulaangom** Uvs, NW Mongolia 49°56′N 92°06′E
162 D5 **Ulaanhus** *var.* Bilüü. Bayan-Ölgiy, W Mongolia 48°54′N 89°40′E
**Ulaantolgoy** *see* Möst
**Ulaan-Uul** *see* Öldziyt, Bayanhongor, Mongolia
**Ulaan-Uul** *see* Erdene, Dornogovĭ, Mongolia
162 M14 **Ulan** *var.* Otog Qi. Nei Mongol Zizhiqu, N China 39°05′N 107°58′E
159 R10 **Ulan** *var.* Xireg; *prev.* Xiligou. Qinghai, C China 36°59′N 98°21′E
**Ulan Bator** *see* Ulaanbaatar
162 L13 **Ulan Buh Shamo** *desert* N China
**Ulanhad** *see* Chifeng
163 T8 **Ulanhot** Nei Mongol Zizhiqu, N China 46°02′N 122°E
127 Q14 **Ulan Khol** Respublika Kalmykiya, SW Russia 45°27′N 46°48′E
163 P13 **Ulan Qab** *var.* Jining. Nei Mongol Zizhiqu, N China 40°59′N 113°08′E
162 M13 **Ulansuhai Nur** ◎ N China
123 N14 **Ulan-Ude** *prev.* Verkhneudinsk. Respublika Buryatiya, S Russia 51°55′N 107°40′E
159 N12 **Ulan Ul Hu** ◎ C China
187 N9 **Ulawa Island** *island* SE Solomon Islands
138 J7 **'Ulayyānīyah, Bi'r al** *var.* Al Hilbeh. *well* S Syria
123 S12 **Ul'banskiy Zaliv** *strait* E Russia
**Ulbo** *see* Olib
113 J18 **Ulcinj** S Montenegro 41°56′N 19°14′E
**Uldz** *see* Norovlin
**Uleåborg** *see* Oulu
**Uleälv** *see* Oulujoki
95 G16 **Ulefoss** Telemark, S Norway 59°17′N 09°15′E
**Uleträsk** *see* Oulujärvi
113 L19 **Ulëz** *var.* Ulëza. Dibër, C Albania 41°42′N 19°52′E
**Ulëza** *see* Ulëz
95 F22 **Ulfborg** Midtjylland, W Denmark 56°16′N 08°21′E
98 N13 **Ulft** Gelderland, E Netherlands 51°53′N 06°23′E
162 G7 **Uliastay** *prev.* Jibhalanta. Dzavhan, W Mongolia 47°47′N 96°53′E
188 F8 **Ulimang** Babeldaob, N Palau
67 T10 **Ulindi** ≈ W Dem. Rep. Congo
188 H14 **Ulithi Atoll** *atoll* Caroline Islands, W Micronesia
112 N10 **Uljma** Vojvodina, NE Serbia 45°04′N 21°08′E
**Ul'kayak** *see* Ol'keyyek
145 Q7 **Ul'ken-Karaoy, Ozero** *prev.* Ul'ken-Karoy, Ozero. ◎ N Kazakhstan
**Ul'ken-Karoy, Ozero** *see* Ul'ken-Karaoy, Ozero
**Ülkenözen** *see* Karaozen
**Ülkenqobda** *see* Kobda
104 G3 **Ulla** ≈ NW Spain
**Ulla** *see* Ula
183 S10 **Ulladulla** New South Wales, SE Australia 35°21′S 150°25′E
153 T14 **Ullapara** Rajshahi, W Bangladesh 24°20′N 89°34′E
96 H7 **Ullapool** N Scotland, United Kingdom 57°54′N 05°10′W
95 J20 **Ullared** Halland, S Sweden 57°07′N 12°45′E
105 T7 **Ulldecona** Cataluña, NE Spain 40°36′N 00°27′E
92 I9 **Ullsfjorden** *fjord* N Norway
97 K15 **Ullswater** ◎ NW England, United Kingdom
101 I22 **Ulm** Baden-Württemberg, S Germany 48°24′N 09°59′E
33 R8 **Ulm** Montana, NW USA 47°27′N 111°32′W
183 V5 **Ulmarra** New South Wales, SE Australia 29°37′S 153°06′E
116 K13 **Ulmeni** Buzău, C Romania 45°08′N 26°43′E
116 K14 **Ulmeni** Călăraşi, S Romania 44°08′N 26°43′E
42 L7 **Ulmukhuás** Costa Caribe Norte, NE Nicaragua 14°20′N 84°30′W
188 C8 **Ulong** *var.* Aulong. *island* Palau Islands, N Palau
83 N14 **Ulonguè** *var.* Ulongwé. Tete, NW Mozambique 14°34′S 34°21′E
**Ulongwé** *see* Ulonguè
95 K19 **Ulricehamn** Västra Götaland, S Sweden 57°47′N 13°25′E
98 N5 **Ulrum** Groningen, NE Netherlands 53°24′N 06°20′E
163 Z16 **Ulsan** *Jap.* Urusan. SE South Korea 35°33′N 129°19′E
94 D10 **Ulsteinvik** Møre og Romsdal, S Norway 62°21′N 05°53′E
97 D15 **Ulster** ◈ *province* Northern Ireland, United Kingdom/Ireland
171 Q10 **Ulu** Pulau Siau, N Indonesia 02°46′N 125°22′E
123 Q11 **Ulu** Respublika Sakha (Yakutiya), NE Russia 60°18′N 127°27′E
42 H5 **Ulúa, Río** ≈ NW Honduras
136 D12 **Ulubat Gölü** ◎ NW Turkey
136 E12 **Uludağ** ▲ NW Turkey 40°08′N 29°13′E
158 D7 **Ulugqat** Xinjiang Uygur Zizhiqu, W China 39°45′N 74°10′E
136 J16 **Ulukışla** Niğde, S Turkey 37°33′N 34°29′E
189 O15 **Ulul** *island* Caroline Islands, C Micronesia
83 L22 **Ulundi** KwaZulu/Natal, E South Africa 28°18′S 31°26′E
158 M3 **Ulungur He** ≈ NW China
158 K2 **Ulungur Hu** ◎ NW China
181 P8 **Uluru** *var.* Ayers Rock. *monolith* Northern Territory, C Australia
97 K16 **Ulverston** NW England, United Kingdom 54°13′N 03°08′W
183 O16 **Ulverstone** Tasmania, SE Australia 41°09′S 146°10′E
94 D13 **Ulvik** Hordaland, S Norway 60°34′N 06°53′E
93 J18 **Ulvila** Satakunta, W Finland 61°26′N 21°55′E
**Ul'yanovka** *see* Blahovishchens'ke
127 Q5 **Ul'yanovsk** *prev.* Simbirsk. Ul'yanovskaya Oblast', W Russia 54°17′N 48°21′E
127 Q5 **Ul'yanovskaya Oblast'** ◈ *province* W Russia
**Ul'yanovskiy** *see* Botakara
**Ul'yanovskiy Kanal** *see* Ul'yanow Kanali
146 M13 **Ul'yanow Kanali** *Rus.* Ul'yanovskiy Kanal. *canal* Turkmenistan/Uzbekistan
**Ulyshylanshyq** *see* Uly-Zhylanshyk
26 H6 **Ulysses** Kansas, C USA 37°36′N 101°23′W
145 O12 **Ulytau, Gory** ▲▲ C Kazakhstan
145 N11 **Uly-Zhylanshyk** *Kaz.* Ulyshylanshyq. ≈ C Kazakhstan
112 A9 **Umag** *It.* Umago. Istra, NW Croatia 45°25′N 13°32′E
**Umago** *see* Umag
41 W12 **Umán** Yucatán, SE Mexico 20°51′N 89°43′W
117 O7 **Uman'** *Rus.* Uman. Cherkas'ka Oblast', C Ukraine 48°45′N 30°10′E
189 V13 **Uman** *atoll* Chuuk Islands, C Micronesia
**'Umān** *see* Oman
**Uman** *see* Uman'
**Umanak/Umanaq** *see* Uummannaq
**'Umān, Khalīj** *see* Oman, Gulf of
**'Umān, Salṭanat** *see* Oman
154 K10 **Umaria** Madhya Pradesh, C India 23°34′N 80°49′E
149 R16 **Umarkot** Sindh, SE Pakistan 25°22′N 69°48′E
188 B17 **Umatac** SW Guam 13°17′N 144°40′E
188 A17 **Umatac Bay** *bay* SW Guam
139 S6 **Umayqah** Şalāḩ ad Dīn, C Iraq 34°32′N 43°45′E
124 J5 **Umba** Murmanskaya Oblast', NW Russia 66°39′N 34°24′E
138 I8 **Umbāshī, Khirbat al** *ruins* As Suwaydā', S Syria
80 A12 **Umbelasha** ≈ W South Sudan
106 H12 **Umbertide** Umbria, C Italy 43°16′N 12°21′E
61 B17 **Umberto** *var.* Humberto. Santa Fe, C Argentina 30°52′S 61°19′W
186 E7 **Umboi Island** *var.* Rooke Island. *island* C Papua New Guinea
124 J4 **Umbozero, Ozero** ◎ NW Russia
106 H13 **Umbria** ◈ *region* C Italy
**Umbrian-Machigian Mountains** *see* Umbro-Marchigiano, Appennino
106 I12 **Umbro-Marchigiano, Appennino** *Eng.* Umbrian-Machigian Mountains. ▲▲ C Italy
93 J16 **Umeå** Västerbotten, N Sweden 63°50′N 20°15′E
93 H14 **Umeälven** ≈ N Sweden
39 Q5 **Umiat** Alaska, USA 69°22′N 152°09′W
83 K23 **Umlazi** KwaZulu/Natal, E South Africa 29°58′S 30°50′E
139 X10 **Umm al Baqar, Hawr** *var.* Birkat ad Dawaymah. *spring* S Iraq
**Umm al Faṭūr** *see* Umm al Fuṭūr
139 Q5 **Umm al Fuṭūr** *var.* Umm at Tūz, Umm al Faṭūr. Şalāḩ ad Dīn, C Iraq 34°53′N 42°42′E
141 U12 **Umm al Ḩayt, Wādī** *var.* Wādī Amilḩayt. *seasonal river* SW Oman
**Umm al Qaiwain** *see* Umm al Qaywayn
143 R15 **Umm al Qaywayn** *var.* Umm al Qaiwain. Umm al Qaywayn, NE United Arab Emirates 25°43′N 55°55′E



◆ Country
● Country Capital
◇ Dependent Territory
○ Dependent Territory Capital
◈ Administrative Regions
✈ International Airport
▲ Mountain
▲▲ Mountain Range
⛰ Volcano
≈ River
◎ Lake
⊠ Reservoir
337

UMM ʻĀMŪD – VAISON-LA-ROMAINE


138 *J3* **Umm ʻĀmūd** Ḥalab, N Syria *35°57′N 37°39′E*
141 *Y10* **Umm ar Ruṣāṣ** ***var.*** Umm Ruṣayṣ. W Oman *20°26′N 58°48′E*
141 *X9* **Umm as Samīn** *salt flat* C Oman
**Umm at Tūz** *see* Umm al Fuṭūr
141 *V9* **Umm az Zumūl** *oasis* E Saudi Arabia
80 *A9* **Umm Buru** Western Darfur, W Sudan *15°01′N 23°36′E*
80 *A12* **Umm Dafag** Southern Darfur, W Sudan *10°28′N 23°20′E*
**Umm Durmān** *see* Omdurman
138 *F9* **Umm el Fahm** Haifa, N Israel *32°30′N 35°06′E*
80 *F9* **Umm Inderab** Northern Kordofan, C Sudan *15°12′N 31°54′E*
80 *C10* **Umm Keddada** Northern Darfur, W Sudan *13°36′N 26°42′E*
140 *J7* **Umm Lajj** Tabūk, W Saudi Arabia *25°02′N 37°19′E*
138 *L10* **Umm Maḥfur** ≈ N Jordan
139 *Y13* **Umm Qaṣr** Al Baṣrah, SE Iraq *30°02′N 47°55′E*
**Umm Ruṣayṣ** *see* Umm ar Ruṣāṣ
80 *F11* **Umm Ruwaba** ***var.*** Umm Ruwābah, Um Ruwāba. Northern Kordofan, C Sudan *12°54′N 31°13′E*
**Umm Ruwābah** *see* Umm Ruwaba
75 *T7* **Umm Sāʻd** ***var.*** Musāʻid, Musaad. NE Libya *31°34′N 23°03′E*
143 *N16* **Umm Saʻīd** ***var.*** Musayʻīd. S Qatar *24°57′N 51°32′E*
139 *Y10* **Umm Sawān, Hawr** ⊛ S Iraq
138 *K10* **Umm Ṭuways, Wādī** *dry watercourse* N Jordan
38 *J17* **Umnak Island** *island* Aleutian Islands, Alaska, USA
32 *F13* **Umpqua River** ≈ Oregon, NW USA
82 *D13* **Umpulo** Bié, C Angola *12°43′S 17°42′E*
154 *I12* **Umred** Mahārāshtra, C India *20°54′N 79°19′E*
**Um Ruwāba** *see* Umm Ruwaba
**Umtali** *see* Mutare
**Umtata** *see* Mthatha
77 *V17* **Umuahia** Abia, SW Nigeria *05°30′N 07°33′E*
60 *H10* **Umuarama** Paraná, S Brazil *23°45′S 53°20′W*
**Umvuma** *see* Mvuma
83 *K18* **Umzingwani** ≈ S Zimbabwe
112 *D11* **Una** ≈ Bosnia and Herzegovina/Croatia
112 *E12* **Unac** ≈ W Bosnia and Herzegovina
23 *T6* **Unadilla** Georgia, SE USA *32°15′N 83°44′W*
18 *I10* **Unadilla River** ≈ New York, NE USA
59 *L18* **Unaí** Minas Gerais, SE Brazil *16°24′S 46°49′W*
39 *N10* **Unalakleet** Alaska, USA *63°52′N 160°47′W*
38 *K17* **Unalaska Island** *island* Aleutian Islands, Alaska, USA
185 *I16* **Una, Mount** ▲ South Island, New Zealand *42°12′S 172°34′E*
82 *N13* **Unango** Niassa, N Mozambique *12°45′S 35°28′E*
**Unao** *see* Unnāo
92 *L12* **Unari** Lappi, N Finland *67°07′N 25°37′E*
141 *O6* **ʻUnayzah** ***var.*** Anaiza. Al Qaṣīm, C Saudi Arabia *26°03′N 44°00′E*
138 *L10* **ʻUnayzah, Jabal** ▲ Jordan/Saudi Arabia *32°09′N 39°11′E*
**Unci** *see* Almería
57 *K19* **Uncía** Potosí, C Bolivia *18°30′S 66°29′W*
37 *Q7* **Uncompahgre Peak** ▲ Colorado, C USA *38°04′N 107°27′W*
37 *P6* **Uncompahgre Plateau** *plain* Colorado, C USA
95 *L17* **Unden** ⊛ S Sweden
28 *M4* **Underwood** North Dakota, N USA *47°25′N 101°09′W*
171 *T13* **Undur** Pulau Seram, E Indonesia *03°41′S 130°38′E*
**Undur Khan** *see* Öndörhaan
126 *H6* **Unecha** Bryanskaya Oblast', W Russia *52°51′N 32°38′E*
39 *N16* **Unga** Unga Island, Alaska, USA *55°14′N 160°34′W*
**Ungaria** *see* Hungary
183 *P8* **Ungarie** New South Wales, SE Australia *33°39′S 146°54′E*
**Ungarisch-Brod** *see* Uherský Brod
**Ungarisches Erzgebirge** *see* Slovenské rudohorie
**Ungarisch-Hradisch** *see* Uherské Hradiště
**Ungarn** *see* Hungary
12 *M4* **Ungava Bay** *bay* Québec, E Canada
12 *J2* **Ungava, Péninsule d'** *peninsula* Québec, SE Canada
**Ungeny** *see* Ungheni
116 *M9* **Ungheni** ***Rus.*** Ungeny. W Moldova *47°13′N 27°48′E*
**Unguja** *see* Zanzibar
146 *G10* **Üngüz Angyrsyndaky Garagum** ***Rus.*** Zaunguzskiye Garagumy. *desert* N Turkmenistan
146 *H11* **Unguz, Solonchakovyye Vpadiny** *salt marsh* C Turkmenistan
**Ungvár** *see* Uzhhorod
60 *I12* **União da Vitória** Paraná, S Brazil *26°13′S 51°05′W*
111 *G17* **Uničov** ***Ger.*** Mährisch-Neustadt. Olomoucký Kraj, E Czechia *49°48′N 17°05′E*
110 *J12* **Uniejów** Łódzkie, C Poland *51°58′N 18°46′E*
112 *A11* **Unije** *island* W Croatia
38 *L16* **Unimak Island** *island* Aleutian Islands, Alaska, USA
38 *L16* **Unimak Pass** *strait* Aleutian Islands, Alaska, USA
62 *J12* **Unión** San Luis, C Argentina *35°09′S 65°55′W*
27 *W5* **Union** Missouri, C USA *38°27′N 91°01′W*
32 *L12* **Union** Oregon, NW USA *45°12′N 117°51′W*
21 *Q11* **Union** South Carolina, SE USA *34°42′N 81°37′W*
21 *R6* **Union** West Virginia, NE USA *37°36′N 80°34′W*
61 *B25* **Unión, Bahía** *bay* E Argentina
31 *Q13* **Union City** Indiana, N USA *40°12′N 84°50′W*
31 *Q10* **Union City** Michigan, N USA *42°03′N 85°06′W*
13 *C12* **Union City** Pennsylvania, NE USA *41°54′N 79°51′W*
20 *G8* **Union City** Tennessee, S USA *36°26′N 89°03′W*
32 *G14* **Union Creek** Oregon, NW USA *42°54′N 122°26′W*
83 *G25* **Uniondale** Western Cape, SW South Africa *33°40′S 23°07′E*
40 *K13* **Unión de Tula** Jalisco, SW Mexico *19°58′N 104°16′W*
30 *M9* **Union Grove** Wisconsin, N USA *42°39′N 88°03′W*
45 *Y15* **Union Island** *island* S Saint Vincent and the Grenadines
46 *K5* **Union Reefs** *reef* SW Mexico
0 *D7* **Union Seamount** *undersea feature* NE Pacific Ocean *49°35′N 132°45′W*
23 *Q6* **Union Springs** Alabama, S USA *32°08′N 85°43′W*
20 *H6* **Uniontown** Kentucky, S USA *37°46′N 87°55′W*
18 *C16* **Uniontown** Pennsylvania, NE USA *39°54′N 79°44′W*
27 *T1* **Unionville** Missouri, C USA *40°28′N 93°00′W*
141 *V8* **United Arab Emirates** ***Ar.*** Al Imārāt al ʻArabīyah al Muttaḥidah, ***abbrev.*** UAE; ***prev.*** Trucial States. ◆ *federation* SW Asia
**United Arab Republic** *see* Egypt
97 *H14* **United Kingdom** ***off.*** United Kingdom of Great Britain and Northern Ireland, ***abbrev.*** UK. ◆ *monarchy* NW Europe
**United Kingdom of Great Britain and Northern Ireland** *see* United Kingdom
**United Mexican States** *see* Mexico
**United Provinces** *see* Uttar Pradesh
16 *L10* **United States of America** ***off.*** United States of America, ***var.*** America, The States, ***abbrev.*** U.S., USA. ◆ *federal republic* North America
**United States of America** *see* United States of America
124 *J10* **Unitsa** Respublika Kareliya, NW Russia *62°31′N 34°31′E*
11 *S15* **Unity** Saskatchewan, S Canada *52°27′N 109°10′W*
80 *D13* **Unity** ***var.*** Wahda. ◈ *state* N South Sudan
105 *Q8* **Universales, Montes** ▲▲ C Spain
27 *X4* **University City** Missouri, C USA *38°40′N 90°19′W*
187 *Q13* **Unmet** Malekula, C Vanuatu *16°09′S 167°16′E*
101 *F15* **Unna** Nordrhein-Westfalen, W Germany *51°32′N 07°41′E*
**Unnan** *see* Kisuki
152 *L12* **Unnão** ***prev.*** Unao. Uttar Pradesh, N India *26°32′N 80°30′E*
187 *R15* **Unpongkor** Erromango, S Vanuatu *18°48′S 169°01′E*
**Unruhstadt** *see* Kargowa
96 *M1* **Unst** *island* NE Scotland, United Kingdom
101 *K16* **Unstrut** ≈ C Germany
**Unterdrauburg** *see* Dravograd
**Unterlimbach** *see* Lendava
101 *L23* **Unterschleissheim** Bayern, SE Germany *48°16′N 11°34′E*
101 *H24* **Untersee** ⊛ Germany/Switzerland
100 *O10* **Unterueckersee** ⊛ NE Germany
55 *N12* **Unturán, Sierra de** ▲▲ Brazil/Venezuela
159 *N11* **Unuli Horog** Qinghai, W China *35°10′N 91°50′E*
136 *M11* **Ünye** Ordu, W Turkey *41°08′N 37°14′E*
**Unza** *see* Unzha
125 *O14* **Unzha** ***var.*** Unza. ≈ NW Russia
79 *E17* **Uolo, Río** ***var.*** Eyo (lower course), Mbini, Uele (upper course), Woleu; ***prev.*** Benito. ≈ Equatorial Guinea/Gabon
55 *Q10* **Uonán** Bolívar, SE Venezuela *04°33′N 62°10′W*
161 *T12* **Uotsuri-shima** ***Chin.*** Diaoyu Dao. *island* (disputed) China/Japan/Taiwan
165 *M11* **Uozu** Toyama, Honshū, SW Japan *36°50′N 137°25′E*
42 *L12* **Upala** Alajuela, NW Costa Rica *10°52′N 85°W*
55 *P7* **Upata** Bolívar, E Venezuela *08°02′N 62°25′W*
79 *M23* **Upemba, Lac** ⊛ SE Dem. Rep. Congo
145 *R11* **Upenskoye** ***prev.*** Uspenskiy. Karaganda, C Kazakhstan *48°45′N 72°46′E*
197 *O12* **Upernavik** ***var.*** Upernivik. Avannaata, C Greenland *73°06′N 55°42′W*
**Upernivik** *see* Upernavik
83 *F22* **Upington** Northern Cape, W South Africa *28°28′S 21°14′E*
**Uplands** *see* Ottawa
192 *I16* **ʻUpolu** *island* SE Samoa
38 *G11* **ʻUpolu Point** ***var.*** Upolu Point. *headland* Hawaiʻi, USA, C Pacific Ocean *20°15′N 155°51′W*
**Upper Austria** *see* Oberösterreich
**Upper Bann** *see* Bann
14 *M13* **Upper Canada Village** *tourist site* Ontario, SE Canada
18 *I16* **Upper Darby** Pennsylvania, NE USA *39°57′N 75°15′W*
28 *L2* **Upper Des Lacs Lake** ⊠ North Dakota, N USA
185 *L14* **Upper Hutt** Wellington, North Island, New Zealand *41°06′S 175°06′E*
29 *X11* **Upper Iowa River** ≈ Iowa, C USA
32 *H15* **Upper Klamath Lake** ⊛ Oregon, NW USA
34 *M6* **Upper Lake** California, W USA *39°07′N 122°53′W*
35 *Q1* **Upper Lake** ⊛ California, W USA
10 *K9* **Upper Liard** Yukon, W Canada *60°01′N 128°59′W*
97 *E16* **Upper Lough Erne** ⊛ SW Northern Ireland, United Kingdom
80 *F12* **Upper Nile** ◈ *state* NE South Sudan
29 *T3* **Upper Red Lake** ⊛ Minnesota, N USA
31 *S12* **Upper Sandusky** Ohio, N USA *40°49′N 83°16′W*
**Upper Volta** *see* Burkina Faso
95 *O15* **Upplands Väsby** ***var.*** Upplandsväsby. Stockholm, C Sweden *59°29′N 18°04′E*
**Upplandsväsby** *see* Upplands Väsby
95 *O15* **Uppsala** Uppsala, C Sweden *59°52′N 17°38′E*
95 *O14* **Uppsala** ◈ *county* C Sweden
38 *J12* **Upright Cape** *headland* Saint Matthew Island, Alaska, USA *60°19′N 172°15′W*
20 *K6* **Upton** Kentucky, S USA *37°25′N 85°53′W*
33 *Y13* **Upton** Wyoming, C USA *44°06′N 104°37′W*
141 *N7* **ʻUqlat aṣ Ṣuqūr** Al Qaṣīm, W Saudi Arabia *25°51′N 42°13′E*
**Uqsuqtuuq** *see* Gjoa Haven
**Uqturpan** *see* Wushi
54 *C7* **Urabá, Golfo de** *gulf* NW Colombia
**Uracas** *see* Farallon de Pajaros
**Uradarʼya** *see* Oʻradaryo
**Urad Qianqi** *see* Xishanzui, N China
165 *U5* **Urahoro** Hokkaidō, NE Japan *42°47′N 143°41′E*
165 *T5* **Urakawa** Hokkaidō, NE Japan *42°11′N 142°42′E*
**Ural** *see* Zhayyk
183 *T6* **Uralla** New South Wales, SE Australia *30°39′S 151°30′E*
**Ural Mountains** *see* Ural'skiye Gory
144 *F8* **Ural'sk** ***Kaz.*** Oral. Zapadnyy Kazakhstan, NW Kazakhstan *51°12′N 51°17′E*
**Ural'skaya Oblast'** *see* Zapadnyy Kazakhstan
127 *W5* **Ural'skiye Gory** ***var.*** Ural'skiy Khrebet, ***Eng.*** Ural Mountains. ▲▲ Kazakhstan/Russia
**Ural'skiy Khrebet** *see* Ural'skiye Gory
138 *I3* **Urām aṣ Ṣughrá** Ḥalab, N Syria *36°10′N 36°55′E*
183 *P10* **Urana** New South Wales, SE Australia *35°22′S 146°16′E*
11 *S10* **Uranium City** Saskatchewan, C Canada *59°30′N 108°46′W*
58 *F10* **Uraricoera** Roraima, N Brazil *03°26′N 60°54′W*
47 *S5* **Uraricoera, Rio** ≈ N Brazil
**Ura-Tyube** *see* Istaravshan
165 *O13* **Urawa** ***var.*** Saitama. Saitama, Honshū, S Japan *35°52′N 139°40′E*
122 *H10* **Uray** Khanty-Mansiyskiy Avtonomnyy Okrug-Yugra, C Russia *60°07′N 64°38′E*
141 *R7* **ʻUrayʻirah** Ash Sharqīyah, E Saudi Arabia *25°59′N 48°52′E*
30 *M13* **Urbana** Illinois, N USA *40°06′N 88°12′W*
31 *R13* **Urbana** Ohio, N USA *40°04′N 83°46′W*
29 *V14* **Urbandale** Iowa, C USA *41°37′N 93°42′W*
106 *I11* **Urbania** Marche, C Italy *43°40′N 12°33′E*
106 *I11* **Urbino** Marche, C Italy *43°45′N 12°38′E*
57 *H16* **Urcos** Cusco, S Peru *13°40′S 71°38′W*
105 *N10* **Urda** Castilla-La Mancha, C Spain *39°25′N 03°43′W*
**Urda** *see* Khan Ordasy
**Urdgol** *see* Chandmanĭ
105 *O3* **Urduña** ***var.*** Orduña. País Vasco, N Spain *43°00′N 03°00′W*
**Urdzhar** *see* Urzhar
97 *L16* **Ure** ≈ N England, United Kingdom
119 *K18* **Urechcha** ***Rus.*** Urech'ye. Minskaya Voblasts', S Belarus *52°57′N 27°54′E*
**Urech'ye** *see* Urechcha
127 *P2* **Uren'** Nizhegorodskaya Oblast', W Russia *57°30′N 45°48′E*
122 *J9* **Urengoy** Yamalo-Nenetskiy Avtonomnyy Okrug, N Russia *65°52′N 78°42′E*
184 *K10* **Urenui** Taranaki, North Island, New Zealand *38°59′S 174°25′E*
187 *Q12* **Ureparapara** *island* Banks Islands, N Vanuatu
40 *G5* **Ures** Sonora, NW Mexico *29°26′N 110°24′W*
**Urfa** *see* Şanlıurfa
**Urga** *see* Ulaanbaatar
162 *F6* **Urgamal** ***var.*** Hungiy. Dzavhan, W Mongolia *48°31′N 94°15′E*
146 *H9* **Urganch** ***Rus.*** Urgench; ***prev.*** Novo-Urgench. Xorazm Viloyati, W Uzbekistan *41°40′N 60°32′E*
**Urgench** *see* Urganch
136 *J14* **Ürgüp** Nevşehir, C Turkey *38°39′N 34°55′E*
147 *O12* **Urgut** Samarqand Viloyati, C Uzbekistan *39°26′N 67°15′E*
158 *K3* **Urho** Xinjiang Uygur Zizhiqu, W China *46°05′N 84°51′E*
152 *G5* **Uri** Jammu and Kashmir, NW India *34°05′N 74°03′E*
108 *G9* **Uri** ◈ *canton* C Switzerland
54 *F11* **Uribe** Meta, C Colombia *03°01′N 74°33′W*
54 *H4* **Uribia** La Guajira, N Colombia *11°45′N 72°19′W*
116 *G12* **Uricani** ***Hung.*** Hobicaurikány. Hunedoara, SW Romania *45°18′N 23°03′E*
57 *M21* **Uriondo** Tarija, S Bolivia *21°43′S 64°40′W*
40 *I7* **Urique** Chihuahua, N Mexico *27°16′N 107°51′W*
40 *I7* **Urique, Río** ≈ N Mexico
56 *E9* **Uritiyacu, Río** ≈ N Peru
**Uritskiy** *see* Sarykol'
98 *K8* **Urk** Flevoland, N Netherlands *52°40′N 05°35′E*
136 *B14* **Urla** İzmir, W Turkey *38°19′N 26°47′E*
116 *K13* **Urlaţi** Prahova, SE Romania *44°59′N 26°15′E*
127 *V4* **Urman** Respublika Bashkortostan, W Russia *54°53′N 56°52′E*
147 *P12* **Urmetan** W Tajikistan *39°27′N 68°13′E*
**Urmia** *see* Orūmīyeh
**Urmia, Lake** *see* Orūmīyeh, Daryācheh-ye
**Urmiyeh** *see* Orūmīyeh
**Uroševac** *see* Ferizaj
**Ŭroteppa** *see* Istaravshan
54 *D8* **Urrao** Antioquia, W Colombia *06°16′N 76°10′W*
**Ursat'yevskaya** *see* Xovos
**Urt** *see* Gurvantes
127 *X7* **Urtazym** Orenburgskaya Oblast', W Russia *52°12′N 58°48′E*
59 *K18* **Uruaçu** Goiás, C Brazil *14°38′S 49°06′W*
40 *M14* **Uruapan** ***var.*** Uruapan del Progreso. Michoacán, SW Mexico *19°26′N 102°04′W*
**Uruapan del Progreso** *see* Uruapan
57 *G15* **Urubamba, Cordillera** ▲▲ C Peru
57 *G14* **Urubamba, Río** ≈ C Peru
58 *G12* **Urucará** Amazonas, N Brazil *02°30′S 57°45′W*
61 *E16* **Uruguaiana** Rio Grande do Sul, S Brazil *29°45′S 57°05′W*
**Uruguai, Rio** *see* Uruguay
61 *E18* **Uruguay** ***off.*** Oriental Republic of Uruguay; ***prev.*** La Banda Oriental. ◆ *republic* E South America
61 *E15* **Uruguay** ***var.*** Rio Uruguai, Río Uruguay. ≈ E South America
**Uruguay, Oriental Republic of** *see* Uruguay
**Uruguay, Río** *see* Uruguay
**Urukthapel** *see* Ngeruktabel
**Urumchi** *see* Ürümqi
**Urumi Yeh** *see* Orūmīyeh, Daryācheh-ye
158 *L5* **Ürümqi** ***var.*** Tihwa, Urumchi, Urumqi, Urumtsi, Wu-lu-k'o-mu-shi, Wu-lu-mu-ch'i; ***prev.*** Ti-hua. Xinjiang Uygur Zizhiqu, NW China *43°52′N 87°31′E*
**Urumtsi** *see* Ürümqi
**Urundi** *see* Burundi
183 *V6* **Urunga** New South Wales, SE Australia *30°33′S 152°58′E*
188 *C15* **Uruno Point** *headland* NW Guam *13°37′N 144°50′E*
123 *U13* **Urup, Ostrov** *island* Kuril'skiye Ostrova, SE Russia
141 *P11* **ʻUruq al Mawārid** *desert* S Saudi Arabia
**Urusan** *see* Ulsan
127 *T5* **Urussu** Respublika Tatarstan, W Russia *54°34′N 53°23′E*
184 *K10* **Uruti** Taranaki, North Island, New Zealand *38°57′S 174°32′E*
57 *K19* **Uru Uru, Lago** ⊛ W Bolivia
55 *P9* **Uruyén** Bolívar, SE Venezuela *05°40′N 62°26′W*
149 *O7* **Uruzgān** ; ***prev.*** Orūzgān. Uruzgān, C Afghanistan *32°58′N 66°39′E*
149 *N6* **Uruzgān** ***prev.*** Orūzgān. ◈ *province* C Afghanistan
165 *T3* **Uryū-gawa** ≈ Hokkaidō, NE Japan
165 *T2* **Uryū-ko** ⊛ Hokkaidō, NE Japan
127 *N8* **Uryupinsk** Volgogradskaya Oblast', SW Russia *50°51′N 41°59′E*
145 *X12* **Urzhar** ***prev.*** Urdzhar. Vostochnyy Kazakhstan, E Kazakhstan *47°06′N 81°33′E*
125 *R16* **Urzhum** Kirovskaya Oblast', NW Russia *57°09′N 49°56′E*
116 *K13* **Urziceni** Ialomiţa, SE Romania *44°43′N 26°39′E*
164 *E14* **Usa** Ōita, Kyūshū, SW Japan *33°31′N 131°22′E*
125 *T6* **Usa** ≈ NW Russia
136 *E14* **Uşak** ***prev.*** Ushak. Uşak, W Turkey *38°42′N 29°25′E*
136 *D14* **Uşak** ***var.*** Ushak. ◈ *province* W Turkey
83 *C19* **Usakos** Erongo, W Namibia *22°01′S 15°32′E*
81 *J21* **Usambara Mountains** ▲▲ NE Tanzania
81 *G23* **Usangu Flats** *wetland* SW Tanzania
65 *D24* **Usborne, Mount** ▲ East Falkland, Falkland Islands *51°35′S 58°57′W*
100 *O8* **Usedom** *island* NE Germany
99 *M24* **Useldange** Diekirch, C Luxembourg *49°47′N 05°59′E*
119 *L16* **Usha** ≈ C Belarus
**Ushachi** *see* Ushachy
118 *L13* **Ushachy** ***Rus.*** Ushachi. Vitsyebskaya Voblasts', N Belarus *55°11′N 28°37′E*
**Ushak** *see* Uşak
122 *L4* **Ushakova, Ostrov** *island* Severnaya Zemlya, N Russia
**Ushant** *see* Ouessant, Île d'
145 *W13* **Usharal** ***prev.*** Ucharal. Almaty, E Kazakhstan *46°08′N 80°55′E*
164 *B15* **Ushibuka** ***var.*** Usibuka. Kumamoto, Shimo-jima, SW Japan *32°12′N 130°00′E*
**Ushi Point** *see* Sabaneta, Puntan
145 *V14* **Ushtobe** ***Kaz.*** Üshtöbe. Almaty, SE Kazakhstan *45°15′N 77°59′E*
**Üshtöbe** *see* Ushtobe
63 *I25* **Ushuaia** Tierra del Fuego, S Argentina *54°48′S 68°19′W*
39 *R10* **Usibelli** Alaska, USA *63°54′N 148°41′W*
**Usibuka** *see* Ushibuka
186 *D7* **Usino** Madang, N Papua New Guinea *05°40′S 145°31′E*
125 *U6* **Usinsk** Respublika Komi, NW Russia *66°01′N 57°37′E*
97 *K22* **Usk** ***Wel.*** Wysg. ≈ SE Wales, United Kingdom
**Uskočke Planine/Uskokengebirge** *see* Gorjanci
**Uskoplje** *see* Gornji Vakuf
**Üsküb/Üsküp** *see* Skopje
114 *M11* **Üsküpdere** Kırklareli, NW Turkey *41°41′N 27°21′E*
126 *L7* **Usman'** Lipetskaya Oblast', W Russia *52°04′N 39°41′E*
118 *D8* **Usmas Ezers** ⊛ NW Latvia
125 *U13* **Usol'ye** Permskiy Kray, NW Russia *59°27′N 56°33′E*
41 *T16* **Uspanapa, Río** ≈ SE Mexico
**Uspenskiy** *see* Upenskoye
103 *O11* **Ussel** Corrèze, C France *45°33′N 02°18′E*
163 *Z6* **Ussuri** ***var.*** Usuri, Wusuri, ***Chin.*** Wusuli Jiang. ≈ China/Russia
123 *S15* **Ussuriysk** ***prev.*** Nikol'sk, Nikol'sk-Ussuriyskiy, Voroshilov. Primorskiy Kray, SE Russia *43°48′N 131°59′E*
136 *J10* **Usta Burnu** *headland* N Turkey *41°58′N 34°30′E*
149 *P13* **Usta Muhammad** Baluchistan, SW Pakistan *28°07′N 68°00′E*
123 *V11* **Ust'-Bol'sheretsk** Kamchatskiy Kray, E Russia *52°48′N 156°12′E*
127 *N9* **Ust'-Buzulukskaya** Volgogradskaya Oblast', SW Russia *50°12′N 42°06′E*
111 *C16* **Ustecký Kraj** ◈ *region* NW Czechia
108 *G7* **Uster** Zürich, NE Switzerland *47°21′N 08°49′E*
107 *I22* **Ustica, Isola d'** *island* S Italy
122 *M11* **Ust'-Ilimsk** Irkutskaya Oblast', C Russia *57°57′N 102°30′E*
111 *C15* **Ústí nad Labem** ***Ger.*** Aussig. Ústecký Kraj, NW Czechia *50°41′N 14°04′E*
111 *F17* **Ústí nad Orlicí** ***Ger.*** Wildenschwert. Pardubický Kraj, C Czechia *49°58′N 16°24′E*
**Ustinov** *see* Izhevsk
113 *J14* **Ustiprača** ◈ Republika Srpska, SE Bosnia and Herzegovina
122 *H11* **Ust'-Ishim** Omskaya Oblast', C Russia *57°42′N 70°58′E*
110 *G6* **Ustka** ***Ger.*** Stolpmünde. Pomorskie, N Poland *54°35′N 16°50′E*
123 *V9* **Ust'-Kamchatsk** Kamchatskiy Kray, E Russia *56°14′N 162°28′E*
145 *X9* **Ust'-Kamenogorsk** ***Kaz.*** Öskemen. Vostochnyy Kazakhstan, E Kazakhstan *49°58′N 82°36′E*
123 *T10* **Ust'-Khayryuzovo** Krasnoyarskiy Kray, E Russia *57°07′N 156°37′E*
122 *I14* **Ust'-Koksa** Respublika Altay, S Russia *50°15′N 85°45′E*
125 *S11* **Ust'-Kulom** Respublika Komi, NW Russia *61°42′N 53°42′E*
123 *Q8* **Ust'-Kuyga** Respublika Sakha (Yakutiya), NE Russia *69°59′N 135°27′E*
126 *L14* **Ust'-Labinsk** Krasnodarskiy Kray, SW Russia *44°40′N 40°46′E*
123 *R10* **Ust'-Maya** Respublika Sakha (Yakutiya), NE Russia *60°27′N 134°28′E*
123 *R9* **Ust'-Nera** Respublika Sakha (Yakutiya), NE Russia *64°28′N 143°01′E*
123 *P12* **Ust'-Nyukzha** Amurskaya Oblast', S Russia *56°30′N 121°32′E*
123 *O7* **Ust'-Olenëk** Respublika Sakha (Yakutiya), NE Russia *73°03′N 119°34′E*
123 *T9* **Ust'-Omchug** Magadanskaya Oblast', E Russia *61°07′N 149°17′E*
122 *M13* **Ust'-Ordynskiy** Irkutskaya Oblast', S Russia *52°50′N 104°42′E*
125 *N8* **Ust'-Pinega** Arkhangel'skaya Oblast', NW Russia *64°09′N 41°55′E*
122 *K8* **Ust'-Port** Krasnoyarskiy Kray, N Russia *69°42′N 84°25′E*
114 *L11* **Ustrem** ***prev.*** Vakav. Yambol, E Bulgaria *42°01′N 26°28′E*
111 *O18* **Ustrzyki Dolne** Podkarpackie, SE Poland *49°26′N 22°36′E*
**Ust'-Sysol'sk** *see* Syktyvkar
125 *R7* **Ust'-Tsil'ma** Respublika Komi, NW Russia *65°25′N 52°09′E*
**Ust Urt** *see* Ustyurt Plateau
125 *O11* **Ust'ya** ≈ NW Russia
124 *K6* **Ust'ye Varzugi** Murmanskaya Oblast', NW Russia *66°16′N 36°47′E*
123 *V10* **Ust'yevoye** ***prev.*** Kirovskiy. Kamchatskiy Kray, E Russia *54°06′N 155°48′E*
117 *R8* **Ustynivka** Kirovohrads'ka Oblast', C Ukraine *47°58′N 32°32′E*
144 *H15* **Ustyurt Plateau** ***var.*** Ust Urt, ***Uzb.*** Ustyurt Platosi. *plateau* Kazakhstan/Uzbekistan
**Ustyurt Platosi** *see* Ustyurt Plateau
124 *K14* **Ustyuzhna** Vologodskaya Oblast', NW Russia *58°50′N 36°25′E*
158 *J4* **Usu** Xinjiang Uygur Zizhiqu, NW China *44°27′N 84°37′E*
171 *O13* **Usu** Sulawesi, C Indonesia *02°34′S 120°58′E*
164 *E14* **Usuki** Ōita, Kyūshū, SW Japan *33°07′N 131°48′E*
42 *G8* **Usulután** Usulután, SE El Salvador *13°20′N 88°26′W*
42 *B9* **Usulután** ◈ *department* SE El Salvador
41 *W16* **Usumacinta, Río** ≈ Guatemala/Mexico
**Usumbura** *see* Bujumbura
**Usuri** *see* Ussuri
**U.S./USA** *see* United States of America
171 *W14* **Uta** Papua, E Indonesia *04°28′S 136°03′E*
36 *K5* **Utah** ***off.*** State of Utah, ***also known as*** Beehive State, Mormon State. ◈ *state* W USA
36 *L3* **Utah Lake** ⊛ Utah, W USA
**Utaidhani** *see* Uthai Thani
93 *M14* **Utajärvi** Pohjois-Pohjanmaa, C Finland *64°45′N 26°25′E*
**Utamboni** *see* Mitemele, Río
**Utaradit** *see* Uttaradit
165 *T3* **Utashinai** ***var.*** Utasinai. Hokkaidō, NE Japan *43°32′N 142°03′E*
**Utasinai** *see* Utashinai
193 *Y14* **ʻUta Vavaʻu** *island* Vavaʻu Group, N Tonga
37 *V9* **Ute Creek** ≈ New Mexico, SW USA
118 *H12* **Utena** Utena, E Lithuania *55°30′N 25°34′E*
118 *H12* **Utena** ◈ *province* Lithuania
37 *V10* **Ute Reservoir** ⊠ New Mexico, SW USA
167 *O10* **Uthai Thani** ***var.*** Muang Uthai Thani, Udayadhani, Utaidhani. Uthai Thani, W Thailand *15°22′N 100°03′E*
149 *O15* **Uthal** Baluchistan, SW Pakistan *25°53′N 66°37′E*
**uThongathi** *see* oThongathi
18 *I10* **Utica** New York, NE USA *43°06′N 75°15′W*
105 *R10* **Utiel** Comunitat Valenciana, E Spain *39°33′N 01°13′W*
11 *O13* **Utikuma Lake** ⊛ Alberta, W Canada
42 *I4* **Utila, Isla de** *island* Islas de la Bahía, N Honduras
**Utina** *see* Udine
59 *O17* **Utinga** Bahia, E Brazil *12°05′S 41°07′W*
**Utirik** *see* Utrik Atoll
95 *M22* **Utlängan** *island* S Sweden
117 *U11* **Utlyuts'kyy Lyman** *bay* S Ukraine
95 *P16* **Utö** Stockholm, C Sweden *58°55′N 18°19′E*
25 *Q12* **Utopia** Texas, SW USA *29°30′N 99°31′W*
98 *J11* **Utrecht** ***Lat.*** Trajectum ad Rhenum. Utrecht, C Netherlands *52°06′N 05°07′E*
83 *K22* **Utrecht** KwaZulu/Natal, E South Africa *27°40′S 30°20′E*
98 *I11* **Utrecht** ◈ *province* C Netherlands
104 *K14* **Utrera** Andalucía, S Spain *37°10′N 05°47′W*
189 *V4* **Utrik Atoll** ***var.*** Utirik, Utrōk, Utrōnk. *atoll* Ratak Chain, N Marshall Islands
**Utrōk/Utrōnk** *see* Utrik Atoll
95 *B16* **Utsira** *island* SW Norway
92 *L8* **Utsjoki** ***N. Sami*** Ohcejohka. Lappi, N Finland *69°54′N 27°01′E*
165 *O12* **Utsunomiya** ***var.*** Utunomiya. Tochigi, Honshū, S Japan *36°36′N 139°53′E*
127 *P13* **Utta** Respublika Kalmykiya, SW Russia *46°22′N 46°03′E*
167 *O8* **Uttaradit** ***var.*** Utaradit. Uttaradit, N Thailand *17°38′N 100°05′E*
152 *J9* **Uttarākhand** ◈ *state* N India
152 *J8* **Uttarkāshi** Uttarākhand, N India *30°45′N 78°19′E*
152 *K11* **Uttar Pradesh** ***prev.*** United Provinces, United Provinces of Agra and Oudh. ◈ *state* N India
45 *T5* **Utuado** C Puerto Rico *18°17′N 66°41′W*
158 *K3* **Utubulak** Xinjiang Uygur Zizhiqu, W China *46°50′N 86°15′E*
39 *N5* **Utukok River** ≈ Alaska, USA
**Utunomiya** *see* Utsunomiya
187 *P10* **Utupua** *island* Santa Cruz Islands, E Solomon Islands
**Utva** *see* Shyngyrlau
189 *Y15* **Utwe** Kosrae, E Micronesia
189 *X15* **Utwe Harbor** *harbor* Kosrae, E Micronesia
**Uubulan** *see* Hayrhan
163 *O8* **Uulbayan** ***var.*** Dzüünbulag. Sühbaatar, E Mongolia *46°30′N 112°22′E*
118 *G6* **Uulu** Pärnumaa, SW Estonia *58°15′N 24°32′E*
197 *N13* **Uummannaq** ***var.*** Umanak, Umanaq. ◈ Avannaata, C Greenland
**Uummannarsuaq** *see* Nunap Isua
162 *E4* **Üüreg Nuur** ⊛ NW Mongolia
**Uusikaarlepyy** *see* Nykarleby
93 *J19* **Uusikaupunki** ***Swe.*** Nystad. Varsinais-Suomi, SW Finland *60°48′N 21°25′E*
127 *S2* **Uva** Udmurtskaya Respublika, NW Russia *56°41′N 52°15′E*
155 *K25* **Uva** ◈ *province* SE Sri Lanka
113 *L14* **Uvac** ≈ W Serbia
25 *Q12* **Uvalde** Texas, SW USA *29°14′N 99°49′W*
119 *O18* **Uvaravichy** ***Rus.*** Uvarovichi. Homyel'skaya Voblasts', SE Belarus *52°36′N 30°44′E*
54 *J11* **Uvá, Río** ≈ E Colombia
**Uvarovichi** *see* Uvaravichy
127 *N7* **Uvarovo** Tambovskaya Oblast', W Russia *51°58′N 42°13′E*
122 *H10* **Uvat** Tyumenskaya Oblast', C Russia *59°11′N 68°37′E*
190 *G12* **Uvea, Île** *island* N Wallis and Futuna
81 *E21* **Uvinza** Kigoma, W Tanzania *05°08′S 30°23′E*
79 *O20* **Uvira** Sud-Kivu, E Dem. Rep. Congo *03°24′S 29°05′E*
162 *E5* **Uvs** ◈ *province* NW Mongolia
162 *F5* **Uvs Nuur** ***var.*** Ozero Ubsu-Nur. ⊛ Mongolia/Russia
164 *F14* **Uwa** ***var.*** Seiyo. Ehime, Shikoku, SW Japan *33°22′N 132°29′E*
164 *F14* **Uwajima** ***var.*** Uwazima. Ehime, Shikoku, SW Japan *33°13′N 132°32′E*
80 *B5* **ʻUwaynāt, Jabal al** ***var.*** Jebel Uweinat. ▲ Libya/Sudan *21°51′N 25°01′E*
**Uwazima** *see* Uwajima
**Uweinat, Jebel** *see* ʻUwaynāt, Jabal al
14 *H14* **Uxbridge** Ontario, S Canada *44°07′N 79°07′W*
**Uxellodunum** *see* Issoudun
**Uxin Qi** *see* Dabqig, N China
41 *X12* **Uxmal, Ruinas** *ruins* Yucatán, SE Mexico
129 *Q5* **Uy** ≈ Kazakhstan/Russia
144 *K15* **Uyaly** Kzylorda, S Kazakhstan *44°22′N 61°16′E*
123 *R8* **Uyandina** ≈ NE Russia
162 *J8* **Uyanga** ***var.*** Ongi. Övörhangay, C Mongolia *46°30′N 102°18′E*
**Üydzen** *see* Manlay
**Uyeda** *see* Ueda
122 *K5* **Uyedineniya, Ostrov** *island* N Russia
77 *V17* **Uyo** Akwa Ibom, S Nigeria *05°00′N 07°57′E*
162 *D8* **Üyönch** Hovd, W Mongolia *46°04′N 92°05′E*
**Uyuk** *see* Oyyk
141 *V13* **ʻUyūn** SW Oman *17°19′N 53°50′E*
57 *K20* **Uyuni** Potosí, W Bolivia *20°27′S 66°48′W*
57 *J20* **Uyuni, Salar de** *wetland* SW Bolivia
146 *I9* **Uzbekistan** ***off.*** Republic of Uzbekistan, ***Uzb.*** Oʻzbekiston, Oʻzbekiston Respublikasi. ◆ *republic* C Asia
**Uzbekistan, Republic of** *see* Uzbekistan
158 *D8* **Uzbel Shankou** ***Rus.*** Pereval Kyzyl-Dzhiik. *pass* China/Tajikistan
146 *B11* **Uzboý** ***prev. Rus.*** Imeni 26 Bakinskikh Komissarov, ***Turkm.*** 26 Baku Komissarlary Adyndaky. Balkan Welaýaty, W Turkmenistan *39°24′N 54°04′E*
119 *J17* **Uzda** Minskaya Voblasts', C Belarus *53°29′N 27°10′E*
103 *N12* **Uzerche** Corrèze, C France *45°24′N 01°35′E*
103 *R14* **Uzès** Gard, S France *44°00′N 04°25′E*
147 *T10* **Uzgen** ***Kyr.*** Özgön. Oshskaya Oblast', SW Kyrgyzstan *40°42′N 73°17′E*
117 *O3* **Uzh** ≈ N Ukraine
**Uzhgorod** *see* Uzhhorod
116 *G7* **Uzhhorod** ***Rus.*** Uzhgorod; ***prev.*** Ungvár. Zakarpats'ka Oblast', W Ukraine *48°36′N 22°19′E*
**Uzi** *see* Uji
112 *K13* **Užice** ***prev.*** Titovo Užice. Serbia, W Serbia *43°52′N 19°51′E*
**Uzin** *see* Uzyn
126 *L5* **Uzlovaya** Tul'skaya Oblast', W Russia *54°01′N 38°15′E*
108 *H7* **Uznach** Sankt Gallen, NE Switzerland *47°12′N 09°00′E*
**Uzunagach** *see* Uzynagash
136 *B10* **Uzunköprü** Edirne, NW Turkey *41°18′N 26°40′E*
118 *D11* **Užventis** Šiaulai, C Lithuania *55°49′N 22°38′E*
117 *P5* **Uzyn** ***Rus.*** Uzin. Kyivs'ka Oblast', N Ukraine *49°52′N 30°27′E*
145 *U16* **Uzynagash** ***prev.*** Uzunagach. Almaty, SE Kazakhstan *43°08′N 76°20′E*
145 *N7* **Uzynkol'** ***prev.*** Lenīn, Leninskoye. Kustanay, N Kazakhstan *54°05′N 65°23′E*


# V


**Vääksy** *see* Asikkala
83 *H23* **Vaal** ≈ C South Africa
93 *M14* **Vaala** Kainuu, C Finland *64°34′N 26°49′E*
93 *N19* **Vaalimaa** Etelä-Karjala, SE Finland *60°34′N 27°49′E*
99 *M19* **Vaals** Limburg, SE Netherlands *50°46′N 06°01′E*
93 *J16* **Vaasa** ***Swe.*** Vasa; ***prev.*** Nikolainkaupunki. Österbotten, W Finland *63°07′N 21°39′E*
98 *L10* **Vaassen** Gelderland, E Netherlands *52°18′N 05°59′E*
118 *G11* **Vabalninkas** Panevėžys, NE Lithuania *55°59′N 24°45′E*
**Vabkent** *see* Vobkent
111 *J22* **Vác** ***Ger.*** Waitzen. Pest, N Hungary *47°46′N 19°08′E*
61 *I14* **Vacaria** Rio Grande do Sul, S Brazil *28°31′S 50°52′W*
35 *N7* **Vacaville** California, W USA *38°21′N 121°59′W*
103 *R15* **Vaccarès, Étang de** ⊛ SE France
114 *I11* **Vacha** ***var.*** Vŭcha. ≈ SW Bulgaria
44 *L10* **Vache, Île à** *island* SW Haiti
173 *Y16* **Vacoas** W Mauritius *20°18′S 57°29′E*
155 *F21* **Vadakara** ***var.*** Badagara. Kerala, SW India *11°36′N 75°34′E*
32 *G10* **Vader** Washington, NW USA *46°23′N 122°58′W*
94 *D12* **Vadheim** Sogn Og Fjordane, S Norway *61°12′N 05°48′E*
121 *Q2* **Vadili** ***Gk.*** Vatylí. C Cyprus *35°09′N 33°39′E*
154 *D11* **Vadodara** ***prev.*** Baroda. Gujarāt, W India *22°19′N 73°14′E*
92 *M8* **Vadsø** ***Fin.*** Vesisaari. Finnmark, N Norway *70°07′N 29°47′E*
95 *L17* **Vadstena** Östergötland, S Sweden *58°26′N 14°55′E*
108 *I8* **Vaduz** ● (Liechtenstein) W Liechtenstein *47°08′N 09°32′E*
**Vág** *see* Váh
125 *N12* **Vaga** ≈ NW Russia
94 *G11* **Vågåmo** Oppland, S Norway *61°52′N 09°06′E*
112 *D12* **Vaganski Vrh** ▲ W Croatia *44°24′N 15°32′E*
95 *A19* **Vágar** ***Dan.*** Vågø. *island* W Faroe Islands
**Vágbeszterce** *see* Považská Bystrica
95 *L19* **Vaggeryd** Jönköping, S Sweden *57°30′N 14°10′E*
137 *T12* **Vagharshapat** ***var.*** Ejmiadzin, Ejmiatsin, Etchmiadzin, ***Rus.*** Echmiadzin. W Armenia *40°10′N 44°17′E*
95 *O16* **Vagnhärad** Södermanland, C Sweden *58°57′N 17°32′E*
**Vågø** *see* Vágar
104 *G7* **Vagos** Aveiro, N Portugal *40°33′N 08°42′W*
**Vágsellye** *see* Sal'a
92 *H10* **Vågsfjorden** *fjord* N Norway
94 *C10* **Vågsøy** *island* S Norway
**Vágújhely** *see* Nové Mesto nad Váhom
111 *I21* **Váh** ***Ger.*** Waag, ***Hung.*** Vág. ≈ W Slovakia
93 *K16* **Vähäkyrö** Österbotten, W Finland *63°04′N 22°05′E*
147 *P13* **Vahdat** ***prev.*** Kofarnikhon, Ordzhonikidzeabad, Yangi-Bazar, ***Taj.*** Orjonikidzeobod. W Tajikistan *38°32′N 68°56′E*
191 *X11* **Vahitahi** *atoll* Îles Tuamotu, E French Polynesia
**Váhtjer** *see* Gällivare
190 *C9* **Vaiaku** Funafuti Atoll, SE Tuvalu *08°31′N 179°11′E*
**Vaidei** *see* Vulcan
22 *L4* **Vaiden** Mississippi, S USA *33°19′N 89°42′W*
155 *I23* **Vaigai** ≈ SE India
191 *V16* **Vaihu** Easter Island, Chile, E Pacific Ocean *27°10′S 109°22′W*
118 *I6* **Väike Emajõgi** ≈ S Estonia
118 *I4* **Väike-Maarja** ***Ger.*** Klein-Marien. Lääne-Virumaa, NE Estonia *59°07′N 26°16′E*
**Väike-Salatsi** *see* Mazsalaca
37 *R4* **Vail** Colorado, C USA *39°36′N 106°20′W*
193 *V15* **Vaina** Tongatapu, S Tonga *21°12′S 175°10′W*
118 *E5* **Väinameri** ***prev.*** Muhu Väin, ***Ger.*** Moon-Sund. *sea* E Baltic Sea
93 *N18* **Vainikkala** Etelä-Karjala, SE Finland *60°54′N 28°18′E*
118 *D10* **Vaiņode** SW Latvia *56°25′N 21°52′E*
155 *H23* **Vaippār** ≈ SE India
191 *W11* **Vairaatea** *atoll* Îles Tuamotu, C French Polynesia
191 *R8* **Vairao** Tahiti, W French Polynesia *17°48′S 149°17′W*
103 *R14* **Vaison-la-Romaine** Vaucluse, SE France *44°15′N 05°04′E*




◆ Country
● Country Capital
◇ Dependent Territory
○ Dependent Territory Capital
◈ Administrative Regions
✈ International Airport
▲ Mountain
▲▲ Mountain Range
⛰ Volcano
≈ River
⊛ Lake
⊠ Reservoir

VAITUPU – VELKÉ MEZIŘÍČÍ


190 *G11* **Vaitupu** Île Uvea, E Wallis and Futuna *13°14′S 176°09′W*
190 *F7* **Vaitupu** *atoll* C Tuvalu
**Vajdahunyad** *see* Hunedoara
**Vajdej** *see* Vulcan
78 *K12* **Vakaga** ⬖ *prefecture* NE Central African Republic
114 *H10* **Vakarel** Sofia, W Bulgaria *42°35′N 23°40′E*
**Vakav** *see* Ustrem
137 *O11* **Vakfıkebir** Trabzon, NE Turkey *41°03′N 39°19′E*
122 *J10* **Vakh** ≈ C Russia
**Vakhon, Qatorkŭhi** *see* Nicholas Range
147 *P14* **Vakhsh** SW Tajikistan *37°46′N 68°48′E*
147 *Q12* **Vakhsh** ≈ SW Tajikistan
127 *P1* **Vakhtan** Nizhegorodskaya Oblast', W Russia *58°00′N 46°43′E*
94 *C13* **Vaksdal** Hordaland, S Norway *60°29′N 05°45′E*
**Valachia** *see* Wallachia
108 *D11* **Valais** *Ger.* Wallis. ⬖ *canton* SW Switzerland
113 *M21* **Valamarës, Mali i** ▲ SE Albania *40°48′N 20°31′E*
127 *S2* **Valamaz** Udmurtskaya Respublika, NW Russia *57°36′N 52°07′E*
113 *Q19* **Valandovo** SE North Macedonia *41°20′N 22°33′E*
111 *I18* **Valašské Meziříčí** *Ger.* Wallachisch-Meseritsch, *Pol.* Wałeckie Międzyrzecze. Zlínský Kraj, E Czechia *49°29′N 17°57′E*
115 *I17* **Valáxa** *island* Vóreies Sporádes, Greece, Aegean Sea
95 *K16* **Vålberg** Värmland, C Sweden *59°24′N 13°12′E*
116 *H12* **Vâlcea** *prev.* Vîlcea. ⬖ *county* SW Romania
**Vălčedrăm** *see* Valchedram
114 *G7* **Valchedram** *var.* Vălčedrăm, Vŭlchedrŭm. Montana, NW Bulgaria *43°42′N 23°25′E*
63 *J16* **Valcheta** Río Negro, E Argentina *40°42′S 66°08′W*
114 *N8* **Valchi Dol** *var.* Vŭlchidol; *prev.* Kurt-Dere. Varna, E Bulgaria *43°25′N 27°33′E*
15 *P12* **Valcourt** Québec, SE Canada *45°28′N 72°18′W*
**Valdai Hills** *see* Valdayskaya Vozvyshennost'
104 *M3* **Valdavia** ≈ N Spain
124 *I15* **Valday** Novgorodskaya Oblast', W Russia *57°57′N 33°20′E*
124 *I15* **Valdayskaya Vozvyshennost'** *var.* Valdai Hills. *hill range* W Russia
104 *L9* **Valdecañas, Embalse de** ⊠ W Spain
118 *E8* **Valdemārpils** *Ger.* Sassmacken. NW Latvia *57°23′N 22°36′E*
95 *N18* **Valdemarsvik** Östergötland, S Sweden *58°13′N 16°35′E*
105 *N8* **Valdemoro** Madrid, C Spain *40°12′N 03°40′W*
105 *O11* **Valdepeñas** Castilla-La Mancha, C Spain *38°46′N 03°24′W*
104 *L5* **Valderaduey** ≈ NE Spain
104 *L5* **Valderas** Castilla y León, N Spain *42°05′N 05°27′W*
105 *T7* **Valderrobres** *var.* Vall-de-roures. Aragón, NE Spain *40°53′N 00°08′E*
63 *K17* **Valdés, Península** *peninsula* SE Argentina
56 *C5* **Valdéz** *var.* Limones. Esmeraldas, NW Ecuador *01°13′N 79°00′W*
39 *S11* **Valdez** Alaska, USA *61°08′N 146°21′W*
**Valdia** *see* Weldiya
103 *U11* **Val d'Isère** Savoie, E France *45°23′N 07°03′E*
63 *G15* **Valdivia** Los Ríos, C Chile *39°50′S 73°13′W*
**Valdivia Bank** *see* Valdivia Seamount
65 *P17* **Valdivia Seamount** *var.* Valdivia Bank. *undersea feature* E Atlantic Ocean *26°15′S 06°25′E*
103 *N4* **Val-d'Oise** ⬖ *department* N France
14 *J8* **Val-d'Or** Québec, SE Canada *48°06′N 77°42′W*
23 *U8* **Valdosta** Georgia, SE USA *30°49′N 83°16′W*
94 *G13* **Valdres** *physical region* S Norway
32 *L13* **Vale** Oregon, NW USA *43°59′N 117°15′W*
116 *F9* **Valea lui Mihai** *Hung.* Érmihályfalva. Bihor, NW Romania *47°31′N 22°08′E*
11 *N15* **Valemount** British Columbia, SW Canada *52°46′N 119°17′W*
59 *O17* **Valença** Bahia, E Brazil *13°22′S 39°06′W*
104 *F4* **Valença do Minho** Viana do Castelo, N Portugal *42°02′N 08°38′W*
59 *N14* **Valença do Piauí** Piauí, E Brazil *06°26′S 41°46′W*
103 *N8* **Valençay** Indre, C France *47°10′N 01°31′E*
103 *R13* **Valence** *anc.* Valentia, Valentia Julia, Ventia. Drôme, E France *44°56′N 04°54′E*
105 *S10* **Valencia** Comunitat Valenciana, E Spain *39°29′N 00°24′W*
54 *K5* **Valencia** Carabobo, N Venezuela *10°12′N 68°02′W*
105 *R10* **València** *var.* Valencia. ⬖ *province* Comunitat Valenciana, E Spain
105 *S10* **Valencia** ✈ Valencia, E Spain
104 *I10* **Valencia de Alcántara** Extremadura, W Spain *39°25′N 07°14′W*
104 *L4* **Valencia de Don Juan** Castilla y León, N Spain *42°17′N 05°31′W*
105 *U9* **Valencia, Golfo de** *var.* Gulf of Valencia. *gulf* E Spain
**Valencia, Gulf of** *see* Valencia, Golfo de
97 *A21* **Valencia Island** *Ir.* Dairbhre. *island* SW Ireland
105 *R10* **Valenciana, Comunitat** *var.* Valencia, València; *anc.* Valentia. ⬖ *autonomous community* NE Spain
**Valencia/València** *see* Valenciana, Comunitat
103 *P2* **Valenciennes** Nord, N France *50°21′N 03°32′E*
116 *K13* **Vălenii de Munte** Prahova, SE Romania *45°11′N 26°02′E*
**Valentia** *see* Valence, France
**Valentia** *see* Valenciana, Comunitat
**Valentia Julia** *see* Valence
103 *T8* **Valentigney** Doubs, E France *47°27′N 06°49′E*
28 *M12* **Valentine** Nebraska, C USA *42°53′N 100°31′W*
24 *J10* **Valentine** Texas, SW USA *30°35′N 104°30′W*
**Valentine State** *see* Oregon
106 *C8* **Valenza** Piemonte, NW Italy *45°01′N 08°37′E*
94 *I13* **Våler** Hedmark, S Norway *60°39′N 11°52′E*
54 *I6* **Valera** Trujillo, NW Venezuela *09°21′N 70°38′W*
192 *M11* **Valerie Guyot** S Pacific Ocean *33°00′S 164°00′W*
**Valetta** *see* Valletta
118 *I7* **Valga** *Ger.* Walk, *Latv.* Valka. Valgamaa, S Estonia *57°48′N 26°04′E*
118 *I7* **Valgamaa** *var.* Valga Maakond. ⬖ *province* S Estonia
**Valga Maakond** *see* Valgamaa
43 *Q15* **Valiente, Península** *peninsula* NW Panama
103 *X16* **Valinco, Golfe de** *gulf* Corse, France, C Mediterranean Sea
112 *L12* **Valjevo** Serbia, W Serbia *44°17′N 19°54′E*
**Valjok** *see* Válljohka
118 *I7* **Valka** *Ger.* Walk. N Latvia *57°48′N 26°01′E*
**Valka** *see* Valga
93 *L18* **Valkeakoski** Pirkanmaa, W Finland *61°17′N 24°05′E*
93 *M19* **Valkeala** Kymenlaakso, S Finland *60°55′N 26°49′E*
99 *L18* **Valkenburg** Limburg, SE Netherlands *50°52′N 05°50′E*
99 *K15* **Valkenswaard** Noord-Brabant, S Netherlands *51°21′N 05°29′E*
119 *G15* **Valkininkai** Alytus, S Lithuania *54°22′N 24°51′E*
117 *U5* **Valky** Kharkivs'ka Oblast', E Ukraine *49°51′N 35°40′E*
41 *Y12* **Valladolid** Yucatán, SE Mexico *20°39′N 88°13′W*
104 *M5* **Valladolid** Castilla y León, NW Spain *41°39′N 04°45′W*
104 *L5* **Valladolid** ⬖ *province* Castilla y León, N Spain
103 *U15* **Vallauris** Alpes-Maritimes, SE France *43°34′N 07°03′E*
**Vall-de-roures** *see* Valderrobres
**Vall D'Uxó** *see* La Vall d'Uixó
95 *E16* **Valle** Aust-Agder, S Norway *59°13′N 07°33′E*
105 *N2* **Valle** Cantabria, N Spain *43°14′N 04°16′W*
42 *H8* **Valle** ⬖ *department* S Honduras
105 *N8* **Vallecas** Madrid, C Spain *40°23′N 03°37′W*
37 *Q8* **Vallecito Reservoir** ⊠ Colorado, C USA
106 *A7* **Valle d'Aosta** *Fr.* Vallée d'Aoste. ⬖ *region* NW Italy
41 *O14* **Valle de Bravo** México, S Mexico *19°19′N 100°08′W*
55 *N5* **Valle de Guanape** Anzoátegui, N Venezuela *09°54′N 65°41′W*
54 *M6* **Valle de La Pascua** Guárico, N Venezuela *09°15′N 66°00′W*
54 *B11* **Valle del Cauca** *off.* Departamento del Valle del Cauca. ⬖ *province* W Colombia
**Valle del Cauca, Departamento del** *see* Valle del Cauca
41 *N13* **Valle de Santiago** Guanajuato, C Mexico *20°25′N 101°15′W*
40 *J7* **Valle de Zaragoza** Chihuahua, N Mexico *27°25′N 105°50′W*
54 *G5* **Valledupar** Cesar, N Colombia *10°31′N 73°16′W*
**Vallée d'Aoste** *see* Valle d'Aosta
76 *G10* **Vallée de Ferlo** ≈ NW Senegal
57 *M19* **Vallegrande** Santa Cruz, C Bolivia *18°30′S 64°06′W*
41 *P8* **Valle Hermoso** Tamaulipas, C Mexico *25°39′N 97°49′W*
35 *N8* **Vallejo** California, W USA *38°08′N 122°16′W*
62 *G8* **Vallenar** Atacama, N Chile *28°35′S 70°44′W*
95 *O15* **Vallentuna** Stockholm, C Sweden *59°32′N 18°05′E*
121 *P16* **Valletta** *prev.* Valetta. ● (Malta) E Malta *35°54′N 14°31′E*
27 *N6* **Valley Center** Kansas, C USA *37°49′N 97°22′W*
29 *Q5* **Valley City** North Dakota, N USA *46°57′N 97°58′W*
32 *I15* **Valley Falls** Oregon, NW USA *42°28′N 120°16′W*
**Valleyfield** *see* Salaberry-de-Valleyfield
21 *S4* **Valley Head** West Virginia, NE USA *38°33′N 80°01′W*
25 *T8* **Valley Mills** Texas, SW USA *31°36′N 97°27′W*
75 *W10* **Valley of the Kings** *ancient monument* E Egypt
29 *R11* **Valley Springs** South Dakota, N USA *43°34′N 96°28′W*
20 *K5* **Valley Station** Kentucky, S USA *38°06′N 85°52′W*
11 *O13* **Valleyview** Alberta, W Canada *55°02′N 117°17′W*
25 *T5* **Valley View** Texas, SW USA *33°27′N 97°08′W*
61 *C21* **Vallimanca, Arroyo** ≈ E Argentina
92 *L9* **Válljohka** *var.* Valjok. Finnmark, N Norway *69°40′N 25°52′E*
107 *M19* **Vallo della Lucania** Campania, S Italy *40°13′N 15°15′E*
108 *B9* **Vallorbe** Vaud, W Switzerland *46°43′N 06°21′E*
105 *V6* **Valls** Cataluña, NE Spain *41°18′N 01°15′E*
94 *N11* **Vallsta** Gävleborg, C Sweden *61°30′N 16°25′E*
94 *N12* **Vallvik** Gävleborg, C Sweden *61°10′N 17°15′E*
11 *T17* **Val Marie** Saskatchewan, S Canada *49°15′N 107°44′W*
118 *H7* **Valmiera** *Est.* Volmari, *Ger.* Wolmar. N Latvia *57°34′N 25°26′E*
105 *N3* **Valnera** ▲ N Spain *43°08′N 03°39′W*
102 *J3* **Valognes** Manche, N France *49°31′N 01°28′W*
**Valona** *see* Vlorë
**Valona Bay** *see* Vlorës, Gjiri i
104 *G6* **Valongo** *var.* Valongo de Gaia. Porto, N Portugal *41°11′N 08°30′W*
**Valongo de Gaia** *see* Valongo
104 *M5* **Valoria la Buena** Castilla y León, N Spain *41°48′N 04°33′W*
119 *J15* **Valozhyn** *Pol.* Wołożyn, *Rus.* Volozhin. Minskaya Voblasts', C Belarus *54°05′N 26°32′E*
104 *I5* **Valpaços** Vila Real, N Portugal *41°36′N 07°17′W*
62 *G11* **Valparaíso** Valparaíso, C Chile *33°05′S 71°18′W*
40 *L11* **Valparaíso** Zacatecas, C Mexico *22°49′N 103°28′W*
23 *P8* **Valparaiso** Florida, SE USA *30°30′N 86°28′W*
31 *N11* **Valparaiso** Indiana, N USA *41°28′N 87°04′W*
62 *G11* **Valparaíso** *off.* Región de Valparaíso. ⬖ *region* C Chile
**Valparaíso, Región de** *see* Valparaíso
**Valpo** *see* Valpovo
112 *I9* **Valpovo** *Hung.* Valpo. Osijek-Baranja, E Croatia *45°40′N 18°25′E*
103 *R14* **Valréas** Vaucluse, SE France *44°22′N 05°00′E*
**Vals** *see* Vals-Platz
154 *D12* **Valsād** *prev.* Bulsar. Gujarāt, W India *20°40′N 72°55′E*
**Valsbaai** *see* False Bay
171 *T12* **Valse Pisang, Kepulauan** *island group* E Indonesia
108 *H9* **Vals-Platz** *var.* Vals. Graubünden, S Switzerland *46°39′N 09°09′E*
171 *X16* **Vals, Tanjung** *headland* Papua, SE Indonesia *08°26′S 137°35′E*
93 *N15* **Valtimo** Pohjois-Karjala, E Finland *63°39′N 28°49′E*
115 *D17* **Váltou** ▲▲ C Greece
127 *O12* **Valuyevka** Rostovskaya Oblast', SW Russia *46°48′N 43°49′E*
126 *K9* **Valuyki** Belgorodskaya Oblast', W Russia *50°11′N 38°07′E*
36 *L2* **Val Verda** Utah, W USA *40°51′N 111°53′W*
64 *N12* **Valverde** Hierro, Islas Canarias, Spain, NE Atlantic Ocean *27°48′N 17°55′W*
104 *I13* **Valverde del Camino** Andalucía, S Spain *37°35′N 06°45′W*
95 *G23* **Vamdrup** Syddanmark, C Denmark *55°26′N 09°18′E*
94 *L12* **Våmhus** Dalarna, C Sweden *61°07′N 14°30′E*
93 *K18* **Vammala** Pirkanmaa, SW Finland *61°20′N 22°55′E*
**Vámosudvarhely** *see* Odorheiu Secuiesc
137 *S14* **Van** Van, E Turkey *38°30′N 43°23′E*
25 *V7* **Van** Texas, SW USA *32°31′N 95°38′W*
137 *T14* **Van** ⬖ *province* E Turkey
137 *T11* **Vanadzor** *prev.* Kirovakan. N Armenia *40°49′N 44°29′E*
25 *U5* **Van Alstyne** Texas, SW USA *33°25′N 96°34′W*
33 *W10* **Vananda** Montana, NW USA *46°22′N 106°58′W*
116 *I11* **Vânători** *Hung.* Héjjasfalva; *prev.* Vînători. Mureş, C Romania *46°14′N 24°56′E*
191 *W12* **Vanavana** *atoll* Îles Tuamotu, SE French Polynesia
**Vana-Vändra** *see* Vändra
122 *M11* **Vanavara** Krasnoyarskiy Kray, C Russia *60°19′N 102°19′E*
15 *Q8* **Van Bruyssel** Québec, SE Canada *47°56′N 72°08′W*
27 *R10* **Van Buren** Arkansas, C USA *35°28′N 94°25′W*
19 *S1* **Van Buren** Maine, NE USA *47°07′N 67°57′W*
27 *W7* **Van Buren** Missouri, C USA *37°00′N 91°00′W*
19 *T5* **Vanceboro** Maine, NE USA *45°31′N 67°25′W*
21 *W10* **Vanceboro** North Carolina, SE USA *35°16′N 77°06′W*
21 *O4* **Vanceburg** Kentucky, S USA *38°36′N 84°40′W*
45 *W10* **Vance W. Amory** ✈ Nevis, Saint Kitts and Nevis *17°08′N 62°36′W*
**Vanch** *see* Vanj
10 *L17* **Vancouver** British Columbia, SW Canada *49°13′N 123°06′W*
32 *G11* **Vancouver** Washington, NW USA *45°38′N 122°39′W*
10 *L17* **Vancouver** ✈ British Columbia, SW Canada *49°03′N 123°00′W*
10 *K16* **Vancouver Island** *island* British Columbia, SW Canada
**Vanda** *see* Vantaa
171 *X13* **Van Daalen** ≈ Papua, E Indonesia
30 *L15* **Vandalia** Illinois, N USA *38°57′N 89°05′W*
27 *V3* **Vandalia** Missouri, C USA *39°18′N 91°29′W*
31 *R13* **Vandalia** Ohio, N USA *39°53′N 84°12′W*
25 *U13* **Vanderbilt** Texas, SW USA *28°45′N 96°37′W*
31 *Q10* **Vandercook Lake** Michigan, N USA *42°11′N 84°23′W*
10 *L14* **Vanderhoof** British Columbia, SW Canada *53°54′N 124°00′W*
18 *K8* **Vanderwhacker Mountain** ▲ New York, NE USA *43°54′N 74°06′W*
181 *P1* **Van Diemen Gulf** *gulf* Northern Territory, N Australia
**Van Diemen's Land** *see* Tasmania
118 *H5* **Vändra** *Ger.* Fennern; *prev.* Vana-Vändra. Pärnumaa, SW Estonia *58°39′N 25°00′E*
**Vandsburg** *see* Więcbork
34 *L4* **Van Duzen River** ≈ California, W USA
118 *F13* **Vandžiogala** Kaunas, C Lithuania *55°07′N 23°55′E*
41 *N10* **Vanegas** San Luis Potosí, C Mexico *23°53′N 100°55′W*
**Vaner, Lake** *see* Vänern
95 *K17* **Vänern** *Eng.* Lake Vaner; *prev.* Lake Vener. ⊚ S Sweden
95 *J18* **Vänersborg** Västra Götaland, S Sweden *58°16′N 12°22′E*
94 *F12* **Vang** Oppland, S Norway *61°07′N 08°34′E*
172 *I7* **Vangaindrano** Fianarantsoa, SE Madagascar *23°21′S 47°35′E*
137 *S14* **Van Gölü** *Eng.* Lake Van; *anc.* Thospitis. *salt lake* E Turkey
186 *L9* **Vangunu** *island* New Georgia Islands, NW Solomon Islands
24 *J9* **Van Horn** Texas, SW USA *31°03′N 104°51′W*
187 *Q11* **Vanikolo** *var.* Vanikoro. *island* Santa Cruz Islands, E Solomon Islands
**Vanikoro** *see* Vanikolo
186 *A5* **Vanimo** West Sepik, NW Papua New Guinea *02°40′S 141°17′E*
123 *T13* **Vanino** Khabarovskiy Kray, SE Russia *49°10′N 140°18′E*
155 *G19* **Vānīvilāsa Sāgara** ⊚ SW India
147 *S13* **Vanj** *Rus.* Vanch. S Tajikistan *38°22′N 71°27′E*
116 *G14* **Vânju Mare** *prev.* Vînju Mare. Mehedinţi, SW Romania *44°25′N 22°52′E*
15 *N12* **Vankleek Hill** Ontario, SE Canada *45°32′N 74°39′W*
**Van, Lake** *see* Van Gölü
93 *I16* **Vännäs** Västerbotten, N Sweden *63°54′N 19°43′E*
93 *I15* **Vännäsby** Västerbotten, N Sweden *63°55′N 19°53′E*
102 *H7* **Vannes** *anc.* Dariorigum. Morbihan, NW France *47°40′N 02°45′W*
92 *I8* **Vannøya** *island* N Norway
103 *T12* **Vanoise, Massif de la** ▲▲ E France
83 *E24* **Vanrhynsdorp** Western Cape, SW South Africa *31°36′S 18°45′E*
21 *P7* **Vansant** Virginia, NE USA *37°13′N 82°03′W*
94 *L13* **Vansbro** Dalarna, C Sweden *60°32′N 14°15′E*
95 *D18* **Vanse** Vest-Agder, S Norway *58°04′N 06°40′E*
9 *P7* **Vansittart Island** *island* Nunavut, NE Canada
93 *M20* **Vantaa** *Swe.* Vanda. Uusimaa, S Finland *60°18′N 25°01′E*
93 *L19* **Vantaa** ✈ (Helsinki) Uusimaa, S Finland *60°18′N 25°01′E*
32 *J9* **Vantage** Washington, NW USA *46°55′N 119°55′W*
187 *Z14* **Vanua Balavu** *prev.* Vanua Mbalavu. *island* Lau Group, E Fiji
187 *R12* **Vanua Lava** *island* Banks Islands, N Vanuatu
187 *Y13* **Vanua Levu** *island* N Fiji
**Vanua Mbalavu** *see* Vanua Balavu
187 *R12* **Vanuatu** *off.* Republic of Vanuatu, *Fr.* République de Vanuatu, *Bis.* Ripablik blong Vanuatu; *prev.* New Hebrides. ◆ *republic* SW Pacific Ocean
175 *P8* **Vanuatu** *island group* SW Pacific Ocean
**Vanuatu, Republic of** *see* Vanuatu
**Vanuatu, République de** *see* Vanuatu
**Vanuatu, Ripablik blong** *see* Vanuatu
31 *Q12* **Van Wert** Ohio, N USA *40°52′N 84°34′W*
187 *Q17* **Vao** Province Sud, S New Caledonia *22°40′S 167°29′E*
**Vapincum** *see* Gap
117 *N7* **Vapnyarka** Vinnyts'ka Oblast', C Ukraine *48°31′S 28°44′E*
103 *T15* **Var** ⬖ *department* SE France
103 *U14* **Var** ≈ SE France
95 *J18* **Vara** Västra Götaland, S Sweden *58°16′N 12°57′E*
**Varaďinska Županija** *see* Varaždin
118 *J10* **Varakļāni** C Latvia *56°36′N 26°40′E*
106 *C7* **Varallo** Piemonte, NE Italy *45°51′N 08°16′E*
143 *O5* **Varāmīn** *var.* Veramin. Tehrān, N Iran *35°19′N 51°40′E*
153 *N14* **Vārānasi** *prev.* Banaras, Benares, *hist.* Kasi. Uttar Pradesh, N India *25°20′N 83°E*
125 *T3* **Varandey** Nenetskiy Avtonomnyy Okrug, NW Russia *68°48′N 57°54′E*
92 *M8* **Varangerbotn** *Lapp.* Vuonnabahta. Finnmark, N Norway *70°09′N 28°28′E*
92 *M8* **Varangerfjorden** *Lapp.* Várjjatvuotna. *fjord* N Norway
92 *M8* **Varangerhalvøya** *Lapp.* Várnjárga. *peninsula* N Norway
**Varannó** *see* Vranov nad Topl'ou
107 *M15* **Varano, Lago di** ⊚ SE Italy
118 *J13* **Varapayeva** *Rus.* Voropayevo. Vitsyebskaya Voblasts', NW Belarus *55°09′N 27°13′E*
**Varasd** *see* Varaždin
116 *K3* **Varash** *prev.* Kuznetsovs'k. Rivnens'ka Oblast', NW Ukraine *51°21′N 25°51′E*
112 *E7* **Varaždin** *Ger.* Warasdin, *Hung.* Varasd. Varaždin, N Croatia *46°18′N 16°21′E*
112 *E7* **Varaždin** *off.* Varaďinska Županija. ⬖ *province* N Croatia
106 *C10* **Varazze** Liguria, NW Italy *44°21′N 08°35′E*
95 *J20* **Varberg** Halland, S Sweden *57°06′N 12°15′E*
114 *J11* **Varbitsa** *var,* Vŭrbitsa; *prev.* Filevo. Haskovo, S Bulgaria *42°02′N 25°25′E*
114 *J12* **Varbitsa** ≈ S Bulgaria
113 *Q19* **Vardar** *Gk.* Axiós. ≈ North Macedonia/Greece *see also* Axiós
**Vardar** *see* Axiós
95 *F23* **Varde** Syddtjylland, W Denmark *55°38′N 08°31′E*
137 *V12* **Vardenis** E Armenia *40°11′N 45°43′E*
92 *N8* **Vardø** *Fin.* Vuoreija. Finnmark, N Norway *70°22′N 31°06′E*
115 *E18* **Vardoúsia** ▲▲ C Greece
**Vareia** *see* Logroño
100 *G10* **Varel** Niedersachsen, NW Germany *53°24′N 08°07′E*
119 *G15* **Varėna** *Pol.* Orany. Alytus, S Lithuania *54°13′N 24°35′E*
15 *O12* **Varennes** Québec, SE Canada *45°42′N 73°25′W*
103 *P10* **Varennes-sur-Allier** Allier, C France *46°17′N 03°24′E*
112 *I12* **Vareš** Federacija Bosne I Hercegovine, E Bosnia and Herzegovina *44°12′N 18°19′E*
106 *D7* **Varese** Lombardia, N Italy *45°49′N 08°50′E*
116 *J12* **Vârful Moldoveanu** *var.* Moldoveanul; *prev.* Vîrful Moldoveanu. ▲ C Romania *45°35′N 24°48′E*
**Varganzi** *see* Warganza
95 *J18* **Vårgårda** Västra Götaland, S Sweden *58°00′N 12°49′E*
54 *L4* **Vargas** *off.* Estado Vargas. ⬖ *state* N Venezuela
95 *J18* **Vargön** Västra Götaland, S Sweden *58°21′N 12°22′E*
95 *C17* **Varhaug** Rogaland, S Norway *58°37′N 05°39′E*
**Várjjatvuotna** *see* Varangerfjorden
93 *N17* **Varkaus** Pohjois-Savo, C Finland *62°20′N 27°50′E*
92 *J2* **Varmahlíð** Norðurland Vestra, N Iceland *65°32′N 19°33′W*
95 *J15* **Värmland** ⬖ *county* C Sweden
95 *K16* **Värmlandsnäs** *peninsula* S Sweden
114 *N8* **Varna** *prev.* Stalin; *anc.* Odessus. Varna, E Bulgaria *43°14′N 27°56′E*
114 *N8* **Varna** ⬖ *province* E Bulgaria
114 *N8* **Varna** ✈ Varna, E Bulgaria *43°16′N 27°52′E*
95 *L20* **Värnamo** Jönköping, S Sweden *57°11′N 14°03′E*
114 *N8* **Varnenski Zaliv** *prev.* Stalinski Zaliv. *bay* E Bulgaria
114 *N8* **Varnensko Ezero** *estuary* E Bulgaria
118 *D11* **Varniai** Telšiai, W Lithuania *55°45′N 22°22′E*
**Várnjárga** *see* Varangerhalvøya
**Varnoús** *see* Baba
111 *D14* **Varnsdorf** *Ger.* Warnsdorf. Ústecký Kraj, NW Czechia *50°57′N 14°35′E*
111 *I23* **Várpalota** Veszprém, W Hungary *47°12′N 18°08′E*
**Varshava** *see* Warszawa
114 *G8* **Varshets** *var.* Vŭrshets. Montana, NW Bulgaria *43°14′N 23°20′E*
118 *K6* **Värska** Põlvamaa, SE Estonia *57°58′N 27°37′E*
98 *N12* **Varsseveld** Gelderland, E Netherlands *51°55′N 06°28′E*
115 *D19* **Vartholomió** *prev.* Vartholomión. Dytikí Elláda, S Greece *37°52′N 21°12′E*
**Vartholomión** *see* Vartholomió
137 *Q14* **Varto** Muş, E Turkey *39°10′N 41°28′E*
95 *K18* **Vartofta** Västra Götaland, S Sweden *58°06′N 13°40′E*
93 *O17* **Värtsilä** Pohjois-Karjala, E Finland *62°10′N 30°35′E*
**Värtsilä** *see* Vyartsilya
117 *R4* **Varva** Chernihivs'ka Oblast', NE Ukraine *50°31′N 32°43′E*
59 *H18* **Várzea Grande** Mato Grosso, SW Brazil *15°39′S 56°08′W*
106 *D9* **Varzi** Lombardia, N Italy *44°51′N 09°13′E*
**Varzimanor Ayni** *see* Ayní
124 *K5* **Varzuga** ≈ NW Russia
103 *P8* **Varzy** Nièvre, C France *47°22′N 03°22′E*
111 *G23* **Vas** *off.* Vas Megye. ⬖ *county* W Hungary
**Vasa** *see* Vaasa
190 *A9* **Vasafua** *island* Funafuti Atoll, C Tuvalu
111 *O21* **Vásárosnamény** Szabolcs-Szatmár-Bereg, E Hungary *48°10′N 22°18′E*
104 *H13* **Vascão, Ribeira de** ≈ S Portugal
116 *G10* **Vaşcău** *Hung.* Vaskoh. Bihor, NE Romania *46°28′N 22°30′E*
**Vashess Bay** *see* Vaskess Bay
125 *O8* **Vashka** ≈ NW Russia
**Vāsht** *see* Khāsh
**Vasilevichi** *see* Vasilyevichy
115 *G14* **Vasiliká** Kentrikí Makedonía, NE Greece *40°28′N 23°08′E*
115 *C18* **Vasilikí** Lefkáda, Iónia Nisiá, Greece, C Mediterranean Sea *38°36′N 20°37′E*
115 *K25* **Vasilikí** Kríti, Greece, E Mediterranean Sea *35°04′N 25°49′E*
119 *G16* **Vasilishki** *Pol.* Wasiliszki. Hrodzyenskaya Voblasts', W Belarus *53°47′N 24°51′E*
**Vasil Kolarov** *see* Pamporovo
**Vasil'kov** *see* Vasyl'kiv
119 *N19* **Vasilyevichy** *Rus.* Vasilevichi. Homyel'skaya Voblasts', SE Belarus *52°15′N 29°50′E*
191 *Y3* **Vaskess Bay** *var.* Vashess Bay. *bay* Kiritimati, E Kiribati
**Vaskoh** *see* Vaşcău
**Vaskohsziklás** *see* Ştei
116 *M10* **Vaslui** Vaslui, C Romania *46°38′N 27°44′E*
116 *L11* **Vaslui** ⬖ *county* NE Romania
**Vas Megye** *see* Vas
31 *R8* **Vassar** Michigan, N USA *43°22′N 83°34′W*
95 *E15* **Vassdalsegga** ▲ S Norway *59°47′N 07°07′E*
60 *P9* **Vassouras** Rio de Janeiro, SE Brazil *22°24′S 43°38′W*
95 *N15* **Västerås** Västmanland, C Sweden *59°37′N 16°33′E*
93 *G15* **Västerbotten** ⬖ *county* N Sweden
94 *K12* **Västerdalälven** ≈ C Sweden
95 *O16* **Västerhaninge** Stockholm, C Sweden *59°07′N 18°06′E*
94 *M10* **Västernorrland** ⬖ *county* C Sweden
95 *N19* **Västervik** Kalmar, S Sweden *57°44′N 16°40′E*
95 *M15* **Västmanland** ⬖ *county* C Sweden
107 *L15* **Vasto** *anc.* Histonium. Abruzzo, C Italy *42°07′N 14°43′E*
95 *J19* **Västra Götaland** ⬖ *county* S Sweden
95 *J16* **Västra Silen** ⊚ S Sweden
111 *G23* **Vasvár** *Ger.* Eisenburg. Vas, W Hungary *47°03′N 16°48′E*
117 *U9* **Vasylivka** Zaporiz'ka Oblast', SE Ukraine *47°26′N 35°18′E*
117 *O5* **Vasyl'kiv** *var.* Vasil'kov. Kyivs'ka Oblast', N Ukraine *50°12′N 30°18′E*
117 *V8* **Vasyl'kivka** Dnipropetrovs'ka Oblast', E Ukraine *48°12′N 36°00′E*
122 *I11* **Vasyugan** ≈ C Russia
103 *N8* **Vatan** Indre, C France *47°06′N 01°49′E*
**Vaté** *see* Efate
115 *C18* **Vathy** *prev.* Itháki. Itháki, Iónia Nisiá, Greece, C Mediterranean Sea *38°22′N 20°43′E*
107 *G15* **Vatican City** *off.* Vatican City State, *It.* Città del Vaticano, Stato della Città del Vaticano, *var.* Holy See. ◆ *papal state* S Europe
**Vatican City State** *see* Vatican City
107 *M22* **Vaticano, Capo** *headland* S Italy *38°37′N 15°49′E*
**Vaticano, Città del** *see* Vatican City
**Vaticano, Stato della Città del** *see* Vatican City
92 *K3* **Vatnajökull** *glacier* SE Iceland
95 *P15* **Vätö** Stockholm, C Sweden *59°48′N 18°55′E*
187 *Z16* **Vatoa** *island* Lau Group, SE Fiji
172 *J5* **Vatomandry** Toamasina, E Madagascar *19°20′S 48°58′E*
116 *J9* **Vatra Dornei** *Ger.* Dorna Watra. Suceava, NE Romania *47°20′N 25°21′E*
116 *J9* **Vatra Moldoviţei** Suceava, NE Romania *47°37′N 25°36′E*
**Vatter, Lake** *see* Vättern
95 *L18* **Vättern** *Eng.* Lake Vatter; *prev.* Lake Vetter. ⊚ S Sweden
187 *X5* **Vatulele** *island* SW Fiji
117 *P7* **Vatutine** Cherkas'ka Oblast', C Ukraine *49°01′N 31°04′E*
187 *W15* **Vatu Vara** *island* Lau Group, E Fiji
**Vatyli** *see* Vadili
103 *R14* **Vaucluse** ⬖ *department* SE France
103 *S5* **Vaucouleurs** Meuse, NE France *48°37′N 05°38′E*
108 *B9* **Vaud** *Ger.* Waadt. ⬖ *canton* SW Switzerland
15 *N12* **Vaudreuil** Québec, SE Canada *45°24′N 74°01′W*
37 *T12* **Vaughn** New Mexico, SW USA *34°36′N 105°12′W*
54 *I14* **Vaupés** *off.* Comisaría del Vaupés. ⬖ *province* SE Colombia
**Vaupés, Comisaría del** *see* Vaupés
54 *J13* **Vaupés, Río** *var.* Rio Uaupés. ≈ Brazil/Colombia *see also* Uaupes, Rio
**Vaupés, Río** *see* Uaupés, Rio
103 *Q15* **Vauvert** Gard, S France *43°42′N 04°16′E*
11 *R17* **Vauxhall** Alberta, SW Canada *50°05′N 112°09′W*
99 *K23* **Vaux-sur-Sûre** Luxembourg, SE Belgium *49°55′N 05°34′E*
172 *J4* **Vavatenina** Toamasina, E Madagascar *17°25′S 49°11′E*
193 *Y14* **Vava'u Group** *island group* N Tonga
76 *M16* **Vavoua** W Ivory Coast *07°23′N 06°29′W*
127 *S2* **Vavozh** Udmurtskaya Respublika, NW Russia *56°48′N 51°53′E*
155 *K23* **Vavuniya** Northern Province, N Sri Lanka *08°45′N 80°30′E*
119 *G17* **Vawkavysk** *Pol.* Wołkowysk, *Rus.* Volkovysk. Hrodzyenskaya Voblasts', W Belarus *53°10′N 24°28′E*
119 *F17* **Vawkavyskaye Wzvyshsha** *Rus.* Volkovyskiye Vysoty. *hill range* W Belarus
95 *P15* **Vaxholm** Stockholm, C Sweden *59°25′N 18°21′E*
95 *L21* **Växjö** *var.* Vexiö. Kronoberg, S Sweden *56°52′N 14°50′E*
125 *T1* **Vaygach, Ostrov** *island* NW Russia
137 *V13* **Vayk'** *prev.* Azizbekov. SE Armenia *39°41′N 45°28′E*
**Vazáš** *see* Vittangi
125 *P8* **Vazhgort** *prev.* Chasovo. Respublika Komi, NW Russia *64°06′N 46°44′E*
45 *V10* **V. C. Bird** ✈ (St. John's) Antigua, Antigua and Barbuda *17°07′N 61°49′W*
167 *R13* **Véal Rénh** *prev.* Phumĭ Veal Renh. Kampot, SW Cambodia *10°43′N 103°49′E*
29 *Q7* **Veblen** South Dakota, N USA *45°50′N 97°17′W*
98 *N9* **Vecht** *Ger.* Vechte. ≈ Germany/Netherlands *see also* Vechte
**Vecht** *see* Vechte
100 *G12* **Vechta** Niedersachsen, NW Germany *52°44′N 08°16′E*
100 *E12* **Vechte** *Dut.* Vecht. ≈ Germany/Netherlands *see also* Vecht
**Vechte** *see* Vecht
118 *I8* **Vecpiebalga** C Latvia *57°03′N 25°47′E*
118 *G9* **Vecumnieki** C Latvia *56°36′N 24°30′E*
95 *C16* **Vedavågen** Rogaland, S Norway *59°18′N 5°13′E*
**Vedāvati** *see* Hagari
95 *J20* **Veddige** Halland, S Sweden *57°16′N 12°19′E*
116 *J15* **Vedea** ≈ S Romania
127 *P16* **Vedeno** Chechenskaya Respublika, SW Russia *42°57′N 46°02′E*
95 *C16* **Vedvågen** Rogaland, S Norway *59°18′N 05°13′E*
98 *O6* **Veendam** Groningen, NE Netherlands *53°05′N 06°53′E*
98 *K12* **Veenendaal** Utrecht, C Netherlands *52°03′N 05°33′E*
99 *E14* **Veere** Zeeland, SW Netherlands *51°33′N 03°40′E*
24 *M2* **Vega** Texas, SW USA *35°14′N 102°26′W*
92 *E13* **Vega** *island* C Norway
45 *T5* **Vega Baja** C Puerto Rico *18°27′N 66°23′W*
38 *D17* **Vega Point** *headland* Kiska Island, Alaska, USA *51°49′N 177°19′E*
95 *F17* **Vegår** ⊚ S Norway
99 *K14* **Veghel** Noord-Brabant, S Netherlands *51°37′N 05°33′E*
**Veglia** *see* Krk
114 *E13* **Vegorítida, Límni** *var.* Límni Vegorítis. ⊚ N Greece
**Vegorítis, Límni** *see* Vegorítida, Límni
11 *Q14* **Vegreville** Alberta, SW Canada *53°30′N 112°02′W*
95 *K21* **Veinge** Halland, S Sweden *56°33′N 13°04′E*
61 *B21* **Veinticinco de Mayo** *var.* 25 de Mayo. Buenos Aires, E Argentina *35°27′S 60°11′W*
63 *I14* **Veinticinco de Mayo** La Pampa, C Argentina *37°45′S 67°40′W*
119 *F15* **Veisiejai** Alytus, S Lithuania *54°06′N 23°42′E*
95 *F23* **Vejen** Syddtjylland, W Denmark *55°29′N 09°13′E*
104 *K16* **Vejer de la Frontera** Andalucía, S Spain *36°15′N 05°58′W*
95 *G23* **Vejle** Syddanmark, C Denmark *55°43′N 09°33′E*
114 *M7* **Vekilski** Shumen, NE Bulgaria *43°33′N 27°19′E*
54 *G3* **Vela, Cabo de la** *headland* NE Colombia *12°14′N 72°13′W*
**Vela Goa** *see* Goa
113 *F15* **Vela Luka** Dubrovnik-Neretva, S Croatia *42°57′N 16°43′E*
61 *G19* **Velázquez** Rocha, E Uruguay *34°05′S 54°16′W*
101 *E15* **Velbert** Nordrhein-Westfalen, W Germany *51°22′N 07°03′E*
109 *S9* **Velden** Kärnten, S Austria *46°37′N 13°59′E*
**Veldes** *see* Bled
99 *K15* **Veldhoven** Noord-Brabant, S Netherlands *51°24′N 05°24′E*
112 *C11* **Velebit** ▲▲ C Croatia
114 *N11* **Veleka** ≈ SE Bulgaria
109 *V10* **Velenje** *Ger.* Wöllan. N Slovenia *46°22′N 15°07′E*
190 *E12* **Vele, Pointe** *headland* Île Futuna, S Wallis and Futuna
113 *O18* **Veles** *Turk.* Köprülü. C North Macedonia *41°43′N 21°49′E*
113 *M20* **Velešta** SW North Macedonia *41°16′N 20°37′E*
115 *F16* **Velestíno** *prev.* Velestínon. Thessalía, C Greece *39°23′N 22°45′E*
**Velestínon** *see* Velestíno
**Velevshchina** *see* Vyelyewshchyna
54 *F9* **Vélez** Santander, C Colombia *06°02′N 73°43′W*
105 *Q13* **Vélez Blanco** Andalucía, S Spain *37°43′N 02°07′W*
104 *M17* **Vélez de la Gomera, Peñon de** *island group* S Spain
105 *N15* **Vélez-Málaga** Andalucía, S Spain *36°47′N 04°06′W*
105 *Q13* **Vélez Rubio** Andalucía, S Spain *37°39′N 02°04′W*
**Velha Goa** *see* Goa
**Velho** *see* Porto Velho
112 *E8* **Velika Gorica** Zagreb, N Croatia *45°43′N 16°03′E*
112 *C9* **Velika Kapela** ▲▲ NW Croatia
**Velika Kikinda** *see* Kikinda
112 *D10* **Velika Kladuša** Federacija Bosne I Hercegovine, NW Bosnia and Herzegovina *45°10′N 15°48′E*
112 *N11* **Velika Morava** *var.* Glavn'a Morava, Morava, *Ger.* Grosse Morava. ≈ C Serbia
112 *N12* **Velika Plana** Serbia, C Serbia *44°20′N 21°01′E*
109 *U10* **Velika Raduha** ▲ N Slovenia *46°24′N 14°46′E*
123 *V7* **Velikaya** ≈ NE Russia
124 *F15* **Velikaya** ≈ W Russia
**Velikaya Berestovitsa** *see* Vyalikaya Byerastavitsa
**Velikaya Lepetikha** *see* Velyka Lepetykha
**Veliki Bečkerek** *see* Zrenjanin
112 *P12* **Veliki Krš** *var.* Stol. ▲ E Serbia *44°10′N 22°09′E*
114 *L8* **Veliki Preslav** *prev.* Preslav. Shumen, NE Bulgaria *43°09′N 26°50′E*
112 *B9* **Veliki Risnjak** ▲ NW Croatia *45°30′N 14°31′E*
109 *T13* **Veliki Snežnik** *Ger.* Schneeberg, *It.* Monte Nevoso. ▲ SW Slovenia *45°36′N 14°25′E*
112 *J13* **Veliki Stolac** ▲ E Bosnia and Herzegovina *43°55′N 19°15′E*
**Velikiy Bor** *see* Vyaliki Bor
124 *G16* **Velikiye Luki** Pskovskaya Oblast', W Russia *56°20′N 30°27′E*
124 *H14* **Velikiy Novgorod** *prev.* Novgorod. Novgorodskaya Oblast', W Russia *58°32′N 31°15′E*
125 *P12* **Velikiy Ustyug** Vologodskaya Oblast', NW Russia *60°46′N 46°18′E*
112 *N11* **Veliko Gradište** Serbia, NE Serbia *44°46′N 21°28′E*
155 *I18* **Velikonda Range** ▲▲ SE India
114 *K9* **Veliko Tarnovo** *prev.* Tirnovo, Trnovo, Tŭrnovo, *var.* Veliko Tărnovo, Veliko Tŭrnovo. Veliko Tarnovo, N Bulgaria *43°05′N 25°40′E*
114 *K8* **Veliko Tarnovo** *var.* Veliko Tŭrnovo. ⬖ *province* N Bulgaria
**Veliko Tărnovo** *see* Veliko Tarnovo
**Veliko Tŭrnovo** *see* Veliko Tarnovo
**Veliko Tŭrnovo** *see* Veliko Tarnovo
**Velikovec** *see* Völkermarkt
125 *R5* **Velikovisochnoye** Nenetskiy Avtonomnyy Okrug, NW Russia *67°13′N 52°00′E*
76 *H12* **Vélingara** C Senegal *15°00′N 14°39′W*
76 *H11* **Vélingara** S Senegal *13°12′N 14°05′W*
114 *H11* **Velingrad** Pazardzhik, C Bulgaria *42°01′N 24°00′E*
126 *H3* **Velizh** Smolenskaya Oblast', W Russia *55°30′N 31°06′E*
111 *F16* **Velká Deštná** *var.* Deštná, Grosskoppe, *Ger.* Deschnaer Koppe. ▲ NE Czechia *50°18′N 16°25′E*
111 *F18* **Velké Meziříčí** *Ger.* Grossmeseritsch. Vysočina, C Czechia *49°22′N 16°02′E*


◆ Country
● Country Capital
◇ Dependent Territory
○ Dependent Territory Capital
⬖ Administrative Regions
✈ International Airport
▲ Mountain
▲▲ Mountain Range
Ж Volcano
≈ River
⊚ Lake
⊠ Reservoir

Velkomstpynten – Vila Rial


92 N1 **Velkomstpynten** headland NW Svalbard 79°51′N 11°37′E
111 K21 **Veľký Krtíš** Banskobystrický Kraj, C Slovakia 48°13′N 19°21′E
186 J8 **Vella Lavella** var. Mbilua. island New Georgia Islands, NW Solomon Islands
107 I15 **Velletri** Lazio, C Italy 41°41′N 12°47′E
95 K23 **Vellinge** Skåne, S Sweden 55°29′N 13°00′E
155 I19 **Vellore** Tamil Nādu, SE India 12°56′N 79°09′E
**Velobriga** see Viana do Castelo
115 G21 **Velopoúla** island S Greece
98 M12 **Velp** Gelderland, SE Netherlands 52°00′N 05°59′E
**Velsen** see Velsen-Noord
98 H9 **Velsen-Noord** var. Velsen. Noord-Holland, W Netherlands 52°27′N 04°40′E
125 N12 **Vel'sk** var. Velsk. Arkhangel'skaya Oblast', NW Russia 61°03′N 42°01′E
**Velsuna** see Orvieto
98 K10 **Veluwemeer** lake channel C Netherlands
28 M3 **Velva** North Dakota, N USA 48°03′N 100°55′W
**Velvendos/Velvendós** see Velventós
115 E14 **Velventós** var. Velvendos, Velvendós. Dytikí Makedonía, N Greece 40°15′N 22°04′E
117 S5 **Velyka Bahachka** Poltavs'ka Oblast', C Ukraine 49°46′N 33°44′E
117 S9 **Velyka Lepetykha** Rus. Velikaya Lepetikha. Khersons'ka Oblast', S Ukraine 47°09′N 33°59′E
117 O10 **Velyka Mykhaylivka** Odes'ka Oblast', SW Ukraine 47°07′N 29°49′E
117 W8 **Velyka Novosilka** Donets'ka Oblast', E Ukraine 47°49′N 36°49′E
117 S9 **Velyka Oleksandrivka** Khersons'ka Oblast', S Ukraine 47°17′N 33°16′E
117 T4 **Velyka Pysarivka** Sums'ka Oblast', NE Ukraine 50°25′N 35°28′E
116 G6 **Velykyy Bereznyy** Zakarpats'ka Oblast', W Ukraine 48°54′N 22°27′E
117 W4 **Velykyy Burluk** Kharkivs'ka Oblast', E Ukraine 50°04′N 37°25′E
**Velykyy Tokmak** see Tokmak
173 P7 **Vema Fracture Zone** tectonic feature W Indian Ocean
65 P18 **Vema Seamount** undersea feature SW Indian Ocean 31°38′S 08°19′E
93 F17 **Vemdalen** Jämtland, C Sweden 62°26′N 13°50′E
95 N19 **Vena** Kalmar, S Sweden 57°31′N 16°00′E
41 N11 **Venado** San Luis Potosí, C Mexico 22°56′N 101°05′W
62 L11 **Venado Tuerto** Entre Ríos, E Argentina 33°45′S 61°56′W
61 A19 **Venado Tuerto** Santa Fe, C Argentina 33°46′S 61°57′W
107 K16 **Venafro** Molise, C Italy 41°28′N 14°03′E
55 Q9 **Venamo, Cerro** ▲ E Venezuela 05°56′N 61°25′W
106 B8 **Venaria** Piemonte, NW Italy 45°09′N 07°40′E
103 U15 **Vence** Alpes-Maritimes, SE France 43°45′N 07°07′E
104 H5 **Venda Nova** Vila Real, N Portugal 41°40′N 07°58′W
104 G11 **Vendas Novas** Évora, S Portugal 38°41′N 08°27′W
102 J9 **Vendée** ◈ department NW France
103 Q6 **Vendeuvre-sur-Barse** Aube, NE France 48°08′N 04°17′E
102 M7 **Vendôme** Loir-et-Cher, C France 47°48′N 01°04′E
**Venedig** see Venezia
**Vener, Lake** see Vänern
106 I8 **Veneta, Laguna** lagoon NE Italy
**Venetia** see Venezia
39 S7 **Venetie** Alaska, USA 67°00′N 146°25′W
106 H8 **Veneto** var. Venezia Euganea. ◈ region NE Italy
114 M7 **Venets** Shumen, NE Bulgaria 43°33′N 26°56′E
126 L5 **Venev** Tul'skaya Oblast', W Russia 54°18′N 38°16′E
106 I8 **Venezia** Eng. Venice, Fr. Venise, Ger. Venedig; anc. Venetia. Veneto, NE Italy 45°26′N 12°20′E
**Venezia Euganea** see Veneto
**Venezia, Golfo di** see Venice, Gulf of
**Venezia Tridentina** see Trentino-Alto Adige
54 K8 **Venezuela** off. Bolivarian Republic of Venezuela, Sp. República Bolivariana de Venezuela; prev. Republic of Venezuela, United States of Venezuela. ◆ republic N South America
**Venezuela, Bolivarian Republic of** see Venezuela
**Venezuela, Cordillera de** see Costa, Cordillera de la
54 I4 **Venezuela, Golfo de** Eng. Gulf of Maracaibo, Gulf of Venezuela. gulf NW Venezuela
**Venezuela, Gulf of** see Venezuela, Golfo de
64 F11 **Venezuelan Basin** undersea feature E Caribbean Sea
**Venezuela, República Bolivariana de** see Venezuela
**Venezuela, Republic of** see Venezuela
**Venezuela, United States of** see Venezuela
155 D16 **Vengurla** Mahārāshtra, W India 15°55′N 73°39′E
39 O15 **Veniaminof, Mount** ▲ Alaska, USA 56°12′N 159°24′W
23 V14 **Venice** Florida, SE USA 27°06′N 82°27′W
22 L10 **Venice** Louisiana, S USA 29°15′N 89°20′W
**Venice** see Venezia
106 J8 **Venice, Gulf of** It. Golfo di Venezia, Slvn. Beneški Zaliv. gulf N Adriatic Sea
**Venise** see Venezia
94 K13 **Venjan** Dalarna, C Sweden 60°58′N 13°55′E
94 K13 **Venjanssjön** ◎ C Sweden
155 J18 **Venkatagiri** Andhra Pradesh, E India 14°00′N 79°39′E
99 M15 **Venlo** prev. Venloo. Limburg, SE Netherlands 51°22′N 06°11′E
**Venloo** see Venlo
95 E18 **Vennesla** Vest-Agder, S Norway 58°15′N 08°00′E
107 M17 **Venosa** anc. Venusia. Basilicata, S Italy 40°57′N 15°49′E
**Venoste, Alpi** see Ötztaler Alpen
**Venraij** see Venray
99 M14 **Venray** var. Venraij. Limburg, SE Netherlands 51°32′N 05°59′E
118 C8 **Venta** Ger. Windau. ≈ Latvia/Lithuania
**Venta Belgarum** see Winchester
40 G9 **Ventana, Punta Arena de la** var. Punta de la Ventana. headland NW Mexico 24°03′N 109°49′W
**Ventana, Punta de la** see Ventana, Punta Arena de la
61 B23 **Ventana, Sierra de la** hill range E Argentina
**Ventia** see Valence
191 S11 **Vent, Îles du** var. Windward Islands. island group Archipel de la Société, W French Polynesia
191 R10 **Vent, Îles Sous le** var. Leeward Islands. island group Archipel de la Société, W French Polynesia
106 B11 **Ventimiglia** Liguria, NW Italy 43°47′N 07°37′E
97 M24 **Ventnor** S England, United Kingdom 50°36′N 01°11′W
18 J17 **Ventnor City** New Jersey, NE USA 39°19′N 74°27′W
103 S14 **Ventoux, Mont** ▲ SE France 44°12′N 05°21′E
118 C8 **Ventspils** Ger. Windau. NW Latvia 57°22′N 21°34′E
54 M10 **Ventuari, Río** ≈ S Venezuela
35 R15 **Ventura** California, W USA 34°15′N 119°18′W
182 F8 **Venus Bay** South Australia 33°15′S 134°42′E
**Venusia** see Venosa
191 P7 **Vénus, Pointe** var. Pointe Tataaihoa. headland Tahiti, W French Polynesia 17°28′S 149°29′W
41 V16 **Venustiano Carranza** Chiapas, SE Mexico 16°21′N 92°33′W
41 N7 **Venustiano Carranza, Presa** ⊠ NE Mexico
61 B15 **Vera** Santa Fe, C Argentina 29°28′S 60°10′W
105 Q14 **Vera** Andalucía, S Spain 37°15′N 01°51′W
63 K18 **Vera, Bahía** bay E Argentina
41 R14 **Veracruz** var. Veracruz Llave. Veracruz, E Mexico 19°10′N 96°09′W
41 Q13 **Veracruz** prev. Veracruz-Llave. ◈ state E Mexico
**Veracruz-Llave** see Veracruz
**Veracruz Llave** see Veracruz
43 Q16 **Veraguas** off. Provincia de Veraguas. ◈ province W Panama
**Veraguas, Provincia de** see Veraguas
**Veramin** see Varāmīn
154 B12 **Verāval** Gujarāt, W India 20°54′N 70°22′E
106 C6 **Verbania** Piemonte, NW Italy 45°56′N 08°34′E
107 N20 **Verbicaro** Calabria, SW Italy 39°44′N 15°51′E
108 D11 **Verbier** Valais, SW Switzerland 46°06′N 07°14′E
**Vercellae** see Vercelli
106 C8 **Vercelli** anc. Vercellae. Piemonte, NW Italy 45°19′N 08°25′E
103 S13 **Vercors** physical region E France
**Verdal** see Verdalsøra
93 E16 **Verdalsøra** var. Verdal. Nord-Trøndelag, C Norway 63°47′N 11°27′E
**Verde, Cabo** see Cape Verde
44 J5 **Verde, Cape** headland Long Island, C The Bahamas 22°51′N 75°50′W
104 M2 **Verde, Costa** coastal region N Spain
**Verde Grande, Río/Verde Grande y de Belem, Río** see Verde, Río
100 H11 **Verden** Niedersachsen, NW Germany 52°55′N 09°14′E
57 P16 **Verde, Río** ≈ Bolivia/Brazil
59 J19 **Verde, Rio** ≈ SE Brazil
40 M12 **Verde, Río** var. Río Verde Grande, Río Verde Grande y de Belem. ≈ C Mexico
41 Q16 **Verde, Río** ≈ SE Mexico
36 L13 **Verde River** ≈ Arizona, SW USA
**Verdhikoúsa/Verdhikoússa** see Verdikoússa
27 Q8 **Verdigris River** ≈ Kansas/Oklahoma, C USA
115 E15 **Verdikoússa** var. Verdhikoúsa, Verdhikoússa. Thessalía, C Greece 39°47′N 21°59′E
103 S15 **Verdon** ≈ SE France
15 O12 **Verdun** Québec, SE Canada 45°27′N 73°36′W
103 S4 **Verdun** var. Verdun-sur-Meuse; anc. Verodunum. Meuse, NE France 49°09′N 05°25′E
**Verdun-sur-Meuse** see Verdun
83 J21 **Vereeniging** Gauteng, NE South Africa 26°41′S 27°56′E
**Veremeyki** see Vyeramyeyki
125 T14 **Vereshchagino** Permskiy Kray, NW Russia 58°06′N 54°38′E
76 G14 **Verga, Cap** headland W Guinea 10°12′N 14°27′W
61 G18 **Vergara** Treinta y Tres, E Uruguay 32°58′S 53°54′W
108 G11 **Vergeletto** Ticino, S Switzerland 46°13′N 08°34′E
18 L8 **Vergennes** Vermont, NE USA 44°09′N 73°13′W
**Veria** see Véroia
104 I5 **Verín** Galicia, NW Spain 41°55′N 07°26′W
**Verin T'alin** see T'alin
118 K6 **Veriora** Põlvamaa, SE Estonia 57°57′N 27°23′E
117 T7 **Verkhivtseve** Dnipropetrovs'ka Oblast', E Ukraine 48°27′N 34°15′E
**Verkhnedvinsk** see Vyerkhnyadzvinsk
122 K10 **Verkhneimbatsk** Krasnoyarskiy Kray, N Russia 63°06′N 88°03′E
124 I3 **Verkhnetulomskiy** Murmanskaya Oblast', NW Russia 68°37′N 31°46′E
124 I3 **Verkhnetulomskoye Vodokhranilishche** ⊠ NW Russia
**Verkhneudinsk** see Ulan-Ude
123 P10 **Verkhnevilyuysk** Respublika Sakha (Yakutiya), NE Russia 63°44′N 119°59′E
127 W5 **Verkhniy Avzyan** Respublika Bashkortostan, W Russia 53°31′N 57°26′E
127 Q11 **Verkhniy Baskunchak** Astrakhanskaya Oblast', SW Russia 48°14′N 46°43′E
127 W3 **Verkhniye Kigi** Respublika Bashkortostan, W Russia 55°25′N 58°40′E
117 T9 **Verkhniy Rohachyk** Khersons'ka Oblast', S Ukraine 47°16′N 34°16′E
123 Q11 **Verkhnyaya Amga** Respublika Sakha (Yakutiya), NE Russia 59°34′N 127°07′E
125 V6 **Verkhnyaya Inta** Respublika Komi, NW Russia 65°55′N 60°07′E
125 O10 **Verkhnyaya Toyma** Arkhangel'skaya Oblast', NW Russia 62°12′N 44°57′E
126 K6 **Verkhov'ye** Orlovskaya Oblast', W Russia 52°49′N 37°20′E
116 I8 **Verkhovyna** Ivano-Frankivs'ka Oblast', W Ukraine 48°09′N 24°48′E
123 P8 **Verkhoyanskiy Khrebet** ▲▲ NE Russia
117 T7 **Verkn'odniprovs'k** Dnipropetrovs'ka Oblast', E Ukraine 48°40′N 34°17′E
101 G14 **Verl** Nordrhein-Westfalen, NW Germany 51°52′N 08°30′E
92 N1 **Verlegenhuken** headland N Svalbard 80°03′N 16°15′E
82 A9 **Vermelha, Ponta** headland NW Angola 05°40′S 12°09′E
103 P7 **Vermenton** Yonne, C France 47°40′N 03°43′E
11 R14 **Vermilion** Alberta, SW Canada 53°21′N 110°52′W
31 T11 **Vermilion** Ohio, N USA 41°25′N 82°21′W
22 I10 **Vermilion Bay** bay Louisiana, S USA
29 V4 **Vermilion Lake** ◎ Minnesota, N USA
14 F9 **Vermilion River** ≈ Ontario, S Canada
30 L12 **Vermilion River** ≈ Illinois, N USA
29 R12 **Vermillion** South Dakota, N USA 42°46′N 96°55′W
29 R12 **Vermillion River** ≈ South Dakota, N USA
15 O9 **Vermillon, Rivière** ≈ Québec, SE Canada
115 E14 **Vérmio** ▲▲ N Greece
18 L8 **Vermont** off. State of Vermont, also known as Green Mountain State. ◈ state NE USA
113 K16 **Vermosh** var. Vermoshi. Shkodër N Albania 42°37′N 19°42′E
**Vermoshi** see Vermosh
37 O3 **Vernal** Utah, W USA 40°27′N 109°31′W
14 G11 **Verner** Ontario, S Canada 46°24′N 80°04′W
102 M5 **Verneuil-sur-Avre** Eure, N France 48°44′N 00°55′E
114 D13 **Vérno** ▲▲ N Greece
11 N17 **Vernon** British Columbia, SW Canada 50°17′N 119°19′W
102 M4 **Vernon** Eure, N France 49°04′N 01°28′E
23 N3 **Vernon** Alabama, S USA 33°45′N 88°06′W
31 P15 **Vernon** Indiana, N USA 38°59′N 85°39′W
25 Q4 **Vernon** Texas, SW USA 34°11′N 99°17′W
32 G10 **Vernonia** Oregon, NW USA 45°51′N 123°11′W
14 G12 **Vernon, Lake** ◎ Ontario, S Canada
22 G7 **Vernon Lake** ⊠ Louisiana, S USA
23 Y13 **Vero Beach** Florida, SE USA 27°38′N 80°24′W
**Verőcze** see Virovitica
**Verodunum** see Verdun
115 E14 **Véroia** var. Veria, Vérroia, Turk. Karaferiye. Kentrikí Makedonía, N Greece 40°32′N 22°11′E
106 E8 **Verolanuova** Lombardia, N Italy 45°20′N 10°06′E
14 K14 **Verona** Ontario, SE Canada 44°30′N 76°42′W
106 G8 **Verona** Veneto, NE Italy 45°27′N 11°E
29 P6 **Verona** North Dakota, N USA 46°19′N 98°03′W
30 L9 **Verona** Wisconsin, N USA 42°59′N 89°33′W
61 E20 **Verónica** Buenos Aires, E Argentina 35°25′S 57°16′W
22 J9 **Verret, Lake** ◎ Louisiana, S USA
**Vérroia** see Véroia
103 N5 **Versailles** Yvelines, N France 48°48′N 02°08′E
31 P15 **Versailles** Indiana, N USA 39°04′N 85°16′W
20 M5 **Versailles** Kentucky, S USA 38°02′N 84°45′W
27 U5 **Versailles** Missouri, C USA 38°25′N 92°51′W
31 Q13 **Versailles** Ohio, N USA 40°13′N 84°28′W
**Versecz** see Vršac
108 A10 **Versoix** Genève, SW Switzerland 46°17′N 06°10′E
15 Z6 **Verte, Pointe** headland Québec, SE Canada 48°36′N 64°10′W
111 I22 **Vértes** ▲▲ NW Hungary
44 G6 **Vertientes** Camagüey, C Cuba 21°18′N 78°11′W
114 G13 **Vertískos** ▲▲ N Greece
102 I8 **Vertou** Loire-Atlantique, NW France 47°10′N 01°28′W
**Verulamium** see St Albans
99 L19 **Verviers** Liège, E Belgium 50°36′N 05°52′E
103 Y14 **Vescovato** Corse, France, C Mediterranean Sea 42°30′N 09°27′E
99 L20 **Vesdre** ≈ E Belgium
117 U10 **Vesele** Rus. Veseloye. Zaporiz'ka Oblast', S Ukraine 47°00′N 34°52′E
111 D18 **Veselí nad Lužnicí** var. Weseli an der Lainsitz, Ger. Frohenbruck. Jihočeský Kraj, S Czechia 49°11′N 14°40′E
114 M9 **Veselinovo** Shumen, NE Bulgaria 43°01′N 27°02′E
126 L12 **Veselovskoye Vodokhranilishche** ⊠ SW Russia
**Veseloye** see Vesele
117 Q9 **Veselynove** Mykolayivs'ka Oblast', S Ukraine 47°21′N 31°15′E
**Veseya** see Vyasyeya
126 M10 **Veshenskaya** Rostovskaya Oblast', SW Russia 49°37′N 41°43′E
127 Q5 **Veshkayma** Ul'yanovskaya Oblast', W Russia 54°04′N 47°06′E
**Vesisaari** see Vadsø
**Vesontio** see Besançon
103 T7 **Vesoul** anc. Vesulium, Vesulum. Haute-Saône, E France 47°37′N 06°09′E
95 J20 **Vessigebro** Halland, S Sweden 56°58′N 12°40′E
95 D17 **Vest-Agder** ◈ county S Norway
23 P4 **Vestavia Hills** Alabama, S USA 33°27′N 86°47′W
84 F6 **Vesterålen** island NW Norway
92 G10 **Vesterålen** island group N Norway
87 V3 **Vestervig** Midtjylland, NW Denmark 56°46′N 08°20′E
92 H2 **Vestfirðir** ◈ region NW Iceland
92 G11 **Vestfjorden** fjord C Norway
95 G16 **Vestfold** ◈ county S Norway
**Vestmanhavn** see Vestmanna
95 B18 **Vestmanna** Dan. Vestmanhavn. Streymoy, N Faroe Islands 62°09′N 07°11′W
92 I4 **Vestmannaeyjar** Suðurland, S Iceland 63°26′N 20°14′W
94 E9 **Vestnes** Møre og Romsdal, S Norway 62°39′N 07°00′E
92 H3 **Vesturland** ◈ region W Iceland
92 G11 **Vestvågøya** island C Norway
**Vesulium/Vesulum** see Vesoul
**Vesuna** see Périgueux
107 K17 **Vesuvio** Eng. Vesuvius. Ѫ S Italy 40°48′N 14°29′E
**Vesuvius** see Vesuvio
124 K14 **Ves'yegonsk** Tverskaya Oblast', W Russia 58°40′N 37°13′E
111 I23 **Veszprém** Ger. Veszprim. Veszprém, W Hungary 47°06′N 17°54′E
111 H23 **Veszprém** off. Veszprém Megye. ◈ county W Hungary
**Veszprém Megye** see Veszprém
**Veszprim** see Veszprém
**Vetka** see Vyetka
95 M19 **Vetlanda** Jönköping, S Sweden 57°26′N 15°05′E
127 P1 **Vetluga** Nizhegorodskaya Oblast', W Russia 57°51′N 45°45′E
125 P14 **Vetluga** ≈ NW Russia
125 O14 **Vetluzhskiy** Kostromskaya Oblast', NW Russia 58°21′N 45°25′E
127 P2 **Vetluzhskiy** Nizhegorodskaya Oblast', W Russia 57°10′N 45°07′E
107 H14 **Vetralla** Lazio, C Italy 42°18′N 12°03′E
**Vetrino** see Vyetryna
122 L7 **Vetrovaya, Gora** ▲ N Russia 73°54′N 95°00′E
**Vetter, Lake** see Vättern
106 J13 **Vettore, Monte** ▲ C Italy 42°49′N 13°15′E
99 A17 **Veurne** var. Furnes. West-Vlaanderen, W Belgium 51°04′N 02°40′E
31 Q15 **Vevay** Indiana, N USA 38°45′N 85°08′W
108 C10 **Vevey** Ger. Vivis; anc. Vibiscum. Vaud, SW Switzerland 46°28′N 06°51′E
**Vexiö** see Växjö
103 S13 **Veynes** Hautes-Alpes, SE France 44°33′N 05°51′E
103 N11 **Vézère** ≈ W France
114 I9 **Vezhen** ▲ C Bulgaria 42°45′N 24°22′E
136 K11 **Vezirköprü** Samsun, N Turkey 41°09′N 35°27′E
57 J18 **Viacha** La Paz, W Bolivia 16°40′S 68°17′W
27 R10 **Vian** Oklahoma, C USA 35°30′N 94°56′W
**Viana de Castelo** see Viana do Castelo
104 H12 **Viana do Alentejo** Évora, S Portugal 38°20′N 08°00′W
104 I4 **Viana do Bolo** Galicia, NW Spain 42°10′N 07°06′W
104 G5 **Viana do Castelo** var. Viana de Castelo; anc. Velobriga. Viana do Castelo, NW Portugal 41°41′N 08°50′W
104 G5 **Viana do Castelo** var. Viana de Castelo. ◈ district N Portugal
98 J12 **Vianen** Utrecht, C Netherlands 52°N 05°06′E
167 Q8 **Viangchan** Eng./Fr. Vientiane. ● (Laos) C Laos 17°58′N 102°38′E
167 P6 **Viangphoukha** var. Vieng Pou Kha. Louang Namtha, N Laos 20°41′N 101°03′E
104 K13 **Viar** ≈ SW Spain
106 E11 **Viareggio** Toscana, C Italy 43°52′N 10°15′E
103 O14 **Viaur** ≈ S France
**Vibiscum** see Vevey
95 G21 **Viborg** Midtjylland, NW Denmark 56°28′N 09°25′E
29 R12 **Viborg** South Dakota, N USA 43°10′N 97°04′W
107 N22 **Vibo Valentia** prev. Monteleone di Calabria; anc. Hipponium. Calabria, SW Italy 38°40′N 16°06′E
105 W5 **Vic** var. Vich; anc. Ausa, Vicus Ausonensis. Cataluña, NE Spain 41°56′N 02°16′E
102 K16 **Vic-en-Bigorre** Hautes-Pyrénées, S France 43°23′N 00°04′E
40 K10 **Vicente Guerrero** Durango, C Mexico 23°30′N 104°24′W
41 P10 **Vicente Guerrero, Presa** var. Presa de las Adjuntas. ⊠ NE Mexico
**Vicentia** see Vicenza
106 G8 **Vicenza** anc. Vicentia. Veneto, NE Italy 45°32′N 11°31′E
**Vich** see Vic
54 J10 **Vichada** off. Comisaría del Vichada. ◈ province E Colombia
**Vichada, Comisaría del** see Vichada
54 K10 **Vichada, Río** ≈ E Colombia
61 G17 **Vichadero** Rivera, NE Uruguay 31°45′S 54°41′W
**Vichegda** see Vychegda
124 M16 **Vichuga** Ivanovskaya Oblast', W Russia 57°13′N 41°51′E
103 P10 **Vichy** Allier, C France 46°08′N 03°26′E
26 K9 **Vici** Oklahoma, C USA 36°09′N 99°18′W
95 I19 **Vickan** Halland, S Sweden 57°25′N 12°00′E
31 P10 **Vicksburg** Michigan, N USA 42°07′N 85°31′W
22 J5 **Vicksburg** Mississippi, S USA 32°21′N 90°52′W
103 O12 **Vic-sur-Cère** Cantal, C France 45°00′N 02°36′E
59 I21 **Víctor** Mato Grosso do Sul, SW Brazil 21°39′S 53°21′W
29 X14 **Victor** Iowa, C USA 41°45′N 92°18′W
182 I10 **Victor Harbor** South Australia 35°33′S 138°37′E
61 C18 **Victoria** Entre Ríos, E Argentina 32°40′S 60°10′W
10 L17 **Victoria** province capital Vancouver Island, British Columbia, SW Canada 48°25′N 123°22′W
45 R14 **Victoria** NW Grenada 12°12′N 61°42′W
42 H6 **Victoria** Yoro, NW Honduras 15°01′N 87°28′W
121 O15 **Victoria** var. Rabat. Gozo, NW Malta 36°02′N 14°14′E
116 I12 **Victoria** Ger. Viktoriastadt. Braşov, C Romania 45°44′N 24°41′E
172 H17 **Victoria** ● (Seychelles) Mahé, SW Seychelles 04°38′S 28°28′E
25 U13 **Victoria** Texas, SW USA 28°47′N 96°59′W
183 N12 **Victoria** ◈ state SE Australia
174 K7 **Victoria** ≈ Western Australia
**Victoria** see Labuan, East Malaysia
**Victoria** see Masvingo, Zimbabwe
**Victoria Bank** see Vitória Seamount
11 Y15 **Victoria Beach** Manitoba, S Canada 50°40′N 96°30′W
**Victoria de Durango** see Durango
**Victoria de las Tunas** see Las Tunas
83 I16 **Victoria Falls** Matabeleland North, W Zimbabwe 17°55′S 25°51′E
83 I16 **Victoria Falls** waterfall Zambia/Zimbabwe
83 I16 **Victoria Falls** ✕ Matabeleland North, W Zimbabwe 18°03′S 25°48′E
**Victoria Falls** see Iguaçu, Salto do
63 F19 **Victoria, Isla** island Archipiélago de los Chonos, S Chile
8 K6 **Victoria Island** island Northwest Territories/Nunavut, NW Canada
182 L8 **Victoria, Lake** ◎ New South Wales, SE Australia
68 I12 **Victoria, Lake** var. Victoria Nyanza. ◎ E Africa
195 S13 **Victoria Land** physical region Antarctica
187 X14 **Victoria, Mount** ▲ Viti Levu, W Fiji 17°37′S 178°00′E
166 L5 **Victoria, Mount** ▲ W Myanmar (Burma) 21°13′N 93°53′E
186 E9 **Victoria, Mount** ▲ S Papua New Guinea 08°51′S 147°36′E
81 F17 **Victoria Nile** var. Somerset Nile. ≈ C Uganda
**Victoria Nyanza** see Victoria, Lake
42 G3 **Victoria Peak** ▲ SE Belize 16°50′N 88°38′W
185 H16 **Victoria Range** ▲▲ South Island, New Zealand
181 O3 **Victoria River** ≈ Northern Territory, N Australia
181 P3 **Victoria River Roadhouse** Northern Territory, N Australia 15°37′S 131°07′E
15 Q11 **Victoriaville** Québec, SE Canada 46°04′N 71°57′W
**Victoria-Wes** see Victoria West
83 G24 **Victoria West** Afr. Victoria-Wes. Northern Cape, W South Africa 31°25′S 23°08′E
62 J13 **Victorica** La Pampa, C Argentina 36°15′S 65°25′W
**Victor, Mount** see Dronning Fabiolafjella
35 U14 **Victorville** California, W USA 34°32′N 117°17′W
62 G9 **Vicuña** Coquimbo, N Chile 30°00′S 70°44′W
62 K11 **Vicuña Mackenna** Córdoba, C Argentina 33°53′S 64°25′W
**Vicus Ausonensis** see Vic
**Vicus Elbii** see Viterbo
33 X7 **Vida** Montana, NW USA 47°52′N 105°30′W
23 V6 **Vidalia** Georgia, SE USA 32°13′N 82°24′W
22 J7 **Vidalia** Louisiana, S USA 31°34′N 91°25′W
95 F22 **Videbæk** Midtjylland, C Denmark 56°08′N 08°38′E
60 I13 **Videira** Santa Catarina, S Brazil 27°00′S 51°08′W
116 J14 **Videle** Teleorman, S Romania 44°15′N 25°27′E
**Videm-Krško** see Krško
**Vídeň** see Wien
104 H12 **Vidigueira** Beja, S Portugal 38°12′N 07°48′W
114 J9 **Vidima** ≈ N Bulgaria
114 G7 **Vidin** anc. Bononia. Vidin, NW Bulgaria 44°00′N 22°52′E
114 F8 **Vidin** ◈ province NW Bulgaria
154 H10 **Vidisha** Madhya Pradesh, C India 23°30′N 77°50′E
25 Y10 **Vidor** Texas, SW USA 30°07′N 94°01′W
95 L20 **Vidöstern** ◎ S Sweden
92 J13 **Vidsel** Norrbotten, N Sweden 65°49′N 20°31′E
118 H9 **Vidzemes Augstiene** ▲▲ C Latvia
118 J12 **Vidzy** Vitsyebskaya Voblasts', NW Belarus 55°24′N 26°38′E
63 L16 **Viedma** Río Negro, E Argentina 40°50′S 62°58′W
63 H22 **Viedma, Lago** ◎ S Argentina
45 O11 **Vieille Case** var. Itassi. N Dominica 15°36′N 61°24′W
104 M2 **Vieja, Peña** ▲ N Spain 43°09′N 04°47′W
24 J10 **Vieja, Sierra** ▲▲ Texas, SW USA
40 E4 **Viejo, Cerro** ▲ NW Mexico 30°16′N 112°18′W
56 B9 **Viejo, Cerro** ▲ N Peru 04°54′S 79°24′W
118 E10 **Viekšniai** Telšiai, NW Lithuania 56°14′N 22°33′E
105 U3 **Vielha** var. Viella. Cataluña, NE Spain 42°41′N 00°47′E
**Viella** see Vielha
99 L21 **Vielsalm** Luxembourg, E Belgium 50°17′N 05°55′E
**Vieng Pou Kha** see Viangphoukha
23 T6 **Vienna** Georgia, SE USA 32°05′N 83°48′W
30 L17 **Vienna** Illinois, N USA 37°24′N 88°55′W
27 V5 **Vienna** Missouri, C USA 38°12′N 91°59′W
21 Q3 **Vienna** West Virginia, NE USA 39°19′N 81°33′W
**Vienna** see Wien, Austria
**Vienna** see Vienne, France
103 R11 **Vienne** anc. Vienna. Isère, E France 45°32′N 04°53′E
102 L10 **Vienne** ◈ department W France
102 L9 **Vienne** ≈ W France
**Vientiane** see Viangchan
**Vientos, Paso de los** see Windward Passage
45 V6 **Vieques** var. Isabel Segunda. E Puerto Rico 18°08′N 65°25′W
45 V6 **Vieques, Isla de** island E Puerto Rico
45 V6 **Vieques, Pasaje de** passage E Puerto Rico
45 V5 **Vieques, Sonda de** sound E Puerto Rico
**Vierdörfer** see Săcele
93 M15 **Vieremä** Pohjois-Savo, C Finland 63°42′N 27°02′E
99 M14 **Vierlingsbeek** Noord-Brabant, SE Netherlands 51°36′N 06°01′E
101 G20 **Viernheim** Hessen, W Germany 49°32′N 08°35′E
101 D15 **Viersen** Nordrhein-Westfalen, W Germany 51°16′N 06°24′E
108 G8 **Vierwaldstätter See** Eng. Lake of Lucerne. ◎ C Switzerland
103 N8 **Vierzon** Cher, C France 47°13′N 02°04′E
40 L8 **Viesca** Coahuila, NE Mexico 25°25′N 102°45′W
118 H10 **Viesīte** Ger. Eckengraf. S Latvia 56°21′N 25°30′E
107 N15 **Vieste** Puglia, SE Italy 41°52′N 16°11′E
167 T8 **Vietnam** off. Socialist Republic of Vietnam, Vtn. Công Hòa Xã H i Ch Nghĩa Vi t Nam. ◆ republic SE Asia
**Vi t Nam, Công Hòa Xã H i Ch Nghĩa** see Vietnam
**Vietnam, Socialist Republic of** see Vietnam
167 S5 **Viêt Quang** Ha Giang, N Vietnam 22°24′N 104°48′E
**Vietri** see Viêt Tri
167 S6 **Viêt Tri** var. Vietri. Vinh Phu, N Vietnam 21°20′N 105°26′E
30 L4 **Vieux Desert, Lac** ◎ Michigan/Wisconsin, N USA
45 Y13 **Vieux Fort** S Saint Lucia 13°43′N 60°57′W
45 X6 **Vieux-Habitants** Basse Terre, SW Guadeloupe 16°04′N 61°45′W
119 G14 **Vievis** Vilnius, S Lithuania 54°46′N 24°51′E
171 N2 **Vigan** Luzon, N Philippines 17°34′N 102°21′E
106 D8 **Vigevano** Lombardia, N Italy 45°19′N 08°51′E
107 N18 **Viggiano** Basilicata, S Italy 40°21′N 15°54′E
58 L12 **Vigia** Pará, NE Brazil 0°50′S 48°07′W
41 Y12 **Vigía Chico** Quintana Roo, SE Mexico 19°49′N 87°31′W
45 T11 **Vigie** prev. George F L Charles. ✕ (Castries) NE Saint Lucia 14°01′N 60°59′W
102 K17 **Vignemale** var. Pic de Vignemale. ▲ France/Spain 42°48′N 00°06′W
**Vignemale, Pic de** see Vignemale
106 G10 **Vignola** Emilia-Romagna, C Italy 44°28′N 11°00′E
104 G4 **Vigo** Galicia, NW Spain 42°15′N 08°44′W
104 G4 **Vigo, Ría de** estuary NW Spain
94 D9 **Vigra** island S Norway
95 C17 **Vigrestad** Rogaland, S Norway 58°34′N 05°42′E
93 L15 **Vihanti** Pohjois-Pohjanmaa, C Finland 64°29′N 25°E
149 U10 **Vihari** Punjab, E Pakistan 30°03′N 72°32′E
102 K8 **Vihiers** Maine-et-Loire, NW France 47°09′N 00°37′W
111 O19 **Vihorlat** ▲ E Slovakia 48°54′N 22°09′E
114 G11 **Vihren** var. Vikhren. ▲ SW Bulgaria 41°45′N 23°24′E
93 L19 **Vihti** Uusimaa, S Finland 60°25′N 24°16′E
**Viipuri** see Vyborg
93 M16 **Viitasaari** Keski-Suomi, C Finland 63°05′N 25°52′E
118 K3 **Viivikonna** Ida-Virumaa, NE Estonia 59°19′N 27°41′E
155 F16 **Vijayāpura** prev. Bijāpur. Karnātaka, C India 16°50′N 75°42′E
155 K16 **Vijayawāda** prev. Bezwada. Andhra Pradesh, SE India 16°34′N 80°40′E
**Vijosa/Vijosë** see Aóos, Albania/Greece
**Vijosa/Vijosë** see Vjosës, Lumi i, Albania/Greece
92 J4 **Vík** Suðurland, S Iceland 63°25′N 18°58′W
**Vik** see Vikøyri
94 L13 **Vika** Dalarna, C Sweden 60°55′N 14°30′E
92 L12 **Vikajärvi** Lappi, N Finland 66°37′N 26°10′E
94 L13 **Vikarbyn** Dalarna, C Sweden 60°57′N 15°00′E
95 J22 **Viken** Skåne, S Sweden 56°09′N 12°36′E
95 L17 **Viken** ◎ C Sweden
95 G15 **Vikersund** Buskerud, S Norway 59°58′N 09°59′E
**Vikhren** see Vihren
11 R15 **Viking** Alberta, SW Canada 53°07′N 111°50′W
84 E7 **Viking Bank** undersea feature N North Sea 60°35′N 02°35′E
95 M14 **Vikmanshyttan** Dalarna, C Sweden 60°19′N 15°55′E
94 D12 **Vikøyri** var. Vik. Sogn Og Fjordane, S Norway 61°04′N 06°34′E
93 H17 **Viksjö** Västernorrland, C Sweden 62°45′N 17°30′E
**Viktoriastadt** see Victoria
**Vila** see Port-Vila
**Vila Arriaga** see Bibala
**Vila Artur de Paiva** see Cubango
**Vila Baleira** see Porto Santo
**Vila Bela da Santissima Trindade** see Mato Grosso
58 B12 **Vila Bittencourt** Amazonas, NW Brazil 01°25′S 69°24′W
**Vila da Ponte** see Cubango
64 O2 **Vila da Praia da Vitória** Terceira, Azores, Portugal, NE Atlantic Ocean 38°44′N 27°04′W
**Vila de Aljustrel** see Cangamba
**Vila de Almoster** see Chiange
**Vila de João Belo** see Xai-Xai
**Vila de Macia** see Macia
**Vila de Manhiça** see Manhiça
**Vila de Manica** see Manica
**Vila de Mocímboa da Praia** see Mocímboa da Praia
83 N16 **Vila de Sena** var. Sena. Sofala, C Mozambique 17°25′S 34°59′E
104 F14 **Vila do Bispo** Faro, S Portugal 37°05′N 08°53′W
104 G6 **Vila do Conde** Porto, NW Portugal 41°21′N 08°45′W
**Vila do Maio** see Maio
64 P3 **Vila do Porto** Santa Maria, Azores, Portugal, NE Atlantic Ocean 36°57′N 25°10′W
83 K15 **Vila do Zumbo** prev. Vila do Zumbu, Zumbo. Tete, NW Mozambique 15°36′S 30°30′E
**Vila do Zumbu** see Vila do Zumbo
105 T8 **Vilafamés** prev. Villafamés. Comunitat Valenciana, E Spain 40°07′N 00°03′W
104 I6 **Vila Flor** var. Vila Flôr. Bragança, N Portugal 41°18′N 07°09′W
105 V6 **Vilafranca del Penedès** var. Villafranca del Panadés. Cataluña, NE Spain 41°21′N 01°42′E
104 F10 **Vila Franca de Xira** var. Vilafranca de Xira. Lisboa, C Portugal 38°57′N 08°59′W
**Vila Gago Coutinho** see Lumbala N'Guimbo
104 G3 **Vilagarcía** var. Villagarcía de Arosa. Galicia, NW Spain 42°35′N 08°45′W
**Vila General Machado** see Camacupa
**Vila Henrique de Carvalho** see Saurimo
102 I7 **Vilaine** ≈ NW France
**Vila João de Almeida** see Chibia
118 K8 **Viļaka** Ger. Marienhausen. NE Latvia 57°12′N 27°43′E
104 I2 **Vilalba** Galicia, NW Spain 43°17′N 07°41′W
**Vila Marechal Carmona** see Uíge
**Vila Mariano Machado** see Ganda
172 G3 **Vilanandro, Tanjona** prev./Fr. Cap Saint-André. headland W Madagascar 16°10′S 44°27′E
**Vilanculos** see Vilankulo
118 J10 **Viļāni** E Latvia 56°33′N 26°55′E
83 N19 **Vilankulo** var. Vilanculos. Inhambane, E Mozambique 22°01′S 35°19′E
**Vila Norton de Matos** see Balombo
104 G6 **Vila Nova de Famalicão** var. Vila Nova de Famalicao. Braga, N Portugal 41°24′N 08°31′W
104 I6 **Vila Nova de Foz Côa** var. Vila Nova de Fozcôa. Guarda, N Portugal 41°05′N 07°09′W
**Vila Nova de Fozcôa** see Vila Nova de Foz Côa
104 F6 **Vila Nova de Gaia** Porto, NW Portugal 41°08′N 08°37′W
**Vila Nova de Portimão** see Portimão
105 V6 **Vilanova i La Geltru** Cataluña, NE Spain 41°15′N 01°42′E
**Vila Pereira de Eça** see Ondjiva
104 H6 **Vila Pouca de Aguiar** Vila Real, N Portugal 41°30′N 07°38′W
104 H6 **Vila Real** var. Vila Rial. Vila Real, N Portugal 41°17′N 07°45′W
105 T9 **Vila-real** var. Vila-real de los Infantes; prev. Villarreal. Comunitat Valenciana, E Spain 39°56′N 00°08′W
104 H6 **Vila Real** ◈ district N Portugal
**Vila-real de los Infantes** see Vila-real
104 H14 **Vila Real de Santo António** Faro, S Portugal 37°12′N 07°25′W
104 J7 **Vilar Formoso** Guarda, N Portugal 40°37′N 06°50′W
**Vila Rial** see Vila Real




◆ Country
● Country Capital
◇ Dependent Territory
○ Dependent Territory Capital
◈ Administrative Regions
✕ International Airport
▲ Mountain
▲▲ Mountain Range
Ѫ Volcano
≈ River
◎ Lake
⊠ Reservoir

Vila Rica – Vóreioi Sporádes


59 J15 **Vila Rica** Mato Grosso, W Brazil 09°52′S 50°44′W
**Vila Robert Williams** see Caála
**Vila Salazar** see N'Dalatando
**Vila Serpa Pinto** see Menongue
**Vila Teixeira da Silva** see Bailundo
**Vila Teixeira de Sousa** see Luau
104 H9 **Vila Velha de Ródão** Castelo Branco, C Portugal 39°39′N 07°40′W
104 G5 **Vila Verde** Braga, N Portugal 41°39′N 08°27′W
104 H11 **Vila Viçosa** Évora, S Portugal 38°46′N 07°25′W
57 G15 **Vilcabamba, Cordillera de** ▲▲ C Peru
**Vilcea** see Vâlcea
122 J4 **Vil'cheka, Zemlya** Eng. Wilczek Land. island Zemlya Frantsa-Iosifa, NW Russia
95 F22 **Vildbjerg** Midtjylland, C Denmark 56°12′N 08°47′E
**Vileyka** see Vilyeyka
93 H15 **Vilhelmina** Västerbotten, N Sweden 64°38′N 16°40′E
59 F17 **Vilhena** Rondônia, W Brazil 12°40′S 60°08′W
115 G19 **Vília** Attikí, C Greece 38°09′N 23°21′E
119 I14 **Viliya** Lith. Neris. W Belarus
**Viliya** see Neris
118 H5 **Viljandi** Ger. Fellin. Viljandimaa, S Estonia 58°22′N 25°30′E
118 H5 **Viljandimaa** var. Viljandi Maakond. ◆ province SW Estonia
**Viljandi Maakond** see Viljandimaa
119 E14 **Vilkaviškis** Pol. Wyłkowyszki. Marijampolė, SW Lithuania 54°39′N 23°03′E
118 F13 **Vilkija** Kaunas, C Lithuania 55°02′N 23°36′E
197 V9 **Vil'kitskogo, Proliv** strait N Russia
**Vilkovo** see Vylkove
57 L21 **Villa Abecia** Chuquisaca, S Bolivia 21°00′S 65°18′W
41 N5 **Villa Acuña** var. Ciudad Acuña. Coahuila, NE Mexico 29°18′N 100°58′W
40 J4 **Villa Ahumada** Chihuahua, N Mexico 30°38′N 106°30′W
45 O9 **Villa Altagracia** C Dominican Republic 18°43′N 70°13′W
56 L13 **Villa Bella** Beni, N Bolivia 10°21′S 65°25′W
104 J3 **Villablino** Castilla y León, N Spain 42°55′N 06°21′W
54 K6 **Villa Bruzual** Portuguesa, N Venezuela 09°20′N 69°06′W
105 O9 **Villacañas** Castilla-La Mancha, C Spain 39°38′N 03°20′W
105 O12 **Villacarrillo** Andalucía, S Spain 38°07′N 03°05′W
104 M7 **Villacastín** Castilla y León, N Spain 40°46′N 04°25′W
**Villa Cecilia** see Ciudad Madero
109 S9 **Villach** Slvn. Beljak. Kärnten, S Austria 46°36′N 13°49′E
107 B20 **Villacidro** Sardegna, Italy, C Mediterranean Sea 39°28′N 08°43′E
44 E5 **Villa Clara** ◆ province N Cuba
**Villa Concepción** see Concepción
104 L4 **Villada** Castilla y León, N Spain 42°15′N 04°59′W
40 M10 **Villa de Cos** Zacatecas, C Mexico 23°20′N 102°20′W
54 L5 **Villa de Cura** var. Cura. Aragua, N Venezuela 10°00′N 67°30′W
**Villa del Nevoso** see Ilirska Bistrica
**Villa del Pilar** see Pilar
104 M13 **Villa del Río** Andalucía, S Spain 37°59′N 04°17′W
**Villa de Méndez** see Méndez
42 H6 **Villa de San Antonio** Comayagua, W Honduras 14°24′N 87°37′W
105 N4 **Villadiego** Castilla y León, N Spain 42°31′N 04°01′W
**Villafamés** see Vilafamés
41 U16 **Villa Flores** Chiapas, SE Mexico 16°12′N 93°16′W
104 J3 **Villafranca del Bierzo** Castilla y León, N Spain 42°36′N 06°49′W
105 S8 **Villafranca del Cid** Comunitat Valenciana, E Spain 40°25′N 00°15′W
104 J11 **Villafranca de los Barros** Extremadura, W Spain 38°34′N 06°20′W
105 N10 **Villafranca de los Caballeros** Castilla-La Mancha, C Spain 39°26′N 03°21′W
**Villafranca del Panadés** see Vilafranca del Penedès
106 F8 **Villafranca di Verona** Veneto, NE Italy 45°22′N 10°51′E
107 J23 **Villafrati** Sicilia, Italy, C Mediterranean Sea 37°53′N 13°30′E
**Villagarcía de Arosa** see Vilagarcía
41 O9 **Villagrán** Tamaulipas, C Mexico 24°29′N 99°30′W
61 C17 **Villaguay** Entre Ríos, E Argentina 31°55′S 59°01′W
62 O6 **Villa Hayes** Presidente Hayes, S Paraguay 25°05′S 57°25′W
41 U15 **Villahermosa** prev. San Juan Bautista. Tabasco, SE Mexico 17°56′N 92°50′W
105 O11 **Villahermosa** Castilla-La Mancha, C Spain 38°46′N 02°52′W
64 O11 **Villahermoso** Gomera, Islas Canarias, Spain, NE Atlantic Ocean 38°46′N 02°52′W
**Villa Hidalgo** see Hidalgo
105 T12 **Villajoyosa** var. La Vila Joíosa. Comunitat Valenciana, E Spain 38°31′N 00°14′W
**Villa Juárez** see Juárez
**Villalba** see Collado Villalba
41 N8 **Villaldama** Nuevo León, NE Mexico 26°29′N 100°27′W
104 L5 **Villalón de Campos** Castilla y León, N Spain 42°05′N 05°03′W
61 A25 **Villalonga** Buenos Aires, E Argentina 39°55′S 62°35′W
104 L5 **Villalpando** Castilla y León, N Spain 41°51′N 05°25′W
40 K9 **Villa Madero** var. Francisco I. Madero. Durango, C Mexico 24°28′N 104°20′W
41 O9 **Villa Mainero** Tamaulipas, C Mexico 24°32′N 99°39′W
**Villamaña** see Villamañán
104 L4 **Villamañán** var. Villamaña. Castilla y León, N Spain 42°19′N 05°35′W
62 L10 **Villa María** Córdoba, C Argentina 32°23′S 63°15′W
61 C17 **Villa María Grande** Entre Ríos, E Argentina 31°39′S 59°54′W
57 K21 **Villa Martín** Potosí, SW Bolivia 20°46′S 67°45′W
104 K15 **Villamartín** Andalucía, S Spain 36°52′N 05°38′W
62 J8 **Villa Mazán** La Rioja, NW Argentina 28°43′S 66°25′W
62 J11 **Villa Mercedes** var. Mercedes. San Luis, C Argentina 33°40′S 65°25′W
**Villamil** see Puerto Villamil
**Villa Nador** see Nador
54 G5 **Villanueva** La Guajira, N Colombia 10°37′N 72°58′W
42 H5 **Villanueva** Cortés, NW Honduras 15°14′N 88°00′W
40 L11 **Villanueva** Zacatecas, C Mexico 22°24′N 102°53′W
42 I9 **Villa Nueva** Chinandega, NW Nicaragua 12°58′N 86°46′W
37 T11 **Villanueva** New Mexico, SW USA 35°18′N 105°20′W
104 M12 **Villanueva de Córdoba** Andalucía, S Spain 38°20′N 04°38′W
105 O12 **Villanueva del Arzobispo** Andalucía, S Spain 38°10′N 03°00′W
104 K11 **Villanueva de la Serena** Extremadura, W Spain 38°58′N 05°48′W
104 L5 **Villanueva del Campo** Castilla y León, N Spain 41°59′N 05°25′W
105 O11 **Villanueva de los Infantes** Castilla-La Mancha, C Spain 38°45′N 03°01′W
61 C14 **Villa Ocampo** Santa Fe, C Argentina 28°28′S 59°22′W
40 J8 **Villa Ocampo** Durango, C Mexico 26°29′N 105°30′W
40 J7 **Villa Orestes Pereyra** Durango, C Mexico 26°30′N 105°38′W
105 N3 **Villarcayo** Castilla y León, N Spain 42°56′N 03°34′W
104 L5 **Villardefrades** Castilla y León, N Spain 41°43′N 05°15′W
105 S9 **Villar del Arzobispo** Comunitat Valenciana, E Spain 39°44′N 00°50′W
105 Q6 **Villaroya de la Sierra** Aragón, NE Spain 41°28′N 01°46′W
**Villarreal** see Vila-real
62 P6 **Villarrica** Guairá, SE Paraguay 25°45′S 56°28′W
63 G15 **Villarrica, Volcán** S Chile 39°28′S 71°57′W
105 P10 **Villarrobledo** Castilla-La Mancha, C Spain 39°16′N 02°36′W
105 N10 **Villarrubia de los Ojos** Castilla-La Mancha, C Spain 39°14′N 03°36′W
18 J17 **Villas** New Jersey, NE USA 39°01′N 74°54′W
105 O3 **Villasana de Mena** Castilla y León, N Spain 43°05′N 03°16′W
107 M23 **Villa San Giovanni** Calabria, S Italy 38°12′N 15°39′E
61 D18 **Villa San José** Entre Ríos, E Argentina 32°01′S 58°20′W
**Villa Sanjurjo** see Al-Hoceïma
105 P6 **Villasayas** Castilla y León, N Spain 41°19′N 02°36′W
107 C20 **Villasimius** Sardegna, Italy, C Mediterranean Sea 39°10′N 09°30′E
41 N6 **Villa Unión** Coahuila, NE Mexico 28°18′N 100°43′W
40 K10 **Villa Unión** Durango, C Mexico 23°59′N 104°01′W
40 J10 **Villa Unión** Sinaloa, C Mexico 23°10′N 106°12′W
62 K12 **Villa Valeria** Córdoba, C Argentina 34°21′S 64°56′W
105 N8 **Villaverde** Madrid, C Spain 40°21′N 03°43′W
54 F10 **Villavicencio** Meta, C Colombia 04°09′N 73°38′W
104 L2 **Villaviciosa** Asturias, N Spain 43°29′N 05°26′W
104 L12 **Villaviciosa de Córdoba** Andalucía, S Spain 38°04′N 05°00′W
57 L22 **Villazón** Potosí, S Bolivia 22°05′S 65°35′W
14 J8 **Villebon, Lac** ◎ Québec, SE Canada
**Ville de Kinshasa** see Kinshasa
102 J5 **Villedieu-les-Poêles** Manche, N France 48°51′N 01°12′W
**Villefranche** see Villefranche-sur-Saône
103 N16 **Villefranche-de-Lauragais** Haute-Garonne, S France 43°24′N 01°42′E
103 N14 **Villefranche-de-Rouergue** Aveyron, S France 44°21′N 02°02′E
103 R10 **Villefranche-sur-Saône** var. Villefranche. Rhône, E France 46°00′N 04°40′E
14 H9 **Ville-Marie** Québec, SE Canada 47°21′N 79°26′W
102 M15 **Villemur-sur-Tarn** Haute-Garonne, S France 43°50′N 01°32′E
105 S11 **Villena** Comunitat Valenciana, E Spain 38°39′N 00°52′W
**Villeneuve-d'Agen** see Villeneuve-sur-Lot
102 L13 **Villeneuve-sur-Lot** var. Villeneuve-d'Agen, hist. Gajac. Lot-et-Garonne, SW France 44°24′N 00°43′E
103 P6 **Villeneuve-sur-Yonne** Yonne, C France 48°04′N 03°21′E
22 H8 **Ville Platte** Louisiana, S USA 30°41′N 92°16′W
103 R11 **Villeurbanne** Rhône, E France 45°46′N 04°54′E
101 G23 **Villingen-Schwenningen** Baden-Württemberg, S Germany 48°04′N 08°27′E
29 T15 **Villisca** Iowa, C USA 40°55′N 94°58′W
**Villmanstrand** see Lappeenranta
**Vilna** see Vilnius
119 H14 **Vilnius** Pol. Wilno, Ger. Wilna; prev. Rus. Vilna. ● (Lithuania) Vilnius, SE Lithuania 54°41′N 25°20′E
119 H14 **Vilnius** ✈ Vilnius, SE Lithuania 54°33′N 25°17′E
117 S7 **Vil'nohirs'k** Dnipropetrovs'ka Oblast', E Ukraine 48°31′N 34°01′E
117 U8 **Vil'nyans'k** Zaporiz'ka Oblast', SE Ukraine 47°56′N 35°22′E
93 L17 **Vilppula** Pirkanmaa, W Finland 62°02′N 24°30′E
101 M20 **Vils** SE Germany
118 C5 **Vilsandi** island W Estonia
117 P8 **Vil'shanka** Rus. Olshanka. Kirovohrads'ka Oblast', C Ukraine 48°12′N 30°54′E
101 O22 **Vilshofen** Bayern, SE Germany 48°36′N 13°10′E
155 J20 **Viluppuram** Tamil Nādu, SE India 12°54′N 79°40′E
113 I16 **Vilusi** W Montenegro 42°44′N 18°34′E
99 G18 **Vilvoorde** Fr. Vilvorde. Vlaams Brabant, C Belgium 50°56′N 04°25′E
**Vilvorde** see Vilvoorde
119 J14 **Vilyeyka** Pol. Wilejka, Rus. Vileyka. Minskaya Voblasts', NW Belarus 54°30′N 26°55′E
122 V11 **Vilyuchinsk** Kamchatskiy Kray, E Russia 52°55′N 158°28′E
123 P10 **Vilyuy** NE Russia
123 P10 **Vilyuysk** Respublika Sakha (Yakutiya), NE Russia 63°42′N 121°20′E
123 N10 **Vilyuyskoye Vodokhranilishche** ⊠ NE Russia
104 G2 **Vimianzo** Galicia, NW Spain 43°06′N 09°03′W
95 M19 **Vimmerby** Kalmar, S Sweden 57°40′N 15°50′E
102 L5 **Vimoutiers** Orne, N France 48°56′N 00°10′E
93 L16 **Vimpeli** Etelä-Pohjanmaa, W Finland 63°10′N 23°50′E
79 G14 **Vina** Cameroon/Chad
62 G11 **Viña del Mar** Valparaíso, C Chile 33°02′S 71°35′W
19 R8 **Vinalhaven Island** island Maine, NE USA
105 T8 **Vinaròs** Comunitat Valenciana, E Spain 40°29′N 00°28′E
**Vînători** see Vânători
31 N15 **Vincennes** Indiana, N USA 38°42′N 87°30′W
195 Y12 **Vincennes Bay** bay Antarctica
25 O7 **Vincent** Texas, SW USA 32°30′N 101°10′W
95 H24 **Vindeby** Syddtjylland, C Denmark 54°55′N 11°09′E
93 I15 **Vindeln** Västerbotten, N Sweden 64°11′N 19°45′E
95 F21 **Vinderup** Midtjylland, C Denmark 56°29′N 08°48′E
**Vindhya Mountains** see Vindhya Range
153 N14 **Vindhya Range** var. Vindhya Mountains. ▲▲ N India
**Vindobona** see Wien
20 K6 **Vine Grove** Kentucky, S USA 37°48′N 85°58′W
18 J17 **Vineland** New Jersey, NE USA 39°29′N 75°02′W
116 E11 **Vinga** Arad, W Romania 46°00′N 21°14′E
95 M16 **Vingåker** Södermanland, C Sweden 59°02′N 15°52′E
167 S8 **Vinh** Nghê An, N Vietnam 18°42′N 105°41′E
104 I5 **Vinhais** Bragança, N Portugal 41°50′N 07°00′W
**Vinh Linh** see Hô Xa
**Vinh Loi** see Bac Liêu
167 S14 **Vinh Long** var. Vinhlong. Vinh Long, S Vietnam 10°15′N 105°59′E
**Vinhlong** see Vinh Long
113 Q18 **Vinica** NE North Macedonia 41°53′N 22°30′E
109 V13 **Vinica** SE Slovenia 45°28′N 15°12′E
114 G8 **Vinishte** Montana, NW Bulgaria 43°30′N 23°04′E
27 Q8 **Vinita** Oklahoma, C USA 36°38′N 95°09′W
**Vinju Mare** see Vânju Mare
98 I11 **Vinkeveen** Utrecht, C Netherlands 52°13′N 04°55′E
116 L6 **Vin'kivtsi** Khmel'nyts'ka Oblast', W Ukraine 49°02′N 27°13′E
112 I10 **Vinkovci** Ger. Winkowitz, Hung. Vinkovcze. Vukovar-Srijem, E Croatia 45°18′N 18°45′E
**Vinkovcze** see Vinkovci
**Vinnitsa** see Vinnytsya
**Vinnitskaya Oblast'/Vinnytsya** see Vinnyts'ka Oblast'
116 M7 **Vinnyts'ka Oblast'** var. Vinnytsya, Rus. Vinnitskaya Oblast'. ◆ province C Ukraine
117 N6 **Vinnytsya** Rus. Vinnitsa. Vinnyts'ka Oblast', C Ukraine 49°14′N 28°30′E
117 N6 **Vinnytsya** ✈ Vinnyts'ka Oblast', N Ukraine 49°13′N 28°40′E
**Vinogradov** see Vynohradiv
194 L8 **Vinson Massif** ▲ Antarctica 78°45′S 85°19′W
94 G11 **Vinstra** Oppland, S Norway 61°36′N 09°45′E
116 K12 **Vintilă Vodă** Buzău, SE Romania 45°28′N 26°43′E
29 X13 **Vinton** Iowa, C USA 42°10′N 92°01′W
22 F9 **Vinton** Louisiana, S USA 30°10′N 93°37′W
155 J17 **Vinukonda** Andhra Pradesh, E India 16°03′N 79°41′E
**Vioara** see Ocnele Mari
83 E23 **Vioolsdrif** Northern Cape, SW South Africa 28°50′S 17°38′E
82 M13 **Viphya Mountains** ▲▲ C Malawi
171 Q4 **Virac** Catanduanes Island, N Philippines 13°39′N 124°17′E
124 K8 **Virandozero** Respublika Kareliya, NW Russia 63°59′N 36°00′E
137 P16 **Viranşehir** Şanlıurfa, SE Turkey 37°13′N 39°32′E
154 D13 **Virār** Mahārāshtra, W India 19°30′N 72°48′E
11 W16 **Virden** Manitoba, S Canada 49°50′N 100°57′W
30 K14 **Virden** Illinois, N USA 39°30′N 89°46′W
**Virdois** see Virrat
102 J5 **Vire** Calvados, N France 48°50′N 00°53′W
102 J4 **Vire** N France
83 A15 **Virei** Namibe, SW Angola 15°43′S 12°54′E
**Virful Moldoveanu** see Vârful Moldoveanu
35 R5 **Virginia Peak** ▲ Nevada, W USA 39°46′N 119°26′W
45 U9 **Virgin Gorda** island C British Virgin Islands
83 I22 **Virginia** Free State, C South Africa 28°06′S 26°53′E
30 K13 **Virginia** Illinois, N USA 39°57′N 90°12′W
29 W4 **Virginia** Minnesota, N USA 47°31′N 92°32′W
21 T6 **Virginia** off. Commonwealth of Virginia, also known as Mother of Presidents, Mother of States, Old Dominion. ◆ state NE USA
21 Y7 **Virginia Beach** Virginia, NE USA 36°51′N 75°59′W
33 R11 **Virginia City** Montana, NW USA 45°17′N 111°54′W
35 Q6 **Virginia City** Nevada, W USA 39°19′N 119°39′W
14 H8 **Virginiatown** Ontario, S Canada 48°09′N 79°35′W
**Virgin Islands** see British Virgin Islands
45 T9 **Virgin Islands (US)** var. Virgin Islands of the United States; prev. Danish West Indies. ◇ US unincorporated territory E West Indies
**Virgin Islands of the United States** see Virgin Islands (US)
45 T9 **Virgin Passage** passage Puerto Rico/Virgin Islands (US)
35 Y10 **Virgin River** Nevada/Utah, W USA
**Virihaur** see Virihaure
92 H12 **Virihaure** Lapp. Virihávrre, var. Virihaur. ◎ N Sweden
**Virihávrre** see Virihaure
167 T11 **Virôchey** Ratanakiri, NE Cambodia 13°59′N 106°49′E
93 N19 **Virolahti** Kymenlaakso, S Finland 60°33′N 27°37′E
30 J8 **Viroqua** Wisconsin, N USA 43°33′N 90°54′W
112 G8 **Virovitica** Ger. Virovititz, Hung. Verőcze; prev. Ger. Werowitz. Virovitica-Podravina, NE Croatia 45°49′N 17°25′E
112 G8 **Virovitica-Podravina** off. Virovitičko-Podravska Županija. ◆ province NE Croatia
**Virovitičko-Podravska Županija** see Virovitica-Podravina
**Virovititz** see Virovitica
113 J17 **Virpazar** S Montenegro 42°15′N 19°06′E
93 L17 **Virrat** Swe. Virdois. Pirkanmaa, W Finland 62°14′N 23°50′E
95 M20 **Virserum** Kalmar, S Sweden 57°17′N 15°18′E
99 K25 **Virton** Luxembourg, SE Belgium 49°34′N 05°32′E
118 F5 **Virtsu** Ger. Werder. Läänemaa, W Estonia 58°35′N 23°33′E
56 C12 **Virú** La Libertad, C Peru 08°24′S 78°40′W
**Virudhunagar** see Virudunagar
155 H23 **Virudunagar** var. Virudhunagar; prev. Virudupatti. Tamil Nādu, SE India 09°35′N 77°57′E
**Virudupatti** see Virudunagar
118 I3 **Viru-Jaagupi** Ger. Sankt-Jakobi. Lääne-Virumaa, NE Estonia 59°14′N 26°29′E
57 N19 **Viru-Viru** var. Santa Cruz. ✈ (Santa Cruz) Santa Cruz, C Bolivia 17°49′S 63°12′W
113 E15 **Vis** It. Lissa; anc. Issa. island S Croatia
**Vis** see Fish
118 I12 **Visaginas** prev. Sniečkus. Utena, E Lithuania 55°36′N 26°22′E
35 R11 **Visalia** California, W USA 36°19′N 119°19′W
**Vişău** see Vişeu
95 P19 **Visby** Ger. Wisby. Gotland, SE Sweden 57°37′N 18°20′E
197 N9 **Viscount Melville Sound** prev. Melville Sound. sound Northwest Territories, N Canada
99 L19 **Visé** Liège, E Belgium 50°44′N 05°42′E
112 K13 **Višegrad** Republika Srpska, SE Bosnia and Herzegovina 43°46′N 19°18′E
58 L12 **Viseu** Pará, NE Brazil 01°10′S 46°09′W
104 H7 **Viseu** prev. Vizeu. Viseu, N Portugal 40°40′N 07°55′W
104 H7 **Viseu** var. Vizeu. ◆ district N Portugal
**Visó** see Vişeu
116 I8 **Vişeu** Hung. Visó; prev. Vişău. NW Romania
116 I8 **Vişeu de Sus** var. Vişeul de Sus, Ger. Oberwischau, Hung. Felsővisó. Maramureş, N Romania 47°43′N 23°24′E
**Vişeul de Sus** see Vişeu de Sus
155 M15 **Vishākhapatnam** var. Vishakhapatnam. Andhra Pradesh, SE India 17°45′N 83°19′E
**Vishakhapatnam** see Vishākhapatnam
125 R10 **Vishera** NW Russia
95 J19 **Viskafors** Västra Götaland, S Sweden 57°37′N 12°50′E
95 J20 **Viskan** S Sweden
95 L21 **Vislanda** Kronoberg, S Sweden 56°46′N 14°30′E
**Vislinskiy Zaliv** see Vistula Lagoon
**Visó** see Vişeu
112 H13 **Visoko** ◆ Federacija Bosne I Hercegovine, C Bosnia and Herzegovina
106 A9 **Viso, Monte** ▲ NW Italy 44°42′N 07°04′E
108 E10 **Visp** Valais, SW Switzerland 46°18′N 07°53′E
108 E10 **Vispa** S Switzerland
95 M21 **Vissefjärda** Kalmar, S Sweden 56°31′N 15°34′E
100 I11 **Visselhövede** Niedersachsen, NW Germany 52°58′N 09°36′E
95 G23 **Vissenbjerg** Syddtjylland, C Denmark 55°23′N 10°08′E
35 U17 **Vista** California, W USA 33°12′N 117°14′W
58 C11 **Vista Alegre** Amazonas, NW Brazil 01°23′N 68°13′W
114 J13 **Vistonída, Límni** ◎ NE Greece
**Vistula** see Wisła
119 A14 **Vistula Lagoon** Ger. Frisches Haff, Pol. Zalew Wiślany, Rus. Vislinskiy Zaliv. lagoon Poland/Russia
114 I8 **Vit** NW Bulgaria
**Vitebsk** see Vitsyebsk
**Vitebskaya Oblast'** see Vitsyebskaya Voblasts'
107 H14 **Viterbo** anc. Vicus Elbii. Lazio, C Italy 42°25′N 12°08′E
112 H12 **Vitez** Federacija Bosne I Hercegovine, C Bosnia and Herzegovina 44°08′N 17°47′E
167 S14 **Vi Thanh** Cân Thơ, S Vietnam 09°45′N 105°28′E
**Viti** see Fiji
186 E7 **Vitiaz Strait** strait NE Papua New Guinea
104 J7 **Vitigudino** Castilla y León, N Spain 41°00′N 06°26′W
175 Q9 **Viti Levu** island W Fiji
187 W15 **Viti Levu** island W Fiji
123 O11 **Vitim** C Russia
123 O12 **Vitimskiy** Irkutskaya Oblast', C Russia 58°12′N 113°10′E
109 V2 **Vitis** Niederösterreich, N Austria 48°45′N 15°09′E
59 O20 **Vitória** state capital Espírito Santo, SE Brazil 20°19′S 40°21′W
**Vitoria** see Vitoria-Gasteiz
**Vitoria Bank** see Vitória Seamount
59 N18 **Vitória da Conquista** Bahia, E Brazil 14°53′S 40°52′W
105 P3 **Vitoria-Gasteiz** var. Vitoria, Eng. Vittoria. País Vasco, N Spain 42°51′N 02°40′W
65 J16 **Vitória Seamount** var. Victoria Bank, Vitoria Bank. undersea feature C Atlantic Ocean 18°48′S 37°24′W
112 F13 **Vitorog** ▲ SW Bosnia and Herzegovina 44°06′N 17°03′E
102 J6 **Vitré** Ille-et-Vilaine, NW France 48°07′N 01°12′W
103 R5 **Vitry-le-François** Marne, N France 48°43′N 04°36′E
114 D13 **Vitsi** var. Vítsoi. ▲ N Greece 40°39′N 21°23′E
**Vítsoi** see Vitsi
118 N13 **Vitsyebsk** Rus. Vitebsk. Vitsyebskaya Voblasts', NE Belarus 55°11′N 30°10′E
118 K13 **Vitsyebskaya Voblasts'** Rus. Vitebskaya Oblast'. ◆ province N Belarus
92 J11 **Vittangi** Lapp. Vazáš. Norrbotten, N Sweden 67°40′N 21°39′E
103 R8 **Vitteaux** Côte d'Or, C France 47°24′N 04°31′E
103 S6 **Vittel** Vosges, NE France 48°13′N 05°57′E
95 N15 **Vittinge** Västmanland, C Sweden 59°52′N 17°04′E
107 K25 **Vittoria** Sicilia, Italy, C Mediterranean Sea 36°56′N 14°30′E
**Vittoria** see Vitoria-Gasteiz
106 I7 **Vittorio Veneto** Veneto, NE Italy 45°59′N 12°18′E
175 Q7 **Vityaz Trench** undersea feature W Pacific Ocean
108 G8 **Vitznau** Luzern, W Switzerland 47°01′N 08°28′E
104 I1 **Viveiro** Galicia, NW Spain 43°39′N 07°35′W
105 S9 **Viver** Comunitat Valenciana, E Spain 39°55′N 00°36′W
103 Q13 **Viverais, Monts du** ▲ C France
122 L9 **Vivi** N Russia
22 F4 **Vivian** Louisiana, S USA 32°52′N 93°59′W
29 N10 **Vivian** South Dakota, N USA 43°53′N 100°16′W
103 R13 **Viviers** Ardèche, E France 44°31′N 04°40′E
**Vivis** see Vevey
83 K19 **Vivo** Limpopo, NE South Africa 22°58′S 29°13′E
102 L10 **Vivonne** Vienne, W France 46°25′N 00°15′E
**Vizakna** see Ocna Sibiului
**Vizcaya** see Bizkaia
**Vizcaya, Golfo de** see Biscay, Bay of
136 C10 **Vize** Kırklareli, NW Turkey 41°34′N 27°45′E
122 K4 **Vize, Ostrov** island Severnaya Zemlya, N Russia
**Vizeu** see Viseu
155 M15 **Vizianagaram** var. Vizianagram. Andhra Pradesh, E India 18°07′N 83°25′E
**Vizianagram** see Vizianagaram
103 S12 **Vizille** Isère, E France 45°05′N 05°46′E
125 R11 **Vizinga** Respublika Komi, NW Russia 61°06′N 50°09′E
116 M13 **Viziru** Brăila, SE Romania 45°00′N 27°43′E
113 K21 **Vjosës, Lumi i** var. Vijosa, Vijosë, Gk. Aóos. Albania/Greece see also Aóos
**Vjosës, Lumi i** see Aóos
99 H18 **Vlaams Brabant** ◆ province C Belgium
99 G18 **Vlaanderen** Eng. Flanders, Fr. Flandre. ◆ Belgium/France
98 G12 **Vlaardingen** Zuid-Holland, SW Netherlands 51°55′N 04°21′E
116 F10 **Vlădeasa, Vârful** prev. Virful Vlădeasa. ▲ NW Romania 46°45′N 22°46′E
**Vlădeasa, Virful** see Vlădeasa, Vârful
113 P16 **Vladičin Han** Serbia, SE Serbia 42°44′N 22°04′E
127 O16 **Vladikavkaz** prev. Dzaudzhikau, Ordzhonikidze. Respublika Severnaya Osetiya, SW Russia 42°58′N 44°41′E
126 M3 **Vladimir** Vladimirskaya Oblast', W Russia 56°09′N 40°21′E
**Vladimirets** see Voldymyerets'
144 M7 **Vladimirovka** Kostanay, N Kazakhstan 53°30′N 64°02′E
**Vladimirovka** see Yuzhno-Sakhalinsk
126 L3 **Vladimirskaya Oblast'** ◆ province W Russia
126 I3 **Vladimirskiy Tupik** Smolenskaya Oblast', W Russia 55°45′N 33°25′E
**Vladimir-Volynskiy** see Volodymyr-Volyns'kyy
123 Q7 **Vladivostok** Primorskiy Kray, SE Russia 43°09′N 131°53′E
117 U13 **Vladyslavivka** Avtonomna Respublika Krym, S Ukraine 45°09′N 35°25′E
98 P6 **Vlagtwedde** Groningen, NE Netherlands 53°02′N 07°07′E
**Vlajna** see Kukavica
112 J12 **Vlasenica** ◆ Republika Srpska, E Bosnia and Herzegovina
112 G12 **Vlašić** ▲ C Bosnia and Herzegovina 44°18′N 17°40′E
111 D17 **Vlašim** Ger. Wlaschim. Středočeský Kraj, C Czechia 49°42′N 14°54′E
113 P15 **Vlasotince** Serbia, SE Serbia 42°58′N 22°07′E
123 Q7 **Vlasovo** Respublika Sakha (Yakutiya), NE Russia 70°41′N 134°49′E
98 I11 **Vleuten** Utrecht, C Netherlands 52°07′N 05°01′E
98 I5 **Vlieland** Fris. Flylân. island Waddeneilanden, N Netherlands
98 I5 **Vliestroom** strait NW Netherlands
99 J14 **Vlijmen** Noord-Brabant, S Netherlands 51°42′N 05°14′E
99 E15 **Vlissingen** Eng. Flushing, Fr. Flessingue. Zeeland, SW Netherlands 51°26′N 03°34′E
**Vlodava** see Włodawa
**Vlonë/Vlora** see Vlorë
113 K22 **Vlorë** prev. Vlonë, It. Valona, Vlora. Vlorë, SW Albania 40°28′N 19°31′E
113 K22 **Vlorë** ◆ county SW Albania
113 K22 **Vlorës, Gjiri i** var. Valona Bay. bay SW Albania
**Vlotslavsk** see Włocławek
111 C16 **Vltava** Ger. Moldau. W Czechia
126 K3 **Vnukovo** ✈ (Moskva) Gorod Moskva, W Russia 55°30′N 36°52′E
146 L11 **Vobkent** Rus. Vabkent. Buxoro Viloyati, C Uzbekistan 40°01′N 64°25′E
25 Q9 **Voca** Texas, SW USA 30°58′N 99°09′W
109 R5 **Vöcklabruck** Oberösterreich, NW Austria 48°01′N 13°38′E
112 D13 **Vodice** Šibenik-Knin, S Croatia 43°46′N 15°46′E
124 K10 **Vodlozero, Ozero** ◎ NW Russia
112 A10 **Vodnjan** It. Dignano d'Istria. Istra, NW Croatia 44°57′N 13°51′E
125 S9 **Vodnyy** Respublika Komi, NW Russia 63°31′N 53°21′E
145 V15 **Vodokhranilishche Kapshagay** Kaz. Qapshagay Böyeni; prev. Kapchagayskoye Vodokhranilishche. ⊠ SE Kazakhstan
124 I6 **Vodokhranilishche, Kumskoye** ◎ NW Russia
95 G20 **Vodskov** Nordjylland, N Denmark 57°07′N 10°02′E
92 H4 **Vogar** Suðurnes, SW Iceland 63°58′N 22°20′W
**Vogelkop** see Doberai, Jazirah
77 X15 **Vogel Peak** prev. Dimlang. ▲ E Nigeria 08°16′N 11°44′E
101 H17 **Vogelsberg** ▲ C Germany
106 D8 **Voghera** Lombardia, N Italy 44°59′N 09°01′E
112 I13 **Vogošća** Federacija Bosne I Hercegovine, SE Bosnia and Herzegovina 43°55′N 18°20′E
101 M17 **Vogtland** historical region E Germany
125 V12 **Vogul'skiy Kamen', Gora** ▲ NW Russia 60°10′N 58°41′E
187 P16 **Voh** Province Nord, C New Caledonia 20°57′S 164°41′E
**Vohémar** see Iharaña
172 H8 **Vohimena, Tanjona** Fr. Cap Sainte Marie. headland S Madagascar 25°20′S 45°06′E
172 J6 **Vohipeno** Fianarantsoa, SE Madagascar 22°21′S 47°51′E
118 H5 **Võhma** Ger. Wõchma. Viljandimaa, S Estonia 58°37′N 25°34′E
81 J20 **Voi** Taita/Taveta, S Kenya 03°23′S 38°35′E
76 K15 **Voinjama** N Liberia 08°25′N 09°42′W
103 S12 **Voiron** Isère, E France 45°22′N 05°35′E
109 V8 **Voitsberg** Steiermark, SE Austria 47°04′N 15°09′E
95 F24 **Vojens** Ger. Woyens. Syddanmark, SW Denmark 55°15′N 09°19′E
112 K9 **Vojvodina** Ger. Wojwodina. Vojvodina, N Serbia
15 S6 **Volant** Québec, SE Canada
**Volaterrae** see Volterra
43 P15 **Volcán** var. Hato del Volcán. Chiriquí, W Panama 08°45′N 82°38′W
**Volcano Islands** see Kazan-rettō
**Volchansk** see Vovchans'k
**Volchya** see Vovcha
94 D10 **Volda** Møre og Romsdal, S Norway 62°07′N 06°04′E
116 K3 **Voldymyerets'** Russ. Vladimirets. Rivnens'ka Oblast', NW Ukraine 51°24′N 25°52′E
98 J9 **Volendam** Noord-Holland, C Netherlands 52°30′N 05°04′E
124 L15 **Volga** Yaroslavskaya Oblast', W Russia 57°56′N 38°23′E
29 R10 **Volga** South Dakota, N USA 44°19′N 96°55′W
122 C11 **Volga** NW Russia
**Volga-Baltic Waterway** see Volgo-Baltiyskiy Kanal
**Volga Uplands** see Privolzhskaya Vozvyshennost'
124 L13 **Volgo-Baltiyskiy Kanal** var. Volga-Baltic Waterway. canal NW Russia
126 M12 **Volgodonsk** Rostovskaya Oblast', SW Russia 47°35′N 42°03′E
127 O10 **Volgograd** prev. Stalingrad, Tsaritsyn. Volgogradskaya Oblast', SW Russia 48°42′N 44°29′E
127 N9 **Volgogradskaya Oblast'** ◆ province SW Russia
127 P10 **Volgogradskoye Vodokhranilishche** ⊠ SW Russia
101 J19 **Volkach** Bayern, C Germany 49°51′N 10°15′E
109 U9 **Völkermarkt** Slvn. Velikovec. Kärnten, S Austria 46°40′N 14°38′E
124 I12 **Volkhov** Leningradskaya Oblast', NW Russia 59°56′N 32°19′E
101 D20 **Völklingen** Saarland, SW Germany 49°15′N 06°51′E
**Volkovysk** see Vawkavysk
**Volkovyskiye Vysoty** see Vawkavyskaye Wzvyshsha
83 K22 **Volksrust** Mpumalanga, E South Africa 27°22′S 29°54′E
98 L8 **Vollenhove** Overijssel, N Netherlands 52°40′N 05°58′E
119 L16 **Volma** C Belarus
**Volmari** see Valmiera
117 W9 **Volnovakha** Donets'ka Oblast', SE Ukraine 47°36′N 37°32′E
116 K6 **Volochys'k** Khmel'nyts'ka Oblast', W Ukraine 49°32′N 26°14′E
117 O6 **Volodarka** Kyïvs'ka Oblast', N Ukraine 49°31′N 29°55′E
**Volodars'ke** see Nikol's'ke
127 R13 **Volodarskiy** Astrakhanskaya Oblast', SW Russia 46°23′N 48°39′E
**Volodarskoye** see Saumalkol'
117 N8 **Volodars'k-Volyns'kyy** Zhytomyrs'ka Oblast', N Ukraine 50°37′N 28°28′E
116 I3 **Volodymyr-Volyns'kyy** Pol. Włodzimierz, Rus. Vladimir-Volynskiy. Volyns'ka Oblast', NW Ukraine 50°51′N 24°19′E
124 L14 **Vologda** Vologodskaya Oblast', W Russia 59°10′N 39°55′E
124 L12 **Vologodskaya Oblast'** ◆ province NW Russia
126 K3 **Volokolamsk** Moskovskaya Oblast', W Russia 56°03′N 35°57′E
126 K9 **Volokonovka** Belgorodskaya Oblast', W Russia 50°30′N 37°54′E
115 G16 **Vólos** Thessalía, C Greece 39°21′N 22°58′E
124 M11 **Voloshka** Arkhangel'skaya Oblast', NW Russia 61°19′N 40°06′E
**Vološinovo** see Novi Bečej
116 H7 **Volovets'** Zakarpats'ka Oblast', W Ukraine 48°42′N 23°12′E
**Volozhin** see Valozhyn
127 Q7 **Vol'sk** Saratovskaya Oblast', W Russia 52°04′N 47°20′E
77 Q17 **Volta** SE Ghana
**Volta Blanche** see White Volta
77 P16 **Volta, Lake** ⊠ SE Ghana
**Volta Noire** see Black Volta
60 O9 **Volta Redonda** Rio de Janeiro, SE Brazil 22°31′S 44°05′W
**Volta Rouge** see Red Volta
106 F12 **Volterra** anc. Volaterrae. Toscana, C Italy 43°23′N 10°52′E
107 K17 **Volturno** S Italy
113 I15 **Volujak** ▲▲ NW Montenegro
**Volunteer Island** see Starbuck Island
65 F24 **Volunteer Point** headland East Falkland, Falkland Islands 51°32′S 57°44′W
114 H13 **Vólvi, Límni** ◎ N Greece
**Volyn** see Volyns'ka Oblast'
116 I3 **Volyns'ka Oblast'** var. Volyn, Rus. Volynskaya Oblast'. ◆ province NW Ukraine
**Volynskaya Oblast'** see Volyns'ka Oblast'
127 Q3 **Volzhsk** Respublika Mariy El, W Russia 55°53′N 48°21′E
127 O10 **Volzhskiy** Volgogradskaya Oblast', SW Russia 48°49′N 44°40′E
172 I7 **Vondrozo** Fianarantsoa, SE Madagascar 22°50′S 47°20′E
39 P10 **Von Frank Mountain** ▲ Alaska, USA 63°36′N 154°29′W
115 C17 **Vónitsa** Dytikí Elláda, W Greece 38°55′N 20°53′E
118 J6 **Võnnu** Ger. Wendau. Tartumaa, SE Estonia 58°17′N 27°06′E
98 G12 **Voorburg** Zuid-Holland, W Netherlands 52°04′N 04°22′E
98 H11 **Voorschoten** Zuid-Holland, W Netherlands 52°08′N 04°26′E
98 M11 **Voorst** Gelderland, E Netherlands 52°10′N 06°10′E
98 K11 **Voorthuizen** Gelderland, C Netherlands 52°12′N 05°36′E
92 L2 **Vopnafjörður** bay E Iceland
92 L2 **Vopnafjörður** Austurland, E Iceland 65°45′N 14°51′W
**Vora** see Vorë
119 H15 **Voranava** Pol. Werenów, Rus. Voronovo. Hrodzyenskaya Voblasts', W Belarus 54°09′N 25°19′E
108 I8 **Vorarlberg** off. Land Vorarlberg. ◆ state W Austria
**Vorarlberg, Land** see Vorarlberg
109 X7 **Vorau** Steiermark, E Austria 47°22′N 15°55′E
98 N11 **Vorden** Gelderland, E Netherlands 52°07′N 06°18′E
108 H9 **Vorderrhein** SE Switzerland
95 I24 **Vordingborg** Sjælland, SE Denmark 55°01′N 11°55′E
92 J2 **Vorðufell** ▲ N Iceland 65°42′N 18°45′W
113 K19 **Vorë** var. Vora. Tiranë, W Albania 41°23′N 19°37′E
115 H17 **Vóreies Sporádes** var. Vóreioi Sporádhes, Eng. Northern Sporades. island group E Greece
115 J17 **Vóreio Aigaío** Eng. Aegean North. ◆ region SE Greece
**Vóreioi Sporádes** see Vóreies Sporádes



◆ Country ● Country Capital ◇ Dependent Territory ○ Dependent Territory Capital ◆ Administrative Regions ✈ International Airport ▲ Mountain ▲▲ Mountain Range Volcano River ◎ Lake ⊠ Reservoir

341

Walvis Ridge – Wenquan


65 O17 **Walvis Ridge** *var.* Walvish Ridge. *undersea feature* E Atlantic Ocean 28°00′S 03°00′E
171 X16 **Wamal** Papua, E Indonesia 08°00′S 139°06′E
171 U15 **Wamar, Pulau** *island* Kepulauan Aru, E Indonesia
79 O17 **Wamba** Orientale, NE Dem. Rep. Congo 02°10′N 27°59′E
77 V15 **Wamba** Nassarawa, C Nigeria 08°57′N 08°35′E
79 H22 **Wamba** *var.* Uamba. ≈ Angola/Dem. Rep. Congo
27 P4 **Wamego** Kansas, C USA 39°12′N 96°18′W
18 I10 **Wampsville** New York, NE USA 43°03′N 75°40′W
42 K6 **Wampú, Río** ≈ E Honduras
171 X16 **Wan** Papua, E Indonesia 08°15′S 138°00′E
**Wan** *see* Anhui
183 N4 **Wanaaring** New South Wales, SE Australia 29°42′S 144°07′E
185 D21 **Wanaka** Otago, South Island, New Zealand 44°42′S 169°09′E
185 D20 **Wanaka, Lake** ◎ South Island, New Zealand
171 W14 **Wanapiri** Papua, E Indonesia 04°21′S 135°52′E
14 F9 **Wanapitei** ≈ Ontario, S Canada
14 F10 **Wanapitei Lake** ◎ Ontario, S Canada
18 K14 **Wanaque** New Jersey, NE USA 41°02′N 74°17′W
171 U12 **Wanau** Papua Barat, E Indonesia 01°20′S 132°40′E
185 F22 **Wanbrow, Cape** *headland* South Island, New Zealand 45°07′S 170°59′E
**Wancheng** *see* Wanning
**Wanchuan** *see* Zhangjiakou
171 W13 **Wandai** *var.* Komeyo. Papua, E Indonesia 03°35′S 136°15′E
163 Z8 **Wanda Shan** ▲▲ NE China
197 R11 **Wandel Sea** *sea* Arctic Ocean
160 D13 **Wanding** *var.* Wandingzhen. Yunnan, SW China 24°01′N 98°00′E
**Wandingzhen** *see* Wanding
99 H20 **Wanfercée-Baulet** Hainaut, S Belgium 50°27′N 04°37′E
184 L12 **Wanganui** Manawatu-Wanganui, North Island, New Zealand 39°56′S 175°02′E
184 L11 **Wanganui** ≈ North Island, New Zealand
183 P11 **Wangaratta** Victoria, SE Australia 36°22′S 146°17′E
160 J8 **Wangcang** *var.* Donghe; *prev.* Fengjiaba, Hongjiang. Sichuan, C China 32°15′N 106°16′E
**Wangda** *see* Zogang
101 I24 **Wangen im Allgäu** Baden-Württemberg, S Germany 47°40′N 09°49′E
**Wangerin** *see* Węgorzyno
100 F9 **Wangerooge** *island* NW Germany
171 W13 **Wanggar** Papua, E Indonesia 03°22′S 135°15′E
160 J13 **Wangmo** *var.* Fuxing. Guizhou, S China 25°08′N 106°08′E
**Wangolodougou** *see* Ouangolodougou
161 S9 **Wangpan Yang** *sea* E China
163 Y10 **Wangqing** Jilin, NE China 43°19′N 129°42′E
167 P8 **Wang Saphung** Loei, C Thailand 17°18′N 101°45′E
167 O6 **Wan Hsa-la** Shan State, E Myanmar (Burma) 20°27′N 98°39′E
55 W9 **Wanica** ◈ *district* N Suriname
79 M18 **Wanie-Rukula** Orientale, C Dem. Rep. Congo 0°13′N 25°34′E
**Wankie** *see* Hwange
**Wanki, Río** *see* Coco, Río
81 N17 **Wanlaweyn** *var.* Wanle Weyn, *It.* Uanle Uen. Shabeellaha Hoose, SW Somalia 02°36′N 44°47′E
**Wanle Weyn** *see* Wanlaweyn
180 I12 **Wanneroo** Western Australia 31°40′S 115°35′E
160 L17 **Wanning** *var.* Wancheng. Hainan, S China 18°55′N 110°27′E
167 Q8 **Wanon Niwat** Sakon Nakhon, E Thailand 17°39′N 103°45′E
155 H16 **Wanparti** Telangana, C India 16°19′N 78°06′E
**Wansen** *see* Wiązów
160 L11 **Wanshan** Guizhou, S China 27°45′N 109°12′E
99 M14 **Wanssum** Limburg, SE Netherlands 51°31′N 06°04′E
184 N12 **Wanstead** Hawke's Bay, North Island, New Zealand 40°09′S 176°31′E
**Wanxian** *see* Wanzhou
188 F16 **Wanyaan** Yap, Micronesia
160 K8 **Wanyuan** Sichuan, C China 32°05′N 108°08′E
161 O11 **Wanzai** *var.* Kangle. Jiangxi, S China 28°06′N 114°27′E
99 J20 **Wanze** Liège, E Belgium 50°32′N 05°16′E
160 K9 **Wanzhou** *var.* Wanxian. Chongqing Shi, C China 30°48′N 108°21′E
31 R12 **Wapakoneta** Ohio, N USA 40°34′N 84°11′W
12 D7 **Wapaseese** ≈ Ontario, C Canada
32 I10 **Wapato** Washington, NW USA 46°27′N 120°25′W
29 Y15 **Wapello** Iowa, C USA 41°10′N 91°13′W
11 N13 **Wapiti** ≈ Alberta/British Columbia, SW Canada
27 X7 **Wappapello Lake** ▣ Missouri, C USA
18 K13 **Wappingers Falls** New York, NE USA 41°36′N 73°54′W
29 X13 **Wapsipinicon River** ≈ Iowa, C USA
14 L9 **Wapus** ≈ Québec, SE Canada
160 H7 **Waqên** Sichuan, C China 33°05′N 102°34′E
21 Q7 **War** West Virginia, NE USA 37°18′N 81°39′W
**Warab** *see* Warrap
155 J15 **Warangal** Telangana, C India 18°N 79°35′E
**Warasdin** *see* Varaždin
183 O16 **Waratah** Tasmania, SE Australia 41°28′S 145°34′E
183 O14 **Waratah Bay** *bay* Victoria, SE Australia
101 H15 **Warburg** Nordrhein-Westfalen, W Germany 51°30′N 09°11′E
182 I1 **Warburton Creek** *seasonal river* South Australia
180 M9 **Warburton** Western Australia 26°17′S 126°18′E
99 M20 **Warche** ≈ E Belgium
**Wardag/Wardak** *see* Wardak
149 P5 **Wardak** *prev.* Vardak, Wardag. ◈ *province* E Afghanistan
32 K9 **Warden** Washington, NW USA 46°58′N 119°02′W
154 I12 **Wardha** Mahārāshtra, W India 20°41′N 78°40′E
**Wardija Point** *see* Wardija, Ras il-
121 N15 **Wardija, Ras il-** *var.* Ras il- Wardija, Wardija Point. *headland* Gozo, NW Malta 36°03′N 14°11′E
**Wardija, Ras il-** *see* Wardija, Ras il-
139 P3 **Wardīyah** Ninawá, N Iraq 36°18′N 41°45′E
185 E19 **Ward, Mount** ▲ South Island, New Zealand 43°49′S 169°54′E
10 L11 **Ware** British Columbia, W Canada 57°26′N 125°41′W
99 D18 **Waregem** *var.* Waereghem. West-Vlaanderen, W Belgium 50°53′N 03°26′E
99 J19 **Waremme** Liège, E Belgium 50°41′N 05°15′E
100 N10 **Waren** Mecklenburg-Vorpommern, NE Germany 53°32′N 12°42′E
171 W13 **Waren** Papua, E Indonesia 02°13′S 136°21′E
101 F14 **Warendorf** Nordrhein-Westfalen, W Germany 51°57′N 08°00′E
21 P12 **Ware Shoals** South Carolina, SE USA 34°24′N 82°15′W
98 N4 **Warffum** Groningen, NE Netherlands 53°22′N 06°34′E
81 O15 **Wargalo** Mudug, E Somalia 06°06′N 47°40′E
146 M12 **Warganza** *Rus.* Varganzi. Qashqadaryo Viloyati, S Uzbekistan 39°18′N 66°00′E
**Wargla** *see* Ouargla
183 T4 **Warialda** New South Wales, SE Australia 29°34′S 150°35′E
154 F13 **Wāri Godri** Mahārāshtra, C India 19°28′N 75°43′E
167 R10 **Warin Chamrap** Ubon Ratchathani, E Thailand 15°11′N 104°51′E
25 R11 **Waring** Texas, SW USA 29°56′N 98°48′W
39 O8 **Waring Mountains** ▲▲ Alaska, USA
110 M12 **Warka** Mazowieckie, E Poland 51°45′N 21°12′E
184 L5 **Warkworth** Auckland, North Island, New Zealand 36°23′S 174°42′E
171 U12 **Warmandi** Papua Barat, E Indonesia 0°21′S 132°38′E
83 E22 **Warmbad** //Karas, S Namibia 28°29′S 18°41′E
98 H8 **Warmenhuizen** Noord-Holland, NW Netherlands 52°43′N 04°45′E
110 M8 **Warmińsko-Mazurskie** ◈ *province* C Poland
97 L22 **Warminster** S England, United Kingdom 51°13′N 02°12′W
18 I15 **Warminster** Pennsylvania, NE USA 40°11′N 75°04′W
35 V8 **Warm Springs** Nevada, W USA 38°10′N 116°21′W
32 H12 **Warm Springs** Oregon, NW USA 44°51′N 121°24′W
21 S5 **Warm Springs** Virginia, NE USA 38°03′N 79°48′W
100 M8 **Warnemünde** Mecklenburg-Vorpommern, NE Germany 54°10′N 12°03′E
27 Q10 **Warner** Oklahoma, C USA 35°29′N 95°18′W
35 Q2 **Warner Mountains** ▲▲ California, W USA
23 T5 **Warner Robins** Georgia, SE USA 32°38′N 83°38′W
57 N18 **Warnes** Santa Cruz, C Bolivia 17°30′S 63°11′W
100 M9 **Warnow** ≈ NE Germany
**Warnsdorf** *see* Varnsdorf
98 M11 **Warnsveld** Gelderland, E Netherlands 52°08′N 06°14′E
154 I13 **Warora** Mahārāshtra, C India 20°12′N 79°01′E
182 L11 **Warracknabeal** Victoria, SE Australia 36°17′S 142°26′E
183 O13 **Warragul** Victoria, SE Australia 38°11′S 145°55′E
80 D13 **Warrap** Warrap, W South Sudan 08°08′N 28°37′E
81 D14 **Warrap** *var.* Warab. ◈ *state* W South Sudan
183 O4 **Warrego River** *seasonal river* New South Wales/Queensland, E Australia
183 Q6 **Warren** New South Wales, SE Australia 31°41′S 147°51′E
11 X16 **Warren** Manitoba, S Canada 50°05′N 97°33′W
27 V14 **Warren** Arkansas, C USA 33°38′N 92°05′W
31 S10 **Warren** Michigan, N USA 42°29′N 83°02′W
29 R3 **Warren** Minnesota, N USA 48°12′N 96°46′W
31 U11 **Warren** Ohio, N USA 41°14′N 80°49′W
18 D12 **Warren** Pennsylvania, NE USA 41°52′N 79°09′W
25 X10 **Warren** Texas, SW USA 30°33′N 94°24′W
97 G16 **Warrenpoint** *Ir.* An Pointe. SE Northern Ireland, United Kingdom 54°07′N 06°16′W
27 S4 **Warrensburg** Missouri, C USA 38°46′N 93°44′W
83 H22 **Warrenton** Northern Cape, N South Africa 28°07′S 24°51′E
23 U4 **Warrenton** Georgia, SE USA 33°24′N 82°39′W
27 W4 **Warrenton** Missouri, C USA 38°48′N 91°08′W
21 V8 **Warrenton** North Carolina, SE USA 36°24′N 78°11′W
21 V4 **Warrenton** Virginia, NE USA 38°43′N 77°48′W
77 U17 **Warri** Delta, S Nigeria 05°26′N 05°34′E
97 L18 **Warrington** C England, United Kingdom 53°24′N 02°37′W
23 O9 **Warrington** Florida, SE USA 30°22′N 87°16′W
23 P3 **Warrior** Alabama, S USA 33°49′N 86°49′W
182 L13 **Warrnambool** Victoria, SE Australia 38°23′S 142°30′E
29 T2 **Warroad** Minnesota, N USA 48°55′N 95°18′W
183 S6 **Warrumbungle Range** ▲▲ New South Wales, SE Australia
154 J12 **Wārsa** Mahārāshtra, C India 20°42′N 79°58′E
31 P11 **Warsaw** Indiana, N USA 41°13′N 85°52′W
20 L4 **Warsaw** Kentucky, S USA 38°47′N 84°55′W
27 T5 **Warsaw** Missouri, C USA 38°14′N 93°23′W
18 E10 **Warsaw** New York, NE USA 42°44′N 78°06′W
21 V10 **Warsaw** North Carolina, SE USA 35°00′N 78°05′W
21 X5 **Warsaw** Virginia, NE USA 37°57′N 76°46′W
**Warsaw/Warschau** *see* Warszawa
81 N17 **Warshiikh** Shabeellaha Dhexe, C Somalia 02°22′N 45°52′E
101 G15 **Warstein** Nordrhein-Westfalen, W Germany 51°27′N 08°21′E
110 M11 **Warszawa** *Eng.* Warsaw, *Ger.* Warschau, *Rus.* Varshava. ● (Poland) Mazowieckie, C Poland 52°15′N 21°E
110 J13 **Warta** Sieradz, C Poland 51°43′N 18°37′E
110 D11 **Warta** *Ger.* Warthe. ≈ W Poland
**Wartberg** *see* Senec
20 M9 **Wartburg** Tennessee, S USA 36°08′N 84°37′W
108 J7 **Warth** Vorarlberg, NW Austria 47°16′N 10°11′E
**Warthe** *see* Warta
169 U12 **Waru** Borneo, C Indonesia 01°24′S 116°37′E
171 T13 **Waru** Pulau Seram, E Indonesia 03°24′S 130°38′E
139 N6 **Wa'r, Wādī al** *dry watercourse* E Syria
183 U3 **Warwick** Queensland, E Australia 28°12′S 152°E
15 Q11 **Warwick** Québec, SE Canada 45°55′N 72°00′W
97 M20 **Warwick** C England, United Kingdom 52°17′N 01°34′W
18 K13 **Warwick** New York, NE USA 41°15′N 74°21′W
29 P4 **Warwick** North Dakota, N USA 47°49′N 98°42′W
19 O12 **Warwick** Rhode Island, NE USA 41°40′N 71°21′W
97 L20 **Warwickshire** *cultural region* C England, United Kingdom
14 G14 **Wasaga Beach** Ontario, S Canada 44°30′N 80°00′W
77 U13 **Wasagu** Kebbi, NW Nigeria 11°25′N 05°48′E
36 M2 **Wasatch Range** ▲▲ W USA
35 R12 **Wasco** California, W USA 35°34′N 119°20′W
29 V10 **Waseca** Minnesota, N USA 44°04′N 93°30′W
14 H13 **Washago** Ontario, S Canada 44°46′N 78°48′W
19 S2 **Washburn** Maine, NE USA 46°46′N 68°08′W
28 M5 **Washburn** North Dakota, N USA 47°15′N 101°02′W
30 K3 **Washburn** Wisconsin, N USA 46°41′N 90°53′W
31 S14 **Washburn Hill** *hill* Ohio, N USA
154 H13 **Wāshīm** Mahārāshtra, C India 20°06′N 77°08′E
97 M14 **Washington** NE England, United Kingdom 54°54′N 01°31′W
23 U3 **Washington** Georgia, SE USA 33°44′N 82°44′W
30 L12 **Washington** Illinois, N USA 40°42′N 89°24′W
31 N15 **Washington** Indiana, N USA 38°40′N 87°10′W
29 X15 **Washington** Iowa, C USA 41°18′N 91°41′W
27 O3 **Washington** Kansas, C USA 39°49′N 97°03′W
27 W5 **Washington** Missouri, C USA 38°31′N 91°01′W
21 X9 **Washington** North Carolina, SE USA 35°33′N 77°04′W
18 B15 **Washington** Pennsylvania, NE USA 40°11′N 80°16′W
25 V10 **Washington** Texas, SW USA 30°18′N 96°08′W
36 J8 **Washington** Utah, W USA 37°07′N 113°30′W
21 V4 **Washington** Virginia, NE USA 38°43′N 78°11′W
32 I9 **Washington** *off.* State of Washington, *also known as* Chinook State, Evergreen State. ◈ *state* NW USA
**Washington** *see* Washington Court House
31 S14 **Washington Court House** *var.* Washington. Ohio, NE USA 39°32′N 83°29′W
21 W4 **Washington DC** ● (USA) District of Columbia, NE USA 38°54′N 77°02′W
31 O5 **Washington Island** *island* Wisconsin, N USA
**Washington Island** *see* Teraina
19 O7 **Washington, Mount** ▲ New Hampshire, NE USA 44°16′N 71°18′W
26 M11 **Washita River** ≈ Oklahoma/Texas, C USA
97 O18 **Wash, The** *inlet* E England, United Kingdom
32 L9 **Washtucna** Washington, NW USA 46°44′N 118°19′W
**Wasiliszki** *see* Vasilishki
110 P9 **Wasilków** Podlaskie, NE Poland 53°12′N 23°15′E
39 R11 **Wasilla** Alaska, USA 61°34′N 149°26′W
139 V9 **Wāsiț** *off.* Muḩāfaẓat Wāsiț, *var.* Al Kūt. ◈ *governorate* E Iraq
**Wāsiț, Muḩāfaẓat** *see* Wāsiț
55 U9 **Wasjabo** Sipaliwini, NW Suriname 05°09′N 57°09′W
12 I10 **Waskaganish** *prev.* Fort Rupert, Rupert House. Québec, SE Canada 51°30′N 79°45′W
11 X11 **Waskaiowaka Lake** ◎ Manitoba, C Canada
11 T14 **Waskesiu Lake** Saskatchewan, C Canada 53°56′N 106°05′W
25 X7 **Waskom** Texas, SW USA 32°28′N 94°03′W
110 G13 **Wąsosz** Dolnośląskie, SW Poland 51°36′N 16°30′E
42 M6 **Waspam** *var.* Waspán. Costa Caribe Norte, NE Nicaragua 14°41′N 84°04′W
**Waspán** *see* Waspam
165 T3 **Wassamu** Hokkaidō, NE Japan 44°01′N 142°25′E
108 G9 **Wassen** Uri, C Switzerland 46°42′N 08°34′E
98 G11 **Wassenaar** Zuid-Holland, W Netherlands 52°09′N 04°23′E
99 N24 **Wasserbillig** Grevenmacher, E Luxembourg 49°43′N 06°30′E
**Wasserburg** *see* Wasserburg am Inn
101 M23 **Wasserburg am Inn** *var.* Wasserburg. Bayern, SE Germany 48°02′N 12°12′E
101 I17 **Wasserkuppe** ▲ C Germany 50°30′N 09°55′E
103 R5 **Wassy** Haute-Marne, N France 48°32′N 04°54′E
171 N14 **Watampone** *var.* Bone. Sulawesi, C Indonesia 04°33′S 120°20′E
171 R13 **Watawa** Pulau Buru, E Indonesia 03°36′S 127°13′E
**Watenstedt-Salzgitter** *see* Salzgitter
18 M13 **Waterbury** Connecticut, NE USA 41°33′N 73°01′W
21 R11 **Wateree Lake** ▣ South Carolina, SE USA
21 R12 **Wateree River** ≈ South Carolina, SE USA
97 E20 **Waterford** *Ir.* Port Láirge. Waterford, S Ireland 52°15′N 07°08′W
31 S9 **Waterford** Michigan, N USA 42°42′N 83°24′W
97 E20 **Waterford** *Ir.* Port Láirge. *cultural region* S Ireland
97 E21 **Waterford Harbour** *Ir.* Cuan Phort Láirge. *inlet* S Ireland
98 G12 **Wateringen** Zuid-Holland, W Netherlands 52°02′N 04°16′E
99 G19 **Waterloo** Walloon Brabant, C Belgium 50°43′N 04°24′E
14 F16 **Waterloo** Ontario, S Canada 43°28′N 80°32′W
15 P12 **Waterloo** Québec, SE Canada 45°20′N 72°28′W
30 K16 **Waterloo** Illinois, N USA 38°20′N 90°09′W
29 X13 **Waterloo** Iowa, C USA 42°31′N 92°16′W
18 G10 **Waterloo** New York, NE USA 42°54′N 76°51′W
30 L4 **Watersmeet** Michigan, N USA 46°16′N 89°10′W
23 V9 **Watertown** Florida, SE USA 30°11′N 82°36′W
18 I8 **Watertown** New York, NE USA 43°37′N 75°56′W
29 R9 **Watertown** South Dakota, N USA 44°54′N 97°07′W
30 M8 **Watertown** Wisconsin, N USA 43°12′N 88°44′W
22 L3 **Water Valley** Mississippi, S USA 34°09′N 89°37′W
27 O3 **Waterville** Kansas, C USA 39°41′N 96°45′W
17 V6 **Waterville** Maine, NE USA 44°34′N 69°41′W
29 V10 **Waterville** Minnesota, N USA 44°13′N 93°34′W
18 I10 **Waterville** New York, NE USA 42°55′N 75°18′W
14 E16 **Watford** Ontario, S Canada 42°57′N 81°51′W
97 N21 **Watford** E England, United Kingdom 51°39′N 00°24′W
28 K4 **Watford City** North Dakota, N USA 47°48′N 103°16′W
141 X12 **Wāṭif** S Oman 18°34′N 56°31′E
18 G11 **Watkins Glen** New York, NE USA 42°23′N 76°53′W
**Watlings Island** *see* San Salvador
171 U15 **Watnil** Pulau Kai Kecil, E Indonesia 05°45′S 132°39′E
26 M10 **Watonga** Oklahoma, C USA 35°52′N 98°26′W
11 T16 **Watrous** Saskatchewan, S Canada 51°40′N 105°29′W
37 T10 **Watrous** New Mexico, SW USA 35°48′N 104°58′W
79 P16 **Watsa** Orientale, NE Dem. Rep. Congo 03°00′N 29°31′E
31 N12 **Watseka** Illinois, N USA 40°46′N 87°44′W
79 J19 **Watsikengo** Equateur, C Dem. Rep. Congo 0°49′S 20°34′E
182 C5 **Watson** South Australia 30°32′S 131°29′E
11 U15 **Watson** Saskatchewan, S Canada 52°13′N 104°30′W
195 O10 **Watson Escarpment** ▲▲ Antarctica
10 K9 **Watson Lake** Yukon, W Canada 60°05′N 128°47′W
35 N10 **Watsonville** California, W USA 36°53′N 121°43′W
167 Q8 **Wattay** ✈ (Viangchan) Viangchan, C Laos 18°03′N 102°36′E
109 N7 **Wattens** Tirol, W Austria 47°18′N 11°37′E
20 M9 **Watts Bar Lake** ▣ Tennessee, S USA
108 H7 **Wattwil** Sankt Gallen, NE Switzerland 47°18′N 09°06′E
171 T14 **Watubela, Kepulauan** *island group* E Indonesia
101 N24 **Watzmann** ▲ SE Germany 47°32′N 12°56′E
186 E8 **Wau** Morobe, C Papua New Guinea 07°22′S 146°40′E
81 D14 **Wau** *var.* Wāw. Western Bahr el Ghazal, W South Sudan 07°43′N 28°01′E
29 Q8 **Waubay** South Dakota, N USA 45°19′N 97°18′W
29 Q8 **Waubay Lake** ◎ South Dakota, N USA
183 U7 **Wauchope** New South Wales, SE Australia 31°30′S 152°46′E
23 W13 **Wauchula** Florida, SE USA 27°33′N 81°48′W
30 M10 **Wauconda** Illinois, N USA 42°15′N 88°08′W
182 J7 **Waukaringa** South Australia 32°19′S 139°27′E
31 N10 **Waukegan** Illinois, N USA 42°21′N 87°50′W
30 M9 **Waukesha** Wisconsin, N USA 43°01′N 88°14′W
29 X11 **Waukon** Iowa, C USA 43°16′N 91°28′W
30 L8 **Waunakee** Wisconsin, N USA 43°13′N 89°28′W
30 L7 **Waupaca** Wisconsin, N USA 44°23′N 89°04′W
30 M8 **Waupun** Wisconsin, N USA 43°40′N 88°43′W
26 M13 **Waurika** Oklahoma, C USA 34°10′N 98°00′W
26 M12 **Waurika Lake** ▣ Oklahoma, C USA
30 L6 **Wausau** Wisconsin, N USA 44°58′N 89°40′W
31 R11 **Wauseon** Ohio, N USA 41°33′N 84°08′W
30 L7 **Wautoma** Wisconsin, N USA 44°05′N 89°17′W
30 M9 **Wauwatosa** Wisconsin, N USA 43°03′N 88°03′W
22 L9 **Waveland** Mississippi, S USA 30°17′N 89°22′W
97 Q20 **Waveney** ≈ E England, United Kingdom
184 L11 **Waverley** Taranaki, North Island, New Zealand 39°45′S 174°35′E
29 W12 **Waverly** Iowa, C USA 42°43′N 92°28′W
27 T4 **Waverly** Missouri, C USA 39°12′N 93°31′W
29 R15 **Waverly** Nebraska, C USA 40°56′N 96°27′W
18 G12 **Waverly** New York, NE USA 42°00′N 76°33′W
20 H8 **Waverly** Tennessee, S USA 36°04′N 87°49′W
21 W7 **Waverly** Virginia, NE USA 37°02′N 77°06′W
99 H19 **Wavre** Walloon Brabant, C Belgium 50°43′N 04°37′E
166 M8 **Waw** Bago, SW Myanmar (Burma) 17°26′N 96°40′E
**Wāw** *see* Wau
14 B7 **Wawa** Ontario, S Canada 47°59′N 84°43′W
77 T14 **Wawa** Niger, W Nigeria 09°52′N 04°33′E
75 Q11 **Wāw al Kabīr** S Libya 25°21′N 16°41′E
43 N7 **Wawa, Río** *var.* Rio Huahua. ≈ NE Nicaragua
186 B8 **Wawoi** ≈ SW Papua New Guinea
25 T7 **Waxahachie** Texas, SW USA 32°23′N 96°52′W
158 L9 **Waxxari** Xinjiang Uygur Zizhiqu, NW China 38°43′N 87°11′E
**Wayaobu** *see* Zichang
23 V7 **Waycross** Georgia, SE USA 31°13′N 82°21′W
180 K10 **Way, Lake** ◎ Western Australia
31 P9 **Wayland** Michigan, N USA 42°40′N 85°38′W
29 R13 **Wayne** Nebraska, C USA 42°13′N 97°01′W
18 K14 **Wayne** New Jersey, NE USA 40°57′N 74°16′W
21 P5 **Wayne** West Virginia, NE USA 38°14′N 82°27′W
23 V4 **Waynesboro** Georgia, SE USA 33°04′N 82°01′W
22 M7 **Waynesboro** Mississippi, S USA 31°40′N 88°39′W
20 H10 **Waynesboro** Tennessee, S USA 35°20′N 87°49′W
21 U5 **Waynesboro** Virginia, NE USA 38°04′N 78°54′W
18 B16 **Waynesburg** Pennsylvania, NE USA 39°51′N 80°10′W
27 U6 **Waynesville** Missouri, C USA 37°48′N 92°11′W
21 O10 **Waynesville** North Carolina, SE USA 35°29′N 82°59′W
26 L8 **Waynoka** Oklahoma, C USA 36°36′N 98°53′W
**Wazan** *see* Ouazzane
**Wazima** *see* Wajima
**Wāzin** *see* Dhēhiba
149 V7 **Wazirabad** Punjab, NE Pakistan 32°28′N 74°04′E
**Wazzan** *see* Ouazzane
110 I8 **Wda** *var.* Czarna Woda, *Ger.* Schwarzwasser. ≈ N Poland
187 Q16 **Wé** Province des Îles Loyauté, E New Caledonia 20°55′S 167°15′E
97 O23 **Weald, The** *lowlands* SE England, United Kingdom
186 A9 **Weam** Western, SW Papua New Guinea 08°33′S 141°10′E
97 L15 **Wear** ≈ N England, United Kingdom
**Wearmouth** *see* Sunderland
26 L10 **Weatherford** Oklahoma, C USA 35°31′N 98°42′W
25 S6 **Weatherford** Texas, SW USA 32°47′N 97°48′W
34 M3 **Weaverville** California, W USA 40°42′N 122°57′W
27 R7 **Webb City** Missouri, C USA 37°07′N 94°28′W
192 G8 **Weber Basin** *undersea feature* S Ceram Sea
**Webfoot State** *see* Oregon
18 F9 **Webster** New York, NE USA 43°12′N 77°25′W
29 Q8 **Webster** South Dakota, N USA 45°19′N 97°31′W
29 V13 **Webster City** Iowa, C USA 42°28′N 93°49′W
27 X5 **Webster Groves** Missouri, C USA 38°32′N 90°20′W
21 S4 **Webster Springs** *var.* Addison. West Virginia, NE USA 38°29′N 80°52′W
171 S11 **Weda, Teluk** *bay* Pulau Halmahera, E Indonesia
65 B25 **Weddell Island** *var.* Isla de San Jorge. *island* W Falkland Islands
65 K22 **Weddell Plain** *undersea feature* SW Atlantic Ocean 65°00′S 40°00′W
65 K23 **Weddell Sea** *sea* SW Atlantic Ocean
65 B25 **Weddell Settlement** Weddell Island, W Falkland Islands 52°53′S 60°54′W
182 M11 **Wedderburn** Victoria, SE Australia 36°26′S 143°37′E
100 I9 **Wedel** Schleswig-Holstein, N Germany 53°35′N 09°42′E
92 N3 **Wedel Jarlsberg Land** *physical region* SW Svalbard
100 I12 **Wedemark** Niedersachsen, NW Germany 52°33′N 09°43′E
10 M17 **Wedge Mountain** ▲ British Columbia, SW Canada 50°10′N 122°43′W
23 R4 **Wedowee** Alabama, S USA 33°16′N 85°28′W
171 U15 **Weduar** Pulau Kai Besar, E Indonesia 05°55′S 132°51′E
35 N2 **Weed** California, W USA 41°26′N 122°24′W
15 Q12 **Weedon Centre** Québec, SE Canada 45°40′N 71°28′W
18 E13 **Weedville** Pennsylvania, NE USA 41°15′N 78°28′W
100 F10 **Weener** Niedersachsen, NW Germany 53°09′N 07°19′E
29 S16 **Weeping Water** Nebraska, C USA 40°52′N 96°08′W
99 L16 **Weert** Limburg, SE Netherlands 51°15′N 05°43′E
98 I10 **Weesp** Noord-Holland, C Netherlands 52°18′N 05°03′E
183 S5 **Wee Waa** New South Wales, SE Australia 30°16′S 149°27′E
110 N7 **Węgorzewo** *Ger.* Angerburg. Warmińsko-Mazurskie, NE Poland 54°12′N 21°49′E
110 E9 **Węgorzyno** *Ger.* Wangerin. Zachodnio-pomorskie, NW Poland 53°34′N 15°35′E
110 N11 **Węgrów** *Ger.* Bingerau. Mazowieckie, C Poland 52°22′N 22°00′E
98 N5 **Wehe-Den Hoorn** Groningen, NE Netherlands 53°20′N 06°29′E
98 M12 **Wehl** Gelderland, E Netherlands 51°58′N 06°13′E
**Wehlau** *see* Znamensk
168 F7 **Weh, Pulau** *island* NW Indonesia
**Wei** *see* Weifang
161 P1 **Weichang** *prev.* Zhuizishan. Hebei, E China 41°55′N 117°45′E
**Weichang** *see* Weishan
**Weichsel** *see* Wisła
101 M16 **Weida** Thüringen, C Germany 50°46′N 12°05′E
**Weiden** *see* Weiden in der Oberpfalz
101 M19 **Weiden in der Oberpfalz** *var.* Weiden. Bayern, SE Germany 49°40′N 12°10′E
161 Q4 **Weifang** *var.* Wei, Wei-fang; *prev.* Weihsien. Shandong, E China 36°44′N 119°10′E
161 S4 **Weihai** Shandong, E China 37°30′N 122°04′E
160 K6 **Wei He** ≈ C China
**Weihsien** *see* Weifang
101 G17 **Weilburg** Hessen, W Germany 50°31′N 08°18′E
101 K24 **Weilheim in Oberbayern** Bayern, SE Germany 47°50′N 11°09′E
183 P4 **Weilmoringle** New South Wales, SE Australia 29°13′S 146°51′E
101 L16 **Weimar** Thüringen, C Germany 50°59′N 11°20′E
25 U11 **Weimar** Texas, SW USA 29°42′N 96°46′W
160 L6 **Weinan** Shaanxi, C China 34°30′N 109°30′E
108 H6 **Weinfelden** Thurgau, NE Switzerland 47°33′N 09°09′E
101 I24 **Weingarten** Baden-Württemberg, S Germany 47°49′N 09°37′E
101 G20 **Weinheim** Baden-Württemberg, SW Germany 49°33′N 08°40′E
160 H11 **Weining** *var.* Caohai, Weining Yizu Huizu Miaozu Zizhixian. Guizhou, S China 26°51′N 104°16′E
**Weining Yizu Huizu Miaozu Zizhixian** *see* Weining
181 V2 **Weipa** Queensland, NE Australia 12°43′S 142°01′E
11 Y11 **Weir River** Manitoba, C Canada 56°44′N 94°06′W
21 R1 **Weirton** West Virginia, NE USA 40°24′N 80°37′W
32 M13 **Weiser** Idaho, NW USA 44°15′N 116°58′W
160 F12 **Weishan** *var.* Weichang. Yunnan, SW China 25°22′N 100°19′E
161 P6 **Weishan Hu** ◎ E China
101 M15 **Weisse Elster** *Eng.* White Elster. ≈ Czechia/Germany
**Weisse Körös/Weisse Kreisch** *see* Crișul Alb
108 L7 **Weissenbach am Lech** Tirol, W Austria 47°27′N 10°39′E
**Weissenburg** *see* Wissembourg, France
**Weissenburg** *see* Alba Iulia, Romania
101 K21 **Weissenburg in Bayern** Bayern, SE Germany 49°02′N 10°59′E
101 M15 **Weissenfels** *var.* Weißenfels. Sachsen-Anhalt, C Germany 51°12′N 11°58′E
109 R9 **Weissensee** ◎ S Austria
**Weissenstein** *see* Paide
108 E11 **Weisshorn** *var.* Flüela Wisshorn. ▲ SW Switzerland 46°06′N 07°43′E
**Weisskirchen** *see* Bela Crkva
23 R3 **Weiss Lake** ▣ Alabama, S USA
101 Q14 **Weisswasser** *Lus.* Běła Woda. Sachsen, E Germany 51°30′N 14°37′E
99 M22 **Weiswampach** Diekirch, N Luxembourg 50°08′N 06°05′E
109 U2 **Weitra** Niederösterreich, N Austria 48°41′N 14°54′E
161 O4 **Weixian** *var.* Wei Xian. Hebei, E China 36°59′N 115°15′E
**Wei Xian** *see* Weixian
159 V11 **Weiyuan** *var.* Qingyuan. Gansu, C China 35°07′N 104°12′E
**Weiyuan** *see* Shuangjiang
160 F14 **Weiyuan Jiang** ≈ SW China
109 W7 **Weiz** Steiermark, SE Austria 47°13′N 15°38′E
**Weizhou** *see* Wenchuan
160 K16 **Weizhou Dao** *island* S China
110 I6 **Wejherowo** Pomorskie, NW Poland 54°36′N 18°12′E
27 Q8 **Welch** Oklahoma, C USA 36°52′N 95°06′W
24 M6 **Welch** Texas, SW USA 32°52′N 102°06′W
21 Q6 **Welch** West Virginia, NE USA 37°26′N 81°36′W
45 O14 **Welchman Hall** C Barbados 13°10′N 59°34′W
80 J11 **Weldiya** *var.* Waldia, *It.* Valdia. Āmara, N Ethiopia 11°45′N 39°39′E
21 W8 **Weldon** North Carolina, SE USA 36°25′N 77°36′W
25 V9 **Weldon** Texas, SW USA 31°00′N 95°33′W
99 M19 **Welkenraedt** Liège, E Belgium 50°40′N 05°58′E
193 O2 **Welker Seamount** *undersea feature* N Pacific Ocean 55°07′N 140°18′W
83 I22 **Welkom** Free State, C South Africa 27°59′S 26°44′E
14 H16 **Welland** Ontario, S Canada 42°59′N 79°14′W
14 G16 **Welland** ≈ Ontario, S Canada
97 O19 **Welland** ≈ C England, United Kingdom
14 H17 **Welland Canal** *canal* Ontario, S Canada
155 K25 **Wellawaya** Uva Province, SE Sri Lanka 06°44′N 81°07′E
**Welle** *see* Uele
181 T4 **Wellesley Islands** *island group* Queensland, N Australia
99 J22 **Wellin** Luxembourg, SE Belgium 50°06′N 05°05′E
97 N20 **Wellingborough** C England, United Kingdom 52°19′N 00°42′W
183 R7 **Wellington** New South Wales, SE Australia 32°33′S 148°59′E
14 J15 **Wellington** Ontario, SE Canada 43°59′N 77°21′W
185 L14 **Wellington** ● Wellington, North Island, New Zealand 41°17′S 174°47′E
83 E26 **Wellington** Western Cape, SW South Africa 33°39′S 19°00′E
37 T2 **Wellington** Colorado, C USA 40°42′N 105°00′W
27 N7 **Wellington** Kansas, C USA 37°17′N 97°25′W
35 R7 **Wellington** Nevada, W USA 38°45′N 119°22′W
31 T11 **Wellington** Ohio, N USA 41°10′N 82°13′W
25 P3 **Wellington** Texas, SW USA 34°52′N 100°13′W
36 M4 **Wellington** Utah, W USA 39°31′N 110°45′W
185 M14 **Wellington** *off.* Wellington Region. ◈ *region* (New Zealand) North Island, New Zealand
185 L14 **Wellington** ✈ Wellington, North Island, New Zealand 41°19′S 174°48′E
**Wellington** *see* Wellington, Isla
63 F22 **Wellington, Isla** *var.* Wellington. *island* S Chile
183 P12 **Wellington, Lake** ◎ Victoria, SE Australia
**Wellington Region** *see* Wellington
29 X14 **Wellman** Iowa, C USA 41°27′N 91°50′W
24 M6 **Wellman** Texas, SW USA 33°03′N 102°25′W
97 K22 **Wells** SW England, United Kingdom 51°13′N 02°39′W
29 V11 **Wells** Minnesota, N USA 43°45′N 93°43′W
35 X2 **Wells** Nevada, W USA 41°07′N 114°58′W
25 W8 **Wells** Texas, SW USA 31°28′N 94°54′W
18 F12 **Wellsboro** Pennsylvania, NE USA 41°43′N 77°39′W
21 R1 **Wellsburg** West Virginia, NE USA 40°15′N 80°37′W
184 K4 **Wellsford** Auckland, North Island, New Zealand 36°17′S 174°30′E
180 L9 **Wells, Lake** ◎ Western Australia
181 N4 **Wells, Mount** ▲ Western Australia 17°39′S 127°08′E
97 P18 **Wells-next-the-Sea** E England, United Kingdom 52°58′N 00°48′E
31 T15 **Wellston** Ohio, N USA 39°07′N 82°31′W
27 O10 **Wellston** Oklahoma, C USA 35°41′N 97°03′W
18 E11 **Wellsville** New York, NE USA 42°06′N 77°55′W
31 V12 **Wellsville** Ohio, N USA 40°36′N 80°39′W
36 L1 **Wellsville** Utah, W USA 41°38′N 111°55′W
36 I14 **Wellton** Arizona, SW USA 32°40′N 114°09′W
109 S4 **Wels** *anc.* Ovilava. Oberösterreich, N Austria 48°10′N 14°02′E
99 K15 **Welschap** ✈ (Eindhoven) Noord-Brabant, S Netherlands 51°27′N 05°22′E
100 P10 **Welse** ≈ NE Germany
22 H9 **Welsh** Louisiana, S USA 30°12′N 92°49′W
97 K19 **Welshpool** *Wel.* Y Trallwng. E Wales, United Kingdom 52°38′N 03°06′W
97 O21 **Welwyn Garden City** E England, United Kingdom 51°48′N 00°13′W
79 K18 **Wema** Equateur, NW Dem. Rep. Congo 0°25′S 21°33′E
81 G21 **Wembere** ≈ C Tanzania
11 N13 **Wembley** Alberta, W Canada 55°07′N 119°12′W
12 I9 **Wemindji** *prev.* Nouveau-Comptoir, Paint Hills. Québec, C Canada 53°00′N 78°42′W
99 G18 **Wemmel** Vlaams Brabant, C Belgium 50°54′N 04°18′E
32 J8 **Wenatchee** Washington, NW USA 47°50′N 120°48′W
160 M17 **Wenchang** Hainan, S China 19°34′N 110°46′E
161 R11 **Wencheng** *var.* Daxue. Zhejiang, SE China 27°48′N 120°01′E
77 P16 **Wenchi** W Ghana 07°45′N 02°02′W
**Wen-chou/Wenchow** *see* Wenzhou
160 H8 **Wenchuan** *var.* Weizhou. Sichuan, C China 31°29′N 103°39′E
**Wendau** *see* Võnnu
**Wenden** *see* Cēsis
161 S4 **Wendeng** Shandong, E China 37°10′N 122°00′E
81 J14 **Wendo** Southern Nationalities, S Ethiopia 06°34′N 38°28′E
36 J2 **Wendover** Utah, W USA 40°41′N 114°00′W
14 D9 **Wenebegon** ≈ Ontario, S Canada
14 D8 **Wenebegon Lake** ◎ Ontario, S Canada
108 E9 **Wengen** Bern, W Switzerland 46°38′N 07°57′E
161 O13 **Wengyuan** *var.* Longxian. Guangdong, S China 24°22′N 114°06′E
189 P15 **Weno** *prev.* Moen. Chuuk, C Micronesia
189 V12 **Weno** *prev.* Moen. *atoll* Chuuk Islands, C Micronesia
158 N13 **Wenquan** Qinghai, C China 33°16′N 91°44′E
159 H4 **Wenquan** *var.* Arixang, Bogeda'er. Xinjiang Uygur Zizhiqu, NW China 45°00′N 81°02′E
**Wenquan** *see* Yingshan


◆ Country
● Country Capital
◇ Dependent Territory
○ Dependent Territory Capital
◈ Administrative Regions
✈ International Airport
▲ Mountain
▲▲ Mountain Range
Volcano
≈ River
◎ Lake
▣ Reservoir

WENSHAN – WILLISTON

160 H14 **Wenshan** *var.* Kaihua. Yunnan, SW China 23°22′N 104°21′E
158 H6 **Wensu** Xinjiang Uygur Zizhiqu, W China 41°15′N 80°11′E
182 L8 **Wentworth** New South Wales, SE Australia 34°04′S 141°53′E
27 W4 **Wentzville** Missouri, C USA 38°48′N 90°51′W
159 V12 **Wenxian** *var.* Wen Xian. Gansu, C China 32°57′N 104°42′E
**Wen Xian** *see* Wenxian
161 S10 **Wenzhou** *var.* Wen-chou, Wenchow. Zhejiang, SE China 28°02′N 120°36′E
34 L4 **Weott** California, W USA 40°19′N 123°57′W
99 I20 **Wépion** Namur, SE Belgium 50°24′N 04°53′E
100 O11 **Werbellinsee** ◎ NE Germany
99 L21 **Werbomont** Liège, E Belgium 50°22′N 05°43′E
83 G20 **Werda** Kgalagadi, S Botswana 25°13′S 23°16′E
81 N14 **Werder** Sumalē, E Ethiopia 06°59′N 45°20′E
**Werder** *see* Virtsu
**Werenów** *see* Voranava
171 U13 **Weri** Papua Barat, E Indonesia 03°10′S 132°39′E
98 I13 **Werkendam** Noord-Brabant, S Netherlands 51°48′N 04°54′E
101 M20 **Wernberg-Köblitz** Bayern, SE Germany 49°31′N 12°10′E
101 J18 **Werneck** Bayern, C Germany 50°00′N 10°06′E
101 K14 **Wernigerode** Sachsen-Anhalt, C Germany 51°51′N 10°48′E
**Werowitz** *see* Virovitica
101 J16 **Werra** ≈ C Germany
183 N12 **Werribee** Victoria, SE Australia 37°55′S 144°39′E
183 T6 **Werris Creek** New South Wales, SE Australia 31°22′S 150°40′E
**Werro** *see* Võru
**Werschetz** *see* Vršac
101 K23 **Wertach** ≈ S Germany
101 I19 **Wertheim** Baden-Württemberg, SW Germany 49°45′N 09°31′E
98 J8 **Wervershoof** Noord-Holland, NW Netherlands 52°43′N 05°09′E
**Wervicq** *see* Wervik
99 C18 **Wervik** *var.* Wervicq, Werwick. West-Vlaanderen, W Belgium 50°47′N 03°03′E
**Werwick** *see* Wervik
101 D14 **Wesel** Nordrhein-Westfalen, W Germany 51°39′N 06°37′E
**Weseli an der Lainsitz** *see* Veselí nad Lužnicí
**Wesenberg** *see* Rakvere
100 H12 **Weser** ≈ NW Germany
**Wes-Kaap** *see* Western Cape
25 S17 **Weslaco** Texas, SW USA 26°09′N 97°59′W
14 J13 **Weslemkoon Lake** ◎ Ontario, SE Canada
181 R1 **Wessel Islands** *island group* Northern Territory, N Australia
29 P9 **Wessington** South Dakota, N USA 44°27′N 98°40′W
29 P10 **Wessington Springs** South Dakota, N USA 44°02′N 98°33′W
25 T8 **West** Texas, SW USA 31°48′N 97°05′W
**West** *see* Ouest
30 M9 **West Allis** Wisconsin, N USA 43°01′N 88°00′W
182 E8 **Westall, Point** *headland* South Australia 32°54′S 134°04′E
194 M10 **West Antarctica** *prev.* Lesser Antarctica. *physical region* Antarctica
14 G11 **West Arm** Ontario, S Canada 46°16′N 80°25′W
**West Australian Basin** *see* Wharton Basin
**West Azerbaijan** *see* Āžarbāyjān-e Gharbī
11 N17 **Westbank** British Columbia, SW Canada 49°50′N 119°37′W
138 F10 **West Bank** *disputed region* SW Asia
14 E11 **West Bay** Manitoulin Island, Ontario, S Canada 45°48′N 82°09′W
22 L11 **West Bay** *bay* Louisiana, S USA
30 M8 **West Bend** Wisconsin, N USA 43°26′N 88°13′W
153 R16 **West Bengal** ◈ *state* NE India
**West Borneo** *see* Kalimantan Barat
29 Y14 **West Branch** Iowa, C USA 41°40′N 91°21′W
31 R7 **West Branch** Michigan, N USA 44°16′N 84°14′W
18 F13 **West Branch Susquehanna River** ≈ Pennsylvania, NE USA
97 L20 **West Bromwich** C England, United Kingdom 52°29′N 01°59′W
19 P8 **Westbrook** Maine, NE USA 43°42′N 70°21′W
29 T10 **Westbrook** Minnesota, N USA 44°02′N 95°26′W
29 Y15 **West Burlington** Iowa, C USA 40°49′N 91°09′W
96 L2 **West Burra** *island* NE Scotland, United Kingdom
30 J8 **Westby** Wisconsin, N USA 43°39′N 90°52′W
44 L6 **West Caicos** *island* W Turks and Caicos Islands
185 A24 **West Cape** *headland* South Island, New Zealand 45°51′S 166°26′E
174 L4 **West Caroline Basin** *undersea feature* SW Pacific Ocean 04°00′N 138°00′E
18 I16 **West Chester** Pennsylvania, NE USA 39°56′N 75°35′W
185 E18 **West Coast** *off.* West Coast Region. ◈ *region* South Island, New Zealand
**West Coast Region** *see* West Coast
25 V12 **West Columbia** Texas, SW USA 29°08′N 95°39′W
29 W10 **West Concord** Minnesota, N USA 44°09′N 92°54′W
29 V14 **West Des Moines** Iowa, C USA 41°33′N 93°42′W
37 Q6 **West Elk Peak** ▲ Colorado, C USA 38°43′N 107°12′W
44 F1 **West End** Grand Bahama Island, N The Bahamas 26°36′N 78°55′W
44 F1 **West End Point** *headland* Grand Bahama Island, N The Bahamas 26°40′N 78°58′W
93 O7 **Westerbork** Drenthe, NE Netherlands 52°49′N 06°36′E
93 N3 **Westereems** *strait* Germany/Netherlands
93 O9 **Westerhaar-Vriezenveensewijk** Overijssel, E Netherlands 52°28′N 06°38′E
100 G6 **Westerland** Schleswig-Holstein, N Germany 54°54′N 08°19′E
99 I17 **Westerlo** Antwerpen, N Belgium 51°05′N 04°55′E
19 N13 **Westerly** Rhode Island, NE USA 41°22′N 71°45′W
153 N11 **Western** ◈ *zone* C Nepal
186 A8 **Western** *var.* Fly River. ◈ *province* SW Papua New Guinea
186 K9 **Western** ◈ *province* S Solomon Islands
186 J8 **Western** *off.* Western Province. ◈ *province* NW Solomon Islands
155 J26 **Western** ◈ *province* SW Sri Lanka
83 G15 **Western** ◈ *province* SW Zambia
180 K8 **Western Australia** ◈ *state* W Australia
80 A13 **Western Bahr el Ghazal** ◈ *state* W South Sudan
**Western Bug** *see* Bug
83 F25 **Western Cape** *off.* Western Cape Province, *Afr.* Wes-Kaap. ◈ *province* SW South Africa
**Western Cape Province** *see* Western Cape
80 A11 **Western Darfur** ◈ *state* W Sudan
**Western Desert** *see* Aş Şaḩrā' al Gharbīyah
118 G9 **Western Dvina** *Bel.* Dzvina, *Ger.* Düna, *Latv.* Daugava, *Rus.* Zapadnaya Dvina. ≈ W Europe
81 D15 **Western Equatoria** ◈ *state* SW South Sudan
155 E16 **Western Ghats** ▲▲ SW India
186 C7 **Western Highlands** ◈ *province* C Papua New Guinea
**Western Isles** *see* Outer Hebrides
21 T3 **Westernport** Maryland, NE USA 39°29′N 79°03′W
**Western Province** *see* Western
**Western Punjab** *see* Punjab
74 B10 **Western Sahara** ◇ *disputed territory* N Africa
**Western Samoa** *see* Samoa
**Western Sayans** *see* Zapadnyy Sayan
**Western Scheldt** *see* Westerschelde
**Western Sierra Madre** *see* Madre Occidental, Sierra
99 E15 **Westerschelde** *Eng.* Western Scheldt; *prev.* Honte. *inlet* S North Sea
31 S13 **Westerville** Ohio, N USA 40°07′N 82°55′W
101 F17 **Westerwald** ▲▲ W Germany
65 C25 **West Falkland** *var.* Gran Malvina, Isla Gran Malvina. *island* W Falkland Islands
29 R5 **West Fargo** North Dakota, N USA 46°49′N 96°51′W
188 M15 **West Fayu Atoll** *atoll* Caroline Islands, C Micronesia
18 C11 **Westfield** New York, NE USA 42°18′N 79°34′W
30 L7 **Westfield** Wisconsin, N USA 43°56′N 89°31′W
**West Flanders** *see* West-Vlaanderen
27 S10 **West Fork** Arkansas, C USA 35°55′N 94°11′W
29 P16 **West Fork Big Blue River** ≈ Nebraska, C USA
29 U12 **West Fork Des Moines River** ≈ Iowa/Minnesota, C USA
25 S5 **West Fork Trinity River** ≈ Texas, SW USA
30 L16 **West Frankfort** Illinois, N USA 37°54′N 88°55′W
98 I8 **West-Friesland** *physical region* NW Netherlands
**West Frisian Islands** *see* Waddeneilanden
19 T5 **West Grand Lake** ◎ Maine, NE USA
18 M12 **West Hartford** Connecticut, NE USA 41°44′N 72°45′W
18 M13 **West Haven** Connecticut, NE USA 41°16′N 72°57′W
27 X12 **West Helena** Arkansas, C USA 34°33′N 90°38′W
28 M2 **Westhope** North Dakota, N USA 48°54′N 101°01′W
195 Y8 **West Ice Shelf** *ice shelf* Antarctica
47 R2 **West Indies** *island group* SE North America
**West Irian** *see* Papua
**West Java** *see* Jawa Barat
36 L3 **West Jordan** Utah, W USA 40°37′N 111°55′W
**West Kalimantan** *see* Kalimantan Barat
99 D14 **Westkapelle** Zeeland, SW Netherlands 51°32′N 03°26′E
**West Kazakhstan** *see* Zapadnyy Kazakhstan
31 O13 **West Lafayette** Indiana, N USA 40°24′N 86°54′W
31 T13 **West Lafayette** Ohio, N USA 40°16′N 81°45′W
**West Lake** *see* Kagera
29 Y14 **West Liberty** Iowa, C USA 41°34′N 91°15′W
21 O5 **West Liberty** Kentucky, S USA 37°56′N 83°16′W
**Westliche Morava** *see* Zapadna Morava
10 J13 **Westlock** Alberta, SW Canada 54°12′N 113°50′W
14 E17 **West Lorne** Ontario, S Canada 42°36′N 81°35′W
96 J12 **West Lothian** *cultural region* S Scotland, United Kingdom
99 H16 **Westmalle** Antwerpen, N Belgium 51°18′N 04°40′E
192 G6 **West Mariana Basin** *var.* Perece Vela Basin. *undersea feature* W Pacific Ocean 15°00′N 137°00′E
97 E17 **Westmeath** *Ir.* An Iarmhí, Na H-Iarmhidhe. *cultural region* C Ireland
27 Y11 **West Memphis** Arkansas, C USA 35°09′N 90°11′W
21 W2 **Westminster** Maryland, NE USA 39°34′N 77°00′W
21 O11 **Westminster** South Carolina, SE USA 34°39′N 83°06′W
22 I5 **West Monroe** Louisiana, S USA 32°31′N 92°09′W
18 D15 **Westmont** Pennsylvania, NE USA 40°16′N 78°55′W
27 O3 **Westmoreland** Kansas, C USA 39°23′N 96°30′W
35 W17 **Westmorland** California, W USA 33°02′N 115°37′W
186 E6 **West New Britain** ◈ *province* E Papua New Guinea
**West New Guinea** *see* Papua
83 K18 **West Nicholson** Matabeleland South, S Zimbabwe 21°06′S 29°25′E
29 T14 **West Nishnabotna River** ≈ Iowa, C USA
175 P11 **West Norfolk Ridge** *undersea feature* W Pacific Ocean
25 P12 **West Nueces River** ≈ Texas, SW USA
**West Nusa Tenggara** *see* Nusa Tenggara Barat
29 T11 **West Okoboji Lake** ◎ Iowa, C USA
33 R16 **Weston** Idaho, NW USA 42°01′N 119°29′W
21 R4 **Weston** West Virginia, NE USA 39°03′N 80°28′W
97 J22 **Weston-super-Mare** SW England, United Kingdom 51°21′N 02°59′W
23 Z14 **West Palm Beach** Florida, SE USA 26°43′N 80°03′W
**West Panamá** *see* Panamá Oeste
**West Papua** *see* Papua Barat
**West Papua** *see* Papua
188 E9 **West Passage** *passage* Babeldaob, N Palau
23 O9 **West Pensacola** Florida, SE USA 30°25′N 87°16′W
27 V8 **West Plains** Missouri, C USA 36°44′N 91°51′W
35 P7 **West Point** California, W USA 38°21′N 120°33′W
23 R5 **West Point** Georgia, SE USA 32°52′N 85°10′W
22 M3 **West Point** Mississippi, S USA 33°36′N 88°39′W
29 R14 **West Point** Nebraska, C USA 41°50′N 96°42′W
21 X6 **West Point** Virginia, NE USA 37°31′N 76°48′W
182 G10 **West Point** *headland* South Australia 35°01′S 135°58′E
65 B24 **Westpoint Island Settlement** Westpoint Island, NW Falkland Islands 51°21′S 60°41′W
23 R4 **West Point Lake** ⊠ Alabama/Georgia, SE USA
97 B16 **Westport** *Ir.* Cathair na Mart. Mayo, W Ireland 53°48′N 09°32′W
185 G15 **Westport** West Coast, South Island, New Zealand 41°46′S 171°37′E
32 F10 **Westport** Oregon, NW USA 46°07′N 123°22′W
32 F9 **Westport** Washington, NW USA 46°53′N 124°06′W
31 S15 **West Portsmouth** Ohio, N USA 38°45′N 83°01′W
**West Punjab** *see* Punjab
11 V14 **Westray** Manitoba, C Canada 53°30′N 101°19′W
96 J4 **Westray** *island* NE Scotland, United Kingdom
14 F9 **Westree** Ontario, S Canada 47°25′N 81°32′W
97 L16 **West Riding** *cultural region* N England, United Kingdom
**West River** *see* Xi Jiang
30 J7 **West Salem** Wisconsin, N USA 43°54′N 91°04′W
65 H21 **West Scotia Ridge** *undersea feature* W Scotia Sea
186 B5 **West Sepik** *prev.* Sandaun. ◈ *province* NW Papua New Guinea
173 N4 **West Sheba Ridge** *undersea feature* W Indian Ocean 12°45′N 48°15′E
**West Siberian Plain** *see* Zapadno-Sibirskaya Ravnina
31 S11 **West Sister Island** *island* Ohio, N USA
**West-Skylge** *see* West-Terschelling
**West Sumatra** *see* Sumatera Barat
98 J5 **West-Terschelling** *Fris.* West-Skylge. Fryslân, N Netherlands 53°23′N 05°15′E
64 J7 **West Thulean Rise** *undersea feature* N Atlantic Ocean
29 X12 **West Union** Iowa, C USA 42°57′N 91°48′W
31 R15 **West Union** Ohio, N USA 38°47′N 83°33′W
21 R3 **West Union** West Virginia, NE USA 39°18′N 80°47′W
31 N13 **Westville** Illinois, N USA 40°02′N 87°38′W
21 R3 **West Virginia** *off.* State of West Virginia, *also known as* Mountain State. ◈ *state* NE USA
99 A17 **West-Vlaanderen** *Eng.* West Flanders. ◈ *province* W Belgium
35 R7 **West Walker River** ≈ California/Nevada, W USA
35 P4 **Westwood** California, W USA 40°18′N 121°02′W
183 P9 **West Wyalong** New South Wales, SE Australia 33°56′S 147°10′E
171 Q16 **Wetar, Pulau** *island* Kepulauan Damar, E Indonesia
**Wetar, Selat** *see* Wetar Strait
171 R16 **Wetar Strait** *var.* Selat Wetar. *strait* Nusa Tenggara, S Indonesia
11 Q15 **Wetaskiwin** Alberta, SW Canada 52°57′N 113°20′W
81 K21 **Wete** Pemba, E Tanzania 05°03′S 39°41′E
166 M4 **Wetlet** Sagaing, C Myanmar (Burma) 22°43′N 95°22′E
37 T6 **Wet Mountains** ▲▲ Colorado, C USA
101 E15 **Wetter** Nordrhein-Westfalen, W Germany 51°22′N 07°24′E
101 H17 **Wetter** ≈ W Germany
99 F17 **Wetteren** Oost-Vlaanderen, NW Belgium 51°06′N 03°59′E
108 F7 **Wettingen** Aargau, N Switzerland 47°28′N 08°20′E
27 P11 **Wetumka** Oklahoma, C USA 35°14′N 96°14′W
23 Q5 **Wetumpka** Alabama, S USA 32°32′N 86°12′W
108 G7 **Wetzikon** Zürich, N Switzerland 47°19′N 08°48′E
101 G17 **Wetzlar** Hessen, W Germany 50°33′N 08°30′E
99 C18 **Wevelgem** West-Vlaanderen, W Belgium 50°48′N 03°12′E
38 M6 **Wevok** *var.* Wewuk. Alaska, USA 68°52′N 166°05′W
23 R9 **Wewahitchka** Florida, SE USA 30°06′N 85°12′W
186 C6 **Wewak** East Sepik, NW Papua New Guinea 03°35′S 143°35′E
27 O11 **Wewoka** Oklahoma, C USA 35°09′N 96°30′W
**Wewuk** *see* Wevok
97 F20 **Wexford** *Ir.* Loch Garman. SE Ireland 52°21′N 06°31′W
97 F20 **Wexford** *Ir.* Loch Garman. *cultural region* SE Ireland
30 L7 **Weyauwega** Wisconsin, N USA 44°16′N 88°54′W
11 U17 **Weyburn** Saskatchewan, S Canada 49°39′N 103°51′W
**Weyer** *see* Weyer Markt
109 U5 **Weyer Markt** *var.* Weyer. Oberösterreich, N Austria 47°52′N 14°39′E
100 H11 **Weyhe** Niedersachsen, NW Germany 53°00′N 08°52′E
97 L24 **Weymouth** S England, United Kingdom 50°36′N 02°28′W
19 P11 **Weymouth** Massachusetts, NE USA 42°13′N 70°56′W
99 H18 **Wezembeek-Oppem** Vlaams Brabant, C Belgium 50°51′N 04°28′E
98 M9 **Wezep** Gelderland, E Netherlands 52°28′N 06°E
184 M9 **Whakamaru** Waikato, North Island, New Zealand 38°27′S 175°48′E
184 O8 **Whakatane** Bay of Plenty, North Island, New Zealand 37°58′S 177°E
184 O8 **Whakatane** ≈ North Island, New Zealand
9 O9 **Whale Cove** *var.* Tikirarjuaq. Nunavut, C Canada 62°14′N 92°10′W
96 M2 **Whalsay** *island* NE Scotland, United Kingdom
184 L11 **Whangaehu** ≈ North Island, New Zealand
184 M6 **Whangamata** Waikato, North Island, New Zealand 37°13′S 175°54′E
184 Q9 **Whangara** Gisborne, North Island, New Zealand 38°34′S 178°12′E
184 K3 **Whangarei** Northland, North Island, New Zealand 35°44′S 174°18′E
184 K3 **Whangaruru Harbour** *inlet* North Island, New Zealand
25 V12 **Wharton** Texas, SW USA 29°19′N 96°08′W
173 U8 **Wharton Basin** *var.* West Australian Basin. *undersea feature* E Indian Ocean
185 E18 **Whataroa** West Coast, South Island, New Zealand 43°17′S 170°20′E
8 K10 **Wha Ti** *prev.* Lac la Martre. Northwest Territories, W Canada 63°10′N 117°12′W
8 J9 **Wha Ti** Northwest Territories, W Canada 63°10′N 117°12′W
184 K6 **Whatipu** Auckland, North Island, New Zealand 37°17′S 174°44′E
33 Y15 **Wheatland** Wyoming, C USA 42°03′N 104°57′W
14 D18 **Wheatley** Ontario, S Canada 42°06′N 82°27′W
30 M10 **Wheaton** Illinois, N USA 41°52′N 88°06′W
29 R7 **Wheaton** Minnesota, N USA 45°48′N 96°30′W
37 T4 **Wheat Ridge** Colorado, C USA 39°44′N 105°06′W
25 P2 **Wheeler** Texas, SW USA 35°26′N 100°17′W
23 O2 **Wheeler Lake** ⊠ Alabama, S USA
35 Y6 **Wheeler Peak** ▲ Nevada, W USA 39°00′N 114°17′W
37 T9 **Wheeler Peak** ▲ New Mexico, SW USA 36°34′N 105°25′W
31 S13 **Wheelersburg** Ohio, N USA 38°43′N 82°51′W
21 R2 **Wheeling** West Virginia, NE USA 40°05′N 80°43′W
97 L15 **Whernside** ▲ N England, United Kingdom 54°13′N 02°27′W
182 F9 **Whidbey, Point** *headland* South Australia 34°36′S 135°08′E
180 I7 **Whim Creek** Western Australia 20°51′S 117°54′E
10 L17 **Whistler** British Columbia, SW Canada 50°07′N 122°57′W
21 W8 **Whitakers** North Carolina, SE USA 36°06′N 77°43′W
14 H15 **Whitby** Ontario, S Canada 43°52′N 78°56′W
97 N15 **Whitby** N England, United Kingdom 54°29′N 00°37′W
10 G6 **White** ≈ Yukon, W Canada
13 T11 **White Bay** *bay* Newfoundland, Newfoundland and Labrador, E Canada
20 I8 **White Bluff** Tennessee, S USA 36°06′N 87°13′W
28 J6 **White Butte** ▲ North Dakota, N USA 46°23′N 103°18′W
19 R5 **White Cap Mountain** ▲ Maine, NE USA 45°33′N 69°15′W
22 J9 **White Castle** Louisiana, S USA 30°10′N 91°09′W
182 M5 **White Cliffs** New South Wales, SE Australia 30°52′S 143°04′E
31 P8 **White Cloud** Michigan, N USA 43°34′N 85°47′W
11 P14 **Whitecourt** Alberta, SW Canada 54°10′N 115°38′W
25 O2 **White Deer** Texas, SW USA 35°26′N 101°10′W
**White Elster** *see* Weisse Elster
24 M5 **Whiteface** Texas, SW USA 33°36′N 102°36′W
18 K7 **Whiteface Mountain** ▲ New York, NE USA 44°22′N 73°54′W
29 W5 **Whiteface Reservoir** ⊠ Minnesota, N USA
33 O7 **Whitefish** Montana, NW USA 48°24′N 114°20′W
31 N9 **Whitefish Bay** Wisconsin, N USA 43°09′N 87°54′W
31 Q3 **Whitefish Bay** *lake bay* Canada/USA
14 E11 **Whitefish Falls** Ontario, S Canada 46°06′N 81°42′W
14 B7 **Whitefish Lake** ◎ Ontario, S Canada
29 U6 **Whitefish Lake** ◎ Minnesota, C USA
31 Q3 **Whitefish Point** *headland* Michigan, N USA 46°46′N 84°57′W
31 O4 **Whitefish River** ≈ Michigan, N USA
25 O4 **Whiteflat** Texas, SW USA 34°06′N 100°55′W
27 V12 **White Hall** Arkansas, C USA 34°18′N 92°05′W
30 K14 **White Hall** Illinois, N USA 39°26′N 90°24′W
31 O8 **Whitehall** Michigan, N USA 43°24′N 86°21′W
18 L9 **Whitehall** New York, NE USA 43°33′N 73°24′W
31 S13 **Whitehall** Ohio, N USA 39°58′N 82°53′W
30 J7 **Whitehall** Wisconsin, N USA 44°22′N 91°20′W
97 J15 **Whitehaven** NW England, United Kingdom 54°33′N 03°35′W
10 I8 **Whitehorse** *territory capital* Yukon, W Canada 60°41′N 135°08′W
184 O7 **White Island** *island* NE New Zealand
14 K13 **White Lake** ◎ Ontario, SE Canada
22 H10 **White Lake** ◎ Louisiana, S USA
186 G7 **Whiteman Range** ▲▲ New Britain, E Papua New Guinea
183 Q15 **Whitemark** Tasmania, SE Australia 40°10′S 148°01′E
35 S9 **White Mountains** ▲▲ California/Nevada, W USA
19 N7 **White Mountains** ▲▲ Maine/New Hampshire, NE USA
80 F11 **White Nile** ◈ *state* C Sudan
81 E14 **White Nile** *Ar.* Al Baḩr al Abyaḑ, An Nīl al Abyaḑ, Bahr el Jebel. ≈ NE South Sudan
67 U7 **White Nile** *var.* Bahr el Jebel. ≈ S Sudan
25 W5 **White Oak Creek** ≈ Texas, SW USA
10 H9 **White Pass** *pass* Canada/USA
32 I9 **White Pass** *pass* Washington, NW USA
21 O9 **White Pine** Tennessee, S USA 36°06′N 83°17′W
18 K14 **White Plains** New York, NE USA 41°01′N 73°45′W
37 N13 **Whiteriver** Arizona, SW USA 33°50′N 109°57′W
28 M11 **White River** South Dakota, N USA 43°34′N 100°45′W
27 W12 **White River** ≈ Arkansas, SE USA
37 P3 **White River** ≈ Colorado/Utah, C USA
31 N15 **White River** ≈ Indiana, N USA
31 O8 **White River** ≈ Michigan, N USA
28 K11 **White River** ≈ South Dakota, N USA
25 O5 **White River** ≈ Texas, SW USA
18 M8 **White River** ≈ Vermont, NE USA
25 O5 **White River Lake** ⊠ Texas, SW USA
32 H11 **White Salmon** Washington, NW USA 45°43′N 121°29′W
18 I10 **Whitesboro** New York, NE USA 43°07′N 75°17′W
25 T5 **Whitesboro** Texas, SW USA 33°39′N 96°54′W
21 O7 **Whitesburg** Kentucky, S USA 37°07′N 82°52′W
**White Sea** *see* Beloye More
**White Sea-Baltic Canal/White Sea Canal** *see* Belomorsko-Baltiyskiy Kanal
63 I25 **Whiteside, Canal** *channel* S Chile
33 S10 **White Sulphur Springs** Montana, NW USA 46°33′N 110°54′W
21 R6 **White Sulphur Springs** West Virginia, NE USA 37°48′N 80°18′W
20 J6 **Whitesville** Kentucky, S USA 37°40′N 86°48′W
32 I10 **White Swan** Washington, NW USA 46°22′N 120°46′W
21 U12 **Whiteville** North Carolina, SE USA 34°20′N 78°42′W
20 F10 **Whiteville** Tennessee, S USA 35°19′N 89°09′W
77 Q13 **White Volta** *var.* Nakambé, *Fr.* Volta Blanche. ≈ Burkina Faso/Ghana
30 M9 **Whitewater** Wisconsin, N USA 42°51′N 88°43′W
37 P14 **Whitewater Baldy** ▲ New Mexico, SW USA 33°19′N 108°38′W
23 X17 **Whitewater Bay** *bay* Florida, SE USA
31 Q14 **Whitewater River** ≈ Indiana/Ohio, N USA
11 V16 **Whitewood** Saskatchewan, S Canada 50°19′N 102°16′W
28 J9 **Whitewood** South Dakota, N USA 44°27′N 103°38′W
25 U5 **Whitewright** Texas, SW USA 33°30′N 96°23′W
97 I15 **Whithorn** S Scotland, United Kingdom 54°44′N 04°26′W
184 M6 **Whitianga** Waikato, North Island, New Zealand 36°50′S 175°42′E
19 N11 **Whitinsville** Massachusetts, NE USA 42°06′N 71°40′W
20 M8 **Whitley City** Kentucky, S USA 36°45′N 84°29′W
21 Q11 **Whitmire** South Carolina, SE USA 34°30′N 81°36′W
31 R10 **Whitmore Lake** Michigan, N USA 42°26′N 83°44′W
195 N9 **Whitmore Mountains** ▲▲ Antarctica
14 I12 **Whitney** Ontario, SE Canada 45°29′N 78°11′W
25 T8 **Whitney** Texas, SW USA 31°56′N 97°20′W
25 S8 **Whitney, Lake** ⊠ Texas, SW USA
35 S11 **Whitney, Mount** ▲ California, W USA 37°45′N 119°55′W
181 Y6 **Whitsunday Group** *island group* Queensland, E Australia
25 S6 **Whitt** Texas, SW USA 32°55′N 98°01′W
29 U12 **Whittemore** Iowa, C USA 43°03′N 94°25′W
39 R12 **Whittier** Alaska, USA 60°46′N 148°40′W
35 T15 **Whittier** California, W USA 33°58′N 118°01′W
83 I25 **Whittlesea** Eastern Cape, S South Africa 32°08′S 26°51′E
20 K10 **Whitwell** Tennessee, S USA 35°12′N 85°31′W
8 L10 **Wholdaia Lake** ◎ Northwest Territories, NW Canada
182 H7 **Whyalla** South Australia 33°04′S 137°34′E
**Whydah** *see* Ouidah
14 F13 **Wiarton** Ontario, S Canada 44°44′N 81°10′W
171 O13 **Wiau** Sulawesi, C Indonesia 03°08′S 121°22′E
111 H15 **Wiązów** *Ger.* Wansen. Dolnośląskie, SW Poland 50°49′N 17°13′E
33 Y8 **Wibaux** Montana, NW USA 46°57′N 104°11′W
27 N6 **Wichita** Kansas, C USA 37°42′N 97°20′W
25 R5 **Wichita Falls** Texas, SW USA 33°55′N 98°30′W
26 L11 **Wichita Mountains** ▲▲ Oklahoma, C USA
25 R5 **Wichita River** ≈ Texas, SW USA
96 K6 **Wick** N Scotland, United Kingdom 58°26′N 03°06′W
36 K13 **Wickenburg** Arizona, SW USA 33°57′N 112°41′W
24 L8 **Wickett** Texas, SW USA 31°34′N 103°00′W
180 I7 **Wickham** Western Australia 20°40′S 117°11′E
182 M14 **Wickham, Cape** *headland* Tasmania, SE Australia 39°36′S 143°55′E
20 G7 **Wickliffe** Kentucky, S USA 36°58′N 89°04′W
97 G19 **Wicklow** *Ir.* Cill Mhantáin. E Ireland 52°59′N 06°03′W
97 F19 **Wicklow** *Ir.* Cill Mhantáin. *cultural region* E Ireland
97 G19 **Wicklow Head** *Ir.* Ceann Chill Mhantáin. *headland* E Ireland 52°57′N 06°00′W
97 F18 **Wicklow Mountains** *Ir.* Sléibhte Chill Mhantáin. ▲▲ E Ireland
14 H10 **Wicksteed Lake** ◎ Ontario, S Canada
**Wida** *see* Ouidah
65 G15 **Wideawake Airfield** ✕ (Georgetown) SW Ascension Island
97 K18 **Widnes** NW England, United Kingdom 53°22′N 02°44′W
110 H9 **Więcbork** *Ger.* Vandsburg. Kujawsko-pomorskie, C Poland 53°21′N 17°31′E
101 E17 **Wied** ≈ W Germany
101 F16 **Wiehl** Nordrhein-Westfalen, W Germany 50°57′N 07°33′E
111 L17 **Wieliczka** Małopolskie, S Poland 50°N 20°02′E
110 H12 **Wielkopolskie** ◈ *province* SW Poland
111 J14 **Wieluń** Sieradz, C Poland 51°14′N 18°33′E
109 X4 **Wien** *Eng.* Vienna, *Hung.* Bécs, *Slvk.* Vídeň, *Slvn.* Dunaj; *anc.* Vindobona. ● (Austria) Wien, NE Austria 48°13′N 16°22′E
109 X4 **Wien** *off.* Land Wien, *Eng.* Vienna. ◈ *state* NE Austria
109 X5 **Wiener Neustadt** Niederösterreich, E Austria 47°49′N 16°08′E
**Wien, Land** *see* Wien
110 G7 **Wieprza** *Ger.* Wipper. ≈ NW Poland
98 O10 **Wierden** Overijssel, E Netherlands 52°22′N 06°35′E
98 I7 **Wieringerwerf** Noord-Holland, NW Netherlands 52°51′N 05°01′E
**Wieruschow** *see* Wieruszów
111 I14 **Wieruszów** *Ger.* Wieruschow. Łódzkie, C Poland 51°18′N 18°09′E
109 V9 **Wies** Steiermark, SE Austria 46°40′N 15°16′E
**Wiesbachhorn** *see* Grosses Wiesbachhorn
101 G18 **Wiesbaden** Hessen, W Germany 50°06′N 08°14′E
**Wieselburg and Ungarisch-Altenburg/Wieselburg-Ungarisch-Altenburg** *see* Mosonmagyaróvár
**Wiesenhof** *see* Ostrołęka
101 G20 **Wiesloch** Baden-Württemberg, SW Germany 49°18′N 08°42′E
100 F10 **Wiesmoor** Niedersachsen, NW Germany 53°22′N 07°46′E
110 I7 **Wieżyca** *Ger.* Turmberg. *hill* Pomorskie, N Poland
97 L17 **Wigan** NW England, United Kingdom 53°33′N 02°38′W
37 U3 **Wiggins** Colorado, C USA 40°11′N 104°03′W
22 M8 **Wiggins** Mississippi, S USA 30°50′N 89°09′W
**Wigorna Ceaster** *see* Worcester
97 I14 **Wigtown** S Scotland, United Kingdom 54°53′N 04°27′W
97 H14 **Wigtown** *cultural region* SW Scotland, United Kingdom
97 I15 **Wigtown Bay** *bay* SW Scotland, United Kingdom
98 L13 **Wijchen** Gelderland, SE Netherlands 51°48′N 05°44′E
92 N1 **Wijdefjorden** *fjord* NW Svalbard
98 M10 **Wijhe** Overijssel, E Netherlands 52°22′N 06°07′E
98 J12 **Wijk bij Duurstede** Utrecht, C Netherlands 51°58′N 05°21′E
98 J13 **Wijk en Aalburg** Noord-Brabant, S Netherlands 51°46′N 05°06′E
99 H16 **Wijnegem** Antwerpen, N Belgium 51°13′N 04°32′E
14 E11 **Wikwemikong** Manitoulin Island, Ontario, S Canada 45°46′N 81°43′W
108 H7 **Wil** Sankt Gallen, NE Switzerland 47°28′N 09°03′E
29 R16 **Wilber** Nebraska, C USA 40°28′N 96°57′W
32 K8 **Wilbur** Washington, NW USA 47°45′N 118°42′W
27 Q11 **Wilburton** Oklahoma, C USA 34°57′N 95°20′W
182 M6 **Wilcannia** New South Wales, SE Australia 31°34′S 143°23′E
18 D12 **Wilcox** Pennsylvania, NE USA 41°34′N 78°40′W
**Wilczek Land** *see* Vil'cheka, Zemlya
109 U6 **Wildalpen** Steiermark, E Austria 47°40′N 14°54′E
31 O13 **Wildcat Creek** ≈ Indiana, N USA
108 L9 **Wilde Kreuzspitze** *It.* Picco di Croce. ▲ Austria/Italy 46°53′N 10°51′E
**Wildenschwert** *see* Ústí nad Orlicí
98 O6 **Wildervank** Groningen, NE Netherlands 53°04′N 06°52′E
100 G11 **Wildeshausen** Niedersachsen, NW Germany 52°54′N 08°26′E
108 D10 **Wildhorn** ▲ SW Switzerland 46°21′N 07°22′E
11 R17 **Wild Horse** Alberta, SW Canada 49°00′N 110°19′W
27 N12 **Wildhorse Creek** ≈ Oklahoma, C USA
28 L14 **Wild Horse Hill** ▲ Nebraska, C USA 41°52′N 101°56′W
109 W8 **Wildon** Steiermark, SE Austria 46°53′N 15°29′E
24 M2 **Wildorado** Texas, SW USA 35°12′N 102°10′W
29 R6 **Wild Rice River** ≈ Minnesota/North Dakota, N USA
**Wilejka** *see* Vilyeyka
195 Y9 **Wilhelm II Coast** *physical region* Antarctica
195 X9 **Wilhelm II Land** *physical region* Antarctica
55 U11 **Wilhelmina Gebergte** ▲ C Suriname
18 B13 **Wilhelm, Lake** ⊠ Pennsylvania, NE USA
92 O2 **Wilhelmøya** *island* C Svalbard
**Wilhelm-Pieck-Stadt** *see* Guben
109 W4 **Wilhelmsburg** Niederösterreich, E Austria 48°07′N 15°37′E
100 G10 **Wilhelmshaven** Niedersachsen, NW Germany 53°31′N 08°07′E
**Wilia/Wilja** *see* Neris
18 H13 **Wilkes Barre** Pennsylvania, NE USA 41°15′N 75°50′W
21 R9 **Wilkesboro** North Carolina, SE USA 36°08′N 81°09′W
195 W15 **Wilkes Coast** *physical region* Antarctica
189 W12 **Wilkes Island** *island* N Wake Island
195 X12 **Wilkes Land** *physical region* Antarctica
11 S15 **Wilkie** Saskatchewan, S Canada 52°27′N 108°42′W
194 I6 **Wilkins Ice Shelf** *ice shelf* Antarctica
182 D4 **Wilkinsons Lakes** *salt lake* South Australia
**Wiłkomierz** *see* Ukmergė
182 K11 **Willalooka** South Australia 36°24′S 140°20′E
32 G11 **Willamette River** ≈ Oregon, NW USA
183 O8 **Willandra Billabong Creek** *seasonal river* New South Wales, SE Australia
32 F9 **Willapa Bay** *inlet* Washington, NW USA
27 T7 **Willard** Missouri, C USA 37°18′N 93°25′W
37 S12 **Willard** New Mexico, SW USA 34°36′N 106°01′W
31 S12 **Willard** Ohio, N USA 41°03′N 82°43′W
36 L1 **Willard** Utah, W USA 41°23′N 112°01′W
186 G6 **Willaumez Peninsula** *headland* New Britain, E Papua New Guinea 05°03′S 150°04′E
37 N15 **Willcox** Arizona, SW USA 32°13′N 109°49′W
37 N16 **Willcox Playa** *salt flat* Arizona, SW USA
99 G17 **Willebroek** Antwerpen, C Belgium 51°04′N 04°22′E
45 P16 **Willemstad** ○ Curaçao 12°07′N 68°54′W
99 G14 **Willemstad** Noord-Brabant, S Netherlands 51°40′N 04°27′E
11 S11 **William** ≈ Saskatchewan, C Canada
23 O6 **William "Bill" Dannelly Reservoir** ⊠ Alabama, S USA
182 G3 **William Creek** South Australia 28°55′S 136°23′E
181 T15 **William, Mount** ▲ South Australia
36 K11 **Williams** Arizona, SW USA 35°15′N 112°11′W
29 X14 **Williamsburg** Iowa, C USA 41°39′N 92°00′W
20 M8 **Williamsburg** Kentucky, S USA 36°44′N 84°10′W
31 R15 **Williamsburg** Ohio, N USA 39°00′N 84°02′W
21 X6 **Williamsburg** Virginia, NE USA 37°17′N 76°43′W
10 M15 **Williams Lake** British Columbia, SW Canada 52°08′N 122°09′W
21 P6 **Williamson** West Virginia, NE USA 37°42′N 82°16′W
31 N13 **Williamsport** Indiana, N USA 40°18′N 87°18′W
18 G13 **Williamsport** Pennsylvania, NE USA 41°16′N 77°03′W
21 W9 **Williamston** North Carolina, SE USA 35°53′N 77°05′W
21 P11 **Williamston** South Carolina, SE USA 34°37′N 82°28′W
20 M4 **Williamstown** Kentucky, S USA 38°39′N 84°32′W
18 L10 **Williamstown** Massachusetts, NE USA 42°41′N 73°11′W
18 J16 **Willingboro** New Jersey, NE USA 40°01′N 74°52′W
11 Q14 **Willingdon** Alberta, SW Canada 53°49′N 112°08′W
25 W10 **Willis** Texas, SW USA 30°25′N 95°28′W
108 F8 **Willisau** Luzern, W Switzerland 47°07′N 08°00′E
83 F24 **Williston** Northern Cape, W South Africa 31°20′S 20°52′E
23 V10 **Williston** Florida, SE USA 29°23′N 82°27′W
28 J3 **Williston** North Dakota, N USA 48°07′N 103°37′W



◆ Country ● Country Capital ◇ Dependent Territory ○ Dependent Territory Capital ◈ Administrative Regions ✕ International Airport ▲ Mountain ▲▲ Mountain Range ∆ Volcano ≈ River ◎ Lake ⊠ Reservoir

WILLISTON – XAI


21 Q13 **Williston** South Carolina, SE USA 33°24′N 81°25′W
10 L12 **Williston Lake** ▣ British Columbia, W Canada
34 L5 **Willits** California, W USA 39°24′N 123°22′W
29 T8 **Willmar** Minnesota, N USA 45°07′N 95°02′W
10 K11 **Will, Mount** ▲ British Columbia, W Canada 57°31′N 128°48′W
31 T11 **Willoughby** Ohio, N USA 41°38′N 81°24′W
11 U17 **Willow Bunch** Saskatchewan, S Canada 49°30′N 105°41′W
32 J11 **Willow Creek** ≈ Oregon, NW USA
39 R11 **Willow Lake** Alaska, USA 61°44′N 150°02′W
8 I9 **Willowlake** ≈ Northwest Territories, NW Canada
83 H25 **Willowmore** Eastern Cape, S South Africa 33°18′S 23°30′E
30 L5 **Willow Reservoir** ▣ Wisconsin, N USA
35 N5 **Willows** California, W USA 39°28′N 122°12′W
27 V7 **Willow Springs** Missouri, C USA 36°59′N 91°58′W
182 I7 **Wilmington** South Australia 32°42′S 138°08′E
21 Y2 **Wilmington** Delaware, NE USA 39°45′N 75°33′W
21 V12 **Wilmington** North Carolina, SE USA 34°14′N 77°55′W
31 R14 **Wilmington** Ohio, N USA 39°27′N 83°49′W
20 M6 **Wilmore** Kentucky, S USA 37°51′N 84°39′W
29 R8 **Wilmot** South Dakota, N USA 45°24′N 96°51′W
**Wilna/Wilno** *see* Vilnius
101 G16 **Wilnsdorf** Nordrhein-Westfalen, W Germany 50°49′N 08°06′E
99 G16 **Wilrijk** Antwerpen, N Belgium 51°11′N 04°25′E
100 I10 **Wilseder Berg** *hill* NW Germany
67 Z12 **Wilshaw Ridge** *undersea feature* W Indian Ocean 17°30′S 56°30′E
21 V9 **Wilson** North Carolina, SE USA 35°43′N 77°56′W
25 N5 **Wilson** Texas, SW USA 33°21′N 101°44′W
182 A7 **Wilson Bluff** *headland* South Australia/Western Australia 31°41′S 129°01′E
35 Y7 **Wilson Creek Range** ▲▲ Nevada, W USA
23 O1 **Wilson Lake** ▣ Alabama, S USA
26 M4 **Wilson Lake** ▣ Kansas, SE USA
37 P7 **Wilson, Mount** ▲ Colorado, C USA 37°50′N 107°59′W
183 P13 **Wilsons Promontory** *peninsula* Victoria, SE Australia
29 Y14 **Wilton** Iowa, C USA 41°35′N 91°01′W
19 P7 **Wilton** Maine, NE USA 44°35′N 70°15′W
28 M5 **Wilton** North Dakota, N USA 47°09′N 100°46′W
97 L22 **Wiltshire** *cultural region* S England, United Kingdom
99 M23 **Wiltz** Diekirch, NW Luxembourg 49°58′N 05°56′E
180 K9 **Wiluna** Western Australia 26°34′S 120°14′E
99 M23 **Wilwerwiltz** Diekirch, NE Luxembourg 49°59′N 06°00′E
29 P5 **Wimbledon** North Dakota, N USA 47°08′N 98°25′W
42 K7 **Wina** *var.* Güina. Jinotega, N Nicaragua 14°00′N 85°14′W
31 O12 **Winamac** Indiana, N USA 41°03′N 86°37′W
81 G19 **Winam Gulf** *var.* Kavirondo Gulf. *gulf* SW Kenya
83 I22 **Winburg** Free State, C South Africa 28°31′S 27°01′E
19 N10 **Winchendon** Massachusetts, NE USA 42°41′N 72°01′W
14 M13 **Winchester** Ontario, SE Canada 45°07′N 75°19′W
97 M23 **Winchester** *hist.* Wintanceaster, *Lat.* Venta Belgarum. S England, United Kingdom 51°04′N 01°19′W
32 M10 **Winchester** Idaho, NW USA 46°13′N 116°35′W
30 J14 **Winchester** Illinois, N USA 39°38′N 90°28′W
31 Q13 **Winchester** Indiana, N USA 40°11′N 84°57′W
20 M5 **Winchester** Kentucky, S USA 38°00′N 84°10′W
18 M10 **Winchester** New Hampshire, NE USA 42°46′N 72°21′W
20 K10 **Winchester** Tennessee, S USA 35°11′N 86°06′W
21 V3 **Winchester** Virginia, NE USA 39°11′N 78°12′W
99 L22 **Wincrange** Diekirch, NW Luxembourg 50°03′N 05°55′E
10 I5 **Wind** ≈ Yukon, NW Canada
183 S8 **Windamere, Lake** ◎ New South Wales, SE Australia
**Windau** *see* Ventspils, Latvia
**Windau** *see* Venta, Latvia/Lithuania
18 D15 **Windber** Pennsylvania, NE USA 40°12′N 78°47′W
23 T3 **Winder** Georgia, SE USA 33°59′N 83°43′W
97 K15 **Windermere** NW England, United Kingdom 54°24′N 02°54′W
14 C7 **Windermere Lake** ◎ Ontario, S Canada
31 U11 **Windham** Ohio, N USA 41°14′N 81°03′W
83 D19 **Windhoek** *Ger.* Windhuk. ● (Namibia) Khomas, C Namibia 22°34′S 17°06′E
83 D20 **Windhoek** ✈ Khomas, C Namibia 22°31′S 17°04′E
**Windhuk** *see* Windhoek
15 O8 **Windigo** Québec, SE Canada 47°45′N 73°19′W
15 O8 **Windigo** ≈ Québec, SE Canada
**Windischfeistritz** *see* Slovenska Bistrica
109 T6 **Windischgarsten** Oberösterreich, W Austria 47°42′N 14°21′E
**Windischgraz** *see* Slovenj Gradec
37 T16 **Wind Mountain** ▲ New Mexico, SW USA 32°01′N 105°35′W
29 T10 **Windom** Minnesota, N USA 43°52′N 95°07′W
37 Q7 **Windom Peak** ▲ Colorado, C USA 37°37′N 107°35′W
181 U9 **Windorah** Queensland, C Australia 25°25′S 142°41′E
37 O10 **Window Rock** Arizona, SW USA 35°40′N 109°03′W
31 N9 **Wind Point** *headland* Wisconsin, N USA 42°46′N 87°46′W
33 U14 **Wind River** ≈ Wyoming, C USA
13 P15 **Windsor** Nova Scotia, SE Canada 45°00′N 64°09′W
14 C17 **Windsor** Ontario, S Canada 42°18′N 83°W
15 Q12 **Windsor** Québec, SE Canada 45°34′N 72°00′W
97 N22 **Windsor** S England, United Kingdom 51°29′N 00°39′W
37 T3 **Windsor** Colorado, C USA 40°28′N 104°54′W
18 M12 **Windsor** Connecticut, NE USA 41°51′N 72°38′W
27 T5 **Windsor** Missouri, C USA 38°31′N 93°31′W
21 X9 **Windsor** North Carolina, SE USA 36°00′N 76°57′W
18 M12 **Windsor Locks** Connecticut, NE USA 41°55′N 72°37′W
25 R5 **Windthorst** Texas, SW USA 33°34′N 98°26′W
45 Z14 **Windward Islands** *island group* E West Indies
**Windward Islands** *see* Barlavento, Ilhas de, Cape Verde
**Windward Islands** *see* Vent, Îles du, Archipel de la Société, French Polynesia
44 K8 **Windward Passage** *Sp.* Paso de los Vientos. *channel* Cuba/Haiti
55 T9 **Wineperu** C Guyana 06°10′N 58°34′W
23 O3 **Winfield** Alabama, S USA 33°55′N 87°49′W
29 Y15 **Winfield** Iowa, C USA 41°07′N 91°26′W
27 O7 **Winfield** Kansas, C USA 37°14′N 97°00′W
25 W6 **Winfield** Texas, SW USA 33°10′N 95°06′W
21 Q4 **Winfield** West Virginia, NE USA 38°30′N 81°54′W
29 N5 **Wing** North Dakota, N USA 47°06′N 100°16′W
183 U7 **Wingham** New South Wales, SE Australia 31°52′S 152°24′E
12 G16 **Wingham** Ontario, S Canada 43°54′N 81°19′W
33 T8 **Winifred** Montana, NW USA 47°33′N 109°26′W
12 E9 **Winisk Lake** ◎ Ontario, C Canada
24 L8 **Wink** Texas, SW USA 31°45′N 103°09′W
36 M14 **Winkelman** Arizona, SW USA 32°59′N 110°46′W
11 X17 **Winkler** Manitoba, S Canada 49°12′N 97°55′W
109 Q9 **Winklern** Tirol, W Austria 46°54′N 12°54′E
**Winkowitz** *see* Vinkovci
32 G9 **Winlock** Washington, NW USA 46°29′N 122°56′W
77 P17 **Winneba** SE Ghana 05°22′N 00°38′W
29 U11 **Winnebago** Minnesota, N USA 43°46′N 94°10′W
29 R13 **Winnebago** Nebraska, C USA 42°14′N 96°28′W
30 M7 **Winnebago, Lake** ◎ Wisconsin, N USA
30 M7 **Winneconne** Wisconsin, N USA 44°07′N 88°44′W
35 T3 **Winnemucca** Nevada, W USA 40°59′N 117°44′W
35 R4 **Winnemucca Lake** ◎ Nevada, W USA
101 H21 **Winnenden** Baden-Württemberg, SW Germany 48°52′N 09°22′E
29 N11 **Winner** South Dakota, N USA 43°22′N 99°51′W
33 U9 **Winnett** Montana, NW USA 47°00′N 108°18′W
14 I9 **Winneway** Québec, SE Canada 47°35′N 78°33′W
22 H6 **Winnfield** Louisiana, S USA 31°55′N 92°38′W
29 U4 **Winnibigoshish, Lake** ◎ Minnesota, N USA
25 X11 **Winnie** Texas, SW USA 29°49′N 94°22′W
11 Y16 **Winnipeg** *province capital* Manitoba, S Canada 49°53′N 97°10′W
11 X16 **Winnipeg** ✈ Manitoba, S Canada 49°56′N 97°16′W
0 J8 **Winnipeg** ≈ Manitoba, S Canada
11 X16 **Winnipeg Beach** Manitoba, S Canada 50°25′N 96°59′W
11 W14 **Winnipeg, Lake** ◎ Manitoba, C Canada
11 W15 **Winnipegosis** Manitoba, S Canada 51°36′N 99°59′W
11 W15 **Winnipegosis, Lake** ◎ Manitoba, C Canada
19 O8 **Winnipesaukee, Lake** ◎ New Hampshire, NE USA
22 I6 **Winnsboro** Louisiana, S USA 32°09′N 91°43′W
21 R12 **Winnsboro** South Carolina, SE USA 34°22′N 81°05′W
25 W6 **Winnsboro** Texas, SW USA 33°01′N 95°16′W
29 X10 **Winona** Minnesota, N USA 44°03′N 91°37′W
22 L4 **Winona** Mississippi, S USA 33°30′N 89°42′W
27 W7 **Winona** Missouri, C USA 37°00′N 91°19′W
25 W7 **Winona** Texas, SW USA 32°29′N 95°10′W
18 M7 **Winooski River** ≈ Vermont, NE USA
98 P6 **Winschoten** Groningen, NE Netherlands 53°09′N 07°03′E
100 J10 **Winsen** Niedersachsen, N Germany 53°22′N 10°13′E
36 M11 **Winslow** Arizona, SW USA 35°01′N 110°42′W
19 Q7 **Winslow** Maine, NE USA 44°33′N 69°35′W
18 M12 **Winsted** Connecticut, NE USA 41°55′N 73°03′W
32 F14 **Winston** Oregon, NW USA 43°07′N 123°24′W
21 S9 **Winston Salem** North Carolina, SE USA 36°06′N 80°15′W
98 N5 **Winsum** Groningen, NE Netherlands 53°20′N 06°31′E
**Wintanceaster** *see* Winchester
23 W11 **Winter Garden** Florida, SE USA 28°34′N 81°35′W
10 J16 **Winter Harbour** Vancouver Island, British Columbia, SW Canada 50°28′N 128°03′W
23 W12 **Winter Haven** Florida, SE USA 28°01′N 81°43′W
23 X11 **Winter Park** Florida, SE USA 28°36′N 81°20′W
25 P8 **Winters** Texas, SW USA 31°57′N 99°57′W
29 U15 **Winterset** Iowa, C USA 41°19′N 94°00′W
98 O12 **Winterswijk** Gelderland, E Netherlands 51°58′N 06°44′E
108 G6 **Winterthur** Zürich, NE Switzerland 47°30′N 08°43′E
29 U9 **Winthrop** Minnesota, N USA 44°32′N 94°22′W
32 J7 **Winthrop** Washington, NW USA 48°28′N 120°13′W
181 V7 **Winton** Queensland, E Australia 22°22′S 143°04′E
185 C24 **Winton** Southland, South Island, New Zealand 46°08′S 168°20′E
21 X8 **Winton** North Carolina, SE USA 36°24′N 76°57′W
101 K15 **Wipper** ≈ C Germany
101 K14 **Wipper** ≈ C Germany
**Wipper** *see* Wieprza
182 G6 **Wirraminna** South Australia 31°10′S 136°13′E
182 F4 **Wirrida** South Australia 29°34′S 134°33′E
182 F7 **Wirrulla** South Australia 32°27′S 134°33′E
**Wirsitz** *see* Wyrzysk
**Wirz-See** *see* Võrtsjärv
97 O19 **Wisbech** E England, United Kingdom 52°39′N 00°08′E
**Wisby** *see* Visby
19 Q8 **Wiscasset** Maine, NE USA 44°01′N 69°41′W
**Wischau** *see* Vyškov
30 J5 **Wisconsin** *off.* State of Wisconsin, ***also known as*** Badger State. ◆ *state* N USA
30 L8 **Wisconsin Dells** Wisconsin, N USA 43°37′N 89°43′W
30 L8 **Wisconsin, Lake** ▣ Wisconsin, N USA
30 L7 **Wisconsin Rapids** Wisconsin, N USA 44°24′N 89°50′W
30 L7 **Wisconsin River** ≈ Wisconsin, N USA
33 P11 **Wisdom** Montana, NW USA 45°36′N 113°27′W
21 P7 **Wise** Virginia, NE USA 37°00′N 82°36′W
39 Q7 **Wiseman** Alaska, USA 67°24′N 150°06′W
96 J12 **Wishaw** W Scotland, United Kingdom 55°47′N 03°56′W
29 O6 **Wishek** North Dakota, N USA 46°12′N 99°33′W
32 I11 **Wishram** Washington, NW USA 45°40′N 120°53′W
111 J17 **Wisła** Śląskie, S Poland 49°39′N 18°50′E
110 K11 **Wisła** *Eng.* Vistula, *Ger.* Weichsel. ≈ C Poland
**Wiślany, Zalew** *see* Vistula Lagoon
111 M16 **Wisłoka** ≈ SE Poland
100 L9 **Wismar** Mecklenburg-Vorpommern, N Germany 53°54′N 11°28′E
29 R14 **Wisner** Nebraska, C USA 41°59′N 96°54′W
103 V4 **Wissembourg** *var.* Weissenburg. Bas-Rhin, NE France 49°03′N 07°57′E
30 J6 **Wissota, Lake** ▣ Wisconsin, N USA
97 O18 **Witham** ≈ E England, United Kingdom
97 O17 **Withernsea** E England, United Kingdom 53°46′N 00°01′W
37 Q13 **Withington, Mount** ▲ New Mexico, SW USA 33°52′N 107°29′W
23 U8 **Withlacoochee River** ≈ Florida/Georgia, SE USA
110 H11 **Witkowo** Wielkopolskie, C Poland 52°27′N 17°49′E
97 M21 **Witney** S England, United Kingdom 51°47′N 01°30′W
101 E15 **Witten** Nordrhein-Westfalen, W Germany 51°25′N 07°19′E
101 N14 **Wittenberg** Sachsen-Anhalt, E Germany 51°53′N 12°39′E
30 L6 **Wittenberg** Wisconsin, N USA 44°53′N 89°20′W
100 L11 **Wittenberge** Brandenburg, N Germany 52°59′N 11°45′E
103 U7 **Wittenheim** Haut-Rhin, NE France 47°49′N 07°19′E
180 I7 **Wittenoom** Western Australia 22°17′S 118°22′E
**Wittingau** *see* Třeboň
100 K12 **Wittingen** Niedersachsen, C Germany 52°42′N 10°43′E
101 E18 **Wittlich** Rheinland-Pfalz, SW Germany 49°59′N 06°54′E
100 F9 **Wittmund** Niedersachsen, NW Germany 53°34′N 07°46′E
100 M10 **Wittstock** Brandenburg, NE Germany 53°10′N 12°29′E
186 F6 **Witu Islands** *island group* E Papua New Guinea
110 O7 **Wiżajny** Podlaskie, NE Poland 54°22′N 22°51′E
55 W10 **W. J. van Blommesteinmeer** ▣ E Suriname
110 L11 **Wkra** *Ger.* Soldau. ≈ C Poland
110 I6 **Władysławowo** Pomorskie, N Poland 54°48′N 18°25′E
**Wlaschim** *see* Vlašim
111 E14 **Wleń** *Ger.* Lähn. Dolnośląskie, SW Poland 51°00′N 15°39′E
110 J11 **Włocławek** *Ger./Rus.* Vlotslavsk. Kujawsko-pomorskie, C Poland 52°39′N 19°03′E
110 P13 **Włodawa** *Rus.* Vlodava. Lubelskie, SE Poland 51°33′N 23°31′E
**Włodzimierz** *see* Volodymyr-Volyns'kyy
111 K15 **Włoszczowa** Świętokrzyskie, C Poland 50°51′N 19°58′E
83 C19 **Wlotzkasbaken** Erongo, W Namibia 22°26′S 14°30′E
15 R12 **Woburn** Québec, SE Canada 45°22′N 70°52′W
19 O11 **Woburn** Massachusetts, NE USA 42°28′N 71°09′W
**Wocheiner Feistritz** *see* Bohinjska Bistrica
**Wöchma** *see* Võhma
147 S11 **Wodil** *var.* Vuadil'. Far'gona Viloyati, E Uzbekistan 40°10′N 71°43′E
181 V14 **Wodonga** Victoria, SE Australia 36°11′S 146°55′E
111 I17 **Wodzisław Śląski** *Ger.* Loslau. Śląskie, S Poland 49°59′N 18°27′E
98 I11 **Woerden** Zuid-Holland, C Netherlands 52°06′N 04°54′E
98 I8 **Wognum** Noord-Holland, NW Netherlands 52°40′N 05°01′E
**Wohlau** *see* Wołów
108 F7 **Wohlen** Aargau, NW Switzerland 47°21′N 08°17′E
195 R2 **Wohlthat Massivet** *Eng.* Wohlthat Mountains. ▲▲ Antarctica
**Wohlthat Mountains** *see* Wohlthat Massivet
**Wojerecy** *see* Hoyerswerda
**Wōjjā** *see* Wotje Atoll
**Wojwodina** *see* Vojvodina
171 V15 **Wokam, Pulau** *island* Kepulauan Aru, E Indonesia
97 N22 **Woking** SE England, United Kingdom 51°20′N 00°34′W
**Woldenberg Neumark** *see* Dobiegniew
188 K15 **Woleai Atoll** *atoll* Caroline Islands, W Micronesia
**Woleu** *see* Uolo, Río
79 E17 **Woleu-Ntem** *off.* Province du Woleu-Ntem, *var.* Le Woleu-Ntem. ◆ *province* W Gabon
**Woleu-Ntem, Province du** *see* Woleu-Ntem
32 F15 **Wolf Creek** Oregon, NW USA 42°40′N 123°22′W
26 K9 **Wolf Creek** ≈ Oklahoma/Texas, SW USA
37 R7 **Wolf Creek Pass** *pass* Colorado, C USA
19 O9 **Wolfeboro** New Hampshire, NE USA 43°34′N 71°10′W
25 U5 **Wolfe City** Texas, SW USA 33°22′N 96°04′W
14 L15 **Wolfe Island** *island* Ontario, SE Canada
101 M14 **Wolfen** Sachsen-Anhalt, E Germany 51°40′N 12°16′E
100 J13 **Wolfenbüttel** Niedersachsen, C Germany 52°10′N 10°33′E
109 T4 **Wolfern** Oberösterreich, N Austria 48°06′N 14°16′E
109 Q6 **Wolfgangsee** *var.* Abersee, St Wolfgangsee. ◎ N Austria
39 P9 **Wolf Mountain** ▲ Alaska, USA 65°20′N 154°08′W
33 X7 **Wolf Point** Montana, NW USA 48°05′N 105°40′W
22 L8 **Wolf River** ≈ Mississippi, S USA
30 M7 **Wolf River** ≈ Wisconsin, N USA
109 U9 **Wolfsberg** Kärnten, SE Austria 46°50′N 14°50′E
100 K12 **Wolfsburg** Niedersachsen, N Germany 52°25′N 10°47′E
57 B17 **Wolf, Volcán** Ѫ Galapagos Islands, Ecuador, E Pacific Ocean 0°01′N 91°22′W
100 O8 **Wolgast** Mecklenburg-Vorpommern, NE Germany 54°04′N 13°47′E
108 F8 **Wolhusen** Luzern, W Switzerland 47°04′N 08°06′E
110 D8 **Wolin** *Ger.* Wollin. Zachodnio-pomorskie, NW Poland 53°52′N 14°35′E
109 Y3 **Wolkersdorf** Niederösterreich, NE Austria 48°24′N 16°31′E
**Wołkowysk** *see* Vawkavysk
**Wöllan** *see* Velenje
8 J6 **Wollaston, Cape** *headland* Victoria Island, Northwest Territories, NW Canada 71°00′N 118°21′W
63 J25 **Wollaston, Isla** *island* S Chile
11 U11 **Wollaston Lake** Saskatchewan, C Canada 58°05′N 103°38′W
11 T10 **Wollaston Lake** ◎ Saskatchewan, C Canada
8 J6 **Wollaston Peninsula** *peninsula* Victoria Island, Northwest Territories/Nunavut NW Canada
**Wollin** *see* Wolin
183 S9 **Wollongong** New South Wales, SE Australia 34°25′S 150°52′E
**Wolmar** *see* Valmiera
100 L13 **Wolmirstedt** Sachsen-Anhalt, C Germany 52°15′N 11°37′E
110 M11 **Wołomin** Mazowieckie, C Poland 52°20′N 21°11′E
110 G!3 **Wołów** *Ger.* Wohlau. Dolnośląskie, SW Poland 51°21′N 16°40′E
**Wołożyn** *see* Valozhyn
14 G11 **Wolseley Bay** Ontario, S Canada 46°05′N 80°16′W
29 P10 **Wolsey** South Dakota, N USA 44°22′N 98°28′W
110 F12 **Wolsztyn** Wielkopolskie, C Poland 52°07′N 16°07′E
98 M7 **Wolvega** *Fris.* Wolvegea. Fryslân, N Netherlands 52°53′N 06°E
**Wolvegea** *see* Wolvega
97 K19 **Wolverhampton** C England, United Kingdom 52°36′N 02°08′W
**Wolverine State** *see* Michigan
99 G18 **Wolvertem** Vlaams Brabant, C Belgium 50°55′N 04°19′E
99 H16 **Wommelgem** Antwerpen, N Belgium 51°12′N 04°32′E
186 D7 **Wonenara** *var.* Wonerara. Eastern Highlands, C Papua New Guinea 06°46′S 145°54′E
**Wonerara** *see* Wonenara
**Wongalara Lake** *see* Wongalarroo Lake
183 N6 **Wongalarroo Lake** *var.* Wongalara Lake. *seasonal lake* New South Wales, SE Australia
163 Y15 **Wonju** *Jap.* Genshū; *prev.* Wŏnju. N South Korea 37°21′N 127°57′E
**Wŏnju** *see* Wonju
10 M12 **Wonowon** British Columbia, W Canada 56°46′N 121°54′W
163 X13 **Wŏnsan** SE North Korea 39°11′N 127°21′E
183 O13 **Wonthaggi** Victoria, SE Australia 38°38′S 145°37′E
23 N2 **Woodall Mountain** ▲ Mississippi, S USA 34°47′N 88°14′W
23 W7 **Woodbine** Georgia, SE USA 30°58′N 81°43′W
29 S14 **Woodbine** Iowa, C USA 41°44′N 95°42′W
18 J17 **Woodbine** New Jersey, NE USA 39°12′N 74°47′W
21 W4 **Woodbridge** Virginia, NE USA 38°40′N 77°17′W
183 V4 **Woodburn** New South Wales, SE Australia 29°07′S 153°23′E
32 G11 **Woodburn** Oregon, NW USA 45°08′N 122°51′W
20 K9 **Woodbury** Tennessee, S USA 35°49′N 86°06′W
183 V5 **Wooded Bluff** *headland* New South Wales, SE Australia 29°24′S 153°22′E
183 V3 **Woodenbong** New South Wales, SE Australia 28°24′S 152°39′E
35 R11 **Woodlake** California, W USA 36°24′N 119°06′W
35 N7 **Woodland** California, W USA 38°41′N 121°46′W
19 T5 **Woodland** Maine, NE USA 45°10′N 67°25′W
32 G10 **Woodland** Washington, NW USA 45°54′N 122°44′W
37 T5 **Woodland Park** Colorado, C USA 38°59′N 105°03′W
186 I9 **Woodlark Island** *var.* Murua Island. *island* SE Papua New Guinea
**Woodle Island** *see* Kuria
11 T17 **Wood Mountain** ▲▲ Saskatchewan, S Canada
30 K15 **Wood River** Illinois, N USA 38°51′N 90°06′W
29 P16 **Wood River** Nebraska, C USA 40°48′N 98°33′W
39 R9 **Wood River** ≈ Alaska, USA
39 O13 **Wood River Lakes** *lakes* Alaska, USA
182 C1 **Woodroffe, Mount** ▲ South Australia 26°19′S 131°42′E
21 P11 **Woodruff** South Carolina, SE USA 34°44′N 82°02′W
30 K4 **Woodruff** Wisconsin, N USA 45°55′N 89°41′W
25 T14 **Woodsboro** Texas, SW USA 28°14′N 97°19′W
31 U13 **Woodsfield** Ohio, N USA 39°45′N 81°07′W
181 P4 **Woods, Lake** ◎ Northern Territory, N Australia
11 Z16 **Woods, Lake of the** *Fr.* Lac des Bois. ◎ Canada/USA
25 Q6 **Woodson** Texas, SW USA 33°00′N 99°01′W
13 N14 **Woodstock** New Brunswick, SE Canada 46°10′N 67°38′W
14 F16 **Woodstock** Ontario, S Canada 43°07′N 80°46′W
30 M10 **Woodstock** Illinois, N USA 42°18′N 88°27′W
18 M9 **Woodstock** Vermont, NE USA 43°37′N 72°33′W
21 U4 **Woodstock** Virginia, NE USA 38°55′N 78°31′W
19 N8 **Woodsville** New Hampshire, NE USA 44°08′N 72°02′W
184 M12 **Woodville** Manawatu-Wanganui, North Island, New Zealand 40°22′S 175°59′E
22 J7 **Woodville** Mississippi, S USA 31°06′N 91°18′W
25 X9 **Woodville** Texas, SW USA 30°47′N 94°26′W
26 K9 **Woodward** Oklahoma, C USA 36°26′N 99°25′W
29 O5 **Woodworth** North Dakota, N USA 47°06′N 99°19′W
171 W12 **Wool** Papua, E Indonesia 01°38′S 135°34′E
183 V5 **Woolgoolga** New South Wales, E Australia 30°04′S 153°09′E
182 H6 **Woomera** South Australia 31°12′S 136°52′E
19 O12 **Woonsocket** Rhode Island, NE USA 41°58′N 71°27′W
29 P10 **Woonsocket** South Dakota, N USA 44°03′N 98°16′W
31 T12 **Wooster** Ohio, N USA 40°48′N 81°56′W
80 L12 **Woqooyi Galbeed** *off.* Gobolka Woqooyi Galbeed. ◆ *region* NW Somalia
**Woqooyi Galbeed, Gobolka** *see* Woqooyi Galbeed
108 E8 **Worb** Bern, C Switzerland 46°54′N 07°36′E
83 F26 **Worcester** Western Cape, SW South Africa 33°41′S 19°22′E
97 L20 **Worcester** *hist.* Wigorna Ceaster. W England, United Kingdom 52°11′N 02°13′W
19 N11 **Worcester** Massachusetts, NE USA 42°17′N 71°48′W
97 L20 **Worcestershire** *cultural region* C England, United Kingdom
32 H16 **Worden** Oregon, NW USA 42°04′N 121°50′W
109 O6 **Wörgl** Tirol, W Austria 47°29′N 12°04′E
171 V15 **Workai, Pulau** *island* Kepulauan Aru, E Indonesia
97 J15 **Workington** NW England, United Kingdom 54°39′N 03°33′W
98 K7 **Workum** Fryslân, N Netherlands 52°58′N 05°25′E
33 V13 **Worland** Wyoming, C USA 44°01′N 107°57′W
*see* São João de Cortes
**Wormatia** *see* Worms
99 N25 **Wormeldange** Grevenmacher, E Luxembourg 49°37′N 06°25′E
98 I9 **Wormer** Noord-Holland, C Netherlands 52°30′N 04°50′E
101 G19 **Worms** *anc.* Augusta Vangionum, Borbetomagus, Wormatia. Rheinland-Pfalz, SW Germany 49°38′N 08°22′E
**Worms** *see* Vormsi
101 K21 **Wörnitz** ≈ S Germany
25 U8 **Wortham** Texas, SW USA 31°47′N 96°27′W
101 G21 **Wörth am Rhein** Rheinland-Pfalz, SW Germany 49°04′N 08°16′E
109 S9 **Wörther See** ◎ S Austria
97 O23 **Worthing** SE England, United Kingdom 50°48′N 00°23′W
29 S11 **Worthington** Minnesota, N USA 43°37′N 95°37′W
31 S13 **Worthington** Ohio, N USA 40°05′N 83°01′W
35 W8 **Worthington Peak** ▲ Nevada, W USA 37°57′N 115°32′W
171 Y13 **Wosi** Papua, E Indonesia 03°55′S 138°54′E
171 V13 **Wosimi** Papua Barat, E Indonesia 02°44′S 134°34′E
189 R5 **Wotho Atoll** *var.* Wōtto. *atoll* Ralik Chain, W Marshall Islands
189 V5 **Wotje Atoll** *var.* Wōjjā. *atoll* Ratak Chain, E Marshall Islands
**Wotoe** *see* Wotu
**Wottawa** *see* Otava
**Wōtto** *see* Wotho Atoll
171 O13 **Wotu** *prev.* Wotoe. Sulawesi, C Indonesia 02°34′S 120°46′E
98 K11 **Woudenberg** Utrecht, C Netherlands 52°05′N 05°25′E
98 I13 **Woudrichem** Noord-Brabant, S Netherlands 51°49′N 05°E
43 N8 **Wounta** *var.* Huaunta. Costa Caribe Norte, NE Nicaragua 13°30′N 83°32′W
171 P14 **Wowoni, Pulau** *island* C Indonesia
81 J17 **Woyamdero Plain** *plain* E Kenya
**Woyens** *see* Vojens
**Wozrojdeniye Oroli** *see* Vozrozhdeniya, Ostrov
**Wrangel Island** *see* Vrangelya, Ostrov
39 Y13 **Wrangell** Wrangell Island, Alaska, USA 56°28′N 132°22′W
38 C15 **Wrangell, Cape** *headland* Attu Island, Alaska, USA 52°55′N 172°28′E
39 S11 **Wrangell, Mount** ▲ Alaska, USA 62°00′N 144°01′W
39 T11 **Wrangell Mountains** ▲▲ Alaska, USA
197 S7 **Wrangel Plain** *undersea feature* Arctic Ocean
96 H6 **Wrath, Cape** *headland* N Scotland, United Kingdom 58°37′N 05°01′W
37 W3 **Wray** Colorado, C USA 40°01′N 102°12′W
44 K13 **Wreck Point** *headland* C Jamaica 17°50′N 76°55′W
83 C23 **Wreck Point** *headland* W South Africa 28°52′S 16°17′E
23 V4 **Wrens** Georgia, SE USA 33°12′N 82°23′W
97 K18 **Wrexham** NE Wales, United Kingdom 53°03′N 03°W
27 R13 **Wright City** Oklahoma, C USA 34°03′N 95°00′W
194 J12 **Wright Island** *island* Antarctica
13 N9 **Wright, Mont** ▲ Québec, E Canada 52°36′N 67°40′W
25 X5 **Wright Patman Lake** ▣ Texas, SW USA
36 M16 **Wrightson, Mount** ▲ Arizona, SW USA 31°42′N 110°51′W
23 U5 **Wrightsville** Georgia, SE USA 32°43′N 82°43′W
21 W12 **Wrightsville Beach** North Carolina, SE USA 34°12′N 77°48′W
35 T15 **Wrightwood** California, W USA 34°21′N 117°37′W
8 H9 **Wrigley** Northwest Territories, W Canada 63°16′N 123°39′W
111 G14 **Wrocław** *Eng./Ger.* Breslau. Dolnośląskie, SW Poland 51°07′N 17°01′E
110 F10 **Wronki** *Ger.* Fronicken. Wielkopolskie, C Poland 52°42′N 16°22′E
110 H11 **Września** Wielkopolskie, C Poland 52°19′N 17°34′E
110 F12 **Wschowa** Lubuskie, W Poland 51°49′N 16°15′E
**Wsetin** *see* Vsetín
161 O5 **Wu'an** Hebei, E China 36°45′N 114°12′E
180 I12 **Wubin** Western Australia 30°05′S 116°43′E
163 W9 **Wuchang** Heilongjiang, NE China 44°55′N 127°13′E
**Wuchang** *see* Wuhan
**Wu-chou/Wuchow** *see* Wuzhou
160 M16 **Wuchuan** *var.* Meilu. Guangdong, S China 21°28′N 110°49′E
160 K10 **Wuchuan** *var.* Duru, Gelaozu Miaozu Zhizhixian. Guizhou, S China 28°40′N 108°04′E
163 O13 **Wuchuan** Nei Mongol Zizhiqu, N China 41°04′N 111°28′E
163 V6 **Wudalianchi** *var.* Qingshan; *prev.* Dedu. Heilongjiang, NE China 48°40′N 126°06′E
159 O11 **Wudaoliang** Qinghai, C China 35°16′N 93°03′E
141 Q13 **Wuday'ah** *spring/well* S Saudi Arabia 17°03′N 47°06′E
77 V13 **Wudil** Kano, N Nigeria 11°46′N 08°49′E
160 G12 **Wuding** *var.* Jincheng. Yunnan, SW China 25°30′N 102°21′E
182 G8 **Wudinna** South Australia 33°06′S 135°30′E
**Wudu** *see* Longnan
160 L9 **Wufeng** Hubei, C China 30°09′N 110°31′E
161 O11 **Wugong Shan** ▲▲ S China
157 P7 **Wuhai** *var.* Haibowan. Nei Mongol Zizhiqu, N China 39°40′N 106°48′E
161 O9 **Wuhan** *var.* Han-kou, Han-k'ou, Hanyang, Wuchang, Wu-han; *prev.* Hankow. *province capital* Hubei, C China 30°35′N 114°19′E
**Wu-han** *see* Wuhan
161 Q7 **Wuhe** Anhui, E China 33°05′N 117°55′E
**Wuhsien** *see* Suzhou
**Wuhsi/Wu-his** *see* Wuxi
161 Q8 **Wuhu** *var.* Wu-na-mu. Anhui, E China 31°23′N 118°25′E
**Wūjae** *see* Ujae Atoll
160 K11 **Wu Jiang** ≈ C China
**Wujlān** *see* Ujelang Atoll
77 W15 **Wukari** Taraba, E Nigeria 07°51′N 09°49′E
**Wulan** *see* Jingyuan
152 H4 **Wular Lake** ◎ NE India
160 H11 **Wulian Feng** ▲▲ SW China
160 F13 **Wuliang Shan** ▲▲ SW China
160 K11 **Wuling Shan** ▲▲ S China
109 Y5 **Wulka** ≈ E Austria
**Wulkan** *see* Vulcan
109 T3 **Wullowitz** Oberösterreich, N Austria 48°37′N 14°27′E
**Wu-lu-k'o-mu-shi/Wu-lu-mu-ch'i** *see* Ürümqi
79 D14 **Wum** Nord-Ouest, NE Cameroon 06°24′N 10°04′E
160 H12 **Wumeng Shan** ▲▲ SW China
160 K14 **Wuming** Guangxi Zhuangzu Zizhiqu, S China 23°12′N 108°11′E
100 I10 **Wümme** ≈ NW Germany
**Wu-na-mu** *see* Wuhu
171 X13 **Wunen** Papua, E Indonesia 03°40′S 138°31′E
12 D9 **Wunnummin Lake** ◎ Ontario, C Canada
80 D13 **Wun Rog** Warap, W South Sudan 09°00′N 28°20′E
101 M18 **Wunsiedel** Bayern, E Germany 50°02′N 12°00′E
100 I12 **Wunstorf** Niedersachsen, NW Germany 52°25′N 09°25′E
166 M3 **Wuntho** Sagaing, N Myanmar (Burma) 23°52′N 95°43′E
101 F15 **Wupper** ≈ W Germany
101 E15 **Wuppertal** *prev.* Barmen-Elberfeld. Nordrhein-Westfalen, W Germany 51°16′N 07°12′E
160 K5 **Wuqi** Shaanxi, C China 36°57′N 108°15′E
161 P4 **Wuqiao** *var.* Sangyuan. Hebei, E China 37°40′N 116°21′E
101 L23 **Würm** ≈ SE Germany
77 T12 **Wurno** Sokoto, NW Nigeria 13°15′N 05°24′E
101 I19 **Würzburg** Bayern, SW Germany 49°48′N 09°56′E
101 N15 **Wurzen** Sachsen, E Germany 51°21′N 12°48′E
160 L9 **Wu Shan** ▲▲ C China
158 G7 **Wushi** *var.* Uqturpan. Xinjiang Uygur Zizhiqu, NW China 41°07′N 79°09′E
**Wusih** *see* Wuxi
65 N18 **Wüst Seamount** *undersea feature* S Atlantic Ocean 32°00′S 00°06′E
**Wusuli Jiang/Wusuri** *see* Ussuri
161 N3 **Wutai Shan** *var.* Beitai Ding. ▲ C China 39°00′N 114°00′E
160 H10 **Wutongqiao** Sichuan, C China 29°21′N 103°48′E
159 P6 **Wutongwozi Quan** *spring* NW China
99 H15 **Wuustwezel** Antwerpen, N Belgium 51°24′N 04°34′E
186 B4 **Wuvulu Island** *island* NW Papua New Guinea
159 U9 **Wuwei** *var.* Liangzhou. Gansu, C China 37°58′N 102°40′E
161 R8 **Wuxi** *var.* Wuhsi, Wu-hsi, Wusih. Jiangsu, E China 31°35′N 120°19′E
**Wuxing** *see* Huzhou
160 L14 **Wuxuan** Guangxi Zhuangzu Zizhiqu, S China 23°40′N 109°41′E
**Wuyang** *see* Zhenyuan
160 K11 **Wuyang He** ≈ S China
163 X6 **Wuyiling** Heilongjiang, NE China 48°36′N 129°24′E
161 Q11 **Wuyishan** *prev.* Chong'an. Fujian, SE China 27°48′N 118°03′E
157 T12 **Wuyi Shan** ▲▲ SE China
162 M13 **Wuyuan** Nei Mongol Zizhiqu, N China 41°05′N 108°15′E
160 L17 **Wuzhishan** *prev.* Tongshi. Hainan, S China 18°37′N 109°34′E
160 L17 **Wuzhi Shan** ▲ S China 18°52′N 109°36′E
159 W8 **Wuzhong** Ningxia, N China 37°58′N 106°09′E
160 M14 **Wuzhou** *var.* Wu-chou, Wuchow. Guangxi Zhuangzu Zizhiqu, S China 23°30′N 111°21′E
18 H12 **Wyalusing** Pennsylvania, NE USA 41°40′N 76°13′W
182 M10 **Wycheproof** Victoria, SE Australia 36°06′S 143°13′E
97 K21 **Wye** *Wel.* Gwy. ≈ England/Wales, United Kingdom
**Wyłkowyszki** *see* Vilkaviškis
97 P19 **Wymondham** E England, United Kingdom 52°29′N 01°10′E
29 R17 **Wymore** Nebraska, C USA 40°07′N 96°39′W
182 E5 **Wynbring** South Australia 30°34′S 133°27′E
181 N3 **Wyndham** Western Australia 15°28′S 128°08′E
29 R6 **Wyndmere** North Dakota, N USA 46°16′N 97°07′W
27 X11 **Wynne** Arkansas, C USA 35°14′N 90°48′W
27 N12 **Wynnewood** Oklahoma, C USA 34°39′N 97°09′W
183 O15 **Wynyard** Tasmania, SE Australia 40°57′S 145°33′E
11 U15 **Wynyard** Saskatchewan, S Canada 51°46′N 104°10′W
33 V11 **Wyola** Montana, NW USA 45°07′N 107°23′W
182 A4 **Wyola Lake** *salt lake* South Australia
31 P9 **Wyoming** Michigan, N USA 42°54′N 85°42′W
33 V14 **Wyoming** *off.* State of Wyoming, ***also known as*** Equality State. ◆ *state* C USA
33 S15 **Wyoming Range** ▲▲ Wyoming, C USA
183 T8 **Wyong** New South Wales, SE Australia 33°18′S 151°27′E
110 G9 **Wyrzysk** *Ger.* Wirsitz. Wielkopolskie, C Poland 53°09′N 17°15′E
**Wysg** *see* Usk
110 O10 **Wysokie Mazowieckie** Łomża, E Poland 52°54′N 22°34′E
110 M11 **Wyszków** *Ger.* Probstberg. Mazowieckie, NE Poland 52°36′N 21°28′E
110 L11 **Wyszogród** Mazowieckie, C Poland 52°24′N 20°14′E
21 R7 **Wytheville** Virginia, NE USA 36°57′N 81°07′W
111 L15 **Wyżyna Małopolska** *plateau*


# X


80 Q12 **Xaafuun** *It.* Hafun. Bari, NE Somalia 10°25′N 51°17′E
80 Q12 **Xaafuun, Raas** *var.* Ras Hafun. *cape* NE Somalia
**Xabia** *see* Jávea
42 C4 **Xaclbal, Río** *var.* Xalbal. ≈ Guatemala/Mexico
137 Y10 **Xaçmaz** *Rus.* Khachmas. N Azerbaijan 41°26′N 48°47′E
80 O12 **Xadeed** *var.* Haded. *physical region* N Somalia
159 O14 **Xagquka** Xizang Zizhiqu, W China 31°47′N 92°46′E
**Xai** *see* Oudômxai


◆ Country
● Country Capital
◇ Dependent Territory
○ Dependent Territory Capital
◆ Administrative Regions
✈ International Airport
▲ Mountain
▲▲ Mountain Range
Ѫ Volcano
≈ River
◎ Lake
▣ Reservoir

346

Ýdras, Kólpos – Žabalj


115 G20 **Ýdras, Kólpos** *strait* S Greece
167 N10 **Ye** Mon State, S Myanmar (Burma) *15°15′N 97°50′E*
183 O12 **Yea** Victoria, SE Australia *37°15′S 145°27′E*
167 P13 **Yéay Sén** *prev.* Phumĭ Yeay Sên. Koh Kong, SW Cambodia *11°09′N 103°09′E*
**Yebaishou** *see* Jianping
78 I5 **Yebbi-Bou** Tibesti, N Chad *21°12′N 17°55′E*
158 F9 **Yecheng** *var.* Kargilik. Xinjiang Uygur Zizhiqu, NW China *37°54′N 77°26′E*
105 R11 **Yecla** Murcia, SE Spain *38°36′N 01°07′W*
40 H6 **Yécora** Sonora, NW Mexico *28°23′N 108°56′W*
**Yedintsy** *see* Edineţ
117 V12 **Yedy-Kuyu** *prev.* Lenine. Avtonomna Respublika Krym, S Ukraine *45°18′N 35°47′E*
124 J13 **Yefimovskiy** Leningradskaya Oblast', NW Russia *59°32′N 34°34′E*
126 K6 **Yefremov** Tul'skaya Oblast', W Russia *53°10′N 38°02′E*
159 T11 **Yêgainnyin** *var.* Henan Mongolzu Zizhixian. Qinghai, C China *34°42′N 101°36′E*
137 U12 **Yegbhegis** *Rus.* Yekhegis. ≈ C Armenia
137 U12 **Yeghegnadzor** C Armenia *39°45′N 45°20′E*
145 T10 **Yegindybulak** *Kaz.* Egindibulaq. Karaganda, C Kazakhstan *49°45′N 75°45′E*
126 L4 **Yegor'yevsk** Moskovskaya Oblast', W Russia *55°29′N 39°03′E*
**Yehuda, Haré** *see* Judaean Hills
81 E15 **Yei** ≈ S South Sudan
161 P8 **Yeji** *var.* Yejiaji. Anhui, E China *31°52′N 115°58′E*
**Yejiaji** *see* Yeji
122 G10 **Yekaterinburg** *prev.* Sverdlovsk. Sverdlovskaya Oblast', C Russia *56°52′N 60°35′E*
**Yekaterinodar** *see* Krasnodar
**Yekaterinoslav** *see* Dnipro
123 R13 **Yekaterinoslavka** Amurskaya Oblast', SE Russia *50°23′N 129°03′E*
127 O7 **Yekaterinovka** Saratovskaya Oblast', W Russia *52°01′N 44°11′E*
76 K16 **Yekepa** NE Liberia *07°35′N 08°32′W*
**Yekhegis** *see* Yegbhegis
145 T8 **Yekibastuz** *prev.* Ekibastuz. Pavlodar, NE Kazakhstan *51°42′N 75°22′E*
127 T3 **Yelabuga** Respublika Tatarstan, W Russia *55°46′N 52°07′E*
**Yela Island** *see* Rossel Island
127 O8 **Yelan'** Volgogradskaya Oblast', SW Russia *51°00′N 43°40′E*
117 Q9 **Yelanets'** *Rus.* Yelanets. Mykolayivs'ka Oblast', S Ukraine *47°40′N 31°51′E*
144 I9 **Yelek** *Kaz.* Elek; *prev.* Ilek. ≈ Kazakhstan/Russia
126 L7 **Yelets** Lipetskaya Oblast', W Russia *52°37′N 38°29′E*
125 W4 **Yeletskiy** Respublika Komi, NW Russia *67°03′N 64°05′E*
76 J11 **Yélimané** Kayes, W Mali *15°06′N 10°43′W*
**Yelisavetpol** *see* Gäncä
**Yelizavetgrad** *see* Kropyvnyts'kyy
123 T12 **Yelizavety, Mys** *headland* SE Russia *54°20′N 142°39′E*
**Yelizovo** *see* Yalizava
127 S5 **Yelkhovka** Samarskaya Oblast', W Russia *53°51′N 50°16′E*
96 M1 **Yell** *island* NE Scotland, United Kingdom
155 E17 **Yellāpur** Karnātaka, W India *15°06′N 74°50′E*
11 U17 **Yellow Grass** Saskatchewan, S Canada *49°51′N 104°09′W*
**Yellowhammer State** *see* Alabama
11 O15 **Yellowhead Pass** *pass* Alberta/British Columbia, SW Canada
8 K10 **Yellowknife** *territory capital* Northwest Territories, W Canada *62°30′N 114°29′W*
8 K9 **Yellowknife** ≈ Northwest Territories, NW Canada
23 P8 **Yellow River** ≈ Alabama/Florida, S USA
30 J4 **Yellow River** ≈ Wisconsin, N USA
30 K7 **Yellow River** ≈ Wisconsin, N USA
30 J6 **Yellow River** ≈ Wisconsin, N USA
**Yellow River** *see* Huang He
157 V8 **Yellow Sea** *Chin.* Huang Hai, *Kor.* Hwang-Hae. *sea* E Asia
33 S13 **Yellowstone Lake** ◎ Wyoming, C USA
33 T13 **Yellowstone National Park** *national park* Wyoming, NW USA
33 Y8 **Yellowstone River** ≈ Montana/Wyoming, NW USA
96 L1 **Yell Sound** *strait* N Scotland, United Kingdom
27 U9 **Yellville** Arkansas, C USA *36°12′N 92°41′W*
122 K10 **Yeloguy** ≈ C Russia
**Yëloten** *see* Ýolöten
119 M20 **Yel'sk** Homyel'skaya Voblasts', SE Belarus *51°48′N 29°09′E*
**Yeltyop'iya Fēdēralawī Dēmokrasīyawī Ripeblik** *see* Ethiopia
77 T13 **Yelwa** Kebbi, W Nigeria *10°52′N 04°46′E*
21 R15 **Yemassee** South Carolina, SE USA *32°41′N 80°51′W*
141 O15 **Yemen** *off.* Republic of Yemen, *Ar.* Al Yaman, Al Jumhūrīyah al Yamanīyah. ◆ *republic* SW Asia
**Yemen, Republic of** *see* Yemen
116 M4 **Yemil'chyne** Zhytomyrs'ka Oblast', N Ukraine *50°51′N 27°49′E*
124 M10 **Yemtsa** Arkhangel'skaya Oblast', NW Russia *63°04′N 40°18′E*
124 M10 **Yemtsa** ≈ NW Russia
125 R10 **Yemva** *prev.* Zheleznodorozhnyy. Respublika Komi, NW Russia *62°38′N 50°59′E*
77 U17 **Yenagoa** Bayelsa, S Nigeria *4°58′N 6°16′E*
117 X7 **Yenakiyeve** *Rus.* Yenakiyevo; *prev.* Ordzhonikidze, Rykovo. Donets'ka Oblast', E Ukraine *48°13′N 38°13′E*
**Yenakiyevo** *see* Yenakiyeve
166 L6 **Yenangyaung** Magway, W Myanmar (Burma) *20°28′N 94°54′E*
167 S5 **Yên Bai** Yên Bai, N Vietnam *21°43′N 104°54′E*
183 P9 **Yenda** New South Wales, SE Australia *34°16′S 146°15′E*
77 Q14 **Yendi** NE Ghana *09°30′N 00°01′W*
**Yêndum** *see* Zhag'yab
158 E8 **Yengisar** Xinjiang Uygur Zizhiqu, NW China *38°50′N 76°11′E*
136 H11 **Yenice Çayı** *var.* Filyos Çayı. ≈ N Turkey
121 R1 **Yenierenköy** *var.* Yialousa, *Gk.* Aigialoúsa. NE Cyprus *35°33′N 34°13′E*
**Yenipazar** *see* Novi Pazar
136 E12 **Yenişehir** Bursa, NW Turkey *40°17′N 29°38′E*
**Yenisei Bay** *see* Yeniseyskiy Zaliv
122 K12 **Yeniseysk** Krasnoyarskiy Kray, C Russia *58°23′N 92°06′E*
197 W10 **Yeniseyskiy Zaliv** *var.* Yenisei Bay. *bay* N Russia
127 Q12 **Yenotayevka** Astrakhanskaya Oblast', SW Russia *47°16′N 47°01′E*
124 L4 **Yenozero, Ozero** ◎ NW Russia
**Yenping** *see* Nanping
39 Q11 **Yentna River** ≈ Alaska, USA
180 M10 **Yeo, Lake** *salt lake* Western Australia
163 Z15 **Yeongcheon** *Jap.* Eisen; *prev.* Yŏngch'ŏn. SE South Korea *35°56′N 128°55′E*
163 Y15 **Yeongju** *Jap.* Eishū; *prev.* Yŏngju. C South Korea *36°48′N 128°37′E*
163 Y17 **Yeosu** *Jap.* Reisui; *prev.* Yŏsu. S South Korea *34°45′N 127°41′E*
**Yeotmāl** *see* Yavatmāl
183 R7 **Yeoval** New South Wales, SE Australia *32°45′S 148°39′E*
97 K23 **Yeovil** SW England, United Kingdom *50°57′N 02°39′W*
40 H6 **Yepachic** Chihuahua, N Mexico *28°27′N 108°25′W*
181 Y8 **Yeppoon** Queensland, E Australia *23°05′S 150°42′E*
126 M5 **Yeraktur** Ryazanskaya Oblast', W Russia *54°45′N 41°09′E*
**Yeraliyev** *see* Kuryk
146 F12 **Yerbent** Ahal Welaýaty, C Turkmenistan *39°19′N 58°34′E*
123 N11 **Yerbogachën** Irkutskaya Oblast', C Russia *61°07′N 108°03′E*
137 T12 **Yerevan** *Eng.* Erivan. ● (Armenia) C Armenia *40°12′N 44°31′E*
137 U12 **Yerevan** ✈ C Armenia *40°07′N 44°34′E*
145 R9 **Yereymentau** *var.* Jermentau, *Kaz.* Ereymentaū. Akmola, C Kazakhstan *51°38′N 73°10′E*
145 R9 **Yereymentau, Gory** *prev.* Gory Yermentau. ▲ C Kazakhstan
127 O12 **Yergeni** *hill range* SW Russia
**Yeriho** *see* Jericho
35 R6 **Yerington** Nevada, W USA *38°58′N 119°10′W*
136 J13 **Yerköy** Yozgat, C Turkey *39°39′N 34°28′E*
114 L13 **Yerlisu** Edirne, NW Turkey *40°45′N 26°38′E*
**Yermak** *see* Aksu
**Yermentau, Gory** *see* Yereymentau, Gory
125 R5 **Yërmitsa** Respublika Komi, NW Russia *66°57′N 52°15′E*
35 V14 **Yermo** California, W USA *34°54′N 116°49′W*
123 P13 **Yerofey Pavlovich** Amurskaya Oblast', SE Russia *53°58′N 121°49′E*
99 F15 **Yerseke** Zeeland, SW Netherlands *51°30′N 04°03′E*
127 Q8 **Yershov** Saratovskaya Oblast', W Russia *51°18′N 48°16′E*
145 S7 **Yertis** *Kaz.* Ertis; *prev.* Irtyshsk. Pavlodar, NE Kazakhstan *53°21′N 75°27′E*
129 R5 **Yertis** *var.* Irtish, *Kaz.* Ertis; *prev.* Irtysh. ≈ C Asia
125 P9 **Yërtom** Respublika Komi, NW Russia *63°27′N 47°52′E*
56 D13 **Yerupaja, Nevado** ▲ C Peru *10°23′S 76°58′W*
**Yerushalayim** *see* Jerusalem
105 R4 **Yesa, Embalse de** ⊠ NE Spain
144 F11 **Yesbol** *prev.* Kulagino. Atyrau, W Kazakhstan *48°30′N 51°33′E*
144 F9 **Yesensay** Zapadnyy Kazakhstan, NW Kazakhstan *49°58′N 51°19′E*
144 F9 **Yesensay** Zapadnyy Kazakhstan, NW Kazakhstan *49°59′N 51°19′E*
145 V15 **Yesik** *Kaz.* Esik; *prev.* Issyk. Almaty, SE Kazakhstan *42°23′N 77°25′E*
145 O8 **Yesil'** *Kaz.* Esil. Akmola, C Kazakhstan *51°58′N 66°24′E*
129 R6 **Yesil'** *Kaz.* Esil. ≈ Kazakhstan/Russia
136 K15 **Yeşilhisar** Kayseri, C Turkey *38°22′N 35°08′E*
136 L11 **Yeşilırmak** *var.* Iris. ≈ N Turkey
37 U12 **Yeso** New Mexico, SW USA *34°25′N 104°36′W*
**Yeso** *see* Hokkaidō
127 N15 **Yessentuki** Stavropol'skiy Kray, SW Russia *44°06′N 42°51′E*
122 M9 **Yessey** Krasnoyarskiy Kray, N Russia *68°18′N 101°49′E*
105 P12 **Yeste** Castilla-La Mancha, C Spain *38°21′N 02°18′W*
**Yesuj** *see* Yāsūj
183 T4 **Yetman** New South Wales, SE Australia *28°56′S 150°47′E*
76 L4 **Yetti** *physical region* N Mauritania
166 M4 **Ye-u** Sagaing, C Myanmar (Burma) *22°49′N 95°26′E*
102 H9 **Yeu, Île d'** *island* NW France
**Yevlakh** *see* Yevlax
137 W11 **Yevlax** *Rus.* Yevlakh. C Azerbaijan *40°36′N 47°10′E*
117 S13 **Yevpatoriya** Avtonomna Respublika Krym, S Ukraine *45°12′N 33°23′E*
**Ye Xian** *see* Laizhou
126 K12 **Yeya** ≈ SW Russia
158 I10 **Yeyik** Xinjiang Uygur Zizhiqu, W China *36°44′N 83°14′E*
126 K12 **Yeysk** Krasnodarskiy Kray, SW Russia *46°41′N 38°15′E*
**Yezd** *see* Yazd
**Yezerishche** *see* Yezyaryshcha
**Yezhou** *see* Jianshi
**Yezo** *see* Hokkaidō
118 N11 **Yezyaryshcha** *Rus.* Yezerishche. Vitsyebskaya Voblasts', NE Belarus *55°50′N 29°59′E*
**Yialí** *see* Gyalí
**Yialousa** *see* Yenierenköy
163 V7 **Yi'an** Heilongjiang, NE China *47°52′N 125°13′E*
**Yiannitsá** *see* Giannitsá
160 I10 **Yibin** Sichuan, C China *28°50′N 104°35′E*
158 K13 **Yibug Caka** ◎ W China
160 M9 **Yichang** Hubei, C China *30°37′N 111°02′E*
160 L5 **Yichuan** *var.* Danzhou. Shaanxi, C China *36°05′N 110°02′E*
157 W3 **Yichun** Heilongjiang, NE China *47°41′N 129°10′E*
161 O11 **Yichun** Jiangxi, S China *27°45′N 114°22′E*
160 M9 **Yidu** *prev.* Zhicheng. Hubei, C China *30°21′N 111°27′E*
**Yidu** *see* Qingzhou
188 C15 **Yigo** NE Guam *13°33′N 144°53′E*
161 Q5 **Yi He** ≈ E China
163 X8 **Yilan** Heilongjiang, NE China *46°18′N 129°36′E*
136 C9 **Yıldız Dağları** ▲ NW Turkey
136 L13 **Yıldızeli** Sivas, N Turkey *39°52′N 36°37′E*
163 U4 **Yilehuli Shan** ▲ NE China
163 S7 **Yimin He** ≈ NE China
159 W8 **Yinchuan** *var.* Yinch'uan, Yin-ch'uan, Yinchwan. *province capital* Ningxia, N China *38°30′N 106°19′E*
**Yinchwan** *see* Yinchuan
**Yindu He** *see* Indus
**Yingcheng** *see* Yingde
161 N14 **Yingde** *var.* Yingcheng. Guangdong, S China *24°08′N 113°21′E*
161 O7 **Ying He** ≈ C China
163 U13 **Yingkou** *var.* Ying-k'ou, Yingkow; *prev.* Newchwang, Niuchwang. Liaoning, NE China *40°40′N 122°17′E*
**Yingkow** *see* Yingkou
161 P9 **Yingshan** *var.* Wenquan. Hubei, C China *30°45′N 115°41′E*
161 Q10 **Yingtan** Jiangxi, S China *28°17′N 117°03′E*
**Yin-hsien** *see* Ningbo
158 H5 **Yining** *var.* I-ning, *Uigh.* Gulja, Kuldja. Xinjiang Uygur Zizhiqu, NW China *43°53′N 81°18′E*
160 K11 **Yinjiang** *var.* Yinjiang Tujiazu Miaozu Zizhixian. Guizhou, S China *28°22′N 108°07′E*
**Yinjiang Tujiazu Miaozu Zizhixian** *see* Yinjiang
**Yinmabin** *see* Yinmarbin
166 L4 **Yinmarbin** *var.* Yinmabin. Sagaing, C Myanmar (Burma) *22°05′N 94°57′E*
163 N13 **Yin Shan** ▲ N China
**Yinshan** *see* Guangshui
**Yin-tu Ho** *see* Indus
159 P15 **Yi'ong Zangbo** ≈ W China
**Yióura** *see* Gyáros
81 J14 **Yirga 'Alem** *It.* Irgalem. Southern Nationalities, S Ethiopia *06°43′N 38°24′E*
61 E19 **Yí, Río** ≈ C Uruguay
81 E14 **Yirol** Lakes, C South Sudan *06°34′N 30°33′E*
163 S8 **Yirshi** *var.* Yirxie. Nei Mongol Zizhiqu, N China *47°16′N 119°51′E*
**Yirxie** *see* Yirshi
**Yishan** *see* Guanyun
**Yishi** *see* Linyi
161 Q5 **Yishui** Shandong, E China *35°50′N 118°39′E*
**Yisra'el** *see* Israel
**Yisra'el, Medinat** *see* Israel
**Yíthion** *see* Gýtheio
**Yitiaoshan** *see* Jingtai
163 W10 **Yitong** *var.* Yitong Manzu Zizhixian. Jilin, NE China *43°23′N 125°19′E*
**Yitong Manzu Zizhixian** *see* Yitong
159 P5 **Yiwu** *var.* Aratürük. Xinjiang Uygur Zizhiqu, NW China *43°16′N 94°38′E*
163 U12 **Yiwulü Shan** ▲ N China
163 T12 **Yixian** *var.* Yizhou. Liaoning, NE China *41°29′N 121°21′E*
159 R15 **Yixing** Jiangsu, China *31°14′N 119°18′E*
161 N10 **Yiyang** Hunan, S China *28°39′N 112°10′E*
161 Q10 **Yiyang** Jiangxi, S China *28°21′N 117°23′E*
161 N13 **Yizhang** Hunan, S China *25°24′N 112°51′E*
**Yizhou** *see* Yixian
93 K19 **Yläne** Varsinais-Suomi, SW Finland *60°51′N 22°26′E*
93 L14 **Yli-Ii** Pohjois-Pohjanmaa, C Finland *65°21′N 25°55′E*
93 L14 **Ylikiiminki** Pohjois-Pohjanmaa, C Finland *65°00′N 26°10′E*
92 N13 **Yli-Kitka** ◎ NE Finland
93 K17 **Ylistaro** Etelä-Pohjanmaa, W Finland *62°58′N 22°30′E*
92 K13 **Ylitornio** Lappi, NW Finland *66°19′N 23°40′E*
93 L15 **Ylivieska** Pohjois-Pohjanmaa, W Finland *64°05′N 24°30′E*
93 L18 **Ylöjärvi** Pirkanmaa, W Finland *61°31′N 23°37′E*
95 N17 **Yngaren** ◎ C Sweden
25 T12 **Yoakum** Texas, SW USA *29°17′N 97°09′W*
77 X13 **Yobe** ◈ *state* NE Nigeria
165 R3 **Yobetsu-dake** ▲ Hokkaidō, NE Japan *43°15′N 140°27′E*
80 L11 **Yoboki** C Djibouti *11°30′N 42°04′E*
22 M4 **Yockanookany River** ≈ Mississippi, S USA
22 L2 **Yocona River** ≈ Mississippi, S USA
171 Y15 **Yodom** Papua, E Indonesia *07°12′S 139°24′E*
169 Q16 **Yogyakarta** *prev.* Djokjakarta, Jogjakarta, Jokyakarta. Jawa, C Indonesia *07°48′S 110°24′E*
169 P17 **Yogyakarta** *off.* Daerah Istimewa Yogyakarta, *var.* Djokjakarta, Jogjakarta, Jokyakarta. ◈ *autonomous district* S Indonesia
**Yogyakarta, Daerah Istimewa** *see* Yogyakarta
165 Q3 **Yoichi** Hokkaidō, NE Japan *43°11′N 140°45′E*
42 G6 **Yojoa, Lago de** ◎ NW Honduras
79 G16 **Yokadouma** Est, SE Cameroon *03°26′N 15°06′E*
164 K13 **Yokkaichi** *var.* Yokkaiti. Mie, Honshū, SW Japan *34°58′N 136°38′E*
**Yokkaiti** *see* Yokkaichi
79 E15 **Yoko** Centre, C Cameroon *05°29′N 12°19′E*
165 V15 **Yokoate-jima** *island* Nansei-shotō, SW Japan
165 R6 **Yokohama** Aomori, Honshū, C Japan *41°04′N 141°14′E*
165 O14 **Yokosuka** Kanagawa, Honshū, S Japan *35°18′N 139°39′E*
164 G12 **Yokota** Shimane, Honshū, SW Japan *35°10′N 133°03′E*
165 Q9 **Yokote** Akita, Honshū, C Japan *39°20′N 140°33′E*
77 Y14 **Yola** Adamawa, E Nigeria *09°08′N 12°24′E*
79 L19 **Yolombo** Equateur, C Dem. Rep. Congo *01°36′S 23°13′E*
146 J14 **Ýolöten** *Rus.* Yëloten; *prev.* Iolotan'. Mary Welaýaty, S Turkmenistan *37°15′N 62°18′E*
165 Y15 **Yome-jima** *island* Ogasawara-shotō, SE Japan
76 K16 **Yomou** SE Guinea *07°30′N 09°13′W*
171 Y15 **Yomuka** Papua, E Indonesia *07°25′S 138°36′E*
188 C16 **Yona** E Guam *13°24′N 144°46′E*
164 H12 **Yonago** Tottori, Honshū, SW Japan *35°30′N 134°15′E*
165 N16 **Yonaguni** Okinawa, SW Japan *24°29′N 123°00′E*
165 N16 **Yonaguni-jima** *island* Nansei-shotō, SW Japan
165 T16 **Yonaha-dake** ▲ Okinawa, SW Japan *26°43′N 128°13′E*
163 X14 **Yŏnan** SW North Korea *37°50′N 126°15′E*
165 P10 **Yonezawa** Yamagata, Honshū, C Japan *37°56′N 140°06′E*
161 Q12 **Yong'an** *var.* Yongan. Fujian, SE China *25°58′N 117°26′E*
**Yong'an** *see* Fengjie
159 T9 **Yongchang** Gansu, N China *38°15′N 101°56′E*
161 P7 **Yongcheng** Henan, C China *33°56′N 116°21′E*
**Yŏngch'ŏn** *see* Yeongcheon
160 J10 **Yongchuan** Chongqing Shi, C China *29°27′N 105°56′E*
159 U10 **Yongdeng** Gansu, C China *35°58′N 103°27′E*
**Yongding** *see* Yongren
129 W9 **Yongding He** ≈ E China
161 P11 **Yongfeng** *var.* Enjiang. Jiangxi, S China *27°19′N 115°23′E*
158 L5 **Yongfeng** *var.* Yongfengqu. Xinjiang Uygur Zizhiqu, W China *43°28′N 87°09′E*
**Yongfengqu** *see* Yongfeng
160 L13 **Yongfu** Guangxi Zhuangzu Zizhiqu, S China *24°57′N 109°59′E*
163 X13 **Yŏnghŭng** E North Korea *39°31′N 127°14′E*
159 U10 **Yongjing** *var.* Liujiaxia. Gansu, C China *36°00′N 103°30′E*
**Yongjing** *see* Xifeng
**Yŏngju** *see* Yeongju
**Yongle Qundao** *see* Crescent Group
**Yongning** *see* Xuyong
160 E12 **Yongping** Yunnan, SW China *25°30′N 99°28′E*
160 G12 **Yongren** *var.* Yongding. Yunnan, SW China *26°09′N 101°40′E*
160 L10 **Yongshun** *var.* Lingxi. Hunan, S China *29°02′N 109°46′E*
161 P10 **Yongxiu** *var.* Tujiabu. Jiangxi, S China *29°09′N 115°47′E*
**Yongzhou** *see* Lingling
**Yongzhou** *see* Zhishan
18 K14 **Yonkers** New York, NE USA *40°56′N 73°51′W*
103 Q7 **Yonne** ◈ *department* C France
103 P6 **Yonne** ≈ C France
54 H9 **Yopal** *var.* El Yopal. Casanare, C Colombia *05°20′N 72°19′W*
158 E8 **Yopurga** *var.* Yukuriawat. Xinjiang Uygur Zizhiqu, NW China *39°13′N 76°44′E*
147 S11 **Yordon** *var.* Iordan, *Rus.* Jardan. Farg'ona Viloyati, E Uzbekistan *39°59′N 71°44′E*
180 J12 **York** Western Australia *31°55′S 116°52′E*
97 M16 **York** *anc.* Eboracum, Eburacum. N England, United Kingdom *53°58′N 01°05′W*
23 N5 **York** Alabama, S USA *32°29′N 88°18′W*
29 Q15 **York** Nebraska, C USA *40°52′N 97°35′W*
18 G16 **York** Pennsylvania, NE USA *39°57′N 76°44′W*
21 R11 **York** South Carolina, SE USA *34°59′N 81°14′W*
14 J13 **York** ≈ Ontario, SE Canada
15 X6 **York** ≈ Québec, SE Canada
181 V1 **York, Cape** *headland* Queensland, NE Australia *10°40′S 142°36′E*
182 I9 **Yorke Peninsula** *peninsula* South Australia
182 I9 **Yorketown** South Australia *35°01′S 137°38′E*
19 P9 **York Harbor** Maine, NE USA *43°10′N 70°37′W*
**York, Kap** *see* Innaanganeq
21 X6 **York River** ≈ Virginia, NE USA
97 M16 **Yorkshire** *cultural region* N England, United Kingdom
97 L16 **Yorkshire Dales** *physical region* N England, United Kingdom
11 V16 **Yorkton** Saskatchewan, S Canada *51°12′N 102°29′W*
25 T12 **Yorktown** Texas, SW USA *28°58′N 97°30′W*
21 X6 **Yorktown** Virginia, NE USA *37°14′N 76°32′W*
30 M11 **Yorkville** Illinois, N USA *41°38′N 88°27′W*
42 I5 **Yoro** Yoro, C Honduras *15°08′N 87°10′W*
42 H5 **Yoro** ◈ *department* N Honduras
165 T16 **Yoron-jima** *island* Nansei-shotō, SW Japan
77 N13 **Yorosso** Sikasso, S Mali *12°21′N 04°47′W*
35 R8 **Yosemite National Park** *national park* California, W USA
127 Q3 **Yoshkar-Ola** Respublika Mariy El, W Russia *56°38′N 47°54′E*
**Yösönbulag** *see* Altay
162 K8 **Yösöndzüyl** *var.* Mönhbulag. Övörhangay, C Mongolia *46°48′N 103°25′E*
171 Y16 **Yos Sudarso, Pulau** *var.* Pulau Dolak, Pulau Kolepom; *prev.* Jos Sudarso. *island* E Indonesia
**Yŏsu** *see* Yeosu
165 R4 **Yotei-zan** ▲ Hokkaidō, NE Japan *42°50′N 140°46′E*
97 D21 **Youghal** *Ir.* Eochaill. Cork, S Ireland *51°57′N 07°50′W*
97 D21 **Youghal Bay** *Ir.* Cuan Eochaille. *inlet* S Ireland
18 C15 **Youghiogheny River** ≈ Pennsylvania, NE USA
160 K14 **You Jiang** ≈ S China
183 Q9 **Young** New South Wales, SE Australia *34°19′S 148°20′E*
11 T15 **Young** Saskatchewan, S Canada *51°44′N 105°44′W*
61 E18 **Young** Río Negro, W Uruguay *32°44′S 57°36′W*
182 G5 **Younghusband, Lake** *salt lake* South Australia
182 J10 **Younghusband Peninsula** *peninsula* South Australia
184 Q10 **Young Nicks Head** *headland* North Island, New Zealand *39°38′S 177°03′E*
185 D20 **Young Range** ▲ South Island, New Zealand
191 Q15 **Young's Rock** *island* Pitcairn Island, Pitcairn Islands
11 R16 **Youngstown** Alberta, SW Canada *51°32′N 111°12′W*
31 V12 **Youngstown** Ohio, N USA *41°06′N 80°39′W*
159 N9 **Youshashan** Qinghai, C China *38°12′N 90°58′E*
**Youth, Isle of** *see* Juventud, Isla de la
77 N11 **Youvarou** Mopti, C Mali *15°19′N 04°15′W*
160 K10 **Youyang** *var.* Zhongduo. Chongqing Shi, C China *28°48′N 108°48′E*
163 Y7 **Youyi** Heilongjiang, NE China *46°51′N 131°54′E*
147 P13 **Yovon** *Rus.* Yavan. SW Tajikistan *38°19′N 69°02′E*
136 J13 **Yozgat** Yozgat, C Turkey *39°49′N 34°48′E*
136 K13 **Yozgat** ◈ *province* C Turkey
62 O6 **Ypacaraí** *var.* Ypacaray. Central, S Paraguay *25°23′S 57°16′W*
**Ypacaray** *see* Ypacaraí
62 P5 **Ypané, Río** ≈ C Paraguay
**Ypres** *see* Ieper
114 I13 **Ypsário** *var.* Ipsario. ▲ Thásos, E Greece *40°43′N 24°39′E*
31 R10 **Ypsilanti** Michigan, N USA *42°12′N 83°36′W*
34 M1 **Yreka** California, W USA *41°43′N 122°39′W*
**Yrendagüé** *see* General Eugenio A. Garay
144 L11 **Yrghyz** *prev.* Irgiz. Aktyubinsk, C Kazakhstan *48°36′N 61°14′E*
186 G5 **Ysabel Channel** *channel* N Papua New Guinea
14 K8 **Yser, Lac** ◎ Québec, SE Canada
147 Y8 **Yshtyk** Issyk-Kul'skaya Oblast', E Kyrgyzstan *41°34′N 78°21′E*
**Yssel** *see* IJssel
103 Q12 **Yssingeaux** Haute-Loire, C France *45°09′N 04°07′E*
95 K23 **Ystad** Skåne, S Sweden *55°25′N 13°51′E*
**Ysyk-Köl** *see* Issyk-Kul', Ozero
**Ysyk-Köl** *see* Balykchy
**Ysyk-Köl Oblasty** *see* Issyk-Kul'skaya Oblast'
96 L8 **Ythan** ≈ NE Scotland, United Kingdom
**Y Trallwng** *see* Welshpool
94 C13 **Ytre Arna** Hordaland, S Norway *60°28′N 05°25′E*
94 B12 **Ytre Sula** *island* S Norway
93 G17 **Ytterhogdal** Jämtland, C Sweden *62°10′N 14°55′E*
**Yu** *see* Henan
**Yuan** *see* Red River
**Yuancheng** *see* Heyuan, Guangdong, S China
**Yuan Jiang** *see* Red River
161 N3 **Yuanping** Shanxi, C China *38°26′N 112°42′E*
**Yuanquan** *see* Anxi
**Yuanshan** *see* Lianping
161 O11 **Yuan Shui** ≈ S China
35 O6 **Yuba City** California, W USA *39°07′N 121°40′W*
35 O6 **Yuba River** ≈ California, W USA
80 H13 **Yubdo** Oromīya, C Ethiopia *09°05′N 35°28′E*
41 X12 **Yucatán** ◈ *state* SE Mexico
47 O3 **Yucatan Basin** *var.* Yucatan Deep. *undersea feature* N Caribbean Sea *20°00′N 84°00′W*
**Yucatán, Canal de** *see* Yucatan Channel
41 Y10 **Yucatan Channel** *Sp.* Canal de Yucatán. *channel* Cuba/Mexico
**Yucatan Deep** *see* Yucatan Basin
**Yucatan Peninsula** *see* Yucatán, Península de
41 X13 **Yucatán, Península de** *Eng.* Yucatan Peninsula. *peninsula* Guatemala/Mexico
36 I11 **Yucca** Arizona, SW USA *34°49′N 114°06′W*
35 V15 **Yucca Valley** California, W USA *34°06′N 116°30′W*
161 P4 **Yucheng** Shandong, E China *37°01′N 116°37′E*
**Yuci** *see* Jinzhong
129 X5 **Yudoma** ≈ E Russia
161 P12 **Yudu** *var.* Gongjiang. Jiangxi, C China *26°02′N 115°24′E*
**Yue** *see* Guangdong
**Yuecheng** *see* Yuexi
160 M12 **Yuecheng Ling** ▲ S China
**Yuegai** *see* Qumarlêb
**Yuegaitan** *see* Qumarlêb
181 P7 **Yuendumu** Northern Territory, N Australia *22°19′S 131°51′E*
**Yue Shan, Tai** *see* Lantau Island
160 H10 **Yuexi** *var.* Yuecheng. Sichuan, C China *28°50′N 102°36′E*
161 N10 **Yueyang** Hunan, S China *29°24′N 113°08′E*
125 U14 **Yug** Permskiy Kray, NW Russia *57°49′N 56°08′E*
125 P13 **Yug** ≈ NW Russia
123 R10 **Yugorënok** Respublika Sakha (Yakutiya), NE Russia *59°46′N 137°36′E*
122 H9 **Yugorsk** Khanty-Mansiyskiy Avtonomnyy Okrug-Yugra, C Russia *61°17′N 63°25′E*
122 H7 **Yugorskiy Poluostrov** *peninsula* NW Russia
**Yugoslavia** *see* Serbia
146 K14 **Yugo-Vostochnyye Garagumy** *prev.* Yugo-Vostochnyye Karakumy. *desert* E Turkmenistan
**Yugo-Vostochnyye Karakumy** *see* Yugo-Vostochnyye Garagumy
**Yuhu** *see* Eryuan
161 S10 **Yuhuan Dao** *island* SE China
160 L14 **Yu Jiang** ≈ S China
**Yujin** *see* Qianwei
159 P9 **Yuka** Qinghai W China *38°03′N 94°45′E*
123 S7 **Yukagirskoye Ploskogor'ye** *plateau* NE Russia
159 P9 **Yuke He** ≈ C China
118 L11 **Yukhavichy** *Rus.* Yukhovichi. Vitsyebskaya Voblasts', N Belarus *56°02′N 28°39′E*
126 J4 **Yukhnov** Kaluzhskaya Oblast', W Russia *54°43′N 35°15′E*
**Yukhovichi** *see* Yukhavichy
79 J20 **Yuki** *var.* Yuki Kengunda. Bandundu, W Dem. Rep. Congo *03°57′S 19°30′E*
**Yuki Kengunda** *see* Yuki
26 M10 **Yukon** Oklahoma, C USA *35°30′N 97°45′W*
10 I5 **Yukon** *prev.* Yukon Territory, *Fr.* Territoire du Yukon. ◈ *territory* NW Canada
0 F4 **Yukon** ≈ Canada/USA
39 S7 **Yukon Flats** *salt flat* Alaska, USA
**Yukon, Territoire du** *see* Yukon
**Yukon Territory** *see* Yukon
137 T16 **Yüksekova** Hakkâri, SE Turkey *37°35′N 44°17′E*
123 N10 **Yukta** Krasnoyarskiy Kray, C Russia *63°16′N 106°04′E*
165 O13 **Yukuhashi** *var.* Yukuhasi. Fukuoka, Kyūshū, SW Japan *33°41′N 131°00′E*
**Yukuhasi** *see* Yukuhashi
**Yukuriawat** *see* Yopurga
125 O9 **Yula** ≈ NW Russia
181 P8 **Yulara** Northern Territory, N Australia *25°15′S 130°57′E*
127 W6 **Yuldybayevo** Respublika Bashkortostan, W Russia *52°22′N 57°55′E*
23 W8 **Yulee** Florida, SE USA *30°37′N 81°36′W*
158 K7 **Yuli** *var.* Lopnur. Xinjiang Uygur Zizhiqu, NW China *41°24′N 86°12′E*
161 T14 **Yuli** *prev.* Yüli. C Taiwan *23°23′N 121°18′E*
160 L15 **Yulin** Guangxi Zhuangzu Zizhiqu, S China *22°37′N 110°08′E*
160 L4 **Yulin** Shaanxi, C China *38°14′N 109°48′E*
161 T14 **Yuli Shan** *prev.* Yüli Shan. ▲ E Taiwan *23°23′N 121°14′E*
160 F11 **Yulong Xueshan** ▲ SW China *27°09′N 100°10′E*
36 H14 **Yuma** Arizona, SW USA *32°40′N 114°38′W*
37 W3 **Yuma** Colorado, C USA *40°07′N 102°43′W*
54 K5 **Yumare** Yaracuy, N Venezuela *10°37′N 68°41′W*
63 G14 **Yumbel** Bío Bío, C Chile *37°05′S 72°40′W*
79 N19 **Yumbi** Maniema, E Dem. Rep. Congo *01°14′S 26°14′E*
159 Q7 **Yumen** *prev.* Yumenzhen. Gansu, N China *40°19′N 97°12′E*
159 R8 **Yumendong** *prev.* Laojunmiao. Gansu, N China *39°49′N 97°47′E*
**Yumenzhen** *see* Yumen
158 J3 **Yumin** *var.* Karabura. Xinjiang Uygur Zizhiqu, NW China *46°14′N 82°52′E*
**Yun** *see* Yunnan
136 G14 **Yunak** Konya, W Turkey *38°50′N 31°42′E*
45 O8 **Yuna, Río** ≈ E Dominican Republic
38 I17 **Yunaska Island** *island* Aleutian Islands, Alaska, USA
160 M6 **Yuncheng** Shanxi, C China *35°07′N 110°45′E*
**Yuncheng** *see* Yunfu
161 N14 **Yunfu** *var.* Yuncheng. Guangdong, S China *22°56′N 112°02′E*
57 L18 **Yungas** *physical region* E Bolivia
**Yungki** *see* Jilin
**Yung-ning** *see* Nanning
160 I12 **Yungui Gaoyuan** *plateau* SW China
**Yunjinghong** *see* Jinghong
160 M15 **Yunkai Dashan** ▲ S China
**Yunki** *see* Jilin
161 S13 **Yunlin** *Jap.* Unrin; *prev.* Yuanlin. C Taiwan *23°57′N 120°33′E*
160 E11 **Yun Ling** ▲ SW China
**Yunling** *see* Yunxiao
161 N9 **Yunmeng** Hubei, C China *31°04′N 113°45′E*
157 N14 **Yunnan** *var.* Yun, Yunnan Sheng, Yünnan, Yun-nan. ◈ *province* SW China
**Yunnan** *see* Kunming
**Yunnan Sheng** *see* Yunnan
**Yünnan/Yun-nan** *see* Yunnan
165 P15 **Yunomae** Kumamoto, Kyūshū, SW Japan *32°16′N 131°00′E*
161 N8 **Yun Shui** ≈ C China
182 J7 **Yunta** South Australia *32°37′S 139°33′E*
161 Q14 **Yunxiao** *var.* Yunling. Fujian, SE China *23°56′N 117°16′E*
160 K9 **Yunyang** Sichuan, C China *31°03′N 109°43′E*
**Yunzhong** *see* Huairen
193 S9 **Yupanqui Basin** *undersea feature* E Pacific Ocean
**Yuping** *see* Libo, Guizhou, China
**Yuping** *see* Pingbian, Yunnan, China
**Yuratishki** *see* Yuratsishki
119 I15 **Yuratsishki** *Pol.* Juraciszki, *Rus.* Yuratishki. Hrodzyenskaya Voblasts', W Belarus *54°02′N 25°56′E*
**Yurev** *see* Tartu
122 J12 **Yurga** Kemerovskaya Oblast', S Russia *55°42′N 84°59′E*
**Yurihonjō** *see* Honjō
56 E10 **Yurimaguas** Loreto, N Peru *05°54′S 76°07′W*
127 P3 **Yurino** Respublika Mariy El, W Russia *56°19′N 46°15′E*
41 N13 **Yuriria** Guanajuato, C Mexico *20°12′N 101°09′W*
125 T13 **Yurla** Komi-Permyatskiy Okrug, NW Russia *59°18′N 54°19′E*
**Yuruá, Río** *see* Juruá, Rio
114 M13 **Yürük** Tekirdağ, NW Turkey *40°58′N 27°09′E*
158 G10 **Yurungkax He** ≈ W China
125 Q14 **Yur'ya** *var.* Jarja. Kirovskaya Oblast', NW Russia *59°01′N 49°22′E*
**Yur'yev** *see* Tartu
125 N16 **Yur'yevets** Ivanovskaya Oblast', W Russia *57°19′N 43°01′E*
126 M3 **Yur'yev-Pol'skiy** Vladimirskaya Oblast', W Russia *56°28′N 39°39′E*
117 V7 **Yur"yivka** Dnipropetrovs'ka Oblast', E Ukraine *48°45′N 36°01′E*
42 I7 **Yuscarán** El Paraíso, S Honduras *13°55′N 86°51′W*
161 P12 **Yu Shan** ▲ S China
124 I7 **Yushkozero** Respublika Kareliya, NW Russia *64°46′N 32°13′E*
124 I7 **Yushkozerskoye Vodokhranilishche** *var.* Ozero Kujto. ⊠ NW Russia
159 R13 **Yushu** *var.* Gyêgu. Qinghai, C China *33°04′N 97°E*
127 P12 **Yusta** Respublika Kalmykiya, SW Russia *47°06′N 46°16′E*
124 I10 **Yustozero** Respublika Kareliya, NW Russia *62°44′N 33°31′E*
137 Q11 **Yusufeli** Artvin, NE Turkey *40°50′N 41°31′E*
164 F14 **Yusuhara** Kōchi, Shikoku, SW Japan *33°22′N 132°52′E*
125 T14 **Yus'va** Permskiy Kray, NW Russia *58°48′N 54°59′E*
**Yuta** *see* Yatta
161 P2 **Yutian** Hebei, E China *39°52′N 117°44′E*
158 H10 **Yutian** *var.* Keriya, Mugalla. Xinjiang Uygur Zizhiqu, NW China *36°49′N 81°31′E*
62 K5 **Yuto** Jujuy, NW Argentina *23°35′S 64°28′W*
62 P7 **Yuty** Caazapá, S Paraguay *26°31′S 56°20′W*
160 G13 **Yuxi** Yunnan, SW China *24°22′N 102°28′E*
161 O2 **Yuxian** *prev.* Yu Xian. Hebei, E China *39°50′N 114°33′E*
**Yu Xian** *see* Yuxian
165 Q9 **Yuzawa** Akita, Honshū, C Japan *39°11′N 140°29′E*
125 N16 **Yuzha** Ivanovskaya Oblast', W Russia *56°34′N 42°00′E*
**Yuzhno-Alichurskiy Khrebet** *see* Alichuri Janubí, Qatorkŭhi
**Yuzhno-Kazakhstanskaya Oblast'** *see* Turkestan
123 T13 **Yuzhno-Sakhalinsk** *Jap.* Toyohara; *prev.* Vladimirovka. Ostrov Sakhalin, Sakhalinskaya Oblast', SE Russia *46°58′N 142°45′E*
127 P14 **Yuzhno-Sukhokumsk** Respublika Dagestan, SW Russia *44°43′N 45°32′E*
145 Z10 **Yuzhnyy Altay, Khrebet** ▲ E Kazakhstan
**Yuzhnyy Bug** *see* Pivdennyy Buh
123 U10 **Yuzhnyy, Mys** *headland* E Russia *57°44′N 156°49′E*
122 H6 **Yuzhnyy, Ostrov** *island* NW Russia
127 W6 **Yuzhnyy Ural** *var.* Southern Urals. ▲ W Russia
159 V10 **Yuzhong** Gansu, C China *35°52′N 104°09′E*
**Yuzhou** *see* Chongqing
103 N5 **Yvelines** ◈ *department* N France
108 B9 **Yverdon** *var.* Yverdon-les-Bains, *Ger.* Iferten; *anc.* Eborodunum. Vaud, W Switzerland *46°47′N 06°38′E*
**Yverdon-les-Bains** *see* Yverdon
102 M3 **Yvetot** Seine-Maritime, N France *49°37′N 00°48′E*
**Ýylanly** *see* Gurbansoltan Eje


# Z


147 T12 **Zaalayskiy Khrebet** *Taj.* Qatorkŭhi Pasi Oloy. ▲ Kyrgyzstan/Tajikistan
**Zaamin** *see* Zomin
**Zaandam** *see* Zaanstad
98 I10 **Zaanstad** *prev.* Zaandam. Noord-Holland, C Netherlands *52°27′N 04°49′E*
**Zabadani** *see* Az Zabdānī
**Zabalatstsye** *see* Zabolottsye
112 L9 **Žabalj** *Ger.* Josefsdorf, *Hung.* Zsablya; *prev.* Józseffalva. Vojvodina, N Serbia *45°22′N 20°01′E*


◆ Country ● Country Capital ◇ Dependent Territory ○ Dependent Territory Capital ◈ Administrative Regions ✈ International Airport ▲ Mountain ▲ Mountain Range ▲ Volcano ≈ River ◎ Lake ⊠ Reservoir

ZABALOTSTSYE – ZHETYSUSKIY ALATAU


119 L18 **Zabalotstsye** *prev.* Zabalatstsye, *Rus.* Zabolot'ye. Homyel'skaya Voblasts', SE Belarus *52°40′N 28°34′E*
**Zāb aş Şaghīr, Nahraz** *see* Little Zab
123 P14 **Zabaykal'sk** Zabaykal'skiy Kray, S Russia *49°37′N 117°20′E*
123 O12 **Zabaykal'skiy Kray** ◈ *autonomous district* S Russia
**Zāb-e Kūchek, Rūdkhāneh-ye** *see* Little Zab
**Zabeln** *see* Sabile
**Zabéré** *see* Zabré
**Zabern** *see* Saverne
141 N16 **Zabīd** W Yemen *14°N 43°E*
141 O16 **Zabīd, Wādī** *dry watercourse* SW Yemen
**Żabinka** *see* Zhabinka
**Ząbkowice** *see* Ząbkowice Śląskie
111 G15 **Ząbkowice Śląskie** *var.* Ząbkowice, *Ger.* Frankenstein, Frankenstein in Schlesien. Dolnośląskie, SW Poland *50°35′N 16°48′E*
110 P10 **Zabłudów** Podlaskie, NE Poland *53°00′N 23°21′E*
112 D8 **Zabok** Krapina-Zagorje, N Croatia *46°00′N 15°48′E*
143 W9 **Zābol** *var.* Shahr-i-Zabul, Zabul; *prev.* Nasratabad. Sīstān va Balūchestān, E Iran *31°N 61°32′E*
**Zābol** *see* Zābul
143 W13 **Zābolī** Sīstān va Balūchestān, SE Iran *27°09′N 61°32′E*
**Zabolot'ye** *see* Zabalotstsye
77 Q13 **Zabré** *var.* Zabéré. S Burkina Faso *11°13′N 00°34′W*
111 G17 **Zábřeh** *Ger.* Hohenstadt. Olomoucký Kraj, E Czechia *49°52′N 16°53′E*
111 J16 **Zabrze** *Ger.* Hindenburg, Hindenburg in Oberschlesien. Śląskie, S Poland *50°18′N 18°47′E*
149 O7 **Zābul** *prev.* Zābol. ◈ *province* SE Afghanistan
**Zabul/Zābul** *see* Zābol
42 E6 **Zacapa** Zacapa, E Guatemala *14°59′N 89°33′W*
42 A3 **Zacapa** *off.* Departamento de Zacapa. ◈ *department* E Guatemala
**Zacapa, Departamento de** *see* Zacapa
40 M14 **Zacapú** Michoacán, SW Mexico *19°49′N 101°48′W*
41 V14 **Zacatal** Campeche, SE Mexico *18°40′N 91°52′W*
40 M11 **Zacatecas** Zacatecas, C Mexico *22°46′N 102°33′W*
40 L10 **Zacatecas** ◈ *state* C Mexico
42 F8 **Zacatecoluca** La Paz, S El Salvador *13°29′N 88°51′W*
41 P15 **Zacatepec** Morelos, S Mexico *18°40′N 99°11′W*
41 Q13 **Zacatlán** Puebla, S Mexico *19°56′N 97°58′W*
144 F8 **Zachagansk** *Kaz.* Zashaghan. Zapadnyy Kazakhstan, NW Kazakhstan *51°04′N 51°13′E*
115 D20 **Zacháro** *var.* Zaharo, Zakháro. Dytikí Elláda, S Greece *37°29′N 21°40′E*
22 J8 **Zachary** Louisiana, S USA *30°39′N 91°09′W*
117 U6 **Zachepylivka** Kharkivs'ka Oblast', E Ukraine *49°13′N 35°15′E*
**Zachist'ye** *see* Zachystsye
110 E9 **Zachodnio-pomorskie** ◈ *province* NW Poland
119 L14 **Zachystsye** *Rus.* Zachist'ye. Minskaya Voblasts', NW Belarus *54°24′N 28°45′E*
40 L13 **Zacoalco** *var.* Zacoalco de Torres. Jalisco, SW Mexico *20°14′N 103°33′W*
**Zacoalco de Torres** *see* Zacoalco
41 P13 **Zacualtipán** Hidalgo, C Mexico *20°39′N 98°42′W*
112 C12 **Zadar** *It.* Zara; *anc.* Iader. Zadar, SW Croatia *44°07′N 15°15′E*
112 C12 **Zadar** *off.* Zadarsko-Kninska Županija, Zadar-Knin. ◈ *province* SW Croatia
**Zadar-Knin** *see* Zadar
**Zadarsko-Kninska Županija** *see* Zadar
166 M14 **Zadetkyi Kyun** *var.* St.Matthew's Island. *island* Mergui Archipelago, S Myanmar (Burma)
67 Q9 **Zadié** *var.* Djadié. ≈ NE Gabon
159 Q13 **Zadoi** *var.* Qapugtang. Qinghai, C China *32°56′N 95°21′E*
126 L7 **Zadonsk** Lipetskaya Oblast', W Russia *52°25′N 38°55′E*
**Za'farâna** *see* Za'farānah
75 X8 **Za'farānah** *var.* Za'farâna. E Egypt *29°06′N 32°34′E*
149 W7 **Zafarwal** Punjab, E Pakistan *32°20′N 74°53′E*
121 Q1 **Zafer Burnu** *var.* Cape Andreas, Cape Apostolos Andreas, *Gk.* Akrotírio Apostólou Andréa. *cape* NE Cyprus
107 J23 **Zafferano, Capo** *headland* Sicilia, Italy, C Mediterranean Sea *38°06′N 13°31′E*
114 M7 **Zafirovo** Silistra, NE Bulgaria *44°00′N 26°51′E*
**Záfora** *see* Sofraná
104 J12 **Zafra** Extremadura, W Spain *38°25′N 06°27′W*
110 E13 **Żagań** *var.* Zagań, Żegań, *Ger.* Sagan. Lubuskie, W Poland *51°37′N 15°20′E*
118 F10 **Žagarė** *Pol.* Żagory. Šiaulai, N Lithuania *56°22′N 23°16′E*
**Zagazig** *see* Az Zaqāzīq
74 M5 **Zaghouan** *var.* Zaghwān. NE Tunisia *36°26′N 10°05′E*
**Zaghwān** *see* Zaghouan
115 G16 **Zagorá** Thessalía, C Greece *39°27′N 23°06′E*
**Zagorod'ye** *see* Zaharoddzye
**Żagory** *see* Žagarė
**Zágráb** *see* Zagreb
112 E8 **Zagreb** *Ger.* Agram, *Hung.* Zágráb. ● (Croatia) Zagreb, N Croatia *45°48′N 15°58′E*
112 E8 **Zagreb** *prev.* Grad Zagreb. ◈ *province* N Croatia
142 L7 **Zāgros, Kūhhā-ye** *Eng.* Zagros Mountains. ▲▲ W Iran
**Zagros Mountains** *see* Zāgros, Kūhhā-ye
112 O12 **Žagubica** Serbia, E Serbia *44°13′N 21°47′E*
**Zagunao** *see* Lixian
111 L22 **Zagyva** ≈ N Hungary
**Zaharo** *see* Zacháro
119 G19 **Zaharoddzye** *Rus.* Zagorod'ye. *physical region* SW Belarus
143 W11 **Zāhedān** *var.* Zahidan; *prev.* Duzdab. Sīstān va Balūchestān, SE Iran *29°31′N 60°51′E*
**Zahidan** *see* Zāhedān
**Zaḩlah** *see* Zahlé
138 H7 **Zahlé** *var.* Zaḩlah. C Lebanon *33°51′N 35°54′E*
146 J14 **Zähmet** *Rus.* Zakhmet. Mary Welaýaty, C Turkmenistan *37°48′N 62°33′E*
111 O20 **Záhony** Szabolcs-Szatmár-Bereg, NE Hungary *48°26′N 22°11′E*
141 N13 **Z̧ahrān** 'Asīr, S Saudi Arabia *17°48′N 43°28′E*
139 R12 **Z̧ahrat al Baţn** *hill range* S Iraq
120 H11 **Zahrez Chergui** *var.* Zahrez Chergúi. *marsh* N Algeria
**Zainlha** *see* Xinjin
127 S4 **Zainsk** Respublika Tatarstan, W Russia *55°12′N 52°01′E*
82 A10 **Zaire** *prev.* Congo. ◈ *province* NW Angola
**Zaire** *see* Congo (river)
**Zaire** *see* Congo (Democratic Republic of)
112 P13 **Zaječar** Serbia, E Serbia *43°54′N 22°16′E*
83 L18 **Zaka** Masvingo, E Zimbabwe *20°20′S 31°29′E*
122 M14 **Zakamensk** Respublika Buryatiya, S Russia *50°18′N 102°57′E*
116 G7 **Zakarpats'ka Oblast'** *Eng.* Transcarpathian Oblast, *Rus.* Zakarpatskaya Oblast'. ◈ *province* W Ukraine
**Zakarpatskaya Oblast'** *see* Zakarpats'ka Oblast'
**Zakataly** *see* Zaqatala
117 O9 **Zakharivka** *prev.* Frunzivka. Odes'ka Oblast', SW Ukraine *47°19′N 29°46′E*
**Zakháro** *see* Zacháro
**Zakhidnyy Buh/Zakhodni Buh** *see* Bug
**Zakhmet** *see* Zähmet
**Zākhō** *see* Zaxo
**Zākhū** *see* Zaxo
**Zákinthos** *see* Zákynthos
111 L18 **Zakopane** Małopolskie, S Poland *49°17′N 19°57′E*
78 J12 **Zakouma** Salamat, S Chad *10°47′N 19°51′E*
115 L25 **Zákros** Kríti, Greece, E Mediterranean Sea *35°06′N 26°12′E*
115 C19 **Zákynthos** *var.* Zákinthos. Zákynthos, W Greece *37°47′N 20°54′E*
115 C20 **Zákynthos** *var.* Zákinthos, *It.* Zante. *island* Iónia Nísoi, Greece, C Mediterranean Sea
115 C19 **Zakýnthou, Porthmós** *strait* SW Greece
111 G24 **Zala** *off.* Zala Megye. ◈ *county* W Hungary
111 G24 **Zala** ≈ W Hungary
138 M4 **Zalābiyah** Dayr az Zawr, C Syria *35°39′N 39°51′E*
111 G24 **Zalaegerszeg** Zala, W Hungary *46°51′N 16°49′E*
104 K11 **Zalamea de la Serena** Extremadura, W Spain *38°38′N 05°37′W*
104 J13 **Zalamea la Real** Andalucía, S Spain *37°41′N 06°40′W*
**Zala Megye** *see* Zala
163 U7 **Zalantun** *var.* Butha Qi. Nei Mongol Zizhiqu, N China *47°58′N 122°44′E*
111 G23 **Zalaszentgrót** Zala, SW Hungary *46°57′N 17°05′E*
**Zalatna** *see* Zlatna
116 G9 **Zalău** *Ger.* Waltenberg, *Hung.* Zilah; *prev. Ger.* Zillenmarkt. Sălaj, NW Romania *47°11′N 23°03′E*
109 V10 **Žalec** *Ger.* Sachsenfeld. C Slovenia *46°15′N 15°08′E*
110 K8 **Zalewo** *Ger.* Saalfeld. Warmińsko-Mazurskie, NE Poland *53°54′N 19°39′E*
141 N9 **Z̧alim** Makkah al Mukarramah al Mukarramah, W Saudi Arabia *22°46′N 42°12′E*
80 A11 **Zalingei** *var.* Zalinje. Central Darfur, W Sudan *12°51′N 23°29′E*
**Zalinje** *see* Zalingei
116 K7 **Zalishchyky** Ternopil's'ka Oblast', W Ukraine *48°40′N 25°43′E*
**Zallah** *see* Zillah
**`Załni Pjašaci** *see* Zlatni Pyasatsi
98 J13 **Zaltbommel** Gelderland, C Netherlands *51°49′N 05°15′E*
124 H15 **Zaluch'ye** Novgorodskaya Oblast', NW Russia *57°40′N 31°45′E*
**Zamak** *see* Zamakh
141 Q14 **Zamakh** *var.* Zamak. N Yemen *16°26′N 47°35′E*
136 K15 **Zamantı Irmağı** ≈ C Turkey
**Zambesi/Zambeze** *see* Zambezi
83 G14 **Zambezi** North Western, W Zambia *13°34′S 23°08′E*
83 G17 **Zambezi** ◈ *region* NE Namibia
83 K15 **Zambezi** *var.* Zambesi, *Port.* Zambeze. ≈ S Africa
83 O15 **Zambézia** *off.* Província da Zambézia. ◈ *province* C Mozambique
**Zambézia, Província da** *see* Zambézia
83 I14 **Zambia** *off.* Republic of Zambia; *prev.* Northern Rhodesia. ◆ *republic* S Africa
**Zambia, Republic of** *see* Zambia
171 O8 **Zamboanga** *off.* Zamboanga City. Mindanao, S Philippines *06°56′N 122°03′E*
**Zamboanga City** *see* Zamboanga
54 E5 **Zambrano** Bolívar, N Colombia *09°45′N 74°50′W*
110 N10 **Zambrów** Łomża, E Poland *52°59′N 22°14′E*
83 L14 **Zâmbuè** Tete, NW Mozambique *15°03′S 30°49′E*
77 T13 **Zamfara** ≈ NW Nigeria
**Zamkog** *see* Zamtang
56 C9 **Zamora** Zamora Chinchipe, S Ecuador *04°04′S 78°52′W*
104 K6 **Zamora** Castilla y León, NW Spain *41°30′N 05°45′W*
104 K5 **Zamora** ◈ *province* Castilla y León, NW Spain
**Zamora** *see* Barinas
56 A13 **Zamora Chinchipe** ◈ *province* S Ecuador
40 M13 **Zamora de Hidalgo** Michoacán, SW Mexico *20°N 102°18′W*
111 P15 **Zamość** *Rus.* Zamoste. Lubelskie, E Poland *50°44′N 23°16′E*
**Zamoste** *see* Zamość
160 G7 **Zamtang** *var.* Zamkog; *prev.* Gamba. Sichuan, C China *32°19′N 100°55′E*
75 O8 **Zamzam, Wādī** *dry watercourse* NW Libya
79 F20 **Zanaga** Lékoumou, S Congo *02°50′S 13°53′E*
41 T16 **Zanatepec** Oaxaca, SE Mexico *16°28′N 94°24′W*
105 P9 **Záncara** ≈ C Spain
**Zancle** *see* Messina
158 G14 **Zanda** Xizang Zizhiqu, W China *31°29′N 79°50′E*
98 H10 **Zandvoort** Noord-Holland, W Netherlands *52°22′N 04°31′E*
39 P8 **Zane Hills** *hill range* Alaska, USA
31 T13 **Zanesville** Ohio, N USA *39°55′N 82°02′W*
**Zanga** *see* Hrazdan
**Zangoza** *see* Sangüesa
142 L4 **Zanjān** *var.* Zenjan, Zinjan. Zanjān, NW Iran *36°40′N 48°30′E*
142 L4 **Zanjān** *off.* Ostān-e Zanjān, *var.* Zenjan, Zinjan. ◈ *province* NW Iran
**Zanjān, Ostān-e** *see* Zanjān
**Zante** *see* Zákynthos
81 J22 **Zanzibar** Zanzibar, E Tanzania *06°10′S 39°12′E*
81 J22 **Zanzibar** ◈ *region* E Tanzania
81 J22 **Zanzibar** *Swa.* Unguja. *island* E Tanzania
81 J22 **Zanzibar Channel** *channel* E Tanzania
161 N8 **Zaoyang** Hubei, C China *32°10′N 112°45′E*
165 P10 **Zaō-zan** ▲ Honshū, C Japan *38°06′N 140°27′E*
124 J2 **Zaozërsk** Murmanskaya Oblast', NW Russia *69°25′N 32°25′E*
161 Q6 **Zaozhuang** Shandong, E China *34°53′N 117°38′E*
28 L4 **Zap** North Dakota, N USA *47°18′N 101°55′W*
112 L13 **Zapadna Morava** *Ger.* Westliche Morava. ≈ C Serbia
124 H16 **Zapadnaya Dvina** Tverskaya Oblast', W Russia *56°17′N 32°03′E*
**Zapadnaya Dvina** *see* Western Dvina
**Zapadno-Kazakhstanskaya Oblast'** *see* Zapadnyy Kazakhstan
122 I9 **Zapadno-Sibirskaya Ravnina** *Eng.* West Siberian Plain. *plain* C Russia
**Zapadnyy Bug** *see* Bug
144 E9 **Zapadnyy Kazakhstan** *off.* Zapadno-Kazakhstanskaya Oblast', *Eng.* West Kazakhstan, *Kaz.* Batys Qazaqstan Oblysy; *prev.* Ural'skaya Oblast'. ◈ *province* NW Kazakhstan
122 K13 **Zapadnyy Sayan** *Eng.* Western Sayans. ▲▲ S Russia
63 H15 **Zapala** Neuquén, W Argentina *38°54′S 70°06′W*
62 I4 **Zapaleri, Cerro** *var.* Cerro Sapaleri. ▲ N Chile *22°51′S 67°10′W*
25 Q16 **Zapata** Texas, SW USA *26°57′N 99°17′W*
44 D5 **Zapata, Península de** *peninsula* W Cuba
61 G19 **Zapicán** Lavalleja, S Uruguay *33°31′S 54°55′W*
65 J19 **Zapiola Ridge** *undersea feature* SW Atlantic Ocean
65 L19 **Zapiola Seamount** *undersea feature* S Atlantic Ocean *38°15′S 25°15′W*
124 I2 **Zapolyarnyy** Murmanskaya Oblast', NW Russia *69°24′N 30°53′E*
117 U8 **Zaporizhzhya** *Rus.* Zaporozh'ye; *prev.* Aleksandrovsk. Zaporiz'ka Oblast', SE Ukraine *47°47′N 35°12′E*
**Zaporizhzhya** *see* Zaporiz'ka Oblast'
117 U9 **Zaporiz'ka Oblast'** *var.* Zaporizhzhya, *Rus.* Zaporozhskaya Oblast'. ◈ *province* SE Ukraine
**Zaporozhskaya Oblast'** *see* Zaporiz'ka Oblast'
**Zaporozh'ye** *see* Zaporizhzhya
40 L14 **Zapotiltic** Jalisco, SW Mexico *19°40′N 103°29′W*
158 G13 **Zapug** Xizang Zizhiqu, W China
137 V10 **Zaqatala** *Rus.* Zakataly. NW Azerbaijan *41°38′N 46°38′E*
159 P13 **Zaqên** Qinghai, W China *33°23′N 94°31′E*
159 Q13 **Za Qu** ≈ C China
136 M13 **Zara** Sivas, C Turkey *39°55′N 37°44′E*
**Zara** *see* Zadar
**Zarafshan** *see* Zarafshon
147 P12 **Zarafshon** *Rus.* Zeravshan. W Tajikistan *39°12′N 68°36′E*
146 L9 **Zarafshon** *Rus.* Zarafshan. Navoiy Viloyati, N Uzbekistan *41°33′N 64°09′E*
**Zarafshon** *see* Zeravshan
147 O12 **Zarafshon, Qatorkŭhi** *Rus.* Zeravshanskiy Khrebet, *Uzb.* Zarafshon Tizmasi. ▲▲ Tajikistan/Uzbekistan
**Zarafshon Tizmasi** *see* Zarafshon, Qatorkŭhi
54 E7 **Zaragoza** Antioquia, N Colombia *07°30′N 74°52′W*
40 I5 **Zaragoza** Chihuahua, N Mexico *29°36′N 107°41′W*
41 N6 **Zaragoza** Coahuila, NE Mexico *28°31′N 100°54′W*
41 O10 **Zaragoza** Nuevo León, NE Mexico *23°59′N 99°49′W*
105 R5 **Zaragoza** *Eng.* Saragossa; *anc.* Caesaraugusta, Salduba. Aragón, NE Spain *41°39′N 00°54′W*
105 R6 **Zaragoza** ◈ *province* Aragón, NE Spain
105 R5 **Zaragoza** ✈ Aragón, NE Spain *41°38′N 00°53′W*
149 O6 **Zaŗah Sharan** Dāykundī, SE Afghanistan *33°28′N 66°19′E*
143 S10 **Zarand** Kermān, C Iran *30°50′N 56°35′E*
148 J9 **Zaranj** Nīmrōz, SW Afghanistan *30°59′N 61°54′E*
118 I11 **Zarasai** Utena, E Lithuania *55°44′N 26°17′E*
62 N12 **Zárate** *prev.* General José F.Uriburu. Buenos Aires, E Argentina *34°06′S 59°03′W*
105 Q2 **Zarautz** *var.* Zarauz. País Vasco, N Spain *43°17′N 02°10′W*
**Zarauz** *see* Zarautz
**Zaravecchia** *see* Biograd na Moru
**Zarāyīn** *see* Zarēn
126 L4 **Zaraysk** Moskovskaya Oblast', W Russia *54°48′N 38°54′E*
55 N6 **Zaraza** Guárico, N Venezuela *09°23′N 65°20′W*
**Zarbdar** *see* Zarbdor
147 P11 **Zarbdor** *Rus.* Zarbdar. Jizzax Viloyati, C Uzbekistan *40°04′N 68°10′E*
142 M8 **Zard Kūh** ▲ SW Iran *32°19′N 50°03′E*
124 I5 **Zarechensk** Murmanskaya Oblast', NW Russia *66°39′N 31°27′E*
127 P6 **Zarechnyy** Penzenskaya Oblast', W Russia *53°12′N 45°12′E*
**Zareh Sharan** *see* Sharan
39 Y14 **Zarembo Island** *island* Alexander Archipelago, Alaska, USA
139 V4 **Zarēn** *var.* Zarāyīn. As Sulaymānīyah, E Iraq *35°16′N 45°43′E*
149 Q7 **Zarghūn Shahr** *var.* Katawaz. Paktīkā, SE Afghanistan *32°40′N 68°20′E*
77 V13 **Zaria** Kaduna, C Nigeria *11°06′N 07°42′E*
116 K2 **Zarichne** Rivnens'ka Oblast', NW Ukraine *51°49′N 26°09′E*
122 J13 **Zarinsk** Altayskiy Kray, S Russia *53°34′N 85°22′E*
116 J12 **Zărnești** *Hung.* Zernest. Brașov, C Romania *45°34′N 25°18′E*
115 J25 **Zarós** Kríti, Greece, E Mediterranean Sea *35°08′N 24°54′E*
100 O9 **Zarow** ≈ NE Germany
**Zarqa** *see* Az Zarqā'
**Zarqa/Muḩāfazat az Zarqā'** *see* Az Zarqā'
111 G20 **Záruby** ▲ W Slovakia *48°30′N 17°24′E*
56 B8 **Zaruma** El Oro, SW Ecuador *03°46′S 79°38′W*
110 E13 **Żary** *Ger.* Sorau, Sorau in der Niederlausitz. Lubuskie, W Poland *51°44′N 15°09′E*
54 D10 **Zarzal** Valle del Cauca, W Colombia *04°24′N 76°01′W*
42 I7 **Zarzalar, Cerro** ▲ S Honduras *14°15′N 86°49′W*
**Zashaghan** *see* Zachagansk
152 I5 **Zāskār** ≈ NE India
152 I5 **Zāskār Range** ▲▲ NE India
**Zaslavl'** *see* Zaslawye
119 K15 **Zaslawye** *Rus.* Zaslavl'. Minskaya Voblasts', C Belarus *54°01′N 27°16′E*
116 K7 **Zastavna** Chernivets'ka Oblast', W Ukraine *48°30′N 25°51′E*
111 B16 **Žatec** *Ger.* Saaz. Ústecký Kraj, NW Czechia *50°20′N 13°35′E*
**Zaumgarten** *see* Chrzanów
**Zaunguzskiye Garagumy** *see* Üngüz Angyrsyndaky Garagum
25 X9 **Zavalla** Texas, SW USA *31°09′N 94°25′W*
99 H18 **Zaventem** Vlaams Brabant, C Belgium *50°53′N 04°28′E*
99 H18 **Zaventem** ✈ (Brussel/Bruxelles) Vlaams Brabant, C Belgium *50°55′N 04°28′E*
**Zavertse** *see* Zawiercie
114 L7 **Zavet** Razgrad, NE Bulgaria *43°46′N 26°40′E*
127 O12 **Zavetnoye** Rostovskaya Oblast', SW Russia *47°10′N 43°54′E*
156 M3 **Zavhan Gol** ≈ W Mongolia
112 H12 **Zavidovići** Federacija Bosne I Hercegovine, N Bosnia and Herzegovina *44°26′N 18°07′E*
123 R13 **Zavitinsk** Amurskaya Oblast', SE Russia *50°23′N 128°57′E*
117 S4 **Zavods'ke** *prev.* Chervonozavods'ke. Poltavs'ka Oblast', C Ukraine *50°24′N 33°22′E*
**Zawia** *see* Az Zāwiyah
111 K15 **Zawiercie** *Rus.* Zavertse. Śląskie, S Poland *50°29′N 19°24′E*
75 P11 **Zawīlah** *var.* Zuwaylah, *It.* Zueila. C Libya *26°10′N 15°07′E*
138 I4 **Zāwīyah, Jabal az** ▲▲ NW Syria
139 Q1 **Zaxo** *Ar.* Zākhū, *var.* Zākhō. Dahūk, N Iraq *37°09′N 42°40′E*
109 Y3 **Zaya** ≈ NE Austria
166 M8 **Zayatkyi** Bago, C Myanmar (Burma) *17°48′N 96°27′E*
145 Y11 **Zaysan** Vostochnyy Kazakhstan, E Kazakhstan *47°30′N 84°55′E*
**Zaysan Köl** *see* Zaysan, Ozero
145 Y11 **Zaysan, Ozero** *Kaz.* Zaysan Köl. ◎ E Kazakhstan
159 R16 **Zayü** *var.* Gyigang. Xizang Zizhiqu, W China *28°36′N 97°25′E*
**Zayyq** *see* Zhayyk
44 F6 **Zaza** ≈ C Cuba
116 K5 **Zbarazh** Ternopil's'ka Oblast', W Ukraine *49°40′N 25°47′E*
116 J5 **Zboriv** Ternopil's'ka Oblast', W Ukraine *49°40′N 25°07′E*
111 F18 **Zbraslav** Jihomoravský Kraj, SE Czechia *49°13′N 16°19′E*
116 K6 **Zbruch** ≈ W Ukraine
**Žd'ár** *see* Žd'ár nad Sázavou
111 F17 **Žd'ár nad Sázavou** *Ger.* Saar in Mähren; *prev.* Žd'ár. Vysočina, C Czechia *49°34′N 16°00′E*
116 K4 **Zdolbuniv** *Pol.* Zdolbunów, *Rus.* Zdolbunov. Rivnens'ka Oblast', NW Ukraine *50°33′N 26°15′E*
**Zdolbunov/Zdolbunów** *see* Zdolbuniv
110 J13 **Zduńska Wola** Sieradz, C Poland *51°37′N 18°57′E*
117 O4 **Zdvizh** ≈ N Ukraine
**Zdzięciół** *see* Dzyatlava
111 I16 **Zdzieszowice** *Ger.* Odertal. Opolskie, SW Poland *50°24′N 18°06′E*
**Zealand** *see* Sjælland
188 K6 **Zealandia Bank** *undersea feature* C Pacific Ocean
63 H20 **Zeballos, Monte** ▲ S Argentina *47°04′S 71°32′W*
83 K20 **Zebediela** Limpopo, NE South Africa *24°16′S 29°21′E*
113 L18 **Zebës, Mali i** *var.* Mali i Zebës. ▲ NE Albania *41°57′N 20°16′E*
**Zebës, Mali i** *see* Zebës, Mali i
21 V9 **Zebulon** North Carolina, SE USA *35°49′N 78°19′W*
112 K8 **Žednik** *Hung.* Bácsjózseffalva. Vojvodina, N Serbia *45°58′N 19°40′E*
99 C15 **Zeebrugge** West-Vlaanderen, NW Belgium *51°20′N 03°13′E*
183 N16 **Zeehan** Tasmania, SE Australia *41°54′S 145°19′E*
99 L14 **Zeeland** Noord-Brabant, SE Netherlands *51°42′N 05°40′E*
29 N7 **Zeeland** North Dakota, N USA *45°57′N 99°49′W*
99 E14 **Zeeland** ◈ *province* SW Netherlands
83 I21 **Zeerust** North-West, N South Africa *25°33′S 26°06′E*
98 K10 **Zeewolde** Flevoland, C Netherlands *52°20′N 05°32′E*
**Zefat** *see* Tsefat
**Żegań** *see* Żagań
**Zehden** *see* Cedynia
100 O11 **Zehdenick** Brandenburg, NE Germany *52°58′N 13°19′E*
**Zē-i Bādīnān** *see* Great Zab
**Zeiden** *see* Codlea
146 M14 **Zeidskoye Vodokhranilishche** ⊠ E Turkmenistan
**Zē-i Kōya** *see* Little Zab
181 P7 **Zeil, Mount** ▲ Northern Territory, C Australia *23°31′S 132°41′E*
98 J12 **Zeist** Utrecht, C Netherlands *52°05′N 05°15′E*
101 M16 **Zeitz** Sachsen-Anhalt, E Germany *51°03′N 12°08′E*
159 T11 **Zêkog** *var.* Zequ; *prev.* Sonag. Qinghai, C China *35°03′N 101°30′E*
**Zelaya Norte** *see* Costa Caribe Norte
**Zelaya Sur** *see* Costa Caribe Sur
99 F17 **Zele** Oost-Vlaanderen, NW Belgium *51°04′N 04°02′E*
110 N12 **Żelechów** Lubelskie, E Poland *51°49′N 21°57′E*
113 H14 **Zelena Glava** ▲ SE Bosnia and Herzegovina *43°32′N 17°55′E*
113 P20 **Zelen Breg** ▲ S Macedonia *41°10′N 22°14′E*
113 I14 **Zelengora** ▲▲ S Bosnia and Herzegovina
124 I5 **Zelenoborskiy** Murmanskaya Oblast', NW Russia *66°52′N 32°25′E*
127 R3 **Zelenodol'sk** Respublika Tatarstan, W Russia *55°52′N 48°49′E*
117 S9 **Zelenodols'k** Dnipropetrovs'ka Oblast', E Ukraine *47°38′N 33°41′E*
122 J12 **Zelenogorsk** Krasnoyarskiy Kray, C Russia *56°08′N 94°29′E*
126 K3 **Zelenograd** Moskovskaya Oblast', W Russia *56°02′N 37°08′E*
118 B13 **Zelenogradsk** *Ger.* Cranz, Kranz. Kaliningradskaya Oblast', W Russia *54°58′N 20°30′E*
127 O15 **Zelenokumsk** Stavropol'skiy Kray, SW Russia *44°22′N 43°48′E*
165 X4 **Zelënyy, Ostrov** *var.* Shibotsu-jima. *island* NE Russia
**Železna Kapela** *see* Eisenkappel
**Železna Vrata** *see* Demir Kapija
112 L11 **Železniki** Serbia, N Serbia *44°45′N 20°23′E*
98 N12 **Zelhem** Gelderland, E Netherlands *52°00′N 06°21′E*
113 N18 **Želino** NW North Macedonia *42°00′N 21°06′E*
113 M14 **Željin** ▲▲ C Serbia
101 K17 **Zella-Mehlis** Thüringen, C Germany *50°40′N 10°40′E*
109 P7 **Zell am See** *var.* Zell-am-See. Salzburg, S Austria *47°19′N 12°47′E*
**Zell-am-See** *see* Zell am See
109 N7 **Zell am Ziller** Tirol, W Austria *47°13′N 11°52′E*
**Zelle** *see* Celle
109 W2 **Zellerndorf** Niederösterreich, NE Austria *48°40′N 15°57′E*
109 U7 **Zeltweg** Steiermark, S Austria *47°12′N 14°46′E*
119 G17 **Zel'va** *Pol.* Zelwa. Hrodzyenskaya Voblasts', W Belarus *53°09′N 24°49′E*
118 H13 **Želva** Vilnius, C Lithuania *55°13′N 25°07′E*
**Zelwa** *see* Zel'va
99 E16 **Zelzate** *var.* Selzaete. Oost-Vlaanderen, NW Belgium *51°12′N 03°49′E*
118 E11 **Žemaičių Aukštumas** *physical region* W Lithuania
118 C12 **Žemaičių Naumiestis** Klaipėda, SW Lithuania *55°22′N 21°39′E*
119 L14 **Zembin** *var.* Zyembin. Minskaya Voblasts', C Belarus *54°22′N 28°13′E*
127 N6 **Zemetchino** Penzenskaya Oblast', W Russia *53°31′N 42°35′E*
79 M15 **Zémio** Haut-Mbomou, E Central African Republic *05°04′N 25°07′E*
41 R16 **Zempoaltepec, Cerro** ▲ SE Mexico *17°04′N 95°54′W*
99 G17 **Zemst** Vlaams Brabant, C Belgium *50°59′N 04°28′E*
112 L11 **Zemun** Serbia, N Serbia *44°52′N 20°25′E*
**Zendajan** *see* Zindah Jān
**Zendeh Jān** *see* Zindah Jān
**Zengg** *see* Senj
112 H12 **Zenica** Federacija Bosne I Hercegovine, C Bosnia and Herzegovina *44°12′N 17°53′E*
**Zenjan** *see* Zanjān
**Zen'kov** *see* Zin'kiv
**Zenshū** *see* Jeonju
**Zenta** *see* Senta
82 B11 **Zenza do Itombe** Kwanza Norte, NW Angola *09°22′S 14°10′E*
112 H12 **Žepče** Federacija Bosne I Hercegovine, N Bosnia and Herzegovina *44°26′N 18°00′E*
23 W12 **Zephyrhills** Florida, SE USA *28°13′N 82°10′W*
158 F9 **Zepu** *var.* Poskam. Xinjiang Uygur Zizhiqu, NW China *38°10′N 77°18′E*
**Zequ** *see* Zêkog
147 Q12 **Zeravshan** *Taj./Uzb.* Zarafshon. ≈ Tajikistan/Uzbekistan
**Zeravshan** *see* Zarafshon
**Zeravshanskiy Khrebet** *see* Zarafshon, Qatorkŭhi
101 M14 **Zerbst** Sachsen-Anhalt, E Germany *51°57′N 12°05′E*
**Zerenda** *see* Zerendy
145 P8 **Zerendy** *prev.* Zerenda. Akmola, N Kazakhstan *52°56′N 69°09′E*
110 H12 **Żerków** Wielkopolskie, C Poland *52°03′N 17°33′E*
108 E11 **Zermatt** Valais, SW Switzerland *46°00′N 07°45′E*
**Zernest** *see* Zărnești
108 J9 **Zernez** Graubünden, SE Switzerland *46°42′N 10°06′E*
126 L12 **Zernograd** Rostovskaya Oblast', SW Russia *46°52′N 40°13′E*
**Zestafoni** *see* Zest'aponi
137 S9 **Zest'aponi** *Rus.* Zestafoni; *prev.* Zestap'oni. C Georgia *42°09′N 43°00′E*
**Zestap'oni** *see* Zest'aponi
98 H12 **Zestienhoven** ✈ (Rotterdam) Zuid-Holland, SW Netherlands *51°57′N 04°30′E*
113 J16 **Zeta** ≈ C Montenegro
8 L6 **Zeta Lake** ◎ Victoria Island, Northwest Territories, N Canada
98 L12 **Zetten** Gelderland, SE Netherlands *51°55′N 05°43′E*
101 M17 **Zeulenroda** Thüringen, C Germany *50°40′N 11°58′E*
100 H10 **Zeven** Niedersachsen, NW Germany *53°17′N 09°16′E*
98 M12 **Zevenaar** Gelderland, SE Netherlands *51°55′N 06°05′E*
99 H14 **Zevenbergen** Noord-Brabant, S Netherlands *51°39′N 04°36′E*
129 X6 **Zeya** ≈ SE Russia
**Zeya Reservoir** *see* Zeyskoye Vodokhranilishche
143 T11 **Zeynalābād** Kermān, C Iran *29°56′N 57°29′E*
123 R12 **Zeyskoye Vodokhranilishche** *Eng.* Zeya Reservoir. ⊠ SE Russia
104 H8 **Zêzere, Rio** ≈ C Portugal
**Zgerzh** *see* Zgierz
138 H6 **Zgharta** N Lebanon *34°24′N 35°54′E*
110 K12 **Zgierz** *Ger.* Neuhof, *Rus.* Zgerzh. Łódź, C Poland *51°55′N 19°20′E*
111 E14 **Zgorzelec** *Ger.* Görlitz. Dolnośląskie, SW Poland *51°10′N 15°E*
119 F19 **Zhabinka** *Pol.* Żabinka. Brestskaya Voblasts', SW Belarus *52°12′N 24°01′E*
**Zhaggo** *see* Luhuo
159 R15 **Zhag'yab** *var.* Yêndum. Xizang Zizhiqu, W China *30°42′N 97°33′E*
**Zhailma** *see* Zhayylma
145 N14 **Zhalagash** *prev.* Dzhalagash. Kzylorda, S Kazakhstan *45°06′N 64°40′E*
145 V16 **Zhalanash** Almaty, SE Kazakhstan *43°04′N 78°08′E*
145 S7 **Zhalauly, Ozero** ◎ NE Kazakhstan
145 W10 **Zhalgyztobe** *prev.* Zhangiztobe. Vostochnyy Kazakhstan, E Kazakhstan *49°15′N 81°16′E*
144 E9 **Zhalpaktal** *Kaz.* Zhalpaqtal; *prev.* Furmanovo. Zapadnyy Kazakhstan, W Kazakhstan *49°43′N 49°28′E*
**Zhalpaqtal** *see* Zhalpaktal
119 G16 **Zhaludok** *Rus.* Zheludok. Hrodzyenskaya Voblasts', W Belarus *53°36′N 24°59′E*
**Zhaman-Akkol', Ozero** *see* Akkol', Ozero
145 Q14 **Zhambyl** *off.* Zhambylskaya Oblast', *Kaz.* Zhambyl Oblysy; *prev.* Dzhambulskaya Oblast'. ◈ *province* S Kazakhstan
**Zhambyl** *see* Taraz
**Zhambyl Oblysy/Zhambylskaya Oblast'** *see* Zhambyl
**Zhamo** *see* Bomi
145 S12 **Zhamshy** ≈ C Kazakhstan
144 M15 **Zhanadariya** *prev.* Zhanadar'ya. Kzylorda, S Kazakhstan *44°41′N 64°39′E*
**Zhanadar'ya** *see* Zhanadariya
144 E10 **Zhanakazan** *prev.* Novaya Kazanka. Zapadnyy Kazakhstan, W Kazakhstan *48°57′N 49°34′E*
145 O15 **Zhanakorgan** *Kaz.* Zhangaqorghan. Kzylorda, S Kazakhstan *43°57′N 67°14′E*
159 N16 **Zhanang** *var.* Chatang. Xizang Zizhiqu, W China *29°15′N 91°20′E*
145 T12 **Zhanaortalyk** Karaganda, C Kazakhstan *47°31′N 75°42′E*
144 F15 **Zhanaozen** *Kaz.* Zhangaözen; *prev.* Novyy Uzen'. Mangistau, W Kazakhstan *43°22′N 52°50′E*
145 Q16 **Zhanatas** Zhambyl, S Kazakhstan *43°36′N 69°43′E*
**Zhangaözen** *see* Zhanaozen
**Zhangaqazaly** *see* Ayteke Bi
**Zhangaqorghan** *see* Zhanakorgan
161 O2 **Zhangbei** Hebei, E China *41°13′N 114°43′E*
**Zhang-chia-k'ou** *see* Zhangjiakou
**Zhangdian** *see* Zibo
**Zhanggu** *see* Danba
163 X9 **Zhangguangcai Ling** ▲▲ NE China
**Zhanghua** *see* Changhua
**Zhangiztobe** *see* Zhalgyztobe
159 W11 **Zhangjiachuan** Gansu, N China *34°55′N 106°26′E*
160 L10 **Zhangjiajie** *var.* Dayong. Hunan, S China *29°10′N 110°22′E*
161 O2 **Zhangjiakou** *var.* Changkiakow, Zhang-chia-k'ou, *Eng.* Kalgan; *prev.* Wanchuan. Hebei, E China *40°48′N 114°51′E*
161 Q13 **Zhangping** Fujian, SE China *25°21′N 117°29′E*
161 Q13 **Zhangpu** *var.* Sui'an. Fujian, SE China *24°08′N 117°36′E*
163 U11 **Zhangwu** Liaoning, NE China *42°21′N 122°32′E*
159 S8 **Zhangye** *var.* Ganzhou. Gansu, N China *38°58′N 100°30′E*
161 Q13 **Zhangzhou** Fujian, SE China *24°31′N 117°40′E*
163 W6 **Zhan He** ≈ NE China
**Zhänibek** *see* Dzhanibek
160 L16 **Zhanjiang** *var.* Chanchiang, Chan-chiang, *Cant.* Tsamkong, *Fr.* Fort-Bayard. Guangdong, S China *21°10′N 110°20′E*
145 V14 **Zhansugirov** *prev.* Dzhansugurov. Almaty, SE Kazakhstan *45°23′N 79°29′E*
163 V8 **Zhaodong** Heilongjiang, NE China *46°03′N 125°58′E*
**Zhaoge** *see* Qixian
160 H11 **Zhaojue** *var.* Xincheng. Sichuan, C China *28°03′N 102°50′E*
161 N14 **Zhaoqing** Guangdong, S China *23°08′N 112°26′E*
**Zhaoren** *see* Changwu
158 H5 **Zhaosu** *var.* Mongolküre. Xinjiang Uygur Zizhiqu, NW China *43°09′N 81°07′E*
160 H11 **Zhaotong** Yunnan, SW China *27°20′N 103°29′E*
163 V9 **Zhaoyuan** Heilongjiang, NE China *45°30′N 125°05′E*
163 V9 **Zhaozhou** Heilongjiang, NE China *45°42′N 125°11′E*
145 X13 **Zharbulak** Vostochnyy Kazakhstan, E Kazakhstan *46°04′N 82°05′E*
158 J15 **Zhari Namco** ◎ W China
144 I12 **Zharkamys** *Kaz.* Zharqamys. Aktyubinsk, W Kazakhstan *47°58′N 56°33′E*
145 W15 **Zharkent** *prev.* Panfilov. Taldykorgan, SE Kazakhstan *44°10′N 80°01′E*
124 H17 **Zharkovskiy** Tverskaya Oblast', W Russia *55°51′N 32°19′E*
145 W11 **Zharma** Vostochnyy Kazakhstan, E Kazakhstan *48°48′N 80°55′E*
144 F14 **Zharmysh** Mangistau, SW Kazakhstan *44°12′N 52°27′E*
**Zharqamys** *see* Zharkamys
118 L13 **Zhary** Vitsyebskaya Voblasts', N Belarus *55°05′N 28°40′E*
**Zhaslyk** *see* Jasliq
158 J14 **Zhaxi Co** ◎ W China
127 X6 **Zhayyk** *Kaz.* Zayyq, *var.* Ural. ≈ Kazakhstan/Russia
144 L9 **Zhayylma** *prev.* Zhailma. Kostanay, N Kazakhstan *51°34′N 61°39′E*
**Zhdanov** *see* Beylăqan
**Zhdanov** *see* Mariupol'
**Zhe** *see* Zhejiang
161 R10 **Zhejiang** *var.* Che-chiang, Chekiang, Zhe, Zhejiang Sheng. ◈ *province* SE China
**Zhejiang Sheng** *see* Zhejiang
145 S7 **Zhelezinka** Pavlodar, N Kazakhstan *53°35′N 75°16′E*
119 C14 **Zheleznodorozhnyy** *Ger.* Gerdauen. Kaliningradskaya Oblast', W Russia *54°21′N 21°17′E*
**Zheleznodorozhnyy** *see* Yemva
122 K12 **Zheleznogorsk** Krasnoyarskiy, C Russia *56°20′N 93°36′E*
126 J7 **Zheleznogorsk** Kurskaya Oblast', W Russia *52°22′N 35°21′E*
127 N15 **Zheleznovodsk** Stavropol'skiy Kray, SW Russia *44°12′N 43°01′E*
**Zhëltyye Vody** *see* Zhovti Vody
**Zheludok** *see* Zhaludok
144 H12 **Zhem** *prev.* Emba. ≈ W Kazakhstan
160 K7 **Zhenba** Shaanxi, C China *32°42′N 107°55′E*
160 I13 **Zhenfeng** *var.* Mingu. Guizhou, S China *25°27′N 105°38′E*
**Zhengjiatun** *see* Shuangliao
159 X10 **Zhengning** *var.* Shanhe. Gansu, N China *35°29′N 108°21′E*
**Zhengxiangbai Qi** *see* Qagan Nur
161 N6 **Zhengzhou** *var.* Ch'eng-chou, Chengchow; *prev.* Chenghsien. *province capital* Henan, C China *34°45′N 113°38′E*
161 R8 **Zhenjiang** *var.* Chenkiang. Jiangsu, E China *32°08′N 119°30′E*
163 U9 **Zhenlai** Jilin, NE China *45°52′N 123°11′E*
160 I11 **Zhenxiong** Yunnan, SW China *27°31′N 104°52′E*
160 K11 **Zhenyuan** *var.* Wuyang. Guizhou, S China *27°07′N 108°33′E*
161 R11 **Zherong** *var.* Shuangcheng. Fujian, SE China *27°16′N 119°54′E*
145 U15 **Zhetigen** *prev.* Nikolayevka. Almaty, SE Kazakhstan *43°39′N 77°10′E*
**Zhetiqara** *see* Zhitikara
144 F15 **Zhetybay** Mangistau, SW Kazakhstan *43°35′N 52°05′E*
145 P17 **Zhetysay** *var.* Dzhetysay. Turkestan *40°45′N 68°18′E*
145 W14 **Zhetysuskiy Alatau** *prev.* Dzhungarskiy Alatau. ▲▲ China/Kazakhstan




◆ Country
● Country Capital
◇ Dependent Territory
○ Dependent Territory Capital
◈ Administrative Regions
✈ International Airport
▲ Mountain
▲▲ Mountain Range
Volcano
≈ River
◎ Lake
⊠ Reservoir

160 M11 **Zhexi Shuiku** ⬚ C China
145 O12 **Zhezdy** Karaganda, C Kazakhstan 48°06´N 67°01´E
145 O12 **Zhezkazgan** *Kaz.* Zhezqazghan; *prev.* Dzhezkazgan. Karaganda, C Kazakhstan 47°49´N 67°44´E
**Zhezqazghan** *see* Zhezkazgan
**Zhicheng** *see* Yidu
**Zhidachov** *see* Zhydachiv
159 Q12 **Zhidoi** *var.* Gyaijêpozhanggê. Qinghai, C China 33°55´N 95°39´E
122 M13 **Zhigalovo** Irkutskaya Oblast´, S Russia 54°47´N 105°00´E
127 R6 **Zhigulevsk** Samarskaya Oblast´, W Russia 53°24´N 49°30´E
118 D13 **Zhilino** *Ger.* Schillen. Kaliningradskaya Oblast´, W Russia 54°55´N 21°54´E
**Zhiloy, Ostrov** *see* Çilov Adası
127 O8 **Zhirnovsk** Volgogradskaya Oblast´, SW Russia 51°01´N 44°49´E
160 M12 **Zhishan** *prev.* Yongzhou. Hunan, S China 26°12´N 111°36´E
**Zhishan** *see* Lingling
144 L8 **Zhitikara** *Kaz.* Zhetiqara; *prev.* Džetygara. Kostanay, NW Kazakhstan 52°14´N 61°12´E
**Zhitkovichi** *see* Zhytkavichy
**Zhitomir** *see* Zhytomyr
**Zhitomirskaya Oblast´** *see* Zhytomyrs´ka Oblast´
126 J5 **Zhizdra** Kaluzhskaya Oblast´, W Russia 53°38´N 34°39´E
119 N18 **Zhlobin** Homyel´skaya Voblasts´, SE Belarus 52°53´N 30°01´E
116 M7 **Zhmerinka** *Rus.* Zhmerinka. Vinnyts´ka Oblast´, C Ukraine 49°00´N 28°02´E
149 R9 **Zhob** *var.* Fort Sandeman. Baluchistan, SW Pakistan 31°21´N 69°31´E
149 R8 **Zhob** ↷ C Pakistan
119 L15 **Zhodina** *see* Zhodzina
119 L15 **Zhodzina** *Rus.* Zhodino. Minskaya Voblasts´, C Belarus 54°06´N 28°21´E
123 Q5 **Zhokhova, Ostrov** *island* Novosibirskiye Ostrova, NE Russia
**Zholkev/Zholkva** *see* Zhovkva
**Zhondor** *see* Jondor
158 I15 **Zhongba** *var.* Tuoji. Xizang Zizhiqu, W China 29°37´N 84°11´E
**Zhongba** *see* Jiangyou
**Zhongdian** *see* Xamgyi´nyilha
**Zhongduo** *see* Youyang
**Zhonghe** *see* Xiushan
**Zhonghua Renmin Gongheguo** *see* China
**Zhongjian Dao** *see* Triton Island
159 V9 **Zhongning** Ningxia, N China 37°26´N 105°40´E
**Zhongping** *see* Huize
161 N15 **Zhongshan** Guangdong, S China 22°30´N 113°20´E
195 X7 **Zhongshan** *research station (China)* Antarctica 69°23´S 76°34´E
160 M6 **Zhongtiao Shan** ▲ C China
159 V9 **Zhongwei** Ningxia, N China 37°31´N 105°10´E
160 K9 **Zhongxian** *var.* Zhongzhou. Chongqing Shi, C China 30°16´N 108°03´E
161 N9 **Zhongxiang** Hubei, C China 31°12´N 112°35´E
161 T14 **Zhongyang Shanmo** *Chin.* Taiwan Shan, *var.* Chungyang Shanmo. ▲ C Taiwan
**Zhongzhou** *see* Zhongxian
144 M14 **Zhosaly** *prev.* Dzhusaly. Kzylorda, SW Kazakhstan 45°29´N 64°04´E
161 O7 **Zhoukou** *var.* Zhoukouzhen. Henan, C China 33°32´N 114°40´E
**Zhoukouzhen** *see* Zhoukou
161 S9 **Zhoushan** Zhejiang, S China
**Zhoushan Islands** *see* Zhoushan Qundao

161 S9 **Zhoushan Qundao** *Eng.* Zhoushan Islands. *island group* SE China
116 I5 **Zhovkva** *Pol.* Żółkiew, *Rus.* Zholkev, Zholkva; *prev.* Nesterov. L´vivs´ka Oblast´, NW Ukraine 50°04´N 24°E
117 S7 **Zhovti Vody** *Rus.* Zhëltyye Vody. Dnipropetrovs´ka Oblast´, E Ukraine 48°24´N 33°30´E
117 Q10 **Zhovtnevoye** *Rus.* Zhovtnevoye. Mykolayivs´ka Oblast´, S Ukraine 46°50´N 32°00´E
**Zhovtnevoye** *see* Zhovtneve
114 K9 **Zhrebchevo, Yazovir** ⬚ C Bulgaria
163 V13 **Zhuanghe** Liaoning, N China 39°42´N 123°00´E
159 W11 **Zhuanglang** *var.* Shuiluo; *prev.* Shuilocheng. Gansu, C China 35°06´N 106°21´E
145 P15 **Zhuantobe** *Kaz.* Zhüantöbe. Turkestan, S Kazakhstan 44°45´N 68°50´E
161 Q5 **Zhucheng** Shandong, E China 35°58´N 119°24´E
159 V12 **Zhugqu** Gansu, C China 33°51´N 104°14´E
161 N15 **Zhuhai** Guangdong, S China 22°16´N 113°30´E
**Zhuizishan** *see* Weichang
126 I5 **Zhukovka** Bryanskaya Oblast´, W Russia 53°33´N 33°48´E
161 N7 **Zhumadian** Henan, C China 32°58´N 114°03´E
161 S13 **Zhunan** *prev.* Chunan. N Taiwan 24°44´N 120°51´E
161 O3 **Zhuozhou** *prev.* Zhuo Xian. Hebei, E China 39°22´N 115°40´E
162 L14 **Zhuozi Shan** ▲ N China 39°28´N 106°58´E
113 M17 **Zhur** *Serb.* Žur. S Kosovo 42°10´N 20°37´E
**Zhuravichi** *see* Zhuravichy
119 O17 **Zhuravichy** *Rus.* Zhuravichi. Homyel´skaya Voblasts´, SE Belarus 53°15´N 30°33´E
145 Q8 **Zhuravlevka** Akmola, N Kazakhstan 52°00´N 69°59´E
117 Q4 **Zhurivka** Kyyivs´ka Oblast´, N Ukraine 50°28´N 31°48´E
144 J11 **Zhym** Aktyubinsk, W Kazakhstan 49°13´N 57°36´E
145 T15 **Zhusandala, Step´** *grassland* SE Kazakhstan
160 L8 **Zhushan** Hubei, C China 32°11´N 110°05´E
**Zhushan** *see* Xuan´en
**Zhuyang** *see* Dazhu
161 N11 **Zhuzhou** Hunan, S China 27°52´N 112°52´E
116 I6 **Zhydachiv** *Pol.* Żydaczów, *Rus.* Zhidachov. L´vivs´ka Oblast´, NW Ukraine 49°20´N 24°08´E
144 G9 **Zhympity** *Kaz.* Zhympity; *prev.* Dzhambeyty. Zapadnyy, NW Kazakhstan 50°16´N 52°34´E
119 K19 **Zhytkavichy** *Rus.* Zhitkovichi. Homyel´skaya Voblasts´, SE Belarus 52°14´N 27°52´E
117 N4 **Zhytomyr** *Rus.* Zhitomir. Zhytomyrs´ka Oblast´, NW Ukraine 50°17´N 28°40´E
116 M4 **Zhytomyrs´ka Oblast´** *var.* Zhytomyr, *Rus.* Zhitomirskaya Oblast´. ◆ *province* N Ukraine
153 U15 **Zia** ✈ (Dhaka) Dhaka, C Bangladesh
111 J20 **Žiar nad Hronom** *var.* Svätý Kríž nad Hronom, *Ger.* Heiligenkreuz, *Hung.* Garamszentkereszt. Banskobystrický Kraj, C Slovakia 48°36´N 18°52´E
161 Q4 **Zibo** *var.* Zhangdian. Shandong, E China 36°51´N 118°01´E
160 L4 **Zichang** *prev.* Wayaobu. Shaanxi, C China 37°08´N 109°40´E
**Zichenau** *see* Ciechanów
111 J15 **Ziębice** *Ger.* Münsterberg in Schlesien. Dolnośląskie, SW Poland 50°37´N 17°01´E

**Ziebingen** *see* Cybinka
**Ziegenhals** *see* Głuchołazy
110 E12 **Zielona Góra** *Ger.* Grünberg, Grünberg in Schlesien, Grünberg. Lubuskie, W Poland 51°56´N 15°31´E
99 F14 **Zierikzee** Zeeland, SW Netherlands 51°39´N 03°55´E
160 I10 **Zigong** *var.* Tzekung. Sichuan, C China 29°20´N 104°48´E
76 G12 **Ziguinchor** SW Senegal 12°34´N 16°20´W
41 N16 **Zihuatanejo** Guerrero, S Mexico 17°39´N 101°33´W
**Ziketan** *see* Xinghai
**Zilah** *see* Zalău
127 W7 **Zilair** Respublika Bashkortostan, W Russia 52°12´N 57°15´E
136 L12 **Zile** Tokat, N Turkey 40°18´N 35°52´E
111 J18 **Žilina** *Ger.* Sillein, *Hung.* Zsolna. Zlínský Kraj, N Slovakia 49°13´N 18°44´E
111 J19 **Žilinský Kraj** ◆ *region* N Slovakia
75 Q9 **Zillah** *var.* Zallah. C Libya 28°30´N 17°33´E
**Zillenmarkt** *see* Zalău
109 N7 **Ziller** ↷ W Austria 109 N8 **Zillertal Alpen** *Ger.* Zillertal Alps, *It.* Alpi Aurine. ▲ Austria/Italy
118 K10 **Zilupe** *Ger.* Rosenhof. E Latvia 56°10´N 28°06´E
41 O13 **Zimapán** Hidalgo, C Mexico 20°45´N 99°21´W
83 I16 **Zimba** Southern, S Zambia 17°20´S 26°11´E
83 J17 **Zimbabwe** *off.* Republic of Zimbabwe; *prev.* Rhodesia. ◆ *republic* S Africa
**Zimbabwe, Republic of** *see* Zimbabwe
116 H10 **Zimbor** *Hung.* Magyarzsombor. Sălaj, NW Romania 47°00´N 23°16´E
**Zimmerbude** *see* Svetlyy
116 H13 **Zimnicea** Teleorman, S Romania 43°39´N 25°21´E
114 L9 **Zimnitsa** Yambol, E Bulgaria 42°34´N 26°37´E
127 N12 **Zimovniki** Rostovskaya Oblast´, SW Russia 47°07´N 42°29´E
128 J5 **Zindah Jān** *var.* Zendajan, Zindajān; *prev.* Zendeh Jān. Herāt, NW Afghanistan 34°55´N 61°53´E
**Zindajān** *see* Zindah Jān
77 V12 **Zinder** Zinder, S Niger 13°47´N 09°02´E
77 W11 **Zinder** ◆ *region* S Niger
77 P12 **Zindijaré** C Burkina Faso 12°35´N 01°18´W
141 P16 **Zinjibār** SW Yemen 13°08´N 45°23´E
117 T4 **Zin´kiv** *var.* Zen´kov. Poltavs´ka Oblast´, C Ukraine 48°41´N 32°40´E
110 H10 **Żnin** Kujawsko-pomorskie, C Poland 52°50´N 17°41´E
111 F19 **Znojmo** *Ger.* Znaim. Jihomoravský Kraj, SE Czech Republic 48°52´N 16°04´E
79 N16 **Zobia** Orientale, N Dem. Rep. Congo 02°57´N 25°55´E
83 N15 **Zóbuè** Tete, NW Mozambique 15°36´S 34°26´E
98 G12 **Zoetermeer** Zuid-Holland, W Netherlands 52°04´N 04°30´E
108 E7 **Zofingen** Aargau, N Switzerland 47°18´N 07°57´E
109 Q7 **Zolling** Bayern, SE Germany 48°27´N 11°46´E
160 M11 **Zi Shui** ↷ C China
109 Y3 **Zistersdorf** Niederösterreich, NE Austria 48°32´N 16°45´E
41 O14 **Zitácuaro** Michoacán, SW Mexico 19°28´N 100°21´W
**Zito** *see* Lhorong
101 O15 **Zittau** Sachsen, E Germany 50°53´N 14°48´E
112 I12 **Živinice** Federacija Bosne I Hercegovine, E Bosnia and Herzegovina 44°26´N 18°39´E
81 J14 **Ziwa Magharibi** *see* Kagera

161 N12 **Zixing** Hunan, S China 26°01´N 113°25´E
127 W7 **Ziyanchurino** Orenburgskaya Oblast´, W Russia 51°36´N 56°58´E
160 K8 **Ziyang** Shaanxi, C China 32°33´N 108°27´E
111 I20 **Zlaté Moravce** *Hung.* Aranyosmarót. Nitriansky Kraj, SW Slovakia 48°24´N 18°20´E
112 K13 **Zlatibor** ▲ W Serbia
114 L9 **Zlati Voyvoda** Sliven, C Bulgaria 42°36´N 26°13´E
116 G11 **Zlatna** *Ger.* Kleinschlatten, *Hung.* Zalatna; *prev. Ger.* Goldmarkt. Alba, C Romania 46°08´N 23°11´E
114 I8 **Zlatna Panega** Lovech, N Bulgaria 43°07´N 24°09´E
114 N8 **Zlatni Pyasatsi** *var.* `Załni Pjašaci, Zlatni Pyasŭtsi, Golden Sands. Varna, NE Bulgaria 43°19´N 28°03´E
**Zlatni Pyasŭtsi** *see* Zlatni Pyasatsi
122 F11 **Zlatoust** Chelyabinskaya Oblast´, C Russia 55°12´N 59°33´E
111 M19 **Zlatý Stôl** *Ger.* Goldener Tisch, *Hung.* Aranyosasztal. ▲ C Slovakia 48°45´N 20°39´E
113 P18 **Zletovo** NE North Macedonia 42°00´N 22°14´E
111 H18 **Zlín** *prev.* Gottwaldov. Zlínský Kraj, E Czechia 49°14´N 17°40´E
111 H19 **Zlínský Kraj** ◆ *region* E Czechia
75 O7 **Zlīṭan** W Libya 32°28´N 14°34´E
110 F9 **Złocieniec** *Ger.* Falkenburg in Pommern. Zachodniopomorskie, NW Poland 53°31´N 16°01´E
110 J13 **Złoczew** Sieradz, S Poland 51°24´N 18°36´E
**Złoczów** *see* Zolochiv
111 F14 **Złotoryja** *Ger.* Goldberg. Dolnośląskie, SW Poland 51°08´N 15°57´E
110 G9 **Złotów** Wielkopolskie, C Poland 53°23´N 17°02´E
110 G13 **Żmigród** *Ger.* Trachenberg. Dolnośląskie, SW Poland 51°31´N 16°55´E
126 J6 **Zmiyevka** Orlovskaya Oblast´, W Russia 52°39´N 36°20´E
117 V5 **Zmiyiv** Kharkivs´ka Oblast´, E Ukraine 49°40´N 36°22´E
**Zna** *see* Tsna
126 M7 **Znamenka** Tambovskaya Oblast´, W Russia 52°24´N 42°28´E
119 C14 **Znamenka** Astrakhanskaya Oblast´, W Russia 54°37´N 21°13´E
127 P10 **Znamensk** *Ger.* Wehlau. Kaliningradskaya Oblast´, W Russia 48°33´N 46°18´E
117 R7 **Znam"yanka** *Rus.* Znamenka. Kirovohrads´ka Oblast´, C Ukraine 48°41´N 32°40´E
112 E10 **Zrinska Gora** ▲ C Croatia
101 N16 **Zschopau** ↷ E Germany
101 N16 **Zschopau** Sachsen, E Germany 50°45´N 13°04´E
141 V13 **Zufār** *Eng.* Dhofar. *physical region* SW Oman
108 G8 **Zug** *Fr.* Zoug. Zug, C Switzerland 47°11´N 08°31´E

116 J5 **Zolochiv** *Pol.* Złoczów, *var.* Zolochev. L´vivs´ka Oblast´, W Ukraine 49°48´N 24°51´E
117 X7 **Zolote** *Rus.* Zolotoye. Luhans´ka Oblast´, E Ukraine 48°42´N 38°33´E
117 Q6 **Zolotonosha** Cherkas´ka Oblast´, C Ukraine 49°39´N 32°05´E
**Zolotoye** *see* Zolote
83 N15 **Zomba** Southern, S Malawi 15°22´S 35°23´E
**Zombor** *see* Sombor
99 D17 **Zomergem** Oost-Vlaanderen, NW Belgium 51°07´N 03°31´E
147 N17 **Zomin** *Rus.* Zaamin. Jizzax Viloyati, C Uzbekistan 39°56´N 68°16´E
79 I15 **Zongo** Equateur, N Dem. Rep. Congo 04°18´N 18°42´E
136 G10 **Zonguldak** Zonguldak, NW Turkey 41°26´N 31°47´E
136 H10 **Zonguldak** ◆ *province* NW Turkey
99 K17 **Zonhoven** Limburg, NE Belgium 50°59´N 05°22´E
142 J2 **Zonūz** Āžarbāyjān-e Khāvari, NW Iran 38°32´N 45°54´E
103 Y16 **Zonza** Corse, France, C Mediterranean Sea 41°49´N 09°13´E
77 Q13 **Zorgo** *var.* Zorgho. C Burkina Faso 12°15´N 00°37´W
**Zorgho** *see* Zorgo
104 K10 **Zorita** Extremadura, W Spain 39°18´N 05°42´W
**Zor Köl, Köl-ye** *see* Zorkūl
147 U14 **Zorkūl** *Rus.* Ozero Zorkul´, *Afg.* Köl-ye Zor Köl. ☉ SE Tajikistan/ NE Afghanistan
56 A8 **Zorritos** Tumbes, N Peru 03°43´S 80°42´W
111 J16 **Żory** *var.* Zory, *Ger.* Sohrau. Śląskie, S Poland 50°04´N 18°42´E
76 K15 **Zorzor** N Liberia 07°46´N 09°28´W
77 R15 **Zou** ◆ S Benin
78 H6 **Zouar** Tibesti, N Chad 20°25´N 16°28´E
76 J6 **Zouérat** *var.* Zouérate, Zouīrât. Tiris Zemmour, N Mauritania 22°44´N 12°29´W
**Zouérate** *see* Zouérat
**Zoug** *see* Zug
**Zouīrât** *see* Zouérat
76 M10 **Zoukougbeu** C Ivory Coast 09°47´N 06°50´W
98 M5 **Zoutkamp** Groningen, NE Netherlands 53°22´N 06°17´E
99 J18 **Zoutleeuw** *Fr.* Léau. Vlaams Brabant, C Belgium 50°49´N 05°06´E
112 L9 **Zrenjanin** *prev.* Petrovgrad, Veliki Bečkerek, *Ger.* Grossbetschkerek, *Hung.* Nagybecskerek. Vojvodina, N Serbia 45°23´N 20°24´E
112 E10 **Zrinska Gora** ▲ C Croatia
**Zsablya** *see* Žabalj
101 N16 **Zschopau** ↷ E Germany
101 N16 **Zschopau** Sachsen, E Germany 50°45´N 13°04´E
55 N7 **Zuata** Anzoátegui, N Venezuela 08°24´N 65°13´W
105 N14 **Zubia** Andalucía, S Spain 37°08´N 03°27´W
65 P16 **Zubov Seamount** *undersea feature* E Atlantic Ocean 20°45´S 08°45´E
124 I16 **Zubtsov** Tverskaya Oblast´, W Russia 56°10´N 34°34´E
142 M10 **Zohreh, Rūd-e** ↷ SW Iran
160 H7 **Zoigê** *var.* Dagcagoin. Sichuan, C China 33°44´N 102°57´E
76 M16 **Zuénoula** C Ivory Coast 07°26´N 06°03´W
105 S5 **Zuera** Aragón, NE Spain 41°52´N 00°47´W
**Zug** *Fr.* Zoug. Zug, C Switzerland 47°11´N 08°31´E

108 G8 **Zug** *Fr.* Zoug. ↷ *canton* C Switzerland
137 R9 **Zugdidi** W Georgia 42°30´N 41°52´E
108 G8 **Zuger See** ☉ NW Switzerland
101 K25 **Zugspitze** ▲ S Germany 47°25´N 10°58´E
117 X8 **Zuhres** *Rus.* Shakhtërsk. Donets´ka Oblast´, SE Ukraine 48°01´N 38°16´E
99 E15 **Zuid-Beveland** *var.* South Beveland. *island* SW Netherlands
98 K10 **Zuidelijk-Flevoland** *polder* C Netherlands
**Zuider Zee** *see* IJsselmeer
98 G12 **Zuid-Holland** *Eng.* South Holland. ◆ *province* W Netherlands
98 N5 **Zuidhorn** Groningen, NE Netherlands
98 O6 **Zuidlaardermeer** ☉ NE Netherlands
98 O6 **Zuidlaren** Drenthe, NE Netherlands 53°06´N 06°41´E
99 K14 **Zuid-Willemsvaart Kanaal** *canal* S Netherlands
98 N8 **Zuidwolde** Drenthe, NE Netherlands
105 O14 **Zújar** Andalucía, S Spain 37°32´N 02°52´W
104 L11 **Zújar** ↷ W Spain
104 L11 **Zújar, Embalse del** ⬚ W Spain
112 J12 **Zvornik** E Bosnia and Herzegovina 44°24´N 19°07´E
98 M5 **Zwaagwesteinde** *Fris.* De Westerein. Fryslân, N Netherlands 53°16´N 06°08´E
98 H10 **Zwanenburg** Noord-Holland, C Netherlands 52°22´N 04°44´E
98 L8 **Zwarte Meer** ☉ N Netherlands
98 M9 **Zwarte Water** ↷ N Netherlands
98 M8 **Zwartsluis** Overijssel, E Netherlands 52°39´N 06°04´E
76 L17 **Zwedru** *var.* Tchien. E Liberia 06°04´N 08°07´W
98 O8 **Zweeloo** Drenthe, NE Netherlands
101 E20 **Zweibrücken** *Fr.* Deux-Ponts, *Lat.* Bipontium. Rheinland-Pfalz, SW Germany 49°15´N 07°22´E
108 D9 **Zweisimmen** Fribourg, W Switzerland 46°33´N 07°22´E
101 M15 **Zwenkau** Sachsen, E Germany 51°11´N 12°19´E
109 V3 **Zwettl** Wien, NE Austria 48°28´N 14°17´E
109 T3 **Zwettl an der Rodl** Oberösterreich, N Austria 48°28´N 14°17´E
99 D18 **Zwevegem** West-Vlaanderen, W Belgium 50°48´N 03°20´E
101 M17 **Zwickau** Sachsen, E Germany 50°43´N 12°31´E
101 N16 **Zwickauer Mulde** ↷ E Germany
101 O21 **Zwiesel** Bayern, SE Germany 49°02´N 13°14´E
99 H13 **Zwijndrecht** Zuid-Holland, SW Netherlands 51°49´N 04°39´E
110 N13 **Zwoleń** Mazowieckie, SE Poland 51°21´N 21°37´E
98 M9 **Zwolle** Overijssel, E Netherlands 52°31´N 06°06´E
22 G6 **Zwolle** Louisiana, S USA 31°37´N 93°38´W
110 K12 **Żychlin** Łódzkie, C Poland 52°15´N 19°38´E
**Zydaczów** *see* Zhydachiv
**Zyembin** *see* Zembin
**Zyôetu** *see* Jôetsu
110 L12 **Zyrardów** Mazowieckie, C Poland 52°02´N 20°28´E
123 S8 **Zyryanka** Respublika Sakha (Yakutiya), NE Russia 65°45´N 150°43´E
145 Y9 **Zyryanovsk** Vostochnyy Kazakhstan, E Kazakhstan 49°45´N 84°16´E

# PICTURE CREDITS

*Every effort has been made to trace the copyright holders and we apologize in advance for any unintentional omissions. We would be pleased to insert the appropriate acknowledgment in any subsequent edition of this publication.*

**Adams Picture Library:** 86CLA; **G Andrews:** 186CR; **Ardea London Ltd:** K Ghana 15CC; M Iijima 132TC; R Waller 148TR; Art Directors **Aspect Picture Library:** P Carmichael 160TR; 131CR(below); G Tompkinson 190TRB; **Axiom:** C Bradley 148CA, 158CA; J Holmes xivCRA, xxivBCR, xxviiCRB, 150TCR, 166TL; J Morris 75TL, 77CRB, J Spaull 134BL; **Bridgeman Art Library, London / New York:** Collection of the Earl of Pembroke, Wilton House xxBC; **The J. Allan Cash Photolibrary:** xlBR, xliiCLA, xlivCL, 10BC, 60CL, 69CLB, 70CL, 72CLB, 75BR, 76BC, 87BL, 109BR, 138BCL, 141TL, 154CCR, 178BR, 181TR; **Bruce Coleman Ltd:** 86BC, 98CL, 100TC; S Alden 192BC(below); Atlantide xxviiTCR, 138BR; E Bjurstrom 141BR; S Bond 96CRB; T Buchholz xvCL, 92TR, 123TCL; J Burton xxiiiC; J Cancalosi 181TRB; J Coates xxvBL, 192CL; B Coleman 63TL; B & C Colhoun 2TR, 36CB; A Compost xxiiiCBR; Dr S Coyne 45TL; G Cubitt xviTCL, 169BR, 178TR, 184TR; P Davey xxviiCLA, 121TL(below); N Devore 189CBL; S J Doye e xxiiCRR; H Flygare xviiCRA; M P L Fogden 17C(above) ; Jeff Foott Productions xxiiiiCRB, 11CRA; M Freeman 91BRA; P van Gaalen 86TR; G Gualco 140C; B Henderson 194CR; Dr C Henneghien 69C; HPH Photography, H Van den Berg 69CR; C Hughes 69BCL; C James xxxixTC; J Johnson 39CR, 197TR; J Jurka 91CA; S C Kaufman 28C; S J Krasemann 33TR; H Lange 10TRE, 68CA; C Lockwood 32BC; L C Marigo xxiiiBC, xxiiiCLA, 49CRA, 59BR; M McCoy 187TR; D Meredith 3CR; J Murray xvCR, 179BR; Orion Press 165CR+above); Orion Services & Trading Co. Inc. 164CR; C Ott 17BL; Dr E Pott 9TR, 40CL, 87C, 93TL, 194CLB; F Prenzel 186BC, 193BC; M Read 42BR, 43CRB; H Reinhard xxviiTR, xxviiTR, 194BR; L Lee Rue III 151BCL; J Shaw xixTL; K N Swenson 194BC; P Terry 115CR; N Tomalin 54BCL; P Ward 78TC; S Widstrand 57TR; K Wothe 91C, 173TCL; J T Wright 127BR; **Colorific:** Black Star / L Mulvehil 156CL; Black Star / R Rogers 57BR; Black Star / J Rupp 161BCR; Camera Tres / C. Meyer 59BRA; R Caputo / Matrix 78CL; J. Hill 117CLB; M Koene 55TR; G Satterley xliiCLAR; M Yamashita 156BL, 167CR(above); **Comstock:** 108CRB; Corbis UK Ltd: 170TR, 170BL; **D Cousens:** 147 CRA; **Corbis:** Bob Daemmrich 6BL; Bryan Denton xxxCBL; Julie Dermansky / Julie Dermansky xxviiiiTC; Everett Kennedy Brown / Epa 165CB; Kimimasa Mayama / Reuters 168CL(above); mosaaberizing / Demotix xxxCBR; Ocean 60BL; Ocean 135CL; Sucheta DAS / Reuters xxviBCR; Rob Widdis / epa 30CA; **Sue Cunningham Photographic:** 51CR; S Alden 192BC(below) **James Davis Travel Photography:** xxxviTCB, xxxviTR, xxxviCL, 13CA, 19BC, 49TLB, 56BCR, 57CLA, 61BCL, 93BC, 94TC, 102TF, 120CB, 158BC, 179CRA, 191BR; **Dorling Kindersley:** Paul Harris xxiiTR; Nigel Hicks xxiiBM; Jamie Marshall 181TR; Bharath Ramamrutham 155BR; Colin Sinclair 133BMR; George Dunnet: 124CA;

**Environmental Picture Library:** Chris Westwood 126C; **Eye Ubiquitous:** xlCA; L. Fordyce 12CLA; L Johnstone 6CRA, 28BLA, 30CB; S. Miller xxiCA; M Southern 73BLA; **Chris Fairclough Colour Library:** xliiBR; **Ffotograff:** N. Tapsell 158CL; **FLPA -Images of nature:** 123TR; **Geoscience Features:** xv:BCR, xviBR, 102CL, 108BC, 122BR; Solar Film 64TC; **Getty Images:** Kim Steele 161BCL; **gettyone stone:** 131BG, 133BR, 164CR(above); G Johnson 130BL; R Passmore 120TR; D Austen 187CL; G Allison 186CL; L Ulrich 17TL; M Vines 17BL; R Wells 193BL; **Robert Harding Picture Library:** xviiTC, xxivCR, xxxC, xxxvTC, 2TLB, 3CA, 15CRB, 15CR, 37BC, 38CRA, 50BL, 95BR, 99CR, 114CR, 122BL, 131CLA, 142CB, 143TL, 147TR, 168TR, 168CA, 166BR; P G. Adam 13TCB; D Atchison-Jones 70BLA; J Bayne 72BCL; B Schuster 80CR; C Bowman 50BR, 53CA, 62CL, 70CRL; C Campbell xxiBC; G Corrigan 159CRB, 161CRB; P Craven xxxvBL; R Cundy 69BR; Delu 79BC; A Durand 111BR; Financial Times 142CR; R Frerck 51BL; T Gervis 3BCL, 7CR; I Griffiths xxxCL, 77TL; T Hall 166CRA; D Harney 142CA; S Harris xliiiBCL; G Hellier xvCRB, 135BL; F Jackson 137BCR; Jacobs xxxviiTL; P Koch 139TR; F Joseph Land 122TR; Y Marcoux 9BR; S Massif xvBC; A Mills 88CLB; L Murray 114TR; R Rainford xlivBL; G Renner 74CB, 194C; C Rennie 48CL, 116BR; R Richardson 118CL; P Van Riel 48BR; E Rooney 124TR; Sassoon xxivCL, 148CLB; Jochen Schlenker 193CL; P Scholey 176TR; M Short 137TL; E Simanor xxviiCR; V Southwell 139CR; J Strachan 42TR, 111BL, 132BR; C Tokeley 131CLA; A C Waltham 161C; T Waltham xviiBL, xxiiCLLL, 138CRB; Westlight 37CR; N Wheeler 139BL; A Williams xxxviiiBR, xlTR; A Woolfitt 95BRA; Paul Harris: 168TC; **Hutchison Library:** 131CR (above) 6BL; P. Collomb 137CR; C. Dodwell 130TR; S Errington 70BCL; P. Hellyer 142BC; J. Horner xxxiTC; R. Ian Lloyd 134CRA; J.Nowell 135CLB, 143TC; A Zvoznikov xxiiCL; **Image Bank:** 87BR; J Banagan 190BCA; A Becker xxivBCL; M Khansa 121CR, M Isy-Schwart 193CR(above), 191CL; Khansa K Forest 163TR; Lomeo xxivTCR; T Madison 170TL(below); C Molyneux xxiiCRRR; C Navajas xviiiTR; Ocean Images Inc. 192CLB; J van Os xviiTCR; S Proehl 6CL; T Rakke xixTC, 64CL; M Reitz 196CA; M Romanelli 166CL(below); G A Rossi 151BCR, 176BLA; B Roussel 109TL; S Satushek xviiBCR; Stock Photos / J M Spielman xxivTRL; **Images Colour Library:** xxiiCLL, xxxixTR, xliCR, xliiiBLL, 3BR, 19BR, 37TL, 44TL, 62TC, 91BR, 102CLB, 103CR, 150CL, 180CA; 164BC, 165TL; **Impact Photos:** J & G Andrews 186BL; C. Bluntzer 156BR; Cosmos / G. Bathaud 65BC; S Franklin 134CRB; A. le Garsmeur 131C; C Jones xxxiCB, 70BL; V. Nemirousky 137BR; J Nicholl 76TCR; C. Penn 187C(below); G Sweeney xviiBR, 196CB, 196TR, J & G Andrews 186TR; **JVZ Picture Library:** T Nilson 135TC; **Frank Lane Picture Agency:** xxiTCR, xxiiiiBL, 93TR; A Christiansen 58CRA; J Holmes xivBL; S. McCutcheon 3C; Silvestris 173TCR; D Smith xxiiiBC; W Wisniewsli 195BR; **Leeds Castle Foundation:** xxxviiBC; **Magnum:** Abbas 83CR, 136CA; S Franklin 134CRB; D Hurn 4BCL; P. Jones-Griffiths 191BL; H Kubota xviBCL, 156CLB; F Mayer xviBL; S McCurry 73CL, 133BCR; G. Rodger 74TR; C Steele Perkins 72BL; **Mountain**

**Camera / John Cleare:** 153TR; C Monteath 153CR; **Nature Photographers:** E.A. Janes 112CL; **Natural Science Photos:** M Andera 110C; **Network Photographers Ltd.:** C Sappa / Rapho 119BL; **N.H.P.A.:** N. J. Dennis xxiiiCL; D Heuchlin xxiiiCLA; S Krasemann 15BL, 25BR, 38TC; K Schafer 49CB; R Tidman 160CLB; D Tomlinson 145CR; M Wendler 48TR; **Nottingham Trent University:** T Waltham xvCL, xvBR; **Novosti:** 144BLA; **Oxford Scientific Films:** D Allan xxiiTR; H R Bardarson xviiiBC; D Bown xxiiiCBLL; M Brown 140BL; M Colbeck 147CAR; W Faidley 3TL; L Gould xxiiiBR; D Guravich xxiiiTR; P Hammerschmidy / Okapia 87CLA; M Hill 57TL, 195TR; C Menteath ; J Netherton 2CRB; S Osolinski 82CA; R Packwood 72CA; M Pitts 179TC; N Rosing xxiiiCBL, 9TR, 197BR; D Simonson 57C; Survival Anglia / C Catton 137TR; R Toms xxiiiBR; K Wothe xxiBL, xviiCLA; **Panos Pictures:** B Aris 133C; P Barker xxivBR; T Bolstao 153BR; N Cooper 82CB, 153TC; J-L Dugast 166C(below), 167BR; J Hartley 73CA, 90CL; J Holmes 149BC; J Morris 76CLB; M Rose 146TR; D Sansoni 155CL; C Stowers 163TL; **Edward Parker:** 49TL, 49CLB; **Pictor International:** xivBR, xvBRA, xixTCL, xxCL, 3CLA, 17BR, 20TR, 20CRB, 23BCA, 23CL, 26CB, 27BC, 33TRB, 34BC, 34BR, 34CR, 38CB, 38CL, 43CL, 63BR, 65TC, 82CL, 83CLB, 99BR, 107CLA, 166TR, 171CL(above), 180CLB, 185TL; **Pictures Colour Library:** xxiBCL, xxiiiBR, xxviBCL, 6BR, 15TR, 8TR, 16CL(above), 19TL, 20BL, 24C, 24CLA, 27TR, 32TRB, 36BC, 41CA, 43CRA, 68BL, 90TCB, 94BL, 99BL, 106CA, 107CLB, 107CR, 107BR, 117BL, 164BC, 192BL, K Forest 165TL(below); **Planet Earth Pictures:** 193CR(below); D Barrett 148CB, 184CA; R Coomber 16BL; G Douwma 172BR; E Edmonds 173BR; J Lythgoe 196BL; A Mounter 172CR; M Potts 6CA; P Scoones xxTR; J Walencik 110TR; J Waters 53BCL; **Popperfoto:** Reuters / J Drake xxxiiCLA; **Rex Features:** 165CR; Antelope xxxiiiCLB; M Friedel xxiCR; J Shelley xxxCR; Sipa Press xxxCR; Sipa Press / Chamussy 176BL; **Robert Harding Picture Library:** C. Tokeley 131TL; J Strachan 132BL; Franz Joseph Land 122TR; Franz Joseph Land 364/7088 123BL, 169C(above), 170C(above), Tony Waltham 186CR(below), Y Marcoux 9BR; **Russia & Republics Photolibrary:** M Wadlow 118CR, 119CL, 124BC, 124CL, 125TL, 125BR, 126TCR; **Science Photo Library:** Earth Satellite Corporation xixTRB, xxxiCR, 49BCL; F Gohier xiCR; J Heseltine xviTCB; K Kent xvBLA; P Menzell xvBL; N.A.S.A. xBC; D Parker xivBC; University of Cambridge Collection Air Pictures 87CLB; RJ Wainscoat / P Arnold, Inc. xiBC; D Weintraub xiBL; **South American Pictures:** 57BL, 62TR; R Francis 52BL; Guyana Space Centre 50TR; T Morrison 49CRB, 49BL, 50CR, 52TR, 54TR, 61C; **Southampton Oceanography:** xviiiBL; **Sovofoto / Eastfoto:** xxiiCBR; **Spectrum Colour Library:** 50BC, 160BC; J King 145BR; **Frank Spooner Pictures:** Gamma-Liason/Vogel 131CL(above); 26CRB; E. Baitel xxxiiBC; Bernstein xxxiCL; Contrast 112CR; Diard / Photo News 113CL; Liaison / C. Hires xxxiiTCB; Liaison / Nickelsberg xxxiiTR; Marleen 113TL; Novosti 116CA; P. Piel xxxCA; H Stucke 188CLB, 190CA; Torrengo / Figaro 78BR; A Zamur 113BL; **Still Pictures:** C Caldicott 77TC; A Crump

189CL; M & C Denis-Huot xxiiBL, 78CR, 81BL; M Edwards xxiCRL, 53BL, 64CR, 69BLA, 155BR; J Frebet 53CLB; H Giradet 53TC; E Parker 52CL; M Gunther 121BC; **Tony Stone Images:** xxviTR, 4CA, 7BL, 7CL, 13CRB, 39BR, 58C, 97BC, 101BR, 106TR, 109CL, 109CRB, 164CLB, 165C, 180CB, 181BR, 188BC, 192TR; G Allison 18TR, 31CRB, 187CRB; D Armand 14TCB; D Austen 180TR, 186CL, 187CL; J Beatty 74CL; O Benn xxviBR; K Biggs xxiTL; R Bradbury 44BR; R A Butcher xxviTL; J Callahan xxviiCRA; P Chesley 185BCL, 188C; W Clay 30BL, 31CRA; J Cornish 96BL, 107TL; C Condina 41CB; T Craddock xxivTR; P Degginger 36CLB; Demetrio 5BR; N DeVore xxivBC; A Diesendruck 60BR; S Egan 87CRA, 96BR; R Elliot xxiiBCR; S Elmore 19C; J Garrett 73CR; S Grandadam 14BR; R Grosskopf 28BL; D Hanson 104BC; C Harvey 69TL; G Hellier 110BL, 165CR; S Huber 103CRB; D Hughs xxxiBR; A Husmo 91TR; G Irvine 31BC; J Jangoux 58CL; D Johnston xviiiTR; A Kehr 113C; R Koskas xviTR; J Lamb 96CRA; J Lawrence 75CRA; L Lefkowitz 7CA; M Lewis 45CLA; S Mayman 55BR; Murray & Associates 45CR; G Norways 104CA; N Parfitt xxviiCL, 68TCR, 81TL; R Passmore 121TR; N Press xviBCA; E Pritchard 88CA, 90CLR; T Raymond 21BL, 29TR; L Resnick 74BR; M Rogers 80BR; A Sacks 28TCB; C Saule 90CR; S Schulhof xxivTC; P Seaward 34CL; M Segal 32BL; V Shenai 152CL; R Sherman 26CL; H Sitton 136CR; R Smith xxvBLA, 56C; S Studd 108CLA; H Strand 49BR, 63TY; P Tweedie 177CR; L Ulrich 17BL; M Vines 17TC; A B Wadham 60CR; J Warden 63CLB; R Wells 23CRA, 193BL; G Yeowell 34BL; **Telegraph Colour Library:** 61CRB, 61TCR, 157TL; R Antrobus xxxixBR; J Sims 26BR; **Topham Picturepoint:** xxxiCBL, 162BR, 168TR, 168BC; **Travel Ink:** A Cowin 88TR; **Trip:** 140BR, 144CA, 155CRA; B Ashe 159TR; D Cole 190BCL, 190CR; D Davis 89BL; I Deineko xxxiTR; J Dennis 22BL; Dinodia 154CL; Eye Ubiquitous / L Fordyce 2CLB; A Gasson 149CR; W Jacobs 43TL, 54BL, 177BC, 178CLA, 185BCR, 186BL; P Kingsbury 112C; K Knight 177BR; V Kolpakov 17BL; T Noorits 87TL, 119BR, 146CL; R Power 41TR; N Ray 166BL, 168TC; C Rennie 116CLB; V Sidoropolev 145TR; E Smith 183BC, 183TL; **Woodfin Camp & Associates:** 92BLR; **World Pictures:** xvCRA, xviiCRA, 9CRB, 22CL, 23BC, 24BL, 35BL, 40TR, 51TR, 71BR, 80TCR, 82TR, 83BL, 86BCR, 96TC, 98BL, 100CR, 101CR, 103BC, 105TC, 157BL, 161BCL, 162CLB, 172CLB, 172BC, 179BL, 182CB, 183C, 184CL, 185CR; 121BR, 121TT; **Zefa Picture Library:** xviBLR, xviiBCL, xviiiCL, 3CL, 8BC, 8CT, 9CR, 13BC, 14TC, 16TR, 21TL, 22CRB, 25BL, 32TCR, 36BCR, 59BCL, 65TCL, 69CLA, 79TL, 81BR, 87CRB, 92C, 98C, 99TL, 100BL, 107TR, 118CRB, 120BL; 122C(below), 124CA, 164BR, 183TR; Anatol 113BR; Barone 114BL; Brandenburg 5C; A J Brown 44TR; H J Clauss 55CLB; Damm 71BC; Evert 92BL; W Felger 3BL; J Fields 189CRA; R Frerck 4BL; G Heil 56BR; K Heibig 115BR; Heilman 28BC; Hunter 8C; Kitchen 10TR, 8CL, 8BL, 9TR; Dr H Kramarz 7BLA, 123CR(below); Mehlio 155BL; J F Raga 24TR; Rossenbach 105BR; Streichan 89TL; T Stewart 13TR, 19CR; Sunak 54BR, 162TR; D H Teuffen 95TL; B Zaunders 40BC. **Additional Photography:** Geoff Dann; Rob Reichenfeld; H Taylor; Jerry Young.

# MAP CREDITS

**World Population Density map, page xxiv**

Source:LandScanTM Global Population Database. Oak Ridge, TN; Oak Ridge National Laboratory. Available at http://www.ornl.gov/landscan/.

◆ COUNTRY  ◇ DEPENDENT TERRITORY  ◈ ADMINISTRATIVE REGION  ▲ MOUNTAIN  ⛰ VOLCANO  ⊚ LAKE
● COUNTRY CAPITAL  ○ DEPENDENT TERRITORY CAPITAL  ✕ INTERNATIONAL AIRPORT  ▲ MOUNTAIN RANGE  ⋙ RIVER  ▣ RESERVOIR